P9-DZN-149

Who's Who in the South and Southwest ®

Biographical Reference Works
Published by Marquis Who's Who

Who's Who in America

Who Was Who Historical Volume (1607-1896)

Who Was Who Volume I (1897-1942)

Who Was Who Volume II (1943-1950)

Who Was Who Volume III (1951-1960)

Who Was Who Volume IV (1961-1968)

Who Was Who Volume V (1969-1973)

Who's Who in the East

Who's Who in the Midwest

Who's Who in the South and Southwest

Who's Who in the West

Who's Who in Government

Who's Who of American Women

World Who's Who in Finance and Industry

World Who's Who in Science

Directory of Medical Specialists

Who's Who in the South and Southwest

Including Alabama, Arkansas, the District of Columbia, Florida, Georgia, Kentucky, Louisiana, Mississippi, North Carolina, Oklahoma, South Carolina, Tennessee, Texas, Virginia, Puerto Rico and the Virgin Islands.

13th edition
1973-1974

MARQUIS
Who's Who

Marquis Who's Who, Inc.
200 East Ohio Street
Chicago, Illinois 60611 U.S.A.

Library of Congress Catalog Card Number 50-58231
ISBN 0-8379-0813-2

Printed and bound at St. Louis by The Von Hoffmann Press, Inc.

Table of Contents

Preface

During the past decade, the Southern and Southwestern areas of the United States have witnessed some startling increases in population and in commercial and industrial activity. Population in these areas has grown at the rate of 13 per cent according to one report. Numerous nationally recognized industrial corporations and financial institutions have expanded their operations in the South and Southwest so that today Atlanta, Miami, Houston, Dallas, Jacksonville, and Mobile are among the fastest growing business centers in the country. This progress could not have been accomplished without the work of educated, experienced, responsible individuals who are concerned on a daily basis with solving the problems of a complex urban and suburban environment as well as solving the problems that arise in their professional fields. Thus, it is appropriate to record in the pages of this new edition of *Who's Who in the South and Southwest* the biographies of those men and women who have made outstanding contributions to their professional fields and to the communities in which they live.

This Thirteenth Edition represents the most diligent, systematic and perceptive effort in the book's history to recognize particular merit and reference interest of persons from the entire spectrum of professional endeavor. Notables from the fields of science, medicine, law, government, religion, education, business, entertainment, and the fine arts are included in this volume. Included are more than 19,000 men and women from the region embracing Alabama, Arkansas, the District of Columbia, Florida, Georgia, Kentucky, Louisiana, Mississippi, North Carolina, Oklahoma, South Carolina, Tennessee, Texas, Virginia, Puerto Rico, and the Virgin Islands. In addition, Mexico, because of its own importance and its contiguity to the the southwestern United States, is also covered in this volume.

Frequently, Marquis Who's Who editors are asked: "How do people get into any Who's Who volume?" Selection is based on the fundamental principle of reference value. Many individuals are eligible by virtue of positions achieved through election or appointment to office; others have distinguished themselves by continuous achievement in their respective careers. Once these individuals have been identified, biographical information about them is collected in two ways. The vast majority of the biographees furnish information by means of biographical data forms. However, shoulα a very prominent citizen fail to furnish his own data, Marquis staff members compile the information through careful and original research.

The task of editing this volume demands a keen knowledge not only of the region covered, but of the entire continent. The people of a region, to be truly evaluated, must be viewed objectively in their universal context. Marquis Who's Who is uniquely qualified to provide this combined knowledge—as publishers of *Who's Who in America* (thirty-seven editions since 1899); *Who Was Who in America* (a six-volume set of notables of America's past); and six specialized reference works of national or international scope. In addition, the company publishes four regional biographical directories, of which, *Who's Who in the South and Southwest* is one.

The people whose biographies appear in *Who's Who in the South and Southwest* can be classified into two basic categories: (1) persons who are of regional reference importance to colleagues, librarians, researchers, scholars, the news media, historians, biographers, participants in business and civic affairs, and others with particular inquiry needs; and (2) persons of national reference interest who are of such regional or local importance that their inclusion in the book is appropriate. There is a bare minimum of duplication between this volume and *Who's Who in America*.

In the editorial evaluation that resulted in the ultimate selection of approximately 19,000 names, an individual's desire to be listed was not sufficient reason for inclusion; rather it was the individual's demonstrated merit that determined inclusion. Similarly, wealth or social position was not a criterion; only occupational stature or achievement in some field affecting the development of the southern and southwestern regions of the United States influenced selection. Indeed, many of the biographees are engaged in fields marked far more by service than by monetary reward. And, of course, this volume lists worthy individuals regardless of their race or ethnic origin.

Thus, on every level, this Thirteenth Edition of *Who's Who in the South and Southwest* carries on the tradition of excellence established 75 years ago with the publication of the first edition of *Who's Who in America.* The essence of that tradition is Marquis's unceasing effort to produce reference works responsive to the needs of their users throughout the world.

Standards of Admission

The foremost consideration in determining who will be admitted to the pages of *Who's Who in the South and Southwest* is the extent of an individual's reference interest. Such reference interest is judged on either of two factors: (1) the position of responsibility held or (2) the level of significant achievement attained by the individual.

Admissions based on the factor of position are absolutely objective. All persons residing or conducting a significant amount of business in the area covered by this volume, and occupying the following positions are automatically eligible for inclusion:

Key members of the Executive Department of the Federal Government.
Members of the U.S. Congress.
Federal judges.
Governors of states.
State attorneys general.
Judges of state and territorial courts of highest appellate jurisdiction.
U.S. ambassadors and ministers plenipotentiary.

Heads of the major universities and colleges.
Living authors of books of more than ephemeral interest or value.
Officers on active duty beginning with the rank of major general in the Army, Air Force, and Marine Corps; and with rear admiral in the Navy.
Heads of leading philanthropic, educational, and scientific societies.
Selected members of the national Academy of Sciences, the National Academy of Design, the American Academy of Arts and Letters, and the National Institute of Arts and Letters.
Bishops and chief ecclesiastics of the principal religious denominations.
Principal officers of national and international businesses.
Others chosen because of incumbency, authorship, or membership.

Admissions based on individual achievement, on the other hand, must be decided by a judicious process of evaluating subtle, qualitative factors. To be selected on this basis, a person must have accomplished some conspicuous achievement—something that distinguishes him from the vast majority of his contemporaries. He or she may scarcely be known in his (or her) own community, but may be widely recognized in some special field of endeavor. Such a person often is one whose work is better known than he is himself.

Key to Information in this Directory

❶ **FULTON, Samuel Gardner,** ❷ banker; ❸ b. Roanoke, Va., May 9, 1923; ❹ s. Oliver and Lorraine (Gardner) F.; ❺ B.A., Furman U., 1944; ❻ m. Rachel Harrison, Dec. 24, 1946; ❼ children—Sallie Jo (Mrs. Garrett Potter), Walter James, Frances Ruth, Cecily Louise. ❽ Teller Union Nat. Bank, Decatur, Ga., 1947-50, trust officer, 1950-57, v.p. trusts, 1957-65, pres., 1965—, ❾ also dir. Lectr. banking Decatur Jr. Coll., 1968—. ❿ Chmn. Decatur United Fund, 1969; active Decatur chpt. A.R.C. ⓫ Mem. Decatur City Council, 1965-68. ⓬ Bd. dirs. Salvation Army Home. ⓭ Served with USNR, 1944-46; PTO. ⓮ Named Man of Year, Decatur Jaycees, 1969; decorated Bronze Star. ⓯ Mem. Am. Banker's Assn., A.I.M., Decatur Banker's League (pres. 1967-68), Phi Delta Theta. ⓰ Democrat. ⓱ Baptist. ⓲ Mason (Shriner). ⓳ Clubs: Decatur Country, Decatur Athletic. ⓴ Contbr. articles profl. jours. ㉑ Home: 28 Hidden Hollow Rd. Decatur, Ga. 30032. ㉒ Office: 350 Peachtree St., Decatur, Ga. 30034

Key

❶ Name
❷ Position
❸ Vital statistics
❹ Parents
❺ Education
❻ Marital status
❼ Children
❽ Career
❾ Career related activities
❿ Civic activities
⓫ Political activities
⓬ Non-professional directorships
⓭ Military record
⓮ Decorations and awards
⓯ Professional and other memberships
⓰ Political affiliation
⓱ Religion
⓲ Lodges
⓳ Clubs
⓴ Writings
㉑ Home address
㉒ Office address

The biographical listings in *Who's Who in the South and Southwest* are arranged in alphabetical order according to the first letter of the last name of the biographee. Each sketch is presented in a uniform order as in the sample sketch above. The many abbreviations used in the sketches are explained in the Table of Abbreviations.

Table of Abbreviations

The following abbreviations and symbols are frequently used in this Directory

*Following a sketch indicates that it was researched and written by the Marquis Who's Who editorial staff and has not been verified by the biographee.

A.A., Associate in Arts.
A.A.A., Agricultural Adjustment Administration; Anti-Aircraft Artillery.
A.A.A.S., American Association for the Advancement of Science.
AAC, Army Air Corps.
A. and M., Agricultural and Mechanical.
AAF, Army Air Force.
A.A.H.P.E.R., American Association for Health, Physical Education, and Recreation.
A.B., Bachelor of Arts.
ABC, American Broadcasting Company.
A.,B.&C.R.R., Atlanta, Birmingham & Coast R.R.
AC, Air Corps.
acad., academy; academic.
A.C.L. R.R., Atlantic Coast Line R.R.
A.C.P., American College of Physicians.
A.C.S., American College of Surgeons.
a.d.c., aide-de-camp.
adj., adjutant; adjunct.
adm., admiral.
adminstr., administrator.
adminstrn., administration.
administrv., administrative.
adv., advocate; advisory.
advt., advertising.
A.E., Agricultural Engineer.
A.E. AND P., Ambassador Extraordinary and Plenipotentiary.
AEC, Atomic Energy Commission.
AEF, American Expeditionary Forces.
aero., aeronautical, aeronautic.
AFB, Air Force Base.
A.F.D., Doctor of Fine Arts.
AFL (or **A.F. of L**), American Federation of Labor.
A.F.T.R.A., American Federation TV and Radio Artists.
agr., agriculture.
agrl., agricultural.
agt., agent.
agy., agency.
A.I.A., American Institute of Architects.
AID, Agency for International Development.
A.I.M., American Institute of Management.
AK, Alaska
AL, Alabama
Ala., Alabama.
A.L.A., American Library Association.
Alta., Alberta.
Am., American, America.
A.M., Master of Arts.
A.M.A., American Medical Association.
A.M.E., African Methodist Episcopal.
Am. Inst. E.E., American Institute of Electrical Engineers.
Am. Soc. C.E., American Society of Civil Engineers.
Am. Soc. M.E., American Society of Mechanical Engineers.
A.N.A., Associate National Academician.
anat., anatomical.
ann., annual.
ANTA, American National Theatre and Academy.
anthrop., anthropological.
A.P., Associated Press.
apptd., appointed.
apt., apartment.
AR, Arkansas
A.R.C., American Red Cross.
archeol., archeological.
archtl., architectural.
Ariz., Arizona.
Ark., Arkansas.
ArtsD., Doctor of Arts.
arty., artillery.
AS, Air Service.
A.S.C.A.P., American Society of Composers, Authors and Publishers.
ASF, Air Service Force.
assn., association.
asso., associate; associated.
asst., assistant.
astron., astronomical.
astrophys., astrophysical.
ATSC, Air Technical Service Command.
A., T. & S. F. Ry., Atchison, Topeka & Santa Fe Ry.
atty., attorney.
AUS, Army of the United States.
Aux., Auxiliary
Av., Avenue.
AZ, Arizona

b., born.
B., Bachelor.
B.A., Bachelor of Arts.
B.Agr., Bachelor of Agriculture.
Balt., Baltimore.
Bapt., Baptist.
B.Arch., Bachelor of Architecture.
B. & A. R.R., Boston & Albany R.R.
B.A.S., Bachelor of Agricultural Science.
B.B.A., Bachelor of Business Administration.
BBC, British Broadcasting Corp.
B.C., British Columbia.
B.C.E., Bachelor of Civil Engineering.
B.Chir., Bachelor of Surgery.
B.C.L., Bachelor of Civil Law.
B.C.S., Bachelor of Commercial Science.
bd., Board.
B.D., Bachelor of Divinity.
B.Di., Bachelor of Didactics.
B.E., Bachelor of Education.
B.E.E., Bachelor of Electrical Engineering.
BEF, British Expeditionary Force.
B.F.A., Bachelor of Fine Arts.
bibl., biblical.
bibliog., bibliographical.
biog., biographical.
biol., biological.
B.J., Bachelor of Journalism.
Bklyn., Brooklyn.
B.L., Bachelor of Letters.
bldg., building.
B.L.S., Bachelor of Library Science.
Blvd., Boulevard.
B. & M. R.R., Boston & Maine R.R.
Bn., Battalion.
B.O., Bachelor of Oratory.
B. & O. R.R., Baltimore & Ohio R.R.
bot., Botanical.
B.P., Bachelor of Painting.
B.P.E., Bachelor of Physical Education.
B.Pd., Bachelor of Pedagogy.
B.Py., Bachelor of Pedagogy.
br., branch.
B.R.E., Bachelor of Religious Education.
brig. gen., brigadier general.
Brit., British; Britannica.
Bro., Brother.
B.S., Bachelor of Science.
B.S.A., Bachelor of Agricultural Science
B.S.D., Bachelor of Didactic Science.
B.S.T., Bachelor of Sacred Theology.
B.Th., Bachelor of Theology.
bull., bulletin.
bur., bureau.
bus., business.
B.W.I., British West Indies.

CA, California
Cal., California.
C.Am., Central America.
CAA, Civil Aeronautics Adminstrn.
CAB, Civil Aeronautics Board.
CAC, Coast Artillery Corps.
Can., Canada.
capt., captain.
Cath., Catholic.
cav., cavalry.
CBI, China, Burma, India Theatre of Operations.
C.,B. & Q. R.R., Chicago, Burlington & Quincy R.R. Co.
CBS, Columbia Broadcasting System.
CCC, Commodity Credit Corporation.
C.,C.,C. & St.L. Ry., Cleveland, Cincinnati, Chicago & St. Louis Ry.
C.E., Civil Engineer, Corps of Engineers.
CEF, Canadian Expeditionary Force.
C. & E.I. R.R., Chicago & Eastern Illinois R.R.
C.G.W. R.R., Chicago Great Western Ry.
ch., church.
Ch.D., Doctor of Chemistry.
chem., chemical.
Chem.E., Chemical Engineer.
Chgo., Chicago.
Chirurg., Chirurgical.
chmn., Chairman.
chpt., Chapter.
Cla. (Spanish), Company.
CIA, Central Intelligence Agency.
CIC, Counter Intelligence Corps.
C.,I. & L. Ry., Chicago, Indianapolis & Louisville Ry.
Cin., Cincinnati.
CIO, Congress of Industrial Organizations.
Cleve., Cleveland.
climatol., Climatological.
clin., clinical.
clk., clerk.
C.L.U., Chartered Life Underwriter.
C.M., Master in Surgery.
C.,M., St.P. & P. R.R., Chicago, Milwaukee, St. Paul & Pacific R.R. Co.
C. & N.-W. Ry., Chicago & Northwestern Ry.
CO, Colorado
Co., Company, County.
C. of C., Chamber of Commerce.
C.O.F., Catholic Order of Foresters.
C. of Ga. Ry., Central of Georgia Ry.
col., colonel.
coll., college.
Col., Colorado.
com., committee.
comd., commanded.
comdg., commanding.
comdr., commander.
comdt., commandant.
commd., commissioned.
comml., commercial.
commn., commission.
commr., commissioner.
condr., conductor.

TABLE OF ABBREVIATIONS

conf., conference.
Congl., Congregational; Congressional.
Conglist., Congregationalist.
Conn., Connecticut.
cons., consulting, consultant.
consol., consolidated.
constl., constitutional.
constn., constitution.
constrn., construction.
contbd., contributed.
contbg., contributing.
contbn., contribution.
contbr., contributor.
conv., convention.
coop. (or **co-op**), cooperative.
corp., corporation.
corr., correspondent; corresponding; correspondence.
C. & O. Ry., Chesapeake & Ohio Ry. Co.
C.P.A., Certified Public Accountant.
C.P.C.U., Chartered Property and Casualty Underwriter.
C.P.H., Certificate of Public Health.
cpl., corporal.
C.P. Ry., Canadian Pacific Ry. Co.
C.,R.I. & P. Ry., Chicago, Rock Island & Pacific Ry. Co.
C.R.R. of N.J., Central Railroad Co. of New Jersey.
C.S., Christian Science.
C.S.B., Bachelor of Christian Science.
C.S.D., Doctor of Christian Science.
C. & S. Ry. Co., Colorado & Southern Ry. Co.
C.,St.P.,M. & O. Ry., Chicago, St. Paul, Minneapolis & Omaha Ry. Co.
ct., court.
C.T., Candidate in Theology.
CT , Connecticut
C.Vt. Ry., Central Vermont Ry.
C. & W.I. R.R., Chicago & Western Indiana R.R. Co.
CWS, Chemical Warfare Service.
cyclo., cyclopedia.
C.Z., Canal Zone.
CZ , Canal Zone

d., daughter.
D., Doctor.
D.Agr., Doctor of Agriculture.
D.A.R., Daughters of the American Reveolution.
dau., daughter.
D.A.V., Disabled American Veterans.
D.C., District of Columbia.
DC , District of Columbia
D.C.L., Doctor of Civil Law.
D.C.S., Doctor of Commercial Science.
D.D., Doctor of Divinity.
D.D.S., Doctor of Dental Surgery.
DE , Delaware
dec., deceased.
Def., Defense.
Del., Delaware.
del., delegate.
Dem., Democratic; Democrat.
D.Eng., Doctor of Engineering.
denom., denominational.
dep., deputy.
dept., department.
dermatol., dermatological.
desc., descendant.
devel., development.
D.F.C., Distinguished Flying Cross.
D.H.L., Doctor of Hebrew Literature.
D. & H. R.R., Delaware & Hudson R.R. Co.
dir., director.
disch., discharged.
dist., district.
distbg., distributing.
distbn., distribution.
distbr., distributor.
div., division; divinity; divorce proceedings.
D.Litt., Doctor of Literature.
D., L. & W. R.R., Delaware, Lackawanna & Western R.R. Co.
D.M.D., Doctor of Medical Dentistry.
D.M.S., Doctor of Medical Science.
D.O., Doctor of Osteopathy.
DPA. Defense Production Administration.
D.P.H., Diploma in Public Health.
Dr., Doctor, Drive.
D.R., Daughters of the Revolution.
D.R.E., Doctor of Religious Education.
D. & R.G.W. R.R. Co., Denver & Rio Grande Western R.R. Co.
Dr.P.H., Doctor of Public Health; Doctor of Public Hygiene.
D.Sc., Doctor of Science.
D.S.C., Distinguished Service Cross.
D.S.M., Distinguished Service Medal.
D.S.T., Doctor of Sacred Theology.
D.T.M., Doctor of Tropical Medicine.
D.V.M., Doctor of Veterinary Medicine.
D.V.S., Doctor of Veterinary Surgery.

E., East.
E. and P., Extraordinary and Plenipotentiary.
ECA, Economic Cooperation Administration.
eccles., ecclesiastical.
ecol., ecological.
econ., economic.
ECOSOC, Economic and Social Council (of the UN).
ed., educated.
E.D., Doctor of Engineering.
Ed.B., Bachelor of Education.
Ed.D., Doctor of Education.
edit., edition.
Ed.M., Master of Education.
edn., education.
ednl., educational.
E.E., Electrical Engineer.
E.E. and M.P., Envoy Extraordinary and Minister Plenipotentiary.
Egyptol., Egyptological.
elec., electrical.
electrochem., electrochemical.
electrophys., electrophysical.
E. M., Engineer of Mines.
ency., encyclopaedia.
Eng., England.
engr., engineer.
engring., engineering.
entomol., entomological.
ethnol., ethnological.
ETO, European Theater of Operations.
Evang., Evangelical.
exam., examination; examining.
exec., executive.
exhbn., exhibition.
expdn., expedition.
expn., exposition.
expt., experiment.
exptl., experimental.

F.A., Field Artillery.
FAA, Federal Aviation Agency.
FAO, Food and Agriculture Organization (of the UN).
FBI, Federal Bureau of Investigation.
FCA, Farm Credit Administration.
FCC, Federal Communications Commission.
FCDA, Federal Civil Defense Administration.
FDA, Food and Drug Administration.
FDIA, Federal Deposit Insurance Administration.
F.E., Forest Engineer.
Fed., Federal.
Fedn., Federation.
Fgn., Foreign.
FHA, Federal Housing Administration.
FL , Florida
Fla., Florida.
FOA, Foreign Operations Administration.
Found., Foundation.
frat., fraternity.
FSA, Federal Security Agency.
Ft., Fort.
FTC, Federal Trade Commission; Federal Tariff Commission.

G.-1 (or other number), Division of General Staff.
GA , Georgia
Ga., Georgia.
gastroent., gastroenterological.
GATT, General Agreement on Tariffs and Trade.
G.,C. & S.F. Ry., Gulf, Colorado & Santa Fe Ry. Co.
G.D., Graduate in Divinity.
gen., general.
geneal., genealogical.
geod., geodetic.
geog., geographical; geographic.
geol., geological.
geophys., geophysical.
G.H.Q., General Headquarters.
G.,M. & N. R.R., Gulf, Mobile & Northern R.R. Co.
G.,M. & O. R.R., Gulf, Mobile & Ohio R.R. Co.
G.N. Ry., Great Northern Ry. Co.
gov., Governor.
govt., government.
govtl., governmental.
grad., graduated; graduate.
Gt., Great.
G.T. Ry., Grand Trunk Ry. System.
GU , Guam
G.W. Ry. of Can., Great Western Ry. of Canada.
gynecol., genecological.

Hdqrs., Headquarters.
H.H.D., Doctor of Humanities.
HHFA, Housing and Home Finance Agency.
H.I., Hawaiian Islands.
HI , Hawaii
H.M., Master of Humanics.
hist., Historical.
HOLC, Home Owners Loan Corporation.
homeo., Homeopathic.
hon., Honorary; honorable.
Ho. of Dels., House of Delegates.
Ho. of Reps., House of Representatives.
Hort., Horticultural.
hosp., hospital.
H.T., Territory of Hawaii.
Hwy., Highway.
hydrog., hydrographic.

IA , Iowa
Ia., Iowa.
IAEA, International Atomic Energy Agency.
IBM, International Business Machines Corp.
ICA, International Cooperation Administration.
ICC, Interstate Commerce Commn.
I.C. R.R., Illinois Central R.R. System.

TABLE OF ABBREVIATIONS

ID, Idaho
Ida., Idaho.
I.E.E.E., Institute of Electrical and Electronics Engineers.
IFC, International Finance Corp.
I.G.N. R.R., International - Great Northern R.R.
IGY, International Geophysical Year.
IL, Illinois
Ill., Illinois.
illus., illustrated.
ILO, International Labor Orgn.
IMF, International Monetary Fund.
IN, Indiana
Inc., Incorporated.
Ind., Indiana.
ind., independent.
Indpls., Indianapolis.
indsl., industrial.
inf., infantry.
ins., Insurance.
insp., inspector.
inst., institute.
instl., institutional.
instn., institution.
instr., instructor.
instrn., instruction.
internat., international.
intro., introduction.
I.R.E., Institute of Radio Engineers.

J.B., Jurum Baccalaureus.
J.C.B., Juris Canonici Bachelor.
J.C.L., Juris Canonici Lector.
J.D., Doctor of Jurisprudence.
j.g., junior grade.
jour., journal.
jr., junior.
J.S.D., Doctor of Juristic Science.
jud., Judicial.
J.U.D., Juris Utriusque Doctor: Doctor of Both (Canon and Civil) Laws.

Kan., Kansas.
K.C., Knight of Columbus.
K.P., Knight of Pythias.
K.C.S. Ry., Kansas City Southern Ry.
KS, Kansas
K.T., Knight Templar.
KY, Kentucky
Ky., Kentucky.

LA, Louisiana
lab., laboratory.
lang., language.
laryngol., laryngological.
lectr., lecturer.
L.H.D., Doctor of Humane Letters.
L.I., Long Island.
L.I. R.R., Long Island R.R. Co.
lit., literary: literature.
Litt.B., Bachelor of Letters.
Litt.D., Doctor of Letters.
LL.B., Bachelor of Laws.
LL.D., Doctor of Laws.
LL.M., Master of Laws.
L. & N. R.R., Louisville & Nashville R.R.
L.R.C.P., Licentiate Royal Coll. Physicians.
L.R.C.S., Licentiate Royal Coll. Surgeons.
L.S., Library Science.
lt., lieutenant.
Ltd., Limited.
Luth., Lutheran.
L.V. R.R., Lehigh Valley R.R. Co.

m., marriage ceremony.
M., Master.
MA, Massachusetts
M.A., Master of Arts.
mag., magazine.
M.Agr., Master of Agriculture.
maj., major.
Man., Manitoba.
M.Arch., Master in Architecture.
Mass., Massachusetts.
math., mathematical, mathematics.
M.B., Bachelor of Medicine.
M.B.A., Master of Business Administration.
MBS, Mutual Broadcasting System.
M.C., Medical Corps.
M.C.S., Master of Commercial Science.
M.C.E., Master of Civil Engineering.
mcht., merchant.
M.C. R.R., Michigan Central R.R.
MD, Maryland
Md., Maryland.
M.D., Doctor of Medicine.
M.Di., Master of Didactics.
M.Dip., Master in Diplomacy.
mdse., merchandise.
M.D.V., Doctor of Veterinary Medicine.
ME, Maine
Me., Maine.
M.E., Mechanical Engineer.
mech., mechanical.
M.E. Ch., Methodist Episcopal Church.
M.Ed., Master of Education.
med., medical.
Med. O.R.C., Medical Officers' Reserve Corps.
Med. R.C., Medical Reserve Corps.
M.E.E., Master of Electrical Engineering.
mem., member.
Meml., Memorial.
merc., mercantile.
met., metropolitan.
metall., metallurgical.
Met.E., Metallurgical Engineer.
meteorol., meteorological.
Meth., Methodist.
metrol., metrological.
M.F., Master of Forestry.
M.F.A., Master of Fine Arts (carries title of Dr.).
MI, Michigan
mfg., manufacturing.
mfr., manufacturer.
mgmt., management.
mgr., manager.
M.H.A., Master of Hospital Administration.
M.I., Military Intelligence.
Mich., Michigan.
micros., microscopical.
mil., military.
Milw., Milwaukee.
mineral., mineralogical.
Minn., Minnesota.
M.-K.-T. R.R., Missouri-Kansas-Texas R.R. Co.
M.L., Master of Laws.
M.L.D., Magister Legnum Diplomatic.
M.Litt., Master of Literature.
Minn., Minnesota.
Miss., Mississippi.
Mlle., Mademoiselle
M.L.S., Master of Library Science.
Mme., Madame
M.M.E., Master of Mechanical Engineering.
MN, Minnesota
mng., managing.
MO, Missouri
Mo., Missouri.

Moblzn., Mobilization.
Mont., Montana.
M.P., Member of Parliament.
M.Pd., Master of Pedagogy.
M.P.E., Master of Physical Education.
M.P.H., Master of Public Health.
M.P.L., Master of Patent Law.
Mpls., Minneapolis.
M.P. R.R., Missouri Pacific R.R.
M.R.E., Master of Religious Education.
MS, Mississippi
M.S., Master of Science.
M.Sc., Master of Science.
M.S.F., Master of Science of Forestry.
M.S.T., Master of Sacred Theology.
M. & St. L. R.R., Minneapolis & St. Louis R.R. Co.
M.,St.P. & S.S.M. Ry., Minneapolis, St. Paul & Sault Ste. Marie Ry.
M.S.W., Master of Social Work.
MT, Montana
Mt., Mount.
MTO, Mediterranean Theater of Operations.
mus., museum; musical.
Mus.B., Bachelor of Music.
Mus.D., Doctor of Music.
Mus. M., Master of Music.
Mut., Mutual.
mycol., mycological.

N., North.
N.A., National Academician; National Army.
N.A.A.C.P., National Association for the Advancement of Colored People.
NACA, National Advisory Committee for Aeronautics.
N.A.D., National Academy of Design.
N.Am., North America.
N.A.M., National Association of Manufacturers.
NASA, National Aeronautics and Space Administration.
nat., national.
NATO, North Atlantic Treaty Organization.
NATOUSA, North African Theater of Operations, U.S. Army.
nav., navigation.
N.B., New Brunswick.
NBC, National Broadcasting Company.
NC, North Carolina
N.C., North Carolina.
N.,C. & St.L. Ry., Nashville, Chattanooga & St. Louis Ry.
ND, North Dakota
N.D., North Dakota.
NDRC, National Defense Research Committee.
NE, Nebraska
N.E., Northeast.
N.E.A., National Education Association.
Neb., Nebraska.
neurol., neurological.
Nev., Nevada.
New Eng., New England.
Nfld., Newfoundland.
N.G., National Guard.
NH, New Hampshire
N.H., New Hampshire.
NIH, National Institutes of Health.
NJ, New Jersey
N.J., New Jersey
NLRB, National Labor Relations Bd.
NM, New Mexico
N.M., New Mexico.
No., Northern.
NPA, National Production Authority.
N.P. Ry., Northern Pacific Ry.

TABLE OF ABBREVIATIONS

nr., near.
NRA, National Recovery Administrn.
NRC, National Research Council.
N.S., Nova Scotia.
NSC, National Security Council.
NSF, National Science Foundation.
NSRB, National Security Resources Board.
N.T., New Testament.
numis., numismatic.
NV , Nevada
N.W., Northwest.
N. & W. Ry., Norfolk & Western Ry.
N.W.T., Northwest Territories.
NY , New York
N.Y., New York.
N.Y.C., New York City.
N.Y.C. RR., New York Central R.R. Co.
N.Y.,C. & St.L. R.R., New York, Chicago & St. Louis R.R. Co.
N.Y.,N.H. & H. R.R., New York, New Haven & Hartford R.R. Co.
N.Y.,O. & W. Ry., New York, Ontario & Western Ry.

O., Ohio.
OAS, Organization of American States.
O.B., Bachelor of Oratory.
obs., observatory.
obstet., obstetrical.
OCDM, Office of Civil and Defense Mobilization.
ODM, Office of Defense Mobilization.
OECD, Organization European Cooperation and Development.
OEEC, Organization European Economic Cooperation.
ofcl., official.
OH , Ohio
OK , Oklahoma
Okla., Oklahoma.
Ont., Ontario.
OPA, Office of Price Administration.
ophthal., ophthalmological.
OPM, Office of Production Management.
OPS, Office of Price Stabilization.
O.Q.M.G., Office of Quartermaster General.
OR , Oregon
O.R.C., Officers' Reserve Corps.
orch., orchestra.
Ore., Oregon.
orgn., organization.
ornithol., ornithological.
O.S.L. R.R., Oregon Short Line R.R.
OSRD, Office of Scientific Research and Development.
OSS, Office of Strategic Services.
osteo., osteopathic.
O.T., Old Testament.
O.T.C., Officers' Training Camp.
otol., Otological.
otolaryn., otolaryngological.
O.T.S., Officers' Training School.
O.U.A.M., Order United American Mechanics.
OWI, Office of War Information.
O.-W. R.R. & N. Co., Oregon-Washington R.R. & Navigation Co.

PA , Pennsylvania
Pa., Pennsylvania.
paleontol., paleontological.
Pa. R.R., Pennsylvania R.R.
path., pathological.
Pd.B., Bachelor of Pedagogy.
Pd.D., Doctor of Pedagogy.
Pd.M., Master of Pedagogy.
P.E., Protestant Episcopal.
Pe.B., Bachelor of Pediatrics.
P.E.I., Prince Edward Island.
P.E.N., Poets, Playwrights, Editors, Essayists and Novelists (Internat. Assn.).
penol., penological.
pfc., private first class.
PHA, Public Housing Administration.
pharm., pharmaceutical.
Pharm.D., Doctor of Pharmacy.
Pharm.M., Master of Pharmacy.
Ph.B., Bachelor of Philosophy.
Ph.C., Pharmaceutical Chemist.
Ph.D., Doctor of Philosophy.
Ph.G., Graduate in Pharmacy.
Phila., Philadelphia.
philol., philological.
philos., philosophical.
photog., photographic.
phys., physical.
Phys. and Surg., Physicians and Surgeons (College at Columbia U.).
physiol., physiological.
P.I., Philippine Islands.
Pitts., Pittsburgh.
Pkwy., Parkway.
Pl., Place.
P. & L.E. R.R., Pittsburgh & Lake Erie R.R.
P.M. R.R., Pere Marquette R.R. Co.
P.O., Post Office.
polit., political.
poly., polytechnic; polytechnical.
pomol., pomological.
PR , Puerto Rico
P.R., Puerto Rico.
prep., preparatory.
pres., president.
Presbyn., Presbyterian.
presdl., presidential.
prin., principal.
proc., proceedings.
prod., produced (play production).
prodn., production.
prof., professor.
profl., professional.
prog., progressive.
propr., proprietor.
pros. atty., prosecuting attorney.
pro tem, pro tempore (for the time being).
psychiat., psychiatric.
psychol., psychological.
P.T.A., Parent-Teacher Association.
PTO, Pacific Theater of Operations.
pub., public; publisher; publishing; published.
publ., publication.
pvt., private.
PWA, Public Works Administration.

q.m., quartermaster.
Q.M.C., Quartermaster Corps.
Q.M.O.R.C., Quartermaster Officers' Reserve Corps.
quar., quarterly.
Que., Quebec (province)

radiol., Radiological.
RAF, Royal Air Force.
R.C., Roman Catholic.
RCA, Radio Corporation of America.
RCAF, Royal Canadian Air Force.
Rd., Road.
R.D., Rural Delivery.
R.E., Reformed Episcopal.
rec., recording.
ref., reformed.
regt., regiment.
regtl., regimental.
rehab., rehabilitation.
Rep., Republican.
rep., representative.
Res., Reserve.
ret., retired.
rev., review, revised.
RFC, Reconstruction Finance Corp.
R.F.D., Rural Free Delivery.
rhinol., rhinological.
RI , Rhode Island
R.I., Rhode Island.
R.N., Registered Nurse.
rontgenol., rontgenological
R.O.S.C., Reserve Officers' Sanitary Corps.
R.O.T.C., Reserve Officers' Training Corps.
R.P., Reformed Presbyterian.
R.R., Railroad.
R.T.C., Reserve Training Corps.
Ry., Railway.

s., son.
S., South.
S.A., (Spanish) Sociedad Anonima; (French) societe Anonyme.
SAC, Strategic Air Command.
S.A.L. Ry., Seaboard Air LIne Ry.
S.Am., South America.
san., sanitary.
S.A.R., Sons of the Am. Revolution.
Sask., Saskatchewan.
S.A.T.C., Student's Army Training Corps.
Sat. Eve. Post, Saturday Evening Post.
savs., savings.
S.B., Bachelor of Science.
SC , South Carolina
S.C., South Carolina
SCAP, Supreme Command Allies Pacific.
Sc.B., Bachelor of Science.
ScD., Doctor of Science.
S.C.D., Doctor of Commercial Science.
sch., school.
sci., science; scientific.
S.C.V., Sons of Confederate Veterans.
SD , South Dakota
S.D., South Dakota
S.E., Southeast.
SEATO, Southeast Asia Treaty Organization.
SEC, Securities and Exchange Commn.
sec., secretary.
sect., section.
seismol., seismological.
sem., seminary.
sgt., sergeant.
SHAEF, Supreme Headquarters, Allied Expeditionary Forces.
SHAPE, Supreme Headquarters Allied Powers in Europe.
S.I., Staten Island.
S.J., Society of Jesus (Jesuit).
S.J.D., Doctor Juristic Science.
S.M., Master of Science.
So., Southern.
soc., society.
social., sociological.
SOS, Services of Supply.
s.p. Co., Southern Pacific Co.
spl., special.
splty., specialty.
Sq., Square.

sr., senior.
S.R., Sons of the Revolution.
S.S., Steamship.
SSS, Selective Service System.
St., Saint; Street.
sta., station.
statis., statistical.
S.T.B., Bachelor of Sacred Theology.
Stblzn., Stabilization.
S.T.D., Doctor of Sacred Theology.
S.T.L., Licentiate in Sacred Theology; Lector of Sacred Theology.
St.L.-S.F. R.R., St. Louis-San Francisco Ry. Co.
supr., supervisor.
supt., superintendent.
surg., surgical.
S.W., Southwest.

T.A.P.P.I., Technical Association Pulp and Paper Industry.
Tb, Tuberculosis.
tchr., teacher.
tech., technical; technology.
technol., technological.
Tel. & Tel., Telephone and Telegraph.
temp., temporary.
Tenn., Tennessee.
Ter., Territory.
Tex., Texas.
T.H., Territory of Hawaii.
Th.D., Doctor of Theology.
Th.M., Master of Theology.
theol., theological.
TN , Tennessee
tng., training.
topog., topographical.
T. & P. Ry., Texas & Pacific Ry. Co.
trans., transactions; transferred.
transl., translation.
transp., transportation.
treas., treasurer.
TV, Television.
TVA, Tennessee Valley Authority.
Twp., Township.
TX , Texas
Ty., Territory.

typog., typographical.

U., University.
UAR, United Arab Republic.
U.A.W., International Union United Automobile, Aircraft, and Agricultural Implement Workers of American-AFL-CIO.
U.B., United Brethren in Christ.
U.D.C., United Daughters of the Confederacy.
U.K., United Kingdom.
UN, United Nations.
UNESCO, United Nations Educational, Scientific and Cultural Organization.
UNICEF, United Nations International Childrens Emergency Fund.
univ., university.
UNRRA, United Nations Relief and Rehabilitation Administration.
U.P., United Presbyterian.
U.P.I., United Press International.
U.P. R.R., Union Pacific R.R.
urol., urological.
U.S., United States.
U.S.A., United States of America.
USAAF, United States Army Air Force.
USAC, United States Air Corps.
USAF, United States Air Force.
USCG, United States Coast Guard.
USCGR, U.S. Coast Guard Reserve.
USES, United States Employment Service.
USIA, United States Information Agency.
USIS, United States Information Service.
USMC, United States Marine Corps.
USMCR, U.S. Marine Corps Reserve.
USMHS, United States Marine Hospital Service.
USN, United States Navy.
U.S.N.A., United States National Army.
U.S.N.G., United States National Guard.
USNR, United States Naval Reserve.
USNRF, United States Naval Reserve Force.
U.S.O., United Service Organizations.
USOM, United States Operations Mission.
USPHS, United States Public Health Service.
U.S.S., United States Ship.
USSR, Union of Soviet Socialist Republics.
U.S.V., United States Volunteers.

UT , Utah

VA , Virginia
Va., Virginia.
VA, Veterans Administration.
vet., Veteran; veterinary.
V.F.W., Veterans of Foreign Wars.
VI , Virgin Islands
V.I., Virgin Islands.
vice pres., vice president.
vis., visiting.
vol., volunteer; volume.
v.p., Vice president.
vs., versus.
VT , Vermont
Vt., Vermont.

W., West.
WA , Washington
WAC, Women's Army Corps.
Wash., Washington (state).
WAVES, Womens Reserve, U.S. Naval Reserve.
W.C.T.U., Women's Christian Temperance Union.
WHO, World Health Organization (of the UN).
WI , Wisconsin
W.I., West Indies.
Wis., Wisconsin.
W. & L.E. Ry., Wheeling & Lake Erie Ry. Co.
WPA, Works Progress Administration.
WPB, War Production Board.
W.P. R.R. Co., Western Pacific R.R. Co.
WSB, Wage Stabilization Board.
WV , West Virginia
W. Va. West Virginia.
WY , Wyoming
Wyo., Wyoming.

YMCA, Young Men's Christian Assn.
YMHA, Young Men's Hebrew Assn.
YM and YWHA, Young Men's and Young Women's Hebrew Assn.
Y. & M.V. R.R., Yazoo & Mississippi Valley R.R.
Y.T., Yukon Territory.
YWCA, Young Women's Christian Assn.

zool., zoological.

ALPHABETICAL PRACTICES

Names are arranged alphabetically according to the surnames, and under identical surnames according to the first given name. If both surname and first given name are identical, names are arranged alphabetically according to the second given name. Where full names are identical, they are arranged in order of age—those of the elder being put first.

Surnames, beginning with De, Des, Du, etc., however capitalized or spaced, are recorded with the prefix preceding the surname and arranged alphabetically under the letter D.

Surnames beginning with Mac are arranged alphabetically under M. This likewise holds for names beginning with Mc; that is, all names beginning Mc will be found in alphabetical order after those beginning Mac.

Surnames beginning with Saint or St. all appear after names that would begin Sains, and such surnames are arranged according to the second part of the name, e.g., St. Clair would come before Saint Dennis.

Surnames beginning with prefix Van are arranged alphabetically under letter V.

Surnames containing the prefix Von or von are usually arranged alphabetically under letter V; any exceptions are noted by cross references (Von Kleinsmid, Rufus Bernhard; see Kleinsmid, Rufus Bernhard von).

Compound hyphenated surnames are arranged according to the first member of the compound.

Compound unhyphenated surnames common in Spanish are not rearranged but are treated as hyphenated names.

Since Chinese names have the family name first, they are so arranged, but without comma between family name and given name (as Lin Yutang).

Parentheses used in connection with a name indicate which part of the full name is usually deleted in common usage. Hence Abbott, W(illiam) Lewis indicates that the usual form of the given name is W. Lewis. In alphabetizing this type, the parentheses are not considered. However if the name is recorded Abbott, (William) Lewis, signifying that the entire name William is not commonly used, the alphabetizing would be arranged as though the name were Abbott, Lewis.

Who's Who in the South and Southwest

AARON, STUART ROSEN, banker; b. Dallas, May 19, 1938; s. Leon S. and Etta (Rosen) A.; B.S., U. Pa., 1959; m. Barbara Ann Tucker, October 17, 1967; children—Kayla Lyn, Blythe Leigh. Began career with Republican Nat. Bank, Dallas, 1959-67, asst. cashier, 1962, asst. mgr. credit dept., 1962-63, mgr. credit dept., 1963, comml. loan officer, asst v.p., 1964-67; v.p., comml. loan officer Houston Nat. Bank, Houston, 1967-71, sr. v.p., 1971—. Counselor, chmn. Southwestern Grad. Sch. Banking, So. Meth. U., Dallas, summers 1966-72. Bd. dirs. Jewish Community Council Houston; bd. dirs., treas. loan fund bd. Jewish Family Service; bd. dirs. Jewish Home for Aged, Joint Distbn. Com. United Jewish Appeal; chmn. local alumni ann. giving U. Pa., 1967-68; adv. dir. Anti-Defamation League Houston; trustee Huston-Tillotson Coll., Austin. Served to 2d lt. AUS, 1959-60; capt. Res. Mem. Am. Inst. Banking, Robert Morris Assos., U. Pa. Dallas Alumni Assn. (pres. 1965-66). Jewish religion (bd. dirs. synagogue). Club: Westwood Country (bd. govs.) (Houston). Home: 12342 Longworth Lane Houston TX 77024 Office: 1010 Milam St Houston TX 77001

ABBEE, JAMES GIBSON, pub. relations cons.; b. Norman, Okla., Aug. 25, 1932; s. Alfred and Naomi (Gibson) A.; B.A., U. Okla., 1956; M.A., Am. U., 1970; m. Catherine N. Walters, June 14, 1956 (div. Sept. 1963); children—Twyla Star, James Gibson, Michelle N.; m. 2d, Gillian Barbara Christi, Sept. 1, 1968; 1 son, James M. Mgr. pub. relations and advt. Anchorage Natural Gas Corp. (Alaska), 1961-62; dir. pub. relations and advt. Lowell Thomas, Jr. for Congress Com., Anchorage, 1962; owner, mgr. Jim Abbee Pub. Relations and Advt., Anchorage, 1962-67; pub. relations cons. speech writer Office of Sec., Dept. Transp., Washington, 1969—. Counselor Air Force Acad., Colorado Springs. Dir. pub. relations Heart Fund, Anchorage, 1963, 64; statewide campaign dir. Am. Fedn. Blind Fund Drive, 1966. Served with USAF, 1956-59. Mem. Fed. Editors Assn., Pub. Relations Soc. Am., Air Force Assn., Res. Officers Assn., Sigma Delta Chi. Clubs: Capitol Hill, Nat. Press, Washington Shrine. Home: 3901 Mill Creek Dr Annandale VA 22003 Office: Office of Sec 5-80 Dept Transp 400 7th St Washington DC 20590

ABBITT, GEORGE FRANCIS, JR, judge; b. Newport News, Va., Aug. 6, 1906; s. George Francis and Otway (Moorman) A.; LL.B., U. Richmond, 1931; m. Josephine Cundiff, Mar. 3, 1935; children—Frances A. (Mrs. David W. Quarrier), Nancy A. (Mrs. Robert E. Torrence). Admitted to Va. bar, 1931; practiced in Appomattox, Va., 1931-64; judge 5th Judicial Circuit Ct. of Va., Appomattox, 1964—; dir. Farmers Nat. Bank, Appomattox, Va. Trustee, Va. Bapt. Hosp. Mem. Va., 5th Circuit bar assns. Baptist. Club: Lions. Home: 125 S Church St Appox VA 24522 Office: 121 Court St Appomattox VA 24522

ABBITT, WATKINS (MOORMAN), congressman; b. Appomattox, Va., May 21, 1908; s. George Francis and Otway C. (Moorman) A.; LL.B., U. Richmond, 1931, LL.D., (hon.), 1965; m. Corinne Hancock, March 20, 1937; children—Anne Culvin Abbitt (Mrs. William S. Kerr), Watkins Moorman, Corrine Hancock. Admitted to Va. bar, 1930, and practiced since in Appomattox; commonwealth's atty. for Appomattox County, 1932-48; mem. 80th to 92d congresses from 4th Va. Dist.; mem. agr. com., mem. house adminstrn. com., com. on standards of ofcl. conduct. Del. State Dem. Convs., 1932—; chmn. Appomattox County Dem. Com., 1937—; Democratic elector, 1944; mem. Va. Constl. Conv., 1945. Dir. Farmers Nat. Bank of Appomattox. Mem. Va. Democratic State Central Com., 1964-72. Mem. Va. Bar Assn., Woodmen of the World, Delta Theta Phi, Omicron Delta Kappa. Democrat. Baptist. Elk, Moose. Clubs: Ruritan (pres. 1940-41), Lions (pres. 1942-43). Home: Appomattox VA 24522 Office: Rayburn House Office Bldg Washington DC 20515

ABBOT, W. ROBERT, lawyer, banker; b. Fayetteville, W.Va., Nov. 24, 1923; s. Alois Bahlmann and Nona (Reynolds) A.; student The Citadel, 1942; grad. U. Wis., 1946; J.D., U. Va., 1949; m. Mary Withers Dempsey, Mar. 11, 1949; children—W. Robert, Alois Bahlmann III, J. Matthew. Admitted to W.Va. bar; since practiced in Fayetteville; mem. firm Love, Abbot & Hill. Chmn. bd. Fayette County Nat. Bank. Mem. W.Va. Bd. Edn., 1965—, v.p., 1967, pres., 1968-69. Served with inf. AUS, World War II; PTO. Decorated Combat Infantryman's Badge. Mem. Am., W. Va bar assns., W.Va. State Bar. Democrat. Episcopalian. Mason. Clubs: Edgewood Country, Hawks Nest Country. Author: Write Me A Verbal Contract, 1961. Home: Abbott Addition Fayetteville WV 25840 Office: PO Box 356 Fayetteville WV 25840

ABBOTT, BENJAMIN EDWARD, JR., corp. exec.; b. Washington, Dec. 7, 1928; s. Benjamin Edward and Agnes (Campbell) A.; B. Indls. Engring., U. Fla., 1953; m. Ellianna Gray, May 22, 1955; children—Celeni, Dawn, Mark, Scott. Began career as industrial engineer with E. I. DuPont de Nemours & Company, Martinsville, Va., 1951, Allis Chalmers, Milw., 1953, Pensacola (Fla.) Naval Air Sta., 1955-61; mem. exec. staff Dr. Wernher von Braun, Marshall Space Flight Center, NASA, Huntsville, Ala., 1961-68; v.p., dir. Investors Corp. of Am., Birmingham, 1968—, Internat. Resorts, Inc., 1970—; dir. Pacific Am. Corp., San Francisco, Life Ins. Co. of Am., Birmingham, Ala. Served to lt. (j.g.) USNR, 1953-55. Registered profl. engr., Ala., Fla. Mem. Am. Inst. Indsl. Engrs. (sr.), Nat. Soc. Profl. Engrs., Ret. Officers Assn., Am. Inst. Aeros. and Astronautics, Pi Kappa Phi. Home: Rt 2 Box 116-B Alpine AL 35014 Office: Investors Corp Am 1545 Montgomery Hwy Birmingham AL 35216

ABBOTT, CHARLES CORTEZ, univ. dean; b. Lawrence, Kan., Oct. 30, 1906; s. Wilbur Cortez and Margaret Ellen (Smith) A.; A.B., Harvard, 1928; A.M., 1930; Ph.D., 1933; M. Louise Slocum, 1934; children— Margaret Ellen, Louise Austin, Charles C., William S., Preston II. Instr. econs. Harvard, 1931-37, asst. prof. bus. econ., grad. sch. bus. adminstrn., 1937-40, asso. prof., 1940-46, prof., 1946-54; dean grad. sch. bus. adminstrn. U. Va., 1954—; War Shipping Adminstrn., 1942-43; dir. indsl. Relations Counselors, Inc., Keystone Custodian Funds, Inc., Miller and Rhoads, Chesapeake Corp. of Va. Adv. council Indsl. Coll. Armed Forces. Mem. Am. Finance Assn., Am. Econ. Assn., Phi Beta Kappa. Clubs: Harvard (N.Y.C.); Farmington (Charlottesville); Union (Boston). Author: The New York Bond Market, 1920-30, 1937; Financing Business During the Transition, 1946; Management of the Federal Debt, 1946. Editor: Basic Financial Research: Needs and Prospects, 1966. Contbr. sci. and tech. jours. Home: Pavilion VI East Lawn Charlottesville VA 22903

ABBOTT, CHARLES WARREN, lawyer; b. Miami, Fla., Jan 16, 1930; s. Voyle Eben and Katherine (Paschall) A.; B.S., U. Fla., 1951 LL.B., 1953; m. Betty Jo Eckholdt, Jan. 9, 1959; children—Brenda Jean, Katherine Louise, Abigail Jill. Admitted to Fla. bar, 1953; practiced in Orlando, Fla., 1955—; mem. firm Maguire, Voorhis and Wells, 1955—. Commr., Goldenrod-Dommerich Fire Control Dist., 1966—. Dir. Orange County Assn. for Retarded Children, 1971—. Served with USAF, 1953-55. Mem. Am. Bar Assn., Fla. Bar, Alpha Tau Omega, Fla. Blue Key, Phi Delta Phi. Clubs: University (Orlando, Fla.); Sertoma (Winter Park, Fla.) Home: 515 Lightning Maitland FL 32751 Office: 135 Wall St Orlando FL 32802

ABBOTT, PRESTON SARGENT, research psychologist; b. Peabody, Mass., Nov. 26, 1922; s. George W. and Dorothy (Kelley) A.; A.B., Bates Coll., 1947; M.A., U. Hawaii, 1948 Ph.D., Brown U., 1953; m. Barbara Beattie, Aug. 27, 1947; children—Judith Tracey, David Monroe, Mark Bunker. Research psychologist U.S. Air Force, Air Force Personnel and Tng. Research Center, Sacramento, 1950-55; sr. research scientist Tng. Methods div. Human Resources Research Office, Washington, 1955-57; dir research Inf. div. Human Resources Research Office, Ft. Benning, Ga., 1957-60; program dir. Human Ecology Fund, N.Y.C., Washington, 1960-65; asst. dir. for rev. and analysis Human Resources Research Office, George Washington U., Alexandria, Va., 1965-66; dir. Am. Insts. for Research, Kensington, Md., 1966—. Cons. to USAF Psychol. Assessment Assos., Music Research Found. Served with USAAF, 1942-45. Decorated D.F.C., Air medal, Purple Heart. Fellow Am. Psychol. Assn.; mem. Sigma Chi. Home: 1305 Namassin Rd Alexandria VA 22308 Office: Am Inst Research 10605 Concord St Kensington MD 20795

ABBOTT, ROBERT FRANKLIN, educator; b. Nashville, Oct. 19, 1927; s. Henry Preston and Nuffie Mae (Allen) A.; B.A., Cumberland U., 1951; M.A., George Peabody Coll., 1952; Ed.D., U. Tenn., 1963; m. Betty Blanche Sullivan, July 7, 1950; children—Robert Preston, Gerald Franklin. Tchr., prin. pub. schs. Maury County, Davidson County, Tenn., 1952-55; counselor, state supr. div. Vocational Rehab. Tenn., 1955-59; mem. faculty Middle Tenn. State U. 1959-67; prof., chmn. counselor edn. and psychology div. Ark. State U., Jonesboro, 1967—. Sch. psychologist Tenn. Dept. Edn., 1965-67; lectr. grad. studies McGill U., 1966. Scoutmaster, chmn. troop coms., dist. chmn. tng. Middle Tenn. council Boy Scouts Am., 1949-67, recipient Scoutmasters key, 1966, Long Rifle, 1967. Mem. Am. Personnel and Guidance Assn., Am. Psychol. Assn., Ark. Edn. Assn., Nat. Rehab. Assn. Home: 1107 Thrush Rd Jonesboro AR 72401

ABDUL-MAGID, KHAMIS, educator; b. Jerusalem, Palestine, Sept. 7, 1928; s. Adib and Fatima Khalil (Gouseh) A.; B.A., Am. U. at Cairo, Egypt., 1950; B.A., U. Tex., 1952; Ph.D., U. Pa., 1963; m. Zahia Goushe, Oct. 24, 1952; 1 dau., Najat. Came to U.S., 1950. Instr. econs. Drexel Inst. Tech., Phila., 1956-62; asst. prof. econs. William and Mary Coll., Williamsburg, Va., 1962-64, asso. prof., 1964-67; econ. and financial adv. Ministry of Finance and Oil, Govt. Kuwait, 1965-67; Dana prof. econs., chmn. econs. dept. Guilford Coll., Greensboro, N.C., 1967—. Econ. adviser to govt. Mem. Am., So. econs. assns., Inst. Home: 728 Westminster Dr Greensboro NC 27410

ABELLA, ROSA MARGARITA, librarian; b. Havana, Cuba, Feb. 13, 1920; d. Faustino and Rosa (Schmidt) Abella; Tecnica Bibliotecarria, U. Habana, 1956, Dr. Filosofia y Letras, 1958. Came to U.S., 1961, naturalized, 1969. Librarian, Biblioteca Instituto de la Habana, 1952-59; head librarian circulation dept. Biblioteca Nacional Jose Marti, Havana, 1959-61; asso. prof., librarian Otto G. Richter Library, U. Miami, Coral Gables, Fla., 1961—. Mem. Inst. Internat. Edn. Club: Cuban Women's. Contbr. articles to profl. jours. Home: 335 SW 47th Av Miami FL 33134 Office: University of Miami Library Coral Gables FL 33124

ABERCROMBIE, RALPH MCCALL, JR., hosp. adminstr.; b. Charlotte, N.C., Sept. 26, 1928; s. Ralph McCall and Mamie (Schenck) A.; A.B., U. N.C., 1958; m. Elizabeth Joann Hovis, Feb. 7, 1953; children—Ralph M. III, Jeffrey H., James M., Anne Elizabeth. Preceptorship hosp. adminstrn. Charlotte (N.C.) Meml. Hosp., 1958-60; asst. adminstr. Spartanburg (S.C.) Gen. Hosp., 1960-63; adminstr. Tuomey Hosp., Sumter, S.C., 1963—. Mem. bd. dirs. Carolinas Hosp. and Health Service, Carolinas Virginas Hosp. Conf., Blue Cross of S.C., Sumter, Clarendon, Kershaw Mental Health Bd., Hosp. Edn. and Research Found. of S.C. Served with AUS, 1950-52. Mem. Am. Coll. Hosp. Adminstrs., S.C. Hosp. Assn. Assn. (pres. 1969-70), Alpha Phi Omega (state chmn. 1964-66). Methodist. Rotarian (pres. 1971-72). Home: 84 Nash St Sumter SC 29150 Office: 16-18 W Calhoun St Sumter SC 29150

ABERNATHY, JACK, bus. exec. Pres. Big Chief Drilling Co., Oklahoma City. Office: 601 NE 63d St Oklahoma City OK 73100*

ABERNATHY, LEWIS MCLAURINE, educator; b. McComb, Miss., June 15, 1932; s. Andrew Hawkins and Marianna Haley (McLaurine) A.; B.B.A., U. Miss., 1954, M.B.A., 1959; Ph.D., U. Okla., 1967; m. Kathryn Louise Rodgers, Mar. 11, 1956; children—Lewis McLaurine, Marifrances, Matthew Rodgers. Teaching asst. econs. U. Okla., 1959-62, instr. econs. and bus., 1962-63; instr. econs. North Tex. State U., Denton, 1963-67, asst. prof., 1967-69, asso. prof., 1969—. Dir. Manpower Inst., 1970—. Cons. econ. problems for various pvt. and pub. agys. Served as lt. (j.g.), USNR, 1954-57. Dept. Health Edn. and Welfare grantee, 1969. Mem. Am. Econ. Assn., Am. Assn. U. Profs., Southwestern Social Sci. Assn., Indsl. Relations Research Assn., Am. Vocational Edn. Research Assn., Am. Soc. Tng. Dirs., Omicron Delta Epsilon, Sigma Chi. Methodist (bd. stewards 1970-73). Home: 1807 Locksley St Denton TX 76201

ABERNATHY, RALPH DAVID, clergyman; b. Linden, Ala., Mar. 11, 1926; s. W. L. and Louivery (Bell) A.; B.S., Ala. State Coll., 1950; M.A. in Sociology, Atlanta U., 1951; LL.D., Allen U., Columbia, S.C., 1960; m. Juanita Odessa Jones, Aug. 31, 1952; children— Juandalynn Ralpheda, Donzaleigh Avis, Ralph David III. Personnel counselor, instr. social sci. Ala. State Coll., 1951; ordained to ministry Baptist Ch., 1948; pastor Eastern Star Bapt. Ch., Demopolis, Ala., 1950-51, 1st Bapt. Ch., Montgomery, Ala., 1951-61; organizer Montgomery Improvement Assn., 1955; initiator bus boycott, Montgomery, 1955; home and church dynamited, 1957; an organizer 1957, since financial sec.- treas. So. Christian Leadership Conf., v.p. at large 1965-67, pres., 1967—; pastor West Hunter St. Bapt. Ch., Atlanta, 1961—. Mem. Atlanta Ministers Union; organizer, chmn. Operation Breadbasket, Atlanta; mem. adv. com. Congress Racial Equality. Active local A.R.C., Am. Cancer Soc., YMCA. Bd. dirs. Indsl. Areas Found., Chgo. Mem. N.A.A.C.P., Kappa Alpha Psi, Phi Delta Kappa. Mason (32 deg.). Home: 76 Cerro St SW Atlanta GA 30314 Office: 334 Auburn Av NE Atlanta GA 30303 also 775 Hunter St NW Atlanta GA 30314

ABERNATHY, WILL TERRY, govt. ofcl.; b. Selmer, Tenn., Sept. 4, 1911; s. Terry and Addie (Darby) A.; B.A., U. Tenn., 1934; m. Lucille Purser, Oct. 16, 1942 (dec. 1951); children—Mary Jane, Terry. Admitted to Tenn. bar, 1934; practiced in Selmer, Tenn., 1934-39; asst. gen. counsel Tenn. Dept. Employment Security, Nashville, 1939-42, appeals referee, 1942-43, 46-53; practiced in Selmer, Tenn., 1953-58; dist. atty. gen. 16th Jud. Circuit Tenn., Selmer, 1958—. Served with CIC, AUS, 1943-46. Mem. Bar Assn. Tenn., Sigma Chi. Democrat. Mem. Christian Ch. Lions. Home: 224 Court Av Selmer TN 38375 Office: Courthouse Selmer TN 38375

ABERNETHY, DONALD DOUGLAS, supt. schs..; b. Newton, N.C., Aug. 8, 1931; s. Ernest Glenn and Lottie Elizabeth (Shaw) A.; B.A., Lenoir Rhyne Coll., 1953; M.Ed., Appalachian State U., 1958, East Carolina U., 1962, Mich. State U., 1967, Duke, 1959; postgrad. U. Ga., 1968; m. Iris Buford Grigg, June 17, 1956; children—Douglas, Jeffrey, Jonathan, Beth, Robert. Tchr., prin. Catawba (N.C.) Elementary Sch., 1955-60; prin. Wallace-Rose Hill High Sch., Teachey, N.C., 1960-64, Hoke County High Sch., 1964-67; dir. student teaching Pembroke (N.C.) State U., 1967; supt. Hoke County Schs., Raeford, N.C., 1967—. Mem. budget com. United Fund, 1968-71; chmn. Hoke County Bd. Health, 1971-73. Bd. dirs. Region N Health Planning Council. Served with AUS, 1953-55. Mem. Horace Mann League, N.C. Assn. Edn. (pres. dist. supts. div. 1971-72), Grange. Democrat. Baptist. Kiwanian. Home: 603 N Fulton St Raeford NC 28376 Office: 109 E Edinboro Av Raeford NC 28376

ABERNETHY, FRANCIS EDWARD, educator; b. Altus, Okla., Dec. 3, 1925; s. Talbot and Aileen (Cherry) A.; B.A., Stephen F. Austin State U., 1949; postgrad. U. Neuchatel (Switzerland), 1949; M.A., La. State U., 1951, Ph.D., 1956; m. Hazel Shelton, June 12, 1948; children— Luanna Cherry, Robert Morris, Sarah Elizabeth, Margaret Leslie, Benjamin Talbot. Tchr. Woodville (Tex.) High Sch., 1951-53; teaching fellow La. State U., Baton Rouge, 1953-56; asso. prof. English, Lamar State Coll., Beaumont, Tex., 1956-65; prof. Stephen F. Austin State U., Nacogdoches, Tex., 1965—. Served with USNR, 1943-46. Francis E. Abernethy Poetry award established in his honor Poetry Soc. Tex., 1969; recipient Distinguished Prof. award, 1970. Mem. Tex. Folklore Soc. (sec., editor, past pres.), Am. Folklore Soc., Tex. Herpetological Soc., South-Central Renaissance Soc., South-Central Modern Lang. Assn., Coll. Conf. Tchrs. English, E. Tex. Hist. Assn., Assn. Mexican Cave Studies. Democrat. Mason. Author: Popular Literature and Social Protest, 1458-1558, 1962; Tales From the Big Thicket, 1966; J. Frank Dobie, 1967. Home: 210 S Lanana St Nacogdoches TX 75961

ABERNETHY, GEORGE LAWRENCE, educator; b. West Orange, N.J., Aug. 23, 1910; s. John and Lydia (Johnson) A.; A.B., Bucknell U., 1932; M.A., Oberlin Coll., 1933; Ph.D., U. Mich., 1936; postgrad. U. Wis., 1933-34, (Ford Found. faculty fellow) Columbia, 1952-53; m. Helen Sarah McLandress, Aug. 25, 1936; children—Robert John, Jean Helen (Mrs. Thomas H. Poston). Faculty, Culver-Stockton Coll., Canton, Mo., 1936-40, U. S.D., 1940-46; prof. philosophy Davidson (N.C.) Coll., 1946—, Richardson prof. philosophy, 1967—. Vis. prof. Coll. Charleston (S.C.), summer 1951; faculty U. N.C., Charlotte, part-time 1947-48, Barber-Scotia Coll., Concord, N.C., part-time 1951-52; fellow in coop. humanitites program U. N.C.-Duke, 1967-68. Mem. regional selection com. Woodrow Wilson Fellowships Found., 1960-62. Recipient Thomas Jefferson award McConnell Found., 1962; Bucknell U. Alumni medal award, 1969. Mem. N.C. Philosophy Soc. (pres. 1951-52), Am. Assn. U. Profs., Am. Philos. Assn., Am. Social. Soc., Assn. Asian Studies, So. Soc. Philosophy and Psychology, Phi Beta Kappa, Omicron Delta Kappa. Author: Pakistan-A Selected, Annotated Bibilography, 1957, 3d rev. edit., 1968; The Idea of Equality, 1959; Living Wisdom From The World's Religions, 1965, paperback edit., 1969; (with T. A. Langford) Philosophy of Religion, 1962, 2d edit., 1968; History of Philosophy-Selected Readings, 1965; Introduction to Western Philosophy-Thales to Mill, 1970. Contbg. editor Presbyn. Outlook, 1963—. Home: 100 Hillside Dr Davidson NC 28036

ABERNETHY, THOMAS GERSTLE, congressman; b. Eupora, Miss., May 16, 1903; s. Thomas Franklin and Minnie Agnes (Jenkins) A.; student U. of Ala., 1920-23; LL.B., Cumberland U., 1924; spl. student U. Miss. Law Sch., 1924-25; m. Alice Margaret Lamb, July 5, 1936; children—Margaret Gail Abernethy (Mrs. Arthur W. Doty), Thomas, Alice Kay (Mrs. James L. Martin). Admitted to Miss. State bar, 1924, practiced law in Eupora, Miss., 1925-29, Okolona, Miss., 1929—. Mayor, Eupora, Miss., 1927-29; elected dist. atty. 3d Jud. Dist. of Miss., 1935, re-elected, 1939; mem. 76th to 82d congresses from 4th Miss. Dist., 83d to 92d congresses from 1st Miss. Dist. Bd. dirs. Northeast Miss. Council. Mem. Okolona C. of C. (pres.), Miss. State, Chickasaw County bar assns., Lambda Chi Alpha. Democrat. Methodist. Mason (Shriner). Club: Okolona Exchange. Home: Okolona MS 38860 Office: House Office Bldg Washington DC 20036

ABERNETHY, WILBUR MURRAH, dentist; b. Troy, Miss., June 28, 1910; s. Bobby Luster and Nelle Olive (Dunlap) A.; student Chickasaw Coll., Pontotoc, Miss., 1929; B.A., U. Miss., 1933, postgrad., 1958; D.D.S., U. Tenn., 1942; m. Jamie C. Hickman, July 24, 1941; children— Sylvia Nelle (Mrs. William Byron Harvey), Wilbur Murrah. Individual practice dentistry, Pontotoc, summer 1942, Oxford, Miss., 1946—. Served to maj. AUS, 1942-46. Mem. Lafayette County Alumni Assn. U. Miss. (past pres.), Oxford Jr. C. of C., Psi Omega, Pi Kappa Alpha. Baptist. Rotarian. Home: 1949 Douglass Dr Oxford MS 38655 Office: 419 S Lamar St Oxford MS 38655

ABERNETHY, WILLIAM HUBERT, pipe and foundry co. exec.; b. Dora, Ala., Jan. 3, 1920; s. Nathan Hubert and Sarah Haskell (Betts) A.; B.S., Auburn U., 1942; m. Robert Dean Lightfoot, Dec. 23, 1941; children—Celia (Mrs. C. T. Benedict), William Dean. Chemist Goodyear Tire & Rubber Co., Akron, O., 1942-46; dist. mgr. chem.

div., Atlanta, 1949-52; chemist So. Research Inst., Birmingham, Ala., 1946-48; supt. paint plant Sloss Sheffield Steel & Iron Co., Birmingham, 1948-49; sales mgr. chem. div. U.S. Pipe & Foundry Co., Birmingham, 1952—. Active Boy Scouts Am. Mem. Am. Chem. Soc., Am. Inst. Chemists, Pi Kappa Alpha, Phi Psi. Methodist (steward 1943-71). Clubs: Optimist, Vestavia Country, Downtown (Birmingham). Home: 2904 Ryecroft Rd Birmingham AL 35223 Office: 3300 1st Av N Birmingham AL 35202

ABETTI, PIER ANTONIO, elec. co. exec.; b. Florence, Italy, Feb. 7, 1921; s. Giorgio and Anna (Garrino) A.; Dr. Engring., U. Pisa (Italy), 1946; M.S. in E.E., Ill. Inst. Tech., 1948, Ph.D. in E.E., 1952; m. Elizabeth Burr Nelson, June 11, 1948; children—George Ernest, Frank Anthony. Came to U.S., 1946, naturalized, 1951. Engr. Italian State Rys., 1945-46; mgr. operations integration and programming power transformers Gen. Electric Co., Pittsfield, Mass., 1953-57, mgr. extra high voltage project, Pittsfield, 1957-60, mgr. elec. and information engring. lab., Schenectady, 1961-63, mgr. data communications project information systems, Phoenix, 1967-70, project mgr. new ventures communications systems, Lynchburg, Va., 1971—; asst. mng. dir. Univac div. Sperry Rand Internat., Lausanne, Switzerland, 1967-70; instr. Ill. Inst. Tech., 1946-48; adj. prof. Rensselaer Poly. Inst., 1951; non-resident instr. Mass. Inst. Tech., 1952-59; instr. Berkshire Community Coll., 1959-60. Pres. Berkshire Film Soc., 1953-58; chmn. Volta Scholarship bd. trustees 1953-71. Recipient Coffin award Gen. Electric Co., 1952; Recognition award Eta Kappa Nu, 1953, Internat. prize Montefiore, Belgium, 1956. Mem. I.E.E.E., Nat. Ry. Hist. Soc. Club: Oakwood Country (Lynchburg). Contbr. articles profl. jours. Home: Apt 421 5001 Boonsboro Rd Lynchburg VA 24503 Office: Gen Electric Communication Systems Div Mountain View Rd Lynchburg VA 24502

ABIDIN, RICHARD ROBERT, JR., psychologist, educator; b. N.Y.C., Sept. 5, 1938; s. Richard S. and Anna (Gennaro) A.; B.A., Rutgers U., 1960, M.Ed., 1962, Ed.D., 1964; m. Mary Louise Caiaccio, May 30, 1958; children—Richard Robert, Lynn, Michael, Joseph. Clin. sychologist USAF Wilford Hall Hosp., San Antonio, 1964-67; asst. prof. U. Va., Charlottesville, 1967—; child-clin. psychologist Bexar County Guidance Center, San Antonio, 1965-67; cons. Va. Dept. Edn., 1967-69, U.S. Office Edn., 1969—. Mem. Charlottesville-Albemarle Mental Health Bd., 1969-70. Bd. dirs. Oakland Farm Sch. Served to capt. USAF, 1964-67. Diplomate Am. Bd. Psychologists. Mem. Am., Va. psychol. assns., Internat. Soc. Study Symbols (treas., dir.), Beta Theta Pi, Phi Delta Kappa, Kappa Delta Pi. Home: 2915 Idlewood Dr Charlottesville VA 22901

ABLON, ARNOLD NORMAN, accountant; b. Ft. Worth, July 21, 1921; s. Esir R. and Hazel (Dreeben) A.; B.S., La. State U., 1941; M.B.A., Northwestern, 1942; m. Carol Sarbin, July 25, 1962; children—Jan Ellen, Elizabeth Jane, William Neal, Robert Jack. Lectr. accounting So. Methodist U., 1946-47; auditor Levine's Dept. Stores, 1947-49; accountant Peat, Marwick, Mitchell & Co., 1946-47; sr. partner Arnold N. Ablon and Co., C.P.A.'s, Dallas, 1949—; partner Troth & Ablon, investments; dir. Mangum Mfg. Co., Troth Enterprises, Inc., 1st Continental Enterprises, Inc., Wolf Textile Co. Served as capt. F.A., AUS, World War II. Mem. Am. Inst. C.P.A.'s, Tex. Soc. C.P.A.'s, Nat. Assn. Accountants. Mason (Shriner). Clubs: Variety International, Dallas Athletic, Columbian. Home: 6929 Prestonshire Lane Dallas TX 75225 Office: Republic Nat Bank Bldg Dallas TX 75201

ABNEY, JAMES MARION, JR., dentist; b. Macon, Ga., Oct. 14, 1939; s. James Marion and Mae (Lockeby) A.; A.B., Emory U., 1961, D.D.S., 1966; m. Sandra Stewman, June 22, 1963; children—Marian Lynn, Mary Kate. Individual practice dentistry, Smyrna, Ga., 1968—; asso. prof. Emory U. Sch. Dentistry, 1968-70; asst. chief dental service Cobb Gen. Hosp., 1971—, cons. gen. dentistry cleft palate team. Mem. Cobb County C. of C., Am., Ga. dental assns., Northwestern Dist., Cobb County dental socs., Atlanta Gnathological Soc., Psi Omega, Sigma Alpha Epsilon. Republican. Episcopalian. Club: Indian Hills Golf and Country (Marietta, Ga.). Home: 333 Hunters Ridge Marietta GA 30060 Office: 2131 Old Concord Rd Smyrna GA 30080

ABOUSSIE, TANAL ALBERT, audiovisual co. exec.; b. Duke, Okla., Jan. 27, 1918; s. Albert M. and Kamala (Haddad) A.; pre-law degree, Hardin, 1939; student Tex. U., 1939-41; m. Gloria Jabara, Apr. 25, 1945; children—Richard, Patricia and Pamela (twins). Dispatcher, Victory Field, Vernon, Tex., 1940-42; agt. OPA, 1942-45; owner retail Childrens Wear & Shoe Store, Wichita, Kan., 1945-55; pres. Jet, Inc., Wichita, 1955-58; pres. Aboussie Bros. Audio-Visual Systems, Inc., Wichita, 1958-67, firm merged with Sylvania Co., 1967, nat. sales mgr., 1967-68; co. merged with LTV Edn. Systems, Inc., 1968, pres., 1968—. Pres., Arotex Uniform Co., Wichita; pres. Community Devel. Co., Wichita. Bd. dirs. Arthritis and Rheumatism Found. Active Boy Scouts Am. Mem. C. of C., YMCA. Mason (Shriner), Moose, Lion. Research in physiological monitoring and devel. of special patient to nurse hosp. communications; research and devel. ednl. TV systems and ednl. TV distbn. systems. Home: Preston Towers Suite 2801 6211 W Northwest Hwy Dallas TX 75201 Office: Suite 502 Fidelity Union Tower Dallas TX 75201

ABRAHAM, CLAUDE KURT, educator; b. Lorsch, Germany, Dec. 13, 1931; s. Siegmund and Johanna (Wachenheimer) A.; brought to U.S., 1946, naturalized, 1952; A.B., U. Cin., 1953, M.A., 1956; Ph.D., Ind. U., 1959; m. Marcia Edythe Phillips, June 3, 1956; children—Susan, Stephen, Catherine, Linda. Instr. French, U. Ill., 1959-62, asst. prof., 1962-64; asso. prof. French, U. Fla., Gainesville, 1964-70, prof., 1970—. Served with AUS, 1953-55. Nat. Endowment for the Humanities grantee, 1969; recipient award South-Atlantic Modern Language Assn., 1970. Mem. Modern Lang. Assn. (bibliography com. 1960-66), Midwest Modern Lang. Assn. (chmn. French I, 1964), South-Atlantic Modern Lang. Assn. (chmn. French I, 1969), Am. Assn. Tchrs. French (chpt. pres. 1971—), Am. Council Teaching Fgn. Langs. (adv. assembly 1968-69), Conf. on 17th Century French Lit. (exec. council 1972). Author: Gaston d'Orleans et sa cour, 1963, rev. 1964; The Strangers, 1966, Enfin Malherbe, 1971. Contbr. articles to profl. pubs. Home: 1820 N W 46th St Gainesville FL 32601

ABRAHAM, MALOUF, JR., physician; b. Canadian, Tex., Mar. 29, 1939; s. Malouf and Iris (Lewis) A.; B.S., Trinity U., 1960; M.D., U. Tex., 1964; m. Therese Ann Browne, Dec. 28, 1963; children—Edward, Salem, Jason. Intern Meml. Hosp. of Chatham County, Savannah, Ga., 1964-65; individual practice medicine, Canadian, 1968—. Dir. 1st State Bank of Canadian. Active conservation and restoration of hist. sites. Served with USAF, 1965-67. Named outstanding young man of year, Canadian, 1970. Mem. A.M.A., Tex. Med. Assn., Am. Acad. Family Practice, Canadian C. of C. (dir.). Republican. Episcopalian. Home: 1519 Willard St Canadian TX 79014 Office: 720 Ash St Canadian TX 79014

ABRAHAMSON, JOHN DEINHART, govt. ofcl.; b. Chisholm, Minn., Oct. 10, 1909; s. John C. and Ida Mary (Koponen) A.; student Eastern Mont. State Coll., 1929-31; A.B., U. Chgo., 1935, S.M., 1936; postgrad. U. Wis., 1936-37, U. Mich., 1940-41; m. Erna Emelia Kuehn, June 12, 1938; 1 dau., Karen Elaine. Econ. geologist Ogden Engring. Co., 1934-40; chief div. maps and graphics OSS and Fgn. Econ. Adminstrn., 1942-45; chief econ. resources br. Mo. River Basin, U.S. Bur. Reclamation, Billings, Mont., 1946-53, economist econ. div. project devel., Washington, 1953-55; economist area devel. div. U.S. Dept. Commerce, 1956-58; asst. chief economist econs. br. U.S. Bur. Comml. Fisheries, 1958-62; asst. chief project devel. staff Bur. Indian Affairs, Washington, 1962-65, economist, 1965—, dir. Indian Bus. Devel. Fund, 1970-71. Professorial lectr. George Washington U., 1954-55; cons. Fed. Field Com. for Devel. Planning in Alaska, 1967; cons. to minister Dept. Industry and Commerce, Prov. Man., Can., 1964, 68. Mem. Am. Geog. Soc. N.Y., Assn. Am. Geographers, Internat. Platform Assn., Am. Econs. Assn., Phi Beta Kappa, Sigma Xi. Mason (Shriner). Conglist. (chmn. bd. trustees 1969). Author: (with Carl Hoffman) Exempt Trucking Fresh and Frozen Fish and Shellfish in Interstate Commerce, 1960; A Program for Economic Development Involving People of Indian Ancestry in Northern Manitoba, 1964; Westward Alaska, The Native Economy And Its Resource Base, 1968. Home: 3127 Patterson Pl NW Washington DC 20015 Office: 1951 Constitution Av NW Washington DC 20240

ABRAHAMSON, LAWRENCE PAUL, research entomologist; b. Sturgeon Bay, Wis., Oct. 9, 1941; s. Walter Herman and Muriel (Potier) A.; B.S. in Forestry with honors, Mich. Technol. U., 1964; M.S. in Entomology, U. Wis., 1967, Ph.D., 1969; m. Margaret Mary LaTendresse, Sept. 7, 1963; children—Maria Jean, Teri Ann, Ann Marie. Research asst. Mich. Technol. U., Houghton, 1962-64; grad. research asst. U. Wis., Madison, 1964-68; research entomologist hardwood entomology Forest Service So. Hardwoods Lab., U.S. Dept. Agr., Stoneville, Miss., 1968—. NSF grantee, 1963-64; named Outstanding Sr. Forestry Student, 1964. Mem. Am., Can. entomol. socs., Soc. Am. Foresters, Sigma Xi, Gamma Sigma Delta. Roman Catholic. Home: 105 Lysbeth St Leland MS 38756 Office: So Woods Lab Forest Service Stoneville MS 38776

ABRAMS, MAYNARD ALVIN, lawyer; b. Chgo., Nov. 15, 1916; s. Isador John and Pauline (Feldman) A.; student U. Fla., 1934-36; J.D., U. Miami, 1950; m. Gertrude Mendelson, Apr. 11, 1945; children—Michael Lee, Susan (Mrs. Kenneth Heyder), Jeffrey Alan. Owner, prin. Hollywood Airport (Fla.), 1946-50; admitted to Fla. bar, 1950; since practiced in Hollywood; partner firm Abrams, Anton, Robbins, Resnick and Schneider. Chmn. bd. 1st Nat. Bank Hollywood, 1st Nat. Bank Hallandale (Fla.); dir. Lawyers' Title Services, Fort Lauderdale, Fla., 1967-69. Pres. Broward County League Municipalities, 1959-60. Commr. City Hollywood, 1959-66, mayor, 1966-69. Mem. exec. bd. So. Fla. council Boy Scouts Am., 1968—. Served with AAC, 1943-45. Named Hon. Seminole Chief, 1969; recipient Citizen Year award Hollywood, 1963; Eleanor Roosevelt Israel Humanitarian award, 1964. Mem. S. Broward Bar Assn. (past bd. dirs.), Am. Legion, Tau Epsilon Phi. Democrat. Elk. Club: Civitan (Hollywood). Home: 1231 Adams St Hollywood FL 33020 Office: PO Box 650 1720 Harrison St Hollywood FL 33022

ABRAMSON, DEBORA ROSE, librarian; b. Baton Rouge, Dec. 20, 1902; d. Abe and Mathilde (Mendelsohn) Abramson; B.A., La. State U., 1924; B.L.S., Columbia, 1929. Tchr., Istrouma High Sch., Baton Rouge, 1925-28; librarian Univ. Lab. High Sch., Oxford, Miss., 1929-30; asst. state librarian La. State Library (La. Library Commn. until 1946), Baton Rouge, 1930-69. Instr. in L.S., Tulane U., summers 1930, 31; mem. La. State Bd. Library Examiners, 1933-65. Mem. A.L.A. (past mem. membership com., Lippincott award com.), La. (pres. 1938-39, mem. various coms.), Southwestern library assns., Am. Assn. State Libraries (nominating com. 1962, legislation liaison com. 1963-66). Home: 833 N 11th St Baton Rouge LA 70802

ABRAMSON, MORRIE KAPLAN, electronics co. exec.; b. Houston, Dec. 28, 1934; s. Albert and Pearl (Kaplan) A.; student U. Tex., 1952-54; B.B.A., U. Houston, 1956; m. Rolaine Segal, July 1, 1962; children—Karen Hope, Beth Ellen. With Sterling Electronics Corp., Houston, 1954—, sales tng., 1954-56, field sales work, 1956-58, sales mgr., 1958-61, v.p., sec., 1961-67, exec. v.p., 1967—, dir., 1963—. Campaign worker United Fund, 1962-63, United Jewish Appeal, 1962-65. Mem. Houston C. of C., Nat. Electronic Distbrs. Assn., Phi Sigma Delta. Jewish religion. Club: Westwood Country. Home: 5622 Jackwood St Houston TX 77035 Office: 4201 Southwest Freeway PO Box 1229 Houston TX 77027

ABRAMSON, SAMUEL RALPH, physician; b. Lafayette, La., Mar. 12, 1917; s. Nathan and Ula (Coronna) A.; B.S., U. Southwestern La., 1937; M.D., Tulane U., 1939; m. Gwen Daly, Oct. 19, 1953; children—Ralph Keith, Robert Coronna, Suzanne Denise. Intern Touro Infirmary, New Orleans, 1939, resident in surgery, 1940-41; gen. practice medicine, Marksville, La., 1946—. Vice pres. Union Bank, Marksville, 1968—. Mem. Avoyelles Parish Sch. Bd., 1960-66, pres., 1960-62. Chmn. State Central Com. Am. party of La., 1969—; coordinator Wallace campaign for Pres., La., 1968. Served with M.C., AUS, 1941-46; MTO. Diplomate Am. Bd. Family Practice. Mem. A.M.A., Am. Assn. Physicians and Surgeons, Am. Physicians Guild, La. Physicians Guild, Am. Assn. Ry. Surgeons, So. Med. Assn., La., Avoyelles Parish med. socs., La. Acad. Gen. Practice, John Birch Soc. (chpt. leader). Home: 608 S Washington Marksville LA 71351 Office: 423 N Washington Marksville LA 71351

ABREGO, GILBERT FREDERICK, JR., accountant; b. Mission, Tex., Jan. 5, 1934; s. Gilbert Frederick and Geraldine (Meister) A.; B.S. in Indsl. Engring. and Indsl. Mgmt., U. Ark., 1956; m. Mary Ann Walker, June 15, 1956; children—Frederick Douglas, Anne Meister. Jr. accountant Douglas Walker & Co., Fort Smith, Ark., 1959-64, jr. partner, 1964-65, gen. partner, 1965—. Finance officer Fort Smith Civil Air Patrol, 1965—; treas., dir. Fort Smith Art Center, 1967; mem. Western Ark. Estate Planning Council, 1967—; coach Ch. League Baseball, 1967; mem. finance com. Mt. Magazine council Girl Scouts U.S.A., 1967-68. Served to capt. USAFR, 1956-59. C.P.A., Ark. Mem. Am. Inst. C.P.A.'s (financial mgmt. and controls com. 1968-69), Ark. Soc. C.P.A.'s (dir. 1969-71, pres. western Ark. chpt. 1967-68), C.P.A. Assos. (practice mgmt. com. 1968-69), Nat. Assn. Accountants (treas., dir. 1966-67), Air Force Assn., Fort Smith C. of C. (vice chmn. aviation com. 1966-67), Sigma Nu. Lutheran. Clubs: Town of Fort Smith, Hardscrabble Country (Fort Smith). Home: 4325 S P St Fort Smith AR 72901 Office: Mchts Bank Bldg Fort Smith AR 72901

ABSHER, LEE ALTON, physician; b. Sugar Grove, Tenn., Jan. 26, 1905; s. Lytle Asberry and Ella Harriet (Perdue) A.; B.S., U. Tenn., 1927, M.D., 1928; m. Della Lucille Cathey, Mar. 25, 1931 (dec. Jan. 1952). Extern Shelby County Hosp., Memphis, 1926-28; intern Knoxville (Tenn.) Gen. Hosp., 1928-29; surg. preceptor, Newport News, Va., 1929-30; practice medicine and surgery, Portland, Tenn., 1931-38; practice medicine and surgery, Midland, Tex., 1938-42, also part owner Western Clinic Hosp.; practice medicine and surgery, Knoxville, 1946—; mem. staff Ft. Sanders Presbyn. Hosp., Knoxville, St. Mary's Meml. Hosp., Knoxville, East Tenn. Bapt. Hosp., Knoxville, U. Tenn. Meml. Hosp., Knoxville. Served from capt. to maj., M.C., AUS, World War II; ETO. Mem. Am. Acad. Gen. Practice, A.M.A., So., Tenn. med. assns., Knoxville Acad. Medicine, Tenn. Soc. S.O.R., Scabbard and Blade, Sigma Nu, Alpha Kappa Kappa. Democrat. Baptist. Mason. Clubs: University Tennessee President's (founding mem.), Cherokee Country (Knoxville). Editor: Some Early Settlers of Upper Sumner County, Tennessee, 1966. Office: 3501 Broadway NE Knoxville TN 37917 Home: 2408 N Park Blvd Knoxville TN 37917

ABSHIRE, DAVID MANKER, govt. ofcl.; b. Chattanooga, Apr. 11, 1926; s. James Ernest and Edith Manker (Patten) A.; B.A., U.S. Mil. Acad., 1951; Ph.D., Georgetown U., 1959; m. Carolyn Lamar Sample, Sept. 7, 1957; children—Lupton, Anna, Mary Lee, Phyllis. Dir. research Republican policy com. Ho. of Reps., Washington, 1958-60; dir. spl. projects Am. Enterprise Inst., Washington, 1961-62; exec. dir. Center for Strategic and Internat. Studies, Georgetown U., Washington, 1962-70; asst. sec. state for congl. relations State Dept., Washington, 1970—. Served to 1st lt. AUS, 1951-55; capt. Res. Decorated Bronze Star with oak leaf cluster. Mem. Fgn. Policy Assn., Am. Acad. Polit. and Social Scis. Episcopalian. Clubs: Chevy Chase, International, Army and Navy (Washington); Metropolitan (N.Y.C.). Author: The South Rejects a Prophet: The Life of Senator D.M. Key 1824-1900, 1967; (with R.V. Allen) National Security: Political, Military and Economic Strategies in the Decade Ahead, 1963; editor, author Portuguese Africa: A Handbook, 1969. Home: 311 S St Asaph St Alexandria VA 22314 Office: Dept State Room 7256 21st & C Sts NW Washington DC 20520

ACCHIARDO, SERGIO ROBERTO, physician; b. Santiago, Chile, Nov. 17, 1933; s. Roberto and Carmela (Montenegro) A.; student Nat. Inst., Santiago, 1945-51, Sch. Medicine, U. Chile, 1952-58; m. Maria Angelica Rojas, Jan. 9, 1960; children—Maria Dolores, Sergio Rodriego, Maria Soledad, Roberto Jose. Came to U.S., 1967. Intern Salvador Hosp., Santiago, 1959, resident, 1960-62, physician, 1957-62, 65-66; physician Cleve. Clinic, 1967-70; dir. Artificial Kidney Center, U. Tenn., Memphis, 1970—, asst. prof. medicine, 1970—. Mem. sci. adv. bd. Kidney Found. Tenn., 1970—; mem. Nat. Kidney Found., 1969—. Served with Chilean Army, 1963-66. Mem. Am. Soc. Nephrology, Internat. Soc. Nephrology, European Dialysis and Transplantation Soc. Home: 2295 Lancashire Cove Germantown TN 38138 Office: 951 Court Av Memphis TN 38103

ACHEE, ROLAND JOSEPH, lawyer; b. New Orleans, Dec. 12, 1922; s. Benjamin Elphege and Marie J. (Cazenave) A.; B.A., Centenary Coll., 1944; LL.B., La. State U., 1949; m. Jean W. Lant, Feb. 19, 1955; 1 dau., Marie Alaine. Admitted to La. bar, 1949; practiced in Shreveport, 1949—; partner Ferris & Achee, attys., 1952—. Chmn. Draft Bd., Shreveport, 1964-67, vice chmn., 1967—. Served to lt. (j.g.) USNR, 1944-46. Mem. Am., La., Shreveport (exec. com. 1964-65) bar assns., La. State Law Inst. (jr. hon.), Centenary Coll. Alumni Assn. (dir. 1969—), 40 and 8, Am. Legion (post comdr. 1961-62), Order of Coif, Omicron Delta Kappa. Elk (Shreveport exalted ruler 1958-59, trustee 1959-69). Editor-in-chief La. Law Review, 1948. Home: 182 Bruce Av Shreveport LA 71101 Office: Johnson Bldg Shreveport LA 71101

ACHENBACH, GERALD HOPE, food chain exec.; b. Deer Lodge, Mont., June 9, 1910; s. Hope Francis and Martha Jane (Wood) A.; B.A., U. Wash., 1934; m. Sara Dean Jones, Dec. 25, 1945; children—Charles Henry II, Gerald Hope, Mary Dean, Ann Towers, John Wood. Partner A Vere Shaw & Co., investment counsel, N.Y.C., 1937-42; pres. Piggly Wiggly So., Inc., Vidalia, Ga., 1942—, Ga. Sales Co., Vidalia, 1943—, Green Realty Co., Vidalia, 1953—; dir. Seaboard Coastline Industries, Richmond, Va., Citizens & So. Nat. Bank, Atlanta. Chmn. bd. trustees Paul Anderson Youth Home, Inc., Vidalia; trustee Aiken Prep. Sch., Columbia Theol. Sem. Mem. Nat. Assn. Food Chains (chmn. bd. dirs. 1958-59, exec. com. 1952—), Nat. Piggly Wiggly Operators Assn. (pres. 1952-53), President's Assn., Am. Mgmt. Assn. (dir.), Southeastern Chain Store Council (pres. 1948-49), Nat. Assn. Food Research (pres. 1963-64), Ga. (dir.) Vidalia (pres. 1949, citizen of year 1949) chambers commerce, Amateur Field Trial Clubs Am. (pres. 1956-57), Presbyn. (elder 1945-68, trustee 1951-68, pres. Men Savannah Presbytery 1954). Clubs: Capital City (Atlanta); Oglethorpe (Savannah, Ga.); Vidalia Golf; Augusta (Ga.) Nat. Golf; Pine Valley Golf; Royal and Ancient (St. Andrews, Scotland). Home: Rocky Creek Farm Vidalia GA 30474 Office: 100 Brinson Rd Vidalia GA 30474

ACHESON, DAVID CAMPION, lawyer, former govt. ofcl.; b. Washington, Nov. 4, 1921; s. Dean G. and Alice (Stanley) A.; B.A., Yale, 1942; LL.B., Harvard 1948; m. Patricia Castles, May 1, 1943; children— Eleanor Dean, David Campion, Peter Wesley. Admitted to D.C. bar, U.S. Supreme Ct. bar; with Office Gen. Counsel, AEC, 1948-49; with firm Covington & Burling, Washington, 1949-61, mem. firm, 1958-61; U.S. atty. for D.C., 1961-65; spl. asst. to sec. treasury, 1965-67; v.p., gen. counsel Communications Satellite Corp., Washington, 1967—. Mem. Democratic Central Com. D.C., 1960-61. Democrat. Episcopalian. Clubs: Metropolitan, Yale (Washington); Century Assn. Home: 3101 Garfield St NW Washington DC 20008 Office: Comsat L'Enfant Plaza Washington DC 20024

ACKEL, FRED JOHN, dentist; b. Gloversville, N.Y., Mar. 28, 1927; s. Fred and Anna Azar (Ackel) A.; student Clarkson Coll. Tech., 1944-45, U.S. Merchant Marine Acad., 1945-46; B.S., Hartwick Coll., 1950; D.D.S., Georgetown U., 1954; m. Mildred Krause, July 15, 1950 (div. Oct. 1969); children—Debra Ann, Gary Fredric, Kimberly Jean. Individual practice dentistry, Ft. Lauderdale, Fla., 1957—. Mem. Fla. State Bd. Health, 1967-68; mem. Fla. State Racing Commn., 1968-71. Pres. Broward County Young Republicans, 1961-63; chmn. Young Ams. for Freedom, 1962-65; del. Rep. Nat. Conv., 1964; chmn. Citizens for Goldwater-Miller, Nat. Draft Goldwater Com., Broward County, 1964; chmn. Rep. Citizens Com., Broward County, 1965-71. Trustee Coral Oaks Med. Dental Bldg. Enterprises. Served from 1st lt. to capt. USAF, 1954-56. Mem. Acad. Gen. Dentistry, Am. Dental Assn. (chmn. dels. ann. meeting 1969), Navy League, Broward County Dental Soc. (pres. 1965-66), Fla. Dental Assn. Roman Catholic. K.C. Club: Coral Ridge Country (Ft. Lauderdale). Editor Broward County Dental Review, 1968—. Home: 4821 NE 26th Av Fort Lauderdale FL 33308 Office: 2655 E Oakland Park Blvd Fort Lauderdale FL 33306

ACKELL, EDMUND FERRIS, educator; b. Danbury, Conn., Nov. 29, 1925; s. Ferris M. and Barbara (Elias) A.; B.S., Holy Cross Coll., 1949; D.M.D., Tufts Coll., 1953; M.D., Western Res. U., 1962. Faculty Western Res. U., Cleve., 1957-66, asso. dean Sch. Dentistry, also chief, dental service, 1960-66, chmn. dept. oral surgery, 1962-66, asst. prof. oral pathology, 1960-66; dean Coll. Dentistry, U. Fla., 1966-69, v.p. for health affairs, U. Fla. Health Center, 1969—, also prof. surgery. Mem. Com. Health Professions Ednl. Facilities Program, USPHS; mem. Nat. Adv. Council on Edn. for Health Professions, Fla. Health Adv. Council for Comprehensive Health Planning. Served to lt. AC, USNR, 1943-46. Diplomate Am. Bd. Oral Surgery. Mem. Am. Dental Assn., A.M.A., Fla. Med. Assn., Fla. Dental Soc., Am. Pub. Health Assn. Home: 4341 Newberry Rd Gainesville FL 32601

ACKER, CHARLES EDWARD, airline exec.; b. Dallas, Apr. 7, 1929; s. Edward Morgan and Lois Jane (McCallum) A.; student North Tex. State U., 1945-46; B.A., So. Meth. U., 1950; m. Norma Higginbotham, Sept. 5, 1952; children—Richard Morgan, Mitchell Taylor, Nell. Vice pres. Lionel D. Edie & Co., Inc., 1958-64; v.p.

finance Gt. Am. Corp., Dallas, 1964—, also dir.; sr. v.p. planning and adminstrn. Braniff Internat., 1965—, also dir., exec. v.p. Braniff Airways, Inc., 1967-70, pres., chmn. operating officer, 1970—; dir. Am.-Amicable Life Ins. Co., Franklin Life Ins. Co., Gulf Life Ins. Co. Higginbotham Corp. Mem. All Sports Assn. Dallas, Dallas Good Neighbor Council. Mem. Dallas Assn. Investment Analysts, Dallas C. of Co., Newcomen Soc. N.Am., Alpha Tau Omega. Episcopalian. Clubs: Terpsichorean; Idlewild; Dallas Country; Brook Hollow Golf; Petroleum; Preston Trail Golf; Imperial. Home: 6023 St Andrew St Dallas TX 65205 Office: PO Box 35001 Dallas TX 75235

ACKER, WARREN HARLAN, petroleum co. exec.; b. Junction City, Kan., Mar. 21, 1919; s. Samuel and Anna (Jolitz) A.; B.S. in Chem. Engring., Kan. State Coll., 1942; m. Jacqueline Ann Folck, May 17, 1942; children—Mark E., Michael W. With Phillips Petroleum Co., Borger, Tex., 1946—, supt. mfg. Philback plant, 1964-65, mgr. plant, 1965—. Bd. dirs. A.R.C. Hutchinson County, United Fund, Borger. Served to lt. USNR, 1943-45. Mem. C. of C. (pres.). Methodist (past pres. bd. stewards). Patentee in field. Home: 305 Riney Dr Phillips TX 79071 Office: Box 1526 Borger TX 79007

ACKERMAN, DOROTHY ANNE PETERSEN, librarian; b. Richmond, Va., July 31, 1926; d. Arthur and Augusta (Geier) Petersen; B.A., McGill U., 1947; B.L.S., U. Chgo., 1948; M.A., Northwestern U., 1952; Diplome Sup. de Bibliothecaire (Fulbright scholar), Bibliotheque Nationale Academie de Paris, 1954; postgrad. Ohio State U., 1952-55; m. Stephen Hamilton Ackerman, Aug. 7, 1954. Asst. cataloger Evanston (Ill.) Pub. Library, 1948-52; modern lang. librarian Ohio State U. Library, Columbus, 1952-55; asst. Fort Jackson (S.C.) Post Library, 1955—. Instr. dept. fgn. langs. U. S.C., 1952-53, 54-55. Mem. Southeastern, S.C. library assns., Alpha Omicron Pi. Presbyn. Compiler: Catalog of the Talford P. Linn Collection, Ohio State U. Library, 1963. Home: 4141 Pinehaven Ct Columbia SC 29205 Office: Post Library Fort Jackson SC 29207

ACKERMAN, RICHARD HENRY, bishop; b. Pitts., Aug. 30, 1903; s. John and Josephine (Richard) A.; B.A., Duquesne U., 1923, Litt. D., 1961; student St. Mary's Seminary, Norwalk, Conn., U. Fribourg, Switzerland, U. Mich.; LL.D., Niagara U., 1953. Ordained priest Roman Cath. Ch., 1926; prof. philosophy, 1930-35, prin. high sch., 1935-40; nat. dir. Pontifical Assn. of Holy Childhood, internat. papal mission-aid soc. for benefit underprivileged children, 1940-56, pres. bd. dirs., v.p. superior council, Paris, France; consecrated titular bishop of Lares, auxiliary bishop of San Diego, 1956; vicar gen. Diocese of San Diego; bishop Covington, Ky., 1960—. Decorated Pro Ecclesiae et Pontifice, 1947. K.C. (4 deg.). Clubs: New York Athletic; Pittsburgh Athletic. Editor: The Paraclete, 1928-30; Annals of Holy Childhood, 1940-56. Address: 1140 Madison Av Covington KY

ACOSTA-MARTINEZ, FELIX, agriculturist; b. Vieques, P.R., Mar. 31, 1918; s. Juan Acosta Robertin and Teresa Martinez (Yimes) A.; B.S. in Agr., Mayaguez (P.R.) Coll. Agr., 1940; M.S. (C.A.A.M. fellow), Mich. State U., 1958; m. Carmen L. Santini, July 3, 1944; 1 dau., Carmen T. With Soil Conservation Service, U.S. Dept. Agr., Rio Piedras, P.R., 1941-42; agrl. agt., Barranquitas, Naguabo, Fajardo, P.R., 1942-57, asst. regional dir. Fajardo Dist., 1960—, counsellor com. in charge preparing overall socio-econ. devel. program, 1963. Recipient Outstanding Service award Agrl. Extension Service, 1962. Mem. Agronomist Coll. P.R. (pres., treas. Fajardo chpt. 1962-69), Epsilon Sigma Phi. Lion (pres. Fajardo, 1965; zone chmn. of P.R., 1970). Club: Cuna de Munoz Rivera Lodge (Barranquitas). Home: 174 9th St Fajardo PR 00648 Office: 6 Union St Fajardo PR 00648

ACREE, WILLIAM BYRNES, physician; b. Memphis, Dec. 8, 1919; s. George T. and Helen Hunt (Byrnes) A.; M.D., U. Tenn., 1942; m. Eva Kersenia McClintock, Dec. 20, 1942; children—William B., George Michael. Intern, Knoxville (Tenn.) Gen. Hosp., 1943; individual practice medicine, Ridgely, Tenn., 1946—. Pres. West Tenn. Heart Assn., 1966-67. Alderman City of Ridgely, 1961-71, vice mayor, 1966-71; magistrate Lake County, Tenn., 1966-71. Served to capt., M.C. AUS, 1942-46. Named Man of Year Ridgely, 1969. Mem. A.M.A., Am. Assn. Family Practice, N.Y. Acad. Scis., Tenn. Med. Assn., N.W. Tenn. Acad. Medicine (pres. 1965—), Royal Soc. Health. Mason, Rotarian (pres. 1956). Home: Hwy 78 Ridgely TN 38080 Office: 115 S Main Ridgely TN 38080

ACUFF, FREDERICK GENE, educator; b. Stinesville, Ind., Sept. 13, 1931; s. George and Beryl (Canada) A.; B.A., Manhattan Christian Coll., 1957; M.S., Kan. State U., 1959 Ph.D., U. Mo., 1967; m. Phyllis Jo Surface, June 3, 1962; children—Jo Shelley (Mrs. Thomas Friedemann), Rod Worth Smith, Gene Taylor. Teaching asst., research asso. Kan. State U., 1958-60; instr. sociology U. Mo., 1959-60: asst. prof. sociology Phillips U., 1960-62; asst. prof. sociology Okla. State U., Stillwater, 1962-67, asso. prof., 1968-69, prof., 1969—, acting chmn. dept. sociology, 1967-68, chmn., 1968—. Faculty Midwest Council Social Research In Aging. Served with AUS, 1952-54. NSF fellow, 1966-67. Mem. Am. Sociol. Assn., Mid-West, S.W. sociol. socs. Mem. Disciples of Christ Ch. (lay minister). Contbr. articles to profl. jours. Home: 10 Canyon Rim Pl Stillwater OK 74074

ADAIR, C. H., hosp. adminstr. Adminstr. G. Pierce Wood Meml. Hosp., Arcadia, Fla. Address: G Pierce Wood Meml Hosp Arcadia FL 33821*

ADAIR (WILLIAM) RALPH, cafeteria chain exec.; b. Temple, Okla., Apr. 19, 1908; s. James Williams and Margaret (Verhines) A.; student Southwestern Coll. Okla., 1925-28, Okla. U., 1931; m. Verna Elizabeth Pulley, May 4, 1933; children—James William, Gerald Paul, Reba Jane. Sales mgr. New State Ice Co., Oklahoma City, 1929-37; owner, gen. mgr. Eastside Ice Co., Oklahoma City, 1938-60, Bethany Ice Co., Oklahoma City, 1938-60; owner Ralph's Supermarket, Oklahoma City, 1948—. Oklahoma county commr., 1953—. Contbr. articles, polit. cartoons to newspapers. Home: 106 Lake Aluma St Oklahoma City OK 73121 Office: 320 Robert S Kerr St Oklahoma City OK 73102

ADAM, WALTER ERNEST, constrn. exec.; b. Stuart, Okla., Oct. 15, 1936; s. Herman Ernest and Jessie (Mason) A.; student Okla. U., 1955-56; B.S., Okla. State U., 1961; m. Carol Kay Durst, June 30, 1961; 1 dau., Erica Dianne. Constrn. engr. City of Ft. Worth, 1961-62; estimator Standard Industries, Tulsa, 1962; design engr. C.E., Tulsa, 1962-63; v.p. All-States Utilities, Inc., Tulsa, 1964—. Mem. Am. Soc. C.E., Okla. Soc. Profl. Engrs., Okla. Municipal Contractors (dir.). Democrat. Elk. Home: 11705 E First St Tulsa OK 74128 Office: Route 13 Box 413 Tulsa OK 74107

ADAMEC, CHARLES JOSEPH, former educator; b. N.Y.C., June 7, 1895; s. Vincent and Antoinette (Skokan) A.; B.A., Yale, 1917, Ph.D., 1921; m. Edith Beatrice Teal, June 19, 1926. Asst. prof. Classical langs., Alfred (N.Y.) U., 1921-23, prof., 1923-25; asst. prof. classics, Knox Coll., 1925-29, prof. 1929-60, chmn. dept. classics, 1929-36, 46-60, admissions officer, 1928-34, dean freshmen, 1930-36, dean, 1936-46, civilian instr. math. A.A.F. Tech. Tng. Comd., 1943-46; study and travel in Italy, 1949-50, Greece and the Mediterranean Area, 1956-57. Served in U.S. Army, 1917-18. Mem. Am. Philol. Assn., Linguistic Soc. Am., Classical Assn. of Middle West and South, Ill. Classical Conf., Scabbard and Blade, Phi Beta Kappa, Phi Sigma Kappa. Conglist. Home: Calzada Obrero Mundial 155-402 Colonia del Valle Mexico City 12 Mexico

ADAMS, ADDISON (ADDIE) FRANK, land title abstracter; b. Abbott, Texas, Jan. 3, 1904; s. John Blair and Addie Frances (Forrest) A.; student Baylor U., Waco, Tex., 1922-24; grad. Sch. Social Sci., Civic Fedn., Dallas, 1937; m. Iva Dell Miller, Oct. 14, 1928 (div. 1930); 1 son John Blair; m. 2d Beulah Grace Jenkins, Dec. 26, 1938; children—Forrest Jenkins, Alice Ann. Resident mgr. R. C. Winters and Co., C.P.A.'s, McCamey, Tex., 1926-30; asso. F. A. Hornbeck, gen. land agt. Kansas City, Mexico and Orient R.R., 1926-30; pub. accountant, 1930-36; investigator Tex. Old Age Assistance Commn., 1936-40; sec.-mgr. Bastrop County Abstract Co., Bastrop, Tex., 1940-59, pres., 1960—. Mem. Am., Tex. land title assns., Am. Assn. Petroleum Landmen, Tex. Geneal. Soc. Baptist. Address: 1707 Pecan St Bastrop TX 78602

ADAMS, A(LFRED) HUGH, coll. pres.; Punta Gorda, Fla., Mar. 8, 1928; s. Alfred and Irene (Gatewood) A.; B.S., Fla. State U., 1950, M.S., 1956, Ed.D., 1962; m. Joyce Morgan, Nov. 11, 1954; children—Joy, Al, Paul. Asst. dean of men, asst. prof. edn. Fla. State U., 1962-64; supt. pub. instrn. Charlotte County, Fla., 1965-68; vice chmn., coordinator Gov.'s Commn. for Quality Edn., 1968; pres. Broward Community Coll., Ft. Lauderdale, Fla., 1968—. Founding pres. Educators Investment Corp. Fla.; mem. regional council Southeastern Edn. Corp., 1966-69; trustee South Fla. Edn. Center, Inc., Pub. Service TV. Del. U.S. Dept. State Nat. Fgn. Policy Conf. for Edn. Leaders, 1968; mem. Fla. State Tchr. Edn. Adv. Council, Profl. Practices Commn.; mem. Fla. Inter-agy. Law Enforcement Planning Council. Bd. dirs. United Fund, Broward chpt. A.R.C. Served to comdr. USNR, 1945-72. Mem. N.E.A., Am. Assn. Sch. Adminstrs., Fla. Assn. Deans and Counselors, Greater Ft. Lauderdale C. of C. (dir.), Omicron Delta Kappa. Kiwanian. Club: Metropolitan Dinner (Ft. Lauderdale). Home: 105 N Victoria Park Fort Lauderdale FL 33301

ADAMS, ALLEN THOMAS, textile co. exec.; b. Commerce, Ga., Oct. 3, 1922; s. Lloyd Thomas and Elizabeth (Allen) A.; B.S., Clemson Coll., 1945; m. LaVera Blankenship, Jan. 19, 1946; children—Dana Thomas, Bryan Stephan. Trainee, J.P. Stevens & Co., Greenville, S.C., 1946-50, textile designer, 1950-57; plant engr. Calloway Mills, LaGrange, Ga., 1957-62, plant supt., 1962-63; plant supt. Chicopee Mfg. Co., textiles, Cornelia, Ga., 1963-65, plant mgr., 1965—. Instl. rep. N.E. Ga. council Boy Scouts Am., 1969-72; finance chmn. Habersham County YMCA, 1970-72. Bd. dirs. Habersham County Cancer Crusade, chmn. bd., 1971. Served with AUS, 1943. Mem. Clemson Alumni Assn., Alpha Phi Omega. Baptist (chmn. bd. deacons 1970-72). Mason. Club: Skitt Mountain Country (Cleveland, Ga.). Home: Route 2 Box 271 Cornelia GA 30531 Office: Chicopee Mfg Co Cornelia GA 30531

ADAMS, CURTIS HARPER, educator; b. DeKalb, Miss., Sept. 12, 1917; s. Samuel Gully and Ada Pearl (Peden) A.; B.S. with highest honors, Miss. State U., 1941; grad. Army Command and Gen. Staff Coll., 1944; M.S. in Edn., Henderson State U., 1963; Ph.D. in Entomology, Miss. State U., 1965; m. Billie Louise Watson, Aug. 8, 1942; 1 son, Curtis Harper. Entomol. field asst. U.S. Dept. Agr., State College, Miss., 1938; entomol. field aide Miss. Plant Bd., State College, 1939; owner-mgr. Adams Exterminating Co., Columbia, S.C., 1946-48; post comdr. Fuesson (Germany) Post, U.S. Army, 1949-51; asso. prof. mil. sci. The Citadel, Charleston, S.C., 1951-54; chief logistics officer Ft. Richardson, Alaska, 1955-56; inf. bn. comdr., Ft. Lewis, Wash., 1957; sr. adviser inf. div., Korea, 1958; dep. post Comdr. Schofield Barracks, 1959-60; prof., head dept. mil. sci. Henderson State Coll., Adelphia, Ark., 1961-63; research asst. Boll Weevil research lab. U.S. Dept. Agr., State College, Miss., 1963-65; asso. prof. biology U. Ala., Huntsville, 1965—. Cons. test reliability lab. Army Missile Command, Redstone Arsenal, Huntsville, 1967—. Mem. nursing edn. adv. com. John C. Calhoun Jr. Coll., Decatur, Ala., 1967-70, Regional Comprehensive Health Planning Council, Top of Ala. Regional Council Govts., 1970—, Health Career Council Ala., 1969—, Ala. Environmental Edn. Adv. Council, 1972—. Mem. Huntsville Opera Soc., 1968—, Huntsville Community Concert Assn., 1969—. Bd. dirs. Huntsville Symphony Assn. Served with AUS, 1941-46, 48-63. Mem. Am. Inst. Biol. Sci., Entomol. Soc. Am., Wildlife Soc., A.A.A.S., Assn. Southeastern Biologists, Ala. Acad. Sci., Ala. Wildlife Fedn., North Ala. Conservation League (pres. 1970—), Ala. Conservancy, Smithsonian Assos., Res., Ret. Officers assns., Nat. Assn. Uniformed Services, Sigma Xi, Phi Kappa Phi. Mason (Shriner), Kiwanian. Contbr. articles to profl. jours. Home: 1703 Stonehurst Dr Huntsville AL 35801 Office: PO Box 1247 Huntsville AL 35807

ADAMS, CYRIL SAMUEL, cons. engr.; b. Austin, Tex., Oct. 2, 1938; s. Cyril S. and Ida (Goldberg) A.; B.S. in Civil Engring., Texas. A. and M. U., 1961, B.B.A., 1961; m. Michelle Vergara, Sept. 14, 1962; children—Simone Louise, Susan Michelle. Engr. Cyril S. Adams Inc., Houston, 1963-64, pres., 1964—; dir. Insular Products, Houston, 1968—. Mem. Am. Soc. C.E., Cons. Engrs. Council. Address: 11703 Flintwood St Houston TX 77024

ADAMS, DONALD JOE, geologist; b. Lyons, Kan., Sept. 7, 1935; s. Arthur Lincoln and Frances Irene (Robbins) A.; B.S., U. Kan., 1958, M.S., 1959; m. Kathryn Sue Sieckmann, Nov. 16, 1963; children—Amy Elizabeth, Stephanie Kay. Geologist, Phillips Petroleum Co., 1959-66, Amarillo, Tex., 1961-62, Denver, 1962-64, Bartlesville, Okla. 1964-65, Oklahoma City, 1965-66; sr. geologist Monsanto Co., Oklahoma City, 1966—. Served with AUS, 1959. Mem. Oklahoma City Geol. Soc., Am. Assn. Petroleum Geologists, Sigma Xi, Phi Kappa Psi. Republican. Methodist. Home: 2517 NW 117th St Oklahoma City OK 73120 Office: 3545 NW 58th St Oklahoma City OK 73112

ADAMS, DONALD PAUL, banker; b. Chauvin, La., Mar. 31, 1939; s. Clarence J. and Thelma (Pellegrin) A.; grad. Dale Carnegie Course, 1958; grad. Sch. of Banking of South, La. State U., 1972; m. Loretta Roberts, Dec. 28, 1957; children—Bryan, Debra, Lisa, Keith. Bookkeeper Terrebonne & Trust Co., Houma, La., 1957, teller, 1958, exchange window teller, 1959, note teller, 1960, asst. br. mgr., 1961, br. mgr., 1962, asst. cashier, 1963-68, asst. v.p., 1968-69, sr. v.p., br. bank adminstr., 1971—; owner Goodwill Advt. Co., 1965—, Bankers Advt. Service, 1967—, House of Gifts, 1968—, Income Protection Plan, 1967—, Adams Pub. House, 1969— (all Chauvin, La.); v.p. Adams & Lecompte Inc., Chauvin, 1966—, Co-chmn. Terrebonne Parish March of Dimes, 1968—; dir. Terrebonne Parish Recreation Dist. 7, 1966—. Mem. Advt. Specialty Inst., Houma-Terrebonne C. of C. Roman Catholic (chmn. finance com.). K.C. (4 deg.). Home: Rte 1 Box 362-A Chauvin LA 70344 Office: PO Box 173 Chauvin LA 70344

ADAMS, EDWARD, wholesale trade co. exec.; b. Bay City, Tex., Mar. 27, 1925; s. Robert Edward and Allie May (Worrell) A.; student pub. schs.; m. Emily Ruth Francis, Jan. 16, 1945; children—Gloria (Mrs. James Buchanan), Robert, Barbara (Mrs. Michael Skehan), Patricia, Betty, Trudy, Sherry, Marie. Foreman, Centeral Power & Light Co., Bay City, 1947-49; terminal mgr. Newsom Truck Line, Lake Charles, La., 1950-56; traffic mgr. Tex-Tube Mfg. Co., Houston, 1957-60, mgr. Pipe Distributors, Inc., 1960—, v.p., 1972—; chmn. bd. ABA Enterprizes, Inc., Houston; partner Lakewood Coin Co., Houston, 1970—. Pastor, Faith Temple, Houston, 1960-64. Served with AUS, 1945. Mem. Internat. Ministerial Assn. (credential com. 1968—). Club: President's Health (Houston). Home: 4706 Hollybrook St Houston TX 77039 Office: 5400 Mesa St Houston TX 77028

ADAMS, ELIE MAYNARD, educator; b. Clarkton, Va., Dec. 29, 1919; s. Wade Hampton and Bessie (Calloway) A.; B.A., U. Richmond, 1941; M.A., 1944; B.D., Colgate-Rochester Div. Sch., 1944; M.A. (Colgate-Rochester grad. scholar 1944-45, Ayer fellow from Colgate-Rochester 1945-47, James H. Woods fellow 1944-46), Harvard, 1947, Ph.D., 1948; m. Phyllis Margaret Stevenson, Dec. 22, 1942; children—Steven Maynard, Jill Elaine. Asst. prof. philosophy Ohio U., 1947-48; asst. prof. U. N.C., 1948-53, asso. prof., 1953-58, prof., 1958-71, Kenan prof., 1971—, chmn. dept. philosophy, 1960-65, dir. curriculum on peace, war and def., 1970-72, dir. Free World Inst., 1951; vis. prof. U. So. Cal., 1966, State U. N.Y., 1971. Recipient Thomas Jefferson award U.N.C., 1971. Mem. Mind Assn., Am. Philos. Assn. (mem. exec. com. Eastern div. 1961-64, chmn. program com. 1965), N.C. Philos. Soc. (past pres.), So. Soc. Philosophy and Psychology (exec. council 1963-66, pres. 1968-69). Author: The Fundamentals of General Logic, 1954; Logic Problems, 1954; The Language of Value (with others), 1957; Ethical Naturalism and the Modern World View, 1960; articles in philos. jours. Editor: Categorical Analysis: Selected Essays of Everett W. Hall on Philosophy, Value, Knowledge and Mind, 1964 Commonsense Realism, 1966. Home: 813 Old Mill Rd Chapel Hill NC 27515 Office: 109 B Caldwell Hall Chapel Hill NC 27515

ADAMS, ELIZABETH KNOWLES, physician; b. Fitzgerald, Ga., Dec. 3, 1923; d. Franklin Armstrong and Viola (Paulk) Knowles; B.S. in Edn., Ga. State Coll. for Women, 1945; postgrad. Emory U., 1946-47, M.D., 1951; m. Dr. Charles Pulliam Adams, Sept. 4, 1948; children—Cheryl Elizabeth, Charles Pulliam, Arthur Franklin. Postgrad. tng. internal medicine Emory U. Hosp., 1951-54, intern, 1951-52, resident, 1952-54; fellow internal medicine Emory U. Sch. Medicine, 1954-55; physician dept. student health Emory U., 1955—, clin. instr. Sch. Medicine, 1954—, lectr. in health and phys. edn., drug abuse edn., 1967—; instr. dept. health and physical edn. Ga. State Coll. Women, 1945-46. State chmn. project on smoking A.A.H.P.E.R.-N.E.A., 1968. Recipient Edn. award Chi Omega Atlanta Alumnae, 1970, Alumni Achievement award Ga. Coll., 1971. Mem. A.M.A., Med. Assn. Atlanta, Am. Women's Med. Assn., Ga. Med. Assn., Am. Coll. Health Assn., Atlanta Women's Med. Assn. (treas. 1964-66, pres.-elect 1966-67, pres. 1968-69), Am. Sch. Health Assn. Methodist. Home: 1685 Mason Mill Rd NE Atlanta GA 30329 Office: Emory U Student Infirmary Atlanta GA 30322

ADAMS, ERNEST CORTLAND, cons. engr.; b. Dieterich, Ill., May 31, 1913; s. Ernest and Ollie (Higgins) A.; B.S., U. Ill., 1937; M.S., Harvard, 1947; student U.S. Army War Coll., 1957-58; m. Dorothy Sims, Feb. 12, 1965; children—James E., Richard B., Daniel E., Stephen C. Commd. 2d lt. C.E., U.S. Army, 1937, advanced through grades to col., 1952; exec. officer amphibious brigade, World War II, regimental comdr. Korean War, dep. engr. Hdqrs. 2d Army, dist. engr., Kansas City, Mo., chief of constrn. div. Dept. Army, chief logistics officer, Alaskan Command; ret., 1964; cons. engr. Frank G. Bryant & Assos., Austin, Tex., 1964—, exec. v.p., dir., 1965—. Decorated Legion of Merit with 2 oak leaf clusters, Bronze Star medal; Croix de Guerre (France). Registered profl. engr., Tex., D.C. Mem. Am. Soc. C.E., Nat. Soc. Profl. Engrs., Soc. Am. Mil. Engrs., Sigma Xi, Tau Beta Pi, Phi Kappa Phi. Patentee in field. Home: 305 Briarwood Trail Austin TX 78746 Office: 1107 W Gibson St Austin TX 78704

ADAMS, EZRA JOHN, educator; b. Darnell, La., Aug. 30, 1923; s. John Washington and Corinne (Hargrove) A.; B.A. in Journalism, N.E. La. State Coll., 1956; M.A., La. State U., 1964; m. Catherine Geraldine Ward, Nov. 2, 1956; children—(adopted) Janet (Mrs. Glen Edward Hawsey), Gayla Dawn. Reporter, state editor Morning World, Monroe, La., 1954-56; pub. relations dir. Parish Recreation and Parks Commn., Baton Rouge, La., 1956-57; salesman, newsman WJBO-Radio, Baton Rouge, 1957-58; reporter Morning Adv., Baton Rouge, 1958; mng. editor Rural La., Assn. La. Elec. Coops., Opelousas, 1959-63; pub. information rep. La. Dept. Agr., Baton Rouge, 1963-64; dir. pubis. Southeastern La. Coll., Hammond, 1964-66, asst. prof. journalism, 1964-66; pub. relations rep. Internat. Paper Co., Bastrop, La., 1966-68; student Am. history doctoral program Northwestern State U. La., Natchiochoes, 1968-69, asso. prof. journalism, 1969—, also dir. La. Studies Inst. Served with USAAF, 1942-46, USAF, 1951-53. Mem. Assn. Edn. in Journalism (charter mem. newspaper div.), Sigma Delta Chi. Tau Kappa Epsilon. Democrat. Baptist. Lion, Mason.‡

ADAMS, FAYE CARR, bus. exec.; b. Lavon, Tex.; d. George W. and Ada Belle (Starnes) Adam high sch. grad. With Morgan Express, Inc., Dallas, 1943—, sec., 1958—, office mgr., 1958-62, adminstrv. v.p., 1962—. Apptd. Poet Laureate of Tex., alternate, 1970. Recipient Lily Peter HemisFair Poetry award with poem Legacy of the Land. Mem. Poetry Soc. Tex. (corr. sec. 1956—), Tex. Hist. Soc. Presbyn. Club: Women's Transportation (Dallas). Author: Sweet is the Homing Hour, 1948; author-illustrator: More Than a Loaf (poetry), 1968; As Seasons Pass. Home: 4244 Skillman St Dallas TX 75206

ADAMS, FRANCIS BOWEN, JR., physician; b. Florence, S.C., Oct. 2, 1925; s. Francis Bowen and Norma (Gignilliat) A.; student Clemson Coll., 1942-43; M.D., Emory U., 1948; m. Gloria Cox Poitevint, Oct. 2, 1948; children—Norma (Mrs. A. L. King, Sr.), Frank Bowen III. Intern, Pledmont Hosp., 1948-49; gen. practice medicine, Kingsport, Tenn., 1950-52, Seneca, S.C., 1954—; mem. staff Meml. Clinic, Seneca; chief medicine Oconee Meml. Hosp., 1945-48, chief obstetrics, 1970—. Chmn. Oconee County chpt. A.R.C., 1955-56, Am. Heart Assn., 1970-72. Served with M.C., USNR, 1949-50, 52-54. Diplomate Am. Bd. Family Practice. Mem. A.M.A., Am. Assn. Family Practice, So. Med. Assn., Oconee County Med. Soc. (pres. 1957-58). Presbyn. Home: 401 S Pine Circle Seneca SC 29678 Office: PO Box 1174 Seneca SC 29678

ADAMS, FRANK JACKSON, JR., judge; b. Cornelia, Ga., July 15, 1916; s. Frank Jackson and Julia (Littlefield) A.; student Piedmont Coll.; LL.B., Atlanta Law Sch., 1940; m. Joye Hipps, Apr. 4, 1941; 1 son, Steven Charles. Admitted to Ga. bar, 1940; law practice, Clarkesville and Cornelia, Ga., 1945—; judge State Ct. of Habersham County, 1947—. Mem. Govs. Commn. on Jud. Selection, 1972—, Commn. on State Compensation, 1971—. Served with USAAF, 1942-45. Decorated D.F.C., Air medal with three clusters. Mem. C. of C. (past pres.), Am. Legion (past comdr.), Am., Ga. (gov. 1961—, exec. com. 1963-64, 67—, pres. elect 1972-73) bar assns., Jud. Council Ga., Am. Judicature Soc. Baptist. Kiwanian (past pres.). Address: Cornelia GA 30531

ADAMS, GEORGE COTTON SMITH, educator; b. N.Y.C., June 1, 1911; s. Edward Leverett and Amanda (Smith) A.; student U. S.C., 1929-30, Middlebury Coll. (Ecole Francaise), summer 1935; A.B., U. N.C., 1933, A.M., 1934, Ph. D., 1950; certificate La Sorbonne, Paris, 1951; m. Adaline Holaday, Aug. 31, 1940 children—Charles Edward, George Holaday. Tchr. French, English, Dunbarton, S.C., 1935; service fellowship dept. romance langs. U. N.C., 1936-38, instr. French, 1938-39; instr. Spanish, English Tusculum Coll., 1939-40; asst. prof. romance langs. W. Ga. Coll., 1940-50, prof., head dept., 1950-52; asso. prof. Wofford Coll., 1952-56, prof. romance langs., 1957—, chmn. dept. fgn. langs., 1960—; prof. Spanish, U. Ariz., summer 1962. Recipient Cristobal Colon award Sigma Delta Pi. Mem. Modern Lang. Assn., Am. Assn. Tchrs. French (pres. Ga. chpt. 1950-51, pres. S.C. chpt. 1964-66), South Atlantic Modern Lang. Assn. (chmn. folklore sect. 1952, 56, 59, mem. exec. com. 1968-71), Southeastern Folklore Soc. (past pres.), Linguistic Soc. Am., Am. Assn. Tchrs. Spanish and Portuguese (past pres. S.C. chpt., state coordinator, Cervantes award 1970), Am. Assn. U. Profs., Phi Beta Kappa. Episcopalian (vestryman). Clubs: Sunrise Civitan (editor Civitan Notes 1965-72, pres. 1967-68) (Spartanburg, S.C.) University (N.Y.). Home: 100 Swansea Rd PO Box 3161 Spartanburg SC 29302

ADAMS, GEORGE HACKNEY, wholesale trade co. exec.; b. Wilson, N.C., Mar. 17, 1920; s. William Dennis and Bess Acra (Hackney) A.; A.B., U.N.C., 1939-43; m. Hennie Green Wallace, May 6, 1942; children— George, Jr., Hennie (Mrs. A. J. Gregory), Acra (Mrs. R. H. Kluttz). Sec., treas. Hackney Wagon Co., Wilson, 1946-63; pres. Wilson Oil Corp., 1963—; v.p., dir. Goldsboro Coca Cola Bottling Co. (N.C.), 1951—. Trustee Atlantic Christian Coll., 1954—. Served with AUS, 1942-45. Decorated Bronze Star, Silver Star. Elk. Club: Wilson (N.C.) Country. Home: 1716 Brentwood Circle Wilson NC 27893 Office: PO Box 1196 Wilson NC 27893

ADAMS, HARRY WESLEY, civil engr.; b. Muncie, Ind., July 10, 1908; s. Curtis Elva and Anna Josepha (Madden) A.; student U. Tenn. Jr. Coll., 1926-27, U. Chgo., 1927-29, U. Cin., 1942; m. Sarah Elizabeth Irwin, Nov. 24, 1934; children—Judith (Mrs. Albert L. Goldsmith, Jr.) and Janet (Mrs. Gilbert Resnik) (twins). With U.S. Army C.E., Louisville, 1930-37, Ohio River Div., Cin., Columbus, O., 1937-46, spl. engring. div. Panama Canal, Diablo Heights, Canal Zone, 1946-48, with Engring. Div., Civil Works, Office of Chief of Engrs., Washington, 1948-54, asst. chief, planning div., 1954-59, asst. exec. dir. U.S. Study Commn., S.E. River Basins, Atlanta, 1959-62; cons. on nat. and fgn. water resources devel. to various pvt. and pub. engring. agys., cons. cos., 1963—. Mem. engring. adv. com. Lake-Sumter Community Coll., Leesburg, Fla., 1970—. Registered profl. engr., Ohio, Va., Fla. Fellow Am. Soc. C.E.; mem. Am. Geophys. Union (life), Internat. Commn. on Irrigation and Drainage, Nat. Soc. Profl. Engrs., Fla. Engring. Soc. (sr. mem.), Alpha Tau Omega. Contbr. articles to profl. lit. Address: 1522 Park Dr Leesburg FL 32748

ADAMS, HAZEL GREENLEE REDFEARN (MRS. PAYTON F. ADAMS II), educator; b. Monroe, N.C., Nov. 12, 1905; d. Ephraim Eugene and Rebecca (Laney) Redfearn; student Radford Coll., 1924; A.B., U. Ky., 1940, M.A., 1953; postgrad. U. Neb., 1955; m. Payton F. Adams II, July 11, 1928; children—Payton F. III, Juliette Greenlee (Mrs. J. B. Hawk). Elementary tchr. Larchmont Sch., Norfolk, Va., 1924-28, Winchester (Ky.) City Schs., 1943-53; supr. Clark County (Ky.) Schs., 1953-61; supr. student tchrs. Ky. Wesleyan Coll., 1945-48; instr. Wesleyan Coll., Macon, Ga., 1960; named asst. prof. edn. Dakota Wesleyan U., Mitchell, S.D., 1961, asso. prof. edn. and psychology, 1961-70; asso. prof. early childhood edn. Pfeiffer Coll., Misenheimer, N.C., 1970—, adviser Student Edn. Assn., 1972-73. Chmn., Clark County Community Council, 1950-52, Clark County Recreation Bd., 1955-60; supr. Teen-Town, Winchester, 1954-60. Mem. Am. Assn. U. Women, Am. Assn. U. Profs., N.E.A., S.D. Edn. Assn., D.A.R., Assn. Supervision Curriculum Devel., Assn. for Childhood Edn., Mitchell Bus. and Profl. Women, Albemarle Bus. and Profl. Women (pres. 1972-73), Phi Kappa Phi (pres. 1964-66), Delta Kappa Gamma (pres. 1964-66), Pi Gamma Mu. Methodist. Mem. Order Eastern Star. Author: The Inimitable Educator: Robert E. Lee. Home: 136 College St Winchester KY 40391 Office: Pfeiffer Coll Misenheimer NC 28109

ADAMS, HELLEN ANNE HUTCHINSON, educator; b. Hamilton, Miss., Aug. 25, 1935; d. James Perry and Lois (Wright) Hutchinson; student Miss. State U., 1953-54; B.S., Miss. State Coll. Women, 1956; M.Ed., Duke, 1957; Ed.D., U. Miss., 1966; postgrad. U. Ga., 1966-67; m. Charles Floyd Adams, June 27, 1959; (div. 1970); son, Charles Floyd. Elementary tchr., Atlanta, 1957-59, Tampa, 1959-60, Hattiesburg, Miss., 1960-61, Oxford, Miss., 1961-64; dir. elementary edn., Columbus, Ga., 1965-67; dir. edn. LeFlore County Sch. Dist., Greenwood, Miss., 1967-69; asst. prof. edn., asso. dir. staff tng. of exemplary early edn. centers U. Tex., Austin, 1969-71; asso. prof. edn. Duke U., Durham, N.C., 1971—. Mem. faculty U. Miss., 1964, U. Ga., 1966; mem. nat. adv. bd. J. B. Lippincott Co., 1966—; reading cons., Ga., Miss., Ala., La.; dir. Diagnostic and Remedial Reading Center, Columbus, 1967—, Duke U. Reading Clinic, 1971—. Named Outstanding Young Woman of Am., Miss. State Coll. Women, 1967, one of Outstanding Personalities of the South, 1966. Mem. Internat. Platform Assn., Phi Delta Epsilon, Alpha Delta Kappa, Pi Gamma Mu, Chi Omega. Author: The Reading Clinic, 1971; The Random House Reading Program, 1969; Threshold Learning Abilities for Children With Handicaps, 1972; Sounds for Me, 1971; also scripts for The Look at you series of films. Contbr. articles to profl. jours. Home: Valley Terrace Apt 28C Durham NC 27707

ADAMS, HENRY BETHUNE, psychologist; b. Charlotte, N.C., Aug. 26, 1925; s. Hal Bethune and Mabel (Cooper) A.; A.B., U. N.C., 1949; M.A., Duke, 1953; Ph.D., Purdue U., 1956. Trainee VA Hosp., Marion, Ind., 1954-55, VA Regional Office, Indpls., 1955-56; instr. med. psychology U. Neb. Coll. Medicine, Omaha, 1956-59; psychologist Neb. Psychiat. Inst., 1956-59; research psychologist VA Hosp., Richmond, Va., 1959-63; psychologist Nat. Tng. Sch., Washington, 1963-64; chief psychol. services Fed. Reformatory, Alderson, W.Va., 1964-67; clin. asso. dept. psychology W.Va. U., Morgantown, 1965-67; chief psychologist Alcoholism and Drug Addiction Service, Area C Community Health Center, 1967—. Served with AUS, 1943-46. Fellow Internat. Council Psychologists; mem. Am., D.C. (treas. 1970—), Richmond (past pres.) psychol. assns. Contbr. articles to profl. jours. Home: 3001 Branch Av SE Washington DC 20031 Office: 1905 E St SE Washington DC 20001

ADAMS, HERSHELL GARLAND, ednl. adminstr.; b. Richland Springs, Tex., Nov. 5, 1917; s. Matt and Eura (Hagar) A.; B.A., Daniel Baker Coll., 1940; M.E., Hardin-Simmons U., 1953; m. Iris Novella Maedgen, Sept. 5, 1940; children—Leslie Garry, Constance Sue. Prin., coach LaVernia (Tex.) High Sch., 1940-41; prin. Oakville (Tex.) Pub. Schs., 1941-43; elementary prin. West Ward Sch., Coleman (Tex.) Pub. Schs., 1943-45; supt. Novice Pub. Schs., 1945-55; prin. high sch., asst. supt. Rankin (Tex.) Pub. Schs., 1955-58; supt. Marfa (Tex.) Pub. Sch., 1958-69; supt. Rankin (Tex.) Independent Sch. Dist., 1969—. Mem. Tex. Textbook Com., 1966-67; mem. exec. council W. Tex. Edn. Center. Active A.R.C.; chmn. W.Tex. Innovative Edn. Center; mem. Selective Service Bd., Salvation Army. Recipient Distinguished Service award Future Farmers Am.; award spl. merit Tex. Tchrs. Assn. Mem. Tex. State Tchrs. Assn., Am., Tex. assns. sch. adminstrs., N.E.A. Lion. Contbr. articles to profl. jours. Home: 601 Elizabeth Rankin TX 79778 Office: Adminstrn Bldg 206 W 12th St Rankin TX 70778

ADAMS, HOWARD, state legislator. Mem. Ariz. Ho. of Reps. Address: The Capitol 1700 W Washington St Phoenix AZ 85007*

ADAMS, J. MARION, state ofcl. Asso. commr. vocational edn. Ark. Dept. Edn., Little Rock. Address: Educational Bldg Little Rock AR 72203*

ADAMS, JAMES LLEWELLYN, lawyer; b. Atlanta, Aug. 19, 1937; s. Oscar Llewellyn and Katherine (Crawford) A.; B.A., Emory U., 1959, LL.B., 1962-3m. Marilynn Elizabeth Pulliam, Aug. 22, 1959; children—Lisa Louise, James Benjamin, Dennis Paul. Admitted to Ga. bar, 1961; practiced in Atlanta, 1961-71; asso. Arnall, Golden & Gregory, Atlanta, 1962-67, partner, 1967-71; pres. AMI Realty & Mortgage Investors & Advisors, Inc., Shreveport, La., 1971—, also dir. gen. counsel; dir.; gen. counsel AMI, Inc.; dir., chmn. exec. com. Bossier Bank and Trust Co.; pres. Mobile Home Service Co. of South. Bd. dirs. Ga. Conservancy. Mem. Ga. bar Assn., Atlanta Lawyers Club, Atlanta Jr. C. of C., Ga. Sportsmen's Fedn. (pres. 1966-68, exec. sec.-treas. 1968-70), Alpha Tau Omega, Phi Delta Phi. Clubs: Cherokee Appaloosa, Kadodacho Appaloosa; Atlanta Brittany, Atlanta Retriever. Home: 480 Railsback Rd Shreveport LA 71106 Office: 6001 Financial Plaza Shreveport LA 71130

ADAMS, JAMES WALTER, educator; b. Meansville, Ga., Aug. 11, 1933; s. James Samuel and Bertha (Brown) A.; B.B.A., Ga. State Coll., 1959, M.B.A., 1962, D.B.A., 1972; m. Carolyn Burnette, June 4, 1961; children—James Samuel, Daniel E., David W. Personal asst. to gen. freight traffic mgr. So. Ry. Co., Atlanta, 1961-62; Regents' fellow in econs. Ga. State U., 1962-63; instr. econs. and statistics U. Ga., 1963-66; asst. prof. econs. W. Ga. Coll., 1966-69; asso. prof. marketing and transp. Auburn (Ala.) U., 1969—. Mem. Am. Soc. Traffic and Transp., So. Econ. Assn., Beta Gamma Sigma, Delta Mu Delta, Delta Sigma Pi. Mem. Pentecostal Holiness Ch. Author: Transportation Cost Control in the Industrial Enterprise, 1962; Role of Economics in Community Development, 1968; Effect of Government Aid and other Factors on Economic Development of three Selected Areas in Georgia, 1972. Home: 1312 Sycamore Dr Auburn AL 36830

ADAMS, JAMES WAYNE, JR., dentist; b. South Boston, Va., Dec. 26, 1934; d. James Wayne and Dorothy (Evans) A.; B.S., Coll. William and Mary, 1957; D.D.S., Med. Coll. Va., 1968; m. Janet Lee Lloyd, June 27, 1959; 1 dau., Anne Livingston. Comml. mgr. Chesapeake & Potomac Telephone Co., Balt., 1957-62; salesman Shaw Real Estate Co., Alexandria, Va., 1962-64; pvt. practice dentistry, South Boston, Va., 1968—. Mem. South Boston (Va.) City Sch. Bd., 1970—. Mem. Am., Va. State dental assns., Va. Assns. Professions, Piedmont Dental Soc., Delta Sigma Delta, Alpha Sigma Chi. Presbyn. (deacon 1972). Clubs: Sertoma (v.p. 1969-70, dir. 1970-72) (South Boston, Va.); Halifax Country (dir. 1970—). Office: Profl Bldg South Boston VA 24592

ADAMS, JESSE EARL, physician, surgeon; b. Lexington, Ky., Dec. 5, 1925; s. Jesse E. and Esther Francis (Nicholson) A.; B.S., U. Ky., 1945; M.D., Harvard, 1948; m. Hattie Boeswetter, Feb. 21, 1959; 1 son, Jesse Earl III. Rotating intern Harper Hosp., Detroit, 1948-49; intern in surgery Vanderbilt Hosp., 1949-50, resident, 53-55; resident Med. Coll. Va. Hosp., 1950-51, U. Va. Hosp., 1955-56; vis. surgeon Rigshospitolet, Copenhagen, Denmark, 1956; asst. prof. surgery Vanderbilt U. Sch. Medicine, Nashville, 1956-60, dir. S.R. Light Lab. for Surg. Research, 1958-60; mem. Assn. Thoracic and Cardiovascular Surgery, Chattanooga, 1961—. Pres. bd. dirs. Chattanooga Area Heart Assn; vice-chmn. Chattanooga-Hamilton County Air Pollution Control Bd. Served with USAF, 1951-52. Diplomate Am. Bd. Surgery, Am. Bd. Thoracic Surgery. Fellow A.C.S.; mem. Am. (rep. councilor), So. thoracic socs., Am. Coll. Chest Physicians, A.M.A., Tenn. Med. Assn., Am. Assn. Thoracic Surgery, Southeastern Surg. Congress, Soc. Thoracic Surgeons, Tenn thoracic Soc. (past pres., mem. exec. com.), Tenn. Tb and Respiratory Disease Assn. (mem. exec. com., pres. elect), Tenn. Heart Assn. (dir., chmn. program com.). Contbr. articles on cardiac surgery to med. jours. Home: 224 N Crest Rd Chattanooga TN 37404 Office: 1000 E 3d St Chattanooga TN 37403

ADAMS, JOHN AMOS, JR., govt. ofcl.; b. Albuquerque, Mar. 27, 1915; s. John Amos and Helen (Shields) A.; student Antioch Coll., 1932-35, U. N.M., 1940; m. Lucille S. Simmons, June 24, 1940; children—Thomas L., John Amos, III, Lucille Anne. Agrl. engr. Soil Conservation Service, U.S. Dept. Agr., Albuquerque, 1935-42; civil engr. U.S. Engrs., Albuquerque, 1942-44; hydraulic engr. Office Chief of Engrs., Washington, 1944-46; hydraulic engr. Intermountain Forest and Range Expt. Sta., U.S. Forest Service, Ogden, Utah, 1946-53, civil engr. U.S. Forest Service, Flagstaff, Ariz., 1953-55, chief rds. and trails Region 3, Albuquerque, 1955-61, then staff engr., asst. regional engr., Region 1, Missoula, Mont., staff engr. Rossyln Bldg., Va.; regional engr. So. region U.S. Forest Service, U.S. Dept. Agr., Atlanta, 1969—. Registered profl. engr., Mont. Mem. Washington Soc. Engrs., Am. Soc. C.E. (mem. hydraulics com.), Geophys. Union. Author: (with Merril Bernard and others) Hydrology Manual, 1943. Contbr. articles to profl. jours. Home: 3946 Brown Rd Tucker GA 30084 Office: 1720 Peachtree Rd NE Atlanta GA 30309

ADAMS, K.S., JR., bus. exec.; b. Bartlesville, Okla., 1923; ed. U. Kan., 1943. Chmn., pres. Ada Oil Co., Houston, Ada Oil Co. of Can. Ltd., Ada Oil Co. of Greece, Ltd., Ada Oil Co. Turkey, Ada Oil Exploration Corp., Ada Securities Corp., Adams Petroleum Center, Inc., Hayou Refining Co., Hud Adams Ranches, Houston Oilers Profl. Football Team, Inc., Internat. Land Resources, Inc., QuicKick Internat. Co., River Garden Farms, S.W. Lincoln-Mercury, Inc., S.W. Motor Leasing, Texoma Petroleum Marketers, Western Tire & Supply Co.; adv. dir. First City Nat. Bank of Houston, Am. Bank & Trust Co., Houston. Address: 6910 Fannin St Houston TX 77001

ADAMS, KIRKWOOD FLOYD, paper mfg. exec.; b. Greenville, Tenn., Jan 29, 1904; s. Thomas Tunstall and Annie (Stokes) A.; student Va. Mil. Inst., 1920-22; B.S. in Commerce and Sci., U. Va., 1925; spl. extension courses, William and Mary Coll.; m. Sarah Anne Chaney, May 17, 1947; children—Kirkwood Floyd, Anne Stokes, Margaret Leigh. Clk. C. & O. Ry., 1925-26; successively clk., splty. sales, prodn.-sales coordinator, prodn. mgr. The Albemarle Paper Mfg. Co., 1926-45, v.p., 1950-63, div. mgr., exec. v.p., dir., 1963—; bd. mgrs. Planters Nat. Bank & Trust Co., Roanoke Rapids, N.C.; dir. Seaboard Mfg. Co., Raymond Bag Co., Halifax Timber Co.; dir., mem. exec. com. Pulp and Paper Found., Inc. Mayor of Roanoke Rapids, N.C., 1969—. Bd. dirs. Roanoke River Basin Assn.; pres. N.C. Traffic League; mem. Roanoke Rapids Zoning Com. Review Bd. Mem. T.A.P.P.I., Am. Pulpwood Assn., Am. Paper and Pulp Assn. (mem. forest policy com.), S.A.R., Newcomen Soc. N.Am., Alpha Kappa Psi. Episcopalian. Clubs: Kiwanis, Chockoyotte County (dir.) (Roanoke Rapids). Home: 240 White Av Roanoke Rapids NC 27870 Office: Albemarle Paper Mfg Co Roanoke Rapids NC 27870

ADAMS, LILLIAN LOYCE, educator; b. Cadiz, Tex., Jan. 10, 1912; d. Marvin Rice and Emma Agnes (Scarborough) A.; B.B.A., Tex. A. and I. U., 1931; M.B.A., U. Tex., 1935, Ph.D., 1959 Auditor, asst. to registrar, bus. mgr. Tex. A. and I. U., Kingsville, 1931-37; instr. bus. Hardin-Simmons U., Abilene, Tex., 1937-42; prof. bus. adminstrn. Sam Houston State U., Huntsville, Tex., 1942—; tchr. Heidelberg Am. Sch., Germany, 1952-53. Mem. Nat. Bus. Edn. Assn., Tex. Bus. Edn. Assn. (pres. 1961-62), Am. Assn. U. Women, Tex. State Tchrs. Assn., Am. Bus. Writing Assn., Alpha Chi, Beta Gamma Sigma, Delta Pi Epsilon, Phi Chi Theta, Pi Omega Pi, Sigma Iota Epsilon. Author: Quaking Leaves, 1940; Three Wishes, 1947; The Three T'S: Teach, Travel and Tell, 1960; Managerial Psychology, 1965; articles in profl. jours. and mags. Home: 216 Elmwood St Huntsville TX 77340

ADAMS, NON QUINCY, banker; b. Mobile, Ala., June 1, 1925; s. Samuel Boyd and Dora (Williams) A.; B.S., U. Ala., 1949, LL.B., 1950; m. Eran Izard Jobe, Nov. 26, 1952; children—Laura A., Samuel Russell. Admitted to Ala. bar, 1950; practice law, Mobile, 1950-51; trust officer 1st Nat. Bank Mobile, 1951-55, asst. v.p., trust officer, 1955-62, v.p., trust officer, 1962-69, sr. v.p., 1969-72, exec. v.p., 1972—. Chmn., Allied Arts Drive, 1969; pres. Mobile chpt. A.R.C., 1969-71; co-chmn. indsl. div. United Fund, 1971—. Bd. dirs., sec. Gordon Smith Center, 1969—; bd. dirs. Community Chest Mobile. Served to lt. (j.g.), USNR, 1943-46. Hon. fellow Mobile Coll. Mem. Ala. Bankers Assn. (pres. trust div.), C. of C. (chmn. legislative com.). Kiwanian. Clubs: Mobile Country (pres. 1967), Athelstan Bienville (Mobile); Lakewood Golf (Point Clear, Ala.). Office: PO Drawer 1467 Mobile AL 36601 Home: 58 Clarise Circle Mobile AL 36608

ADAMS, PAUL LIEBER, child psychiatrist, educator; b. Broken Bow, Okla., Jan. 22, 1924; s. Moses Robert and Beulah (Lieber) A.; A.B., Centre Coll. of Ky., 1943; M.A. (Rosenwald fellow), Columbia, 1948, M.D., 1955; postgrad. Fisk U., 1943, N.Y. U., 1945-55, Duke, 1956-60; m. Evelia Valdes-Rodriguez, Jan. 31, 1953; children—Christine Beate Lieber Adams Tucker (by previous marriage), Gabrielle Lieber, Gerald Berwin Lieber. Instr. social scis. Bennett Coll., Greensboro, N.C., 1947-51; asst. in psychiatry Duke, 1956-58, instr. psychiatry, 1958-60; dir. Cumberland County (N.C.) Guidance Center, 1956-58; vis. prof. sociology N.C. Coll. Grad. Sch., Durham, 1957-60; vis. prof. U. N.C. Coll. Dentistry, Chapel Hill, 1965-66, U. Oslo, Norway, 1971; vis. fellow Hampstead Child Therapy Clinic, London, Eng., 1966; from asst. prof. to prof. psychiatry and pediatrics Fla. Coll. Med., Gainesville, 1960—; chief div. child psychiatry, dir. children's mental health unit U. Fla., Gainesville, 1960—; cons. Fla. Div. Youth Services. Fellow Am. Coll. Psychiatrists, Am. Acad. Child psychiatry (sec.), Am. Psychiat. Assn., Am. Orthopsychiat. Assn.; mem. World Congress Psychiatry, Am. Assn. Psychiat. Clinics for Children (nat. dir. 1969-71), Am. Fedn. Tchrs., Am. Assn. U. Profs. (mem. exec. com. 1968-70). Mem. Soc. of Friends. Contbr. articles to profl. jours. Home: 1116 NW 60th St Gainesville FL 32601 Office: HD 30 U Fla Med Center Gainesville FL 32601

ADAMS, PERRY RONALD, coll. pres.; b. Parkersburg, W.Va., Sept. 16, 1921; s. Russell Douglas and Beulah Grace (Cunningham) A.; A.B., U. Ky., 1943, M.A., 1948; Ed.D. (Kellogg fellow), U. Fla., 1965; m. Ann Mallory Gillespie, Dec. 25, 1943; children—Suzanne, Sally (Mrs. Robert Barrios). Instr., U. Ky., 1948-53; dir. music U. Fla., 1953-63; dean instrn. Polk Jr. Coll., Winter Haven, Fla., 1965-69; provost No. Va. Community Coll., Annandale, 1969-70; pres. Paul D. Camp Community Coll., Franklin, Va., 1970—. Adjudicator various high sch. music contests, 1953—; mem. finance adv. com. Va. Council Higher Edn., 1970—. Served with USNR, 1942-47; MTO, ETO, PTO. Mem. Am. Assn. Jr. Colls., So. Assn. Colls. and Schs. (accreditation com.), Phi Mu Alpha (nat. councilman), Phi Delta Kappa, Kappa Delta Pi. Baptist. Rotarian. Home: 117 Beechwood Dr Franklin VA 23851 Office: PO Box 611 Franklin VA 23851

ADAMS, RALPH WYATT, SR., univ. pres., lawyer; b. Samson, Ala., June 4, 1915; s. Alfred E. and Eunice M. (Clements) A.; A.B., Birmingham-So. Coll., 1937; LL.B., U. Ala., 1940, J.D., 1965; postgrad. U. Colo., 1958, George Washington U., 1960; m. Dorothy Kelly, Sept. 5, 1942; children—Ralph Wyatt, Kelly Clement, Samuel. Admitted to Ala. bar, 1940, also U.S. Supreme Ct. bar; atty., dep. supt. Dept. Ins., State of Ala., 1945-46; judge, Tuscaloosa, Ala., 1946-47; founder Adams Life Ins. Co. Am., 1950, merged with Western Bankers Life; founder Acad. Life Ins. Co., Denver, 1957; lectr. life ins. U. Colo. Dep. dean, acting dean Air Force Law Sch., Maxwell AFB, Ala.; pres. Troy State U., 1964—. Dir. Bankers Credit Life Ins. Co., Am. Educators Life Ins. Co., 1st Farmers & Mchts. Nat. Bank, Kinston Bank (Ala.). Mem. State Personnel Bd. Ala., State Ins. Bd. Ala.; pres.-elect Ala. Assn. Colls. and Univs. Trustee Lyman Ward Mil. Acad., Camp Hill, Ala. Served to capt. USAAF, 1941-45; brig. gen. Ala. Air N.G. Mem. Am. Legion, Phi Alpha Delta, Kappa Delta Pi, Pi Delta Phi, Kappa Phi Kappa, Lambda Chi Alpha, Phi Kappa Phi. Methodist. Mason. Clubs: Alexandria Civitan (past pres.), Army-Navy Country (Alexandria, Va.); Rotary; Montgomery (Ala.) Country; Troy Country. Home: President's Mansion Troy State U Troy AL 36081

ADAMS, R(ICHARD) M(CGARY), oceanographer; b. Vincennes, Ind., Apr. 30, 1928; s. Yula Ulysses and Evelyn I. (McGary) A.; A.A., Vincennes U., 1947; B.S., Tex. A. and M.U., 1949, M.S., 1951; m. Jane Charlene Rodgers, Dec. 22, 1957; children—Jenny Lee, John David. Research scientist and adminstrv. asst. Tex. A. and M.U., College Station, 1951-57, adminstrv. scientist dept. oceanography and meteorology, 1959-64; chief, computations div. Smithsonian Astrophys. Obs., Cambridge, Mass., 1957-59; br. head U.S. Naval Oceanographic Office, Washington 1965-66; mgr. oceanographic programs br. Tex. Instruments Inc., Dallas, 1966—. Cons. in field. Mem. Am. Geophys. Union, A.A.A.S., Marine Tech. Soc., Am. Soc. Oceanography. Presbyn. Mason, Lion (past v.p.). Contbr. articles to profl. jours. Home: 7806 Fallmeadow Lane Dallas TX 75240 Office: 13500 N Central Expressway Dallas TX 75222

ADAMS, SALVATORE CHARLES, lawyer; b. N.Y.C., July 10, 1934; s. Charles Joseph and Rose (Scala) A.; B.C.E., Rensselaer Poly. Inst., 1955; M.S., U. Conn., 1961; J.D., U. Miami, 1968; m. Ann Mary Shepherdson, Aug. 3, 1957; children—Mark Charles, Scott Shepherd, David James, Christopher Amos. Constrn. estimator Bechtel Corp., San Francisco, 1957-58; planning and econ. feasibility cons., Hartford, Conn., 1958-63; faculty U. Conn., Storrs, 1958-63; project mgr. Rader & Assos., cons. engrs., Miami, Fla., 1963-65; pres. Motivation Cons., Miami, 1965-68; admitted to Fla. bar, 1968, practiced in Miami, 1968-70, Ft. Lauderdale, Fla., 1971—; mem. firm Weiner & Rubin, Miami, 1968-70, DiGuilian & Spellacy, Ft. Lauderdale, 1971, Adams & Harris, Ft. Lauderdale, 1971; dir. Exposition Corp. Am., Miami, Lambert Credit Control Systems, Miami, Internat. Francorp, Inc., Miami. Served with USNR, 1955-57. Mem. Am. Trial Lawyers Assn., Am., Fla. bar assns., Lambda Chi Alpha, Delta Theta Phi. Author: Land Use and Municipal Finance, 1961. Home: 7920 SW 53d Av Miami FL 33143 Office: 208 SE 6th St Fort Lauderdale FL 33301

ADAMS, TOM, lt. gov. Florida; b. Jacksonville, Fla., Mar. 11, 1917; s. Thomas Burton and Carolyn (Hamilton) A.; grad. The Hill Sch., Pottstown, Pa., 1936; A.B., U. Mich., 1940; student U. Fla. Law Sch., 1948; D. Space Edn., Brevard Engring. Coll.; H.H.D., Trinity Coll.;

m. Helen Brown, July 30, 1939; children—Carolyn (Mrs. James A. DeHaven, Jr.), Augusta (Mrs. T. Buckingham Bird), Frances. Real estate, property mgmt. H. P. Holmes, Inc. Detroit, 1940-42; plant supt. Foremost Dairies, Jacksonville and Daytona Beach, Fla., 1942-44; owner, operator dairy farm, Orange Park, 1944-48; timber dealer, property mgmt. Orange Park Properties (Fla.), 1948-61; farmer, Fla., 1942-61; mem. Fla. Senate, 29th Dist., 1956-60, chmn. com. reorgn. Fla. Dept. Agr.; sec. state Florida, 1961-70, now lt. gov., also sec. commerce. Pres. Leon County United Fund, 1964; state campaign chmn. Fla. Mental Health Assn., 1964. Decorated Order of San Carlos (Colombia); named most outstanding freshman senator 1957 Session, Fla. Legislature, also recipient agrl. award 1957 Session; named most valuable mem. legislature 1959 Session, named most effective state adminstr. 1961, 63, 65. Mem. U.S. Commn. Southeast River Basins (mem. resources adv. bd.), Nat. Rivers and Harbors Congress (dir.), Nat. Waterways Conf. (chmn. 1964-65, pres. 1965-67), Miss. Valley Assn. (pres. 1968, dir.), Fla. Colombia Alliance (founder 1963), Fla. State U. Gold Key Soc., Newcomen Soc., U. Fla. Alumni Assn., Blue Key, Phi Delta Theta, Alpha Kappa Psi. Baptist. Moose (state pres. 1966-67), Rotarian. Home: Magnolia Dr Tallahassee FL 32304 Office: State Capitol Tallahassee FL 32304

ADAMS, WILLIAM CARROLL, educator; b. Star City, Ark., July 15, 1930; s. Allie L. and Ila (Miles) A.; B.A. in Econs., State Coll. Ark., 1951; M.A., U. Ark., 1953, Ph.D. (Gen. Elec. fellow), 1963. With Graybar Elec. Co., St. Louis, 1953-54; instr. U. Ark., 1957-60; faculty E. Tex. State U., Commerce, 1960-—, prof. bus. adminstrn., 1965-—. Pub. utility cons. Bd. dirs. Commerce Pub. Library, Carmichael Found., Conway Ark. Served with AUS, 1954-57. Bus. Exchange fellow, 1964; Ill. Bell fellow, 1966. Mem. Am., So., Western econ. assns., Beta Gamma Sigma. Author: The Inflationary Erosion of Capital—A Case Study, 1964; A Checklist for Acquisitions, 1964. Home: Box 3064 ET Station Commerce TX 75428

ADAMS, WILLIAM MARSHALL, hosp. adminstr.; b. Estancia, N.M., Nov. 30, 1936; s. William Feldon and Maurine (Shoemaker) A.; B.A., Tex. Wesleyan, 1964; M.S., Trinity U., 1971; m. Edna Jean Thomason, Oct. 17, 1958; children—Clint, Crystal. Dist. exec. Boy Scouts of Am., San Angelo, Tex., 1965-67; adminstr. Uvalde (Tex.) Hosp. Authority, 1967-71; adminstr. Doctors Hosp., Houston, 1971-—. Vice chmn. Alamo Area Hosp. Div., 1971-72; dist. chmn. leadership tng. Boy Scouts of Am., 1969-—. Bd. dirs. Uvalde Retail Mchts., Uvalde chpt. A.R.C. Served with USAF, 1957-61. Graduate fellow Tex. Christian U., 1964. Mem. Am. Coll. Hosp. Adminstrs., Am. Acad. Med. Adminstrs., Tex. Hosp. Assn. (del. 1970-71). Mason, Rotarian. Home: 231 Weeping Oak St Spring TX 77373 Office: 5815 Airline St Houston TX 77022

ADAMS, WILLIAM YEWDALE, educator; b. Los Angeles, Aug. 6, 1927; s. William F. and Lucy M. (Wilcox) A.; A.B., U. Cal. at Berkeley, 1948; Ph.D., U. Ariz., 1958; m. Nettie Alice Kesseler, June 7, 1955; children— Ernest W., Edward K. Dir., Glen Canyon archeol. salvage project Mus. No. Ariz., Flagstaff, 1957-59; dir. Sudan Antiquities Service archeol. salvage program, liaison officer UNESCO, 1959-66; prof. anthropology U. Ky. at Lexington, 1966-—; vis. lectr. Archeol. Inst. Am., 1968-72. Served with USNR, 1945-46. Fellow A.A.A.S., Am. Anthrop. Assn., Soc. for Applied Anthropology. Author: Shonto: A Study of the Role of the Trader in a Modern Navaho Community, 1963. Home: 957 Wolf Run Rd Lexington KY 40504

ADAMSON, DOUGLAS VAN FLEET, computer co. exec.; b. Houston, Sept. 26, 1930; s. Arthur Douglas and Nora Maud (Harriman) A.; B.B.A., Tex. A. and M. U., 1952; M.S., So. Meth. U., 1962; m. Martha Lynn Kelfer, May 27, 1966; children—Douglas, Elaine, Mary, Marshall. Jr. salesman IBM, 1954-56, sr. salesman, 1957-63; trust officer Rep. Nat. Bank, 1964-65; sales mgr. Mgmt. Assistance Inc. Equipment Corp., 1966-67, gen. br. mgr., 1967-68; exec. v.p. Data Automation Services, 1969-70; v.p. marketing Gen. Computer Systems, Dallas, 1971-72; dir. bus. and product planning UCC Communications Systems, Inc., 1972-—. Served from 2d lt. to 1st lt. USAF, 1952-54. Mem. Data Processing Mgmt. Assn. Episcopalian. Clubs: Corinthian Sailing, Martha Turner Reilly Dads (pres. 1963) (Dallas). Home: Route 1 Argyle TX 76226 Office: 7220 N Stemmons Freeway Dallas TX 75247

ADANALIAN, ALICE ARAXIE, research scientist; b. Turkey; d. Garabed and Vartouhie (Manisalian) Adanalian; came to U.S., 1920, naturalized, 1927; student U. Pa., 1926-28; B.A., Northwestern U., 1930; M.A., Columbia, 1935; post-grad. Johns Hopkins, 1954, 57. Exec. sec. Bus. and Profl. Women's Program YWCA, Yonkers, N.Y., 1930-37; dir. Cleve. Guidance Service, 1937-39; exec. sec. group work-recreation employment-guidance div. Welfare Council N.Y., 1939-44; welfare specialist Middle East mission UNRRA, Egypt, Italy, 1944-45; chief liaison officer UN mission, Austria, 1946-47; head leaders and specialist div. Inst. Internat. Edn., 1948-51; Africa-Middle East specialist U.S. Govt., Washington, 1951-67; dep. chief Middle East Africa br. Center Research of Social Systems, Am. U., Washington, 1967-69; cons. Am. Inst. for Research, 1969-—. Sec. exec. com. Community Chest, Yonkers, 1936-37; mem. program planning bd. Nat. Youth Adminstrn., Yonkers, 1936-37; sec. Fair Employment Practice Com. N.Y., 1943-44. Bd. missions Meth. Ch., 1960-68. Mem. Nat. Vocational Guidance Assn. (chmn. internat. relations com. 1949-51), Am. Personnel and Guidance Assn., Africa Studies Assn., Johns Hopkins U. Alumni Assn., Columbia U. Tchrs. Coll. Alumni Assn., Am. Political Social Sci. Assn., Nat. Capital Area Councilors Assn. (dir.), Acad. Am. Polit. and Social Scis. Contbr. articles to profl. jours. Home: 4600 Connecticut Av NW Washington DC 20008 Office: Kenwood MD 04102

ADCOCK, BILL ARTHUR, mfg. exec.; b. Chariton, Ia., Oct. 21, 1933; s. William A. and Golda (Preva) A.; student Ia. State U., 1952-54; m. Mary Ream, Dec. 20, 1953; children—Debra, David, Diane. Mgr., Miller Garment Co., Chariton, 1954-58; mgr., co-owner Unionville Garment Co. (Mo.), 1958-61, All-Wear Mfg. Co., Newbern, Tenn., 1961-67; pres., co-owner Troy Mfg. Co. (Tenn.), 1967-—; owner Adcock Fabrics & Outlet Store, 1971-—; dir. B. &M. Stamp Co., Newbern. Chmn. Newbern Planning Commn., 1969-72; mem. Dyer County Cancer Bd., 1969-72, Dyer County Bd. Alcoholism and Drugs, 1969-71; active Boy Scouts Am., 1969-—. Bd. dirs. Newbern Library. Served with AUS, 1953-55. Mem. Am. Apparel Mfrs. Assn., Tenn. Mfrs. Assn., C. of C. (dir.), Tenn. Indsl. Engrs. Assn. Baptist (deacon). Mason, Rotarian, Lion (pres. 1962-64, dir. 1966-67). Home: 322 Flora Circle Newbern TN 38059 Office: 2000 Grayson St Newbern TN 38059

ADCOCK, THOMAS WAYNE, former naval officer, assn. exec.; b. Indpls., Dec. 20, 1930; s. Thomas Abram and Dorothy (Sullivan) A.; student pub. schs.; m. Erma Jo Pittman, Jan. 5, 1952; children—Debra Lynne, Thomas Wayne, Gary Alan, Tamara Jo. Enlisted U.S. Navy, 1948, advanced through the grades to lt. comdr., 1969; instrumentalist, also drum major, and the asst. leader, leader Navy bands throughout continental U.S., overseas bases, various aircraft carriets, 1949-60; asst. head music br. Bur. Naval Personnel, 1961-65; comdg. officer Sch. Music, Little Creek, Norfolk, Va., 1967-71; music dir. Internat. Azalea Festival, 1968-70. Adv. board All Am. Band, 1967-—, Am. Youth Symphony and Chorus, 1968-—. Cub scout committeeman Boy Scouts Am., 1962-65. Bd. dirs. Va. Beach Friends of Music, United Communities Fund. Mem. Nat. Band Assn. (dir. 1965-—, v.p. 1968-70), Music Educators Nat. Conf., Va. Music Educators Assn. Mason. Club: Circus Saints and Sinners (Norfolk). Home and office: 1913 Horseshoe Bend Virginia Beach VA 23455

ADDEN, ROBERT SPENCER, educator; b. Orangeburg, S.C., Jan. 1, 1923; s. John Augustus and Mary Elizabeth (Heggie) A.; B.S., The Citadel, 1947; M.B.A., U. Pa., 1948; Ph.D., U. N.C., 1954; m. Sue Sligh, Dec. 27, 1953; children—Carolyn, Robert Spencer, Virginia. Mem. faculty dept. bus. adminstrn. The Citadel, Charleston, S.C., 1947-—, prof., 1962-—, head dept., 1962-—. Lecr. Sch. for Bank Adminstrn., 1970-71. Bd. advisers Salvation Army, Charleston. Served with AUS, 1943-46. Decorated Bronze Star, Purple Heart. Mem. So. Econ. Assn., Am. Accounting Assn. Rotarian. Home and Office: The Citadel Charleston SC 29409

ADDISCOTT, DEREK HERBERT, publisher; b. Plymouth, Eng., Apr. 14, 1910; s. Herbert C. and Claire (Roberts) A.; student Oundle Coll., Eng., 1924-28, Stevens Inst. Tech. 1928-29; m. Katharine W. Bray, Nov. 23, 1944: children—Gayle K., Lynn C. Office mgr. Hamilton Watch Co., Lancaster, Pa., 1939-41; mgr. orgn. planning and procedures div. RCA, Camden, N.J., 1941-50; mgr. indsl. engring. PanAm. Airways, Cape Kennedy, Fla., 1954-58, mgr. data processing, 1958-67; pub. Eau Gallie, Fla., 1967-—. Councilman, Town of Palm Shores, Fla., 1960-61, vice mayor, 1961-63, mayor, 1963-—. Mem. Planning Zoning Commn., Palm Shores, Brevard County Civilian-Mil. Relations Council. Mem. Am. Mgmt. Assn., Nat. Office Mgmt. Assn., Moonwalk Commemorative Assn. (pres. 1972), Sigma Nu. Democrat. Episcopalian. Home: Box 76 Route 1 Palm Shores FL 32935 Office: PO Box 399 Eau Gallie FL 32935

ADDISON, STAYTON DOUGLAS, hotel exec.; b. Toledo, May 13, 1935; s. John Nelson and Florence Mae (Smith) A.; B.A., Mich. State U., 1959; m. Joan Ellen Kohrman, Sept. 4, 1959; children—Stayton Douglas, Rodger Alan. Dir. of food Sheraton Hawaii Corp., Honolulu, 1960-63; resident mgr. Bismarck Hotel, Chgo., 1963-65; mgr. Hospitality Motor Inns, Columbus, O., 1965-69; v.p. Gardens Services, Inc., Pine Mountain, Ga., 1969-—. Served with AUS, 1954-56. Mem. Am., Ga. (v.p. 1971) hotel and motel assns., Hotel Sales Mgrs. Assn. Home: PO Box 512 Pine Mountain GA 31822 Office: Callaway Gardens Pine Mountain GA 31822

ADDISON, WILLIAM PIERCE, physician; b. Ida, La., Apr. 6, 1909; s. William Pierce and Susan (Antony) A.; B.A., La. Coll., 1927; M.D., Tulane U., 1931; student Mass. Inst. Tech., summer 1953, U. Chgo., 1961-62; m. Edelweiss Buswell, June 6, 1938; 1 dau., Mary Elise (Mrs. J. G. Dupree). Intern, Tri-State Hosp., Shreveport, La., 1931-32; practice medicine, Shreveport, La., 1932-51; resident Langley Porter Psychiat. Inst. 1955-57; dir. Lake County Mental Health Clinic, Painesville, O., 1957; asst. supt. State Hosp., Columbus, O., 1957-60; asst. commr. Ohio Div. Mental Hygiene, Columbus, 1960-64; dir. Baton Rouge Regional Mental Health Center, 1964-66; commr. Mental Health State of La., Baton Rouge, 1966-—; clin. prof. psychiatry Tulane U., 1964-—, La. State U., 1971-—; staff psychiatrist La. State U. Student Mental Health, 1965-—. Served from lt. to lt. col. USAAF, 1942-46. Diplomate Am. Bd. Psychiatry and Neurology. Mem. Am. La. Psychiat. Assns., A.M.A., La. Med. Soc., Pi Kappa Phi, Phi Chi. Democrat. Home: 3719 Jolly Dr Baton Rouge LA 70808 Office: 655 N 5th St Baton Rouge LA 70804

ADEN, ROBERT CLARK, educator; b. Paris, Tenn., Jan. 13, 1927; s. Robert Franklin and Esther (Clark) A.; B.A., U. N.M., 1947; M.A., Murray State U., 1953; Ph.D., George Peabody Coll. for Tchrs., 1955; m. Martha Elizabeth Irby, Apr. 4, 1958; children—Robert Paul, Martha Lucille. Vis. prof. Bemidji (Minn.) State Coll., summer 1955; head dept. edn. and psychology Bethel Coll., McKenzie, Tenn., 1955-60; asst. prof. edn. N. Tex. State U., Denton, 1960-63, asso. prof., 1963-67; prof. edn. Middle Tenn. State U., Murfreesboro, 1967-—, dean of the graduate school, 1968-—. Cons. Cal. Test Bur., 1961-—, Tex. Small Schs. Assn., 1960-67; asso. dir. N. Tex. area Met. Center Supplementary Ednl. Services, 1966-67. Served with AUS, 1950-52. Mem. N.E.A., Nat. Soc. Study Edn., Tenn. Edn. Assn., Phi Delta Kappa, Pi Gamma Mu, Phi Kappa Phi, Kappa Delta Pi. Author: Teacher Training in Guatemala, 1955; (with Crosthwait) Adolescent Psychology Achievement Test, 1963; Status of the Social Studies in Texas Secondary Schools in 1964-65, 1966. Contbr. articles to profl. jours. Home: 419 Minerva Dr Murfreesboro TN 37130

ADERHOLT, HARRY CHANEY, physician; b. Birmingham, Ala., Jan. 22, 1938; s. William Lewis and Lempi (Pernu) A.; B.S., U. Ala., 1960; M.D., U. Ala. Med. Center, 1964; m. Sandra Joy Doyle, Sept. 8, 1958; children—Mark C., Ashley Ayn. Intern Brooke Gen. Hosp., San Antonio, 1964; resident radiology U. Ala., 1968-71; practice medicine specializing in radiology, Winfield, Ala., Guin, Ala., Hamilton, Ala., Haleyville, Ala.; mem. staffs Rankin Fite Meml. Hosp., Winfield, Burdick West Meml. Hosp., Haleyville. Served with AUS, 1964-68. Mem. Phi Beta Kappa, Sigma Phi Epsilon, Phi Eta Sigma. Baptist. Home: 3341 Stone Ridge Lane Birmingham AL 35243 Office: 1529 N 25th St Birmingham AL 35233

ADKINS, CEPHAS JOE, JR., psychologist, educator; b. Gainesville, Fla., Apr. 18, 1925; s. Cephas Joe and Eloise (Cox) A.; B.A., U. Fla., 1946, M.A., 1947; Ph.D., Ohio State U., 1957. Asst. prof. psychology Bridgewater (Va.) Coll., 1948-51; asso. prof. psychology Carsen-Newman Coll., Jefferson City, Tenn., 1954-57; asso. prof. psychology High Point (N.C.) Coll., 1957-61; asso. prof. psychology Old Dominion U., Norfolk, Va., 1961-66, prof., 1966-—. Organist High Point Friends, 1960-61, Second Presbyn. Ch., Norfolk, 1968-—. Fellow A.A.A.S.; mem. Am. Psychol. Assn., Am. Assn. U. Profs., So. Soc. for Philosophy and Psychology, Va. Acad. Sci., Psi Chi, Theta Chi. Presbyn. Home: 7832 Sea Wolf Dr Norfolk VA 23518

ADKINS, GEORGE BOZEMAN, JR., technical adviser; b. Ft. Worth, July 30, 1921; s. George Bozeman and Ethel (Hough) A.; B.S., U. Mo., 1950, M.A.,; m. Edith G. Mercer, Aug. 16, 1958; 1 dau., Virginia Ann. Chief statistician Gen. Motors Corp., Kansas City, Kan., 1951-53, dept. Air Force, Kansas City, Mo., 1952-54, Dept. Def., 1953-56 chief math. statistics br. AEC, Washington, 1956-60; chief operation and intelligence br. Strategy and Tactics Analysis Group, Dept. Army, 1960-62; charge operations research group FAA, Washington, 1962-66; tech. adviser Defense Communication Agy., 1966-—. Served with USN, 1940-46. Recipient Outstanding award Navy Dept., 1955, Superior Performance award, 1955. Mem. A.A.A.S., Inst. Math. Statistics. Author: (with others) The Management of Nuclear Materials, 1960; Operational Evaluation of Flight Inspections of Instrument Landing Systems, 1968. Research in electronics, ship propulsion, nuclear materials mgmt. Home: 4801 Kenmore Av Alexandria VA 22304 Office: Pentagon Washington DC 20301

ADKINS, JAMES CALHOUN, JR., judge; b. Gainesville, Fla., Jan. 18, 1915; s. James C. and Elizabeth (Edwards) A.; LL.B., U. Fla., 1938; m. Ethel Mae Fox, July 15, 1952; children—James Calhoun, III, Linda Rae. Admitted to Fla. bar, 1938; research atty. Supreme Ct. Fla., 1938; asst. atty. gen. Fla. 1939-41; practice law, Gainesville, 1941-57; asst. state atty., Gainesville, 1957-59; judge Ct. Record, 1959-61; circuit judge, Gainesville, 1964-69; justice Fla. Supreme Ct., Tallahassee, 1969-—. Mem. Fla. Council on Crime and Delinquency, 1961-69, Alachua County Mental Health Assn., 1957-69, Fla. Council on Criminal Justice, 1971-—, Fla. Hwy. Safety Commn., 1971-—, Fla. Alcoholism Adv. Council, 1971-—, Criminal Justice Information System Adv. Council, 1971-—; pres. Alachua County Taxpayers Assn., 1962-63; mem. adv. bd. Boys Club of Gainesville, 1958-69, pres., 1966-68, bd. dirs. Leon County chpt., 1969. Served with Inf. AUS, 1945. Mem. Am. Bar Assn., Fla. Bar, Am. Legion, Scribes, Forty and Eight, Phi Delta Phi. Democrat. Methodist. Lion, Moose, Elk, Woodmen of World. Author: Florida Criminal Law and Procedure, 1954; Florida Real Estate Law and Procedure, 1959; Florida Pleading, Practice and Legal Forms, 1964; Florida Civil and Criminal Discovery, 1970; also articles in Fla. law and practice. Home: 1111 Mimosa Dr Tallahassee FL 32303 also PO Box 427 Tallahassee FL 32302 Office: Supreme Ct Bldg Tallahassee FL 32304

ADKINSON, BURTON WILBUR, geographer; b. Everson, Wash., Mar. 5, 1909; s. Jason H. and Clara Fannie (Warriner) A.; student Western Wash. Coll. Edn., Bellingham, 1926-29, summers, 1932, 34; A.B. in edn., U. Wash., Seattle, 1936, M.A. in geography, 1939; Ph.D., Clark U., Worcester, Mass., 1942; m. Margaret Louise Klock, Sept. 10, 1942; children—Karen Louise, Margaret Jane. Tchr. pub. schs., Wash., 1929-39; asso. regional asst. Office of Geography, Dept. State, 1942-43; asst. dir. U.S. Bd. Geog. Names, 1943-44; asst. chief map intelligence sect., map div. OSS, 1944-45; asst. chief, acting chief map div. Library of Congress, Washington, 1945-47, chief, 1947-49, dir. reference dept., 1949-57, head Sci. Information Service (formerly Office Sci. Information), NSF, 1957-—. Fellow A.A.A.S.; mem. Am. Geog. Soc., Am. Documentation Inst. Internat. Fedn. for Documentation (past pres.), A.L.A., Spl. Libraries Assn. (treas. 1954-56, 1st v.p., pres. 1959-60), Assn. Am. Geographers (sec. 1954-57). Club: Cosmos (Washington). Contbr. articles to profl. jours. Home: 5907 Welborn Drive Washington DC 20016 Office: Nat Sci Found Washington DC 20550

ADKISSON, DAVID FLINTOFF, coll. pres.; b. Ashland City, Tenn,. Aug. 21, 1912; s. Samuel Henry and Ruth (Flintoff) A.; B.S., Middle Tenn. State Coll., 1935; M.A., George Peabody Coll., 1946; Ed.D., U. Tenn., 1960; m. Odessa Duncan, Feb. 2, 1940; 1 dau., Barbara Ann. Tchr. pub. schs., Cheatham County, Tenn., 1935-42, prin., South Fulton, Tenn., 1942-44, Bristol, Tenn., 1946-50; supt. schs., Watertown, Tenn., 1944-46, Bristol, Tenn., 1956-67; regional supr. Tenn. Dept. Edn., 1950-53; county dir. instrn. Knox County, Tenn., 1953-55; instr. U. Tenn., 1955-56; pres. Cleveland (Tenn.,) State Community Coll., 1967-—. Mem. Nat. (life), Tenn. (life) congresses parents and tchrs., Nat., Tenn., edn. assns., Phi. Kappa Phi, Phi Delta Kappa. Methodist. Mason, Rotarian. Home: 1211 Greenwood Trail Cleveland TN 37311

ADKISSON, PERRY LEE, educator; b. Hickman, Ark., Mar. 11, 1929; s. Robert Louis and Imogene (Perry) A.; B.S., U. Ark., 1950, M.S., 1954; Ph.D. in Entomology, Kan. State U., 1956; m. Frances Rozelle, Dec. 29, 1956; 1 dau., Jean Amanda. Asst. prof. U. Mo., 1956-58; asso. prof. Tex. A. and M. U. at College Station, 1958-63, prof. entomology, 1963-—, head dept., 1967-—. Cons. Internat. AEC, Vienna, Austria, 1969, Hazardous Materials Adv. Com. and Office Water Programs Environmental Protection Agy., 1971-—; chmn. sci. adv. panel to Gov. Tex. on Agrl. Chems., 1970-—; chmn. Tex. Pesticide Adv. Com., 1971-—; mem. panel experts on integrated pest control UN/FAO, Rome, Italy, 1971-—; mem. Structural Pest Control Bd. Tex., 1971-—; So. Agrl. Expt. Sta. Dirs. rep. to So. Regional Pest Mgmt. Working Group. Served with M.C., AUS, 1951-53. USPHS spl. post-doctoral fellow Harvard, 1963-64. Fellow A.A.A.S.; mem. Entomol. Soc. Am. (mem. governing bd. 1971-73, Bussart Meml. award 1967), Kan. Entomol. Soc., Sigma Xi. Contbr. numerous articles profl. jours. Research in insect photoperidism, integrated control of cotton insects. Home: 305 W Brookside St Bryan TX 77801

ADLER, LAWRENCE, educator; b. N.Y.C., June 6, 1923; s. Bertram and Serena (Katz) A.; A.B., N.Y.U., 1946; B.S., Columbia, 1949; M.S., U. Utah, 1953; Ph.D., U. Ill., 1964; m. Joan M. Anderson June 29, 1957; children—Charles, Lauri Jo, Albert. Jr. engr. N.Am. Aviation Co. Los Angeles, 1951; asst. civil engr. City Los Angeles, 1952-55; asst. prof. mining engring. U. Mo., Rolla, 1955-56, Lehigh U., Bethlehem, Pa., 1956-58, Mich. Technol. U., Houghton, 1958-61; asso. prof. mining engring. Va. Poly. Inst. and State U., Blacksburg, 1963-69, prof., 1969-—, pres. engring. faculty orgn., 1971-72; cons. Rand Corp., Calumet & Hecla Co., Freeport Mining Co., Nat. Gypsum Co., U.S. Gypsum Co. Served with USAAF, 1943-45. Decorated Air medal, Purple Heart with one oak leaf cluster. Registered profl. engr., Va. Mem. Am. Soc. C.E., Am. Inst. Mining, Metall. and Petroleum Engrs., Sigma Xi. Mem. Disciples of Christ Ch. (deacon). Author: Ground Control; Excavation and Materials Handling. Contbr. articles to profl. jours. Patentee field roof support device. Home: 600 Preston Av Blacksburg VA 24060

ADMAS, EDWARD JAMES, ofcl. Nat. Gallery Art; b. Los Angeles, Oct. 31, 1916; s. Edward James and Nelle Marie (Platt) A.; B.A., U. Mich., 1938, J.D., 1941; m. Kathryn Porter Johnson, June 28, 1941; children—Linda A. (Mrs. Russell Holland Bronstein), Douglas J., Brian R. Admitted to Ohio bar, 1941, D.C. bar, 1951; gen. atty. Treasury Dept., Washington, 1946-50; asst. sec., asst. gen. counsel Nat. Gallery Art, 1950-65, asst. treas., 1962-65, adminstr., 1965-71, sec., gen. counsel, 1971-—. Hon. trustee Greater Washington Ednl. TV Assn. Served with USCGR, 1942-46. Decorated Bronze Star. Mem. Fed. Bar Assn., Nat. Lawyers Club. Home: 12809 Spring Dr Rockville MD 20850 Office: National Gallery of Art Constitution at 6th St Washington DC 20565

ADREON, HARRY BARNES, JR., architect; b. Norfolk, Va., July 18, 1929; s. Harry Barnes and Helen (Medairy) A.; student Coll. William and Mary, 1947-48; B.S., Va. Polytech. Inst., 1950, M.S., 1952; m. Beatrice M. Rice, Dec. 27, 1952. Mem. firms Keyes, Smith, Satterlee & Lethbridge, Washington, 1954-56, Keyes, Lethbridge, &Condon, Washington, 1956-61; partner Cross & Adreon, Washington, 1961-—; pres. Auto World, Inc., Newbern, N.C. Served with USMCR, 1952-54. Recipient Design awards Nat. Assn. Home Builders 1965, 66; award for Architecture, Washington Bd. Trade, 1965; Design award Bethesda-Chevy Chase C. of C., 1966-67; House and Home Nat. awards A.I.A., 1966-67, Honor award Mid Atlantic Region, 1967, Nat. A.I.A. Honor award, 1968; Nat. Honor award Am. Inst. Steel Constrn., 1967. Registered profl. architect, Md., Va., D.C. Mem. A.I.A., Washington Bldg. Congress, Constrn. Specifications Inst. (bd. dirs. 1969-—, chpt. pres. 1972-—), Washington Episcopal Diocesan Archtl. Commn., Tau Sigma Delta. Episcopalian (vestryman 1961-63, 67-—). Home: 4524 N 19th Rd Arlington VA 22207 Office: 901 27th St NW Washington DC 20037

ADRIANCE, ROBERT ALLAN, found. exec.; b. N.Y.C., Oct. 22, 1917; s. Thomas Floy and Grace (Underwood) A.; B.S., Georgetown U., 1950; m. Isabelle Y. Long, Jan. 17, 1942; children—Robert Allan, Grace A. (Mrs. William D. Frierson III), Carol Long. Asst. treas., treas., 2d v.p. United Services Life Ins. Co., Washington, 1950-56; bus. mgr., treas. Assn. for Research and Enlightenment, Edgar Cayce Found., Virginia Beach, Va., 1956-61, pres. found., 1961-—, also trustee; dir. Cavalier Birdneck Land Corp. Trustee, Tidewater Westminster Homes, Atlantic U. Served with Md. N.G., 1940-41; to 1st lt. AUS, 1941-45; ETO. Mem. Spiritual Frontier Fellowship, Huguenot Soc., Soc. Mayflower Descs., U.S. Power Squadrons, Archeol. Inst. Am. Presbyn. (elder 1967—). Home: 1212 Kittiwake Ct Virginia Beach VA 23451 Office: 215 67th St Virginia Beach VA 23451

ADRIANI, JOHN, physician; b. Bridgeport, Conn., Dec. 2, 1907; s. Nicola and Lucia (Caseria) A.; A.B., Columbia, 1930, M.D., 1934; m. Eleanor Anderson, Dec. 1936 (div. Feb. 1947); 1 son, John Nicolas; m. 2d, Irene Miller, Sept. 7, 1953. Intern surgery French Hosp., N.Y.C., 1934-36; resident anesthesiology Bellevue Hosp., N.Y.C., 1936-37; fellow N.Y. U., 1937-39, instr. anesthesiology dept. surgery, 1939-41; asst., then asso. clin. prof. surgery La. State U. Sch. Medicine, 1941-54, clin. prof. surgery and pharmacology 1954, clin. prof. oral surgery Sch. Dentistry, 1971—; asst. prof., later asso. prof. anesthesiology Loyola Sch. Dentistry, New Orleans, 1945-56, prof. gen. anesthesiology, 1956-71; prof. surgery Tulane U., 1947—, dir. dept. anesthesiology, 1941—, dir. dept. inhalation therapy, 1941-70, dir. blood plasma bank, 1944-70, asst. dir., 1960-64; asso. dir. Charity Hosp., 1966—, center chmn. regional med. program, 1967—; cons. anesthesiologist Flint-Goodridge, VA, USPHS, Ochsner Found. hosps., Hotel Dieu, New Orleans; cons. to Touro Infirmary, New Orleans, also FDA. Mem. adv. com., div. investigational drugs FDA, 1963-71; chmn. adv. com. on anesthetic and respiratory drugs, 1966-71; mem. founders group expansion program Holy Cross Coll., 1963; mem. revision com., chmn. com. on anesthesia, subcom. on scope U.S. Pharmacopoela, 1960-70, mem. com. admissions nat. formulary, 1970—. Bd. dirs. Cancer Soc. of New Orleans. Named hon. col. Staff Gov. La., 1965; recipient Distinguished Service award Am. Soc. Anesthesiologists, 1949, Internat. Anesthesiology Research Soc., 1957; Guedel medal for anesthesiology, 1959; Gold medal Assn. Alumni Coll. Phys. and Surg., Columbia, 1967; Silver medal for achievements in medicine Columbia U. Sch. Medicine; Ralph M. Waters award internat. achievements in anesthesiology, 1968; Horace Wells award in anesthesiology Horace Wells Soc., 1969; decorated knight comdr. Order of Merit (Italy), 1969; named Nat. Italian Am. of Year, 1969. Diplomate Am. Bd. Anesthesiology (dir. 1960, chmn. exams. com. 1963—, pres. 1967-68). Fellow Am. Soc. Clin. Pharm. and Chemotherapy, Am. Soc. Clin. Pharm. and Therapy, Am. Coll. Anesthesiologists (gov. 1944-50, 56-60); mem. Am. Heart Assn., Assn. Colonic Surgeons, A.A.A.S., Soc. Exptl. Biology and Medicine, So. Soc. Clin. Research, Internat. Anesthesia Research Soc., (Baxter Travenol lectr. 1972), NRC, Columbia U. Alumni Assn., Am. Hosp. Assn., Assn. U. Anesthesiologists (pres. 1955), Assn. Univ. Anesthesiology Departmental Chmn., A.M.A. (chmn. council on drugs 1968—, vice chmn. 1967, chmn. 1967-70, chmn. ad hoe editorial com. to write drug evaluations 1971), Internat. Soc. Comprehensive Medicine, Am., La. (1950), So. (pres. 1952—), Cuban (hon.), Venezuelan (hon.) socs. anesthesiologists, So. Med. Assn., Southeastern Surg. Congress, Am. Acad. Anesthesiology, Am. Coll. Angiology, Am. Surg. Assn., Mexican Soc. Anesthesiology (hon. pres. 1954), La. Thoracic Soc., Yucatan Soc. Anesthesiology (hon. pres. 1966), Civil Service League La., (bd. dirs.), Assn. Wildlife and Fisheries La. (asso. mem.). Clubs: Thoracophilis, Horse Shoe. Author: Pharmacology of Anesthetic Drugs, rev. edit. 1970; Chemistry of Anesthesia, 1946; Techniques and Procedures of Anesthesia, 3d edit., 1964; Nerve Blocks, 1954; Selection of Anesthesia, 1955; General Anesthesiology For Students and Practitioners of Dentistry, 1958; The Recovery Room, 1958; Chemistry and Physics of Anesthesia, 1962; Appraisal-Current Concepts Anesthesiology (Mosby), Vol. 1, 1961, Vol. 2, 1964, Vol. 3, 1966, Vol. 4, 1969; Revision of Labat's Regional Anesthesia, 1967; also scientific and med. papers. Editor: American Lecture Series in Anesthesiology; cons. editor, Surgery, The Resident G. P. Survey Anesthesiology; editor Anesthesiology, 1964—; cons. editor Excerpta Medica, Audiodigest, Dorland's Illustrated Med. Dictionary, 1969—, Internat. Corr. Soc. Anesthesiology. Home: 67 N Park Pl New Orleans LA 70124 Office: Charity Hosp New Orleans LA 70140

AFFLECK, BERT, educator; b. Childress, Tex., Apr. 22, 1934; s. Bert and Reba Marie (Wilson) A.; B.A., McMurry Coll., 1955; B.D., Perkins Sch. Theology, 1958; Ph.D. (Grad. fellow 1958-59), Drew U., 1968; m. Patsy Green, Dec. 27, 1955; children—Ellen Marie, Scott. Ordained to ministry Methodist Ch., 1956; asst. minister St. Mark's Meth. Ch., Midland, Tex., 1955-57, First Meth. Ch., Big Spring, Tex., 1957; minister Andover (N.J.) Meth. Ch., 1959-61; minister, asst. prof. religion McMurry Coll., Abilene, Tex., 1961-64, minister, asso. prof. religion, 1968—; minister United Meth. Ch., Pond Eddy, N.Y., 1964-68. Vol. co-pastor St. James United Meth. Ch., 1968-69; cons. multi-media team teaching in religion, 1968—; mem. bd. ministry N.W. Tex. conf. United Meth. Ch., 1968—, chmn. ministerial recruitment, 1969—. Recipient Selecman Greek award Perkins Sch. Theology, 1958. Jesse Jones Edn. grantee, 1964-65, 65-66. Mem. Soc. Ch. History, Am. Acad. Religion, Am. Assn. U. and Coll. Chaplains, West Tex.-N.M. Philos. Soc., Fellowship Christian Athletes, Alpha Chi. Democrat. Methodist. Home: 1601 Sayles Blvd Abilene TX 79605

AGAMEMNON, GEORGE JOSEPH, transp. co. exec.; b. N.Y.C., Dec. 20, 1916; s. Emmanuel G. and Margaret (Rein) A.; student N.Y.U., 1944, Alexander Hamilton Inst., 1948, U.N.C., 1954, LaSalle Extension U., 1962, U. Mich., 1967; m. Helen A. Preston, Oct. 10, 1942 children—G. Richard, John Paul. Rate clk. Horton Motor Lines, N.Y.C., 1939-41 (merged with Asso. Transport, Inc 1941), sales asst., 1943-44, asst. to v.p., 1946-59; asst. mgr. trucking Burlington Industries Inc. (N.C.), 1959-62, mgr., 1962—, v.p. trucking and warehousing, 1968—. Lectr. in field. Vice pres. Am. Cancer Soc., Alamance County, N.C., 1969-70; chmn. campaign United Fund, Alamance County, 1967-68; mem. Alamance County Civil Def. Commn., 1969-72. Mem. Am. Trucking Assn. (indsl. relations com. 1964—), Am. Mgmt. Assn. (planning council 1968—), Pvt. Carrier Conf. (dir.), Burlington C. of C., N.C. Motor Carriers Assn., Va. Hwy. Users Assn., Burlington Traffic Club, Internat. Platform Assn., Central Motor Freight Assn. Roman Catholic. Elk, K.C. (4 deg.). Home: Rt 7 Box 114 Collingwood Dr Burlington NC 27215 Office: Tucker St Extension PO Box 691 Burlington NC 27215

AGEE, WARREN KENDALL, educator; b. Sherman Tex., Oct. 23, 1916; s. Frederic M. and Minnie E. (Logsdon) A.; B.A. cum laude, Tex. Christian U., 1937; M.A., U. Minn., 1949, Ph.D., 1955; m. Edda Robbins, June 1, 1941; children—Kim Kathleen, Robyn Kendall. Mem. editorial staff Ft. Worth Star-Telegram, 1937-48; instr. journalism Tex. Christian U., 1948-50, asst. prof. 1950-55, asso. prof., 1955-57, prof., 1957-58, chmn. dept., 1950-58, faculty adviser student publs., 1949-58, prof. journalism, dean Evening Coll., 1962-65; prof. journalism, dean sch. journalism W.Va. U., 1958-60, mem. edn!. adv. com. WJPB-TV, Fairmont and Weston, W.Va., 1959-60; nat. exec. officer Sigma Delta Chi, 1960-62; prof. journalism, dean William Allen White School of Journalism, U. Kan., Lawrence, 1965-69; dean Henry W. Grady Sch. Journalism, U. Ga., 1969—. Pub. information splst. USCG Res. Hdqrs., 1944-45. Mem. adv. screening com. journalism, com. internat. exchange of persons Conf. Bd. of Asso. Research Councils, Washington, 1958-62; mem. Am. Council on Edn. for Journalism, 1955-60, 65-67, mem. accrediting com., 1969—. Mng. dir. William Allen White Found., 1965-69, trustee, 1970—; mng. dir. George Foster Peabody Radio and TV awards, 1969—. Recipient Journalism award from the Ft. Worth Press, 1936; outstanding News Writing award Ft. Worth Professional chpt. Sigma Delta Chi, 1946; Carl Towley award, Journalism Edn. Assn., 1969. Mem. Assn. Edn. in Journalism (pres. 1958), Am. Studies Assn., Sigma Delta Chi (pres. Fort Worth professional chpt. 1954-55; sec. Tex. 1957-58; nat. v.p. campus chpt. affairs 1966-69), Kappa Tau Alpha, Alpha Chi, Phi Kappa Sigma, Alpha Sigma Lambda. Mem. Christian Church. Rotarian. Clubs: Gridiron (Ft. Worth); University (Athens, Ga,). Author: (with Edwin Emery and Phillip H. Ault) Introduction to Mass Communications, 1960, rev. edit., 1965, 70; also articles. Editor: The Press and the Public Interest, 1968; Mass Media In A Free Society, 1969. Asso. editor, bus. mgr. The Quill, 1960-62; adv. editorial bd. Journalism Quar., 1955-60. Home: 130 Highland Dr Athens GA 30601 Office: Henry W Grady Sch Journalism U Ga Athens GA 30601

AGLIO, THOMAS JOSEPH, social agy. exec.; b. Boston, Nov. 22, 1931; s. Joseph Michael and Mary (Rossetti) A.; B.S., Boston Coll., 1953, M.S.W., 1955; m. Margaret Mary Cronin, Sept. 17, 1955; children—Susan M., Teresa E., Mariana, Stephen J., Elizabeth J. Philip G. Caseworker, acting dir. social service Albany (N.Y.) Med. Center, 1955-58; supr. social service St. Vincent Hosp., Worcester, Mass., 1958-61; adminstr. Camp St. John for Cuban Refugees, Jacksonville, Fla., 1962; dir. Catholic Social Services, Inc., Orlando, Fla., 1962, asso. diocesan dir., 1968—; adminstr. Maris Stella Villa Maternity Home, Winter Park, Fla., 1964-69. Instr. Albany Med. Coll., Union U., Albany, N.Y., 1957-58; lectr. Russell Sage Sch. Nursing, Albany, N.Y., 1956-58; cons. Catholic Charities Diocese, Worcester, Mass., 1961. Mem. Acad. Certified Social Workers, Nat. Assn. Social Workers, Fla. Community Services Assn., Fla. Health and Welfare Council, Am. Pub. Health Assn., Profl. Community Service League, Nat. Conf. Catholic Charities. Home: 367 Fitzhugh Rd Winter Park FL 32789 Office: 550 N Bumby Av Orlando FL 32803

AGNEW, DONALD BURNS, govt. ofcl.; b. Ogden, Ill., Aug. 10, 1922; s. Theodore Lee and Agnes (Faris) A.; B.S. (Sears Roebuck scholar 1938-1940), U. Ill., 1941; postgrad. Am. U., 1955, U. Md., 1957-65; m. Virginia L. Penn, Feb. 14, 1946 (div. June 1966); children— Donald Burns Lee, Melissa Louise; m. 2d, Joan Lee Parker, June 28, 1969; one daughter, Leslye Ann. Began career as research asst. econ. entomology Ill. Natural History Survey, Urbana, 1940-41; economist Bur. Land Mgmt., U.S. Interior Dept., Cheyenne, Wyo., also Washington, 1946-48, with U.S. Dept. Agr., 1948—, economist Agrl. Marketing Service, also Prodn. and Marketing Administrn., 1948-62, economist Econ. Research Service, Washington, 1962—; dir. Spl. Econ. Surveys, Washington, 1954-58; econ. cons. U.S. AID Mission in Panama, 1972; cons. on food irradiation studies to Atomic Energy Commn. and the food industry; lectr. various univs., dairy and livestock industry meetings; instr. econs. U. Md., 1969—. Served with inf. AUS, 1941-46; PTO. Recipient citation for meritorious research U.S. Dept. Agr., 1952, 72; commendation Nat. Commn. Food Marketing, 1966. Mem. A.A.A.S., Am. Farm Econ. Assn., Canadian Agrl. Econ. Soc., Am. Marketing Assn., Western Farm Econs. Assn., Anteaters Assn., Internat. Assn. Agrl. Economists, Orgn. Profl. Employees Dept. Agr., Alpha Zeta. Contbr. to Readings in Agricultural Marketing, 1954; also articles in profl. jours. Compiler: Readings in Linear Programming: Applications to Agricultural Problems, 1956. Home: 6108 Rivanna Dr Springfield VA 22150 Office: South Agriculture Bldg 14th and C Sts SW Washington DC 20250 also 500 C St SW Washington DC

AGNEW, SPIRO THEODORE, vice pres. of U.S.; b. Balt., Nov. 9, 1918; s. Theodore S. and Margaret (Akers) A.; student Johns Hopkins; LL.B., U. Balt.; m. Elinor Isabel Judefind, May 27, 1942; children—James Rand, Pamela Lee (Mrs. Robert DeHaven), Susan Scott, Elinor Kimberly. Formerly claims adjuster Lumbermens Mut. Casualty Co., then personnel mgr. Shreiber Food Stores; admitted to Md. bar; formerly engaged in pvt. practice in Balt. and Balt. County; then mem. firm Karl F. Steinmann; chmn. Balt. County Bd. Appeals, 1958-61; chief exec. Balt. County, 1962-66; chmn. transp. com. Nat. Assn. Counties, 1963; gov. of Md., 1967-69; vice pres. of U.S., 1969—. Served as officer AUS, 1942-45, 51. Decorated Bronze Star medal, Combat Inf. badge. Mem. Md., Balt. county bar assns. Republican. Episcopalian. Kiwanian. Address: 2660 Woodley Rd Washington DC 20008

AGNEW, MRS. SPIRO THEODORE, wife of vice pres. U.S.; b. Balt.; d. W. Lee and Ruth Elinor (Schafer) Judefind; m. Spiro T. Agnew, May 27, 1942; children—Pamela Lee (Mrs. Robert DeHaven), James Rand, Susan Scott, Elinor Kimberly. Address: 2600 Connecticut Av NW Washington DC 20008

AGNEW, THEODORE LEE, JR., historian; b. Ogden, ILL., Dec. 21, 1916; s. Theodore Lee and Agnes (Faris) A; B.A., U. Ill., 1937, M.A., 1938; A.M., Harvard U., 1939, Ph.D., 1954; M. Jeanne Starrett LeCaine, Dec. 25, 1942; children—Theodore (dec.), Theodore Lee III, Susan Elizabeth, Hugh LeCaine, Peter Wallace, Marion Jeanne. Grad. research asst. U. Ill., 1938; asst. prof. history Okla. State U., 1947-54, asso. prof., 1954-60, prof., 1960—; vis. prof. history Emory U., 1964, 1966-67. Served with USNR, 1942-46. Mem. Am. Hist. Assn., Orgn. Am. Historians, So. Hist. Assn., Western History Assn., Am. Soc. Ch. History, Ill., Okla. hist. socs., Am. Assn. U. Profs. (mem. council 1960-63), Am. Studies Assn., Phi Beta Kappa, Phi Kappa Phi, Phi Alpha Theta, Alpha Kappa Lambda, Omicron Delta Kappa. Democrat. Methodist. Home: 1216 N Lincoln St Stillwater OK 74074

AGRONSKY, MARTIN ZAMA, radio, TV news analyst; b. Phila., Jan. 12, 1915; s. Isador Nathan and Marcia (Dvorin) A.; B.S., Rutgers U., 1936, M.A. (hon.), 1949; m. Helen Smathers, Sept. 1, 1943 (dec. Feb. 1969); children—Marcia, Jonathan, David, Julie. Gen. reporter Palestine Post, Jerusalem, 1936-37; free lance contbr. newspapers, mags., 1937-40; NBC corr. Geneva, Belgrade, Sofia, Ankara, 1940-43; war corr. Libya, Greece, Singapore, Java, Australia, Pacific, 1940-43; Washington corr. ABC, 1943-64; former NBC radio and TV corr., Washington corr. Today Show; Washington corr. for CBS, 1964, Paris corr., bur. chief CBS, 1964-69; TV commentator Washington Post-Newsweek stas., Washington, 1969—. Recipient Peabody award for distinguished reporting, 1952; Heywood Broun award for radio reporting Am. Newspaper Guild, 1948; Alfred Dupont award for distinguished reporting and commentary, TV, 1962; Nat. Headliners award TV reporting, 1962; Venice Film Festival award for documentary Polaris Submarine—Journal of an Undersea Voyage, 1963; TV Emmy for CBS Special, 1969. Mem. Congl. Radio-TV Corrs. Assn. (pres. 1953), Omicron Delta Kappa (hon. mem.). Clubs: Federal City, Overseas Writers, Nat. Press (Washington). Home: 2605 Tilden Pl NW Washington DC 20008 Office: Broadcast House Washington DC 20005 also 3620 27th St SArlington VA 22206

AGUAYO, JORGE, librarian; b. Havana, Cuba, Dec. 4, 1903; D.C.L., U. Havana, 1925; certificate librarianship (Rockefeller fellow) Columbia, 1941. Asst. dir. gen. library U. Havana, 1937-59, dir. gen. library, 1959-60, prof. cataloging and classification, 1950-60; head br. librarian Pan Am. Union, Washington, 1962—. Mem. Am., D.C. library assns. Contbr. articles to profl. jours. Address: Pan Am Union 2800 Quebec St Washington DC 20008*

AGUILAR, ABRAHAM, lawyer, legislator; b. Mexico, 1912; ed. Nat. U. Mexico. Admitted to Mexican bar, 1937; mem. firm Hardin, Hess, Santos Galindo & Hanhausen, Mexico City; mem. Mexican Chamber Deps. Address: Hardin Hess Santos Galindo & Hanhausen Calle Lopez 1 Mexico DF Mexico*

AGUILAR, RODOLFO JESUS, architect, engr.; b. San Jose, Costa Rica, Sept. 28, 1936; s. Hector Jesus and Nora Noemi (Espinosa) A.; student U. Santo Domingo, Dominican Republic, 1953-55; B.S. in Archtl. Engring., La. State U., 1958, M.S. in Civil Engring. (Latin-Am. fellow), 1960, B.Arch., 1961; postgrad. Ill. Inst. Tech., summer 1962; Ph.D. in Civil Engring. (Ford Found. fellow), N.C. State U., 1964; m. Nellyn Mariana Carias, Oct. 5, 1956; children—Rodolfo J., Ricardo A., Roberto J., Nora N. Came to U.S., 1955, naturalized, 1966. Architect, engr. Bodman, Murrell and Smith, Baton Rouge, La., summer 1959; architect, structural engr. J. Wesley Leake and Assos., Baton Rouge, 1959-62; cons. engr. Kahn &Furbush, Raleigh, N.C., summer 1964, Alfred G. Rayner, Baton Rouge, 1964; v.p. Systems Analysis and Design Optimization, Inc., Baton Rouge, 1966-70; pres. A.D.H. Systems, Inc., Baton Rouge, 1970—. Structural examiner La. State Bd. Archtl. Examiners, 1965-66. Recipient Halliburton award for Excellence in Teaching Halliburton Co. and La. State U., 1967. NSF grantee, 1962, 65, 66; Ford Found. fellow, grantee, 1962-64. Mem. Am. Soc. C.E., A.I.A., Am. Soc. Engring. Edn., Operations Research Soc. Am., La. Engring. Soc. (certificate of Merit, 1958), Sigma Xi, Tau Beta Pi, Phi Kappa Phi, Chi Epsilon. Author: Systems Analysis and Design in Engineering, Architecture, Construction and Planning. Contbr. articles to tech. jours. Home: 4866 Whitehaven Baton Rouge LA 70808 Office: 3104 Convention Baton Rouge LA 70806

AGUIRRE, RAFAEL ANGEL, educator; b. Havana, Cuba, Mar. 1, 1925; s. Rafael Angel and Raquel (Rencurrell) A.; B.A., Colegio de Belen, 1942; LL.D., Havana U., 1947; M.A., Middlebury Coll. (Vt.), 1967; m. Olga Psychol. Assn. (chmn. legal Rueda, Nov. 11, 1945; 1 dau., Ivonne (Mrs. Bruce W. Deal). Came to U.S., 1960, naturalized, 1969. Dir. law firm Havana, Cuba, 1947-60; counselor Ministry of Labor, Havana, 1952-59; prof. Spanish and Spanish lit. Stratford Coll., Danville, Va., 1963—, chmn. dept. Spanish, 1965—. Prof. philosophy law Jose Marti U., Havana, 1956-58. Mem. Colegio de Abogados de la Habana, Colegio de Abogados de Cuba, Colegio de Notarios, Comision Permanente de Derecho Penal del Colegio de Abogados de la Habana, Comision Permanente de Derecho Laboral, Colegio Abogados de la Habana. Home: 137 Briarcliff Lane Danville VA 24541

AHLGREN, FRANK RICHARD, editor; b. Superior, Wis., June 25, 1903; s. Oscar John and Beatrice Marie (Gibson-Taylor) A.; student Superior (Wis.) State Tchrs. Coll., 1922-25, Memphis U. Law Sch., 1926-28; D.C.L., Southwestern Coll.; m. Elizabeth Alley, Feb. 25, 1932; children—Frank Richard, Gibson-Taylor, Calvin Lane. Reporter Superior Eve. Telegram, 1923-24, Duluth (Minn.) Herald, 1924-25, Milw. Jour., 1925-26, Memphis Eve. Appeal, 1926-33, Tex. Newspaper Pubs. Assn., Houston, 1934-36, Cleve. Press, 1936-37; editor Memphis Comml. Appeal, 1937-69. Trustee U. Tenn.; bd. dirs. Meth. Hosp., Memphis Pub. Library, Memphis-Ark. Bridge Commn. Mem. Sigma Delta Chi, Kappa Tau Alpha. Episcopalian. Mason, Rotarian. Clubs: Tennessee, Memphis Country, Hunt and Polo (Memphis). Home: 2714 Lombardy Memphis TN 38111 Office: Box 3120 100 N Main St Memphis TN 38101

AHOUA, TIMOTHEE N'GUETTA, diplomate of Ivory Coast; b. Aboisso, Ivory Coast, Apr. 25, 1931; s. Moise N'Guetta and Assan (Aka) A.; bachelor degree in Pub. Law and Polit. Sci., U. Paris, 1961; student Nat. Sch. French Magistracy of Paris, 1959-62; diploma Inst. Overseas Higher Studies, U. Paris, 1963. Tng. in French embassy, Bonn, Germany, Acad. Internat. Law, Hague, Netherlands, WHO, ILO, Geneva, Switzerland, 1962-63; 1st counselor Ivory Coast, Washington, 1964-65; ambassador of Ivory Coast to Morocco, 1965-66, to U.S., 1966—, to Can., 1967—. Home: 5111 Broad Branch Rd NW Washington DC 20008 Office: 2424 Massachusetts Av NW Washington DC 20008

AIKEN, BEDFORD ELIAS (DICK), JR., advt. agy. exec.; b. Rocky Mount, N.C., July 30, 1916; s. Bedford Elias and Anna (Simmons) A.; student, Rollins Conservatory of Music (Winter Park, Fla.), 1947; m. Anne Shepherd Wright, July 2, 1939; children—Dian Shepherd (Mrs. Paul Leslie Martz), Bedford Elias III, Anne Wright (Mrs. Charles Denver Hayes, Jr.), John Charles, David Sutherland, Margaret Ava, Dick Seaborn, Michael Hamilton, Timothy Clay, Mary Simmons. Wholesale produce broker, Winston Salem, N.C. and Sanford, Fla., 1932-47; profl. singer (tenor), 1947-52; comml. mgr. WTRR Radio, Sanford, Fla., 1950-52; owner, operator Aiken Advt. Agy., Sanford, Fla., 1952—; spl. promotion adviser Sanford Herald, 1961-65. Winner, all-Florida Talent Contest, 1947, Arthur Godfrey Talent Scout Show, 1947. Mason (Shriner). Home: 444 Elliott Av Sangford FL 32771 Office: 110 S Palmetto St Sanford FL 32771

AIKMAN, LEO, journalist; b. Dana, Ind., Dec. 22, 1908; s. Clarence Burch and Gertrude (James) A.; A.B., DePauw U., 1930; M.A. in History, U. Mich., 1936; m. Ira Irby, July 12, 1941; 1 dau., Susan Kathleen. High sch. tchr., 1930-39; historian Nat. Park Service, 1939-44; editor Cobb County Times. Marietta, Ga., 1944-50; columnist Atlanta Constitution, 1950—; dir. community services Atlanta Newspapers. Mem. Ga. Press Assn. (bd. mgrs.), Phi Beta Kappa. Presbyn. (elder). Rotarian. (dist. gov.). Home: 268 Vance Circle Marietta GA 30060 Office: PO Box 4689 Atlanta GA 30302

AINSWORTH, H. GARDNER, fgn. service officer; b. Charleston, S.C., Mar. 15, 1917; s. Walden Lee and Katharine (Gardner) A.; student St. Paul's Sch., Concord, N.H., 1933-35; A.B., Princeton, 1939; spl. studies Harvard, 1948-49; m. Helen Louise Reed, Aug. 25, 1940; children—Linda Gardner, Lee Thornton (Mrs. Keith C. Johnson). Apptd. fgn. service officer, 1940; service in Winnipeg, 1940, San Salvador, 1941-44, Rome, 1944-48, Washington, 1949-51; 1st sec., Paris, 1951-54, Helsinki, 1954-57, Washington, 1957-60; Nat. War Coll., 1960; econ. counselor Rome, 1960-63, AID Regional Office Central Am., Guatemala, 1964-65; adviser to asst. sec. commerce for sci. and tech., 1965-66; econ. counselor AID dir., Mexico City, 1966-69; dir. Office Maritime Affairs Dept. State, Washington, 1969—. Mem. Soc. Cin. Club: Chevy Chase (Md.). Address: 7711 Brookville Rd Chevy Chase MD 20015

AINSWORTH, ROBERT ANDREW, JR., U.S. judge; b. Gulfport, Miss., May 10, 1910; s. Robert Andrew and Catherine (Wursch) A.; LL.B., Loyola U., New Orleans, 1932, LL.D., 1967; LL.D. (hon.), Xavier U., New Orleans, 1953; m. Elizabeth Hiern, Oct. 14, 1933; children— Elisabeth (Mrs. Clarence Rareshide), Robert Andrew III, Leslie. Admitted to La. bar, 1932; practice in New Orleans, 1932-61; U.S. judge Eastern Dist. La., 1961-66; judge 5th circuit U.S. Ct. Appeals, 1966—. Chmn. bd. mgrs. Council State Govts., 1955-56; mem. Charter Com. City New Orleans, 1951-52; founder La. Legislative Council, 1952; pres. Nat. Legislative Conf., 1955-56. Mem. La. Senate from Orleans Parish, 1950-61, pres. pro tem, 1952-56, 60-61. Mem. Presdl. Commn. Govt. Relations, 1961. Mem. exec. com., bd. dirs. Internat. House, 1951-58. Recipient Weiss award Nat. Conf. Christians and Jews, 1966; St. Mary's Dominican Coll.

medal, 1971. Mem. Blue Key. Democrat. Author: La. Civil Service Act, also Annual Fiscal Session Law. Home: 1776 Arabella St New Orleans LA 70115 Office: 400 Royal St New Orleans LA 70130

AKER, GEORGE FREDERICK, educator; b. Fort Wayne, Ind., June 2, 1927; s. George Mosier and Elvira (Marten) A.; B.S. with distinction, Purdue U., 1950; M.S., U. Wis., 1958, Ph.D. (U. fellow), 1962; postgrad. U. Chgo., 1958-59; m. Patricia Lou Lawson, Nov. 16, 1946; children—Linda Lou, Kathy Ann, Jon Kent, Susan Nanette. Instr., research asso. U. Mo., Columbia, 1950-51; agrl. extension agt. Purdue U., 1951-59; asst. prof. edn., dir. studies and tng. in continuing edn. U. Chgo., 1962-63; faculty Fla. State U., Tallahassee, 1963—, prof., head dept. adult edn., 1965—; v.p. Research Tech. Corp., 1969—; pres. Action Research Corp.; dir. Multi-Racial Corp., 1970—. Vis. prof. edn. U. Wis., Madison, 1963-66; dir. tng. Fla. Inst. Continuing U. Studies, Tallahassee, 1963-65; cons. Fla. Dept. Edn., 1963-67, Ednl. Projects, Inc., 1966-67, U.S. Office Edn., 1969—, Ednl. Systems Corp.; dir. Nat. Seminar Adult Edn. Research, 1964, 65; mem. Joint Commn. Tng. of Correctional Manpower, Washington, 1966-69; mem. Fla. adv. com. Higher Edn. Act, 1965-72. Served with USNR, 1945-50. Mem. Adult Edn. Assn. U.S.A. (pres. 1969-70), Nat. Assn. Pub. Continuing and Adult Edn., Fla. Adult Edn. Assn., Nat. Commn. Profs. Adult Edn., Phi Delta Kappa. Mason (Shriner). Author: Adult Education Procedures, 1965. Co-editor: Handbook of Adult Edn., 1970. Contbr. articles to profl. jours. Home: 3333 Lakeshore Dr Tallahassee FL 32303

AKERMAN, JOSEPH LAX, physician; b. Savannah, Ga., June 24, 1921; s. Walter E. and Marian (Lax) A.; student Vanderbilt U., 1940-42; M.D., Tulane U. Sch. Medicine, 1951; m. Orfa Mae Palko, Jan. 2, 1950; children—Joseph Lax, Marian Beth, Amos Tappan, John Michaels, Mary Louise. Intern USPHS, Galveston, Tex., 1951-52; resident USPHS Hosp., Memphis, 1952, med. staff, 1952; individual practice medicine, Apopka, Fla., 1953—; physician Plymouth Citrus Products Coop. plant, 1958-71, Plymouth Citrus Growers Assn. (Fla.), 1958-71, Gen. Electric Lamp Plant, Plymouth, 1969-71; cons. physician for numerous owners in foliage plant industry. Pres. Central Fla. council Boy Scouts Am., 1968, 69, 70, council commr., 1966, 67, 71, mem. nat. council, 1965-71; mem. nat. council Cub Scout Com., 1968-71. Served with AUS, 1943-46, USAF, 1946-51; ATO, ETO. Recipient Silver Beaver award Fla. council Boy Scouts Am., Vigil Honor, Order of Arrow, 1968, named Man of Yr. Orange County YMCA, 1969, 1 of Top 10 Citizens Apopka, 1968, 69, 70. Mem. Kappa Alpha. Presbyn. (ruling elder). Club: Apopka Sertoma (charter pres.; chmn. bd. 1969-70, 70-71; named Distinguished Club pres., gov. N.E. Fla. dist. 1972-73). Home: 220 N Washington St Apopka FL 32703 Office: 125 S Park PO Box 1107 Apopka FL 32703

AKERMAN, MILDRED STALNAKER, lawyer, former judge; b. Ft. Valley, Ga., Dec. 11, 1908; d. James William and Minnie Lee (Fountain) Stalnaker; student Mchts. and Bankers Bus. Coll., N.Y., 1935; LL.B., U. Miami, 1955; m. Frank Bruce Akerman, Dec. 24, 1955 (dec.). Comptroller Loudee Iron & Metal Co., Ltd., N.Y.C., 1938-40; office mgr. Hubbard & Carr, attys., also Sen. Claude Pepper, Miami, Fla., 1940-52; admitted to Fla. bar; asst. atty. gen. to atty. gen. of Fla., 1955-57, also atty. to 8 state agys.; judge Small Claims Ct., Broward County, Fla., 1959-71; practice law, Tavernier, Fla., 1971—. Mem. Fla. Gov.'s Commn. on Status of Women. Bd. dirs. A.R.C. Recipient certificate of service State of Fla.; certificate of service to law sch. U. Miami. Mem. Am., Broward County bar assns., Fla. Bar, Am. Judicature Soc., Internat., Nat., Fla. (pres. 1957-58) assns. women lawyers, Bus. and Profl. Womens Clubs, Am. Assn. U. Women, Kappa Beta Pi (past pres. local chpt.). Conglist. Clubs: Soroptimist, Isla morada Fishing. Home: Fontaine Lake Estates Plantation Key FL 33314 Fontaine Lake Estates Plantation Key FL 33314 Office: Profl Bldg Tavernier FL 33070

AKIN, HENRY DAVID, JR., lawyer; b. Amarillo, Tex., Apr. 30, 1927; s. Henry D. and Catherine (Clark) A.; B.A., U. Tex., 1946, LL.B., 1950; m. Mary Ella Jones, Sept. 2, 1949; children—Catherine Anita, Henry David, John Stewart, Matthew Clark, Mary Haydon, Admitted to Tex. bar, 1950; practice law firm Leachman, Matthews, Gardere, Akin & Porter, 1950-53; partner Williams & Akin, 1953-57, Akin, Viai, Hamilton, Koch & Tubb, (all Dallas), 1957—; dir. Capital S.W. Corp., Dallas, 1962-65, 1st Bank & Trust, Richardson, Tex., 1964—, Richardson Savs. & Loan Assn., 1957—, Federated Financial Corp., (both Dallas), 1961—, Vice pres. bd. Richardson Ind. Sch. Dist., 1958-64; active Baylor U. Hosp. Dr., 1967—, Meth. Hosp., Dallas, 1967—, Goals for Dallas Dr., 1968—, Dallas United Fund, 1968—; bd. dirs. YMCA, Richardson, 1965-71, Girls, Dallas, 1966-71. Judge, Richardson, 1956-57. Served with Campfire USNR, 1944-46. Named Outstanding Young Lawyer Dallas Jr. Bar Assn., 1967. Mem. Dallas (dir. 1958-59, 68-69, 2d v.p. 1967), Richardson (dir. 1956), Am. bar assns., Southwestern Legal Found., Tex. Bar Found. Methodist (chmn. bd.). Clubs: Northwood (Dallas), Dallas Gun. Home: 7249 Elmridge Dr Dallas TX 75240 Office: Republic Nat Bank Tower Dallas TX 75201

AKIN, J. REGINALD, elec. machinery mfg. co. exec.; b. Carrollton, Ga., Aug. 29, 1936; s. T. Roy and Virginia (Tant) A.; student Atlanta Sch. Electronics, 1954-55; m. Betty Jean Allen, June 18, 1955; children—Deborah Lynne, Donna Leigh. Dealer rep. Economy Auto Stores Inc., Atlanta, 1954-60; territory mgr. Westinghouse Appliance Sales Co., Macon, Ga., 1960-62, 65-66; pres. Elec. Appliance, Inc., Atlanta, 1962-65; mgr. So. div. Kelvinator, Inc., Atlanta, 1966-69; v.p., mgr. appliance div. Carolina Sales Corp., Greenville, N.C., 1969—. Pres. Akin Appliance, Inc., Macon, Ga., 1962-65. Republican. Mem. Christian Ch. (deacon, bd. dirs.). Mason (32 deg., Shriner). Club: Greenville Golf and Country. Home: 201 W Martinsborough Rd Greenville NC 27834 Office: PO Box 1927 Greenville NC 27834

AKIN, MARGARET CATHERINE ROUSE (MRS. AUSTIN FRANKLIN AKIN), physician; b. Boone, Ia., Apr. 18, 1913; d. Martin Francis and Margaret (Conry) Rouse; B.S. in Medicine, State U. Ia. 1936, M.D., 1936; m. Austin Franklin Akin, July 22, 1933; children—Mary Patricia (Mrs. Charles Gordon Cloutier, Jr.), John Rouse. Intern Tri-State Hosp., Shreveport, La., 1936-37; practice medicine, Iowa, La., 1937-41, Shreveport, 1941—; partner Family Clinic, Shreveport, 1964—; mem. staff Physicians and Surgeons Hosp., Shreveport, staff pres., 1960; mem. staff Schumpert Hosp., Shreveport; mem. staff Willis Knighton Hosp., Shreveport, staff pres. 1958; clin. asst. prof. medicine La. State U. Sch. Medicine, Shreveport. Mem. La. Bd. Practical Nurse Examiners, 1962—. Chmn. Com. Health Care of Religious and Clergy of Diocese of Alexandria, 1962—; bd. mem. Holidays for Humanity, 1964—. Bd. dirs. Cath. Charities Diocese of Alexandria. Mem. A.M.A., Am. Acad. Gen. Practice (dist. treas. 1966-68), La., Shreveport (rep. to internat. tb conf. 1965, v.p. 1954, dir.) med. assns., Am. Assn. U. Women, Pan-Pacific Surg. Assn., League Women Voters (pres. Shreveport 1948), Cath. Physicians Guild, Alpha Omega Alpha, Theta Phi Alpha. Democrat. Roman Catholic. Club: Altrusa. Home: 2828 Thornhill Av Shreveport LA 71104 Office: 838 Margaret Pl Shreveport LA 71101

ALANDER, ROBERT JOHN, newspaper exec.; b. Oak Park, Ill., Aug. 10, 1908; s. John William and Gunhild (Anderson) A.; student pub. schs. Chgo.; m. Nena A. Anderson, Apr. 24, 1929; 1 dau., Roberta Ann (Mrs. Douglass Phillips). Media dir. Montgomery Ward & Co., Chgo., 1929-36; retail advt. mgr. Birmingham (Ala.) Post, 1936-38; advt. dir. Miami (Fla.) Daily News, 1946-49; advt. dir. Columbus Ledger-Enquirer, 1940-46; advt. mgr. Observer-News, Charlotte, N.C., 1949-65, advt. dir., 1965—. Hon. life mem. Alpha Delta Sigma, Pi Sigma Epsilon. Mem. Newspaper Advt. Execs. Assn. (dir., past pres. art council), Carolina Carroussell Assn. (pres.). Elk (pres. George Elks Assn.). Kiwanian (lt. gov.). Home: 4920 Carmel Club Dr Charlotte NC Office: 600 S Tryon St Charlotte NC 28202

ALARIO, ROBERT JOSEPH, off-shore marine contracting co. exec.; b. Golden Meadow, La., June 3, 1938; s. Juan Victor and Victoria (Rebstock) A.; B.A. (Univ. scholar), U. Southwestern La., 1959; student Law Sch., La. State U., 1959-61; M.S. in Fgn. Service, Georgetown U., 1963; postgrad. in bus. Tulane U., 1968; m. Joan Carole Whitman, Jan. 21, 1961; children—Mitzi Louise, Robert Christopher. Clk., asso. dir. publs. Com. on Un-American Activities, U.S. Ho. of Reps., Washington, 1962-63; with Texaco Inc., various internat. locations, 1963-68, asst. to mgr., Port-au-Prince, Haiti, 1964-66, acting mgr., Conakry, Guinea, 1963-64; asst. to pres. Nolty J. Theriot, Inc., New Orleans, 1968-70, v.p., sec., 1970—, also dir.; pres., chmn. bd. Offshore Tugs Inc., New Orleans, 1971—; dir. Internat. Hotel Corp., New Orleans; pres. Internat. Imports Inc., New Orleans, 1972—. Mem. subcom. on manning, licensing and stability Nat. Offshore Operations Adv. Panel, 1969—; tech. adviser La. Adv. Commn. Coastal and Marine Resources, 1972—. Bd. dirs., vice chmn. Indsl. Found. South; bd. dirs. Council for Devel. French in La.; pres., chmn. bd. dirs. Offshore Marine Service Assn. Edn. Fund. K.C. fellow, 1962; Ill. Central R.R. fellow, 1956. Mem. Offshore Marine Service Assn. (chmn. 1970—), Pi Sigma Alpha, Kappa Sigma. K.C., Toastmaster. Clubs: Colonial Gulf and Country (Metairie, La.); Mystic Krewe of Louisianians (Washington). Office: 706 Odeco Bldg 1600 Canal St New Orleans LA 70112 Home: 16 Colonial Lane Harahan LA 70123

ALBERT, CARL BERT, congressman; b. McAlester, Okla., May 10, 1908; s. Ernest Homer and Leona Ann (Scott) A.; A.B., U. Okla., 1931; B.A. (Rhodes scholar), Oxford U., Eng., 1933, B.C.L., 1934; m. Mary Harmon, Aug 20, 1942; children—Mary Frances, David. Admitted to Okla. bar, legal clk. FHA, 1934-37; atty., accountant Sayre Oil Co., Oklahoma City, 1937-38; legal dept. Ohio Oil Co., Marshall, Ill., Findlay, O., 1939-40; gen. practice law, Oklahoma City, 1938, Mattoon, Ill., 1938-39, McAlester, Okla., 1946-47; mem. 80th to 92d congresses from 3d Okla. Dist., majority leader. Served from pvt. to lt. col. 3d U.S. Army, 1941-46. Decorated Bronze Star. medal. Democrat. Methodist. Home: 827 E Osage McAlester OK 74501 Address: Capitol Bldg Washington DC 20515

ALBERT, EMIL RICHARD, JR., engr., equipment co. exec.; b. Tulsa, Feb. 17, 1913; B.S. in Geol. Engring., U. Tulsa, 1935; m. Mary Katherine McCarhty, Sept. 1, 1936; children—Judith (Mrs. Harold John Haus, Jr.), Emil Richard III. Engr. Midcontinent div. Gulf Oil Corp., 1935-39; midcontinent div. engr. Baroid Sales div. Nat. Lead Co., 1939-46; pres., gen. mgr. Mud Products, Inc., Bomund Co., Beaumont Cement Sales Co. La., Mudco Equipment Co., 1946-56; pres., dir. Rubarite, Inc., 1956-57; organizer ERA Corp., 1957, pres., gen. mgr.; dealer prin. Albert & Harlow, Tulsa, 1959—, now chmn. bd. Bd. dirs. Southwestern Art Assn., Tulsa Opera and Philharmonic Assn., Tulsa Arts Council; trustee U. Tulsa. Mem. Am. Inst. Mining and Metall. Engrs., Am. Assn. Petroleum Geologists, Am. Petroleum Inst., Midcontinent Oil and Gas Assn., Tulsa Geol. Soc., Ind. Petroleum Assn. Am., Tulsa C. of C. (pres., dir. 1964). Presbyn. Clubs: Southern Hills, Tulsa, Summit (Tulsa). Home: 2300 Riverside Dr Penthouse Apt 4 Tulsa OK Office: 6650 Evanston Av Tulsa OK

ALBERT, IRENE HOLT, journalist, author; b. Moline, Ill., Jan. 4, 1910; d. George Edmund and Jean (Cox) Holt; student pvt. tutors and Internat. Sch. of Tangier, Morocco, schs. in N.Y. and Ill.; student Sorbonne U., 1927-30; m. John Jacob Albert III, June 10, 1939; 1son, John J. IV (dec.). Staff writer Moline (Ill.) Dispatch, 1925-26, fgn. corr., 1927-30; accredited corr. U.S. Senate Press Gallery, 1926-27; contbr. to Paris edits. N.Y. Herald Tribune, Paris Times, 1927-30; contbr. book reviews Washington Post, 1937-39, short stories and poetry to nat. publs., 1940—; stringer for Time, Inc., 1957-58; spl. news reporter, art and music reviewer and columnist, feature writer Clearwater (Fla.) Sun, 1955—; pub. relations Fla. Gulf Coast Art Center, 1958-68; pub. relations counselor Jr. Ballet Guild Found. Fla., 1964-70. Recipient first prize McCall's Home of Tomorrow, 1945; 2d pl. pub. short story Nat. League Am. Pen Women, 1962; 2d place interview Fla. Women's Press Club, 1959; spl. award Fla. State Poetry Contest, 1961; Press award Cuban Resistance, 1963; award in features, A.P. (Fla), 1964; award for interviews, Fla. Women's Press Club, 1964; biennial awards lyrics Nat. League Am. Pen Women, 1965; Hadassah award for contbn. to journalism, 1966; Merit award Am. Heart Assn.; Grand prize Poetry Americana Folk Festival, 1970; poetry prize Fla. competition, 1971, others. Mem. Nat. Soc. Arts and Letters, Fla. Working Press Club, Nat. League Am. Pen-women (pres. Clearwater br. 1958-60). Nat. League Women Voters, Am. Assn. UN, Fla. Gulf Coast Art Center, St. Petersburg Mus. Fine Arts, Womens Aux. A.I.A., Theta Sigma Phi. Club: Washington Press. Home: 1321 Murray Av Clearwater FL 33515 Office: Clearwater Sun Clearwater FL 33516

ALBERTS, HAROLD, lawyer; b. San Antonio, Apr 3, 1920; s. Bernard H. and Rose (Cassel) A.; LL.B., U. Tex., 1942; m. Rose M. Gaskin, Mar. 25, 1945; children—Linda Rae, Barry Lawrence. Tchr., U. Tex., 1942; admitted to Tex. bar, 1943; gen. practice law, Corpus Christi, Tex., 1946—. Pres., Jewish Welfare Fund Corpus Christi, 1948; charter vice chmn. of the Southwest Regional Anti-Defamation League, 1953, chmn., 1969-72; also chmn. Brotherhood Week, 1957; chmn Nueces County chpt. A.R.C., 1959-61; mem. campaign exec. com., chmn. meetings United Community Services, 1961; vice chmn. Coastal Bend Council on Alcoholism; v.p. Combined Jewish Appeal, 1972; v.p. Little Theatre Corpus Christi, 1964—. Chmn. Corpus Christi Nat. Conf. Christians and Jews, 1967-69; bd. dirs. Tex. State Assn. for Mental Health. Served to lt. USNR, 1942-46. Mem. Am., Tex., Nueces County bar assns. Mason, Kiwanian (pres. 1962); mem. B'nai B'rith (pres. 1955, past v.p. Tex.). Home: 618 Dolphin Pl Corpus Christi TX 78411 Office: Wilson Tower Corpus Christi TX 78401

ALBERTSON, FRED WOODWARD, lawyer, radio engr.; b. Fairgrove, Mich., Sept. 29, 1908; s. Charles Elton Eugene and Helen Louise (Woodward) A.; A.B., U. Mich., 1931, LL.B., 1934; m. Catherine Frances Dolan, June 10, 1942; children—Fred Woodward, Helen Dolan. Engineered constrn. and operation several broadcast and radio telegraph stas., 1925-27; radio equipped and handled communications with remote meterol. expdns. and stas., U. Mich., 1927-34; admitted to Mich. bar, 1934, D.C. bar, 1935; gen. law practice, 1935—; engaged as radio and communications legal counsel for radio, TV telegraph, television and broadcast cos. and stas., 1935—; partner Dow, Lohnes & Albertson, specializing in communications, radio and air law, 1944—; licensed radio operator, 1924-; owner, operator amateur radio sta. W3GZ. Trustee, bd. dirs. Delta Theta Phi Found., 1945-46. Registered profl. elec. communications engr., D.C. Life fellow Am. Bar Found.; mem. I.E.E.E. (sr. mem.; chmn. Washington sect. 1946-47, mem. adminstrv. com. 1943-; bd. editors proc. 1946-54), Broadcast Pioneers, Fed. Communications; (pres. 1953-54), Am. (ho. dels. 1953-54, chmn. standing com. on communications 1957-58), D.C. bar assns., Am. Judicature Soc., Delta Theta Phi. Clubs: Engineers (co-founder, life mem.), Washington Radio (past pres.), Congressional Country, Broadcasters, Capitol Hill, National Lawyers (Washington); University Michigan Radio (co-founder, past pres.) (Ann Arbor, Mich.). Home: 3753 Jenifer St Washington DC 20015 also 240 West Wood Dr Key Biscayne FL 33149 Office: 1225 Connecticut Av Washington DC 20036

ALBOHM, JOHN C., supt. schs. City sch. supt. Alexandria (Va.) Bd. Edn. Office: Alexandria Bd Edn Alexandria VA 22314*

ALBREN, EDWARD JOSEPH, govt. ofcl.; b. Manchester, N.H., Oct. 10, 1919; s. Frank and Anna (Wyderka) Albrewczenski; student St. Anselm's Coll., 1945-46; B.S., U. N.H., 1949; postgrad. U. Ala., 1948, George Washington U., 1950, Md. U., 1964; m. Mary Helen Stevenson, Sept. 24, 1959. Asst. head atomic energy and applied sci. br. Naval Facility Engring. Command, Washington, 1959-61, head nuclear, biol. and chem. def. br., 1961—. Served to capt. AUS, 1940-46. Decorated Purple Heart. Mem. Soc. Am. Mil. Engrs. Home: 1003 Robroy Dr Silver Spring MD 20903 Office: Navy Dept Washington DC 20390

ALBRIGHT, ARNOLD DEWALD, ednl. adminstr.; b. Washington, Mar. 6, 1913; s. Earl J. and Elizabeth (Welch) A.; Rector scholar DePauw U., 1931-32; A.B. (honor scholar 1934-37), Milligan Coll., 1937; M.S. (grad. fellow 1937-38), U. Tenn., 1938; Ph.D. (Gen. Edn. Bd. fellow 1949-50), N.Y.U., 1950; m. Grace Carroll, June 23, 1939; children—Carl Wesley, Earl Thomas. Field worker U.S. Bur. Plant Industry, 1932-34; supr. Chattanooga pub. schs., 1938-39; supr. Tenn. Dept. Edn., then dir. research, chmn. staff, asst. state commr. edn., 1939-49; prof. edn. George Peabody Coll., 1950-54; asso. dir. So. States Coop. Program in Ednl. Aminstrn., 1950-54; dir. bur. sch. service, chmn. div. ednl. adminstrn., prof. edn. U. Ky., 1954-57, exec. dean extended programs, 1957-61, provost, 1960-62, exec. v.p., 1962-69, v.p. instnl. planning, 1970—; asso. dir. Asso. Programs in Ednl. Adminstrn., Auburn U., 1954-57; cons. So. Regional Edn. Bd. Atlanta, 1958; cons. local Edn. Commn. Atlanta and Fulton County, 1959; study dir. W.Va. Bd. Edn., 1960. Cons. Tenn. Commn. on Children, 1949. Conn. Gov.'s Fact Finding Commn., 1950, So. Edn. Found., 1954—; cons. Ashmore Study (Fund for Advancement of Edn.), 1952-54; asso. dir. study higher edn. Tenn. Legislative council, 1956-58; Tenn. edn. chmn. A.R.C., 1948. Mem. Nat. Conf. Profs. Ednl. Adminstrn. (chmn. 1957), Nat. Council Chief State Sch. Officers, N.E.A., John Dewey Soc., Am. Assn. Sch. Adminstrs., Assn. Higher Edn., Phi Delta Kappa, Sigma Nu, Omicron Delta Kappa. Methodist. Club: Donelson Civic (pres. 1945-47). Author: (with Truman M. Pierce) A Profession in Transition, 1960. Editor: Administrative Leadership, 1952. Adv. editorial bd. The School Executive, 1957-59. Home: 791 Chinoe Rd Lexington KY 40502

ALBRIGHT, BENJAMIN PHILLIPS, textile exec.; b. Grantville, Ga., Mar. 18, 1912; s. James Oscar and Jennie Mae (Couch) A.; student Mercer U., 1929; B.S., Ga. Inst. Tech., 1931; m. Loula Callaway, Jan. 2, 1937; children—Benjamin Phillips, Robertson Callaway, Stuart Alan, Jane, Meredith. Mgr., Bibb Mfg. Co., Macon, Ga., 1931-33; asst. v.p. Callaway Mills, LaGrange, Ga., 1933-61; v.p. Textiles, Inc., Gastonia, N.C., 1961—. Past pres. LaGrange Concert Council. Bd. dirs. United Appeal, Gaston Day Sch. Mem. Gen. Arbitration Council Textile Industry, C. of C. (dir. 1963-69). Methodist. Rotarian. Club: Gaston Country. Home: Club Colony Dr Gastonia NC 28052 Office: PO Box 699 Gastonia NC 28052

ALBRIGHT, BOYCE SINGLETON, supt. schs.; b. Haleyville Ala., Apr. 27, 1924; s. Virgie Hugh and Tiney (Posey) A.; student U. Ala., 1943; B.A., Howard Coll., 1948; M.A., George Peabody Coll., 1952. Head coordinator Vets. Tng. Program, Haleyville, 1948-61; tchr. Haleyville Schs., 1952-61, supt. schs., 1971—; coordinator trade and indsl. edn. Haleyville High Sch., 1960-61; supt. schs. Winston County (Ala.), 1961-71; state chmn. Profl. Relations and Tchr. Welfare Com. Mem. Ala. Com. for Better Schs., 1961—. Trustee N.W. Ala. State Jr. Coll. Served with AUS, World War II. Mem. Ala. Edn. Assn. (mem. state legislative com.; dist. pres. elect, state chmn. joint com.), Ala. Assn. Sch. Adminstrs. (state exec. com.), N. E. A., Distributive Edn. Clubs Am. (hon. life), Alabama Congress Parents and Tchrs. (hon. life), Internat. Platform Assn., Am. Legion, V.F.W., C. of C., Kappa Phi Kappa. Alpha Phi Omega, Omicron Delta Kappa, Pi Kappa Alpha. Mason., Lion (pres., dep. dist. gov., zone chmn.). Home: PO Box 149 Haleyville AL 35565 Office: 1800 E 20th St Haleyville AL 35565

ALBRIGHT, GEORGE JACOB, JR., ins. co. exec.; b. Weirsdale, Fla., Sept. 24, 1931; s. George Jacob and Julia (Martin) A.; B.S. in Bus. Adminstrn., U. Fla., 1954; m. Linda Austin, June 19, 1954; children—George Jacob III, David Austin, Robert Clayton. With Nat. Standard Life Ins. Co., various locations, 1954—, v.p., agy. dir., Orlando, Fla., 1966-70, exec. v.p. marketing, 1970—, also dir. Sec.-treas. Lake Weir High Sch. Booster Club, 1970-71; pres. Weirsdale Elementary Sch. PTA, 1968-70; mem. pres.'s round table Fla. Presbyn. Coll., St. Petersburg, 1970-71. C.L.U. Mem. Central Fla. Life Underwriters Assn. (asso.), Fla. Assn. Life Underwriters (named man of year 1971), Pi Kappa Alpha. Presbyn. Kiwanian, Elk. Club: Silver Springs Shores Country (Ocala, Fla.). Home: PO Box 36 Weirsdale FL 32695 Office: PO Box 991 Orlando FL 32802

ALBRIGHT, JOSEPH LINDSAY, ins. agt.; b. Greensboro, N.C., Nov. 18, 1927; s. Jacob Mack and Bessie (Moore) A.; B.S. in Bus. Adminstrn., U. N.C., 1951; m. Sarah Long Allison, Nov, 26, 1955; children—Mary Allison, Joseph Lindsay, Sarah Long, James Lowry. Asst. mgr. S & W Cafeteria chain, Greensboro, 1951-56; area mgr. Penn Mut. Life Ins. Co., Greensboro, 1956-59, Greensboro Nat. Ins. Co., 1959-62; unit mgr. Guardian Life Ins. Co., Greensboro, 1962-63; gen. agt. Am. Nat. Inst. Co., Greensboro, 1963—. Mem. Greensboro Estate Planning Council, 1969—. Served with Army Security, 1946-47. C.L.U. Mem. Greensboro Assn. Life Underwriters (past pres.), Central Carolina Chpt. C.L.U.'S, Piedmont Sales Execs. (pres. 1968). Presbyn. (deacon). Kiwanian (pres. Gate City club 1970). Club: Green Valley Park (Greensboro). Home: 1103 McDowell Dr Greensboro NC 27408 Office: 1842 Banking St Greensboro NC 27408

ALBRIGHT, SPENCER DELANCEY, JR., educator; b. Nashville; s. Spencer Delancey and Sarah Anne (Lang) A.; B.A., U. Ark., 1922; A.M., U. Chgo., 1932; Ph. D., U. Tex., 1940; m. Margaret McCain Hyatt, July 23, 1929; children—Spencer Delancey III, Sarah Katherine (Mrs. William Karl Sipfle). Tchr. high sch., Earle, 1922-23, Fayetteville, Stuttgart, 1925-30 (all Ark.); faculty Crane Coll., Chgo., 1930-32, George Williams Coll., 1933-34, Central YMCA Coll., Chgo., 1934-35, U. Ark., 1935-37, U. Tex., Austin, 1937-39, Tex. Technol. Coll., 1939-40, Reed Coll., Portland, Ore., 1940-42, U. Wash., Seattle, 1942-43, U. Wis., summer 1946; prof. polit. sci. U. Richmond (Va.), 1946—, chmn. dept. history and polit. sci., 1967—; tchr. summer sessions U. S.D., 1947-49, Emory U., 1950, 52, 57, 61,

64. Served with U.S. Army, 1918; to capt. USAF, 1943-46. Mem. Am., So. polit. sci. assns., Am. Acad. Polit. and Social Sci., Va. Social Sci. Assn., Am. Soc. Pub. Administrn., N.E.A., Scabbard and Blade, Pi Sigma Alpha, Omicron Delta Kapa, Kappa Delta Pi, Pi Delta Epsilon, Phi Alpha Theta, Tau Kappa Alpha. Democrat. Baptist. Author: The American Ballot, 1942. Contbr. articles to profl. publs. Home: 6611 Three Chopt Rd Richmond VA 23226

ALBRIGHT, W(ILLIAM) DOUGLAS, lawyer; b. West Lafayette, Ind., Jan. 19, 1939; s. William Purvis and Dorothy (Wilbanks) A.; A.B., Duke, 1961; LL.B., Am. U., 1964; m. Mary Egerton,Apr. 1, 1961; children—Jon Douglas, David Erik, Robert Stuart, Lawrence Ethan. Admitted to N.C. bar, 1964; pvt. practice law, Greensboro, N.C., 1964-66; asst. solicitor Guilford County Superior Ct., Greensboro, 1966-68; chief dist. prosecutor 18th Jud. Dist., Greensboro, N.C., 1968-69; dist. solicitor, 12th Solicitorial Dist., 1969—. Mem. N.C., Greensboro bar assns., N.C. State Bar, Optimist Internat., Phi Beta Kappa. Home: Red Forest Ct Greensboro NC 27410 Office: Guilford County Courthouse Greensboro NC 27408

ALBRITTON, ROBERT BYNUM, lawyer; b. Andalusia, Ala., Feb. 1, 1905; s. William Harold and Anne (Mashburn) A.; LL.B., U. Ala, 1930; m. Carrie Veal, Aug. 16, 1928; 1 son, William Harold III. Admitted to Ala. bar, 1930; practiced in Andalusia, 1930—. mem. firm Albrittons & Rankin, 1930—. Mem. bd. dirs. U. Ala. Law Sch. Found. Fellow Am. Coll. Probate Counsel; mem. Am., Ala., (pres. 1971-72), Covington County (pres. 1955) bar assns., Fedn. Ins. Counsel, Assn. Ins. Attys., Ala. Law Inst., Am. Judicature Soc., Farrah Law Soc., Kappa Sigma, Phi Delta Phi. Presbyn. (deacon). Clubs: Rotary (pres. 1969-70), Ft. Walton Yacht, Andalusia Country. Home: 723 Albritton Rd Andalusia AL 36420 Office: 109 Opp Av Andalusia AL 36420

ALBRITTON, WILLIAM HAROLD, III, lawyer; b. Andalusia, Ala., Dec. 19, 1936; s. Robert Bynum and Carrie (Veal) A.; diploma Marion Inst. (Ala.), 1955; A.B., U. Ala., 1959, LL.B., 1960; m. Jane Rollins Howard, June 2, 1958; children—William Harold IV, Benjamin Howard, Thomas Bynum. Admitted to Ala. bar, 1960, since practice law firm Albrittons & Rankin, Andalusia, 1962—, asso., 1962-66, partner, 1966—. Dir. TV Cable Co., Andalusia. Chmn. Andalusia Bd. Zoning Adjustment, 1963-64. Mem.Ala., Covington County Republican party exec. coms., 1967—. Served to capt. AUS, 1960-62. Mem. Am., Ala. (mem. exec. council young lawyers 1965-70), Covington County bar assns., Andalusia C. of C. (pres. 1967-68), Nat. Assn. R.R. Trial Counsel, Am. Judicature Soc., Phi Beta Kappa, Phi Delta Phi, Omicron Delta Kappa, Alpha Tau Omega. Presbyn. (deacon). Rotarian. Home: 730 Albritton Rd Andalusia AL 36420 Office: 109 Opp Av Andalusia AL 36420

ALBURY, CHARLES BAUGHMAN, pub., editor, writer; b. Millersburg, O., Aug. 17, 1925; s. Charles R. and Ruth (Baughman) A.; B.A., Bowling Green State U., 1950; m. Maxine Marie Finley, June 11, 1955; children— Janice Michelle, Suzanne Marie, Cherie Babette, Charles Lloyd. Asst. sports editor Mansfield (O.) News-Jour., 1950-55; feature writer, photographer Lakeland (Fla.) Ledger, 1955; Clearwater bur. chief St. Petersburg (Fla.) Times, 1956-60, Enterprise writer, 1960—; editor, pub. Sr. Golfer mag., 1964—, also pres. Sr. Golf Publs. Co., 1964—; contbr. to Golf Digest, Book of Golf, Golf World; pub. Am. Srs. Golf Assn. yearbook, Fla. Profl. Golfers Assn. Sect. Annual. Served as sgt., AUS, 1943-45. Mem. Golf Writers Assn. Am., Softball Writers and Broadcasters Assn., YMCA, Clearwater C. of C., Clearwater Advt. Club. Republican. Methodist. Home: 1716 Verde Dr Clearwater FL 33515 Office: 311 S Osceola Av Clearwater FL 33516

ALCIATORE, JULES C(ESAR), educator; b. New Orleans, Nov. 18, 1901; s. Jules L. and Marie Althea (Roy) A.; A.B., Tulane U., 1922; A.M., U. of Ill., 1929; Ph.D., Univ. Chicago, 1938; m. Miss Audrey S. Bond, June 11, 1929; 1 son, Jules L. Asst. in French, U. of Ill., 1927-29; instr. French, Northwestern, 1929-31, 1934-35; instr. Romance lang., Catholic U. of Am., 1938-41; asso. prof. French, U. of Ga. 1947-49, prof., 1959-64, Alumni Found. prof., 1957, emeritus, 1964; vis. lectr. U. Chgo., summer 1948, vis. asso. prof., summer 1950. Served at lt. (s.g.), USNR, 1943-46. Recipient Carnegie grant-in-aid. 1951; M. G. Michael award, 1953. Mem. Modern Lang. Assn. (chmn. French VI 1958), S. Atlantic Modern Lang. Assn. (v.p. 1960), Am. Assn. Tchrs. of French, Societe d Histoire Litteraire de la France, Am. Assn. Teachers Italian, Am. Assn. U. Profs., Sigma Phi Epsilon, Phi Kappa Phi, Pi Delta Phi. Author: Abstract of dissertation; Stendhal et Helvetius; Les Sources de la philosophie de Stendhal (Geneve: Librairie Droz. 1952) Stendhal et Maine de Biran (Geneve Librarie Droz, 1954). Home: 118 Mulberry Dr Metairie LA 70005

ALCIATORE, ROY LOUIS, restaurateur; b. New Orleans, Dec 19, 1902; s. Jules Louis and Marie Althea (Roy) A.; student St. Aloysius Coll., New Orleans, 1913-17, Spring Hill Coll., Mobile, Ala., 1917-18, Chenet Inst., New Orleans, 1918-19, Tulane U., 1919; m. Mary Pearl Duggan, Apr. 9, 1932; 1 dau., Yvonne Elaine; m. 2d, Mrs. Fred N. Blount, Jr. Apprentice restaurant worker Pension Alciatore, New Orleans, 1920-23; continued studies in famous restaurants, France, 1923-30; mgr. Antoine's (founded by grandfather in 1840, formerly Pension Alciatore), 1930, now propr. Bd. commrs. New Orleans Pub. Belt R.R. Mem. Mardi Gras carnival orgns., also New Orleans Conv. and Visitors Bur. Bd. curators La. State Mus., 1937-41. Served with USCG. Decorated grand officer Confrerie du Tastevin (Nuits-Saint-Georges, France); named chevalier du Merite Touristique, France, chevalier Du Merite Commercial, France. Mem. New Orleans Assn. Commerce (mem. council), Nat. (dir.), New Orleans (pres. 1937) restaurant assns., Wine and Food Soc. of London, Les Amis D'Escoffier Soc., Gourmet Soc. of N.Y. Clubs: Young Men's Business, Southern Yacht, New Orleans Athletic. Home: 5700 Canal Blvd New Orleans LA 70124 Office: 713 St Louis Street New Orleans LA 70130

ALCOCK, JAMES L., judge, 1933; B.A., Loyola U., New Orleans, LL.B., 1963. Formerly asst. dist. atty., New Orleans; now criminal dist. ct. judge. Address: 1337 Rapides Dr New Orleans LA 70122*

ALCORN, CHARLES WILLIAM, JR., mining co. exec.; b. Nov. 23, 1927; s. Charles William and Lexey Jane (Cragin) A.; B.S., U. Tex., 1952; m. Dorothy Jean Walston, Sept. 27, 1952; children—Anne, Lexey, Charles William III. Dist. geologist Warren Petroleum Corp., Abilene, Tex., 1952-58; geologist Gulf Oil Co., Midland, Tex., 1958-66; pres. Spears Alcorn Well Service, Inc., Victoria, Tex., 1966—. Served with USNR, 1946-48. Mem. Am. Petroleum Inst. (chpt. v.p. 1971-72). Presbyn. (ruling elder 1970—). Club: Victoria Country (pres. 1970-71). Home: 406 Tampa Dr Victoria TX 77901 Office: Box 3187 Victoria TX 77901

ALCORN, ROY ANVIL, ednl. adminstr.; b. Williamsville, Mo., Dec. 3, 1925; s. Scott and Dealia Ann (Boxx) A.; B.S. in Edn., Southeast Mo. State Coll., 1955; M.A., George Peabody Coll. for Tchrs., 1958, Ed.D. in Edn., 1963; m. Virgie Lois Carter, Oct. 23, 1953; children—Martha Lynn, Daniel Sheridan, Joseph Dean, Elizabeth Ann, Walter Lee. Tchr. Mo. pub. schs., 1946-51; congl. aide to Mo. congressman, 1953-56; prin., high sch. Waynesville, Mo., 1956-58; supt. of schs., Eminence, Mo., 1958-61; asst. supt. schs., Wilmington, Del., 1963-65; supt. schs., Chesterfield County, Va., 1965-69, Roanoke City, 1969—. Mem. exec. bd. Central Va. Ednl. TV, 1965-69. Served with AUS, 1944-46, USAF, 1950-52. Recipient Freedom's Found. award, 1969. Mem. Am. Assn. Sch. Adminstrs., Va. Edn. Assn., N.E.A., Phi Delta Kappa, Kappa Delta Pi. Rotarian. Home: 2702 Creston Av Roanoke VA 24015 Office: 40 Douglas Av NW Roanoke VA 24009

ALDERDICE, NOMER WOODROW, retail trade exec.; b. nr. Mayfield, Ky., Feb. 23, 1913; s. Calvin Arnie and Bertha Alma (Foy) A.; student Murray State Tchrs. Coll., 1930-31, 32-33; m. Grace W. Boulton, Aug. 15, 1936; children—Jimmy, Donna (Mrs. Scott Lingo). Tchr. Graves County (Ky.) Sch. System, 1931-32, 34-37; prodn. worker B.F. Goodrich Co., Akron, O., 1933-34; mgr. Western Auto Store, Mayfield, 1937-38, 45-49, mgr. Marion, Ky., 1938-42, owner, mgr., 1949—; prodn. supr. Nat. Fireworks 20MM Plant, Viola, 1942-45; dir. Peoples Bank, Marion. Mayor, City of Marion, 1956-58. Democrat. Mem. Ch. of Christ (tchr., treas. 1949—). Rotarian (pres. 1956-57). Home: Gum St Marion KY 42064 Office: 103 W Bellville St Marion KY 42064

ALDERDICE, ROBERT, research instrn. exec. Dep. dir. adminstrn. Flower Garden Ocean Research Center U. Tex. Med. Sch. at Galveston. Address: Flower Garden Ocean Research Center U Tex Med Branch Galveston TX 77550*

ALDERDICE, ROBERT JAMES, architect; b. Pitts., Jan. 29, 1929; s. William Patterson and Hilda (Karlen) A.; B.Arch., Carnegie Inst. Tech. (now Carnegie-Mellon U.), 1952; m. Jane M. Hanley, Jan. 23, 1957. With Tasso Katselas, Architect, Pitts., 1953-54, Rene O. Ramirez, A.I.A., Santurce, P.R., 1955-57, Schmidt & McDade, Architects, Santurce, 1957-58; architect Robert J. Alderdice, A.I.A. & Assos., Santurce, San Juan, P.R., 1958—. Served with USAF, 1946-49. Mem. A.I.A. (chpt. sec. 1966), Ingenieros y Agrimensores, Colegio de Arquitectos, Nat. Council Archtl. Registration Bds. Rotarian. Club: San Juan Exchange (Condado, Santurce, P.R.). Archtl. works includes El Conquistador Hotel, Gen. Foods, Inc., San Juan Star newspaper plant. Home: PO Box 41G RFD 3 Beverly Hills Rio Piedras PR 00928 Office: 1351 Ashford Av Condado San Juan PR 00907

ALDERSON, CARLTON O., cons. engr.; b. Childress, Tex., July 20, 1922; s. Patrick Andrew and Esther (Simmons) A.; B.S., So. Meth. U., 1951; m. Doris Jeanne Melliff, Nov. 26, 1950; children—Glen Randal, Dean Thomas. Test and mech. engr. Gen. Electric Co., Dallas and Schenectady, 1951-55; chief mech. engr. Civil Engring. div. Kelly AFB, San Antonio, 1955-67; chief mech. engr. Simpson, Ng, Pratt & Assos., San Antonio, 1967-69; v.p., dir., chief mech. engr. K.M. Ng and Assos., 1969—; pres., chmn. Olmos Supply Co., Inc. Com. chmn. Cub Scouts, San Antonio, 1962-67. Served as combat pilot USAAF, 1940-45; MTO. Decorated Purple Heart, Air medal with oak leaf clusters. Registered profl.engr., Tex. Mem. Am. Soc. Heating, Refrigerating and Air Conditioning Engrs., Am. Soc. M.E., Tex. Soc. Profl. Engrs., Nat. Soc. Profl. Engrs. Home: 219 Inspiration Dr San Antonio TX 78228 Office: KM Ng and Assos Broadway Nat Bank Bldg Loop 410 and Nacogdoches Rd San Antonio TX 78209

ALDERSON, HARRY ORVILLE, city ofcl.; b. Stratford, Tex., Feb. 12, 1923; s. Walter Gene and Ora (Simmons) A.; B.S. in Civil Engring., Tex. Technol. Coll., 1947; m. Negella Jeanne Abrams, Mar. 20, 1948; children—Ronald Craig, Bruce Douglas, Vance Irvin, Anita Kay. Asso. engr. City of Lubbock, Tex., 1950-52, chief paving engr., 1952-56, dir. planning and traffic, 1956-57, exec. dir. Urban Renewal Agy., 1957—. Pres., YMCA, Lubbock, 1964-65; mem. Community Planning Council United Fund, Lubbock, 1956-57; pres. Lubbock chpt. World Neighbors. Served with AUS, 1943-46; ETO. Recipient 20 Year Pin, City of Lubbock, 1967. Mem. Nat. Assn. Housing and Redevel. Ofcls., Tex. Soc. Profl. Engrs., Phi Delta Theta. Democrat. Methodist. Lion. Home: 3307 56th St Lubbock TX 79413 Office: 907 Texas Av Lubbock TX 79401

ALDERSON, VETTRA GLENN, lawyer; b.Oxford, Miss., Oct. 10, 1940; s. Vettra Curtis and Louise (Mathis) A.; B.P.A., U. Miss., 1963, J.D., 1966; m. Jackie Lovell, Aug. 11, 1961; children—Vettra Glenn, Laura Lovell. Admitted to Miss. bar, 1966; pvt. practice law, Oxford, 1966—, also pros. atty. Lafayette County, City of Oxford, 1968—. Pres. Lafayette County Heart Assn., 1967-68. Mem. Lafayette County (pres.), Miss. Jr. (dir.), Am., Miss., 5th Circuit bar assns., Oxford Jr. C. of C. (dir.), Kappa Sigma, Phi Alpha Delta. Baptist. Mason. Home: 314 Garner Oxford MS 38655 Office: 1120 1/2 Van Buren Av Oxford MS 38655

ALDERSON, WILLIAM THOMAS, JR., assn. dir.; b. Schenectady, May 8, 1926; s. William Thomas and Helen Martha (Knowlton) A.; student Howard Coll., 1944-45, Tulane U., 1945-46; A.B., Colgate U., 1947; M.A., Vanderbilt U., 1949, Ph.D., 1952; m. Sylvia Caldwell Farrell, Sept. 14, 1953; children—William Thomas III, Virginia Ann, Rebecca Louise. Asst. archivist Tenn. State Library and Archives, 1952-57; asst. state librarian and archivist, 1959-61; exec. sec. Tenn. Hist. Commn., 1957-61, state librarian and archivist, chmn. commn., 1961-64; dir. Am. Assn. for State and Local History, editor History News, Nashville, 1964—. Asst. editor Tenn. Hist. Quar., 1953, asso. editor, 1954-55, editor, 1956-65; adv. com. Library of Congress Nat. Union Catalog Manuscript Collections, 1965-70; adv. council Historic Am. Bldgs. Survey, 1968-71; adv. com. hist. socs. and humanistic museums Nat. Endowment for Humanities, 1966—; instr. extension div. U. Tenn., 1954-61; vis. asst. prof. history Vanderbilt U., 1955-56; mem. adv. council for Nat. Mus. Act, Smithsonian Instn., 1971—. Dir. Am. Heritage Pub. Co. Mem. Hist. Commn. Met. Nashville and Davidson County, 1966-70. Served with USNR, 1943-46 Fellow Soc. Am. Archivists (council 1963-67); mem. Am. Assn. State and Local History (council 1959-64), Am. Records Mgmt. Assn. (pres. S.E. chpt. 1963-64), Tenn. Assn. Mus. (pres. 1965-67), Assn. Preservation Tenn. Antiquities (trustee 1964-70), Colgate U. Alumni Assn. (pres. Tenn. 1962-66), Nashville Rose Soc. (pres. 1963), So. Hist. Assn., Orgn. Am. Historians, National Trust Historic Preservation, Historic Sites Fedn. Tenn. (treas. 1968-72), Tenn. Hist. Soc. (v.p. 1969-71), Am. Assn. Museums (chmn. accreditation commn. 1970—). Republican. Methodist. Author: Tennessee Historical Markers 1958; (with R. H. White) A Guide to the Study and Reading of Tennessee History, 1959; (with R. M. McBride) Tennessee Historical Markers, 1962; (with H. G. Thomas) Historic Sites in Tennessee, 1963; Tennessee, A Student's Guide to Localized History, 1966. Co-editor: Landmarks of Tennessee History, 1965. Contbr. encys., profl. jours. Home: 124 Taggart Av Nashville TN 37205 Office: 1315 8th Av S Nashville TN 37203

ALDRED, WILLIAM HUGHES, educator; b. Thomson, Ga., Dec. 16, 1927; s. Fred Lovett and Willie (Connell) A.; B.S. in Agrl. Engring., U. Ga., 1951; M.S., Tex. A. and M.U., 1956; m. Evelyn C. Campbell, Mar. 11, 1953; children—Barbara, Bill. Instrumentation engr. E.I. DuPont de Nemours & Co., Inc., 1951-52; instr. N.M. State U., 1952-53; instr. agrl. engring. dept. Tex. A. and M. U., College Station, 1953—, asst. prof., 1957—. Served with USNR, 1946-48. Mem. Am. Soc. Agrl. Engring., Am. Soc. Engring. Edn. Baptist. Home: 310 Day St Bryan TX 77801 Office: Tex A and M U College Station TX 77843

ALDRICH, WILLIE L. B. (MRS. THOMAS N. ALDRICH), librarian; b. Cleve, Sept. 9, 1924; d. Alfred and Hattie Ross (Batts) Banks; B.S., Coll. Livingstone, Salisbury, N.C., 1945, C.R.E., 1949 M.S. in L.S., Atlanta U., 1964; m. Thomas N. Aldrich, Feb. 11, 1947. Tchr. Bible pub. schs., Salisbury, 1953-54, asst. librarian Rowan County Br. Library, 1955-58; tchr., librarian Cleveland High Sch., Shelby, N.C., 1957-58; librarian Dunbar High Sch., East Spencer, N.C., 1958-60; asst. librarian Carnegie Library, Livingstone Coll., 1960-62; hood seminarian librarian W. J. Walls Center, 1962—; curator Heritage Hall. Mem. N.C. Tchrs. Assn., A.L.A., Am. Assn. U. Women, Rowan County Citizens for Better Libraries, Rowan-Salisbury Library Assn., Delta Sigma Theta Home: 919 W Marsh St Salisbury NC 28144

ALDRIDGE, JACK HILTON, paper products co. exec.; b. Huntington, W.Va., Jan. 2, 1928; s. Jesse Hilton and Glenys Faire (Runyon) A.; B.A. in Psychology, Marshall U., 1950; postgrad. U. Cin., 1952-54; M.B.A., Xavier U., 1955; m. Patricia Ann Riley, Sept. 20, 1952. Salaried personnel interviewer Crosley-Bendix divs. Avco Mfg. Corp., Cin., 1952-55, sr. interviewer, 1952-53, coordinator employee benefits, 1953-55; with Monsanto Co., Cin., East St. Louis, Ill., Trenton, Mich., Anniston, Ala., 1955-66; with Xerox, Atlanta, Ft. Lauderdale, Fla., Washington, 1966-67; v.p. indsl. relations Package Products Co., Inc., Charlotte, N.C., 1967—. Seminar and conf. leader Am. Mgmt. Assn. seminars, 1960—; instr. Internat. Mgmt. Council, 1968-72, pres., 1970, mem. top mgmt. adv. com., 1971-72; Instr. extension div. Central Pledmont Community Coll., 1971-72. Bd. dirs. Friends U. N.C., at Charlotte, 1970-72, resources chmn., 1971-72. Served with USMCR, 1945-46. Mem. Charlotte Personnel Dirs. Assn. (treas. 1971-72), Am. Soc. Tng. and Devel., Am. Soc. Personnel Adminstrs., Internat. Mgmt. Council. Kiwanian. Home: 2300 Thornridge Rd Charlotte NC 28211 Office: 1930 Camden Rd Charlotte NC 28201

ALDRIDGE, JAMES MILTON, elec. engr.; b. Starkville Miss., Oct. 23, 1921; s. Hugh M. and Carrie M. (Ashmore) A.; B.S., Miss. State U., 1952; student Clemson Coll., 1957-58; m. Mary Keller, Sept. 18, 1942; children—Josephine K. (Mrs. Eddy Cox) James V. Owner Aldridge Radio Service, Baldwin, Miss., 1945-49; transmission engr. So. Bell Tel & Tel. Co., Jackson, 1952-59; applications engr. Collins Radio Co. Dallas, 1959-60, mgr. sage transmission, 1960-62, asst. dir. Middle and Far East Projects div., Richardson, Tex., 1962-63, mgr. Internat. Systems div. 1963-64, dir. subdiv. III A, 1964-69, regional mgr., Alaska, 1969-72, mgr. govt. and internat. systems engring., 1972—; asst. instr. physics Miss. State U., 1950-51. Served with Signal Corps, AUS, 1940-43; with USAAF, 1943-45; ETO. Registered profl. engr., Tex. Mem. I.E.E.E., Tex. Soc. Profl. Engrs. Home: 420 Royal Crest Dr Richardson TX 75030 Office: 820 E Arapaho Rd Richardson TX 75030

ALEPA (FRANCIS) PAUL, physician; b. Bronx, N.Y., Dec. 29, 1932; s. Frank P. and Carmelina (Maiuzzo) A.; B.S., Lebanon Valley Coll., Anniville, Pa., 1954; M.D., Georgetown U., 1958. Intern, Cin. Gen. Hosp., 1958-59; resident D.C. Gen Hosp., Washington, 1959-60, resident internal medicine VA Hosp., Washington, 1960-62 postdoctoral fellow Nat. Inst. Arthritis Metabolic Diseases, NIH, Bethesda, Md., 1962-64, sr. investigator, acting asst., chief arthritis and rheumatism br., 1964-65; med. attendant VA Hosp., Washington, 1962—; asst. prof. medicine Georgetown U., 1965-71, asso. prof., 1971—. Mem. D.C. Rheumatism Soc., (pres. 1971-72), Am. Rheumatism Assn. Home: 7211 Barnett Rd Bethesda MD 20034 Office: Georgetown U Hosp Washington DC 20007

ALESSANDRO, VICTOR NICHOLAS, symphony condr.; b. Waco, Tex., Nov. 27, 1915; s. Victor and Josephine (Kemendo) A.; Mus. B., U. Rochester, 1937, Mus.D. (hon.), 1948; L.H.D., So. Meth. U., 1956; student Mozarteum Acad., Salzburg, Austria, 1937, Santa Cecilia Acad., Rome, Italy, 1938; m. Ruth Drisko, May 1, 1955; children—Victor Tabbut, Ruth Ann. Musical dir. Oklahoma City Symphony, 1938-51, San Antonio Symphony Orch. and San Antonio Grand Opera Festival, 1951—; European conducting debut with Oslo Philharmonic, 1968. Trustee U. Rochester. Decorated cavalier Order Star of Solidarity (Italy); recipient Alice M. Ditson award Columbia, 1956; citation for outstanding service to Am. music Nat. Music Council, 1964. Mem. Internat. Alliance Theatrical and Stage Employees (hon.), Am. Fedn. Musicians (hon.), Phi Mu Alpha (hon.). Club: Torch (San Antonio). Home: 711 Garraty Rd San Antonio TX 78209 Office: Symphony Soc of San Antonio 600 Hemisfair Plaza Way San Antonio TX 78209

ALEXANDER, A. E., mfg. co. exec.; b. Kirksville, Mo., Apr. 23, 1913; s. George A. and Ettie (Hammond) A.; student Drake U., 1931-36; LL.B., So. Meth. U., 1937; m. Charlotte Agnus, Sept. 3, 1937; children—Jane, Nancy Ruth. Various positions The Cal. Co., New Orleans, 1937-50; v.p. Hibernia Nat. Bank, New Orleans, 1950-64; vice chmn. bd. La. Delta Offshore, New Orleans, 1964-65; pres. Crestwave Offshore Services, Inc., New Orleans, 1966—; pres. Crestwave Internat., Inc., Crestwave Overseas, Ltd.; dir. Tex. Gas Transmission Corp.; trustee Grandison Land Co. Bd. mem. Tb Assn. Greater New Orleans, 1951—, pres., 1968-69. Mem. New Orleans C. of C. (com. chmn. 1962-64). Methodist (bd. mem. 1963-66, 67-70). Mason (Jester). Clubs: New Orleans Country (bd. mem. 1959-67); Houston; Plimsoll (New Orleans). Home: 25 Versailles Blvd New Orleans LA 70125 Office: PO Drawer J 500 Vets Memorial Blvd Metairie LA 70005

ALEXANDER, DOROTHY MOSES, ballet dancer, choreographer; b. Atlanta, Apr. 22, 1904; d. Frank Hamilton and Cora Mina (Thibadeau) Moses; A.B., Oglethorp U., 1930; postgrad. U. Ga., Sadlers Wells Ballet Sch., Eng., others U.S.; m. Marion Davis Alexander, June 1926 (dec.). Concert dancer in early 20's and 30's; founder Atlanta Ballet Co., 1929, now cons.; founder Atlanta Sch. Ballet, 1922, now cons.; spearheaded Regional Ballet Movement in Am., 1956; introduced, supervised phys. fitness through dance program Atlanta Pub. Schs.; choreographer numerous ballets, 1929-69. Mem. dance com. Atlanta Arts Council, 1970; Pres., v.p. nat. bd. dirs. Regional Ballet; trustee Atlanta Arts Alliance. Recipient Nat. Dance Mag. award, 1960; named Atlanta's Woman of Year in Arts, 1947. Mem. Assn. Am. Dance Cos. (Nat. Distinguished Service award 1971), Atlanta Symphony Womens Assn., High Mus. Art, Phi Sigma Alpha. Episcopalian. Contbr. articles profl. jours. Home: 9 Ansley Dr Atlanta GA 30309 Office: 3215 Cains Hill Pl NW Atlanta GA 30305

ALEXANDER, EVA ETHEL GALLMAN, bus. exec.; b. Spartanburg, S.C., Feb. 23, 1898; d. Joe and Etta Emily (Lancaster) Gallman; m. George F. Alexander, Apr. 24, 1923 (div. June 1930); children—Frank Harold, Wilbur Gallman, Mary Fay (Mrs. Jay Bodenheimer). With accounting dept. City of High Point, N.C., 1930-35; sec. bookkeeper Rhodes Press, 1935-56; owner, operator Arts by Alexander, High Point, 1956—; pres., treas. Alexander Press, Inc., High Point, 1960—. Chmn., High Point Crippled Children and Adults Soc., 1959; hon. mem. Boy's Home of Lake Waccamaw, N.C., 1963; treas. High Point Fine Arts Guild, 1969-70. Mem. Democratic Com., 1964. Recipient Medallion award for oil Guildford County Fine Arts Exhbn., 1956; silver cup for oil Sears Traveling Exhibit, 1964; 1st prize in High Point Fine Art Juried Show, 1967. Mem. Am., N.C. iris socs., Carolina Club Printing House Craftsmen, Printing Industry High Point (sec.-treas. 1958—), High Point C. of C. (civic com. 1964-68), Nat. Home Fashions League. Baptist. Club: Pilot (pres. High Point 1962, chmn. extension com. 1964-66, dist. extension chmn. 1965-66, internat. extension com. mem. 1966-68, chmn. safety com.). Home: 708 Willoubar Terrace High Point NC 27262 Office: 701 Greensboro Rd High Point NC 27262

ALEXANDER, FRED J., coll. adminstr.; b. Childress, Tex., May 14, 1935; s. E. C. and Tillie (Branum) A.; B.S., Abilene Christian Coll., 1958, M.Ed., 1959; postgrad. U. Mich., 1962-63; m. Claudette Harris, May 31, 1957; children—Joe Frederick, Beverly Ellen, Denise Kay. Instr. Moran (Tex.) High Sch., 1956-58, Baird (Tex.) High Sch., 1958-59; instr. Mich. Christian Jr. Coll., Rochester, 1959-64, registrar, dir. admissions, 1964-68; dir. jr. coll. relations Harding Coll., Searcy, Ark., 1968-69, dir. admissions, 1969—. Served with USNR, 1953-60. Mem. Am., Mich. assns. collegiate registrars and admissions officers. Home: 15 Indian Trail Searcy AR 72143

ALEXANDER, HOLMES, editor; b. Tampa, Fla., Aug. 7, 1921; s. Thomas Ferdinand and Annie (Holmes) A.; B.A. with honors, U. Fla., 1942; grad. U.S. Army Command and Gen. Staff Coll.; m. Lilia R. Guerra, May 18, 1946; children—Thomas Jefferson, Linda Lilia, Michael Holmes, Lycia Lucia. Reporter, Tampa (Fla.) Times, 1942-46; staff Tampa Tribune, 1946—, state editor, 1949-59, asso. editor, book editor, 1959—. Served with USNR, 1942-46. Mem. Phi Beta Kappa, Kappa Tau Alpha, Phi Eta Sigma. Roman Catholic. Home: 2103 E 109th Av Tampa FL 33612 Office: PO Box 191 Tampa FL 33601

ALEXANDER, JAMES ATWELL, poultryman; b. Stony Point, N.C. July 23 1911; s. J. Will and Mary Emma (Alexander) A.; A.B. Davidson Coll., 1929, M.A., 1931; student Colo. Sch. Mines, 1930, postgrad. U. N.C., 1932-34; m. Anna Pauline Hill, Dec. 23, 1938; children—Mary Anna, Eva Pauline. Seismologist Shell Oil Co., Houston, 1937-40; owner, mgr. Alexander Poultry Farm, Stony Point, 1940— bd. of dirs. Alexander County Water Corp. Chmn. Alexander County Poultry Council, 1953-55, Catawaba Soil Conservation Dist. Conservation Dist. Suprs., 1949-51; mem. adv. com. poultry test, 1958—; mem. gen. bd. Northwestern Bank, 1971—. Mem. Bd. Commrs., Alexander County, 1950-54, Welfare Bd., 1952-54, Alexander County Planning Bd., 1969—; mem. N.C. State Bd. Agr., 1955—; mem. Gov's. Adv. Com. Nuclear Energy, N.C., 1957—; mem. N.C. Gov.'s Council on Occupational Health, N.C. Gov.'s Council on Rehabilitation; chmn. N.C. Gov.'s Adv. Com. Agr., 1965—; mem. exec. com. Gov's Council for Econ. Devel. Mem. Fair Commn., Dixie Classic Fair, Winston-Salem, N.C. Bd. dirs. Alexander County Hosp.; exec. com. N.C. Agricultural Found., 1965—, v.p., 1967; adv. com. Sch. Agr. N.C. State U. Named Man of the year by Grange of Alexander County, N.C., 1957, BY Alexander County C. of C., 1967; N.C. Outstanding Farm Manager, 1965, N.C. County Agrl. Agts. award, 1971. Mem. N.C. Acad. Science, N.W. N.C. Devel. Assn. (pres., chmn agrl. div. award 1969), C. of C. (dir.), N.C. Egg Marketing Assn. (pres. 1961-62), N.C. Poultry Council (pres. 1963), N.C. Agribusiness Council (exec. com.), Sigma Xi, Gamma Sigma Epsilon, Sigma Gamma Epsilon. Democrat. Lion (charter mem., zone chmn.). Home: Stony Point NC 28678

ALEXANDER, JAMES HENRY, ins. broker, state ofcl.; b. McKenzie, Tenn., Jan. 2, 1922; s. E. Marvin and Lillis (McElroy) A.; student Bethel Coll., 1939-41; B.S. in Bus. Administrn., U. Tenn., 1943; m. Lola Diuguid Chestnut, Dec. 21, 1945; children—Anne Elizabeth, James Henry, Jean. Engaged in gen. ins. bus., McKenzie, 1946—; treas. State of Tenn., Nashville, 1963-67; gov.'s staff dir. for indsl. devel., 1967-71; exec. dir. Insurors of Tenn., 1971—. Pres. Tenn. Sch. Bd. Assn., 1961; chmn. Tenn. Heart Fund, 1963-64. Sec., Tenn. Bd. Elections, 1953; campaign mgr. Gov. Frank Clement for gov., 1962, for U.S. Senate, 1964; alternate del. Dem. Nat. Conv., 1956. Trustee Lambuth Coll., Jackson, Tenn. Served to lt. (j.g.) USNR, 1943-46. Mem. Insurors of Tenn. (v.p.), Am. Legion (dist. comdr. 1950), V.F.W. Elk, Rotarian. Home: 714 Stonewall St McKenzie TN 38201 Office: Broadway St McKenzie TN 38201 also 1412 Parkway Towers Nashville TN 37219

ALEXANDER, JOHN DAVID, JR., coll. pres.; b. Springfield, Tenn., Oct. 18, 1932; s. John David and Mary Agnes (McKinnon) A.; B.A., Southwestern at Memphis, 1953; student Louisville Presbyn. Theol. Sem., 1953-54; D.Phil., Oxford (Eng.) U., 1957; m. Catharine Coleman, Aug. 26, 1956; children—Catharine McKinnon, John David III, Julia Mary. Asso. prof. San Francisco Theol. Sem., 1957-65, dean summer session, 1958, acting sec. in-parish profl. doctorate program, 1962-63; pres. Southwestern at Memphis, 1965—. Pres. Univ. Council Edn. Pub. Responsibility, 1966—; mem. commn. liberal learning Assn. Am. Colls., 1966—; mem. commn. colls. So. Assn. Colls. and Schs., 1966—. Bd. dirs. Louisville Presbyn. Theol. Sem. Mem. bd. Rhodes Scholars, 1954, Mem. Am. Oriental Soc., Soc. Bib. Lit., Soc. Religion in Higher Edn., The Egyptians, Newcomen Soc., Phi Beta Kappa, Omicron Delta Kappa, Sigma Nu. Rotarian. Home: 671 West Dr Memphis TN 38112

ALEXANDER, JOSEPH EUGENE, aerospace co. exec.; b. Tampa, Fla., Jan. 11, 1925; s. Thomas Ferdinand and Annie (Holmes) A.; B.E.E., Ga. Inst. Tech., 1948; M.S. in Elec. Engring., La. State U., 1949; Ph.D., Northwestern U., 1953; m. Ann Elizabeth Jackson, Sept. 3, 1948; children—James Porter, Diane Marshall, Thomas Eugene, Leann Jackson, Lisa Lynn. Engr. automatic control E.I. Dupont Co., Orange, Tex., 1953-56; sect. head electronics system Lockheed Aircraft Co., Marietta, Ga., 1956-57; mgr. advanced design Martin-Co., Orlando, Fla., 1957-62; mgr. systems analysis dept. Aerospace Corp., El Segundo, Cal., 1962-66; head systems analysis dept. TRW Systems, Houston, 1966—. Instr. elec. engring. La. State U., 1947-50, Northwestern U., 1950-53. Asst. scout master Boy Scouts Am., Palos Verdes, Cal., 1962-65. Served with AUS, 1943-44. Mem. I.E.E.E., Inst. Nav., Soc. Plastic Engrs., Am. Legion, Sigma Xi, Phi Kappa Phi. Phi Eta Sigma, Eta Kappa Nu, Kappa Alpha. Episcopalian. Author: (with J. M. Bailey) Systems Engineering Mathematics, 1962. Home: 18610 Martinique Dr Houston TX 77058 Office: Space Park Dr Houston TX 77058

ALEXANDER, KENNETH DEEDES, JR., ter. senator; b. Chgo., 1921; s. Kenneth Deedes and Mollie (King) A.; grad. Lawrenceville Sch. (N.J.), 1940; grad. Brit. Commonwealth Air Tng. Coll., 1942; m. Peggy French; children— Laurie King, Katherine Virginia. Account exec. J. Walter Thompson Co., N.Y.C., 1946-51; v.p., dir. Columbia Artists and Mgmt. Inc., Community Concerts, Inc., 1951-53; pres. French-Alexander Real Estate Co., St. Thomas, V.I., 1959—; a founder, 1st pres. St. Thomas-St. John Real Estate Bd., 1961—; mem. V.I. Senate, 1966—. Mem. Gov.'s Commn. on Rent Control, 1964, Gov.'s Commn. on Economy Opportunity, 1964; mem. V.I. Police Commn.; mem. 59th Gov.'s Conf., 1968; commr. real estate Ter. of V.I., 1969. Served with USAF. Decorated Air medal with three oak leaf clusters, Bronze Star (3), Brit. Empire medal. Mem. Nat. Rifle Assn., Am. Contract Bridge League, C. of C. of V.I., Humane Soc. V.I. Democrat. Rotarian, Lion (founder St. Thomas club, charter mem.). Clubs: Virgin Islands Pistol and Rifle; Sleepy Hollow Country (Tarrytown, N.Y.). Address: PO Box 1488 St Thomas Virgin Islands 00801*

ALEXANDER, LOUIS, writer, educator; b. N.Y.C., Mar. 15, 1917; s. Louis I. and Gertrude (Seydel) A.; B.S. in Marketing, U. Newark, 1941; M. Letters in Journalism, U. Houston, 1961 m. Paulette Marlowe, Dec. 23, 1948 (div. Dec. 20, 1968); children—Kathryn, Marjory Lynn. Reporter, county editor Houston Chronicle, 1947-57; free-lance writer for mags. and newspapers including Sat. Eve. Post, N. Am. Newspaper Alliance, Popular Sci., others, 1957—; instr. journalism U. Houston, 1954-69, asst. prof. journalism, 1969—. Corr., Wall Street Jour., 1959—, Nat. Observer, 1961—. Mem. Bellaire Parks and Recreation Commn., 1957-60, vice chmn., 1960. Served with USAAF, 1942-45; to capt. USAF, 1951-52; lt. col. Res. Decorated D.F.C., Air medal with three oak leaf clusters. Mem. Aviation/Space Writers Assn. (gen. chmn. nat. conv. 1958), Assn. Petroleum Writers, Assn. Edn. in Journalism, Sigma Delta Chi. Club: Press (Houston). Contbr. to Historic Decade, 1960. Home: 704 Mulberry Lane Bellaire TX 77401 Office: Communications Dept U Houston TX 77004

ALEXANDER, MARY LOUISE, educator; b. Ennis, Tex., Jan. 15, 1926; d. Emmett F. and Florence (Hill) Alexander; B.A., U. Tex., 1947, M.A., 1949, Ph.D., 1951. Instr., research asst. Genetics Found., U. Tex., Austin, 1944-51, postdoctoral research fellow, 1952-55, research scientist Genetics Found., 1962-68; postdoctoral fellow biology div. AEC, Oak Ridge, 1951-52; research asso. U. Tex.-M.D. Anderson Hosp. and Tumor Inst., Houston, 1956-58, asst. biologist, 1959-62; asso. prof. biology S.W. Tex. State U., San Marcos, 1967-69, prof., 1969—. Research cons. Brookhaven Nat. Lab., Upton, N.Y., 1955; research participant Oak Ridge Inst. Nuclear Studies, Tenn., 1951—. Nat. Cancer Inst. fellow Inst. Animal Genetics, Edinburgh, Scotland, 1960-61. Mem. Genetics Soc. Am., Radiation Research Soc., Am. Soc. Human Genetics, Sigma Xi, Gamma Phi Beta, Phi Sigma, Alpha Epsilon Delta. Home: Hunter's Glen Route 2 Box 119 San Marcos TX 78666

ALEXANDER, PAULINE HILL (MRS. JAMES ATWELL ALEXANDER), educator, clubwoman; b. Stony Point, N.C., Apr. 7, 1916; d. James Lolo and Eva (Shuford) Hill; student Mitchell Coll., 1932-34, Lenoir Rhyne Coll., 1935-36, Western Carolina Tchrs. Coll., 1937, U. Houston, 1939; m. James Atwell Alexander, Dec. 23, 1938; children—Mary Anna, Eva Pauline. Tchr. Central High Sch., Statesville, N.C., 1934-45, dramatics coach, 1939-41. Leader Stony Point Council Girl Scouts U.S., 1951-60; adult leader 4-H Clubs, Alexander County, N.C., 1958-61; 4-H Club sponsor, 1967—; area chmn. Mitchell Coll. Endowment, 1956; choir dir. Elk Shoals A.R. Presbyn. Ch., 1958-64. Recipient oratorical and essay awards Am. Legion, 1931, W.C.T.U., 1933; named Woman of the Year, Alexander County, 1959. Mem. D.A.R. (dir., chpt. conservation chmn. chpt. regent 1965, local nat. def. chmn. 1967—), Mitchell Coll. Alumni Assn. (pres. 1963-64). Democrat. Presbyn. (home mission sec. Women of Ch.) Club: Stony Point Woman's (pres. 1953-54). Home: Stony Point NC 28678

ALEXANDER, RAYMONDE ALWYN, journalist; b. Ogelthorpe, Ga., June 6, 1921; d. William Linton and Dade (Partee) Alexander; student Central Mo. State Coll., 1939-40; A.B. in Journalism, U. Ga., 1943. Fashion copywriter Davison-Paxon Co., Atlanta, 1943-48; freelance copywriter, Atlanta, 1948-54; copywriter Atlanta Rich's, Inc., 1955-57; fashion editor The Atlanta Constitution, 1957—. Mem. Atlanta Civic Ballet, Atlanta Art Assn., Fashion Group Atlanta (dir. 1961-62), Theta Sigma Phi (pres. Atlanta Alumni Chpt. 1953-54), Sigma Sigma Sigma. Club: Atlanta Music (Atlanta, Ga). Democrat. Methodist. Home: 3083 Andrews Dr NW Atlanta GA 30305 Office: 72 Marietta St NW Atlanta GA 30303

ALEXANDER, RICHARD GERALD, orthodontist; b. Lubbock, Tex., Feb. 25, 1936; s. Jenkins Charles and Geraldine (Smith) A.; B.A., Tex Technol. U., 1958; D.D.S., U. Tex., 1962, M.S.D., 1964; m. Janna Dean Murray, June 20, 1959; children—Charles Dean, James Moody, Shanna. Pvt. practice orthodontics, Arlington, Tex., 1964—; asso. prof. orthodontics Baylor U.; cons. Scottish Rites Crippled Children's Hosp. (Dallas). Pres. Arlington Boys Club, 1969. Bd. dirs. Am. Cancer Soc., 1969—; bd. dirs. Tex. Found. for Dental Health and Edn.; city councilman, Arlington, 1971—; trustee Tex. Technol. Ex. Students Assn. Recipient Milo Hellman research award, Am. Assn. Orthodontists, 1965, C.T. Rowland award C.H.Tweed Orthodontic Group of Tex., 1968; named Outstanding Young Man of Arlington, 1969. Diplomate Am. Bd. Orthodontics, 1971. Mem. Ft. Worth Dist. Dental Soc. (del.), Edward H. Angle Soc., Charles H. Tweed Orthodontic Group Tex., Am. Dental Assn., Am. Assn. Orthodontics, Arlington C.of C. (dir. 1968-69). Republican. Methodist (chmn. bd. trustees). Rotarian (pres. Arlington 1971-72). Editor of 12th Night Dental Jour., 1969-71. Home: 4013 Shady Valley Dr Arlington TX 76013 Office: 840 W Mitchell Arlington TX 76013

ALEXANDER, ROBERT HOUSTON, geographer; b. Griswold, Ia., Apr. 20, 1927; s. George H. and Ann Ella (Reynolds) A.; B.S., Ia. state Coll. 1950; M.S., Cal. Inst. Tech., 1953; postgrad. Trinity Coll, U. of Dublin, U. Wash. 1 dau., Maura. Geophys. aide Socony-Vacuum Oil Co., Venezuela, 1951; geologist Shell Oil Co., So. Cal., 1953-56; geographer Office of Naval Research, Washington, 1960-67, U.S. Geological Survey. Washington, 1967—. Served with AC, AUS, 1945-46. Mem. Assn. Am. Geographers, Regional Sci. Assn. Home: PO Box 2301 Washington DC 20013 Office: US Geol Survey Washington DC 20242

ALEXANDER, ROBERT HUGH, symphony exec.; b. Wichita Falls, Tex., June 12, 1933; s. Elijah Oscar and Ida Lucille (Johnston) A.; B.A., Midwestern U., Wichita Falls, 1955; m. Jean Ann Fulfs, May 3, 1958; children—Lynn, Lisa. Mgr. Fort Worth Symphony Orch., 1958-69, Arts Council Greater Fort Worth, Inc., 1963-69, Youth Orch. Greater Fort Worth, 1965-69; pub. relations dir. Dallas Symphony Orch., 1969-71, dir. devel., 1971—. Home: 10843 Camellia Dr Dallas TX 75230 Office: PO Box 8472 Dallas TX 75205

ALEXANDER, S. M., state ofcl. Asst. supt. pub. instrn. State of Ky., Frankfort. Address: State Dept Edn Frankfort KY 40601*

ALEXANDER, WILLIAM MORTIMER, educator; b. Jacksonville, Fla., Dec. 5, 1928; s. Leon Wilson and Ruth Louise (Chesebrough) A.; A.B., Davidson Coll., 1950; B.D., Louisville Presbyn. Sem., 1953; S.T.M., Harvard, 1957; Th.D., Princeton, 1961; m. Katherine Alice Fryer, June 5, 1953; children—John Edward, Susan Dorman, David Leon. Asst. prof. St Andrews Coll., Laurinburg, N.C., 1961-63, asso. prof., 1963-67, prof. religion and philosophy, 1967—. Served with AUS, 1953-56. Research grantee Am. Council Learned Socs., 1966. Piedmont U. Center, 1969-71. Mem. Am. Philos. Assn., Am. Acad. Religion, Am. Assn. U. Profs., Soc. for Philosophy and Pub. Affairs, N.C. Council Human Relations. Presbyn. Author: Johann Georg Hamann: Philosophy and Faith, 1966. Home: Shepherd Av Laurinburg NC 28352

ALEXANDER, WILLIAM VOLLIE, JR., congressman; b. Memphis, Jan. 16, 1934; s. William V. and Spencer (Buck) A.; student U. Ark., 1951-53; B.A., Southwestern, Memphis, 1957; LL.B Vanderbilt U., 1960; m. Marjorie Gwendolyn Haven, Feb. 5, 1957; one dau., Alyse Haven. Admitted to Tenn. bar, 1960, Ark. bar, 1963; law clk. to chief judge U.S. Dist. Ct., Memphis, 1960-61; asso. Montedonico, Bonne, Gilliland, Heiskell & Loch, Memphis, 1961-63; partner Swift & Alexander, Osceola, Ark., 1963-69; former dir. Osceola Riverport Authority; former commr., Arkansas Waterways Commn. Mem. 91st, 92d Congress 1st dist. Arkansas. Mem. bd. dirs. Osceola YMCA; dir. Mississippi County YMCA; dir. East Ark. Council Boy Scouts Am. Bd. dirs. Southwestern at Memphis. Mem. Am. Acad. Polit. and Social Sci., Kappa Sigma, Phi Delta Phi. Episcopalian. Mason. Clubs: Rotary (pres., dir.). Office: Cannon House Office Bldg Washington DC 20515

ALEXANDRIDES, COSTAS GEORGE, educator; b. Athens, Greece, Sept. 28, 1929; s. George Alexander and Maria C. (Papadopoulos) A.; came to U.S., 1948, naturalized, 1968; B.A., U. Ga., 1951; Ph.D., New York U., 1961; m. Sophia Macris, Jan. 27, 1952. Chmn. UN Series, N.Y. U., 1961-63; dir. UN Studies, New Sch. for Social Research, 1963-67; asso. prof. of mgmt., Ga. State U., Atlanta, 1967—. Economic reports officer, UN, 1952-55; exec. asst. to pub. Atlantis, 1957-58; adv. Cyprus Delegation to UN, 1960-63; adjunct asso. prof. L.I.U., 1965-66, Coll. City N.Y., 1966; sec. treas. So. Consortium for Internat. Edn., 1969—; chmn. Atlanta Export Trade Workshop, 1970. Aide to Gov. Nelson Rockefeller of N.Y., 1966. Recipient State Tech. Services Grant, Ga. State U., 1969-71. Mem. Acad. Mgmt., Assn. Edn. in Internat. Bus., Nat. Soccer Coaches Assn., Omigran Delta Epsilon, Delta Sigma Pi. Author: Global Markets for Georgia Products, 1971. Editor Internat. Bus. Systems, 1970, The Challenge of Exports, 1971, Computerization of Internat. Market Research, 1970, State of Ga. in World Trade 1968. Home: 3433 Paces Forest Rd NW Atlanta GA 30327

ALFARO, VICTOR RICARDO, physician; b. Panama, 1907; M.D., Georgetown U., 1929. Intern Hosp. Santo Tomas, Panama, 1928; tng. otology U. Pa., 1930-31; surgeon Washington Hosp. Center; now prof. emeritus Georgetown U. Served to lt. col. M.C., AUS, 1942-46. Diplomate Am. Bd. Otolaryngology. Fellow Am. Laryngol., Rhinol. and Otol. Soc. (pres.); mem. Am. Acad. Ophthamology and Otolaryngology, Am. Otol. Soc., So. Med. Assn., Am. Laryngol. Assn. Address: 916 19th St NW Washington DC 20006

ALFORD, HOWARD, assn. exec. Pres., Plains Cotton Co-op. Assn. Inc. Office: 3301 E 50th St Lubbock TX 79408*

ALFORD, MARION ELMER, supt. schs.; b. Perry, Fla., Dec. 29, 1919; s. William D. and Jessie (McHargue) A.; B.S., Middle Tenn. State Coll., 1941; M.A., George Peabody Coll., 1947; Ed.D., U. Va., 1958; m. Eva Davis, Sept. 18, 1944; 1 son, William Andrew. Tchr. pub. schs., Taylor County, Fla., 1941-42, Portsmouth, Va., 1946-47, Hickory, Va., 1947-48; prin. demonstration sch. Ala. State Coll. for Women, 1948-49; prin. pub. schs., Great Bridge, Va., 1949-51; dir. instrn., Norfolk County, Va., 1951-56, asst. supt. schs., Norfolk County, 1957-60; prof. George Peabody Coll., 1960-61, asso. dir. div. surveys and field services, 1961-62; pres. Frederick Coll., Portsmouth, Va., 1962-65; supt. Portsmouth City Schs., 1965—; instr. extension div. Coll. William and Mary, 1956, U. Va., 1953-54. Trustee Ferrum Jr. Coll., 1968—; chmn. bd. trustees Tidewater Community Coll. Served ensign to lt. USNR, 1942-46; now lt. comdr. Res. Mem. Am. Assn. U. Profs. (asso.), Am. Assn. Sch. Administrs., Assn. Supervision and Curriculum Devel., Phi Delta Kappa, Kappa Delta Pi. Methodist (mem. Va. conf. bd. edn. 1964—). Contbr. articles to profl. jours. Office: Board Edn Portsmouth VA

ALFORD, SAMUEL JACKSON, JR., physician; b. Orlando Fla., June 10, 1923; s. Samuel Jackson and Ada Lee (Jacobs) A.; student So. Jr. Coll., Collegedale, Tenn., 1942-43, Washington Missionary Coll., 1943-44; M.D., Med.-Coll. of Med. Evangelists, 1949; m. Margie LaVerne Morgan, June 19, 1945; children—Michael Lee, Stephen Douglas, Joni Gail. Intern St. Luke's Hosp., Jacksonville, Fla., 1948-49, resident, 1949-50; practice medicine, specializing in obstetrics, also family practice, Jacksonville, Fla., 1953—; mem. staff St. Luke's Hosp., Jacksonville, 1953—, chmn. emergency room dept., 1960-72, pres. staff, 1965-66. Pilot, group flight surgeon Civil Air Patrol, Jacksonville, 1953-72. Served to capt. M.C., USAF, 1951-53. Mem. Fla. Acad. Gen. Practice (bd. dirs. 1966-72, editor jour. 1966-72). Club: Jacksonville Police Pistol (pres. 1955-71). Home: 1035 Rio St Johns Jacksonville FL 32211 Office: 33 W Ashley St Jacksonville FL 32202

ALFRIEND, SUE LANDON, banker, advt. exec.; b. North Wilkesboro, N.C.; d. Henry Clayton and Sue (Ennis) Landon; student Salem Coll., 1944-46; A.B., Randolph-Macon Woman's Coll., 1948; M.S., U. N.C., 1951; postgrad. Northwestern U., 1962; m. Richard Jeffrey Alfriend III, Jan. 12, 1952 (div. July 1958); 1 dau., Sue Landon. Tchr., Norfolk (Va.) City Schs., 1953-55, elementary Sch., Princess Anne County, Va., 1955-56; advt. mgr. Northwestern Bank, North Wilkesboro, N.C., 1958-61, asst. treas., 1961-62, assistant vice president in charge advt. dept., 1962-69, vice president, 1969—. Chmn. publicity Wilkes United Fund, 1962-63, mem. publicity com., 1965. Mem. bd. Tarheel Triad council Girl Scouts, U.S.A. Mem. Bank Marketing Assn., N.C. Bankers Assn., Wilkes C. of C. (chmn. mchts. div.), Delta Delta Delta. Presbyn. Home: 611 8th St North Wilkesboro NC 28659 Office: 924 B St North Wilkesboro NC 28659

ALISON, JAMES CONRAD, city ofcl.; b.Dyersburg, Tenn., Sept. 7, 1922; s James Dailey Jr. and Gladys Beatrix (Sudbury) A.; student Fla. Mil. Inst., Haines City, 1937, Gordon Mil. Coll., Barnesville, Ga., 1938-40, Officer Tng. Sch. USMC, Quantico, Va., 1945, Naval Law Sch., Port Hueneme, Cal., 1946, Staff and Command Sch., 1959; m. Emma Faye Shelton, Aug. 22, 1942; 1 son, Conrad Daley. Enlisted U.S. Marine Corps, 1940, Commd. 2d lt. U.S. Marine Corps, 1945, advanced through grades to lt. col.; various assignments including comdg. officer automotive maintenance, Tientsin, China, 1947-48, comdg. officer tng. center, Memphis, 1962-66, ret., 1966; dir. maintenance, head municipal maintenance dept. City of St. Petersburg, Fla., 1966—. Recipient Nat. award Am. Cities Mag. for leadership in field of automotive and equipment maintenance, 1968. Mason. Home: 100 Ricardo Way NE St Petersburg FL 33704 Office: Municipal Maintenance Dept 619 19th St N St Petersburg FL 33713

ALLAN, ROGER DEMUTH, profl. assn. exec.; b. Waterloo, Ia., Oct. 12, 1933; s. Stuart Eugene and Clara (Demuth) A.; B.A., U. Notre Dame, 1957; m. Catherine Justine Baumann, Oct. 29, 1960; children— Theresa Joan, Susan Marie. Journalist, Covington (Va.) Virginian, 1957-59; with Homestead Hotel, Hot Springs, Va., 1959-61, Nat. Assn. Real Estate Bd., Washington, 1961-63, Asso. Gen. Contractors, 1963-66, C. of C. of U.S., 1966-67; account exec., pub. relations Ketchum McLeod & Grove, Pitts., 1967-68; pub. relations mgr. Electronic Industries Assn., Washington, 1968—. Active United Givers Fund, Washington, 1971-72. Served with AUS, 1956. mem. Pub. Relations Soc. Am. (chmn. chpt. publicity com. 1971—). Democrat. Roman Catholic. Club: Nat. Press (profl. relations com. 1971-72) (Washington). Home: 1903 Windmill Lane Alexandria VA 22307 Office: 2001 I St NW Washington DC 20006

ALLBAUGH, LELAND GIRARD, econ. cons.; b. Leon, Ia., Oct. 6, 1896; s. William Alvin and Laura (Gammon) A.; B.S., Ia. State U., 1919, M.S., 1928; Ph.D., Harvard, 1951; m. Cora Emelia Oleson, Dec. 24, 1919; children—Robert Dean, James William. Asst. farm mgmt. demonstrator Ia. State U., 1918-19, extension 1964-72, Ensco, Cocoa

Beach, Fla., 1972—. prof. agrl. econs., 1922-30, asso. prof., 1931-41; farmer, Humboldt County, Ia., 1920; county agt., Carroll County, Ia., 1921; chief farm plan and loan sect. FSA, Washington, 1941-42; asso. dir. Agrl. Extension Service, Ames, Ia., 1942-43; chief agrl. supplies Fgn. Econ. Adminstrn., Washington, 1944; dir. agrl. subcommn. Allied Control Commn., Rome, Italy, 1944-45; chief test-demonstration br. TVA, Knoxville, Tenn., 1946-47, dir. div. agrl. relations, 1952-61; econ. cons. UN Spl. Fund, Afghanistan, in 1963, FAO, Taiwan and Egypt, Korea, Ethiopia, 1964, Korea, Rome, Sudan, 1965, Tanzania, 1966, UNDP, Sudan, 1966, UNDP, Sudan, Iraq. West Irian, Indonesia, and Geneva, 1967; assistant dir. social scis. Rockefeller Found., N.Y.C., 1948-50; agrl. economist Inst. InterAm. Affairs, Washington, Asuncion, Paraguay, Port-au-Prince, Haiti, 1951-52. Lectr. agrl. econs. So. Ill. U., 1962. Served with U.S. Army, 1918. Recipient Medal of Freedom, U.S. Army, 1945; Distinguished Achievement citation Ia. State U. Alumni Assn., 1969. Mem. Am. Farm Econ. Assn., Internat. Assn. Agrl. Economists; Am. Forestry Assn., Am. Soc. Agronomy, Phi Kappa Phi, Gamma Sigma Delta, Lambda Chi Alpha. Methodist. Mason. Club: Torch (Knoxville). Author: Crete, 1953; also numerous articles in profl. jours. Address: 6830 Sheffield Dr Knoxville TN 37919

ALLBRITTON, JOE LEWIS, banker, ins. co. exec.; b. D'Lo, Miss., Dec. 29, 1924; s. Lewis A. and Ada (Carpenter) A.; LL.B., Baylor U., 1949, LL.D. (hon.), 1964, J.D., 1969; m. Barbara Jean Balfanz, Feb. 23, 1967; 1 son, Robert Lewis. Admitted to Tex. bar, 1949; practiced in Houston, 1949—; mem. firm Clawson, Allbritton & Clawson, 1950-53, Allbritton, McGee & Hand, 1961-64; chmn. bd., chief exec. officer Pierce Nat. Life Ins. Co., 1958—; chmn. bd. Pierce Bros., 1958—; dir Perpetual Corp., 1958—, pres., 1965— (all Los Angeles); chmn. bd. Mineral Oil Refining Co., Dickinson, Tex., 1963-68; pres., dir. San Jacinto Savs. Assn., 1956-68; dir. Bank of Southwest Nat. Assn., 1964-69, mem. exec. com., 1965-69; chmn. exec. com., dir. Houston Citizens Bank & Trust Co., 1969—, pres., chief exec. officer, 1970—; dir. Southwestern Pub. Service Co., Dallas, 1965—, First Fed. Savs. &Loan, Dallas, 1971—. Mem. hosp. adv. council Tex. State Dept. Health, Austin, 1965-66; mem. fgn. mission bd. So. Bapt. Conv., Richmond, Va., 1966—. Trustee, Baylor U., Waco, Tex., 1959-68, mem. exec. com., 1960-68, vice chmn. bd., 1965-68; trustee Baylor U. Coll. Medicine, Houston, 1959-68, chmn., 1965-68; trustee Mus. Fine Arts, Houston; mem. council Tulane U. Bus. Shc., New Orleans, 1972—; mem. nat. bd. dirs. Inst. Internat. Edn., N.Y.C., 1972—, bd. dirs. So. region, Houston, 1972—; v.p., bd. dirs., treas. Houston Symphony Soc., 1972—. Served with USNR, 1943-46. Recipient Distinguished Alumni award Pi Kappa Delta, 1963. Mem. Am. Bar Assn., State Bar Tex. Baptist (chmn. trustees 1953-71). Home: Warwick Hotel Houston TX 77001 Office: Houston Citizens Bank Bldg Houston TX 77002

ALLDERDICE, JACK HARRY, chem. co. exec.; b. Coldwater, Kan., Nov. 19, 1917; s. Charles E. and Burdee P. (Rucker) A.; A.B., U. Kan., 1940; m. Rose Mary Mulvihill, Apr. 26, 1942; children—J. Douglas, Michael B. Chemist, prodn. supr. E.I. DuPont de Nemours and Co., Chgo., 1940-46; splty. chemist Bell Co. Inc., Chgo., 1946-52; mem. sales staff Chem. div. Gen. Mills Inc., Kankakee, Ill., 1952-57; dist. mgr. Humko div. Kraft Co., Chgo., 1957-63, nat. marketing mgr., Memphis, 1963—. Mem. Chem. Spltys. Mfrs. Assn., Fatty Acid Producers Council, Kappa Sigma. Home: 190 E Cherry Circle Memphia TN 38117 Office: 5050 Poplar St Memphis TN 38117

ALLEGER, DANIEL E(UGENE), agrl. economist; b. East Stroudsburg, Pa., Oct. 18, 1903; s. Frank H. and Lena (Ruff) A.; B.S. in Agrl. Econs., Pa. State Coll., 1926, M.S. in Rural Sociology, 1943; m. Carolyn Breckenridge, May 6, 1933; 1 dau., Martha Alice. Agrl. prodn. and research United Fruit Co. in Honduras and Guatemala, 1926-31; agt. Met. Life Ins. Co., 1931-41; product supr. shells Bethlehem Steel Co., 1942-45; asso. agrl. economist Fla. Agrl. Expt. Sta., U. Fla., 1945—. Cons. agrl. econs. to Govt. of Costa Rica, 1956; chief of party U. Fla. Mission to Costa Rica, 1960. Mem. Rural Sociol. Soc., Am. Agrl. Econ. Assn., Internat. Assn. Agrl. Economists, So. Agrl. Econs. Assn., Omicron Delta Epsilon, Gamma Sigma Delta. Editor: Fertile Lands of Friendship, 1963; Social Change and Aging in the Twentieth Century, 1964; Adventures on the Mosquito Shore (by Samuel Bard 1855), 1965. Compiler: The Genesis of the Allegers, 1970. Home: 1710 SW 49th Pl Gainesville FL 32601

ALLEN, ALFRED KEYS, constrn. co. exec.; b. Birmingham, Ala., Feb. 18, 1914; s. Charles Morhead and Nannie (Thompson) A.; B.S., Auburn U., 1935; postgrad. Birmingham Law Sch., 1939; m. Barbara Moose, Sept. 15, 1938; children—Charles M. II, Louise Condon, Alfred Keys, Barbara Marie. Vice pres. Dunn Constrn. Co., Birmingham 1945-57, Utah Constrn. Co., San Francisco, 1957-59, Blount Bros., Montgomery, Ala., 1959-62; pres. South Engring. & Constrn. Co., Montgomery, 1954—; v.p., dir. Perini Corp. San Francisco, 1963-69, exec. v.p., dir., Miami, Fla., 1969-70; pres. dir. Jahncke Service, Inc., Metairie, La., 1970—; v.p., dir. OKC Corp., Dallas, 1970—. Served to lt. col. C.E., AUS, 1940-45; CBI. Decorated Order of Cloud and Banner (China); Legion of Merit (U.S.). Mem. Moles, Beavers, New Orleans C. of C. Home: 5101 Cleveland Pl Metairie LA 70003 Office: 4001 Division St Metairie LA 70002

ALLEN, ANITA FORD, edn. ofcl.; b. Washington, Feb. 13, 1925; d. Leonard Guy and Jerlean (Reynolds) Ford; B.A., Howard U., 1941-45; M.A., U. Chgo., 1946; postgrad. Am. U. Grad. Sch. Pub. Adminstrn., 1955-57; m. Willie Berkeley Allen, Dec. 28, 1959; children— George Ferguson III, Stephen Ferguson; step-children—Willie Allen, Vincent Allen. Instr., Howard U., Washington, 1946-48; preliminary cataloger Library of Congress, 1953-56; participant 7th Jr. Mgmt. Intern Program, 1955-56; mgmt. analyst Dept. Army, 1956-63; tng. instr. Gen. Services Adminstrn. Inst., 1963-65; program specialist U.S. Office Edn., Washington, 1965—. Mem. Tech. Adv. Com. on Adult Illiteracy, 1956; v.p. D.C. Bd. Edn., 1967-70, pres., 1970-72. Recipient Outstanding Performance award Gen. Services Adminstrn. Inst., 1964. Mem. D.C. Council Adminstrv. Women in Edn. (v.p. 1969-70), Am. Inst. Parliamentarians, Nat. Com. Support Pub. Sch., Nat. Assn. Ministers Wives (dist. body), Bapt. Ministers Wives Washington and Vicinity, Progressive Nat. Bapt. Assn. (women's div.), Howard U. Alumni Assn., Delta Sigma Theta. Baptist (com. wider cooperation). Home: 5701 Moreland St NW Washington DC 20015 Office: 7th and D Sts SW Washington DC 20202

ALLEN, ARTHUR WRIGHT, JR., govt. ofcl.; b. Washington, Ind. Nov. 2, 1915; s. Arthur Wright and Willoughby (Stamper) A.; student Ind. U., 1933-35; B.S., U.S. Mil. Acad., 1939; grad. Command and Gen. Staff Coll, 1944; m. Mary Virginia Welsh, Mar. 14, 1940. Commd. 2d lt. U.S.Army, 1939, advanced through grades to col., 1954; troop officer, also regimental staff officer 12th U. S. Cav., 1939-42; gen. staff officer 102d Inf. Div., Europe, 1942-45; exec. asst. to under sec. war, also mil. aide to sec. war, 1945-48; armored staff officer, then bn. comdr. 14th Armored Cav., Germany, 1948-51; assigned Armed Forces Staff Coll., also Army War Coll., then gen. staff officer Dept. Army, 1951-56; hospitalized, 1957-60; mil. asst., also spl. asst. to sec. army, 1960-63; retired, 1963; dep. under sec. army, 1963-68; dep. asst. sec. army (manpower and res. affairs), 1968—. Dir. Home Bldg. Savs. & Loan Assn., Washington, Ind. Decorated D.S.M., Legion of Merit, Bronze Star medal with oak leaf cluster; Order Orange-Nassau (Netherlands) named Sagamore of the Wabash, State of Indiana. Mem. Indiana Soc. Washington, Ind. U. Alumni Assn., Assn. U.S. Army, Assn. Grads. U.S.Mil. Acad., Army Athletic Assn. (hon. v.p.), U.S. Armor Assn., 102d Inf. Div. Assn., Phi Gamma Delta, Kappa Kappa Psi. Clubs: Army Navy, Army Navy Country (Washington); Indiana University (Bloomington, Ind.). Home: 510 N St SW Washington DC 20024 Office: Office Asst Sec Army (Manpower and Res Affairs) The Pentagon Washington DC 20310

ALLEN, BARRY WILBURN, veterinarian; b. Rotan, Tex., May 19, 1925; s. Arnold W. and Dollie (Schieck) A.; student John Tarlton Agr. Coll., 1942-43, 46-47; D.V.M., Tex. A. and M. Coll., 1951; m. Sarah Ann Keith, Nov. 9, 1946 (div. Dec. 1966); children—Susan Ann, Cathy Lynn, Barry Keith; m. 2d, Mildred Marie Graves Ashbrook, June 3, 1967; 1 son, Gerald Q. Vet. meat insp. Bur. of Animal Industry, Meat Insp. dv., Ft. Worth, 1951-52; pvt. veterinary practice, 1952—. Mem. Bd. of Edn., Rotan, 1956-62, pres. bd., 1958-62. Served from pvt. S/Sgt. AUS, 1943-46. Decorated Purple Heart. Mem. Am., Tex. (dist. dir. 1959—, mem. pharmacy com.) vet. med. assns., Am. Assn. Bovine Practitioners, Am. Assn. Equine Practitioners. Home: 411 N McKinley St Rotan TX 79546 Office: 1101 Cleveland St Rotan TX 79546

ALLEN, BENJAMIN HARRISON, state ofcl.; b. Goldsboro, N.C., Apr. 7, 1931; s. Benjamin Harrison and Nancy (Jones) A.; A.B. magna cum laude, Wofford Coll., 1956; M.A., Peabody Coll., 1957, Ph.D., 1962; m. Martha L. Payne, Aug. 10, 1952; children—Martha Jean and Mary Joan (twins), John Charles. Psychologist, City Schs., Nashville, 1959-61; cons. mental health Dept. Pub. Health, Wilmington, N.C., 1961-63; asso. prof. psychology East Carolina Coll., 1963-65; asst. prof. spl. edn. Fla. State U., 1965-68, U. Ga., 1968-69; dir. Div. Mental Retardation, Ala. Dept. Mental Health, Montgomery, 1969-70; program cons. Fla. Div. Retardation, 1970; dir. programs and services Sunland Tng. Center, Fort Meyers, Fla., 1971—. Evaluator div. Mental Retardation, Social Rehab. Services, Washington, 1965-68. Served with USN, 1949-53. Mem. Am. Psychol. Asson., Am. Assn. Mental Deficiency, Phi Beta Kappa. Home: 4028 Manning Av Fort Myers FL 33902 Office: Sunland Tng Center Fort Myers FL 33901

ALLEN, CARROLL RANDOLPH, automobile dealer; b. Georgetown, Tex., May 5, 1898; s. Henry Young and Ida (Rivers) A.; B.B.A., U. Tex., 1920; m. Elizabeth Ann Christian, Dec. 29, 1937; children—Mary Ann (Mrs. Roy B. Johnson), David. Head dept. Ford Motor Co., Dallas, 1922-33; head dept. Chevrolet Motor Co., Dallas, 1933-37, New Orleans, 1937-40, Houston, 1940-43; pres. Allen Chevrolet Co., Gonzales, Tex., 1943—. Chmn., Housing Authority, Gonzales, 1951-72. Bd. dirs. Tex. Rehab. Center, Gonzales. Served with USN, World War I. Mem. Tex. Automobile Dealers Assn. (area bd. dirs.), Am. Legion, Phi Gamma Delta. Methodist. Rotarian. Home: 1803 Contour Dr Gonzales TX 78629 Office: PO Box 38 Gonzales TX 78629

ALLEN, CHARLES ANTHONY, operations research analyst; b. Rochester, Minn. May 16, 1933; s. Raymond Bernard and Dorothy (Sheard) A.; student U. Wash., 1951-55; B.S., U So Cal., 1956, M.S., 1959; m. Susan Sadri Volkmann, Aug. 29, 1959; 1 son, Charles Anthony II. Archtl. planner and designer firm Pereira & Luckman, Los Angeles, 1952-57; pub. relations rep. Welton Becket & Assos., Los Angeles, 1957-59; research engr. operations research Convair div. Gen. Dynamics Corp., Pomona, Cal., 1959-61; sr. research engr. systems analysis Norair div. Northrop Corp., Hawthorne, Cal., 1961-64; mem. tech. staff, project chmn., program mgr. sci. and engring. Research Analysis Corp., McLean, Va., 1964—. Mem. Los Angeles Recreation Council, 1963-64. Fellow A.A.A.S.; mem. Operations Research Soc. Am., Am. Ordnance Assn., U.S. Armor Assn., Phi Gamma Delta. Episcopalian. Home: 4420 Briarwood Ct N Annandale VA 22003 Office: Old Springhouse Rd McLean VA 22101

ALLEN, CHARLES GUY, physician; b. Denison, Tex., Aug. 9, 1923; s. Charlie Guy and Minnie Pearl (Church) A.; B.A., Union Coll., Lincoln, Neb., 1944; M.D., Loma Linda U., 1948; m. Cordelia Williamson, Sept. 30, 1945; children—Larry Guy, Jackie Charles. Intern, Loma Linda Sanitarium and Hosp., 1947-48, resident obstetrics and gynecology, 1948-50; gen. practice medicine, Strong, Ark., 1950-51, Itasca, Tex., 1953—, also owner clinic. City health officer, Itasca, 1967—. Served with AUS, 1951-53. Mem. Com. of 100 Southwestern Union Coll., Keene, Tex. 7th Day Adventist (elder). Club: 500 (Itasca). Home and office: Box 147 Itasca TX 76055

ALLEN, CLIFTON JUDSON, clergyman, editor; b. Latta, S.C., Nov. 7, 1901; s. William Benjamin and Theodosia (Cox) A.; B.A., Furman U., 1923, D.D., 1960; Th.M., So. Baptist Theol. Sem., 1928, Ph.D., 1932; m. Hattie Bell McCracken, Aug. 22, 1930; children—Judson Boyce, Rosalind (Mrs. John C. Barker), Robert Moore. Prin., Minturn (S.C.) High Sch., 1923-25; tutor Greek N.T., So. Bapt. Theol. Sem., 1928-31; ordained to ministry So. Bapt. Ch., 1926; pastor in McHenry, Ky., 1926-29, Utica, Ky., 1929-32, Fairmont, N.C., 1932-36, Statesville, N.C., 1936-37; asso. editorial sec. Sunday sch. bd. So. Bapt. Conv., 1937-44, editorial sec., 1945-68; rec. sec. So. Bapt. Conv., 1966—. Sec. commn. Christian teaching and tng. Bapt. World Alliance, 1957-65, chmn., 1965-70; mem. exec. com. Bapt. Conv. N.C., 1935-37; mem. internat. Sunday sch. lesson com. div. Christian edn. Nat. Council Chs., 1942-68, chmn., 1960-67, mem. div. assembly. div., 1957-63; radio broadcaster, 1945—. Recipient E.Y. Mullins Denominational Service award So. Baptist Theol. Sem., 1970. Democrat. Rotarian. Quarternion. Author: The Gospel According to Paul, 1956; Points for Emphasis (annual) 1953—; Affirmation of Our Faith, 1972; also curricular materials. Chmn. editorial com. Ency. of Southern Baptists, 1958; gen. editor Broadman Bible Commentary, 12 vols., 1969-72. Home: 4215 Harding Rd Nashville TN 37205 Office: 460 James Robertson Pkwy Nashville TN 37219

ALLEN, DONALD COLE, mfg. exec.; b. Dallas, Sept. 9, 1922; s. Raymond Daniel and Anne Elizabeth (Cole) A.; student Murray State Tchrs. Coll., 1943, U. Ga., 1945, So. Meth. U., 1948; J.D., LaSalle U., 1968; A.B., B.L.S., Syracuse U., 1972; m. Mary Jane Dunn, July 11, 1942; children—Dianne (Mrs. Charles Taylor Ashworth), Cynthia (Mrs. Phil Messer). Sales rep. Rice Stix Co., St. Louis. 1950-55; terr. mgr. Ely & Walker Co., Memphis, 1955-62, regional sales mgr., 1962-65, 1st v.p., gen. sales mgr., 1965-69, pres., 1969—. Asso. mem. Field Sales Mgmt. Inst., Syracuse U., 1962-63; research asso. So. Meth. U., 1950-65. Served with USNR, 1942-45. Mem. Sales Exec. Club, Sales and Marketing Execs. Internat. Methodist. Contbr. articles in field to profl. jours. Home: 3641 Woodglade Cove Memphis TN 38116 Office: 823 E Holmes Rd Memphis TN 38116

ALLEN, EDMUND ELMER, educator; b. Oneida, N.Y., Aug. 2, 1919; s. Barnard L. and Mary Ethel (Reynolds) A.; B.S., Norwich U., 1941; postgrad. Northwestern U., 1949, Rensselaer Poly. Inst., 1951; M.E., Birmingham So. Coll., 1957; postgrad. E. Carolina Coll., 1960-61; Ed.D., U. Fla., 1964; m. Ruth M. Strachen, Sept. 1944; children—Thomas, Brian, Susan, Barbara, Edmund. Commd. 2d lt. USMC, 1941, advanced through grades to lt. col., 1961; instr. Gunfire Support Sch., Little Creek, Va., 1946-49; naval and mil. sci. Rensselaer Poly. Inst., 1949-52; supt. instrn. Res. Tng. Unit, Birmingham, Ala., 1953-57; comdr. 10th Marine Regt., 1961; ret., 1961; intern, counselling psychologist, dir. Counseling Center for Human Devel., asst. prof., asso. prof., prof. statistics U. So. Fla., Tampa, 1963—, research asst., prin. investigator Fed. grants, 1964-68. Mem. Am. Univ. and Coll. Counseling Center Dirs. (exec. dir.), Am. Personnel and Guidance Assn., Fla., Tampa Bay psychol. assns., Interam. Soc. Psychology. Mason. Contbr. chpt. to The Student in Society, 1969; articles to profl. jours. Home: 201 Willowick Av Temple Terrace FL 33617 Office: Univ South Fla 4202 Fowler Av Tampa FL 33620

ALLEN, EDWARD HAMILTON, educator; b. Vernal, Miss., Nov. 16, 1921; s. Charles H. and Winnie (McLeod) A.; B.S., La. State U., 1946, M.S., 1953; Ph.D., Miss. State U., 1967; m. Frances Barnes, Mar. 23, 1945; children—Edward H., Betty Marie, Barbara Melissa. Mem. staff, Vet. farm tng. Farmers Home Adminstrn., Warren County, Vicksburg, Miss., 1946-48, Humphrey's County, Belzoni, Miss., 1948-51, Smith County, Raleigh, Miss., 1953; prof. animal sci. N.E. La. U., Monroe, 1953—. Served with USNR, 1942-45. Mem. Am. Soc. Animal Sci., La. Tchrs. Assn., Agr. Tchrs. Assn., La. Farm Bur., La. Cattlemens' Assn., La. Animal Sci. Assn., Ouachita Pork Producers Assn. Baptist. Home: 4100 Blanks St Monroe LA 71201

ALLEN, EDWARD PATRICK, scientist; b. Dallas, Sept. 20, 1943; s. Jack Christopher and Dorothy (Holloway) A.; student So. Meth. U., 1961-65; D.D.S., Baylor U., 1969, Ph.D. (NIH fellow 1969-72), 1972; m. Joe Karen Callaway, Mar. 5, 1965; children—Karen Elizabeth, Edward Patrick, Everett Hunter. Research asso. endrocinrology Baylor U. Med. Center, Dallas, 1966-69. Vice pres. Specialized Biomed. Testing, Inc., Dallas, 1972—. Mem. Park Cities Com. for Water Fluoridation, 1971—. Recipient Joe H. Smith award S.W. Soc. Periodontists, 1969. Mem. Am. Acad. Periodontology, Am., Tex. dental assns., Dallas County Dental Soc., Internat. Assn. Dental Research, Sigma Xi. Methodist. Contbr. articles to profl. lit. Home: 3209 Cornell Dallas TX 75205 Office: 800 Hall St Dallas TX 75226

ALLEN, GEORGE, football coach; b. Detroit, Apr. 29, 1922; s. Earl R. and Loretta (Hannigan) A.; B.A., M.A., U. Mich.; postgrad. U. So. Cal.; m. Etty L. Lumbroso, May 26, 1951; children—George, Gregory, Gerald, Jennifer. Formerly football coach Morningside Coll., Sioux City, Ia., Whittier (Cal.) Coll.; defensive coach Chgo. Bears, 1958-65; head coach Los Angeles Rams, 1966-70; head coach Washington Redskins, 1970—. Served with USNR, 1943-46. Author books. Office: Washington Redskins 1835 K St NW Washington DC 20006

ALLEN, GEORGE L., city ofcl. Mem. Dallas City Council. Address: Gt Liberty Life Ins Co 2527 Ross Av Dallas TX 75201*

ALLEN, HERBERT, steel works exec.; b. Ratcliff, Tex., May 2, 1907; s. Jasper and Leona (Matthews) A.; B.S. in Mech. Engring., Rice Inst., 1929; m. Helen Daniels, Aug. 28, 1937; children—David Daniels, Anne (Mrs. Jonathan Taft Symonds), Michael Herbert. Engaged in miscellaneous research, 1929-31; chief engr. Abercrombie Pump Co., Houston, 1931-35; chief engr. Cameron Iron Works, Inc., 1935-41, v.p. engring. and mfg., 1942-50, v.p., gen. mgr., 1950-66, pres., 1966—, also dir.; dir. Tenneco Inc., Tex. Commerce Bank. Bd. dirs. Tex. Tech. U., 1963-69, Houston Symphony Soc., 1971—; trustee St. Stephen's Episcopal Sch., S.W. Research Inst., 1956-64; trustee, chmn. bd. William Marsh Rice U. Named Engr. of Year, San Jacinto chpt. Tex. Soc. Profl. Engrs. Registered profl. engr., Tex. Fellow Am. Soc. M.E., mem. C. of C. (bd. dirs. 1952-54, 62, v.p. 1954-55), Am. Inst. Mining, Metall. and Petroleum Engrs., Am. Petroleum Inst., Philos. Soc. Tex., Newcomen Soc. N. Am., Tex. Soc. Profl. Engrs., Houston Engring. and Sci. Soc., Houston Philos. Soc., Tau Beta Pi, Episcopalian. Clubs: Ramada, River Oaks Country, Petroleum, Houston, Bayou. Patentee in field. Home: 3262 Huntington Pl Houston TX 77019 Office: PO Box 1212 Katy and Silber Rds Houston TX 77001

ALLEN, HERBERT CLIFTON, JR., physician; b. Richmond, Va., Jan. 7, 1917; s. Herbert C. and Josephone (Myers) A.; B.S., U. Richmond, 1937; M.D., Med. Coll. Va., 1941; m. Elisabeth Hunt, Feb. 1, 1949; children—Dana Lee, Debra Lynn, Herbert Clifton III, Steven Hunt, Cynthia Jo, Jullie Myers. Intern, Phila. Gen. Hosp., 1941-42; resident pathology Pa. Hosp., Phila., 1946; resident medicine Med. Coll. Va. Hosp., Richmond, 1947; practice medicine specializing in nuclear medicine, Houston, 1952—; asst. prof. medicine Baylor U. Houston, 1951-71, asso. prof., 1971—; asst. chief radioisotope sect. VA, Washington, 1947-48; chief metabolic service, asst. dir. radioisotope unit Birmingham VA Hosp., Van Nuys, Cal., 1948-49; asst. dir. unit Wadsworth VA Hosp., Los Angeles, 1949-50; dir. unit VA. Hosp., Houston, 1951-55, Meth. Hosp., Houston, 1952-60; dir. Nuclear Medicine Labs. Tex., Houston, 1960—; dir. dept. nuclear medicine Hermann Hosp., Houston, 1956—, Meml. Bapt. Hosp., Houston, 1965-71; pres. Atomic Engergy Indsl. Labs of S.W. Houston, 1960—; Atomic Food Processing Corp. Am., Houston, 1966—. Sec., Tex. Radiation Adv. Bd., 1961-65. Trustee Med. Coll. Va., Mus. Med. Sci., Houston, 1970. Served to maj. USAAF, 1942-46; ETO. Decorated Air medal with 2 bronze oak leaf clusters. Recipient pharm. research grants, AEC grants. Mem. A.M.A., A.A.A.S., Tex. Med. Assn. (council sci. advancement 1959-67), S.W. Soc. Nuclear Medicine (pres. 1958-59, treas., sec. 1966-72, trustee 1970—), Soc. Nuclear Medicine (v.p. 1961-62, trustee 1960-67), Harris County (Tex.) Med. Soc. (chmn. radiation med. adv. com. 1959—, alternate del. 1962—), Houston Thyroid Club (sec. treas. 1960-62), Royal Soc. Medicine (London, Eng.), Am. Thyroid Assn., others. Home: 4010 Martinshire St Houston TX 77025 Office: 100 Hermann Profl Bldg Houston TX 77025

ALLEN, HOMER ELMORE, hosp. adminstr.; b. Johnson City, Tenn., Aug. 11, 1914; s. William Jackson and Cherrie Elizabeth (Musser) A.; grad. Mars Hill Coll., 1937; certificate Am. Coll. Hosp. Adminstrs., Duke, 1948, Colo. Coll. of Edn., 1943; postgrad. Internat. Accountant Soc., 1942-43, 46, Va. Poly. Tech. Inst., 1935, 68, Med. Coll. Va., 1968, Am. Coll. Hosp. Adminstr.-Fedn. Am. Hosp. Inst., 1972, Va. Hosp. Assn.-Ga. Hosp. Assn. Inst., 1964; m. Evelyn Marie St. Clair, Jan. 3, 1940; children—Patricia Carol, Barbara Diane. Head bookkeeper W.B.F. White & Sons, Richlands, Va., 1937-41; asst. cashier Richlands Nat. Bank, 1941-42, 46; adminstr. Clinch Valley Clinic Hosp., Richlands, 1947—. Vice pres. Richland Area Indsl. Devel. Corp., 1968—; mem. com. on health Cumberland Plateau Econ. Devel. Corp.; mem. Gov.'s Adv. Council on Hosps., 1971—. Adminstr., Civil Def. Hosp. of Tazewell County, 1966; active Boy Scouts Am. Chmn. bd. trustees Barker Youth Center, 1955, Bluefield (Va.) Coll., 1957—; mem. adv. bd. health careers S.W. Va. Community Coll., bd. dirs. Roanoke Blue Cross, Va. Health and Edn. Found., Council of S.W. Va. Hosps., Tazewell Meth. Dist. Bd.; preceptor U. Ala. Sch. Health Services Adminstrn. City recorder Town of Richlands, 1946-48. Served with USAAF, 1942-46. Mem. Am. Coll. Hosp. Adminstrs., Royal Soc. Health (London), Fedn. Am. Hosps. (vice chmn. legislative com. 1967-71, mem. FHA mortgage com. 1970-71, mem. finance com. 1971-72, mem. bur. health ins. liaison com. 1970-71, vice chmn. com. FHA mortgage ins. 1971, state membership chmn. 1967-72), Nat. League Nursing, Am. Pub. Health

Assn., Am. Vocational Assn. Va. Hosp. Assn. (dir. 1964-66, 70-71, mem. council legislative and govtl. relations), Richlands C. of C. (past v.p.). Methodist (dist. lay leader 1966-71, certified lay speaker 1963-72; tchr. Sunday and Ch. schs.; chmn. finance com. 1968-72). Kiwani Club: De-Do of America. Home: 1 Rogers Circle Highland Park Richlands VA 24641 Office: Clinch Valley Clinic Hosp Richlands VA 24621

ALLEN, IVAN, JR., merchant; b. Atlanta, Mar. 15, 1911; s. Ivan and Irene (Beaumont) A.; grad. Ga. Inst. Tech., 1933; m. Louise Richardson, Jan. 1, 1936; children—Ivan III, Inman, Beaumont. With Ivan Allen Co., Atlanta, 1933-—, pres. 1946-57, became vice chmn. bd., 1957, now chmn. bd.; dir. Mead Corp., Rich's Inc., So. Airways, So. Bell Tel. & Tel., Equitable Life Ins. Soc. U.S., Cox Broadcasting Corp., Atlanta Braves. Scout, scoutmaster, area pres., regional committeeman, mem. nat. exec. bd. Boys Scouts Am.; chmn. Greater Atlanta Community Chest, 1949. Lt. col. Gov's Staff, 1936; treas. Ga. State Hosp. Authority, 1936; sec. exec. dept. State Ga., 1945-46; mayor City of Atlanta, 1961-69. Trustee Ga. Found., Spelman Coll., Agnes Scott Coll.; chmn. Police Found. Served to maj. inf. AUS, World War II. Recipient Armin Maier award Atlanta Rotary Club, 1952; Silver Beaver, Silver Antelope, Silver Buffalo awards Boy Scouts Am. Mem. Ga. Tech Alumni Assn. (pres. 1953-54), Ga. C. of C. (pres. 1956-57, dir.). Atlanta C. of C. (pres. 1961, dir.), Nat. Stationery and Office Euipment Assn. (dist. gov. 1938-40, pres. 1955-56), Sigma Alpha Epsilon. Rotarian. Home: 3700 Northside Dr Atlanta GA 30305 Office: 221 Ivy St Atlanta GA 30303

ALLEN, JAMES BROWNING, U.S. senator; b. Gadsden, Ala., Dec. 28, 1912; s. George C. and Mary Ethel (Browning) A.; student U. Ala., 1928-31, U. Ala. Law Sch., 1932-33; m. Marjorie Jo Stephens, Mar. 16, 1940 (dec. Jan. 1956); children—James Browning, Mary Rebecca, Debbie; m. 2d, Maryon Pittman Mullins, Aug. 7, 1964; stepchildren—J. Sanford Mullins III, John Pittman Mullins, Maryon Foster Allen. Admitted to Ala. bar, 1935, since practiced in Gadsden; mem. Ala. Legislature from Etowah County, 1939-43, mem. Ala. Senate, 1947-51; lt. gov. Ala., 1951-55, 63-67; senator from Ala., 1968-—. Del. Democratic Nat. Conv., 1952. Served to lt. (j.g.) USNR, 1943-46. Home: 1321 Bellevue Dr Gadsden AL 35901 also 7405 Hallcrest Dr McLean VA 22101 Office: 6313 New Senate Office Bldg Washington DC 20510

ALLEN, JAMES SCRIBNER, assn. exec.; b. Proctor, Vt., Oct. 6, 1919; s. Sinclair Tousey and Katharine (Scribner) A.; B.S., Norwich U., 1943; postgrad. N.Y. Law Sch., 1953, Alexander Hamilton, 1954; m. Virginia James Claudon, Mar. 5, 1947; children—Pamela Beckwith, Jeffrey James. Design engr. Gen Electric Co., Pittsfield, Mass., 1946-49, product application engr., N.Y.C., 1949-52, Gen. Electric Internat., 1952-56; econ. devel. cons. Ebasco Internat., 1956-59; mgr. Edison Electric. Inst., Washington, 1959-71; mgr. Electric Enery Assn., Washington, 1971-—, Treas., Community Westmoreland Citizens Assn., 1968-70. Served with Signal Corps, AUS, 1943-47; PTO. Mem. Washington Soc. Assn. Execs., Producers Council (past pres.), Am. Marketing Assn. (dir. 1963-65), I.E.E.E., Soc. Am. Mil Engrs. Clubs: Washington Coal (pres. 1969), University (Washington); Chevy Chase. Home: 5208 Portsmouth Rd Washington DC 20016 Office: 1015 18th St Washington DC 20036

ALLEN, J(ESSE) DANIEL, printing sales exec.; b. Louisville, Aug. 6, 1921 Thomas Conway and Bettie (Kincheloe) A.; student pub schs.; m. Ester McKinney, Sept. 17, 1948; 1 dau., Dana Dee. With Courier-Jour. Lithographing Co., Louisville, 1939-—, asst. v.p., 1962-63, v.p. sales, 1963-—, also dir.; v.p. dir. Courier-Jour. Job Printing Co., Louisville, 1965-—, Ins. Field Co., Louisville, 1965-—; pres., dir. Courier-Jour. Lithographing Co. of Ga., Inc., Atlanta; dir. Clothiers, Ltd., Inc. Served with USMCR, 1942-46, 1951-52. Mem. Printing Salesmens Club Atlanta (past pres.), Lithograph Mfrs. Assn. (past pres.), Bank Stationers Assn. (past pres.). Methodist. Clubs: City (Charlotte, N.C.); Louisville Boat; International Trade (Mobile, Ala.); Jefferson (Louisville). Home: 515 Blankenbaker Lane Louisville KY 40207 Office: PO Box 18245 Louisville KY 40218

ALLEN, JESSIE SPANN, librarian; b. Rushville, Ind., Mar. 14, 1907; d. Harvey Dinwiddie and Winifred Pugh (Spann) Allen; student Dickinson Secretarial Sch., Waterloo, Ia., 1942, Ia. U., 1943. Asst. librarian, Cedar Falls, Ia., 1928-42, head librarian, Cedar Falls, 1943; asst. librarian USAF, Wendover Field, Utah, 1943-44; librarian Hosp. Library, Walter Reed Gen. Hosp., Washington, 1944-—. Mem. Am. Library Assn., P.E.O., D.A.R. Republican. Presbyn. Club: Brooke Manor Country (Rockville, Md.). Home: 2205 Washington Av Silver Spring MD 20910 Office: Walter Reed Army Hosp Washington DC 20012

ALLEN, JOHN ALEXANDER, educator; b. Chevy Chase, Md., Apr. 25, 1922; s. Emanuel Alexander and Ann (Allen) Goldenweiser; B.A., Swarthmore Coll., 1943; B.A., Oxford U., 1948, M.A., 1952; Ph.D., U. N.C., 1954; m. Josephine Haynes, June 2, 1951; children—Margaret Haynes, Elizabeth Alexander. Instr. English, U. Rochester, 1952-55; asst. prof. English, Hollins Coll., Va., 1955-60, asso. prof., 1960-67, prof., 1967-—, chmn. dept. English, 1967-70. Served to lt. (j.g.) USNR, 1943-46. Mem. Modern Lang. Assn. Am., Renaissance Soc. Am. Author: The Lean Divider, 1968; Hero's Way: Contemporary Poems, 1971. Address: Hollins Coll Hollins College VA 24020 Hollins Coll Hollins College VA 24020

ALLEN, JOHN BOYD, hotel exec.; b. Salyersville, Ky., Feb. 14, 1916; s. Troy Crowe and Lou Ellen (Rudd) A.; B.A., Berea Coll., 1940; postgrad. Cornell U., 1944-45; m. Eva B. Britton, Oct. 23, 1943; children—Jonathan Benson, James Kevin. Beverage purchasing agt. Statler Hotel, Detroit, 1946-50; food and beverage dir. Book Cadillac Hotel, Detroit, 1950-56; gen. mgr. Pier 66 Hotel & Marina, Ft. Lauderdale, Fla., 1957-—; dir. Ocean First Nat. Bank, Ft. Lauderdale. Mem. adv. bd. Hotel Adminstrn. Sch., Broward Community Coll., Broward County Adult-Vocational Edn. Program; bd. dirs. Broward County Safety Council; mem. adv. bd. Ft. Lauderdale U. Served with AUS, 1940-43, PTO. Decorated Bronze Star medal. Mason. Club: Lago Mar Hotel Beach (Ft. Lauderdale). Home: 2029 NW 14th Av Ft Lauderdale FL 33311 Office: Pier 66 PO Drawer 9177 Fort Lauderdale FL 33010

ALLEN, JOHN ELDRIDGE, hist. researcher; b. Morehead City, N.C., Sept. 11, 1911; s. Arthur Vincent and Annie (Willis) A.; B.B.A., U. Miami (Fla.), 1934; M.A., George Washington U., 1937; postgrad. Am. U., 1937; m. Mary Josephine Edwards, June 11, 1949, 1 son, Mark Edwards. Information aid NRA, Washington, 1935; tech. aid Dept. Treasury, 1935-39; records asst. Dept. Agr., 1940-41; social research supr. Works Progress Adminstrn. Fed. Works Agy., 1941-42; analyst Depts. Army and Defense, 1948-57; asst. exec. dir. Lincoln Sesquicentennial Commn., 1958-59; research, writer Lincoln Sesquicentennial Tributes, 1959-61; instr. social sciences U. Miami, 1961-62, asst. Office Residence Halls, 1963-—; research and writing, 1962-—. Served from ensign to lt. comdr., USNR, 1942-46. Recipient Lincoln medallion Lincoln Sesquicentennial Commn., 1960. Mem. Columbia Hist. Soc. (past v.p.), Lincoln Group (past pres.), S.A.R. (past pres. D.C.; nat. trustee 1953-54), Am. Econ. Assn., U.S. Capitol Hist. Soc. (founding mem.), George Washington Law Assn. U. Miami Gen. Alumni Assn. (bd. dirs., 1961-64, chmn. Spring reunion 1962; chmn. devel. council 1962-63). Democrat. Methodist. Clubs: University of Miami (Fla.) Faculty; University (sec. 50th Anniversary Celebration com. 1954) (Washington). Home: 5520 SW 78th St South Miami FL 33143

ALLEN, JOSEPH PERCIVAL, astronaut; b. Crawfordsville, Ind., June 27, 1937; s. Joseph P. and Harriet (Taylor) A.; B.A., DePauw U., 1959; student Christian Albrechts U., Kiel, Germany, 1959-60; M.S., Yale, 1961, Ph.D., 1965; m. Bonnie Jo Darling, July 9, 1961. Guest research asso. Brookhaven Nat. Lab., 1962-65; staff physicist Nuclear Structure Lab., Yale, 1965; research asso. U. Wash., 1966; scientist-astronaut NASA-Manned Spacecraft Center, Houston, 1967-—. Rector scholar, 1955-59; Fulbright scholar, 1959-60. Mem. Am. Phys. Soc., Am. Astronautical Soc., N.Y. Acad. Scis., Am. Astron. Soc., A.A.A.S., Phi Beta Kappa, Sigma Xi, Beta Theta Pi, Phi Eta Sigma. Author articles in field. Home: 1410 Antigua Lane Nassau Bay TX 77058 Office: NASA Manned Spacecraft Center CB Houston TX 77058

ALLEN, L. SCOTT, clergyman. Ordained to ministry Methodist Ch., now bishop, Knoxville, Tenn. Address: 502 Gay St SW Knoxville TN 37902*

ALLEN, LAURENCE EDMUND (LARRY), war corr.; b. Mt. Savage, Md., Oct. 19, 1908; s. Laurence Bernard and Mary Caroline (Crowe) A.; student schools of several states; grad. high sch.; m. Helen Fazakerley Quisenberry. Reporter Balt. News, 1926, later on Washington Herald and Huntington (W.Va.) Evening Herald; reporter, telegraph editor Charleston (W.Va.) Daily Mail, 1927-33; with Asso. Press, 1933-60, as reporter and state editor Charleston bur., 1933-35 reporter Washington bur., 1935-37, fgn. cables desk, N.Y.C., 1937-38, European war corr., 1938-44, corr. Poland, 1945, 47, 49, chief Moscow bur., 1949, in Tel Aviv, 1950, war corr., S.E. Asia, Singapore, 1951, French Union and Vietminh Indochina, 1951-55, Malaya, Thailand, Burma, 1956, Caribbean area, 1957-61; organized Am. Press Service specializing Latin Am., 1960-—. Recipient Bronze Star for defending freedom press as prisoner of war, 1945; Croix de Guerre Fr. High Command, Indo China, frontline reporting, Nov. 1952. Received first award Nat. Headliners Club, 1941, for best news-reporting in covering Brit. Fleet operations; awarded Pulitzer prize for reporting on internat. affairs, May 5, 1942; decorated Order of British Empire by King George VI, 1947. Republican. Contbr. many short stories to various publs., 1925-33. Home: Rio Amazonas 78 Mexico City 5 Mexico

ALLEN, MACK KENT, banker; b. Columbus, Tex., Sept. 9, 1924; s. Dee Hansworth and Anna (Hemans) A.; B.S., Tex. A. and M. U., 1950; m. Lillian Rodgers, Aug. 18, 1946; children—David Kent, Tricia Lynn, Nancy Kathryn. Tchr. agr. Vets. Vocational Tex. Edn. System, 1950-55; salesman Met. Life Ins. Co., Houston, 1955-61, cons., 1958-62; appraiser and loan officer Colo. County Fed. Savs. and Loan, Columbus, Tex., 1962-67; cashier Katy Nat. Bank (Tex.), 1967-69, v.p., 1969-71; dir. North Shore Bank of Houston, 1968-70. Tchr., Savs. and Loan Inst., 1962-63. Cons. soil conservation Boy Scouts of Am., 1953-64; adviser, coordinator Jr. Achievement, Katy, 1967-69; chmn. Colorado County (Tex.) chpt. Red Cross, 1962-67; Bd. dirs., trustee Houston Harris County United Fund; bd. dirs. Houston Harris County Red Cross 1968-71. Served with USNR, 1943-46, PTO. Methodist (trustee 1963-67). Mason, Rotarian (pres. 1971-—), Lion (pres. Columbus 1966-67). Home: 809 Aster St Katy TX 77450 Office: 5622 3rd St Katy TX 77450

ALLEN, MARSHALL EDMUNDE, ednl. TV exec.; b. Chgo., Sept. 20, 1937; s. Marshall C. and Mildred (Zabel) A.; B.A., Miami U., Oxford, O., 1959, M.A., 1961; m. Joyce Sylvia Huff, Nov. 28, 1959; children—Terri Sue, David Marshall. Stage mgr. sta. WLWI-TV, Indpls., 1959-60; supr. closed circuit TV operations So. Ill. U., 1961-67; head ednl. TV services Okla. State U., 1967-—; cons. Okla. Ednl. TV Authority, 1968-—, Okla. Consortium on Research Devel., 1969. Mem. Nat. Assn. Ednl. Broadcasters, Town and Gown Community Theater. Home: 2702 Fox Ledge Dr Stillwater OK 74074 Office: 307 Communications Bldg Stillwater OK 74074

ALLEN, MARYON PITTMAN (MRS. JAMES BROWNING ALLEN), columnist; b. Meridian, Miss., Nov. 30, 1925; d. John D. and Tellie (Chisms) Pittman; student U. Ala., 1944-47; m. Joshua Sanford Mullins, Jr., Oct. 17, 1946 (div. Jan. 1959); children—Joshua Sanford, III, John Pittman, Maryon Foster; m. 2d, James Browning Allen, Aug. 7, 1964; 1 stepson, James Browning Allen. Office mgr. Dr. Alston Callahan, Birmingham, Ala., 1959-60; bus. mgr. psychiat. clinic U. Ala. Med. Center, Birmingham, 1960-61; agt. Protective Life Ins. Co., Birmingham, 1961-62; women's editor Sun Newspapers, Birmingham, 1962-64; staff writer, columnist The Birmingham News, 1964-—; v.p. Emerald Valley Corp., partner J. D. Pittman Partnership Co., Birmingham. Mem.-at-large Ala. Hist. Commn. Democratic presdl. elector Dem. primary, 1968. Bd. dirs. Children's Fresh Air Farm, Birmingham, Mamie Fogarty com. Birmingham Festival of Arts. Recipient 1st place award Ala. Press Assn. 1962, 63; also various awards in typography, fashion writing, food pages. Mem. Birmingham Com. 100 for Women, Ala. Writers Conclave, Antiquarian Soc. Assn., Relay House. Methodist. Clubs: Gadsden Music; Mountain Laurel Garden. Home: 7405 Hallcrest Dr McLean VA 22101 also 1321 Bellevue Dr Gadsden AL 35901

ALLEN, MATTHEW CARTWRIGHT, JR., cotton compressing co. exec.; b. Dallas, Dec. 3, 1934; s. Matthew Cartwright and Flossie Cleona (Davis) A.; B.S., West Tex. State U., 1958; m. Teddie Jean Trulove, May 30, 1959; children—Sandra Kay, Sue Lynn. With Memphis Compress Co. (Tex.), 1959-—, crew pusher, 1959-60, supt., 1961-65, v.p. and gen. mgr., 1966-—; dir. First Nat. Bank. Mem. Memphis Vol. Fire Dept., 1967-—, chmn. Girl Scout Fund drive, 1970. Mem. Memphis Sch. Bd., 1971-—. Bd. dirs. Hall County Indsl. Found, treas., 1968-—. Recipient Community Service award radio sta. KCTX, 1970. Mem. Southwestern Cotton Compress and Warehouse Assn. (dir. 1961-71, pres. 1970-71), Nat. Cotton Council (del. 1968-70), C. of C. (dir. 1966-68, 70-—). Mem. Ch. of Christ (deacon 1964-—). Lion (dir. 1965-67). Home: 910 North 18th St Memphis TX 79245 Office: 820 Lucille St Memphis TX 79245

ALLEN, MELBA TILL (MRS. MARVIN E. ALLEN), state ofcl.; b. Butler County, Ala., Mar. 3, 1933; d. Samuel Ben and sch.; m.Gertrude (Johnson) Till; grad. high sch.;; m. Marvin E. Allen, Dec. 24, 1950; children—Judy Kathryn, Randy Earl. With Hass-Davis Packing Co., Mobile, Ala., 1951-52, W. T. Smith Lumber Co., Chapman, Ala., 1953-54, Cooper Stevedoring Co., Mobile, 1956-63, Algernon Blair Inc., Montgomery, Ala., 1963-66; now auditor State of Ala., Montgomery. Mem. Bus. Women's Assn. Democrat. Baptist. Mem. Order Eastern Star. Home: Box 3 Route 1 Grady AL 36036 Office: State Capitol Bldg Montgomery AL 36104

ALLEN, NELL RUTH, speech pathologist, audiologist; b. Winnfield, La.; d. Columbus Willma and Caroline (Long) Allen; B.A., Northwestern State Coll., 1950; M.Ed., Wayne U., 1957; postgrad. N.Y. U. at Buffalo, summer 1951, Tulane U., 1957, La State U. Med. Sch., 1963-66, 66. Dept. head, speech therapist La. Spastic Sch., Alexandria, 1950-51, Detroit Cerebral Palsy Center, 1951-54, N.E. Cerebral Palsy Sch., Monroe, La., 1954-55, Rapides Parish Rehab. Center, Alexandria, 1955-57; dept head., dir. speech and hearing clinic. Crippled Children's Hosp., New Orleans, 1959-—; spl. lectr. speech La. State U., 1963; instr. speech pathology and audiology Tulane U., 1966-—; supr. speech therapy majors St. Mary's Dominican Coll., New Orleans, Northwestern State Coll., Nathitoches, La., Tulane U., 1960-—; lectr. civic orgns. Recipient scholarship United Cerebral Palsy Assn. La., 1954, scholarship Office Vocational Rehab., 1957; awarded clin. competence in speech pathology, audiology Am. Speech and Hearing Assn., 1965, 67. Mem. Am., La. (past pres.) speech and hearing assns., Internat. Platform Assn. Research pertaining to hearing acuity of muscular dystrophic individuals. Home: 6755 River Rd New Orleans LA 70123 Office: 200 Henry Clay Av New Orleans LA 70118

ALLEN, OLLIE JAMES, supt. schs.; b. nr. Clayhole, Ky., Oct. 20, 1911; s. Ethan and Elizabeth (Combs) A.; B.S., Murray (Ky.) State U., 1941, M.A., 1958; m. Ruth Wallis, Feb. 11, 1940; children—Maura (Mrs. John A. Armes), J. Phillip, Jeanne A. (Mrs Darry A. Lieb). Tchr. pub. schs., Breathitt County, Ky., 1932-39, Trigg County, Ky., 1940, Ohio County, Ky., 1957; tchrs., coach, Ballard County, Ky., 1941-44; prin. Cunningham (Ky.) High Sch., 1944-57; prin., coach Fordsville (Ky.) High Sch., 1957-58; supt. schs. Breckinridge County Sch., Hardinsburg, 1958-—. Bd. dirs. North Central Found., J. Town Vocational Area Sch. Mason, Rotarian, Lion. Address: Hardinsburg KY 40143

ALLEN, PHILLIP ELWOOD, lawyer; b. Joplin, Mo., Jan. 18, 1931; s. Elwood A. and Opal (Calhoun) A.; B.S., U. Ark., 1959, J.D., 1962; m. Lorraine V. Miller, July 12, 1952; children—Linda Denise, Karen Diane, Bradley Phillip. Admitted to Ark. bar, 1962, Ky. bar, 1971; asso. Rose, Meck, partner firm Allen, Dahlen & Young, Little Rock, Ark., 1968-71; pvt. practice law, Louisville, 1971-—. Served with AUS, 1949-52, 52-57. Mem. Am., Ark., Ky bar assns., Tau Kappa Alpha, Beta Gamma Sigma Omicron Delta Kappa, Phi Eta Sigma, Delta Theta Phi. Home: 4720 Fox Den Ct Louisville KY 40222 Office: 400 Sherburn Lane Louisville Ky 40207

ALLEN, R. EARL, clergyman; b. Fort Worth, May 26, 1922; s. James Roy and Mary (Coker) A.; B.A., Howard Payne Coll., 1946, D.D., 1952; B.S., Midwestern U., 1947; postgrad. Southwestern Baptist Theol. Sem., 1947-49; LL.D., Atlanta Law Sch. L.H.D., Linda Vista Baptist Coll.; Litt.D., John Brown U.; m. Joyce Lovelace, Dec. 25, 1941; children—Norma Allene (dec.) James Todd, Joy Earline. Ordained to ministry Bapt. Ch., 1940; asso. dist. missionary Tex. Bapt. Conv., 1945; pastor 1st Bapt. Ch., Archer City, Tex., 1945-47, Seagraves, Tex., 1947-50, Floydada, Tex., 1950-56, Rosen Heights Bapt. Ch., Fort Worth, 1956-—. Mem. So., (Sunday sch. bd. 1959-66, mem. home mission bd.), Tex. (mem. exec. bd. mem. Christian edn. commn. 1962) Bapt. convs. Author: Bible Paradoxes, 1963; Memorial Messages, 1964; Trials, Tragedies, and Triumphs,1965; Christian Comfort, 1965; Strength From Shadows, 1967; The Sign of the Star, 1968; Silent Saturday, 1968; The Personal Jesus, 1972. Home: 2523 Prairie St Fort Worth TX 76106 Office: 2524 Roosevelt St Fort Worth TX 76106

ALLEN, RICHARD SWEETNAM, educator; b. Pekin, Ill., Nov. 9, 1896; s. William Henry and Margaret Anne (Olt) A.; student U. Chgo., 1917-18, 26-27, 36-37; B.S., U. Rochester, 1922, M.S., 1925; m. Leone M.S. McLoughlin, Aug. 23, 1924; 1 son, William Henry II. Research asso. U. Rochester, 1922-23, asst., 1923-25; physiol. chemist Wilson Research Lab., Chgo., 1923; phys. chemist Western Elec. Co., Chgo., 1924; instr. Coll. Medicine, U. Tenn., 1925-26; asst. prof. anatomy and physiology U. Ky., Lexington, 1927-29, asso. prof., 1929-36, prof., 1936-67, head dept., 1931-67, prof. physiology Med. Sch., 1960-67, prof. emeritus, 1967-—, faculty asst. to dean Coll. Arts and Scis., 1966-67. Served with U.S. Army, 1918-19. Mem. Assn. Am. Med. Colls., A.A.A.S., Am. Genetic Soc., Nat. Geog. Soc., Am. Legion (chmn. jr. athletic coms. local and state 1941-49), U. Ky. Research Club (sec. 1931-36), Sigma Xi, Alpha Epsilon Delta. Democrat. Contbr. articles to profl. jours. Home: 1836 McDonald Rd Lexington KY 40503

ALLEN, ROBERT DEE, lawyer; b. Tulsa, Oct. 13, 1928; s. Harve and Olive Jean (Brown) A.; B.A., U. Okla., 1951, LL.B., 1955, J.D., 1970; m. Mary Latimer Conner, May 18, 1957; children—Scott, Randy, Blake. Admitted to Okla. bar, 1955; asso. Abernathy & Abernathy, Shawnee, Okla., 1955; law clk. for Hon. A. P. Murrah, judge 10th U.S. Ct. Appeals, Denver, 1956, Hon. Ross Rizley, judge Western Dist. Okla., 1956-57; asst. ins. commr., counsel Okla. Ins. Dept., 1957-63; partner firm DeBois, Allen & Batchelor, Oklahoma City, 1963-65, DeBois & Allen, 1965-66; counsel Am. Tel. & Tel., Washington, 1966-67, gen. atty. Southwestern Bell Telephone Co., Okla., 1967-—. Exec. com. local council Boy Scouts Am.; mem. Gov.'s Ad Valorem Tax Structure and Sch. Finance Commn., 1972. Served to sgt. AUS, 1946-48; maj. Res. Mem. Am., Okla., Oklahoma County bar assns., Order of Coif, Phi Delta Phi, Sigma Phi Epsilon (dir.). Presbyn. Home: 3021 Robin Ridge Rd Oklahoma City OK 73120 Office: 707 N Robinson Oklahoma City OK 73102

ALLEN, ROBERT G., physician; b. Memphis, June 14, 1928; student Southwestern at Memphis, Johns Hopkins, 1945-47; M.D., U. Tenn., 1950. Intern John Gaston Hosp., Memphis, 1951-52, now mem. staff; resident Boston Children's Hosp., 1952-53, sr. resident, 1956-57, cheif resident, 1957-58; resident Kennedy Vets. Hosp., 1953-54; dir. cardiovascular surgery Le Bonheur Children's Hosp., Memphis, 1959-—, chief surgery, 1964-68; mem. active staff W.F. Bowld Hosp.; mem. courtesy staff Bapt. Meml. Hosp., Meth. Hosp., St. Joseph Hosp. Served with USNR, 1954-56. Diplomate Am. Bd. Surgery. Mem. A.C.S., Am. Acad. Pediatrics, Am. Coll. Cardiology, A.M.A., Am. Pediatric Surg. Assn. (charter), Lilliputian Surg. Soc. (founder), Bowers Surg. Soc. (founder), Memphis, Shelby County med. socs., Memphis Thoracic Soc., Memphis Pediatric Soc., Memphis (pres. 1963), Research. Staff and Serpent Jour. Club, Alpha Omega Alpha. Contbr. articles to profl. jours. Address: 4111 Gwynne Rd Memphis TN 38117

ALLEN, ROBERT LEWIS, physician; b. Spartanburg, S.C., Feb. 13, 1930; s. Dudley Allen and Edna (Moore) A.; B.S. magna cum laude, Wofford Coll., 1951; M.D., Tulane U., 1955; m. Sterling Peebles, May 31, 1955; children—Elizabeth, Catherine, Deborah. Intern, Meyer Meml. Hosp., Buffalo, 1955-56; resident Kennedy Vets. Hosp., Memphis, 1956-59; pvt. practice internal medicine, Cleveland, Tenn., 1961-—; dir. nuclear medicine Bradley Meml. Hosp., Cleveland Bd. dirs. YMCA. Mem. Cleveland City Planning Commn., 1966-—. Served to capt. AUS, 1959-61. Diplomate Am. Bd. Internal Medicine. Mem. A.M.A., Am. Heart Assn., Soc. Nuclear Medicine, Bradley County Med. Soc. (pres. 1968), Phi Beta Kappa, Nu Sigma Nu. Home: 3545 Edgewood Circle Cleveland TN 37311 Office: 755 Broad St Cleveland TN 37311

ALLEN, ROBERT SHARON, writer; b. Latonia, Ky.; student U. Wis., 1923, U.S. Cavalry Sch., Ft. Riley, Kan., 1922, U. Munich, Germany, 1923-24; George Washington U., 1927-28; m. Ruth Finney, Mar. 30, 1929. Reporter, Capital Times, Madison, Wis., 1919; successively reporter Wis. State Jour., Milw. Jour., United Press Assn., Christian Science Monitor, Internat. News Service; Washington corr. Phila. Record. Served with U.S. Army, 1916, 2d lt.

1918; also capt. Wis. N.G., 1921-27; recalled to active duty AUS, July 1942, with rank of maj. Cav., Graduate Command and General Staff Coll., Ft. Leavenworth, Kans., Jan. 1943; promoted to lt. col., May 1943, col., Mar. 1945; operations exec. G-2 Sect. Hdqrs. 3d Army, throughout its combat operations ETO. Decorated Silver Star, Legion of Merit, Bronze Star, Purple Heart, Commendation Ribbon with cluster, French Legion of Honor, Croix de Guerre with palm and gold star. Mem. Sigma Delta Chi. Club: National Press (Washington). Author: Washington Merry-Go-Round, 1931; Why Hoover Faces Defeat, 1932; More Washington Merry-Go-Round, 1932; Nine Old Men, 1936; Nine Old Men at the Crossroads, 1937; Our Fair City, 1946; Lucky Forward, 1947; Our Sovereign State, 1949; The Truman Merry-Go-Round, 1950. Contbr. to mags. Home: 1525 28th St NW Washington DC Office: National Press Bldg Washington DC 20004

ALLEN, ROBERT WILSON, lawyer, educator; b. Los Angeles, Sept. 13, 1919; s. Albert V. and Myrtle Isabel (Hogg) A.; A.B., U. Cal. at Los Angeles, 1942; M.A., So. Meth. U., 1947; Dr. de L'Univ. de Paris, 1952; LL.B., John Marshall U., 1961, J.D., 1962. Instr. fgn. langs. Oxford Coll., Emory U., 1953-57, chrmn. div., 1957-67; admitted to Ga. bar, 1963; gen. practice Oxford, Ga., 1963-—. Justice 1525th Dist. Ga. Militia, Newton County, 1965-—. Served with AUS, 1942-46. Mem. Am. Trial Lawyers Assn., Ga. State Bar, Covington Bar, Nat., Ga. edn. assns., Alliance Francaise, Atlanta Symphony Guild, Pi Delta Phi, Alpha Mu Gamma, Lambda Phi Alpha. Democrat. Methodist. Mason. Contbr. articles to profl. jours. Home: 309 W Stone St Oxford GA 30267 Office: Starr Bldg Covington GA 30209

ALLEN, ROBERTA ETHRIDGE (MRS. ARTHUR ABELE ALLEN), writer; b. Sandersville, Miss., Nov. 9, 1908; d. Mark Dee and Mary Elizabeth (Bostick) Ethridge; B.A., Miss. Woman's Coll., 1928; postgrad. Columbia, 1937; m. Arthur Abele Allen, Oct. 20, 1934; children—Arthur Mark, James Charles. Tchr. English, Hintonville Consol. Sch., Richton, Miss., 1928-29; billing clk. Buick-Olds-Pontiac Zone Office, Memphis, 1929-33, Weathersby-Brunner Coffee Co., Memphis, 1933-36; stenographer, clk. Community Motors, Inc., Little Rock, 1936-38, Fred Murray Motor Co., Miami, Fla., 1940; substitute tchr. Little Rock Pub. Schs., 1951-54; free-lance writer, Little Rock, 1954-—. Block warden Civil Def., Miami, 1941-43, Cammack Village, Little Rock 1954-—; fund raiser numerous nat. health drives, Little Rock 1954-—. Recipient various writing awards. Mem. Nat. League Am. Pen Women (pres. Ark. Pioneer br. 1962-64), Ark. Writer's Conf. (mem. bd., registrar), Women's Nat. Book Assn. (charter mem. Little Rock chpt.), Am. Assn. U. Women, Poets Roundtable Ark. (pres. 1971-72), Baptist (asso. Bible tchr. 1947-—). Author: The Cammack Village Story, 1963; God With Us-Immanuel Baptist Church, Little Rock, Arkansas, 1892-1967, 1967. Contbr. articles and poems to mags., newspapers. Address: 6604 Kenwood Rd Little Rock AR 72207

ALLEN, ROGER WILLIAMS, coll. dean; b. Birmingham, Ala., Mar. 29, 1897; s. Charles Morehead and Nannie Arabella (Thomson) A.; B.S., Auburn U., 1918, M.S., 1919; A.M., U. Mich., 1921; Ph.D., Columbia, 1927; m. Margaret Ann Chruch, Nov. 22, 1927; children—Patsy Jane, Roger W. Chemist, D. C. Pickard, cons. chemists, summer 1917, with E. I. du Pont de Nemours & Co., Washburn, Wis., summer 1918; with U.S. Chem. Warfare Service, Cleve., 1918; chemist Ala. State Chem. Lab., Auburn, 1919, U.S. Dept. Entomology, summer 1921; prof. chemistry Howard Coll., Birmingham, Ala., 1921-22, 1923-26; chemist Inecto, Inc., and Marinello Co., N.Y.C., 1926-28; prof. chemistry Auburn (Ala.) U., 1928-41, dean sch. sci. and lit., 1941-67, dean emeritus, 1967-—. Dir. Auburn Community Chest Drive, 1940. Mem. Ala. Acad. Sci., Ala. Ednl. Assn., Sigma Xi, Phi Kappa Phi, Phi Lambda Upsilon, Omicron Delta Kappa, Delta Sigma Pi, Alpha Epsilon Delta, Pi Kappa Alpha, Phi Eta Sigma. Author: Fundamentals of Chemistry, 1930. Home: 572 Wright's Mill Rd Auburn AL 36830

ALLEN, ROLAND HAROLD, asst. atty. gen. Tex.; b. Waco, Tex., Apr. 16, 1921; s. Albert Sidney and Ida (Neel) A.; J.D., Baylor University, Waco, Tex., 1951; m. Elnora Lee Daniel, July 18, 1953; children—Donna Carol, James Edwin, William Harold. Admitted to Tex. bar, 1951; law clk., liaison with mil. and vets. reps. Office U.S. Congressman, Washington, 1951-52; asso. firm Eugene E. Piper, Borger, Tex., 1953; partner Gassaway & Allen and predecessor firms, Borger, 1954-68; asst. atty. gen. of Tex., Austin, 1969-—. Engaged in oil gas bus., Borger, 1955-—, real estate investments, 1958-—; sec., dir. Indsl. Dynamics, Inc., Borger, 1961-69; atty. Panhandle Bank & Trust Co., Borger, 1954-68, 1st Savs. & Loan Assn., Borger, 1955-68. Dist. chmn. Nat. Fedn. Ind. Bus., 1963-68; mem. Tax Equalization Bd., Borger, 1965-67, chmn., 1967. Precinct chmn. Democratic party, 1960-62. Bd. dirs. Hutchinson County Child Welfare, 1967-69; trustee land trust, Amarillo, Tex., 1965-69; trustee, sec. N.W. Tex. Masonic Home and Sch. Ednl. Found. 1963-—. Served with USMC, 1942-46; PTO. Decorated Purple Heart. Mem. Am., Borger (pres. 1957), Travis County bar assns., State Bar Tex., Am. Judicature Soc., Am. Legion, Delta Theta Phi. Baptist. Mason (Shriner, 32 deg.). Clubs: Exchange (pres. 1957), Country (Borger, Tex.). Home: 2903 Clarice Ct Austin TX 78731 Office: Supreme Ct Bldg Austin TX 78711

ALLEN, ROY, state ofcl. Dir. div. corps. State of Fla., Tallahassee. Address: The Capitol Tallahassee FL 32304*

ALLEN, SIDNEY MITCHELL GREMILLION (MRS. JOHN HORTON ALLEN), civic worker; b. Alexandria, La., Nov. 8, 1921; d. Forrest and Neta Belle (Mitchell) Gremillion; B.A. Northwestern State Coll., Natchitoches, La., 1942; M.Ed., La. State U., 1951; m. John Horton Allen, July 14, 1943; children—John Horton, Lisa Jane. Elementary tchr. Caddo Parish Schs., La., 1942-44, 46-47; supervising tchr., instr. edn. Southeastern La. Coll., Hammond, 1947-51; summer workshop cons. La. State U., 1950-51, supervising tchr. Coll. Area Joint Schs., State Coll., Pa., 1951-52; prin. supervising tchr. Primary Sch., 1952-53; cons., supervising tchr. Pa. State U., 1952, 53, in service tchr. tng. cons., 1952, 53; elementary tchr. Hattiesburg (Miss.) Pub. Schs., 1954, 57-60. Vol. tchr. art appreciation Hattiesburg, (Miss.) Pub. Schs., 1964-69. Vice pres., bd. dirs. Shreveport Art Guild; bd. dirs. Shreveport Symphony Guild, Shreveport Civic Opera Assn., Northwest La. Heart Assn., YWCA, Caddo chpt. A.R.C. Mem. Am. Assn. U. Women (past br. pres.), Nat. Assn. Jr. Auxilaries (chpt. pres.), Hattiesburg. Panhellenic Assn., Alpha Sigma Alpha, Phi Alpha Theta, Kappa Delta Pi, Phi Kappa Phi, Delta Kappa, Gamma, Alpha Sigma Alpha (nat. alumnae dir.). Home: 254 Rutherford Shreveport LA 71104

ALLEN, STANLEY FRANKLIN, coll. exec.; b. Holly Springs, Ga., July 26, 1905; s. John Robert and Lula (Franklin) A.; A.B., N. Ga. coll., 1926; M.A., Columbia, 1935; m. Harriett McMorrough, Dec. 21, 1937; children—Bettie Laura (Mrs. Edward M. Fore), Mary Francis, Farmer nr. Goodman, Miss., 1938-—; tchr. pub. schs., Ga., 1926-28, Va., 1928-35, N.J., 1935-36; business mgr. with Holmes Jr. Coll., Goodman, Miss., 1937-—; pres. Magmolia Chem. Co., Jackson, Miss., 1953-55; dir. Holmes County Bank and Trust Co. (Lexington, Miss.). Home: Goodman MS 39079 Office: Holmes Jr Coll Goodman MS 39079

ALLEN, WILLIAM E., labor union ofcl. Sec.-treas. Fla. Federated Labor Council, Miami. Office: 1400 NW 36th St Miami FL 33142*

ALLEN, WILLIAM GROVER, orthodontist; b. Prestonsburg, Ky., Jan. 1, 1934; s. Claude C. and Bertha B. (Bradley) A.; student Pikeville Coll., 1952-54, Morehead Coll., 1956; B.S. in Anatomy and Physiology, U. Ky., 1958, A.B. in Chemistry, 1959; D.M.D., U. Louisville, 1965; M.S. IN Orthodontics, U. Tenn., 1967; m. Anita Ann Lankford, Dec. 19, 1959; children—Francis Michellen, Lynda Ann, Pamela Sue. Individual practice orthodontics, Ashland, Ky., 1967-—. Served with AUS, 1952-54. Mem. Am. Dental Assn., Ky., Eastern Ky. (pres. elect 1972-73) dental socs., Am., So. orthodontic socs., Beta Delta, Omicron Delta Kappa, Phi Kappa Phi, Alpha Omega, Phi Delta, Omicron Kappa Upsilon. Home: 601 Amanda Dr Ashland KY 41101 Office: 1506 Winchester Av Ashland KY 41101

ALLEN, WILLIAM SAMUEL, agrl. engr.; b. Watertown, Tenn., Nov. 23, 1919; s. Matt Martin and Mamie (Routin) A.; B.S, U. Tenn., 1947; M.S., Tex. A and M U., 1964; m. Betty Eng, Aug. 31, 1946; children—Lisbeth Elaine, Baldwin Kaye. Extension agrl. engr. Tex. A. and M U., College Station, 1947-50, 52-—, tchr. adult edn.; dir., officer H& A Constrn. Co., Bryan, Tex., 1954-72; grain storage operator Mid-Brazil Valley Industries, Inc., Bryan, 1959-70; dir. officer Crimpomatic Mill & Equipment Co., 1961-— Cons. agrl. engr., 1960-—. Served from pvt. to capt. AUS, 1943-46 from capt to maj., 1950-52; now col. Res. Decorated Bronze Star medal with oak leaf cluster. Mem. Am. Soc. Agr. Engrs., Nat., Tex. socs. profl. engrs., Tex. Agr. Workers Assn., Profl. Engrs. in Pvt. Practice. Baptist. Mason. (Shriner). Contbr. articles to profl. jours. Home: 521 Moran St Bryan TX 77801 Office: Box 304 Tex A and M U College Station TX 77840

ALLERS, JOHN CHRISTIAN, broadcasting co. exec.; b. New Milford, N.J., Jan. 15,, 1918; s. John Christian and Edna Susan (Reeve) A.; student N.C. State Coll., 1936-38; certificate N.Y. State U., Morrisville, 1939; m. Lorraine Humphrey, July 7, 1942; children—Katherine Lee, Susan Carol (Mrs. Paul Frizell Miller). Salesman, Copeland &Thompson, Inc., N.Y.C., 1939-41, Manhattan Soap Co., Raleigh, 1952-53; asst. mgr. Kimbrell's Furniture Co., Raleigh, N.C., 1945-50; sales mgr. Capital Broadcasting Co., Raleigh, 1960-68; with Durham Life Broadcasting Service, Raleigh, 1968-—, gen. sales mgr., 1969-—. Pres. P.T.A., 1963-65; chmn. Millbrook Adv. Council, 1964-69. Bd. dirs. Wake Found Inc., pres. 1969-71. Served to 1st lt. AUS, 1941-45. Mem. Assn. Nat. Farm Broadcasters, Nat. Agrl. Advt. and Marketing Assn., Sales and Marketing Execs. Club, Raleigh Advt. Club (sec. 1971-72). Baptist (deacon 1969-71). Clubs: Raleigh Sports (dir. 1970-73), Civitan (Raleigh). Home: 3315 Baugh St Raleigh NC 27604 Office: 410 S Salisbury St Raleigh NC 29602

ALLEY, J. T., JR., city ofcl.; b. Lubbock, Tex., June 26, 1923; s. J.T. and Edna Ann (Mullins) A.; student FBI Nat. Acad., 1952, Tex. Technol. U., 1955-56, U. Okla., 1962, U. Louisville, 1963, U. Tex., 1967; m. Dorris D'Arlene Reed, Jan. 8, 1944; children— Mary Ann (Mrs. David Andy Wilkinson), Patricia K. (Mrs. Robert Seiter), Billie D'Arlene, Jaye Tori. Patrolman, Lubbock Police Dept., 1946-47, Sgt., 1947-51, capt., 1951-57, chief of police 1957-—. Served with USMCR, 1942-46. Mem. Am. Fedn. Police, Internat. Assn. Chiefs of Police (vice chmn. emergency planning com. 1968-—). Methodist Rotarian (dir. 1968-70). Home: 4207 39th St Lubbock TX 79413 Office: Box 2000 Lubbock TX 79457

ALLGEIER, ROBERT KEITH, aerospace engr.; b. Albany, Ga., Oct. 14, 1941; s. Robert Keith and Mary Ann (Johnson) A.; student Adams State Coll., Colo., 1959-60; B.S., N.M. State U., 1964; postgrad. U. Houston, 1968-72. Aerospace engr., contract adminstr. NASA, Manned Spacecraft Center, Houston, 1964-—. Recipient Apollo Achievement award, Apollo Group Achievement award NASA, 1969; NASA Patent award, 1970. Registered profl. engr., Tex. Mem. Pi Tau Sigma, Sigma Tau. Republican. Author: The Development of Cryogenic Storage Systems for Spaceflight, 1971. Patentee in field. Home: 2001 San Sebastian Ct Houston TX 77058 Office: 2101 Nasa Blvd Houston TX 77058

ALLGOOD, CLARENCE WILLIAM, U.S. judge; b. Birmingham, Ala., Sept. 12, 1902; s. Robert Veneable and Patricia (Robinson) A.; student Howard Coll., 1921-23; B.S., Ala. Poly. Inst., 1926; LL.B., Birmingham Sch. Law, 1941; m. Marie Maxwell, June 27, 1927 1 son, Clarence William. Referee in bankruptcy U.S. Dist. Ct. No. Ala., 1937-61; admitted to Ala. bar, 1941; U.S. dist. judge No. Dist. Ala., 1961-—. Dir. Fidelity Mortgage Co. Ala., Fidelity Fed. Savs. and Loan Assn. Mem. counsel profl. relations Am. Hosp. Assn., 1950-52; chmn. Ala. Hosp. Trustees Assn., 1951. Chmn. bd. trustees S. Highland Infirmary, Birmingham, 1945-55; trustee Crippled Childrens Hosp. and Clinic, 1941-—, pres., 1958; trustee Ala. Soc. Crippled Children and Adults, 1946-48. Mem. Am., Ala., Birmingham bar assns., Pi Kappa Alpha, Sigma Delta Kappa, Blue Key. Elk. Club: Civitan (Birmingham). Author articles, contbr. textbooks. Home: 3524 Brookwood Rd Birmingham AL 35223 Office: PO Box 155 Birmingham AL 35202

ALLIN, JOHN MAURY, clergyman; b. Helena, Ark., Apr. 22, 1921; s. Richard and Dora (Harper) A.; B.A., U. South, 1943, B.D., 1945; M.Ed., Miss. Coll., 1960; m. Frances Ann Kelly, Oct. 18, 1949; children—Martha May, John Maury, Kelly Ann, Frances Elizabeth. Ordained to ministry Protestant Episcopal Ch.; vicar St. Peter's Mission, Conway, Ark., vicar of chs., Harrison, Euraka Springs, Russellville (all Ark.), 1945-49; curate St. Andrews Ch., New Orleans, 1950-52; rector Grace Ch., Monroe, La., 1952-58; pres., rector All Saints' Jr. Coll., Vicksburg, Miss., 1958-61; consecrated bishop coadjutor Episcopal Diocese Miss., 1961-66, diocesan bishop, 1966-—. Chmn. dept. Christian edn. Diocese La.; v.p. dept. Christian edn. Province of Sewanee; mem. joint com. on ecumenical relations; adv. com. on deaconesses House of Bishops; pres. Com. of Concern, 1966-67. Bd. regents U. South; trustee All Saints' Sch.; chmn. bd. dirs. Sewanee Summer Tng. Sch. Mem. Newcomen Soc., St. Luke's Alumni Assn. U. South, Kappa Sigma. Home: 3775 Old Canton Rd Jackson MS 39216 Office: 112 S West St Jackson MS 39201

ALLISON, FRANK EDWARD, SR.,, architect, planner; b. San Saba, Tex., Nov. 7, 1929; s. Benjamin Rush and Gladys Mae (Karnes) A.; B. Arch., A. and M. Coll. Tex., 1951; m. Maxine G. Nickles, Nov. 26, 1952; children—Ta'na Denise, Brenda Day, Frank Edward, Melissa Dawn. Engr. draftsman H.E. Bovay Engrs., Houston, 1953-54; project architect firm Pitts Mebane & Phelps, Beaumont, Tex., 1954-59; prin. Allison & Assos. Architects/Planners, Beaumont, 1959-61; dir. planning, project architect Welton Becket, Houston, N.Y.C., 1961-66; prin. Allison Assos. AIA Architects Planners, Houston, 1966-—; partner Developments/Dynamics, Houston, 1970-—; sr. v.p. Three-O-One Corp., Multi-D Inc. (both Houston), 1971-—; cons. in field. Served with USNR, 1952-53; PTO. Registered architect, Tex. Mem. A.I.A., Tex. Soc. Architects, A.M. Soc. Planning Ofcls., Urban Land Inst. Home: 7151 Edgemoor Dr Houston TX 77036 Office: 5555 W Loop South Houston TX 77401

ALLISON, IRL, pianist, music educator; b. Warren, Tex., Apr. 8, 1896; s. John Van and Mary Cleona (Richardson) A.; A.B., Baylor U., 1915, A.M., 1922; Dr. Music, Southwestern Conservatory, Dallas, 1947; LL.D., Hardin-Simmons U., 1954; attended Chgo. Mus. Coll., summer 1919, Columbia U., 1920-21, summers 1942, U. Tex., 1943; Dr. Music (hon.), Houston Conservatory, 1954; piano study Ezra Rachlin, Rudolph Hoffman, Josef Evans, Percy Grainger, Ernest Hutcheson, Harold von Mickwitz, Walter Gilewicz; m. Jessie Johnson, July 3, 1918; children—Mary J. (dec.), John (dec.), Irl, Lucille (Mrs. Therl Ockey). Dean music, Rusk Coll., 1918-19; instr. piano Baylor Coll. Women, 1921-23; dean fine arts Montezuma Coll., 1923-27; dean music Hardin-Simmons Univ., 1927-34. Founder, pres. Nat. Guild Piano Tchrs.; pres. Am. Coll. Musicians, 1934-60; founder Golden Rule Peace Movement and originator World Peace Programs (radio), 1948; mgr. Nat. Piano-Playing Auditions (founder), 1929-60; editor Piano Guild Notes, 1951-—. Mem. Music Tchrs. Nat. Assn., Music Educators Nat. Conf., Nat. Music Council, Author: Through the Years; Our George. Compiler editor Irl Allison Piano Library, 33 vols. Contbr. to newspapers, music publications. Co-founder, donor grand prize Van Cliburn Internat. Quadrennial Piano Competition. Home: 1500 Murray Lane Austin TX 78703

ALLISON, JULIAN TRACY, real estate broker; b. Greer, S.C., Dec. 24 934; s. Tracy H. and Nell (Whitlock) A.; B.S., U.S.C., 1959; postgrad. U. Tenn., 1959-61; m. Kaye Turbyfill, Sept. 1, 1956; children—Julian Tracy II, Jason Whitlock. Real estate broker, 1962-—; organizer United State Acres, Ltd., 1964; organizer, chmn. bd. Security Fed. Savs. & Loan Assn., Alcoa, Tenn., 1967-—; owner Julian T. Allison Enterprises, Maryville, Tenn., 1964-—; organizer, pres. Allied Realty, Inc.; partner Modular Structures Tenn.-Ky., Smoky Mountain Trailer Sales; chmn. bd. Concepts, Inc.; sec.-treas. Univ. Devel. Corp. Served with USNR, 1952-55. Mem. Maryville-Alcoa (past pres.), Knoxville (past dir.) homebuilders assns., Maryville Bd. Realtors (past v.p., dir.). Home: 1818 E Westwood Dr Maryville TN 37801 Office: Alcoa Hwy at Lakemont Box 1026 Maryville TN 37801

ALLISON, MARSHALL L., lawyer; b. Lavonia, Ga., Mar. 3, 1897; s. Thomas F. and Gertrude (Bost) A.; B.S., Young Harris Coll., 1915-3m. Marion W. Willbanks, Aug. 27, 1919; 1 dau., Julia Carolyn (Mrs. Robert J. Urick). Admitted to Ga. bar, 1926, practiced in Lavonia, 1926-36, city atty., 1926-36; asst. atty. gen. of Ga., Atlanta, 1937-38, 1938-41, 1943-45; judge No. Jud. Circuit of Ga., Lavonia, 1938; law asst. to chief justice of Ga. Supreme Court, 1941-42; pvt. practice of law under own name, Atlanta, 1945-53; in law practice, Lavonia, Ga., 1953-—; apptd. mem. Jud. Council Ga., 1962-64. U.S. Supreme Court, 1936. Trustee Young Harris Coll., 1942-—. Served with F.A., U.S. Army, World War I. Mem. Am., Ga. bar assn's., Bar Assn. No. Jud. Circuit Ga., Am. Legion (1st comdr.). Methodist (steward). Lion (1st pres.). Author: Compiled Opinions of Attorney General of Georgia, 1939-41, 1941-43. Address: 55 Bowman St Lavonia GA 30553

ALLISON, NOAH DWIGHT, former editor; b. Spencer, Ind., Feb. 9, 1899; s. Clayton Benbridge and Pearl (Coble) A.; A.B., DePauw U., 1921; grad. Command and Gen. Staff Sch., Brit. Sr. Staff Coll.; m. Tomi Charpentier, July 3, 1923 (dec.). Reporter, 1921; news editor Post-Enquirer, Oakland, Cal., 1922-24; Sunday editor The Record, Fort Worth, 1925; mng. editor The Light, San Antonio, 1928-67; Lozano prof. journalism Trinity U., 1967-68. Served as 2d lt. RAF, Gt. Britain, World War I; lt. col. Mil. Intelligence Res., AUS, World War II; 36th Div. V Corps, Hdqrs. ETO, 12th Army Group; chief liaison officer, 12th to 21st Army Group (Brit.) in continental operations; campaigns: Normandy, No. France, Ardennes, Rhineland, Central Europe, brig. gen. AUS (ret.). Decorated Bronze Star, Bronze Service Arrowhead, Order of British Empire. Mem. Tex. Cavaliers, Sigma Delta Chi, Beta Theta Pi. Democrat. Mason. Club: Argyle. Home: 102 Allson Dr San Antonio TX 78212

ALLISON, WILLIAM BURGESS, coal co. exec.; b. Monteray, Tenn., Sept. 5, 1925; s. Virgil Croft and Anna M. (Copeland) A.; student U. South, 1943-44, Princeton, 1944, Columbia, 1945; B.S. Tenn. Tech. U., 1948; m. Katy Helen Garner, Aug. 25, 1963; children—Ann Grier, William Kenneth, Mrs. Larry Wayne Thomas. Accountant, Central Coal Co., Monteray, Tenn., 1948-49; chief accountant, dept. mgr. Cumberland Elec. Membership Corp., 1949-50; U.S. govt. cost accountant Arnold Engring. Devel. Center, Tullahoma, Tenn., 1951; pub. accountant, Fayetteville, Tenn., 1951-54; owner, operator Largin Motor Inn and Restaurant, Fayetteville, 1954-60; v.p. treas., asst. sec. Tenn. Consol. Coal Co., Tenn. Consol. Coal Co. Internat., Nashville, Tracy City and Jasper, 1960-—, also dir.; dir. cos. including Grundy Mining Co., Mary Lee Coal Co., Va. Mining Co., Walnut Coal Co., Whitewell Coal Corp. Lectr., Austin Peay State Coll., Clarksburg, Tenn., 1949-50. Active various civic drives; mem. Marion County Indsl. Adv. Bd., Jasper, Tenn., 1968-—. Served to lt. (j.g.) USNR, 1943-46; PTO. Mem. Lincoln County C. of C. (dir. 1953-57). Presbyn. (deacon 1952-61). Kiwanian. Home: PO Box 865 Victoria Av Jasper TN 37347 Office: PO Box 878 Betsy Pack Dr Jaser TN 37347

ALLRED, DEWITT TALMAGE, physician; b. Caseyville, Miss., July 27, 1890; s. John Sylvester and Alla (McLaurin) A.; B.S., U. Miss., 1916; M.D., Tulane U., 1918; m. Velma Ann Watkins, Dec. 1, 1920; children— DeWitt Talmage, Doris Mae (Mrs. C.E. Bane, Jr.), Anne (Mrs. G.H. Bethea). Intern, Charity Hosp., New Orleans, 1918-19; practice medicine, Collins, Miss., 1919-—. Examiner, SSS, 1940-—. Served with USNR, 1918-20. Recipient Presdl. citation for 30 years service to SSS, 1970. Mem. A.M.A., Miss. Med. Assn., S. Miss. Med. Soc. Mason, Rotarian. Address: PO Box 302 Collins MS 39428

ALLSBROOK, OGDEN OLMSTEAD,, JR., educator; b. Wilmington, N.C., July 1, 1940; s. Ogden Olmstead and Elizabeth Barringer (Warren) A.; A.B., Wake Forest U., 1962; Ph.D., U. Va., 1966. Asst. prof. econs. U. Miami, Coral Gables, Fla., 1965-66; operations research analyst U.S. Dept. Def., Washington, 1966-68; asst. prof. econs. U. Ga., Athens, 1968-—. Lectr. U. Md., College Park, 1967-68. Served to capt. AUS, 1966-68. Decorated Army Commendation medal. Mem. Am., So. econs. assns., Pub. Choice Soc., Omicron Delta Epsilon, Lambda Chi Alpha. Lutheran. Author: The Utilization of Military Resources, 1968; A Survey of Army Automated Cost Models, 1968. Home: 107 Ashley Circle Apt 6 Athens GA 30601

ALLUISI, EARL ARTHUR, psychologist, educator; b. Richmond, Va., June 11, 1927; s. Humbert Peter and Elizabeth Mary (Dini) A.; B.S., Coll. William and Mary, 1949; M.A., Ohio State U., 1950, Ph.D., 1954; m. Mary Jane Boyle, Dec. 16, 1954; children—John, Jean, Paul, Janet. Research psychologist Army Med. Research Lab., Ft. Knox, 1951-52; vis. instr. psychology dept. Coll. William and Mary, summers 1953-54; research asso., lectr. Ohio State U., 1954-57; head environmental factors sect. U.S. Army Med. Research Lab., 1957-58; head engring. psychology Stanford Research Inst., 1958-59; from asst. prof. to asso. prof. psychology Emory U., 1959-61; asso. scientist human factors research lab. Lockheed-Ga. Co., 1961-63; lectr. Ga. Inst. Tech., 1962-63; prof. psychology U. Louisville, 1963-—, asst. dean Grad. Sch., 1966-67, asso. dean Grad. Sch., 1970-71, exec. officer for planning and devel., 1967-69, dir. performance research lab., 1968-72, research prof., 1968-—, v.p. planning and instnl. research, 1971-—; with I.D.A., 1969-70. Served as capt. AUS, 1944-47, 50-52, 57-58. Fellow Am., Ky. (pres. 1966-67) psychol.

assns., A.A.A.S.; mem. Psychonomic Soc., Psychometric Soc., So. Soc. Philosophy and Psychology (sec. 1962-65, councilman 1965-66, pres. 1967-68), Ky. Acad. Sci. (chmn. psychol. sect. 1964-65), Am. Assn. U. Profs., Am. Council for Higher Edn., Ky. Sci. and Tech. Adv. Council, Ky. Humanities Council (chmn. 1972—), Factors Soc., Ky. Civil Liberties Union (dir. 1964—, chmn. 1972—), Phi Beta Kappa, Sigma Xi, Psi Chi, Alpha Psi Delta, Phi Kappa Phi Club: Lakeside. Home: 4093 Gilman Av Louisville KY 40207

ALLYN, KENNETH HERSCHEL, city ofcl.; b. Elyria, O., Feb. 17, 1912; s. Richard H. and Frances Hanna (Briggs) A.; student U. Mich., 1930-32, LaSalle U., 1938-40; m. Mabel Christine Walsh, July 25, 1938; children—John Kenneth, Joyce (Mrs. Robert E. Coleman). Accountant, City of Coral Gables (Fla.), 1935-40, purchasing agt., 1940-45, chief accountant, 1945-56, asst. finance dir., 1956-59, finance dir., 1959—. Recipient Good Government award Jr. C. of C., 1968-69. Mem. Municipal Finance Officers Assn. U.S. and Can. (Fla. chpt. pres. 1954-55, Fla. chmn. 1956-71, exec. bd. 1971—, dir. 1971, mem. Hall of Fame), Fla. Soc. Ins. Buyers (pres. 1966-67). Office: PO Drawer 1549 Coral Gables FL 33134

ALMACK, DON LEE, banker; b. Tonkawa, Okla., July 7, 1927; s. Dennis F. and Juanita (McBride) A.; grad. high sch.; m. Beryle D. Dingler, July 12, 1947; 1 son, Glenn A. Loan officer First Nat. Bank & Trust Co., Oklahoma City, 1947-55; v.p. Capitol Hill State Bank, Oklahoma City, 1955-63, 64—; pres. Grant Sq. Bank & Trust Co., Oklahoma City, 1963-64. Sec., v.p., bd. dirs. Okla. Goodwill Industries. Served with USAAF, 1945-46, USAF, 1951-52. Mem. Christian Ch. Club: Capitol Hill Sertoma (sec., past chmn. bd., pres.). Home: 2109 SW 71st St Oklahoma City OK 73159 Office: 700 SW 29th St Oklahoma City OK 73109

ALMAND, BOND, judge; b. Lithonia, Ga., Jan. 13, 1894; s. Alexander James and Clara Emily (Bond) A.; Ph.B., Emory U., 1913; LL.B., Columbia, 1916, A.M., 1916; m. Helen Whitefoot Barnett, June 18, 1932; children—Helen (Mrs. Roy F. Morgan, Jr.), Bond. Admitted to Ga. bar, 1916; practiced in Atlanta, 1916-42; asst. city atty., 1939-42; judge Fulton County Superior Ct., 1942-43, 1945-49, asso. justice Supreme Ct. of Ga., 1949-69; chief justice Supreme Ct. of Ga., 1969—; solicitor Criminal Ct. Fulton County, 1939-42; lectr. Emory U. Sch. Law, 1951—. Rep. Ga. Gen. Assembly, 1935-38. Served as 1st lt., Inf., U.S. Army, with 82d and 9th divs., A.E.F., World War I. Mem. Am. Bar Assn., Inst. Jud. Adminstrn., Phi Beta Kappa, Sigma Nu, Phi Alpha Delta, Omicron Delta Kappa. Episcopalian. Home: 3291 Rilman Rd NW Atlanta GA 30305 Office: Judicial Bldg Atlanta GA 30303

ALMODOVAR, LUIS RAUL, biologist, educator; b. San German, P.R., Jan. 19, 1931; s. Pablo and Elisa (Almodovar) A.; B.A., Poly. Inst. P.R., 1950; M.S., Fla. State U., 1955, Ph.D., (grad. fellow), 1958. Tchr., Fajardo High Sch., P.R., 1950-51; grad. asst. Oceanographic Inst., Fla. State U., Tallahassee, 1953-54, grad. teaching asst. dept. biol. scis., 1955-57; instr. Inst. Marine Biology, U. P.R., Mayaguez, P.R., 1958-60, asst. prof., 1960-63, asso. prof. dept. marine scis., 1964-67, prof. 1967—. Served with USMCR, 1951-53. Am. Acad. Arts Scis. fellow, 1961, Guggenheim Found. fellow, 1969-70. Mem. N.Y. Acad. Scis., Bot. Soc. Am., Phycological Soc. Am., Brit., Internat. phycological socs., Internat. Assn. Plant Taxonomists, Assn. Island Marine Labs., P.R. Acad. Arts Scis., Internat. Oceanographic Found., Torrey Bot. Club, Fla. Acad. Scis., Sigma Xi, Phi Sigma, Beta Beta Beta. Contbr. articles to profl. jours. Home: Box 286 San German PR 00753 Office: Dept Marine Scis U PR Mayaguez PR 00708

ALMOND, JAMES LINDSAY, JR., judge; b. Charlottesville, Va., June 15, 1898; s. James Lindsay and Eddie Nicholas (Burgess) A.; LL.B., U. Va., 1923; LL.D., Coll. William and Mary; m. Josephine Katherine Minter, Aug. 15, 1925. Admitted to Va. bar, 1921, practiced in Roanoke, 1923-32; prin. Zoar High Sch., 1921-22; asst. pros. atty., Roanoke, 1930-33; judge Hustings Ct., Roanoke, 1933-45; mem. 79th and 80th Congresses from Va., mem. post office and civil service com.; atty. gen. Va., 1948-57, gov., 1958-62; asso. judge U. S. Ct. Customs and Patent Appeals, Washington, 1962—. Served with U.S. Army, World War I. Recipient Distinguished Service medal Va. Mem. Am., Va., Roanoke bar assns., United Comml. Travelers, Raven Soc., Omicron Delta Kappa, Alpha Kappa Psi, Delta Theta Phi. Democrat. Lutheran (tchr. Men's Bible Class 20 yrs.). Mason (Shriner, past potentate). Home: 208 Wexleigh Dr Richmond VA 23229 Office: U S Ct of Customs and Patent Appeals Bldg 717 Madison Pl NW Washington DC 20439

ALMY, PATTY CARPENTER (MRS. LIONEL A. ALMY), librarian; b. Eatonton, Ga., Mar. 10, 1926; d. Clyde and Erma (Dunn) Carpenter; B.A. in Journalism, U. Ga., 1947; postgrad. Ga. Coll., 1957-58; M.A. in L.S., George Peabody Coll., 1964; m. Lionel A. Almy, June 13, 1948; children—Clyde Carpenter, Lee Andrade. Feature writer Athens (Ga.) Banner Herald, 1946-47, Atlanta Jour.-Constn. Mag., 1958-59; radio continuity WGGS, Tifton, GA., 1947-48; publicity dir. Uncle Remus Regional Library, Madison, Ga., 1958-60; librarian Putnam County High Sch., 1960-61; dir. Sibley Cone Meml. Library, Ga. Coll., Milledgeville, 1961—. Speaker women's clubs, Central Ga., 1960—. Active P.T.A. Mem. Am., Ga., Southeastern library assns., Nat., Ga. edn. assns., Am. Assn. U. Women, Delta Delta Delta. Temporary editor Eatonton Messenger (Ga.). Home: 203 Carriage Way Eatonton GA 31024

ALPER, ARTHUR EUGENE, psychologist, educator; b. Bklyn., Jan 5, 1928; s. Leonard and Rose (Kaplan) A.; B.A., U. Fla., 1949, M.A., 1950, Ph.D., 1960; m. Lee Wray, Apr. 3, 1953; children—David Bruce, Carl Edwin. Psychologist, Sunland (Fla.) Tng. Center, 1954-59; psychologist Med. Coll, Ga., 1960-62; dir. clin. psychology doctoral tng. program Milledgeville (Ga.) State Hosp., 1962-64; asso. prof. Coll. Edn., U. Fla., 1965-68, chmn. Exceptional Children Tng. Program, 1967-68; prof., head Edn. Disturbed Children Program, Coll. Edn., U. Ga., Athens, 1968—; research field reader U.S. Office Edn.; pvt. practice clin. psychology; spl. edn. cons. Fla. Dept. Edn. Served to 2d lt. USAF, 1951-53. Diplomate Am. Bd. Profl. Psychologists. Mem. Am., S.E., Ga. psychol. assns., Council for Exceptional Children, Phi Delta Kappa. Home: 545 Cedar Creek Dr Athens GA 30601

ALPERT, ESTHER SHIRLEY OFFERMAN (MRS. BARNETT ALPERT), civic worker; b. N.Y.C.; d. Samuel and Sadie (Meyers) Offerman; B.A., Hunter Coll., 1930, postgrad., 1933-36; m. Barnett Alpert, June 17, 1932; children—Michael Allen, Judith Ruth. Substitute tchr. N.Y.C. Sch. System, 1940-45; caseworker Dept. Welfare, N.Y.C., 1933-38. Vice-pres. Mental Health Assn. Broward County, Fla., 1961, pres., 1962-65; coordinator vol. services South Fla. State Hosp., 1963-65; mem. Coummunity Mental Health Planning Com., 1964—; chmn. South br. Broward County Med. Aux., 1965-66; state chmn. mental health Fla. Med. Aux., 1966-68; v.p. Henderson Clinic Broward County, 1965-66, pres., 1966-67, corr. sec., 1967-68, bd. dirs., 1971—; mem. exec. com. N.Y. Philanthropic League, N.Y.C., 1952-56; rec. sec. Fla. Adv. Council on Mental Health, 1968-69, vice chmn., 1969—; mem. Com. on Aging, 1964-65; founder, adviser Mental Health Forum, Broward County, 1961—. Recipient Bronze plaque for services rendered to mentally ill Mental Health Assn. Fla., 1965. Mem. Nat. Council Jewish Women (exec. com. 1958-60), Hadassah (pres. United Order True Sisters 1950-51), Hunter Coll. Alumni Assn., Am. Jewish Congress. Jewish religion. Home: 1135 N North Lake Dr Hollywood FL 33020

ALSBROOK, ELEANOR ANNICE YOUNG, educator, coll. dean; b. Lincoln Ridge, Ky.; d. Whitney M. and Laura (Ray) Young; A.B., Ky. State Coll., 1944; B.L.S., Atalnta U., 1946; M.Ed., U. Louisville, 1965, advanced certificate in edn., 1967; D.Ed., U. Ill.; m. James Alsbrook, Sept. 14, 1965 (div.); 1 dau., Laura E. Librarian, Fla. A. and M. U., Tallahassee, 1946-51, Bergen Jr. Coll., Teaneck, N.J., 1951-53; librarian Lincoln Inst., Lincoln Ridge, Ky., 1953-61, guidance counselor, 1961-64, prin., 1964-66; dir. student personnel, asst. dean U. Coll., U. Louisville, 1966—, from 1966, now prof. edn.; dir. Upward Bound, 1966-67. Cons. Head Start, Volt Tech. Corp., 1967—, Black Econ. Union, 1969—. Chmn., United Negro Coll. Fund Ky., 1966-67, United Appeal U. Coll., 1966-67; mem. curriculum com. Loretta High Sch., 1969—; mem. selection com. Nat. Achievement Scholars, 1967—. Bd. dirs. Ky. Youth Conf., Lincoln Found., Vis. Nurses Assn. Recipient Outstanding Citizens award Newburg Sch. Library, 1968. Gen. Electric fellow, 1965; Nat. Def. Edn. Assn. fellow, 1968-69. Mem. Urban League, Nat., Ky. edn. assns., Am. Personnel Guidance Assn., Am. Coll. Personnel Assn., Kappa Delta Pi, Alpha Sigma Lambda. Democrat. Episcopalian. Home: 749 S 43d St Louisville KY 40211

ALSETH, CHARLES ALBERT, transp. exec.; b. Lake Preston, S.D., Aug. 12, 1919; s. Charles Albert and Ida (Brooks) A.; B.A. in Bus. Adminstrn., Yankton Coll., 1941; postgrad. in bus. U. Minn., 1941-42, Northwestern U., 1946-47, U. Chgo., 1960-61; m. Joanna Gregory Maneras, Apr. 3, 1944. Exec. trainee 1st Nat. Bank of Mpls., 1941-42; sales rep. Richards Boggs and King, Chgo., 1946-48; sales rep. Victor Comptometer Corp., Chgo., 1948-49, nat. sales trainer, 1949-51, br. mgr., Dallas, 1951-58, dir. sales tng., Chgo., 1958-63; dir. sales and marketing Lustra Corp. Am., Carle Place, L.I., N.Y., 1963-65, v.p. sales, 1965-68; v.p. sales Lustra Lighting, ITT Lamp div. Internat. Tel. & Tel. Corp., 1968-69; 1st v.p. Am.-Mayflower, Dallas, 1969—. Instr., Sales Tng. Mgmt. Clinic, U. Wis., 1961, Cornell U., 1963; cons. sales and mgmt. devel. to various domestic and internat. cos. Active Boy Scouts Am. Bd. dirs. Jr. Achievement, Dallas, 1957-58. Served to lt. USNR, 1942-46. Mem. Nat. Soc. Sales Tng. Execs., Yankton Coll. Alumni (pres. Chgo., 1950), Navy League, Illuminating Engring, soc., Toronto (Ont., Can.) Bd. Trade. Republican. Congregationalist, Clubs: Sertoma (pres. Dallas 1954-55, gov. N. Tex. dist. 1955-56, recipient Distinguished Gov.'s award 1956), Dallas Sales Marketing Executives (dir. 1954-58), Brookhaven Country (Dallas), Sales Marketing Executives of Chicago (pres. 1961-62), Executives of Chicago, Sales Executives of N.Y. Contbr., cons. to profl. publs. on sales mgmt. and tng. Home: 7325 Meadow Rd Dallas TX 75230 Office: 950 W Mockingbird Lane Dallas TX 75247

ALSOBROOK, JAMES SAMUEL, JR., interior designer; b. Rossville, Ga., June 21, 1918; s. James S. and Ettie (Hullender) A.; B.S., U. Chattanooga, 1939; postgrad. U. Ga., U. Ala., N.Y. Sch. Interior Design; m. Alice E. Jobron, July 15, 1945; 1 dau., Lynn. Gen. practice interior design, Chattanooga, 1948-50; pres. Alsobrook Decor, Chattanooga, 1953—; chmn. bd. ADX Corp., 1966—; design. cons. to bd. Caldsted Found. Bd. dirs. Houston Mus. Served with USAAF, 1942-45. Fellow Inst. Profl. Designers London; mem. Am. Inst. Interior Designers (state bd. dirs.), Pi Kappa Alpha, Gamma Sigma Epsilon, Phi Chi. Presbyn. Patentee in field. Home: 1619 Fairydell Trail Lookout Mountain TN 37350 Office: 900 Mcalle Av Chattanooga TN 37403

ALSOP, JOSEPH WRIGHT, newspaperman, author; b. Avon, Conn., Oct. 11, 1910; s. Joseph Wright and Corinne Douglas (Robinson) A.; grad. Groton Sch., 1928; A.B., Harvard, 1932; m. Susan Mary Jay Patten, Feb. 16, 1961. Mem. N.Y. Herald Tribune staff, N.Y.C., 1932-35, Washington, 1936-37; with Robert E. Kintner, author of syndicated column on politics, The Capital Parade, for N.Am. Newspaper Alliance, 1937-40; commd. lt., U.S. Navy, 1940; sent to India; resigned from Navy, joined Am. Vol. Air Force as aide to Gen. Chennault; captured by Japanese at Hong Kong and held prisoner until 1942, exchanged and returned to U.S.; became chief of Lease Lend Mission to China at Chunking, 1942; capt. 14th Air Force and mem. staff of Gen. Chennault, 1943-45. Recipient Legion of Merit; Chinese Cloud Banner. Clubs: Links (N.Y.C.); Turf (London); Travellers' (Paris, France); Metropolitan (Washington). Author; (with Turner Catledge) The 168 Days, 1938; (with Robert E. Kintner) Men Around the President, 1938, American White Paper, 1940; (with Stewart Alsop) We Accuse, 1955; The Reporter's Trade, 1958; From the Silent Earth, 1964. Author (with brother, Stewart J. O. Alsop) column Matter of Fact, syndicated through N.Y. Herald Tribune Syndicate, 1945-58, sole author, through Los Angeles Times Syndicate, 1964—. Contbr. Life, Atlantic Monthly, New Yorker, New Republic. Home: 2720 Dumbarton Av Washington DC 20007

ALSOP, STEWART JOHONNOT OLIVER, columnist; b. Avon, Conn., May 17, 1914; s. Jospeh Wright and Corinne Douglas (Robinson) A.; grad. Groton Sch., 1932; A.B., Yale, 1936; m. Patricia Hankey, Oct. 1944; children—Joseph Wright, Ian Alexander Douglas, Elizabeth Winthrop, Stewart Johonnot Oliver, Richard Nicholas, Andrew Christian. Editor, Doubleday Doran, N.Y.C.; after World War II, partner with brother, Joseph, to write column Matter of Fact for N.Y. Herald Tribune Syndicate, 1945-48; nat. affairs contbg. editor Saturday Eve. Post, 1958-68, Washington editor, until 1968; now columnist staff Newsweek Mag., 1968—. Enlisted Kings Royal Rifle Corps, British Army, 1942; commd. 2d lt., 1943, promoted capt., 1944; transferred to Am. Army as parachutist OSS, 1944; took Jedburgh tng. course; parachuted into France to join Maquis shortly after D-Day; resigned commn., 1945. Decorated Croix de Guerre with palm (France). Clubs: River (N.Y.C.); Metropolitan (Washington). Author: (with Thomas Braden) Sub. Rosa, 1945. Contr. articles to Sat. Eve. Post, Life, Atlantic Monthly mags. Author (with Joseph Alsop) We Accuse, 1955; The Reporter's Trade (with Joseph Alsop); Nixon and Rockefeller, 1960; The Center, 1968. Home: 3520 Springland Lane NW Washington DC 20008 Office: 1750 Pennsylvania Av NW Washington DC 20006

ALSPAUGH, J. FRANK, state ofcl.; b. Winston-Salem, N.C., Feb. 23, 1921; s. William T. and Elizabeth (Hester) A.; B.S. in Bus. Adminstrn., U. N.C., 1947; m. Frances Rousseau, Mar 1, 1952; children—John, Nancy, David. Indsl. relations, personnel adminstrn. staff Western Electric Co., 1947-49; sales rep. Nat. Cash Register Co., 1949-54; mgr. indsl. dept. Winston-Salem C. of C., 1954-60; exec. dir. Va. Peninsula Indsl. Com. and Peninsula Ports Authority of Va., Newport News, 1960-67; dir. Va. Div. Indsl. Devel., Richmond, 1967—. Served to capt. USMCR, 1943-46; PTO. Mem. Am. (dir.), So. indsl. devel. councils, Indsl. Devel. Research Council, Nat. Assn. State Devel. Agys. (pres.), So. Assn. State Planning and Devel. Agys. Methodist. Clubs: Downtown, Kanawha. Home: 208 Santa Clara Dr Richmond VA 23229 Office: Div Indsl Devel State Office Bldg Richmond VA 23229

ALSTON, CLARENCE WYATT, banker; b. Richmond, Va., June 12, 1926; s. Joseph John and Elizabeth (Alston) A.; student U. Richmond, 1943-44, 46-47; B.B.A., Emory U., 1949; m. Anne Elizabeth Simpson, Aug. 21, 1954; children—Allen Davies, Charles Wyatt, Joanne Elizabeth, Susan Douglas. Supr., Miller & Rhoads, Richmond, 1949-50; asst. cashier Bank Va., Richmond, 1950-60, sr. v.p., 1962—; bank examiner U.S. Treasury Dept., Charlotte, N.C., 1960-62. Pres. Richmond chpt. Easter Seal Soc., 1965-67. Served with USNR, 1944-45. Mem. Richmond C. of C., Va. C. of C., Am. Inst. Banking (pres. Richmond chpt. 1956-57, mem. adv. bd.), Va. (chmn. installment credit com. 1965-67), Am. (adv. bd. installment credit com. 1967—) bankers assns., Alpha Kappa Psi, Phi Gamma Delta. Republican. Presbyn. Clubs: Civitan (pres. Richmond 1968-69), Bull and Bear; Salisbury Country. Home: 2436 Chancellor Rd Richmond VA 23235 Office: 800 E Main St Richmond VA 23214

ALTERMAN, JACK, govt. ofcl.; b. N.Y.C., Sept. 11, 1917; s. David and Frieda (Spitzer) A.; B.S., N.Y. City Coll., 1940; postgrad. Am. U., 1941-42, 46-48; m. Toby Gilman, Oct. 9, 1946; children—David, William. Research asst. Nat. Resource Planning Bd., 1941-42; economist FCC, 1946-48; chief br. analysis and evaluation div. interindustry econs. Bur. Labor and Statistics, Dept. Labor, Washington, 1948-53, asst. chief div. productivity and tech. devels., 1953-62, chief div. econ. growth, 1962-68, dir. econ. growth studies, 1968-71, asst. commr. Office Econ. Trends and Labor Conditions, 1971—. Served to 1st lt. USAAF, 1942-45. Recipient Meritorious Service award Dept. Labor, 1961, Commr's award Bur. Labor and Statistics, 1967. Fellow Am. Statis. Assn.; mem. Am. Econ. Assn., Conf. on Research in Income and Wealth, Internat. Assn. Research on Income and Wealth. Contbr. articles to profl. publs. Home: 9015 Garland Av Silver Spring MD 20901 Office: Bureau of Labor Statistics US Dept of Labor Washington DC 20212

ALTHAUS, VOY ERNST, geologists; b. Fredericksburg, Tex., Oct. 3, 1926; s. Marlin Ernst and Lena (Reams) A.; student Okla. A. and M. U., 1944, Rutgers U., 1945; B.S. in Geology, Tex. U., 1949; postgrad. Tulane U., 1964-65;; m. Betty Lord, Dec. 16, 1950; children— Voy Ernst, Bess, Ellen. Petroleum geologist Humble Oil & Refining Co., New Orleans, 1949-67, computer geologist in charge Tex. geol. computer operations, Houston, 1967—. Bd. dirs., treas. Tchefuncta Club Estates, New Orleans; 1964-66. Served with AUS, 1945-47. Mem. Am. Assn. Petroleum Geologists, Soc. Profl. Well Log Analysts, Houston Geol. Survey. Home: 331 Patchester St Houston TX 77024 Office: Box 2180 Houston TX 77001

ALTHOUSE, GERALD FREDERICK, city ofcl.; b. Danbury, Conn., May 9, 1920; s. Gerald and Margaret (Goebel) A.; grad. high sch.; m. Joanne Elizabeth Novak, Aug. 18, 1945; children—Gerald Frederick, Margaret Marilyn. Asst. mgr. Thom McAn Shoe Co., Danbury, Conn., 1938-39; prodn. and control supr. Sikorsky div. United Aircraft, 1940-41; owner, operator hotel, Ormond Beach, Fla., 1946-66; water clk. City of Ormond Beach, 1946-53, bookkeeper-accountant, 1953-56, city auditor and clk., 1956—, personnel dir., 1959-67, dir. city operations, 1956-63, city adminstr., 1963-64, city mgr., 1964—. Treas. Ormond Beach Community Fund, 1957—. Trustee Ormond Beach War Meml. Corp. Served with AUS, 1941-45. Recipient Good Govt. award Ormond Beach C. of C., 1958, Daytona Beach Jr. C. of C., 1966; award of merit Ormond Beach post Am. Legion, 1962; award Civitan Club, Ormond Beach, 1966; civic achievement award Masonic Lodge, 1965. Mem. Internat. City Mgrs. Assn., Internat. Inst. Municipal Clks., Nat. Municipal League, Pub. Works Assn., Fla. City Mgrs. Assn. (sec.-treas.), Am. Legion. Episcopalian. Mason (treas. 1958-59, 62, 63). Clubs: Ormond Beach Veterans (pres. 1953-54, treas. 1952-53), Oceanside, Tomoka Oaks Country (Ormond Beach, Fla.). Home: 251 Riverside Dr Ormond Beach FL 32074 Office: 22 S Beach St Ormond Beach FL 32074

ALTMAN, JAMES ESTON, machine co. exec.; b. Manatee, Fla., Jan. 23, 1938; s. Eston and Alma (Bland) A.; B.Mech. Engring., Ga. Inst. Tech., 1960; m. Lois Elaine Middlebrooks, June 15, 1958; children—April Elaine, Allison Leigh, Adriane Ermine. Vice pres. 1960—. Past pres. Gray P.T.A. Treas., Jones County Devel. Commn., 1963; mayor pro-tem City of Gray, 1965-69; Chmn., Jones County Republican Com., 1966-70. Registered profl. engr., Ga. Mem. Ga. Soc. Profl. Engrs., Jones County Jr. C. of C. (past pres.), Com. of 150 Macon. Baptist. Kiwanian (past pres.). Inventor freestone peach split-pit remover, pepper coring machine knife; automatic feed for freestone peach-pitting machine; co-inventor numerical product flow meter for fruits, vegetables, etc. Home: 501 Fraley St Gray GA 31032 Office: Gray GA 31032

ALTMAN, MARVIN, hosp. adminstr. Adminstr. Sparks Regional Med. Center, Ft. Smith, Ark. Address: 1311 S Eye St Fort Smith AR 72901*

ALTON, LOUISE MILLER, educator; b. Donaldsonville, La.; d. William Hugh and Annie (Evans) Miller; Mus.B., La. State U., 1936; Mus.M.Edn., Northwestern U., 1940; Ed. D., Columbia, 1960; m. Charles Irving Alton, Jan. 10, 1947 (dec. Sept. 1950). Tchr. vocal music Gonzales, La., 1936-37; tchr. vocal and instrumental music, St. Francisville, La., 1937-41, Thibodaux, La., 1941-42; recreation dir. A.R.C. Mil. Hosps., 1942-47; music supr. Mobile County, Ala., 1947-48; supr., tchr. vocal music Opelika (Ala.) City Schs., 1948-50; music supr. elementary sch., Artesia, N.M., 1951-52; tchr. vocal music, Ruston, La., 1952-54; dir. vocal music, Lafayette, La., 1955-57, Westdale Jr. and Broadmoor Sr. High Sch., Baton Rouge, 1957-62; chmn. music edn. La. Poly. Inst., Ruston, 1962-68. North Tex. State U., 1968—. Dir. Music Edn. Workshops and Clinics, La., Ala., Tex. Mem. La. Music Educators Assn. (mem. exec. bd. 1958-66, sec. 1958-62, pres. 1962-66), Fedn. Music Clubs La. (state bd. 1964-68), Pilot Internat., Tex. Music Educators Assn., Music Educators Nat. Conf., Internat. Soc. Music Edn., Phi Mu, Delta Kappa Gamma, Sigma Alpha Iota. Episcopalian. Home: 315 Delgado Dr Baton Rouge LA 70808 Office: School of Music North Texas State Univ Denton TX 76203

ALTWEGG, AL, bus. and financial editor Dallas Morning News. Address: Dallas News Dallas TX 75222*

ALVARADO-TIZOL, HECTOR MANUEL, dentist; b. Carolina, P.R., Mar. 26, 1935; s. Antonio Benito and Amina (Tizol) Alvarado; B.S., The Citadel Mil. Coll. S.C., 1956; D.M.D., U. P.R., 1961; m. Carmen Theresa Munoz, Dec. 28, 1957; children—Maria Victoria, Antonio Ramon, Carmen Teresa, Maria Larissa. Research asso. Univ. Hosp., San Juan, P.R., 1963-64; resident oral surgery San Juan Municipal Hosp., 1964-67, attending oral surgeon, 1967—. Served to capt. AUS, 1961-63. Mem. Am. Dental Assn., P.R. Soc. Oral Surgeons, Phi Delta Gamma. Democrat. Roman Catholic. Club: Exchange (pres. 1969—) (San Francisco); Santa Maria (Rio Piedras, P.R.). Contbr. articles to profl. jours. Home: B 20 Rufino Rodriquez Villa Clementina Guaynabo PR 00657 Office: 1452 Ashford Av Condominio Ada Ligia 408 Condado PR 00907

ALVAREZ, ANSELMO SEGUNDO, physician; b. Sangti-Spiritus, Cuba, Nov. 25, 1920; s. Anselmo C. and Brigida J. (Gomez) A.; B.S., Instituto Havan, Cuba, 1938; M.D., Havana U., 1948; m. Caridad M. Sanchez, Sept. 14, 1946; children—Laura M., George L. Came to U.S., 1961, naturalized, 1967. Intern, Univ. Hosp., Havana, 1947-48; chief interns and residents Dependientes Med. Center, Havana, Cuba, 1960-61; house physician Hillsborough County Hosp., Tampa, Fla., 1961-67; pvt. practice gen. medicine, Tampa, 1967—; mem. staffs

Univ. Community Hosp., Tampa, Tampa Gen. Hosp., Hillsborough County Hosp., Tampa, Centro Asturiano Hosp., Tampa, Centro Espanol Hosp., Tampa; med. dir. Cambridge Convalescent Center, Tampa, 1971-72; asst. dir. Havana Plaza Nursing Center, Tampa, 1971-72. Mem. Fla., Hillsborough County, So. med. assns., A.M.A., Assn. Fgn. Med. Grads., Cuban Med. Assn. Exile, Am. Acad. Family Physicians. Roman Catholic. Home: 2708 N Dundee St Tampa FL 33609 Office: 8003 9th St Tampa FL 33604

ALVERSON, LUTHER, superior ct. judge; b. East Point, Ga., Aug. 13, 1907; s. James Carroll and Minnie (Flemning)A.; student Emory U., LL.B., Atlanta Law Sch. 1941; m. Ruth Long, Mar. 21, 1942; children—Elizabeth (Mrs. Richard P. Heist), Patricia (Mrs. Robert M. Kelly). Admitted to Ga. bar, 1941; practiced in Atlanta, 1941-52; mem. firms Hooper, Hooper & Miller, 1941-43, Woodruff, Alverson & O'Neal, 1946-48; mem. Ga. Ho. of Reps., 1948-52; judge Fulton County Criminal Ct., Ga., 1952-56, Atlanta Jud. Circuit Superior Ct., 1957—. Bd. dirs., pres. YMCA; bd. dirs. Community Council, Ga. Assn. Mental Health, Family Service Soc., Atlanta; mem. exec. com. Joint Information Service; chmn. joint information service Am. Psychiat. Assn. and Nat. Assn. for Mental Health. Chmn. bd. dirs., exec. com. Nat. Assn. for Mental Health, 1953-60, pres., 1957-59, bd. dirs., 1966-69, 69-72, v.p. region, 1967-69. Served from pvt. to 1st lt., AUS, 1943-45. Mem. Ga. Council Superior Ct. Judges (pres. 1965-66), Am. Ga., Atlanta bar assns., Atlanta Lawyers Club, Delta Theta Phi (dean alumni senate). Democrat. Baptist. Clubs: Atlanta Athletic, Buckhead Civitan, Piedmont Driving, Druid Hills Golf (Atlanta). Home: 3635 Rembrandt Rd Atlanta GA 30327 Office: Fulton County Ct House Atlanta GA 30303

ALVES, JOHN JOSEPH, JR., petroleum co. exec.; b. Provincetown, Mass., Aug. 16, 1900; s. John Joseph and Rose Francis (Deking) A.; B.M.E., Northeastern U., 1922; m. Marie A. Duffley, June 6, 1923; children—John Joseph III, Robert Paul. With Worthington Corp., various locations, 1922-66, v.p., Buenos Aires, Argentina, 1962-65, gen. mgr. internat. sales, Harrison, N.J., 1965-66; v.p., Knight Industries, Inc., Tulsa, 1966-70, also dir.; v.p. Topper Oil Co., Tulsa, 1967—. Home: 4645 S Norwood Tulsa OK 74135 Office: 2300 E 14th St Tulsa OK 74104

ALVEY, BERNARD EUGENE, lumber co. exec.; b. Owensboro, Ky., Mar. 24, 1931; s. Bernard A. and Eugenia B. (Busam) A.; B.S., St. Louis U., 1953; m. JoAnn Temborn, Nov. 26, 1963; children—Miriam B., Berdette A., Bernard T. Sales mgr. Arnolt Corp., Los Angeles, 1956-64; pres. Alvey Bros. Lumber Co., Inc., Owensboro, 1964—; pres. Nanco Corp., Owensboro, 1966—, also dir.; pres. Breckinridge Enterprises, Owensboro, 1969—, also dir.; owner United Ins. Agy., Owensboro, 1965—; dir. Lastet Corp. Bd. dirs. Owensboro Symphony Orch. Served with USAF, 1953-56. Mem. Homebuilders Assn. (pres. 1970—, dir. 1969-72), St. Stephens Cathedral Council (dir. 1971-72). Club: Owensboro Country. Home: 2415 N Stratford St Owensboro KY 42301 Office: 425 Leichfield Rd Owensboro KY 42301

ALVIS, JAMES CHESTER, former ednl. adminstr.; b. Thomas, Okla., July 29, 1903; s. William Elmer and Effie (Falen) A.; grad. Southwestern State Tchrs. Coll., 1928; M.A., N. Tex. State Coll., 1943; m. Fairy Jewel McCain, July 20, 1928; 1 dau., Chestella Ann (Mrs. William A. Hudel). Athletic coach, tchr., Crescent, Okla., 1926-27, 28-29, Weatherford, Okla., 1927-28; prin. high sch., Temple, Okla., 1929-39; supt. schs., Byers, 1939-43, Springlake, 1943-45, Bandera, 1945-57, Nordheim, 1957-68 (all Tex.), ret., 1968; dir. Dist. III Soil and Water Conservation. Mayor, Nordheim, Tex. Active Boy Scouts; life mem. Parent Tchrs. Assn. Mem. N.E.A., Am., Tex assns. sch. adminstrs. Lion, Mason; mem. Order Eastern Star. Home: PO Box 158 Nordheim TX 78141 Office: 500 N Broadway Nordheim TX 78141

AMACKER, DAVID MUIR, educator, planter; b. East Carroll Parish, La., Feb 26, 1897; s. Amos Kent and Elizabeth Chalmers (Muir) A.; student Miss. Coll., 1912-13; A.B., Princeton, 1917; B.A. (Rhodes scholar), Oxford U., 1922, M.A., 1927. YMCA relief worker, Germany, summer 1920; researcher Inquiry, N.Y.C., spring 1923; instr. Culver (Ind.) Mil. Acad., 1923-26; instr. polit. sci. Dartmouth, 1926-30, asst. prof., 1930-36; asso. prof. history La. Poly. Inst., 1927-28; prof. polit. sci. Southwestern U. at Memphis, 1936-67, emeritus, 1967—, vis. prof., 1967-69; pres., dir. Hollybrook Land Co., Inc., Lake Providence, La., 1947—. Mem secretariat Am. Commn. to Negotiate Peace, Paris, 1919; interpreter League of Nations Commn., Paris, 1919. Dir. La. Delta Council, 1949-50; mem. Beltwide Cotton Acreage Conf., 1949. Alt. N.H. del. Dem. Nat. Conv., 1936. Served with AEF, 1917-19. Mem. Phi Beta Kappa. Methodist Home: 600 1st St Lake Providence LA 71254 Office: Hollybrook Land Co Lake Providence LA 71254

AMADEO, JOSE H., physician, educator; b. N.Y.C., July 16, 1928; s. H. R. and Carmen (Nigaglioni) A.; B.Sc., Ursinus Coll., 1948; M.D., Jefferson Med. Coll., 1952; m. Patricia Carron; children—Jose F. Javier, Luis Robert; children (by previous marriage)—Mary Martha, Jose H., John Michael, Jennifer. Intern Jefferson Med. Coll. Hosp., Phila., 1952-53, resident surgery, 1953-57, Am. Cancer Soc. fellow, 1956-57; instr. surgery Jefferson Med. Coll., 1959-61; chief surg. service San Juan (P.R.) VA Hosp., 1961—, prof. surgery U. P.R. Sch. Medicine, San Juan, 1961—. Mem. Phila. Dist. Health and Welfare Council, 1960-61. Served to capt. M.C., USAF, 1957-59; now lt. col. Res.; med. adviser to state dir. Selective Service. Diplomate Am. Bd. Surgery, Am. Bd. Thoracic Surgery, Nat. Bd. Med. Examiners. Fellow A.C.S., Internat. Soc. Surgery; mem. A.M.A., Pan Am. Med. Assn., Soc. Thoracic Surgery, Assn. Mil. Surgeons U.S., Am. Fedn. Clin. Research, Res. Officers Assn., Alpha Omega Alpha, Alpha Kappa Kappa. Republican. Roman Catholic. Contbr. articles to med. and surg. publs. Home: PO Box 10837 Caparra Heights PR 00922 Office: VA Hospital San Juan PR 00936

AMADOR, FRANCISCO ALBERTO, dentist; b. Quebradillas, P.R., Dec. 6, 1935; s. Alberto and Carmen Luisa (Rodriguez) A.; A.A., Sunflower Jr. Coll., 1953-55; predental student U. Md., 1955-57; D.M.D., U. P.R., 1961; m. Xochitl G. Aznar, June 20, 1959; children—Marissa C., Francisco A., Jorge A., Xochitl G. Individual practice dentistry, Camuy, P.R., 1964—; No. regional dir. Oral Health, Areclbo, P.R., 1963—. Mem. dental com. State Health Bd. P.R. Served with USAF, 1961-63, now maj. Res. Fellow Am. Pub. Health Assn.; mem. Colegio de Cirujanos Dentistas de P.R. (auditor 1969), Asociacion Dentistas Salud Publica de P.R. (pres. 1966-68), Am. Dental Assn., Am. Acad. Gen. Dentistry, Phi Eta Mu. Rotarian (pres. 1969-70), Lion (v.p. 1970-71). Home: Bo Terranova Quebradillas PR 00742 Office: District Hospital Arecibo PR 00612

AMARAL, JESUS EDUARDO, architect; b. Humacao, P.R., Oct. 13, 1927; s. Jesus and Ana Maria (Carmona) A.; B.C.E., Cornell U., 1948, B.Arch., 1951; m. Maria L. Bibloni, Apr. 11, 1953; children—Ana Maria, Maria Luisa, Maria Teresa, Eduardo Jose. Civil engr. P.R. Housing Authority, 1948; constrn. insp.-asst. to Miguel Ferrer Caribe Hilton Hotel Project; archtl. designer with office Rene Ramirez-Architect, 1953; individual practice architecture, 1954-55; architect with Urban Renewal Br. San Juan Municipal Housing Authority, 1955; partner firm Amaral y Morales-Arquitectos, Hato Rey, P.R., 1956-69; prin. J.E. Amaral-Arquitecto, Hato Rey, 1970—. Cons. architect for Instituto de Cultura de P.R. on historic restoration Old City San Juan, 1962-65; in charge orgn. new Sch. Architecture U. P.R., 1965-66; dir. Sch. Architecture, 1966-69; lectr. Sch. Engring. U. P.R. Mayaguez campus, 1964, 68. Mem. Com. on Hist. Monuments P.R., 1962-65; mem. com. to advise Instituto on Hist. Zone City Ponce, 1965; mem. P.R. Com. Soc. Archtl. Historians Tour Leeward Islands, V.I., P.R., 1967; tech. adviser to Spl. Com. on Natural Resources Chamber Reps. P.R., 1967-68. Mem. alumni secondary schs. com. Cornell U., 1966—. Served to 1st lt. USAF, 1951-53. Archtl. works include pvt. and pub. housing, apt. in condominium, apt. bldgs., hotels and motels, office, comml., indsl., ednl., sci., cultural, religious bldgs., also med., recreational, govtl. and transp. bldgs., sports complexes. Home: 578 Maximo Gomez St Hato Rey PR 00918 Office: Box 896 Hato Rey PR 00919

AMBERG, JACOB HENRY, dentist; b. Oklahoma City, Mar. 24, 1928; s. Jacob Henry and Courteney Delores (Herpin) A.; student Oklahoma City U., 1984-51; D.D.S., U. Kansas City, 1955; m. Claudine Myers, Apr. 23, 1971; children from previous marriage—Jacob Henry IV, Catherine Ann. Individual practice dentistry, Oklahoma City, 1955—. Served with USNR, 1946-48. Mem. Psi Omega (chaplain 1953-54). Lion. Home: 10917 Blue Stem Backroad Oklahoma City OK 73114 Office: 2546 NW 23d St Oklahoma City OK 73107

AMBROSE, CHARLES EDWARD, artist, educator; b. Memphis, Jan. 6, 1922; s. William Thomas and Minnie (Langdon) A.; B.F.A., U. Ala., 1949, M.A., 1950; m. Betty Carol Rainer, Oct. 21, 1950; children—Charles Edward, Michael Rainer, Marc Carroll, Jamie Elizabeth. Prof. art, resident artist U. So. Miss. at Hattiesburg, 1950-70; chmn. art dept. Miss. State Coll. Women, 1970—; exhibited in major cities of S.W.; art cons. U.S. Govt. programs. Pres., S. Miss. Art Assn.; mem. gov.'s staff State of Miss., 1969—; mem. adv. com. Miss. Art Assn.; trustee Hattiesburg Acad. Served with USMCR, 1941-45. Mem. Miss. Edn. Assn., La. Watercolor Soc., Internat. Platform Assn., S.E. Coll. Art Conf., So. Assn. Sculptors, Civitan Internat. (dist. gov. 1967-68). Elk. Home: 1907 Hwy 45 N Columbus MS 39701 Office: Box 70 MSCW Columbus MS 39701

AMBROSE, JOHN AUGUSTINE, chem. geneticist; b. Fort Dodge, Ia., Feb. 15, 1923; s. Abraham T. and Josephine (Vega) A.; student Marquette U., 1944-45, U. Wis., summers 1947-48; B.A., Johns Hopkins, 1948, postgrad (U. fellow), 1957-58; M.S., Marquette U., 1951; postgrad (USPHS fellow), Ind. U., 1958-60; Ph.D. (U. fellow), U. Miami (Fla.), 1965; m. Edith Louise Brockman, June 27, 1964; 1 dau., Dianne Louise. Research chemist Ore. State U., 1951-52; research biochemist Chgo. Med. Sch., 1952-54, Johns Hopkins Med. Sch., 1954-57; research chemist Metabolic Disorders Lab., Nat. Communicable Disease Center, USPHS, Atlanta, 1964-65, chief Mental Retardation Lab., 1965-67, chief Chem. Genetics Lab., 1967-70, chief Biochem. Genetics Metabolic Disorders Lab., Center for Disease Control USPHS, 1970-72, chief pediatric and Genetic chemistry unit, 1972—. Cons. state health depts., mental retardation activities. Mem. Atlanta chpt. Nat. Assn. for Retarded Children, 1967—. Fellow Am. Inst. Chemists; mem. Am. Pub. Health Assn., mem. A.A.A.S., Am. Chem. Soc., Am. Soc. Microbiology, N.Y. Acad. Sci., Sigma Xi, Phi Kappa Phi, Sigma Phi Epsilon. Moose. Research in enzymology, radiation chemistry, protein structure, microbiology, others. Home: 126 Surrey Circle NE 1 Chamblee GA 30341 Office: 1600 Clifton Rd Atlanta GA 30333

AMBURN, LUTHER FRANKLIN, JR., publisher; b. Boonville, N.C., Sept. 10, 1932; s. L. F. and Martha (Oakley) A.; grad. Mitchell Coll., 1952; postgrad. U. N.C., 1952-53; m. Emily Ann Greer, June 1, 1957; children— Martha Ruth, Melissa, Luther Franklin III, Paul, Emily. Rural carrier, circulation dept. Statesville Record Landmark, 1950-53, reporter, 1953-58, news editor, 1958-62; pres., gen. mgr., pub. Chowan Herald, Inc., 1965—; exec. dir. Edenton Housing Authority, 1968—; pres. Eden Press, Inc; co-mgr. Vance Motor Inn: 1962-64. Apptd. U.S. commr. Statesville div. Western Dist. Ct. of N.C., 1953-64; founder, 1st pres. Statesville Town Affiliation Council, 1961-62; sec.-treas. Iredell County Jr. Dept. Sheriff's League; pres. lo-County Albemarle Area Devel. Assn., 1972. Served with AUS, 1954-56. Mem. Edenton C. of C., Eastern N.C. Press Assn. (pres. 1971-72), Pi Kappa Phi. Democrat. Methodist. Elk. Clubs: Statesville City, Civitan (past pres.); Chowan Golf and Country. Home: 104 W Gale St Edenton NC 27932 Office: 421-425 S Broad St Edenton NC 27932

AMES, MRS. BOBBIE HACKNEY, civic worker, former mem. Republican Nat. Com.; b. Washington, N.C., July 23, 1930; d. James Acra and Mae (Ayers) Hackney; student Greensboro (N.C.) Coll., 1948-49, East Carolina coll., Greenville, N.C., 1949-50; m. John Brewer Ames, Dec. 30, 1950; children—Elizabeth, John Brewer II, Laurie and David (twins), James Hackney. Prin. Perry Christian Sch., Marion, Ala., 1965-66, 69, dir. boarding div., 1972—; dir. Ames Bag & Packaging Corp., Marion; elementary curriculum cons. Ala. Pvt. Sch. Assn. Pres. Ala. Fedn. Republican Women, 1965-67; mem. Rep. Nat. Com. for Ala., 1968-72. Pres. Dallas County Fedn. Ch. Women, 1952. Chmn. bd., sec. Perry County Crippled Children and Adults; bd. dirs. Central Ala. Occupational Rehab., Central Ala. Rehab. Facilities; chmn. bd. dirs. Ala. Recipient Woman of Year award Rep. Women of Ala., 1967, Woman of Achievement award Bus. and Profl. Women's Club, 1969. Mem. Nat. Assn. Pro America (chmn. bd. Ala. chpt.), Ala. Hist. Soc., Blackbelt Antiquarian Soc. Republican. Mem. Westminster Community Ch. Club: Selma (Ala.) Garden (past pres.). Home: Amesmont Marion AL 36756 Office: Box 670 Marion AL 36756

AMES, EDWARD ALMER, JR., banker; b. Onley, Va., Jan. 22, 1903; s. Edward Almer and Lena (Trower) A.; student Randolph Macon Coll., 1919-21; A.B., Washington and Lee U., 1924; LL.B., 1925; m. Elizabeth Johnson Melson, Jan. 8, 1936; 1 son, Edward Almer III. Admitted to Va. bar, 1924, since practiced in Accomack County; commonwealth's atty., Accomack County, 1943-55; dir. First Nat. Bank, Onanock, Va., 1953—, v.p., 1956-69, pres., 1969—. Mem. Va. Senate, 1956-68; chmn. Accomack County Democratic Com., 1948-69; mem. State Central Dem. Com. Va., 1956-72. Mem. Am., Va., Accomack County (pres. 1956-57) bar assns., Order of Coif, Phi Beta Kappa, Phi Delta Phi. Democrat. Presbyn. Mason, Rotarian. Clubs; Ruritan; Eastern Shore Yacht and Country; Downtown of Richmond. Home: Accomac VA 23301 Office: Onancock VA 23417

AMES, RICHARD KINGLEY, county ofcl., dentist; b. Daytona Beach, Fla., Mar. 16, 1936; s. Orris Kingsley and Helen Margaret (Reed) A.; A.A., U. Fla., 1957; D.D.S., Med. Coll. of Fla., 1961; m. Sheila Ann Jacob, Aug. 6, 1960; children—Richard Kingsley, Ramon Anthony, Sheryl Lynn, Christie Marie. Individual practice denistry, Pahokee, Fla., 1961-70; dental dir. Broward County Health Dept., Fort Lauderdale, Fla., 1971—; dental cons. Broward County, 1970—. Mem. Charter Revision Bd., City of Pahokee, 1969—. Mem. Am. (student clinician 1960), Fla. dental assns., Atlantic Coast Dist. Dental Soc., Am. Soc. Dentistry for Children, Am. Soc. Preventive Dentistry, C. of C. (v.p. 1967). Elk. Office: 2421 SW 6th Av Fort Lauderdale FL 33302

AMIR-MOEZ, ALI REZA, mathematician, educator; b. Teheran, Iran, Apr. 7, 1919; s. Mohammad and Fatema (Gorgestani)A-M.; B.A., U. Teheran, 1942; M.A., U. Cal. at Los Angeles, 1951, Ph.D., 1955. Came to U.S., 1947, naturalized, 1961. Instr. math. Teheran Tech. Coll., 1942-46; asst. prof. math. U. Ida., 1955-56, Queens Coll., N.Y.C., 1956-60, Purdue U., 1960-61; asso. prof. U. Fla., Gainesville, 1961-63; prof. math. Clarkson Coll., Potsdam, N.Y., 1963-65; prof. math. Texas Tech U., Lubbock; 1965—. Served to 2d lt. Persian Army, 1936-38. Decorated Honor emblem Persian Royal Ct. Mem. Am. Math. Soc., Math. Assn. Am., Soc. Indsl. and Applied Math., Sigma Xi, Pi Mu Epsilon. Author: Elements of Linear Space, 1961; (play) Kaleeheh & Demneh, 1962; Three Persian Tales, 1961, Matrix Techniques Trigonometry and Analytic Geometry, 1964; Mathematics and String Figures, 1966; Classes Residues et Figures ovec Fuelle, 1968; Extreme Properties of Linear Transformations and Geometry in Unitary Spaces, 1971. Contbr. articles to math. jours. on proper and singular values of linear operators and matrices.Office: Dept Math Texas Tech U Lubbock TX 79409

AMIS, GUY BALLARD, banker; b. Juno, Tenn., Dec. 11, 1897; s. August Joseph and Bettie (Ballard) A.; student W. Tenn. Tchrs. Coll., 1921, Union U., 1960-33; m. Dora Alberta Holmes, Dec. 24, 1923; 1 dau., Carol Ann (Mrs. William Thomas Stone). Tchr. and ins. salesman, 1921-30; sec.-treas., dir. Lexington Amusement Co., Inc. (Tenn.), 1930—; supt. Lexington City Schs; 1933-41; cashier Central State Bank, 1941-62, pres., 1962—; pres. Lexington Broadcasting Service, 1957-71, dir., 1957—; pres. Amis & Stone, Inc., 1960—. Bd. dirs. Lexington Indsl. Improvement Assn., Inc., 1946—, pres., 1970—; bd. dirs. Henderson County Fair Assn., 1960—; chmn. bd. dirs., v.p. W. Tenn. Indsl. Assn., Inc., 1956-62; chmn. Lexington Indsl. Com., 1941—; mem. Tenn. Indsl. and Agrl. Devel. Commn., 1967-71; mem. bd. Lexington Municipal Gas System. Served with Tenn. State Guard, 1941-45. Named Rotarian of Yr., 1969. Mem. Am., Tenn. (mem. legislative com. 1961-69, mem. exec. council 1964-67) bankers assns., Am. Judicature Soc. Democrat. Methodist. Rotarian (dir. 1955-56, 61-62). Club: Summit. Home: 208 Monroe St Lexington TN 38351 Office: Church and Monroe St Lexington TN 38351

AMLEY, EDWARD ARNOLD, dentist; b. Portland, Me., July 6, 1942; s. Arnold O. and Beth M. (Kehler) A.; B.A. in History, Duke, 1963; D.D.S., Emory U., 1967; certificate in orthodontics U. Pa., 1968; m. Margaret M. Shedd, June 18, 1966; 1 son, Edward A., Jr. Pvt. practice orthodontics, St. Petersburg, Fla., 1969—. Chmn. orthodontic sect. Pinellas County Dental Research Clinic, 1970-71; lectr. practice mgmt. U. Pa., 1971-72, Emory U., 1971-72. Chmn. Children Dental Health Week Com., 1971. Mem. C. of C. (mem. leadership seminar 1971-72), Pinellas County Dental Soc. Emory U. Alumni Soc. (pres. Pinellas County chpt. 1969-70). Conglist. Home: 1771 Serpentine Dr St Petersburg FL 33712 Office: 1751 66th St N St Petersburg FL 33710

AMONTREE, EDWARD JOSHUA, dentist; b. N.Y.C., May 2, 1919; s. Max and Elaine (Neger) Mandelbaum; A.B., Columbia Coll., 1941; A.B., Columbia Sch. of Dental and Oral Surgery; D.D.S., U. Chgo., 1944-45; m. Eva Johanna Hagenstein, July 17, 1955; children—Michael Joshua, Madelaine, Thomas Samuel. Practice of dentistry, N.Y.C., 1945-52; Sarasota, Fla., 1954—; mem. staff Sarasota Meml. Hosp.; pres. Shamont Corp., dental dir. Environmental Health and Light Inst. Served to capt., Dental Corps, AUS, 1942-44, 52-54. Mem. Fla., West Coast Dist., Manatee-Sarasota dental socs., First Dist. Dental Soc. of N.Y. Sarasota Power Squadron. Elk. Clubs: Ivy League, Bath and Racquet (Sarasota). Home: 3850 Tangier Terrace Sarasota FL 33579 Office: 3100 South Gate Circle Sarasota FL 33579

AMOS, MABEL SANDERS, state ofcl.; b. Brooklyn, Ala.; d. James Sanders and Hattie (Bethea) Sanders; ed. Ala. Coll. at Montavallo, State Tchrs. Coll. at Troy, Peabody Coll. Tchr. pub. schs.; stenographer State Tax Commn., Ala., 1931; rec. sec. to gov., 1939-66; sec. of state, Ala., 1967—. Vice pres. Interassn. Commns. Status of Women, 1970—. Mem. Bus. and Profl. Women's Club (exec. sec., commn. on status of women), Zonta. Democrat. Baptist. Address: Office of Sec of State State Capitol Montgomery AL 36104*

AMSLER, HENRY MOORE, banker, business exec.; b. Marienville, Pa., Mar. 20, 1896; s. Cornelius Washington and Ida (Moore) A.; student U. Pa., 1915; m. Jean Wilson, Sept, 27, 1918 (dec.); children—Henry C., E. Wilson; m. 2d, Hannah Goheen, Aug. 4, 1967. Mgr. New Wellsboro Store, Tioga W. Va., 1917 asst. supt., Birch Lumber Co., 1918-19; supt. mgr., dir., pres. Hamler Coal Co., Inc. and affiliated cos., Clarion, Pa., 1919-37; dir. emeritus First Seneca Bank & Trust Co., Oil City, Pa., 1932—; dir. Alta Co., Inc., Clarion, Pa.; owner Amsler Co., Clarion; partner Fishwell Co., Clarion, H &H Co., St. Petersburg, Fla. Mem. Clarion Town Council, 1930-42, pres., 1934-42. Trustee Polk State Sch., 1938-42, Clarion State Coll., 1946-58. Served as lt. comdr. USCG Res., World War II, dist. officer 7th Naval Dist., USCG Aux., 1942-45. Mem. St. Petersburg Power Squadron (comdr. 1944-46), Delta Phi Delta, Phi Sigma Kappa. Presbyn. (trustee). Mason. Clubs: St. Petersburg Yacht (Fla.); Oil City (Pa.); Classics Car Club Am.; Antique Automobile Am., Auburn Cord Duesenberg, Inc. Cal. Home: 707 Main St Clarion PA 16214 also 105 2d St N St Petersburg FL 33701 Office: 2 Grant St Clarion PA 16214 also 103 2d St N St Petersburg FL 33701

AMUSSEN, THEODORE S., museum ofcl., editor. Editor publs. Nat. Gallery of Art, Washington. Home: 3133 University Blvd Kensington MD 20795 Office: Nat Gallery of Art 6th St and Constitution Av Washington DC 20565*

ANDERLE, RICHARD JOHN, mathematician; b. N.Y.C., Oct. 8, 1926; s. Joseph and Jennie (Styskal) A.; B.A., Bklyn. Coll., 1948; postgrad. Am. U., 1957-58; m. Fay A. Leitch, June 12, 1960. Mathematician, Naval Weapons Lab., Dahlgren, Va., 1948-59, head, exterior ballistics br., 1959-60, head, astronautics div., 1960—. Lectr. math. Am. U., 1964—. Recipient Superior Civilian Service award Dept. Navy, 1960. Mem. Am. Inst. Aeronautics and Astronautics, Am. Geophys. Union, A.A.A.S. Lutheran (treas. 1963-64, councilman 1963-65). Contrb. to sci. textbooks. Home: 1320 Parcell St Fredericksburg VA 22401 Office: Naval Weapons Lab Dahlgren VA 22448

ANDERS, SARAH FRANCES, educator; b. Monroe, La.; d. Edward Eugene and Malda M. (Elliott) Anders; A.B., La. Poly. Inst., 1945; M.R.E., So. Bapt. Theol. Sem., 1948; M.A., Fla. State U., 1952, Ph.D., 1955; postdoctoral Rensselaer Poly Inst., 1965, U. N.H., 1968. Ednl. dir. 1st Bapt. chs., Quincy, Fla., 1948-52, Gadsden, Ala., 1952-53; asst. dir. research lab. Fla. State U., Tallahassee, 1953-55; faculty, chmn. sociology dept. Mary Hardin Baylor Coll., Belton, Tex., 1955-62; prof. sociology, head dept. La. Coll., Pineville, 1962—; vis. prof. So. Meth. U., summer 1961. Mem. Tex. Gov.'s Com. on Children and Youth, 1959; treas. La. Council Family Relations. Bd. dirs. Rapides YWCA; pres. bd. dirs. Cenla Community Action, 1966—; mem. bd. Family Service Agy., Child Guidance Center. Named Piper prof., State of Tex., 1959; NSF fellow, 1965, 1968. Mem. Am. Assn. U. Women, Southwestern Religious Research Assn. (past pres.), Nat., Tex. (past pres.) councils on family relations,

Southwestern Social Sci. Assn., Am. Sociol. Assn. Contbr. numberous articles to profl. jours. Home: 111 Mary St Pineville LA 71360

ANDERS, WILLIAM A., astronaut; b. Hong Kong, Oct. 17, 1933 (parents Am. citizens); s. Arthur F. and Muriel Anders; B.S., U.S. Naval Acad., 1955; M.S. in Nuclear Engring., Air Force Inst. Tech.; m. Valerie Elizabeth Hoard; children—Alan Frank, Glen Thomas, Gayle Alison, Gregory Michael, Eric William, Diana Elizabeth. Commd. 2d lt. USAF, 1955, advanced through grades to lt. col.; nuclear engr., also instr. polit. Air Force Weapons Lab., Kirtland AFB, N.M.; astronaut with Manned Spacecraft Center, NASA; exec. sec. Nat. Aeros. and Space Council, Washington. Mem. Am. Nuclear Soc., Tau Beta Pi. Office: New Exec Office Bldg Washington DC 20502

ANDERSEN, DANIEL JOHANNES, lawyer; b. Jamestown, N.Y., Nov. 3, 1909; s. Christian J. and Maria (Hansen) A.; A.B., George Washington U., 1937, J.D., 1940; postgrad. Army War Coll., 1965; m. Alice Klopstad, June 29, 1937; 1 dau., Dianne Marie (Mrs. Paul L. Tecklenberg). With U.S. Dept. Labor, Washington, 1933-37; statis, clk., procedures analyst-job analyst Social Security Adminstrn., U.S. Employment Service, Washington, 1937-40; admitted to D.C., U.S. Supreme Ct. bars, 1940; mem. firm Baker, Beedy & Magee, Washington, 1940-42, Magee, Bulow & Andersen, Washington, 1946-58; individual practice law, Washington, 1958—. Mem. men's bd. Florence Crittenton Home and Hosp., 1963—. Bd. dirs. Gettysburg Coll., 1963—, chmn. devel. com., mem. exec. com., 1965—; bd. dirs. Dr. O. E. Howe Found. Served with USAAF, 1941-46; ETO, MTO. Mem. Judge Advs. Assn. (pres.), Delta Phi Epsilon, Sigma Chi. Clubs: Newcomers (Washington); Chevy Chase (Md.); Nat. Lawyers, Nat. Press. Author: Job Descriptions and Code Manual, 1937. Home: 4441 Lowell St NW Washington DC 20016 Office: Woodward Bldg Washington DC 20005

ANDERSON, AMOS MILLEDGE, judge; b. Houston County, Ga., Dec. 7, 1908; s. Amos Milledge and Irene (Phillips) A.; student Emory U., 1926-28; J.D., Mercer (now Walter F. George) Sch. Law; 1932; m. Laura Killen Gilbert, July 18, 1930; children—Angela (Mrs. Fred M. Hasty), Laura Killen (Mrs. Laura A. Hedgepeth), Phyllis Irene (Mrs. Irvin G. Bullock), Amos Milledge III. Admitted to Ga. bar, 1931; practiced in Perry, 1931-39; Ga. dir. penal adminstrn., 1938-39; judge Superior Cts., Macon Jud. Circuit, 1939-44, 46-61, now emeritus; practiced law in Perry and Macon, 1945-46; v.p., trust officer The 1st Nat. Bank & Trust Co., Macon, 1961-71. Mem. Jud. Council Ga., 1956—; mem. rules com. Ga. Supreme Ct., 1954—. Mayor, Perry, 1934-39. Bd. dirs. Ga. Municipal Assn., 1936-39; trustee Mercer U., 1950-56, Ga. Indsl. Home; bd. govs. Stratford Acad. Chmn. Houston County Democratic Exec. Com., 1934-39. Served from apprentice seaman to lt. USNR, 1944-45. Mem. Am., Ga., Macon bar assns., Ga. Council Superior Ct. Judges, Am. Judicature Soc., Inst. Jud. Adminstrn. Rotarian. Home 1293 S Jackson Springs Rd Macon GA 31201

ANDERSON, BRUCE ROY, architect, artist; b. Newport, Ark., Oct. 7, 1907; s. George Roy and Ameila (Frei) A.; B.S., Auburn U., 1929; M. Arch., Harvard, 1936; m. Helen Venus McClain, Dec. 25, 1930; 1 son, Bruce Roy. Practice architecture, 1938—. Bd. dirs. Ark. Childrens Hosp., Little Rock. Served to capt. CWS, AUS, 1942-45. Mem. A.I.A., S.W., La. water color socs., Midsouthern Watercolorists, Harvard Grad. Sch. Design Assn., Cal. Water Color Soc., Sigma Nu. Methodist. Mason. Clubs: Harvard, Pleasant Valley Country; Spl. works include various colls., chs., hosps. Exhibited paintings nationally, including many one-man shows. Home: 320 Ridgeroad Little Rock AR 72207 Office: Comml Nat Bank Bldg Little Rock AR 72201

ANDERSON, CHARLES DARWIN, newspaper editor; b. Lakeville, Minn., Sept. 6, 1916; s. Paul H. and Mabel G. (Johnson) A.; student Ft. Dodge Jr. Coll., 1934-36; B.A., State U. Ia., 1938; m. Louise Elisabeth Wigdahl, Dec. 14, 1942. News editor Pierre (S.D.) Daily Capital Journal, 1938-52, Iowa City (Ia.) Press-Citizen, 1952-54; editorial asso. Sioux City (Ia.) Journal, 1954-60, Sunday editor, 1960-68; Sunday editor Dallas Morning News, 1968—. Served to lt. comdr., USNR, 1942-46, 50-51. Mem. S.D. Jr. C. of C. (nat. dir. 1950-51), Navy League, Retired Officers Assn. Elk. Office: Dallas Morning News Communications Center Dallas TX 75222

ANDERSON, CHARLES HILL, govt. ofcl.; b. Chattanooga, June 16, 1930; s. Ray and Lois (Entrekin) A.; J.D., U. Tenn., 1953; m. Virginia R. Baker, May 5, 1956; children—Eric Scott, Alicia Lea, Burton Hill. Admitted to Tenn. bar, 1953; practice law, Chattanooga, 1953-60; asso. gen. counsel Life & Casualty Ins. Co. Tenn., Nashville, 1960-69; U.S. atty. Middle Dist. of Tenn., Nashville, 1969—. Del. Tenn. Constl. Conv., 1965; chmn. Davidson County, (Tenn.) Republican party, 1965-66; mgr., Nixon-Agnew Campaign, Davidson County, 1968. Served to maj. AUS. Mem. Am., Tenn., Nashville bar assns., Assn. Life Ins. Counsel, Phi Delta Phi, Phi Kappa Phi. Republican. Presbyn. Editor: Tenn. Law Rev., 1951-53. Home: 4704 Granny White Pike Nashville TN 37220 Office: Room 879 US Courthouse Nashville TN 37203

ANDERSON, CHARLES KELLER, Air Force officer; b. Rochester, Minn., Feb. 2, 1920; s. Herman Edgar and Florence (Keller) A.; B.A., U. Wis., 1941; M.S., Mass. Inst. Tech., 1953; Ph.D., U. Colo., 1965; m. Doris Michell, Nov. 21, 1941 (div.); 1 son, Stephen R.; m. 2d, Pearl Mary Tracy, Feb. 2, 1950; children—Donna R., Grady C., Dewey K. Accountant Gen. Electric Co., Schenectady, 1941-42, 46-47; commd. 2d lt. USAF, 1943, advanced through grades to col., 1965; navigator, combat operations officer, Mediterranean, World War II; meteorologist, weather reconnaissance officer, Cal., Mass., Fla., Bermuda, 1947-52; weather staff officer, advanced meteorologist, tech. cons., Japan, Md., 1953-58, research geophysicist, Mass., 1959-62, astro-geophysicist, facility dir., Colo., 1962-68, ionospheric research dir., Va., 1968—. Decorated D.F.C., Air Medal with five oak leaf clusters, Commendation Medal. Mem. Am. Astron. Soc., Am. Geophys. Union, A.A.A.S., Am. Meteorol. Soc., Air Force Assn., Sigma Xi, Beta Alpha Psi, Phi Eta Sigma. Home: 8817 Gateshead Rd Alexandria VA 22309 Office: Air Force Tech Applications Center 6801 Telegraph Rd Alexandria VA 22313

ANDERSON, CHARLES WEBSTER, mdse. broker; b. Greenville, Ga., June 7, 1929; s. Charlie W. and Myrtice (James) A.; ed. pub. schs., corr. courses; m. Barbara June Colwell, Aug. 21, 1949; children—Barbara Cherry, Richard Charles, Scott Jay. Jr. draftsman Tovell Constrn. Co., 1946-47; freight agt. A.C.L. R.R. Co., 1949-53; spl. salesman Internat. Salt Co., 1953-61; owner C.W. Anderson & Co., Dublin, Ga., 1961—. Active Boy Scouts Am. Baptist (deacon). Mason (Shriner), Moose, Elk. Home: 1601 Roberson St Dublin GA 31021 Office: PO Box 905 303 5th Jefferson St Dublin GA 31021

ANDERSON, CLARENCE ALFRED, II, coll. dean; b. Randolph, N.Y., Oct. 14, 1921; s. Clarence Alfred and Grace (Vanderhoof) A.; B.A., St. John's Coll., Annapolis, Md., 1949; M.A. in Philosophy, U. Va., 1951; m. Irene Eleanor Webb, June 21, 1945; children—Erik V., Reilly R., John V., Dorothy Jo. Accountant, Kesler & Robinson, C.P.A.'s, Charlottesville, Va., 1953-58; accountant U. Va., Charlottesville, 1958-67; chief bus. officer, asst. prof. philosophy Patrick Henry Coll., U. Va., 1967-71; dean financial and adminstrv. services, asso. prof. Patrick Henry Community Coll., Martinsville, Va., 1971—. Scuba leader examiner YMCA, 1970—; scuba diver Nat. Assn. Underwater Instrs., 1967—; water safety instr. A.R.C., 1960—. Served to 1st lt. USAAF, 1942-45; MTO; ETO. Decorated Air medal with 1 silver and 4 bronze oak leaf clusters. Originator coll. seminar in creative morality. Home: 724 Beechnut Lane Martinsville VA 24112

ANDERSON, CLINTON PRESBA, U.S. senator; b. Centerville, S.D., Oct. 23, 1895; s. Andrew Jay and Hattie Belle (Presba) A.; student Dakota Wesleyan U., 1913-15, U. Mich., 1915-16; L.H.D., Dakota Weslyan U., 1933; D.Agr. (hon.), N.M. Coll. Agr. and Mechanic Arts, 1946; LL.D., U. Mich., 1946, St. Lawrence U., 1946, Mo. Valley Coll., 1949, U. Alaska, 1965; m. Henrietta McCartney, June 22, 1921; children—Sherburne, Presba, Nancy (Mrs. Ben L. Roberts). Reporter, editor, Albuquerque, N.M., 1918-22; mgr. ins. dept. N.M. Loan & Mortgage Co., 1922-24; owner ins. agy., Albuquerque, 1925-63. Treas. State of N.M., 1933-34; mem. 77th to 79th U.S. Congresses from New Mexico at large; sec. U.S. Dept. Agr., June, 1945-May 1948; U.S. senator from N.M., Profl. 1948—. Mem. Sears-Roebuck Found. Mem. Delta Theta Phi. Democrat. Presbyterian. Mason, Elk. Club: Rotary (pres. Rotary Internat. 1932-33). Home: 3621 Camino Alameda SW Albuquerque NM 87105 also Wesley Circle NW Washington DC 20016 Office: 215 5th SW Albuquerque NM 87101 also Senate Office Bldg Washington DC 20510

ANDERSON, CONWELL AXEL, coll. pres.; b. Sister Bay, Wis., May 24, 1926; s. Arthur J. and Amy (Seaquist) A.; grad. Bethel Jr. Coll., 1947; B.A., U. Ala., 1949, M.A., 1950, Ph.D.,1954; m. Marjorie Jean Erickson, Aug. 29, 1947; children—Sheryl Lorraine, Susan Lynn, Steven Conwell. Mem. faculty U. Ala., 1950-54; dean of coll., prof. history Mary Hardin-Baylor Coll., Belton, Tex., 1954-60; pres. Judson Coll., Marion, Ala., 1960-65, Md. Bapt. Coll., 1965; asso. dir. Inst. Higher Edn., U. Ga., Athens, 1966; pres. Averett Coll., Danville, Va., 1966—. Chmn. Pub. Sch. Week, 1960; mem. City Sch. Bd., Marion, Ala., 1965; Va. mem. membership council Regional Edn. Lab. for Carolinas and Va., 1968-71; pres. Danville Theatre Prodns., Inc., 1967-69; bd. dirs. Nat. Tobacco-Textile Mus., 1971—; bd. dirs. Danville YMCA, 1968—, pres., 1970-71; mem. edn. and culture com. Citizens Adv. Com., 1968-69; budget and planning com. Danville United Fund, 1968—; mem. City Beautiful Com., 1970—. Served with USNR, 1944-46. Decorated Purple Heart. Mem. Assn. So. Bapt. Colls. and Schs., Latin Am. Conf., So. Assn. Colls. for Women (pres. 1963-64), Ala. Edn. Assn. (pres. div. higher edn. 1963-64), Ala. Assn. Coll. Administrs. (pres. 1965), Ala. Assn. Ind. Colls. (v.p. 1963-65), Danville Hist. Soc. Baptist (deacon). Mason, Lion (dir. 1955-56, 59-60, tail twister 1963), Rotarian (dir. 1970—). Contbr. articles periodicals. Home: 174 Mountain View Av Danville VA 24541

ANDERSON, DARRELL RAYMOND, army officer; b. Red Wing, Minn., Mar. 2, 1930; s. Raymond O. and Florence (Voth) A.; B.S., U.S. Mil. Acad., 1954; M.S. in Civil Engring., U. Ill., 1960, M.S. in Nuclear Engring., 1960; m. Mary Grace Pelgrin, Dec. 21, 1954; children—Karen Marie, Linda Jean, Patricia Mary. Commd. 2d lt. U.S. Army, 1954, advanced through grades to lt. col., 1968; various engring. units, Germany, 1955-58, Korea, 1961-62; with Def. Intelligence Agy., 1962-65; with U.S. Army Command and Gen. Staff Coll., 1965-66; Anchorage area engr., dep. dist. engr. Alaska Dist., 1966-68; exec. officer Engr. Group, Vietnam, 1968-69; br. chief Combat Devel. Command Engr. Agy., Ft. Belvoir, Va., 1969-71, comdg. officer 1st Battalion USAESBDE, 1971—. Decorated Bronze Star medal, Army Commendation medal with oak leaf cluster, Meritorious Service medal. Registered profl. engr., Vt. Mem. Soc. Am. Mil. Engrs. Home: 6401 Twin Ct Springfield VA 22150 Office: 1st BN USAESBDE Ft Belvoir VA 22060

ANDERSON, DELIA MAY CASH (MRS. MACK HARVIE ANDERSON), librarian; b. Collins, Ark.; d. Hogan Allen and Carrie (Oliver) Cash; A.B., Ark. A. and M. Coll., 1938; M.S., U. Ark. 1952, La. State U., 1955; m. Mack Harvie Anderson, June 20, 1925; children—Mack Hogan, Alice Carolyn (Mrs. Earl Craig Beard). Tchr., DeSota Sch., Arkansas City, Ark., 1923-24, Yancopin Sch., Watson, Ark., 1924-26, Neal Sch., McGehee, Ark., 1926-27, 31-35, McGehee Pub. Schs., 1938-46; tchr.-librarian Desha Central Sch., Rowher, Ark., 1946-54; librarian Delhi (La.) High Sch., 1954-70, Dermott (Ark.) Pub. Schs., 1970—; vis. librarian, cataloger Ark. State U., summer 1964; instr. N.E. La State U., summer 1965-67, 68. Mem. N.E.A., Ark. Library Assn., A.L.A., Ark. Classroom Tchrs., Ark. Tchrs. Assn., Ark. Sch. Librarians Assn., Bus. and Profl. Women's Club (pres. 1948-49), Kappa Delta Pi, Delta Kappa Gamma. Baptist. Mem. Order Eastern Star. Home: RFD 1 Box 61 McGehee AR 71654 Office: Dermott High Sch Dermott AR 71638

ANDERSON, DICK EDWARD, banker; b. Chgo., May 1, 1930; s. Ocar E. and Hilma M. (Anderson) A.; B.S. in Bus. Adminstrn., U. Fla., 1957; postgrad. Sch. Banking of South, La. State U., 1962-64; m. Evelyn Joan Frank, June 9, 1956; children—Derek Edward, Stephanie Marie. Vice pres. 1st Nat. Bank of Miami (Fla.), 1957—; v.p., cashier Coral Way Nat. Bank, Miami, 1966; v.p. S.E. Data Processing, Inc., Miami, 1970—. Served with USNR, 1950-54. Mem. Am. Inst. Banking, Greater Miami C. of C. Home: 9245 SW 97th Av Miami FL 33156 Office: 100 S Biscayne Blvd Miami FL 33131

ANDERSON, EDWARD EUGENE, physician; b. Jackson, Miss., Sept. 19, 1936; s. William Eugene and Mabel (Koenig) A.; B.A., Vanderbilt U., 1957, M.D., 1961; m. Kay Klemens Kratz, June 14, 1969. Intern, resident in internal medicine Vanderbilt U. Hosp., 1961-63, clin. instr., 1971—; fellow in cardiology U. Va. Hosp., 1966-69; dir. coronary care unit St. Thomas Hosp., Nashville, 1969-71, cardiologist cardiovascular lab., 1969—; cons. disability determination sect. Social Security Adminstrn. Served with USNR and USMC, 1963-66. Mem. Aerospace Med. Assn., Am. Heart Assn., Phi Beta Kappa, Alpha Tau Omega. Roman Catholic. Home: 3503 Woodmont Lane Nashville TN 37215 Office: 21st and Hayes Med Bldg Nashville TN 37203

ANDERSON, ESTHER SANFREIDA, educator, orgn. exec.; b. Lincoln, Neb.; d. Frank H. and Anna (Swenson) Anderson; B.S., U. Neb., 1915, M.A., 1917; postgrad. U. Wis., 1921-22; Ph.D. (fellow), Clark U., 1932. Instr. geography U. Neb., 1918-21, 22-29, 30-36, asst. prof., 1936-42, 46-58; asso. geographer, geog. sect. M.I., War Dept., 1942-43; econ. statistician fgn. div. Bur. Planning and Statistics, WPB, 1943-45; economist, chief cordage unit, program br. Bur. Textile, Clothing and Leather, Civilian Prodn. Adminstrn., 1945-46; geographer, geography div. U.S. Bur. Census, 1958-61; cons. div. earth scis. Nat. Acad. Scis.-NRC, 1963-64. Fellow A.A.A.S. (mem. council 1958-60); mem. Nat. League Am. Pen Women (state and br. pres. 1952-54, br. treas. 1943-45, nat. treas. 1964-68, br. registrar 1968-69, auditor 1969-72, D.C. br. pres. 1972—), Am. Assn. U. Women, Am. Assn. U. Profs., Assn. Am. Geographers, Nat. Council Geog. Edn. (2d v.p. 1941-42, state dir. and coorinator 1932-39, 49-58, editor state bull. 1948-51), Soc. Woman Geographers, Internat. Geog. Union, Neb. Writers Guild, Sigma Xi, Delta Kappa Gamma, Gamma Theta Upsilon (2d nat. v.p., editor 1955-57), Sigma Delta Epsilon (nat. pres. 1959, dir. 1957-60, chmn. awards. com. 1951-53), Phi Sigma. Author, co-author various publs. including: Regions and Nations of the World (text); also articles. Home: PO Box 28004 Central Sta Washington DC 20005

ANDERSON, FELIX SYLVESTER, bishop; b. Wilmington, N.C., Oct 3, 1893; s. Charles and Betty (Foye) A.; A.B., Livingstone Coll., 1920; postgrad. Hood Theol. Sem., 1920-21, Western Theol. Sem., 1922-24; m. Bessie Bezzell, Apr. 28, 1920; children—Felix Sylvester, Herman L., Mrs. Wright P. Robinson, Joseph D., Theodore M., Mrs. Alfred Haney. Ordained to ministry A.M.E. Zion Ch.; pastor in N.C., Ala., R.I., and Ky., 1916-60; bishop of Louisville, 1960—; tchr. P.W. Moore High Sch., Elizabeth City, N.C., 1929-31. Pres. Mobile Civic Orgn., 1942-48; chmn. Louisville Civic Orgn., 1950-54. Mem. Ky. Ho. of Reps., 1954-60. Recipient plaque for service Ky. Gen. Assn. A.M.E. Zion Ministerial Alliance, 1954-58. Mem. N.A.A.C.P. (life), Ky. Tchrs. Assn., Ky. Fraternal Police Officers. Democrat. Home: 741 S 44th St Louisville KY 40211

ANDERSON, FRANK JOHN, librarian; b. Chgo., Jan. 29, 1919; s. Charles Emil and Alida (Solomon) A.; student U. Conn., 1947-48; A.B., Ind. U., 1950; M.S., Syracuse U., 1951; m. Jeanette Irene Rioux, Feb. 17, 1944; 1 dau., Maria Alida. Librarian, Kan. Wesleyan U., 1952-56; br. head East Chicago (Ind.) Pub. Library, 1956-57; dir. Submarine Library, Groton, Conn., 1957-60; librarian Kan. Wesleyan U., Salina, 1960-66, Wofford Coll., Spartanburg, S.C., 1966—. Owner, mgr. Kitemaug Books, Spartanburg, 1959—, Kitemaug Press, 1965—. Served with submarine service USNR, 1943-45, 51-52. Mem. Spl. Libraries Assn., Southeastern, S.C. (chmn. coll. and univ. sect. 1970-72) library assns., Am. Assn. Prof. (chpt. sec. 1968—), Am. Civil Liberties Union, U.S. Naval Inst., Amalgamated Printers Assn. Author: Submarines, Submariners and Submarining, 1963. Book reviewer Library Jour., 1954—. Contbr articles to profl. publs. Home: 229 Mohawk Dr Spartanburg SC 29301

ANDERSON, FRITHIOF BERTRAM, communications engr; b. Phila., Dec. 27, 1903; s. George and Louise (Michaelis) A.; B.S., in Elec. Engring., U. Pa., 1926, E.E., 1934; m. Dorothy Harp Smalley, Apr. 4, 1931; (dec. 1967); 1 dau., Ruth (Mrs. Arthur Andrew Trimble); m. 2d, Flora Truett Ross, Oct. 23, 1971. Mem. tech. staff Bell Telephone Labs., Inc., N.Y.C., 1926-64, communications engr. Bradenton, Fl., 1964-67, Chamblee, Ga., 1967—; newspaper columnist, 1970—. Mem. Mensa, Atlanta Writers Club, Dixie Council Authors and Journalists, Theosophical Soc., Eta Kappa Nu. Mason. Author: Upsidown, 1966; Stay A Notion Ahead:, 1967—; Jesus Started Something:, 1969. Home: 3361 Chamblee-Tucker Rd Chamblee GA 30341

ANDERSON, GEORGE DAVID, JR., dentist; b. Fort Valley, Ga., Dec. 17, 1935; s. George David and Ethel (Taylor) A.; B.S., U. N.C., 1958, D.D.S., 1961, certificate in orthodontics, 1969; m. Carolyn Frances Bennett, Oct. 12, 1957; children—Jo Ellen, Pamela Leigh, Julie Lynn. Individual practice gen. dentistry, So. Pines, N.C., 1961-67; practice dentistry limited to orthodontics, Pinehurst, 1969—; dir. VAN, Inc., So. Pines. Cons. and part time instr. U. N.C. Served with AUS, 1961-62. Mem. Am. Dental Assn., Am. Assn. Orthodontists, So. Soc. Orthodontists, N.C. Orthodontic Soc., N.C. Dental Soc. Elk, Kiwanian. Home: 145 Highland Rd Southern Pines NC 28387 Office: Pinehurst Medical Center Pinehurst NC 28374

ANDERSON, GERALDINE ANN MCMURRY (MRS. JAMES LAVERNE ANDERSON), educator; b. Corpus Christi, Tex., Jan. 18, 1941; d. Allen Turk and Mary Louise (Smith) McMurry; B.S., East Tex., State U., 1963, M.S., 1964, Ph.D., 1967; m. James LaVerne Anderson; children—Robert Joseph, William Turk. Asst. prof. counselor edn. U. Ga., Athens, 1967—, coordinator tutorial enrichment program, 1969-71, coordinator field experience I, elementary edn. program, 1971—. Mem. Am. Personnel and Guidance Assn., N.E.A., Assn. for Counselor Edn. Supervision, Student Personnel Assn. for Tchr. Edn., Am. Coll. Personnel Assn., Ga. Edn. Assn., Kappa Delta Pi. Home: 135 Cedar Creek Dr Athens GA 30601

ANDERSON, HERSCHEL VINCENT, librarian; b. Charlotte, N.C., Mar. 14, 1932; s. Paul Kemper and Lillian (Johnson) A.; B.A., Duke, 1954; M.S.; Columbia 1959. Librarian, Bklyn. Pub. Library, 1954-55, 57-59; asst. bookmobile librarian King County Pub. Library, Seattle, 1959-67; asst. librarian Longview (Wash.) Pub. Library, 1962-63; librarian N.C. Mus. Art, Raleigh, 1963-64; audio-visual cons. N.C. State Library, Raleigh, 1964-68; dir. Sandhill Regional Library, Rockingham, N.C., 1968-70; asso. state librarian Tenn. State Library and Archives, Nashville, 1970—. Served with AUS, 1955-57. Mem. Am., Southeastern, Tenn. library assns., Tenn. Hist. Soc., N.C. Art Soc., N.C. Lit. and Hist. Soc., Phi Kappa Psi. Episcopalian. Home: Box 1623 Nashville TN 37202 Office: Tennessee State Library and Archives Nashville TN 37219

ANDERSON, JACK NORTHMAN, newspaper columnist; b. Long Beach, Cal., Oct. 19, 1922; s. Orlando N. and Agnes (Mortensen) A.; student U. Utah, 1940-41, Georgetown U., 1947-48, George Washington U., 1948; m. Olivia Farley, Aug. 10, 1949; children—Cheri, Lance F., Laurie, Tina, Kevin N., Randy, Tanya, Rodney, Bryan. Reporter, Salt Lake Tribune, 1939-41; war corr. Deseret News, 1945; reporter Washington Merry-go-Round, 1947—, partner, 1965—; Washington editor Parade mag., 1954-68, bur. chief, 1968—. Missionary in So. states for Church of Jesus Christ of Latter Day Saints, 1941-44; sec., trustee Chinese Refugee Relief, 1962—. Served with U.S. Mcht. Marine, 1944-45; with AUS, 1946-47. Mem. White House Corr. Assn. Club: Nat. Press (Washington). Author: (with Ronald May) McCarthy the Man, the Senator, the Ism, 1952; (with Fred Blumenthal) The Kefauver Story, 1956; (with Drew Pearson) U.S.A. Second Class Power, 1958; Washington Expose, 1966. Home: 7300 Burdette Ct Bethesda MD 20034 Office: 1612 K St NW Washington DC 20006

ANDERSON, JACK R., physician; b. New Orleans, 1917; M.D., La. State U., 1942. Intern Norfolk Naval Hosp., Protsmouth, Va., 1942-43; resident Eye, Ear, Nose and Throat Hosp., New Orleans, 1947-49, now mem. active staff; chief otolaryngology ind. service Charity Hosp. New Orleans, 1955-61; asst. prof. Tulane U., 1949—. Served to lt. comdr. M.C., USN, 1942-46. Diplomate Am. Bd. Otolaryngology. Fellow Internat. Coll. Surgeons; mem. A.C.S., A.M.A., Am. Soc. Ophthalmology and Otolaryngology, Am. Acad. Facial Plastic and Reconstructive Surgery (pres. 1963-64; sec. 1964-69; pres. elect 1971), So. Med. Assn., Am. Acad. Ophthalmology and Otolaryngology. Contbr. articles to profl. jours. Home: 481 Fairfield Av Gretna LA 70053 Office: 1111 Tulane St New Orleans LA 70112*

ANDERSON, JAMES BYRD, JR., fashion designer; b. Columbia, S.C., Nov. 1, 1921; s. James Byrd and Louise (Miller) A.; A.B., U. S.C., 1941; postgrad. Traphagen Sch. Fashion, U. Miami. Designer, Maurice Rentner of N.Y., 1941-42; pres., treas. Posh, Inc., Miami, Fla., 1955—. Served to capt. AUS, 1942-46. Decorated Bronze Star. Recipient Resort Fashion award 1958. Home: 943 N Venetian Dr Miami FL 33139 Office: 50 NW 10th St Miami FL 33136

ANDERSON, JAMES FRANKLIN, librarian; b. Prairie, Miss., May 22, 1941; s. Robert Alonzo and Elizabeth (Black) A.; B.S., Miss. State U., 1963; M.S. in L.S., La. State U., 1966; M.B.A., Ark. State U., 1971; m. Mary Alice Colvert, July 12, 1969; children (by previous marriage)--Lee, Tracy, Glen, Nancy. Head cataloger Dean B. Ellis Library, Ark. instr. library sci., 1967-71; dir. First Regional Library, Hernando, Miss., 1972-—. Served with AUS, 1964. Mem. A.L.A., Southwestern, Ark. (pres. resources and tech. services div. 1971), N.E. Ark. library assns. Methodist. Contbr. articles to profl. jours. Home: 69 North St Hernando MS 38632 Office: First Regional Library 59 Commerce St Hernando MS 38632

ANDERSON, JEFF LENVOL, mfr.; b. Carthage, Tex., May 11, 1923; s. Abner Lenvol and Willard (Wall) A.; B.S., U. Houston, 1950; postgrad. W. Tex. State U., 1966-—; m. Kathleen Reagan, Jan. 20, 1946; children—Timothy Warren, Karen Teresa, Sandra Jean. Materials and prodn. control mgr. Lone Star Boat Co., Plano, Tex., 1960-64; plant mgr. Metal Structures Corp., Grapevine, Tex., 1964; prodn. control mgr. Load Craft, Inc., Brady, Tex., 1964-65; material mgr. machinery div. Cabot Corp., Pampa, Tex., 1965-—; instr. U. Houston, 1953. Served with USCG, 1942-46. Registered profl. engr., Okla. and Kan. Mem. Am. Inst. Indsl. Engrs. (past pres. Wichita chpt.). Republican. Methodist. Club: Pampa Kiwanis (dir. 1967-69). Home: 1916 Lynn St Pampa TX 79065 Office: PO Box 1101 Pampa TX 79065

ANDERSON, JERRY DEAN, basketball coach; b. Lexington, Okla., Dec. 2, 1927; s. Perry D. and Grace (King) A.; B.S., E. Central State Coll., Ada, Okla., 1951; M.S., Okla. U., 1955; m. Letitia M. Swoap, Jan. 20, 1950; children—Michael David, Ronald Kent. Basketball coach Stratford (Okla.) High Sch., 1951-52, Blackwell (Okla.) High Sch., 1952-56, Panhandle State Coll., Goodwell, Okla., 1956-67; basketball coach E. Central State Coll., Ada, 1967-—. Active various civic and ch. groups. Served with AUS, 1946-47. Recipient Outstanding Citizen award C. of C., 1967. Mem. Nat. Basketball Coaches Assn., Okla. Tchrs. Assn., Okla. Coaches Assn. Democrat. Methodist. Elk, Kiwanian. Home: 1600 S Broadway Blvd Ada OK 74820

ANDERSON, JOHN CECIL, educator; b. Waterview, Ky., Aug. 23, 1918; s. Leslie C. and Ruby (Anderson) A.; diploma Moody Bible Inst., 1941; B.A., U. Ill., 1948; postgrad., 1963; Th.M., Dallas Theol. Sem., 1952, Th.D., 1959; m. Harriet Lucille Van Order, Nov. 23, 1945; children—John Douglas, Anita Ellen, James Carroll. Teaching fellow Dallas (Tex.) Theol. Sem., 1952-55; prof. Greek and Hebrew, William Jennings Bryan Coll., Dayton, Tenn., 1955-—. Bd. dirs. Rhea-Dayton-Bryan Credit Union, Dayton. Served with USNR, 1942-46. Mem. Evang. Theol. Soc. (pres. So. sect. 1966). Home: Hwy 27 S Dayton TN 37321

ANDERSON, JOHN EDWIN, JR., coll. adminstr.; b. Akron, O., Jan. 26, 1932; s. John Edwin and Ella (Kennedy) A.; B.A., U. Akron, 1953; Ph.D., Ohio State U., 1957; m. Joyce E. Querry, June 11, 1956; children—Christie Lynn, John Edwin III, Karen Joyce. Instr. Rochester Inst. Tech., 1957-58; asst. to asso. prof. psychology Fla. State U., 1958-63; prof. psychology, dean of coll. Columbus (Ga.) Coll., 1963-—. Chmn. bd. dirs. Brookstone Sch.; adv. com. div. vocational rehab. Ga. Dept. Edn. Registered psychologist, Ga.; certified psychologist, Fla. Mem. Am. Psychol. Assn. Rotarian. Home: 3411 Cambridge Dr Columbus GA 31906 Office: Columbus College Columbus GA 31907

ANDERSON, JOHN PALMER, coll. adminstr.; b. New Orleans, Mar. 27, 1939; s. William Wyatt and Lottie Palmer (Johnson) A.; B.S., Ga. Inst. Tech., 1961, M.S. in Engring. Mechanics, 1963, M.S. in Math., 1964, Ph.D., 1966; m. Mary Agnes Harris, June 16, 1962; children— Deborah Louisa, Michael Gary. Asst. prof. Ga. Inst. Tech., Atlanta, 1965-66; asst. prof. U.S. Air Force Acad., Colorado Springs, Colo., 1966-67, asso. prof., 1967-68; asso. prof. engring. and math. U. Ala., Birmingham, 1968-71, asst. to v.p., 1971-—. Served to capt., AUS, 1966-68. Mem. Am. Soc. M.E., Am. Soc. C.E., Am. Soc. Engring. Edn. (sec. mechanics div. 1968-—), Sigma Xi, Tau Beta Pi, Pi Mu Epsilon, Phi Kappa Phi. Methodist. Home: 3424 Brookwood Rd Mt Brook Alabama 35223 Office: Office Vice Pres U Alabama Birmingham AL 35233

ANDERSON, JOHN QUINCY, educator; b. Wheeler, Tex., May 30, 1916; s. Albert Slayton and Emily (Grant) A.; B.A., Okla. State U., 1939; M.A., La. State U., 1948; Ph.D., U.N.C., 1952; m. Marie Loraine Epps, Aug. 24, 1946. Asst. prof. McNeese State Coll., 1952-53; faculty Tex. A. and M. U., College Station, 1953-66, prof. English, 1959-66, head dept., 1962-66; prof. English, U. Houston, 1966-—. Served to capt. AUS, 1940-46. Decorated French Medaille de la Reconnaissance. Mem. Modern Lang. Assn., S. Central Modern Lang. Assn., Am. Studies Assn. Tex. (pres. 1963-64), Am. Studies Assn. (exec. council 1964-67), Southwestern (editor 1970-—), Western Am. lit. assns., Am., Tex. (pres. 1955-56) folklore socs. Author: Brokenburn: The Journal of Kate Stone, 1955; A Texas Surgeon in the C.S.A., 1957; Louisiana Swamp Doctor: The Life and Writings of Henry Clay Lewis, 1962; Tales of Frontier Texas, 1966; Campaigning with Parsons' Texas Cavalry, C.S.A., 1967; John C. Duval, First Texas Man of Letters, 1967; With the Bark On: Popular Humor of the Old South, 1967; Texas Folk Medicine, 1970; The Liberating Gods: Emerson on Poets and Poetry, 1971. Mem. editorial bd. Miss Quar., 1963-—; Computer Studies in Verbal Behavior and the Humanities, 1966-—, Paisano Books, Tex. Folklore Soc., 1968-—. Contbr. numerous articles to profl. jours. Home: 11327 Gaymoor St Houston TX 77035

ANDERSON, JOHN WEIR, newspaper editor; b. Phila., Sept. 29, 1928; s. Henry Ince and Marian (Carter) A.; A.B., Williams Coll., 1950; m. Madelyn Anne Streeter, Apr. 28, 1956; children—Hilary Elissa, Adam Weir. Reporter, York (Pa.) Dispatch, 1953-55, Reading (Pa.) Times, 1955-56 Congl. fellow Am. Polit. Sci. Assn. 1956-57; reporter Washington Post, 1957-61, 67-68, editorial writer, 1961-67, city editor, 1968-70, fgn. editor, 1970-71, editorial writer, 1971-—. Served with AUS, 1946-48. Author: Eisenhower, Brownell and the Congress: The Origins of the Civil Rights Bill of 1956-57, 1964. Home: 514 Prince St Alexandria VA 22314 Office: 1515 L St NW Washington DC 20005

ANDERSON, LARRY VANCE, librarian; b. Gorman, Tex., Oct. 16, 1935; s. Herman Asa and Winnie Davis (Morgan) A.; student Tarleton State Coll., 1958-59; B.A., U. Tex. at Austin, 1961; M.S. in L.S., East Tex. State U., 1967; m. Elsie Jean Miners, Dec. 23, 1961; children— Winifred Jean, Margaret Elizabeth. Tchr. English, New Braunfel (Tex.) Ind. Sch. Dist., 1961-62, Desdemona, 1962-64, Kopperl, 1964-65; acquisitions librarian E. Tex. State U., 1965-67; head librarian Laredo (Tex.) Jr. Coll., 1967-72; head librarian Western Tex. Coll., Snyder, 1972-—. Farmer and rancher, Comanche, Tex., 1957-—. Served with AUS, 1954-57. Mem. Tex. Library Assn., Tex. State, Tex. Jr. Coll. tchrs. assns., Tex. Sheep and Goat Raiser Assn., Rhodesians Soc. Baptist. Mason; mem. Order Eastern Star (asso. patron 1962-—). Home: 600 29th St Snyder TX 70549

ANDERSON, LEE STRATTON, newspaper editor; b. Trenton, Ky., Dec. 15, 1925; s. Herbert Love and Corinne (Kirkpatrick) A.; A.B., U. Chattanooga, 1948; m. Elizabeth McDonald, June 10, 1950; children—Corinne Elizabeth, Mary Stewart. Reporter, Chattanooga News-Free Press, 1942-48, asso. editor, 1948-58, editor, 1958-—; pres. Trail of Tears Inc., Gatlinburg, Tenn., Anderson-Meyers Enterprises, Inc., operator Confederama. Pres. Chattanooga Conv. and Visitor's Bur., 1958; chmn. Chattanooga chpt. Visitor's Bur., 1958. Chmn. Chattanooga chpt. A.R.C., 1969-71. Served with USAAF, World War II. Recipient Freedoms Found. award for editorial writing, 1959, 60, 63, 64, 65, 66, 67, 68, 69, 71, Freedoms Found. award for speech 1962, Liberty Bell award Chattanooga Bar Assn., 1968. Mem. Sigma Chi. Presbyn. (elder). Rotarian (pres. Chattanooga 1964-65). Author: Valley of the Shadow: Battles of Chickamauga and Chattanooga 1863. Home: 220 N Crest Rd Chattanooga TN 37404 Office: 400 E 11th St Chattanooga TN 37401

ANDERSON, MABLE BELL, educator; b. Birmingham, Ala., Sept 7, 1930; d. I. C. and Beatrice (Craddock) Bell; B.S. (inst. scholar), Tuskegee Inst., 1950; M.A. (univ. scholar), Mich. State U., 1952; Ed.D., Pa. State U., 1965; postgrad. Grambling Coll., summer 1960, Bank St. Coll. Edn., summer 1967, Yeshiva U., summer 1967; m. Furman C. Anderson, June 9, 1958 (div. May 1965). Instr. home econs. and health Fayette County Tng. Sch., Fayette, Ala., 1950-51; tchr.-trainer in home econs. edn. and child devel. Grambling Coll., 1952-54; mem. faculty child devel. and family relationships Miles Coll., Birmingham, 1954-60; presch. asst. tchr. Pa. State U., 1961-62; dir. Migrant Day Care Center, Dept. Child and Family Welfare, Harrisburg, Pa., summer 1961, social caseworker, summer 1962; prof. child devel., chmn. grad. studies in home econs. Tenn. A. and I. State U., 1963-66; prof. elementary edn. Western Ky. U., Bowling Green, 1966-69, supr. student tchrs. in elementary edn., 1966; prof. Center for Early Childhood Personnel Devel., State Coll. Ark., Conway, 1969-70; prof. edn., coordinator early childhood edn., asso. dir. tchr. corps. Albany (Ga.) State Coll., 1970-—. Instr., guest lectr. Head Start Tchr. Tng. programs George Peabody Coll., Pa. State U., 1965; workshop leader TACUS tchrs., Chattanooga and Knoxville, Tenn., 1966, 67; rep. Ky. Com. on Early Childhood Edn., 1966-70; adviser, cons. kindergartens, day care centers, Bowling Green, 1967-70; mem. com. Ga. Comprehensive Early Childhood Devel. programs; chmn. Dougherty County Task Force in comprehensive Early Childhood Devel. programs cons. Warren County-Bowling Green Assn. Mental Retardation, 1966-70, Coll. of Ozarks, Clarksville, 1969-—; lectr., cons. P.R. Dept. Edn., San Juan; mem. Ark. Gov.'s Task Force Com. on Early Childhood, 1969-—; bd. dirs., tech. adv. So. Ky. Econ. Opportunity Council, 1967-—. Mem. Soc. Research in Child Devel., Assn. Childhood Edn. Internat. (dir. 1970-—), Nat. Council Family Relations (dir. 1969-70), Ky. Edn. Assn., Nursery-Kindergarten Nat. Edn. Assn., Am. Home Econs. Assn., Am. Assn. U. Women, Am. Assn. U. Profs., Groves Conf. Family Life. Home: PO Box 876 Albany GA 31702

ANDERSON, MARIAN MCCUTCHEN (MRS. WILLIAM WHITE ANDERSON), hosp. adminstr.; b. Bishopville, S.C., June 2, 1913; d. Robert Othello and Florence (Jenkins) McCutchen; student U. S.C., 1930-32, 36; grad. Draughan's Bus. Coll. 1936; m. William White Anderson, May 30, 1941 (dec. May 1949); children—Susan Anderson (Mrs. Donald Eugene Mathis), McCutchen Brooks. Chief clk. Selective Service Bd., 1941-42; sec.-bookkeeper Ashwood Area Vocational Sch., Bishopville, 1949-50; bookkeeper Lee County Meml. Hosp., Bishopville, 1950-58, adminstr., 1958-—. Mem. Santee-Wateree Health Planning Council. Bd. dirs. Lee County Mental Health Assn., Lee County chpt. A.R.C., Mem. Am., S.C. hosp. assns., Hosp. Financial Mgmt. Assn. (Follmer award for outstanding service S.C. chpt. 1966, sec. 1966-—), Internat. Platform Assn., French Huguenot Soc., Soc. Magna Charta Dames. Presbyn. Home: 211 S. Heyward St Bishopville SC 29010 Office: Church St Extension Bishopville SC 29010

ANDERSON, MAURICE GEORGE, photog. mfg. co. exec.; b. Rochester, N.Y., Mar. 16, 1911; s. George Perry and Emma (Converse) A.; B.A., Oberlin (O.) Coll., 1934; postgrad. Rochester Inst. Tech., 1947; m. Helen Stolarcyk, Aug. 26, 1939; 1 dau., Beatrice (Mrs. Waldo Hunter Allen). Mgr. paper quality control; mgr. film quality control, gen. mgr. quality control, dir. product operation tech. Gen. Aniline & Film Corp., Binghamton, N.Y., 1935-62; dir. quality control, mgr. operations, v.p. operations Kalvar Corp., New Orleans, 1962-—, now exec. v.p. Pres. bd. dirs. Social Welfare Planning Council New Orleans; vice chmn., bd. dirs. Welfare Planning Council Broome County. Mem. Soc. Photog. Scientists and Engrs., Soc. Photog. Instrumentation Engrs., A.A.A.S., Am. Soc. Testing Materials. Rotarian. Home: 300 Spencer Av New Orleans LA 70124 Office: 907 S Broad St New Orleans LA 70125

ANDERSON, RALPH E., baking co. exec.; b. Manor, Tex., Jan. 26, 1919; s. Ralph E. and Ruth (Widen) A.; m. Margaret Droemer, May 21, 1939; children—Gary, David, Kathy. Route salesman Richter's Bakery, San Antonio, 1943-47; sales supr. Richter Baking Co., Corpus Christi, Tex., 1947-51, gen. sales mgr., 1951-66, now dir.; v.p., gen. mgr. Austin Baking Co. (Tex.), 1967-—, also dir. Served with AUS, 1943-46. Mem. Tex. Bakers Assn. (pres., dir.). Lutheran. Lion, Rotarian. Home: 8711 Tallwood Dr Austin TX 78759 Office: 5800 Airport Blvd Austin TX 78752

ANDERSON, ROBERT CLETUS, educator; b. Birmingham, Ala., July 18, 1921; s. Allie Cletus and Dana (Hilliard) A.; B.S., Auburn U., 1942; M.A., U. N.C., 1947; Ph.D., N.Y.U., 1950; m. Margaret Campbell Spidle, June 2, 1942; children—Margaret Campbell, William Robert. Research asst. Inst. for Research in Social Sci., U. N.C., 1946-47; Gonoraf Edn. Bd. fellow, 1947-48; asst. to dean Sch. of Edn., N.Y.U., 1948-50; dir. The Grad. Sch., Memphis State U., 1950-53; exec. asso., So. Regional Edn. Bd., 1953-55, asso. dir. 1955-57, dir. 1957-61; exec. v.p. Auburn U., 1961-65; v.p. research U. Ga., Athens, 1965-—. Dir. So. Regional Project on Ednl. TV, So. Regional Edn. Bd., 1952, So. Regional Conf. on Edn. Beyond the High Sch., 1957; mem. nat. council Nat. Planning Assn., 1958-—; mem. Surgeon Gen.'s cons. group on Med. Edn., 1958-59; mem. W. K. Kellogg Found. Ednl. Adv. com., 1960-64, Joint Council on Ednl. Telecommunications, 1961-69 (v.p. 1965-67); chmn. council for research policy and adminstrn. Nat. Assn. State Univs. and Land-Grant Colls., 1965-67. Chmn. exec. com. Skidaway Inst. Oceanography, 1968-69. Served from 2d lt. to capt. AUS, 1942-46, ETO. Decorated Purple Heart. Mem. Am. Council on Edn. (mem. council on fed. relations 1963-67), Am. Assn. for Higher Edn. (com. on research and devel. 1967-68), Phi Kappa Phi, Alpha Tau Omega, Alpha Kappa Delta, Kappa Delta Pi, Omicron Delta Kappa, Phi Delta Kappa, Pi Gamma Mu, Phi Eta Sigma. Democrat. Presbyn. Home: 640 Glenwood Dr Athens GA 30601

ANDERSON, ROBERT THOMAS, educator; b. Seale, Ala., Dec. 25, 1926; s. Samuel Pitts and Allie Rebecca (Dixon) A.; B.S., Troy (Ala.) State U., 1951; M.S., Auburn U., 1954; Ed.D., George Peabody Coll. for Tchrs., 1964; m. Betty Ann Ransom, June 3, 1951; children—Elizabeth Ann, Robert Thomas. Tchrs., Montgomery, Ala., 1951-54, elementary prin., 1954-58, jr. high prin., 1958-62; supr. lang. arts, asst. dir. instrn., Richmond, Va., 1964-66; asst. supt. for curriculum and instruction, Chesterfield, County, Va., 1966-68; asst. dir. Tennessee Valley Edn. Center, Huntsville, Ala., 1968-69; asso. prof. of adminstrn. supervision and curriculum devel. U. Ala., Tuscaloosa, 1969-—. Cons. to numerous sch. systems in Va. and Ala. Served with AUS, 1946-48. Mem. Am. Assn. Sch. Adminstrs., Assn. Supervision and Curriculum Devel., Nat. Assn. Elementary Sch. Prins., Ala. Edn. Assn., Ala. Assn. Sch. Adminstrs., Ala. Dept. Elementary Sch. Prins. (exec. dir. 1971-—), Phi Delta Kappa. Home: 8 Woodland Pines Tuscaloosa AL 35401

ANDERSON, SAM OTEY, telephone co. exec.; b. Little Lot, Tenn., Mar. 14, 1923; s. Elbert Nelson and Elizabeth (Baker) A.; grad. high sch.; m. Mary Elizabeth Strode, June 19, 1943; 1 dau., Carol Ann. Mgr., Ben Baugh Co., Livingston, Tenn., 1946-47; supr. Montgomery Electric & Heating Co., Gainsboro, Tenn., 1947-52; equipment supr. Twin Lakes Telephone Coop., Gainesboro, 1952-56, mgr., 1956-—; dir. Jackson County Bank. Chmn. Planning Commn. Gainesboro, 1966; sec. Jackson County Recreation Assn., 1968-69. Served with USAF, 1943-46. Recipient Mgr. of Year award Nat. Telephone Coop. Assn., 1967. Mem. Tenn. Telephone Assn. (dir.). Rotarian. Address: Gainesboro TN 38562

ANDERSON, SAMUEL ARMISTEAD, III, architect; b. Richmond, Va., Dec. 18, 1933; s. Samuel and Frances Gertrude (Webster) A.; B.A., U. Va., 1955; B.Arch., U. Pa., 1961; m. Alice Gordon Childs, Mar. 24, 1956; children— Sarah Gordon, Ann Starling, Lucy Daniel, Susannah Webster. Designer, Venturi & Rauch, Phila., 1962; project designer Ballinger Co., Phila., 1963, Harbeson, Hough, Livingston, Larsen, Phila., 1964; project design coordinator Llewelyn-Davies Weeks & Partners, London, Eng., 1965-66; staff architect Rawlings & Wilson, Richmond, Va., 1967-68; partner Glave Newman Anderson, Richmond, 1969-—. Lectr. Bartlett Sch. Arch., Univ. Coll. U. London, 1965; tech. adviser Richmond Regional Planning Dist. Commn., 1969-—, John Tyler Community Coll., Chesterfield County, Va., 1970-71. Vice chmn. Chesterfield County A.R.C., 1968-71; mem. West Philadelphia Neighborhood Resources Bd., 1964. Bd. dirs. Spruce Hill Community Assn., Phila., 1962-64, Richmond Scenic James Council, 1971. Served to lt. USNR, 1955-58. Mem. A.I.A. (pres. Richmond sect. 1970), Am. Inst. Planners (asso. mem.), Council Ednl. Facilities Planners, Central Richmond Assn., Zeta Psi. Democrat. Clubs: Country Virginia, Engineers (Richmond). Architect Basingstoke (Eng.) Town Center Redevel., 1964-66, Va. Commonwealth U. Master Plan, 1970. Home: 8511 Ben Nevis Dr Bon Air VA 23235 Office: 2 S Foushee St Richmond VA 23220

ANDERSON, WALTER CLINTON, economist; b. Erie, Pa., May 14, 1923; s. Walter O. and Marie (Trimble) A.; B.S., Pa. State U., 1948, M.S., 1950, Ph.D., 1966; m. Shirley Kathryn Zeitler, Aug. 28, 1948; children—Lawrence, Gail, Karen. Jr. forester Southeastern forest exptl. sta. U.S. Forest Service, Asheville, N.C., 1953-54, forest economist, 1954-66, prin. economist Southern forest exptl. sta., New Orleans, 1966-—. Served with AUS, 1943-46. Mem. Soc. Am. Foresters (group chmn. 1967-68), Am. Agr. Econ. Assn., Am. Econ. Assn., Xi Sigma Pi, Tau Phi Delta. Baptist. Club: Toastmasters (pres. 1970, area. gov. 1970-71) (New Orleans). Contbr. articles to profl. pubs. Home: PO Box 53153 New Orleans LA 70153 Office: 701 Loyola Av New Orleans LA 70113

ANDERSON, W(ALTER) E. (ANDY), writer; b. Carlinville, Ill., Dec. 2, 1903; s. Crittenden Henry Crawford and Nellie (Patchen) A.; ed. Tex. A. and M. Coll.; m. Mabel Mae Rooks, Nov. 15, 1930. With Nat. Life & Accident Ins. Co., Dallas, 1933-54; gen. partner Adventurers Assos., producer hunting films; producer, narrator, participant Hollywood prodn. Big Game Hunting in North America; dir., producer, narrator Wildlife and Mem. hunting film Big Game Trails, 1971. Leader's Round Table of Tex., 8 yrs. Past dir. YMCA, West Dallas Social Center. Mem. S.A.R. Methodist (mem. adminstrv. bd., finance com., chmn. new pledge com., stewardship com.). Clubs: Oak Cliff Lions (past chmn. membership com., health and welfare com., civic improvement com., interstate and internat. pub. relations com.), Oak Cliff Country (charter), Dallas Woods and Water (charter; past chmn. big game hunting com.). Author poem: The Hunter's Dream; stories: Bushytails of the Llano; Duke, the Story of a Bird Dog; with Deep in the Heart of Texas; Johnnie's Lucky Day, with illustrations; Skyline Meadows, 1954; King Caribou, 1954; Sleek and Glossy, 1954; A Texan Meets a Silvertip, 1957; Five from Which to Choose, 1957; various other stories in Sports Afield. Guns mag., Alaskan Sportsman, Am. Rifleman, Field and Stream, Outdoor Life mag. Home: 955 Sam Dealey Dr Dallas TX 75208

ANDERSON, WILLIAM ALBION, JR., investment banker; b. Paris, Ark., July 12, 1939; s. William A. and Maud (Rodgers) A.; B.S., U. Ark., 1962; M.B.A., Harvard, 1963; m. Patricia E. Puterbaugh, July 5, 1968; step-children—Charles L. Kuehn, Jr., Cynthia P. Kuehn. Corporate finance asso. Eastman Dillon, Union Securities & Co., Inc., N.Y.C., 1963-67, corporate finance asso., Houston, 1967-68, v.p., 1968-69, gen. partner, 1969-71, 1st v.p., 1971-—. Mem. Phi Delta Theta. Home: 3661 Ella Lee St Houston TX 77027 3661 Ella Lee St Houston TX 77027 Office: 2000 Houston Natural Gas Bldg Houston TX 77002

ANDERSON, WILLIAM HINTON WILDER, assn. exec.; b. Washington, Nov. 27, 1914; s. Parker Richardson and Katharine Wilder (Fort) A.; A.B., U. N.C., 1936; M.S., Columbia, 1937; m. Mary Elizabeth Ferguson, July 5, 1939; children—William Hinton Wilder, Jr., Margaret (Mrs. John Harrelson McGee), David Ira Fort. Reporter, Washington Daily News, 1937-38; reporter, copy editor News and Observer, 1938-42; night editor Asso. Press, 1946-48; copy editor Richmond Times Dispatch, 1948-50; information officer Va. Dept. Hwys., 1950-53; dir. pub. relations and travel promotion Va. State C. of C., 1953-57; mng. dir., exec. sec, treas. Tobacco Growers' Information Com., Raleigh, N.C., 1957-—. Mem. Gov's. Adv. Com. Jamestown (Va.) Festival, 1956-57. Trustee, v.p. Va. Episcopal Sch., 1960-66. Served with USNR, 1942-46; lt. comdr. ret. Mem. Pub. Relations Soc. Am., Richmond (pres. 1956-57), Raleigh (pres. 1970) pub. relations assns., Raleigh C. of C., Va. Soc., S.A.R., Sigma Nu. Democrat. Episcopalian. Clubs: Carolina Country, City (Raleigh, N.C.). Editor: Virginia Highway Needs During the National Defense Era, 1952; First American Heritage, 1959; Pride of Kentucky, 1965. Home: 2607 St Marys St Raleigh NC 27609 Office: PO Box 12046 Raleigh NC 27605 also 2016 Cameron St Raleigh NC 27605

ANDERSON, WILLIAM MCREE, III, hardware co. exec.; b. Hot Springs, Ark., Feb. 24; s. William McRee and Mary Elizabeth (Stafford) A.; B.S., U. Ark., 1960; m. Salli Jo Rager, Jan. 27, 1968; children— Kimberly Anderson, William McRee IV. Warehouse employee F. C. Stearns Hardware Co., Inc., Hot Springs, 1963, salesman, 1964-65, buyer, 1965-69, v.p., 1969-—; pres. Entertainment Ltd., Inc., Hot Springs, 1966-—. Co-chmn. Garland County Heart Fund, 1966, chmn., 1967. Served to 2d lt. USAF, 1960-63. Mem. Musicians Protective Union, Hot Springs Jr. C. of C., Kappa Sigma, Presbyn. Elk. Home: 621 Prospect Av Hot Springs AR 71901 Office: PO Box 940 Hot Springs AR 71901

ANDERSON, WILLIAM ROBERT, congressman; b. Bakerville, Tenn., June 17, 1921; s. David Hensley and Mary (McKelvey) A.; B.S. in Elec. Engring., U.S. Naval Acad., 1942; D.Sc., Defiance Coll., 1958; m. Yvonne Etzel, June 10, 1943; children—Michael David,

William Robert. Commd. ensign, U.S. Navy, 1942, advanced through grades to capt., 1960; assigned submarines Tarpon, Narwhal, Trutta, Pacific combat patrols, World War II, postwar service submarines Sarda, Trutta, Tang; comdr. attach submarine U.S.S. Wahoo. Pearl Harbor; 1953-55; head tactical dept. Submarine Sch., 1955-56; staff naval reactors br. AEC. Washington, 1956-57; comdr. U.S.S. Nautilus, 1957-59; ret. 1962; v.p. Freedoms Found., until 1964; mem. 89th-92d Congress, 6th Tenn. Dist. Candidate for gov. Tenn., 1962. Decorated Bronze Star medal, Legion of Merit recipient Stephen Decatur prize Navy League U.S., Distinguished Service award N.Y.C., Christopher Columbus medal Genoa, Italy, Elisha Kent Kane medal Geog. Soc. Phila., 1959, Patron's medal Royal Geog. Soc., 1959, Leadership award Freedom's Found., 1960. Mem. Am. Legion, Amvets. Club: Explorers (N.Y.C.). Author: Nautilus 90 North 1959; First Under the North Pole, 1959; The Useful Atom, 1966; also articles in national mags. Home: Waverly TN 37185 Office: House Office Bldg Washington DC 20515

ANDERSON, WILTON THOMAS, educator; b. Richland, Tex., Nov. 29, 1916; s. William Nix and Ruth (Skipper) A.; B.S., Northwestern State Coll., Alva, Okla., 1938; M.C.E., U. Okla., 1941; Ed.D., U. Colo., 1953; m. Gwendolyn Hollis, Dec. 10, 1938; children—Kaye Lynn, Wilton Thomas. Bus. tchr. Cyril (Okla.) High Sch., 1938-40; asso. prof., head dept. bus. No. Okla. Jr. Coll., 1940-46; prof., head dept. bus. adminstrn. Bowling Green Coll. Commerce, 1946-47; asso. prof. accounting U. Colo., 1947-57; dir. edn. Am. Inst. C.P.A.'s, N.Y.C., 1957-60; prof., head dept. accounting Okla. State U., 1960—. Named Outstanding Bus. Adminstrn. Tchr., Okla. State U., 1963, 64, 70, Outstanding U. Tchr., 1970. C.P.A., Okla., Colo. Mem. Am. Inst. C.P.A.'s, Okla. Soc. C.P.A.'s, Am. Accounting Assn. (v.p. 1964-65), Beta Gamma Sigma, Beta Alpha Psi (nat. council 1964-68, nat. pres. 1966-67), Delta Sigma Pi. Author: (with C.A. Moyer and A.R. Wyatt) Accounting: Basic Financial Cost and Control Concepts. Contbr. articles to profl. publs. Home: 60 Yellowbrick Rd Stillwater OK 74074

ANDERSSON, KINGSLEY SHERMAN, ret. operations research co. exec.; b. Big Rapids, Mich., Apr. 7, 1902; s. Gustav Edmund and Karen Hansina (Johansson) A.; B.S., U. Mich., 1923; m. Laurella Florence Hollis, Nov. 3, 1923; children—Gunnar Einar, Merry Lusinn (Mrs. Elmer Henry Strathman). Commd. 2d lt. U.S. Army, 1923, advanced through grades to col., 1942; asst. prof. mil. sci. and tactics Tex. A. and M. Coll., College Station, 1932-34; engr. in charge fortification works, Corregidor, Phillipines, 1936-39; asst. dist. engr. Detroit, acting dist. engr., Lake Survey, Detroit, officer in charge St. Mary's Falls and Locks, Sault Ste Marie, Mich., 1939-41; div. engr. 79th Div., 1942; comdg. officer engr. combat group, Africa, Italy, 1943-44; operations officer engr. div. 6th Army Group, France, 1944-45; engr. Replacement Tng. Center, Ft. Belvoir, Va., 1946, comdg. officer, 1952-53; operations officer engring. div., Eucom., Heidelberg, Germany, 1948-50; engr. U.S. Constabulary, Stuttgart, Germany, 1950, 7th Army, 1951-52; resident mem. Engr. Devel. Bd., 1953; chief staff, Ft. Belvoir, 1953-54; ret., 1954; mem. combat operations research group Tech. Operations, Inc., Burlington, Mass., 1955-63, chief war gaming and tactical analysis, 1955-56, spl. asst. to dir., 1956-58, mgr. profl. placement, 1958-62. Decorated Silver Star, Bronze Star (2), Purple Heart (2), Legion of Honor (France), Croix de Guerre with Palm (France). Registered profl. engr., Mich. Fellow Am. Soc. C.E., Explorers Club; mem. Operations Research Soc. Am., Sci. Research Soc. Am., Soc. Mil. Engrs., Nat. Assn. Profl. Engrs., Ret. Officers Assn., Army and Navy Club Washington, Scabbard and Blade, Lambda Chi Alpha. Republican. Home: Reveille Chase City VA 23924

ANDOLSEK, LUDWIG JOHN, govt. ofcl.; b. Denver, Nov. 6, 1910; s. Ludvig and Frances (Gouze) A.; B.Ed., St. Cloud (Minn.) State Tchrs. Coll., 1935; m. Regina A. Burnett, Nov. 25, 1945; 1 dau., Kathryn M. With Nat. Youth Adminstrn., 1936-42, area dir., No. Minn., 1940-42; asst. to personel officer charge personal relations and grievance procedures VA Hosp., St. Cloud, 1947-50; civilian personnel officer Ellsworth AFB, Weaver, S.D., 1950-51; adminstrv. asst. to Congressman J.A. Blatnik, 1951-62; chief clk. com. pub. works Ho. of Reps., 1963; commr. U.S. Civil Service, 1963—, vice chmn. commn., 1963-69. Served to capt. AUS, 1942-46. Recipient Silver Helmet, Civil Servant of Year, Amvets, 1966. Mem. Am. Legion, Amvets (life). Eagle (dist. dir. central Minn. 1948-50). Home: 9609 Bulls Run Pkwy Bethesda MD 20034 Office: 1900 E St NW Washington DC 20415

ANDRE, JOHN JOSEPH, research co. exec.; b. New Bedford, Mass., Nov. 17, 1916; s. John Sylvia and Agnes Veronica (Power) A.; Ph.B., Providence Coll., 1939; m. Alyce May Mello, June 7, 1943; 1 son, Stephen V. Personnel asst. VA, Los Angeles, 1946-49; bus. mgr. Pacific Schs. Langs., 1949-52; personnel adminstr. aircraft div. Northrop Corp., Hawthorne, Cal., 1952-67; personnel dir Research Analysis Corp., McLean, Va., 1967—. Lectr. Am. Mgmt. Assn. and Manpower Planning seminars. Served with AUS, 1942-46. Mem. Washington Personnel Assn., Washington Tech. Personnel Forum, So. Cal. Tech. Personnel Assn. (chmn. 1963-64), Am. Mgmt. Assn. Home: 367 Park St NE Vienna VA 22180 Office: Old Springhouse Rd McLean VA 22101

ANDRE, WILLIAM JOSEPH, carpet mfg. co. exec.; b. Croghan, N.Y., Aug. 4, 1926; s. E. A. and Madeline Cecilia (Clark) A.; B.S. in Mgmt. Engring., Rensselaer Poly, Inst., 1950; m. Vesta Helen Powers, Nov. 12, 1949; children—Judith (Mrs. Dwight Gatlin), Janet, Robert, Nancy, Sarah, Mary, William. Tech. asst. Mohawk Carpet Mills, Amsterdam, N.Y., 1950-58; asst. plant supt. Mohasco Industries, Inc., Amsterdam, 1959-62, asst. gen. mgr., Laurens, S.C., 1962-64, gen. mgr., 1964-65, gen. mgr., Dublin, Ga., 1965—. Pres. Dublin Central P.T.A., 1968. Bd. dirs. A.R.C., 1968-69. Served with USNR, 1944-46, 50-51. Mem. Ga. Textile Mfrs. Assn., Ga., Dublin (v.p.) chambers commerce, Epsilon Delta Sigma. Democrat. Roman Catholic. Rotarian (pres. 1970), Elk. Club: Dublin Country (pres. 1969). Home: 1705 Meadowdale Dr Dublin GA 31021 Office: PO Box 430 Dublin GA 31021

ANDREWS, ALFRED STOKES, bus. exec.; b. Dayton, O., Jan. 16, 1903; s. Harry Caho and Clare Margaruite (Stokes) A.; B.S., Carnegie Inst. Tech., 1926; postgrad. Cleve. Marshall Law Sch., 1929-30; m. Estelle Garibaldi, Sept. 2, 1926. Supt., Walker & Weeks, Architects, Cleve., 1926-28; dist. engr. for N.E. Ohio, U.S. Fidelity & Guaranty Co., Cleve., 1929-34; pres. Great Lakes Box Co. (now St. Regis subsidiary), Cleve., 1934-38; owner Am. Flag & Decorating Co., also gen. mgr. Cleve. Aircraft Products Co., 1940-45; pres. Andrews-Bartlett & Assos., Inc., Cleve., 1945-68, chmn. bd., 1968—. Cons. 15 bldg. supply dealers, Cleve. area, 1940-42. Chmn., Ohio City Planning Sponsors and Near West Devel. Assn., 1958-67; v.p. West Side Civic Council, 1960-66; chmn. vis. com. Margaret Morrison Coll., 1960-68; pres., exec. dir. Cuyahoga County Assn. for Retarded, 1965-67. Trustee, Carnegie Mellon U., 1960, life trustee, 1969—. Recipient Raphael award for work with retarded Cleve. Raphael Soc., 1967, Distinguished Service award Carnegie-Mellon, 1968. Mem. Am. Soc. C.E. (life), Cleve. C. of C. (chmn. lakefront com. 1954-58), Cleve. Engring. Soc., Cleve. Advt. Club, Area Council Cleve. Welfare Assn., Carnegie Tech. Alumni (pres. fedn. 1960), Sigma Alpha Epsilon. Presbyn. Club: Clifton (Lakewood, O.). Author: Carnegie Song Book, 1924; Andrews-Wright Genealogy, 1970. Home: Marine Tower 2500 E Las Olas Fort Lauderdale FL 33301 Office: 1849 W 24th St Cleveland OH 44113

ANDREWS, ALLIE ELDON, JR., radiologist; b. Jonesboro, Ark., Jan. 18, 1927; s. Allie Eldon and Lillian (Kerl) A.; B.S.M., U. Ark., 1951, M.D., 1952; m. Johnnie Mae Scott, Apr. 30, 1948; children—Susan Diane, Helen Lee, Jennifer Lynn, David Allen. Intern Ark. Baptist Hosp., Little Rock, 1952-53; resident radiology U. Tenn. Hosp., 1966-69; gen. practice medicine, Paragould, Ark., 1953-66; head dept. radiology St. Michael Hosp., Texarkana, Ark., 1969—. Electric utility commnr., Paragould, 1962-66. Served with USNR, 1945-46. Mem. Ark., Miller County med. socs., A.M.A., Am. Coll. Radiology. Methodist. Mason (Shriner). Lion (pres. Paragould 1956-57; v.p. Mid South Sight Service 1963-64). Home: 1311 Rio Grande Texarkana TX 75501 Office: 315 E 5th St Texarkana AR 75501

ANDREWS, CHARLES HAYNES, economist, educator; b. Waycross, Ga., Nov. 30, 1937; s. Charles Haynes and Louise (McQuaig) A.; A.B., Mercer U., 1960; Ph.D., Vanderbilt U., 1967; m. Susan Gahan, Aug. 29, 1961; children—Charles Haynes, William. Asso. prof. econs. Stetson U., DeLand, Fla., 1964—, chmn. dept. econs., 1967—. Mem. West Volusia Council on Human Relations. Woodrow Wilson fellow, 1960-61, Earhart fellow, 1961-62, Fgn. Area Fellowship Program fellow, 1963-65. Mem. Am., So. econ. assns., Assn. Comparative Econs. Democrat. Presbyn. (deacon). Author: The Economic Performance of the Compania de Acero del Pacifico, S.A., 1970. Home: 2232 Mimosa Lane DeLand FL 32720

ANDREWS, CYRIL BLYTHE, pub. co. exec.; b. Apalachicola, Fla., July 6, 1901; s. William Wallace and Henrietta Geneva (Smith) A.; B.A., Atlanta U., 1925; postgrad. U. Chgo., 1925-26; LL.D., Fla. Meml. Coll., 1970; m. Johna Belle Thompson, Apr. 20, 1929; children—Cyril Blythe, William Wallace. Journalism intern Chgo. Defender, 1925-26, Chgo. Bee, 1926-29; agt. Afro-Am. Life Ins. Co., Jacksonville, Fla., 1930; agt. insp. Central Life Ins. Co., Fla., 1931-33, sec.-treas., 1933-39; real estate broker, Tampa, 1939-45; founder Fla. Sentinel, Tampa, 1945-58, owner, editor Fla. Sentinel-Bull (merger Fla. Sentinel and Tampa Bull.), 1958—. Chmn. Negro Adv. Com., 1954-58; mem. Mayor's Bi-Racial Com., Tampa, 1959-72; mem. Mayor's Commn. on Human Relations, 1964-72; mem. Pres.'s Fla. Commn. on Civil Rights, 1958-66; apptd. mem. Hillsboro County Civil Service Bd., 1966—; mem. Hillsboro County Health Planning Commn., 1971—. Recipient numerous citations Fla. A. and M. U., Edward Waters Coll., Bethune-Cookman Coll., Fla. Normal Coll., others. Mem. N.A.A.C.P., Frontiers of Am. (founder, pres. Tampa 1956—), Lily White Soc. (grand pres. 1939—), Alpha Phi Alpha. Baptist (deacon). K.P., Mason (Shriner, 32deg.), Elk. Odd Fellow. Home: 2216 23d Av Tampa FL 33605 Office: Fla Sentinel Bulletin Tampa FL 33601

ANDREWS, DONALD HATCH, chemist; b. Southington, Conn., June 11, 1898; s. Russell Gad and Mary Boles (Hatch) A.; grad. Phillips Acad., Andover, Mass., 1916; B.A., Yale, 1920, Ph.D., 1923; m. Josephine Adair Veeder, June 20, 1939 (div. 1950); m. 2d, Elizabeth Howland, Sept. 23, 1950; 1 son, Donald Hatch. Research asst. in chemistry, Yale, 1923; nat. research fellow U. Cal., 1924-25; internat. research fellow U. Leiden, 1925-26; research fellow, Bartol Research Found., 1926-27; with Johns Hopkins U., 1927—, prof. chemistry, 1930—, chmn. dept., dir. chem. lab., 1936-44, dir. Cryogeny Lab., 1943-48, B. N. Baker prof. chemistry, 1957-63, prof. emeritus, 1963—; prof. chemistry Fla. Atlantic U., Boca Raton, 1963-64, distinguished prof. of chemistry, 1964-67, distinguished prof. emeritus, 1967—, distinguished prof. biophysics, 1968-70. Mem. chemistry div. NRC, 1933; chmn. Calorimetry Conf., 1957-58. Mem. 1st sci. commn. L'Inst. Internationale de Froid. Fellow Royal Chem. Soc. (Eng.), N.Y. Acad. Scis., A.A.A.S., Am. Philos. Soc.; mem. Am. Chem. Soc. (sec. div. phys. and inorganic chemistry, 1932, vice chmn., 1933, chmn. 1934), Am. Math. Assn., Am. Phys. Soc., Philosophy of Sci. Assn., British Assn. Philosophy Sci., Phi Beta Kappa, Sigma Xi. Republican. Episcopalian. Club: Appalachian Mountain. Author: Fundamental Chemistry, 1962, 2d edit., 1965; Quimica Fundamental, 1964; Symphony of Life, 1967; Quimica Geral, 1968; Notiones Fundamentales de Chimie, 1968; Introductory Physical Chemistry, 1970. Home: 750 NE 33d St Boca Raton FL 33432

ANDREWS, EARL PRENTICE, JR., banker; b. Montgomery, Ala., May 12, 1928; s. Earl Prentice and Olive Lucille (Smith) A.; B.S., Auburn U., 1949; postgrad. Stonier Grad. Sch. Banking, Rutgers U., 1965, Grad. Sch. Credit and Financial Mgmt. Harvard, 1969; m. Verda Louise Bethea, Oct. 22, 1949; children—Earl Prentice III, Ellen B. Announcer, WSFA Radio, Montgomery, 1949-50; program dir. WAUD Radio, Auburn, Ala., 1950-53; salesman WABB Radio, Mobile, Ala., 1953-55; with Mchts. Nat. Bank Mobile, 1955—, v.p., 1965-72, sr. v.p., 1972—, head marketing div., 1969-71. Pres., Mobile Azalea Trail, 1958; pres. Am. Jr. Miss Pageant, 1959. Bd. dirs., treas. Mobile Gen. Hosp., 1968-71. Named Outstanding Young Man Ala., Ala. Jaycees, 1958. Mem. Am. Marketing Assn., Bank Marketing Assn., So. Indsl. Devel. Council, Sigma Chi. Presbyn. Lion (past pres.). Clubs: Mobile Country, Athelstan. Home: 2502 Oak View Dr Mobile AL 36606 Office: PO Drawer 2527 106 St Francis St Mobile AL 36622

ANDREWS, FREDERICK RANDOLPH, librarian; b. Madison, Fla., Dec. 15, 1937; s. Zack Marion and Iva Calvin (Hamilton) A.; B.A., Fla. State U., 1959, M.A., 1970; m. Flora Lee Warner, Sept. 18, 1960; 1 dau., Tracy Lynn. Spl. services librarian U.S. Army, Fairbanks, Alaska, 1961-63; dir. Clay County Libraries, Green Cove Springs, Fla., 1963-67, Suwannee River Regional Library, Live Oak, 1967—. Sponsor, Leo Club, Live Oak, Fla., 1970-72. Mem. Am., Fla. (vice-chmn. pub. libraries div.) library assns., Beta Phi Mu. Methodist. Lion. Home: 406 E Duval St Live Oak FL 32060 Office: Pine St Live Oak FL 32060

ANDREWS, GEORGE FRASER, JR., electronics engr., scientist; b. Balt., Mar. 5, 1931; s. George F. and Violet (Nicely) A.; m. Rita Ann Mundy, Aug. 19, 1948; children—Brenda Joyce, Melody Ann. Teresa Marie, Angela Helen, George F. III, Mary Grace. Electronic engr. Fed. Aviation Agy., 1957-67; research scientist U. Miami, 1967—; cons. engr. electronic circuit design industry and govt. Recipient outstanding fed. service award, Fed. Aviation Agy., 1965. Registered profl. engr., Fla. Mem. Nat. Soc. Profl. Engrs., Fla. Engring. Soc., I.E.E.E., A.A.A.S., Soc. Photo-Optical Instrumentation Engrs., Eta Kappa Nu. Contbr. articles profl. jours. Inventor lightning display device, radar sea-state analyzer. Research on radar, remote sensing of atmosphere, solar radiation. Home: 11800 SW 87th Av Miami FL 33156 Office: University of Miami Radar Laboratory PO Box 8003 Coral Gables FL 33124

ANDREWS, HARVEY WELLINGTON, chem. co. exec; b. Stowe Twp., Pa., Sept. 9, 1928; s. Robert W. and Theresa R. (Reis) A.; B.B.A. cum laude, U. Pitts., 1952; M.B.A., Harvard, 1957; m. Jane Garland, Aug. 9, 1969. With Gen. Electric Co., Syracuse, N.Y., 1952-55, Scovill Mfg. Co., Waterbury, Conn., 1957; comptroller Alcon Labs., Inc., Ft. Worth, 1958-61, comptroller, treas., 1961-65, v.p. finance, 1964-68; pres. Medimation, Inc., Ft. Worth, 1968—; v.p. finance, dir. Poly-co, Inc., Service Engrs., Inc., Conal Pharmacal, Inc., Highland Terrace Park, Alcom Universal Ltd., Lawton Co.; dir. Internat. Chem. & Nuclear Corp., Union Bank of Ft. Worth. Gen. chmn. Ft. Worth Opera Ball; dir., mem. exec. com. Fort Worth Opera Assn. Trustee Alcon Labs. Employees Profit Sharing Trust. Served with AUS, 1946-48. Mem. Financial Execs. Inst., Am. Acad. Polit. and Social Scis., Pharm. Mfrs. Assn. (steering com. financial sect.), Am. Accounting Assn., Ft. Worth C. of C., Soc. Advancement Mgmt., Order Artus, Scabbard and Blade, Sigma Alpha Epsilon. Republican. Lutheran. Mason. Clubs: Fort Worth Boat, Economic, Colonial Country, Casa del Sol. Home: PO Box 1786 4906 Arborlawn Dr Fort Worth TX 76109 Office: Continental Life Bldg Fort Worth TX 76102

ANDREWS, JAMES CLAIRE, physician; b. Pleasant Plain, Ia., Mar. 7, 1921; s. Claire H. and Lola E. (Crew) A.; student Upper Ia. U., 1940-42; B.S., U. Notre Dame, 1945; M.D., U. Mich., 1949; m. Katherine P. McGinnis, June 21, 1947; 1 son, John C. Intern, St. Joseph's Hosp., Lexington, Ky., 1949-50; resident U. Va. Hosp., 1950, 52-55; practice medicine, specializing in dermatology, Charlottesville, Va., 1955—, mem. staff Martha Jefferson Hosp., Charlottesville. Served with USNR, 1942-46; as capt. M.C., USAF, 1950-52. Mem. A.A.A.S., Am. Acad. Dermatology, Am., So. med. assns., Washington Dermatol. Assn., Va., Albemarle County med. socs., Soc. Investigative Dermatology, Internat. Soc. Tropical Dermatology, Va. Dermatol. Soc. Presbyn. (elder). Home: Woodland, RFD 6 Box 303 Charlottesville VA 22901 Office: Doctor's Bldg 801 E High St Charlottesville VA 22901

ANDREWS, JAMES LEWIS, army officer, oral surgeon; b. Canton, O., June 7, 1929; s. Lloyd F. and Gertrude (Griggs) A.; D.D.S. cum laude, Ohio State U., 1953; postgrad. Northwestern U., 1961-62; m. Joanne Mary Jenkins, Aug. 2, 1952; children—Susan L., Ellen J., David L. Intern oral surgery Univ. Hosps., Columbus, O., 1953-54; commd. 1st lt. U.S. Army, 1954, advanced through grades to col. 1971; stationed Ft. Knox, Ky., 1954-57; oral surgeon U.S. Army Hosp., Berlin, Germany, 1958-61; resident oral surgeon Letterman Gen. Hosp., San Francisco, 1962-64, asst. chief oral surgery, 1956-66, chief oral surgery, 1966-68; chief dental services 106th Gen. Hosp., 1968-70; chief clinician dental clinic Camp Zama, Japan, 1970-71; oral surgeon Darnall Army Hosp., Ft. Hood, Tex., 1971—. Diplomate Am. Bd. Oral Surgery. Fellow Am. Coll. Dentists; mem. Am. Soc. Oral Surgeons, Am. Acad. Oral Pathology, Am. Dental Assn., Omicron Kappa Upsilon. Mason. Contbr. articles to profl. jours. Address: Darnall Army Hosp Fort Hood TX 76544

ANDREWS, JOE WILLIAM, JR., assn. exec.; b. Blanton, Ala., Feb. 14, 1926; s. J.W. and Charlie Belle (Williams) A.; A.B., Mercer U., 1948, postgrad., 1949-50; student Southeastern Inst. Comml. Orgn. Execs., 1955-56; m. Virginia Garland, Apr. 22, 1951; children—Joe W. III, Laura. Editorial dept. Macon (Ga.) Telegraph & News, 1943-49; dir. pub. relations S.C. Farm Bur., Anderson, 1949-51, WMAZ Radio and TV, Macon, 1951-62; pres. So. Assn. Services, Inc., Macon, also Southeastern Services, Inc., Macon, 1963—; owner J & L Prodns.; pres. Builders Mortgage Corp.; dir. Carlisle Investment Co., Inc., Train, Inc. Served as lt. inf. AUS, World War II. Mem. Am. Soc. Assn. Execs., Multiple Assn. Mgmt. Assn., Sales Execs. Club Macon (pres. 1959), Distributive Edn. Club Am. (hon. life), Sigma Delta Chi, Phi Delta Theta. Baptist. Clubs: Macon Farmers (pres. 1958), Kiwanis (Macon). Home: 720 Forest Ridge Dr W Macon GA 31208 Office: 654 1st St Macon GA 31204

ANDREWS, JOHN LEWIS, educator, design engr.; b. Bloomington, Ind., Dec. 28, 1897; s. William McCoy and Jennie (Hanson) A.; B.S., Sch. Mines, U. Mo., 1924; student Gen. Electric Advanced Mgmt. Sch., 1957;; m. Mary Evelyn Ray, Jan. 3, 1924; children—John Lewis, Peter Hanson, Thomas Warren. Asst. engr. Am. Steel Foundry Co., Granite City, Ill., 1924-25; head phys. and elec. lab. Stewart Warner Corp., Chgo., 1925-29; engring. supr. Edison Gen. Electric Appliance Co., Chgo., 1929-42; acting mgr. mech. engring. Naval Ordnance Lab., Washington, 1942-44; dir. engring. and research Airtex Products, Fairfield, Ill., 1944-48; individual practice patent research and cons., Fairfield, 1948-49; mgr. engring. Hotpoint div. Gen. Electric Co., Chgo., 1949-59; prof. mech. engring. U. Miss., University, 1959—; pres. Research Assos. Miss., Inc., University. Chmn. orgn. and extension Boy Scouts Am., Wayne, Edwards Counties, So. Ill., 1944-49. Registered profl. engr., Miss. Mem. Am. Soc. M.E., Miss., Nat. socs. profl. engrs., Am. Soc. Engring. Edn. Methodist. Mason, Elk. Home: PO Box 276 University MS 38677

ANDREWS, JOHN ROBERT, physician; b. Kent, O., June 10, 1906; s. William Baird and Anna (Doyle) A.; Ph.B., Brown U., 1928; M.D., Western Res. U., 1932; D.Sc. in Medicine, U. Pa., 1948; m. Anne Cosgrove, June 15, 1935; children—Catherine Firth (Mrs. Albert Kapikian), William Baird, John Robert; m. 2d. Jeannette Welsh, Mar. 7, 1951; m. 3d, Nicole Crozier, Dec. 31, 1962. Intern Cleve. City Hosp., 1932-33; resident U. Pa. Hosp., 1933-35, Meml. Hosp., N.Y.C., 1937; prof., dir. radiology Bowman Gray Sch. Medicine, 1950-55; with Nat. Cancer Inst., NIH, 1955-64, chief radiation br., 1955-64; clin. prof. oncology Georgetown U. Sch. Medicine, 1958-64, prof. radiology, 1964—; dir. radiotherapy Georgetown U. Hosp., 1964—; cons. Sibley Meml., Providence hosps., Washington, Clin. Center of NIH, Gordon Friesen Assos.; chief radiotherapy service Washington VA Hosp. Mem. A.M.A., Am. Roentgen Ray Soc., Radiol. Soc. N.A., Am. Radium Soc., Am. Coll. Radiology, D.C. Med. Soc., Radiation Research Soc., Am. Assn. Cancer Research, Am. Assn. for Cancer Edn. Author: The Radiobiology of Human Cancer Radiotherapy, 1968. Contbr. articles to profl. jours. Home: 4428 Volta Pl NW Washington DC 20007 Office: 3800 Reservoir Rd NW Washington DC 20007

ANDREWS, RAWLE, physician; b. Grenada, W.I., Feb. 4, 1929; s. Lawrence and Adina (Gibbes) A.; came to U.S., 1952, naturalized, 1969; B.S. with honors, Hampton Inst., 1956; postgrad. U. R.I., U. Mich., 1956-58; M.D., Meharry Med. Coll., 1963; m. Naomi Cox, Aug. 17, 1963; children—Rawle, Rhetta, Ronald. Intern Los Angeles County Gen. Hosp., 1963-64; gen. practice medicine, Houston, 1964—. Sch. physician Charles R. Drew Sch., Houston, 1964, William Jr.-Sr. High, Houston, 1965-67; mem. adv. bd. Riverside Nat. Bank, Houston. Pres., Houston Med. Forum, 1970, 71-72; v.p. Acres Home Citizens Council, 1969-70, pres., 1970-72. Bd. dirs. Operation Breadbasket, co-chmn. task task force com. Houston Galveston Area council, 1970—; bd. dirs. So. Christian Leadership conf.; mem. adv. bd. Eliza Johnson Center for Aged, Martin Luther King Center; v.p., trustee Montessori Sch., Houston, 1970-71. Recipient Humanitarian award Antioch Bapt. Ch., 1969. Mem. A.M.A., Nat. Med. Assn. (bd. dirs.). Mason (med. dir. lodge). Home: 5325 Blythewood Houston TX 77021 Office: 7901 W Montgomery Rd Houston TX 77088

ANDREWS, ROBERT CHARLES, owner pub. co.; b. Rockford, Ill., Oct. 15, 1911; s. Charles and Maria (Zuck) A.; student U. Wis., 1928-31; m. Margaret Erminie Meier, Sept. 14, 1958; children—Louise R. (Mrs. Art Sams), Edward C., James F.; stepchildren—Richard M. and Veachel W. Davis. Editor, East Tex. Press, Buna, 1966-67; owner, pub. editor East Tex. News, Buna, 1967—; co-organizer, dir. Sabine Neches Press, Inc., Newton, Tex. Active Boy Scouts Am., 1949, 68-70; pres. P.T.A., Phoenix, Ariz.,

1950. Recipient pub. service award U.S. Post Office Dept., 1969. Mem. Prodn. Engrs. Rock River Valley (pres. 1937). Unitarian. Lion (deputy dist. gov. 1962-63). Address: 6345 Daisy Dr Beaumont TX 77706

ANDREWS, VICTOR L(EE), educator; b. Huntington, W. Va., June 23, 1930; s. Victor L. and Louise Gerding (King) A.; B.A., U. Chgo., 1951, M.A., 1953, M.B.A., 1954; Ph.D., Mass. Inst. Tech., 1958; m. Elaine Bernasek, July 9, 1954. Research asso. Indsl. Relations Center, U. Chgo., 1953-55; instr. Mass. Inst. Tech., 1957-58, asst. prof. finance, 1958-61; asst. prof. bus. adminstrn. Harvard Bus. Sch., 1961-64, asso. prof., 1964-68; Mills Lane prof. banking and finance Ga. State U., Atlanta, 1968—; dir. Concept Industries, Inc., Atlanta; faculty asso. Mgmt. Analysis Center, Inc., Boston. Mem. Am. Econ. Assn., Am. Finance Assn., Financial Mgmt. Assn., Am. Inst. Decision Scis., Appalachian Finance Assn., Soc. Financial Analysts. Clubs: Commerce Atlanta City. Author: (with Pearson Hunt) Financial Management: Cases and Readings. Editor jour. Financial Mgmt. Assn., 1972—. Home: 4625 Jettridge Dr N W Atlanta GA 30327

ANDREWS, WALLACE CHRISTOPHER, supt. schs.; b. Weatherford, Tex., Apr. 30, 1917; s. George Wallace and Rue Eddith (Hardman) A.; A.A., Weatherford Jr. Coll., 1939; B.S., U. Tex., 1942; M.S., Tex. Arts and Industry U., 1951; m. Violet Fletcher, Sept. 7, 1939; children—Martha Sue (Mrs. Joe Andrews), Elizabeth Ann (Mrs. James Bockholt), Wallace Christopher. Tchr., Brock Pub. Sch., Weatherford, 1940-41, Springtown (Tex.) Pub. Schs., 1941-42; with Gregory (Tex.) Portland Pub. Schs., 1942—, supt. schs., 1945—. Bd. dirs. Gregory Housing Authority. Mem. N.E.A. (life mem.), Am. (adv. council 1968-72), Tex. (life mem., pres. 1968-69) assns. sch. adminstrs., Tex. Tchrs. Assn. (life), Phi Delta Kappa. Methodist (chmn. ofcl. bd. 1949-50). Mason, Kiwanian. Home: Box 336 Gregory TX 78359 Office: Box 338 Gregory TX 78359

ANDREWS, WILLIAM CLAUD, state ofcl.; b. Tampa, Fla., Jan. 24, 1934; s. Claud Fleming and Agatha (Leeuwenburg) A.; B.S., U. Fla., B.A., 1955, LL.B., 1958; m. Cedora Platt, June 25, 1955; children—Claudia Lynn, William Claud, Suzanne Marie. Admitted to Fla. bar; now state atty., dist. 19, Fla. Dir. Bank Hawthorne. Mem. Fla. Ho. of Reps., from 1966. Served with AUS, 1958-59. Mem. Am., Fla. bar assns., Jr. C. of C. Methodist. Kiwanian, Mosse. Address: PO Box 1036 Gainesville FL 32601*

ANDREWS, WILLIAM FREDERICK, mfg. co. exec.; b. Easton, Pa., Oct. 7, 1931; s. William Frederick and Lydia Nielson (Cross) A.; B.S., U. Md., 1953; M.B.A., Seton Hall U., 1961; m. Carol Meadow Beaman, Feb. 8, 1962; children—William, Whitney, Carter, Clayton, Sloane. Mgmt. trainee W.R. Grace & Co., N.Y.C., 1956-57; salesman Kaiser Aluminum Co., N.J., 1957-58; salesman Scovill Mfg. Co., Mills div., N.Y. and N.C., 1958-62, dist. mgr., Southeast, 1962-65; product mgr. rod and wire, Waterbury, Conn., 1965-68, gen. mgr. fluid power div., Raleigh, N.C., 1968—. Dist. finance chmn. Occoneechee council Boy Scouts Am., Raleigh, N.C., 1971-72. Bd. trustees United Fund, Raleigh, N.C. Served to capt. USAF, 1953-56. Mem. Nat. Fluid Power Assn. (bd. dirs. 1970—), Machinery and Allied Products Inst. (marketing council 1969—), Fluid Power Found. (bd. trustees 1970—, v.p. 1971—), Fluid Power Soc., Am. Supply and Machinery Mfg. Assn., Power Transmission Dist. Assn., Am. Mgmt. Assn., Sigma Chi, Gate and Key. Republican. Episcopalian. Rotarian. Club: Carolina Country (Raleigh). Home: 100 Perquimans Dr Raleigh NC 27609 Office: Route 1 Wake Forest NC 27587

ANDREWS, WILTON WAYLAND, former geophysicist; b. Collins, Miss., Sept. 17, 1906; s. Charles Forrest and Annis (Speed) A.; student Baylor U., 1923-24; B.A., Sam Houston State U., 1926; postgrad. U. Cal. at Los Angeles, 1929; B.S., Tex. A. and M. U., 1933; m. Mary Reed, July 6, 1936; children—Wilton Wayland, Mary Catherine (Mrs. John W. Bahr), Eleanor Sherrell. High sch. prin. and coach, Madisonville, Tex., 1926-29; high sch. prin., West Columbia, Tex., 1929-30; field seismic interpreter, Humble Oil Co., 1933-43, hdqrs. office seismic interpreter, Houston, 1943-53, supervisory seismic interpreter all Gulf Offshore explorations, 1953-56, div. supervisory seismic interpreter, 1956-64, sr. staff geophysicist, 1964-66, sr. geophysical specialist, 1966-71, ret., 1971. Treas., dir. United Cerebral Palsy Assn. Houston and Harris County, 1958-65; worker-coordinator Houston United Fund, 1958-70, Easter Seal Soc., 1958—. Tax assessor, councilman City of Southside Place, 1960-65. Served with AAC, 1931. Mem. Soc. Exploration Geophysicists, Am. Assn. Petroleum Geologists, Geophys. Soc. Houston, Geol. Soc. Houston. Baptist (Sunday sch. tchr., deacon). Home: 6534 Auden St Houston TX 77005

ANDRUS, CHARLES ELMER, educator, clergyman; b. Atchison, Kan., July 8, 1912; s. Charles Linden and Libbie Gertrude (Harris) A.; A.B., Park Coll., 1937; M. Div., Louisville Presbyn. Sem., 1940; M.Th., St. Andrew's 1963, Th.D., 1964, Ph.D., 1968; m. Bernece Aileen Lindsey, May 30, 1932; children—Charles E., George Linden, Sarah Katherine (Mrs. Kendall D. Ramey), John C., David Mark. Ordained to ministry U.P. Ch., 1940; minister, Ashland, Kan., 1940-44, Butler, Mo., 1947-49, Hannibal, Mo., 1951-59, Fayetteville, Ark., 1959-64, Lawton, Okla., 1964-68, Chattanooga, Okla., 1968; prof. philosophy and social sci. Cameron Coll., Lawton, Okla., 1967—. Cons., Model Cities, Lawton, 1968—. Chmn. Comanche County chpt. A.R.C., 1966—; mem. Guidance Council for Mental Health, Comanche County, Okla., 1966—. Bd. dirs. Salvation Army, Lawton, 1966—, pres., 1967—. Served as chaplain USNR, 1943-47. Mem. Higher Edn. Council, Okla. Edn. Assn. Mason, Rotarian. Club: Hi-Twelve (Hannibal, Mo.). Author: Manual for Marital Instruction, 1964. Home: 807 NW 48th St Lawton OK 73501 Office: Cameron College 2200 Gore Blvd Lawton OK 73501

ANDRUS, GERALD (LOUIS), utilities exec.; b. Crowley, La., Nov. 15, 1904; s. Charles D. and Rosa C. (Ramoin) A.; B.B.A., Tulane, 1928; m. Lucile G. Isacks, Apr. 22, 1930; 1 dau., Marion L. (Mrs. Andrew McCollam, Jr.). With New Orleans Pub. Service Inc., 1928-62, comptroller, 1947-52. v.p., 1952-59, pres., 1959-62, dir. 1959—; dir. New Orleans br. Fed. Res. Bank of Atlanta, 1959-61, chmn., 1960; pres. Middle S. Utilities, Inc., N.Y.C., 1962-70, chmn. bd., 1970—, dir., 1960—; pres., dir. Middle South Services, Inc., New Orleans, 1963-70, chmn. bd., dir., 1970—; dir. Ark. Power & Light Co., Ark.-Mo. Power Co., La. Power & Light Co., Miss. Power & Light Co. Chmn. United Fund campaign, 1954; bd. adminstrs. Tulane U., 1960—. King of 1960 New Orleans Carnival (Mardi Gras). C.P.A. Clubs: New Orleans Country (pres. 1959-60), Pickwick, Boston (pres. 1967-68), Stratford (New Orleans); Racquet and Tennis, Blind Brook, Links, Recess (N.Y.C.). Home: 1309 Nashville Av New Orleans LA 70115 Office: 225 Baronne St New Orleans LA 70161 also 280 Park Av New York City NY 10017

ANDUJAR, JOHN J., physician; b. Chgo., Jan. 26, 1912; s. M.A. and Lily (Kurzenknabe) A.; B.S., Pa. State Univ., 1930; M.D., Temple U., 1934; postgrad. Union U., 1935-36, Cornell U., 1942; m. Elizabeth Richards, Aug. 16, 1935; children—Betty Jo, Linda Lee. Intern Harrisburg Gen. Hosp., 1934-35, Memorial Hosp., N.Y. C., 1942-43, Bender Hygienic Lab., Albany, N.Y., 1935-36; asso. prof. U. Ark., 1937-38; practice of medicine, Ft. Worth, 1938—; prof. med. technology Tex. Christian U., 1938-50; dir. Ft. Worth Med. Labs., Doctors Hosp. Labs., Ft. Worth Dept. Health Labs., Texas Dept. Health Regional Labs.; cons. pathologist USPHS, John Peter Smith hosps., Carswell AFB Sta. Hosp. Past pres. Tarrant County Crime Commn. Past. pres. Am Pathology Found.; pres. World Pathology Found. Diplomate Nat. Bd. Med. Examiners, Am. Bd. Pathology (past pres.). Fellow Am. Soc. Clin. Pathologists (past. pres.), A.C.P., Coll. Am. Pathologists (founder); mem. A.A.A.S., A.M.A., Am. Assn. Blood Banks (founder), Am. Assn. Phys. and Surg., Am. Cancer Soc., Soc. Am. Bacteriologists, Pan-Am. Tex. Acad. Internal Medicine, Assn. Mil. Surgeons U.S., Internat. Acad. Pathology, Am. Public Health Assn., Tex. Acad. Sci., Tex. Hosp. Assn., Tex. Pub Health Assn., Tex. Soc. Pathologists (past pres.), Tarrant County Med. Soc. (past pres.), Internat. Council Soc. Pathology, Royal Soc. Health, World Assn. Soc. Pathology (pres. 1969-72), Tarrant County Mental Health Soc., Phi Beta Pi. Presbyterian. Clubs: Fort Worth Boat, Peninsula Country, Torch. Address: PO Box 1118 Fort Worth TX 76101

ANGEL, W.G., petroleum co. exec. Sec. exec. and mem. financial com. Phillips Petroleum Co. Office: Phillips Bldg Bartlesville OK 74003*

ANGELE, GUSTAVE JOHN, SR., civil engr.; b. Balt., Mar. 30, 1906; s. John and Emma Anna (Wirth) A.; student Internat. Corr. Schs., 1920-24, Johns Hopkins, 1927-30; m. Myrtle Marie Sauer, June 19, 1935; 1 son, Gustave John, Jr. Sr. design engr. Union Carbide Nuclear div. Union Carbide Corp., Oak Ridge, 1944-71; plant san. engr., Oak Ridge, 1971. Chmn. bd. plumbing examiners City Oak Ridge, 1961-71; mem. U.S. Power Squadron, 1947—. Registered profl. engr., Tenn. Mem. Am. Water Works Assn. (chmn. backflow com.; moderator cross connection control seminars), Am. Soc. San. Engrs., Am. Soc. C.E. Mason. Contbr. articles to profl. jours. Home: 120 Porter Rd Oak Ridge TN 37830 Office: PO Box 237 Oak Ridge TN 37830

ANGELL, J(OHN) WILLIAM, educator; b. Mocksville, N.C., Feb. 29, 1920; s. John Tilden and Juanita (Hanes) A.; student Mars Hill Coll., 1937-39; B.A., Wake Forest Coll., 1941; Th.M., So. Bapt. Theol. Sem., 1945, Th.D., 1949; S.T.M., Andover Newton Theol. Sch., 1948; postgrad. U. Zurich, 1962; m. Marjorie Sutterlin, June 6, 1944; children—John William, George Sutterlin. Ordained to ministry Bapt. Ch., 1945; pastor Buies Creek Ch., also chaplain Campbell Coll., 1949-52; asso. prof. religion Stetson U., 1952-55; prof. religion Wake Forest U., Winston-Salem, N.C., 1955—, dir. Ecumenical Inst., 1970—. Mem. order of bus. com. So. Bapt. Conv., 1968—; mem. commn. on coop. Christianity, Bapt. World Alliance, 1972—. Fellow Ministers Research Found.; mem. Soc. Bibl. Lit., Am. Acad. Religion, N.C. Tchrs. Religion, Assn. Bapt. Profs. Religion, Delta Kappa Alpha. Democrat. Author: Can the Church Be Saved: How the Insights of Kierkegaard Speak to Present Needs, 1967. Contbr. articles profl. jours. Home: 108 Belle Vista Ct Winston-Salem NC 27106 Office: Wake Forest University Winston-Salem NC 27109

ANGELO, BONNIE (MRS. HAROLD R. LEVY), newspaper corr.; b. Winston-Salem, N.C.; d. Ernest J. and Ethel (Hudgins) Angelo; B.A., U. N.C.; m. Harold R. Levy, Aug. 19, 1950; 1 son, Charles Christopher. Reporter, women's editor Winston-Salem Jour. & Sentinel. 1944-50; women's editor Richmond Times-Dispatch, 1950; feature writer Newsday, 1952-55, Washington corr., 1955-63; syndicated columnist Newhouse Nat. News Service, 1963-66; Washington corr. Time mag., 1966—. Featured performer Channel 5 TV, 1967—. Pres. Women's Nat. Press Club, 1961-62. Recipient distinguished reporting in civil rights Paul Tobenkin Meml. Found., 1961. Mem. White House Corr. Assn. Club: Washington Press. Home: 5401 Edgemoor Lane Bethesda MD 20014 Office: 888 16th St NW Washington DC 20006

ANGER, CHARLES LEROY, educator; b. Balt., May 13, 1912; s. Charles P. and Catherine (Kemp) A.; B.S., U. Va., 1932, M.S., 1933, Ph.D., 1940; m. Elizabeth Abbey Foy, Oct. 4, 1963. Asst. prof. The Citadel, Charleston, S.C., 1941-44, asso. prof., 1946-55, prof., head dept. history, 1955—. Chmn., S.C. Commn. Archives and History, 1965—, S.C. bd. review Nat. Register Historic Places, 1969—. Mem. Am. (life), S.C. (pres. 1959-61), So. hist. assns. Episcopalian. Clubs: Carolina Yacht, Charleston. Home: 843 Sheldon Rd Charleston SC 29407

ANGERMAYER, KARL, metals co. exec.; b. Neu-Isenburg, West Germany, May 24, 1912; s. Karl and Franziska (Ziegler) A.; Mech. and Structural Engr., Engring Coll. Bingen, 1933; m. Anna Maria Schoenbein, Aug. 28, 1937; 1 dau., Hannelore (Mrs. Michael Adam Glagola). Came to U.S., 1953, naturalized, 1959. Engr., then chief engr. I.G. Farbenindustrie AG, Bitterfeld, Germany, 1933-45; chief engr. Stahlbau Rademacher, Kreuznach, 1946-49, Hombak Maschinenfabrik, Kreuznach, 1949-53; chief design engr. Reynolds Metals Co., Louisville, 1953-68, dir. design engring., Richmond, Va., 1968—. Served with German Army, 1944-45. Registered profl. engr., Va. Mem. Am. Soc. Metals, Am. Soc. C.E. Home: 7702 Brookside Rd Richmond VA 23229 Office: 6601 W Broad St Richmond VA 23218

ANGLEMYER, MARY, librarian; b. Chelan, Wash., Aug. 4, 1909; d. Thaddeus Delos and Philinda (Rand) Anglemyer; A.B., Radcliffe Coll., 1931; B.S. in L.S., Columbia, 1936. Asst., Elizabeth (N.J.) Pub. Library, 1931-34; asst. librarian Pace Inst., N.Y.C., 1934-36; library asst. N.Y. Pub. Library, N.Y.C., 1937; cataloger, asso. Bar of City of N.Y., 1937-38; asst. librarian Div. Placement and Unemployment Ins., N.Y.C., 1938-42, librarian, 1946-48; librarian U.S. Army, Mitchel Field, N.Y., Atlantic City, also Eng., Germany, 1942-46; dir. library service USIA, Bangkok, Thailand, 1949-53; asst. editor Dewey Decimal Classification, Library of Congress, Washington, 1954-56; library expert Thailand-UNESCO Fundamental Edn. Centre, Ubol, Thailand, 1957; librarian Mil. Assistance Inst., Arlington, Va., 1958-66; selection officer Library Dept. Interior, Washington, 1966-68; information specialist Engr. Agy. Resources Inventories, Washington, 1968-70; librarian Woodrow Wilson Internat. Center for Scholars, Washington, 1970—. Cons. on Thailand to research orgns., 1953—. Vice chmn. Thai Library Coordinating Com., Bangkok, 1951-53; mem. com. vis. fgn. librarians Council Nat. Library Orgns., 1956-68; chmn. Inter-Agy. Library Group, 1961—. Hon. mem. Siam Soc., Thai Library Assn.; mem. A.L.A.; Spl. Libraries Assn., D.C. Library Assn. Contbr. articles to profl. jours. Home: 2035 Trumbull Terrace Washington DC 20011 Office: Smithsonian Instn Bldg 1000 Jefferson Dr SW Washington DC 20560

ANGLIN, ROBERT HENRY, accountant; b. Richmond, Va., Feb. 23, 1913; s. Robert Henry and Clelia (Keeton) A.; student U. Va., 1947, 59, U. Tex., 1965, 66; m. Minnie Louise Milstead, Jan. 5, 1933 (div. June 1943); 1 son, Robert Henry III (dec.). Timekeeper, Danville Knitting Mills (Va.), 1929-33; law clk. J. William Scruggs, Atty., Danville, 1933-36; prodn. clk. Dan River Mills, Danville, 1936-37, timekeeper, 1937-42, cost accountant, 1942-68, cost analyst, 1968-71, cost engr., 1971—. Lectr. on cost control, optimum machinery assignments Dan River Textile Sch., 1945-52. Treas., Republican Com., Danville, 1964-68. Recipient Civilian Merit citation for setting up radio communications USAF, 1964. Mem. Am. Radio Relay League, A.A.A.S., Math. Assn. Am., Fibonacci Assn. Contbr. articles to profl. jours. Home: 833 Noble Av Danville VA 24541 Office: Dan River Mills Danville VA 24541

ANGLIN, W(ILLIAM) E(NGLISH), lawyer; b. Burnsville, N.C., Oct. 24, 1907; s. Geo. W. and Carrie (English) A.; B.S., U. N.C., 1934, LL.B. 1934. Admitted to N.C. bar, 1934, practiced under own name in Burnsville, 1934-42, 46-65; resident superior ct. judge, 1965—. Served to comdr. USNR, 1942-46; PTO. Mem. N.C. Bar Assn., Theta Chi, Phi Delta Phi. Office: Law Bldg Burnsville NC 28714

ANIGSTEIN, DOROTHY MCCARTNEY WHITNEY (MRS. LUDWIK ANIGSTEIN), research scientist; b. Salina, Kan.; d. William Russell and Faye (McCartney) Whitney; A.B., U. Kan., 1926, M.A., 1932; m. Ludwik Anigstein, May 2, 1958. Asst. bacteriology U. Kan., 1926-34; bacteriologist Charles S. Wilson Meml. Hosp., Johnson City, N.Y., 1934-41, Pillsbury Research Lab., Mpls., 1941-45; research scientist immunology, chemotherapy, exptl. tumors U. Tex. Med. Br., Galveston, 1945—. Mem. Art League Galveston (pres. 1950-55), Sigma Xi. Contbr. articles to sci. publs. Home: 28 Manor Way Galveston TX 77550 Office: U Tex Med Br Dept Preventive Medicine and Community Health Galveston TX 77550

ANKRUM, WARD ELWOOD, educator; b. Danville, Ill., Mar. 2, 1910; s. Wesley Jay and Margaret Elizabeth (Ward) A.; student Wabash Coll., 1929-32; B.S. in Edn., U. Ill., 1934, M.S. in Edn., 1941; student U. Denver, 1942-43; Ed.D., U. Mo., 1951; m. Wilma Mooney Walloch, May 30, 1965. Instr. speech and English, Danville High Sch., 1938-42; ednl. specialist, div. instr. tng. USAAF, 1942-44; instr. speech and English, U. Denver, 1943-44; chmn. English dept. Coronado (Cal.) High Sch., 1944-45; instr. div. communications Stephens Coll., Columbia, Mo., 1945-52, dir. audio-visual library, 1952-57; asso. prof., dir. audio-visual edn. Henderson State Tchrs. Coll., Arkadelphia, Ark., 1957-63, prof., dir. audio visual edn., 1963—; Ford Found. lectr. Ark. A. and M. Coll., 1953; co-dir. Grad. and Undergrad. Credit Workshop, Northeast Mo. State Tchrs. Coll., Kirksville, 1954-58, 62, 64, 66; asst. dir. Ednl. Media Inst. Ark. State Coll., summer 1967; special research influence selected television programs on preservice teachers, fundamental factors in reading rate acceleration. Charter pres. Columbia (Mo.) Art Theatre Adv. Council, 1955-58; chmn. audiovisual services Mo. P.T.A., 1955-58; del. from Mo. nat. conv. P.T.A., 1957; chmn. audio-visual services Ark. P.T.A., 1958-61; pres. dept. audio visual services Mo. Tchrs. Assn., 1955-56; juror Golden Reel Film Festival, N.Y.C., 1955, juror, chmn. motion pictures in edn., 1956. Mem. Nat. (parliamentarian dept. audio visual instrn. 1960—), Ark. (pres. Ark. audio visual assn. 1959-61, treas. 1971—) edn. assns., Ark. Ednl. TV Assn. (v.p. 1961—), Phi Delta Kappa, Tau Kappa Epsilon. Republican. Presbyn. Mason. Contbr. profl. jours. Co-author: Utilization of Audio-Materials in Missouri, 1955. Home: 309 Riverside Dr Arkadelphia AR 71923

ANNIS, EDWARD ROLAND, physician; b. Detroit, Mar. 27, 1913; s. Edward Roland and Ethel Mary (Graham) A.; B.S., U. Detroit, 1933; M.D., Marquette U., 1938; postgrad. Cook County Grad. Sch., Chgo.; D. Sc., U. San Diego, U. Detroit, 1963, Hahnemann Med. Coll.; LL.D., U. Scranton; Litt.D., Barry Coll. Miami, 1966; m. Betty McCue Starck, June 16, 1941; children—Joseph Payne, Brian Roland, Paul Starck, Barbara Mary, Marjorie Joan, Kathleen Deborah, Timothy John, Roberta Marie. Intern Milwaukee County Hosp., Milw., 1937-38; practice of medicine, specializing surgery, Tallahassee, 1938-46, Miami, Fla., 1946—; chief dept. gen. surgery Mercy Hosp., 1953-63; med. cons. Home Life Ins. Co. N.Y.; attending surgeon North Shore Hosp.; vis. surgeon Jackson Meml. Hosp., Variety Children's Hosp., Christian Hosp. (all Miami), St. Francis Hosp., Miami Beach, Fla. Dir., Blvd. Nat. Bank; Royal Resources Exploration, Inc., Regency Income Corp., Inc. (Denver), Medequip Corp., Chgo.; pres. Denver Corp., 1969-71. Chmn. Fla. Gov.'s Citizens Med. Com. on Health, 1959. Trustee Nat. Assn. Interns and Residents; bd. dirs. Imperial-Am. Resources Fund Inc. Recipient Distinguished Service award Creighton U., 1963, Outstanding Alumnus of Year award Marquette U., 1964. Fellow Internat. Coll. Surgeons (pres. U.S. sect. 1964-65), Am. Acad. Gen. Practice (hon. life), Air Force Soc. Clin. Surgeons (hon.), Flying Physicians Assn. (hon.), Am. Profl. Practice Assn. (chmn.), Southeastern Surg. Soc.; mem. A.M.A. (trustee), World (pres. 1963-64, council emissary 1964-66), Fla. (chmn. legislative com. 1960-65), Dade County med. assns., U.S. (dir.), Miami chambers commerce, Nat. Assn. Professions (dir.). Roman Catholic. K.C. Clubs: Bath (Miami Beach); Palm Bay, Jockey (Miami). Home: 4425 Banyan Lane Bay Point Miami FL 33137 Office: 2121 Biscayne Blvd Miami FL

ANSLEY, JOSEPH ALBERT, banker; b. Americus, Ga., Feb. 24, 1906; s. Joseph A. and Jessie (Whitaker) A.; student Stetson U., 1925-26, Am. Inst. Banking, 1948, Sch. Financial Pub. Relations, Northwestern U., 1950, Grad. Sch. Banking, Rutgers, The State U., 1953; m. Barbara Jean Holmes, Nov. 13, 1943; children—Barbara Jean, Mary Elizabeth. Advt. dir. Ft. Myers News-Press, 1927-42; with Lee County Bank, Ft. Myers, Fla., 1945—, pres., 1966—, chmn. bd., 1967—. Pres., Lee Meml. Hosp., Ft. Myers, Fla., 1963-65, bd. dirs., 1947—. Served with USNR, 1942-45. Recipient citations Bankings Forum in Print, 1951, 52, 53. Mem. Am. Inst. Mgmt. (fellow pres.'s council 1967—), Am. Bankers Assn. (mem. exec. council 1970-71), Fla. Bankers Assn. (pres. 1957), Financial Pub. Relations Assn., 40 and 8, Am. Legion (comdr. 1947), Fla., Ft. Myers chambers commerce; Am. Orchid Soc. Presbyn. Mason. Clubs: Kiwanis (pres. 1937), Royal Palm Yacht (commodore 1966); Mountain City (Asheville, N.C.). Home: 3310 Hibiscus Dr Fort Myers FL 33901 Office: 1st and Monroe Sts Fort Myers FL 33902

ANTHONY, JACK RAMON, mech. engr.; b. Hobbs, N.M., Dec. 9, 1932; s. Wadie Fowler and Zelma (Allen) A.; B.S., U. N.M., 1959; postgrad. Tex. Tech. U., 1969—; m. Peggy Lou Berryhill, July 17, 1953; children— Vera Lynn, Michael Ray. Engr. Controls Co. Am., Santa Fe, 1959-61; project engr. Eberline Instrument Corp., Santa Fe, 1961-63; engr. space div. Chrysler Corp., New Orleans, 1963-65; design engr. Dresser Co., Houston, 1965-67; project engr. Mason &Hanger, Amarillo, Tex., 1967—. Mem. Sheriff's Posse Hutchison County, 1968—. Served with AUS, 1953-55. Registered profl. engr., Tex. Mem. Tex. Soc. Profl. Engrs., Pi Tau Sigma. Toastmaster. Home: PO Box 3389 Borger TX 79007 Office:PO Box 647 Amarillo TX 79105

ANTHONY, WALTER PHILIP, JR., surgeon; b. Princeton, Ind., May 1, 1919; s. Walter Philip and Lois (Fowler) A.; B.S., Purdue U., 1941; M.D., Ind. U., 1943; M.S., U. Minn., 1951; m. Dora Kell, Nov. 12, 1943; children—Philip Fowler, Laura. Resident, Mayo Clinic, Rochester, Minn., 1948-51; pvt. practice surgery, Ft. Worth, 1951—, specializing in ear surgery and disease, 1961—; mem. staffs Harris, All Saints, St. Joseph, Peter Smith, Cook Childrens hosps. (all Ft. Worth); faculty U. Tex. Southwestern Med. Sch., 1962—, clin. asst. prof. otolaryngology, 1964—. Cons. Tex. Christian Speech and Hearing Clinic, Otosclerosis Study Group of Am. Acad. Ophthalmology and Otolaryngology. Mem. com. services for deaf Tex. Legislative Council, 1965-67. Served to lt. M.C. USNR, 1943-47. Mem. Am. Otol. Soc., Am. Acad. Ophthalmology and Otolaryngology, Am. Triological Soc., Sigma Xi, Pi Kappa Alpha, Phi Chi. Clubs: Rivercrest Country, Fort Worth Boat, Fort Worth. Contbr.

articles to profl. jours. Home: 321 N Bailey Av Fort Worth TX 76107 Office: 622 S Henderson St Fort Worth TX 76104

ANTIL, JEROME MARK, marketing cons.; b. Cortland, N.Y., Apr. 9, 1941; s. Michael Charles and Mary Margaret (Holman) A.; student Xavier U., Cin., 1958-61; m. Andrea Jocelyn Lyster, Aug. 24, 1968. Sales promotion and pub. relations cons. Antil Studios, Inc., Cin., 1961-67; with Aamco Transmissions, franchising, King of Prussia, Pa., 1968-69; with Bonanza Internat., fast food franchising, Dallas, 1969-71, cons., coordinator marketing activities, 1970—; marketing services cons. Jerry Antil, Inc., Dallas, 1971—. Cons., coordinator marketing Steamatic, Inc., Ft.Worth, Internat. Music Centers, Dallas, Security Electronic and Engring., Dallas; cons. to city Ogdensburg, N.Y., also coordinator maj. rehab. program, 1967. Asso. adviser Explorer Post, Boy Scouts Am., Dallas, 1969—. Recipient various awards, including Kodak Film Festival award, 1964, Best Advt. Program Dallas Ad League, 1969, Best Packaging Internat. Paper Council, 1969, Best TV Comml. Phila. Festival, 1971; commended by editorial and Gov. Rockefeller for achievement in Ogdensburg, 1966. Mem. Dallas Advt. League. Roman Catholic. Writer 47 indsl. motion pictures. Home: 4522 Arcady Av Dallas TX 75205 Office: 6116 N Central Expressway Dallas TX 75206

ANTO, JOHN, city ofcl.; b. Manifolk, Pa., Aug. 30, 1910; s. George and Ann (Repka) A.; grad. high sch.; m. Virginia A. Williams, Oct. 25, 1946; children—John M., Mary P., Paul S. Joined U.S. Navy, 1928; commd. ensign, 1942, advanced through grades to comdr., 1956; officer-in-charge ship dept. U.S. Naval Sta., Green Cove Springs, Fla., 1951-54; comdg. officer U.S.S. Skywatcher, 1954-56; ret., 1956; civil engr. Dept. Pub. Works, City of Norfolk (Va.), 1957-62, asst. hwy. supt., 1962-64, hwy. supt., 1964—. Decorated Bronze Star medal. Home: 257 Louvick St Norfolk VA 23503 Office: City Hall Bldg St Paul's Blvd Norfolk VA 23510

ANTON, PAUL NAJIB, engr.; b. Jerusalem, Palestine, Dec. 19, 1934; s. Nicola Najib and Mary Michail (Salama) A.; diploma St. George's Coll., Heliopolis, Egypt, 1951; B.A., U. Tex., 1960; postgrad. St. Mary's U., San Antonio, 1960-62; m. Margaret Jean Welch, Jan. 26, 1958; 1 dau., Cybele Najib. Came to U.S., 1954, naturalized, 1962. Various banking duties Alamo Nat. Bank, San Antonio, 1959-61; sci. programming analyst Lockheed Missiles and Space Co., Sunnyvale, Cal., 1962-70; sr. devel. engr. Well Services div. Schlumberger Tech. Corp., Houston, 1970—. Mem. Am. Math. Soc., Mat. Assn. Am., Assn. Computing Machinery. Republican. Home: 1923 South Blvd Houston TX 77006 Office: PO Box 2175 Houston TX 77001

ANTRIM, HARRY THOMAS, educator; b. Richmond, Va., Feb. 17, 1936; s. Robert Emmett and Eliza (Eldridge) A.; A.B., Davidson Coll., 1957; M.A., U. Fla., 1962, Ph.D., 1967; m. L. Self; children—Donald and Terry. Asst. curator John and Mable Ringling Mus. Art, Sarasota, Fla., 1957-58; instr. English, U. Fla., 1962-64; asst. prof. English, U. Va., Charlottesville, 1965-71; asso. prof. English, asst. dean Coll. Arts and Scis. Fla. Internat. U., Miami, 1971—. Cons. lang. and linguistics U. Va. Sch. Gen. Studies, 1969-71; chmn. selection com. W. Faulkner Found. 1st Novel award, 1966-70. Bd. dirs. William Faulkner Found. Served to 1st. AUS, 1958-60. Mem. Modern Lang. Assn. Am., Southeastern Modern Lang. Assn., Modern Humanities Research Assn., Kappa Alpha, Phi Kappa Phi. Author: T.S. Eliot's Concept of Language, 1971. Contbr. articles to lit. jours. Home: 9341 SW 106th Av Miami FL 33156 Office: Fla Internat U Tamiami Trail Miami FL 33154

APINIS, JOHN, chemist; b. Katvari, Latvia, Mar. 20, 1933; s. Augusts and Marta (Gravelsins) A.; B.S., Clemson U., 1960; m. Johnnie Verena Burden, Feb. 6, 1960. Came to U.S., 1949, naturalized, 1954. Apprentice, Am. Thread Co., Willimantic, Conn., 1951-52, Leiss Velvet Mfg. Co., Willimantic, 1952-53; asst. plant chemist Burlington Industries, Wake Finishing Co., Raleigh, N.C., 1960-65, plant chemist, 1965—. Served with AUS, 1953-55. Mem. Am. Assn. Textile Chemists and Colorists. Elk, Rotarian (v.p. 1963-64, pres. 1964-65, dir. 1963-66). Research in textile color computer and chromosorter. Home: Route 7 Box 497 Millbrook Rd Raleigh NC 27609 Office: Box 2748 Raleigh NC 27607

APONTE, MARTINEZ LUIS, archbishop; b. Lajas, P.R., Aug. 4, 1922; s. Santiago E. Aponte and Rosa Martinez; student San Ildefonso Sem., San Juan, P.R., 1944, St. John's Sem., Boston, 1950; LL.D. (hon.), Fordham U., 1965. Ordained priest Roman Cath. Ch., 1950; asst. in Patillas, P.R.; pastor in Maricao, P.R., Sta. Isabel, P.R., 1953-55; sec. to bishop of Ponce, P.R., 1955-57; pastor in Aibonito, P.R., 1957-60; aux. bishop of Ponce, 1960-63, bishop, 1963-64; archbishop of San Juan, 1964—. Chancellor Cath. U. P.R., Ponce, 1963—. Served as chaplain P.R. N.G., 1957-60. Lion. Address: 50 Cristo St PO Box 1967 San Juan PR 00907

APONTE-PEREZ, FRANCISCO, labor lawyer; b. Barranquitas, P.R., Sept. 17, 1928; s. Delfin and Catalina (Perez) Aponte; B.A. magna cum laude, U. P.R., 1950; LL.B., U. Kan., 1958; m. Ana C. Alicea, Oct. 27, 1957; children—Liza, Maria, Emma. Admitted to P.R. bar; adminstrv. technicial P.R. Bur. Budget, San Juan, 1951-53; labor mediator and arbitrator P.R. Dept. Labor, San Juan, 1953-58; trial examiner P.R. Labor Relations Bd., San Juan, 1958-60; practiced labor law, Santurce, P.R., 1960—. Lectr. U. P.R., mem. bd. bar examiners P.R. Supreme Ct. Served as 1st lt. AUS. Recipient citations Interam. U., Govt. of V.I., Am. Trial Lawyers Assn. Mem. P.R. Bar Assn. (pres. 1970—). Contbr. articles to law revs. Home: A-1 Montebello Gardens Hills PR 00619 Office: 607 Condado Av Santurce PR 00908

APPEL, WILLIAM GEORGE, assn. exec.; b. Pitts., Dec. 13, 1925; s. Ellwood and Charlotte (Wiertheimer) A.; student Inst. Orgn. Mgmt., Mich. State U., 1968-70; m. Frances Christine Dunagan, Sept. 15, 1950; 1 son, Robert William. Shipping clk. Paramount Pictures, Pitts., 1948-50, booker, Atlanta, 1950-51; booker Universal Pictures, Atlanta, 1951-54, salesman, Cin., 1954-57; sales engr. Shower Door Co. Am., Atlanta, 1958-61; v.p. sales A-B Real Estate & Constrn. Co., Smyrna, Ga., 1961-63; gen. sales mgr. King-Williams Land Co., Smyrna, 1963-64; asst. v.p. Potter &Co., Smyrna, 1964-66; exec. dir. Ga. Automotive Wholesalers Assn., Atlanta, 1966—. Mem. Heart Assn. Fund, 1965. Served with AUS, 1944-46; ETO. Recipient Distinguished Service award So. Automotive Show, 1969. Mem. Automotive Wholesalers Trade Assn. Execs. (chmn. liaison com. 1971-72, chmn. edn. com. 1970—, sec. 1969-70, v.p. 1970-71, pres. 1971-72), Ga. Soc. Assn. Execs. (sec. treas. 1968-71, exec. com.), Automotive Booster Club, Am. Soc. Assn. Execs., Cobb County C. of C., Internat. Platform Assn., Airline Passengers Assn. Contbg. columist Automotive Aftermarket News, 1971-72, Cotton Pickers jour. Atlanta Automotive Boosters, 1970—. Home: 3893 West Lane Dr SE Smyrna GA 30080 Office: 148 Cain St NE Atlanta GA 30303

APPERSON, CLEO NORMAN, city ofcl.; b. Mayfield, Ky., July 27, 1904; s. Will Lee and Ida May (Cosby) A.; student LaSalle U., 1935; m. Mary Kate Kennedy, Sept. 16, 1928; children—Barbara (Mrs. Harold St. Aubin), William, Walter. With Baker, Yates & McGeehee, Mayfield, 1918-28, Sinclair Oil Co., Detroit, 1928-29, Shell Oil Co., 1929-49; station mgr. Gulf Oil Co., Mayfield, Ky., 1949-51; with City of Mayfield, 1951—, city clk., 1951—, city councilman, 1949, city sch. tax collector, 1952—. Asso., Graves County Woodrow Wilson Found., 1956—, chmn., 1957—; team chmn. United Fund, 1955-70. Named Man of Year, Young Democrats Club, 1969. Mem. Mayfield C. of C., USAF Air Def. (life mem.). Mem. Disciples of Christ Ch. (elder). Mason, Lion (sec. 1952-58). Home: 506 Jones St Mayfield KY 42066 Office: City Hall Mayfield KY 42066

APPLEGATE, CHARLES STANLEY, JR., physician; b. Fort Smith, Ark., June 23, 1920; s. Charles Stanley and Helen Louise (Parmelee) A.; B.S., U. Ark., 1942, M.D., 1945; m. Annabel Applegate, Apr. 3, 1954; children—Jo Anne (Mrs. Chester Vogt), Charles Stanley III. Intern, Univ. Hosp., Little Rock, 1945-46; gen. practice medicine, Springdale, Ark., 1949—. Pres., dir. Springdale Savs. & Loan Assn., 1960—. Chmn. adv. com. to mayor of Springdale, 1969—. Chmn. Springdale Housing Authority, 1967—. Served with M.C., AUS, 1946-48. Mem. A.M.A., Ark. (pres. 1971-72), Washington County med. socs., Am. Assn. Family Practice, Springdale C. of C. (pres. 1969-70, chmn. indsl. com. 1966—). Home: 322 S Pleasant St Springdale AR 72764 Office: 220 Meadow Av Springdale AR 72764

APPLEGATE, WILLIAM ARTHUR, physician; b. Sharon, Pa., Sept. 7, 1904; s. Harry Abner and Elizabeth Meldrum (MacDonald) A.; A.B., U. W.Va., 1926, B.S. in Medicine, 1927; M.D., U. Pa., 1929; m. Nell Christine Stillstrom, July 2, 1930; children—Donna Jean (Mrs. David White), William Karl. Intern Allegheny Gen. Hosp., Pitts., 1929-30; practice medicine, Sharon, Pa., 1930-45, surgery, 1945-51; in charge clinics for V.I. Govt., St. John, V.I., 1959—. Ship surgeon Am. Export Lines, 1956-57. County coroner Mercer County, Pa., 1932-40. Mem. A.M.A., Am. Acad. Family Physicians, V.I. Med. Soc. Republican. Mason, Elk. Founder birth control clinic in V.I. Address: Cruz Bay St John VI 00830

APPLETON, JON GILBERT, clergyman; b. Louisville, Aug. 9, 1934; s. Zack Yergan and Kate (Chappell) A.; A.B., Samford U., 1955; B.D., So. Bapt. Theol. Sem., 1959; M.A., Auburn U., 1968; m. Virginia Bell, Aug. 19, 1956; 1 dau., Catherine Anne. Ordained to ministry Bapt. Ch., 1953; minister edn. and youth First Bapt. Ch., Gadsden, Ala., 1959-61; pastor First Bapt. Ch., Opelika, Ala., 1961-68; sec. adminstrn. com. Ala. Bapt. State Exec. Bd., Montgomery, 1962-68, dir., sec. campus ministry dept., 1968—; sec.-treas. So. Bapt. Conv. State Campus Ministers Dirs., 1969—. Trustee Am. Bapt. Theol. Sem., Nashville. Am.-Scottish Pastoral Exchange scholar U. Glasgow, summer 1965. Mem. Omicron Delta Kappa, Phi Alpha Theta. Writer religious column Truth Triumphant editorial page Gadsden Times, 1960-61. Home: 1234 Primrose Lane Montgomery AL 36111 Office: 2001 E South Blvd Montgomery AL 36111

APTON, RALPH JULIUS, govt. ofcl.; b. Cologne, Germany, Oct. 16, 1930; s. Adolph A. and Erna (Neu) A.; brought to U.S. 1935, naturalized, 1940; B.A., U. Chgo., 1950, M.B.A., 1954; m. Renate Sickinger, Dec. 30, 1959; 1 dau., Kory Kim. Fgn. trade and investment asst. AID, Washington, 1954; asst. indsl. analyst, New Delhi, India, 1955-57; dep. regional tech. aids coordinator for Latin Am., Mexico City, 1957-59; dep. exec. sec. Pres. Task Force for Fgn. Econ. Assistance, Washington, 1960-61; chief mgmt. analysis br. Bur. for Latin Am. Affairs, Washington, 1962; devel. loan officer, Quito, Ecuador, 1963-65, AID del. to Ecuadorian Hwy. Transp. Com., 1963-65; chief preinvestment loans Inter-Am. Bank, Washington, 1966—; real estate operator. Trustee Stonewall Dairy Farm. Mem. Am. Finance Assn., Am. Marketing Assn., Psi Upsilon. Clubs: U. Chgo. of Washington (dir.), River Bend Country (Va.), Quito Golf and Tennis. Home: 9610 Beach Mill Rd Great Falls VA 22066 Office: 808 17th St NW Washington DC 20577

AQUILINA, SAM ANTHONY, hotel exec.; b. Port Arthur, Tex., July 8, 1914; s. Marion and Angela A.; grad. high sch. Co-owner, v.p. Aquilina's Food Store, Port Arthur, 1932-63; pres. AORA Devel. Corp., 1960-71; co-owner, pres. Holiday Motor Hotel, Port Arthur, 1963—; partner M. Aquilina and Sons. Dir. First Nat. Bank, Port Arthur, Beaumont (Tex.) Savs. Bd. dirs. Goodwill Industries, Port Arthur; trustee St. Mary's Hosp. Mem. Port Arthur C. of C. (pres. 1971), Retail Mchts. Assn. (dir. 1964—). Kiwanian (pres. 1955). Club: Serra (pres. 1959—) (Port Arthur). Home: 100 Eddingston Ct Port Arthur TX 77640 Office: 3889 Gulfway St Port Arthur TX 77640

ARANGO, JORGE SANIN, architect; b. Bogota, Colombia, Nov. 29, 1916; s. Fernando Arango and Maria Sanin; student Sch. Architecture, Universidad Catolica de Chile, 1935-42; postgrad. Harvard Grad. Sch. Design, 1942-43; m. Judith Wolpert, Dec. 14, 1952; children— Richard, Virginia; 1 son, Pedro (by previous marriage). Came to U.S., 1957, naturalized, 1963. Practice architecture, Bogota, 1945-57, Caracas, Venezuela, 1957-59, Miami, Fla., 1959—. Prof. archtl. design Nat. U. Colombia, 1946-48; vis. lectr. Coll. Architecture, U. Cal. at Berkeley, 1954,56. Adminstr. pub. bldgs. Colombia, 1948-49 U.S. Dept. State, N.Y. Mus. Modern Art guest to U.S., 1943-44. Mem. A.I.A. Author: The Urbanization of the Earth, 1971; (with C. Martinez) Architecture in Colombia, 1952. Home: 3920 Wood Av Miami FL 33133 Office: 3141 Commodre Plaza Miami FL 33133

ARANT, JOHN AMOS, automobile agy. exec.; b. Pageland, S.C., Apr. 14, 1913; s. Peter May and Lottie Ann (McManus) A.; student Clemson U., 1930-32; m. Pearl Sowell, Dec. 3, 1935; children—Joan (Mrs. Owen W. Cook), Judy (Mrs. Curtis Lackey), John Amos. Pres., Arant Motor Co., Pageland, S.C., 1945—; owner, operator 3000 acre farm, Pageland, 1940—; dir., mem. finance bd. Peoples Bank & Trust Co., Pageland, 1937—; dir. S.C. Farm Bur. Ins. Co., 1st Citizens Bank & Trust Co. S.C.; sec., treas. Pageland Industries, 1946-57. Mem. Chesterfield County Bd. of Equalization for Taxes, 1940-65; county chmn. Agrl. Stablzn. and Conservation Service, 1962-69. Mem. City Council, 1947-70, mayor pro-tem, 1962-70. Bd. visitors Clemson U. Recipient award of merit Clemson U., 1970. Mem. Farm Bur. (county dir. 1945—, state dir. 1955—, exec. com. 1971—), S.C. Cotton Ginners (pres. 1938-40). Methodist (chmn. ofcl. bd. 1955-66). Home: 501 W McGregor St Pageland SC 29728 Office: 229 W McGregor St Pageland SC 29728

ARBINGAST, STANLEY ALAN, educator; b. Lisbon, Ia., Sept. 26, 1910; s. Clarence Earle and Faye (Oxley) A.; B.E., Winona State Coll., 1934; M.A., U. Wash., Seattle, 1948, Ph.D., 1956. Tchr., Minn. pub. schs., Lewisville, 1929-33, Lewiston, 1934-38, Duluth, 1938-42, 45-46; acting instr. U. Wash., 1948-49; asst. prof. resources U. Tex., Austin, 1949-53, asso. prof., 1953-59, prof. marketing adminstrn., 1959—, resources specialist Bur. Bus. Research, 1949—, asst. dir., 1951-60, asso. dir., 1960-69, dir., 1969—. Served with USAAF, 1942-45. Fellow Am. Geographic Soc.; mem. Am. Assn. Geographers (chmn. Southwestern div. 1968,69), A.A.A.S., Regional Sci. Assn., Am. Assn. U. Profs., Southwestern Social Sci. Assn. (2d v.p. 1958-59, 1st v.p. 1959-60, pres. 1960-61), Associated Univ. Burs. Bus. and Econ. Research (sec.-treas. 1961-64, pres. 1968), Phi Kappa Phi, Phi Kappa Sigma, Delta Sigma Pi, Omicron Delta Kappa. Episcopalian. Author: (with J. R. Stockton) Water Requirements Survey, Texas High Plains, 1952; (with J.R. Stockton and W.B. Moore) Water Requirements Survey, Red River Basin, Texas, 1953; (with L.G. Kennamer and Roberta Steele) Texas Resources and Industries, Selected Maps of Distribution, 1958; (with others) Water for the Future, 4 vols., 1959; The Texas Economy to 1975; (with Lorrin Kennamer) Atlas of Texas, 1963, (with Lorrin Kennamer and Michael Bonine), 1967; (with others) Texas 90, 1968; (with others) Atlas of Mexico, 1970. Editor: Tex. Bus. Rev., 1963—, Tex. Indsl. Expansion, 1950—. Contbr. numerous articles and monographs to profl. publs. Home: 3208 Duval St Austin TX 78705

ARBOGAST, RICHARD TERRENCE, entomologist; b. Freeport, Ill., Aug. 7, 1937; s. Raymond Dale and Virginia Mabel (Edler) A.; B.S., U. Ill., 1959; postgrad. U. Chgo., 1959-60, Ariz. State U., 1961; Ph.D. (Nat. Def. Edn. Act fellow), U. Fla., 1965; m. Helen Dee Fortney, Dec. 21, 1958; children—James Raymond, Kimberly Ann, Timothy Scott, Stephanie Ann. Research entomologist, stored product insects research and devel. lab. Market Quality Research div. Agrl. Research Ser., U.S. Dept. Agr., Savannah, Ga., 1965—. Cubmaster Coastal Empire council Boy Scouts Am., 1968-69, asst. scoutmaster, asst. cubmaster, 1970-72. Served to 1st lt. USAF, 1959-62. Mem. Entomol. Soc. Am., Lepidopterists' Soc., Ga. Entomol. Soc., Sigma Xi, Phi Sigma, Alpha Zeta. Contbr. to profl. jours. Home: 114 Monica Blvd Savannah GA 31406 Office: PO Box 5125 Savannah GA 31403

ARBOLEYA QUIROS, CARLOS J., banker; b. Havana, Cuba, Feb. 1, 1929; s. Fermin and Ana (Quiros) Arboleya; ed. Havana U.; advanced courses Systems and Research, Mgmt., Personnel; m. Martha Quintana, Aug. 29, 1954; 1son, Carlos. Came to the United States, 1960, naturalized, 1969. Employed with 1st Nat. City Bank of N.Y., in Havana, 1946-57, advancing to asst. head collection dept.; asst. mgr. trust and securities dept. Trust Co. of Cuba, Havana, 1957-59, also examiner and auditor, now mem. Employees in Exile Assn.; chief auditor controller's div. Banco Continental Cubano, Havana, 1959-60; from clk. to office mgr. and controller Allure Shoe Corp., Miami, Fla., 1960-62; v.p. operations and personnel, cashier, sec. Blvd. Nat. Bank Miami, 1962-66; exec. v.p., chief exec. officer, sec. Fidelity Nat. Bank South Miami (Fla.), 1966-69, president, chief exec. officer, 1969—, also dir. Tchr. banking operations Am. Inst. Banking, Miami, City Bank Club, Havana. Acting pres. Sts. Peter and Paul Parents Assn., Miami; co-chmn. Latin-Am. div. United Fund; adviser Greater Miami Jr. Achievement; mem. Latin Am. Affairs Commn. of Fla.; mem. internat. affairs action com. City of Miami; mem. citizens adv. planning com. City of South Miami; asst. council commr. Boy Scouts Am. Bd. dirs. Cuban Little League, Miami. Recipient Diploma of Honor Lincoln-Marti, Fed. Govt.; various awards for work in community and civic affairs. Mem. Bank Adminstrn. Inst. (pres. 1967-68, dir.; (pres. S. Fla. chpt., ofcl. rep. from Fidelity Nat. Bank South Miami, recipient Distinguished Service award S. Fla., 1965), Am. Inst. Banking (v.p. and gov. Miami), Nat. Amateur Athletic Union Havana (past bd. dirs.), Quivican Amateur Athletic Union Havana (past bd. dirs.), Nat. Softball Assn. (past del.), Havana U. Honor Athletes Assn., Inter-Am. Assn. Bus. Men in Miami, Latin C. of C. (pres. banker's adv. bd.), Dade County Bankers Assn. (mem. bd.), Kiwanian. Clubs: City Bank (past pres., past sports commnr., past bd. dirs.) (Havana); Bankers (past bd. dir., past del. to Cuban Olympic Com., past sports commnr.) (Havana). Home: 1941 SW 23d St Miami FL 33145 Office: Fidelity Nat Bank of South Miami PO Box 7397 Laudlaw Station South Miami FL 33143

ARCENEAUX, GEORGE, JR., lawyer; b. New Orleans, May 17, 1928; s. George and Louise (Austin) A.; B.A., La. State U., 1949; LL.B., Am. U., 1957; m. Mary Elizabeth Martin, Aug. 17, 1954; children—Mary Elizabeth, George III, Robert Martin. Program dir. Radio Sta. KCIL, Houma, La., 1949; state editor Daily Advertiser, Lafayette, 1949-50; legislative asst. Senator Allen J. Ellender, Washington, 1952-56, adminstrv. asst., 1957-60; admitted to La. bar, 1959; practiced in Houma, 1960—; mem. firm Duval, Arceneaux, Lewis & Gaidry, 1960—. Chmn., Houma-Terrebonne Regional Planning Commn., 1963—. Served with AUS, 1950-51. Mem. Am., La., Terrebonne Parish (pres. 1964-65) bar assns., C. of C. (dir. 1963, pres. 1966-67). Methodist. Clubs: Plimsoll, International House (New Orleans); University (Washington); Rotary (dir. 1963, pres. 1966, dist. gov. 1971-72). Home: 2 El Paso Dr Houma LA 70360 Office: 504 Belanger St PO Box 1568 Houma LA 70360

ARCHBOLD, RICHARD, mammalogist, explorer; b. N.Y.C., Apr. 9, 1907; s. John F. and May (Barron) A.; ed. pvt. schs. and spl. studies at Columbia; unmarried Mammalogist, Mission Zoologique Franco-Anglo-Americaine a Madagascar, 1929-31; leader and sponsor New Guinea Expdn., 1933-34, 1936-37; leader Indisch-Amerikaansche Expeditie (in cooperation with Netherlands Indies Govt.) 1938; pres. Archbold Expeditions; resident dir. Archbold Biol. Sta.; research asso. in mammalogy Am. Mus. Natural History. Trustee John D. Archbold Memorial Hosp., Thomasville, Ga. Officer, Order of Orange Nassau, 1940. Mem. N.Y. Acad. Scis., Inst. Aero. Scis., Am. Mammalogists Soc., Am. Ornithologists Union. Clubs: Explorers, American Alpine (N.Y.). Contbr. to sci. jours. Home and Office: Route 2 Box 380 Lake Placid FL 33852

ARCHER, ALFORD, geographer; b. Garrettsville, O., Apr. 11, 1908; s. John Clark and Cathaline (Alford) A.; student Hiram Coll., 1925-26, Carnegie Inst. Tech., 1927-29; B.S., Columbia, 1935, M.S., 1936; Ph.D., Ohio State U., 1962; m. Barbara Kathleen Dietrich, Oct. 14, 1938; children—John Clark, Joan Elizabeth. Asst. dept. geography Ohio State U., 1936-41; instr. geology and geography Ind. State Tchrs. Coll., 1941-42; asst. prof. commerce and geography, Toledo U., 1942-46, asst. dir. summer session, 1946; with U.S. Bur. Census, 1946—, geographer geography div., 1946-49, 55-59, 68-71, chief cartographic methods br., 1959-61, Internat. Statis. Programs as census geography adviser Republics of Panama, 1949-50, Bolivia, 1950, Honduras, 1951-55, 60, Costa Rica, 1952-54, El Salvador, 1953-55, 61, Thailand, 1961-63, Iran, 1966-68, Argentina, 1969, Paraguay, 1971-72, chief fgn. census research br., 1963 to 1966. Occasional instr. George Washington U., Am. U. Mem. adv. com. to Pan-Am. Inst. Geography and History, Nat. Acad. Scis., 1959-62. Pres. Rolling Terrace Civic Assn., Silver Spring, 1958-59, 64-65. Recipient Meritorious Service award from sec. commerce, 1956. Mem. Assn. Am. Geographers, Congress on Surveying and Mapping, Population Assn., Am. Statis. Assn. Home: 711 Forston Dr Takoma Park MD 20012 Office: Internat Statis Programs Div Bur of Census Washington DC 20233

ARCHER, CASS LOUIS, educator; b. nr. Spearman, Tex., June 1, 1924; s. Charles Otis and Jessie (Karr) A.; B.S., U. Tex., 1950, M.Ed., 1954, M.A., 1959, Ph.D., 1967; m. Irma Ruth Fulbright, July 25, 1953; children—Laura, Deborah, Timothy. High sch. tchr. Beeville (Tex.) Pub. Schs., 1950-51, Seminole (Tex.) Pub. Schs., 1951-58; prof., chmn. math. dept. Angelo State U., San Angelo, Tex., 1959—. Cons. math. Tex. Edn. Agy., 1962-64; speaker Conf. Advancement Math. Teaching, 1966, 67. Vice pres. P.T.A., 1967-68, pres., 1966-67. Served with USAAF, 1943-46. NSF fellow, 1958-59. Mem. Math. Assn. Am. (rep.), Tex. Assn. Coll. Tchrs., Nat. Council Tchrs. Math., Am. Math. Soc., Seminole Jr. C. of C. (past dir.), Phi Delta Kappa (pres. 1970-71), Pi Mu Epsilon, Rotary Internat. Home: 2810 Vista del Arroyo San Angelo TX 76901

ARCHER, DAVID RUSSELL, librarian; b. Phila., Mar. 6, 1943; s. William Andrew and Marcia Leona (Anderson) A.; A.B. (Augustus Trask Ashton scholar), U. Pa., 1963; M.L.S., Rutgers U., 1964. Audio-visual cataloger Miami-Dade Jr. Coll., 1965-66; audio-visual librarian Rockland (N.Y.) Community Coll., 1966-67; asso. prof., dir. library Cleveland (Tenn.) State Community Coll., 1967—. Mem. Miami Civic Chorus, 1966, Cleveland Civic Chorus, 1967—. Mem. Am. (mem. coms. 1969—), Southeastern, Tenn., Chattanooga (pres. 1969-70) library assns., Kappa Phi Kappa, Sigma Delta Pi. Home: 1100 20th St NW Cleveland TN 37311

ARCHER, WILLIAM REYNOLDS, JR., congressman; b. Houston, Mar. 22, 1928; s. William Reynolds and Eleanor (Miller) A.; student Rice U., 1945-46; B.B.A., U. Tex., 1949, LL.B., 1951; m. Patricia Moore, Nov. 21, 1953; children—William Reynolds III, Richard Moore, Sharon Leigh, Elizabeth Ann, Barbara Elise. Admitted to Tex. bar; pres. Uncle Johnny Mill, Inc., Houston, 1959-61, W.R. Archer, Inc., 1961—; partner firm Harris, Archer Parks & Graul, 1967—; dir. Heights State Bank, 1967-71; mem. 92d congress from 7th Tex. Dist. councilman, mayor pro-tem City of Hunters Creek Village, Tex., 1955-62. Bd. dirs. Houston Soc. for Prevention of Cruelty to Animals; trustee Houston Fund for Mental Research. Served from pvt. to 1st lt. USAF, 1951-53. Recipient Man of Yr. award Sigma Alpha Epsilon, 1969. Mem. Houston Bar Assn., Phi Delta Phi. Republican. Roman Catholic. Home: 3127 Avalon St Houston TX 77019

ARCHIBALD, JOHN CHRISTIE, JR.,, mining engr.; b. San Luis Potosi, Mexico, Mar. 16, 1916 (parents Am. citizens); s. John Christie and Edith Bell (Mangum) A.; student Columbia, 1932-34; B.S., Mont. Sch. Mines, 1938, Geol. Engr., 1951; m. Fontella Eunice Baird, Jan. 2, 1955; children—John Christie III, Wendy (Mrs. David Hulen), Robert Maro. With various mining cos., Mont., 1938-42; with Fgn. Econ. Adminstrn., Washington, 1944-45; chief mining operations Nat. Lead Co., Mexico, 1946-52, mgr. Tex. Mining & Smelting div., Laredo, 1952—. Campaign chmn. Webb County (Tex.) Republican Com., 1960. Mem. Am. Mining Congress (bd. govs. Western div. 1954-69), Am. Inst. Mining, Metall. and Petroleum Engrs., Tex. Soc. Profl. Engrs., Mensa, Laredo C. of C. (dir. 1962—), Sigma Alpha Epsilon. Republican. Christian Scientist. Clubs: Rotary (pres. 1955-56), Knife and Fork (pres. 1956-57) (Laredo). Address: Box 559 Laredo TX 78040

ARDOIN, JOHN LOUIS, newspaper music editor; b. Alexandria, La., Jan. 8, 1935; s. Louis and Ruth (Herren) A.; Mus.B., U. Tex., 1955; Mus.M., U. Okla., 1956; postgrad. Mich. State U., 1958-59. Asst. editor Mus. Am. mag., 1959-63, asso. editor, 1963-64, editor, 1964; mng. editor Philharmonic Hall program, mem. music staff Saturday Rev., 1965-66; music editor, amusements critic Dallas Morning News, 1966—. Mem. N.Y. Music Critics' Circle, 1960-64; N.Y. music critic London Times, 1964-66, Opera mag., 1965-66; guest lectr. music criticism Ind. U., 1971, 72. Contbr. articles to publs. Home: 4318 Abbott Av Dallas TX 75205 Office: Communications Center Dallas TX 75222

ARENS, JAMES FREDERICK, physician; b. Hamel, Minn., Apr. 20, 1934; s. Frederick John and Aurelia Marie (Buldoc) A.; M.D., Creighton U., 1959; m. Mary Helen Brown, Feb. 4, 1960; children—Patricia A., James F. Intern Tripler Army Hosp., Honolulu, 1959-60; resident in anesthesiology Charity Hosp., New Orleans, 1960-62; chief dept. anesthesia U.S. Air Force Burdrop Hosp., Swindon, Eng., 1962-65, Travis AFB, Fairfield, Cal., 1965-66; chief dept. anesthesia Ochsner Clinic, New Orleans, 1966—, med. dir. inhalation therapy and intensive care unit, 1970—; asso. prof. anesthesiology Tulane U., New Orleans, 1970—; cons. Keesler AFB, Biloxi, Miss. Diplomate Am. Bd. Anesthesiology. Mem. La. Soc. Anesthesia (pres. 1970-71), So. Soc. Anesthesiologists (v.p. 1969-70), A.M.A., Am. Soc. Anesthesiologists, So. Med. Assn., Internat. Research Soc., Phi Rho Sigma, Alpha Sigma Nu. Club: Colonial Country (New Orleans). Invented Ochsner cuff inflator, 1970. Home: 338 Garden Rd New Orleans LA 70121 Office: 1514 Jefferson Hyw New Orleans LA 70121

ARENS, RICHARD, commnr. U.S. Ct. Claims; b. Kansas City, Mo., Aug. 3, 1913; s. Ollie L. and Hazel (Payne) A.; A.B., Baker U., 1934; J.D., Washington U., St. Louis, 1937; m. Margaret Marie Stark, Sept. 13, 1941 (dec. Jan. 1952); children—Margaret Ann, Janice Marie; m. 2d, Mary Jane MacDevitt, June 29, 1955; children— Elizabeth Jane, Richard Thomas. Admitted to Mo. bar, 1937, also U.S. Supreme Ct.; gen. practice, Kansas City, Mo., 1937-41; legal sec. gov. Mo., 1941-45; mem. Mo. Pub. Service Commn., 1945-46; dir. reorgn. exec. depts. Mo., 1946-47; staff dir. immigration subcom. U.S. Senate, 1947-52, internal security subcom. U.S. Senate, 1947-52, internal security subcom., 1952-56; staff dir. com. un-Am. activities Ho. of Reps., 1956-60; commr. U.S. Ct. Claims, 1960—. Lectr. Communism; bd. mgrs. Council State Govts., 1941-45. Recipient Certificate of Merit, Patriotic Order Sons Am., 1953; Citation of Merit and Commendation, Am. Legion, 1954; citation Am. Coalition Patriotic Societies, 1958; Medal of Honor, Order Founders and Patriots Am., 1954; Citation of Merit and Distinction, Nat. Women's patriotic Conf. Nat. Def.; Certificate of Merit, D.A.R., 1956; Vigilant Patriot award All-Am. Conf. Combat Communism, 1960; Freedom award Order Lafayette, 1961. Mem. Delta Theta Phi. Methodist. Home: 10 Briggs Ct Wheaton MD 20906 Office: US Court Claims Washington DC 20006

AREY, WILLIAM GRIFFIN, JR., govt. ofcl.; b. Shelby, N.C., Feb. 18, 1918; s. William Griffin and Catherine (Roberts) A.; A.B., U. N.C., 1939; m. Louise Turner Craft, Mar. 7, 1942; children—William Griffin III, John Gordon Craft. Reporter, Daily Star, Shelby, N.C., 1939-41; co-pub., editor The Cleveland Times, Shelby, 1941-48; pub. affairs officer U.S. Embassies in Bogota, Colombia and Panama, Republic of Panama, 1948-54; asst. to the pres. Panama Canal Co., Balboa Heights, C.Z., 1954-62; exec. officer U.S. Travel Service, U.S. Dept. Commerce, Washington, 1963—. Served to 1st lt. USAAF, 1942-45. Recipient Commerce Gold Key, Shelby and Cleveland County C. of C., N.C., 1941. Mem. Pub. Relations Soc. Am. (chpt. pres. 1956), Pacific Area Travel Assn. (dir. 1972—), Internat. Union Ofcl. Travel Orgns. (v.p. 1968), Sigma Nu. Methodist. Rotarian (pres. 1946-47). Home: 2700 Virginia Av NW Washington DC 20037 Office: US Travel Service Department of Commerce 14th and Constitution Av NW Washington DC 20230

ARGYLL, MARION H. G., real estate broker; b. New Orleans, Jan 29, 1912; d. Franklin Johns and Sarah (Henry) Gustine;; attended pvt. schs.; widow 1 son, James E. Med. records librarian Doctors Hosp., Washington, 1944-47; asst. to neurosurgeon VA, Washington, 1948-51; electro-encephalographic tech. service NIH, 1952-55; tchr. real estate Washington Real Estate and Ins. Sch., 1958-60; real estate broker, Washington, 1958—, Va., 1958—, Md., 1959—. Recipient award in recognition of services to Nation, Pres. U.S., 1940, award for vol. work with United China Relief, 1942. Mem. So. Electro-encephaology Soc. Club: Kenwood Golf and Country (Bethesda, Md.). Author: Moonlight Poems; also scenarios under pseudonym Julie de Quistine. Patentee san. disposable baby bottle, payroll safety box, adjustable automobile seat, protective garment. Creator Argyll mortgage plan. Home: 15 E Irving St Chevy Chase Village MD 20015 Office: 810 18th St Washington DC 20006

ARIAS, TEODORO A., physician, C.Z. govt. ofcl. Pres. elect C.Z. Address: Balboa Heights Canal Zone*

ARKIN, STANLEY HERBERT, gen. contractor; b. N.Y.C., Aug. 28, 1932; s. Joseph L. and Mildred (Neidenberg) A.; B.B.A. cum laude, U. Miami, 1954; m. Jill Theo Flitman, June 21, 1958; children—Bradley, Robert, Gregory. Vice pres. Arkin Constrn. Co., Inc., Miami Beach, Fla., 1954—. Mem. sustaining bd. fellows Mt. Sinai Hosp. Miami Beach Exec. Bd.; v.p., dir. Island View Hosp. Mem. City of Miami Beach Planning Commn.; chmn. Metro-Dade County Contractors Trade Qualifying Bd.; former chmn. Miami Beach Devel. Commn. Mem. Fraternal Order of Police Assos. (state conductor 1961, pres. Fla. state lodge 1962-64), Phi Eta Sigma, Alpha Delta Sigma, Alpha Epsilon Pi, Alpha Sigma Upsilon. Mason (Shriner). Club: University of Miami Alumni (dir.). Home: 333 S Hibiscus Dr Hibiscus Island Miami Beach FL 33139 Office: 1827 Purdy Av Miami Beach FL 33139

ARLEN, CHARLES HUGH, constrn. co. exec.; b. Tulsa, Dec. 23, 1927; s. Hugh Charles and Edna Margaret (Swanson) A.; B.S. in Petroleum Engring., U. Tulsa, 1950; m. Shelley Ann Boyd, Aug. 4, 1950; children— Shelley A., Paul A. Petroleum engr. Gulf Oil Co., San Tome, Venezuela, 1954-60; self-employed home builder, 1960—; pres. Arlen Constrn. Co., Tulsa, 1961—; dir. Edgewater Beach Corp., Oklahoma City. Served to 1st lt., USAF, 1951-54. Mem. Okla. (area v.p. 1971—), Tulsa (pres. 1971) homebuilders assns., Lambda Chi Alpha. Republican. Christian Scientist. Home and office: 7444 E 68th Tulsa OK 74133

ARLT, HELEN, museum ofcl. Pres. New Orleans Jazz Mus. and Archives. Address: 1913 Valance St New Orleans LA 70115*

ARMAN, ARA, educator; b. Istanbul, Turkey, Sept. 12, 1930; s. Hayg and Marie (Papazian) A.; B.S. in Civil Engring., Robert Coll. (Istanbul), 1955; M.S., U. Tex., 1956; m. Claudia Catherine Carr, Nov. 31, 1963; children—Eric Hayg, Michelle Marie. Came to U.S., 1955, naturalized, 1961. With La. Dept. Hwys., Baton Rouge, 1956-63, dist. lab. engr., 1958-61, soils-design engr., 1961-63; mem. faculty La. State U., Baton Rouge, 1963—, asso. prof. civil engring., 1967-70, prof., 1970—, asst. dir. div. engring. research, 1965—. Vice pres. Shelltech Engrs., Baton Rouge, 1964-68, Systems Analysis & Design Optimization, Inc., Baton Rouge, 1968—; cons. civil engring., 1963—. Mem. Nat. Acad. Scis. (mem. maintenance bituminous pavements com. 1965—, soil cement stblzn. com. 1966—), Am. Road Builders Assn. (v.p. nat. edn. div. 1970, pres. nat. edn. div. 1972-73), Hwy. Research Bd. (com. soil-cement stblzn.), Am. Soc. C.E., Internat. Soc. Soil Mechanics and Found., Am. Soc. Engring. Edn., Am. Soc. Testing and Materials, Internat. Peat Soc. Club: Piedmont (Baton Rouge). Contbr. profl. jours. Home: 1148 Verdun Dr Baton Rouge LA 70810

ARMBRECHT, WILLIAM HENRY, lawyer; b. Mobile, Ala., Nov. 1, 1908; s. William Henry and Anna Bell (Paterson) A.; student Spring Hill Coll., 1927-29; LL.B., U. Ala., 1932; m. Katherine Little, Oct. 8, 1927; children—William Henry III, Elizabeth A. (Mrs. J. D. Brown), Anna Bell (Mrs. William Bru), Conrad P. II, Clara L. Admitted to Ala. bar, 1932; since practiced in Mobile; partner firm Armbrecht, Jackson & DeMouy; gen. counsel McLean Industries; chmn. bd., dir. 1st Nat. Bank, Mobile; dir. Title Ins. Co. Mobile, So. Industries Corp., Grand Hotel Co., Mem. Mobile Indsl. Devel. Bd. Bd. dirs. Found. for Pub. Higher Edn.; bd. regents Spring Hill Coll. Mem. Am., Ala., Mobile (pres. 1954) bar assns., Ala., Phi Delta Phi, Alpha Tau Omega. Episcopalian. Kiwanian. Clubs: Lakewood Country (Point Clear, Ala.); Mobile Country, Athelstan, Propeller; Lunch (N.Y.C.). Home: 112 Pinebrook West Mobile AL 36608 Office: 1101 Mchts Bank Bldg Mobile AL 36602

ARMBRECHT, WILLIAM HENRY, III, lawyer; b. Mobile, Ala., Jan. 13, 1929; s. William Henry and Katherine (Little) A.; B.S., U. Ala., 1950, J.D., 1952; m. Dorothy Jean Taylor, Sept. 1, 1951; children—Katherine Handley, William Taylor, Alexander Paterson. Admitted to Ala. bar, 1952; asso. firm Inge, Twitty, Armbrecht & Jackson, Mobile, 1952-56; partner Armbrecht, Jackson, McConnell & DeMouy, Mobile, 1956-65, Armbrecht, Jackson & DeMouy, Mobile, 1965—; dir. Spanish Fort Estates, Inc.; dir., v.p. Landel, Inc. Served to 1st lt. AUS, 1952-54. Mem. Am., Ala. (mem. exec. council jr. bar sect. 1957-58, mem. grievance com. 1970—, Mobile (mem. exec. council 1960, pres. jr. bar sect. exec. council corp., partnership and bus. law sect. 1972—), 1960), bar assns., Mobile C. of C. (vice chmn. community planning com. 1969-70), Southeastern Corporate Law Inst. (mem. planning com.), Phi Delta Phi, Delta Kappa Epsilon. Episcopalian. Clubs: Mobile Country, Athelstan, International Trade (Mobile). Home: 600 Fairfax Rd East Mobile AL 36608 Office: 1101 Mchts Nat Bank Bldg 61 St Joseph St Mobile AL 36601

ARMENDAREZ, PETER X., educator; b. San Pedro, Cal., Sept. 7, 1930; s. Pedro M. and Carmen (Miranda) A.; B.S., Loyola U. of Los Angeles, 1952; M.S., Washington U., 1954; Ph.D., U. Ariz., 1963; m. Charlene Towery, Oct. 23, 1954; children—Mary Agnes, Peter, Patrick, Philip, John, Lawrence, William. Instr. Odessa Coll., 1958-59; asst. prof. U. Tenn. at Martin, 1963-65, Brescia Coll., Owensboro, Ky., 1965-67; prof., chmn. dept. physics Brescia Coll., 1968—; research asso. Ill. Inst. Tech., summers 1964-66. Served as capt., USAF, 1954-57. Mem. Am. Chem. Soc., Am. Crystallog. Assn. Research and publs. on molecular spectroscopy and structure of inorganic complexes. Home: 1224 Parrish Av Owensboro KY 42301 Office: Brescia College Owensboro KY 42301

ARMISTEAD, MOSS WILLIAM, III, newspaper exec.; b. Suffolk, Va., Sept. 7, 1915; s. Moss William and Mary Judith (Smith) A.; student Randolph-Macon Coll., 1933-36; LL.D., Washington and Lee U., 1967; m. Mary Ragan Bridges, Dec. 30, 1939; 1 dau., Elfleda Bridges (Mrs. Peter Huff Ring). Reporter, Covington Virginian, 1936; reporter, state editor, utility editor, legislative corr. Roanoke (Va.) Times, 1936-42; exec. sec. to Gov. of Va. and Sec. of Commonwealth, 1946-47; asst. to pub. Times & World-News, Roanoke, 1947-51, asso. pub., 1951, v.p., pub., 1954; pres., dir. Times-World Corp.; pres., pub. Roanoke Times and World-News, 1954—, chmn. bd., 1955-69; pres. Roanoke Valley Devel. Corp., 1957-59; dir. Nelson-Roanoke Corp., 1st Nat. Exchange Bank, Landmark Communications, Inc., Norfolk, Va., Dominion Bankshares Corp., Roanoke, Chesapeake and Potomac Telephone Co. Mem. Va. Bd. Welfare and Instns., 1947-51. Pres. Roanoke Community Fund, 1952, Central YMCA, 1957-58; pres. Community Hosp. Roanoke Valley. Mem. Va. Port Authority, Norfolk, 1959-71. Served from pvt. to 1st lt. inf., AUS, 1942-46. Decorated Purple Heart. Mem. U.S., Va. (v.p.), Roanoke (pres. 1953) chambers commerce, Va. Press Assn., Am. Newspaper Pubs. Assn. (dir., sec.), So. Newspaper Pubs. Assn. (dir., sec.), Phi Kappa Sigma, Sigma Delta Chi, Alpha Kappa Psi. Club: Shenandoah (Roanoke). Office: 201-209 W Campbell Av Roanoke VA 24010

ARMISTEAD, THEUS NICHOLSON, hosp. supt.; b. Shreveport, La., Aug. 5, 1916; s. William Wilchia and Lillian (Willis) A.; student Acad. Sch., Centenary Coll., Shreveport, 1934-37; M.D., La. State U., 1946; M.P.H., Tulane U., 1960; m. Lola Pearl Horton, Nov. 26, 1947; children—William Clinton, Susan Garland, John Nicholson. Intern Tri-State Hosp., Shreveport, 1946-47; gen. practice State Line Clinic, Waskom, Tex., 1947-48; dir. Webster Parish Health Unit, Minden, La., 1950-51; gen. practice Plain Dealing, La., 1951-56; dir. Red River, DeSoto and Claiborne Parish Health Units, 1955-60; area med. cons. parishes N.W. La., 1960-64; La. health officer, pres. La. Bd. Health, 1964-66; supt. East La. State Hosp., Jackson, 1966—. Surgeon, USPHS, 1962, sr. surgeon, 1964. Served to capt. AUS, 50. Episcopalian. Address: East Louisiana State Hosp Jackson LA 70748

ARMOUR, THOMAS SCOTT, JR., elec. engr.; b. Columbia, S.C., Mar. 24, 1923; s. Thomas Scott and Elisabeth (Rivers) A.; B.E.E., Clemson U., 1947; M.S., La. State U., 1950; m. Irene Blair Watson, Feb. 14, 1947; children—Irene Elisabeth, Thomas Scott III. Elec. engr. Plantation Pipe Line Co., Atlanta, Baton Rouge, 1947-49; teaching fellow La. State U., 1949-50; engr. Patchen & Zimmerman, engrs., Augusta, Ga., 1950-53; engr. Lyles, Bissett, Carlisle & Wolff, architects and engrs., 1953-63; v.p., dir., gen. mgr. operations Jones & Assos., Augusta, then Jones & Fellers, architects, engrs. and planners, Augusta and Savannah, Ga., Columbia, S.C., 1963-70; self-employed as elec. design cons., Columbia, S.C., 1970—. Pres. Sr. Citizens Council of Augusta and Richmond County. Served with AUS, World War II. Registered profl. engr., S.C., Ga., Tex. Mem. Nat., Ga., S.C. socs. profl. engrs., Constrn. Specifications Inst. (past. chpt. pres.), Soc. Mil. Engrs., Assn. U.S. Army, Illuminating Engring. Soc., Congaree Power Squadron. Episcopalian. Elk. Club: Augusta Country. Home: 2166 Shady Lane Columbia SC 29206 Office: 4445 Devine St Columbia SC 29205

ARMSTRONG, A(LBERT) FRED, JR., ins. exec.; b. Dallas, Apr. 21, 1918; s. A. F. and Mayme (Miller) A.; student So. Meth. U., 1935-36; m. Ernestine Dublin, Aug. 17, 1940; 1 dau., Tina. With Employers Casualty Co., Dallas and Houston, 1935-43, gen. agt., Houston, 1946-54; pres., dir. Am. Capitol Ins. Co., 1954—; dir. Nat. Assn. of Life Cos., Chem. Bank, Houston. Served with USAAF, 1943-46. Mem. Tex. Legal Res. Ofcls. Assn. (dir., past pres.). Methodist. Mason. Home: 10603 Gawain St Houston TX 77024 Office: 3839 Buffalo Speedway Houston TX 77006

ARMSTRONG, ANNE LEGENDRE (MRS. TOBIN ARMSTRONG), Republican nat. committeewoman; b. New Orleans, Dec. 27, 1927; d. Armant and Olive (Martindale) Legendre; grad. Vassar Coll., 1949; m. Tobin Armstrong, Apr. 12, 1950; children—John Barclay, Katharine A., Sarita S., Tobin and James L. (twins). Trustee Kenedy County (Tex.) Sch. Bd., 1968—. Chmn., Kenedy County Rep. Party, 1958-61; mem. Tex. Rep. Exec. Com. from 20th dist., 1961-66; Rep. dep. vice chmn., 1965-66; Rep. state vice chmn., 1966-68; del., mem. platform com. Rep. Nat. Conv., 1964, 68; mem. Nat. Rep. Com. from Tex., 1968—, steering com. Women for Nixon, 1968, mem. exec. com. Rep. Nat. Com., 1969—, co-chmn. Nat. Com., 1971—. Home: Armstrong Ranch Armstrong TX 78338

ARMSTRONG, ARTHUR ALEXANDER, chem. engr., educator; b. Gastonia, N.C., July 13, 1921; s. Arthur Alexander and Julia T. (Compton) A.; student Belmont Abbey Coll., 1938-40; B.Chem. Engring., N.C. State U., 1947, M.S., 1949, Ph.D., 1957; m. Helene Adele Payet, June 15, 1956; children—Alexander Charles, Richard George. Chem. engr. Gen. Electric Co., Pittsfield, Mass., 1947, Duke Power Co., Charlotte, N.C., 1949-50, Chemstrand Corp., Pensacola, Fla., 1953-54; tech. supt. Celanese Corp., Rock Hill, S.C., 1954-58; asso. prof. U. S.C., Columbia, 1958-59, N.C. State U., Raleigh, 1959-65, U. N.M., Albuquerque, 1965-68; engring. fellow Chemstrand Research Center, Inc., Durham, N.C., 1968—; cons. chem. engr., 1959—. Served to lst lt. USAAF, 1943-45. Mem. Am. Inst. Chem. Engrs., Am. Soc. for Engring. Edn., Sigma Xi. Home: 219 Rose St Cary NC 27511 Office: PO Box 731 Durham NC 27702

ARMSTRONG, DICKWIN DILL, assn. exec.; b. Muncie, Ind., Aug. 18, 1934; s. Colby C. and Elizabeth A. (Houck) A.; B.S., Ind. U., 1956; m. Janice Flora, June 2, 1957; children—Brent D., Stacey J. Mgr., Madison (Ind.) C. of C., 1959-61; exec. v.p. Frankford (Ind.) C. of C., 1961-63, Marion (Ind.) C. of C., 1963-66, Lakeland (Fla.) C. of C., 1966—. Served with AUS, 1957-59. Mem. Ind. Exec. Assn. (v.p. 1966), Fla. C. of C. Execs. (pres. 1972—), Ind. U. Alumni Assn. Methodist. Rotarian. Home: Route 1 Box 355 Lakeland FL 33803 Office: 35 Lake Morton Dr Lakeland FL 33801

ARMSTRONG, ELMER E., accountant; b. Monmouth, Ill., Dec. 20, 1904; s. Elmer Ellsworth and Alice (Logan) A.; A.A., Kansas City Jr. Coll., 1921; postgrad. Centenary Coll., 1942-43; m. Ruth Marie Dale, July 25, 1925; children—Dale E., Lenora Ann (Mrs. Steven Cowel). Mem. editorial staff Kansas City Jour., 1920-22, Kansas City Kansan, 1922-25; editor Alva Record, Okla., 1922; account specialist Burroughs Adding Machine Co., 1925-45; with Armstrong & Armstrong, C.P.A.'s, Shreveport, La., 1945—, sr. partner, 1952—; treas. Honor Oil Co., Inc., Shreveport, 1951—. Lectr. advanced accounting Centenary Coll. of La., 1950-52, So. States Accounting Conf., Savannah, Ga., Conf. Lawyers and C.P.A.'s, U. Miss. at Hattiesburg, 1951; dean Shreveport Sch. Theology, 1968-69. Mem. Nat. Conf. Christians and Jews, Shreveport, 1968—, dir. Speakers Bur., 1969—, chmn. Brotherhood Week, 1972; chmn. Shreveport Housing Authority, 1967-72. C.P.A., La., Tex. Mem. Soc. La. C.P.A.'s (pres. Shreveport 1967-68), Am. Inst. C.P.A.'s, Shreveport C. of C., Internat. Platform Assn., Am. (dist. treas.), Shreveport (v.p. 1970-71) rose socs. Methodist (steward; dir. adult tchrs. 1963-66; dist. dir. adult ministries Shreveport dist. 1968—). Kiwanian (treas. 1952-56, bd. dirs. 1969-71, Shreveport), Toastmaster (dist. gov. 1952). Clubs: Shreveport Petroleum, Metropolitan Dinner. Home: 1402 Audubon Pl Shreveport LA 71105 Office: Armstrong & Armstrong Pioneer Center 1400 Line St Shreveport LA 71101

ARMSTRONG, FRANK, III, apple processing co. exec.; b. Winchester, Va., Oct. 31, 1936; s. Frank and Margaret (Tweltridge) A.; B.S., U. N.C., 1960; m. Sandra Lineburg, Nov. 28, 1959; 1 dau., Katherine Neil. With Nat. Fruit Product Co., Inc., Winchester, Va., 1960—, technician, lab., 1960, asst. in engring., 1960-61, salesman sales service, 1961-62, coordinator capital expenditures prodn. supervision, 1962-63, v.p., 1964-68, exec. v.p., 1968—. Mem. bd. dirs. Farmers & Mchts. Bank, Winchester, Winchester Equipment Co., Winchester-Frederick County Indsl. Devel. Corp. Div. chmn. United Fund, Winchester, 1967—; treas. Shenandoah Apple Blossom Festival, 1965-67, pres., 1968-69; mem. exec. bd. Shenandoah Area council Boy Scouts Am., 1968—, chmn. Eagle Scout recognition dinner, 1966-67, finance chmn., 1967—. Trustee, Found. for Ind. Jr. Colls. of Va. Served with AUS, 1959-60. Recipient Distinguished Service award Winchester Jr. C. of C., 1969. Mem. Shenandoah Valley Mfrs. Assn., Va. Mfrs. Assn., Nat. Canners Assn., Processed Apples Inst., Judges Athletic Assn., Va., W.Va., Md., Mich. state hort. socs., C. of C., Winchester Jr. C. of C. Episcopalian. Rotarian. Home: 416 Briarmont Dr Winchester VA 22601 Office: PO Box 609 Winchester VA 22601

ARMSTRONG, NEIL A., astronaut; b. Wapakoneta, O., Aug. 5, 1930; s. Stephen Armstrong; B.S. in Aero. Engring., Purdue U., 1955; postgrad. student U. So. Cal.; m. Janet Shearon; children—Eric, Mark. With Lewis Flight Propulsion Lab., NACA, 1955; then aero. research pilot for NACA, later NASA, High Speed Flight Sta., Edwards, Cal.; now astronaut Manned Spacecraft Center, NASA, Houston, Texas, back-up command pilot Gemini 5; command pilot Gemini 8, March 1966; backup command pilot Gemini 11; backup comdr. Apollo VIII; Spacecraft comdr. Apollo XI, July 1969, 1st man to walk on moon. Served as aviator with USNR, 1949-52; Korea. Recipient Octave

Chanute award Inst. Aero. Scis., 1962; John J. Montgomery award, 1962; AIAA Astronautics award, 1966; NASA Exceptional Service medal; Presdl. Medal for Freedom, 1969. Fellow Soc. Exptl. Test Astronautics; mem. Soaring Soc. Am. Office: Manned Spacecraft Center NASA Houston TX 77058

ARMSTRONG, OLIVER WENDELL (JACK), oil co. exec.; b. Mound Valley, Kan., July 13, 1919; s. Charles Eugene and Elva (Williams) A.; student Kan. State U., Manhattan, 1937-40; B.S., Kan. State Coll., Pittsburg, 1941; m. Betty Jane Nichols, June 24, 1945; 1 dau., Julia Anne. With Phillips Petroleum Co., 1944—, div. credit mgr., Chgo., 1951-55, regional credit mgr., Bartlesville, Okla., 1955-59, adminstrv. asst., 1959-60, asst. treas., 1960-65, sec., treas., 1965-71, v.p., treas., 1971—. Mem. Am. Petroleum Inst. Republican. Presbyn. Elk, Mason (Shriner, Jester), Rotarian. Home: 2000 Skyline Dr Bartlesville OK 74003 Office: Phillips Bldg Bartlesville OK 74004

ARMSTRONG, SINCLAIR WALKER, banker; b. Okemah, Okla., Aug. 1, 1905; s. Robert Walker and Margaret June (Edmundson) A.; student Okla. U., 1926-27; m. Lola Irene Aston, June 9, 1929; children—Ann (Mrs. Archie Farmer), Robert A., Sinclair Walker. With Vian State Bank (Okla.), 1922—, pres., 1965—. Trustee City of Vian, 1933—, mayor, 1950—. Chmn., Sequoyah County Democratic central com., 1945-47. Trustee Cookson Hills Electric Co-op. Baptist. Mason (32 deg., Shriner, Jester). Address: Vian OK 74962

ARMSTRONG, THOMAS HARPER, dentist; b. Mesa, Ariz., June 12, 1912; s. Thomas Ackerman and Mabel (Harper) A.; student Eldorado Coll., 1931-32; D.D.S., Northwestern U., 1942; postgrad. Harvard, 1942-43; m. Vara Marie Freeman, Sept. 5, 1935; children—Thomas W., John Harper. Individual practice dentistry, Lebanon, Tenn., 1945—; prof., chmn. dept. aux. personnel U. Tenn. Sch. Dentistry, 1969—. Active orgn. Little League Softball, Lebanon, 1955; active vocational guidance program for high sch. Served to capt. Dental Corps, AUS, 1943-45. Recipient Fellowship Key Outstanding Dentist Tenn., 1965; award Ohio Sch. Journalism for Sci. Writing, 1970. Fellow Am. Coll. Dentists (council 1959), Internat. Coll. Dentists; mem. Am. Dental Assn. (council journalism 1970—), Tenn. Dental Assn., Am. Assn. Dental Editors (pres. 1965; Man of Year award 1970), Pierre Fauchard Acad., Omicron Kappa Upsilon. Kiwanian (pres. 1954-55). Club: Exchange (pres. 1946). Editor: Tenn. Dental Assn. 1955—. Home: 220 S McLean St Memphis TN 38104 Office: 847 Monroe St Memphis TN 38103

ARMSTRONG, WALLACE FARIS, chem. co. exec.; b. Castor, Alta., Can., Apr. 26, 1915; s. George A. and Margaret (Faris) A.; U.S. citizen, came to U.S., 1922; B.S., U. Fla., 1938, M.S., 1940; postgrad. Harvard, 1954; m. Eileen Ratterree, Aug. 15, 1941; children—Betty Eileen (Mrs. Michael E. Kirby), George Alexander, Robert Calvin, William Wallace. With Ethyl Corp., Baton Rouge, 1939—, resident mgr., 1956-66, gen. mgr. mfg., 1966, v.p., gen. mgr. mfg., 1967—. Pres. United Givers Fund; mem. adv. council La. State U. Coll. Bus. Adminstrn. Bd. dirs., council trustees Gulf South Research Inst.; bd. dirs. Pub. Affairs Research Council La., Council for A Better La. Mem. Am. Chem. Soc., Am. Inst. Chem. Engrs., Am. Petroleum Inst., Chlorine Inst., Baton Rouge C. of C., Phi Kappa Phi, Sigma Tau, Gamma Sigma Epsilon. Presbyn. (elder). Rotarian. Clubs: Country, City, Camelot (Baton Rouge). Home: 7375 Boyce Dr Baton Rouge LA 70809 Office: Ethyl Corp 451 Florida Baton Rouge LA 70801

ARMSTRONG, WALTER PRESTON, JR., lawyer; b. Memphis, Oct. 4, 1916; s. Walter Preston and Irma Lewis (Waddell) A.; grad. Choate Sch., Wallingford, Conn., 1934; A.B., Harvard, 1938, J.D., 1941; D.C.L. (hon.), Southwestern at Memphis, 1961; m. Alice Kavanaugh McKee, Nov. 3, 1949; children—Alice Kavanaugh, Walter Preston III. Admitted to Tenn. bar, 1940, practiced in Memphis, 1941—; asso. Armstrong, Allen, Braden, Goodman, McBride & Prewitt, and predecessor law firms, Memphis, 1941—, partner, 1948—. Commr. for Promotion Uniformity of Legislation in U.S. for Tenn., 1947-67 mem. Tenn. Hist. Commn., 1969— pres. bd. edn. Memphis City Schs., 1956-61; mem. Tenn. Higher Edn. Commn., 1967—. Served from pvt. to maj. AUS, 1941-46. Fellow Am. Bar Found. (sec. 1960-62), Am. Coll. Trial Lawyers; mem. Am. (mem. ho. of dels.), Tenn. (pres. 1972—), Memphis and Shelby County, Inter-Am., Internat. bar assns., Assn. Bar City N.Y., Am. Law Inst., Am. Judicature Soc., Nat. Conf. Commns. on Uniform State Laws (exec. com., 1959-61, pres. 1961-63), Harvard Law Sch. Assn., Order of Coif, Scribes (pres. 1960-61), Omicron Delta Kappa. Author articles in field. Home: 1530 Carr Av Memphis TN 38104 Office: Commerce Title Bldg Memphis TN 38103

ARNESON, ANNE M. (MRS. R. GORDON ARNESON), social scientist; b. Monticello, Ark.; d. Walter Fagan and Alma (Shadow) McClerkin; B.A., Mary Washington Coll. of U. Va., 1951; postgrad. Am. U., 1952, 63—; m. Jack H. Jonas, Nov. 5, 1952 (dec. Aug. 1968); m. 2d, R. Gordon Arneson, June 16, 1972. Producer ednl. radio program Careers in New Orleans, 1950; social sci. research and propaganda analysis Rand Corp., Washington, 1951-61; profl. staff Weapons Systems Evaluation Div., Inst. Def. Analyses, Washington, 1961-65; polit. scientist Strategic Studies Center, Stanford Research Inst., Washington, 1965-67, editor Cameo of Zeta Phi Eta, 1958-59; cons., author politico-mil. affairs, 1968—. Instr. swimming and water safety A.R.C., 1946-51. Mem. Am. Assn. Advancement Slavic Studies, Acad. Polit. Sci., Am. Acad. Polit. and Social Sci., D.A.R., Zeta Phi Eta (pres. D.C. Alumnae chpt. 1953-54, nat. officer 1958-59, alumnae adviser Alpha Mu chpt. 1961-70). Democrat. Author articles in field. Address: 11633 North Shore Dr Reston VA 22070

ARNETT, ALVIN CREWS, food broker; b. nr. Hamilton, Tex., Apr. 13, 1922; s. Alvin Green and Minnie (Harlien) A.; ed. pub. schs., spl. courses; m. Lottie Jean Rheubotham, Nov. 30, 1957; children—Alvin Crews, Allison Jean. Store mgr. Great A & P Tea Co., 1945-50; div. sales mgr. Austex Foods, Inc., Austin, Tex., 1950-57; pres. Arnett Brokerage Co., Lubbock, Tex., 1957—; pres. Globe Trailers, Inc., 1968-69; v.p. Bachelor Burgers, Inc. Trustee The Brokers Trust, 1961—. Served with USCG, 1942-45. Mem. Lubbock Food Brokers Assn. (pres. 1960), Food Buyers and Drummers Club (dir. 1962). Republican. Mem. Ch. of Christ. Rotarian. Club: Lubbock Country. Home: 4915 19th St Lubbock TX 79407 Office: PO Box 1856 Lubbock TX 79408

ARNETT, EUGENE BRITTON, JR., dentist; b. Lexington, Ky., Nov. 1, 1929; s. Eugene and Frances (Kirk) A.; B.S., Georgetown Coll., 1951; D.M.D., U. Louisville, 1956; m. Sharkey Utley, Oct. 31, 1953; children— Eugene Britton III, Allison Sharkey, Claire Elisabeth. Pvt. practice dentistry, Louisville, 1956-60, Owens Med. Center, 1960—. Mem. Ky. Bd. Dental Examiners; v.p. Ky. State Bd. Dentistry, 1971, pres., 1972. Served from A/b to A/2c, USAF, 1951-52. Mem. Louisville Dist., Ky., Am. dental socs., Order Ky. Colonels, Pierre Fauchard Acad., Kappa Alpha (life), Delta Sigma Delta (life), Phi Delta. Democrat. Baptist (deacon). Clubs: Hurstbourne Country; Lions. Charter mem. Ky. Athletic Hall of Fame. Home: 2802 Lime Kiln Lane Louisville KY 40222 Office: 4122 Shelbyville Rd Louisville KY 40207

ARNETT, FOSTER D., lawyer; b. Knoxville, Tenn., Nov. 28, 1920; s. Foster Greenwood and Edna (Deaver) A.; B.A., U. Tenn., 1946; LL.B., U. Va., 1948; m. Jean Medlin, Mar. 3, 1951; children—Melissa Lee, Foster Deaver. Admitted to Va. and Tenn. bars, 1948; with firm Cates, Dowler, Long & Fowler, Knoxville, 1948-55; partner firm Arnett, Draper & Hagood, and predecessors, Knoxville, 1955—. Pres. Knox Children's Found., 1959-61, U. Tenn. Hearing and Speech Center, 1963-65; chmn. nat. alumni ann. giving program U. Tenn., 1962-63. Bd. dirs. E. Tenn. Children's Rehab. Center, Knoxville chpt. A.R.C., Knoxville Cerebral Palsy Center, Knoxville chpt. Am. Cancer Soc. Del. Republican Nat. Conv., 1964. Served to 1st lt. AUS, 1942-46; lt. col. U.S. Army Res. ret. Decorated Silver Star, Purple Heart. Fellow Am. Coll. Trial Lawyers, Internat. Soc. Barristers; mem. Soc. Hosp. Attys., Scribes, Knoxville (pres. 1959-60, Tenn. (pres. 1968-69), Am. (vice chmn., mem. numerous coms., adv. com. to standing com. traffic ct. program 1960—, life ins. com. 1966—) bar assns., U. Tenn. Gen. Alumni Assn. (pres. 1961-62), Internat. Assn. Ins. Counsels, Fedn. Ins. Counsels, Am. Trial Lawyers Assn., Scarrabbean, Phi Delta Phi, Phi Gamma Delta, Omicron Delta Kappa. Home: 4636 Alta Vista Way SW Knoxville TN 37919 Office: Arnett Draper & Hagood Hamilton Nat Bank Bldg Knoxville TN 37902

ARNETT, HALBURN CLINTON, dentist; b. Mayfield, Ky., May 29, 1928; s. Samuel Clinton and Lola Belle (Allen) A.; student U. Louisville, 1947-49, D.M.D., 1954; B.S., Western Ky. U., 1950; m. Theresa Ann Kuhn, June 28, 1952; children—Karen Lynn, Martin Allen, Bryan Clinton. Intern Walter Reed Hosp., Washington, 1954-55; gen. practice dentistry, Louisville, 1957—; dir. Nat. Chem. Corp., Louisville, Dart Industries, Morganfield, Ky., Ky. Resorts, Inc., Louisville. Served with USAF, 1954-57. Mem. Louisville Dental Soc., Ky., Am. dental assns., Lambda Chi Alpha, Delta Sigma Delta, Omicron Delta Kappa, Phi Delta. Mason, Kiwanian. Club: Louisville Boat. Home: 3409 Nandina Dr Louisville KY 40222 Office: Starks Bldg Louisville KY 40202

ARNETT, JOHN LESLIE, lawyer, city ofcl.; b. Paintsville, Ky., Feb. 3, 1936; s. Eugene Britton and Frances (Kirk) A.; B.A., U. Ky., 1959; J.D., U. Louisville, 1963; m. Annette Violet Pemberton, May 4, 1956; children—Deborah Lynn, Timothy Lee. Admitted to Ky. bar, 1963; with FBI, Washington, 1954-56; partner Faurest, Collier, Arnett, Hensley & Coleman, Elizabethtown, Ky., 1963—; city atty. City of Elizabethtown, 1967—. Instr. U. Ky. Community Coll., Elizabethtown, 1964-66. Leader Boy Scouts Am., Elizabethtown, 1967-69; chmn. Hardin County (Ky.) Blood Program, 1966-68. Precinct chmn. Democratic Party County Com., 1964-68, sec. 26th legislative dist. of Ky., 1964-68; vice chmn. Young Democrats, 1966-69. Mem. Am., Ky., Hardin County bar assns., Elizabethtown-Hardin County C. of C. (bd. dirs. 1966-69), Omicron Delta Kappa. Methodist. Club: Lions (pres.). (Elizabethtown, Ky.). Home: 622 El Dorado Dr Elizabethtown KY 42701 Office: 128 W Dixie Av Elizabethtown KY 42701

ARNHOLT, WALDON SYLVESTER, artist; b. Nankin, O., Jan. 1, 1909; student C. Fritz Hoelzer, N.Y.C., 1932-38; m. Helen Mayflower Howman, Sept. 6, 1938. Pvt. art tchr., O., N.Y., 1929-61, Clearwater, Fla.; artist-lithographer A.L. Garber Co., Ashland, O., 1931-61; one-man shows in Ashland, Cleve., Parthenon Gallery, Nashville, Municipal Gallery, Tampa, Fla., Fla. Fedn. Arts Hdqrs. and Mus., DuBarry, Tampa, Clearwater, Lakeland, St. Petersburg, Dunedin, Fla.; exhibited in group shows in Ashland, Mansfield, O., Tampa, Clearwater, Lakeland, St. Petersburg, Dunedin; cons. Mus. Sci. and Natural History, Tampa. represented in permanent collections Mus. Sci. and Natural History, also various chs. Recipient ribbons, medals, certificates for art. Mem. Ohio, Fla. fedns. art. Home and studio: 1224 Sunset Point Rd Clearwater FL 33515*

ARNIM, SUMTER SMITH, educator; b. Hallettsville, Tex., Oct. 9, 1904; s. Charles William and Kate (Smith) A.; B.A. in Bacteriology, Rice Inst., 1926; D.D.S. (Montgomery Ward fellow), Northwestern U., 1930; Ph.D. in Pathology (Rockefeller Found. fellow), Yale, 1935; m. Dorothy Mildred Brownlee, Sept. 8, 1945; children—Susan Smith (Mrs. Leonard Campbell Smyth II), Leslie Ann. Instr. dental surgery Yale Sch. Medicine, 1934-35; asst. prof., acting head, dept. operative dentistry U. Ill., 1936-39; asst. prof. operative dentistry Med. Coll. Va., 1939-40, asso. prof. operative dentistry and pathology, 1941-42, prof., 1942-43, chmn. grad. study and research, 1942-45; prof. periodontics and operative dentistry Ohio State U., 1945-47; prof. pathology U. Tex. Dental Br., Houston, 1947—, chmn. pathology, 1954-66, asso. dean. grad. studies, 1964-66, dean. Grad. Sch. Biomed. Scis., 1966-70. Gen. practice dentistry, New Haven, 1935-37, Houston, 1953-56. Cons. Regional Conf. on Edn., Atlanta, 1948, VA Hosp., Houston, 1951—, VA Center, Temple, Tex., 1951-57, Tex. Children's Hosp., Houston, 1954—, St. Luke's Episcopal Hosp., Houston, 1954—, M.D. Anderson Hosp. and Tumor Inst., 1955—, drug products div. Procter & Gamble Co., Cin., 1957—, VA Central Office, 1966—, Ciba Pharm. Co., N.J., 1960, dental service USAF Hosp., Lackland AFB, Tex., 1961—, U.S. Sch. Aerospace Medicine, Brooks AFB, Tex., 1963—, Humble Oil Co., Houston, 1963—, U. Tex. Radio Sta. KLRN, KUT-FM, TEMP, Austin, 1965—; nat. cons. U.S. Air Force, 1967-72. Recipient Gold medal award Am. Soc. Periodontists, 1967. Fellow Va., Ohio, Tex. acads. sci., A.A.A.S., Am. Acad. Oral Pathology; mem. Am. Dental Assn., Internat. Assn. Dental Research, Am. Assn. U. Profs., Sigma XI, Omicron Kappa Upsilon. Author: Laboratory Manual for Airbrasive Technic, 1951; A Study of Dental Caries, 1953; A Study of Periodontal Disease, 1953; also articles. Editorial bds. Dentistry, A Digest of Practice, 1940-47, jour. Dental Research, 1941-52. Home: 2600 Bellefontaine Houston TX 77025

ARNOLD, DAVID JAMES, architect; b. Charleston, W.Va., Jan. 1, 1933; s. Joseph Nation, Jr. and Florence Elizabeth (Morgan) A.; B.S. in Architecture, U. Cin., 1958; m. Barbara Jean Tucker, Aug. 9, 1957; children—Valerie Lee, David James. Archtl. trainee various firms, Ohio, W.Va., N.C., 1958-68; prin. firm David J. Arnold, Asheboro, N.C., 1968—. Part-time tchr. Randolph Tech. Inst., 1968—. Served with AUS, 1953-55. Registered prof. architect, W.Va., N.C.; Certificate Nat. Council Architecture Registration Bds. Mem. A.I.A. (corporate mem.), N.C. chpt. A.I.A. (dir. Piedmont sect. 1971). Republican. Methodist (chmn. furnishings com. ch., ofcl. bd.). Mason (32 deg.). Prin. archtl. works include 1st United Ch. Christ, Asheboro, United Parcel Service Package Delivery Center, Kinston, N.C., Fire Sta. 2, Asheboro. Home and office: 932 Parkview St Asheboro NC 27203

ARNOLD, DAVID SCOTT, editor; b. Findlay, O., Aug. 16, 1920; s. Ed Samuel and Florence (Adams) A.; A.B., Lafayette Coll., 1942; M.S., Syracuse U., 1943; m. Catherine Rose Fury, Apr. 18, 1953; children—Susan Scott, David Fury. Field cons. Pub. Adminstrn. Service, Chgo., 1943-49; staff mem., asst. dir. publications Internat. City Mgmt. Assn., Washington, 1949—. Mem. Am. Soc. for Pub. Adminstrn. (chpt. pres. 1961-62). Home: 3303 Brandy Ct Falls Church VA 22042 Office: 1140 Connecticut Av NW Washington DC 20036

ARNOLD, EDGAR FRANK, JR., real estate broker; b. Madisonville, Ky., Sept. 29, 1925; s. Edgar F. and Caroline (Long) A.; student Kan. State Tchrs. Coll., 1943-44, U. Ky., 1946-47; m. Ruby Jarvis Mitchell, June 20, 1948 (div. June 1965); children—Frank Edgar, Gillis Mitchell, Brian Bowen; m. Jeanne Campbell Hannah, Mar. 11, 1966. With Madisonville (Ky.) Messenger, 1946-70, editor, pres. Madisonville Pub. Co., 1963-70; past editor Ky. State Democrat; real estate broker, Madisonville, 1970—. Mem. Ky. Athletic Commn., 1964-68. Sec. Madisonville Coll. Found., Hopkins County-Madisonville Hosp. Corp. Dep. sheriff Hopkins County, 1954-58; mem. Ky. Ho. of Reps., 1958-59; mem. Ky. Democratic Exec. Com., 1966—. Served from pvt. to flight officer USAAC, 1943-45. Mem. Madisonville Bd. Realtors, Asso. Press Mng. Editors Assn., Asso. Press, Am. Newspaper Pubs. Assn., C. of C. (pres. 1970), Sigma Delta Chi. Rotarian. Home: 62 E Broadway St Madisonville KY 42431 Office: 221 S Main St Madisonville KY 42431

ARNOLD, JAMES ANGUS, trust co. exec.; b. Palmer, Tex., Jan. 18, 1917; s. Angus Allen and Alice Mamie (Wheeler) A.; grad. high sch. Asst. cashier, dir. First Nat. Bank, Nowata, Okla., 1935-51; office mgr. Forest Oil Co., 1951-52, J. Wood Glass Trust Co., Nowata, 1952—; trustee H.W. Reed Trust Co., 1963—, W.W. Warner Trust Co., 1964—; v.p., dir. Panhandle Producing Co., San Antonio, 1965—; dir. Victory Nat. Bank, Nowata. Active chmn. A.R.C. Nowata, Okla.; active as county chmn. Am. Cancer Soc., various times. Served with USNR, 1942-45. Mem. Nowata C. of C. (bd. dirs. 1972). Methodist. Home: 324 W Davis St Nowata OK 74048 Office: 114 E Delaware St Nowata OK 74048

ARNOLD, LYNWOOD FREDERICK, real estate broker, state senator; b. Jacksonville, Fla., Oct. 6, 1916; s. Columbus Washington and Margaret (Lee) A.; B.A., Seetson U., 1941; postgrad. Princeton, 1942; m. Elsie Ferguson, May 30, 1947; children—Lynwood Frederick, Pamela Hope. Real estate broker; pres. Statewide Sales & Services, Jacksonville; mem. Fla. Ho. of Reps., 1963-70, Fla. Senate, 1971—. Served to lt. USNR, 1941-46; PTO. Mem. Southside, Northside bus. men's clubs, Sigma Nu. Episcopalian. Mason (Shriner), Elk, Lion. Home: 1504 Harbor Oaks Rd Jacksonville FL 32207 Office: PO Box 5062 Jacksonville FL 32207*

ARNOLD, PHILIP MILLS, chem. engr.; b. Springfield, Mo., Feb. 9, 1911; s. Anthony L. and Mary Genevieve (Hodnett) A.; B.S., Washington U., 1932, Chem. E., 1941; Chem. engr. research div. Phillips Petroleum Co., 1937-48, asst. mgr. chem. dept., 1948-50, mgr. research and devel. dept., 1950-64, v.p. research and devel., 1964—. Fellow Am. Inst. Chemists; mem. NRC (div. chemistry and chem. tech. 1959-68, div. engring. and indsl. research 1965-68), Indsl. Research Inst. (pres. 1964-65), Am. Inst. Chem. Engrs., Am. Chem. Soc., A.A.A.S., Coordinating Research Council (dir. 1964—, pres. 1969-71), Internat. Union Pure and Applied Chemistry (chmn. finance com. 1963-71, mem. bur. 1969—, exec. com. 1971—), World Petroleum Congress (mem. permanent council 1965-71), Am. Petroleum Inst., Am. Soc. Testing and Materials, Atomic Industrial Forum (dir. 1966-69), Soc. Chem. Industry (mem. exec. com. 1967-70), Independent Natural Gas Assn., Ind. Petroleum Assn., Nat. Acad. Engring., Tau Beta Pi, Alpha Chi Sigma, Sigma Chi. Republican. Home: Box 1457 Bartlesville OK 74003 Office: Phillips Petroleum Co Bartlesville OK 74004

ARNOLD, RICHARD L., lawyer; b. Texarkana, Ark., Dec. 30, 1906; grad. Phillips-Exeter Acad., Exeter, N.H., 1925; A.B., Harvard, 1929, LL.B., 1932. Admitted to Ark. bar, 1931; mem. firm Arnold & Arnold, Texarkana. Mem. Am., Ark., Miller County bar assns. Office: 507 Hickory St Texarkana AR 75501*

ARNOLD, ROGER MURRAY, tool co. exec.; b. Glastonbury, Conn., Feb. 3, 1934; s. William Milton and Evelyn (Mahorney) A.; B.S., U. Houston, 1959; m. Wanda Ruth Webb, Feb. 13, 1953; children—Wanda Sue, Roger David, William Clyde. Asst. to v.p. mfg. and engring. Mission Mfg. Co., Houston, 1957-60; cons. Bonner & Moore Engring. Assos., 1960; pres. Diatron Electronics Corp., Houston, 1961; mgr. information systems and diversified products Hughes Tool Co., Houston, 1964-69, group mgr. diversified prodn., 1969—. Standard Oil Acad. scholar U. Houston, 1957-58; Franklin Found. fellow U. Houston, 1955-56. Mem. Assn. for Systems Mgmt. (dir. 1967, 68), Systems and Procedures Assn. (dir. 1965, 66), Am. Mgmt. Assn. (mem. continuing systems seminar; mem. exec. com.). Home: 15721 Juneau Lane Houston TX 77040 Office: 5425 Polk Av Houston TX 77001

ARNOLD, WILLIAM BUCK, lawyer; b. Houston, Nov. 18, 1919; s. Thomas J. and Georgia (Buck) A.; B.B.A., U. Tex., 1942, LL.B., 1949; m. Lucy Gray, May 30, 1948; children—Lucinda Gray, Georgia Anne, Mary Virginia. Admitted to Tex. bar, 1949; mem. law firm Vinson, Elkins, Weems and Searls, Houston, 1949—. Dir. South Main Bank, Tex. Electric Steel Casting Co., Quintana Petroleum Corp. (Houston), A-V Corp. Chmn. bd. trustees Kinkaid Sch. Served as pvt. AUS; then to lt. comdr., USNR, 1942-46. Mem. Am., Tex., Harris County bar assns., Am. Judicature Soc., Order of Coif, Phi Delta Phi, Phi Gamma Delta. Methodist. Clubs: Houston Country (dir.); Ramada. Home: 3440 Ella Lee Lane Houston TX 77027 Office: First City Nat Bank Bldg Houston TX 77002

ARNOLD, WILLIAM H., JR., lawyer; b. Texarkana, Ark., Jan. 30, 1893; grad. Phillips-Exeter Acad., Exeter N.J.; A.B., Harvard, 1914; M.A. (Rhodes scholar), Oxford (Eng.) U., 1918. Admitted to Ark. bar, 1916, La. bar, 1932, Tex. bar, 1937; mem. firm Arnold & Arnold, Texarkana. Mem. Am., Ark. bar assns., State Bar Tex. Office: 507 Hickory St Texarkana AR 75501*

ARNOLD, WILLIAM S., lawyer; b. Yonkers, N.Y., Feb. 5, 1921; A.B., U. Ark., 1942, J.D., 1947; LL.M., Columbia U., 1948. Admitted to Ark. bar, 1947, U.S. Dist. Ct., Western Dist. Ark. bar, U.S. Ct. Appeals, 8th circuit, U.S. Supreme Ct. bar. Instr. comml. law U. Ark., 1946-47; mem. firm Arnold, Hamilton & Streetman, Hamburg, Ark., also Crossett, Ark.; dep. pros. atty., 1949-60; atty. City of Crossett, 1959-66. Ark. commr. Nat. Conf. on Uniform State Law, 1969—. Fellow Am. Coll. Probate Counsel; mem. Am., Ark. (pres. 1967-68), Ashley County (v.p. 1960-63, pres. 1963—) bar assns., Am. Judicature Soc., Internat. Assn. Ins. Counsel, Delta Theta Phi. Mem. bd. editors Ark. Law Rev., 1947. Office: 110 N Main St Hamburg AR 71646 also 302 Main St PO Drawer A Crossett AR 71635*

ARNOLDY, ROMAN F., corp. exec.; b. Clements, Minn., Aug. 5, 1911; s. Frank Joseph and Magdalen (Zettel) A.; student St. Thomas Coll., 1928-30; M.E., U. Minn., 1933; m. Lillian Ethyl Joint, May 2, 1947; children—John, Susan. Salesman, Standard Oil Co. (Ind.), Mason City, Ia., 1933-34; self employed oil refining, Savage, Minn., 1934-36; supt. ind. survey U. Minn., 1936; devel. engr. Union Carbide Corp., Newark, 1936-39, dist. engr., Houston, 1939-44; founder, pres. Houston Heat Treating Co., 1944-46; founder, v.p. Houston Grinding & Mfg. Co., 1944-46; founder, pres. Tex. Alloy Products, Houston, 1946—. Mem. C. of C., Am. Welding Soc. (dir.), Am. Soc. for Engring. Edn., N.A.M., Tex. Mfrs. Assn., Breakfast Assn. Clubs: Rotary, Warwick, Lakeside Country, University. Contbr. articles to profl. jours. Inventor Bulkweld Process. Home: 225 Millbrook Lane Houston TX 77024 Office: 1403 N Post Oak Rd Houston TX 77055

ARNOW, WINSTON EUGENE, U.S. judge; b. Micanopy, Fla., Mar. 13, 1911; s. Joseph Leslie and Mable (Thrasher) A.; B.S. in Bus. Adminstrn., U. Fla., 1932, J.D., 1933; m. Frances Day Cease, Jan. 11, 1941; 1 dau., Ann Winston. Research clk. Supreme Ct. of Fla., 1933; admitted to Fla. bar, 1933; gen. practice Gainesville, 1935-42; mem. firm Clayton, Arnow, Duncan, Johnston, Clayton & Quincey, Gainesville, 1946-67; chief judge U.S. Dist. Ct., No. Dist. Fla., Pensacola, 1968—. Chmn. steering com. Fla. Civil Practice Before Trial. Served to maj. AUS, 1942-46. Recipient Distinguished Alumnus award U. Fla., 1972. Fellow Am. Coll. Probate Counsel; mem. Am. Bar Assn., Fla. Bar, Am. Law Inst., Soc. Bar 1st Jud. Circuit, Am. Judicature Soc., Order of Coif, Scabbard and Blade, Fla. Blue Key, Sigma Phi Epsilon, Phi Delta Phi, Tau Kappa Alpha, Pi Delta Epsilon. Clubs: Pensacola Country, Rotary. Contbr. articles profl. jours. Home: San Carlos Hotel Pensacola FL 32502 Office: US Dist Ct Pensacola FL 32502

ARONOW, SAUL, geologist, educator; b. Bklyn., Dec. 10, 1923; B.A., Bklyn. Coll., 1945; M.S., State U. Ia., 1946; postgrad. Yale, 1946-47; Ph.D., U. Wis., 1955; m. 1948; 3 children. Draftsman, Army Map Service, 1945; geologist U.S. Geol. Survey, 1948-52; asst. in geology U. Wis., Madison, 1953-54; prof. geology Lamar U., Beaumont, Tex., 1955—. Mem. A.A.A.S., Geol. Soc. Am., Am. Assn. Geology Tchrs. Research on geomorphology, glacial geology, ground water, Pleistocene age, Gulf Coast region. Home: 5590 Frost St Beaumont TX 77706*

ARPER, WILLIAM BURNSIDE, educator; b. Duluth, Minn., Dec. 10, 1915; s. William B. and Alice (Webster) A.; B.S., U. Okla., 1940, M.S., 1942; Ph.D., U. Kan., 1953; m. Elizabeth Jane Pearce, Nov. 6, 1942. Geologist, Phillips Petroleum Co., Shreveport, La., 1946-48; asst. instr. U. Kan., 1948-50; instr. U. Mo., 1950-53; asst. prof. geology Tex. Technol. U., Lubbock, 1953-56, asso. prof., 1956-60, prof., 1960—. Served with C.E., AUS, 1943-45. Fellow Geol. Soc. Am.; mem. Am. Assn. Petroleum Geologists, Soc. Econ. Paleontologists and Mineralogists, A.A.A.S., Am. Chem. Soc., Geo-chem. Soc., Southwestern Fedn. Geol. Socs. (sec.-treas. 1965-66), Lubbock Geol. Soc. (pres. 1967-68), Nat. Assn. Geology Tchrs., Sigma Xi. Home: 2117 31st St Lubbock TX 79411

ARRINGDALE, WALLACE JOHN, physician; b. Boone, Ia., Oct. 31, 1937; s. John Bertrum and Carolyn Anna (Leininger) A.; B.S., Ia. State U., 1960, postgrad., 1960-61; M.D., U. Neb., 1965. Intern Immanuel Deaconess Inst., Omaha, 1965-66; gen. surgery resident St. Joseph's Hosp., Houston, 1968-72; resident thoracic and cardiovascular surgery St. Luke's Hosp., Tex. Heart Inst., Houston, 1972—; dir. med. edn. Career Acad., Houston, 1969-71. Served with M.C., AUS, 1966-68. Mem. Phi Rho Sigma. Home: 2200 Fountainview 49 Houston TX 77027 Office: Texas Heart Inst Houston TX 77501

ARRINGTON, ALYNE ROGERS (MRS. JAMES D. ARRINGTON), newspaper editor; b. Collins, Miss., Feb. 9, 1911; d. Thomas Carter and D. L. O. (Buchanan) Rogers; student pub. schs.; m. James D. Arrington, Oct. 8, 1931 (dec. 1957); children—Analyn (Mrs. James Rogers Goff), Carol Jeanne (Mrs. Albert Sidney Gooch, Jr.), James D. Asst. editor The News Commercial, 1931-57, editor, owner, 1957—; owner, editor-Mt. Olive Tribune, weekly, 1960—. Active A.R.C., Am. Heart Assn., Mental Health Assn., Nat. Found., Easter Seal group. Sec. Covington County Democratic exec. com., 1950—. Mem. Miss. Press Women (v.p. 1956-57, 65—), D.A.R. (treas. 1962-70), Nat. Fedn. Press Women, Nat. Editorial Assn., Miss. Press Assn., C. of C. Baptist. Address: Collins MS 39428

ARRINGTON, JOHN LESLIE, JR., lawyer; b. Pawhuska, Okla., Oct. 15, 1931; s. John Leslie and Grace Louise (Moore) A.; grad. Lawrenceville Sch., 1949; A.B., Princeton, 1953; LL.B., Harvard, 1956, LL.M., 1957; m. Elizabeth Anne Waddington, July 21, 1956 (div. Jan. 1972); children—Elizabeth Anne, John Leslie III, Winifred Louise, Katherine Moore; m. 2d, Linda Vance Mullendore, 1972. Admitted to Okla. bar, 1956; with Huffman, Arrington, Scheurich & Kihle and predecessor firms, Tulsa 1957—, partner, 1961—. Bd. dirs. Tulsa County Legal Aid Soc., pres., 1967-69; bd. dirs. Family and Children's Service, Tulsa; trustee Holland Hall Sch., Tulsa. Recipient Jr. award for service to profession Tulsa County Bar Assn., 1962; named Outstanding Young Man, Tulsa Jr. C. of C., 1963. Mem. Okla., Tulsa County (pres. 1970), Am. Fed. Power bar assns., Am. Soc. Internat. Law, Harvard Law Sch. Assn. Okla (pres. 1961) Phi Beta Kappa. Republican. Episcopalian (vestryman). Clubs: Tulsa, Southern Hills Country, Princeton (pres. 1964-65) (Tulsa). Home: 2219 E 45th Pl Tulsa OK 74105 Office: Okla Natural Bldg Tulsa OK 74119

ARROWOOD, FRANCES ELIZABETH, Social worker; b. Union, S.C., Sept. 6, 1939; d. Robert Henry and Mary (Hall) Arrowood; student Isabella Thoburn Coll., Lucknow, India, 1959-60; B.A., Winthrop Coll., 1961; M.S.W., Fla State U., 1963. Psychiat. social worker Spartanburg (S.C.) Mental Health Clinic, 1963-65, Childrens Psychiat. Center, Miami, Fla., 1965-67, VA Hosp., Miami, 1967-71, VA Hosp., New Orleans, 1971—; social worker Big Bros. Am., 1967-71. Field instr. grad. students Fla. State U., 1969-71. Mem. Acad. Certified Social Workers, Nat. Assn. Social Workers, (sec. Piedmont chpt. 1964), Council Social Work Edn., Alpha Kappa Delta. Home: 1205 Dauphine St Apt 3 New Orleans LA 70116 Office: VA Hosp 1601 Perdido St New Orleans LA 70146

ARTERBURY, BRYANT PLATT, tool co. exec.; b. Houston, May 27, 1923; s. Roy L. and Hazel (Platt) A.; student Rice Inst., 1941-42, Tex. U., 1943, 46-47; m. Jacquelyn Jones, Oct. 10, 1947; children—Roy S., Bryant Alan. Service engr. Cavins Corp., oil well cleanout tool splty. co., Houston, 1947-56, asst. mgr., 1956-57, mgr., 1958—, dir., 1960—. Pres., Millbrook Subdiv. Improvement Fund, 1955-63; active Cub Scouts Am. Served with AUS, 1943-46. Mem. Sigma Chi. Methodist. Clubs: Pine Forest Country (Houston); Grapeland (Tex.) Country. Patentee in field. Home: 201 Millbrook Lane Houston TX 77024 Office: 6215 Thomas Rd Houston TX 77040

ARTHUR, RICHARD, state ofcl. Dir. Dept. Aeronautics, Ala. Office: State Office Bldg Montgomery AL 36104*

ARTHUR, SUSAN, librarian; b. nr. Pineville, Ky.; d. John M. and Lettie (McKeehan) Arthur; student Cumberland Coll., 1932-34, A.B. Berea Coll., 1936; B.S. in L.S., U. Ky., 1948. High sch. tchr. English and social studies, Pineville, 1937-41; high sch. librarian, 1941-48; asst. librarian Henderson State Tchrs. Coll., Arkadelphia, Ark., 1951-52; asst. librarian Union Coll., Barbourville, Ky., 1952-54; tchr. English, Barbourville High Sch., 1954-56; serials librarian, instr. library sci. Berea Coll., 1956-60; classified librarian in tech. manuals Transp. Research Center, U.S. Army, Ft. Eustis, Va., 1960-61; librarian, Barbourville City Schools, 1969—. Mem. pub. library bd. for Knox County, 1953-55. Mem. Am. Assn. U. Women (local br. pres. 1965-67), Am. Assn. U. Profs. Mem. Disciples of Christ Ch. Club: Barbourville, Garden (pres. 1969—). Home: 601 N Main St Barbourville KY 40906

ARTLEY, MALVIN NEWTON, educator; b. Newark, Aug. 17, 1921; s. Norman M. and Marion L. (Bisbing) A.; Mus.B., Shenandoah Conservatory Music, 1943; Mus.M., Cin. Conservatory Music, 1947; D.F.A., Roosevelt U., 1955; m. Joan Brown, Aug. 16, 1953; children—Malvin Newton, Nathan Monroe, Kevin Craig, Melanie Sue. Faculty, Brevard (N.C.) Coll., 1947-49, Bethany (W.Va.) Coll., 1949-53, W. Liberty (W.Va.) State Coll., 1953-54; dir. instrumental music Burlington (N.C.) City Schs., 1955-64, Greensboro (N.C.) City Schs., 1964-65; prof. music Elon Coll., Elon College, N.C., 1965—. Adminstrv. dir. Guilford Mus. Arts Center, Greensboro, 1962-69. Served with AUS, 1943-46. Mem. Am. String Tchrs. Assn. (state pres. 1965-68), Am. Musicological Soc., N.E.A., N.C. Edn. Assn., Nat. Sch. Orch. Assn. (nat. treas. 1963-67, pres. 1969-71), N.C. Symphony Soc. (trustee), Music Educators Nat. Conf. (named Outstanding Am. Educator 1971), N.C. Music Educators Conf. Home: Foster Dr Elon College NC 27244

ARTUSY, RAYMOND LONGINO, cons. geologist, cons. economist; b. Galveston, Tex., July 25, 1916; s. Max and Lena (Magee) A.; A.B., U. So. Cal., 1937, M.S., 1939; A.B., St. Mary's U., San Antonio, 1952; postgrad. (Stanolind fellow 1952-54) La. State U., 1952-55, Ph.D., 1960; postdoctoral studies in Econs., U. Colo., 1964-68; m. Jane Burks Cox, Oct. 7, 1937; 1 son, Max. Research geologist Tidewater Assn. Oil Co., 1937-38; sr. research geologist Union Producing Co., 1939-41; pilot Pan Am. World Airways, 1945-47; capt. AVIANCA, 1946-47; regional geologist Ryan, Hays & Burke, 1949-50; asst. prof. geology St. Mary's U., San Antonio, 1950-52; asst. prof. Tex. Christian U., Ft. Worth, 1955-56; v.p. Univ. Oil & Gas Corp., Houston, 1956-57; asst. prof. geology N.Y. U., N.Y.C., 1957-59; chief geologist Dorfman Prodn. Co., Dallas, 1959-61; pvt. cons. geologist, Boulder, Colo., and Texas City, Tex., VAM Co., 1950—; prof. econs. Black Hills State Coll., Spearfish, S.D., 1970—; asso. prof. econs. No. State Coll., Aberdeen, S.D., 1968-70; research asso. geology Pa. State U., 1961-62; fellow geography U. Cal., Berkeley, 1962-63; lectr. geography U. Ore., Eugene, 1963-64. Bd. govs. St. Marys U., 1950-59. Served to maj. USAAF, 1941-45, 47-49. Decorated D.F.C. Mem. Am. Assn. Petroleum Geologists, Soc. Econ. Paleontologists and Mineralogists, Paleontol. Soc., Geol. Soc. Am., Am. Assn. U. Profs., Assn. Am. Geographers, Air Force Assn., Am. Geog. Soc., Nat. Rifle Assn., N.Y. Acad. Scis., Am. Econs. Assn., Sigma Xi, Alpha Tau Omega, Phi Delta Kappa, Phalanx Frat. Republican. Baptist. Mason, Eagle. Home: 815 Sul Ross Houston TX 77006 Office: 250 Fair Pl Boulder CO 80302 also Box 961 Aberdeen SD 57401 also 1870 California St Mountain View CA 94040

ASBILL, DAVID ST. PIERRE, SR., physician; b. Ridge Spring, S.C., Oct. 23, 1901; s. Fletcher Gladstone, M.D., D.D.S. and Miranda (Du Bose) A.; B.S., The Citadel, Charleston, S.C., 1922; M.D., Med. Coll. S.C., 1926; course in surg. pathology, Mayo Clinic, 1925; m. Pauline Porter, Feb. 9, 1928; 1 son, David St. Pierre. Intern Roper Hosp., Charleston, 1925-27; resident in ophthalmology and otolaryngology Harlem Eye and Ear Hosp., N.Y.C., 1927-28; resident in ophthalmology Manhattan Eye, Ear, Throat Hosp., N.Y.C., 1928-29; physician in charge eye, ear, nose and throat dept. Davis Hosp., Statesville, N.C., 1929-33, charge teaching Sch. Nursing, 1929-33; practice ophthalmology and otolaryngology, Columbia, S.C. 1934—; in charge of teaching ophthalmology and otolaryngology Columbia Hosp. Sch. Nursing, 1935-43, S.C. Bapt. Hosp. 1935—; lectr. U. S. C., 1951-53; staff Columbia Hosp., S.C. Bapt. and Providence Hosps.; surgeon oculist, Seaboard Air Lines R.R. Co.; co. oculist, So. Rys. System. Founder S.C. Eye-Bank, Inc. Served as capt. M.C., AUS, 1943-44; student otolaryngology, Ind. U. Indpls., 1944. First award Eye-Bank Assn. Am. Diplomate Am. Bd. Ophthalmology. Fellow A.C.S.; mem. A.M.A., So. Med. Assn., Am. Acad. Ophthalmology and Otolaryngology, S.C. Soc. Ophthalmology and Otolaryngology (pres. 1953-54), Pan-Am. Ophthal. Soc., Columbia Med. Soc., Tri-Co. Med. Soc., S.C. Med. Assn., Tri-State Med. Assn., Soc. Ex-House-Surgeons of Manhattan Eye, Ear and Throat Hosp., Soc. Surgeons of So. Rys. System, Soc. Surgeons of Seaboard Air Lines R.R. Co., Am. Assn. Ry. Surgeons. S.C., Cal., Am. Camellia Soc., Am. Iris Soc., Am. Hemerocallis Soc., Assn. Citadel Men, Nat. Rifle Assn., The French Huguenot Soc. S.C., Columbia, S.C. C. of C. Mason, Lion. Clubs: Medical, Men's Garden, Forest Lake Country, White Pond Fishing. Episcopalian. Died Feb. 28, 1970, nr. Ridge Spring, S.C. Home: 419 Eisto Av Columbia SC 29205 Office: 1417 Barnwell St Columbia SC 29201

ASBILL, PAULINE PORTER(MRS. DAVID ST. PIERRE ASBILL), office mgr.; b. Royston, Ga., Sept. 19, 1906; d. James Alexander and Ophelia Kathryn (Fowler) Porter; R.N., Med. Coll. S.C. Sch. Nursing, 1926; m. David St. Pierre Asbill, Feb. 9, 1928; 1 son, David St. Pierre. Nurse charge pediatrics dept. Roper Hosp., Charleston, S.C., 1926-28; nurse obstet. dept. N.Y. Polyclinic Med. Sch. and Hosp., N.Y.C., 1928-29; mgr. physician's office, Columbia, S.C., 1934—. State of S.C. Civil Def. nurse in Richland County Civil Def. Council, 1953—. Mem. Woman's Aux. Assn. Surgeons So. Ry. and S.A.L. R.R. Systems, Woman's Aux. Columbia Med. Soc. (chmn. decorations 1948-55, v.p. 1942), Woman's Aux. S.C. Med. Assn. (charge decoration 1952-55), Internat. Platform Assn., Intercontinental Biog. Assn., Columbia Art Assn. (mem. art com. 1935-36), Delphian Soc. Episcopalian. Clubs: Columbia Woman's (publicity chmn. 1940; decorations com. 1939), Altrusa Forest Lake Country (Columbia). Home: Senate Plaza 1520 Senate St Columbia SC 29201 Office: 1417 Barnwell St Columbia SC 29201

ASBILL, SMITH LANGFORD, JR., physician, anesthesia assn. exec.; b. Tipton, Okla., Oct. 10, 1931; s. Smith Langford and Lois (Gilliland) A.; B.A. in Chemistry, Tex. Technol. U., 1957; M.D., U. Tex. Southwestern Med. Sch., 1961; m. Marjorie Ann Smith, Mar. 23, 1951; children—Lisa Ann, Leslie Annette, Robert Lawrence, Lea Anne, Laurel Allison. Intern Meth. Hosp., Dallas, 1962-64; resident Parkland Meml. Hosp., Dallas; individual practice medicine specializing in anesthesiology, Lubbock, Tex., 1964—; with Lubbock Anesthesia Assos., Lubbock, 1964—, v.p., bus. mgr., 1970-72; chief anesthesia Meth. Meml. Hosp., Lubbock, 1968-69, now mem. staff. Cartoonist Tex. Soc. Anesthesiologist Newsletter, 1970—. Served with USNR, 1951-54. Decorated Korean Presidential Unit Citation, Korean Service Ribbon Star. Mem. Am., Tex. socs. anesthesiologists, Phi Rho Sigma, Alpha Epsilon Delta. Methodist (mem. adminstrv. bd. 1969—). Home: 4418 10th St Lubbock TX 79416 Office: 3709 21st St Lubbock TX 79410

ASBURY, LOUIS HUMBERT, JR., architect; b. Charlotte, N.C., May 17, 1912; s. Louis Humbert and Mary Whitmore (Crosby) A.; student Duke, 1931-33; B. Archtl. Engring., N.C. state U., 1939; m. Helen Lee Eighme, Nov. 11, 1939; children—Kathryn (Mrs. Dennis G. Dease), Louis Humbert III. With firms Louis H. Asbury, Charlotte, 1939-42, Louis H. Asbury & Son, Charlotte, 1946-55; owner Louis H. Asbury & Assos., Charlotte, 1956—. Mem. Bishop's Com. on Ch. Architecture. Mem. exec. com. Charlotte chpt. Am. Cancer Soc., Charlotte Dist. Mission Soc. Mem. Mecklenburg County (N.C.) Bd. Adjustment. Bd. dirs. Methodist Home for Aged. Mem. A.I.A., Charlotte Exchange Club (sec. 1970-71). Clubs: Charlotte City, Carmel Country (Charlotte). Home: 4312 Tottenham Rd Charlotte NC 28211 Office: 1600 E 5th St Charlotte NC 28204

ASCHER, BERNARD, govt. economist; b. Bklyn., Dec. 7, 1933; s. Nelson Nathan and Ida (Buchwald) A.; B.A., Bklyn. Coll., 1956; M.B.A., City Coll. N.Y., 1962; m. Elinor Hirsch, Aug. 12, 1956; children— Scott, Ruth, Mark. With Aero Sea Shipping Corp., export-import, N.Y.C., 1950-57, Continental Grain Co., 1959-60, Jack Liss & Sons Co., exporters, textiles and fashions, 1960-62; commodity analyst U.S. Tariff Commn., Washington, 1962-65; sr. economist, dir. import policy staff and legislation and tariff analysis div. Bur. Internat. Commerce, U.S. Dept. Commerce, 1965-71, dir. Indsl. Products div. Office Import Programs, Washington, 1971—. Instr. Econs. U. Balt., 1966-70; credit analyst R.H. Macy & Co., N.Y.C., 1960-62; v.p. Forest Knolls Pool, Silver Spring, Md., 1970, pres., 1971. Active Forest Knolls Boys Club. Served with AUS, 1957-59. Recipient medallion Am. Marketing Assn., 1962. Mem. Am. Econ. Assn., City Coll. N.Y. Alumni Assn., Bklyn. Coll. Alumni Assn., Beta Gamma Sigma. Contbr. articles to profl. pubs. Home: 811 Caddington Av Silver Spring MD 20901 Office: Main Commerce Bldg Washington DC 20230

ASELTINE, HERSCHEL EDWARD, educator; b. Richford, Vt., Dec. 28, 1915; s. William Henry Edward and Lucy (Fuller) A.; B.A. McMaster U., 1951, B.D., 1952; M.A., U. Chgo., 1955; Ph.D., So. Ill. U., 1963; m. Gwendolyn Ruth Pamenter, June 11, 1948; children—Edward George, Richard Malin, Alice Lynne. Ordained to ministry Baptist Ch., 1949; pastor various chs., 1945-56; asst. prof. sociology Elmhurst Coll., 1958-61; mem. faculty So. Ill. U., 1961-63, U. So. Fla., 1963-67; prof. sociology Middle Tenn. State U., Murfreesboro, 1967—, chmn. sociology, 1967-70. Served with RCAF, 1940-45. Mem. So. Sociol. Soc. Home: 1919 Riverview Dr Murfreesboro TN 37130

ASHBROOK, ARTHUR GARWOOD, JR., economist; b. Pitts., Jan. 30, 1921; s. Arthur Garwood and Theodora (Hoerle) A.; B.S., Haverford Coll., 1941; Ph.D., Mass. Inst. Tech., 1947; m. Cecilia Garcia, June 20, 1964; children—Marina-Yolanda, Alexandra. Asst. prof. econs. Duke, 1947-51, Carnegie Inst. Tech., 1953-54; economist U.S. Govt., Washington, 1954—. Served with USAAF, 1943-45. Research on Chinese Communist economy. Home: 2925 39th St NW Washington DC 20016 Office: National War College Washington DC 20315

ASHBY, KEITH HAMILTON, architect; b. Hanson, Ky., Sept. 15, 1921; s. Ossie Aubrey and Ruth Annette (Weir) A.; B.S., Ga. Inst. Tech., 1948, B.Arch., 1949. Asso. architect Lawrence Casner, Architect, Madisonville, Ky., 1949-52; architect K. H. Ashby, Architect, Madisonville, 1952-54, 57-60; partner Ashby & Bond, Architects, Madisonville, 1955-56; architect Engring. div. Ky. Dept. Finance, Frankfort, 1961—, chief architect, 1964-70, asso. dir. for planning, 1970—. Served with Seabees, USNR, 1942-45. Mem. A.I.A., Ky. Hist. Soc., Tau Beta Pi, Phi Kappa Phi, Chi Epsilon, Phi Eta Sigma. Kiwanian (Key club dist. bd. 1958—). Home: 530 Capitol Av Frankfort KY 40601 Office: New Capitol Annex Frankfort KY 40601

ASHBY, LYLE WALTER, ednl. assn. exec.; b. Guide Rock, Neb., May 16, 1905; s. Ernest W. and Virginia (Walsh) A.; B.A., Hastings Coll., 1927, LL.D., 1949; M.A., American U., 1931; Ph.D., Columbia, 1936; m. Annetta Anderson, July 20, 1928; children—Harold, Lyle Walter, Coralyn Virginia. Field man Hastings Coll., 1927; tchr. Kearney Sr. High Sch., 1927-28; asst. dir. div. publs. N.E.A., 1928, asst. editor jour., 1942-48, asst. sec. profl. relations, 1948-55, asst. exec. sec. ednl. services, 1955-58, dep. exec. sec., 1959-70; vis. instr. Wash. State Coll., 1937. Chmn. Conf. Nat. Orgns., White House Conf. on Edn., 1960-62; chmn. Nat. Com. on Children and Youth, 1967-69; mem. exec. com. Joint Council on Ednl. Television, 1957-61; cons. to profl., ednl. orgns. in India on short term Fulbright Scholarship, 1961-62. Mem. Nat. Commn. on TV, Radio and Films, Meth. Ch., 1960-64, Commn. on Higher Edn., Balt. Conf., 1963—. Trustee Am. U., 1944—. Mem. N.E.A., Nat. Conf. Social Work (dir. 1955-58), Ednl. Press Assn. Am. (sec. treas. 1935-45, v.p. 1947-48); Fed. Schoolmen's Club (pres. 1971-72). Methodist. Author: The Efforts of the States to Support Education, 1936; also articles various mags. Editor: The Public and Edn., 1945-48. Observer Bikini atomic bomb tests, 1946. Home: 540 N St SW Washington DC 20024

ASHCRAFT, CHARLES HUGHES, clergyman; b. Poyen, Ark., Dec. 19, 1916; s. Henry Harrison and Ida Mae (Mathis) A.; A.B., Ouachita Bapt. U., 1939; Th.M., So. Bapt. Theol. Sem., Louisville, 1942; D.D., Ouachita Bapt. University, 1969; m. Sarah Eunice Bell, May 20, 1942; children—Charles H., James Quintin, Harry Samuel. Ordained to ministry Bapt. Ch., 1935; brotherhood and found. sec. N.M. Bapt. Found., Albuquerque, 1946-51, exec. sec., 1947-51; pastor 1st Bapt. Ch., Los Alamos, N.M., 1951-55, 1st So. Bapt. Ch., Las Vegas, Nev., 1955-65; exec. sec.-treas. Utah-Ida. So. Bapt. Conv., Salt Lake City, 1965-69; exec. sec. Ark. Bapt. Conv., 1969—. Trustee Southwestern Bapt. Theol. Sem., Fort Worth, 1958-65, Grand Canyon Coll., 1958-65; pres. Ariz.-So. Bapt. Conv., 1963-65, chmn. exec. bd., 1963-65. Served to maj. Chaplains Corps, AUS, 1943-46. Decorated Bronze Star medal. Home: 2010 Gristmill St Little Rock AR 72207 Office: 525 West Capitol St Little Rock AR 72201

ASHE, ARTHUR, tennis player; b. Richmond Va., 1944; grad. U. Cal. at Los Angeles, 1966. Winner two U.S. Inter-collegiate championships during coll.; winner U.S. Men's Hard Court Championship, 1963, U.S. Amateur title, 1968, U.S. Open championship, 1968; now mem. U.S. Davis Cup Team; Australian open winner U.S. Men's Clay Ct., 1967; pres. Players Enterprises, Inc., Washington. Served with AUS. Address: 888 17th St NW Washington DC 20006

ASHER, BUD, motel exec.; b. Atlanta, May 27, 1925; s. Baron H. and Erna (Fromme) A.; J.D., U. Ga., 1950; m. Rebecca Jane Sheets, Dec. 30, 1955; children—Ron, Marybeth. Admitted to Ga. bar, 1950; practiced in Atlanta, 1951-58; pres., gen. mgr. Daytona Safari Motel, Inc., Daytona Beach, Fla., 1958—; head coach, gen. mgr. Orlando (Fla.) T-Birds, 1962-64; head football coach, athletic dir. Father Lopez High Sch., Daytona Beach, 1964-68; head offensive coach Bethune Cookman Coll., Daytona Beach, 1969-70; area scout San Diego Chargers, 1963-66, Cin. Bengals, 1967-68, Oakland Raiders, 1969—; head football coach New Smyrna Beach (Fla.) High Sch., 1971—. Chmn., Daytona Beach Easter Affairs Com., 1970—. Bd. dirs. Holiday Football Clinic. Served with A.C., USNR, 1942-46. Decorated Air medal with gold star. Named Coach of Year, St. Johns River Conf., 1967. Mem. Daytona Beach Jr. (v.p. 1958-60), Daytona Beach (mem. accomodations com. 1970—) chambers commerce, Fla. Athletic Coaches Assn. (Dist. 5 Coach of Year 1968), Am. Football Coaches Assn., Fla. Hotel and Motel Assn., Ga. Bar Assn. Home: 5 Tropical Lane Daytona Beach FL 32018 Office: 357 S Atlantic Av Daytona Beach FL 32018

ASHER, DAVID COLSON, physician; b. Pineville, Ky., Feb. 1, 1927; s. Thomas Jefferson and Effie Catherine (Colson) A.; B.S., U. Ky., 1948; M.D., U. Louisville, 1953; m. Marjorie Ann Smith, May 28, 1965; children—David Michael, Georgianna, Sharon Louise, Byron Patrick. Intern Good Samaritan Hosp., Lexington, Ky., 1953-54, resident in surgery, 1954-55; practice medicine specializing in gen. medicine and surgery, Pineville, Ky., 1955—; staff Pineville Community Hosp., 1955—, chief of surgery, 1955-71, bd. dirs., 1955—. Vice pres. Colonel Drive Inn, Richmond, Ky., 1959—; dir. First State Bank, Pineville. Mem. Pineville Sch. Bd., 1963—; chmn.

sch. bd. Pineville Ind. Sch., 1969—. Served with USNR, 1945. Mem. Pineville Jr. C. of C. (pres. 1959), Ky. C. of C. (state health chmn. 1961), Jr. C. of C. of U.S. (internat. senator 1960—), Belle County Med. Soc. (pres. 1958), A.M.A., Ky. Med. Assn., Alpha Kappa Alpha. Club: Pineville Athletic Boosters (pres. 1961-63). Presbyn. (deacon 1968—; elder 1972). Home: Box 507 Pineville KY 40977 Office: Asher Bldg Pineville KY 40977

ASHER, JOSEPH F., dept. store exec.; b. Augusta, Ga., 1901. Former vice pres., sec. Rich's Inc., Atlanta, now dir. Home: 359 Blackland Rd NW Atlanta GA 30305 Office: Broad Alabama Forsyth and Hunter Sts Atlanta GA 30302*

ASHFORD, THEODORE ASKOUNES, chemist, educator; b. Greece, Feb. 27, 1908 (came to U.S. 1922, naturalized 1930); s. Nicholas and Catherine (Togias) Askounes; B.S., U. Chgo., 1932, M.S., 1934, Ph.D., 1936; m. Venette Tomaras, Sept. 3, 1933; children—Nicholas, Theodore II, Bobby. Tchr. math., chemistry and physics Chgo. pub. schs., 1932-36; instr., then asst. prof. chemistry U. Chgo., 1936-50; asso. prof., then prof. chemistry St. Louis U., 1950-60; prof. chemistry, dir. div. natural scis. and math. U. So. Fla., Tampa, 1960-66, prof. chemistry, asso. dean Coll. Liberal Arts, 1966-71, prof. chemistry, dean Coll. Natural Sci., 1971—. Mem. Bd. Basic Scis., State of Fla., 1963—. Bd. dirs. Fla. Found. Future Scientists. Recipient citation Nat. Sci. Tchrs. Assn., 1971. Fellow A.A.A.S.; mem. Am. Chem. Soc. (chmn. exams. com. 1946; recipient award chem. edn. 1965), N.E.A., Fla. Edn. Assn., Am. Assn. U. Profs., Am. Assn. Higher Edn., Fla. Acad. Sci., Sigma Xi. Author: From Atoms to Stars, 1960; The Structure of the Atom, the Mystery of Matter, 1965; The Physical Sciences, 1967. Editor numerous tests Am. Chem. Soc., U.S. Armed Forces Inst. Contbr. articles to profl. jours. Home: 1832 Bearss Av Tampa FL 33612

ASHLER, PHILIP FREDERIC, ednl. adminstr.; b. N.Y.C., Oct. 15, 1914; s. Philip and Charlotte (Barth) A.; B.B.A. cum laude, St. John's Coll., 1935; M.B.A., Harvard, 1937; postgrad. Indsl. Coll. Armed Forces, 1956; Sc.D., Fla. Inst. Tech., 1969; LL.D., U. W.Fla., 1969; m. Jane Porter, Mar. 4, 1942 (dec. 1968); children—Philip Frederic, Robert Porter, Richard Harrison; m.2d, Elise Barrett Duvall, June 21, 1969; stepchildren—Richard Edward Duvall, Jeffries Harding Duvall. Enlisted USMCR, 1932; commd. ensign U.S. Navy, 1938, advanced through grades to rear adm., 1959; dir. Office of Small Bus. Dept. Def., Washington, 1948-51; mem. joint staff Joint Chiefs of Staff, Washington, 1957-59; ret., 1959; dir. devel. Pensacola Jr. Coll., 1960-68; vice chancellor adminstrn. State U. System Fla., Tallahassee, 1968-70, exec. vice chancellor, 1970—. Mem. Fla. Edn. Council, 1967-68; commr. from Fla., Edn. Commn. of States, 1967-68; mem. legislative adv. council So. Regional Edn. Bd., 1966-68; chmn. Fla. Civil Def. Adv. Council, 1966-69; mem. State Bd. Ind. Colls. and Univs. Fla.; mem. Select Council on Post-High Sch. Edn., 1967-68. Mem. Fla. Ho. of Reps., 1963-68. Bd. dirs. Fla. Heart Assn., 1963—, chmn., 1969-71; bd. dirs. Am. Heart Assn., LeMoyne Art Found., Tallahassee Meml. Hosp. Decorated Bronze Star medal with Combat V; recipient Kiwanis Internat. Distinguished Service award, 1965, Am. Heart Assn. Distinguished Service award, 1965, 71, St. Petersburg Times Legislative award, 1967. Mem. Kappa Delta Pi. Democrat. Episcopalian (lay reader). Mason (32 deg., Shriner), Elk, Rotarian. Clubs: National Sojourners, Capital City Country, Capital City Tiger Bay (v.p.) (Tallahassee). Home: 1506 Argonne Rd Tallahassee FL 32303 Office: Bd Regents 107 W Gaines St Tallahassee FL 32304

ASHLEY, CHARLES GARY, assn. exec.; b. Greenville, S.C., Aug. 7, 1934; s. Lee Roy and Vivian Katherin (Jordan) A.; B.S., Fla. State U., 1956; M.Ed., Ga. So. Coll., 1965; m. Barbara Yost, May 28, 1955; children—Demi Dee, Wynters Lee, Irie Laine. Asst. coach Stranahan High Sch., Ft. Lauderdale, Fla., 1955-56; head coach, athletic dir. Mowat Jr. High Sch., Pahama City, Fla., 1960-62, Ridgeland (S.C.) High Sch., 1962-63; prin. Ridgeland High Sch., 1963-65; coordinator Title I ESEA of S.C. Dept. Edn., Columbia, 1965-69; supt. Darlington (S.C.) Area Schs., 1969-71; exec. dir. S.C. Sch. Bds. Assn., Columbia, 1971—. Served with AUS, 1957-59. Recipient Citizenship award Am. Legion, 1952, Distinguished Service award, Young Man of Year award Columbia Jr. C. of C., 1968. Mem. S.C. Soc. Exec. Dirs., Am., S.C. assns. sch. adminstrs., S.C. Assn. Sch. Supts., Fellowship Christian Athletes. Lion, Sertoma, Rotarian. Home: 6557 Eastshore Rd Columbia SC 29206 Office: 1401 Hampton St Columbia SC 29201

ASHLEY, EDWARD EVERETT, III, economist; b. Palisade, N.J., Apr. 27, 1906; s. Edward Everett, Jr. and Lillian (Shaw) A.; Ph.B., Yale, 1929; M.B.A. with distinction, Harvard, 1931; m. Mary Josephine Callahan, Apr. 3, 1965; children—Susan Joyce (Mrs. David A. Rounds), Peter Shaw. Constrn. economist Tri Continental Corp., N.Y.C., 1931-41; chief cons. to Def. Housing Coordinator, Washington, 1941-42; dir. statistics and reports Nat. Housing Agy., Washington, 1942-46; dir. econ. research Housing and Home Finance Agy., Washington, 1947-54, dir. statis. reports and analysis, 1954-65; dir. statis. reports and devel. Dept. Housing and Urban Affairs, Washington, 1965-68; exec. asst. Health and Welfare Council, Washington, 1968-69; self employed as cons. economist, Arlington, Va., 1969—; mem. housing adv. com. Arlington, (Va.) Bd. of Suprs., 1971—. Vis. lectr. housing and urban devel. U. Mich., 1960—, Howard U., 1958—. Pres. Nat. Capital Area council Girl Scouts Am., 1962-64, Arlington Community Chest and Council, 1963-65; chmn. Arlington Health and Welfare Council, 1963-65; v.p. Health and Welfare Council Greater Washington, 1963-65; bd. dirs. Health and Welfare Council of Nat. Capital Area, 1963-67. Mem. A.A.A.S., Gerontol. Soc., Com. of 100, Order of Chamaro (Guam), Alpha Sigma Phi. Clubs: Torch, Yale (Washington); Harvard Business School. Author books including: A Happy Home for the Later Years, 1962; How and Where to Live When You Retire, 1971; Choosing the Right Housing Arrangements Home: 2604 Arlington Blvd Arlington VA 22204 for the Later Years, 1972. Office: 2604 Arlington Blvd Arlington VA 22204 also Box 442 Indian Lake NY 12842

ASHLEY, JERRY SHELTON, automobile dealer, state legislator; b. nr. Orr, Okla., Jan. 20, 1906; s. Jerry and Ida Pearl (Cobb) A.; student Cameron Coll., 1923, Okla. State U., 1924-25; m. Thelma Townsend, June 25, 1932. Tchr. pub. schs., Bee, Okla., 1922; clk. Peden Iron & Steel Co., San Antonio, 1926; territorial mgr. Rayvac Co., 1927-30; dist. mgr. Chevrolet Motor div. Gen. Motors Corp., 1931-34, sales promotion mgr., 1935-36, divisional used car mgr., 1937; owner, pres. Jerry Ashley Chevrolet, Inc., Crowley, La., 1938—; pres. Rice Belt Ins. Co., Crowley, 1946—, Ashley Oil Co., Crowley, 1957—; treas. Republic Wholesale Parts Co., Crowley, 1945—; mem. La. Ho. of Reps., 1960—. Mem. La. Bd. Nuclear Energy, 1962-63. Finance officer Crowley Little Theatre, 1947—; pres. Internat. Rice Festival, 1941, 46; chmn. Crowley Indsl. Devel. Bd., 1963; mem. Acadia Parish Sch. Bd., 1952-56; mem. automobile dealers planning com. Chevrolet div. Gen. Motors Co., 1954-60. Bd. dirs. Found. of La. State U. Served to lt. col. AUS, 1942-45; ETO. Recipient 25 year Plaque Chevrolet Motor Div., 1963. Mem. Nat., La. (pres. 1963-64) automobile dealers assns., Am. Legion (La. legislative chmn.), Crowley C. of C. (pres. 1948-49). Democrat. Mem. Disciples of Christ Ch. (chmn. bd. deacons and elders). Mason (Shriner). Club: Crowley Business (pres. 1941). Home: 1701 N Parkerson Av Crowley LA 70526 Office: 919 W 2d St Crowley LA 70526

ASHLEY, THELMA TOWNSEND (MRS. JERRY ASHLEY), club woman; b. Frederick, Okla., Nov. 10, 1904; d. Jay E. and Anna (McGuire) Townsend; B.S., U. Okla., 1927; postgrad. U. Colo., summer 1928; m. Jerry S. Ashley, June 25, 1932. Tchr. home econs. high schs., Temple, Walters and Lawton, Okla., 1923-24, 28-32; mgr. Jerry Ashley Chevrolet, Inc., Crowley, La., 1941-47, now v.p. Pres. Crowley Little Theater, 1949; v.p. Community Concert, 1950; asso. dir. Girls State of State of La., Inc., 1972, bd. dirs., 1972—. Mem. Am. Legion Aux. (nat. exec. committeewoman 1955, nat. v.p., 1957, nat. vice chmn. nat. security 1959-61, nat. chmn. edn. scholarships 1962, state historian 1951, 1st v.p. 1952, 2d v.p. 1953, pres. 1954, state asso. dir. La. Girls State 1954—, state finance chmn. 1960—, mem. joint child welfare com. 1953—, regional chmn. legislation 1958, nat. div. chmn. national civil defense), Crowley Business and Profl. Women (pres. 1958), Delta Zeta (province dir. 1951, 52). Democrat. Mem. Christian Ch. Home: 11601 N Parkerson AV Crowley LA 70526

ASHMORE, FRANK LEON, univ. ofcl.; b. Greenville, S.C., Dec. 12, 1925; s. Frank Little and Lemma Leone (Burdette) A.; student Duke, 1943-44; A.B., Furman U., 1947; student Candler Sch. Theology, Emory U., 1950-53; m. Nancy Price Hall, Sept. 4, 1948; children—Elaine Anne, Hall Burdette, Louise Leona. Asst. news editor Greenville News, 1947-49; life ins. salesman, 1949-50; theol. student assigned also to churches in S.C. Ann. Conf., 1951-53; copy editor Atlanta Jour., 1953; staff pub. relations and devel. Emory U., 1953-57, asst. dir. devel. and pub. relations, 1956-57; dir. devel. and pub. relations Randolph-Macon Woman's Coll., 1957-59; exec. dir. Am. Coll. Pub. Relations Assn., Washington, 1959-61; asst. v.p. for devel. Duke, Durham, N.C., 1961-63, v.p. instl. advancement, 1963—. Mem. nat. adv. com. Council Advancement Small Colls.; pub. relations adv. com. So. Regional Edn. Bd. 1959-62, chmn., 1961-62. Trustee Bennett Coll., Paine Coll.; trustee N.C. Symphony. Served to ensign USNR, 1943-45. Mem. Am. Coll. Pub. Relations Assn., Am. Alumni Council, Delta Tau Delta. Democrat. Methodist. Kiwanian. Contbr. articles to profl. publs. Home: 2637 McDowell St Durham NC 27705

ASHMORE, HENRY LUDLOW, coll. pres.; b. Tallahassee, July 4, 1920; s. John Henry and Nursie (Whaley) A.; B.A. with honors, U. Fla., 1942, Ed.M., 1948, Ed.D. (grad. fellow 1947-50), 1950; m. Clarice Langston, Aug. 16, 1946; children—Randan Ludlow, Jerri. Prin., St. Marks (Fla.) Sch., 1946-47; dir. student teaching Ga. Tchrs. Coll., 1950-53; pres. Pensacola Jr. Coll., 1954-64; pres. Armstrong State Coll., Savannah, Ga., 1964—. Dir. Candler Hosp., Savannah. Served from pvt. to 1st lt., AUS, 1942-46. Mem. Kappa Delta Pi, Phi Delta Kappa, Phi Kappa Phi. Democrat. Baptist (chmn. bd. deacons). Rotarian. Home: 1416 N Camden Circle Savannah GA

ASHMORE, WILLIAM THOMAS, JR., candy mfr.; b. Batesburg, S.C., Feb. 14, 1912; s. William Thomas and Carrie Bryson (Glenn) A.; grad. Jr. Coll. of Augusta, 1932; A.B., LL.B., Mercer U., 1935, J.D., 1970; m. Sara Marbut Zealy, Dec. 17, 1942; children—Sara (Mrs. Kenneth W. Parrish), Martha (Mrs. John H. Burton), Elizabeth (Mrs. John P. Turner, Jr.). Editor alumni mag. Mercer U., 1935-37; asst. trust dept. 1st Nat. Bank of Macon, 1937-41; v.p., sec., dir. Fine Products Co., Inc., Augusta, Ga., 1944—; dir. Richmond Bonded Warehouse Co., Inc. Dir. Augusta-Richmond County Pub. Library, 1961-70, pres. bd., 1966-68; dir. A.R.C., 1961-67; dir. Augusta Opera Assn., Augusta Symphony League. Mem. Augusta City Council, 1959-63, 68—. Mem. Ga. Bar Assn., Augusta Coll. Alumni Assn. (pres. 1965-66), Mercer U. Alumni Assn. (dir.), Phi Alpha Delta, Alpha Tau Omega. Clubs: Exchange (pres. 1958), Augusta Country, Pinnacle (Augusta). Home: 2429 McDowell St Augusta GA 30904 Office: 833 Telfair St Augusta GA 30903

ASHTON, ALBERT A., mech. engr.; b. Adana, Turkey, Feb. 16, 1908; s. Hampar H. and Esther (Haleblian) Ashjian; student Am. U. Beirut, 1924-26, Los Angeles Poly. U., 1926-30; m. Elizabeth Carson Leland, May 16, 1934; children—Denis Leland, Bruce Leland. Engr., Hallet Mfg. Co., Los Angeles, 1930-32; engr. Emsco Derrick & Equipment Co., Los Angeles, 1936-52; chief engr. Emsco Mfg. Co., Houston, 1942-52; dir. engring. Continental-Emsco, Dallas, 1952—. Lectr. oilwell drilling machinery U. Tex. Extension Div., 1952-56, Tex. A. and M. U., 1961-62. Recipient Spl. Citation for Meritorious Service, Am. Petroleum Inst., 1961. Mem. Am. Soc. M.E., Am. Gear Mfg. Assn. (chmn. oilfield gears com. 1958-66), Am. Petroleum Inst. (chmn. mfrs. sub.-com. 1954-68), Am. Inst. Mining, Metall. and Petroleum Engrs., Am. Ordnance Assn., Am. Inst. Aeros. and Astronautics, Am. Soc. Metals. Republican. Conglist. Patentee in field. Home: 6920 Midbury Dr Dallas TX 75230 Office: Box 359 Dallas TX 75221

ASHWORTH, MAYNARD RICHARD, newspaper publisher; b. Holden, Mo., July 21, 1894; s. Henry Brinkley and Eunice Mary (West) A.; ed. State Tchr. Coll., Warrensburg, Mo., 1912-15, U. Chgo., summer 1916, U. Minn., summer, 1917; m. Annie Laurie Page, Jan. 26, 1926; children— Maynard R. Jr., Peggy. Tchr. pub. schs., Guthrie, Okla., 1915-16, Mpls., 1917; dept. store work, Pitts., 1919-24; real estate, Pitts., Los Angeles, Miami, 1924-26; in newspaper work since 1926, with Ledger-Enquirer, Columbus, Ga., 1927-28, Durham (N.C.) Sun, 1929; gen. mgr. Wilmington (N.C.) Star-News, 1929-30, Long Beach (Cal.) Sun, 1930-31; newspaper broker, Los Angeles, 1932; with San Pedro News Pilot, 1932-34; gen. mgr. Ledger-Enquirer, Columbus, Ga., 1934-36; pub. Columbus Ledger and Columbus Enquirer, 1936—; pres. R. W. Page Corp., dir. Columbus Bank & Trust Co.; sec.-treas. Columbus Broadcasting Co. Inc. Served from pvt. to 2d lt. U.S. Army, 1917-19; commd. 1st lt. Inf. Reserve Corps, 1919, capt., 1924. Served in World War II, Aug. 1941-Oct. 1944; capt. to lt. col. Inf.; 17 mos. Africa and Italy. Democrat. Methodist. Mason (32 deg., Shriner). Clubs: Rotary (dist. gov. 165th dist. 1939-40), Columbus Country, Big Eddy (Columbus); Officers' (Fort Benning, Ga.). Home: 821 Peachtree Dr Columbus GA 31520 Office: Ledger-Enquirer Columbus GA

ASHWORTH, ROBERT RALPH, supt. schs.; b. Hunt County, Tex., Nov. 20, 1913; s. John Townsend and Beaulah (Rnadle) A.; B.A., E. Tex. State U., 1934; M.A., So. Methodist U., 1939; postgrad. U. Tex., 1950-51; m. Mabel Elizabeth Miracle, July 17, 1940; children—Anne Elizabeth, Larry Robert. Tchr., Josephine (Tex.) High Sch., 1934-36, Kilgore (Tex.) High Sch., 1936-45; counselor Tyler (Tex.) High Sch., 1945-47, prin., 1947-52; supt. Kilgore Pub. Schs., 1952-56; supt. Corsicana (Tex.) Pub. Schs., 1956-58; supt. Amarillo (Tex.) Pub. Schs., 1958—. Served with USAAF, 1943-44, Mem. N.E.A., Am., Tex. (pres. 1957-58) assns. sch. adminstrs., Tex. Tchrs. Assn. Home: 3902 Lynette Amarillo TX 79109 Office: 910 W 8th St Amarillo TX 79101

ASKEW, HUBERT CARL, dentist; b. Houston, Sept. 30, 1939; s. Hubert Carl and Mary Eugiene (Philip) A.; B.S., U. Tex., 1962, D.D.S., 1966; m. Rebecca Ann Beckering, June 15, 1963. Individual practice dentistry, Houston, 1968—; asst. Meml. Bapt. Hosp., 1969—; mem. staff Meml. City Hosp.; cons. VA Hosp., Houston, 1969—. Served to capt., Dental Corps, AUS, 1966-68. Recipient children's dental health week citation USPHS, 1969. Mem. Am., Tex. dental assns., Xi Psi Phi, Phi Sigma Kappa. Home: 14527 Kellywood St Houston TX 77024 Office: 902 Frostwood St Houston TX 77024

ASKEW, J(OSEPH) THOMAS, educator; b. Carrollton, Ga., Mar. 15, 1903; s. Charles O. and Ada (Daniel) A.; Ph.B., Piedmont Coll., 1924, LL.D., 1943; M.A., U. Ga., 1930; postgrad. U. Chgo., 1935, U. London, 1939; m. Anne Sherman McMillan, June 18, 1925; 1 dau., Julia Ellen (Mrs. Raymond Weathers Stephens, Jr.). With Miami (Fla.) Herald, 1924-27; tchr. history 9th Dist. A. and M., Clarkesville, Ga., 1927-29; dean Armstrong Jr. Coll., Savannah, Ga., 1935-40, pres., 1940-43; instr. history and polit. sci. U. Ga., Athens, 1929-32, asst. prof., 1932-35, asso. prof. polit. sci., dir. vets. div., 1945-55, registrar, dir. admission, 1947-49, asst. to pres., dir. pub. relations, 1949-51, dean students, 1949-55, acting dir. U. Center, 1956, prof. polit. sci., 1956—. Pres., Savannah Community Forum, 1940-42; Savannah Inst. Citizenship. Trustee Rotary Internat. Edn. Fund Savannah. Served to lt. comdr. USNR, 1943-46. Mem. N.E.A., Ga. Edn. Assn. (pres. dept. higher edn. 1956-57), Am., So. (sec.-treas. 1931-32) polit. sci. assns., Nat. Assn. Student Personnel Adminstrs. (exec. com. 1955-56), Phi Beta Kappa, Phi Kappa Phi, Pi Sigma Alpha. Author: Savannah: The Political Community, 1963; (with Merritt B. Pound) The Government of Georgia, 1959. Editor: (with Malcolm H. Bryan) Book of Readings in Contemporary Georgia, 1935. Editor: Georgia Local Govt. Jour., 1959-60. Contbr. chpts. to polit. sci. texts, articles to profl. jours. Home: 260 Southview Dr Athens GA 30601

ASKEW, RUEBEN, gov. of Fla. Office: Capitol Bldg Tallahassee FL 32304*

ASKEW, THURMAN EDWARD, oil co. exec.; b. nr. Jackson, N.C., Feb. 16, 1929; s. James Joshua and Gladys Jesse (Askew) A.; student Internat. Accountants Sch., 1955, East Carolina U., 1969; m. Janie Mae Hale, Aug. 17, 1949; children—Wanda (Mrs. James Alderman Westbrook, III), Thurman Edward. With Newsom Oil Co., Inc., Roanoke Rapids, N.C., 1949—, sec.-treas. 1958—, gen. mgr., 1960—, dir., 1954—; dir. Bell's Shoe & Clothing Store, Inc., Jan's Inc., Newsom Realty Co., Newsom Transports, Inc. Mem. Roanoke Rapids Planning Bd., 1964-69, William R. Davie Sch. Bd., 1956-61. Councilman, Roanoke Rapids, 1969—. Named oil man of the year N.C. Oil Jobbers, 1968. Mem. Choanoke Area Devel. Assn. (pres. 1971), Roanoke Rapids C. of C. (pres. 1967-68). Methodist (ofcl. bd. 1956-71). Home: 150 Valley Dr Roanoke Rapids NC 27870 Office: 1503 W 10th St Roanoke Rapids NC 27870

ASKIN, WILLIAM DAVIS, sulphur co. exec.; b. Denver, Apr. 25, 1924; s. Thomas Barwiss Hagstoz and Lucille Anne (Thorsen) A.; B.J., U. Mo., 1950; m. Patricia Ann Neale, June 9, 1956; children—Brett Davis, Martha Lynn. With Denver Post, 1950-53, Norman (Okla.) Transcript., 1954-55; editor Shell Pipe Line Corp., Houston, 1955-56; mgr. pub. relations Robert H. Ray Geophys. Co., Houston, 1956-61, Tex. Gulf Sulphur Co., Houston, 1961—. Mem. pub. relations com. A.R.C., 1961—; chmn. pub. information group Am. Cancer Soc., 1969-70, 70-71, state pub. information com. 1971; mem. Publs. com. U. Mo., 1970. Served with USNR, 1942-46. Mem. Pub. Relations Soc. Am. (dir. Houston chpt. 1971-73), Internat. Assn. Bus. Communicators (Editor of Year Houston Chpt. 1971), Houston C. of C. (pub. relations com. 1963—), U. Mo. Aplumni Assn. (pres. 1969), Sigma Delta Chi (past pres.), Sigma Alpha Epsilon. Clubs: Press., Tejas Golf (Houston). Home: 5615 Dumfries Dr Houston TX 77035 Office: 1740 Houston Club Bldg Houston TX 77002

ASKINS, KNOX WINFRED, lawyer; b. Houston, July 19, 1937; s. Elgie Joseph and Geneva (Rulison) A.; B.F.A., U. Houston, 1958, J.D., 1962; student Blinn Jr. Coll., 1955-56; m. Augusta Ann Thomas, Sept. 13, 1958; children—Diane, Suzanne, Sally Ann, James Paul, Clark. Admitted to Tex. bar, U.S. Dist. Ct. bar, 1962, U.S. Supreme Ct. bar, 1970; practice law, La Porte, Tex., 1962—; gen. counsel, dir. Bayshore Nat. Bank of La Porte, 1966—; city atty., City of La Porte, 1965—; govt. appeal agt. Selective Service Local Bd., 1970—; legal counsel Bay Area Fine Arts Assn., 1970—. Me. La Porte Welfare Com., 1965—, La Porte Council for Retarded Children, 1965—. Mem. Am., Tex., Houston bar assns., Am. Judicature Soc., Texas City Atty.'s Assn., Nat. Inst. Municipal Legal Officers, Order of the Barons, Delta Theta Phi. Club: Houston Yacht. Office: 122 S Broadway La Porte TX 77571 Home: 1010 S Country Club Dr La Porte TX 77571

ASSAF, RONALD GEORGE, electronics co. exec.; b. Akron, O., June 2, 1935; s. Jaleel and Bernice (St. John) A.; student U. Akron, 1958; m. Nancy Jean Wooddell, June 10, 1955; children—Kimberley Marie, Timothy Patrick, Ronald James. Store mgr. Kroger Co., Solon, O., 1954-67; exec. v.p. Sensormatic Electronics Corp., Hollywood, Fla., 1967—, chmn. bd. 1971—; pres., dir. RWA Co. Ltd., Nassau, Bahamas. Mem. Phi Sigma Kappa. Republican. Roman Catholic. Home: 4240 NW Riverside Av Coral Springs FL 33060 Office: 2040 Sherman St Hollywood FL 33020

ASTIN, ALEXANDER WILLIAM, ednl. researcher; b. Washington, May 30, 1932; s. Allen Varley and Margaret (Mackenzie) A.; A.B., Gettysburg Coll., 1953; M.A., U. Md., 1956, Ph.D., 1957; m. Helen P. Stavridou, Feb. 11, 1956; children—John, Paul. Dep. chief Psychology Service, USPHS Hosp., Lexington, Ky., 1957-59; asst. chief psychology research unit VA Hosp., Balt., 1959-60; dir. research Nat. Merit Scholarship Corp., Evanston, Ill., 1960-64; dir. research Am. Council on Edn., Washington, 1965—; lectr. U. Ky., 1958-59, U. Md., 1959-60, Northwestern U., 1961-63; cons. Surgeon Gen.'s Adv. Com. on Smoking and Health, 1962-63, NIH study sect. on med. edn., 1965-66, IBM Corp., 1966-67, U.S. Office Edn., 1971—, NIH, 1971—. Recipient award for outstanding research Am. Personnel and Guidance Assn., 1965. Fellow Center for Advanced Study in Behavioral Scis., 1967-68. Mem. Am. Psychol. Assn., Am. Ednl. Research Assn., A.A.A.S., Am. Personnel and Guidance Assn., Assn. Instl. Research, Psi Chi. Author: Who Goes Where to College, 1965; The College Environment, 1968; The Educational and Vocational Development of College Students, 1969; Predicting Academic Performance in College, 1971; The Invisible Colleges, 1971; The Disadvantaged Student in Higher Education, 1972. Home: 4829 Chevy Chase Blvd Chevy Chase MD 20015 Office: 1 DuPont Circle Washington DC 20036

ASTLER, VERNON BENSON, physician; b. Wyoming, O., Sept. 5, 1925; s. Vernon Wolfert and Blanche (Benson) A.; student Miami U., 1943-45; M.D., Temple U., 1949; M.S., U. Mich., 1953; m. Louise Menge, Aug. 9, 1949 (div.); children—Kim Louise, Kristy Lee, Douglas Vernon; m. 2d, Diane Rosacker, Dec. 31, 1969. Intern Univ. Hosp., Ann Arbor, Mich., 1949-50, resident, 1950-57; practice medicine, specializing in surgery, Boynton Beach, Fla., 1958—; mem. staff Bethesda Hosp., Boca Raton Hosp., Lake Worth Gen. Hosp. Mem. Fla. State Bd. Med. Examiners (pres. 1971-72). Served with M.C., AUS, 1953-55. Diplomate Am. Bd. Surgery. Fellow A.C.S., Southeastern Surg. Congress; mem. Fla. Med. Assn. (gov. 1971—), Frederick A. Coller Surg. Soc., A.M.A., Delray Beach C. of C., Sigma Nu, Phi Chi. Mason (Shriner), Kiwanian (dir.). Home: 3268 N Ocean Blvd Gulfstream FL 33444 Office: Med Arts Center 2800 S Seacrest Blvd Boynton Beach FL 33435

ASTON, FLOYD DWIGHT, oil co. exec.; b. Sherman, Tex., Nov. 20, 1905; s. John Elmore and Permelia (Outhouse) A.; B.A., Austin Coll., 1927; C.P.A., LaSalle Extension U., 1935; m. Marguerite Stuart

Stokes, June 23, 1951; 1 son, Dwight Stuart; 1 stepson, Joseph Morgan Stokes, Jr. Accountant, traveling auditor Tex. Power & Light Co., Dallas, 1927-36; accountant Haskins & Sells, Dallas, 1936, Houston, 1937-40; sec., chief accountant Berkshire Oil Co., Houston, 1940-62; chief accountant Frankel Oil & Gas Co., Houston, 1963-—; sec. Cove Oil, Inc., Houston, 1966-—, also dir. Sec.-treas. Maurice Frankel Found., 1963-—. Mem. Am. Inst. C.P.A.'s, Tex. Soc. C.P.A.'s, Am. Accounting Assn., Petroleum Accountants Soc. Houston. Methodist. Club: Valley Lodge (Simonton, Tex.). Home: 3301 Bluebonnet St Houston TX 77025 Office: 815 Walker St Houston TX 77002

ASTON, JAMES W(ILLIAM), banker; b. Farmersville, Tex., Oct. 6, 1911; s. Joe A. and Jimmie Gertrude (Jackson) A.; B.S. in C.E., A & M. Coll. Tex., 1933; m. Sarah Camilla Orth, June 29, 1935; 1 son, James William. Asst. city mgr., Dallas, 1935-39, city mgr., 1939-41; city mgr., Bryan, Tex., 1939; v.p. Republic Nat. Bank of Dallas 1945-55, exec. v.p., 1955-57, dir., pres., 1957-65, chmn., chief exec. officer, dir., 1965-—; dir. Am. Airlines, Inc., Lone Star Steel Co., Gen. Portland Cement Co., Times Mirror Co., Zale Corp., Group Hosp. Service, Inc., Group Med. & Surg. Service, Group Life & Health Ins. Co., Neuhoff Brothers Packers, Dallas Times Herald. Mem. Greater Dallas Planning Council; treas. City of Dallas. Trustee Tex. Research Found., Southwestern Med. Found., Southwest Research Inst., Wadley Inst. of Molecular Medicine, S.W. Legal Found., Hoblitzelle Found.; bd. dirs. State Fair Texas; bd. govs. So. Meth. U., United Way of Am. Served from lt. to col. USAAF, 1941-45. Decorated D.S.M., Legion of Merit. Registered profl. engr. Mem. Assn. Res. City Bankers, Trinity Improvement Assn. (v.p.), Internat. C. of C. (dir. U.S. council), Newcomen Soc. N. Am., Am. (exec. council 1965-68), Tex. bankers assns., Tau Beta Phi. Mem. Christian Ch. Clubs: City, Dallas, Northwood Country, Athletic, Petroleum Country, Dallas Country (Dallas); Army-Navy Country (Washington); Brook, Marco Polo (N.Y.C.); Tres Vidas (Acapulco, Mexico); Chaparral, Southwest; Cherokke Lancers; Las Colinas Country; Preston Trail Golf. Home: PO Box 5961 Dallas TX 75222

ASTROP, WILLIAM BOWEN, investment co. exec.; b. Charleston, S.C., Sept. 22, 1929; s. Robert Collins and Arretha Robertson (Bowen) A.; B.A., U. Richmond, 1950, M.B.A. (J.Spencer Love fellow), Harvard, 1953; m. Jean Anne Trimmer, Sept. 18, 1963; 1 son, William B. Vice pres. Fla. Capital Corp., Palm Beach, 1960-63, Stone & Webster Securities, N.Y.C., 1963-68, UniCapital Corp., Atlanta, 1968-70; partner Post & Astrop, investment counsel, Atlanta, 1970-—; dir. Kem Mfg. Corp., Atlanta, Founders Corp., Palm Beach, Cavalier Corp., Chattanooga; chmn. bd. Charlotte House Mgmt. Co., N.Y., 1972-—. Instr. U. Richmond, eves. 1958-60. Mem. Com. of 100, Emory U., 1971-—. Served with USNR, 1953-56. Chartered financial analyst. Mem. N.Y., Atlanta socs. security analysts, Clubs: Harvard (Atlanta, Palm Beach); Commerce, Piedmont Driving (Atlanta). Home: 2415 Hanover W Lane N W Atlanta GA 30327 Office: 134 Peachtree St Atlanta GA 30303

ASTUDILLO SANDOVAL, HOMERO, lawyer, Mexican govt. ofcl.; b. Mexico, D.F., Mexico, 1940; Atty. at Law, Nat. Autonomous U. Mexico; Diploma in Social Policy, Inst. Social Studies, The Hague; Diploma in Pvt. Internat. Law, Internat. Ct. Justice; Diploma, Inst. Labor Studies, Geneva, Switzerland. Admitted to Mexico bar, 1962; asst. chief social security dept. Labor Union of Mexican Republic, Mexico D.F. Mem. Studies Assn. Mexican Social Security (pres. 1971). Address: Paseo de la Reforma 116-404 Mexico DF Mexico*

ASUNCION, JUAN SANTOS, physician; b. Philippines, June 12, 1932; s. Eustaquio Mateo and Leoncia (Santos) A.; A.A., Manila Central U., 1953, M.D., 1958; m. Margaret Ann James, Oct. 1, 1960; children—Kimberly, Terri, Alesia, Christine. Intern Sts. Mary & Elizabeth Hosp., Louisville, 1958-59, dir. house physicians, 1971-72, med. dir. inhalation therapy, 1969-73, chmn. dept. anesthesia, 1969-73; resident in surgery Norton Meml. Infirmary, Louisville, 1959-63; resident in anesthesia Balt. City Hosps., 1964-67, asst. chief anesthesiologist, 1967-68; instr. anesthesiology Johns Hopkins Med. Sch., 1967-68, U. Md. Sch. Medicine, 1967-68. Mem. ch. council Our Lady Mt. Carmel Cath. Ch., Louisville, 1971-73. Mem. A.M.A., Am. Soc. Anesthesiologists, Ky. Med. Assn., Med. and Chirurgical Soc. Md., Jefferson County Med. Soc. Louisville, Louisville, Ky. Socs. anesthesiologists. Home: 501 Wilderness Rd Louisville KY 40214 Office: 4602 Southern Pkwy Louisville KY 40214

ATCHESON, JAMES EDWARD, architect; b. Terrell, Tex., Jan. 26, 1906; s. Frank and Bessie (Barton) A.; B. Arch., Tex. Technol. Coll., 1936; m. Armista Lucille Heggen, June 20, 1936; children—Michael Edward, Daniel Benn, Timothy Jon, Anne Louise. Draftsman, Eickenroht & Cocke, architects, San Antonio, also part-time instr. Tex. Technol. Coll., 1928-34; designer O.R. Walker, architect, Lubbock, Tex., 1935-40; asso. archtl. engr., C.E., U.S. Army, Albuquerque and Pyote, Tex., 1942-44; partner Walker &Atcheson, architects, Lubbock, 1941-46; prin. James Atcheson, architects, Lubbock, 1947-48; partner Atcheson & Atkinson architects, Lubbock, 1949-55, Atcheson, Atkinson & Cartwright, architects and engrs., Lubbock, 1956-—; prin. works include Lubbock Country Club, 1960, Citizens Nat. Bank, Lubbock, 1963, First Christian Ch., Lubbock, 1964, Bell System Telephone Bldg., Lubbock, Tex. (merit award for architectural excellence), 1967, Am. State Bank, Lubbock, 1969, Courthouse and Fed. office bldg., Lubbock, 1971. Mem. A.I.A. (pres. Panhandle chpt. 1945, Lubbock chpt. 1963), Tex. Soc. Architects (v.p. 1960); Constn. Specifications Inst. (pres. Lubbock chpt. 1966), Phi Delta Theta. Lutheran (pres. 1966-67). Kiwanian. Club: Lubbock Country. Home: 3203 26th St Lubbock TX 79410 Office: 1214 14th St Lubbock TX 79401

ATCHLEY, EDWARD NOAH, boat mfg. co. exec.; b. Knoxville, Tenn., Mar. 27, 1935; s. Curtis Bentley and Alma Ada (Wells) A.; B.B.A., U. Tenn., 1956; m. Sharon Ester Thompson, Aug. 16, 1963; children—Teresa Lynne, Edward Scott, Stanley Dean. Dist. mgr. McCulloch Corp., Los Angeles, 1958-63; v.p., gen. mgr. Stowaway Marinas Inc., St. Petersburg, Fla., 1963-67; field salesman Cobia Boats, Inc. div. Ashland Oil Co., Inc., Sanford, Fla., 1967-69, v.p. marketing, 1969-—. Bd. dirs. St. Petersburg Boat Show, 1964-67. Served with USNR, 1953-61. Mem. Boating Industry Assos., Nat. Assn. Engine and Boat Mfrs., St. Petersburg Beach C. of C. (chmn. marine com. 1964-67). Home: 516 Tivoli Ct Altamonte Springs FL 32701 Office: 100 Silver Lake Rd Sanford FL 32771

ATHANASIOU, BETTYE, pub. relations exec., editor; b. Dallas, June 15, 1923; d. J.L. and Edythe (Stewart) Raiden; student Massey Bus. Sch., 1947 div.; children—Rolanette (Mrs. Fred J. MacKie III), Susan Saul. Pvt. sec. to sec.-treas. Mission Mfg. Co., Houston, 1947-49; pvt. sec. to pres. Marine Exploration Co., Houston, 1949-52; sec., editor, pub. relations Robert H. Ray Co., Houston, 1952-56; mgr. pub. relations, editor Geo. Space Corp., Houston, 1963-—; co-chmn. publicity 36th Ann. Internat. Soc. Exploration Geophysicists Meeting, 1966. Gen. chmn. Gov. Bill Daniels Ann. Crippled Childrens Party, 1956-69; capt. Pin Oaks Charity Horse Show, 1959-64. Pres. Hedgecroft Hosp. Aux., President's Council Houston Hosp. Aux.; bd. dirs. Tex. Hosp. Auxs. Recipient Service award Geophys. Soc. Houston, 1968. Mem. Am. Bus. Womens Assn. (charter pres. Houston), Soc. Exploration Geophysicists, Geophys. Soc. Houston (publicity chmn. 1971-—), Internat. Council Indsl. Editors, Internat. Assn. Bus. Communicators, Am. Soc. for Oceanography, European Assn. Exploration Geologists, Houston C. of C. (mem. communications and information com. 1972-—), Asociacion Mexicana de Geofisicos de Exploracion. Home: 3102 Suffolk St Houston TX 77027 Office: 5803 Glenmont Dr Houston TX 77036

ATHERTON, JAMES CHRISTIAN, educator; b. Bolivar, La., Aug. 4, 1915; s. James G. and Mary (Matthews) A.; B.S., La. State U., 1935, M.S., 1947; Ed.M., U. Ill., 1949, Ed.D., 1950; m. Ruth Victoria Cash, Nov. 26, 1937; children—James Christian, George A., Ruth V. Tchr., Loranger (La.) High Sch., 1935-42, 45-46, prin., 1946-48; prof. agrl. edn. U. Ark., Fayetteville, 1950-65, La. State U., Baton Rouge, 1965-—. Pres. tchr. tng. sect. So. Regional Conf. Agrl. Edn., 1957-58. Vice pres. So. Agrl. Edn. Conf., 1971-72. Served to lt. col. AUS, 1942-45. Recipient Distinguished Service award in agrl. edn. So. Regional Conf. Agrl. Edn., 1962; outstanding service citation, Nat. Vocational Agrl. Tchrs. Assn., 1968; hon. state farmer degree, Ark., La. Future Farmers Am., 1955, 67. Mem. Am. Vocational Assn., Nat. Vocational Agr. Tchrs. Assn., Am. Assn. Tchr. Educators in Agr. editor Jour. 1966-70, Alpha Tau Alpha (nat. 1st v.p. 1965-69), Phi Kappa Phi, Alpha Zeta, Gamma Sigma Delta, Phi Delta Kappa. Democrat. So. Baptist. Co-author: Essential Aspects of Career Planning and Development, 1969. Editor Ark. Service Bull., 1955-65; regional editor Agrl. Edn. mag., 1955-62, 64-—. Contbr. articles to profl. jours. Home: 6099 S Pollard Pkwy Baton Rouge LA 70808

ATKIN, JOHN THATCHER, retail sales co. exec.; b. Georgetown, Tex., Apr. 21, 1904; s. Samuel Thatcher and Sallie (Mason) A.; A.B., Southwestern U., Georgetown, 1925; M.A., U. Tex., Austin, 1930; m. Genevieve Critz, June 11, 1931; children—Richard T., John M. Tchr. math. Southwestern U., 1926, 37-38; tchr. math. U. Miss., 1927-29, U. Tex., 1930; instr. U.S. Treasury Dept., San Antonio, 1935; auditor U.S. Dept. Labor, Georgetown, 1936; with S.T. Atkin Furniture Co., Georgetown, 1931-35, 37-—, now owner, mgr.; dir. Georgetown Savs. & Loan Assn. Chmn. United Fund Drive, Georgetown, 1967. Mem. City Council, mayor, Georgetown, 1947-58; mem. Gov.'s Statewide Water Com., 1952-57; precinct chmn. Williamson County Democratic Exec. Com., 1950-72. Pres., bd. dirs. Williamson County Tb. Assn., Georgetown Library; bd. dirs. Tex. United Fund. Served with Tex. N.G., 1941-47. Recipient Silver Beaver award Boy Scouts Am., 1962, Most Worthy Citizen award, Georgetown, 1971. Mem. Tex. Retail Furniture Assn., Pi Kappa Alpha. Methodist. Mason (Shriner), Rotarian. Club: Georgetown Country (dir.). Home: 1108 Church St Georgetown TX 78626 Office: 701-05 Main St Georgetown TX 78626

ATKINS, ANTHONY PAUL, rancher; b. El Dorado, Kan., Nov. 26, 1902; s. James and Eva Jane (Pool) A.; B.S. in Agr., Kan. State U., 1924; m. Winifred Blanche Rhodes, Aug. 15, 1924; children—Marcia (Mrs. Richard L. Walden), James Robert. Owner, operator cattle ranches in Okla., Tex. Panhandle, S.W. Kan., Texas County, Okla., 1924-—; dir. City Nat. Bank, Guymon, Okla. Pres., Guymon Meml. Found., 1962-—. Mayor, City of Guymon, 1959-62. Mem. Am. Soc. Range Mgmt. (life; pres. 1955-56), Okla. Assn. Conservation Dists. (pres. 1948-51), Nat. Assn. Conservation Dists. (dir. 1954-55), Am. Nat., Okla. cattlemen's assns., Okla. Farm Bur. (charter). Democrat. Methodist. Mason (33 deg., Shriner), Lion (pres. Guymon 1946-47). Address: PO Box 470 (801 W 1st St Guymon OK 73942

ATKINS, C(ARL) CLYDE, judge; b. Washington, Nov. 23, 1914; s. C. C. and Marguerite (Criste) A.; student U. Miami (Fla.), 1931-32; LL.B., U. Fla., 1936, LL.D., 1968; LL.D., Barry Coll. at Miami Shores, 1966, Biscayne Coll., Miami, 1970; m. Esther Castillo, Jan. 18, 1937; children—Sister Julie, Carla Schulte, Carl Clyde. Admitted to Fla. bar, 1936; practice in Stuart, 1936-41, Miami, 1941-66; partner firm Walton, Lantaff, Schroeder, Atkins, Carson & Wahl, and predecessors, 1941-66; U.S. dist. judge So. dist. Fla., 1966-—. Founder-trustee Lawyers Title Guaranty Fund, 1948-60, treas., 1963-66. Pres. St. Augustine Diocesan Union Holy Name Socs., 1950-51, Miami Diocesan Council Cath. Men, 1959-69. Trustee Biscayne Coll., Miami. Recipient Outstanding Cath. award Nat. Conf. Christians and Jews, 1959. Fellow Am. Coll. Trial Lawyers; mem. Fedn. Ins. Counsel, Am. (ho. of dels. 1960-66), Dade County (pres. 1953-54) bar assns., Fla. Bar (bd. govs. 1954-59, pres. 1960-61), Internat. Assn. Ins. Counsel, Tau Kappa Alpha, Phi Kappa Tau, Phi Alpha Delta. Kiwanian (past dir. Miami). Clubs: Miami; Coral Gables Country. Author articles profl. jours. Home: 2040 Country Club Prado Coral Gables FL 33134 Office: US Ct House Box 3009 Miami FL 33130

ATKINS, CRAIG STARBUCK, judge, lawyer; b. Greensboro, N.C., Aug. 17, 1903; s. Benjamin F. and Neva O. (Starbuck) A.; student U. N.C., 1920-21; A.B., George Washington U., 1923, LL.B., 1925; m. Margaret Elinor Denty, June 30, 1926; children—Craig Starbuck, Constance (Mrs. John E. McShulskis). Admitted to D.C. bar, 1925; atty. U.S. Bd. Tax Appeals, 1927-37; atty. Office of Chief Counsel, Internal Revenue Service, 1937-49, asst. chief counsel, 1954-55; tax adviser to Greek Govt. and ECA Mission to Greece, 1949-51; judge Tax Ct. of U.S., 1955-—. Mem. Am. Bar Assn., Sigma Phi Epsilon. Mason. Home: 7004 Florida St Chevy Chase MD Office: Tax Ct of US Washington DC 20025

ATKINS, HARDIN LOUIS, JR., agriculturist; b. Asheville, N.C., Nov. 7, 1898; s. Hardin Louis and Elizabeth (Whitaker) A.; B.S. in Animal Husbandry, Tex. A. and M. Coll., 1922; m. Elizabeth Buford Beasley, Mar. 18, 1926; children—Hardin Louis III, Joseph Noble, Elizabeth (Mrs. Charles Alan Bray), Lydia (Mrs. Lydia L. Canterbury). Asst. in cane cultivation Russell & Co., Fortuna, P.R., 1922-23; county agrl. agt. Mitchell County, Colorado City, Tex., 1924-26, Midland County, Tex., 1926-28; asso. editor Progressive Farmer, Dallas, 1928-32; field agt. emergency feed and seed loans U.S. Dept. Agr., Dallas, 1932-33; county agrl. agt. for Andrews, Crane, Ector counties, Odessa, Tex., 1933-48; div. mgr., dir. McElroy Ranch Co., Midland, Tex., 1949-54; mgr. personal investments oil royalties, ins. stocks, 1954-—. Founding incorporator San Hills Hereford Show, Odessa, Tex. Past dir. Black Gold dist. Boy Scouts Am. Mem. Selective Service Bd., 1961-72. Mem. Odessa C. of C. (past dir. Tex. County Agts. Assn. (pres. 1941). Methodist (ofcl. bd. 1933-—). Mason (32 deg., K.T.), Rotarian (pres. Odessa 1947-48). Home: 1409 Byron Av Odessa TX 79760

ATKINS, OLIVER (OLLIE) F., photographer; b. Hyde Park, Mass., Feb. 18, 1916; s. Oliver Fraser and Annie Sally (McLeod) A.; grad. Huntington Sch. for Boys, Boston; A.B., U. of Ala., 1938; m. Marjorie Neola Deakin, Aug. 10, 1940; children—Randle Claire (Mrs. Shumate), Dale Ann (Mrs. Wheeler). Staff and chief photographer for the Birmingham (Ala.) Post, 1939-40; staff photographer, Washington Daily News, 1940-42; fgn. corr. photographer 1942-45; Washington photographer, Sat. Eve. Post, Washington office, 1945-68, fgn. corr., photographer, Japan, Korea, other countries for Sat. Eve. Post.; photography columnist, Washington Post, 1947-50; personal photographer to Pres. Richard M. Nixon; photography 2 photo books, Washington Portrait and Potomac Portrait. Recipient citation from A.R.C. for overseas service; Sprague award Nat. Press Photographers Assn., 1969. Mem. White House News Photographers Assn. (pres. 1964, 65), Am. Overseas Assn. (pres.). Author: Camera on Assignment; Home: 1364 MacBeth St McLean VA 22101 Office: The White House Washington DC 20500

ATKINS, ORIN ELLSWORTH, oil co. exec.; b. Pitts., June 6, 1924; s. Orin E. and Dorothy (Whittaker) A.; student Marshall U., Huntington, W.Va., 1942-43, 46-47, LL.D., 1970; student U. Pa., 1943-44; LL.B., U. Va., 1950; m. Kathryn Agee, Nov. 25, 1950; children—Randall, Charles. Admitted to W. Va. bar, 1950, Ky. bar, 1952; with Ashland Oil & Refining Co. (Ky.), 1950-—, exec. asst., 1956-59, adminstrv. v.p., 1959-65, pres., chief exec. officer, 1965-72, chmn. bd., chief exec. officer, 1972-—, dir.; dir. Cin. br. Fed. Res. Bank Cleve., 1968-71. Mem. Nat. Pub. Adv. Com. on Regional Econ. Devel., 1970-—; mem. Nat. Indsl. Pollution Control Council; mem. Nat. Petroleum Council Ky., chmn. com. on factors affecting U.S. refining, 1972-—; mem. Council Econ. Advisers. Chmn. bd. advisers Marshall U. Served with AUS, 1942-46. Mem. Am., W.Va., Ky. bar assns., Conf. Bd., Nat. Planning Assn. (nat. council), Nat. Petroleum Refiners Assn., Am. Petroleum Inst. Presbyn. Home: 602 Amanda Dr Bellefonte Ashland KY 41101 Office: Bellefonte Ashland KY 41101

ATKINS, ROBERT MARSH, dentist, county ofcl.; b. Tampa, Fla., June 28, 1939; s. Cedric Donald and Martha Kathryn (Marsh) A.; student Emory U., 1957, 58, U. Fla., 1958, 59; D.D.S., Emory U., 1963; m. Janis Amanda Dodson, Nov. 27, 1961; children—James Donald, Linda Kay, Kenneth Edwin. Individual practice dentistry, Frostproof, Fla., 1963-69; dental dir. Palm Beach County Health Dept., West Palm Beach, Fla., 1969-—. Dental cons. Palm Beach County Home and Gen. Care Facility, Palm Beach County Bd. Pub. Instrn.; asso. prof. dept. community dentistry U. Fla. Spl. dep. sheriff Palm Beach and Polk counties. Mem. Am. Dental Assn., Fla., Am. pub. health assns., Am. Assn. Pub. Health Dentists, Fla. Pub. Health Assn., Fla. Dental Assn., Am. Profl. Practice Assn., Atlantic Coast Dist., Palm Beach County dental socs., Xi Psi Phi. Home: 7715 St Andrews Dr Lake Worth FL 33460 Office: 826 Evernia St West Palm Beach FL 33402

ATKINSON, CARROL HOLLOWAY, educator; b. Fairbury, Neb., Oct. 24, 1896; s. Charles Raymond and Florence (Bennie) Atkinson; A.B., Lawrence Coll., 1920; student U. Grenoble (France), 1919, Pacific U., 1922, U. Ore., 1922, U. Wash., 1923, U. Cal. at Los Angeles, 1926, U. Tex., 1937; M.A., U. So. Cal., 1929; Ph.D., George Peabody Coll. for Tchrs., 1938; m. Ruby Baker, Aug. 23, 1921 (dec. 1925) children—Yvonne Dorothy, Carroll Holloway; m. 2d, Mary Hansen, 1926 (dec. 1941); m. 3d, Carol Mary Gonzales, 1959; children—Ardith Anne, Alicia Arthurita, Arthur Amigo. Jr. clerk Met. Life Ins. Co., 1915-16; steno. Sheridan (Wyo.) Iron Works, 1917-18; statistician Kimberly-Clark Paper Co., Wis., 1920-21; athletic coach Lawrence Coll., 1915-17 and 1919-21; prof. and athletic coach Coll. of Ida., 1921-22; prin. and coach, Forest Grove, Ore., 1922-23, Thorp, Wash., 1923-24, North Bend. Ore., 1924-25; salesman Acme Fast Freight Service, 1925-26; tchr. Pasadena Pub. Schs., 1926-30; prin. and coach San Luis Obispo, Cal., 1930-35; ednl. advisor CCC, 1935-36; asso. prof. N. Tex. State Tchrs. Coll., 1936-37, Edinboro (Pa.) State Tchrs. Coll., 1938-39; asso. prof. and dir. radio Jersey City and Newark State Tchrs. colls., 1939-41; dir. Nelson and McLucas Meml. Libraries, Detroit, 1941-45; pub. relations dept. Key System, Oakland, Cal., 1945-46; columnist Honolulu Star-Bulletin and radio producer, 1946-47; columnist Santa Fe New Mexican, 1951-52; dean men Southwestern U., 1947-49; dir. tchr. tng. Dakota Wesleyan U., 1949-51; lectr. St. Michaels Coll., Santa Fe, 1951-54, also summer; supervising prin. pub. schs., Pojoaque, N.M.; tchr. summer sch. U. Wash., 1940, U. Wyo., No. Mont. Coll. and Eastern Mont. State Normal Sch., 1941, U. Utah, 1943, N.M. Highlands U., 1949, supervising prin. Belen (N.M.) Pub. Schs., 1954-57; tchr. pub. schs., Grants, N.M., 1957-60; prof. edn. and psychology Tex. Luth. Coll., Sequin, Tex., 1960-61; chmn. psychology dept. Pacific U., 1961-64; vis. prof. history Fla. Meml. Coll., 1964-66; asso. prof. edn. Bethune-Cookman Coll., 1966-72, Extension staff faculty N.M. Western Coll., 1954-57; radio producer, 1931-—; promotion mgr. The Three Young Atkinsons, 1967-—. Mem. exec. com. Boy Scouts Am. Served with A.E.F., World War I. Life mem. N.E.A.; mem. A.A.A.S., Tex. Acad. Scis., Texas Psychol. Assn., Am. Assn. Sch. Adminstrs., Soc. Advancement Learning, Am. Legion, Acad. Polit. Sci., United Comml. Travelers, Portland Psychol. Assn., Am. Assn. of Croix de Guerre, Vets. Fgn. Wars, Am. Assn. U. Profs., Daytona Beach Psychol. Assn., Advt. Club; C. of C., Jr. C. of C. (asso.). Methodist. Author 19 books, 1928-—, including: Intellectual Tramp, 1955; Story of Education, 2d edit., 1965; True Confessions of a Ph.D., 1938. Home: 3021 N Oleander Av Daytona Beach FL 32018

ATKINSON, HENRY ALEXIS, II, dentist; b. Belvidere, Tenn., Nov. 11, 1919; s. Henry Alexis and Nelle Gray (Mason) A.; B.S., U. of the South, 1943; D.D.S., U. Tenn., 1947; m. Elizabeth Frances Ruch, June 30, 1946; children—Henry Alexis III, Bette Nelle, Richard Samuel. Individual practice gen. dentistry, Winchester, Tenn., 1948-51, 53-—. Mem. Tenn. Dental Health Council, 1963-69. Trustee Franklin County Resource Devel. Assn., Maxwell Cemetary. Served with Dental Corp AUS, 1951-53. Mem. 4th Dist. Dental Soc. (pres. 1960-61), Pierre Fauchard Acad. Baptist (deacon 1971). Lion (pres. 1950). Club: Maxwell Community (pres. 1962-63). Home: 2 RFD Belvidere TN 37306 Office: 214 1st Av S E Winchester TN 37398

ATKINSON, JAMES HAROLD, coll. pres.; b. Liberty Hill, Tex., Feb. 22, 1918; s. Harold and Olivia Mae (Powell) A.; B.A. cum laude, Southwestern U., 1938; M.Ed., U. Houston, 1948; postgrad. A. and M. U. Tex., U. Tex.; Litt.D., Houston Bapt. Coll., 1970; m. Katherine Louise Smith, Aug. 25, 1945 (dec.); children—James Durham, David Harold. High sch. coach, tchr., La Grange, Tex., 1939-41, Llano, Tex., 1941-42; prin. high sch. Cypress-Fairbanks High Sch., Cypress, Tex., 1946-47; athletic dir., head coach Blinn Coll., Brenham, Tex., 1947-49, dean, 1949-57, pres., 1957-—. Dir. Consol. Funds of Washington County, Tex., 1957-—, pres., 1965-71; chmn. City Brenham Planning and Zoning Com. Served from pvt. to lt. col. USAAF, 1942-46; ETO. Mem. Tex. Jr. Coll. Athletic Assn. (pres. 1954-55, 58-59), Tex. Jr. Coll. Football Fedn. (pres.), Washington County Tchrs. Assn. (pres. 1958-59), Am. Legion (comdr. 1949), Southwestern Sci. Soc., C. of C., V.F.W., Tex. Jr. Coll. Agrl. Assn. (hon.), Alpha Chi, Phi Delta Kappa, Phi Theta Kappa Frats. Methodist (chmn. ofcl. bd. 1959-60). Mason, Rotarian, Lion. Club: The Red Red Rose. Home: 906 Green St Brenham TX 77833

ATKINSON, JAMES THOMAS, pedodontist; b. Six Mile, S.C., July 25, 1937; s. Thomas Benson and Jessie Mae (Sullivan) A.; B.S., Furman U., 1958; D.D.S., Med. Coll. Va., 1962, postgrad. pedodontics, 1962; resident pedodontics Children's Hosp., Washington, 1964-65; m. Sherry Jones Atkinson, Aug. 23, 1958; children—James Thomas, Tara Leslie, Paul Benson. Pvt. practice specializing pedodontics, Greenville, S.C., 1962-—. Dental dir. United Fund of Greenville County, 1968; dir. Citizens for Community Action Council, 1968-—. Recipient Spoke award, U.S. Jr. C. of C., 1964, award for service to mankind, Sertoma, 1968. Mem. Pedodontic Assos. Profl. Assn. (pres.), Am. Dental Assn., Greenville County, S.C. dental socs., Am., S.C. socs. dentistry for children, Piedmont Dist. Dental Soc., Am., Internat. acads. orthodontics, Begg Study Group, Alpha Epsilon Delta, Xi Psi Phi. Clubs: Paladin of Furman University (dir.), Gamecock (Greenville County). Home: 1201 Parkins Mill Rd Greenville SC 29607 Office: 410 Pelham Rd Greenville SC 29607

ATKINSON, JOHN LITTLETON BOONE, educator; b. Vance, Miss., May 11, 1918; s. Thomas Robinson and Sallie (Prescott) A.; B.A., La State U., 1939, M.A., 1941; Ph.D., U. Pa., 1951; m. Gloria Jean Lewis, July 20, 1965; children by previous marriage—Judith, Prescott, John, William. Prof. history Air U., 1949-62; prof. internat. affairs, dir. George Washington U. Center, 1962-67; chmn. dept. history Miss. State Coll. for Women, Columbus, 1967—. Lectr., European history, 1952-57. Served with USAAF, 1942-46. Mem. Am. Hist. Assn., Soc. French Hist. Studies. Home: 905 6th Av S Columbus MS 39701

ATKINSON, MALLORY COOK, lawyer, jurist, educator; b. Newnan, Ga., Feb. 23, 1906; s. Theodore Ellis and Mary Lou (Cook) A.; Ph.B., Emory U., 1926, LL.B., 1930; m. Gertrude Gist Gee, June 9, 1928; children— Bettie A. (Mrs. James D. Lawrence), Jane A. (Mrs. Henry Middlebrooks), Mallory Cook. Admitted to Ga. bar, 1930; practiced law in Macon, 1930-44, 55—; lectr. Walter F. George Sch. Law, Mercer U., Macon, 1954, prof., 1955-68; gen. counsel State Bar Ga., 1965-72; judge Superior Cts., Macon Circuit, 1944-54. Mem., v.p., past sec. Bibb County Bd. Edn., Macon, 1944-67. Bd. dirs., past pres. Macon YMCA. Mem. Am., Ga., Macon bar assns., Am. Judicature Soc., Sigma Alpha Epsilon. Democrat. Methodist (chmn. bd. trustees, past chmn. administrv. bd. local church). Mason, Lion (past pres., past sec.). Home: 294 Corbin Av Macon GA 31204 Office: First Nat Bank Bldg Macon GA 31201

ATKINSON, PAUL TULANE, JR., supt. schs.; b. Staunton, Va., Oct. 9, 1920; s. Paul Tulane And Margaret Esther (Thomas) A.; B.S., Hampden-Sydney Coll., 1941; M.Ed., Coll. of William and Mary, 1952; m. Margaret Ruth Whittle, Dec. 20, 1047; children—Paul Tulane III, Margaret W., Francis B., Robert B. Tchr., Amelia County, Va., 1941-42, Greensville City, Va., 1946; prin. Clover (Va.) High Sch., 1946-47, Alleghany Central High Sch., (Low Moor, Va., 1948-49, Fieldale (Va.) High Sch., 1949-52, Northampton High Sch., Eastville, Va., 1953-61; supt. schs., Amelia County, Va., 1961-65, Caroline County, Bowling Green, Va., 1965—. Mgr. Little League, Eastville and Amelia, 1959-62; chmn. March of Dimes, Caroline County, 1966-72. Mem. Eastville Town Council, 1958-61; dir. Caroline County Civil Def., 1967—. Served with USAAF, 1941-46. Mem. Tappahanock Supts. Assn. (sec. 1970—). Presbyn. (elder 1955-72, pres. elders, 1966). Club: Ruritan (sec. 1961-72) (Amelia and Caroline County). Home: Milford VA 22514 Office: Box 526 B Bowling Green VA 22427

ATKINSON, TROY CARROLL, JR., city ofcl.; b. Marion, S.C., Feb. 5, 1923; s. Troy Carroll and Evelyn (Rowell) A.; B.S., Clemson U., 1945; m. Lucia O. Oliver, Mar. 10, 1945; children—Troy Carroll III, John Wyatt. Founder, Atkinson Implement Co., Marion, 1945, mgr., 1945—; mayor, Marion, 1952-58, 67—; dir. Marion Nat. Bank. Apptd. by Pres. Nixon to Fed. Farm Credit Bd., 1969—; mem. City Council, Marion, 1950-52; mem. S.C. Ho. of Reps., 1958-60. Served with AUS, 1943. Recipient Gov.'s award for Contbn. to Agr., 1962. Mem. S.C. Municipal Assn., Am. Legion (comdr. 1950), Carolina Farm Equipment Dealers Assn. (pres. 1960, dir. 1965-68). Mason, Rotarian (named Citizen of Year 1952-69). Club: Dusty Hills Country (dir.) (Marion). Home: 1102 N Main St Marion SC 29571 Office: Conway Hwy Marion SC 29571

ATRIA, NICHOLAS FRED, physician; b. West Orange, N.J., Dec. 1, 1906; s. James V. and Catherine D. (Stefano) A.; B.A., Washington and Lee U., 1928; M.D., Tulane U., 1932; m. Ethel Davis, May 21, 1937; children—James Adrian, Nicholas Davis, Mark Stewart. Intern, Med. Center, Jersey City, 1932-33, resident, 1933-35; commd. 1st lt. USAF, 1936, advanced through ranks to col.; grad. Army Med. Field Service Sch., Carlisle Barracks, Pa., 1937-38, USAF Sch. Aerospace Medicine, Randolph Field, Tex., 1942; instr. physiology Tulane Sch. Medicine, 1947-48; instr. mil. medicine USAF Sch. Aerospace Medicine, 1948-49; asst. air attache US embassy and exchange officer, London, 1949-51; ret., 1959; dep. commr. mental health Tenn., 1959-63; supr. Kan. Neur. Inst., Topeka, 1963-64; chief med.-surg. service Crafts-Farrow State Hosp., Columbia, S.C., 1964—. Decorated Bronze Star medal with six battle stars; recipient Arrow Head A.M.A., 1936. Diplomate Am. Bd. Preventive Medicine. Mem. Am. Pub. Health Assn., Aerospace Med. Assn., Am. Coll. Preventive Medicine, Am. Geriatrics Soc., Royal Soc. Health, Phi Rho Sigma. Home: 3160 Travis Ct Columbia SC 29204 Office: Craft-Farrow State Hosp Columbia SC 29203

ATTAWAY, DOUGLAS F., publisher; b., 1910. Pres., pub. Shreveport (La.) Journal. Home: 957 Sheridan St Shreveport LA 71102 Office: 222 Lake St Shreveport LA 71102*

ATTAWAY, HUGH ELDON, dentist; b. Aransas Pass, Tex., Jan. 5, 1931; s. Hugh Milton and Lela Evelyn (Chambers) A.; student Tex. A. and I. U., 1948-50; D.D.S., Baylor U., 1954; M.S.D., U. Neb., 1961; m. Joan Elizabeth Evans, Sept. 17, 1955; children—Leigh, Linda, Douglas. Instr. crown and bridge Baylor U. Coll. Dentistry, 1958-59; pvt. practice orthodontics, Irving, Tex., 1961—. Asso. prof. orthodontics Baylor U. Coll. Dentistry, 1962—. Served with Dental Corps, AUS, 1954-58. Mem. Am. Assn. Orthodontists, Am., Tex. dental assns., Dallas County Dental Soc., Charles H. Tweed Tex. Orthodontic Study Group (C. T. Roland award 1965). Rotarian. Home: 2909 Pacific Ct Irving TX 75062 Office: 801 N O'Connor Rd Irving TX 75061

ATTERBERRY, ANN DONALDSON (MRS. PHILIP ATTERBERRY), reporter; b. Jackson, Miss., Apr. 13, 1937; d. Frank and Agnes (Hunt) Donaldson; B.A., La. State U., 1959; m. Philip Atterberry. Society editor Jackson (Miss.) Daily News, 1959-60; Dallas Morning News, 1960—, reporter, 1960-63, society editor, 1963-69, reporter Austin bur., 1970—. Mem. Theta Sigma Phi (v.p. Dallas profl. chpt. 1968—). Home: Route 3 Leander TX 78641 Office: Dallas Morning News Austin Bureau Box 12097 Austin TX 78711

ATWATER, JOHN SPENCER, physician; b. Cin., Oct. 12, 1913; s. Carleton William and May (Spencer) A.; student Western Res. U., 1931-32; A.B., Denison U., 1935; student Ind. U. Sch. Medicine, 1934-36; M.D., Johns Hopkins, 1939, M.S. in Medicine, U. Minn., 1944; m. Laura Virginia Zipplies, July 29, 1939; children—John Spencer, Paul Carleton, Elizabeth Baron. Intern medicine U. Chgo. Clinics. 1939-40, asst. resident medicine, 1940-41; fellow Mayo Found., 1941-44, 1st asst. medicine Mayo Clinic, Rochester, Minn., 1943-44; pvt. practice medicine, specializing in internal medicine and gastroenterology, Atlanta, 1946—; mem. staffs Ga. Bapt. Hosp., Crawford W. Long Meml. Hosp., Atlanta Hosp.; asso. chief medicine Ga. Bapt. Hosp., 1948-57, acting chief medicine, 1958-60, pres. staff, 1962, mem. exec. com., 1961-64, chmn. exec. com., 1963, chief gastroent. sect., 1948—; chief dept. medicine Atlanta Hosp., 1968-69, chief medicine, 1969—, mem. exec. com., 1968—, chmn. credentials com., 1968-69, mem. utilization rev. com., 1968-69, mem. med. recs. com., 1968, mem. joint conf. com., 1970—; cons. in gastroenterology Robert T. Jones Meml. Hosp., Canton, Ga., 1962—, Cobb Gen. Hosp., Austell, Ga., 1968—; instr. in medicine U. Minn., 1943-44; instr. in medicine Emory U., 1946-54, asso. in medicine, 1954-65; cons. internal medicine VA, Ga. Dept. Edn., Fgn. Mission Bd. So. Bapt. Conv., U.S. Dept. State. Chmn. Atlanta Grad, Med. Assembly, 1958-59, exhibit chmn., 1960, mem. adv. com., 1961, mem. emergency care service com., 1964-65; mem. Gov.'s Commn. on Aging, 1959-62, chmn. health com., 1959-62; del. White House Conf. on Aging, 1961; chmn. Gov.'s Conf. on Aging, 1960, Ga. Joint Council to Improve Health Care of Aged, 1959—; mem. health adv. com. Ga. Commn. on Aging, 1964—; mem. clin. lab., blood bank and tissue bank com. Ga. Dept. Pub. Health, 1971—. Partner, Caduceus Properties, 1969—; dir. So. Gen. Ins. Co., Stuyvesant Ins. Co., Stuyvesant Life Ins. Co., Jersey Ins. Co. N.Y., 1st Ga. Bank, Peoples Am. Bank Atlanta. Bd. dirs. Atlanta Boys Club, med. dir., 1953-65, mem. endowment com., 1970—; bd. dirs. Atlanta Girls Club, vice chmn., 1957-58, chmn. bd. 1958-59, 3d v.p., 1960. Served as lt. M.C., USNR, 1944-46. Recipient Certificate of Appreciation, Fulton County Med. Soc., 1960, 63; Aven Citizenship award, 1961; Award of Recognition, Atlanta Boys Club, 1966; Keystone Bronze award Boys Clubs Am., 1968; Letter of Appreciation, Med. Assn. Ga., 1969, Certificate of Appreciation, 1970. Diplomate Am. Bd. Internal Medicine, Am. Bd. Gastroenterology. Fellow A.C.P., Am. Geriatrics Soc.; mem. A.M.A. (cons. council med. services 1960—, chmn. reference com. med. edn. 1969, mem. reference com. financing med. care 1967, mem. reference com. ins. and med. services 1971), Med. Assn. Ga. (chmn. bd. spl. activites 1961—, treas. 1962—, mem. publs. com. jour. 1962—, mem. exec. com. 1962—, mem. finance com. 1962—, mem. spl. finance, central billing, hdqrs. expansion and bldg. coms., chmn. awards com.), Fulton County (chmn. com. on aging 1959, 60, 61), 5th Dist. med. socs., So. Med. Assn. (past chmn.), Am. Gastroent. Assn., Am. Gastroscopic Soc., Am. Soc. for Gastrointestinal Endoscopy, World Congress Gastroenterology, N.Y. Acad. Scis., Am. Heart Assn., Alumni Assn. Mayo Found. Med. Edn. and Research, Mayo Gastrointestinal Alumni Assn., Johns Hopkins Med. and Surg. Soc., U. Chgo. Med. Alumni Assn. Am., Ga. socs. internal medicine. Johns Hopkins Alumni Assn. (past pres. Ga. soc., past nat. v.p.), Atlanta C. of C., S.A.R., Phoenix Soc., Phi Gamma Delta, Nu Sigma Nu, Baptist. Kiwanian (mem. boys and girls work com. 1966-70, fund-raising com. 1969-70, vocational guidance com. 1969, operation drug alert com. 1970-71. Clubs: Commerce, Atlanta City (charter mem.). Author numerous articles in field; sci. exhibits at med. meetings (with others); films, TV demonstrations in field. Home: 2625 Howell Mill Rd NW Atlanta GA 30327 Office: 478 Peachtree St NE Atlanta GA 30308

ATWOOD, SANFORD SOVERHILL, univ. pres.; b. Janesville, Wis., Dec. 3, 1912; s. C. Starr and Cora (Soverhill) A.; B.A., U. Wis., 1934, M.A., 1934, Ph.D., 1937; L.H.D., Gettysburg Coll., 1966;; m. Nora Elizabeth Long, Aug. 15, 1936; children—Charles Starr, Elizabeth Ann, Phoebe Ellen, Richard Jay. Teaching fellow, asst. U. Wis., 1934-37; asst., asso. agronomist U.S. Regional Pasture Research Lab., State Coll., Pa., 1937-44; asst. prof., asso. prof. plant breeding Cornell U., Ithaca, N.Y., 1944-48, prof., 1948-63, head dept. plant breeding, 1949-53, dean grad. sch., 1953-55, provost, 1955-63; now pres. Emory U., Atlanta. Fellow Am. Soc. Agronomy, N.Y. Acad. Sci., A.A.A.S.; mem. Am. Soc. Naturalists, Am. Genetic Assn., Am. Assn. U. Profs., Genetics Soc. Am., Bot. Soc. Am., Biometrics Soc., Phi Beta Kappa, Sigma Xi, Phi Kappa Phi, Phi Sigma, Gamma Alpha, Phi Eta Sigma, Alpha Chi Rho. Clubs: Atlanta Athletic, Piedmont Driving, Capital City (Atlanta); Cosmos (Washington); University (N.Y.C.). Rotarian. Contbr. articles sci. jours., books. Home: 1463 Clifton Rd NE Atlanta GA 30329

ATYEO, WARREN THOMAS, educator; b. Highland Park, Mich., Feb. 15, 1927; s. Albert J. and Grace (McGinnis) A.; student Northwestern U., 1946-48; B.S., Western Ill. U., 1952, M.S., 1953; Ph.D., U. Kan., 1959; m. Marilyn Jeanne Rogers, June 4, 1954; children—Thomas Warren, Timothy Rogers. Asst. to prof. U. Neb., Lincoln, 1958-67; Grants asso. NIH, Bethesda, Md., 1967-68; prof. entomology U. Ga., Athens, 1968—. Served with USNR, 1945-46, 50-52. Mem. Entomol. Soc. Am., Kan., Ga. entomol. socs., Am. Inst. Biol. Scis., Soc. Study Evolution. Contbr. articles to profl. jours. Home: 160 Pioneer Ct Athens GA 30601

AUCOIN, PASCHAL JOSEPH, pub. and printing co. exec; b. New Orleans, Oct. 18, 1906; s. Alvin J. and Ruth (Paschal) A.; B.B.A., S. Tex. Sch. Commerce, 1935; postgrad. U. Houston, 1958-60; m. Gladys Blazek, May 24, 1930; children—Paschal J., James B., David J. (dec.), Anne Marie (Mrs. John R. Jordan, Jr.). Accountant, Gulf Pub. Co., Houston, 1929-38, asst. treas., 1938-44, treas., dir., 1944—; treas., dir. Gulf Printing Co., Houston, 1954—. Trustee Gulf Pub. Trust, Gulf Printing Trust, Gulf Pub. and Printing Found. C.P.A., Tex. Mem. Tex. Soc. C.P.A.'s, Nat. Assn. Accountants. Roman Catholic. Club: Serra (Houston). Home: 6154 Ella Lee Lane Houston TX 77027 Office: 3301 Allen Pkwy Houston TX 77001

AUERBACH, STANLEY IRVING, ecologist; b. Chgo., May 21, 1921; s. Abraham and Carrie (Friedman) A.; B.S., U. Ill., 1946, M.S., 1947; Ph.D., Northwestern U., 1949; m. Dawn Patricia Davey, June 12, 1954; children—Andrew J., Anne B., Jonathan B., Alison M. Instr., then asst. prof. Roosevelt U., Chgo., 1950-54; asso. scientist, then scientist health physics div. Oak Ridge Nat. Lab., 1954-59, sr. scientist, sect. leader, 1959-70, dir. ecol. scis. div., 1970-72, dir. environmental scis. div., 1972—; lectr. radioecology U. Tenn., 1958—; adj. research prof. radiation ecology U. Ga., 1963—. Mem. U.S. nat. com. Internat. Biol. Program, co-chmn. program coordinating com. dir. deciduous forest biome project, 1969—; mem. Nat. Acad. Scis. exec. com. for Internat. Biol. Program, 1969-72. Mem. bd. ecol. advisers Bur. of Reclamation, 1971—; mem. spl. com. on biol. water quality of Ohio River Valley Water Sanitation Com., 1971—; mem. power plant siting program com. Nat. Acad. Engring., 1970—. Bd. dirs., treas. Oak Ridge Nursery Sch.; trustee Inst. of Ecology; bd. dirs. Oak Ridge Civic Music Assn., 1963-66, Tenn. Citizens Wilderness Planning, 1968. Served to 2d lt. AUS, 1942-44. Fellow A.A.A.S.; mem. Soc. Zoology (chmn. ecology div. 1967-68), Am. Soc. Agronomy, Planned Parenthood Assn., Brit. Ecol. Soc., Health Physics Soc., Entomol. Soc. Am., Am. Inst. Biol. Scis. (bd. govs.), Research Soc. Am., Soc. Systematic Biology, Ecol. Soc. Am. (pres. 1971-72), Sigma Xi, Alpha Epsilon Pi Spl. research ecology centipedes, radioecology and radioactive waste disposal, environmental behavior of radionuclides. Home: 24 Wildwood Dr Oak Ridge TN 37830 Office: PO Box X Oak Ridge TN 37830

AUG, ROBERT GAENGE, educator, psychiatrist; b. Cin., Sept. 13, 1930; s. George Christian and Gertrude (Gaenge) A.; student U. Cin., 1947-49, M.D., 1955; A.B. magna cum laude, Whitman Coll., 1951; m. Lois Marie Edelen, Jan. 14, 1956; children—Lisa Marie, Suzanne Yvette. Intern Cin. Gen. Hosp., 1955-56; resident psychiatry U. Cin., 1956-58, fellow child psychiatry, 1958-60; asst. prof. psychiatry U. Ky. Med. Center, 1962-64; asso. clin. prof. psychiatry Marquette U. Med. Sch., 1964-68; dir. tng. child psychiatry Milw. County Mental Health Center, 1964-68, dir. children's inpatient service, 1967-68; asso. prof. psychiatry U. Ky. Med. Center, Lexington, 1968-72, prof. psychiatry, 1972—, dir. div. child psychiatry, 1968—; mem. staff University Hosp. Founder, organizer, first dir. grad. and undergrad. tng. programs child psychiatry Milw. County Mental Health Center, 1965. Served to capt. M.C., 1960-62. Diplomate in psychiatry and child psychiatry Am. Bd. Psychiatry and Neurology (examiner in child psychiatry 1969—). Fellow Am. Acad. Child Psychiatry; mem. Am. Psychiat. Assn., A.M.A., Milw. (co-founder 1965, pres. 1966-67), Cin. councils child psychiatry, Phi Beta Kappa, Delta Tau Delta, Phi Chi. Presbyn. Home: 432 Kingsway Dr Lexington KY 40502 Office: U Ky Med Center Lexington KY 40506

AUGSBURGER, MYRON SHENK, clergyman, educator, coll. pres.; b. Elida, O., Aug. 20, 1929; s. Clarence Aaron and Estella (Shenk) A.; B.A., Eastern Mennonite Coll., 1955, Th.B., 1958; B.D., Coshen Coll., 1959; Th.M., Th.D., Union Theol. Sem., 1964; postgrad. George Washington U., 1964-65; m. Esther Louise Kniss, Nov. 28, 1950; children—John, Michael, Marcia. Ordained to ministry Mennonite Ch., 1951; pastor of students Eastern Mennonite Coll., Harrisonburg, Va., 1953-54, asst. prof. theology, 1962-65, prof. theology, pres., 1965—. Dir., Valley Nat. Bank, Harrisonburg, Shenandoah Valley Ednl. TV. Corp. Mem. council Mennonite Colls., higher edn. council Mennonite Ch. Mem. Nat. Assn. Evangelicals (bd. adminstrn. 1969-73). Author: Called to Maturity, 1963; Quench Not the Spirit, 1964; Plus Living, 1965; Invitation to Discipleship, 1966; Principles of Biblical Interpretation, 1966; Pilgrim Aflame, 1967; Faith for a Secular World, 1968; The Broken Chalice, 1971. Home: 1539 Hillcrest St Harrisonburg VA 22801

AUGUST, JAMES DAVIS, govt. ofcl.; b. Denver, July 17, 1940; s. James Perry and Catherine (Davis) A.; A.B., Georgetown U., 1962, Ph.D. (H.B. Earhart fellow), 1968; m. Susan Louise Hurley, Aug. 24, 1963; children—Jeffrey, Gregory. Staff supr. Chesapeake & Potomac Telephone Cos., Washington, 1965-69; economist, bd. govs. Fed. Res. System, Washington, 1969—. Mem. Am., Western econ. assns. Home: 1643 N Woodstock St Arlington VA 22207 Office: Fed Reserve System 20th St and Constitution Av NW Washington DC 20551

AULTMAN, DONALD SARRELL, coll. adminstr.; b. Gadsden, Ala., Sept. 22, 1930; s. Leonard H. and Jewell Esther (Barnwell) A.; B.A., Samford U., 1954; Ed.D. (Grad. instr. 1967-68), U. Tenn., 1969; m. Winona Cook, June 7, 1950; children—Melodie Dawn, Melissa Diane. Asst. gen. dir. youth and Christian edn. Ch. of God, Cleveland, Tenn., 1960-64, gen. dir. youth and Christian edn., 1964-68; pres. Denominational Exec. Sunday Schs. Secs., Wheaton, Ill., 1966; bd. dirs. Nat. Sunday Sch. Assn., Wheaton, 1964-68; v.p., dean Lee Coll., Cleveland, Tenn., 1968—. Coordinator ednl. gifts Cleveland Community Chest, 1968-70. Bd. dirs. YMCA, Cleveland, Cleveland Community Concert Assn. Mem. Am. Psychol. Assn., Am. Assn. Higher Edn., Phi Delta Kappa. Rotarian (sec. 1968). Club: Cleveland (Tenn.). Author: Learning Christian Leadership, 1959; Guiding Youth, 1965; The Ministry of Christian Teaching 1966; Contemporary Christian Education, 1968. Home: 1480 Church St Cleveland TN 37311

AUR, RHOMES JOAO S., physician. Diplomate Am. Bd. Pediatrics. Research on leukemia. Office: St Jude Children's Research Hospital 332 N Lauderdale St PO Box318 Memphis TN 38117*

AUSBAND, JOHN RUFUS, physician; b. Winston-Salem, N.C., Oct. 14, 1920; s. Charles Clarence and Estelle (Crowell) A.; B.A., Asbury Coll., 1940; M.D., Bowman Gray Sch., Wake Forest Coll., 1943; m. Geraldine Belva Trent, June 25, 1949; children—Leigh Trent, Elinor Ann. Intern, Hartford (Conn.) Hosp., 1944; resident N.C. Bapt. Hosp., Winston-Salem, 1944-46, 49-52, now mem. staff; practice medicine, specializing in otolaryngology, Winston-Salem, 1952—; instr., asst. prof., asso. prof. otolaryngology Bowman Gray Sch. Medicine, 1952-67, prof., 1967—. Trustee Med. Found. N.C. Bapt. Hosp., Bowman Gray Sch. Medicine. Served from 1st lt. to capt. M.C., AUS, 1946-48. Diplomate Am. Bd. Otolaryngology. Mem. N.C. Soc. Ophthalmology and Otolaryngology (past pres.), Am. Broncho Esophagological Assn. (pres. 1971), A.M.A., Med. Soc. State N.C., Internat. Broncho Esophagological Soc., Am. Acad. Ophthalmology and Otolaryngology, Am. Laryngol., Rhinological and Otological Soc., Am. Laryngol. Assn., Forsyth County Med. Soc., Phi Rho Sigma (grand chpt. pres. 1966-70). Home: 909 Goodwood Rd Winston-Salem NC 27106 Office: Bowman Gray Sch Medicine Winston-Salem NC 27103

AUSERE, JOE MORRIS, food co. exec.; b. Miami, Ariz., Sept. 29, 1929; s. Joe P. and Josephine (Sanez) A.; student Phoenix Jr. Coll., 1948, U. So. Cal., 1949; B.S. in Indsl. Engring., Ariz. State U., 1951; m. Elizabeth Ann Oxford, Dec. 19, 1959; children—Melinda Jo, Leigh Ann, Michael Joseph. Sales and prodn. supr. Rainbo Baking Co., Phoenix, 1941-51; prodn. and engring. cons. Campbell- Taggart Asso. Bakeries, Dallas, 1951-60; v.p. mfg. and sales Am. Foods, Inc., Atlanta, 1960-65; exec. v.p., dir. Merico, Inc., Dallas 1965-70, pres., dir., 1970—. Dist. Sec. Tex. Republican Com., 1968-69. Served with AUS, 1955-58. Mem. Phi Sigma Kappa. Republican. Baptist. Kiwanian. Home: 4415 Myerwood Lane Dallas TX 75234 Office: 1820 N Josey Lane Dallas TX 75234

AUSLEY, METT BAGLEY, dentist; b. Micro, N.C,, Sept. 1, 1926; s. Lillian Merritt and Leoria Adina (Bagley) A.; student N.C. State U. at Raleigh, 1943-44, 47-48; A.B., U. N.C. at Chapel Hill, 1950, D.D.S., 1954; m. Margaret Edriel Knight, Apr. 8, 1950; children—Mett Bagley, Margaret Glenn. Practice dentistry, Warsaw, N.C., 1954—. Mem. Town Council, 1969-71, mayor, 1971-73. Served with AUS, 1944-47. Pres., P.T.A., 1964-65; Active Tuscalola council Boy Scouts Am., 1955-71, nat. rep., 1967-70. Mem. N.C., Am. dental assns., Assn. Profls., Demeritt Pedodontic Study Club, Delta Sigma Phi, Xi Psi Phi. Baptist (deacon; tchr.). Rotarian. Home: 803 Memorial Dr Warsaw NC 28398 Office: 602 College St Warsaw NC 28398

AUSTIN, CLARENCE WESLEY, JR., metallurgist; b. Amsterdam, N.Y., Nov. 29, 1935; s. Clarence W. and Beulah (Weaver) A.; B.Metall. Engring., Rensselaer Poly. Inst., 1957 Materials research engr. U.S. Army Ballistic Missile Agy., Redstone Arsenal, Ala., 1957-60; research asso. metallurgy Am. Dental Assn. research div. Nat. Bur. Standards, Washington, 1960; sr. research phys. metallurgist, phys. scis. lab. U.S. Army Missile Command, Redstone Arsenal, Ala., 1961—. Mem. Am. Soc. Metals, Am. Soc. Testing and Materials, Internat. Metallographic Soc., Electron Probe Analysis Soc. Am. Contbr. articles to profl. jours. Home: 404 Hillmont Circle NW Huntsville AL 35805 Office: US Army Missile Command Redstone Arsenal AL 35809

AUSTIN, ELEANOR LOUISE SEGO (MRS. JAMES LLOYD AUSTIN), club woman; b. Florence, Ala., Nov. 16, 1911; d. John Thomas and Lillie (Blair) Sego; grad. S.W. Bapt. Coll., 1931-33; student Florence State Coll., 1934-35; m. James Lloyd Austin, May 6, 1934; 1 son, James Lloyd. Tchr. Lauderdale County Schs., Ala., 1935-43. Mem. women's com. Birmingham Symphony; vol. Bapt. Med. Center, Montclair; patron Civic Ballet; mem. womens aux. Salvation Army. Mem. Montgomery Fedn. Women's Clubs (publicity chmn. 57-59, asst. treas. 1959-60), Arlington Hist. Assn., Birmingham Mus. Art, Mothers Circle of Montgomery (mem. exec. bd. 1959-65, corr. sec. 1959-61, prospectus chmn. 1960-61, fedn. dir. 1961-63, pres. 1963-65), Samford U. Aux. (corr. sec.). Baptist. Democrat. Clubs: Woman's Civic (exec. bd., bd. dirs. 1972—, corr. sec.) (Birmingham); Normandale Garden (rec. sec. 1964-65). Home: 3744 Crestbrook Rd Birmingham AL 35223

AUSTIN, HARRY GUIDEN, engring. co. exec.; b. Belton, Tex., Dec. 10, 1917; s. Harry Guiden and Emma Lena (Brown) A.; B.S. in Elec. Engring., Tex. A. and M. U., 1938; M.B.A., Harvard, 1940; m. Elizabeth Ann Heard, Aug. 31, 1940; children—Lucy Ann, Elizabeth (Mrs. Page), Catherine Marshall. With Pan Am. Airways, Miami, Fla., 1940-41, elec. engr. Brown Shipbldg. Co., Houston, 1941-45; with Brown & Root, Inc., Houston, 1945-—, sr. v.p., 1965-70, exec. v.p. constrn., 1970-—, dir.; dir. Atlas Travel, Inc., Highland Ins. Co. (both Houston); chmn. bd. Bank Harris County. Adv. bd. Houston Salvation Army, Registered profl. engr., Tex. Mem. Nat. Soc. Profl. Engrs., I.E.E.E., Houston Engring. and Sci. Soc., (past pres.), Houston Com. Fgn. Relations, Harris County Heritage Soc., Museum Natural Sci., Mus. Fine Arts. Methodist. Clubs: Petroleum, World Trade, Houston Country, Ramada, University (Houston). Home: 267 Pine Hollow Lane Houston TX 77027 Office: PO Box 3 Houston TX 77001

AUSTIN, J(AMES) LLOYD, ins. exec.; b. Cloverdale, Ala., Oct. 7, 1909; s. James R. and Minnie (Koonce) A.; student Florence State Tchrs. Coll., 1932-33; m. Eleanor Sego, May 6, 1934; 1 son, James Lloyd. With Lauderdale Country Bd. Edn., 1932-37; agt. So. Life & Health Ins. Co., Florence, Ala., 1937-39, asst. mgr., 1939-41, auditor, insp., 1941-45, mgr. Jacksonville (Fla.) dist., 1945-55, div. mgr., 1955-65, agy. sec., 1965-70, field v.p., 1970-—, also trustee profit sharing. Mem. adv. bd. Bapt. Home for Children, Jacksonville; trustee So. Life and Health Ins. Co. Mem. Jacksonville Life Underwriters Assn. (past pres.), Gen. Agts. and Mgrs. Assn. (pres.), C. of C., Jacksonville Civil Round Table, Nat. Assn. Life Underwriters) charter builder, com. 100, bd. dirs.), Baptist (deacon, supt. Sunday Sch., pres. Men's Fellowship). Democrat. Clubs: South Montgomery Exchange (bd. dirs.); Ponte Vedra; So. Montgomery Exchange (pres.); Executive (Birmingham). Home: 3744 Crestbrook Rd Mountain Brook Birmingham AL 35223 Office: 2121 Highland Av Birmingham AL 35205

AUSTIN, JAMES WESCOAT, dentist; b. Cottage Grove, Tenn., Aug. 20, 1920; s. Dudley Emerson and Sally Maggie (Wescoat) A.; B.S., Abilene Christian Coll., 1946; D.D.S., Tex. U., 1950; m. Julia Hill, Feb. 22, 1946; children—Miriam, Alan, Ray. Individual practice dentistry, Corpus Christi, Tex., 1952-—. Mem. adv. bd. Abilene Christian Coll., 1970-—. Served to capt., Dental Corps, AUS, 1950-52. Mem. Am., Tex. dental assns., Nueces Valley Dist. Dental Soc. (pres. 1970-71). Kiwanian. Home: 433 Cape Henry Corpus Christi TX 78412 Office: 4141 Gollihar St Corpus Christi TX 78411

AUSTIN, JOHN PAUL, beverage co. exec.; b. La Grange, Ga., Feb. 14, 1915; s. Samuel Yates and Maude (Jernigan) A.; A.B., Harvard, 1937, LL.B., 1940; m. Jeane Weed, July 14, 1950; children—John Paul, Samuel Weed. Admitted to N.Y. bar, 1940; practiced in N.Y.C., 1940-41, 45-49; mem. legal dept. Coca-Cola Co., 1949-50, exec. v.p., 1961-62, pres., dir., 1962-—, chief exec. officer, 1966-—; exec. v.p. Coca-Cola Export Corp., 1958-59, pres., dir., 1959-—; dir. Continental Oil Co., Morgan Guaranty Trust Co., N.Y.C., Gen. Elec. Co., Trust Co. Ga., Atlanta, Ga. Served as lt. comdr. USNR, 1942-45. Clubs: Racquet and Tennis, Links (N.Y.C.); Blind Brook Golf (Purchase, N.Y.); Capital City, Peachtree Golf (Atlanta). Office: PO Box 1734 Atlanta GA

AUSTIN, OLIVER L., JR., museum ofcl.; author. With Fla. State Mus., Gainesville. Author: Birds of the World; Families of Birds. Home: 205 SE 7th St Gainesville FL 32601 Office: Fla State Museum Gainesville FL 32601*

AUTEN, PAUL PAGE, gas co. exec.; b. Collinsville, Okla., Apr. 9, 1918; s. Robert Franklin and Lenora Mae (Taylor) A.; student East Central State Coll., 1935-37; m. Myrtle Wray Underwood, Oct. 29, 1937; children—Barbara (Mrs. William B. Shives), Carol (Mrs. A. W. Hampf), Paul Wayne. Asst. circulation mgr. Tulsa Daily World, 1933-37; asst. circulation mgr. Ada (Okla.) Evening News, 1937-39; plant operations Carbide Carbon & Chem. Co., 1940-44; pres. Automatic Butane Gas Co., Houston, 1946-—; dir., chmn. bd. Pinemont Bank. Mem. fire prevention com., City of Houston, 1969-—, mem. transp. study com., 1971-—. Served with inf., AUS, 1944-45. Decorated Purple Heart. Mem. Tex. LP Gas Assn. (v.p. 1958). Club: Racquet. Office: 4722 W 18th St Houston TX 77018

AUTHEMENT, RAY, ednl. adminstr.; b. Chauvin, La., Nov. 19, 1929; s. Elios Lawrence and Ephia (Duplantis) A.; B.S., U. Southwestern La., 1950; M.S., La. State U., 1952, Ph.D., 1956; m. Barbara B. Braud, June 1, 1950; children—Kathleen Elizabeth, Julie Ann. Instr. La. State U., Baton Rouge, 1952-56; asso. prof. McNeese State Coll., Lake Charles, La., 1956-57; asso. prof. U. Southwestern La., 1957-59, prof. math., 1957-—, acad. v.p., 1966-—; vis. prof. U. N.C., Chapel Hill, 1960-61. Mem. Sch. bd. Fatima Parish, Lafayette, 1963-65. Mem. Math. Assn. Am., A.A.A.S., Phi Kappa Phi, Kappa Mu Epsilon, Sigma Pi Sigma, Phi Kappa Theta. Rotarian. Home: 609 Landry Dr Lafayette LA 70501

AUTRY, MAYME BLANKINSHIP (MRS. DAVID EDGAR AUTRY), employment agy. exec.; b. Stephenville, Tex., Nov. 2, 1896; d. Martin Dawson and Dora Leona (Hickey) Blankinship; student Brantley Draughon Coll., 1916; m. David Edgar Autry, Jan. 20, 1917 (dec. 1944). Tchr. pub. schs., 1914-16; editor Hartley County News, Channing, Tex., 1926-37; bus. mgr., advt. mgr. Dalhart Pub. Co. (Tex.), Dalhart Texan, 1926-37; advt. mgr. Liberal (Kan.) News, 1937-39, Ochiltree County Herald, Perryton, Tex., 1937-39; owner, mgr. Autry Co., advt., Ft. Worth, 1939-45; owner, mgr. Autry Employment Service, Ft. Worth, 1943-72, mgr., Dallas, 1956-65; v.p. Acme-Autry Personnel Service, Ft. Worth, 1972-—; owner, pub. Mansfield (Tex.) News, 1940-45; mgr. Kelly Services, Inc., Ft. Worth, Tex., 1955-—, Dallas, 1956-66. Dir., Nat. Employment Bd., 1959-60. Pres. Women's Civic Club Council, Ft. Worth, 1950; chmn. Bus. Owners Group, 1947; commr. Tex. Centennial of Statehood, 1945; mem. Ft. Worth Mayor's Com. on Status of Women, also chmn. speakers bur.; mem. Pan Am. Round Table No. 1. Recipient Pub. Relations award Kelly Girl Service, Inc., 1960, Silver medal award, Citizen of Year, 1961. Mem. Assn. pvt. Employment Services (pres. Ft. Worth 1960-61), S.W. Employment Bd. (pres. 1958-59, editor Tall Tales 1963-64, Outstanding Service award 1959), Internat. Platform Assn., Adminstrv. Mgmt. Soc. (dir. 1959-60, 63-64, chmn. 5-state conf. 1963), Nat. Employment Assn., Tex., Fort Worth pvt. employment assns., Better Bus. Bur. (chmn. woman's div. 1957, Distinguished Service award 1957), Ft. Worth C. of C., Retail Mchts. Assn., Ft. Worth Bus. and Profl. Women's Club (dir. 1946), Alpha Iota. Mem. Order Eastern Star. Clubs: Woman's Zonta (pres. 1947-50, dir. 1963-65, 71-—) (Ft. Worth). Home: 2014 6th Av Fort Worth TX 76110 Office: Sinclair Bldg Fort Worth TX 76102

AUTRY, OTWA TILDEN, supt. schs.; b. Gracemont, Okla., Jan. 7, 1910; s. Samuel Tilden and Sarah Jane (Mays) A.; B.A., Phillips U., 1932, M.A., 1935, LL.D., 1965; m. Esther Alma Bank, Jan. 9, 1932; children—Barbara Jo (Mrs. Floyd Stroup), Richard Bank, Steven Tilden. Instr., Phillips U., 1932-34; tchr., coach Emerson Jr. High Sch., 1934-35, prin., 1953-59; tchr., coach Enid (Okla.) High Sch., 1935-40, 45-53, prin. 1959-64; supt. Enid Pub. Schs., 1964-—. Served with AUS, 1940-45, 50-52. Decorated Silver Star, Bronze Star medal with oak leaf cluster. Mem. N.G. Assn. (div. pres. 1946-47), N.E.A., Am., Okla. assns. sch. adminstrs., Okla., Enid edn. assns. Presbyn. (deacon 1934-51, elder 1953-62, trustee 1969-72). Lion. Home: 1310 Ramona Dr Enid OK 73701 Office: 500 S Independence St Enid OK 73701

AVANT, WILLIAM EARL, dentist; b. Georgetown, S.C., Aug. 28, 1919; s. Landy Wood and Mary Ella (Grier) A.; A.B., Duke, 1954; student U. Ga., 1955-56; B.S., Med. Coll. Va. (A.D. Williams scholarship award; NIH student fellow), 1959, D.D.S., 1960; M.S. (and certificate prosthodontics), Ohio State U., 1967; m. Annie Eleanor Duke, June 2, 1951; children—Alan Berry, David Keith. Dental intern USPHS Hosp., Balt., 1960-61; gen. practice dentistry, Georgetown, Columbia, S.C., Union, S.C., 1961-64; instr. prosthodontics U. Md. Sch. Dentistry, 1964-65; grad. research asst., tchr. Ohio State U. Coll. Dentistry, 1965-67; individual practice orthodonitcs, Columbia, S.C., 1967-—. Served with USNR, 1940-45. Tng. fellow Nat. Inst. Dental Research, 1965-67. Mem. Am. Assn. Orthodontists (certificate 1970), Am., S.C., Greater Columbia dental assns., So. Soc. Orthodontists, S.C. Orthodontic Assn., Central Dist. Dental Soc., Phi Beta Kappa, Omicron Kappa Upsilon, Sigma Zeta, Alpha Sigma Chi. Methodist. Contbr. articles to profl. jours. Home: 8004 Pinelake Rd Columbia SC 29204 Office: 2827 Millwood Av Columbia SC 29205

AVANTS, MACK, exec. asst. to supt. La. Dept. Edn., Baton Rouge. Address: State Education Bldg Baton Rouge LA 70804*

AVE, PAUL E., business exec.; b. Clinton, Ind., 1933; grad. Ind. U., 1954, J.D., 1959. Vice pres., sec., gen. counsel Altec Corp. Office: 1st Bank & Trust Bldg Richardson TX 75080

AVEN, ALEXANDER PHIPPS, mgmt. cons. exec.; b. San Antonio, Aug. 23, 1929; s. William Ralph and Rhoma (Phipps) A.; B.S., U. Okla., 1951; M.B.A., Harvard, 1955; m. Camilla Lytle, Dec. 26, 1951; children— William Cobb, Margaret Farrar. Geologist, Brit. Am. Oil Producing Co., Denver, Casper, Wyo., 1951-55, Continental Oil Co., 1955-57; v.p., dir. Eason Oil Co., Oklahoma City, 1957-64; petroleum cons., 1964-69; sr. partner Resource Analysis & Mgmt. Group, Oklahoma City, 1969-—. Asso. bus. Oklahoma City U., 1964-71; dir. Bandera, Inc., Internat. Pacific Exploration Co. Ltd., Tolbert Co.; cons. to adminstr. NASA, 1966-70. Served with USAF, 1955-57. Mem. Am. Assn. Petroleum Geologists, Am. Assn. Petroleum Landmen, Am. Soc. Photogrammetry. Democrat. Episcopalian. Clubs: Economic, Men's Dinner, Beacon, Harvard Business School Oklahoma (pres. 1965; dir. 1964-67) Oklahoma City Golf and Country; University (Washington). Home: 1213 Larchmont Lane Oklahoma City OK 73116 Office: First Nat Center Oklahoma City OK 73201

AVERA, WILBUR KAY, city ofcl.; b. Powersville, Ga., Aug. 26, 1924; s. Cornelius Marion and Victoria Elberta (Pyles) A.; diploma Ga. Southwestern Jr. Coll., 1950; B.S. in Edn., Fla. State U., 1952; m. Jane Benefield, Aug. 2, 1953; children—Mathew Wilbur, Rosemary Benefield. Postman, U.S. P.O., Ft. Valley, Ga., 1953-55; auditor Ga. Dept. Revenue, Atlanta, 1955-59; city clk., treas. city Ft. Valley, 1959-—. Chmn., United Givers Fund, 1964; committeeman Central Ga. council Boy Scouts Am., 1970-71; adminstr. finance Lula Thomas Library Trust Fund, Ft. Valley, 1959-—. Served with USNR, 1942-43. Named certified municipal clk. Internat. Inst. Municipal Clks., 1971. Mem. Ga. Municipal Assn. (dir. state at large 1971), Ga. Municipal Clks. and Finance Officers Assn. (pres. 1971), U.S. Municipal Treas. Assn., Municipal Finance Officers Assn. Baptist (Sunday sch. tchr.). Kiwanian (pres. 1965). Home: 418 W Church St Fort Valley GA 31030 Office: PO Box 956 Fort Valley GA 31030

AVERITT, FRANKLIN MURPHY, lawyer; b. Fayetteville, N.C., Dec. 12, 1911; s. Herschel Strange and Cornelia (Culbreth) A.; B.A., Wake Forest Coll., 1932, LL.B., 1936; m. Carolyn Wooten Council, Feb. 1, 1936; children—Cornelia A. (Mrs. Charles Sugg Fox), Franklin M., Carolyn Council. Tchr. pub. schs. Columbus County (N.C.), 1932-34; admitted to N.C. bar, 1936; gen. practice law Fayetteville, 1936-—. Mem. Gen. Assembly of N.C., 1945-49. Mem. Am., N.C. bar assns. Democrat. Episcopalian. Mason. Club: Highland Country. Home: 303 Sylvan Rd Fayetteville NC 28305

AVERY, NATHAN MARK, petroleum equipment mfg. co. exec.; b. Tulsa, May 6, 1934; s. Nate and Rena Marie (Dean) A.; Profl. Engring. degree in Petroleum Engring., Colo. Sch. Mines, 1956; m. Sally Jean Galbreath, Feb. 5, 1957; children—Mark Galbreath, Paige Elizabeth, Jonathan Stuart. Petroleum engr. Cable and Stephens, Cons. Engrs., Wichita Falls, Tex., 1957-59, Schultz & Brannan Drilling, Wichita Falls, 1959-60; ind. petroleum engr. cons., Wichita Falls, 1961-64; pres. Power Generation, Inc., Houston, 1964-66; self-employed cons. engr., Houston, 1966-67; pres. Mattco, Inc., Houston, 1967-—, also dir.; pres., dir. Tex. Tech. Enterprises, Inc., 1968-—; dir. Communications Properties, Inc. Served to lt. C.E. AUS, 1957. Mem. Soc. Petroleum Engrs., Am. Soc. Metals, Am. Petroleum Inst., Am. Inst. Mining, Metall. and Petroleum Engrs., Colo. Sch. Mines Alumni Assn., Sigma Alpha Epsilon. Club: Petroleum, Racquet, University (Houston). Home: 1014 Briar Ridge Dr Houston TX 77027 Office: 219 Baywood St Houston TX 77011

AVERY, PARNELL NAPOLEON, surgeon; b. Henderson, N.C., Feb. 18, 1931; s. Napoleon and Hazel (Bing) A.; B.S., Va. State Coll., 1952, M.S., 1958; M.D., Meharry Med. Coll., 1962; m. Gloria Magdalene Reid, July 12, 1954; children—Natalie Sherena, Sibyl Charlene, Vida Letitia. Tchr. biology Burley High Sch., Charlottesville, Va., 1954-56, Carver High Sch., Chesterfield, Va., 1957; intern Hubbard Hosp. of Meharry Med. Coll., Nashville 1962-63, extern, summer 1965, resident surgery, 1966-—; extern Walter Reed Army Hosp., summer 1964; resident surgery USPHS Hosp., Seattle, 1967-68. Served as capt. M.C., AUS, 1952-54. Decorated Bronze Star medal. Mem. A.M.A., Nat. Med. Assn., Harris County, Old North State, R.F. Boyd med. socs., Am. Geriatric Soc., Houston Med. Forum, Omega Psi Phi. Contbr. arcitles to profl. jours. Home: 4014 Woodmont Dr Houston TX 77045 Office: 8109 Cullen Blvd Houston TX 77057

AVERY, WILFRED MABRY, investment mgmt. co. exec.; b. Hammon, Okla., May 17, 1920; s. James F. and Neil (Mabry) A.; B.A., U. Okla., 1943, J.D., 1947; m. Mary Elizabeth Falter, Dec. 3, 1943; 1 son, Robert David. Admitted to Okla. bar, 1943; adminstr. Blackwood & Nichols Co., Oklahoma City, 1950-56; exec. v.p. Mid.-Am. Minerals, Inc., Oklahoma City, 1957-64; pres. Sahara Oilfield Services, Ltd. S.A., Libya, 1963-65, Avery-Laurence, Ltd. S.A., engring cons., mfrs. rep., Singapore, Djakarta, Indonesia, Oklahoma City, 1964-—, Delta Bldg. & Devel. Co., residential housing, Oklahoma City, 1961-—; pres. Falter Plantation, Inc., farming operation, 1968-—; chmn. Avery-Laurence (Singapore) Pte. Ltd., Singapore and Djakata, 1964-—. Served to capt. AUS, 1943-46, 51-52. Decorated Bronze Star, Air medal. Mem. Okla. Bar Assn., Oklahoma City C. of C., Delta Tau Delta. Clubs: Quail Creek Golf and Country; Nomads (Oklahoma City and Tulsa); Petroleum (Oklahoma City). Home: 5609 NW 36th St Oklahoma City OK 73122 Office: 710 National Found Life Bldg 3535 NW 58th St PO Box 12609 Oklahoma City OK 73112

AVERYT, GAYLE OWEN, ins. co. exec.; b. Montgomery, Ala., Oct. 13, 1933; s. Edwin Franklin and Asenath Pratt (Murfee) A.; B.S. cum laude, Davidson Coll., 1955; M.B.A., Harvard, 1958; m. Margaret Rosborough Finlay, June 15, 1963; children—Caroline Elliott, Margaret McQueen. Asst. v.p. Colonial Life & Accident Ins. Co., Columbia, S.C., 1958-60, v.p., dir., 1960-69, exec. v.p., 1969-70, chmn. bd., chief exec. officer, 1970-—; dir. Citizens & So. Nat. Bank S.C. Mem. adv. bd. Aurora Club for Blind, 1968-—; treas. United Community Services, 1961-64, bd. dirs., 1961-64, 67-70; mem. exec. com. Central S.C. council Boy Scouts Am., 1960-64; mem. Kanuga Confs. Finance Com., 1971. Committeeman, S.C. Republican Com., 1962-64. Bd. dirs. Columbia Music Festival Assn., 1965-71, pres., 1969-70. Served to 2d lt. AUS, 1955-56. Mem. Columbia Jr. C. of C. (dir. 1961-63), Phi Beta Kappa, Sigma Alpha Epsilon, Omicron Delta Kappa. Episcopalian (chmn. every mem. canvass 1969). Rotarian (dir. 1961-67, pres. 1965-66). Clubs: Palmetto, Forest Lake Country, Spring Valley Country (Columbia); Litchfield Country (Litchfield Beach, S.C.). Home: 1717 Green St Columbia SC 29201 Office: 1612 Marion St Columbia SC 29201

AVILES, ANGEL NEGRON, architect; b. San Juan, P.R., Feb. 10, 1913; s. Manuel and Gregoria (Negron) A.; m. Iraida Toro, Mar. 1, 1954; 1 son, Angel. Asst. project planner FSA, Phila., 1942-44, Nat. Housing Adminstrn., Washington, 1944-45; architect Govt. P.R., 1945-47; pvt. archtl. practice, Santurce, P.R., 1947-—. Mem. A.I.A., Navy League, U.S. Power Squadron. Clubs: Nautico, Congrejos Yacht, Casino (Santurce). Address: 22 Yardley Pl Santurce PR 00911

AVINGER, WILLIAM HERSCHEL, coll. ofcl.; b. Brownwood, Tex., Aug. 6, 1915; s. Willie Barnard and Dora Ethel (Hutcherson) A.; B.A., Howard Payne Coll., 1937; M.A., U. Tex., 1943; Ed.D., Tex. Technol. U., 1965; m. Ora Juanita Hunt, Aug. 26, 1939; children—James Hershel, John Ross. Tchr., prin., Coleman, Tex., 1937-45; prin. high sch., Marfa, Tex., 1945-47; prin., supt., Electra, Tex., 1947-49; supt. schs., Plainview, Tex., 1949-53; dir. pupil personnel services, Lubbock, Tex., 1953-65; dir. grad. studies in edn. Abilene (Tex.) Christian Coll., 1965-—. Dir. Lubbock Child Guidance Clinic, 1962-65; mem. Lubbock Community Planning Council, 1960-65. Mem. Am., West Tex. (pres. 1951-52) assns. sch. adminstrs., Internat. Assn. Pupil Personnel Workers (dir. 1964-65), Lubbock C. of C., Phi Delta Kappa. Mem. Ch. of Christ. Kiwanian (pres. Lubbock 1962). Home: 910 Harwell St Abilene TX 79601

AVIZONIS, ANGELE (MRS. KONSTANTINAS AVIZONIS), educator; b. Alvitas, Lithuania; d. Tomas and Magdalena (Matulaitis) Asevicius; M.A., U. Lithuania, 1929; advanced studies U. Berlin, Munich and Vienna, 1932-35; B.S., in L.S., U. N.C., 1953; m. Konstantinas Avizonis, Dec. 19, 1942. Prof. German lang. and lit. State Gymnasiums in Kaunas and Vilnius, Lithuania, 1927-44; pvt. tchr. German and Russian langs., Germany and U.S., 1945-52; asst. cataloger, library U. N.C., Chapel Hill, 1953-59, sr. cataloger, library, 1960-68; asst. prof. German, Elon (N.C.) Coll., 1968-—. Mem. Am., Southeastern, N.C. library assns., Am. Assn. Tchrs. German, Am. Assn. U. Women, So. Conf. Slavic Studies. Translator into Lithuanian, editor: Der moralische Schwachsinn, 1930, German Short Stories, 1930-32. Contbr. articles to profl. jours. Home: 420 Smith Av Chapel Hill NC 27514

AVRETT, ROBERT, author, ret. educator, publs. counselor; b. nr. Rockdale, Tex., Dec. 1, 1901; s. Cary Collins and Lillie Araminta (Griffith) A.; A.B., U. Texas, 1927, A.M., 1928; Harrison fellow Romanics, U. Pa., 1936-37; m. Mindora Bagby, 1928 (div. 1940); m. 2d, Lucile Dutton Kershner, Dec. 14, 1955. Instr. Spanish, Edinburg (Tex.) Coll., 1928; instr., asst. prof. modern langs. Tex. Coll. Mines and Metallurgy (now U. Tex.-El Paso), El Paso, 1928-45; dir. Instituto Cultural Argentino-Norteamericano, Buenos Aires, 1945-46; asst. prof. Romance langs. and lits. U. Tenn., Knoxville, 1947-51, asso. prof., 1951-66, prof., 1966-72; ret., 1972; lectr., publs. counselor Huckleberry Mountain Workshop Camp, Hendersonville, N.C., summer 1957, Camp Cherryfield for Adults, Brevard, N.C., summer 1959, Critical Exploration Inst., Dixie Council Authors and Journalists, Epworth-by-the-Sea, St. Simons Island, Ga., summer 1968. Recipient Bellamann Found. award, 1960; Order Don Quijote, 1966. Mem. Internat. Acad. Poets (life), Am. Assn. Tchrs. Spanish and Portuguese, Poetry Soc. Am., East Tenn. Edn. Assn. (chmn. modern lang. sect.), S. Atlantic Modern Lang. Assn. (chmn. nominating com.), Authors League of Am., The Authors Guild, Sigma Delta Pi (acting exec. sec. 1951-52; editor Entre Nosotros 1951-52), Pi Delta Phi, Phi Delta Kappa, Omicron Delta Kappa, Phi Kappa Tau. Author: Outline Spanish Review Grammar, 1940; The Dream Comes First, 1949; Spanish in Review, 1959; Against the Dark, 1961; The Timid Pup, 1964; also poems, book revs., articles in misc. publs. Asst. mng. editor The Modern Language Jour., 1951-56; editor The Lyric, 1957-58; poetry editor Author and Journalist, 1965-66; bd. reviewers The World in Books, 1966-—. Address: U Tenn Knoxville TN 37916

AWAD, JOHN MICHAEL, mental health adminstr.; b. Jackson, Miss., Jan. 4, 1934; s. Samuel and Lena (Katool) A.; B.A., Millsaps Coll., 1956; M.S.W., Tulane U., 1961; Ph.D., Fla. State U., 1972. Child welfare worker Miss. Dept. Pub. Welfare, Greenville, 1959-60; caseworker Family Counseling Center, Mobile, Ala., 1961-63; asst. planning coordinator Miss. Mental Health and Retardation Planning Program, Jackson, 1963-66; chief social work cons. Fla. Div. Mental Health, 1966-68, adminstr. mental health program grants, 1968-70, dep. dir., 1970-—; cons. in field. Served with AUS, 1956-58. Mem. Nat. Assn. Social Workers, Acad. Certified Social Workers, Millsaps Coll. Alumni Assn., (dir. 1962-64, v.p. 1965-66), Kappa Sigma. Episcopalian. Home: 2020 Continental Av Tallahassee FL 32304 Office: 200 E Gaines St Tallahassee FL 32304

AWAD, JOSEPH FREDERICK, metals co. exec.; b. Shenandoah, Pa., May 17, 1929; s. Fred A. and Helen (Dwyer) A.; student Corcoran Sch. Art, 1946-47; B.A., Georgetown U., 1951; postgrad. George Washington U., 1951-52; m. Doris C. Brown, Dec. 28, 1950; children—Michael J., Jean M., Patricia A., Mary T., Judith A., Marguerite F., Timothy A., Clare P., Ann E., Christopher P. Asst. dir. pub. relations and advt. Dave Herman Assos., Washington, 1950-57; mem. pub. relations staff Reynolds Metals Co., Richmond, Va., 1957-—, gen. dir. pub. relations, 1968-—. Mem. pub. relations panel U.S. Treasury, 1969-—. Mem. Pub. Relations Soc. Am. (pres. Old Dominion chpt. 1971), Internat., Richmond (pres. 1970-71) pub. relations assns., Aluminum Assn. (communications policy com. 1968-—). Club: Executives (Richmond). Home: 1909 Nortonia Rd Richmond VA 23229 Office: 6601 W Broad St Rd Richmond VA 23218

AXBERG, DONALD EDWARD, food co. exec.; b. Lincoln, Neb., Dec. 21, 1932; s. George Theodore and Alta Margaret (Butts) A.; B.S. in Bus. Adminstrn., U. Neb., 1958, M.B.A. (Regents scholar), 1959; postgrad. Northwestern U., 1961-62, Purdue U., 1962-64, U. Minn., 1967-69; m. Mary Lou Richie, June 30, 1957; children—William Christopher, Thomas Charles, John R. Auditor, Gen. Mills, Inc., Chgo., 1959-61, plant personnel mgr., Chgo., 1961-65, div. tng. mgr., Mpls., 1965-66, personnel mgr. mfg. div., 1966-68, div. controller, 1968-69, v.p. finance and personnel Goodmark div., Raleigh, N.C., 1969-—. Instr. econs. U. Neb., 1958-59; partner, dir. Mgmt. and Tax Cons., Inc., Raleigh, 1970-—; dir., sec. United Investors of Chapel

Hill, Inc. (N.C.), 1971—. Chmn., Crusade of Mercy, South Chgo., 1965. Active Young Republicans of Ill., 1960-64; block capt. Rep. party, Minn., 1966, 67. Bd. dirs. Jr. Achievement. Served with AUS, 1951-54. Mem. Raleigh C. of C., Delta Sigma Pi. Roman Catholic. Kiwanian, K.C., Lion. Club: Raleigh Racquet. Author tech. and tng. manuals for employer. Home: 1008 Pebblebrook Dr Raleigh NC 27609 Office: 3825 Barrett Dr Raleigh NC 27609

AXTON, WILLIAM FITCH, educator; b. Louisville, Sept. 24, 1926; s. Edwin Dymond and Blanche Thompson (Miller) A.; B.A., Yale, 1948; M.A., U. Louisville, 1951; Ph.D., Princeton, 1961; m. Joanne Virginia Lewis, June 23, 1951 (dec. Aug. 1965); children—Blanche Miller, Lucy Riggs, Belle Sherlock; m. 2d, Anne Elizabeth Millano, Aug. 5, 1967. Instr. Brown U., Providence, 1957-61; asst. prof. U. Ky., Lexington, 1961-66, asso. prof. English, 1966-67; asso. U. Louisville, 1967-68, prof. English, 1968—, chmn. dept., 1971. Served with USNR, 1944-46. Mem. Modern Lang. Assn., Victorian Soc. in Am. (adviser 1971—), Dickens Soc. (v.p. 1971), Tennyson Soc., Ky. Hist. Soc. Clubs: Polo (Lexington); Harmony Landing Country, Filson (Louisville). Editor: Melmoth the Wanderer (C.R. Maturin), 1961; Circle of Fire: Dickens' Vision and Style and the Nineteenth Century Theater (W.F. Axton), 1966; asso. editor Dickens Studies Annual, 1969—; rev. editor Dickens Newsletter, 1969—. Home: 2421 Cherokee Pkwy Louisville KY 40204

AYCOCK, CLARENCE C. (TADDY), lt. gov. La.; b. Franklin, La., 1916; LL.B., Loyola U. of South, 1937; m. 6 children. Mem. La. Ho. of Reps., 1952-60, speaker, 1952-60; lt. gov. State La., 1960—. Mem. La. Bar Assn. Home: 608 Palfrey St Franklin LA 70538 Office: State Capitol Baton Rouge LA 70804

AYCOCK, EZRA KENNETH, physician, state ofcl.; b. Pinewood, S.C., Mar. 23, 1927; s. Robert James and Helen B. (Geddings) A.; A.B., Duke, 1950; M.D., S.C. Med. Coll., 1954; M.P.H., Harvard, 1964; m. Mary Echo Cook, June 4, 1954; children—Doris Dawson, Ezra Kenneth. Intern Columbia (S.C.) Hosp., 1954-55; resident in pediatrics Childrens Hosp., Los Angeles, 1955-56, S.C. Med. Coll. Hosp., Charleston, 1956-57; practice medicine, specializing in pediatrics, Columbia, 1957-63; chief pediatrics depts. Baptist, Hosp., Columbia Hosp., Providence Hosp., 1957-63; asst. dir. Maternal and Child Health div. S.C. Bd. Health, 1963-65, also dir. Child Evaluation Clinics; dir. Charleston County Health Dept., 1965-66, S.C. health officer, 1967—. Chmn. S.C. Child Devel. Council, 1971—. Served with USNR, 1944-46. Diplomate Am. Bd. Preventive Medicine, Am. Acad. Pediatrics (mem. S.C. chpt.). Fellow Am. Coll. Preventive Medicine; mem. Am., S.C. med. assns., Columbia, Charleston med. socs., S.C. Pediatric Assn., Am. (pres. so. br. 1972-73), S.C. (pres. 1970) pub. health assns., S.C. Mental Health Assn. (dir.), Assn. State and Territorial Health Officers (exec. com. 1970, sec. 1971—), S.C. Assn. Retarded Children (dir.), State Employees Assn. (pres. Charleston County chpt. 1966-67), Alpha Omega Alpha. Episcopalian. Rotarian. Contbr. articles profl. jours. Home: 1401 Kathwood Dr Columbia SC 29206 Office: State Bd Health Columbia SC 29201

AYCOCK, WILLIAM FRANK, JR., newspaper pub. co. exec.; b. Selma, Ala., Jan. 6, 1909; s. William Frank and Mamie (Finlayson) A.; B.S., Sanford U., 1930; m. Margaret O'Dell, June 15, 1935; 1 dau., Peggy (Mrs. Malcolm L. Prewitt, Jr.). With Birmingham News Co. (Ala.), 1937-56; v.p., asst. to gen. mgr., Memphis Pub. Co., 1956-57, pres., bus. mgr., 1957—. Mem. exec. com. Future Memphis. Bd. dirs. Danny Thomas Memphis Classic Golf Tournament, Memphis Cotton Carnival Assn., Mid-South Fair, Better Bus. Bur., adv. com. Baptist Meml. Hosp., Memphis; trustee So. Newspaper Pub. Assn. Found. Served as lt. (j.g.) USNR, World War II. Decorated Legion of Merit. With V device, Air medal with gold star, Purple Heart. Mem. So. Newspaper Publs. Assn. (treas., exec. com.), Navy League of Memphis, Pi Kappa Alpha. Baptist. Rotarian. Home: 50 Cherry Rd Memphis TN 38117 Office: 495 Union Av Memphis TN 38101

AYCOCK, WILLIAM JASPER, physician; b. Phoebe, Miss., Oct. 8, 1888; s. William Jefferson and Rosie (Wooten) A.; student Miss. Coll., 1906-07; M.D., U. Tenn., 1912; postgrad. Postgrad. Sch. N.Y., 1919, Tulane U., 1938; m. Marian Denley, June 12, 1919; children—Josephine (Mrs. R. E. Anderson), Bobbie Ruth (Mrs. Bernard Senter), Willie Rose (Mrs. R. L. Liddell), Nancy (Mrs. R. P. Rogers). Individual practice gen. medicine, Smithville, Miss., 1912-16, Derma, Miss., 1919-34, Calhoun City, Miss., 1934—. Pres. Sch. Bd., Agrl. Sch., Derma, Miss., 1924-34, Calhoun City Pub. Schs., 1934-47; col. Gov.'s Staff, 1942-50. Mem. Bd. of Aldermen, 1920-34. Trustee Houston Hosp., 1924-42. Served with inf. U.S. Army, 1917-18. Recipient Robins award Miss. Med. Soc., 1970. Mem. N.E. Miss. Med. Soc. (pres. 1928, 43). Baptist (deacon). Mason (32 degree, Shriner), Rotarian. Club: Country (Calhoun City). Home: Calhoun City MS 38916

AYENSU, EDWARD SOLOMON, botanist; b. Sekondi, Ghana, Aug. 28, 1935; B.A. (Ghana Govt. scholar), Miami U., Oxford, O., 1961; M.Sc. (Ghana Govt. scholar), George Washington U., 1963; Ph.D. (Ghana Govt. scholar), U. London, 1966; postgrad. on bot. histo-chemistry U. Cal. at Berkeley, 1967; m. Dinah Ameley. Asso. curator dept. botany Smithsonian Instn., Washington, 1966-69, curator, 1970—, chmn. dept. botany, 1970—. Vis. prof. U. Ghana, 1969—; mem. adv. panel for systematic biology NSF; mem. U.S. com. Internat. Union Biol. Scis. Trustee, InterFuture, Princeton, N.J. Fellow Ghana Acad. Arts Scis., Linnean Soc. London, Washington Acad. Scis.; mem. Bot. Soc. Am., Internat. Assn. Plant Taxonomy, West African, Ghana sci. assns., A.A.A.S., Am. Inst. Biol. Scis., Assn. for Tropical Biology (exec. dir. 1969-71), Bot. Soc. Wash., Internat. Soc. Tropical Ecology, Internat. Assn. Wood Anatomists, Assn. for Advancement Agrl. Scis. in Africa. Club: Cosmos (Washington). Author: Anatomy of the Monocotyledons, 1972. Contbr. articles to profl. jours. Research on comparative anatomy and phylogeny of angiosperms, vascular architecture and histology of monocotyledons, tropical biology, behavior of fruit-eating bats. Home: 103 G St SW Washington DC 20024 Office: Nat Museum of Natural History Constitution at 10th St Washington DC 20560*

AYER, HUGH MASON, educator, historian; b. Livia, Ky., Mar. 8, 1924; s. Henry Cashman and Myrtle (Thomasson) A.; A.B., Western Ky. State Coll., 1948; M.A., Ind. U., 1950, Ph.D., 1957; m. Elizabeth Heisler, Aug. 17, 1946; children—Margaret Mason, David Hugh. Instr. history Culver Mil. Acad., 1952-58; mem. faculty N. Tex. State U., Denton, 1958—, prof. history, 1960—, chmn. div. social sci., 1965-69, asso. dean Coll. Arts and Scis., 1969—. Mem. Denton Planning and Zoning Commn., 1962-66, chmn., 1964-66; mem. Denton City Council, 1969-72. Served with USNR, 1943-45; PTO. Mem. Am. Hist. Assn., Orgn. Am. Historians, Ind. Hist. Soc., Am. Assn. U. Profs., So. Hist. Assn., Southwestern Social Sci. Assn., Danforth Assos. Mem. Christian Ch. Home: 425 Mimosa Dr Denton TX 76201

AYERS, DONALD LEWIS, supt. schs.; b. Linden, Tex., Aug. 15, 1926; s. Jesse Franklin and Robena (Goodson) A.; B.S., Tex. A. and M. U., 1950; M.Ed., East Tex. State U., 1955; m. Ruby Sessums, Feb. 14, 1952; children—Michael Jess, Kitsy. Tchr., Avinger (Tex.) Ind. Sch. Dist., 1950-61, supt., 1961-67; supt., Hughes Springs (Tex.) Ind. Sch. Dist., 1967—. Served with USNR, 1945-46. Mem. Am., Tex. assns. sch. adminstrs., Tex. State Tchrs., Assn. Baptist. Lion. Home: Harris Chapel Rd Hughes Springs TX 75656 Office: Box 398 Hughes Springs TX 75656

AYERS, HARRY BRANDT, pub. co. exec.; b. Anniston, Ala., Apr. 8, 1935; s. Harry M. and Edel (Ytterboe) A.; A.B., U. Ala., 1959; m. Josephine Peoples Ehringhaus; 1 dau., Margaret. Capitol and legislative reporter Raleigh (N.C.) Times, 1960-62; Washington corr. Timmons Agy., 1962-64; mng. editor Anniston Star, 1964-68, editor, pub., 1968—; treas. Piedmont Pub. Co., 1964—, Talladega Pub. Co., 1965—; v.p. Anniston Broadcasting Co., 1964—. Mem. adv. bd. U. Ala., Birmingham, 1967—; pres. Ala. Press Assn. Journalism Found., 1968-70. Served with USNR, 1956-58. Recipient Nat. Headliner award, 1968, Distinguished Alumnus award Journalism Dept. U. Ala., 1967. Nieman fellow Harvard, 1967-68. Mem. Lamar Soc. (pres. 1971-72), Nat. Conf. Christians and Jews. Soc. Nieman Fellows, Newcomen Soc. N.Am., Nat. Press Club, Sigma Delta Chi. Episcopalian. Home: 501 Keith Av Anniston AL 36201 Office: 210 W 10th St Anniston AL 36201

AYERS, JAMES WILSON, pub. relations exec.; b. Washington, N.C., Oct. 10, 1923; s. James Cleveland and Ethel (Wilson) A.; student Asheville-Biltmore Coll., 1956-62, Western Carolina Coll., 1956-62; m. Alice Keuling, Mar. 28, 1948; children—Linda Diane, Nancy Elaine. Staff writer Times-News, Hendersonville, N.C., 1941-44; with Am. Enka Co. (N.C.), 1944—, now mgr. pub. relations, employee communications. Nat. chmn. Indsl. Publs. Brotherhood Week, 1960. Mem. Am. Assn. Indsl. Editors (dir.), Appalachian Indls. Editors Assn. (past pres.), Indsl. Editing Inst. U. Tenn. (past chmn.). Republican. Lutheran. Elk, Kiwanian. Editor: Enka Voice, 1954—. Home: 103 Bent Creek Rd Asheville NC 28806 Office: Enka NC 28728

AYRES, RICHARD, mech. engr.; b. England, Ark., Mar. 17, 1915; s. Gold and Georgia (Walker) A.; B.S. in Mech. Engring., U. Ark., 1936; married. Engr., Fuel Process Co., South Charleston, W.Va., 1937-40, E.I. du Pont de Nemours & Co., Inc., Charleston, 1940-42, Magnolia Petroleum Co., Dallas, 1942-46; plant engr. Rohm & Haas Co., Houston, 1946—. Councilman, City of West University Place (Tex.), 1961-65. Registered profl. engr., Tex. Mem. Nat., Tex. (state chmn. employment practices com. 1958-59, ins. adv. com. 1971-73) socs. profl. engrs., C. of C. Houston (water conservation com. 1969-70, 71-72), Sigma Chi. Republican. Presbyn. Home: 2723 University Blvd Houston TX 77005 Office: PO Box 672 Deer Park TX 77536

AZAR, SHIBLEY, JR., nut processing co. exec.; b. El Paso, Tex., July 25, 1920; s. Shibley and Emaline (Abdou) A.; B.S. with honors in Accounting and Statistics, Tex. A. and M. U., 1942; m. Doris Jean Isaacs, Sept. 8, 1951; children—Laurie, Ricky, Patti. With Azar Nut Co., El Paso, 1946—, chmn. bd., 1970—. Bd. dirs. El Paso Mental Health, Central YMCA, Child Guidance Center, Radford Sch. for Girls. Served from 2d lt. to maj., USAAF, 1942-46. Decorated Bronze Star medal; recipient 1st pl. YMCA membership drs. for several years. Mem. El Paso C. of C., Nat. Pecan Shellers Assn. (v.p., dir.), Episcopalian (vestryman). Mason (Shriner). Clubs: Coronado Country (El Paso), El Paso Tennis. Home: 4304 Park Hill El Paso TX 79902 Office: 1900 Mills El Paso TX 79901

AZPEITIA, MARIO, labor ofcl.; b. Key West, Fla., Nov. 22, 1899; s. Armando H. and Andrea (Esquinaldo) A.; student San Carlos Sch., Key West; m. Eleodora Toledo, Oct. 5, 1918; children—Mario, Jr., Armando., Evelio, Eloy. Mem. Cigar Makers Internat. Union, A. F. of L., pres., 1948—. Home: 2703 St John St Tampa FL 33607 Office: 815 15th St Washington DC 20005

BABB, BARBARA CAROLINE, state bar exec.; b. Fountain Inn, S.C., Dec. 16, 1933; d. Victor Morgan, Jr. and Ida Kate (Morrison) Babb; student Sweet Briar Coll., 1951-53; B.A., U. N.C., 1959, postgrad., 1963, J.D., 1968. Admitted to S.C. bar, 1968, also Fed. Dist. Ct. bar; sec. Woodside div. Dan River Mills, Greenville, S.C., 1954-58, 60-65, indsl. and pub. relations artist, 1954-70; spl. instr. for prospective legal secs. Greenville Tech. Inst., 1969-70; exec. dir. S.C. Bar Assn., Columbia, 1970-71; exec. sec.-treas. S.C. State Bar, Columbia, 1970—. Spl. cons. Appalachian Regional Commn., Greenville, 1970; mem. Chief Justice's Com. to Study S.C. Ct. System, 1970-71. Mem. Am., S.C. bar assns., S.C. State Bar, Am. Judicature Soc., Nat. Assn. Bar Execs. Home: 407 S Main St Fountain Inn SC 29644 Office: South Carolina Supreme Court Bldg PO Box 11297 Capitol Station Columbia SC 29211

BABB, HAROLD THOMAS, utility exec.; b. Eastanollee, Ga., Jan. 26, 1930; s. Z. T. and Eva (Camp) B.; B.S. in Physics, N. Ga. Coll., 1950; m. Peggy Watson, Apr. 4, 1952; children—Karen, Martin. Nuclear and instrument automatic control engring. E. I. duPont de Nemours & Co., Aiken, S. C., 1954-60; design engr. instrument and control Carolina Virginia Nuclear Power Assn., 1960—, mgr., 1963-69, pres., 1969—; dir. power resources S. C. Electric & Gas Co., Columbia, 1967-71; tchr. So. Meth. Coll., Aiken, 1956-57. Vice chmn. S. C. Water Resources Commn., 1970—. Served with AUS, 1950-54. Decorated Bronze Star, Purple Heart (2), Battle Stars (7). Mem. Instrument Soc. Am., Am. Nuclear Soc. (dir. reactor operations div. 1967-70), Edison Electric Inst. (chmn. nuclear plant design and operations task force). Baptist. Mason. Clubs: Palmetto (Columbia); University (Washington). Contbr. articles to profl. jours. Home: 341 Tram Rd Columbia SC 29210 Office: 328 Main St Columbia SC 29201

BABB, HERBERT EUGENE, ednl. inst. exec.; b. McDonough, Ga., Aug. 25, 1922; s. Archie Tye and Maud Alma (Foster) B.; student West Ga. Coll., 1939-41; B.A., Emory U., 1943; M.S., Ph.D., U. Ky., 1955; m. Evelyn Marie Riley, Oct. 30, 1948; children—Franklin Tye, Mary Riley. Claims adjuster Liberty Mutual Ins. Co., Roanoke, Va., 1947-50; sr. psychologist Milledgeville (Ga.) State Hosp., 1955-57; instr. U. Ky., Lexington, 1959; asst. prof. Queens Coll., Charlotte, N.C., 1957-58, asso. prof., head dept., 1958-61, prof., dean coll., 1961-70; dir. programs N.C. Leadership Inst., Greensboro, 1970-71, v.p., 1971—; vis. prof. Guilford Coll., Greensboro, part-time, 1971—. Recipient scholarship K.T., Masonic Order, 1941. Mem. Am. Psychol. Assn., Zeta Sigma Pi, Pi Sigma Alpha. Democrat. Methodist. Rotarian (bd. dirs. 1967-70). Home: 1106 McDowell Dr Greensboro NC 27408 Office: PO Box 1439 Greensboro NC 27402

BABIN, CLAUDE HUNTER, univ. adminstr.; b. Baton Rouge, Feb. 6, 1924; s. Ventress Victor and Essie (Bond) B.; B.A., La. State U., 1945; M.A., U. Wis., 1946; Ph.D., Tulane U., 1954; LL.D., Hendrix Coll., 1965; m. Barbara Ann Murphy, Dec. 29, 1947; 1 son, Claude Hunter. Instr. history U. Miami (Fla.), 1946-49; grad. fellow Tulane U., 1949-54; asst. prof., asso. prof., then prof. history Ark. A. and M. Coll., 1954-60, acad. dean, 1960-62, pres., 1962-71, chancellor, 1972—. Ford fellow, 1951-52. Mem. Ark. Creed Selection Com. Mem. Am., So. hist. assns., Am. Assn. Univ. Profs. (asso.), Ark. Edn. Assn., State Coll. Presidents Orgn., Assn. State Colls. and Univs., Ark. Farm Bur. Fedn., Acad. Polit. Sci., C. of C., Phi Alpha Theta, Pi Sigma Alpha. Methodist. Democrat. Kiwanian. Home: Monticello AR 71655

BACH, FREDERICK CHARLES, microbiologist; b. Watertown, N.Y., Dec. 10, 1923; B.A., Utica Coll., 1950; M.S., Syracuse U., 1953, Ph.D., 1960. Asst. microbiology, biochemistry Biology and Food Labs., Syracuse (N.Y.) U., 1956-60; group leader Fleischmann Labs., Stamford, Conn., 1960-62; research scientist marine microbiology Lamont Geol. Obs., Columbia, N.Y.C., 1962-64; head microbiology Alcon Labs., Inc., Ft. Worth, 1964-70; cons., 1971—; asso. dir. Dalwarth Clinic Labs., Ft. Worth, 1972—. Served with AUS, 1945-46. Mem. Am. Soc. Microbiology, Am. Chem. Soc., A.A.A.S., N.Y. Acad. Sci., Sigma Xi. Home: 2008 Hemphill St Fort Worth TX 76110 Office: 7th Av and Rosedale St PO Box 1691 Fort Worth TX 76101

BACHI, MICHAEL MARIO, artist, educator; b. Genoa, Italy, Mar. 1, 1920 (parents Am. citizens); s. Angelo Luigi and Alcisa (Cardinale) B.; B.A., Oklahoma City U., 1951; M.F.A., U. Okla., 1953, postgrad., 1953; postgrad. Southeastern State Coll., Durant, Okla., 1954, Instituto de Allende, San Miguel De Allende, Gt., Mexico, 1964; m. Mable Naomi Baker, Apr. 5, 1947. Tchr. art McAlester (Okla.) Jr. and Sr. High Schs., 1953-56; prof., head dept. art Rio Grande (O.) Coll., 1956-57; asst. prof. art Wis. State Coll., Superior, 1957-60; asst. prof. art Chadron (Neb.) State Coll., 1960-62; asst. prof. art Central State U., Edmond, Okla., 1962—, mem. faculty governance com., 1968-69, senator Faculty Senate, 1969-70; exhibited in one man shows Henson Gallery, Yukon, Okla., 1966, Ballet Theatre Sch., Oklahoma City, St. Pauls Cathedral, Oklahoma City, 1968; exhibited in group shows Philbrook Mus., Tulsa, 1953, Okla. U. Show at Forum Gallery, N.Y.C., 1954, Tweed Gallery, Duluth, Minn., 1959, galleries Superior, Wis., 1958, Norman, Okla., 1963, Yukon, 1966, Oklahoma City, 1967. Faculty Show, Okla. Sci. and Arts Found., 1965, Okla. Painting and Sculpture Biennial, 1971, Balcony Art Gallery, Oklahoma City, 1971; executed mural Midland Coop. Supermarket, Superior, 1959; tchr. water color Okla. Sci. and Art Found. Faculty, 1965-66. Mem. Gov.'s Council on Arts and Humanities, 1966. Served with USAAF, 1941-45. Decorated Bronze Star medal with five clusters. Mem. Contemporary Art Found. of Oklahoma City, Am. Assn. U. Profs. (exec. com. local chpt.), Kappa Pi, Delta Phi Delta. Democrat. Home: 5008 White Oak Rd Edmond OK 73034

BACK, EDWARD WILLIAM, JR., banker; b. Cin., Aug. 5, 1926; s. Edward William and Mary Marcella (Trimbur) B.; B.S. cum laude, Xavier U., 1950; postgrad. Grad. Sch. Banking, U. Wis., 1963, U. N.C., 1967; m. Mary Elizabeth Zur Schmiede, Nov. 28, 1957; children—Edward W., III, Mary Susan, Carolyn Elizabeth. Asst. treas. Provident Bank, Cin., 1953-63; with Central Carolina Bank & Trust Co., Durham, 1963—, sr. v.p., 1967—. Pres., co-founder Goodwill Industries Research Triangle Inc., Durham, 1968-69; treas., bd. dirs. United Fund Durham and Durham County, Inc., 1968-71. Served with AUS, 1945-47. Mem. Robert Morris Assos. (gov. Carolina Vas. chpt. 1970-72), Cin. Jr. C. of C. Clubs: Hope Valley Country, Tobac (Durham). Home: 18 Kimberly Dr Durham NC 27707 Office: PO Box 931 Durham NC 27702

BACK, KENNETH CAMERON, govt. ofcl.; b. Whitesburg, Ky., Feb. 23, 1919; s. Kennon and Mary Ann (Adams) B.; A.B., Transylvania Coll., 1948; M.A., U. Ky., 1949; m. Marie Shepherd, Nov. 23, 1942; children— Kenneth M., Stephen A., Janet M. Asst. commr. revenue State of Ky., 1950-54; acting exec. dir. Nat. Assn. Assessing Officers, Chgo., 1954-56; research cons. Dept. Finance and Revenue, D.C. Govt., 1956, dep. finance officer, 1956-57, finance officer, 1957-69, dir., 1969—. Tchr. course George Washington U., 1958-62; cons. taxation State of Ohio, 1967-68. Bd. dirs. Lincoln Found. Served to maj. AUS, 1939-45. Recipient Louis Brownlow award Am. Soc. Pub. Adminstrn., 1969, Outstanding Mem. of the Year award Internat. Assn. Assessing Officers. Mem. Nat. Tax Assn. (pres. 1971), Internat. Assn. Assessing Officers (pres. 1964). Home: 4620 Brandywine St NW Washington DC 20016 Office: Room 4136 Municipal Center 300 Indiana Av NW Washington DC 20001

BACKLUND, ALVIN LORENZO, JR., geologist; b. Omaha, Oct. 19, 1912; s. Alvin Lorenzo and Florence (Elmgren) B.; B.S., U. Neb., 1949, M.S., 1953. Jr. geologist Magnolia Petroleum Co., Morgan City, La., 1950-51, asst. geologist, Lake Charles, La., 1951-54; with Mobil Oil Co., Lafayette, La., now New Orleans, 1954—, asso. prodn. geologist, 1966-68, 70—, asso. exploration geologist, 1968-70. Served with USAAF, 1942-45. Mem. A.A.A.S., Am. Assn. Petroleum Geologists, Am. Geophys. Union, Am. Inst. Profl. Geologists, Geol. Soc. Am., Soc. Econ. Paleontologists and Mineralogists, Geol. Socs., Phi Beta Kappa, Sigma Xi, Sigma Gamma Epsilon. Home: 1205 St Charles Av New Orleans LA 70130 Office: 1001 Howard Av New Orleans LA 70113

BACKSTROM, MARTHA CAROLYN MURPHREE (MRS. JAMES WALTON BACKSTROM), educator; b. Pittsboro, Miss., Aug. 20, 1916; d. Stanley Thomas and June Elizabeth (Byars) Murphree; B.A. cum laude, Miss. State Coll. for Women, 1937; m. James Walton Backstrom, May 22, 1938; 1 son, James Walton. Tchr. pub. schs., Greene County, Miss., 1937-64; coordinator Elementary and Secondary Edn. Act. Program, Greene County Sch. Dist., Leakesville 1966—. Sec., Backstrom Timber Co. Mem. fund raising coms. Nat. Found., Cancer Fund, A.R.C., Tb Soc.; mem. Leakesville Beautification Com., 1966; mem. Inter-Alumni Council for Instns. Higher Learning in Miss. Mem. D.A.R. (chpt. chmn. 1963-71, state chmn. 1965-68, sec. 1966-69, chpt. vice regent 1969-71, chpt. regent 1971—), Miss State Coll. for Women Alumnae Assn. (dir. 1967-69), Murphree Geneal. Soc., Miss. Hist. Soc., Miss., Nat. edn. assns., Pi Gamma Mu. Methodist; also active Baptist Ch. Clubs: Three Arts (pres. 1941-42, 65-66)(Leakesville). Home: PO Box 108 Leakesville MS 39451 Office: Dept Edn Greene County Sch Dist Leakesville MS 39451

BACON, ANALEE ELIZABETH CAMP (MRS. KARL F. HAUSAUER), educator, musician; b. Mountain View, Cal., June 16, 1913; d. Wilbur L. and Elizabeth (Burns) Camp; B.A. Mills Coll., 1935, Mus.B., 1935; Mus.M., Syracuse U., 1958, Ph.D., 1962; m. Ernst Bacon, June 12, 1937 (div. Feb. 1952); children—Paul, Arthur; m. 2d, Karl F. Hausauer, Feb. 25, 1971. Concert cellist solo tours, U.S. and Europe, 1938—; prof. cello Converse Coll., Spartanburg, S.C., 1939-45, Syracuse (N.Y.) U., 1945-62; prof. humanities and music U. Miami, Coral Gables, Fla., 1962-71. Prof. cello Bennington (Vt.) Coll., 1951-52; prin. cellist Buffalo Philharmonic Orch., 1952-55; dir. music Syracuse (N.Y.) Psychopathic Hosp., 1951-52; vis. prof. Univ. Ga., Athens, 1968-69. Recipient Humanities award U. Miami, 1966. Mem. Am. Musicological Soc. (pres. Fla.-Ga. 1967-68). Author books including History of Violoncello as a Solo Instrument, 1967; Realizations and Accompaniments to 3 Sonatas for Cello and Piano by A. Scarlatti, 6 Sonatas for Cello and Piano by L. Boccherini, 6 Sonatas for Cello and Piano by Marcello. Editor: Suite for Strings (G.B. Vitali), 1970. Home: The Billows B7 Rural Route 2 Box 4J Vero Beach FL 32960

BACON, DONALD CONRAD, journalist; b. Jacksonville, Fla., Jan. 15, 1935; s. Francis H. and Myrtis (Gunter) B.; B.S. in Journalism, U. Fla., 1957; m. Barbara Lee Barnwell, June 22, 1957; 1 dau., Elizabeth. Staff writer Wall St. Jour., 1957-61; Ford Found. congl. fellow, 1961-62; with Washington Evening Star, 1962-63; congl. corr. Newhouse Nat. News Service, Washington 1963-68, White House corr., 1968-—, sr. corr., 1971-—. Congl. fellow Am. Polit. Sci. Assn.; mem. White House Corrs. Assn., Fla. Blue Key, Beta Theta Pi, Sigma Delta Chi. Club: Internat. Author: Congress and You, 1969; (with others) The New Millionaires, 1961. Home: 3514 Livingston St NW Washington DC 20015 Office: 1750 Pennsylvania Av NW Washington DC 20006

BACON, DONALD WALTER, bus. exec.; b. Cin., Aug 28, 1914; s. Frank B. and Laura (Claassen) B.; A.B., Antioch Coll., 1939; m. Lois Neuhart, June 8, 1946; children—Janet, Anne, David, Susan. With Lybrand, Ross Bros. & Montgomery, C.P.A.'s, Chgo., 1939-40; asst. budget dir. Studebaker Corp., South Bend, Ind., 1940-42; staff Office Comptroller Gen., Washington, 1946-53, Dept. Army, Washington, 1953-54; with Internal Revenue Service, 1954-71, regional commr., 1956-62, asst. commr., 1962-71; dir. taxes Gulf & Western Industries, Inc., Washington, 1971-—. Served as lt. comdr. USNR, 1942-46. Mem. Am. Inst. C.P.A.'s, Mass. Soc. C.P.A.'s, Fed. Govt. Accountants Assn. (nat. pres. 1962-63), D.C. Inst. C.P.A.'s, Tax Execs. Inst., Internat. Fiscal Assn. Club: Internat. (Washington). Home: 1440 Cola Dr McLean VA 22101 Office: Gulf & Western Industries Inc Room 920 600 New Hampshire Av NW Washington DC

BACON, DOUGLAS EUGENE, geologist; b. Boone, Ia., June 11, 1925; s. Raymond H. and Lola M (Adams) B.; student Millsaps Coll., 1943-44, Miami U., 1944-45; B.S., U. Ark., 1948, M.S., 1949; m. Emily Jane Coghlan, Oct. 15, 1949; children—S. Douglas, Robert M., Barbara S. Tchr., U. Ark., 1948-49; geologist Atlantic Refining Co., Wichita, Kan., 1949-52, dist. geologist, Bismarck, N.D., 1952-55, asst. to chief geologist, Dallas, 1955-56, dist. geologist, Houston, 1956-60; cons. geologist, Houston, 1960-—. Chmn. phys. com., bd. dirs. YMCA, 1967-69; mem. Meadowbrook Civic Club, 1957-—. Served with USMCR, 1943-46. Mem. Am. Assn. Petroleum Geologists (dist. rep.), Soc. Ind. and Earth Scientists (chpt. v.p., dir., nat. treas.), Am. Geol. Inst., Houston Geol Soc. Methodist (dir.). Club: Crude (pres., dir.) (Houston). Home: 8307 Glenvista St Houston TX 77017 Office: 3110 SW Freeway Houston TX 77006

BACON, FRANKLIN CAMP, mining co. exec.; b. White Springs, Fla., July 30, 1919; s. Nathaniel Hunter and Elizabeth Brett (Camp) B.; A.B. in Journalism, U. Ga., 1940; m. Marjorie Edna Caldwell, Feb. 28, 1942; children—Franklin Camp, Paul Caldwell, John Lee. Editorial asst. Douglas (Ga.) Enterprise, 1940; city reporter Columbus (Ga.) Enquirer, 1940-41; commd. 2d lt. USMC, 1941, advanced through grades to col., 1962; ret., 1967; mgr. pub. relations Freeport Sulphur Co., New Orleans, 1968-—. Mem. Devel. Council, Sara Mayo Hosp., 1970-71. Bd. dirs. La. Assn. for Mental Health; mem. exec. com. Explorers, New Orleans Area council Boy Scouts Am. Decorated Legion of Merit, Bronze Star medal, Purple Heart. Mem. La. Assn. Broadcasters (asso. mem., dir. 1971-—), Marine Corps Res. Assn. (pres., chmn. bd. New Orleans chpt.), Press Club New Orleans (v.p. 1969-70), Mil. Order World Wars. Home: 2725 Prancer St New Orleans LA 70114 Office: Box 61520 New Orleans LA 70161

BACON, PHILLIP, educator, author; b. Cleve., July 10, 1922; s. Hollis Phillip and Emma (Schneider) B.; student The Citadel, 1940-41; A.B., U. Miami, 1946; M.A., George Peabody Coll. for Tchrs., 1951, Ed.D., 1955; m. Dorothy Willey, Aug. 16, 1951; children— Laura Jane (Mrs. Robert C. Fraser), Phillip Everett. Tchr. social studies Castle Heights Mil Acad., Lebanon, Tenn., 1946-47, Army and Navy Acad., Carlsbad, Cal., 1948-53; grad. asst. geography George Peabody Coll. for Tchrs., 1953-55, dean Grad. Sch. 1963-64; asst. prof. geography U. Pitts., 1955-57; vis. asst. prof. geography Columbia Tchrs. Coll., 1956-57, asso. prof., 1957-60, prof., 1960-63, 64-66; prof. geography U. Wash., Seattle, 1966-71, co-dir. tri-univ. project in elementary edn., 1967-71; prof. geography U. Houston, 1971-—. Mem. editorial adv. bd. World Book Ency., 1965-—; bd. cons. World Book Atlas, 1965-70; cons. editor Golden Press, 1958-61; cons. book div. Time, Inc., 1960-69; cons. social sci. project Ednl. Research Council Am., 1962-70; mem. steering com. High Sch. Geography Project, 1965-70; cons. U.S. Office Edn., 1964-—; mem. Wash. Social Studies Adv. Commn., 1968-71; curriculum cons. Served with USNR, 1942-45. Fellow Royal Geo. Soc. Am., Geog. Soc. N.Y.; mem. Assn. Am. Geographers, Nat. Council for Geog. Edn. (pres. 1966), Nat., Wash. edn. assns., Am. Assn. Higher Edn., Assn. Pacific Coast Geographers, Nat., Tex. councils social studies, Sigma Xi, Sigma Alpha Epsilon, Phi Delta Kappa, Kappa Delta Pi, Pi Gamma Mu. Presbyn. Clubs: Men's Faculty of Columbia; Mercer Island Country; Bay Area Racket. Author: Australia, Oceania, and the Polar Lands, 1961, North America, 1961; Children's Picture Atlas of the World, 1966; (with Norman Carls and Frank E. Sorenson) Knowing Our Neighbors in the United States, 1966; Knowing Our Neighbors in the United States and Canada, 1966; Regions Around The World, 1970; (with R.R. Boyce) Towns and Cities, 1970; (with others) The United States and Canada, 1970; (with P.V. Greco) The Story of Latin America, 1970. Editor: Focus on Geography, Key Concepts and Teaching Strategies, 1970; co-editor: Foundations of World Regional Geography Series, 1970-—. Cons editor Life Pictorial Atlas of the World, 1961, Jour. of Geography, 1967-70, Where and Why, 1972. Co-dir. Field Elementary Social Studies Series. Contbr. articles to profl. jours. Home: 18601 Point Lookout Dr Nassau Bay Houston TX 77058

BACON, SYLVIA, judge; b. Watertown, S.D., July 9, 1931; d. Julius Franklin and Ann Rae (Hyde) Bacon; A.B., Vassar Coll., 1952; certificate London Sch. Econs., 1953; LL.B., Harvard, 1956; LL.M., Georgetown U., 1959. Admitted to D.C. bar, 1956; law clk. fed. dist. ct., Washington, 1956-57; asst. U.S. atty., 1957-63, exec. asst. atty., 1969-70; asso. dir. Pres. Commn. on Crime D.C., 1965-67; trial atty. criminal div. Justice Dept., 1967-69; asso. judge D.C. Superior Ct., 1970-—. Mem. Am. Bar Assn., Am. Judicature Soc. Republican. Home: 2500 Q St NW Washington DC 20007 Office: 613 G St NW Washington DC 20001

BACON, WILLIAM ARTHUR, lawyer; b. Durant, Miss., Feb. 8, 1912; s. James Webster and Zouella (Guess) B.; LL.B., U. Miss., 1935; m. Carolee Meyer Pratt, Mar. 15, 1941; 1 son, William A. Admitted to Miss. bar, 1935; city atty., Durant, Miss., 1935-40; asst. U.S. dist. atty., So. Dist., Miss., 1942, 46; state bond atty., Miss., 1951-—. Mem. Miss. Ho. of Reps., 1936-40. Pres. Crestview Home, 1957-64; pres. Miss. Children's Home Soc, 1964-—; pres. Jackson YMCA 1963-64. Served as lt. USNR, 1942-46. Mem. Am., Miss., Hinds County (pres. 1959-60) bar assns., Jackson Photog. Soc. (pres 1957), Miss. State Bar (pres. 1970-71), Fed. Bar Assn., Am. Judicature Soc. Democrat. Episcopalian (vestryman). Clubs: Gulf States Camera (pres. council), Men's Y (pres. 1947); Kiwanis (pres. 1956), Jackson Country, River Hills (dir.). Home: 3909 Pinewood Dr Jackson MS 39211 Office: Bankers Trust Plaza Bldg PO Box 15 Jackson MS 39205

BACOTE, CLARENCE ALBERT, educator; b. Kansas City, Mo., Feb. 24, 1906; s. Samuel William and Lucy (Bledsoe) B.; A.B., U. Kan., 1926, M.A., U. Chgo., 1929, Ph.D., 1955; m. Lucia Moore, Aug. 3, 1931; children—Lucia Jean (Mrs. Charles James II), Samuel William. Tchr. Kansas City (Mo.) 1926-27; prof. history Fla. A. and M. Coll., 1927-30; asst. prof. history Atlanta U., 1930-39, prof., 1939-—. Mem. Ga. adv. com. U.S. Civil Rights Commn.; jury commr. Fulton County, 1965-70; mem. Atlanta Charter commn. Mem. Am., So. hist. assns., Orgn. Am. Historians, Atlanta Negro Voters League, Assn. Study Negro Life and History, Alpha Phi Alpha, Sigma Pi Phi. Baptist. Club: 27. Author: The History of Atlanta University 1865-1965. Contbr. articles profl. jours. Home: 478 Thackeray Pl SW Atlanta GA 30311

BADER, FRANZ, gallery dir.; b. Vienna, Austria, Sept. 19, 1903; s. David and Elsa (Steindler) B.; ed. Vienna; m. Antonia Blaustein, Dec.2, 1928; m. 2d, Virginia Forman, July 31, 1971. Owner, Wallishausser Book Shop, Vienna; v.p., gen. mgr. Whyte Gallery, Washington, 1939-53; pres. Franz Bader Gallery, Washington, 1953-—; cons. for collectors, art appraisals for mus. and pvt. collectors. Mem. Print Council Am., Am. Book Sellers Assn., Friends of Music at Dumbarton Oaks, Mus. of Modern Art. Club: George Washington Univ. Home: 2242 48th St NW Washington DC 20007 Office: 2124 Pennsylvania Av NW Washington DC 20037

BADILLO, SAMUEL, advt. agy. exec. Chmn. bd., chief exec. officer Badillo-Compton, Inc. Office: PO Box F Caparra Heights PR 00922*

BADOUD, JOHN JAMES, labor union exec.; b. McDonald, Pa., Feb. 11, 1912; s. James J. and Maggie (James) B.; student Kiski Prep Sch., Saltsburg, Pa., 1932; m. Agnes Marie Rodichok, June 7, 1934; children— Constance Margaret (Mrs. Richard B. Parks), Gary David, John James, Dale Thomas, Karen Louise (Mrs. Terrell B. Bridges), William Alan, Keith Lynn. Truck driver, lab. technician Am. Briquet Co., Lykens, Pa., 1934-42; mem. United Mine Workers Am., 1937, pres. local union 13010, dist. 50, 1940-42, traveling auditor dist. 50, 1942, regional dir. Mich. dist. 1944-54, asst. to pres. dist. 50, Washington, 1954-57, sec.-treas. distr. 50, 1957-—. Mem. labor panel region II, NWLB, 1944-45. Mem. Mich. Commn. Study Problems of Aging, 1951-52. Home: 3945 Military Rd NW Washington DC 20015 Office: 1435 K St NW Washington DC 20005

BAER, ALFRED, physician; b. Strasbourg, France, Mar. 15, 1917; s. Arthur and Frances (Cohn) B.; student Sorbonne, U. Paris, 1937-39; A.B., Ohio State U., 1942; M.D., Johns Hopkins, 1945; m. Eva Rosenberg, Aug. 28, 1949; children—Barbary, Alan. Came to U.S., 1939, naturalized, 1945. Intern pathology Montefiore Hosp., N.Y.C., 1946; intern Lincoln Hosp., N.Y.C., 1945-46, resident, 1948-50; practice medicine, specializing in internal medicine and rheumatology, Washington, 1950-—; mem. staffs George Washington U. Med. Center, Washington Hosp. Center; asso. clin. prof. medicine George Washington U. Sch. Medicine, Washington, 1966-—. Bd. dirs., mem. med. adv. com. various times Arthritis and Rheumatism Assn. Met. Washington. Diplomate Am. Bd. Internal Medicine. Fellow A.C.P.; mem. A.M.A., Am. Rheumatism Assn., Am. Heart Assn., N.Y. Acad. Scis., Phi Beta Kappa. Home: 4400 Springdale St NW Washington DC 20016 Office: 730 24th St NW Washington DC 20037

BAER, GEORGE MARTIN, veterinarian; b. London, Eng., Jan. 12, 1936; s. Curtis Otto and Catherine Gertrude (Meyer) B.; came to U.S., 1940, naturalized, 1946; D.V.M., Cornell U., 1959; M.P.H., U. Mich., 1961; m. Maria Olga Lara, July 2, 1960; children—Katherine, Yvette. Pvt. practice vet. medicine, Beaumont, Cal., 1959-60; with N.Y. State Dept. Health, 1961-63; acting chief Rabies Investigations Lab., Atlanta, 1963-64; chief Southwest Rabies Investigations Lab., Las Cruces, N.M., 1964-66; cons. Nat. Communicable Disease Center, Pan Am. Health Orgn., Mexico, 1966-69; chief lab. investigating unit Viral Zoonoses sect. Viral Diseases br. Epidemic Program, Communicable Disease Center, Lawrenceville, Ga., 1969-—. Mem. N.Y. Acad. Sci., Am. Pub. Health Assn. Home: 5462 Rosser Rd Stone Mountain GA 30083 Office: Box 363 Communicable Disease Center Lawrenceville GA 30245

BAETZ, ERNEST ARTHUR, banker; b. San Antonio, Feb. 28, 1898; s. Max and Clara (Giesen) B.; student Wharton Sch. Finance and Commerce, U. Pa., 1916-17; m. Frances Helen Lucas, June 28, 1921; children— Dorothy (Mrs. Kenneth E. Jackson), Ernest Arthur, Jr., Barbara. Asst. cashier Bexar County Nat. Bank, San Antonio, chmn. bd., 1968-—, pres., 1946-—. Chmn. bd. San Antonio Portland Cement Co., 1968-—, also dir.; dir. Roegelein Provision Co., San Antonio. Served with U.S. Army, 1917-18. Recipient Silver Beaver award Boy Scouts Am., 1955; citation Nat. Conf. Christians and Jews, 1967. Mem. San Antonio Zool. Soc. (sec. 1960). Mason (33 deg., Shriner), Kiwanian. Club: San Antonio Country. Home: 524 Tuxedo Av San Antonio TX 78209 Office: Travis and St Marys San Antonio TX 78291

BAGBY, GEORGE LEWIS, elec. products co. exec.; b. nr. South Boston, Va., Apr. 6, 1909; s. Samuel Lewis and Ruth Lillian (Oliver) B.; B.S., U. N.C., 1931; m. Sara Kimbrough Jenkins, June 11, 1941; children—Katherine (Mrs. Ivon D. Rohrer), George Lewis, Sara Jenkins, Ruth Oliver. With S. L. Bagby Co., mfrs. agts. elec. products, Charlotte, N.C., 1931-—, chief exec. officer, 1959-—; dir. Bank of Commerce, Charlotte, Ga. Theater Co., Atlanta. Served to maj. C.E., AUS, 1953. Mem. Illuminating Engring. Soc. Mason (Shriner). Clubs: Charlotte Country, Charlotte City, Quail Hollow Country (Charlotte). Home: 2645 Beverwyck Rd Charlotte NC 28211 Office: 822 W Morehead St Charlotte SC 28201

BAGBY, WILLIAM RARDIN, lawyer; b. Grayson, Ky., Feb. 19, 1910; s. John Albert and Nano (Rardin) B.; A.B., Cornell U., 1933; LL.B., U. Mich., 1936; postgrad. Northwestern U., 1946-47; m. Mary Carpenter, Sept. 4, 1939; 1 son, John Robert. Admitted to Ky. bar, 1937, Ohio bar, 1952; practiced in Grayson, Ky., 1937-43; city atty., Grayson, 1939-41, judge, 1941-43; counsel U.S. Treasury, 1946-54; practiced law, Lexington, Ky., 1954-—. Prof. law U. Ky., 1956-57; pub. Enquirer, Grayson, 1937-43. Mem. Lexington County Bd. Adjustment, 1965-67, Lexington Mayor's Adv. Com., 1963-—. Trustee Bagby Music Lovers' Found., N.Y.C. Served as lt. USNR, 1944-46. Mem. Am., Ky., Ohio, Fed. bar assns., Kappa Sigma, Democrat, Episcopalian, Rotarian. Clubs: Spindletop, Lexington. Home: 228 Market St Lexington KY 40508 Office: First Nat Bldg Lexington KY 40507

BAGDIKIAN, BEN HAIG, writer; b. Marash, Turkey, Jan. 30, 1920 (came to U.S. 1920, naturalized 1926); A.B., Clark U., 1941, D.Litt., 1963; L.H. D., Brown U., 1961; m. Elizabeth Ogasapian, Oct. 2, 1942; children—Christopher Ben, Frederick Haig. Reporter, Springfield (Mass.) Morning Union, 1941-42; asso. editor Periodical House, Inc., N.Y.C., 1946; successively reporter, fgn. corr., chief Washington corr. Providence Jour., 1947-62; contbg. editor Sat. Eve. Post, 1963-67; project dir. study of future U.S. news media Rand, 1967-69; asst. mng. editor Fox Mut. News, The Washington Post, 1970-—. Trustee Clark U., 1964-—; bd. dirs. Nat. Capital Area Civil Liberties Union, 1964-66); pres. Lowell Mellett Fund for Free and Responsible Press, 1965-—. Served with USAAF, 1942-45, Recipient George Foster Peabody award, 1951, Sidney Hillman Found. award, 1956; Ogden Reid Found. fellow, 1956; Guggenheim fellow, 1961-62. Mem. Overseas Writers, Authors League. Democrat. Unitarian. Club: Nat. Press (Washington). Author: In The Midst of Plenty: The Poor in America, 1964; The Information Machines: Their Impact on Men and the Media, 1971; also pamphlets. Contbr.: The Kennedy Circle, 1961. Editor: Man's Contracting World in an Expanding Universe, 1959. Office: 1515 L St NW Washington DC 20005

BAGERT, BERNARD J., judge; b., 1913; LL.D., Loyola U. Admitted to La. bar, 1935; now criminal dist. ct. judge, New Orleans. Office: Criminal Cts Bldg 2700 Tulane Av New Orleans LA 70119

BAGGETT, AGNES, state ofcl.; b. Columbus, Ga.; d. John R. and Leila (Thomason) Beahn; student pub. schs., Columbus, Ga., Jones Law Sch., Montgomery, Ala.; m. George Lamar Baggett, Oct. 14, 1926 (dec. 1949). With L.& N. R.R., 1925-27; various positions sec. state's office, Montgomery, Ala., 1927-46, sec. state, 1951-55, state auditor, 1955-58, state treas., 1959-63, 67-—, sec. of state, Ala., 1963-67. Mem. Am. Legion Aux. (chmn. Girls State, Ala.; state legislative chmn.), Bus. and Profl. Women's Club (past state pres.). Mem. Order Eastern Star. Club: Altrusa (pres.). Home: 3202 Montezuma Rd Montgomery AL 36104 Office: State Capitol Montgomery AL 36104

BAGGETT, BRYCE ALLEN, lawyer, state senator; b. Oklahoma City, June 4, 1932; s. James Everett and Esther (Tippens) B.; A.B., U. Okla., 1954, LL.B., 1956; m. Barbara Jean Bolton, Dec. 21, 1953; children—Bryce Allen, Breene Everett, Barbara Lynn. Admitted to Okla. bar, 1956, since practiced in Oklahoma City; mem. Okla. Ho. of Reps., 1958-64; mem. Okla. Senate, 1964-—. Dir., Capitol Hill State Bank & Trust Co. Okla. commr. Nat. Conf. Commrs. Uniform State Laws; mem. steering com. Edn. Commn. States. Named Outstanding Young Man of Okla., Okla. Jr. C. of C., 1961, Outstanding Young Man Oklahoma City, Oklahoma City Jr. C. of C., 1967. Mem. Am., Okla. Oklahoma County bar assns. Home: 2620 NW 109th St Oklahoma City OK 73120 Office: 1st Nat Bldg Oklahoma City OK 73102

BAGGETT, JERRELL PINKEY, oilwell drilling contractor; b. Corsicana, Tex., Nov. 26, 1917; s. Hub Brewer and Sadie Gay (Butler) B.; grad. high sch.; m. Lois Annice Cooper, Oct. 28, 1937; children—Carolyn (Mrs. Jay Terry O'Brien), Linda Lou, Jerrell David. Roughneck, Magnolia Oil Co., 1940-47; tool pusher Hondo Oil Co., Dixon, Tex., 1947-60, drilling supt., 1960-65; owner, pres. Baggett Drilling Co., Eagle Pass, Tex., 1965-—. Mem. Am. Assn. Oilwell Drilling Contractors. Mason (32deg., Shriner). Home: Golden Eagle Ranch Eagle Pass TX 78852 Office: PO Box 526 489 Main St Eagle Pass TX 78852

BAGGS, LEAH L. BATES (MRS. LINTON DANIEL BAGGS, JR.), social leader; b. Franklinville, N.Y.; d. William Henry and Arlie Mae (Bozworth) Bates; A.B., Barnard Coll., 1922; student spl. courses various univs.; m. Linton Daniel Baggs, Jr., Oct. 1, 1926; children—Joan Bates (Mrs. Herbert A. McKenzie, Jr.), Linton Daniel III. Hon. bd. dirs. Macon Community Concert Assn., 1968-—, pres., 1959-64; bd. dirs. Middle Ga. Camellia Soc., v.p. Macon Grand Opera Assn., 1954-—; vice regent Ga. div. Magna Charta Dames, 1968-69, regent, 1970-—; hon state regent Daus. Am. Colonists, 1962, nat. chmn. colonial heritage com., 1962-64; com. chmn. Ga. br. Sons and Daus. of Pilgrims Soc., 1954-55. Mem. Am. Assn. U. Women, Ga. Soc. Mayflower Descs. (corr. sec. 1960-62), Pilgrim John Howland Soc., D.A.R., Middle Ga. Hist. Soc. (charter mem.). Am., Ga. camellia socs., Nat. Trust for Historic Preservation, Sigma Alpha Iota. Presbyn. Clubs: Barnard College (Atlanta, v.p. 1967-—). Morning Music (pres. 1951-53), Atlanta Music, Capitol City Atlanta, Idle Hour Country (Macon, Ga.). Home: 1137 N Jackson Springs Rd Macon GA 31201

BAGGS, LINTON DANIEL, JR., corp. exec.; b. Bainbridge, Ga., Dec. 27, 1902; s. Dr. Linton Daniel and Madge Ione (Morgan) B.; student Mercer U., 1920-21, Pace Inst., 1921-22; m. Leah Bates, Oct. 1, 1926; children—Linton Daniel III, Joan Bates (Mrs. Herbert Alonzo McKenzie, Jr.). Accountant, L. D.Baggs & Co., Macon, Ga., 1923-46; v.p. Jacksonville Broadcasting Co. (Fla.), 1942-52; pres. Community Broadcasting Co., Asheville, N.C., 1946-49, Bibb Transit Co., Macon, 1949-67, Coca Cola Bottling Co., Hannibal, Mo., Coca Cola Bottling Co., Kankakee, Ill., Coca Cola Bottling Co., Dubuque, Ia., all until 1967; sec.-treas. Brower-Baggs Press, Inc., North Miami; Fla., 1967-—; dir. Ga. Bank & Trust Co., Macon, Peeler Hardware Co. Mem. Ga. Bd Accountants, 1953-58. Bd. regents Univ. System of Ga. C.P.A., Ga. Mem. Ga. Soc. C.P.A.'s, Am. Inst. C.P.A.'s, Am., Middle Ga. (pres. 1961-62, dir. 1968-—) camellia socs., Sigma Nu. Presbyn. Mason, Rotarian (pres. 1957-58), Elk. Clubs: Idle Hour (Macon); Capitol City (Atlanta). Home: 1137 N Jackson Springs Rd Macon GA 31201 Office: 1137 N Jackson Springs Rd Macon GA 31201 also 12365 W Dixie Hwy North Miami FL 33161

BAGLEY, WILLIAM BLAKE, iron and steel co. exec.; b. Oxford, Ala., July 9, 1914; s. Floyd Charles and Mary Etta (Disharoon) B.; student Internat. Corr. Schs., 1936-37, Auburn U. Extension Sch., 1945, U. Ala. Extension Sch., 1946; m. Emma John Angle, Oct. 11, 1938; children—Barbara Anne (Mrs. Boone), Brenda (Mrs. Mac Simmon Dunaway). Billing clk. Anniston Foundry Co., (Ala.), 1936-40, purchasing agt., 1940-46, sec., 1946-61, v.p. sales, 1961-62, pres., 1962-66; v.p. marketing Woodward Co. (Ala.), 1966-72, group v.p. soil pipe and related products, pres. Soil Pipe Group, 1972-—. Past chmn. membership com. Anniston YMCA. Mem. Asso. Industries Ala., Am. Marketing Assn., Ala., Anniston (past dir.) chambers commerce, Birmingham Art Assn., Cast Iron Soil Pipe Inst. (pres.) Baptist. Rotarian. Clubs: N.Y. Athletic; Anniston Country; Downtown; The Club; Relay House, Woodward Golf and Country. Home: 2540 Mountain Brook Circle Birmingham AL 35223 Office: Woodward Co Woodward AL 35189

BAGWELL, CHARLES MALCOLM, civil engr.; b. Lawrenceville, Ga., May 25, 1934; s. John Danial and Julia Ellen (Morcock) B.; B.C.E., Ga. Inst. Tech., 1959; m. Susan Grovia Brender, Nov. 8, 1964; children—Jennifer Ann, Tyler Ernst. Civil engr. Ga. Hwy. Dept., Atlanta, 1959-63, Dept. Housing and Urban Devel., Atlanta, 1963-65; civil engr. Urban Renewal, Atlanta, 1965-67; civil engr., planner Dept. Health, Edn. and Welfare, Constrn. Services, Office of Edn., Atlanta, 1967-71; civil engr. Fac. Engring. Constrn. Agy., Dept Health, Edn. and Welfare, Atlanta, 1971-—. Registered prof. engr., Ga. Served with AUS, 1954-56. Mem. Am. Soc. C.E. Home: 123 Lancelot Way Lawrenceville GA 30245

BAGWELL, ISAIAH WILLIAM, III, wholesale oil co. exec.; b. Onancock, Va., May 2, 1921; s Isaiah William and Eugenia (Taylor) B.; grad. Randolph Macon Acad., 1938; student Va. Poly Inst., 1939-40; grad. U.S. Mcht. Marine Acad., 1944; m. Anne Virginia Nelson, Jan. 25, 1947; children—Linda (Mrs. Henry Custis, Jr.), Bill, Jean. Pres., Bagwell Oil Co., Inc., Onancock, 1946-—, jobber Union Oil Co., Onancock, 1946-—; sec. Bayshore CATV, Inc., 1971-—; pres. Bagwell Terminal and Transp. Corp., 1961-—. Served with U.S. Mcht. Marine, 1942-45. Presbyn. Lion. Home: 2 Mt Prospect Av Onancock VA 23417 Office: 35 Market St Onancock VA 23417

BAHAN, ROLAND ALOYSIUS, JR., hotel mgr.; b. New Orleans, Nov. 2, 1930; s. Roland Aloysius and Marie Adele (Munch) B.; B.A., Tulane U., 1951; m. Patricia Jane Murphy, Oct. 22, 1952; children—Shelley, Sharon, Laurie. Mgr., Lasalle Hotel, New Orleans, 1953-—. Bd. dirs. Greater New Orleans Tourist and Convention Com., 1970-—. Served to lt. (j.g.) USNR, 1951-53. Mem. La. (chmn. ednl. com. 1968-—), New Orleans (treas. 1968-69) hotel and motel assns., Internat. House, Delta Tau Delta. Home: 5225 Bancroft Dr New Orleans LA 70122 Office: 1113 Canal St New Orleans LA 70112

BAHNER, THOMAS MAXFIELD, lawyer; b. Little Rock, Nov. 26, 1933; s. Carl Tabb and Catharine (Garrott) B.; B.S., Carson Newman Coll., 1954; B.D., So. Bapt. Theol. Sem., 1957; LL.B., U. Va., 1960; m. Sara Minta McIntyre, Sept. 28, 1957; children—Maxfield Tabb, Minta Susan, Margaret Catharine. Admitted to Va., Tenn. bars, 1960, asso. firm Kefauver, Duggan and McDonald, Chattanooga, 1960-62; partner firm Duggan, McDonald and Bahner, Chattanooga, 1962-64, firm Chambliss, Bahner and Crawford, Chattanooga, 1964—; dir. Apollo Inc., Chattanooga, 1964—. Pres. United Cerebral Palsy Greater Chattanooga, 1966-67; mem. allocations steering com. United Fund Greater Chattanooga, 1970—. Bd. dirs. Chattanooga Council Alcoholism, 1964-65, Team Evaluation Center Inc., Chattanooga, 1965-70, Orange Grove Sch., Chattanooga; mem. Hamilton County Sch. Bd., 1969—; mem. adv. bd. Carson-Newman Coll., Jefferson City, Tenn., 1969—; mem. Tenn. and Am. Sch. Bds. Assn. Mem. Chattanooga (pres. 1969-70), Tenn. (lectr. 1965, bd. govs. local bar conf. 1969-71, chmn. legal aid and referral com. 1971-72), Am. bar assns., Va. State Bar, Am. Judicature Soc., Estate Planning Council (bd. dirs. 1971-72), Baptist (deacon). Clubs: Civitan, Mountain City (Chattanooga). Home: Route 1 Parsons Lane Chattanooga TN 37377 Office: Maclellan Bldg 721 Broad St Chattanooga TN 37402

BAHR, GORDON JOHN, educator; b. Berlin, Wis., Oct. 4, 1926; s. John Ernst and Anna Bertha (Braun) B.; B.A., Wartburg Coll., 1951; B.D., Wartburg Theol. Sem., 1954; postgrad. U. Gottingen, 1954-56; Ph.D., Hebrew Union Coll., 1962. Instr., Wartburg Coll., Waverly, Ia., 1956; asst. prof. Wayne State U., Detroit, 1963-65, Marquette U., Milw., 1965-69; prof. religion Claflin Coll., Orangeburg, S.C., 1969—. Marquette U. Research grantee, 1967. Mem. Soc. Bibl. Lit. Home: 967 Carolina St Orangeburg SC 29115

BAHR, GUNTER F., biophysicist; b. Altona, Germany, Oct. 10, 1922; s. Karl and Elfriede (Wedekind) B.; M.D., U. Wurzburg, 1952, Karolinska Inst., Stockholm, 1957; m. Karina Edblad, Mar. 6, 1960; children—Josephine, Nina. Asst., Nobel Inst. Cell Research and Genetics, Stockholm, 1950-57; asst. prof. Nobel Inst., Karolinska Inst., 1957-58, Inst. Pathology of Karolinska Inst., 1957-60; chief biophysics br. Armed Forces Inst. Pathology, Washington, 1960—; clin. prof. pathology Georgetown U., 1963—; vis. prof. dept. pathology Northwestern U., 1958. Scandinavian rep. to UNESCO Com. on Animal Resources, 1955. Recipient Maurice Goldblatt Cytology award Internat. Acad. Cytology, 1966; recipient Meritorious Service award, 1965, Distinguished Civilian Service award, 1967, Army Research Team award, 1967. Hon. fellow Internat. Acad. Reproductive Medicine; hon. mem. Mil. Surgeons of U.S.; mem. Internat. Acad. Cytology, Electron Microscopy Soc. Am., Soc. Exptl. Pathology and Biology, Histochem. Soc., Am. Soc. Cell Biology, Internat. Acad. Pathology; Scandinavian Soc. Electron Microscopy. Author numerous sci. papers in field. Major work in quantitative electron microscopy, malaria, chromosomes, pattern recognition. Address: Armed Forces Inst Pathology Washington DC 20305

BAIAR, JOHN MOULTON, utility exec.; b. Johnston City, Ill., May 4, 1922; s. Ben L. and Ora L. (Moulton) B.; student So. Ill. U., 1940-42, U. Miami (Fla.), 1950-52;; m. Mary Frances Gillespie, Feb. 21, 1945; 1 dau., Sharon Kaye. Mng. editor Riviera-Times, Coral Gables, Fla., 1952-53; editorial writer Miami News (Fla.), 1953-60; account exec. E.A. Clay Pub. Relations, Coral Gables, 1960-67; exec. v.p. Greater Miami Ins. Bd., 1967-70; account exec. Bishopric & Fielden Advt., Miami, 1970-71; pub. relations rep. Fla. Power & Light Co., Miami, 1971—. Chmn. Paint Up, Fix Up, Clean Up com. City of Miami Beautification Com., 1964; mem. commr.'s staff S. Fla. council Boy Scouts Am., 1970—. Served with USAAF, 1943-46. Mem. Omicron Delta Kappa, Sigma Delta Chi, Sigma Alpha Epsilon. Baptist (deacon). Home: 7425 S W 34th Terrace Miami FL 33155 Office: 4200 W Flagler St Miami FL 33101

BAIER, A. LEIGH, bus. exec.; b. White Plains, N.Y., July 1, 1941; grad. Taft Sch., Watertown, Conn., 1959; B.A. in Polit. Economy, Williams Coll., 1963; LL.B., Duke, 1966; m. Alyse Gautier Lucas Corcoran. Admitted to Ga. bar; with firm Hansell, Post, Brandon &Dorsey, Atlanta, 1966-69; now pres., chmn. bd. Baier Corp., Atlanta; chmn. bd. First Atlanta Equity Corp., Restoration Atlanta, Inc. Bd. dirs. Atlanta Council Internat. Visitors; bd. sponsors Atlanta Symphony Orch. Mem. Atlanta Arts Alliance, Atlanta, Ga. bar assns., Atlanta Music Club (mem. men's adv. com.). Kiwanian. Clubs: Atlanta Polo, Commerce, Capital City, Lawyers (Atlanta); Carolina Yacht (Charleston, S.C.). Home: Glenwoods 1632 Ponce de Leon Av NE Atlanta GA 30307 Office: Baier Corp Equitable Bldg 100 Peachtree St NW Atlanta GA 30303

BAILES, PORTER M., JR., physician, state ofcl.; b. Greer, S.C., 1918; M.D., Baylor U., 1942. Intern Parkland Hosp., Dallas, 1942-43, asst., then sr. resident gen. surgery, 1946-49; mem. attending staff Med. Center Hosp., Tyler, Tex., Mother Frances Hosp., Tyler; cons. surgeon East Tex. Tb Hosp. Exec. officer Tex. Bd. Edn., Austin. Served to capt. AUS, 1943-46. Diplomate Am. Bd. Surgery. Fellow A.C.S.; mem. A.M.A., So. Med. Assn. Address: State Bd Edn State Capitol Austin TX 70761

BAILEY, AMOS PURNELL, clergyman; b. Grotons, Va., May 2, 1918; s. Louis William and Evelyn (Charnock) B.; B.A., Randolph-Macon Coll., 1942, D.D., 1956; B.D., Duke, 1948; Th.M., Union Theol. Sem., 1957;; m. Ruth Martin Hill, Aug. 22, 1942; children—Carol (Mrs. Thomas T. Harriman), Anne Ruth (Mrs. Peter S. Page), Joyce Elizabeth, Jeanne Purnell. Ordained to ministry United Methodist Ch., 1942; student pastor, Emporia, Va., 1938; pastor Richmond (Va.), Beulah Ch., 1938-43, New Kent (Va.) Circuit, 1943-44, Oak Grove Ch., Norfolk, Va., 1948-50, Grace Ch., Newport News, Va., 1950-54, Centenary Ch., Richmond, 1954-61; dist. supt. Richmond dist. Meth. Ch., 1961-67; sr. minister Reveille Ch., Richmond, 1967-70; exec. sec. Commn. on Chaplains, United Meth. Ch., Washington, 1970—. Mem. Meth. Commn. Higher Edn. 1960—, v.p. 1961; mem. Meth. Interbd. Council, 1960-70, Meth. Chaplains Commn., 1964—; mem. World Meth. Council; del. S.E. Jurisdictional Confs. Methodist Ch., 1964, 68; mem. Gen. Conf., 1964, 66, 68, 70 World Meth. Conf., London, Eng., 1966, Denver, 1971; mem. com. pastoral care, com. on ministry to servicemen Nat. Council Chs.; pres. joint radio com. S.E. Jurisdiction and S.C. Jurisdiction, 1968—, S.E. Jurisdiction Communications Commn., 1968—; mem. program and coordinating councils United Meth. Ch.; mem. family life com. Meth. Hist. Soc., mem. Council of secs., Dir. Interpretation, Interagy. Staff Com. on Research. Mem. adv. bd. VA Chaplaincy; mem. Armed Forces chaplains Bd.; trustee, mem. exec. com. trustees Randolph-Macon Coll.; trustee, mem. exec. com. So. Sem.; bd. dirs. Va. Meth. Advocate, 1952-66; bd. visitors Duke Div. Sch., 1962-68; bd. mgrs. Richmond YMCA. Served with Chaplain Corps, AUS, 1945-47. Mem. Duke Div. Alumni Assn. (past pres.), Coll. Chaplains, Assn. Mental Health Chaplains. Kiwanian. Author: syndicated column Bread of Life, 1945—; syndicated radio devotional Daily Bread, 1945—; The Night Pastor, religious counseling radio stas., 1955-69, Sunshine and Shadows, 1967-70. Meth. speaker on The Protestant Hour, 1962, 71. Contbr. articles to profl. publs. in U.S., Can., Eng., Australia, Japan; contbr. to Ency. of World Methodism. Home: 7815 Falstaff Rd McLean VA 22101 Office: 3900 Wisconsin Av NW Washington DC 20016

BAILEY, BOB GIPSON, bridge constrn. co. exec.; b. Vernon, Tex., Oct. 5, 1930; s. Earl M. and Mildred G. (Gipson) B.; B.A., Abilene Christian Coll., 1952; m. Ruth Heggie, Aug. 23, 1952; children—Becky, Lynn, Bryan. Partner, E. M. Bailey, contractor, Abilene, Tex., 1955-67; exec. v.p. Bailey Bridge Co., Abilene 1967—; co-owner Towne Crier Steakhouse, Lubbock, Tex.; dir. Bank of Commerce, Abilene. Pres., Highland Found., 1966-69; co-chmn. adv. bd. dirs. Abilene Christian Coll. Mem. Asso. Gen. Contractors, Tex. Restaurant Assn., Abilene C. of C. (bd. dirs. 1970—, v.p. 1972). Mem. Church of Christ. Kiwanian. Home: 1501 Hillview Rd Abilene TX 79601 Office: Box 3115 Abilene TX 79604

BAILEY, DANIEL MILTON, gas co. exec.; b. Marshall, Ill., May 9, 1908; s. Clarence Grover and Edith (Bush) B.; A.B., U. Okla., 1931, LL.B., 1930; grad. Advanced Mgmt. Program, Harvard, 1948; m. Miriam Nicholas, Apr. 15, 1933; children—Daniel Nicholas, Lynne Bailey. Admitted to Okla. bar, 1930, Tex. bar, 1934; with Continental-Emsco Co., Dallas, 1931-61, gen. counsel, 1937-61; v.p., 1950-61; exec. v.p. So. Union Gas Co., Dallas, 1961—, also dir. Served to maj. USAAF, 1942-45. Mem. Am. Bar Assn., Am. (dir.) So. (dir.) gas assns., Mid-Continent Oil and Gas Assn., Delta Upsilon, Phi Delta Phi. Clubs: Petroleum (dir.), Dallas, Northwood Country (Dallas). Home: 3549 Marquette St Dallas TX 75225 Office: Fidelity Union Tower Dallas TX 75201

BAILEY, GEORGE OSGOOD, physician; b. Sheboygan, Wis., Mar. 6, 1932; s. Morton Stevens and Fern Jeanette (Snow) B.; B.S., Furman U., 1956; M.D., Med. Coll. S.C., 1959; m. Joan Beverly Powell, Feb. 21, 1953; children—Dawn Marie, Steven Powell, George Osgood. Intern, Greenville (S.C.) Gen. Hosp., 1959-60; gen. practice medicine, Greenville, 1960—; chmn. family practice dept. Greenville Gen. Hosp., 1969—. Served with USNR, 1951-53. Diplomate Am. Bd. Family Practice. Mem. Am. Acad. Family Practice, A.M.A., So., S.C. med. assns., Greenville County Med. Soc., Assn. Am. Physicians and Surgeons, Greenville Jr. C. of C., Phi Rho Sigma, Chi Delta Phi. Rotarian. Home: 5 Barksdale Rd Greenville SC 29607 Office: 12 Greenacre Rd Greenville SC 29607

BAILEY, GUY VERNIE, transp. co. exec.; b. Alexander, N.C., Aug. 7, 1929; s. Allen Lee and Lydia (Bradshaw) B.; A.A., Asheville-Biltmore Coll., 1954; B.S., U. Tenn., 1957; m. Weyburn Lewis Reid, Aug. 6, 1955; children—Kay Lynn, Barry Douglas, Mgmt. trainee R. C. Motor Lines, Jacksonville, Fla., 1957-60; v.p. Valley Transfer, Inc., Lenoir, N.C., 1960-66, pres., 1966—, chmn. bd. dirs., 1966-69. Precinct chmn. Republican Party, 1967. Served with AUS, 1951-53. Mem. N.C. Motor Carriers Assn. Baptist (trustee, deacon). Republican. Rotarian (pres. 1965-66, dist. chmn. 1969-70). Home: Moore-Lan Park PO Box 88 Granite Falls NC 28630 Office: 233 Country Side Dr PO Box 26 Lenoir NC 28645

BAILEY, HERBERT JOHN, banker; b. Anderson, Ala., Oct. 4, 1907; s. Henry Dee and Edna Frances (Dunkle) B.; grad. high sch.; m. Mabel Anne Jordan, Mar. 3, 1934. Asst. mgr. Planters & Mchts. Bank, Minor Hill, Tenn., 1928-31; cashier, dir. East Lauderdale Banking Co., Rogersville, Ala., 1932-42; v.p., cashier, dir. Parker Bank & Trust Co., Cullman, Ala., 1946—. Registered Angus cattle breeder, Cullman, 1961—. Served with AUS, 1942-45. Named County Key Banker, Ala. Bankers Assn., 1970. Mem. Ala. Bankers Assn. (group chmn. 1969—), Am. (conv. del. 1970), Ala. angus assns. Presbyn. Club: Civitan (v.p. 1936). Address: PO Box 615 Cullman AL 35055

BAILEY (EDWARD) JAMES, journalist; b. Klamath Falls, Ore., Sept. 18, 1932; s. Merrill Leon and Lillian (Smith) B.; B.S., Armstrong Coll., Berkeley, Cal., 1953; m. Joan Madeleine Henrion, Nov. 7, 1959; 1son, Christopher Franklin. Asso. editor Daily Pacific Builder, San Francisco, 1954-59; exec. asst. Cal. Council, A.I.A., San Francisco, 1959-62, dir. Information Services, Washington, 1962-65; sr. editor Archtl. Forum mag., N.Y.C., 1965-69; dep. dir. Urban Information Center, also mng. editor City, Urban Am., Inc., Washington, 1969—. Home: 4317 Stanford Ct Chevy Chase MD 20015 Office: 1717 Masssachusetts Av NW Washington DC 20036

BAILEY, JAMES DONALD, dentist; b. Cleburne, Tex., Dec. 30, 1929; s. Harold B. and Roxa Ann (Young) B.; student N. Tex. State Coll., 1949-53; B.S., Tex. Wesleyan Coll., 1956; D.D.S., Baylor U., 1960, M.S. in Dentistry, 1962; m. Betty Sue Seawright, Aug. 1, 1953; children—Rebecca Sue, Jerry Dale, Cathy Gale. Pvt. practice pediatric dentistry, El Paso, Tex., 1962—; chief dental service R. E. Thomason Hosp., El Paso, 1964-65, Sun Towers Hosp., El Paso, 1969-70, Providence Meml. Hosp., El Paso, 1964-65, 71-72; cons. pedodontics William Beaumont Army Hosp., 1963—; clin. instr. Baylor U. Coll. Dentistry, 1960—; treas., dir. Normac, Inc., El Paso, 1967—. Served with AUS, 1953-55. Mem. Am. Soc. Dentistry for Children (pres. Tex. chpt. 1969-70), S.W. Soc. Pedodontics (dir. 1969-70), Am. Dental Assn., Tex., El Paso (pres. 1968-69) dental socs., Xi Psi Phi. Mason. Home: 5200 Yucca Pl El Paso TX 79932 Office: 2101 N Oregon St El Paso TX 79902

BAILEY, JAMES EDWARD, architect; b. Birmingham, Ala., Jan. 7, 1932; s. Clifton Owen and Ila Browning (Ayers) B.; B. Arch., Auburn U., 1955; m. Myrtle Elizabeth Jone, Sept. 8, 1951; 1 son, Daniel Edwin. Architect, Charles McCauly, 1957-58; with H.S. Long, Architect, Birmingham, 1958-65; pvt. practice architecture, Birmingham, 1965—. Served with AUS, 1955-57. Mem. A.I.A. Baptist (deacon). Club: Civitan (pres. Green Acres club 1958-59). Home: 3324 Stoneridge Dr Birmingham AL 35223 Office: 200 Office Park Dr Birmingham AL 35223

BAILEY, JAMES EVERETT, chem. co. exec.; b. nr. Kosciusko, Miss., Nov. 13, 1923; s. Everett E. and Gladys Estelle (O'Briant) B.; B.S., Miss. State U., 1949, M.S., 1951; m. Mary Louise Kuykendall, Dec. 24, 1943; children—James Everett, Wesley Wayne, Lou Anne. Spl. agt. FBI, N.Y.C., 1950-54; salesman Chapman Chem. Co., Memphis, 1954-60, Chemagro Corp., Kansas City, Mo., Memphis, 1960-69; salesman Occidental Chem. Co. div. Occidental Petroleum Co., Houston, 1971—. Tchr., Miss. State U., 1948, 49. Served with USNR, 1944-46. Mem. Am. Legion, V.F.W., Soc. Former FBI Agts., Pi Kappa Alpha, Omicron Delta Kappa, Blue Key. Republican. Episcopalian. Mason. Home: 5440 Braesvalley Houston TX 77035 Office: Box 1185 Houston TX 77001

BAILEY, JAMES HINTON POU, judge; b. Balt., Aug. 14, 1917; s. Josiah W. and Edith (Pou) B.; grad. Woodberry Forest Sch., 1935; A.B., U. N.C., 1940, J.D., 1941; m. Marie Fiquet Pate, Aug. 1, 1945 (dec. Oct. 1968); children—James H. Pou, Edwin Pate; m. 2d, Ann T. 1941; practiced in Raleigh, N.C., 1946-65; mem. firm Bailey & Bason, 1954-62, Bailey & Ragsdale, 1962-65; resident judge Superior Ct., 10th Jud. Dist., 1965—; gen. counsel N.C. Bankers Assn., 1953-65; spl. agt. Washington, FBI, 1941; mem. faculty Nat. Coll. State Trial Judges, 1968. Active, Occoneeche council Boy Scouts Am., 1953-60; chmn. Raleigh Traffic Safety Council. Mem. N.C. State Senate, 1950-54; mem. N.C. Gen. Statutes Commn., 1953-59; chmn. Senate Judiciary Com., 1953. Served from pvt. to capt. AUS, 1942-46. Mem. Am., N.C., Wake County (mem. exec. com 1947-49), 10th Dist. (pres. 1963-64) bar assns., C. of C. (mem. exec. com. 1952-53)., Nat. Rifle Assn. (life), US Power Squadrons (rear comdr. 1971—), Alpha Tau Omega. Democrat. Presbyn. Home: 1509 Chester Rd Raleigh NC 27608 Office: Wake County Court House Raleigh NC 27602

BAILEY, JAMES LOVELL, state ofcl.; b. Portland, Tenn., Dec. 18, 1907; s. James Johnson and Annie May (Lovell) B.; student Bowling Green U., 1925, Middle Tenn. State Tchrs. Coll., 1926-29, Western Ky. State Coll., 1929-30, George Washington U., 1931-33, U. Tenn., 1938-41; m. Fairrelle Brown, June 1, 1940; 1 dau., Annie Elizabeth. With U.S. Bur. of Census, 1930-32, U.S. Dept. of Agr., 1933-37; with Tenn. Dept. Conservation, Nashville 1937—, dir. ednl. service, 1957—. Pres. Davidson County (Tenn.) chpt. Muscular Dystrophy Assn., 1957. Mem. edn. com. Tenn. Bot. Gardens and Fine Arts Center, Nashville, 1969—. Trustee Southeastern Indian Antiquities Survey; charter mem., bd. dirs. Tenn. Environmental Council, 1970— Tenn. Beautiful, 1972—. Served with USNR, 1942-45. Recipient awards including Cartter Patten award Tenn. Conservation League, 1963, Key Man award Conservation Edn. Assn., 1967, Gov.'s Conservationist of Year award, 1971. Fellow Soil Conservation Soc. Am. (pres. Tenn council chpts. 1961); mem. Middle Tenn. Conservancy Council, E. Tenn. Edn. Assn., Nat. Assn. Conservation Edn. and Publicity, Conservation Edn. Assn., Keep Tenn. Green Assn., Tenn. Hist. Soc., Nat. Wildlife Fedn., Tenn. Assn. Preservation Antiquities, Tenn. Fedn. Garden Clubs Inc. (life). Club: Nashville Torch (pres. 1963-64). Author: Our Land and Our Living, 1940. Asso. editor Tenn. Conservationist, 1959—. Home: 450 Moss Trail Goodlettsville TN 37072 Office: 2611 West End Av Nashville TN 37203

BAILEY, JOE HARDEN, librarian; b. Dallas, Jan. 16, 1918; s. David Joseph and Minnie Belle (Perry) B.; B.A., N. Tex. State Coll., 1938, M.A., 1941; B.S., George Peabody Coll. for Tchrs., 1946, postgrad., 1951-53; m. Elizabeth Lloyd DeBrohun, July 26, 1946; children—Elizabeth Lloyd, Margaret Anne. Prin. Carrollton Elementary Sch., 1939-41; librarian Union Grove High Sch., Gladewater, Tex., 1941-42; periodicals and ref. librarian So. Meth. U., 1946-47; librarian, head library sch. Murray State Coll., 1947-51; grad. asst. library sch. George Peabody Coll. for Tchrs., 1951-53; librarian W. Tex. State Coll., Canyon, 1953-57, N. Tex. State U., Denton, 1957—. Served as sgt. M.C., AUS, 1942-45. Mem. A.L.A., Southwestern (treas.), Ky. (dir. 1949-51), Tex. library assns., Western Ky. Ednl. Assn., Tex. Edn. Assn., Tex. Panhandle Audubon Soc. (pres. 1955, dir. 1956), Am. Ornithologist Union, Pi Delta Kappa, Kappa Delta Phi. Author: (with Elizabeth L. Bailey) Checklist of the Birds of the Panhandle of Texas, 1956. Contbr. to library lit. Home: 2010 N Locust St Denton TX 76201

BAILEY, JOSEPH PEDEN, physician; b. Liberty, S.C., June 4, 1917; s. John Crooks and Annie Mabel (Cantey) B.; B.S., Davidson Coll., 1938; M.D., Med. Coll. S.C., 1943; m. Louise King Howe, Sept. 16, 1944; children—Joseph Peden, William Howe, Robert Woodward. Intern St. Francis Xavier Hosp., Charleston, S.C., 1943; intern Greenville (S.C.) Gen. Hosp., 1944, resident, 1945; student Sch. Mil. Neuropsychiatry, Mason Gen. Hosp., Brentwood, L.I., N.Y., 1945; gen. practice medicine, Hendersonville, N.C., 1947—; mem. staff Pardee Meml. Hosp. Served to capt. M.C., AUS, 1945-47. Mem. Henderson County Med. Soc. (pres. 1954), A.M.A. Presbyn. (elder 1955-65). Home: PO Box 241 Flat Rock NC 28731 Office: 559 N Justice Hendersonville NC 28739

BAILEY, LLOYD WHITFIELD, physician; b. Phila., Mar. 24, 1928; s. Clarence Whitfield and Olive (Magnusson) B.; B.S., Wake Forest Coll., 1949; M.D., Jefferson Med. Coll. Phila., 1953; postgrad. U. Pa., 1957-58; m. Ann Witherspoon Lewis, July 29, 1955; children—Lloyd Whitfield, Linda Lee, Joan Lewis, Intern, Jefferson Med. Coll. Hosp., Phila., 1953-54; resident Wills Eye Hosp., Phila., 1958-60; practice medicine, specializing in ophthalmology, Rocky Mount, N.C., 1960—; mem. staff Park View Hosp., Nash Gen. Hosp., Rocky Mount Sanatorium. Chmn. disaster com. A.R.C., Rocky Mount, 1963-69; mem. Nash County Republican Exec. Com., 1966-68; Presdl. elector for 2d Congl. Dist. N.C., 1968; mem. exec. com. Am. party of N.C., 1970-71. Served with USAF, 1955-57. Mem. So. Med. Assn. (life), Med. Soc. State N.C., Nash County Med. Soc., Am. Assn. Ophthalmology, Wills Eye Hosp. Soc., N.C. Soc. Ophthalmology and Otolaryngology, Am. Assn. Phys. and Surg., U.S. Power Squadron, Ducks Unltd., John Birch Soc. (life), Kappa Alpha, Phi Chi. Baptist. Home: 3813 Hawthorne Rd Rocky Mount NC 27801 Office: 147 NE Main St Rocky Mount NC 27801

BAILEY, PAUL EDWIN, dentist; b. nr. Huntington, Ind., Apr. 14, 1912; s. George Albert and Elmina (Myers) B.; B.S., Marion Coll., 1933, A.B., 1934; D.D.S., Ind. U., 1950; m. Mildred Elizabeth Gillis, Jan. 23, 1943; children—James Malcolm, Paul Edwin, Robert Eugene. Chemist Anaconda Wire & Cable Co., 1935-41; gen. practice dentistry, Hattiesburg, Miss., 1950—; mem. staff Meth. Hosp. Mem. adv. bd. Salvation Army; committeeman Boy Scouts Am. Sec. Forrest County Republican Exec. Com., chmn., 1972—. Served with AUS, 1941-46. Fellow Internat. Coll. Dentists; mem. Am., Miss. (trustee) dental assns., Forrest County, East Dist. dental socs., Assn. Am. Dentists, Acad. Gen. Dentistry, Am. Profl. Practice Assn., Am. Legion, V.F.W., Am. Numismatic Assn., Hattiesburg C. of C., Delta Sigma Delta. Presbyn. Elk. Home: 122 Short Bay St Hattiesburg MS 39401 Office: 509 Main St Hattiesburg MS 39401

BAILEY, ROBERT WILSON, army officer, optometrist; b. Bellefountaine, O., Oct. 7, 1920; s. James Edgar and Myrtle L. (Wilson) B.; B.S., Ohio State U., 1950, M.S., 1968; postgrad. Ind. U., 1963; m. Jeanne Irene Denser, Dec. 26, 1942; children—James E., Robert P., Barbara J., Diana E. Commd. 2d lt. U.S. Army, 1939, advanced through grades to col., 1969; active duty, 1939-46; optometrist Walter Reed Army Hosp., Washington, 1950-51, Army Navy Hosp., Hot Springs, Ark., 1951-54, Army Environmental Health Lab., Md., 1954-57, Army Med. Research Lab., Ft. Knox, Ky., 1958-60, Army Aeromed. Research Lab., Ft. Rucker, Ala., 1963—. Decorated Legion of Merit. Recipient Safety award McClellan Aviation, 1970. Fellow Aerospace Med. Assn., Am. Acad. Optometry; mem. Am. Helicopter Soc. (pres. Jake Fortner chpt. 1969-72), Am. Optometric Assn., Nat. Research Council (mem. com. on vision, and com. on hearing and bioacoustics 1959-72). Editorial council Am. Jour. Optometry, 1969-72. Contbr. articles to profl. jours. Home: 17 Ferguson St Fort Rucker AL 36360 Office: PO Box 577 Fort Rucker AL 36360

BAILEY, SCOTT FIELD, bishop; b. Houston, Oct. 7, 1916; s. William Stuart and Tallulah (Smith) B.; B.A., Rice U., 1938; student U. Tex. Law Sch., 1938-39; B.D., Va. Theol. Sem., 1942, D.D., 1965; D.D., U. of South, 1965; m. Evelyn Williams, Dec. 11, 1943; children—Louise (Mrs. Allen C. Taylor), Nicholas, Scott Field, Sarah. Ordained to ministry Episcopalian Ch., 1942; pastor in Waco, Lampasas, San Augustine and Austin, Tex., 1942-61; asst. to bishop of Tex., 1961-64; suffragan bishop of Tex., 1964—. Sec. house of bishops Episcopal Ch., 1967—. Served as chaplain USNR, World War II. Fellow Coll. Preachers; mem. Phi Delta Theta. Home: 5309

Mandell St Houston TX 77005 Office: 520 San Jacinto Houston TX 77002

BAILEY, THOMAS EDWARD, engring. co. exec.; b. Milw., Oct. 25, 1930; s. Thomas Johnson and Adele Louise (Doering) B.; B.S., Northwestern U., 1953; m. Betty Lou Wells, Sept. 21, 1957; children—Thomas Mark, Thomas Alan, Thomas Lynn. Test engr. Soil Testing Services, Inc., Chgo., 1953, 56; structural engr. Stearns Roger Mfg. Co., Denver, 1956-58; with Reed-Mullins & Assos., architects and engrs., Fayetteville, Tenn., 1958-72, v.p., 1969-72; with Teledyne Engring. Co., Huntsville, Ala., 1972—. Task force chmn. Elk River Devel. Assn., 1970-71; chmn. Fayetteville Regional Planning Commn., 1963-69, sec., 1970-72; mem. Fayetteville Gas Bd., 1970-72. Vice chmn. bd. dirs. Multi County Mental Health Center, Tullahoma, Tenn., 1969-72. Served with AUS, 1953-55. Recipient poetry prize Tenn. Poetry Contest, 1970. Mem. Am. Soc. C.E., Nat. Model R.R. Assn. (regional sec. 1970-72, regional v.p. 1972, various awards 1964-70). Presbyn. (mem. session 1967-72). Home: Route 1 Fayetteville TN 37334 Office: Research Park Huntsville AL 35807

BAILEY, WILLIAM DAVID, orgn. exec.; b. Jackson, Miss., Oct. 30, 1935; s. Charles E. and Emmie (Roberts) B.; student Millsaps Coll., 1953-55, U. Houston, summers 1961-66; m. Sylvia Royce Golmon, July 18, 1956; 1 son, Charles Alan. Instr. choral music Jackson Pub. Sch. System, 1956-57; adminstrv. asst. IBM Corp., Jackson, 1957-59; dir. pub. relations and advt. 1st Miss. Corp., Jackson, 1959-60; asso. dir. pub. relations Lamar Life Ins. Co., Jackson, 1960-61; exec. v.p. Pascagoula (Miss.) C. of C., 1961-69; exec. v.p. Dothan (Ala.) C. of C., 1969-72; cons. Tri-Rivers Devel. Assn., 1972—. Sec., Pascagoula Planning Commn., 1964-66; chmn. water safety com. Jackson County chpt. A.R.C., 1962, asso. chmn., disaster com., 1963-67. Mem. Am., Miss. (pres. 1967-68), So. (dir. 1964-66) assns. chamber commerce execs. Home: 213 Junaluska Dothan AL 36301 Office: PO Box 1406 Dothan AL 36301

BAILEY, WILLIAM S., elec. contracting exec.; b. Calvert, Tex., Aug. 13, 1907; s. William S. and Tallulah (Smith) B.; B.A., Rice U., 1930; m. Jessie Jones, Oct. 1, 1931; children—William S., Margaret Elizabeth. With Jesse Jones Interests, Tex., 1930-42; v.p. corporate sales client devel. program dir. Fischbach & Moore, Inc., Houston, 1946-69, sr. v.p., 1969—; dir. MacGregor Park Nat. Bank. Bd. dirs. Air Force Acad. Served with USAAF, 1942-46. Episcopalian. Clubs: Houston, Petroleum, Old Capitol, Fort Worth, University, Lakeside Country. Home: 5552 Tupper Lake Rd Houston TX 77027 Office: Gulf Bldg Houston TX 77002

BAILEY, WILSON MONROE, mfg. co. exec.; b. Altha, Fla., Mar. 1, 1897; s. David Samuel and Ella M. (Coxwell) B.; student pub. schs.; m. Thelma Clary, May 22, 1919; children—Inez (Mrs. M. C. Eldridge), Wilson L., Betty Jo (Mrs. Tommy Miller). Pres., Coastal Variety Works, Inc., Blountstown, Fla., 1960—. Dir. Calhoun County Indsl. Commn., county commr., 1939-52. Mason (Shriner), Lion. Home: 1106 S Pearl St Blountstown FL 32424 Office: 2 1/2 MS Hwy 71 Blountstown FL 32424

BAILY, NATHAN A(RIEL), govt. ofcl., educator; b. N.Y.C., July 19, 1920; s. Saul and Eleanor (Mintz) B.; B.S.S., Coll. City N.Y., 1940; M.A., Columbia, 1941; Ph.D., 1946; m. Judith Bernstein, June 20, 1946; children—Alan Eric, Lawrence Joel. Economist OPA; sr. editor-economic analyst Research Inst. Am. moderator District Viewpoint, weekly TV program; faculty Advanced Sch. Retail Mgmt. Nat. Sales Execs., Rutgers U., Stonier Grad. Sch. Banking; hon. faculty mem. U.S. Army Mgmt. Sch.; instr., hon. dean faculty Washington chpt., mem. nat. ednl. adv. com. Am. Inst. of Banking; mem. history and econs. dept. Coll. City N.Y.; instr. Fashion Inst. Tech. and Design, N.Y.C.; faculty Am. U. Sch. Bus. Adminstrn., 1946—, prof. bus. adminstrn. and finance, 1953—, dean, 1955-70; mem. Postal Rate Commn., 1970—; dir. Washington Mut. Investors Fund, Carl M. Freeman & Assos., Carrols Devel. Corp., Am. Wholesalers, Inc.; bd. advisers Columbia Realty Trust, Fed. Realty Investment Trust; ednl. cons. Nat. Appliance-Radio-TV Dealers Assn., Inst. Indsl. Launderers; editorial adv. bd. Internat. Classics Press; cons., participant tng. programs Milk Industry Found., Social Security Adminstrn., Electric Inst. of Washington, Internat. Bank for Reconstrn., IBM. Gen. Electric; ednl. cons. WDCA-TV. Mem. D.C. Small Bus. Adv. Council; mem D.C. adv. council for State Tech. Services Act; mem. Commn. on Ch. Family Financial Planning; nat. mgmt. selection bd. U.S. Post Office. Trustee Council on Opportunities in Selling; bd. dirs. Friends of U.S. Latin Am., Pioneer Found., Homer Hovt. Inst.; chmn. Invest-In-Am. nat. adv. council on econ. edn. Recipient fellowship E. I. duPont de Nemours, Swift & Co., Danforth Found. Harvard Bus. Sch., Volker Fund U. N.C. Mem. A.I.M., Am. Econ. Assn., Am. Assn. U. Profs., Middle Atlantic Assn. Colls. of Bus. Adminstrn. (pres. 1964-65), Washington Sales Execs. Club (dir. 1962-63), Washington Bd. Trade, Washington Real Estate Bd. (affiliate mem.), Suburban Md. Builders Assn. (hon. mem., econ. cons.), U.S. C. of C. (com. anti-trust and trade regulation, dir. 1969-71), Phi Beta Kappa, Omicron Delta Kappa. Editor: Marketing Profitably Under the Robinson-Patman Act, 1963. Contbg. editor: Modern Security Services. Office: Postal Rate Commn Washington DC 20068

BAIN, HELEN LORENE PATE (MRS. D. F. BAIN), educator; b. Nashville, May 9, 1924; d William Buford and Florence (Whitt) Pate; B.A., Peabody Coll., 1945; M.A., U. Mich., 1948; m. D. F. Bain, June 25, 1946; children—Kenneth Pate, David Oscar. Tchr. English and speech Cohn High Sch., Nashville, 1947—. Mem. Peabody Coll. Devel. Council, Nashville, 1966—; bd. dirs. Nashville Sr. Citizens' Com., 1966—; mem. Citizens and Politics, 1965—; pres. Met. Nashville Tchrs. Apart, Inc.; mem. Nat. Adv. Council or Supplementary Centers and Service, 1968—. Mem. N.E.A. (past pres.). Baptist. Home: 4427 Lealand Lane Nashville TN 37204 Office: 4805 Park Av Nashville TN 37209

BAINBRIDGE, THOMAS RUTHERFORD, textile mfg. exec.; b. Savannah, Ga., May 22, 1917; s. Herbert Bartholomew and Edith Davis (Nichols) B.; B.S., Clemson Coll., 1939; m. Clyde Hellen Schuler, Sept. 15, 1940; children—Carl Davis, Steven Nichols. With acetate yarn div. Tenn. Eastman Co., Kingsport, 1939—, lab. supr., 1947-48, supr. quality inspection, 1948-53, asst. supt. quality and standards, 1953-62, supt. quality and standards, 1962—. Moderator Holston Prebytery, Presbyn. Ch., 1969, central treas. benevolences Holsten Presbytery, 1958-63, chmn. com. on women's work, 1968, chmn. com. on stewardship, 1969, chmn. com. on restudy and reorgn., 1969-71, chmn. com. on crisis, 1971. Trustee Presbyn. Sch. of Christian Edn. Served to maj. AUS, 1942-46. Recipient Braumbaugh award Am. Soc. for Quality Control, 1966. Fellow Am. Soc. Quality Control; mem. Am. Soc. Testing and Materials, Phi Kappa Phi, Alpha Chi Sigma. Home: 4527 Timberlake Lane Kingsport TN 37664 Office: Tenn Eastman Co Kingsport TN 37662

BAIRD, DUKE BARNETT, orthopedic surgeon; b. Oklahoma City, Dec. 3, 1921; s. Duke and Margaret (Galyon) B.; student U. Miss., 1943-44; M.D., Med. Coll. Ala., 1949; m. Nadine Blackwood, June 29, 1946; children—Daren, Duke II, Nini, John Henry; m. 2d, Cheryl Gorman, June 11, 1971. Orthopedic resident N.Y. Orthopedic Hosp., Columbia Presbyn. Med. Center, N.Y.C., 1954-57; gen. practice orthopedic surgery, Hialeah, Fla., 1957—; asst. prof. orthopedic surgery U. Miami Med. Sch., 1954—. Bd. dirs. Am. Cancer Soc. Served with AUS, 1942-45, USNR, 1949-50, 51-52, USAF, 1952-54. Diplomate Am. Bd. Orthopedic Surgeons. Fellow Am. Acad. Orthopaedic Surgery; mem. Am. So., Fla. med. assns. Home: 828 Lake Dr Miami Springs FL Office: 2825 E 4th Av Hialeah FL 33012

BAIRD, EDWARD ALLEN, basso, educator; b. Kansas City, Mo., Mar. 18, 1933; s. Edward Allen and Mary Sue (Bradley) B.; B.A., U. Mo. Kansas City, 1955, M.A., 1957; D.Mus. Arts, 1962; m. Shirley Jean Vedder, June 29, 1952; 1 son, Keith Allen. Supr. music recreation div. of Kansas City (Mo.) Welfare Dept., 1954-56; instr. music Midland Coll., Fremont, Neb., 1956-59, asst. prof. music, 1959-60, chmn. dept. fine arts, 1957-60; grad. teaching fellow U. Mich., 1960-62; instr. voice Nat. Music Camp, Interlochen, Mich., 1962; asst. prof. music N. Tex. State U., Denton, 1962-64, asso. prof., 1964-68, prof., 1968—. Basso with orchestras, operas, recitals including Houston Grand Opera, San Diego (Cal.) Opera, Kansas City Lyric Opera, Fort Worth Opera, St. Louis Opera Theater, Corpus Christi Opera, New Orleans Opera, Beaumont Opera; guest soloist Dallas, Chgo. symphonies, Kansas City Philharmonic, New Orleans Symphony, San Angelo (Tex.) Symphony, Corpus Christi Symphony. Mem. Am. Assn. U. Profs., Tex. Music Educators Assn., Tex. Assn. Coll. Tchrs., Nat. Assn. Tchrs. Singing (gov Southwestern region), Am. Choral Dirs. Assn., Tex. Choral Dirs. Assn. Pi Kappa Lambda, Omicron Delta Kappa, Phi Mu Alpha, Tau Kappa Epsilon. Presbyn. Home: 2602 Woodhaven Dr Denton TX 76201

BAIRD, JAMES OSCAR, coll. pres.; b. Lebanon, Tenn., Jan. 16, 1920; s. James O. and Harriet (Morrow) B.; student Freed-Hardeman Coll., Henderson, Tenn., 1938-40; B.A., George Peabody Coll. for Tchrs., 1941, M.A., 1942, Ph.D., 1948; student Princeton Theol. Sem., 1943-44, Rutgers U., 1940-41; m. Mary Avanelle Elliott, May 31, 1946; children—Harriet Adelle, Lynn M., Elisa F., James, Morrow Beth. Prof. Bible and sociology David Lipscomb Coll., Nashville, 1944-50; dean Okla. Christian Coll., Oklahoma City, 1950-54, pres., 1954—; staff The Ministers Monthly, 20th Century Christian, Teenage Christian; speaker, lecturer. Pres. Council for Advancement Small Colls. Mem. N.E.A., Newcomen Soc., C. of C., Phi Delta Kappa, Kappa Delta Pi, Kappa Delta Kappa, Pi Gamma Mu. Kiwanian. Author: The Life and Times of Charles Edgar Little, 1948. Contbr. articles religious jours. Home: Route 3 Box 243 B Edmond OK 73034

BAIREY, W(OLFGANG) ZEV BRONNER, educator; b. Vienna, Austria, Mar. 11, 1920; s. Jacob Hirsch Bronner and Edith S. (Epstein) B.; B.Sc., U. Cal. at Berkeley, 1940; M.A., U. of Americas (Mexico), 1968; m. Gloria Elana Haydis, Sept. 21, 1946; children—Daniel, Miryam Seona, Ariela Raquel, Guita Zivia. Dir. research Matmor Canning Co., Inc., Woodland, Cal., 1944-47; 1st dep. dir. Govt. Israel Investment Center, 1950-53; investment adviser for various cos., also self-employed, N.Y., Houston, Mexico, 1954-68; chmn. dept. econs. U. of Americas, Cholala, Mexico, 1970—. Econ. cons. Pres., Beth Israel Community Center, Mexico City, 1960-64; chmn. Commn. on Edn., S.W. Region, United Synagogue of Am., 1968—. Served with Israel Def. Forces, 1948-49. Mem. A.A.A.S., Am. Econ. Assn., Omicron Delta Epsilon. Asso. editor Tlaltelolco Monographs, 1968—. Home: Montes Urales 610 Mexico City 10 D F Mexico Office: Apartado 10-756 Mexico City 10 D F Mexico

BAKER, BENJAMIN RIVES, dentist; b. Durham, N.C., July 25, 1928; s. Newell Edward and Edith (Rives) B.; A.B., Guilford Coll., 1951; M.Ed., U. N.C., 1952, D.D.S., 1961, M.S., 1964; m. Mary Elizabeth Barney, July 30, 1949; children—Drury Penn, Mary Bennett. Coach, tchr. Liberty (N.C.) High Sch., 1952-53; recreation dir., Liberty, 1952-53; coach, instr. phys. edn. Guilford Coll., 1953-57; instr. pedodontics U. N.C., Chapel Hill, 1961-62, asst. prof. pedodontics, 1964-68, dir. dental aux. tchr. edn., 1966-68; pvt. practice pedodontics, Kinston, N.C., 1968—. Served with M.C., AUS, 1945-47. Recipient Nat. Sci. Writing award for corr. textbooks, 1969. NIH fellow Lancaster Cleft Palate Clinic, 1964. Mem. Am. Acad. Pedodontics, Am. Dental Assn., Royal Soc. Health, N.C. Dental Soc., N.C. Soc. Dentistry for Children (pres. 1970-71). Southeastern, N.C. socs. pedodontics, Xi Psi Phi, Phi Delta Kappa, Econodontic Study Club, Demerit Study Club, Yaupon Soc., C. of C. Rotarian. Clubs: Kinston (dir. 1970—), Kinston (N.C.) Country. Co-author: (textbooks) Clinical Sciences, 1970, Clinical Application, 1970; contbg. author Dental Assistant, 1970. Editor N.C. Dental Jour., 1969-72. Home: 1709 Cambridge Dr Kinston NC 28501 Office: 2101 N Herritage St Kinston NC 28501

BAKER, BILL BERT, coll. adminstr.; b. Gilbert, Ark., July 19, 1932; s. Noel Riley and Lucille (Moore) B.; B.S., Ark. Tech., 1953; M.S., U. Ark., 1954, Ed.D., 1962; m. Bonnie Jean King, July 13, 1953; children—Bill Bert II, Joe Brian, Julia Jane. Coach, West Fork (Ark.) High Sch., 1953-54; asst. coach, instr. Ark. Tech., Russellville, 1957-59, dir. pub. relations, 1960-68, dean students, athletic dir., 1968—. Cons. Ark. Sch. Bd. Assn. Mem. Govs. Adv. Council on Childhood Edn., 1967—; v.p. West Ark. council Boy Scouts of Am., 1967-69. Bd. dirs. Wesley Found., Ark. Jr. Miss. Served with AUS, 1955-57. Mem. Nat. Assn. Student Personnel Adminstrs., N.E.A., Ark. Edn. Assn., Ark. Sch. Adminstrs. Assn., Nat. Assn. Coll. Athletic Dirs., Ark. High Sch. Coaches Assn., Phi Delta Kappa. Methodist. Mason (32 deg.); mem. Order Eastern Star (past patron). Home: 1414 W 2d Pl Russellville AR 72801

BAKER, BROUGHTON LEONARD, educator; b. Columbia, S.C., July 26, 1912; s. Andrew Charles and Lilliam (Yarbrough) B.; B.S. in Chem. Engring., U.S.C., 1933 Ph.D., in Chem. Engring., N.C. State Coll., 1955; m. Mary Rawls, Oct. 22, 1952; children—Thomas, Julianne. Chem. engr. Gen. Chem. Co., 1935-40, C.W.S., 1940-42; plant mgr. Naylee Chem. Co., 1942-44; sec. Elliott Labs., Inc., 1944-46; with U. S.C., Columbia, 1946—, successively asso. prof. chmn. div. chem. engring, 1946-56, prof., head dept. chem. engring., 1956-68, prof. engring., 1968—; research participant Oak Ridge Inst. Nuclear Studies, 1951. Mem. S.C. Bd. Engring. Examiners. Registered profl. engr., S.C. Mem. Am. Inst. Chem. Engrs., Am. Chem. Soc., Am. Soc. for Engring. Edn., Nat. Soc. Profl. Engrs., S.C. Soc. Engrs. (pres. 1965), S.C. Acad. Scis., Sigma Xi, Tau Beta Pi, Omicron Delta Kappa. Baptist. Kiwanian. Address: 819 Burwell Lane Columbia SC 29205

BAKER, CHARLES BELK, structural engr.; b. Sumter, S.C., Aug. 4, 1933; s. John Henry and Charlotte M. (Belk) B.; B.S., The Citadel, 1955; m. Stephanie Jeanne Counts, Oct. 28, 1962; children—Charles Belk II, John Steven, Charlotte Suzanne, Shannon Elizabeth. Design engr., civil engring. dept., dept. pub. works U.S. Navy, Charleston, S.C., 1955-58; chief engr., prodn. supr. Perma-Stress, Inc., Daytona Beach, Fla., 1958-62; asst. chief engr. So. Prestressed Concrete, Inc., Pensacola, Fla., 1963-71, chief structural devel. engr., 1971—. Served to 1st lt. C.E., AUS, 1955-57. Registered profl. engr., Ala., Fla. Mem. Nat. Soc. Profl. Engrs., Fla. Engring. Soc. (chpt. pres. 1969; outstanding mem. award 1967), Prestressed Concrete Inst. Baptist. Kiwanian (pres. 1971—). Home: 3885 Summer Dr Pensacola FL 32504 Office: So Prestressed Concrete Inc PO Box 2338 Pensacola FL 32503

BAKER, CLIFFORD HOWARD, marketing research co. exec.; b. Paoli, Ind., Oct. 14, 1932; s. James A. and Alice (Limeberry) B.; B.S., U.S. Mil. Acad., 1956; M.S., Purdue U., 1965; m. Joan B. Meyer, Feb. 4, 1958; children—Steven Conrad, Bradford Nelson, Paul Milton, Jeffrey Todd, Douglas Ross. Indsl. marketing exec. Tex. Instruments, Dallas, 1959-61; market research exec. Gen. Motors Corp., Kokomo, Ind., 1961-65; supr. market analysis Corning Glass Works, Raleigh, N.C., 1965-70; pres. Market Research & Statistics Co., Raleigh, 1970—. Served with AUS, 1956-59. Recipient Nat. Def. Service medal West Point, 1956. Mem. I.E.E.E., Assn. Grads. West Point, Adminstrv. Mgmt. Soc. Mem. Ch. of Christ. Republican. Home: 4816 Deerwood Dr Raleigh NC 27609 Office: 3901 Barrett Dr Raleigh NC 27609

BAKER, DANIEL RICHARD, systems analyst; b. nr. Rostock, Denmark, Mar. 19, 1932; s. Arthur and Molly (Needman) B.; Came to U.S., 1936, naturalized, 1945; student Tufts Coll., 1949-51; B.A., Bklyn. Coll., 1957; m. June Ellin Nebenzahl, Oct. 2, 1960; children—David Charles, Jill Alison. Math tchr. Bd. Edn., N.Y.C., 1958-59; computer programmer Systems Devel. Corp., Paramus, N.J., 1959-61; programmer analyst I.T&T., Paramus, 1961-64; sr. mathematician Melpar, Falls Church, Va., 1964-65; systems analyst Wolf Research & Devel. Corp., Bladensburg, Md., 1965-66, ARIES Corp., McLean, Va., 1966-68; sr. systems analyst N. Am. Rockwell Corp., Roslyn, Va., 1968-70; pres. Baker & Baker Data Assos., North Springfield, Va., 1970—. Served with AUS, 1954-55. Mem. Am. Math. Soc., Math. Assn. Am., Soc. Indsl. and Applied Math., Am. Soc. Cybernetics. Home: 5624 Heming Av Springfield VA 22151 Office: Baker & Baker Data Assos North Springfield VA 22150

BAKER, DAVID, architect; b. Chgo., Feb. 7, 1917; s. A. Josiah and Sarah (Gross) B.; B.S., Ill. Inst. Tech., 1938; postgrad. (scholar), Ill. Inst. Tech. 1938-39; M. Arch. (Kendall grad. scholar), Harvard, 1942; Diploma, Ship Constrn., George Washington U., 1943; m. Beverly L. Brody, Nov. 25, 1951; children—Jonathan Brody, Stuart Glenn. Researcher in historic Am. bldg. for Earl Reed, architect, Chgo.; archtl. designer Alphonso Iannelli, sculptor and indsl. designer, Park Ridge; archtl. designer Thomas Shaver, engr. Chgo.; Samuel A. Marx, architect; urban planner Chgo. Housing Authority, 1936-40; asst. field rep. architect's supt. James Gamble Rogers, architect, N.Y.C., architect Neiler, Rich & Bladen, engrs., Chgo., 1940-41; archtl. designer Shaw, Naess & Murphy, Chgo., 1941-42; Walter Bogner, Cambridge, Mass., 1942; archtl. and engring. designer Naval Ordnance Lab., Washington, 1942-43; naval architect, engr. Bur. Ships, Navy Dept., 1943-45; architect for electronics div. Dept. Navy, 1945-49, for Hdqrs. Command USAF, 1950-51; architect Solar-Space House, built and exhibited, Washington, 1952; cons. architect 1952—. Trustee Boys Club Greater Washington. Registered architect, Ill., Mass., D.C., Md., Va.; registered profl. engr. Ill.; Nat. Council Archtl. Registration Bds., 1948. Recipient 1st Medals Beaux Arts Inst. Design Competitions, 1937, 38; prize Insulux Glass Block Competition, 1939; beneficial tech. award Bur. Ships, USN, 1945; A.I.A. award for Scholarship; Charles L. Hutchinson medal for highest record in archtl. design; award of merit Georgetown Progressive Citizens Assn., 1954; plaque for design Pres.'s Com. on Beautification of Nation's Capitol, 1966. Mem. Ill. Inst. Technology Alumni Association. (pres. chpt. 1961), A.I.A. (corporate mem.; chmn. pub. relations com. Washington-Met. 1950). Club: Harvard (Washington). Contbr. articles profl. jours. Office: 2141 Sudbury Pl Washington DC 20012

BAKER, DAVID LLOYD, univ. adminstr.; b. Louisville, Nov. 23, 1940; s. David Lloyd and Evelyn Diana (Beville) B.; B.A., U. Louisville, 1964, J.D., 1969; m. Mary Anne King, Sept. 4, 1962; 1 son, David Lloyd III. Dir. news bur. U. Louisville, 1962-64, asst. dir. pub. information, 1964-65, dir. pub. information, 1965—. Sec. Toward Greater Quality Com., 1969-71. Mem. Pub. Relations Soc. Am., Am. Coll. Pub. Relations Assn., Am., Ky., Louisville bar assns., Ky. Civil Liberties Union. Democrat. Baptist. Home: 1837 Lauderdale Rd Louisville KY 40205

BAKER, DILLARD WOODWARD, lawyer; b. Coleman, Tex., Oct. 7, 1912; s. Jesse Kirkland and Willie (Woodward) B.; LL.B., U. Tex., 1936; m. Mary Margaret Thomas, Jan. 30, 1938; children—Jesse Kirkland, Roger Thomas. Admitted to Tex. bar, 1936; gen. atty. Humble Oil & Refining Co., Houston, 1956—. City councilman, Bunker Hill Village, Tex., 1955-57. Mem. Am., Houston bar assns., State Bar of Tex., Am. Coll. Trial Lawyers, Houston C. of C., Kappa Sigma. Methodist. Clubs: Houston Hereferd (pres.), World Trade (Houston); Houston, Austin. Home: 4 Pine Forest Circle Houston TX 77027 Office: PO Box 2180 Houston TX 77001

BAKER, DONALD LEE, civil engr.; b. Sealy, Tex., Aug. 16, 1930; s. Thomas John and Alma (Hartmann) B.; B.S., Tex. A. and M. Coll., 1960; m. Mary Beth Gregory, May 22, 1963; children—John Donald, Wilber Lee. Engring. asst. Tex. Hwy. Dept., Houston, 1960-64, designing engr., 1964—. Served with AUS, 1953-55. Mem. Am. Soc. C.E., Am. Soc. Testing and Materials, Tau Beta Pi, Phi Kappa Phi. Lutheran. Home: Box 33 Brookshire TX 77423 Office: Box 656 Bellville TX 77418

BAKER, EVERARD GREEN, chem engr., educator; b. Natchez, Miss., Feb. 19, 1922; s. Everard Green and Josephine (Balfour) B.; B.S., Miss. State U., 1943, postgrad., 1948-49; M. Chem. Engring. (Inst. Indsl. Research fellow), U. Louisville, 1949; m. Lillian Louise Wheeler, Nov. 23, 1947; children—Everard Green III, Francis Lee. Jr. chemist Miss. State Chem. Lab., State College, 1943-44, asso. chemist, 1950-53, chemist, instr. chemistry and chem. engring., 1953-60, chemist, asst. prof., 1960-63, asso. prof. chem. engring., 1963—; research engr. U. Louisville, 1949-50. Tchr., Natchez (Miss.) High Sch., 1946-48; cons. Humble Oil & Refining, S.E. Esso region, summer 1963. Served with AUS, 1944-46; lt. col. USPHS Res. NASA-Am. Soc. Engring. Edn. fellow Marshall Space Flight Center, summer 1965, 66. Registered profl. engr., Miss., Ala., La. Mem. Am. Inst. Chem. Engrs. (asso.), Am. Chem. Soc. (past sec. Miss. sect.), Nat., Miss. (past pres. Tombigbee chpt.) socs. profl. engrs., Tombigbee Chem. Engr. Club (past pres.), Am. Soc. Engring. Edn., Tau Beta Pi. Presbyn. Home: 205 White Dr Starkville MS 39759

BAKER, FRANCIS WILLIAM, lawyer; b. Victoria, Tex., May 30, 1924; s. William Westhoff and Marguerite (Golke) B.; B.S. in Commerce with high honors, St. Mary's U., San Antonio, 1948, J.D. with highest honors, 1949; m. Mary Johnson, May 3, 1952; children—Susan Judith, Stephen Francis, Patricia Ann, Matthew William. Admitted to Tex. bar, 1949; asst. criminal dist. atty. San Antonio, 1950-51; with Eaton & Huddle, C.P.A.'s, San Antonio, 1952-55; partner law firm Matthews, Nowlin, Macfarlane & Barrett, San Antonio, 1956—. Lectr., St. Mary's U. Law Sch., 1956-63; dir. Southwell Co., San Antonio. Served with AUS, World War II; now col. USAFR. Decorated Bronze Star medal. Mem. Am., San Antonio (pres. 1971-72) bar assns., State Bar Tex., Order of Alhambra, Delta Theta Phi. Democrat. Roman Catholic. K.C. (state adv. 1965-67). Home: 323 Royal Oaks Dr San Antonio TX 78209 Office: Alamo Nat Bldg San Antonio TX 78205

BAKER, FRANK COKE, dentist; b. Corinth, Miss., Aug. 4, 1934; s. John Armstrong and Beatrice Mildred (Coke) B.; student U. Miss., 1952-55; D.D.S., U. Tenn., 1959; postgrad. U. Mich., 1960, 65, U. Miss., 1960-71, U. Ala., 1969, 71, Ohio State U., 1968; m. Bernice Settle, June 20, 1958; children—Frank Coke, John Albert. Rotating intern Kennedy med. teaching group VA Hosp., Memphis, 1960; pvt. practice dentistry, Tupelo, Miss., 1960—. Dental cons. Regional Child Devel. Clinic, Tupelo, 1962—. Dist. commr. Yocona council Boy Scouts Am., 1966-70; active Community Devel. Found. Bd. dirs. Lee United Neighbors. USPHS fellow in pharmacology, 1957-58. Mem. Pierre Fouchard Acad., Fedn. Dentaire Internat., Am. Assn. Endodontists, Am. Assn. Dental Editors, Southeastern Acad. Prosthodontics, So. Acad. Oral Surgery, Miss. Dental Assn. (trustee 1968-71), N.E. Miss. Dental Soc. (pres. 1972), Psi Omega. Presbyn. (deacon 1962—). Kiwanian. Club: Tupelo (Miss.) Country. Editor Jour. Miss. Dental Assn., 1968—. Home: 314 Willow Rd Tupelo MS 38801 Office: 810 Garfield Dr Tupelo MS 38801

BAKER, FRANK LEE, dentist, army officer; b. Pontiac, Mich., Mar. 20, 1930; s. Ivyn Lee and Sue (Young) B.; D.M.D., U. Louisville, 1955; m. Lillian Jane McClung, Dec. 21, 1957; children—Patricia Ann, Cynthia Jane. Commd. 1st lt. Dental Corps, U.S. Army, 1955, advanced through grades to col., 1972; chief dental lab. sect. Med. Field Service Sch., Ft. Sam Houston, Tex., 1969-72; assigned 86th Med. Detachment, Giessen, Germany, 1972—. Decorated Army Commendation ribbon. Fellow Internat. Coll. Dentists; mem. Am., Ky. dental assns., Am. Prothodontic Soc., Louisville Dental Soc., Nat. Rifle Assn., Delta Sigma Delta. Mason (Shriner). Home: APO New York City NY 09169

BAKER, GEORGE WALTER, govt. ofcl., educator; b. Seaford, Del., June 15, 1915; s. Walter and Mary (Hill) B.; B.A., U. Del., 1939; M.A., U.N.C., 1947, Ph.D., 1952; postgrad. Princeton Mil Govt. Sch., 1944, Brookings Instn. Fed. Sci. Exec. Tng., 1965; m. S. Louise Krok, May 29, 1958; 1 dau., Mary Louise Baker. Program officer to sr. task scientist U.S., Air Force human factors programs, 1951-57; team chmn. spl. operations research Office Am. U., 1957-59; tech. dir. disaster research group Nat. Acad. Scis.-NRC, 1959-63; asso. program dir. to program dir. for behaviorial scis. facilities to staff asso. U. Sci. Devel. NSF, 1963—. Cons. to Office Emergency Planning, 1959-63; Westbrook lectr., 1963; cons. to Canadian, Swedish and French offcls. on Disaster Research, also White House conf. Internat. Disaster Relief. Served from pvt. to 1st lt. AUS, 1942-46. Fellow A.A.A.S., Am. Anthropol. Assn., Am. Sociol. Assn., Soc. for Applied Anthropology. Club: Cosmos (Washington). Co-author: The Occasion Instant: The Structure of Social Responses to Unanticipated Air Raid Warnings, 1961. Sr. editor: Human Problems in the Utilization of Fallout Shelters, 1960; Behavioral Science and Civil Def., 1962; Man and Society in Disaster, 1962. Home: 7502 Nevis Rd Bethesda MD 20034 Office: NSF 1800 G St Washington DC

BAKER, GEORGE WILBER, curator; b. Lansing, Mich., Apr. 21, 1927; s. Donald Howard and Harriett (Root) B.; B.A. in Landscape Architecture, Mich. State U., 1949; m. Ara Marie Schultz, Sept. 1, 1961. Partner, Lakeview Garden Center, landscape nursery, Ypsilanti, Mich., 1953-57; supr. maintenance Dearborn campus U. Mich., 1957-65; curator Norfolk (Va.) Bot. Gardens, 1965—; garden columnist Virginian-Pilot newspaper, 1967-71; tchr. gardening adult edn. Old Dominion U., 1967—. Served with AUS, 1945. Mem. Am. Bonsai Soc. (pres. 1971). Rotarian. Home: 2407 Blueberry Rd Norfolk VA 23518 Office: Norfolk Botanical Gardens Airport Rd Norfolk VA 23518

BAKER, HOUSTON ALFRED, hosp. adminstr.; b. Louisville, May 6, 1908; s. Harry W. and Susie (Talley) B.; B.S. in Bus. Adminstrn., W.Va. State Coll., 1931; M.B.A., U. Pa. Wharton Sch. Finance, 1937; M.H.A., Northwestern U., 1948; m. Viola Smith, June 11, 1938; children—John, Houston Alfred, William. Tchr., Louisville pub. schs., 1933-44; adminstr. Red Cross Hosp., Louisville, 1944-52; asst. supt. Freedmen's Hosp., Washington, 1953, 61-66, dep. supt., 1966-70, acting hosp. dir., 1970-71, asso. hosp. dir., 1971—; dir. personnel Mammoth Life Ins. Co., Louisville, 1954, adminstrv. asst. to pres., 1955-56. Chmn. Vocational Ednl. Adv. Council to Bd. Edn., Washington, 1967-69. Trustee 12th St. YMCA, Washington, 1962-65. Named Indsl. Man of Year, Vocational Ednl. Adv. Council to Washington Bd. Edn., 1969. Mem. Assn. Asst. Adminstrs. Nat. Capital Area, Boule. Presbyn. (mem. dept. ministerial relations). Home: 1441 Manchester Lane NW Washington DC 20011 Office: Freedmen's Hospital 6th and Bryant Sts NW Washington DC 20001

BAKER, HOWARD HENRY, JR., U.S. senator, lawyer; b. Huntsville, Tenn., Nov. 15, 1925; s. Howard Henry and Dora (Ladd) B.; grad. McCallie Sch., 1943; student U. of South, Tulane U.; J.D., U. Tenn., 1949; LL.D., Tusculum Coll.; D.C.L., Southwestern U., Memphis; m. Joy Dirksen, Dec. 22, 1951; children—Darek, Cynthia. Practice law, Knoxville, Tenn.; formerly partner firm Baker, Worthington, Barnett & Crossley; formerly chmn. bd. First Nat. Bank, Oneida, Tenn.; U.S. senator from Tenn., 1966—. Served to lt. (j.g.) USNR, 1943-46. Chmn. Tenn. delegation Republican Nat. Conv., 1968. Mem. Am., Knoxville, Scott County bar assns., Bar Assn. Tenn., Scarabbean Soc., Phi Delta Phi, Pi Kappa Phi. Presbyn. Home: Huntsville TN 37756 Office: Huntsville TN also US Senate Washington DC 20510

BAKER, IRA LEE, educator; b. Fairwood, Va., Sept. 5, 1915; s. Joseph Franklin and Celia (Blackburn) B.; B.A., Wake Forest Coll., 1936; M.A., Columbia, 1952; postgrad. U. Ill., U. Wis., U. Tenn., Syracuse U.; M.Sc. in Journalism, U. Ill., 1963. Instr. English, N.C. State Coll., Raleigh, 1946-50, asst. extension editor State Coll. Extension Service and mng. editor Extension Farm-News, 1950-51; head journalism dept. Furman U., Greenville, S.C., 1951-65; asso. prof. journalism and English, High Point (N.C.) Coll., 1965-68; prof. journalism East Carolina U., Greenville, 1968—. Corr. for the Religion News Service, 1953—. Publicity chmn. Wake County council N.C. Symphony Orch., 1947-51; permanent advisor S.C. Collegiate Press Assn.; active Raleigh Music Club, Raleigh Little Theatre, 1946-51, Greenville Little Theater, 1951—; mem. alumni council Wake Forest Coll., 1964. Del., S.C. Republican Conv., 1958. Served with USAAF, 1942-44. Recipient Scholastic Pioneer award Nat. Scholastic Press Assn., 1970. Mem. Am. Assn. Coll. and U. Profs. (v.p. Furman U. chpt.), Am. Assn. Tchrs. Religious Journalism, Assn. Ednl. Journalism, S.C. Press Assn., Nat. Council Coll. Publs. Advisers (membership chmn. dist. III 1967-68), S.C. Assn. Coll. Publs. Advisers (pres. 1957—), South Atlantic Modern Lang. Assn., Pitt County (N.C.) Hist. Soc., (publicity chmn.) S.A.R., Sigma Delta Chi, Tau Kappa Epsilon, Alpha Phi Gamma (nat. pres. 1968-70). Baptist. Co-author: Modern Journalism, 1961. Mem. adv. bd. Student Writer; chmn. adv. bd. Cerebral Palsy News of S.C.; mem. bd. editors Scholastic Mag.; mem. book reviewing staff Greensboro News, 1960; editor The Collegiate Journalist. Contbr. to Ency. So. Bapts., 1958. Address: Box 2707 East Carolina U Greenville NC 27834

BAKER, JEFFERSON TASWELL, JR., lawyer, real estate broker; b. Cedar Hill, Tex., Mar. 25, 1900; s. Jefferson T. and Georgia Thalia (Strauss) B.; student North Tex. Agrl. Coll., 1925-26, S.W. Tex. Tchrs. Coll., 1926-27, Jefferson U. Law Sch., 1928-30; J.D. Dixie U., 1932, J.D., 1965; postgrad. U. Houston, 1940-41; B.S., Northwestern U., 1945; m. Doris Mae Upton, Oct 10, 1921 (dec. 1945); 1 son, Reginald Gordon; m. 2d, Claribel Victoria Vinas, Oct. 15, 1941; children—Charlotte Diane (Mrs. Nathan Camarda), Jefferson Taswell III. Mem. faculty various schs., 1932-44; instr. USN Radio Sch., Northwestern U., 1944-45; admitted to Ark. bar, 1933; practiced in Texarkana, Ark, 1933; real estate and mortgage loan broker Baker Real Estate & Mortgage Co., Pasadena, Tex., 1933—; chmn. bd. Alcanus, Inc., 1959—, McSaib, Inc., 1959—. Mem. City Charter Com., Pasadena, 1952. Served to capt. AUS, 1933-34. Named Ky. col., 1971, adm. Tex. Navy, 1972. Fellow Internat. Acad. Forensic Pathology; mem. Alpha Beta Sigma (charter mem., chancellor 1928—, pres. 1968—). Roman Catholic. Club: Sports Car of Am. (competition driver 1958-71). Address: 713 Armor Av Pasadena TX 77502

BAKER, JOANNE THERESE KAYE (MRS. HOWARD MICHAEL BAKER), librarian; b. Chgo., July 21, 1927; d. Thomas and Cecilia (Keil) Kaye; B.A. DePaul U., 1962; A.M. in L.S. Rosary Coll., 1964; m. Howard Michael Baker, Nov. 30, 1963; 1 dau., Cecilia Mary. Tchr. pub. schs., Chgo., 1948-61; librarian, Oak Lawn, Ill., 1961-63; head librarian St. Joseph's Coll., East Chicago, Ind., 1963-65, Upper Ia. Coll., Fayette, 1965-68, Lea Coll. on Lake Chapeau, Albert Lea, Minn., 1968-70, Pikeville (Ky.), 1970—. Vol., A.R.C. Mem. A.L.A., Ill library assns. Home: PO Box 196 Pikeville Coll Pikeville KY 41501

BAKER, JOHN WESLEY, educator; b. Austin, Tex., Aug. 6, 1920; s. William Loyd and Edith (Mosher) B.; B.A., U. Tex., 1942; Ph.D. in Polit. Sci., U. Cal., Berkeley, 1953; m. Mary Ethel Posey, Jan. 8, 1943; children—Robert Shelton, Frederick, Brian, John Preston. Instr., Trinity U., 1947-49, asso. prof. polit. sci., 1951; asst. prof. polit. sci. U. Fla., 1952-53; asso. prof. polit. sci. Humboldt State Coll., 1953-58; prof., chmn. dept. polit. sci. Coll. Wooster, 1958-69; asso. exec. dir., dir. research Bapt. Joint Com. on Pub. Affairs, Washington, 1969—; vis. scholar U. Cal. at Berkeley, 1962-63, vis. prof., summer 1966; vis. scholar Brookings Instn., Washington, 1967-68; vis. prof. Am. U., 1968, 69—. Mem. Democratic Central Com., Humboldt County, Cal., 1954-58. Served from pfc. to maj. USMCR, 1942-46. Decorated Purple Heart. Mem. Am., So. polit. sci. assns., Am. Acad. Polit. and Social Sci., Acad. Polit. Sci., Am. Soc. Pub. Adminstrn., Pi Sigma Alpha. Baptist. Author: (with Clem Miller) Member of the House, 1962; author monograph. Editor: Dissent in Church and State, 1970; Religious Liberty and the Bill of Rights, 1972. Contbr. articles profl. jours. Home: 6414 Crane Terrace Bethesda MD 20034 Office: 200 Maryland Av NE Washington DC 20002

BAKER, JOHN WILLIS, newspaper editor; b. Granite, Okla., Oct. 27, 1908; s. Roscoe C. and Anna G. (Jung) B.; student Okla. A. and M. Coll., 1930-34; m. Ruby Elithe Martin, June 2, 1934. Owner-operator advtg. firm, Enid, Okla., 1928-43; reporter Enid News-Eagle, 1943-44; with Okla. Pub. Co., Oklahoma City, 1944—, financial editor, 1954—. Chmn. Ind. Securities Study Com., 1957—. Named Hon. Prof., Sch. Bus., Okla. City U., 1958. Mem. Oklahoma City C. of C., Okla. Soc. Financial Analysts, Investment Securities Assn. Oklahoma City, Econ. Club Okla., Sigma Delta Chi. Republican. Methodist (chmn. bd. stewards 1961-63, charge lay leader 1964-69, trustee 1965-69). Home: 333 NW 5 Oklahoma City OK 73102 Office: 500 N Broadway Oklahoma City OK 73125

BAKER, MRS. JOHN (MAXINE BAKER), state legislator, civic worker; b. Berwyn, Md.; d. Maurice Owen and Bertha (Stier) Eldridge; A.B., Radcliffe Coll., 1920; m. John Adams Baker, June 25, 1921; children—Grover Eldridge, Douglas Allen, Martha Anne (Mrs. Erhard Fritz Hoegger). Sec.-treas. Baker's Carpet Co., Inc., Miami; mem. Fla. Ho. of Reps., 1963—. Sec.-treas. Met. Charter Bd. of Dade County, 1955-57, drafter home rule county charter adopted in referendum, 1957. Mem. Dist. Welfare Bd., 1953-62; dir. Citizens Const. Com. of Fla., 1950-58; mem. Gov's. Adv. Com. on Constl. Revision, 1958-59; mem. State Capitol Bldg. Com., 1959—. Trustee Mental Health Services, Inc.; bd. dirs. United Health Found. of Dade County, Assn. Child Guidance Clinics, Dade County, Welfare Planning Council. Recipient Community Headliner award Theta Sigma Phi; Pub. Service award Dem. Women's Club, Dade County; Alumnae Recognition award Radcliffe Coll., 1967; Meritorious Service award Fla. Psychiat. Soc. Mem, Am. Assn. U. Women (pres. Miami 1934-35), League Women Voters (pres. Miami 1945-47, 53-54, pres. Fla. 1947-49), Hist. Assn. So. Fla., Fla. Nature Conservancy, Daus. Am. Colonists. Democrat. Episcopalian. Home: 1782 Opechee Dr Miami FL 33133

BAKER, KARLO LIVINGSTON, textile co. exec.; b. Mt. Croghan, S. C., Mar. 20, 1927; s. Wilson Joyce and Ethel Cleo (Atkinson) B.; B.S., Wake Forest U., 1948; m. Eleanor Lois McBride, Sept. 7, 1950; children— Beth, Elyse, Stephen, Eleanor. Chief chemist Delta plant J. P. Stevens, Cheraw, S.C., 1951-54, gen. supt. Delta finishing plant, Cheraw, 1958-65; tech. dir. Amerotron Corp., Clarksville, 1954-56; founder, pres. Cheraw Dyeing & Finishing Co., Inc. (S.C.), 1965—, also dir.; dir. S.C. Nat. Bank of Cheraw. Mem. Chesterfield County Bd. Health, Cheraw, 1957-61; trustee pub. schs., Cheraw, 1964-68. Bd. dirs. Matheson Meml. Library, Cheraw, 1960-64; trustee Cheraw (S.C.) Acad., 1967-71. Served with USNR, 1945-47. Mem. Am. Assn. Textile and Colorists, S.C., Cheraw (dir. 1960-62) chambers commerce. Baptist (trustee 1956-60). Mason. Club: Cheraw (S.C.) Country; Florence (S.C.) Country; Stadium (Wake Forest U.). Home: 303 Sliding Hill Rd Cheraw SC 29520 Office: Jersey at W Greene St Cheraw SC 29520

BAKER, LAMAR, congressman; b. Chattanooga, Dec. 29, 1915; student David Lipscomb Coll.; B.S., Harding Coll., 1940; m. Sue Batey; children—Edward L., Susan. Owner Comml. Janitors, Inc., Floormaster Rug Cleaning Co.; mem. 92d Congress from 3d Tenn. dist. Mem. Chattanooga Safety Council, Chattanooga Citizens' Good Govt. League. Formerly mem. Tenn. Ho. of Reps., Tenn. Senate. Bd. dirs. U. Tenn. at Chattanooga Christian Student Center; trustee Boyd Buchana Sch. Mem. Greater Chattanooga C. of C., Am. Legion. Republican. Club: Civitan. Home: 2324 Roosevelt Blvd Chattanooga TN 37412

BAKER, LEONARD STANLEY, author; b. Pitts., Jan. 24, 1931; s. Charles and Bess (Schwartz) B.; B.A., U. Pitts., 1952; M.S., Columbia, 1955; m. Liva Weil, Aug. 1, 1958; children—David, Sara. Reporter, St. Louis Globe-Democrat, 1955-56, Newsday, L.I., N.Y., 1956-65; author: The Johnson Eclipse, 1966; Back to Back, 1967; The Guaranteed Society, 1968; Roosevelt and Pearl Harbor, 1970; Brahmin in Revolt, 1972. Served with AUS, 1952-54. Address: 606 4th Pl SW Washington DC 20024

BAKER, LISLE, JR., newspaper exec.; b. Monticello, Ky., Apr. 11, 1902; s. Walter Lisle and Zona (Ramsey) B.; A.B., Centre Coll., 1922; m. Mary Elizabeth Turner, May 24, 1930; children—Elizabeth Maddox, Louise Ramsey, Robert Lisle, Mary Stuart. Asst. sec., later sec.-treas. Capital Trust Co., Frankfort, Ky., 1922-34; cashier, trust officer, dir. State Nat. Bank, Frankfort, 1934-36; past. chmn. finance com., dir. Louisville Courier-Journal, Louisville Times Co., and affiliated Standard Gravure Corp., WHAS, Inc.; past pres. Bus. Devel. Corp. Ky.; dir. Photon, Inc. Mem. Ky. Council for Public Higher Edn. Past dir. Audit Bur. Circulations. Past trustee Centre Coll. (Danville, Ky.); past chmn. Louisville R.R. Planning Commn.; past pres. Louisville Fund Am. Newspaper Pubs. Assn. Research Inst. Mem. So. Newspaper Publishers Assn. (pres., 1947-48), Louisville Philharmonic Soc. (past pres. and dir.), Louisville Com. on Fgn. Relations, English Speaking Union, Delta Kappa Epsilon, Omicron Delta Kappa. Clubs: Pendennis, Country (Louisville). Home: 330 Mockingbird Valley Rd Louisville KY Office: Courier-Journal Louisville KY

BAKER, MARGARET V., librarian; b. Savannah, Ga.; d. Clarence Edwin and Carrye (Keller) Baker; student Randolph-Macon Womans Coll., 1929-31; A.B., Valdosta State Coll., 1933; A.B. in L.S., U. N.C., 1939. Librarian, Valdosta (Ga.) High Sch., 1934-40; cataloger, reference librarian Gen. Library, U. Ga., Athens, 1940-43; librarian Washington Sem., Atlanta, 1943-45; with reference dept. main library U. Fla., Gainesville, 1946; librarian Emory Jr. Coll., Valdosta, 1946-48; dir. S. Ga. Regional Library, Valdosta, 1948-71; library cons. South Ga. Med. Center, Valdosta, 1972—. Bd. dirs. Civic Music Assn., 1955-60. Mem. Ga., Southeastern library assns., Lowndes County Hist. Assn. (bd. dirs. 1967-72), Am. Assn. U. Women, D.A.R. (auditor 1957-62), Delta Kappa Gamma, Phi Mu. Club: Valdosta. Home: 1017 Slater St Valdosta GA 31601 Office: South Ga Med Center Valdosta GA 31601

BAKER, MARILYN JEANINE MILLER (MRS. ALLYN LEE BAKER), journalist, editor; b. Chickasha, Okla., July 13, 1934; d. Basil Eugene and Vivian (Townsend) Miller; A.A., Tex. Southmost Coll., 1954; B.J., U. Tex., 1956; m. Allyn Lee Baker, Aug. 31, 1956; children—Lisa Denise, Darryl Allyn. Reporter, Brownsville Herald, 1956-57; women's editor Denton (Tex.) Record-Chronicle, 1956-57; asst. editor Tex. Press Messenger, Tex. Press Assn., 1959-60; asst. editor Tex. State Jour. Medicine, Tex. Med. Assn., 1960-62; mng. editor Tex. State Jour. Medicine, 1962—. Mem. Soc. Austin Indsl. Editors (pres. 1971), Theta Sigma Phi. Methodist. Home: 8904 Currywood Dr Austin TX 78759 Office: 1801 N Lamar Blvd Austin TX 78701

BAKER, OLLIE MARIE OSBORN (MRS. RUSSELL MONTEZ BAKER, SR.), civic worker; b. Texarkana, Ark., Feb. 13, 1909; d. Charles Westly and Harriett V. (Raney) Osborn; student Celeste Morton Sch. Voice, 1926-27; m. Russell Montez Baker, Aug. 26, 1927; children—Harriett Kay (Mrs. William Frank Bain), Russell Montez. Dir. Blue Birds Bradfield Sch., Dallas, 1943-44, room mother, 1944-45; den mother Shady Brook Manor Sch. Club Scouts Am., Dallas, 1945-46; capt. polio dr., Dallas, 1950, block worker, 1950—, chmn. rummage sale Cosmo-Pal Club, 1951-52, pres. 1952; v.p. Gamma Phi Beta Mother's Club, 1953-54; mem. White Contemporary Group, 1958-63; vol. worker Thrift House and Altar Guild. Ch. of Incarnation; corr. sec. Tuesday study dept. Dallas Woman's Forum, 1960; block worker Heart Dr., Cancer Dr., Muscular Distrophy Dr., 1955—. Mem. Dalla Lawyer's Wives Club, Laurel Book Club, Women's Aux. Nat. Assn. Claimants' Counsel of Am., Dallas Theatre Guild State Fair Tex., Dallas Athletic Club, Dallas Athletic Country Club. Home: 6256 Lupton Dr Dallas TX 75225

BAKER, PAUL, theatre dir., educator; b. Hereford, Tex., July 24, 1911; s. William Morgan and Retta (Chapman) B.; student U. Wis., 1929; B.A., Trinity U., Waxahachie, Tex., 1932, D.F.A. (hon.), 1958; M.F.A., Yale 1939; student of Elsie Fogarty, Central Sch. Speech, London, Eng., 1932; studied, observed theater in Eng., Germany, Russia, Japan; m. Sallie Kathryn Cardwell, Dec. 21, 1936; children—Robyn Cardwell, Retta Chapman, Sallie Kathryn. Chief entertainment br. spl. services div. U.S. Army, ETO, 1944-45; prof. drama, chmn. dept. Baylor U., 1934-63; dir. Dallas Theater Center, 1959—; prof. drama, chmn. dept. Trinity U., San Antonio, 1963—; lectr. Am. Theatre, Salzburg (Austria) Seminar in Am. Studies, summer 1968; organized S.W. Summer Theater, Waco, 1939, also built theater inside Waco Hall, Baylor U., 1939; designed Studio I, Baylor U., 1942; dir. exptl. prodn. Othello, 1953; co-designer Weston Theater addition to Baylor Theater, 1954; dir. A Different Drummer, Baylor U. and CBS-TV, 1955, Hamlet with Burgess Meredith and Charles Laughton, Baylor Theater, 1956; promoted bldg., founding Kalita Humphreys Theater designed by Frank Lloyd Wright in Dallas, 1959, also establishment permanent sch. and repertory co. for Am. in Dallas, 1959. Mem. Texas Fine Arts Commn.; bd. govs. Am. Playwrights Theater, 1967—. Served to rank of maj. AUS, 1943-45; ETO. Rockefeller Found. fellow, 1937-39, 41, 46, 59; recipient Rodgers and Hamerstein award for outstanding theatrical contbr. in S.W., 1961. Mem. Nat. Theatre Conf. (pres. 1958-62), S.W. Theatre Conf. (pres. 1956), ANTA (corr. mem. bd. standards and planning for the living theater), Am. Ednl. Theatre Assn., Tex. Inst. Letters. Presbyn. (past elder). Author chpts. in books. Office: Trinity Univ San Antonio TX 78284

BAKER, RAY ROBERT, music pub. co. exec.; b. San Antonio, Dec. 24, 1937; s. E. Jack and Irene (Roberts) B.; student San Antonio Coll., 1956-58; m. Barbara Ferguson, Feb. 11, 1959; children—Deborah Anne, Dawn Alaine. Radio announcer KVOU, Uvalde, Tex., KENS, San Antonio, 1959-62; bus. mgr. Jim Reeves, Nashville, 1962-65; pres. Blue Crest Music, Inc., Madison, Tenn., 1965—, Jaray Music, Inc., 1969—, Dalray Jingle Co., 1967. Writer various songs including Theres A Heartache Following Me. Home: 816 Sylvania Av Nashville TN 37207 Office: PO Box 162 Madison TN 37115

BAKER, RAYMOND DEAN, mobile and modular homes mfg. co. exec.; b. Correctionville, Ia., Oct. 6, 1927; s. Charles Bartin and Clara Dorothea (Bice) B.; B.S., Ia. State U., 1951; m. Esther Waddell, Oct. 15, 1946; children—Charles Dean, Christine Jo, Jana Kay. Indsl. engr. Maytag Co., Newton, Ia., 1951-53; prodn. mgr. Maytag Carver Pump Co., Muscatine, Ia., 1953-55; plant mgr. Modern Homes Corp., Dearborn, Mich., 1955-57; v.p. mgr. Home Bldg. Corp., Sedalia, Mo., 1957-65; gen. mgr. Knox Mobile Homes, Thomson, Ga., 1965-68; v.p. operations Brigadier Industries, Thomson, 1968—, also mem. exec. com. Mem. Thomson Ten-Seventies. Served with AUS, 1946-47. Mem. Southeastern Mobile Housing Inst. (dir. 1967-68). Methodist (ofcl. bd. 1967-71, chmn. stewardship com. 1970-71). Mason. Home: PO Box 463 Thomson GA 30824 Office: PO Box 954 Thomson GA 30824

BAKER, RETA NEIL (MRS. WEBSTER B. BAKER, SR.), banker; b. Tampa, Fla., Oct. 15, 1929; d. Matthew and Edna (Seivers) Neil; grad. high sch.; m. Webster Bedorial Baker, Sr., Oct. 3, 1946; children—Webster Bedorial, W. Everett, Bernice A., Brenda Sue. Clk.-typist Thurow Electronics, Lakeland, Fla., 1958; bookkeeper, teller First State Bank of Lakeland, 1959-61; bookkeeper, teller First State Bank of Lakeland, 1963-66, head bookkeeper, 1966-67, asst. cashier, 1967-71, asst. v.p., 1971—. Mem. Nat. Assn. Bank Women Officers, Credit Women Internat. (Lakeland 3d v.p. 1969). Home: 307 Woodstock Av Eaton Park FL 33840 Office: 2211 S Florida Av Lakeland FL 33803

BAKER, REX GAVIN, JR., lawyer, savs. and loan exec.; b. Beaumont, Tex., Apr. 22, 1920; s. Rex Gavin and Edna (Heflin) B.; B.A., U. Tex., 1941, LL.B., 1947; m. Jeannette M. Russell, Sept. 6, 1947; children—Jeannette (Mrs. Anthony Masraff), Bess (Mrs. John L. Sharman), Ann (Mrs. Jack G. Wise), Rex Gavin III. Admitted to Tex. bar, 1946; practice law, Houston, 1947—; partner Berry,

Richards & Baker, 1947-57, Roberts, Baker, Richards, Elledge & Heard, 1957-62, Baker, Heard, & Elledge, 1962-70, Baker, Heard & Brunson, 1970—. Pres., Southwestern Savs. Assn., Blanca Devel. Co., Southwest Group Investors, Inc., Baker Properties, Inc.; dir. Holly Resources, Inc., Lake Telephone Co.; dir., gen. counsel Western Nat. Bank; Mem. Tex. Finance Commn. Councilman, Bellaire, Tex., 1948-49; mem. Houston Juvenile Delinquency and Crime Commn., 1955-56; mem. Tex. Hi-Y Council, 1957-61. Bd. dirs. Holly Hall, Inst. Religion. Served to lt. USNR, 1942-46. Mem. Am., Tex., Houston bar assns., Nat. League Insured Savs. Assns. (past pres.), Kappa Sigma. Baptist (past chmn. bd. deacons). Home: 3747 Chevy Chase Dr Houston TX 77019 Office: 3300 Main St Houston TX 77002

BAKER, ROBERT CALHOUN, banker; b. Everett, Pa., May 22, 1902; s. Francis and Jennie (Calhoun) B.; B.S., U. Pa., 1927. Vice pres., dir. Central Nat. Bank, Richmond, Va., 1935-45; v.p. Columbia Nat. Bank, Washington, 1945-46; v.p. Am. Security & Trust Co., Washington, 1946-49, dir., 1948—, exec. v.p., 1949-59, pres., 1959-69, chmn. bd., 1962—; pres., dir. Am. Security Corp., 1959—; dir. Burlington Industries, Greensboro, N.C., Peoples Drug Stores, Inc., Washington Gas Light Co., Peoples Life Ins. Co., mem. adv. bd. Washington Mut. Investors Fund. Chmn., Nat. Capital Downtown Com. Bd. dirs. United Givers Fund; trustee Juniata Coll., Fed. City Council, George Washington U. Mem. Assn. Res. City Bankers (past dir.). Clubs: University (N.Y.C.); Chevy Chase, 1925 F St., Nat. Press, University, City Tavern, Capitol Hill, Metropolitan, Burning Tree (Washington); Everglades, Bath and Tennis (Palm Beach, Fla.), Lyford Cay (Hassau, Bahamas). Home: 2500 Calvert St NW Washington DC 20008 Office: 15th and Pennsylvania Av Washington DC 20013

BAKER, ROBERT DONALD, educator; b. Chico, Cal., Dec. 7, 1927; s. Lester W. and Wilma (Vitzthum) Baker; B.S. in Forestry, U. Cal. at Berkeley, 1951, M.F., 1952; Ph.D., State U. N.Y., 1957; m. Mary Ann Brooks, Sept. 6, 1958; 1 dau., Allison. Asst. prof. Stephen F. Austin State U. Sch. Forestry, Nacogdoches, Tex., 1956-59. asso. prof., 1959-68, prof., 1968—. Cons. forestry and photogrammetry. Served with USAAF, 1946-47. Danforth asso. Danforth Found. Mem. Am. Soc. Photogrammetry (regional pres., chmn. nat. edn. com. 1970-72), Soc. Am. Foresters (chpt. pres. 1968-69), Tex. Forestry Assn. (dir. 1969-70), Sigma Xi, Chi Eta Sigma, Alpha Zeta, Xi Sigma Pi. Kiwanian (pres. club 1971-72). Home: 3705 Raguet St Nacogdoches TX 75961 Office: Stephen F Austin State U Sch Forestry Nacogdoches TX 75961

BAKER, ROGER CARROLL, JR., physician; b. N.Y.C., June 18, 1919; s. Roger Carroll and Mary Berry (Lawrence) B.; student Seton Hall Coll., 1937-39; B.S., Boston Coll., 1939-41; M.D., Tufts U., 1944; Ph.D., U. Chgo., 1952; m. Genevieve Eremich, Jan. 4, 1946; children— Susan Lawrence, Leslie Greenberry, Abigail Kindley, Roger Carroll III, Alexander Cruise. Intern, St. Vincent's Hosp., N.Y.C., 1944-45, asst. resident gen. surgery, 1945-46; resident urology USN, 1947-48, Mass. Meml. Hosp., Boston, 1948-49; fellow urology U. Chgo., 1949-50, head div. urology, 1949-53; prof., dir. urology Georgetown U. Hosp., Washington, 1953—; practice medicine, Washington, 1953—. Bd. dirs. Am. Urol. Research Found., Inc., 1957—. Served as lt (j.g.) USNR, 1944-48. Recipient Am. Assn. Urol. Research award, 1950, Research Exhibit awards Am. Urol. Assn., A.M.A., 1955. Fellow A.C.S.; mem. A.A.A.S., Am. Urologic Assn., Am. Assn. Cancer Research, Soc. Exptl. Biology and Medicine, Sigma Xi. Club: Cosmos. Home: 1133 Chain Bridge Rd McLean VA 22101 Office: Georgetown U Hosp Washington DC 20007

BAKER, RUSSELL MONTEZ, lawyer; b. Celeste, Tex., Mar. 11, 1906; s. William Perry and Kathleen (Bolte) B.; grad. So. Meth. U., 1928; m. Ollie Marie Dedman, Aug. 26, 1927; children—Harriet Kay, Russell Montez. Admitted Tex. bar, 1929, asso. Caldwell, Gillen, Francis & Gallagher, Dallas, 1929-32; jr. partner Caldwell, Gillen, Francis & Gallagher, 1932-38; mem. firm Caldwell, Baker &Jordan, Dallas, 1938-59; now sr. mem. firm Baker, Jordan & Foreman. Research fellow Southwestern Legal Found. Fellow Am. Coll. Trial Lawyers, Tex. Bar Found.; mem. Am., Tex. trial lawyers assns., Am. Judicature Soc., Law Science Acad., Law Sci. Found. of Am., Internat. Acad. Trial Lawyers, Tex. Assn. Plaintiff Attys. (pres.), Internat. (patron), Am., Tex., Dallas bar assns., Delta Chi. Clubs: Dallas Athletic. Dallas Athletic Country, Cosmopolitan (internat. pres. 1950-51). Editor Am. Trial Lawyers Assn. Law Jour. Home: 6256 Lupton Dr Dallas TX 75225 Office: 1907 Elm St Dallas TX 75201

BAKER, RUSSELL WAYNE, newspaperman; b. Loudoun County, Va., Aug. 14, 1925; s. Benjamin Rex and Lucy Elizabeth (Robinson) B.; B.A., Johns Hopkins, 1947; m. Miriam Emily Nash, Mar. 11, 1950; children—Kathleen Leland, Allen Nash, Michael Lee. With Balt. Sun, 1947-54; mem. Washington bur. N.Y. Times, 1954-62, author-columnist, Observer, editorial page, 1962—. Served with USNR, 1943-45. Author: An American in Washington, 1961; No Cause for Panic, 1964; All Things Considered, 1965; Our Next President, 1968; Poor Russell's Almanac, 1972. Home: 5211 39th St NW Washington DC 20015 Office: 1920 L St Washington DC 20036

BAKER, SENA CAROLYN, mfr. hearing aids.; b. McLean County, Ill., May 5, 1912; d. Jerry C. and Hulda A. (Tetzlaff) Sampson; B.S., Ill. State Normal U., 1931; m. Russell Lewis Baker, Dec. 10, 1938. Personnel dir., sec.-treas. Electone, Inc., Fern Park, Fla., 1965—. Republican. Lutheran. Mem. Order Eastern Star. Club: Rio Pinar Country (Orlando, Fla.). Home: 528 Park North Ct Winter Park FL 32789 Office: 110 Atlantic Dr Fern Park FL 32737

BAKER, STUART LISLE, JR., newspaper pub. exec.; b. Monticello, Ky., Apr. 11, 1902; s. Waller Lisle and Zona (Ramsey) B.; student Centre Coll., Danville, Ky., 1919-22; A.B., Rutgers U., 1937; m. Mary Elizabeth Turner, May 24, 1930; children—Elizabeth (Mrs. William Harmon Leete), Louise Ramsey (Mrs. John G. Seiler, Jr.), Mary Stuart (Mrs. William A. Pike), Robert Lisle. Asst. sec. Capital Trust Co., Frankfort, Ky., 1923-24; sec.-treas., trust officer, dir. State Nat. Bank, 1924-36; chmn. finance com. Courier-Jour. & Louisville Times Co.-WHAS, Inc., Standard Gravure Corp., 1936—; dir. Photon, Inc., North Wilmington, Mass., Fed. Res. Bank, Bus. Devel. Corp. Mem. Council Pub. Higher Edn., Am., So. (past pres.) newspaper pubs. assns., English-Speaking Union. Clubs: Pendennis, Louisville Country. Home: 330 Mockingbird Valley Rd Louisville KY 40207 Office: 525 W Broadway Louisville KY 40202

BALANCY, PIERRE GUY GIRALD, ambassador of Mauritius; b. Mauritius, Apr. 8, 1924; s. Pierre Rene and Marie Alix (Herse) B.; student Royal Coll., 1939-42, Bhujoharry Coll., 1943-44; m. Therese Louis, July 14, 1947; children—Pierre Gervais, Gerard, Anne-Marie Jacqueline Clairette, Marie-France Janine Josianne, Marie Therese Renee Ginette, Philippe Gaetan Gilles. Local govt. officer, 1946-63; founder, chief editor daily newspaper l'Express, 1963-64; joined Diplomatic Service, 1968; ambassador of Mauritius to U.S., also high commr. to Can., 1968—. Mem. Mauritius Legislative Council, 1963-68; municipal councillor, 1963-64; parliamentary sec. Ministry Edn. and Cultural Affairs, 1963-65; minister of information, posts and telegraphs, 1965-67, of works, 1967-68. Sec. Cercle Litteraire de Port Louis, 1962, Cercle Remy Ollier, 1955-59, Action Sociale, 1959-60; mem. com. direction Centre Cultural Francais. 1967-68. Recipient Cercle Litteraire de Port Louis award, 1956. Mem. Internat. Platform Assn. Mem. Labour Party (exec. com. 1961-68). Roman Catholic. Club: Internat. (Washington). Author: Human Brotherhood in a Modern Multi-Racial Society, 1956. Home: 2308 Wyoming Av NW Washington DC 20008

BALCH, LEON CRAWFORD, clergyman, educator; b. Notasulga, Ala., June 23, 1916; s. Berta Leon and Martha (Crawford) B.; B.S., Auburn U., 1937; B.D., U. of South, 1962, S.T.M., 1965; m. Laura Ruth Hindman, Aug. 18, 1945; children—Laura Lee, Thomas Crawford, Martha Lynn. Application engr. Westinghouse Electric Corp., East Pittsburgh, Pa., 1937-42; elec. engr. Kingsport Electric Co., 1948-53; ordained to ministry Episcopal Ch., 1953; rector Grace Ch., Chattanooga, 1957—. Evening faculty Chattanooga State Tech. Inst. Coordinator Chattanooga Area Suicide Prevention Service; mem. Chattanooga Area Council on Alcoholism and Other Drug Abuse; co-founder Hillandale Center. Served to lt. comdr. USNR, 1942-46. Profl. engr., Tenn. Mem. I.E.E.E. (sr.), Nat. Soc. Profl. Engrs., Phi Kappa Phi. Tau Beta Pi, Eta Kappa Nu. Club: Torch (past pres.) (Chattanooga). Home: 120 Tuxedo Circle Chattanooga TN 37411 Office: 4010 Brainerd Rd Chattanooga TN 37411

BALD, MARGARET, librarian; b. Pitts., Sept. 3, 1913; d. Edmond James and Margaret (Siemon) Bald; A.B., Asbury Coll., 1934; B.S., Carnegie Inst. Tech., 1935. Asst. Carnegie Library, Pitts,, 1935-37; asst. librarian Carnegie Steel Corp., 1937-40; asst. Pasadena Pub. Library, 1940-44; various positions U.S. Navy Dept., 1944-48; librarian Bob Jones U., Greenville, 1948—. Mem, Am., S.C. library assns. Home: Bob Jones Univ Greenville SC 29614

BALDOWSKI, CLIFF, cartoonist. Cartoonist Atlanta Jour. & Constn. Office: 10 Forsyth St Atlanta GA 30303*

BALDRIDGE, JOSEPH FILMORE, JR., banker; b. Ft. Worth, July 30, 1931; s. Joseph Filmore and Frances Maybell (Gunter) B.; B.B.A. in Personnel Adminstrn., U. Tex., 1953; postgrad. Grad. Sch. Bus., Tex. Christian U., 1959-60; m. Barbara Ann Sanguinet, June 7, 1952; 1 son, Joseph Filmore III. With Ft. Worth Nat. Bank, 1957—, mgr. systems and procedures dept., 1967—. Bd. dirs. Trinity Valley Sch., Ft. Worth. Served with USAF, 1953-57. Mem. Am. Inst. Banking, Assn. Systems Mgmt. (pres. Ft. Worth 1971-72), Tex. Bankers Assn. (chmn. records retention com.), Kappa Sigma. Methodist. Kiwanian. Home: 4800 Winthrop St E Fort Worth TX 76116 Office: PO Box 2050 Fort Worth TX 76101

BALDRIDGE, WILLIAM KARNES, lawyer, county judge; b. Bartlett, Tex., Aug. 13, 1908; s. William and Cora (Karnes) B.; student N. Tex. State U., 1929-31; LL.B., So. Methodist U., 1942; m. Catherine Martin, Apr. 10, 1930; children—Betty, Barbara (Mrs. C.E. Hesse). Admitted to Tex. bar, 1940; pvt. practice, Denton, 1940—; asst. dist. atty., 1941-45, dist. atty., 1945-51, county judge, 1955-69, judge county ct. at law, 1969-71. Mem. C. of C., State Bar Tex., Denton County Bar Assn. Kiwanian. Home: 2015 Locksley Lane Denton TX 76201 Office: 300 E McKinney St Denton TX 76201

BALDWIN, CLAUDE DAVID, economist, govt. ofcl.; b. Wellington, Colo., May 29, 1917; s. John Edwin and Eva I. (Hoflund) B.; B.S., U. Denver, 1937; M.S., U. Ill., 1938, Ph.D., 1940; m. Velma Neville Wilson, Jan. 31, 1942. Instr. W.Va. U., 1940-41, Kan. U., 1941-42; asst. prof. Ind. U., 1946-47; v.p. Jefferson County Bank of Lakewood, Colo., 1948-50; mng. dir. Met. State Bank, Derby, 1950-51; fiscal economist Bur. of Budget, 1951-52; chief fiscal analysis br. Office Asst. Sec. Def., 1952-55; asst. comptroller (systems) USAF, 1955-61; asst. dir. research div. Internal Revenue Service, Washington, 1962—. Served with Supply Corps, USNR, 1943-46. Mem. Am. Econ. Assn., Phi Beta Kappa, Beta Gamma Sigma, Phi Kappa Phi. Author: Economic Planning: Its Aims and Implications, 1942. Home: 2234 49th St NW Washington DC 20007

BALDWIN, DAVID GILMORE, assn. exec.; b. New Orleans, Mar. 28, 1918; s. David Gilmore and Adele (Ziegler) B.; student Tulane U., 1938, New Sch. for Social Research, 1946; m. Mildred Lyons, Dec. 9, 1945; children—Stephen Brooks, Geoffrey S.J. Reporter, New Orleans Item, 1935-36, 46-50, New Orleans Tribune, 1936-37, N.Y. Daily News, 1938-39, Louisville Courier Jour., 1950-52; pub. relations exec., New Orleans, 1952-55; asst. press sec. Gov. of Pa., 1955-58; with A.M.A., Chgo., 1959-69, dir. communications dept., Washington, 1969—. Served to flight lt. RCAF, 1939-45. Decorated D.F.C. and Bar. Mem. Am. Assn. Polit. Consultants, Am. Assn. Med. Execs., Pub. Relations Soc. Am., Sigma Chi. Democrat. Clubs: University, Nat. Press, Capitol Hill (Washington). Home: 3018 44th Pl NW Washington DC 20016 Office: 1776 K St NW Washington DC 20006

BALDWIN, DONALD EARL, veterinarian; b. Kansas City, Mo., Jan. 25, 1930; s. Charles Joseph and Bertha (Schweddi) B.; student Kansas City Jr. Coll., 1952-53; B.D., D.V.M., Kansas State U., 1958; M.S. in Microbiology, Ohio State U., 1962; m. Gloria Ermatinger, Apr. 26, 1952; children—Deborah, Eric, Marianne. Animal disease research U.S. Dept. Agr., Plum Island, N.Y., 1958-60; instr. Ohio State U., 1960-62; animal disease research U.S. Dept. Agr., Ames, Ia., 1962-65; tech. dir. research and prodn. Affiliated Labs., White Hall, Ill., 1965-71; tech. adviser Ft. Dodge-Nova Lab., Mexico City, Mexico, 1971—. Served with USCG, 1948-52. Mem. Am. Vet. Med. Assn., Am. Soc. Microbiology, Tissue Culture Assn., Am. Legion, Phi Zeta. Lion. Address: Fort Dodge-Nova Lab Mexico City D F Mexico

BALDWIN, DONALD KRING, newspaper editor; b. Vermillion, S.D., Dec. 10, 1917; s. Ernest Joy and Madge (Kring) B.; student Ida. So. U., 1939; m. Madalyn Leah Cope, May 3, 1940; children—Steven Worth, Lori Ann. Reporter, Pocatello (Ida.) Tribune, 1939-40; city editor Idaho Falls (Ida.) Post-Register, 1940-41; copy editor Santa Barbara (Cal.) News-Press, 1941-42; with A.P., 1942-58, news editor, Tokyo, Japan, 1955-58; mng. editor St. Petersburg (Fla.) Times & Independent, 1958-61, exec. editor, 1961-69, editor, 1969—; exec. v.p. Times Pub. Co., 1967-69, pres., 1969—. Mem. Am. Soc. Newspaper Editors. Sigma Delta Chi. Home: 1000 Brightwaters Blvd St Petersburg FL 33704 Office: PO Box 1121 St Petersburg FL 33731

BALDWIN, ESTHER LILLIAN, pianist, composer; b. Chgo.; d. George and Minnie (Neidigh) Baldwin; pvt. study Dr. Francis Hemington, Chgo.; Mus. B., Columbia Sch. Music and Art, in 1946; Mus. D.; widow. Tchr., dir. Baldwin Music Studios, Columbia, S.C., 1927—, concert pianist, 1946—; composer Sonata in C Major; Sonata in D Major. Adjudicator Nat. Guild Piano Tchrs. Bd. govs. Exec. and Profl. Hall of Fame. Fellow Internat. Inst. Arts and Letters; mem. Internat. Pianist's Guild, Nat. Guild Piano Tchrs. (chmn. Columbia, S.C. chpt.), Internat. Platform Assn., Musicians Club Am. Home: Box 114 Apt. 118 Davis Hotel Columbia SC 29202 Studio: 1712 Sumter St Columbia SC 29201

BALDWIN, GARZA, JR., lawyer; b. Litchfield, Ill., Mar. 10, 1921; s. Garza and Hazel (Saterlee) B.; student Vincennes U., 1938-39; B.S., Ind. U., 1942, J.D., 1948; m. Margaret Jean Skinner, Sept. 7, 1946; children—Deborah Allen, Garza III, Mary Beth, Daniel David, Benjamin Willis. Admitted to Ind. bar, 1948, N.C. bar, 1959; practiced in Sullivan, Ind., Indpls., 1948-57; city atty. Sullivan, 1951-55; asso. counsel Olin Mathieson Chem. Corp. (name changed to Olin Corp.), Pisgah Forest, N.C., 1957-58, div. counsel, 1958-63, sr. counsel, 1963-69, group v.p., 1969-71, group pres., 1971—; dir. Asheville office Wachovia Bank & Trust Co. Dir. Pub. Works and Safety, Sullivan, 1951-55; trustee, sec. Sullivan Sch. Bd. 1956-57; pres. N.C. Indsl. Council, 1965-67; dir. Ednl. Found., Commerce and Industry N.C., Inc., 1965—; mem. N.C. Gov.'s Council Econ. Devel., 1967-68. Trustee Transylvania Community Hosp.; bd. dirs., v.p., mem. exec. com. N.C. Citizens Assn.; bd. dirs. U. N.C. at Asheville Found. Served to lt. (j.g.) USNR, 1942-45. Mem. Am., Ind., N.C. State bar assns., Western Carolina Mfrs. Assn. (pres. 1963-70), Order of Coif, Am. Legion, Kappa Sigma, Phi Delta Phi. Republican. Presbyn. Mason (32 deg.). Clubs: Asheville (N.C.) Country, Asheville City, Biltmore Forest Country. Home: 18 Beaverdr n Knoll Asheville NC 28804 Office: PO Box 200 Pisgah Forest NC 28768

BALDWIN, JAMES W., govt. ofcl. Exec. dir. D.C. Human Relations Commn., Washington. Home: 3818 Pope St Washington DC 20020 Office: DC Human Relations Commn Dist Bldg 11th and E Sts Washington DC 20004*

BALDWIN, PHILLIP BENJAMIN, U.S. judge; b. Marshall, Tex., Dec. 23, 1924; s. Jack B. and Lucille (Jones) B.; student U. Tex., 1942-43; B.A. in Biology, N. Tex. State Tchrs. Coll., 1949; student E. Tex. Bapt. Coll., 1949, Baylor U. Law Sch., 1950-51, S. Tex. Sch. Law, 1951-52; m. Mertie Bellamy, July 2, 1948; children—Rebecca, Nancy, Jane, Phillip Benjamin. Admitted to Tex. bar, 1952; asst. dist. atty., Marshall, 1953-54; criminal dist. atty. Harrison County, Tex., 1954-58; practice in Marshall, 1958-68; U.S. asso. judge Ct. Customs and Patent Appeals, 1968—. Served with USAAF, 1943-46; PTO. Mem. Am., Tex., N.E. Tex., Harrison County (sec. 1957, pres. 1958-60) bar assns., Tex. Trial Lawyers Assn., Nat. Assn. Def. Lawyers in Criminal Cases, Am. Legion, V.F.W., Alpha Tau Omega, Phi Delta Phi. Episcopalian. Elk. Home: 3409 Willow Tree Lane Falls Church VA Office: 717 Madison Pl NW Washington DC 20439

BALDWIN, VELMA NEVILLE WILSON (MRS. CLAUDE DAVID BALDWIN), govt. ofcl.; b. Meade, Kan., Aug. 31, 1918; d. Charles Chester and Anna Velma (Neville) Wilson; A.B., U. Kan., 1940; m. Claude David Baldwin, Jan. 31, 1942. Placement working students U. Kan., 1940-41; personnel War Dept., Washington, 1942-45; research asst. Dr. A.C. Kinsey, Ind. U., 1946; with Carter Oil Co., Denver, 1948-50; personnel Bur. of Budget, Washington, 1951-55; asst. to dir. personnel Treasury Dept., 1955-59; personnel officer, dir. adminstrn. Office Mgmt. and Budget, 1959—. Mem. Am. Soc. Pub. Adminstrn. (past mem. exec. bd.), Soc. for Personnel Adminstrn. (mem. exec. bd.). Home: 2234 49th St NW Washington DC 20007 Office: Office of Mgmt and Budget Washington DC 20503

BALE, DON, state ofcl. Asst. supr. Ky. Dept. Edn., Frankfort. Address: Bur Instrn Ky Dept Edn Frankfort KY 40601*

BALES, RICHARD HENRY HORNER, condr., composer; b. Alexandria, Va., Feb. 3, 1915; s. Henry Ahijah and Henrietta Wyeth (Horner) B.; Mus.B., Eastman Sch. Music, U. Rochester, 1936; student Julliard Grad. Sch., 1938-41; pvt. pupil Serge Koussevitzky, 1940; m. Mary Elizabeth Starley, Nov. 7, 1942; 1 dau., Mary Starley. Debut as condr. with Nat. Symphony Orch., 1935; condr. Va.-N.C. Symphony, 1936-38; music dir. Nat. Gallery Art, condr. Nat. Gallery Orch., Washington, 1943—; condr. Washington Cathedral Choral Soc., 1945-46, Eastman Chamber Orch., Rochester, N.Y., 1965-67; music dir. Nat. Symphony Orch., summer 1947; guest condr. orchs. in U.S. including Phila., N.Y.C., St. Louis, San Antonio, Cleve., Am. Little Symphony, Naumburg Orch.; tchr. Mass. State Tchrs. Coll., summer 1941, George Washington U., 1953; lectr. music. Recipient 1st prize string composition Arts Club Washington, 1940; Alice M. Ditson award Columbia, 1960, Acad. of Achievement, Monterey, Cal., 1961; Distinguished Service award Sons of Confederate Vets., 1965. Life fellow Internat. Inst. Arts and Letters; mem. Nat. Assn. Am. Composers and Condrs. (dir.; award of merit 1959), Am. Fedn. Musicians, Soc. Cincinnati, Bruckner Soc. Am. (hon.), Civil War Round Table D.C. (Gold medal 1960, pres. 1960-61), U.S. Navy Band (hon. life), Md. Hist. Soc., Kindler Found. (pres. 1959-62), Alexandria Library Co. (life mem., pres. 1962-63), S.C.V. (hon. life). Episcopalian. Clubs: Internat., Cosmos (Washington). Composer various orchestral, instrumental, and choral selections. Home: 6022 Pike Branch Dr Alexandria VA 22310 Office: Nat Gallery of Art Washington DC 20565

BALKUS, KOZMAS, educator; b. Lithuania, USSR, Aug. 13, 1920; s. Aleksas and Ona (Burzdzius) B.; B.S. in C.E., Poly. Inst. Bklyn., 1952; M.S. in Urban Planning, N.Y. U., 1964, Ph.D., 1968; m. Meila Kairiukstis, Jan. 17, 1947; 1 dau., Daiva. Came to U.S., 1948, naturalized, 1953. Design engr. Am. Electric Power Co., N.Y.C., 1953-64; supr. research and analysis urban travel Tri-State Transp. Commn., N.Y.C., 1964-68; Regional Sci. Assn. Post-doctoral fellow regional sci. Harvard, 1968-69; asso. prof. urban planning Fla. State U., Tallahassee, 1969—, dir. Transp. Center, 1971—. Research cons. Lab. for Computer Graphics and Spatial Analysis, Harvard, 1969. Chmn. long range planning com. Community Planning Bd. 7, N.Y.C., 1966-68. Bd. dirs. Lithuanian Relief Fund BALF, 1949-51. Recipient Founder's Day Certificate for Outstanding Acad. Achievement, N.Y. U., 1968. Mem. Am. Acad. Polit. and Social Scis., Am. Soc. Pub. Adminstrn., Am. Soc. C.E. (mem. exec. com. N.Y. Met. region 1966-68), Am. Inst. Planners, A.A.A.S., World Future Soc., Soc. Gen. Systems Research. Club: Tennis (Tallahassee, Fla.). Home: 1701 W Pensacola St Tallahassee FL 32304

BALL, CHARLES DENVER, supt. schs.; b. Mattie, Ky., May 16, 1917; s. Greenville and Virginia (Moore) B.; B.S., Morehead State U., 1946; M.A., Marshall U., 1959; postgrad., U. Ky., 1965-67; m. Kathryn Wolford, Dec. 4, 1937; children—Denny James, Jenny (Mrs. Buford Crager). Tchr. math. and physics pub. schs., Russell, Ky.; 1946-47; Raceland, Ky., 1947-48; Ashland, Ky., 1949-51; dean boys Ashland High Sch., 1954-55; prin. Raceland High Sch., 1954-58; supt. schs. Fairview Ind. Schs., Ashland, 1959—. Mem. Ashland Bd. Edn., 1952-53. Mem. N.E.A., Am., Ky. assns. sch. adminstrs., Nat. Assn. Sch. Execs. (acad. leader 1969-71). Home: 1428 Wurts Av Ashland KY 41101 Office: Fairview Schools Ashland KY 41101

BALL, CLAYTON GARRETT, JR., physician; b. Evanston, Ill., June 28, 1939; s. Clayton Garrett and Una L. (Brown) B.; B.S., Yale, 1961; M.D., Northwestern U., 1965; m. Anne F. Morrison, June 27, 1962; children—Martha Anne, Clayton Garrett III, Jennifer Corrine. Intern, Evanston Hosp., 1965-66; resident anesthesiology U. Va. Med. Center, Charlottesville, Va., 1968-71; asst. prof. anesthesiology, 1971—. Served with USNR, 1966-68. Fellow Am. Coll. Anesthesiology; mem. Va., Albermarle County med. socs., Am., Va. socs. anesthesiologists. Home: 632 Preston Pl Charlottesville VA 22903

BALL, EDWARD, chmn. Fla. East Coast Ry. Co. pres., dir. Jacksonville Properties, Inc., St. Joseph Tel. & Tel. Co., Port St. Joe Dock &Terminal Ry., Apalachicola No. R.R., Wakulla Edgewater Co., Almours Securities, Inc. of Va., St. Joseph Land and Devel. Co., Fla. Nat. Realty Co., Keystone Sand Co., Silver Glenn Springs Co.,

Ballynahinch Castle, Inc.; chmn. exec. com., pres., dir. St. Joe Paper Co., Jacksonville; dir. Fla. Nat. Bank of Jacksonville, Fla. Nat. Bank & Trust Co. at Miami, Fla. Nat. Bank at Orlando. Sec., treas., dir. Nemours Found.; dir. Alfred I. DuPont Found. Office: Florida East Coast Ry Co 1 Malaga St St Augustine FL 32084*

BALL, FRANK J., scientist. Mem. WESCAVO sulphur dioxide team. Address: 4 Atlantic St Charleston SC 29401*

BALL, GENE V., med. educator; b. Rivesville, W. Va., June 28, 1931; s. John Franklin and Rebecca E. (Rush) B.; M.D., Vanderbilt U., 1959; m. Sara Jane Clark, June 6, 1959; children—Rebecca Anne, Hilary Elizabeth. Intern, Cin. Gen. Hosp., 1959-60; resident U. Pa. Hosp., Phila., 1960-61, U. Miami-Jackson Meml. Hosp., 1961-65; instr. U. Ala. Sch. Medicine, 1965-66, asst. prof., 1966-68, asso. prof., 1968-71, prof. internal medicine, 1971—. Pres. Ala. chpt. Arthritis Found., 1969-71. Served with AUS, 1952-54. Fellow A.C.P.; mem. Ala. Zool. Soc. (v.p. 1969-71). Republican. Episcopalian. Clubs: Mt. Brook Swim and Tennis, Relay House (Birmingham). Home: 3516 Springvalley Ct Birmingham AL 35223 Office: 1919 7th Ave S Birmingham AL 35223

BALL, IVAN ESTUS, utility co. exec.; b. Ages, Ky., July 5, 1923; s. Alex and Maude (Crider) B.; student Eastern Ky. State Tchrs. Coll., 1939-41; B.S. in Accounting, Bowling Green Coll. Commerce, 1948; m. Madaline Cornett, Oct. 18, 1946 (div. 1952); 1 dau., Lynn Estes (Mrs. George John Hume); m. 2d, Mona Elizabeth Gilbert, Sept. 25, 1954; 1 stepdau., Penelope Elizabeth (Mrs. Burton G. Goldstein). With Peoples Water & Gas Co., Miami Beach, Fla., 1948-58, financial v.p., 1957-58; with Tampa Gas Co. (Fla.), 1955-57, financial v.p., 1957; controller So. Gulf Utilities, 1959-60; controller City Gas Co. Fla., Hialeah, 1961—, financial v.p., 1966—; mgmt. cons. S & W Service Corp., 1962. Served with USAAF, 1941-45. Decorated Bronze Star medal. Mem. Gas Inst. Greater Miami, Am. Gas Assn., C. of C., Beta Pi. Democrat. Clubs: Miami Shores Country, Basset Hound (Am.), Southern Fla. Basset Hound, Greater Miami Dog. Home: 800 NE 97th St Miami Shores FL 33138 Office: 955 E 25th St Hialeah FL 33013

BALL, JOHN WILLIS, lawyer; b. Jacksonville, Fla., Jan. 22, 1910; s. Philip Manville and Anna McNeill (Bullock) B.; A.B. magna cum laude, Washington and Lee U., 1932, J.D., 1935; m. Margaret Ann Moreland, Apr. 11, 1936; children—Haywood Moreland, John Willis, Margaret Ann. Admitted to Fla. bar, 1935, since practiced in Jacksonville; mem. law firm Ulmer, Murchison, Ashby & Ball, 1947—; spl. atty. lands div. Dept. Justice, 1937-54. Mem. 5th Circuit Fed. Jud. Com., Am. Bar Assn., 1963-69. Bd. dirs. Family Consultation Service, Jacksonville. Fellow Am. Bar Found., Am. Coll. Probate Counsel; mem. Am. (com. jud. selection, compensation and tenure 1959-63, 69—, chmn. 1972-73, ho. dels. 1964-67), Jacksonville bar assns., Am. Judicature Soc., Am. Law Inst., Inst. Judicial Adminstrn., Fla. Bar, Phi Beta Kappa, Order of Coif, Phi Gamma Delta, Omicron Delta Kappa, Phi Delta Phi. Home: 4730 Arapahoe Av Jacksonville FL 32210 Office: PO Box 479 Jacksonville FL 32201

BALL, MICHAEL FRANCIS, JR., med. educator, assn. exec.; b. N.Y.C. Dec. 27, 1933; s. Michael Francis and Rita Patricia (Klipper) B.; B.S. St. Peter's Coll., 1955; M.D., Georgetown U., 1959; m. Janet Margaret deGroot, June 18, 1960; children—Michael F., Frederick A., Margaret J., Joseph A., Patricia K., Edward C. Intern, Georgetown U. Hosp., Washington, 1959-60; resident Duke Med. Center, Durham, N.C., 1960-62, fellow, 1962-63; research fellow Georgetown U., Washington, 1963-64, instr. dept. medicine, 1964-67, asst. prof., 1967-72, asso. prof., 1972—; asst. dir. biomed. research and faculty devel. Assn. Am. Med. Colls., Washington, 1972—. Established investigator Am. Heart Assn., 1968-72. Recipient Research and Devel. award Am. Diabetic Assn., 1966-67. Fellow A.C.P.; mem. Am. Fedn. Clin. Research (pres. 1972-73), Am. Diabetic Assn., Endocrine Soc., So. Soc. Clin. Investigation. Editor Clin. Research, 1969-71. Home: 6201 Kellogg Dr McLean VA 22101 Office: Assn Am Med Colls 1 Du Pont Circle Washington DC 20036

BALL, NEAL, govt. ofcl. Dep. press sec. to Pres. Nixon. Address: The White House Washington DC 20500*

BALL, ROBERT M., social security specialist; b. N.Y.C., Mar. 28, 1914; s. Archey Decatur and Laura Elizabeth (Crump) B.; A.B., Wesleyan U., 1935, M.A., 1936; m. Doris Jacqueline McCord, June 30, 1936; children—Robert Jonathan, Jacqueline Elizabeth. With Bur. Old Age and Survivors Ins., Social Security Bd., 1939-46; asst. dir. com. on edn. and social security Am. Council on Edn., 1946-49; staff dir. adv. council on social security to U.S. Senate Finance Com., 1947-48; asst. dir. Bur. Old Age and Survivors Ins., 1949-52, dep. dir., 1953-62; commr. Social Security, 1962—; staff dir. pension study Nat. Planning Assn., 1950-52. Bd. govs. Internat. Social Security Assn.; mem. com. social ins. experts ILO. Recipient Distinguished Service award Dept. Health, Edn. and Welfare, 1954; Career Service award Nat. Civil Service League, 1958; Rockefeller Public Service award, 1961. Mem. Am. Pub. Welfare Assn., Am. Soc. Public Adminstrn., Nat. Acad. of Public Adminstrn., Nat. Conf. Social Welfare (mem. bd.), Phi Beta Kappa, Delta Kappa Epsilon. Club: International (Washington). Author: Pensions in the United States, 1952; also articles. Home: 4009 Villa Nova Rd Baltimore MD 21207 Office: Social Security Adminstrn Washington DC 20201

BALL, WILLIAM KENNETH, lawyer; b. DeQueen, Ark., Jan. 15, 1927; s. William P. and Lucille (Jeter) B.; LL.B., U. Ark., 1953; m. Ella Hubbard Scaife, Dec. 28, 1950; children—Lucy Jane, William Ramsay, Charles Scaife. Admitted to Ark. bar, 1953; law clk. George Rose Smith, Asso. Justice of Ark. Supreme Ct., Little Rock, 1953-54; practiced in Monticello, Ark., 1954—; mem. firm Williamson, Ball and Bird, 1954—, City atty., Monticello, Ark., 1961—. Served with Signal Corps, AUS, 1945-47, 50-52. Mem. Am., Ark., S.E. Ark. (pres. 1957-58) bar assns., Kappa Sigma, Delta Theta Phi. Presbyn. Rotarian (pres. 1962-63). Home: 7 Westwood Dr Monticello AR 71655 Office: 701 N Main St Monticello AR 71655

BALLANCE, PAUL SALEN, librarian; b. Maple, N.C., Sept. 7, 1906; s. Frank and Laura (Griggs) B.; B.S., N.C. State U., 1929; B.L.S., Columbia, 1932; m. Susan Covington, Sept. 24, 1932; 1 son, Frank Covington. Reference asst. N.Y. Pub. Library, 1929-36; head sci. and tech. div. Rochester (N.Y.) Pub. Library, 1936-42; librarian Tex. Engrs. Library, 1943-49; librarian Tex. A. and M. Coll., 1944-49, Greensboro (N.C.) Pub. Library, 1949-51, Winston-Salem (N.C.) Pub. Library, 1951-71; ret., 1971; cons. in field, 1948—. Mem. N.C. Library Commn., 1953-70; cons. N.C. Library Bd., 1953-70, vice chmn., 1968-70; chmn. N.C. Library Certification Bd., 1968-70. Mem. Am. (chmn. coms.), N.C. (chmn. coms. 1965-67), Southeastern (chmn. coms.), Tex. (past treas.) library assns., Winston-Salem C. of C. Contbr. to profl. jours. Editor: North Carolina Index, 1955—. Compiler: First Fifty Years of Public Library Service in Winston-Salem, 1906-56, 1956; List of Books in Texas Engineers Library, 1945; Union List of Periodicals in Selected North Carolina Libraries, 1959. Home: Route 8 Winston-Salem NC 27106

BALLANTINE, DUNCAN SMITH, educator; b. Garden City, N.Y., Nov. 5, 1912; s. Raymond and Amy (Smith) B.; student Deerfield Acad., 1928-30; Ph.D., Harvard, 1947; B.A., Amherst Coll., 1934, LL.D., 1959; m. Saffeti Acele, Dec. 24, 1962; children—Katharine (Mrs. Bruce Davy), Duncan Ahmet, Andrea Shirin. With Aetna Surety & Casualty Co., Hartford, Conn., 1934-35; tchr. Gow Sch., South Wales, N.Y., 1936-39; instr. history Mass. Inst. Tech., 1939-42, asso. prof., 1947-52; pres. Reed Coll., 1952-55, Robert Coll., Istanbul, 1955-61; research asso. Harvard U., 1961-62; dir. edn. projects dept. World Bank, Washington, 1962—. Trustee Robert Coll., Istanbul. Served from lt. (j.g.) to comdr. USNR, 1942-46. Mem. Soc. Internat. Devel., Middle E. Inst. Home: 5306 Blackistone Rd Washington DC 20016 Office: 1818 H St NW Washington DC 20433

BALLANTYNE, ROBERT HUBBARD, educator; b. Kansas City, Mo., Aug. 2, 1932; s. Robert Law and Ruth (Hubbard) B.; B.A., U. Ia., 1954, M.A., 1958; Ed.D., Wash. State U., 1962; m. Mary Ann Olsen, Sept. 30, 1956; children—Shelli Ann, Kerri Lynn, Robbi Kay, Brian Robert. Instr. edn. Wash. State U., 1961-62; faculty edn. Duke, 1962, sr. counselor, 1962-64, coordinator instl. studies, 1964-66, asst. to pres., 1966-67, dir. admissions, 1967—, asso. prof. edn., 1967—. Served with USAF, 1954-57. Mem. Am. Psychol. Assn., Am. Personnel and Guidance Assn. Home: 2510 Wrightwood St Durham NC 27705

BALLARD, CLAUDE KAY, chem. co. exec.; b. Mineral, Tex., July 16, 1912; s. Chester E. and Lela A. (Smith) B.; B.Chem. Engring., Tex. Coll. Arts and Industries, 1934; m. Dorothy Lee Wells, May 6, 1940; children—Douglas Alan, Charles Lee. With chem. div. Pitts. Plate Glass Co., 1934-42, 46-52, dist. sales mgr., Houston, 1955-62; pres. Columbia Nitrogen Corp., Augusta, Ga., 1962—, also dir. Served to capt., Chem. Corps, AUS, 1942-46. Mem. Am. Inst. Chem. Engrs. Methodist. Home: 2281 Overton Rd Augusta GA 30904 Office: PO Box 1483 Augusta GA 30903

BALLARD, EDWIN DAVIDSON, state ofcl.; b. Lancaster, Ky., Aug. 17, 1917; s. George Thomas and Elizabeth (Buchanan) B.; student U. Ky., 1938-39; m. Mary Nancy Gray, Sept. 19, 1942; children—Patricia Carol, Elizabeth Ann. Civilian flight instr. USAAF Res., 1942-45; comml. pilot, 1945-47; bur. mgr. Van Winkle & Arhold, auto agy., Lancaster, Ky., 1947-50; with Ky. Dept. Revenue, Frankfort, 1950—, supr., 1956-60, asst. dir., 1960-62, dir. tax div., 1962—. Instr., Internat. Assn. Assessing Officers, 1960—; Latin Am. tax assistance res. Internal Revenue Service, 1963—. Recipient Donohoo essay award Internat. Assn. Assessing Officers, 1966. Mem. Internat. Assn. Assessing Officers (editorial bd. 1968-70), Soc. Real Estate Appraisers (past pres. Lexington, dir.). Democrat. Author: Manual on Tax Maps, 1960; Property Tax Administration Manual, 1957; Real Property Appraisal Manual, 1962. Home: 235 Pepper Dr Lexington KY 40505 Office: Capitol Annex Frankfort KY 40601

BALLARD, NELSON LEON, dept. store co. exec.; b. Winchester, Ky., Nov. 29, 1918; s. Walter Nelson and Sophia (Witt) B.; student various profl. courses; 1 son, Nelson Leon. Salesman, J.C. Penney Co., Winchester, Ky., 1945-48, St. Louis, Mo., 1949-52, asst. mgr., Bedford, Ind., 1952-53, asst. mgr., Clinton, Ia., 1953-55; with Belk Simpson, Winchester, Ky., 1955-59, Parks Belks, Danville, Ky., 1959-60; mgr. Parks Belk Co., London, Ky., 1960—. Mem. Cumberland Valley Devel. Council, 1968-69; mem. Ky. Extension Council, 1968-72; pres. leaders council Ky. 4-H Club, 1970-72. Served with USAAF, 1943-45. Mem. Ky. Retail Mchts. Assn. (chpt. pres. 1965-70), Retail Mchts. Assn. (pres. 1968-69), C. of C. London (pres. 1968-69, dir. 1970-71). Mem. Christian Ch. (elder). Kiwanian (pres. 1966). Home: 420 Bomont St London KY 40741 Office: 249 N Main St London KY 40741

BALLARD, WILEY PERRY, JR., petroleum co. exec.; b. Birmingham, Ala., Oct. 23, 1922; s. Wiley Perry and Helen (McCary) B.; student U. N.C., 1940-43; m. Anne Hart Equen, Sept. 12, 1947; children—Anne McCary, Wiley Perry. Pres. Ballard Corp., Atlanta, 1948—, Ballard & Curren Corp., Atlanta, 1948—, Ballard & Cordell Corp., Atlanta, 1958—, Perco Products, Atlanta, 1950—; dir. Road Atlanta, Inc., Phenix Supply Co. (both Atlanta), Phenix Supply Co., Tampa, Fla., W.P. Ballard Co., Greensboro, N.C. and Washington, Phenix Supply, Birmingham. Mem. Mineral Leasing Commn. Ga., 1968-71. Served with USAAF, 1943-45. Mem. Oil Investment Inst. (gov.), Phi Delta Theta. Episcopalian. Clubs: Atlanta Country, Peachtree Golf, Commerce, Piedmont Driving, Capital City (Atlanta). Home: 2576 Howell Mill Rd NW Atlanta GA 30327 Office: 1608 Peachtree Center Towers 230 Peachtree St NW Atlanta GA 30303

BALLARD, WILLIAM THOMAS, chem. engr.; b. Mt. Pleasant, Tex., Dec. 22, 1923; s. William T. and Jeanie (Jackson) B.; B.S., U. Tex., 1946; M.S., Ga. Inst. Tech., 1950; m. Marian LaVerne Ehlers, May 3, 1947; children—William Brian, Bruce Thomas, Barbara Ann. Dist. engr. Tex. Dept. Health, Tyler, 1946-58; process engr. LaGloria Oil & Gas Co., Tyler, 1958-65, chief engr., 1965-69, gen. supt., 1969-70; regional dir. environmental health Tex. Dept. Health, Tyler, 1970—. Fellow Tex. Pub. Health Assn (pres. 1956-57); mem. Nat., Tex. socs. profl. engrs. Mason (Shriner). Club: Optimist. Home: 1015 N Azalea Dr Tyler TX 75701 Office: PO Box 2003 Tyler TX 75701

BALLINGER, JAMES N., rancher; b. Hanna, Okla., Apr. 1, 1914; s. George H. and Millie J. (McClain) B.; B.S. in Agr., Okla. State U., 1937; m. Mary Katherine Henson, Jan. 1, 1938; children—Barbara (Mrs. Paul Moore), James N., George C., Amelia Kay (Mrs. James Pearce). Asst., county supr. Farm Security Adminstrn. (now Farmers Home Adminstrn.), Okla., 1937-43; farmer, Eufaula, Okla., 1943—; dairy farmer, 1953-66; tchr. vets. agr. Eufaula Sch. System, 1946-57; land appraiser Eufaula Lake Project, 1958-60; mem. Okla. Bd. Agr., Oklahoma City, 1964—, pres., 1966-71; dir. Canadian Valley Elec. Co-op. Mem. McIntosh County Republican Com., 1960—. Chmn. bd. dirs. Eufaula Indsl. Found.; McIntosh County Soil and Water Conservations Dists. Named Hon. State Farmer, County 4-H Club. Mem. Farm Bur., Eufaula C. of C. (dir.), McIntosh County Dairy Herd Improvement Assn. (sec.-treas.), Alpha Zeta. Baptist (deacon). Lion (dir.). Home: Route 3 Eufaula OK 74432

BALLON, DAVID, lawyer; b. Memphis, Sept. 27, 1907; student Washington and Lee U.; LL.B., Vanderbilt U., 1932. Admitted to Tenn. bar, 1931; spl. judge Memphis Municipal Ct., 1939-42, circuit ct. and gen. sessions ct., 1957, probate ct., 1959, criminal ct., 1960-64; now mem. firm Glasscock, Ballon, Vorder Bruegge & Friedman, Memphis. Chmn. Memphis City Traffic Adv. Commn., 1958-60. Bd. dirs. Mid-South Fair, 1948-66. Mem. Memphis, Shelby County (dir. 1965-68), West Tenn. (v.p. 1968-69), Tenn. (gov. 1959-67), Am. (mem. resolutions coms. 1965-66) bar assns. Address: 2424-100 N Main Bldg Memphis TN 38103*

BALMAN, SIDNEY, constrn. co. exec.; b. Mpls., Mar. 19, 1919; s. Max and Lea (Goodman) B.; student U. Minn., 1937-40; B.B.A., So. Meth. U., 1952; m. Patricia Ann Papert, Nov. 29, 1952; children—Beth Leigh, Sidney, Jr. Owner, chief exec. officer Tex. Builders Devel. Co., Dallas, 1950-67; owner, pres. Sidney Balman, Inc., Dallas, 1965—; gen. partner Sidney Balman, Ltd., Dallas, 1965—; mem. nat. operators marketing com. Howard Johnson Co., 1970—; partner, operations exec. Preston Alpha Properties. Capt., Presbyn. Hosp. Bldg. Drive, 1962; vol. solicitor United Fund, 1960; mem. jr. bd. Jewish Welfare Assn., 1955-56; mem. Cotton Bowl Council, Dallas, 1969-72; hon. councilman Circle 10 council Boy Scouts Am., 1972—; asso. bd. mem. Girl's Town U.S.A., Austin, 1972—; active fund-raising Nat. Jewish Hosp., Denver, 1960-72, Children's Med. Center, Dallas, 1965—, Dallas Symphony Assn., 1970-71, Dallas Civic Opera Assn., 1970, 71; orgn. worker N. Tex. Devel. Council, 1971—. Trustee St. Mark's Sch., Dallas, pres. Dads Club, 1968-69. Served with USAAF, 1941-45; ETO. Decorated Air medal with 4 oak leaf clusters, D.F.C. Mem. N. Dallas C. of C. (v.p.), Hotel Sales Mgmt. Assn., Nat., Tex. hotel-motel assns., UN Assn. U.S. (mem. UN Day com.). Jewish religion (trustee temple). Mason (Shriner). Clubs: T Bar M Tennis, Sportsmen's of Tex., Dallas Woods and Water (Dallas). Home: 4645 Park Lane Dallas TX 75220 Office: 10333 N Central Expy Dallas TX 75231

BALMER, GLENN GRAVES, scientist; b. Woodston, Kan., Dec. 24, 1914; s. Clarence A. and Myrtle W. (Graves) B.; A.B., Ft. Hays, Kan. State Coll., 1937; M.S., State U. Ia., 1939; postgrad. U. Mich., Summer 1940, U. Colo., evenings 1950-54, Northwestern U., evenings 1955-56; m. Mary F. Neely, Dec. 25, 1942; children—Darrell G., Glenn B. Grad. asst. State U. Ia., Iowa City, 1937-39; tchr. Estherville (Ia.) Jr. Coll., 1939-41; physicist engring., research lab. Bur. Reclamation, Denver, 1945-54; sr. devel. engr. research, devel. lab., Portland Cement Assn., Skokie, Ill., 1955-66, highway research engr., Fed. Hwy. Adminstrn., Washington, 1966—. Served with AUS 1941-45; PTO; lt. col. Res. Decorated Air medal. Mem. Nat. Safety Council (com. on winter driving hazards), Am. Soc. Testing Materials, Am. Concrete Inst., Hwy. Research Bd., Sigma Xi, Delta Epsilon. Contbr. articles tech. lit. Home: 11128 Hunt Club Dr Potomac MD 20854 Office: Fed Hwy Adminstrn Washington DC 20590

BALNICKY, ROBERT GABRIEL, clergyman; b. Elizabeth, N.J., Apr. 18, 1922; s. Harry and Irene (Sawicky) B.; student Pensacola Jr. Coll., 1949, Emory U., 1950. Columbia Theol. Sem., Decatur, Ga., 1952; m. Elizabeth Marie Hartenstein, Apr. 18, 1943; children—Richard Ozzie, Barbara Gail. With Merck & Co., Rahway, N.J., 1939-42; pastor Troy (N.C.) Presbyn. Ch., 1952-55, 1st Presbyn. Ch., Ocean Drive Beach, S.C., 1955-56, McCutchen Meml. Ch., Union, S.C., 1956-60, Fairfield Presbyn. Ch., Pensacola, Fla., 1960-64; founder, pastor Trinity Bible Ch., Pensacola, 1964-70; pastor Inskip Presbyn. Ch., Knoxville, Tenn., 1970-72; pres. Robert G. Balnicky Evang. Assn., Inc., Pensacola. Pres. Union County (S.C.) Ministers Assn., 1957; chmn. Enoree Presbytery Com. Evangelism, 1956-60; mem. com. evangelism S.C. Synod, 1956-60; chmn. bd. dirs. Pensacola Youth for Christ; bd. dirs. Fla. Alcohol-Narcotics, Inc., Fla. United Christian Action, Inc.; mem. adv. bd. Community Action Program, Am. Security Council. Lt. col., chaplain Fla. Civil Air Patrol, 1965-70; dep. wing chaplain Tenn. Civil Air Patrol 1970—. Served as aviation machinist's mate, flight engr. 1st class USN, 1942-49. Recipient Four Chaplains citation Chapel Four Chaplains, Phila., 1960. Mem. Am. Legion (state chaplain S.C. 1956-58, post comdr. 1953-54; grad. Am. Legion Coll., Indpls. 1954; mem. nat. press assn.; chmn. S.C. religious emphasis com. 1956-58, mem. nat. comdr.'s flying squadron; mem. Century Club 1954-55), 40 and 8 (grand aumonier S.C.; state chaplain 1957-59, aumonier nat., nat. chaplain 1959-60; local chaplain 1961-70), Navy League, World Ministry Fellowship (pres. 1966-68), Nat. Assn. Evangs., Internat. Order St. Luke the physician. Mason (32 deg.). Office: PO Box 12228 Knoxville TN 37912

BALSA, CESAR, hotel exec.; b. Barcelona, Spain, June 21, 1923; s. Antonio and Elisa (Carralero) B.; ed. in Spain; m. Carmen Cruz, July 16, 1948; children—Carmen Cesar, Elena, Elisa, Cristina, Monica, Antoineta. Bell boy Oriental Hotel, Barcelona, 1938; mgr. food services Palace Hotel, Madrid, 1945; mgr. Tampico Club, Mexico City, 1949; opened Focolare Restaurant, beginning of Balsa Chain, Mexico City, 1952; pres. Nacional Hotelera, S.A., Mexico City, 1956—; dir. Eastern Airlines, Inc. Bd. dirs. Maxican Council Businessmen of Mexico. Mem. Young Pres. Orgn. Catholic. Home: Calzada del Desierto 24 San Angel Inn Mexico DF Mexico Office: Hamburgo 135 Mexico 6 DF Mexico

BALSLEY, HOWARD LLOYD, educator; b. Chgo., Dec. 3, 1913; s. Elmer Lloyd and Katherine (McGlashing) B.; A.B., Ind. U., 1946, M.A., 1947, Ph.D., 1950; postgrad. John Hopkins, 1947-48, U. Chgo., summer 1948; m. Irol Verneth Whitmore, Aug. 24, 1947. Asst. prof. econs. U. Utah, Salt Lake City, 1949-50; asso. prof. econs., dir. Sch. Bus., Russell Sage Coll., Troy, N.Y., 1950-52; asso. prof. econs. Washington and Lee U., Lexington, Va., 1952-54; prof. bus. statistics, head dept. bus. and econ. research La. Tech. U., Ruston, 1954-65; prof. marketing statistics Tex. Tech. U., Lubbock, 1965—. Served with USAAF, 1943-46. Mem. Am. Econ. Assn., Am. Statis. Assn., Southwestern Social Sci. Assn., Am. Inst. Decision Scis. Club: Lubbock (Tex.) Country. Author: (with James Gemmell) Principles of Economics, 1953; Readings in Economic Doctrines, vols. 1 and 2, 1961; Introduction to Statistical Method, 1964; Quantitative Research Methods for Business & Economics, 1970. Home: 2609 Ridge Rd Lubbock TX 79409

BALSLEY, IROL WHITMORE (MRS. HOWARD L. BALSLEY), educator; b. Venus, Neb., Aug. 22, 1912; d. Sylvanus Bertrand and Nanna (Carson) Whitmore; B.A., Neb. State Tchrs. Coll., Wayne, 1933; M.S., U. Tenn., 1940; Ed.D., Ind. U., 1952; m. Howard Lloyd Balsley, Aug. 24, 1947. Tchr. high schs., Osmond and Walthill, Neb., 1934-37, VanSant Sch. Bus., Omaha, 1938; asst. prof., Ind. U., 1942-49; lectr. U. Utah, 1949-50, Russell Sage Coll., 1953-54; prof. office adminstrn. La. Tech. U., 1960-65, also head dept. office adminstrn.; prof. bus. edn. Tex. Technol. Univ., 1965—; coordinator of USAF clk.-typist tng. program Pa. State U., 1951, inst., head office tng. sect. TVA, 1941-42; editorial asst. South-western Pub. Co., 1940-41. Mem. Nat. Bus. Edn. Assn. (past pres. research found.), Nat. Bus. Tchrs. Edn. Assn., Adminstrv. Mgmt. Soc., N.E.A., Nat. Collegiate Assn. Secs. (co-founders, past pres.), Pi Lambda Theta, Delta Pi Epsilon (past nat. sec.), Beta Gamma Sigma, Pi Omega Pi, Sigma Tau Delta, Alpha Psi Omega. Author: (with Wanous) Shorthand Transcription Studies, 1968; (with Robinson) Integrated Secretarial Studies, 1963. Home: 2609 Ridge Rd Lubbock TX 79403

BALTZ, RICHARD BRUCE, educator, economist; b. St. Louis, July 27, 1930; s. Arthur William and Ollie May (Batdorf) B.; student Belleville Jr. Coll., 1948-50, St. Louis U., 1950; B.B.A., Baylor U., 1955, M.S., 1957; Ph.D., U. Ark., 1962; m. Nancy Jane Cozort, Aug. 26, 1958; 1 dau., Cynthia Lynn. Security salesman Clisbee & Co., Waco, Tex., 1955-57; instr. Baylor U., 1957-58, U. Ark., 1958-62; asst. prof. U. Ark., 1962-63; asst. prof. econs. St. Louis U., 1963-65; asso. prof. econs. and finance N.E. La. State Coll., Monroe, 1965-66; chmn. dept. econs. and bus. adminstrn. Millsaps Coll., Jackson, Miss., 1966—. Served with USAF, 1951-55. Mem. So., Ozark econ. assns., Beta Gamma Sigma, Omicron Delta Epsilon. Author: (with Howard B. Baltz) Fundamentals of Business Analysis. Contbr. articles to profl. jours. Address: PO Box 15497 Millsaps Coll Jackson MS 39210

BAMBER, JOHN IRVING, city ofcl.; b. Plaucheville, La., Aug. 20, 1921; s. James Deway and Mary Madeline (Ducote) B.; student La. State U., 1939-41, Internat. Corr. Schs., 1960; m. Arclie Phrozine McMaster, Nov. 9, 1941; 1 son, Deway James. Forms rep. Economy Forms Corp., Des Moines, 1941-45; with Stearns Rogers Co., Denver, 1945-50; heavy constrn. supt. R.P. Farnsworth, New Orleans, 1950-56; asst. city engr., Marshall, Tex., 1956-67; dir. pub. works, Nederland, Tex., 1967—. Profl. handwriting analyst; personnel cons., marriage and teaching counselor; tchr. Am. Banking Inst., Lamar U., 1971-72. Mem. Internat. Graphoanalysis Soc., Inst. Certification Engring. Technicians, Am. Water Works Assn., Am., Tex. (membership com. 1967-72) pub. works assns. Episcopalian. Mason (Shriner); mem. Order Eastern Star. Home: 1420 Chicago Av Nederland TX 77627 Office: PO Box 967 Nederland TX 77627

BANDROFCHECK, JOSEPH, mfg. co. exec.; b. Hunker, Pa., Sept. 1, 1920; s. Paul and Catherine (Kukla) B.; student Internat. Accountants Soc., 1948-53, U. Pitts. Extension, 1950-54; m. Mary Kay Wesbecher, Oct. 27, 1951; children—Charles Paul, Susan Kathleen, Mark Joseph. Accountant, Robertshaw Controls Co., Youngwood, Pa., 1941-57, Richmond, Va., 1957-59, asst. controller, 1959-68, asst. treas., 1968-69, treas. 1969—. Served with USNR, 1944-46. Mem. Nat. Assn. Accountants (pres. Richmond chpt. 1967-68), Financial Execs. Inst., Planning Execs. Inst. (pres. Richmond chpt. 1964-65), West Richmond Bus. Men's Assn. Home: 3705 Shore Dr Richmond VA 23225 Office: 1701 Byrd Av Richmond VA 23226

BANDY, OLIE SHERMAN, educator; b. Lafayette, Tenn., May 22, 1904; s. Freely Skyles and Dolly (Jenkins) B.; A.B., Western Ky. State Tchrs. Coll., 1928; M.A., Rollins Coll., 1930; Ed.D., U. Fla., 1960; m. Emily Whitmore, June 1, 1929; children—Ruth (Mrs. W. T. Howard), Lynn Sherman, Louie Albra, Mary Juanita, Joyce Elisabeth. Tchr. pub. schs., Orlando, Fla., 1928-30, Atlanta, 1930-47; head Spanish dept. Fla. So. Coll., 1947-51; gen. supt. instrn. Pasco County, 1951-52; prin. Pasco High Sch., 1952-58, dir. edn., 1958-64; acting chmn. fgn. langs. dept., asso. dean DeKalb Coll., Clarkston, Ga., 1964-71; acad. dean Atlanta Bapt. Coll., 1971—. Bd. dirs. Hispanic Inst. Fla., 1955-64. Mem. Nat., Fla. edn. assns., Nat. Assn. Secondary Prins., Am. Assn. Tchrs. Spanish and Portuguese (pres. Fla. chpt. 1948-49), Pan Am. League (past pres. Atlanta br.), Kappa Phi Kappa, Phi Delta Kappa. Baptist. Rotarian (past pres.). Home: 142 Alpine Dr Lilburn GA 30247 Office: 3000 Flowers Rd NE Atlanta GA 30341

BANDY, WILLIAM HENRY, physician; b. Maiden, N.C., July 25, 1917; s. William Gaither and Myrtle (Daniel) B.; B.S., Appalachian State U., 1937; M.D., Med. Coll. Va., 1941; M.P.H., Johns Hopkins, 1952; m. Pauline Pope, June 21, 1941; children—Margaret Elizabeth (Mrs. Albert Barnes Marshall), William Hollis. Intern, City Hosp., Winston Salem, 1941-42; resident Watts Hosp., Durham N.C., 1946-49; practice medicine, specializing in preventive medicine, Georgetown, Del., 1949-56, Hickory, N.C., 1956-66, Williamsburg, Va., 1966—; dep. state health dir., Georgetown, 1949-56; dist. health dir., Hickory, 1956-66; dir. pub. health Colonial Health Dist., 1966-71; dir. Hampton Health Dept. (Va.), 1972—. Served from 1st lt. to maj. M.C., AUS, 1942-46. Diplomate Am. Bd. Preventive Medicine. Fellow Am. Coll. Preventive Medicine; mem. A.M.A., Va., James Hampton med. socs. Am. Pub. Health Assn. Home: 207 Watkins Dr Hampton VA 23369 Office: 3130 Victoria Blvd Hampton VA 23361

BANG, GARY RACH, dentist; b. Chgo., July 19, 1941; s. Olaf Edward and Orpha Agatha (Hulteen) B.; A.B., U. Richmond, 1963; D.D.S., Med. Coll. Va., 1967; m. Susan Stitley Block, Aug. 14, 1965; children—Michael Edward, Eric Riley. Pvt. practice dentistry, Staunton, Va., 1969—; mem. dental staff Kings Daus. Hosp., Staunton, 1969—, sec., 1971-72. Bd. dirs. Staunton-West Augusta County unit Am. Cancer Soc. Served with Dental Corps, AUS, 1967-69. Mem. Am. Dental Assn., Va. Gun Owners and Sportsmens Alliance (dir. 1972—), Nat. Rifle Assn., Amateur Trapshooting Assn., N.G. Assn. U.S., Alumni Assn. Med. Coll. Va., Delta Sigma Delta (life), Sigma Alpha Epsilon. Presbyn. Mason, Elk, Kiwanian. Clubs: Stonewall Rifle and Pistol (sec. 1970-71), Rockbridge Baths Hunt, Westside Swim. Home: 502 Robin St Staunton VA 24401 Office: Profl Bldg W Frederick St Staunton VA 24401

BANISTER, JOHN ROBERT, librarian; b. Saginaw, Mich., Feb. 5, 1912; s. John Lansing and Agnes (Bell) B.; A.A., Bay City (Mich.) Jr. Coll., 1934; A.B., U. Mich., 1936; B.S. in L.S., U. Ill., 1937; m. Nancy Simpson, Sept. 9, 1944; 1 dau., Nancy Anne (Mrs. Edmund Alan Attebury, Jr.). Asst. reference librarian Mich. State Library, Lansing 1936-41; order librarian, tech. library TVA, 1942-44; extension librarian Lansing Pub. Library, 1944-46; regional librarian Ill. State Library, Mt. Carmel, 1946-48; pub. library cons. gen. extension div. U. Fla., 1948-50; dir. libraries Chattahooches Valley Regional Library, Columbus, Ga., 1951—; cons. in field, 1960—. Del. Assembly Libraries of Ams., 1946; chmn. jr. mems. round table Mich. Library Assn., 1941, Ill. Library Assn., 1946. Chmn. Muscogee County (Ga.) chpt. Am. Heart Assn., 1952, Community Services Assn. Columbus, 1956-58; bd. dirs. Columbus Symphony Guild, 1962—, Columbus United Givers, 1957-59. Mem. Am. (council 1940-41, chmn. jr. mems. round table 1946), Ga. (v.p. 1960), Southeastern (chmn. pub. libraries sect. 1948) library assns. Presbyn. Rotarian (dir. Columbus 1963—), Club: Columbus Country. Editor: The Junior Librarian, 1939-41; The Florida Public Library News-Letter, 1948-50. Contbr. articles to profl. jours. Home: 2952 Roswell Lane Columbus GA 31906 Office: W C Bradley Mem Library Columbus GA 31906

BANKS, EUGENE PENDLETON, educator; b. Florence, S.C., Nov. 5, 1923; s. Walter Dickson and Constance (Pendleton) B.; student Brevard Coll., 1939-41; B.A., Furman U., 1943; postgrad. U. N.M., 1946-48; A.M., Harvard, 1950, Ph.D., 1954; m. Catherine Barber, June 28, 1945; children—Philip P., James B., John M., Kate D. Instr., Duke, 1953-54; asst. prof. to prof. anthropology Wake Forest U., Winston-Salem, N.C., 1954—; vis. prof. Rangoon U., 1960-61, Zagreb U., 1966-67; vis. lectr. Am. Anthrop. Assn.; vis. scientist Nat. Acad. Sci. Bd. dirs. Assn. for Handicapped, Gallery Contemporary Art, Bethabara Hist. Soc. Served to comdr. USNR, 1943-46. Fellow Am. Anthrop. Soc.; mem. Am. Ethnol. Soc., So. Anthrop. Soc. (pres. 1972—), A.A.A.S., Am. Assn. U. Profs. (past chpt. pres.). Author: Methodology of the Behavioral Sciences, 1971. Contbr. articles profl. jours. Home: Route 3 Pfafftown NC 27040 Office: Dept Sociology and Anthropology Wake Forest U Winston-Salem NC 27109

BANKS, RALPH ROUNDTREE, JR., lawyer; b. Eutaw, Ala., June 20, 1924; s. Ralph R. and Sarah (Minor) B.; A.B., U. Ala., 1946, LL.B., 1948; m. Sara Henry Reynolds, June 1, 1949; children—Jamie R., Ralph Roundtree III. Admitted to Ala. bar, 1948; practiced in Eutaw, 1948—; atty., dep. solicitor Greene County (Ala.), 1957—. Dir. Mchts. and Farmers Bank of Greene County. Served with USNR, 1943-45. Mem. Ala. Bar Assn. Episcopalian. Home: 854 Boligee Rd Eutaw AL 35462 Office: 106 Main St Eutaw AL 35462

BANKS, RICHARD GRIFFIN, army officer, ednl. adminstr.; b. Montgomery, Ala., Oct. 12, 1912; s. Richard Griffin and Blanche (Cartter) B.; B.A.E., U. Fla., 1934; M.A., U. Va., 1949; m. Isabel Gwendolyn Day, July 26, 1942; children—Ann Cartter, Barbara Jane. Tchr. pub. schs., Fla., 1935-40; commd. 1st lt. U.S. Army, 1940, advanced through grades to col., 1960; dir. instrn. Arty. Sch., 1954-57, polit. rep. U.S. Forces Germany to German Govt., 1958-61, prof. mil. sci. U. Miami, 1964-67, ret. 1967; research scientist U. Miami, Coral Gables, Fla., 1967-71, asst. dean Coll. Arts and Scis., 1971—. Decorated Legion of Merit, Bronze Star with oak leaf cluster, Purple Heart; Order of Ulchi (Korean). Mem. Delta Tau Delta, Phi Kappa Phi, Kappa Delta Pi, Phi Delta Kappa, Pi Delta Epsilon. Democrat. Episcopalian. Club: Army Navy of Coral Gables. Co-author articles pattern analysis of disturbed coll. students. Home: 14320 SW 86th Av Miami FL 33158 Office: U Miami Coral Gables FL 33146

BANKS, ROBERT BLACKBURN, found. exec.; b. Wichita, Kan., Oct. 12, 1922; s. Bernard T. and Georgia (Corley) B.; B.S., Northwestern U., 1947, M.S., 1948; Ph.D. (Hilp fellow), U. Cal., 1951; D.I.C., U. London, 1952; m. Gunta Matisons, Dec. 25, 1960 children—Steven, Erik. Research engr. U. Cal., 1949-51, Infilco, Inc., Tucson, 1952-54; asso. prof. civil engring., Northwestern U., 1954-59, chmn. sci.-engring. com., 1955-57, chmn. dept. civil engring., 1956-59, asst. dean research and grad. studies, prof. engring. sci., 1959-61; dean engring. U. Ill., Chgo., 1963-67; adviser sci. and engring. Ford Found., Mexico and C.Am., 1967—; vis. prof. Grad. Sch. Engring., Nat. Univ. of Mexico, 1967—; dir. of research SEATO Grad. Sch. Engring., Bangkok, Thailand, 1961-63. Cons., McDonnell Aircraft Corp., 1958, Space Tech. Labs, Inc., 1960. Served from ensign to lt. (j.g.), USNR, 1943-46. Fulbright fellow, 1951-52. Mem. Am. Inst. Aeros. and Astronautics, Am. Soc. C.E., Internat. Hydraulics Research Assn., A.A.A.S., Am. Geophys. Union, Am. Soc. Engring. Edn., Sigma Xi, Tau Beta Pi, Pi Mu Epsilon, Delta Nu Alpha, Sigma Chi. Home: Meseta 111 Pedregal Mexico City 20 Mexico Office: Ford Found Reforma 243 Mexico City 5 Mexico

BANKSTON, JESSE H., state ofcl.; b. Mt. Hermon, La.; B.A., La. State U., also M.A. in Pub. Adminstrn.; postgrad. U. N.C.; m. Ruth Paine; 4 children. Formerly cons. Griffenhagen and Assos., Chgo.; research supr. La. Dept. Revenue, Baton Rouge; adminstrv. asst. La. Dept. Civil Service, Baton Rouge; exec. asst. La. Dept. Instns., then dir.; hosp. dir. La. Hosp Bd.; exec. sec. La. Hosp Assn.; dir. La. Dept. Hosps., Baton Rouge; now mem. La. Bd. Edn. Sec.-treas. Bankston Enterprises, Inc.; dir. Baton Rouge Bank and Trust Co. Pres. YMCA, Baton Rouge, chmn. fund-raising com.; chmn. fund-raising com. Baton Rouge Gen. Hosp.; mem. fund-raising coms. Our Lady of the Lake Hosp., Salvation Army; mem. White House Conf. Children and Youth, 1950, 60, White House Conf. on Aging, 1960-61. Former mem. La. Democratic central com. Bd. dirs. La. Tb Assn., Baton Rouge Community Chest. Mem. Baton Rouge C. of C., Assn. Mental Health, La., Am. hosps assns., Am. Soc. Pub. Adminstrn., Acad. Hosp. Counselors (pres.), Internat. inst. Hosp. Cons. Baptist (trustee). Mason (Shriner). Address: La Dept Edn Box 44064 Baton Rouge LA 70804

BANNERMAN, ARTHUR MARLING, ret. coll. pres.; b. Juneau, Alaska, May 26, 1900; s. William S. and Grace (Mitchell) B.; A.B., Lafayette Coll., 1922, L.H.D., 1945; A.M., U. N.C., 1940; LL.D., Berea Coll., Johnson C. Smith U., Warren Wilson Coll., 1971; summer student, U. Wis., Middlebury Coll.; m. Lucile Patton, Nov. 27, 1930; children—Janet Patton, Mary Mitchell. Instr. Asheville (N.C.) Farm Sch., 1928-42, prin., 1930-38, supt., 1940-42; pres. Warren Wilson Coll., 1942-71, pres. emeritus, 1971—. Dir. Swannanoa Bank & Trust Co. Mem. adv. bd. Asheville Country Day Sch. Trustee James G. K. McClure Devel. and Ednl. Fund. Pres. Swannanoa Community Council. Greater Asheville Council; pres. bd. dirs. United Fund of Asheville and Buncombe County, 1957-58; mem. Buncombe County Planning Council; mem. Buncombe County Hosp. Authority Bd., 1971—. Treas. N.C. Found. Ch. Related Colls., 1959-60; pres. N.C. Council Ch. Related Colls., 1959-60; trustee Asheville City Libraries. Recipient Award of Merit, Asheville Sch., 1971. Mem. So. Mountain Workers (past pres. council), United Church Men (bd. mgrs.). Nat. Council Presbyn. Men (pres.), Sigma Alpha Epsilon. Presbyn. Clubs: Civitan of Asheville (past pres.); Biltmore Forest Country. Address: Warren Wilson College Swannanoa NC 28778

BANUELOS, ROMANA ACOSTA (MRS. ALEJANDRO BANUELOS), treas. U.S.; b. Miami, Ariz., Mar. 20, 1925; d. Juan Francisco and Teresa (Lugo) Acosta; ed. elementary sch., Mexico; m. Alejandro Banuelos, Dec. 31, 1949; children—Martin Torres, Carlos Torres, Ramona. Founder, Ramona's Mexican Food Products, Inc., Los Angeles, 1949; founding dir. Pan Am. Nat. Bank, East Los Angeles, Cal., 1964, chmn. bd. dirs., 1969—; treas. U.S., Washington, 1971—. Founder, Ramona's Mexican Food Products Scholarship Found., Inc., 1970. Named Outstanding Businesswoman of Year Mayor of Los Angeles, 1969; recipient Commendation award Bd. Suprs. County Los Angeles, certificate of merit Mexican-Am. agy. Met. Los Angeles, 1971. Home: 2500 Virginia Av Washington DC 20037 Office: Treasury Dept Office of Treasurer Washington DC 20220

BARAFF, ALVIN SIDNEY, clin. psychologist; b. Washington, Apr. 22, 1935; s. Abraham and Betty (Zuckerman) B.; B.A., U. Md., 1957; M.S., U. Miami (Fla.), 1959; Ph.D., U. Ky., 1963 children—Ramie Lynn, Todd Mitchell. Clin. trainee VA Hosps., Lexington, Ky., Cin., 1960-63; child psychologist Woods Schs., Langhorne, Pa., 1959; asst. prof. Emory U., Atlanta, 1963-66; clin. psychotherapist, Atlanta, 1966-69; supervisory clin. psychologist Rehab. Center for Alcoholics, Occoquan, Va., 1969—; pvt. practice psychotherapy, Washington, 1969—. Pres., dir. Career Planning, Inc., Atlanta, 1967—. Mem. Am., Ga., D.C., Va., Md., Southeastern psychol. assns. Home: 1400 S Joyce St Arlington VA 22202 Office: 2430 Pennsylvania Av NW Washington DC 20037

BARANCO, RAPHAEL ALVIN, dentist; b. Baton Rouge, La., Nov. 19, 1932; s. Beverly Victor and Evelyn Gertrude (Edmond) B.; B.S. in Biology, Xavier U., 1956; D.D.S., Meharry Med. Coll., 1961; m. Terry Bryant, June 10, 1961; children—Angela, Rachel, Raphael. Intern, Jersey City Med. Center, 1961-62; pvt. practice dentistry, Baton Rouge, 1962-63 instr. prosthetic dentistry Meharry Med. Coll., Nashville, 1963-64; dir. clin. dentistry VA Hosp., Tuskegee, Ala., 1964-68; individual practice dentistry, Lafayette, La., 1968—. Mem. Lafayette Council on Human Relations, 1968—; chmn. Lafayette Parish Community Action Council, 1971-72. Mem. Sheriffs' Adv. Commn., 1968—. Bd. dirs. Tri-Parish Community Action Agy.; pres., bd. dirs. Holy Family Sch., 1971—. Served with AUS, 1953-55. Mem. N.A.A.C.P. (chmn. housing com.), Am. Dental Assn., Alpha Phi Alpha, Alpha Phi Omega, Chi Delta Mu. Democrat. Roman Catholic. Home: 200 Alfred St Lafayette LA 70501 Office: 120 Louisiana Av Lafayette LA 70501

BARBEE, JAMES DORRIS, textile co. exec.; b. Carthage, Tenn., Oct. 2, 1912; s. Joe Dorman and Willie (Smith) B.; B.S. in Elec. Engring., U. Tenn., 1933; m. Lois Beatrice Dunn, Nov. 10, 1935; children—James Dorris, Linda Bruce. With Brookside Mills, Knoxville, Tenn., 1933-40, 42-45, Dan River Mills, Danville, Va., 1940-41, Borden Mills, Kingsport, Tenn., 1945-46; with Burlington Industries, Inc., 1946—, exec. v.p., 1963-72, sr. v.p., 1972—, mem. mgmt. policy com., dir.; dir. Northwestern Ry. Bd. dirs. So. States Indsl. Council, Nat. Cotton Council; Bd. advisers N.C. Vocational Textile Sch., 1954-60, Belmont Abbey Coll., 1958—; trustee Lenoir Rhyne Coll.; chmn. devel. bd. U. Tenn. Mem. N.A.M. (dir.), Yarn Spinners Assn. (past dir.), Gastonia (N.C.) C. of C. (past 1st v.p.). Presbyn. Kiwanian. Clubs: Charlotte (N.C.) Textile (past pres., dir.); Greensboro Country; University (N.Y.C.). Home: 105 Elmwood Terrace Greensboro NC 27408 Office: 3330 W Friendly Av Greensboro NC 27410

BARBER, BYRON EDWARD, music co. exec.; b. Chico, Cal., Oct. 31, 1946; s. Ernest E. and Janice (Carmack) B.; student Tex. Technol. Coll., 1965-66, Odessa Coll., 1966-67; B.B.A., S.W. Tex. State U., 1970; m. Sandra Kay Oliver, Jan. 21, 1967. Drummer dance bands, 1960-66; founder Bo Barber Prodns., Midland, Tex., 1966, Byron Talent Mgmt., Byron Records and ByBar Pub. Co., Midland, 1967; chief exec. officer Byron-Wayne Assos., San Marcos, Tex., 1969-70; staff announcer radio sta. KJBC, Midland, 1964-65, radio sta. KWEL, Midland, 1965-66, radio sta. KBST, Big Spring, Tex., 1966, radio sta. KBYG, Big Spring, 1966-67, radio sta. KCNY, San Marcos, 1967-70. Served with USAF, 1970—. Mem. Lambda Chi Alpha. Home: 127 N 11th St Enid OK 73701

BARBER, MONTY CLYDE, cosmetic co. exec.; b. Rockdale, Tex., Jan. 12, 1931; s. Clyde and Hattie Estelle (Montague) B.; B.B.A., LL.B., U. Tex., 1955; m. Kay Wallace, June 29, 1963; children—Kelty Lynn, Brandon Chase. Admitted to Tex. bar, 1955; mem. firm Biggers, Baker, Lloyd & Carver, Dallas, 1957-67; v.p. Liquid Paper Corp., Dallas, 1967; v.p., sec., gen. counsel Mary Kay Cosmetics, Inc., Dallas, 1968—. Bd. mgrs. The Mary Kay Found. Served with AUS, 1955-57. Mem. Silver Spurs, Phi Delta Phi, Alpha Tau Omega. Home: 3508 Crescent St Dallas TX 75205 Office: 8900 Carpenter Freeway Dallas TX 75247

BARBER, N. LYNN, librarian; b. Mont Belvieu, Tex., Oct. 16, 1923; s. Arthur Elmer and Thelma (Carmody).; B.A., U. Tex., 1945; M.S., U. Houston, 1948; M.A., U. Denver, 1959. Tchr., librarian pub. schs. Tex., Md., 1946-53, 62; supr. practice teaching Eastern Ill. U., 1954-55; bookmobile librarian Tex. State Library, 1957-58; head librarian Ark. State Coll., 1958-59; circulation librarian Trinity U., 1959-60; head librarian Atlantic Christian Coll., 1960-61; dir. St. Lucie-Okeechobee Regional Library, 1961-62; pub. services librarian Washington and Lee U., 1962-63; acquisitions librarian S.E. Mo. State Coll., 1963-65; reference librarian N. Tex. State U., 1965-66; documents librarian Tarlton Law Library, University Tex., 1968-69; head librarian Paul Quinn Coll., 1967-69; cons. James Connally Tech. Inst., 1968; asst. law librarian Coll. William and Mary, 1969-71; asst. law librarian U. Ala., 1971; chief librarian St. Edward's U., 1971-72; reference librarian Nev. So. U.; dir. Bristol (Va.) Pub. Library; documents librarian Sch. Law, U. Va. Mem. A.L.A., Am. Assn. U. Profs., Tex., Southeastern library assns., Tex. Assn. Coll. Tchrs., Ex-Students Assn. U. Tex., Sertoma Internat., Am. Assn. Law Libraries, Delta Upsilon, Alpha Beta Alpha. Club: Forty Acres. Address: PO Box 205 Mont Belvieu TX 77580

BARBER, RICHARD LESLIE, coll. dean; b. Northeast, Pa., Apr. 22, 1920; s. Chester Clifford and Agnes (Leslie) B.; A.B. in Philosophy and Math., Ohio U., 1940; postgrad. U.S. Naval Acad., 1944-45; M.A. in Philosophy, Ind. U., 1948; Ph.D., Yale, 1950; m. Frances Pardue McCutchon, Aug 1, 1944; children—Richard Leslie, Frances Edith. Grad. asst., all univ. fellow, teaching asst. Ind. U., 1941, 46-48; asst. instr. Yale, 1948-50; asst. prof., asso. prof. philosophy, coordinator ednl. TV prodn. Tulane U., 1950-59; prof. philosophy, dean Coll. Arts and Scis., U. Louisville, 1959—. Vice pres. Ky. Youth Devel. Found. Served to lt. (s.g.) USNR, 1941-45; ETO, PTO. Mem. Am. Assn. U. Profs. (pres. Tulane 1954), Am. (exec. com. 1965—), Ky. confs. acad. deans, Assn. Higher Edn., Nat. Soc. Study Edn., Assn. American Colleges, Conference Acad. Deans So. States (pres. 1970), English-Speaking Union (dir. 1969—), Metaphys. Soc. Am. (charter), So. Soc. Philosophy and Psychology, Southwestern, Ky. (pres. 1965) philos. assns., Louisville Com. Fgn. Relations, Delta Tau Delta, Omicron Delta Kappa, Phi Eta Sigma, Alpha Phi Omega, Kappa Delta Pi, Phi Mu Alpha, Phi Kappa Phi. Methodist. Kiwanian. Clubs: Jefferson, Filson, Conversation, Helium (Louisville). Author numerous articles, revs. Home: 2431 Top Hill Rd Louisville KY 40206

BARBER, WILLIAM GILBRETH, III, lawyer; b. Austin, Tex., Dec. 14, 1931; s. William Gilbreth and Mildred (Williams) B.; B.A., U. Tex., 1954; LL.B., Harvard, 1957; m. Patricia Leonore Wallum, June 28, 1958; children—Mary Elizabeth, William Gilbreth, John Patrick, Katherine Marie. Admitted to Tex. bar, 1958; briefing atty. Supreme Ct. Tex., Austin, 1958-59; practice law firm Brown, Maroney, Rose, Baker & Barber, Austin, 1959—. Mem. Citywide Com. Human Rights, Austin, 1970—. Served with AUS, 1957. Mem. State Bar Tex., Travis County Bar Assn., Tex. Assn. Def. Counsel, Fedn. Ins. Counsel, Am. Arbitration Assn., Def. Research Inst., Lay Cath. Speakers Guild, Austin Deanery Council Cath. Men, Phi Beta Kappa, Phi Eta Sigma, Beta Theta Pi. Rotarian. Contbr. articles legal jours. Home: 3500 Scenic Hills Dr Austin TX 78703 Office: 900 Brown Bldg Austin TX 78701

BARBLES, EUGENE ANTHONY, savs. and loan exec.; b. Houston, Nov. 24, 1922; s. Nick and Anna (Barretta) B.; student Tex. A. and M. Coll., 1939-40, U. Houston, 1941; m. Dorothy Cecile Block, Jan. 17, 1943; children—Gary Eugene, Larry Drew. Asst. chief engr. Rice Hotel, 1946-52; bldg. mgr. San Jacinto Bldg., 1952-60; bldg. mgr. Main Bldg., from 1960; partner, dir. Bonded Maintenance Co., Dallas, also Ft. Worth; partner B & D Laundromats; dir. Milam Co., Inc., N.G.L. Corp.; now v.p. Am. Savs. and Loan Assn., Houston; pres. Am. Place Land Co., also dir.; pres. ASLA, Inc.; sec., treas. Staff Inc., also dir.; dir. Main Bank Houston. Mem. Houston Examining Bd. for Stationary Engrs., 1958—, Houston Code Com., 1958—; founder Stationary Engrs. Apprenticeship Tng. Sch., 1956, chmn., 1956—. Served from ensign to lt. (j.g.), U.S. Maritime Service, 1942-45. Mem. Internat. (sec.-treas. 1971—), Nat., Tex. (past pres.), Houston (past pres.) Southwest conf. (v.p.) assns. bldg. owners and mgrs., Am. Savs & Loan Assn. Club: Rams. Home: 5034 Tangle Lane Houston TX Office: PO Box 948 Main and Polk Sts Houston TX 77001

BARBOUR, OFFIE ALMON, JR., publicist; b. Benson, N.C., Sept. 20, 1916; s. Offie Almon and Emily (Canaday) B.; student Boiling Springs Jr. Coll., 1934, U. N.C., 1935-39; m. Frances Margaret Lewis, Feb. 9, 1957; children—Frances Lewis, Nancy Spence, Aubrey Elizabeth, Margaret Adams, Emily Sharon. Reporter, staff writer The Raleigh (N.C.) Times, 1941; pub. information officer N.C. Dept. of Labor, Raleigh, 1942—. Served with USNR, 1944-46. Mem. Oratorio Soc. (past pres.), Raleigh Pub. Relations Soc. (past treas.). Club: Wake County Young Democrat. Editor North Carolina Labor and Industry, monthly bull., 1941—. Home: 2710 Kittrell Dr Raleigh NC 27608 Office: Box 1151 Raleigh NC 27602

BARCELLONA, MATTHEW ROBERT, helicopter co. exec.; b. Buffalo, May 31, 1911; s. Frank and Mary (Frisa) B.; student Carnegie Inst. Tech. 1930-32, U. Buffalo, 1934-42; m. Alice Edmere Cabana, Sept. 12, 1936; 1 dau., Marianne. Auditor, N.Y. State Labor Dept. Buffalo, 1938-42; mgr. indsl. engring. Bell Aircraft Co., Buffalo, 1942-50; v.p. mgmt. engring. Bell Helicopter Co., Ft. Worth, 1968-70; v.p. materiel, 1970—, also mem. exec. com. Bd. dirs. Hillcrest High Sch. P.T.A., Dallas, 1961-62. Mem. Am. Helicopter Soc., Am. Inst.

Indsl. Engrs., Assn. U.S. Army. Republican. Roman Catholic. Club: Dallas Athletic. Home: 5707 Watson Circle Dallas TX 75225 Office: Bell Helicopter Co Box 482 Fort Worth TX 76101

BARCLAY, CARL ARCHIE, physician; b. Nanticoke, Md., July 30, 1922; s. Souvenir Archie and Viola Victoria (Elsey) B.; B.S., Hampton Isnt., 1942; M.D., Howard U., 1947; m. Mae Neece Hodge, June 4, 1949; children—Carl Archie, Kenneth Dale. Teaching asst. Hampton Inst., 1942-44; intern Homer G. Phillips Hosp., St. Louis, 1947-48; house physician Edwards Meml. Hosp., Oklahoma City, 1948-51; sch. physician Oklahoma City Bd. Edn., 1949-59; gen. practice, Oklahoma City, 1951—; physician Guthrie (Okla.) Job Corps Center for Women, 1971—. Dir., treas., mng. officer M-D-P Investment Fund, Inc. Chmn. met. outreach dept. Greater Oklahoma City YMCA, 1971—. Mem. Nat. Med. Assn., Oklahoma City Med-De-Phar Soc. (pres. 1962-65), Okla. Med., Dental and Pharm. Assn. (pres. 1965-66), Oklahoma City Urban League, N.A.A.C.P. (life). Democrat. Mem. A.M.E. Ch. Home: 2813 NE 19th St Oklahoma City OK 73111 Office: 215 N Walnut Av Oklahoma City OK 73104

BARCLAY, ELTON WILLIAM, hosp. adminstr.; b. Camden, N.J., Nov. 11, 1915; s. William Henry and Anna (Knox) B.; student U. Fla., 1943; m. Laura Fenton, Feb. 14, 1941; children—Bonnie Susan (Mrs. Merwyn Delano Rimel), Leslie Benton (Mrs. Crawford Raymond Lord). Commd. 2d lt., Med. Service Corps, U.S. Army, 1943, advanced through grades to maj., 1953; company officer, ETO, 1943-45; exec. officer Army Hosp., Carlisle, Pa., 1945-48; dir. personnel 22d Gen. Hosp., Guam, 1948-50; liaison officer Navy Hosp., Phila., 1950-52; comdg. officer detachment of patients Valley Force (Pa.) Army Hosp., 1952-54; registrar Army Hosp., Ft. Hood, Tex., 1954-56; ret., 1956; adminstr. Stetson Hosp., Phila., 1956-60, Croxer Hosp., Chester, Pa., 1960-63, Crozer-Chester Med. Center, 1963-68; exec. dir. Phila. Gen. Hosp., 1968-71; exec. dir. Doctors Hosp., Lake Worth, Fla., 1971—. Dist. commr. Boy Scouts Am., 1963-67. Bd. dirs. Delaware County Health and Welfare Council, 1962-65, Delaware Valley Hosp. Council, 1967—, Inter-County Hosp. Plan, 1966-68. Recipient Achievement award Olney High Sch. Alumni Assn., 1968. Fellow Am. Coll. Hosp. Adminstrs.; mem. Am. Hosp. Assn., Hosp. Assn. Pa. Home: 248 N Country Club Dr Atlantis FL 33462 Office: Doctors Hosp 2829 10th Av N Lake Worth FL 33460

BARD, EDWIN JAY, dentist; b. Mpls., Apr. 6, 1924; s. Samuel David and Edith Sophia (Carlson) B.; student Washington U., St. Louis, 1943; B.S., U. Minn., 1950, D.D.S., 1952; m. Barbara Jeanne Hultgren, Mar. 17, 1949; children—Ann Elizabeth (Mrs. Charles Oswald), Nancy Leigh, Brian Jay, Irene Dell, David Jay, Barbara Claire, James Jay, April Jeanne. Dentist, State Bd. Health Dental Services, Jacksonville, Fla., 1952; pvt. practice dentistry, Jacksonville, 1952—; dir. Hayes Oil & Gas Co. Active Am. Cancer Soc. Trustee Trinity Rescue Mission, Jacksonville. Served with USAAF, 1943-46. Decorated D.F.C., Purple Heart (5), Air medal. Mem. Am. Dental Assn., N.E., Jacksonville dental socs., D.A.V., Parington Study Group, Psi Omega. Democrat. Baptist (deacon 1967—, trustee 1967-72). Mason (Shriner). Home: 8568 San Jose Blvd Jacksonville FL 32217 Office: 50 W 8th St Jacksonville FL 32206

BAREFOOT, ALDOS CORTEZ JR., educator; b. Angier, N.C., Feb. 25, 1927; s. Aldos Cortez and Eva (Benson) B.; student Wake Forest Coll., 1945-47; B.S., N.C. State Coll., 1950, M.W.T., 1951; D. Forestry, Duke, 1958; m. Naomi Gertrude Pugh, Aug. 6, 1949; children—Aldos Cortez III, James Eric, Rebecca Jane. Quality control engr. Henry County Plywood Corp., Ridgeway, Va., 1951; grad. asst. statistics N.C. State Coll., 1952-54, asst. prof., 1954-59; forestry adviser I.C.A., U.S. Govt., Chittagong, E. Pakistan, 1959-61; asso. prof. N.C. State U., Raleigh, 1961-68, prof., 1968—, chmn. univ. adv. council, 1970-71, leader Wood Products Extension, 1972—; wood technologist cons.; cons. industry and Winchester (Eng.) excavations. Chmn. Tchrs. and State Employees Study Commn. for N.C. Gen. Assembly. Served with USNR, 1945-46. Fellow Inst. Wood Sci.; mem. Forest Products Research Soc., Internat. Assn. Wood Anatomists, Soc. Wood Sci. and Tech., T.A.P.P.I., Sigma Xi, Alpha Zeta, Phi Kappa Phi, Xi Sigma Pi. Democrat. Baptist. Mason. Contbr. articles to profl. jours. Home: 3401 Hampton Rd Raleigh NC 27607

BAREFOOT, GARY FENTON, librarian; b. nr. Smithfield, N.C., May 13, 1939; s. Willard and Mary Catherine (Barbour) B.; A.A., Mount Olive Jr. Coll., 1959; A.B., U. N.C. at Chapel Hill, 1961, M.S. in L.S., 1968. Librarian jr. high sch., High Point, N.C., 1961-63; librarian, elementary sch. Mount Olive, 1963-65; cataloger Moye Library, Mount Olive Coll., 1964-65, head librarian, 1965—. Mem. exec. com. Heart Fund, 1967, 71. Inst. Training Learning Resource Personnel fellow, 1970. Mem. Am., Southeastern, N.C. (sec. 1971-73) library assns., U.S. Jr. C. of C. (chpt. pres. 1970-72), Phi Theta Kappa, Beta Phi Mu. Democrat. Baptist. Lion. Home: 302 N Church St Mount Olive NC 28365

BAREFOOT, SHERWOOD WASHINGTON, physician; b. Benson, N.C., July 24, 1913; s. Allen Leon and Emma Kitsey (Tart) B.; B.S., U. N.C., 1936; M.D., Duke, 1938; m. Christine Long, Mar. 20, 1937; children—Sherwood Washington, Susan Waters. Intern, resident Duke Hosp., 1938-40, fellow in dermatology, 1946-47; research fellow Bellevue Hosp., N.Y.C., 1940-41; practice medicine, specializing in dermatology, Greenboro, N.C., 1947—; mem. staff Moses H. Cone Meml. Hosp., pres. Med. bd., 1972-73; mem. staff Wesley Long Hosp.; instr. dermatology Duke Med. Sch., 1947-65, clin. asso. dermatology, 1967—; clin. asso. prof. medicine U. N.C. Sch. Medicine, 1968—. Served from 1st lt. to maj. M.C., AUS, 1941-46. Fellow Am. Acad. Dermatology; mem. N.Am. Clin. Dermatologic Soc., Guildford County Med. Soc. (pres. 1969), C. of C. Lutheran. Kiwanian (dir. 1963-66). Contbr. articles profl. jours. Home: 3107 Madison Av Greensboro NC 27403 Office: 1030 Professional Village Greensboro NC 27401

BARES, RUDOLPH, JR., hotel exec.; b. Chgo., Feb 1, 1915; s. Rudolph and Pauline (Stepanik) B.; B.S.C., Northwestern U., 1937; postgrad. Cornell U., 1955; m. Elizabeth Houston Raymond, May 15, 1943; children—Robert Edward, Barbara Houston, David Raymond. Sales research dir. Ditto, Inc., Chgo., 1937-40, br. mgr., Norfolk, Va., 1940-42; dir. mgmt. engring. sect. Bur. Ships, Navy Dept., 1945-51; asso. Cresap, McCormick & Paget, mgmt. cons., N.Y.C., 1951-53; asst. dir. hotel operations Williamsburg Restoration, Inc. (Va.), 1953-56; v.p., sec., exec. asst. to pres. Colonial Williamsburg, Inc. and Williamsburg Restoration, Inc., 1956-63, v.p., dir. hotel operations and mdsg., 1963—. Served to lt. comdr. USNR, 1942-45. Mem. Am. (chmn. quality environment com. 1967-70, chmn. resort com. 1972), Va. (pres. 1968, chmn. quality environment com. 1972—) hotel and motel assns., Williamsburg C. of C. (v.p., dir. 1965-67), Delta Sigma Pi. Episcopalian. Contbr. articles in field. Home: Ludwell-Paradise House Williamsburg VA 23185 Office: Colonial Williamsburg Found Williamsburg VA 23185

BARGEON, HERBERT ALEXANDER, JR., lawyer; b. Fayetteville, N.C., May 23, 1934; s. Herbert Alexander and Violet (Geilfuss) B.; B.S. in Bus. Adminstrn., U. Va., 1956; LL.B., U. Fla., 1968; m. Gail Freer, Mar. 14, 1963; children—Brett Elizabeth (by previous marriage), Herbert Alexander III, Violet Gail. Admitted to Fla. bar; partner firm Anderson & Rush, Orlando. Pres. bd. trustees Orlando Pub. Library. Served to 2d lt. AUS, 1957. Mem. Am. Bar Assn., Orlando C. of C. Republican. Presbyn. Club: University (Orlando). Home: 1314 Chichester Rd Orlando FL 32803 Office: 322 E Central Blvd Orlando FL 32801

BARGER, ALPHONSO SLEDGE, lawyer; b. York, Ala., May 6, 1908; s. Eugene E. and Frances (Jackson) B.; B.S., Howard Coll., 1932; LL.B., George Washington U., 1939; m. Edith Christine Smith, Dec. 25, 1935; children—Alphonso S., Ken, Edith Ann. Admitted to D.C. bar, 1938, Tenn. bar, 1948; scientist Bur. Ordnance, U.S. Navy, 1934-39; atty. Social Security Bd., 1939-41; commr. U.S. Conciliation Service, 1946-48; pvt. practice, Chattanooga, 1948—; asst. city atty., 1962—. Active Boy Scouts Am.; sec. Hamilton County Election Commn., 1952-58. Served as maj. AUS, 1941-46. Decorated Victory medal. Mem. Fed., Am., D.C., Tenn., Chattanooga bar assns., V.F.W. (trustee 1948-60, state judge advocate 1957-58). Democrat. Presbyn. Mason (Shriner; merit award 1967). Club: Yacht (dir. 1967). Home: 401 Talley Rd Chattanooga TN 37411 Office: Hamilton Bank Bldg Chattanooga TN 37402

BARGER, BENJAMIN, clin. psychologist, educator; b. The Congo, Africa, Oct. 26, 1920; s. Gervase James P. and Myrtle (King) B.; A.B., George Washington U., 1947; Ph.D., Duke, 1952; m. Marilyn Eloise McDaniel, Nov. 28, 1946; children—Lynn Marie, Janette Arlene, Karen Sue. Came to U.S., 1931. Chief psychologist Mental Hygiene Clinic, Ohio State U., Coll. Medicine, Columbus, 1952-55, dir. psychol. services Columbus Psychiat. Inst. and Hosp., 1955-59, instr., asst. prof. dept. psychiatry, 1953-59; co-dir., dir. student mental health projects, dept. student health U. Fla., Gainesville, 1959—, lectr., asst. prof., asso. prof., 1959-65, prof. dept. psychology, 1965—. Cons., Project on Student Devel. in Small Colls., Plainfield, Vt., 1966-70; mem. juvenile problems research review com. Nat. Inst. Mental Health, Bethesda, Md., 1968-71, mem. adv. bd. strategies for change and knowledge utilization, 1971—. Served with AUS, 1943-46. Decorated Bronze Star Medal. Diplomate Am. Bd. Examiners Profl. Psychology. Fellow Am. Psychol. Assn., A.A.A.S., Am. Coll. Health Assn.; mem. Southeastern, Fla. psychol. assns. Home: 3029 NW 2d Av Gainesville FL 32601 Office: U Fla Infirmary Gainesville FL 32601

BARGFREDE, JAMES ALLEN, lawyer; b. Seguin, Tex., Sept. 10, 1928; s. Herman Fred and Elsie (Vorpahl) B.; B.S., Tex. A. and M. U., 1950; postgrad. Ohio State U., 1952-53; J.D., St. Mary's U., 1957; m. Virginia Felts, Nov. 27, 1970. Engr., Signal Corps, San Antonio, 1950-52; elec. engr. San Antonio Pub. Service Bd., 1953-58; admitted to Tex. bar, 1957; patent counsel Hubbard & Co., Chgo., 1958-59; practiced in Chgo., 1959-60, Houston, 1960—; mem. firm Butler, Binion, Rice, Cook & Knapp, 1960-68; pvt. practice law, 1968—. Served with USAF, 1952-53. Mem. Am., Houston (chmn. automated equipment com. 1971-72) bar assns., State Bar of Tex., Houston Patent Law Assn., Former Students Tex. A. and M. U., Am. Patent Law Assn., Tex. Soc. Profl. Engrs., Houston Livestock Show and Rodeo, Delta Theta Phi. Democrat. Baptist. Home: 5649 Piping Rock Lane Houston TX 77027 Office: 1923 Bank SW Bldg Houston TX 77002

BARHAM, CHARLES, found. exec.; b. Nashville, Oct. 18, 1903; s. Charles and Mary Hannah (Wilkinson) B.; B.A., Vanderbilt U., 1924; m. Emmalou Wheeler, Oct. 10, 1928; children—Frank Wheeler, Charles III. Teller, First Nat. Bank, Nashville, 1924-31, br. mgr., 1931-32; sec.-treas. Modern Bread Co., Nashville, 1932-40; owner Radio Sta. WCHV, Charlottesville, Va., 1940-59; developer Bellair Estates, Charlottesville, Va., 1946—; pres. Thomas Jefferson Meml. Found., Charlottesville, 1967—; dir. Va. Nat. Bank, Norfolk. Pres. beautification com., Charlottesville, 1962; chmn. Albemarle Planning Com. Mem. C. of C. (pres. 1946). Clubs: Farmington Country (Charlottesville); Harbor (Norfolk, Va.). Home: 3 Lake Rd Charlottesville VA 22903

BARHAM, MACK ELWIN, judge, justice; b. Bastrop, La., June 18, 1924; s. Henry A. and Lockie (Harper) B.; J.D., La. State U., 1946; postgrad. U. Colo., 1966; m. Ann LeVois, June 3, 1946; children—Bret, Megan. Admitted to La. bar, 1946; practiced in Bastrop, La.; judge Bastrop City Ct., 1949-61, Fourth Jud. Dist. Ct., 1961-68; asso. justice La. Supreme Ct., New Orleans, 1968—. Mem. White House Conf. on Youth, 1960; chmn. Boy Scouts Am., Bastrop, 1950—, United Fund Campaign, Bastrop, 1952—. Vice pres., dir. S. Central Region Edn. Lab., Ark., La., Miss., Kan., Okla., 1966-68, Mem. La. Juvenile Ct. Judges Assn., Am., Fourth Dist., La. State bar assns., Am. Judicature Soc., Lambda Chi Alpha, Omicron Delta Kappa, Phi Delta Phi. Kiwanian. Home: 5837 Bellaire Dr New Orleans LA 70124 Office: 301 Loyola Av New Orleans LA 70112

BARKAN, ALEXANDER ELLAS, labor ofcl.; b. Bayonne, N.J., Aug. 9, 1909; s. Jacob and Rachel (Perelmen) B.; Ph.B., U. Chgo., 1933; m. Helen Stickno, May 10, 1942; children—Lois, Carol. With Textile Workers Organizing Com., 1937; organizer Textile Workers Union Am., 1938, sub-regional dir., 1938-42, polit. action dir., 1947-55; vets. dir. CIO community services dir., 1945; exec. dir. N.J. CIO Council, 1946; asst. dir. com. polit. edn. AFL-CIO, Washington, 1955-57, dep. dir. com. polit. edn., 1957-63, dir., 1963—. Served with USNR, 1942-45. Home: 6515 E Halbert Rd Bethesda MD 20034 Office: 815 16th St NW Washington DC 20006

BARKAS, EDWARD, mfg. co. exec.; b. Atlanta, July 28, 1925; s. Alexander and Marie (Dreyfus) B.; B.S., The Citadel, 1950; m. Kathleen Prolman, Aug. 3, 1951; children—Marilyn, Daniel. Salesman, Morgan Mfg. Co., Chattanooga, 1951-55; sales mgr. Lindheimer Mfg. Co., Hillsborough, N.C., 1955-58, v.p. sales, 1958—. Active Boy Scouts Am. Trustee Central Bapt. Hosp. Served with AUS, 1941-45; ETO. Decorated Purple Heart. Mem. Hillsborough C. of C., N.A.M., Nat. Assn. Sales Execs. Democrat. Home: Box 365-A Route 3 Hillsborough NC 27278

BARKDULL, THOMAS H., JR., dist. judge; b., 1925; grad. U. Fla. Law Sch., 1949. Judge 3d Fla. Appellate dist. ct., Miami. Home: 7500 Old Cutler Rd Miami FL 31343 Office: 1350 NW 12th St Miami FL*

BARKER, CARL LEON, educator, civil engr.; b. Parksville, Tenn., June 27, 1902; s. Joseph Mark and Kate (Lillard) B.; student Tenn. Poly. Inst., 1922-24; B.S., U. Ala., 1932, C.E., 1937; m. Frances Dyer, Oct. 18, 1924; children—Mark, Sharon (Mrs. Roy Lee Tunnell). Insp., Robert W. Hunt Co., Birmingham, Ala., 1924-30; dist. mgr., 1937-45; instr. civil Engring. U. Ala., 1932-34; resident engr. PWA, 1934-37; chief insp. Crane Co., Chattanooga, 1945-51; specifications engr. TVA, 1951-61, chief procurement planning staff, 1961-66; head civil engring. tech. Chattanooga State Tech. Inst., 1966—. Active Boy Scouts Am. Registered profl. engr., Tenn., Ala. Mem. Nat. Soc. Profl. Engrs., Tau Beta Pi. Presbyn. Mason. Home: 3216 Pinewood Av Chattanooga TN 37411

BARKLEY, ROBERT EMMANUEL, city ofcl.; b. Cleve., Sept. 24, 1927; s. E. Ray and Nelle (Doke) B.; B.S. in Civil Engring. with honors, Case Inst. Tech., 1949; M.S. in Civil Engring., Purdue U., 1950; certificate in hwy. transp., Yale, 1951; m. Brenda Voit, Aug. 14, 1954; children—Bryan, Bradford. Prin. asso. Wilbur Smith & Assos., New Haven, 1951-54; asst. dir. City-County Planning Bd., Winston-Salem, N.C., 1954-56; dir. Urban Renewal, Chattanooga, 1956-58; exec. dir. Redevel. Commn. Greensboro (N.C.), 1958—. Sec.-treas. Cumberland Cts., Inc., Greensboro, 1962—; chmn. legislative com. Carolinas Council Housing and Redevel. Ofcls. Hon. trustee Old Salem (North Carolina) Restoration Project. Recipient Outstanding Service award Phi Beta Sigma, 1966. Registered profl. engr., Ohio, N.C. Mem. Am. Soc. C.E. (sect. v.p. 1967—), Sigma Xi. Baptist (mem. finance com. 1967-69). Author: Origin-Destination Surveys and Traffic, 1951. Contbr. articles profl. publs. Home: 3314 Northampton Dr Greensboro NC 27401 Office: Southeastern Bldg Greensboro NC 27401

BARKLIS, SAM STEVEN, scientist; b. Geneva, Ill., May 19, 1925; s. Steven E. and Georgia (Jiokaris) B.; student Wright Coll., 1941-43; M.D., U. Chgo., 1947, B.S., 1944; m. Ingrid Lid, June 14, 1947; children—Steven, Georgia, Eric, Nina. Instr. microbiology Western Reserve U., Cleve., 1951-53; intern Univ. Chgo. Clinics, 1947-48; asst. prof. biochemistry U. Ill., Chgo., 1953-59; dir. microbiological research CIBA Pharm. Co., Summit, N.J., 1959-66; dir. research St. Barnabas Med. Center, Livingston, N.J., 1966-68; v.p., gen. mgr. Sci. & Tech. div. Alcon Labs., Ft. Worth, 1968—. Mem. N.J. Council on Med. and Dental Edn., 1965-68. Chmn., Chatham Democratic Com., 1960-63. Trustee, sec. bd. N.J. Coll. Medicine and Dentistry, 1965-68. Served with AUS, 1943-46. Mem. A.A.A.S., Am. Soc. Microbiology, Infectious Disease Soc. Am., Sigma Xi, Alpha Kappa Kappa. Contbr. numerous articles in field to profl. jours. Home: 3497 South Hills Av Fort Worth TX 76109 Office: 6200 S Freeway Fort Worth TX 76101

BARKSDALE, A.R., state ofcl. Mem. Ga. Bd. Edn., Atlanta. Office: State Office Bldg Bd Edn Atlanta GA 30303*

BARKSDALE, ETHELBERT COURTLAND, educator; b. Athens, La., Oct. 24, 1905; s. Ethelbert Courtland and Eliza (Wellborn) B.; B.A., U. Tex., 1928, M.A., 1931, Ph.D., 1941; m. Marjorie Miller, June 12, 1937; children—Ethelbert Courtland, Stephen Webb. Tchr. Tex. Pub. Schs., 1926-39; tchr. U. Tex., Austin, 1940-41, prof. history, Arlington, 1942—, head dept. history and philosophy, 1954-71. Mem. adv. com. Civil War Centennial, 1961-65, Kennedy U.S. Senate com. selection outstanding U.S. Senators, 1958. Pres. San Antonio Young Democrats, 1934, Baytown (Tex.) Young Democrats, 1937. Mem. Orgn. Am. Historians, Acad. Am. Polit. Social Sci., Am., So., Western, Tex. State hist. assns., Southwestern Social Sci. Assn. (gen. program chmn. 1964-65, mem. exec. bd. 1965-67). Methodist. Author: Financing a System of State Highways, 1935; The Art and Science of Speech, 1937; Genesis of Texas Aviation, 1957; The Meatpackers Come to Texas, 1959; Southern Governatorial Elections, 1969. Editor: Unpublished Writings of W. P. Webb, 1969: History As High Adventure, 1969. Mem. editorial bd., Texana, 1967; mem. adv. editorial bd., Ency. Brit. Contbr. articles Ency. Brit. Home: 1333 S Pecan St Arlington TX 76010

BARKSDALE, HIRAM COLLIER, educator; b. Sandersville, Ga., Dec. 4, 1921; s. William Henry and Maude (Smith) B.; B.B.A., U. Ga., 1948; M.S., N.Y.U., 1949, Ph.D., 1955; m. Jeanne Epp, July 22, 1950; children— Hiram Collier, Beverly Jeanne, Sally Braswell, Addison Andrew. Instr., Washburn Municipal U., 1949-51; projects mgr. Advt. Research Found., 1952-56, asst. to pres., 1956-60; mem. faculty N.Y.U., 1956-65, asso. prof. Sch. Commerce and Grad. Sch. Bus., 1956-60, prof., chmn. dept. marketing Sch. Commerce, 1960-65; prof. Coll. Bus. Adminstrn., U. Ga., Athens, 1965—, chmn. marketing dept., 1968—. Served with AUS, 1943-46. Ford Found. grantee Harvard Bus. Sch., summer 1957, Carnegie Inst. Tech., summer 1962. Mem. Am. Marketing Assn., Inst. Mgmt. Scis., A.A.A.S., Soc. for History of Tech., Phi Beta Kappa, Beta Gamma Sigma. Author: The Use of Survey Research Findings as Legal Evidence, 1957; Problems in Marketing Research: In-Basket Simulation, 1963; co-author: Marketing Research, 1966. Editor: Marketing in Progress Patterns and Potentials, 1964; Marketing Change and Exchange, 1964. Book rev. editor: Media/scope mag., 1964-69. Editorial bd. Jour. of Marketing, 1965—. So. Jour. of Bus., 1968—. Home: 340 Cedar Creek Dr Athens GA 30601

BARKSDALE, JAMES ALTON, educator; b. McKenzie, Tenn., Nov. 29, 1904; s. James Monroe and Judith Ada (Esch) B.; A.B., Bethel Coll., 1925, D.Litt., 1959; A.M., U. Colo., 1936; student Peabody Coll., 1927; Ed.D., U. Tenn., 1954; m. Eleanor Herrin, May 18, 1928. Tchr., prin. Charlotte (Tenn.) High Sch., 1925-35; prin. Central High Sch., Ashland City, Tenn., 1935-41, E. W. Grove High Sch., Paris, Tenn., 1941-43, Tenn. High Sch., Bristol, 1943-46; supt. pub. schs., Union City, 1946-49; dir. Tenn. Dept. Personnel, 1949-50; commr. edn. State of Tenn., 1950-53; v.p. Cumberland Bd. Edn., 1949-51, pres., 1951-57; acting asso. prof. edn. U. Tenn. Coll. Edn., Knoxville, 1953-55; dean Tenn. Poly. Inst., 1955-60; adviser higher edn. U.S. Overseas Mission, ICA, Ankara, Turkey, 1960-62; chief edn. adviser U.S. AID, Am. Embassy, Amman, Jordan, 1963-65; prof. history Bethel Coll., McKenzie, Tenn., 1965—, interim pres., 1969; vis. prof. Memphis State U., 1967. Cons., Henry County (Tenn.) Sch. System, 1967-68; mem. Tenn. Gen. Assembly Commn. for State Compensation, 1969; del. Carroll and Benton counties Tenn. Ltd. Constl. Conv., 1972. Mem. Am., Tenn. (pres. 1959) edn. assns., Tenn. Coll. Assn. (pres. 1959). Democrat. Presbyn. Mason, Rotarian. Home: Highland Dr McKenzie TN 38201

BARKSDALE, MARY MORTON, librarian; b. Randolph, Va., Aug. 12, 1911; d. William Sydnor and Frances (Lovelace) Barksdale; A.B., Randolph-Macon Woman's Coll., 1932; B.L.S., Columbia U., 1939; postgrad. Temple U., 1957, U. N.C. Grad. Sch., 1962, William and Mary Coll., 1968; m. Frederick H. M. S. Farley, Feb. 23, 1948 (div. July 1950). Prin. elementary schs., Charlotte County, Va., 1932-37; librarian Charlotte County (Va.) Pub. Library, 1937-40; library supr. WPA, Ga. and Va., 1940-42; circulation librarian Va. Poly. Inst. Blacksburg, Va., 1942-43; analyst U.S. Air Force Intelligence, Washington, 1944-45; reference librarian Enoch Pratt Free Library, Balt., 1945-49; librarian Randolph-Henry High Sch., Charlotte Court House, Va., 1951-68; coordinator library services Danville (Va.) Community Coll., 1968—, instr. edn. Longwood Coll., 1954, 55, Madison Coll., 1961-62, U. Va. Sch. Gen. Studies, 1962-66, Richmond Profl. Inst., 1967; sec. William S. Barksdale Co., Inc., Randolph, 1950-56. Mem. evaluating com., Va. Bd. Edn., 1954, 66; chmn. scholarship com. Patrick Henry Boys' Plantation, Brookneal, Va. Bd. dirs. Danville YWCA. Mem. Va. Edn. Assn., Va. (past pres.), Southeastern library assns., Va. Mus. Fine Arts (dir. Danville chpt.), Randolph-Macon Woman's Coll. alumnae Assn., N.E.A., A.L.A., Alumnae Assn. Columbia U., Delta Kappa Gamma. Presbyn. Contbr. articles in field to profl. jours. Home: Windemere Randolph VA 23962 Office: Danville Community Coll 1009 Bonner Av Danville VA 24541

BARLEMANN, ARTHUR, JR., county agrl. agt.; b. San Antonio, Sept. 5, 1922; s. Arthur and Olga (Ackermann) B.; B.S., Tex. A. and M. Coll., 1951, postgrad., 1966; m. Halley Grace Doree, Aug. 8, 1953. With Tex. Agrl. Extension Service and Tex. A. and M. Coll., 1951—, asst. county agrl. agt. Van Zandt County, 1951-54, Tom Green County, 1954-56, county agrl. agt. Sterling County, Sterling City, 1956—. Served with AUS, 1944-46; PTO. now maj. Res. Mem. Nat.,

Tex. (dist. dir., bd. dirs. 1970—, Distinguished Service award 1971) county agrl. agts. assns., Am. Legion (comdr. Canton, Tex. 1953). Methodist (chmn. ofcl. bd. 1965—). Lion (pres. 1964). Address: Box 337 Sterling City TX 76951

BARLEY, GEORGE EMERSON MCKIM, fertilizer co. exec.; b. Manassas, Va., Oct. 23, 1904; s. John McKim and Lida Estelle (Finch) B.; grad. high sch.; m. Mary Elizabeth Daly, Oct. 29, 1925; children—Charles McKim, George Emerson McKim, Elizabeth Anne, John David. Office boy R. G. Dun & Co., Jacksonville, Fla., 1918-21; asst. bookkeeper Nitrate Agys. Co., 1925-35; sec. Atlantic & Gulf Fertilizer Co., 1935-39; with Am. Potash & Chem. Corp., Travelling, Fla., 1939-41; Fla. rep. Ashcraft-Wilkinson Co., Atlanta, 1941-48; asst. mgr. Wheeler Fertilizer Co., Oviedo, Fla., 1948-50; v.p., mgr. Diamond R. Fertilizer Co., Winter Garden, Fla., 1950—. Chmn. council local govts. Orange County, Fla., 1970-71. Commr. City of Winter Garden, Fla., 1952-58, mayor, 1967—, mem. water adv. bd., 1968-69. Mem. Fla. Agrl. Research Inst. (pres. 1971-72). Episcopalian (treas. 1961-72). Elk, Rotarian (pres. 1962). Clubs: University (Orlando, Fla.); West Orange Country (Winter Garden, Fla.). Home: 115 Temple Grove Dr Winter Garden FL 32787 Office: Hennis Rd PO Box 1137 Winter Garden FL 32787

BARLOW, THOMAS JAMES, indsl. corp. exec.; b. Houston, June 22, 1922; s. Thomas Jefferson and Dorothy (James) B.; B.S., Tex. A. and M. Coll., 1943; postgrad. Harvard, 1962; m. Billye Louise Sears, May 31, 1944; children—Lance, Lynne. Trainee, Western Cottonoil Co., Abilene, Tex., 1946-47, asst. gen. mgr., 1958-59; constrn. engr. San Joaquin Cottonoil Co., Bakersfield, Cal., 1948; supt. Western Cotton Products Co., Phoenix, 1949-50; prodn. mgr. Nile Ginning Co., Minia, Egypt, 1951-55; process engr. Anderson, Clayton & Co., Houston, 1956-57, now pres., dir.; dir. Pan Am. Ins. Cos., Anderson, Clay & Hunt Pty., Ltd., 1st Nat. Bank Abilene, Central & S.W. Corp., Ranger Ins. Co. Mem. Chgo. Bd. Trade, N.Y. Produce Exchange, Memphis Bd. Trade. Mem. Houston C. of C., Newcomen Soc. N.Am., Tex. Research League (dir.). Home: 35 Willowend St Houston TX 77024 Office: Box 2538 Houston TX 77001

BARMETTLER, RICHARD OTTO, JR., petroleum co. exec.; b. Omaha, Nov. 28, 1928; s. Richard Otto and Jane (Harvey) B.; student Springhill Coll., 1946-47; B.S., Auburn U., 1950; m. Joyce McCrory, Apr. 15, 1955; 1 dau. Valerie Anne. Sales engr. Chevron Asphalt Co., Mobile, Ala., 1953-64, sales mgr., 1964-69; sales mgr. Seminole Asphalt Refining Co., St. Marks, Fla., 1969—. Served with AUS, 1950-52. Mem. Am. Soc. C. E., Soc. Am. Mil. Engrs., Kappa Alpha. Democrat. Roman Catholic. Elk. Home: 2808 Roscommon Dr Tallahassee FL 32303 Office: Seminole Asphalt Refining Co Main Hwy St Marks FL 32355

BARNARD, BILLINGS, editor; b. Abilene, Tex., Apr. 30, 1926; s. Bernie D. and Lora (Billings) B.; B.A., U. Tex., 1952, B.J., 1952, M.A., 1959; m. Billie Kathryn Roche, July 28, 1947; 1 dau., Kathryn Annabel. Editor Alice (Tex.) News, 1952-54, Gulf Pub. Co., Houston, 1954-56, Martin-Marietta Corp., Denver, 1958-60, Gen. Dynamics Co., San Diego, 1960-65; editor Stanford Research Inst., Menlo Park, Cal., 1965-67; editor, economist Fed. Res. Bank of Chgo., 1967-69; sr. editor, economist Fed. Res. Bank of Dallas, 1969—; cons. Gulf Pub. Co., Houston, 1956-57. Served with USNR, 1944-46. Mem. Am. Econ. Assn., A.A.A.S. Democrat. Contbr. articles to profl. jours. Home: 1636 Russell Glen Lane Dallas TX 75232 Office: Fed Reserve Bank of Dallas Station K Dallas TX 75202

BARNARD, JOHN FLOYD, JR., accountant; b. Charleston, Ark., June 10, 1927; s. John F. and Helen (Hawkins) B.; B.S., U. Ark., 1956;; m. Betty Jo Culbertson, Dec. 17, 1966; stepchildren—Patricia Ann Goodin, Janet Kay Goodin. With Douglas Walker & Co., 1956—, resident partner Russellville (Ark.) office, 1967—. Served with AUS, 1951-54. Mem. Beta Alpha Psi. Lion. Home: 237 Beaumont Dr Russellville AR 72801 Office: 305 W 2d St Russellville AR 72801

BARNARD, LESLIE RAYDENE, gas co. exec.; b. Mitchellville, Tenn., Apr. 24, 1929; s. Marvin S. and Tallie Mai (McCombs) B.; B.S., U. Tenn., 1959; m. Pauline Sue Paul, Dec. 26, 1952; children—Paulla Rei, Melody Ann, Roma Leigh, Jeffrey. With E. Tenn. Natural Gas. Co., Knoxville, 1955-68, chief engr., 1964-68; gen. mgr. Natural Gas Utility Dist., Rogersville, Tenn., 1968—. Served with AUS, 1951-53. Mem. Am. Soc. C.E., Nat. Soc. Profl. Engrs., Rogersville Area C. of C. (pres. 1971—). Rotarian (Rogersville pres. 1969-70). Home: PO Box 128 Rogersville TN 37857 Office: 850 W Main St Rogersville TN 37857

BARNARD, THOMAS ELLIOTT, educator, clergyman; b. Glendale, Cal., Aug. 30, 1931; s. Malcolm Bower and Goldie (Drake) B.; A.B., Pasadena Coll., 1958; M.R.E., Fuller Theol. Sem., 1960; M.A., Bethany Nazarene Coll., 1971; postgrad. Okla. State U., 1972; m. Madeline Newcomer, May 3, 1957; children—Bruce Kendall, Gaylene. Ordained to ministry Ch. of the Nazarene, 1960; minister edn. Ch. of Nazarene, Upland, Cal., 1960-62; asso. minister First Ch. of Nazarene, San Diego, 1962-64, Whittier, 1964-66; asso. prof. religion Bethany (Okla.) Nazarene Coll., 1966—, dean students, 1972—. Minister edn. Bethany First Ch. of Nazarene, 1966-70; mem. dist. ch. sch. bd., N.W. Okla. dist. Bd. Ministerial Studies, 1967—. Served with USAF, 1951-54. Mem. Nazarene Dirs. of Christian Edn. Fellowship. Author: The Adult Class in Action, 1970. Home: 7508 NW 21st St Bethany OK 73008

BARNDS, WILLIAM PAUL, bishop; b. Sweet Springs, Mo., Aug. 5, 1904; s. William Tyson and Virginia (Larsen) B.; B.A., Mo. Valley Coll., 1925, D.D. (hon.), 1947; M.A., U. Mo., 1927; Ph.D., U. Neb., 1949; B.D., U. Chgo., 1940; S.T.M., Seabury-Western Sem., 1944; S.T.D. (hon.), 1967; D.D. (hon.), U. of South, 1967; m. Ida Lou Sterrett, June 30, 1930; children—William Joseph, Mary Ida (Mrs. James W. Garrard), Virginia Lou (Mrs. Nicholas George Albanese, Jr.). Ordained deacon Episcopal Ch., 1932, priest, 1933, bishop, 1966; rector in Mo., Kan., Neb. and Ind., 1933-56; lectr. philosophy and lit. Ind. U. extension at S. Bend, 1954-56; rector Trinity Ch., Ft. Worth, 1956-66; suffragan bishop Diocese Dallas, 1966—; adj. prof. philosophy Tex. Christian U., 1956—. Chmn. dept. Christian edn. Diocese Kan., 1939-44, dept. Christian social relations Diocese Neb., 1945-48, dep. promotion, also mem. bishop and council Diocese No. Ind., 1954-56; mem. exec. council depts. Christian edn., promotion and div. missions Diocese Dallas, 1956-66, mem. standing com., 1958-61; dep. to gen. convs., 1937, 43, 46, 49, 52, 55, 58, 61, 64. Club: Torch. Author articles. Home: 3533 Stadium Dr Fort Worth TX 76109 Office: 1630 N Garrett Dallas TX 75206

BARNES, ASA, physician; b. Marston, Mo., Mar. 20, 1904; s. Charles Merlin and Emma (Atkins) B.; B.S. in Edn., S.E. Mo. State Coll., 1925; A.B., B.S. in Medicine, U. Mo., 1929; M.D., U. Tenn., 1931; M.P.H., Johns Hopkins, 1940; m. Elizabeth Dickey Pruitt, June 5, 1931; children—Asa, Robert Pruitt. Intern Marine Hosp., USPHS, New Orleans, 1931-32; practice medicine, Dexter, Mo., 1932-37; asst. dir., local health adminstr. Mo. Dept. Health, 1937-41; Med. adminstr. Pacific area A.R.C., 1946-49; area med. adminstr. United Mine Workers Am. Welfare and Retirement Fund, Louisville, 1948-63, Beckley and Charleston, W.Va., 1963-69, asst. exec. med. officer, Washington, 1969-70; county health officer Nassau-Baker Counties, Fla., 1971—. Asso. prof. U. Louisville, 1951-64; asst. clin. prof. U. Cin., 1958-63; mem. staff Beckley Appalachian Regional Hosp., Raleigh Gen. Hosp., Beckley. Chmn. pub. health com. Appalachian Regional Commn., 1965—; mem. W. Va. Comprehensive Health Planning Council, 1968—; mem. Citizens' Com. for Better Health, W. Va., 1964—; mem. med. quality bd. Mountaineer Family Health Plan, Beckley, 1968—; mem. other health coms. and councils. Bd. dirs. Raleigh Co. Tb and Health Assn. Served from maj. to col. M.C., AUS, 1940-46. Diplomate Am. Bd. Preventive Medicine and Pub. Health. Fellow Am. Pub. Health Assn., Indsl. Med. Assn. (past dir.), Am. Coll. Preventive Medicine; mem. Group Health Assn., Assn. Mil. Surgeons, A.M.A., W.Va. State Med. Assn., other local and nat. med. socs. Presbyn. Mason. Abstractor Jour. Occupational Medicine, 1959—; contbr. to profl. jours. Home: 101 S 18th St Fernandina Beach FL 32034 Office: 4th and Ash Sts Fernandina Beach FL 32034

BARNES, BEN F., state ofcl.; b. Gorman, Tex., Apr. 17, 1938; s. B.F. Barnes; student Tarleton State Coll., Tex. Christian U., U. Tex. at Austin; LL.D., McMurry Coll., Tex. Tech U., St. Edwards U.; m. Nancy Sayers; children—Greg, Amy. Lt. gov. State of Tex., 1969—. Mem. Tex. Ho. of Reps., 1960-68, chmn. rules com., 1963, speaker, 1965-68. Chmn. Tex. legislative council and legislative budget bd., 1969—; chmn. So. conf. Council State Govts., 1967-68, mem. exec. com., 1968-70; pres. Nat. Legislative Conf., 1968-69. Named one of 10 outstanding young men in U.S., U.S. Jr. C. of C., 1970. Mem. Tex. Jr. C. of C. (one of 5 outstanding young Texans 1965), S.W. Cattle Growers Assn. Methodist. Elk. Office: Office of Lt Gov Austin TX 78711 Home: De Leon TX 76552

BARNES, BENNY BLAIR, educator, elec. engr.; b. Gadsden, Ala., Mar. 7, 1935; s. Newton Eldridge and Sara (Roach) B.; student Jacksonville (Ala.) State U., 1952-53; B.S., Ala. Poly. Inst., 1956; M.S., U. Ala., 1962; Ph.D., Auburn U., 1965; m. Patsy Harris Barnes, June 3, 1956; 1 son, Douglas. Design engr. Chance Vought Aircraft, Dallas, 1956-57; instrument engr. E. I. duPont de Nemours, Aiken, S.C., 1957-59; aerospace technologist NASA, Huntsville, Ala., 1959-63; instr. elec. engring. Auburn (Ala.) U., 1963-65, asso. prof., 1970—, dir. computer center, 1970—; asst. prof. Va. Poly. Inst., 1965-66; mgr. simulation dept. Computer Scis. Corp., Huntsville, 1966-67; asso. prof. elec. engring., U. Tenn., Knoxville, 1967-70, asso. prof. computer sci., 1969-70, asst. dean Coll. Engring., 1967-69. Served with AUS, 1957. Registered profl engr., Tenn., Ala. Mem. I.E.E.E., A.A.A.S., Simulation Councils, Assn. for Computing Machinery, Tau Beta Pi, Eta Kappa Nu, Pi Mu Epsilon, Sigma Pi Sigma.Home: 323 Carter St Auburn AL 36830

BARNES, DOUGLAS ROGER, educator; b. Mobile, Ala., May 6, 1921; s. Charles Harrison and Dora (Heeden) B.; B.A., Emory U., 1950; M. Div., Candler Sch. Theology, 1953; M.Ed., Auburn U., 1965, postgrad., 1965—; m. Mildred Bowman, Aug. 18, 1953; 1 son, Neil Vance. Ordained to ministry Meth. Ch., 1950; minister United Meth. Ch., Preston, Graves and Edison, Ga., 1950-58; salesman Albany Typewriter Exchange (Ga.), 1958-63; faculty dept. religion Andrew Coll., Cuthbert, Ga., 1963-64, dean of students, 1964-66, acad. dean, 1966—; supply minister United Meth. Ch., Ga., 1964—. Served with USAAF, 1942-45. Mem. So. Conf. Deans Faculties and Acad. Vice Presidents, Assn. Continuing Edn. and Pub. Service Adminstrs., Ga. Adult Edn. Council, Inc., Am. Assn. Higher Edn., Ga. Edn. Assn., Ga. Assn. Collegiate Registrars and Admissions Officers. Home: 325 College St Cuthbert GA 31740

BARNES, EDWARD MARCELLUS, JR., aero. engr.; b. Stillwater, Okla., Jan. 29, 1932; s. Edward Marcellus and Edna (Morris) B.; B.S., Okla. State U., 1954, M.S., 1961; m. Cynthia Lou Canfield, June 1, 1954; children— Edis Ann, Barbara Lou, Warren Edward. Engring. trainee Gen. Electric Co., Ft. Wayne, Ind., Phila., 1954; staff engr. McDonnell Douglas Corp., Douglas Aircraft Co., Tulsa, 1956-62, chief electronics engring. sect., 1962-65, dir. Apollo/Range instrumented aircraft program, 1965-67, dir. engring., 1967—. Mem. Gilcrease Inst., 1965—. Mem. adv. bd. Coll. Engring. and Phys. Scis., U. Tulsa. Served with USAF, 1954-56. Registered profl. engr., Okla. Mem. Tulsa C. of C., Tulsa Philharmonic Soc., Nat. Mgmt. Assn., I.E.E.E. Home: 7824 E 22d Pl Tulsa OK 74129 Office: 2000 N Memorial Dr Tulsa OK 74115

BARNES, EVA LOUISE BLUM (MRS. MALCOLM LYNN BARNES), civic worker; b. Ellsworth, Kan.; d. Samuel and Emma Lena (Kunz) Blum; M.A., U. Cal. at Berkeley, 1939; m. Malcolm Barnes, June 10, 1946; children—Marsha Evangeline, Malcolm Samuel John. Counselor, Oakland (Cal.) Pub. Sr. High Sch., 1939-42; club dir. A.R.C., Eng. and France, 1942-46; civilian club dir., Germany, 1946. Publicity chmn. lit. events Golden Gate Expn., 1940-41; publicity chmn. Writers Conf. of West, 1941; mem. Louisville com. Nat. Conf. Christians and Jews, 1960—; mem. com. for passing new Ky. Constn., League of Women Voters, 1966. Bd. dirs. Library Assos. Louisville, 1963—. Life mem. Filson Club, Speed Mus., Women's Aux. of Orch. Assn. Louisville, U. Cal. Alumni Assn. (br. pres. Santa Barbara Bay area 1938-40); mem. Women's Aux. Jefferson County Med. Soc. (publicity chmn. 1950-51), Women's Aux. Ky. Med. Soc. (chmn. aux. conv. 1953, chmn. cancer sta. wagon drive 1953-54), Aux. U. Louisville (v.p., program chmn. 1951-52), Assn. Sch. Adminstrs. (asso.), English-Speaking Union, Internat. Platform Assn. Cleve., Chgo. Council on Fgn. Relations, Phi Lambda Theta, Lambda Kappa Sigma, Delta Chi Delta. Clubs: Louisville Boat, Pendennis (Louisville), California Writers (dir.), University Women's (life mem.) (Washington). Art work exhibited in many galleries in Cal. Home: 425 Country Lane Louisville KY 40207

BARNES, FANNIE BURRELL (MRS. RICHARD ALEXANDER BARNES), librarian; b. New Orleans; d. Alexander and Lorenza (Nicholas) Burrell; A.B., Dillard U., 1945; M.S., Atlanta U., 1950; m. Roscoe Ross, May 18, 1962 (div.); children—Erica Arnetta, Maria Monique; m. 2d, Richard Alexander Barnes, May 29, 1968. Tchr. English, Gilbert Acad., New Orleans, 1945-49; asst. librarian Atlanta U., summer 1950, 57-61, 67; head librarian Claflin Coll., Orangeburg, S.C., 1950-54; head librarian Clark Coll., Atlanta, 1954—, tchr. children's lit., 1957—; childrens librarian Atlanta Pub. Library Bookmobile, summer 1961. Mem. A.L.A., N.E.A., N.A.A.C.P., Alpha Kappa Alpha. Baptist. Home: 1981 Valley Ridge Dr SW Atlanta GA 30331 Office: 240 Chestnut St SW Atlanta GA 30314

BARNES, GEORGE ERIC, civil engr.; b. Washington, Apr. 17, 1898; s. Raymond Friend and Mattie (Van Slyck) B.; B.S. in Civil Engring., Mass. Inst. Tech., 1923; M.A. in Romance Langs., Western Res. U., 1954; C.E. (hon.), Case Inst. Tech., 1935; m. Mary Magdalene O'Hara, Sept. 23, 1920; children—Mary Loretta (Mrs. Garland Swaggerty), Dorothy Vera (Mrs. Thomas Whitaker), Janet Isabel (Mrs. Arthur Macias). Instr. to asso. prof. civil engr. U. Fla., 1923-29; jr. partner George A. Main Engrs., Daytona Beach, Fla., 1923-29; design engr. Metcalf & Eddy, Boston, 1927; cons. engr. Standard Fruit & S.S. Co. New Orleans, 1927; design engr. Fuller & McClintock, N.Y.C., 1929-33, N.Y.C. Dept. Sanitation, Ward Island, 1929-33; prof., head dept. civil engring. and engring. mechanics Case Inst. Tech., Cleve., 1933-55, prof. hydraulic and san. engring., 1955-63, prof. emeritus, 1963—; prof. environmental engring. U. N.C., Chapel Hill, 1963-70, prof. emeritus, 1970—; cons. to internat. program in san. engring. design, 1970—. Cons. to Parsons, Brinckerhoff, Hall and McDonald on devel. Juramento River, Argentina, 1949 (on leave from Case Inst.); vis. prof. san. engring. Universidad Central de Venezuela, Caracas, 1961; cons. to fed., state and municipal agys., engring. firms and industries on hydraulic and san. engring. projects, 1955—. Vice chmn. N.C. Wastewater Treatment Plant Operators Bd. Certification, 1970—. Served to 2d lt., U.S. Army, 1918-19. Mem. Am. Soc. C.E. (life, past pres. Cleve. chpt.), Nat. Soc. Profl. Engrs. (past pres. Cleve. chpt.), Am. Soc. M.E. (life), Am. Water Works Assn. (life), Water Pollution Control Fedn. (life), Am. Assn. Engring. Edn. (life), Am. Inst. Cons. Engrs., Am. Pub. Health Assn., Interam. Assn. San. Engring., Internat. Assn. Hydraulic Research, Venezuela Soc. San. Engrs. (hon.). Contbr. articles to engring. textbooks, profl. jours. Home: 1303 Willow Dr Chapel Hill NC 27514 Office: Sch Pub Health U NC Chapel Hill NC 27514

BARNES, GEORGE H., supt. schs., state ofcl.; b. Ripley, Tenn., May 26, 1905; B.S., U. Ill., 1928; M.A., Memphis State U., 1952; m. 1937; 2 children. Tchr. English Ripley High Sch., 1928-29, Whitehaven High Sch., Shelby County, Tenn., 1929-35; financial sec. Shelby County Schs., 1935-50, supr., 1951—. Mem. Tenn. Bd. Edn., 1969—. Mem. Tenn. Edn. Assn. (pres. 1957), N.E.A., Am. Assn. Sch. Adminstrs. Address: 4262 Chamwil Pl Memphis TN 38117*

BARNES, JOHN EVAN, JR., clergyman; b. Pratt City, Ala., July 9, 1911; s. John Evan and Hattie (Pollard) B.; A.B., Samford U., 1934; Th.M., So. Bapt. Theol. Sem., 1937; D.D., Miss. Coll., 1948; m. Maron Stallworth, Aug. 25, 1936; children—Frances Marilyn, John Evan III, Elizabeth Carson. Ordained to ministry Bapt. Ch., 1932; pastor 1st Bapt. Ch., Atmore, Ala., 1937-42, West Point, Miss., 1942-44, Main St. Bapt. Ch., Hattiesburg, Miss., 1944—. Pres. Miss. Bapt. Conv., 1953-54, chmn. edn. commn., 1965—, chmn. commn. on bds., 1956—; pres. So. Bapt. Sunday Sch. Bd., 1964—; pres. bd. dirs. So. Bapt. Hosp. Commn., 1957—. Co-chmn. United Gives Fund, Hattiesburg, 1955—. Kiwanian (dir. 1946). Writer tract, Is it Right, 1951; also articles. Home: 1000 Estelle St Hattiesburg MS 39401 Office: 1101 Main St Hattiesburg MS 39401

BARNES, JOHN POTTS, lawyer; b. Montgomery, Ala., Aug. 13, 1902; s. Justus McDuffie and Ethel (Rawdon) B.; student U. Va., 1918, U. Ala., 1919-21; Ph.B., U. Chgo.,1923, J.D. cum laude, 1924; m. Thelma Jeannette Boyd, Oct. 18, 1926; children—Thelma (Mrs. Edward Keith Banker), Judith. Admitted to Ala. bar, 1925, Ill. bar, 1933, Cal. bar, 1944, D.C. bar, 1964; practice in Chgo., 1929-61, Washington, 1962—; mem. firms MacLeish, Spray, Price & Underwood, 1957-61, Reavis, Pogue, Neal & Rose, 1962—. Mem. vis. com. U. Chgo. Law Sch., 1962-68; prof. law U. Va., 1961-65. Mem. Am., Ill., Cal., D.C. bar assns., U. Chgo. Alumni Assn., Phi Alpha Delta. Home: Stanford Hall Farm Keswick VA 22947 Office: 1100 Connecticut Av NW Washington DC 20036

BARNES, MADELINE ADELE, educator; b. San Antonio, May 6, 1919; d. William L. and Lydia (O'Bannon) Barnes; B.S., B.A., Tex. Women's U., 1941; M.A., N. Tex. State U., 1944; postgrad. U. Mich., U. Colo., U. Oslo (Norway), Rocky Mountains Biol. Lab. Tchr. trainer W. Tex. U., Canyon, 1942-46; tchr. Tex. Wesleyan Coll., summer 1955; prof. biology, chmn. dept. biol. scis. Amarillo (Tex.) Coll., 1946—. Mem. Nat., Tex. Panhandle (past pres.) Audubon socs., Tex. State, Tex. Jr. Coll. (Tchr. of Year 1966) tchrs. assns., A.A.A.S., Am. Assn. U. Profs., Am. Assn. U. Women, Am. Inst. Biol. Scis., Nat. Assn. Biol. Tchrs., Tex. Acad. Sci., Southwestern Assn. Naturalists, Delta Kappa Gamma (chpt. pres. 1968-70, Alpha State Achievement award 1972). Home: 3625 Doris Dr Amarillo TX 79109

BARNES, SAMUEL, educator; B.A., Oberlin Coll., then M.A.; Ph.D., Ohio State U. Chmn. dept. phys. edn. Howard U. Office: Howard U Washington DC 20001*

BARNES, WELDEN FAIRBANKS, JR., univ. ofcl.; b. Oklahoma City, Apr. 11, 1911; s. Welden F. and Mary (Gill) B.; B.A., Okla. State U., 1938; m. Arlene Alicia White, Mar. 3, 1936; children—Frank W., Mary A., Ann E. Mem. sports staff Tulsa Daily World, 1929-31; sports publicity dir. Okla. State U., 1935-42; insp. Douglas Aircraft Co., Tulsa, 1942-45; mem. sports staff Daily Oklahoman, Oklahoma City, 1945-46; pub. relations writer Okla. State U., Stillwater, 1946-48, sec. to pres., 1948-54, dir. pub. information, 1954—. Mem. Am. Coll. Pub. Relations Assn. (S.W. dist. dir. 1958-59), Am. Assn. Agrl. Coll. Editors' Am. Assn. Land-Grant Colls and Univs. (pub. relations com. 1959-62), So. Regional Edn. Bd. (pub. relations adv. bd. 1959-61), Okla. Edn. Assn., Kappa Sigma, Sigma Delta Chi. Presbyn. (elder). Rotarian (pres. 1952, v.p. 1953, dir. 1951-54). Home: 1809 W 4th St Stillwater OK 74074

BARNES, WILLIAM P., oil co. exec.; b. Marlin, Tex., May 31, 1920; s. William P. and Katharine E. (Horne) B.; B.A., So. Meth. U., 1947, LL.B., 1949; m. Sally Temple, Oct. 20, 1950; children—William P., Joseph L., James H., Thomas L. Admitted to Tex. bar, 1949, practiced in Dallas, 1949-53; atty. Gen. Am. Oil Co. Tex., 1953-54, v.p., 1955-60, now pres., dir.; pres. Meadows Bldg. Corp. 1963-66, chmn. bd., 1966—; dir. Stockton, Whatley, Davin &Co., Premier Petrochem Co. Served from pvt. to maj. AUS, 1942-46. Mem. Am., Tex., Dallas bar assns., Kappa Sigma, Phi Alpha Delta, Blue Key. Clubs: Petroleum, City, Texas (Dallas); Deerwood; Ponte Vedra (Jacksonville, Fla.). Editor in chief Southwestern Law Jour., 1948. Home: 3629 Princeton Av Dallas TX 75205 Office: Meadows Bldg Dallas TX 75206

BARNETT, BENJAMIN LEWIS, JR., physician; b. Woodruff, S.C., July 22, 1926; s. Benjamin Lewis and Mattie Bernice (Skinner) B.; B.S., Furman U., 1946; M.D., U. S.C., 1949; m. Annalyne Louise Hall, Oct. 25, 1958; children—Benjamin Lewis III, Jane Kristen. Intern, Protestant Episcopal Hosp., Phila., 1949-50; pvt. practice gen. medicine, Woodruff, 1950-70; asso. prof. family practice Med. U. S.C., Charleston, 1970—, asst. dir. family practice residency program, 1970—; mem. clin. staff Med. U. Hosp., Charleston County Hosp., 1970—; chief of staff Woodruff Hosp., 1966-69. Health officer Town of Woodruff, 1950-54. Mem. Spartanburg County Bd. Edn., 1968-70, sec., 1969-70. Trustee, Bethea Bapt. Home for Aged, Darlington, S.C. Served with USNR, 1954-56. Named Citizen of Year, Woodmen of World, 1968. Diplomate Am. Bd. Family Practice. Mem. A.M.A., So., S.C. med. assns., Charleston County Med. Soc., Soc. Tchrs. Family Practice, Am. Acad. Gen. Practice, Spartanburg County Med. Soc. (v.p. 1968), S.C. Thoracic Assn., Am. Philatelic Soc., Am. Manuscript Soc., Alpha Omega Alpha, Alpha Kappa Kappa, Kappa Alpha. Baptist (deacon, chmn. bd.). Mason (32 degree). Contbr. articles to med. jours. Home: 673 Pawley Rd Mount Pleasant SC 29464

BARNETT, BERNARD HARRY, lawyer; b. Helena, Ark., July 13, 1916; s. Harry and Rebecca (Grossman) B.; student U. Mich., 1934-36; J.D., Vanderbilt U., 1940; m. Marian Spiesberger, Apr. 9, 1949; 1 son, Charles Dawson. Admitted to Ky. bar, 1940; pvt. practice, Louisville, 1940-42; asso. Woodward, Dawson, Hobson & Fulton, 1946-48; partner Bulitt, Dawson & Tarrant, 1948-52, Greenebaum, Barnett, Wood & Doll, 1952-70; partner Barnett & McConnell, 1972, Barnett, Greenebaum, Martin & McConnell, 1972—. Chmn. exec. com. Nat. Industries, Inc.; dir. Bank of

Louisville, Madison Fund, Inc., Paz Oil Co., Ltd. Mem. adv. group Joint Com. on Internal Revenue Taxation, U.S. Congress 1953-55, Com. on Ways and Means, U.S. Ho. of Reps. 1956-58. Chmn. Louisville Fund, 1952-53; mem. nat. exec. com., nat. campaign cabinet United Jewish Appeal, 1959—, nat. chmn., 1967—; chmn. Louisville United Jewish Appeal, 1968-69. Mem. Louisville and Jefferson County Republican Exec. Com., 1954—; chmn. Ky. Rep. Finance Com., 1955-60. Served as lt. USNR, 1942-45. Mem. Am., Ky., Louisville bar assns. Home: Apt 2706 800 S 4th St Louisville KY 40203 Office: 510 W Broadway Louisville KY 40202

BARNETT, BURLEIGH FRANCIS, banker; b. Osceola, Mo., Jan. 6, 1896; s. John Carter and Mary Jane (Rothgeb) B.; student pub. schs. of Osceola; m. Mary Nanon Linney, June 24, 1916; children—Leigh Frances (Mrs. G. M. Baccash), George C. Clk., Farmers & Mchts. Bank, Osceola, 1915-16, Internat. State Bank, Trinidad, Colo., 1917; v.p. First Nat. Bank of Tulsa, 1918-49; pres. Comml. Nat. Bank of Shreveport, La., 1949-52; pres. Citizens First Nat. Bank of Tyler (Tex.), 1952-67, chmn. bd., 1967-69, cons., 1969—; dir. Cooperative Savs. & Loan Assn., Tyler. Mem. Robert Morris Assos., C. of C. (pres. 1957-58). Mason. Home: 1521 S College St Tyler TX 75705 Office: Citizens First Nat Bank Tyler TX

BARNETT, CHARLES DARWIN, govt. ofcl.; b. Little Rock, July 9, 1935; s. Ernest L. and Lola E. (Herrin) B.; B.S., U. S.C., 1953, M.A., 1954; Ph.D. (fellow 1956-58), George Peabody Coll. for Tchrs., 1959; m. Emmala Ward Evins, Mar. 15, 1954; children—Laura, Patricia, Nancy. Instr. psychology U. S.C., 1954-55; psychometrist S.C. Mental Health Commn., Columbia, 1955; psychol. intern State Colony and Tng. Sch., Pineville, La., 1957-58, exptl. psychologist, 1958-60, acting dir. psychology, 1958-59; part-time instr. La. Coll., 1958-60; dir. psychology Austin State Sch., 1960-61, coordinator student services, 1961, asst. supt., 1961-62; asso. dir. So. Regional Edn. Bd., Atlanta, 1962-63; asst. dir. spl. schs. Bd. for Tex. State Hosps. and Spl. Schs., Austin, 1963-65; asso. clin. prof. psychology, dept. psychiatry Baylor U. Med. Sch., 1963—; dep. commr. for mental retardation Tex. Dept. for Mental Health and Mental Retardation, Austin, 1965-69; commr. S.C. Dept. Mental Retardation, Columbia, 1969—; clin. prof. psychology Med. U. S.C., 1971—. Pres. Nat. Assn. Coordinators State Programs Mentally Retarded, 1969-71; cons. Pres. Com. Mental Retardation, 1969-71; mem. Nat. Adv. Council on Developmental Disabilities, 1971—. Mem. Am. Assn. on Mental Deficiency. Contbr. articles profl. jours. Home: 4915 Landrum Dr Columbia SC 29206 Office: 2414 Bull St Columbia SC 29201

BARNETT, CRAWFORD FANNIN, JR., physician; b. Atlanta, May 11, 1938; s. Crawford Fannin and Penelope Hollinshead (Brown) B.; student Taft Sch., 1953-56, U. Minn., 1957; A.B. magna cum laude, Yale, 1960; postgrad. (Davison scholar) Oxford (Eng.) U., 1963; M.D. (Trent scholar), Duke, 1964; m. Elizabeth McCarthy Hale, June 6, 1964; children—Crawford Fannin III, Robert Hale. Intern internal medicine Duke U. Med. Center, Durham, N.C., 1964-65, resident, 1965; resident internal medicine Wilmington (Del.) Med. Center, 1965-66; dir. Tenn. Heart Disease Control Program, Nashville, 1966-68; practice medicine, specializing in internal medicine, Atlanta, 1968—; mem. staff Crawford Long, Northside, Ga. Bapt., Grady Meml., Jessie Parker Williams, Doctors Meml., West Paces Ferry Hosp., Atlanta hosps. (all Atlanta); mem. teaching staff Vanderbilt Med. Center, Nashville, 1966-68, Crawford Long Meml. Hosp., 1969—; clin. instr. internal medicine, dept. medicine Emory U. Med. Sch., Atlanta, 1969—. Vice pres., dir. Preferred Equities Corp., 1970—; med. dir., v.p., dir. Med. Data Acquisition Corp., 1971—. Mem. Good Govt. Atlanta. Bd. govs. Doctors Meml. Hosp., 1971—. Served as surgeon USPHS, 1966-68. Fellow Am. Geog. Soc.; mem. Am. Fedn. Clin. Research, Council Clin. Cardiology, A.A.A.S., Am., Ga., Fulton County med. assns., Am., Ga. heart assns., Am., Ga. socs. internal medicine, Am. Assn. History Medicine, Ga., Atlanta hist. socs., Nat. Trust for Historic Preservation, Internat. Hippocratic Found. Cos (Greece), Faculty of History of Medicine and Pharmacy Worshipful Soc. Apothecaries of London (Eng.), Atlanta Com. on Fgn. Relations (chmn. exec. com.), Atlanta Clin. Soc., Victorian Soc. Am. (bd. advisers Atlanta chpt. 1971—), Internat. Platform Assn. Mensa, Gridiron, Phi Beta Kappa. Episcopalian. Clubs: Piedmont Driving, Yale (dir. 1970—), Nine O'Clocks (Atlanta); Pan Am. Doctors (Hidalgo, Mexico). Contbr. articles to profl. publs. Home: 2739 Ramsgate Ct NW Atlanta GA 30305 Office: 490 Peachtree St NW Atlanta GA 30308

BARNETT, DAVID L(EON), editor; b. Savannah, Ga., Jan. 21, 1922; s. Jack and Ida (Levy) B.; B.S. with honors in Govt., Harvard, 1943; M.S., Columbia, 1947; m. Jeanne Kahn, Dec. 29, 1946; children— Randel, Megan, Jane. Mem. staff Richmond (Va.) News Leader, 1947-54, chief statehouse bur. and polit. corr., 1950-51, asst. city editor, 1951-54; regional corr. Business Week mag., 1951-54; Washington corr. N.Am. Newspaper Alliance, 1954-55, chief Washington bur., columnist, 1955-65; Washington news editor Hearst Newspapers, 1966—. Served with USAAF, 1943-46. Mem. White House Corrs. Assn. Clubs: Harvard, Federal City, Internat., Nat. Press (Washington). Contbr. articles to mags. Home: 7218 Beechwood Rd Alexandria VA 22307 Office: 1701 Pennsylvania Av NW Washington DC 20006

BARNETT, FRANK ELLIOTT, lawyer; b. Atlanta, July 20, 1933; s. Jack W. and Erline (Harville) B.; J.D., Univ. Tenn., 1959; m. Adrienne A. Cross, Dec. 15, 1956; 1 son, Brian Lee. Asst. swimming coach U. Tenn., 1957-59; admitted to Tenn. bar, 1960, Fed. Dist. Ct. bar, 1965; landman Standard Oil Co. Cal., Los Angeles, Jackson, Miss., 1959-60; agt. FBI, Washington, Kansas City, Mo., 1960-61; atty. E. Tenn. Natural Gas Co., Knoxville, 1961-64; atty. Baker, Worthington, Barnett & Crossley, Knoxville, 1964-70; exec. asst. to Gov. of Tenn., Nashville, 1970—. Propr., Barnett Real Estate Co., Knoxville, 1963—; chmn. bd. Olympic Devel. Co. Served with USMCR, 1953-55. Mem. Am., Fed. Power, Knoxville bar assns., Bar Assn. Tenn., Club: Knoxville Racquet (dir.). Home: 1500 Agawela Knoxville TN 37919 Office: State Capitol Bldg Nashville TN 37219

BARNETT, JAMES ARDEN, lawyer, judge; b. Miss., Aug. 4, 1924; s. Arden and Vera (Turner) B.; B.B.A., U. Miss., 1948, LL.B., 1949; m. Lucy Lee Owen, Mar. 4, 1945; children—Ruth Elizabeth, James Arden, Vera Susan. Admitted to Miss. bar, 1949; mem. firm Barnett, Montgomery, McClintock and Cunningham, Jackson, 1949-65; partner Barnett & Barnett, Jackson, 1965-70; individual practice, 1970-71; mem. Miss. Ho. of Reps., 1964-68; mem. Miss. Senate, 1968-71; chancery judge, Jackson, 1971—. Mem. Hinds County Sch. Bd., 1954-64. Served with USNR, 1943-45. Decorated D.F.C., Air medal. Mem. Am., Miss., Hinds County bar assns. Baptist. Republican. Lion (past pres.). Home: 710 E Leake Clinton MS 39056 Office: Chancery Ct Jackson MS 39201

BARNETT, JAMES E., sch. supt.; b. Flo, Tex., Apr. 26, 1927; s. William Wade and Sally (Owens) B.; B.S., Sam Houston State U., 1949, M.Ed., 1958; m. Joann Cecelia Perryman, Jan. 18, 1951; children—Barry, Kevin. Tchr. coach Oakwood (Tex.) Ind. Sch. Dist., 1949-51, Woodhouse Sch., 1951-60; supt. Leverett Chapel schs., Overton, Tex., 1960—. Served with USNR, 1945-46; PTO. Mem. Am., Tex. assns. sch. adminstrs., N.E.A., Tex. Tchrs. Assn. Rotarian. Home and office: Route 2 Overton TX 75684

BARNETT, PATRICIA GLOVER (MRS. ROBERT WARREN BARNETT), govt. ofcl.; b. White Plains, N.Y., June 22, 1914; d. Patrick W.R. and Louise A. (Miller) Glover; A.B., Vassar Coll., 1935; m. Robert Warren Barnett, Apr. 26, 1940; children—Dickson G., Robert Warren, Clare Elizabeth, Eugenia Lois. Research asst. Inst. Pacific Relations, N.Y.C., 1938-41; adminstrv. asst. United China Relief, Inc., N.Y.C., 1941-42; econ. analyst OSS, Washington, 1943-44, chief E. Asia econ. sect., 1945; fgn. affairs specialist, chief S.E. Asia sect., Dept. States Office of Intelligence Research, Washington, 1945-49; intelligence analyst on S.E. Asia, Bur. Intelligence and Research, Dept. State, Washington, 1949-56, 62—. Home: 5205 Abingdon Rd NW Washington DC 20016 Office: Dept of State Washington DC 20521

BARNETT, ROBERT JAMES, ballet sch. exec.; b. Okanogan, Wash., May 6, 1925; s. James Garfield and Vera (Berry) B.; dance tng. with Bronislava Nijinska, Lubov Egorova, Olga Preobrajenska, Sch. Am. Ballet; m. Virginia Gleaves Rich, July 20, 1967; children—Robert James, David Michael. With Original Ballet Russe, Europe, 1948-49, N.Y.C. Ballet, 1950-58; dir. Atlanta Ballet Inc., 1958—; part owner, co. exec. Atlanta Sch. Ballet, 1969—. Served with USNR, 1943-46. Mem. South Eastern Regional Ballet Assn. (coordinator), Nat. Assn. for Regional Ballet, Inc. (v.p.), Pacific Regional Ballet Assn. (ajudicator), South West Regional Festival Assn. Choreographer: The Nutcracker, La Valse, Fate, Pas de Trois, Quatre Vignettes, Suite Brilliante, Waltz Pas de Deux, Divertimento. Ballet master: Swan Lake, Sleeping Beauty, Giselle. Home: 27 W Andrews Dr NW Atlanta GA 30305 Office: 3215 Cains Hill Pl N W Atlanta GA 30305

BARNETT, ROBERT WARREN, assn. exec.; b. Shanghai, China, Nov. 6, 1911 (parents Am. citizens); s. Eugene Epperson and Bertha Mae (Smith) B.; A.B., U. N.C., 1933, M.A., 1934; B.A. (Rhodes scholar), Oxford U., 1936, B.Litt., 1937; Gen. Edn. Bd. fellow, Yale, 1937-39; postgrad. U. Mich., 1938, Universita per Stranieri, Perugia, Italy, 1935; Rockefeller Found. fellow, 1940-41; m. Patricia Robertson Glover, Apr. 26, 1940; children—Dickson Glover, Robert Warren, Clare, Eugenia. Mem. staff Inst. Pacific Relations, exec. sec. program com. United China Relief, 1941-42; U.S. mem. econs. and reparations coms. Far Eastern Commn. representing U.S. Dept. State, Japan, 1945-49, officer charge China econ. affairs, 1949-51, charge Western European econ. affairs, 1951-54, charge European econ. orgns., 1954-56, econ. counselor Am. embassy, The Hague, The Netherlands, 1956-60, counselor U.S. Mission European Communities, Brussels, Belgium, 1960-61; dep. dir. fgn. econ. adv. staff. Dept. State, Washington, 1961-62, dep. asst. sec. state for Far Eastern Affairs (now East Asian and Pacific Affairs), 1963-70; v.p. Asia Soc., dir. Washington Center, 1970—. Fellow Center Internat. Affairs, Harvard, 1959-60. Served 1st lt. to maj. USAAF, 1943-45; PTO. Decorated Legion Merit, 1945. Harvard U. fellow Harvard, 1959-60. Mem. Council Fgn. Relations, Far Eastern Assn., Am. Rhodes Scholar Assn., Washington Inst. Fgn. Affairs, Phi Beta Kappa, Beta Theta Pi. Methodist. Clubs: Chevy Chase, Cosmos (Washington). Author: Economic Shanghai: Hostage to Politics, 1941; Orientation Booklet for U.S. Military Personnel in China, 1945. Contbr. to U.S. Economic Foreign Policy, 1948. Home: 5205 Abingdon Rd NW Washington DC 20016 Office: 1785 Massachusetts Av NW Washington DC 20036

BARNETT, ROSS R., lawyer; b. Carthage, Miss., 1898; B.A., Miss. Coll.; postgrad. Vanderbilt U.; LL.B., U. Miss. Admitted to Miss. bar, 1926; mem. firm Barnett, Montgomery, McClintock & Cunningham, Jackson, Miss. Gov. Miss., 1960-64. Mem. Jackson, Hinds County (pres. 1940-43, 47-49), Am. (mem. law reform com. 1945—; com. legal aid and lawyer reference 1951—) bar assns., Miss. State Bar (pres. 1943-44). Address: Barnett Bldg Suite 315 Jackson MS 39205*

BARNETT, WILLIAM HALBERT, architect; b. Lewisburg, Tenn., July 11, 1915; s. William Lee and Erma (Halbert) B.; B.S. in Architecture, Ga. Inst. Tech., 1940, B.Arch., 1941; m. Norma Cook, June 12, 1942; children—Thomas Vance, Andrew Preston, Mary Cecille. With Burge &Stevens, Atlanta, 1938-40, Perkins & Will, Chgo., 1946; with Stevens & Wilkinson, Architects, Atlanta, 1947—, pres., 1972—. Served with USNR, 1941-46. Mem. A.I.A. Club: Cherokee Town & Country (Atlanta). Home: 5550 Dupree Dr N W Atlanta GA 30327 Office: 100 Peachtree St N W Atlanta GA 30303

BARNETT, WILLIAM RANDLE, banker; b. Jacksonville, Fla., Oct. 15, 1908; s. Harlow and Marian (Speers) B.; B.B.A., Emory U., 1932; m. Frances H. Boykin, Apr. 11, 1933; children—William B., Anne A., Marian R. With Barnett Nat. Bank, Jacksonville, 1932—, became pres., 1958, chmn. bd., 1964—, also dir.; chmn. bd. Barnett Nat. Bank, Deland, Fla., 1959—; treas., dir. Barnett Nat. Securities Corp., 1948—; dir. Jacksonville Ice & Cold Storage Co. Trustee Jacksonville U. Home: 4915 Morven Rd Jacksonville FL 32210 Office: Barnett Nat Bank Jacksonville FL

BARNETT, WILLIAM WOODSON, JR., ednl. adminstr.; b. Lexington, Mo., Oct. 23, 1920; s. William Woodson and Elizabeth (Slusher) B.; A.A., Wentworth Mil. Acad., 1939; B.S., U. Mo., 1941, M.A., 1949; m. Ann Mahler, Oct. 29, 1946; 1 son, Theodore Mahler. Accounting clk. Gen. Electric Co., Bridgeport, Conn., 1941-42; commd. 2d lt. U.S. Army, 1942, advanced through grades to lt. col., 1954, ret., 1965; instr. Wentworth Mil. Acad., Lexington, 1965-67; dir. publicity and student publs. Schreiner Inst., Kerrville, Tex., 1967—, asso. prof. journalism, 1967—. Decorated Bronze Star medal with oak leaf cluster. Presbyn. Kiwanian. Home: Schreiner Campus Kerrville TX 78028 Office: Schreiner Institute Kerrville TX 78028

BARNHARDT, WILLIAM MCLAUGHLIN, textile co. exec.; b. Latrobe, Pa., July 29, 1928; s. William Horace and Margaret (McLaughlin) B.; grad. Woodberry Forest Sch., 1946; student Princeton, 1947; B.S., N.C. State U., 1950; m. Harriet Oehler Bangle, Sept. 7, 1949; children— William Bangle, Richard Alan, Steven Fredric. With textile fibers dept. E. I. duPont de Nemours & Co., Wilmington, Del., 1950-52; v.p. Barnhardt Elastic Corp., Charlotte, N.C., 1952-58, area sales mgr., 1958-66, v.p. sales, 1967—; v.p., dir. So. Webbing Mills, Am. Textile Corp., Barnhardt Bros. Co., Tryon Processing Co.; dir. Riverview Acres, Thomas Constrn. Corp. Pres. Blue Ridge Assembly, YMCA, 1969—. Commr. Charlotte (N.C.) Housing Authority, 1968—. Bd. dirs. Charlotte (N.C.) YMCA, 1966—; nat. bd. dirs. YMCA, 1970—; mem. exec. bd. Mecklenburg council Boy Scouts Am., 1960—; mem. adv. bd. Salvation Army, 1964-67; bd. mgrs. Camp Thunderbird, 1954—; bd. dirs. Mecklenburg chpt. A.R.C., 1962-65, Greater Charlotte Found., Charlotte Choral Soc., 1966-71; bd. dirs., v.p. Barnhardt Found.; bd. visitors Davidson Coll.; trustee Presbyn. Hosp. Recipient Silver Beaver award Boy Scouts Am., 1966. Mem. Internat. Brotherhood Magicians, Soc. Am. Magicians, Charlotte Sales and Mgmt. Execs., Charlotte Textile Club (dir. 1956-57), Charlotte C. of C. (dir. 1965-67). Rotarian (dir. 1972—). Clubs: Quail Hollow Country, City (Charlotte, N.C.). Home: 3921 Arborway St Charlotte NC 28211 Office: NC Nat Bank Bldg Charlotte NC 28202

BARNHART, HARRY BASCOMB, JR., ind. oil producer; b. Austin, Tex., Aug. 9, 1911; s. Harry Bascomb and Nelle (Sterzing) B.; student U. Tex., 1929-32. Self employed as investor, independent oil and gas producer, 1948—. Mem. Mus. of Fine Arts, Houston Symphony Soc. Served from pvt. to 1st lt., AUS, 1942-45; PTO. Mem. Am. Petroleum Inst., Ind. Petroleum Assn. Am., Tex. Mid-Continent Oil and Gas Assn., Sigma Nu. Presbyn. Clubs: Petroleum, River Oaks Country. Office: Post Oak Bank Bldg Houston TX 77027

BARNHART, RALPH CLAYTON, univ. dean; b. nr. Springfield, O., Oct. 18, 1905; s. Charles Anthony and Adell (Patterson) B.; student Battle Creek Coll., 1927-30; A.B., Simpson Coll., 1931; LL.B., U. Cin., 1934; m. Mary Elizabeth Gerber, Aug. 26, 1930; children—Lloyd, Daniel, Clayton. Admitted to Ohio bar, 1934, Ark. bar, 1958; practiced in Cin., 1934-37; mem. editorial staff Lawyers Coop. Pub. Co., Rochester, N.Y., 1937-42; atty. War Relocation Authority, Dept. Interior, 1942-46; prof. law U. Ark., 1946—, dean Sch. Law 1958—. Chmn. Ark. Statute Revision Commn. Mem. Am., Ark. bar assns., Nat. Acad. Arbitrators. Unitarian. Home: 634 Oliver Av Fayetteville AR 72701

BARNHILL, JOHN HENRY, univ. athletic dir.; b. Savannah, Tenn., Feb. 21, 1903; s. James Monroe and Alice (Bryan) B.; B.S.A., U. Tenn., 1928; m. Katherine Peeler, Aug. 28, 1930; 1 dau., Nancy (Mrs. Ellis Trumbo). Coach, Bristol (Tenn.) High Sch., 1928-31; athletic dir., football coach U. Tenn., 1931-46; athletic dir., football coach U. Ark., Fayetteville, 1946-49, dir. athletics, 1949—. John Barnhill Fieldhouse named in his honor at U. Ark., 1958. Mem. Alpha Tau Omega. Methodist. Mason (Shriner), Rotarian. Home: 1425 Markham Rd Fayetteville AR 72701

BARNS, PAUL DRYDEN, JR., lawyer; b. Miami, Fla., Feb. 17, 1924; s. Paul D. and Victoria (Coleman) B.; B.S. in Bus. Adminstrn., Washington and Lee U., 1944; LL.B., U. Fla., 1948; m. Katherine Ghislane Hall, Jan. 26, 1961 (dec. Nov. 1967); m. 2d, Carol Ann Powelson, June 13, 1970. Admitted to Fla. bar, 1948; individual practice law, Miami, 1948-49; v.p., trust officer Security Trust Co., Miami, 1949-65; partner firm, Salley, Barns & Pajon, Miami, 1965—, Dir. Paek, Madrid, Spain. Served to lt. USNR, 1944-46. Mem. Am., Dade County bar assns., Fla. Bar (chmn. state tax com. 1969-71). Democrat. Presbyn. Home: 3941 Park Av Miami FL 33133 Office: 100 Biscayne Tower Miami FL 33132

BARON, HOWARD NAFTALI, citrus fruit co. exec.; b. Berlin, Germany, June 16, 1922; s. Leon Y. and Friede (Kohane) B.; student U. London, Eng., 1936-39; m. Rebecca Zimerman, Dec. 5, 1950; children—Allen, Martin, Michael-Lesley. Came to U.S., 1954, naturalized, 1960. Mgr. internat. div. Fla. Citrus Exchange (now known as Seald-Sweet Growers, Inc.), Tampa, Fla., 1954—; consul of Finland, 1966—. Sr. v.p. Tampa World Trade Council. Pres. Tampa Consular Corps, 1967-70, now v.p. Served with Israeli Army, 1947-49. Decorated Officier de Merit Agricole (France). Mem. Tampa Greater C. of C. Clubs: Commerce, University, Palma Golf and Country (Tampa). Contbr. articles profl. jours. Home: 528 Riviera Dr Tampa FL 33606 Office: Florida and Oak Av Tampa FL 33602

BAROODY, WILLIAM JOSEPH, research inst. exec.; b. Manchester N.H., Jan. 29, 1916; s. Joseph Assad and Helen (Hasney) B.; B.A., St. Anselm's Coll., Manchester, N.H., 1936; postgrad. U. N.H., 1937-38, Am. U., 1938; m. Nabeeha Marion Ashooh, Oct. 15, 1935; children—Anne Mary (Mrs. John G. Gallagher), William Joseph, Joseph D., Helene (Mrs. Michael Payne), Michael E., Mary Frances, Kathryn Jane. Asst. statistician N.H. Unemployment Compensation Div., 1937-40, supr. fiscal, research and legislative planning sects., 1941-44; dir. statis. div. N.H. War Finance Com., 1943-44; research asso. N.H. Legislative Commn. on Disability Benefits, 1940-44; chief research and statistics div. readjustment allowance service VA, Washington, 1946-49; exec. sec. com. on econ. security U.S. C of C., asso. editor Am. Econ. Security, 1950-53; exec. v.p. Am. Enterprise Assn. (name now Am. Enterprise Inst. for Pub. Policy Research), 1954-62, pres., 1962—; bd. overseers Hoover Instn. Stanford U., 1960—. Founding mem. exec. bd. Georgetown Center for Strategic Studies; mem. adv. bd. DeSales Sch. Theology; mem. bishop's liturgical commn. Diocese Richmond (Va.); bd. dirs. Herbert Hoover Birthplace Found., Cath. Virginian, Nr. East Found.; treas., trustee Inst. Social Sci. Research, Washington, 1957—; trustee St. Anselm's Coll., chmn. bd. trustees Woodrow Wilson Internat. Center for Scholars. Served as lt. (j.g.) USNR, 1944-45. Mem. Acad. Polit. Sci., John Carroll Soc., Newcomen Soc., K.C. Clubs: Army-Navy, Carleton (Washington); Belle Haven Country (Alexandria, Va.). Author articles on employment security, ecumenism, Eastern rites. Home: 1111 Francis Hammond Pkwy Alexandria VA 22302 Office: 1150 17th St NW Washington DC 20036

BARR, GLADYS H. HUTCHISON (MRS. THOMAS C. BARR), author; b. Butte, Mont., Dec. 19, 1904; d. David and Laura (Mooney) Hutchison; student State U. N.Y., 1924-25; LL.B., Albany Law Sch., 1926; m. Thomas C. Barr, Oct. 27, 1928; children—Thomas C., Ann (Mrs. Donald A. Weems), Jane, William Hune. Admitted to N.Y. bar, 1927; practiced in N.Y.C., 1926-29. Lectr. schs., colls., womens clubs, others. Vice chmn. bd. Pub. Libraries of Met. Govt. of Nashville and Davidson County, Tenn., 1959—. Mem. Am., Tenn., Southeastern library assns., Women's-Nat. Book Assn., Authors Guild, Authors League of Am., English Speaking Union. Democrat. Presbyn. Clubs: Centennial, Ladies of Richland Country. Author: Monk in Armour, 1950; Cross, Sword and Arrow, 1955; Master of Geneva and the Tinker's Armor, 1961; The Pilgrim Prince, 1963; Famous Witches and Ghost Series, 1969; The Bell Witch at Adams, 1969; The Ghost at Epworth Rectory, 1970; various stories and articles. Home: Apt 6F Georgetown 5025 Hillsboro Rd Nashville TN 37215 Office: Box 706 Nashville TN 37215

BARR, HOWARD RAYMOND, architect; b. Pitts., Feb. 15, 1910; s. Robert Wesley and Myrtle (Hockensmith) B.; B. Arch., U. Tex., 1934; m. Margaret Claire Pressler, Apr. 30, 1938; children—Richard Stuart, Alan Robert. Gen. practice architecture, Austin, Tex., 1939-42, 46; asso. Giesecke, Kuehne & Brooks, Architects, 1946-50; partner Kuehne, Brooks & Barr, 1950-60, Brooks & Barr, 1960-64, Brooks, Barr, Graeber & White, 1964—; dir. First Fed. Savs. of Austin. Sec., Tex. Bd. of Plumbing Examiners, 1961-67; mem. City of Austin Parks and Recreation Bd., 1966-70; commr. Tex. Urban Devel. Commn., 1970—. Served to lt. comdr. USNR, 1942-46. Fellow A.I.A.; mem. Tex. Soc. Architects (pres. 1969). Tex. Ex-Students Assn., Tau Sigma Delta, Phi Kappa Psi, Sphinx. Methodist. Clubs: Forty Acres, Citadel, Headliners. Works include: U.S. Embassy Bldg., Mexico; Manned Spacecraft Center, Houston; Lyndon B. Johnson Library and East Campus Library and Research Bldg., Austin; U.S. Dept. Labor Bldg., Washington; S.W. Tex. Med. Sch., U. Tex., San Antonio; FAA Communications and Control Bldgs., San Juan, P.R., Balboa, C.Z. Home: 4602 Ridge Oak Dr Austin TX 78731 Office: Perry-Brooks Bldg Austin TX 78701

BARR, JAY DAVID ADELSTON, retail store exec.; b. Norfolk, Va., Nov. 30, 1936; s. Phillip and Dena (Adelston) Barr; B.A., U. Va., 1958, LL.B., 1964; M.A., U. London, 1961; m. Clay Hofheimer, Dec.

21, 1962; children—Philippa Elise, Elena Ann Hofheimer. Asso., Etheridge Baylor Hofheimer, Inc., Norfolk, Va., 1963-69; sec.-treas. Barr Corp., real estate devel., 1963—; pres. Cofers, Inc., interior design studios, 1969—; dir. Barr Bros., Inc., jewelers, 1966—. Bd. dirs. Feldman Chamber Music Soc. Served to lt. USNR, 1958-60. Republican. Clubs: Harbor (Norfolk, Va.); Raffles (N.Y.C.); St. James (London, Eng.). Home: Meadowbrook Point Norfolk VA 23505 Office: 1611 Colley Av Norfolk VA 23517

BARR, JESSE ALFRED, banker; b. Cleveland, Miss., Dec. 19, 1936; s. Jesse Coleman and Arlene (Shaffer) B.; B.S., Delta State Coll., 1959; postgrad. Rutgers U., 1970—; m. Connie Buckels, Jan. 24, 1960; children—Anne Louise, Sarah Catherine. With Union Planters Nat. Bank, Memphis, Tenn., 1961—, sr. v.p., sr. loan officer, 1970—. Tchr., Am. Inst. Banking, 1966-67. Mem. Memphis Cotton Carnival Assn., 1967-68; treas. Citizens-Police Community Relations Com., 1968-69. Bd. dirs. Chickasaw Council Boy Scouts Am., dist. chmn., 1966-67, commr., 1963-66; bd. dirs. Delta State Coll. Found. Served with AUS, 1959-61. Recipient Distinguished Service award Memphis Jr. C. of C., 1965. Mem. Am. Inst. Banking (consul 1966-68), Nat. Assn. Credit Men, Robert Morris Assos., Delta State Coll. Alumni Assn. (pres. 1971—). Home: 6227 Quince St Memphis TN 38117 Office: 67 Madison St Memphis TN 38103

BARRANGER, DALTON JOSEPH, lawyer; b. Houma, La., Feb. 6, 1901; s. Harry and Mathilde (Dupuis) B.; student Coll. S.W. La., 1915-17; J.D., Loyola U. (New Orleans), 1927; m. Miriam Ruth Garic, Sept. 12, 1928; 1 son, Garic Kenneth. Admitted to La. bar, 1927; practiced in New Orleans, 1927-37, Covington, 1937—; mem. firm. Ellis & Ellis, Ellis & Barranger, Ellis, Barranger & Suthon, 1937-47, D. J. Barranger, 1947-62, Barranger, Barranger, Jones & Fussell, 1962—. Dir. Comml. Bank & Trust Co. City atty., Covington, La., 1949—; town atty., Mandeville, La., 1962—; chmn. St. Tammany Parish chpt dr. A.R.C., 1957; govt. appeal atty. St. Tammany Parish (La.) Draft Bd., 1941—. Dir. Playmakers, Inc., 1962-68. Mem. Am., La., St. Tammany Parish bar assns., Delta Theta Phi. Democrat. Mason (32 deg.). Clubs: Covington Country (dir. 1958-62), Lions (pres. 1959). Home: Folsom Rd PO Box 1268 Covington LA 70433

BARRANGER, MIRIAM RUTH GARIC(MRS. DALTON JOSEPH BARRANGER), artist, craftsman; b. New Orleans; d. Henry Lawson and Lilly (Guedry) Garic; student Tulane U., 1927-28, 62-63; m. Dalton Joseph Barranger, Sept. 12, 1928; 1 son, Garic Kenneth. Exhibited one-man shows Isaac Delgado Mus. Art, New Orleans, 1951, Carl Barnetts, Inc., Dallas, 1952, La. Art Commn. Gallery, 1952, Mus. Art, Columbia, S.C., 1953, 331 Gallery, New Orleans, 1959, St. Tammany Art Assn., Covington, La., 1964, Foster Art Gallery, Baton Rouge, 1965, La. Crafts Council, New Orleans, 1970; exhibited in numerous shows, New Orleans, 1970; exhibited in numerous group shows including La. Art Commn. Galleries, Baton Rouge, 1953, 63, 65, 66, Isaac Delgado Mus., 1950-53, 58, New Orleans Downtown Gallery, 1961-63, Mint Mus. Art, Charlotte, N.C., 1966, 67 (hon. mention 1966), Mus. Contemporary Crafts, N.Y.C., 1963, N.C. Mus. Art, Raleigh, 1963, 66, Brooks Meml. Art Gallery, Memphis, 1965, La. Craft Council Gallery, New Orleans, 1965, Cabild. Presbytere, New Orleans, 1966. Chmn., St. Tammany Parish Welfare Bd., 1943-48; mem. adv. bd. La. Mental Health, 1959-61; chmn. home nursing, supr. surg. dressings groups A.R.C., 1942-45; vol. occupational therapist S.E. La. Hosp., Mandeville, La., 1962-63; membership chmn., editor Newsletter, La. Assos. Acad. Religion and Mental Health, 1962-65; chmn. St. Tammany Parish (La.) Tb Assn., 1942-48. Bd. dirs. New Orleans Tourist and Conv. Commn.; mem. nat. adv. com. Am. Crafts Council Devel. Fund. Recipient 1st prize in crafts New Orleans Art Assn., 1951; hon. mention Ann. Juried Show, La. Crafts Council, New Orleans, 1969, 70, 1st prize jewelry, 1972; 1st prize crafts Hodges Gardens Art Festival. Dir., v.p. Playmaker's Inc., Covington, 1966-67. Mem. St. Tammany Art Assn. (1st prize crafts 1971, (founder, past pres.) Am. Craftsmen's Council (La. rep. S.E. region), La. Craft Council (bd. mem., chmn. pub. relations 1966-70), Theosophical Soc. (past pres. Covington lodge). Designed, executed murals Comml. Bank and Trust Co., Covington, La., 1962. Address: Red Bluff Box 1268 Covington LA 70433

BARRERA GRAF, GUSTAVO A., lawyer; b. Toluca, Mexico, June 8, 1914; student Instituto Cientifico y Literario, Toluca; LL.B., Nat. U. Mexico. Admitted to Mexican bar, 1938; dist. atty., Tlainepantla and Toluca, 1937-39; under-sec. govt, State of Mexico, 1940-41, pres. local electoral commn., 1946, del. of sec. industry and trade, 1949-54, sec. gen., 1963-69; asst chief legal dept. Banco Nacional de Creditor Ejidal S.A., 1961-63; now mem. firm Gaxiola y Barrera, Toluco. Procurer Toluca City Hall, 1942-43, 55-57. Address: Gaxiola y Barrera Constitucion 104 Toluco Mexico*

BARRERA GRAF, JORGE, lawyer; b. Toluca, Mexico, Feb. 10, 1918; ed. U. Mexico Law Sch., U. Mich. Law Sch. Admitted to Mexican bar, 1943; mem. firm Hidalgo, Barrera, Siqueiros y Torres Landa, Mexico City. Mexican rep. UN Commn. Internat. Trade Law, 1968-69. Mem. Counseil de Direction of Internat. Inst. Unification Pvt. Law. Address: Hidalgo Barrera Siqueiros y Torres Landa Torre latinoamericana Mexico 1 DF Mexico*

BARRET, WILLIAM MORRIS, geophysicist; b. Shreveport, La., May 2, 1898; s. Thomas Charles and Lillian (Hollingsworth) B.; student U. of South, 1916-17, Columbia, 1919-20; B.Engring., Tulane U., 1923, E.E., 1932; m. Lola Belle Holloway, May 4, 1938. Student engr. Gen. Electric Co., Schenectady, 1923; owner, operator electric utilities, 1923-27; cons. geophysicist, 1927-30; founder, pres. Engring. Research Corp., Shreveport, 1930—, William M. Barret, Inc., Shreveport, 1931—. Mem. Soc. Exploration Geophysicists, European Assn. Exploration Geophysicists, Am. Assn. Petroleum Geologists, Am. Inst. Mining, Metal, and Petroleum Engrs., A.A.A.S., La. Acad. Scis., Franklin Inst., Am. Geol. Inst. (sustaining founder), Acad. Applied Scis., Ark.-La.-Tex. Geophys. Soc., Shreveport Geol. Soc., Sigma Alpha Epsilon. Democrat. Episcopalian. Club: Tennis. Contbr. articles to profl. jours.; numerous tech. papers on application and instrumentation of geophys. methods for locating econ. mineral deposits. U.S., fgn. patentee in geophys. methods and apparatus. Home: 2524 Fairfield Av Shreveport LA 71104 Office: Linwood at Dalzell Sts Shreveport LA 71103

BARRETT, ARNOLD LANKFORD, economist, educator; b. Clover, S.C., Mar. 8, 1916; s. Hugh David and Elizabeth (Clinton) B.; A.B., U. Ga., 1937; M.A., U. Va., 1947, Ph.D., 1957; m. Sarah Margaret Counts, Dec. 18, 1948; children—Cynthia Elizabeth, Layne Arnold, Margaret Counts. Asso. prof., head Howard Coll., 1947-54; prof. King Coll., 1954-57; asso. prof. U. Ala., 1957-63; prof. Western Carolina U., Cullowhee, N.C., 1963—. Served with USAAF, 1942-46. Mem. Royal Econ. Soc., Acad. Mgmt., Am. Assn. U. Profs., Alpha Kappa Psi. Contbr. articles to profl. jours. Home: Box 25 Webster NC 28788

BARRETT, CHARLES HENRY, transp. co. exec.; b. N.Y.C., June 7, 1914; s. Charles H. and Isabelle (Lee) B.; student Trenton Bus. Coll., 1932-34; Sparton Sch. Engring., 1942-43; grad., Drake U., 1947; m. Ruth Mary McClean, Sept. 13, 1947; children—Victoria Marie, Charles Michael, Robert McClean, Thomas Henry. Pres., Refrigerated Motor Carrier Tank Transp. System, 1934-42; pres., owner White Line A Motor Carrier, 1946-52; founder, pres., owner Van-Pak Inc., 1952-64; pres., dir., owner U.S. Van Line, Washington, 1964—; pres. Ind. Uniment, Inc., Mishawaka, 1972—; dir. Manley Industries, Areon Corp. Financial cons. motor carriers, 1960—. Served with USAF, 1942-46; CBI. Decorated Legion of Merit. Mem. House Hold Goods Forwarded Assn. (dir. 1963-66), Movers and Warehouse Assn. Am. (1964—, dir.), Am. Movers Conf. (dir. 1968—), Internat. Gold Flow Com. (dir. 1964-66), Movers Tarriff Com. (dir. 1965—). Home: 51312 Mayflower Rd South Bend IN 46628 Office: 1523 L St NW Washington DC 20026

BARRETT, CLIFTON WALLER, author, lectr., bibliophile; b. Alexandria, Va., June 1, 1901; s. Robert S. and Annie Viola (Tupper) B.; student U. Va., 1917-20; Litt.D., Clark U., 1966; L.H.D., Brown U., 1966; m. Cornelia C. Hughes, Apr. 24, 1924; children—Clifton Waller, William Hughes, Jon Sherwood, Robert Paul, Richard Tupper, Kate Waller. Asst. to v.p. Munson S.S. Line, N.Y.C., 1920-32; co-founder, v.p., dir. North Atlantic & Gulf S.S. Co., Inc., N.Y.C., 1932-52, pres., 1952-54; pres., chmn. Norgulf Corp.; dir. Eastern Broadcasting Corp., Alexandria Improvement Corp., 620 Park Avenue Corp., Henry Holt & Co. Pres. bd. edn. Garden City, N.Y., 1945-46; mem. N.Y.C. Art Commn.; regent's lectr. Am. lit. U. Cal., 1959; chmn. fellows Pierpont Morgan Library. Bd. dirs. Barrett Found., Beekman Downtown Hosp.; trustee exec. com., pres. Lake Placid Edn. Found.; trustee McGregor Library, U. Va., U. Va. Alumni Fund; chmn. Friends of Columbia Libraries; mem. council Princeton Library Assos.; trustee N.Y. Pub. Library, Sweet Briar Coll., Clark U., Thomas Jefferson Found., John Carter Brown Library, Mt. Vernon Jr. Coll.; adv. bd. Mt. Vernon (Washington Homestead); chmn., bd. regents James Monroe Meml. Library; bd. visitors U. Va. Decorated comdr., Order Cespedes (Cuba). Mem. Poetry Soc. Am. (trustee), Cuban C. of C. U.S. (pres. 1949-55), Am. Antiquarian Soc. (pres.), Fgn. Policy Assn. N.Y. (dir., exec. com.), Bibliographical Soc. Am. (pres. 1962-64), Am.- Italy Soc. (dir.), Century Assn., Mass., Va. (exec. com.) hist. socs., Phi Beta Kappa. Episcopalian (vestryman) Clubs: Downtown Assn., Grolier (pres. 1957-61), Union (library com.) (N.Y.C.); Lake Placid (pres. 1960-63); Cosmos (Washington); Corinthian Yacht (Oyster Bay, L.I.); Rowfant (Cleve.); Southampton (L.I.); Odd Volumes (Boston). Author: Bibliographical Adventures in Americana, 1950; Henry Admas, 1951; American Fiction, The First Seventy-Five Years, 1954; John Greenleaf Whittier Politician. Antiquarian. Poet: Henry Adams and The Making of a History; Italian Influence on American Literature, 1962; The American Writer in England; also author govtl. monographs on sugar transp. Editor: The Anatomy of Freedom by Judge Medina, 1959. Founder Clifton Waller Barrett Library Am., Lit., U. Va. Home: Arcadia Farmington Charlottesville VA 22901

BARRETT, EDWARD, geologist; b. West Frankfort, Ill., Jan. 26, 1921; s. Edward and Margaret (Stefan) B.; student So. Ill. U., 1939-42; B.S., U. Neb., 1948; m. Valerie Louise Horvat, Jan. 14, 1957; children—Monica Lisa, Jeb Elia. With Continental Oil Co., Oklahoma City, 1948-70, regional research geologist, 1953-65, regional stratigrapher, sr. geologist, 1965-70; v.p., mgr. exploration Dublin Corp., Oklahoma City, 1970—. Founder (with wife) day care center, Warr Acres, Okla., 1965—. Councilman, Warr Acres, 1957-69, vice-mayor, 1957, budget dir., 1957-69, mayor, 1967-69. Served with USAAF, 1942-45. Fellow Geol. Soc. Am., A.A.A.S., Sigma Xi; mem. Am. Assn. Petroleum Geologists, Am. Geol. Inst., Oklahoma City Geol. Soc., Oklahoma City Geol. Soc. Study Group (charter), Phi Beta Kappa, Gamma Theta Upsilon, Sigma Gamma Epsilon. Contbr. articles to profl. publs. Home: 5705 N MacArthur Oklahoma City OK 73132 Office: Fidelity Plaza Robinson at Robert S Kerr St Oklahoma City OK 73102

BARRETT, GEORGE DICKEY, architect; b. Cornelia, Ga., Jan. 25, 1910; s. George W. and Nellie (Fox) B.; B.S. with honors in Architecture, Ga. Inst. Tech., 1931, postgrad. in engring.; m. Mary Carolyn Burns, July 27, 1935; children—Elizabeth, Richard Fox. Engr. and architect Cooper & Cooper, architects, 1936-42, Corps Engrs., War Dept., 1942-44; v.p., dir. Cooper, Bond & Cooper, architects and engrs., 1945-52; exec. v.p., dir. Cooper, Barrett, Skinner, Woodbury & Cooper, Inc., architects and engr., 1952-64, pres., 1964— (all Atlanta). Mem. A.I.A., Am. Concrete Inst. Kiwanian. Principal archtl. works: Coll. Vet. Medicine. U. Ga., 1948. Atlanta Masonic Temple, 1959. Home: 885 St Charles Av NE Atlanta GA 30306 Office: Carnegie Bldg Atlanta GA 30303

BARRETT, HENRY, educator. Prof. music, chmn. strings div. U. Ala., University. Author: The Viola. Address: Sch Music U Alabama University AL 35486*

BARRETT, JERRY WAYNE, educator; b. Marshall, Tex., Apr. 29, 1936; s. Earl and Gladys (Gilstrap) B.; A.A., Kilgore Coll., 1959; B.S., East Tex. Bapt. Coll., 1961; Ph.D., Baylor U., 1968; m. Rebecca Lynn Madison, Aug. 28, 1959; children—Patrick Sean, Leigh Erin. Research asst. Baylor U., 1961-64, Robert A. Welch fellow, 1964-66; asst. prof. chemistry Samford U., Birmingham, Ala., 1966-69, asso. prof. chemistry, 1969—, chmn. health programs, 1969—, chmn. univ. discipline com., 1970—; vis. prof. chemistry Hong Kong Bapt. Coll., 1972-73. Served with AUS, 1954-57. Mem. Am. Chem. Soc., Electrochem. Soc., Ala. Acad. Scis., Sigma Xi, Alpha Epsilon Delta. Baptist. Contbr. articles profl. jours. Home: Samford Univ Birmingham AL 35209

BARRETT, LAWRENCE JAMES, JR., banker; b. Butler, Okla., Oct. 25, 1923; s. Lawrence James and Olive (Bovey) B.; B.S., U. Okla., 1947; m. Marion Eleanor Law, Aug. 4, 1956; children—Diane, Judy, Randy. With Watonga (Okla.) State Bank, 1947—, pres., chmn., 1963—. Served to 1st lt. USAAF, 1942-45. Decorated Air medal, D.F.C. Mem. C. of C. (past pres.). Home: 1005 N Forrest St Watonga OK 73772 Office: 101 W Main St Watonga OK 73772

BARRETT, ROBERT EARL, rubber co. exec.; b. Wooster, O., Mar. 8, 1923; s. Clarence Dale and Cathryn Ann (DeChant) B.; B.S., Mich. State U., 1947; M.S., Ohio State U., Ph.D., 1951; m. Dorothy Jean Brown, Mar. 27, 1944; children—Steven, Cathy, Michael, Susan, Peggy. Prin. chemist Visking Corp., Chgo., 1951-52; prin. chemist Battelle Meml. Inst., Columbus, O., 1952-57; supr., asst. to v.p. research and devel. Copolymer Rubber & Chem. Corp., Baton Rouge, 1957—. Scoutmaster Boy Scouts Am., Baton Rouge, 1958—; mem. Broadmoore Citizens Assn., 1965-66. Served with AUS, 1943-46. Recipient Silver Beaver award Boy Scouts Am., 1970. Mem. Am. Chem. Soc. Presbyn. (deacon, elder). Patentee in field. Home: 9545 Southmoor Dr Baton Rouge LA 70815 Office: PO Box 2591 Baton Rouge LA 70821

BARRETT, RUSSELL HUNTER, educator; b. Cottonwood Falls, Kan., Dec. 30, 1919; s. Raymond John and Mabel Adele (Hunter) B.; B.A., U. Kan., 1946, M.A., 1947; Ph.D., U. Melbourne, 1952; postgrad. (East Asian Studies fellow) Harvard, 1958-59; m. Alamada Orpha Bollier, June 17, 1947; children—Valerie Sue, Pamela Anne. Instr., U. Kan. at Lawrence, 1947-50, U. Cal. at Berkeley, 1952-53, San Francisco State Coll., 1953-54; asst. prof. polit. sci. U. Miss., University, 1954-57, asso. prof., 1957-61, prof., 1961—. Mem. Miss. adv. com. U.S. Commn. on Civil Rights, 1965-66. Served with USAAF, 1942-45. Rockefeller Found. Travel grantee, 1966; Social Sci. Research Council Research grantee, 1964. Mem. Am. Assn. U. Profs. (mem. nat. council 1965-67), Am., So. polit. sci. assns., Phi Beta Kappa, Pi Sigma Alpha, Phi Kappa Phi. Author: Integration at Ole Miss, 1965; Promises and Performances in Australian Politics, 1959, rev. edit., 1963. Home: 544 N 9th St Oxford MS 38655 Office: Deupree Hall University MS 38677

BARRETT, ST. JOHN, govt. ofcl. Dep. gen. counsel Dept. Health, Edn. and Welfare, Washington. Address: Dept Health Edn and Welfare 330 Independence Blvd SW Washington DC 20201*

BARRETT, THOMAS WILLIAM, mech. engr.; b. Barnesville, Ohio, Jan. 2, 1930; s. Robert Morris and Minnie (Morgan) B.; B.M.E., Tex. A. and M. U., 1956; m. Mary Glynn Sanders, June 9, 1951; children—David William, Glynn Ellen. Test engr. ARO, Inc., Tullahoma, Tenn., 1956-58; analysis engr. Martin Co., Denver, 1959-61; engr., sect. chief, project leader NASA, George C. Marshall Space Flight Center, Huntsville, Ala., 1962—. Served with USAF, 1948-52. Registered profl. engr. Mem. Am. Inst. Aeros. and Astronautics, Am. Soc. M.E. Mason. Clubs: Redstone Yacht (vice comdr. 1969), Poseidon Scuba (pres. 1969-70). Patentee personal propulsion unit. Home: 500 Seaborn Dr Huntsville AL 35806 Office: PD SA Marshall Space Flight Center AL 35812

BARRETT, WILLIAM ARVEL, hosp. exec.,; b. Bluefield, W.Va., Aug. 16, 1919; s. Lawrence Witten and Beatrice (Massey) B.; B.B.A., Ga. State Coll., 1957; m. Dorothy Clements, Sept. 21, 1947 (div); children—William Arvel III (dec.), Johnny, Perry, Joy; m. 2d, Frances S. Whitley, Oct. 24, 1970. Asst. adminstr. Ga. Bapt. Hosp., Atlanta, 1955-58; adminstr. Athens (Ga.) Gen. Hosp., 1958-72; pres. Heritage Nursing & Convalescent Center, Inc., 1965—, Barrett Convalescent Center, Inc., 1966, Spring Valley Convalescent Center, Elberton, Ga., Medic Corp., Atlanta. Partner B & G Farm. Past trustee Ga. Hosp. Assn. Served with Med. Service Corps, AUS, 1943-46, 51-54. Mem. Am. Coll. Hosp. Adminstrs., Ga. Hosp. Service Assn. (past (trustee Columbus). Baptist. Home: 515 Highland Av Athens GA 30601 Office: 797 Cobb St Athens GA 30601

BARRETT, WILLIAM ERVAN, accountant; b. Lexington, S.C., Aug. 14, 1928; s. John Edward and Harriet (Harmon) B.; B.S., U.S.C., 1951, postgrad., 1951-52; m. Joan Elizabeth Copeland, June 21, 1952; children—William E., Lauralee. Chief accountant WIS Radio WIS-TV Corp., Columbia, S.C., 1953-55; accountant Robert A. Bruce & Co., Camden, S.C., 1955-62, J.W. Hunt & Co., Columbia, 1962-63; chief accountant S.C. Industries, Inc., Florence, 1963—. Served with AUS, 1946-47. C.P.A., S.C. Mem. Am. Inst. C.P.A.'s, S.C. Assn. C.P.A.'s, Phi Kappa Sigma, Delta Sigma Pi, V.F.W., Jaycees. Methodist. Mason. Clubs: Elks, Toastmasters. Home: 1204 Pinckney Av Florence SC 29501 Office: PO Box 4000 Florence SC 29501

BARRINGER, PAUL BRANDON, lumber co. exec.; b. Sumter, S.C., Aug. 22, 1930; s. Victor Clay and Gertrude (Hampton) B.; B.S., U. Va., 1952; student George Washington U., 1954; m. Merrill Underwood, May 27, 1957; children—Merrill U., Victor Clay, Ann Hampton. With Human Relations Lab., Washington, 1954; with Coastal Lumber Co., Weldon, N.C., 1954—, pres., treas., dir., 1967—; pres., treas., dir. Dubarco Lumber Co., Havana, Fla., 1967—; 1st v.p., dir., exec. com. State Record Co., Columbia, S.C., 1966—, Gulf Pub. Co., Biloxi, Miss., 1967; dir. Bestway Express, Wrenn Tools, Inc., State Printing Co., Caro Craft, Inc., Columbia Newspapers, Inc., State Telecasting Co. Inc., State Record Pub. Co. Regional fund chmn. A.R.C., 1960, dir., 1962-66; vice chmn. bd. visitors Louisburg Coll. Pres., trustee Enfield Acad.; trustee Brandon Ednl. Found. Served with USAF, 1952-54. Mem. Eastern N.C. Lumber Mfg. Assn. (sec.-treas. 1957—), Nat. Assns. Mfrs., Nat. Lumber Mfrs. Assn., Zeta Psi, Sigma Delta Psi, Lambda Chi. Episcopalian. Clubs: Clockoyotte Country, Farmington Country, Downtown. Home: Country Club Rd Weldon NC 27809 Office: PO Box 231 Weldon NC 27890

BARROLL, JOHN LEEDS, educator; b. Lausanne, Switzerland, July 20, 1928 (parents Am. citizens); s. John Leeds and Mary Hargrove (Bellamy) B.; A.B. cum laude, Harvard, 1950; M.A., Princeton, 1955, Ph.D., 1956; m. Rayna Sue Klatzkin, Mar. 17, 1951; children—John Leeds, James Edmondson, Ellen. Asst. prof. English, U. Tex., Austin, 1956-60; asso. prof. U. Cin., 1960-64, prof., 1964-67, asst. dean Grad. Sch., 1965-66, asso. dean Grad. Sch., 1966-67; vis. prof. English lit. U. Newcastle upon Tyne (Eng.), 1967-68; prof. English, Vanderbilt U., Nashville, 1968-69, dir. Center for Shakespeare Studies, 1968—; dean arts and scis. William Paterson Coll., Wayne, N.J., 1969-70; prof. English lit. U. S.C., Columbia, 1970—. Served with AUS, 1946-48. Huntington Library fellow, 1957, 59, Folger Shakespeare Library fellow, 1958; recipient Sachs award Cin. Inst. Fine Arts, 1966. Mem. Shakespeare Council Am. (chmn. bd. trustees 1970—), Modern Lang. Assn., Malone Soc., Internat. Assn. U. Profs., Modern Humanities Research Assn. Episcopalian. Clubs: D.U., Hasty Pudding (Harvard). Author: (with Austin Wright) The Art of the Short Story, 1969 Editor: Shakespeare Studies, ann., 1965; Shakespeare Studies Monograph Series, 1969—; The Blackfriars Shakespeare, 1969; gen. editor: The South Carolina Shakespeare, 1972. Home: 4853 Forest Ridge Rd Columbia SC 29208

BARRON, BRYTON, book editor; b. Doon, Ia., Dec. 6, 1898; s. Hiram H. and Emma J. Barron; A.B., Sioux Falls Coll., 1922; B. Litt. (Rhodes scholar at Pembroke Coll. 1920-23), Oxford U. (Eng.), 1923, diploma in econ. and polit. sci., 1922; m. Ella Rosalie Lillibridge, Dec. 31, 1922; children—Bebe (Mrs. Edgar Carl Seward, Jr.), Roger L. Editorial writer Daily Argus-Leader, Sioux Falls, S.D., 1923-25; ednl. work, P.I., 1925-28; asst. editor Dept. State, Washington, 1929, chief pub. sect., 1929-40, asst. chief div. research and publs., 1940-44, chief treaty staff, adviser on treaty affairs, 1944-50, research historian, 1950-56; pub. Crestwood Books, 1962-66, sr. editor, 1966—; lectr. on fgn. affairs throughout U.S., 1956-65. Founder. treas., gen. mgr. Dept. of State Fed. Credit Union, 1935-42; founder, pres. Dept. of State Recreation Assn., 1935. Barron papers preserved Library U. Ore. Active in numerous conservative causes. Recipient award Am. Acad. Pub. Affairs of Los Angeles, 1964; Liberty award Congress Freedom, 1959; award Young Americans Against Communism, 1964; Distinguished Alumni award Sioux Falls Coll., 1972. Mem. Acad. Model Aeros. (nat. sec. 1952), Fla. Modelers Assn. (sec.-treas. 1969—). Author: Inside the State Department, 1956; The Untouchable State Department, 1962, rev. as State Department; Blunders or Treason, 1965. Co-author: Dream Becomes a Nightmare: The UN Today, 1964; The Inhumanity of Urban Renewal, 1965. Compiler: Trouble Abroad: An Independent Survey of World Affairs, 1965. Contbr. articles to mags. and newspapers. Co-author series of grammar textbooks. Address: 7710 NW 8th St Pembroke Pines Hollywood FL 33024

BARRON, DEMPSEY J., state senator; b. Andalusia, Ala., Mar. 5, 1922; s. Jessie Carl Dempsey and Minnie (Brown) B.; B.S., Fla. State U.; LL.B., U. Fla.; m. Louverne Hall, Jan. 27, 1952; children—Stephen C., Stuart J. Atty. firm Barron, Redding & Boggs, 1954—; owner D Bar Ranch; mem. Fla. Ho. of Reps., 1956-60; mem. Fla. senate, 1960—, pres. pro tem, 1967—. Dir. Panama City and Bay Co. Chmn.

Panama City (Fla.) Heart Fund Drive, United Fund, Bd. Dirs. Boys Club Am. Served with USNR, 1942-47; PTO, ETO. Named one of 10 outstanding mems. Fla. legislature by press, 1957-—, one of 2 outstanding mems. Fla. senate, 1965. Mem. Panama City C. of C. (bd. dirs). Methodist. Home: 224 Woodlawn Dr Panama City FL 32406 Office: Box 1638 Panama City FL 32401

BARRON, ORAN JAMES, JR., rancher; b. Athens, Tex., May 29, 1916; s. Oran James and Mavit (Hardin) B.; student U. Ariz., 1933, Tex. Western U,, 1934-35; m. Eleonora Prudence Swenson, Feb. 20, 1942; children—Oran James III, Helen Mavit, Amanda Hope. Owner Spur Hdqrs. Ranch, Spur Tex., 1946-—; pres. Caprock Telephone Co. Inc., Spur 1955-—; dir. Swenson Land & Cattle Co., N.Y.C., 1959-—. Mem. Tex. Water Resources Research Adv. Com., 1968-71; mem. Tex. Brush and Range Improvement Com., 1969-—. Chmn. Dickens County (Tex.) bd. edn., 1956-—; pres. Dickens County Water Control and Improvement Dist. 1, 1962-70. Dir. Tex. Exptl. Ranch Com., 1958-—. Served to maj. AUS, 1941-45. Decorated Bronze Star with oak leaf cluster. Mem. Am. Soc. Animal Sci., Am. Soc. Range Mgmt., Tex. Cattle Feeders Assn. (dir. 1967-—). Methodist. Address: Route 1 Spur TX 79370

BARRON, RANDALL FRANKLIN, educator; b. Many, La., May 16, 1936; s. Benjamin Franklin and Inez (Norseworthy) B.; B.S., La. Poly. Inst., 1958; M.S., Ohio State U., 1961, Ph.D., 1964; m. Shirley Estelle McDuffie, Mar. 14, 1958; children—Randall Franklin, Donna Carol, Steven Dale, Brian Richard. Instr. dept. mech. engring. Ohio State U., Columbus, 1958-64, asst. prof., 1964-65; prof. mech. engring. La. Tech. U., Ruston, 1965-—. Cons. AMF Beaird, Inc., Shreveport, La., 1966-—. Recipient R.M. Teetor Outstanding Educator award Soc. Automotive Engrs., 1966; award of merit La. Engring. Soc., 1967; Gold Medal award Pi Tau Sigma, 1968; Research award Sigma Xi, 1971. Mem. Am. Soc. M.E., Am. Soc. Engring. Edn., A.A.A.S., La. Engring. Soc., La. Acad. Sci., Sigma Xi, Phi Kappa Phi, Tau Beta Pi, Pi Tau Sigma. Mason (K.T.). Author: Cyrogenic Systems, 1966. Contbr. chpt. Cryogenics in Surgery, 1971. Home: 2202 Greenbriar Dr Ruston LA 71270

BARROS-LOUBRIEL, ULISES, bldg. mgmt. exec.; b. San Juan, P.R., July 4, 1928; s. Ulises Barros and Lolin Loubriel; B.S. in Civil Engring., U. P.R., 1950; B.S. in Bldg. Engring. and Constrn., Mass. Inst. Tech., 1955, M.S., 1955; m. Madeleine Carrero, June 6, 1960; children—Marinilka, Ulises Barros-Carrero. Planner engr. P.R. Planning Bd., 1952-55, dir. bldg. permit appeals bd., 1955-58, dir. Bldg. Permit Bur., 1958-60; exec. dir. Pub. Bldgs. Authority, 1960-69; cons. engr., gen. mgr. Marmoles de P.R., Santurce, 1969-—. Mem. Bd. Realtors P.R., 1967. Served with AUS, 1960-62. Mem. Colegio de Ingenieros, Arquitectos y Agrimensores de P.R., Am. Concrete Inst., Am. Soc. C.E., Inst. Real Estate Mgmt. (Chgo.), Bldg. Research Inst. (Washington), Nat. Inst. Real Estate Brokers. Home: FO No 12 Urd Villamar Carolina PR 00914 Office: Box 12086 Loizoi Sta Santurce PR 00914

BARROW, ALLEN EDWARD, U.S. judge; b. Okemah, Okla., Jan 22, 1914; s. Alfred E. and Minnie Lee (Coffelt) B.; student Okla A. and M. Coll., 1935-36; B.A., U. Okla., 1936; postgrad. U. Tulsa; LL.B., Southwestern Coll., 1942; m. Dorothy Elaine Dalton, Oct. 2, 1942; children—Allen Edward, Karla Elaine, Mary Celeste. With FBI, 1940-42; admitted to Okla. bar, 1942, U.S. Supreme Ct. bar; practice law, Tulsa, 1946-50, 54-62; counsel Southwestern Power Adminstrn., Dept. Interior, Tulsa, 1950-54; formerly judge U.S. Dist. ct. for No. Dist. Okla., now chief judge. Adv. bd. Tulsa Salvation Army, 1956-—. Bd. dirs. A.R.C. Served to maj. AUS, 1942-46. Mem. Am., Okla. (Outstanding Service award 1959) bar assns., S.A.R. (pres. Okla. 1954), Delta Theta Phi, Phi Eta Sigma, Sigma Chi (pres. alumni assn. 1950). Democrat. Mem. Christian Ch. Home: 2142 E 25th Pl Tulsa OK 74114 Office: Fed Bldg 333 W 4th Tulsa OK 74103

BARROW, THOMAS LEE, statistician; b. Beaumont, Tex., Aug. 5, 1913; s. Jesse and Mary Ann (Tatum) B.; student Tex. Christian U., 1949; m. Ann Mae Thompson, Jan. 2, 1953; 1 dau., Janice (Mrs. Elmer Grape). Labor market analyst Tex. Employment Commn., Austin, 1936-63, dir. research and statistics, 1963-—. Served with AUS, 1943-46. Mem. Internat. Assn. Personnel in Employment Security, Tex. Pub. Employees Assn., Am. Statis. Assn. Home: 11804 Oak Trail Austin TX 78753 Office: TEC Bldg Austin TX 78701

BARRY, JAMES JOSEPH, retail business exec.; b. Charleston, S.C., Sept. 25, 1907; s. James Thomas and Charlotte (Thweatt) B.; student pub. schs.; m. Katherine Mims, Jan. 8, 1936; children—James Joseph, Katherine Mims. Owner, Barry's Dept. Store, St. Stephen, S.C., 1929-—; pres. Berkeley Radio & Furniture Co., St. Stephen, 1936-—; pres. Indsl. Devel. Corp., St. Stephen, L. Mendel Rivers Indsl. Park, Inc.; dir. Bank Berkeley. Mem. South Carolina Hwy. Commn. from 9th Dist. 1946-50; 54-58.; adv. com. Charleston Area Comprehensive Health Planning; mem. Berkeley County Bd. Edn., Monoks Corner, S.C., 1958-—; vice chmn. Berkeley County Area Redevel. Adminstrn., 1962-—. Bd. dirs. Berkeley County Hosp. Mem. Hibernian Soc., S.C. C. of C. (dir. 1959-60). Roman Catholic. Lion (charter pres. St. Stephen 1958-59). Address: PO Box 606 St Stephen SC 29479

BARRY, WILLIAM LOGAN, lawyer, ex-state legislator; b. Lexington, Tenn., Feb 9, 1926; s. Henry Daniel and Mary (Logan) B.; B.A., Vanderbilt U., 1947; LL.B., 1950; M. Joanne Coffman, 1966. Admitted to Tenn. bar, 1950; practiced in Lexington; mem. firm Barry & Walker; mem. Tenn. Ho. of Reps., 1955-67, speaker, 1963-67; exec. asst. to gov. Tenn., 1967-71; asst. atty. gen. State of Tenn., Nashville, 1971-—. Chmn. Tenn. Legislative Council 1965-67. Served as 1st lt. AUS, 1951-53. Mem. Am. Legion, V.F.W. Democrat. Baptist. Lion. Elk, K.P. Home: RFD 1 Lexington TN 38351 Office: Supreme Ct Bldg Nashville TN

BART, JEROME BARRY, physician; b. Glens Falls, N.Y., Mar. 28, 1938; s. Abraham and Pearl N. (Schwartz) B.; A.B., Dartmouth, 1960, B.Med.Sci., 1961; M.D., Harvard, 1963; m. Sandra Seibel, June 13, 1965; children—Aaron, Joelle. Intern, Buffalo Gen. Hosp., 1963-64, resident, 1964-66; practice medicine, specializing in hematology, Houston, 1969-—; chief sect. hematology Kelsey-Seybold Clinic, Houston, 1969-—; mem. staff hematology sect. M.D. Anderson Hosp., Houston, 1970-—; asst. prof. medicine Baylor U., 1971-—; sect. head hematology sect. St. Lukes Episcopal Hosp., Houston. Served with USAF, 1967-69. Mem. A.C.P., Am., Tex. med. assns., Am. Soc. Hematology, Houston Soc. Internal Medicine. Home: 5242 Loch Lomond St Houston TX 77025 Office: 6624 Fannin St Houston TX 77035

BARTELMES, RAYMOND FREDERICK, civil engr.; b. Washington, Sept. 24, 1912; s. Frederick Armisted and Annie May (Stipe) B.; B.S. in Civil Engring. with honors, U. Md., 1936; M.Civil Engring., Cath. U., 1959; m. Constance Audrey Hampton, Feb. 12, 1936; children—Barbara (Mrs. Edward Surovel), Bette Jean, Robert F., William R. Bonnie L. Engr., D.C. Govt., 1937-40, Navy Dept., 1940-41; with Dist. Engring. Office, B.W.I., 1941-42; engr., br. and div. chief Army Engr. Research and Devel. Labs., Ft. Belvoir, Va., 1945-—. Pres., Citizens Assn., Groveton, Va., 1952-—. Served to lt. AUS, 1936-37; served to capt. C.E., AUS, 1942-45; PTO; lt. col. Res. ret. Mem. Am. Soc. C.E., Sci. Research Soc. Am., Scabbard and Blade, Tau Beta Pi. So. Baptist. Mason. Project engr. for Atomic Weapons Assembly Bldg., Missile Gantry for Juno and medium range missiles. Home: 3304 Arundel Av Alexandria VA 22306 Office: US Army Mobility Equipment Research and Devel Center Fort Belvoir VA 22060

BARTENFELD, WILLIAM CHELSEA, textile co. exec.; b. Dalton, Ga., May 27, 1920; s. Joseph Cleve and Isabella (Hill) B.; student Internat. Corr. Sch., 1949, Advanced Mgmt. Program, Emory U., 1972; m. Mildred Virginia Stanfield, Sept. 13, 1941; 1 son, Chelsea Levone. With textile div. Cabin Crafts, Dalton, Ga., 1939-—., mgr. mfg., 1961-—. Served with AUS, 1943-45. Baptist (deacon 1956, finance chmn. 1959). Elk. Home: Audubon Dr Dalton GA 30720 Office: Springdale Rd Dalton GA 30720

BARTH, ALAN, editorial writer; b. N.Y.C., Oct. 21, 1906; s. Jacob and Flora (Barth) Lauchheimer; Ph.B., Yale 1929; Nieman fellow, Harvard, 1948-49; m. Adrienne Mayer, July 1, 1939; children—Flora, Andrew. Reporter, Beaumont (Tex.) Enterprise, 1936; editorial writer Beaumont Jour., 1937-38; Washington corr. McClure Newspaper Syndicate, 1938-41; editorial asst. Sec. Treasury, 1941-42; editor reports OWI, 1942-43; editorial writer Washington Post, 1943-—; vis. prof. govtl. affairs U. Cal. at Berkeley, 1958-59. Recipient Sigma Delta Chi award, distinguished service Am. journalism 1947; Am. Newspaper Guild award, distinguished editorial writing, 1948, Sidney Hillman Found., 1952; Oliver Wendell Holmes Bill of Rights award, 1964, Lasker Civil Liberties award, 1967. Mem. Am. Acad. Arts and Scis. Author: The Loyalty of Free Men, 1951; Government By Investigation, 1955; The Price of Liberty, 1961; Heritage of Liberty, 1965. Contbr. articles to popular mags. Home: 3520 Rodman St NW Washington DC 20008 Office: Washington Post Washington DC 20005

BARTH, ALF OTTO, architect; b. Risor, Norway, Aug. 5, 1921; s. Haakon Hjalmar and Emilie (Gisslerud) B.; came to U.S., 1929, naturalized, 1943; B.Arch. with honors, U. Fla., 1953; m. Mary Jayne Ingram, Apr. 28, 1951; children—Kathleen Elizabeth, Paul Haakon. Architect, dir. sch. planning Polk County, Fla., 1956-60; asso. dir. sch. planning Dade County, Fla., 1960-64; coordinating architect Orange County (Fla.) schs., 1964-65; architect in charge Charles W. Cole & Son, South Bend, Ind., 1966; chief architect Dade County, 1968-—; cons. architect, 1956-—; prin. works include Oakland Elementary Sch., Haines City, Fla., 1960; Sanctuary for Grace Lutheran Ch., Winter Haven, Fla., 1960, ednl. bldg., 1967; addition Redeemer Luth. Ch., Miami Shores, Fla., 1961; Immanuel Luth. Ch., Tavernier, Fla., 1967; ednl. bldg. Concordia Luth. Ch., Miami, 1966. Chmn. Dade County Archtl. Selection Com., 1968-—. Bd. dirs. Eastridge Retirement Village, Miami, 1963-64. Served with USNR, 1943-46; AUS, 1947-50. Mem. A.I.A. (dir. local chpt. 1964), Nat. Council Archtl. Registration Bds., Am. Arbitration Assn., Am. Pub. Works Assn., Gargoyle (historian), Phi Kappa Phi. Lutheran (chmn. trustees 1961-65). Mason, Odd Fellow. Home: 7581 SW 58th St Miami FL 33143 Office: 1351 NW 12th St Miami FL 3125

BARTH, PIUS JOSEPH, clergyman, educator; b. Chgo., Mar. 6, 1908; A.B., St. Joseph Coll., 1930; S.T.B., St. Joseph Sem., 1934; M.A., Case Western Res. U., 1938; postgrad. Harvard, 1940, Catholic U., 1940; Ph.D. in Higher Edn., U. Chgo., 1945. Tchr. Quincy Coll. Acad., 1934-38; dean Quincy Coll., 1938-45; chmn. dept. edn. DePaul U., 1945-54; provincial Franciscan Midwest province, 1954-60; pres. Internat. Pedagogical Inst., Rome, Italy, 1960-67; dean grad. studies Cath. U., P.R., 1967-—, provost, 1969-—. Examiner North Central Assn. Colls. and Univs., 1944-60. Fulbright prof. and adviser, Philippines, 1950-51. Mem. N.E.A., Nat. Cath. Edn. Assn. Phi Delta Kappa. Contbr. articles to profl. jours. Office: Office of Provost and Dean Grad Studies Catholic U Ponce PR 00731*

BARTHA, LOUIS ALEXANDER, accountant; b. Toledo, June 18, 1917; s. Stephen Joseph and Susan (Piszkaly) B.; student Berea Coll., 1935-36, Ohio State U., 1936, U. Ill., 1936-39, 40; m. Ruth Kathryn Woodson, May 18, 1942; 1 son, Gregory Woodson. Accountant Louis A. Bartha C.P.A., Midland, Tex., 1945-—; sec.-treas., dir. Palafox Exploration Co., Midland, 1957-—; v.p., dir. Scharbauer Cattle Co., Midland, 1958-—; sec.-treas., dir. Scharbauer Bros. & Co., 1958-—, Alamositas Cattle Co., 1958-—; sec., dir. Ranching Enterprises, Inc., 1966-70. Mem. Tex. State Bd. Pub. Accountancy, 1958-67. Chmn. Midland County Democratic Exec. Com., 1948-52. Sec., dir. Midland Fair, Inc., 1950-65; treas., dir. Midland Indsl. Plan, Inc., 1954-65; sec., dir. Prairie Found., Midland, Tex., 1957-—; chmn. Midland County Draft Bd., 1966-—. C.P.A., Tex. Trustee Midland Ind. Sch. Dist., 1957-63, sec., 1959-63. Served to capt. USAAF, 1941-45. C.P.A., Tex. Mem. Am. Inst. C.P.A.'s, Tex. Soc. C.P.A.'s, Accounting Research Assn., Am. Accounting Assn. Rotarian. Home: 905 Bedford Dr Midland TX 79701 Office: 1st Nat Bank Bldg Midland TX 79701

BARTHEL, WILLIAM FREDERICK, chemist; b. Arbutus, Md., Mar. 12, 1915; s. Robert Amthor and Caroline (Coulbourne) B.; student U. Md., 1936-41, Johns Hopkins, 1955-56; m. Eva Buday, June 6, 1938; 1 son, William Frederick. Chemist, U.S. Dept. Agr., Beltsville, Md., 1936-45; supervisory chemist Victor Products Corp., Hagerstown, Md., 1946-47; supervisory chemist Edco Corp., Elkton, Md., 1947-48; supervisory chemist Innis Speiden & Co., N.Y.C., 1949-51; chemist U.S. Dept. Agr., Beltsville, Md., 1951-57, Gulfport, Miss., 1957-67; chief toxicology lab. Nat. Communicable Disease Center, USPHS, Atlanta, 1967-68; chief Atlanta Toxicology Br., U.S. FDA; 1968-71; chief clin. toxology lab. Center for Disease Control, Atlanta, 1971-—. Fellow Am. Inst. Chemists (chmn. Piedmont chpt.);mem. Am. Chem. Soc., Entomol. Soc. Am., Sci. Research Soc. Am., Assn. Food and Drug Ofcls., Assn. Food and Agrl. Chemists, Alpha Chi Sigma. Home: 1529 Jennings Way Norcross GA 30071 Office: 1600 Clifton Rd NE Atlanta GA 30333

BARTHELD, ROBERT LYLE, dentist; b. McAlester, Okla., Jan. 4, 1933; s. Floyd Thomas and Nedra (Ackors) B.; student N.M. Mil. Inst., 1950-52; B.S., U. Okla., 1954; D.D.S., U. Kansas City, 1958; m. Patricia E. McCann, June 10, 1956; children—Thomas M., William E., Joseph L. Dentist Okla. Dept. Health, 1958; pvt. practice dentistry, McAlester, 1960-61, 62-—. Mem. Okla. Health Planning Council, 1969-—. Served with AUS, 1958-60, 61-62. Mem. Okla. State Dental Assn. (trustee, ho. of dels.), Soc. Dentistry for Children, Fedn. Dentaire Internationale, Eastern Dist. Dental Soc. (pres. 1968-—), Navy League (2d v.p., bd. dirs.), Pierre Fouchard Acad., McAlester C. of C., Beta Theta Pi, Delta Sigma Delta. Episcopalian (sr. warden 1969-—, mem. vestry). Mason (32 deg., Shriner, Jester). Clubs: Lion's (pres. 1967-68), McAlester Country (bd. dirs.). Home: 1317 Mac Arthur Lane McAlester OK 74501 Office: Med Arts Bldg McAlester OK 74501

BARTHELEMY, JOSEPH EDWARD, JR., geophysicist; b. Jackson, Miss., Oct. 18, 1927; s. Joseph Edward and Lessie (Hooper) B.; B.S., St. Louis U., 1949; m. Mary Jean DeLisle, Apr. 15, 1961; children—Lora Ann, Jean Louise, Joseph Edward III, Ross Alan. With Western Geophys. Co., 1949-63, supr., Canada, 1951-53, Rocky Mountain area, West Coast, Alaska, 1953-54, 55-63; sr. staff geophysicist Superior Oil Co., Houston, 1963-66; operations mgr. Western Geophys. Co., Houston, 1966-69; chief geophysicist Ocean Drilling & Exploration, New Orleans, 1969-—. Served with AUS, 1954-55. Mem. Soc. Exploration Geophysicists, Am. Assn. Petroleum Geologists, Alpha Sigma Nu, Pi Mu Epsilon. Home: 5204 Haring Ct Metairie LA 70002 Office: 1600 Canal St New Orleans LA 70121

BARTHOLOMEW, ALBERT WAYNE, educator; b. Chico, Cal., Sept. 18, 1941; s. Roy Martin and Hazel Ivy (Hufford) B.; B.S., Cal. State Poly. Coll., San Luis Obispo 1963; M.S., Cornell U., 1965, Ph.D., 1968; m. Judy Lee Kilpatrick, April 22, 1967. Faculty prof. econs. Benedict Coll., Columbia, S.C., 1968-—, dir. econs. and bus. 1968-—. Campaign worker for Senator Robert Kennedy, 1968. Mem. Am. Econs. Assn., Am. Agrl. Econs. Assn., Alpha Zeta, Phi Kappa Phi. Home: 2537 Midland Dr Columbia SC 29204

BARTHOLOMEW, FLETCHER LAVALLEE, meteorologist; b. Mpls., Nov. 24, 1918; s. Frederick Roscoe and Stella (LaVallee) B.; B.S. in Meteorology, Mass. Inst. Tech., 1950; m. Cynthia Louise Turek, July 10, 1943; children— Ann, John Fletcher, Mary Christine, Gregory Turek, Gail Pepin. Meteorologist, Pan Am.-Grace Airways, Lima, Peru, 1950-51; sr. scientist Gen. Mills, Mpls., 1951-58; sr. specialist engr. Boeing Corp., Seattle, 1958-70; sr. research scientist Center for Environment and Man, Hartford, Conn., 1970-71; sr. environmental specialist Northrop Airport Devel. Corp., Vienna, Va., 1971-—; staff Free Europe Com., 1954-56; tech. staff Research Analysis Corp., Washington, 1964. Served to capt. USAAF, 1942-46. Mem. Am. Meteorol. Soc., Operations Research Soc. Am. (asso. mem., sec., v.p. N.W. chpt. 1962-63). Office: Northrop Page Technology Park Vienna VA 22180

BARTLETT, ALBERT CHARLES, banker; b. Portsmouth, Va., Jan. 14, 1907; s. Charles Albert and Frances Lee (Pettit) B.; student Grad. Sch. Banking, Rutgers U., 1939-41; m. Mildred Antoinnette Barrett, Mar. 4, 1933; children—Charles A., Richard B., Robert L. Clk., Citizens Trust Co., Portsmouth, Va., 1924-26, teller, 1926-37, asst. treas., 1937-45, treas., 1945-50, v.p., 1950-52; v.p. Bank Va., 1952-60; sr. v.p. Am. Nat. Bank, Portsmouth, 1960-61, exec. v.p., 1961-63, pres., 1963-72, now only dir.; chmn. bd. Fidelity Am. Bankshares, Lynchburg, Va. Active United Fund, Portsmouth. Mem. City Council, Portsmouth, 1956-60, mayor, 1956-58. Trustee Old Dominion U. Found., Portsmouth Community Trust; bd. dirs., mem. finance com. Portsmouth Gen. Hosp. Mem. Portsmouth C. of C. (pres. 1955-56), Portsmouth Execs. Club. Mason, Kiwanian. Methodist. Home: 4706 Westmoreland Terrace Portsmouth VA 23707

BARTLETT, CHARLES LEFFINGWELL, newspaperman; b. Chgo., Aug. 14, 1921; s. Valentine C. and Marie (Frost) B.; student St. Mark's Sch., Southboro, Mass., 1934-39; A.B., Yale, 1943; m. Josephine Martha Buck, Dec. 16, 1950; children—Peter B., Michael V., Robert S., Helen B. Reporter Chattanooga Times, 1946-63, Washington corr., 1948-63; editor News Focus Service, 1958-63; columnist Chgo. Sun-Times, 1963-—. Served as lt. USNR, 1943-46. Recipient Pulitzer prize for nat. reporting, 1955. Roman Catholic. Clubs: National Press, Gridiron, Federal City. Author: (with Edward Weintal) Facing the Brink, 1957. Home: 4615 W St NW Washington DC 20007 Office: Nat Press Bldg Washington DC 20004

BARTLETT, DEWEY FOLLETT, gov. Okla.; b. Marietta, O., Mar. 28, 1919; s. David A. and Jessie (Follett) B.; grad. Lawrenceville (N.J.) Sch., 1938; B.S. in Geol. Engring., Princeton, 1942; m. Ann C. Smith, Apr. 2, 1945; children—Dewey Follett, Joan, Mike. Partner, Keener Oil Co., Tulsa, 1951-—; pres. Dewey Supply Co. (Okla), 1953-56; owner-operator ranch in Wagoner County, Okla., 1958-64, in Delaware County, 1958-—. Mem. Okla. Senate from Tulsa County, 1962-66; gov. of Okla, 1967-—. State chmn. Ozarks Regional Commn., 1968-69; chmn. Interstate Oil Compact Commn., 1970-—. Bd. dirs. Tulsa County chpt. A.R.C. Served as pilot USMCR, World War II. Decorated Air medal. Mem. Ind. Petroleum Assn. Am. (bd. dirs.), Okla. Ind. Producers Assn. (bd. dirs). Republican. Roman Catholic. Home: 2462 E 30th St Tulsa OK 74114 Office: National Bank of Tulsa Bldg Tulsa OK 74103

BARTLETT, DOROTHY LUCILLE WOOD (MRS. KENNETH FRANKLIN BARTLETT), librarian; b. Richmond, Va.; d. Wilfred Walton and Maude (Robins) Wood; B.A., Randolph-Macon Woman's Coll., 1932; B.A. in L.S., Emory U., 1933; m. Kenneth Franklin Bartlett, Oct. 20, 1945. Library asst., head children's dept. Richmond Pub. Library, 1933-40; map asst., archives div. Va. State Library, Richmond, 1940-42; chief circulation dept. City Library Assn., Springfield, Mass., 1942-43; map curator Nat. Archives, Washington, 1943-44; map analyst, chief map research sect. Fgn. Econ. Adminstrn., Washington, 1944-45; map analyst Dept. Agr., Beltsville, Md., 1946; chief reference sect., map library Dept. State, Washington, 1946-47; map librarian CIA, Washington 1948-61; head reference and bibliography sect., geography and map div. Library Congress, Washington, 1962-70, bibliographer of div., 1970-—. Mem. Spl. Libraries Assn. (chpt. vice chmn. geography and map group 1964-66, chmn. 1966-67, nominating com. 1967), Jamestowne Soc., U. D.C., Assn. Am. Geographers, Am. Assn. U. Women, Assn. Preservation Va. Antiquities, Carto-Philatelists, Va. Library Assn. Methodist. Contbr. articles to profl. jours. Home: 1713 Wainwright Dr Reston VA 22070 Office: Library Congress Washington DC 20540

BARTLETT, EUGENE MONROE, JR., ch. musician, composer; b. Greenwood, Ark., May 4, 1918; s. Eugene Monroe and Joan (Tatum) B.; B.A., John Brown U., 1940; Mus.B., Okla. Baptist U., 1954, Mus.D., 1971; m. Emma Jeanne Stephens, Aug. 25, 1940; children—Larry Eugene, Frances Maurine (Mrs. David Lawrence Myers), Reginald. Dir. music Baptist Chs., Ark. and Okla., 1941-54; sec. ch. music Bapt. Gen. Conv. of Okla., Oklahoma City, 1954-—; dir. music Falls Creek Bapt. Assembly. Served with USNR, 1944-45. Mem. So. Bapt. Ch. Music Conf. (past pres.). Baptist (deacon). Composer numerous anthems, hymns, gospel songs and youth folk songs. Home: 2612 NW 52d St Oklahoma City OK 73112 Office: 1141 N Robinson St Oklahoma City OK 73103

BARTLETT, EVE (MRS. MOODY W. BARTLETT), journalist, postmaster; b. Norton, Kan., July 26, 1909; d. Hiram Isaac and Georgia Ann (McDaniel) White; student U. Houston, 1939-40, U. Chgo., 1944-45; m. Moody Wayne Bartlett, Jan. 30, 1943 (dec. Nov. 1962); 1 dau., Lannie Bartlett (Mrs. Robert Dayvault Williams). Columnist, feature writer San Antonio Express-News, 1954-59. Mem. Wharton County Hist. Survey Com.; founding pres., bd. dirs. Girls' Council; sponsoring mem. Assn. for Research and Enlightment. Recipient awards Pan-Am. Round Table, 1955, Bus. and Profl. Women's Club, San Antonio, 1955, San Antonio Council Pres.'s, 1956, Tex. A.P. award for ednl. club project, 1956, 1st place awards Tex. Women's Press Assn., 1955-59, Headliner award San Antonio chpt. Theta Sigma Phi, 1960, named Ky. Col., 1968; Order of the Vest. Smithsonian Asso. Mem. Tex. Press Women's Assn. (pres. 1959-61), Nat. Fedn. Press Women San Antonio Press Club (charter mem.), Spiritual Frontiers Fellowship, Nat. Assn. Postmasters (exec. com.), Tex. Hist. Found., Theta Sigma Phi (pres. 1958-60). Democrat. Presbyn. Clubs: Zonta, Port Lavaca Stamp, Pa. Dutch Beam. Editor: Lone Star Postmaster (1st place NAPUS award 1966). Home: 10 Pecan Rd Glen Flora TX 77443 Office: Post Office Glen Flora TX 77443

BARTLETT, JOSEPHINE MARTHA BUCK (MRS. CHARLES L. BARTLETT), interior decorator; b. N.Y.C., Jan. 7, 1926; d. Leonard J. and Helen (Rouss) Buck; student Finch Coll., 1944-47; m. Charles L. Bartlett, Dec. 16, 1950; children—Peter, Michael, Robert, Helen. Interior decorator J.M. Bartlett, Inc., Washington, 1955—. Trustee Sheridan Sch., Washington. Home: 4615 W St Washington DC 20007

BARTLETT, WILLIAM MARCUS, broadcasting co. exec.; b. Richland, Ga., Aug. 19, 1910; s. William Mercer and Eula Mae (Bell) B.; A.B. in Journalism, Emory U., 1939; m. Mamie Ruth Baggott, Dec. 18, 1943; children—Ann (Mrs. Cecil Cannon), Bill, Bruce, Blair, Brian. Announcer, musician, sportscaster, musical dir., prodn. mgr., program dir. radio sta. WSB, Atlanta, 1930-48; program dir., sta. mgr., gen. mgr. WSB-TV, 1948-64; v.p. Cox Broadcasting Co., Atlanta, 1964-69, exec. v.p., 1969—; dir. United Tech. Publs., Cox Cable Communications, Bing Crosby Prodns., Manheim Services Corp. Lectr. Emory U., 1941-42, 46. Bd. dels. NBC-TV Affiliates, 1959-63, sec.-treas., 1963. Chmn. bd. visitors Emory U., 1969-70; mem. adv. bd. Atlanta Salvation Army; bd. dirs. Fulton-Dekalb County chpt. Nat. Found. Served to lt. USNR, 1943-45. Mem. Nat. Cable Television Assn. (sec. 1969-70), Ga. Assn. Broadcasters (v.p. for TV 1961-62, dir. 1960-61), Phi Beta Kappa, Sigma Chi, Omicron Delta Kappa, Di Gamma Kappa (named Broadcast Pioneer of Year 1965), Sigma Delta Chi. Baptist (ch. organist 1960—). Clubs: Atlanta Athletic, Cherokee Town and Country, Commerce (Atlanta). Home: 4694 Tall Pines Dr NW Atlanta GA 30327 Office: 1601 W Peachtree St NE Atlanta GA 30309

BARTLEY, ERNEST R., educator, urban planning cons.; b. Lincoln, Neb., May 11, 1919; s. James Earl and Neva Leona (McNiel) B.; A.B. with distinction, Neb. Wesleyan U., 1940; M.A., U. Neb., 1941; Ph.D., U. Cal. at Berkeley, 1948; m. Ruth Arline Nielsen, Apr. 17, 1942; children—Susan Kay, Deborah Dell. Instr. polit. sci. Ore. State Coll., 1948-49; instr. polit. sci. U. Fla., 1949-51, asso. prof., 1951-55, prof. 1955—; acting dir. U. Fla. Pub Adminstrn. Clearing Service, 1950, dir., 1957-58; adviser com. adminstr. law and procedure Fla. Bar Assn., 1952-58; lectr. legal insts. Fla. Bar Assn., 1952-58; fellow Fund Advancement Edn., 1954-55; cons. Alaska Statehood Com., Pub. Adminstrn. Service on Alaska Constl. Conv., 1955; cons. numerous cities and counties; dir. research Fla. Constl. Adv. Commn., 1955-56. Served from 2d lt. to maj. 21st Bomber Command, USAAF, 1941-45. Decorated 3 battle stars, Air medal; recipient Freedom Found. award, 1956. Mem. Am. Inst. of Planners (pres. Fla. chpt. 1972—), Am. So. polit. soi. assns., Am. Soc. Planning Ofcls., Fla. Planning and Zoning Assn. (pres. 1970-71), Am. Assn. U. Profs., Pi Sigma Alpha, Pi Kappa Delta, Pi Gamma Mu, Phi Kappa Phi, Phi Kappa Tau. Democrat. Methodist. Mason. Author: Municipal Zoning: Florida Law and Practice (with William W. Boyer, Jr.), 1950; Principles and Problems of American National Government (with John M. Swarthout), 1951; The Tidelands Oil Controversy, 1952; Principles and Problems of State and Local Govt. (with John M. Swarthout), 1958; A Model Zoning Ordinance for Small and Medium-Sized Cities (with Fred H. Bair, Jr.), 1958, rev. edit., 1965, 3d edit., 1967; Mobile Home Parks and Comprehensive Planning (with Fred H. Bair, Jr.), 1961. Editor: Materials on American National Government (with John M. Swarthout), 1952; Papers on Florida Administrative Law, 1952. Contbr. profl. jours. Home: 1050 SW 11th St Gainesville FL 32601

BARTLEY, JERALD HOWARD, oil co. exec.; b. Springtown, Tex., Nov. 25, 1913; s. Hugh Thomas and Emma (Johnson) B.; B.S. in Geology, U. Tex., 1937; m. Bernice O. Lonsdorf, Jan. 19, 1946; children—Bruce Howard, Steven Charles, Ann Marie. Geologist, U.S. Geol. Survey, 1937-38, Tex. Univ. Lands, Midland, 1938-49; cons. geologist, ind. oil operator, Midland, 1949—; exec. v.p., chief geologist Tex. Am. Oil Corp., Midland, 1955-66; partner Autograph Driltime Corp., Midland, 1961-66, Broxson-Bartley Ins. Agy., Midland, 1966-69; v.p., dir. Pacific Union Gas Co., Midland, 1961-66, Western Oil Shale Corp., Midland, 1964—. Served to lt. USNR, 1942-46. Mem. Geol. Soc. Am., Am. Assn. Petroleum Geologists, Soc. Ind. Profl. Earth Scientists (dir.), Ind. Petroleum Assn. Am., Mid-Continenta Oil and Gas Assn., Tex. Ind. Producers and Royalty Owners Assn., Tex. Acad. Sci. Roman Catholic. Elk. Author Bulls. Patentee in field. Home: 1705 W Illinois St Midland TX 79701 Office: 300 W Wall St Midland TX 79701

BARTLEY, JOHN COLEMAN, engring. constrn. co. exec.; b. New Orleans, Feb. 13, 1916; s. John Coleman and Pearl (Forsyth) B.; B.Engring. in Civil Engring., Tulane U., 1936; m. Doris Rosalie Parham, Nov. 11, 1944; children—John Coleman, Kathleen (Mrs. Clayton Claverie Bohn), William P. (dec.), D. Patrick, Marianne D. Partner firm Bartley & Binnings, New Orleans, 1946-54; pres. Bartley, Inc., New Orleans, 1954—; pres. Bartley Engring. Corp., New Orleans, 1957—; pres. Interstate Devel. Co., Inc., New Orleans, 1947—, West End Landing, Inc., New Orleans, 1969—. Fellow Am. Soc. C.E. (mem. estimating, cost control com.); mem. Consulting Contractor's Council Am., Asso. Gen. Contractors Am. (nat. bd. dirs.), La. Engring. Soc. (life mem.), Tulane U. Alumni Assn. (dir.). Roman Catholic. Clubs: International House, Southern Yacht, Metairie Country, Bienville (New Orleans). Home: 778 Amethyst St New Orleans LA 70124 Office: 415 N St Patrick St New Orleans LA 70179

BARTLEY, LEO SHERMAN, electronics engr; b. Bonneville, Ark., Apr. 23, 1919; s. Finis Euing and Maud (Ragsdale) B.; A.A., Ventura Coll., 1950; B.S., Okla. State U., 1958; m. Virginia Deane Bailey, Nov. 12, 1943; children—Cynthia Ann (Mrs. Frank Nolan Cornett), Joyce Lynn, Kenneth Leo, Carol Deane. Commd. lt. USAF, 1943, advanced through grades to lt. col., 1966; research specialist Lockheed Missiles & Space Co., Sunnyvale, Cal., 1966-67; mem. engring. staff, mgr. Continental Electronics, Dallas, 1967—. Adviser, Boy Scouts Am., 1964. Decorated D.F.C., Air medal. Registered profl. engr., Okla. Mem. I.E.E.E. (certificate appreciation 1965, chmn. Holloman-Alamogordo sect. 1964-65). Republican. Mem. Ch. of Christ. Mason. Home: 1516 Fairfield Dr Plano TX 75074 Office: 4212 S Buckner Blvd Dallas TX 75217

BARTOLO, ADOLPH MARION, food co. exec.; b. Cairo, Egypt, Apr. 12, 1929; s. Edgar Charles and Emma C. (Borrelli) B.; came to U.S., 1947, naturalized, 1953; B.S. in Chem. Engring., La. State U., 1950; m. Joycelyn Mary Bergeron, June 7, 1950; children—Pamela Bridget, Edgar Charles II, Janice Ann, Mary Elizabeth. From chem. engr. to asst. supt. Southdown Sugar, Inc., Houma, La., 1951-58; with Imperial Sugar Co., Sugarland, Tex., 1958—, v.p. refinery operations, 1968—, also dir.; dir. Cane Sugar Refiners Research Project, 1965—; dir., mem. exec. com. Sugar Industry Technologists, Inc. Mem. La. State U. Found., 1966-68. Mem. Am. Inst. Chem. Engrs., Internat. Sugar Research Found., U.S. Nat. Com. Sugar Anaylsis. Catholic. Lion (pres. Sugarland 1960-61). Club: Riverbend Country (Sugarland). Home: 303 S Belknap St Sugarland TX 77478 Office: PO Box 9 Sugarland TX 77478

BARTON, DON FREDERICK, advt. agy. exec.; b. Anderson, S.C., Aug. 19, 1924; s. David J. and Harriet (Crouch) B.; A.B., U. S.C., 1949; m. Betty Kneece, Aug 7, 1955; 1 dau., Mary Elizabeth. Pub. relations U. S.C., Columbia, 1950-56, 58-60; sports editor Columbia (S.C.) Record, 1949, 56-58; sec. Rodgers-Newman-Barton Advt., Columbia, 1960-62; dir. pub. relations WIS-TV, Columbia, 1963-65; pres. Barton-Blair-Coreton Advt. Agy., Columbia, 1965—. Chpt. chmn. A.R.C., Richland County, S.C., 1966-67; chmn. Riverbanks Park Commn., 1964—. Pres., S.C. Speech and Hearing Clinic, 1969-70. Served with USAAF, 1943-45. Mem. Alpha Delta Sigma, C. of C. Presbyn. Clubs: Forest Lake Country, Columbia Touchdown (pres. 1963), Sertoma (pres. 1968-69). Author: The Carolina-Clemson Game-1896-1966, 1967. Home: 117 Spring Lake Rd Columbia SC 29206 Office: 2512 Devine St Columbia SC 29206

BARTON, ELEANOR KEESE (MRS. WILLIAM P. BARTON), newspaperwoman; b. Walhalla, S.C., May 31, 1901; d. John Perry and Soula T. (Reeder) Keese; B.A., Greenville Woman's Coll., 1921; postgrad. Cornell U., 1923; m. William P. Barton, July 19, 1924; 1 dau., Eleanor Sue (Mrs. John O. Allen). Instr. Greenville Woman's Coll., 1921-24, pub. relations work, 1921-29; woman's editor Greenville (S.C.) Piedmont, 1929-51, columnist, 1951—; feature writer, 1951—; radio news commentator, 1956-62. Pres., Crescent Music Club, 1939-41, now hon. life mem., Community Concert Assn., 1953-55; mem. vol. corps U.S.O., 1951-63, chmn., 1959-61; chmn. Greenville County chpt. A.R.C., 1956-57; pres. Crescent Community Club, 1953-55; v.p. Better Govt. Assn., 1956-57; mem. Greenville Symphony Assn., 1949-65; mem. Greenville County Heart Council; adv. bd. S.C. div. Nat. Found.; bd. dirs. S.C. div. Am. Cancer Soc.; pres. Crescent Literary Club, 1961-63; v.p. Greenville County Fedn. Women's Clubs, 1965-66, chmn. Diamond Jubilee, Gen. Fedn. Women's Clubs; helped establish S.C. Commn. on Aging; pres. Myrtle Hall Fund for Scholarships; adv. com. Palmetto Outdoor Hist. Drama Assn.; mem. S.C. Tricennial Adv. Com. Recipient Nat. Bus. and Profl. Women's Club award, 1932; Certificate Appreciation, Boys' Club Am., 1956; Nat. Recreation Assn. citation, 1961; Plaque from Greenville Symphony Assn., 1966. Gen., and State Fedns. Women's Clubs citation, 1955-56; Nat. Community Achievement citation, 1956. Mem. Furman U. Alumni Council, Hand and Torch, Nat. Fedn. Music Clubs (hon. life), Sigma Iota Chi. Democrat. Baptist. Club: Woman's (dir. 1951-61, 63—). Author: History of the Crescent Music Club. 1956; History of Greenville Woman's Club. 1960; also papers, reports, brochures. Editor: U.S.O. Volunteer, 1959-61. Home: 208 McIver St Greenville SC 29602 Office: The Greenville Piedmont PO Box 1688 Greenville SC 29602

BARTON, FRANK LEWIS, agrl. banker; b. Tigerville, S.C., Feb. 9, 1917; s. Hovey Goodlet and Anne (McKinney) B.; B.S., Berea Coll., 1937; postgrad. U. Ky., 1937, Clemson U., 1940, 50; M.Ed., U. S.C., 1952; m. Margaret Ettie Coggins, June 5, 1939; children— Lollie, Frank Lewis, Nancy. Tchr. agr. Spartanburg County (S.C.), 1937-48; supr. agrl. edn. S.C. Dept. Edn., 1948-59; dir. information Farm Credit Banks, Columbia, S.C., 1959-66; v.p. Fed. Land Bank, Columbia, 1966-69, v.p., sec., 1969—. Mem. exec. com., trustee Am. Inst. Coop. Recipient awards including Hon. Degree of Am. Farmer Future Farmers Am., 1960. Mem. Pub. Relations Soc. Am. (pres. S.C. chpt. 1970, assembly del. 1968-72), S.C. Vocational Assn., S.C. Farm Bur. Fedn., Am. Berkshire Assn. (pres. 1954-56), S.C. Livestock Assn. (sec. 1950-56), S.C. Grange, S.C. Livestock Council (sec. 1956-61), S.C. Agrl. Council (sec. 1968), Block and Bridle. Baptist. Rotarian. Clubs: Columbia, Woodruff. Contbr. articles to publs. Home: 2119 Dalloz St Columbia SC 29204 Office: 1401 Hampton St Columbia SC 29202

BARTON, JACK QUINN, lawyer, instr., police chief; b. Denison, Tex., Nov. 27, 1932; s. Joseph R.T. and Marion (Quinn) B.; B.A., U. Tex., 1960, J.D., 1962; m. Jane Thomas, Aug. 30, 1958; children—Robert Barry, Catherine Eileen, Joseph Lawrence, Raymond Edward, Jerry Quinn. With Corpus Christi (Tex.) Police Force, 1956-57; admitted to Tex. bar, 1962; practiced in San Francisco, 1962-63; law book editor Matthew Bender Co.; city atty. Denton, Tex., 1963-72; instr., dir. police N. Tex. State U., Denton, 1972—. cons. municipal law to various cities. Mem. Decisions for Denton Com., 1969—; chmn. Denton March of Dimes, 1969. Trustee Optimist Meml. Found., Fairhaven Home for Aged, Denton; bd. dirs., chmn. finance com. Cross Timbers council Girl Scouts Am. Served with AC, USNR, 1951-55. Mem. Am., Tex., Denton County bar assns., Tex. Trial Lawyers Assn. K. C. Home: 124 Mill Pond Rd Denton TX 76201 Office: 1603 W Hickory St Denton TX 76201

BARTON, JAMES HOWARD, physician; b. Murphy, N.C., Apr. 14, 1931; s. Guy Arvil and Esta (Swaim) B.; B.A., U. N.C., 1953, M.S. in Pub. Health, 1958; M.D., Med. Coll. Ga., 1962; m. Barbara Nell Brown, June 18, 1957; children—Gregory Jay, Steven Lyle, Leslie Kay. Intern, Spartanburg Gen. Hosp., 1962-63; gen. practice medicine, Social Circle, Ga., 1963—. Mem. Walton County Bd. Health, Walton County Hosp. Bd. Authority, Social Circle Bd. Edn. Served with AUS, 1954-56. Mem. Am., Ga. med. assns. Methodist (trustee 1970). Lion (pres. Social Circle 1965). Home: 356 N Cherokee St Social Circle GA 30279 Office: PO Box 468 Social Circle GA 30279

BARTON, J(OHN) CLIB, lawyer; b. Antoine, Ark., July 9, 1903; s. Clib and Etta (Hardin) B.; student Hendrix Coll., 1922-23, U. Ark., 1923-24, George Peabody Coll., 1924-25, Vanderbilt U., 1925-26; LL.B., Cumberland Law Sch., 1927; m. Wilma Stone, Feb. 14, 1929; children—Patsy (Mrs. Ralph McDonald), John Clib, James Grover. Admitted to Ark. bar, 1927; partner firm Barton & Armstrong, Ft. Smith, 1927-29, Hardin, Barton & Shaw, 1952-62, Hardin, Barton, Hardin & Jesson, 1962—. Vice pres. Alma Canning Co., Ft. Smith, 1942-62, Good Canning Co., Charleston Canning Co., Ft. Smith, 1945-52; chmn. bd. dirs. Superior Fed. Savs. & Loan Assn., Ft. Smith, 1932—; organizer, pres. bd. dirs. Harbor House, Inc., Western Ark., 1965—. Mem. Sebastian County Welfare Bd., 1952—; mem. bd. Sebastian County chpt. A.R.C., 1942-49. Chmn., Young Democrats Orgn., 1927-34. Chmn. bd. dirs. Doss T. Sutton Charitable Found.; pres. Tabitha Godrey and Maude J. Thomas Charitable Found. Recipient Silver Beaver award Westark council Boy Scouts Am., 1955. Mem. Ft. Smith C. of C., Sigma Chi. Methodist (ofcl. bd.). Clubs: Town, Hardscrabble Country (Ft. Smith). Author: (pamphlet) How to Dismantle a Corporation, 1946. Home: 1236 Elizabeth Lane Ft Smith AR 72901

BARTON, MAURICE ARTHUR, physician; b. London, Eng., Feb. 25, 1897; s. Abraham and Mary (Gardner) B.; M.D., Boston Coll. Physicians and Surgeons, 1927; m. Marianne Helen Wrba, Nov. 28, 1940; children—Jackson Arthur, William Karl, Bert Kaufmann, James (dec.), Joan. Intern Boston City Hosp., 1927-28, Waltham Hosp., 1928-29; resident Waltham Hosp., 1929; practice medicine specializing in surgery, Boston, 1930-42; chief varicose vein clinic Boston Evening Clinic and Hosp., 1931-45, asso., 1945— tchr. Mound Park Hosp., St. Petersburg, Fla., 1944-45, hon. mem. staff, pres., chmn. bd. trustees Mound Park Hosp. Found., 1956—, mem. med. sci. adv. bd., 1956—, dir. Inst. Geriatrics, 1956—, dir. Inst. Med. Research and Edn. 1960—, dir. postgrad. med. edn.; hon. staff mem., hon. life dir. All Children's Hosp.; clin. asso. prof. psychiatry and medicine Coll. Medicine, U. Fla.; clin. asso. prof. internal medicine U.S. Fla.; pres. Childrens Hosp. Chmn. Tampa Bay Area Council for Research in Aging, U. So. Fla., 1962-63; chmn. gerontology sect. Community Welfare Council, St. Petersburg, 1961-62, bd. dirs., 1961-62; mem. adv. com. Pinelas County Bd. Health, 1959—; del. White House Conf. on Aging, 1971. Recipient accolade Mound Park Hosp. Found., 1958; Art of Medicine award, Fla. Acad. Gen. Practice, 1970; Physicians Recognition award A.M.A., 1969 Bd. dirs. Crippled Childrens Hosp. 1st hon. v.p. Fla. div. Leukemia Soc. Fellow Am. Geriatrics Soc., Gerontological Soc., Internat. Acad. Law and Sci., A.A.A.S.; mem. Am. Acad. Gen. Practice (asso. mem., hon.), Am. Thoracic Soc., Pan Am. Med. Assn., Pinneilas County Med. Soc. (hon.), Fla. Acad. Scis. (chmn. med. scis. sect.; pres. 1969, Scientist of Yr. award 1971), Am., Fla. med. assns., N.Y. Acad. Scis., Assn. Schs. Allied Health Professions. Democrat. Methodist. Mason (Shriner). Clubs: St. Petersburg Bath, St. Petersburg Yacht. Contbr. over 150 articles and monographs to profl. publs. Home: 1900 Almeria Way South St Petersburg FL 33712 Office: Mound Park Hosp Found St Petersburg FL 33701

BARTON, NELDA ANN(MRS. HAROLD BRYAN BARTON), Republican nat. committeewoman; b. Providence, Ky., May 12, 1929; d. Eulis Grant and Rubie (West) Lambert; student Western Ky. U., 1947-49; grad. Norton Meml. Infirmary Sch. Med. Tech., Louisville, 1950; m. Harold Bryan Barton, May 11, 1951; children—Barbara Lynn, Harold Bryan, Stephen Lambert, Suzanne. Med. technologist, 1950-53; v.p. Newcomers Club, New Albany, Ind., 1953; dist. chmn. P.T.A., 1958-59; vice-gov. 9th Dist. Ky. Fedn. Woman's Club, 1962-64; gov. 5th Dist. Ky. Fedn. Republican Women, 1963-67; Ky. councilor Woman's Aux. So. Med. Assn., 1965-66, Southeastern councilor, 1966-67; health career chmn. Woman's Aux. Ky. Med. Assn., 1965-68; chairwoman 5th Dist. Rep. Campaign, 1967; Whitley County Rep. chairwoman, 1968-72; 2d v.p. Ky. Fedn. Rep. Women, 1968-70, conv. chmn., 1970; Rep. Nat. Committeewoman for Ky., 1968—; chmn. Nat. Rep. Women's Conf., Ky., 1969; mem. del. selection and orgn. com. Rep. Nat. Com., 1969-72; mem. arrangements com. Rep. Nat. Conv., 1971-72; mem. Gov.'s Commn. on Women, Ky., 1968—; mem. Corbon Adv. Bd., 1969-70; co-chmn. for Corbin: Urban Renewal and Community Devel., 1970—. Pres. Woman's Aux. Whitley County Med. Soc., 1959-60, Ossoil Woman's Club, 1961-62, Corbin Central Elementary P.T.A., 1963-65, Corbin Rep. Woman's Club, 1968; charter mem. Fine Arts Assn. Southeastern Ky. Recipient life membership award P.T.A., 1964; named Ky. Rep. Woman of Yr., 1968-69; named Ky. col. Mem. Christian Ch. (circle chmn. 1964-65, youth fellowship leader 1965-68). Home: 1311 7th St Rd Corbin KY 40701

BARTON, RANDOLPH, toy co. exec. Exec. v.p. Parker Bros. & Co., Inc., Houston. Address: Parker Bros & Co Inc Box 107 Houston TX 76101*

BARTON, WILLIAM BRYAN, JR., educator; b. Oklahoma City, Oct. 6, 1923; s. William Bryan and Alma (Brundege) B.; B.A. cum laude, Abilene Christian Coll., 1944; B. Systematic Theology, Harvard, 1947, M. Systematic Theology, 1948, Ph. D., 1955; m. Mary Elizabeth Sturgeon, Aug. 11, 1946; children—John Bryan, Laura Alison, Rebecca Ann, Sylvia Jeanne. Instr., Cath. U. Am., Washington, 1948-49, Simmons, Coll., Boston, 1949-50; asso. prof. Harding Grad. Sch., Memphis, 1955-57; prof., chmn. dept. philosophy Memphis State U., 1958—. Bd. mem. Barth House (Episcopal), 1964-67. Mem. Am. Philos. Assn., So. Soc. Philosophy and Psychology, Metaphys. Soc. Am., Internat. Soc. Phenomenological Research. Democrat. Episcopalian (bd. edn. Diocese Tenn. 1965-67). Author: Emerson's Method as a Philosopher, 1971. Founder, editor: So. Jour. Philosophy, 1963—. Co-translator: Martin Heidegger's Die Frage nach dem Ding (What is a Thing) 1967. Editor: Emerson's Unpublished Sermons, 1971—. Home: 4020 Mickey Dr Memphis TN 38116

BARTON, WILLIAM LAMAR, civil engr.; b. Alton, Ill., Sept. 4, 1939; s. Lamar C. and Bernice (Witthofft) B.; B.S., Auburn U., 1961; m. Patricia Joan Mead, June 12, 1959; children—William B., Tracy, Berne. Asso. engr. Smally, Wellford, & Nalven, Sarasota, Fla. 1962-65; head engring. Tri-County Engring., Inc., Naples, Fla., 1965-66; v.p. HOB Labs., Inc., Naples, 1965-66, pres., 1966-67; v.p. Harlan & Barton Engring. Labs., Lakeland, Ft. Myers and Naples, 1967-69, Wilson, Miller, Barton & Soll, Naples, 1969—. Engring. cons. City of Naples, Collier County, Lee County, Fla. Registered profl. engr., Fla. Mem. Nat. Soc. Profl. Engrs., Fla. Engring. Soc. (pres. Calusa chpt. 1972—), Greater Naples C. of C. (dept. v.p. 1971-72), Am. Soc. Testing and Materials. Kiwanian. Home: 1161 Diana Av Naples FL 33940 Office: 665 5th Av S Naples FL 33940

BARTON, WILLIAM LAWRENCE, physician; b. Macon, Ga., Nov. 16, 1909; s. William and Mary (Cherry) B.; B.S., Mercer U., 1932; M.D., Med. Coll. Ga., 1935; m. Rebecca Griffin, June 20, 1942 (dec. Dec. 1954); 1 dau., Mary Lynn; m. 2d, Carol Balkcom, Oct. 8, 1955; 1 son, William Lawrence. Intern Macon City Hosp., 1935-36; resident Columbia-Presbyn. Med. Center, N.Y.C., 1936-39; practice medicine specializing otolaryngology, Macon, 1940—; attending Parkview Pvt. Hosp., Coliseum Park Hosp.; cons. Med. Center Central Ga., Baldwin County Hosp. Served as maj. Ga. State Guard, World War II, Recipient award for outstanding service YMCA, 1954. Diplomate Am. Bd. Served as maj. Ga. State Guard, World War II. Recipient Otolaryngology. Fellow A.C.S., Internat. Coll. Surgeons; mem. A.M.A., So., Ga., 6th Dist., Bibb County med. socs., Am. Acad. Otolaryngology and Ophthalmology, Pan-Am. Assn. Otorhinolaryngology and Bronchoesophagology, Alpha Omega Alpha. Methodist. Mason (Shriner, 32 deg.), Elk, Moose, Kiwanian. Clubs: Idle Hour Golf and Country, Macon Touchdown, Centurion. Home: 1588 Waverland Dr Macon GA 31201 Office: 744 1st St Macon GA 31201

BARTOS, BRUCE LOUIS, dentist; b. Cleve., Nov. 10, 1942; s. Louis and Eva (Barabasoff) B.; student Case-Western Res. U., 1961-62, Kent State U., 1962-64; D.D.S., Ohio State U., 1968. Practice dentistry, Fort Lauderdale, Fla., 1968—; partner B & D Speed Marine, Fort Lauderdale, 1971—, B. & W. Marine, Independence, O., 1968—. Active Head Start project, Fort Lauderdale, 1971—. Mem. Young Republicans Club, Columbus, O., 1967-68. Mem. Am., East Coast dental assns., Cleve. Dental Soc., Delta Sigma Delta. Republican. Club: Bachelor's (Fort Lauderdale, Fla.). Home: 1311 W Lake Dr Fort Lauderdale FL 33316 Office: 5241 W Broward Blvd Fort Lauderdale FL 33313

BARTSCHT, HERI BERT, sculptor, educator; b. Breslau, Germany, Aug. 30, 1919; s. Richard and Emma (Philipp) B.; student Acad. Fine Arts, Munich, Germany, 1946-52; m. Waltraud Erika Gutensohn, Mar. 31, 1950; 1 son, Martin Donald. Came to U.S., 1952, naturalized, 1959. Prof. sculpture, U. Dallas, 1961—, head div. art, music, speech and drama, 1965—. One-man shows, including Dallas, Oklahoma City, Austin, Tex.; exhibited in group shows, 1951—, including Ball State Tchrs. Coll. Muncie, Ind., 1959, Univ. Ill., 1961, Cranbrook Academy Art, Mich., 1969; important works include Pieta, Ch. in Munich, 1952, Stas. of Cross, Jesuit High Sch., Dallas, 1963, library sculpture The Graduate, Tex. A. and M. U., 1968, sanctuary embellishment First Meth. Ch., Alexandria, La. Mem. Council for German Day in Tex., 1963; mem. condrs. com. Dallas Symphony, 1963. Pres., Dallas Goethe Center, 1971—. Served with German Army, 1939-45. Mem. Am. Soc. Ch. Architecture, Nat. Art Edn. Assn., Ch. Archtl. Guild, Dallas Fine Arts Assn., Dallas Soc. Contemporary Arts (founder, dir., trustee 1955-61), Guild Religious Architecture. Author: Twenty Years of My Sculpture, 1969, Research on Bronze Casting. Home and studio: 1125 N Canterbury Ct Dallas TX 75208

BARZE, KEITH EGBERT, television exec.; b. Winter Park, Fla., Feb. 19, 1928; s. Roland Detling and Marguerite (Enlow) B.; A.B., U. Ala., 1950, M.A., 1956; m. Nancy Ruth Hendrix, Oct. 11, 1953; children— Sandra Suzanne, Beverly Roxanne, Stacy Yvonne. Announcer, engr., various radio stas., 1947-54; instr. dept. radio-television U. Ala., 1950-52, vis. lectr., 1970-71; engr. WBRC-TV, Birmingham, Ala., 1954-57, program dir., head program prodn. depts., 1957—. Mem. pub. relations council A.R.C., 1963-65; dir. Festival of Arts, 1964-65; mem. Jefferson County Radio and TV Council, 1957—; treas. Bd. of Missions, Ala., Fla, Miss. Synod, Cumberland Presbyn. Ch.; adviser Jr. Achievement Co., 1966—. Served with AUS, 1946-47. Mem. Ala. Broadcasters Assn. (dir. 1963-67, v.p. TV 1966-67, chmn. edn. com. 1971-72), Birmingham Advt. Fedn., Birmingham C. of C., Nat. Assn. TV Program Execs., Faith and Patiotism Soc. Am. (exec. council 1970—), Delta Chi, Alpha Epsilon Rho. Republican. Presbyn. (elder, dir. Birmingham council Christian edn. 1968—). Kiwanian (pres. Birmingham 1971-72). Clubs: Mountain Brook Swim and Tennis, Birmingham Press, Birmingham Amateur Radio. Home: 3581 Spring Valley Rd Birmingham AL 35223 Office: PO Box 6 Birmingham AL 35201

BASCO, FREDERICK, educator; b. Derry, La., Oct. 30, 1922; s. Fred and Artemise (Kerry) B.; B.S., Northwestern State Coll. La., 1948; M.S., U. Ark., 1949; postgrad. U. Miss, 1958, 62, 67; Ph.D., Ohio Christian Coll., 1969; m. Inez Marie Setliff, Dec. 13, 1943; 1 dau., Anita Marie. Cargo clk. Port of New Orleans, 1944-48; tchr. bus., also prin. high sch., Barton, Ark., 1948; instr. bus. edn. State Coll. Ark., 1949-54; asst. prof., 1954-59, asso. prof. bus. 1959—. Mem. Conway (Ark.) Cath. Sch. Bd., 1966—. Served with AUS, 1940-44. Named Ark. Bus. Tchr. of Year, Ark. Bus. Edn. Assn., 1962-63. Decorated Silver Star medal. Mem. Nat., Ark. (past pres.) bus. edn. assns., Ark. Coll. Tchrs. Econs. and Bus. (past pres.), D.A.V. (past comdr. Conway), Pi Omega Pi, Delta Pi Epsilon, Kappa Delta Pi, Phi Delta Kappa. K.C. Author: (with others) College Typewriting, 1961. Co-editor: Business Education Handbook for Arkansas Secondary Schools, 1956. Home: 325 Augusta Av Conway AR 72032

BASH, JAMES HAVENS, educator; b. Fort Wayne, Ind., June 28, 1924; s. Carl Edward and Maud (Trabue) B.; student Pa. State U., 1941; B.S., U. Va., 1949, M.Ed., 1953, Ed.D., 1960; m. Jean McNett, Aug. 13, 1946; children—Bonnie Jean, Michael McNett. Tchr., Lane High Sch., Charlottesville, Va., 1949; prin. Highland View Elementary Sch., Bristol, Va., 1949-52, Brosville Sch., Pittsylvania County, Va., 1952-54, Farmville (Va.) High Sch., 1954-55; instr. edn. U. Va., Charlottesville, 1956-60, asst. prof., 1960-62, asso. prof. edn., 1964-69, prof., 1969—, asso. dir. div. tchr. placement and field services, 1963-64, asso. dir. Office Instnl. Analysis, 1964-65, dir. div. field services Sch. Edn., 1966-70, dir. Consultative Resource Center on Sch. Desegregation, 1967-72; program asso. So. Regional Edn. Bd. Atlanta, 1962-63; exec. sec. Assn. Sch. Coll. and Univ. Staffing, 1959-64; cons. Spong Commn. on Pub. Edn. in Va., 1959-62. Served with USNR, 1942-46. Recipient U. Va. Phi Delta Kappa award, 1962. Mem. Va. Edn. Assn., N.E.A., Phi Delta Kappa (mem. commn. edn., human rights and responsibilities 1962-69), Nat. Assn. Secondary Sch. Prins.. Researcher sch. desegregation, 1965-66. Home: 1508 Jamestown Dr Charlottesville VA 22901 Office: Sch Edn U Va Charlottesville VA 22903

BASHFUL, EMMETT WILFORT, ednl. adminstr.; b. New Roads, La., Mar. 12, 1917; s. Charles and Mary (Walker) B.; student Leland Coll., 1936-37; B.S., So. U., 1940; M.A., U. Ill., 1947, Ph.D., 1955; m. Juanita Jones, Aug. 16, 1941; 1 dau., Cornell (Mrs. Charles Nugent). Tchr. Allen Parish (La.) Sch., 1940-41; asst. mgr. Keystone Co., 1941-42; mem. faculty Fla. A. and M. U., 1948-58, prof. polit. sci., 1955-58, head dept., 1950-58; prof. polit. sci. So. U., Baton Rouge, 1958-59; dean So. U., New Orleans, 1959-69, v.p., 1969—. Chmn. John Albert dist. Boy Scouts Am., New Orleans., 1965-67, mem. exec. bd., 1965—; mem. La. Youth Commn., 1965—. Bd. dirs. Community Relations Council, New Orleans, Frey Found. Served to 1st lt. AUS, 1942-46. Recipient Silver Beaver award Boy Scouts Am., 1967; Ford Found. fellow, 1954-55. Mem. Am., So. polit. sci. assns., Assn. Social Sci. Tchrs., Alpha Phi Alpha, Alpha Pi Omega, Sigma Rho Sigma, Pi Gamma Mu. Author: The Florida Supreme Court: A Study in Judicial Selection, 1958. Home: 5808 Lafaye St New Orleans LA 70122

BASINGER, JAMES MAYHEW, advt. agy. exec.; b. Aliceville, Ala., July 26, 1923; s. Albert Hunter and Mary (Mayhew) B.; B.S., U. Ala., 1949, postgrad., 1949-50; m. Ruth Wilson, Dec. 27, 1954; children— James M., Brian Hunter. Quality control engr. Westinghouse Electric Corp., Reform, Ala., 1951-53; dir. advt. U.S. Pipe & Foundry Co., Birmingham, Ala., 1954-65; pres. Basinger & Sankey, Inc., Birmingham, 1966—. Served with AUS, 1942-45. Mem. Chi Phi. Methodist (bd. stewards). Clubs: Downtown, Altadena Valley Country. Home: 2707 Lakeland Trail Birmingham AL 35243 Office: 13 Office Park Circle Birmingham AL 35243

BASKIN, CLARENCE LEE, dentist; b. Apopka, Fla., Feb. 27, 1927; s. Horace and Carrie Belle (Weathers) B.; B.S., Morehouse Coll., 1948; D.D.S., Howard U., 1953; m. Thelma Erline Cobb, July 21, 1956; 1son, Clarence Lee. Pvt. practice dentistry, Atlanta, 1954-56, Columbus, Ga., 1957—. Chmn. adv. bd. Washington Shores Fed. Savs. & Loan Assn., Orlando, Fla. Served with USNR, 1945-46. Mem. Am., Nat., Ga. dental assns., Western Dist. Dental Soc., Kappa Alpha Psi. Home: 4539 Kerz Court Columbus GA 31907 Office: 500 1/2 9th St Columbus GA 31901

BASKIN, EVERETT ROY, advt. exec.; b. McAlester, Okla., Oct. 21, 1927; s. Everett Edmond and Lottie (Hattery) B.; B.S., Southeastern State Coll., 1952; m. Wanda Joy Major, Feb. 19, 1949; children—Rhonda Lea, Janice Lynn. Dept. head J. C. Penny Co., McAlester, Durant, Okla., 1943-50; asst. mgr. Duke & Ayres, Inc., Durant, 1950-54; account exec. McAlester News Capital, 1954-59; real advt. mgr. Donrey Operating Co., Ft. Smith, Ark., 1959-60, advt. and acting plant mgr., Okmulgee, Okla., 1960-61, plant mgr., Rogers, Ark., 1961-62; sales mgr. Mena (Ark.) Star, 1963-64; store mgr. Montgomery Ward & Co., Ft. Smith, 1964-66; advt. mgr. McAlester Democrat, New Offset Daily, 1966—. Served with USNR, 1945-46. Mem. Red Red Rose, Kappa Delta Pi, Sigma Tau Gamma, Pi Omega Pi. Democrat. Presbyn. Mason, Eagle. Home: 201 W Madison St McAlester OK 74501 Office: 106 E Cherokee St McAlester OK 74501

BASKIN, WADE J., educator; b. Harmony, Ark., July 27, 1924; s. Dewey Buchanan and Essie (Jacobs) B.; B.A., Coll. of the Ozarks, 1947; certificat d'etudes Sorbonne, U. Paris, 1946; M.A., Columbia, 1951, Ed.D., 1956; m. Vlasta Kolena, Jan. 1, 1949; children— Wade J., Daniel Gregory, Michael Kenmar. Instr. Romance langs. Coll. of the Ozarks, Clarksville, Ark., 1947-49; dir., instr. Acad. Applied Linguistics, N.Y.C., 1951-57; asst. prof. fgn. langs. So. State Coll., Magnolia, Ark., 1957-59; asso. prof. fgn. langs., head. dept. Southeastern State Coll., Durant, Okla., 1959-62, prof., 1962—, adviser fgn. students, 1959-71. Cons. Okla. State Dept. Edn., 1962-71; originator and linguistics cons. Choctaw Bilingual Edn. Program, 1968-71. Mem. bd. higher edn. Presbyn. Ch. of U.S.A. Served with AUS, 1943-46. Named Tchr. of Year, Southeastern State Coll., 1963; U.S. Dept. State grantee, 1947. Mem. Am. Assn. Tchrs. French (chpt. pres. 1963), Am. Assn. Tchrs. Spanish and Portuguese (chpt. pres. 1962), Am. Assn. Tchrs. German, Modern Lang. Assn., South Central Modern Lang. Assn., Linguistic Circle of N.Y., Am. Council on Teaching of Fgn. Langs., Okla. Edn. Assn., Alpha Chi. Author: Classics in Education, 1966; Dictionary of Satanism, 1971; Classics in Chinese Philosophy, 1972; Dictionary of the American Negro, 1972; The Wisdom of Jean Paul Sartre; (with G. Pat Powers) New Outlooks in Psychology, 1968; (with G. Pat Powers) Sex Education, 1969; (with H. E. Wedeck) Dictionary of Pagan Religions, 1971; (with H. E. Wedeck) Dictionary of Spiritualism, 1971. Translator numerous books including Course in General Linguistics (F. de Saussure), 1959; History of Philosophy (Emile Brehier), 1965-69. Home: 1730 Oak Hills Dr Durant OK 74701

BASKIN, WILLIAM P., lawyer, banker; b. Bishopville, S.C., Apr. 27, 1904; s. William P. and Esther (Fleming) B.; A.B., U. S.C., 1925, LL.B., 1927; m. Margaret E. Pittman, June 14, 1932; children—William P., Emsley P., Sylvia Elaine. Admitted to S.C. bar, 1927, since practiced in Bishopville; sr. member Baskin & Baskin; former chmn. bd., dir., gen. counsel Peoples Bank; state counsel Nat. Assn. Ind. Insureres; dir. Home Fed. Savs. & Loan Assn., Bishopville. Mem. S.C. Senate from Lee County, 1938-58. Mem. Lee County, S.C. State, Am. bar assns., S.C. Bankers Assn. (pres. 1965-66). Democrat (state chmn. 1947-52). Home: 324 S Main St Bishopville SC 29010 Office: Farmers Trust Bldg Bishopville SC 29010

BASORE, BENNETT LEE, educator; b. Oklahoma City, Aug. 31, 1922; s. Warren L. and Marie (Bump) B.; B.S. in Math., Okla. State U., 1948, B.S. in Elec. Engring., 1948; Sc.D., Mass. Inst. Tech., 1952; m. Wandalee Hinkle, June 1, 1948; children—Paul Alan, Peggy Ann, Polly Marie. Asst. group leader Lincoln Lab., Lexington, Mass., 1952; staff mem. Sandia Corp., Albuquerque, 1952-57; div. head, asso. tech. dir. Dikewood Corp., Albuquerque, 1957-63; phys. sci. officer U.S. Arms Control and Disarmament Agy., Washington, 1963-67, cons., 1968; prof. Okla. State U., Stillwater, 1967—; cons. USAF, 1958, 68—. Served with USNR, 1942-46. Decorated Bronze Star medal, Gold Star. Mem. I.E.E.E. (past sect. chmn.), Sigma Xi, Phi Kappa Phi, Sigma Alpha Epsilon. Presbyn. Home: 924 Will Rogers Dr Stillwater OK 74074

BASS, BOB EUGENE, basketball coach; b. Big Spring, Tex., Jan. 28, 1929; s. William A. and Dovie (Law) B.; B.S., Okla. Bapt. U., 1950; M.P.E., Okla. U., 1954; m. Billie Pat Phelps, Aug. 6, 1950; children—Kelly E., Kip E. Athletic dir., basketball coach Okla. Bapt. U., Shawnee, 1952-67; head basketball coach Denver Rockets, Am. Basketball Assn., 1967-69, Tex. Tech. U., Lubbock, 1969-71; coach, gen. mgr. Floridians of Am. Basketball Assn., Miami, 1971—. Named Coach of Year, Nat. Assn. Inter-collegiate Athletics, 1967. Home: 13200 Coronado Lane North Miami FL 33161

BASS, CALVIN G., air force officer, educator; b. Okla.; B.S., U. Md., 1959; M.A., U. Colo., 1963; m. Hannah Bass; children—Janet, James, Julia. Commd. officer U.S. Air Force, advanced through grades to col.; flight instr., 1943—; comdr. 309th Air Commando Troop Carrier Squadron, Tan San Nhut, Vietnam; chief mobility planning Pacific Air Force hdqrs., Hickman AFB, Hawaii; now prof. aerospace studies R.O.T.C. detachment U. Tulsa. Mem. Exptl. Aircraft Assn., Internat. Aero. Club. Address: 6111 S Joplin Av Tulsa OK 74135*

BASS, CORNELIUS GRAHAM, oil jobber exec.; b. Latta, S.C., May 28, 1918; s. Howard H. and Sarah (Carmichael) B.; B.S. in Bus. Adminstrn., U. S.C., 1940; m. Ann Blair, May 23, 1942 children—Ann Blair (Mrs. James E. Crowder, III), AND Cornelius Graham. With The Latta Cotton Co., 1940-41; asst. mgr. Dilmar Oil Co., Latta, 1941-42; mgr. Santee Oil Co., 1945-47, sec.-treas., 1947-71, v.p., 1971—, gen. mgr., 1947—; partner, gen. mgr. S & P Tire Co., Kingstree, S.C., 1949—; sec.-treas., gen. mgr. Services, Inc., Kingstree, 1950-71; pres. Warsaw Mfg. Co., Kingstree, 1958-63: pres. Bass Farms, Inc., Latta. 1963—, pres. Santee Broadcasting Co., Inc. (radio sta. WDKD), 1965-69, treas., 1970—; pres. Kingstree Indsl. Devel. Corp., 1958—; sec.-treas. King's Tree Inn, Inc., 1967-70. Mem. Williamsburg Planning Commn., 1967—; chmn. Williamsburg County Bd. Edn., 1957-62. Served with AUS, World War II. Decorated Bronze Star. Mem. Kingstree C. of C. (v.p. 1956-58), S.C. Oil Jobbers Assn. (pres. 1954-55). Moose (past gov. Kingstree). Clubs: Kingstree Country (pres.), Optimist (past pres.), Lions (past pres.). Home: 1601 Fulton Av Kingstree SC 29556 Office: Santee Oil Co Inc Hwy 52 N Kingstree SC 29556

BASS, MILTON GERSON, revenue ofcl.; b. Phila., Jan. 8, 1914; s. Joseph H. and Ruth (Back) B.; student Drexel Inst. Engring., 1931-32; B.C.S., Benjamin Franklin U., 1941, M.C.S., 1942; postgrad. George Washington U., 1942-43, U. Hawaii, 1944-45; m. Ernestine Shute, Aug. 14, 1946; 1 dau., June Yvonne. Various positions Fed. Govt., 1935-55; supr. Internal Revenue Service, Baton Rouge, 1955-58, chief rev. staff, New Orleans, 1958—. Served with USNR, 1942-45. C.P.A., Md., La. Mem. Am. Inst. C.P.A.'s, La. Soc. C.P.A.'s, Am. Legion. Baptist. Mason (32 deg.). Home: 17 Tennyson Pl New Orleans LA 70114 Office: Fed Bldg 600 South St New Orleans LA 70130

BASS, ROBERT E., profl. basketball coach; grad. Okla. Bapt. U., 1950; m. Billie Pat; children—Kip. Coach Cromwell (Okla.) High Sch., 1950-52; coach Okla. Bapt. U., 1952-67; coach profl. basketball team Denver Rockets, 1967-69; head basketball coach Tex. Technol. U., 1969-71; head coach, gen. mgr. Miami Floridians, 1971—. Coach Am. Athletic Union team Dept. State, South Am. and Caribbean, 1964, Southeastern Asia, 1966. Address: Miami Floridians 1175 NE 125th St North Miami FL 33161

BASS, SAMUEL EARL, banker; b. Mount Calm, Tex., Mar. 23, 1930; s. Wayne Earl and Alyne (Ferguson) B.; B.B.A., Baylor U., 1951; M. Profl. Accounting, U. Tex., 1961; LL.B., So. Meth. U., 1964; postgrad. Southwestern Grad. Sch. Banking, 1969; m. Vilma A. Vieira, Feb. 25, 1965; children—Vivienne Kay, Rochelle Andrea. Bldg. contractor, 1951-56; with Hunt Oil Co., 1958-62, Haskins & Sells, C.P.A.'s, 1962-63, Mobil Oil Co., 1963-64; admitted to Tex. bar, 1964; with First Nat. Bank, Dallas, 1964—, v.p., trust officer, 1964—. C.P.A., Tex. Mem. Tex. Soc. C.P.A.'s, Tex. Bar Assn., Am. Inst. C.P.A.'s, Dallas Estate Council, Accounting Research Assn., Am. Accounting Assn., Am. Civil Liberties Union, Delta Theta Phi. Clubs: Dallas Baylor, German-American (Dallas). Home: 4716 Homer St Dallas TX 75204 Office: Room 673 First Nat Bank Bldg Dallas TX 75222

BASS, TERENCE PATRICK, civil engr., govt. ofcl.; b. Little Rock, Jan. 19, 1939; s. Terence Patrick and June (Meroney) B.; B.S., U. Ark., 1961; m. Mary Carolyn Robnett, Aug. 8, 1958; children—Elizabeth, Mary, Martha, Patricia, Deborah. With Ark. Hwy. Dept., 1961; with Soil Conservation Service, U.S. Dept. Agr., 1961—, project engr., Wilburton, Okla., 1965—. Served with N.G. Registered profl. engr., Okla. Mem. Soil Conservation Soc. Am., Am. Soc. Agrl. Engrs., Jr. C. of C. K.C. Home: PO Box 6 Wilburton OK 74578 Office: PO Box 368 Wilburton OK 74578

BASS, THOMAS HUTCHESON, III, educator; b. Houston, Jan. 11, 1927; s. Thomas Hutcheson and Mary Lee (Scoggins) B.; B.A., U. Tex. 1950; M.Ed., U. Houston, 1954, postgrad., 1959—; m. Mary Ann King, Sept. 2, 1950; children—Patricia, Martin, Paul, Rita, Amy, Victoria, Robert, Daniel, Laura, David. Retail store mgr. Western Auto Supply Co., Houston, 1951-52; tchr. Houston Ind. Sch. Dist., 1952-60; asst. prof. polit. sci. Sacred Heart Dominican Coll., Houston, 1960-67; prof. U. St. Thomas, Houston, 1967—, chmn. dept. polit. sci., 1968—; mem. Tex. Legislature from Harris County, 1963-72. Guest lectr. ednl. and religious instns. Chmn. social action dept. Tex. Cath. Conf.; mem. Cath. interracial com. and supervisory com. Houston Tchrs. Credit Union. Served with AUS, 1945-47. Named Outstanding Religious Layman, Houston Jr. C. of C., 1961. Mem. Am. Polit. Sci. Assn., Am. Assn. U. Profs., Res. Officers Assn., Nat. Catholic Edn. Assn. (sec. adv. com. on history 1962-63), Phi Delta Kappa, Kappa Delta Pi. Democrat. Roman Catholic. Home: 3437 N Parkwood St Houston TX 77021 Office: 3812 Montrose Blvd Houston TX 77006

BASS, WILLIAM MARVIN, III, educator; b. Staunton, Va., Aug. 30, 1928; s. William Marvin and Jennie (Hicks) B.; B.A., U. Va., 1951; M.S., U. Ky., 1956; Ph.D., U. Pa., 1961; m. Mary Anna Owen, Aug. 8, 1953; children—Charles E. II, William Marvin IV, James O. Instr. Grad. Sch. Medicine, U. Pa., Phila., 1956-59; instr. dept. anthropology U. Neb., Lincoln, 1959-60; from instr. to prof. U. Kan., Lawrence, 1960-71; prof., head dept. anthropology U. Tenn., Knoxville, 1971—. Served with AUS, 1951-53. Recipient Hill Tchr. award U. Kan., 1965. Author: The Leavenworth Site Cemetery: Archaeology and Physical Anthropology, 1971; Human Osteology: A Laboratory and Field Manual of the Human Skeleton, 1971; also contbr. articles to profl. jours. Home: 8201 Bennington Dr Knoxville TN 37919

BASSET, GENE, editorial cartoonist; b. Bklyn., July 24, 1927; student U. Mo., 1946-47, Cooper Union, 1947-50; B.A., Bklyn. Coll., 1950; student Pratt Inst., 1954, Art Students League N.Y., 1953-54; m. Charlotte Goldenberg, July 8, 1951; children—Darien, Roger, Brian. Sketch artist Indpls. Times, 1951-53; theatrical and sports cartoonist Bklyn. Eagle, 1953-54; sports cartoonist Boston Post, 1955-56; tchr. Famous Artists Sch., Westport, Conn., 1957-62; editorial cartoonist Honolulu Star-Bull., 1962, Scripps-Howard Newspapers, 1962—. Served with USCGR, 1944-46. Mem. Nat. Cartoonist Soc., Assn. Am. Editorial Cartoonists, Sigma Delta Chi. Home: 8106 Birnam Wood Dr McLean VA 22101 Office: 1013 13th St NW Washington DC 20005

BASSETT, HARRY H(OOD), banker; b. Flint, Mich., May 6, 1917; s. Harry Hoxie and Jessie Marie (Hood) B.; B.S., Yale, 1940; children—Harry Hood, George Rodney, Patrick Glenn; m. 2d, Florence Schust Knoll, June 22, 1958. Asst. trust officer First Nat. Bank, Palm Beach, Fla., 1940-42; asst. v.p. First Nat. Bank, Miami, 1947-48, dir., 1947—, v.p., 1948—, asst. to pres., 1951—; chmn. exec. com., 1959—, pres., 1962-66, chmn. bd., 1966—; chmn. bd. 1st Nat. Bank in Palm Beach, 1965—; mem. Assn. Res. City Bankers, 1958—; dir. Wometco Enterprises, Gen. Devel. Corp., Eastern Airlines, Inc., Maule Industries; chmn. bd. S.E. Banking Corp. Mem. Orange Bowl Com. Chmn. bd. trustees U. Miami. Served as pilot Civil Coastal Patrol (anti-submarine), 1941-42; 1st lt. USAAF, 1944-46. Decorated Air Medal. Mem. Fla. Bankers Assn., Am. Inst. Banking, Assn. Registered Bank Holding Cos. (dir.). Episcopalian. Clubs: Bath, LaGorce Country (Miami Beach, Fla.); Miami, Palm Bay (Miami, Fla.); Yale, River (N.Y.C.); Lyford Cay, East Hill Club (Nassau, Bahamas); Everglades (Palm Beach, Fla.); Bohemian (San Francisco); Metropolitan (Washington). Home: 1801 W 27th St Sunset Island 2 Miami Beach FL 33140 Office: 100 S Biscayne Blvd Miami FL 33131

BASSETT, NORMAN, editor; b. Dover, N.J., Mar. 22, 1917; s. Edward T. and Edith (Tompkins) B.; A.B., U. Ala., 1940; m. Alva Hilbish, Dec. 25, 1940; children—Mary Alva (Mrs. Victor T. Stark), Howard, Elizabeth, William, Charles. Reporter Lakeland News, Dover, 1940; telegraph editor Tuscaloosa (Ala.) News, 1940, Rome (Ga.) News-Tribune, 1940-41; telegraph editor, mng. editor, editor Tuscaloosa News, 1941-46; asso. dir., acting dir. U. Ala. News Bur., 1946-50; acting field mgr. Ala. Press Assn. 1949-50; mng. editor, editor, exec. editor, v.p. Tuscaloosa News, 1950—. Bus. mgr. Tuscaloosa Civic Chorus. Bd. dirs. Warrior-Tombigbee Devel. Assn. Recipient Freedoms Found. citation, 1956; named Lion of the Year, Tuscaloosa Lions Club, 1963. Mem. Ala. AP Assn. (treas.), Tuscaloosa Civic Chorus (pres.), Internat. Platform Assn., Tuscaloosa County Preservation Soc. (dir., v.p. 1971—). Club: Lions (dep. gov. internat. 1964-65). Office: 2001 6th St Tuscaloosa AL 35401

BASSHAM, HUGH ALLEN, veterinarian; b. nr. Bethel Springs, Tenn., June 12, 1907; s. Edgar Eugene and Lela (Wilson) B.; student Union U., 1926, Memphis State Tchrs. Coll., 1927, Freed-Hardeman Coll., 1927-28, U. Tenn. Jr. Coll., 1930-31; D.V.M., Ala. Poly. Inst., 1941; m. Bertha Jean Harris, Aug. 12, 1936; children—Hugh Harris, Nancy (Mrs. Neal Weigmun), Dennie McCaskill. Tchr. pub. schs., Bethel Springs, 1926-28; basketball coach high schs., Adamsville, Tenn., 1929-30, 36-38, Finger, 1931-36; practice veterinary medicine, Quitman, Ga., 1941—. Brooks County coroner, Quitman, 1961—. Lt. col., a.d.c. Gov.'s staff Ga., 1968—. Mem. Am., Ga. vet. med. assns., Continental Field Trial Assn. (v.p. 1950). Home: PO Box 471 Quitman GA 31643

BASTIAN, WALTER MAXIMILLIAN, judge; b. Washington, Nov. 16, 1891; s. Charles Sandal and Katherine (Draeger) B.; LL.B., Georgetown U., 1913; LL.D., Nat. U., 1953, George Washington U., 1958; m. Eva E. Alger, July 3, 1914; children—Walter M., David C. Admitted to D.C. bar, 1913, practiced law in D.C., 1915-50; U.S. Dist. Judge, Dist. Ct. of U.S. for D.C., 1950-54, circuit judge, U.S. Ct. of Appeals, D.C. Circuit, 1954-68, sr. judge U.S. Ct. of Appeals for D.C., 1968— lectr. Nat. U. Sch. of Law, 1918-48. Served as 1st lt. CWS, World War I. Trustee George Washington U. Mem. Bar Assn. of D.C. (treas., past pres.), Am. Bar Assn. (treas. 1945-50; ho. of dels. 1936-53, 56—), Order of Coif. Republican. Methodist, Mason (past master). Clubs: Metropolitan, Columbia Country, Lawyers, Alfalfa (Washington). Contbr. articles to profl. jours. Home: 1533 4th Av W Bradenton FL 33505 Office: US Court House Washington DC 20543

BASTNAGEL, CHARLES ERWIN, JR., fabricated metals mfg. co. exec.; b. Memphis, Aug. 6, 1942; s. Charles Erwin and Emily Rebeccah (Perry) B.; student Southwestern U., Memphis, 1960-61, Memphis State U., 1961-64; m. Jennifer Kay Ottenville, May 30, 1964; children—Charles Erwin III, Daniel Showin, Beatrice Jane. Adminstrv. asst. to pres., purchasing agt. aluminum products div. The Jordan Cos., Memphis, 1964-69, operations mgr., 1969—. Active Boy Scouts Am.; mem. Whitehaven Community Council, 1969—, v.p., 1969, pres., 1970. Recipient Key Man award Whitehaven Jr. C. of C., 1970, Distinguished Service award, 1970. Mem. Archtl. Aluminum Mfrs. Assn. (chmn. tech. com. 1970-71), Soc. Mfg. Engrs., Whitehaven Jr. C. of C. (v.p., 1968-70), Sigma Phi Epsilon, Club: Graceland Recreation (bd. dirs. 1970). Home: 1387 Mary Gene Dr Memphis TN 38116 Office: 4656 Hungerford Rd Memphis TN 38118

BATCHELDER, ORLAND RALPH, electronics engr.; b. Dresden, Kan., June 12, 1924; s. Ralph William and Lillian (Petracek) B.; B.S., Tex. A. and M. U., 1949; postgrad. So. Meth. U., 1955-59; m. Betty Lou Rosenboom, Oct. 12, 1946; children—Joyce Elaine (Mrs. William Clarence Newland, Jr.), Michael Kerin. With Gen. Dynamics, Ft. Worth, 1949—, group engr., 1959-63, design group engr., 1963-65, design specialist, 1965—. Scoutmaster, Boy Scouts Am., 1950-55. Served with USNR, 1943-46. Profl. engr., Tex. Mem. Nat. Mgmt. Assn., I.E.E.E. (sr. mem.). Asso. editor Aerospace and Electronic systems Group Transactions. Home: 517 Merrill Dr Bedford TX 76021 Office: Box 748 Fort Worth TX 76101

BATCHELDER, ROBERT, JR., radio field engr.; b. Cleve., Dec. 12, 1912; s. Robert and Hazel E. (Kullman) B.; student Ohio U., 1931; m. Aldonna A. Kersis, Feb. 26, 1944; children—Robert A., Sheldon J. Vice pres. Foote Printing Co., Cleve., 1938-42; v.p. Acad. Film Service Co., Cleve., 1942-44; engr. WJW Broadcasting Co., Cleve., 1944-47, 47-55, Evening Star Broadcasting Co., Washington, 1947; with USIA-Voice of Am., Washington, 1955—, radio field engr., 1960—. Recipient certificate of merit Dept. Def., 1954. Mem. Washington Audio Video Engrs. Soc. (pres. 1970-71). Home: 308 Burnt Mills Av Silver Spring MD 20901 Office: 330 Independence Av Washington DC 20547

BATCHELLER, DAVID SPRINGSTEEN, lawyer; b. Miami, Fla., May 28, 1928; s. George Ellinwood and Ella (Springsteen) B.; LL.B., U. Fla., 1950; m. Joe Ann Deming, Aug. 8, 1957; children—David S., Elizabeth St. Claire, Osmer, John A. Admitted to Fla. bar, 1950, partner Smathers, Thompson. Mem. adv. bd. Pan Am. Bank of Miami; dir. Pan Am. Bank of Dade County (Fla.). Bd. dirs., Dade County chpt. A.R.C., chmn., 1971-72; bd. dirs. Miami Heart Inst. Mem. Fla. Bd. Pilot Commrs. and Port Wardens of Port Miami, 1956-64. Served with USNR. Mem. Am., Dade County (dir. 1957-60) bar assns., Fla. Bar, Internat. Assn. Ins. Counsel, Maritime Law Assn., Phi Delta Phi. Episcopalian. Home: 4595 Sabal Palm Rd Bay Point Miami FL 33137 Office: DuPont Bldg Miami FL 33131

BATCHELLER, JOE ANN DEMING (MRS. DAVID SPRINGSTEEN BATCHELLER), business exec.; b. Jacksonville, Fla., Dec. 11, 1932; d. Osmer St. Clair and Lorena (Jones) Deming; A.A., Stephens Coll., 1952; B.A., U.N.C., 1955; m. David Springsteen Batcheller, Aug. 8, 1957; children—Elizabeth St. Clair, Osmer Deming, John Alden. Sec., Seminole Oil Co., Miami, 1957, pres., dir., 1961—; sec., dir. Blue Grass Plant Foods, Inc., Cynthiana, Ky., 1958; chmn. bd. dirs. Superior Plant Foods, Inc., Lakeland, Fla., 1958; v.p., dir. Pensacola Petroleum Co., Inc. (Fla.), 1961—, Top Power Stations, Inc., Miami, 1961—; chmn. bd. Blue Water Mobile Home Subdiv., Inc. Travernier, Fla., 1967—; pres. Blue Waters Mobile Home Sales, Inc. Bd. dirs. Miami Heart Inst., 1970—, v.p. aux., 1970—. Mem. Young Patronesses of Opera, Symphony Club, Beaux Arts, Opera Guild, Vizcayans, Pi Beta Phi. Republican. Episcopalian. Home: 4595 Sabal Palm Rd Bay Point Miami FL 33137 Office: Blue Waters Trailer Village Inc Travernier FL 33070

BATEMAN, DOTTYE JANE SPENCER (MRS. JOSEPH E. LINDSLEY), realtor; b. Athens, Tex.; d. Charles Augustus and Lillie (Freeman) Spencer; student Fed. Inst., 1941-42, So. Meth. U., Dallas Coll., 1956-58; m. George Truitt Bateman, 1947 (div. Apr. 1963); children—Kelly Spencer, Bethena Bateman.; m. 2d, Joseph Eric Lindsley, 1968. Sec. to state senator, Tyler, Tex., 1941-42; sec. to pres. Merc. Nat. Bank, Dallas, State Fair of Tex., Dallas, 1942-48; realtor, broker, Garland, Tex., 1956—; co-partner Play-Shade Co.; appraiser Asso. Soc. Real Estate Appraisers; auctioneer, 1963—; developer Stonewall Cave, 1964—. Pres. Central Elementary Sch. P.T.A., 1955-56, Bussey Jr. High P.T.A., 1956-57; den mother Cub Scouts Am., 1957-59; chmn. Decent Lit. Com., 1956-58; chmn. P.T.A.'s council 1958; dir. Dallas Heart Assn., 1960, local chmn., 1955-57 county chmn., 1957-60; spl. dir. Henderson County Red Cross, 1945; local chmn. March of Dimes, 1961-63; mem. Dallas Civic Opera Com., 1963-64. Named Outstanding Tex. Jaycee-Ette Pres., 1953, hon. Garland Jay-Cee-Ette, 1956, hon. Sheriff, Dallas County, 1963. Mem. Garland Dallas (chmn. reception com., past dir.) real estate bds., Auctioneers Assn., Nat. Farm and Land Brokers, Internat. Platform Assn., Soc. Prevention Cruelty to Animals, Dallas Women's (charter mem., project chmn.), Garland (chmn. ministerial alliance com. 1955-56) chambers commerce, Nat. Audubon Soc., Wilderness Soc., Consejo Internacional De Buena Vecindad, Delphian Study Club, Eruditis Study Club. Methodist (chmn. membership and evangelism com.). Clubs: Garland (past v.p., pres.), Tex. (past treas., ofcl. hostess) Jaycee-Ettes, Garland Fedn. Women's (past pres.), Garland Garden, Trinity dist. Feds. Women's (past pres.), Press Pub. Affairs Luncheon. Home: 1140 Rock Creek Dr Garland TX 75040 Office: 5518 Dyer St Dallas TX 75206

BATEMAN, ROBERT EDWARD, real estate broker; b. Wauchula, Fla., July 27, 1907; s. Wiley Wallace and Sophronia Cordelia (Hoard) B.; B.S.A., U. Fla., 1929; m. Elizabeth Lane Bryan, June 11, 1938; children— Elizabeth Anne (Mrs. Ray Blesi West), Alice Cordelia (Mrs. Earl Clifford Catron), Virginia Jean (Mrs. Ronald Mack Sinderud). Insp., Mediterranean fruit fly eradication U.S. Dept. Agr., Fla., 1929-31; various capacities Fed. Land Bank of Columbia (S.C.), 1932-37; salesman Barrett div. Allied Chem. & Dye Corp., 1938-42; real estate broker, ins. agt., citrus grower, land developer, Pompano Beach, Fla., 1946—; developer Lighthouse Point and Coconut Creek subdivs., Pompano Beach; pres. Bateman & Co., Winter Haven Corp.; pres. Golden Gate Land Co.; chmn. bd. Bateman, Gordon & Sands, Inc.; founder, dir. 1st Nat. Bank of North Broward County, 1st Nat. Bank of Margate, 1st Nat. Bank of Pompano Beach, 1st Nat. Bankshares Fla. Inc. Served to lt. comdr. USNR, 1942-46; ETO. Mem. Pompano Beach C. of C. (past pres.), Alpha Zeta, Gamma Sigma Delta. Presbyn. Home: 935 Hillsboro Beach Pompano Beach FL 33062 Office: 2401 Atlantic Blvd Pompano Beach FL 33061

BATES, ALFRED SCOTT, educator, poet; b. Evanston, Ill., June 13, 1923; s. Alfred R. and Eleanor (Fulchar) B.; B.A., Carleton Coll., 1947; M.A., U. Wis., 1948, Ph.D., 1954; m. Phoebe Strehlow, Apr. 17, 1948; children—Robin Ricker, Jonathan Reed, David Scott, Samuel Jackson. Prof. French, U. of the South, Sewanee, Tenn., 1954—. Chmn. bd. dirs. Highland Center, Knoxville, Tenn., 1968—. Served with AUS, 1943-46. Fulbright scholar, 1951-53. Author: Guillaume Apollinaire, 1967; poems pub. in various jours. and mags. Editor: Poems of War Resistance, from 2300 B.C. to Present, 1969. Home: Sewanee TN 37375

BATES, ARTHUR RAYMOND, restaurant owner; b. Ludlow, Ky., Feb. 6, 1904; s. Arthur Hubert and Delia (Frency) B.; grad. high sch.; m. Hetty Maudine Denton, Apr. 18, 1948; 1 dau. (by previous marriage), Mrs. Don Davry. Asst. mgr. Gibson Hotel, Cin., 1925; asst. mgr. Severin Hotel, Indpls., 1926; lessee restaurant Kaufmann's Dept. Store, Pitts., 1927-29; food controller Baker Hotels, Dallas, 1930-36; owner restaurant N.Y. World's Fair, 1939-40; pres. Arthur's Restaurant Inc., Dallas, 1948—. Served to maj. USMC, 1942-45. Mem. Heroes of 76, Sojourners. Mason (32 deg., Shringer). Clubs: President's (Washington); World Travellers (Kansas City, Mo.); Ky. Home: 5200 Milam St Dallas TX 75206 Office: 3701 McKinney Av Dallas TX 75204

BATES, BURWELL MILLARD, mining co. exec.; b. Konawa, Okla., Jan. 18, 1921; s. Samuel Walter and Bertha (Rudell) B.; B.A., U. Okla., 1942; m. Elaine Lucas, Dec. 11, 1943; children—Craig Laird, Carla (Mrs. Leaford L. Blevins III). Owner, pres. Johnson-Bates Drilling Co., Konawa, Okla., 1953—; owner Bates Limousin Ranch, 1948—; dir. Fed. Nat. Bank, Shawnee, Okla., Okla. State Bank, Konawa. Mem. Sch. Bd., Konawa, 1948-60; active Boy Scouts Am., Future Farmers Am., P.T.A. Sec., North Am. Limousin Found., 1969—. Served to lt. (j.g.) USNR, 1942-45. Mem. Okla. Limousin Breeders (pres. 1970—), Petroleum Club, Am. Legion, Pi Delta Theta. Baptist. Mason, Lion (pres. 1949-50). Clubs: Tulsa, South Hills Country (Tulsa). Home: Route 2 Konawa OK 74849 Office: 107 S Broadway Box 55 Konawa OK 74849

BATES, CARL ELKANAH, clergyman; b. Miss., Sept. 5, 1914; s. Richard Elkanah and Caroline (Brabham) B.; student S.W. Miss. Jr. Coll., Miss. Coll.; B. Theology, So. Bapt. Theol. Sem., Louisville, also M. Theology; D.D., Baylor U.; LL.D., Miss. Coll.; D.H., Judson Coll.; m. Myra Mae Gray, Nov. 15, 1939; 1 dau., Judith Hampton. Ordained minister Bapt. Ch.; pastor, Winchester, Ky., Leesburg, Fla., Texarkana, Tex., Amarillo, Tex., until 1959; pastor First Bapt. Ch., Charlotte, N.C., 1959—. Chmn. gen. bd. Tex. Bapt. Conv., also pres.; pres. N.C. Bapt. Conv., mem. gen. bd., pres. So. Bapt. Pastors Conf., So. Bapt. Conv., 1970—. Home: 844 Hempstead Pl Charlotte NC 28207 Office: 318 Tryon St Charlotte NC 28202

BATES, CHARLES CARPENTER, oceanographer; b. nr. Harrison, Ill., 1918; s. Carl Albert and Vera Elizabeth (Carpenter) B.; grad. (Rector scholar 1936-39). DePauw U., 1939; M.A., U. Cal. at Los Angeles, 1944, Ph.D. in Geol. Oceanography, Tex. A. and M. Coll., 1953; postgrad. Cath. U., 1947-48, Johns Hopkins, 1951, George Washington U., 1954; m. Pauline Barta; children—Nancy Ann, Priscilla Jane, Sally Jean. Geophys. trainee Carter Oil Co., 1939-41; spl. asst. to pres. Am. Meteorol. Soc., 1945-46; mem. survey phys. and geol. environment Marshall Is. relative to pending Bikini atomic bomb tests, 1946; with div. oceanography U.S. Navy Hydrographic Office, 1946-57, dep. dir. div., 1953-57; part-time cons. in field to govt. and industry, 1946-52; environmental surveillance coordinator, Office Devel. Coordinator, Office Naval Research, 1957-60; chief VELA uniform br. Advanced Research Projects Agy., Office Sec. Def., 1960-64; sci. and tech. dir. U.S. Naval Oceanographic Office, 1964-68; sci. adviser to comdt., also chief scientist Office Research and Devel., USCG, 1968—. Mem. Bd. Expert Civil Service Examiners, 1954-60; mem. adv. com. postdoctoral awards for Fullbright grants NRC, 1957-60, chmn., 1959-60; vis. geoscientist Am. Geol. Inst., 1959-60; mem. meteorology panel, space sci. bd. Nat. Acad. Sci., 1959-61; mem. Mcht. Marine Council, 1968-71, Nat. Transp. Research Bd., 1968-71; mem. sea grant adv. council La. State Univ. System, 1968—. Served to capt. USAAF, 1941-45. Decorated Bronze Star; recipient U.S. Navy Meritorious Civilian award, 1962. Mem. Am. Geophys. Union (chmn. com. interaction sea and atmosphere 1950, mem. council 1964-67), Soc. Exploration Geophysicists (council 1963-67, v.p. 1965-66). Am. Meteorol. Soc. (chmn. com. indsl. bus. and agrl. meteorology 1946-48), Am. Assn. Petroleum Geologists (President's award 1954), Geol. Soc. Washington. Seismological Soc. Washington, Sigma Xi. Author numerous articles, reports in field. Editor meteorol. terms Glossary of Geology and Related Items, 1957. Home: 5807 Massachusetts Av NW Washington DC 20016 Office: Hdqrs US Coast Guard Washington DC 20590

BATES, CLYDE THOMAS, educator; b. Sadieville, Ky., June 6, 1933; s. Thomas Marion and Carrie Josephine (Gillespie) B.; B.S., U. Ky., 1960, M.S. 1961, Ph. D., (Water Resources Inst. grantee), 1969; m. Frances Ruth Phillips, July 10, 1956; children—Bobby Gene, Calvin Thomas. Instr. econs. Western Ky. Coll., Bowling Green, 1961-63; research asst. U. Ky., Lexington, 1964; asso. prof. econs. Georgetown Coll., 1965—. Served with AUS, 1954-56. Mem. Appalachian Finance Assn., So. Econ. Assn., Omicron Delta Epsilon, Beta Gamma Sigma, Lambda Chi Alpha (hon.). Mem. Church of Christ (elder). Club: Optimist (pres. 1970-71) (Georgetown). Home: 619 Pueblo Trail Georgetown KY 40324

BATES, HAROLD MARTIN, lawyer; b. Glamorgan, Va., Mar. 11, 1928; s. William Jennings and Reba (Williams) B.; B.A., Coll. William and Mary, 1952; LL.B., Washington and Lee U., 1961; m. Audrey Rose Doll, Nov. 1, 1952; children—Linda, Carl. Spl. agt. FBI, Newark, N.Y.C., 1952-56; tech. sales rep. Hercules Powder Co., Wilmington, Del., 1956-58; admitted to Ky. bar, 1961; practiced in Louisville, 1961-62; sec.-treas., house counsel Life Ins. Co. of Ky., Louisville, 1962-67, also dir.; pvt. practice law, Roanoke, Va., 1967—; mem. firm Bates, Cruey & Lee. Served with AUS, 1946-47. Mem. Va., Roanoke bar assns., Phi Alpha Delta, Sigma Nu. Democrat. Presbyn. Kiwanian. Club: Hidden Valley Country. Home: 2602 Sharmar Rd SW Roanoke VA 24018 Office: Shenandoah Bldg Roanoke VA 24011

BATES, JEWEL LANE, JR., accountant; b. Baton Rouge, Sept. 6, 1915; s. Jewel Lane and Elizabeth (Bradley) B.; B.S., La. State U., 1935; M.B.A., Northwestern U., 1937; m. Joy Annise Bernhardt, July 31, 1949; children—Beverly Annise, Frederick Lane, Robert Parker. Partner, Bates, Buras & Assos., New Orleans, 1941—. Served with AUS, 1941-46. Mem. Internat. House. Club: Bierville. Home: 210 Vincent Av Metairie LA 70005 Office: Maritime Bldg New Orleans LA 70130

BATES, JOHN WALTER, trans. planner; b. Bainbridge, Ga., Sept. 24, 1939; s. Clarence Floyd and Lillian (Drake) B.; B.C.E., Ga. Inst. Tech., 1962; M.B.A., Ga. State Coll., 1967; m. Martha Harriet Smith, July 1, 1961; children—Andrew John, Robin Elizabeth. With Ga. State Hwy. Dept., Atlanta, 1962-71, successively trainee, hwy. planning engr., asst. chief of urban planning, 1962-68, chief planning and operations research, 1968-71; sr. transp. planner Met. Atlanta Rapid Transit Authority, 1971-72, acting dir. planning, 1972—. Prin., Transp. Hwy. Econ. Planning Assos., Inc., Atlanta, 1967—. Sec.-treas. Alpha Nu Home Owning Corp., 1964-66, 68-70, chmn. bd., 1967. Registered profl. engr., Ga., Fla. Mem. Am. Soc. C.E. (sect. dir. 1969, 72), Am. Inst. Planners (asso.), Inst. Traffic Engrs. (sec.-treas. Ga. div. 1972), Phi Kappa Sigma. Presbyn. Mason (K.T.). Home: 4303 Rocking Chair Lane Stone Mountain GA 30083 Office: Suite 1300 100 Peachtree St NW Atlanta GA 30303

BATES, JOSEPH HENRY, physician; b. Little Rock, Sept. 19, 1933; s. Henry Ermer and Susan Elizabeth (Wallis) B.; B.S., U. Ark., 1954, M.D., 1957, M.S., 1963; m. Patsy McGinnis, Aug. 5, 1955; children— Patricia, Susan Elizabeth, Joseph Henry III, Elisabeth Lee. Intern, U. Ark. Med. Center, Little Rock, 1957-58, resident, 1958-61; instr. dept. medicine U. Ark., 1961-63, asst. prof., 1963-68, asso. prof., 1968-71, prof. medicine microbiology, 1971—; chief medicine VA Hosp., Little Rock, 1967—. Cons. Ark. State Health Dept., 1965—; mem. com. for phage typing mycobacteria WHO, 1965—. Royal Coll. Physicians (London) fellow, 1971. Fellow A.C.P., Am. Coll. Chest Physicians; mem. Infectious Disease Soc., So. Soc. Clin. Investigation, Pulaski County Tb and Respiratory Disease Assn. (pres. 1968-71). Club: Racquet (Little Rock). Home: 5 Glenridge Rd Little Rock AR 72207 Office: 300 E Roosevelt Rd Little Rock AR 72206

BATES, ROBERT LOUIS, JR., civil engr.; b. Waycross, Ga., Sept. 10, 1937; s. Robert Louis and Virginia (Carswell) B.; B.C.E., Ga. Inst. Tech., 1959, M.S., 1967; m. Frances Elon Sasser, Feb. 1, 1958; children—Virginia Elizabeth, Robert Louis III, Matthew Bowen. Engring. designer Robert & Co. Assos., Atlanta, 1961-65; sr. water quality control engr. Ga. Water Quality Control Bd., Atlanta, 1965-67, chief plans and reports sect., 1967-68; asso. Flood & Assos., Inc., Jacksonville, Fla., 1968-69, v.p., 1969—. Mem. Glynlea-Holiday Hills Civic Assn., 1969. Registered profl. engr., Ga., Fla. Mem. Nat. Soc. Profl. Engrs., Fla. Engring. Soc., Ga. Water and Pollution Control Assn., Water Pollution Control Fedn., Delta Tau Delta, Chi Epsilon. Baptist. Home: 706 Trinidad Rd Jacksonville FL 32216 Office: 934 Arlington Rd Jacksonville FL 32211

BATES, SHIRLEY SCHULZ (MRS. C. ALBERT BATES), dietitian, ednl. adminstr.; b.Lockhart, Tex., Mar. 23, 1920; d. Harry G. and Freda (Kuse) Schulz; B.S., S.W. Tex. State Coll., 1940; postgrad. U. Tex.; m. C. Albert Bates, Feb. 3, 1961. Asst. bus. dir. Women's Residence Halls, U. Tex., 1944-48; dietitian, women's residence halls, Tex. Technol. Coll., Lubbock, 1948-51, dir. food service, 1951—. Mem. Am., Tex. (pres. 1961-62) dietetic assns., Tex. Nat. Restaurant Assn., Am., Tex. home econs. assns., A.A.A.S., Assn. Coll. and Univ. Housing Officers, Nat. Assn. Coll. and Univ. Food Service (pres. 1969-70). Home: 3112 46th St Lubbock TX 79413

BATES, THOMAS ISAAC, JR., civil engr.; b. Charleston, Tenn., June 29, 1913; s. Thomas I. and Margaret (Bates) B.; B.C.E., Tenn. Tech. U., 1936; grad., U. Tenn., 1948; postgrad. Mass. Inst. Tech., 1961. Engr. aid Soil Conservation Service, U.S. Dept. Agr., 1938; with Bur. Pub. Rds., various states, 1938-43; sr. engr. Dept. Commerce. Civil Aeros. Adminstrn., 1943-47; with Republic Steel Corp., 1947-54; with Fla. Dept. Transp., Tallahassee, 1954—, asst. state traffic and planning engr., 1955—. Pres. Young Democrats of Tenn., 1936—. Registered profl. engr., Fla. Mem. Am. Soc. C.E., Nat. Soc. Profl. Engrs., Fla. Engring. Soc., Inst. Traffic Engrs., Engrs. Joint Council. Episcopalian. Mason, Kiwanian (bd. dirs.). Home: PO Box 1321 Tallahassee FL 32302 Office: Dot Bldg Tallahassee FL 32304

BATES, WILL LEWIS, realtor; b. Corpus Christi, Tex., Aug. 8, 1923; s. Will Lewis and Agnes (McAllister) B.; student pub. schs.; m. Cherry Dugger, July 6, 1943; children—William Glenn, Dan Mac, Mary Ann, Terri Elizabeth. Pres., W.L. Bates Co., Six Hundred Corp., Met. Land Co., 1969—, Coastal Bend Oil Co., 1960—, Bacor, Inc., 1967—. Past dir., v.p. Goodwill Industries; bd. dirs. Better Bus. Bur. Served with USNR, 1941-45. Mem. Soc. Indsl. Realtors, Tex. Assn. Realtors, Urban Land Inst., Corpus Christi Bd. Realtors (past pres.), Tex. Indsl. Council, C. of C., Am. Orchid Soc. (trustee). Mem. Christian Ch. Mason (32 deg., Shriner). Club: Corpus Christi Country. Home: 238 Cape Cod Corpus Christi TX 78412 Office: Box 909 Park Towers Bldg 720 Buffalo St Corpus Christi TX 78403

BATES, WILLIAM FULTON, JR., civil engr.; b. Greenville, Miss., Nov. 8, 1938; s. William Fulton and Alice (Outland) B.; B.S., Ga. Inst. Tech., 1962; m. Martha Bernice Hammonds, June 21, 1959; children—William Fulton III, Patrick Hammonds, Holly Diane. With Lockheed Ga. Co., Marietta, Ga., 1961—, group engr., structural integrity devel. group, 1969—; dir. Mgmt. Systems Inc. of Am., Atlanta. Asso. mem. Am. Soc. C.E. Baptist. Home: 116 Annette Lane Austell GA 30001 Office: S Cobb Dr Marietta GA 30060

BATES, WILLIAM LEROY, JR., land devel. co. exec.; b. Columbia, S.C., Mar. 8, 1921; s. William LeRoy and Ruth (Hawley) B.; B.B.A., Emory U., 1941; postgrad. U. Pa., 1941; m. Valerie Ogden Bates, Jan. 5, 1946 (div. Jan. 1965); 1 dau., Catherine (Mrs. Akin); m. 2d, Charlotte Louise Starr Bagley, Jan. 1970; 1 dau., Claire Starr Bagley. Commd. 2d lt. USMC, 1941, advanced through grades to col., 1962; comdg. officer Marine detachment U.S.S. Lexington, 1944-45; co. comdr. 1st Marine Div., Korean War; strategic planner U.S. European Command, 1952-54; head Marine Corps tng., 1954-58; acad. head Amphibious Warfare Coll., 1960-62; bn. comdr. Parris Island, S.C., 1962-63; controller Parris Island, 1964-65; ret., 1965; v.p. Gen. Am. Devel. Corp., Atlanta, 1970—; pres. Bates Bldg. Supply Co., Atlanta, 1972—; sr. v.p. Asso. Distbrs. Inc., Atlanta, 1965-70. Decorated Silver Star medal, Bronze Star medal, Air medal, Navy Commendation medal, Presdl. Unit citation. Mem. Mil. Order World Wars, Am. Legion, Kappa Alpha, Alpha Kappa Psi. Republican. Episcopalian. Kiwanian. Home: 3155 Verdun Rd NW Atlanta GA 30305 Office: Suite 700 84 Peachtree St Atlanta GA 30303

BATES, WILLIAM WANNAMAKER, JR., chemist; b. Orangeburg, S.C., Oct. 12, 1919; s. William W. and Ethel (Smith) B.; B.S., The Citadel, 1941; Ph.D., Duke, 1951; m. Anne Johnson Clarkson, Apr. 15, 1942; children—Mary Douglas (Mrs. David Taliaferro Wells), Elizabeth Wannamaker (Mrs. Steven Wayne Harkins), William Wannamaker III, Emily Heyward, Anne Clarkson. Research chemist Liggett & Myers Tobacco Co., Durham, N.C., 1950-53, asst. dir. research, 1953-60, asso. dir., 1960-64, dir., 1964—. Served to capt. USAAF, 1941-45; ETO. Decorated D.F.C., Air medal with oak leaf cluster, Purple Heart. Mem. Am. Chem. Soc., A.A.A.S., N.C. Acad. Sci. Episcopalian. Home: 2420 Alpine Rd Durham NC 27707 Office: Box 341 Durham NC 27702

BATLLE, JOSEFINA OJEDA (MRS. SALVADOR BATLLE), Puerto Rican govt. ofcl.; b. Fajardo, P.R., June 1, 1910; d. Juan and Baudilia (Trevino) Ojeda; grad. U. P.R.; m. Salvador Batlle, June 1, 1928; children—Josefina, Carmen, Salvador, Teresita, Jose Austin, Jorge Fernando. Formerly tchr. pub. schs.; mem. Bd. Commrs., San Juan, P.R., 1948-52; v.p. San Juan City Council, 1952-64; mem. P.R. Senate, 1964-69; pres. Edn. Com.; v.p. Pub. Order Com.; sec. Work and Labor Com.; mem. Coms. on Health, State and Municipal Govt. Mem. Nat. Order Women Legislators, United Women of Am., Inter-Am. Alliance (pres., hon. pres.), UN Assn., Zonta. Democrat. Roman Catholic. Address: Rampia del Admirante 61 Santurce PR 00901*

BATSON, BLAIR EVERETT, physician, educator; b. Hattiesburg, Miss., Oct. 24, 1920; s. Claud L. and Mary Eaton (Bryan) B.; B.A., Vanderbilt U., 1941, M.D., 1944; M.P.H., Johns Hopkins, 1954; m. Margaret Donovan Bailly, Oct. 2, 1954. Intern dept. pediatrics Vanderbilt U. Hosp., 1944-45, asst. resident, 1948-49, resident pediatrician, 1949-50; instr. pediatrics Vanderbilt U. Sch. Medicine, 1949-52; asst. resident dept. pediatrics Johns Hopkins Hosp., 1945-46; instr. pediatrics Johns Hopkins Sch. Medicine, 1952-54, asst. prof., 1954-55, instr. pub. health adminstrn., div. maternal and child health Sch. Hygiene and Pub. Health, 1952-54, asst. prof. pub. health adminstrn., 1954-55; prof. pediatrics, chmn. dept. U. Miss. Sch. Medicine, Jackson, 1955—. Chmn. health com., adv. council Miss. Children's Code Commn., 1958-61; chmn. Miss. Conf. on Handicapped Children, 1960-61; nat. adviser children, pub. children's bur. Dept. Health Edn. and Welfare; ofcl. examiner Am. Bd. Pediatrics, 1963—. Trustee Easter Seal Research Found., 1969—. Served to capt. M.C., AUS, 1946-48. Diplomate Am. Bd. Pediatrics. Mem. Am. Acad. Pediatrics (Mead Johnson awards com. 1958-61; exec. com. child devel. sect. 1964-67; charter mem. sect. on community pediatrics 1968, hosp. car com. 1970), A.M.A., So. Soc. Pediatric Research, Am. Assn. Med. Colls., So. Med. Assn. (sec. pediatric sec. 1956-58, pres. 1959), Vanderbilt Alumni Club (pres.

Jackson 1960-64), Am. Pediatric Soc., Sigma Chi, Phi Chi. Home: 4157 Crane Blvd Jackson MS 39216

BATSON, CHARLES ALVIN, broadcasting exec.; b. Greenville, S.C., Aug. 14, 1916; s. Charles Austell and Bessie (McCauley) B.; B.A., Furman U., 1938; 1 son, Reginald Fleming. Program dir. radio sta. WFBC, Greenville, 1938-41; dir. information and dir. TV, Nat. Assn. Broadcasters, Washington, 1946-51, now mem. adv. com. Corp. for Pub. Broadcasting, TV Code Rev. Bd.; dir. TV Broadcasting Co. of the South (now Cosmos Broadcasting Corp.), Columbia, S.C., 1951-53, pres., 1968—, now chmn. exec. com., also dir.; gen. mgr. sta. WIS-TV, Columbia, 1953-66; gen. mgr. sta. WTOL-TV, Toledo, 1966-68; dir. Liberty Corp., TV Stas., Inc.; mem. Columbia adv. bd. Citizens & So. Nat. Bank. Mem. NBC TV Bd. Dels., 1962-66. Vice chmn. A.R.C., Columbia, 1963-66; chmn. pub. information com. United Community Services, 1961, trustee, 1969—. Bd. dirs. Better Bus. Bur., 1963-64, Columbia Area Mental Health Center, 1969-70, S.C. Easter Seal Soc. for Crippled Children and Adults, 1970-73. Served with AUS, 1941-46. Recipient Abe Lincoln award So. Bapt. Radio and TV Commn., 1971. Mem. S.C. Broadcasters Assn. (pres. 1957), Greater Columbia C. of C. (pres. 1965). Presbyn. (former deacon, chmn. finance com.). Clubs: Palmetto; Forest Lake; Summit (dir. 1971—). Author series: Television: A Report on the Visual Broadcasting Art, 1948-49. Home: 1623 Milford Rd Columbia SC 29206 Office: PO Box 367 Columbia SC 29202

BATSON, FRANK OTERI, JR., dentist; b. Greenville, Miss., Sept. 27, 1940; s. Frank Oteri and Hoyett (Wheat) B.; student U. Miss., 1958-60; D.D.S., Loyola U., New Orleans, 1964; m. Katherine Crosson Downing, Nov. 24, 1961; children—Megan Michelle, Allyson Leigh. Pvt. practice dentistry, Laurel, Miss., 1966, Columbus, Miss., 1966—; mem. dental staff Lowndes Gen. Hosp., Columbus Hosp., dental cons. Columbus Med. Center. Dir. Piedmont Investment Securities, Inc. City councilman, Columbus, 1969-73. Bd. dirs. Miss. Elected Rep. Assn., 1971. Served with USAF, 1964-66. Recipient Certificate of Recognition, Am. Acad. Roentgenology, 1964; Distinguished Service award, Columbus Man of Year award Columbus Jr. C. of C., 1971. Mem. Columbus C. of C., Am., Miss. Northeast Miss. dental assns., Phi Delta Theta, Delta Sigma Delta. Republican. Methodist (steward 1968-71). Kiwanian (chmn. operation drug alert 1971-72). Club: Columbus (Miss.) Country. Home: 337 Williamsburg Rd Columbus MS 39701 Office: 501 7th St N Columbus MS 39701

BATSON, HOKE WADDY, pub. relations exec.; b. Greenville, S.C., June 10, 1936; s. Waddy Smith and Edna (McAlister) B.; B.A., Clemson Coll., 1958; postgrad. Furman U., 1958-59, Fla. Inst. Tech., 1962-63; m. Nelle Hill, June 12, 1959; 1 son, Kevin Tallysmith. With Dun & Bradstreet, Jacksonville, Fla., 1959-60, Ciba Pharm. Co., Montgomery, Ala., 1960-64, Spitz Electric Co., Melbourne, Fla., 1964-68; partner Allen-Batson, Melbourne, 1968—. Sec. Day-Nite Flyers, Inc., Melbourne, 1966—. Founder Brevard County Fair, 1968, v.p., 1967—; bd. dirs. Brevard County Mental Health Assn.; founder Indian River County Fair, 1969. Mem. City Council, Melbourne, 1968—; mayor City of West Melbourne, 1969-71. Trustee Melbourne Teen Town. Served with AUS, 1959-60. Named U.S. Jaycee Ambassador, 1967. Mem. Fla. Pub. Relations Assn., Illuminating Engring. Soc., Fla. League Municipalities, Jr. C. of C. (local pres. 1966—, nat. dir.). Democrat. Baptist. Elk, Kiwanian. Home: 716 Debra Lynn Dr Brandon FL 33511 Office: 680 Fairville Rd Orlando FL 32808

BATTAGLIA, GASPARE FRANCIS, JR., agr. bus. exec.; b. Troy, N.Y., Mar. 1, 1910; s. Gaspare and Antonina (Caruso) B.; student Syracuse U., 1929; m. Catherine Wherrett, June 15, 1935; children—Gaspare Francis III, Catherine (Mrs. John Haley), Robert, Christine (Mrs. William Macchia), Mary (Mrs. James Welborn), Julia, Paul. Pres., Krisp-Pak Co., Inc., Norfolk, Va., 1954—, Battaglia Produce Shippers, Inc., Norfolk, 1955—, Farmers Potato Distbg. Co., Inc., Norfolk, 1958—. Mem. Va. State Commn. of Industry of Agr., 1964—, Va. Bd. Agr. and Commerce, 1967—, Va. Seed Potato Commn., 1960—. Vice pres. Catholic Charities Diocese of Richmond. Bd. dirs. Norfolk Little Theatre, 1938—, pres., 1957; bd. dirs. Tidewater Regional Health Planning Council, Health, Welfare, Recreation Planning Council, 1960—, Southeastern Tidewater Opportunity Poverty Project, 1966—, St. Marys Infant Home; United Community Fund; trustee De Paul Hosp.; pres., 1963, meml. lay bd., 1954—. Mem. Va. Assn. Vegetable and Potato Growers (pres. 1962). Roman Catholic. Home: 1331 Willowwood Dr Norfolk VA 23509 Office: PO Box 1852 Norfolk VA 23501

BATTAILE, WILLIAM MCCAULEY, automobile dealer; b. Fredericksburg, Va., Jan. 7, 1913; s. Lawrence C. and Blanche M. (McCauley) B.; grad. high sch.; m. Virginia Burke, June 5, 1941; children—John William, Janet White, Jeannie Burke, Lawrence Gordon. Farmer, Westmoreland County, Va., 1933-35; field rep. Chevrolet div. Gen. Motors Co., 1935-41; dealer Chevrolet-Cadillac, Winchester, Va., 1945—. Pres. Indsl. Devel. Corp., 1959-66. Mem. city council, Winchester, 1964, mayor, 1964—. Served with USNR, 1929-33, USCGR, 1942-45. Named Outstanding Young Man, Winchester Jr. C. of C., 1946, Outstanding Boss, 1956; Outstanding Citizen, Winchester C. of C., 1952. Mason (Shriner), Moose, Elk, Lion. Clubs: Winchester (Va.) White Point Yacht (Kinsale, Va.). Home: 638 Tennyson Av Winchester VA 22601 Office: 2700 Valley Av Winchester VA 22601

BATTE, GEORGE ALBERT, JR., textile co. exec.; b. Greensville County, Va., Sept. 12, 1906; s. George Albert and Fannie (Mallory) B.; A.B., Davidson Coll., 1927; m. Cynthia Louise Thompson, May 6, 1939; children—Cynthia Anne, Frances Mallory. With Cannon Mills Co., Kannapolis, N.C., 1927—, v.p., 1959-63, treas., 1962—, exec. v.p., 1963—, also dir.; sec., treas., dir. Imperial Cotton Mills., 1960—; sec., treas., dir. Social Circle Cotton Mills Co., 1960—; v.p., dir. Brown Mfg. Co., 1956—, Roberta Mfg. Co., 1956—; asst. sec. Cannon Mills Inc., 1962-66, sec., 1966—; also dir.; asst. sec., dir. Wiscassett Mills Co.; dir. Cabarrus Bank & Trust Co. Chmn. trustees, chmn. exec. com. Cabarrus Meml. Hosp.; treas., dir. Cannon Meml. YMCA. Mem. Kappa Alpha, Knights of York Cross of Honour. Methodist (trustee). Mason. Home: 70 Spring St NW Concord NC 28025 Office: Cannon Mills Co Kannapolis NC 28081

BATTE, JAMES HERBERT, state ofcl.; b. Concord, N.C., July 8, 1913; s. George Albert and Fannie (Mallory) B.; B.S., Davidson Coll., 1935; student U.S. Mil. Acad., 1935-36; M.B.A., Harvard, 1950; m. Elenita Dyer, June 17, 1948. Commd. 2d lt. U.S. Army, 1940, advanced through grades to brig. gen., 1966; faculty Indsl. Coll. Armed Forces, 1958-61; spl. asst. congl. affairs Army Materiel Command, Washington, 1962-64; comdr. Edgewood (Md.) Arsenal Complex, 1965-66; sr. logistics adviser to Korean Army, 1967-68; asst. chief logistics Hdqrs. Continental Army Command, 1969-70; ret., 1970; exec. asst. to gen. mgr., dir. adminstrn. S.C. Pub. Service Authority, Moncks Corner, 1970—. Decorated D.S.M., Silver Star, Legion of Merit with 2 oak leaf clusters, Bronze Star with cluster, Purple Heart (U.S.); Fourragere (France). Mem. Interserv Financial Assn. (dir. 1970—), Am. Soc. Mil. Comptrollers, Kappa Alpha, Gamma Sigma Epsilon. Home: 115 Briarwood Lane Summerville SC 29483 Office: South Carolina Public Service Authority Moncks Corner SC 29461

BATTELL, WILLIAM PUTNAM, ret. marine corps officer; b. Mediapolis, Ia., Dec. 26, 1906; s. Frederick Louis and Harriet Elizabeth (Chapman) B.; student Ia. State Coll., 1924-27, also marine corps, army and navy profl. schs.; m. Esther Lillian Martin, Feb. 15, 1930. Enlisted in USMC, 1927, commd. 2d lt., 1930, advanced through grades to maj. gen.; assigned communications and electronics, 1927-48, supply, 1948-65; Q. M. Gen. Marine Corps, 1963-65; ret., 1965; now pres., dir. Sun City Center Bank (Fla.). Mem. corp. Nat. Capitol USO Club. Organizer, pres. S.W. Ga. Cerebral Palsy Assn.; mem. adv. com. Hillsborough County Charter Commn., v.p. Sun City Center Civic Assn., 1969-70, pres. 1971. Mem. Nat. Def. Transp. Assn. (v.p.), Def. Supply Assn. (hon. pres.), Armed Forces Mgmt. Assns. (bd. govs.), Am. Legion, Ret. Officers Assn., Old Timer Communicators of So. Cal., Am. Inst. Banking. Rotarian. Club: Sun City Center Men's (pres.). Home: 1006 La Jolla Av Sun City Center FL 33570

BATTEN, FRANK, newspaper publisher, broadcaster;; b. Norfolk, Va., Feb. 11, 1927; s. Frank and Dorothy (Martin) B.; A.B., U. Va., 1950; M.B.A., Harvard, 1952; m. Jane Neal Parke; children—Frank, Mary, Dorothy. Pub. Norfolk Virginian-Pilot, Norfolk Ledger-Dispatch, also Portsmouth Star, 1954—; chmn. bd. Greensboro (N.C.) Daily News, Greensboro Record, also WFMY-TV, Greensboro, 1965—; chmn. bd. Landmark Communications, Inc., 1967—; chmn. dir. WTAR Radio-TV Corp.; chmn. bd. Roanoke Times and World-News, Telecable Corp.; dir. Va. Nat. Bank. Trustee Norfolk Acad. Chmn., 1957 Internat. Naval Rev., Hampton Roads, Va. Pres. Norfolk Area United Fund, 1964. Bd. dirs. Norfolk Gen. Hosp.; trustee Hollins Coll.; chmn. bd. Old Dominion U., 1962-70. Recipient Norfolk's First Citizen award, 1966. Mem. Asso. Press, Bur. Advt. (chmn. bd. 1972-74), Norfolk C. of C. (pres. 1961), Delta Kappa Epsilon. Episcopalian. Clubs: Princess Anne Country, Norfolk Yacht. (Norfolk); Farmington Country (Charlottesville, Va.). Home: Holly Lane North Shore Point Norfolk VA 23505 Office: 150 W Brambleton Av Norfolk VA 23501

BATTEN, JAMES WILLIAM, educator; b. Goldsboro, N.C., Aug. 5, 1919; s. Albert LeMay and Lydia Annie (Davis) B.; A.B., U. N.C., 1940, M.A., 1947, Ed.D., 1960: postgrad. Columbia, 1942; m. Sara Magdalene Storey, June 1, 1945. Tchr., Glendale High Sch., Kenly, N.C., 1940-41, Wilmington Jr. Coll., 1946-47; tchr., coach Princeton (N.C.) High Sch., 1947-50; prin. Micro (N.C.) High Sch., 1950-58; teaching fellow, narrator Morehead Planetarium, Chapel Hill, N.C., 1958-60; asso. prof. E. Carolina U., Greenville, N.C., 1960-62, prof. edn., 1962—, chmn. dept. secondary edn., 1967—, also asst. dean Sch. Edn. Active in civic affairs. Served to lt. comdr. USNR, 1941-46. Mem. N.E.A., N. C. edn. Assn. (chpt. pres. 1961-62), Nat. Sci. Tchrs. Assn., Assn. for Supervision and Curriculum Devel., Phi Delta Kappa (pres. 1961-62), Horace Mann League, Nat. Soc. Study of Edn., Am. Ednl. Research Assn., Internat. Platform Assn., Nat. Assn. Tchrs. French, Kappa Delta Pi. Democrat. Baptist (deacon). Lion (pres. 1949-51). Author: Our Neighbors in Space, 1962, rev. edit., 1969; Research as a Tool for Understanding, 1965; Stars, Atoms, and God, 1968; (with J. Sullivan Gibson) Soils, 1970; Understanding Research, 1970, rev. edit., 1972. Contbr. numerous articles profl. jours. Home: 1014 E Wright Rd Greenville NC 27835

BATTEN, SARA STOREY (MRS. JAMES WILLIAM BATTEN), librarian; b. Murfreesboro, N.C., Nov. 6, 1915; d. Gladstone Bunn and Eldorado (Whitley) Storey; A.B., Chowan Coll., 1936; M.S. in L.S., U. N.C., 1960; m. James William Batten, June 1, 1945. Tchr. pub. high sch., Enfield, N.C., 1937; tchr., librarian Glendale Sch., Kenly, 1937-45, Micro, N.C., 1945-46; tchr. high sch. New Hanover Sch., Wilmington, 1946-47; tchr., librarian, Micro, 1947-48; cataloger Joyner Library, E. Carolina U., Greenville, N.C., 1960—. Established Hugo E. Miller scholarships E. Carolina U., 1963. Mem. N.C., Southeastern library assns., N.C. Assn. Educators, E. Carolina U. Women's Club, Beta Phi Mu. Baptist. Home: 1014 E Wright Rd Greenville NC 27834

BATTIN, ROSABELL HARRIET RAY (MRS. TOM C. BATTIN), psychologist, audiologist; b. Rock Creek, O.; d. Harry Walter and Sophia (Boldt) Ray; student Kent State U., 1944-45, U. Cal. at Los Angeles, 1946-47; A.B., U. Denver, 1948; M.S., U. Mich., 1950; Ph.D., U. Fla., 1959; m. Tom C. Battin, Aug. 27, 1949. Instr. speech pathology U. Denver, 1949-50; clin. asst. speech pathology U. Fla., 1952-54; audiologist Houston Speech and Hearing Center, 1954-56; dir. speech pathology-psychology Hedgecroft Hosp. and Rehab. Center, Houston, 1956-59; audiologist Drs. Guilford, Wright and Draper, Houston, 1959-63; practiced in speech pathology-audiology, psychology Houston, 1959—; dir. speech and hearing div. Houston Ear, Nose and Throat Hosp. Clinic, 1963—; clin. instr. dept. otolaryngology U. Tex., 1964—. Chmn. med. profl. adv. bd. Cerebral Palsy Treatment Center, Houston, 1965-69. Diplomate Am. Bd. Examiners in Speech Pathology and Audiology (mem. profl. services bd. 1967-70). Fellow Am. Speech and Hearing Assn.; mem. Am., Tex., Houston psychol. assns., Academy of Aphasia, Internat. Assn. Logopedics and Phoniatrics, Tex. Speech and Hearing Assn., Am. Acad. Speech Pathologists-Audiologists in Pvt. Practice (pub. bd. 1965-70, pres. 1968-70). Co-author: Speech and Language Delay, a Home Training Program, 1964. Home: 2130 Willowick Houston TX 77027 Office: 3931 Essex Lane Houston TX 77027

BATTISTE, EDWIN LINUS, govt. ofcl.; b. Pueblo, Colo., Aug. 13, 1926; s. Linus Edwin and Dorothy (Colgin) B.; B.A., Western State Coll. of Colo., 1949, M.A., 1955; postgrad. U. Denver, 1949, U. Colo., 1965; m. Lida Dean Milliken, Aug. 20, 1949; children—Michele Lynn, Patricia Ann, Michael Patrick. Salesman, Cudahy Packing Co., Denver, 1950-54; classroom tchr. schs. in Colo., 1954-57, Guam, 1957-60; prin. Jr.-Sr. High Sch., Ty. Guam, 1960-63, supt. schs., 1963-65; dir. extension Western State Coll. of Colo. at Gunnison, 1966-68; edn. specialist U.S. Office Edn., Washington, 1968—. Mem. Bd. Control Apprentice Tng., 1964, Bd. Control Manpower Devel. Tng., 1965 (both Ty. Guam). Mem. Community Children and Youth Com.-Juvenile Delinquency, 1963-65, Joint Mil. Civilian Traffic Safety Council, 1964-65 (both Ty. Guam). Served with USNR, 1944-46. Recipient Hon. Chamorro citation Gov. of Guam, 1965. Mem. Nat., Guam (pres. 1959) edn. assns., Theta Chi. Elk. Home: 9024 Brook Ford Rd Burke VA 22051 Office: DSAC/BESE/USOE 400 Maryland Av SW Washington DC 20201

BATTLE, JEAN ALLEN, educator; b. Talladega, Ala., June 15, 1914; s. William Raines and Lemerle McLemore (Allen) B.; student Birmingham So. Coll., 1932-33; B.S., Middle Tenn. State Coll., 1937; M.A., U. Ala., 1941; Ed.D., U. Fla., 1952; m. Lucy Troxell, Aug. 25, 1940; 1 dau., Helen Carol. Dept. chmn., dean students Fla. So. Coll., 1940-55, dean coll., 1956-59; dean coll. edn. U.S. Fla., Tampa, 1959-71. Editor, pub. Tennessee Valley News. Chmn. personnel and unification coms. Univ. Chapel Fellowship. Mem. steering com. Gov.'s Conf. on Edn., Fla. Mem. Fla. Tchr. Edn. Adv. Council, Fla. Continuing Edn. Council, Fla. Courses Study Com.; cons. Sarasota County Pub. Sch. System, Gov.'s Commn. on Quality Edn., Fla., 1967-68. Mem. adv. com. Hillsborough County Hosp.; bd. dirs. Southeastern Edn. Lab., Atlanta, World Trade Council. Served from pvt. to capt. USAAF, 1942-46. Recipient Distinguished Service awards Fla. So. Coll., 1952, Fla. Citizenship Clearing House, 1957. Mem. S.A.R., Fla. Hist. Soc., N.E.A., Fla. Edn. Assn. (co-chmn. tchr. recruitment com.), Omicron Delta Kappa, Pi Gamma Mu, Kappa Delta Pi, Phi Delta Kappa, Sigma Alpha Epsilon. Methodist. Rotarian. Co-author: New Idea in Education, 1968. Author: Culture and Education for the Contemporary World. Author papers in field. Home: 11011 Carrollwood Dr Tampa FL 33618

BATTLE, JOE MARSHALL, state ofcl.; b. Uvalde, Tex., Apr. 2, 1915; s. Ligon M. and Chloe (Shearer) B.; student N.Tex. Agrl. Coll., 1932-37; B.S. in Civil Engring., Tex. U., 1940; m. Nuggie Law, Mar. 21, 1940; children—Marie J. (Mrs. Eric R. Nye), Marshall Lee. Insp. Tex. Hwy. Dept., Mt. Pleasant, 1940-42, resident engr. to asst. engr. mgr., Houston, 1943-63, dist. engr., El Paso, 1963—; engr. U.S. Corp Engrs., Houston, 1942-43. Chmn. Wapaha dist. Boy Scouts Am., 1969. Mem. Nat., Tex. socs. profl. engrs. Methodist (steward). Home: 10121 Honolulu St El Paso TX 79925 Tex Hwy Dept 212 N Clark St El Paso TX 79994

BATTLE, LUCY TROXELL (MRS. J. A. BATTLE), educator; b. Bridgeport, Ala., June 28, 1916; d. John Price and Emily Florence (Williams) Troxell; student Ala. Coll., 1934-35; B.S., Fla. So. Coll., 1949; postgrad. U. Fla., 1950, 52; Fla. State U., 1963; m. Jean Allen Battle, Aug. 25, 1940; 1 dau., Helen Carol (Mrs. George Clipper Salmon, Jr.). Asst. postmaster, Bridgeport, Ala., 1936-40; asst. dir. personnel office Sebring (Fla.) AFB, 1942-44; tchr. Cleveland Court Sch., Lakeland, Fla., also Forest Hill Sch., Carrollwood Sch., Tampa, Fla., 1949-64; dean of girls Greco Jr. High Sch., Tampa, 1964-67. Bd. dirs. Tampa Oral Sch. for Deaf. Recipient Outstanding Service award Fla. So. Coll. Woman's Club, 1942. Mem. N.E.A. Am. Childhood Edn. Internat., Am. Assn. U. Women, Delta Kappa Gamma, Kappa Delta Pi, Phi Mu. Methodist. Club: Carrollwood Golf and Tennis. Contbr. articles to profl. jours. Home: 11011 Carrollwood Dr Tampa FL 33618 Office: 2517 S Himes Av Tampa FL 33609

BATTLE, TURNER WESTRAY, assn. exec.; b. Rocky Mount, N.C. Nov. 30, 1921; s. Turner Westray and Helen (Staats) B.; B.S. in Engring., U.S. Naval Acad., 1942; m. Francesca Barksdale Shackelford, June 22, 1942; children—Turner Westray, Stephen Shackelford, Richard Staats. Pres., N. State Constrn. Co., Inc, Rocky Mount, 1948-65; exec. dir. N.C. Wildlife Fedn., 1959—; v.p. Westwood Lumber Co., Inc., 1951-71, N.C. rep. to Nat. Wildlife Fedn., 1958-72, nat. dir., 1972—; mem. N.C. Aquatic Recreation Study Commn., 1963, Gov.'s Com. on Water Safety, 1965; vice chmn. Pesticide Adv. Com., mem. spl. adv. bd. N.C. Dept. Natural and Econ. Resources; mem. adv. bd. Water Resource Inst., U. N.C. Mem. nat. council Boy Scouts Am., Pres. Rocky Mount Acad. trustee, sec. N.C. Conservation Edn. Found. Served with USN, 1942-46; PTO. Recipient Silver Beaver award Boy Scouts Am., 1964; Distinguished Conservation Service award Nat. Wildlife Fedn., 1965; Nat. Conservation award Am. Motors Corp., 1971; named Ky. col, Hon. Citizen of Tex. Mem. Nat. Rifle Assn. (life), Am. Philatelic Soc. (life), Outdoor Writers of Am., Wilderness Soc., Nat. Audubon Soc., Nat., N.C. wildlife fedns., Southeastern, Tar Heel outdoor press assn., Am. Forestry Assn., Trout Unltd., Ducks Unltd., Save-the-Redwood League (life), U.S. Naval Acad. Alumni Assn. (life). Democrat. Episcopalian. Clubs: Jones Hill Gun, Roanoke and Tar River Gun, Benvenue Country. Kiwanian. Editor; Friend of Wildlife, 1959—. Home: 1633 Pinecrest Rd Rocky Mount NC 27801 Office: 109 S Main St Rocky Mount NC 27801

BATTLE, WILLIAM RAINEY, ins. co. exec.; b. Santa Anna, Tex., July 10, 1924; s. Fred and Margaret (Rainey) B.; student U. Tex., El Paso, 1941-43; B.A., U. Ia., 1947, M.S., 1948; m. Jane Nichol Brown, Jan. 6, 1951; children—Rebecca Brown, William Lee. Mgr. actuarial dept. Nat. Life & Accident Ins. Co., Nashville, 1948-51; asso. actuary Southwestern Life Ins. Co., Dallas, 1951-58; actuary Shenandoah Life Ins. Co., Roanoke, Va., 1959-62, v.p., actuary, 1962-70, v.p. financial operations, 1970-71, exec. v.p., 1971—. Pres. bd. dirs. Jr. Achievement; chmn. bd. trustees Employees Retirement System, City of Roanoke; mem. adv. bd. Salvation Army. Served to 1st lt. USAAF, 1943-46. Fellow Soc. Actuaries; mem. Middle Atlantic Actuarial Club (pres. 1967), Am. Acad. Actuaries, Newcomen Soc., Roanoke Valley C. of C. (v.p., dir.). Home: 3221 Fordham Rd Roanoke VA 24014 Office: 2301 Brambleton Av SW Roanoke VA 24015

BATTLE, WILLIAM ROBERT, newspaper exec.; b. Nolensville, Tenn., Dec. 25, 1927; s. William Robert and Cleo (Smith) B.; student George Peabody Coll., 1946-49; m. Elizabeth Ogilvie, Dec. 23, 1948; children—Valerie Elizabeth, William Robert III. With Nashville Banner, 1943—, police beat, county polit. beat, 1943-53, city editor, 1953-64, mng. editor, 1964-71, movie columnist, 1955—, exec. editor, 1971—; editor Hurst Constrn News; corr. Nat. Enquirer, Lantana, Fla.; Tenn. rep. Screen Daily. Supt. gates and admissions Tenn. State Fair, 1953-64; mem. Middle Tenn. council Boy Scouts Am. Bd. dirs. Boys Club, also mem. exec. com., chmn. camping com.; bd. dirs. Women Execs. Internat.; mem. Nat. 4-H Found. Recipient Big Story award NBC TV, 1956. Appeared in movie as a newspaperman in Teacher's Pet, 1957; appeared in movie Country Music on Broadway, 1963. Mem. Nashville Area C. of C., Tenn. Press Assn., A.P. Mng. Editors Assn., Nat. Screen Council, Sigma Delta Chi. Methodist. Mason (32 deg., Shriner, Jester), Elk. Clubs: Colemere Country; Admiral's; Nashville City. Contbr. numerous articles to nat. publs. Home: 4108 Crestridge Dr Nashville TN 37202 Office: 1100 Broadway Nashville TN 37202

BATTS, B.F. (JERRY), city ofcl.; b. St. Louis, July 11, 1921; s. Bascom Franklin and Lila May (Bartlett) B.; B.S., U. Mo., 1942; postgrad., Harvard, Mass. Inst. Tech.; m. Edna Helen Vahrenkamp, Sept. 1, 1951. Edn. dir. Tex. Coll. Tech., San Antonio, 1948-51; sr. research engr. Southwest Research Inst., San Antonio, 1951-55, mgr., 1955-58; sect. head Motorola Inc., Phoenix, 1958-60; program mgr. LTV Continental Electronics, Dallas, 1960-65, F&M Systems Co., Dallas, 1965-68 dir., systems engring. div., Def. Electronics, Inc., Rockville, Md., 1968-69; v.p. systems Nat. Data Controls, Inc., Dallas, 1969-70; tech. and research coordinator City of Dallas, 1971—. Served to 1st lt. Signal Corp, AUS, 1942-46: ETO. Registered profl. engr., Tex. Mem. Nat., Tex. socs. profl. engrs., I.E.E.E., Eta Kappa Nu, Pi Mu Epsilon, Phi Kappa Psi. Kiwanian. Home: 9308 Vinewood Dr Dallas TX 75228 Office: 1500 W Mockingbird Lane Dallas TX 75247

BAUCOM, MARGARET DEAN (MRS. H. BASCOM BAUCUM), newspaper worker, feature writer, poet; b. Charlotte, N.C., Sept.25, 1909; d. John Calvin and Lelia (Robinson) Dean; student pub. schs.; m. Hiram Bascom Baucom, Sept. 20, 1927 (dec.); 1 dau., Joan (Mrs. James Preston Brown, Jr.). Automobile dealer B & M Motor Co., Monroe, N.C., 1950-53; now free lance writer for newspapers and others; society editor The Monroe Enquirer. Bd. dirs. Mecklenburg-Union Tb and Respiratory Disease Assn. Founder Marshville Pub. Library. Recipient Etta Caldwell Harris Poetry award; 1st prize Ill. Poetry Soc., 1972. Mem. N.C. Hist. Soc., U.D.C. (pres. 1956-58, state chmn. patriotic service), Colonial Dames 17th Century, D.A.R. (publicity chmn.), Union County Hist. Soc., Little Theatre (v.p. and rule regulation), Women's Golf Assn., Monroe Opera Guild (charter), Carolinas Geneal. Soc. (co-editor bull.), Daus.

Am. Colonists, Huguenot Soc., Internat. Platform Assn. (mem. publicity com. 1966-—), Nat. Fedn. Press Women, N.C. Press Women, Nat. League Am. Pen Women, Cal. Fedn. Chaparral Poets, Ill. Poetry Soc., World Poetry Soc. Internat., Am. Poets Fellowship Soc. Presbyn. Clubs: Monroe Woman's Golf (charter mem., past pres.), Monroe Woman's (past pres.), Monroe Garden (past pres.), Monroe Music (past pres.), N.C. Press Woman's (dist. chmn. 1965-66), Silhoutte Dance. Contbr. to poetry mags. Address: 710 S Hayne Monroe NC 28110

BAUER, JOHN ALDEN, JR., educator; b. Boise, Ida., Oct. 6, 1932; s. John Alden and Gladys C. (Hall) B.; B.Mus., Yale, 1954, M. Mus., 1955; D.Mus., Fla. State U., 1969; postgrad. Ind. U.; m. R. Ann Hutchings, June 8, 1963; children—John Alden III, Burgin Ann. Concertmaster, Robert Shaw Chorale & Orch., 1955, Mantovani Orch., 1958; asst. prof. Wesleyan Coll., 1959-62; asst. prof. U. S.C., 1962-71; asso. prof., 1971-—; guest condr. Columbia Philharmonic Orch., 1963-—, acting mus. dir., 1970-—; condr. Columbia Jr. Orch., 1965-—; 1st violinist Columbia String Quartet; dir. music div. Summer Sch. Arts, Hilton Head Island, S.C.; dir., founder U.S. Carolina Chamber Music Series, 1963-—; choirmaster St. Martins Episcopal Ch. Bd. dirs. Columbia Mus. Fine Art. Served with AUS, 1956-58. Mem. Phi Mu Alpha, Pi Kappa Lamda. Numerous concerts in 14 countries, 1954-—. Author: Scale System for Violin, 1969. Contbr. articles to newspapers. Home: 6431 Briarwood Columbia SC 29206

BAUER, MELVIN BLOOM, retail exec.; b. Alexandria, La., July 26, 1902; s. Achille Soloman and Hortense (Schmalinski) B.; student Vanderbilt U., 1920-21; m. Freida Belle Goldberg, Jan. 19, 1927; children— Melvin Bloom Jr., Bobette Joan (Mrs. Lowell Friedman). Dep. collector Internal Revenue Service, La., 1924-27; comptroller United Shoe Stores Co. of La. Inc., Shreveport, 1930-—. Jewish religion (trustee 1943-57, pres. 1948-49, 1956). Home: 3845 Creswell St Shreveport LA 71106 Office: 2901 Linwood Av Shreveport LA 71103

BAUGHMAN, RONALD ADRIAN, educator; b. Palatka, Fla., Aug. 25, 1939; s. Warner Cecil and Lavonia Flourella (Larkins) B.; student Stetson U., 1957-60; B.A., U. Fla., 1963; D.D.S., Med. Coll. Va., 1967; M. Oral Pathology, Ind. U., 1969; m. Mary Jean Downs, Aug. 12, 1960; children—Rhonda Jeanene, Kent Adrian. Asst. prof. oral pathology Coll. Dental Medicine, Med. U. S.C., 1969-71; asst. prof. oral pathology Coll. Dentistry, U. Fla., Gainesville, 1971-—, dir. forensic odontology consultation service, 1971-—. Mem. profl. information com. Am. Cancer Soc., Charleston, S.C., 1970-71. Am. Cancer Soc. Research fellow, 1967-69. Fellow Am. Acad. Oral Pathology; mem. Am., S.C. dental assns., Am. Soc. Forensic Odontology, Omicron Kappa Upsilon, Zeta Eta. Mason. Home: 1608 N W 26th Way Gainesville FL 32601

BAUMBERGER, THEODORE SHRIVER, state agy. exec.; b. Glasgow, Ky., Aug. 28, 1925; s. Perry Alvin and Helen (Shriver) B.; B.A., U. Louisville, 1949, M.A., 1950; Ph.D., U. Okla., 1961; m. JoAnn Dodson, Apr. 12, 1948; children—Erick Theodore, Andrea Leigh, Brent Lane. Exec. sec. Ky. Com. for Children and Youth, Mid-Century White House Conf., Louisville, 1950-51; adminstrv. asst., acting dir. div. sch. health Ky. Dept. Health, Louisville, 1951-52; supr. psychol. unit Okla. Dept. Pub. Welfare, 1954-59, supr. div. state homes and schs., 1960-68, acting supr. psychol. unit, 1960-68, adminstrv. asst., 1968-—; practicum supr. Psychol. Clinic, U. Okla., 1953-54, 58-68, staff psychologist Guidance Service, 1959-60, cons. Psychol. Clinic, 1961-68, adj. asst. prof., 1963-68; pvt. practice clin. psychology, Norman, Okla., 1962-—; cons. psychologist Okla. Bd. Pub. Affairs, 1956-59, Peace Corps Tng. Program, U. Okla., 1965-67, Oklahoma City Bd. Edn., 1966-69, Griffin Meml. Central State Hosp., 1968-—, Fed. Bur. Prisons, El Reno Reformatory 1969-—; profl. adv. bd. North Oklahoma City Mental Health Center. Sec. Okla. Bd. Examiners Psychologists, 1965-67, chmn., 1967-68. Mem. Gov.'s Com. on Vocational Rehab., 1966-67; mem. Okla. Crime Commn. coms. juvenile delinquency and corrections. Mem. adv. council Okla. Council on Crime and Delinquency; mem. adv. com. Okla. Congress Parents and Tchrs. Served with USAAF, 1943-45. Mem Am., Southwestern, Okla. (past pres.) psychol. assns., Am. Acad. Psychotherapists, Am. Group Psychotherapy Assn., Southwestern Group Psychotherapy Soc., Am. Pub. Welfare Assn., Nat. Assn. Tng. Schs. and Juvenile Agys., Nat. Council on Crime and Delinquency, Okla. Psychiat. Soc., Okla. Group Process Soc., Okla. Health and Welfare Assn., Sigma Chi Sigma, Delta Upsilon, Psi Chi, Delta Phi Alpha. Democrat. Methodist. Home: 616 NW 41st St Oklahoma City OK 73118 Office: PO Box 25352 Oklahoma City OK 73125

BAUMERT, JOHN BENJAMIN, lawyer; b. McAlester, Okla., June 26, 1921; s. Charles Carter and Maude (Evans) B.; student N.M. Mil. Inst., 1939; B.S., U. Okla., 1943, LL.B., 1948; m. Suzanne Loveall, May 6, 1950; children—Charles Loveall, John L., Carter L. Admitted to Okla. bar, 1948; partner Cornish and Baumert, McAlester, 1948-52; pvt. practice, 1952-—; gen. counsel Elsing Mfg. Co., 1956-—, dir., 1956-—; dir. Doss Oil Co., Choctaw Petroleum Corp., Arrowhead Petroleum Inc., Thunderbird Royalty Corp. Bd. dirs. McAlester Gen. Hosp. Served as capt., U.S. Army, 1943-46; PTO. Fellow Am. Coll. Probate Counsel; mem. Am., Okla., Pittsburg County bar assns., Southwestern Legal Found., Okla. U. Law School Assn (dir. 1961-—, chmn. bd. trustees 1963, past pres.), Beta Theta Pi. Methodist (dir. McAlester Dist. Bd. of Missions). Mason (33 deg., Shriner), United Comml. Traveler (grand counselor 1956, chmn. com. on jurisprudence for supreme counsel 1961, supreme page 1965,) supreme jr. counselor 1967-68), supreme counselor, 1968-69, chmn. bd., 1969-70), Lion (pres. 1955). Home: 1842 Wood Rd McAlester OK 74501 Office: McMurray Bldg McAlester OK 74501

BAUMGARDNER, JOHN HENRY, educator; b. Wellington, Tex., May 15, 1916; s. Joseph Bailey and Eva Lyle (Godfrey) B.; B.S., Tex. Tech. U., 1939, M.S., 1940; m. Maretta Frank Holloway, Aug. 21, 1941; children—John Rudolph, Sharon Ann, Alice Camille, Rebecca Jane. Tech. adviser Nat. Cottonseed Products Assn., Dallas 1940-42; prof. animal sci. Tex. Tech. U. Lubbock, 1945-—. Nutrition cons., Plainview, Tex., 1956-—. Served with USAAF, 1942-45, with USAF, 1951-56. Decorated D.F.C., Air medal with three clusters. Mem. Am. Soc. Animal Prodn., Sigma Xi, Phi Kappa Phi. Mason (32 degree, K.T.). Home: Olton Route Plainview TX 79072

BAUMGARTEN, PHILLIP STANLEY, investment co. exec.; b. Hillsdale, Mich., June 1, 1924; s. Joseph and Gertrude (Langendorf) B.; grad. U. Ariz., 1944; m. Joanie B. Baumgarten; children—Lang Elton, Mari Lee. Pres., Baumgarten Investment Co., Chgo., 1946-—, North Miami Motors Inc. (Fla.), 1966-—, Jensen Lincoln-Mercury Inc., Jackson, Mich., 1963-—, Baumgarten Transp. Co., Jackson, Mich., 1946-—, Master Devel. Corp., South Bend, Ind., 1960-—, Trans-Air Inc., Eng., Chgo., 1967-—, v.p. Baumgarten Found. Inc., Chgo., 1960-—. Served with AUS, 1943-46. Home: 24 Isla Bahia Dr Ft Lauderdale FL 33316 Office: 277 SW 33d Ct Ft Lauderdale FL 33315

BAVOUSETT, GLENN BYRON, investor; b. Fort Worth, Dec. 31, 1926; s. Glenn Lanham and Ruth Mae (Morris) B.; grad. high sch.; m. Jennie Stevens, Dec. 3, 1966; children—Byron, Ferris, Leslie. Pres. Illus. Publs. Service, Inc., Dallas, 1958-60, Foto-Listing Service, Inc., Dallas, 1960; gen. mgr. Volt Tech. Corp., Fort Worth, 1960-66; pres. NHA, Inc., Fort Worth, 1969-71, dir. 1968-71. Bd. dirs. Case Manana Musicals, 1971; served with USNR, 1944-46, 48, 50-52. Mem. Confederate Air Force (adv. council 1971-72), Air Force Assn., Soc. Tech. Writers and Pubs., Assn. U.S. Army. Mason, Elk. Home: Route 1 Box 33D Keller TX 76248

BAWER, ROBERT, electronic co. exec.; b. Ellenville, N.Y., Feb. 12, 1925; s Abraham and Minnie (Slutsky) B.; B.E.E., U. Fla., 1947; M.S., Mass. Inst. Tech., 1949; postgrad. George Washington U., 1956-61; m. Norma Haas, Sept. 11, 1949; children—Joyce, Kenneth, Paula. Project engr. Melpar, Inc., Falls Church, Va., 1949-56; prin. engr. Emerson Research Labs., Washington, 1956-58; asst. dir. research Aero Geo Astro Corp., Alexandria, Va., 1958-60; with Radiation Systems, Inc., McLean, Va., 1960-—, pres., 1963-—. Mem. I.E.E.E., Electronic Industries Assn., Sigma Tau, Phi Kappa Phi, Sigma Xi. Home: 3529 Glenbrook Rd Fairfax VA 22030 Office: 1755 Old Meadow Rd McLean VA 22101

BAXLEY, HUGH FRANCIS, accountant; b. Plaquemine, La., Aug. 10, 1933; s. Lester Leo and Vera (Gamble) B.; B.S., La. State U., 1955; m. Gwendolyn Ann Didier, Jan. 19, 1957; children—Francis Ghent, Janina Joyce. Staff accountant Peat, Marwick, Mitchell, C.P.A.'s, New Orleans, 1957-58; budget examiner State of La., Baton Rouge, 1959-61; partner Baxley & Swetman, C.P.A.'s, Plaquemine, 1961-70; Hugh F. Baxley, C.P.A.'s, Plaquemine, 1970-—. Cons., Parish Indsl. Devel. Bd. dirs. Pvt. Sch. Iberville, 1969-—. Served with USNR, 1955-57. Mem. Am. Inst. C.P.A.'s, Soc. La. C.P.A.'s, Am. Accounting Assn., La. State U. Alumni Fedn., Plaquemine-Iberville C. of C. (dir. 1967-70). Democrat. Baptist. Clubs: Rotary (pres. 1969-70); Westside Golf (Brusly, La.). Home: 306 Erwin Dr Plaquemine LA 70764 Office: Earle Dr Plaquemine LA 70764

BAXLEY, KEENER, judge; b. Dothan, Ala., Dec. 6, 1899; s. William Joseph Baxley and Mary Josephine (Folkes) B.; LL.B., U. Ala., 1926; m. Lemma Rountree, May 8, 1929; children—William Joseph, Wade Hampton. Admitted to Ala. bar, 1925; practiced in Dothan, 1926-39; circuit solicitor 20th Jud. Circuit of Ala., 1939-57; circuit judge, 1957-—. Democrat. Methodist. Home: 200 E Woodland Dr Dothan AL 36301 Office: County Court House Dothan AL 36301

BAXTER, ALLIN PRESTON, securities co. exec.; b. Sanitary Springs, N.Y., May. 1, 1929; s. Preston Lee and Violette Cordella (Regal) B.; B.A., U. Va., 1952; LL.B., George Washington U., 1957; m. Diana Hopkins, Nov. 26, 1953; children—Audrey McNair, David Hopkins. Admitted to U.S. Dist. Ct. bar, 1957, U.S. Ct. Appeals bar, 1965; atty. SEC, Washington, 1957-61; v.p., sec. Steadman Security Corp., Aberdeen Mgmt. Corp., Asso. Fund Mgmt. Corp., Asso. Mut. Funds, Washington, 1961-70; partner Jones and Baxter, Attys., Washington, 1970-—; pres. Baxter, Blyden, Selheimer & Co., Inc., Washington, 1970-—. Seminar speaker Mut. Fund Seminar Assos., 1971-—. Served to 1st lt. AUS, 1952-54. Mem. Fed., D.C. bar assns., Nat. Lawyers Club. Clubs: Metropolitan (Washington); Monterey Country (pres. 1970-72) (Blue Ridge Summit, Pa.). Home: 4643 Kenmore Dr NW Washington DC 20007 also Monterey Circle Blue Ridge Summit PA Office: 1775 K St NW Washington DC 20006

BAXTER, E.R., state ofcl. Dir. vocational rehab. services Ark. Dept. Edn., Little Rock. Address: Ednl Bldg Ark Dept Edn Little Rock AR 72203*

BAXTER, GEORGE WILLIAM, JR., educator; b. Moresville, Tenn., Oct. 8, 1925; s. George William and Lenora (Long) B.; A.B., Emory U., 1946; M. Div. cum laude, Yale, 1951; M.A., George Peabody Coll., 1968, Ph.D., 1969; m. Jane Elizabeth Farrar, Aug. 28, 1959; children—George William III, Elizabeth Lynne. Instr. religion Fla. So. Coll., Lakeland, 1959-60, asst. acad. dean, registrar, 1960-66; prof., chmn. dept. psychology King Coll., Bristol, Tenn., 1969-—, Mary Reynolds Babcock prof. pscyhology, 1970, chmn. div. social scis., 1970-—. Served with USNR, 1943-45. Mem. Am. Assn. Higher Edn., Am. Assn. U. Profs., Am., Southeast psychol. assns., Soc. Psychol. Study Social Issues, Soc. Scientific Study Religion, Va. Archeol. Assn., Phi Beta Kappa. Methodist (adminstrv. bd. 1970). Contbr. articles to profl. publs. Home: 928 Florida Av Bristol TN 37620

BAXTER, HARRY STEVENS, lawyer; b. Ashburn, Ga., Aug. 25, 1915; s. James Hubert and Anna (Stevens) B.; A.B. summa cum laude, U. Ga., 1936, LL.B. summa cum laude, 1939; postgrad. Yale, 1939-40; m. Edith Ann Teasley, Apr. 4, 1943; children—Anna Katherine (Mrs. Paul Worley) (dec.), Nancy Julia (Mrs. John Adams Sibley III). Admitted to Ga. bar, 1941; instr. U. Ga. Law Sch., Athens, 1941; asso. Smith Kilpatrick, Cody, Rogers & McClatchey, Atlanta, 1942-51; partner Kilpatrick, Cody, Rogers, McClatchey & Regenstein, Atlanta, 1951-—. Mem. State Bd. Bar Examiners Ga., 1960-66, chmn., 1961-66. Dir. Latex Contrns. Co., Atlanta, Thompson Co., Atlanta. Pres., Atlanta Community Chest, 1963; mem. bd. visitors U. Ga. Law Sch., 1965-68, chmn., 1965-66, chmn. alumni adv. com. on reorgn., 1962-64; chmn. chancellor's alumni adv. com. on selection of pres. U. Ga., 1966-67; gen. co-chmn. Joint Ga. Tech.-Ga. Devel. Fund, 1967. Trustee U. Ga. Found., William E. Honey Found. Served with AUS, 1942-45. Recipient Distinguished Alumnus award U. Ga. Law Sch., 1967. Fellow Am. Bar Found.; mem. Am. Law Inst., Am., Ga., Atlanta bar assns., Atlanta C. of C. (dir. 1959-62), Atlanta Legal Aid Soc. (pres. 1956-57), U. Ga. Alumni Soc., Phi Beta Kappa, Phi Beta Kappa Assos., Phi Kappa Phi, Omicron Delta Kappa, Phi Delta Phi, Clubs: Capital City (pres. 1965-67), Lawyers (pres. 1958-59), Piedmont Driving, Commerce, University Yacht (all Atlanta). Home: 3197 Chatham Rd NW Atlanta GA 30305 Office: Equitable Bldg 100 Peachtree St NW Atlanta GA 30303

BAXTER, L. C., hosp. adminstr.; b. Sherman, Tex., Mar. 22, 1917; s. Thomas Andrew and Ethel (Hartwig) B.; grad. Dallas Inst. Mortuary Sci., 1946; m. Caromae Reese, Apr. 10, 1937; children—Thomas Reese, L.C. Embalmer, funeral dir. Guardian Funeral Home, Ft. Worth, 1934-48; adminstr. Ft. Worth Osteo. Hosp., 1948-53, Okla. Osteo. Hosp., Tulsa, 1953-—. Med. adv. com. Dept. Pub. Welfare, Okla., vice chmn., 1964-—; mem. health facilities adv. bd. Okla. Dept. Health; mem. Tulsa Hosp. Council, pres., 1964-66. Trustee, sec.-treas. Tulsa Area Health & Hosp. Council. Served AUS, World War II. Mem. Okla. Hosp. Assn. (trustee 1967-—), Am. Osteo. Hosp. Assn. (trustee 1955-—, pres. 1963-64, merit award), Am. Coll. Osteo. Hosp. Adminstrn., C. of C., Osteo. Hosp. Founders Assn. (treas.). Mem. Christian Ch. Clubs: Petroleum, Tulsa, University. Home: 1722 S Carson Tulsa OK 74119 Office: 9th and Jackson Sts Tulsa OK

BAXTER, MARY KATHERINE, educator; b. Rockdale, Tex., Feb. 11, 1915; d. Lee Allen and Nettie (Colbert) Baxter; student Blinn Jr. Coll., 1931-33; B.A., S.W. Tex. State Coll., 1936; M.Ed., U. Tex., 1944. Tchr. Rockdale (Tex.) pub. schs., 1937-42, Beaumont, Tex., 1942-69; dir. secondary instrn. Beaumont Ind. Sch. Dist., 1969-—. Mem. Tex. (pres. 1958), Sabine Area (local pres. 1961-62) councils social studies, Tex. Tchrs. Assn. (sec. dist. V 1969-—, exec. bd. dist I 1961-62), Tex. Edn. Agy. (social studies curriculum commn. 1958-59), Tex. (adv. bd. 1953-54), Beaumont (pres. 1967-69) classroom tchrs. assns., Am. Assn. U. Women (pres. Beaumont 1957-59, state topic chmn. 1971-—), N.E.A., Beaumont C. of C. (chmn. edn. com. 1970-71), Alpha Chi, Pi Gamma Mu, Pi Lamba Theta, Delta Kappa Gamma (v.p. Beaumont chpt. 1956-58, pres. 1964-66, state chmn. com. personal growth and services 1969-71), Alpha Delta Kappa (chpt. pres. 1966-68). Methodist (life mem. Wesleyan Service Guild). Home: 5730 Duff Av Beaumont TX 77706 Office: 820 Neches St Beaumont TX 77701

BAXTER, OSCAR FITZ-ALAN, IV, real estate and ins. broker; b. Norfolk, Va., Aug. 29, 1917; s. Alan Leonidas and Vivian (Wright) B.; student Coll. William and Mary, 1956, U. Richmond, 1948; m. Lucy Gordon Bailey, Sept 3, 1941; children—Oscar Fitz-Alan V, Pamela A., Stephen H. Salesman, O. F. Baxter & Co., Norfolk, 1935-38, property mgr., 1938-45, partner, 1945-51, pres., owner, 1951-53; pres. Baxter & Wood, Inc., Norfolk, 1953-—. Treas., Norfolk Republican Com., 1952-53; sec. Princess Anne County Republican Com., 1956, chmn., 1958; chmn. 1st Dist. Republican Com., 1958-59; mem. Republican State Central Com., 1960-66. Served with AUS, 1942-45. Decorated Bronze Star medal. Mem. Norfolk Bd. Realtors, Inst. Real Estate Mgmt. (chpt. pres. 1967), Norfolk Bd. Realtors (pres. 1968). Episcopalian. Clubs: Kiwanis, Harbor, Cavalier Beach. Home: 3757 Lynnfield Dr Virginia Beach VA 23452 Office: 328 Boush St Norfolk VA 23510

BAXTER, RICHARD DUNCAN, purchasing exec.; b. Fort Payne, Ala., May 6, 1918; s. Stephen Elisha and Jessie (Duncan) B; student pub. schs.; m. Viola Nancy Ellis, Mar. 11, 1947; children—Ellis Fielding, Stephen Tyrus. Clk., So. Ry., 1936-54; traffic mgr. Kingsberry Homes Corp., 1954-56, purchasing agt., traffic mgr., 1956-64, v.p., purchasing and traffic, 1964-67; dir. purchasing and traffic Kingsberry Homes div. Boise Cascade Corp., 1967. Councilman, Fort Payne, 1948-52. Mem. DeKalb County (Ala.) Democratic Exec. Com., 1950-63, vice chmn., 1956-60. Served with USNR, 1941-46. Baptist. Author: A History of the Baxter Family of DeKalb County, Alabama, 1957; Annals of Fort Payne Baptist Church, 1964. Home: 1890 Gainsborough Dr Chamblee GA 30341 Office: 61 Perimeter Park E Chamblee GA 30341

BAYER, ALVIN, III, dentist; b. Jacksonville, Fla., Dec. 31, 1935; s. Alvin and Margaret (Patterson) B.; A.A. Jacksonville U., 1957; D.D.S., Emory U., 1962; student U. Fla., 1957-58; m. Renia Catherine Poe, June 17, 1961; children—Michael Alvin, Allison Marie, Renia Catherine. Practice dentistry, Fernandina Beach, Fla., 1964-—; mem. staff Humphreys Meml. Hosp. Pres., Nassau Food Services, Inc., Fernandina Beach, 1965-—. Asst. fund dr. chmn. Nassau County Cancer Soc., 1968, dir., 1967-69; co-chmn. Nassau County United Fund, 1971. Served to lt. Dental Corps, USNR, 1962-64. Mem. Acad. Gen. Dentistry (Fla. pres. 1969-70), Am., Fla., N.E. Dist., Jacksonville dental assns., Am. Soc. Dentistry for Children, Am. Analgesia Soc., Am. Soc. for Preventive Dentistry, Internat. Assn. for Orthodontics, Fernandina Beach Golf Assn. (v.p. 1970, sec. 1971, dir. 1969-70), Psi Omega. Democrat, Rotarian (dir.). Home: 1803 Parkway Fernandina Beach FL 32034 Office: 1014 Atlantic Av Fernandina Beach FL 32034

BAYER, THOMAS STEELE, JR., real estate co. exec.; b. Houston, Dec. 4, 1938; s. and Hazel Francis (Reid) B.; B.A., So. Methodist U., 1961; m. Elizabeth Sadler Steinmetz, July 15, 1972; stepchildren—James Michael, Jeffrey Edward. Adminstrv. asst. Southwestern Grad. Sch. Banking, So. Methodist U., Dallas, 1961; dir. pub. relations Robert Morris Assos., Phila., 1965-69; dir. pub. relations Sch. Business, So. Methodist U., 1969-72; dir. pub. relations Henry S. Miller Cos., Dallas, 1972-—. Active Common Cause. Served to lt. (j.g.) USNR, 1961-65; lt. comdr. Res. Mem. Pub. Relations Soc. Am., Dallas Advt. League, Delta Sigma Pi. Methodist. Home: 5920 Village Glen Dr Dallas TX 75206 Office: 1 Main Pl Suite 2500 Dallas TX 75250

BAYES, RONALD HOMER, author, educator; b. Milton, Ore., July 19, 1932; s. Floyd Edgar and Mildren (Cochran) B.; M.S., Eastern Ore. Coll., 1956; postgrad. U. Pa., 1959-60, U.B.C., 1963, Trinity Coll., Dublin, Ireland, 1966, Colo. State U. at Greeley, 1955-61, Woodrow Wilson nat. fellow, 1959-60. Asso. prof. English Eastern Ore. Coll., 1956, 60-68; lectr. English U. Md., 1958-59, 66-67; writer-in-residence St. Andrews Coll., Luarinburg, N.C., 1968-—. Independent. Episcopalian. Mason. Author: History of The Turtle, 4 vols.; 1964, 65, 66; X-ing Warm, 1968, John Reed and Limits of Idealism, 1968; The Casketmaker: Selected Short Poems 1960-70, 1972. Contbr. articles profl. jours. Address: St Andrews Coll Laurinburg NC 28352

BAYLESS, ROBERT PAUL, civil engr.; b. Cullman, Ala., Feb. 3, 1932; s. Clarence M. and Myrtle (Silvey) B.; B.C.E., U. Fla., 1959; m. Florence Emily Pace, Dec. 24, 1954; children—Catherine Jane, Stephanie Jo. with Rader & Asso. Engrs., St. Petersburg, Fla., 1959-61, Misener Marine Constrn., Inc., St. Petersburg, 1961-62; project engr. Black, Crow & Eidsness Assos., Engrs., Clearwater, Fla., 1962-65; designer, project engr. Misener Marine Constrn., Inc., St. Petersburg Beach, 1965-69, v.p. engring. and sales, 1969-—. Served with USNR, 1951-55. Registered profl. engr., Fla., Ga., Tex. Mem. Am. Soc. C.E., Nat. Soc. Profl. Engrs., Fla. Engring. Soc. Democrat. Baptist. Kiwanian. Office: 115 75th Av S St Petersburg Beach FL 33736

BAYLEY, NED DUANE, govt. ofcl.; b. Battle Creek, Mich., Dec. 29, 1918; s. Howard G. and Beulah (Sperry) B.; B.S., Mich. State U., 1940; postgrad. U. Minn., 1940-41; Ph.D., U. Wis., 1950; student pub. adminstrn., Harvard, 1963-64; m. Lillian Joyce Safstrom, June 5, 1943; children—Gwen Ellen, Will Douglas, Fred Wallace. Asst. prof. U. Wis., 1948-53; asso. prof. U. Minn., 1953-55; with Dept. Agr., 1955-—, dir. sci. and edn. Office of Sec., 1968-—. Del. 4th FAO Far East Regional Conf. Animal Prodn. and Health. Ceylon, 1966. Recipient Outstanding Performance award Dept. Agr., 1965. Mem. Am. Dairy Sci. Assn., Am. Soc. Animal Prodn., A.A.A.S. (sec. sect. O, 1966-67). Author papers. Home: 13907 Overton Lane Silver Spring MD 20904 Office: Sci and Edn Office of Secretary Dept Agr Washington DC 20250

BAYNE, JAMES MANUEL, architect; b. Piggott, Ark., Dec. 24, 1928; s. Manley Earl and Mabel (Hodges) B.; B.S. in Archtl. Engring., U. Ill., 1951; postgrad. U. Miami, Coral Gables, Fla., 1955, Lawrence Inst. Tech., 1955; A.M.P., Harvard, 1971; m. Melba Lois Beckmeyer, June 5, 1951; children—Melanie Lee, Melissa Ann. Structural engr. Smith, Hinchman & Grylls, Detroit, 1951-53, architect 1955-61; architect, chief of planning and design Manned Spacecraft Center., NASA, Houston, 1961-66, architect, chief of constrn. Electronics Research Center, NASA, Cambridge, Mass., 1967-70, dir. design and constrn. NASA, Washington, 1970-71, dir. programs and engring., 1971-—. Instr. archtl. design and art Detroit Inst. Tech., 1956-61. Served with C.E., AUS, 1953-55. Mem. A.I.A. (active various nat., state coms.), Tex. Soc. Architects, Mich. Assn. Professions, Pi Kappa Phi (chpt. pres. 1950-51). Home: 4902 Tarheel Way Annandale VA 22003 Office: 600 Independence Av SW Washington DC 20003

BAYNHAM, JAMES COMER, tile mfg. co. exec.; b. Little Rock, May 29, 1924; s. James Dewitt and Agnes (Freyburger) B.; student Texarkana Jr. Coll., 1941-42, Oklahoma City U., 1950-51; m. Frances

Ferguson, Oct. 1, 1943; children—James, David, Patrick, Mary Katherine, Mark, Mary Margaret, John, Timothy. Sales mgr. Continental Baking Co., Oklahoma City and Dallas, 1946-62; v.p. Royal Tile Mfg. Co., Fort Worth, 1962—. In-firm chmn. United Fund, 1970-71. Served to capt. USAAF, 1942-46. Decorated Air medal. Mem. So. Tile Terrazzo and Marble Contractors Assn. (adv. council 1969-71), Tex. Tile Contractors Assn. (asso. dir. 1969-70), Tile Council Am. (marketing advt. com. 1969-71), Sales and Marketing Execs. Club. K.C. Home: 8184 San Leandro St Dallas TX 75218 Office: 3600 Conway St Fort Worth TX 76111

BAZELON, DAVID LIONEL, judge; b. Superior, Wis., Sept. 3, 1909; s. Israel and Lena (Krasnovsky) B.; student U. Ill., 1928-29; B.S. in Law, Northwestern U., 1931; LL.D., Colby Coll., 1966; LL.D., Boston U., 1969; m. Miriam M. Kellner, June 7, 1936; children—James A., Richard Lee. Admitted to Ill. bar, 1932, practiced law, 1932-35; asst. U.S. atty. No. Dist. Ill., in charge fed. tax matters, 1935-40; sr. mem. firm Gottlieb & Schwartz, 1940-46; asst. atty. gen. U.S. Lands Div., 1946-47, Office of Allen Property, 1947-49; judge U.S. Ct. of Appeals for D.C. Circuit, 1949—, chief judge, 1962—. Lectr. law and psychiatry U. Pa. Law Sch., 1957-58, 58-59; Sloan vis. prof. Menninger Found., Topeka, 1961-62; Regent's lectr. U. Cal., Los Angeles, 1964; mem. faculty dept. psychiatry Johns Hopkins U. Sch. Medicine, 1964—; clin. prof. psychiatry George Washington U., 1966—. Chmn. task force on law President's Panel on Mental Retardation; nat. cons. forensic medicine Surgeon Gen. of U.S. Air Force, 1964—; chmn. adv. com., model sch. div. D.C. Pub. Schs., 1964-66; mem. adv. com. Harvard U. Program Tech. and Soc., 1966—; nat. adv. mental health council USPHS, 1967-71; bd. dirs. Joint Commn. Mental Health Children, Inc., 1965—; mem. nat. adv. com. John F. Kennedy Center Research Edn. and Human Devel., 1968—; mem. com. on ethics Am. Heart Assn., 1968—; mem. Battelle-N.W. Behavioral and Social Sci. Cons. Panel, 1970; chmn. adv. bd. Boston U. Center for Law and Life Scis., 1970—; bd. dirs. Citizens Bd. Inquiry into Health Services for Ams., Washington, 1969—; mem. adv. com. on child devel. Nat. Research Council of Nat. Acad. Scis., 1971—; mem. adv. bd. P.R. Inst. Psychiatry, 1971—; mem. Twentieth Century Fund Task Force on Working Women, 1970—; mem. U.S. Mission on Mental Health to USSR, 1967. Bd. overseers Brandeis U. Center for Study of Violence; trustee Salk Inst. Biol. Studies. Recipient Isaac Ray award Am. Psychiat. Assn., 1960. Fellow Am. Psychiat. Assn. (hon.), Am. Acad. Arts and Scis.; mem. Am. Orthopsychiat. Assn. (pres.), Am., Fed. bar assns., Bar Assn. D.C., Nat. Assn. State Mental Health Program Dirs. (adv. council), Am. Psychol. Assn. Democrat. Jewish religion. Club: Cosmos. Home: 2700 Virginia Av NW Washington DC 20037 Office: US Ct House Washington DC 20001

BEACH, BESSIE MAE, physician; b. Seymour, Ind.; d. Omer and Georgia May (Blumer) Beach; B.S., U. Cin., 1929, B.M., 1933, M.D., 1934. Intern, U. Wis. Hosp., 1933-34; resident in pediatrics St. Christopher's Hosp. for Children, Phila., 1934-35, U. Cin., 1935-37; cons. pediatrics Bur. Maternal and Child Health, Wis. Bd. Health, 1937-39; asst. dir. Bur. Maternal and Child Health, Ala. Dept. Health, 1939-41; regional med. cons. U.S. Children's Bur., 1941-43; pvt. practice medicine specializing in pediatrics, Columbus, Ga., 1943-67; med. dir. Maternal and Infant Care Project, Greenville County (S.C.) Pub. Health Dept., 1967—. Mem. Am., N.C. med. assns., Greenville County Med. Soc., Am. Acad. Pediatrics, S.C. State Pediatric Soc., Am. Heart Assn., Am., S.C. pub. health assns., Zonta Internat., Alpha Epsilon Iota. Episcopalian. Mem. Order Eastern Star. Home: 17 Balentine Dr Greenville SC 29605 Office: Maternal and Infant Care Project Greenville Pub Health Dept University Ridge Greenville SC 29602

BEACH, CECIL PRENTICE, librarian; b. Knoxville, Tenn., July 12, 1927; s. Frank Alfred and Lillie Maude (Sims) B.; A.B., U. Chattanooga, 1950; M.A., Fla. State U., 1952; m. Doris Jean Pardue, Apr. 17, 1949 (div. 1968); children—Steven Prentice, Rex, Keven, Kyle, Quentin Anthony; m. 2d, Marcia Gibson, June 20, 1969. Bookmobile librarian Chattanooga Pub. Library, 1948-51; extension librarian Decatur (Ga.)-DeKalb Regional Library, 1952-54; dir. Piedmont Regional Library, Winder, Ga., 1954-60, Gadsden (Ala.) Pub. Library, 1960-64, Tampa (Fla.)-Hillsborough Library System, 1965-72, Tampa Pub. Library; librarian State of Fla., Tallahassee, 1972—. Cons. library bldgs. and service. Pres. Gadsden Community Council, 1963. Served with USNR, 1944-46. Mem Am., Southeastern, Ala., Ga., Fla. (pres. 1969-70) library assns., Adult Edn. Assn. (pres. 1967), Fla. State U. Alumni Assn. (pres. 1967). Democrat. Baptist. Mason. Home: Cline St Tallahassee FL 32303 Office: State Library Bldg Tallahassee FL 32301

BEACH, LOUIS ANDREW, physicist; b. Greenville, Ind., June 2, 1925; s. George Covert and Clara (Kiesler) B.; B.S., Ind. U., 1944, M.S., 1947, Ph.D., 1949; m. Virginia Ann McHugh, Oct. 20, 1956; children— Andrew, Ann Marie, Ruth Christine, Covert John. Research asso. Lab. Nuclear Studies, Cornell U., 1949-51; physicist Naval Research Lab., Washington, 1951—, head shielding sect., 1953-55, head nuclear reactions br., 1955-66, head physics I sect., cyclotron br., 1966-71, head nuclear physics sect., 1971—. Lectr. grad. program nuclear engring. Catholic U. Am., 1960—. Served with AUS, 1944-46. Fellow Washington Acad. Sci.; mem. Am. Phys. Soc., A.A.A.S., Philos. Soc. Wash. Democrat. Roman Catholic. Home: 1200 Waynewood Blvd Alexandria VA 22308 Office: Code 6611 Naval Research Lab Washington DC 20390

BEACH, ROBERT EDWARD, circuit judge; b. Hollywood, Cal., July 26, 1930; s. Kenneth Clyde and Dorothy (Monser) B.; B.A., U. Tampa, 1955; LL.B., Stetson U., 1958; m. Shirley Ann Powers, Sept. 8, 1956; children—Janet Ann, Stephanie Lynn, Patricia Jean, Paul Jonathan. Admitted to Fla. bar, 1958; practiced in St. Petersburg, Fla., 1961-68; circuit judge, St. Petersburg, 1968—. Chmn. Nat. Found. March of Dimes, 1969-70. Lion. Office: 6th Judicial Circuit Ct St Petersburg FL 33704

BEACH, ROBERT OLIVER, computer exec.; b. Washington, June 25, 1932; s. Oliver Fairmont and Aldora (Stone) B.; student George Washington U., 1950-51, 57-62; m. Patricia Carrington, May 9, 1952 (div.); children—Patricia Ann, Robert Edward, Michael Oliver, John Roger. With Engring. Research Corp., 1951-52; design engr. Nems-Clarke, 1952-55; project engr. Frederick Research Corp., 1955-59; project mgr. Am. Machine & Foundry Co., 1959-62; pres., founder SAID, Inc., Falls Church, Va., 1962—; real estate broker; comml. airplane pilot; cons. marketing and finance; v.p. Interstate Service Corp.; high sch. faculty adviser devel. data processing curriculum, 1971. Mem. Data Processing Mgmt. Assn., UNIVAC Users Assn., Aircraft Owners and Pilots Assn. Home: 500 N Roosevelt Blvd Falls Church VA 22044 Office: 1243 W Broad St Falls Church VA 22046

BEACH, WALTER EGGERT, assn. exec.; b. North Adams, Mass., Aug. 24, 1934; s. W. Edwards and Liselotte Josephine Sophie (von Usedom) B.; B.A., Dickinson Coll., 1956; M.A., George Washington U., 1961. Staff asso. Am. Polit. Sci. Assn., Washington, 1965-68, asst. dir., 1968—, editor PS, 1970—. Bd. dirs. Mt. Vernon Coll., Washington; trustee Prevention of Blindness Soc. Met. Washington. Served with AUS, 1956-58. Home: 5719 Chevy Chase Pkwy NW Washington DC 20015 Office: 1527 New Hampshire Av NW Washington DC 20036

BEACHAM, DANIEL WINSTON, physician. Clin. prof. obstetrics and gynecology Tulane U., New Orleans. Editor Synopsis of Gynecology. Address: Tulane U Sch Medicine 4240 Magnolia at Gen Pershing St New Orleans LA 70115*

BEACHAM, WOODARD DAVIS, physician; McComb, Miss., Apr. 10, 1911; s. Woodard D. and Ida (Felder) B.; B.A., U. Miss., 1932; B.S. 1933; M.D., Tulane U., 1935. Intern Charity Hosp. of La., New Orleans, resident obstetrics and gynecology; now sr. vis. surgeon; prof. clin. gynecology and obstetrics Tulane U. Sch. Medicine, 1949—; obstetrician and gynecologist So. Bapt. Hosp., pres. staff, 1961; past pres. surg. staff Charity Hosp., New Orleans; cons. Beacham Meml. Hosp. Magnolia, Miss., Hotel Dieu Sisters Hosp., New Orleans; pvt. practice, 1940—. Pres. Beacham Corp. Recipient A.C.S. medical records prize, 1943. Diplomate Am. Bd. Obstetrics and Gynecology. Fellow A.C.S. (gov. as rep. obstet., gynecol. sect. A.M.A. 1955-60, gov. as rep. Am. Gynecol. Soc. 1961-63; adv. council gynecology and obstetrics 1963-67, chmn. council 1967, past pres. La. chpt., 2d v.p.-elect 1971-72), Am. Gynecol. Soc. (council 1959, 60), Am. Assn. Obstetricians and Gynecologists (com. on material welfare 1960, v.p. 1970-71), Am. Coll. Obstetricians and Gynecologists (first pres., nominating com. 1972); mem. So. Gynecol. and Obstet. Soc. (pres. 1967), Am. (chem. sect. obstetrics and gynecology 1957-58), So. (chmn. sect. on obstetrics 1949, mem. council 1961-63, gen. chmn. arrangements ann. meeting 1972) 1961-63) med. assns., Internat. House, C. of C., La., Orleans Parish med. socs., New Orleans Grad. Med. Assembly (past pres.), New Orleans Gynecol. and Obstet. Soc. (past pres.), Conrad G. Collins Obstetric and Gynecologic Soc. Tulane U. (1st pres.), Central Assn. Obstetricians and Gynecologists (exec. com. 1948-52), Am. Assn. Med. Colls., U. Miss. Alumni Assn. (dir. 1962-65, past pres. New Orleans), Philippine Obstet. and Gynecol. Soc. (hon.), A.A.A.S., Assn. Profs. Gynecology and Obstetrics, Sigma XI, Alpha Omega Alpha, Phi Chi (grand presiding sr., nat. pres.), Beta Theta Pi. Methodist (trustee, mem. adminstrv. bd.) Clubs: Plimsoll, New Orleans Country. Author: (with Robert J. Crossen and Dan W. Beacham) Synopsis of Gynecology (5th edit.), (with Dan W. Beacham) 6th edit., 1963, 7th edit., 1967, 8th edit., 1972. Editor for gynecology and obstetrics Stedman's Med. Dictionary, 23d edit. Contbr. to publs. in field. Home: 1527 S Carrollton Av New Orleans LA 70118 Office: 4240 Magnolia at General Pershing St New Orleans LA 70115

BEACHUM, PEARL BOWERS, JR., dist. ct. judge; b. Wadesboro, N.C., Dec. 18, 1910; s. Pearl Bowers and Mary (Gaddy) B.; B.S., Davidson Coll., 1933; LL.B., George Washington U., 1939, J.D., 1939; m. Anne Thomason, Apr. 16, 1938; children—James Tyson, Susan Anne. Admitted to bar, 1939; with U.S. Fed. Land Bank Bd., 1933-34; accountant, Dept. of Agr., Columbia, S.C., 1934-39; with FBI, 1939-61; ret.; work in fields adminstrn., pub. relations, also instr. internal security law, 1942-61; judge Recorder's Ct., Charlotte, N.C., 1961-68; judge N.C. Gen. Ct. Justice, 1968—. Active Mecklenburg (N.C.) council Boy Scouts Am., Mecklenburg Council P.T.A.'s, Nat. Council Alcoholism (past bd. chmn. Charlotte). Bd. dirs. Goodwill Industries, Blind Assn., Family and Children Service, A.R.C. (all Charlotte). Mem. Am., N.C., D.C. bar assns., N.C. State Bar, N. Am. Judges Assn. (bd. govs. 1967—), Am. Judicature Soc., Soc. Former FBI Agts. Presbyn. (past pres. Men of Church). Rotarian. (bd. dirs. 1964-68, 70-71). Home: 2112 Beverly Dr Charlotte NC 28207 Office: Mecklenburg County Court House Charlotte NC 28207

BEACOM, JOHN PATRICK, broadcasting exec., mayor; b. St. Joseph, Mo., May 27 905; s. Timothy Patrick and Mary (Davies) B.; student Omaha U., 1923-25, U. Tulsa, 1925-27; B.A., Marshall Coll., 1930; m. Emily May Peed, July 15, 1955; children—Mary Davies, George Patrick. U.S. Army Sch. Mil. Govt., Charlottesville, Va., 1942—; pres., owner Beacom Broadcasting Enterprises, WDTV, Fairmont, W. Va., WTVX, Ft. Pierce, Fla., WVVW, Grafton, W. Va., WETZ, New Martinsville, W. Va., WBUT AM-FM, Butler, Pa., WAC-Y, Kissimee, Fla.; pub. pres. Mannington (W. Va.) Times. Mem. W.Va. Ho. of Reps., 1933-35, W.Va. Senate 1935-40; city dir., mayor, Fairmont, 1955-60; mayor City of St. Lucie (Fla.), 1965—. Mem. W. Va. Athletic Commn., 1950-53. Chmn., St. Lucie County Republican Exec. Com., 1971—. Mem. C. of C. (dir.). Clubs: University Nat. Broadcasters (Washington); Variety (Pitts.); Pelican Yacht, St. Lucie Country (Ft. Pierce). Home: 2811 N Indian River Dr St Lucie FL 33450 Office: Beacom Bldg 101 Atlantic Av Fort Pierce FL 33450

BEADLES, JACK ANDREWS, banker; b. Union City, Tenn., Oct. 20, 1914; s. Arleigh Joe and Mary (Stephens) B.; grad. Am. Inst. Banking, 1942; m. Jenny Eunice Jones, Nov. 20, 1951. With First Am. Nat. Bank, Nashville, 1937—, auditor, 1952—, v.p., 1962—, v.p., controller, since 1968—. Served with USAAF, 1942-45. Mem. Nat. Assn. Bank Audit, Control and Operation (pres. Nashville 1953-54), Nat. Assn. Accountants. Presbyn. Mason (32 degree). Home: 4210 Hillcrest Av Nashville TN 37204 Office: 326 Union St Nashville TN 37202

BEADLES, NICHOLAS ASTON, educator; b. Asheville, N.C., Nov. 28, 1918; s. Nicholas N. and Mary (Stikeleather) B.; A.B., U. N.C., 1940; M.A., U. Colo., 1957; Ph.D., Harvard, 1965; m. Cornelia Pegram, June 24, 1950; children—Mary Jane, Nicholas Aston II, Jessica Stuart, Samuel Jay Pegram. Instr., U. Colo., 1945-47, Wellesley Coll., 1950-52, Auburn U., 1954-55; faculty U. Ga., Athens, 1955—, prof. econs., 1966—, dir. supervisory and mgmt. devel. programs, 1960—. Dir. Asheville Coca-Cola Bottling Co.; Mem. Am. Arbitration Panel of Arbitrators, 1967—, Panel Mediation and Conciliation Service Arbitrators, 1969—; cons. indsl. relations and mgmt. devel. Served to 1st lt. AUS, 1942-45. Mem. Am., So. econs. assns., Indsl. and Labor Relations Research Assn., Am. Assn. U. Profs., Beta Gamma Sigma, Sigma Chi, Pi Gamma Mu. Episcopalian. Home: 113 Inverness Rd Athens GA 30601

BEAIRD, CHARLES T., machinery co. exec., educator; b. Shreveport, La., July 17, 1922; s. James Benjamin and Mattie Connell (Fort) B.; B.A., Centenary Coll., 1966; Ph.D. in Philosophy Columbia, 1972; m. Carolyn Williams, Feb. 6, 1943;children—Susan (Mrs. George M. McCormick), Marjorie (Mrs. M. Buie Seawell, Jr.), John B. Vice pres., gen. mgr. J.B. Beaird Corp., Shreveport, 1946-57; self employed in oil and investments, Shreveport, 1957-59; pres. Beaird-Poulan Inc., Shreveport, 1959—; dir. Westport Devel. Corp.; asst. prof. Centenary Coll., Shreveport, 1969—. Chmn. United Fund Campaign, 1962; mem. Caddo Parish Police Jury, 1956-60; active Young Presidents Orgn., 1961-68. Chmn. Caddo Parish Republican Exec. Com., 1952-56; del. Rep. Nat. Conv., 1956. Pres. Charles T. Beaird Found. Served to capt. USMCR, 1943-46. Decorated D.F.C., Air medal. Mem. C. of C. (v.p. 1965-66). Clubs: Shreveport, Shreveport Country, Demolselle (Shreveport) Home: 7030 E Ridge Dr Shreveport LA 71106 Office: P O Box 9329 Shreveport LA 71109

BEALE, BETTY (MRS. GEORGE K. GRAEBER), columnist; b. Washington; d. William Lewis and Edna (Sims) Beale; A.B., Smith Coll. Columnist Washington Post, 1937-40; reporter and columnist Evening Star, Washington, 1945—; weekly columnist Pubs. Hall Syndicate, Washington, 1953—; lectr. Named Am. Woman of Accomplishment, Multiple Sclerosis Soc.; recipient Assn. Fed. Investigator Spl. Act award, 1968, Freedom Found. award, 1969. Clubs: Washington Press, 1925 F Street (Washington). Home: 2926 Garfield St NW Washington DC 20008

BEALL, BILL, football coach Baylor U. Office: Athletic Dept Baylor U Waco TX 76706*

BEALL, PAUL RENSSELAER, aerospace cons.; b. Des Moines, Aug. 28, 1909; s. Ollie Monroe and Helen May (Paul) B.; A.B., Grinnell Coll., 1932; postgrad. in law Harvard, 1935-36; A.M., U. Mich., 1940; Ph.D., Pa. State U., 1948, spl. courses indsl. engring., 1948-50; m. Helen Minerva Wadsworth, Sept. 18, 1937; children—Helen (Mrs. Paul Gerken), Sarah, Christopher Wadsworth Paul, Nancy P. Eastern states sales mgr. Morrison-Shults Mfg. Co., leather products, 1932-39; teaching fellow speech U. Mich., 1939-41; from instr. to asso. prof. speech and rhetoric Pa. State U., 1941-50, lectr. indsl. engring. extension, 1941-50, summer sch. lectr. in communications problems in mgmt., 1951-57; dir. information, research and devel. bd. Dept. of Defense, 1950-51; sci. adviser to comdg. gen. Air Research and Devel. Command, 1952, to comdg. gen. for operations-USAF, 1953, to comdg. gen. USAF-Far East, 1955, 57; lectr. Joint U.S.-NATO commands in Europe, intermittently, 1955-58, cons. to founding faculty USAF Acad.; communications cons. in indsl. and mil. mgmt., 1953—; pres. Oglethorpe Coll., Atlanta, 1964-67; cons. aerospace industries, 1953—. Trustee, Aerospace Edn. Found. Cons., Community Welfare Drive, Greater Balt., 1955-57; mem. president's council Rollins Coll., Winter Park, Fla.; mem. visitors adv. council Grinnell Coll., 1962—; mem. tech. adv. com. Atlanta-Fulton County Econ. Opportunity Authority, 1965—. Mem. Speech Assn., Am. Arbitration Assn., Nat. Conf. Adminstrn. Research (pres. 1961), Air Force Assn. Episcopalian. Mason. Rotarian. Clubs: Cosmos (Washington) Racquet. Contbr. to tech. mags. Address: 323 Trismen Terrace Winter Park FL 32789

BEALLE, JOHN RUFUS, lawyer, univ. ofcl.; b. Tuscaloosa, Ala., May 6, 1918; s. John Rufus and Josie (Bell) B.; A.B., U. Ala., 1940, J.D., 1942; m. Elizabeth Ann Turner. Oct 26, 1948; children—John Rufus, Sally Hays. Admitted to Ala. bar, 1942, partner firm Davis and Bealle, Tuscaloosa, 1946-49; county solicitor, Tuscaloosa County, 1949-51; city atty., Northport, Ala., 1952-54; atty., land commr., sec. bd. trustees U. Ala., 1953-69, exec. sec. bd. trustees, gen. counsel, 1969—. Supr. in bankruptcy Western div. No. Dist. Ala., 1946-48. Past chmn. Tuscaloosa County Bd. Pub. Welfare. Pres. Black Warrior council Boy Scouts Am., 1961; v.p. Tuscaloosa County United Fund, 1962. Mem. exec. com., Tuscaloosa County Democratic Com., 1946-60, sec., 1947-60, chmn., 1946-47. Treas. U. Ala. Law Sch. Found. Served from 2d lt. to maj. A.A.A., AUS, 1942-46: now col. Res. ret. Past chmn. Ala. Jr. Bar Assn. Mem. Nat. Assn. Coll. and Univ. Attys. (dir. 1962-72, v.p. 1966, pres. 1969-70), U. Ala. Law Sch. Alumni Assn. (sec., treas. 1949). Res. Officers Assn. (pres. Tuscaloosa 1947, pres. Ala. dept. 1962), Am. Bar Assn., Newcomen Soc. N. Am., Omicron Delta Kappa, Pi Kappa Alpha, Phi Delta Phi. Presbyn. (elder). Home: 194 The Highlands Tuscaloosa AL 35401 Office: U Ala University AL 35486

BEAMAN, NATHANIEL, III, banker; b. Norfolk, Va., Apr. 29, 1925; s. Robert P. and Salome (Slingluff) B.; A.B. Duke, 1945, J.D., 1949; m. Elizabeth Middleton Dashiell, Dec. 28, 1950; children—Nathaniel IV, Elizabeth Johns, William Prentis. Admitted to Va. bar, 1949; practiced in Norfolk, 1949-50, 62-66, asso. firm Breeden & Hoffman, 1949-50; asso. trust officer First Citizens Bank & Trust Co., Raleigh, N.C., 1952-54; v.p., trust officer So. Bank of Norfolk, 1955-62; v.p., trust officer First & Mchts. Nat. Bank, Norfolk, 1966—, dir., Norfolk adv. bd. 1967—; pres., dir. So. Ins. Agy. Treas. DePaul Hosp. Bldg. Fund; bd. dirs. Tidewater (Va.) Heart Assn.; trustee Norfolk Found.; vice chmn. bd. Norfolk City Employees Retirement Trust. Served to lt. USNR, 1943-46, 50-52. Mem. Tidewater Duke Alumni Assn. (v.p.), Am., Va., Norfolk-Portsmouth bar assns., Va. Bankers Assn., Norfolk Assembly, Navy League, English Speaking Union, Kappa Alpha, Phi Delta Phi. Episcopalian. Clubs: Norfolk German (sec.), Norfolk Yacht and Country, Harbor (Norfolk). Home: 5220 Edgewater Dr Norfolk VA 23508 Office: One Bank St Norfolk VA 23510

BEAMS, JESSE WAKEFIELD, educator; b. Belle Plaine, Kan., Dec. 25, 1898; s. Jesse Wakefield and Kathryn (Wylie) B.; A.B., Fairmount (Kan.) Coll., 1921; M.A., U. Wis., 1922; Ph.D., U. Va., 1925; Sc.D., William and Mary Coll., 1941; Sc.D., U. N.C., 1946; Sc.D., Washington and Lee U., 1949; Sc.D., Fla. Inst. Tech., 1969; m. Maxine Sutherland, June 16, 1931. Instr. physics and math. Ala. Poly. Inst., 1922-23; Nat. Research fellow U. Va., 1925-26, Yale, 1926-27; instr. physics Yale, 1927-28; asso. prof. physics U. Va., Charlottesville, 1928-30, prof., 1930-69, prof. emeritus, 1969—, Francis H. Smith prof. physics, chmn. dept. physics, 1948-62. Recipient Potts med. Franklin Inst., 1942; John Scott award, 1956; Alumni Achievement award U. Wichita; Thomas Jefferson award, Nat. medal Sci., 1967. Fellow Am. Phys. Soc. (pres. 1958-59), A.A.A.S. (chmn. sect. B., 1943); mem. Am. Acad. Arts and Scis., Am. Philos. Soc. (Lewis award 1958, v.p. 1960-62), Am. Optical Soc., Va. Acad. Sci. (pres. 1947), Am. Physics Tchrs. Assn., Am. Assn. U. Profs., Nat. Acad. Scis., Phi Beta Kappa, Sigma Xi, Sigma Pi Sigma (hon.), Raven Soc. Club: Colonnade. Author numerous articles. Home: 1705 Kenwood Lane Charlottesville VA 22901

BEAN, ALAN L., astronaut; b. Wheeler, Tex., Mar. 15, 1932; s. Arnold H. Bean; B.S. in Aero. Engring., U. Tex., 1955; grad. U.S. Navy Test Pilot Sch.; postgrad. U. So. Cal. Sch. Aviation Safety; m. Sue Ragsdale; children—Clay, Amy Sue. Commd. ensign U.S. Navy, 1955, advanced through grades to capt.; project officer various aircraft for preliminary evaluation, initial trials, final bd. inspection and survey trials. Patuxent, Md., 1960-63; replacement pilot Attack Squadron 44, Cecil Field, Fla., 1963, then Attack Squadron 172; astronaut with Manned Spacecraft Center, NASA, 1963—; lunar module pilot Apollo XII flight to moon, 1969. Decorated D.S.M.; recipient Distinguished Service medal NASA, Man of Year award Tex. Press Assn., 1969, Rear Adm. William S. Parsons award for sci. and tech. progress, 1970; Distinguished Grad. award U. Tex., 1970, Distinguished Alumnus award, 1970; Godfrey L. Cabot award, 1970, Spl. Trustees award Nat. Acad. Television Arts and Scis., 1970. Fellow Am. Astronautical Soc.; mem. Soc. Exptl. Test Pilots, Delta Kappa Epsilon. Home: 18706 Point Lookout Dr Houston TX 77058 Office: Manned Spacecraft Center NASA Houston TX 77058

BEAN, WILLIAM RUSSELL, architect; b. Erwin, Tenn., Oct. 26, 1930; s. Joseph and Beryl (Franks) B.; B.S. in Archtl. Engring., U. Miami (Fla.), 1958; certificate in architecture and city planning Ecole de Beaux Arts, Fontainebleu, France, 1958; m. Sally Ann Neumann, Aug. 27, 1955; children—Jennifer Ann, Alison Scott. Draftsman, designer Stefan H. Zachar, A.I.A., Miami Beach, Fla., 1955-59, Hugh J. Leitch, A.I.A., Pensacola, Fla., 1959-60, Barron, Heinberg & Brocato, Pensacola, 1960-62; individual practice as architect, Pensacola, 1962—. Mem. bd. supervising architects Fla. Hotel and Restaurant Commn., 1967-71. Mem. N.W. Fla. Regional Health Planning Council, 1968-71; bd. advisers Pensacola Acad. Arts and Scis., 1968—; bd. dirs. Pensacola Arts Council, 1971—. Served with

USNR, 1950-54. Mem. A.I.A. (corporate mem., chpt. sec. 1966-67), Fla. Assn. Architects, Navy League, Pensacola C. of C. Rotarian. Home: 2740 Bayou Blvd Pensacola FL 32503 Office: Davis Office Park 5514 N Davis Hwy Pensacola FL 32503

BEANE, JOHN WALTERS, dentist; b. Lake Worth, Fla., Dec. 4, 1928; s. Edgar Graham and Virginia Kathryn (Priddy) B.; B.S., Fla. So. Coll., 1951; D.D.S. (Research fellow), Emory U., 1957; m. Mary Sue Weathersbee, Nov. 18, 1950; children—Alden Graham, John Dale. Tchr. Northside High, Atlanta, 1951-52; teaching fellow in biochemistry Emory U., 1954-55; practice of dentistry, Lake Worth, Fla., 1957—; dir. Fed. Savs. and Loan Assn. Mgr. Youth Baseball Assn., 1968—; pres. R. Kent Smith Meml. Scholarship Fund, 1968—. Served with AUS, 1946-48. Mem. Am., Fla., Palm Beach County dental assns., S.A.R., Atlantic Coast Dental Research Clinic (charter mem.), C. of C. Presbyn. Rotarian (treas. 1965-66). Home: 2301 N Federal Hwy Lake Worth FL 33460 Office: 509 Lake Av Lake Worth FL 33460

BEARD, G.W., univ. ofcl.; B.S., Auburn U. Faculty, Auburn (Ala.) U., 1937—, athletic dir., 1951—. Address: Athletic Dept Auburn University Auburn AL 36830*

BEARD, MARION FOREE, physician; b. Shelbyville, Ky., Nov. 29, 1905; s. Samuel Lowery and Jessie L. (McClure) B.; A.B., U. Louisville, 1927, M.D., 1930; m. Margaret Jefferson, Dec. 26, 1930. Intern, resident pathology Louisville Gen. Hosp., 1930-32; instr. pathology U. Louisville, 1932-34, asso. prof. medicine, 1953-65, clin. prof., 1965—; practicing medicine, specializing internal medicine, Louisville, 1935-40, specializing hematology, Louisville, 1941—; instr. research hematology Ohio State U., 1940-41; pres. staff Ky. Bapt. Hosp., 1967. Recipient Gold medal Am. Soc. Clin. Pathologists, 1940; citation Transylvania Coll., 1956, U. Louisville, 1956. Fellow A.C.P., Internat. Soc. Hematology; mem. Am. Fedn. Clin. Research, N.Y. Acad. Scis., A.A.A.S., Am. Soc. Hematology, Sigma Xi, Alpha Omega Alpha. Clubs: Louisville Boat, Pendennis (Louisville). Home: 9 Woodhill Rd Louisville KY 40207 Office: Medical Towers Louisville KY 40202

BEARD, RICHARD, state ofcl.; b. Nashville, Apr. 9, 1903; s. Richard Beard and Lillian (Yeagrin) B.; ed. Washington and Lee U.; m. Mary Emma Pope; children—Richard, Edward Ewing. Pres. Nat. Distbrs., Inc., 1938-42; owner Glendale Mills & Supply Co., Trussville, Ala., 1942-67; commr. Ala. State Dept. Agr. and Industries, 1967—. Councilman, Trussville, 1947-56. Mem. Ala. Cattlemen's Assn., Am. Cattlemen's Assn., Kappa Sigma. Address: 2776 S Colonial Dr Montgomery AL 36111*

BEARD, RICHARD LEONARD, educator; b. Findlay, O., Dec. 10, 1909; s. Jesse William and Mae (Leonard) B.; A.B., Findlay Coll., 1936; M.A., Bowling Green State U., 1936; Ph.D., Ohio State U., 1943; m. Reva Leona Coleman, July 3, 1937; children—Elaine Louise (Mrs. A.W. Pinkerton, Jr.), John Coleman. Tchr. English, Elida (O.) pub. schs., 1936-37; head English dept. Whitmer High Sch., Toledo, 1937-42; asst., then instr. Ohio State U., Columbus, 1942-43; asst. prof. edn. U. No. Ia., Cedar Falls, 1946-48; prof. edn. Marshall U., Huntington, W.Va., 1948-52; asso. prof. edn. U. N.C., Chapel Hill, 1952-57; head counselor tng. N.C. Coll. at Durham, 1952-56; chmn., prof. edn., counselor edn. dept. U. Va., Charlottesville, 1957—. Lectr. radio sta. KXEL, Waterloo, Ia., 1947-48; TV instr. WUNC, Chapel Hill, N.C., 1954-57; ednl. cons. Served to 1st lt. AUS and USAAF, 1943-46; CBI. Mem. Am., Va. (Career Service award 1967) personnel and guidance assns., Am. Assn. Counselor Edn. and Supervision, Nat. Vocational Guidance Assn., N.E.A., Va. Edn. Assn., Nat. Soc. for Study Edn., Phi Delta Kappa (Distinguished Service award Va. chpt. 1966). Home: 1812 Meadowbrook Heights Rd Charlottesville VA 22901

BEARD, MRS. SAMUEL CLEMENS (MATTIE CARSON DUNCAN BEARD), ret. assn. exec.; b. Leesburg, Tenn., Feb. 28, 1888; d. Joseph Barkley and Mattie Elizabeth (Carson) Duncan; A.B., Stonewall Jackson Coll., 1911; m. Samuel Clemens Beard, Feb. 25, 1914; children—Samuel Clemens. Ruth Duncan (Mrs. Clarence K. Farris), Mattie Louise (Mrs. Robert N. Reams), Anna Lynn (Mrs. Wesley V. Haddock). Dir. legislation Tenn. W.C.T.U., 1950-51, rec. sec., 1951-53, pres. 1953-71; sec. missionary edn. Holston Conf., Woman's Soc. Christian Service, 1940-46; mem. Civil Defense Com. of Tenn.; Bible tchr., pulpit and chapel guest speaker. Mem. bd. edn. Holston Conf. Meth. Ch., 1942-46, bd. temperance, 1954-60; accredited dean, Christian Worker's Schs., Holston Conf. Mem. W.C.T.U. (life; pres. Jonesboro 1965-68, nat. chmn. lit. com. 1955-71), Internat. Platform Assn., Women's Soc., Christian Service (life), Gamma Delta. Methodist (ofcl. bd. mem., chmn. commn. Christian social concerns). Clubs: Federated, Music, Garden Tenn. Women's Press and Authors. Author: The WCTU in the Volunteer State: Handbook of Tenn. WCTU, 1951; 2d edit., 1967; Historical Pageant-On Sun-Crowned Heights; We Build for Tomorrow; Frances Willard Day in Public Schools; also booklets in field; poems. Editor: The Open Door, 1953—. Home: 102 N Cherokee Av Jonesboro TN 37659

BEARD, WINSTON CLINGAN, economist, educator; b. Camden, Ark., Apr. 17, 1930; s. Cleburne M. and Ruby (Bullock) B.; B.A., Ouachita Baptist U., 1953; M.B.A., U. Ark., 1954; Ph.D., U. Ill., 1961; m. Mildred Shaffer, June 25, 1955; children—Jon Winston, Kevin David. Research economist Indsl. Research Center, U. Ark., 1958-62; asst. prof. finance U. Tex., 1962-65; prof. econs., chmn. dept. Baylor U., 1965-67; exec. dir. Ark. Planning Commn., 1967-69; prof. econs. and finance, head dept. U. Ark., Little Rock, 1969—. Mem. Am. Econ. Assn., Am. Finance Assn., Financial Analysts Fedn., Inst. Chartered Financial Analysts, Beta Gamma Sigma, Omicron Delta Epsilon, Alpha Kappa Psi. Home: 1112 Yosemite Valley Dr Little Rock AR 72207

BEARDEN, HARLIE, physician; b. Claremore, Okla., Sept. 3, 1924; s. Buchanon H. and Rilla (Newport) B.; B.S., Centenary Coll., 1953; M.D., La. State U., 1957; m. Mary Jane Marine, Dec. 23, 1947; children—William H., Robin Jean. Intern USPHS Hosp., New Orleans, 1957-58; gen. practice resident Charity Hosp., Lafayette, La., 1958; pvt. practice medicine, specializing in family practice, Jennings, La., 1958—; mem. staff Am. Legion Hosp., Jennings; med. examiner FAA. Pres., bd. dirs. Southwest La. Tb-RD Assn., 1968—. Served with USAF, 1943-50; PTO. Recipient Air medal with three oak leaf clusters; recipient 12 Battle Stars. Diplomate Am. Bd. Family Practice. Mem. Am. Acad. Family Practice, Alpha Omega Alpha, Phi Kappa Phi, Omicron Delta Kappa, Alpha Sigma Chi, Lambda Chi Alpha. Kiwanian (pres. 1967). Home: 410 Decker St Jennings LA 70546 Office: 711 N Main St Jennings LA 70546

BEARDEN, JAMES HUDSON, ednl. adminstr.; b. Marion, Ala., Sept. 25, 1933; s. Joseph N. and Lulu (Worrell) B.; A.A., Marion Inst., 1953; B.S., Centenary Coll. La., 1956; M.A., E. Carolina U., 1959; Ph.D. (Grad. fellow), U. Ala., 1966; m. Pauline Larkins, Mar. 31, 1961; children—James Hudson, Pauline Larkins. Bus. mgr. Marion Inst., 1959-60; instr. E. Carolina U., Greenville, N.C., 1959-61, asst. prof. bus., 1961-63, asso. prof., 1963-64, prof., 1964—, dir. bur. business research, 1964-68, asst. dean, 1967-68, dean, 1968—. Chmn. tchr. edn. com. State Dept. Pub. Instrn., 1970—; vice chmn. Gov.'s Adv. Com. Econs. and Environment, 1970—; econ. adv. Gov.'s Com. on Indsl. Devel., 1969—. Mem. Bd. Edn., Greenville City Schs., 1969—. Bd. dirs. Pitt County United Fund, Tar River Basin Devel. Assn.; trustee N.C. Council Econ. Edn. Served with AUS, 1956-58. Nat. Assn. Purchasing Agts. Research fellow, 1962; Birmingham Sales Execs. fellow, 1963. Mem. Am. Assn. U. Profs., Am. Marketing Assn., Assn. Edn. Internat. Business, N.C. World Trade Assn., So. Econ. Assn., So. Marketing Assn., Beta Gamma Sigma, Delta Sigma Pi, Pi Omega Pi. Rotarian (bd. dirs. 1969-70). Author: Personal Selling: Behavioral Science Readings and Cases, 1967; The Environment of Business: Perspectives and Viewpoints, 1969. Home: 106 Crown Point Rd Greenville NC 27834 Office: School of Business East Carolina University Greenville NC 27834

BEARDEN, WALTER CHURCHILL, civil engr.; b. Asheville, N.C., Mar. 4, 1898; s. William Rankin and Catherine Madeline (Doherty) B.; ed. pub. schs.; m. Florence Helen Carter, Apr. 11, 1923; children—Florence, Madeline, Walter Churchill. Partner Carter & Bearden, Engrs., Asheville, N.C., 1936-43, 46-50, 62-70; head civil engring. dept. Six Assos., Inc., Asheville, 1957-61; treas. Colburn & Gove Co., Engrs., Asheville, 1961-62; self-employed as cons. engr., Asheville, 1970—. Served with USMC, 1918-19; served to capt. C.E., USNR, 1943-46, 50-57. Decorated Bronze Star medal. Registered profl. engr., N.C., S.C. Fellow Am. Soc. C. E.; mem. Nat. Soc. Profl. Engrs., Profl. Engrs. of N.C., Soc. Am. Mil. Engrs., N.C. Soc. of Engrs., N.C. Soc. Surveyors, Am. Water Works Assn., N.C. Water Pollution Control Assn. Democrat. Episcopalian. Club: Civitan (pres. 1963) (Ashevillle). Home: Bridle Path Asheville NC 28804 Office: Northwestern Bank Bldg Asheville NC 28801

BEARDSLEY, PAUL WESLEY, ednl. adminstr.; b. Newstraitsville, O.; Aug. 20, 1921; s. Arthur Hiram and Hazel (Murray) B.; student Kemper Sch., Boonville, Mo., 1939-41, Okla. Bapt. U., 1941-42; B.A., Centenary Coll., Shreveport, La., 1948; M.A., U. Okla., 1949; Ph.D., U. Colo., 1966; m. Bonnie Jean Smith, June 13, 1942; children—Michael Paul Wesley, Mark Arthur, Christopher Murray. Chief announcer, asst, program dir. KWKH, Shreveport, La., 1945-48; grad. asst., instr. U. Okla., 1948-50; prof., chmn. dept. speech-theatre Austin Coll., Sherman, Tex., 1950-66, adminstrv. dean, 1967-68, exec. dean, 1968-72, dean continuing edn., 1972—. Lectr., communications cons., performer. Active United Fund, Sherman, 1960—. Served to 1st lt. AUS, 1942-46. Recipient United Fund award, 1962, Lions Club award, 1954. Mem. Speech Communications Am., Southwestern Theatre Conf., Am., Tex. ednl. theatre assns., Tex. Speech Assn., Tex. Ednl. Television Assn., Nat. Soc. Study Communication, Sherman C. of C., Alpha Psi Omega, Pi Delta Phi. Democrat. Episcopalian. Rotarian. Analytical studies of utilization of ednl. media in current speech programs of colls. and univs. in Tex.; devel. ednl. arena theatre in Tex.; devel. religious drama in S.W. Home: 1102 N Grand Av Sherman TX 75090

BEARSE, GEORGE FRANCIS, dentist; b. South Harwich, Mass., Apr. 19, 1895; s. David Wilmot and Florine Frances (Nickerson) B.; D.M.D., Tufts U., 1917; postgrad. Harvard, 1927; m. Vema Helen Pace, Sept. 21, 1920; 1 dau., Nancy (Mrs. Thomas Ackroyd Clingan, Jr.). Pvt. practice prosthetic dentistry, Cambridge, Mass., 1920-61. Rep. Milton (Mass.) Town Meeting, 1930-51. Served to capt. Dental Corps, U.S. Army, 1917-19. Decorated French Marne medal, Verdun medal. Fellow Am. Acad. Dental Sci.; mem. Sr. Soc. Harvard Sch. Dental Medicine, Mass. Dental Soc., Am. Dental Assn., Am. Legion (del. 1st Mass. conv. 1919), World War I Vets. Assn., Ret. Physicians and Dentists Club (co-organizer 1966, 1st pres. 1966), Delta Sigma Delta (grand master Boston chpt. 1933). Republican. Presbyn. Mason. Club: Colony Cabana (Delray Beach, Fla.). Home: 661 SW 4th St Boca Raton FL 33432

BEASLEY, CHARLES ARTHUR, banker, lawyer; b. Garland, Ark., Mar. 13, 1918; s. Charles Arthur and Susie (Moore) B.; student Ouachita Coll., 1935-37; J.D., U. Ark., 1940; m. Mary Frances Romaine, Jan. 11, 1942; children—Charles Arthur, Robert Burke, John Romaine. Admitted to Ark. bar, 1940; practiced in Texarkana, Ark., 1940-41; asst. U.S. atty., Fort Smith, Ark., 1941-53; practiced in Fort Smith, Ark., 1953-62; v.p., trust officer 1st Nat. Bank Fort Smith; 1962—; dir. 1st Fed. Savs. and Loan Assn. Fort Smith, Bank of Mulberry. Bd. dirs. Fort Smith Pub. Library, Salvation Army, Bost Sch. for Limited Children, Inc., Harbor House, Inc., A.R.C. Served with USNR, 1942-46. Mem. C. of C., Kappa Sigma. Methodist (chmn. bd. 1966-67, dist. lay leader, 1963-65). Mason (32 degree). Club: Exchange (Fort Smith). Home: 613 Clifton Ct Fort Smith AR 72901 Office: 6th and Garrison Sts Fort Smith AR 72901

BEASLEY, JAMES ALLEN, mech. engr.; b. Indpls., June 29, 1929; s. Price and Viola (Beck) B.; B.S.M.E., Purdue U., 1958; m. Mary Helen Glende, Sept. 29, 1950; children—Michele (Mrs. Haco Wilhelm Detlof von Hacke), Bryan Edward, Elizabeth Monroe, Bradford Palmer. Mfg. engr. Boeing Corp., Seattle, 1958-62, asst. project mgr., New Orleans, 1962-65, mgr., mfg. devel. Huntsville, Ala., 1965-69, mgr. engring. lab., 1969—. Co-sponsor Youth Cultural Exchanges Guatemala and Huntsville, Ala., 1967-68. Finance chmn. Madison County Republican Com., 1969. Registered profl. engr., Ala. Mem. Am. Rocket Soc., Soc. Aerospace Materials and Process Engrs., Huntsville Assn. Tech. Socs., Internat. Assn. of Educators for World Peace (dir. Huntsville chpt. 1970-71), Delta Tau Kappa. Club: Boeing Mgmt. (exec. v.p. 1970-71). Home: 1116 Brookmeade St Huntsville AL 35805 Office: Huntsville Indsl Council Bldg Oakwood Huntsville AL 35801

BEASLEY, JOHN HARVEY, loan co. exec.; b. Hart County, Ga., Apr. 26, 1901; s. John Bart and Effie (Smith) B.; student pub. schs.; m. Lucile Elizabeth Brown, Apr. 5, 1921; 1 son, Walter George. Farmer, Lavonia, Ga., 1941—; with Lavonia Mfg. Co., 1925—, laborer, yard foreman, mgr. Girmery, v.p., 1945—; pres., treas. Farmers Equipment Co., Lavonia, 1945—; pres. Franklin Bldg. & Loan Assn., Lavonia, 1948—. Ga. Coins, Inc. Trustee, Truett-McConnell Coll. Lt. col. Ga. Gov's Staff, 1959-67. Recipient Sr. Dealer award Internat. Harvester Co., 1970. Mem. Ga. Farm Equipment Assn. (life dir., pres. 1962), Ga. Sheriff's Assn., Farm Bur., U.S. Jaycees (hon. life), Lavonia C. of C. Baptist. Mason (Shriner). Home: RFD 2 Lavonia GA 30553 Office: S Main St Lavoina GA 30553

BEASLEY, JOHN SNODGRASS, II, lawyer, banker; b. Franklin, Tenn., Oct. 2, 1930; s. Thomas Earl and Elsie (Eggleston) B.; B.A., Vanderbilt U., 1952, J.D., 1954; m. Mary D. Allison Tidman, Sept. 4, 1958; children—John Snodgrass III, Eleanor Christensen. Admitted to Tenn. bar, 1954; practiced in Franklin, 1957-58; exec. sec. Vanderbilt U. Alumni Assn., 1958-62; asst. dean, asst. prof. law Vanderbilt U. Law Sch., Nashville, 1962-64, asso. dean, asst. prof. law, 1964-66, asso. dean, asso. prof. law, 1966-69, asso. dean, prof. law, 1970-71; sr. v.p., head trust dept. Commerce Union Bank, Nashville, 1971—; pres., dir. Pebblestone Ct., Inc., Franklin; sec., dir. Cumberland Machinery Co., Nashville. Mem. bd. Franklin Spl. Sch. Dist. Trustee Battle Ground Acad., Tenn. Bot. Gardens and Fine Arts Center; pres. Coverdale Scholarship Found., 1965-67. Bd. dirs. Nashville Symphony Assn., 1959-65, pres., 1962-64; bd. dirs. Heritage Found. of Franklin and Williamson County (pres. 1968). Served with USNR, 1954-57. Mem. Am., Tenn. bar assns., Assn. Preservation Tenn. Antiquities (trustee 1962-70), Order of Coif, Phi Beta Kappa, Omicron Delta Kappa, Sigma Chi, Pi Delta Epsilon, Phi Delta Phi. Republican. Episcopalian. Clubs: Carnton (Franklin); University, Nashville City, Cumberland (Nashville). Home: 335 4th Av S Franklin TN 37064 Office: Commerce Union Bank 400 Union St Nashville TN 37219

BEASLEY, PERCY EUGENE, supt. schs.; b. Rocky Ford, Ga., Oct. 23, 1914; s. Stephen Enoch and Lillia Jane (Fennell) B.; A.B., Furman U., 1938; M.Ed., U. S.C., 1947; m. Amelia Evangeline Schroder, May 31, 1938; children—Stephen Tully, Frederick Alexander, James Fennell. Prin., coach Springfield (S.C.) High Sch., 1938-42; supt. schs., Salley, S.C., 1943-50; supt. Salley and Windsor Area Schs., 1950-54; supervisory prin. elementary schs., Aiken, S.C., 1954-58, supt. schs. adminstrv. area 1, Aiken, 1968—. Mem. state Com. Accreditation Elementary Schs., 1948-49. Served as lt. (j.g.) USNR, 1943-46. Mem. Nat., S.C., Aiken County (pres. 1948) edn. assns., Am., S.C. assns. sch. adminstrs. Mason, Lion. Home: 205 Barnard Av SE Aiken SC 29801 Office: Box 657 Aiken SC 29801

BEASLEY, WILLIAM ROBERT, dentist; b. Richmond, Va., Aug. 22, 1927; s. Joseph Dewitt and Jenneill (Allison) B.; B.S., U. Richmond, 1953; D.D.S., Med. Coll. Va., 1957; m. Betty Bolling Hurt, Dec. 27, 1952; children—Mark Dewitt, Jenneill Allison, John Stringfellow, James Thornton. Intern oral surgery Med. Coll. Va. Hosp., 1957-58; resident oral surgery U. Ia. Hosp., 1958-60, asst. prof. oral surgery, 1960-64; pvt. practice dentistry, specializing in oral surgery, Harrisonburg, Va., 1964—; cons. oral surgery VA Hosp., Iowa City, Ia., 1960-64. Pres. local unit Am. Cancer Soc., 1971-72; pres. Shenandoah Valley Choral Soc., 1970—; pres. Valley Players, 1967-68; scoutmaster Cub Scouts Am., 1967-68. Bd. dirs. Shenandoah Valley Music Festival, 1970—. Served with USNR, 1945-48. Diplomate Am. Bd. Oral Surgery. Mem. Am., Southeastern, Va. (pres. 1971-72) socs. oral surgeons. Elk, Rotarian. Contbr. articles to dental jours. Home: Route 1 Forest Hills Harrisonburg VA 22801 Office: 725 S Mason St Harrisonburg VA 22801

BEATCHFORD, JOSEPH H., govt. ofcl. Dir. ACTION, Washington. Home: 125 Queen St Alexandria VA 23314 Office: 806 Connecticut Av SW Washington DC 20006

BEATTIE, JACK ROBERT, dentist; b. Bay City, Mich., Oct 2, 1934; s. Aaron Joseph and Sadie Evelyn (Young) B.; B.A., Mich. State U., 1956; D.D.S., U. Mich., 1960; M.S., Western Reserve U., 1963; m. Ernestine Linda Johnson, June 27, 1959; children—John Robert, Jeffrey Lind, Kimberly Young, Beattie. Orthodontist, Orlando, Fla., 1963—. Guest lectr. Internat. Acad. Stomatology, Lima, Peru, 1965. Chmn. Orange County (Fla.) Republican Exec. Com., 1968—; mem. Fla. delegation Rep. Nat. Conv., 1968, 72. Recipient Milo Hellman Research award Am. Assn. Orthodontists, 1964. Mem. Am., Fla., Central Dist., Orange County dental assns., Fla. Orthodontic Soc., Am. Assn. Orthodontists, So. Soc. Orthodontists. Mem. All-Am. Collegiate Swimming Team, 1955. Home: 561 Via Lugano Winter Park FL 32789 Office: 618 E South St Orlando FL 32801

BEATTY, BEULAH LEE COOPER (MRS. JOHN DAY BEATTY), club woman, genealogist; b. Louisburg, N.C., May 28, 1901; d. Willie Jackson and Annie Laura (Bowden) Cooper; student Louisburg Coll., 1918-19, 25-26; m. John Day Beatty, July 14, 1926; children—Laura Day (Mrs. Clyde Buchanan Rosser), Beulah (Mrs. Andrews), Neill McLaurin. Genealogist, 1959—. Historian, Bladen County Hist. Soc., 1963—; pres. Bladen Stars chpt. U.D.C., 1961-64, N.C. div. v.p., 1964-66, treas. N.C. div., 1966-68; dir. dist. 3, Wilmington Presbytery Women Ch., 1966-68; pres. Lord Craven chpt. Colonial Dames 17th Century, 1964-66, registrar, 1966-72. Active civic, polit. affairs of Bladen County. Mem. Daus. Founders and Patriots Am. (registrar N.C. Soc. 1970—). D.A.R. (regent Battle of Elizabethtown chpt. 1971—), Huguenot Soc. S.C., Nat. Geneal. Soc., New Eng. Historic Geneal. Soc. N.C. Soc. County and Local Historians. Democrat. Presbyn. Home: PO Box 905 Elizabethtown NC 28337

BEATTY, FLOY WARD (MRS. RICHMOND CROOM BEATTY), book editor; b. Birmingham, Ala., Apr. 25, 1908; d. Walter Rowland and Monica (Morris) Ward; A.B., Birmingham So.-Coll., 1928; m. Richmond Croom Beatty, May 7, 1927 (dec. Oct. 1961). Asso. book editor and youth columnist Nashville Tennessean, 1959-61, book editor, 1961—. Mem. Theta Sigma Phi. Home: 1808 Lombardy Lane Nashville TN 37215 Office: Nashville Tennessean 1100 Broadway Nashville TN 37201

BEATTY, JAMES TULLY, indsl. chem. and equipment exec., state ofcl.lb. N.Y.C., Oct. 28, 1934; s.; Henry Elder and Mary (Guccione) B.; A.B., U. N.C., 1957; m. Barbara Ann Harmon, Feb. 20, 1960; children— James Tully, Mary Kathleen. With Harmon Products Co., Inc., Gastonia; mem. N.C. Ho. of Reps., 1966—. Guest commentator ABC-TV Wide World of Sports, 1964—; mem. U.S. Olympic Com., 1965—; alumni rep. U. N.C. Athletic Council, 1967—. Served with AUS, 1957-58. Recipient Sullivan award as Am.'s amateur athlete of year Amateur Athletic Union U.S., 1962; named one of Am.'s Ten Outstanding Young Men of Year U.S. Jr. C. of C., 1962; charter mem. N.C. Sports Hall of Fame, 1963. Democrat. Roman Catholic. Home: 1609 Scotland Av Charlotte NC 28207 Office: PO Box 1122 Gastonia NC 28052

BEATTY, KENNETH ORION, JR., educator; b. East Lansdowne, Pa., Dec. 18, 1913; s. Kenneth Orion and Ada Pearl (Marshall) B.; B.S., Lehigh U., 1935, M.S., 1937; Ph.D., U. Mich., 1946; m. Mary Catharine Carter, Aug. 8, 1936; children—Susan (Mrs. Peter W. Woodruff), Prudence (Mrs. Sam L. Abram), Lucy Margaret (Mrs. Mark Heideman). With Dow Chem. Co., Midland, Mich., 1937-39; asst. prof. chem. engring. U. R.I., Kingston, 1939-44; research asso. U. Mich., Ann Arbor, 1944-46; faculty N.C. State U., Raleigh, 1946—, Reynolds prof. chem. engring., 1961—. Vis. prof. Ohio State U., Columbus, 1949; resident cons. Nat. Lead Co. of Ohio, 1952; design engr. spl. project CANEL, Pratt & Whitney, 1957; Univ. fellow Princeton, 1967; U.S. rep. to Assembly for Internat. Heat Transfer Confs., 1968-72; mem. sci. council Internat. Center for Heat and Mass Transfer, Yugoslavia, 1969—; mem. coordinating com. Nat. Heat Transfer Conf., 1965—, chmn., 1967. NASA Research grantee, 1960, 64; NSF grantee, 1960-62; AEC grantee, 1956-61. Registered profl. engr., N.C. Mem. Am. Inst. Chem. Engrs. (chmn. heat transfer div. 1966, mem. exec. com. div. heat transfer and energy conversion 1964—, Am. chem. Soc., A.A.A.S. Democrat. Mem. United Ch. of Christ. Contbr. articles to profl. jours. Home: 323 Shepherd St Raleigh NC 27607

BEATTY, PAUL COUSART, textile mill products co. exec.; b. Beverly, N.J., Mar. 1, 1918; s. Albert Edwin and Florence (Perkins) B.; T.E., Phila. Textile Inst., 1939; grad. Advanced Mgmt. Program, Harvard, 1954; m. Moselle Olive Butterworth, Dec. 4, 1943; children—Sherryl Ann, Paul Craig. Mgr. Watertown Woolen Mills, Millbury, Mass., 1940-41; woolen supt. Beacon Mfg. Co., Swannanoa, N.C., 1941-42; instr. Phila. Textile Inst., 1942-43; technician Am. Viscose Corp., Marcus Hook, Pa., 1943-46; mgr. Pacific Mills, Halifax, Va., 1946-59; v.p. Record Advertiser, South Boston, Va.,

1959-60; gen. mgr. Halifax Cotton Mills, South Boston, 1960-62; pres. Danville Industries, Inc. (Va.), 1963-—, also dir. Pres. Halifax United Fund, 1960-61; chief Halifax Vol. Fire Dept., 1947-52. Chmn. Halifax County Sch. Bd., 1966-70. Bd. dirs. Red Cross Bloodmobile, Halifax County Little Theatre. Recipient Outstanding Citizen award Woodmen of the World, 1951; named Outstanding Citizen of Halifax County, Boston Jaycees, 1960. Mem. Nat. Assn. Hosiery Mfrs. (dir. 1967-—), The Carded Yarn Assn. (dir. 1966-70) Newcomen Soc. N. Am. Episcopalian (vestryman 1959-68). Lion (pres. 1952-53). Home: 421 Lakeside Dr Halifax VA 24558 Office: 525 Lynn St Danville VA 24541

BEATTY, ROBERT O., govt. ofcl. Asst. sec. for pub. affairs Dept. Health, Edn. and Welfare, Washington. Address: Dept Health Edn and Welfare 330 Independence Blvd SW Washington DC 20201*

BEATTY, ROY P., ret. army officer; b. Mexico, Mo., Oct. 26, 1923; s. James E. and Bessie Lee (Daniel) B.; student U. Mo., 1941, 42; B.S., U.S. Mil. Acad., 1946; M.S. in Civil Engring., U. Ia., 1950; student Command and Gen. Staff Coll., 1960; m. Bonniejean Miller, June 16, 1946; children—Keith G., Gary L. Commd. 2d lt. C.E., U.S. Army, 1946, advanced through grades to lt. col., 1963, col., 1968; ret., 1970; asst. air installations officer, Tachikawa, Japan, 1947-49; instr. fixed and floating bridges Engr. Sch., Ft. Belvoir, Va., 1951-52; unit comdr. Karlsruhe, Germany, 1952-55; engr. officer Army Ballistic Missile Agy., 1956-59; asst. area engr. Nike Zeus facility, Kwajalein Atoll, 1961-62; dep. dist. engr., Honolulu, 1962-64; area engr. Miss. test facility NASA, Bay St. Louis, 1964-67; exec. officer engring. and constrn. bur. Panama Canal Co., C.Z., 1967-68; area engr. Sentinel and Safeguard Anti-Ballistic Missile Systems, Boston and Omaha, 1968-70. Decorated Legion of Merit, Meritorious Service medal. Registered profl. engr., Ala. Home: 711 Beresford Circle Stone Mountain GA 30083

BEAUCHAMP, RAYMOND ORVAL, dentist; b. Monett, Mo., July 26, 1906; s. William Harry and Annie Maude (Bell) B.; B.S., U. Ark., 1929; D.D.S., U. Mo., 1935; m. Helen Ruth Pennington, Mar. 12, 1938; 1 son, James Harry. Student asst. biology U. Mo. Dental Coll., Kansas City, 1932-34; pvt. practice dentistry, Broken Bow, Okla., 1935-38, Stillwater, 1938-43, 46-—. Bd. dirs. YMCA, 1969-70, Partners in Prayer. Served with AUS, 1943-46; lt. col. ret. Mem. Am., Okla. (ho. dels. 1966-68) dental assns., Payne County Dental Soc. (pres. 1946-47), Delta Sigma Delta, Sigma Nu. Presbyn. (elder). Elk, Kiwanian (pres. 1957). Club: Stillwater Golf and Country. Home: 4824 Woodland Dr Stillwater OK 74074 Office: 119 W 7th St Stillwater OK 74074

BEAUDOIN, KENNETH LAWRENCE, poet, genealogist; b. Elmira, Mich., Dec. 12, 1913; s. Arthur Joseph and Ruth Helen Marie Derrer (Boyce) B.; B.S., Memphis State Coll., 1935. Editor and pub. Iconograph (quar.), 1940-47; dir. Galerie Neuf, N.Y.C., 1944-47; editor Archangel Press, 1947-48; chief clk. criminal intelligence Memphis Police Dept. Pres. Nodena Found. Recipient Ruth Forbes Sherry award, 1967; S. and W. Silver Trophy award for contbn. to Am. poetry, 1967, citation for distinguished service World Poetry Soc., 1971. Mem. Shelby County Hist. Com. (sec. 1965), Societe Genealogique Francaise-Canadienne, Montreal, Memphis Archaeol. and Geol. Soc. (founder), Tenn. Poetry Soc. (v.p., workshop dir.). Author: (poems City Suite, 1940; Boll Weevils and Butterflies, 1936; Incunabula, 1943; Six Eye Poems, 1947; The First Encrustation, 1949; Two Suites for Manhattan, 1949; Strange April, 1950; (trans.) Four Sioux Myths, 1950; The Papago Genesis, 1950; (other pubs.). The Family of Napoleon Beaudoin I, 1949; The Wuwuchim (translation), 1950; Hot Springs Holiday (poems), 1950; Elegy for a Southern Poet (poems), 1951; The Christ Urge, 1952; Pavanne for Gorley Dead (poem), 1953; Beloved Kinsman, 1953; On Hot Summer Afternoons (poems), 1953; Bayou Gayoso (poem), 1954, Japanese translation 1958; Memphis Haiku (poems), 1960; 16 Eye Poems, 1963; Mississippi River Suite, 1964; A Book of the Hours (holograph), 1965; The Rhythmic Landcape, 1968; Discourses in Poetry, 1965-70; New Look Trio-South and West Inclusive, 1969; Selected Poems, 1970. Home: 1298 Jefferson Av Memphis TN 38104

BEAUDREAU, DAVID EUGENE, educator; b. Plummer, Ida., May 30, 1929; s. Arthur T. and Ada (Olmstead) B.; student Eastern Wash. Coll., 1947-49; D.D.S., U. Wash., 1954; M.S.D., U. Pa., 1963; m. Leah Hardin, Dec. 17, 1950; children—Gary Michael, Brian Douglas, Ronald Wayne. Practice of dentistry, Spokane, 1956-61, 63-68; instr. U. Wash., 1956-58, clin. instr., 1958-61; asst. prof., chmn. dept. fixed partial dentures U. Pa., 1963-66; asso. prof., 1966-68, dir. postgrad. periodontal prosthesis, 1967-68; prof., asso. dean, chmn. dept. restorative dentures Sch. Dentistry, Med. Coll. Ga., Augusta, 1968-—. Served with USNR, 1954-56. Fellow Am. Coll. Dentists; mem. Omicron Kappa Upsilon. Contbr. to book Peridontal Therapy, 4th edit., 1968. Contbr. articles to profl. jours. Home: 8146 Sir Lancelot Court Evans GA 30809 Office: Sch Dentistry Med Coll Georgia Augusta GA 30902

BEAUDREAU, THELMA FAY JACKSON (MRS. NED BEAUDREAU), musician, club woman; b. Kiowa, Okla., Nov. 12, 1907; d. George Edmond and Leona May (Harris) Jackson; student San Antonio Coll. Music, 1926-27, Kansas City Conservatory Music, 1929-30, San Angelo Coll., 1948, Tex. Coll. Arts and Industries, 1957-58, 60-61; m. Ned Willard Beaudreau, June 6, 1931; children—Vance Jackson, Marilyn Anne (Mrs. David B. Coulson). Dir., music instr., Lamesa (Tex.) High School Orchestra, 1925-1926; music instr., Big Spring, Tex., 1927-29, 31-34, Corpus Christi (Tex.) pub. schs., 1948-50; tchr. Presbyn. Day Sch., 1952, charter mem. Corpus Christi Symphony, 1945, mem. string sect., 1945-—; mem. Jackson-Wade Trio, Dallas, fall 1930; mem. String Ensemble Driscoll Hotel, Corpus Christi, 1941-42. Rec. sec. Harmony Music Club, 1945-47, pres., 1949-51; jr. scrapbook chmn. 5th Dist. Fedn. Music Clubs, Tex., 1956-57; patron Thursday Music Club, Corpus Christi; rec. sec. Corpus Christi chpt. D.A.R., 1955-57, regent, 1958-60, parliamentarian, 1960-62; chmn. Am. Music com. Tex. Soc. D.A.R., 1961-64, chaplain Regents Club, 1964-66. Recipient 25 year award Corpus Christi Symphony. Mem. Internat. Platform Assn., Nueces County Hist. Survey Com., Nueces County Hist. Soc., Nat. Assn. Music Tchrs., Corpus Christi Symphony Guild, Corpus Christi Music Tchrs. Assn., Episcopalian. Clubs: Harmony Music (corr. sec. 1965-67, v.p. 1972-—); Thursday Music. Address: 109 E Vanderbilt St Corpus Christi TX 78415

BEAUFORT, C.W., state senator. Mem. Fla. Senate. Address: Box 2221 2861 College St Jacksonville FL 32203*

BEAVER, PAUL CHESTER, educator; b. Glenwood, Ind., Mar. 10, 1905; s. John Chester and Blanche Emma (Murphy) B.; A.B., Wabash Coll., 1928, D.Sc., 1963; M.S., U. Ill., 1929, Ph.D., 1935; m. Lela E. West, Oct. 16, 1931; 1 dau., Paula Jean (Mrs. David Ross Chipman). Asst. in zoology U. Ill., 1928-29, 31-34; instr. zoology U. Wyo., 1929-31; instr. biology Oak Park Jr. Coll., 1934-37; asst. prof. biology Lawrence Coll., 1937-42; biologist Ga. Dept. Pub. Health, 1942-45; asst. prof. parasitology Tulane U. Med. Sch., 1945-47, asso. prof., 1947-52, prof., 1952-—, head dept. parasitology, 1956-—, William Vincent prof. tropical diseases and hygiene, 1958-—; vis. prof. Eastern Mont. Normal Sch., summers 1935-37, Colo. State Coll., 1940, U. Mich., 1954-56, 58, U. Natal Med. Sch., Durban, South Africa, 1957; hon. vis. prof. U. del Valle, Cali, Colombia, 1970-—. Cons. Ga. Dept. Pub. Health, 1946-53, USPHS Hosp., New Orleans, 1949-—, WHO, 1960-—; mem. com. standards and exams. Am. Bd. Microbiology, 1960-67; mem. commn. parasitic diseases Armed Forces Epidemiological Bd., 1953-—, dir. commn., 1967-—; mem. Am. Found. for Tropical Medicine, 1961-66; microbiology fellowships rev. panel NIH, 1960-63; mem. WHO expert com. on intestinal helminths, 1963, WHO expert panel on parasitic diseases, 1963-—; bd. sci. counselors Nat. Inst. Allergy and Infectious Diseases, NIH, 1966-68, mem. parasitic diseases panel U.S.-Japan Cooperative Med. Sci. program, 1965-69; mem. adv. sci. bd. Gorgas Meml. Inst. Tropical and Preventive Medicine, 1970-—. Diplomate Am. Bd. Microbiology. Fellow Am. Acad. Microbiology (gov.), A.A.A.S., Am. Soc. Tropical Medicine and Hygiene (councilor 1956-57, v.p. 1958, pres. 1969); mem. Internat. Filariasis Assn., Royal Soc. Tropical Medicine and Hygiene, Am. Soc. Parasitologists (past counselor, pres. 1968), Am. Micros. Soc. (2d v.p. 1953, exec. com. 1955-59, 61-62), Am. Pub. Health Assn., Soc. Exptl. Biology and Medicine, Sociedad Mexicana de Parasitologia (hon.), New Orleans Acad. Sci., Societe de Pathologie Exotique Paris (hon.), Brazilian Soc. Tropical Medicine (hon.), Sigma Xi, Delta Omega. Clubs: Internat. House, Round Table (New Orleans). Co-author: Faust's Animal Agents and Vectors of Human Disease, rev. edit. Contbg, author: Mitchell-Nelson's Pediatrics, Meakins' Practice of Medicine, Diagnostic Procedures and Reagents. Mem. editorial bd. Am. Jour. Tropical Medicine and Hygiene, 1958-60, 67-—, editor-in-chief, 1960-66, 72-—; asso. editor Am. Jour. Hygiene, 1961-64, Jour. Parasitology, 1965-—, Am. Jour. Epidemiology, 1967-—; editorial bd. Trans. Am. Micros. Soc., Ceskoslovenska Parasitologie. Author sci. papers. Home: 1416 Cadiz St New Orleans LA 70115 Office: 1430 Tulane Av New Orleans LA 70112

BEAVER, RUBY CARROLL, elec. engring. cons.; b. Chidester, Ark., Aug. 21, 1931; s. Ruby H. and Ollie (Haddox) B.; A.A., So. State Coll., 1951; B.S., U. Ark., 1954; postgrad. So. Meth. U., 1956-57, U. Houston, 1962-63; m. Virginia Josephine Carrington, June 15, 1958; children—William Hardey, Joseph Gregory. Design engr. Chance Vought Aircraft Corp., Dallas, 1956-57; plant engr. Dierk's Forest, Inc., Hot Springs, Ark., 1957-61; engring. mgr. pipeline services div. AMF-Tuboscope, Houston, 1961-69; cons. engr., Marshall, Tex., 1969-—. Coach Little League Baseball, Houston, 1969-—. Served to lt. (j.g.) USNR, 1954-56. Registered profl. engr., Tex., Ark. Mem. Theta Tau, Alpha Tau Omega. Presbyn. (elder). Patentee in field. Address: Rt 3 Box 304 Marshall TX 75670

BEBB, HERBERT BARRINGTON, lab. dir.; b. Wichita Falls, Tex., June 22, 1935; s. Edwin and Hester Ann (Allyn) B.; student Midwestern U., 1955; B.S., U. Okla., 1959; M.S., Syracuse U., 1964; Ph.D., U. Rochester, 1965; m. Neva Sue Robison, Dec. 21, 1958; children—Byran Timothy, Deanna. Asso. physicist Fed. Systems div. IBM, 1959-61, research staff T.J. Watson Research Center, 1961-62; theoretical physicist Tex. Instruments, Inc., Dallas, 1966-69, mgr. applied optics br. Advanced Tech. Lab., 1969, dir., 1969-—. Am. Optical Co. fellow, 1962-63; NASA fellow, 1963-65. Mem. Am. Phys. Soc., Optical Soc. Am., Math. Assn. Am., Sigma Xi. Contbr. articles profl. jours. Patentee in field. Office: PO Box 5936 Dallas TX 75222

BECHARA, JOSE ANTONIO, corp. exec.; b. Mayaguez, P.R., Jan. 17, 1917; s. Jose Antonio and Nacira (Galib) B.; B.S., Duke, 1939; B.S.A., U. P.R., 1942; m. Zaida M. Bravo, July 27, 1942; children—Eileen, Jose Antonio, Dennis. Dir., Mayaguez Sugar Co., 1942-—; pres. Gen. Auto Sales Corp., Mayaguez, 1946-50, radio sta. WKJB, Mayaguez, 1946-—, WKJB-FM, 1961-—, P.R. Gases Corp., Mayaguez, 1949-—, Gravero Mayaguezano, Inc., Hormigonera Mayaguezana Inc., 1949-—, Asfalto Mayaguezano, Inc., 1963-—; treas. Western Broadcasting Corp. P.R., Mayaguez, 1959-70, WOLE-TV,Aguadilla, also Mayaguez, 1959-70, v.p., 1970-—; sec. Mayaguez Ready Mix Concrete, Inc., 1955-70; dir. San Juan Cement Co., Inc. Mem. Internat. Advt. Assn. N.Y., U.S. Coast Guard Aux., P.R., Southwestern indsl. assns., Navy League U.S., Casino de Mayaguez, Phi Sigma Alpha. Clubs: Nat. Press (Washington); Lions, Rifle and Pistol Shotgun, Western Hunting and Fishing, Hilton Tennis and Swimming (Mayaguez); Sales Executives (San Juan, P.R.). Home: Las Mesas Mayaguez PR 00708 Office: WKJB Bldg 637 S Post St Mayaguez PR 00708

BECHTEL, ROBERT WARREN, banker; b. Slaton, Tex., July 29, 1933; s. Robert B. and Esther (Heatherly) B.; B.S., Okla. U., 1957, LL.B., 1961; m. Joan Morrison, Jan. 28, 1955; children—Susan, Amy. Field engr. Halliburton Co., Midland, Tex., 1957-58; admitted to Tex. bar, 1961; title analyst Shell Oil Co., Midland, 1961-62; trust officer First Nat. Bank of Midland, 1962-68, head financial and planning dept., 1969-—; pres., dir. Eagle Computing Corp., 1970-—. Bd. dirs. Chapparal dist. Boy Scouts Am. Beal Found. Potts & Sibley Found. Served with AUS, 1955-56. Mem. Midland, Tex., Am. bar assns., Delta Theta Phi. Author: Uniform Commercial Code in Texas, 1966. Home: 10 Cambridge Ct Midland TX 79701 Office: 303 Wall St Midland TX 79701

BECHTLER, CHARLES MONROE, paper mfg. co. exec.; b. York, S.C., Nov. 30, 1924; s. Luther Bryant and Eurah (Rich) B.; B.S., U. S.C., 1949; m. Peggy Rolston, July 17, 1946 (div. Mar. 1968); children— Charmaine (Mrs. T. David Jordon, Jr.), Charles Monroe, Noel; m. 2d, Betty Mitchell, May 11, 1968. Singing entertainer WRHI Radio, Rock Hill, S.C., 1943; chem. technologist Tenn.-Eastman Corp., Oak Ridge, 1944; with Standard Paper Mfg. Co., Richmond, Va., 1949-56, 57-—, v.p. sales promotion and product devel., 1967-—; mfr.'s rep. Christian Co., Richmond, 1956-57. Served with AUS, 1944-47. Recipient Pres.'s award Southeasterners, Inc., 1963. Baptist (deacon, dir. music 1953-65). Home: 3701 Cedar Grove Rd Richmond VA 23235 Office: PO Box 1554 Richmond VA 23212

BECK, CURT BUXTON, chem. engr.; b. Dallas, Aug. 6, 1924; s. Curt Walter and Anne (Buxton) B.; B.S., Mass. Inst. Tech., 1945, M.S., 1952; m. Wilhelmina P. V.W. Kuhr, Nov. 5, 1957; children—Curt Emile, Anna Catherine, Paul Buxton. With Cabot Corp., 1945-—, successively chem. engr., group leader, 1945-57, adminstrn. asst. research and devel. dept., 1957-65, asso. dir. research, 1965-—. Active Cub Scouts. Diplomate Am. Acad. Environmental Engrs. Registered profl. engr., Tex., La., W.Va., Ill. Mem. Am. Chem. Soc., Air Pollution Control Assn., Am. Inst. Chem. Engrs. Patentee in field to profl. jours. Home: 1940 Fir St Pampa TX 79065 Office: Box 1101 Pampa TX 79065

BECK, EARL RAY, educator; b. Junction City, O., Sept 8, 1916; s. Ernest Ray and Mary Frances (Helser) B.; A.B., Capital U., 1937; M.A., Ohio State U., 1939, Ph.D., 1942; m. Marjorie Culbertson, Nov. 7, 1944; children—Ann, Mary Sue. Instr., Capital U., 1942-43, Ohio State U., 1946-49; asst. prof. Fla. State U., Tallahassee, 1949-52; asso. prof., 1952-60, prof., 1960-—, chmn., 1967-72. Vis. prof. La. State U., summer 1955, Tulane U., summer 1959, Duke, summer 1966. Mem. com. on library research sources European history sect. So. Hist. Soc., 1959-66, chmn., 1963-64. Served with AUS 1946-49. Mem. Am., So. hist. assns., Conf. Group for Central European History. Presbyn. Author: Verdict on Schacht, 1956; The Death of the Prussian Republic, 1959; Contemporary Civilization I, 1959; Germany Rediscovers America, 1968.*

BECK, GEORGE PRESTON, physician; b. Wichita Falls, Tex., Oct. 21, 1930; s. George P. and Amanda (Wilbanks) B.; B.S., Midwestern U., 1951; M.D., U. Tex., 1955; m. Constance Carolyn Krog, Dec. 22, 1953; children—Carla Elizabeth, George P., Howard W. Intern, John Sealy Hosp., 1955-56; resident anesthesiology Parkland Meml. Hosp., Dallas, 1959-62, vis. staff, 1964-—; practice medicine, specializing in anesthesiology, Lubbock, Tex., 1964-—; chief staff Meth. Hosp., Lubbock, 1967-68; asst. prof. anesthesiology Southwestern Med. Sch., Dallas, 1962-64, asst. clin. prof., 1964-—. Owner, Gt. Plain Ballistics Corp., 1967-—. Served with USAF, 1956-59. Diplomate Am. Bd. Anesthesiology. Fellow Am. Coll. Anesthetists; mem. Am., Tex socs. anesthesiologists, Tex. Med. Assn., Lubbock County Med. Soc., Lubbock Surg. Soc. Lutheran (pres. ch. council 1965-66, pres. congregation 1965-66). Author: The Ideal Anesthesiologist, 1960; Mnemonics as an Aid to the Anesthesiologist, 1961; Anterior Approach to Sciatic Nerve Block, 1962. Home: 4601 W 18th St Lubbock TX 79416 Office: PO Box 3326 Lubbock TX 79410

BECK, NANCY MANN MCCONNICO (MRS. EARL C. BECK, JR.), distbg. co. exec.; b. Memphis, Aug. 31, 1930; d. John Davis and Pauline (Hilton) McConnico; grad. So. Sem. and Jr. Coll., 1949; m. Dean Carlton Dubois, Aug. 19, 1950 (div. Nov. 1963); children—Denise Hilton, Dean Carlton; m. 2d, Earl C. Beck, Jr., Jan. 31, 1971. Asst. buyer, sportswear John Gerber Co., Memphis, 1949-50; fashion coordinator J. Hilton McConnico, Designer, Memphis, 1963-65; buyer, mgr. Bridal Salon, Goldsmiths, Memphis, 1965-70, French Room, 1970-71; v.p. Beck Distbg. Co., 1970-—. Press relations Hunter Lane for mayor, 1967. Mem. Memphis Arts Council, Internat. Platform Assn., Memphis Symphony League. Episcopalian. Home: Casa Lorraine Plantation Hughes AR 72348

BECK, RALPH ARTHUR, ednl. adminstr.; b. N.Y.C., Mar. 22, 1922; s. Ralph Fernando and Ethel Victoria (Aplustille) B.; B.A., Fordham U., 1943; m. Gwendolyn Farrar, Sept. 20, 1947; 1 dau., Suzanne Farrar. Advt. mgr. Thalhimers Dept. Store, Richmond, Va., 1946-51; sales promotion dir. Mabley & Carew, Dept. store, Cin., 1957-59; v.p. sales promotion Davison's Dept. Store Atlanta, 1959-71; dir. devel. Ga. State U., Atlanta, 1971-—. Vice-pres., Atlanta Community Chest, 1964. Mem. exec. bd. Atlanta Area council Boy Scouts Am., commr., 1971-—, nat. bd., 1971-—; bd. dirs. Atlanta chpt. A.R.C., Community Council Atlanta; bd. sponsors Atlanta Art Sch.; sec. Ga. State U. Found., Inc., 1971-—. Served with AUS, 1942-46, 51-52. Decorated Bronze Star; recipient Silver Beaver award Boy Scouts Am., 1966, Outstanding Pub. Service award Ga. Pub. Relations Soc. Am., 1969. Mem. Atlanta C. of C. Home: 4350 Harris Valley Rd Atlanta GA 30327

BECK, SISTER RICHARD MARIE, coll. adminstr.; b. N.Y.C., May 19, 1935; d. Richard Joseph and Mary (Cody) Beck; B.A., Marymount Manhattan Coll., 1956; M.A., Marquette U., 1961. Registrar, dir. admissions Marymount Coll., Arlington, Va., 1958-60; tchr. Marymount Coll., Quebec, Que., Can., 1961-62; dir. admissions Marymount Coll., Tarrytown, N.Y., 1962-66; acad. dean Marymount Coll., N.Y.C., 1966-67; dean of admissions Marymount Coll., Boca Raton, Fla., 1967-—. Mem. Coll. Entrance Exam. Bd. Mem. Fla. Personnel Guidance Assn., Assn. Coll. Admission Counselors, Am. Assn. Collegiate Registrars and Admission Officers. Address: Marymount Coll Boca Raton FL 33432

BECK, THEODORE DEWEES, JR., computer co. exec.; b. Washington, May 2, 1933; s. Theodore Dewees and Ella Sandborn (Sanborn) B.; student Miss. State U., 1950-51; B.S. in Aero. Engring., U. Ill., 1959; post grad. in Mech. Engring., Seattle U., 1962; postgrad. Loyola U., New Orleans, 1963-64; m. Jacqueline Phylis Elliott, Jan. 23, 1954; children—Theodore Dewees III, Denise Lynn, Thomas Sanborn. Engr., Boeing Co., Seattle, 1959-62, engring. mgr., Huntsville, Ala., 1964-71, supr., New Orleans, 1962-64; marketing mgr. Boeing Computer Services, Inc., Huntsville, 1971-—; cons. for environmental control, heating, air-conditioning and mgmt. Plantation Community Center, New Orleans, 1962-64. Mem. Willowbrook Civic Assn., 1964-68, pres., 1967. Served with USNR, 1951-55. Recipient Key to City, City of New Orleans, 1964, Registered profl. engr., Ala. Mem. Boeing Huntsville Mgmt. Assn. (1st v.p. 1972-—), V.F.W., Amvets. Club: Willowbrook Country, Valley Hill Country (chmn. jr. golf) (Huntsville); Burning Tree Country (Decatur, Ala.). Home: 728 Lily Flagg Rd SE Huntsville AL 35802 Office: PO Box 1470 Huntsville AL 35807

BECK, W.M., state ofcl. Mem. Ala. Bd. Edn., Montgomery. Address: State Bd Edn Montgomery AL 36104*

BECK, WILLIAM, clergyman, educator. Supt. Catholic schs. of Ark., Little Rock. Address: 2500 N Tyler St Little Rock AR 72207*

BECKER, ARTHUR MARVIN, lawyer; b. N.Y.C., Aug. 30, 1908; s. Charles and Frances (Blumberg) B.; student Fordham U., 1925-26 B.A., N.Y.U., 1929; LL.B., Columbia U., 1931; m. Faye Elizabeth Samples, Nov. 20, 1953; 1 son, Francis Evans. Admitted to N.Y. State bar, 1932, D.C., bar, 1946; practiced in N.Y.C., 1932-35, Washington, 1946-—; sr. atty. U.S. Dept. Agr., 1935-41; prin. atty. WPB, 1941-42; asst. gen. counsel War Shipping Adminstrn., 1942; sr. asst. gen. counsel U.S. Maritime Commn., 1945-46; partner firm Mudge, Rose, Guthrie and Alexander, and predecessors, N.Y.C., Washington and Paris, 1964-—. Dir., 1st Nat. Bank of Washington; mem. Pres.'s Commn. Am. Shipbldg. Bd. dirs. Washington Internat. Horse Show. Served to comdr. USNR, 1942-45. Mem. Am., Fed. bar assns., Bar Assn. D.C. Clubs: Propeller, Nat. Lawyers, Army-Navy, Columbia University, International, 1925 F St (Washington); Potomac Hunt; India House (N.Y.C.). Home: 8800 Bradley Blvd Bethesda MD 20034 Office: Paris France also 20 Broad St New York City 10005 also 1701 Pennsylvania Av NW Washington DC 20006

BECKER, CHARLES HENRY, educator; b. Chgo., May 26, 1914; s. Stanley Frank and Katherine (Kwiatkowska) B.; B.S. in Pharmacy, U. Ill., 1937; M.S., U. Fla., 1939, Ph.D., 1940; m. Katherine E. Tomkies, July 27, 1940; children—Nancy K. (Mrs. DeWayne Tucker), Ann T. From asst. prof. to prof. Sch. Pharmacy, Duquesne U., 1940-47; dir. research Balch Flavor Co., Pitts., 1942-47; mem. faculty U. Fla., Gainesville, 1947-—, prof. pharmacy, 1954-—, chmn. dept. 1961-—. cons. in field, 1941-—. Mem. Am., Fla. pharm. assns., Sigma Xi, Sigma Phi Epsilon, Phi Kappa Phi. Rho Chi. Rho Pi Phi, Kappa Psi. Author, patentee in field. Home: 2235 NW 5th Pl Gainesville FL 32601

BECKER, EUGENE MATTHEW, govt. ofcl., banker; b. St. Paul, Sept. 1, 1930; s. John Joseph and Evelyn (Patterson) B.; B.A., Colgate U., 1952; M.A., U. Chgo., 1953; Fulbright scholar, U. Paris, 1953-54; M.F.A., Princeton, 1958, Ph.D., 1959. Research asst., lectr. Frick Collection, N.Y.C., 1959-60; dir. information municipal securities Investment Bankers Assn. Am., 1960-61; asst. v.p. First Nat. City Bank, N.Y.C., 1962-65; dir. budget N.Y.C., 1966; asst. sec. army for financial mgmt., Washington, 1967-—. Trustee Carnegie Hall Corp., Carnegie Hall Soc., 1966-—; v.p., exec. com. Carnegie Hall Corp., 1968-—; v.p. Carnegie Hall Soc., 1968-—. Served with AUS, 1954-56.

Recipient Distinguished Civilian Service award Dept. Army. Mem. Army Finance Assn. (hon. pres. 1967—), Phi Beta Kappa. Clubs: Princeton (N.Y.C.); Army and Navy (Washington). Home: 2440 Virginia Av NW Washington DC 20037 Office: The Pentagon Washington DC 20310

BECKER, HAL CLARENCE, educator; b. New Orleans, July 12, 1922; s. Clarence E. and Louise (Nusloch) B.; B.E. in Elec. Engring., Tulane U., 1942, M.S. in Physics, 1953; postgrad. Princeton, 1953-55; m. Elizabeth Patricia Tobin, May 9, 1949; 1 dau., Louise Nan. Research asso. radiation lab., Mass. Inst. Tech., 1942-46; research engr. Bendix Radio, Balt., 1946-47; asst. prof. exptl. neurology Tulane U. Sch. Medicine, New Orleans, 1949-58, asso. prof. radiology, 1964-69, prof., 1969—; systems engineer IBM Corp., 1960-64; v.p. research Precon Process & Equipment Corp., New Orleans, 1955—. Cons. to X-Scope Corp., Charity Hosp., New Orleans, Eastern Pa. Psychiat. Inst. Recipient Outstanding Tech. Contbn. award IBM, 1963. Registered profl. engr., La. Mem. I.E.E.E. (founder profl. tech. group 1966, chmn. group 1966-68), A.A.A.S., Soc. Nuclear Medicine, La. Radiol. Soc., La. Engring. Soc., Nat. Rifle Assn., Civil Air Patrol (La. Wing communications officer 1950-52). Club: Engineers (New Orleans). Author: (with others) A Programmed Introduction in Differential Diagnosis of Lung Diseases, 1964; also chpts. in books. Home: 4801 Green Acres Ct Metairie LA 70003

BECKER, MARY LOUISE, polit. scientist; b. St. Louis; d. W. R. and Evelyn (Thompson) Becker; B.S., Washington U., St. Louis, 1949, M.A. (Blewett fellow), 1951; Ph.D. (resident fellow 1952-56), Radcliffe Coll., 1957; postgrad. (Fulbright scholar) U. Karachi, Pakistan, 1953-54. Intelligence research analyst Dept. State, Washington, 1957-59; internat. relations officer Agy. for Internat. Devel., Washington, 1959-64, community relations officer, 1964-66, sci. research officer, 1966-71, UN relations officer, 1971—. Lectr. internat. relations civic orgns., student groups, 1954—. Mem. adv. bd., chmn. student placement Washington Citizenship Seminar, Nat. YMCA-YWCA, Washington, 1961—. Mem. Am. Polit. Sci. Assn., Am. Acad. Polit. and Social Sci., Assn. Asian Studies, Am. Soc. Pub. Adminstrn., Am. Friends Middle East, Am. Assn. U. Women, Mo. Soc. Washington (sec. 1959-60), Mortar Bd., Chimes, Alpha Lambda Delta, Beta Gamma Sigma, Eta Mu Phi, Pi Sigma Alpha. Presbyn. Club: International (Washington). Author: Muhammed Iqbal, 1965. Contbr. articles to govt. publs. Office: Agy for Internat Devel Washington DC 20523

BECKETT, FLOSSIE LEE EATON (MRS SI BECKETT), educator; b. Mounds, Okla., Apr. 8, 1910; d. Danial J. and Mattie (Cumbey) Eaton; student Northeastern State Coll., Tahlequah, Okla., 1928-29; B.S. in Edn., East Central State Coll., Okla., 1947; M.Ed., U. Okla., 1951; postgrad. various colls., univs.; m. Si Beckett, Sept. 1, 1929 (dec.); children—Jo Anne (Mrs. Thomas L. Phillips), Peggy Jean Cochran, Si Dean. Tchr., prin. Tate Sch., Wewoka, Okla., 1943-48, Mountain View Sch., Seminole, 1948-49, Hilltop Sch., Wewoka, 1949-53; tchr. Central Elementary Sch., Wewoka, 1953-55; tchr. Lindsay (Okla.) Elementary Sch., 1955-67, elementary librarian, dir. instructional media center 1967—. Various positions N.E.A.-Okla. Edn. Assn. leadership workshops, 1951-67, N.E.A. Regional Classroom Tchrs. Confs., 1960-67; mem. Okla. Tchr. Edn. and Profl. Standards Commn., 1961-65, Okla. Curriculum Improvement Commn., 1961-66; mem. Gov.'s Phys. Fitness Council and Phys. Fitness Commn., 1965-69; mem. Okla. Dept. Edn. Profl. Practices Commn., 1965-73, vice chmn., 1969-70; del. tchr., edn. convs. Organizer various 4-H Clubs, Little Theatre groups; mem. state com. Oklahomans for Better Edn., 1964-65. Precinct insp. Seminole County (Okla.) Democratic Com., 1953-55; mem. Okla. Acad. for State Goals, 1966-68. Named Garvin County's Tchr. of Year, 1961, Okla. Tchr. of Yr., 1961; Nat. Tchr. of Yr. Honor Roll, 1962; recipient award Gov. of Okla., meritorious service award Lindsay C. of C. Mem. Am. Assn. U. Women, (pres. Chickasha br. 1971-73), N.E.A., Garvin County Tchr. Assn., Okla. (sect. state pres. 1953-54, county unit treas. 1956-61, mem. constn. revision com. 1965-68), Lindsay (chmn. pub. relations com. 1970—) edn. assns., East Central Dist. (pres. 1959, chmn. program com. 1968—), Lindsay (organizer 1957, exec. bd. 1957-67) classroom tchrs. assns., State (exec. com. 1961-67, state pres. 1964-66), South Central Regional (resolution com. 1966-68) depts. classroom tchrs., Kappa Kappa Iota (Okla. pres. 1969-70, projects com. 1966-71), Gamma Theta (conclave treas. 1967-69), Alpha Delta Kappa (election com. Eta chpt.; pres. 1972—). Mem. Rebekah Lodge (chmn. edn. com. 1960-61). Contbr. articles to publs. Home: 420 Garrett Av Lindsay OK 73052

BECKETT, WILLIAM WADE, lawyer; b. Charleston, S.C., Feb. 2, 1928; s. Theodore Ashe and Mary (Scroggs) B.; B.S., The Citadel, 1948; J.D. George Washington U., 1956; m. Kathryn Rae Sims, June 4, 1955; children—Kathryn Elizabeth, Nancy Ellen, Mary Sims, Engr., Am. Bridge Co., Ambridge, Pa., 1948; with Burns, Doane, Benedict & Irons, 1953-60; mem. firm Irons, Birch Swindler & McKie, Washington, 1960-69, Schuyler, Birch, Swindler, McKie & Beckett, 1969—. Trustee Internat. Students, Inc., 1962-65. Served to 1st lt. AUS, 1948-53. Mem. Am., D.C. bar assns., Am. Patent Law Assn., Washington Patent Lawyers Club (sec. 1965-66, pres. 1966-67, mem. businessmen's com. young life campaign 1965-71), Delta Theta Phi, Presbyn. (elder 1972—). Home: 9300 Renshaw Dr Bethesda MD 20034 Office: 1000 Connecticut Av Washington DC 20036

BECKHAM, ANN LEE (MRS. WILLIAM THEO BECKHAM), librarian; b. Wilmington, N.C., July 10, 1909; d. Dennis H. and Katherine (Beckwith) Lee; B.S., George Peabody Coll., 1932, B.S. in L.S., 1933; student Winthrop Coll., summber 1954, U. S.C., summer 1955-57; m. William Theo Beckham, July 1, 1937; 1 dau., Ann (Mrs. James E. Shealy). Librarian, Dentsville High Sch., Columbia, S.C., 1953-66; dist. librarian Sch. Dist. No. 2, Richland County, Columbia, 1953-66; cataloger U. S.C., Columbia, 1966—. Mem. A.L.A., S.C., Southeastern library assns. Baptist (supt. Adult II Dept.). Home: 111 Marietta St Columbia SC 29204 Office: U SC Columbia SC 29204

BECKHAM, JOE WARREN, engring exec.; b. Brownwood, Tex., Mar. 31, 1922; s. Ernest A. and Mae (Blair) B.; B.A., Daniel Baker Coll., 1943; B.S. in Civil Engring., Tex. U., 1948; m. Marjorie Ann Chambers, Oct. 23, 1948; children—Carol G., Blair W., Phillip C. Asst. research engr. Tex. Foundries, Inc., Lufkin, 1948-52, design engr., 1952-55, product devel. engr., 1955-58, research and design supt., 1958—, also dir.; dir. Am. Pole Structures Corp. Mem. finance com. Diocese Tex. (Episcopal Ch.), 1966-69. Bd. dirs. Wilson McKewen Treatment Center. Served to 1st lt. USAAF, 1942-45; PTO. Mem. Soc. for Exptl. Stress Analysis, Am. Soc. for Testing and Materials, Am. Foundrymen's Soc. (dir. Tex. chpt. 1962-67, 70—, internat. dir. 1967-70), Phi Gamma Delta, Chi Epsilon. Clubs: Lufkin (dir.), Lufkin Country. Patentee in field. Home: 1017 West Grove Lufkin TX 75901 Office: PO Box 1608 Lufkin TX 75902

BECKHAM, LACY CALDWELL, periodontist; b. Abilene, Tex., Jan. 30, 1930; s. Lacy Hiram and Agnes (Caldwell) B.; B.A., Hardin-Simmons U., 1951; D.D.S., Baylor U., 1955; certificate Periodontology, Columbia, 1959.; m. Joanne Blunk, June 18, 1952; children—Mildred Karen, Steven Caldwell. Practice limited to periodontics, Amarillo, Tex.; asst. clin. prof. periodontics Coll. Dentistry, Baylor U., Dallas; lectr., clin. instr. Amarillo Coll. Cons. Amarillo AFB. Bd. dirs. United Fund Amarillo. Served to capt., Dental Corps, USAF, 1955-57. Fellow Acad. Internat. Dentistry; mem. Am. Acad. Periodontology, Am. Dental Assn., Am. Soc. Periodontology (charter), S.W. Soc. Periodontics (sec.-treas.), Psi Omega. Presbyn. (elder). Rotarian. Contbr. articles to profl. publs. Home: 3003 Harmony St Amarillo TX 79101 Office: 1422 Tyler St Amarillo TX 79101

BECKLER, DAVID Z(ANDER), govt. ofcl., chem. engr.; b. Detroit, June 29, 1918; s. William J. and Thekla (Levy) B.; B.S. in Chem. Engring., U. Rochester, 1939; J.D., George Washington U., 1943; m. Harriet Levy, Aug. 1, 1943; children—Stephen, Paul, Rochelle. Admitted to D.C. bar, 1942; patent atty. Pennie, Davis, Marvin & Edmonds, Washington, 1939-42; tech. aide Fgn. Liaison Office, Office Sci. Research and Devel., 1942-44, chief tech. intelligence group, 1945; patent atty. Eastman Kodak Co., Rochester, N.Y., 1946; dep. tech. historian Joint Task Force One (Operation Crossroads), Joint Chiefs of Staff, 1946; chief tech. intelligence br. Research and Devel. Bd., Office Sec. Def., 1947-49; mem. internat. sci. policy survey group Dept. of State (on leave from Research and Devel. Bd.), 1949-50; exec. dir. com. atomic energy Research and Devel. Bd., 1950-52; asst. dir. Office Indsl. Devel., AEC, 1952-53; exec. officer Pres.'s Sci. Adv. Com., 1953—; spl asst. dir. Office Def. Moblzn., 1954-57; asst. to spl. asst. Pres. for sci., technology, 1957-62; asst. to dir. Office Sci. and Tech., Exec. Office Pres., 1971—. Recipient Certificate of Appreciation for services rendered during World War II (War and Navy depts.). Registered patent atty. U.S. Patent Office. Home: 8709 Duvall St Fairfax VA 22030 Office: Exec Office Bldg Washington DC 20506

BECKLES, FRANK N., govt. ofcl. Dir. Family Planning Nat. Center, Health Services and Mental Health Adminstrn., Dept. Health, Edn. and Welfare, Rockville, Md. Address: Health Services and Mental Health Adminstrn 5600 Fishers Lane Rockville MD 20852*

BECKMAN, FRANCES WALTERS, business exec.; b. Austin, Tex., Feb. 7, 1918; d. Sidney Francis and Ruth (Lawrence) Walters; student pub. schs.; m John B. Beckman, 1936 (div. 1949); children—Patricia Boykin (Mrs. Douglas Ian McCall), John Cornelius III; m. 2d, Peter Antone Dworaczyk, July 2, 1965 (div. 1966). Writer copy, layouts, sales space various weekly publs. Savannah Pub. Co. (Ga.), 1943; asst., sec. to advt. mgr. So. States Iron Roofing Co., 1944; free-lance copy and advt. service, 1946; owner-pres. Adcraft Advt. Agy., Inc., Corpus Christi, Tex., 1946—. Bd. dirs. Corpus Christi Area Tourist Bur., Corpus Christi Better Bus. Bur. Mem. Advt. Fedn. Am (Printer's Ink Silver medal award 1967), Southwestern Assn. Advt. Agys. (pres. 1972-73). Address: 538 S Tancahua Corpus Christi TX 78403

BECKMANN, GEORGE CLAUS, JR., hosp. adminstr.; b. Savannah, Ga., Aug. 16, 1922; s. George Claus and Lucile (North) B.; B.S., Ga. Inst. Tech., 1951; m. Mary Helen Scranton, Sept. 19, 1944; children—Barbara Ann, Nancy Ann. Marine draftsman Savannah Machine & Foundry, 1945-46; asst. to exec. dir. Elks Aidmore Inc., Atlanta, 1947-50; asst. adminstr. Emory U. Hosp., Atlanta, 1951-53; adminstr. med. services Ga. Warm Springs Found., 1953-66, adminstr., 1967—. Guest lectr., preceptor grad. program in hosp. and health adminstrn. U. Fla., 1967—; mem. Ga. Joint Council To Improve Health Care for Aged; mem. Ga. Gov.'s Com. on Arthritis, Com. on Employment of Handicapped, 1970—. Trustee Nat. Amputee Golf Scholarship Fund. Served with USAAF, 1942-45. Mem. Am. Coll. Hosp. Adminstrs., Am. Acad. Health Adminstrs., Am. (alternate del 1972—, chmn.-elect governing council sect. for rehab. and chronic disease hosps. 1971), Ga. (treas. 1970-71) hosp. assns., W. Central Ga. Hosp. Council (pres. 1958), Ga. Gerontology Soc. (v.p. 1965-66), Ga. Hosp. Service Assn. (trustee 1963—), Am. Rehab. Centers, Nat., Ga. (pres. 1961). rehab. assns. Nat. Amputee Golf Assn. (trustee). Rotarian (pres. 1956). Home: 105 Oak Rd Warm Springs GA 31830 Office: Warm Springs Found Hosp Warm Springs GA 31830

BECKNER, DAVID STUART, banker; b. Roanoke, Va., Sept. 5, 1911; s. Alexander Lyle and Ida Belle (Davis) B.; grad. Sch. Banking U. Wis., summer, 1960; m. Dorothy Gertrude Rhodes, Oct. 15, 1938; children— Dorothy (Mrs. James A. McClung), David Stuart. With Va. Nat. Bank, Norfolk, 1930-45, bookkeeper, 1940-43; chief clk., 1940-45; with Bank of Va., Norfolk, 1945—, asst. v.p., 1959-67, v.p. 1967—. Mem. Norfolk, Norfolk Jr. (past pres.) chambers commerce, Am. Inst. Banking, Hampton Roads Maritime Assn., Hampton Roads Fgn. Commerce Club. Baptist (deacon). Kiwanian. Home: 3715 Wedgefield Av Norfolk VA 23502 Office: 500 Plume St E Norfolk VA 23501

BECKWITH, BOSWORTH CLIFTON, architect; b. Raleigh, N.C., Dec. 10, 1921; s. Clifton Warren and Annie Herndon (Willson) B.; student U. N.C., 1945-46; B.Arch., N.C. State U., 1952; m. Elizabeth Dickson Dunn, Apr. 21, 1955; children—Bosworth Clifton III, Elizabeth Willson. Designer draftsman William Henley Deitrick, architect, Raleigh, 1952-56, architect, 1956-59; architect Lemmon, Freeth, Haines & Jones, Architects, Ltd., Honolulu, 1959-62; partner Dodge and Beckwith, architects, Raleigh, 1962—. Cons. architect. Active United Fund. Served with AUS, 1940-43, USAAF, 1943-45. Decorated D.F.C., Air Medal with four oak leaf clusters. Mem. A.I.A. (v.p. Raleigh sect. 1971, pres. 1972), N.C. Assn. of Professions, Raleigh Council of Architects, Raleigh C. of C. Democrat. Methodist. Kiwanian. Home: 329 Transylvania Av Raleigh NC 27609 Office: 611 Tucker St Raleigh NC 27603

BEDELL, CATHERINE DEAN (MRS. DONALD W. BEDELL), govt. ofcl.; b. Yakima, Wash., May 18, 1914; s. Charles Henry and Pauline (Van Loon) Barnes; B.A., U. Wash., 1936, edn. degree, 1937; m. James O. May, Jan. 18, 1943 (div. May 1970); children—James C. May, Melinda E. May; m. 2d, Donald W. Bedell, Nov. 14, 1970. Tchr., Chehalis, Wash., 1937-40; writer, commentator radio sta. KMO, Tacoma, 1940-41; writer radio sta. KOMO, Seattle, 1941-42; head radio dept. Strang-Prosser Advt. Agy., Seattle, 1942-43; radio writer sta. WEAF, N.Y.C., 1944-46; radio braodcaster sta. KIT, Yakima, Wash., 1948-56; mem., incorporator Nat. R.R. Passenger Corp., Washington, 1970-71; chmn. U.S. Tariff Commn., Washington, 1971—. Mem. Nat. Commn. Food Marketing, 1964-66. Mem. Wash. Ho. of Reps., 1952-58; mem. 86th to 91st congresses from 4th Wash. dist. Mem. Alpha Chi Omega. Republican. Home: 4101 Cathedral Av Apt 610 NW Washington DC 20016 Office: US Tariff Commn 8th and E Sts NW Washington DC 20436

BEDENBAUGH, AMON LYTTLETON, city ofcl.; b. Lake City, Fla., Jan. 16, 1919; s. Amon Lyttleton and Lila Belle (Allen) B.; grad. high sch.; m. Mary Kathleen Atkinson, Aug. 11, 1940; 1 son Kirk Lyttleton. With Jacksonville (Fla.) Fire Dept., 1942-65; chief Ocala (Fla.) Fire Dept., 1965—. Chmn. Fla. Fire Service Tng. Improvement Conv., 1966-68. Pres. Central Fla. Greyhound Coll. Corp., 1971—; mem. adv. bd. Salvation Army. Served with USCGR, 1942-45. Mem. Fla. Fire Chiefs Assn. (pres. 1970). Democrat. Baptist (deacon). Kiwanian (v.p. Ocala 1966, dir. 1967-71). Home: 1833 NE 5th St Ocala FL 32670 Office: 235 NE Watula Av Ocala FL 32670

BEDFORD, MADELEINE ALANN PECKHAM (MRS. CHARLES FRANCIS BEDFORD) civic worker; b. Ontario, Cal., Jan. 25, 1910; d. Allen Lewis and Madeleine (Elliott) Peckham; A.B., U. Cal. at Berkeley, 1930, M.A., 1937; m. Charles Francis Bedford, Dec. 30, 1930; children—Madeleine Alann, Frances Ellen, Charlotte Jean. Supr. tchr. tng. and counseling, in charge testing Univ. High Sch., U. Cal. at Berkeley, 1931-38; tchr. English to fgn. born San Leandro (Cal.) Evening Schs., 1931-38. Treas., Tarrant County Day Care Assn., 1953-54; pres. Ft. Worth and Tarrant Co. council Camp Fire Girls, 1961-63, pres. nat. council, 1965-68; pres. Ft. Worth Lit. Council, 1963-65; v.p. Tarrant Co. United Fund and Community Council, 1963-66, mem. exec. com. bd. dirs., 1963—; pres. Ft. Worth chpt. Am. Field Service, 1964-66; chmn. budget sub-com. United Fund, 1959-68; sec. Tex. United Community Services, 1968-70, v.p., 1970—; Tex. rep. for UNICEF, 1969—; mem. gov's steering com. White House Conf. on Children and Youth, 1970, chmn. task force com. for Tex. on internat. relations, 1970; chmn. Met. div. Crusade of Hope campaign; chmn. Mayor's Council Youth Opportunity, Fort Worth, 1971—. Bd. dirs. Tarrant County chpt. A.R.C. united Cerebral Palsy, Tarrant County Community Action Agy., Tarrant Co. Community Council, Tex. Social Welfare Assn.; trustee Assn. for Grad. Edn. and Research North Tex., 1971—; bd. visitors Add-Ran Coll., Tex. Christian U., 1971—. Recipient Gulick award Camp Fire Girls, 1961, Wo-He-Lo award 1968; award of Excellence for Outstanding Leadership and Service Tarrant Co. Community Council, 1964, Civic award First Lady Ft. Worth Altrusa, 1966. Mem. Ft. Worth Lecture Found., Mortar Board, Phi Beta Kappa (pres. Ft. Worth 1958-59), Alpha Chi Omega, Pi Sigma Alpha. Episcopalian. Club: Ft. Worth Woman's (past pres. history sect.). Home: 7 Westover Rd Fort Worth TX 76107

BEDGOOD, WILLIAM RANDALL, JR., devel. co. exec., state legislator; b. Athens, Ga., May 26, 1917; s. William Randall and Melba (McGowan) B.; B.S. in Bus. Adminstrn., U. Ga., 1937; m. Eleanor Louise Banks, Dec. 9, 1939; children—William Randall III, Diane Banks, Richard Coe, James David, Glyn Parmalee, Robert Eugene. Vice pres. Bedgood Lumber & Coal Co., Athens, 1937-50, City Wholesale Co., Inc., Griffin, Ga., 1951-60; pres. Athens Devel. Co., Inc., 1949—, Circle B Ranch, Inc., Athens, 1948—; owner, mgr. Univ. Hotel Ct., Athens, 1954—; mem. Ga. Ho. of Reps., 1963—. Chmn. N.E. Ga. Planning and Devel. Commn.; pres. Athens YMCA, 1961-62, bd. dirs., 1948—. Commr. rds. and revenues Clarke County, 1959—. Bd. dirs. Athens Indsl. Devel. Authority; trustee Ga. Bapt. Childrens Home. Served from 1st lt. to lt. col. AUS, 1937-45, USAAF, 1945. Decorated Silver Star, D.F.C. with oak leaf cluster, Air medal with five oak leaf clusters. Mem. Athens C. of C. (dir.), Am. Legion, Sigma Xi, Kappa Delta Pi. Democrat. Baptist. Elk, Rotarian. Club: Athens Country. Home: 375 West View Dr Athens GA 30601 Office: PO Box 886 Athens GA 30601

BEDINI, SILVIO A., museum dir.; b. Ridgefield, Conn., Jan. 17, 1917 s. Vincent and Cesira (Stefanelli) B.; student Columbia U.; LL.D., U. Bridgeport; m. Gerda Hintz, Oct. 20, 1951; children—Leandra, Peter. Self-employed in Ridgefield, 1945-61; spl. research history of horology, 1950—; curator div. mech. and civil engring. U.S. Nat. Mus., Smithsonian Instn., 1961-65, asst. dir. Mus. History and Tech., 1965-71, dep. dir., 1971—. Dir., mem. exec. com. Ridgefield Library and Hist. Assn., 1959—, mem. exec. council Soc. History Tech., 1963—. Chmn. U.S. nat. com. UNESCO world inventory sci. instruments. Served with AUS, 1942-45. Fellow Washington Acad. Scis.; mem. Soc. History Discoveries, Soc. Am. Historians, Am. Hist. Assn., Internat. Council Museums, Am. Assn. Mus. History Sci. Soc., A.A.A.S. Roman Catholic. Club: Cosmos (Washington). Author: Ridgefield in Review, 1958; The Scent of Time, 1963; Early American Scientific Instruments and Their Makers, 1964; Mechanical Universe, 1966; (with Wernher von Braun and Fred L. Whipple) Moon, Man's Greatest Adventure, 1970; The Life of Benjamin Banneker, 1972. Home: 4303 47th St NW Washington DC 20016 Office: Smithsonian Instn Washington DC 20560

BEDSAUL, WOODROW WILSON, land surveyor engr.; b. Lambsburg, Va., Nov. 5, 1912; s. Peter Brazzleton and Dora Bell (Hawks) B.; student E.C. Glass Bur. Sch., Lynchburg, Va., 1933, King Coll., 1934-35; spl. student U. Va., 1935-36; engring. and surveying courses Va. Mil. Inst., 1965, 66, 68; m. Lillian Savada Easter, June 14, 1948; children—Ann (Mrs. Rufus Franklin Hawks), George Allen. With Va. Forestry Office, Charlottesville, 1937-42; field engr. airport constrn. U.S. Engring. Dept., Trinidad, B.W.I., 1942-43; owner Bedsaul Surveying and Mapping, Lambsburg, Va., 1948—. Mem. Ednl. TV Com., 1967-69. Mem. Carroll County Sch. Bd., 1951-69; mem. Carroll County Democratic Com., 1966-71. Trustee, mem. Cana Vol. Fire Dept., 1965-71. Served with AUS, 1943-46; PTO. Mem. Va. Edn. Assn., Va. Assn. Surveyors (dir. 1966, chpt. pres. 1967, chpt. sec.-treas. 1965, 70, 71), Am. Congress Surveying and Mapping, N.C. Soc. Surveyors. Address: PO Box 14 Lambsburg VA 24351

BEDWELL, EDWARD ELISHA, lawyer; b. Ft. Smith, Ark., Jan. 21, 1921; s. Maurice D. and Edna (Carver) B.; B.A., U. Okla., 1941; J.D., U. Ark., 1948; m. Eloise Stuckey, Aug. 29, 1946; children—Anne, Barbara, Edward Elisha, Elise. Admitted to Ark. bar, 1948; since practiced in Ft. Smith; asst. pros. atty., 1948-50; pvt. practice, 1951—. Dir. City Nat. Bank, Ft. Smith. Served to capt. USAAF, 1943-45. Mem. Sebastian County Bar Assn. (pres. 1957), Phi Delta Theta, Omicron Delta Kappa. Presbyn. (elder). Rotarian. Home: 2200 S 46th St Fort Smith AR 72901 Office: 24 N 7th St Fort Smith AR 72901

BEE, FANNA MAI KEES (MRS. EUGENE SEAVEY BEE), librarian; b. Fair River, Miss., Aug. 18, 1899; d. Leondias Polk and Florence Laperl (Maxwell) Kees; student Whitworth Coll., 1916-19; m. Eugene Seavey Bee, May 5, 1921 (dec. Sept. 1946); children—Alon Wilton, Gwendolyn (Mrs. Robert Melbourne Haynes), Gene Pearl (Mrs. Cecil Howard Reid). Office sec., librarian Birmingham (Ala.) Sunday Sch. Council, 1946-52; library cons. Sunday Sch. Bd. So. Bapt. Conv., Birmingham, 1952-58; spl. collection librarian Howard Coll. (now Samford U.), Birmingham, 1958—, faculty Geneal. Inst., 1963-72. Speaker to clubs, chs.; library cons. Bapt. Sunday Sch. Bd., 1952-58. Dir. Hosp. Library, 1955-58. Mem. Ala. Bapt. Hist. Soc. (sec.), Ala. Bapt. Library Assn. (historian), Pi Gamma Mu, Phi Alpha Theta. Club: Shakespeare Fortnightly. Author: (with Lee N. Allen) Sesquicentennial History Ruhama Baptist Church 1819-1969, 1969 (Am. Assn. State and Local History award 1971); (with Simon J. Smith) Canaan: Garden Spot by the Cuttacochee, 1971. Contbr. hist. articles to profl. publs. Home: 1630 Ridge Top Circle Birmingham AL 35206

BEEBE, GEORGE HOLLIS, newspaper editor; b. Pittsfield, Mass., Mar. 1, 1910; s. George Hatch and Lila (Brainard) B.; B.S., Boston U. 1932; m. Helen Plato Lewis, Aug. 14, 1938. With Billings (Mont.) Gazette, 1933-43, city editor, 1939-43; telegraph editor Jacksonville Times-Union, 1943; joined Miami (Fla.) Herald, 1944, now sr. mng. editor. Mem. Am. Soc. Newspaper Editors. Am. Assn. Sunday and Feature Editors (pres. 1950), A.P. Mng. Editors Assn. (pres. 1964-65), A.P. Assn. Fla. (pres. 1958-59), Inter-Am. Press Assn. (dir. 1963—). Home: 650 NE 52d St Miami FL 33137 Office: Miami Herald Miami FL 33131

BEEBE, GILBERT WHEELER, med. statistician; b. Mahwah, N.J., Apr 3, 1912; s. Edwin P. and Gertrude (Gilbert) B.; A.B., Dartmouth Coll., 1933; A.M., Columbia, 1938, Ph.D., 1942; m. Ruth Lillian White, Dec. 29, 1933; children—Alfred S., Beatrice A., Brian G., Christopher A. Statistician, Nat. Com. Maternal Health, N.Y.C., 1934-41; research asso. Milbank Meml. Fund, N.Y.C., 1939-41, mem. tech. staff, 1941-46; chief reports and analysis br., control div. Office Surgeon Gen., U.S. Army, 1943-46; cons. to chief hist. div. U.S. Army, 1946-50; statistician div. med. scis. Nat. Acad. Scis., Washington, 1946—. Chief statistics dept. Atomic Bomb Casualty Commn., Hiroshima, Japan, 1958-60, 66-68. Served from 1st lt. to capt., AUS, 1943-46. Mem. A. A.A.S., Inst. Math. Statistics, Population Assn. Am., Am. Sociol. Soc., Am. Statis. Assn., Am. Pub. Health Assn., Am. Epidemiological Soc., Biometric Soc., Radiation Research Soc. Home: 7311 Stafford Rd Alexandria VA 22307 Office: 2101 Constitution Av NW Washington DC 20418

BEEBE, WILLIAM THOMAS, airline exec.; b. Los Angeles, Jan. 26, 1915; s. Dewey Sheldon and Elsie (Thomas) B.; B.B.A., U. Minn., 1937; m. Nancy Lee Gragg, Feb. 3, 1951; children—Marshall J., Linda Lee, Deborah Susan. With Gen. Electric Co., 1938-40; personnel mgr. United Aircraft Corp., Hartford, Conn., 1940-46; in charge personnel adminstrv. and labor relations Pratt & Whitney Aircraft Co., Kansas City, Mo., World War II; in charge personnel and labor relations Chgo. and So. Air Lines (merged with Delta Air Lines, Inc., 1953), 1947-51, v.p., 1951-53, personnel dir. Delta Air Lines, Inc., Atlanta, 1953-54, v.p., 1954-67, dir., 1966—, sr. v.p. for adminstrn., 1967-70, pres., 1970-71, chmn. bd. dirs., chief exec. officer, 1971—; dir. Citizens & So. Realty Investors, Provident Life & Accident Ins. Co. Past mem. Atlanta Bd. Edn.; mem. Gov.'s Goals for Ga. Program. Mem. Air Transport Assn. (dir.), Ga. (dir.), Atlanta (dir.) chambers commerce, Am. Saddlebred Horse Assn. Ga. (dir.), Nat. Alliance Businessmen (chmn. region IV). Episcopalian. Kiwanian. Office: Delta Air Lines Inc Hartsfield Atlanta Internat Airport Atlanta GA 30320

BEEGHLY, BERT EUGENE, mech. engr.; b. Olathe, Kan., Sept. 26, 1924; s. Albert Welch and Hazel (Ferguson) B.; student Baker U., 1947; B.S., Kan. State U., 1951; m. Mary Rae Rogers, Dec. 28, 1946; children—Victoria Jean (Mrs. David Housh), Mark William, Mary Jeannette, Jennifer Rae. With Phillips Pipe Line Co. div. Phillips Petroleum Co., Bartlesville, Okla., 1951—, design and devel. engr., 1954-55, mech. supt., 1955—. Served with USMCR, World War II, to maj., 1952-54; Korea. Mem. Am. Soc. M.E., Nat. Soc. Profl. Engrs., Profl. Engrs. Okla., Pipe Liners Club, Pi Tau Sigma, Sigma Tau. Patentee in surges control in liquid pipeline. Home: 112 Brahma St Dewey OK 74029 Office: 132 Phillips Annex Bartlesville OK 74003

BEELER, JAMES RUSH, educator; b. Pensacola, N.C., May 27, 1921; s. Wilkes S. and Dora (Riddle) B.; A.B., U. N.C., 1942, M.A., 1949, Ph.D., 1964; m. Anne Rose Morton Norman, Dec. 18, 1961; 1 son, James Rose Bolling. Asso. in French, U. Cal. at Los Angeles, 1952-57; instr. U. N.C., Chapel Hill, 1961-64; asst. prof. Coll. William and Mary, Williamsburg, Va., 1964-67, asso. prof. modern langs., 1967-69; prof. French, U. N.C. at Wilmington, 1969—. Served with USAAF, 1942-46. Mem. Alliance Francaise, Am. Assn. U. Profs., Assn. Preservation Va. Antiquities, Botetourt Bibliog. Soc., N.C. State Art Soc., Renaissance Soc. Am., South Atlantic Modern Lang. Assn. Republican. Episcopalian. Contbr. articles to profl. publs. Home: 1419 Market St Wilmington NC 28401

BEENE, GEORGE PATTON, JR., dentist; b. Jasper, Tenn., Apr. 8, 1933; s. George Patton and Anna Lee (Walker) B.; D.D.S., U. Tenn., 1959; m. Barbara Jean Stanfield, Nov. 27, 1953; children—Betsy, Charles, Carol. Pvt. practice dentistry, Trumann, Ark., 1959-61, Little Rock, 1961—. Bd. dirs. Little Rock Sch. Dist., sec., 1970—. Served with AUS, 1954-56. Mem. Ark. Dental Assn., Central Dist. Dental Soc. Lion. Home: 3421 Happy Valley Rd Little Rock AR 72207 Office: 5606 W Markham St Little Rock AR 72205

BEENE, WOODIE EUGENE, supt. schs.; b. Hillsboro, Tex., Aug. 16, 1916; s. Wood and Jessie (Hunt) B.; A.A., Hill Jr. Coll., 1935; B.S., North Tex. State U., 1938; M.Ed., West Tex. State U., 1950; m. Corrie Luzelle Bryan, June 1, 1954; children—Richard Eugene, Judith Ann. Tchr. pub. schs. Sunray, Tex., 1938-41, supt., 1941-45; tchr. pub. schs. Panhandle, Tex., 1946; program sec. YMCA, Amarillo, Tex., 1946-47; ednl. therapist VA Hosp., Amarillo, 1947-50; prin. pub. schs., Claude, Tex., 1950-51, supt., 1951-55; supt schs., Canadian, Tex., 1955-66, Stamford, Tex., 1966—. Mem. Am., Tex. assns. sch. adminstrs., Tex. Tchrs. Assn., Panhandle Sch. Leaders Assn. (past pres.), Red Red Rose. Mason. Lion. Home: 1406 Bartley St Stamford TX 79553 Office: PO Box 1238 Stamford TX 79553

BEESON, CLARENCE EARL, wholesale distbg. co. exec.; b. Winston-Salem, N.C., June 14, 1901; s. Charles H. and Zena (Berrier) B.; grad. Evans Bus. Coll., Winston-Salem, 1921; m. Ruth V. Ransom, Mar. 21, 1945; children—Clarence Earl, Carolyn Ruth. Owner, City Retreading and Vulcanizing Co., N. Wilkesboro, N.C., 1918-20; bookkeeper So. Bearings and Parts Co., Inc., Charlotte, N.C., 1922-26, sec., treas., 1927-40, v.p., treas., 1940-48, pres., 1948-72, chmn. bd., chief exec. officer, 1972—; pres., treas. Charlotte Appliance Service, Inc., 1948—, Carolina Nurseries, Inc., Charlotte, 1950-65; dir. N.C. Nat. Bank. Mem. Masons, 1928—, pres. Masonic Fellowship Luncheon Club (Charlotte) 1949-50; mem. Shriners, 1929—; gen. chmn. Shrine Bowl of Carolinas, Inc., 1944-45, pres., 1946-47, chmn. bd., 1957-72; potentate Oasis Temple of Shrine, Charlotte, 1956, chmn. bd. trustees, 1956; bd. govs. Shriners Hosp. Crippled Children, 1958—; mem. Jesters, formerly dir. Trustee Charlotte Rehab. Hosp., Pfeiffer Coll., Misenheimer, N.C. Mem. Southeastern Parts Jobbers Assn. (sec., treas. 1927-29), Va.-Carolinas Wholesalers Assn. (past dir.), Motor and Equipment Wholesalers Assn. (past dir.), Charlotte C. of C. (past dir.). Methodist (trustee). Lion. Clubs: Myers Park Country (dir., pres.) Red Fez Country (Charlotte); Country of N.C. (Pinehurst, N.C.) Charlotte Yacht (commodore); Grandfather Golf and Country (charter mem.) (Linville, N.C.). Home: 2400 Woodhaven Rd Charlotte NC 28211 Office: 500 N College St Charlotte NC 28201

BEEUWKES, LAMBERT BAER, engr. and mgmt. cons.; b. Balt., May 6, 1907; s. John Christian and Elizabeth (Baer) B.; student, grad. Balt. Poly. Inst., 1922-26, Johns Hopkins, 1926-28; m. M. Eleanor Byerly, Oct. 14, 1936; 1 son, Foster L. Aero. Design exptl. aircraft Ford-Stout, Fokker, Glenn L. Martin, 1928-33; radio sta. mgmt. and cons. KYW, WXYZ, WLAW, Mut. Network, sales dir. NBC Radio Network, 1936-56; personal mgr. The Lone Ranger, 1942-45; mgmt. and engr. cons., 1956—. Inventor retractable wing, boundary layer laminar flow control; pioneer broadcast techniques such as telephone giveaway, continuous news program, guarantee compensation. Home: 4596 Mountain Creek Dr Roswell GA 30075

BEGGIANI, SEELY JOSEPH, clergyman, educator; b. Youngstown, O., June 23, 1935; s. Joseph and Sada (Seely) B.; student John Carroll U., 1953-54, 56-57; A.B., Borromeo Sem. Ohio, 1956; postgrad. Universite de S. Joseph, Beyrouth, Lebanon, 1957-58; S.T.L., Cath. U., 1961, S.T.D., 1963. Ordained priest Roman Cath. Ch., 1961; prof. religion St. John Coll., Cleve., 1962-67, chmn. arts and scis., 1967; prof. religion John Carroll U., 1964-67; prof. religion and religious edn. Cath. U. Am., Washington, 1967—; rector Maronite Sem., 1968—. Mem. Cath. Theol. Soc. Am., Cath. Biblical Assn., Coll. Theology Soc., Mensa. Address: 7164 Alaska Av NW Washington DC 20012

BEGLEY, MICHAEL J., clergyman. Ordained priest Roman Catholic Ch., 1934; apptd. bishop, Charlotte, N.C., 1971, consecrated, 1972. Address: Rectory St Peter's Cath Ch 507 S Tryon St Charlotte NC 28202*

BEHAR, LENORE BALSAM (MRS. VICTOR SAMUEL BEHAR), educator; b. Pitts., Oct. 6, 1938; d. Fred and Sara (Rosenzweig) Balsam; student U. Pitts., 1956-57; A.B. with high honors, Duke, 1959, Ph.D., 1963; m. Victor Samuel Behar, Aug. 31, 1958; children—Marcy Lynn, Jeffrey Victor, Susan Rebecca. USPHS fellow, 1959-62; research asso. dept. psychology Duke, 1962-63; staff psychologist Community Guidance Center, San Antonio, 1963-65; asst. prof. psychology, dept. psychiatry and psychology, coordinator presch. services U.N.C. Sch. Medicine, Chapel Hill, 1965—, dir. presch. services, 1968—, chief child psychiatry, 1969—. Cons. Wake County Mental Health Clinic, Raleigh, N.C., 1962-63; clin. psychologist psychiat. outpatient clinic Duke Med. Center, 1962-63; chief adminstr. Project Early-Aid, 1969—. Mem. Am., N.C. psychol. assns., Am. Orthopsychiat. Assn., Soc. for Research in Child Devel. Home: 1821 Woodburn Rd Durham NC 27705 Office: Dept Psychiatry NC Meml Hosp Chapel Hill NC 27514

BEIDLER, WILLIAM, educator; b. Los Angeles, Dec. 28, 1928; s. William and Leila Belle (Warner) B.; B.S., U. Cal., 1950; M.A., U. N.C., 1956; Ph.D. (Fulbright scholar), Osmania U., Hyderabad, India, 1958; m. Anne Corpening Morrison, June 10, 1967; children—Ben, Tina, Emily. Control chemist Technicolor Motion Picture Co., Hollywood, Cal., 1953; asst. prof. philosophy Elon Coll., 1958-59; chmn. philosophy dept. Queens Coll., 1959-70; asso. prof. philosophy, dir. intercultural studies Guilford Coll., Greensboro, N.C., 1970—. Pres. Charlotte Symposium on World Affairs, 1963-65; mem. exec. com. Am. Friends Service Commn. S.E. Region, 1964-70. Served with Chem. Corps, AUS, 1950-52. Recipient Distinguished Tchr. award Queens Coll., 1964. Mem. N.C. Philos. Soc. (pres. 1962), Assn. for Asian Studies, Soc. for Asian and Comparative Philosophy, Am. Acad. Religion, Am. Philos. Assn., Am. Soc. Psychical Research. Contbr. articles to profl. jours. Home: 922 Woodbrook Dr Greensboro NC 27410

BEIRNE, JOSEPH ANTHONY, labor union ofcl.; b. Jersey City, Feb. 16, 1911; s. Michael Joseph and Annie T. (Giblin) B.; evening student Hudson Coll. of St. Peter, Jersey City, 1933-37, N.Y.U., 1937-39; m. Anne M. Abahaze, July 2, 1933; children—Carole Anne (Mrs. James McDonald, III), Maureen Anne (Mrs. Clifford Houston), Bren Anne (Mrs. Robert Leiss). Utilities, instrument repairman Western Electric Co. N.J. and N.Y., 1928-39; pres. Western Electric Employees, N.Y., 1937-38; organized Nat. Assn. Tel. Equipment Workers, 1937, nat. pres., 1938-45; v.p. Nat. Fedn. Tel. Workers, 1940-43, pres., 1943-47, pres. Communications Workers Am. (successor union), 1947—; v.p. CIO, 1949-55, v.p. AFL-CIO, 1955—. Vice pres., dir. United Community Funds and Councils of Am., Inc., 1956—. Mem. adv. council, career planning bd., Peace Corp. Councilman City of Fairview, N.J., 1941-46; mem. WSB, 1951-52. Dir. Religion and Labor Council Am., bd. visitors U.S Mil. Acad., West Point. Named one of 10 outstanding men of year Jr. C. of C., 1946; recipient Quadregisimo Anno medal Assn. Cath. Trade Unionists, 1950; Bicentennial medal Columbia U. N.Y. Sch. Social Work, 1955. Mem. Am. Arbitration Assn. (dir.). Democrat. Roman Catholic. Elk. Author: New Horizons for American Labor, 1962. Home: 3103 Cummings Lane Chevy Chase MD 20015 Office: 1925 K St NW Washington DC 20006

BEISWANGER, GEORGE, educator, govt. ofcl.; b. Balt.; Ph.D., U. Ia., 1928. Prof. philosophy, chmn. div. fine arts Ga. State Coll. for Women, Milledgeville, 1944-63; mem. faculty Ga. State U., 1963-66, prof. emritus, 1969—. Dance critic Atlanta Jour. and Atlanta Sunday Jour. Constn. Chmn. dance com. Greater Atlanta Arts Council; mem. dance panel Nat. Council on the Arts; chmn. Ga. Commn. Arts, 1970—. Bd. dirs. Sponsors High Museum Art. Dance editor Theatre Arts mag., 1939-44. Contbr. articles to dance mags., profl. jours. Address: 2109 Spring Creel Rd Decatur GA 30033*

BEKY, ZOLTAN BISHOP, clergyman; b. Hernadszentandras, Hungary, June 21, 1903; s. Alexander and Yolanda (Szabo) B.; grad. Theol. Acad. Sarospatak (Hungary), 1927; student Rutgers U., 1928-30; B.D., Div. Theol. Sem. Phila., 1930; m. Margaret Zombory, Oct. 11, 1929; children—Yolanda Margaret, Mary Gloria. Came to U.S., 1928, naturalized, 1940. Ordained to ministry Free Magyar Ref. Ch., 1928; pastor Free Magyar Ref. Ch., Trenton, N.J. 1928-33, gen. Sec. Eastern Classic, 1933, gen. sec. Diocese, 1936-39, Free Magyar Ref. Ch. in Am., 1939-44; hon. prof. Theol. Acad. of Sarospatak, Hungary, 1948; arch dean Ref. Ch. in Am., Trenton, 1954-58, bishop Hungarian Ref. Ch. in Am., Trenton, 1958-61; v.p. Hungarian Ref. Fedn. Am., Washington, 1956-64, pres., 1964—, chmn. bd. dirs. Am.-Hungarian Fedn., 1965—. Mem. Presdl. adv. bd. Small Bus. Adminstrn., 1970—. Recipient Washington award, 1969. Author: The Immortality of the Soul in the Theology of Paul Stoics and Plato, 1930; The Theology of Calvin and Barth, 1936; Last Theological Thinking, 1937; Faith of Gabor Bethlen of Transylvania, 1958; Contemporary Theolgical Thinking and Calvin in the Theology of the Hungarian Reformed Ch., 1958; Sermons, 1938 (in Hungary), Sermons, 1958 (in Am.). Contbr. numerous articles to religious, scholastic, polit. jours. Home: 5221 Massachusetts Av Washington DC 20016 Office: 3216 New Mexico Av NW Washington DC 20016

BELCHER, ARLIE GLENN, ret. editor, publisher; b. Pine, Mo., Oct. 20, 1897; s. Alanson Niffin and Margaret (Crane) B.; student Columbia, 1932-35; m. Harriet Knopfler, Dec. 9, 1949; children—Carol, Marilynn, Clifford Samuel. Salesman, McCray Refrigerator Co., Nat. Cash Register Co., 1919-27; printing salesman, N.Y.C., 1927-34; insp. Internal Revenue Service, U.S. Treasury Dept., N.Y.C., 1934-50; prodn. mgr. Brooks-Pollard Co., Little Rock, 1950-54; advt. mgr. Tandy Leather Co., Tulsa, 1954-56; pub. Leathercraftsman, Inc., Ft. Worth, 1956-72. Served with U.S. Army, 1916-19; to capt. AUS, 1942-46. Mem. Internat. Council Indsl. Editors (pres. Ft. Worth chpt. 1960). Home: 4404 Diaz Av Fort Worth TX 76107

BELCHER, JEWELL GREEN, JR., mech. engr.; b. El Dorado, Ark., May 19, 1934; s. Jewell Green and Lera (Allman) B.; B.M.E., Auburn U., 1959; m. Barbara Ann Mears, Sept. 5, 1955; children—Deborah Diane, Geri Lynn. Design draftsman Tenn. Coal and Iron div. U.S. Steel Corp., Fairfield, Ala., 1960; jr. engr. Ala. Power Co., Birmingham, 1960-63; sr. project engr. Brown Engring., Teledyne Co., Huntsville, Ala., 1963-68; mech. engr. U.S. Army Corps Engrs., Huntsville div., 1968-69; aerospace engr. NASA, Marshall Space Flight Center, Ala., 1969—. Served with AUS, 1954-56. Mem. Nat., Ala. socs. profl. engrs., Am. Soc. M.E., (chmn. North Ala. sect. 1969-70), Ala. Inventors Assn. Baptist. Home: 3609 Wilbur Av Huntsville AL 35810 Office: NASA George C Marshall Space Flight Center AL 35812

BELCHER, PAGE, congressman; b. Jefferson, Okla., Apr. 21, 1899; s. George Harvey and Jessie (Ray) B.; student Friends U., U. Okla.; LL.D., Oklahoma City U.; m. Gladys Collins, June 16, 1922; children—Page, Jr., Carol Jean (Mrs. Clyde V. Collins). Admitted to Okla. bar, 1936; ct. clk. Garfield County, Okla., 1934-38; municipal judge, Enid, Okla., 1938; sec. to Congressman Ross Rizley, 8th dist. Okla., 1941; pvt. practice law, Enid. Mem. 82d-92d U.S. Congresses from 1st Okla. Dist. Mem. Great Salt Plains council Boy Scouts Am. Recipient Silver Beaver award Boy Scout Council, 1948. Mem. Okla., Garfield County bar assns., Enid C. of C., Am. Legion (comdr. 1947). Methodist. Odd Fellow. Clubs: Kiwanis, Varsity O. Home: Dorchester House 2480 16th NW Washington DC 20009 Office: House Office Bldg Washington DC 20515

BELCHER, WILLIAM ALVIS, rancher, veterinarian; b. Del Rio, Tex., Aug. 25, 1918; s. Clifton C. and Willie (Cochran) B.; D.V.M., Tex. A. and M. U., 1943; postgrad. Mich. State U., Colo. State U.; m. Hazel Arledge, Sept. 8, 1937; children—Willie Ellen (Mrs. Lindsay L. Langham), Madge Elizabeth (Mrs. Samuel M. Rhoades). Gen. practice vet. medicine, Crystal City, Tex., 1943-46; rancher, Brackettsville, Tex., 1946—; owner, operator Shirley Comm. Co.-Ft. Worth Stockyard 1956-59; area veterinarian Tex. Animal Health Commn., 1965—; 1st v.p. Del Rio Wool and Mohair Co., 1950—; chmn. bd. dirs. San Antonio br. Dallas Fed. Res. Bank. County chmn. screw worm eradication program, 1961—. Mem. Am. Vet. Med. Assn., Tex., S.W. cattle raiser's assn., Tex. Sheep and Goat Raiser's Assn. (dir.), Tex. Angus Assn. (dir.). Address: Box 588 Bracketville TX 78832

BE LIEU, KENNETH EUGENE, govt. ofcl.; b. Portland, Ore., Feb. 10, 1914; s. Perry Gordon and Ilia Jean (Rood) BeL.; B.A., U. Ore., 1937; grad. Advanced Mgmt. Program, Harvard, 1955; m. Margaret Katherine Waldhoff, Dec. 22, 1951; children—Kenneth Eugene, Christopher Michael. Bus. exec., Portland, Ore., 1937-40; staff Senate Armed Services Com., 1955-58; staff dir. Preparedness Sub-Com., staff dir. Senate Com. on Aero. and Space Sci., 1958-61; asst. sec. for installations and logistics Navy Dept., Washington, 1961-65, under-sec. navy, 1965; bd. advisers Ryan Aero. Co., 1965-69; dep. asst. to Pres. U.S., 1969-71; under sec. of army, 1971—. Mem. Def. Sci. Bd., 1966-68. Served to col. U.S. Army, 1940-55. Home: 1214 Westgrove Blvd Alexandria VA 22307 Office: The Pentagon Washington DC 20310

BELITSKY, ABRAHAM HARVEY, research economist; b. Brockton, Mass., Aug. 27, 1929; s. Aaron and Bertha (Yarmalowsky) B.; B.A., U. Wis., 1952; postgrad. Brown U., 1952; M.A., Syracuse U., 1953; Ph.D., Harvard, 1960; m. Helen Roslyn Mintz, Mar. 10, 1968. Asst. prof. econs. Rutgers U., New Brunswick, N.J., 1959-62, Lawrence Coll., Appleton, Wis., 1962-64; research economist Upjohn Inst. for Employment Research, Washington, 1964—. Served to lt. USNR, 1954-57. Mem. Am. Econ. Assn., Indsl. Relations Research Assn., Assn. for Evolutionary Econs. Author: (with Harold L. Sheppard) The Job Hunt, 1966; Private Vocational Schools and their Students, 1969. Home: 7821 Morningside Dr NW Washington DC 20012 Office: 1101 17th St NW Washington DC 20036

BELK, FREDERICK MCKINNEY, JR., lawyer; b. Memphis, Aug. 20, 1937; s. Frederick M. and Letitia (Ellis) B.; student Millsaps Coll., 1955-58; B.A., U. Miss., 1961, LL.B., 1963; m. Linda Kay Moore, July 3, 1960; children—Letitia Linda, Frederick McKinney III, William Fielding. Admitted to Miss. bar, 1963, Tenn. bar, 1972; pvt. practiced in Holly Springs, Miss. 1963-65; mem. firms Fant &* Crutcher, 1965-69, Rather & Belk, 1970-72; asst. gen. counsel Peoples Protective Corp., Jackson, Tenn., 1972—. Mem. Miss. Senate, 1968-72, vice chmn. judiciary B. com. 1968-72, vice chmn. pub. property com. 1968-72, Chmn., Holly Springs Planning Commn., 1965-71. Served with USMCR, 1958-60. Recipient Distinguished Service award Holly Springs Jr. C. of C., 1965. Mem. Am., Marshall County bar assns., Miss. State Bar, U. Miss. Alumni Assn., Holly Springs C. of C. (pres. 1971-72), Kappa Sigma. Democrat. Methodist. Rotarian, Lion. Clubs: Holly Springs Country, Millsaps College M. Home: 127 Chickering Rd Jackson TN 38301 Office: PO Box 1 Jackson TN 38301

BELK, HENRY, newspaper editor, coll. trustee; b. Monroe, N.C., May 8, 1898; s. Robert Lee and Lula (Rape) B.; A.B., Duke, 1923; m. Lucile Marie Bullard, Oct. 7, 1923; 1 dau., Marie (Mrs. Edgar L. Lipton) (dec.). Publicity dir. Trinity Coll. of Duke, 1920-23; instr. English, publicity dir. Wake Forest Coll., 1923-25; lectr. journalism New Rochelle (N.Y.) Coll., 1924-25; editor Goldsboro (N.C.) News, 1926-29; mng. editor Goldsboro News-Argus, 1929-55, editor, 1949-68; editor emeritus, columnist editorial page, 1968—; columnist Greensboro Daily News, 1956—. Mem. Pres.'s Com. Employment Physically Handicapped, 1960—, N.C. Citizens Commn. Better Schs., 1957—, vice chmn., 1962—; trustee E. Carolina Coll., 1947—, chmn. 1963-64; mem. N.C. Gov.'s Study Com. Vocational Rehab. Sec. N.C. R.R. Bd., 1942; mem. Commn. Monument 3 Native N.C. U.S. Presidents, 1945-48; mem. Gov. Aycock Meml. Commn., 1949-67; life mem. adv. bd. Goldsboro Salvation Army. Bd. dirs. Bib. Recorder, 1959-62, Homes for Aging, 1963—, N.C. Baptist Homes for the Aging, Wayne County (N.C.) Coll. Aid, Inc., 1954—; named Foremost Handicapped Man of Year in N.C., Gov. Commn. Employment Handicapped, 1960; recipient Citizenship award Goldsboro Rotary Club, 1956. Mem. N.C. (pres. 1950-51), Eastern N.C. (pres. 1944) press assns., Goldsboro Jr. C. of C. (hon. life mem. 1957), A.P. Council N.C. (pres. 1953; hon. plaque 1964), Am. Soc. Newspaper Editors, N.C. Lit. and Hist. Assn. (pres. 1962-63), Sigma Delta Chi, Alpha Phi Gamma. Baptist. Mason. Elk. Home: 1409 E Walnut St Goldsboro NC 27530 Office: 310 N Berkeley Blvd Goldsboro NC 27530

BELK, IRWIN, merchant, ex-state senator; b. Charlotte, N.C., April 4, 1922; s. William Henry and Mary Leonora (Irwin) B.; student Davidson Coll., U. N.C., 1946; m. Carol Grotnes, Sept. 11, 1948; children—William, Irene, Marilyn, Carl. Trained in mdse. field since childhood; pres. Monroe Hardware Co.; pres. Belk Enterprises, Inc., Brothers Investment Co.; v.p., dir. Belk Group of Stores, Charlotte, P.M.C., Inc., Raleigh, N.C.; exec. v.p. finance Belk Stores Services, Inc., Charlotte; dir. First Union Nat. Bank, Highland Park Mfg. Co., Stonecutter Mills, Spindale, N.C., Fidelity Bankers Life Ins. Co., Richmond, Va., Henry River Mills Co., Adams-Millis Corp., Lumbermen's Mut. Casualty Co., Park Yarn Mill, Pilot Realty Co., Union Mills Co. Chmn. bd. Belk Found. Mem. N.C. Ho. of Reps., 1959-60, 61-62; N.C. state senator, 1960-61, 63-66; mem. N.C. Lesgislative Council, 1963-64, Legislative Research Commn., 1965-66; del. Nat. Democratic Conv., 1956, 60, 64, 68, 72; Democratic nat. committeeman, 1969-72. Mem. finance com., trustee U. N.C.; trustee, mem. finance com. Queens Coll.; dir. Bus. Found. N.C.; local dir. Am. Heart Assn.; mem. ho. of dels., local dir. Am. Cancer Soc.; bd. dirs. N.C. Med. Adv. Council U. N.C.; mem. Gov.'s Commn. to Study Cause and Control Cancer; co-chmn. N.C. Symphony Ball Com., Edenton and Chowan County Historic Commn.; past pres. Carolinas Carrousel; bd. dirs. Charlotte Opera Assn. (mem. finance bd.), Hist. Found. Presbyn. and Reformed Chs.; chmn. bd. advisers Chowan Coll.; mem. adv. council Wingate Coll.; bd. visitors Appalachian State Tchrs. Coll.; bd. assos. Meredith Coll.; bd. counselors Erskine Coll.; bd. dirs., past pres. N.C. Soc. Prevention

Blindness; bd. dirs. Bus. Found. N.C., Ednl. Found., Inc. (both Chapel Hill); mem. bd. Wake Forest U. Sch. Bus. Served as sgt., 8th Air Force, World War II. Named One of 10 Outstanding Young Men in Charlotte, 1954, 55, 56, 57. Mem. N.C. Mchts. Assn. (past pres., state dir.), C. of C. (dir.), Charlotte Mchts. Assn., Kappa Alpha, Delta Sigma Pi. Presbyn. (deacon; past pres. men's council Synod of N.C.). Mason (shriner), Lion (dist. gov.). Clubs: Executives (dir., past pres.), Charlotte Country, Myers Park Country, Charlotte City (Charlotte); Raleigh City; Sky, Lotos (N.Y.C.). Home: 400 Eastover Rd Charlotte NC 28207 Office: 308 E 5th St Charlotte NC 28201

BELK, JOHN MONTGOMERY, dept. store exec., mayor; b. Charlotte, N.C., Mar. 29, 1920; s. William Henry and Mary (Irwin) B.; B.S. in Econs., Davidson Coll., 1941; m. Claudia Watkins, Feb. 20, 1971. With Belk Stores Services, Inc., Charlotte, N.C., 1941-—, pres., 1955-—, also dir; dir. Wachovia Bank & Trust Co., Charlotte, Winston-Salem, N.C., Integon Inc., Winston-Salem. Mem. exec. bd. Region 6 Boy Scouts Am., 1958-—. Mayor of Charlotte, 1969-—. Trustee Davidson Coll.; bd. dirs. Found. U. N.C., Charlotte, N.C. Research Triangle Found., Tom Haggai & Assos. Found., N.C. Sports Hall Fame, Mint Mus. Served to capt. AUS, 1943-45. Recipient Silver Beaver award Boy Scouts Am., 1955, Silver Antelope award, 1962. Mem. Charlotte C. of C. (pres. 1964), Am. Mgmt. Assn., Nat. Retail Mchts. Assn. (dir.), World Bus. Council, Omicron Delta Kappa, Mason (Shriner). Home: 2318 Beverly Dr Charlotte NC 28207 Office: 308 E 5th St Charlotte NC 28201

BELKIN, ARNOLD, painter; b. Can.; student Nat. Poly. Inst., Mexico City, Mexico. Asst. prof. mural techniques, U. of Ams., Mexico City, 1953-60; prof. theatre design U. Motolinia, Mexico City, 1954-60; guest instr. painting Pratt Inst., N.Y.C., 1967-71. One-man shows, 1952-—, latest being Phoenix Art Mus., 1967, Ankrum Gallery, Los Angeles, 1967, Galeria Jack Misrachi, Mexico City, 1969, 10 Downtown, N.Y.C., 1970, Jack Misrachi Gallery, N.Y.C., 1970, London Arts, Detroit, 1971, Galeria Pecanins, Mexico City, 1971, Midtown Gallery, Atlanta, 1971, Lerner-Misrachi Gallery, N.Y.C., 1972; exhibited in numerous group shows, 1959-—, latest being Expo '67, Montreal, Que., Can., 1967, U. Tex. Art Mus., Ausitn, 1967, Hemisfair '68, San Antonio, 1968, I Salon de Independientes, Mexico City, 1968, IX Internat. Arts Festival, Cali, Colombia, 1969, Internat. Graphics Biennale, San Juan, P.R., 1969, I Panam. Biennale Graphics, Cali, 1970, Lerner-Misrachi Gallery, N.Y.C., 1971, 72, II Latin Am. Graphics Biennale, San Juan, 1971, Bienal de Arte Coltejer, Medellin, Colombia, 1972; murals executed at Nat. Poly. Inst., Mexico City, 1952, Continental Hilton Hotel, Mexico City, 1956, Casa de Piedra, Cuernavaca, Mexico, 1957, Jewish Community Center, Vancouver, B.C., Can., 1959, Fed. Penitentiary, Mexico City, 1961, Sch. for Rehab. Handicapped Children, Mexico City, 1963, Jewish Cultural Center, Mexico City, 1967, Mexican Pavillion, Expo '67, Hemisfair '68, Lock Haven (Pa.) State Coll., 1971; represented in permanent collections Mus. Modern Art, Mexico City, Phoenix Art Mus., Betzalel Nat. Mus., Jerusalem, Israel, Los Angeles County Mus., Mass. Inst. Tech., Gen. Motors Collection Mexican Graphics, Austin, Club de Industriales, Mexico City, Queens Coll., Des Moines Mus., Nat. Mus., New Delhi, India, Pitts. Mus., USIS, Kresge Internat. Collection, Detroit, Bank of Chgo. Lectr. on Mexican art in Can., U.S., Mexico, to museums and cultural insts., on radio and TV. Recipient purchase prize II Latin Am. Graphics Bienal, San Juan, 1971. Founder, co-editor Neuva Presencia, 1961-64. Contbr. numerous articles on Mexican artists of 5th generation to profl. publs. Address: Pecanins Gallery Mexico City DF Mexico*

BELL, AUBREY BLAN, reprodn. co. exec.; b. Center, Tex., May 26, 1909; s. Dan Marion and Edna (Adams) B.; B.S., U. Tex., 1938; m. Vera Catherine McDaniel, Nov. 22, 1928 (dec. July 10, 1971); m. 2d, Mary Jane Dulaney Shultz, May 1, 1972. Rodman, then asst. engr. City of Abilene (Tex.), 1928-31; prin. asst. H.L. Thackwell, cons. engr., Longview, Tex., 1938-39; sales engr. Keuffell & Esser Co., Austin, Tex., 1939-42; pres., chmn. bd. Bell Reprodn. Co., Ft. Worth, 1946-—, Active YMCA. Served from 1st lt. to maj. San. Corps, AUS, 1942-46. Decorated Bronze Star; named Boss of Year, Exec. Secs., Ft. Worth, 1966. Registered profl. engr., Tex. Mem. Nat., Tex. (past pres. Ft. Worth, Richard Van Trump award 1972) socs. profl. engrs., S. Mid Continent Blue Print Assn. (past pres.), Am. Soc. C.E. (pres. Ft. Worth 1951), Internat. Soc. Blue Print and Allied Industries (dir. 1956-59). Home: 37 Brenton Rd Fort Worth TX 76134 Office: 907 Throckmorton St Fort Worth TX 76124

BELL, CHARLES ELWOOD, JR., agrl. cons.; b. Jacksonville, Fla., June 20, 1908; s. Charles Elwood and Annie Elizabeth (Nooney) B.; B.S. in Agr. with honors, U. Ga., 1931, postgrad., 1950-53; diploma Command and Gen. Staff Coll., 1943; m. Mary Lucy Gholston, June 16, 1932; children—Charles H., Mary Ann (Mrs. Walter Aubrey Lundy, Jr.). Mgr., Gaymont Dairy, Atlanta, 1932-34; asst. county agt. Ga. Extension Service, Ellijay, 1935, county agt., Fayetteville, Ga., 1936-38, livestock specialist, Tifton, Ga., 1939-40, extension livestock specialist U. Ga., Athens, 1946-54; chief, animal industry br., Fed. Extension Service, U.S. Dept. Agr., Washington, 1955-60, dir. agr. div., 1961-67, dep. adminstr., 1968-69; cons. FAO, Nigeria, 1961, AID, Korea, 1967, Uganda, 1969, World Bank, Brazil, 1969, Jamaica and Malaysia, 1970, Thailand, 1971. Vice pres. Arlington Rose Found. Served to lt. col., AUS, 1941-45; ETO. Decorated Bronze Star medal (U.S.), Croix de Guerre (France); recipient Pfizer Extension award Am. Soc. Animal Sci., 1964; named to Livestock Industry Hall of Fame U. Ga., 1956. Mem. Am. Soc. Animal Sci. (chmn. extension sect. 1956), Seduroc Breeders Assn. (sec. 1945-54), Ga. Livestock Assn. (sec. 1953-55), Am. Vet. Med. Assn. (hon. life), Am. Soc. Agrl. Cons. (hon. life), Ga. State Soc. (v.p. Washington 1971-72), Phi Kappa Phi, Alpha Zeta, Epsilon Sigma Phi, Methodist (trustee 1967-72, pres. Men's Club 1969-70). Contbr. articles to profl. jours. Home and office: 904 Janneys Lane Alexandria VA 22302

BELL, C(LYDE) RITCHIE, botanist; b. Cin., Apr. 10, 1921; s. William Harold and Mary Edith (Spielman) B.; A.B., U. N.C., 1947, M.A., 1949; Ph.D., U. Cal. at Berkeley, 1953; m. Sarah Foushee Fore, Jan. 14, 1943. Instr., U. Ill., 1953-55; asst. prof. U. N.C., Chapel Hill, 1955-59, asso. prof., 1959-66, prof. botany, 1966-—. Dir. N.C. Bot. Garden. Served to 1st lt. USAAF, 1942-45. Decorated Air medal. Fellow A.A.A.S.; mem. Am. Inst. Biol. Scis. (governing bd. 1970-—), (Commn. on Undergrad. Edn. in Biol. Scis. (exec. com. 1970), Bot. Soc. Am (program dir. 1967-69), Am. Soc. Plant Taxonomists (sec. 1959-62, council 1962-68), Soc. for Study Evolution, Internat. Assn. Plant Taxonomists, Assn. Southeastern Biologists (exec. com. 1963-65). Co-author: Wild Flowers of North Carolina, 1968; Manual of the Vascular Flora of the Carolinas, 1968. Home: 1122 Sourwood Dr Chapel Hill NC 27514

BELL, CRAIG THOMAS, pulp and paper co. exec.; b. Easthampton, N.Y., Oct. 8, 1929; s. Willard Conklin and Eleanor (Thomas) B.; B.S., Syracuse U., 1953; m. Patricia Bushnell Bates, Jan. 30, 1951 children—Willard B., Serena B., Stephanie T. Forester N.C. Forest Service, Newton, 1953-55, Canal Wood Corp., Conway, S.C., 1955-57, Elizabethtown, N.C., 1957-58; area rep, Container Corp. Am., Kissimmee, Fla., 1958-—. Active Boy Scouts Am.; dir. Osceola County United Appeal, 1966-67; chmn. Osceola County Recreation Commn., 1966; mem. Gov's. Task Force on Recreation, 1969; mem. Osceola County Bd. Edn., 1971-—. County campaign mgr. Gov. Haydon Burns, 1964-66, U.S. Senator Edward Gurney, 1968. Served with USMCR, 1950-52. Recipient Silver Beaver award Boy Scouts Am., 1964. Mem. Soc. Am. Foresters (Fla. sect. chmn. 1966), Nat. Recreation and Parks Assn. (Fla. rep. to nat. citizens com. 1969), Fla. Bd. Forestry (pres. 1968-70), Fla. Forestry Assn. (dist. dir. 1964-—), Fla. Conservation Council (mem. exec. com. 1968-—), Fla. Audubon Soc. (v.p. Kissimmee Valley chpt. 1968), Fla. Conservation, Beta Theta Pi. Republican. Methodist. Kiwanian. Home: PO Drawer 640 Kissimmee FL 32741 Office: N 8th St Fernandina Beach FL 32034

BELL, DANIEL JOSEPH, JR., food co. exec.; b. Corsicana, Tex., Mar. 7, 1914; s. Daniel Joseph and Mary (Rucker) B.; student U. Wash., 1945, So. Methodist U., 1966; m. Ella Ruth Sims, July 19, 1937; children—Betty Jo, Ruth Ann. Accountant, Am. Well & Prospecting Co., Corsicana, 1933-41; insp. U.S. Dept. Labor, Little Rock, 1941-44; with Gen. Accounting Office, U.S. Navy, Seattle, 1944-46; plant mgr. Wolf Brand Products, Inc., Corsicana, 1948-—. Chmn. City Beautification, 1965-67; chmn. Corsicana Citizen Com., 1965-67; mem. adv. bd. Salvation Army, 1971-—. Commr. City of Corsicana, 1967-—. Served with USNR, 1944-46. Recipient Pub. Service award City of Corsicana, 1968. Mem. Nat. Inst. Food Technologists, Nat. Canners Assn., Tex. Mfrs. Assn., Tex. Food Processors Assn. Methodist. Club: Corsicana Country (dir.). Home: 1704 Sycamore St Corsicana TX 75110 Office: 416 S Main St Corsicana TX 75110

BELL, DOROTHY MAYS (MRS. JACK C. BELL), educator; b. Denton, Tex., Dec. 9, 1909; d. Charles and Lucile (Rogers) Mays; B.S., U. Tex., 1932; M.A., U. Denver, 1954, Ph.D., 1958; m. Jack C. Bell, 1936; children—Jackie Anne (Mrs. Byron Bohnn), Judie Kaye (Mrs. Paul Fruge). With Tex. Christian U., 1949-—, dir. speech and hearing clinic, 1951-—; head div. communication pathology. Profl. cons. Easter Seal Soc. for Crippled Children and Adults, Inc. of Ft. Worth and Tarrant County, Ft. Worth Child Study Diagnostic Clinic, dept. spl. edn. Arlington Ind. Sch. Dist.; reasearch speech and lang. disorders in cooperation with Ft. Worth Ind. Sch. Dist. Mem. Am., Tex. (sec.) speech and hearing assns., Council Exceptional Children, Am. Ednl. Research Assn., Speech and Hearing Assn. of N. Texas, Am. Assn. U. Women, Council of Administrv. Women in Edn., Alpha Delta Pi, Alpha Lambda Delta, Psi Chi, Sigma Alpha Eta. Contbr. articles to profl. jours. Home: 2314 Fairmount Av Fort Worth TX 76110

BELL, GEORGE, govt. ofcl. Spl. asst. to Pres. Nixon, Washington. Office: White House Washington DC 20500*

BELL, GEORGE A., assn. exec.; b. Bklyn., Aug. 2, 1914; s. Stephen M. and Madeleine (Clark) B.; A.B., U. Newark, 1936; M.A., N.J. State Tchrs. Coll., 1940; Ph.D., U. Mich., 1955; m. Marian Yerzley, Aug. 31, 1940; children—Nancy Louise (Mrs. Garry M. Short), Constance E. (Mrs. Howard C. Hein), George Alfred. Asst., Newark Library, 1936-40; tchr. Briarley Mil. Acad., Beltsville, Md., 1940-41, Pentecost Garrison Sch., Memphis, 1941-42, S.I. (N.Y.) Acad., 1942-44, Va. Episcopal Sch., Lynchburg, 1944-46; instr., asst. prof. govt. Asso. Colls. Upper N.Y., Plattsburgh, 1946-52; instr. U. Mich., Ann Arbor, 1954-55; research asso. U. Md., 1955-57; asst. budget dir. State of Mo., Jefferson City, 1957-62; budget dir. State of Vt., Montpelier, 1962-65; research dir. Council of State Govts., Chgo., 1965-69, Lexington, Ky., 1969. Mem. Am. Polit. Sci. Assn., Am. Soc. Pub. Adminstrn. Home: 2121 Nicholasville Rd Lexington KY 40503 Office: Council of State Governments PO Box 5377 Lexington KY 40505

BELL, GRIFFIN B., U.S. judge; b. Americus, Ga., Oct. 31, 1918; s. A.C. and Thelma (Pilcher) B.; student Ga. Southwestern Coll. LL.B. cum laude, Mercer U., 1948, LL.D. (hon.), 1967; m. Mary Foy Powell, Feb. 20, 1943; 1 son, Griffin B. Admitted to Ga. bar 1947; practice law, Savannah and Rome, 1947-53; partner firm King & Spalding, Atlanta, 1953-59, mng. partner, 1959-61; judge U.S. Ct. of Appeals, 5th Circuit, Atlanta, 1961-—. Chief of staff gov. of Ga., 1959-61; chmn. Atlanta Commn. on Crime and Delinquency, 1965-66; chmn. com. on innovation Fed. Jud. Center, 1968. Trustee Ga. Inst. Continuing Legal Edn., Mercer U. Served to maj. AUS, 1941-46. Mem. Am. Law Inst., Order of Coif. Democrat. Baptist. Home: 3100 Habersham Rd NW Atlanta GA 30305 Office: US Court House Atlanta GA 30303

BELL, HENRY MARSH, JR., banker; b. Tyler, Tex., Jan. 23, 1928; s. Henry Marsh and Elizabeth (Loftin) B.; B.S. in Indsl. Adminstrn., Yale, 1948; m. Dorothy N. Allen, Dec. 8, 1951; children—Henry Marsh III, John Allen. With Citizens First Nat. Bank of Tyler, 1948-—, v.p. and trust officer, 1955-62, sr. v.p., 1962-65, exec. v.p., 1965-68, pres., 1968-—, also dir. Regional chmn. A.R.C.; exec. bd. Episcopa! Diocese Tex.; bd. dirs. Tyler YMCA; trustee Tex. Tchr. Retirement System. Mem. E. Tex. (dir.), Tyler (pres. 1966-67) chambers commerce, Newcomen Soc. N.A. Episcopalian (vestry, finance com. Diocese Tex.). Mason (32 degree, Shriner, Jester). Clubs: Tyler, Willow Brook Country, Tyler Petroleum. Home: 2725 Pecan Dr Tyler TX 75701 Office: 100 E Ferguson St Tyler TX 75701

BELL, JACK L., newspaperman; b. Yates Center, Kan., July 24, 1904; s. John H. and Anna J. (Peterson) B.; A.B., U. Okla., 1925; m. Helen Morey, Aug. 21, 1926; 1 son, Stratton Morey. Head U.S. Senate staff and chief polit. writer for A.P., 1937-68; columnist Gannett Newspapers; city editor, Washington corr. Daily Oklahoman, also Oklahoma City Times. Mem. Phi Beta Kappa, Pi Kappa Alpha. Clubs: Nat. Press, Gridiron, International, Chevy Chase. Author: The Splendid Misery; Mr. Conservative: Barry Goldwater; The Johnson Treatment; The Presidency: Office of Power. Home: 4000 Cathedral Av NW Washington DC 20016 Office: Nat Press Bldg Washington DC 20004

BELL, JAMES VINCENT, microbiologist; b. Chgo., Apr. 2, 1919; s. James Vincent and Madeline Nanette (Klinker) Bellizzi; student San Diego State Coll., 1946-47; B.A., Denver U., 1948; M.S., U. Mich., 1951; m. Marie Charlotte Larkin, Sept. 19, 1950; children—James Vincent, Brian Gregory. Horticulturist, Denver Forestry Dept., 1949-50; insect pathology technician U. Cal. at Riverside, 1959-66; microbiologist insect pathology U.S. Dept. Agr., Charleston, S.C., 1966-—. Served with USNR, 1943-46. Mem. Soc. Invertebrate Pathology, Internat. Orgn. Biol. Control, Audubon Soc., Smithsonian Instn., Nat. Geog. Soc., Phi Sigma. Home: 650 Cornell St Charleston SC 29407 Office: PO Box 3187 St Andrews Dr Charleston SC 29407

BELL, J(ESSE) SPENCER, judge; b. Charlotte, N.C., 1906; s. James Ardrey and Jessie Mable (Spencer) B.; A.B., Duke, 1927; postgrad. Law Sch., Harvard, 1929; LL.B., U. N.C., 1930; LL.D., Catawba Coll., 1960; m. Katherine Castellett, May 8, 1943. Admitted to N.C. bar, 1929, since practiced in Charlotte; mem. firm Bell, Bradley, Gebhardt & Delaney, 1952; judge U.S. Ct. Appeals, 4th Circuit, 1961-—. State senator, 1957-61; del. Democratic Nat. Conv. 1960. Mem. Am., N.C. (pres. 1953-54), Mecklenberg County bar assns. Home: 6121 Providence Rd Charlotte NC 28202 Office: US Court of Appeals Charlotte NC 28202

BELL, JOHN ALTON, dentist; b. Roanoke, Va., May 20, 1909; s. John Henry and Madie (Likens) B.; student Emory and Henry U., 1929-32; M.C.S., Benjamin Franklin U., 1939; postgrad. George Washington U., 1942; D.D.S., Georgetown U., 1946; m. Mary Lou Ruth, July 15, 1939; children—Susan, John Alton. Practice gen. dentistry, Arlington, Va., 1946-—; asso. prof. operative dentistry Georgetown U., Washington, 1947-51, 53-57. Mem. Va. Bd. Dental Examiners, 1971-—. Mem. Arlington County Youth Commn., 1967-69. Bd. dirs. Mt. Olivet Found. Fund. Served to capt. USAAF, 1951-53. Fellow Internat. Coll. Dentists, Va. State Dental Assn.; mem. Am., Va. dental assns., No. Va. Dental Soc. (pres. 1965-66), Georgetown Alumni Assn., Pan Am. Med. Soc., Old Dominion Study Club, Arlington C. of C., Omicron Kappa Upsilon, Psi Omega. Methodist (mem. adminstrv. bd.). Mason, Kiwanian (pres. 1962). Clubs: Washington Golf and Country; Northern Virginia Acquatic, Better Sports (pres. 1968-69) (Arlington). Home: 4710 N 33d St Arlington VA 22207 Office: 4625 Old Dominion Dr Arlington VA 22207

BELL, JOHN WILLIAM, state senator; b. N.Y.C., Sept. 16, 1916; s. George William and Ethel (Ryder) B.; B.A., Columbia, 1938, LL.B., 1941 children—Douglas R., Susan Heather, Holli Lei. Practice law, 1946-—; mem. Fla. Senate, 1967-—. Chmn. Broward County (Fla.) Port Authority, 1953-57, Broward County Commn., 1957-60; mem. Fla. Ho. of Reps., 1963-64, 66-67. Served to lt. comdr. USNR, 1943-46. Mem. Am. Legion, Res. Officers Assn., Navy League, Am. Bar Assn., Phi Delta Phi, Sigma Alpha Epsilon. Episcopalian. Kiwanian. Club: Propeller. Address: 100 S E 6th St Fort Lauderdale FL 33301*

BELL, LLOYD RAYMOND, assn. exec.; b. Independence, Kan., Apr. 6, 1926; s. Warren James and Cleo Elizabeth (Jackson) B.; B.A., U. Mo., 1948; E.Edn., So. Meth. U., 1955; m. Betty Lou Verlaine, June 29, 1947; children—Mary Lynn (Mrs. Raymond Peterson Smith), Michael Warren, Janet Lea. Speech, debate and drama tchr. Joplin (Mo.) pub. schs., 1948-50; speech tchr. Forest Av. High Sch., Dallas, 1952-56; prin. Nathaniel Hawthorne Elementary Sch., Dallas, 1956-61, Benjamin Franklin Jr. High Sch., Dallas, 1961-65; asst. dir. pub. relations Tex. State Tchrs. Assn., Austin, 1965-—. Mem. pub. affairs panel U.S. Office Edn., 1971-72. Served to lt.(j.g.) USNR, 1943-46. Mem. N.E.A., Am. Assn. Sch. Adminstrs., Nat. Sch. Pub. Relations Assn. (v.p. South Central region 1968-70, mem. exec. com. 1970-71 pres. 1971-72), Tex. Elementary Prins. and Suprs. Assn. (pres. 1963-64), Alliance Assns. Advancement Edn. (pres. 1971-72), Tex. Congress Parents and Tchrs., Tex. Tchrs. Assn., Phi Gamma Delta. Home: Apt 117 E E Anderson Lane Austin TX 78759 Office: 316 W 12th St Austin TX 78701

BELL, PAUL BUCKNER, lawyer; b. Charlotte, N.C., July 29, 1922; s. George Fisher and Carrie (Savage) B.; B.S., Wake Forest U., 1947, J.D., cum laude, 1948; m. Betty Sue Trulock, May 3, 1952; children—Paul B., Morris Trulock, Betty Fisher, Douglas Savage. Admitted to N.C. bar, 1948; patent atty.; pres. firm Parrott, Bell, Seltzer, Park & Gibson, Charlotte, 1948-—. Dir. Pilot Research Corp., Southland Investors, Inc., Idlewild Farms, Inc., Consol. Credit Realty Co., Inc. Trustee Mecklenbury Presbetery, Alexander Children's Center, Presbyn. Home of Charlotte, Mountain Retreat Assn. Served to 1st lt. USAAF, 1943-46. Mem. Am. N.C., Mecklenburg bar assns., Am. Patent Law Assn., Licensing Execs. Soc., Sigma Phi Epsilon, Phi Alpha Delta. Presbyn. (elder). Club: Charlotte Textile (past pres.). Home: 4001 Foxcroft Rd Charlotte NC 28211 Office: 1211 E Morehead St PO Box 10337 Charlotte NC 28201

BELL, WARREN EARL, lodge and country club exec.; b. Findlay, O., Jan. 26, 1922; s. Charles Omar and Mearl Marie (Alheim) B.; student Ohio State U., 1941-42; m. Peggy Kirk, Aug. 18, 1953; children— Bonnie, Peggy Ann, Kirk. Distbr. salesman Krantz Brewing Corp., Findlay, 1944-49; with sales and promotion dept. A. G. Spalding &Bros., Chgo., 1949-53; designer, builder, owner, operator Pine Needles Lodges and Country Club, Southern Pines, N.C., 1953-—. Served with AUS, 1942-43. Elk. Home: Grove Dr Southern Pines NC 28387 Office: Midland Rd Southern Pines NC 28387

BELL, WILLIAM JACK, educator; b. nr. Norcatur, Kan., Nov. 1, 1915; s. James S. and Ruth (Diefendorf) B.; B.A., B.S., Emporia Kan. State Tchrs. Coll., 1937, M.S, 1940; Ph. D., U. Mo., 1949; m. Marjorie May Andrews, May 9, 1942. Tchr. high sch., Colby, Kan., 1937-42; reporter-editor Colby Free Press-Tribune, 1937-42; grad. asst., instr. U. Mo. Sch. Journalism, 1946-49; asst. prof. U. Okla. Sch. Journalism, 1949-51; photographer Daily Oklahoman, Oklahoma City, summer 1951; prof. journalism, head journalism and graphic arts dept. East Tex. State U., Commerce, 1951-—. City commr., Commerce, 1960-64, mayor pro-tem, 1964-66, mayor, 1967-70; chmn. Airport Adv. Bd., 1971-—. Bd. dirs. Sulphur River Municipal Water Dist., 1971-72. Mem. exec. com. NetSeO Trails council Boy Scouts Am., 1953-57. Served with USNR, 1942-45. Mem. Am. Soc. Journalism Sch. Adminstrs., Sports Information Dirs. (coordinator 68-—; nat. pres. 1965-67) Nat. Assn. Intercollegiate Athletics (Hall of Fame 1970), C. of C. (dir. 1955-57, 59-62; 69-72), Tex. Journalism Edn. Council (exec. com. 1972-—); Phi Delta Kappa (historian 1957-69), Sigma Delta Chi (chpt. 50). Lion (pres. 1959-60, dep. dist. gov. 1962-64). Home: 2500 Washington St Commerce TX 75428

BELLAH, CHARLIE LEWIS, architect, structural engr.; b. Corpus Christi, Tex., Feb. 26, 1937; s. Doy B. and Pearl (Boswell) B.; B. Arch., Tex. Technol. Coll., 1961; postgrad. in planning, structural, civil and soil engring.; m. Dixie Darlyne Hulsey, Jan. 29, 1960; children—Anthony Todd, Barry Kip. Asso. R.S. Colley & Assos., Corpus Christi, 1961-69; partner Valentine & Bellah, architects, engrs., Corpus Christi, 1969-70; owner, prin. Charlie L. Bellah, architects, engrs., planners, Corpus Christie, 1970-—. Mem. A.I.A. adv. com. to Del Mar Technol. Sch., Corpus Christi, 1968-—, guest lectr., instr., spring 1971. Registered architect, Tex., Okla. Mem. A.I.A. (chpt. v.p. 1972-73), Tex. Soc. Architects, Constrn. Specification Inst. (chpt. v.p. 1969-70 pres., chmn. bd. dirs. 1970-71), Soc. Am. Mil. Engrs., Nat., Tex. (Young Engr. of Year Nueces chpt. 1972) socs. profl. engrs., Soc. Am. Mil. Engrs. (pres., dir. 1971-72). Home: 1009 Stirman St Corpus Christi TX 78411 Office: 4517 S Staples St Woodbury Sq Corpus Christi TX 78411

BELLERINO, FRANK ANTHONY, JR., geologist; b. New Orleans, Aug. 28, 1928; s. Frank Anthony and Dora (Hansen) B.; B.S., La. State U. 1952; m. Frances Louise Young, Dec. 29, 1951; children—Kathryn M., Patricia L., Michael T. With Western Co., Midland, Tex., 1952, El Capitan Oil Co., Midland, 1952-53, Forest Oil Co., Midland, 1953-56, Am. Trading Oil Co., Midland, 1956; geologist W.M. & A.P. Fuller, Midland, also New Orleans, 1956-65; petroleum cons., New Orleans, 1965-—; dir. G.T.C. Corp., Micro-Tec, Inc. (both New Orleans). Served with USMCR, 1948-52. Mem. Am. Assn. Petroleum Geologists, Internat. Oil Scouts, New Orleans Geol. Soc., Soc. Econ. Paleontologists and Mineralogists, Am. Inst. Mining, Metall. and Petroleum Engrs., Phi Gamma Delta. Presbyn. (chmn. bd. deacons 1966). Mason. Home: 984 Chapelle St New Orleans LA 70124 Office: Pere Marquette Bldg New Orleans LA 70112

BELLHORN, E.L., religious adminstr. Sec. Synod Evang. Luth. Chs., Oveido, Fla. Address: Route 1 Box 92 Slavia Oviedo FL 32765*

BELLINGER, EDGAR THOMSON, lawyer; b. N.Y.C., Sept. 23, 1929; s. John B. and Margaret (Thomson) B.; B.A., Haverford Coll., 1951; J.D., George Washington U., 1955; m. Adrian J. Dunn, Nov. 23, 1957; children—Edgar, Robert, Margaret. Admitted D.C., Md. bars, 1955; law clk. to chief judge U.S. Dist. Ct. for D.C., 1955-57; asst. U.S. atty. for D.C., 1957-59; partner firm Pope Ballard and Loos, Washington, 1959—. Bd. dirs. DC chpt. A.R.C., Children's Hosp D.C., Mem. Am., D.C., Md. bar assns., The Barristers, Phi Alpha Delta. Episcopalian. Clubs: Chevy Chase, Metropolitan. Home: 28 Quincy St Chevy Chase MD 20015 Office: 888 17th St NW Washington DC 20006

BELLMON, HENRY, U.S. senator; b. Tonkawa, Okla., Sept. 3, 1921; s. George and Edith (Caskey) B.; B.S. in Agr., Okla. State U., Stillwater, 1942; m. Shirley Osborn, Jan. 24, 1947; children—Patricia (Mrs. Larry Lewis), Gail (Mrs. John Hal Wynne), Ann. Engaged in farming, Billings, Okla., 1946—; mem. Okla. Ho. of Reps. from Noble County, 1946-48; gov. State of Okla., 1962-66; U.S. senator from Okla., 1968—. Past chmn. Interstate Oil Compact Commn.; past mem. exec. com. Nat. Gov.'s Conf. Chmn. Okla. Republican Com., 1960-62; past nat. chmn. Nixon-for-Pres. Com. Served with USMCR, 1942-46. Presbyn. Home: Route 1 Red Rock OK 74651

BELLOMY, BRUCE BEN, pathologist; b. La Feria, Tex., Sept. 28, 1927; s. Frank Ray and Grace (Ashworth) B.; student U. Cal. at Berkeley, 1945-48; M.D., George Washington U., 1952; m. Eleanor Marie Tiley, May 29, 1952; children—Ray Michael, Barbara Ann, Rex Robert. Intern, Vanderbilt U. Hosp., Nashville, 1952-53; USPHS Hosp., Seattle, 1953-54; fellow in pathology U. Va., 1954-55; resident in pathology Clin. Center, NIH, Bethesda, Md., 1955-57; sr. surgeon USPHS, 1956-58; asso. pathologist Bapt. Hosp., Nashville, 1958-61; chief of pathology Ft. Sanders Presbyn. Hosp., Knoxville, Tenn., 1961—, East Tenn. Children's Hosp., Knoxville, 1961—. Instr. pathology U. Tenn., Knoxville, 1963—; dir. Knoxville City Sch. System Sch. of Certified Lab. Assts., 1968—. Pres. bd. Helen Ross McNabb Mental Health Center, Knoxville, 1969—. Served with USPHS, 1956-58; now comdr. Res. Mem. A.M.A., Tenn. Med. Assn., Coll. Am. Pathologists, Am. Soc. Clin. Pathologists, Knoxville Acad. Medicine, Tenn. Soc. Pathologists. Home: 3600 Montlake Dr Knoxville TN 37920 Office: 1909 W Clinch Av Knoxville TN 37916

BELLOS, JACK FRANK, dentist; b. San Antonio, Aug. 20, 1939; s. Photios Peter and Aphrodite (Varessis) B.; B.S., U. Tex. at Austin, 1962; D.D.S., U. Tex. at Houston, 1969; m. Mary Jane Beck, July 26, 1969. Pharmacist, Sommers Drug Stores, San Antonio, 1962-63, Univ. Drug Store, San Antonio, 1963-65; practicing dentist, San Antonio, 1969—. Mem. Psi Omega, Kappa Psi. Mem. Greek Orthodox Ch. (v.p. bd. dirs.). Mem. Order DeMolay. Home: 415 Rockhill St San Antonio TX 78209 Office: 7411 Broadway PO Box 6574 San Antonio TX 78209

BELLOWS, THOMAS JOHN, educator; b. Chgo., Aug. 15, 1935; s. Charles Everett and Dorothy (Morrison) B.; student Am. U., 1956, U. Cal. at Los Angeles, 1956-57; B.A., Augustan Coll., 1957; M.A., U. Fla., 1958; M.A., Yale, 1960, Ph.D., 1968; m. Mellie Joyce Spencer, July 12, 1956; children—Roderick Alan, Adrienne Marie, Jeannine Louise, Derek John. Asst. prof. polit. sci. West Ga. Coll., Carrollton, 1962-64, 66; asst. to asso. prof. polit. sci. U. Ark., Fayetteville, 1967—, chmn. dept., 1971—. Vis. lectr. depts. history, polit. sci. Nanyang U., Singapore, 1965. Mem. Am. Polit. Sci. Assn., Assn. Asian Studies, Brit. Assn. of Malaysia and Singapore, Phi Beta Kappa, Phi Alpha Theta. Methodist. Author: (with S. Erikson and H. Winter) Political Science: Introductory Essays and Readings, 1971; The People's Action Party of Singapore: Emergence of a Dominant Party System, 1970. Home: 2327 Berry St Fayetteville AR 72701

BELSER, JAMES EDWIN, lawyer; b. Columbia, S.C., Nov. 13, 1912; B.A., Washington and Lee U., 1934; LL.B., U. S.C., 1936; LL.M., Harvard, 1937. Admitted to S.C. bar, 1936; now mem. firm Belser & Kemmerlin, Columbia; asso. prof. U. S.C. Law Sch., 1946-51. Mem. Richland County, S.C., Am. bar assns., Phi Delta Phi. Address: Belser & Kemmerlin 1408 Hampton St Columbia SC 29201*

BELTRAN, ALBERTO, artist; b. Mexico City, Mexico, Mar. 22, 1923; ed. Escuela Libre de Publicidad y Arte Commercial, Mexico City, Escuela Nacional de Artes Plasticas, San Carlos. Works exhibited, Mexico, U.S., Europe, Russia; illustrator books; contbr. daily polit. cartoon La Prensa, Mexico; founder, editor, illustrator satirical polit. mags. Ahi va el Golpe and El Coyote emplumado. Recipient numerous award including prize Art Dirs. Club Chgo., 1952, Premio Nacional de Grabado, Mexico, 1954—, first prize Inter-Am. Biennale of Painting and Engraving, 1958. Address: 71-7 Revilla Gigedo Mexico DF Mexico*

BELZILE, JOSEPH DANIEL, dentist, army officer; b. Van Buren, Me., May 9, 1930; s. Joseph Paul and Anne Elizabeth (Cyr) B.; B.S., Coll. Holy Cross, Worcester, Mass., 1953; D.D.S., U. Pa., 1957; Ph.D., Georgetown U., 1965; m. Beverly Renee Bernier, Aug. 10, 1963; children—Joseph Daniel, Michael William. Commd. 2d lt. U.S. Army, 1956, advanced through ranks to col., 1972; intern Tripler U.S. Army Hosp., Honolulu, 1957-58; periodontist 25th Inf. div. Schofield Barracks, Hawaii, 1958-60; post dental surgeon U.S. Army Garrison, Fort Totten, N.Y., 1960-62; resident pathology Armed Forces Inst. Pathology, Washington, 1965-66; researcher U.S. Army Inst. Dental Research, Washington, 1966-69; oral pathologist Ireland Army Hosp., Fort Knox, Ky., 1969—. Asst. prof. oral pathology Georgetown U., 1965-71; cons. oral pathology 1st Army Dental Surgeon, Reynolds Army Hosp., Fort Sill, Okla., U.S. Army Hosp., Fort Campbell, Ky., U.S. Army Hosp., Fort Jackson, S.C. Diplomate Am. Bd. Oral Pathology, Am. Bd. Oral Medicine. Fellow Am. Acad. Oral Pathology; mem. Am. Dental Assn., Psi Omega. Roman Catholic. Home: 1462 A 5th Av Fort Knox KY 40121 Office: US Ireland Army Hosp Fort Knox KY 40121

BENAVIDES, JAIME MIGUEL, physician; b. Chuquicamata, Chile, Oct. 20, 1923; s. Jaime and Elena (Spikula) B.; came to U.S., 1926, naturalized, 1934; A.B., Duke, 1943; M.D., U. Pa., 1947; m. Nela Montejo, May 14, 1947 children—Suzanne, Maria, Jaime Manuel. Intern, resident Lutheran Hosp., Cleve., 1947-49; resident orthopaedics U.S. Naval Hosp., Phila., 1953-55, asst. chief orthopedics, Newport, R.I., 1955-56; resident Newington (Conn.) Hosp. Crippled Children, 1957; asst. chief orthopedics U.S. Navy Hosp., Phila., 1958-61, chief orthopaedics, Key West, Fla., 1961-66; chief of staff Monroe Gen. Hosp., Key West, 1966-70; chief staff, chief surgery Fla. Keys Meml. Hosp., 1972—; chmn. bd. Lower Fla. Keys Hosp. Dist., 1970-71, (Mem. med. adv. council Fla. Easter Seal Soc. Bd. dirs. Monroe County Health Planning Council. Diplomate Am. Bd. Orthopedic Surgeons. Fellow A.C.S., Am. Acad. Orthopedic Surgeons, Internat. Coll. Surgeons, Am. Orthopedic Foot Soc., N.Y. Acad. Scis.; mem. Monroe County Med. Soc. (pres. 1971), Fla., Miami, Eastern orthopedic socs., A.M.A., Fla. Med. Assn., Acad. Sports Medicine,Kappa Sigma, Phi Rho Sigma. Roman Catholic. Home: PO BOX 124013 Hilton Haven Key West FL 33040 Office: 638 United St Key West FL 33040

BENBOW, CHARLES FRANK, business exec.; b. Winston-Salem, N.C., Aug. 22, 1924; s. Charles Frank and Ruth (Harper) B.; B.S., U. N.C., 1947; grad. Sch. Credit and Financial Mgmt., Amos Tuck Sch., Dartmouth, 1951, 52, 54; m. Mary Elizabeth Baxter, Sept. 13, 1947; children—Shirley, Martha, Mary. With R.J. Reynolds Industries (formerly R.J. Reynolds Tobacco Co.), Winston-Salem, 1947—, asst. credit mgr., 1948-56, asst. sec., 1956-58, credit mgr., 1958-68, asst. treas., 1961-68, treas., 1968-70, v.p. finance, 1969, dir., 1971—; chmn. bd. Reynolds Leasing Corp., 1969—; treas., dir. Archer Products, Inc., Winston-Salem, 1966-71; treas. R.J. Reynolds Foods, Inc., 1967-70; dir. N.C. Nat. Bank, Winston-Salem, 1967-71, Pennick & Ford Ltd., 1970-71, Charlotte br. Fed. Res. Bank Richmond. Episcopalian. Home: Route 8 Winston-Salem NC 27106 Office: PO Box 2943 Winston-Salem NC 27102

BENDER, ARTHUR STILLMAN, physician; b. Springfield, Mass., July 7, 1938; s. Theodore George and Faye Dorothy (August) B.; B.A., Yale, 1959; M.D., U. Va., 1963; m. Susan K. Gabroy, Nov. 2, 1963; children—Penelope Ann, Arthur Kenneth. Intern, resident U. Va. Hosp., 1963-68; pvt. practice medicine, specializing in internal medicine and hematology, Charlottesville, Va., 1970—; asst. clin. prof. medicine U. Va., 1970—. Served from capt. to maj. M.C., AUS, 1968-70. Diplomate Am. Bd. Internal Medicine. Mem. A.C.P. Home: 404 Key West Dr Charlottesville VA 22901 Office: 400 10th St NE Charlottesville VA 22901

BENDER, ERNEST LINWOOD, JR., business exec.; b. New Bern, N.C., July 21, 1923; s. Ernest Linwood and Mary (Strother) B.; student N.C. State Coll., 1941-43, 46; m. Mary Catherine Brinson, Mar. 14, 1948; children—Ernest Linwood III, Brian B. With A.H. Robins Co., Inc., Richmond, Va., 1947—, field sales mgr., 1963-67, asst. v.p., 1967-69, v.p., 1969—. Served to 1st lt. USAAF, 1943-45. Mem. Sales and Marketing Execs. Richmond, Am. Marketing Assn. (dir.), Sigma Nu. Episcopalian. Mason. Clubs: Rotunda, Country of Va. (Richmond). Home: 6130 St Andrews Circle Richmond VA 23229 Office: 1407 Cummings Dr Richmond VA 23220

BENDER, RICHARD NELSON, clergyman, ednl. adminstr.; b. Red Key, Ind., Apr. 18, 1913; s. Orlo O. and Iva E. (Giddings) B.; student Earlham Coll., 1938-40; A.B., Boston U., 1942, M.A., 1943, Ph.D., 1952; postgrad. Harvard; m. Rosalie Jurgle, Feb. 2, 1935; 1 dau., Jacqueline (Mrs. Pier H. Morgan, Jr.). Ordained to ministry Methodist Church, 1943; pastor Meth. chs., Geneva Circuit, Ind., 1936-38, Chester, Ind., 1938-40, Acushnet, Mass., 1940-45; prof. philosophy Baker U., Baldwin, Kan., 1945-53, dir. religious life, 1948-53; dir. religion in higher edn. Meth. Bd. Edn., Nashville, 1953-68; dir. dept. ednl. instns. United Meth. Bd. Edn., Nashville, 1969-72. Exec. dir. Assn. Colls. and Univs. for Internat.-Intercultural Studies, Inc., 1967—, Council on Ch.-Related Colls., 1966-72. Trustee St. Paul Sch. Theology. Mem. Am. Assn. U. Profs., Am. Philos. Assn. Author: A Philosophy of Life, 1949; Called To Be Relevant, 1964. Editor: Faculty Forum jour., 1957-68; The Church Related College Today: Anachronism or Opportunity, 1971. Home: 5062 Lakeview Dr Nashville TN 37220 Office: PO Box 872 Nashville TN 37202

BENDHEIM, LEROY S., lawyer; state senator; b. Alexandria, Va., Feb. 12, 1906; s. Charles and Edith (Schwarz) B.; A.B., George Washington U., 1928, J.D., 1929; grad. Provost Marshall Gen. Sch. for Mil. Govt., 1944; m. Ethel Colman, June 10, 1934. Admitted to D.C., Va. bars, 1929; pvt. practice law, 1929—; mem. firm Bendheim & Ratner; instr. George Washington U., 1949-50; mem. Va. Senate, 1963—. dir. 1st Fed. Savs. & Loan Assn. of Alexandria, Park & Shop, Alexandria Corp., Downtown Garage, Inc., Columbia Bldg. Products Co., Inc., 1st Va. Bank. Mem. Alexandria Bd. Edn., 1934-43, chmn., 1934-40; mem. city council 1948-61; vice mayor 1952-55, mayor, 1955-61. Former bd. dirs. Alexandria dist. Boy Scouts Am., Nat. Capital area council; dir. B'nai B'rith Found., United Jewish Appeal; mem. adv. council Nat. Community Relations; hon. chmn. Jewish Welfare Bd. Asso. adv. mem. Alexandria Selective Service Bd., 1934-43; asst. staff member NRA Rev. Bd., 1935-36. Served with AUS, 1943-45. Mem. Am., Alexandria (pres. 1951-52), Va. bar assns., Bar Assn. D.C., C. of C., V.F.W. (past dept. comdr. Va.), Am. Legion, Nat. Assn. of Army (adv. com. George Washington chpt.). Jewish religion (hon. pres. Beth El congregation). Mason, Elk, Odd Fellow (grand master Va., 1955-56), Eagle, Lion. Contbg. editor Probate Law Digest for State Va. Home: 309 Mansion Dr Alexandria VA 22302 Office: 718 Jefferson St Alexandria VA 22314

BENEDICT, ANDREW BELL, JR., banker; b. Nashville, July 6, 1914; s. Andrew B. and Anne Hillman (Scales) B.; student Wallace U. Sch., Nashville; B.A., Vanderbilt U., 1935; grad. Rutgers U. Grad. Sch. Banking, 1944; m. Sarah Richardson Bryan, Apr. 17, 1937; children—Henriette Richardson (Mrs. Russell F. Morris, Jr.), Andrew Bell III. With First Am. Nat. Bank, 1935—, beginning as runner, successively asst. cashier, asst. v.p., v.p., 1938-51, exec. v.p., 1951-60, pres., 1960-69, chmn. bd., 1969—. Commr., Nashville Municipal Auditorium, Bd. dirs. United Givers Fund, Nashville YMCA; trustee Meharry Med. Col., Vanderbilt U. Mem. Am. Inst. Banking, Assn. Res. City Bankers (past pres., dir.), Phi Delta Theta, Omicron Delta Kappa. Methodist (mem. bd. publ.). Mason (Shriner, 33 1/2, mem. Supreme Council), Rotarian. Home: Curtiswood Lane Nashville TN 37204 Office: First American Nat Bank Nashville TN 37237

BENEFIELD, JUNE, newspaper columnist; b. Gorman, Tex., 1921; student U. Tex. News reporter Houston Press; columnist Houston Chronicle, 1956—. Recipient Matrix award, Houston, 1965, News award Tex. Bar Assn., 1971, Houston Bar Assn., 1971. Mem. Theta Sigma Phi. Office: 512-30 Travis St Houston TX 77002

BENEFIELD, LLOYD, broadcasting exec. Pres. KOFM-FM, Oklahoma City. Office: 1200 NE Britton Rd Oklahoma City OK 73101*

BENENATI, JOSEPH ANGELO, physician; b. Bklyn., Nov. 4, 1920; s. Francis and Margaret (Leonardi) B.; B.S., Fordham U., 1941; M.D., U. State N.Y. at Bklyn., 1950; m. Virginia Angela Scileppi, July 11, 1953; children—Joseph Michael, James Francis, Margaret Anne, Laura Marie. Intern, St. Vincent's Hosp., N.Y.C., 1950-51, resident, 1951-52; pvt. practice medicine, specializing in family medicine, Massapequa, N.Y., 1952-66, Ft. Lauderdale, Fla., 1966—; med. dir. Grumman Aerospace Corp., Bethpage, N.Y., 1955-66; attending physician Holy Cross Hosp., Ft. Lauderdale, Fla. Served with AUS, 1942-46. Diplomate Nat. Bd. Med. Examiners; charter diplomate Am. Bd. Family Practice. Fellow Indsl. Med. Assn.; mem. Am. Acad. Family Practice, A.M.A., Fla., Broward County med. assns., Phi Chi. Office: 2940 E Commercial Blvd Fort Lauderdale FL 33308

BENHAM, DAVID BLAIR, cons. engr.; b. Ft. Riley, Kan., Nov. 11, 1918; s. Webster Lance and Margaret L. (Drake) B.; student Oklahoma City U., 1937; B.S., U.S. Naval Acad., 1941, Naval Architect, 1942; m. Betty Louise Prichard, June 29, 1950; children—Barbara Lee (Mrs. John L. Tracy), Suzanne Lance (Mrs. Suzanne Murch), Nancy Ann, David Blair II. Joined Benham Engring Co., Oklahoma City, 1946, jr. partner, 1947-52; sr. mng. partner Benham Engring Co. and Affiliates, Oklahoma City, also Phoenix, 1952-63, sr. mng. partner Benham-Blair & Affiliates, 1963-67, inc., 1967, pres. chmn. bd. 1967—; dir. Acad. Computing Corp., 1967-72, Technology Research & Devel. Co., 1970—; cons. engr. to U.S. cities; dir. Fidelity Bank, N.A., Oklahoma City. Chmn. Bd. Registration for Profl. Engrs., Okla., 1963-64. Vice chmn. Okla. Mental Health Bd., 1958-59. Past mem. exec. com. Frontiers of Sci. Found.; trustee U.S. Naval Acad. Found.; bd. dirs. Salvation Army; bd. visitors Okla. State U. Served to lt. comdr. USN, World War II. Recipient citation for work in naval constrn. U.S. sec. navy, 1944. Registered profl. engr., 22 states and D.C. Diplomate Am. Acad. Environmental Engrs. Mem. Am. Soc. C.E. (past pres. Okla. sect.), Cons. Engrs. Assn. Okla. (past dir.), Nat. Soc. Profl. Engrs., Soc. Am. Mil. Engrs. (Outstanding Service award), Okla. (past dir.), Oklahoma City (past dir.) chambers commerce, Navy League (past Okla. pres., past nat. dir.), Oklahoma City Downtown Assn. (past dir.), U.S. Naval Acad. Alumni Assn. (v.p. Central area), Newcomen Soc. Presbyn. (elder). Mason (32 deg., Shriner, Jester); mem. Order Red, Red Rose. Clubs: Optimist (past pres.), Economic, Embassy (pres.), Men's Dinner (Oklahoma City). Contbr. papers and articles to tech. jours. Home: 6621 Hillcrest St Oklahoma City OK 73116 Office: 6323 N Grand Blvd Oklahoma City OK 73118

BENINTENDE, ALFRED JOSEPH, JR., communications co. exec.; b. New Orleans, Apr. 9, 1936; s. Alfred Joseph and Anna Elizabeth (Becker) B.; B.S., La. State U., 1962; postgrad. Bell System Communications Engring. Sch., Clemson U., 1963-64; m. Virginia Lucean Rhudy, July 27, 1957; children—Alfred Joseph III, Cheryl Suzanne. Student engr. So. Bell Telephone Co., Baton Rouge, 1962-65, engr., New Orleans, 1965-67; project engr. So. Central Bell Telephone Co., Birmingham, Ala., 1967-70, audit supr. accounting, 1970-71, Bell-ind. relations mgr., New Orleans, 1971—; v.p. City News, Kenner, La.; 1972—. Pres. Birmingham Interclub Council, 1970-71; vice chmn. County Cancer Crusade, 1970. Bd. dirs. Operation New Birmingham, 1969-71, Birmingham Jaycee Found., 1969-71. Served with USAF, 1954-58. Named Gold Key Man, New Orleans Jr. C. of C., 1967, Jaycee of Yr., Birmingham Jr. C. of C., 1970, Outstanding Local Jaycee Pres. in Dist., Ala. Jr. C. of C., 1970. Registered profl. engr., Ala., La. mem. I.E.E.E. (vice chmn. New Orleans communicaton tech. group 1966-67), La. Telephone Assn. (dir. 1971—). Home: 2101 Comet St New Orleans LA 70114 Office: 1215 Prytania St New Orleans LA 70140

BENITEZ, JAIME, univ. pres.; b. Vieques, P.R., Oct. 29, 1908; s. Luis and Candida (Rexach) B.; LL.B., Georgetown U., 1930, LL.M., 1931; A.M., U. Chgo., 1939; LL.D., Polytech. Inst., P.R., 1950, N.Y.U., 1960, Fairleigh Dickinson U., 1961, Cath. U. P.R., 1965, U. West Indies, 1969, U. Miami, 1970; Litt.D., Temple U., 1969; m. Luz A. Martinez, Aug. 15, 1941; children—Clotilde, Jaime N., Margarita. Instr. polit. sci. U. P.R., 1931-41, asso. prof., 1941-42, chancellor univ., 1942-66, pres., 1966—. Head hearings officer Nat. War Labor Bd., Washington. Del. to Gen. Conf. UNESCO, Paris, 1951; mem. U.S. Nat. Commn. UNESCO, 1951-55; pres. com. of Bill of Rights, P.R. Constl. Conv., 1951; U.S. del. Conf. of Univs., Utrecht, Holland, 1948; mem. adv. com. on coll. housing program Housing and Home Agy., 1957; co-chmn. Caribbean Conf. P.R., 1960; pres. Assn. Caribbean Univs., 1969. Named Citizen of Year, Inst. of P.R. in N.Y., 1958; Distinguished Citizen award Soc. Knights of St. John, Chgo., 1959. Mem. Am. Acad. Arts and Scis., P.R. Tchrs. Assn., Nat. Assn. State Univs. (pres. 1958), Georgetown U., U. Chgo. alumni assns., Am. Acad. Polit. and Social Scis., Fed. Bar Assn., Colegio de Abogados de Puerto Rico, Assn., Insular Employees. Clubs: Cosmos (Washington); Berwind's Country; Bankers (San Juan). Author: The Concept of the Family in Roman and Common Law Jurisprudence, 1931; Political and Philosophical Theories of Jose Ortega Y Gasset, 1939; Reflexiones Sobre el Presente, 1950; La Iniciacion Universitaria Y las Ciencias Sociales, 1952; The United States, Cuba and Latin America, 1961; Junto a La Torre, 1963; La Universidad del Futuro, 1964; Sobre el Futuro Cultural y Politico de Puerto Rico, 1965; 25 Anos de Direccion Universitario, 1967; Crisis enel Mundo y en La Educacion, 1968; with the Odds Against Us, 1969; Los Colegios Regionales en La Vida Universitaria, 1969; Where is Our Courage 1970. Home: House of Pres Univ Puerto Rico Rio Piedras PR 00931

BENITEZ, SISTER MARIA MARGARITA, supt. schs. Supt., Catholic Schs., San Juan, P.R. Address: PO Box 1967 San Juan PR 00903*

BENITO, LOUIS, advt. agy. exec.; b. Tampa, Fla., Nov. 23, 1914; s. Luis and Concha (Bonera) B.; grad. high sch.; m. Helen Canedo, Nov. 19, 1944; children—John, Mary Charles, Cristina, Conchita, Louis, Olga, Davian. With R.E. McCarthy Advt. Agy., 1934-54; chmn. bd. Louis Benito Advt. Agy., Inc., Tampa, 1954—. Sr. v.p. Tampa World Trade Council. Trustee, Tampa Childrens Home; bd. counselors U. Tampa; mem. bd. Tampa Pub. Library. Served with AUS, 1942-46. Recipient Top Mgmt. award Sales and Marketing Execs., 1965; named Tampa Advt. Man of Year, 1954, 59. Mem. Am. Assn. Advt. Agys. (past sec.-treas.), Affiliated Advt. Agys. Internat., Fla. (sec.), Greater Tampa chambers commerce, Alpha Delta Sigma, Roman Catholic. Rotarian. Clubs: Palma Ceia Golf and Country, University (Tampa). Home: 200 Corsica St Tampa FL 33606 Office: PO Box 3382 915 Ashley Dr Tampa FL 33602

BENJAMIN, BLANCHE STERNBERGER, civic worker; b. Mayesville, S.C., May 15, 1901; d. Emanuel and Bertha (Strauss) Sternberger; student Wellesley Coll., 1920-21; m. Edward B. Benjamin, Oct. 19, 1921; children—Edward B., W. Mente, Jonathan S. Vice pres. Starmount Co., Greensboro, N.C. 1930-67, Friendly Center, Inc., Greensboro, 1955-67; dir. Benjamin Minerals, Inc., New Orleans, 1947—. Vice pres. New Orleans Garden Soc., 1927-30, New Orleans Philharmonic Soc., 1928-51; mem. orgn. com. Newcomb Presch. and Metairie Park Country Day Sch.; bd. dirs. Isaac Delgado Museum, New Orleans, 1958-72; v.p. Benjamin Fund, New Orleans Symphony Soc.; co-founder (with husband) Sternberger Hosp. (now Guilford Welfare Center), Starmount Forest Country Club; co-founder Emanuel Sternberger Ednl. Fund, Greensboro. Mem. Jr. League. Clubs: Orleans (corr. sec. 1947-49), Garden Soc., New Orleans Country, Southern Yacht (New Orleans); Greensboro Country, Assembly, Dogwood Garden (Greensboro); Saratoga Golf (Saratoga Springs, N.Y.). Address: 383 Walnut St New Orleans LA 70118

BENJAMIN, EDWARD B., corp. exec.; b. New Orleans, Nov. 18, 1897; s. Emanuel Victor and Rachel (Goldsmith) B.; A.B. magna cum laude, Harvard, 1918; D.H.L., U. Rochester, 1960; m. Blanche Sternberger, Oct. 19, 1921; children—Edward Bernard Jr., William Mente Sternberger, Jonathan Sternberger. Began with family interests, 1919; v.p. E.V. Benjamin Co., Inc., 1919-29, pres., 1939-47; pres. Bay Chem. Co., 1938-47, Myles Salt Co., 1940-47; pres. Starmount Co., 1929-67, Friendly Center, Inc., 1953-67, Benjamin Minerals Co. Bd. dirs. U.S. Coast Guard Acad. Found., Grayson Found; pres. Benjamin Fund. Donor Benjamin Awards for Restful Music. Trustee, founder (with Mrs. Benjamin) Sternberger Children's Hosp. (now Guilford County Welfare Center), Greensboro, N.C.; mem. vis. com. dept. biology Harvard, 1953-59; export adv. com. U.S. Dept. Commerce, 1946; orgn. com. New Orleans Community Chest, New Orleans Welfare Com., 1930-32; bd. dirs. New Orleans Opera House Assn.; chmn. organizing com., 1st pres. Cultural Attractions Fund Greater New Orleans, 1960-61; pres. Community Concert

Assn. New Orleans, 1960-68. Served with Harvard ROTC, 1917, Camp Lee, Va., 1918. Clubs: Round Table, Southern Yacht (New Orleans); Merchants and Manufacturers (Greensboro); Turf and Field; Bankers (N.Y.C.); New Orleans Country; Greensboro Country; Saratoga Golf. Author: The Larger Liberalism, 1918. Home: 383 Walnut St New Orleans LA 70118 Office: Whitney Bldg New Orleans LA 70130

BENJAMIN, EDWARD BERNARD, JR., lawyer; b. New Orleans, Feb. 11, 1923; s. Edward Bernard and Blanche (Sternberger) B.; B.S., Yale, 1944; LL.M., Tulane U., 1952; m. Adelaide Wisdom, May 11, 1957; children—Edward Wisdom, Mary Dabney, Ann Leith, Stuart Minor. Admitted to La. Bar, 1952, since practiced in New Orleans; now partner firm Jones, Walker, Waechter, Poitevent, Carrere & Denegre. Chmn. bd. Starmount Co., Greensboro, N.C. Lectr. fed. taxation Tulane Tax Inst., N.Y.U. Inst. Fed. Taxation, others. Trustee Hollins Coll., mem. bd. Southwestern Legal Found. Research Fellows, Salvation Army Adv. Bd., Bur. Govtl. Research New Orleans. Served from 2d lt. to 1st lt., AUS, 1943-47. Mem. Am. (sec. sect. taxation 1967-69), La. (chmn. sect. taxation 1959-60), New Orleans bar assns., Am., La. law insts. Episcopalian (vestryman). Clubs: New Orleans Country, New Orleans Law Tennis, Greensboro Country, Southern Yacht, Plimsoll, Petroleum, Internat. House (New Orleans). Home: 1837 Palmer Av New Orleans LA 70118 Office: 225 Baronne St New Orleans LA 70112

BENJAMIN, PAUL RAYMOND, sales exec.; b. Wellsboro, Pa., Nov. 24, 1914; s. Raymond Mortica and Neva (Jackson) B.; grad. high sch.; m. Sarah Ellen Williamson, Dec. 21, 1947; children—Paul Raymond, Ellen Blair. With Dept. Mil. Affairs, State of Pa., 1936-41; owner Paul R. Benjamin Assos., advt., 1951-66; account exec., 1969-—; account exec. First Financial Marketing Group, 1966-67, Bankers Systems, Memphis, 1967-—. Served with AUS, 1941-47. Decorated Bronze Star medal with oak leaf pendulant. Methodist (steward), Club: Lost Chord (bd. dirs 1960-62, pres. 1962-—). Address: 1759 Eastmoreland St Memphis TN 38104

BENKEN, EUGENE EDWIN, lawyer, certified public accountant; b. Savannah, Ga., Dec. 9, 1889; s.Eugene Edwin and Effie (Strobhar) B.; grad. Walton Sch. Commerce, Chgo., 1924; LL.B., Blackstone Coll. Law, 1935; m. Elsie Ehler, Sept. 15, 1932. Accounting dept. So. Cotton Oil Co., Savannah, 1911-24; certified pub. accountant, Savannah, 1925-—; admitted to Ga. bar, 1936; practiced in Savannah, 1937-—; partner firm Thompson and Benken, attys.-C.P.A.'s. Served in Armed Forces, World War I. C.P.A., Ga., Ind., Tenn. Mem. Am. Inst. C.P.A.'s, Ga. Soc. C.P.A.'s (v.p. 1930-31), Am., Ga. Savannah bar assns., Telfair Acad. Arts and Scis., S.R. (treas., mgr.), Am. Legion, S.C.V., Soc. Colonial Wars, Ga. Assn. Atty.-C.P.A.'s. Baptist. Mason (32 deg., Shriner), Elk. Home: 735 E 40th St Savannah GA 31401 Office: 144 Drayton St Savannah GA 31401

BENNACK, FRANK ANTHONY, JR., newspaper exec.; b. San Antonio, Feb. 12, 1933; s. Frank Anthony and Lula Wardell (Connally) B.; student U. Md., Germany, 1954-55, St. Mary's U., 1956-57; m. Luella Smith, Sept. 1, 1951; children—Shelley, Laura, Diane, Cynthia, Julie. With classified advt. dept. San Antonio Light, Hearst Corp., 1950-54, with retail advt. dept., 1956-58, retail advt. mgr., 1961-65, asst. pub., 1965-67, pub., v.p., 1967-—; dir. sales and advt. Jorrie Furniture Co., San Antonio, 1958-61; dir. Alamo Nat. Bank. Bd. dirs. S.W. Found. for Research and Edn.; vice chmn. bd. dirs. Symphony Soc. San Antonio; trustee Witte Meml. Mus., Our Lady of Lake Coll. Served with AUS, 1954-56. Mem. Tex. Daily Newspaper Assn. (v.p.), Greater San Antonio C. of C. (pres. 1971). Roman Catholic. Rotarian. Home: 106 Villa Ann San Antonio TX 78213 Office: PO Box 161 San Antonio TX 78291

BENNER, CLAUDE JACOB, aerospace co. exec.; b. Wilkes-Barre, Pa., Sept. 16, 1917; s. Rollie O. and Blanche (Engler) B.; certificate in aero. engring. Casey Jones Sch. Aero., 1940; m. Marie M. Meaney, June 14, 1947; children—Susan (Mrs. Michael E. O'Neill), Linda Joy, Patricia Lee. With LTV Aerospace Corp., Dallas, 1940-—, dir. adminstrn., 1965-68, v.p. adminstrn., 1968-—. Bd. dirs. Jr. Achievement, Dallas. Mem. Am. Inst. Aeros. and Astronautics. Independent. Lutheran (supt. Sunday Sch. 1967-70). Club: Royal Oaks Country (Dallas). Home: 4535 Mill Creek Rd Dallas TX 75234 Office: PO Box 5003 Dallas TX 75222

BENNETT, ALLYN CHARLES, civil engr.; b. Mart, Tex., Jan. 6, 1916; s. Luther Estes and Arlye (Allen)B.; B.S., Tex. A. and M. U., 1939; m. Margaret Thurston, Jan. 22, 1943; children—Allyn C., James T., Stephen E., Kenneth R., Margaret K. Engr., Soil Conservation Service, Tex., 1939-42, civil engr., 1945-—. Served to lt. col. USAAF 1942-45. Decorated Air Medal with oak leaf cluster, D.F.C. Registered profl. engr., Tex. Mem. Nat., Tex. socs. profl. engrs., Am. Soc. Agrl. Engrs. (nat. drainage com.), Soil Conservation Soc. Am., Air Force Assn. Am. Heritage Soc. Episcopalian. Home: 2 East Walker Temple TX 76501 Office: PO Box 95 Temple TX 76501

BENNETT, ARTHUR GORDON, educator; b. Jackson, Mich., Jan. 2, 1929; s. Arthur Gordon and Collette Jeanette (McEachern) B.; B.S., U. Mich., 1951; M.S., Purdue U., 1958, Ph.D., 1964; m. Virginia Vogelsang, May 23, 1959; children—John, Barbara. Engr., ARO, Inc., Tullahoma, Tenn., 1951-53; project engr. Brown Engring. Co., Huntsville, Ala., 1953-55; instr. engring. sci. dept. Purdue U., Lafayette, Ind., 1955-64; supr. engring. research Boeing Co., Seattle, 1964-65, Huntsville, Ala., 1965-68; asso. prof. aerospace engring. Auburn (Ala.) U., 1968-—. NSF grantee 1962, 63; recipient New Tech. award NASA, 1968, awards for tech. briefs, 1968, 69, 71. Registered profl. engr., Ala. Mem. Am. Astronautical Soc. (sr. mem.; mem. nat. bd. 1969-71, vice chmn. S.E. sect. 1968-—), Ala. Acad. Sci. (v.p. engring. 1968-69). Home: 543 Auburn Dr Auburn AL 36830

BENNETT, BRADLEY FREDERICK, research adminstr.; b. New Milford, Conn., Aug. 29, 1911; s. Frederick Lum and Florence (Bradley) B.; B.S., U.S. Naval Acad., 1935; M.S., Mass. Inst. Tech., 1940, M.S. in Physics, 1953; student U. Md. Extension, 1947-50, 62-63; m. Virginia K. White, Dec. 22, 1956; children—Bradley R., Bruce R. Commd. ensign, USN, 1935, advanced through grades to capt., 1953-65; with U.S.S. Saratoga, 1935-37, Norfolk Navy Yard, 1940-44; hull supt. Pearl Harbor Shipyard, 1944-47; engring. services officer Naval Research Lab., 1947-50; repair supt. Ship Repair Facility, Yokosuka, Japan, 1950-51; dir. materials devel. Bur. Ships Navy Dept., 1953-57; comdg. officer Naval Research Br. Office, London, Eng., 1957-60, dir. adminstrn. Naval Research Lab., Washington, 1960-63, dir., 1963-65; sci. and tech. cons. Office Chief Naval Operations, Washington, 1965-67; asst. to pres. Univs. Research Assn., Washington, 1967-68, v.p. adminstrn., 1968-—. Decorated Bronze Star Medal. Fellow Royal Soc. Medicine; mem. A.A.A.S., Am. Inst. Biol. Sci., N.Y. Acad. Scis., Philos. Soc. Washington, Br. Inst. Radiology, Am. Phys. Soc., Am. Soc. Metals, Am. Geophys. Union, Am. Numis. Assn. Clubs: Cosmos, Explorers. Home: 3301 Macomb St NW Washington DC 20008 Office: 2100 Pennsylvania Av NW Washington DC 20037

BENNETT, CALDWELL TUCKER, lawyer; b. Louisville, June 16, 1918; s. James Charles and Mary (Caldwell) B.; student U. Ark. Law Sch., 1946-49; m. Pauline Parker Gay, Feb. 18, 1943; children—Nancy Caldwell (Mrs. Michael Hilliard), Marion Gay, Mary Rebecca. Admitted to Ark. bar, 1941; enlisted as pvt. U.S. Army, 1941, advanced through grades to maj., 1956; comdg. officer 2472 Q.M. Truck Co., CBI, 1943-45, 312th M.I., 1961-64; ret., 1964; practiced in Batesville, Ark., 1949-—; dep. pros. atty. 3d Jud. Dist., 1950-—. Pres. 8th Chancery Bar, 1965-66. Mem. Independence Bar Assn. (pres. 1953-54), Phi Alpha Delta. Club: Batesville Civitan (pres. 1968-69). Home: 1401 Byers St Batesville AR 72501 Office: 106 S 3d St Batesville AR 72501

BENNETT, CHARLES EDWARD, congressman; b. Canton, N.Y., Dec. 2, 1910; s. Walter James and Roberta Augusta (Broadhurst) B.; A.B., U. Fla., 1934, J.D., 1934; H.H.D., U. Tampa, 1950; m. Jean Bennett; children—Bruce, Charles, James, Lucinda. Admitted to Fla. bar, 1934, practiced in Jacksonville, until 1949; mem. 81st-92d congresses from 3d Fla. Dist., mem. armed services com. Mem. Fla. Ho. of Reps., 1941. Dir. Boys' Home, A.R.C., Tb Assn. Council Social Agencies (Jacksonville). Multiple Sclerosis Assn.; trustee Lynchburg Coll. Served from pvt. to capt., inf., AUS, 1942-47; New Guinea, including guerrilla fighting in Luzon. Decorated Silver Star, Bronze Star: Phillippine Legion Honor and Gold Cross; recipient Certificate of Merit, Freedoms Found., 1951, 56, Good Govt. award, Jr. C. of C., 1952, Good Citizenship gold medal Nat. S.A.R., 1959. Mem. D.A.V., V.F.W., Fla. Bar. Am. Legion, Fleet Res. Assn. (hon.), Jacksonville Bar Assn., Jr. C. of C. (pres. 1939). Democrat. Mem. Disciples of Christ Ch. (elder). Mason. Author: Laudonniere, 1964; Settlement of Florida, 1967; also hist. papers. Home: 2130 Riverside Av Jacksonville FL 32204 Office: Rayburn House Office Bldg Washington DC 20515

BENNETT (SILAS) FLEMING, librarian; b. Everson, W.Va., Aug. 20, 1910; s. Jonathan Lloyd and Beulah Gertrude (McIntire) B.; A.B., Fairmont State Coll., 1931; B.L.S., Western Res. U., 1941; student Grad. Library Sch., U. Chgo., 1947-50; m. Violet Marie Mackey, Oct. 20, 1943; children—Carole Roxane, Richard Fleming. Librarian Fairmont Jr. High Sch., 1934-40, Findlay (O.) Sr. High Sch., 1941-42; asst. reference librarian W.Va. U. Library, 1942, 1945-46, chief audio-visual aids librarian, 1946-47; head acquisitions dept. Columbia U. Libraries, 1950-52; univ. librarian U. Ariz., 1952-64; librarian Inst. Food and Agrl. Scis., U. Fla., 1964-69, asst. dir. libraries U. Fla., 1969-—. Pres. bd. trustees Tucson Pub. Library, 1961-64. Mem. A.L.A. (council 1954-59), Assn. Coll. and Research Libraries (chmn. agrl. and biol. scis. 1965-66, chmn. Oberly Meml. award com. 1968-71), Ariz. Library Assn. (pres. 1956-58), Am. Assn. U. Profs. Alpha Psi Omega. Asso. editor Ariz. Librarian, 1959-60, editor, 1962-64. Contbr. articles library jours. Home: 318 SW 40th Terrace Gainesville FL 32601

BENNETT, FRANKLIN DAVIS, hardware co. exec.; b. Sanford, Fla., Jan. 25, 1916; s. John Croswell and Mary Anne (Wall) B.; B.S. in Bus. Adminstrn., U. Fla., 1937; m. Ann Wells, Aug. 21, 1941 (div. 1961); children— John Franklin, William Wall. Comptroller Race & Race, Inc., aluminum irrigation, Winter Haven, Fla., 1945-46; with Baird Hardware Co., wholesalers, Gainesville, 1946-—, treas., 1948-—, v.p., 1950-—, dir., 1948-—. Served with AUS, 1941-45. Mem. Phi Kappa Tau. Democrat. Kiwanian (treas. 1955-72). Home: 1014 NE 3d St Gainesville FL 32601 Office: PO Drawer B Gainesville FL 32601

BENNETT, GARLAND BRAXTON, clergyman; b. Greensboro, N.C., Aug. 25, 1929; s. George Robert and Thama (Carter) B.; B.A., Elon Coll., 1958; B.D., Duke U., 1963; m. Peggy Matherly, Mar. 25, 1949; children— Cindy (Mrs. Brantley Powell), Lynn (Mrs. Charles Mangum), Robin, Susan. Called to ministry Christian Ch., 1953; pastor Zion Christian Ch., Burlington, N.C., 1954-55, Ramseur (N.C.) Christian Ch., 1955-62, Great Bridge Christian Ch., Chesapeake, Va., 1962-66, Wake Chapel Christian Ch., Fuquay-Varina, N.C., 1966-—. Tchr. 7th grade pub. sch., Franklinville, N.C., 1957-58, Police Sch., Chesapeake. Mem. fund-raising team Duke U., 1965-69, Elon Coll., 1970. Mason (Shriner). Home: Wake Chapel Rd Fuquay-Varina NC 27526 Office: Box 307 Fuquay-Varina NC 27526

BENNETT, GORDON RICHARD, coll. pres.; b. Stamford, Tex., Sept. 22, 1904; s. George William and Ella (Reilly) B.; student Wayland Coll., 1922-24; B.A., Baylor U., 1926; postgrad. Tex. Technol. Coll., 1928, U. Tex., 1931; M.A., Hardin-Simmons U., 1944; LL.D., Midwestern U., 1953; m. Lola Juanita McElhaney, May 17, 1930; children— Patricia Lee, Richard Michael. Prin. high sch., Whireflat, Tex., 1928-31; supt. schs., Avoca, Tex., 1931-34; prin. high sch., Hamlin, Tex., 1935-39, supt. schs., 1939-45; mgr. Hamlin Hatchery, 1945-48; v.p. McMurry Coll., Abilene Tex., 1948-58, acting pres., 1958, pres., 1958-—. Mem. sch. bd., Hamlin, Tex., 1945-—, councilman, 1946-48; mem. Jurisdictional Bd. Edn., 1960-64. Mem. com. on interdenominational coop. conf. bd. edn. N.W. Tex. Conf. Meth. Ch. Del. N.W. Tex. Ann. Conf., 1950-—; Gen. Conf., 1960, Jurisdictional Conf., 1960. Mem. Tex. Council Church-Related Colls. (pres. 1962-63), Tex. Meth. Coll. Assn. (pres. 1961-63). Club: Lions (pres. 1957-58). Home: 1632 Sayles Blvd Abilene TX 79605

BENNETT, HOWARD ALLEN, physician; b. Mt. Vernon, Ia., Jan. 1, 1919; s. Joseph and Belle A. (Turner) B.; B.A., Cornell Coll., Mt. Vernon, 1941; M.D., U. Ia., 1943; m. Margaret A. Christensen, Apr. 10, 1943; children—Howard Allen, Barbara Lynn (Mrs. Henry Eddins), Nancy Gayle (Mrs. Gerald W. Shonkwiler). Intern, Louisville Gen. Hosp., 1943-44; resident anesthesiology U. Ia. Hosp., Iowa City, 1946-48; prof., chmn. dept. anesthesiology U. Okla. Sch. Medicine and Univ. Hosp., Oklahoma City, 1948-55, clin. prof. anesthesiology Sch. Medicine, Tulsa, 1955-70; mem. staff Jane Phillips Meml. Hosp. and Med. Center, Bartlesville. Served to maj. M.C., AUS, 1944-46; ETO. Mem. Am. (dir. 1950-73), Okla. (founding pres. 1949, pres. 1952) socs. anesthesiologists, Okla. Med. Assn., Washington County Med. Soc. Alpha Omega Alpha, Phi Beta Pi. Republican. Methodist. Elk. Club: Hillcrest Country (Bartlesville, Okla.). Home: 2824 Redhawe Ct Bartlesville OK 74003 Office: 3325 E Frank Phillips Blvd Bartlesville OK 74003

BENNETT, HOWARD CLIFTON, coll. pres.; b. Cleburne, Tex., June 13, 1910; s. Howard C. and Lillie (Freeman) B.; student U. Tenn., 1928-29; B.A., Union U., Jackson, Tenn., 1936; Th.M., So. Baptist Theol. Sem., 1939; D.D. (hon.), E. Tex. Bapt. Coll. Marshall, 1948; m. Mary Lee Hurt, May 6, 1935; children—Marilyn (Mrs. Bill Hillyer), Kate (Mrs. John E. Fite), Susan (Mrs. Kenneth B. Livingston). Ordained to ministry Bapt. Ch., 1935; pastor in Carthage, Tenn., 1939-41, Vivian, La., 1941-43, Kilgore, Tex., 1943-60; pres. E. Tex. Bapt. Coll., 1960-—, trustee coll., 1944-53. Mem. exec. bd. Bapt. Gen. Conv. Tex., 1943-52; mem. Tex. Bapt. Edn. Commn., 1953-60, chmn., 1959-60. Chmn. Gregg County chpt. A.R.C., 1945. Trustee So. Bapt. Theol. Sem., 1958-68; chmn. bd. Roy H. Laird Meml. Hosp., Kilgore, 1952-58; bd. dirs. Kilgore Little League Baseball, 1952. Mem. Marshall C. of C., Sigma Alpha Epsilon. Rotarian. Home: 701 East Av Marshall TX 75670

BENNETT, HUBERT DOUGLAS, state ofcl.; b. nr. Danville, Va., Nov. 18, 1906; s. Coleman Douglas and Sallie (Hogan) B.; B.S., U. Va., 1933, LL.B., 1938; m. Georgean Cameron Phillips, Dec. 30, 1938. Tchr. pub. schs., Pittsylvania County, Va., 1931-33; mem. Va. Ho. of Dels., 1934-36; admitted to Va. bar, 1937; judge Pittsylvania County C., Chatham, Va., 1938-52; exec. sec. Supreme Ct. Appeals of Va., Richmond, 1952-—. Served with USNR, 1942-45. Mem. Am., Va. bar assns., Nat. Conf. Ct. Administrv. Officers. Methodist. Home: 38 Locke Lane Richmond VA 23226 Office: Supreme Ct Bldg 11th and Broad Sts Richmond VA 23219

BENNETT, J. RICHARDSON, JR., mem. Ala. Republican Com.; b. Georgiana, Ala., Oct. 12, 1922; s. Julius Richardson and Jennie (Brock) C.; ed. U. Ala.; m. Margery Cameron Carey, Aug. 25, 1947; children—Jean Cameron, Bruce. Pres., Bennett Timber Co. Chmn. Greenville (Ala.) Indsl. Devel. Bd. Mem. Ala. Republican Exec. Com., 1954-—, v.p., 1962-66, chmn., 1966-—; del. Rep. Nat. Conv., 1956-64. Served to 2d lt. AUS, 1942-45. Presbyn. Rotarian. Address: PO Box 188 Greenville AL 36037*

BENNETT, JAMES BAXTER, geologist; b. Houston, Jan. 5, 1935; s. James Benjamin and Mary (Baxter) Mauldin; B.S., U. Tex., 1961; m. Kathryn Adele Giddens, Jan. 28, 1961; 1 dau., Kathryne Alison. Oil scout Tex. Eastern Transmission Corp., Shreveport, La., 1960-63, exploration geologists, 1964-67; exploration petroleum geologist Skelly Oil Co., Shreveport, 1967-70; area geologist Champlin Petroleum Co., Shreveport, 1970, Houston, 1970-—. Served with AUS, 1957-59. Mem. Am. Assn. Petroleum Geologists, Shreveport (2d. v.p. 1969-70), Houston geol. socs., Sigma Nu. Republican. Home: 10930 Burgoyne St Houston TX 77042 Office: 700 Houston Natural Gas Bldg Houston TX 77002

BENNETT, JAMES GORDON, JR., ship bldg. co. exec.; b. Wilkinsburg, Pa., Dec. 5, 1921; s. James Gordon and Evalina Parks (Miller) B.; B.A., Westminster Coll., 1947; m. Marjorie Ruth Beck, Mar. 20, 1948; children— Karen Holly, Janine Gordon. Instr., Westminster Coll., New Wilmington, Pa., 1947; chief accountant McCrady-Rogers, Pitts., 1948-52; office mgr. Rinker Materials, West Palm Beach, Fla., 1953-54; v.p. finance Spencer Boat Co., West Palm Beach, 1955-—, dir., 1956-—. Served with USNR, 1942-46; now comdr. Res. ret. Mem. Navy League U.S. (founding council pres. 1966-67), Soc. Preservation and Encouragement Barber Shop Quartet Singing in Am., Am. Legion, Nat. Office Mgmt. Assn., Alpha Sigma Phi. Presbyn. (elder 1971-73). Lion (dep. dist. gov. 1963-64). Home: 1569 40th St West Palm Beach FL 33407 Office: 4000 N Dixie St West Palm Beach FL 33407

BENNETT, J(AMES) MURRELL, architect.; b. Dallas, Aug. 22, 1904; s. Edward C. and Maude (Ramsey) B.; B.A., So. Meth. U., 1923; B.Arch. with honors, Washington U., St. Louis, 1927; m. Juanita Morgan. Jan. 2, 1926; children—Elizabeth (Mrs. David Schultz), Edward. With archtl. firms, St. Louis, 1926-37; partner charge design Gill & Bennett, Dallas, 1938-42; archtl. rep. in Dallas and Houston, J. Gordon Turnbull, Inc., Cleve., 1942-44; partner Bennett & Crittenden, Dallas, 1945-64; partner Bennett & Bennett, Dallas, 1965-—; specializing in design of churches; prin. works include Fain Meml. Presbyn. Ch., 1948, Floral Heights Meth. Ch., Wichita Falls, Tex., 1949, Flow Meml. Hosp., Denton, Tex., 1950, Highland Park Meth. Ch., 1951, Kessler Park Meth. Ch., 1952, Restland Mortuary, 1957, Lovers Lane Meth. Ch., 1958, Zion Luth. Ch., Dallas, 1958, Rowsey Meml. Chapel, Muskogee, Okla., 1960, 1st Presbyn. Ch., Irving, 1st Meth. Ch., Alexandria, La. Mem. city plan com-Tex., mn. Univ. Pk., Tex., 1956-—, chmn., 1962-—; mem. city zone commn. University Park, 1956-62. James Harrison Steedman travelling fellow, Europe, 1928. Fellow A.I.A. (pres. N. Tex. chpt. 1946. Dallas chpt. 1947); mem. Tex. Soc. Architects (chmn. com. archtl. practice 1953-58). Methodist. Club: Lions. Home: 3717 University Blvd Dallas TX 75205 Office: 3308 Oak Grove Dallas TX 75204

BENNETT, JAMES THOMAS, cons. statistician, educator; b. Memphis, Oct. 19, 1942; s. Louie Edward and Carrie (Tunnell) B.; B.S., Case Inst. Tech., 1964, M.S., 1966, Ph.D., 1970; m. Sara Ellen Dorman, Sept. 2, 1967. Operations research analyst, finance central staff Ford Motor Co., Dearborn, Mich., 1964-65; cons. econ. statistician Chesapeake & Ohio Ry. Co., 1966-70; research asso. Case Inst. Tech., 1965-67; asst. prof. indsl. mgmt. Cleve. State U., 1967-70; asst. prof. econs. George Washington U., 1970-—, also sr. staff scientist program in logistics; cons. Cleve. Transit System. Trustee Ohio Epsilon Corp. Research fellow Fed. Res. Bank Cleve., 1969-70. Mem. Am. Econ. Assn., Am. Statis. Assn., Econometric Soc., Phi Kappa Psi, Tau Beta Pi. Democrat. Presbyn.. Home: 8702 Bluedale St Alexandria VA 22308 Office: George Washington Univ Washington DC 20006

BENNETT, (JAMES) JEFFERSON, univ. pres.; b. Owensboro, Ky., June 8, 1920; s. James Henry and Amelia (Brownfield) B.; B.S., U. Ala., 1941, LL.B., 1948, LL.D., 1966; m. Christine Thaxton, Oct. 21, 1941; 1 son, James Jefferson. Admitted to Ala. bar, 1948; practiced in Birmingham, 1948, Fairhope, 1948-50; asst. prof. U. Ala. Sch. Law, University, 1950-52, asso. prof., 1952-53, asst. to dean, 1952-54, prof., 1953-69, asst. to pres. for devel. U. Ala., 1954-56, adminstrv. asst. to pres., 1956-60, adminstrv. v.p., 1960-68, provost, 1968; asst. adminstr. for legislation and pub. policy, health service and mental health adminstrn. U.S. Dept. Health, Edn. and Welfare, 1968-69; exec. dir. Health Edn. Authority of La., New Orleans, 1969-71; vice chancellor, pres. U. of South, Sewanee, Tenn., 1971-—. Dir. City Nat. Bank, Tuscaloosa, Ala., 1962-68. Served to maj. USMCR, 1942-46; maj. Res. Recipient Algernon Syndey Sullivan award, 1964. Mem. Farrah Order Jurisprudence, Sigma Chi, Omicron Delta Kappa, Phi Delta Phi. Episcopalian (sec. standing com. Ala. Diocese 1958-65, pres. Episcopal Churchmen Ala. 1955-67). Club: AEDC (Tullahoma, Tenn.). Home: Fulford Hall Sewanee TN 37375

BENNETT, JOHN CARLYLE, accountant; b. Doyle, Tenn., Sept. 11, 1910; s. John P. and Florence (Parker) B.; student Duke, 1929-31, Cecil's Bus. Coll., Ashville, N.C., 1932-33, corr. course I.A.S., 1934-40; m. Betty E. Strunk, Dec. 1, 1943; children—Gloria Louise, John Richard, William Gordon, Charlotte Emily. Accountant, So. Dairies, Inc., Asheville, N.C., 1933-35; head accounting 15th Naval Dist., Panama C.Z., 1938-39, auditor Panama Canal, constrn. foreman Army Engrs., 1939-42; accountant, auditor, mem. staff Ernst & Ernst, C.P.A.'s, Detroit, 1943-45; chief accountant Alexander Tool & Mfg. Co., Detroit, 1945; internal revenue agt., 1945-48; practice as C.P.A., 1948-—. Played with Ringling Bros. Circus Band; mem. Charlotte Symphony Orch.; bus. mgr. Charlotte Community Band Assn. Served with AUS, 1935-38, USNR, 1943. Mem. Am. Fedn. Musicians, Nat. Small Business Assn. Mason (32 deg., Shriner). Club: Red Fez Country. Author: Book of Income Tax Rates, Federal Income Tax Calculator (pub. annually); Outlaws in Swivel Chairs, 1958; also articles and legal actions on polit sci. under Article III of Constn. Address: 2245 Chambwood Dr Charlotte NC 28205

BENNETT, JOHN LOOKER, physician; b. High Point, N.C., Nov. 28, 1904; s. Ernest and Florence Mabel (Barker) B.; B.S., U. N.C., 1924; postgrad., U. Va., 1925-27, U. Ala. Med. Sch., 1927-29; M.D., U. Tenn., 1931; m. Louise Lubkin, Jan. 1, 1936; children—John Ernest, Julie Louise. Intern, resident internal medicine Univ. Hosp., U. Ga. Med. Sch., 1931-34; practice medicine, specializing in internal medicine and pediatrics, St. Augustine, Fla., 1935-36; resident surgery Logan (W.Va.) Gen. Hosp., 1936-37; mem. staff Trion Hosp. (Ga.), 1937-38; individual practice, Acworth, Ga., 1938-40; gen. practice medicine, Tallassee, Ala., 1940-—; mem. staff Community Hosp., East Tallassee, 1941-—. Chief staff Tuckabatchic council Boy Scouts Am., 1954-64; pres., founder Little League, Tallassee, 1952-55. Examiner, SSS, World War II; mem. City Council, 1952-62, also mayor pro-tem. Mem. A.M.A., So., Ala. med. assns., Tallapoosa County Med. Soc., Phi Chi. Democrat. Presbyn. (deacon, elder). Mason, Rotarian (pres. 1957). Home: 101 Freeman Av East Tallassee AL 36023 Office: 103B Freemon Av East Tallassee AL 36023

BENNETT, LESLIE HERMAN, newspaper exec.; b. Monroe, La., Oct. 20, 1925; s. Leslie Herman and Mildred (Howell) B.; B.A., La. State U., 1948; m. Margaret Ann Chiaborel, Apr. 14, 1946; 1 son, Bruce. Reporter, Galveston (Tex.) News, 1948-49; news editor New Orleans Item, 1950-57; with Houston Chronicle, 1957-—, city editor, 1963-71, sr. asso. editor, 1972-—. Served with USAAF, 1943-46. Mem. New Orleans, Houston press clubs, Sigma Delta Chi. Methodist. Home: 9011 Bintliff Houston TX 77036 Office: 512 Travis St Houston TX 77001

BENNETT, LUTHER ALCORN, librarian; b. Smithville, Miss., Aug. 22, 1909; s. James C. and Roxie (Evans) B.; B.S., Millsaps Coll., 1934; B.D., Duke, 1947; M.A., George Peabody Coll., 1954; m. Mary Kathryn Burchette, Sept. 11, 1937; children—Elizabeth Anne (Mrs. John C. Perry), Luther Alcorn. Ordained to ministry Methodist Ch., 1937; minister, No. Miss. Conf., 1937-52; instr., Brevard Coll., 1939-42; asst. librarian Western Carolina Coll., Cullowhee, N.C., 1952; librarian, instr. Union Coll., Barbourville, Ky., 1953-57; librarian, Greensboro (N.C.) Coll., 1957-—. Home: 1012 Guilford Av Greensboro NC 27401

BENNETT, MICHAEL MOFFETT, coll. pres.; b. Westfield, Ill., May 30, 1916; s. Clayton Moffett and Iva (Phillips) B.; B.S., U. Fla., 1940; M.A., Fla. State U., 1949, Ed.D., 1955; m. Beverly Ann Backus, June 21, 1942; children—Charles, William, Registrar, St. Petersburg (Fla.) Jr. Coll., 1940-49, dean of men, 1949-50, pres., 1950-—. Dir. South Pinellas chpt. A.R.C.; dir. Community Welfare Council, St. Petersburg chpt. Am. Cancer Soc., United Fund. Mem. Phi Delta Kappa. Episcopalian. Rotarian. Home: 300 Lake Shore Dr N St Petersburg FL 33710

BENNETT, RICHARD HOWELL, JR., sales exec.; b. Chgo., Aug. 10, 1916; s. Richard Howell and Beatrice (Schieberl) B.; student U. Ill., 1935-37; m. Dorothy Caroline Brain, Dec. 28, 1940; children—Carol Ann (Mrs. Robert V. Matenaer), Richard Edwin, Dorothy Marion. Buyer coll. textbook dept. Wilcox & Follett, Chgo., 1937-42; salesman Bauer-Black, Oshkosh, Wis., Detroit, 1942-47; salesman, dist. mgr., regional mgr., nat. sales mgr. U.S. Time Corp., N.Y.C., 1947-54; gen. sales mgr. Amity Leather Products, West Bend, Wis., 1954-64; mdse. coordinator Am. Optical Co., Boston, 1964-65; nat. sales mgr. Bentley Lighter Corp., N.Y.C., 1965-69; Fla. regional mgr. Garrity Industries, Inc., Stamford, Conn., 1969-—; chmn. bd. Bennett Industries, Inc., Naples, Fla., 1969-—. Mem. Fed. Wholesale Druggists Assn., Nat. Assn. Tobacco Distbrs., Nat. Assn. Chain Drug Stores, Mawanda Assn. of U. Ill., Delta Alpha Epsilon. Clubs: Boston Skating, Glades Country (Naples). Home: 626 Park Shore Dr Naples FL 33940

BENNETT, THOMAS LYNDON, ret. civil engr.; b. Greensboro, N.C., Mar. 16, 1905; s. Thomas Monroe and Maud (Fields) B.; B.S., N.C. State U., 1926; m. Louise Egerton McComb, Jan. 8, 1929; 1 son, Thomas Lyndon. Municipal engring. City of Greensboro, 1926-30; hwy. design La. Hwy. Commn., Baton Rouge, 1930-32; civil engring., and surveying, Hickory, N.C., 1932-33; with TVA, 1933-—, hwy. design, land acquistion studies, report preparation, writing and editing and administrv. duties, 1933-51, utility relocation engring., 1951-65, head utility relocation sect., 1965-70. Mem. Am. Soc. C.E., Soc. Am. Mil. Engrs., A.A.A.S., Phi Kappa Phi. Presbyn. Club: Chattanooga Engineer's. Home: 307 Guild Dr Chattanooga TN 37421

BENNETT, WALTER EDWARD, photojournalist; b. London, Eng., Aug. 16, 1921; s. Walter Albert Edward and Gladys Mae (Bulger) B.; grad. high sch.; m. June Anne Whittaker, Sept. 11, 1942 (div. 1965); children—Vicki June, Craig Walter; m. 2d, Joy Lynn Furry, Feb. 21, 1970; 1 dau., Lisa Lynn. Came to U.S., 1930, naturalized, 1943. Free-lance photographer, 1939-42, 46-52; staff photographer Time mag., 1952-—. Served with USAAF, 1942-46. Mem. White House News Photographers Assn., Nat. Press Photographers Assn., U.S. Senate Photographers Gallery. Club: Nat. Press. Co-discoverer Wreck of Mantaceros off southern coast Quintana Roo, Mexico, 1957. Photographer for Diving for Treasure and Pleasure, 1960. Home: 4711 47th St Washington DC 20016 Office: 888 16th St NW Washington DC 20006

BENNETT, WILLARD HARRISON, physicist, educator; b. Findlay, O., June 13, 1903; s. Harry and Elsie (Ward) B.; student Carnegie Inst. Tech., 1921-22; A.B., Ohio State U., 1924; M.S., U. Wis., 1926; Ph.D., U. Mich., 1928; m. Mona D. Sheets, Sept. 8, 1928; children—Willard Harrison, Barbara, Bruce Stephan; m. 2d, Helen Mae Sawyer, Oct. 24, 1948; children—Charles, Ward, Rebecca. Nat. research fellow Cal. Inst. Tech., 1929-30; instr. to asst. prof. physics Ohio State U., 1930-38; dir. research Electronics Research Corp., 1939-41; dir. applied research Inst. Textile Tech., 1945; physicist, sect. chief Nat. Bur. Standards, 1946-50; prof. physics U. Ark., 1950-51; br. head, div. cons. U.S. Naval Research Lab., 1951-61; Burlington Prof. physics N.C. State U. at Raleigh, 1961-—. Served from maj. to lt. col., AUS, 1941-45. Fellow Am. Physics Soc., Wash. Acad. Sci. Contbr. articles to profl. jours. Home: 604 Appleton Dr Raleigh NC 27606

BENNETT, WILLIAM BATCHELDER, govt. ofcl.; b. Hillsboro, N.H., Jan. 4, 1914; s. William Frank and Bella (Kendall) B.; B.S., U. N.H., 1935; M.A., La. State U., 1936, Ph.D., 1941; LL.B., George Washington U., 1953; postgrad. Harvard, summer, 1949; m. Anne Louise Rutherford, Jan. 1, 1944; 1 son, William Batchelder. Admitted to Va. bar, 1953; claim adjustor New Amsterdam Casualty Co., Balt., Phila., 1936-38; statistician OPA, Washington, 1941; supervisory economist War Assets Administrn., Washington, 1945-48; requirements specialist Munitions Bd., U.S. Dept. Def., 1948, supervisory procurement specialist, 1949-51, chief fgn. procurement and prodn. Office Asst. Sec. Def. for Internat. Security Affairs, 1951-59; fgn. excess property officer Bus. and Def. Services Administrn., Dept. Commerce, Washington, 1959, dir. fgn. activities staff, 1959-61, spl. asst. to adminstr., 1962, acting dir. Office Distbn. Services, 1962-63, program coordinator bus. and govt. services, 1963-64, dir. bus. relations staff, 1964-66, dir. food industries div., 1966-68; dep. dir. Office Moblzn. Plans, 1968-71; spl. asst. Office Indsl. Moblzn., Bur. Domestic Commerce, 1971-—. instr. econs. and bus. law A. and M. Coll. Tex., also La. State U., 1938-41. Mem. appeals bd. Dept. Commerce, 1965-—. Founding dir. sec.-treas. Teke Scholarship Fund, Inc., 1958-62. Served from lt. to lt. col. gen. staff AUS, 1941-45; col. Res. ret. Mem. Am. Econ. Assn., Am. Bar Assn., Va. State Bar, Fed. Bar Assn., Beta Gamma Sigma, Phi Kappa Phi. Conglist. Club: Nat. Lawyers. Author: The American Patent System, 1943; Industry Views Concerning Military Procurement Methods, 1950. Home: 3318 Rose Lane Falls Church VA 22042 Office: Bureau of Domestic Commerce US Dept Commerce Washington DC 20230

BENNIGHT, J.D., elec. engr.; b. Steepcreek, Tex., Oct. 14, 1920; s. Jerome Willie and Allie Faye (Coats) B.; B.S., Rice U., 1943; m. Gaye Charlene Whitaker, Sept. 17, 1943; children—James Dennis, Susan Winnette, Debora Gay. Elec. engr. Reed Roller Bti Co., Houston, 1946-47; field engr. Schlumberger Well Surveying Corp., Houston, Liberty, Tex., 1947-49; sales engr. Gulf Coast Electronics, Houston, 1949-50; elec. engr. Red River Arsenal, Texarkana, Tex., 1950-54, Redstone Arsenal, Huntsville, Ala., 1954-56; supervisory elec. engr. Army Ballistic Missile Agy., Huntsville, 1956-60; br. chief Marshall Space Flight Center, NASA, Huntsville, 1960-—. Mem. com. Boy Scouts Am., 1965-67. Served to 1st lt. Signal Corps, AUS, 1943-46. Registered profl. engr., Ala. Mem. Gideons Internat. Methodist (asso. dist. lay leader; chmn. ch. adminstrv. bd.). Home: 3904 Thomas Rd SW Huntsville AL 35805 Office: Marshall Space Flight Center Huntsville AL 35812

BENNISON, ALLAN PARNELL, geologist; b. Stockton, Cal., Mar. 8, 1918; s. Ellis and Cora (Parnell) B.; A.B., U. Cal. at Berkeley, 1940; m. DeLeo Smith, Sept. 4, 1941; children—Victor, Christina, Mary. Geology fellow Antioch Coll., 1940-42; photogrammetrist U.S. Geol. Survey, Arlington, Va., 1942-45; stratigrapher, asst. chief geologist Companias Unidas de Petroleos, Cartagena, Colombia, S. Am., 1945-49; staff stratigrapher Sinclair Oil & Gas Co., Tulsa, 1949-68; geol. cons., 1968-—. Pres., Tulsa Sci. Found., 1965-66, dir., 1966-—. Mem. Tulsa Geol. Soc. (v.p. 1964, pres. 1965), Geol. Soc. Am., Tulsa Met. C. of C., Sigma Xi. Clubs: Astronomy, Tulsa (v.p. 1967-68). Editor: Tulsa Geol. Digest, 1969. Contbr. articles to profl. jours. Discovered 1st known dinosaur in Cal., 1935. Home: 1410 Terrace Dr Tulsa OK 74104 Office: Beacon Bldg 4th St and Boulder Av Tulsa OK 74103

BENNS, IRALEE W., broadcasting exec. Pres. WVOK, Birmingham, Ala. Office: PO Box 1926 Birmingham AL 35201

BENNY, ROBERT IRVING, JR., computer co. economist; b. Cushing, Okla., June 5, 1934; s. Robert Irving and Marguerite Dorothy (Hill) B.; B.A., U. Okla., 1957; M.A., Georgetown U., 1965; m. Maria Katharina Mollemeier, Oct. 6, 1967. Economist, So. Railway Corp., Washington, 1963-65, United Aircraft Corp., East Hartford, Conn., 1965-68, Computer Scis. Corp., Falls Church, Va., 1968-—. Cons. Hoover Instn. on War Revolution and Peace. Mem. bd. finance Town of Rocky Hill, Conn., 1967; mem. bd. edn. Town of Rocky Hill, 1967-68. Mem. Am. Econ. Assn., Nat. Assn. Bus. Economists, Transp. Research Forum. Roman Catholic. Home: 303 Valeview Court Vienna VA 22180 Office: 6565 Arlington Blvd Falls Church VA 22046

BENOIT, EMILE, educator, economist; b. N.Y.C., July 14, 1909; s. Isadore and Rosina (Freeman) Benoit-Smullyan; B.A., Harvard, 1932, M.A., 1933, Ph.D., 1938; m. Mary Louise Mincher, Mar. 13, 1936; 1 son, Jon; m. 2d, Etta Leist Fleming, Feb. 11, 1959. Mem. faculty Harvard, 1934-36, U. Ill., 1938-39, Wells Coll., 1939-42; prof. internat. bus. Grad. Sch. Bus. and Sch. Internat. Affairs, Columbia, N.Y.C., 1956-—; sr. economist Labor Dept., 1943-47; attache Am. embassy, London, 1948-51, Vienna, 1951-53; economist McGraw Hill Pub. Co., 1954-56; cons. Dept. Def., State Dept., Pfizer Internat. Corp. Dir. research program on econs. arms control Ford Found., Carnegie Corp., and U.S. Arms Control and Disarmament Agy.; dir. research project Effects of Nat. Def. on Devel. Econs., 1968-69, Vice chmn. Ams. for Democratic Action, 1964-—. Bd. dirs. N.Y. Friends Group, Soc. Family of Man. Mem. Am. Econs. Assn., Am. Finance Assn., A.A.A.S. Author: Europe at Sixes and Sevens, 1961; Disarmament and the Economy, 1963. Editorial bd. Columbia Jour. World Bus., 1964-—; The Internat. Exec., 1962-—; Disarmament and Arms Control, 1963-—; Jour. of Arms Control, 1963-64, Jour. Conflict Resolution, 1966-—, Am. Rev. of East West Trade, 1968-—. Editor, contbr. Disarmament and World Economic Interdependence, 1966. Contbr. chpts. to books, articles to profl. jours. Home: 39 Claremont Av New York City NY 10027 also Elka Park Greene County NY 12427

BEN-RUBIN, JACK, economist; b. N.Y.C., June 7, 1929; s. Max and Esther (Allalouf) B-R.; B.S., Columbia, 1954, M.A., 1959; postgrad, N.Y. U.; m. Phyllis A. Huene, Sept. 15, 1962. Economist, Real Estate Research Corp., Washington, 1963-64, U.S. C. of C., 1964-65; economist U.S. Dept. Agr., Washington, 1965-—. Lectr. econs. George Washington U., 1964-—. Served with AUS, 1954-56. Mem. Am. Econ. Assn., Am. Statis. Assn., Regional Sci. Assn. Mason. Club: Columbia University (v.p.). Author: An Economic Indicator System for Measuring Progress in Rural Renewal Areas, 1967. Home: 3804 Howard St Annandale VA 22003 Office: US Dept Agr Washington DC 20250

BENRUD, CHARLES HARRIS, economist; b. Goodhue, Minn., Apr 30, 1921; s. Ole Christian and Edna (Bollum) B.; B.S. with high distinction, U. Minn., 1948, M.S., 1949, Ph.D., 1963; postgrad. N.C. State U., 1959, U. Fla., 1960, Ia. State U., 1961; m. Audrey Elaine Anderson, Oct. 1, 1949; children—Edith Audrey, Kurt Michael, Erik Charles. Asst. agrl. agt. Fairbault County, Blue Earth, Minn., 1949-50; club agt. Hennepin County, Mpls., 1950-53; Ramsey County agrl. agt., St. Paul, 1953-55; asst. prof., asst. economist S.D. State U., Brookings, 1955-58, asso. prof., asso. economist, 1958-63; sr. statistician, chief of party Research Triangle Inst., U.S. AID Contract Group, Lagos, Nigeria, 1963-67; economist Research Triangle Inst., Research Triangle Park, N.C., 1967-—, Adviser explorer post Boy Scouts Am., Cary, N.C., 1969-—. Mem. Am. Agrl. Econs. Assn., Alpha Gamma Rho, Alpha Zeta, Gamma Sigma Delta (chpt. pres. 1960-61), Pi Gamma Mu. Lutheran. Home: 929 Warren Av Cary NC 27511 Office: PO Box 12194 Research Triangle Park NC 27709

BENSMAN, MARVIN ROBERT, educator; b. Two Rivers, Wis., Sept. 18, 1937; s. David A. and Rose (Swerdlow) B.; B.S., U. Wis., 1960, M.S., 1964, Ph.D., 1969; m. Harriet Landsman, Aug. 21, 1965; children—David, Lauren. Program dir., announcer, newsman Sta. WSHE, Sheboygan, Wis., 1955-57; announcer Wis. radio network, Madison, 1957-58, WLHA student carrier sta., Madison, 1958-59, Sta. WMAD, Madison, 1964; tchr. West High Sch., Green Bay, Wis., 1960-62, North High Sch., Sheboygan, 1962-63; teaching asst. U. Wis., 1964-67, summer, 1968; instr. U. Vt., Burlington, 1967-69, acting head mass communication div., 1967-68, gen. mgr. WRUV-FM, 1967-69, adviser WRUV-AM, 1967-69; asst. prof. dept. speech and drama Memphis State U., 1969-—, dir. grad. studies in radio-TV-film. Mem. editorial bd. for radio-TV history series Arno Press, 1971. Mem. Speech Communication Assn., So. States Communication Assn. (chmn. mass media div.), Assn. for Profl. Broadcast Edn. (vice chmn. com. history broadcasting 1972-—). Contbr. articles to profl. jours. Home: 3672 Ironwood Dr Memphis TN 38118

BENSON, HAROLD AUGUSTUS, JR., social worker; b. Poughkeepsie, N.Y., Aug. 19, 1933; s. Harold Augustus and Helen (Cole) B.; A.B., Colgate U., 1955; postgrad. Syracuse U., 1956; M.S., Columbia, 1957. Social worker Travelers Aid Soc. N.Y., 1957-60; psychiat. social worker Yale, 1960-63; chief social worker Child Guidance Clinic, Winston-Salem, N.C., 1963-64, dir., 1966-69; clinic coordinator Clinic for Retarded, East Orange, N.J., 1964-66; asst. commr. N.C. Dept. Mental Health, Raleigh, 1969-72; dep. commr. children and youth, 1972-—; counseling cons. Geneva Sch. Bus., N.Y.C. Mem. Gov.'s Adv. Council Mental Health, 1966-69, N.C. Child Day Care Licensing Bd., 1971-—, Gov.'s Adv. Commn. on Children and Youth, 1972-—. Mem. Nat. Assn. Social Workers, Am. Orthopsychiat. Assn., Am. Group Psychotherapy Assn., Am. Assn. for Mental Deficiency, Am. Pub. Health Assn., Assn. Mental Health Clinics N.C. (pres.), Columbia U. Sch. Social Work Alumni Assn. (dir. 1972-—). Home: Chalet Apts No I Green St Chapel Hill NC 27514 Office: Box 26327 325 N Salisbury St Raleigh NC 27611

BENSON, HARRY DONALD, lumber co. exec.; b. Pawhuska, Okla., Mar. 1, 1931; s. Harry Garfield and Louella (Parrott) B.; B.S. in Commerce, Okla. A. & M. Coll., 1953; m. Mary Karen Emery, Sept. 19, 1953; children—Harry Emery, Anne Elizabeth, Ruth Louise, Catherine Lou, Nancy. Vice pres. Benson Lumber Co., Pawhuska, 1953-69, pres., 1969-—. Served to lt. USAF, 1955-57. Mem. Okla., Kan., Southwestern lumbermens assns. Am. Legion, Pawhuska C. of C., Sigma Chi, Alpha Kappa Psi. Democrat. Presbyn. Mason, Rotarian (pres. 1962-63). Home: Route 1 Pawhuska OK 74056 Office: 5th and Osage Sts Pawhuska OK 74056

BENSON, JAMES MILLER, physicist; b. Dayton, Tenn., Dec. 31, 1907; s. King Mathias and Edna Cora (Miller) B.; B.S., East Tenn. State Coll., 1929; M.S., Tenn. U., 1932, Ph.D., 1950; m. Rosalie Hooper, Sept. 17, 1938; children—Rosalie Irwin, James Franklin, Maureen Healy. Head hydrodyn analysis Langley Aero. Lab., NACA, Hampton, Va., 1940-45, instrument research, 1945-48; instr. physics U. Tenn., 1948-50; v.p., dir. research Hastings-Raydist, Inc., Hampton, Va., 1950-—; v.p. Offshore-Raydist, Inc., New Orleans, 1956-—. Mem. Am. Phys. Soc., I.E.E.E., Inst. Nav. Vacuum Soc., Newcomen Soc., Sigma Xi. Home: 2210 Chesapeake Av Hampton VA 23361 Office: Newcomb Av Hampton VA 23361

BENSON, JOHN, JR., ins. co. exec.; b. Durant, Okla., Sept. 14, 1918; s. Tom and Eunice (Boston) B.; B.S. in Econs., U. Pa., M.B.A. in Accounting, U. Tex., 1947; grad. Advanced Mgmt. Program, Harvard, 1957; m. Betty Mitchell, Apr. 4, 1942; children—John III, Sally, Elizabeth. Supr. prodn. control Lockheed Aircraft Co., Burbank, Cal., 1940-41; instr. U. Tex., Austin, 1946-48; mgr. Tenn. Life Ins. Co., Houston, 1948-56, dir. ins., 1956-59, v.p., 1959-61, sr. v.p., 1961-69, exec. v.p., 1969-—. Served to capt. USAF, 1941-46. C.P.A., Tex., Okla., C.L.U. Fellow Life Office Mgmt. Assn. Presbyn. (elder 1965-68). Rotarian. Club: Racquet (Houston). Home: 11111 Wickway St Houston TX 77024 Office: 8th Floor Chamber of Commerce Bldg Houston TX 77001

BENSON, KENNETH EDWARD, indsl. research exec.; b. DeKalb, Ill., Sept. 6, 1911; s. John Edward and Mary (Johnson) B.; student U. Akron, 1934-37; m. Anita Mae Foust, Jan. 15, 1939; children—Kenneth Edward, Anita Joan (Mrs. Wade Phillips Young, Jr.), Mary Andrea (Mrs. Joel Douglas Eaton), Barbara Jean (Mrs. Kermit Stuart Taylor); m. 2d, Leona Schaefer Smith, Aug. 2, 1968. Mgr. dept. Akron (O.) C. of C., 1937-39; sales mgr. Textilite Corp., 1939-41; owner Benson Fotocopist Co., Orlando, Fla., 1941-42; 1st lt. intelligence officer Civil Air Patrol, Coastal Patrol, Sarasota, Fla., 1942-43; sales engr. Communications Co., Inc., Coral Gables, Fla., 1944-45; dept. mgr. Ackerman Ins. Co., Miami Fla., 1946-52; exec. v.p. Nat. Union Life Ins. Co., 1953-56; real estate broker Benson & Smith Realty, 1956-64; bus. cons. aviation industry, 1965-72; exec. v.p. Energy Research, Inc., Coral Gables, 1964-71; dir. Riddle Airlines 1953-57. So. Region v.p. NAA, Washington, 1963-71; citizens aviation adv. bd. Dade County Port Authority, 1957-65. Lt. col., Fla. Wing. Civil Air Patrol, 1967-71. Recipient Dedicated Service award City of Miami, 1961, certificate of honor Nat. Aero. Assn., 1964, Distinguished Service award Greater Miami Aviation Assn., 1970. Mem. Greater Miami Aviation Assn. (pres. 1954-71, life pres. emeritus 1970-—), Air Force Assn., Am. Inst. Aeros. and Astronautics, Nat. Aerospace Edn. Council, Aircraft Owners and Pilots Assn., Internat. Platform Assn., Miami Bookfellows, Nat. Hist. Soc., Smithsonian Assos., Silver Wings Fraternity, Solar Energy Soc. Mason (32 deg., Shriner, K.T.). Clubs: Ambassadors, Admiral, Clipper, Three Coast, Florida Alligator, Birmingham Aero, OX5; LaGorce Country; Miami Beach Rod and Reel; Miami Acacia, Miami Millionaires, Around the World, Bal Harbour Yacht, Bal Harbour Beach, Circus Saints and Sinners. Home: 9064 Garland Av Surfside FL 33154 Office: PO Box 6641 Surfside FL 33154

BENSON, PAUL HARRISON, JR., radio station exec.; b. Simpsonville, S.C., Apr. 18, 1915; s. Paul Harrison and Lucille (Woodside) B.; student U. S.C., 1932-33; A.A., Anderson Coll., 1934; student High Mus. Sch. Art (Atlanta), 1934-36; m. Sara D'Oyley Croft, Nov. 6, 1937; children—Paul Harrison III, George Laurence, Sara Legere, Peter Woodside. Mgr., partner Atlantic Outdoor Advt. Co., Florence, S.C., 1936-47; mng. dir. Radio Sta. WJMX, Florence, 1948-—; sec.-treas. Atlantic Broadcasting Co., 1947-—; dir. Darlington Raceway Radio Network. Mem. Florence County Selective Service Bd., 1946-49, chmn. bd., 1948-49. Bd. dirs. Florence County chpt. A.R.C., 1972; dir.-at-large Pee Dee council Boy Scouts Am., 1971-72. Served with USNR, 1945. Recipient Honor Certificate for editorial comment Freedoms Found. at Valley Forge, 1966; George Washington Honor medal, 1967, Honor certificate, 1968, 69. Mem. Florence C. of C. (dir. 1960-63), Assn. of Broadcasters (charter), S.C. Broadcasters Assn. (dir. 1970-72). Rotarian (sec. Florence 1942-44). Home: Black Creek Rd Florence SC 29501 Office: PO Box 1211 Florence SC 29501

BENSON, STANLEY HUGH, librarian; b. Sparta, Ill., Oct. 1, 1930; s. Edward Hugh and Laurence (Sanders) B.; B.S., So. Ill. U., 1951; B.D., Southwestern Bapt. Theol. Sem., 1956, Th.D., 1964; M.L.S., U. Tex. at Austin, 1965; m. Sara Elizabeth Collins, Dec. 28, 1959; children—Andrew, Raymond. Library asst. Tex. Christian U., 1959-61; head librarian Ky. So. Coll., 1964-68, Gardner-Webb Coll., 1968-69, Berry Coll., 1969-71, Okla. Bapt. U., Shawnee, 1971-—. Instr. library sci. and religion, part-time 1964-—. Lilly Endowment fellow Am. Theol. Library Assn., 1963. Mem. Am. Theol. Library Assn., Okla. Library Assn. Baptist. Home: 3907 N Chapman St Shawnee OK 74801 Office: Oklahoma Baptist University Library Shawnee OK 74801

BENSON, STEPHEN DAVID, research psychologist; b. Phila., June 14, 1936; s. Louis E. and Esther (Sacks) B.; diploma, U. Vienna, 1955 B.Sc., Dickinson Coll., 1956 M.A., U. Pa., 1958; Ph.D., Etudes Universitaires Internationales, 1965; m. Ann H. Mallan, Mar. 7, 1969; children—Jennifer E., Josh, Mark. Research asso. Applied Psychol. Services, Phila., 1958-59; research psychologist Franklin Inst. Labs., Phila., 1959-62, engring. psychologist, 1962-63; tech. head engring. psychology United Aircraft Corp., Conn., 1963-65; sr. asso. Operations Research Inc., Silver Spring, Md., 1965-67; sr. staff Planning Research Corp., Washington, 1967; v.p. Eastern operations Behavior Scis. Corp., Washington, 1967-69; pres. Synergy, Reston,

Va., 1969-70, dir., 1970-72; v.p. Assos. for Research in Behavior, Inc., Phila., 1972—. Asst. adj. prof. dept. psychology U. Hartford, 1963-67. Mem. Am. Eastern psychol. assns., Soc. Engring. Psychologists, Human Factors Soc. Home: 1333 Deep Run Lane Reston VA 22070

BENSON, THOMAS DEAN, state ofcl.; b. Ethridge, Tenn., Feb. 14, 1932; s. Robert Millard and Nell (Kitchen) B.; B.S., U. Tenn., 1958; LL.B., YMCA Night Law Sch., 1963; m. Mary Elizabeth White, June 17, 1956; children—Mary Kathleen, David Michael. Asst. field dir. A.R.C., Ft. Campbell, Ky., 1958-59; admitted to Tenn. bar, 1963; dir. regulatory bds. Tenn. Dept. Ins. and Banking, 1959-62; adminstrv. asst. Tenn. Commn. Purchasing, Nashville, 1962-63; dep. commr. Tenn. Dept. Finance and Adminstrn., Nashville, 1963-67; commr. Tenn. Dept. Revenue, Nashville, 1967—. Mem. com. on jurisdictional standards (income tax) Multistate Tax Commn. Served with USAF, 1951-54. Mem. Nat. Assn. State Budget Ofcls. (asso.), Am. Bar Assn., Bar Assn. Tenn., Fedn. Tax Adminstrs. (trustee), Am. Assn. Motor Vehicle Administrs., Internat. Assn. Assessing Officers, Southeastern, Nat. (mem. exec. com., pres.) assns. tax adminstrs., Alpha Gamma Rho. Methodist. Democrat. Home: 3614 Woodlawn Dr Nashville TN 37215 Office: Andrew Jackson State Office Bldg Nashville TN 37219

BENSON, WILLIAM ARCHIBALD, JR., printing co. exec.; b. Nashville, Apr. 30, 1917; s. William Archibald and Florence (Riddle) B.; B.A. Vanderbilt U., 1938; m. Jeanne Elizabeth Donavan, Mar. 12, 1944; children—William Archibald IV, Robert Donavan, Stephen Alexander. Vice pres. Benson Printing Co., Nashville, 1938-41, 46—, salesman, 1946-64, partner, 1947-66. Past mem. bd. dirs. Printing Industry of Nashville. Mem. C. of C., Sigma Alpha Epsilon (province gov. 1966-70). Rotarian. Clubs: Nashville Quarterback (sec. 1968-69); Commodore Boosters (bd. dirs. 1964—); Belle Meade Country. Home: 307 Jackson Blvd Nashville TN 37205 Office: 136 4th Av Nashville TN 37219

BENT, ROY SUMNER, JR., educator; b. Westfield, Mass., Mar. 31, 1927; s. Roy Sumner and Kathleen Frances (Watkins) B.; B.A., Hofstra U., 1950; postgrad. Boston U., 1950-51; M. Div., Episcopal Theol. Sch., 1956; postgrad. (Martin Luther fellow) Emory U., 1961-63; m. Elinor Cornelia Bell, Aug. 27, 1950; children—Matthew David, Stephanie Kathryn. Asst. dept. philosophy Boston U., 1950-51, Emory U., Atlanta, 1961-63; master English and Latin, Va. Episcopal Sch., Lynchburg, Va., 1956-58; mem. faculty dept. philosophy and religion Roanoke Coll., Salem, Va., 1958—. Moderator, panelist TV program Discourse, WRFT-TV, 1969—; tchr. humanities Upward Bound program, summers 1970, 71; faculty summer session Luth. theol. So. Sem. at Roanoke Coll., 1972; mem. Commn. on Ministry, Episcopal Diocese Southwestern Va. Served with USNR, 1945-46. Mem. So. Soc. Philosophy Religion, Va. Philos. Assn., Am. Civil Liberties Union, Roanoke Valley Council Human Relations, Sigma Kappa Alpha, Delta Epsilon Beta, Pi Lambda Phi. Episcopalian (lay reader, vestryman). Home: 840 Red Lane Salem VA 24153

BENTLEY, T. KEILOR, museum ofcl. Dir. Explorers Hall Nat. Geog. Soc., Washington. Home: 9251 Lowlston Rd McLean VA 22101 Office: Nat Geog Soc 17th and M St NW Washington DC 20036*

BENTON, MORRIS CAREY, JR., trucking exec.; b. Kenansville, N.C., Oct. 25, 1917; s. Morris Carey and Mattie (Grady) B.; B.S. in Commerce, U. N.C., 1938; m. Elizabeth Holmes, Dec. 25, 1939; children—William Grady, Kathryn Stuart (Mrs. Broadhurst), Carey Elizabeth, Alice Holmes. Accountant, W.M. Russ & Co., Raleigh, N.C., 1939; exec. v.p., treas. McLean Trucking Co., 1939-71; chmn. bd. dir. Benton-Spry, Inc., 1971—; chmn. bd., chief. exec. officer, dir. Hennis Freight Lines, Inc., 1971—; pres., dir. Salem Ventures, Inc., 1970—; mayor, Winston-Salem, N.C., 1963-70; dir. Hercules Steel Corp., N.C. Nat. Bank, Integon Corp. Chmn., Winston-Salem Bd. Edn., 1957-63; past pres., dir. N.C. League of Municipalities. Served to 1st lt. USAF, 1943-45; ETO. Decorated Air medal with three oak leaf clusters, D.F.C. Mem. Am. Trucking Assn. (past pres., dir., nat. accounting and finance com.), N.C. Motor Carriers Assn. (past. pres., (dir.), Gen. Alumni Assn. U. N.C. (past. pres.); YMCA, Winston-Salem Traffic Club, Winston-Salem C. of C. (dir.) Democrat, Presbyn. (elder). Moose, Elk, Lion (past pres.). Clubs: Forsyth Country, Bermuda Run Country, Twin City. Home: 2901 Country Club Rd Winston-Salem NC 27104 Office: City Hall Winston-Salem NC 27101*

BENTON, WILLIAM JOSEPH, constrn. co. exec.; b. Verbena, Ala., Dec. 29, 1921; s. William Joseph and Lovie (Holdbrooks) B.; student Marion Inst., 1948-50; m. Baroness Waldtraut Hilda Von Den Brincken, Dec. 19, 1959. Various engring. positions, constrn. div. E.I. duPont de Nemours & Co., Inc., Ala., Wash. and Tex., 1941-48; various mgmt. positions to v.p. fgn. subsidiaries heavy marine constrn. J. Ray McDermott & Co., Inc., La. and Netherlands, 1950-64; with Ingram Corp., Harvey, La., 1964—, sr. v.p., 1969—, chief operating officer world constrns. operations, 1966—, corp. dir., 1967—, exec. v.p. various operating subsidiaries, 1966—, also dir. subsidiaries. Trustee Tommy C. Turner Meml. Found. Served with AUS, 1943-45. Decorated Purple Heart, Bronze Star medal, Silver Star. Life fellow Internat. Oceanographic Found.; mem. A.I.M., New Orleans C. of C. Club: Timberlane Country (Gretna, La.). Office: 2800 Internat Trade Mart New Orleans LA 70130

BENTRUP, MAUD MERRITT COOK, librarian; b. Baton Rouge, Mar. 25, 1908; d. John Brown and Fannie Elam (Merritt) Cook; A.B., La. State U., 1929, summer student, 1961; B.S. in L.S., U. Ill., 1931; summer student Columbia, 1937, U. S.C., 1950; m. Walter Carl Bentrup, Apr. 15, 1944. Cataloger, La. State U., 1929-43, instr. Library Sch., summer 1939; head cataloger, asso. prof. Stephens Meml. Library, U. Southwestern La., 1943-49, acting head librarian, 1948-49; librarian McMaster and Hamrick schs., Columbia, S.C., 1950-54; asso. prof. Sandel Library, Northeast La. State Coll., 1954-66, librarian, prof., 1966—. Mem. Am., La. (pres. 1961-62, chmn. coll. and reference sect. 1959-60), Southwestern library assns., La. Coll. Conf. (chmn. coll. sect. 1957, 71), Am. Assn. U. Women, Delta Kappa Gamma, Sigma Tau Delta, Kappa Delta. Home: 305 K St Monroe LA 71204

BENZ, EDMUND WOODWARD, surgeon; b. Nashville, May 8, 1911; s. Max and Angie (Hudson) B.; student Wallace U. Sch., 1931-33; A.B., Vanderbilt U., 1937, M.D., 1940; m. Elizabeth Ann McElroy, June 16, 1945; children—Edmund Woodward, Angela H., Charles McChord, Yarrott McElroy. Intern Vanderbilt U. Hosp. 1940-41; asst. resident surgery Vanderbilt U. Hosp., Nashville, 1941-44; resident, 1944-45; practice medicine specializing in surgery, Nashville, 1945—; attending surgeon Vanderbilt U. Hosp., St. Thomas Hosp., Bapt. Hosp., Met. Nashville Gen. Hosp., Park View Hosp.; research asst. dept. physiology Vanderbilt U. Sch. Medicine, Nashville, 1937-39, mem. faculty, 1945—, asso. clin. prof., 1969—. Mem. Gov.'s Adv. Com. for Med. Emergency Services in Tenn., 1968—; chmn. cancer study group Tenn.-Mid South Regional Med. Program, 1968—, mem. adv. com., 1968—. Fellow Tenn. Acad. Sci.,A.C.S.; mem. Tenn. Trauma Com., A.A.A.S., Nashbille Surg. Soc. (pres. 1970—), Am. Cancer Soc. (unit pres. 1964-65, div. bd. dirs.), A.M.A., Tenn., So. med. assns., Vanderbilt Med. Alumni Assn. (mem. governing council 1969—, Phi Beta Kappa, Alpha Omega Alpha. Home: 1120 Tyne Blvd Nashville TN 37220 Office: 1211 21st Av S Med Arts Bldg Nashville TN 37212

BENZ, GEORGE ALBERT, educator; b. St. Louis, Feb. 21, 1926; s. George and Genevieve B. (Klueg) B.; B.B.A., N. Tex. State U., 1953, M.S., 1955; Ph.D., U. Okla., 1969; m. D. Jean Tabor, Apr. 14, 1951; children—Lynda, Kaye. Grad. asst. U. Okla., 1957-59; asst. prof. Central State U., 1959-66; asso. prof., chmn. dept. econs. St. Mary's U., San Antonio, 1966—, acting dir. U. Research Center, 1971—, dir. urban studies dept., 1972—. Cons. several poverty projects. Chmn., San Antonio Civil Liberties Union, 1970-71; mem. Tex. State adv. com. U.S. Civil Rights Comm., 1969—. Served with Paratroops 11th Airborne Div., AUS, 1943-49. Decorated Bronze Star medal. Mem. Assn. of U. Profs. (v.p. Tex. chpt. 1970-71), Am., So. econ. assns., Southwest Social Science Assn. Home: 206 E Sunshine St San Antonio TX 78228 Office: 2700 Cincinnati St San Antonio TX 78284

BERESFORD, JOHN CLINTON, information industry exec.; b. St. Paul, Mar. 11, 1930; s. Howard Clinton and Vivian (Brand) B.; B.A., Antioch Coll., 1951; M.A., U. Mich., 1953; m. Nancy Harris, Mar. 29, 1951; children—Alison, John Roderic. Market research asst. Nat. Cash Register Co., Dayton, O., 1949-50; factory sales engr. Gates Rubber Co., Denver, 1950-51; teaching fellow, research asst. U. Mich., Ann Arbor, 1955-58; fertility specialist Bur. of Census, Washington, 1959, household statistics specialist, 1960-63, staff asst. population div., 1964-66, spl. asst. to asso. dir., 1967, chief data access and use lab., 1967-69; pres. Data Use and Access Labs., Inc., Washington, 1969—. Served with AUS, 1953-55. Mem. Am. Statis. Assn., Am. Sociol. Assn., Population Assn. Am., Council Social Sci. Data Archives, Am. Soc. Information Scis.; Urban and Regional Information Systems Assn. (pres. 1971-72; Internat. Union Sci. Study Population. Home: 1317 Alexandria Av Alexandria VA 22308 Office: 1601 N Kent St Suite 900 Arlington VA 22209

BERESFORD, SPENCER MOXON, lawyer, govt. ofcl.; b. Los Angeles, Dec. 2, 1918; s. Frank Moxon and Gail (Fitch) B.; B.S., Harvard, 1939, J.D., 1942; m. Helen Ann Lincoln, Aug. 13, 1955; children—Richard Ellsworth, Gail Freeman, Thomas Newell, Douglas Lincoln, Annette Diana. Chem. research engr. Dewey & Almy Chem. Co., Cambridge, Mass., 1942-43; admitted to Mass. bar, 1947, U.S. Supreme Ct. bar, 1953, D.C. bar, 1956; practiced in Boston, 1947-52; mem. faculty U.S. Naval Intelligence Sch., Washington, 1950-52; govt. ofcl., 1952-62; asst. chief Am. law div. Legislative Reference Service, Library of Congress, Washington, 1957-58, sr. specialist Am. pub. law, 1958-59; spl. counsel U.S. Ho. of Reps. Select Com. Astronautics and Space Exploration, 1958; spl. counsel House Com. Sci. and Astronautics, 1959-62; partner vom Baur, Beresford & Coburn, 1962-67, Batzell & Nunn, Washington, 1967-69; gen. counsel NASA, Washington, 1969—. Gen. counsel Nat. Space Club, 1962-65; adviser U.S. Dept. Transp., 1967-68; mem. U.S. delegation to UN Gen. Assembly, 1969—; mem. President's Com. on Govt. Patent Policy, 1969—. Rep. town meeting, Wellesley, Mass., 1948-52. Served from ensign to lt., USNR, 1942-46, lt. to lt. comdr., 1950-52. Recipient Ford Found. award in internat. law, Am. Soc. Internat. Law, 1962. Mem. Am. (com. oceanography, sect. internat. and comparative law 1967-69), Fed., Boston bar assns., Internat. Astronautical Fedn., Am. Inst. Aeros. and Astronautics. Internat. Inst. Space Law (chmn. liability com.) Am. Astronautical Soc. (chmn. com. internat. law and cooperation). Home: 8304 Thoreau Dr Bethesda MD 20034 Office: NASA Washington DC 20546

BERG, IRWIN AUGUST, educator, univ. dean; b. Chgo., Oct. 9, 1913; s. Bertil Sigfried and Clara (Anderson) B.; A.B. cum laude, Knox Coll., 1936; A.M., U. Mich. 1940, Ph.D., 1942; m. Sylvia Maria Taipale, Mar. 4, 1939; 1 dau., Karen Astrid (Mrs. A. C. Kirby). Asst. prof. psychology U. Ill., 1942-47; asso. prof. Pomona Coll., 1947-48; asso. prof. Northwestern U., 1948-55; chmn. dept., prof. psychology La. State U., Baton Rouge, 1955-66, dean Coll. Arts and Scis., prof. psychology, 1965—. Spl. cons. U.S. Dept. Labor, VA, La. Dept. Hosps. Mem. La. Commn. on Law Enforcement and Adminstrn. Criminal Justice, 1968—; mem La. Bd. Licensing for Sanitarians, Nat. Commn. on Arts and Scis., 1971—. Mem. Am. (pres. div. counseling psychology 1964), Southeastern (pres. 1963), Southwestern (pres. 1963-64) psychol. assns., A.A.A.S., Am. Assn. U. Profs. Phi Beta Kappa, Sigma Xi, Phi Kappa Phi, Phi Beta. Author: Workbook in Psychology, 1961; Response Set and Personality Assessment, 1967. Co-editor: Conformity and Deviation, 1961; An Introduction to Clinical Psychology, 3d edit., 1966. Home: 853 DuBois Dr Baton Rouge LA 70808

BERG, JOSEPH WILBUR, JR., geophysicist; b. Essington, Pa., Oct. 6, 1920; s. Joseph Wilbur and Anne (Fullerton) B.; B.S., U. Ga., 1948; M.S., Pa. State U., 1952, Ph.D., 1954; m. Lillian Miriam Douglas, June 26, 1950; children—Anne Lillian, Joseph Wilbur III, Frederick Douglas. Instr., Armstrong Coll., Savannah, Ga., 1948-49; research asst. Pa. State U., 1949-55; asst. prof. dept. physics and geophysics U. Tulsa, 1954-55; asso. prof. dept. geophysics U. Utah, Salt Lake City, 1955-60; geophysicist Inst. for Def. Analyses, Washington, 1960-61; prof. dept. oceanography Ore. State U., Corvallis, 1961-66; exec. sec. div. earth scis. Nat. Acad. Sci., Washington, 1966—. Vis. prof. dept. geol. scis. Cornell U., 1969-70. Fellow Geol. Soc. Am.; mem. Geophys. Soc. Am., Soc. Exploration Geologists, Seismol. Soc. Am. Research, publs. in generation and propagation of seismic waves, determination of earth structure from transit times of seismic waves, interpretation of earth gravity in terms geol. structure, conduction of electricity by rocks. Home: 8904 Gallant Green Dr McLean VA 22101 Office: 2101 Constitution Av Washington DC 20418

BERGAMASCHI, ADONAY, architect; b. Aracatuba, Brazil, Dec. 31, 1926; s. Humberto and Maria Dias (Gocen) B.; came to U.S., 1950, naturalized, 1963; student Ypiranga Call., Sao Paulo, Brazil, 1946-48; B.S. in Archtl. Engring., U. Miami, Coral Gables, Fla., 1961; m. Dorothy Hildegarde Eden, Dec. 18, 1952; children—Paul Adonay, Frank Adonay, Brian Adonay. Archtl. liaison Brazilian Air Force, 1947-50; archtl. designer Robert M. Nordin, architect, Miami, Fla., 1952-57; partner Anderson & Bergamaschi, Miami, 1957-61; archtl. cons., structural engr. H.J. Ross Assos., engrs., Miami, 1961-63; project architect Herbert H. Johnson Assos., architects, Miami, 1963-66; prin. A. Bergamaschi Assos., Miami, 1966—. Instr. art Escola de Artes, Aracatuba, Brazil, 1944-45. Recipient Rotary scholarship, 1950-54. Mem. A.I.A. (corporate mem. Fla. assn.). Constrn. Specifications Inst. (dir.). Prin. works include Miami (Fla.) Serpentarium Labs. and Facilities, 1961, Sunderland residence, 1967, Quick residence, 1958, Golubovic residence, 1960, Cannon residence, 1966. Home: 7550 SW 60th St Miami FL 33143 Office: 1460 Brickell Av Miami FL 33131

BERGE, TRUMAN KENT, air force officer; b. Erskine, Minn., Sept. 2, 1922; s. Thor Knute and Pauline (Larson) B.; student U. Minn., 1939-42; B.S., U.S. Mil. Acad., 1946; M.S., Purdue U., 1952; m. Genevieve Medlin, May 15, 1948; children—Karen, Pamela, Thomas Kent, David Medlin, Heidi Ann. Commd. 2d lt. U.S. Army, 1946, advanced through grades to col., U.S. Air Force, 1968; reconnaissance pilot, flight test maintenance officer Brooks AFB, Tex., Langley AFB, Va., Yokota AFB, Japan, Itazuke AFB, Japan, Taegu, Korea, 1946-50; instr., asst. prof. physics U.S. Mil. Acad., West Point, N.Y., 1952-55; research and devel. administr., Brussels, Belgium, 1955-58; asst. prof., asso. prof. physics U.S. Air Force Acad., Colorado Springs, Colo., 1958-61; student Armed Forces Staff Coll., 1962; physicist, research and devel. administr. Patrick AFB, Fla., 1962-65; dep. dir. Tactical Operations, Air Forces Korea, 314th Air Div., 1965; dep. comdr. 343d Fighter Group, Duluth, Minn., 1965-66; student Air War Coll., 1966-67; flight comdr. 361st Tactical Electronic Warfare Squadron, Nha Trang, Vietnam, 1967-68; staff scientist and chief computation div., data services center Hdqrs. U.S. Air Force, Waslngton, 1968-72; comdr. Fed. Automated Data Processing Simulation Center, 1972—. Decorated D.F.C. with oak leaf cluster, Air medal with ten oak leaf clusters. Fellow Brit. Phys. Soc.; mem. Am. Phys. Soc., Am. Soc. Physics Tchrs., A.A.A.S. Assn. Grads. U.S. Mil. Acad., Sci. Research Soc. Am., Sigma Xi (asso.), Sigma Pi Sigma. Lutheran. Home: 4610 Mansfield Manor Dr Washington DC 20022 Office: FEDSIM 2461 Eisenhower Av Alexandria VA 22314

BERGEN, JOSEPH BODELL, lawyer; b. Savannah, Ga., Mar. 12, 1925; s. Cletus William and Hildegarde (Blake) B.; student Mich. State Coll., 1943, Ga. Inst. Tech., 1945-48; J.D., U. Ga., 1950; m. Shirley Shearouse, Feb. 2, 1952; children—Elizabeth Blitch, Virginia Blake, Frederick Shearouse. Admitted to Ga. bar, 1951, D.C. bar, 1960; asst. U.S. atty. So. Dist. Ga., 1953-57, U.S. commr., 1959-63; practiced in Savannah Ga., 1951—. Served to lt. col., judge adv. USAF, 1943-45, 1951-52. Mem. Savannah Area C. of C., Civitan Club, Am. Legion, Mil. Order World Wars, S.A.R., Holland Soc. (N.Y.C.), Hibernian Soc., Am., Fed. (pres. Savannah chpt. 1967-68), Ga., Savannah bar assns., Am. Judicature Soc., Judge Advs. Assn., Sigma Alpha Epsilon, Delta Theta Phi. Elk, K.C. Clubs: University of Ga., Savannah Yacht & Country, Savannah Golf, Forest City Gun. Home: 3 E 49th St Savannah GA 31405 Office: 125 Habersham St Savannah GA 31401

BERGER, BRUCE, investment co. exec.; b. Omaha, June 10, 1939; s. Alvin Sanford and Marjorie (Frieden) B.; B.S., U. Pa., 1961; J.D., Harvard, 1964; m. Jean Karen Levendula, Sept. 9, 1961; 1 dau., Lauren Beth. Admitted to Ohio bar, 1964, D.C. bar, 1968; atty.-adviser to judge Tax Ct. U.S., Washington, 1964-66; atty. Office Tax Legislative Counsel, U.S. Treasury Dept., Washington, 1966-68; sec.-treas., chmn. bd. Network Mgmt. Corp., Washington Investment Network, Inc., 1968—; pres., treas. U.S. Land Resources, Inc., Washington, 1971—; dir. Shareholder Investment Advisers, Inc., U.S. Land Fund N.V., Landco, Ltd. C.P.A., Md. Mem. Am. Bar Assn., Am. Inst. C.P.A.'s. Democrat. Jewish religion. Home: 1721 Chesterford Way McLean VA 22101 Office: 1700 K St NW Washington DC 20006

BERGER, NORMAN JACK, dentist; b. Mobile, Ala., Jan. 19, 1929; s. Nathan and Leah (Mattes) B.; B.S., Spring Hill Coll., 1950; M.S., U. Ala., 1952; D.D.S., Loyola U., New Orleans, 1957; m. Ruth Miriam Rosen, Aug. 10, 1952; children—Karen, Harry David. Tchr., Vigor High Sch., Prichard, Ala., 1952-53; gen. practice dentistry, Mobile, Ala., 1959—. Second v.p. Mobile Mental Health Assn., 1971. Mem. Mobile County Sch. Bd., 1970—. Bd. dirs. Fonde Sch. P.T.A., 1959-63, pres., 1961-62. Served with USPHS, 1957-59. Mem. Am., Ala. dental assns., Am. Soc. Dentistry for Children, Mobile C. of C., Blue Key, Omicron Kappa Upsilon, Xi Psi Phi, Zeta Beta Tau. Clubs: Mobile Touchdown, Civitan (dir. 1960-65). Home: 4454 Airport Blvd Mobile AL 36608 Office: 266 S McGregor Av Mobile AL 36608

BERGER, WILLIAM ERNEST, newspaper pub.; b. Ferris, Ill., June 6, 1918; s. William George and Ethel (Nelson) B.; student Carthage Coll., 1935-38; m. Jerry June Barnes, Feb. 26, 1943; children—William Edward, Barbara, John Jeffrey. Newspaper editor and pub., Hondo, Tex., 1946-65; commr. Tex. Water Rights Commn., Austin, 1965-69; pres. Asso. Tex. Newspapers, Inc., 1957—; v.p. Tex. Offset Printing Service, Inc., Seguin, 1966—; owner radio sta. KRME Hondo 1969—; co-founder Tex. Star, 1970—. Treas., Medina Meml. Hosp., Hondo, 1962-64. Del., Tex. Democratic Conv., 1962, 64, 66, 68, Nat. Dem. Conv., 1968. Served with AUS, 1942-46. Mem. Tex. (pres. 1963), South Tex. (pres. 1954) press assns., Sigma Delta Chi (chpt. treas. 1967-69). Methodist. Lion (Hondo past pres.). Clubs: Headliners Westwood Country (Austin). Home: 1801 Exposition Blvd Austin TX 78703 Office: 1801 Exposition Blvd Austin TX 78703

BERGERON, WILTON LEE, physician; b. Scott, La., Feb. 13, 1933; s. Lee and Ida Ruby (Duhon) B.; B.S., U. Southwestern La., 1956; M.D., La. State U., 1958; m. Juanita Marie Landry, Aug. 3, 1957; children— David, Marcel, Rene, Jeanne. Intern, Confederate Meml. Med. Center, 1959; resident Lafayette Charity Hosp., 1959-60; gen. practice medicine, Scott, La., 1960-68; Mead Johnson fellow in allergy Tulane Med. Center, 1968-69; practice medicine, specializing in allergy and related skin diseases, Lafayette, La., 1969—; cons., dir. allergy clinic Lafayette (La.) Charity Hosp., 1969—. Mem. A.M.A., Am. Cath. Physicians, Am. Coll. Allergists, Am. Acad. Family Practice, So. Med. Assns., La. State Med. Soc., Cursillio in Christianity. Roman Catholic. Lion. Home: PO Box 98 Scott LA 70583 Office: 105 St Joseph St Lafayette LA 70501

BERGIDA, HAL, writer; b. N.Y.C., June 25, 1922; s. William and Dorothy (White) B.; B.A., in Journalism, U. Miami, 1952.; m. Messica R. Reynolds, 1966. Pub. relations cons. 1st motion picture unit USAAF, Culver Cal., 1942-44; free lance writer, 1944-48; editor Tamiami News, Miami, Fla., 1953-54, mem. staff Miami Beach Daily Sun, 1954-55; exec. sec. Greater Miami Beach Motel Assn., 1955-59; editorial rep. nat. mags., 1960—; daily columnist Miami Review, 1965—; polit. commentator sta. WOCN. Lobbyist foreign aid bill, 1961. Served with USAAF, 1942-44. Mem. Am. Legion, Internat. Platform Assn., D.A.V., Sigma Delta Chi. Clubs: Toastmasters, Tiger Bay (exec. sec.). Home: 3301 NE 5th St Miami FL 33137 Office: Ainsley Bldg Miami FL 33132

BERGLIN, MARVIN OSCAR, business exec.; b. Fairhope, Ala., Apr. 29, 1908; s. Adolph O. and Eva Mary (La Vigne) B.; LL.B., Cumberland Law Sch., 1932; m. Mary Pitman, Feb. 1, 1947 (dec. 1970); 1 dau., Becky (Mrs. James H. Tait, Jr.). Pres., Fairhope Ice & Creamery Co. (Ala.), until 1961; treas. Fairhope Single Tax Corp., 1964—; owner Fairhope Motor Co., 1967—; dir. 1st Nat. Bank Fairhope. Mem. Gov.'s Com. Hire the Handicapped, 1964. Mem. Fairhope City Council, 1936-44, Baldwin County Jury Commn., 1963—. Bd. govs. Organic Sch., 1964—. Served with USNR, 1944-45. Mem. U.S. Power Squadron (comdr. 1960). Mason (Shriner), Rotarian (pres. 1962). Clubs: Fairhope Yacht (commodore 1960), Jubilee Saddle (pres. 1965). Home: Sea Cliff Dr Fairhope AL 36532 Office: 422 Fairhope Av Fairhope AL 36532

BERGMAN, WARREN CARL, dentist; b. Boston, June 17, 1923; s. Carl Leonard and Signe (Tornbloom) B.; B.S., Northeastern U., 1950; D.M.D., Tufts U., 1954; M.P.H., Harvard, 1965; m. Elaine Ruth Johnson, June 26, 1954; children—Joan Elaine, Jeffrey Carl. Pvt. practice dentistry, East Bridgewater, Mass., 1954-59, Braintree, Mass., 1956-59, Brockton, Mass., 1959-66; dentist Brockton Pub. Schs., 1954-66; dir. dental pub. health, Anne Arundel County, Md., 1966—. Served with AUS, 1942-45. Decorated Purple Heart, Bronze

Star, Silver Star. Mem. U.S. Power Squadron, Am. Dental Assn., So. Md. Dental Soc., Royal Soc. Health, Delta Sigma Delta. Methodist. Home: 2100 Bay Front Terrace Annapolis MD 21401 Office: 6827 Annapolis Rd Landover Hills MD 30784

BERHEL, MARTHA MARIE, librarian; b. Baton Rouge, June 22, 1917; d. Aby Cornelous and Bettie E. (Collins) Berhel; B.S., So. U., 1936; B.S. in L.S., Hampton Inst., 1937; postgrad. N.Y. U., 1954, U. Fla. Asst. librarian So. U., librarian Demonstration High Sch., tchr. library service courses, summers 1937-40; tchr. library service Grambling Coll., summer 1939; organizer libraries T. J. Harris High Sch., Meridian, Miss., 1937, Sands Springs (Okla.) High Sch., 1942; librarian Edward Waters Coll., Jacksonville, Fla., 1940-42; asst. clk. Ration Bd., Jacksonville, Fla., 1942; head librarian Bethune-Cookman Coll., Daytona Beach, Fla., 1942—. Asso. prof. instructional materials center classes for state certification, summers 1950—; cons. library services; mem. state evaluation team for high sch. libraries So. Assn. Schs. and Colls. Sec., Daytona Beach chpt. A.R.C., 1949, now mem. bd. dirs. Volusia-Flagler Counties; mem. library com., City Daytona Beach. Mem. N.A.A.C.P., A.L.A., Fla. Library Assn. (past treas.), Am. Tchrs. Assn., Fla. Tchrs. Assn., Asso. Mid-Fla. Colls. (sec.), Delta Sigma Theta (past chpt. pres.), Beta Kappa Chi. Home: 217 Garden St Daytona Beach FL 32015 Office: Bethune-Cookman Coll Daytona Beach FL 32015

BERING, CONRAD, realtor; b. Houston, Dec. 20, 1895; s. August C. and Josephine (Pauska) B.; student U. Tex., 1914-17; m. Lorene Rogers, July 8, 1920 (dec. Nov. 1965); children—Conrad, Donald Rogers, Barbara (Mrs. Garrett S. Dundas). Owner, operator Conrad Bering Co., Houston, 1922—; pres. Longwoods Corp., Houston, 1952—; sec.-treas. Bering Realty Corp., Houston, 1952—, Rogers Investment, Inc., Austin, Tex. Life mem. bd. Methodist Hosp., Houston; founder mem. Naval War Coll. Found., Inc., U.S. Naval War Coll., Newport, R.I. Mem. Houston Bd. Realtors, Tex. Real Estate Assn., Navy League U.S. (hon. life pres. Houston council), Nat. Assn. Real Estate Bds., Houston C. of C. Methodist (mem. bd., bd. missions and land devel.). Clubs: Houston, Kiwanis (Houston). Home: 306 Fall River Ct Houston TX 77024 also Box 128 Route 5 Long Island Dr Lake Hamilton Hot Springs AR Office: Conrad Bering Co 6002 Wodway Dr Houston TX 77027

BERKELEY, FRANCIS LEWIS, JR., archivist, univ. adminstr.; b. Albemarle County, Va., Apr. 9, 1911; s. Francis Lewis and Ethel (Crissey) B.; B.S., U. Va., 1934, M.A., 1940; m. Helen Wayland Sutherland, June 12, 1937. Tchr. Va. pub. schs., 1934-38; asst. In charge manuscripts U. Va. Library, Charlottesville, 1938-41, curator manuscripts and univ. archivist, 1946-63, asso. librarian, 1957-63, sec. of Rector and Visitors, 1953-58, exec. asst. to pres., 1963—; council Inst. Early Am. History and Culture. Fulbright research fellow U. Edinburgh, 1952; Guggenheim fellow U. London, Eng., 1961-62; sec. of navy adv. com. on naval history, 1958—. Vice pres. Thomas Jefferson Meml. Found.; mem. adv. com. Papers of Thomas Jefferson; mem. Va. Com. on Colonial Records, 1955—. Served with USNR, 1942-46. Fellow Soc. Am. Archivists; mem. Am. Artiquarian Soc., Mass., Va., (v.p. 1970—), and other hist. socs., Colonial Soc. Mass., Walpole Soc., Raven Soc., Phi Beta Kappa, Omicron Delta Kappa. Democrat. Episcopalian. Clubs: Colonnade, Farmington Country (Charlottesville). Editor and compiler: Dunmore's Proclamation of Emancipation, 1941; Annual Reports on Historical Collections, University of Virginia Library, 1945— with cumulative indexes, 1945, 50); Jefferson Papers of the University of Virginia, 1950; Papers of John Randolph of Roanoke, 1950; John Rolfe's True Relation. 1951; Introduction to Thomas Jefferson's Farm Book, 1953. Editorial bd. Va. Quarterly Review, 1961—. Contbr.: Dictionary of Biography, Ency. Brit., Collier's Nat. Am. Cyclopedia; and other reference works. Home: 1927 Thomson Rd Charlottesville VA 22903

BERKELEY, MARVIN H., instrument co. exec.; B.A. in Pre-Medicine and Edn., Ph.D. in Psychology, Washington U. (St. Louis); m. 4 children. Asst v.p., dir. pub. affairs Tex. Instruments, Inc., Dallas, Pres. Dallas Ind. Sch. Dist. Bd. Edn., 1967-70; bd. dirs. Dallas Family Service, Dallas Community Action Program; former pres. Dallas Council on Alcoholism, Assn. Mental Health Dallas County; rep. to Goals for Dallas. Mem. Presdl. Task Force Career Advancement in Fed. Service; mem. adv. com. Manpower Devel. and Tng. Act; adviser to job corps Camp Gary, Tex.; mem. regional panel White House Fellows; mem. exec. com. Big City Bds. Edn.; v.p. Tex. Instruments Found.; mem. Tex. Urban Devel. Commn. Bd. dirs. Tex. United Community Services, sta. KERA, ednl. TV, Dallas Symphony Orch. Mem. Am. Psychol. Assn. Methodist (former chmn. ofcl. bd.). Office: PO Box 5474 Dallas TX 75222

BERKMAN, DAVE, educator, govt. ofcl.; b. Bklyn., May 6, 1934; s. Henry and Edna (Berkowitz) B.; B.A., cum laude, L.I. U., 1955; M.S., Syracuse U., 1956; Ed.D., N.Y. U., 1963; m. Jo Castellucci, June 29, 1963; children—Linda, Elena, Neil. Producer, dir. WHIZ-TV, Zanesville O., 1956-57, ednl. TV sta. WTVS, Detroit, 1957-59, instr. radio-TV, N.Y. Inst. Tech., 1960-61; tchr. N.Y.C. High Sch., 1961-63; pub. relations and edn. dir. Dist. 65, AFL-CIO, N.Y.C., 1963-64; asst. prof. speech Nassau (N.Y.) Community Coll., 1964-65; communications media coordinator Kingsborough Community Coll. City U. N.Y., 1966-67; sr. media systems specialist, edn. div. Xerox Corp., 1967-68; edn. systems cons. Xerox Edn. Group Hdqrs., Stamford, Conn., 1968-70; v.p. Ergonomics, Inc., 1970; asso. prof. mass communication Am. U., 1970-71; edn. program specialist TV Task Group Nat. Center Ednl. Tech., U.S. Office Edn., 1971—. Mem. Am. Civil Liberties Union; bd. mem. Fairfield County Civil Liberties Union; state bd. Conn. Civil Liberties Union, 1969-70. Mem. Nat. Assn. Ednl. Broadcasters, Nat. Acad. TV Arts and Scis., Am. Assn. U. Profs., Am. Fedn. Tchrs., Am. Fedn. Govt. Employees, Authors League of Am., N.Y. State Ednl. Radio-TV Assn. Club: Roosevelt Reform Democratic Party of Bklyn. (past pres.). Cons. editor: Ednl. Television mag., 1968-70. Contbr. articles in field to profl. jours. Home: 1816 Ivy Oak Sq Reston VA 22070 Office: Nat Center Ednl Tech US Office Edn Washington DC 20202

BERKOWITZ, SAMUEL, orthodontist; b. N.Y.C., Aug. 31, 1928; s. Morris and Goldie (Berkowitz) B.; B.A., N.Y. U., 1949, D.D.S., 1954; M.S., U. Ill., 1959; m. Lynn I. Schwartz, Mar. 5, 1960; children—David, Beth Jo, Debra. Clin. practice orthodontia, Miami, Fla., 1959-71; cons. Center for Cranio-Facial Anomalies U. Ill., 1959-71; asst. clin. prof. pediatrics Birth Defects Center, Sch. Medicine, U. Miami, 1968-71; asst. dir. Cleft Palate Clinic So. Fla., South Miami, 1971—. Cons. Fla. Crippled Children's Commn., 1960-71. Pres. Miami Cranio-Facial Anomalies Found., 1971. Bd. dirs. Am. Jewish Com. Served with Dental Corps, USNR, 1954-56. Recipient Spl. Merit award in research Am. Assn. Orthodontists, 1970. Mead-Johnson Research grantee, 1971. Mem. Internat. Assn. Dental Research, Am. Bd. Orthodontists, Am. Assn. Orthodontists, Am. Dental Assn., Angle Soc. Office: 6601 SW 80th St South Miami FL 33143

BERKOWITZ, SIDNEY ADRIAN, govt. ofcl.; b. Phila., Dec. 24, 1913; s. Morris Emanuel and Rose (Unglicht) B.; student Newark Coll. Engring., 1931-32; B.S. in Civil Engring., U. Fla., 1935; M.S., Harvard, 1950; m. Frances Mazo, Sept. 27, 1936; 1 dau., Judith (Mrs. Stanley Edward Jacobs). Operator sewage treatment plant U. Fla., 1933-35; survey party chief, jr. engr. sewerage project WPA, Key West, Fla., 1935-38; engring. aide Corps Engrs., U.S. Army, Sardis, Miss., 1938-39; jr. hydraulic engr. U.S. Geol. Survey, Jackson and Oxford, Miss., 1939-41; with Bur. San. Engring. Fla. Div. Health, 1946—, asst. dir., Jacksonville, 1958-68, dir., 1968—. Mem. vis. com. dept. environmental engring. U. Fla., Gainesville, 1971—, also vis. lectr., mem. standing adv. com. Environmental Protection Agy., 1968—; chmn. Conf. State San. Engrs., 1972, Duval Air Authority, 1968. Served to lt. comdr. USNR, 1941-45; PTO. Recipient Arthur Sidney Bedell award Water Pollution Control Fedn., 1964, Distinguished Service award in water pollution control Nat. Clay Pipe Inst. 1969. Registered profl. engr., Fla. Diplomate Am. Acad. Environmental Engrs. Fellow Fla. Engring. Soc.; mem. Water Pollution Control Fedn. (pres. 1968), Fla. Pollution Control Assn. (pres. 1958-59), Am. Water Works Assn., Harvard Engring. Soc., Fla. Pub. Health Assn., Nat. Soc. Profl. Engrs., Delta Omega. Home: 7061 Olk Kings Rd Jacksonville FL 32217 also PO Box 210 Jacksonville FL 32201

BERLE, ANTON ALOIS, editor; b. Switzerland, Dec. 26, 1919; s. John Emille and Mary (Steckenbiller) B.; B.A., U. Conn., 1945; M.A., N.Y. U., 1948; postgrad. Johns Hopkins, 1948-50; m. Beatrice Conrath, Feb. 17, 1945; children—Margaret (Mrs. Stefan Dasho), Isobel, Jenifer, David. Asso. prof. U. Balt., 1947-50; writer, editor Civic Edn. Service, Washington, 1950-69, editor Civic Leader mag., 1965-69; editor Civic Leader mag. Scholastic Mags., Inc., N.Y.C., 1969—; prof. govt. and econs. Benjamin Franklin U., Washington, 1951-72. Ednl. cons.-writer Changing Times Edn. Service, Washington, 1970-72, mem. editorial bd., 1970-72. Recipient Vigilant Patriot award All-Am. Conf. to Combat Communism, 1963; Eleanor Fishburn award Ednl. Press Assn. 1969. Mem. Nat. Council for Social Studies, Ednl. Press Assn., Am. Hist. Assn., Am. Polit. Sci. Assn. Contbr. to Am. Observer. Address: 4201 Duncan Dr Annandale VA 22003

BERLINER, ARTHUR KERMIT, social worker; b. Bklyn, July 4, 1920; s. Max and Bertha (Goldstein) B.; B.S., City Coll. N.Y., 1940; M.S., Case Western Reserve U., 1942; m. Miriam Hamilton, Nov. 14, 1942; children—Susan Ruth (Mrs. Michael Guerrero), Sharon Mae, Debra Lu. Social case worker, Dcase supr. VA Hosp., Cleve., 1946-49; chief social work service Nat. Inst. Mental Health, Clin. Research Center, Ft. Worth, 1949-71; dir. alcoholism treatment unit Fed. Correction Inst., 1971—. Adj. asst. prof. psychology and sociology Tex. Christian U., 1950—; case cons. Jewish Social Service Agy., Ft. Worth. Bd. dirs. Tarrant County Child Study Center. Served with USAAF, 1943-46. Mem. Nat. Assn. Social Workers (Tex. council pres. 1966-68), Acad. Certified Social Workers, Am. Pub. Health Assn. Contbr. articles to profl. jours. Home: 2312 San Jose Dr Fort Worth TX 76112 Office: 3150 Horton Rd Fort Worth TX 76119

BERLY, ROBERT HERMAN, JR., elec. engr.; b. Elloree, S.C., Oct. 20, 1924; s. Robert Herman and Cecile Claudius (Adams) B.; B.S., Clemson U., 1948; m. Opal Newkirk Buie, Aug. 20, 1947; children—Barbara, Kathryn. Dist. engr. Carolina Power & Light Co., Marion, S.C., 1948-51, dist. engr., Sumter, S.C., 1951-65, sr. engr. div. office, Wilmington, N.C., 1965-67, sr. engr. planning and gen. engring. sect., Raleigh, N.C., 1967-68, distbn. planning engr., Raleigh, 1968-72, prin. engr. distbn. planning, Raleigh, 1972—. Mem. adv. bd. Salvation Army, Sumter, 1963-66. Served with USAAF, 1942-45; now lt. col. USAF Res. ret. Named Sumter Man of Yr., Civitan Club, 1962. Registered profl. engr., N.C. Mem. Raleigh Engrs. Club. Presbyn. (deacon 1966-67, elder 1971—). Club: Civitan (pres. Sumter club 1960-61, zone lt. gov. 1960-61, dir. membership S.C. club 1961-62, dir. Wilmington, N.C. club 1966-67) (Raleigh, N.C.). Home: 4104 Southall Rd Raleigh NC 27604 Office: Box 1551 Raleigh NC 27602

BERMAN, DONALD ABEL, physician; b. Wildwood, N.J., Oct. 23, 1932; s. Louis and Isabel (Dresnick) B.; B.S. cum laude, U. Miami, 1953; M.D., Tulane U., 1957; m. Frona Lee Sherman, Aug. 15, 1954; children—Lynn Daryl, Marla Sharon, Jill Mallorie. Intern, Walter Reed Army Med. Center, 1957-58; practice medicine, specializing in family practice, Hollywood, Fla., 1961—; mem. staff Hollywood Meml. Hosp.; med. dir. Med. Exam. Centers, Inc., 1971—; clin. instr. U. Fla. Sch. Medicine, 1971—. Served with AUS, 1957-61. Diplomate Am. Bd. Family Practice. Mem. A.M.A., Am., Fla. acads. gen. practice, So., Fla. med. assns., Broward County Med. Assn., Hollywood Hills Homeowners Assn., Phi Delta Epsilon, Alpha Epsilon Pi. Mason (32 deg.). Club: Graduate. Home: 2941 Fairway Dr Hollywood FL 33021 Office: 3301 Johnson St Hollywood FL 33021

BERMAN, DONALD CHARLES, indsl. engr.lb. N.Y.C., May 18, 1931; s.; Sol and Sue (Orzach) B.; student Carnegie Inst. Tech., 1949-53; B.S., N.Y.U., 1958; m. Harriet Hope Waldbaum, Sept. 13, 1958; children—David Shawn, Daniel Ross. Project engr. Artisan Electronics, Morristown, N.J., 1953-54; indsl. engr. Emerson Radio, Jersey City, 1954; mgr. engring. quality control Polarad Electronics, L.I., N.Y., 1956-59; head reliability assurance dept. Olympic div. Siegler Corp., L.I., 1959; reliability project engr. Astrionics div. Fairchild Stratas Corp., L.I., 1959-61; supr. components and standards Aeronutronics div. Philco Corp., Newport Beach, Cal., 1961-63; chief components and standards Northrop Space Labs. Hawthorne, Cal., 1963-64; head vendor reliability control TRW Systems, Redondo Beach, Cal., 1964-66, engring. sect. head, reliability and systems assurance, 1966-68; dir. product assurance TRACOR, Inc., Austin, Tex., 1968—. Chmn. Austin regional group Sierra Club; program chmn., mem. exec. com. Tex. Environmental Coalition; mem. Austin Town Lake Beautification Com.; mem. com. Chmn. Citizens Environmental Bd., City of Austin. Bd. govs. Environmental Action for Tex. Served with AUS, 1954-56. Mem. Am. Soc. Quality Control. Contbr. articles in field to profl. jours. Home: 7608 Rustling Rd Austin TX 78731 Office: 6500 Tracor Lane Austin TX 78721

BERMAN, HOWARD BENJAMIN, dentist; b. N.Y.C., Jan. 8, 1939; s. Hyman and Evelyne Pearl (Bernstein) B.; student Emory U., 1956-57, U. Miami, 1957-58; D.D.S., U. Md., 1962; M.S., Goergetown U., 1967; m. Drazia Schacter, June 11, 1961; children—Marcie, Robin, Steven Barry. Intern Jackson Meml. Hosp., Miami, Fla., 1962-63, chief resident oral surgery, 1963-64; pvt. practice oral surgery, Hollywood, Fla., 1967—. Mem. Dade County Dental Research Clinic, Miami, Fla., 1967-71; lectr. Miami-Dade Jr. Coll. Sch. Dental Hygiene, 1971-72; sr. attending oral surgeon Meml. Hosp., Hollywood, Fla., 1967—. Served to capt. AUS, 1964-66. Mem. Fla. (del. 1971-72), East Coast Dist. (exec. bd. 1971-72), Greater Hollywood (pres. 1971-72) dental socs., Am., Fla. socs. oral surgeons, Am. Soc. Dental Anesthesiology, Young Leadership Group Jewish Welfare Fedn. (adviser 1971-72). Jewish religion (bd. dirs. temple 1971-72). Home: 3500 N 33d Terrace Hollywood FL 33021 Office: 4410 Sheridan St Hollywood FL 33021

BERMAN, MILTON S., mcht.; b. Rochester, N.Y., Sept. 29, 1907; s. Julius and Annie (Schooler) B.; ed. U. Rochester, 1929, Harvard, 1931; m. Ruth Kasdan, Jan. 17, 1936; children—William, Susan, David. With Jordan Marsh Co., Boston, 1931-45, successively trainee, buyer, divisional mdse. mgr.; with Abraham & Straus, Bklyn., 1945-64, successively divisional mdse. mgr., merchandising v.p., v.p., gen. mdse. mgr.; pres. Foley's Houston, (became div. Federated Dept. Stores, Inc., 1945), chmn. bd., 1967—, also v.p. parent co. Bd. dirs. Assn. Community TV (Channel 8), Houston Housing Devel. Corp., Houston Symphony Soc., Tex. Bill of Rights Found., Asso. Credit Services, Inc.; trustee Bus. Resource Devel. Center; founding dir. Soc. Performing Arts; patron Mus. Fine Arts Houston, Houston Contemporary Arts Mus., Alley theatre. Mem. Houston C. of C., Am. Civil Liberties Union. Clubs: Houston, Houston Racquet, Houston Yacht, Harvard of Houston. Home: 2200 Willowick Houston TX 77027 Office: 1110 Main St Houston TX 77001

BERMAN, SIDNEY ARTHUR, social worker; b. Chgo., June 18, 1924; s. Joseph A. and Nettie (Roth) B.; B.S., DePaul U., 1949; M.A., U. Fla., 1951; M.S., U. Tenn., 1958; student Tulane U., 1955-56; m. Carol Siegel, July 20, 1956; children—Steven, Adrian, Welfare visitor Fla. Dept. Pub. Welfare, Jacksonville, 1952-55, unit supr., Ft. Pierce, 1956-57; psychiat. social worker Nashville Mental Health Center, 1958-61; chief social worker Bristol (Va.) Mental Health Clinic, 1961-64; dir. profl. service Peninsula Family Service & Travel Aid, Newport News, Va., 1964-70; exec. dir. No. Va. Family Service, Falls Church, 1970—. Instr. U. Va. Extension, 1968-69. Pres., Bristol Mental Health Assn., 1963, Va. Council on Social Welfare, 1966-67, Peninsula Council on Human Relations, 1967, Reston Community Assn., 1971. First v.p. Nat. Conf. Christians and Jews, 1968-69. Served to 2d lt. USAAF, 1944-45. Mem. Nat. Assn. Social Workers, Am. Orthopsychiat. Assn. Democrat. Home: 1721 Wainwright Dr Reston VA 22070 Office: 803 W Broad St Falls Church VA 22046

BERMAN, STANLEY MARC, govt. ofcl.; b. Akron, O., Sept. 27, 1938; s. Leonard J. and Anna M. (Dasch) B.; student U. Wis., 1958; B.A., U. Akron, 1960; M.A., Washington U., St. Louis, 1963; m. Carole M. Limbert, June 24, 1962; children—Bruce Rand, Jeri Lyn. Research asst. Inst. Urban and Regional Affairs, Washington U., 1961-63; mgmt. intern U.S. Dept. Labor, Washington, 1963-64, asst. to adminstr. Neighborhood Youth Corps, 1964-67; budget examiner natural resources programs div. Office Mgmt. and Budget, Exec. Office of Pres., Washington, 1967—. Mem. Bd. Civil Service Examiners, 1966—. Mem. Am. Econ. Assn. Home: 2721 Washington Av Chevy Chase MD 20015 Office: Executive Office of President Office of Management and Budget Washington DC 20503

BERNAL Y DEL RIO, VICTOR, physician; b. Sebastian, P.R., 1917; M.S., U. Coimbra (Portugal), 1941. Intern Arecibo Municipal Hosp., P.R., 1941-42, resident surgery, 1942-44; resident psychiatry N.Y. State Psychiat. Inst., N.Y.C., 1950-53; grad. tng. Columbia Psychoanalytic Clin., 1953; med. dir. State Psychiat. Hosp., P.R., 1953-59; dir. tng. P.R. Inst. Psychiatry, 1959—; asst. clin. prof. psychiatry Hato Rey (P.R.) Psychiat. Hosp., 1958-64; cons. San Patricio VA Hosp., 1962—. Diplomate in psychiatry Am. Bd. Neurology and Psychiatry. Mem. Assn. Psychoanalytic Medicine, Am. Psychiat. Assn., Am. Psychol. Assn. Address: 300 Franklin Roosevelt Av Roosevelt San Juan PR 00918*

BERNAL Y GARCIA PIMENTEL, IGNACIO, archaeologist; b. Paris, Feb. 13, 1910; s. Rafael Bernal and Rafaela Garcia Pimentel; M.A. in Anthropology, Escuela Nacional de Antropologia, 1946; Ph.D. in Archaeology, U. Nacional Autonoma de Mexico, 1949; L.H.D. (hon.), U. Am., 1967; L.H.D., U. Cal. at Berkeley, 1969; m. Sofia Verea Corcuera, Oct. 14, 1944; children—Ignacio, Rafaela, Carlos, Concepcion. Prof. U. Nacional Autonoma de Mexico, 1948—; dir. anthropology Mexico City Coll., 1948-59; cultural attache Mexican embassy, Paris, 1955-56, also permanent del. Mexico to UNESCO; mem. Internat. Commn. Monuments, UNESCO, 1956—; dir. Teotihuacan Project, 1962-64, Nat. Museum Anthropology, 1962-68; pres. Soc. Am. Archaeology, 1969-70; dir. gen. Inst. Nacional de Antropologia e Historia, 1968-70; dir. Nat. Museum Anthropology, 1970—. Decorated officer Royal Order Orange-Nassau (Netherlands); officer Legion of Honor (France); comdr. Order of Merit (Italy); officer Royal Order of Crown (Belgium); comdr. Order of Merit (Germany); officer Royal Order Dannebrog (Denmark). Fellow Am. Anthrop. Assn., Am. Acad. Arts and Scis. regular mem. Mexican Acad. History; mem. Colegio Nacional (Mexico), Brit. Acad., Soc. Am. Archaeology, Acad. Nacional de Ciencias, Soc. des Americanistes de Paris, Soc. Mexicana de Antropologia, Acad. Nacional de la Investigacion Cientifica. Author: (with Alfonso Caso) Urnas de Oaxaca, 1952; Bibliografia de Arqueologia y Etnografia, Mesoamerica y Norte de Mexico, 1514-1960, 1962; La Ceramica de Monte Alban, 1967; El Museo Nacional de Antropologia, 1967; El Mundo Olmeca, 1968; Ancient Mexico in Colour, 1968; The Olmec World, 1969. Home: 65 Tres Picos Mexico 5 DF Mexico Office: Nat Museum Anthropology Mexico 5 DF Mexico

BERNARD, CHARLES TAYLOR, dry cleaning co. exec.; b. Helena, Ark., Sept. 10, 1927; s. Charles L. and Sallie (Eakin) B.; B.A., Baylor U., 1950; LL.B., Shorter Coll., Little Rock, 1969; m. Betty Ann Hill, Nov. 26, 1953; children—Sallie Hill, Mary Troy, Charles Taylor, David Wesley, John Harbert. Self employed in field agr., cotton ginning and elevator operation, 1950—; owner, operator Bernard Manor One Hour Dry Cleaning Chain, Erle, Ark., 1957—; dir. Earle State Bank. Del. to Nat. Cotton Council, 1971—. Chmn., Ark. Bank Commn., 1971. Vice pres., mem. exec. bd. Eastern Ark. Area council Boy Scouts Am., mem. exec. com. Region 5; mem. exec. com. Ark. region Nat. Conf. Christians and Jews; Ark fund raising chmn. Nat. Cystic Fibrosis Research Found., 1970. Mem. Earle City Council, 1956-62; chmn. Crittenden County Republican Party, 1966-68; finance dir., mem. exec. com. Ark. Rep. Com., 1966—, now chmn.; Rep. candidate U.S. Senate, 1968; mem. Rep. Nat. Com. Bd. dirs. Memphis Area chpt. A.R.C.; trustee So. Bapt. Coll.; mem. exec. bd. Bapt. State Conv. Ark. Served with USNR, 1944-45. Recipient Silver Beaver and Silver Antelope awards Boy Scouts Am. Mem. Ark.-Mo. Ginners Assn. (pres.), So. Cotton Ginners Assn. (pres.), Delta Sigma Pi. Baptist (deacon). Mason (32 deg., Shrine), Rotarian. Home: Bernard Farms Earle AR 72331 Office: 1000 Main St Earle AR 72331

BERNARD, CICERO HENRY, ret. educator; b. Rush Springs, Okla., May 18, 1906; s. Cicero Edgar and Helen Gertrude (Sperling) B.; A.B., Phillips U., 1928; M.S., U. Ky., 1931; postgrad. U. Okla., 1934-35, Okla. State U., 1938, U. Tex., 1939-40, Tex. A. and M. U., 1942-58; m. Maxie Ruola Travis, Dec. 24, 1927; 1 dau., Dormalee Maxine (Mrs. Bill T. Cummins). Tchr. sci. and math. high sch., Miami, Okla., 1927-29; instr. physics and mathematics Lees Jr. Coll., Jackson, Ky., 1931-33, Altus (Okla.) Jr. Coll., 1935-37; head phys. sci. dept. Seminole (Okla.) Jr. Coll., 1937-41; instr. physics Tex. A. and M. U., College Station, 1941-43, asst. prof., 1943-47, asso. prof., 1947-61; prof., chmn. dept. physics Midwestern U., Wichita Falls, Tex., 1961-71. Sr. nuclear engr. Convair div. Gen. Dynamics, Ft. Worth, 1951-53, summers 1954-56; asso. faculty engr. Lockheed Aircraft, Marietta, Ga., summer 1957; health physics research Oak Ridge Nat. Lab., summers 1958-59. Recipient Hardin Prof. award Midwestern U., 1964. Mem. Am. Assn. Physic Tchrs., Sigma Pi Sigma. Mem. Ch. of Christ (elder). Lion. Author: Laboratory Experiments in College Physics, 1949, 1957, 1964, 72. Research in gamma ray scattering, radiation effects, radiation dosimetry. Home: PO Box 156 Rush Springs OK 73082

BERNARD, HAROLD GRADY, state ofcl.; b. Jamestown, Ky., Apr. 3, 1938; s. Byron H. and Creola (Foley) B.; B.S., Eastern Ky. State Coll., 1962; m. Nancy Hunter Prather, June 16, 1962; children—Lisa Jean, Andrew Coleman. Auditor, Ky. Dept. Revenue, Bowling Green, 1962-66, audit supr., 1966-68; dir. div. rates and services, rate specialist Ky. Dept. Motor Transp., Frankfort, 1968—. Served with AUS 1955-58. Mem. V.F.W. Episcopalian. Home: 233 Rancho Dr Frankfort KY 40601 Office: New State Office Bldg Frankfort KY 40601

BERNARD, HUGH YANCEY, JR., librarian, educator; b. Athens, Ga., July 17, 1919; s. Hugh Yancey and Marguerite (Vonderau) B.; student Piedmont Coll., 1937-38; A.B., U. Ga., 1941; B.S., Columbia, 1947; J.D., George Washington U., 1961. Tchr. high schs., Moultrie, Ga., 1941 acting supr. VA, Atlanta, 1946; cataloger, copyright office Library of Congress, Washington, 1947-52, reviser, 1952-59, sr. cataloger manuscripts sect., Descriptive Cataloging Div., 1959-60; librarian Law Library, George Washington U., Washington, 1960—; lectr., 1962-66, asst. prof. law, 1966-68, asso. prof., 1968-70, prof., 1970—; admitted to D.C. bar, 1961; dir. 381 Southern Av., S.E., Inc., Washington, 1952-55, pres., 1955. Founding dir., incorporator Women's Home, Alexandria, Va., 1963; pres. Robinson Farm, Inc., Alexandria, 1970—. Mem. corp. Luther Rice Coll., Franconia, Va., 1967—, bd. dirs., 1972—. Served with USAAF, 1942-46. Mem. Bar Assn. D.C., Spl. Libraries Assn., Am. Bar Assn., Am. Judicature Soc., Law Librarians Soc. Washington (v.p. 1964-66, pres. 1966). Am. Assn. Law Libraries, Order of Coif, Phi Beta Kappa, Kappa Delta Pi, Phi Alpha Delta. Baptist (deacon). Mason (Shriner). Club: Nat. Lawyers (Washington). Author: The Law of Death and the Disposal of the Dead, 1966; Public Officials, Elected and Appointed, 1968. Home: 1911 Paul Spring Pkwy Alexandria VA 22308 Office: 716 20th St NW Washington DC 20006

BERNARDIN, WILLARD, bank holding co. ofcl.; b. Silverton, Colo., Apr. 25, 1943; s. Otokar Franz and Ruth Caryl (Thwing) B.; B.A., Purdue U., 1965; postgrad. U. N.C., 1965-66; M.A., Johns Hopkins, 1967; m. Maren Anne Nelson, June 26, 1965. Sci. writer U. N.C., Chapel Hill, 1965-66, Johns Hopkins, Balt., 1966; securities analyst Bache & Co., N.Y.C., 1967-68; treas., sec. Ocean Sci. & Engring., Inc., Bethesda, Md., 1968-72, asst. to pres. 1st Va. Bankshares Corp., Falls Church, 1972—. Mem. Marine Tech. Soc., Nat. Assn. Sci. Writers, Johns Hopkins, Purdue U. alumni assns., Delta Upsilon. Republican. Home: 2325 37th St NW Washington DC 20007 Office: 1 First Virginia Plaza 6400 Arlington Blvd Falls Church VA 22042

BERNARDS, VOLDERMARS THEODORE, educator; b. Riga, Latvia, Oct. 1, 1907; s. Voldemars and Eva (Simons) B.; B.A., State U. Latvia, 1938, M.A., 1944; postgrad U. Tubingen, Germany, 1948-49; Ph.D., Columbia, 1958 Came to U.S., 1950, naturalized, 1956. Coll. prof., Riga, Esslingen and Stuttgart, Germany, 1944-49; lexicographer, etymologist Merriam Webster Dictionary Co., Springfield, Mass., 1958; asso. prof. linguistics and classical langs. Lenoir Rhyne Coll., Hickory, N.C., 1959—. Bible translator Brit. and Fgn. Bible Soc., London. Mem. Linguistic Soc. Am., Assn. for Advancement Baltic Studies; Cactus and Succulent Soc. Am., Am. Assn. U. Profs. Lutheran. Home: Lenoir Rhyne Coll Hickory NC 28601

BERNAT, HARRY, govt. ofcl.; b. St. Paul, May 16, 1924; s. Maier and Bertha (Weiss) B.; student Reed Coll., 1944, Harvard, 1945; B. Elec. Engring. with distinction, U. Minn., 1949, B.B.A. with distinction, 1949, M.A. in Pub. Adminstrn., 1951; postgrad. polit. sci. Johns Hopkins, 1951-53; m. Frances Lorraine Simon, Sept. 2, 1951; children—Renae Ellyn, Corey Mitchell, Donna Jeanne. Tech. plans, program officer hdqrs. air research and devel. command U.S. Air Force, Balt., 1951-58, mgmt. systems engr. Systems Command, Andrews AFB, Md., 1958-63; research and devel. program mgr. Def. Communications Agy., Dept. Def., Washington, 1963—. Vice pres., account exec., ins. agt. Manna Financial Planning Corp., Falls Church, Va., 1962—, also dir.; dir. Manna Equities Corp., Falls Ch.; instr. adult edn. program Prince George's County, Md., 1970—. Mem. Greater S.E. Community Hosp. Found., Inc., Washington, 1960—; treas. Troop 205, Nat. Capital council Boy Scouts Am., 1966-68. Bd. dirs. River Ridge Recreation Council, Oxon Hill, Md., (pres. 1971). Served with AUS, 1943-46. Congl. fellow Am. Polit. Sci. Assn., 1968-69. Mem. Am. Polit. Sci. Assn., Eta Kappa Nu, Tau Beta Pi, Beta Gamma Sigma, Sigma Alpha Sigma. Toastmaster (distinguished award 1972). Home: 6202 Cloverdale Dr Oxon Hill MD 20021 Office: Research and Devel Div (Code 340) Directorate of Plans Def Communications Agy Dept Def Washington DC 20305

BERND, JOSEPH LAURENCE, polit. scientist, educator; b. Macon, Ga., Dec. 8, 1923; s. Laurence Joseph and Eva (Bloom) B.; B.A., Mercer U., 1945; M.A., Boston U., 1953 Ph.D., Duke, 1957; m. Ruth Audrey Brady, July 2, 1960; 1 dau., Alison Ruth. Instr. polit. sci. Boston, U., 1952-53; asst. prof., High Point (N.C.) Coll., 1957-59; asst. prof., asso. prof. So. Meth. U., 1959-65; prof. Va. Poly. Inst., Blacksburg, 1965—, chmn. dept., 1965-70. Cons. former gov. Ga., 1949-50, 54, U.S. Commn. Civil Rights, 1958, NSF, 1965. Duke U. Press, 1966, plaintiffs brief in Sanders v. Gray U.S. Supreme Ct., 1963. Myer & Rubin in case on election law; polit. reporter, analyst, cons. to TV and radio stas.; lectr., New Orleans, Vienna, Austria, Lexington, Lynchburg, Va., Atlanta. Founder Young Peoples League for Better Govt., 1947; wage analyst WSB, 1951. Fellow Social Sci. Research Council, 1956-57. Grad. Council Humanities So. Meth. U., 1962-63. Mem. Am., So. (mem. exec. com. 1966-69) polit. sci. assns., Am. Assn. U. Profs. Jewish religion. Author: Grass Roots Politics in Georgia, 1960. Editor: Mathematical Applications in Political Science, Vols. II-IV, 1965-69, co-editor Vol.I, V, VI; 1971. Contbr. articles to profl. jours. Home: 502 Stonegate Dr Blacksburg VA 24060

BERNE, ROBERT M(ATTHEW), physician; b. Yonkers, N.Y., Apr. 22, 1918; A.B., U. N.C., 1939; M.D., Harvard, 1943; m. 1944; 4 children. Instr. physiology Case Western Res. U., 1949-50, sr. instr., 1950-52, asst. prof., 1952-55, asso. prof., 1955-61, prof., 1961-66, asst. prof. medicine, 1957-66; prof. physiology, chmn. dept. U. Va. Sch. Medicine, 1966—. Served with M.C. AUS, 1944-46. Mem. Am. Physiol. Soc. (pres. elect. 1972), A.A.A.S., Soc. Clin. Investigation, Soc. Exptl. Biology, Fedn. Clin. Research, Am. Heart Assn. Address: U Va Sch Medicine Charlottesville VA 22903*

BERNER, LEWIS, biologist, educator; b. Savannah, Ga., Sept. 30, 1915; s. Joseph Benjamin and Frances (Lax) B.; B.S., U. Fla., 1937; M.S., 1939, Ph.D., 1941; m. Amelia Pauline Brenn, Oct. 7, 1945; children—Roberta Jacqualyn, Cheryl Brenna. Asst. prof. biol. sci. U. Fla., 1946-51, asso. prof., 1951-54, prof., 1954—, chmn. biol. sci. dept., 1959-71; acting dir. div. biol. scis., 1970—; prof. entomology U. Minn., Lake Itasca, summers 1958-60, 62, 68, 69; entomologist Volta River Project, Govt. of Gold Coast, Brit. W. Africa, 1950, Shire River Project, Govt. Nyasaland, Brit. Central Africa, 1952. Vice pres., bd. dirs. Highlands Biol. Sta. Served to lt. col. Med. Service Corps, AUS, 1941-46; col. Res. Decorated Legion of Merit; recipient Phi Sigma medal, 1941; Distinguished Service award Fla. Entomol. Soc., 1963, Distinguished Faculty award Blue Key Honor Soc., 1967. Mem. Entomol. Soc. Am. (past sect. chmn.), Assn. Southeastern Biologists, Fla. Entomol. Soc. (past pres., editor 1950-63), Entomol. Soc. Washington, Midwest Benthological Soc. Phi Beta Kappa, Sigma Xi, Phi Kappa Phi, Phi Sigma, Alpha Epsilon Delta. Rotarian. Author: The Mayflies of Florida, 1950. Contbr. articles profl. jours. Home: 7080 NW 23D Av Gainesville FL 32601

BERNHARDT, JOHN BOWMAN, banker; b. Norton, Va., Aug. 7, 1929; s. Claude Bowman and (Dixon) B.; B.A., U. Va., 1954, LL.B., 1957; postgrad. Rutgers U., 1965-67; m. Ada Nuckels, Aug. 29, 1952; children—Jared B., J. Carter. With Peoples Nat. Bank, Charlottesville, 1957-63; asst. v.p. Va. Nat. Bank, Norfolk, 1963-64, v.p., 1964-68, sr. v.p., 1968-69, exec. v.p., 1969—, sec., exec. com., 1972—; sec., asst. treas. Va. Nat. Bankshares, Inc., 1972—; dir. Mortgage Investment Corp. Treas., trustee Chrysler Mus., Norfolk, 1971—; mem. Norfolk Bd. Sinking Fund Commrs., 1969—; mem. regional adv. council Small Bus. Adminstrn., 1970—. Bd. dirs. Urban Coalition Norfolk, 1970-72; trustee Leigh Meml. Hosp., Va. Wesleyan Coll., Eastern Va. Med. Sch. Found. Mem. Navy League U.S., Newcomen Soc. N.Am., Hampton Roads Maritime Assn., Nat. Alliance Businessmen (metro chmn. 1970-72), Am., Va. bankers assns., Va., Norfolk Chamber Commerces. Presbyn. Clubs: Cedar Point (Crittenden, Va.); Harbor, Norfolk Yacht and Country. Home: 925 Hanover Av Norfolk VA 23508 Office: 1 Commercial Pl Norfolk VA 23510

BERNI, RALPH JOHN, chemist; b. New Orleans, Nov. 1, 1931; s. Louis A. and Victorie (Parr) B.; B.S., La. State U., 1954; M.S., Tulane U., 1961, Ph.D., 1966; m. Joan McGuire, Oct. 17, 1957; children—Ann L., Ralph H., Erin E. Research chemist So. Regional Research Lab., U.S. Dept. Agr. Agrl. Research Service, New Orleans, 1955—. Instr. chemistry Tulane U. and Loyola U., 1960-68. Served with AUS, 1955-57. Fellow Am. Inst. Chemists (chmn. La. chpt. 1970); mem. Am. Chem. Soc. (treas. La. sect. 1969—), Research Soc. Am. (chmn.-elect 1972, Am. Assn. Textile Chemists and Colorists, Orgn. Profl. Employees of Dept. Agr., Sigma Xi. Contbr. articles to profl. jours. Patentee in field. Home: 645 Aris Av Metairie LA 70005 Office: PO Box 19687 New Orleans LA 70179

BERNSTEIN, JOSEPH, lawyer; b. New Orleans, Feb. 12, 1930; s. Eugene Julian and Lola (Schlemoff) B.; B.S., U. Ala., 1952; LL.B., Tulane U., 1957; m. Phyllis Maxine Askanase, Sept. 4, 1955; children—Jill, Barbara, Elizabeth R., Jonathan Joseph. Clk. to Justice E. Howard McCaleb of La. Supreme Court, 1957; admitted to La. bar, 1957; asso. firm Jones, Walker, Waechter, Poitevent, Carrere & Denegre, 1957-60, partner, 1960-65; gen. practice New Orleans, 1965—. Pres. CATV Systems of Jefferson, Inc. Pres., New Orleans Jewish Community Center. Served to 2d lt. AUS, 1952-54. Mem. Am., La., New Orleans bar assns., Phi Delta Phi, Zeta Beta Tau. Democrat. Jewish religion. Home: 5705 St Charles Av New Orleans LA 70115 Office: 310 Security Homestead Bldg Veterans Blvd Metairie LA 70002

BERNSTEIN, MARK RICHARD, lawyer; b. York, Pa., Apr. 7, 1930; s. Phillip G. and Evelyn (Greenfield) B.; A.B. cum laude, U. Pa., 1952; LL.B., Yale U., 1957; m. Ellen Louise Kaufman, Aug. 21, 1955; children—Phillip G., Cary Jane, Adam, Andrew William, Jonathon, Evan. Admitted to N.C. bar, 1957; asso. in firm Kennedy, Covington, Lobdell & Hichman, Charlotte, N.C., 1957-60; pvt. law practice, 1960-61; partner firm Haynes & Bernstein, Charlotte, 1961-62; partner Haynes, Graham & Bernstein, Charlotte, 1962-64; partner Haynes, Graham, Bernstein & Baucom, Charlotte, 1965-70, Grier, Parker, Poe, Thompson, Bernstein, Gage and Preston, Charlotte, 1970—. Pres. Charlotte Temple Beth El, 1963-65; pres. Charlotte Civitan Club, 1965-66; chmn. long-range planning com. Charlotte Symphony Orch., 1965—, also bd. dirs.; bd. dirs. Charlotte Area Fund. Served as lt. AUS, 1952-54. Recipient Distinguished Service award Charlotte Jr. C. of C., 1961. Mem. Am., N.C. bar assns. 26th Jud. Bar Assn. (exec. com.), C. of C. (chmn. legislation com., dir.), Phi Epsilon Pi, Phi Alpha Delta. Jewish religion. Mem. B'nai B'rith (pres. lodge 1961). Home: 6619 Burlwood Dr Charlotte NC 28202 Office: Wachovia Bldg Charlotte NC 28202

BERNSTROM, RICHARD EDWARD, dentist; b. Nutley, N.J., Oct. 5, 1930; s. Harry Oscar and Marie (Housselle) B.; student Colgate U., 1949-50, U. Va., 1950-51, 58-60; D.D.S., Fairleigh Dickinson U., 1964; m. Beverly Arabelle Todd, July 15, 1959; children—Kimberly Anne, Maurine Marie. Practice dentistry, Richmond, Ky., 1964—. Dir. 1st Fed. Savings & Loan Assn., Richmond, Ky. Served with Dental Corps. AUS, 1956-57. Mem. Am., Ky., Madison County dental assns., Am. Soc. Dentistry for Children, Study Group Dentistry for Children, Madison County Hist. Soc., Blue Grass Dental Soc., Alpha Tau Omega. Methodist (chmn. bd. 1969-71). Rotarian (dir. 1967-68, pres. Richmond 1970-71). Home: Bel-Air Richmond KY 40475 Office: 1st Fed Savings & Loan Bldg Richmond KY 40475

BERREY, BEDFORD HUDSON, govt. ofcl.; b. Carrollton, Mo., Apr. 20, 1922; s. Robert Wilson and Elizabeth Mary (Hudson) B.; B.S., U. Mo., 1943; M.D., U. Colo., 1944-45; M.A., Am. U., 1968; m. Marcia Lois Bagley, May 22, 1943; children—Elizabeth Jane (Mrs. Craig E. O'Connor), Barbara Lynn, Bedford Hudson, Christopher Lee, Michael David. Intern, Kansas City (Mo.) Gen. Hosp., 1945-46; resident Children's Hosp., Denver, 1946-47, Ocshner Clinic, New Orleans, 1949; pvt. practice medicine, specializing in pediatrics, Kansas City, Mo., 1947-48, Harlingen, Tex., 1950-51; commd. capt. U.S. Army, 1951; advanced through ranks to col., 1967; various assignments world wide including asst. army attache Am. embassy, New Delhi, India, 1963-65; dir. for personnel Office Asst. Sec. Def., for Health and Environment, Washington, 1970-72; dep. chief surgeon Hdqrs. U.S. Army Pacific, 1972—. Pres., P.T.A., Denver, 1952, Am. Sch., Berlin, Germany, 1954; pres. San Antonio Commn., S. Tex. Am. Athletic Union, 1961-62; referee Indian Nat. Swimming Championship, India, 1964. Decorated meritorious Service medal with 1 oak leaf cluster. Diplomate Am. Bd. Pediatrics. Fellow A.C.P.; Mem. Am. Med. Assn., Assn. Mil. Surgeons U.S., Am. Polit. Sci. Assn., Com. Internat. Child Health, Am. Acad. Pediatrics, Nat. Council Internat. Health, Sigma Nu, Phi Beta Pi, Pi Sigma Alpha. Mason (32 deg.). Clubs: National Sojourners, Army-Navy (Washington). Contbr. articles to profl. pubs. Home: 4212 23d St N Arlington VA 22207 Office: Dep Chief Surgeon Hdqrs US Army Pacific APO San Francisco CA 96558

BERRIER, JOE HERMAN, city ofcl.; b. Lexington, N.C., Jan. 23, 1925; s. David Lee and Claudia Jane (Sink) B.; B.S. in Civil Engring., N.C. State U., 1948; m. Mary Frances Clodfelter, July 11, 1947; children— Frances (Mrs. Dermont Morris), Sarah, Robert, Patricia, Martha. Jr. engr. Frank T. Miller, cons. engrs., Greensboro, N.C., 1948-49; jr. resident engr. State Hwy. Commn., 1949-57; street supt. City of Winston-Salem, N.C., 1957-63, asst. dir. pub. works, 1963-65, dir. pub. works, 1965—. Served with AUS, 1944-46. Recipient George C. Franklin Meml. award N.C. League Municipalities, 1959. Mem. Am. Roadbuilders Assn. (v.p. municipal and airport div. 1970-71), Am. Pub. Works Assn. (pres. N.C. chpt. 1968), N.C. Soc. Engrs. (dir. 1968-69), C. of C. Lion. Home: 3205 Nottingham Rd Winston-Salem NC 27104 Office: Box 2511 Winston-Salem NC 27102

BERRONG, HARTRIDGE JACKSON, civil engr.; b. Hiawassee, Ga., Jan. 17, 1909; s. Edward Carlton and Cora Alvey (Blalock) B.; diploma Draughons Bus. Coll., 1927; certificate U. Ala. Extension Center, 1942; m. Sue Mary Gammons, Feb. 17, 1929; children—Mary Elizabeth, Nelson Green. With U.S. C.E., 1929-33, TVA, 1933-45; with Ga. Testing Labs., Inc., Atlanta, 1945—, pres., 1963—. Mem. Am. Soc. C.E., Am. Concrete Inst., Am. Soc. Testing and Materials. Elk. Home: 767 Gresham Av SE Atlanta GA 30316 Office: 1130 Hemphill Av NW Atlanta GA 30318

BERRY, AMOS NELSON, SR., elementary sch. prin.; b. Fort Gaines, Ga., Sept. 27, 1919; s. Will and Loucresia (Peterson) B.; A.A., Albany State Jr. Coll., 1940; B.S., Albany State Coll., 1945; M.Ed., Tuskegee Inst., 1953; postgrad. Fort Valley (Ga.) State Coll., Wayne U., N.Y. U., U. P.R.; LL.D., Union Baptist Sem., 1967; m. Leavie Chandle, Apr. 2, 1966; children—Astria Ruth, Loucresia Vivian, Amos Nelson. Prin. pub. schs., Tifton, Ga., 1941-47, Hahira, Ga., 1947-48; asst. prin., dir. audio-visual aids Barbour County Schs., Eufaula, Ala., 1948-50; prin. Arlington (Ga.) Vocational High Sch., 1950-54, Flintside Elementary Sch., Albany, Ga., 1954—. Dir. Harlem Cut Rate Drug Store, Albany. Pres. Dougherty County Band Boosters, 1957-60; asst. pres. Dougherty County Resource Devel. Com., 1959-61, treas., 1961-62; chmn. Dougherty County Art Fair, 1965-67; pres. Flintside Community Improvement Assn., 1966-68; mem. higher edn. council Albany (Ga.) State Coll., 1966-68, Albany Coll. Student Tchr. Assn., 1967-68. Recipient certificates appreciation Bur. Census, 1970, March of Dimes, 1971; named Prin. of Year, Lowndes, 1946. State Prin. scholar, 1945, State Health scholar, 1954, Audio-Visual scholar, 1948. Mem. Dougherty County Prin.'s Council, Dougherty County Classroom Tchrs. Assn., Ga. Tchrs. Assn., Ga., Dist. 2 Elementary, Nat. elementary prins. assns., Omega Psi Phi. Baptist (mem., financial sec. Ga. Missionary Sunday Sch. Bd.). Mason. Clubs: 26, Criterion (Albany, Ga.). Home: 813 Cherry Av Albany GA 31701 Office: 2610 S Jackson St Albany GA 31701

BERRY, CHARLES EDWARD, trust co. exec., state legislator; b. Columbus, Ga., July 16, 1908; s. Turner E. and Annie Belle (Lynch) B.; B.A., U. of South, 1929; m. Martha L. Bartlett, Apr. 28, 1933 (dec. Nov. 1967); children—Charles Edward, William, Mary; m. 2d, Mildred H. Holleman, Oct. 13, 1968; stepchildren—Ralph M., Mildred (Mrs. J. M. Dean). Basement mdse. mgr. J.A. Kirven Co., Columbus, 1931-41, asst. mgr., 1941-44; partner and office mgr. Columbus Fixture Mfg. Co., 1944-68, was v.p. and sec., now ret.; v.p. Trust Co. Columbus, 1969—; mem. Ga. Ho. of Reps., 1966—. Trustee Ga. Hosp. Service Assn. Mem. City-County Planning Bd., Columbus Water Bd., 1955, mem. city council, 1954-60, mayor, 1955; mem. Ga. Democratic Exec. Com.; mem. exec. bd. emeritus City of Columbus; lt. col. Gov.'s Staff; mem. gov.'s staff Ga. and Ala. Dir. United Cerebral Palsy Muscogge County; bd. mgmt. Armed Services YMCA, chmn., 1955; vice chmn. Ga. Commn. Devel. Chattanoochee River Basin. Mem. Ga. Sheriff's Assn. (hon.), Nat. Soc. State Legislators, Third Congl. Legislative Assn., 40 and 8, Am. Legion (comdr. 3d dist. 1950; life mem.; Ga. legislative chmn.), Assn. U.S. Army, Am. Ch. Union, Am. Numis. Assns., C. of C., Asso. Industries of Ga., Ga. Municipal Assn. (hon. life), Delta Tau Delta. Episcopalian (vestryman 1952-55, jr. warden 1954-55). Mason, Moose, Elk. Clubs: The '49 Er, Lions. Home: 2516 Harding Dr Columbus GA 31906 Office: Trust Co of Columbus PO Box 57 Columbus GA 31902

BERRY, DALE, machinery co. exec.; b. Mesquite, Tex., Sept. 3, 1928; s. Roscoe Shelby and Ida Myrl (Ellis) B.; student Draugons Bus. Coll., 1948; m. Dorothy Louise Lewis, Jan. 25, 1946; children—Susan Dee, Robin Dale, Mark Wayne. Country Western radio star, touring U.S. with Grand Ol' Opry, 1945-48; performed as singer, guitarist, actor in motion pictures, including Hidden Valley Days, 1946; Free White and 21, 1960; TV appearances include Route 66 series, 1966; exec. v.p. Transcontinental Artists Corp., 1962-71, Berry Bros. Machinery, Inc., Mesquite, Tex. 1971—. Home: 2655 Lanecrest St Dallas TX 75228 Office: 2615 Big Town Blvd Mesquite TX 75223

BERRY, FRANK LAFAYETTE, bank exec.; b. Columbia, Miss., Jan. 11, 1899; s. James Russell and Mollie Elmira (Riley) B.; student U. Miss., 1916-17; grad. pharmacist Atlanta Coll. Pharmacy, 1919-21; m. Pearl Chesnut, July 22, 1961; 1 stepdau., Cheryl Miller Guynn. Owner Berry's Drug Stores, Gaffney, S.C., 1922-27; salesman E.R. Squibb & Sons, N.Y.C., 1928-58; owner Real Estate Investments, 1958—; organizer, dir. Citizens and So. Bank Chamblee (Ga.), 1968—; dir. Chamblee (Ga.) Nat. Bank. Tchr. chemistry Atlanta Sch. Pharmacy, 1920-21. Served with AEF, 1917-19. Mem. Ga. Pharm. Assn. (pres. traveling men's aux. 1948-49), DeKalb C. of C., DeKalb Hist. Soc., Chamblee-Doraville Bus. Men's Assn., English Speaking Union U.S. Democrat. Methodist (chmn. bd. trustees 1969-70). Mason, Rotarian. Club: Dunwoody (Atlanta). Home: 1734 Dunridge Ct Atlanta GA 30338 Office: PO Box 80424 Atlanta GA 30341

BERRY, LEWIS EDWARD, editor; b. Crystal Springs, Ark., Sept. 11, 1914; s. Charles Lucien and Minerva (Lewis) B.; student Southeastern U., 1935-37; m. Gertrude Louise Allen, May 23, 1942; children—Zora Margaret (Mrs. Richard R. Wilcoxen), Lewis Edward, Susan Elizabeth (Mrs. William J. Matthews), Patricia Ann (Mrs. William Harmon Simmons, Jr.). Hwy. patrolman Tex. Dept. Pub. Safety, 1941-42, pub. information officer, 1949-52, 1952-57; detective Met. Police Dept., Washington, 1942-48; officer regional police coordinator Fed. Civil Def. Adminstrn., 1952; editor Tex. Lawman, 1956—; exec. sec. Sheriffs' Assn. of Tex., 1957-72. Served with USMC, 1934-37; asso. editor Leatherneck Mag.; col. Tex. State Guard, 1950—. Recipient Tex. Medal of Merit, 1965. Mem. Sigma Delta Chi. Mason, K.P. Home: 5501 Caprice Dr Austin TX 78731 Office: 5520 N Lamar Blvd Austin TX 78751

BERRY, LOREN MURPHY, business exec.; b. Wabash, Ind., July 24, 1888; s. Charles D. and Elizabeth (Murphy) B.; student Northwestern U., 1909-10; LL.D., Rio Grande (Ohio) Coll.; m. Lucile Kneipple, June 9, 1909 (dec.); children—Loren Murphy, Martha Sue Fraim, John William, Elizabeth Anne Fox; m. 2d, Helen Anderson Henry, Aug. 28, 1938; 1 son, Leland. Newspaper reporter, Wabash, Ind., Joliet, Ill., Chgo.; sold telephone directory advt., Marion, Ind., 1910, St. Louis, Louisville, Indpls., which developed into nat. sales orgn. of L. M. Berry & Co., main office, Dayton, O., now chmn. bd., chief exec. officer; dir. United Telecommunications, Inc., Kansas City, Mo., Mut. Broadcasting Corp., N.Y.C., Super Food Services, Inc., Dayton, Fla. Telephone Corp., Ocala, Laughter Corp., Dayton, Hulman Realty Co., Dayton, Edison Nat. Bank, Ft. Myers, Fla. Mem. Republican Nat. Finance Com., Washington. Bd. dirs. Jr. Achievement, Dayton; trustee Rio Grande Coll. Mem. U.S. Ind. Telephone Pioneers (pres. 1938-39), Bell Telephone Pioneers Assn. (v.p. N.C. Kingsbury chpt. 1939-40). Republican. Episcopalian. Mason (32 deg., Shriner). Clubs: Dayton City, Engineers, Kiwanis, Dayton Country, Moraine Country, Bicycle (Dayton); Surf (gov.), Committee of 100, Indian Creek (Miami Beach, Fla.); Bohemian (San Francisco); Capitol Hill (Washington). Home: 1155 Ridgeway Rd Dayton OH 45419 also Surf Club Apts 9133 Collins Av Miami Beach FL 33154 Office: 3170 Kettering Blvd PO Box 6000 Dayton OH 45401 also 3818 Bay Vista Av Tampa FL 33611

BERRY, MARVIN ALBERT, physician; b. Pampa, Tex., Jan. 14, 1940; s. Albert Eura and Bessie Mae (Chatwell) B.; B.S., W. Tex. State U., 1962; M.D., U. Tex., 1965; m. Kathleen Ann Knox, Dec. 27, 1966; 1 son, Robb Marvin. Intern, John Peter Smith Hosp., Fort Worth, 1965-66; gen. practice resident, 1966-67; gen. practice medicine Pampa (Tex.) Clinic, 1967-68, Lubbock, Tex., 1971—; dir. dept. gen. practice and emergency services John Peter Smith Hosp., Fort Worth, 1968-71. Mem. Fort Worth Emergency Med. Services Com., 1970; med. cons. Fort Worth Fire Dept., 1970-71; coordinator emergency med. technician-ambulance course Tarrant County Jr. Coll., 1970-71; instr. cardiopulmonary resuscitation Lubbock Dept. Pub. Safety and Fire Dept, 1971. Served to capt., M.C., USAFR, 1966-71. Recipient award for leadership S.A.R., 1961. Service award Fort Worth Fire Dept., 1971. Diplomate Am. Bd. Family Practice. Mem. Am. Acad. Family Practice, A.M.A., Am. Coll. Emergency Physicians, Tex. Acad. Gen. Practice, Tex. Med. Assn., Tarrant County, Lubbock-Garza-Crosby med. socs., Am. Rifle Assn., Red Helmets, Kappa Alpha, Phi Chi, Alpha Chi. Mem. Ch. of Christ. Died Sept. 8, 1971. Home: 3704 66th St Lubbock TX 79413 Office: 4501 50th St Lubbock TX 79414

BERRY, PAUL LUCIEN, librarian; b. San Jose, Cal., Sept. 4, 1921; s. Elmer Garfield and Nellie (Bush) B.; B.A., Am. U., 1943, postgrad., 1957-63; postgrad. Yale U., 1943-44, Cath. U. Am., 1946-50; m. Doris M. Patterson, Apr. 14, 1945; children—Marsha Joan, Donald Lucien. With D.C. Pub. Library, 1944-45; with Library of Congress, Washington, 1945—, chief serial div., 1953-61, coordinator reference dept., 1961-64, asso. dir. adminstrv. dept., 1964-67, dir., 1967-68, asso. dir. reference dept., 1968-69, dir. reference dept., 1969—. Mem. Am., D.C. library assns., Nat. Microfilm Assn., Am. Soc. Information Sci., Am. U. Alumni Assn. (pres. 1958-60), Omicron Delta Kappa, Alpha Tau Omega. Contbr. to profl. jours. Home: 2104 Cascade Rd Silver Spring MD 20902 Office: Library of Congress Washington DC 20540

BERRY, THOMAS SENIOR, educator; b. Holyoke, Mass., Nov. 21, 1906; s. James and Mary Elizabeth (Senior) B.; S.B. cum laude, Harvard, 1927, M.A., 1932, Ph.D., 1938; m. Hazel Lillian Marsh, June 23, 1930 (dec. 1948); m. 2d, Mary Ellen Palmer, Mar. 2, 1951; children—John Paul, Margaret Elizabeth (Mrs. Kenneth Collins), Mary Elizabeth (Mrs. R. Wayne White), Charles Palmer, David Holmes, Thomas Senior. Instr., Oxford Sch., Cambridge, Mass., 1929-32; mem. research staff Harvard Bur. Econs. Research in Latin Am., Internat. Sci. Com. on Price History, 1932-35; instr. econs. Duke, 1935-43; sr. economist Atlanta OPA, 1943-45; field office economist PHA, 1945-47, 1949-53; prof. econs. Millsaps Coll. (Miss.), 1947-49; asso. prof. Sch. Bus., U. Richmond (Va.), 1953—. Mem. Am., So. econ. assns., Econ. History Assn., Am. Hist. Assn., Va. Hist. Soc., Phi Beta Kappa, Beta Gamma Sigma. Club: Harvard of Virginia. Author: Western Prices Before 1861, 1943; Estimated GNP, 1789-1909, 1968. Editor: (with C.H. Haring and Miron Burgin) Economic Literature of Latin America, 1935-36. Home: 5 Bostwick Lane U Richmond PO Richmond VA 23173

BERRY, WENDELL, poet, educator; b. Henry County, Ky., Aug. 5, 1934; A.B., M.A., U. Ky.; m. Tanya Berry; children—Mary Dee, Pryor Clifford. Mem. faculty English dept U. Ky. at Lexington; author novels: Nathan Coulter, A Place on Earth; poetry collections: The Broken Ground, Findings, Openings, Farming: A Handbook, 1970; essays: The Long-Legged House. Home: Port Royal KY 20058 Office: English Dept U Ky Lexington KY 50406*

BERRY, WILLIAM AYLOR, chief justice Okla. Supreme Ct.; b. Ripley, Okla., Dec. 28, 1915; s. Thomas Nelson and Harriett Virginia (Patton) B.; B.A., Okla. State U., 1939; LL.B., Okla. U., 1940; m. Carolyn Burwell, Jan. 2, 1947; children—Elizabeth Patton, Nichols Burwell. Admitted to Okla. bar, 1940; county atty. Payne County, 1940-41; asst. U.S. dist. atty. for Western Dist., Oklahoma City, 1947-50; Oklahoma County judge, Oklahoma City, 1953-59; asso. justice of Supreme Ct. of Oklahoma, 1959— vice chief justice, 1967-70, chief justice, 1970—. Nat. comdr. Am. Ex-Prisoners of War, Inc., 1953, nat. judge advocate, 1955—; chmn. com. on cooperation between state and fed. judges, 1960. Bd. dirs. Oklahoma County chpt. A.R.C., 1956-60; bd. dirs. Salvation Army. Served from ensign to lt. comdr. USNR, 1941-46. Decorated Purple Heart. Mem. Am. Bar Assn. (chmn. com. coop. between state and fed. judges), Okla. C. of C. (dir.), Sigma Nu, Phi Delta Phi. Home: 1706 Wilshire Blvd Oklahoma City OK 73116 Office: State Capitol-Supreme Ct Oklahoma City OK 73105

BERRYHILL, EARL JOHN, educator; b. Thrall, Tex., June 25, 1908; s. Charles Monroe and Juanita (Inabinet) B.; B.S., Tex. A. and M. U., 1931; M.A., U. Phillippines, 1954; postgrad. Trinity U., 1962-63; Ed.D., U. Houston, 1969; m. Helen Parkhurst, Apr. 13, 1935; children— Barbara Ann (Mrs. John R. Murray), Maria Elizabeth. Commd. 2d lt., inf. U.S. Army Res. 1931, transferred to USAF, 1947, advanced through grades to col., 1951; exec. officer 398th Bomb Group, Europe, World War II; comdr. U.S. Mil. Port Manila, P.I., 1953-54; prof. air sci. Lehigh U., Bethlehem, Pa., 1954-57; dir. tng. Air Force Systems Command, Andrews AFB, Md., 1957-60; plans and programs officer Aerospace Studies Inst., Maxwell AFB, Ala., 1960-62; ret., 1962; asso. prof. edn. The Citadel, Charleston, S.C., 1965—. Decorated Legion of Merit, Commendation medal with oak leaf cluster. Mem. Air Force Assn., S.A.R., Assn. Former Students Tex. A. and M. U. Clubs: Century (charter), Aggie, Reveille. Home: 225 Rosemary Av San Antonio TX 78209 Office: The Citadel Charleston SC 29409

BERRYHILL, WALTER REECE, educator; b. Charlotte, N.C., Oct. 14, 1900; s. Samuel Reece and Minnie Eugenia (Scott) B.; B.A., U. N.C. at Chapel Hill., 1921, student Med. Sch., 1923-25; M.D., Harvard, 1927; D. Sci., Davidson Coll., 1956; m. Norma Mae Connell, Aug. 2, 1930; children—Jane Carol (Mrs. John Small Neblett), Catherine Brewer (Mrs. Clawson Williams, Jr.). Intern, 4th Med. Service, Boston City Hosp., 1927-29; resident medicine Univ. Hosps., Cleve., 1930-31; instr. medicine Western Res. U., asst. physician Lakeside Hosp. Cleve., 1931-33; physician-in-chief Univ. Infirmary and dir. student health service, U. N.C. at Chapel Hill, 1933-41, asso. prof. medicine, 1935-41, asst. dean, sch. medicine, 1937-41, prof. medicine, 1941-71, dean sch. medicine, 1941-64, dean emeritus, 1964—, dir. div. edn. and research in community med. care, 1965-69, Sarah Graham Kenan prof. medicine, 1968-71, Sarah Graham Kenan prof. emeritus of medicine, 1971—. Cons. Brown U. Med. Study Commn., Med. Coll. S.C. Study, Norfolk Gen. Hosp., 1965, Josiah Macy Found., N.Y.C., 1966-68, S.C. Adv. Commn. on Higher Edn., 1967-68, coordinating bd. Tex. Coll. and University System, 1968. Former trustee, Watts Hosp., Durham, N.C., Moses Cone Hosp., Greensboro, N.C.; bd. visitors Peace Coll., Raleigh, N.C. Recipient distinguished service award U. N.C. Sch. Medicine, 1965, O. Max Gardner award Bd. trustees, U. N.C., 1964, distinguished Citizen award Gov. N.C., 1964. Mem. Am. Coll. Physicians, So. Med. Assn., Assn. Am. Med. Colls., Med. Soc. N.C., N.C. Acad. Gen. Practice (hon.), N.C. Acad. Sci., N.C. Thoracic Soc., Elisha Mitchell Sci. Soc., Chapel Hill-Carbboro C. of C. (dir. 1966-69), Phi Beta Kappa, Sigma Xi, Alpha Omega Alpha. Club: Harvard of Eastern N.C. Home: PO Box 866 Chapel Hill NC 27514 Office: Box 35 North Carolina Hosp Chapel Hill NC 27514

BERRYMAN, JACK HOLMES, govt. ofcl.; b. Salt Lake City, July 28, 1921; s. Richard G. and Theo (Anderson) B.; A.A. with honors, Westminster Coll., 1940; B.S., U. Utah, 1941, M.S. with honors, 1947; m. Juanita Nussbaum, Aug. 9, 1941; children—Marjorie Sharon, Richard Gordon. Research and devel. staff Utah Dept. Fish and Game, 1947-50; asst. regional supr. U.S. Fish and Wildlife Service, Albuquerque, 1950-53, Mpls., 1953-59, chief div. wildlife services Bur. Sport Fisheries and Wildlife, Washington, 1965—; asso. prof. wildlife scis. Utah State U., 1959-65; cons. U.S. Sec. Interior, 1960-64, Shade Rivers Wonderland, O., 1964-65; participant White House Conf. Conservation, 1962, Nat. Acad. Sci. Symposium Pesticides, 1963, Agrl.-Wildlife Relationships, 1965—; chmn. legislative com. Utah Wildlife Fedn., 1963-65. Served with USMC, 1941-45. Decorated Silver Star, Purple Heart; recipient Minn. award outstanding service wildlife, 1960. Mem. Wildlife Soc. (pres. 1964-65), Washington Biologists Field Club, N.Y. Acad. Scis., Sigma Xi, Xi Sigma, Xi Sigma Pi. Presbyn. (mem. ministerial com.). Contbr. articles to profl. jours. Home: 10503 Linfield St Fairfax VA 22030 Office: Dept Interior Washington DC 20240

BERRYMAN, JAMES CLEO, educator; b. Russellville, Ark., Sept. 28, 1935; s. H. Cleo and Corinne (Swearengen) B.; B.A., Ouachita Bapt. U., 1957; B.D., Southwestern Bapt. Theol. Sem., 1960, Th.D., 1964; m. Mary Anne Pierce, Aug. 5, 1961; children—James Andrew, Cathryn Anne, Dir. sem. extension Southwestern Bapt. Theol. Sem., Ft. Worth, 1959-61; v.p. Book Nook, Inc., Ft. Worth, 1958-63; prof. religion and philosophy Ouachita U., Arkadelphia, Ark., 1964—, acting v.p. for academics, 1969-71; vis. prof. St. Johns Sem., 1967, Henderson State Coll., 1968. Chmn. bd. dirs. Central Ark. Devel. Council, 1969-72; chmn. bd. dirs. West Central Ark. Housing Devel. Corp., 1972—. Mem. Am. Acad. Religion, Am. Assn. U. Profs., Ark. Philos. Assn., So. Hist. Assn. Democrat. Baptist. Club: Civitan (lt. gov. Ozark dist. 1970-72, gov. elect 1972-73). Home: Box 833 OBU Arkadelphia AR 71923

BERRYMAN, MACON MOORE, welfare agy. ofcl.; b. Lexington, Ky., Feb. 17, 1908; s. James Henry and Elizabeth (Bridges) B.; B.A., Lincoln U., 1930, postgrad., 1931, D.C.L., 1967; grad. Atlanta U. Sch. Social Work, 1933; m. Dortha Alice Hackett, June 19, 1943; 1 son, James Henry. Investigator, Emergency Relief Adminstrn., Burlington County, N.J., 1933-34, dist. adminstr., case supr., 1934-36; social worker, parole officer N.Y. State Tng. Sch. Boys, N.Y.C., 1936-45; exec. dir. Sunnycrest Farm for Boys, Cheyney, Pa., 1945-50; dir. insular div. child welfare Dept. Social Welfare, St. Thomas, V.I., 1950-58, acting commr. social welfare, 1958-59, commr. 1959—. An organizer, chmn. bd. People's Bank of V.I., 1971—. Cons. V.I. Commn. on Aging, 1959-67, V.I. Insular Commn. on Children and Youth, 1950-67. Chmn. Gov.'s Com. on Employment Handicapped, 1959-67; vice chmn. Gov.'s Commn. Human Resources, 1964-69; mem. local bd. no. 1 SSS, 1964—; mem. V.I. dist. com. Boy Scouts Am., 1964-66, pres. V.I. council, 1966-69, Nat. council rep., 1964-67, 69—, mem. Region II com., 1968— (all St. Thomas). Bd. dirs. St. Thomas chpt. Hands Across Sea Scholarship Com. (treas. 1955-60), St. Thomas Community Chest (treas. 1960—), St. Thomas U.S.O. Recipient Alumni award Lincoln U., 1954. Mem. Am. Pub. Welfare Assn. (welfare policy com. 1959—, nat. membership com. and chmn. V.I. membership com. 1959-68), Nat. Assn. Social Workers (mem. cabinet div. social policy and action 1967—), Acad. Certified Social Workers, Lincoln U. Alumni Assn. (pres. V.I. chpt. 1964-67), Alpha Phi Alpha. Anglican. Mason, Rotarian (pres. St. Thomas 1966-67). Home: 26 AC Lindberg Bay St Thomas VI 00801 Office: Dept Social Welfare St Thomas VI 00801

BERRYMAN, ROBERT LEE, drilling co. exec.; b. nr. Palestine, Tex., Oct. 11, 1899; s. Lee J. and Cora (Hathcock) B.; student Washington and Lee U., 1919-20, Tex. U., 1920-21; m. Juanita McPherson, Sept. 26, 1955; children—John Robert, Hugh Lee, Lee Howard. With Wheless Drilling Co., Shreveport, La., 1925—, sec.-treas., 1941—, dir., 1941—. Trustee, treas. Southfield Sch., Shreveport, 1936-46. Served with U.S. Army, 1918-19. Clubs: Shreveport, Shreveport Country. Home: 532 Monrovia St Shreveport LA 71106 Office: 920 Commercial Nat Bank Bldg Shreveport LA 71166

BERTHRONG, MERRILL GRAY, librarian, educator; b. Cambridge, Mass., July 18, 1919; s. Louis Paul and Helen Clifton (Gray) B.; A.B., Tufts U., 1941; M.A., Fletcher Sch. Law and Diplomacy, 1947; Ph.D., U. Pa., 1958; m. Geraldine Merritt Brock, June 9, 1945; children—Peter Gray, Paul Merritt, Stephen Clark. Instr., U. Conn., 1947-50, Rutgers U., 1952-55, Drexel Inst., 1953-55; Fulbright scholar, France, 1955-56; head research and circulation dept. U. Pa. Library, 1956-58, librarian adminstr., 1958-64; dir. libraries, asso. prof. history, Wake Forest U., Winston-Salem, N.C., 1964—. Served to capt. AUS, 1942-45. Decorated Air Medal. Mem. Am. Hist. Soc., Am., Southeastern, N.C. library assns., Am. Assn. U. Profs., N.C. Hist. and Lit. Soc., Delta Upsilon. Editor: Library Chronicle, 1960-64. Home: 2032 Faculty Dr Winston-Salem NC 27106

BERTRAN, CARLOS ENRIQUE, physician; b. Santurce, P.R., July 4, 1926; s. Juan Manuel and Pilar (Margarida) B.; B.A., Cornell U., 1945, M.D., 1948; m. Patrice Minette Neve, Sept. 6, 1952; children—Patrice Minette, Muriel Pilar, Carlos Enrique, Michele, Alexandra, John, Charlotte. Intern, Lincoln Hosp., N.Y.C., 1948-49; resident in medicine Bellevue Hosp., N.Y.C., 1949-52; clin. asst. in medicine N.Y.U. Postgrad. Med. Sch., 1951-52; asst. prof. medicine U. P.R., 1952-56, asst. clin. prof. medicine Sch. Medicine, 1958-66, Sch. Dentistry, 1959—; practice medicine, specializing in internal medicine, cardiology, Santurce, 1958—; asst. clin. prof. medicine U. P.R., 1958—; dir. Cardiac Clinic, Rio Piedras Municipal Hosp., 1958-66; mem. staff Presbyn. Hosp., 1961—, dir. cardiac clinic, 1966—, dir. coronary care unit, 1967—; mem. staff Doctors, Auxilio Mutuo, San Juan City hosps. Mem. P.R. Bd. Med. Examiners, 1961-66. Bd. dirs. P.R. Heart Assn., 1960—, chmn. com. research, postgrad. edn., 1960-62, pres., 1965-66; trustee Presbyn. Hosp., Santurce. Served as maj. M.C., USAF, 1956-58. Diplomate Am. Bd. Internal Medicine. Fellow A.C.P., Am. Coll. Cardiology; mem. A.M.A., Am. Heart Assn., P.R. Med. Assn. (chmn. sci. council; pres. 1963-64). Research in gastrointestinal bleeding, chronic ulcerative colitis, hepatitis, cardiac arrhythmias. Home: 1468 Ashford Av Santurce PR 00907 Office: Ashford Med Center San Juan PR 00907

BERTRAND, JOHN AVERY, supt. schs.; b. Corsicana, Tex., Oct. 27, 1925; s. Joseph Avery and Anaise (Boone) B.; B.A. summa cum laude, U. Southwestern La., 1950; M.S., La. State U., 1952; Ph.D., U. Tex., 1966; m. Ella Mae Simar, June 1, 1946; children—Ronald Joseph, Linda Gail (Mrs. John Steib, Jr.), Darlene Frances, Angela Michelle. Tchr. pub. schs., Acadia Parish, La., 1950-52, Calcasieu Parish, La., 1952-53; prin. Starks (La.) High Sch., 1953-56; prin. College Oaks Elementary Sch., Lake Charles, La., 1956-58, F.K. White Jr. High, Lake Charles, 1958-65; supt. schs. Acadia Parish, Crowley, La., 1965—. Asst. prof. U. Southwestern La., Lafayette, summer, 1954; dir. So. Educators Corp., Baton Rouge. Served with USCGR, 1943-46; ETO; PTO. Mem. Crowley Commerce and Agr. Chamber (dir. 1968—), La. Tchrs. Assn., La. Supts. Assn., Am. Assn. Sch. Adminstrs., N.E.A., Kappa Delta Pi, Pi Gamma Mu, Phi Delta Kappa. Roman Catholic. K.C. Home: 1505 North Av D Crowley LA 70526 Office: PO Box 309 Crowley LA 70526

BERTRAND, JOHN RANEY, coll. pres.; b. Gray County, Tex., Aug. 3, 1914; s. Bell Otis and Eugenia Theresa (Studer) B.; student West Tex. State Coll., 1933-34; B.S., Tex. Technol. U., 1940, M.S., 1941; postgrad. U. Mo., 1941-42; Ph.D., Cornell U., 1950; m. Annabel Lee Hodges, Oct. 23, 1942; children—John Thomas, Diana Carroll, Karen Elizabeth, Janet May. Farmer, White Deer, Tex., 1932-37; vocational agr. tchr., Claude, Tex., 1940; asso. prof., acting dean men Sam Houston State U., 1945-46; asst. prof. rural sociology Tex. A. and M. U., 1946-47, asso. prof., asst. dean agr., 1947-50, dean basic div., 1950-54; dean Max C. Fleischmann Coll. Agr., U. Nev., 1954-56, dir. Nev. Agrl. Expt. Sta., Nev. Agrl. Extension Service, 1954-56; staff study needs and resources for higher edn. ICA, Libya, 1955; pres. Berry Coll., Mt. Berry, Ga., 1956—, Berry Acad., 1956—. Trustee Ga. Found. for Ind. Colls., 1967-70; bd. visitors U.S. Naval Acad.; past pres. N.W. Ga. council Boy Scouts Am. Served as submarine officer USNR, 1942-45; comdr. Ret. Res. Decorated Silver Star twice, Presdl. Unit Citation. with oak leaf Mem. Am. Coll. Personnel Assn., Am. Sociol. Soc., Am. Ednl. Research Assn., Assn. Am. Colls., Assn. Higher Edn., Assn. Pvt. Colls. and Univs. Ga. (pres. 1969-70), Fedn. State Assns. Ind. Colls. and Univs. (dir., exec. com.), Phi Delta Kappa, Pi Gamma Mu. Phi Eta Sigma, Alpha Chi. Methodist. Rotarian. Club: Army and Navy. Address: Berry Coll Mount Berry GA 30149

BERZAK, WILLIAM PETER, govt. ofcl.; b. Czechoslovakia, Mar. 23, 1914; s. Michael F. and Anna (Matlon) B.; came to U.S., 1920; B.S.L., U. Minn., 1938, J.D., 1940; M.P.A., St. Louis U., 1960; m. Maurine McCaskill, Jan. 4, 1947: children—Susan, William, Frank. Admitted to Minn. bar, 1940, also U. S. Supreme Ct. bar; with U. S. Civil Service Commn., 1946—. dep. chmn. Bd. Appeals and reviewer Internat. Orgns. Employees Loyalty Bd., 1966, chmn., 1966—. Served to capt. AUS, 1941-46. Mem. Minn., Fed. bar assns., Bar Assn. D.C., Am. Soc. Pub. Adminstrn., Pub. Personnel Assn., Soc. Personnel Adminstrn., Am. Legion, Delta Theta Phi. Home: 1416 Carrington Lane Vienna VA 22180 Office: 1900 E St NW Washington DC 20415

BESEMANN, EBERHARD FRANZ, physician; b. Wolfen, Germany, May 2, 1923; s. Franz and Luzie (Schmidt) B.; M.D., U. Frankfort (Germany), 1952; m. Johanna M. Giorgi, Oct. 26, 1955; children—Hans, Klaus. Came to U.S., 1954. Intern, St. Mary's Hosp., East St. Louis, Ill., 1954-55; resident Mo. Pacific Hosp., St. Louis, 1955-57, St. Louis City Hosp., 1957-60; practice medicine, specializing in radiology, Bellevue, Wash., 1960-63, Chattanooga, 1963—; mem. staff Erlanger Hosp. Served with M.C., German Army, 1940-45. Diplomate Am. Bd. Radiology. Mem. East Tenn. Radiol. Soc. (sec.-treas. 1968-70). Lutheran. Translator, editor profl. books from German into English. Contbr. articles to profl. jours. Home: 41 Carriage Hill Signal Mountain TN 37377 Office: Erlanger Hosp Chattanooga TN 37403

BESS, WILLIAM LAFAYETTE, JR., architect; b. El Paso, Tex., Oct. 22, 1927; s. William Lafayette and Rose (Backler) B.; m. Ridla French, June 21, 1948; 1 dau., Lisa Denise. Draftsman C.E., U.S. Army, 1948-49; designer NASA, 1949-51; chief draftsman aviation and meteorology Dept. Army, 1951-53; C.E. Armstrong, architects, Fort Worth, 1953-56; chief designer R.L. Brown, architects, Roanoke, Va., 1956-59; asso. Preston M. Geren, architects and engrs., Fort Worth, 1959-69, project architect, 1969-72; partner Dockstader & Partners, Architects and Planners, Ft. Worth, 1972—. Mem. bldg. code bd. appeals, Fort Worth, 1971-73. Bd. dirs. Fort Worth Community Theatre. Served with USMC, 1946-47. Mem. A.I.A. (treas. Fort Worth chpt. 1968-69, sec. 1972), Nat. Council Archtl. Registration Bds., Tex. Christian U. Alumni Assn., English Speaking Union. Republican. Episcopalian (mem. com. on ch. architecture and applied arts 1971-73). Rotarian. Home: 3574 Dryden Rd Fort Worth TX 76109 Office: Bank of Commerce Bldg Fort Worth TX 76102

BEST, FRANK MILTON, publisher; b. N.Y.C., Dec. 26, 1930; s. Frank M. and Mary (Leitner) B.; B.A., Cath. U. Am., 1952, M.S., 1957, postgrad., 1957-58; m. Princess Susanne Schachowskoi, Dec. 29, 1971. Staff, Nat. Conf. Cath. Welfare News Service 1951-54; staff Army-Navy Jour./Jour. Armed Forces, 1957-65, asso. editor, 1962-65; pub. U.S. Medicine, Washington, 1965—, U.S. Transport, Washington, 1966-69; pres. Profl. Lithography, Inc., Washington, 1967—. Served with AUS, 1955-56. Mem. Am. Med. Writers Assn., Nat. Press Club, Phi Beta Kappa. Address: 1601 18th St NW Washington DC 20009

BEST, HERMAN EUGENE, city ofcl.; b. Maryville, Tenn., May 4, 1930; s. George D. and Sina E. (Fields) B.; B.S., U. Tenn., 1960; m. Betty June Boone, Sept. 4, 1959; children—Elaine Rae, Sarah Kathryn. Farmer, Blount County, Tenn., 1948-53; instrumentman Batson & Himes, engrs., Knoxville, Tenn., 1959; asst. city engr. City of Maryville, 1960-61, city engr., dir. pub. works, 1961—. Served with AUS, 1953-55. Registered profl. engr., Tenn. Mem. Am. Soc. C.E., Chi Epsilon. Baptist (deacon 1963—). Mason. Club: Civitan (Maryville-Alcoa). Home: Route 10 Peterson Lane Maryville TN 37801 Office: 400 W Broadway Av Maryville TN 37801

BEST, WILLIE DEAN, architect; b. Goldsboro, N.C., Jan. 22, 1938; s. Cornelius Jackson and Wilda May (Bartlette) B.; B.Arch., N.C. State U., 1966; m. Anne Spencer, Aug. 3, 1958; children—Matthew Spencer, Melissa Noble. Chief designer, office mgr. Simpson-Savage, architects, Raleigh, N.C., 1964-65; project architect, asso. Leif Valand & Assos., architects, Raleigh, 1965-68; v.p., partner in charge archtl. practice, dir. Hakan-Best & Assos., Inc., architects and engrs., Chapel Hill, N.C., 1968-71; pvt. practice architecture, Raleigh, 1971—. Gen. partner Bolinwood Assos., Chapel Hill, 1970—, HBM Properties, Chapel Hill, 1970—, Peachtree Devel., Goldsboro, 1969—. Mem. N.C. Campaign Planning Com., 1967-69. Recipient 3d prize Southeast region Chemstrand Design Competition, 1963. Mem. A.I.A. (mem. com. 1970-72), Raleigh Council Architects. Clubs: North Ridge Country, City (Raleigh, N.C.); Tennis (Chapel Hill, N.C.). Maj. archtl. works include: Crabtree Valley Mall, Raleigh, NCNB Plaza, Chapel Hill; various others throughout South and Southeast. Home: 2200 White Oak Rd Raleigh NC 27608 Office: 2610 Wycliff Rd Raleigh NC 27607

BETHANY, FRANK MILAS, social worker; b. DeKalb, Miss., Sept. 19, 1928; s. Shade Albert and Frances (Clark) B.; B.S., Miss. State U., 1951; M.S.W., Fla. State U., 1958; student Tulane U., 1954; m. Virginia Dare Donovan, Sept. 3, 1954; children—Virginia Renee, Frank Todd. Sales rep. Am. Hosp. Supply Corp., Dallas, 1951-52; child welfare worker, supr. orientation, dist. child welfare supr. Miss. Dept. Pub. Welfare, Jackson, 1953-61; psychiatric social worker VA Hosp., Jackson, Miss., 1961-62; dir. social service dept. Childrens Home, Inc., Tampa, Fla., 1962-64; div. exec. Childrens Home Soc. Fla., West Palm Beach., 1964—. Asst. prof. U. Miss., 1960-62. Pres., Community Services Council Palm Beach County, 1968, dir., 1964—; dir. S.W. Palm Beach Exchange. Served with AUS, 1946-48. Mem. Nat. Assn. Social Workers (chpt. pres. 1970-71). Mason (32 deg.). Democrat. Methodist. Home: 4306 Althea Way Palm Beach Gardens FL 33403 Office: 3600 Broadway West Palm Beach FL 33401

BETHEA, BARRON, lawyer, state legislator, elec. hardware mfr.; b. Birmingham, Ala., May 20, 1929; s. Malcolm and Wilma (Edwards) B.; student U. of South, 1948-50; B.S., U. Ala., 1952, LL.B., 1953. Admitted Ala. bar, 1953; practiced in Birmingham, 1953-54; founder Barron Bethea Co., Inc., elec. hardware mfrs., Birmingham, 1957, pres., sec., treas. 1957—. Mem. Ala. Democratic Exec. Com., 1958-62—; mem. Ala. Ho. of Reps., 1962—. Mem. mgmt. bd. Five Points YMCA, 1962—. Served as 1st lt. USAF, 1954-56. Mem. Ala. State Bar, Birmingham Bar Assn., Asso. Industries Ala., Birmingham C. of C., Scabbard and Blade, Phi Gamma Delta, Phi Alpha Delta. Methodist. Elk. Home: PO Box 2202 Birmingham AL 35201 Office: 1625 Carolina Av Bessemer AL 35020

BETHEL, MILLARD BAIMBRIDGE, physician; b. Elizabethtown, Ky., Apr. 12, 1911; s. William Robert and Rebecca (Jenkins) B.; student Vanderbilt U., 1930-33; M.D., U. Tenn., 1936; M.P.H. U. N.C., 1941; m. Elizabeth Newell Roach, May 10, 1938; children—Brenda Gwynn, Rebecca, Thomas. Dir. Mecklenburg County Health Dept., Charlotte, N.C., 1945-59; prof. pub. health adminstrn., asst. dean Sch. Pub. Health, U. N.C., Chapel Hill, 1959-62; dir. dept. environmental health A.M.A., Chgo., 1962-64; dir. Wake County Health Dept., Raleigh, N.C., 1964—. Fellow Am. Pub. Health Assn., Am. Acad. Preventive Medicine and Pub. Health; mem. A.M.A. Home: 2231 Whitman Rd Raleigh NC 27607 Office: 3010 New Bern Av Raleigh NC 27610

BETHMANN, ERICH WALDEMAR, educator; b. Berlin, Germany, Sept. 4, 1904; s. Carl Louis and Anna Elise (Muller) B.; B.D., Theol. Sem., Friedensau, Germany, 1925; postgrad. Livingstone Coll., London, 1925, Am. U., Cairo, Egypt, 1926-27; M.A., Theol. Sem., Takoma Park, Md., 1949; m. Zora Kaludjerski, Nov. 1927 (div. 1953); children— Erika (Mrs. Marcus Schaaf), Claus W., Hans G.; m. 2d, Olivia Lattof, Aug. 1954. Mem. ednl. mission, Egypt., 1927-33, Transjordan, 1933-37; with Iraq Div. of Mission, 1937-39, Brit. India, 1940-46; dir. research and publs. Am. Friends of the Middle East, N.Y.C. and Washington, 1951-59; tchr. oriental art and Islamics, Trinity Coll., Washington, 1969—. Organizer, Muslim-Christian Convocations, Bhamdoun, Lebanon, 1954, 56, Alexandria, Egypt, 1955. Mem. Am. Oriental Soc., Middle East Inst., Iran Am. Soc. Author: Bridge to Islam, 1951, Yemen on the Threshold, 1960, Steps Toward Understanding Islam, 1966. Editor: Basic Facts Series on Middle East, 1956-62. Home: 1830 R St NW Washington DC 20009

BETO, GEORGE JOHN, state ofcl.; clergyman; b. Hysham, Mont., Jan. 19, 1916; s. Louis H. and Margaret (Witsma) B.; student Concordia Coll., Milw., 1930-35, Concordia Sem., St. Louis, 1935-37, 38-39; B.A., Valparaiso U., 1938; M.A., U. Tex., 1944, Ph.D., 1955; m. Marilynn Knippa, Mar. 5, 1943; children—Dan, Lynn, Mark, Beth. Instr., Concordia Coll., Austin, Tex., 1939-49, pres., 1949-59; vis. instr. U. Tex., 1944; pres. Concordia Theol. Sem., Springfield, Ill., 1959-62; dir. Tex. Dept. Corrections, Huntsville, 1962—. Dir. Huntsville Nat. Bank, First Nat. Bank Palestine. Sec. Tex. Bd. Corrections, 1953-59, mem. Ill. Parole and Pardon Bd., 1961-62; mem. Nat. Adv. Council on Correctional Manpower and Tng.; cons. President's Commn. on Law Enforcement and Adminstrn. of Justice; mem. Commn. on Correctional Facilities and Services, Am. Bar Assn. Recipient Tex. Heritage Found. medal for devel. ednl. system Tex. Prison System; named Distinguished Alumnus, U. Tex., 1971. Mem. Am. Soc. Ch. History, Am. Correctional Assn. (pres. 1969-70). Lutheran. Clubs; Old Capitol (Houston); 40-Acres, Citadel (Austin). Home: 1206 Av I Huntsville TX 77340 Office: Tex Dept of Corrections Box 99 Huntsville TX 73340

BETTERSWORTH, JOHN K(NOX), educator; b. Jackson, Miss., Oct. 4, 1909; s. Horace Greely and Annie McConnell (Murphey) B.; B.A. magna cum laude. Millsaps Coll., 1929; Ph.D. (grad. fellow), Duke, 1937; m. Ann L. Stephens, Oct. 28, 1943; 1 dau., Nancy Elizabeth. Tchr., Jackson Central High Sch., 1930-35; vis. prof. Duke, summer 1940; vis. instr. Asheville (N.C.) Normal, summer 1937; instr. history Miss. State U., State College, 1937, asst. prof., 1938-42, asso. prof., 1945-48, prof., 1948—, head dept. history and govt., 1948-61, dir. Social Sci. Research Center, 1950-60, asso. dean liberal arts, Coll. Arts and Sci., 1956-61, acad. v.p., 1961—, dean faculty, 1966—; text editor Miss. Hist. Commn., 1948-68. Chmn. Miss. Research Clearing House, 1953-55; pres. Mississippians for Ednl. Television, 1971-72. Trustee Miss. State Dept. Archives and History, 1955—. Served as lt. (j.g.) USNR, 1942-45; instr. Naval Indoctrination Sch., Tucson. Mem. Miss. Hist. Soc. (dir. 1963—, pres. 1963-64), Orgn. Am. Historians., Am., So. hist. assns., Phi Beta Kappa, Phi Kappa Phi, Phi Alpha Theta, Alpha Tau Omega, Omicron Delta Kappa. Democrat. Episcopalian. Rotarian (pres. Starkville 1951-52). Author: Confederate Mississippi, The People and Policies of a Cotton State in Wartime 1943; People's College: A History of Mississippi State, 1953; Mississippi: A History, 1959; Mississippi in the Confederacy, vol. 1, 1967; co-author South of Appomattox, 1959; Your Old World Past, 1961; Mississippi Yesterday and Today, 1964; co-author This Land of Ours. 1965; New World Heritage, 1969. Contbr. articles profl. publs. Home: 401 Broad St Starkville MS 39759 Office: Drawer B State College MS 39762

BETTIS, JOHN RANDOLPH, city ofcl.; b. Greenville, S.C., Aug. 20, 1917; s. Zeb Vance and Alice (Reamey) B.; B.S. in M.E., Clemson U., 1940; m. Louise Murray Cauthen, June 17, 1941; children—Anne Louise, John R., Vance Jackson, Susan Cauthen. With Commrs. Pub. Works, Charleston, S.C., 1940—, asst. mgr., engr., 1947-54, chief exec. officer, 1954—. Chmn. adv. bd. Salvation Army, Charleston, 1968—. Bd. dirs. Water Pollution Control Fedn., 1967-70. Served with AUS, 1942-46; ETO. Mem. Am. Water Works Assn. (chmn. Southeastern sect. 1959; recipient Water Utility Man Year award 1961, Herman F. Wiedeman award 1965), St. Andrews Soc., Mech. Engs. Club Charleston (past chmn.). Methodist (past chmn. bd. trustees). Rotarian. Contbr. profl. jours. Home: 179 3d Av Charleston SC 29403 Office: 14 George St Charleston SC 29402

BETTON, TEE ROY, extension agt.; b. Cotton Plant, Ark., July 3, 1912; s. Farrish Roy and Ora Mary (Dean) B.; B.S., Agrl. Mech. and Normal Coll., 1937; M.A., Mich. State U., 1952; postgrad. U. Wis., 1960; m. Thelma Odom, July 16, 1936; children—June Renee (Mrs. Wilford Glenn, Teroy, Robert Louie (dec.), Farrish, Carol Lee (Mrs. Robert Evans), Harold, William. Tchr. vocational agr. Bradley County Tng. Sch., Warren, Ark., 1937; dir. Nat. Youth Adminstrn. Camp, Agrl. Mech. and Normal Coll., Pine Bluff, Ark., 1937-39; tchr. vocational agr. Lincoln Jr. High Sch., Fayetteville, Ark., 1939-42; county extension agt. Agrl. Extension Service, Coll. Agr., U. Ark., Little Rock, Noward and Nevada ~~Counties~~, 1942, Negro county agt., 1943, Negro movable sch. agt., 1943-46, Negro dist. agt., 1946-53, Negro agrl. agt., 1953-62, agrl. agt. for Negro work, 1962-64, area agrl. agt., 1964, extension specialist farm safety programs, 1967-69, extension specialist, 1969—; tech. leader AID, Washington, 1966-67. Organizer Eastern Ark. Alliance for Minority Enterprise, 1971; bus. mgmt. cons. Minority Enterperneurship, Pine Bluff, Ark., 1969-71; Ark. personnel cons. Opportunities Industrialization Center, Little Rock, 1968-71. Merit badge counselor Mt. Pleasant council Boy Scouts Am., 1947-49; chmn. State Health Com., 1948-50. Recipient Citation CAMPS Com., 1970. Mem. Ark. Farm Bur. Fedn. Democrat. Baptist. Home: 2505 Ringo St Little Rock AR 72206 Office: 1201 McAlmont St Little Rock AR 72203

BETTS, CAROLYN MCILVAINE WELCH (MRS. EMMETT ALBERT BETTS), educator, author; b. Phila., Dec. 28, 1915; d. Wilbur Short and Eula May (McIlvaine) Welch; B.S., Beaver Coll., 1937; M.S., Pa. State U., 1942; m. Emmett Albert Betts, July 15, 1950. Tchr. pub. schs., Lewistown, Pa., 1937-39, 39-40; dir. reading clinic and supr. Benjamin Franklin Tng. Sch., State Tchrs. Coll., Bloomsburg, Pa., 1940-42 reading cons. Scott, Foresman & Co., N.Y., 1942-43; supr. reading clinic Lab. Sch., Reading Clinic, Pa. State U. Sch. Edn., 1943-45; acting supr. Reading Clinic, Balt. Dept. Edn., 1945-46; lectr., supr. publs. Reading Clinic, dept. psychology Temple U., Phila., 1946-54; supr. in-service tchr. edn. Betts Reading Clinic, Haverford, Pa., 1954-61; reading cons. Henry S. West Lab. Sch., U. Miami, Coral Gables, Fla., 1961—. Served as lt. USAF, 1952-57. Mem. Am. Assn. U. Women, Assn. for Childhood Edn., Internat. Reading Assn., Nat. Council Tchrs. English, Internat. Soc. for Gen. Semantics, Phi Kappa Phi, Pi Lambda Theta, Psi Chi, Delta Kappa Gamma. Author: Betts Basic Readers, 1965; Betts New Reading-Study Program: Pre-reading Through First Reader, 1970. Contbr. articles to profl. jours. Home and office: 12255 SW 73rd Av Miami FL 33156

BETTS, CHARLES O., judge; b. Centenary, S.C., Aug. 17, 1907; s. William A. and Lula Frances (Young) B.; student Schreiner Inst., 1925-27, U. Tex., 1927-32, Cumberland U., 1932-33; m. Eula Lea Kohn, Oct. 6, 1934; children—Charles Adolph, Cheryl Frances. Admitted to Tex. bar, 1933, practiced in Austin, Tex., 1934-41, judge, County Ct., 1941-46, Dist. Ct., 1946—. Bd. dirs. Tex. Inst. Children and Youth; mem. bd. Travis County Child Welfare Unit; dir. Tex. Inst. Children and Youth, chmn., 1960; mem. adv. council judges Nat. Council Crime and Delinquency; chmn. lay adv. bd. Seton Hosp., Austin; chmn. com. on adjudication and appeals So. Dist. American Lutheran Ch., mem. bd. theol. edn. 1968—; mem. Central Tex. Comprehensive Health Planning Commn., 1969—. Bd. dirs. Capital Area Radiation and Research Found. Served with AUS, 1944-45. Mem. Am., Travis County (past pres.) bar assns., State Bar Tex. (chmn. com. on adoption, family law sect.), Am. Judicature Soc., Nat. Council Juvenile Ct. Judges, Tex. Probation and Parole Assn. (exec. com.), Nat. Assn. State Trial Judges, Tex. Juvenile Officers Assn., Tex. Social Welfare Assn., Am. Legion, C. of C., Tex. State Guard Assn., Delta Theta Phi. Lutheran. Mason (32 deg., Shriner), K.P. Home: 5422 Shoalwood Av Austin TX 78756 Office: Travis County Courthouse PO Box 1748 Austin TX 78767

BETTS, DORIS JUNE WAUGH, author; b. Statesville, N.C., June 4, 1932; d. William Elmore and Mary Ellen (Freeze) Waugh; student Woman's Coll. U. N.C., 1950-53, U. N.C., 1954; m. Lowry Matthews Betts, July 5, 1952; children—Doris LewEllyn, David Lowry, Erskine Moore II. Newspaperwoman, Statesville Daily Record, 1950-51, Chapel Hill (N.C.) Weekly and News-Leader, 1953-54, Sanford Daily Herald, 1956-57; Guggenheim fellow, 1958-59; editorial staff N.C. Democrat, newspaper, 1961-62, editor Sanford (N.C.) News Leader, 1962-67; lectr. creative writing, English dept. U. N.C., Chapel Hill, 1966—. Mem. N.C. Tercentenary Commn., 1961-62. Mem. Sanford City School Board. Recipient short story prize Mademoiselle mag., book-length fiction prize G. P. Putnam-U. N.C., 1954. Mem. N.C. Writers Assn., Am. Philatelic Soc. Author: (story collection) The Gentle Insurrection, 1954; (novel) Tall Houses in Winter (Sir Walter Raleigh award for best fiction by Carolinian 1957), 1957; The Scarlet Thread (Sir Walter Raleigh award 1965); The Astronomer & Other Stories, 1966. Contbr. stories collections, anthologies. Editor: Young Writer at Chapel Hill, 1968. Office: Dept English U NC Chapel Hill NC

BETTS, DWIGHT BARTON, constrn. co. exec.; b. Raleigh, N.C., Dec. 22, 1919; s. Dwight Fairfax and Dessie (Wellons) B.; B.S. in Civil Engring., N.C. State U., 1940; m. Frances Ray Williams, June 8, 1942; children—Donald Barton, Marianne Fairfax, Richard Wellons, Katherine Ray. With J.A. Jones Constrn. Co., Charlotte, N.C., 1940—, v.p., 1967—; v.p., dir. constrn. firm, Teheran, Iran, 1960-61. Bd. dirs. N.C. State U., 1958-59. Served to lt. col. AUS, 1942-46. Mem. C. of C., Execs. Club, Newcomen Soc., Knights of Carrousel, Mil. Order World Wars, Soc. Am. Mil. Engrs. Democrat. Baptist (deacon). Mason, Lion. Club: Myers Park Country. Home: 4108 Foxcroft Rd Charlotte NC 28211 Office: 521 E Morehead St Charlotte NC 28201

BETTS, EMMETT ALBERT, psychologist, educator, author; b. Elkhart, Ia., 1903; s. Albert Henry and Grace L. (Greenwood) B.; B.S., Des Moines u., 1925; M.S., U. Ia., 1928, Ph.D., 1931; LL.D. (hon.), Sioux Falls (S.D.) Coll., 1972. Vocational dir. indsl. arts and agr., Orient, Ia., 1922-24; staff physics dept. Des Moines U., 1924-25; supt. schs., Northboro, Ia., 1925-29; research asst. U. Ia., 1929-31; sch. psychologist, elementary prin., Shaker Heights, O., 1931-34; dir. tchr. edn., dir. summer sessions State Tchrs. Coll., Oswego, N.Y., 1934-37; research prof. dir. reading clinic sch. edn. Pa. State Coll., 1937-45; prof. psychology, dir. reading clinic, dept. psychology Temple U., 1945-54; dir. Betts Reading Clinic, Haverford, Pa., 1954-61; research prof., lectr. psychology U. Miami, Coral Gables, Fla., 1961—, also dir. Reading Research Library. Vis. prof. numerous colls. and univs. U.S., 1930—; cons. state and nat. orgns. Recipient Apollo award Am. Optometric Assn., 1962; Founders award and citation of merit Internat. Reading Assn., 1971; named Ky. Col. Vice pres., dir. Nat. Aviation Edn. Council. Lt. col., nat. comdr.'s ednl. adv. com. USAF-Civil Air Patrol, Maxwell AFB. Fellow Distinguished Service Found. Optometry, Grad. Soc. Optometry; mem. Soc. Advancement Edn., Nat. Council Research in English (chmn. editorial com.), Nat. Conf. on Research Elementary Sch. English, Nat. Soc. Study Edn., Internat. Reading Assn., Nat. Aerospace Ednl. Council (v.p., dir.), Linguistic Soc. Am., Nat. Council Tchrs. of English, Am., Southeastern, Fla. psychol. assns., Internat. Council for Improvement Reading Instrn., Internat. Council Exceptional Children (adv. com.), N.E.A., Am. Assn. U. Profs., Am. Assn. Sch. Adminstrs., Am. Assn. Applied Psychology, Am. Psychol. Assn., Phoemic Spelling council (pres. 1967—), Assn. Childhood Edn., Am. Edn. Research Assn., Nat. Aeronautics Assn., Aircraft Owners and Pilots Assn., A.A.A.S., Phi Delta Kappa, Beta Sigma Kappa (hon.), Phi Theta Pi (hon.), Psi Chi. Mason (Shriner), Elk. Club: Aero (Pa.). Author numerous books, including Foundation of Reading Instruction, rev. edit., 1963; Betts Basic Readers, 1970; also author vision tests. Editorial advisor My Weekly Reader; editor-in-chief Edn.; asso. editor Jour. Ednl. Research; contbg. editor Jour. Exptl. Edn. Contbr. articles to profl. jours. Home: Royal Caribbean Club 1150 Av Madruga Coral Gables FL 33146 Office: U Miami Sch Edn Coral Gables FL 33124

BEVILL, TOM, lawyer, congressman; b. Townley, Ala., Mar. 27, 1921; s. Herman and Fannie Lou (Fike) B.; B.S., U. Ala., 1943, LL.B., 1948; m. Lou Betts, June 24, 1943; children—Susan B., Donald H., Patricia Lou. Admitted to Ala. bar, 1949; practiced in Jasper, Ala., 1949-1967; past mem. Ala. Ho. of Reps.; mem. 90th-92d congresses from 7th Ala. Dist. Mem. Am., Ala., Walker County (pres. 1954-55) bar assns., Am. Judicature Soc. Home: 1600 Alabama Av Jasper AL 35501 Office: Longworth House Office Bldg Washington DC 20515

BEVINGTON, HELEN SMITH (MRS. MERLE M. BEVINGTON), educator, author; b. Afton, N.Y., Apr. 2, 1906; d. Charles Wesley and Elizabeth (Raymond) Smith; Ph.B., U. Chgo., 1926; M.A., Columbia, 1928; m. Merle M. Bevington, June 1, 1928 (dec. Aug. 1964); children—David M., Philip R. Faculty Duke U., 1943—, prof. English, 1970—. Recipient Roanoke-Chowan award, 1956, 62, Mem. Am. Assn. U. Profs., Phi Beta Kappa. Author: Dr. Johnson's Waterfall, 1946; Nineteen Million Elephants, 1950; A Change of Sky, 1956; When Found, Make a Verse Of, 1961; Charley Smith's Girl, 1965; A Book and a Love Affair, 1968; The House Was Quiet and the World Was Calm, 1971; poems pub. in popular mags. including New Yorker, Atlantic Monthly, N.Y. Times Book Review. Home: 4428 Guess Rd Durham NC 27705

BEVINS, KARL ALTEN, traffic engr.; b. Wellman, Ia., May 30, 1915; s Daniel James and Jean (Alten) B.; B.S. in Elec. Engring., Ga. Inst. Tech., 1939; postgrad. (fellow) Yale, 1941; m. Blanche Albert, June 3, 1944; 1 dau., Jean Marie. Asst. engr. Ga. Power Co., Atlanta, 1940, traffic engr., 1941-49; also tech. adviser Atlanta C. of C.; city traffic engr. City of Atlanta 1949—. Chmn. Atlanta Traffic Commn., 1949-54. Registered profl. engr., Ga. Mem. Inst. Traffic Engrs. (pres. so. sect. 1955, dir. 1955-56), Ga. Soc. Profl. Engrs., Ga. Archtl. and Engring. Soc., Atlanta Fedn. Musicians (pres.), I.E.E.E. Kiwanian. Club: Ga. Motor (pres.). Home: 110 Laurel Forest Circle NE Atlanta GA 30305 Office: 68 Mitchell St SW Atlanta GA 30303

BEVIS, HERBERT ANDERSON, educator; b. Perry, Fla., Sept. 28, 1929; s. Herbert Urlin and Jenny Thomas (Anderson) B.; B.C.E., U. Fla., 1951, M.S. in San. Engring., 1952, Ph.D., 1963; M.S. in Physics, U.S. Naval Postgrad. Sch., 1958; m. Cotella Marie Ingle, Aug. 24, 1952; children—John H., Gerald C. San. engr. region II USPHS, N.Y.C., 1952-53, san. engring. cons. to Nat. Park Service, Washington, 1953-54, staff officer radiol. health program San. Engring. Services div. Bur. State Services, Washington, 1954-55; instr. radiol. health tng. sect. Robert A. Taft San. Engring. Center, Cin., 1955-56; sr. USPHS officer Joint Task Force 7, Pacific Nuclear Test Site, Eniwtok, Marshall Is., 1958; chief ionizing radiation program Occupational Health div. Tex. State Dept. Health, 1958-61; teaching asso. civil engring. U. Fla. at Gainesville, 1961-63, asso. prof. civil engring., 1963-66, asso. prof. environmental engring., grad. coordinator, 1966—. Prin., dir. Water and Air Research, Inc. Registered profl. engr., Fla., Tex. Diplomate Am. Acad. Environmental Engrs.; certified health physicist Am. Bd. Health Physics. Club: Civitan (dep. gov. Fla. dist. 1971-72). Home: 3414 NW 7th Pl Gainesville FL 32601

BEYER, W. F., JR., state ofcl. Asst. supt. curriculum La. Dept. Edn., Baton Rouge. Address: Dept Edn State Ednl Bldg Baton Rouge LA 70804*

BIANCHI, AL, basketball coach; b. Long Island City, N.Y., Mar. 26, 1932; s. Alfred and Rose (Sciallo) B.; grad. Bowling Green State U., 1954; children—Mark, children—Mark, Al, Shireen, Carol, Leah. Player basketball Syracuse (N.Y.) Nats., 1956-63, Phila. 76ers, 1963-66; asst. coach Chgo. Bulls, 1966-67; coach Seattle Supersonics, 1967-69, Washington Caps, 1969-70, Va. Squires, 1970—. Served with M.C., AUS, 1954-56. Named to Bowling Green State U. Hall of Fame, 1965. Mem. Sigma Alpha Epsilon. Roman Catholic. Office: 300 Boush St Norfolk VA 23510

BIANCHI, EUGENE CARL, educator; b. Oakland, Cal., May 5, 1930; s. Natale and Catherine (Mangini) B.; B.A., Gonzaga U., 1954, M.A., 1955; postgrad. Coll. St. Albert de Louvain, 1958-62; Ph.D., Union Theol. Sem., Columbia, 1966; m. Cathryn A. Cummings, July 4, 1969. Tchr., St. Ignatius High Sch., San Francisco, 1955-58; asst. editor America mag., N.Y.C., 1963-66; asst. prof. theology U. Santa Clara (Cal.), 1966-68; asso. prof. religion Emory U., Atlanta, 1968—. Vis. prof. summers U. San Francisco, 1966, 68, Stanford, 1969; Danforth Underwood fellow, 1972-73. Mem. Am. Civil Liberties Union (dir.), Soc. Priests for a Free Ministry, Catholic Theol. Soc. Am., Am. Assn. U. Profs., Am. Acad. Religion, Common Cause. Democrat. Roman Catholic. Author: John XXIII and American Protestants, 1968; Reconciliation: The Function of the Church, 1969; The Religious Experience of Revolutionaries, 1972. Home: 454 Emory Circle NE Atlanta GA 30307

BIASCO, FRANK, educator, social worker, psychologist; b. Chgo., Jan 15, 1928; s. Joseph and Mary (Pernini) B.; A.B., Wheaton Coll., 1953; M.S.W., Loyola U., 1956; Ed.D., Ind. U., 1965; m. Nancy Ellen Oplinger, Jan. 30, 1953; children—Richard Alan, James Randal, Constance Marie, Thomas Edward, Gary David. Tchr., counselor Park Forest (Ill.) Pub. Schs., 1959-64; asst. prof. dept. counseling and guidance Ind. U., Bloomington, 1964-66; asso. prof. psychology State U. N.Y. at Oswego, 1966-68; asso. prof. Fla. State U., Tallahassee, 1968-70; dir. pupil personnel services Jacksonville (Fla.) Pub. Schs., 1970-71; coordinator counselor edn. U. West Fla., Pensacola, 1971—. Cons. U.S. Office of Edn., State Dept. Edn., Leon County Pub. Schs. Served with USNR, World War II, Korea. Mem. Nat. Assn. Social Workers, N.E.A., Am. Assn. U. Profs., Council Social Work Edn., Am. Psychol. Assn., Am. Personnel and Guidance Assn., Am. Ednl. Research Assn., Am. Rehab. Counseling Assn., Southeastern, Fla. psychol. assns., Am. Orthopsychiat. Assn., Am. Legion, Pi Gamma Mu, Phi Delta Kappa. Home: 9759 Pickwood Dr Pensacola FL 32504

BIBB, WILLIAM ROBERT, immunobiologist, govt. ofcl.; b. Salisbury, N.C., May 28, 1932; s. Claude Robert and Ann Margaret (Carter) B.; B.S., U. N.C., 1957, M.S., 1959, Ph.D., 1962; m. Patty Lu McDuffie, June 11, 1955; children—William Robert, Susan Ann. Research asst. U. N.C. at Chapel Hill, 1957-59, USPHS trainee, 1959-62, research asso. Virus Lab., 1962-63, asst. prof., 1964-65; immunobiologist div. biology and medicine AEC, Washington, 1965-71, tech. asst. to commr., 1971—. Recipient Spl. Achievement award AEC, 1970. Mem. Am. Soc. for Microbiology, Elisha Mitchell Sci. Soc., Electron Microscopy Soc. Am., Reticuloendothelial Soc., Am. Nuclear Soc., N.C. Soc. Bacteriologists, Sigma Xi. Contbr. articles to profl. jours. Home: 19018 Stedwick Dr Gaithersburg MD 20760 Office: Office Commn AEC Washington DC 20545

BICE, LORIN TRESSLAR, citrus grower; b. Winnemucca, Nev., Oct. 25, 1903; s. Samuel Otis and Clara (Schwartz) B.; student U. Fla., 1923-24; m. Ruth Cramer, Sept. 18, 1924; children—Doris Jean (Mrs. R. T. Stalnaker), William Thomas, Judy Catherine. (Mrs. E. W. Winchester). Engaged in Fla. citrus industry, 1918—; plant supt. Florence Citrus Growers Assn., 1924-35; gen. mgr. Haines City Citrus Growers Assn., 1935-43; exec. v.p., gen. mgr. Lake Hamilton Coop, Inc., 1943-51; pres. West Coast Growers Coop., 1947-51, 59-60, dir., 1946-70; chmn. Farm Credit Bd., Columbia, S.C., 1960, dir., 1956-63; dir. Central Bank Coops., Washington, 1961-63; mem. Fed. Farm Credit Bd., Wash., 1963-69, chmn. 1968-69. Mem. Fla. Citrus Commn., 1949-50, Citrus Marketing Agreement Coms., 1941-44, 52-54; v.p. Fed. Land Bank Assn. of Lakeland, 1952-63, Fla. Citrus Prodn. Credit Assn., 1945-63; mem. gov. com. re-writing and enacting Fla. Citrus Code, 1948-49; dir. State Bank Haines City. Chmn. bd. trustees Polk Jr. Coll., 1968-69. Mem. Haines City C. of C. Methodist. Rotarian. Address: 1107 Peninsular Dr Box 1477 Haines City FL 33844

BICHSEL, GEORGE, city ofcl. Chief police San Antonio. Address: 414 W Nueva St San Antonio TX 78207*

BICKEL, WILLIAM CROFT, oil co. exec.; b. Pitts., Feb 20, 1918; s. William Foreman and Florence (Croft) B.; A.B., Princeton, 1939; m. Minnette Chapman Duffy, Jan. 3, 1947; children—Minnette Chapman, Susan Croft. With Pure Oil Co. So. Ill., 1941-—; with Gulf Oil Corp., 1946-—, div. mgr., Syracuse, N.Y., 1962, div. mgr., New Orleans, 1962-65, v.p., Tulsa, 1965-—. Bd. dirs. Tulsa Community Chest, Better Bus. Bur. Tulsa, Tulsa Opera, Inc.; trustee U. Tulsa, Tulsa Charity Horse Show. Mem. Hamilton (Mass.) Republican Town Com., 1956. Served to capt. USMC, World War II; PTO. Decorated D.F.C., Air Medal. Mem. La. (dir.), Ark. (dir.), Okla. (dir.) petroleum councils. Presbyn. Clubs: Cottage (Princeton); Hyannisport, Tulsa, Southern Hills Country; Boston (New Orleans). Home: 2430 E 29th St Tulsa OK 74114 Office: 1350 S Boulder St Tulsa OK 74102

BICKERSTAFF, CLYDE LESTER, govt. ofcl.; b. Oxford, Miss., Sept. 4, 1921; s. Andrew Mitchell and Lula (Arnold) B.; B.B.A., U. Tex., 1948; m. Mary Beverly Ashworth, Oct. 30, 1948; children—William D., Brian C., Beverly Ann. With Internal Revenue Service, 1948-—, asst. dir., Albuquerque, 1959-60, dir., 1960-64, dist. dir., Oklahoma City, 1964-—. Chmn. Albuquerque Fed. Plan Coordinating Com., 1960-61; vice chmn. Fed. Agys. Readiness Com., 1962, budget com. Albuquerque United Community Fund, 1963-64; pres. exec com. Okla. Interagency Bd., 1966-—. Served to lt. col. USAAF, World War II. Decorated Air medal with four oak leaf clusters. Mem. Albuquerque-Santa Fe Fed. Exec. Assn. (pres.), Oklahoma City C. of C. (dir.). Home: 6805 N Shawnee Dr Oklahoma City OK 73116 Office: Fed Bldg Office Dist Dir Internal Revenue Oklahoma City OK 73101

BICKERSTAFF, THOMAS ALTON, educator; b. Tishomingo, Miss., Sept. 5, 1904; s. John Ramsey and Mary (Blunt) B.; student U. Miss., 1924-29, A.B., 1928; A.M., 1929; Ph.D., U. Mich., 1948; m. Lillian Josephine Russell, Aug. 26, 1933; children—Thomas Alton, David Russell, Carolyn Josephine. Instr. math. U. Miss., 1928-30, asst. prof., 1930-36, asst. prof. and registrar, 1936-47, prof., chmn. dept. math., 1947-—, faculty chmn. athletics, 1937-—, sec. Southeastern Conf., 1957, spl. coordinator STAR unit Army Specialized Tng. Program, 1942-44; spl. instr. Navy V-12 program U. Mich., 1944-45. Mem. Math. Assn. Am. (past pres. La.-Miss. sect.), Am. Math. Soc., Inst. Math. Statistics, Miss. Acad. Sci., Miss. Ednl. Assn., Sigma Xi, Omicron Delta Kappa, Pi Kappa Alpha, Pi Mu Epsilon. Democrat. Baptist. Mason, Rotarian (past pres.). Home: Box 262 University MS 38677

BICKFORD, JAMES VAN ALLEN, III, realtor; b. Norfolk, Va., Sept. 28, 1939; s. James Van Allen and Margaret Snyder (Wakefield) B.; B.S. in Civil Engring., Va. Mil. Inst., 1961; M. Regional Planning, U. N.C., 1965; postgrad. Old Dominion U., 1968; m. Elizabeth Blair Kelsey, June 30, 1961; children—James Van Allen IV, Christopher West, Nathan Taylor. Space technologist NASA, Langley Field, 1965; asst. gen. mgr. constrn. Tidewater Homes, 1965-67; pres. land devel. Urban Planning Assos., 1967-70; v.p. property mgmt. and devel. Larasan Realty Corp., Norfolk, Va., 1970-—; treas., bus. cons. Downstairs Corp., Shack Inc., 1969-—; exec. v.p. Chesapeake Bay Marine Industries, 1970-—. Chmn. Norfolk Citizens Adv. Com., 1971, Tidewater Heart Fund, 1971-72. Mem. alumni bd. Norfolk Acad., 1969-71. Served to 1st lt. AUS, 1962-63. Mem. Urban Land Inst., Tidewater Assn. Home Builders (dir. 1969-70), Norfolk Va. Mil. Inst. Alumni Assn. (v.p. 1971), Kappa Alpha. Episcopalian (vestryman 1968-—). Clubs: Norfolk (Va.) Yacht, Norfolk German, Norfolk Assembly. Home: 7220 Shirland Av Norfolk VA 23505 Office: 3401 Virginia Beach Blvd Virginia Beach VA 23452

BICKLEY, N. ALEX, city ofcl.; b. Abilene, Tex., Mar. 7, 1918; s. W.C. and Frankie (Alexander) B.; student McMurry Coll., 1935-38; LL.B., U. Tex., 1941; m. Dorothy Hennegas, Feb. 12, 1943; children— Barbara Ann, Lynn Denise, Neil Alexander. Asso. firm Smith, Eplen & Bickley Attys., Abilene, 1946-50; city atty., Abilene, 1955-58; then mem. firm Smith, Bickley & Pope, Attys., Abilene, 1st asst. city atty., Dallas, 1958-65, city atty., 1965-—. Prof. oil and gas legislation McMurry Coll., 1956-57; chmn. Inst. Condemnation S.W. Legal Found., 1964; prof. law Acad. Am. and Internat. Law So. Meth. U. Council commr. Circle Ten council Boy Scouts Am., 1956-57; pres. YMCA, Abilene, 1957. Legislation liaison City of Dallas with Tex. Legislature. Served with USN, 1941-46, 50-51. Decorated Bronze Star. Named Outstanding Man of Abilene, 1947. Mem. Nat. Inst. Municipal Law Officers (dir.), Tex. City Attys. Assn. (pres. 1965-66). Democrat. Methodist (chmn. bd. stewards; mem. Dallas Council Ch. Bds.). Mason (32 deg.). Contbr. articles to profl. jours. Home: 3558 Waldorf St Dallas TX 75229 Office: 501 City Hall Dallas TX 75201

BIEGEL, HERMAN CHARLES, lawyer; b. N.Y.C., Aug. 5, 1909; s. David and Tillie (Nusim) B.; B.S.S. cum laude, Coll. City N.Y., 1930; LL.B. (editor Law Jour.), Yale, 1933; m. Shirley Gubert, June 24, 1934; children—Richard, Judy. Admitted to N.Y. bar, 1933, D.C. bar, 1938; with office Chief Counsel, Bur. Internal Revenue, 1934-37; pvt. practice, Washington, 1937-—; partner firm Alvord &Alvord, 1942-50, Lee, Toomey & Kent, 1950-—; lectr. Tax and Law Insts. Legal adviser Council Profit-Sharing Industries, 1950-—; pension research council Wharton Sch. Finance, U. Pa., 1958-—. Served as lt. comdr. USNR, 1944-46. Mem. Am. Bar Assn., Phi Beta Kappa. Author articles law jours., contbr. periodicals. Home: 2838 Chesterfield Pl NW Washington DC 20008 Office: 1200 18th St NW Washington DC 20006

BIEGELEISEN, HYMAN IRVING, physician; b. N.Y.C., June 4, 1904; s. Max and Fannie (Plancher) B.; student Columbia, 1923, M.D., L.I. Coll., 1927; postgrad. U. Vienna (Austria), 1933; m. Dorothy Rich, Aug. 17, 1947; children—Robert, Ken, Joyce, Wanda. Intern, York (Pa.) Hosp., 1927-28; resident Kingston Av. Hosp., Bklyn., 1928-29; chief peripheral vascular clinic Beth David Hosp., N.Y.C., 1937-47; chief varicose vein clinic Stuyvesant Polyclinic, N.Y. C., 1933-58; exec. dir. Sclerotherapy Research Found., 1956-—; founder, exec. dir. Peripheral Vascular Soc., Am., Inc., 1962-—. Mem. A.M.A., N.Y. Cardiol. Soc. Author: Injection Treatment, 1934-1962. Contbr. articles to profl. jours. Home: 3181 S Ocean Dr Hallandale FL 33009 Office: 26 Gables Blvd East Setauket NY 11733

BIELEY, PEGGY MOSES, economist; b. N.Y.C., June 5, 1929; d. Louis and Bella (Kenarik) Moses; B.S. magna cum laude, N.Y.U. Sch. Commerce, 1950; M.A., Stanford U., 1953; student Columbia U., 1952-53; m. Alfred D. Bieley, Dec. 25, 1953; children—Harlan C., Lily Beth. Economist Nat. Indsl. Conf. Bd., N.Y.C., 1949; economist Jules Backman Asso., N.Y.C., 1949-50; teaching fellow Stanford, 1950-51; economist Nat. Manpower Council, Columbia, 1951-53; instr. econs. U. Miami, 1954-55; v.p., chief economist Juliam Langner Research, Inc., Miami, 1955-60; pres., chief economist Bieley, Wagner & Assos., Miami, 1960-—, Econ. Data Bank, Inc., Miami, 1970-—; cons. economist savs. and loan assns., comml. banks. Mem. Am. Econ. Assn., Am. Statis. Assn. Econ. Soc. So. Fla., Beta Gamma Sigma, Contbr. articles to tech. jours., nat. mags. Home: 11601 SW 64 Av Miami FL 33156 Office: 7300 SW 62 Av Miami FL 33143

BIEMILLER, ANDREW J(OHN), labor union ofcl., ex-congressman; b. Sandusky, O., July 23, 1906; s. Andrew Frederick and Pearl (Weber) B.; A.B., Cornell U., 1926; grad. study U. Pa., 1928-32; m. Hannah Perot Morris, Dec. 20, 1929; children—Andrew John, Nancy Barbara. Tchr. history Syacuse U., U. Pa., 1926-32; newspaper and labor relations positions, 1932-42; mem. Wis. legislature, 1936-42; with WPB, 1942-44; mem. 79th, 81st U.S. congresses, 5th Wis. Dist.; pub. relations counsellor, lectr., writer; spl. asst. to sec. interior, 1951-52; dir. dept. legislation AFL-CIO, 1956-—, chmn. staff com. on atomic energy. Mem. labor-mgmt. advisory com. AEC; mem. mgmt.-labor textile advisory com. Dept. Commerce, 1961-—; mem. Presidential Task Force on Career Advancement, 1966-67; mem. consumer com. on automobile ins. and compensation Dept. Transp.; labor adviser Am. delegation GATT Conf., 1957, 61. Mem. Am. Fedn. Tchrs., Delta Kappa Epsilon. Democrat. Mem. Soc. Friends. Clubs: Kenwood Golf and Country, Nat. Press. Home: 6805 Glenbrook Rd Bethesda MD 20014 Office: 815 16th St NW Washington DC 20006

BIER, JUSTUS, art historian; b. Nuremberg, Germany, May 31, 1899; s. Jacob and Minna (Honig) B.; student univs. of Munich, Erlangen, Jena, Bonn, Zurich, 1918-24; Ph.D. magna cum laude, U. Zurich, 1924; D.F.A., Duke, 1970; L.H.D., U. Louisville, 1972; m. Senta Dietzel, Mar. 17, 1931; 1 son, Max Robert. Came to U.S., 1937, naturalized, 1944. Docent Inst. Art History, Municipal U., Nuremberg, 1925-30; traveling fellow Notgemelinschaft der Deutschen Wissenchaft, 1928; dir., curator Kestner-Gesellschaft Art Inst., Hannover, Germany, 1930-36; founder, dir. Mus. fur das vorbildliche Serienprodukt, 1930-36; asst. prof. art history, acting head dept. fine arts U. Louisville, 1937-41, asso. prof., 1941-46, head dept., 1941-60, prof., 1946-60; Fulbright lectr. and vis. prof. U. Wurzburg Germany, 1960-61; dir., curator research N.C. Museum of Art, Raleigh, 1961-70, dir. emeritus, curator research, 1970-—; dir. Allen R. Hite Art Inst., U. Louisville, 1946-60; Guggenheim fellow, 1953-54, 56-57; mem. Inst. for Advanced Study, Princeton, N.J., 1953-54; art editor, art critic The Courier-Jour., Louisville, 1944-56; vis. prof. Free U. Berlin, 1956, U. So. Cal., 1958. Bd. mem. Deutscher Werkbund, Berlin, 1931-34; adv. bd. art edn. U. of Ky., 1947; adv. com. Ky. State Fair and Expn. Center, 1949; bd. dirs. Louisville Art Center Assn., 1940-60, Jr. Art Gallery, Louisville, 1949-60, Louisville Council Historic Sites and Bldg., 1950-53; profl. adviser Jr. League Louisville 1945-60. Awarded Notgemeinschaft der deutschen Wissenschaft research grant, 1928; Durer Medal, City of Nuremberg, 1928; August Kestner medal Kestner-Gesellschaft, Hannover, 1938. Mem. Coll. Art Assn. Am., Southeastern Coll. Art Conf. (chmn. nominations com.), Midwestern Coll. Art Conf. (pres. 1951-52), Am. Soc. Aesthetics, So. Art Mus. Dirs. Assn., Internat. Art Critics Assn. (asso. Am. sect.), Assn. German Art Historians (hon.), Friends of Art and History in Mainfranken at Wurzburg (hon. mem.), Delta Phi Alpha, Kappa Pi Epsilon, Phi Kappa Phi. Club: Filson (Louisville). Author: Tilmann Riemenschneider Ein Gedenkbuch, 6th edit. 1948, and other books and articles. Mem. editorial council Jour. Aesthetics and Art Criticism, 1951-53, lectr. in Germany, Austria, Switzerland, U.S. Home: PO Box 14182 Raleigh NC 27610 Office: NC Museum of Art Raleigh NC 27611

BIGBY, MARY FRANCES WILSON (MRS. LUTHER S. BIGBY), county ofcl., civic worker; b. Williamston, S.C.; d. James G. and Mary (Cason) Wilson; B.S., Greenville Woman's Coll., 1932; m. Luther S. Bigby, Oct. 12, 1935; children—Luther, James. Tchr. pub. sch., Pelzer, S.C., 1932-33; saleslady J. C. Penney Co., Greenville, 1933-34; caseworker Emergency Relief Adminstrn., Greenville, 1934-42; dept. head Greenville Army Air Base, 1942-45; retirement clk. Greenville County Dept. Edn., 1946-53; 1st clk. Office County Supr., Greenville, 1953-—. Corr. sec. S.C. Conf. on Status of Women, 1964-66, chmn. nominating com., 1966-—, treas., 1969-70, 2d v.p., 1970-72, 1st v.p., 1972-—; mem. S.C. Council for Common Good, 1960-—; mem. S.C. Gov's. Commn. on Status of Women, 1965-70; membership chmn. Greenville Forum on World Affairs, 1967-—; residential chmn. Cancer Crusade, 1969; chmn. camp com. Salvation Army Aux.; mem. County Home Aux., Greenville County Mental Health, Friends of Library. Named Woman of Yr., Greenville Bus. and Profl. Woman's Club, 1968. Mem. Greater Greenville Women's Div. of C. of C. (1st v.p. 1965, pres. 1966), Order Eastern Star, S.C. Fedn. Bus. and Profl. Women's Clubs (corr. sec. 1959-61, rec. sec. 1961-62, 2d v.p. 1962-64, 1st v.p. 1964-66, pres. 1966-68, nat. contact. chmn. 1959-60, nat. bd. 1966-68, parliamentarian 1970-72; dir. Edn. Found. 1970, pres. 1972-73), Greenville Bus. and Profl. Women's Club (pres. 1958-59, chmn. nominating com. 1970-72), Nat. Secs. Assn. (local coms.). Baptist (pres. Sunday Sch. class). Clubs: Altrusa (pres. 1970-72, mem. bd.), Blue Ridge (presiding partner 1971-72). Home: 9 W Augusta Pl Greenville SC 29605 Office: Courthouse Greenville SC 29601

BIGGERS, JANE RICHARDSON, fashion editor; b. Johnson City, N.Y., May 12, 1926; d. William Sentell and Marian (Yetter) Richardson; A.A., Stephens Coll., 1946; grad., Tobe-Coburn Sch. for Fashion Careers, N.Y.C., 1947; m. William Michael Biggers, Sept. 18, 1949; children—William Michael, Robert Allen. Dept. mgr. McLean's Dept. Store, Binghamton, New York, 1947-49; engaged as womens feature editor for The Greenwood (Miss.) Commonwealth, 1949-—, Jackson (Miss.) State Times, 1957-60; women's editor Greenwood Commonwealth, 1960-—, broadcaster radio and TV, Lamar Broadcasting Co., Jackson, 1955-—; fashion cons., 1957-—; free-lance lectr. Mem. bd. dirs. Commonwealth Publishing Co. Bd. dirs. local cancer soc., County Heart Assn., Cerebral Palsy, Leflore County Arts Festival. Mem. women's exec. com. Delta Council, 1960-67. Recipient Miss. Press awards, 1957-68, 7 first place awards Miss. Press Women's Contest, 1964. Nat. Pres. awards, 1958, 60, 63, 64, 68; named Woman of Yr., 1962; Asso. Press Hon. Mention award, 1964; Inky award journalism Miss. State Coll. Women; named Outstanding Woman Achievement Leflore County. Mem. Bus. and Profl. Women (pres. Greenwood), D.A.R., Miss. Little Theatre, Miss. Press Women's Assn., Nat. Fedn. Press Women, Tobe-Coburn Alumni Assn., Fashion Group (treas. Jackson-Delta), Nat. Assn. Jr. Auxiliaries, Miss. Art Assn., Nat. Assn. Am. Pen Women, Bus. and Profl. Women's Clubs (found. chmn. 1968). Episcopalian. Club: Town and Country Garden. Home: 404 E Park Av Greenwood MS 38930 Office: 209 W Market St Greenwood MS 38930

BIGGERS, NEAL BROOKS, JR., lawyer; b. Corinth, Miss., July 1, 1935; s. Neal B. and Sara (Cunningham) B.; B.A., Millsaps Coll., 1957; LL.B., U. Miss., 1963; Admitted to Miss. bar, 1963; pvt. practice, Corinth, 1963-—; county atty. Alcorn County, 1964-68; dist. atty. 1st Judicial Dist. Miss., 1968-—. Served to lt. comdr. USNR, 1957-60. Mem. Miss., Am. bar assns., Nat. Dist. Atty. Assn. Home: 818 Shilon Rd Corinth MS 38824 Office: 402 Franklin St Corinth MS 38824

BIGGS, E. GLENN, banker; b. San Angelo, Tex., June 10, 1933; s. Bennie Austin and Clara (Stucke) B.; B.A., Baylor U., 1956; m. Ann Carolyn Dendy, July 29, 1955; children—Barry, Brian. Partner, real estate ins. firm, Abilene, Tex., 1956-65; exec. aide to speaker Tex. Ho. Reps., 1965-67; exec. v.p. Nat. Western Life Ins., Auston, Tex., 1968-70, pres., 1968-70; also dir.; chmn. bd. Stockman Nat. Life, Rapid City, 1968-70; pres. Aberdeen Petroleum Inc., Tulsa, 1968-70, also dir.; pres., dir. 1st Nat. Bank, San Antonio. Mem. Gov.'s Com. on Lang. Disabilities, 1968-—; chmn. Tex. Conservation Found. Bd. dirs. Harry Jersig Lang. Center, San Antonio; trustee Hendrick Meml. Hosp., Abilene, Hardin-Simmons U., Abilene, Tex. State Hist. Found. Home: 603 Cave Lane San Antonio TX 78209 Office: 231 E Travis St San Antonion TX 78205

BIGGS, JAMES ELBERT, architect; b. Atlanta, Dec. 31, 1926; s. James Elbert and Anna Louise (Berlin) B.; B.S., Ga. Inst. Tech., 1950, B.Arch., 1951; m. Ellen Shuford Cowan, Oct. 23, 1955; children—William, Anna, David. Draftsman A.L. Aydelott & Assos., architects and engrs., Memphis, 1951-52; designer William J.J. Chase, architect, Atlanta, 1952-53, Harold Woodward & Assos., architects, Spartanburg, S.C., 1953-54; partner Abee & Biggs, architects, Hickory, N.C., 1954-62; prin. James E. Biggs, architect, Hickory, 1963-67; partner Architecture III, Hickory, 1967-—. Pres. Cripple Creek Corp., 1967-—. Mem. Hickory Community Relations Council, 1965-68, chmn., 1967-68. Served with USAAF, 1945-46. Recipient Distinguished Merit citation Nat. Council Christians and Jews, 1968, awards of merit N.C. chpt. A.I.A., 1961, 63. Mem. A.I.A. Club: Lake Hickory (Hickory). Home: 234 3d Av NW Hickory NC 28601 Office: 361 2d St NW PO Box 1953 Hickory NC 28601

BIGGS, JOHN HUMPHREYS, III, dentist; b. Norfolk, Va., Dec. 5, 1935; s. John Humphreys and Eva Frances (Bailey) B.; student William and Mary Coll., 1954-56; B.S., Ohio U., 1958; D.D.S., Med. Coll. Va., 1961; m. Nancy Louise Dick, July 6, 1956 (div. July 1971); children—Randolph Ward, Karen Lee. Dentist, Fla. State Bd. Health, 1963-64; pvt. practice dentistry, Lake Worth, Fla., 1964-—. Served to capt. Dental Corps, AUS, 1961-63. NIH Research grantee, 1959, 60. Mem. Am., Fla., Atlantic Dist. dental assns., Sigma Zeta, Omicron Kappa Upsilon, Psi Omega, Sigma Alpha Epsilon. Home: 717 Flamingo Dr West Palm Beach FL 33401 Office: 3150 Congress Av Lake Worth FL 33460

BIGGS, RONALD EVERETT, mirror mfg. co. exec.; b. Ft. Smith, Ark., May 11, 1940; s. James Everett and Aleyene Idessa (Cauthron) B.; B.S., Okla. State U., 1961, B.E., 1961, M.S., 1962. Tchr., coach Cushing (Okla.) High Sch., 1962-63, Ponco City High Sch., 1963-64; purchasing agt. Willard Mirror Co., Ft. Smith, Ark., 1964-69, sales mgr., 1969-—, dir., 1968-—; pres. Biggs Oil and Gas Co., Ft. Smith, 1971-—, H & B Distbg. Co., Rogers, Ark., 1971-—. Dir. spl. events United Fund, 1971, key man, 1967-70. Sebastian County campaign chmn. McClerkin for Gov., 1970. Bd. dirs. Viking Corp. Served with AUS. Mem. Sigma Alpha Epsilon. Baptist. Home: 6723 S T St Fort Smith AR 72901 Office: 5023 Old Greenwood Rd Fort Smith AR 72901

BIGGS, WELLINGTON ALLEN, journalist; b. Platteville, Colo., Mar. 9, 1923; s. Wellington H. and Adeline (Brown) B.; B.A. in Journalism, U. Colo., 1949; m. Laura Jean Mowrey, Dec. 7, 1951; children— Catherine, Joseph, Lorraine, Louise, Jeffrey. Asst. editor Brighton (Colo.) Blade, 1949-50; editor Haywood Pub. Co., Chgo., 1950-52; asst. editor Alamosa (Colo.) Daily Courier, 1952, Wyo. State Jour., Lander, 1952; dir. publs. U. Colo., 1952-56; editor Rocky Mountain Teamster, Denver, 1956-61; pub. relations cons. Colo. Freedom to Bargain Com., 1958; dir. pub. relations, editor Internat. Teamster mag., Washington, 1961-—. Precinct committeeman, dist. capt., publicity chmn., pub. relations cons. Boulder County (Colo.) Democratic Party, 1952-61. Served with USNR, 1942-46; PTO. Mem. Sigma Delta Chi, Pi Kappa Alpha. Methodist. Home: 500 Valleybrook Dr Silver Spring MD 20904 Office: 25 Louisiana Av NW Washington DC 20001

BIGGS, WILLIAM ARCHIBALD, JR., chemist; b. Lincolnton, N.C., Sept. 9, 1907; s. William Archibald and Mattie (Gay) B.; B.S., U. N.C., 1931; m. Sarah Hough Fletcher, July 30, 1938; children—William Archibald III, Robert Fletcher. Research chemist Sonoco Products Co., Hartsville, S.C., 1935-50, group leader, research and devel., 1951-67, chem. research coordinator, 1968-—. Mem. Hartsville Bd. Health, 1950-55. Fellow Am. Inst. Chemists; mem. Am. Chem. Soc., T.A.P.P.I., Forest Products Research Soc., S.C. Acad. Sci., Alpha Chi Sigma, Phi Mu Alpha. Episcopalian. Patentee in field. Home: Woodland Dr Hartsville SC 29550 Office: Sonoco Products Co Hartsville SC 29550

BILES, GEORGE LACEY, physician; b. Sumner, Miss., Mar. 2, 1907; s. James David and Willie Benny (Lacey) B.; A.B., U. Miss., 1927; M.D., Columbia, 1931; m. Lucie Evaline Dewees, Apr. 15, 1936; children—George Lacey, Anne Fairfax (Mrs. Dumas Ponder). Intern, Meth. Hosp., Bklyn., 1931-33; practice medicine, specializing in family practice, Sumner, Miss., 1933-—; mem. staff Coahoma Hosp., Tallahatchie County Hosp. Med. examiner Selective Service Bd., 1943-—; vice pres., dir. Grenada Bank, Bank Sumner. Mem. Tallahatchie County Library Bd., 1964-70. Mem. Tallahatchie County Bd. Edn., 1954-62, pres., 1958-59; mayor, Sumner, 1948-—. Served with AUS, 1942-44. Diplomate Nat. Bd. Med. Examiners. Mem. A.M.A., Am. Assn. Gen. Practice, So., Miss. State med. assns., Clarksdale (pres. 1953-54), Six Counties (pres. 1955-57), Tallahatchie County (pres. 1940-48) med. socs., Am. Legion (comdr. 1953-—), U. Miss. Alumni Assn., Federated Bd. State Med. Examiners, Sigma Chi, Phi Chi. Mem. Christian Ch. Club: Bayou Bend Country (Sumner, Miss.). Home: 106 N Cassidy St Sumner MS 38957 Office: 1 Court Square Sumner MS 38957

BILGER, DONALD EARL, lawyer; b. Lewistown, Pa., Mar. 7, 1920; s. John Nevin and Verna (Collins) B.; student Bucknell U., 1938-40; B.S., U. Colo., 1951; J.D., George Washington U., 1954, LL.M., 1955, J.S.D., 1957; m. Irene F. Rasmussen, June 1, 1946; children— Nancy Margaret, Donald Earl II. Admitted to D.C. bar, Fed. bar, Va. bar, 1954; law clk. U.S. Dist. Ct., Washington, 1954-56; asst. U.S. Atty., Washington, 1956-57; practiced in Fairfax, Va., 1955-57, Washington, 1957-—; mem. firm Welch, Mott & Morgan, 1957-63, Smith & Pepper, 1963-68, Bilger & Glaser, 1968-70, Bilger & Blair, 1970-—. Served to lt. col. USAF, 1940-52. Decorated Purple Heart. Mem. Bar Assn. D.C., Fed., Fed. Communications, Am., Va. State, Fairfax County bar assns., Va. State Bar, Am. Judicature Soc., Barristers Inn, Order of Coif, Phi Delta Phi. Clubs: Broadcasters, Touchdown (Washington); Chantilly National Golf and Country (Va.). Home: 9301 Hamilton Dr Fairfax VA 22030 Office: Bilger & Blair 1730 M St NW Washington DC 20036

BILL, DORA COX, govt. ofcl., civic worker; b. Knoxville, Tenn., Apr. 18, 1911; d.Charles Fred and Imogene (Masters) Cox; student LaGrange Coll., 1928, 29; flower show judging degree U. Ga., 1950; m. C. R. Dodson, May 1930; M. 2d, Clayton Justin Cosse, Apr. 9, 1950; 1 dau., Jeanie Cox (Mrs. Albert A. Price, Jr.); m. 3d, Russell W. Bill, June 20, 1969. Gen. mgr. So. office J. H. McGillvra Co. of N.Y., Atlanta, 1948-49; formed Dora Dodson Radio Rep. Agy., 1949, So. mgr. Forjoe Co., Atlanta, 1949; formed Dora-Clayton Agy., Inc., 1950, v.p., treas., 1950-68; pub. information specialist S.E. regional office Office Econ. Opportunity, Atlanta, 1968-71; pub. information officer ACTION, Atlanta, 1971-—. Active in Cerebral Palsy, A.R.C. drives; pres. Civitan Aux., 1955-56; mem. Atlanta Symphony Guild, Atlanta Opera Guild; nat. bd. Heart Assn. Recipient silver medal Printers Ink, 1968. Mem. Am. Women in Radio and Television (nat. local boards, chpt. pres., nat. pres. 1965-66; trustee Ednl. Found. 1966-72), Broadcast Execs. Club, Internat. Platform Assn., Internat. Soc. Radio and Television, C. of C., Am. Fedn. Advt. Clubs, Atlanta Advt. Club, League of Women Voters. English-Speaking Union, Atlanta Art Assn., Am. Soc. for Pub. Adminstrn., Am. Acad. Polit. and Social Sci., Presidents Council Atlanta, UN Council. Episcopalian. Clubs: Atlanta Press, Atlanta Women's Golf Assn., East Lake Golf Assn. (sec. 1956-58), Atlanta Variety (women's com.),

Parkwood Garden (sec.), Atlanta Athletic, East Lake Country (all Ga.); Ponte Vedra (Fla.) Country; Highlands (N.C.) Country. Home: 6851 Roswell Rd Apt B14 Atlanta GA 30328 Office: ACTION 730 Peachtree St Atlanta GA 30308

BILL, HARTHON LEWIS, ret. govt. ofcl.; b. Bridgeport, Conn., May 12, 1911; s. Charles Lewis and Grace (Munson) B.; B.A., Middlebury Coll., 1934; M.F., Yale, 1935; m. Jane Haines, June 20, 1935 1 son, Harthon H. With Nat. Park Service, 1935-72, asst., then chief park ranger Grand Canyon Nat. Park, 1935-46, asst. supt. Mt. Rainier Nat. Park, 1947-52, asst. supt. Yosemite Nat. Park, 1952-55, asst. regional dir. S.W. region, Santa Fe, N.M., 1955-59, supt. Grand Teton Nat. Park, 1960-63, supt. Glacier Nat. Park, 1963-64, chief, resources mgmt. and visitor protection, Washington, 1964-66, dep. asst. dir., asst. dir. operations, 1966-67, dep. dir. Nat. Park Service, Washington, 1967-72. Recipient Distinguished Service award Dept. Interior, 1966, Cornelius Amory Pugsley gold medal, 1970. Mem. Soc. Am. Foresters, Ecol. Soc. Am., Nat. Recreation and Park Assn. Nat. Trust for Historic Preservation. Mason. Club: Yale (Washington). Home: 5008 Dodson Dr Annandale VA 22003

BILLETT, ROY OREN, educator; b. Martel O., June 17, 1891; s. Edward Elmore and Ida Lenora (Earley) B.; ed. Bliss Bus. Coll., 1917; Bowling Green State Normal Sch., 1918; B.S., Ohio State U., 1923, M.A., 1927, Ph.D., 1929; Ed.D. (hon.), R.I. Coll. Edn., 1958; m. Edna Mae Cunningham, Sept. 14, 1912; 1 dau., Evelyn Margaret. Tchr., supt., village schs., Morrow County, O., 1912-18; supt, New Bloomington centralized schs., Marion County, O., 1918-22; prin., Thomas W. Harvey Meml. High Sch., Painesville. O., 1923-28; instr. Ohio State U., 1929; specialist in sch. adminstrn. U.S. Office of Edn., 1930-32; professorial lectr. on edn. Grad. Sch., Am. U., 1930-32, George Washington U., 1931-32; mem. staff, Ark. Survey Higher Instns. Learning, 1930; mem. staff Nat. Survey Secondary Edn., 1930-32; asso. prof. secondary edn., supr. practice teaching Ill. State Normal U., 1932-33; lectr. edn. Grad. Sch. Edn., Harvard U., 1933-34; asso. prof. edn. Boston U., 1934-35, prof., 1935-57, prof. edn. emeritus, 1957-—; became chmn. dept edn. Grad Sch., 1944. Mem. staff Survey Pub. Schs., Cin., 1935; dir., Survey Pub. Edn., Harford County, Md., 1945-46; lectr. edn. U. B.C., 1946, 51; vis. prof. U. So. Cal., 1948, Duke, 1955, U. Fla., 1959 Fla. State U., 1960, Fla. Atlantic U., 1967-68; dir. Two-Year Revision Program, Co-op. Study Secondary Standards, 1948. Mem. Nat., Fla. assns. secondary sch. prins., International Reading Assn., Nat. Council Measurement in Edn., Am. Assn. U. Profs., Am. Ednl. Research Assn., Nat. Soc. Study Edn. (yearbook com., 1936). Phi Delta Kappa. Club: Boston Authors'. Author: Administration and Supervision of Homogeneous Grouping; Aims and Activities of Supervisors; Provisions for Individual Differences, Marking and Promotion: Fundamentals of Secondary School Teaching; Growing up and related manuals; Youth Problem Inventories; Teaching in Junior and Senior High Schools; Preparing Theses and Other Typed Manuscripts; Improving the Secondary-School Curriculum; also articles, periodicals, chpts. in books. Home: 5921 NE 15th Av Fort Lauderdale FL 33308

BILLIG, OTTO, psychiatrist; b. Vienna, Austria, Aug. 10, 1910; s. Neure and Ottilie (Butschowitz) B.; B.A., Fed. Realschule (Austria), 1929; M.D., U. Vienna, 1937;; m. Sebby Orr, Oct. 5, 1943; 1 dau., Martha Gwen. Came to U.S., 1939, naturalized, 1944. Intern, U. Vienna Hosp., 1934-36, resident, 1936-38; asst. neurology Rothschild Hosp., Vienna, 1938-39; clin. dir. Highland Hosp., Asheville, N.C., 1939-46; instr. psychiatry Duke, 1941-43, asso. psychiatry Duke Univ., 1943-46, asst. prof. neuropsychiatry, 1946-48; dir. mental health clinic Vanderbilt U. Hosp., Nashville, 1948-60, asso. prof., 1952-69, clin. prof. psychiatry, 1969-—; acting chmn. dept. psychiatry Meharry Med. Coll., Nashville, 1952-66, prof. clin. psychiatry, 1967-—. Lectr., U. Tenn. Sch. Social Work, Nashville, 1952-—, VA Hosp., Murfreesboro, Tenn., 1949-—; mem. Met. Bd. Health Nashville-Davidson County, 1963-—, chmn., 1969-—. Pres., Nashville Art Council, 1961-63. Bd. dirs. Peabody Coll. Art Mus., Nashville. Diplomate Am. Bd. Psychiatry and Neurology. Mem. A.M.A., Am. Psychiat. Assn., Internat. Soc. Psychopath. Expression, (hon., mem. council), Soc. Projective Techniques, World Congress Psychiatry. Contbr. articles to profl. jours. Home: 1050 Overton Lea Rd Nashville TN 37220 Office: 2011 Ashland Av Nashville TN 37212

BILLINGS, CLAUDE, used car dealer; b. Traphill, N.C., June 18, 1918; s. John and Flora (Lyon) B.; grad. high sch.; m. Emma Jane Lyon, Sept. 11, 1943; children—Brenda Carole (Mrs. John R. Ratledge), Vivian Lynn, Daniel Claude, Philip Ray. Owner, operator Traphill Motors, used cars, 1946-—; dir. Northwestern Bank, Wilkesboro, N.C. Mem. Stone Mountain Park and Preservation Commn., 1968-—; mem. N. High Sch. Adv. Bd., 1960-71; chmn. Wilkes County Bd. Commrs., 1956-58, mem., 1959-60; chmn. Appalachian Regional Library, 1968-71. Republican precinct chmn., 1960-71; mem. N.C. Ho. Reps., 1967-68, 69-70. Served with AUS, 1940-42. Recipient Wilkes Citizenship award, 1971. Baptist (deacon 1946-—). Mason (past dist. dep. grand master). Home: Route 1 Box 45 Traphill NC 28685 Office: Route 1 Box 2-A Traphill NC 28685

BILLINGS, FREDERIC TREMAINE, JR., physician, educator; b. Pitts., Feb. 22, 1912; s. Frederic Tremaine and Romaine (LeMoyne) B.; A.B., Princeton, 1933; B.Sc., (Rhodes scholar), Balliol Coll., Oxford, Eng., 1936; M.D., Johns Hopkins, 1938; m. Ann Howe, Feb. 21, 1942; children—Frederic Tremaine III, Ann Howe (Mrs. Harwell), John Howe. Postgrad. tng. medicine Johns Hopkins, Vanderbilt U. hosps., 1938-42; instr. medicine Vanderbilt U. Sch. Medicine, 1946-49, asst. prof., 1949-53, asso. prof., 1953-63, clin. prof. medicine, 1963-—, dean students, 1960-67, asso. dean for Med. Center Devel., 1967-—; prof. med. Meharry Med. Coll., 1950-65, chmn, dept., 1950-57, also trustee. Sec., State Selection Com. Rhodes Scholars, Tenn. Past dir. Nat. Med. Fellowships, Inc.; trustee Princeton, 1956-60, Choate Sch. Served from capt. to lt. col., AUS, 1942-46; asst. med. cons. S.W. Pacific area, 1944; chief gen. medicine br. med. consultants div., Office Surgeon Gen., 1945-46. Diplomate Am. Bd. Internal Medicine, 1946. Fellow A.C.P., A.M.A.; mem. Assn. Am. Rhodes Scholars (past dir.), Am. Clin. and Climatol. Assn. (sec.-treas. 1958-68, pres. 1969), Assn. Am. Physicians, Soc. U.S. Med. Consultants Armed Forces, A.A.A.S., Am. Heart Assn., Am. Fedn. Clin. Research, Phi Beta Kappa, Alpha Omega Alpha. Clubs: Ivy; Rolling Rock (Ligonier, Pa.); Belle Meade Country (Nashville). Contbr. articles to profl. publs. Home: 3906 Woodlawn Dr Nashville TN 37205 Office: Med Arts Bldg Nashville TN 37212

BILLINGS, SAMUEL CLARK, entomologist; b. Cambridge, Mass. Mar. 21, 1908; s. John Davis and Katherine (Wight) B.; B.S., U. Mass., 1930; M.S., U. Md., 1939; m. Lucille Francis Pemberton, June 27, 1937 (dec. June 1966); 1 son, Ronald Samuel. Entomologist insecticide div. FDA, U.S. Dept. Agr., 1930-42, 46-50, chief staff officer insecticides evaluation staff, pesticides regulation div. agrl. research service, 1950-70; chief entomologist pesticides regulation div. U.S. Environmental Protection Agy., Washington, 1971-—. Served from 1st lt. to maj., Med. Service Corps, AUS, 1942-46. Mem. Entomol. Soc. Am., Entomol. Soc. Washington, Am. Inst. Biol. Scis. Methodist. Home: 1110 Fidler Lane Silver Spring MD 20910 Office: Dept Agr South Bldg Washington DC 20250

BILLINGS, WILLIAM DWIGHT, ecologist, educator; b. Washington, Dec. 29, 1910; s. William Pence and Mabel (Burke) B.; B.A., Butler U., 1933; D.Sc., 1955; M.A., Duke, 1935; Ph.D., 1936;; m. Shirley Ann Miller, July 29, 1958. Instr. botany U. Tenn., 1936-37; instr. biology U. Nev., 1938-40, asst. prof., 1940-43, asso. prof., 1943-49, prof., chmn. biology dept., 1949-52; asso. prof. botany Duke, Durham, N.C., 1952-58, prof., 1958-67, James B. Duke prof. botany, 1967-—. Mem. adv. panels NSF, Washington, 1954-57. Fulbright research scholar, New Zealand, 1959. Mem. Ecol. Soc. Am. (v.p. 1960, Mercer award 1962), Brit. Ecol. Soc., Bot. Soc. Am. (certificate of merit 1960). Author: Plants, Man, and the Ecosystem, 1970. Editor: Ecology, 1952-57; Ecological Monographs, 1969. Contbr. articles to tech. jours. Home: 1628 Marion Av Durham NC 27705

BILLINGSLEY, HASCAL SANDERS, beverage co. exec.; b. Wylie, Tex., Dec. 26, 1905; s. James Clement and Eva (Sanders) B.; student Advanced Accounting Sch., U. Tex., 1926-27; m. Mary Louise Bruss, Nov. 15, 1935; children—Hascal Bruss, Martha Joan (Mrs. Ralph D. Bowman). Accountant, Peat, Marwick, Mitchell & Co., C.P.A.'s. Dallas, 1927-30; with Dr. Pepper Co., Dallas, 1931-—, pres., 1966-69, chmn. bd., 1969-—. Mem. Salesmanship Club Dallas (bd. dirs. 1953-54, sec. 1953-54), All Sports Assn., Beta Alpha Psi. Club: Dallas City. Home: 4818 Melissa Lane Dallas TX 75229 Office: 5523 E Mockingbird Lane Dallas TX 75222

BILLINGSLEY, WILLIAM EVERETT, univ. ofcl.; b. Hamlet, N.C., July 9, 1930; s. James Marcus and Lula (Gibson) B.; B.S. with honors, N.C. State Coll., 1957; M.S. in Commerce, U. Richmond, 1966; postgrad. U. N.C. 1967; m. Kay Frances Hargett, June 5, 1955; children—Andrew Everett, William Lawrence, Melinda Kay. Began career as apprentice carman with the Seaboard Air Line R.R. Co., Hamlet, N.C., 1948-51, mech. engr., Richmond, Va., 1957-67; supt. bldgs. Phys. Plant div. U. N.C., Chapel Hill, 1967-68, operations engr., 1969-70, supt. elec. and water distbn. Univ. Service plants, 1970-—. Mem. Chapel Hill Bd. Edn., 1969-71. Served from pvt. to sgt. M.C., AUS, 1951-53. Registered profl. engr., N.C., Fla., Va. Mem. of Am. Soc. M.E., Am. Ry. Engrs. Assn., Tau Beta Pi, Pi Tau Sigma, Phi Kappa Phi, Phi Eta Sigma, Theta Tau, Methodist. Clubs: Toastmasters (pres. Chapel Hill club 1971), Sertoma (pres. Meridian club 1971). Author articles in field. Home: 317 Barclay Rd Chapel Hill NC 27514 Office: Utilities Div PO Box 540 Univ North Carolina Chapel Hill NC 27514

BILLINGTON, TED FRANKLIN, cons. engr.; b. Almo, Ky., Now. 22, 1938; s. Eldred Guy and Lurline (Morris) B.; student Murray State U., 1956-59; B.S. in C.E., U. Ky., 1961; m. Joan Patricia Baker, Apr. 25, 1961; children—Julia Kathryn, Claudia Joan, Cheryl. Assn. resident engr. Ky. Dept. Hwy., Ashland, 1961-62; chief structural engr. Lee Potter Smith & Assos., architects, Paducah, Ky., 1962-67; cons. engr. Ted F. Billington, Murray, Ky., 1967-—, prin. cons. services civil and structural engring., land surveying. Registered profl. engr., land surveyor, Ky.; registered profl. engr., Tenn. Mem. Am. Soc. C.E., Nat. Soc. Profl. Engrs., Am. Soc. Testing Materials, Am. Concrete Int., Ky. Soc. Profl. Engrs. Baptist. Rotarian. Home: 505 Whitnell St Murray KY 42071 Office: Johnson Blvd Box 422 Murray KY 42071

BILLIONS, GERALD FREEMAN, dentist; b. Memphis, Oct. 14, 1939; s. Robert Edward and Rosa Louise (Humphries) B.; student Memphis State U., 1957-61; D.D.S., U. Tenn., 1965; m. Barbara Ann Robins, Nov. 25, 1961; children—Jeffrey Lowell, David Andrew. Asso. O.C. Faulkner, Memphis, 1968; instr. operative dentistry U. Tenn., 1969-70; pvt. practice, Memphis, 1970-—. Served to capt. AUS, 1965-67. Mem. Memphis, Tenn. dental socs., Am. Dental Assn., Memphis Dental Legion, Delta Sigma Delta. Republican. Baptist. Club: Optimist (Memphis). Home: 2702 Kelmscott Cove Germantown TN 38138 Office: 4676A Knight Arnold Rd Memphis TN 38118

BINDER, LEONARD JAMES, editor; b. Jackson, Mich., June 21, 1926; s. Leonard George and Ethel Cecille (Lilly) B.; B.S., Central Mich. U., 1952; m. Margery Elizabeth Rose, Sept. 7, 1950; children—Timothy James, Michael Paul, Douglas Harold. Editor Wingfoot Clan, Goodyear Tire & Rubber Co., Jackson, 1952-54; editor-in-chief Wayne (Mich.) Eagle, 1954-55; news editor Pontiac (Mich.) Press, 1955-57; editor AP, Detroit, 1957-60; state editor Detroit News, 1960-67; editor-in-chief Army Mag., Washington, 1967-—. Spl. writer, book reviewer Nat. Observer, 1967-70. Bd. dirs. Central Mich. U. Devel. Fund. Served with USNR, 1944-46. Mem. Central Mich. U. Alumni Assn. (v.p. Detroit chpt. 1966-67), Methodist (adminstrv. bd. 1969-—). Clubs: Nat. Press, Detroit Press. Home: 304 Lewis St Vienna VA 22180 Office: 1529 18th St NW Washington DC 20036

BINFORD, WILLIAM FRANCIS, judge; b. Disputanta, Va., Mar. 19, 1903; s. John Henry and Elizabeth Johnson (Binford) B.; student Va. Tech. Inst., 1920-21; LL.B., Eastman Coll., 1924; m. Sue Burrow, June 18, 1927; 1 son, William Francis. Admitted to Va. bar, 1931; practiced in Southside, Va., 1931-—; judge, Prince George (Va.) County Ct., 1930-—. Dir. Bank Waverly, Va. Sec.-treas. Prince George County, Democratic Com., 1940-70. Mem. Am., Va., Petersburg (pres. 1959), 3d Circuit bar assns., Assn. Judges Va. (sec.-treas. 1930-70), Va. Trial Lawyers Assn. Methodist (trustee ch. 1935-71). Moose. Club: Ruritan (Disputanta, Va.). Home: RFD 1 Box 141 Disputanta VA 23842 Office: Prince George VA 23845

BINGHAM, BARRY, editor; b. Louisville, Feb. 10, 1906; s. Robert Worth and Eleanor (Miller) B.; student Middlesex Sch., Concord, Mass., 1921-23; A.B. magna cum laude, Harvard, 1928; LL.D., U. Ky., Kenyon Coll., Centre Coll.; Litt.D., U. Louisville, U. Cin.; m. Mary Clifford Caperton, June 9, 1931; children—Worth (dec.), Barry, Sarah (Mrs. Micheal Iovenko), Eleanor. With Courier-Jour. and Louisville Times Co., 1930-—, reporter, sec., asso. pub., pub., 1930-45, editor, pub., until 1971, now chmn. bd.; chmn. bd. WHAS, Inc., Standard Gravure Corp. Chmn. bd. dirs. Historic Homes Found.; trustee Berea Coll., Pine Mountain Settlement Sch.; overseer U. Louisville; bd. dirs. Asia Found.; past chmn. Internat. Press Inst. Chief of mission to France, ECA, 1949-50. Nat. chmn. Vols. for Stevenson-Kefauver, 1956. Served with USNR, 1941-45; comdr., 1945; ETO, PTO. Decorated comdr. Order Brit. Empire, comdr. Legion of Honor; recipient Sullivan award U. Ky. Mem. Sigma Delta Chi (hon. nat. chmn.), Omicron Delta Kappa. Democrat. Episcopalian. Clubs: Pendennis, River Valley, Wynn-Stay, Louisville Country (Louisville); Century Assn. Home: Glenview KY 40025 Office: Courier-Journal and Times Louisville KY 40202

BINGHAM, BARRY, JR., broadcasting exec. Vice pres. radio sta. WHAS, Louisville. Office: 520 W Chestnut St Louisville KY 40202*

BINGHAM, MARY CAPERTON (MRS. BARRY BINGHAM), newspaper exec.; b. Richmond, Va., Dec. 24, 1904; d. Clifford R. and Helena (Lefroy) Caperton; B.A., Radcliffe Coll., 1928; postgrad. (Charles Eliot Norton fellow) Am. Sch. Classical Studies, Athens, 1929; D.Litt., U. Louisville, 1954; m. Barry Bingham, June 9, 1931; children—Robert W. (dec.), G. Barry, Sarah (Mrs. Michael Iovenko), Jonathan W. (dec.), Eleanor M. Vice pres., dir. Courier-Jour. and Louisville Times, WHAS, Inc., 1942-—; editor World of Books column Louisville Courier Jour., 1943-67. Mem. library servies com. Nat. Book Com. 1956-57; dir. Council Basic Edn., Washington; mem. Ky. Arts Com. Trustee Radcliffe Coll., 1942-60. Recipient Margaret Douglas Conservation award Garden Club Am., 1972. Mem. Colonial Dames. Clubs: River Valley, Louisville Country (Louisville): Cosmopolitan (N.Y.C.); Glenview (Ky.) Garden. Home: Glenview KY 40025 Office: 525 W Broadway Louisville KY 40202

BINGHAM, MARY JOSEPHINE HOLMES (MRS. JAMES GREER BINGHAM), artist; b. Detroit, Aug. 22, 1923; d. Arthur Mudge and Alice (Leonard) Holmes; student U. Mich., 1941-44; B.A. in Humanities, U.S. Fla., 1970; m. James Greer Bingham, Nov. 4, 1944; children—John Greer, David Hartman, Betsy Josephine. Sec.-treas. Castle Homes Pa., Inc., Beaver Falls, Pa., 1955-59; v.p. Caribbean Homes, Inc., Ft. Meyers, Fla., 1961-62, represented S.W. Fla. Art Council Sears Show, 1966, 1st Nat. Cape Coral Art Show, 1967. Mem. Art League Ft. Myers (v.p.), Port Edison Civic Assn. (co. fdr., sec.), Gamma Phi Beta, Phi Kappa Phi. Clubs: Republican (Greenhills, O.); Lee County Republican (rec. sec., Ft. Myers). Christian Scientist. Home: 1270 Sunrise Dr North Ft Myers FL 33903 also 405 Royal Palm Way Tampa FL 33609

BINGHAM, REBECCA JOSEPHINE TAYLOR (MRS. WALTER D. BINGHAM), librarian; b. Indpls., July 14, 1928; d. George Edward and Lalla (Bass) Taylor; B.S., Ind. U., 1950, M.L.S., 1969; M.A., U. Tulsa, 1962; m. Louis J. Simmons, July 28, 1950 (div. Dec. 1954); children—Gail Elaine, Louis Edward; m. 2d, Walter D. Bingham, Oct. 27, 1957. Asst. librarian Alcorn (Miss.) A. and M. Coll., 1950-51; asst. serials librarian Tuskegee (Ala.) Inst., 1952-53; asst. librarian Jarvis Christian Coll., Hawkins, Tex., 1955-57; librarian Carver Jr. High Sch., Tulsa, 1960-62; tchr. English, Russell Jr. High Sch., Louisville, 1962-63; librarian Jackson Jr. High Sch., Louisville, 1963-66; supr. library services Louisville Pub. Schs., 1966-70, dir. media services, 1970-—. Mem. Ky. Library Adv. Council. Mem. Louisville and Jefferson County (Ky.) Health and Welfare Council, 1970-—. Bd. dirs. Louisville Children's Theatre; mem. alumni bd. Ind. U. Grad. Library Sch., 1971. Named Outstanding Sch. Librarian, Ky. Library Trustees, 1969. Mem. A.L.A., Am., Ky. (editor Bull. 1967-68) assns. sch. librarians, Nat., Ky., Louisville edn. assns., Ky. Library Assn. (pres. 1971), Pi Lambda Theta, Kappa Delta Pi. Episcopalian (pres. Episcopal Churchwomen 1969-70). Home: 3608 Dumesnill St Louisville KY 40211 Office: Brown Edn Center Fourth and Broadway Louisville KY 40202

BINION, WILLIE CLAYTE, JR., newspaper editor; b. Houston, June 7, 1912; s. Willie Clayte and Mattie (Sayers) B.; student Southwestern U., Georgetown, Tex., 1929-31, Stephen F. Austin Coll., Nacogdoches, Tex., 1931-32, U. Tex., 1932-35; m. Sara Dell Newson, Mar. 28, 1937; children—Clayte III, Jack Russell, Emma Lee (Mrs. David V. Wilson), Tommy Sayers. With Lufkin (Tex.) Daily News, 1937-42, 45-48, mng. editor, 1942, 47-48; mem. pub. relations dept. Jefferson Amusement Co., Beaumont, Tex., 1942-43; with sports copy desk Beaumont Enterprise, 1948-49; with Houston Chronicle, 1949-—, mng. editor, dir., 1965-71, exec. editor, dir., 1971-—. Mem. Pulitzer Prize Jury, 1969-70; mem. Harris County Hist. Com.; mem. newspapers editors com. U. Tex. Mem. publs. com. Tex. United Methodist Ch. Bd. dirs. U.S.O., Houston. Served with USMCR, 1944-46; PTO. Named Distinguished Alumnus, Southwestern U., Georgetown, Tex., 1967. Mem. Nat., Tex. (pres. 1971-72), U.P.I. editors assns., Nat., Tex. (pres. 1969-70) A.P. mng. editors assns., Am. Soc. Newspaper Editors, Houston C. of C., S.A.R., Sons Republic Tex., Kappa Sigma, Sigma Delta Chi (dir. 1969). Methodist. Clubs: Houston, Yacht, Old Capitol, Press, Farm and Ranch (Houston). Home: 5502 Pebble Springs St Houston TX 77040 Office: Houston Chronicle Travis St Houston TX 77001

BINKLEY, FLOYD HALIE, dentist; b. Corydon, Ind., July 26, 1898; s. George W. and Anna Elizabeth (Davidson) B.; D.D.S., Kansas City Dental Sch., 1924; m. Faye Sincle Keller, Oct. 30, 1924; children—James Edgar, LaGay (Mrs. Donald Hill), Louise (Mrs. Terry Brown). Pvt. practice dentistry, Hennessey, Okla., 1924-—. Mem. Hennessey Sch. Bd., 1930-55, pres., 1935-50. Named Man of Year, Okla. State Dental Assn., 1963-64. Fellow Am. Coll. Dentists; mem. Am. Dental Assn. (life mem.), Okla. Dental Assn. (sec.-treas. 1948-50), N.W. Dist. Dental Assn. (sec.-treas. 1930-36, councilman, 1940-48). Mem. Christian Ch. (deacon 1930-70, elder 1970-—). Mason, Lion (1st pres. 1934). Home: 402 E Oklahoma St Hennessey OK 73742 Office: 120 E Oklahoma St Hennessey OK 73742

BINKLEY, LOWELL, educator; b. Lima, O., Oct. 3, 1914; s. Wilfred Ellsworth, Dora (Stotts) E.; A.B., Ohio No. U. 1935 M.A., Wittenberg U., 1947; postgrad. Ohio State U., U. Tenn.; m. Edith Emily Knipp, July 2, 1960. Field biologist Ohio Dept. Agr., 1939-47; asst. prof. biology Bethany (W. Va.) Coll., 1947-50; asso. prof. biology, dept. head Tusculum Coll., Greeneville, Tenn., 1950-52; asst. prof. bacteriology Albany (N.Y.) Coll. Pharmacy, 1952-60; prof. biology dept. head Lenoir Rhyne Coll., Hickory, N.C., 1960-—; lectr. Russell Sage Coll., Albany, 1958-60. Cons. W.Va. Conservation Commn., 1948-50. Pres., Town View Manor, Loudonville, N.Y., 1958-60. Mem. A.A.A.S., Am. Soc. Mammalogists, N.C. Acad. Sci., Am. Assn. U. Profs., Beta Beta Beta, Alpha Epsilon Delta, Chi Beta Phi, Phi Lambda Pi. Home: 431 8th St NW Hickory NC 28601

BINKLEY, OLIN TRIVETTE, clergyman, sem. pres.; b. Harmony, N.C., Aug. 4, 1908; s. Joseph and Minnie (Trivette) B.; A.B. magna cum laude, Wake Forest (N.C.) Coll., 1928; D.D., 1951; Th.B., So. Bapt. Theol. Sem., 1930; B.D., Yale, 1931; Ph.D., 1933; D.D., U. N.C., 1964; m. Pauline Eichmann, Aug. 24, 1933; children—Pauline Edith, Janet Margaret. Ordained to ministry Baptist Ch., 1928; asso. pastor Calvary Bapt. Ch., New Haven, 1931-33; pastor Chapel Hill (N.C.) Bapt. Ch., 1933-38; lectr. sociology U. N.C., 1937-38; head dept. religion Wake Forest (N.C.) Coll., 1938-44; asso. prof., acting head dept. ethics and sociology So. Bapt. Theol. Sem., 1944-46, prof., head dept., 1946-52; prof. Christian sociology and ethics Southeastern Bapt. Theol. Sem., Wake Forest, 1952-—, dean, 1958-63, pres., 1963-—. Vis. fellow Yale Div. Sch., 1951. Pres. N.C. Conf. Social Service, 1957-58. Pres. bd. mgrs. Louisville Children's Agy., 1948-50; trustee Ministry Studies Bd., Children's Homes Soc. N.C., Bapt. Children's Homes of N.C., Meredith Coll. Mem. Am. Assn. Marriage Counselors, Am. Assn. Theol. Schs. (pres. 1964-66), Am. Social. Soc., So. Bapt. Conv. (Christian life and social service commns.), Phi Beta Kappa. Clubs: Rotary (past pres.), Louisville Torch. Author: Frontiers for Christian Youth, 1942; From Victory Unto Victory, 1945; The Churches and the Social Conscience, 1948; How to Study the Bible, 1969. Home: Durham Rd Wake Forest NC 27587

BIRD, FRANCIS MARION, lawyer; b. Comer, Ga., Sept. 4, 1902; s. Henry Madison and Minnie Lee (McConnell) B.; A.B., U. Ga., 1922, LL.B., 1924; LL.M., George Washington U., 1925; m. Mary Adair Howell, Jan. 30, 1935; children—Francis Marion, Mary Adair, Elizabeth Howell, George Arthur. Admitted to Ga. bar, 1924, D.C. bar, 1925, since practiced in Atlanta; with Senator Hoke Smith, 1925, pvt. practice, 1930-45, Bird & Howell, 1945-49, now Jones, Bird & Howell; served as part-time U.S. referee in bankruptcy, 1945-54; spl. asst. to atty. gen. as hearings officer Nat. Selective Service Act. Mem. commn. for preparation plan of govt. City of Atlanta and county in which located; mem. permanent rules com. Ga. Supreme Ct.; chmn.

Met. Atlanta Commn. on Crime and Juvenile Delinquency, 1969-70; co-chmn. Tech-Ga. Devel. Fund. Trustee Young Harris Coll., U. Ga. Found., Atlanta Lawyers Found., Interdenominational Theol. Center; trustee, exec. com. Emory U. Chmn. Ga. Bd. Bar Examiners, 1954-61; mem. Permanent Editorial Bd. Uniform Comml. Code, Fed. Jud. Conf., 5th Circuit. Recipient Distinguished Service citation U. Ga. Law Sch., Alumni Achievement award George Washington U., 1965. Fellow Am. Bar Found.; mem. Am. Judicature Soc. (dir.) Am. Law Inst. (council), Am., Ga. (past pres.), Atlanta (past pres.) bar assns., Assn. Bar City N.Y., Atlanta C. of C. (past pres., dir. Atlanta Civic Service award 1957), U. Ga. Alumni Assn. (past pres., Certificate merit, 1952), Sigma Chi, Phi Kappa Phi, Phi Delta Phi. Meth. Clubs: Peachtree Golf, Piedmont Driving, Capitol City, Lawyers (past pres.). Atlanta Athletic (pres.), Kiwanis (dir. Atlanta); Augusta (Ga.) Nat. Golf. Home: 89 Brighton Rd NE Atlanta GA 30309 Office: Haas-Howell Bldg Atlanta GA 30303

BIRD, JORGE, legislator; b. Guayama, P.R., Aug. 23, 1910; s. Agustin and Angelica Fernandez (Citron) Bird Elias; ed. U. P.R.; m. Victoria L. Vilella, Dec. 23, 1934; children—Luisa Angelica (Mrs. Roberto Inclan), Victoria Josefina (Mrs. Jose Antonio Saenz de Ormijana), Nellie Aurora, Agustin Jorge, Jorge Pablo. Owner, pres. Bird Restaurants Inc., Jorge Bird Elec. Appliances, Inc., P.R. Airways; dir. Amstell Brewery Corp., P.R. Investment Corp.; founder, 1st pres. P.R. Conv. Bur.; dir. Marriott Corp.; pres., owner Jorge Bird Travel Service, Inc., Bird Gasoline Sta., Real Estate and Farming. Mem. P.R. Ho. of Reps. Mem. adv. com. P.R. Devel. Bank; mem. Sch. Bd. P.R. Vocational Tng. Courses; mem. Citizens Com. on Improvement of Relations Between P.R. Citizenship and Govt.; adviser Sec. of Commerce; mem. Tourism Adv. Com. Trustee, Inst. Am. World U. P.R. Named Man of Year, P.R. C. of C. Mem. P.R. Travel Agts. Assn. (pres.), Inter-Am. C. of C., Sales Execs. Club. Democrat. Roman Catholic. Elk, Lion. Address: P O Box BA Rio Piedras PR 00928*

BIRD, ROBERT JAMES, lawyer; b. Milw., July 3, 1911; s. Robe and Gertrude (Trainor) B.; A.B., Vanderbilt U., 1934, LL.B., 1937; m. Charla Coleman, July 25, 1940; children—Nancy (Mrs. Frank B. McKown, Jr.), Coleman, Barbara. Admitted to Ill. bar, 1938, D.C. bar, 1946; practiced in Chgo., 1938-44, Washington, 1953—; with govt. and pvt. industry, 1944-53. State chmn. for Md. Republican Nat. Finance Com., 1969—. Mem. Am., D.C. bar assns. Roman Catholic. Clubs: University (Washington); Chevy Chase (Md.). Home: 5 Quincy St Chevy Chase MD 20015 Office: 1140 Connecticut Av NW Washington DC 20036

BIRD, ROBERT MONTGOMERY, physician, univ. dean; b. Charlottesville, Va., Feb. 1, 1915; s. Robert Montgomery and Caroline (Reid) B.; B.S., U. Va., 1937, M.D., 1939. Intern, N.Y. Hosp., 1939-40, asst. resident medicine, 1940-42; Am. Cancer Soc. fellow Cornell U. Med. Coll., 1946-48; research asso., 1946-47, asst. prof. physiology, 1947-50, instr. medicine, 1947-52, asst. physician to outpatients, 1946-48, physician, 1948-52; practice medicine specializing in internal medicine, N.Y.C., 1950-52; asso. prof. medicine U. Okla Coll. Medicine, Oklahoma City, 1952-61, prof., 1961—, prof. physiology, 1962—, vice-chmn. dept. medicine, 1961-65, asso. dean planning and devel., 1965-70, dean Coll. Medicine, 1970—; attending Oklahoma City VA Hosp., 1953-68, cons., 1953—. Cons., U.S. Dept. Health, Edn. Welfare, 1967-70, mem. Constrn. Sch. Medicine Rev. Com., 1967-70, cons. Div. Physician Manpower, 1967—; chmn. com. B. instnl. research program evaluation VA, 1970-71; Mem. Okla. Sci. and Arts Found., Okla. Zool. Soc., Oklahoma City Symphony Soc. Served to maj., M.C., AUS, 1942-46. Recipient Regents award U. Okla., 1969. Diplomate Am. Bd. Internal Medicine, Fellow A.C.P. (state gov. 1970—); mem. Am. Physiology Soc., Am. Soc. Hematology, A.A.A.S., Am. Clin. and Climatol. Assn., A.M.A., Central Soc. Clin. Research, Harvey Soc. N.Y., So. Soc. Clin. Investigation, N.Y. Acad. Scis., Oklahoma City Acad. Medicine, Assn. U. Okla. Med. Faculty, Sigma Xi, Alpha Omega Alpha, Omicron Delta Kappa. Club: Sierra. Contbr. articles to profl. jours. Home: 205 NE 28th St Oklahoma City OK 73105 Office: 800 NE 13th St Oklahoma City OK 73104

BIRDSALL, WILLIAM CHAULK, govt. ofcl.; b. Deadwood, S.D., Oct. 7, 1933; s. Edward Morrow and Temple (Chaulk) B.; student Marquette U., 1951-53; B.A., St. Louis U., 1958, Licentiate Phil., 1959; Ph.D. (NSF fellow; Resources for Future fellow), Johns Hopkins U., 1963; B.Th., Woodstock Coll., 1966, Licentiate Theol. 1967; m. Olivia Kilbourn, Aug. 9, 1969; 1 dau., Moira Kilbourn. Research economist, div. econ. and long range studies Office Research and Statis. Social Security Adminstrn., Washington, 1967—. Lectr. econs. Georgetown U., Washington, 1964, Boston Coll., 1965, 66, Trinity Coll., Washington, 1968. Mem. Am. Econ. Assn. Democrat. Roman Catholic. Home: 1016 Massachusetts Av NE Washington DC 20002 Office: Social Security Adminstrn 1875 Connecticut Av Washington DC 20009

BIRDSONG, ANDREW WILLIS, JR., juvenile judge; b. LaGrange, Ga., Jan. 30, 1925; s. Andrew Woodie and Bessie (Cofield) B.; J.D., U. Ga., 1951; m. Sarah Elizabeth Cliatt, Sept. 16, 1948; children—Nancy Leslie, Sarah Elizabeth, Katherine Guinn. Admitted to Ga. bar, 1950; practiced in LaGrange, 1951-55; partner firm Richter & Birdsong, LaGrange, 1955—; Troup County (Ga.) juvenile judge, 1958—.Organizer, dir., sec. RSB Fiberglass Forms, Inc.; partner K & B Farms; organizer, dir., mem. exec. com. Peoples Bank of LaGrange. Chmn. Troup County Democratic Com., 1962. Trustee Camp Viola, La Grange. Served with AUS, 1943-47. Mem. Am., Ga. hereford assns., Am. Judicature Soc., Am., Ga. bar assns., Assn. Ins. Attys., Phi Delta Theta, Phi Alpha Delta. Baptist (chmn. bd. deacons). Moose, Elk, Lion (pres. LaGrange 1965-66). Club: Highland Country (pres., gov.). Home: Lakeshore Dr LaGrange GA 30240 Office: 306 N Lewis St LaGrange GA 30240

BIRD-SOTO, HECTOR MANUEL, physician; b. Santurce, P.R., Apr. 21, 1928; s. Modesto Bird and Agustina Soto; B.A., Emory U., 1949; M.T., P.R. Sch. Medicine, 1951; M.D., U. de Zaragoza, Spain, 1961; m. Iraida Hernandez Terre Forte, Aug. 29, 1954; children—Hector Manuel, Alberto Modesto, Mirena Maria, Jose Agustin, Juan Carlos. Intern, Arecibo Dist. Hosp., 1961-62; physician Dorado Health Center, 1962-63; house physician Hosp. Pavia, 1963; physician Bayamon Health Center, 1964-67, U. Dist. Hosp., 1967-69; physician family planning project U. P.R. Sch. Medicine, 1969-70, instr. family planning, 1970; resident in neuropsychiatry VA Hosp., San Juan, P.R., 1971—; mem. faculty Pub. Health Sch., Dept. Human Devel., U. P.R., 1971. Mem. A.M.A. Roman Catholic. Elk. Club: Casa de Espana de P.R. (San Juan, P.R.). Home: 1-15 Hucare Caparra Hills San Juan PR 00920 Office: VA Hosp Rio Piedras PR 00936

BIRKS, LAVERNE STANFIELD, govt. ofcl.; b. Rockford, Ill., Feb. 4, 1919; s. LaVerne Stanfield and Kathryn (Ross) B.; B.S., in Physics, U. Ill., 1942; M.S. in Physics, U. Md., 1951; m. Mary-Jane McIntosh, Oct. 2, 1942; children—Jeanne Kathryn, James Norman, Charles William. Jr. physicist electron optics Naval Research Lab., Washington, 1942-44, physicist, x-ray, 1945-49, sect. head, x-ray, 1949-58, physicist, head x-ray optics br., 1958—. Cons. x-ray optics, 1945—. Pres., Sligo Citizens' Assn., Takoma Park, Md., 1954-55. Served as ensign USNR, 1944-45; lt. comdr. Res. Recipient Spectroscopy Soc. award, Pitts., 1965; gold medal award N.Y. Soc. for Applied Spectroscopy, 1967, E.O. Hulburt award Naval Research Lab., 1970. Fellow Washington Acad. Sci.; mem. Internat. Union Pure and Applied Chemistry, Am. Phys. Soc., Electron Microscope Soc. Am., Am. Soc. Testing Materials (chmn. x-ray spectroscopy subcom. 1957-60, electron probe subcom. 1960-62), Research Soc. Am. (applied sci. award 1961; pres. sect. 1972), Electron Probe Analysis Soc. Am. (pres. 1968), Soc. for Applied Spectroscopy (chmn. Balt.—Washington sect. 1972), U.S. Power Squadron, Sigma Xi, Tau Beta Pi, Phi Kappa Phi, Pi Mu Epsilon. Author: X-Ray Spectrochemical Analysis, 1959, 2d edit., 1969; Electron Probe Microanalysis, 2d edit., 1971. Patentee x-ray optics. Home: 11908 Ledgerock Ct Potomac MD 20854 Office: Code 6680 US Naval Research Lab Washington DC 20390

BIRNBAUM, OWEN, govt. atty.; b. N.Y.C., Mar. 1, 1925; s. Alvin Jerome and Mildred (Safferstone) B.; A.B., Cornell U., 1945; LL.B., Yale, 1947; m. Claire Weil, Oct. 14, 1950; children—Jane Ellen, Andrew Jon. Admitted to N.Y. State bar, 1948, D.C. bar; practiced in N.Y.C., 1948-51; atty. govt. contracts Dept. Army, 1951-59; with Office of Gen. Counsel, FAA, 1960—, asso. gen. counsel, 1968—. Mem. Yale Law Sch. Alumni Assn., Fed. Bar Assn. (chmn. civil rights com. 1964-66; chmn. govt. contracts com. 1962-64), Scribes, Bar Assn. City N.Y., Beta Sigma Rho. Club: Yale (Washington). Contbr. articles to profl. jours. Home: 6431 Bannockburn Dr Bethesda MD 20034 Office: Fed Aviation Agy Washington DC 20590

BIRNIE, JOSEPH EARLE, banker; b. Greenville, S.C., Nov. 30, 1903; s. James and Annie Curran (Earle) B.; student Washington and Lee U., 1923-24; grad. cum laude, Am. Inst. Banking Sch., Richmond, Va., 1929; grad. Naval Tng. Sch., Quonset Point, R.I., 1943; m. Octavia Norfleet Riley, June 4, 1941; 1 dau., Ada Lea Norfleet (Mrs. Larry M. Dew, Jr.). Clk., Alexander Nat. Bank, St. Petersburg, Fla., 1925-27; clk., later officer Bank of Va., Richmond, 1927-33; exec. sec. and treas. Morris Plan Bankers' Nat. Assn., 1933-38, pres., 1945-46; pres. and dir. Nat. Bank Ga. (formerly Bank of Ga.), Atlanta, 1940—, now chmn. exec. com.; dir. Abbey Internat. Corp., Ga. Internat. Life Ins. Co. Apptd. by FDIC, Washington, as mem. 3-man bd. to examine applicants for FDIC examiners, 1942. Nat. treas. Washington and Lee Univ. Bicentennial. Trustee Met. YMCA, A.R.C., Washington and Lee U., Met. Found. Atlanta; nat. dir. Jr. Achievement, Inc.; trustee Atlanta Art Mus.; hon. life trustee, past pres. Atlanta Tb Assn.; life trustee Atlanta Music Festival Assn.; pres. Atlanta Symphony Orch.; mem. adv. council Furman U. Comdg. officer of Aeronautics Rep. Mid-Western Procurement Dist., U.S. Navy, 1943-44. Recipient commendation from U.S. Navy for meritorious performance of duty, 1946. Mem. Am. Bankers Assn. (v.p. Ga. savs. div. 1940, mem. exec. council 1965-68), Consumer Bankers Assn. (Pres. 1945-47), Newcomen Soc. Am., Soc. Cincinnati, Soc. Colonial Wars in Va., Nat. Alumni Assn. of Washington and Lee U. (1st v.p. 1931), Alumni Assn. of Richmond (pres. 1935), of Atlanta (pres. 1946), Mil. Order World Wars, Ga. State C. of C. (dir.), Sigma Alpha Epsilon, Omicron Delta Kappa. Southern Republican. Episcopalian (vestryman). Clubs: Piedmont Driving, Capital City, The Nine O'Clocks (Atlanta); Commonwealth (Richmond). Contbr. numerous articles on banking subjects to nat. publs. Home: 3130 Habersham Rd Atlanta GA 30305 Office: 34 Peachtree St Atlanta GA 30305

BIRO, CARLOS E., physician. Dir. dept. immunology, dir. anti-viral drug research Instituto Nacional de Cardiologia, Mexico City, Mexico. Address: Instituto Nacional de Cariologia Mexico DF Mexico*

BISH, HUGH WILLIS, supt. schs.; b. Okeene, Okla., Dec. 15, 1911; s. Robert Conrad and Laura (Willis) B.; student Okla. State U., 1930-31; A.B., N.M. Highlands U., 1934, M.A., 1941; m. Marion Elizabeth Knox, Nov. 6, 1937; 1 dau., Billie Ruth (Mrs. Wilson David Fargo). Tchr., Wheatland High Sch., Cameron, N.M., 1934-35; prin. high sch., Nara Visa, N.M., 1935-38, supt. schs., 1938-42; tchr. Lawton (Okla.) Pub. Schs., 1945-46, prin. jr. high sch., 1946-47, prin. high sch., 1947-62, asst. supt. schs., 1962-66, supt. schs., 1966—. vice pres. YMCA, Lawton, 1952—. Served with USNR, 1942-45. Mem. Nat., Lawton edn. assns., Nat., Okla. assns. sch. adminstrs., Assn. Supervision and Curriculum Devel. (state pres. 1965-66), Secondary Sch. Prins. Assn. (state pres. 1954-55), Okla. North Central Assn. (state exec. com. 1964-70), C. of C. (bd. dirs. 1969-70). Mason, Lion (pres. 1956-57). Home: 1008 Kingswood Rd Lawton OK 73501 Office: 753 Fort Sill Blvd Lawton OK 73501

BISHER, JAMES FURMAN, journalist; b. Denton, N.C., Nov. 4, 1918; s. Chisholm and Mamie (Morris) B.; student Furman U., 1934-36; A.B., U. N.C., 1938; children—Roger, James Furman, Monte. Editor, Lumberton (N.C.) Voice, 1938-39; mem. editorial staff High Point (N.C.) Enterprise, 1939-40; reporter, state editor Charlotte (N.C.) News, 1940-42, sports editor, 1946-50; sports editor Atlanta Constn. 1950-57, Atlanta Jour., Sunday Jour.-Constn., 1957—. Vice pres. Bisher Hosiery Mill, Denton; dir. Putt-Putt Golf, Inc., Fayetteville, N.C. Chmn. Ga. chpt. Nat. Tb Christmas Seal Campaign, 1961; mem. adv. bd. Salvation Army. Bd. dirs. Ga. Easter Seal Soc., Easter Seal Rehab. Center. Served with USNR, 1943-46. Recipient Ga. A.P. Sports-Writing awards, 1951, 53-55, 57-59, 61-63, 65-68, 71; Ga. Sportswriter of Yr., 7 times. Mem. Football Writers Assn. Am. (past pres.), Nat. Left-Handers Golf Assn. (dir.), Baseball Writers Assn. Am. (chpt. chmn.), Gridiron Soc., Chi Psi. Presbyn. Clubs: Atlanta County; Druid Hills Golf; Capital City; Jockey (Miami, Fla.). Author: With A Southern Exposure, 1962 (Grantland Rice prize); Miracle in Atlanta; Strange But True Baseball Stories; Aaron, RF; Arnold Palmer—The Golden Year. Contbr. to popular mags., anthologies. Moderator TV show, Football Rev. Home: 3135 Rilman Rd NW Atlanta GA 30327 Office: 10 Forsyth St Atlanta GA 30303

BISHOP, BARRY LEE, journalist; b. Floresville, Tex., Oct. 7, 1906; s. Charles Milton and Zella (Riggs) B.; student U. Tex., 1923-28; m. Josephine Foester, Dec. 1, 1929 1 son, Barry Louis (dec.). Asst. state house corr. Dallas Morning News, 1926-29, reporter, staff writer, corr. specializing city planning and racial integration progress, 1929-45, Latin Am. corr., 1945-50, staff corr. Washington bur., 1951; press-information officer Am. embassy, Mexico City, 1951-54; chief Latin Am. press service USIA, Washington, 1955-58; information officer Am. embassy, Buenos Aires, Argentina, 1958-59; pub. affairs officer-attache Am. embassy, La Paz, Bolivia, 1959-62; attache Am. embassy, Madrid, Spain, 1962; Latin Am. corr. Chgo. Tribune Press Service, Mexico City, 1967—. Mem. Sigma Delta Chi. Mason (Shriner). Clubs: Overseas Press (N.Y.C.); Nat. Press (Washington); American (Buenos Aires). Office: care Chgo Tribune Press Service 435 N Michigan Av Chicago IL 60611 also Paseo de la Reforma 46-6 Mexico City 1 Mexico

BISHOP, CARRIE LEE (MRS. JOHN G. BISHOP), ednl. adminstr.; b. Port Lavaca, Tex., May 10, 1907; d. James Monroe and Ida (Dobbins) Carruth; student Tex. Tech. Coll., 1925-26, B.S., 1941, M.S., 1949; m. John Gaston Bishop, July 24, 1928; children—Cara Juan (Mrs. Jack Schuster), James Gaston. Tchr. elementary edn., Fairview, Tex., 1927-28, Circle Back, Tex., 1936-37, Longview, Tex., 1937-40; vocational home econs. tchr. Roaring Springs, Tex., 1941-42; Seagraves, Tex., 1942-45, Lubbock, Tex., 1945-50; counselor Lubbock pub. schs. and housing authority, 1945-49; area supr. vocational home econs. Tex. Edn. Agy., Kingsville, 1950-51; dean women Tex. Coll. Arts and Industries, 1951—. Mem. exec. com. Kenedy Kleberg County Tb Assn., 1951-56. Mem. Am. Assn. U. Women (local pres. 1954-56, mem. state legislative com. 1956-57), Nat., Tex. (sec. 1956-58) assns. women deans and counselors, Tex. Tchrs. Assn., Delta Kappa Gamma. Baptist. Contbr. to Forecast for Home Economics. Home: 526 William St Kingsville TX 78363

BISHOP, COWAN EDWARD, profl. engr.; b. Harlan, Ky., May 4, 1922; s. Cowan Calhoun and Sue (Garrett) B.; B.Arch. Engring., Va. Polytech. Inst., 1948; B.C.E., Auburn U., 1952; m. Virginia Ruth Owens, Aug. 31, 1952; children—Garrett, Dane, Stephen, Elizabeth. Constrn. laborer Jack Kelly, contractor, Harlan, Ky., 1940; jr. engr., acting project engr. Reynolds Alloys Co., Listerhill, Ala., 1949-51; office engr. Vinson & Co., Architects and Engrs., Atlanta, 1952-53; planning engr. Municipal Planning Bd., Atlanta, 1953; hydraulic engr. Jacksonville Dist., U.S. Corps of Engrs., Fla., 1954; design engr., project engr. Reynolds, Smith & Hills, Cons. Engrs., Jacksonville, Fla., 1954-56; civil engr. Brown Engring. Co., Huntsville, Ala., 1957; constrn. engr. Dow Chem. Co., Freeport, Tex., 1957-58; asso. research engr. Boeing Airplane Co., Wichita, Kan., 1958; cons. engr., Lake Jackson, Tex., 1959; civil engr. Bowaters Engring. & Devel., Calhoun, Tenn., 1959-62; project engr., constrn. project engr., activation team chmn. Boeing Co., New Orleans 1962-64; sr. constrn. supr. Dow Chem. Co., Corp. Engring. and Constrn. Services, Freeport, Tex., 1964-67; sr. project engr. Atlas Chem. Industries Inc., Chattanooga, 1967-70; cons. engr., Chattanogga, 1970—. Active Boy Scouts Am. Served with AUS, 1942-46. Registered profl. engr. Tenn., Ga., Fla., Tex., Ohio. Mem. Am. Soc. C.E., Chattanooga Engrs. Club, Nat. Rifle Assn. Home: 1714 Clayton Av Chattanooga TN 37412 Office: PO Box 2593 Chattanooga TN 37407

BISHOP, GEORGE WILLIAMS, III, bus. exec.; b. Williamson, W.Va., May 11, 1936; s. George Williams and Dorothy (Scott) B.; student Va. Mil. Inst., 1955-58; B.E.E., U. Va., 1959; m. Harriett Ann Kaminsky, Dec. 29, 1962; children—George Williams IV, Dale Scott. Gen. mgr. Elec. div. Buchanan-Williamson Supply Co., Grundy, Va., 1962-64, exec. v.p., 1964—, also dir.; v.p., gen. mgr. Wingfield & Hundley, Inc., Richmond, Va., 1966-69, pres., 1969—, also chmn. bd. dirs.; dir. Grundy Coal & Dock Corp. Served to capt. USAF, 1959-62. Presbyn. Rotarian (local pres. 1965-66). Home: 2845 Bicknell Rd Richmond VA 23235 Office: S 17th Richmond VA 23205

BISHOP, JIM, author; b. Jersey City, Nov. 21, 1907; s. John Michael and Jenny Josephine (Tier) B.; student Drakes Secretarial Coll., 1923; Litt.D., St. Bonaventure U., 1958, Belmont Abbey Coll., 1968; m. Elinor Margaret Dunning, June 14, 1930 (dec. Oct. 1957); children—Virginia Lee, Gayle Peggy; m. 2d, Elizabeth Kelly Stone, May 1961; children—Karen, Kathleen. Copy boy N.Y. News, 1929-30; reporter N.Y. Daily Mirror, 1930-32, asst. to Mark Hellinger, columnist, 1932-34, rewrite man feature writer Daily Mirror, 1934-43; asso. editor Colliers mag., 1943-44, war editor, 1944-45; exec. editor Liberty mag., 1945-47; dir. lit. dept. Music Corp. Am., 1947-49; founding editor Gold Medal Books, 1949-51; exec. editor Catholic Digest, founding editor Catholic Digest Book Club, 1954-55. Author: The Glass Crutch, 1945; The Mark Hellinger Story, 1952; Parish Priest, 1953; The Girl in Poison Cottage, 1953; The Making of a Priest, 1954; The Day Lincoln Was Shot, 1955; The Golden Ham, 1956; The Day Christ Died, 1957; Go With God, 1958; Some of My Very Best; 1960; The Day Christ Was Born, 1960; The Murder Trial of Judge Peel, 1962; Honeymoon Diary, 1963; A Day in the Life of President Kennedy, 1964; Jim Bishop: Reporter, 1965; A Day in the Life of President Johnson, 1967; The Day Kennedy was Shot, 1968; The Days of Martin Luther King, Jr., 1971. Columnist, King Features Syndicate. Contbr. to nat. mags. Home: Golden Isles Hallandale FL 33009

BISHOP, MARGARET STEARNS (MRS. BARTON PHELPS BISHOP), educator, author; b. Lewiston, Mich., June 21, 1906; d. Harry Lindley and Lizzie (Christman) S.; A.B., U. Mich., 1929, M.S., 1931, Ph.D., 1933; m. Barton Philips Bishop, Aug. 14, 1937; children—Harry Barton, Richard Stearns. Jr. geologist Pure Oil Co., 1929-30, 33-35, asst. to chief geologist, 1935-38, cons., 1938-53; asst. prof. U. Houston, 1953-57, asso. prof., 1957-65, prof., 1965-71, prof. emerita, 1971—; dir. Earth Sci. Insts., 1965-71. Mem. Am. Assn. Petroleum Geologists, Nat. Assn. Geology Tchrs., Geol. Soc. Am., Tex. Acad. Sci., Houston Geol. Soc. Phi Beta Kappa, Sigma Xi, Phi Kappa Phi. Author: Subsurface Mapping, 1960; Focus on Earth Science, 1965. Home: A125 17th St N Texas City TX 77590

BISHOP, ROBERT JEFFERSON, lawyer, public relations cons, state ofcl.; b. Bishopville, Fla., Mar. 25, 1913; s. Stephen Ward and Archie (Mills) B.; B.S.A., U. Fla., 1935, LL.B., 1943; m. Edna Yacobian, June 1, 1939; children—Carol (Mrs. John J. Phifer), Judith (Mrs. Errol L. Greene). Admitted to Fla. bar, 1943, practiced law before state and fed. cts., 1943—; pub. relations counsel to chain store industry, Fla., 1944-48; exec. sec. Lawyers Title Guaranty Fund, 1948-49; exec. dir. Atlantic Union Com., Inc., 1949-50, bd. govs., 1950; dir. consumer services State of Fla.; exec. sec. Fla. Consumers Council. Chmn. Fla. Scholarship and Loan Commn. Designated One of 5 Outstanding Young Men in Fla., 1948. Mem. Am. Bar Assn., Fla. Bar, Am. Judicature Soc., Am. Acad. Polit. Sci., Tallahassee Jr., Fla. Jr. (pres. 1946-47), U.S. Jr. (v.p. 1947-48), Internat. Jr. (treas. 1948-49) chambers commerce, U. Fla. Alumni Assn. (v.p. 1943-52, pres., 1952), Fla. Blue Key, Alpha Gamma Rho. Alpha Zeta, Phi Alpha Delta. Democrat. Episcopalian. Mason (Shriner), Elk. Club: Rio Pinar Country. Home: 1215 Munster Av Orlando FL 32803 Office: State Capitol Tallahassee FL 32304

BISHOP, THOMAS RAY, mech. engr.; b. Hutchinson, Kan., Oct. 26, 1925; s. Orren E. and Myrtle (Dale) Bish; student California (Pa.) State Tchrs. Coll., 1947-48; B.S., U. Houston, 1953; postgrad. U. Wash., 1960-61; m. Mary Lou Nesmith, Sept. 1, 1951 children—Thomas Ray II, Frances Joann. Research engr. Boeing Co., Seattle, 1953-69, research engr. Apollo program, 1964-69; asst. chief engr. Product div. Bowen Tools, Inc., Houston, 1969—; pres. Bishop & Assos., mech. engring. consultants, Houston, 1970—. Precinct committeeman King County Democratic Com., 1960. Served with USMCR, 1944-46. Decorated Purple Heart; named Engr. of Year, Boeing Aerospace Co., 1966. Registered profl. engr., Ala., La., Tex. Mem. Tex. Soc. Profl. Engrs. Democrat. Unitarian. Mason. Contbr. articles to profl. jours. Home: 8411 Delwin St Houston TX 77034 Office: 2429 Crockett St Houston TX 77001

BISHOP, VANCE DAVIS, dentist; b. Ocoee, Tenn., Nov. 6, 1924; s. John and Gussie (Wilson) B.; student U. Chattanooga, 1946-49; D.D.S., U. Tenn., 1953; m. Isabel Gordo, Oct. 22, 1949. Dentist, VA Hosp., Bay Pines, Fla., 1953-55; pvt. practice dentistry, St. Petersburg, Fla., 1955—. Pres. Re-Bi Corp.; partner Club Redington Trust, Howard Johnson Restaurant, Econo Motel Corp. Served with USCG, 1942-45; ETO. Mem. Am. Dental Assn., Internat., Fla., Tenn., West Coast of Fla., Pinellas County dental socs., Com. 100, C. of C., Pinellas County Med. Soc., Pi Kappa Alpha, Delta Sigma Delta. Clubs: Quarterback; St. Petersburg (Fla.) Yacht; Racquet (Miami); Circus Saints and Sinners. Home: 1234 Park St N St Petersburg FL 33710 Office: 5922 9th Av N St Petersburg FL 33710

BISHOP, WILLIAM ERNEST, constrn. co. exec.; b. Melrose, Mass., July 24, 1910; s. Jerden Everett and Annie Blanche (Quimby) B.; B.S., Northeastern U., 1934; m. Kathryn M. Lane, Jan. 28, 1944; children—William L., Jerden A., Michael D., Thomas D., Kathryn A. Constrn. engr. Tidewater Constrn. Co., Norfolk, Va., 1935-46; dist. mgr. Texas Constrn. Co., Dallas, 1946-52; v.p., partner Gulf States Marine Constrn. Co., Beaumont, Tex., 1952-65; v.p. Tellepsen Constrn. Co., Houston, 1965, also dir. Instl. dir. Neclies council Boy Scouts Am., 1961-64; mgr. Little League, Beaumont, 1962. Served with USNR, 1942-46. Mem. Am. Soc. C.E. (state bd. dirs. 1962, 64). Methodist. Home: 931 Wycliffe Dr Houston TX 77024 Office: 1710 Telephone Rd Houston TX 77001

BISSELL, CHARLES OVERMAN, editorial cartoonist; b. Nashville, June 29, 1908; s. Charles Jay and Adelaide (Overman) B.; ed. pub. schs.; m. Lolita Hannah, June 5, 1943; 1 son, Charles William. Lithographic artist, 1924-45; mem. staff Nashville Tennessean, 1943—, art dir. Sunday mag., 1945-70, editorial cartoonist, 1943—. Recipient Cartoon award Nat. Headliners Club, 1963. Distinguished Service award Sigma Delta Chi, 1964; Pub. Service award Nat. Safety Council, 1966. Mem. Assn. Am. Editorial Cartoonists, Nat. Cartoonist Soc. Creator cartoon feature Bissell's Brave New World, 1962. Home: 4221 Farrar Av Nashville TN 37215 Office: 1100 Broadway Nashville TN 37202

BISSO, LOUIS CLARENCE, civil engr.; b. New Orleans, Oct. 3, 1915; s. Alexander Louis and Elfrida Margaret (Geier) B.; B.C.E., Tulane U., 1936; m. Vivian Clare Cairns, June 16, 1937; children—Sally (Mrs. Louis Linton Morgan), Regel, Ellen (Mrs. John Devereaux O'Reilly III). Resident engr. Farnsworth Constrn. Co., New Orleans, 1936; dir., engr. City Planning Commn., New Orleans, 1936-58; pres. Planning Services, Inc., New Orleans, 1958—; pvt. practice as city planning cons., New Orleans, 1958—. Prof. city planning Archtl. Sch., Tulane U., 1959, prof. Archtl Sch. Urban Design, 1962-64. Recipient Plaque for Outstanding Service, Mayor and City Council New Orleans, 1953; named Architect of Year, Sch. Architecture, Tulane U., 1955. Mem. Am. Pub. Works Assn. (pres. local chpt. 1950-51), Am. Soc. C.E. (mem. bd. city planning div. 1959-60), Am. Soc. Planning Ofcls., Am. Planning and Civic Assn. (dir. 1957-58), Am. Inst. Planners, Tau Beta Pi, Delta Sigma. Club: Valencia (dir. 1959-61) (New Orleans). Home: 5238 Marcia Av New Orleans LA 70124 Office: 1100 Royal St New Orleans LA 70116

BIVINS, DANIEL EUGENE, III, univ. adminstr.; b. Monroe, La., July 14, 1932; s. Daniel Eugene and Carmen (Anderson) B.; B.A., La. State U., 1954, postgrad., 1957, 60; postgrad. U. Chgo., 1955; m. Claudia Faye Atkins, Feb. 5, 1971; children (by previous marriage)—Barbara, Stephan, Lawrence; stepchildren—Jeffrey, Christie. Reporter, Monroe Morning World, 1956, Baton Rouge Morning Adv., 1957; with sales promotion dept. Caterpillar Tractor Co., Peoria, Ill., 1957; sales promotion mgr. Boyce-Harvey Machinery, Inc., Baton Rouge, 1958; asst. dir. alumni affairs La. State U., Baton Rouge, 1959-67, dir. alumni affairs, 1968—; exec. dir. La. State U. Alumni Fedn., 1968—. Bd. dirs. A.R.C., 1965—, chmn. pub. information, 1965-66, treas., 1968-69; bd. dirs. Greater Baton Rouge Safety Council, 1966-69. Served with AUS, 1954-56. Recipient editorial awards Am. Alumni Council, 1962, 64, 65, 67. Mem. Sigma Delta Chi, Omicron Delta Kappa (dir. alumni 1969-71), Phi Kappa Phi, Sigma Chi, Phi Sigma Iota, Pi Alpha Mu. Roman Catholic. Rotarian (chmn. Rotaract 1969-70). Home: 7322 Sheffield Ct Baton Rouge LA 70806

BIXBY, TAMS, III, publishing co. exec.; b. Muskogee, Okla., Dec. 10, 1918; s. Tams and Esther (Bailey) B.; student U. Pa., 1938; m. Oleta Belle Roller, Jan. 21, 1962; 1 son, Tams IV. With Okla. Press Pub. Co., Muskogee, 1946—, gen. mgr., 1955-70, pres., 1970—; with Springfield Newspapers, Inc., 1949—, v.p., 1970—, gen. mgr., 1970—, dir., 1941— dir. Okla. Printing Co., 1942-71, pres., 1970—; dir. Phoenix Improvement Co., 1942—, pres., 1970—; dir. Springfield TV. Co., 1st Nat. Bank. Chmn. Muskogee Met. Area Planning Commn., 1960-63; pres. Muskogee County Polio Found., 1949-59; chmn. Muskogee County chpt. A.R.C., 1956-58, Nat. vice-chmn., 1959; gen. chmn. Muskogee United Fund, 1955; chmn. Urban Renewal, 1969—. Bd. dirs. Okla. Med. Research Found., Okla. Crippled Childrens Soc. Served with USAAF, 1941-45. Mem. A.P., So. Newspaper Pubs. Assn. (dir. 1967-69), Am. Newspaper Pubs. Assn., Muskogee C. of C. (dir. 1961-69), Newcomen Soc., Am. Legion, V.F.W. Republican. Episcopalian (warden 1971-72). Kiwanian. Clubs: Muskogee Country (pres. 1971), Southern Hills Country (Tulsa); Hickory Hills Country (Springfield, Mo.). Home: Route 3 Box 129 Muskogee OK 74401 Office: PO Box 1968 Muskogee OK 74401

BJORK, PAUL ANDREW, hosp. adminstr.; b. Sterling, Ill., Mar. 1, 1919; s. Otto Victor and Julia (Buckley) B.; student Milw. State Tchrs. Coll., 1939-40; B.S., Marquette U., 1949; m. Laura Jean Scovel, Dec. 23, 1942; children—Donald, Laura, Barbara, Cynthia. Asst. adminstr. Kenosha (Wis.) Hosp., 1949-52; adminstr. Community Gen. Hosp., Sterling, Ill., 1952-59; exec. dir. Oak Ridge Hosp. of Methodist Ch., 1959-67, Methodist Hosp., New Orleans, 1967—; v.p. Hosp. Services, Inc., New Orleans. Adj. asst. prof., dept. health services Tulane U. Trustee Tenn. Blue Cross, New Orleans Hosp. Service Assn. (Blue Cross). Trustee Tenn. Edn. and Research Found. Preceptor George Washington U. Served to 1st lt. AUS, 1941-46. Fellow Am. Coll. Hosp. Adminstrs., Royal Soc. Health - Eng.; mem. Tenn. (dir. 1967-69), Ill. (dir. 1957-59), La. (trustee 1970-71) hosp. assns. Home: 13018 Deauville Ct New Orleans LA 70129 Office: 5620 Read Blvd New Orleans LA 70127

BLACK, CHARLES ALVIN, cons. engr.; b. Gainesville, Fla., July 7, 1920; s. Alvin Percy and Lillian Barnes (Russell) B.; B.S., U. Fla., 1947; m. Elizabeth Beck, Sept. 12, 1943; children—Charles Russell, Elizabeth Ann. Pres., Black Labs., Inc., Gainesville, Fla., 1947—; pres. Black, Crow and Eidsness of Ga. v.p. Black, Crow & Eidness, Inc., 1950—, Black & Assos. Land Planning & Engrng. Co., Clearwater, Fla., 1959—, Engrng. Devel. Co., Boca Raton, Fla., 1950—. San. engr. USPHS, 1959—; mem. Fla. Gov.'s Task Force for Water, Minerals and Solid Fuels for Civil. Served AUS, 1944-45. Recipient U.S.A. citation for outstanding pub. service. Registered profl. engr., Fla., Ga., S.C., Ala. Mem. Am. Water Works Assn. (chmn. purification div. 1951, chmn. Fla. sect. 1962; George Warren Fuller award 1961, nat. dir. 1966—, nat. v.p. 1969-70, nat. pres. 1971-72), Cons. Engrs. Council, Cons. Engrs. Fla., Am. Soc. C.E., Royal Soc. Health, Nat. Soc. Profl. Engrs., Am. Pub. Health Assn., Fla. Pollution Control Assn., Soc. Am. Mil. Engrs., Alpha Tau Omega. Episcopalian. Elk. Contbr. articles to profl. jours. Home: 2941 NW 21st Av Gainesville FL 32601 Office: SE 3d St Gainesville FL 32601

BLACK, DAVID LUTHER, research inst. exec.; b. Plainview, Tex., Apr. 3, 1934; s. Mac Truman and Wilma Louise (Bailey) B.; A.B., Baylor U., 1954; postgrad. U. Tex., 1956-59; m. Julia Virginia Williams, Nov. 17, 1956; stepchildren—Barry Snell, Whitfield Snell; 1 son, R. David. Asso. dir. exec. devel. program U. Tex., 1957-59; asst. dir. pub. relations S.W. Research Inst., San Antonio, 1959-64, dir. spl. programs, 1967-72, dir. spl. programs, also asst. to the pres., 1972—; dir. pub. relations HemisFair 1968, 1964-65; pres., David Black & Assos., 1965-67. Cons. UN Indsl. Devel. Orgn., Vienna, Austria, 1971. Bd. dirs. Planned Parenthood Assn., 1966-69, San Antonio Chamber Music Soc. (pres. 1972—), First Repetory Theater, San Antonio. Mem. A.A.A.S., Am. Soc. for Metals, Nat. Assn. Sci. Writers. Episcopalian. Contbr. articles to profl. jours. Home: 213 Allen St San Antonio TX 78209 Office: Box 28510 San Antonio TX 78284

BLACK, EMERSON PAUL, county ofcl.; b. Shamrock, Okla., July 29, 1926; s. Carmon Otis and Essie Opal (Ingram) B.; B.S., Okla. A. and M. U., 1951; M.S., Okla. State U., 1963; m. Wanda Lorene Collum, May 29, 1944; children—Sharon Ann (Mrs. Alan T. McKay), Paula Lorene (Mrs. Frank Riddle), Jay Emerson. Instr. agr. Vets. Class, Dorchester, Neb., 1951; instr. vocational agr., Lewiston, Neb., 1951-53, Alma, Neb., 1953-57; with Okla. State U. Extension Service, 1957—, asso. county Pontotoc County, Ada, 1957-65, county agt., county extension dir. Jefferson County, Waurika, 1965—; founded (with others) Republican Chem. Corp., Alma, 1955, v.p., 1955-56. Sec. Jefferson County Fair Bd., 1965—, County Beef Cattleman's Assn., 1965—. Bd. dirs. United Fund, Waurika, Okla., 1966-67. Served with USAAF, 1945. Mem. Nat., Okla. county agts. assns., Waurika C. of C., Phi Kappa Phi, Alpha Zeta. Methodist (bd. ofcls.). Kiwanian, Lion. Home: 103 E Monroe St Waurike OK 73573 Office: Courthouse Bldg Waurika OK 73573 Died May 2 1968

BLACK, FISCHER SHEFFEY, utility co. exec.; b. Bryson City, N.C., Jan. 27, 1911; s. Stanley Warren and Marianna (Fischer) B.; grad. Riverside Mil. Acad., Gainesville, Ga. 1929; B.S., U. N.C., 1933; LL.B., Nat. U. Law Sch., Washington, 1939, M.P.L., 1939; m. 2d, Elizabeth Clark Zemp, June 20, 1936; children—Fischer S., Janice Blakeney, Louis Engleman. With Nantahala Power & Light Co., Franklin, N.C., 1933-34; eng. Potomac Elec. Power Co., Washington, 1934-42; asst. system planning engr., 1942-46, asst. to pres., 1946-48; editor Elec. World, McGraw-Hill Pub. Co., N.Y.C., 1948-54, pub., editor, 1954-59; v.p. adminstrn. Tampa Electric Co. (Fla.), 1959-61, exec. v.p., 1961-67, pres., 1967-71, vice chmn., 1971—; chmn. bd. Founders Financial Corp., George Thompson Corp.; dir. First Equity Financial Corp., Registered profl. engr., Va. Mem. I.E.E.E., Beta Theta Pi, Alpha Sigma Phi, Delta Theta Phi. Presbyn. Rotarian. Clubs: Palma Ceia Golf; University; Tampa Yacht and Country. Home: 930 Golfview Av Tampa FL 33609 Office: 111 N Dale Mabry Highway Tampa FL 33609

BLACK, GEORGE WASHINGTON, civil engr.; b. Giddings, Tex., Mar. 6, 1917; s. George W. and Mary (Dodd) B.; B.S. in Civil Engring., U. Tex., 1951; m. Opal House, Oct. 20, 1946; children—Beth Ann, Patrick. Insp., Tex. Hwy. Dept., Giddings, 1934-39, party chief, Austin, 1940-42, sr. resident engr., 1946-48, supervising resident engr., Fort Worth, 1951-59, civil engr., Stephenville, Tex., 1959—. Active Boy Scouts Am. Served with USNR, 1942-46. Recipient Safety award Tex. Hwy. Dept., 1964; Community Improvement award Dublin (Tex.) C. OF C., 1966. Registered profl. engr., Tex. Mem. Tex. Soc. Profl. Engrs. (edn. com. 1968); Stephenville C. of C. (dir. 1968), Soc. Profl. Engrs., Tex. Soc. Registered Pub. Surveyors, Tex. Pub. Employees (pres. Ft. Worth chpt. 1955). Baptist (chmn. bd. deacons 1967). Mason, Rotarian (pres. 1972). Home: 1271 Wildwood Dr Stephenville TX 76401 Office: Morgan Mill Rd Stephenville TX 76401

BLACK, GLADYS CHRISTINE WILLIAMS, lawyer; b. Spencer County, Ky., June 30, 1921; d. Amos Snider and Edith (Snider) Williams; J.D., U. Louisville, 1942; m. David M. Black, May 29, 1963 (dec. Mar. 1971). Admitted to Ky. bar, 1941, U.S. Supreme Ct. bar, 1951; city atty. Taylorsville, Ky., 1944-60; atty. Spencer County Flood-Wall Dist. 1, Taylorsville, 1958-63; county atty. Spencer County, 1962—. Mem. Ky. Commn. on Children and Youth, 1969—. Mem. Ky. (mem. dist. ho. dels.), Am. bar assns., Internat., Nat. assns. women lawyers, Am. Judicature Soc., Acad. Politics and Sci., Internat. Platform Assn., Bus. and Profl. Women's Clubs (pres. Spencer County 1963-64). Home: Taylorsville KY 40071 Office: Box 337 Taylorsville KY 40071

BLACK, INA GRIFFITH, pharmacist, educator; b. Mulvane, Kan., Jan. 30, 1906; d. George Clarence and Pearl (Shade) Griffith; Ph.C., U. Okla., 1927, B.S., 1930, M.S., 1931; m. Joseph Brundidge Black, Nov. 8, 1944 (dec. June 1966). Tchr. Sch. Pharmacy, U. Okla., Norman, 1929-44; pharmacist Liberty Drug Store, Chickasha, Okla., 1945-50, Owl Pharmacy, Chickasha, 1950-54, Green's Prescription Shop, Chickasha, 1954-61; asso. prof. pharmacy Southwestern State Coll. Sch. Pharmacy, Weatherford, 1961—, asso. dean Sch. Pharmacy, 1970—. Co-chmn. pharmacists fund-raising campaign for Okla. Med. Research, 1952. Recipient award for service to pharmacy Okla. U. Alumni Assn., 1959, Grad. award Kappa Psi. Mem. Okla. Pharm. Assn. (exec. council), P.E.O., Sigma Xi, Rho Chi (past nat. sec.), Iota Sigma Pi, Phi Sigma, Lambda Kappa Sigma, Alpha Xi Delta. Methodist (ofcl. bd.). Contbr. articles to profl. jours. Home: 715 Eureka St Weatherford OK 73096

BLACK, JACK ELLIOTT, banker; b. Norman, Okla., Nov. 6, 1921; s. Herman Eugene and Lela Bell (Jack) B.; B.S., U. Okla., 1949; postgrad. So. Meth. U., summer 1968, 69, 70; m. Claudia Mae Jones, Apr. 1, 1944; 1 dau., Sally Lou. Owner, mgr. Finance Co., Norman, Okla., 1952-64; pres., chief exec. officer Am. Exchange Bank & Trust Co., Norman, 1964—, also dir.; dir. Am. Exchange Center Corp., Colonial Estates. Bd. mem. Okla. Banking Commn., 1969—. Chmn. county chpt. A.R.C., 1965-68; mem. hosp. health and planning exec. com. Oklahoma Met. Area, 1969—; mem. Okla. U. Alumni Devel. Fund Bd., 1970—; county rep. Frontiers of Sci., 1969—; mem. adv. bd. U. Okla. Sch. Geology and Geophysics, 1971—; mem. vis. com. U. Okla. Sch. Bus., 1969—. Served with USAAF, 1943-45, USAF, 1951-52. Mem. Conf. State Bank Suprs. (mem. adv. council 1971—), Okla. Assn. State Banks (pres. 1969), Norman C. of C. (pres. 1964). Mason (Shriner), Lion (pres. 1962). Home: 2438 Smoking Oak Rd Norman OK 73069 Office: Box BB Norman OK 73069

BLACK, JAMES HAY, educator; b. Pitts., Aug. 14, 1921; s. Alexander and Ruth (Hay) B.; A.B., Cornell U., 1943; B.S., U. Pitts., 1948, M.S., 1949, Ph.D., 1954; hon. alumnus Carnegie-Mellon U., 1954; m. Mary Lucretia Garland, Feb. 4, 1950; children—Ruth Hay (Mrs. Charles Linden Vess), Alexander Chisholm, Patricia Anne. Research chemist Koppers Co., Inc., Pitts., 1943; instr. U. Pitts., 1950-52; fellow Mellon Inst. Indsl. Research, Pitts., 1952-54; asst. project engr. Standard Oil Co., Whiting, Ind., 1954-55; sr. technologist, supervising technologist U.S. Steel Corp., Monroeville, Pa., 1955-62; prof. chem. engring., head dept. U. Ala., 1962—. Cons. chem. engr. various cos. and govt. agys. including Tuscaloosa (Ala.) Environmental Quality Control Com., 1970—. Mem. Nat. Air Pollution Techniques Adv. Com., Dept. Health Edn. and Welfare, Washington, 1968-69; mem. tech. panel U.S. Office Coal Research, Washington. Served to 1st lt. AUS, 1943-46. Registered profl. engr., Pa., Ala. Mem. Am. Chem. Soc., Am. Inst. Chemists, Am. Inst. Chem. Engrs., Am. Assn. Cost Engrs. (exec. sec. 1964-70, bd. dirs. 1963-64), Soc. History of Tech. Sigma Xi, Sigma Tau, Phi Lambda Upsilon, Tau Beta Pi, Omega Chi Epsilon. Episcopalian. Clubs: Tuscaloosa (Ala.) Racquet, University (Tuscaloosa). Home: 96 Arcadia Dr Tuscaloosa AL 35401 Office: PO Box 6312 University AL 35486

BLACK, JOHN LARRY, educator; b. McKenzie, Tenn., Apr. 16, 1942; s. Hulon Thompson and Maggie Lois (Rucker) B.; B.S., U. Tenn., 1964, M.S., 1965, Ph.D. (Nat. Defense Edn. Act fellow), 1967; m. Carey Jeanne Duncan, June 2, 1963; 1 dau., Robyn Valerie. Asst. prof. biology Union U., Jackson, Tenn., 1967-68; asst. prof. chemistry Jackson State Community Coll., 1968-70; prof. biology, chmn. div. sci. and math. Bethel Coll., McKenzie, 1970—. Chmn., Jackson State Community Coll. Faculty Council, 1968-69. Mem. Tenn. Acad. Sci., Alpha Gamma Rho, Gamma Sigma Delta, Omicron Delta Kappa, Alpha Zeta. Home: Route 2 McKenzie TN 38201

BLACK, KENNETH, JR., coll. adminstr.; b. Norfolk, Va., Jan. 30, 1925; s. Kenneth and Margaret (Wolf) B.; A.B., U.N.C., 1948, M.S., 1951; Ph.D., (S.S. Huebner Found. for Ins. Edn. fellow), U. Pa., 1953; m. Mabel Llewellyn Folger, Sept. 20, 1948; children—Kenneth III, Kathryn Anne. Partner Colonial Ins. Agy., Chapel Hill, N.C., 1948-50; instr. U. Pa., 1952-53; chmn. ins. dept. Ga. State U., Atlanta, 1953-69, Regents' prof. ins., 1959—, dean Sch. Bus. Adminstrn., 1969—. Dir. N.Am. Reassurance Co., N.Am. Reins. Corp., U.S. Life Ins. Co. Trustee, Griffith Found. for Ins. Edn.; trustee, exec. dir. Ednl. Found., Inc., Harold T. Dillon Found.; bd. govs. Internat. Ins. Seminars, Inc., 1968—; mem. lay adv. bd. Marist Sch., Atlanta, 1967—. Trustee Village of St. Joseph, Atlanta, 1969—. Served with USNR, 1944-46. Recipient Paul Speicher award Am. Soc. Chartered Life Underwriters, 1958. Mem. Am. (pres. 1964-65), So. (pres. 1968-69) risk and ins. assns., Soc. Chartered Property and Casualty Underwriters (regional v.p. 1960-61), Am. Soc. Chartered Life Underwriters, So. Econ. Assn., Ins. Library Assn. Atlanta (mem. exec. com. 1953—), Ga. State U. Athletic Assn. (trustee 1965—), Order Golden Fleece, Phi Beta Kappa, Beta Gamma Sigma, Omicron Delta Kappa, Alpha Kappa Psi. Author: Group Annuities, 1955; (with S. S. Huebner) Property Insurance, 1957; (with G. Hugh Russell) Human Behavior, 1962, Human Behavior and Life Insurance, 1963, Human Behavior and Property and Liability Insurance, 1964; Human Behavior in Business, 1972; (with Jack C. Keir and Sterling Surrey) Cases in Life Insurance, 1965; (with S.S. Huebner and Robert S. Cline) Property and Liability Insurance, 1968; (with S.S. Huebner) Life Insurance, 1972. Editor: Jour. Am. Soc. Chartered Life Underwriters, 1959—; editor ins. series Appleton-Century-Crofts, Inc., 1959—. Home: 2 Hanover West Ct NW Atlanta GA 30327 Office: 33 Gilmer St SE Atlanta GA 30303

BLACK, MALCOLM HILL, ex-hosp. adminstr., reporter; b. Glasgow, Ky., May 7, 1905; s. James and Eya (Redford) B.; grad. high sch.; m. Dorothy Mae Layne, Oct. 2, 1945. Police reporter, sports scribe Louisville Herald, 1922-26; reporter Courier-Jour., 1926-31; various journalistic positions Glasgow Times, 1935-49, Todd County Standard, Elkton, Ky., 1949-50; contbr. Stars and Stripes, 1944-45; bus. mgr. dist. 6, Ky. Tb Hosp., Glasgow, 1950-57, adminstr., 1957-68, ret., 1968; now newspaper reporter. Head Barren County chpt. fund drive A.R.C., 1946. Organizer, past pres. Barren County Young Men's Democratic Club, 1935; campaign chmn.; asst. county dir. F.D. Roosevelt campaign. Served with Signal Corps, AUS, 1942-45. Commd. Ky. col., 1955; Adm. of Ky. Waterways, 1967; named Boss of Year, Glasgow Bus. and Profl. Womans Club, 1966, Glasgow Jr. C. of C., 1969; recipient Fellow Am. Coll. Hosp. Adminstr.; mem. Ky. Hosp. Assn. (life, trustee 1958-60, pres. 1960-61, Distinguished Service trophy 1969), Ky. Pub. Health Assn., Glasgow C. of C. (dir.; pres. 1947), Am. Legion, V.F.W., D.A.V., Travelers Protective Assn. (past pres.). Baptist. Contbr. articles to profl. jours. Died June 2, 1972. Home: Sunny Chat Pl Glasgow KY 42141

BLACK, RALPH POWELL, city mgr.; b. Pulaski, Va., July 20, 1921; s. Ernst Glen and Jennie Lewis (Powell) B.; student pub. schs., Nat. Bus. Coll. Internat. City Mgrs. Assn.; m. Mildred Virginia Webster, Aug. 4, 1942; children—Ralph Powell, Susan Patricia, Maud Ellen, Caroline Lee, Kathryn Page. Mgr. Vets. Housing Authority, Roanoke, Va., 1946-50; asst. to city mgr. Alexandria, Va., 1950; city mgr. Jasper, Ala., 1951-53, Athens, Tenn., 1953-55, Aiken, S.C., 1955-58, Dothan, Ala., 1958-60, Florence, S.C., 1960—. Mem. Smoky Mountain council Boy Scouts Am. Served as comdr. USNR. Mem. Christian Bus. Men's Com. (past chmn.), Internat. (past pres.) city mgrs. assns., Am. Acad. Polit. and Social Sci., Nat. Inst. Govt. Purchasing, Municipal Finance Officers Assn., A.I.M., S.C. Municipal League, Jr. C. of C. (past pres.), Res. Officers Assn. U.S. (pres. S.C. dept. 1972-73). Baptist. Rotarian. Mem. editorial bd. Am. Security Council. Home: 1305 Pinckney Av Florence SC 29501 Office: City Hall Florence SC 29501

BLACK, RICHARD LAWRENCE, county ofcl.; b. Butler, Pa., Dec. 22, 1919; s. Chester Leroy and Hazel (Thompson) B.; student U. Pitts., 1949; A.B., Grove City Coll., 1948; M.G.A., U. Pa., 1950; m. Dorothy Isobel Rumbaugh, Aug. 31, 1943; children—Lawrence Elliott, Richard Gregory, Virginia Louise. Asst. to county mgr. Montgomery County, Rockville, Md., 1949-51; village adminstr., Bronxville, N.Y., 1951-54; city adminstr., Englewood, N.J., 1954-61; city mgr. Webster Groves, Mo., 1961-68; county mgr. Charleston County, Charleston, S.C., 1968—. Served to capt. USAAF, 1942-46. Mem. Internat. City Mgmt. Assn., Municipal Finance Officers Assn., Am. Soc. Pub. Adminstrs. Home: 113 Manchester Rd Charleston SC 29407 Office: 2 Courthouse Square Charleston SC 29401

BLACK, ROBERT PERRY, banker; b. Hickman, Ky., Dec. 21, 1927; s. Burwell Perry and Veola (Moore) B.; B.A., U. Va., 1950. M.A., 1951, Ph.D., 1955; m. Mary Rives Ogilvie, Oct. 27, 1951; children—Patty Rives, Robert Perry. Part-time instr. U. Va., 1953-54; research asso. Fed. Res. Bank, Richmond, Va., 1954-55, asso. economist, 1956-58, economist, 1958-60, asst. v.p., 1960-62, v.p., 1962-68, 1st v.p., 1968—; asst. prof. U. Tenn., 1955-56. Lectr. U. Va., 1956-57. Served with AUS, 1946-47. Mem. Am., So. econ. assns., Am., So. finance assns., Am. Inst. Banking, Raven Soc., Robert Morris Assos., Richmond Soc. Financial Analysts, Phi Beta Kappa, Beta Gamma Sigma, Alpha Kappa Psi, Kappa Alpha. Methodist. Clubs: Bond; Focus; Country of Virginia. Author articles and pamphlets. Home: 10 Dahlgren Rd Richmond VA 23233 Office: Fed Res Bank Richmond VA 23261

BLACK, THOMAS CLAIBORNE, physician; b. Lees Summit, Mo., Oct. 5, 1904; s. Thomas Harvey and Margaret Reid (Porter) B.; A.B., U. Kan., 1926, B.S. 1928, M.D., 1930; m. Susan Terbush, Aug. 27, 1932 1 son, Thomas Claiborne. Intern, St. Luke's Hosp., Kansas City, Mo., 1930-31; resident in chest diseases Glen Lake San., Oak Terrace, Minn., 1932; asso. with U. Kan. outpatient chest dept., 1935-36, staff physician Kan. State Tb San., Norton, 1936-39; resident physician Fla. State Tb San., Orlando, 1939- 42, sr. resident, 1943-45, asst. supt., med. dir., 1945-48; supt., med. dir., 1949-51; supt., med. dir. West Okla. State Tb San., Clinton, 1942-43, Montgomery Tb San., 1943; chief. profl. services Lamar VA Hosp., Memphis, 1948-49; chief Tb service VA Hosp., Alexandria, La., 1951-58; chief of staff VA Center, Temple, 1958-64; chief Tb VA Hosp., Houston, 1964-69; asst. prof. dept. medicine Baylor U. Fellow Am. Geriatrics Soc., Am. Coll. Chest Physicians (charter); mem. Am. Fla., Orange County med. assns., Am. Thoracic Soc., Am. Coll. Hosp. Adminstrs., So. Tb Assn., Tex. Tb Assn., S.A.R., Delta Chi, Phi Chi. Presbyn., Mason (32 deg.). Contbr. numerous articles to profl. jours. Home: 2 E Xavier Temple TX 76501

BLACKARD, WILLIAM GRIFFITH, physician; b. Balt., July 14, 1933; s. Embree Hoss and Margaret Lounsbury (Griffith) B.; M.D., Duke, 1957; m. Attelia Shealy, Oct. 1, 1960; children—Harriet Attelia, William Griffith, Kirland Lounsbury. Intern, N.Y. Hosp., N.Y.C., 1957-58, resident, 1958-59; resident fellow Duke Med. Center, 1960-64; instr. La. State U. Med. Center, New Orleans, 1964-65, asst. prof., 1965-68, asso. prof., 1968-72, prof., 1972-—. Vis. prof U. Geneva, 1971-72. Served with USPHS, 1961-63. Markle Found. scholar, 1968-—; Sinsheimer Found. award, 1971-—; NIH fellow, 1971. Mem. Am. Soc. Clin. Investigation, Am. Fedn. Clin. Research., So. Soc. Clin. Investigations, Endocrine Soc., Am. Diabetes Assn., Sigma Xi, Kappa Alpha. New Orleans Lawn Tennis Assn. Methodist. Contbr. articles and reviewer numerous sci. jours. Home: 1309 Cadiz St New Orleans LA 70115

BLACKBIRD, WILLIAM H., justice; b. Coalgate, Okla., May 26, 1894; s. Robert and Agnes (Phillips) B.; student Okla. Sch. Mines, 1914, Okmulgee Law Sch., 1922-27; m. Anne Courtney, 1915; m. 2d, Daisey Hawley, Dec. 1, 1954. County judge, Okmulgee County, Okla., 1933-43, dist. judge, 1943-53; asso. justice Supreme Ct. Okla. 1953, past chief justice. Mem. Okla. Bar Assn. Mason. Home: Okmulgee OK 74447 Office: PO Box 3122 State Capitol Oklahoma City OK 73105

BLACKBURN, BENJAMIN BENTLEY, III, congressman; b. Atlanta, Feb. 14, 1927; s. Benjamin Bentley, Jr. and Sara (Medlock) B.; B.A., U. N.C., 1947; LL.B., Emory U., 1954; m. Mary A. Pandora, 1952; children—Michael, Robert, Kathryn, David. Admitted to Ga. bar, 1954; practiced in Atlanta, 1956-66; mem. staff Atty. Gen. Ga., 1955-56; partner firm Peck, Whaley & Blackburn, 1963-66; mem. 90th-92d congresses from 4th Dist. Ga., 1966-—. Mem. DeKalb County Republican Exec. Com., 1964-67; sec. 4th Congl. Dist. Rep. Exec. Com., 1966-67. Served with USNR, 1944-46, 50-52. Mem. Am. Ga., Atlanta bar assns., Phi Delta Phi. Episcopalian. Optimist. Club: Lawyers (Atlanta). Home: 9603 Hillridge Dr Kensington MD 20795 Office: Longworth House Office Bldg Washington DC 20515

BLACKBURN, CHARLES LEE, petroleum co. exec.; b. Cushing, Okla., Jan. 9, 1928; s. Sam and Lilliam (Beall) B.; B.S. in Engring. Physics, U. Okla., 1952; m. Jo Ann Benito, Aug. 20, 1950; children—Kern Andrew, Alan Jeffrey. With Shell Oil Co., Houston, New Orleans, 1952-—, gen. mgr., New Orleans, 1968-70, v.p. exploration and prodn., 1970-—. Mem. exec. com. New Orleans Philharmonic Soc., 1971-—; mem. adv. council Grad. Sch. Bus., Tulane U., New Orleans, 1970-—. Vice pres., trustee pub. broadcasting sta. WYES-TV, New Orleans, 1971-—; bd. dirs. Adult Edn. Center, New Orleans, pres., 1971. Mem. Mid-Continent Oil and Gas Assn. (bd. dirs.), Soc. Petroleum Engrs., Petroleum Club of New Orleans. Methodist. Clubs: New Orleans Country, International House, Plimsoll (New Orleans). Home: 412 Country Club Dr New Orleans LA 70124 Office: PO Box 60193 New Orleans LA 70160

BLACKBURN, CHARLES RALPH, II, mgmt. scientist; B.S., Tulane U., 1962, M.B.A., 1964; m. Joanett Rogers, Dec. 22, 1961; children—Charles Ralph III, John Joseph. Systems engr. IBM, New Orleans, 1964-65; project dir. computer system research, instr. Tulane U., New Orleans, 1965-68; sr. operations research analyst Atlantic Richfield, Dallas, 1968-69, project leader, 1969-—. Vis. indsl. asst. prof. So. Methodist U., 1970-—. Recipient Outstanding Contbn. award of systems engring. IBM, 1965. Mem. Operations Research Soc. Am., Assn. for Computing Machinery, Inst. Mgmt. Scis., Math. Programming Soc., Pi Mu Epsilon. Baptist (deacon 1968-—). Home: 7620 LaVerdura Dr Dallas TX 75240 Office: PO Box 2819 Dallas TX 75221

BLACKBURN, DAVID RICHARD, banker; b. Britton, Tex., Mar. 6, 1914; s. Dave E. and Zola Mae Blackburn; ed. pub. schs., Tex.; m. Carmelita Kilp, Dec. 1, 1924. Engaged in constrn. work, 1932-34; bookkeeper Groce Parrish Wholesale Grocery Co., 1934-36; with Victoria Bank & Trust Co. (Tex.), 1936-—, now pres., dir.; dir. First State Bank & Trust Co., Pt. Lavaca, Tex., Jackson County State Bank, Edna, Tex., Bank Southwest N.A., Houston. Served with AUS, World War II. Mem. Am. (bd. govs.), Tex. (exec. com., past v.p., pres.) bankers assns., Assn. State Chartered Banks Tex. (bd. govs.). Home: Arlington Apts Victoria TX 77901 Office: Victoria Bank & Trust Co PO Box 1698 Victoria TX 77901

BLACKBURN, EUGENIA (MRS. SAMUEL EVERETT BLACKBURN), museum exec.; b. Frankfort, Ky., June 4, 1913; d. Charles Walter and Mary Belle (Taylor) Hay; student Sophie Newcomb Meml. Coll.; B. Design, Tulane U.; m. Samuel Everett Blackburn, June 12, 1937; children—Samuel Everett, James Wier, Robert Lyle, Jacob Taylor, Edmund Taylor, Eugenia Crittenden. Curator, Mus. of Ky. Hist. Soc., Frankfort, 1957-—. Exhibited portraits at Constn. Sq. State Park, Danville, Ky., U.S.S. Daniel Boone; tchr. art classes, Frankfort, pottery classes VA Hosp., Lexington, Ky.; scenic cons. Frankfort Little Theatre, Bd. dirs. Franklin County Fall Festival. Mem. Ky. Arts and Crafts, Ky. Hist. Soc., Frankfort Art Club, Chi Omega. Democrat. Episcopalian. Works include watercolor Old Kentucky Home presented to First Lady U.S., 1964. Home: Route 3 Frankfort KY 40601 Office: Old State House Frankfort KY 40601

BLACKBURN, EULESS BERTRAM, JR., educator; b. Decatur, Tex., Aug. 4, 1919; s. Euless Bertram and Annie (Baughier) B.; student Decatur Bapt. Coll., 1937-39; B.S., N. Tex. State U., 1941; M.Ed., Hardin-Simmons U., 1952; Ed.D., U. Colo., 1962; m. Virginia Scruggs, Nov. 19, 1941; children—Velva Ruth, Bert. Tchr. Blooming Grove (Tex.) Ind. Sch. Dist., 1941-42; elementary prin. Forsan (Tex.) Ind. Sch. Dist., 1942-43; civilian mgr. Post Exchange, Big Spring (Tex.) Bombardier Sch., 1943-46; chief clk. Kimball-Midland (Tex.) Co. 1946-47; prin. supr. Big Spring (Tex.) Ind. Sch. Dist., 1947-49, Ballinger (Tex.) Ind. Sch. Dist., 1949-62; prof. edn. Lamar U., Beaumont, Texas, 1962-69. dean grad. sch., 1969-—. Cons. remedial reading program S. Park Ind. Sch. Dist., Beaumont, 1966-—, Silsbee (Tex.) Ind. Sch. Dist., 1966-—. Mem. Tex. Soc. Coll. Profs. Edn., Tex. Assn. Coll. Tchrs. (chpt. pres. 1967-68), Tex. Elementary Prin. and Suprs. Assn., Tex. Assn. for improvement of Reading, Kappa Delta Pi, Phi Delta Kappa. Home: 6350 Arrowhead Dr Beaumont TX 77707

BLACKBURN, FRANCIS MARION, librarian; b. Akron, O., May 31, 1917; s. Chester A. and Angeline (Schumacher) B.; A.B., Kent State U., 1941, M.A., 1946, M.A. in L.S., 1951; m. Geraldine Springer, Mar. 4, 1941 (dec. Dec. 1962); 1 son, Thomas Scott, m. 2d, Carolyn G. Holmes, Sept. 2, 1968. Proprietor Blackburn's Book Store, Akron, 1948-51; acquisitions librarian Matthews Library, Ariz. State Coll., 1951-53; base librarian Sheppard AFB, Wichita Falls, Tex., 1953-56; asst. to librarian U. Mo. Library, 1956-58, librarian West Tex. State U., Canyon, 1958-—. Mem. Tex. librarians com. for Nat. Library Week, 1960. Served with USAAF, 1942-46. Mem. Am., Southwestern, Tex. (chmn. dist. 1, 1960-62) library assns., Am. Assn. U. Profs. Tex. Assn. Coll. Tchrs. Home: 413 Taylor Lane Canyon TX 79015

BLACKBURN, ROBERT ED, JR., govt. ofcl.; b. Tampa, Fla., Dec. 5, 1912; s. R. Ed. and Mary (Edmundson) B.; ed. U. Fla., U. Tampa; m. Frances Catherine Bishop; 1 dau., Barbara (Mrs. Cook). Mcht., Tampa, 1943-50; real estate broker, 1950-52; spl. agt. Bankers Life Ins. Co., 1965-—; now mem. Fla. Ho. of Reps., chmn. citrus fruit subcom. Mem. Hillsbourough County (Fla.) Port Authority, 1949-52; sheriff, Hillsborough County, 1953-65. Trustee emeritus, past chmn. bd. trustees Fla. Sheriffs Boys Ranch. Mem. Fla. Sheriffs Assn. (hon. life; pres. 1964), Future Farmers Am. (hon. life). Methodist. Address: PO Box 16624 Temple Terrace FL 33617*

BLACKLEDGE, HAROLD JOYCE, hosp. adminstr.; b. Laurel, Miss., Sept. 7, 1927; s. Henry B. and Nellie (Mitchell) B.; student Jones County Jr. Coll., 1948-49; B.S., U. Miss., 1951; postgrad. U. So. Miss., 1964; m. Dorothy Anita Sanders, June 6, 1948; children—Rebecca Ann, Debra Lynn. Pharmacist, Wiggins Drug Co., Pascagoula, Miss., 1951; pharmacist Jones County Community Hosp., Laurel, 1952, purchasing agt., 1953, office mgr., 1954-57, asst. adminstr., 1957-63, adminstr., 1963-67, adminstr. Hancock General Hosp., Bay St. Louis, Miss., 1967-—. Pres., Laurel Safety Council, 1963; chmn. prospect devel. com. Laurel Indsl. Com. of 100, 1966; mem. adv. bd. Hearthside Haven Convalescent and Retirement Home, Laurel, 1964-66; past pres. Laurel Teen Center, Inc., established 1st Poison Control Center in Miss., 1960, Jones County Community Nursing Sch. 1964, Sch. Radiol. Tech., 1965, Practical Nurses Tng. Program, 1965. Bd. dirs. Am. Cancer Soc., Jones County Nurses Scholarship Fund. Served with USMCR, 1945-46. Mem. Am. Coll. Hosp. Adminstrs., Am., Miss. hosp. assns., Miss. Pharm. Assn., Southeastern Miss. Hosp. Council, U. Miss. Alumni Assn., Am. Legion, V.F.W. Lion (pres. 1965-66). Home: 141 Fox Dr Bay St Louis MS 39520 Office: Hancock Gen Hosp 725 Dunbar Av Bay St Louis MS 39520

BLACKMAN, CHARLES FRANKLIN, fgn. service officer; b. Kansas City, Mo., May 20, 1911; s. Charles Franklin and Rae (Wood) B.; grad. Nat War Coll., 1958; m. Martha Kearney, Nov. 15, 1946; children—Barbara, Charles III, Susan, Rebecca, Nan. Editorial staff Springfield (Mo.) Leader, 1934-36, Kansas City Star, 1936-42; U.S. resident officer, Heppenheim and Frankfurt, Germany, 1947-49; govt. ofcl. U.S. High Commn. to Germany, 1949-52; dir. Office German Programs, Dept. State, 1953; dep. pub. affairs officer Am. embassy, Rome, Italy, 1955-57; pub. affairs officer U.S. Mission to Berlin, 1958-62; dir. Berlin task force USIA, Washington, 1962-64, pub. affairs adviser AEC, U.S. Maritime Adminstrn., 1964-66; counselor of embassy Am. embassy, Canberra, 1967-70; chief information and edn. div. Office of Population, AID, 1970-—. Served to capt. USAAF, 1942-46. Mem. Am. Fgn. Service Assn. Clubs: Commonwealth, Refugee (Canberra); Journalists (Sydney); Nat. Press (Washington). Home: 3615 Raymond St Chevy Chase MD 20015 also Honeysuckle Hill Box 123 Three Springs PA 17264 Office: Agency Internat Development Washington DC 20523

BLACKMON, BILLY JACK, bus. exec.; b. Vernon, Tex., Dec. 28, 1927; s. Charlie Culberson and Stella Mae (Shirley) B.; A.A., Odessa Coll., 1950; m. Edith Hilda Hezel, Sept. 4, 1949; children—Mark, Brent, Sherrie, Janie, B'Jaye. Pres., Bob's Casing Crews, Inc., Odessa, Tex., 1955-—; chmn. bd. Emco Machine Works Co., Odessa, 1969-—; pres. Ector County Ranch & Cattle Co., Odessa, 1965-—. Sponsor, Troop 876 Buffalo Trail council Boy Scouts Am., 1964-—. Bd. dirs. Indsl. Founds., 1960-70, pres., 1964. Served with USNR, 1945-47. Baptist. Inventor pipe racker. Home: Route 3 Box 1000 Odessa TX 79760 Office: PO Box 2412 Odessa TX 79760

BLACKMON, CHARLES ROBERT, educator; b. Bee Ridge, Fla., Feb. 17, 1925; s. Nelson Samuel and Oma Grace (Walker) B.; student U. Tampa, 1946-47; B.A., Emory U., 1949, M.Ed., 1950; Ednl. Specialist, U. Fla., 1960, Ed.D., 1962; m. Doris Evelyn Hendry, Sept. 25, 1955; 1 dau., Janet Lynn. Machinist, Newport News Shipbldg. Co. (Va.). 1942-43; editor Decatur (Ga.) News, 1949-50; tchr. social studies jr. high sch., Palmetto, Fla., 1950-55; tchr. social studies Sulphur Springs Jr. High Sch., Tampa, 1955-58; asst. prin. Adams Jr. High Sch., 1958-59; instr. Fla. State U., 1959-61, asst. prof. edn., 1961-64; prin. high sch., Stone Mountain, Ga., 1964-65; asso. prof. edn. U. Southwestern La., 1965-69, prof., 1969-71; asso. prof. edn. La. State U., Baton Rouge, 1971-—. Dir., Center for Lab. Sch. Study, Baton Rouge, 1968-—. Served with USNR, 1943-46. Recipient Achievement award Air Force Assn., Tampa, 1958; Sigma Delta Chi scholar, 1949; So. Fund fellow, 1961. Mem. La. Tchrs. Assn., Assn. Supervision and Curriculum Devel., Am. Assn. Sch. Adminstrs., Soc. Research Adminstrs., Am. Ednl. Research Assn., Am. Assn. U. Profs., Internat. Soc. Ednl. Cons. (founder 1969), Nat. Council Measurement Edn., Nat. Conf. Profs. Ednl. Adminstrn., So. Regional Conf. Ednl. Adminstrn., Nat. Orgn. Legal Problems in Edn., Lab. Sch. Adminstrs. Assn., Order of Red Red Rose, Sigma Pi, Sigma Delta Chi. Democrat. Baptist. Mason (Shriner); mem. Order Eastern Star. Author numerous poems. Editor and contbr.: Selected Paper on Values, 1968; Changing Values and Behaviors, 1969; Laboratory Schools, U.S.A., 1970; Procedures in Educational Research, 5 edits., 1966-71. Contbr. articles to profl. jours. Editor: Fla. Aerospace Newsletter, 1962-64, Fla. AST Newsletter, 1962-64, Nat. Lab. Sch. Adminstrs. Newsletter, 1967-69. Home: 2633 June St Baton Rouge LA 70808

BLACKMON, DON E., sch. adminstr.; b. Calion, Ark., July 7, 1913; s. Orland B. and Laura (Hux) B.; A.B., Henderson State Tchrs. Coll., 1937; M.A., U. Ark., 1940; m. Hester Wylie, Aug. 21, 1937; children—Betty Ann (Mrs. R. Wm. Petty), Lynda Janice. Supt., Cotten (Ark.) Pub. Schs., 1937-41; supt. Dyess (Ark.) Pub. Schs., 1941-46; supt. Wynne (Ark.) Pub. Schs., 1946-52; asst. state commr. edn., Little Rock, 1952-55; supt. Dell (Ark.) Pub. Schs., 1955-59; supt. Pulaski County Schs., Little Rock, 1959-—; pres. Asso. Educators. Mem. Ark. Edn. Assn. (past pres.). Lion. Home: 8711 Cantrell Rd Little Rock AR 72207 Office: County Court House Little Rock AR 72201

BLACKMON, JACK, lawyer; m. Margaret McGlaun; children—Robert, Diane, Debbie. Partner firm North, Blackmon & White, Corpus Christi, Tex.; past pres. Municipal Gas Corp.; sec., treas. NBW Bldg. Corp.; mayor, emeritus City of Corpus Christi. Past pres. region 11 Tex. Municipal League; chmn. Corpus Christie Sister City Com. Pres. bd. trustees U. Corpus Christi. Mem. Res. Officers Assn. (pres. local chpt.), Navy League (judge adv. Corpus Christi), Corpus Christi C. of C. (exec. bd.), Naval Res. Law Co. (exec. officer). Club: Civitan (past gov. Tex. dist., judge adv.). Home: 101 Alta Plaza Corpus Christi TX 78411 Office: 419 N Tancahua St Corpus Christi TX 78401

BLACKMORE, JAMES HERRALL, clergyman, ednl. adminstr.; b. Warsaw, N.C., Feb. 15, 1916; s. Willie Richard and Martha Janie (Sansbury) B.; B.A. cum laude, Wake Forest Coll., 1937; B.D. (Rauschenbusch scholar, Colgate-Rochester scholar), Colgate-Rochester Div. Sch., 1940; postgrad. Duke, 1940-41, U. Ia., 1949; Ph.D., U. Edinburgh (Scotland), 1951; m. Ruth May Lillick, Jan. 26, 1945; children—Julia, John. Dir. religious edn. Parsells Av. Bapt. Ch., Rochester, N.Y., 1938-40; ordained to ministry Baptist Ch., 1940; pastor King (N.C.) Bapt. Ch., 1941-43, Masonboro Bapt. Ch., Wilmington, 1947-49, First Bapt. Ch., Spring Hope, 1951-61; dir. pub. relations Southeastern Bapt. Theol. Sem., Wake Forest, N.C., 1963-69, dir. publs., spl. instr., 1969-—, editor Outlook, sem. mag., 1963-—. Pres. Wilmington Ministerial Conf., 1948-49; moderator Tar River Bapt. Assn., 1960-61; sec. bd. dirs. Bibl. Recorder, 1959-62; chmn. hist. com. Bapt. State Conv., N.C., 1970-72. Served to maj. AUS, 1943-46. Mem. Bapt. Pub. Relations Assn., Kappa Delta Alpha, Chi Eta Tau. Lion. Author: The Cullom Lantern, A Biography of W.R. Cullom, 1963; A Preacher's Temptations, 1966; A Reticle, A Collection of Short Stories and Essays, 1969. Contbr. to various religious and learned jours., also encys. Home: 315 S Wingate St Wake Forest NC 27587

BLACKMUN, HARRY ANDREW, justice U.S. Supreme Ct.; b. Nashville, Ill., Nov. 12, 1908; s. Corwin Manning and Theo H. (Reuter) B.; B.A. summa cum laude, Harvard, 1929, LL.B., 1932; m. Dorothy E. Clark, June 21, 1941; children—Nancy Clark, Sally Ann, Susan Manning. Admitted to Minn. bar, 1932; law clk. for John B. Sanborn, judge 8th circuit, U.S. Ct. of Appeals, St. Paul, 1932-33; asso. Dorsey, Colman, Barker, Scott & Barber, Mpls., 1934-38, jr. partner, 1939-42, gen. partner, 1943-50; instr. St. Paul Coll. Law, 1935-41, U. Minn. Law Sch., 1945-47; resident counsel Mayo Clinic, Mayo Assn., Rochester, 1950-59, mem. sect. adminstrn., 1950-59; judge 8th Cir., U.S. Ct. of Appeals, 1959-70; asso. justice U.S. Supreme Ct., 1970-—. Sec., mem. bd. members Mayo Assn., Rochester, 1953-60; bd. dirs., mem. exec. com. Rochester Methodist Hosp., 1954-70. Trustee Hamline Univ., William Mitchell Coll. Law. Mem. Am., Minn., Olmsted County, 3d Jud. Dist. bar assns., Phi Beta Kappa. Methodist. Clubs: Harvard of Minn. (pres. 1940); Rotary (pres. Rochester 1955-56); Minneapolis, Univ. Rochester. Contbr. profl. articles to legal, med. jours. Office: US Supreme Ct Bldg 1 1st St NS Washington DC 20543

BLACKSTOCK, LEROY, lawyer; b. El Reno, Okla., Apr. 19, 1914; s. Herbert Austin and Ethel Mae (Gwin) B.; grad. Draughon's Bus. Inst., Tulsa, 1933; LL.B., U. Tulsa, 1938; m. Virginia Lee Lowman, Dec. 29, 1939; children—Craig, Priscilla, Birch, Lore, Trena. Admitted to Okla. bar, 1938; practice law, Tulsa, 1941-—; sr. partner firm Blackstock, Joyce & Pollard; with Phillips Petroleum Co., Tulsa, 1933-41, asst. credit mgr., 1939-41. Dir. First Bank, Owasso, 1967-70, 1st Nat. Bank of Tulsa; pres. Gt. Western Investments Trust, Skelley Stadium Corp., Jud. Reform Okla., Tulsa Sci. Center, Inc.; dir., gen. counsel Tulsa Home Builders Assn., 1959-68. Pres., Tulsa County Legal Aid Soc., 1961-62, bd. dirs., 1958-66; pres. bd. dirs. Tulsa County Bar Found., 1968-71; chmn. Citizen's Adv. Com. County Commrs., 1963-66; pres. Tulsa Bapt. Laymen's Corp., 1962-66; mem. Mayor's Adv. Com. Community Problems, 1957-58; mem. Gov.'s Acad. State Govt., 1966-68; pres. Tulsa Campire Council, 1971-72; chmn. U. Tulsa Alumni Loyalty Fund, 1969-70. Bd. dirs. Tulsa County Mental Health Assn., 1963-68, Tulsa Psychiat. Found., 1964-67; mem. nat. adv. council Practising Law Inst. Served with USNR, 1943-46. Recipient Distinguished Citizens award Okla. Psychol. Assn., 1963. Mem. Am. (ho. dels 1965-67, mem. com. nat. coordination of disciplinary enforcement), Okla. (pres. 1966), Tulsa County (pres. 1962; Outstanding Atty. award 1961) bar assns. Republican. Baptist (chmn. deacons 1962, chmn. bldg. com. 1951-66). Clubs: Petroleum, Summit, University. Author: Paper Dolls; Lawyers' Fees. Lectr. law offices econs. and mgmt. Home: 3740 Terwilleger St Tulsa OK 74105 Office: 1304 Petroleum Club Bldg Tulsa OK 74119

BLACKSTOCK, VIRGINIA LEE LOWMAN (MRS. LEROY BLACKSTOCK), civic worker; b. Bixby, Okla., July 2, 1917; d. Joseph Arthur and Winifred (Lundy) Lowman; student Tulsa Coll. Bus., 1935-37; m. Leroy Blackstock, Dec. 29, 1939; children—Vincent Craig, Priscilla Gay (Mrs. Richard S. Kurz), Birch Lee, Lore Anne, Trena Jan. Legal sec. law firm, Tulsa, 1937-41. Chmn. program Internat. Students in Tulsa, 1955-65; mem. Tulsa Council Camp Fire Girls, 1963-66; mem. youth com. Tulsa Philharmonic Soc., 1969-70; now mem. women's assn.; pres. Eliot Elementary P.T.A., 1961-62, Edison High Sch. P.T.A., 1971-72; mem. Tulsa Opera Guild. Co-chmn. Democratic precinct No. 132, 1960-67. Mem. Tulsa County Bar Aux. (pres. 1954-55, sec. 1962-63, chaplain 1966-67). Baptist. Clubs: University, Summit, Petroleum. Home: 3740 Terwilleger Blvd Tulsa OK 74105

BLACKSTON, EWING DEVOE, motel exec.; b. Seneca, S.C., Mar. 22, 1941; s. Eddie Devoe and Ruby Mae (Dyar) B.; student Anderson Jr. Coll., 1960-62; B.S., Erskine Coll., 1964. Mem. mgmt. tng. program S.S. Kresge Co., 1965-67; mgr. Seneconee Motel, Seneca, S.C., 1967-—. Coordinator, Seneca High Sch. Track Field, 1969-71; chmn. judges Miss Seneca Pageant, 1968, 69; mem. Oconee County Tax Appeal Bd., 1971-72. Republican precinct pres., Seneca, 1971-72; county coordinator precincts Watson for Gov., 1970. Mem. Am. Hotel and Motel Assn., S.C. Innkeepers Assn., Seneca C. of C. (mem. banquet com. 1970), Seneca Jr. C. of C. (dir. 1968), Oconee Recreational and Hist. Soc., Erskine Coll. Alumni Assn. (chmn. Seneca area 1968, 70), Phi Beta Lambda. Baptist. Kiwanian. Club: Bobcat (mem. speakers com. for ann. banquet 1968-72). Home: N 4th St Extension Seneca SC 29678 Office: 123 Bypass Seneca SC 29678

BLACKSTONE, WILLIAM CRULL, architect; b. Greenwood, Miss., Apr. 16, 1932; s. Edward Hartwell and Louise Elizabeth (Crull) B.; B.Arch., Tulane U., 1958; m. Neita Lorraine Gose, June 20, 1959; children—William Emory, Elizabeth Hartwell. Designer, architect Curtis & Davis, New Orleans, 1958-64; asso. in charge design Neuhaus & Taylor, Houston, 1964-68; partner Hoff, Blackstone, Strode, Houston, 1968-—. Served with AUS, 1953-55. Mem. Nat. Council Archtl. Registration Bds., A.I.A., Tex. Soc. Architects, Sigma Chi. Episcopalian (vestryman 1970-72). Clubs: Century, Carousel, Petroleum (Houston). Home: 1659 South Blvd Houston TX 77006 Office: 930 Park Tower S 1333 W Loop S Houston TX 77027

BLACKSTONE, WILLIAM THOMAS, educator; b. Augusta, Ga., Dec. 8, 1931; s. Thomas and Katie Curtis (Blackstone) Watson; B.A., Elon Coll., 1953; M.A., Duke, 1955, Ph.D., 1957; m. Norma Jean Tew, Mar. 27, 1954; children— Lisa Brooks, Jeffrey Thomas. Asso. prof. philosophy Elon Coll., 1957-58; asst. prof. philosophy U. Fla., 1958-61; faculty U. Ga., Athens, 1961-—, prof., head dept. philosophy and religion, 1964-—, chmn. div. social scis., 1969-—. Mem. So. Soc. for Philosophy and Psychology (sec.). Author: The Problem of Religious Knowledge, 1963; Frances Hutcheson and Contemporary Ethical Theory, 1964; Education and Ethics, 1968; Concept of Equality, 1969; Meaning and Existence, 1970. Contbr. articles profl. jours. Home: Barnett Shoals Rd Athens GA 30601

BLACKWELDER, CHESTER ARTHUR, apparel mfg. co. exec.; b. nr. Taylorsville, N.C., July 9, 1904; s. Carl Columbus and Emma Mae (Campbell) B.; ed. pub. schs.; m. Ruby Lee Adams, Feb. 23, 1929; 1 dau., Venita Lee (Mrs. Billy Lee Dwiggins). With Cannon Mills, Kannapolis, N.C., 1920-22, Dillon-Vitt Underwear Co., Statesville, N.C., 1926-30; plant supt. McNeer-Dillon Co., Statesville, 1930-32; mgr. Marathon Underwear Co., 1933-36; plant mgr. Carolina Underwear Co., Thomasville, 1937-46; organizer, chief exec. officer Monleigh Garment Co., Thomasville, 1946-48, Mocksville, 1948-—; organizer, chief exec. officer Blackwelder Mfg. Co., Inc., Mocksville, 1956-—, Carolina Mfg. Co., Inc., Mocksville, 1957-—, Piedmont Garment Co., Inc., Harmony, N.C., 1961-—; Harmony Sportswear Co., Inc., Mocksville, 1961-—, B & F Mfg. Co., Inc., Mocksville, 1952-—, Edgewood Shirtmakers Ltd., Mocksville, 1970-—; dir. Branch Banking and Trust Co., Mocksville. Baptist. (trustee 1967-—). Rotarian (pres. 1969-70). Address: Box 808 Mocksville NC 27028

BLACKWELL, ANNA MARGARET THOMPSON (MRS. DAMIAN LEE BLACKWELL, JR.), orgn. exec.; b. Ewing, Ill., Aug. 29, 1905; d. Edmund Lee and Effie (Moss) Thompson; student U. Ala., 1926, Watkins Inst., 1936-37, 38; m. Damian Lee Blackwell, Jr., May 22, 1926 (dec. Jan. 1967); children—Evelyn (Mrs. Marvin E. Loney), Sarah (Mrs. Hollis O. Birdwell), Barbara (Mrs. Harold W. Atkinson). Recreation dir. Morgan County, Somerville, Ala., 1938-41; order office mgr. Sears, Roebuck & Co., Decatur, Ala., 1941-53; cashier White Way Pure Milk Co., Decatur, 1953-57; asso. dir. Morgan County United Fund, Decatur, 1957—. Mem. Community Services Planning Council, 1957—, pres., 1962-63, 67. Mem. Ala. Assn. Retarded Children, Morgan County Assn. for Mental Health, Morgan County Soc. Crippled Children and Adults, Internat. Platform Assn., Am. Bus. Women's Assn. (treas., pres. 1972-73), Wesleyan Service Guild (pres. 1964-68). Methodist. Club: Pilot (treas. Decatur 1971-72). Home: Route 1 Box 294 Somerville AL 35670 Office: PO Box 1058 Decatur AL 35601

BLACKWELL, GORDON WILLIAMS, univ. pres.; b. Timmonsville, S.C., Apr. 27, 1911; s. Benjamin L. and Amelia (Williams) B.; A.B., Furman U., 1932, LL.D., 1958; M.A., U. N.C., 1933, LL.D., 1967; A.M., Harvard, 1937, Ph.D., 1940; D.H.L., Rollins Coll., 1961; LL.D., U. Miami (Fla.), 1964, The Citadel, 1968, William Jewell Coll, 1968; m. Elizabeth Blair Lyles, Aug. 21, 1937; children—Gordon Lyles, Randolph Williams, Elizabeth Blair, Amelia Mayo. Research asst. U. N.C., 1932-33; research N.C. Emergency Relief Adminstrn., 1933-34, W.P.A., 1935-36; fellow Harvard, 1936-37; prof. and head dept. sociology Furman U., Greenville, S.C., 1937-41, pres., 1965—; asso. prof. sociology and research asso. Inst. for Research in Social Science, U. N.C., 1941, study of community understanding in teacher edn. Com. on Tchr. Edn. 1942, dir. Inst. for Research in Social Sci., and research prof. sociology U. N.C., 1944-57, became Kenan prof. sociology, 1955, chancellor Woman's Coll., U. N.C., 1957-60; pres. Fla. State U., 1960-65. Field instr. Columbia, summers, 1939-41, vis. prof., summers 1948, 49. Mem. So. Regional Edn. Bd., 1969—. Staff, Greenville County Council for Community Devel., 1937-41; chief, tng. sect. and community problems sect. Civilian War Services br. Office Civilian Defense, 1942-43; mem. adv. com. on computing activities NSF, 1968-72. Trustee Fla. Presbyn. Coll. Named Greenville Man of Yr., Soc. Advancement Mgmt., 1968. Mem. Am., So. (chmn. com. on research 1946; 1st v.p. 1947), Rural (chmn. com. on research 1945, com. on extension 1948, 49, v.p. 1948) sociol. socs., So. Univ. Conf. (v.p. 1972-73), Assn. So. Baptist Colls. (pres. 1971-72), Am. Assn. U. Profs., Phi Beta Kappa, Phi Kappa Phi, Omicron Delta Kappa, Alpha Phi Omega, Kappa Sigma, Alpha Kappa Delta, Pi Gamma Mu, Alpha Kappa Psi. Baptist. Clubs: Quaternion, Poinsett, Green Valley. Author: (with L.M. Brooks and S.H. Hobbs, Jr.) Church and Community in the South, 1949; (with R.F. Gould) Future Citizens All, 1952; (with G. E. Nicholson) Game Theory and Defense Against Community Disaster, 1954; Addresses of Gordon W. Blackwell, 1965. Dir. of Study of College Teaching of Social Sci. in S., for So. Assn. Colls. and Secondary Schs., 1944-48; dir., editor Studies of So. Resources, for So. Assn. Sci. and Industry, 1943-50; library adv. bd. Air U., 1951-54; editor Social Forces, 1954-57; asst. editor Am. Sociol. Rev., 1946-50; com. on adminstrv. affairs Am. Council on Edn., 1962-63, com. on plans and objectives for higher edn., 1965-67; mem. com. on coll. adminstrn. Am. Assn. Colls., 1965-67; pres. S.C. Assn. Colls., 1968-69; adv. bd. Ency. Internat., 1962-65. Contbr. articles to profl. publs. Home: 68 Kensington Rd Greenville SC 29609

BLACKWELL, LUCY WHITE, govt. ofcl.; b. Jackson, Tenn., Apr. 22, 1912; d. William Francis and Ethel (White) Blackwell; A.B., Lambuth Coll., 1933; postgrad. West Tenn. Bus. Coll., 1934-35. Stenographer Tenn. Emergency Relief Adminstrn., Jackson, 1935; accounting clk. FSA, Jackson, Brownsville, Tenn., 1936-39; stenographer Tenn. Dept. Pub. Welfare, Jackson, 1939-40; clk., interviewer, local office mgr. Tenn. Dept. Employment Security, Jackson, 1940—. Comdr. Am. Cancer Soc., Madison County, Tenn., 1943-54, dist. comdr. West Tenn., 1947-48; rec. sec. Tenn. div., 1954-56, bd. dirs., 1945—, organizer Madison County unit, 1954, pres., 1954-55; bd. dirs. Jackson Community Chest, 1955-57; pres. League Women Voters, 1951. Treas., chmn. bd. trustees Jackson Free Library, 1948-57. Recipient R.E. Womack Alumni Achievement award Lambuth Coll. Alumni Assn., 1956; named Jackson-Madison Woman of Year, 1955. Mem. Internat. Assn. Personnel Emloyment Security (pres. Jackson 1956), Lambuth Coll. Alumni Assn. (pres. 1962-63). Presbyn. Clubs: Pilot (past pres. Jackson, dist. gov. Tenn., internat. dir. exec. com.), Altrusa (chmn.). Home: 166 Russell Rd Jackson TN 38301 Office: 416 E Chester St Jackson TN 38301

BLACKWELL, WILLIAM, lawyer, textile co. exec.; b. Richmond, Va., Oct. 22, 1911; s. Benjamin T. and Lola B. (Gary) B.; B.S., U. Va., 1932; LL.B., U. Richmond, 1935; m. Helen L. Dodd, Apr. 22, 1965. Admitted to Va. bar, 1933; partner firm Shewmake & Gary, Richmond, 1937-70, firm Cutchins, Wallinger, Christian & House, Richmond, 1971—. Vice pres. Brooks Warehouse Corp., 1945—; gen. counsel, asst. sec. Ga. Bonded Fibers, Inc., Newark and Buena Vista, Va., 1954—; sec., gen. counsel Henry W. Woody, Inc., Richmond, 1968—; gen. counsel Overnite Transp. Co., Richmond; instr. U. Richmond, 1947-48. Spl. asst. city atty., Richmond, 1938-39; chmn. Bd. Zoning Appeals, Richmond, 1948-52. Trustee Stonewall Found. Served to capt., AUS, 1942-46. Mem. Am., Richmond (pres. 1961-62), Va. State bar assns., Phi Beta Kappa, Delta Sigma Phi, Delta Theta Phi. Episcopalian. Clubs: Country of Virginia (Richmond); Farmington Country (Charlottesville, Va.). Home: 9300 Cragmont Dr Richmond VA 23229 Office: Mutual Bldg Richmond VA 23219

BLACKWELL, WILLIAM HAYDEN, lawyer; b. Pacolet, S.C., Nov. 12, 1916; s. William Joseph and Eva (Genoble) B.; A.B., Wofford Coll., 1938; LL.B., U. S.C., 1939; m. Helene Hickson Carpenter, Nov. 16, 1946; children—Helene Anne, Elizabeth Hayden. Admitted to S.C. bar, 1939; practiced in Florence, S.C., 1939-41, 46—; mem. firm Wright, Scott, Blackwell & Powers, 1959—. Vice pres., dir. Security Savs. & Loan Assn., Florence, 1967—. Served from pvt. to maj., USAAF, 1942-46. Mem. Am., S.C., Florence bar assns., Jud. Council S.C., C. of C. (pres. 1952), Blue Key, Phi Beta Kappa. Clubs: Kiwanis (pres. 1958), Florence Country (dir., sec. bd. 1966-67). Home: 617 Rosewood Av Florence SC 29501 Office: 234 W Cheves St Florence SC 29501

BLACKWOOD, JAMES RUSSELL, clergyman; b. Columbia, S.C., Apr. 30, 1918; s. Andrew Watterson and Carolyn (Philips) B.; B.A., Coll. Wooster, 1941, D.D., 1965; B.D., Princeton Theol. Sem., 1945, Th.M., 1946; m. Louise Ritter, June 30, 1949; children—Paul John, Philip David, Carolyn Louise. Ordained to ministry Presbyn. Ch., 1945; minister chs., St. Charles, Mo., 1947-52, Coll. of Wooster (O.), 1952-61, Winter Haven, Fla., 1962-70, Siesta Key, Fla., 1970—. Moderator Presbytery of St. Louis U.S., 1949-50, The Presbytery of Wooster, 1955-56, Presbytery of W. Fla., 1967-68. Mem. Mayor's Com. on Human Relations, Winter Haven, Fla., 1963-66. Trustee, Fla. Presbyn. Coll., St. Petersburg. Author: The Soul of Frederick W. Robertson, 1947, The House on College Avenue: The Comptons at Wooster, 1968. Editor: College Talks (Howard F. Lowry), 1969. Address: 317 Givens St Sarasota FL 33581

BLAINEY, KEITH DALE, hosp. adminstr.; b. Anamesa, Ia., Feb. 8, 1937; s. Darrell P. and Evelyn (Thompson) B.; B.S., U. Ia., 1959, M.A., 1961, Ph.D., 1966; m. Joyce Ann Bryan, Dec. 1, 1937; children— Michael Bryan, Steven Price. Instr. program in hosp. adminstrn. U. Ia., 1964-66; asst. prof. Sch. Health Services Adminstrn., U. Ala., Birmingham, 1966-67, dir., 1969, dir. U. Ala. Hosps. and Clinics, 1969—. Cons. Appalachian Regional Commn.; mem. Nat. Adv. Allied Health Professions Council. Trustee Ala. Blue Cross-Blue Shield. Served with USAF, 1964-66. Recipient Leadership award U. Ia. Mem. Am. Hosp. Assn., Assn. Am. Med. Colls., Am. Coll. Hosp. Adminstrs. Am. Pub. Health Assn. Republican. Unitarian. Home: 3009 Sterling Rd Birmingham AL 35213 Office: 619 S 19th St Birmingham AL 35233

BLAIR, BARBARA, educator; b. Gastonia, N.C., Oct. 21, 1926; d. James Luther and Maude (Smith) Blair; B.A., Agnes Scott Coll., 1948; M.S., U. Tenn., 1953, Ph.D., 1956. Lab. analyst Union Carbide Corp., Oak Ridge, 1948-49; grad. asst. U. Tenn., Knoxville, 1952, fellow U. Meml. Hosp., 1952-56; research asso. U. Buffalo (N.Y.) Med. Sch., 1956-57, U. Va. Med. Sch. Charlottesville, 1957-59, 59-61; asst. prof. chemistry Wilson Coll., Chambersburg, Pa., 1961-62; asst. prof. chemistry Sweet Briar (Va.) Coll., 1962-67, asso. prof., 1967—, chmn. dept., 1966-68, asst. dean, 1969—. Vis. lectr., acting head chemistry dept. Women's Christian Coll., Madras, India, 1968-69. Fellow Am. Inst. Chemists, A.A.A.S.; mem. Am. Assn. U. Profs., Am. Assn. U. Women, Am. Chem. Soc., N.Y., Va. acads. scis., Phi Beta Kappa, Sigma Xi. Contbr. articles to profl. jours. Address: Sweet Briar Coll Sweet Briar VA 24595

BLAIR, BILL J., architect; b. Kennett, Mo., Aug. 4, 1925; s. Carl B. and Nelle (Brown) B.; B. Archtl. Engring. Okla. State U., 1951, postgrad., 1952-53, 56-59; m. Reva Bernice Hill, Nov. 8, 1946; children—David Keith, Stephen Kent, Paul Kevin. Archtl. engr. Univ. Architect's Office Okla. State U., 1951-54, 56-59; archtl. adv. USOM to Ethiopia, 1954-56; architect Benham Engring. Co., Oklahoma City, 1959-61; partner Bill J. Blair & Assos., Oklahoma City, 1961-63; chief architect, v.p., prin. Benham-Blair and Affiliates, Inc., with offices in Oklahoma City, Phoenix, Los Angeles, Little Rock, Ark., Jackson, Miss., Ft. Lauderdale, Fla., Washington, San Antonio, N.Y. State, 1963—. Bd. dirs. Okla. State U. Devel. Found. Served with USNR, World War II. Registered architect, Okla., S.D., Neb., Ariz., Ark., Cal., Fla., Ill., Tex., N.Y., D.C. Registered profl. engr., Okla., Mem. A.I.A., Am. Soc. Registered Architects, Am. Soc. Profl. Engrs., Am. Protestant, Catholic hosp. assns., Internat. Hosp. Fedn., Okla. Soc. Profl. Engrs., Am. Socs. C.E., Am., So. hosp. assns., Am. Assn. Hosp. Planners, Aircraft Owners and Pilots Assn., Soc. Am. Mil. Engrs., Internat. Inst. Hosp. Consultants, Internat. Platform Assn., Oklahoma City C. of C., Navy League, Acacia. Baptist (chmn. bd. deacons 1966-67, lay minister 1953—). Mason (32 deg., Shriner). Home: 1712 S Rankin St Edmond OK 73034 Office: 6323 N Grand Blvd Oklahoma City OK 73118

BLAIR, FORBES WESLEY, lawyer; b. Chester, W.Va., Dec. 17, 1926; s. Andrew Clark and Edna (McHenry) B. A.B., W.Va. U. 1950; LL.B., 1952;; m Hilma Deem Robbins, June 20, 1954; children—Kristin Robbins, Forbes Robbins. Admitted to W.Va. bar, 1952; law clk. Adminstrv. Office U.S. Cts., Washington, 1952; law clk. to U.S. Atty. for D.C., 1953-54; asst. U.S. atty. for D.C., 1955-57; asso. firm Welch & Morgan, Washington, 1957-66, partner, 1966-69; partner firm Bilger & Blair, 1970—. Mem. Montgomery County (Md.) Charter Revision Commn., 1968. Regional chmn. Montgomery County Republican Com., 1967—; pres. Montgomery County Men's Rep. Club, 1972—. Asso. mem. W.Va. U. Found., 1967—. Served with USNR, 1944-46. Mem. Am. Judicature Soc., Am. Fed., Fed. Communication bar assns., W.Va. U. Alumni Assn. (pres. D.C. chpt. 1960), Phi Alpha Delta. Republican. Presbyn. Mason (32 deg.). Editor: Civitan Bull., Washington, 1965—. Contbr. articles to profl. jours. Home: 13826 Overton Lane Silver Spring MD 20904 Office: 1150 Connecticut Av NW Washington DC 20036

BLAIR, FORREST LLOYD, physician, state regent; b. Jackson County, W.Va., Mar. 26, 1913; s. Samuel F. and Victoria (Lockhart) B.; B.S., W.Va. U., 1936; M.D., U. Louisville, 1938; m. Eveline Salchli, May 1, 1942; children—Marie, David. Intern Louisville City Hosp., 1938-39, resident in gen. surgery, 1939-42; practice medicine specializing in surgery, Parkersburg, W.Va.; mem. staff Camden Clark Hosp.; instr. gen. surgery U. Louisville, 1941-42. Dir. Comml. Banking and Trust Co., Parkersburg. Bd. regents State of W.Va., v.p., 1971-72. Served to 1st lt. M.C., AUS, 1943. Diplomate Am. Bd. Surgery. Fellow A.C.S., Southeastern Surg. Congress; mem. A.M.A., Flying Physicians Assn., Am. Legion, Republican. Methodist. Mason. Office: 1130 Market St Parkersburg WV 26101*

BLAIR, FREDERICK LEE, hosp. adminstr.; b. Banner Elk, N.C., Mar. 13, 1934; s. Charlie Gudger and Beulah Ester (Jones) B.; A.A., Lees McRae Jr. Coll., Banner Elk, 1956; B.S., Appalachian State U., 1960; M.A. East Tenn. State U., 1969; m. Joanne McGuire, Sept 25, 1954; children—Frederick Lee,, Mark, Stephen. Adminstrv. asst. Charles A. Cannon Jr. Meml. Hosp., Banner Elk, 1960-64; elementary sch. prin. Avery County Schs., Newland, N.C., 1964-68; adminstr. Garrett Meml. Hosp., Crossnore, N.C., 1968—. Pres., Blue Ridge Health Council, 1969-71. Bd. dirs. Regional Health Council of Eastern Appalachia. Served with USNR, 1950-54. Mem. Am., N.C. hosp. assns., Hosp. Financial Assn. Home: Route 1 Box 307 Elk Park NC 28622 Office: Box 220 Crossnore NC 28616

BLAIR, HENRY CLAY, lawyer; b. nr. Granite Falls, N.C., Feb. 18, 1913; s. William H. and Mary Lou (Satterwhite) B.; A.B., U. N.C., 1938, J.D. 1941; m. Shirley Miller, Nov. 21, 1945; children—Lucille (Mrs. Clifford L. Coultes), William H. Admitted to N.C. bar, 1941; since practiced in Fayetteville. Mem. Am., N.C. bar assns., N.D. State Bar. Home: 2211 Meadow Wood Rd Fayetteville NC 28301 Office: 104 1/2 Gillespie St Fayetteville NC 28301

BLAIR, MARY ELIZABETH JOHNSON, psychiat. social worker; b. Elizabethtown, N.C., July 18, 1924; d. David Bunyan and Lillian (Horne) Johnson; B.A., Flora Macdonald Coll., 1945; postgrad. Nashville Sch. Social Work, 1950-51; M.S.W., U. Tenn., 1955. Caseworker, Children's Bur., Inc., Memphis, 1951-52; child welfare worker Bladen County Welfare Dept., Elizabethtown, 1952-54; psychiat. social worker, dir. social work services Guilford County Mental Health Centers, Greensboro and High Point, N.C., 1955-69; resident dir. High Point Center, 1969—. Mem. Nat. Assn. Social Workers (charter mem.), Acad. Certified Social Workers (charter), Am. Ortho-psychiat. Assn., N.C. Pub. Health Assn. (sec.-treas. mental health sect. 1963-66), Bus. and Profl. Woman's Club, Elizabethtown Am. League Aux. (charter). Presbyn. Club: Altrusa (rec. sec. 1965-66, pres. 1967-69). Home: William and Mary Apts High Point NC 27262 Office: 404 N Wrenn St High Point NC 27260

BLAIR, SAM, sports editor Dallas Morning News. Office: Communications Center Dallas TX 75222*

BLAIR, W(ILLIAM) FRANK(LIN), zoologist; b. Dayton, Tex., June 25, 1912; s. Percy Franklin and Mona (Patrick) B.; B.S., U. Tulsa, 1934; M.S., U. Fla., 1935; Ph.D., U. Mich., 1938; m. Fern Antell, Oct. 25, 1933. Research asso. Lab. Vertebrate Biology, U. Mich., 1937-46; mem. faculty U. Tex., 1946—, now prof. zoology. Mem. adv. panel environmental biology NSF, 1958-62, mem. adv. com. div. biology and medicine, 1967—; chmn. U.S. nat. com., mem. spl. com. Internat. Biol. Program, 1968—. Fellow A.A.A.S.; mem. Am. Soc. Ichthyologists and Herpetologists (bd. govs. 1951-55, 56-61, 62—, v.p. 1955), Am. Soc. Mammalogists, Am. Soc. Naturalists (editorial bd. 1957-58). Ecol. Soc. Am. (editorial bd. 1960-62, pres. 1963, chmn. pub. affairs com. 1968—), Am. Soc. Zoologists (chmn. ecology sect. 1965), Genetics Soc. Am., Soc. Study Evolution (mem. council 1959-61, pres. 1962, asso. editor 1961-62), Soc. Systematic Zoology (council 1968—). Author: The Rusty Lizard, 1960. Sr. author: Vertebrates of the United States, 1957, rev. edit., 1968. Editor: Vertebrate Speciation, 1961. Home: R 1 Box 197 Austin TX 78702

BLAIR, WILLIAM MELLVILLE, newspaper reporter; b. Cleve., June 14, 1911; s. Mellville Clifton and Margaret (O'Grady) B.; student Ohio State U., 1930-34; m. Helen Stern, Oct. 26, 1936 children—Jonathan Stern, Christopher Jo, Jeffery William. With publicity dept. Ohio State U. radio sta. WEAO, 1933-34; reporter-editor Canton (O.) Repository, 1934-36, Pitts. Sun-Telegraph, 1936-37; with Pitts. Harrisburg and Phila. bureaus A.P., 1937-42; mem. staff N.Y. Times, 1942—, reporter, Washington bur., 1953—. Mem. mgmt. bd. Central br. YMCA, 1968-70, mem. adv. bd., 1970—. Recipient U.S. Navy commendation, 1946, award Nat. Council Farmer Coops., 1950, U.S. Russell Meml. award Newspaper Farm Editors Assn., 1962, Conservation Service award Dept. Interior, 1969. Mem. Sigma Delta Chi. Clubs: Washington Athletic (govs. 1958-61, 64-68), Touchdown, Nat. Press (pres. 1965). (Washington). Home: 5602 Namakagan Rd Washington DC 20016 Office: 1701 K St NW Washington DC 20006

BLAKE, GARTH KERMIT, educator; b. Larned, Kan., Dec. 24, 1919; s. Loyd C. and Velma (Rex Road) B.; student Wheaton Coll., 1937, John Brown U., 1938-39; B.M.E., Okla. State U., 1946; M.Ed., U. Tulsa, 1951, Ed. D., 1956; m. Bonnie Jean Fretwell, Aug.8, 1941; 1 son, Richard G. Music tchr. Strang, Jefferson, Nowata, Okla., 1940-42; dir. music, Sapulpa, Okla., 1946-53, prin. high sch., 1953-57, supt. schs., 1957; asso. prof. edn. Fla. State U., Tallahassee, 1957-59, prof., head dept. student teaching, 1959-67, asst. dean Coll. Edn., 1967—. Served with USNR, 1944-46. Mem. Nat., Fla. edn. assns., Nat. Assn. for Student Teaching, Phi Kappa Phi, Phi Delta Kappa, Phi Beta Mu, Kappa Delta Pi. Rotarian. Home: 902 N Ride Tallahassee FL 32301

BLAKE, JULIUS YOUNG, dentist; b. Houston, Ala., Nov. 30, 1912; s. Isaac Young and Julia Ann (Robinson) B.; student Florence State U., 1928-29, U. Ala., 1930; D.D.S., Emory U., 1935; m. Emma Laura Gunter, Apr. 29, 1935; children—Dollie Ann (Mrs. Donald Glenn Murray), Virginia Kathryn (Mrs. Michael Dale Perren). Pvt. practice dentistry, Russellville, Ala., 1935—. Vol. dentist underprivileged children Franklin County Health Dept., 1960-71. Chmn. Russellville (Ala.) Water Works, 1951-71; treas. Franklin County Tb Assn., 1953-71. Served with Dental Corps, AUS, 1941-46. Mem. Am., Ala. dental assns., 8th Dist. Dental Soc., V.F.W. Baptist (life deacon 1948—). Club: Civitan (Russellville, Ala.). Home: Box 548 Russellville AL 35653 Office: Box 548 Russellville AL 35653

BLAKE, THOMAS MATHEWS, educator; b. Sheffield, Ala., Aug. 4, 1920; s. Jeptha Hill and Edna Austin (Mathews) B.; A.B., U. Ala., 1941; M.D., Vanderbilt U., 1944. Intern medicine Vanderbilt U. Hosp., Nashville, 1944-45, intern in pathology, 1947-48, resident, 1948-49; resident Strong Meml. Hosp., Rochester, N.Y., 1949-50; practice medicine, specializing in cardiology, Jackson, Miss., 1955—; instr. medicine Vanderbilt U., 1952-55; asst. prof. medicine U. Miss., Jackson, 1955-58, asso. prof., 1958-70, prof., 1970—. Served to capt. AUS, 1945-47. Fellow A.C.P., Am. Coll. Cardiology, Am. Coll. Chest Physicians; mem. Council on Clin. Cardiology and Arteriosclerosis, Am. Heart Assn. Home: 4210 Hanover Place Jackson MS 39211

BLAKELEY, ROBERT PHILIP, real estate co. exec.; b. Hampton, Ky., Jan. 3, 1917; s. William Roney and Gladys Mae (Styers) B.; student Dyke Sch. Commerce, 1936-38; m. Evelyn Diane White, Apr. 19, 1941; children—Brent Philip, Diana Gaye. Asst. office mgr. Chandler Products Co., Cleve., 1941-48; sec.-treas., gen. mgr. Plantation Farms, Inc., Plantation, Fla., 1949—; pres., dir. Old Plantation Water Control Dist., 1958—; chmn. governing bd. Central & So. Fla. Flood Control Dist.; dir. Farsouth Growers Coop. Assn., Tropical Agr. Coop. Assn., Plantation 1st Nat. Bank, Security 1st Nat. Bank. Fire chief Plantation Vol. Fire Dept., 1960-62. Bd. dirs. Broward County Indsl. Devel. Bd., 1965-66; co-trustee Plantation Land Trust, 1964-66; dir. Broward County chpt. A.R.C. Mem. C. of C. (dir. 1962-66, past pres.), Aquatic Weed Sci. Soc. (dir.). Kiwanian. Home: 320 E Tropical Way Plantation FL 33314 Office: 7049 NW 4th St Plantation FL 33313

BLAKEY, DURWARD LACEY, physician, pub. health adminstr.; b. Paxton, Fla., Mar. 31, 1922; s. Claude C. and Catherine (Stevenson) B.; B.A., U. Ala., 1943; M.D., La. State U., 1946; M.P.H., Tulane U., 1957; m. Rosemary Nichols, Apr. 7, 1946; 1 son, Kenneth Tyler. Intern Jefferson-Hillman Hosp., Birmingham, Ala., 1946-47; asst. health officer Hinds County Health Dept., Jackson, Miss., 1947; dir. Tri-County Health Dist., Prentiss, Miss., 1947-48; dir. Coahoma County Health Dept., Clarksdale, Miss., 1951-57, acting dir., 1966-70; asst. dir. div. preventable disease control Miss. Bd. Health, Jackson, 1957-58, dir., 1958—, state epidemiologist, 1957—, dir. chronic disease program, 1957-62, dir. cancer control program, 1957-69, dir. Tb control program and Miss. controller, 1957—; asso. clin. prof. pub. health and preventive medicine U. Miss., 1958—; sec. med. staff Coahoma County Hosp., 1952-56; bd. dirs. Jackson Council Alcoholism, Am. Cancer Soc., Jackson, Hinds County chpt. Am. Cancer Soc., Arthritis and Rheumatism Found. Miss., Hinds County Tb Assn., Miss. Clearing House for Poison Control Centers, Migratory Labor Health Program, Venereal Disease Control Program. Served from 1st lt. to maj. M.C., AUS, 1948-51. Mem. Clarksdale and Six Counties (sec. 1952-56), Central med. socs., Miss. Med. Assn. (past mem. com. on aging of council med. service), Am., Miss. pub. health assns., Assn. State and Territorial Epidemiologists, Assn. State and Territorial Chronic Disease Program Dirs., Miss. Thoracic Soc., Mental Health Assn. Miss., A.M.A., Delta Omega. Home: Raymond MS 39154 Office: Miss Bd Health Jackson MS 39216

BLAKLEY, WILLIAM A., lawyer, found. exec.; b., 1898; student U. Okla. Admitted to bar, 1933; part-time lawyer; chmn. bd., dir. Blakley-Braniff Found., Dallas. Trustee Southwestern Med. Found., Inc., Dallas. Mem. Am. Bar Assn. Address: Blakley-Braniff Found PO Box 35212 Exchange Park Dallas TX

BLALOCK, CARLISLE, lawyer; b. New Willard, Tex., Jan. 24, 1922; s. Phillip Horace and Louise (Mann) B.; student Lamar Coll., 1938-40; J.D. with honors, U. Tex., 1945; m. Sally Reed Anderson, Feb. 9, 1952; children—Sally Hudson, Patricia Louise, Carol Anderson, Lyle Roberts. Jr. airport mgr. Pan Am. Airways, Brownsville, Tex., 1942-44; admitted to Tex. bar, 1945; practiced in Dallas, 1945-58, 59—, Houston, 1958-59; mem. firm Carrington, Gowan, Johnson & Walker, 1945-52, Carrington, Gowan, Johnson, Bromberg &Leeds, 1952-58, Tobolowsky, Hartt, Schlinger & Bialock, 1959-68, Tobolowsky, Schlinger & Bialock, 1968—. Vice pres., dir. He-Po

Gas, Inc., Cairo, Ga., 1946-67; sec. dir. H.J. Gruy & Assos., Inc., 1961-70; v.p., sec., dir. Gruy Mgmt. Service Co., 1961-70, Presidio Corp., 1962 (all Dallas), Gruy Engring. Corp., Monrovia, Liberia, 1963-70. Trustee Childrens Med. Center, Dallas. Presbyn. Clubs: Dervish (pres. 1950), Calyx (pres. 1951), Terpsichorean, Northwood Country, Chaparral, Dallas. Home: 7011 Desco Dr Dallas TX 75225 Office: 1900 Southland Center Dallas TX 75201

BLALOCK, DANIEL BRAXTON, JR., constrn. machinery co. exec.; b. Atlanta, July 22, 1912; s. Daniel Braxton and Estelle (Zellars) B.; B.S., Ga. Inst. Tech., 1934; m. Dorothy Eleanor Pettus, Nov. 12, 1945; children—Mary Estelle, Daniel Braxton III, William Pettus. With Austin Western Machinery Co., Harvey, Ill., 1934-35; with Blalock Machinery & Equipment Co., Atlanta, 1935-41, 46-—, salesman, partner, v.p., 1935-61, pres., 1961-—. Mem. Ga. Democratic Exec. Com., 1951-54, 59-62. Served to lt. col. C.E., AUS, 1941-46. Mem. Ga. Bus. and Industry Assn. (vice chmn. 1969-70), Ga. Inst. Tech. Nat. Alumni Assn. (pres. 1969-70), Asso. Equipment Distbrs. (nat. pres. 1962), Kappa Alpha. Episcopalian. Clubs: Capitol City, Piedmont Driving, Commerce, Cherokee Town and Country, Atlanta Country. Home: 1224 Johnson Ferry Rd NE Atlanta GA 30319 Office: 225 Forsyth St SW Atlanta GA 30302

BLALOCK, JOHN VERNON, tobacco co. exec.; b. Durham, N.C., Aug. 1, 1921; s. Reuben Allen and Lelia Pearl (Goss) B.; B.A., Duke, 1944; m. Kathleen Glymph, Apr. 6, 1947; children—Kathleen (Mrs. Alexander Prescott IV), Barry Vernon. Various positions Durham Morning-Herald, 1942-48; asst. dir. pub. relations Seaboard R.R., Norfolk, Va., 1948-49; asst. v.p. advt. and pub. relations Liberty Life Ins. Co., Greenville, S.C., 1949-61; dir. pub. relations Brown & Williamson Tobacco Corp., Louisville, 1961-—. Guest lectr. U. Louisville. Active United Way, Louisville Devel. Com.; commr. Commonwealth of Ky. Hist. Commn. Bd. dirs. Louisville Fund, Greater Louisville Conv. Assn., Parkhill Community Council, Sts. Mary and Elizabeth Hosp. Recipient medal of honor Freedoms Found., 1954, medal of merit Jewish War Vets. U.S., 1971, Human Relations Leadership award Am. Jewish Com., 1971. Mem. Pub. Relations Soc. Am. (local pres., del. nat. assembly), Louisville Area C. of C., Phi Kappa Sigma. Presbyn. Clubs: Jefferson, Hurstbourne Country (Louisville). Home: 4907 Clovernook Rd Louisville KY 40207 Office: 1600 W Hill St Louisville KY 40201

BLALOCK, THOMAS CARLTON, univ. adminstr.; b. Lucama, N.C., Oct. 6, 1924; s. Walter Henry and Pearl Lee (Barnes) B.; B.S., N.C. State U., 1948, M.S., 1952; Ph.D. (Kellogg fellow), U. Wis., 1963; m. Alva Cornelia Peacock, June 8, 1947; children—Thomas Carlton, Walter Douglass, Phyllis Leigh. Instr., N.C. State U., Raleigh, 1949-50, extension specialist, 1951-59, specialist in charge, 1959-63, dist. agt., 1963-64, asst. dir. 1964-70, asst. dir. adminstrn., 1970-72, asso. dir., 1972-—; mgr. Wis. Sci. Breeding Inst., 1950-51. Cons. Peruvian Govt. on Yough Programs, 1966; chmn. Nat. 4-H Sub-Com. of Extension Com. on Organization and Policy, Mem. adv. council N.C. Gov's. Com. for Children and Youth, 1968-70. Served with Signal Corps, AUS, 1943-46. Mem. Assn. So. Agrl. Workers (pres. youth sect. 1968-69), N.C. Adult Edn. Assn., N.C. Rural Safety Council (award chmn. 1970-72), Epsilon Sigma Phi, Alpha Zeta. Baptist (deacon 1962-65, 67-70). Club: Faculty (v.p. 1966-67). Home: 1315 Brooks Av Raleigh NC 27607

BLANCHARD, CAREY EDWARD, hosp. adminstr.; b. Boyce, La., Aug. 24, 1917; s. Carey Edward and Perla Greenville (Carter) B.; student Charity Hosp., New Orleans, 1946, Gradwohls Sch., 1947, U. Ala., 1971; m. Evelyn Louise Corley, Oct. 25, 1945; 1 son, Carey Edward IV. Dir., lab. x-ray technician, anesthetist Broyles Hosp., Leesville, La., 1948-50, Carthage (Tex.) Panola Clinic, 1950-68; adminstr. Hartner Med. Center, Urania, La., 1968-69, Merryville (La.) Gen. Hosp., 1970-—; dir. Respiratory Service, Inc., Merryville; pres. Merryville (La.) Indsl. Corp., 1971-—. Served with inf., M.C., AUS, 1940-45. Fellow Am. Coll. Med. Technicians; mem. Am. Acad. Hosp. Adminstrs., Am. Radiol. Technicians. Methodist (bd. dirs. 1970-71). Mason (Shriner, K.T.); mem. Order Eastern Star, Lion. Address: Drawer C Merryville LA 70653

BLANCHARD, HUBERT HOWARD, edn. assn. exec.; b. Sulphur Rock, Ark., July 21, 1920; s. Hubert H. and Van (Martin) B.; B.S., U. Ark., 1943, M.S., 1951, diploma Sch. Adminstrn., 1966; m. Janive Segraves, June 14, 1946; children—Warren Martin, Charles Howard. High sch. tchr., Strawberry, Ark., 1946-51; supt. schs., Strawberry, 1951-54; supr. schs., Lawrence County, 1954-59; asst. exec. sec. Ark. Edn. Assn., Little Rock, 1959-—. Mem. White House Conf. Edn., 1960; treas. Ark. Com. for Pub. Schs., 1962-—, mem. Ark. Polit. Action Com. for Edn. Lawrence County chmn. March of Dimes, 1958. Served with USNR, 1943-46. Mem. Ark. Edn. Assn., N.E.A., Am. Assn. Sch. Adminstrs., Phi Delta Kappa. Democrat. Methodist (chmn. ofcl. bd. 1957-59, chmn. com. edn. 1967-70). Mason (32 deg.). Home: 3417 Pope Av North Little Rock AK 72116 Office: 1500 W 4th St Little Rock AR 72201

BLANCHARD, JOHN MICHAEL, lawyer; b. New Orleans, Jan. 16, 1932; s. John H. and Adismae (McWilliams) B.; B.A., So. U., 1954 M.A., Xavier U., 1960; J.D., Loyola U., New Orleans, 1968; m. Regina Oliver, June 26, 1954 children—Jonilyn, John, Reginald. Tchr., Orleans Parish Sch. Bd., New Orleans, 1954-60, Chgo. Bd. Edn., 1960-65; admitted to La. bar, 1969; practiced in New Orleans, 1969-—. Vice Pres. Young Democrats, New Orleans, 1969-70; candidate Orleans Parish Dem. Com. Wards, 1967. Served with AUS, 1954-56. Mem. New Orleans Civic Assn., La. Edn. Assn., Am. Fedn. Tchrs., Am., La. bar assns., La. Civic Assn., Kappa Alpha Psi. Elk. Home: 6109 Campus Blvd New Orleans LA 70126 Office: 2108 Dryades St New Orleans LA 70113

BLANCHARD, PHYLLIS EDRA WALTERS, foods co. exec.; b. Dallas, Sept. 29, 1914; d. Edward D. and Rhoda (Dennison) Walters; student U. Houston, 1931-32, evenings 1947-49; LaSalle Extension U., 1944-46; m. Hillis Robert Blanchard, Mar. 16, 1935 (dec. 1957). With Herrin Transp. Co., Houston, 1932-38; with Maxwell House div. Gen. Foods Corp., Houston, 1938-—, traffic mgr., 1948-—. Named Woman of Year in Transp., Traffic Club Houston, Houston Freight Carriers Assn., Women's Traffic Club Houston, 1960. Mem. Traffic Club Houston (dir. 1952-53, 54), Women's Traffic Club Houston (pres. 1952-53), Houston Freight Carriers (assoc.), S.W. Shippers (adv. bd.), Bus. and Profl. Women's Club Houston (pres. 1964-65). Mem. Order Eastern Star. Club: Flagg (v.p. Houston 1964-65). Home: 3224 Amherst St Houston TX 77005 Office: 3900 Harrisburg Blvd Houston TX 77001

BLANCHARD, RUSSELL A., banker; b. Camak, Ga., Oct. 2, 1908; s. Walter and Rachel (Chapman) B.; ed. Stonier Grad. Sch. Banking, Rutgers U., 1947; m. Catherine Jones, Dec. 22, 1932; children—Russell A., Jr., Thomas W. and John Richard (twins). With Ga. R.R. Bank & Trust Co., Augusta, 1928-—, asst. cashier, 1944-47, cashier, 1947, v.p., cashier, 1948-57, exec. v.p., 1957-66, 1st v.p., 1966-69, pres., 1969-—; also dir.; dir. Ga. R.R. and Banking Co., 1st R.R. & Banking Co. Ga., Bankers Trust of S.C., 1st Ga. Devel. Corp., Profl. Bldg., Inc., Riverside Mills Inc., Hamburg Industries Inc. Past pres., chmn. loan execs. United Fund of Augusta-North Augusta; chmn. nominating com. Jr. Achievement, 1969-—. Bd. dirs. Ga. Banking Sch. of U. Ga.; trustee Tuttle-Newton Home; trustee, chmn. Augusta Coll. Found., Ga. Bapt. Found. Recipient Outstanding Alumnus award Augusta Coll., 1959. Mem. Am. (past pres. state bank div.), Ga. (past pres.) bankers assns. Baptist. Clubs: Augusta Country, Pinnacle (Augusta). Home: 3027 Bransford Rd Augusta GA 30904 Office: 699 Broad St Augusta GA 30904

BLANCHARD, WILLARD JACKSON, coll. pres.; b. Whaleyville, Va., 1919; B.A. cum laude, Wake Forest Coll., 1941; M.A. in Ednl. Adminstrn., U. N.C., 1949; m. Crotia Ila Bass; 2 sons, 2 daus. Instr., Pineland Coll.-Edwards Mil. Inst., Salemburg, N.C., 1941-43, dean, registrar, 1945-49, pres., 1949-57; pres. Frederick Mil. Acad. and Jr. Coll., Portsmouth, Va., 1957-62; pres. Southwood Coll. (formerly Pineland Coll.-Edwards Mil. Inst.), Salemburg, 1962-—. Served to 1st lt. USAAF, World War II. Baptist (chmn. bd. deacons.). Lion (dist. gov.). Address: Southwood Coll Salemburg NC 28385*

BLANCHARD, WILLIAM WARD, civil engr.; b. Wallace, N.C., Sept. 26, 1926; s. Ward Caswell and Pearl (Carr) B.; B.C.E., N.C. State Coll. of U. N.C., 1950; m. Catherine LeGwin, Sept. 22, 1951; adopted children—Julia Catherine, William David. With J.E. Sirrine Co., engring. design, 1951; pvt. practice as civil engr., Wallace, 1951-—; pres. William W. Blanchard, Inc., engring. and surveying, Wallace. Served with USNR, 1945. Registered profl. engr., N.C., S.C., Va. Mem. Nat. Soc. Profl. Engrs., Profl. Engrs. N.C. (past pres. S.E. chpt.), N.C. Soc. Engrs., Am. Congress Surveying and Mapping. Presbyn. (past chmn. bd. deacons; Sunday sch. tchr.). Mason (32 deg. past master), Lion (past pres.). Club: Rockfish Country. Home: Friendly Acres Wallace NC 28466 Office: 215 NE Railroad St PO Box 208 Wallace NC 28466

BLANCHET, WALDO WILLIE EMERSON, coll. pres.; b. New Orleans, Aug. 6, 1910; s. Louis Alexander and Hattie (D'Astugue) B.; A.B., Talladega Coll., 1931; M.S., U. Mich., 1936, Ph.D., 1946; m. Josephine Lavizzo, Oct. 13, 1943; children—Geri Therese, Waldo Willie Emerson. Tchr. sci. Fort Valley (Ga.) Normal and Indsl. Sch., 1932-35, dean, 1936-38; instr. Fort Valley State Coll., 1939, prof. phys. sci., 1939-—, adminstrv. dean, 1939-66, pres. coll., 1966-—. Cons. sci. edn. Ga. Dept. Edn. NSF Sci. Insts. in Albany and Atlanta, 1960-61. Mem. Nat. Adv. Council on Edn. of Disadvantaged Children. Mem. Assn. Higher Edn., Nat. Assn. Research Sci. Teaching (pres. 1956-57), Nat. Inst. Sci., A.A.A.S., Phi Kappa Phi, Phi Delta Kappa. Contbr. articles to tech. lit. Home: 110 Lamar St Fort Valley GA 31030

BLANCO-LUGO, LUIS, justice P.R. Supreme Ct.; b., 1921; B.A., LL.B., U. P.R. Admitted to bar, 1943; now asso. justice Supreme Ct. P.R., San Juan. Address: Av Ponce de Leon Parada 8 Puerta Tierra PR 00906*

BLANDFORD, JOHN RUSSELL, lawyer; b. Buffalo, Feb. 20, 1918; s. Raymond S. and Mary (Perkins) B.; B.A. cum laude, Hobart Coll., 1939 LL.B., Yale, 1946; m. Barbara Jane Waterhouse, July 28, 1944 1 dau., Marcia Ann (Mrs. Irwin Raymond Hoener II). Admitted to N.Y. State bar., 1947, D.C. bar, 1957, U.S. Supreme Ct. bar; practiced in Buffalo, 1947; counsel com. armed services U.S. Ho. of Reps., Washington, 1947-63, chief counsel, 1963-72. Served to maj. USMCR, 1941-46; PTO. Recipient Rockefeller Pub. Service award, 1966; Distinguished Pub. Service award U.S. Navy; Outstanding Civilian Service award U.S. Air Force; Legion of Merit award U.S. Army, 1972. Mem. Phi Beta Kappa, Tau Kappa Alpha. Methodist. Mason. Home: 4520 N 39th St Arlington VA 22907 Office: Rayburn House Office Bldg Washington DC 20515

BLANDING, WARREN, publishing exec.; b. Providence, Dec. 9, 1921; s. Percy Howard and Helen (Eddy) B.; grad. Phillips Acad., Andover, Mass., 1939; A.B. cum laude, Harvard, 1943; m. Betty Estelle Lightfoot, Nov. 27, 1947 (div. 1965); children—India, Brett (dec.). Pres. Wayward Printers, Inc., Washington, 1947-51; asst. to pres. Directorios Publicitarios, Mexico, 1951-52; asst. to pres., dir. marketing, editor and asso. pub. Traffic Service Corp., Washington 1953-65; exec. v.p. Marketing Publs., Inc., Washington, 1965-67, pres., 1967-—; v.p. Schuyler Hopper Co., N.Y. Mem. U.S. Dept. Agr. Market Research Adv. Com., 1965-—. Served with AUS, 1943-46. Clubs: Nat. Press, Harvard of N.Y.C. Contbr. articles to profl. jours. Home: 1829 Parkside Dr NW Washington DC 20012 Office: Nat Press Bldg Washington DC 20004

BLANK, RALPH JOHN, JR., banker; b. Lake City, Fla., Apr. 2, 1922; s. Ralph John and Stella Pauline (Kleinbeck) B.; B.S., B.A., U. Fla., 1942; m. Merry Lake, May 17, 1952; children—Pamela Hellin, Liisa Pauline, Michelle Susan. Admitted to Fla. bar, 1948; asso. mem. firm Moorehead, Pallot, Smith, Green & Phillips, Miami, 1948-49; home office counsel Am. Fire & Casualty Co., Orlando, Fla., 1950-51; individual practice law, West Palm Beach, Fla., 1952-—; chmn. bd. Citizens Bank Palm Beach County, West Palm Beach, 1963-—. Mem. Fla. Ho. of Reps., 1956-60, Fla. Senate, 1960-64; mem. Civil Service Bd. West Palm Beach, 1965-—. Trustee Fla. Atlantic U. Endowment Corp., Boca Raton, 1960-—. Served with Arty., AUS, 1942-45; ETO; lt. col. Res. ret. Decorated Air medal with 5 oak leaf clusters. Presbyn. Home: 122 Forest Hill Blvd West Palm Beach FL 33405 Office: 316 Pan American Bldg West Palm Beach FL 33401

BLANK, ROBERT J., dentist; b. Newark, Aug. 23, 1934; s. Samuel and Mary (Solodar) B.; A.A., U. Fla., 1954 D.D.S., Northwestern U., 1958; postgrad. Marquette U., 1969; m. Diane Roberta Perkus, July 3, 1960; children—Stephen Gary, Keith Stuart, Valerie Lyn. Pvt. practice dentistry, Miami Beach, Fla., 1958-60, Miami, 1960-—. Sec.-treas. Lemostron Corp., treas. CBR Mfg. Corp. Cons. Sherwood Med., div. Brunswick Corp., 1967-—; coordinator dental edn. N.W. Dade County Elementary Schs., 1964-68. Recipient Certificate of Merit and Appreciation E. Coast Dental Soc., 1967, United Fund of Dade County, 1965. Mem. Am. Dental Assn., Fla. State, E. Coast, North Dade, Hollywood dental socs., Alpha Omega, Tau Epsilon Phi. Jewish religion. Patentee in field. Home: 4002 Buchanan St Hollywood FL 33021 Office: 2734 NW 183d St Miami FL 33054

BLANKENSHIP, GEORGE TONY, JR., state govt. ofcl.; b. Oklahoma City, Mar. 11, 1928; s. George Tony and Daisy (Dean) B.; B.A., U. Okla., 1951, LL.B., 1954; m. Elizabeth Katherine Warren, June 8, 1951; children— Matthew Steven, Elizabeth Ann, Julie Kay. Owner Blankenship Properties, 1956-—; partner firm Lampkin, Wolfe and Blankenship, 1961-65; atty. gen. Okla., 1967-—. Vice chmn. Okla. Young Republicans, 1957-59; Rep. nat. committeeman, 1959-61; mem. Okla. Ho. of Reps., 1960-66. Served to 1st lt. USAF, 1954-56. Mem. Okla., Am. bar assns., Phi Alpha Delta Sigma Nu. Methodist. Mason (32 deg., Shriner). Address: 1600 Elmhurst St Oklahoma City OK 73120

BLANKENSHIP, LILLIAN BARTLETT (MRS. HARVEY TAYLOR BLANKENSHIP), social worker; b. Dallas, Jan. 20, 1932; d. James Lloyd and Grace (McCormack) Naylor; student Blinn Coll., 1949-51; A.B., U. Houston, 1953; M.S.W., La. State U., 1959; m. Harvey Taylor Blankenship, May 20, 1968. Psychiat. social worker Child Guidance Clinic of Fort Worth and Tarrant County, 1959-65, Child Guidance Center, Houston, 1965-66; asso. dir. Child Guidance Clinic of Ft. Worth and Tarrant County, 1966-—; field instr. U. Tex. Sch. Social Work; pvt. practice social work Psychotherapy Inst. of Ft. Worth. Recipient Outstanding Scholastic Achievement award La. State U., 1959. Mem. La. State U. Alumni Council, Acad. Certified Social Workers, Am. Orthopsychiat. Assn., Nat. Assn. Social Workers (sec. Fort Worth 1962-63), Tex. Social Welfare Assn., Nat. Conf. on Social Work, Council on Social Work Edn., Tarrant County Assn. for Mental Health (com. on childhood mental illness, sec. 1963-65), Mental Health Assn. Houston and Harris County. Episcopalian. Clubs: Fort Worth Skiers, Space City Ski (Houston). Home: PO Box 17101 Fort Worth TX 76102 Office: 1300 W Lancaster St Fort Worth TX 76102 also 927 8th Av Fort Worth TX 76104

BLANKENSHIP, MRS. WAYNE GOVAN, club woman; b. Pensacola, N.C., Dec. 25, 1906; d. Welzie Hampton and Emma (Wilson) Hensley; grad. Opportunity Bus. Coll, 1931; m. Wayne Govan Blankenship, May 3, 1930; children—Emma Mae, Wayne Govan. Tchr. Pensacola Hich Sch., 1926-30; sec. Home Fed. Savs. and Loan Assn., Knoxville, Tenn., 1937-40, sec. to pres., 1940-—. Mem. fine arts com. Ossoll Circle Club, 1960-62, mem. ways and means com., 1964-65, mem. pub. affairs com., 1965-66; rec. sec. Knoxville Woman's Club, 1951-52, pres., 1965-66; dist. treas. Tenn. Fedn. Women's Clubs, 1960-62, Tenn. music chmn., 1962-64, dist. v.p., 1970-72; state rec. sec. Tenn. W.C.T.U., 1959-62, dist. chmn., 1961-63, corr. sec., 1962-64, Tenn. promotion sec., 1964-65, local pres., 1965-66, promotion sec., 1966-68, state v.p., 1969-70, state pres., 1971-72; pres. Frances Willand W.C.T.U., 1966-72; historian Tenn. Fedn. Music Clubs, 1962-64, East Tenn. v.p. 1964-66, 68-70, corr. sec., 1966-68; v.p. City Assn. Women's Clubs, 1964-65; treas. Knoxville area chpt. Am. Assn. UN, 1962-64; historian Exchangette Club, 1964-65, parliamentarian, 1965-66, pres., 1968-69; conservation chmn. Flower Lovers Club, 1963-64, treas., 1970-72; v.p. Tuesday Morning Musical Club, 1960-62, pres., 1962-64; dist. sec. Christian social relations Woman's Soc. Christian Service, 1961-64, local pres., 1959-60, treas. local dist., 1964-65. Methodist (steward). Home: 5107 Holston Dr Knoxville TN 37914

BLANKINSHIP, LESLIE CHARLES, govt. ofcl.; b. Buckongham, Va., Mar. 23, 1909; s.Herman and Minnie (McCraw) B.; A.B., Lynchburg Coll., 1932; grad. study U. Va., 1936; m. Elizabeth Hoye, June 9, 1934; children—Martha Elizabeth, Leslie Scott. Tchr., coach Gordonsville (Va.) High Sch., 1932-36, Randolph-Macon Acad. Fort Royal, Va., 1936-41, Lexington (N.C.) High Sch., 1941-42; dir. phys. edn. YMCA, Roanoke and Lynchburg, Va., 1946-51; gen. sec. YMCA, Daytona Beach, Fla., 1951-53; pres. Millersburg Mil. Inst., 1953-62; founder, pres., Carolina Mil. Acad., Maxton, N.C., 1962-68; dir. Jarvis Sch. Bur.; Atlanta; 1969-70; program officer U.S. Office Edn., Atlanta, 1970-—. Founder, Vardell Hall, Red Springs, N.C., 1964, Highlands Sch., Avon Park, Fla., 1966. Served with AUS, 1942-46. Presbyn. Mason (32 deg.), Rotarian. Home: 4167 Rue St Michel Stone Mountain GA 30083 Office: US Office of Education 50 7th St Atlanta GA 30323

BLANKS, CHARLES PRESTON, JR., state ofcl.; b. Meridian, Miss., June 27, 1913; s. Charles Preston and Mary Eleanor (Pumphrey) B.; B.S. Miss. State Coll., 1940 M.S. Harvard, 1947; M.P.H., U. N.C., 1957; m. Shirley Rue Dumas, Aug. 20, 1932. Chief, pub. health div. AID, Nicaragua, 1960-63, chief pub. health div., Columbia, 1963-65, chief malaria adviser, Pakistan, 1965-67; health planning adminstr. Ala. Dept. Pub. Health, Montgomery, 1968-—. Served with AUS, 1942-46. Mem. Nat. Soc. Profl. Engrs., Harvard Soc. Engrs. and Scientists, Inter-Am. Soc. San. Engrs., Tau Beta Pi, Delta Omega. Home: 3315 Walton Dr Montgomery AL 36102 Office: State Office Bldg Montgomery AL 36104

BLANKS, JAMES BAILEY, educator; b. Clarksville, Va., Aug. 6, 1903; s. Lyddall Bailey and Isabelle (McBriety) B.; B.B.A., U. Richmond, 1926; M.A., Wake Forest (N.C.) Coll., 1929; grad. student in guidance, Columbia; m. Margaret Earle, Sept. 10, 1932; children—Margaret Elizabeth, Mary Isabelle. (Mrs. Aubrey A. West). Prin. schs., Va. 1925-27; prof. edn. and acting dean Boiling Springs Jr. Coll., 1929-30; asso. prof. edn. and psychology Limestone Coll., 1930-31; prof. edn. and psychology La Grange (Ga.) Coll., 1932-57, prof. psychology social sci., 1957-—, chmn. dept. psychology 1957-67, chief examiner grad. record examination, 1949-57; lectr. hist. and econs., 1943; guidance and mental hygiene cons., 1937; dir. Vets. Guidance Center, Furman U., Greenville, S.C., 1945-47; vis. prof. U. Ga. Off-Campus Center, Columbus, 1947-57, Carson-Newman Coll., 1956, summer session 57; cons. Troup County Family and Children Services, Ga. Dept. Edn. Mem. Ga. Mental Health Assn., Ga. Psychol. Assn. (chmn. legal affairs com.), So. Council on Tchr. Edn., Am. Acad. Polit. and Social Sci., Ga. Edn. Assn., N.E.A., Southeastern Assn. Geographers, Pi Gamma Mu (sec.) Democrat. Baptist. Mason. Licensed to practice applied psychology Ga. Bd. Examiners of Psychologists, 1951. Surveyor ednl. systems, both plant and curriculum, Ga. Contbr. psychol. articles to newspapers and other publs. Home: 114 College Av LaGrange GA 30240 Office: La Grange Coll LaGrange GA 30240

BLANTON, HOOVER CLARENCE, lawyer; b. Green Sea, S.C., Oct. 13, 1925; s. Clarence Leo and Margaret (Hoover) S.; J.D., U. S.C., 1953; m. Cecilia Lopez, July 31, 1949; children—Lawson Hoover, Michael Lopez. Admitted to S.C. bar, 1953; since practiced in Columbia; mem. firm Whaley & McCutchen, 1953-66, Whaley, McCutchen, Blanton & Richardson, 1967-—. Dir. Legal Aid Service Agy., Columbia, chmn., 1972. Gen. counsel S.C. Republican Com., 1963-66; pres. Richland County Rep. Conv., 1962; del. Rep. State Convs., 1962, 64, 66, 68, 70. Bd. dirs. Midlands Community Action Agy., Columbia, vice chmn., 1972. Served with USNR, 1942-46, 50-52. Mem. Am., S.C., Richland County bar assns., S.C. State Bar (historian 1969-—), S.C. Def. Attys. Assn., Assn. Ins. Attys. (state chmn. 1971-—), Phi Delta Phi. Baptist. Clubs: Toastmasters (pres. 1959), Columbia Young Lawyers. Home: 3655 Deerfield Dr Columbia SC 29204 Office: 1414 Lady St Columbia SC 29201

BLANTON, LEONARD RAY, congressman; b. Hardin County, Tenn., Apr. 10, 1930; s. Leonard and Oea (DeLaney) B.; B.S. (Danforth Found. award), U. Tenn., 1951; m. Betty Littlefield; children—Debbie, Jane, David, Paul. Tchr. pub. schs., Moresville, Ind., 1951-58; with B.B. Constrn. Co., Adamsville, Tenn., 1954-67; mem. Tenn. Ho. of Reps. from McNairy County, 1965-66; mem. 91st-92d congresses from 7th Dist. Tenn. Mem. U. Tenn. Alumni Assn., Tenn. Plant Mix Asphalt Assn. (past v.p.). Methodist (chmn. bd.). Lion, Moose, Mason (Shriner). Home: Old Shilo Rd Adamsville TN 38310 also 12313 Arron Park Dr Oxon Hill MD 20002 Office: Longworth House Office Bldg Washington DC 20515

BLASDELL, JONATHAN HIRAM, electric co. exec.; b. Kyle, Tex., Jan. 30, 1905; s. Jonathan Hiram and Martha Rose (Capers) B.; student U. Houston, 1936; m. Gladys Viola Fruzia, May 21, 1927; children— Jonathan Hiram, James Edward, Taneen Bentrup (Mrs. Arlie Bentrup). Engr., Houston Electronics, 1925; contractor Compton Electric, 1926-27, Caywood Electric, 1935-41; v.p. Fisk Electric Co., contractors, engrs., Houston, 1942-—. Mem. Ch. of Christ (elder 1950-—). Club: Atascocito Country (Houston). Home: 312 Eleanor St Houston TX 77009 Office: 3102 Milam St Houston TX 77006

BLASICK, HANK, state librarian Fla. Office: Supreme Ct Bldg Tallahassee FL 33204*

BLATCHFORD, NICHOLAS, journalist; b. Winnetka, Ill., May 6, 1919; s. Nathaniel Hopkins and Margaret (Copeland) B.; B.A., Harvard, 1940; m. Lois Greeley, June 3, 1944; children—Anne Hathaway (Mrs. Albert), Kim Copeland, Nicholas Mark. With Washington Daily News, 1940—, asst. mng. editor, 1958-66, mng. editor, 1966-68, asso. editor, 1968—. Served with AUS, 1941-45. Recipient Ernie Pyle Meml. award, 1969. Home: 2945 Cedar Lane Fairfax VA 22030 Office: 1013 13th St NW Washington DC 20005

BLATT, SOLOMON, lawyer, state legislator; b. Blackville, S.C., Feb. 27, 1896; s. Nathan and Mollie (Blatt) B.; LL.B., U. S.C., 1917; m. Ethel Green, Mar. 18, 1920. Mem. firm Blatt, Fales, Peeples, Bedingfield and Loadholt, Barnwell, S.C.; mem. S.C. Ho. of Reps., Columbia, 1933—, speaker, 1935-45, 51—. Trustee, Barnwell Sch., U. S.C., 1936-48. Served with U.S. Army, World War I. Address: SC House of Representatives State Capitol Columbia SC 29201

BLAUSTEIN, SAUL J., economist; b. N.Y.C., July 30, 1924; s. David and Ester (Kahane) B.; B.S., City Coll. N.Y., 1948 postgrad. U. So. Cal., 1948-50, George Washington U., 1951-53; m. Renee Liebman, June 18, 1949; children—Michael, Jonah. Price and cost living economist Bur. Labor Statistics, U.S. Dept. Labor, Washington, 1951-55, dir. unemployment ins. program research Bur. Employment Security, 1955-67; sr. staff economist unemployment and related manpower research W.E. Upjohn Inst. for Employment Research, Washington, 1967—. Tchr. econs. George Washington U., 1953-55. Served with USAAF, 1943-45. Recipient Meritorious Service award U.S. Dept. Labor, 1959. Mem. Indsl. Relations Research Assn., Am. Econ. Assn., Phi Beta Kappa. Jewish religion. Home: 9308 Compton St Silver Springs MD 20901 Office: 1101 17th St NW Washington DC 20036

BLAYNEY, KEITH DALE, univ. dean; b. Anamosa, Ia., Feb. 8, 1937; s.Darrell P. and Evelyn (Thompson) B.; B.S., U. Ia., 1959, M.A., 1961, Ph.D., 1966; m. Joyce Ann Bryan, Sept. 14, 1958 children—Michael Bryan, Steven Price. Adminstrv. resident Trumbull Meml. Hosp., Warren, O., 1960; instr. Program in Hosp. Adminstrn., U. Ia., 1964-66; asst. prof. Sch. Health Services Adminstrn., U. Ala., Birmingham, 1966-67, asso. prof., 1967-68, acting dir. Regional Tech. Inst. for Health Occupations, 1966-67, dir. Bur. Research and Community Service, 1967-69, dir. Sch. Health Services Adminstrn., 1969-70, adminstr. U. Hosps. and Clinics, 1969-71, dean Sch. Community and Allied Health Resources, 1971—; prof. dept. pub. health and epidemiology Med. Coll. Ala., 1969. Cons., Nat. Center for Health Scis. Research and Devel., Health Activities; mem. Nat. Adv. Allied Health Professions Council; co-chmn. health research com. Community Service Council Jefferson County, Inc. Served to capt. USAF, 1961-64. Recipient U. Ia. Leadership award, 1959, Outstanding Pub. Speaking award, 1963. Mem. Am., Ala. hosp. assns., Am. Coll. Hosp. Adminstrs., Am. Pub. Health Assn. Mem. editorial adv. bd. Ala. Jour. of Med. Scis., 1967—. Contbr. articles to profl. jours. Home: 3009 Sterling Rd Birmingham AL 35213 Office: 619 S 19th St Birmingham AL 35233

BLAZEK, STEPHEN MILAN, govt. ofcl.; b. Uniontown, Pa., Apr. 22, 1929; s. Stephen and Helen (Adamovich) B.; B.S. in M.E., Carnegie Inst. Tech., 1951; m. Woodrith Inez Richardson, Oct. 6, 1956. With Navy Dept., Washington, 1951—, dir. research and devel. programs on mech. impedance, shipboard vibration, 1958-61, head tech. planning and evaluation, ship acoutical signatures Nav. Ships Systems Command, 1961—, also prin. cons. on ship quieting, 1965—. Mem. Nav. Ships System Assn. Sr. Engrs. (Profl. Achievement award 1969). Home: 1641 Evers Dr McLean VA 22101 Office: Navships 0371 National Center No 3 Washington DC 20360

BLAZER, JOHN ALLISON, clin. psychologist; b. Nashville, Apr. 18, 1930; s. John Payne and Henryetta (Rowland) B.; B.A., Andrew Jackson U., 1954; A.B., Cumberland U., 1958; B.S., Coll. William and Mary, 1959; M.S., 1960; Ph.D., Episcopal U., 1962; Sc.D., Burton Coll., 1965; postgrad. U. Tenn., 1958, Vanderbilt U., 1960; U. Miami, 1961, U. London, 1962, Sorbonne, U. Paris, 1962; Ph.D. (hon.), Ohio Christian Coll., 1970; m. Judith Kristine Rosen, Mar. 28, 1964; 1 dau., Allison Kristine. Individual practice psychology, Dallas, 1962; staff psychologist Bristol Mental Health Clin., Meml. Hosp. Bristol, Va.-Tenn., 1963-64; dir. Bristol (Va.) Family Guidance Center, 1964; clin. psychologist mental health clin. Chatham County Health Dept., Savannah, Ga., 1964—, acting dir., 1971; pres. Psychol. Press, Savannah, 1962—; sch. psychologist Bristol (Tenn.) Bd. Edn., 1963-64; cons. Bayview Psychol. Services, Portsmouth, Va., 1964—; instr. Am. U. Savannah, 1966—, Med. Coll. Ga. Savannah, 1966; dir. Children's Learning Center, 1969—, Savannah Reading Center, 1970—; personnel dir. Wachtel's Physician Supply Co., 1968-69; personnel cons. Candler Gen. Hosp., 1969-70; asso. psychologist Marion F. Smith and Assos., psychol. consultants, 1969—. Served with USMCR, 1948-53. Decorated Purple Heart. Mem. Am. Assn. for Humanistic Psychology, Am. Sociol Assn., Am. Assn. Criminology (chmn. Com. crime prevention, psychology criminality 1964—, v.p. Ga. chpt. 1966—), Ga. mental health sect. (chmn. 1967-68) Ga. Pub. Health Assn., Ga. Psychol. Assn., Nat. Council Family Relations, Am. Assn. Sex Educators and Counselors, Am. Assn. Suicidology, Am. Counselors Soc., Am. Personnel and Guidance Assn., Ga. Sch. Psychol. Services Assn., Internat. Assn. Hypnotists, Nat. Assn. Sch. Psychologists, Nat. Assn. Social Workers, Soc. for Sci. Study Sex, Am. Acad. Mental Health Technicians, Southeastern Council on Family Relations. Luthern. Editor Psychology—A Journal of Human Behavior, 1963; editorial adviser Edn., 1970; cons. editor Psychologists and Educators Press, 1970. Contbr. articles to profl. jours, poems to lit. mags. Home: 308 Kensington Dr Savannah GA 31405 Office: Chatham County Health Dept Savannah GA 31405

BLAZER, REXFORD S(YDNEY), oil exec.; b. Aledo, Ill., Sept. 1, 1907; s. Frederick B. and Elizabeth E. (Niederlander) B.; A.B., U. Ill., 1928; D.Sc., (hon.), Pikeville Coll., 1969; m. Mary Elizabeth Vary, 1935 (dec.); 1 dau., Mary Linda; m. 2d, Frances Montross Green, 1942 (div.); 1 son, Richard M.; m. 3d, Lucile Thornton Scott, 1954; 1 son, Rexford Sydney; stepchildren—Dan W. Scott III, W. Thornton Scott. Joined Allied Oil Co., Inc., Cleve., 1928, dir., 1935-59, v.p., 1938, pres., 1948-59; dir. Ashland Oil, Inc. (Ky.) (formerly Ashland Oil & Refining Co.), 1949—, pres., 1951-57, chmn. bd. 1957-72, chmn. exec. com., 1972—; dir. 3d Nat. Bank of Ashland. Bd. dirs. U. Ill. Found.; mem. exec. com. U. Ky. Devel. Council; trustee Ky. Ind. Coll. Found., 1952-64; regent, trustee U. of South; bd. dirs. Spindletop Research Center. Mem. Ky. Indsl. Devel. Bd., 1956-69, East Ky. Regional Planning Commn., 1960-64 chmn. adv. council Ohio Valley Improvement Assn.; mem. adv. com. Nat. Waterways Conf. Recipient Illini Achievement award U. Ill., 1968. Mem. Nat. Petroleum Assn. (past pres.), Western Petroleum Refiners Assn. (v.p. 1957-61), Nat. Petroleum Refiners Assn. (dir., mem. exec. and finance coms.), Am. Petroleum Inst. (dir., mem. exec. com., past v.p. transp., mem. asphalt com.), Asphalt Inst. (past dir.), 25 Year Club of Petroleum Industry (pres.), Hwy. Users Fedn. for Safety and Mobility, (past chmn.), Ky. (pres. 1955-56), Ohio (dir. 1960—) chambers commerce, Ky. Oil and Gas Assn. (dir.), Psi Upsilon (chmn. bd. govs. Omicron chpt., v.p. exec. council). Episcopalian (sr. warden Ashland 1959; mem. exec. council Lexington Diocese 1958-62). Rotarian. Clubs: Bellefonte Country (Ashland); Idle Hour Country (Lexington); Westwood Country (Cleve.); Pendennis (Louisville); Filson. Home: 2711 Seminole Av Ashland KY 41101 Office: 1409 Winchester Av Ashland KY 41101

BLECHER, MELVIN, educator; b. Rahway, N.J., July 19, 1922; s. Jacob and Tessie (Katzman) B.; B.S., Rutgers U., 1949; Ph.D., U. Pa., 1954; m. Doris Burton, 1950; children—Marjorie Ellen, Jonathan Burton; m. 2d, Marlene Selmer, 1963. Research asso. Columbia Coll. Phys. and Surg., N.Y.C., 1954-56; instr. Albert Einstein Coll. Medicine, N.Y.C., 1956-57, asst. prof., 1957-61; asso. prof. biochemistry Georgetown U. Sch. Medicine and Dentistry, Washington, 1961-68, prof., 1968—. Mem. Am. Soc. Biol. Chemists, Endocrine Soc., Soc. Exptl. Biology and Medicine, A.M.A., Am. Assn. U. Profs., Assn. Am. Med. Colls., A.A.A.S. Contbr. articles to profl. jours. Home: 4000 Tunlaw Rd NW Washington DC 20007

BLECHMAN, WILBUR JORDAN, physician; b. Washington, May 7, 1932; s. Charles and Florence (Goodman) B.; B.S., Yale, 1954; M.D., Med. Coll. Va., 1957; m. Sidell Ray Cohen, June 26, 1955; children—Michele Ilene, Michael Howard, Ivy Beth. Intern, Med. Coll. Va., 1957-58; resident Jackson Meml. Hosp., 1958-60, Johns Hopkins Hosp., 1960-61; practice medicine, specializing in internal medicine and rheumatology, North Miami Beach, Fla., 1961—; sec. North Dade Med. Group, 1965-68; asst. prof. rheumatology U. Miami Med. Sch., 1970—. Pres. Andover Golf Estates Civic Assn., 1964; mem. med. adv. com. Crippled Children's Soc. Dade County, 1971—. Bd. dirs. Fla. Arthritis Found.; pres. The Dade County Arthritis Found., 1967-70. Recipient certificate of appreciation City of North Miami Beach, 1969; Distinguished Service award The Arthritis Found., 1971. Mem. A.C.P., Am., S. Fla. (pres. 1963) rheumatism assns. Kiwanian (pres. 1966). Home: 2200 NE 201st St Miami FL 33160 Office: 909 Interama Blvd North Miami Beach FL 33162

BLECKNER, EDWARD, JR., data communications co. exec.; b. Pompano, Fla., June 30, 1933; s. Edward and Emma (DeLozier) B.; B.E.E., U. Fla., 1954; m. Sondra Marie Roush, June 25, 1954; children—Karen Marie, Laura Louise. Sr. engr. Melpar Inc., Falls Church, Va., 1956-59; staff engr. Aero Geo Astro Corp., Alexandria, Va., 1959; with Milgo Electronic Corp., Miami, 1960—, mgr. Data Communications div., 1966-67, v.p., 1970—, pres. subsidiary Internat. Communications Corp., Miami, 1967—; pres. Milgo-IDAB Corp., Miami, 1966-67; dir. Racal-Milgo Ltd., Reading, Berkshire, Eng. Served with USAF, 1954-56. Mem. Sigma Chi. Republican. Methodist. Patentee in field. Office: 7620 NW 36th Av Miami FL 33147

BLEE, MYRON ROY, educator; b. Paw Paw, Ill., Feb. 25, 1917; s. Roy T. and Martha (Fox) B.; B.Ed., No. Ill. State Tchrs. Coll., 1938; M.A. in Polit. Sci., U. Ill., 1939, D.Ed., 1958; m. Charlotte Marie Leverenz, Jan. 1, 1941; 1 dau., Kathleen Marie. Tchr., also teaching prin. elementary schs., Lake County, Ill., 1939-42; asso. dean men, instr. Am. Govt. No. Ill. State Tchrs. Coll., 1946-48; asst. supt. instrn. Community Unit Sch. Dist. 271, Ashton, Ill., 1948-52; asso. dir. Fla. Legislative Reference Bur., Tallahassee, 1952-54, Council Study Higher Edn. in Fla., 1954-56; ednl. and research officer Fla. Bd. Control Higher Edn., 1956-62; pres. Fla. Inst. Continuing Univ. Studies, Tallahassee, 1962-65; asso. dean acad. affairs Fla. Atlantic U., 1965-66; dep. dir. Office Emergency Planning, Exec. Office Pres., 1966-67; pres. Jr. Coll. Broward County, Ft. Lauderdale, Fla., 1967-68; pres. Asso. Consultants in Edn., Inc., 1968—; academic affairs adminstr. Div. Community Colls., Fla. Dept. Edn., 1972—. Mem. Fla. Ednl. TV Commn., 1960-66; bd. edn. Fla. Ann. Conf. Methodist Ch., 1960—. Trustee Bethune Cookman Coll., Daytona Beach, 1961-68. Served to lt. comdr. USNR, 1942-46; PTO. Mem. Am. Assn. Sch. Adminstrs., N.E.A., Fla. Adult Edn. Assn., Kappa Delta Pi, Phi Delta Kappa. Democrat. Club: Internat. Torch. Home: 1447 Marion Av Tallahassee FL 32303 Office: Knott Bldg Tallahassee FL

BLEEMER, ROBERT R., interior designer; b. N.Y.C., July 8, 1931; s. Alfred I. and Fay (Niemer) B.; student Washington U., St. Louis, 1951-52; B.Arch., U. Fla., 1958; m. Mary Ann Brown, June 22, 1964. Designer, planner Victor Gruen, N.Y.C., 1959-60; project designer, planner Morris Lapidus Assos., Miami Beach, Fla., 1960-62; project designer, planner Henry End Assos., Miami, Fla., 1963-65; pres. Bleemer & Levine, Miami, 1965—. Mem. Lowe Art Mus. Assn. Served with USNR, 1952-55. Mem. Designers and Decorators Guild Miami, Am. Inst. Interior Designers. Club: Jockey (Miami). Home: 4717 N Bay Rd Miami Beach FL 33140 Office: 64 NE 40th St Miami FL 33137

BLESSING, BERWYN MARSHALL, pub. co. exec.; b. Farmington, Ill., Feb. 6, 1910; s. George Richard and Hazel (Snell) B.; student Bradley Coll., 1929-31, Chrysler Engring. Sch., 1942-44, Columbia U., 1968; m. Mary Ann Roberts, Mar. 25, 1965; children—(by previous marriage) Susan E., Robert W., Wynn (Mrs. Morris Weeks). With Peoria (Ill.) Star Pub. Co., 1921-36, Chgo. Tribune, 1936-37; asst. press supt. Detroit Free Press, 1937-59, press supt. Columbia (S.C.) Newspapers, Inc., 1959-67, prodn. dir., 1968—. Mem. Columbia Artist Guild, C. of C. Lutheran. Club: Spring Valley Country (Columbia, S.C.). Home: 4210 Willingham Dr Columbia SC 29202 Office: Box 1333 Stadium Rd Columbia SC 29202

BLEVINS, BRYAN O'DONNELL, dentist; b. Baytown, Tex., July 19, 1939; s. Arthur Bustor and Ollie Marie (Norris) B.; student Panola Coll., 1957-59, Northeast State U., 1959-61; B.S., D.D.S., Baylor U., 1965; m. Doris Jeanne Vaughn, Feb. 15, 1964; children—Bryan O'Donnell, Jaime D'Lea. Pvt. practice dentistry, Lufkin, Tex., 1965—. Mem. Am. Acad. Cold Foil Operators, Am., Tex. dental assns., East Tex. Dental Soc., Am. Acad. Gen. Dentistry, Am. Soc. Preventive Dentistry, Internat. Acad. Orthodontics, Jr. C. of C., C. of C., Psi Omega. Baptist. Home: 1407 Oak Hill St Lufkin TX 75901 Office: 105 E Bremond St Lufkin TX 75901

BLEVINS, JAMES VICTOR, internat. trade co. exec.; b. Birmingham, Ala., Jan. 10, 1912; s. James Edward and Gertrude (Stewart) B.; student Ga. Sch. Tech., 1929-30; m. Patty Louise Hester, Feb. 17, 1933; children—Betty (Mrs. Peter A. Jensen, Jr.), James William. Founder, pres. J.V. Blevins Co., Nashville, 1945—; organizer Blevins Popcorn Co. (merged with Conwood Corp., 1961), Nashville, 1948, chmn. bd., 1961—; founder Marble Co., Nashville, 1952, pres., 1962—; dir. Third Nat. Bank, Australian Popcorn Co., Mobile Home Parts Co., Abbott Corp. Bd. dirs. Cordell Hull Found., Jim Blevins Found., Big Bros. Served with USCGR, 1941-45. Presbyn. (elder 1952—). Mason (32 deg., Shriner, Jester), Rotarian. Home: 5350 Hillsboro Rd Nashville TN 37215 Office: PO Box 7893 Nashville TN 37209

BLEWER, JOHN RANDALL, gas pipeline co. exec.; b. Shreveport, La., Sept. 9, 1929; s. Edwin Laurine and Mildred (Sewall) B.; B.S., La. State U., 1950; m. Nancy Harper, Feb. 28, 1959; children—John Randall, Susan Elizabeth. Mgr. community and stockholder relations Tex. Eastern Transp. Corp., Shreveport, 1952-59; mgr. financial relations Bozell & Jacobs, Inc., N.Y.C., 1959-60; dir. pub. relations Tex. Gas Transmission Corp., Owensboro, Ky., 1960-71, v.p. pub. relations, financial relations and advt., 1971—. Mem. adv. bd. Salvation Army, chmn. 1971-72; mem. adv. bd. Jr. Service League; bd. dirs., mem. exec. com. United Fund. Served to capt. AUS, 1951-52. Mem. Am., So. gas assns., Ind. Natural Gas Assn., Mid-Continent, Ky. Oil and gas assns., Ohio Valley Improvement Assn., So. States Indsl. Council, Pub. Relations Soc. Am., Assn. Petroleum Writers. Clubs: Campbell (dir. 1969-72, pres. 1970), Owensboro Country (Owensboro). Home: 1805 Littlewood Dr Owensboro KY 42301 Office: 3800 Frederica St Owensboro KY 42301

BLINN, C. J., judge. Formerly judge Oklahoma County, Oklahoma City, now asso. dist. judge. Office: Courthouse and County Bldg 321 Park Av Oklahoma City OK 73102*

BLISS, DONALD T., JR., govt. ofcl. Spl. asst. to Sec., Dept. Health, Edn. and Welfare. Office: 330 Independence Blvd SW Washington DC 20201*

BLISSITT, CHARLES ASH, elec. engr.; b. Andrews, S.C., July 1, 1922; s. Grover Cleveland and Mary Fay (Delk) B.; student Internat. Corr. Schs.; m. Vivian C. Vinson, Apr. 13, 1941; children—Barbara Jean (Mrs. Phelix D. Welch), Charles Vernon. Various positions, 1940-43; with St. Johns River Shipbldg. Co., 1943-45, Jax Ice & Cold Storage Co., 1946-50; with Electric and Water Engring. Dept., Jacksonville, Fla., 1950-68, engr. in charge water sect., 1964-68, profl. engr. in charge water activity engring. div. Pub. Works Dept., 1968—; asso. in design. cons. comml., Indsl. power lighting Evans & Hammond, engrs., Jacksonville, 1962—. Served with USNR, 1945-46. Registered profl. engr., Fla. Mem. Nat. Soc. Profl. Engrs., I.E.E.E. (sect. sec.-treas. 1965-66, sect. chmn. 1966-67). Am. Water Works Assn., Am. Pub. Works Assn., Engineering Professions (pres. 1962). Presbyn. Mason. Home: 1017 Ashton St Jacksonville FL 32208 Office: City Hall Jacksonville FL 32202

BLITCH, JAMES BUCHANAN, architect; b. Charleston, S.C., Sept. 2, 1923; s. Norman Henry and Louise (Buchanan) B.; student Loyola U. of South, 1943; B.Arch., Tulane U., 1950; m. Hilda Goodspeed Mouledoux, Nov. 24, 1945; children—James Buchanan, John Crandell, Ronald Buchanan, Judith Ann (dec.), Courtney Ann, David Alan, Leslie Ann, Lisl Maria. Profl. asst. Ricciuti, Stoffle & Asso., 1950-54; partner Ricciuti Asso., 1954-58; owner J. Buchanan Blitch & Asso., 1958-66; pres. J. Buchanan Blitch & Asso., Inc., 1966—, Blitch Assos., Ltd. (Miss.), 1971—. Chmn., East Jefferson Hosp. Found., 1971-72. Trustee Asso. Catholic Charities, St. Elizabeth's Home for Girls (v.p.). Served with USNR, 1943-45. Decorated Knight Equestrian Order of Holy Sepulchre; recipient honor awards for excellence in design Gulf. States region A.I.A., 1962-69, La. Architects Assn., 1964-69. Fellow A.I.A.; mem. La. Architects Assn. (v.p. 1969-70, pres. 1971-72, dir.), New Orleans C. of C., Phi Kappa Theta, Omicron Delta Kappa, Tau Beta Pi. Democrat. Roman Catholic. K.C. Home: 1703 Haring Rd Metairie LA 70001 Office: 1070 St Charles Av New Orleans LA 70130

BLIVEN, FLOYD EDWARD, JR., physician, educator; b. Erie, Pa., May 20, 1921; s. Floyd Edward and Margaret (Willis) B.; A.B., U. Rochester, 1942, M.D., 1945; m. Hester DuPuy Spencer, July 29, 1950; children—Caroline DuPuy, Andrew Willis II, Rachel Davis, Lydia Colwell, James Spencer, Amy Somerville. Intern Strong Meml. Hosp. Rochester, N.Y., 1945-46, resident in surgery, orthopedics, 1948-51; practice medicine specializing in surgery, Rochester, 1952-56, Augusta, Ga., 1956—; mem. faculty U. Rochester Sch. Medicine, 1952-56; prof. orthopedic surgery Med. Coll. of Ga.; chief orthopedics Eugene Talmadge Meml. Hosp., Augusta, 1956—; cons. Ga. Dept. Pub. Health, Battey State Hosp., Rome, Ga., Crippled Children's Service, Waycross, Ga., VA Hosp., 1956—, Milledgeville (Ga.) State Hosp., 1958-68, U.S. Army Hosp., Ft. Gordon, Ga., 1963—. Bd. dirs. United Cerebral Palsy Assn., 1958-59, pres. Easter Seal Soc., Augusta, 1964-65; trustee, Augusta Prep. Sch., 1966; bd. dirs. Episcopal Day Sch., Augusta, 1964-67, 71—; Friends of Augusta Library. Diplomate Am. Bd. Othopedic Surgery. Fellow Am. Coll. Surgeons; mem. Am., So. med. assns., Orthopedic Research Soc., Am. Acad. Orthopedic Surgeons. Home: 619 Scotts Way Augusta GA 30904

BLOCK (EDWARD) BATES, lawyer; b. Atlanta, Aug. 16, 1918; s. E. Bates and Julia (Porter) B.; A.B., Emory U., 1940 LL.B., U. Ga., 1942; m. Margaret Ann Davison, Dec. 18, 1956; foster children—Julia, Baxter, Douglas Jones. Admitted to Ga. bar, 1942; partner firm Hansell, Post, Brandon & Dorsey, Atlanta; sec., dir. So. Syndicate, Inc., Ga. Capital Corp.; pres., dir. Valley Devel. Corp., 1954-71, Woodlands, Inc. Mem. Ga. Student Loan Commn., 1964-70. Trustee Chi Phi Ednl. Trust. Mem. Ga. Geneal. Soc. (pres. 1965-66), Atlanta Hist. Assn., Atlanta Art Assn., Ga., Atlanta (sec. 1943-49) bar assns., Atlanta Lawyers Club, Motor Carrier Lawyers Assn., Phi Beta Kappa, Omicron Delta Kappa, Chi Phi (nat. v.p.). Presbyn. Clubs: University Yacht; Capital City, Nine O'Clocks, Piedmont Driving (Atlanta). Editor: Atlanta Lawyer, 1956-62, Ga. Bar News, 1963-64. Home: 25 Valley Rd NW Atlanta GA 30305 Office: First Nat Bank Bldg Atlanta GA 30303

BLOCK, HERBERT LAWRENCE (HERBLOCK), editorial cartoonist; b. Chgo., Oct. 13, 1909; s. David Julian and Tessie (Lupe) B.; student Lake Forest (Ill.) Coll., 1927-29, L.L.D. (hon.), 1957; student Art Inst. Chgo. (part time classes); unmarried. Editorial cartoonist Chgo. Daily News, 1929-33, NEA Service, 1933-43, U.S. Army, 1943-45; editorial cartoonist The Washington Post, 1946—. Recipient Pulitzer prize, 1942, 54; Am. Newspaper Guild award, 1948; Heywood Broun award, 1950; Sigma Delta Chi Nat. Editorial Awards, 1949, 50, 52, 57; Sidney Hillman award (for book), 1953; Reuben award Nat. Cartoonists Soc., 1957; Lauterbach award for civil liberties union, 1960; Distinguished Service Journalism award U. Mo., 1961. Fellow Am. Acad. Arts and Scis. Club: Cosmos (Washington). Author: The Herblock Book, 1952; Herblock's Here and Now, 1955; Herblock's Special for Today, 1958. Address: The Washington Post 1515 L St NW Washington DC 20005

BLOCK, IRVIN SEYMOUR, wholesale paper trade exec.; b. San Antonio, Jan. 3, 1927; s. Al and Metha (Wolff) B.; student San Antonio Coll., 1945-47; m. Laurile Michelson, Aug. 14, 1955; children—Jack, Molly. Purchasing agt. Westinghouse Electric Supply Co., San Antonio, 1945-51, Corpus Christi (Tex.) Electric Co., 1953-61; real estate broker Block Realty Co., San Antonio, 1951-53; purchasing mgr. Century Papers, Inc., Corpus Christi, 1961—. Owner, Irv Block Orch., 1969—, Irv Block Rare Coins, 1971—. Active Boy Scouts Am. Democrat, Jewish religion, Mem. B'nai B'rith (bd. dirs. 1969-70). Home: 734 Meadowbrook Dr Corpus Christi TX 78412 Office: PO Box 4788 Corpus Christi TX 78408

BLOCK, WILLIAM JOSEPH, JR., physician; b. San Antonio, Tex., Oct. 3, 1921; s. William Joseph and Mary Irene (McNelly) B.; B.A., St. Mary's U., San Antonio, 1942; M.D., U. Tex. at Galveston, 1945; M.S., U. Minn., 1952; m. Mary Patricia O'Daniel, Aug. 18, 1949; children—Patricia Irene, Susan Kearney, Mary Kathleen, Martha Terry, Sharon Ann, William Joseph III, Michael Alfred. Intern, Robert B. Green Hosp., San Antonio, 1945-46; resident medicine Boston City Hosp., 1948-49, Mayo Clinic, 1949-52; pvt. practice medicine, specializing in cardiology, San Antonio, 1952—; clin. prof. medicine U. Tex. at San Antonio; cons. cardiology to Surgeon Gen.; mem. staff Nix Meml., Robert B. Green Meml., Bexar County Teaching hosps.; mem. courtesy staff S.W. Tex. Meth., Bapt. Meml., Santa Rose, St. Benedict's, Grace Gen. hosps.; cons. cardiology San Antonio State TB Hosp. Active San Antonio A.R.C. Bd. dirs. Travelers Aid Soc.; trustee S.W. Research Found. Served with AUS, 1946-48. Diplomate Am. Bd. Internal Medicine. Fellow A.C.P., Am. Heart Assn., Am. Coll. Chest Physicians, Am. Coll. Cardiology (past gov.); mem. Tex. (past pres.), San Antonio (past pres.) heart assns., Tex. Acad. Internal Medicine (past pres.), Tex. Club Cardiologists (past pres.), San Antonio Club Internal Medicine (past pres.), Tex. Soc. Internal Medicine (past dir.), San Antonio C. of C., Sigma Xi, Alpha Omega Alpha. Rotarian (dir.). Clubs: Christmas Cotillion, Town, German, Order of Alamo, Texas Cavaliers, San Antonio Country, Argyle, University, St. Anthony (San Antonio). Home: 407 Elizabeth Rd San Antonio TX 78209 Office: Nix Professional Bldg San Antonio TX 78205

BLOCKER, RICHARD DANIEL, JR., ednl. adminstr.; b. Jacksonville, Fla., Nov. 25, 1931; s. Richard Daniel and Claudis Mary (Webb) B.; B.S., U. Fla. 1954, M.Ed., 1958; Ed.D., Am. U., 1968; m. Martha M. Johnston, Aug. 24, 1963; children—Richard Daniel III, Mark Franklin. Tchr., John Gorrie Jr. High Sch., Jacksonville, 1958-62; tchr. Washington-Lee High Sch., Arlington, Va., 1962-63, asst. prin., 1964-69; tchr. McLean (Va.) High Sch., 1963-64; dir. secondary edn. Prince William County Schs., Manassas, Va., 1969-71; dir. gen. programs Arlington County Schs., Arlington, 1971—. Lectr. applied linguistics Georgetown U., Washington, 1969—. Served with AUS, 1954-56; maj. Res. Mem. N.E.A. (life), Nat. Assn. Pupil Personnel Adminstrs., Council for Exceptional Children, Phi Delta Kappa. Home: 3156 Kenney Dr Falls Church VA 22042 Office: 1426 N Quincy St Arlington VA 22207

BLOCKER, WILLIAM PRESTON, JR., physician; b. Eagle Pass, Tex., July 21, 1918; s. William Preston and Joy Ovada (Johnston) B.; B.S., U. Tex., 1939, M.D., 1944; postgrad. U. Cal. at Los Angeles, 1965; m. Anna Katherine Roberts, June 18, 1944; 1 son, William Preston, III. Intern, Baylor U. Hosp., Dallas, 1944-45; resident internal medicine Scott-White Hosp.-Clinic, Temple, Tex., 1945-47; pvt. practice medicine, owner Donna (Tex.) Clinic, 1950-60; resident neurology and phys. medicine and rehab. Baylor Med. Coll. Hosp. System, 1960-64, chief phys. medicine and rehab., Dallas, 1964-66; chief policy VA Central Office, Washington, 1966-68; chief, rehab. medicine VA Hosp., Houston, 1968—; clin. prof. rehab. medicine U. Tex. Med. Sch., Dallas, 1964-66; asst. prof. rehab. medicine Baylor Coll. Medicine, Houston, 1968—. Served to capt. M.C., AUS, 1942-45, 48-50. Fellow A.C.P., Am. Acad. Phys. Medicine, Am. Geriatric Soc.; mem. A.M.A., Mil. Surgeons Assn. Lion, Elk. Clubs: Toastmasters, Run for Life (Houston). Contbr. articles to profl. jours. Producer numerous med. video and audio tapes. Home: 5102 Sanford St Houston TX 77035 Office: 2002 Holcombe St Houston TX 77031

BLOMME, CARLYLE WHITNEY, JR., educator; b. Wilmington, N.C., Oct. 14, 1933; s. Carlyle Whitney and Vivian Inez (Darden) B.; A.A., Wilmington Jr. Coll., 1957; B.A., U. N.C., 1971; m. Dorothy Blount Anderson, June 8, 1960; 1 son, Carlyle Anderson. Chief survey party John B. Davis, Jr., surveyor, Wilmington, 1956-57; partner Davis & Blomme Surveying Co., Wilmington, 1957-59; owner Blomme Surveying Co., Wilmington, 1959-68; instr. engring. tech., chmn. civil tech. div. Coastal Carolina Community Coll., Jacksonville, 1969—; instr., Cape Fear Tech. Inst., Wilmington, 1965-67. Engring. adviser to exec. com. Wilmington Presbytery, Presbyn. Ch., Synod N.C., 1967—. Served with USCGR, 1952-55. Mem. Am. Congress Surveying and Mapping, Am. Soc. Engring. Edn., N.C. Soc. Surveyors (chpt. pres. 1962, chmn. edn. com. 1972), V.F.W. Democrat. Home: Route 3 Box 282 Richlands NC 28574 Office: 222 Georgetown Rd Jacksonville NC 28540

BLOODWORTH, JAMES NELSON, justice; b. Decatur, Ala., Jan 21, 1921; s. Benjamin M. and Marguerite (Nelson) B.; student Athens Coll., 1938-39; B.S., U. Ala. Sch. Commerce, 1942; LL.B., U. Ala., 1947; m. Mary Jean Gregg, Sept. 27, 1963; children—Catherine, Sandra, Jean Marguerite. Admitted to Ala. bar, 1947; mem. firm Calvin & Bloodworth, Decatur, 1947-58; judge, Recorder's Ct., Decatur, Ala., 1948-51; solicitor Morgan County, Decatur, 1951; judge Circuit Ct. Ala., 8th Jud. Circuit, Decatur, 1959-68; asso. justice Ala. Supreme Ct., 1968—. Co-chmn. Circuit Judges' Seminars Ala., 1960-66; lectr. before judges, solicitors assns., seminars, 1963—; chmn. Ala. Pattern Jury Instr. Com., 1966-68. Pres. Morgan County Jury Com., 1966-68. Pres. Decatur Boys Club, 1951; moderator North Ala. Presbytery, 1965; mem. bd. Morgan County chpt. A.R.C., 1959-60. Mem. Bd. Pardons and Paroles Ala., 1951-52; chmn. Ala. Democratic campaign steering com., 1961-63; faculty adviser Nat. Coll. State Trial Judges, 1967, 71; faculty Am. Acad. Jud. Edn., 1970—; lectr. Ala. Police Acad., 1969—. Served from pvt. to captain AUS, lt. col. Reserve retired. Decorated Bronze Star medal, Combat Infantry badge. Mem. Ala. Res. Officers Assn. (pres. chpt. 1959), Morgan County Bar Assn. (pres. 1955), Decatur C. of C., Ala. Bar Assn., Phi Delta Phi, Kappa Alpha Order, Omicron Delta Kappa. Presbyn. (elder). Mason (K.T., Shriner), Rotarian (pres. 1953-54). Home: 3221 Bankhead Av Montgomery AL 36106 Office: Judicial Bldg Capitol Montgomery AL 36104

BLOOM, WALLACE, psychologist; b. N.Y.C., Apr. 9, 1916; s. Irving and Agnes (Weinstein) B.; B.B.A., Coll. City N.Y., 1936; M.S., Trinity U., 1952; Ph.D., U. Tex., 1964; m. Riselle Levis, Dec. 24, 1950; children—Winifred (Mrs. Ralph Bengis), Michael. Interviewer, N.Y. State Labor Dept., 1936-39; commd. 2d lt. USAF, 1937, advanced through grades to lt. col., 1947; personnel officer Wheeler Field, Hawaii, 1941-42; research psychologist Kirtland AFB 1959-60; ret., 1960; human factors psychologist United Tech. Corp., Cal., 1963-64; staff clin. psychologist Porterville State Hosp., Cal., 1964-66; chief psychologist Child Guidance Clinic, Wilford Hall USAF Hosp., Tex., 1966—; lectr. Fresno State Coll. Extension, 1965-66, Our Lady of Lake Coll., Tex., 1967—. Mem. Am., N.M. (past treas.) psychol. assns., San Antonio Assn. for Children With Learning Disorders, San Antonio Assn. for Mental Retardation, Am. Assn. on Mental Deficiency. Contbr. chpt. Studies in Personnel and Industrial Efficiency, 1961. Home: 133 Twinleaf Lane San Antonio TX 78213 Office: Child Guidance Clinic Wilford Hall USAF Hosp San Antonio TX 78236

BLOOMER, JOHN WELLMAN, newspaper editor; b. Wabash, Ind., Apr. 23, 1912; s. John W. and Floy (Hubbard) R.; student Ind. U., 1932-34; m. Margaret Schornick, Nov. 10, 1935. Editor, Elizabethton (Tenn.) Daily Star, 1935-39; exec. editor Kingsport (Tenn.) Times & News, 1939-42, 46; mng. editor Sarasota (Fla.) Herald-Tribune, 1947-52, Columbus (Ga.) Ledger and Sunday Ledger- Enquirer (Pulitzer prize meritorious pub. service 1955), 1952-56; pub-editor Portsmouth (Va.) Daily Times, 1956-57; state editor Birmingham (Ala.) News, 1957-59, asso. editor, 1959-61, mng. editor, 1961—. Chmn., Adv. Council for Environmental Quality. Bd. dirs. A.R.C., Jefferson County Mental Health Assn., Trio Counties A.R.C., Ala. Tb Assn.; bd. dirs. Nat. Partners of Americas, pres. Ala. chpt. Mem Ala. Press Assn. (dir.), Am. Soc. Newspaper Editors, Newcomen Soc., Ala. Hist. Soc. (mem. exec. com.), Sigma Delta Chi (pres. Ala. profl. chpt. 1963). Episcopalian. Elk, Kiwanian. Author: articles on newspaper problems. Home: 2717 Highland Av Birmingham AL 35205 Office: 2200 4th Av N Birmingham AL 35202

BLOSKAS, JOHN D., editor, pub. relations dir.; b. Waco, Tex., July 13, 1928; s. George and Alvina (Schrader) B.; B.A., Baylor U., 1953; m. Anna Louise Nelson, Feb. 7, 1955; children—Suzanne, John D., Kenneth Douglas. Exec. sec. Waco Jr. C. of C., 1953-55; asso. editor Mexia (Tex.) Daily News, 1955-56; dir. publicity Valley C. of C., Weslaco, Tex., 1956-57; religion editor Houston Chronicle, 1957-58; v.p. pub. relations annuity bd. So. Bapt. Conv., Dallas, 1958—. Served with USNR, 1945-49, 50-51. Mem. So. Bapt. (past pres.), Tex. Bapt. (past pres.) pub. relations assns., Pub. Relations Soc. Am. (accredited), Religious Pub. Relations Council, Fellowship of Christians in Arts, Media and Entertainment. Editor: The Years Ahead. Home: 5816 Clendenin Dallas TX 75228 Office: 511 N Akard Bldg Dallas TX 75201

BLOSSER, DALE ALAN, architect; b. Brussells, Belgium, Oct. 3, 1927; s. (father Am. citizen) Rolland Ernest Blosser and Josephine (My) B.; student Carnegie Inst. Tech., 1947-49; B.Arch., N.C. State Coll., 1956; m. Louise Ann Schultz Pinkerton, May 25, 1967; stepchildren—Stephen R., Susan L., Timothy J., Don Charles, Lizabeth Ann. Architect, Goedesics, Inc., Raleigh, N.C., 1957-60, John D. Latimer & Asso., Durham, N.C., 1960-62, Synergetics, Inc., Raleigh, 1962-65, Dale Blosser & Assos., archtl. constrn. administrn., Raleigh, 1966—. Lectr. profl. practice dept. architecture Sch. Design, N.C. State U. Served with AUS, 1945-47. Registered architect, N.C., S.C., Va. Mem. Am. Soc. Testing Materials (councilor Carolinas dist.), A.I.A. (office procedures com. N.C. 1966—), Constrn. Specification Inst. (Raleigh-Durham chpt. pres. 1967-68), Bldg. Research Inst. (chmn. sect 5.05 constrn. techniques subcom. of Div. V constrn. mgmt. 1969—), N.C. Assn. Professions, Am. Concrete Inst., Am. Inst. Steel Constrn. Unitarian-Universalist (pres. Thomas Jefferson dist. 1968-69). Home: 3008 Ruffin St Raleigh NC 27607 Office: 124 Groveland Av Raleigh NC 27605

BLOUNT, PAUL GROVES, educator; b. Fulton, Mo., Jan. 20, 1919; s. Pearl G. and Daise (Mahoney) B.; A.B., Westminister Coll., 1941; M.A., Emory U., 1942 Ph.D., Cornell U., 1960; m. Mary Elizabeth Galloway, May 9, 1942; 1 dau., Nancy Elizabeth. Instr. to asst. prof. English, Ga. Tech., 1946-50; head dept. English, Ga. State U., Atlanta, 1951—. Served with USNR, 1942-46. Mem. Pi Kappa Alpha, Phi Sigma Iota, Sigma Tau Delta, Omicron Delta Kappa. Contbr. articles to profl. jours. Home: 2022 Briarcliff Rd NE Atlanta GA 30329

BLOUNT, ROBERT WARD, lawyer, banker; b. Hillsboro, Tex., Sept. 10, 1926; s. Robert Clinton and Aaron (Ward) B.; B.A., U. Tex., 1949; J.D., So. Meth. U., 1962; m. Clara Rae Belzner, Oct. 22, 1951; 1son Alan Curtis. Admitted to Tex. bar, 1962; spl. agt. FBI, Washington, 1951-54; security officer Magnolia Petroleum Co., Dallas, 1954-60, Hunt Oil Co., 1960-61; trust officer Merc. Nat. Bank, Dallas, 1961-65; v.p., trust officer Corpus Christi Bank & Trust (Tex.), 1965-69; v.p., trust officer, head trust dept. Exchange Bank and Trust Co., Dallas, 1969-72; v.p., trust officer Preston State Bank, Dallas, 1972—. Active Boy Scouts Am. Served with USNR, 1944-46. Mem. Am. Inst. Banking, Soc. Former F.B.I. Agts. (chmn. Dallas chpt. 1965), Am., Dallas bar assns., State Bar Tex., Phi Delta Phi. Kiwanian. Home: 7772 Querida Lane Dallas TX 75240 Office: Preston State Bank 8111 Preston Rd Dallas TX 75225

BLOUNT, WILLIAM BOYLE, civil engr.; b. Memphis, May 21, 1934; s. Isaac Sylvester and Louise (Townsend) B.; B.S., U. Ky., 1957; m. Shirley Flanagan, Jan. 26, 1957; children—William Boyle, Jane Barlow. Engr., Ruby Precast Concrete Co., Madisonville, Ky., 1957-60; plant mgr. Precision Prestressed Products, Henderson, Ky., 1960-63; exec. v.p. Ky. Prestressed Concrete, Lexington, Ky., 1963—; dir. Dixie Concrete Products Co., Lexington Erecting Co. (both Lexington). Mem. Nat., Ky. socs. profl. engrs. Home: 212 Leawood St Lexington KY 40502 Office: Box 5436 Lexington KY 40505

BLOUNT, WINTON MALCOLM, former postmaster gen. of U.S.; b. Union Springs, Ala., Feb. 1, 1921; s. Winton Malcolm and Clara B. (Chalker) B.; student U. Ala., 1939-41; L.H.D., Judson Coll., 1967; H.H.D., Huntington Coll., 1969; LL.D., Birmingham-So. Coll., 1969; D.C.L., Southwestern U. at Memphis, 1969; m. Mary Katherine Archibald, Sept. 12, 1942; children—Winton Malcolm III, Thomas A., S. Roberts, Katherine, Joseph W. Founder, Blount Bros. Corp., gen. contractors, Montgomery, Ala., 1946, pres., chmn. bd., 1946-69; chmn. bd. Benjamin F. Shaw Co., piping contractors, Wilmington, Del., until 1968; postmaster gen. U.S., Washington, 1969-71. Former bd. dirs. So. States Indsl. Council, So. Research Inst.; trustee U. Ala. Served with USAAF, 1942-45. Named One of 4 Outstanding Young Men of Ala., 1956, Montgomery Man of Year, 1961; recipient Golden Knight of Mgmt. award Ala. council Nat. Mgmt. Assn., 1962, City of Montgomery Distinguished Service citation, 1966, Ct. of Honor award Ala. Exchange Club, 1969, Nat. Brotherhood award Nat. Conf. Christians and Jews, 1970. Presbyn. (deacon) Rotarian. Home: Route 10 Box 43 Vaughn Rd Montgomery AL 36106

BLOXSOM, DANIEL EDGAR, chem. engr., plastics mfr.; b. Houston, Aug. 20, 1904; s. Edgar Daniel and Lillie (Penny) B.; student Rice Inst., 1925; m. Betty Bolton, June 26, 1926; children—Daniel Edgar, Joseph Thomas, and Betty Louise (Mrs. George A. McMoran, Jr.). With Anderson, Clayton and Company, Houston, 1927-42; organizer Southwestern Plastics, Inc., Houston, 1945, pres., 1954—; developed solarlite skylights, 1951, also acrylite plastics, 1945. Served as lt. comdr. USNR, 1941-45, PTO. Mem. N.A.M. (research and market com. patents com.), Soc. Plastics Industry, A.A.A.S., C. of C. Republican. Episcopalian. Patentee electronic communication systems, sky light, polex acrylite plastics. Home: 22 E Shady Lane Houston TX 77042 Office: 5615 Rice Av Houston TX 77036

BLUE, GEORGE R, lawyer, state legislator; b. Dec. 10, 1916; B.A., Tulane U., 1937, LL.B.; m. Catherine E. Colquitt; children—K.F., II, Leslie R., George R. Admitted to La. bar, 1939, practiced in New Orleans; notary public Parish of Orleans, 1938-40, 45-56; spl. agt. FBI, 1940-45; U.S. atty. Eastern Dist. La., 1953-56; mem. firm Beard, Blue, Schmitt & Treen, and predecessor, New Orleans, 1946—; mem. La. Ho. of Reps., 1964—; pres. Found. Plan, Inc. Republican candidate for U.S. Ho. of Reps. Mem. adv. com. on rules of criminal procedure U.S. Supreme Ct., 1960-70; mem. Nixon's Task Force Crime and Adminstrn. Justice. Served 2d lt. USMCR, 1937-41, lt. (j.g.), USNR, O.N.I., 1949-51. Mem. Am. Judicature Soc., Am., La., New Orleans bar assns., Internat. Assn. Ins. Counsel, Soc. Former Spl. Agts. FBI Inc. (former nat. v.p.), Phi Delta Phi. Clubs: Metairie Country, Southern Yacht. Home: 5308 Haring Ct Metairie LA 70002 Office: 833 Howard Av New Orleans LA 70113

BLUE, HERBERT CLIFTON, newspaper publisher, state legislator; b. nr. Vass, N.C., Aug. 28, 1910; s. John Patrick and Christian Ann (Stewart) B.; student pub. schs., Vass; m. Gala Lee Nunnery, July 4, 1937; children—Patricia Joyce (Mrs. David E. Bailey), Herbert Clifton, John Lee, Elizabeth Ann. Founder, owner, pub. The Captain (consol. with Sandhill Citizen 1934), Vass. 1932-36, Aberdeen, N.C., 1936—; owner, pub. Robbins (N.C.) Record, 1958—; dir. Carolina Bank, Pinehurst, N.C., Montgomery Herald, Troy, N.C.; mem. N.C. Ho. of Reps., 1947—, speaker, 1963-64. Pres., N.C. Young Democratic Clubs, 1948-49; sec. N.C. Dem. Exec. Com., 1949-52. Bd. dirs. N.C. Cancer Inst., 1961-64, N.C. Soc. for Crippled Children and Adults; chmn. N.C. Cancer Crusade Campaign, 1966; pres. N.C. div. Am. Cancer Soc., 1968; chmn. bd. trustees Sandhills Community Coll. Mem. N.C. Weekly Newspaper Assn. (pres. 1951-52), N.C. Press Assn. (dir. pres.), Woodman of World. Democrat. Presbyn. (elder, trustee). Mason, Lion. Home: 800 N Poplar St Aberdeen NC 28315 Office: 202 N Sandhills Blvd Aberdeen NC 28315

BLUE, RON B., broadcasting exec. Gen. mgr., sta. mgr. KRMG, Tulsa. Office: 1502 S Boulder St Tulsa OK 74119*

BLUM, ETHEL WIDLUS (MRS. MILTON R. BLUM), editor; b. Cleve., Aug. 16, 1921; d. Abe and Minnie (Cherlin) Widlus; student Ohio State U., 1942; m. Milton R. Blum, Feb. 23, 1942 children—Carol Lynn (Mrs. Gould), Jeffrey D., Roger. Editor for Gen. MacArthur, Japan, 1947-50; free lance travel writer, 1950-64; travel editor, women's editor Miami Beach (Fla.) Daily Sun, 1964-69; editor Travel Publs., Inc., Miami Beach, Fla., 1970—; spl. cons. Diversified Services of Bahama Islands. Pres., Cancer Inst. Miami; mem. adv. bd. Channel 2. Recipient Fla. Press Womens award for best series articles written by a woman, 1966. Mem. Fla. Press Womens Assn., Soc. Am. Travel Writers. (chmn. southeastern U.S.-Caribbean chpt., photography and writing awards 1966, 67, 68). Author, editor: Travel Guides, 1970. Home: 5005 Collins Av Miami Beach FL 33140 Office: 1853 Alton Rd Miami Beach FL 33139

BLUM, FRED, librarian; b. N.Y.C., Nov. 27, 1932; s. Henry and Jeanne (Cohen) B.; B.M., Oberlin Coll., 1954; M.F.A., Ohio U., 1955; Ph.D., State U. Ia., 1959; M.S. in L.S., Cath. U. Am., 1968; postgrad. U. Cologne, 1959-60, Free U. Berlin, 1960-61; m. Beula Eisenstadt, Sept. 24, 1967. Tchr., research asst. State U. Ia., Iowa City, 1955-59; teaching asst. Menzel-Schule, Berlin, Germany, 1960-61; reference librarian Library of Congress, Washington, 1961-66, editor Union catalog div., 1966-67; head spl. service dept. Cath. U., Washington, 1967-71, head tech. service dept., 1971—. Recipient Deutscher Akademischer Austauschdienst, 1959-60, Deutscher Paedagogischer Austauschdienst, 1960-61. Mem. Am., D.C. library assns., Assn. Coll. and Research Libraries (publs. com. 1971—), Music Library Assn. (chpt. chmn. 1964-66, chmn. microform com. 1966—), Internat. Assn. Music Libraries, Am. Nat. Standard Inst. (com. Z-39, 1969—, Beta Phi Mu. Author: Susanne Langer's Music Aesthetics, 1959; Music Monographs in Series: A Bibliography of Numbered Monograph Series in the Field of Music Current since 1945, 1964; Jean Sibelius: An International Bibliography on the Occasion of the Centennial Celebrations, 1965; Guide to Selected Research Material on Microforms, 1968. Editor: National Register of Microform Masters (U.S. Library of Congress), 1966; Theses and Dissertations (Cath. U. Am.), 1970; Nursing Theses (Cath. U. Am.), 1970. Systems design and Fortran programs; Union List of Serials (Consortium of Universities of the Washington Met. Area), 1970. Asst. editor, D.C. Libraries, 1968-70. Contbr. articles to profl. pubs. Home: 2400 Queens Chapel Rd Hyattsville MD 20782 Office: 205 Mullen Library Catholic University Washington DC 20017

BLUM, GERALD S., broadcasting exec. Gen. mgr. WQXI, WQXI-FM, Atlanta. Office: 2970 Peachtree Rd NW Atlanta GA 30305

BLUM, HENRY, physician; b. N.Y.C., July 12, 1899; s. Herman and Rose (Lazarow) B.; M.D., N.Y.U.-Bellevue Med. Coll., 1920; m. Edna Levine, Apr. 15, 1956. Intern, Lincoln Hosp., Bronx, N.Y., 1921-22; resident Kingston Av. Hosp., Bklyn., 1920-21; research work Woods Hole, Mass., Bellevue Hosp. Med. Coll., N.Y.C., 1933-39; practice medicine, Miami Beach, Fla., 1950—; chief surgeon Rosoff Subway Constrn. Co., 1925-33; med. dir. Hollywood (Fla.) Med. Center, 1950-56; police surgeon, Hollywood, 1951-56; med. dir. various spas in Fla.; 1965-69; attending physician Women's House of Detention, N.Y.C., 1933-39. K.P., Elk. Address: 5838 Collins Av Apt 10C Miami Beach FL 33140

BLUM, HERMAN, cons. engring. co. exec.; b. New Orleans, May 12, 1914; s. Herman and Abbie (Jacobs) B.; B.S. in Mech. Engring., Tulane U., 1938; m. Delphine Frances Orlowski, Aug. 6, 1957; children—Andrew Jay, Denise Frances. Engr., estimator, field supr. C. Wallace Plumbing Co., Dallas, 1938-45; pres. Herman Blum Cons. Engrs., Inc., Dallas, 1945—; chmn. bd. APACE (Automated Procedures for Architects, Contractors, Engrs., Inc.), Dallas, 1970—, Herman Blum Cons. Engrs.-Presley Land Surveyors, Inc., Dallas, 1971—; a founder APEC (Automated Procedures for Engring. Consultants), 1966, pres., 1966-67. Recipient Constrn. Industry Brotherhood citation, 1965. Registered profl. engr., Tex., Ariz., Colo., Conn., D.C., Ga., Ill., Ind., Kan., Ky., La., Miss., Mo., N.M., Ohio, Okla., Ore., Pa., Tenn., Va., Wash., Wis. Mem. Nat. Bur. Engring., Cons. Engrs. Council Tex., Nat. Tex. socs. profl. engrs., Am. Soc. Heating, Refrigeration and Air Conditioning Engrs. (pres. Dallas chpt. 1950). Clubs: City, Columbian, Chapparal, Lancers, Engineers. Designer world's 1st computer-controlled bldg. system, 1968. Home: 3708 Lexington St Dallas TX 75205 Office: 1015 Elm St Dallas TX 75202*

BLUM, JOHN CURTIS, govt. ofcl.; b. Terryville, Conn., July 5, 1915; s. John A. and Marion D. (Curtis) B.; B.S., U. Conn., 1937, M.S., 1939; grad. student U. Wis., 1941, Dept. Agr. Grad. Sch., 1946; student Indsl. Coll. Armed Forces, 1965-66; m. Mable L. Brooks, Oct. 21, 1939; children—Joanne M. (Mrs. Kogut), John Curtis, Nancy J. With Dept. Agr., 1939—, asst. dir. dairy div. Agrl. Marketing Service, 1960-61, dir. div., 1961-63, economist Office of Administr., 1963-64, asst. dep. adminstr. Consumer and Marketing Service, 1964-67, dep. adminstr., 1967—. Violinist, Fairfax County (Va.) Symphony Orch., 1957—, bd. dirs., 1957-70, pres., 1959-61, treas., 1965-67; dist. dir. N. Va. dist. P.T.A., 1961-63; treas. Va. Congress Parents and Tchrs., 1963-65, regional v.p., 1965-67, chmn. extension com., 1967-69, chmn. budget com., 1969-71; bd. mgrs. Va. P.T.A., 1961-71. Served to lt. (j.g.) USNR, 1944-46; PTO. Mem. Am. Acad. Polit. and Social Sci., Am. Agrl. Econ. Assn., Grange. Home: 7501 Walton Lane Annandale VA 22003 Office: Dept of Agriculture Washington DC 20250

BLUM, MAURICE DAULTON, interior designer; b. San Francisco, July 27, 1925; s. Julian Jack and Juliette Vivian (Cohen) B.; B.S., U. Cal. at Los Angeles, 1945; postgrad. Rudolph Schaeffer Sch. Design, 1950. Vice-pres. John J. Greer-Maurice D. Blum Assos., Inc., Washington, 1947—; pres. Interior Design Cons., 1955—. Mem. fashion com. Washington Bicentennial, 1971; founder mem. Friends of Kennedy Center; mem. environmental design com. Wolftrap Found. Served with USNR, 1942-45, 47-49. Mem. Am. Inst. Interior Designers, Zeta Beta Tau. Club: Arts (Washington). Address: 1212 Potomac St NW Washington DC 20007

BLUM, WILLIAM, JR., lawyer, corp. exec.; b. Washington, July 6, 1911; s. William and Willetta C. (Baylis) B.; student Swarthmore Coll.; B.S. cum laude, U. Pa., 1932; J.D., Georgetown U., 1942; postgrad. George Washington U., Catholic U., Am. U.; m. Virginia Henry, May

30, 1945 (dec. 1964); children—Margaret L., William M. H.; m. 2d, Ruth M. Truitt, Apr. 9, 1966. With Riggs Nat. Bank, Washington, 1932-34, E.I. du Pont de Nemours & Co., Wilmington, Del., 1934, investment dept. Nat. Savs. & Trust Co., Washington, 1934-40; admitted to D.C. bar, 1942; practiced in Washington, 1945—; mem. firm Blum, Lindsey & Powell, Blum, Olson & Oulihan. Dir., sec. Fed. Bar Building Corp., Washington, 1959-67; mem. council Fed. Bar, 1967—. Bd. dirs., gen. counsel Episcopal House of Mercy, 1947-63; pres., gen. counsel, dir. Columbia Hosp., 1955-65. Trustee D.C. chpt. A.R.C.; bd. dirs. Episcopal Home for Children. Served to lt. comdr. USNR, 1940-45. Mem. Fed., D.C., Am., N.Y. State assns. Episcopalian. Clubs: Nat. Lawyers, University, Metropolitan (Washington); Chevy Chase (Md.); Jefferson Islands (Md.); North Springs (W.Va.); Rolls Royce Owners. Home: 5225 Partridge Lane NW Washington DC 20016 Office: Fed Bar Bldg 1815 H St NW Washington DC 20006

BLUMBERG, DAVID M., ins. exec., religious adminstr. Pres. B'nai Brith, 1971—. Address: 1222 Lakeland Dr SW Knoxville TN 37919*

BLUMBERG, RANDOLPH, ocean engring. co. exec.; b. San Antonio, Feb. 1, 1926; s. Randolph J. and Toni (Wiederstein) B.; B.S. in E. E., Tex. A. and M. U., 1948, M.S., 1950, Ph.D. in Phys. Oceanography, 1955; m. Ann McClellan, Feb. 26, 1955; children—Randolph William, Richard James. With Tex. A. and M. Research Found., College Station, 1948-49; design engr. Fargo Engring. Co., Austin, Tex., 1949-51; research engr. S.W. Research Inst., San Antonio, 1951-52; sr. research engr. Humble Oil & Refining Co., Houston, 1955-62; pres. Am. Sci. & Engring. Co., Houston, 1962—. Asso. prof. ocean engring. U. Houston, 1964—. Chmn., Engrs. Week for Met. Houston Area, 1966. Served with USAAF, 1944-45. Fellow Tex. Acad. Scis., Am. Soc. for Oceanography (v.p., treas. 1966-68), Sigma Xi, Tau Beta Pi. Home: 5533 Redstart St Houston TX 77035 Office: Humble Bldg 800 Bell St Houston TX 77002

BLUME, LOUIS JOHN, univ. pres.; b. Chgo., Dec. 21, 1913; s. John A. and Helen (Berger) B.; B.S., Dayton U., 1933; A.M., Catholic U. Am., 1941; Th.D., St. Meinrad, Ind., 1945. Joined Soc. of Mary, 1931, ordained priest Roman Catholic Ch., 1945; faculty South Side Cath. High Sch., St. Louis, 1934-37; dean men Chaminade Coll., Clayton, Mo., 1937-40; prof. English, St. Anselme, Que., 1941-42; chaplain St. Mary's U., San Antonio, 1945-46, pres., 1947-53, 63—; v.p. Maryhurst Normal, Kirkwood, Mo., 1946-47; pres. Church Related Colls. in Tex., 1952-53; pres. Chaminade Coll. Prep., 1955-61; sabbatical leave, Rome, 1961-62; founder Villa St. Jean Internat. Sch., Fribourg, Switzerland, 1962-63. Chmn. bd. Tex. Found. Voluntarily Supported Colls. and Univs.; past pres. Ch.-Related Colls. in South; mem. cons. com. Coordinating Bd. Tex. Coll. and U. System; mem. bd. Ind. Colls. and Univs. of Tex., Inc.; adv. bd. Arts Council San Antonio; dir. Tex. Systems Natural Labs.; trustee St. Mary's U., U. Dayton. Mem. Nat. Cath. Edn. Assn. (regional del. exec. com.). Tex. Council Chs. (commn. on scholarships), C. of C., Nat. Conf. Christians and Jews, Assn. U.S. Army, Def. Orientation Conf. Assn., Antonians, Delta Epsilon Sigma. K.C. (state comdg. officer; state com. Cath. higher edn). Club.: Torch. Address: St Mary's U San Antonio TX 78284

BLUMHORST, ROY, clergyman; b. Slater, Mo., Oct. 1, 1932; s. Karl and Hulda (Klasing) B.; student St. Paul's Coll., 1950-52 B.D., Concordia Sem., 1957; M.A., St. Louis U., 1959; m. Vernette Rennegarbe, July 7, 1956; children—David, Joy, Hope. Ordained to ministry Luth. Ch., 1959; research asst. Bd. for Higher Edn., Mo. Synod Luth. Ch., St. Louis, 1957-59; pastor Hope Luth. Ch., LaGrange, Ill., 1959-66, First Trinity Luth. Ch., Washington, 1966—; engaged in exploratory mission Mo. Synod Luth. Ch., Marina City Apts., Chgo., 1964-66. Bd. dirs. Ch. Youth Research, Mpls. Author: Design for Family Living, 1963; Faithful Rebels, 1967; collaborator Death and Birth of the Parish, 1964. Home: 907 Massachusetts Av NE washington DC 20002 Office: 309 E St NW Washington DC 20001

BLUMRICH, HENRY CHRYSOLOGUS, dept. store exec.; b. Lockhart, Tex., Sept. 7, 1913; s. Henry Chrysologus and Wiley (Williamson) B.; B.B.A., U. Tex., Austin, 1948; m. Marey Dunlap, Sept. 2, 1939 children—Brenda Nell, Donald Dunlap. Clk., Lockhart Post Office, 1933-43; store controller Sears, Roebuck & Co., Galveston, Tex., 1949, Houston, 1950-56, Pasadena, Tex., 1956—. Served with USCGR, 1943-45. C.P.A. Mem. Am., Tex. socs. C.P.A.'s. Home: 8535 Dover St Houston TX 77017 Office: 1107 S Shaver St Pasadena TX 77502

BLUNCK, HERBERT CHRISTOPHER, hotel exec.; b. Seattle, Oct. 3, 1904; s. John Frederick and Emma Wilhemina (Buttner) B.; student U. Cal.; m. Janet Elizabeth Edwards, Oct. 23, 1932; 1 son, Brooks Edwards. Staff Fairmont Hotel, San Francisco, also Huntington Hotel, Pasadena, Cal., 1925-31; mgr. El Cortez, Bellevue hotels, San Francisco, 1934-39, Hotels Statler Co., Inc., N.Y.C., St. Louis, 1939-41, William Penn Hotel, Pitts., 1941-42; gen. mgr. Detroit Statler, 1942-44, Statler Hilton, Washington, 1944-66, sr. v.p., 1966—; v.p. Hilton Hotels Corp.; dir. No. Va. Bldg. & Loan Assn.; adv. bd. Nat. Bank of Washington. Co-chmn. people to people com. Hotel Industry. Mem. Fed. City Council; pres. Community Chest Fedn., 1954-55; incorporator United Givers Fund. Bd. dirs. Washington chpt. A.R.C., Greater Nat. Capitol Com.; adv. com. mem. Inaugural Com., 1953-57; trustee Washington Hosp. Center. Mem. Hotel Assn. Washington (past pres.), Am. Hotel Motel Assn. (chmn. bd.), Detroit Hotel Assn. (past pres.), Sigma Phi Epsilon. Episcopalian. Mason (Shriner, K.T.) Clubs: Burning Tree Golf, Columbia Country, Loudoun Country (Washington). Address: 1001 16th St NW Washington DC 20036

BOAGNI, ETHEL HAAS, physician; b. Madisonville, La., May 17, 1933; d. Edward Rudolph and Ethel (Oulliber) Haas; B.S., La. State U., 1954, M.D., 1956; m. Edward M. Boagni III, July 7, 1962; children— Thomas Jonathan, Nancy Ann, Robert Edward, Mary Elizabeth. Intern, Touro Infirmary, New Orleans, 1956-57; resident Ochsner Found. Hosp., New Orleans, 1957-59; staff physician Ochsner Clinic, New Orleans, 1959-64; practice medicine, specializing in anesthesiology, Baton Rouge, 1964—; mem. staff Baton Rouge, Our Lady of the Lake hosps.; instr. Med. Sch., La. State U., Baton Rouge, 1971—. Mem. Com. Capital Area Health Planning Commn. Mem. Patroness Vol. of Am., Baton Rouge Symphony Aux., Baton Rouge Hist. Found., A.M.A., La., E. Baton Rouge med. assns., La. Anesthesiology Soc., Am. Soc. Anesthesiologists, Baton Rouge Opera Guild, Baton Rouge Art League, Alpha Chi Omega. Roman Catholic. Home: 3156 McCarroll Dr Baton Rouge LA 70809

BOARDMAN, WILLARD HARLOW, physician; b. Dundee, N.Y., Jan. 6, 1922; s. Warren Milton and Lulu B. (Covert) B.; M.D., U. Buffalo, 1944; m. Jean Elizabeth Moore, Oct. 13, 1956; children—Lori Ann, Lisa Allyn, Lynn Amy. Intern, E.J. Meyer Meml. Hosp., Buffalo, 1944-45, resident, 1945-46, 49-50; fellow in cardiology-vascular diseases U. Buffalo, 1951-52; practice medicine, specializing in cardiology, Lancaster, N.Y., 1953-56, Orlando, Fla., 1956—; mem. staffs Orange Meml. Hosp., Orlando, Fla. Hosp., Orlando, Winter Park (Fla.) Hosp.; pres. staff Fla. Hosp., 1963, chief dept. cardiology, 1971—; v.p. Evans Central Fla. Cardiology Group, 1969—. Bd. dirs. Fla. Heart Assn.; bd. dirs. Central Fla. Heart Assn., pres., 1962. Served with M.C., AUS, 1946-48, 53. Diplomate Am. Bd. Internal Medicine. Fellow Am. Coll. Cardiology and Chest Physicians, A.C.P.; mem. A.M.A., Am. Heart Assn. Presbyn. Clubs: Citrus, Committee of One Hundred (Orlando, Fla.). Home: 701 Balmoral Rd Winter Park FL 32789 Office: 500 E Colonial Dr Orlando FL 32803

BOARDMAN, WILLIAM MORGAN, mech. engr.; b. Manchester, Conn., Mar. 22, 1917; s. Frank Crawford and Jane Adams (Elam) B.; B.S., U. Ala., 1942; postgrad. U. Mich., 1960; m. Jeanne Harriet Melarvie, Nov. 23, 1946; 1 son, James William. Commd. 2d lt. C.E., U.S. Army, 1943, advanced through grades to col., 1965, ret., 1969; supt. bldgs. and grounds Valencia Community Coll., Orlando, Fla., 1971—. Decorated Legion of Merit with oak leaf cluster. Registered profl. engr., Ala. Mem. Soc. Am. Mil. Engrs. (chpt. pres. 1966-67). Home: 5019 St Denis Ct Orlando FL 32809 Office: Valencia Community Coll 1800 S Kirkman Rd Orlando FL 32802

BOBBITT, WILLIAM HAYWOOD, state supreme ct. justice; b. Raleigh, N.C., Oct. 18, 1900; s. James Henry and Eliza May (Burkhead) B.; A.B., U. N.C., 1921, LL.D., 1957; LL.D., Davidson Coll., 1953; m. Sarah Buford Dunlap, Feb. 28, 1924 (dec. Oct. 1965); children—Sarah (Mrs. John W. Carter), William Haywood (dec.), Buford (Mrs. Ekkehart Sachtler), Harriet (Mrs. Dan S. Moss). Admitted to N.C. bar, 1922; practiced in Charlotte, N.C., 1922-38; judge Superior Ct., 14th Jud. Dist., 1939-54; asso. justice Supreme Court of N.C., Raleigh, 1954-69, chief justice, 1969—. Mem. N.C. Jud. Council, 1949-54, chmn., 1966-69. Trustee Brevard (N.C.) Coll., 1933-52. Mem. Am., N.C. bar assns., Am. Judicature Soc., Gen. Alumni Assn. U. N.C. (pres. 1954-55). Methodist. Club: Civitan (past pres. Charlotte). Home: Boylan Apts Raleigh NC 27603 Office: Justice Bldg Raleigh NC 27601

BOBKO, KAROL J., astronaut; b. N.Y.C., Dec. 23, 1937; s. Charles P. and Veronica (Sagatis) B.; B.S., U.S. Air Force Acad., 1959; grad. USAF Aerospace Research Pilot Sch., 1966; M.S., U. So. Cal., 1970; m. Frances Dianne Welsh, Feb. 11, 1961; children— Michelle Ann, Paul Joseph. Commd. officer U.S. Air Force, advanced through grades to maj.; pilot trainee, 1959-61; F-100 tactical fighter pilot, 1961-63; F-105 tactical fighter pilot, 1963-65, test pilot, 1965-67, astronaut, 1967—. Roman Catholic. Office: NASA Manned Spacecraft Center 2101 NASA Blvd Houston TX 77012

BOBO, FRANK EUGENE, JR., hosiery co. exec.; b. Gray Court, S.C., July 21, 1917; s. Frank Eugene and Mittie Lou (Todd) B.; B.S., Clemson U., 1938; postgrad. U. N.C., 1962; m. Reba Elaine Brown, Feb. 21, 1942; children—Ronald Brown. Mgr., Gaybourn Mills, Gainesville, Ga., 1946-59; v.p. Chadbourn Hosiery Co., 1959-69; pres. Chadbourn Industries, 1969-70, Chadbourn Hosiery, Charlotte, N.C., 1970—; dir. Republic Bank & Trust Co. Pres. Ednl. Found. Commerce and Industry, 1969-70; pres. Mecklenburg County council Boy Scouts Am., 1971-72. Trustee Mercer U., 1959. Served with AUS, 1942-45. Named Young Man of Year, Jr. C. of C., 1952, Man of Year, Rotary Club, 1958. Mem. Am. Inst. Chem. Engrs., Nat. Assn. Hosiery Mfg. (chmn. 1970-71), Alpha Chi Sigma. Baptist (chmn. bd. deacons 1969). Mason, Rotarian, Kiwanian. Club: Athletic. Patentee in field. Home: 1227 Coddington Pl Charlotte NC 28211 Office: 712 N Brevard St PO Box 1891 Charlotte NC 28201

BOBO, JAMES ROBERTS, economist, educator; b. Florence, Ala., Aug. 16, 1923; s. Robert Lee and Lenora (Vickery) B.; B.S., Florence State U., 1950; M.A., George Peabody Coll., 1952; Ph.D., La. State U., 1961; m. Cala Sue Reid, Mar. 27, 1969. Prof. econs. La. State U., New Orleans, 1960-63, 67—, dir. div. research, 1964-69, dean, Grad. Sch., 1969-70, 71—; dean Sch. Bus., N.E. La. State Coll., Monroe, 1963-64; exec. dir. Goals Found. Council, 1970-71. Served with AUS, 1943-46. Mem. Am., So. econ. assns., Regional Sci. Assn. Home: 5734 Chatham Dr New Orleans LA 70122

BODDEKER, EDWARD WILLIAM, III, architect, govt. ofcl.; b. Houston, Mar. 22, 1929; s. Edward William and Ruth Margaret (Cook) B.; B.Arch., Tex. A. and M. U., 1952; 1 son, Mark Montagne. Architect, MacKie & Kamrath, architects, Houston, 1960-63; architect Manned Spacecraft Center, NASA, Clear Lake, Tex., 1963—, project design mgr., 1963-65, master planner, 1965-67, head master planning sect., 1967-68, head archtl. civil sect., engring. div., 1968—. Served to 1st lt. Army Security Agy., AUS, 1953-54. Recipient Apollo Achievement award NASA, also NASA group achievement awards. Registered architect, Tex. Mem. A.I.A., Tex. Soc. Architects. Unitarian. Home: 2004 San Sebastion Ct No 313 Houston TX 77058 Office: NASA Manned Spacecraft Center Clear Lake TX 77058

BODIE, BELIN VOORHEES, r.r. exec.; b. Pitts., Jan. 13, 1910; s. Charles William and Edna W. (Cree) B.; B.S. in Engring., Johns Hopkins, 1933; m. Thelma Louise Barbee, Sept. 15, 1940; children—Charles William Belin Frederick. Clk. car service dept. B.&O. R.R., Balt., 1928; rodman U.S. Geodetic Survey, Belair, Md., 1933-34; signalman helper Pa. R.R., Balt., 1934-35; with G., M.&O. R.R. (formerly Alton R.R.), 1935—, successively rodman, instrumentman div. engrs. Eastern div., Bloomington, instrumentman, Chgo., asst. train master, Bloomington, train master, supt., Bloomington, chief engr., Mobile, Ala., asst. v.p. chief engr., gen. mgr., 1935-58, v.p., gen. mgr., 1958—, now exec. v.p., gen. mgr.; v.p. New Orleans Great No. R.R. Co., New Orleans; dir. Joliet Union Depot Co., Gulf Transport Co., Trailer Train Co., Kansas City Terminal Ry. Co., Miss. Export R.R. Co., Gulf, Mobile & Ohio R.R. Co. Bd. dirs., Southwestern at Memphis. Mem. Ala., Ill., Mobile chambers commerce, Am. Ry. Bridge and Bldg. Assn., Am. R.R. Supts. Assn., Am. Ry. Engring. Assn., Roadmasters and Maintenance of Way Assn., Kappa Alpha. Rotarian. Club: Mississippi Valley Maintenance of Way (St. Louis). Home: 4210 Bellevue Lane Mobile AL 36608 Office: 104 St Francis St Mobile AL 36624

BODINE, ROY L., JR., dentist, educator; b. Indpls., Mar. 25, 1911; s. Roy L. and Zelda (Read) B.; D.D.S., U. Ia., 1934; m. Monica Dunn, June 2, 1934; children—Patricia Joan, Ann Mary. Commd. 1st lt. U.S. Army, 1934, advanced through grades to col., 1950; dental officer, 1934-61; assigned to Dental Surgeon Hdqrs. 4th Army, Fort Sam Houston, Tex., 1957-58; dental surgeon Hdqrs. U.S. Army, Pacific, 1958-61; prof. prosthodontics Sch. Dentistry, U. of P.R. 1961-71, dir. grad. prosthodontics, dir. univ. hosp. service, 1963-68; clin. prof. advanced prosthodontics U. So. Cal. Sch. Dentistry, Los Angeles, 1971—. Pioneer in implant dentistry; guest lectr. U. So. Cal., Emory U., U. Cal., U. Tex. Decorated Silver Star medal, Bronze Star medal with combat V, Purple Heart. Diplomate Am. Bd. Prosthodontics. Fellow Am. Coll. Dentists, Am. Acad. Implant Dentistry (charter mem., past pres.; exec. sec. 5 years); mem. Am. Dental Assn., Am. Coll. Prosthodontists, Am. Prosthodontic Soc., Am. Acad. Maxillofacial Prosthetics, Fedn. Dentaire Internationale (co-reporter implant dentures 12th Congress Rome, Italy 1957, Varna, Bulgaria 1968), Am. Soc. Geriatric Dentistry, Pierre Fauchard Acad., Omicron Delta Kappa, Delta Sigma Delta. K.C. (4 deg.). Contbr. articles to profl. jours., chpts. in Current Therapy in Dentistry, also Dental Clinics of North America. Home: 1422 E Grayson St Fort Sam Houston TX 78286 Office: Sch Dentistry University of Southern Cal 925 W 34th St Los Angeles CA 90007

BODNAR, STEPHEN JOHN, chem. co. exec.; b. Carteret, N.J., July 6, 1925; s. Stephen and Helen (Sadowski) B.; B.A., Lafayette Coll., 1951; Ph.D., U. Ill., 1954; m. Louise C. Brechka, Sept. 20, 1947; children— Alison B. (Mrs. Dwight Auckland), Patrice L., Kristin M. Chem. engr. Esso Standard Oil Co., Baton Rouge, La., 1954-60; mgr. process engring. section Tex. U.S. Chem. Co., Port Neches, Tex., 1960—. Served with AUS, 1943-46. Decorated Purple Heart, Metz medal. Mem. Am. Chem. Soc., So. Rubber Group, 95th Inf. Div. Assn., Alpha Chi Sigma, Phi Lambda Upsilon. Patentee in field. Home: 6320 Pansy Dr Beaumont TX 77706 Office: PO Box 846 Port Neches TX 77651

BODO, MATTHEW BELA, architect; b. Temesvar, Hungary, Apr. 28, 1912; s. Matthew and Julianna (Varga) B.; student Royal Tech. Coll. Architecture, Budapest, Hungary, 1929-33; children—Matthew, Attila, Richard. Came to U.S., 1957. Structural engr. Coastal Steel Constrn. Co., St. Petersburg, Fla., 1957-61; pvt. practice structural engring., St. Petersburg, 1961—, architect, 1963—. Mem. bd. adjustment Bldg. Dept. St. Petersburg, 1965—. Mem. A.I.A., Nat. Soc. Profl. Engrs., Fla. Engring. Soc., Nat. Fire Protection Assn., Archtl. Precast Assn. Home: 4692 Dover St NE St Petersburg FL 33703 Office: 101 2d Av N St Petersburg FL 33701

BOECKMAN, DUNCAN E., lawyer; b. Houston, Sept. 17, 1926; B.B.A., U. Tex., 1948, LL.B., 1951. Admitted to Tex. bar, 1951; now mem. firm Golden, Burrow, Potts & Boeckman, Dallas. Gen. counsel Tex. Republican Exec. Com., 1964—. Mem. Am., Dallas bar assns., State Bar Tex., Phi Delta Phi. Office: 2300 Republic Nat Bank Bldg Dallas TX 75201*

BOEGLEN, DURWOOD LOUIS, bldg. supply co. exec.; b. Albany, Ala., Jan. 4, 1917; s. Louis Edward and Vernon Irene (Murphree) B.; student Southwestern U. Accounting, Washington, 1935-37; m. Margaret Cordelia Herron, Nov. 14, 1941; children—Katharine (Mrs. James C. Chapin), Bonnie (Mrs. Gary L. DiGirolamo), Jay Louis. With United Clay Products Co., Washington, 1934-47; with Cushwa Brick & Bldg. Supply Co., Washington, 1947—, pres., 1965—; exec. v.p. Compackager Corp., Washington, 1969—; adv. bd. Suburban Trust Co., Hyattsville, Md., 1959—. Trustee, Nat. Jewish Hosp., Denver, Boys Clubs D.C. Mem. Masonry Isnt. (pres. 1955), Nat. Assn. Distbrs. and Dealers Structural Clay Products (pres. 1957-58), Home Builders Assn. D.C. (pres. 1966-70), Home Builders Met. Washington Found. (pres. 1967—), Washington Bldg. Congress (treas. 1968-69), Met. Washington Builders Assn. (pres. 1972). Methodist. Mason (Shriner), Kiwanian. Clubs: Columbia Country (Chevy Chase, Md.); University (Washington); Congressional Country (pres. 1968-69) (Potomac, Md). Home: 4807 Enfield Rd Bethesda MD 20014 Office: 137 Ingraham St NE Washington DC 20011

BOEHM, JOHN FRANCIS, oil refining co. exec.; b. St. Louis, Nov. 5, 1926; s. Robert Jacob and Isabel Madeline (MacDonald) B.; student U. Mo., 1944-46, Pa. State U., 1967; m. Lois Jeanne Byrne, Jan. 27, 1951; children—Nancy Jean, John Gerard, Robert Charles, Thomas William. Salesman, Standard Oil Co. Ind., St. Louis, 1947-52, Quaker State Oil Refining Corp., Tulsa, 1952-57; sales mgr. R.J. Brown Co., motor oils, St. Louis, 1957-59; div. mgr. Valvoline Oil Co., Cin., 1959-67, v.p., 1968-69, exec. v.p., 1970, pres., Ashland, Ky., 1971—. Served with USNR, 1944-46. Mem. Automotive Warehouse Distbrs. Assn., Automotive Service Industry Assn., Am. Petroleum Inst., Ohio Petroleum Marketers Assn., U.S. Auto Club, Ohio, Ashland chambers commerce. Club: Bellefonte Country (Ashland). Home: 1609 Lexington Av Ashland KY 44101 Office: 1401 Winchester Av Ashland KY 41101

BOELSCHE, EDGAR HENRY, dentist; b. Industry, Tex., Nov. 5, 1905; s. Henry Herman and Minnie (Froelich) B.; diploma Blinn Coll., 1924; D.D.S., U. Tex., 1928; m. Sarah Margaret New, June 16, 1936. Pvt. practice dentistry, Ballinger, Tex., 1928—. Served to maj. Dental Corps, USAAF, 1942-46. Mem. Am. (life mem.), Tex. (life mem.) dental assns., San Angelo Dist. Dental Soc. (pres. 1964-65), Southwestern Soc. Dental Medicine, C. of C. (bd. dirs. 1950-52), Omicron Kappa Upsilon, Pierre Fauchard Acad. Baptist. Rotarian (pres. 1941-42). Office: 702 Park St Ballinger TX 76821

BOENIG, HERMAN, plastics co. exec.; b. Danzig, Poland, Feb. 17, 1919; s. Herman F. and Victoria (Koslowski) B.; B.A., U. Heidelberg (Germany), 1947, Ph.D., 1950; m. Lise A. Sarniski, Jan. 5, 1944; children—Gabrielle (Mrs. James Ransdell), Beata, Robert. Came to U.S., 1956, naturalized, 1961. Plant mgr. I.G. Farben Co., Germany, 1950-53; sr. research chemist Goodyear Tire & Rubber Co., Akron, O., 1953-56; dir. research and devel. Brook Park Inc., Cleve., 1956-58; mgr. chem. research Brunswick Corp., Muskegon, Mich., 1958-64; mgr. research devel. Spindletop Research, Lexington, Ky., 1964-67; pres. R & B Plastics Inc., Lexington, 1967-70, chmn. bd., 1970—; cons. in field. Mem. Am. Chem. Soc., Am. Mgmt. Soc., Soc. Plastics Industry, Soc. Plastics Engrs., N.Y. Acad. Sci. Contbr. articles to profl. jours., books. Home: 416 Lakeshore Dr Lexington KY 40502 Office: 183 Lisle Rd Lexington KY 40505

BOESE, ELSIE JEAN MCGIVNEY (MRS. HERMAN LAMAR BOESE), mem. Republican Nat. Com.; b. New Orleans, Jan. 19, 1925; d. John Roderick and Elsie (Buist) McG.; B.A., Sophie Newcomb Coll., 1945; m. Herman Lamar Boese, May 20, 1946; 1 son, Robert Lamar. Caseworker A.R.C., 1945-46; script writer Tulane U. Ednl. TV, 1954-55; tchr. Sunny Ct. Sch. For Retarded Children, 1954-55. Vice chmn. La. Republican Central Com., 1964-68, mem., 1964—, vice chmn. Rep. Polit. Action Council La., 1965-68, del. nat. conv., 1964, 68; mem. Rep. Nat. Com. of La., 1968—. Legislative chmn. St. Frances Cabrini Hosp. Aux., 1963-68. Recipient Freedom award La. State Farm Bur. Fedn., 1965, Distinguished Service award 12th Dist. V.F.W., 1967. Mem. Central La. Community Theatre, Poets' Circle, Woman's Aux. Rapides Parish Med. Soc. (pres.), Alpha Delta Pi. Roman Catholic. Home: 831 City Park Blvd Alexandria LA 71301

BOGGESS, JOHN P., elec. engr.; b. Demopolis, Ala., Oct. 19, 1914; s. Norman West and Katherine (Thompson) B.; B.S., U. Ala., 1938; m. Dorothy Gaynelle McClusky, Apr. 2, 1941; children—Dorothy Gaynelle, (Mrs. Henry Owen Wharton), Tina Marie. Engr. asst. sub-sta. constrn. Ala. Power Co., Birmingham, 1937-38; operations and maintenance engr. Lakeland (Fla.) Light & Water Plant, 1939-40; owner, mgr. Boggess Florist & Nursery, Demopolis, Ala., 1946-52; chief coordinator Vets. Tng. for Marengo County, Linden, Ala., 1946-51; asst. plant engr. Beaunit Mills, Inc., Childersburg, Ala., 1952-60; elec. engr. Marshall Space Flight Center, Huntsville, Ala. 1960—. Served as capt. Corps of Engrs., 1940-46; ETO, PTO. Mem. Nat., Ala. (chpt. and state dir. 1963—) socs. profl. engrs. Presbyn. Club: Ten/Twenty Stock (pres. 1967-72). Home: 6311 Sheri Dr NW Huntsville AL 35806 Office: S&E-Qual-EX Marshall Space Flight Center Huntsville AL 35812

BOGGS, EDMOND M., state ofcl. Commr., Va. Dept. labor and industry, Richmond. Office: 9th St Office Bldg Richmond VA 23219*

BOGGS, JEAN CASTERTON BULETTE (MRS. LAWRENCE K. BOGGS), civic worker; b. York, Pa.; d. Warren Clifton and Ruth (Casterton) Bulette; B.A., Coll. William and Mary, 1944; m. Lawrence K. Boggs, Oct. 15, 1949; children—Randall and David (twins), Elizabeth. Editorial dept., caption title and subtitle writer Sat. Eve. Post, 1945-50; with research dept. Holiday Mag., 1950-51, asst. editor, 1951-52. Mem. residence com. YWCA, 1958-67; mem. aux. bd. Presbyn. Hosp., 1959-60; sect. chmn. United Appeal, 1962; treas. Med. Aux., 1965-66; co-chmn. Culture Week for State N.C., 1968; publicity chmn. Met. Opera Benefit Concert, 1969. Mem. Soc. for Preservation Antiquities N.C., D.A.R. (regent 1966-68), Delta Delta Delta. Republican. Presbyn. Clubs: Queen of Spades Garden (pres. Charlotte, N.C. 1965-66), Fortnightly Book (pres. 1967-68), Charlotte Guild Debutante (mem. bd. 1969-70, pres. 1971-72), Charlotte Country, N.C. Golddiggers Investment (Charlotte). Address: 2208 Wellesley Av Charlotte NC 28207

BOGGS, LAWRENCE KENNEDY, physician; b. Birmingham, Ala., Feb. 13, 1925; s. Ralph Erwin and Meta (Long) B.; student Davidson Coll., 1943, Duke, 1943-45; M.D., Jefferson Med. Coll., 1949; m. Jean Casterton Bulette, Oct. 15, 1949; children—Randall, David, Elizabeth. Intern, Phila. Gen. Hosp., 1949-51; resident urology Charlotte (N.C.) Meml. Hosp., 1953-56; practice medicine, specializing in urology, Charlotte, 1956—; chief staff dept. urology Presbyn. Hosp., v.p. med. staff, 1966-67, pres. med. staff, 1967; mem. teaching staff dept. urology Charlotte Meml. Hosp., dir. med. assistance, 1960—. Vice chmn. local Boy Scouts Am., dist. chmn., 1963. Bd. dirs. Mecklenburg unit Am. Cancer Soc., Arts Council; mem. adv. bd. Planned Parenthood; coordinator 1968 Culture Week, State of N.C. Republican precinct chmn., 1957-58. Served with USNR, 1943-46, as 1st lt. AUS, 1951-53. Hartford Found. fellow, 1954-55, 55-56. Diplomate Am. Bd. Urology. Fellow A.C.S.; mem. Am. (S.E. sect.), N.C. urologic assns., Mechlenburg County Med. Soc. (pres. 1970), C. of C. Presbyn. (elder 1967). Clubs: Executives, Rotary (pres. 1961—, dir. 1959-61); Goodfellows, London Dinner (pres. 1966-67), Charlotte Country (Charlotte). Home: 2208 Wellesley Av Charlotte NC 28205 Office: Doctors Bldg Charlotte NC 28801

BOGGS, THOMAS HALE, congressman; b. Long Beach, Miss., Feb. 15, 1914; s. William Robertson and Claire Josephine (Hale) B.; B.A., Tulane U., 1935, LL.B., 1937; m. Corinne Claiborne, Jan. 22, 1938; children—Barbara (Mrs. Paul Eugene Sigmund, Jr.), Thomas Hale, Corinne Morrison (Mrs. Steven V. Roberts). Admitted to La. bar, 1937, practiced in New Orleans, 1937-40; mem. 77th (1941-43), 80th-92d congresses from 2d La. Dist., mem. joint econ. com., chmn. subcom. on fgn. econ. policy, dep. whip, 1955-61, majority whip, 1962-71, majority leader, 1971—. Mem. Pres.'s Commn. on Assassination Pres. Kennedy, 1963-65, Pres's Commn. To Study Causes and Prevention Violence, 1968-69. Vice chmn. Dem. Nat. Com., 1956—; chmn. platform com. Dem. Nat. Conv., 1968. Served with USNR, U.S. Maritime Service, 1943-46. Recipient Miss. Valley World Trade Award, 1956; Cunningham award Internat. House, 1958. Mem. Am., La., New Orleans, D.C., Fed. bar assns., New Orleans Chamber Commerce, Am. Judicature Soc., S.A.R., Am. Legion, Am. Vets. World War II, Tulane U. Alumni Assn., Phi Beta Kappa, Beta Theta Pi, Omicron Delta Kappa. Roman Catholic. K.C. Club: Congressional (Washington). Home: 2801 St Charles Av New Orleans LA 70130 Office: Rayburn House Office Bldg Washington DC 20515

BOHANAN, JAMES OVERSTREET, state ofcl.; b. Louisville, June 11, 1935; s. James Otis and Mary Margaret (Overstreet) B.; A.B., Centre Coll. Ky., 1956; M.B.A., Columbia, 1961; m. Jane Georgeann Morris, May 17, 1969; children—Scott James, Amy Jane. Financial analyst Rohm & Haas Co., chem. co., 1961-62; research analyst, Ky. Dept. Commerce, State Indsl. Devel. Agy., Frankfort, 1963-65, dir. research, 1965-67; asst. Ga. field dir. Coastal Plains Regional Commn., Multi-State Regional Planning Agy., Atlanta, 1968-70; dir. research Ga. Dept. Industry and Trade, State Indsl. Devel. Agy., Atlanta, 1970-72, asst. dep. dir., 1972—. Served to lt. USNR, 1956-60. Mem. Am., So. indsl. devel. councils, Ga. Indsl. Developers Assn., Ga. Planning Assn., Sigma Alpha Epsilon. Presbyn. Club: Toastmasters. Home: 1028 W Nancy Creek Dr NE Atlanta GA 30319 Office: 270 Washington St SW PO Box 38097 Atlanta GA 30334

BOHANNON, JAMES ARTICE, hosp. adminstr.; b. Boaz, Ala., Mar. 23, 1924; s. William Thomas and Bertha Mae (Williams) B.; student Auburn U., 1946-47; m. Ann Snead, Dec. 10, 1949; children—Mike, Tony, Judy. Accountant, Jones Constrn. Co., Montgomery, Ala., 1948-56; adminstr. Profl. Center Hosp., Montgomery, 1956—. Bd. dirs. Montgomery Regional Med. Found.; trustee Blue Cross-Blue Shield of Ala. Served with AUS, 1943-46. Mem. Central Ala. Hosp. Council (pres. 1962), Am. Coll. Hosp. Adminstrs., Am., Ala. pub. health assns., Financial Mgmt. Assn., Ala. Sight Conservation Assn., Blue and Gray Assn. Lion (pres. 1969). Home: 321 Grove Park Dr Montgomery AL 36109 Office: 219 Church St Montgomery AL 36104

BOHANON, LUTHER L., U.S. judge; b. Ft. Smith, Ark., Aug. 9, 1902; s. William Joseph and Artelia (Campbell) B.; LL.B., U. Okla., 1927; m. Marie Swatek, July 17, 1933; 1 son, Richard L. Admitted to Okla. bar, 1927, also U.S. Supreme Ct.; gen. practice law, Seminde, Okla. and Oklahoma City, 1927-61; U.S. dist. judge Eastern, Western and No. dists. Okla., 1961—. Mem. platform com. Democratic Nat. Conv., 1940. Served to maj. USAAF, 1942-45. Mem. Oklahoma City C. of C., Sigma Nu, Phi Alpha Delta. Methodist. Mason (Shriner, 32 deg., K.T., Jester), Kiwanian. Home: 1617 Bedford Dr Oklahoma City OK 73116 Office: US Courthouse 4th and Robinson Sts Oklahoma City OK 73102

BOHART, PHILIP HARRIES, JR., petroleum and mining cons.; b. San Antonio, Dec. 28, 1930; s. Philip H. and Margarite (Perron) B.; B.S. in Geology, Okla. U., 1954, B.S. in Petroleum Engring., 1954, M.S. in Geol. Engring., 1958; m. Diane Moserip, Oct. 4, 1969; children—Kevin R. Kennedy, Terry, Lisa, Karin, Kevin, Kelly, Christopher. Individual practice cons., 1954-58, 62-65; area geologist TXL Oil Co., 1958-61; project head Texaco, 1961-62; pres. Devonian Oil Co., 1965-66; v.p., mgr. operations, dir. Tellus Oil, Oklahoma City, 1968—; v.p., mgr. Cimarron Fund, Midland, Tex., 1968—; exec. v.p., dir. Delta Drilling, N.Y.C., 1968—. Served with USMC, 1953-56. Decorated Silver Star (2), Bronze Star, Air medal (2), Purple Heart (2). Mem. Am. Assn. Petroleum Geologists, Am. Inst. Mining, Metall. and Petroleum Engrs., Soc. Econ. Paleontologists, Soc. Mineralogists, West Tex. Geol. Soc. Home: 2817 Maxwell St Midland TX 79701 Office: Midland Savs Bldg Midland TX 79701

BOHLKE, JOHN HENRY, JR., real estate devel. firm exec.; b. New Orleans, Sept. 4, 1937; s. John Henry and Iris Louise (Koebel) B.; B.Arch., Tulane U., 1960; m. Mada Wynne Price, Apr. 5, 1968; children—Peggy, Catherine, Pamela, Thomas, Kathleen, Aimee, Avery, Michael. Architect Koch & Wilson, architects, New Orleans, 1960-65; architect, project mgr. Curtis & Davis, architects, New Orleans, 1965-70; chief exec. officer, founder Garfield Enterprises, Inc., Metairie, La., 1970—. Mem. A.I.A., La. Archtl. Assn., Spring Fiesta Assn., Tau Sigma Delta. Democrat. Roman Catholic. Clubs: New Orleans Lawn Tennis, Ambassador (New Orleans). Home: 1416 Webster St New Orleans LA 70118 Office: 4403 Veterans Blvd Metairie LA 70002

BOHMFALK, BENJAMIN HENRY, clergyman; b. Needville, Tex., Apr. 12, 1907; s. Christian F. and Johanna (Schlechte) B.; B.A., Southwestern U., 1932; B.D., So. Meth. U., 1936; postgrad. Boston U., 1933-34, U. Tex., 1958-59; m. Rubye L. Lindemann, June 20, 1934; children—Barbara Elaine (Mrs. James A. Kendall), Elizabeth Ruth (Mrs. William E. Sterling, Jr.). Ordained to ministry Methodist Ch., 1935; minister, Woodville, Tex., 1933-34, Denton, Tex., 1934-35, Lexington, Caldwell, Tex., 1935-37, Mason, Tex., 1937-40, Bronte, Tex., 1940-42; pastor, San Angelo, Tex., 1947-53, Crystal City, Tex., 1953-56, Trinity Ch., Corpus Christi, Tex., 1956-58, Granger, Tex., 1958-59, Ingleside, Tex., 1959-62, Rockport, Tex., 1962-68, Lampasas, 1968—; tchr. Bible courses San Angelo Coll., 1949-53, Del Mar. Coll., Corpus Christi, 1956-58. Statistician S.W. Tex. Conf., 1947-72, mem. com. on ministerial tng., 1960-64, mem. com. on conf. relations, 1954-60, chmn., 1956-60; vice chmn. Conf. Commn. Archives and History, 1968—. Sec. adv. bd. REACH Child Care Center; mem. local com. United Fund; mem. Mayor's Housing Com. Bd. mgrs. Tex. Pastors Sch., 1960-64. Served with AUS, 1942-47. Mem. Am. Acad. Religion, Am. Legion (chaplain), V.F.W., Lampasas C. of C. Mason (K.T.; past grand prelate Tex.). Home: PO Box 946 Lampasas TX 76550

BOHMFALK, JOHN HENRY, physician; b. Mason, Tex., Sept. 26, 1920; s. Christian F. and Johanna Alvina (Schlechte) B.; B.A., Southwestern U., 1940; M.D., U. Tex. Sch. Medicine, 1945; m. Marjorie Mae Moss, Mar. 15, 1943; children—William H., Thomas C. Intern, Santa Rosa Hosp., San Antonio, 1945-46; practice medicine, specializing in gen. medicine and surgery, San Antonio, 1947—; mem. staffs Bapt. Meml. Hosp., Santa Rosa Hosp., S.W. Meth. Hosp., Nix Hosp. (all San Antonio); chief staff Bapt. Meml. Hosp., San Antonio, 1964, mem. adv. bd., 1965-66; mem. adv. med. staff S.W. Meth. Hosp., San Antonio, 1956-63. Med. dir. Am. Security Life Ins. Co., San Antonio, 1968—, dir., 1969—. Trustee Bettye Thorman Trust for Cancer Research, San Antonio 1971—; hon. mem. B. Thorman Cancer Research Team, Trinity U., San Antonio, 1971. Served with M.C., AUS, 1946-47. Mem. Tex. Med. Assn. (del. 1954-66), Tex. Acad. Gen. Practice (dir. 1960-63), Alamo Acad. Gen. Practice (pres. 1958), Internat. Med. Assembly (pres. 1967), Bexar County Med. Soc. (pres. 1969), A.M.A., Tex. Assn. Med. Dirs., Theta Kappa Psi. Republican. Methodist. Mason. Home: 220 Linda Dr San Antonio TX 78216 Office: 227 E Hildebrand Av San Antonio TX 78212

BOHORFOUSH, JOSEPH GEORGE, physician; b. Birmingham, Ala., Dec. 20, 1907; s. George and Susan (Joseph) B.; A.B., Vanderbilt U., 1929, M.D., 1933; m. Bliss Paige, Feb. 17, 1960; children—David, William, Eugenia Paige Hoffman (Mrs. R. S. Sayers). Intern Hillman Hosp., Birmingham, 1933-34; resident Waverly Hills (Ky.) Sanatorium, 1934-35; asst. med. dir. Lake View Sanatorium, Madison, Wis., 1936-41; med. dir. Jefferson Sanatorium, Birmingham, 1946-47; instr. medicine U. Ala. Med. Coll., 1946-48; chief profl. services VA Hosp., Memphis, 1947-51; asst. prof. medicine U. Tenn., Memphis, 1947, 51; clin. prof. medicine Med. Coll. Ga., 1951-60; chief medicine VA Hosp, Augusta, Ga., 1951-60; dir. phys. health services Central State Hosp., Milledgeville, Ga., 1960-69; dir. Jones Hosp., Milledgeville, 1969-72. Dir. Bohorfoush Corp. Served as maj. M.C., AUS, 1941-45; col. M.C. ret. Diplomate Am. Bd. Internal Medicine, Am. Bd. Pulmonary Diseases. Fellow A.C.P., Am. Coll. Chest Physicians, Am. Fedn. Clin. Research; mem. A.M.A., Med. Assn. Ga., Baldwin County, 10th Dist. med. socs., Am., Ga. thoracic socs., Pan Am., So. med. assns., Ga. Acad. Sci., Ga. Heart Assn., Ret. Officers Assn., Internat. Soc. Internal Medicine. Kiwanian. Clubs: Internationale; Milledgeville Country. Home: 1862 Tanglewood Rd Milledgeville GA 31061 Office: 811 N Cobb St Milledgeville GA 31061

BOHUSLAV, GEORGE FRANK, dentist; b. Hallettsville, Tex., Sept. 16, 1909; s. Adolph Frank and Lillie Matilda (Hajek) B.; B.S., S.W. Tex. State U., 1935; D.D.S., U. Tex., 1942; postgrad. Coll. Physicians and Surgeons, Sch. Dentistry, San Francisco, 1947, U. Mich., 1949, U. Ala., 1959, Boston U., 1969; m. Ella Lillian Stratman, July 27, 1935; children—Jacquelyn Sue (Mrs. Neville B. Graham), Georgia Ellan (Mrs. Willie N. Raven). Prin. Midfields (Tex.) High Sch., 1936-38; cons. dental health edn. Dental div. Tex. Dept. Health, Austin, 1942-46; pvt. practice dentistry, specializing in pedodontics, Austin, 1946—. Chmn. dental div. United Funds, 1969. Named papal knight Temple of Jerusalem. Fellow Am. Acad. Pedodontists; goodfellow Tex. Dental Assn.; mem. Austin Dist. Dental Soc. (pres. 1949-50), Tex. Soc. Dentistry for Children (pres. 1944-46), Southwestern Soc. Pedodontists (pres. 1952), U. Tex. Ex-Student's Assn., Xi Psi Phi. Roman Catholic. K.C. (4 deg.), Lion. Clubs: Serra (pres. 1956-58), Longhorn, Westwood Country (Austin). Home: 2706 Scenic Dr Austin TX 78703 Office: 715 W 34th St Austin TX 78705

BOIRE, HAROLD ARTHUR, govt. ofcl.; b. Mooers, N.Y., May 21, 1914; s. Charles Willis and Eva (Dragoon) B.; J.D., Stetson U., 1940; LL.M., Nat. U., 1949; B.S., Am. U., 1950. Admitted to Fla. bar, 1940, U.S. Supreme Ct. bar, 1944; atty. NLRB, Washington, 1948-56, asst. gen. counsel, 1956-57, regional dir. 12th Region, Tampa, Fla., 1957—. Served with USCGR, 1942-43. Mem. Fla. Bar, Sigma Nu, Phi Alpha Delta. Mason Home: 3905 Pearl Av Tampa FL 33611 Office: 706 Fed Bldg 500 Zack St Tampa FL 33602

BOLAND, THOMAS EDWIN, banker; b. Columbus, Ga., July 8, 1934; s. Clifford E. and Helen M. (Robinson) B.; student Emory U., 1952-54; B.B.A., Ga. State U., 1957; postgrad. Stonier Grad. Sch. Banking, Rutgers U., 1964-66; m. Beth Ann Campbell, May 23, 1959; children— Susan Ann, Thomas E., Jr. With First Nat. Bank Atlanta, 1954—, v.p., 1968—; dir. Aunt Fanny's Baking Co., Atlanta. Trustee Atlanta Baptist Coll., 1970—. Served with AUS, 1957. Named Salesmen of Year, Atlanta Sales and Marketing Execs. Club, 1969. Mem. Am. Bankers Assn. (bank card com. 1964-66). Kiwanian. Club: Cherokee Town and Country (Atlanta). Home: 3603 Embry Circle Atlanta GA 30341 Office: PO Box 4148 Atlanta GA 30302

BOLDEN, DARWIN W., assn. exec. Exec. dir. Interracial Council for Bus. Opportunity, Washington. Address: Interracial Council Bus Opportunity 1200 19th St NW Washington DC*

BOLDEN, JOHN HENRY, ednl. adminstr.; b. River Junction, Fla., Jan. 10, 1922; s. Idell and Eddie L. (Jackson) B.; B.S., Fla. Meml. Coll., 1950; M.S., Fla. A. and M. U., 1952, M.Ed., 1963; Ed. S., Ind. U., 1966, Ed.D., 1968; m. Bertha M. Johnson, Sept. 5, 1942; 1 son, Richard L. Pres., Bolden's Coll. Music, Jacksonville, Fla., 1958-67, chmn. bd. dirs., 1958—; research asst. Ind. U., 1967-68; dean tchr. edn. Cheyney (Pa.) State Coll., 1968-69; area dir. elementary edn. Duval County Schs., Jacksonville, Fla., 1969—. Vis. lectr. Jacksonville U., Fla. A. and M. U.; vis. dir. bands Edward Waters Coll. Bd. dirs. Johnson br. YMCA, 1950—. Served with USNR, 1942-45. Recipient Nathan W. Collier Meritorious Service award Fla. Meml. Coll., Miami, 1968. Mem. Am. Assn. Sch. Adminstrs., Nat., Fla. edn. assns., N.A.A.C.P., Jacksonville Urban League, Phi Delta Kappa, Kappa Delta Pi. Author: Systematic Approach to School Management, 1972; Curriculum Development Module: Designing an Instructional Management System, 1972. Home: 2922 Pearce St Jacksonville FL 32209 Office: 1011 Gilmore St Jacksonville FL 32202

BOLDEN, THEODORE EDWARD, dentist, educator; b. Middleburg, Va., Apr. 19, 1920; s. Theodore D. and Mary E. (Jackson) B.; A.B., Lincoln U., 1941; D.D.S., Meharry Med. Coll., 1947; M.S., U. Ill., 1951, Ph.D., 1958; m. Dorothy M. Forde, June 17, 1952. Asso. prof. oral diagnosis and pathology Seton Hall Coll., 1960-62; prof. dentistry, chmn. dept. oral pathology and oral medicine, dir. research Meharry Med. Coll., 1962-69, prof. dentistry, chmn. dept. oral pathology, dir. research, 1969—, asso. dean Sch. of Dentistry, 1967—. Chmn. health com. Montclair (N.J.) Health Dept., 1959-60; abstractor N.Y. State Dental Jour., 1960; mem. dental edn. rev. com. Dept. Health, Edn. and Welfare, 1969—; cons. dentistry VA Hosps., Tuskegee, Ala., Murfreesboro, Tenn., and Nashville. Served with Dental Corps, AUS, 1951-52. Diplomate Am. Bd. Oral Medicine. Fellow Am. Acad. Oral Pathology; mem. Ewell Neil Dental Soc., Nat. Dental Assn., Capital City (pres.), Lincoln dental socs., Internat. Assn. Dental Research, Northeastern Soc. Periodontists, N.Y. Acad. Scis., Omega Psi Phi. Baptist. Author: (with J. Manhold) Outline of Pathology, 1960; (with E. L. Mobley and E. S. Chandler) Dental Hygiene Examination Review Book, Vol. I, Edit. 2, 1969. Contbr. articles profl. jours. and books. Home: 1419 22d Av N Nashville TN 37208 Office: 1005 18th Av N Nashville TN 37208

BOLDT, ALBERT WALTER, govt. ofcl.; b. Altoona, Pa., Aug. 28, 1904; s. John Henry and Bertha (Seig) B.; B.S., Gettysburg Coll., 1927; M.A., Lehigh U., 1938;21, 1934; children—Jacqueline (Mrs. Robert C. Poor), Sandra (Mrs. Samuel Bockman). Instr. Reading (Pa.) Sch. Dist., 1930-42; chief Vocational Rehab. and Edn. div. VA, Reading, 1945-48; asst. dean men U. Fla., Gainesville, 1948-58; dean students Am U., Washington, 1958-60; dir. div. higher edn. Dept. Health, Edn. and Welfare Region IV, U.S. Office Edn., Atlanta, 1960—. Cons. evaluation sch. dists. Atlanta, Jacksonville, DeLand and Ocala, Fla., 1950-58. Served to lt. comdr. USNR, 1942-45. Mem. Am. Coll. Personnel Assn., Nat. Assn. Student Personnel Adminstrs., Nat. Assn. Sch. and Coll. Placement, N.E.A., Assn. Higher Edn., Nat. Assn. Deans and Advisers Men, Phi Delta Kappa, Phi Kappa Phi, Kappa Delta Pi. Author: Objective Tests in American History, 1940; History of the Schools of Reading from 1748 to 1859, 1938; The Leadership Fraternity in American Society—A Study of the Florida Blue Key, 1956. Editor: Gator Guide. Home: 3804 Briarcliff Rd NE Atlanta GA 30329 Office: 50 7th St NE Atlanta GA 30323

BOLEN, HAROLD JEAN, coll. pres.; b. Wildersville, Tenn., July 3, 1901; s. William R. and Florence (Parish) B.; A.B., Cumberland U., 1925, LL.B., 1926; B.C.S., Am. Bus. U., 1928; B.C.Ed., Haddock Bus. U., 1932; M.S., Cal. Coll. Commerce, 1952, LL.D., 1953; Ph.D., U. of West, 1957; Ed.D., Burton Coll., 1961; m. Lucy Jane Huggins, Aug. 28, 1926; children—Hannah Jean (Mrs. Martin L. Bridges), Martha Jane (Mrs. Charles David Moore), William Harold. Vice-prin. Jasper (Fla.) High Sch., 1928-33; v.p., prin. Draughon's Bus. Coll., Savannah, Ga., 1933-40, pres., 1940-52; pres. Bolen-Draughon Coll., Savannah, 1952—. Bd. dirs. Savannah YMCA; trustee Brewton-Parker Coll., Mt. Vernon, Ga. Mem. So. Bus. Edn. Assn., Nat. Bus. Edn. Assn., Southeastern Bus. Coll. Assn. (pres.), Am. Assn. Comml. Colls. (dir.), Savannah C. of C., Nat. Sales Execs. Club, Pi Rho Zeta. Club: Exchange (Savannah). Home: 3605 Bull St Savannah GA 31405

BOLENE, ROBERT VICTOR, physician; b. Enid Okla., Aug. 31, 1925; s. Victor Emanuel and Alna (Brown) B.; student Phillips U., 1942-43; Northwestern U., 1943, U. N.H., 1943-44; M.D., U. Okla., 1948; m. Margaret Rosalie Steele, Feb. 6, 1948; children—Judith Kay, John Eric, Sally Sue, Janice Lynn, Daniel William. Surg. intern Henry Ford Hosp., Detroit, 1948-49; county health dir. Garvin and Murray County, Okla., 1949-50; chief surgery VA Hosp., Sulphur, Okla. 1950, 1952-53; resident obstetrics and gynecology U. Okla. Med. Center, Oklahoma City, 1953-56, asso. instr., chief resident faculty Sch. Medicine, 1955-56; practice medicine specializing in obstetrics and gynecology, Ponca City, Okla., 1956—; mem. staff Ponca City Hosp., chief dept. obstetrics and gynecology, pres.-elect, 1971, chief staff, 1972; mem. staff Fairfax Hosp. Committeeman, Boy Scouts Am., patron Ponca City Playhouse; sponsor YMCA, 1960-61; rep. Cub Scouts Am., 1959-61. Served from pvt. to pfc Inf., AUS, 1942-46; served from 1st lt. to capt. M.C., USAF, 1950-52. Diplomate Am. Bd. Obstetrics and Gynecology. Fellow A.C.S., Am. Coll. Obstetricians and Gynecologists, Am. Geriatric Soc.; mem. Am. Soc. Study Sterility, Internat. Fertility Assn., Tulsa Obstetrics and Gynecology Soc., A.M.A., Okla., Kay Noble County (pres. 1969) med. socs., C. of C., New Hosp. Devel. Orgn., Phi Chi. Republican. Presbyn. Club: Ponca City Country. Home: 2116 Juanito St Ponca City OK 74601 Office: Ponca Med Arts 1215 E Hartford St Ponca City OK 74601

BOLES, DAVID LAVELLE, lawyer; b. Tulia, Tex., May 2, 1937; s. Jerry Hoytt and Irma Ruth (Walker) B.; student North Tex. State U., 1955-57; B.S., Trinity U., 1959; J.D. (Royston, Rayzor and Cook scholar 1963), U. Tex. Law Sch., 1963; m. Kerstin Gunilla Stenerudh, May 25, 1959; children—David LaVelle, Kerstin Regina, William Gail. Admitted to Tex. bar, 1963; asst. atty. gen. State Tex., Austin, 1963-67; pvt. practice law, Denton, Tex., 1967-69; house counsel Sam P. Wallace Co., Dallas, 1969—; sec. Central Energy Corp. and subsidiaries, Dallas, 1970—; sec., or asst. sec. numerous corps. throughout U.S., P.R., 1970—. Alumni chmn. Trinity U., Austin, 1965-66; counsel Synod Tex. Presbyn. Found., Denton, 1968-69. Mem. Tex., Denton County bar assns., Lancers (pres. 1959). Presbyn. (deacon 1959-71). Home: 1510 Laurelwood St Denton TX 76201 Office: 2102 Proctor St Dallas TX 75235

BOLES, PAUL DARCY, author; b. Auburn, Ind., Mar. 5, 1919; s. Ernest A. and Gwendolyn (Cowan) B.; student pub. schs.; m. Dorothy Kathleen Flory, Dec. 25, 1941; children—Shawn Michael, Terence Ross, Patric Laurence. Vice pres. Liller, Neal, Battle & Lindsey Advt., Atlanta, 1953—. Recipient Friends of Am. Writers Medal and, 000 award, 1958; fiction gold medal Ga. Writers Assn., 1969; award U. Ind., 1969. Author: The Streak, 1953; The Beggars in The Sun, 1954; Glenport, Illinois, 1956; Deadline, 1957; Parton's Island, 1958; A Million Guitars, 1967 (Ind. U. Writers Conf. award 1969); I Thought You Were a Unicorn, 1971; also numerous short stories in maj. mags. Home: 4009 Wieuca Rd NE Atlanta GA 30305 Office: Life of Ga Tower Atlanta GA 30303

BOLEY, ROBERT EUGENE, assn. exec.; b. Washington, Nov. 25, 1925; s. Charles Taylor and Viva (Weightman) B.; A.B., George Washington U., 1953 M.A., 1958; m. Janet Elizabeth McCarty, May 26, 1950; 1 stepson, Stephen C. Sole. Geographer Fed. Govt., 1953-54; research asso. George Washington U., 1954-56; dir. Indsl. Devel. Com. of Prince George County (Md.), 1956-57; with Urban Land Inst., Washington, 1957—, exec. dir., 1969—. Bd. dirs. Urban Land Research Found. Served with AUS, 1943-46. Decorated Air medal. Mem. Assn. Am. Geographers, Am. Indsl. Devel. Council (chmn. research edn. and cons. com. 1969—),Lambda Alpha, Pi Gamma Mu. Contbr. indsl. sect. of Community Builders Handbook, 1969. Home: 3430 N Randolph St Arlington VA 22207 Office: 1200 18th St NW Washington DC 20036

BOLGER, ROBERT JOSEPH, trade assn. exec.; b. Phila., Aug. 9, 1922; s. Harold Stephen and Edna (Adams) B.; B.S., Villanova U., 1943; postgrad. Northwestern U., 1945-46, U. Pa., 1946-47, U. Geneva (Switzerland), 1948-49; m. Helen Siegfried, May 22, 1954; children—Robert, Mary T., Cynthia A., Ann M., Catherine B., David A. Salesman, Container Corp., Phila., 1946; sales supr. Kraft Food Co., Phila., 1949-52; overseas mgr., dir. retail relations Smith, Kline & French Labs., Phila., 1952-62; exec. v.p. Nat. Assn. Chain Drug Stores, Inc., Arlington, Va., 1962-72, pres., 1972—. Bd. dirs. Am. Found. Pharm. Edn., Nat. Drug Trade Conf. Served to lt. comdr., USNR; PTO. Decorated Air medal; named Man of Year Cosmetic and Toiletry Sect. United Jewish Appeal, 1972. Mem. Am. Pharm. Assn., Nat. Assn. Retail Druggists. Clubs: Belle Haven Country (Alexandria); Canadian (N.Y.C.); Army-Navy, Capitol Hill (Washington); Germantown Cricket (Phila.). Contbr. articles to trade publs. Home: 906 Dalebrook Dr Alexandria VA 22308 Office: 1911 Jefferson Davis Hwy Arlington VA 22202

BOLIN, RICHARD ARNOLD, city ofcl.; b. York, S.C., Dec. 24, 1935; s. John Henry and Cora (Clinton) B.; B.S., Appalachian State Tchrs. Coll., 1958; m. Glenda Kay Tucker, Aug. 1, 1964; children—John Patrick, Margaret Lynne. Budget and personnel officer, asst. to city mgr. City of Greenville, S.C., 1962-64; dir. finance City of Brunswick (Ga.), 1964-65; town mgr. Town of Canton (N.C.) 1965-68; city mgr. City of Anderson (S.C.), 1968-70, City of Newnan (Ga.), 1970—. Pres., Canton (N.C.) Bethel-Clyde United Fund, 1968, drive chmn., 1968; 3d v.p. Newnan United Fund, 1972. Bd. dirs. Canton chpt. A.R.C., 1967, Newnan chpt., 1972—, Chat-Flint Area Planning and Devel. Commn., 1971-72. Served to lt. (j.g.) USNR, 1959-62. Mem. Internat. City Mgmt. Assn., Ga. City-County Mgrs. Assn. (sec.-treas. 1971-72, v.p. 1972-73) Am. Judicature Soc. Methodist. Lion. Home: 4 Mansour Circle Newnan GA 30263 Office: 25 Jefferson St Newnan GA 30263

BOLING, EDWARD JOSEPH, univ. adminstr.; b. Sevier County, Tenn., Feb. 19, 1922; s. Sam R. and Nerissa (Clark) B.; B.S. in Accounting, U. Tenn., 1948, M.S. in Statistics, 1950; Ed.D. in Ednl. Adminstrn., George Peabody Coll. Tchrs., 1961; m. Carolyn Pierce, Aug. 8, 1950; children—Mark Edward, Brian Marshall, Steven Clark. With Wilby-Kinsy Theatre Corp., Knoxville, Tenn., 1940-41, Aluminum Co. Am., 1941-42; instr. statistics U. Tenn., 1948-50; research statistician Carbide & Carbon Chem. Corp., Oak Ridge, 1950, supr. source and fissionable materials accounting K-25 plant, 1951-54; budget dir. Tenn., 1955-59, commr. finance and adminstrn., 1959-61; v.p. U. Tenn., 1961—. Dir. Nashville br. Fed. Res. Bank of Atlanta. Chmn. Tenn. Commn. Youth Guidance; mem. Tenn. Commn. on Human Relations; mem. So. Regional Edn. Bd., 1957-61; mem. Nat. Govs. Conf. Good Will Tour to Brazil and Argentina, 1960. Bd. dirs. Knoxville United Fund, E. Tenn. Speech and Hearing Assn., Bill Wilkerson Speech and Hearing Center, Nashville. Served with AUS, 1943-46; ETO. Mem. Am. Statis. Assn., Assn. Higher Edn., Nat. Assn. Land-Grant Colls., Am. Coll. Public Relations Assn. (trustee, chmn. com. on taxation and philanthropy), Am. Alumni Council, Knoxville C. of C. (v.p.), Am. Legion, Phi Kappa Phi (Scholarship award 1948), Beta Gamma Sigma (charter pres. Alpha chpt. 1948), Phi Delta Kappa. Democrat. Author: (with D. A. Gardiner) Forecasting University Enrollment, 1952. Home: 4915 Westover Terrace Knoxville TN 37914

BOLING, JEWELL, govt. ofcl.; b. Randleman, N.C., Sept. 26, 1907; d. John Emmitt and Carrie (Ballard) Boling; student Women's Coll., U. N.C., 1926; Am. U., 1942, 51-52. Interviewer, N.C. Employment Service, Winston-Salem, Asheboro, 1937-41; occupational analyst US. Dept. Labor, Washington, 1943-57, placement officer, 1957-58, employment service adviser, 1959-61, occupational analyst, 1962, employment service specialist counseling and testing, 1963-69, manpower devel. specialist, 1969—. Recipient Meritorious Achievement award Dept. Labor, 1972. Mem. A.A.A.S., Am. Personnel and Guidance Assn. (profl. mem. nat. vocational guidance assn.). Am. Rehab. Counselling Assn. (archivist 1964-67), Assn. Measurement and Evaluation in Guidance, Am. Assn. Humanistic Psychology, Smithsonians, Audubon/Naturalist Soc., Nat. Capital Astronomers (editor Star Dust 1949-58), Internat. Platform Assn., Sierra Club. Author: Counselor's Handbook, Interviewing Guides in Individual Appraisal, 1967; Counselor's Desk Aid, Eighteen Basic Vocational Directions, 1967; Handbook for New Careerists in Employment Security, 1971. Contbr. articles to profl. publs. Home: 1514 17th St NW Washington DC 20036 Office: 1741 Rhode Island Av NW Washington DC 20036

BOLINGER, JOHN MICHAEL, veterinarian; b. E. Dare and Rina (Morrison) B.; student Wofford Coll., 1959-62, Clemson U., 1962-63; D.V.M., Coll. Vet. Medicine, U. Ga., 1963-67; m. E. Marcella Meredith, Nov. 10, 1962; children—Jara, Joy, Jony, Ann, Mike. Veterinarian, Central Soya Co., Decatur, Ind., 1967-69; pvt. practice vet. medicine, Gaffney, S.C., 1969—. Mem. Gaffney Jr. C. of C., Cherokee Sertoma, Am., S.C. vet. med. assns., Alpha Zeta. Home: 308 W Race St Gaffney SC 29340 Office: PO Box 1333 S Granard St Gaffney SC 29340

BOLINO, AUGUST CONSTANTINO, educator; b. East Boston, Mass., Sept. 30, 1922; s. Nicholas and Rose (Capozzi) B.; B.B.A., U. Mich., 1948, M.B.A., 1949; postgrad. U. Wash., 1950-52; Ph.D., St. Louis U., 1957; m. Thora G. Johnson, Sept. 15, 1951; children—Bradlee, Douglas, Jacquelyn, Gregory. Research fellow Bur. Bus., U. Mich., 1949; bookkeeper Libby McNeill & Libby, Seattle, 1950; instr. statistics U. Wash., 1950-51; instr. bus. and econs. Ida. State U., 1952-55; asst. prof. econs. St. Louis U., 1955-60, asso. prof., 1960-62; research asst. James Ford Bell Found., U. Minn., 1957; research asso. W.E. Upjohn Inst. for Employment Research, Kalamazoo, Mich., 1962; lectr. U. Md., 1963; adj. prof. econs. Am. U., 1964-66; asso. prof. econs. Cath. U. Am., Washington, 1966-69, prof., 1970—; faculty fellow Washington Center Met. Studies, 1969-70. Cons., Yellowstone Ins. Co., Pocatello, Ida., 1954-55, Char Travel Bur., Honolulu, 1960-61, Honduras Contingent, U.S. Peace Corps, 1961-62; econ. adviser Mayor's Citizens Com. for Econ. Growth, Webster Groves, Mo., 1961-62; editorial reader Charles E. Merrill Books, Inc., 1961—; dir. div. manpower devel. U.S. Office Edn., 1964-66; chief div. econ. studies U.S. Dept. Labor, 1962-64; tech. asst. expert U.S. Office Econ. Opportunity, 1967-69; prin. investigator Manpower Research Project, U. Md., 1967-69; cons. Program Policy Studies, George Washington U., 1969-70, Automated Systems Corp., Washington, 1970-71. Served to 1st lt. USAAF, 1942-45. Decorated D.F.C., Air medal; recipient Distinguished Service award Silver Degree, Alpha Kappa Psi, 1960. Am. Philos. Soc. grantee, 1960, NSF grantee, 1967, U.S. Manpower Adminstrn. grantee, 1971. Mem. Alpha Kappa Psi. Author: The Development of The American Economy, 2d edit., 1966; Manpower and the City, 1969. Contbr. articles to profl. jours. Home: 11411 Lund Pl Kensington MD 20795 Office: The Catholic University of America 404 McMahon Hall Washington DC 20017

BOLLES, ROBERT STEPHEN, coll. dean; b. McCook, Neb., Oct. 30, 1908; s. Stephen D. and Sarah (Oyster) B.; diploma, Juilliard Grad. Sch., N.Y.C., 1934; B.S., Columbia, 1936, M.A., 1938, Ed.D., 1948; m. Georgia Coy, Aug. 17, 1935 children—Robert C., John L. Instr., Juilliard Sch. Music, N.Y.C., 1936-37; asso. North Tex. State Tchrs. Coll., Denton, 1939; dir. sch. music dept. Peabody Conservatory Music, Balt., 1939-42; instr. Columbia, 1947-48; mem. faculty U. Fla., Gainesville, 1948—, head music div., 1956-60, asst. dean. Coll. Architecture and Fine Arts, 1960-65, acting dean, 1965-66, dean, 1966—. Served with USNR, World War II. Recipient Notable Nebraskan award Neb. Heritage Assn., 1964. Mem. Music Educators Nat. Conf. Kiwanian (dir. 1969). Author: A Compendium of Solo Flute Literature for Teachers and Students of the Flute, 1948; editor, lectr. Office Naval Research, Washington, 1956-64. Home: 2213 NW 11th Av Gainesville FL 32601

BOLLING, BRANTLEY LAMBERD (MRS. A. STUART BOLLING), mem. Democratic Nat. Com.; b. Asheville, N.C., Dec. 1, 1927; d. Charles Ellsworth and Brantley Heartwell (Carter L.;; student The Baldwin Sch., Bryn Mawr, 1943-45; B.A.; Sweet Briar, 1949; m. A. Stuart Bolling, Jr., Sept. 3, 1949 children—Brantley Carter, Mary Stuart. Mem. alumnae council Sweet Briar Coll., 1955—; bd. dirs. Portsmouth Service League, 1956-57, 60-62; bd. dirs. Norfolk Civic Ballet: pres. Portsmouth Child Care Center, 1965-68. Dem. nat. committeewoman, 1968—; del. at large nat. conv., 1968; mem. exec. com. Va. Dem. State Central Com., 1964—. Trustee Portsmouth Hist. Found., Patrick Henry Hosp.; exec. com. Gov.'s Com. Youth, 1962—; mem. Va. Commn. Visually Handicapped, 1965—; bd. visitors Va. Poly. Inst., 1967—. Episcopalian. Club: Cedar Point Country (Portsmouth). Home: 110 Park Rd Portsmouth VA 23707

BOLLINGER, ESTHER HELEN BAKER (MRS. EDWARD ARTHUR BOLLINGER), artist; b. Melvern Square, N.S., Can., July 5, 1907; d. Joseph Edwin and Kathryn (Buchanan) Baker; student Provincial Normal Coll., Truro, N.S., Can., 1924-25, Albright Art Sch., 1926-28, Scott Carbee Sch. Art, 1929-30; m. Edward Arthur Bollinger, July 15, 1933; 1 son, Wynn Buchanan. Comml. artist Boston Herald, 1929-30; fashion illustrating Simpson's, Halifax, N.S., Can., 1931-32; free lance fashion illustrator stores in Buffalo, 1934-39; exhibited in one-man shows at Zwicker Gallery, Halifax, N.S., 1963, Halifax Meml. Library, 1963, 64, Halifax Shopping Center, 1965, 67, Eatons, Halifax, 1968, Neate Gallery, 1970; exhibited in groups shows at Miami Art League's annual shows, 1960—, Am. Artists Profl. League's annual shows, 1962—, Allied Arts of N. Miami annual shows, 1958—, Nat. League Am. Pen Women annual shows, 1960—. Recipient numerous art awards including blue ribbons Nat. League Am. Pen Women, Am. Artists Profl. League. Fellow Am. Artists Profl. League (bd. mem. 1967—, v.p. Miami chpt. 1968—); mem. Allied Arts North Miami (pres. 1962), Miami Art League (treas. 1963; bd. mem. 1967—), Nat. League Am. Pen Women (membership chmn. Greater Miami br. 1962-64, telephone chmn. 1967-68, art chmn. 1970-71). Republican. Address: 1100 NE 153rd Terrace North Miami Beach FL 33162

BOLTON, ARTHUR KEY, state govt. ofcl.; b. Griffin, Ga., May 14, 1922; s. Herbert Alfred and Eunice (Maddox) B.; grad. N. Ga. Coll., 1941; LL.B., U. Ga., 1943; m. Marion Lee Cashen, Sept. 30, 1946; children—Arthur Key, Marian Lee. Judge criminal ct., Griffin, Ga., 1952-65; mem. Ga. Ho. of Reps., 1949-65, floor leader, from 1963, chmn. tax equalization com.; now atty. gen. Ga. Served to capt. AUS; ETO. Decorated Silver Star, Purple Heart, ETO ribbon with 3 battle stars, Am. Def. medal, Victory medal; recipient Statesmanship award GA. Gen. Assembly, 1961-62. Mem. C. of C., V.F.W., Am. Legion. Baptist. Elk. Home: PO Box 252 Griffin GA 30223 Office: State Judicial Bldg Atlanta GA 30334

BOLTON, ELLIS TRUESDALE, research lab. exec.; b. Linden, N.J., May 4, 1922; s. Elliott L. and Elizabeth (Lindsay) B.; B.S., Rutgers U., 1943, Ph.D. in Zoology, 1950; postgrad. Harvard-Mass. Inst. Tech. Radar Sch., 1943-44; m. V. Elaine Alber, Sept. 11, 1943; children—Roger T., Craig E. Instr. zoology Rutgers U., 1946-49; mem. staff Dept. Terrestrial Magnetism, Carnegie Instn., Washington, 1951-64, chmn. biophysics sect., 1961-66, asso. dir., 1964-66, dir., 1966—; vis. investigator Rocky Mountain Lab., NIH, 1956, 57, U. Auckland, New Zealand, 1960-61. Mem. internat. fellowship award panel USPHS, 1964-68. Served to capt. USMCR, World War II. Recipient Washington Acad. Sci. award, 1959. Carnegie Instn. fellow, 1949-51. Mem. A.A.A.S., Biophysics Soc. (council 1964-66), Am. Geophys. Union, Sigma Xi. Club: Cosmos (Washington). Research in devel. of agar technique to immobilize single strands of DNA for studies of hybridezation reactions; pioneer in developing new techniques in field of molecular biology. Home: 1 Briggs Ct Foxhall Silver Spring MD 20906 Office: Dept Terrestrial Magnetism Carnegie Instn 5241 Broad Branch Rd NW Washington DC 20015

BOMAR, HORACE LELAND, lawyer; b.Spartanburg, S.C., May 20, 1912; s. Horace Leland and Mallie (Brown) B.; A.B., Furman U., 1933; LL.B., Duke, 1936; m. Martha Grier, Mar. 20, 1947; children—Horace Leland III, James Grier, Martha Elizabeth. Admitted to S.C. bar, 1936; asso. firm Chadbourne, Wallace, Parke & Whiteside, N.Y.C., 1936-37; practiced in Spartanburg, 1937-42; asst. U.S. atty., 1940-42; partner firm Holcombe, Bomar & Cureton, Spartanburg, 1946—. Pres., Spartanburg Legal Aid Soc., 1967-68; mem. S.C. Bd. Edn., 1968—. Trustee Spartanburg Jr. Coll., Kennedy Library. Served with USNR, 1942-46. Mem. Am., Spartanburg (pres. 1965—), S.C. (v.p. 1967—), bar assns., Spartanburg C. of C. (pres. 1960-61), Order of Coif. Presbyn. Home: 1019 Andrews Farm Rd Spartanburg SC 29302 Office: 305 Montgomery Bldg Spartanburg SC 29301

BOMAR, STEVE HERREN, banker; b. Atlanta, Aug. 13, 1907; s. James Spencer and Iva (Camp) B.; LL.B., Atlanta Law Sch., 1937; grad. Stonier Grad. Sch. Banking, Rutgers U., 1941; m. Reba Murphy, July 3, 1930; children—Steve Herren, William Joseph, Reba Nancy, Lynda Anne. With Trust Co. Ga., 1925—, sr. v.p., treas., 1957-59, sr. v.p., sec.-treas., 1959-64, exec. v.p., sec.-treas., 1964—, also dir.; v.p., sec.-treas. Trust Co. Ga. Assos., 1948—, also dir. Mem. banking com. emergency operations of adv. com. comml. bank preparedness Am. Bankers Assn., 1955; adv. com. to President for improving presentation fed. budget U.S. C. of C., 1962. Admitted to Ga. bar, 1938. Mem. Nat. Assn. Accountants (dir. 1951-52), Bank Adminstrn. Inst. (pres., dir. 1956-58; recipient Key award 1961), Adminstrv. Mgmt. Assn. (Leffingwell award 1968), Financial Execs. Inst. (pres. 1962-63, dir. 1963-66, chmn. bd. 1963-64, dir. research found. 1962-64), Better Bus. Bur. Atlanta (sec.-treas., dir. 1961-63, 68-70), Ga. Bar Assn., Atlanta C. of C., Sigma Delta Kappa. Presbyn. (deacon, past chmn. finance com. and bd. deacons). Mason. Clubs: Capital City, University Yacht, Civitan (Atlanta). Home: 3516 Pace's Place NW Atlanta GA 30327 Office: PO Box 4418 Atlanta GA 30302

BOMBA, JOHN GILBERT, civil engr.; b. Yorktown, Tex., Feb. 8, 1932; s. Vincent Englebert and Regina (Ibrom) B.; student St. Mary's U., San Antonio, 1949-51; B.S. in Petroleum Engring., Tex. A. and M. U., 1954; m. Jane Killingsworth, June 9, 1958; children—Anne Killingsworth, Marian Regina, Beatrice Joan, Norma Jane. Civil engr. Collins Constrn. Co., Port Lavaca, Tex., 1954-61, Sigler, Clark & Assos., Cons. Engrs., Weslaco, Tex., 1961-64; sr. marine engr. Williams Bros. Engring. Co., Tulsa, 1964-71, mgr. marine engring., 1972—. Served with Signal Corps, AUS, 1954-56. Registered profl. engr., Tex., Okla. Mem. Nat., Tex., Okla. socs. profl. engrs., Am. Soc. C.E. (various coms.), Marine Tech. Soc. Toastmaster. Home: 4354 E 57th St Tulsa OK 74135 Office: Resource Scis Center 321 S Boston Av Tulsa OK 74103

BONADIO, FRANK, labor union ofcl.; b. Pitts., Mar. 19, 1904; s. Felice and Amelia (Torchia) B.; ed. pub. schs.; m. Carmela Doccolo, June 1, 1930; children—Felice A., Francis Charles, Joseph James. Bus. agt. local Sheet Metal Workers Union, 1936-48, internat. rep., 1948-54, v.p., 1956-60; v.p., treas. Balt. Bldg. and Trades Council, 1941-42; sec.-treas. bldg. and constrn. trades dept. AFL-CIO, 1954—. Mem. Nat. Joint Bd. Settlement Jurisdictional Disputes, 1949-54. Democrat. Roman Cath. Home: 3203 Beverly Rd Baltimore MD 21212 Office: 815 16th St NW Washington DC 20006

BOND, ALMON DEWEY, trade assn. exec.; b. Willoughby, O., Jan. 3, 1923; s. Forrest H. and Lennah (Battles) B.; B.S., Ohio State U., 1947; M.S., Cornell U., 1948; Ph.D., Mich. State U., 1953; m. Ruth Collar, June 13, 1953; children—Philinda, Laurel, Carolyn, Sylvia. Asst. dir., fruit and vegetable dept. Am. Farm Bur. Fedn., Washington, 1948-50; asst. dir. marketing dept. Am. Meat Inst., Chgo., 1953-56, dir., Washington office, 1956—; exec. sec. Nat. Meat Canners Assn., Washington, 1962—. Mem. adv. com. hog cholera U.S. Sec. Agr. Served with USNR, 1943-46. Mem. Washington Soc. Assn. Execs. (pres. 1971-72), Am. Agrl. Econs. Assn. Clubs: Nat. Press, Nat. Economists. Home: 458 River Bend Rd Great Falls VA 22066 Office: 1243 Nat Press Bldg Washington DC 20004

BOND, BERNARD BATSON, materials engr.; b. Wiggins, Miss., Mar. 28, 1906; s. Willard Faroe and Susie (Graham) B.; B.A., in Chemistry, Miss. Coll., 1926; m. Laura Lee Traylor, Dec. 24, 1931 (div.); 1dau., Myrna Rose; m. 2d Elizabeth Elmore Fisher, July 17, 1953. Chemist testing div. Miss. Hwy. Dept., Jackson, 1936-42; materials engring. supt. overhaul and repair dept. U.S. Naval Air Sta., Pensacola, Fla., 1942-67, dir. materials engring. div. Naval Air Rework Facility, 1967-71; dir. Tech. Support Center, Dept. Def. Equipment Oil Analysis Program, 1971-72; cons. spectrometric wear metal analysis, Warrington, Fla., 1972—. Fellow Am. Inst. Chemists, A.A.A.S.; mem. N.Y. Acad. scis., Am. Chem. Soc., Am. Inst. Aeros. and Astronautics, Navy League U.S., Am. Camellia Soc. Baptist. Mason. Home: 308 E Sunset Av Warrington FL 32507 Office: 308 E Sunset Av Warrington FL 32507

BOND, DANIEL WEBSTER, JR., chem. co. exec.; b. Leesville, La., July 15, 1926; s. Daniel Webster and Alice Belle (McRae) B.; B.S., La. State U., 1950; m. Elaine Vandigriff, Aug. 30, 1947; children—Daniel, James, Suzanne. Various engring. and plant mgmt. positions Cabot Corp., Ville Platte, La., 1950-59, various personnel and labor relations mgmt. positions, Pampa, Tex., 1959—, dir. personnel and indsl. relations, 1965—. Mem. adv. bd. Salvation Army, 1968-71. Bd. dirs. Gray County Hosp., 1969-71, pres. 1971. Served with USNR, 1944-46. Mem. Panhandle Personnel Assn. (pres. 1965), Bur. Nat. Affairs Personnel Policy Forum. Republican. Presbyn. (elder 1966—). Mason, Kiwanian (pres. 1971). Home: 2228 Aspen St Pampa TX 79065 Office: Cabot Corp PO Box 1101 Pampa TX 79065

BOND, GEORGE DOHERTY, educator; b. Hillsboro, Tex., Oct. 23, 1903; s. George Doherty and May (Wigley) B.; A.B., So. Meth. U., 1924, M.A., 1937; Ph.D., U. Mich., 1947; m. Mildred Elizabeth Martin, Sept. 6, 1922; children—Margaret Burke (Mrs. James T. Richmond), Robert Doherty. Instr. English So. Meth. U., 1924-27, 35-41, asst. prof., 1941-47, asso. prof., 1947-50, prof., 1950-69, chmn. dept., 1953-57, of faculty Senate, 1957-58. Mem. Democratic Organizing Com. of Dallas County, Tex., 1953-57, Mem. Modern Lang. Assn., Linguistic Soc. Am., Coll. English Assn. Am. Assn. U. Profs., Tex. Conf. Coll. Tchrs. English (v.p. 1954, pres. 1965-66), Poetry Soc. Tex. (v.p. 1963-66), Tex. Inst. of Letters, Phi Beta Kappa, Kappa Sigma. Democrat. Methodist. Author: Prairie Pegasus (with J.B. Hubbel and M.D. Hemke), 1924; Better College English (with J.W. Bowyer, J.L. Brooks, and I.H. Herron), 1950. Editor: Inter-American Publs., 1941-45. Editor Southwest Review. 1925-27, 44-45, contbg. editor, 1946-63. Home: 3460 Mockingbird Lane Dallas TX 75205

BOND, HORACE MANN, ednl. adminstr.; b. Nashville, Nov. 8, 1904; s. Dr. James and Jane (Browne) B.; A.B., Lincoln U., Pa., 1923, LL.D., 1941; A.M., U. Chgo., 1926, Ph.D., 1936; LL.D., Temple U., 1952; m. Julia Agnes Washington, Oct. 11, 1929; children—Jane Marguerite, Horace Julian, James George. Head dept. of edn. Langston U., Okla., 1924-27; dir. of extension Ala. State Coll., 1927-28; instr. Fisk U., Nashville, Tenn., 1928-29, asst. prof., 1932-34, prof., head dept. of edn., 1937-39; research asst. Julius Rosenwald Fund, 1934-37; pres. Fort Valley State Coll., Ga., 1939-45; pres. Lincoln U., 1945-67, pres. hon., 1957—; dean Sch. Edn., Atlanta U., 1957-66, dir. bur. of ednl. and social research, 1966—; summer lectr. Tuskegee Inst., Ala., 1929, Garrett Biblical Inst., Evanston, Ill., 1943. Mem. Joint Army and Navy Com.; staff mem. UNESCO seminar, Ashridge, Eng., summer 1948; ednl. survey West Africa, 1949, 60-61. Chmn. bd. Am. Soc. African Culture; bd. dirs. Southeastern Ednl. Corp. Recipient Ednl. Research Assn. Am. award for book Education in Ala.; A Study in Cotton and Steel, 1940; Susan Colver Rosenberger prize for outstanding thesis in social science U. Chgo., 1936. Author: The Education of the Negro in the American Social Order, 1934, rev., reprinted, 1966; Education in Alabama: A Study in Cotton and Steel, 1936; The Search for Talent. Contbr. profl. jours. Home: 361 Lee St SW Atlanta GA 30310 Office: 223 Chestnut St SW Atlanta GA 30314

BOND, JOHN RUSSELL, dentist; b. Roseland, La., May 28, 1918; s. Rufus and Mollie Mae (Russell) B.; B.S., Northwestern State U., 1940; postgrad. Tulane U., 1944-45; D.D.S. cum laude, Loyola U., New Orleans, 1950; m. Lillian Alice Bernadas, Jan. 15, 1944 (dec. July 1962); children—Hester Lyn, John Russell; 2d m. Ramona Ellen Goff, May 21, 1966; 1 son, Jonathan Scott. With Burroughs Adding Machine Co., New Orleans, 1950-51; pvt. practice dentistry, New Orleans, 1950—. Instr. bus. adminstrn. Loyola U. of the So.; instr. oral surgery Charity Hosp., New Orleans; mem. staff So. Bapt. Hosp., Ear, Nose, and Throat Hosp. Sec., Young Men's Bus. Club, New Orleans, 1940-42; chmn. dental div. United Fund, 1952-57. Served with USNR, 1942-45. Fellow Internat. Coll. Dentists, Acad. Gen. Dentistry; mem. Royal Soc. St. George, Soc. of War of 1812, New Orleans C. of C., New Orleans Postgrad. Dental Group (pres. 1968-69), Alpha Sigma Nu, Omicron Kappa Upsilon, C. Victor Vignes Soc. Baptist (chmn. bd. deacons 1970). Club: Timberlane Country. Contbr. articles to profl. pubs. Home: 49 Stilt St New Orleans LA 70124 Office: 1035 Maison Blanche Bldg New Orleans LA 70112

BOND, JULIAN, politician, civil rights leader; b. Nashville, Jan. 14, 1940; s. Horace Mann and Julia Agnes (Washington) B.; B.A., Morehouse Coll., 1971; m. Alice Louise Clopton, July 28, 1961; children—Phyllis Jane, Horace Mann, Michael Julian, Jeffrey Alvin, Julia. A founder Com. Appeal for Human Rights, 1960, exec. sec., 1961; a founder Student Nonviolent Coordinating Com., 1960, communications dir., 1961-66; reporter, feature writer Atlanta Inquirer, 1960-61, mng. editor, 1963; mem. Ga. Ho. of Reps. from Fulton County, 1965—; barred from house because of Vietnam statements, 1966; U.S. Supreme Ct. ruled his Constl. rights were violated, 1966. Bd. dirs. So. Conf. Edn. Fund; mem. Robert Kennedy Meml. Fund, Highland Research and Edn. Center. Mem. So. Corr.

Reporting Racial Equality Wars, Phi Kappa (hon.). Author poems, articles. Address: 361 Westview Dr SW Atlanta GA 30310

BOND, RAYMOND THEODORE, dentist; b. Youngstown, O., July 16, 1933; s. Raymond F. and Mary (Harley) B.; D.D.S. cum laude, Ohio State U., 1958; m. Barbara Gay Wall, July 29, 1961; children—Katherine Louise, Susan Gay. Intern USAF Hosp., Lackland AFB, 1958-59; pvt. practice dentistry, Alexandria, Va., 1963-—; sec.-treas. Tralee Devel. Corp.; adviser Community Bank & Trust Co., Springfield, Va. Dental adviser No. Va. Community Coll.; mem. Alexandria Bd. Health; pres. No. Va. Gnathological Research Group. Served with USAF, 1957-63. Mem. Southeastern Acad. Prosthodontics, Am. Acad. Preventive Dentistry, Am. Dental Assn., Va., No. Va. dental socs. Club: Sertoma (Alexandria). Home: 1608 N Frost St Alexandria VA 22304 Office: 101 S Whiting St Alexandria VA 22304

BOND, ROLAND S., corp. exec.; b. Van Alstyne, Tex., 1898. Dir. Consumers Gas Co., Pioneer Am. Ins. Co.; chmn. bd. Bond Oil Corp. Home: 4600 Brookview Dr Dallas TX 75220 Office: Republic Nat Bank Bldg Dallas TX 75201

BONDS, FRANK LANIER, banker; b. Fairfield, Ala., May 25, 1930; s. Erskine Webster and Lois E. (Graham) B.; B.A., Auburn U., 1955; m. Lavada M. Reese, Sept. 28, 1951 children—Cheryl Ann, Frank Lanier, Brian David. Jr. analyst U.S. Steel Corp., Fairfield, Ala., 1955-58, asst. analyst, 1958-61, analyst, 1961-64; dir. market research Birmingham (Ala.) Trust Nat. Bank, 1964-68, v.p., dir. marketing, 1968-—. Served with AUS, 1948-49, 50-51. Recipient Most Valuable Member award Birmingham chpt. Am. Marketing Assn., 1968. Mem. Am. Marketing Assn. (pres. 1968-69), Ala. Bus. Research Council (treas. 1964-67), Birmingham C. of C. (chmn. research com. 1968). Kiwanian. Clubs: Birmingham (Ala.) Advertising (dir. 1969); Green Valley Country. Home: 1831 Thornton Pl Birmingham AL 35226 Office: 112 N 20th Birmingham AL 35202

BONDURANT, GORDON E., pres. emeritus Darlington Sch., Rome, Ga. Office: Darlington Sch Rome GA 30161

BONEBRAKE, MATTHEW HARRY, broadcasting exec.; b. Rolla, Mo., 1907; s. Harry Everett and Alice (Loflin) B.; B.S. in Journalism, U. Mo.; m. Jan. 11, 1938; 1 child, Ronal. Mem. display staff Oklahoman & Times, 1929-30; comml. mgr. radio sta., 1930-38; gen. mgr. radio sta. KOCY, Oklahoma City, 1938-50, pres. radio sta. KOCY AM and FM, 1950-—. Pres. Taxpayers Research. Mem. Nat. Assn. Broadcasters (dir. 1944-48), Oklahoma City C. of C. Club: Oklahoma City Golf and Country. Home: 9 Oakwood Dr Oklahoma City OK 73121 Office: 101 NE 28th St Oklahoma City OK 73105

BONEY, WALTER THOMAS, city ofcl.; b. Savannah, Ga., May 6, 1937; s. Clark Howell and Evelyn (Anderson) B.; B.S., Jacksonville U., 1963; A.A., S. Ga. Coll., 1957; m. Mickey Ogden, July 12, 1958; children— Cheryl Lynn, Walter T., William Henry. Dir. recreation and parks dept. Duval County, Jacksonville, Fla., 1960-68; supt. recreation and pub. affairs dept. Consol. City of Jacksonville, 1968-—. Pres., chmn. bd. Pastime Enterprises, Inc., 1969-—; v.p., dir. Jacksonville Developers, Inc., 1969-—; gen. agt. Am. Heritage Life Ins. Co., 1970-—. Chmn. Cancer Crusade, Duval County Employees, 1966-67; mem. Community Planning Council, 1968-69, dir., 1968-69. Commr., Pop Warner Football Conf., 1962-69. Bd. dirs. Greater Jacksonville Econ. Opportunity, Inc., 1972-—. Fellow Fla., Assn. for Health, Phys. Edn. and Recreation, Fla. Inst. Park Personnel; mem. Fla. Assn. County Park and Recreation Execs. (dir. 1964-69), Nat. Parks and Recreation Assn., Fla. Recreation Assn., Amateur Softball Assn. Am. (dist. commr. 1965-69), Nat. Assn. County Park and Recreation Execs., C. of C. Methodist. Mason (32 deg.). Club: Quarterback (dir. 1968). Home: Route 1 Box 289E Keystone Heights FL 32656 Office: 1245 E Adams St Jacksonville FL 32202

BONEY, WILLIAM JERRY, educator; b. N.Y.C., Nov. 20, 1930; s. Cecil DeWitt and Myrtle Elizabeth (Cox) B.; A.B., Princeton, 1952; B.D., Union Theol. Sem., 1955; postgrad. U. Tubingen, Germany, 1961-62; Ph.D., Drew U., 1963; m. Nancy Jane Dyck, Aug. 23, 1958; children—Elizabeth Jane, William Thomas, Paul DeWitt. Ordained to ministry Presbyn. Ch., 1955; minister to students Blacksburg (Va.) Presbyn. Ch., 1955-58; lectr. religion Douglass Coll., Rutgers U., New Brunswick, N.J., 1962-63; prof. theology Sch. Theology, Va. Union U., Richmond, 1963-—. Minister, Hanover Presbytery, Presbyn. Ch., U.S., 1965-—, inter-church relations com., 1971-—; Protestant cons. to Ecumenical Affairs Commn., Roman Cath. Diocese of Richmond, 1966-—; chmn. Richmond area Consultation On Ch. Union Study Com., 1971-—. Am. Assn. Theol. Schs. fellow, 1968-69. Fellow Inst. Ecumenical and Cultural Research; mem. Am. Acad. Religion, N.Am. Acad. Ecumenists. Democrat. Club: Princeton (N.J.) Quadrangle. Editor: (with L.E. Molumby) The New Day: Catholic Theologians of the Renewal, 1968; (with P.A. Crow, Jr.) Church Union at Mid-Point, 1972. Home: 2904 Noble Av Richmond VA 23222

BONIFAZ L, ROBERTO, Peruvian diplomat, lawyer; m. Blanca M. Bonifaz; children—Roberto, Gonzalo, Rosa. Consul gen. of Peru, Houston. Home: 4034 Falkirk Houston TX 77025

BONIN, GARLAND L., state govt. ofcl.; b. St. Martinville, La., Apr. 2, 1912; s. Luke and Blanche (Durand) B.; grad. U. Southwest La., 1933; m. Aline Lallande, June 13, 1936; 1 dau., Yvette (Mrs. Hargett). Mem. sch. bd. Lafayette (La.) Parish, 1950-62; mem. La. senate, 1962-65; commr. welfare State of La., 1965-—. Mem. Tau Sigma Delta. Roman Catholic. Home: 143 Parduton St Lafayette LA 70501 Office: Div Public Welfare State Welfare Bldg Baton Rouge LA 70801

BONIN, JOSEPH MAURICE, educator; b. LeRoy, La., Mar. 21, 1930; s. E. Whitney and Rita (Villien) B.; B.S., Spring Hill Coll., 1950; M.A., La. State U., 1952, Ph.D., 1960; m. Margie Ann Johnson, Dec. 22, 1956; children—Catherine, Theresa, Elizabeth, Susan, Judith, John, Rita. Instr., La. State U., 1957-58, asst. prof., 1959-60; asst. prof. U. Ark., 1958-59; asso. prof. Auburn U., 1960-63, prof., 1963-66; prof. econs. U. Ga., Athens, 1966-—. Research analyst Soc. Security Adminstrn., Washington, 1964-65. Served to lt. (j.g.), USNR, 1952-55. Earhart Found. fellow, 1956-57; NSF grantee, 1969-71. Mem. Nat. Tax Assn., Am., So. econ. assns., Am. Finance Assn., Am. Statis. Assn., Pi Gamma Mu, Beta Gamma Sigma. Roman Catholic. Contbr. articles to profl. jours. Home: 170 Hunnicutt Dr Athens GA 30601

BONNELL, WILLIAM FREDERIC, dentist; b. Fort Worth, Oct. 28, 1940; s. William Fearnley and Jean (Booth) B.; B.A., Okla. U., 1961; D.D.S., Baylor U., 1965; m. D'Ann Elisabeth Walsh, June 17, 1965; children— William Frederic, Laura Elisabeth, Jonathan Richard. Pvt. practice dentistry, Fort Worth, 1965-66, 68-—. Chmn., Tarrant County chpt. Nat. Children's Dental Health, 1970-72. Served with Dental Corps, AUS, 1966-68. Recipient award of merit Fort Worth Dist. Dental Soc., 1971. Mem. Am., Tex. dental assns., Fort Worth Dist. Dental Soc., Phi Delta Theta. Clubs: Canterbury, Steeplechase. Home: 6120 Curzon St Fort Worth TX 76116 Office: 3403 Hulen St Fort Worth TX 76107

BONNER, ALLAN BAKER, dentist; b. Aurora, N.C., Oct. 28, 1912; s. George Irving and Vesta Catherine (Mooring) B.; student U. N.C., 1933-36, 37-39; D.D.S., U. Tenn., 1943; m. Sally Ballou Jordan, Aug. 14, 1940; children—Allan Baker, Kathryn (Mrs. Robert Levin Reese), James J., Charles M. Pvt. practice dentistry, Hertford, N.C., 1943-—. Chmn., Perquimans County Morehead Found.; chmn. Alcoholic Beverage Control Bd., Town of Hertford, 1961-63; chmn. Perquimans County Sch. Bd., 1963-69. Mem. Am., N.C. dental assns., Phi Chi. Democrat. Episcopalian (sr. warden 1965-66). Mason (Shriner), Rotarian (past pres.). Home: Route 1 Box 284D Hertford NC 27944 Office: 111 Market St Hertford NC 27944

BONNER, EDWIN EUGENE, ednl. adminstr.; b. Dalton, Ga., Sept. 16, 1926; s. Fred Allen and Agnes (Mullinax) B.; A.B., Mercer U., 1951; M.Ed., U. Tenn., 1960; Ed.S., U. Ga., 1963; m. Helen L. Caldwell, May 2, 1947; children—Gregory Allen, Frances Lynn. Tchr., Whitfield County (Ga.) Bd. Edn., 1951-54, tchr., asst. prin., 1954-60, prin., 1961-—. Served with USNR, 1944-46. Coe Found. Am. Studies grantee, summers 1958, 59; Freedom Found. grantee, summer 1971. Mem. Nat. (life mem.), Ga. edn. assns., 7th Dist. Prin. Assn. (sec. 1967-—), Nat. Assn. Secondary Sch. Prins. Democrat. Baptist (minister of music 1951-—). Club: Ruritan. Home: 205 Lowell Dr Dalton GA 30720 Office: Route 8 Dalton GA 30720

BONNER, JAMES CALVIN, educator, author; b. nr. Carrollton, Ga., June 16, 1904; s. William Allen and Sara (Moore) B.; A.B., U. Ga., 1926, M.A., 1936; Ph.D., U. N.C., 1943; m. Ida Gayle Munro, Nov. 23, 1937; children—Page Munro (Mrs. Wm. Warren Craghead), James Calvin, William Allen II. Instr., asst. prof. social sci. W. Ga. Coll., 1933-41; adj. prof. history Randolph-Macon Womans Coll., 1942-44; prof. history Ga. Coll., Milledgeville, 1944-—, chmn. dept. social studies, faculty research and grad. study, 1948-65. Mem. Ga. Hist. Commn., 1965-—. Trustee, sec.-treas. Lockerly Arboretum Found., Elizabeth, N.J., 1965-—. Mem. Am., Ga., So. (editorial bd. jour. 1950-54) hist. assns., Agrl. History Soc. (editorial bd. jour. 1963-67). Author: Studies in Georgia History and Government, 1940; The Georgia Story, 1958; A History of Georgia Agriculture, 1964; The Journal of a Milledgeville Girl, 1861-67; Georgians in Profile, 1957, (with others) Writing Southern History, 1965; Georgia's Last Frontier, 1971; numerous articles profl. jours. Home: 120 S Jackson St Milledgeville GA 31061

BONNER, JOHN S., cons.; b. Houston, May 3, 1927; s. John S. and Virginia (Harrell) B.; S.B., Mass. Inst. Tech., 1950; postgrad. Cal. Inst. Tech., 1950-51; m. Betty Whitefield, July 31, 1948; children—Barbara, John F., Mary Beth, Melissa, Louisa. Engr., Humble Oil & Refining Co., Baytown, Tex., 1951-56; cons. Bonner &Moore Assos., Inc., Houston, 1957-—, exec. v.p., now chmn. bd. Served with AUS, 1945-47. Mem. Am. Inst. Chem. Engrs., Assn. Computing Machinery, Houston Petroleum Club, Phi Delta Theta. Episcopalian (past vestryman). Clubs: Houston Country, Houston Yacht. Home: 655 Hedwig Rd Houston TX 77024 Office: 500 Jefferson St Houston TX 77002

BONNER, MARK HERBERT, JR., journalist, utility exec.; b. Ft. Necessity, La., Aug. 5, 1918; s.Mark Herbert and Emma Dee (Johnson) B.; student La. Poly. Inst., 1938-41, La. State U., 1946-48; m. Janie Lee Coughran, Jan. 10, 1947; children—Janie Dee, Mark H. III. Reporter, Franklin Sun, Winnsboro, La., 1948-52, asso. editor, 1949-50, editor, 1950-52 editor Rural La., Opelousas, 1952-65, mgr. in charge publ., advt., pub. relations, legislative affairs, 1962; gen. mgr. Assn. La. Electric Coops., 1967-—. Pres. Nat. Rural Electric Consumer Publs., 1958-59, 64-65; dir. Central Area Data Processing Corp. Mem. exec. com. Franklin Library, 1948-51; mem. La. Superport Commn., 1972. Bd. dirs. local A.R.C. Served with USAF, 1941-45; CBI. Recipient editorial award of year La. Press, 1951, photography award, 1954, State Future Farmer Award, 1968, Newspaper Service award, 1968. Mem. Nat. Rural Electric Mgrs. Assn. (sec.-treas. 1971-—), La. Partners Alliance (sec. 1967-—), Am. Legion, V.F.W., Pub. Affairs Research Council, La. Wildlife Fedn. Opelousas C. of C., Soil Conservation Soc. Democrat. Methodist. Rotarian. Home: 648 Natchez Blvd Opelousas LA 70570 Office: 755 W Grolee St Opelousas LA 70570

BONNEVILLE, DOUGLAS ALAN, educator; b. Greenfield, Mass., Apr. 30, 1931; s. Joseph Ernest and Dorothy Louise (Wait) B.; A.B., Wesleyan U., Middletown, Conn., 1955; M.A., Ohio State U., 1958, Ph.D., 1961; m. Ellen Ann Bracken, June 10, 1961; children—Anne Louise, Loretta Marie, Raymond Griffith. Instr. French, Kenyon Coll., Gambier, O., 1959-60, Dartmouth, Hanover, N.H., 1961-63; asst. prof. U. Fla., Gainesville, 1963-68, asso. prof., 1968-—. Mem. Am. Assn. U. Profs., Societe francaise d'etude du XVIIIe Siecle, Internat. Soc. 18th Century Studies. Contbr. profl. jours. Home: 600 NE 9th Av Gainesville FL 32601 Office: Box 415 Dept French U Fla Gainesville FL 32601

BONNEY, BENJAMIN, Israeli diplomat; b. Warsaw, Poland, Apr. 30, 1917; s. Manas M. and Bina (Waksman) B.; went to Palestine, 1934; B.A., U. Tours (France), 1934-37; LL.B., Jerusalem Sch. Law, 1937-40; m. Sara Zeiger, Aug. 16, 1956; 1 son, Moddy Daniel. Dir., Lod Internat. Airport, Tel Aviv, Israel, 1956-60; dep. dir. Civil Aviation, Israel, 1961-63; dep. dir. Dept. for Internat. Cooperation, Ministry of Fgn. Affairs, Jerusalem, Israel, 1963-65; counselor Israeli embassy, Rome, Italy, 1965-69; consul gen. of Israel, Houston, 1969-—. Served with RAF, 1940-46, Isreli Air Force, 1947-56. Mem. Inst. Aero. Scis. Rotarian. Home: 3646 Merrick St Houston TX 77025 Office: 230 World Trade Bldg 1520 Texas Av Houston TX 77002

BONNEY, HAL JAMES, JR., lawyer, judge; b. Norfolk, Va., Aug. 27, 1929; s. Hal J. and Mary (Shackelford) B.; B.A., U. Richmond, 1951, M.A., 1953; J.D., Coll. William and Mary, 1969; m. Marie McBee, July 4, 1963; children—David James, John Wesley. Instr. Norfolk pub. schs., 1951-61; supt. Douglas MacArthur Acad., 1961-67; practiced law, 1969-71; law clk. U.S. Dist. Ct., 1969; prof. U. Va., 1964-71, Coll. William and Mary, 1969-71; judge (U.S. referee in bankruptcy, Norfolk, 1971-—. WTAR radio tchr. Wesleymen Bible class, 1962-—. Treas., Wesleymen Found., Inc.; v.p. Va. Methodist Children's Home. Mem. Am., So. hist. assns., Phi Alpha Theta, Pi Sigma Alpha, Phi Alpha Delta. Methodist. Mason (Shriner). Home: 1357 Windsor Point Rd Norfolk VA 23509 Office: 408 US Court House Norfolk VA 23501

BONNEY, ORRIN H., lawyer, writer; b. Idaho Springs, Colo., May 14, 1903; s. Rufus C. and Cliftonia (Hanning) B.; LL.B. U. Colo., 1926; m. Ethel Craik, June 4, 1928 (div. 1955); 1 son, Roger; m. 2d, Lorraine Gagnon, 1955. Admitted to Tex. bar, 1926; asst. probate judge, Harris County, Houston, 1926-30; practiced law, 1930-33, 51-—; mem. firm Mathes Bonney & Clawson, 1933-51; expert in probate and property practice; pres., dir. Sunrise Place Co., 1939-52; sec. Texas Water Wells, Inc., 1943-60. Served as mil. analyst, mil. planning div. Office Q.M. Gen., U.S. Army,1944-45. Mountain climber; leader expdns. in U.S. Mexico, Can. and Europe; 1st ascents, Wind River Range of Wyo., 1939, 40, 41. Mem. State Bar Tex., Houston Bar Assn., Jr. C. of C., Outdoor Writers Assn. Am., Wilderness Soc., Audubon Soc., Delta Sigma Phi. Democrat (past officer Young Dems.). Mason (K.T., Shriner). Clubs: Am. Alpine (past v.p.), Sierra (past nat. council, leader wilderness studies, past chpt. chmn., past chmn. Big Thicket coordinating com., chmn. Gulf Coast regional cons. com.), Scribblers (past pres.), Shrine Luncheon (sec.), Alpine of Canada, de Exploraciones de Mexico. Author (with wife): Guide to Wyoming Mountains and Wilderness Areas (award Wyo. Hist. Soc.); Bonney's Guide to Jackson's Hole and Grand Teton National Park; Field Book, The Wind River Range (Outdoor Writers Assn. Am. award); Field Book, The Teton Range; Field Book, Yellowstone Park and The Absaroka Range; Field Book, Big Horn Range, 1970; Battle Drums and Geysers—The Life and Journals of Lt. G. C. Doane, 1970. (Wyo. Hist. Soc. award). Contbr. articles to Am. Alpine jour. and other periodicals. Home: 625 E 14th St Houston TX 77008 Office: 627-A E 14th St Houston TX 77008

BONTE, FREDERICK JAMES, physician; b. Bethlehem, Pa., Jan. 18, 1922; s. Frederick R. and Harriett (Stoudt) B.; B.S., Western Res. U., 1942, M.D., 1945; m. Mary Helen Hawke, Aug. 31, 1952; 1 son, Frederick William; m. 2d, Mary Cecile Poetzel; children—Therese Anne, Steven James, Suzanne Marie, John Anthony, Anne Elizabeth. Intern, Huntington Meml. Hosp., Pasadena, Cal., 1944-46; resident Univ. Hosp. of Cleve., 1948-52; practice medicine specializing in radiology, Dallas; mem. faculty Western Reserve U. Sch. Medicine, Cleve., 1952-56, asst. prof., 1952-56, chief radiotherapy and nuclear medicine, 1954-56; prof. U. Tex. Southwestern Med. Sch., Dallas, 1956-—, chmn. dept. radiology, 1956-—; dir. dept. radiology Parkland Meml. Hosp., Childrens Med. Center, VA Hosp., Presbyn. Hosp. (all Dallas). Mem. bd. Nat. Council Radiation Protection and Measurements, 1966-71, mem. radiology tng. com. Nat. Insts. Gen. Med. Scis., USPHS, 1966-70; mem. residency rev. com. radiology A.M.A., 1966-69. Pres. Dallas County unit Am. Cancer Soc., 1965-67, bd dirs. Tex. div., 1965-70. Served to capt. USAAF, 1946-48. Diplomate Am. Bd. Radiology (trustee 1969-—), Am. Bd. Nuclear Medicine (founding trustee 1969-—). Fellow Am. Coll. Radiology; mem. Am. Roentgen Ray Soc. (exec. com. 1965-67),Radiol. Soc. N.Am. (counselor 1967-72), Nuclear Med. Soc. dir. 1965-—), Sigma Xi. Contbr. articles to profl. jours. Home: 11138 Wonderland Trail Dallas TX 75229 Office: 5323 Harry Hines St Dallas TX 75235

BOOE, JOHN CHARLES, candy co. exec.; b. Cin., Jan. 19, 1927; s. Charles Douglas and Ruth (Hanly) B.; B.S., U. Ky., 1951; m. Carolyn Smothers, Oct. 3, 1964; children—Martin, Charles, Ruth. Clk., Internat. Freighting Corp., N.Y.C., 1951-54; clk E.I. du Pont de Nemours & Co., Inc., Wilmington, Del., 1954-58, mgr. marine sect., 1958-60, analyst devel. div., 1960-64; pres. Rebecca Ruth Candy, Inc., Frankfort, Ky., 1964-—. Pres., Historic Frankfort, Inc., 1968. Served with AUS, 1945-47. Rotarian (dir. 1966-67). Home: 104 Dakota Rd Frankfort KY 40601 Office: 112 E 2d St Frankfort KY 40601

BOOG, JANET MARGARET, physician; b. Cin., Mar. 4, 1913; d. Fredrick Anthony and Gertrude (Petit) Boog; student U. Cin., 1931-33; M.D., N.Y. Med. Coll., 1939. Intern, Good Samaritan Hosp., Cin., 1939-40; resident N.Y. Infirmary for Women and Children, N.Y.C., 1940-41, Margaret Hague Hosp., Jersey City, 1942-43, Univ. Hosp., Ann Arbor, Mich., 1943-44, Omaha, 1945-46; cons. obstetrics Dept. of Health, Honolulu, 1946-48; practice medicine specializing in gynecology and obstetrics, Lawrence, Mass., 1949-52, Detroit, 1953-57; resident neuropsychiatry VA Hosp., N.Y.C., 1959-62; staff psychiatrist Longview State Hosp., Cin., 1962-66; unit chief psychiatry VA Hosp., Lexington, Ky., 1966-—; clin. instr. psychiatry U. Ky., 1968-—. Diplomate Am. Bd. Obstetrics and Gynecology. Fellow Am. Coll. Obstetrics and Gynecology; mem. Am. Psychiat. Assn., Cin. Soc. Neurology and Psychiatry, Wilderness Soc. Club: Sierra. Contbr. articles in field to profl. jours. Home: 1545 Alexandria Dr Lexington KY 40504 Office: Leestown Pike Lexington KY 40507

BOOHAKER, JOSEPH ALBERT, accountant; b. Birmingham, Ala., Mar. 10, 1931; s. Albert Simon and Nazha (Stephen) B.; B.S., U. Ala., 1959; m. Paulette Moutran, Sept. 24, 1955; children—Saidie, Emily, Maron, Leo. Staff accountant Arthur Anderson & Co., Atlanta, 1959-61; sr. accountant Peat, Marwick, Mitchell & Co., Atlanta, 1961-65; owner Joseph A. Boohaker C.P.A., Birmingham, Ala., 1965-—. Trustee, Knights of St. Maron Charitable Trust; dir. Nat. Apostolate of Maronites. Served with USAF, 1951-55. C.P.A. Mem. Am. Inst. C.P.A.'s, Ala. Soc. C.P.A.'s (chpt. treas. 1969-70), Am.-Lebanese Nat. Com., Beta Gamma Sigma, Beta Alpha Psi, Chi Alpha Phi, Delta Sigma Pi. Home: 4813 Clairmont Av Birmingham AL 35222 Office: 1200 S 20th St Birmingham AL 35205

BOOKER, HENRY MARSHALL, educator; b. Newport News, Va., Jan. 12, 1935; s. William Henry and Mary Evelyn (Wheeler) B.; B.S. cum laude, Lynchburg Coll., 1959; Ph.D., U. Va., 1965; m. Sarah Porter Cheatwood Phillips, June 22, 1963; children—Mary DeMott, Sharon. Sinclair, Paige Meriwether. Teller, Bank Hampton Rds., Hampton, Va., 1951-53; instr. econs. Salem Coll., Winston-Salem, N.C., 1962-64; asst. prof. econs. Frederick Coll., Portsmouth, Va., 1964-65; asso. prof., dir. grad. studies in econs. Old Dominion U., Norfolk, Va., 1965-69; prof., dean faculty Christopher Newport Coll., Newport News, Va., 1969-—. Cons. Bank Hampton Rds., W. A. Norris, Portsmouth, George Washington U., NASA, Langley Field, C. of C., Newport News, Indsl. Coll. Armed Forces. Civilian with USAF, 1953-55. E. I. duPont Nat. fellow U. Va., 1959; Nat. Defense fellow, U. Va., 1959-62; Am. Soc. Engring. Edn. Summer Faculty fellowship NASA, 1968, 69; recipient Achievement award in finance Wall St. Jour., 1959. Mem. Am. Acad. Polit. and Social Sci., Am., So. econs. assns., S.A.R. (sec. Thomas Nelson chpt. 1969-71), Omicron Blue Key, Alpha Kappa Psi. Episcopalian (mem. vestry 1970-—). Contbr. articles to profl. jours. Home: 31 Indian Springs Dr Newport News VA 23606 Office: PO Box 6070 Hidenwood Sta Newport News VA 23606

BOOKER, JOHN PARKS, physician; b. Charlotte, N.C., Dec. 3, 1910; s. James Carter and Belle (Rowland) B.; student Duke, 1929-32; M.D., S.C. Med. U., 1936; m. Frances Louise Schumacher, June 17, 1940; children—John Parks, Robert Leonard, Edward Henry. Intern and resident Gen. Hosp., Greenville, S.C., 1936-38; practice medicine specializing in surgery, Walhalla, S.C., 1938-—; former chief staff, Oconee Meml. Hosp., also chief surgery. Chmn. Oconee County Aeros. Commn. Mayor pro tem Walhalla, Bd. dirs. S.C. Blue Shield, S.C. Regional Med. Program, Appalachian Regional Health Policy and Planning Council; trustee Wickcliffe Fund. Served to col. AUS, World War II. Diplomate Am. Bd. Surgery. Mem. Oconee County Med. Soc. (past pres.) S.C. Med. Assn. (chmn. council 1968-69, pres. 1971-72), Sigma Phi Epsilon, Phi Rho Sigma. Methodist (ch. bd.). Mason. Home: 315 Church St Walhalla SC 29691 Office: Broad and Church Sts Walhalla SC 29691

BOOKHOLT, WILLIAM JOHN, govt. ofcl.; b. Paterson, N.J., Aug. 30, 1916; s. James and Bella (Van Haste) B.; student Pace Inst., 1935-39, Ga. State Coll., 1950-52; LL.B., Woodrow Wilson Coll., 1950; m. Marian Bell, June 30, 1943; children—Robert G., Barbara G. Field auditor Equitable Life Assurance Soc., N.Y.C., 1935-40; regional commnr. U.S. Internal Revenue Service, Atlanta, 1946-—. Served to capt., Ordnance Dept., AUS, 1941-45. C.P.A. Mem. Ga. Soc. C.P.A.s, Ga. Bar Assn. Home: 2435 Tanglewood Rd Decatur GA 30033 Office: PO Box 926 Atlanta GA 30301

BOOKMAN, RONALD WESTMORELAND, JR., editor; b. Houston, July 7, 1941; s.Ronald W. and Martha (Bown) B.; B.A., Tex A. and M. Coll., 1963; m. Sylvia Ann Ideus, Sept. 23, 1961 children—Ronald W. III, William Daniel. Reporter, copy editor Houston Press, 1962-64; reporter Houston Post, 1964; reporter, make-up editor, exec. sports editor Memphis Press-Scimitar, 1964-68; pub. relations dir., profl. tennis tour, 1968-72; asso. publisher World Tennis mag., 1972—. Mem. Sigma Delta Chi. Episcopalian. Club: Houston Press. Home: 18014 Bambriar St Houston TX 77090 Office: 8100 Westglen St Houston TX 77042

BOOMERSHINE, DONALD EUGENE, banker; b. Dayton, O., Oct. 5, 1931; s. Harold Everett and Elsie (Rhoads) B.; B.S., Bowling Green State U., 1953; postgrad. Bank Pub. Relations Grad. Sch., Northwestern U., 1965-66, Stonier Grad. Sch. Banking, Rutgers U., 1969—; m. Marilyn Sullivan, Aug. 29, 1953; children—Jeffrey, Alan. Mem. Gen. Motors jr. exec. program, Frigidaire, Dayton, 1955-57; sales rep. IBM, Dayton, Birmingham, Ala., 1957-61; asst. cashier, bus. devel. rep. Exchange Security Bank, Birmingham, 1963; v.p. nat. accounts div. Birmingham Trust Nat. Bank, 1964—. Chmn. Ala. Bankers Conv., 1972. Mem. ednl. com. Asso. Industries Ala., 1970; pres. N. Central Ala. Muscular Dystrophy, 1966. Bd. dirs. YMCA, Muscular Dystrophy. Served.with USMCR, 1953-55; now lt. col. Res. Mem. Bank Pub. Relations and Marketing Assn. (v.p.), Am. Inst. Banking, Native Sons and Daus. Ala. (coordinator 1972), Bank Marketing Assn. (nat. dir. 1971—), Sigma Chi, Kiwanian. Clubs: Birmingham Touchdown (founder), Downtown, Executive (Birmingham). Home: 3801 Cromwell Dr Birmingham AL 35243 Office: PO Box 2487 112 N 20th St Birmingham AL 35202

BOOMERSHINE, WALTER MCKINLEY, JR., automobile dealer; b. Charlotte, N.C., July 20, 1929; s. Walter McKinley and Nellie (McConnell) B.; B.S., Ga. Inst. Tech., 1951; m. Winifred Forbes, Sept. 9, 1950; children—Linsay Ann, Kathy Renee, Jacquelyn Gay, Joanne Patrice, Walter McKinley III. With Boomershine Pontiac, Inc., Atlanta, 1946—, v.p., gen. mgr., 1959-65, pres. 1965—; pres., dir. Alexander Williams Co., Inc., Atlanta 1960—; pres. Boomershine Agy., Inc., ins. and leasing, 1968—, Boomershine Life Ins. Co., 1970—; dir. Citizens & So. Nat. Bank, Atlanta, Backus Cadillac-Pontiac Co., Savannah. Served with USAF, 1951-53. Mem. Atlanta (pres., dir.), Ga. (dir.) automobile dealer assns., Atlanta C. of C. (tax com.), Chi Phi. Presbyn. (elder). Kiwanian (dir.). Home: 4636 Powers Rd Marietta GA 30060 Office: 390 Spring St Atlanta GA 30308

BOONE, BYRON VEST, newspaper pub.; b. Gainsville, Mo., Feb. 27, 1908; s. George W. and Lu (Comer) B.; student U. Tulsa, 1926, LL.B., 1929; m. Audray Sipes, Feb. 17, 1934; 1 dau., Brenda Jo. Pres., World Publishing Co., Tulsa, 1960—; pub. Tulsa Daily World, 1959—; v.p. dir. Standard Life & Accident Ins. Co.; dir. Farmers & Mchts. Bank & Trust Co., Sloan Oil & Gas Co. Trustee U. Tulsa, Hillcrest Med. Center. Mem. Am., Okla. bar assns. Clubs: Tulsa, Southern Hill Country (Tulsa). Home: 2150 Forest Hill Blvd Tulsa OK 74114 Office: World Bldg 315 S Boulder St Tulsa OK 74102

BOONE, JAMES LEROY, JR., educator; b. Houston, May 15, 1923; s. James Leroy and Mora Evelyn (Waddell) B.; B.S. in Indsl. Edn., Tex. A. and M. U., 1947, M.Ed., 1948, Ed.D., 1966; m. Lillian Vorpahl, May 18, 1944; 1 son, James Leroy III. Tchr. trainer Laredo (Tex.) Jr. Coll., 1948-50, dir. vocational sch., 1950-52; asso. prof. indsl. edn. Tex. A. and M. U., College Station, 1952-69, head dept. indsl. edn., 1969—. Mem. Brazos County (Tex.) Hist. Survey Com., 1967-71, Tex. Adv. Council for Tech.-Vocational Edn., 1971—. Trustee Brazos County (Tex.) Sch. Bd., 1960-71. Served with AUS, 1943-46; now lt. col. Res. Mem. Am. Council Indsl. Arts Tchr. Edn., Am. Indsl. Arts Assn., Am. Vocational Assn., N.E.A., Res. Officers Assn. Am., Phi Delta Kappa, Iota Lambda Sigma. Methodist. Contbr. articles to profl. publs. Home: Route 4 Box 251 Bryan TX 77801 Office: Dept Indsl Edn Tex A and M U College Station TX 77843

BOONE, SISTER JOSEPH ANGELA, educator; b. New Haven, Ky.; d. William Joseph and Mary Josephine (Greenwell) Boone; B.A., Brescia Coll., 1961; M.S., Cath. U. Am., 1963; postgrad. Tulane U., 1965. Tchr. jr. high parochial schs., Owensboro, Louisville, Ky., 1949-61; tchr. math. Brescia Coll., Owensboro, Ky., 1963—, mem. adminstrv. bd., dean of women, 1966-70; treas. Mt. St. Joseph Ursuline Sisters, 1970—. Mem. Nat. Council Tchrs. Math., Math. Assn. Am., Assn. Physics Tchrs. Home: Maple Mount KY 42356

BOONE, SHELLEY SHELTON, ednl. adminstr.; b. Wauchula, Fla., May 7, 1922; s. Falcon B. and Ethel (Clardy) B.; B.S. in Econs., Fla. So. Coll., 1947, M.A., in Pub. Adminstrn. and Supervision, 1949; postgrad. U. Fla., 1949-52; m. Facheon Lee Kirby, Apr. 6, 1947; children— Shelley S. II, James A., William David. Tchr. pub. schs., Auburndale, Fla., 1948-51; prin. schs., Haines City, Fla., 1951-57; supervising prin. Winter Haven (Fla.) area schs., 1958-60; dir. personnel Polk County (Fla.) Sch. Bd., Bartow, Fla., 1960-61, supt. pub. instrn., 1961-68; exec. dir. div. jr. colls. Dept. Edn., State of Fla., 1968-69, dir. div. elementary and secondary edn., 1969-72, dep. commn., 1972—. County supt., Polk County, 1961-68. Served as lt. comdr. USNR, 1942-46. Mem. N.E.A., Fla. Edn. Assn. (past dir.), Fla. Assn. Secondary Sch. Prins. (past dir.), Fla. Congress Parent-Tchrs. Assn., Kappa Sigma. Democrat. Methodist. Rotarian. Clubs: Haines City (pres.); Lakeland (Fla.) (dir.). Home: 901 Chestwood St Tallahassee FL 32303 Office: Room 409 Dept Edn Tallahassee FL 32304

BOONE, WILLIAM GARDNER, JR., lawyer; b. Eufaula, Ala., Sept. 8, 1925; s. William Gardner and Emily (Milton) B.; A.B., Duke, 1948, J.D., 1950; m. Inez F. Rosamond, June 21, 1952 children—Constance Rosamond, Robin Elizabeth, Leslie Allison. Admitted to Tenn. bar, 1950; law clk. U.S. Ct. of Appeals, Cin., 1950-51; asso. or mem. firm Montedonico, Boone, Gilliland, Heiskell and Loch, Memphis, 1951-65, Boone, Boone, Langschmidt and Pemberton, Memphis, 1965—. Sec., gen. counsel, dir. Transmar Downtowner Corp., N.Y.C. Served with AUS, 1943-45. Decorated Purple Heart. Mem. Am., Memphis, Shelby County bar assns., Am. Judicature Soc., Sigma Alpha Epsilon, Phi Delta Phi, Republican. Episcopalian. Clubs: Memphis Country, Memphis University, Memphis Petroleum; Summit; Palm Bay (Miami, Fla.). Home: 1457 Goodbar St Memphis TN 38104 Office: 1st Nat Bank Bldg Memphis TN 38103

BOORAS, THEODORE PETER, banker; b. Pensacola, Fla., July 13, 1918; s. Peter Nick and Melpomeni (Poulos) B.; student La. State U., 1968-70; m. Marion Lois Taranto, Apr. 22, 1941; children—Constance (Mrs. Conrad Borzych), Patricia (Mrs. James Morrison), Theodore Peter. Co-owner Booras & Weidlich, Pensacola, Fla., 1946-56; sales rep. Grice Electronics, Inc., Pensacola, Fla., 1956-65; v.p. First Nat. Bank, Ft. Walton Beach, Fla., 1965—. Committeeman Gulf Coast council Boy Scouts Am., 1966—. Bd. dirs. United Fund, 1967-68, A.R.C. Served with USNR, 1942-46, 51-52. Mason (32 deg., Shriner), Rotarian. Home: 735 Revere Av Fort Walton Beach FL 32548 Office: PO Drawer 1327 Fort Walton Beach FL 32548

BOORD, MILLER, librarian; b. Danville, Ill., Feb. 16, 1910; s. Harry J. and Pauline (Miller) B.; A.B., U. Ill., 1933; M.A., George Peabody Coll., 1951, M.A. in Library Sci., 1952; m. Patricia Anne Romig, Jan. 22, 1944. Indsl. engr. Carnegie-Ill. Steel, Chgo., 1939-41; standards analyst F. L. Jacobs Co., Danville, Ill., 1946-50; asst. to dir. Peabody Library Sch., Nashville, 1951-52; dist. librarian Ill. State Library, 1952-54, regional librarian, 1957-60; librarian Mason City, Ia., 1954-57; dir. Fed. Library Program for So. Ill., 1957-60, chief library service Ill. State Library, 1960-65; head librarian Randolph-Macon Woman's Coll., Lynchburg, Va., 1965—. Served from pvt. to capt. AUS, 1941-46; now maj. Res. ret. Mem. Am., Va. library assns., Phi Delta Kappa, Pi Gamma Mu, Beta Phi Mu. Contbr. profl. mags. Home: Princeton Circle W Lynchburg VA 24503 Office: Randolph-Macon Woman's Coll Lynchburg VA 24504

BOORSTIN, DANIEL J., dir. Nat. Mus. History and Tech., Smithsonian Instn.; b. Atlanta, Oct. 1, 1914; s. Samuel and Dora (Olsan) B.; A.B. summa cum laude, Harvard, 1934; B.A. with 1st class honors (Rhodes scholar), Balliol Coll., Oxford (Eng.) U., 1936, B.C.L. with 1st class honors, 1937; postgrad. in law Inner Temple, London, 1934-37; J.S.D. (Sterling fellow), Yale, 1940; Litt.D., Cambridge (Eng.) U., 1967; m. Ruth Carolyn Frankel, Apr. 9, 1941; children—Paul Terry, Jonathan, David West. Admitted as barrister-at-law to Inner Temple, 1937, Mass. bar, 1942; instr., tutor history and lit. Harvard and Radcliffe Coll., 1938-42, also lectr. legal history Law Sch., Harvard, 1939-42; sr. atty. Office Lend Lease Adminstr., Washington, 1942-43, Office Asst. Solicitor Gen. U.S., 1942-43; asst. prof. history Swarthmore Coll., 1942-44; asst. prof. U. Chgo., 1944-49, asso. prof., 1949-56, Preston and Sterling Morton Distinguished prof. Am. history, 1956-71; dir. Nat. Mus. History and Tech., Smithsonian Instn., Washington, 1971—; Fulbright vis. lectr. Am. history U. Rome (Italy), 1950-51, Kyoto (Japan) U., 1957; cons. social sci. research center U. P.R., 1955; lectr. for State Dept. in Turkey, Iran, Nepal, India, Ceylon, 1959-60, Indonesia, Australia, New Zealand, Fiji Islands, 1968; 1st incumbent of chair Am. history and instns. U. Paris, 1961-62; Pitt prof. Am. history and instns. Cambridge U., also fellow Trinity Coll., 1964-65. Mem. Am. Revolution Bicentennial Commn., 1966—. Mem. bd. visitors U.S. Air Force Acad., 1967—. Mem. Colonial Soc. Mass., Internat. House Japan, Am., Miss. Valley, So. hist. assns., Phi Beta Kappa. Jewish religion. Clubs: Cosmos (Washington); Elizabethan (Yale); Quadrangle (Chgo.); Reform (London). Author: The Mysterious Science of the Law, 1941, Delaware Cases, 1792-1830 (3 vols.), 1943; The Lost World of Thomas Jefferson, 1948; The Genius of American Politics, 1953; The Americans: The Colonial Experience, 1958 (Bancroft award 1959); America and the Image of Europe, 1960, The Image or What Happened to the American Dream, 1962; The Americans; The National Experience, 1965 (Francis Parkman prize 1966); The Landmark History of the American People, 2 vols., 1968, 70; The Solidarity of the Absurd, 1970. Editor: Chicago History of American Civilization, 30 vols., 1951—; An American Primer, 1966; editor for Am. history Ency. Brit., 1951-55. Contbr. articles, book revs. to profl. jours. Home: 3541 Ordway St NW Washington DC 20016 Office: Nat Museum History and Technology Smithsonian Instn Washington DC 20025

BOOSALIS, JAMES JOHN, bus. exec.; b. Mpls., May 27, 1924; s. John James and Stamata (Villas) B.; B.A., U. Minn., 1947; m. Inga Margarita Swanson, Aug. 5, 1941; children—Joanne, John, Julie, Jimmy, Janet. Sales mgr. John Morrell Co., Chgo., 1948-61; dir. sales Am. Bakeries, Chgo., 1961-66; v.p. sales Jeno's, Inc., Duluth, Minn., 1966-69; v.p. marketing sales United Foods, Inc., Memphis, 1969—, also dir.; dir. John Ingles Frozen Food Co. Served with AUS, 1941-45. Club: Colonial (Memphis). Home: 6180 Heather Dr Memphis TN 38138 Office: 1700 White Station Tower 5050 Poplar Ave Memphis TN 38117

BOOTH, ARCH NEWELL, orgn. exec.; b. Wichita, Kan., July 9, 1906; s. Winfield Milton and Laura Belle (Parker) B.; A.B., Wichita State U., 1927; Nat. Inst. Comml. and Trade Orgn. Exec., Northwestern U., 1932-43; LL.D., Hillsdale Coll., Hillsdale, Mich., 1953; m. Wilma Grace Harrison, Feb. 2, 1929; children—Joan, Robert Harrison, Donald A. Spl. rep. Wheeler-Kelley-Hagney Trust Co., Wichita, 1927-29; asst. mgr. Wichita C. of C., 1929-38, gen. mgr., 1938-43; asst. gen. mgr. U.S. C. of C., 1943-47, mgr., 1947-50, exec. v.p., 1950—, chief staff officer, spokesman, 1970— pub. Nations Bus. Mag., 1950—; dir., mem. exec. com. Union Trust Co., Washington; dir. Financial Gen. Corp. Recipient gold medal Freedoms Found., 1952, Spl. Freedom Leadership award, 1963; named Vol. Leader of Year, Am. Assn. Orgn. Execs., 1960. Mem. Pi Kappa Delta. Methodist (trustee). Mason (Shriner). Club: Metropolitan (Washington). Home: 3520 Overlook Lane NW Washington DC 20016 Office: 1615 H St Washington DC 20006

BOOTH, EDGAR CHARLES, lawyer; b. Gainesville, Fla., July 13, 1934; s.Clyde V. and Bertha (Hutchison) B.; B.S., U. Fla., 1956, LL.B., 1962; m. Anne Payne Cawthon, Sept. 6, 1958; children—Rainey Cawthon, Jonn Edgar. Research asst. to G. Harold Carswell, U.S. Dist. Ct., Tallahassee, 1962-63; admitted to Fla. bar, 1962; practiced in Tallahassee, 1963—; mem. firm W. Dexter Douglass, 1963-65, Douglass and Booth, 1965-70; judge Small Claims Ct., Leon County, Fla., 1964-65; municipal judge City of Tallahassee, 1965-71. Chmn. March of Dimes, Tallahassee, 1965; pres. Sigma Nu House Corp.; regional dir. Fla. Drug Abuse Program, 1972—. Sec., bd. dirs. Fla. Heritage Found. Served from 1st lt. to capt., USAF, 1957-60. Mem. Am., Tallahassee (sec.-treas. 1971-72) bar assns., Fla. Bar. Democrat. Episcopalian. Club: Exchange. Home: 402 S Bronough St Tallahassee FL 32301 Office: PO Box 1388 Tallahassee FL 32302

BOOTH, STUART EDGAR, chem. co. exec.; b. Summit, N.J., Nov. 9, 1939; s. John Stuart and Eleanor Frances (Edgar) B.; B.S. in Zoology, Duke, 1962; m. Carol Spence, Sept. 29, 1962; children—Barry Craig, Kimberly Carol. Sales rep. Kerr McGee Chem. Co., Atlanta, 1968-69, mgr. sales adminstrn., Oklahoma City, 1970—. Bd. dirs. YMCA, Oklahoma City, 1971. Served to lt. USNR, 1962-68. Mem. Oklahoma City Jr. C. of C., Alpha Tau Omega. Home: 11433 N May Av Oklahoma City OK 73120 Office: OMB 1002C Kerr McGee Bldg Oklahoma City OK 73102

BOOTHE, LOUIS EARL, grain elevator co. exec.; b. Floydada, Tex., Jan. 27, 1920; s. Joe Franklin and Minnie Lee (Gatewood) B.; student U. Miss., 1943; m. Jean Louise Boen, Sept. 14, 1947; children— Phillis, Lisa. Dep. sec., City of Floydada, 1939-40; jr. accountant Cornell & Co., 1940-41; asst. mgr. Doggett Grain Co., 1945-55; local mgr. Uhlmann Elevators Co., 1955-68; owner, mgr. Boothe Elevators, Anton, Tex., 1968—. City commrs. Anton, 1960-62; fire chief Anton Fire Dept., 1965—, fire marshall, 1963—. Served with AUS, 1941-45. Mem. Panhandle Grain and Feed Assn., West Tex. (dir. 1971-74), Anton (sec. 1951-71) chambers commerce. Mem. Ch. of Christ (deacon 1961-71). Mason, Lion. Home: 606 Lawrence St Anton TX 79313 Office: Santa Fe St Anton TX 79313

BOOTLE, WILLIAM AUGUSTUS, judge; b. Colleton County, S.C., Aug. 19, 1902; s. Philip Loraine and Laura Lilla (Benton) B.; A.B., Mercer U., 1924, LL.B., 1925; m. Virginia Childs, Nov. 24, 1928; children— William Augustus, Ann, James C. Admitted to Ga. bar, 1925, since practiced at Macon; mem. Carlisle & Bootle, 1933-54; U.S. dist. atty. Middle Ga. Dist., 1929-33; acting dean Mercer U. Law Sch., 1933-37, part-time prof. law, 1926-37; sr. judge U.S. Dist. Ct., Middle Dist. Ga., 1954—. Trustee Mercer U., chmn. exec. com. bd. 1941-46, 47-52. Recipient Distinguished Alumni award Mercer U., 1971. Mem. Phi Delta Theta, Phi Alpha Delta. Republican. Baptist. Mason (33 deg., Shriner). Club: Civitan(pres. 1936). Home: 365 Old Club Rd Macon GA 31204 Office: PO Box 36 Macon GA 31202

BOOZER, ALBERT MARION, physician; b. Newberry, S.C., July 24, 1920; s. Alonzo Pinkney and Rhoda (Boozer) B.; B.S. magna cum laude, Newberry Coll., 1942; M.D., U. Tenn., 1945; m. Virginia Ellen Baker, June 20, 1946; children—Albert Marion, Russell Whitman, Lou Ann. Intern, Denver Gen. Hosp., 1945-46; resident in surgery City Hosp., Winston-Salem, N.C., 1948-49; gen. practice medicine and surgery, Dalton, Ga., 1949—; mem. staff Hamilton Meml. Hosp., Dalton, 1949—, pres., 1956, 61, v.p., 1960, dir. tumor clinic, 1958-59. Served to capt. AUS, 1946-48. Mem. A.M.A., Med Assn. Ga., Am. Geriatrics Soc., Am. Acad. Gen. Practice, Whitfield County Med Soc. (pres. 1953, 67-68), Alpha Omega Alpha, Alpha Kappa Kappa, Theta Nu Epsilon. Lion, Elk. Home: 603 Valley Dr Dalton GA 30720 Office: 204 W Waugh St Dalton GA 30720

BOOZER, DARLING GERALDINE RAKESTRAW, psychologist; b. N.Y.C., July 15, 1918; d. Henry Clay and Lee (Hurdus) Rakestraw; certificate diploma N.Y. U., 1939; B.B.A., U. Miami, 1954, M.S., 1957; Ph.D., La. State U., 1961; m. James Corkern Boozer, Apr. 24, 1948 (div. 1966); 1 son, James Corkern. Asst. clin. psychologist Child Clinic, Baton Rouge, 1957-58; Psychology fellow S.E. La. State Hosp., Mandeville, 1958-59; psychology intern La. State Med. Sch. and Charity Hosp., New Orleans, 1958-59; Research fellow USPHS, 1960-61; mem. clin. psychologist staff S. Fla. State Hosp., Hollywood, 1960-65, 1966—; pvt. practice clin. psychology, Miami and Hollywood, Fla., 1961—; clin. asst. prof. psychology U. Miami, Coral Gables, Fla., 1962-66; staff cons. Fla. Gardens Children's Center, Hallandale, 1965—. Cons. various orgns., 1960—; discussant, lectr., panel mem. various groups; exhibited in group art shows at Miami Beach, Fla.; comml. artist Advt. Co., Miami, 1954-63; legal, exec. sec. various attys., N.Y.C. Instr. water safety A.R.C., Miami, 1945-46. Mem. Am., S.E. psychol. assns., Mental Health Soc. Greater Miami, Fla. Council Crime and Delinquency, Internat. Platform Assn., Art Students' League N.Y., Psi Chi. Home: 3419 Acapulco Dr Hollywood FL 33023 Office: South Fla State State Hosp West Hollywood FL 33023

BORBA, DEAN, broadcasting exec. Vice pres., gen. mgr. KHOU-TV, Houston. Office: 1945 Allen Pkwy Houston TX 77019*

BORCHERS, WILLIAM HENRY, lawyer; b. Yoakum, Tex., Aug. 13, 1923; s. Willie Menn and Mary (Schaeg) B.; student Baldwin Bus. Coll., 1940-41, Tex. A. and M. Coll., 1941-42, 47-48; LL.B., Baylor U., 1952; m. Joyce Carl Word, June 30, 1956; children—Mary Marcia, Georgia Bonner. Admitted to Tex. bar, 1954; practiced in New Braunfels, Tex., 1959—; claims adjuster Allstate Ins. Co., Houston, 1952-53; life underwriter S. Coast Life Ins. Co., Yoakum, Tex., 1953-54; asst. dist. atty. Harris County, Houston, 1954-57; atty. Tex. Hwy. Dept., 1957; asso. Carl & Lee, Houston, 1957-59; pres. Oakwood Estates, Inc.; dir. the Guaranty State Bank, New Braunfels. Chmn. Comal County Democratic Exec. Com., 1960-66; city atty., New Braunfels, 1966. Served with AUS, World War II, USAF, 1950-60. Mem. Am., Tex., Tri-County bar assns. Elk, Lion. Clubs: Optimist (New Braunfels, Tex.); San Antonio German, San Antonio Country. Home: 260 Lakeview St New Braunfels TX 78130 Office: 251 S Seguin St New Braunfels TX 78130

BORDELON, DONALD RAY, dept. store exec.; b. Marksville, La., Jan. 26, 1933; s. Hilton and Mary Jane (Bielkiewicz) B.; student La. State U., 1951-52; B.S., U. Southwestern La., 1956; m. Martha H. Campbell, Apr. 23, 1960; children—Donna, Celia, Daryl. Accountant, P. G. Bell, Inc., Houston, 1956; salesman accounting systems Nat. Cash Register, Shreveport, La., 1967; accountant W. F. Beall Co., Shreveport, 1958, Dealers Truck Equipment, Shreveport, 1959; accountant, asst. mgr. Shreveport Cigar & Tobacco Co., Inc., 1960-64; controller Master Packaging, Inc., Shreveport, 1965-70; v.p., controller Palais Royal, Inc., Shreveport, 1970—; pres., dir. Custom Labels, Inc. Mem. steering com. Gillis Long for Gov. Democratic campaign, 1971. Bd. dirs. promotion com. Downtown Shreveport Unltd. Baptist. Mason (32 deg., Shriner). Home: 6036 Dillingham St Shreveport LA 71106 Office: 600 Milam St Shreveport LA 71120

BORDENCA, CARL, chem. co. exec.; b. Birmingham, Ala., Aug. 13, 1916; s. Charles and Anna (Diliberto) B.; B.S. with honors, Howard Coll., 1936; M.S., Ga. Tech. U., 1938; Ph.D., Purdue U., 1941; m. Jennie Tortorici, June 14, 1939; children—Mary Ellen (Mrs. Ralph T. Edwards), Susan Kay (Mrs. Edward A. Chazal, Jr.). Instr. chemistry Auburn U., 1941-43; research chemist Visking Corp., Chgo., 1943-45; research chemist So. Research Inst., Birmingham, Ala., 1945-51, asst. dir., 1951-56; asst. to pres. Newport Industries, Pensacola, Fla., 1956-57; dir. research and devel. Heyden Newport Chem. Corp., 1957-62; dir. research and devel. Glidden-Durkee div. SCM Corp., Jacksonville, Fla., 1962-68, v.p. biochem. dept., 1968—. Mem. Am. Chem. Soc. (chmn. Fla. sect. 1967), Swiss Chem. Soc., Hyacinth Control Soc., So. Weed Sci. Soc., Sigma Xi. Author: (with E. F. Degering) Outline Organic Nitrogen Compounds, 1945. Home: 837 Ponte Vedra Blvd Ponte Vedra Beach FL 32082 Office: Box 389 Jacksonville FL 32201

BORDERS, ROBERT WILLIAM, physician; b. Stratton, Colo., Nov. 17, 1925; s. Herschel C. and Hazel Mae (Harrison) B.; B.S., La. Tech. U., 1949; M.D., Kan. U., 1949; m. Emma Jean Sewell, Oct. 17, 1969; children— Robert, Thomas, Anne, Blaine. Intern New Orleans Charity, 1949-50; resident Duke, 1952-54; pvt. practice medicine, specializing in anesthesiology, Shreveport, La., 1954-66; dir. dept. anesthesiology Bossier City (La.) City Gen. Hosp., 1966—; mem. staff Schumpert Meml. Hosp., Confederate Meml. Hosp., Doctor's Hosp., Willis Knighton Hosp., Highland Hosp., Brentwood Hosp. (all Shreveport); clin. asst. prof. anesthesiology Sch. Med., La. State U., Shreveport. Pres. La. Tennis Assn., 1963-64. Served with USNR, 1943-46, 1950-52. Diplomate Am. Bd. Anesthesiology. Fellow Am. Coll. Anesthesiology; mem. La., Shreveport, 4th Dist. (v.p. 1969) med. socs., Am. Soc. Anesthesiologists, Internat. Anesthesia Soc. Home: 2977 Risinger St Shreveport LA 71109 Office: 2105 Airline St Bossier City LA 71010

BORDERS, WILLIAM D., bishop; b. Washington, Ind., Oct. 9, 1913; ed. St. Meinrad Sem., Notre Dame Sem., U. Notre Dame. Ordained priest Roman Catholic Ch., 1940; rector St. Joseph Cathedral, Baton Rouge; bishop of Orlando (Fla.), 1968—. Address: P O Box 3069 Orlando FL 32802

BOREN, DAVID LYLE, lawyer, state legislator; b. Washington, Apr. 21, 1941; s. Lyle H. and Christine (McKown) B.; B.A. summa cum laude, Yale, 1963; M.A. (Rhodes scholar), Oxford (Eng.) U., 1965; J.D. with honors, U. Okla. 1968; m. Janna Lou Little, Sept. 7, 1968; 1 dau., Carrie Christine. Resident counsellor U. Okla., Norman, 1965-66; practiced in Wewoka and Seminole, Okla., 1968—; prof. polit. sci., chmn. div. social scis., Okla. Baptist U., Shawnee, 1969—; mem. Okla. Ho. of Reps. 1966—. Propaganda analyst USIA,

Washington, 1962—; asst. to liaison dir. OCDM, Washington, 1961. Mem. Okla. Gov.'s Task Force on Tech. Edn., 1967—. Named Outstanding Young Oklahoman, Okla. Jr. C. of C., 1969. Mem. Am., Okla. (vice chmn. law schs. com.) bar assns., Am. Assn. Rhodes Scholars, Seminole, Wewoka, Seminole Jr. Chambers commerce, Order of Coif, Phi Beta Kappa, Phi Delta Phi. Democrat. Methodist. Clubs: Yale (Western Okla.); Seminole Sportsman's. Home: 917 Wilson St Seminole OK 74868 Office: State Capitol Oklahoma City OK 73105

BOREN, JAMES HARLAN, ednl. cons.; b. Wheatland, Okla., Dec. 10, 1925; s. James Basil and Una Lee (Hamilton) B.; student Hardin Coll., 1943-46; A.B. in Econs., U. Tex., 1948, postgrad., 1952-54, Ph.D., 1969; A.B. in Edn., Long Beach (Cal.) State Coll., 1950; A.M. in Econs., U. So. Cal., 1950; L.H.D., Nathaniel Hawthorne Coll., 1967; m. Irene Cheek, Aug. 16, 1946; children—Richard Vincent, James Stanley. Tchr. high sch. night dir. recreation dept., Oxnard, Cal., 1950-52; chief accounting div. Tex. Dept. Agr., 1952-54; prof. edn., head dept. Arlington (Tex.) State Coll., 1954-56; pres. Boren Oil & Gas Corp., 1956-57; adminstrv. asst. to U.S. Senator Yarborough, 1957-61; dep. dir. USOM to Peru, 1961, U.S. AID mission to Peru, 1961-63; spl. asst. to U.S. coordinator The Alliance for Progress, 1963-70; dir. Partners of Alliance Programs, U.S. AID, 1963-70; pres. Boren Assos.-Devel. Services, Washington, 1970—. Chmn. World Tapes for Edn. Pres. U. Tex. Young Democrats, 1952; Dem. presdl. elector, 1956; campaign mgr. Ralph Yarborough for gov. Tex., 1956, for U.S. senator, 1957. Served with USNR, 1943-46; mem. AUS Res. Recipient Outstanding Alumnus award Long Beach State Coll., 1961. Mem. Am. Polit. Sci. Assn., Am. Fgn. Service Assn., Burro Club U.S. (pres. 1960), Soc. for Internat. Devel., Nat. Assn. Profl. Bureaucrats (founder-pres.), Ednl. Communications Assn. (chmn. bd.), Order Artus, Phi Delta Kappa. Methodist. Club: North Austin (Tex.) Exchange (charter, past sec.). Author: When in Doubt, Mumble, 1972. Home: 1803 Paul Spring Pkwy Alexandria VA 22308 Office: 908 Nat Press Bldg Washington DC 20004

BORENSTEIN, EMANUEL, social worker; b. Manchester, N.H., Apr. 11, 1904; s. Solomon and Etta (Salzberg) B.; student Harvard, 1921-22; B.A., Coll. City N.Y., 1925; M.S. in Social Work, Boston U., 1942; m. Gertrude Perlman, Dec. 8; 1 dau., Selma (Mrs. Alvin Milchen). Exec. dir. Montreal (Que., Can.) Hebrew Orphan Home, 1929-30; parole supr. Mass. Dept. Pub. Welfare, Boston, 1931-43; asst. chief Fgn. Inquiry unit A.R.C., Washington, 1943-44; mem. staff War Refugee bd., Washington, 1944; exec. dir. New Eng. Zionist Region, Boston, 1944-48; dir. for Brazil Am. Jewish Joint Distbn. Com., San Paulo, Brazil, 1948-49; chief mission for CARE, Israel, 1949-50; area dir. Israel Bond Orgn., Indpls., Harrisburg, Pa., Boston, 1951-54; exec. dir. Neustadter Convalescent Center, Yonkers, N.Y., 1955-56; psychiat. social worker pub. schs., Wantagh, N.Y., 1958-61; exec. dir. Pride Judea Children's Services, Bklyn., 1961-62; asst. dir., clinic adminstr. Infants Home Bklyn., 1962-64; adminstr. Hempstead (N.Y.) Consultation Service; supr. home health care services Greenpoint Hosp., Bklyn., 1965-67; adminstr. Glen Oaks Nursing Home, 1967-68; social work cons., N.Y., Fla., 1968-71; dir. dept. social work Meml. Hosp., Hollywood, Fla., 1968-72; regional dir. social work Am. Medicorp. Inc., Dr.'s Hosp., Hollywood, 1972—; instr. Boston U., 1935-42, Endicott Jr. Coll., 1946-47; Adelphi Coll. 1957-61. Vice pres. Broward County (Fla.) Service Agy. Sr. Citizens; chmn. adv. bd. Broward County Ret. Sr. Vol. program; v.p. Jewish Family Service Broward County. Mem. Democratic exec. com., Broward County. Bd. dirs. Am. Civil Liberties Union Broward County, Broward Community Concerts Assn. Mem. Nat. Assn. Social Workers (former chmn. L.I. chpt., Soc. Hosp. Social Work Dirs. (chmn. Fla. chpt.), Am. Hosp. Assn. (chmn. Fla. chpt.). Club: Harvard (Broward County). Home: 1701 S Ocean Dr Apt 902 Hollywood FL 33020 Office: Drs Hosp 1859 Van Buren St Hollywood FL 33020

BORG, JOSEPH FRANKLIN, physician; b. St. Paul, Aug. 27, 1898; s. Samuel Andrews and Dorothea Sophia (Youngberg) B.; student MacAlester Coll., 1916-18; B.S., U. Minn., 1920, M.B., 1922, M.D., 1923; m. Esther Lane, Sept. 14, 1948. Intern, Aucker Hosp., St. Paul, 1922, resident, 1923-24; intern City Hosp., Cleve., 1923; practice medicine specializing in cardiology, St. Paul, 1924-66, Tryon, N.C., 1966—; electrocardiographer Bethesda Hosp., St. Paul, 1930-68; clin. asso. prof. internal medicine U. Minn., 1942-68. Served to col. AUS, 1941-46. Decorated Bronze Star medal. Mem. A.M.A., A.C.P., Am. Therapeutic Soc. (pres. 1945), Am. Heart Assn., Ramsey County Med. Soc. (pres. 1941). Rotarian. Home: Box 306 Tryon NC 28782 Office: 100 Jervey Rd Tryon NC 28782

BORG, MATTHEW F., civil engr.; b. N.Y.C., May 12, 1928; s. Herman L. and Pauline (Lehman) B.; B.C.E., Coll. City N.Y., 1950 M.C.E., Catholic U., 1953; M.S. in Civil Engring., Lehigh U., 1959; m. Margot Pappaterra, June 15, 1950; children—Angela Cynthia, Roger Allen. Engr., David Taylor Model Basin, 1951-55, Electric Boat Co., 1959-61, Naval Underwater Sound Lab., 1961-66, Naval Tng. Device Center, Orlando, Fla., 1966—; instr. civil engring. Lehigh U., Bethlehem, Pa., 1955-59. Lectr., U. Conn., 1960-66, Rensselaer Poly. Inst., Hartford, Conn., 1961, Mitchell Coll., New London, Conn., 1960-64; lectr. math. Rollins Coll., Winter Park, Fla., 1967, 68, Fla. Tech. U., 1968—. Mem. Sigma Xi. Research in dynamics, sonar and underwater sound. Home: 668 Darcey Dr Winter Park FL 32789 Office: Naval Tng Device Center Orlando FL 32813

BORGMANN, HERBERT CARL, food co. exec.; b. Athol, Kan., May 20, 1923; s. Lawrence W. and Elisa (Henkel) B.; B.S., U. Kan., 1947; m. Erline Elizabeth Shotwell, Aug. 20; 1944 (div. Dec. 1969); 1 dau., Nancy Jean (Mrs. Charles Raymond Kee, Jr.); m. 2d, Dorothea Nichols, June 15, 1970. With Swift & Co., 1947—, S.W. marketing regional mgr. Swift Edible Oil Co. div., Ft. Worth, 1968—. Served with USAAF, 1942-45. Decorated Air medal with two oak leaf clusters. Home: 1625 Jenson Rd Fort Worth TX 76112 Office: PO Box 265 Fort Worth TX 76101

BORING, GEORGE WALLACE, JR., dentist; b. Arcadia, Fla., Jan. 9, 1939; s. George Wallace and Pearl Lois (Johnston) B.; student Presbyn. Coll., 1957-58; B.S., Fla. State U., 1962; D.M.D., U. Louisville, 1966; m. Nancy Marie Migliore, Dec. 16, 1956; children—Deborah, George Wallace III, Beth, Mary Ann. Pvt. practice dentistry, Brooksville, Fla., 1966—; mem. staff Lykes Meml. Hosp. Dir. Hernando Indsl. Corp. Bd. dirs. Hernando County Guidance Center. Mem. Am., Fla., Lacoochee (pres. 1970-71) dental assns., Hernando County C. of C. (dir. 1968-71), Psi Omega. Presbyn. (deacon 1969-71). Kiwanian (pres.-elect 1971-72). Home: 750 Fernwood Dr Brooksville FL 33512 Office: 609 Lamar Av Brooksville FL 33512

BORK, DUANE LEROY, physician; b. Marcus, Ia., June 17, 1936; s. Roy L. and Clara S. (Sandbeck) B.; B.A., Augustana Coll., 1958; B.S., U. S.D., 1960; M.D., U. Ia., 1962; m. Audrey Ida Wek, Aug. 31, 1956; children—Terence, Trudence, Todd. Intern, U.S. Naval Hosp., Pensacola, Fla., 1962; practice medicine, specializing in family practice, Jacksonville, Fla., 1962—; mem. staff Meml. Hosp., Bapt. Hosp., Beaches Hosps., Hope Haven Hosp.; univ. and team physician Jacksonville U., 1970-71. Bd. dirs. Fla. Tb and Respiratory Disease Assn. Served with USNR, 1962-67. Mem. Duval County Acad. Family Practice (pres. 1970-71). Republican. Lutheran. Clubs: Hidden Hills, University Country (Jacksonville). Home: 5341 Contina St Jacksonville FL 32211 Office: 2732 Trollie Lane Jacksonville FL 32211

BORLAUGH, NORMAN ERNEST, wheat scientist; b. Cresco, Ia., Mar. 25, 1914; s. Henry O. and Clara (Vaala) B.; B.S. in Forestry, U. Minn., 1937, M.S. in Plant Pathology, 1940, Ph.D., 1941; Sc. D. honoris causa, Punjab (India) Agrl. U., 1969; m. Margaret G. Gibson, Sept. 24, 1937; children—Norma Jean (Mrs. Richard H. Rhoda), William Gibson. With U.S. Forest Service, 1938-39; instr. U. Minn., 1941; research scientist DuPont de Nemours Found., 1942-44; research scientist in wheat Rockefeller Found., Mexico, 1944—, Centro Internacional de Mejoramiento de Maiz y Trigo, Mexico, 1966—; Leonard L. Klinck lectr. Agrl. Inst. Can., 1966. Recipient citation and award from govt. and farmers of Tlaxcala, Mexico, 1955, wheat farmers Yacqui Valley Cindad Obregon, Sonora, Mexico, 1962; diplomas of honor Wheat Farmers Queretaro, Mexico, 1956, Wheat Farmers and State of Zacatecas, Mexico, 1958; Outstanding Achievement award U. Minn., 1959, E.C. Stakman award, 1962; Distinguished Citizen award Cresco, 1966; Nat. award Agrl. Editors Assn., 1967; Ann. award Nat. Council Comml. Plant Breeders, 1968; Distinguished Service medal Pakistan, 1968; Internat. Agronomy award Am. Soc. Agronomy, 1968; Nobel Peace prize, 1970. Hon. fellow Indian Soc. Genetics and Plant Breeding; mem. Nat. Acad. Sci. Home: Sierra Gorda 69 Lomas de Chapultepec Mexico City Mexico Office: care CIMHYT Londres 40 Mexico City 6 Mexico Piso Mexico City Mexico*

BORMAN, FRANK, airline exec.; b. Gary, Ind., Mar. 14, 1928; s. Edwin Borman; B.S., U.S. Mil. Acad., 1950; M. Aero. Engring., Cal. Inst. Tech., 1957; grad. USAF Aerospace Research Pilots Sch., 1960; hon. doctorate Ill. Wesleyan Coll., 1969; S.D., Sch. Mines and Tech., 1969, U. Pitts., 1969, U. Houston, 1969, Whittier Coll., 1969, U. Wyo., 1969; m. Susan Bugbee; children—Fredrick, Edwin. Commd. 2d lt. U.S. Air Force, advanced to col., 1965; assigned various fighter squadrons, U.S. and Philippines, 1951-56; instr. thermodynamics and fluid mechanics U.S. Mil. Acad., 1957-60; instr. USAF Aerospace Research Pilots Sch., 1960-62; astronaut with Manned Spacecraft Center, NASA, command pilot on 14 day orbital Gemini 7 flight, Dec. 1965, including rendezvous with Gemini 6, comdr. 6 day Apollo 8 flight, 1st manned lunar orbital mission, 1968, field dir., space sta. task group; v.p. Eastern Air Lines, Inc. Decorated D.F.C., D.S.M.; recipient Distinguished Service award NASA, 1965, also Exceptional Service medal; David C. Schilling trophy Air Force Assn., 1966; Distinguished Alumni Service award Cal. Inst. Tech., 1966, H.H. Arnold trophy Air Force Assn., 1969; Gold medal for achievement Czechoslovakian Acad. Sci., 1969; others; co-recipient Hubbard medal Nat. Geog. Soc., 1969; Flight Achievement award Am. Astronautical Soc., 1968, Robert J. Collier trophy, 1969. Mem. Am. Inst. Aeronautics and Astronautics, Soc. Exptl. Test Pilots. Address: Miami Internat Airport Miami FL 33148

BORNET, DAVID, banker; b. N.Y.C., Apr. 7, 1892; s. Bernard and Katherine (Hellman) B.; LL.B., Georgetown U., 1913; m. Julia Levy, Mar. 23, 1919; children—Barbara (Mrs. Jack Rubin), Paul Leon. With Nat. Savs. & Trust Co., Washington, 1910—, sr. v.p., 1936-66, exec. v.p., 1966-70, sr. cons., 1970—, dir., 1936-66, adv. dir., 1966—; admitted to D.C. bar, 1913. Pres. Jewish Social Service Agy., 1956-59. Bd. dirs. Kent Washington, Inc., 1968-72. Served with U.S. Navy, 1918. Mem. Am., D.C. bar assns., Met. Washington Bd. Trade. Mason. Clubs: Woodmont Country (Rockville, Md.); National Press, Amity, Variety (Washington). Home: 4201 Cathedral Av NW Washington DC 20016 Office: 719 15th St NW Washington DC 20005

BORNMAN, DAVID LOUIS, III, social worker; b. Monroe, La., July 31, 1932; s. David Louis and Lillian (Bryan) B.; B.A., La. State U., 1958, M.S.W., 1962; m. Kemper Fay Luttrell, Dec. 23, 1960; children—David Bryan, Ann Kemper. Welfare visitor La. Dept. Pub. Welfare, Monroe, 1958; chief social worker East La. State Hosp., Jackson, 1962-64; clin. social worker Baton Rouge Mental Health Center, 1964-65; social work cons. spl. edn. services La. State U., Baton Rouge, 1965-66; adminstr. Baton Rouge Mental Health Center, 1966-71; mental health exec. officer La. Dept. Hosps., Baton Rouge, 1971—. Field instr. La. State U. Sch. Social Welfare, 1966—. Served to 1st lt. Mil. Police Corps, AUS, 1955-57. Mem. Nat. Assn. Social Workers (pres. Baton Rouge chpt. 1966-70), Acad. Certified Social Workers. Home: 6048 Chandler Dr Baton Rouge LA 70808 Office: 655 N 5th St Baton Rouge LA 70804

BORNN, EDITH L., lawyer; b. St. Thomas, V.I., Aug. 30, 1922; A.B., Barnard Coll., 1945; LL.B., Columbia U., 1948. Admitted to N.Y. State bar, 1948, V.I. bar, 1952, U.S. Ct. Appeals, 3d circuit, 1952; legal research sec. Caribbean Commn., Trinidad, 1948-51; law clk. to Judge Herman E. Moore, U.S. Dist. Ct., V.I., 1951-55; partner firm Cox & Bornn, 1955-65; practiced in V.I., 1965-69; mem. firm Bornn, McLaughlin & Finucan, Charlotte Amalie, St. Thomas, 1969—. U.S. rep. to UN Seminar on Adminstrv. Law, Buenos Aires, Argentina, 1959; cons. V.I. delegation to W.I. Conf., Caribbean Orgn., 1960-64; mem. Atty. Gen.'s Com. on Juvenile Delinquency, 1963-65. Chmn. Citizens Fire Protection Com., 1953—, Citizens Com. on Youth, 1958-62; pres. Women's League St. Thomas, 1956-58, 69—; mem. econ. stblzn. com. Civil Def., 1961—; mem. Citizens Adv. Com. to Gov. on Community Improvement, 1963-69; chancellor to bishop V.I. Episcopalian Diocese, 1964—, mem. nat. exec. council of Episcopal Ch., 1966-69; pres. All Saints Sch. P.T.A., 1965-67; sec. bd. edn. All Saints Parish Sch., 1966—. Bd. dirs. Bluebeard's Housing Corp., 1963-67, pres., 1969; trustee Caribbean Episcopal Seminar, P.R., 1970—, Mem. Am., Fed., V.I. (bar adv. com. to V.I. Code Commn. 1954-56, bd. govs. 1956-58, sec. 1961-62, chmn. bar examiners com. 1965—) bar assns., Internat. Fedn. Women Lawyers (v.p. for V.I. 1958—), Nat. Council Juvenile Ct. Judges (asso.). Episcopalian (vestrywoman 1958-60). Office: Norre Gade 8 Charlotte Amlie St Thomas VI 00801*

BORSCHOW, RON CLARKE, statis. cons.; b. Houston, Feb. 8, 1933; s. Reuben and Hazel I. (Beatty) B.; B.B.A., U. Houston, 1958 M.B.A., So. Methodist U., 1960; postgrad. Ohio State U., 1958, U. Chgo., 1960-61, U. Houston, 1964—. Market research analyst Toni Co., Chgo., 1960-61; research mgr. Product Acceptance & Research, Evansville, Ind., 1961-63; founder, pres. R. Borschow & Assos., statis. and market research consultants, Houston, 1963—; statis. cons. Houston Health Dept., 1964—. Mem. Am. Marketing Assn., Am. Statis. Assn., Tex. Pub. Health Assn., Houston Symphony Soc., Houston Grand Opera Assn., Phi Theta Kappa. Home: 2422 Albans St Houston TX 77005 Office: 1115 N MacGregor St Houston TX 77025

BORUM, RODNEY LEE, corp. executive; b. nr. High Point, N.C., Sept. 30, 1929; s. Carl Macy and Etta (Sullivan) B.; student U. N.C., 1947-49; B.S., U.S. Naval Acad., 1953; m. Helen Marie Rigby, June 27, 1953; children—Richard Harlan, Sarah Elizabeth. Design-devel. engr. Gen. Electric Co., Syracuse, N.Y., Cape Kennedy, Fla., 1956-58, missile test condr., Cape Kennedy, 1958-60, mgr., ground equipment engr., 1960-61, mgr. Eastern Test Range Engring., 1961-65; adminstr. Bus. and Def. Services Adminstrn. U.S. Dept. Commerce, 1966-69; pres. Printing Industries of Am., Inc., 1969—. Dir. Strangers Cay, Ltd. Dir. United Fund, Brevard County, Fla., 1963—, v.p., 1964-65; exec. council of Cub Scouts Am., 1965; dir. Brevard Beaches Concert Assn., 1964. Republican candidate Fla. Ho. of Reps., 1960. Served to 1st lt. USAF, 1953-56. Named Boss of Yr., Jr. C. of C., 1965; recipient Bausch and Lomb sci. award; award Am. Legion. Mem. I.E.E.E., U.S. Naval Inst., U.S. Naval Acad. Alumni Assn., Phi Eta Sigma. Episcopalian. Clubs: Eau Gallie Yacht, PAFB Officers. Home: 4008 Glenrose St Kensington MD 20795 Office: 1730 N Lynn St Arlington VA 22209

BOSCO, FREDERICK JOHN, educator; b. Bay City, Mich., May 13, 1929; s. Felix and Rosalie (Lupo) B.; A.B., Central Mich. U., 1951 M.A. in French, U. Mich., 1955, M.A. in Linguistics, 1958. Lectr., English Lang. Inst., U. Mich., 1956-61; asst. prof. linguistics Georgetown U., Washington, 1961—, chmn. dept. Italian, 1969—, coordinator TEFL/TESL Peace Corps tng. program, 1962-64. Cons. lang. tng. program Def. Lang. Inst., 1966—; mem. TESL evaluating bd. Bia Navajo Area Schs., 1970-71. Served with USMC, 1951-53. Fulbright lectr. U. Rome, Italy, 1958-59. Mem. Linguistic Soc. Am., Am. Assn. Tchrs. Italian, Washington Linguistics Club, Tchrs. English to Speakers Other Langs. Author: Incontro con l'italiano, 1967; Comprehensive Testing Program in Italian, 1972. Home: 1403 30th St NW Washington DC 20007

BOSHELL, BURIS RAYE, physician, educator; b. nr. Phil Campbell, Ala., Oct. 9, 1926; s. Harvey M. and Lela (Alexander) B.; B.S., Ala. Polytech. Inst., 1947, postgrad., 1947-49; postgrad. Med. Coll. Ala., 1949-51; M.D., Harvard, 1953; m. Martha Sue Johnson, June 4, 1951; children—Patty, Thomas Eppinger. Intern, Peter Bent Brigham Hosp., Boston, 1953-54, resident, 1954-59; practice medicine, specializing in internal medicine, Birmingham, Ala., 1959; mem. staff U. Ala. Hosps. and Clinics; instr. Harvard, 1956-58, asst. in medicine, 1958-59; asst. prof. medicine Med. Coll. Ala, 1959-62, asso. prof., 1962-64, prof., 1964-67, Ruth Lawson Hanson prof. medicine, 1967—; asst. dir., dept. medicine, 1963-69, dir. div. diabetes, endocrinology and related disorders, 1970—. Pres. bd. dirs. Diabetes Trust Fund of Ala.; bd. dirs. Diabetes Research Lab. Diplomate Am. Bd. Internal Medicine. Fellow A.C.P., Am. Coll. Clin. Pharmacology and Chemotherapy; mem. A.M.A., Ala., Jefferson County med. assns., Am. Assn. U. Profs., Birmingham Acad. Medicine, Ala. Acad. Sci., Am., New Eng., N.Y., Ala. diabetes assns., Endocrine Soc., Am. Fedn. for Clin. Research, So. Soc. for Clin. Investigation, Sigma Xi, Omicron Delta Kappa, Phi Kappa Phi, Gamma Sigma Delta, Tau Kappa, Alpha Omega Alpha. Contbr. articles to profl. jours. Home: 3017 Old Ivy Rd Birmingham AL 35210 Office: 2117 8th Av S PO Box 3371-A Birmingham AL 35205

BOSS, HAROLD FRANCIS, life ins. exec.; b. Washington, July 10, 1903; s. Joseph Centennial and Lillie (Bowdler) B.; student Okla. U., 1922-23; B.S., U. Va., 1926; m. Josephine Brodnax, Sept. 17, 1928; children—Bruce Whitaker, Gregory Brodnax. Securities and wholesale glass bus., Va., 1929-33; agt. Universal Life & Accident Ins. Co., Dallas, 1934-35, div. mgr., San Antonio, 1935-43, v.p., Dallas, 1935-68, dir., 1943-68; dir. Southwestern Gen. Life Ins. Co., 1969—; columnist Life Insurer mag. Dir. Dallas Tb. Assn., 1958—, pres., 1962-64; bd. dirs. Tex Tb. Assn., S.W. Area YMCA; bd. dirs. Dallas Services for Blind Children, pres., 1967-69; bd. dirs. Met. YMCA, 1956—, mem. internat. com., 1959—, mem. exec. com., 1969—, chmn. internat. bldg. and capital needs com., 1969—; pres. Dallas Health and Sci. Mus., 1958-60, trustee, 1946—. Recipient Distinguished Service award S.W. Area YMCA, 1967. Mem. Ins. Club (dir.), Lighting Class Assn. (dist. commodore 1959), Phi Beta Kappa, Delta Upsilon. Methodist. Clubs: Corinthian Sailing, Reaugh Art (Dallas). Author: Prospecting—the Fountain of Success, 1946. Home: 3405 Southwestern Blvd Dallas TX 75225 Office: Ross and Akard Sts Dallas TX 75221

BOST, RAYMOND MORRIS, coll. pres.; b. Maiden, N.C., Aug. 18, 1925; s. Loy Robert and Virginia (Anderson) B.; A.B., Lenoir Rhyne Coll., 1949; B.D., Luth. Theol. So. Sem., 1952; M.A., Yale, 1959, Ph.D., 1963; m. Margaret Martha Vedder, Aug. 16, 1947; children—Timothy Lee, Penelope Ruth, Peter Raymond, Jonathan Otto. Ordained to ministry Lutheran Ch., 1952; pastor in Spartanburg, S.C., 1952-53, Raleigh, N.C., 1953-57; prof. ch. history, dir. field work Luth. Theol. So. Sem., 1960-66; acad. dean Lenoir Rhyne Coll., Hickory, N.C., 1966-68, pres., 1968—. Dir. N.C. Nat. Bank, Hickory br., 1971—. Contact minister Nat. Luth. Council, N.C. State U., 1953-57, Yale, 1957-59; part-time instr. sociology Columbia Coll., 1962-65; mem. selection com. Woodrow Wilson Nat. Fellowship Found. Acad. Internship Program, 1971—. Mem. Com. to Implement Refugee Act, 1953; chmn. com. pub. affairs N.C. Council Chs., 1956; pres. Raleigh Ministerial Assn., 1957; treas. N.C. Found. Ch.-Related Colls., 1969; mem. bd. theol. edn. Luth. Ch. Am., 1969-70; del. 1970, 72 convs., mem. standing com. on approaches to unity, 1971—. Bd. dirs. Luth. Ednl. Conf. N.Am., 1970—; bd. dirs. Piedmont U. Center N.C., 1968—, mem. exec. com., 1970—; trustee Luth. Theol. So. Sem., 1969—. Served with USMCR, 1943-47. Luth. Brotherhood Sem. Grad. scholar, 1957-58, Faculty fellow, 1960; Martin Luther fellow Nat. Luth. Ednl. Conf., 1959; Faculty fellow Am. Assn. Theol. Schs., 1959-60. Mem. Am., So. hist. assns., Am. Soc. Ch. History, Orgn. Am. Historians, N.C. Assn. Ind. Colls. and Univs. (exec. bd. 1971—). Rotarian. Clubs: Yale (N.Y.C.); Lake Hickory Country. Home: 741 4th St NE Hickory NC 28601

BOST, ROGER BROWNING, pediatrician, state ofcl.; b. Clarksville, Ark., Oct. 28, 1921; s. Roger Samuel and Fae (Browning) B.; student Okla. State Coll., 1939-40, Coll. of Ozarks, 1941-42; M.D., U. Ark., 1945; m. Kathryn Elizabeth King, June 23, 1944; children—Roger Kingsley, Rebecca, Margaret, Virginia. Intern Santa Rosa Hosp., San Antonio, 1945-46; asst. resident, chief resident pediatrics Duke Hosp., Durham, N.C., 1948-51; practice medicine specializing in pediatrics, Ft. Smith, Ark., 1954-65; instr. pediatrics Duke Sch. Medicine, Durham, N.C., 1950-51, Tulane U. Sch. Medicine, New Orleans, 1951-52, asst. prof. pediatrics, 1952-54; pediatrician Ochsner Clinic and Ochsner Found. Hosp., New Orleans, 1951-54; pediatric cons. Crippled Children's Program Ark., 1954-65, Ark. Tb Sanitorium, Booneville, 1954-65, project head start for Ark, Ark. Mental Retardation Planning Project, 1964-66; dir. birth defects center U. Ark. Med. Center, Little Rock, 1965-70, dir. cystic fibrosis center, 1965-70, acting chmn. dept. pediatrics, prof. pediatrics, 1970-71; dir. Ark. Dept. Social and Rehab. Services, Little Rock, 1971—. Coordinator Ark. Regional Med. Program, 1967-69. Served with M.C., USNR, 1946-48. Diplomate Am. Bd. Pediatrics. Fellow Am. Acad. Pediatrics; mem. A.M.A., So. Soc. for Pediatric Research, Central Ark. Pediatric Soc., Ark. Med. Soc. Methodist. Home: 12 Patricia Lane Little Rock AR 72205

BOSWELL, GARY TAGGART, computer systems co. exec.; b. Ft. Worth, Dec. 24, 1937; s. David W. and Marjory (Taggart) B.; B.A., Tex. Christian U., 1958, M.S., 1965; postgrad. San Diego State Coll., 1960-61; m. Margaret Ruth Yelvington, Sept. 8, 1957; children—Michael David, Margaret McQuiston, Susannah Ruth. Scientist U.S. Govt., White Sands (N.M.) Missile Range, 1958-59; research engr. Gen. Dynamics, San Diego, 1959-60; programmer Bell Helicopter, Hurst, Tex., 1960-63; sect. head Collins Radio Co., Dallas, 1963-68; mgr. Tex. Instruments, Inc., Austin, 1968—. Mem. Am. Nat. Fortran Standards Com., 1970—. Mem. Assn. Computing

Machinery, N.A. Yacht Racing Union. Republican. Episcopalian. Clubs: Austin Yacht; Austin Sailing. Designer several Fortran Compliers. Winner Western Hemisphere Snipe championship, 1970, also other major regattas. Home: 4205 Woodway Dr Austin TX 78731 Office: 2601 N Lamar Austin TX 78767

BOSWELL, GEORGE MARION, JR., surgeon; b. Grand Prairie, Tex., May 12, 1920; s. George Marion and Viola (Scarbrough) B.; B.S., Tex. Tech. Coll., 1940; M.D., U. Tex., 1950; m. Veta M. Fuller, Oct. 30, 1958; children—Brianna Fuller, Kama, Maia. Intern, Parkland Hosp., Dallas, 1950-51; resident surgery and orthopaedic surgery Parkland, Baylor U. Med. Center, and Scottish Rite Hosps., Dallas, 1950-55; practice medicine specializing in surgery, Dallas, 1955—; instr. anatomy U. Tex. Southwestern Med. Sch., 1955—; chief surg. service Garland Hosp., 1960-61; attending staff Baylor U. Med. Center and Doctors Hosp., 1955—. Served from ensign to lt. comdr., USNR, 1940-45. Diplomate Am. Bd. Orthopaedic Surgery. Fellow A.C.S.; mem. Tex., Western orthopaedic assns., Am. Acad. Orthopaedic Surgeons, Tex., Dallas County med. assns., Am. Coll. Traumatology, Tex. Soc. Traumatology, Flying Physicians Assn. (pres. Tex. chpt. 1959, nat. dir.), U. Tex. Southwestern Med. Sch. Alumni Assn. (pres.), Phi Chi. Republican. Methodist (chmn. ofcl. bd., charge lay leader, trustee, del. Gen. Conf. Home: 7249 Wabash St Dallas TX 75214 Office: 4849 W Lawther Dr Dallas TX 75218

BOSWELL, JAMES LOUIS, educator; b. Wynnewood, Okla., Dec. 10, 1911; s. John Everett and Fannie (Cobb) B.; B.S., E. Central State Coll., 1936; M.S., U. Okla., 1938; postgrad. U. Mich., 1940-41; Ph.D., Tex., A. and M. U., 1966; m. Doris Mae Martin, May 24, 1947; children—Linda Lee, Katherine Ann, James Martin. Tchr. sci. Seminole (Okla.) High Sch. and Jr. Coll., 1937-42; asso. prof. biology East Central State Coll., 1942-47; biologist Tex. A. and M. Research Found., Grand Isle, La., 1948-60; instr. Tex. A. and M. U., 1961-65; mem. faculty Midwestern U., Wichita Falls, Tex., 1965—, asso. prof. biology, 1966—. Mem. A.A.A.S., Am. Inst. Biol. Scis., Am. Soc. Limnology and Oceanography (charter), Sigma Xi, Beta Beta Beta, Phi Sigma. Home: 4603 Cascades St Wichita Falls TX 76310

BOSWELL, JAMES MALCOLM, coll. pres.; b. Cynthiana, Ky., Jan. 26, 1906; s. Joseph and Fannie (Thomason) B.; A.B., Georgetown Coll., 1928, LL.D., 1949; M.A., U. Ky., 1931, postgrad. in Math., summers 1937, 38, 40, 41, 1938-39, U. Mich., summer 1930; m. Mary Susan Dudley, Jan. 23, 1932; children—James Malcolm, Frances Louise (Mrs. Hershel Tipton). Instr. math. Georgetown Coll., 1928-31, U. Ky., 1938-39; with Cumberland Coll., Williamsburg, Ky., 1931-38, 40-42, 45—, dean adminstrn., 1945, acting pres., 1946-47, pres., 1947—. Served from lt. to lt. comdr. USNR, 1942-45. Mem. Am. Math. Assn., Ky. Assn. Colls. and Secondary Schs. (past v.p.), So. Assn. Bapt. Colls (past pres.), So. Assn. Jr. Colls. (past pres.). Baptist. Rotarian. Home: 804 Main St Williamsburg KY 40769

BOTHWELL, RUTH DEE, economist, govt. adminstr.; b. Fairbank, Ia., Feb. 19, 1917; d. Clyde Dee and Nell (Everett) Bothwell; B.A., U. Cal. at Los Angeles, 1939. Chief women's placement USES, Richmond, Cal., 1941-43, labor market analyst, San Francisco, 1943-46, Washington, 1946-47; economist women's bur. U.S. Dept. Labor, Washington, 1947-48; chief, current labor force reports Bur. Census, Washington, 1948-54, resource estimates div. dental pub. health and resources USPHS, Washington, 1954-66, chief resource analysis, div. dental health, 1965-67, chief planning officer, 1967—. Recipient Superior Service medal U.S. Dept. Health, Edn. and Welfare, 1962. Fellow Am. Pub. Health Assn. Contbr. articles to profl. jours. Home: 3302 Pendleton Dr Silver Spring MD 20902 Office: Div Dental Health USPHS Dept Health Edn and Welfare Washington DC 20014

BOTKIN, DOROTHY VIRGINIA, educator; b. Lexington, Ky.; d. Daniel Robert and Dooley (Welch) Botkin; B.A., U. Louisville, 1947; B.S., Juilliard Sch. Music, 1950; M.Mus., Ind. U., 1951; postgrad. North Tex. State U., summer 1954, Mozarteum, Salzburg, Austria, summers, 1956, 66, Eastman Sch. Music, summers 1960, 61, Music Acad. West, 1963. Faculty, Mary Hardin-Baylor, Belton, Tex., 1951-53, Del Mar Coll., Corpus Christi, Tex., 1954-58; asst. prof. North Tex. State U., Denton, 1958-70, asso. prof., 1970—. Performed with Dallas Symphony, Ft. Worth Opera Co., Corpus Christi Symphony, Midland-Odessa Symphony, Monroe Symphony Orch., numerous choral socs.; held concerts in Austria, Mexico, Malaysia, West Malaysia, Viet-Nam, U.S.; concert tour Asia; toured Viet-Nam and sang in mil. hosp. wards, chapels, hdqrs. spl. forces camps; gave concerts mission stas., chs. Mem. bd. South Plains area com. Inter-Varsity Christian Fellowship, Tex., Okla., Ark., also faculty adviser. Mem. Tex. Assn. Coll. Tchrs., Am. Assn. U. Profs., Nat. Assn. Tchrs. Singing, Music Tchrs. Nat. Assn., N. Tex. Juilliard Assn., Mu Phi Epsilon (faculty adviser 1959—), Mu Phi Epsilon Alumni, Pi Kappa Lambda (chpt. pres. 1964-66). Presbyn. Republican. Office: Box 5331 North Texas Station Denton TX 76203

BOTSKO, GEORGE EDWARD, newspaper exec.; b. Ambridge, Pa., Dec. 14, 1931; s. Joseph Stephen and Mary (Zilka) B.; B.S. in Indsl. Engring., Geneva Coll., 1958; m. Marjorie R. Miller, Sept. 1, 1955; children— Roy E., Nancy R., Jennifer L. Printer, Daily Citizen, Ambridge, 1949-58; composing foreman Beaver County Times, Beaver, Pa., 1958-61; prodn. mgr. South Dade News Leader, Homestead, Fla., 1961-68, gen. mgr., 1968—. Served with AUS, 1952-54. Republican. Methodist (ofcl. bd. 1966-67). Rotarian. Club: Civitan (sec. 1964-65) (Homestead, Fla.). Home: 18910 SW 309 Homestead FL 33030 Office: 15-17 NE 1st Rd Homestead FL 33030

BOTT, CLAIRE JORGENSEN, dentist; b. Hyrum, Utah, Nov. 23, 1926; s. John Cecil and Nettie B. (Jorgensen) B.; student U. Wyo., 1944-46; B.S., D.D.S., U. Neb., 1954; m. Mary Helen Kuppinger, June 16, 1949; children—Victoria, Deborra, Amy, Lorri. Pvt. practice dentistry, Cheyenne, Wyo., 1956-59, Terrell, Tex., 1968—; pres. Wyo. Monument Co., 1959-68, also dir.; dir. Strata Corp., Astra Corp. Mem. adv. bd. Terrell (Tex.) City Airport, 1972—. Served to capt. Dental Corps, USAF, 1954-56. Mem. Am., Tex. dental assns., 4th Dist. Dental Soc., Alpha Tau Omega, Xi Psi Phi. Mem. Ch. of Jesus Christ of Latter-day Saints. Home: 9 Carl-Lee Circle Terrell TX 75160 Office: 300 N Catherine St Terrell TX 75160

BOTTENBERG, ROBERT ALAN, govt. ofcl.; b. Kansas City, Mo., Sept. 25, 1924; s. J.H. and Grace (Hay) B.; B.A., U. Mo., 1948, M.A., 1950 Ph.D., Stanford, 1957; m. Dorothy Gene Laffoon, Aug. 24, 1946; children—Julia Sue, Ann Christine, Janet Louise. Personnel selection and evaluation psychologist, exptl. research br. Personnel Lab., Lackland AFB, Tex., 1953-58; personnel measurement and evaluation psychologist, statis. analysis br., personnel research div. Air Force Human Resources Lab., Lackland AFB, 1958-59, chief math and statis. analysis sect., 1959-68, chief computer and mgmt. scis. br., personnel research div., 1968—. Cons. statis. applications, computer methods. Bd. mem. Sensory Aids Evaluation and Devel. Center, Mass. Inst. Tech., 1966—. Served with AUS, 1943-46. Named Handicapped Texan of Year by Gov. of Tex., 1964, Handicapped Am. of Year by President's Com., 1971. Mem. Blinded Vets. Assn. (pres. 1960-62), Psychometric Soc., Am. Statis. Assn., Inst. Math. Statistics, Assn. Computing Machinery, Am. Ednl. Research Assn., A.A.A.S. Presbyn. (elder). Kwanian. Contbr. articles to publs. Home: 4014 Fawnridge St San Antonio TX 78229 Office: Personnel Research Div Air Forces Human Resources Lab Lackland AFB Tx 78236

BOTTLE, WILLIAM A., dist. chief judge Macon, Ga. Address: US Courthouse Macon GA 31201

BOTTOMS, WILLIAM RALPH, physician; b. nr. Cumming, Ga., Jan. 14, 1914; s. George Washington and Maude Emily (Hughes) B.; student North Ga. Coll., 1933-34, 1939; B.A. cum laude, Mercer U., 1955; M.D., Med. Coll. Ga., 1959; m. Mildred Mae Heard, May 21, 1935; children—Nancy (Mrs. Donald Ray Jordan), Carol (Mrs. Robert Warren Richter), William Ralph, Jr. Tchr. Forsyth County (Ga.) Sch., 1935-41; methods engr. Sears Roebuck & Co., Atlanta, 1941-44; indsl. engr. Bell Aircraft Corp., Marietta, Ga., 1944-45; indsl. engring. dept. Firestone Tire & Rubber Co., Atlanta, 1944-45; head indsl. engring. dept. Chevrolet plant Gen. Motors Corp., Atlanta, 1945-53; ordained to Ministry Bapt. Ch., 1954; pastor Camak (Ga.) Bapt. Ch., 1953, Haddock (Ga.) Bapt. Ch., 1954-55; intern Midstate Bapt. Hosp., Nashville, 1959-60; pvt. practice medicine, specializing in family practice, Cumming, Ga., 1960-70, Blairsville, Ga., 1970—; chief of staff Union Gen. Hosp., Blairsville, 71—. Med. examiner Union County, 1970—. Med. v.p. Union County Cancer Fund, 1970—; mem. Ga. Heart Assn. Founder Wm. Ralph Bolton Missionary Ednl. Fund. Mem. A.M.A., Med. Assn. Ga., Hall County, 9th Dist. med. assns., Am. Acad. Family Practice. Democrat. Baptist. Kiwanian. Address: Box 506 Blairsville GA 30512

BOUDREAUX, BERNARD EDWARD, JR., lawyer; b. Berwick, La., May 20, 1937; s. B. Edward and Martha (Chapron) B.; B.A., U. Southwestern La., 1960; LL.B., La. State U., 1961; m. Patricia Fitzgerald, Aug. 26, 1961; children—Cynthia Leigh, Jennifer Kay, Bernard Edward III. Admitted to La. bar, 1961; asso. firm M.J. McNulty, Jr., Franklin, La., 1961, Bauer, Darnall, Fleming & McNulty, Franklin, 1964-67; partner firm Bauer, Darnall, McNulty & Boudreaux, Franklin, 1967—; asst. dist. atty. 16th Jud. Dist. La., 1966—; atty. City of Franklin, 1968—. Dir., Franklin Nursing Center, Inc. (La.), Louisa Sugar Coop, Inc., J.C.B. Devel. Corp., Inc., Teche Corp., Inc., Bayou Sale Corp., Inc. (all Franklin), Explo Precision Engring. Corp., Gretna, La. Served to capt., Judge Adv. Gen's Corps, USAF, 1961-64. Mem. Am., La. State bar assns., Franklin C. of C. (v.p. 1966-68), Kappa Sigma, Gamma Eta Gamma. Rotarian. Home: 117 Eastwood Dr Franklin LA 70538 Office: Lawless Bldg Franklin LA 70538

BOUDREAUX, WARREN LOUIS, bishop; b. Berwick, La., Jan. 25, 1918; s. Alphonse Louis and Loretta Marie (Senac) B.; student St. Joseph's Sem., Benedict, La., 1931-36; student Notre Dame Sem., New Orleans, 1937, 42, LL.D., 1963; student Grand Sem. de St. Sulpice, Paris, France, 1938-39; J.C.D., Catholic U. Am., 1946; D.D., Pope John XXIII, 1962. Ordained priest Roman Catholic Ch., 1942; asst. pastor, Crowley, La., 1942-43; vice chancellor Diocese Lafayette, La., 1946-54, officialis, 1949-54; pastor St. Peter's Ch., New Iberia, La., 1954-71; vicar gen. Diocese Lafayette, 1957-71, also diocesan consultor; dean New Iberia Deanery, 1954-71; apptd. aux. bishop Diocese of Lafayette, 1962, bishop Diocese of Beaumont (Tex.), 1971—. Mem. Bishops Com. on Liturgy, Nat. Conf. of Catholic Bishops, 1966-70; mem. U.S. Cath. Conf. Adv. Council, 1969—. Vice pres. S.W. La. Register Newspaper, 1957—. Mem. New Iberia Community Relations Council, 1963—. Bd. dirs. Iberia Paris Youth Home, Consolata Home for Aged, New Iberia, Southwest Ednl. Devel. Lab. Pres. Archdiocesan Conf. Chancery Ofcls., Archdiocese New Orleans, 1950-51, bd. dirs., 1952-55. Address: 703 Archie St Beaumont TX 77701

BOUGH, WAYNE ARNOLD, biochemist; b. Stockton, Mo., Mar. 21, 1943; s. Samuel Junior and Marjorie Evelyn (Baker) B.; B.S., U. Mo., 1965; Ph.D., U. Minn., 1969; m. Viki Charlene Roux, Sept. 13, 1964; children—Thomas Wayne, Stephen Rogers. Research asst. agr. chem. U. Mo., 1965; research asst. biochemistry U. Minn., 1965-69; research dir. Am. Bacteriol. and Chem. Research Corp., Gainesville, Fla., 1969-72; asst. prof. food sci. U. Ga. Expt. Sta., Experiment, 1972—. Vol. worker Hospitality House Boy's Club, Mpls., 1969; clin. asso. Suicide and Crisis Intervention Service, Gainesville, Fla., 1971. Mem. A.A.A.S., Am. Soc. Microbiology, Alpha Gamma Rho, Alpha Chi Sigma. Mem. Ch. of Christ. Home: Route 3 Box 313 B Griffin GA 30223 Office: Dept Food Sci Univ Ga Expt Sta Experiment GA 30212

BOUGHTON, JAMES KENNETH, tire and rubber co. exec.; b. Akron, O., Mar. 22, 1922; s. James Arthur and Louise (Smith) B.; student U. Akron, 1940-42; B.S. in Elec. Engring., Ill. Inst. Tech., 1944; M.S., Lamar Coll. Tech., 1968; m. Evelyn Frances Robottom, Feb. 10, 1945; children—Steven Kent, Susan Lynn, Lisa Jean, Jeffrey Leigh. With Goodyear Tire and Rubber Co., 1942—, machine designer, Akron, 1951, atomic supt. elec. and instrument maintenance, 1953-60, mgr. engring., Beaumont, Tex., 1960—. Instr. U. Akron, 1947-49. Mem. cultural affairs com. Lamar U., 1968—; active Beaumont Symphony, Lamar Philharmonic Orch. Served to lt. comdr. USNR, 1942-45, 51-53; PTO. Registered profl. engr., Ohio. Mem. I.E.E.E., Beaumont C. of C. Republican. Episcopalian (sr. warden 1970-71). Club: Pinewood Country (Pinewood Estates, Tex.). Patentee tire bldg. machines, prodn. counters and controls. Home: Route 1 Box 260 Beaumont TX 77706 Office: Box 3687 Beaumont TX 77704

BOUGHTON, WILLIAM HARRISON, artist, educator; b. Dubuque, Ia., Feb. 19, 1915; s. Richard and Mayme (Pierce) B.; B.A., U. Ia., 1943; M.A., U. Cal. at Berkeley, 1945, fgn. travel and ind. study (James Phelan fellow), 1945-47; m. Leta S. Shelley, July 16, 1971. Asst. prof. Fla. State U., Tallahassee, 1947-54; prof. Lamar U., Beaumont, Tex., 1954—, head art dept., 1954-70; numerous one-man shows; exhibited in group traveling shows in U.S., Europe, Asia, S. Am.; represented in numerous pvt. and pub. collections, including Serigraph Gallery and Meltzer Gallery, N.Y.C., Realities Gallery S. br., Taos, N.M., Gallery Galaxie, Detroit, Joann Scott Gallery, Norfolk, Va., Long Gallery, Houston; slides of paintings in Am. Library Color Slides Co., N.Y.C. Mem. Internat. Acad. Arts and Letters (Rome, Italy), Coll. Art Assn. Home: 4625 Corkwood Lane Beaumont TX 77706 Office: Lamar University Beaumont TX 77705

BOULDIN, WALTER, lawyer, utility exec.; b.Scottsboro, Ala., July 30, 1905; s. Virgil and Irene (Jacoway) B.; A.B., U. Ala., 1925, LL.D., 1966; LL.B., Harvard, 1928; LL.D., Stanford, 1967; m. Elizabeth Donovan, Aug. 27, 1932 (dec. Nov. 21, 1967); 1 son, Walter Virgil. Admitted to Ala. bar, 1928, since practiced in Birmingham; mem. Martin, Turner, Blakey & Bouldin and predecessor firm, 1935-52; financial v.p., Ala. Power Co., Birmingham, 1952-54, exec. v.p., 1955-57, pres., 1957-69, chmn. bd., 1969—; pres. Southeastern Electric Exchange, 1968-69; v.p., dir. So. Electric Generating Co.; dir., mem. exec. com. Warrior-Tombigbee Devel. Assn.; dir. Liberty Nat. Life Ins. Co., So. Services, Inc., Coosa-Ala. River Improvement Assn., Southern Co., 1st Nat. Bank of Birmingham, Ala., Gt. So. R. R. Co. Mem. U.S. Indsl. Payroll Savs. Com., Treasury Dept., 1963-64. Chmn. bd. trustees, mem. exec. com. So. Research Inst.; trustee Birmingham Symphony Assn.; vice chmn. adv. bd. Salvation Army; mem. adv. bd. U. Ala., Birmingham; mem. U. S. com. Internat. Edison Birthday Celebration; trustee Gorgas Scholarship Found., Inc., 1965-66, Tuskegee Inst., 1966-68, Central Ala. Regional Sci. Fair, Thomas Alva Edison Found., Inc., Ala. Acad. Sci.; chmn. Birmingham Centennial Corp.; bd. dirs. Festival of Arts, 1965-67; dir., past pres. Anti-Tb Assn. Jefferson County; Ala. chmn. Crusade for Freedom, 1960. Mem. Edison Electric Inst. (pres. 1963-64, dir. 1961-67), Am. Ordnance Assn. (dir.) Am., Ala., Birmingham bar assns., Ala. (dir., pres. 1967-70, chmn. 1970—), Birmingham (past pres., dir.) chambers commerce, Newcomen Soc. N. Am., Ala. Hist. Soc., Nat. Assn. Electric Cos. (dir. mem. exec. com.), Phi Beta Kappa, Kappa Alpha, Beta Gamma Sigma. Democrat. Presbyn. Clubs: Rotary (bd. dirs. 1965-67) (Birmingham); Mountain Brook (Ala.); The Club, Downtown Relay House; Metropolitan (Washington). Home: 2611 Watkins Rd Birmingham AL 35223 Office: Ala Power Co Birmingham AL 35202

BOULMAY, GARDNER CASTANEDO, motel exec.; b. New Orleans, Dec. 15, 1916; s. Lionel Soniat and Isabell Marie (Castanedo) B.; grad. high sch.; m. Leanora Ann Tedesco, July 1, 1942; children—Gardner Francis, Gregory, Geoffrey, Gerald, Grant, Gigi. Owner, Boulmay's Service Sta., New Orleans, 1935-39; parts mgr. Bert Wells Nash Co., New Orleans, 1939-42; owner Gentilly Appliance Co., New Orleans, 1943-45; self-employed as gen. contractor, 1945-63; mgr., owner Vieux Carre Motor Lodge, New Orleans, 1964—. Mem. Vieux Carre Action Assn. Bd., 1969-72, Vieux Carre Property Owners Bd., 1968-72, Greater New Orleans Tourist and Conv. Bd., 1971-72, New Orleans Food Fest Bd., 1969-71; mem. Super Bowl Task Force, 1970-72. Bd. dirs. La. Tb and Respiratory Disease Assn. Served with AUS, 1942-43. Mem. Greater New Orleans Hotel Motel Assn. (chmn. bd. 1972). Clubs: Krewe of Bacchus (New Orleans); Country (Covington, La.). Home: 187 Country Club Dr Covington LA 70433 Office: 920 N Rampart St New Orleans LA 70116

BOUMA, ARNOLD HEIKO, educator; b. Groningen, The Netherlands, Sept. 5, 1932; s. Pier and Trientje (Eissens) B.; B.S., U. Groningen, 1956; M.S., U. Utrecht (The Netherlands), 1959, Ph.D., 1961; m. Mechelina H. Kampers, Jan. 16, 1960; children—Mark, Nils, Lars. Came to U.S., 1966. Instr., U. Utrecht, 1960-62, chief instr., 1963-66; postdoctoral fellow U. Cal. Scripps Inst. Oceanography, San Diego, 1962-63; asso. prof. oceanography Tex. A. & M. U., College Station, 1966-70, prof., 1970—. Fellow Am. Assn. Petroleum Geologists, Soc. Econ. Paleontologists Mineralogists; mem. Internat. Assn. Sedimentologists, Geol. Soc. Am., Am. Geophys. Union, Sigma Xi. Author: Sedimentology of Flysch Deposits, 1962; Methods for the Study of Sedimentary Structures, 1969. Editor: Turbidites, 1964. Contbr. articles to profl. jours. Home: Route 4 Box 112 A Bryan TX 77801 Office: Dept Oceanography Tex A & M U College Station TX 77843

BOUNDS, LAURENCE HAROLD, gas co. exec.; b. Newcastle, Wyo., Feb. 15, 1922; s. James Henry and Blanche Agnes (McKay) B.; B.S., Simpson Coll., 1943; postgrad. Columbia, 1943; m. Dorothy May Bostrom, Nov. 20, 1965. With comptroller dept. Kemper Ins., Chgo., 1947-51; sec.-treas. W & J Constrn. Co., 1951-64; auditor, Roosevelt Hotel, Jacksonville, Fla., 1964-66; v.p. Western Natural Gas Co., Jacksonville, 1966—. Served to lt. USNR, 1942-46. Mem. Adminstrv. Mgmt. Soc. (asst. treas. 1971), Navy League, Alpha Tau Omega. Episcopalian. Club: Willow Lakes Golf and Country. Home: 1929 Constant Dr Jacksonville FL 32210 Office: 2960 Strickland St Jacksonville FL 32205

BOUNDS, SAM, JR., mech. engr.; b. Florence, Ala., June 23, 1924; s. Sam and Pearl (Huepel) B.; B.M.E., Auburn U., 1948; postgrad. U. Houston, 1949-50, U. Cal. at Los Angeles, 1962, U. Tex. extension, 1952; m. Julia Dixon, Oct. 27, 1951; children— Molly, Beverly, Sarah, Timothy Dixon. Engr. Stanolind Oil & Gas Co., Okla. and Tex., 1948-52, Carter Oil Co., Okla, 1952-54; designer Douglas Aircraft Co., Tulsa, 1954-60; mech. engr. U.S. Army Missile Command, Redstone Arsenal, Ala., 1960—. Served AUS, 1943-45. Decorated Purple Heart. Registered profl. engr. Ala. Mem. Am. Soc. M.E., Am. Legion, Pi Tau Sigma, Tau Beta Pi. Presbyn. Club: Burningtree Country. Home: 2507 College St SE Decatur AL 35601 Office: Bldg 5400 Redstone Arsenal AL 35809

BOURGOYNE, JULIOUS ROY, dentist; b. Beaumont, Tex., Nov. 13, 1914; s. Rene Jules and Ora Lee (Norton) B.; student Tulane U., 1933-34; B.S., Sam Houston Coll., 1936; D.D.S., Loyola U., New Orleans, 1941; m. Helen Ruth Bass, Mar. 15, 1947; children—Ruth Elaine, Lisa Helen, Rene Stephen, Laura Jean. Intern oral surgery Charity Hosp., New Orleans, 1941-42, resident, 1942-44; fellow in pathology Tufts Coll. Dental Sch., Boston, 1944; chief div. oral surgery and anesthesia U. Tenn. Coll. Dentistry, Memphis, 1944-59; individual practice oral surgery, Memphis, 1947—; mem. staff Memphis hosps. Cons. oral surgery VA, USPHS hosps., Memphis, U.S. Naval Air Sta. Hosp., Millington; chmn. Tenn. Hosp. Dental Service Com. Diplomate Am. Bd. Oral Surgery. Mem. Am. Soc. Oral Surgeons, Am. Dental Assn., Memphis Dental Soc. (pres. elect 1972-73), Southeastern Soc. Oral Surgeons, Pierre Fauchard Acad., Dean Odontol. Soc. (charter), Delta Sigma Delta, Omicron Kappa Upsilon. Baptist. Club: Chickasaw Country (Memphis). Author: Surgery of the Mouth and Jaws, 1949, Oral Cancer, 1954; (with Nevin) Conduction, Infiltration and General Anesthesia in Dentistry, 1959, also articles. Home: 310 S Perkins Rd Memphis TN 38117 Office: 1422 Lamar Av Memphis TN 38104

BOURNE, GEOFFREY HOWARD, educator; b. Perth, Western Australia, Nov 17, 1909; s. Walter Howard and Mary Ann (Mellon) B.; B.S. (hon.), U. Western Australia, 1931, M.S., 1932, D.Sc., 1935; Ph.D., Oxford (Eng.) U., 1943; m. Gwen Jones, Dec. 31, 1935 (div. Feb. 1964); children—Peter, Mervyn; m. 2d, Maria Nelly Golartz, Oct. 31, 1964. Biologist Australian Inst. Anatomy, Canberra, 1934-36; biochemist adv. council on nutrition Commonwealth of Australia, 1936-38; Beit Meml. fellow for med. research Oxford (Eng.) U., 1938-41, dept. demonstrator in physiology, 1938-43; Machenzie-Mackinnon research fellow Royal Coll. Surgeons, Royal Coll. Physicians, 1941-43; maj. in charge research and devel. Spl. Forces, S.E. Asia, biology and medicine, Eng., 1943-45; lt. col. and nutritional adv. Brit. Mil. Adminstrn., Malaya, 1945-46; reader histology U. London, 1947-57; chmn. anatomy Emory U., Atlanta, 1957-62, dir. Yerkes Regional Primate Research Center, 1962—. Served to lt. col. Brit. Army, 1943. Fellow Royal Soc. Medicine, Zool. Soc. London, Brit. Interplanetary Soc., Inst. Biology, Am. Gerontological Soc.; mem. Sigma Xi. Author or editor numerous books including: Structure and Function of Muscle, 1963, 2d edit., 1972; Biochemistry and Physiology of Bone, 1956, 2d edit., 1972; Muscular Dystrophy in Man and Animals, 1963. Editor: Internat. Rev. of Cytology, 1950—, World Rev. of Nutrition and Dietetics, 1959—, Structure and Function of Nervous Tissue, 1969, Vols. 4-6, 1972; The Ape People, 1971; Primates in Biomedical Research, 1972. Home: 849 Lullwater Pkwy Atlanta GA 30307 Office: Yerkes Regional Primate Center Emory Univ Atlanta GA 30322

BOURQUE, LESLIE PAUL, JR., real estate broker; b. Gonzales, La., Apr. 4, 1922; s. Leslie P. and Eugenie (Bourque) B.; student Molar Barber Sch., New Orleans, 1940-41, Officer's Candidate Sch., Ft. Benning, Ga., 1945; student real estate course La. State U., 1955; m. Shirley Mire, Jan. 27, 1942; children—Leslie Paul III, Victor, Neal,

Dawn, Stacy. Head barber, shop owner, Gonzales, La., 1947-56; real estate broker, developer Bourque Real Estate, Gonzales, 1956—; v.p. Markets, Inc., 1957—, Chateau Bourque Apts., 1963—; pres. Park Vista Corp., (all Gonzales), 1959—. Served to 2d lt. AUS, 1942-45. Democrat. Roman Catholic. Clubs: Lion's (pres. Gonzales 1948-50, award 1948, sec-treas. 1956-57), Gonzales Quarterback (sec. 1949-51). Address: 1017 Mire St Gonzales LA 70737

BOUTALL, JOHN CHARLES, judge; b. Jefferson Parish, La., Sept. 28, 1920; s. Charles A. and Lillian (Bruning) B.; B.A., Tulane U., 1940, LL.B., 1946; m. Marilyn Margaret Bartol, Mar. 31, 1945; children—Richard John, Katherine E., William C., Charles A. Admitted to La. bar, 1946; practiced in Jefferson Parish, 1946-55; judge 24th Jud. Dist. Ct., Jefferson Parish, 1955-70, Ct. Appeals, 4th Circuit La., New Orleans, 1970—. Past mem. Jud. Council, State of La. Served to lt. USNR, 1942-45. Mem. La., Jefferson Parish bar assns., La., Am. Judicature Soc., Internat. Acad. Law and Sci., Dist. Judges Assn. (pres.). Lion. Home: 1521 Lakeshore Dr Metairie LA 70005 Office: 210 Civil Courts Bldg 421 Loyola Av New Orleans LA 70112

BOUVIER, HELEN SCHAEFER (MRS. JOHN A. BOUVIER, JR.), leasing co. exec.; b. McAlester, Okla., Sept. 11, 1910; d. William John and Anna (Perrin) Schaefer; student U. Fla., 1928-29, Northwestern U., 1929-30; m. John A. Bouvier, Jr., June 6, 1928; children—Helen Elizabeth (Mrs. William Spencer), John A. III, Thomas R. Sec., Sunset Rock & Sand Co., Miami, Fla;, 1939-45, Coral Rock & San Co., 1945-48; now chmn. Nat. Leasing, Inc.; dir. Knight Manor, Inc., Miami, West Kingsway, Inc., Miami, East Kingsway, Inc., Miami, South Kingsway, Inc., Miami, Fiftieth St. Heights, Inc., Miami, Karen Garden, Inc. Ft. Lauderway, Inc., Fiftieth St. Heights, Inc., Miami and N.Y.C.; also mgmt; cons., Miami, N.Y.C., 1945—. Dir., v.p. Ella R. Bouvier Found. Presbyn. (pres. womens auxiliary, pres. womens auxiliary synod). Clubs: Corinthian (Syracuse, N.Y.); Skaneateles (N.Y.) Country; Riveria County (Coral Gables, Fla.), (Surfside, Fla.); Beach Colony (Miami Bleach, Fla.). Home: 2756 NE 17th St Fort Lauderdale FL 33305 Office: Blowing Rock NC also 6888 NW 7th Av Miami FL 33150

BOUVIER, JOHN ANDRE, JR., lawyer, corp. exec.; b. nr. Ocala, Fla., May 16, 1903; s. John Andre and Ella (Richardson) B.; student Davidson Coll., 1922-24; A.B., U. Fla., 1926, LL.B., 1929; M.B.A., Northwestern U., 1930; m. Helen A. Schaefer, June 6, 1928; children—Helen Elizabeth (Mrs. William Spencer), John Andre III, Thomas Richardson. Admitted to Fla. bar, 1929, pvt. practice, Gainesville, 1929, Miami, 1930—, specialist corp., real estate and probate law, cons. atty.; gen. counsel Patterson and Maloney. attys. chmn. exec. com. Permutit Co.; chmn. bd. Prosperity Co. div. vice chmn. bd. Ward Industries Corp., 1958; chmn. bd., pres. Pantex Mfg. Corp., 1958—, Nat. Leasing Corp., Miami; chmn. bd. Knaust Bros., Inc., K-B Products Corp., Iron Mountain Atomic Storage Vaults, Inc.; sec. West Kingsway, Inc., East Kingsway, Inc., South Kingsway, Inc.; sec. Fiftieth Street Hts., Inc. Knight Manor, Inc., Dade Constrn. Co., Farm Industries, Inc., Iron Mountain Atomic Storage Vaults, Inc. (all Miami), Karen Club Apt. Hotel, Ft. Lauderdale; pres. Knaust Bros., Inc., West Coxsackie, N.Y., 1960-64, chmn., 1964—; pres. K-B Products Corp., Hudson, N.Y., 1960-61, chmn., 1964—; dir. the Ocean First Nat. Bank, Farquhar Machinery Co., Consol. Bankshares. Commr. Dade County council Boy Scouts Am.; chmn. Malecon Com. Dade County; dir. Syracuse Govtl. Research Bur., Inc.; mem. Nat. Def. Exec. Res. planning council Zoning Bd. Miami; chmn. Coxsackie-Athens Area Redev. Com.; vice chmn. Nat. Parkinson Found. Trustee Parkinson Rehab., Diagnostic and Research Inst., Windham Coll.; adv. bd. Fla. Meml. Coll.; pres., dir. Ella R. Bouvier Found. Mem. Internat. Platform Assn. N.A.M. (conservation renewable natural resources com.) Mfrs. Assn. Syracuse (dir.), Miami, Auburn civic music assns. Cayuga Mus. History and Art, Am. Acad. Polit. Sci., Am. Judicature Soc., Am., Fla., Broward County, Dade County bar associations, Chamber of Commerce, Sigma Chi. Presbyn. (chmn. bd. trustees). Mason (Shriner), Elk, Rotarian. Clubs: Miami Beach Rod and Reel, Surf, Riveria Country, Skaneateles Country; Ponte Verde; Washington Lawyers; Civitan (dir.). Author monographs, newspaper articles in field. Home: 2756 NE 17th St Fort Lauderdale FL 33305 also Box 14 Climax NY 12042 Office: 6888 NW 7th Ave Miami FL 33150 also Kenann Bldg Fort Lauderdale FL 33306 also Blowing Rock NC 28605

BOW, RUSSELL LEON, clergyman; b. Bow, Ky., Jan. 23, 1925; s. Stephen Tyler and Lula (King) B.; A.A., Lindsey Wilson Coll., 1944; student Union Coll., 1945-46; A.B., Ky. Wesleyan Coll., 1949; B.D., Emory U., 1952; m. Roxie Marie Minton, Sept. 15, 1945; children—Michael, Beverly. Ordained to ministry Methodist Ch., 1952; asst. pastor Settle Meml. Meth. Ch., Owensboro, Ky., 1952-56; pastor, Woodlawn Meth. Ch., Owensboro, Ky., 1956-61, Preston Hwy. Meth. Ch., Louisville, 1961-67, United Meth. Temple, Russellville, Ky., 1967-71, Ogden Meml. United Meth. Ch., Princeton, Ky., 1971—. Bd. dirs. Welsey Found., U. Ky. Mem. Russellville Ministerial Assn. (pres. 1970). Mason, Kiwanian. Club: Civitan (pres. 1954) (Owensboro, Ky). Home: 304 Hospital Dr Princeton KY 42445 Office: W Main at Cave Sts Princeton KY 42445

BOWDEN, EVA, educator, librarian; b. Timberland, N.C., Aug. 9, 1906; d. William David and Mary Eliza (Caddell) Bowden; A.B., U.N.C., 1928; postgrad. Franklin Inst. Corr., 1929-30, U. N.C., Corr., 1930-31; A.B. in L.S., Emory U., 1945; certificate med. librarianship (Med. Library Assn. scholar), 1958; postgrad. U. N.C., summers 1946-48. Tchr., librarian N.C. High Sch. System, 1927-43; asst. librarian Greensboro Coll., 1943-45; with Lander Coll., Greenwood, S.C., 1945-47; asst. librarian Flora McDonald Coll., Red Springs, N.C., 1947-49; asst. supr. card distbn. and indexing sect. Atomic Energy Library, Oak Ridge, summer 1949; head librarian dental br. U. Tex. Houston, 1949-71. Mem. Am. Assn. U. Women, Am. Bus. Women's Assn. (Woman of Jr. award Houston Chpt. 1969-70; numerous offices and coms. Houston chpt.), A.L.A., Med. Library Assn., Tex. Library Assn., Am. Assn. U. Profs. Writer library handbooks for dental students, dental hygiene students, grad. students U. Tex. Home: 4707 Fannin Ct Houston TX 77004

BOWDEN, OSSIE HANSON, assn. exec.; b. Cullman, Ala., Jan 1, 1918; s. Richard E. and Stella (Allgood) B.; grad. with honors, Auburn U., 1941; m. Julia Batastini, Dec. 20, 1941; 1 dau., Sara Beatrice. County agt. Ala. Agrl. Extension Service, Heflin, 1941-44; farm products marketing agt. T.C.I. div. U.S. Steel Corp., Birmingham, Ala., 1944-54; gen. mgr. Farmers Marketing and Exchange Assn., Montgomery, Ala., 1954-60; dir. personnel and mem. relations Gold Kist, Inc. (formerly Cotton Producers Assn.), Atlanta, 1960—. Bd dirs. Associated Coops., Ala. Farmers Coop.; pres. Ga. Council of Farmers Coop. Mem. Atlanta C. of C., Am. Inst. Coops. (trustee), Internat. Platform Assn., Nat. Cooperative Council, Phi Kappa Phi, Gamma Sigma Delta, Kappa Delta Phi. Baptist. Mason. Club: Chattahoochee Plantation. Home: 4686 Brinkley Lane NE Atlanta GA 30342 Office: 3348 Peachtree Rd NE Atlanta GA 30326

BOWDEN, WILLIAM ANTON, JR., architect; b. Memphis, Feb. 25, 1930; s. William Anton and Sybil Naomi (Arnold) B.; B.A., Southwestern U., 1951; B.Arch. with high honor, Auburn U., 1957; m. Janice Swanson Livingston, Mar. 17, 1962; children—Carolyn, Bill (children from previous marriage), Livingston, Max. Apprentice, A.L. Aydelott & Assos., Memphis, 1957-58, Lawrence S. Whitten, Birmingham, Ala., 1958-59, Mann & Harrover, Memphis, 1959-60; jr. mem. firm Eason, Anthony, McKinnie, & Cox, Inc., architects, Memphis, 1960-63; asso. firm Buchmueller, Whitworth, & Assos., Sikeston, Mo., 1963-64; prin. Fischer-Bowden, Inc., Carbondale, Ill., 1964-68; asso. univ. architect Duke U., Durham, N.C., 1968-71; pres., exec. dir. LBC &W Assos. N.C., Inc., Greensboro, 1971—. Active campaign United Fund; mem. Carbondale Pub. Bldgs. Com., 1966-68, sidewalk adv. com., 1966-68, profl. engr. selection com., 1966-68. Served with USMCR, 1947-49, 52-53; now lt. col. Res. ret. Mem. A.I.A., Constrn. Specifications Inst., Nat. Panel Arbitrators, Am. Arbitration Assn., Marine Corps League, Marine Corps Res. Officers Assn., Scarab, Phi Kappa Phi, Sigma Nu, C. of C. (bd. dirs. 1965-68). Episcopalian. Elk. Club: Tennessee (Memphis). Home: 3008 Greenbrook Dr Greensboro NC 27408 Office: 1327 Beaman Place Greensboro NC 27408

BOWDOIN, WILLIAM REDDING, banker; b. Atlanta, July 21, 1913; s. William Henry and Pauline (Collins) B.; LL.B., U. Ga., 1933; LL.D., Emory U., 1970; m. Margaret Stoddard, July 30, 1942; children—William Redding, John Collins. Admitted to Ga. bar, 1934; with Peoples Bank, Winder, Ga., 1936-41; pres. First Nat. Bank, East Point, Ga., 1946-48; with Trust Co. Ga., Atlanta, 1948—, vice chmn. bd., 1964—, also dir.; chmn., pres. Trust Co. Ga. Assos., 1964—; dir. First Nat. Bank & Trust Co., Augusta, Fourth Nat. Bank, Columbus, First Nat. Bank & Trust Co., Macon, First Nat. Bank, Rome, Liberty Nat. Bank & Trust Co., Savannah. Chmn. Ga. Ports Authority, 1953-55, Gov. Ga. Commn. Efficiency and Improvement, 1963-64; supr. purchases Ga., 1959; co-chmn. Atlanta Meml. Cultural Center campaign, 1964; treas. Ga. Assn. Crippled Children, 1964; adv. com. Ga. Vocational Assn., 1963-64. Trustee Emory U., Ga. Found. Ind. Colls.; vice chmn. bd. Berry Schs. Served to maj. AUS, 1941-46. Recipient Ga. Citizen of Year award Ga. Assn. County Commrs., 1963, Nat. Citizenship award Future Farmers Am., 1964; named to Officer Candidate Sch. Hall of Fame, Ft. Benning, Ga., 1970; recipient President's award Assn. Pvt. Colls. and Univs. in Ga., 1972. Mem. Gridiron Secret Soc. (U. Ga.) (hon.), Beta Gamma Sigma, Sigma Alpha Epsilon. Episcopalian. Home: 3845 Club Dr NE Atlanta GA 30319 Office: Trust Co of Georgia Atlanta GA 30302

BOWDRE, CARL EUGENE, banker; b. Champaign, Ill., Oct. 5, 1930; s. Harold Alonzo and Euncie (Perkins) B.; student U. Tex., 1953, 54, Am. Inst. Banking, 1959, 60, 63; m. Mary Virginia Franklin, June 24, 1951; children—Pamela Glen, Stephen Franklin, Linda Ann. With Nat. Bank Monticello (Ill.), 1956-57; with Peoples Group Nat. Banks, Dade County, Fla., 1957-70, pres., North Miami Beach, Fla., until 1970; sr. v.p. Pan Am. Bank of Dade County, North Miami Beach, 1970—. Adviser, Sch. Banking Dade County Jr. Coll., Miami, 1968—. Served with USAF, 1950-54. Mem. North Miami Beach (pres. 1968-69), U.S. chambers commerce, Bank Adminstrn. Inst. S. Fla. (bd. dirs.). Republican. Mem. Ch. of Jesus Christ Latter-day Saints. Kiwanian (pres. 1972—). Home: 6800 SW 22d Ct Miramar FL 33023 Office: PO Drawer 29 North Miami Beach FL 33160

BOWEN, A'DELBERT, lawyer; b. Tuscumbia, Ala., Nov. 13, 1919; s. A'Delbert and Gertrude (Willett) B.; student State Tchrs. Coll., Florence, Ala., 1936-38; LL.B., Atlanta Law Sch., 1954; m. Rebecca Montez Proctor, July 27, 1945; children—A'Delbert III, Lanny Proctor, Montez Elizabeth. Gen. ins. agt. Proctor Ins. Agy., Cuthbert, Ga., 1950—; admitted to Ga. bar, 1954, since practiced in Cuthbert; atty. City of Shellman (Ga.), City of Georgetown (Ga.); county atty. Randolph County, Ga., 1960-71, Quitman County, Ga., 1966—. Mem. Ga. Gen. Assembly, 1959-64. Sec., bd. dirs. Randolph Devel. Corp.; trustee Andrew Coll. Served to maj. USAAF, 1941-47. Decorated Air medal with five oak leaf clusters. Mem. Am., Ga. bar assns., Am. Legion. Republican. Methodist (trustee). Mason. Home: 118 W Harris St Cuthbert GA 31740 Office: 111 Court St Cuthbert GA 31740

BOWEN, CHARLES ELBERT, supt. schs.; b. Austell, Ga., May 10, 1913; s. Urben and Mattie Jane (Bolding) B.; A.B., U. Ga., 1934, M.A., 1939; postgrad. Peabody Coll. for Tchrs.; m. Irene Elizabeth Cooper, June 6, 1942; children—Peggy Ann (Mrs. Charles Green), Charles Elbert. Prin., Weston (Ga.) Sch., 1934-36; asst. prin. Fitzgerald (Ga.) High Sch., 1936-38; asst. math. dept. U. Ga., 1938-39; asst. prin. Sandersville (Ga.) High Sch., 1939-40; prin. Ft. Hill Jr. High Sch., Dalton, Ga., 1940-43; instr. math. Ga. Inst. Tech., 1946; prin. Dalton High Sch., 1946-68; asst. supt. Dalton Pub. Schs., 1968-69, supt., 1969—. Mem., past chmn. N.W. Ga. YMCA; mem. adv. council Cherokee dist. Boy Scouts Am. Chmn. Dalton Planning and Zoning Commn., 1962-67. Bd. dirs. Big Bros. Served to lt. (j.g.), USNR, 1943-46. Mem. N.E.A., Ga., Dalton assns. educators, Ga. Assn. Sch. Supts. (past chmn.), Nat., Ga. assns. secondary sch. prins., So. Assn. Colls. and Schs. (past chmn. Ga. com.), Pi Mu Epsilon (charter). Baptist (deacon). Rotarian (past pres. Dalton). Home: 906 Hillcrest Dr Dalton GA 30720 Office: PO Box 1408 Dalton GA 30720

BOWEN, DEWITT, dentist; b. Florence, Miss., Mar. 6, 1922; s. Drue and Lillie (Harp) B.; student U. Chattanooga, 1946, So. Missionary Coll., 1946-49; D.D.S., U. Tenn., 1953; m. Josie Flevella Newlon, Jan. 27, 1948; children—Bruce DeWitt, JoDee Marie. Pvt. practice dentistry, Chattanooga, 1953—. Served with AUS, 1942-46. Mem. Am., Tenn. State dental assns., So. Missionary Coll. Alumni Assn. (pres. 1967), Delta Sigma Delta. Home: PO Box 7 Collegedale TN 37315 Office: 6781 Lee Hwy Chattanooga TN 37421

BOWEN, FRANK WESTON, physician; b. Memphis, May 5, 1921; s. George Samuel and Virgie (Hamill) B.; B.A., U., Miss., 1948, B.S. 1949; M.D., U. Tenn., 1951; m. Bobbie Elizabeth McPhail, May 1, 1943; 1 son, Frank Weston. Intern, Methodist Hosp., Memphis, 1951-52; practice family medicine, Walnut Grove, Miss., 1952-57, Carthage, Miss., 1957—; chief of staff Leake County Meml. Hosp., Carthage, 1961, 72. Served from pvt. to 2nd lt., MAC, AUS, 1942-46. Diplomate Am. Bd. Family Practice. Fellow Am. Geriatrics Soc., mem. Am. Heart Assn., A.M.A., Am. Acad. Family Practice, Miss. Med. Assn., Central Med. Soc. (pres. 1969), C. of C., N.Y. Acad. Scis., Leake County Hist. Soc., Phi Chi. Methodist. Home: 700 N Pearl St Carthage MS 39051 Office: 303 W Franklin St Carthage MS 39051

BOWEN, TED, hosp. adminstr. Dir. Methodist Hosp., Houston. Office: 6516 Bertner Blvd Houston TX 77025*

BOWEN, WILLIAM JACKSON, gas co. exec.; b. Sweetwater, Tex., Mar. 31, 1922; s. Berry and Annah (Robey) B.; B.S., U.S. Mil. Acad., 1945; m. Annis K. Hilty, June 6, 1945; children—Shelley Ann, Barbara Kay, Berry Dunbar, William Jackson. Petroleum engr. Delhi Oil Corp., Dallas, 1949-57; v.p. Fla. Gas Co., Houston, 1957-60, pres., Winter Park, Fla., 1960—; trustee Barnett Mortgage Trust; dir. First Nat. Bank Orlando. Mem. Orange Bowl Com., 1962—. Trustee Rollins Coll.; bd. dirs. Loch Haven Art Center, Orange Center YMCA, Fla. Council 100. Served with AUS, 1945-49. Registered profl. engr., Tex. Mem. Ind. Natural Gas Assn. (dir. 1961—), Am. Gas Assn. (dir. 1970—), Delta Kappa Epsilon. Presbyn. Home: 1821 Pinetree Rd Winter Park FL 32789 Office: PO Box 44 Orange and Orlando Avs Winter Park FL 32789

BOWEN, WILLIAM STEPHEN, JR., metals co. exec.; b. Blackshear, Ga., Feb. 14, 1938; s. William Stephen and Alafae (Jones) B.; B.M.E., Ga. Inst. Tech., 1961 M.M.E., Stanford, 1962, M.B.A., 1967. Engring. trainee Lockheed Aircraft Corp., 1956-61; prodn. dept. mgr. Procter & Gamble Mfg. Co., 1962-65; asst. v.p., Southwire Co., 1967-69; dir., officer Nat.-Southwire Aluminum Co., 1968-69; chmn., chief exec. officer Wyre Wynd, Inc., Jewett City, Conn., 1969—; founder, pres. Trans-Am. Aviation, Inc., Dallas, 1964—. Registered profl. engr., Cal., Ga., Ky. Mem. Soc. Automotive Engrs., Am. Soc. M.E. Home: Box 57 Carrollton GA 30117 Office: Southwire Co PO Box 1000 Carrollton GA 30117

BOWEN, WILLIAM WARD, physician; b. Grenada, Miss., Nov. 11, 1927; s. Hugh and Myrtle (Stevens) B.; B.S., La. State U., 1950, M.D., 1954; m. Betsy Ann Green, June 29, 1950; children—Charlotte Ann, Cynthia Louise, William Ward, Melinda Rose, Elizabeth Emily, Frederick Carl. Intern, McLeod Infirmary, Florence, S.C., 1954-55; practice gen. medicine, Hartsville, S.C., 1955—; owner Hartsville Hosp., 1956—; founder, pres. Hartsville Convalescent and Nursing Home, 1968—. Mem. Hartsville Bd. Health, 1961—; v.p. S.C. Health Care Plan, 1970-72; mem. S.C. Bd. Examiners for Nursing Home Adminstrs., 1971-74. Vice pres. Hartsville Area Council for Retarded, 1968; bd. dirs., 1st vice chmn. Hartsville A.R.C.; pres. Pee Dee Found. for Handicapped, 1968-71; mem. steering com. White House Conf. on Children and Youth, 1970. Served with USNR, 1945. Named Civitan of Year, Hartsville, S.C. 1967; Honor medal S.C. Civitan Club, 1968; Annual award for outstanding community service, Hartsville, 1969. Mem. Am., So., S.C. med. assns., S.C. Nursing Home Assn. (treas. 1971-72), Darlington County (pres. 1958), Pee Dee (pres. 1962) med. socs., Flying Physicians Med. Assn., S.C. Assn. for Retarded Children (dir.), Nat. Assn. Bds. Examiners for Nursing Home Adminstrs. (dir. 1971-72), Am. Assn. of Mental Deficiency, Kappa Sigma, Nu Sigma Nu. Democrat. Methodist (trustee). Clubs: Hartsville Red Fox (pres. 1960), Hartsville Civitan (v.p. 1959-60). Home: 507 Carolina Av Hartsville SC 29550 Office: 412 Home Av Hartsville SC 29550

BOWERS, ANDREW EUGENE, supt. schs.; b. Fayetteville, Ga., Apr. 2, 1927; s. Joseph Edward and Winnie (Mask) B.; B.S., U. Ga., 1950, M.Ed., 1961, Specialist in Edn., 1970; m. E. Adrian Short, July 30, 1960; children—Andrew Eugene, Adrienne Elyse, Timothy John, Maria Elwin. Tchr. agr., Fayette County, 1950-52, Pike County, 1952-56; asst. supr. Farmers Home Adminstrn., Mitchell County, 1956-58; prin. Fairview Elementary Sch., Stockbridge, Ga., 1958-63; tchr. sci. Fayette County High Sch., 1963-64; supt. Fayette County Schs., 1964—. Mem. Fayette County Bd. Health, 1964—. Served with AUS, 1945-46. Mem. N.E.A., Am. Assn. Sch. Adminstrs., Nat. Soc. Study Edn., Assn. Educators Am. Legion, Fayette County Farm Bur., Fayette County C. of C. Baptist (chmn. deacons 1967-68, brotherhood pres. 1963-64, 71-72, supt. adult dept. 1963-69). Kiwanian (chmn. various local coms.). Home: 250 Forrest Ave Fayetteville GA 30214 Office: County Office Bldg Fayetteville GA 30214

BOWERS, HERBERT EDWIN, librarian; b. Washington, N.J., Mar. 29, 1917; s. Herbert and Cora M. (Raub) B.; A.B., Columbia, 1939; B.S., 1948, M.A., 1955; postgrad. U. Pa., 1966; m. Patricia C. Clark, June 16, 1956; 1 dau., Debbie Lynn. Asst. librarian Hill Sch., Pottstown, Pa., 1948-58; reference librarian Lafayette Coll., Easton, Pa., 1958-59; head audiovisual center Drexel Inst. Tech., 1959-62; librarian Neshaminy Sch. Dist., Langhorne, Pa., 1962-66; dir. library Iolani Sch., Honolulu, 1966-67; librarian periodicals-documents dept. Miami (Fla.)-Dade Jr. Coll., 1967—. Served with USAAF, 1942-46. Mem. Hump Pilots Assn., Am. (life), Fla. library assns., Univ. Profs. for Acad. Order (chpt. treas.), Hollywood Stamp Club. Home: 2810 1st St N St Petersburg FL 33704 Office: 11380 NW 27th Av Miami FL 33167

BOWERS, QUINTON ROOSEVELT, lawyer, state legislator; b. Samson, Ala., Mar. 20, 1921; s. William E. and Mary (Alpin) B.; B.S., U. Ala., 1949; J.D., Birmingham Sch. Law, 1955; m. Betty Mathews, Dec. 5, 1953; one dau., Lita Kay. Salesman, Goodyear Service Store, Gadsden, Ala., 1950-51; adjuster Universal C.I.T. Credit Corp., Birmingham, Ala., 1951-52, Am. Fore Ins. Group, 1953-57; admitted to Ala. bar, 1960; practiced in Birmingham, 1957—; spl. asst. atty. gen. State of Ala., 1967—; mem. Ala. Ho. of Reps., 1962—, mem. com. on local legislation number 2, mem. judiciary com., chmn. com. mil. affairs. Chmn. exec. com. Old Age Pension Inst. of Ala., Birmingham, 1958-59; mem. Ala. Vets.' Affairs Com., 1965-69; mem. Gov.'s Com. Employment of the Physically Handicapped, State of Ala.; mem. permanent study comn. Ala. Judicial Commn., 1971—, chmn. subcom to study coroner system; mem. Continuing Women's Commn. Ala., 1971. Served with USMC, 1939-45. Mem. Am., Ala., Birmingham bar assns., State Ala. Employees Assn., Ala. League Aging Citizens (life), Ala. Peace Officers Assn., Jefferson County Sportsmen's Assn., C. of C., Am. Legion, V.F.W. (comdr. dept. Ala. 1963-64, comdr. Kelly Ingram post 1961-62, mem. all-Am. team of state comdrs. 1964, state comdr. of yr. award 1964, vice chmn. nat. legislative com. 1964-66), Sigma Delta Kappa. Democrat. Methodist. Mason (32 deg., Shriner), Eagle. Club: Civitan. Home: 1528 Shades Crest Rd Birmingham AL 35226 Office: Frank Nelson Bldg Birmingham AL 35203

BOWERS, RONALD WILLIAM, dentist; b. St. Louis, Dec. 10, 1941; s. Paul William and Dorothy Geraldine (Barton) B.; D.D.S., Emory U., 1965; m. Nancy Lee Heath, Apr. 29, 1960; children—Ronald William, Amy Elizabeth, Barton Bentley. Intern Fla. Instnl. Dental Service, 1965-66; pvt. practice dentistry, 1966-70, mem. profl. corp., Augusta, Ga., 1970—; dir. Bowers Finance Co. Vice chmn. adv. bd. Salvation Army; chmn. profl. div. Am. Cancer Soc. Mem. AUS Res. Mem. Augusta Dental Soc. (v.p.), Am., Ga. dental assns., Xi Psi Phi. Methodist. Elk. Clubs: Augusta Country, Augusta Sailing, Highgate Green and Tennis. Home: 3219 Ramsgate Rd Augusta GA 30904 Office: 2701 Washington Rd Augusta GA 30904

BOWERSOX, CLARENCE HOYT, JR., chem. co. exec.; b. Duncan, Okla., Oct. 18, 1918; s. Clarence Hoyt and Stella (Cottle) B.; student Ga. Mil. Acad., 1933-36; B.S., Okla. U., 1941; grad. student U. Pitts., 1957; m. Barbara Jean Ingram, Sept. 19, 1943; children—Stephen Craig, Philip Gordon, James Dudley, Sarah Della. Petroleum engr. Cities Service Gas Co., 1941; with Gulf Oil Corp., 1941-61, operations mgr., 1958-61; pres. Solvent Mfg. Co., Midwest City, Okla., 1961—. Cons. water chemistry. Served from 2d lt. to maj. AUS, 1942-46. Decorated Bronze Star medal with oak leaf cluster. Registered profl. engr., Okla., Colo. Club: Optimist (treas. 1965-66). Home: 617 NW 41st St Oklahoma City OK 73118 Office: 1517 Ocama Blvd Midwest City OK 73110

BOWLES, HARGROVE, JR., business exec.; b. Monroe, N.C., Nov. 16, 1919; s. Hargrove and Kelly (Moneyhun) B.; student U. N.C., 1941; m. Jessamine Woodward Boyce, June 28, 1941; children—Hargrove III, Erskine Boyce, Mary Holland (Mrs. John Geil), Martha Thomas. Pres., Thomas and Howard Co., Greensboro, N.C., 1952-57; dir. First Union Nat. Bank N.C., Charlotte, Northside Devel. Co., Central Carolina Sports, Inc.; vice chmn., dir. Jewel Box Stores Corp., Greensboro, N.C.; formerly dir. Am. Hog Co.,

Bloomfield, Colo., 1st Mortgage Ins. Co., Greensboro. Dir., chmn. bd. dept. conservation and devel. State of N.C., Raleigh, 1961-65. Mem. N.C. Ho. of Reps., 1967-68, N.C. Senate, 1968-70; Democratic candidate for gov. N.C. Active Boy Scouts Am.; pres. Greensboro Heart Assn., 1956; bd. dirs. nat. council U.S.O.; chmn. bd. dirs. N.C. Heart Assn.; bd. dirs. Outward Bound Sch., Inc., N.E. Manpower Devel. Corp., N.C. Engring. Found., Greensboro Cerebral Palsy Sch.; trustee Pfeiffer Coll., Greensboro Coll.; bd. visitors Guilford Coll. Served with AUS, 1943-45. Mem. N.C. Partners of Alliance (chmn.), Beta Theta Pi. Methodist. Club: Country of N.C. (Pinehurst). Home: 2304 Princess Ann Greensboro NC 27408 Office: PO Box 549 Raleigh NC 27602 also Piedmont Bldg Greensboro NC 27401

BOWLES, W(ALTER) DONALD, univ. adminstr.; b. Seattle, Dec. 28, 1923; s. Walter Alexander and Minnie Ellen (Martin) B.; B.A., U. Wash., 1949; M.A., Columbia, 1952, certificate in Soviet Economy, 1952, Ph.D., 1958; m. Vincenza Pompea Galasso, Dec. 22, 1955; children—Ellen Maria, Walter Donald. Editor, Research Program on USSR, N.Y.C., 1953-55; fellow Air U., 1955-57; mem. faculty Am. U., Washington, 1957—, prof., chmn. dept. econs., 1964-65, prof. econs., dean Coll. Arts and Scis., 1965-69, prof. econs., v.p. acad. affairs, 1969—. Bd. dirs. Nat. Inst. Labor Edn., 1965-69, Assn. Colls. and Univs. for Internat.-Intercultural Studies. Served with AUS, 1943-46. Mem. Am., So. econ. assns., Assn. Study Soviet Type Econs., Assn. Advancement Slavic Studies, Assn. Comparative Econ. Systems, Am. Assn. U. Profs., Am. Assn. Higher Edn., Pi Gamma Mu, Omicron Delta Kappa, Omicron Delta Epsilon, Phi Kappa Phi. Home: 6017 Rossmore Dr Bethesda MD 20014 Office: Am U Massachusetts and Nebraska Sts NW Washington DC 20016

BOWLING, WILLIAM LOUIS, mfg. engr.; b. Wilmington, N.C., Jan. 13, 1929; s. Joseph Cary and Vivian Gertrude (Lewis) B.; student Wilmington Coll., 1949-50; B.S., Ind. Inst. Tech., 1953; m. Doris Elaine Wooten, Sept. 3, 1955; children—Kendra Lea, Kirk London, Glen Davis. With Western Electric Co., Burlington, N.C., 1953—, prodn. engr., 1953-58, liaison engr., 1958-60, project engr. various missile guidance systems, 1960-70, sr. engr. in configuration mgmt. engring. for safeguard anti-ballistic missile system, Greensboro, 1970—. Team capt. United Fund Drive, 1967, 68, 69; team capt. membership drive YMCA, 1968, 69, 70. Served with USAF, 1946-49. Registered profl. engr., N.C. Mem. Profl. Engrs. N.C. (chpt. sec. 1971), N.C. Profl. Engrs. in Industry (vice chmn. 1970-71), Burlington-Graham Engrs. Club, Sigma Phi Delta Alumni. Republican. Baptist. Moose. Home: 2807 Charlotte Lane Burlington NC 27215 Office: Western Electric Co Dept 59350 Guilford Center PO Box 20046 Greensboro NC 27420

BOWMAN, A. SMITH, distillery exec.; b. Lexington, Ky., Mar. 26, 1906; s. A. Smith and Katherine L. (DeLong) B.; A.B., Princeton, 1927; M.Arch., Harvard, 1931; m. Kate Hyde Scully, Nov. 17, 1945 (dec.); m. 2d, Mary Walker Lee, Nov. 25, 1960. Pvt. practice of architecture, 1931-35; exec. A. Smith Bowman Distillery, Sunset Hills, Va., 1935—, now chmn. bd., treas., dir.; dir. Colony Hotel, Jamaica; v.p. Internat. Fueling Co. Dir. Distilled Spirits Inst., 1955—, v.p., 1956-60, treas., 1960-71, chmn. exec. com., 1971—. Pres., mem. exec. com. Fairfax Race Assn.; treas., bd. govs. Fairfax Hunt. Mem. exec. bd. Nat. Capital area council Boy Scouts Am., 1953-70, v.p. exec. bd., 1956-66; bd. dirs. United Cerebral Palsy of No. Va., 1954-59, United Givers Fund, Nat. Capital Area, 1961-67. Pres., bd. dirs. Bowman Found., 1958—; v.p., bd. dirs. Garfield Hosp., 1956-62; treas., bd. trustees Fairfax Hosp. Assn., 1956-65; trustee D.C. Presbyn. Home, 1961-68; mem. corp. Washington Hosp. Center, 1958—; trustee St. James (Md.) Sch., London Sch., Bethesda, Md.; bd. regents James Monroe Law Office Museum and Meml. Library, Fredericksburg, Va. Served from lt. to lt. comdr. USNR, 1942-46. Recipient Silver Beaver award Boy Scouts Am., 1960. Mem. Hist. Soc. Fairfax County (bd. dirs., pres. 1964-68), Fairfax County C. of C. (dir. 1959-63), Soc. Cincinnati, S.R., Nat. Steeplechase and Hunt Assn., Am. Legion. Presbyn. (past deacon, past treas., past trustee). Clubs: Metropolitan, Army and Navy, Nat. Press, Princeton, Chevy Chase City Tavern (gov.), Admiral's (Washington); Princeton, Turf and Field (N.Y.C.); Coral Beach and Tennis (Bermuda); Farmington Country (Charlottesville, Va.); Rolling Rock (Ligonier, Pa.); Campus (grad. bd. govs.), Nassau (Princeton, N.J.); Springdale Hall (S.C.). Home: Sunset Hills VA 22070

BOWMAN, ALBERT HALL, historian, educator; b. Evanston, Ill., Jan. 16, 1921; s. Francis Brainerd and Gertrude (Bowman) B.; A.B., Trinity Coll., Hartford, Conn., 1947; M.A., Columbia, 1948, Ph.D., 1954; m. Joyce Adair Duschl, June 5, 1948; children—Victoria Joyce, Elizabeth Ann, Catherine Louise. Instr. history N.Y.U., 1948-49; fgn. affairs analyst U.S. Govt., 1951-57; prof. history, chmn. div. social scis. Tenn. Wesleyan Coll., Athens, 1957-62; prof. history, dir. libraries U. Chattanooga, 1962-69; prof. history U. Tenn. at Chattanooga, 1969—; vis. prof. history L.I.U., summer 1962; Fulbright prof. U. Louvain (Belgium), 1967-68. Served to 1st lt. AUS, 1942-46; mem. N.Y.N.G., 1947-50. Decorated Bronze Star, Purple Heart. Mem. Am., So., Chattanooga hist. assns., Orgn. Am. Historians, Soc. Historians Am. Fgn. Relations, Am. Assn. U. Profs., UN Assn. U.S. (pres. Chattanooga 1963-64), Alpha Delta Phi. Democrat. Episcopalian. Club: Torch. Contbr. profl. and other jours. Editor: The United States and Europe: A Colloquim, 1968. Home: 511 James Blvd Signal Mountain TN 37377 Office: Univ Tenn Chattanooga TN 37401

BOWMAN, DANIEL OLIVER, psychologist, educator; b. Holly Hill, S.C., Feb. 1, 1931; s. John Daniel and Pansy (Mizzell) B.; B.A. in Music, Furman U., 1951; M.Ed., U. S.C., 1952; Ph.D., 1963. Tchr. English and French, Summerville (S.C.) High Sch., 1952-53; sr. guidance counselor, chmn. dept. English, Boys High Sch., Anderson, S.C., 1955-61; instr. psychology U. Ga., 1961-63; asso. prof. psychology, counselor Corps of Cadets, The Citadel, Charleston, S.C., 1963-69, prof. psychology, dir. grad. studies, 1969—. Served with AUS, 1953-55. Mem. Am. Psychol. Assn., Am. Acad. Polit. and Social Sci., Am. Assn. U. Profs., Psi Chi, Phi Delta Kappa, Kappa Delta Pi, Phi Mu Alpha, Phi Kappa Phi. Home: 135 Beaufain St Charleston SC 29401

BOWMAN, EDMUND DELONG, distillery exec.; b. Lexington, Ky., Sept. 13, 1911; s. Abram Smith and Katherine Lyttleton (DeLong) B.; B.A., Princeton, 1934; m. Helen Caldwell Potts, Feb. 17, 1942; children—Katherine (Mrs. W. Frederic Burton, Jr.), Nena (Mrs. John B. Adams, Jr.). Gen. mgr. Sunset Hills (Va.) Farm, 1930-62; gen. mgr. A. Smith Bowman Distillery, Sunset Hills, 1935-49, v.p., 1949-52, pres., 1952—. Trustee Fauquier Hosp., Warrenton, Va., Oatlands, Nat. Trust for Historic Preservation; trustee, v.p. Bowman Found., Inc. Mem. Va. Mfrs. Assn. (dir. 1964-67, 72—). Clubs: Society of Cincinnati (Washington); Chevy Chase, Nat. Lawyers (Chevy Chase, Md.); Commonwealth, Downtown (Richmond, Va.); Fauquier (Warrenton, Va.); Nassau; Princeton (N.Y.C.); Orange County Hunt, Fairfax Hunt, Thoroughbred Am., Press of Va.; Evergreen Country (Haymarket, Va.). Home: Belvoir Farm The Plains VA 22171 Office: A Smith Bowman Distillery Sunset Hills VA 22070

BOWMAN, FOREST JACKSON, state bar exec.; b. Harrisonburg, Va., Apr. 15, 1938; s. Forest Wells and Gladys Mae (Keplinger) B.; B.S. in Bus. Adminstrn., W.Va. U., 1960, LL.B., 1963; m. Myla Francis Woodford, Aug. 27, 1961; children—Gregory Wells, Matthew Thomas. Admitted to W.Va. bar, mem. firm Stone, Bowles, Kauffelt & McDavid, Charleston, W.Va., 1968-69; exec. sec. W.Va. Workmen's Compensation Fund, Charleston, 1969-71; exec. dir. W.Va. State Bar, 1971—. Served with Judge Adv. Gen.'s Corps, AUS, 1963-67. Mem. Phi Kappa Psi. Presbyn. (elder). Author weekly hist. column W.Va. Hillbilly. Contbr. articles to Civil War Times, Illustrated. Home: 1125 Emerald Rd Charleston WV 25314 Office: E-404 State Capitol Charleston WV 25305

BOWMAN, JAMES PENDLETON, social worker; b. Staunton, Va., Oct. 29, 1931; s. Otto Pendleton and Sallie (Thacker) B.; B.A., U. Tenn., 1954; M.S.W., Richmond Profl. Inst., 1960; m. Barbara Jean Reed, Dec. 3, 1956 children—David Pendleton, Diane Pendleton. Chief probation officer Juvenile Ct., City of Staunton, 1957-58; psychiat. social worker U.Va., Charlottesville, 1960-61; cons. regional office Bur. Juvenile Probation and Detention, Staunton, 1961-69; social worker State of Va. Faculty, Bridgewater (Va.) Coll.; pyschotherapist Relationship Therapy Center, Fredericksburg, Va. Chmn. Augusta-Staunton chpt. Planned Parenthood Assn., 1971—. Bd. dirs. Am. Cancer Soc., 1963-64, Community Welfare League, 1969-71. Served to 1st lt. USAF, 1954-56. Presbyn. Home: 7 Woodland Dr Staunton VA 24401 Office: PO Box 350 Verona VA 24482

BOWMAN, JOAN, acting dir. Miss. Council on Human Relations. Address: 1110 Prose Av Jackson MS 39204*

BOWMAN, JOHN FRANCIS, educator; b. Saranac Lake, N.Y., Oct. 24, 1916; s. William Conroy and Mary Belle (Durgan) B.; student St. Lawrence U., 1934-37; D.M.D., Tufts U., 1941, certificate oral prosthetics, 1954; certificate prosthetic dentistry U.S. Navy Dental Sch., 1947; m. Elinore May Whitney, Sept. 25, 1941; children—Dale Anne (Mrs. Frank Laumer), Rhoda (Mrs. Douglas Sheppard Lynn), Penelope Jean (Mrs. Edward Kosheba), Patricia Jane. Asso. prof. Sch. Dental Medicine, U. Pitts., 1963-69; prof. Coll. Dentistry, U. Fla. at Gainesville, 1969—, chmn. div. complete denture prosthodontics, 1969—. Cons. central office VA, various VA Hosps., U.S. Navy Hosp. Diplomate Am. Bd. Prosthodontics. Fellow Am. Coll. Prosthodontists, Am. Coll. Dentists, Internat. Coll. Dentists; mem. Am. Prosthodontic Soc., Am. Assn. U. Profs., Omicron Kappa Upsilon. Author: (with others) Removable Partial Prosthodontics Clinical Procedures and Technology, 1965. Home: 4510 NW 13th Av Gainesville FL 32601

BOWMAN, LINDEN ALLEN, aerospace components mfr.; b. Timberville, Va., Mar. 22, 1932; s. Vernon Erasmus and Cora Ellen (Fansler) B.; student Berea Coll., 1949-50; B.S., Va. Poly. Inst., 1958; m. Nancy Sue Linkous, Mar. 20, 1955; children—Steve Allan, Barry Marvin. With Poly-Sci. div. Litton Industries, Inc., Blacksburg, Va., 1956—, div. pres., 1970—; dir. North br. Nat. Bank of Blacksburg. Bd. dirs. Blacksburg United Fund, Showalter Meml. Hosp. Served with USNR, 1950-54. Mem. Am. Mgmt. Assn., Va. Mfrs. Assn. (taxation com.), U.S., Va. chambers commerce. Republican. Lutheran. Moose. Home: 1412 Palmer Dr Blacksburg VA 24060 Office: 1213 N Main St Blacksburg VA 24060

BOWMAN, RALPH JEROME, city ofcl.; b. Valeda, Kan., Sept. 27, 1925; s. Glenn T. and Vida (Neidigh) B.; B.S. in Bus., U. Kan., 1950; m. Retha J. Burns, Aug. 14, 1953. Cost accountant Carl Bjorkman, C.P.A., Topeka, 1951-52, C. Robert Belt, C.P.A., Coffeyville, Kan., 1952-54: city office mgr., Ponca City, Okla., 1954-59, city treas., 1959—. Served with USNR, 1943-46. C.P.A., Okla. Mem. Am. Inst. C.P.A.'s, Okla. Soc. C.P.A.'s, Am. Legion. Home: 613 E Emporia Av Ponca City OK 74601 Office: 516 E Grand Av Ponca City OK 74601

BOWMAN, ROBERT LEE, dentist; b. Gainesville, Fla., July 11, 1939; s. Robert Lee and Annie Laurie (Arnold) B.; student Emory U., 1957, U. Fla., 1958-61; D.D.S., Loyola U., New Orleans, 1965; m. Elizabeth Ann Taylor, June 3, 1961; children—Natalie Ann, Robert Taylor. Pvt. practice dentistry, Gainesville, Fla., 1967—. Bd. dirs. United Fund. Served to capt. Dental Corps, AUS, 1965-67. La. State Bd. Health grantee, 1966. Mem. Am., Fla., Alachua County dental assns., Am. Small Bus. Fedn., Jr. C. of C., C. of C., Xi Psi Phi, Kappa Alpha, (alumni adviser 1972—). Presbyn. (asst. deacon 1971—). Home: 3321 NW 18th Av Gainesville FL 32601 Office: 112 NE 2d Av Gainesville FL 32601

BOWMER, JIM DEWITT, lawyer; b. Temple, Tex., May 4, 1919; s. DeWitt and Linnie B. (Morgan) B.; A.A., Temple Jr. Coll. (Tex.), 1938; B.A. cum laude, Baylor U., 1940, LL.B. cum laude, 1942;; m. Daurice Spoonts, Mar. 26, 1961; children—Bonnie Nell (Mrs. David Dan Simmonds), Mary Helen. Admitted to Tex. bar, 1942; county atty. Bell County, Tex., 1946-47; lectr. law Baylor U. Law Sch., 1949-50, 56-57; mem. firm Bowmer, Courtney & Burleson, 1964—. Bd. dirs. Nat. Park Found., 1968-69. Served with AUS, 1942-46. Mem. Am. Law Inst., Am. Judicature Soc., Tex. Assn. Def. Counsel, Temple C. of C. (past pres.), Baylor Law Alumni Assn. (past pres.), Bell-Lampasas-Mills Counties Bar Assn. (past pres.), State Bar Tex. (dir. 1968-71, chmn. bd. 1970-71, pres.-elect 1971), Phi Alpha Delta. Democrat. Baptist. Mason (K.T.), K.P. (past grand chancellor Tex.), Kiwanian. Contbr. articles to profl. jours. Home: 618 N 9th St Temple TX 76502 Office: First Nat Bank Bldg Temple TX 76502

BOWRON, RICHARD ANDERSON, utilities exec.; b. Birmingham, Ala., Jan. 18, 1924; s. James Edgar and Mary (Anderson) B.; B.S., U. Ala., 1943; M.B.A., U. Pa., 1948; m. Ruth Womelsdorf Matthews, Dec. 29, 1961; children—Richard Anderson, Mary Anderson, Lee Matthews. With Ala. Power Co., Birmingham, 1948—, asst. sec., 1962, sec., 1963—. Served to 1st lt. AUS, 1943-46, U.S. Army, 1950-52. Mem. Newcomen Soc. N.Am., Ala. Hist. Assn., Phi Delta Theta. Presbyn. Clubs: Exchange, Mountain Brook. Home: 3629 Springhill Rd Birmingham AL 35223 Office: Ala Power Co Birmingham AL 35202

BOX, SAMUEL EUGENE, marine splty. co. exec.; b. Quitman, Miss., July 30, 1917; s. Samuel Eugene and Mattie Omega (Neal) B.; student E. Central Jr. Coll., 1936-37; m. Mary Elizabeth Hughes, Nov. 16, 1946; children—Diana Christine (Mrs. James Lawrence Waters), Shannon Hughes, Simeon Alex, Samuel Lucien. Roughneck, driller Arnold Drilling & Exploration Co., Houston, 1937-40; driller, Failing Exploration Co., Kingsville, Tex., 1942; 3d and 2d engr. Am. Hawaiian S.S., 1946-47; 1st engr. W. R. Grace S.S. Co., N.Y.C., 1947-48; supt. shipping and warehouse Marine Splty. Co., Mobile, Ala., 1948—, v.p., 1971—. Cons. engr. Galanos Ship Supply Co., Mobile, Ala., 1950-72. Councilman, City of Fairhope, Ala., 1968-72, mayor pro tem, 1971-72; mem. Planning and Zoning Bd., City of Fairhope, Ala., 1968-72; adminstrv. mem. Mobile-Baldwin-Escambia counties So. Regional Planning Bd., 1969-72. Served with U.S. Maritime Service, 1942-46. Methodist (chmn. finance 1966-67, 69-71). Mason. Home: 356 N Summit St Fairhope AL 36532 Office: 111 Texas St Mobile AL 36601

BOYAN, CHARLES PAUL, physician, educator; b. Sofia, Bulgaria, 1916; M.D., U. Sofia, 1940. Intern, Univ. Hosp., Sofia, 1940-41; sr. intern Royal Victoria Hosp., Montreal, Que., Can., 1948-49; resident Mass. Meml. Hosp., Boston, 1949-50, N.Y. Hosp., N.Y.C., 1954; fellow Meml. Sloan-Kettering Cancer Center, N.Y.C., 1950-51, former attending anesthesiologist; former asso. Sloan-Kettering Inst. Cancer Research, N.Y.C.; former asso. prof. surgery (anesthesiology) Cornell U. Med. Sch., N.Y.C.; now prof., chmn. dept. anesthesiology Med. Coll. Va., Richmond. Diplomate Am. Bd. Anesthesiology. Mem. A.M.A., Am. Soc. Anesthesiology, Internat. Anesthesia Research Soc. Office: 1200 E Broad St Richmond VA 23219*

BOYCE, EDWARD WAYNE, JR., lawyer; b.Tuckerman, Ark., June 20, 1926; s. Edward Wayne and Sylla (Harvey) B.; student The Citadel, 1943-44; A.B., U. Ark., 1950, LL.B., 1951; m. Phyllis Elayne Williams, Oct. 29, 1951; children—Martha Elayne, Edward Wayne III. Admitted to Ark. bar, 1951; asso. firm Pickens & Pickens, 1951-54; practiced law, 1954-59; mem. firm Pickens, Boyce & McLarty, and predecessor, Newport, Ark., 1959—. Dep. pros. atty., 1951-56, pros. atty., 3d Jud. Circuit, 1957-60. Mem. Ark. Penitentiary Study Commn. Chmn., Jackson County chpt. Nat. Found., 1965-69. Served with 31st Inf. Div., AUS, 1944-47. Mem. Am. (bd. gen. practice sect.), Ark. (exec. com. 1968-71), Jackson County (pres. 1954, 62), 8th Chancery bar assns., Ark. Legal Edn. Council, Am. Law Inst., American Judicature Society, Phi Alpha Theta, Phi Delta Theta. Episcopalian. Home: 7 Pickens St Newport AR 72112 Office: 209 Walnut St Newport AR 72112

BOYCE, ERNEST F., retail exec.; b. Somerville, Mass., 1916; grad. Boston U., 1940; post-grad. Harvard Grad. Sch. Bus. Adminstrn., 1947. Pres., Colonial stores, Inc., East Point, Ga. Home: 5510 Long Island Dr NW Atlanta GA 30327 Office: 2251 N Sylvan Rd East Point GA 30044

BOYCE, MARSHALL HERMAN, city ofcl.; b. Chesapeake, Va., Nov. 24, 1906; s. William Jesse and Nancy (Dail) B.; student pub. schs.; m. Louise G.E. Plummer, Dec. 14, 1927 children—Jane Ray (Mrs. Thomas Gerald Hamer), Dorothy Fay (Mrs. Ray A. Henley). With Virginian Ry. Co., Norfolk, Va., 1925-59; real estate salesman Va. Realty Co., Norfolk, 1960-61; with South Norfolk Redevel. and Housing Authority of Chesapeake, 1961—, exec. dir., 1967—. Mem. Nat. Assn. Redevel. and Housing Ofcls., Va. Assn. Housing and Redevel. Authorities, Notaries Pub. Assn. (charter), Chesapeake C. of C. Home: 2305 Rodgers St Chesapeake VA 23324 Office: 10 Admiral's Rd Chesapeake VA 23324

BOYD, ANN LOUISE STRIPLING, realtor; b. Bonaire, Ga., Apr. 1, 1917; d. John Robert and Estelle (Greene) Stripling; student Piedmont Coll., 1936-40, U. Miami, 1961; student Florida State University, 1970; m. Joseph A. Boyd, Jr., June 6, 1938; children—Joanne, Betty Jean, Joseph, James, Jane. Asst. city clk., Hialeah, Fla., 1945-46; realtor Hialeah, 1947—. Sec., bd. dirs. Hialeah-Miami Springs YMCA, 1958-59, chmn. Mem. Hialeah-Miami Springs Bd. Realtors (dir., treas., past pres.), Fla. Assn. Realtors (dist. v.p. 1967), Hialeah-Miami Springs C. of C. (treas., dir., v.p.), Am. Legion Aux. (past pres., dist. pres.), Dade County Women's Democratic Club. Clubs: Pilot, 8 and 40 (pres. Fla. Chapeau), Bus. and Profl. Women's (past pres., dist. sec.), Womens (Tallahassee). Home: 2210 Monaghan Dr Tallahasse FL 32301 Office: 375 E 1st Av Hialeah FL 33010

BOYD, CLARENCE ELMO, surgeon; b. Leesville, La., Nov. 2, 1911; s. Isaac C. and Ada Lee (Stakes) B.; B.A., U. Tex., 1933, M.D., 1935; m. Emma Sims, Aug. 13, 1937; children—Charles E., Marjorie E., Frances A., James E. Intern, Charity Hosp., New Orleans, 1935-36; resident North La. San. (now Doctors Hosp.), Shreveport, La., 1936-37; gen. practice medicine, Shreveport, 1937-42, specializing in gen. surgery, 1942—; founder, sr. partner C.E. Boyd Clinic, Shreveport, 1942—; vis. surgeon Doctors Hosp., Shreveport, 1937—; jr. vis. surgeon Charity Hosp. (now Confederate Meml. Hosp.), 1937-42; sr. vis. surgeon Confederate Meml. Hosp., Shreveport, 1944—; clin. asst. prof. surgery La. State U. Postgrad. Sch. Medicine, 1957-67, La. State U. Sch. of Medicine, Shreveport, 1967—; teaching faculty Am. Bd. Abdominal Surgeons, 1967; chief surgeon La. and Ark. Ry. Co. Employees' Hosp. Assn. to 1967. Founding dir. Shreveport Bank & Trust Co., 1954—, chmn. investment com., 1954—, chmn. bd. dirs., 1961—. Sponsors com. Shreveport United Fund, 1962-66. Dir. Vols. Am., 1950-58, pres. bd., 1955-57; trustee Pub. Affairs Rev. Council, Shreveport, 1959—; chmn. exec. com., chmn. bd. dirs. Doctors Hosp. and Research Found., Shreveport, 1959—. Fellow A.C.S., Internat. Coll. Surgs., Southwestern Surg. Congress, Am. Soc. Abdominal Surgeons (chmn. com. preparing audio-visual postgrad. program on diseases of gall bladder); mem. A.M.A. (chmn. surg. sect. 1967-68, alternate del. sect. council on surgery 1972—, mem. surg. council 1972—), La. (chmn. pub. policy and legislative com. 1954-57, 4th dist. councilor 1959-66, del. 1945-59, v.p. 1967-68), Shreveport (pres. 1956) med. socs., Am. Cancer Soc. (dir. Caddo br. 1952-58), Surg. Assn. La., So. Med. Assn. (asso. Councilor), Assn. Abdominal Surgeons (founding mem.; pres.), Am. Assn. Physicians and Surgeons (del., mem. chmn., pres. La. chpt. 1972). Rotarian (pres. Cedar Grove, Shreveport, 1940-41, founder and chmn. com. of student loan fund), Mason (32 deg., Shriner). Contbr. articles to profl. jours. Research on operative cholangiography, local hernioplasty with immediate ambulation; producer color film on cholangiogram, 1954, 60. Home: 401 Delaware St Shreveport LA 71106 Office: 6815 Southern Av Shreveport LA 71106

BOYD, CLINTON ARGOLAS, pump co. exec.; b. Arpelar, Okla., May 11, 1925; s. Dee Alan and Emma (Cobbs) B.; B.S., Okla. State U., 1952; m. Lillian Rosetta Turnbow, Jan. 31, 1946; children—Dan Alan, Traci. Design engr. Reda Pump Co., Bartlesville, Okla., 1952-56; chief elec. engr. Sta-Rite Products, Delavan, Wis., 1956-60; v.p., asst. gen. mgr. Byron Jackson Pump Co., Tulsa, 1966—. Mem. Clean Air Rev. Bd., 1968—. Bd. dirs. YMCA. Served with USNR, 1943-45. Mem. Am. Inst. E.E., Okla. Soc. Profl. Engrs., Tulsa C. of C. Patentee in field. Home: 6073 E 56th St Tulsa OK 74135 Office: PO Box 486 Tulsa OK 74135

BOYD, CROSBY NOYES, newspaper exec.; b. Phila., Jan. 2, 1903; s. George W. and Miranda C. (Noyes) B.; grad. St. George's Sch., Newport, R.I., 1920; A.B., Princeton, 1924; m. Elizabeth Utz, Jan. 2, 1932; children—Elizabeth Noyes, Crosby Noyes, Susan Ann. Asst. advt. mgr. Evening Star Newspaper Co., Washington, 1938-44, asst. bus. mgr., 1944-49, also asst. sec.-treas., 1941-49, bus. mgr., treas., 1949-63, exec. v.p., 1955-63, pres., 1963-68, chmn. bd., 1968—, also dir.; dir. Evening Star Broadcasting Co., Washington Star Communications, Inc., Nat. Bank of Washington. Bd. dirs. Bur. Advt. Served to capt. USAAF, 1942-45. Clubs: Metropolitan, Chevy Chase (Washington); Court (Princeton, N.J.). Home: 2801 New Mexico Av NW Washington DC 20007 Office: 225 Virginia Av SE Washington DC 20003

BOYD, CURTIS WAYNE, physician; b. nr. Athens, Tex., Mar. 25, 1937; s. Hubert Lee and Ruth (Trammell) B.; B.S. (Danforth scholar), Tex. A. and M. U., 1959; M.D. (Merck scholar) U. Tex. Southwestern Med. Sch., 1963; m. LaMerle Matthews, Jan. 25, 1959;

children—Curtis Wayne, Jr., Lori Deanne, Kyle Matthew. Intern, John Peter Smith Hosp., Fort Worth, 1963-64; pvt. practice medicine, specializing in family practice, Park Highland Clinic, Athens, Tex., 1964-71, Dallas, 1971—; mem. staff Henderson County Meml. Hosp., Athens. Health officer Henderson County, Athens, Tex., 1964-70. Bd. trustees Athens Ind. Sch. Dist., 1967-70, sec., treas., 1969-70. Bd. dirs. Planned Parenthood, 1970. Mem. Am. Civil Liberties Union, Jr. C. of C., Tex. Med. Assn., Henderson County Med. Soc., Alpha Omega Alpha, Phi Rho Sigma, Phi Kappa Phi. Democrat. Unitarian-Universalist (pres. fellowship 1970-71). Rotarian. Club: Texas A. and M. (pres. 1966-67) (Athens). Home: 9899 Brockbank St Dallas TX 75220 Office: 3614 Fairmount St Dallas TX 75219

BOYD, DANIEL FRANKLIN, mfg. co. exec.; b. Farrell, Miss., Aug. 29, 1922; s. William Franklin and Lola (McDonald) B.; student Johns Hopkins U., 1941-42, Aero Indsl. Tech. Inst., 1943; m. Mary Virginia DuBose, Mar. 5, 1944; children—Daniel Franklin II, Sarah DuBose. Salesman Tuckers Sporting Goods, Sarasota, Fla., 1945-50; sales mgr. So. Mill Creek Products, Tampa, Fla., 1950-53; nat. sales mgr. Silver Creek (N.Y.) Precision, 1953-55, Curtis Automotive Devices, Bedford, Ind., 1955-56, Manatee Corp., Tampa, Fla., 1956-59; v.p. sales Lowndes Engring., Valdosta, Ga., 1960—. Served USAAF, World War II. Mem. Fla. Entomol. Soc., Am. (chmn. coml. com., 1964, 1966), Fla. (chmn. comml. dept. 1963-66) mosquito control assns. Baptist (deacon 1961-67, asst. supt. Sunday sch., 1962-65). Mason (Shriner). Patentee in field. Research thermal aerosol equipment; designed electronic liquid formulating equipment, insecticide dispersant. Home: 203 Avondale Av Temple Terrace FL 33617 Office: 125 Blanchard St Valdosta GA 31601

BOYD, EARL NEAL, univ. dean; b. Trinity, Ky., Dec. 20, 1922; s. Samuel Brady and Gladys (Nash) B.; B.S., Eastern Ky. State U., 1948; M.S., U. Ky., 1949; Ph.D., Ohio State U., 1952; m. Jeanne Ruark, Sept. 1, 1948; 1 son, Michael Neal. Asst. prof. U. Ky., 1952-55; research chemist Swift & Co., Chgo., 1955-57; research adminstr. U.S. Dept. Agr., Washington, 1957-68; head dept. food sci. and tech. Va. Poly. Inst. and State U., Blacksburg, Va., 1968-70, asst. dean, dir. div. basic scis., 1970—. Served with AUS, 1942-46. Mem. Am. Dairy Sci. Assn. (dir. 1971-72), Inst. Food Technologists, Sigma Xi, Phi Lambda Upsilon, Phi Tau Sigma, Gamma Sigma Delta. Presbyn. (deacon 1970-73). Home: 813 McBryde Dr Blacksburg VA 24060

BOYD, HENRY ESTILL, JR., airport mgmt. exec.; b. Portsmouth, Va., May 3, 1912; s. Henry Estill and Ethel (Bryant) B.; student Presbyn. Jr. Coll., 1932-34, Norfolk Coll. Bus. Adminstrn., 1934-36; m. Jean Marie Meharry, Sept. 5, 1948; children—Janet Marie, Nancy Jean. Mgr., New Hanover County Airport, Wilmington, N.C., 1946-52; commr. aviation Schenectady County (N.Y.) Bd. Suprs., 1952-60; mgr. Raleigh(N.C.)-Durham Airport, 1960—. Commr. Boy Scouts Am., Wilmington, N.C., 1934-35. Served with USNR, 1944-46. Mem. Southeastern Airport Mgrs. Assn. (founder 1947, 2d pres. 1949), Am. Assn. Airport Execs. (dir.), N.C. Soc. Profl. Engrs., Am. Soc. Plant Engrs. Mason. Clubs: Kiwanis, Traffic. Home: 737 Currituck Dr Raleigh NC 27609 Office: Raleigh-Durham Airport Raleigh NC 27602

BOYD, HOWARD, gas co. exec.; b. Woodside, Md., 1909; A.B., Georgetown U., 1932, J.D., 1935. Chmn. bd., chief exec. officer El Paso Natural Gas Co., Houston; chmn. Geonuclear Nobel-Paso, S.A.; dir. Beaunit Corp., Phillips Pacific Chem. Co., El Paso Products Co., Greyhound Corp., Armour and Co., Tex. Commerce Bank N.Am., Houston. Mem. Nat. Petroleum Council, Am. Gas Assn., Ind. Natural Gas Assn. Am. (dir.). Home: 6042 Crab Orchard Houston TX 77027 Office: 2727 Allen Pkwy Houston TX 77019

BOYD, JAMES EMORY, coll. pres.; b. Tignall, Ga., July 18, 1906; s. Emory Fortson and Rosa Lee (Wright) B.; A.B., U. Ga., 1927; M.A., Duke U. (fellow), 1928; Ph.D. (Loomis fellow), Yale, 1933; m. Elizabeth Reynolds Cobb, June 2, 1934; children—Betty Cobb, James Fortson. Instr. physics U. Ga., 1928-30; head math. and sci. dept. West Ga. Coll., 1933-35; asst. prof. physics Ga. Inst. Tech., 1935-37, asso. prof., 1937-42, prof. physics, 1946—, dir. microwave propagation and radar research projects Engring. Expt. Sta., 1946-50, head physics div., 1950-55, dir. research projects in radar, nuclear physics and microwave spectroscopy, asst. dir. (research), 1954-55, asso. sta. dir., 1955-57, dir., 1957-61; pres. West Ga. Coll., Carrollton, 1961—. Dir. Peoples Bank of Carrollton. Chmn. Carrollton Payroll Devel. Authority, 1965—; mem. Nuclear Adv. Commn., 1956—, Ga. Sci. and Tech. Commn., 1964—; dir. Sci. Atlanta, Inc., 1952—; trustee Ga. Tech. Research Inst., 1957—. Served from lt. to comdr. USNR, 1942-46, radar research and devel. Bur. Ordnance, Navy Dept., 1942-45, electronics div. Office Chief of Naval Operations, 1945-46; comdg. officer Naval Res. Research Co. 6-1, Atlanta, 1949-57; capt. USNR, 1957—. Mem. I.R.E. (sr.), Am. Phys. Soc., Phi Beta Kappa, Omicron Delta Kappa (hon.), Sigma Xi, Phi Kappa Phi, Gamma Alpha. Episcopalian (dep. gen. conv. 1964, 67). Clubs: Rotary, Sunset Hills. Author sci. articles. Address: West Ga College Carrollton GA 30117

BOYD, JOSEPH ARTHUR, JR., justice Fla. Supreme Ct.; b. Hoschton, Ga., Nov. 16, 1916; s. Joseph Arthur and Esther (Puckett) B.; grad. Piedmont Coll., LL.D., 1963; J.D., U. Miami, 1948; m. Ann Stripling, June 6, 1938 children—Joanne (Mrs. Robert Goldman), Betty Jean (Mrs. David Jala), Joseph, James, Jane. City atty., Hialeah, Fla., 1951-58; commr. Dade County, 1958-68, vice mayor, 1967; chmn. Dade County Commn., 1963; dir. Fla. Assn. County Commrs., 1964-68; justice Fla. Supreme Ct., Tallahassee, 1969—. Served with USMCR, 1943-46; PTO. Decorated Japanese Occupation medal with one star; recipient Top Hat award for advancing status of women U.S. Bus. and Profl. Women's Clubs, 1967. Mem. Am. Fla., Dade County, Hialeah-Miami Springs (pres. 1955) bar assns., Hialeah-Miami Springs C. of C. (pres. 1956), Am. Legion (state comdr. 1953), V.F.W., Pi Kappa Psi, Phi Alpha Delta. Baptist. Mason (Shriner), Lion, Elk, Moose. Home: 2210 Monaghan Dr Tallahassee FL 32302 Office: Supreme Ct Bldg Tallahassee FL 32304

BOYD, LENORE FRANCIS ANGLIN, psychologist; b. Tahoka, Tex., Dec. 3, 1923; d. Walter S. and Fannie (Teague) Anglin; B.A. with honors, Tex. Technol. Coll., 1948; postgrad. Los Angeles State Coll., spring 1951; M.A., N.E. Mo. State Tchrs. Coll., 1955; postgrad. U. Tex., summer 1960, 64-65, Tex. A. and M. U., 1972; m. John H. Boyd, Aug. 18, 1944 (div. Feb. 1970); children—John H. III, Alan R., J. Robin. Tchr. sci. and math. pub. schs., Brownfield, Tex., 1942-43, Uvalde, Tex., 1943-44, Louise, Tex., 1946, 55-57, Wolforth, Tex., 1946-48, Galveston, Tex., 1948-49, Flomot, Tex., 1949-50, Kirksville, Mo., 1951-55; coop. county unit counselor Wharton County Schs., Louise, East Bernard, Hungerford, Tex., 1957-70; spl. edn. counselor, psychologist Lamar Consol. Ind. Sch. Dist., Rosenberg, Tex., 1970—; counselor East Bernard, Tex., 1965-66. Mem. Am., Tex. personnel and guidance assns., Nat. Vocational Guidance Assn., Am. Sch. Counselors Assn. (life), N.E.A. (life), Bus. and Profl. Women's Club (pres. Louise 1969-70), Tex. Tchrs. Assn. (pres. Wharton County 1963-64), Nat. Assn. Sch. Psychologists; Tex. Assn. Osteo. Physicians and Surgeons Aux. (pres. dist. 9, 1957-58, state treas. 1959-61, pres. 1962-63), Tex. Psychol. Assn. Episcopalian. Home: 107 2111 Thompson Rd Richmond TX 77469 Office: Adminstrn Bldg Lamar Consol Ind Sch Dist Rosenberg TX 77471

BOYD, ROBERT FRIEND, lawyer; b. Richmond, Va., May 11, 1927; s. Oscar L. and Ruby (Friend) B.; A.B., Coll. William and Mary, 1950, J.D., 1952; m. Sara Grace Miller, Sept. 20, 1952; children—Robert Friend, David Miller, Mary Elizabeth, James Matheson. Admitted to Va. bar, 1952; practiced in Norfolk, 1955—; sr. partner firm Boyd, Davis & Payne, 1957—; commr. Chancery for Circuit Ct. (Norfolk), Corp. Ct. (Chesapeake, Va.), 1967—. Dir., Santee Portland Cement Corp., Cementon, S.C., Holly Hill Lumber Co. (N.C.); treas., dir. Stewart Sandwiches, Inc. (Va.). Bd. dirs. Union Mission, Am. Heart Assn., Fraternal Order Police Assns.; mem. adv. com. Norfolk city council, 1966-71. Mem. Democratic Exec. Com. of Norfolk, 1965-70. Trustee and mem. exec. com. Va. Wesleyan Coll.; trustee, v.p. Randolph-Macon Acad.; bd. dirs. Coll. William and Mary Law Sch., Norfolk Municipal Hosp., Tidewater Rehab. Inst., Tidewater Health Found., Va. Cultural Found. Served to capt. USMC, 1952-54. Named Outstanding Young Man of City, Norfolk Jr. C. of C., 1959. Mem. Va. Trial Lawyers Assn. (v.p.), Tau Kappa Alpha. (chmn. ofcl. bd.). Mason (Shriner), Kiwanian (bd. dirs., pres. Norfolk, Va.). Clubs: Harbor, Norfolk Yacht and Country. Home: 912 Hanover Av Norfolk VA 23508 Office: Va Nat Bank Bldg Norfolk VA 23510

BOYD, WILLIAM HARDIN, lawyer; b. Cookeville, Tenn., Jan. 30, 1915; s. Ernest Houston and Mattie (Ragland) B.; LL.B., Cumberland U., 1939; certificate in real estate U. Tenn., 1953, certificate in law and appraisal, 1958; m. Alberta Johnson, Aug. 23, 1958. Admitted to Tenn. bar, 1939, Supreme Ct. bar, 1960; practiced in Cookeville, 1939-42; trial atty. VA, Nashville, 1946-67, asst. chief atty., 1967—. Served to 1st lt. AUS, 1942-46. Mem. Am. (mem. com. mortgage law and practice), Fed. (vets. laws, govt. loans and finance coms., pres. Nashville chpt. 1968), Tenn. bar assns., Am. Judicature Soc., Am., Legion, V.F.W., Am. Vets. World War II, Nat. Fedn. Fed. Employees. Democrat. Presbyn. Elk. Home: 5813 Vine Ridge Dr Nashville TN 37205 Office: US Court House 801 Broadway Nashville TN 37202

BOYDSTUN, JACKSON BENJAMIN, architect; b. Natchitoches, La., Feb. 5, 1908; s. Benjamin Kendall and Eunice Augusta (Hargis) B.; grad. high sch.; m. Bernice Erline Hill, Apr. 19, 1930; children—Nelwyn (Mrs. Dan W. Poole, Jr.), Betty Sue (Mrs. Stuart Carpenter), Jackson Benjamin, David H. Constrn. supervising engr. constrn. firms, 1936-46; archtl. asso. Barron, Hienberg & Brocato, architects, Alexandria, La., 1947-50; self-employed as architect, Natchitoches, La., 1960—; dir., chmn. bd. J. B. Boydstun & Assos., Inc. Mem. Constrn. Legislative Council La., 1970-72. Served with AUS, World War II. Mem. A.I.A., Am. Legion (comdr. 1945-46), La. Architects Assn. Democrat. Methodist. Mason (Shriner). Prin. archtl. works include Marthaville Phys. Edn. and Auditorium, St. Matthew High Sch., Elementary Sch. Library, Allen High Sch. Classroom Bldg., Goldonna High Sch. Auditorium and Classroom Bldg., Robeline Phys. Edn. and Classroom Bldg. Home and office: 410 Stephens Av Natchitoches LA 71457

BOYER, JAMES WILLIAM, assn. exec.; b. Washington, Jan. 4, 1921; s. Rudy Wendell and Minnie (Currier) B.; B.S., U. Md., 1955; m. Nannie Louise Sharp, Jan. 1, 1943; children—James Lee, Carolyn Sue (Mrs. Lawrence Lee Cook). With advt. dept. Hecht Co., Washington, 1939-40; with Capital Airlines, Washington, 1940-51; exec. sec. operations council Am. Trucking Assn., Washington, 1955-64; transp. analyst U.S. C. of C., Washington, 1964-65; mng. dir. Contract Carrier Conf., Washington, 1965—. Chmn. pub. service com. Seabrook Acres-Greenwood Forest Civic Assn., 1957-65. Served with USNR, 1942-45. Mem. Washington Soc. Assn. Execs., Nat. Assn. Execs. Club, Potomac River Sailing Assn., Sigma Phi Epsilon. Democrat. Methodist. Home: 11204 Evans Trail Beltsville MD 20705 Office: 1616 P St Washington DC 20036

BOYERS, ROBERT CYRUS, dentist, army officer; b. Morgantown, W.Va., Nov. 15, 1924; s. Fred Earl and Imogene Mary (Harkness) B.; student Duke, 1944-45, W.Va. U., 1947-48; D.D.S., U. Pitts., 1952; M.S., Georgetown U., 1961; m. Nina Helen Ullery, July 26, 1947; children—Barbara (Mrs. Ralph Young), Laura (Mrs. Larry Burt), Janet (Mrs. James Crum), Beverly, Nanette. Commd. 1st lt., Dental Corps, U.S. Army, 1954, advanced through grades to col., 1971; chief dept. pathology Walter Reed Army Inst. Research, 1961; cons. oral pathology to dental surgeon U.S. Army, Europe, 1963-66; asst. chief dept. oral pathology U.S. Army Inst. Dental Research, Walter Reed Army Med. Center, Washington, 1966-69, chief dental and oral pathology div., Armed Forces Inst. Pathology, 1969—, course dir. oral and forensic pathology, 1969—; lectr. oral pathology Sch. Dentistry, W.Va. U., 1968-70; prof. oral pathology Sch. Dentistry, Howard U., 1971; asso. prof. oral pathology Georgetown U., 1968—; asst. prof. George Washington U. Grad. Sch., 1972. Recipient Surgeon Gen.'s award for profl. superiority, 1971. Diplomate Am. Bd. Oral Medicine, Am. Bd. Oral Pathology. Fellow Am. Acad. Pathology; mem. Am. Dental Assn., Am. Soc. Forensic Odontology (pres.), Internat. Acad. Law and Scis., Capitol Order Oral Pathologists (founder 1970). Mason (Shriner). Contbr. articles to profl. jours. Home: 4601 Harling Lane Bethesda MD 20014 Office: Armed Forces Inst Pathology Washington DC 20305

BOYETTE, ISAAC HARMON, banker; b. Lakeland, Ga., Apr. 14, 1907; s. Jessie Thomas and Leona (Crum) B.; student Valdosta Bus. Coll., 1925; m. Sallie Touchton, July 14, 1935; children—Gloria (Mrs. Isaac Harmon, Jr.), Myra, Betty. Tchr. schs. Lowndes County, Ga., 1929-30; bookkeeper Chevrolet Agy., Nashville, Ga., 1930-31; salesman Jewel Tea Co., Jacksonville, Fla., 1932-39, asst. mgr. Jacksonville br., 1933-34, salesman, Birmingham, Ala., 1934-35, Atlanta, 1937-39; owner, mgr. Boyette Motor Co., 1939-56; developer Dairy Queen Ga., 1947-57; dir. First State Bank, Valdosta, Ga., 1951—. Pres. Alapaha Area council Boy Scouts Am., 1965-69. Mem. Valdosta and Lowndes County Planning Commn., 1961—. Trustee Norman Jr. Coll., 1964-69; bd. dirs. Boys Club. Recipient Silver Beaver award Boy Scouts Am., 1968. Baptist (deacon 1929—). Mason (Shriner), Rotarian. Home: Bemis Rd Valdosta GA 31601 Office: Box 668 Valdosta GA 31601

BOYKIN, JOHN CLAUDE, business exec.; b. Crandall, Tex., Jan. 24, 1935; s. Allie C. and Agnes (Henry) B.; student St. Benedicts Coll., 1953-54, Arlington State Coll., 1954-56, So. Meth. U., 1956-57, 63-66; m. Beverley Jo Stillings, Sept. 4, 1954; children—Shean, Kevin, Shannon, Colleen. Mem. engring. staff Gen. Electric Co., Dallas, 1954-56; football coach Jesuit High Sch., Dallas, 1956-57; with Space Corp., Garland, 1957-58; with Geotech, Teledyne Co., Garland, 1959-70, mgr. marketing of instruments, 1966-70; pres., dir. Calcite Crystal Corp., 1966-67; v.p., mem. bd. Rare Minerals Corp., 1967; v.p. Copper-Pitt-Copper Corp., 1967; pres., chief exec. officer Technitron Internat., Inc., Dallas, 1970—. Athletic dir. Dallas-Ft. Worth Diocesan Catholic Youth Orgn., 1967-68; mem. adult bd. dirs. Cath. Youth Orgn., 1967-68. Mem. Petroleum Electric Supply Assn., Am. Geophys. Union, Internat. Union Geodesy and Geophysics, Instrument Soc. Am., Dallas Geophys. Soc. Democrat. Roman Catholic. K.C. Home: 2420 El Cerrito Dr Dallas TX 75228 Office: PO Box 28877 Dallas TX 75228

BOYKIN, NELL GASKIN (MRS. FLOYD HAMILTON BOYKIN), civic worker; b. Dolphin, Va., Nov. 20, 1913; d. William Rufus and Maggie Mason (Lucy) Gaskin; student 20th Century System Bus. Sch., 1934-35; m. Floyd Hamilton Boykin, Sept. 25, 1937; children—Sandra Watson (Mrs. Edward L. Smith), Lucy Mason. Pvt. practice bookkeeping, Camden, S.C., 1937—; co-owner, operator Boykin Furniture Co., Camden, 1939—. Charter mem. Camden Woman's Club, 1956; bd. dirs. Golden Age Council for Sr. Citizens, 1958—; mem. steering com. Community Coll. for Adult Edn., 1952-55; charter mem. Camden Lions Aux., 1954, treas., 1955-56; active Kershaw County Civil Def. Program, 1953—, mem. welfare com., 1954—, rec. sec., 1955, treas., 1962—; charter bd. dirs., mem. exec. com. Thomas Salmond Community Center, 1956—, treas., 1958-60. Named Career Woman of Year, Camden Bus. Profl. Woman Club, 1965. Mem. U.D.C. (past chpt. pres. treas. 1960—, dist. and S.C. nominating com. 1963), Camden Hist. Soc., D.A.R., Exec. Club Bus. and Profl. Women's club (charter Camden, past pres., S.C. dir. 1958-60, mem. S.C. legislative com., chmn. Camden legislative com.). Methodist (past supt. nursery dept., past pres. Women's Soc. Christian Service, now mem. commn. on missions, Ch. Altar Guild, bldg. planning com.). Mem. Order Eastern Star (past worthy matron, chmn. bd. dirs. Rainbow Girls Camden). Home: 1611 Mill St Camden SC 29020 Office: 920-922 Broad St Camden SC 29020

BOYKIN, WILLIAM ANCRUM, JR., beverage co. exec.; b. Atlanta, Sept. 29, 1906; s. William Ancrum and Annie (Smith) B.; LL.B., U. Ga., 1927; postgrad. Columbia, 1927-28. Admitted to Ga. bar, 1927; with Coca-Cola Co., Atlanta, 1928—, asst. treas., 1959-63, treas., 1963-71; v.p., dir. Coca-Cola Internat. Corp., 1947—. Mem. Am. Bar Assn. Home: 3921 Beechwood Dr NW Atlanta GA 30327 Office: 310 North Av NW Atlanta GA 30313

BOYLE, EDWARD JAMES, U.S. dist. judge; b.McDonoghville, La., Oct. 11, 1913; s. Thomas F. and Margaret (Fields) B.; LL.B., Loyola U., New Orleans, 1935; m. Edith Fink, Jan. 29, 1936; children—Edward J., Kathleen A. Admitted to La. bar, 1935; practice in New Orleans, 1935-66; asst. U.S. atty. Eastern Dist. La., 1942-45; now U.S. dist. judge Eastern Dist. La. Mem. Am., La., Fed., New Orleans bar assns., Am. Judicature Soc., Blue Key (hon.). Democrat. Roman Catholic. Home: 7356 Cameo St New Orleans LA 70124 Office: 400 Royal St New Orleans LA 70130

BOYLE, JAMES PRESTON, govt. ofcl.; b. Callao Va., May 15, 1921; s. William Porter and Bertha (Harper) B.; B.C.S., Strayer Coll. Accountancy, 1940; LL.B., Woodrow Wilson Coll. Law, 1950; m. Rosalie Clayton, Dec. 2, 1944; children—Ronald, Gary, Richard, Michael. Admitted to Ga. bar, 1950; with Internat. Revenue Service, 1946— successively internal revenue agt., chief, field audit br., Atlanta, chief, audit div., asst. dist. dir., Nashville dist. dir. Richmond (Va.) Dist., 1965—. State coordinator interdepartmental savs. bonds, Va., 1965—. Chmn., Combined Fed. Campaign, 1967. Bd. dirs. Va. Civil Service Interagy. Bd. Served as comdr. AC, USNR, 1942-45. C.P.A., Ga. Mem. Richmond Fed. Exec. Assn. (pres. 1968-69). Home: 355 N Mooreland Rd Richmond VA 23229 Office: Fed Bldg Richmond VA 23240

BOYLE, JOHN HARTFORD, electronics co. exec.; b.Chattanooga, July 6, 1918; s. Hartford D. and Clementine (Zimmerman) B.; B.B.A., U. Chattanooga, 1941; m. Paty Spearman, Mar. 23, 1946; children—John Michael, Robert Hartford, Patrick Joseph, Timothy Richard, Sharon Paty. Football coach U. Chattanooga, 1940-41; pilot European operations Am. Overseas Airlines, 1946-49; pilot, mgr. European operations Pan Am. World Airways, 1949-52; v.p. corporate marketing Collins Radio Co., Dallas, 1952—. Served to maj. USAAF, 1941-46. Home: Box 87 Route 1 Allen TX 75002 Office: Collins Radio Co Dallas TX 75207

BOYLE, STANLEY EUGENE, educator; b. Sandpoint, Ida., Sept. 4, 1927; s. Stanley Cleveland and Bessie Ethel (Watkins) B.; B.A., Wash. State U., 1954, M.A., 1955; Ph.D., U. Wis., 1959; m. Phyllis Patricia Weiler, Apr. 26, 1949 (dec. Feb. 29, 1972); children—Michael Brian, John Patrick. Asst. prof. St. Louis U., 1958-61, asso. prof., 1961-62; sr. staff economist antitrust div. Dept. Justice, 1962; asst. to dir. Bur. Econs. FTC, 1963, chief div. industry analysis, 1963-66; prof. econs. Va. Poly. Inst. and State U., Blacksburg, 1966—. Asso. dir. Study Export Opportunities for Small Mfg. Firms Mo., Small Bus. Adminstrn., 1960-61; vis. prof. Naval War Coll., Newport, R.I., 1961-62; cons. Law Enforcement Adv. Adminstrn., State Council Higher Edn., Commonwealth Va., 1969-70, Antitrust div. U.S. Dept. Justice, 1969-70, FTC, 1970—. Served with USAAF, 1945-48. Author: County Income Payments in Washington, 1950-52, 1954; (with Joseph P. McKenna) The Participation of Missouri Firms in Export Trade, 1962; Industrial Organization: An Empirical Approach, 1971. Mng. editor Review Regional Studies, 1970—; bd. editors So. Econ. Jour., 1967-70. Contbr. articles to profl. jours. Home: 208 High View Dr NE Blacksburg VA 24061

BOYLE, WILLIAM ANTHONY, labor union exec.; b. Bald Butte, Mont., Dec. 1, 1904; s. James P. and Catherine (Mallin) B.; m. Ethel V. Williams, June 3, 1928; 1 dau., Antoinette. Asst. to internat. pres. United Mine Workers Am., 1948-60, internat. v.p., 1960-63; internat. pres., 1963—. Vice chmn. Nat. Coal Policy Conf.; mem. President's Adv. Com. Labor-Mgmt. Policy. Dir., mem. exec. com. National Bank, Washington. Home: 4422 35th St NW Washington DC 20008 Office: 900 15th St NW Washington DC 20005

BOYLES, CARL LEROY, dentist; b. Hubbard, Tex., July 29, 1924; s. Carl and Eiliese (McWilliams) B.; student Baylor U., 1941-43; D.D.S., U. Tex., 1946; m. Lucy Marie Wiggins, Apr. 21, 1970; children (by previous marriage)—Harriet (Mrs. Leon Berry), Carl Leroy, Elizabeth, William Gilbert, Christopher David. Pvt. practice dentistry, Houston, 1949—; mem. staff Bapt. Meml. Hosp. Postgrad. instr. U. Tex. Dental Sch., 1951-57. Scoutmaster Sam Houston area council Boy Scouts Am., 1950-53; chmn. dental health sub-com. Houston Ind. Sch. Dist., 1970-72. Served to capt. Dental Corps, AUS, 1946-48. Recipient award of merit Houston Ind. Sch. Dist., 1972. Mem. Am. Soc. Preventive Dentistry, Am. Acad. Gold Foil Operators, Am., Tex. dental assns., S.W. Soc. Dental Medicine (pres. 1958-59), Acad. Gen. Dentistry, Houston Dist. Dental Soc. (chmn. preventive dentistry com. 1970-72). Baptist. Home: 4023 Gulf St Houston TX 77017 Office: 8060 Moline St Houston TX 77017

BOYLES, DANIEL FLETCHER, banker; b. Houston, Aug. 23, 1941; s. Howard and Edith (Saxenmeyer) B.; B.A., Washington and Lee U., 1963; postgrad. S.W. Grad. Sch. Banking, 1971-73; m. Martha Ann Masterson, May 1, 1965: 1 son, Daniel Fletcher. Real estate loan officer Robert C. Wilson Mortgage Co., 1965-68; sr. v.p. Republic Nat. Bank of Houston, 1968—; v.p. S.W. Mortgage and Realty Advisors, 1971—; dir. Citizens and So. Life Ins. Co. Served with USAF, 1963-69. Clubs: Racquet, Larchmont Civic (v.p. 1970-71) (Houston). Home: 5522 Schumacher St Houston TX 77027 Office: 5200 N Shepherd St Houston TX 77018

BOYLES, HARLAN EDWARD, SR., state ofcl.; b. Vale, N.C., May 6, 1929; s. Curtis E. and Kate (Scronce) B.; student U. Ga., 1947-48; B.S., U. N.C., 1951; m. Frances Wilder, Feb. 29, 1928;

children—Lynn, Harlan Edward. Auditor, N.C. Dept. Revenue, 1951-56; exec. sec. N.C. Tax Rev. Bd., 1956-60; dep. treas. State of N.C., Raleigh, 1960—, sec. N.C. Local Govt. Commn., 1960—. C.P.A., N.C. Mem. N.C. Assn. C.P.A.'s. Presbyn. (elder). Rotarian. Home: 1924 Fairfield Dr Raleigh NC 27608 Office: State Capitol Bldg Raleigh NC 27602

BOYLES, JAMES EDWARD, indsl. engr.; b. Houston, Aug. 15, 1929; s. Lester Tucker and Hazel Viola (Montgomery) B.; B.S., Tex. A. and M. U., 1951; m. Martha Faye Brannen, Oct. 20, 1961; children—Johnna, William. Home builder, Houston, 1955; indsl. engr. Reed Roller Bit Co., 1956-60; indsl. engr. W.K.M. Valve div. A.C.F. Industries, Houston, 1960-66, head indsl. engring. dept., 1966-69, mgr. indsl. engring., 1970—; lectr. U. Houston. Served from lt. to capt. USAF, 1952-54, now lt. col. Res. Registered profl. engr., Tex. Mem. Am. Inst. Indsl. Engrs. (pres.; nat. gen. conf. chmn. 1969), Res. Officers Assn., Air Force Assn., Armed Forces Communications and Electronics Assn., Tex. Soc. Profl. Engrs. Home: 4415 Woodvalley Dr Houston TX 77035 Office: PO Box 2117 Houston TX 77001

BOYLSTON, SAMUEL LIONEL, assn. exec.; b. Springfield, S.C., May 8, 1923; s. Raymond Powell and Lillie Victoria (Boylston) B.; LL.B., U. S.C., 1950; m. June Christine Busbee, July 3, 1957; stepchildren—Robin Virginia Cheatham, Norma June Cheatham. Admitted to S.C. bar, 1950; atty. City of Springfield, 1950-56; dir. Warehouse div. S.C. Dept. Agr., Columbia, 1956-62; gen. mgr. Motor Transp. Assn. S.C., Columbia, 1963—. Mem. S.C. Ho. of Reps., 1951-56. Served with USAAF, 1943-46. Mem. S.C. Hwy. Users Conf. (pres. 1969), S.C. Soc. Assn. Execs. (pres. 1970). Democrat. Rotarian. Home: 3201 Stepp Dr Columbia SC 29205 Office: 2425 Devine St Columbia SC 29204

BOYNTON, GERALD WAYNE, educator; b. Madison, Tenn., Dec. 13, 1937; s. Gerald Willis and Evelyn (Vaughn) B.; B.A., Columbia Union Coll., 1960; M.S.W., U. Tenn., 1962; m. Phyllis Charlene Byrd, June 12, 1960; children—Colleen Michele, Rebecca Elizabeth. Group worker Sudekum Community Center, Nashville, 1960-61; psychiat. social worker Reception & Diagnostic Center, Columbus, O., 1962-64; chief med. social cons. Team Evaluation Center, Chattanooga, 1964-69; asst. prof. Sch. Social Work, U. Ga., Athens, 1969—; field work supr. Sch. Social Work, Ohio State U., 1964; instr. U. Chattanooga, 1965-69; lectr. So. Missionary Coll., Collegedale, Tenn., 1965-68. Bd. mem. Suicide Prevention Service, 1967-69. Del. Md. Gov. Conf. on Children and Youth, 1959, Tenn. Conf. on Comprehensive Health Planning, 1967. Vice pres. Chattanooga-Hamilton County Mental Health Assn.; bd. dirs., treas. Athens-Clarke County Mental Health Assn., 1969-72. Mem. Nat. Assn. Social Workers (past del.), Acad. Certified Social Workers, Tenn. Council Social Workers, Am. Assn. Mental Deficiency, Athens Jr. C. of C., Sigma Iota Kappa, Delta Sigma Tau. Mem. Seventh Day Adventist Ch. Book reviewer Chattanooga Times, 1967-69. Home: 208 Riverside Dr Athens GA 30601

BOZARTH, HOWARD J., banker; b. Abilene, Tex., Aug. 21, 1906; s. Edgar L. and Ethel (Cannon) B.; student Centre Coll., Danville, Ky., 1924-26; B.S., U. Okla., 1928; m. Zereta Sutton, Nov. 3, 1933; children—Howard J., Betty (Mrs. Rudolph Carl Metzner). With Empire Oil Co., Oklahoma City and Guthrie, Okla., 1928-29; collector Seminole Oil Fields area Comml. Credit Co., 1929-30; with Dun & Bradstreet, 1930; with City Nat. Bank, Oklahoma City, 1930—, exec. v.p., 1955-58, pres., 1958—; dir. Oklahoma City br. Fed. Res. Bank of Kansas City. Pres., bd. dirs. Oklahoma County chpt. A.R.C.; bd. dirs. Better Bus. Bur., Salvation Army. Served to lt. (j.g.) USNR, 1943-46. Mem. Oklahoma City C. of C. (dir.). Episcopalian. Kiwanian. Home: 700 NW 41st St Oklahoma City OK 73118 Office: PO Box 25715 101 W Main St Oklahoma City OK 73125

BRACHMAN, SOLOMON, business exec.; b. Jacobstadt, Latvia, Dec. 15, 1896; s. Marcus and Mindel (Vershok) B.; A.B.,m. Etta L. Katzenstein, Oct. 31, 1921; children—Malcolm K., Marilyn. Came to U.S., 1905, naturalized, 1918. With Producers Supply & Tool Co., Marietta, O., 1918-19. Ft. Worth, 1919—, officer and dir., 1920—, pres., 1934—; chmn. bd. Pioneer Am. Ins. Co., Ft. Worth, 1948—; dir. 1st Nat. Bank, Ft. Worth. Trustee Tex. Christian U., Harris Hosp. Mem. Am. Petroleum Inst. Jewish religion. Mason. Clubs: Ft. Worth, Shady Oak, Columbian, Colonial, Petroleum, Ridglea, Dallas. Office: Trans Am Bldg Fort Worth TX 76102

BRACK, EDYTHE ELLA MULVEYHILL (MRS. REGINALD BRACK), civic worker; b. Kansas City, Kan.; d. William Edward and Easter (Loftus) Mulveyhill; A.B., U. Kan., 1934; m. Reginald Brack, July 28, 1934; children—Reginald, William Dennis, Linda (Mrs. John Samuel McFarland). Bd. mem. Dallas Day Nursery Assn., 1961—, sec. bd., 1967; co-chmn. Southwestern bd. Met. Opera, 1963-69, chmn., 1969—; area adviser Nat. Panhellenic Conf., 1964-69; mem. Caruth Rehab. Center Aux., Dallas. Internat. v.p. Pi Beta Phi, 1964-67, mem. nat. bd. dirs. grand council 1961-67. Mem. Nat. Assn. Women Deans and Counselors, Dallas Art Assn., Art Mus. League. Episcopalian (directress altar guild 1954—, mem. St. Simons day care bd. 1954-62). Clubs: Dallas Woman's (bd. govs. 1970—), Dallas Garden (membership chmn. 1968—), Colony. Home: 6043 Walnut Hill Lane Dallas TX 75230

BRACK, REGINALD KUFELD, SR., airline exec.; b. Radomissl, Russia, Dec. 28, 1910; s. John and Irma (von Liphart) Kufeld; brought to U.S., 1923; B.A., U. Kan., 1935; m. Edythe Ella Mulveyhill, July 28, 1934; children—Reginald Kufeld, Dennis, Linda. Owner, mgr. Brack Ins. Agy., 1935-44; pres. Brack Finance Co., 1935-44 (both Great Bend, Kan.); dist. sales mgr. Braniff Airways, Inc., Kansas City, Mo., 1944-45, regional sales mgr., 1945-47, gen. traffic and sales mgr., Dallas, 1947-53, v.p., 1953-60, sr. v.p., 1961—, also dir.; dir. Air Cargo, Inc. Mem. C. of C., Newcomen Soc., Phi Gamma Delta. Lutheran. Club: Northwood Country (Dallas). Home: 6043 Walnut Hill Lane Dallas TX 75230 Office: Braniff Bldg Exchange Park Dallas TX 75235

BRACKEN, VIRGIL, accountant; b. Sebastian County, Ark., Nov. 1, 1922; s. John C. and Ruby E. (Meeks) B.; B.S. in Bus. Adminstrn., U. Ark., 1950; m. Virginia S. Baker, Sept. 15, 1948; children—Bill, Leslie. Partner firm Bracken and Gardner C.P.A.s, Ft. Smith Ark., 1950—, Pres. Ark. Bd. Accountancy, 1969. Sec. Ft. Smith Parking Authority, 1970. Mem. Ark. Soc. C.P.A.s (pres. 1972). Methodist (ofcl. bd.). Optimist (pres. 1960). Home: 12 Berry Hill Fort Smith AR 72901 Office: 509 Garrison St Fort Smith AR 72901

BRACKEN, WILLIAM EARL, JR., lawyer, city ofcl.; b. Phila., Jan. 25, 1934; s. William Earl and Alabell (Terry) B.; B.B.A., Baylor U., 1956, J.D., 1958; m. Sarah Lou Graves, May 31, 1958; children—Elizabeth Louise, Terry Suzanne, Sarah Lynn. Admitted to Tex. bar, 1958; asso. Bryan, Maxwell, Wilson & Olson, Waco, Tex., 1961-63; asst. city atty. City of Waco, 1963-67, city atty., 1967—. Loan exec. United Fund, 1965—; bd. dirs. Lake Air Little League, 1964-69; pres. Meml. Little League, 1964-66; active various fund-raising drives. Served with USAF, 1958-61. Mem. State Bar Tex., Waco-McLennan County Bar Assn. (sec. treas. 1963), Tex. City Attys. Assn. (pres. 1970-71, dir. 1971-72), Waco-McLennan County Jr. Bd. Assn. (pres. 1969). Baptist. Home: 5000 Ridgeview Waco TX 76710 Office: City Hall PO Box 1370 Waco TX 76703

BRACKETT, JAMES WILLIAM, govt. ofcl.; b. Gastonia, N.C., Oct. 7, 1931; s. Oliver L. and Maggie (Eason) B.; A.B., U. N.C., 1953; m. Joan Weeden, Jan. 29, 1955; children—Benjamin Stuart, Nathaniel Gardner. Chief estimates and projections br., fgn. demographic analysis div. Bur. Census, 1955-67; dep. chief population and program analysis div. AID, Dept. State, Washington, 1967-70, chief analysis and evaluation div. Office of Population, 1970—. Treas. HURELCO Land Devel. Corp., Annandle, Va., 1965-68; cons. UN, U. Md. Mem. Internat. Union for Sci. Study Population, Population Assn. Am. (sec.-treas. 1971—). Home: 2030 N Adams St Arlington VA 22201 Office: Dept State Washington DC

BRACKIN, HENRY BRYAN, JR., psychiatrist; b. Raleigh, N.C., Nov. 3, 1924; s. Henry Bryan and Rachel (Luker) B.; B.A., Vanderbilt U., 1944 M.D., 1947; m. Eva Drucilla Cato, Oct. 15, 1948; children—Henry Bryan III, John Curtis and Robert Lewis (twins). Intern St. Thomas Hosp., Nashville, 1947; surg. resident Nashville Gen. Hosp. 1948-49; psychiatric resident Perry Point (Md.) VA Hosp., 1950, U.S. Naval Hospital, Oakland, Cal., 1951-52, Hosp. U. Pa., Phila., 1952-54; practice medicine specializing in psychiatry, Nashville, 1954—; mem. staff Madison, St. Thomas, Bapt., Met-Nashville Gen., Vanderbilt U. hosp.; clin. instr. psychiatry Vanderbilt Sch. Medicine, 1954-63, asst. clin. prof. psychiatry, 1964—. Mem. Met. Nashville Bd. Hosps., 1963—. Served with USNR, 1943-45; served to lt. M.C., USNR, 1950-52. Diplomate Am. Bd. Psychiatry. Fellow Am. Psychiat. Assn. (dist. pres; alternate area mem. exec. com. assembly), mem. Am., So., Tenn. med. assns., Nashville Acad. Medicine, So. Psychiatry Assn., Phi Beta Kappa, Kappa Alpha, Alpha Kappa Kappa. Methodist. Home: 223 Hillwood Dr Nashville TN 37205 Office: 1918 Church St Nashville TN 37203

BRADBURY, ROBERT WESLEY, economist, educator; b. Louisville, Jan. 3, 1905; s. Herbert Roberts and Kate (Fitch) B.; A.B., Albion Coll., 1926; M.A., U. Mich., 1927, Ph.D., 1937; m. Elizabeth C. Kukst, Jan. 30, 1948; children—Joan Elizabeth, Robert Douglas. Instr. U. Mich., 1927-31; asst. prof. La. State U., 1931-37, asso. prof., 1939-41, prof., dir. div. Latin Am. studies, 1941-42; dir. Bur. Research and Statistics, La. Dept. Labor, 1937-39; econ. attache Am. embassy, Panama City, Panama, 1942-44, attache, Mexico City, 1945-46; polit. economist Dept. State, 1944-45; dean Am. Inst. Fgn. Trade, 1946-47; spl. exec. rep. Pan Am. Airways, 1947-50; prof. econs. U. Fla., Gainesville, 1950—; Am. consul, Sao Paulo, Brazil, 1952-53. Hon. prof. U. Asuncion (Paraguay), U. San Andres, La Paz, Bolivia. Mem. Am., So. econ. assns., Phi Beta Kappa, Sigma Nu. Author: Water-Borne Commerce of New Orleans, 1937; El Comercio Internacional, 1959. Editor: Bolivian Economic Seminar, also Second Bolivian Economic Seminar, 1959-60. Home: 501 SW 21st Av Gainesville FL 32601

BRADDY, HALDEEN, educator; b. Fairlie, Tex., Jan. 22, 1908; s. John Winfield and Lena Moss (Rountree) B.; B.A., East Tex. State U., 1928; M.A., U. Tex., 1929; Ph.D., N.Y.U., 1934; m. Virginia Bell, June 19, 1927. Instr. English, N.Y.U., 1929-38, prof. Tex. Christian U., 1938-42; supr. Tex. Tech. Coll., 1943-44; asso. prof. U. Kan., 1944-45; lectr. Tulane U., 1946, U. So. Cal., 1946; prof. English, U. Tex. at El Paso, 1946—, research prof., 1963-64. Served as 1st lt. USAAF, 1942-43. Am. Council Learned Socs. grantee, 1937. Mem. Tex. Folklore Soc. (pres. 1951-52, program chmn. 1952), Modern Lang. Assn., Westerners, Kappa Sigma. Mem. Christian Ch. Author: Chaucer's Parlement of Foules, 2d edit., 1969; Chaucer and the French Poet Graunson, 2d edit., 1968; Glorious Incense, The Fulfillment of Edgar Allan Poe, 2d edit., 1968; Cock of the Walk, Legend of Pancho Villa, 2d edit., 1970; Hamlet's Wounded Name, 1964; Pershing's Mission to Mexico, 2d edit., 1972; Pancho Villa Rides Again, 1967; Mexico and the Old Southwest, 1971; Geoffrey Chaucer: Literary and Historical Studies, 1971. Rev. editor Jour. Am. Folklore, 1945. Home: 2109 Arizona Av El Paso TX 79930

BRADDY, ROBERT LEWIS, city ofcl.; b.Pavo, Ga., Jan. 30, 1920; s. Robert Lewis and Florence (Rehm) B.; student Ga.-Ala. Sch. Commerce, 1938-39; m. Marie Miller, Apr. 19, 1942; children—Jennifer (Mrs. Charles R. Frost, Jr.), Robert Miller. With Melrose Plantation, Thomasville, Ga., 1939-41; personnel clk. U.S. Engrs., Macon, Ga., 1941-42; electrician Southeastern Shipbldg. Corp., Savannah, Ga., 1942-45; dep. sheriff clk. Thomas County (Ga.), 1946-49; housing mgr. Housing Authority of Thomasville, 1949—; exec. dir. Housing Authority Boston (Ga.), 1958—. Partner Success Club Thomasville 1960—. Served with U.S. Mcht. Marine, 1945-46. Baptist (deacon, chmn. bldg. com. 1964—). Kiwanian (dir.). Home: 125 Grant St Thomasville GA 31792 Office: 216 S College St Thomasville GA 31792

BRADEN, WALDO W., educator; b. Ottumwa, Ia., Mar. 7, 1911; s. Wilburn C. and Stella (Warder) B.; B.A., Penn Coll., 1932; M.A., U. Ia., 1938, Ph.D., 1942; m. Dana Crane, Aug. 18, 1938; 1 dau., Helen Dana. Tchr., Fremont (Ia.) High Sch., 1933-35, Mt. Pleasant High Sch., 1935-38; tchr. speech Ia. Wesleyan Coll., 1938-40, dean of students, 1942-46; asso. prof. speech La. State U., Baton Rouge, U., 1946-51, prof., 1951—, chmn., 1958—. Vis. prof. Washington U., summer 1952, Mich. State U., summer 1953, U. Pacific, summer 1965, Cal. State Coll., Fullerton, summer 1969. Mem. Speech Assn., Am. (council 1954—, exec. sec. 1954-57, pres. 1962), So. Speech Assn., Am. Studies Assn., Pi Kappa Delta, Delta Sigma Rho, Tau Kappa Alpha, Omicron Delta Kappa. Methodist. Author: (with Gray) Public Speaking, 1951, rev. 1963; (with Brandenburg) Oral Decision-Making, 1955; (with Gehring) Speech Practices, 1958; Public Speaking: Essentials, 1966; (with Pennybacker) Broadcasting and the Public Interest, 1969; (with Thonssen and Baird) Speech Criticism, 1970. Editor: Speech Methods and Resources, 1961; revised, 1972; The Speech Teacher, 1967-69; Oratory in the Old South, 1970; Representative American Speeches, 1971. Contbr. articles speech, hist. jours. Home: 535 Ursuline Dr Baton Rouge LA 70808

BRADFIELD, WILLIAM HENRY, JR., publisher; b. Dallas, May 3, 1927; s. William Henry and Lillialma (Boswell) B.; student U. Tex., 1943-45; B.S. in Journalism, So. Meth. U., 1949; m. Clarice Eloise Sargent, Apr. 20, 1952; one son, Clayton Ross. Editor Garland (Tex.) Daily News, 1952-58, Tex. Mesquiter, Mesquite, Texas, 1957-61, pub., 1962-65;pub. Financial Trend, 1970—; chmn. bd. Equity Media Inc.; dir. Garland Bank & Trust. Served with USAAF, World War II. Mem. Sigma Delta Chi. Mem. Ch. of Christ. Rotarian. Home: 7588 Benedict Dr Dallas TX 75214 Office: 7616 LB Johnson Freeway Dallas TX 75240

BRADFORD, ADDISON MORTON, lawyer, corp. exec.; b. Lee County, Ark., Jan. 2, 1918; s. Addison Morton and Olivette (Bonner) B.; B.A., Ark. State Coll., 1939; postgrad. So. Meth. U., 1940-41, J.D., 1948; m. Peggy Caraway, June 18, 1942; children—Paul Randolph, Patricia Gay, Timothy Caraway. Admitted to Tex. bar, 1948; practiced in Dallas, 1948—; partner firm Bradford & Pritchard, Dallas, 1953-68, Anderson, Henley, Shields, Bradford & Pritchard, 1968—; dir. Central Bank & Trust Co.; pres., dir. Trans World Imports, Inc., Wig Outlet Internat., Inc., Di-Cel Corp., O.E.M. Industries, Inc., Tex. Sign Supply Co.; sec., dir. Insta-Forms Corp. Am.; dir. J.T. Chapman Co., Mahard Pullet Farms, Inc., R. B. Wilber Co., Mahard Egg Farm, Inc., Mahard Egg Co., Mahard Feed Mill, Inc., Taylor Enterprises, Inc. Served as finance officer, capt. AUS, 1943-46. Mem. Am., Dallas bar assns., State Bar Tex., Am. Judicature Soc., Delta Theta Phi. Democrat. Methodist. Mason (32 degree, K.T., Shriner). Clubs: Lancers, Knife and Fork (Dallas); Brookhaven Country. Home: 5339 Royal Crest Dallas TX 75229 Office: Fidelity Union Tower Dallas TX 75201

BRADFORD, JAMES CULLEN, accountant, govt. ofcl.; b. Lewisville, Tex., Nov. 21, 1924; s. James Franklin and Lona Virginia (Porter) B.; grad. North State U., Denton, 1959; m. Eva Ernestine Watson, Dec. 14, 1949; 1 dau., Theresa Dawn. Accountant, Am. Maracaibo Oil Co., Dallas, Felmont Oil Corp., Midland, Tex., 1948-56; controller Rocky Ford Transp. Co., Midland, 1956-57; staff accountant Alexander Grant & Co., C.P.A.'s, Dallas, 1959-61; accountant Internal Revenue Service, U.S. Treasury Dept., Dallas, 1962—; asst. to prof. accounting North Tex. State U., 1958-59. Served with AUS, 1943-45; ETO. Decorated Bronze Star medal with three oak leaf clusters. C.P.A. Am. Inst. C.P.A.'s, Tex. Soc. C.P.A.'s, Nat. Assn. Internal Revenue Employees, Alpha Lambda Pi. Republican. Mem. Ch. of Christ. Club: Chapel Downs Country (Dallas). Home: 3107 Ponder Dr Dallas TX 75229 Office: 1114 Commerce St Dallas TX 75202

BRADFORD, TUTT S., publisher; b. Columbia, S.C., Apr. 30, 1917; s. Tutt S. and Zula (Bowen) B.; student Wofford Coll., 1934; m. Elizabeth Hendley, June 30, 1941; children—Nancy, Debbie. Pub. Cleve. Daily Banner, 1948-51; asst. to pres. Gen. Newspapers, 1951; pub. Bristol (Va.) Herald Courier, 1951-55, Maryville (Tenn.) Alcoa Daily Times, 1955—; dir. Cairo (Ill.) Tribune. Pres. Blount County Indsl. Devel. Bd., 1970-72. Mem. bd. Audit Bur. Circulations, 1967-72. Served with AUS, 1943-45; ETO. Recipient Distinguished Service award Bristol Jr. C. of C., 1952, Maryville-Alcoa Jr. C. of C., 1958. Mem. So. Newspaper Pubs. Assn. (dir. 1968-70), Blount County C. of C. (pres. 1960), Tennessee River Valley Assn. (dir.), Sigma Delta Chi. Kiwanian (pres. Maryville 1967). Home: 1901 Westwood St W Maryville TN 37801 Office: 307 E Harper St Maryville TN 37801

BRADLEE, BENJAMIN CROWNINSHIELD, journalist; b. Boston, Aug. 26, 1921; s. Frederick J. and Josephine (deGersdorff) B.; grad. St. Mark's Sch., Southboro, Mass., 1939; A.B., Harvard, 1943; m. Jean Saltonstall, Aug. 8, 1942; 1 son, Benjamin Crowninshield; m. 2d, Antoinette Pinchot, July 6, 1956; children—Dominic, Marina. Reporter, N.H. Sunday News, Manchester, 1946-48, Washington Post, 1948-51; press attache Am. embassy, Paris, France, 1951-53; European corr. Newsweek mag., Paris, 1953-57, reporter Washington bur., 1957-61, sr. editor, chief bur., 1961-65; mng. editor Washington Post, 1965-68, v.p., exec. editor, 1968—. Served to lt. USNR, 1942-45. Author: That Special Grace, 1964. Home: 4521 Dexter St NW Washington DC 20007 Office: 1150 15th St NW Washington DC 20005

BRADLEY, HAROLD WHITMAN, educator, state legislator; b. Greenwood, R.I., July 9, 1903; s. Harold and Lillian (Whitman) B.; A.B., Pomona Coll., 1925, A.M., 1926; Ph.D., Stanford U., 1932; m. Elizabeth Forbes, Aug. 28, 1940; 1 dau., Anne; m. 2d, Pearle E. Quinn, Dec. 5, 1947; 1 son, David. Tchr., Burbank high sch., 1926-27; instr. Santa Barbara State Tchrs. Coll., 1929-30, instr. history, 1930-36; asst. prof. Stanford, 1936-42; asst. prof. history U. Wash., 1938-39; asso. prof. history Stanford, 1942-45; dean and prof. history Claremont (Cal.) Grad. Sch., 1945-53, Clarke prof. history, 1953-54; prof. history Vanderbilt U., Nashville, 1954-72, prof. emeritus, 1972—, chmn. dept., 1954-62; mem. Tenn. Ho. of Reps., 1964—. Mem. Com. on Am. History in Schs. and Colls. Alternate del. Democratic Nat. Conv., 1952; mem. Davidson County Dem. Exec. Com., 1960-62. Recipient Albert J. Beveridge Meml. prize Am. Hist. Assn., 1943. Mem. Am., So. hist. assns., Orgn. Am. Historians, Am. Studies Assn. (pres. Ky.-Tenn. chpt. 1956-57, nat. council 1972—), Phi Beta Kappa. Methodist. Author: The American Frontier in Hawaii, 1942; The United States 1492-1877, 1972. Mem. bd. editors Pacific Hist. Rev., 1940-54, Miss. Valley Hist. Rev., 1946-49. Contbr. Ency. Brit., Collier's Ency. Yearbook. Home: 212 Craighead Av Nashville TN 37205

BRADLEY, HARRY MORRISON, ednl. cons.; b. Floreffe, Pa., Dec. 9, 1908; s. George Morrison and Florence (Laird) B.; B.S., California State Tchrs. Coll. (Pa.), 1931; M.Ed., U. Pitts., 1942; m. Frances Melvena Sargent, Oct. 25, 1969; stepchildren—Ed Lynn, Anne Betts (Mrs. John H. Womack, Jr.), Katherine Florence, Theresa Monroe (Mrs. Charles Embler). Tchr. elementary sch., prin., supervising prin., Pa., 1928-34; tchr. high sch., Ellwood City, Pa., 1934-42; supervising prin. elementary schs., Kissimmee, Fla., 1946-48; prin. A. and M. Consol. Sch., College Station, Tex., 1948-49; dir. instrn. Houston County, Tex., 1949-50; asst. dir. U. Fla., P.K. Yonge Lab. Sch., Gainesville, 1950-51; prof. edn., dir. Peabody Lab. Schs., Ga. State Coll. for Women, Milledgeville, 1951-53; prof., head edn. dept. Tift Coll., Forsythe, Ga., 1953-54; coordinator Eve. Clearwater div. St. Petersburg (Fla.) Jr. Coll., 1954-58; tchr. Edgewater High Sch., Orlando, Fla., 1958-65; prof., head behavioral sci. dept. Polk Jr. Coll., Winter Haven, Fla., 1965-68; dir. adult edn. Va. Western Community Coll., Roanoke, 1968-72; ednl. cons., 1972—. Served with USAAF, 1942-45. Mem. N.E.A., Am. Assn. Sch. Adminstrs., Assn. Supervision and Curriculum Devel., Nat. Council Community Services, Phi Sigma Pi, Phi Delta Kappa. Contbr. articles to profl. jours. Home: Route 3 Box 412A Salem VA 24153

BRADLEY, JAMES CHRISTOPHER, JR., under sec. Smithsonian Instn.; b. Washington, July 11, 1910; s. James Christopher and Josephine (Facer) B.; B.S., Cath. U. Am., 1931; m. Margaret Mary Collins, Sept. 27, 1935; children—James Christopher III, William Joseph, John Collins. Engring. adminstr. D.C. Govt., 1935-45; budget analyst Bur. Budget, 1945-50; prin. asst. to under sec. interior, 1950-53, engring. asst. to asst. sec., 1953-59; asst. to sec. Smithsonian Instn., 1959-60, asst. sec. instn., 1960-70, under sec., 1970—. Recipient Distinguished Service award Interior Dept., 1959; Achievement certificate Smithsonian Instn., 1963, Exceptional Ser. award, 1966. Registered profl. engr., D.C. Home: 9502 Columbia Blvd Silver Spring MD 20910 Office: 1000 Jefferson Dr SW Washington DC 20560

BRADLEY, JOHN DAVID, physician; b. Shawnee, Okla., May 1, 1912; s. William Joseph and Edna (Gurley) B.; A.B. cum laude, Mercer U., 1932, B.S., 1933; M.D., U. Ga., 1936; postgrad. Johns Hopkins U., 1938; m. Mary Elizabeth Ross, Nov. 28, 1955; 1 son, John Peter. Intern, also med. resident, Macon (Ga.) Gen. Hosp., 1936-38; staff physician Milledgeville (Ga.) State Hosp., 1940-44; resident, fellow in psychiatry Duke U., 1944-47; practice medicine specializing in psychiatry, Asheville, N.C., 1948—; mem. staffs Meml. Mission, St. Joseph's Hosp., Aston Park Hosp., (all Asheville); sr. cons. VA Hosp., Oteen, N.C., 1948—; cons. various hosps. Bd. dirs. Blue Ridge Community Health Center, Asheville, 1966—, Buncombe County Mental Health Assn., 1967—, Developmental Evaluation Clinic of West N.C., Inc., Asheville, 1967—; mem. profl. adv. com. Counseling and Consultation Service of West N.C. Episcopal Center, Asheville, 1967—. Diplomate Am. Bd. Psychiatry and Neurology. Fellow Am., N.C., So. psychiat. assns.; mem. A.M.A., N.C., Buncombe County med. assns., Acad. Religion and Mental Health, Alpha Omega Alpha, Sigma Nu, Phi Rho Sigma. Republican. Episcopalian. Contbr. articles to sci. publs. Home: 313 Vanderbilt Rd Asheville NC 28803 Office: 675 Biltmore Av Asheville NC 28803

BRADLEY, MARTHA WASHINGTON NUTTER (MRS. GEORGE WASHINGTON BRADLEY), educator; b. East St. Louis, Ill.; d. Cecil Grafton and Mabel (Hunt) Nutter; B.S. in Edn., U. Va., 1951, M.Ed., 1960; diplome de la langue Francaise, Alliance Francaise, Paris, 1958; Ph.D. (Nat. Def. Edn. Act fellow), Syracuse U., 1967; m. George Washington Bradley, Feb. 20, 1960. Tchr. elementary sch., East St. Louis, 1951-53, Long Beach, Cal., 1953-54, U.S. Army Dependent Schs., Europe, 1954-59, 60-61; reading cons. pub. schs., Fredericksburg, Va., 1961-62; instr. U. Va. Sch. Gen. Studies, 1962-63; asst. prof. edn. E. Tenn. State U., Johnson City, 1967-70, asso. prof. edn., 1970—, faculty adviser Student N.E.A., 1968—. Trustee George and Martha Washington Bradley Found., Johnson City; bd. dirs. People to People, Johnson City. Mem. Nat. (life), Tenn., E. Tenn. edn. assns., Conf. English Edn. evaluator com. to evaluate documents 1968—), Nat. Council Tchrs. English, D.A.R. (chmn. service for vet. patients 1971-74), Daus. Am. Colonists, Internat. Reading Assn. (upper E. Tenn. council research chmn. 1969-70), Bus. and Profl. Womens Club (chmn. personal devel. com. 1969-70), pres. 1971-72, 2d v.p. 1972-73), Am. Ednl. Research Assn., Nat. Soc. Study of Edn., Am. Assn. U. Women (publicity chmn. 1968-70), Am. Assn. U. Profs., Assn. Ednl. Communications and Tech., Unaka Rock and Mineral Soc. (pres. 1969-70), Phi Kappa Phi (charter pres. E. Tenn. State U. chpt. 1970-72), Kappa Delta Pi (counselor Zeta Iota chpt. 1968—), Delta Kappa Gamma (1st v.p. 1972-74). Mem. Christian Ch. (pres. Women's council 1970-72, dir. Bible sch. 1971—). Clubs: Wednesday Morning Music (yearbook com. 1971-72), E. Tenn. State U. Women's Faculty Book (co-chmn. 1969-70), v.p. 1971-72, pres. 1972-73). Home: Box 2757 E Tenn State U Johnson City TN 37601

BRADLEY, NOLEN EUGENE, JR., coll. dean; b. Memphis, Nov. 29, 1925; s. Nolen Eugene and Anice Pearl (Luther) B.; B.S., Memphis State U., 1951, M.A., 1952; Ed.D., U. Tenn., 1966; m. Eloise Mullins, Jan. 7, 1947; children—Sharon (Mrs. Leonard A. Brabson), Diana Elizabeth, Nolen Eugene III, David Lee. Instr. polit. sci. Memphis State U., 1951-52; tchr. English, Messick High Sch., Memphis, 1952-56; asst. dean admissions Memphis State U., 1956-64; dir. State Agy. for Title I, Higher Edn. Act 1965, Div. Continuing Edn., U. Tenn., 1966-70; dean instrn. Vol. State Community Coll., Gallatin, Tenn., 1970—. Served with AUS, 1944-46. Mem. Am. Assn. Sch. Adminstrs., Tenn. Adult Edn. Assn., Tenn. Edn. Assn., Omicron Delta Kappa, Pi Delta Epsilon, Phi Delta Kappa, Phi Kappa Phi. Baptist (deacon 1966—). Lion. Home: 907 Harris Dr Gallatin TN 37066

BRADLEY, (CHARLES) NORMAN, newspaper editor; b. Flora, Miss., Aug. 7, 1913; s. William Hampton and Annie (Lee) B.; B.S. summa cum laude, Millsaps Coll., 1931; m. Mary Frances Weems, June 29, 1936 children— Caroline, William. Reporter Jackson (Miss.) Clarion Ledger, 1934-37; corr. A.P., 1937-47; editorial writer Chattanooga Times, 1947-54; exec. news editor, 1956-57, asso. editor, 1958-71, editor, 1971—; editor-in-chief Jackson (Miss.) State Times, 1954-55, Pres., bd. dirs. Family Service Agy.; charter pres. Adult Edn. Council, 1952; charter dir. Chattanooga Area Literacy Movement, 1960; mem. bd., pres. Chattanooga Symphony; bd. dirs. Chattanooga Art Assn.; trustee Found. World Literary. Mem. Am. Soc. Newspapers Editors, Kappa Alpha, Sigma Delta Chi. Democrat. Methodist. Clubs: Kiwanis, Lookout Mountain Fairyland. Home: 309 W Brow Rd Lookout Mountain TN 37350 Office: 117 E 10th St Chattanooga TN 37402

BRADLEY, ROBERT JAMES, physician, army officer; b. Milw., June 11, 1922; s. Harold A. and Hazel (Bautz) B.; B.S., U. Wis., 1943, M.D., 1945; M.H.A., Baylor U., 1966; m. Charlotte Marie Cornett, Aug. 9, 1947; children—Barbara Janet, Elizabeth Louise. Commd. lt. M.C., U.S. Army, 1946; intern Med. Coll. Va., Richmond, 1945-46; resident internal medicine Fitzsimons Gen. Hosp., Denver, 1947-50; resident hosp. adminstrn. Army-Baylor Program U.S. Army Med. Field Service Sch., San Antonio, 1965-66; chief med. service 34th Gen. Hosp., La Chapelle, St. Mesmin, France, 1953-56, Irwin Army Hosp., Ft. Riley, Kan., 1956-61, Ryukyus Army Hosp., Okinawa, 1961-64; comdg. officer U.S. Army Hosp., Ft. Huachuca, Ariz., 1965-67; dir. Coco Solo Hosp., C.Z., 1967-70; army surgeon N.G. Bur., Washington, 1970—. Mem. A.M.A., Assn. Mil. Surgeons U.S., Med. Assn. Isthmian C.Z., Baylor U.-Army Hosp. Adminstrn. Alumni Assn., U. Wis. Med. Alumni Assn., Am. Numis. Assn., Phi Beta Kappa, Phi Eta Sigma, Alpha Omega Alpha. Methodist (elder). Home: 4206 Adrienne Dr Alexandria VA 22309 Office: Army Surgeons Office Nat Guard Bur Washington DC 20310

BRADLEY, ROLAND EUGENE, grading and paving contractor; b. Gastonia, N.C., Nov. 16, 1922; s. Thomas Wesley and Laura (McArver) B.; grad. high sch.; m. Sara Kate Moore, Dec. 29, 1951; children—Michael Shane, Steven Eugene, Thomas Wesley II. Clk. Gt. Atlantic & Pacific Tea Co., 1937-40; parts room mgr. Textile Parts & Machine Co., 1940-46; v.p., asst. gen. mgr. Gastonia Plumbing & Heating Co., 1946-59; pres., gen. mgr. Bradley-Jenkins, Inc., Gastonia, 1959—. Served with AUS, 1943-46. Republican. Methodist (local trustee 1957—, dist. trustee 1960-63). Mason (32 deg., Shriner), Elk. Club: Optimist (local pres. 1955-56, dist. gov. 1963-64, internat. v.p. 1968-69). Home: 1841 Westbrook Circle Gastonia NC 28052 Office: PO Box 12366 Gastonia NC 28052

BRADSHAW, HERBERT CLARENCE, newspaperman; b. Rice, Va., Nov. 7, 1908; s. Herbert Leslie and Dell Garnett (Weaver) B.; A.B., Hampden-Sydney Coll., 1930, Litt.D., 1967; M.A., U. Va., 1933; m. Mildred Elizabeth Cunningham, June 20, 1936; children—Kate Weaver (Mrs. Charles William Cloninger), Herbert Cunningham, Elizabeth Scott. Instr., McGuire's U. Sch., 1930-32; prin. Darlington Heights (Va.) High Sch., 1933-38; instr. English Hampden-Sydney Coll. summer sessions, 1937,38; prin. Emporia (Va.) pub. schs., 1938-49; Sunday feature editor Durham (N.C.) Morning Herald, 1949-50, asso. editor, 1951-64, editor editorial page, 1964—. Mem. N.C. Commn. for Blind, 1952-70; pres. N.C. Council World Affairs, 1961-63; mem. N.C. Adv. Commn. to Peace Corps, 1963-65; mem. Gov.'s Study Com. in Vocational Rehab., 1967-68; pres. N.C. Soc. for Prevention of Blindness, 1967-69, treas., 1969-71; moderator Yates Bapt. Assn., 1957-59; mem. N.C. Adv. Council on Comprehensive Health Planning, 1968-70; mem. Nat. Policy and Performance Council Rehab. Services Adminstrn., 1968-72. Bd. dirs. Nat. Soc. for Prevention Blindness, Found. for Research on Nature of Man. Recipient Distinguished Service award. N.C. Rehab. Assn., 1967. Mem. S.A.R. (past v.p. N.C.) N.C. Lit. and Hist. Assn. (past v.p.) Huguenot Soc. N.C. (past pres.), Am. Clan Gregor Soc., Va. Hist. Soc., Va. Bapt. Hist. Soc., Phi Beta Kappa, Omicron Delta Kappa, Sigma Upsilon. Democrat. Baptist. Lion (pres.; dist. gov. 1969-70, chmn. state council 1969-70). Author: History of Prince Edward County, Virginia, 1936, rev. edit., 1955; History of Farmville, Va. 1948; Toward the Dawn: History of the First Quarter Century of the N.C. State Assn. for the Blind. 1961; also articles in field. Home: 1107 Vickers Av Durham NC 27707 Office: Herald Sun Bldg Durham NC 27702

BRADSHAW, JUNIE LEROY, lawyer, state legislator; b. Erwin, N.C., Jan. 30, 1930; A.A., William and Mary Coll.; LL.B., T.C. Williams Sch. Law; m. Deirdree Eagle. Admitted to Va. bar; practiced in Richmond, Va.; mem. Va. Ho. of Dels., 1962—. Vice pres. Va. Young Democrats. Served with USNR, Korea. Mem. Am. Legion (post legal officer), Phi Alpha Delta, Phi Theta Kappa. Baptist. Mason (Shriner). Address: 201 North Blvd Richmond VA 23220*

BRADSHAW, LILLIAN MOORE, librarian; b. Hagerstown, Md., Jan. 10, 1915; d. Harry M. and Mabel E. (Kretzer) Moore; B.A., Western Md. Coll., 1937; B.L.S., Drexel U., 1938; m. William Theodore Bradshaw, May 19, 1946. Asst. adult circulation dept. Utica (N.Y.) Pub. Library 1938-41, asst. head, 1941-43; adult librarian Enoch Pratt Free Library, Balt., 1943-44, asst. coordinator work with young adults, 1944-46; br. librarian Dallas Pub. Library, 1946-47, readers adviser, 1947-52, head dept. circulation, 1952-55, coordinator work with adults, 1955-58, asst. dir., 1958-62, dir., 1962—. Mem. steering com. Nat. Library Week; bd. dirs. Dallas County Community Action Program; mem. profl. adv. com. Greater Dallas Community Relations Commn.; mem. adv. bd. Friends Tex. Libraries; conferee, asst. task force leader Goals for Dallas, So. Methodist U. Bd. Publs., 1970-73, vice chmn. goals achievement com. for continuing edn., 1971-72, chmn., 1972—; mem. Gov.'s Commn. on Status of Women; mem. adv. com. U. Tex. at Dallas; library edn. adv. com. Tex. Coll. and U. System Coordinating Bd.; mem. U.S. Com. for Am. Library in Paris, 1970-71; mem. friendship mission to France, 1970; mem. Nat. Reading Council, 1970—. Bd. dirs. Hoblitzelle Found. Named Tex. Librarian of Yr. 1961; recipient Distinguished Alumnus award Drexel Library Sch., 1970, Titche's Arete award, 1970. Mem. A.L.A. (dir. adult services div. 1962-65, pres. adult services div. 1967-68, dir. exec. com. pub. relations sect., library adminstrn. div. 1964-66, chmn. nominating com. 1966-67, mem. council 1968-69, mem. pub. library study com. 1968-69, pres. 1970-71, bd. dirs. Freedom To Read Found. 1969-71), Internat. Fedn. Library Assns. (rep. to revise standards for pub. libraries 1970-72), Tex. (pres. 1964-65, chmn. pub. libraries div.), pub. (service subcom. of com. on standards, 1965-66), library assns., Am. Assn. U. Women, Tex. Municipal League (dir. 1966-68, com. of future 1971—), Assn. Grad. Edn. and Research North Tex. (adv. council bd. trustees), League Women Voters, Beta Phi Mu. Club: Zonta. Bd. cons. Library Jour., 1962-63. Contbr. articles to profl. jours. Home: 6804 Clayton Av Dallas TX 75214 Office: 1954 Commerce St Dallas TX 75201

BRADSHAW, LUCY HYMAN (MRS. JOSEPH ELTON BRADSHAW), librarian; b. Clinton, N.C., July 20, 1922; d. Zachariah Henry and Laura (McCorkle) Hyman; B.S., Winston-Salem State Coll., 1943, B.S. in L.S., Atlanta U., 1946, M.S., 1955; m. Joseph Elton Bradshaw, Dec. 24, 1946; children—Cheryl Yvonne, Joseph Elton. Library asst. Winston-Salem Tchrs. Coll., 1943-45, asst. librarian, 1946-61, acting librarian, 1961-62, librarian, 1962—. Mem. A.L.A., N.C., Southeastern library assns., Urban League Guild, Am. Assn. U. Women, Winston-Salem Symphony Guild, Beta Phi Mu. Baptist. Home: 442 26th St NW Winston-Salem NC 27105

BRADSHAW, RICHARD JETER, civil engr.; b. Birmingham, Ala., May 15, 1924; s. John William and Elloie (Jeter) B.; student U. Ala., 1946-49, U. Tex., 1953-54 B.S., Ala. Poly. Inst., 1951, M.Div., Episcopal Theol. Sem. S.W., 1956; m. Walter Elizabeth Claburn, Jan. 1, 1943; children—Richard Jeter, John William, Walter Claburn, Elizabeth Ann, Howard Lee, Paul Dunlap. Civil engr. Ala. Power Co., Birmingham, 1947-49; chief, survey party Vernon B. Watwood, Auburn, Ala., 1949-51; engr. Humble Oil Refining Co., Houston, 1951-52; asso. engr. Asso. Cons. Engrs., Midland, Tex., 1952-53, Roger L. Erickson, Austin, Tex., 1953-56; ordained to ministry Episcopal Ch., 1956; minister Episcopal Diocese of Tex., Houston, 1956-60; utility engr. Ala. Hwy. Dept., Birmingham and Montgomery, 1961-70, asst. div. engr., 1970—; instr. civil engring. dept. Ala. Poly. Inst., 1951; part time asst. to rector Episcopal Ch., 1966—. Scoutmaster, Boy Scouts Am., 1965—, cubmaster 1964-65, scout committeeman, 1958-64; mem. Berry High Sch. Athletic Assn., 1963—. Served USMC, 1943-46. Recipient Vulcan award Boy Scouts Am., 1968. Mem. Chi Epsilon, Tau Beta Phi, Phi Kappa Phi. Clubs: Civitan (dir. 1966—, chaplain 1968—), Ala. Takedown. Home: 1836 Shade Crest Rd Birmingham AL 35216 Office: State of Ala Hwy Dept PO Box 2745 Birmingham AL 35202

BRADT, KENNETH HAROLD, psychologist, govt. ofcl.; b. Oakfield, N.Y., Mar. 18, 1928; s. Eli Harold and Lucy (Kreckman) B.; A.B., Syracuse U., 1948, M.A., 1950; Ph.D., Northwestern U., 1951; m. Thelma E. Johnson, June 12, 1948; children—Cheryl E., Jeffrey K., Gary H. Teaching asst. Northwestern U. Evanston, Ill., 1949-51; research psychologist Personnel Research br. Adj. Gen. Office, Dept. Army, Washington, 1951; attitude and opinion research psychologist Dept. Def., 1953-54; U.S. Govt., 1955—. Lectr. Am. U., 1958—; asso. professorial lectr. George Washington Univ.; cons. problems personnel selection and exec. devel., 1959—. Served to 1st lt., Med. Service Corps. AUS, 1952-54. Mem. Am., Eastern, D.C. psychol. assns., A.A.A.S., Sigma Xi. Methodist (ch. psychologist). Contbr. numerous articles to psychol. jours. Home: 10115 Blue Coat Dr Fairfax VA 22030

BRADY, A. ROSE MASSEY (MRS. PERSHING R. BRADY), pub., editor; b. Richmond, Mo., June 25, 1923; d. Albert and Opal (Hagans) Massey, Jr.; grad. high sch.; m. Pershing R. Brady, Mar. 15, 1941 (dec. Jan. 1972); children—Patricia Ann (Mrs. Larry Raney), Pershing Edward. Co-pub., editor Westminster Jour., Westminster, Colo., 1954-56, Erie (Kan.) Record, 1957-62, Hooker (Okla.) Advance, 1962—. Mem. Okla. Press Assn., Am. Legion Aux. (pres. 1959), Wesleyan Soc. Christian Service (pres. 1959). Mem. Order Eastern Star. Home: 207 W Main St Hooker OK 73945 Office: Box 367 Hooker OK 73945

BRADY, BENNETT MANNING, mathematician; b. Orangeburg, S.C., Apr. 11, 1943; d. William Ellis and Elizabeth (Mays) Manning; student Agnes Scott Coll., 1961-62; A.B., Vassar Coll., 1965; M.A. (NSF fellow), U. Cal. at Berkeley, 1968; Fulbright fellow Cambridge (Eng.) U., 1965-66. Mathematician Ernst & Ernst, Washington, 1968-70; staff asso. Pres.'s Commn. on Fed. Statistics, 1970-71, analytical statistician White House Office Mgmt. and Budget, 1971—; also mem. faculty George Washington U., 1969—. Model, Cain-Sloan Dept. Store, Nashville, 1963; mathematician USAF, Washington, 1967; mem. Washington Operations Research Council. Mem. Am. Math. Assn., Operations Research Soc. Am., Inst. Mgmt. Scis., D.A.R., Phi Beta Kappa (award for highest acad. record Vassar Coll. 1965). Presbyn. Home: 10401 Grosvenor Pl Rockville MD 20853 Office: 17th and H St NW Washington DC 20503

BRADY, EDWARD LEWIS, govt. ofcl.; b. Charleston, S.C., Apr. 21, 1919; s. Aaron W. and Theresa (Morgenstern) B.; B.A., U. Cal. at Los Angeles, 1940, M.A., 1942 Ph.D., Mass. Inst. Tech., 1948; m. Evelyn G. Padway, Aug. 22, 1944. Research asst. metall. lab. U. Chgo., 1942-43; research asso. Clinton Labs., Oak Ridge, 1943-46, Gen. Elec. Research Lab., Schenectady, 1948-55; mgr. coolant chemistry Knolls Atomic Power Lab., Schenectady, 1955-56, mgr. exptl. equipment devel., 1958-59; U.S. rep. AEC, London, Eng., 1956-58; sci. adv. U.S. mission to IAEA, Vienna, Austria, 1959-61; asst. chmn. chemistry dept. Gen. Atomic div. Gen. Dynamics Corp., San Diego, 1961-63; chief Office of Standard Reference Data, Nat. Bur. Standards, Washington, 1963-69, asso. dir. for information programs, 1969—. Mem. Am. Chem. Soc., Am. Phys. Soc., Am. Nuclear Soc., A.A.A.S., Phi Beta Kappa, Sigma Xi. Home: 4501 Connecticut Av NW Washington DC 20008 Office: Nat Bureau of Standards Washington DC 20234

BRADY, PERSHING R., publisher, editor; b. Richmond, Mo., Dec. 13, 1917; s. B. Bryan and Georgia H. (Endsley) B.; grad. high sch.; student extension courses; m. A. Rose Massey, Mar. 15, 1941; children— Patricia Ann, Pershing Edward. With Richmond Missourian, 1935-39, Leavenworth (Kan.) Chronicle, 1939-41, Liberty (Mo.) Chronicle, 1941-42, Kansas City (Mo.) Star, 1942-51; pub. Rooks County Record, Stockton, Kan., 1951-54, Westminster (Colo.) Jour. 1954-56; with Denver Post, 1956-57; publ., editor Erie (Kan.) Record, 1957-62; editor Hooker (Okla.) Advance, 1962—. Served as sgt. USAAF, World War II; on Guam, 9 mos. Mem. Nat. Editorial Assn., Internat. Platform Assn., Hooker C. of C. (pres.), Am. Legion, V.F.W., Kan. U. Alumni Assn., Okla. Press Assn., 40 and 8. Mason (Shriner), Lion; mem. Order Eastern Star. Died Jan. 17, 1972

BRADY, RUFUS HOLLAND, JR., architect; b. Tryon, N.C., June 21, 1925; s. Rufus Holland and Julia Fort (Carroll) B.; student Clemson U., 1942-43; B.Arch., U. Mich., 1950; m. Carolyn Flynn, May 12, 1951; children—Marcus Fort, Alison Stuart. Instr. architecture U. Mich., 1950; vis. instr. architecture Clemson U., S.C., 1955-57; asso. Shannon Meriwether, architect, Tryon, N.C., 1951-53; pvt. practice Holland Brady, Jr., architect, Tryon, 1953-70; sr. partner Holland Brady, Jr., architect and Michael J. Brannon, A.I.A., asso., 1970—; dir. The Northwestern Bank, Tryon. Pres., Lanier Library Assn., Tryon, 1965; chmn. Tryon Planning Bd., 1968; chmn. Local Selective Service Bd., 1958-71. Served with AUS, 1943-46; ETO. Decorated Purple Heart. Mem. A.I.A., Alpha Rho Chi. Democrat. Conglist. Clubs: Red Fox Country, Tryon (N.C.) Country; Michigan Union (Ann Arbor). Major archtl. works include Presbyn. Ch., Tryon, 1958, parish house Ch. of St. John in Wilderness, Flat Rock, N.C., 1967. Home: Horseshoe Curve Rd Tryon NC 28782 Office: PO Box 1362 114A N Trade St Tryon NC 28782

BRADY, RUPERT JOSEPH, lawyer; b. Washington, Jan. 24, 1932; s. John Bernard and Mary (Rupert) B.; B.E.E., Catholic U. Am., 1953; LL.B., J.D., Georgetown U., 1959; m. Maureen Mary MacIntosh, Apr. 20, 1954; children—Rupert Joseph, Laureen, Kevin, Warren, Jeannine, Jacqueline, Brian, Barton. Elec. engr. Speery Gyroscope Co., L.I., N.Y., 1953-56; patent specification writer John B. Brady, patent atty., 1956-59; patent agt. B. P. Fishburne, Jr., patent atty., Washington, 1959-61; pvt. practice patent agt., Washington, 1961, patent atty., 1961-63; sr. partner firm Brady, O'Boyle & Gates, specializing in patent, trademark, copyright law, Washington, 1963—; admitted to U.S. Ct. Customs and Patent Appeals, 1961, U.S. Supreme Ct., 1969. Mem. Md., D.C. bar assns., Am. Patent Law Assn., Senators Club Alumni. Patentee. Home: 7201 Pyle Rd Bethesda MD 20034 Office: Colorado Bldg 14th & G Sts NW Washington DC 20005

BRADY, THOMAS PICKENS, judge, lawyer; b. New Orleans, Aug. 6, 1903; s. Thomas and Jane Tullia (Smith) B.; A.B., Yale, 1927; LL.B., U. Miss., 1930; m. LaVerne Holmes, July 23, 1929; children—Thomas Pickens, Bruce Holmes. Instr. sociology U. Miss., 1929-30; admitted to Miss. bar, 1930, practiced in Brookhaven, Miss.; mem. firm Brady, Dean &Hobbs, 1930-38; dir. Brookhaven Bank & Trust Co., 1930—, atty., 1947-50; pres. Brookhaven Investment Co., 1934-44; v.p. Arcade Theater, Inc., 1935; pres., atty., Brookhaven Leader Co., 1942-57; dir., atty. Miss. Compress Co., 1947-61; judge Circuit Ct. 14th Dist., 1950-63; asso. justice Miss. Supreme Ct., 1963—. Commr. pub. safety, dir. Miss. Hwy. Safety Patrol, 1940-43, chmn. hwy. traffic adv. com. to War Dept., 1942-43; mem. Miss.-Gettysburg Meml. Commn., 1971-72. Nat. chmn. speakers bur. States' Rights, Democratic party, 1948, mem. exec. com., City of Brookhaven, 1932-53, del. Dem. Nat. Conv., 1940, 48, 60, 64; chmn. Miss. Dem. Nominating Com., 1960; formerly mem. Dem. Nat. Com. Awards judge of Freedoms Found. 1966. Recipient Distinguished Service citation Miss. Legislature, 1956. Mem. Miss. State Bar (v.p. 1954-55), Miss. Gun Collectors Assn. (pres. 1957), Am. Newcomen Soc., Abraham Lincoln Assn., S.A.R., Descs. Colonial Govs., 1st Families Miss., Am. Judicature Soc. Co. Mil. Collectors and Historians, Miss. Poetry Soc. (pres. 1972), U. Miss. Alumni Assn. (dir. 1962-64), Eta Sigma Phi, Phi Delta Phi, Zeta Psi, Sigma Phi, Omicron Delta Kappa. Baptist. Mason (32 deg. K.T., Shriner). Clubs: Summer (Yale); New Orleans Athletic, Boston (New Orleans). Author: South at Bay, 1948; Black Monday, 1954. Home: Natchez Rd Brookhaven MS 39601 Office: Brady Bldg Brookhaven MS 39601 also State Capitol Jackson MS 39205

BRAGG, ALFRED ORMAN, JR., banker; b. Florence, Ala., Apr. 18, 1920; s. Alfred Orman and Martha Henrietta (Veid) B.; B.A., Duke U., 1947; postgrad. Emory U., 1950-53, Rutgers U., 1963-65; m. Martha P. Bragg, Jan. 15, 1945; children—Alfred Orman III, Douglas Nelson, John Geoffrey, Susan Read. Securities analyst Conn. Gen. Life Ins. Co., Hartford, 1947-49; credit mgr. CIT Corp., Atlanta, 1949-51; credit mgr. Rich's, Inc., Atlanta, 1951-53; with Columbus Bank and Trust Co. (Ga.), 1953—, investment officer, 1954-69, v.p., 1970—. Instr. investments Columbus Coll., 1965-66; instr. trusts and investments Am. Inst. Banking, 1967-68. Bd. dirs. Jr. Achievement, 1954-59; trustee St. Thomas Sch.; trustee, dir. Echo Day Care Center. Served to lt. comdr. USNR, 1941-46. Recipient Service award Girl Scouts U.S., 1963. Mem. Atlanta Soc. Financial Analysts, C. of C. Democrat. Episcopalian (vestryman 1958-61, 62-65, 66-69, 70-72). Lion (bd. dirs. 1969-70). Club: Bryan Soc. Home: 2665 Habersham Av Columbus GA 31906 Office: PO Box 120 Columbus GA 31902

BRAIKOVICH, A.C., ins. co. exec. Sec., Am. Nat. Ins. Co., Galveston, Tex. Office: Moody Av at Market St Galveston TX 77550*

BRAILSFORD, JAMES MONCRIEF, state justice; b. Orangeburg, S. C., July 3, 1910; s. James Moncrief and Mary Elizabeth (Bates) B.; A.B., U. S.C., 1932, LL.B., 1934; m. Louise Rook Tompkins, Nov. 5, 1938 (dec. Aug. 1962) children—James Moncrief, Daniel Tompkins, Amelia Tompkins, Martha Aldrich; m. Joan Ward Culler, June 19, 1971. Admitted to S.C. bar, 1934; practiced in Orangeburg, 1934-49; circuit judge S.C., 1949-62; asso. justice Supreme Ct. S.C., 1962—. Mem. S.C. Ho. of Reps. from Orangeburg County, 1939-42, 47-49. Served with AUS, World War II. Mem. Phi Beta Kappa. Address: PO Box 386 Orangeburg SC 29115

BRAINARD, JAYNE DAWSON (MRS. ERNEST SCOTT BRAINARD), club woman; b. Amarillo, Tex., Nov. 1; d. Bill Cross and Evelyn (McLane) Dawson; A.B., Oklahoma City U., 1950; m. Ernest Scott Brainard, Nov. 26, 1950; children—Sydney Jane, Bill Dawson. Guardian Camp Fire Assn., 1960-65; vol. N.W. Tex. Hosp. Aux., 1960-63; state chmn. Am. Heritage, D.A.R., 1963-67, vice regent chpt. 1963-66, regent, 1966-68, state historian Tex. soc., 1967-70, state chmn. marshalls Tex. soc., 1967-70, nat. vice chmn. marshal com., 1969-73, Tex. rec. sec., 1970-73, mem. state organizing com., 1967-70, nat. vice chmn. motion picture commn., 1971—, also organizing pres. Children of Am. Revolution, 1963-66, state chmn.; organizing regent Daus. Am. Colonists, 1972; br. pres. Am. Assn. U. Women, 1963-65, mem. state library com., 1967-69; sec.-treas. group League of Democratic Women, 1964; pres. Amarillo Rep. Women's Club, 1968, v.p., 1972; pres. Panhandle Geol. Soc. Aux., 1959; pres. Speaking of Living Study Club, 1962-63; pres. Starlighters Dance Club, 1963-64; bd. dirs., chmn. pub. relations Amarillo Little Theater; chmn. Leaders Assn. Amarillo Camp Fire Council, 1964-69; mem. steering com. Nat. Library Week, Amarillo, 1964-68; bd. dirs. Amarillo Fine Arts Council, 1966-68; pres. Amarillo Little Theatre, 1968-69; mem. Revitalize Amarillo Com. Mem. U.D.C., Internat. Platform Assn. Home: 2119 S Lipscomb St Amarillo TX 79109 Office: Box 1101 Amarillo TX 79105

BRALLEY, JAMES ALEXANDER, JR., chem. co. exec.; b. Hot Springs, Va., Aug. 18, 1916; s. James Alexander and Daisy Elizabeth (Williams) B.; B.S., U. Va., 1936, Ph.D., 1941; m. Rosemary Kearfott, Aug. 17, 1946; children—Sandra Lynn (Mrs. Henry Claude Billingsley, Jr.), Patricia, James Alexander III. Research chemist B. F. Goodrich Co., Akron, O., 1941-46; devel. chemist Rohm & Haas Co., Phila., 1946-49, sr. devel. chemist, 1949-54, lab. mgr., 1954-56; dir. chem. research A. E. Staley Mfg. Co., Decatur, Ill., 1956-61, v.p., research and tech. dir., 1961-70; v.p., research and tech. dir. Puritan Chem. Co., Atlanta, 1971—. Tech. rep. Corn Industries Research Found., 1957-70. Mem. Mayor's Human Relations Commn., Decatur, Ill., 1962-65. Bd. dirs. Indsl. Research Inst., 1965-69, Ill. Jr. Coll., 1967-71. Mallinckrodt fellow in organic chemistry U. Va., 1938-41. Mem. Am. Chem. Soc., A.A.A.S., Soc. Chem. Industry, Dirs. Indsl. Research, Sigma Xi, Alpha Chi Sigma. Republican. Unitarian. Patentee in field. Home: 5209 Pine Bark Lane Dunwoody GA 30338 Office: 916 Ashby St NW Atlanta GA 30318

BRAMAN, LEONARD, superior ct. judge; b. Phila., Aug. 21, 1925; s. Harry and Katie (Rappaport) B.; B.S., Temple U., 1949; LL.B., U. Va., 1952; m. Joyce J. Roberts, June 22, 1952; children—David Henry, Barrett Andrew. Admitted to D.C. bar, 1952; law clk. U.S. Ct. Appeals for D.C., Washington, 1952-53; asst. U.S. atty. criminal div. D.C., Washington, 1953-54; Bigelow teaching fellow U. Chgo. Law Sch., 1954-55; mem. firms Newmyer & Bress, Washington, 1955-61, David G. Bress, 1961-64, Bress, Braman & Hilmer, 1964-65, Surrey, Karasik, Greene & Hill, 1965-70; asso. judge Superior Ct. D.C., Washington, 1970—. Served with USAAF, 1943-45. Mem. Am., D.C. bar assns., Internat. Platform Assn., Order of Coif. Editorial bd. U. Va. Law Sch., 1952. Home: 12600 Springloch Ct Silver Spring MD 20904 Office: 440 G St NW Washington DC 20001

BRAMBILA, SERGIO, animal nutritionist; b. Mexico City, Mexico, Oct. 21, 1930; s. Aureliano and Teresa (De La Mora) B.; B. Quimico Farmaceutico Biologo, Nat. U. Mexico, 1953; M. Nutrition Sci., Cornell U., 1960; Ph.D., U. Cal. at Davis, 1965; m. Bertila Gomez, Feb. 24, 1957; children—Eduardo, Julieta, Dora. Asst. prof. food analysis Nat. U. Mexico, Mexico City, 1955-56, prof. nutrition and biochemistry, 1961; research asst. biochemistry Mexican Inst. Tech., Mexico City, 1957-58; head dept. animal nutrition Nat. Center for Livestock Research, Mexico City, 1965-67; animal nutritionist Ralston Purina de Mexico, Mexico City, 1967—. Bank of Mexico fellow, 1958-60; Rockefeller Found. fellow, 1962-65. Mem. Chem. Soc. Mexico, Mexican Soc. Animal Prodn., Mexican Soc. Nutritionists, Am. Soc. Animal Sci., Am. Soc. Poultry Sci., World's Poultry Sci. Assn., Am. Oil Chemists Soc., Cal. Avocado Soc., Centro Asturiano de Mexico, Sigma Xi, Phi Kappa Phi. Home: 36 Bugambilia Av Mexico 21 DF Mexico Office: 51-10 piso Reforma Mexico 1 DF Mexico

BRAMBLE, RONALD LEE, educator; b. Pauls Valley, Okla., Sept. 9, 1937; s. Homer Lee and Ethyl Juanita (Stephens) B.; A.A., San Antonio Coll., 1957; B.S., Trinity U., 1959, M.S., 1964; postgrad. St. Mary's Univ. Sch. Law, 1969-71; m. Kathryn Louise Seiler, July 2, 1960; 1 dau., Julia Dawn. Mgr., buyer Fed-Mart, Inc., San Antonio, 1959-61; tchr. bus. San Antonio Ind. Sch. Dist., 1961-65, edn. coordinator, bus. tng. specialist, 1965-67; asso. prof., chmn. dept. mgmt. San Antonio Coll., 1967—. Prin. Ron Bramble Assos., San Antonio, 1967—; lectr. bus., edn. and ch. groups, 1965—; cons. editor Prentice-Hall, Inc., Englewood Cliffs, N.J., 1969-71. Served with AUS, 1959. Recipient Wall Street Jour. award Trinity U., 1959; Distinguished Salesman award Sales and Marketing Execs., 1967; Merit award Adminstrv. Mgmt. Soc., 1968. Mem. San Antonio C. of C. (mem. com. 1967—), Adminstrv. Mgmt. Soc. (pres. 1966-68), Bus. Edn. Tchrs. Assn. (pres. 1964), Sales and Marketing Execs. San Antonio (dir. 1967—), Phi Delta Phi. Republican. Methodist. Lion. Club: San Antonio Advertising. Contbr. articles to profl. jours. Home: 127 Palo Duro San Antonio TX 78216

BRAMLETT, EDWIN C., hosp. adminstr. Adminstr. Mobile (Ala.) Infirmary. Office: Box 4097 Mobile AL 36604*

BRAMLETTE, SELMA GEORGIA MITCHELL (MRS. JAMES D. BRAMLETTE), librarian; b. Centerhill, Ark., July 22, 1893; d. Virgil B. and Sarah L. (Adams) Mitchell; B.A., Tex. Coll. Arts and Industries, 1930; B.S., in L.S., Tex. Woman's U., 1946, M.L.S., 1950; m. James D. Bramlette, July 24, 1912 (dec. Oct. 1967); children—Sarah J. (Mrs. C. A. Buenning), James D., Mary Jane (Mrs. W. D. Hughart). Social studies tchr., Stephenville, Tex., 1924, Waco State Home, 1943-46, Sinton, Tex., 1945-46; librarian Sinton (Tex.) High Sch., 1946-49; supr. libraries Sinton Ind. Sch. Dist., 1949-62; librarian Refugio County Pub. Library, Refugio, Tex., 1962—. Recipient certificate of merit Sinton Pub. Schs., 1962. Mem. N.E.A. (life), Tex. State, Coastal Bend (pres. 1952-53) library assns., Alumni Assn. Tex. Coll. Arts and Industries, Delta Kappa Gamma, Alpha Beta Alpha. (life). Clubs: Sinton Faculty; Century (Stephenville, Tex.). Democrat. Baptist. Home: 214 W Heard St Refugio TX 78377 Office: Commerce St Refugio TX 78377

BRAMLETTE, WILLIAM ALLEN, oil co. exec.; b. Greenville, Tex., Aug. 31, 1911; s. Felix B. and Minnie (Williams) B.; B.S., So. Meth. U., 1932; M.A., U. Tex. at Austin, 1934; Ph.D. in Geology, U. Kan., 1943; m. Roberta Wooten, Apr. 1, 1932; children—William Allen, Sara (Mrs. George Wells), Robert W. Instr. geology U. Tex., 1936-43; from sr. geologist to asst. exploration mgr. Carter Oil Co., Billings, Mont., 1943-47, Denver, 1947-53, Tulsa, Okla., 1953-61; from coordinator spl. exploration studies to mgr. hdqrs. exploration dept. Humble Oil & Refining Co., Houston, 1961-68; exec. v.p. Esso Exploration Inc., N.Y.C., 1968-71, Houston, 1971; v.p. Esso Prodn. Research Co., Houston, 1971—. Mem. adv. bd. dept. geol. scis. U. So. Cal., 1970-72, U. Kan., 1971; mem. tech. subcom. on petroleum resources under ocean floor Nat. Petroleum Council, 1968-69. Recipient Erasmus Haworth Distinguished Alumnus award U. Kan., 1956. Fellow Geol. Soc. Am.; mem. Nat. Security Indsl. Assn. (adv. council ocean scis. and tech. 1970), Soc. Econ. Paleontologists and Mineralogists, Am. Assn. Petroleum Geologists. Home: 11606 Shady Grove Houston TX 77024 Office: 3120 Buffalo Speedway Houston TX 77006

BRANAM, GEORGE CURTIS, educator, univ. ofcl.; b. Amarillo, Tex., July 15, 1923; s. William C. and Mabel (McNutt) B.; B.A., U. Cal. at Berkeley, 1947, M.A., 1949, Ph.D., 1952 Inst. U. Cal. Far East Comd., 1950-52 instr. La. State U., 1952-54; asst. prof. La. State U. at Baton Rouge, 1954-58, asso. prof., New Orleans, 1958-63, prof., 1963—, dir. humanities div., 1958-62, dean Coll. Liberal Arts, 1962-64, dean acad. affairs, 1964-69, vice chancellor, 1969—. Served with AUS, 1943-46. Mem. Modern Lang. Assn., Shakespeare Assn. Am., Bibliog. Soc. Author: Eighteenth Century Adaptations of Shakespearean Tragedy, 1956. Office: Office of Academic Affairs La State U New Orleans LA 70122

BRANCH, HARLLEE, JR., ret. public utility exec.; b. Atlanta, June 21, 1906; s. Harllee and Bernice (Simpson) B; A.B., Davidson Coll., 1927, LL.D., 1962; LL.B., Emory U., 1931, LL.D., 1965; L.H.D., Howard Coll. (now Samford U.), 1965; m. Katherine Quintard Hunter, June 8, 1932; children—Harllee III, Katherine B. McKenzie, Barrington Heath, David Stuart. Reporter Atlanta Jour., 1929-31; admitted to Ga. bar, 1931; publicity dir., radio sta. WSB, 1930-32; lectr. Emory U., 1931-36, U. Ga. Evening Coll., 1929-34, Atlanta Law Sch., 1936-40: asso. firm Colquitt, MacDougald, Troutman & Arkwright, 1931-35; mem. firm MacDougald, Troutman Sams & Branch, 1936-49; v.p., gen. mgr., dir. Ga. Power Co., 1949-50, pres., 1951-56; pres., dir. So. Co. (parent firm Ala., Ga., Gulf and Miss. power cos.), 1957-69, chmn. bd., dir., 1969-71; chmn., dir., chmn. exec. com. So. Services, Inc., 1969-71; v.p., dir. Ala., Ga., Gulf, Miss. power cos., 1951-68; dir., dep. chmn. Fed. Res. Bank of Atlanta, 1953-59; dir. U.S. Steel Corp., Interfinancial, Inc.; former dir. Gen. Motors Corp. Mem. Bus. Council, 1963—; mem. Ga. Sci. and Tech. Commn., 1956-71; mem. president's adv. council Agnes Scott Coll.; mem. Atlanta Found. Mem. Pres.'s Nat. Center for Vol. Action, 1970-71. Trustee, Emory U., Davidson Coll., Ga. Tech. Research Inst., Tax Found., Inc., 1966-71; dir. Ga. 4-H Club, State YMCA Ga., 1939—; trustee United Student Aid Funds, Inc., 1963-71; hon. trustee Ga. Coll. at Milledgeville. Served as lt. (jg.) USNR, 1944-45. Mem. Ga. Bar Assn., Beta Theta Pi, Omicron Delta Kappa, Phi Delta Phi, Alpha Kappa Psi. Independent. Presbyn. (elder). Clubs: Piedmont Driving, Capital City, Peachtree Golf, Homosassa Fishing; Highlands (N.C.) Country. Home: 3106 Nancy's Creek Rd NW Atlanta GA 30327

BRANCH, JAMES W., physician; b. Little Rock, Mar. 26, 1909; s. William Mathew and Rosie (Perkins) B.; B.S., U. Ark., 1931, M.D., 1935; postgrad. Washington U., St. Louis, 1938-39, Cook Grad. Sch. Medicine, 1951-56; m. Nell Wilkes, June 20, 1935; children— James William, Hal W., Marynell. Intern, Charity Hosp. La., New Orleans, 1935-36, U.S. Marine Hosp., New Orleans, 1936; student in surgery and orthopedic surgery under Sir Watson Jones, Sedenham, Eng., 1944; practice medicine, specializing in gen. surgery, Hope, Ark., 1945—; mem. staff Branch Gen. Hosp., Hope, Ark. Served with USMCR, 1941-45. Decorated Bronze Star medal with five oak leaf clusters, Silver Star medal, Purple Heart; Croix de Guerre, Vermillion Star (France). Mem. Am. Acad. Family Practice (pres. Ark. chpt. 1967-68), A.M.A., Am. Soc. Abdominal Surgeons, Internat. Acad. Proctology, So. Med. Assn. (counselor 1968-72), Ark. Med. Soc. (v.p. 1966-67). Presbyn. (elder 1960-72). Home: 1801 S Main St Hope AR 71801 Office: 426 S Main St Hope AR 71801

BRANCH, JOSEPH, justice N.C. Supreme Ct. Asso. Justice N.C. Supreme Ct., Raleigh. Office: Justice Bldg Raleigh NC 27602*

BRAND, PAUL WILSON, surgeon; b. India, July 17, 1914; s. Jesse Mann and Evelyn Constance (Harris) B.; student Univ. Coll. Sch., London, Eng., 1933; M.B., B.S., Univ. Coll. Hosp., London, 1943; LL.D., Wheaton Coll., 1971.; m. Margaret Elizabeth Berry, May 29, 1943; children—Christopher W., Jean M., Constance M., Estelle F., Patricia N., Pauline F. Intern Univ. Coll. Hosp., 1943-44, resident, 1944-45; resident Hosp. for Sick Children, London, 1945-46; tchr. orthopaedic surgery Christian Med. Coll., Vellore, India, 1946-64, prof. surgery, 1954-64, also past pres.; chief rehab. br. USPHS Hosp., Carville, La., 1966—; clin. prof. surgery La. State U. Med. Sch., 1966—; spl. research to correct deformity in leprosy, 1947—; past chmn. world com. Leprosy rehab. Internat. Soc. Rehab. Disabled, 1962-70; Hunterian prof. (reconstructive surgery in leprosy), Royal Coll. Surgeons, 1952, 62. Recipient Lasker award for distinguished services field rehab., 1958, medal Am. Assn. Plastic Surgeons, 1966; decorated comdr. Order British Empire. Fellow Royal Coll. Surgeons, Royal Soc. Medicine, Brit. Orthopaedic Assn., Am. Surg. Assn. (hon.), A.C.S.; hon. mem. Am. Soc. Surgery Hand; corr. mem. Am. Assn. Plastic and Reconstructive Surgery. Address: USPHS Hospital Carville LA 70721

BRAND, VANCE DEVOE, astronaut; b. Longmont, Colo., May 9, 1931; s. Rudolph William and Donna (DeVoe) B.; B.S. in Bus., U. Colo., 1953, B.S. in Aero. Engring., 1960; M.B.A., U. Cal. at Los Angeles, 1964; grad. U.S. Naval Test Pilot Sch., Patuxent River, Md., 1963; m. Joan Virginia Weninger, July 25, 1953; children—Susan Nancy, Stephanie, Patrick Richard, Kevin Stephen. With Lockheed-Cal. Co., Burbank, 1960-66, flight test engr., 1961-62, traveling engr. rep., 1962-63, engring. test pilot, 1963-66; astronaut NASA Manned Spacecraft Center, Houston, 1966—. Served with USMC, 1953-57. Mem. Soc. Exptl. Test Pilots, Am. Inst. Aeros. and Astronautics. Home: 18607 Martinique Houston TX 77058 Office: NASA Manned Spacecraft Center Houston TX 77058

BRANDELL, ROY A., wholesale co. exec.; b. St. Charles, Ill., Oct. 18, 1913; s. G.A. and Hannah (Alexander) B.; ed. Northwestern U., U. Chgo.; m. Blythe Taylor, Nov. 25, 1945; children—John Taylor, Patricia Louise. Office mgr. Forest Milk Co., River Forest, Ill., 1946-50; sr. accountant Wolf & Co., Oklahoma City, 1950-59, partner, 1960-62; sec.-treas. Scrivner-Boogaart, Inc., Oklahoma City, 1962—, also dir. Served to capt. AUS, 1941-46. C.P.A., Ill. Mem. Am. Inst. C.P.A.s, Okla. Soc. C.P.A.s. Club: Quail Creek Golf and Country. Home: 3406 Venice Blvd Oklahoma City OK 73112 Office: Box 26146 Oklahoma City OK 73126

BRANDENBURG, E. CRAIG, clergyman; b. Corydon, Ind., Aug. 26, 1907; s. William S. and Brittie (Breeden) B.; B.A., Ind. Central Coll., 1930, D.D., 1945; B.D., United Theol. Sem., 1935, M.Div., 1972; m. Eva Traylor, Aug. 20, 1933; 1 son, Calvin. Ordained to ministry Evang. U.B. Ch., 1930; pastor First Ch., Evansville, Ind., 1935-44; supt. Ind. Conf., Bedford, Ind., 1944-55; exec. sec. Nat. Bd. Christian Edn., Evang. U.B. Ch., Dayton, O., 1955-68; asso. gen. sec. Bd. Edn., United Meth. Ch., Nashville, 1968—. Trustee Ind. Central Coll., 1937—, United Theol. Sem., Dayton, O., 1947—, Evang. Theol. Sem., 1955-71. Mem. Nat. Council Chs., Trinium, and Div. of Christian Edn., World Council Christian Edn., 1950-68. Home: 26 Williamsburg Circle Brentwood TN 37027 Office: 1001 19th Av S Nashville TN 37202

BRANDENBURG, KURT E., dir. Mus. of Confederacy. Office: 1201 E Clay St Richmond VA 23219*

BRANDLI, JEAN S., telephone co. ofcl.; b. New Haven, Sept. 13, 1918; d. Arthur J. and Beatrice (Murray) Smith; student So. Sem., Jr. Coll.; grad. mgmt. devel. program U. Kan., 1966; grad. engring. mgmt. course U. Mich., 1967; m. Charles J. Augustine, May 14, 1945 (div. 1956); m. 2d, Shumway J. Bird, Feb. 1958 (div. 1964); m. 3d, Henry E. Brandli, Jr., June 28, 1964. Treas., Lexington Telephone Co., 1951-54. pres., 1954-58; pres. Coosa Valley Telephone Co., Pell City, Ala., 1955—, No. Ind. Telephone Co., Wawaka, Ind., 1959-67. Mem. Southeastern telephone exec. delegation to Russia, 1966; leader People to People travel to Russia, 1969. Named Ala. Telephone Woman of Yr., 1966. Mem. C. of C. Greater Pell City (pres.), U.S., Va. ind. telephone assns., Orgn. for Protection and Advancement Small Telephone Cos. (bd. dirs.), Ala.-Miss. Telephone Assn. (bd. dirs., v.p.), Ind. Telephone Pioneers Am., So. Sem. Alumnae Assn. (pres.), U.S. Woman's Club, Bus. and Profl. Women's Clubs (pres. Pell City). Clubs: The Club; Relay House; Pine Harbor Country; Downtown (Birmingham, Ala.). Home: Abbot Dr Rivere Estates Pell City AL 35125 Office: 1700 Cogswell Av Pell City AL 35125

BRANDON, CHARLES LEWIS, assn. exec.; b. Pontotoc, Miss., Sept. 17, 1938; s. William Charles and Lorene Elizabeth (Sneed) B.; B.S., Miss. Coll., 1966; m. Ruth Allon McEarley, Aug. 30, 1961; children—Charles Allen, Bradlea Ann. Tchr., coach Gulf Coast Mil. Acad., Mississippi City, Miss., 1961-62; tchr. St. Mary's Cath. Sch., Jackson, Miss., 1962-64; coach St. Joseph's High Sch., Jackson, Miss., 1963-65; dir. recreational therapy Miss. State Hosp., Whitfield, 1965-68; dir. field services U.S. Jaycees, Tulsa, Okla., 1968—. Cons. Nat. Center Vol. Action, 1970—. Mem. exec. com. Pres's Com. Employment Handicapped, 1969—; mem. Pres. Task Force on Rubella, 1970—; mem. Pres. Listening Post, 1971—; mem. youth com. Nat. Safety Council, 1969—; mem. Tulsa-Police-Community 1970—; Council, 1970—; mem. drug abuse com. Greater Tulsa Community Council, 1970—; mem. adv. com. Okla. Assn. Retarded Children, 1969—. Bd. dirs. On the Bricks Inc. Named Outstanding State Chmn., Miss. Jaycees, 1968. Mem. Fellowship Christian Athletes, Hermenian Lit. Soc., Internat. Platform Assn., Miss. Jr. C. of C. (state chmn. 1967). Baptist. Home: 5634 S Zunis St Tulsa OK 74105 Office: Box 7 Tulsa OK 74105

BRANDON, HEMBREE BEDELL, newspaper editor; b. New Albany, Miss., July 11, 1936; s. Roy Bedell and Pearl (Miller) B.; A.A., N.E. Miss., 1956; m. Gloria Jean Floyd, June 22, 1961; children—Stephen Alan, Lisa Carole. Pub. relations dir. No. dist. Miss. Hwy. Dept., Tupelo, 1956-62; editor Winona (Miss.) Times, 1962—. Mem. Miss. Press Assn. Methodist. Rotarian. Home: 417 Witty St Winona MS 38967 Office: 321 Summitt St Box 151 Winona MS 38967

BRANDON, HENRY (OSCAR), newspaper editor; b. Mar. 9, 1916; s. Oscar and Ida Brandon; student univs. Lausanne (Switzerland), Prague (Czechoslovakia), London (Eng.). With Sunday Times of London, 1939—, war corr. Africa and Europe, then Paris corr., 1945-46, roving diplomatic corr., 1946-49, Washington corr., 1949—, asso. editor, 1963—. Adviser UN Conf. Freedom Information, 1948. Recipient journalistic awards U. Cal. at Los Angeles, 1957, Lincoln U., Jefferson City, Miss., 1962; Hannen Swaffer award Odham Press, London, 1964, 67. Mem. Overseas Writers, Fgn. Press Assn. Clubs: Nat. Press, Federal City (Washington). Author: As We Are, 1961; In The Red, 1966; Conversations with Henry Brandon, 1966; The Anatomy of Error, 1969. Address: 1814 National Press Bldg Washington DC 20004

BRANDON, WILLIAM GERALD, sch. adminstr.; b. Aliceville, Ala., Oct. 5, 1928; s. Ralph Waldo and Winnie Mildred (Russell) B.; B.S., U. Ala., 1952; M.A., 1953; postgrad. U. Ga., 1963-65; m. Polly Ann Parker, Nov. 18, 1948; children—Sharon Kay, Shannon Gerald. Coach, Excel (Ala.) High Sch., 1953-56, prin., 1956-62; tchr. Northwoods Sch., Doraville, Ga., 1962-65; prin. Peachcrest Sch., Decatur, Ga., 1965—. Coach basketball team Midway Recreation Center, 1966-70; coach baseball team Midway Park, 1966-70. Bd. dirs., sec. Midway Football Assn., 1969—. Bd. dirs. Midway Heights Little League, sec. bd. dirs., 1966—. Served with USAF, 1946-49. Mem. Ga. Elementary Assn. (mem. credential com. 1969), Dekalb County Elementary Prins. Assn. (pres. 1969), Phi Delta Kappa. Mason. Home: 1367 Cornwall Rd Decatur GA 20032 Office: 1530 Joy Lane Decatur GA 30032

BRANDT, CARL DAVID, virologist; b. Bridgeport, Conn., Jan. 19, 1928; s. Carl August and Hildur (Wedberg) B.; B.S., U. Conn., 1949; M.S., U. Mass., 1951; Ph.D., Harvard, 1958; m. Elsa Lund Erickson, Apr. 25, 1964; children—Karen Lund, Erik Lund. Instr. vet. sci. U. Mass., Amherst, 1949-52, 54; research virologist biologics research dept. Charles Pfizer and Co., Terre Haute, Ind., 1958-61, research virologist chemotherapy research dept. Pfizer Med. Research Labs., Groton, Conn., 1961-62; asso. dept. epidemiology Pub. Health Research Inst., N.Y.C., 1962-66; research asso. virology sect. Research Found., Children's Hosp. D.C., Washington, 1966—. Instr. pediatrics Georgetown U. Sch. Medicine, 1966-69, asst. prof. pediatrics (microbiology) George Washington U. Sch. Med., 1969-71, asst. prof. child health and devel., 1971—. Served with USAF, 1952-54. Mem. A.A.A.S., Am. Soc. Microbiology, Sigma Xi. Research on epidemiology of respiratory viruses, virus vaccines. Home: 819 E Franklin Av Silver Spring MD 20901 Office: Children's Hosp Research Found 2125 13th St Washington DC 20009

BRANDT, GEORGE FRED, JR., civil engr.; b. Wetumpka, Ala., July 14, 1927; s. George Fred and Alpha (Leonard) B.; student U. Tenn., 1946-48; B.C.E., Clemson Coll., 1951; m. Jo Frances Oulla, June 9, 1951; children—David George, Donna Jo. Constrn. engr. E. I. Dupont Co., Savannah River (S.C.) Plant, S.C., 1951-54, prodn. supr., 1954-59; plant engr. Merry Bros. Brick & Tile Co., Augusta, Ga., 1959-62; head civil engring. dept. Jones & Fellers, Augusta, 1962-66; owner Brandt & Assos., cons. engrs., North Augusta, S.C., 1966—. Served with USNR, 1945-46. Registered profl. engr., Ga., S.C., N.C., Tenn., Fla. Mem. Am. Soc. C.E., S.C. Water and Pollution Control Assn., Nat., Ga. socs. profl. engrs. Baptist. Home: 516 Tanager Rd North Augusta SC 29841 Office: Brandt & Assos 516 Tanager Rd North Augusta SC 29841

BRANDT, HARRY, economist; b. Dresden, Germany, Apr. 13, 1925; s. George and Margarethe (Hamburger) B.; came to U.S., 1938; B.A., U. Wash., 1947; M.S., Columbia, 1949, Ph.D., 1954; m. Frances M. Jacobson, Oct. 29, 1950; children—Stephen J., Douglas M., Sandra J. Instr., Rutgers U., 1949-52, City Coll. N.Y., summer 1951, Ga. State Coll., Atlanta, 1955-59; asst. economist Fed. Res. Bank of Atlanta, 1954, asso. economist, 1955-58, economist, 1958-59, sr. economist, 1959-60, asst. cashier, 1961, asst. v.p., 1962-65, v.p. research, 1965—. Served with AUS, 1944-46. Mem. Am., So. econ. assns., Am., So. (pres. 1971-72) finance assns. Home: 2722 Foster Ridge Rd NE Atlanta GA 30345 Office: 104 Marietta St NW Atlanta GA 30303

BRANDT, PAUL CARL HENRY, educator; b. Indpls., Oct. 26, 1923; s. Carl F. and Alma C. (Schakel) B.; B.S., U. Ill., 1947, M.S., 1948; m. Olga Louise Gates, Nov. 25, 1945; children—Marsha (Mrs. Michael S. Davis), Mark, James, John, Chris. Grad. asst. instr. U. Ill., 1947-48; with Lennox & Matthews & Asso., architects, Indpls., 1948-50, Brandt Bros., & Co., gen. contractors, Indpls., 1950-57, Paul Brandt, architect and engr., Indpls., 1957-60; pres. Brandt & DeLap, Inc., architects, Indpls., 1960-68; prof., head. dept. bldg. tech. Auburn U. (Ala.), 1968—. Del. Ind. State Republican Conv. 1966. Bd. dirs. Asso. Schs. Constrn., 1970-71, v.p., 1972-74. Served with AUS, 1943-46. Mem. A.I.A. (chpt. sec. 1968-70), Alpha Rho Chi, Scarab, Gargoyle. Lutheran (trustee 1958-64, elder 1964-67, sch. bd.

1967-68). Lion. Prin. archtl. works include RCA Tv Assembly Plant, Bloomington, Ind., 1965, Lincoln Elementary Sch., Indpls., 1961, MacArthur Elementary Sch., Indpls., 1963, Pub. Library, Speedway, Ind., 1967. Home: 1248 E Samford Av Auburn AL 36830

BRANNON, GERARD MARION, econ. cons.; b. Manila, P.I., June 28, 1922; s. Ernest M. and Marjorie (Devitt) B.; A.B., Georgetown U., 1943, M.A., 1944; Ph.D., Harvard, 1950; m. Frances M. Maguire, Sept. 7, 1946; children—Michael, Phillip, Richard, Marguerite, Paul. Instr. econs. Boston Coll., 1946-48; asst. prof. U. Notre Dame, 1948-51; economist Joint Congl. Com. Taxation, Washington, 1951-56; economist Ways and Means Com., Ho. of Reps., Washington, 1956-63; economist, asso. dir. to dir. Office Tax Analysis, U.S. Treasury Dept., Washington, 1963-72; professorial lectr. Georgetown U., 1951-71, research prof., 1972-—. Home: 4813 N 24th St Arlington VA 22207 Office: Georgetown Univ Washington DC 20220

BRANSON, ROBERT EARL, market research economist; b. Dallas, Dec. 3, 1918; s. Earl and Gertrude (Smith) B.; B.S. in Bus. Adminstrn., So. Meth. U., 1941; M.A. in Econs., Harvard, 1949, M.A. in Pub. Adminstrn., 1948, Ph.D. in Econs., 1954; m. Ruth Parker, May 18, 1945; children—Donald Elliott, Richard Parker. Economist, U.S. Dept. Agr., 1941-47; asso. dir. market research U. P.R., 1949-50; statistician U.S. Dept. Agr., 1950, economist, 1951-54; prof. econs., chmn. market devel. research, dept. agrl. econs. and sociology Tex. A and M. U., also dir. consumer market research Tex. Agrl. Expt. St., 1954-69, coordinator Tex. Agrl. Market Research and Devel. Center, 1969-—; pres. Branson & Assos., Inc.; cons. economist U.S. AID, Argentina, 1962. Chmn. Bryan City Planning Commn. Served as economist OSS, Hdqr. Detachment, U.S. Army, Washington, World War II. Mem. Urban Land Inst., Am. Marketing Assn., Am. Econ. Assn., Am. Farm Econs. Assn. Democrat. Methodist (bd. dirs). Kiwanian. Author: (with others) Marketing Efficiency in Puerto Rico, 1955. Contbr. articles on consumer marketing. Home: 4008 Culpepper Dr Bryan TX 77801 Office: Dept Agrl Econs Tex A and M Univ College Station TX 77840

BRANSTETTER, GWENDOLYN HARRIS (MRS. CECIL ANDREW BRANSTETTER), artist; b. Beeville, Tex., Oct. 7, 1924; d. William Ward and Pearl (Johnson) Harris; student Tex. Technol. Coll., 1949; m. Cecil Andrew Branstetter, May 24, 1943; children—Ronnie Cecil, Reagan Ecil, Randy Ward. Tchr., Live Oak County, Tex., 1942-44; ednl. sec. Refugio (Tex.) Rural High Schs., 1955-61; bookkeeper B & G Constrn. Co., Sinton, Tex., 1961-71, also pvt. art instr., Refugio and Woodsboro, Tex., 1965-—; artist, works exhibited Sta. KRIS-TV (Corpus Christi, Tex.), Nat. League Am. Pen Women (Dallas), NASA (Houston), Internat. Platform Assn. show, Washington, also Paris and Issoudun, France, 1968; one-man show YWCA, Corpus Christi, Ann Page Art Studio, Corsicana, Tex., Andrews, San Antonio, Corpus Christie, Goliad, Refugio (all Tex.), 1971; art show judge, 1965, 66, 69; chmn. 18th Senatorial Dist. Gov.'s 3d Annual Art Show, 1966; spl. guest artist, Jemez Aprings, N.M., 1971. Recipient awards Corpus Christi Fine Arts, 1957, 1958, South Tex. Traditional Art Assn. exhibit, Corpus Christi, 1959, Nat. League Am. Pen Women, 1966-68. Mem. Refugio Art Guild (pres. 1957-60), Corpus Christi Fine Arts, Nat. League Am. Pen Women, Centro Studi e Scambi Internazionali (Rome, Italy), South Tex. Traditional Art Assn., Traditional Art Club of Woodsboro, Internat. Platform Assn. Home and studio: 1004 Douglas St Refugio TX 78377

BRANTLEY, ALICE VIRGINIA SINGER (MRS. EDWARD FITZROY BRANTLEY), civic worker; b. Muncie, Ind.; d. Harry Dwight and Dessa (Slater) Singer; student Muncie Conservatory Music, 1912-20, Met. Sch. Music, 1920-22; studied harp with Louise Schelschmidt Koehne, Indpls., 1917-22, Henriette Renie, Paris, France, 1922-26, 50; m. Edward Fitzroy Brantley, Sept. 19, 1956. Concert debut, Paris, 1925; mem. Septuor Renie, 1923-26; concerts in Paris, N.Y.C., Chgo., Ft. Wayne, Indpls., St. Petersburg, Fla., 1920-63, with Alice Singer Trio, St. Petersburg, 1933-56; performed with St. Petersburg Symphony, Jacksonville (Fla.) Symphony, Tampa (Fla.) Philharmonic, Fla. Philharmonic, 1950-66; radio program WSUN, St. Petersburg, 1933. Ambassador, People-to-People Goodwill Mission from St. Petersburg to Europe and Middle East, 1960, to Soviet Union and satellites, 1965; mem. Fla. Art Commn., 1964-67; v.p. Suncoast Goodwill Industries, 1965-69, v.p. Aux. Guild, 1965-66; mem. St. Anthony's Hosp. Guild, 1961-—, Children's Home Soc., 1963-—, Suncoast Heart Assn., 1966; chmn. Queen of Hearts Ball, St. Petersburg, 1968; Heart Sunday chmn., 1963. Bd. dirs. Pinellas County Mental Health Assn., Mound Park Hosp. Aux., All Children's Hosp. Guild. Recipient Renie Harp award Paris, 1926, citation Radio Sta. WDAE, Tampa, 1965; named Princess of Royal Ct., St. Petersburg Heart Assn., 1963, Queen of Hearts, 1967; Contessa of Yr., Suncoast Opera Guild, 1970. Mem. Fla. Philharmonic Soc. (charter pres. 1954), Chamber Music Soc. (charter pres. 1966-68), Bel Canto (charter 1956), St. Petersburg opera assns., Fla. Art Council (charter 1963), Lions Club Aux. (past pres.), Soroptimist Internat. (pres. St. Petersburg 1962-63), St. Petersburg Hist. Soc., Mus. Fine Arts. Home: 1910 Brightwaters Blvd NE St Petersburg FL 33704

BRANTLEY, BILLY BURDETTE, supt. schs.; b. McLean, Tex., Nov. 20, 1925; s. Thaddius Frederick and Ada Fern (Robinson) B.; A.B., Panhandle State Coll., 1949; M.Ed., West Tex. State U., 1955; postgrad. U. Tex. 1957-58; m. Margaret Irene Hood, Aug. 7, 1949; children—Janelle, Billy Burdette, Jacalyn, Jerri. Dir. guidance Dumas (Tex.) Ind. Sch. Dist., 1949-64; supt., Claude (Tex.) Ind. Sch. Dist., 1964-68, Kilgore (Tex.) Ind. Sch. Dist., 1968-—. Served with USNR, 1944-46. Mem. Am., Tex. assns. sch. adminstrs., N.E.A. (life), Tex. Tchrs. Assn. (life), Kilgore C. of C. (dir. 1969-72), Phi Delta Kappa. Democrat. Baptist (deacon 1960-72). Lion, Rotarian. Home: 500 Bean St Kilgore TX 75662 Office: PO Box 1541 Kilgore TX 75662

BRANTLEY, EDWARD FITZROY, realtor, bus. exec.; b. nr. St. Petersburg, Fla., Aug. 15, 1893; s. Clarence Beverly and Lula (Dye) B.; student pub. schs., St. Petersburg, Fla.; m. Maude Wisenbaker, June 17, 1914 (div. 1945); children—Mary Estelle (Mrs. Kenneth J. Hedstrom), Edward Fitzroy; m. 2d, Etta Boyd Kneisler (dec.); m. 3d, Virginia Alice Singer, Sept. 19, 1956. Fisherman-seaman Hibbs Fish Co., Favorite Line, 1907-15, Gulf Refining Co., 1915-16; master mariner Clyde Mallory, N.Y.C., U.S. Shipping Bd., Standard Oil N.J., Lykes Bros., Munson SS Co., War Shipping Bd., others, 1917-42; salesman Davis & Davis, real estate, 1943-45, Bud Scott, Realtor, 1946-47; co-owner Brantley &Salinas, Inc., Realtors, 1960-— (all St. Petersburg); founder, owner Nat. Petroleum Corp., St. Petersburg, 1948-60; owner, mgr. Nat. Automotive Service, St. Petersburg, 1949-51; co-owner Pinellas Aviation Service, St. Petersburg, 1951-53; chmn. bd. dirs. Guaranty Fed. Savs. & Loan Assn., St. Petersburg, 1960; chmn. bd. Russell, Brantley & Peterson; pres. Brantley & Salinas & Jackson Estates, Inc., Gainesville, 1960-—; pres. Ed Brantley Assos., Inc.; chmn. adv. bd. Farmers Nat. Life Ins. Co. Mem. Pinellas County Bd. Health, St. Petersburg; pres. Fla. Philharmonic Soc., St. Petersburg, Councilman, City of St. Petersburg, 1953-59, mayor, 1959-61. Bd. dirs. Joe's Creek Indsl. Park; trustee Mound Park Hosp. Found., St. Petersburg. Served as civilian pilot U.S. Naval Convoy Anchorage, Key West, Fla., 1942. Recipient citation for 8 years pub. service City of St. Petersburg, 1961. Mem. St. Petersburg C. of C., Fla. Hist. Soc., Com. of 100, Hon. Order Ky. Cols., Pinellas County Gold Star Pioneers, Internat. Platform Assn. Democrat. Christian Scientist. Mason (Shriner), Lion. Clubs: Commerce; St. Petersburg Yacht, Propeller (pres. St. Petersburg 1958-59). Home: 1910 Brightwaters Blvd NE St Petersburg FL 33704 Office: 5001 Central Av St Petersburg FL 33710

BRANTLEY, LEW, mem. Fla. Senate. Address: 422 Copeland St Jacksonville FL 32204*

BRANTLEY, OLIVER WILEY, lawyer; b. Troy, Ala., Oct. 30, 1915; s. James T. and Julia (Wiley) B.; LL.B., U. Ala., 1939; m. Betty Jane Gaston, Jan. 20, 1936; children—Michael Wiley, Elizabeth Ayers (Mrs. William Maxwell Greshan), Grace Lamar (Mrs. William Garnett Anderson), Oliver Wiley. Admitted to Ala. bar, 1939; law practice, Troy, Ala., 1939-—, Ala. solicitor Pike County, 1947-—. Dir. Cotton States Life Ins. Co.; vice chmn. Ala. Judicial Commn., 1971-—. Bd. commrs. Ala. State Bar, 1952-—; bd. trustees Ala. State Bar Found., 1961-—;bd. dirs. Ala. Law Sch. Found. Served to lt. (jg.) USNR, 1943-46. Fellow Am. Coll. of Probate Counsel, Am. Coll. Trial Lawyers; mem. Am., Ala. State, Pike County bar assns., Farrah Law Soc. (chmn.), Nat. Assn. R.R. Trial Counsel, Delta Kappa Epsilon, Phi Delta Phi, Farrah Order Jurisprudence. Episcopalian. Home: 216 Flavia Circle Troy AL 36081 Office: 220 S Oak St Troy AL 36081

BRANUM, LOWELL EDWIN, drilling co. exec.; b. Memphis, Tex., Oct. 24, 1913; s. Ben Alvin and Eula Jean (Davenport) B.; B.S., Sul Ross State U., 1940; J.D., Georgetown U., 1949; m. Ruth L. Chambers, Dec. 14, 1940 (div. Nov. 1957); 1 dau., Helen Lowella (Mrs. Robert Ellenger). Admitted to D.C bar, 1949, Tex. bar, 1953; with U.S. Civil Service Commn., Washington, 1948-52, U.S. Dept. Justice, Washington, 1948-52; partner McCormick, Branum, Jennings, Cason, Midland, 1952-55; with Tri-Service Drilling Co., Midland, 1952-—, sec.-treas., 1955-—. Served with USMCR, 1943-45. Mem. Marine Corps Res. Officer Assn. (Midland pres. 1969-70), Res. Officers Assn. U.S. (v.p. marines 1971-—). Eagle. Home: 2200 N D St Midland TX 79701 Office: First Nat Bank Bldg Midland TX 79701

BRASWELL, EDWIN MAURICE, judge; b. Rocky Mount, N.C., Dec. 16, 1922; s. Walter R. and Ella (Denson) B.; LL.B., U. N.C., 1950; student Nat. Coll. State Trial Judges, U. Colo., 1966; m. Ruth Cox, Jan. 19, 1945; children—Susan, Edwin, Mark. Admitted to N.C. bar, 1950; practiced in Fayetteville, N.C., 1950-62; solicitor 9th Dist., Fayetteville, 1955-62; judge Superior Ct., 12th Jud. Dist., Fayetteville, 1963-—. Faculty adviser Nat. Coll. State Trial Judges, U. Nev., 1970. Served with USAAF, 1942-45. Decorated Air Medal with three oak leaf clusters, Purple Heart. Democrat. Methodist. Author: Voir Dire-Use and Abuse, 1970; (with Elmer R. Oettinger) Color Me Straight, 1972, Truths and Consequences, 1972. Home: 333 Devane St Fayetteville NC 28305

BRATAGER, PETE (ELLSWORTH), newspaper exec.; b. Miami, Fla., Oct. 11, 1928; s. Ellsworth Victor and Garnet (Severin) B.; B.A., U. Miami, 1951; m. Alicia Helen Radulski, Jan. 10, 1953; children—Stephen Ellis, Daniel Victor, Donald Pete, James Edward, Reid Thomas. Sports writer Miami Herald, 1946-59, night sports slot, 1959-64, Fla. state news editor, 1964-69, photo editor, 1969-—. Served with AUS, 1951-53. Home: 245 E 34th St Hialeah FL 33012 Office: 1 Herald Plaza Miami FL 33101

BRATCHER, RHODES, U.S. dist. judge; s.; Andrew Jackson B.; m. Martha Bratcher children—Thomas, Suzanne, Sarah, William. Admitted to Ky. bar; asst. U.S. atty. Western Ky. Dist., 1953-55; now judge U.S. Dist. Ct., Western Dist. Ky. Republican. Address: Owensboro KY 42301*

BRATTON, FRANK N., lawyer; b. Cowan, Tenn., Dec. 29, 1908; student U. of South, U. Tenn.; LL.B., Cumberland U., 1933. Admitted to Tenn. bar, 1934; practiced in Athens, Tenn. Fellow Am. Bar Found., Am. Coll. Trial Lawyers, Am. Coll. Probate Counsel; mem. Am. (ho. of dels. 1960-—, chmn. com. on lay assts. gen. practice sect. 1968-72, chmn. late reports com. of Ho. of Dels. 1970-71, mem. council gen. practice sect. 1971-—, mem. adv. com. continuing legal edn. of bar com. from Tenn. 1969-70), Internat., Tenn. (central council 1950-52, v.p. 1953-54, chmn. joint com. on ct. modernization 1965-69, pres. 1971-72, award of merit 1967), McMinn County bar assns., Nat. Assn. R.R. Trial Counsel, Am. Judicature Soc. (dir. 1967-71), Internat. Soc. Barristers, Scribes, World Peace through Law Center (charter). Office: 121 N Jackson St Athens TN 37303*

BRATTON, SAMUEL ISAAC, supt. schs.; b. Grenada, Miss., Jan. 7, 1911; s. Amos Gwyn and Minnie Augusta (Harper) B.; B.A., Hendrix Coll., 1933; M.A., George Peabody Coll., 1941; diploma advanced study U. Ark., 1965; m. Pauline Kilgore, May 24, 1940; children—Samuel Isaac, George. Tchr., Earle (Ark.) High Sch., 1933-39, prin., 1939-42, 46-47; supt. Earle Pub. Schs., 1947-—. Served with AUS, 1942-46. Mem. Ark. Sch. Adminstrs. Assn. (pres. 1966-67). Methodist. Rotarian (past pres. Earle). Home: 808 5th Av Earle AR 72331 Office: 1425 2d St Earle AR 72331

BRAUER, ALFRED T(HEODOR), educator; b. Berlin, Germany, Apr. 9, 1894; s. Max and Caroline Lilly (Jacob) B.; student U. Heidelberg, 1913; Ph.D., U. Berlin, 1928; L.L.D. (hon.), U.N.C., 1972; M. Hildegrad Franziska Wolf, Sept. 4, 1934; children—Ellen Evelyn (Mrs. Berton H. Kaplan), Carolyn Toni (Mrs. Richard H. Hudson). Came to U.S. 1939, naturalized, 1944. Asst., U. Berlin, 1926-35, privatdocent, 1932-35; asst. Inst. for Advanced Study, Princeton, N.J., 1939-42; lectr. N.Y. U., 1940-42; instr. U. N.C., 1942, asst. prof., 1942-43, asso. prof., 1943-47, prof. 1947-59, Kenan prof., 1959-66; vis. prof. U. Colo., summer 1962, 67, Wake Forest U., Winston-Salem, N.C., 1965-—. Served with German Army, 1914-19. Recipient Sci. Research award for significant contributions to science in South, Oak Ridge Inst. Nuclear Studies, 1948; Hegel medal Humboldt U., Berlin, 1971. Mem. Am. Math. Soc., Math. Assn. of Am., N.C. Acad. Sci., Elisha Mitchell Sci. Soc., Sigma Xi. Home: 410 Patterson Pl Chapel Hill NC 27514

BRAUER, GEORGE CHARLES, JR., educator; b. Cleve., Aug. 7, 1925; s. George Charles and Hazel (Batig) B.; B.A., Princeton, 1947; M.A., 1949; Ph.D., 1952. Instr. English, U. Tex., Austin, 1952-56; asst. prof. English, U. S.C., Columbia, 1956-60, asso. prof., 1960-69, prof., 1969-—. Recipient Russell award for creative research U. S.C. Mem. Modern Lang. Assn., Istituto di Studi Romani, Am. Schs. Oriental Research, Princeton Alumni Assn., Phi Beta Kappa, Omicron Delta Kappa (faculty adviser 1963-67), Chi Psi (faculty adviser 1964-—). Republican. Lutheran. Club: Campus (Princeton). Author: The Education of a Gentleman: Theories of Gentlemanly Education in England, 1660-1775, 1959; The Young Emperors: Rome, A.D. 193-244, 1967; Judaea Weeping, 1970. Home: Cornell Arms Apts Columbia SC 29201

BRAUER, HARROL ANDREW, JR., TV sta. exec.; b. Richmond, Va., Oct. 17, 1920; s. Harrol Andrew and Bertie (Gregory) B.; B.A., U. Richmond, 1942; m. Elizabeth Anne Hill, May 18, 1946; children—Harrol Andrew III, William Lanier, Gregory Hill. Chief announcer, program dir., account exec. various radio stas. in Va. 1939-42, 45-49; asso. WVEC radio, Hampton, Va. 1949-—; v.p., dir. sales WVEC-TV, Hampton, 1953-—; v.p. Peninsula Cable Corp., 1966-—; dir. Peninsula Broadcasting Corp. Mem. Hampton Sch. Bd., 1963-—, vice chmn., 1964-67, chmn., 1967-—. Trustee, Hampton Roads Ednl. TV Assn., chmn. bd. trustees, 1965-—. pres. Hampton Community Chest, 1951-52; dir. Peninsula unit Am. Cancer Soc., mem. hist. and cultural com. City of Hampton. Dir. YMCA, Va. U.S.O. Served from midshipman to lt., USNR, 1942-45. Mem. Broadcast Pioneers, Hampton Retail Mchts. Assn. (past pres., dir.), Peninsula C. of C. (dir. 1964-—), Jamestowne Soc., Sigma Alpha Epsilon. Episcopalian. Clubs: Peninsula Executive's (past pres., dir.), Kiwanis (past dir., pres., lt. gov.), James River Country; Harbor; Huntington. Home: 35 N Boxwood St Hampton VA 23369 Office: 1930 E Pembroke Av Hampton VA 23363

BRAUGHLER, GUY ERNST, non-powder guns and ammunition mfg. co. exec.; b. Punxsutawney, Pa., Aug. 31, 1932; s. Ernst C. and Wilma (Bortnik) B.; Asso. Mech. Engr., U. Pa., 1958; student Internat. Corr. Schs., 1963, Alexander Hamilton Inst., 1970; m. Alice M. Bretz, July 5, 1958; children—Bonnie Sue, Beth Ann, Amy Marie. Employed various gun shops, Washington, 1951-55; with U. Pa., 1955-58; engr. Crosman Arms Co., Fairport, N.Y., 1958-61; engr. Daisy-Heddon Co., Rogers, Ark., 1961-64, mgr., 1964-—. Served with AUS, 1953-55. Certified Mfg. engr. Mem. Soc. Mfg. Engrs. (chpt. chartering chmn. 1968-70). Home: 1005 S Lakeview Dr Rogers AR 72756 Office: PO Box 220 Rogers AR 72756

BRAUN, ERNEST CARL, petroleum engr.; b. Denver, Oct. 1, 1922; s. Ernest William and Frieda (Muller) B.; B.S., Colo. Sch. Mines, 1949; m. Jean Carol Reilly, June 14, 1958; children—Gregory William, Christopher Ernest. Petroleum engr. trainee Magnolia Petroleum Co., various locations, 1949-50; mem. engring. staff Mobil Oil Co., various internat. locations, 1951-—, reservoir engring. adviser, cons., Celle, Germany, 1961-65, asso. prodn. engr. div., Oklahoma City, 1966-—. Com. chmn. Pack 158, Cub Scouts Am., Oklahoma City, 1968-70. Served with C.E., AUS, 1946-47. Registered profl. engr. Okla., Tex. Mem. Soc. Petroleum Engrs., Am. Inst. M.E. Home: 2716 NW 112 St Oklahoma City OK 73120 Office: PO Box 1934 200 N Harvey St Oklahoma City OK 73101

BRAUN, JOHN WALTER, govt. ofcl., educator; b. Two Rivers, Wis., Oct. 18, 1907; s. Paul and Metta L. (Cole) B.; B.C.S., Benjamin Franklin U., 1943, M.C.S., 1946; J.D., Am. U., 1960; m. Lary H. Dalton, Oct. 31, 1941; children—John F., Gerry C., Lary Ann. With Modern Sch. Supply, 1946-49; with Treasury Dept, Washington, 1949-—, Bur. of Mint, 1949-56, Bur. of Accounts, 1956-67, comptroller of currency, 1967-—. Served with A.R.C., 1943-45. C.P.A., D.C. Mem. Am. Inst. C.P.A.'s. Elks. Home: 2239 N Underwood St Falls Church VA 22043 Office: Comptroller of Currency Washington DC 20220

BRAUN, WARREN L(OYD), radio engr.; b. Postville, Ia., Aug. 11, 1922; s. Karl William and Cornela (Muller) B.; student Valparaiso Tech. Inst., 1940-41, Capitol Engring. Inst., 1946; m. Lillian Carol Stone, May 24, 1942; children—Warren (dec.), Dikki Carol. Chief engr. WKEY, 1941, WSVA, 1941; E.S.M.W.T.P. sect. head, 1942-45; charge installation stas. WSIR, WTOW, WSVA-FM, WJMA, TV stas. WAAM and WSVA-TV, Blue Ridge TV cable facilities, 1945-65; pres. Com Sonics, Inc., Research and Devel. Labs., Warren Braun, cons. engrs. Panel 44 mem. TV allocations study orgn.; v.p. Market Dimensions, Inc. Bd. Salvation Army, 1961-—. Chmn. Harrisonburg-Rockingham County Recreation Study Commn.; mem., sec. Va. Air Pollution Control Bd., 1966-—; pres. Shenandoah Valley Devel. Corp.; mem. Va. Citizens Com. for Va. Outdoor Planning; chmn. Upper Valley Regional Park Authority, 1966-69; mem. Regional Export Expansion Council; mem. Va. Far East Trade Mission, 1972; mem. bd. Tb and Thoracic Soc., Va. state seal chmn., 1967-—. Registered profl. engr. Va. Chmn. bus. relations com. Harrisburg C. of C. 1959-61, mem. bd., 1961-66, pres., 1964. Recipient Jefferson Davis medal U.D.C. 1961; named outstanding engr. of yr. Va. Soc. Profl. Engrs., 1965; man of yr. Harrisonburg and Rockingham County; nat. award, Am. Soc. Engring., 1969, Internat. award, 1969; Rietzke Nat. award, 1972. Fellow Audio Engring. Soc. (membership chmn. 1963-64), Internat. Consular Acad.; mem. I.E.E.E., Soc. Motion Picture and Television Engrs., Acoustical Soc. Am., Nat. Va. (mem. bd. and exec. com. 1963-64, chpt. pres. 1963-64) socs. profl. engrs. Nat. Assn. Broadcasters, Va. C. of C. (chmn. world trade conf. 1968, chmn. world trade com. 1968-—), Presbyn. (deacon). Elk. Club: Engineers (Richmond, Va.). Address: 680 New York Av Harrisonburg VA 22801

BRAWNER, LEE BASIL, librarian; b. Seguin, Tex., May 1, 1935; s. Lee Basil and Thelma (Davenport) B.; student Tex. A. and M. U., 1953-55; B.A., N. Tex. State U., 1957; M.A., George Peabody Coll. Tchrs., 1960; m. Nancy Jayne Wallis, Dec. 6, 1958; children— Betsy Lynn, Allen Lee. Head popular library and circulation dept. Dallas Pub. Library, 1958-60, head Lakewood br., 1961-62, chief br. services, 1964-67; dir. Waco (Tex.) Pub. Library, 1962-64; asst. state librarian Tex. State Library, 1967-71; dir. Oklahoma County Libraries System, Oklahoma City, 1971-—. Chmn. Southwestern Library Interstate Library Coop. Endeavor Project, 1971-72. Served with AUS, 1957-58. Mem. Am., Okla., Southwestern (pres. 1971-72) library assns., Okla. C. of C., Sigma Phi Epsilon. Rotarian. Contbr. articles to profl. jours. Home: 5013 NW 61st Pl Oklahoma City OK 73122 Office: 131 NW 3d St Oklahoma City OK 73102

BRAXTON, HERMAN HARRISON, physician; b. Almanance County, N.C., Nov. 13, 1906; s. James Guy and Nette E. (Guthrie) B.; A.B., U. N.C., 1928; M.D., Johns Hopkins, 1932; m. Anne Norfolk Grimm, June 22, 1935; children—Herman Harrison II, Elizabeth Anne. Mem. house staff Duke Hosp., 1932-33, White Plains (N.Y.) Hosp., 1933-34; gen. practice medicine, Chase City, Va., 1934-—; mem. staffs Community Meml. Hosp., South Hill, Va., Southside Community Hosp. Farmville, Va., local med. dir. Nat. Found.; med. examiner Mecklenburg County, 1947-—; surgeon So. R.R. Bd. dirs. Chase City Indsl. Devel. Corp.; mem. adv. bd. Fidelity Nat. Bank. Mem. local bi-racial commn., 1965-—. Mem. Chase City Town Council, 1955-63. Mem. Va. Med. Soc., A.M.A., Am. Acad. Gen. Practice, Chase City C. of C. (past pres.), Phi Beta Kappa. Episcopalian (sr. warden). Clubs: Lions (past pres., zone chmn.); Mecklenburg Country (past pres.). Home: 440 Walker St Chase City VA 23924 Office: 4th and Main Sts Chase City VA 23924

BRAY, HOWARD, alternate fed. co-chmn. Appalachian Regional Commn. Office: 1666 Connecticut Av NW Washington DC 20235*

BRAY, ROBERT STUART, librarian; b. Cin., Sept. 9, 1915; s. Charles Ayers and Helen Mar (Pollock) B.; B.S., George Washington U., 1941; student library service, Cath. U. Am., 1947-50; m. Virginia Elizabeth Ballard, Oct. 2, 1937; children—Robert Stuart, James Sargent, Paul Charles, Philip Austin. Page, D.C. Library, 1935-40; mem. staff Library of Congress, 1940-44, 46-—, chief div. blind and physically handicapped, 1957-—. Mem. adv. bd. Recording for Blind; chmn. service adv. com., trustee Am. Found. Blind; mem. bd. Nat. Accreditation Council Agys. Serving Blind and Visually Handicapped; chmn. library com. President's Com. Employment

Handicapped. Served to lt. (j.g.) USNR, 1944-46. Recipient Migel medal Am. Found. Blind, 1963; Apollo award Am. Optometric Assn., 1968; Francis Joseph Campbell award, 1968. Mem. Assn. Hosp. and Instn. Libraries (pres. 1968), Adult Edn. Assn., Am. Pub. Health Assn., Council Exceptional Children, A.L.A., Nat. Assn. of the Physically Handicapped, Nat. Braille Assn., Nat. Rehab. Assn., Nat. Soc. Prevention Blindness, Am. Assn. Workers Blind, Am. Assn. Instrs. Blind, Assn. of Edn. of Visually Handicapped. Democrat. Episcopalian. Home: 910 Seneca Rd Herndon VA 22070 Office: 1291 Taylor St NW Washington DC 20542

BRAY, WILLIAM RANDALL, architect; b. Suffolk, Va., Apr. 11, 1938; s. Aleck and Susan Penina (Dail) B.; B.Arch., N.C. State U., 1963; M.Arch., Mass. Inst. Tech., 1964; m. Helen LeDoux, Oct. 10, 1964; children—William Randall II, Zanne Elizabeth. Grad. asst. Mass. Inst. Tech., 1963-64; designer Edward Durrell Stone, architect, N.Y.C., 1960-61, The Architects Collaborative, Cambridge, Mass., 1964-65; project architect Toombs, Amisano & Wells, Atlanta, Ga., 1968-69; asso. Thompson Ventulett & Stainback, Inc., Atlanta, 1969—; founder NBCS Architects Inc., 1972. Second and 3d year design critic Boston Archtl. Center, 1964; design critic Ga. Inst. Tech., 1969; pres. KBG, Inc., Atlanta. Served with USAAF, 1958-60. Mem. A.I.A., Exptl. Aircraft Assn., Aircraft Owners and Pilots Assn. Home: 2570 Drew Valley Atlanta GA 30319

BRAYNON, EDWARD JOSEPH, JR., dentist; b. Miami, Fla., Jan 15, 1928; s. Edward Joseph and May Dell (Jackson) B.; B.S., Howard U., 1949; D.D.S., 1954; student Fisk U., 1945-47; m. Ann Carey, July 24, 1954; children—Edward Joseph III, Keith Warren. Practice dentistry, Miami. Mem. Dade County Youth Adv. Bd. Dir. YMCA, 1957-61. Served as capt., Dental Corps, USAF, 1954-56. Mem. Dade County Acad. Medicine, Am. Dental Soc. Anesthesiology, Fla. Med., Dental and Pharm. Assn., Nat. Dental Assn., Am., East Coast dental assns., Fla., North Dade, South Dade dental socs., Howard U. Alumni Assn. (pres. Miami 1968—), Omega Psi Phi (meritorious service award 1963, 7th Dist. Man of Year 1970, 7th dist. rep.), Chi Delta Mu. Methodist. Club: Century. Home: 2271 NE 191st St North Miami Beach FL 33160 Office: 5594 NW 17th Av Miami FL 33142

BREATHITT, EDWARD THOMPSON, mem. Democratic Nat. com., ry. exec., former gov. of Ky.; b. Hopkinsville, Ky., Nov. 26, 1924; s. Edward T. and Mary Jo (Wallace) B.; B.S., U. Ky., 1948; LL.B., 1950; m. Frances Holleman, Dec. 20, 1948; children—Mary Frances, Linda, Susan, Edward Thompson III. Admitted to Ky. bar, 1950; mem. firm Trimble, Soyars and Breathitt, Hopkinsville, 1952-63; gov. State of Ky., Frankfort, 1963-67; v.p. pub. affairs So. Ry. System, Washington, 1972—. Chmn. Coalition for Rural Am. Personnel commr. State of Ky., 1959-60; mem. Ky. Pub. Service Commn., 1961-62. Pres., Ky. Young Democrats, 1952; mem. Ky. Ho. of Reps., 1952-58; mem. Dem. Nat. Com. for Ky. Served with USAAF, 1942-45. Mem. Omicron Delta Kappa, Sigma Alpha Epsilon. Democrat. Mason, Kiwanian, Elk. Home: 3237 Circle Dr Hopkinsville KY 42240 Office: Planters Bank Bldg Hopkinsville KY 42240

BREAUX, CLARENCE THOMAS, state ofcl.; b. New Iberia, La., Feb. 7, 1917; s. Hypolite A. and Anita M. (Louviere) B.; B.A., St. Mary's U., 1938; postgrad. U. Miami, 1941-42, Northwestern U., 1951-52; m. Edna Mae Broussard, Oct. 17, 1942; children—Kenneth, Norwood. Tchr. pub. high schs., La. and Tex., 1936-41; comml. attache, chief econ. sect. Am. embassy, Buenos Aires, Argentina, 1946-49, Bilbao, Spain, 1949-51, Guatemala City, Guatemala, 1954-57, La Paz, Bolivia, 1957-59, Phnom Penh, Cambodia, 1963-65, Port-au-Prince, Haiti, 1965-67, Addis Ababa, Ethiopia, 1952-54, Dept. State, Washington, 1959-63; dir. research La. Dept. Commerce and Industry, Baton Rouge, 1967-70, dir. internat div., New Orleans, 1970—. Served with USNR, 1941-46. Mem. Am. Fgn. Service Assn., Diplomatic and Consular Officers Ret., Am. Econ. Assn. Home: 219 G West Gatehouse Dr Metairie LA 70001 Office: La Dept Commerce and Industry State Office Bldg New Orleans LA 70112

BREAUX, IVAN JOSEPH, rice processing co. exec.; b. Kaplan, La., Apr. 2, 1925; s. Cladis and Ozite (Trahan) B.; B.S., U. Southwestern La., 1949; m. Geneva Martin, June 22, 1946; children—Thomas, Charlene (Mrs. Randall Villejoin), Bruce, Sandra (Mrs. Allison Gaspard), Brenda, Jacquelin, Kenneth. Vice pres. Kaplan Rice Mill, Inc. (La.), 1949—, also dir. Served with USAAF, 1941-45; ETO. Decorated Air medal. Mem. Rice Millers' Assn. (mem. grade standards com. 1970-71), Woodmen of the World, V.F.W. (comdr. 1970-71). Home: 1200 Church Av Kaplan LA 70548 Office: PO Box 329 Kaplan LA 70548

BREBBIA, JOHN HENRY, lawyer; b. Boston, Feb. 16, 1932; s. Joseph Dante and Gertrude (Hogan) B.; A.B., Stonehill Coll., 1953; LL.B., Boston Coll., 1956; m. Patricia Mary Burke, Jan. 9, 1967. Admitted to Mass. bar, 1957, D.C. bar, 1965; practiced, Boston, 1960-61; trial atty. FTC, Bur. Restraint of Trade, 1961-64; asso. Davies, Richberg, Tydings, Lamda & Duff, Washington, 1965-67; partner Alston, Miller & Gaines, Washington and Atlanta, 1967—, mng. partner Washington office, 1971—; dir., v.p. and gen. counsel First Western Financial Corp., Las Vegas, 1966-67, pres., dir., 1967-69; dir. First Western Savings & Loan Assn., Las Vegas, 1966—. Mem. campaign staff Senator Robert F. Kennedy, 1964. Served from 1st lt. to capt. with Judge Adv. Gen. Corps, AUS, 1957-60. Mem. Am., Fed. bar assns., Bar Assn. D.C. Home: 3232 Kingle Rd NW Washington DC 20008 Office: 1776 K St NW Washington DC 20006

BRECHNER, BEVERLY LORRAINE, educator; b. N.Y.C., May 27, 1936; d. Herman and Goldie (Zimmerman) Brechner; B.S., U. Miami, 1957, M.S., 1959; Ph.D., La. State U., 1964. Instr. La. State U., New Orleans, 1962-64, asst. prof., 1964-68; asst. prof. U. Fla., Gainesville, 1968-71, asso. prof. math., 1971—. Vis. lectr. La. Acad. Sci., 1967-68; reviewer Zentralblatt Fur Maths., 1968—, Math. Reviews, 1971—; mem. Inst. Advanced Grad. Students Topology, U. Ga., Athens, 1961, Topology Manifolds Inst., 1961. Bd. dirs. Fla. Found. Future Scientists. Mem. Am. Math. Soc., Math. Assn. Am., A.A.A.S., Fla. Found. Future Scientists, Sigma Xi. Democrat. Jewish religion. Office: Dept Math Univ Fla Gainesville FL 32601

BRECK, LOUIS WILLIAM, physician, orthopaedic surgeon; b. El Paso, Tex., Mar. 24, 1909; s. Louis M. and Olive Jane (Roblee) B.; B.S., Northwestern U., 1930, M.D., 1933; m. Julia S. North, June 11, 1932; children—Louis W., Julia A., Alan N., Susan M. Rotating intern Mary's Help Hosp., 1932-33, gen. resident, 1933-35; spl. tng. orthopaedic surgery Mayo Clinic, 1935-37; practice medicine, specializing in orthopaedic surgery, El Paso, 1937—; mem. staff Hotel Dieu Sisters Hosp., chief of staff, 1955; cons. Thomason Gen. Hosp., Carrie Tingley Hosp. for Crippled Children; civilian cons. to William Beaumont Gen. Hosp.; orthopaedic cons. S.P. R.R., Tex. Crippled Children's Div., New Mexico Crippled Children's Hosp.; sr. partner El Paso Orthopedic Surgery Group. Mem. med. adv. bd. Tex. Rehab. Commn. Served from capt. to lt. col. AUS, 1942-46; chief orthopaedic sect. Regional Hosp., Camp Swift, Tex. Recipient Legion of Honor Order of DeMolay, 1953. Fellow A.C.S., Am. Writers Assn.; mem. Am., Tex. State, S.W. (pres. 1950-51) med. assns., El Paso County Med. Soc. (pres. 1961), Am. Acad. Orthopaedic Surgeons, Assn. Bone Joint Surgeons (pres. 1955), Western (pres. N.M. chapt. 1958), Texas (pres. 1950) orthopaedic assns., Societe Internationale de Chirurgie et de Traumatologie, Tex. Soc. Athletic Team Physicians (pres. 1965), Tex. Traumatic Surg. Soc. (pres. 1967), Tex. Rehab. Assn. (pres. 1968), Sigma Alpha Epsilon, Phi Beta Pi (Arnold-Surman lectr. U. Tex. 1951). Mason (32 deg., Shriner), Kiwanian. Author: Atlas of the Osteochondroses. Mng. editor Southwestern Medicine. Editorial bd. Clin. Orthopaedics, Jour. Indsl. Medicine. Contbr. articles to profl. jours. Home: 1207 N Kansas St El Paso TX 79902 Office: 1220 N Stanton St El Paso TX 79902

BRECKINRIDGE, JOHN BAYNE, lawyer, state govt. ofcl.; b. Washington, Nov. 29, 1913; s. Dr. Scott Dudley and Gertrude (Ashby-Bayne) B.; A.B., U. Ky., 1937, LL.B., 1939; m. Helen Congleton; children—Knight, John Bayne. Admitted to Ky. bar, 1940; atty. anti-trust div. Dept. Justice, 1940-41; pvt. practice law, 1946—; mem. Ky. Ho. of Reps., 1956-59; atty. gen. of Ky., 1960-64, 67—; corp. counsel for the City of Lexington (Ky.), 1964. Del. to White House Conf. on Children and Youth, 1960; mem. adv. com. state ofcls. AEC; vice chmn. So. Interstate Nuclear Bd.; chmn. Ky. Adv. Com. Nuclear Energy, 1960-64; chmn. Ky. Inter-Agy. Legislative Program Com., 1960-64; bd. trustees Frontier Nursing Service; commr. Nat. Conf. Commns. on Uniform State Laws, 1960-64; mem. Ky. Constn. Rev. Com., 1960-62; counsel Ky. Citizens for Child Welfare, 1956-59. Past vice chmn. Ky. Welfare Assn., v.p. 1962-63; chmn. So. Interstate Nuclear Bd.; vice chmn. Ky. Social Welfare Found.; chmn. Ky. Sci. and Tech. Adv. Council; mem. Ky. Commn. on Children and Youth, 1966—, Ky. Crime Commn., 1967—; chmn. Ky. Water Pollution Control Commn., 1968—; v.p., mem. operating bd. officers, exec. com. United Cerebral Palsy Assn.; past asst. v.p. So. region, past pres. United Cerebral Palsy of Ky., United Cerebral Palsy of Bluegrass. Del., Dem. Nat. Conv., mem. rules com., Los Angeles, 1960. Served from 1st lt. to col. AUS 1941-46; chief projects and indsl. licensing div. Bd. Econ. Warfare, 1941-42, asst. chief internat. div. USAFIME Hdqrs., comdg. officer Mil. Liaison Hdqrs., Albania. Mem. Am. Council for Community (past mem. exec. com., dir.), Am., Ky., Fayette County bar assns., Am. Judicature Soc. (dir. Ky.), Ky. Hist. Soc. (pres. 1962-64), Atlantic Union Com. (pres. Ky. chpt. mem. council), Kentucky Peace officers' Standards and Tng. Council, Kappa Alpha (pres. Theta chpt. 1936-37). Democrat. Contbr. articles to legal jours. Home: 1100 Fincastle Rd Frankfort KY 40601 Office: Office of Atty Gen State Capitol Frankfort KY 40601

BREEDIN, B. BRENT, ednl. adminstr.; b. Beaufort, S.C., Nov. 3, 1925; s. Berryman Brent and Jane (Dixon) B.; B.A., Washington and Lee U., 1947; m. Louise Allain Crenshaw, Sept. 10, 1959; children—David Singleton, Sarah duBois, Amelia Knowles. Reporter, Corpus Christi (Tex.) Caller, 1947; sports editor Anderson (S.C.) Daily Mail, 1949-52; dir. sports publicity Clemson U., 1952-55, univ. editor, 1964-66; resident mgr. Hunt Internat. Petroleum Co., Pakistan, 1955-58; press and research asst. U.S. Senator Strom Thurmond of S.C., 1958-59; pub. relations DuPont Co., 1960-63; editor-pub. South Carolinian, 1963-64; editor Coll. and Univ. Jour., 1966-71; asso. dir. ERIC/Higher Edn., 1971-72; dir. publs. Council on Library Resources, 1972—. Served with USNR, 1944-45. Mem. Am. Coll. Pub. Relations Assn., Ednl. Press Assn., Am. Acad. Polit. and Social Sci., Sigma Delta Chi, Sigma Alpha Epsilon. Episcopalian. Rotarian. Club: Nat. Press. Home: 5419 41st St NW Washington DC 20015 Office: 1 Dupont Circle NW Washington DC 20036

BREEDLOVE, JAMES GERALD, bus. exec.; b. Opp, Ala., Nov. 7, 1920; s. E. Marvin and Mary (Jeffcoat) B.; B. Ceramic Engring., Ga. Inst. Tech., 1950; m. Carolyn Elizabeth Archer, Nov. 27, 1947; children—Mary Carolyn, (Mrs. P. J. Peacock), Sally Elizabeth, Donna Ellen. Ceramic engr. Am. Lava Corp., Chattanooga, 1950-53, mgr. Titania div. lab., 1953-63, mgr. new product devel. lab., 1963-68, research supr., 1968—. Chief aux. police, Signal Mountain, Tenn., 1964—. Served to sgt. AUS, 1941-45. Recipient Distinguished Community Service award Signal Mountain Lions Club, 1968. Mem. Am. Ceramic Soc., Inst. Ceramic Engrs., Chattanooga C. of C., Signal Mountain Sportsman's Assn., Nat. Rifle Assn. Democrat. Episcopalian. Patents and publs. in fields tech. ceramics, dielectrics, procelain enamels. Inventor composite armor plate (ceramic-glass fiber). Home: 804 James Blvd Signal Mountain TN 37377 Office: Am Lava Corp Cherokee Blvd Chattanooga TN 37405

BREEDLOVE, WILLIAM ALFORD, banker; b. nr. Nashville, N.C., May 13, 1928; s. James William and Ellen Louise (Harris) B.; student N.C. State U., 1945-46, Campbell Coll., 1948-49, Smithdeal Massey Bus. Coll., 1949-50, Stonier Grad. Sch. Banking, 1965-68, Nat. Comml. Lending Sch., 1970; m. Bettye Catherine Evans, Dec. 20, 1952; children—William Alford, Laura Lynne. Credit mgr. Universal C.I.T. Corp., Charlotte, N.C., 1951-53, mgr., Fayetteville, N.C., 1951-55; with Planters Nat. Bank and Trust Co., Rocky Mount, N.C., 1955—, sr. v.p., 1970—, sr. v.p., city exec. br. bank, Mt. Airy, N.C., 1971—. Sec., Rocky Mount Human Relations Commn., 1968. Served with USAAF, 1946-47. Mem. Am. Inst. Banking (pres. 1961-62), Bank Adminstrn. Inst. (pres. 1966-67, dir. 1967-71). Democrat. Baptist (deacon 1955—). Elk, Rotarian (dir. 1969-70). Club: Mt. Airy Country. Home: 664 Knollwood Dr Mount Airy NC 27030 Office: 501 N Main St Mount Airy NC 27030

BREELAND, JEWELL JEROME, JR., physician; b. Tylertown, Miss., Jan. 13, 1930; s. Jewell J. and Tressa (Istvan) B.; B.A., U. So. Miss., 1951; M.D., U. Miss., 1960; m. Jane Manning, June 14, 1953; children— Marjorie, Durwood, Jeri, Petty. Intern Chatham County Hosp., Savannah, Ga., 1960-61; pvt. practice medicine, specializing in obstetrics and gynecology, Brookhaven, Miss., 1961—; mem. staff Kings Daus. Hosp., Brookhaven. Served with USAF, 1951-55. Mem. Lincoln County Cancer Soc. (pres. 1968-70), S. Central County Med. Assn., Miss. Med. Assn. Presbyn. Home: S Church Extension Brookhaven MS 39601 Office: 439 N Jackson St Brookhaven MS 39601

BREEN, JAMES LOWELL, educator; b. Charleston, Ill., May 14, 1921; s. Charles C. and Myrtle (Potts) B.; B.S., Eastern Ill. U., 1948; M.S., U. Ill., 1949, Ph.D., 1959; m. Juanita June Chesser, June 6, 1943; children—Suanne, Pamela (Mrs. Henry Koch), Janette Deane, Barbara Jo. Mem. faculty, U. Ill., 1948-57; dir. research Chgo. Nat. League Baseball Club, Inc., 1957-58; faculty Tulane U., 1959-69, head dept. phys. edn., 1960-69; chmn. dept. phys. edn. George Washington U., Washington, 1969—. Co-chmn., mem. exec. com. Greater New Orleans March of Dimes, 1965-67; mem. exec. com. Mus. Therapy Assn., New Orleans, 1968. Served to lt. USNR, 1942-45; now Res. Mem. Am. Coll. Sports Medicine, Am. Personnel and Guidance Assn., Am. Assn. U. Profs., Am. (chmn. phys. fitness sect. 1965-66), La. assns. health, phys. edn. and recreation. Republican. Methodist. Contbr. articles to publs. Producer, dir. ednl. film. Home: 2611 Lemontree Lane Vienna VA 22180 Office: Phys Edn Dept George Washington 817 23d St NW Washington DC 20006

BREESKIN, ADELYN DOHME, art mus. dir.; b. Balt., July 19, 1896; d. Alfred R.L. and Emmie (Blumner) Dohme; grad. Sch. Fine Arts, Crafts and Decorative Design, Boston, 1918; L.D., Goucher Coll., Balt., 1953; D.F.A. (hon.), Washington Coll., 1961, Wheaton Coll., 1964, Hood Coll., 1966, Morgan State Coll., 1966; m. Elias Breeskin, Apr. 12, 1920; children—Jean (Mrs. Clayton Timbrell), Dorothy (Mrs. Samuel E. Brown, Jr.), Gloria (Mrs. Cornelius Peck). Asst. print dept. Met. Mus., N.Y.C., 1918-20; with Baltimore Mus. Art, 1930-62, acting dir., 1942-47, dir., 1947-62; dir. Washington Gallery of Modern Arts, 1962-64; also curator graphic art lectr. U.S.A. and abroad; now spl. cons. Nat. Collection of Fine Arts, Smithsonian Instn., Washington. Decorated Star of Solidarity by Italian Govt., 1954. Recipient Distinguished Service award U. Md., 1962. U.S. Commr. Am. Pavilion, Venice Exhbn., 1960. Mem. Assn. Art Museum Dirs. (sec.-treas. 1953-56, pres. 1956-57), Internat. Graphic Arts Soc. (mem. Am. jury of selection, 1955-65). Author: Catalogue Raisonne, Graphic Works of Mary Cassatt, 1949; Paintings, Pastels, etc. of Mary Cassatt, 1970. Home: 1254 31st NW Washington DC 20007 Office: Nat Collection Fine Arts 8th and G Sts Washington DC 20560

BREESKIN, BARNET, orch. condr.; studied with Leon Barzin, Hans Kindler, Pierre Monteux. Solo violinist; with various symphony orchs.; condr., dir., mgr. Miami Beach (Fla.) Symphony, 1955—. Home: 5301 Alton Rd Miami Beach FL 33140 Office: 420 Lincoln Rd Mall Suite 401 Miami Beach FL 33139*

BREGMAN, JACOB ISRAEL, chemist; b. Hartford, Conn., Sept. 17, 1923; s. Aaron and Jennie (Katzoff) B.; B.S., Providence Coll., 1943; M.S., Poly. Inst. Bklyn., 1948, Ph.D., 1951; m. Mona Madan, June 27, 1948; children—Janet, Marcia, Barbara. Research chemist Fels & Co., 1947-48; head phys. chem. labs. Nalco Chem. Co., Chgo., 1950-59; supr., phys. chemistry research sect. Armour Research Found., Chgo., 1959-63; asst. dir. chemistry research Ill. Inst. Tech. Research Inst., Chgo., 1963-65, dir. chem. scis., 1965-67; dep. asst. sec. U.S. Dept. Interior, 1967-69; pres. WAPORA, Inc., 1969—. Chmn. N.E. Ill. Met. Area Air Pollution Control Bd., 1962-63; chmn. Ill. Air Pollution Control Bd., 1963-67; chmn. adv. bd. on saline water conversion NATO Parliamentarians Conf., 1963; chmn. Water Resources Research Council, 1964-67. Chmn task force on ecology Montgomery County Democratic Central Com., 1971—. Mem. plan commn., Park Forest, Ill., 1956-58, trustee, 1958-62. Served with AUS, 1943-46; ETO. Fellow Am. Inst. Chemists; mem. Am. Chem. Soc., N.Y. Acad. Scis., Midwest Air Pollution Prevention Assn., Sigma Xi, Phi Lambda Upsilon. Author: Corrosion Inhibitors, 1963: Surface Effects in Detection, 1965; The Pollution Paradox, 1966; Contbr. articles to profl. jours. Home: 5630 Old Chester Rd Bethesda MD 20014 Office: 1725 DeSalles St Washington DC 20036

BREHM, THOMAS WALTER, educator; b. Columbus, O., Oct. 14, 1924; s. Walter E. and Helen Lucille (Fountain) B.; student Ohio State U., 1942-44; D.D.S., Ohio State Dental Coll., 1949; postgrad. U. So. Cal., 1955-56; m. Reva Ruth Libby, July 3, 1949; children—Pamela (Mrs. Richard Cheeks), Timothy, Bruce. Dental intern, Walter Reed Gen. Hosp., 1949-50; commd. 1st lt. Dental Corps, AUS, 1948, advanced through grades to col., 1967; dental officer Pentagon Dispensary, Washington, 1950-52, SHAPE, Paris, France, 1952-55; asst. prof., dir. fixed prosthodontics U. Ky. Coll. Dentistry, Lexington, 1969—. Chief fixed prosthodontics Brooke Gen. Hosp., 1956-62, Darnall Gen. Hosp., 1962-66, Tripler Gen. Hosp., 1966-69. Sponsor, Leilehua Choir, Oahu, Hawaii, 1968-69; active P.T.A. Decorated Army Commendation Medal. Diplomate Am. Bd. Prosthodontics. Fellow Am. Coll. Dentistry; mem. Am. Dental Assn., Am. Assn. Dental Schs., Am. Coll. Prosthodontics, Internat. Assn. Dental Research, Blue Grass Dental Soc., Psi Omega, Beta Theta Pi, Phi Eta Sigma, Omicron Kappa Upsilon. Methodist. Home: 3145 Lamar Dr Lexington KY 40502

BRELAND, JABE ARMISTEAD, physician; b. Memphis, Tenn., Dec. 1, 1924; s. Loren Dewey and Gladys Louise (Davenport) B.; M.D., La. State U., 1948; m. Betty Jane Baker, Sept. 16, 1948; children—Jabe Armistead, Thomas Lynn, Margaret Elaine, Henry Baker, Anna Elizabeth. Intern, John Sealy Hosp., U. Tex. Med. Br., Galveston, 1948-49; resident El Paso (Tex.) Gen. Hosp., 1949-50; practice medicine, specializing in family practice, Marianna, Fla., 1950—; chief profl. staff Jackson Hosp.; chmn. cons. med. staff Marianna Convalescent Center; pres. Camp Seclusion, Inc., 1966—; mem. Gov.'s Spl. Edn. Task Force Com., 1972—. Chmn. Selective Service Appeal Bd., No. Fed. Judicial Dist. Fla., 1968—. Served with AUS, 1942-43. Diplomate Am. Bd. Family Practice, 1970. Mem. So., Fla. med. assns., Am., Fla. acads. family practice. Episcopalian (licensed lay reader 1963—). Mason (32 deg., Shriner), Elk. Club: Marianna (Fla.) Country. Home: Country Club Hills Marianna FL 32446 Office: 709 3d Av Marianna FL 32446

BRELAND, WALKER LEE, educator; b. Walterboro, S.C., Nov. 30, 1935; s. Julius Earl and Rebecca (Walker) B.; B.A. in Ch. Music, Furman U., 1958; Mus.M. with high distinction, Ind. U., 1959, postgrad., 1962-65; m. June Price, June 5, 1959; children—Rebecca Elizabeth, Melanie Lynn. Concert organist, profl. accompanist, 1959—; instr. organ Franklin (Ind.) Coll., 1959-60; grad. teaching asst. music edn. Ind. U., 1963-65; asst. prof. music Columbia (S.C.) Coll., 1965—. Organist, dir. music First Bapt. Ch., Greenville, S.C., 1955-58, North Christian Ch., Columbus, Ind., 1959-62, St. John's United Ch. of Christ, Indpls., 1964-65, Cayce Meth. Ch. (S.C.), 1965-67, Trenholm Rd. United Meth. Ch., Columbia, 1967—. Organ cons.; cons. to State Dept. Edn., 1968—. Served to capt. AUS, Mem. Am. Assn. U. Profs., Fellowship Meth. Musicians, Music Educators Nat. Conf. (S.C. coll. div. v.p. 1971—), Am. Guild Organists (sub-dean 1967—), Hymn Soc. Am., Arts Guild, Quaternion, Phi Mu Alpha Sinfonia, Phi Delta Kappa. Methodist (chmn. exec. com. S.C. conf. program council 1968—, exec. com. conf. worship commn. 1968—). Kiwanian. Home: 3711 Oakleaf Rd Columbia SC 29206

BRELSFORD, GEORGE WILLIAM, V, fiberglass co. exec.; b. Bridgeton, N.J., Oct. 5, 1927; s. George William and Jeanette (Brockway) B.; A.B., Vanderbilt U., 1949; m. Patricia Murphy, Oct. 15, 1949; children—George William VI, Kathleen, Robin, Jean Ann, Debbie. Personnel staff asst. Owens-Ill., Bridgeton, N.J., 1949-59, employment mgr., Barrington, N.J., 1959-60, corporate communications supr., Toledo, 1960-63; personnel dir. Owens-Corning Fiberglas Corp., Aiken, S.C., 1963—. Adj. prof. U. S.C., Columbia, 1971—. Pres. Aiken County United Fund, 1970. Bd. dirs. Community Action Commn.; trustee Hopelands Meml. Park. Recipient communications award for mgmt. publs. Internat. Council Indsl. Editors, 1961, 62. Mem. Am. Assn. Indsl. Editors (dir. 1962, 63), Am. Soc. Tng. and Devel. Lion (pres. 1967). Clubs: Pinnacle (Augusta, Ga.); Palmetto Golf, Midland Valley Country (Aiken). Home: 807 Calhoun St Aiken SC 29801 Office: PO Box 499 Aiken SC 29801

BREMER BARRERA, JUAN JOSE, lawyer; b. Monterey, Nuevo Laredo, Mexico, June 29, 1907; LL.B., Nat. U. Mexico. Admitted to Mexico bar, 1933; mem. firm Bremer, Quintana, Vaca, Rocha, Obregon y Mancera, Mexico D.F., Mexico. Sec. faculty law Nat. U. Mexico, 1935, chief clk., sec. council, 1935-38. Mem. Nat. Assn. Lawyers of Mexico. Author: Critical, Axiological and Integral Theory of Law. Translator: Modern Theories of Law and State (Stammler); Law and Ethics (Laun). Office: Paseo de la Reforma 116-404 Mexico 6 DF Mexico*

BRENES, LUIS RIVERA, sec. agr. Commonwealth of P.R. Address: Apartado 10163 Santurce PR 00908*

BRENGELMAN, SARAH TURNLEY PARDUE (MRS. GEORGE D. BRENGELMAN), civic worker; b. Los Angeles; d. Samuel Hollins and Amanda Carney (Turnley) Pardue; ed. Ward-Belmont Coll., 1935, Vanderbilt U., 1938; m. George Dury Brengelman, Oct. 1, 1941 (dec. June 1962); children—Amanda Carney (Mrs. Joseph Ross McBride, Jr.), Edna Armstrong (Mrs. Walter M. Rush, Jr.), Sarah Pardue (Mrs. Robert L. Ritchey, Jr.) George Dury III, Alvin Armstrong. Officer, 1st Nat. Bank Birmingham (Ala.), then asst. v.p., dir. women's div., now ret. Vice pres. Civiettes Inc., 1952; active United Appeal, 1958—, chmn. women's div., 1963, dir. speaker bur., 1966; pres. elementary sch. P.T.A., Mountain Brook, 1956-57, pres. high sch., 1967—; coordinator 1st aid-fall out boot camp Cahaba council Girl Scouts U.S.A., 1962, coordinator Hurrican Betsy, 1965; organizational pres. Friends of Emmet O'Neal Library, Mountain Brook, 1965-66; co-chmn. tickets Beaux Arts Ball, 1964; active A.R.C., Birmingham, guest speaker Ark. conf., 1966; mem. bd. Women's Soc. Christian Service, 1943—, pres. 1959-60, chmn. ann. luncheon and fashion show, 1963, mem. exec. bd. Birmingham dist., 1960-64; mem.-at-large Birmingham dist. Wesleyan Service Guild, 1960-64; mem. Women's Com. of 100; mem. women's com. Birmingham Symphony; mem. Women's com. Birmingham Art Mus. Bd. dirs. YWCA, Birmingham area chpt. A.R.C., Goodwill Industries, Children's Aid Soc., Vis. Nursing Assn., Festival of Arts. Mem. Am. Assn. U. Women, Antiquarian Soc., Birmingham Opera Guild, D.A.R., U.D.C., Vanderbilt U. Class 1938 (sec.), Chi Omega. Methodist. Clubs: Fleur-de-lis Garden (pres. 1960), Zonta, Amaranth Literary (pres. 1965-66). Home: 2608 Heathermoor Rd Birmingham AL 35223

BRENNAN, DAN, broadcasting exec. Program dir. WVOK, Birmingham, Ala. Office: P O Box 2468 Birmingham AL 35201*

BRENNAN, WILLIAM J(OSEPH), JR., justice; b. Newark, Apr. 25, 1906; s. William J. and Agnes (McDermott) B.; B.S., U. Pa., 1928; LL.B., Harvard, 1931; m. Marjorie Leonard, May 5, 1928; children—William Joseph, Hugh Leonard, Nancy. Admitted to N.J. bar, 1931, practiced in Newark, 1931-49, mem. Pitney, Hardin, Ward & Brennan; superior ct. judge, 1949-50; appellate div. judge, 1950-52; justice Supreme Ct. N.J., 1952-56; asso. justice U.S. Supreme Ct., 1956—. Served with Gen. Staff Corps, U.S. Army, World War II. Decorated Legion of Merit. Office: Supreme Ct Bldg Washington DC 20004

BRENNER, EDGAR H(IRSCH), lawyer; b. N.Y.C., Jan. 4, 1930; s. Louis and Bertha (Guttman) B.; B.A., Carleton Coll., 1951; LL.B., Yale, 1954; m. Phyllis Rudstrom, June 2, 1952; children—Charles Sand, David McCaskie, Paul Rudstrom. Admitted to D.C. bar, 1954; mem. legal task force staff Second Hoover Commn., 1954; trial atty. U.S. Dept. Justice, 1954-57; mem. firm Arnold & Porter, Washington, 1957—. Commr. Fairfax County (Va.) Indsl. Devel. Authority, 1963—, chmn., 1964-66, 70—. Bd. dirs. Stella and Charles Guttman Found. Recipient citation of merit Fairfax County C. of C., 1966. Mem Am., Fed. (chmn. ct. of claims com. 1957) bar assns., Bar Assn. D.C. Home: 2205 Marthas Rd Alexandria VA 22307 Office: 1229 19th St NW Washington DC 20036

BRENT, J. ALLEN, beverage co. exec.; b. Carmi, Ill., Nov. 21, 1921; s. J. A. and Mabel C. (Rvg) B.; B.S., Eastern Ill. U., 1943; Ph.D., U. Fla., 1949; m. Norma U. Miller, Jan. 8, 1946; children—Mark Allen, Robert Lee, Karen Ann, William Michael. Chemist Manhattan Project, Tonawanda, N.Y., 1943-46; naval stores research asst. U. Fla., Gainesville, 1946-49; head chemistry dept. Jacksonville U., 1949-51; chief chemistry sect. research and devel. Minute Maid Co. div. Coca-Cola Co., Plymouth, Fla., 1951-62, asso. dir. research, 1962-64, dir. research and devel. carbonated beverages Coca-Cola Co., Atlanta, 1956—; v.p. Coca-Cola U.S.A., 1968—. Mem. Am. Chem. Soc. (chmn. Fla. sect.), A.A.A.S., Inst. Food Technologists. Sigma Xi, Gamma Sigma Epsilon. Roman Catholic. K.C. (4th deg.). Rotarian. Patentee in field. Home: 8900 Huntcliff Trace Atlanta GA 30328 Office: The Coca-Cola Co Atlanta GA 30304

BRESNAHAN, JOHN FRANCIS, librarian; b. Medford, Mass., Sept. 29, 1918; s. Michael J. and Margaret (Campbell) B.; A.B., Villanova, 1942, M.S. in L.S., 1953, M.A., 1961. Librarian Villanova Prep. Sch., Ojai, Cal., 1944-57; asst. librarian Augustinian Coll., Wash., 1958-60, Msgr. Bonner High Sch., Drexel Hill, Pa., 1961-62; librarian Biscayne Coll., Miami, Fla., 1962—. Mem. Am., S.E., Fla., Cath. library assns. Home: 16400 NW 32d Av Miami FL 33054

BRESS, DAVID GERALD, lawyer, educator; b. N.Y.C., June 7, 1908; s. Abraham and Elizabeth (Geto) B.; B.S., U. Va., 1928; LL.B., Harvard, 1931; m. Flora M. Lyon, Sept. 20, 1941; children—Pamela Lyon, David Gerald. Admitted to D.C. bar, 1931, since practiced in Washington; U.S. atty. D.C., 1965-69, 71—; partner law firm Ginsburg, Feldman & Bress, 1969—; mem. faculty Washington Coll. Law, Am. U., 1932-52; prof. law Georgetown U. Law Sch., Washington, 1953-61, U. Va. Law Sch., 1963-64. Mem. adv. bd. dirs. Riggs Nat. Bank. Vice pres. Nat. Capitol Area council Boy Scouts Am. Bd. dirs. Columbia Hosp., Police Boys Club Inst. Criminal Law. Served as comdr. USNR, 1941-45. Fellow Am. Coll. Trial Lawyers, Am. Bar Found.; mem. Am. Bar Assn. (ho. of dels. 1957-64; chmn. com. on uniform rules evidence fed cts. 1958-59, 64-66), Bar Assn. D.C. (pres. 1957-58), Am. Jewish Com. (past pres. Washington chpt.), Am. Judicature Soc. (bd. dirs. 1967-69), Phi Beta Kappa. Jewish religion (pres. congregation). Home: 3126 Ellicott St Washington DC 20008 Office: 1700 Pennsylvania Av NW Washington DC 20006

BRESSLER, BERNARD, educator; b. Milan, Mich., May 22, 1917; s. Samuel and Rose (Grossman) B.; A.B., Washington U., St. Louis, 1938, M.D., 1942; m. Elizabeth Burgess, Aug. 18, 1948; children—Barbara Anne, Robert Burgess, Garrett Schell, Peter Bartlett. Intern St. Louis City Hosp., 1940-43; resident St. Louis City Sanatorium, 1943-44; fellow Michael Reese Hosp., Chgo., 1944-46; practice medicine specializing in psychiatry Duke U. Med. Center, Durham, N.C., prof. psychiatry, 1957—; tng. analyst U. N.C.-Duke U. Psychoanalytic Inst., 1959—. Served to capt. M.C., AUS, 1953-55. Diplomate Pan Am. Med. Assn. Fellow Am. Psychiatric Assn.; mem. A.M.A., Am. Psychoanalytic Assn., Am. Psychosomatic Assn. Home: 2700 Circle Dr Durham NC 27105

BRETT, CHARLES HENRY, educator; b. Lincoln, Neb., July 21, 1909; s. John Howard and Teresa (Price) B.; B.S., U. Neb., 1930; M.S., 1938; Ph.D., Kan. State U., 1946; m. Melba Delores Durst, June 10, 1931; children—Charles Everett, Dewey Howard. Tchr. high sch., Nebraska City, Neb., 1931-43; asst. prof. entomology Okla. State U., 1943-48, asso. prof., 1948-52; prof. N.C. State U., Raleigh, 1952—. Guest lectr. U.S. Dept. Agr. Plant Resistance Sch., Kan. State U., 1966. Fellow Okla. Acad. Sci.; mem. N.C. (pres. award for contbns. to entomology 1971), Kan. entomol. socs., Entomol. Soc. Am., N.C. Acad. Sci., Am. Inst. Biol. Sci., N.C. State U. Faculty Club, Sigma Xi (pres.), Phi Sigma, Gamma Sigma Delta, Phi Kappa Phi, Tau Kappa Epsilon. Contbr. articles in field to profl. jours. Home: 1425 Dixie Trail Raleigh NC 27607

BREUER, LOUIS KARL, III, cons.; b. Kearney, N.J., July 17, 1923; s. Louis Karl and Matilda Anna (Schneider) B.; student N.C. State U., 1941-42, Coe Coll., 1946-48; postgrad. So. Meth. U., 1970-71; m. Elizabeth Ellen Anderson, Nov. 20, 1943; children—Lou Ellen (Mrs. John Rogers), Louis Karl IV, John, Teresa. Asst. city editor Cedar Rapids (Ia.) Gazette, 1948-59; dir. corporate communication Collins Radio Co., 1959-64; corporate dir. Varo, Inc., Dallas, 1964-71; cons., 1971—; mem. exec. com. Montex Devel. Co. Mem. exec. com. Muscular Dystrophy Assn. Am., 1971—; mem. Pres.'s adv. com. U. Dallas, 1968—. Served with USAAF, 1942-46. Decorated Air medal with 15 oak leaf clusters, Silver Star medal, D.F.C. with one oak leaf cluster, Croix de Guerre (Belgium). Mem. Pub. Relations Soc. Am., Thunderbolt Fighter Pilots Assn., Sigma Nu. Episcopalian. Rotarian. Club: Press (Dallas). Home: 808 Belt Line Cove Richardson TX 75080 Office: Rep Bank Tower Dallas TX 75201

BREWER, ALBERT PRESTON, lawyer, former gov. Ala.; b. Bethel Springs, Tenn., Oct. 26, 1928; s. Dan A. and Clara (Yarber) B.; A.B., U. Ala., 1952, LL.B., 1952; m. Martha Farmer, Jan. 31, 1951; children—Rebecca Ann, Beverly Alison. Admitted to Ala. bar, 1952, since practiced in Decatur and Montgomery; mem. Ala. Ho. of Reps., 1955-66, speaker of house, 1963-66; lt. gov. Ala., 1966-68, gov., 1968-71. Named Outstanding Young Man of Decatur, Decatur Jr. C. of C., 1963, one of four outstanding Young Men of Ala., Ala. Jr. C. of C., 1963, Outstanding Mem. Ala. Ho. of Reps., 1963. Mem. Am., Ala. bar assns., Ala. Trial Lawyers Assn., Phi Alpha Delta, Delta Sigma Phi. Baptist. Home: Route 1 Box 40 Pike Road AL 36064 Office: Box 901 Montgomery AL 36102

BREWER, BILL, ins. and real estate exec.; b. Winnsboro, Tex., Dec. 1, 1920; s. Alvie Irwin and Lola Bell (Calwell) B.; B.A., So. Meth. U., 1941; m. Aline Polan, Nov. 27, 1942; children—Ben, Wayne. Mgr., A & P Grocery Store, 1942-44; owner Brewers Gen. Mdse., 1944-45; profl. golfer 1945-60; builder golf courses, 1960-72; developer sub-div., 1960-72; ins. gen. agt. Am. Nat. Ins. Co., 1970-72; pres. State Wide Electroplating, Inc., Longview, Tex., 1960-72; dir. E. Tex. Bank & Trust Co. Pres., Gregg County Water Control Bd., 1949-56. Chmn. Gregg County Democratic Com., 1960-72. Bd. dirs. YMCA, Longview, Tex., Salvation Army. Methodist. Mason (Shriner). Lion. Home: 5803 W Marshall St Longview TX 75601 Office: 5703 W Marshall St Longview TX 75601

BREWER, (MARION) CAREY, coll. pres.; b. Lynchburg, Va., July 8, 1927; s. James Allen and Esther Goode (Leftwich) B.; B.A., Lynchburg Coll., 1949; student Am. U., 1951; M.P.A., Harvard, 1952, Ph.D., 1956; m. Betty Ann Brighton, Sept. 3, 1949; children—Mary Elizabeth, Robert Allen, Ruth Ann, Catherine Lee. Analyst legislative reference service Library of Congress, 1949-56; senior def. specialist mil. operations subcom. Ho. of Reps., 1956-60; mem. staff joint com. atomic energy U.S. Congress, 1960-61; dep. dir. program and policy, later exec. asst. to dir. OCDM, 1961; dir. emergency plans and readiness Office Emergency Planning, Exec. Office Pres., 1961-62, dir. civil affairs, 1962-64; pres. Lynchburg (Va.) Coll., 1964—; lectr. Am. U., 1954-56. Mem. Bd. Higher Education Disciples of Christ. Served with USNR, 1945-46. Littauer fellow Harvard, 1951-53. Mem. Am. Polit. Sci. Assn., Am. Soc. Pub. Adminstrs., Lynchburg Coll. Alumni Assn. (pres. 1963-64). Mem. Christian Ch. (elder). Author numerous articles. Home: 3806 Faculty Dr Lynchburg VA 24501

BREWER, CLYDE SAVAGE (MRS. CLAUDE A. BREWER), educator, civic worker; b. Whitewright, Tex.; d. Charles Edward and Flora Belle (Payne) Savage; grad. North Tex. State U., 1917; B.S., So. Meth. U., 1951; m. Claude A. Brewer, Jan. 13, 1918; children—Bette Belle (Mrs. Carl H. Ingwer, Jr.), James Ashley II, Claude A. Tchr., Jefferson, 1914-15, Sherman, Tex., 1917-18, Dublin, Tex., 1920-21, Ranger, Tex., 1921-22, Big Springs, Tex., 1922-23, Cumby, Tex., 1925-27, Dallas, 1935-38, 1943-44, Dallas Pub. Schs., 1942-43, 1953-54; substitute tchr. Dallas Schs., 1967—. Publicity chmn. Dallas Woman's Forum, 1967—; mem. Local History and Geneal. Soc.-Dallas Pub. Library, 1955—, dir., 1963-69; pres. Clionean Study Club, 1964-65; del. State Federated Clubs, 1915-17; pres. Christian Woman's Fellowship Fowler Homes, 1966-67, 1967-68; mem. P.T.A., Robert E. Lee Elementary Sch., 1927-43, J. L. Long Jr. High Sch., 1933-35, Woodrow Wilson High Sch., 1932-40, Spence Jr. High Sch., 1941-45, North Dallas High Sch., 1946-50; active various fund drives. Mem. D.A.R. (com. chmn. 1965-69), Nat. Soc. China Painters, So. Meml. Assn. Mem. Christian Ch. (pres. Lida C. Walls Bible Class 1956, corr. sec. Christian Women's Fellowship 1969-70). Clubs: Palm (pres. 1956-57) Mary Arden. Address: 6824 Dalhart Lane Dallas TX 75214

BREWER, CURTIS CLAUDE, banker; b. Bonlee, N.C., Aug. 20, 1922; s. Curtis Claude and Mabel (Lambe) B.; B.S. in Commerce, U. N.C., 1943; m. Gladys Ross Smith, June 20, 1942; children—Curtis Claude III, Constance Susan, Ted LeRoy, Barry Dwight. With N.C. Nat. Bank, Greensboro, 1943-44; with First Union Nat. Bank N.C., Charlotte, and predecessors, 1945—, exec. v.p., 1955—; pres. Siler City Devel. Corp (N.C.), 1960—; v.p., dir. Piedmont Cattle Credit Co., Siler City, 1959—. Pres. Chatham Hosp., Siler City, 1959-61. Bd. dirs. Junior Achievement. Served with Transp. Corps. AUS. World War II. Methodist. Mason (Shriner). Clubs: Democratic Men's, Charlotte Executives, Myers Park Country (Charlotte). Home: 4112 Arbor Way Charlotte NC 28211 Office: 301 S Tryon St Charlotte NC 28201

BREWER, EDWIN, art dir. Ark. Dept. Edn. Made trip to Vietnam to paint conflict. Address: 4701 N Lookout St Little Rock AR 72205*

BREWER, EUGENE WILLIAMS, lumber and bldg. materials co. exec.; b. New Castle, Ky., Sept. 29, 1929; s. Eugene Strother and Dora (Williams) B.; B.S., U. Ky., 1952; m. Juanita Lee Tingle, Sept. 13, 1950; children—Eugene Allan, Stephen Leslie. Dist. mgr. Massey Ferguson, Indpls., 1952-55; field sales engr. Brandeis Machine Co., Louisville, 1956-60; sales mgr. Wilson Machinery Co., Lexington, Ky., 1960-62; pres. Brewer Lumber Co., New Castle, Ky., 1962-71; pres., chmn. bd. Weir Magic Pit Corp., New Castle, Ky., 1971—. Chmn. Com. on Health Facilities Planning, Louisville, 1968—; chmn. Municipal Housing Commn., New Castle, 1965—. Pres. Henry County Fair Bd., HOST Community Action, Indsl. Devel. Found. New Castle; v.p. Community Coll. Com. Henry County; bd. dirs. Falls Region Health Council, Louisville. Ky. Col. Methodist (trustee). Home: PO Box 28 New Castle KY 40050 Office: PO Box 296 New Castle KY 40050

BREWER, GEORGE MADISON, hosp. adminstr.; b. Glazier, Tex., Jan. 4, 1916; s. Robert Edward and Blanche Julia (Palmer) B.; B.S., U. Colo., 1947; M.S., Northwestern U., 1957; L.H.D., McMurry Coll., 1964. Mgr., Indsl. Clinic, Pampa, Tex., 1937-42; merchandiser Montgomery Ward & Co., Oakland, Cal., 1947-49; administr. Hansford Hosp., Spearman, Tex., 1949-50, Roosevelt Gen. Hosp., Portales, N.M., 1950-55, Los Alamos (N.M.) Med. Center, 1955-56; asst. adminstr. Presbyn. Hosp. Center, Albuquerque, 1957-58; dir. Louisville Gen. Hosp., 1958-61; adminstr. Meth. Hosp., Lubbock, Tex., 1961-72, pres., 1972—. Prof. hosp., clinic adminstrn. U. Louisville, 1958-61. Dir. N.M. Blue Cross Plan, 1953-56; mem. Tex. Radiation Adv. Bd., 1970-76. Served to lt. (j.g.) USNR, 1942-45. Fellow Am. Coll. Hosp. Admnstrs.; mem. Am., Tex. (chmn. council on profl. service 1964-66; trustee 1966-69, 72—) hosp. assns. Rotarian. Home: 5305 43rd St Lubbock TX 79414 Office: 3615 19th St Lubbock TX 79410

BREWER, JACK ALAN, religious orgn. exec.; b. Elmore City, Okla., Apr. 13, 1933; s. Jesse Elijah and Opal Mae (Brookshire) B.; B.A., E. Central State Coll., 1958; M. Religious Edn., Southwestern Bapt. Theol. Sem., 1960; m. Carolyn Sue Wright, Mar. 15, 1953; children—Lee, Lisa, Lynn. Merchandising rep. Spokane (Wash.) Daily Chronicle; ordained to ministry Baptist Ch., 1970; minister youth First Bapt. Ch., Tulia, Tex., 1960-62, Springfield, Mo., 1962-65, Texarkana, Tex., 1965-67, Tallowood Bapt. Ch., 1967-70; exec. dir. Boys Country, Houston, 1970—, mem. exec. bd. 1971—. Founder Youth Ecol. Soc., Houston, 1971. Active Pres. Youth Employment Campaign, 1966. Served with USAF, 1951-55. Mem. Southwestern Bapt. Religious Edn. Assn. Democrat. Author: Fellowships From A-Z, 1967; Serving In My Community, 1970. Contbr. articles to profl. jours. Home: 12718 Dermott St Houston TX 77040 Office: 18806 Roberts Rd Hockley TX 77447

BREWER, JAMES MALCOLM, dentist; b. Leesburg, Ala., June 24, 1914; s. Murt and Mary Emma (Cartlidge) B.; student High Point Coll., 1939; B.S., Jacksonville State U., 1937; D.D.S., Emory U., 1943; m. Maureen Roberts, Jan. 24, 1969; children by previous marriage—Stephen J., Anne Elizabeth (Mrs. Ray Selvage). Tchr. pub. schs., 1935-38; gen. practice dentistry, Ft. Payne, Ala., 1946—; dir. 1st Fed. Savs. & Loan Assn. Chmn. A.R.C. Bd. dirs. Mountain Manor Nursing Home. Served with AUS, 1943-46. Fellow Internat. Coll. Dentists; mem. Am., Ala. (pres. 1972) dental assns., 5th Dist., Chgo. dental socs., Am. Soc. Dentistry for Children, So. Acad. Oral Surgery, Am. Legion (comdr.). Baptist. Mason (Shriner). Home: 300 16th St NW Ft Payne AL 35967 Office: PO Box 428 Ft Payne AL 35967

BREWER, MICHAEL FRASER, social scientist; b. N.Y.C., May 9, 1929; s.George E. and Ann (Fraser) B.; B.S., Yale, 1953; M.S., U. Mich., 1955; Ph.D., U. Cal. at Berkeley, 1959; m. Charlotte J. Kidder, June 11, 1955; children—Henry, Fraser, Mika, Polly. Asst. prof. U. Cal. at Berkeley, 1959-62; staff economist Council of Econ. Advisers, Exec. Office of Pres., Washington, 1962-63; dir. Natural Resources Policy Center, George Washington U., 1965-67; v.p. Resources for the Future, Inc., Washington, 1967-71; pres. Population Reference Bur., Washington, 1971—. Mem. Am. Econ. Assn., Am. Agrl. Econ. Assn., Student Conservation Assn. (dir. 1969—). Served with AUS, 1950-52. Home: 6817 Connecticut Av Chevy Chase MD 20015 Office: 1755 Massachusetts Av NW Washington DC 20015

BREWER, NORMAN C(RAIG), JR., lawyer, city judge; b. Black Hawk, Miss., Oct. 4, 1913; s. Norman C. and Ella Hunter (Jumper) B.; A.B., U. Miss., 1935, LL.B., 1937; m. Martha Manly. Apr. 12, 1946; children—Martha, Norman III. Admitted to Miss. bar, 1937, since practiced Greenwood; sr. mem. firm Brewer, Deaton & Evans; city judge, 1939-43; 47-57. Commr. Yazoo-Miss. Delta Levee Dist. Mem. adv. bd. Mt. Buelah Christian Center, Edwards, Miss.; treas. Nat. Found. Infantile Paralysis, Inc., Le Flore County, 1948—; state pres. Conv. Christian Chs.; dir. Girl Scout Campers; chmn. bd. Miss. Christian Missionary Soc. Served as lt. comdr. USNR, 1942-46; overseas, 1943-45, comdr., 1953—. La. colonel, 1948-52, Miss., 1952—. Chmn. Bd. Bar Admissions, Miss., 1958-60. Named Ky. Col. Mem. Am. Coll. Probate Counsel, V.F.W., S.A.R. (state pres.), Am. Legion (past comdr.), Internat. Assn. Ins. Counsel, Am. Leflore County bar assns., Miss. Assn. Def. Lawyers, Miss. State Bar, C. of C. (mem. exec. com.), Soc. Colonial Wars (gov.), Sigma Chi (nat. pres.), Omicron Delta Kappa, Phi Delta Phi. Mem. Christian Ch. (chmn. ofcl. bd.). Elk. Clubs: Batteaux Bay (Tobago, B.W.I.); Greenwood (Miss.) Country; Summit (Memphis). Home: W River Rd Greenwood MS 38930 Office: 107 W Market St Greenwood MS 38930

BREWER, PHILIP WARREN, civil engr.; b. Hagerstown, Md., Dec. 18, 1923; s. J. Chester and Ruth (Emmert) B.; B.S., U. Md., 1945; m. Elizabeth Marvel Wynn, Aug. 29, 1947; children—Dorothy Wynn, Bruce Douglas. Hydraulic engr. Water Resources Br., U.S. Geol. Survey, College Park, Md. 1945-47; designing engr. Wash. Suburban San. Commn., Hyattsville, Md., 1947-53; san. engr., civil engr. Bur. of Yards and Docks, Dept. Navy, Washington, 1953-68, head spl. design Naval Facilities Engring. Command, 1968—. Registered profl. engr. Mem. Am. Soc. C.E., Soc. Am. Mil. Engrs. Episcopalian. Home: 12545 Two Farm Dr Silver Spring MD 20904 Office: Code 041B Naval Facilities Enginng Command Washington DC 20390

BREWER, RALPH WRIGHT, JR., lawyer; b. Alexandria, La., Jan. 9, 1928; s. Ralph Wright and Margot (Riviere) B.; B.J., La. State U., 1950, J.D., 1955; m. Peggy Knapps; 1 dau., Margo Beatrice; children (by previous marriage)—David, Daniel, Ralph Wright III, William. Admitted to La. bar, 1955; practice law, Baton Rouge, 1955—. Served with USNR, 1946-48, 1950-52. Mem. Am., La., Baton Rouge bar assns., V.F.W., Amvets, Am., La. trial lawyers assns., Nat. Defender and Legal Aid Assn., Sigma Delta Chi, Sigma Alpha Epsilon. Democrat. Presbyn. (elder). Home: 1023 Waverly Dr Baton Rouge LA 70806 Office: 200 Government St Baton Rouge LA 70802

BREWSTER, LEO, judge; b. Ft. Worth, Oct. 16, 1903; s. C. B. and Mary (Thomas) B.; LL.B., U. Tex, 1926; m. Lois Rice, Mar. 21, 1928; children—Gayle (Mrs. Ben Rollert, Jr.), Sarah (Mrs. Richard Griffith). Admitted to Tex. bar, 1926, since practiced in Fort Worth; U.S. dist. judge No. Dist. Tex., 1961—. First asst. dist. atty., Tarrant County, Tex., 1935-39, mem. ho. of dels. Am. Bar Assn., 1958-61. Fellow Am. Coll. Trial Lawyers; mem. Philos. Society Texas, Ft. Worth Bar Assn. (v.p. 1951, pres. 1952), State Bar Tex. (pres. 1958-59, dir. 1953-60). Clubs: Fort Worth, Ridglea Country. Home: 1700 Ridgmar Blvd Fort Worth TX 76116 Office: US Courthouse Fort Worth TX 76102

BREWSTER, MCCLUER, graphic arts exec.; b. Washington Cane Hill, Ark., Feb. 3, 1919; s. Boudinot and Henrietta (McCluer) B.; grad. high sch.; m. Eleanor Hines, Oct. 15, 1947; 1 dau., Katie. Salesman, Ennis Bus. Forms, Inc. (Tex.), 1940-50, sales mgr. Eastern div., Chatham, Va., 1950-66, v.p., asst. gen. mgr., 1966-69, exec. v.p., Ennis, 1969—, also dir. Chmn., Pittsylvania County (Va.) Safety Council, 1962; mem. Chatham Town Council, 1958-62. Served with AUS, 1942-46; PTO, CBI. Decorated 7 Bronze Star medals. Recipient with Mrs. Brewster Outstanding Citizens' award Chatham C. of C., 1969. Mem. C. of C. (pres. 1960) Methodist. Mason, Lion, Rotarian. Club: Lakeside Country (Ennis, Tex.). Home: 903 N Preston Ennis TX 75119 Office: 214 W Knox St Ennis TX 75119

BREWSTER, ROBERT CHARLES, fgn. service officer; b. Beatrice, Neb., May 31, 1921; s. Charles Lee and Lillian Aseneth (French) B.; student Grinnell Coll., 1939-41; A.B., U. Wash., 1943; postgrad. U. Mexico, summer 1946, George Washington U., summer 1947, Columbia, 1946-48; m. Mary Virginia Blackman, Feb. 22, 1951. Fgn. affairs analyst State Dept., 1948-49; fgn. service officer, 1949—; 3d sec. Am. embassy, Managua, Nicaragua, 1949-51, 2d sec., 1951-52; vice consul Am. consulate gen., Stuttgart, Germany, 1952-55; policy briefing officer ICA, 1956-57; staff asst. to under sec. of state for econ. affairs, 1958, spl. asst., 1959; spl. asst. to under sec. of state, 1959-60;

assigned Nat. War Coll., 1960-61; fgn. service inspector, 1961-63; counselor Am. embassy, Asuncion, 1964-66; dep. exec. dir. Bur. European Affairs, Dept. State, Washington, 1966-67, exec. dir., 1967-69, dep. exec. sec. Dept. State, 1969-71; dep. dir. gen. Fgn. Service, dir. personnel, 1971—. Served to lt. (j.g.) USNR, 1943-46. Mem. Am. Fgn. Service Assn. Home: 2528 Queen Anne's Lane NW Washington DC 20037 Office: Dept of State Washington DC 20520

BREWSTER, W(ILLIAM) HERBERT, clergyman, composer gospel music; b. Somerville, Tenn., July 2, 1899; ed. Roger Williams Coll.; m. Julia Brewster; 1 son, 1 dau. Ordained to ministry Baptist Ch.; pastor Forrest City, Ark., North Memphis, Tenn., East Trigg Av. Bapt. Ch., Memphis, 1930—; mem. staff Am. Bapt. Theol. Sem. Exec. sec. Nat. Bapt. Edn. Bd. U.S., Inc. Composer: Tomorrow, Surely God is Able, Move On Up a Little Higher, How Far Am I From Canaan, God's Amazing Love, numerous others. Address: 1189 E Trigg Av Memphis TN 38106

BREWTON, CHARLES SIDNEY, govt. ofcl.; b. Larkinsville, Ala., Nov. 9, 1913; s. Charles Spurgeon and Ora (Smith) B.; student Birmingham-So. Coll., 1932-35; J.D., U. Ala., 1938; m. Jewell Wann, Oct. 12, 1940; children—Carol Ann, Charles Sidney III. Admitted to Ala. bar, 1938; practice in Scottsboro, Ala., as partner Brewton & Jones, 1938-40; spl. asst. to U.S. atty. gen., 1940-43; staff dir. U.S. Senate Com. Expenditure in Exec. Depts., 1943-44; adminstrv. asst. to U.S. Senator Lister Hill, 1943-56; asso. dir. law and legislation Joint Commn. Mental Illness and Health, Cambridge, Mass., 1956-59; gen. counsel Senate Com. Small Bus., 1959-61; asst. dir. Office Emergency Preparedness Exec. Office President, 1961-69; gen. counsel Joint Com. Def. Prodn., 1969—. Chmn. com. arrangements Nat. Conf. Nat. Def. Exec. Res., 1965. Asst. campaign mgr. presdl. nominee Adlai E. Stevenson, 1952, 56; asst. to chmn. Presdl. Inaugural Com., 1965. Mem. Assn. Senate Adminstrv. Assts. and Exec. Secs. (past pres.), Nat. Grange, Sigma Alpha Epsilon. Clubs: President's; Nat. Capitol Democratic. Author: (with others) Action for Mental Health, 1961. Home: 2206 Belle Haven Rd Alexandria VA 22307 Office: Senate Office Bldg Washington DC 20510

BREWTON, WILLIAM FRANKLIN, lawyer; b. New Port Richey, Fla., Sept. 5, 1932; s. Wade Hampton and Jewell (McLean) B.; B.A., Emory U., 1954; LL.B., U Fla., 1957. Admitted to Fla. bar, 1957; partner Brewton and Brewton, Dade City, 1958-65, owner, 1965—; municipal judge City of Dade City, Fla. Served with AUS, 1957-58. Mem. Fla. Bar, Am., Pasco County (pres. 1964) bar assns., Am. Judicature Soc., Fla. Heart Assn. (parliamentarian for bd. dirs., del. to Am. Heart Conv.), Sigma Nu, Phi Delta Phi, Pi Sigma Alpha. Democrat. Methodist. Mason (Shriner). Home: 123 W Hendley Av Dade City FL 33525 Office: 708 E Meridian Av Dade City FL 33525

BREYERE, EDWARD JOSEPH, biologist, educator; b. Washington, Apr. 25, 1927; s. Edward Joseph and Mollie (Swing) B.; B.S., U. Md., 1951; M.S., U. Md., 1954, Ph.D., 1957; m. Marjorie Louise Gillet, June 16, 1951; 1 son, Edward John. Teaching asst. U. Md., 1954-55; research fellow Nat. Cancer Inst., 1955-57, 57-61; asso. prof. Am. U., Washington, 1961-67, prof. biology, 1967—, dir. Leukemia Research Fund, 1966—; dir. Immunogenetics Lab., Sibley Meml. Hosp., Washington. Served with AUS, 1945-46. Mem. Transplantation Soc., Am. Assn. Cancer Research, A.A.A.S., Am. Inst. Biol. Scis., Am. Genetics Assn., Sigma Xi, Phi Kappa Phi. Contbr. Articles profl. jours. Home: 6707 Sulky Lane Rockville MD 20852 Office: 5255 Loughboro Rd NW Washington DC 20016

BRIAN, ALEXIS MORGAN, JR., lawyer; b. New Orleans, Oct. 4, 1928; s. Alexis Morgan and Evelyn (Thibaut) B.; B.A. in Sociology, La. State U., 1949, J.D., 1956; M.S. in Psychology, Trinity U., 1954; m. Elizabeth Louise Graham, Mar. 17, 1951; children—Robert Morgan, Ellen Graham. Admitted to La. bar, 1956; asso firm Deutsch, Kerrigan & Stiles, New Orleans, 1956-60, partner, 1961—. Mem. com. on bds. So. Bapt. Conv., mem. exec. bd. New Orleans Bapt. Assn. Trustee New Orleans Bapt. Theol. Sem.; pres., 1968—; bd. dirs. Goodwill Industries, New Orleans Bapt. Theol. Sem. Found. Served with USAF, 1951-55. Mem. Am., La., New Orleans bar assns., Internat. Assn. Ins. Counsel, La. Assn. Def. Counsel, Def. Research Inst., Am. Arbitration Assn. (panel of arbitrators); Phi Delta Phi, Theta Xi. Baptist (deacon; trustee; tchr.; lay preacher). Home: 1738 S Carrollton Av New Orleans LA 70118 Office: One Shell Sq New Orleans LA 70130

BRIANS, AUDREY LEE, architect; b. Corsicana, Tex., Aug. 23, 1934; d. Robin Hood and Audrey Mae (Harris) Brians; B.Arch., U. Tex., 1956, postgrad., 1971—. With Nat. Park Service, Phila., 1956; with York & Sawyer, N.Y.C., 1958, Internat. Basic Economy Corp., N.Y.C., 1959-64; with Daniel, Mann, Johnson, & Mendenhall, Madrid, Spain, 1964-68; partner Lammers & Brians, Austin, Tex., 1968-71; pvt. practice architecture, Austin, 1971—. Mem. Community Devel. Corp., Austin, 1969, Laguna Gloria Mus., Austin. Bd. dirs. Zachary Scott Civic Theatre, Austin, 1968-69. Registered landscape architect. Mem. A.I.A., Constrn. Specifications Inst., Alpha Alpha Gamma, Alpha Delta Pi. Home: 1701 Palma Plaza Austin TX 78703 Office: 1306 Woodlawn Blvd Austin TX 78703

BRICE, EDWARD WARNER, govt. ofcl.; b. Hallsboro, N.C., Sept. 25, 1916; s. Jethro E. and Carrie Agnes (Heath) B.; B.S. in Edn., Tuskegee Inst., 1938; M.A., U. Pa., 1947, Ph.D. in Edn. (Rosenwald fellow), 1949; LL.D., Monrovia Coll., 1955; m. Creola L. Lindsay, July 4, 1943; 1 son, Edward Warner. Prin., Treutlen County High Sch., Soperton, Ga., 1938-39; pres. Clinton Coll., Rock Hill, S.C., 1939-42; dean ednl. extension, prof. edn. S.C. State Coll., Orangeburg, 1948-51; pub. affairs officer, attache U.S. embassy, Monrovia, Liberia, 1951-52; chief edn. div., chief ednl. adviser Govt. of Liberia, 1952-56; chief ednl. div. U.S. Operation Mission to Nepal, chief ednl. adviser Govt. of Nepal, 1956-58; edn. program and research specialist U.S. Office Edn., Washington, 1958-61, dir. adult edn. br., 1962-67; confidential asst. to asst. sec. for edn. Dept. Health, Edn. and Welfare, 1967—; edn. adviser Bur. African Affairs, U.S. Dept. State, Washington, 1962-63; pres. Warner & Warner Internat. Assos., Inc. Mem. joint com. on human relations N.E.A.-Am. Tchrs. Assn., 1958—. Trustee Nat. Commn. for Adult Literacy. Served with AUS, 1942-46; ETO. Decorated Bronze Star; recipient George Washington Carver Distinguished Achievement award Phi Beta Sigma, 1950, Distinguished Alumnus award Tuskegee Inst., 1961. Mem. Adult Edn. Assn. U.S.A., N.E.A., Am. Assn. Sch. Adminstrs., Nat. Assn. Pub. Sch. Adult Edn., Am. Acad. Polit. and Social Sci. Author: Education in Africa, 1959; Education in the New Free Societies, 1961; Arithmetic for Adults, 1963; Citizenship for Adults, 1964. Contbr. articles on undereducated, adult migrant, Negro edn. to profl. publs. Home: 7810 14th St NW Washington DC 20012 Office: 1100 17th St NW Washington DC 19802

BRICE, LAURIE SIMONTON, educator; b. Winnsboro, S.C., Apr. 18, 1916; s. Eugene Douglas and Laura Lee (Jamison) B.; A.B., Erskine Coll., 1937; certificate in personnel psychology U. Pitts., 1943; M.Ed., U. S.C., 1948; m. Margaret Mae Hemminger, Sept. 7, 1943; children—Laurie Simonton, James Douglas, Carolyn Ann. Prin. Johnsonville (S.C.) Pub. Schs., 1937-40, Calhoun Falls (S.C.) Pub. Schs., 1940-42; supt. Indiantown Schs., Williamsburg County, S.C., 1946-49; prin., dir. edn. John de la Howe Sch., McCormick, S.C., 1949-67, supt., treas., 1967—. Sec-treas. McCormick County Devel. Bd., 1964-68; mem. commn. Piedmont Tech. Edn. Center. Bd. dirs. Southeastern Child Care Assn. Served with the AUS, 1942-46, PTO, 1944-46. Mem. N.E.A. (life), McCormick County Edn. Assn., Nat. Assn. Secondary Sch. Prins., S.C. Hist. Soc. Democrat. Presbyn. (elder). Lion (pres. 1961-62). Home: McCormick SC 29835 Office: John de la Howe Sch McCormick SC 29835

BRICKER, SHIRLEY ZUBRADT, advt. agy. exec.; b. Alta, Ia., Jan. 10, 1927; d. Theodore William and Mabel (Peterson) Zubradt; grad. high sch. 1 dau., Linda M. Asst. prodn. mgr. Cabell Eanes, Inc., Richmond, Va., 1954-57; v.p., prodn. mgr. Advt. Assos., Inc., Richmond, 1957-60; asst. mgr. research dept. U.S. Fed. Res. Bank, Richmond, 1960-62; media supr. Cargill, Wilson & Acree, Inc., Richmond, 1962-70, advt. cons., 1970; media dir. Lin Lockhart Advt., Inc., 1970-71; media dir. Clinton E. Frank, Inc., 1971—. Mem. Advt. Club Richmond (dir. 1965-68, treas. 1968-69, sec. 1969-70). Club: Press (hon.) (Va.) Address: 501 N Daisy Av Highland Springs VA 23075

BRIDGE, WILLIAM JOHN, govt. ofcl.; b. Ft. Wayne, Ind., Jan. 22, 1942; s. Charles Dwight and Berniece (Hershberger) B.; student Purdue U., 1962-64; A.B. with high distinction, Ind. U., 1967. Planning asst. Model City Program, Norfolk, Va., 1967-69, planning specialist, 1969-70, dir. planning, 1970; economist Norfolk (Va.) Redevel. and Housing Authority, 1970-71, dir. program devel., 1971—. Served with USNR, 1960-62. Mem. Am. Econ. Assn., Am. Soc. Planning Ofcls., Nat. Assn. Housing and Redevel. Ofcls., Phi Beta Kappa. Home: 535 Washington Park Norfolk VA 23517 Office: PO Box 968 Norfolk VA 23501

BRIDGEMAN, BEN DALY, lawyer; b. New Orleans, Nov. 29, 1932; s. Sidney and A. Irene (Daly) B.; B.B.A., Loyola U., New Orleans, 1954; LL.B., Tulane U., 1961; m. Dorothy E. Brennan, Sept. 4, 1954; children—O. Brennan, B. Daly, Bradford D. Admitted to La. bar, 1961; practiced in New Orleans, 1961—; mem. firm Bridgeman & Conway; chmn. bd. Merc. Bank & Trust Co., Gretna, La; partner The Claiborne Co., 1957—; dir. Peoples Bank's Trust Co., Chalmette. Bd. dirs. Vols. Am. Served to 1st lt. AUS, 1954-56. Club: Metairie Country. Home: 105 Mulberry Dr Metairie LA 70005 Office: 747 NBC Bldg New Orleans LA 70112

BRIDGER, JAMES ALBERT, JR., civil engr.; b. Bladenboro, N.C., Jan. 28, 1931; s. James Albert and Elise Fogle (Matthews) B.; student U. N.C., 1946-50, certificate in municipal adminstrn., 1962; B.S., N.C. State U., 1959; m. June Morris, Dec. 19, 1953; children—James Albert III, Matthew Anthony, M. Randall, R. Cameron. Office mgr., estimator Crowell Constrn. Co., Fayetteville, N.C., 1959, gen. supt., field engr., 1959-60; chief inspection div. City of Raleigh, N.C., 1960-64; resident engr. William C. Olsen & Assos., Raleigh, 1964-69; owner J. A. Bridger, Jr., cons. engrs., Raleigh, 1969—; pres., dir. Bridger Motor Co.; v.p., dir. Crowell Constructors; sec., dir. Pait Transfer Co., Kelly Supply Co., So. Builders Equipment Co.; dir. Bank of Bladenboro, Bladenboro Cotton Mills, Bridger Corp. Dist. commr. Boy Scouts Am., 1964. Served to 1st lt. USAF, 1951-56. Mem. Raleigh Engrs. Club, Am. Water Works Assn., N.C. Soc. Engrs. Baptist. Home: Route 1 Apex NC 27502 Office: 3917 Western Blvd Raleigh NC 27606

BRIDGES, ALBERT FOSTER, sch. athletics adminstr.; b. Athens, La., Mar. 17, 1905; s. Milton L. and Minnie Florence (Word) B.; student Bryson Coll., 1922-25; B.S., George Peabody Coll., 1926, M.A., 1932; m. Margaret Burrow, June 2, 1931. Tchr., coach Peabody High Sch., Trenton, Tenn., 1926-30, Milan (Tenn.) High Sch., 1930-31; tchr. Chester County High Sch., Henderson, Tenn., 1931-35, Byars Hall High Sch., Covington, Tenn., 1935-36; supt. Trenton Pub. Schs., 1936-43; supt. Covington City Schs., 1943-46; exec. sec. Tenn. Secondary Sch. Athletic Assn., Trenton, 1946—. Sec.-treas. Girls Nat. Basketball Rules Com., 1952-69. Treas. Laura Harlan Mack Morris Home for Aged. Mem. Tenn. Pub. Sch. Officers Assn. (pres. 1945-46), Gibson County Edn. Assn. (pres. 1936-37). Methodist. Rotarian. Home: 210 10th St Trenton TN 38382 Office: Box 67 Trenton TN 38382

BRIDGES, BENJAMIN, JR., govt. ofcl.; b. Washington, May 21, 1936; s. Benjamin and Laura (Titus) B.; B.A., Duke, 1958; Ph.D., Johns Hopkins U., 1962; m. Ruth Ann Mutchler, Aug. 20, 1960; children—Elizabeth Colleen, Ann Clark. Asst. prof. econs. U. Wis., Madison, 1962-65; vis. lectr. econs. U. Md., College Park, part-time, 1965-66; economist Office Research and Statistics, Social Security Adminstrn., Washington, 1965-68, chief long range research br., 1968—. Mem. Western, Am. econ. assns., Nat. Tax Assn. Contbr. chpt. to book, articles to publs. Home: 809 Grand View Dr Alexandria VA 22305 Office: 1875 Connecticut Av NW Washington DC 20009

BRIDGES, HENRY LEE, state ofcl.; b. Franklin County, N.C., June 10, 1907; s. John Joseph and Ida Loraine (Carroll) B.; A.B., Mars Hill Jr. Coll., 1929; B.A., Wake Forest Coll., 1931; postgrad. in law, 1932-33; m. Clarice Hines, Dec. 12, 1936; children—Joseph Henry, George Hines. Atty. at law; dep. clk. Superior Ct. Guilford County, 1935-40, 41-42, 45-46; aduitor State of N.C., Raleigh, 1947—. Sec., treas. Guilford County Democratic Exec. Com., 1933-40. Trustee Wake Forest U., 1949-52, 55-58, 60-63, 65-68, Southeastern Bapt. Theol. Sem., 1968—. Served with AUS, 1940-41, 42-45. Mem. Nat. Assn. State Auditors, Comptrollers and Treas. (exec. dir. 1958-69), Am. Legion, 40 and 8. Baptist (deacon). Mason (K.T., Shriner), Lion. Home: 2618 Grant Av Raleigh NC 27608 Office: Box 870 Raleigh NC 27602

BRIDGES, WILLIAM RAGAN, community devel. specialist; b. Mount Sterling, Ky., Mar. 17, 1913; s. Walter Hiram and Mayme (Greene) B.; student Centre Coll., 1929-31; A.B., U. Mich., 1933; postgrad. U. Chgo., 1934; M.A., Columbia U., 1936; m. Margaret Bruce Cruise, May 11, 1958 (dec. Dec. 1959). Disability examiner Ky. Dept. Edn., Frankfort, 1958-63; asso. in edn. Peace Corps, Pakistan Acad., Comilla, 1963-65; specialist in community devel. U. Ky., Quicksand, 1965—. Tng. cons. Community Devel. Found., 1968—. Chmn., Mt. Sterling Community House Com., 1935-38; chmn. leadership training Midland Trail dist. Boy Scouts Am., 1946-48; mem. adv. com. Breathitt County Sch., 1967-71. Bd. dirs. Montgomery County chpt. A.R.C.; mem. adv. council Salvation Army, Frankfort, 1960-63. Mem. Rural Sociol. Soc., Community Devel. Soc., Ky. Welfare Assn., Montgomery County Farm Bur., Breathitt County Arts Council. Democrat. Mem. Disciples of Christ Ch. Kiwanian. Author: Community Development What Why How, 1967; Let's Go, Community Leaders, 1968. Address: Robinson Substation Quicksand KY 41363

BRIDGES, WORTH TALMADGE, JR., dentist; b. Hickory, N.C., May 29, 1928; s. Worth Talmadge and Florrie Jane (Jeffcoate) B.; B.S., Wake Forest U., 1954; D.M.D., U. Louisville, 1959; m. Ethel Lawing, Aug. 23, 1953; children—Melissa Kay, Sherri Leigh. Pvt. practice dentistry, Shelby, N.C., 1959, Mooresville, N.C., 1960—. Bd. dirs. Lowrance Hosp., Mooresville. Served with USNR, 1946-51. Mem. Am. Dental Assn., Iredell County Dental Soc. (sec.-treas. 1962-63, pres. 1972), N.C. Dental Soc., Southeast Analgesia Soc. (charter, chmn. N.C. chpt. 1972), Alpha Sigma Phi, Delta Sigma Delta. Republican. Baptist. Mason, Elk. Home: 781 Pinewood Circle Mooresville NC 28115 Office: 213 S Broad St Mooresville NC 28115

BRIEGEL, HEINZ ADOLF, ins. co. exce.; b. Stuttgart, Germany, Jan. 21, 1928; s. Franz Josef and Rosa (Seiz) B.; B.S. in Math. summa cum laude, U. Mass., 1960; m. Dorothy Claire Breynaert, June 30, 1962; children—Karen Anne, Diana Beth, John Rolf. Came to U.S., 1953, naturalized, 1961. Various positions in mfg. industry and comml. enterprises in U.S. and Germany, 1948-56; asst. actuary Monarch Life Ins. Co., Springfield, Mass., 1960-65; v.p., actuary Fidelity Bankers Life Ins. Co., Richmond, Va., 1966—. Served with German Army, 1944-45. Fellow Soc. Actuaries; mem. Am. Acad. Actuaries. Club: Briarwood Swim and Racquet (Richmond, Va). Home: 4602 Butte Rd Richmond VA 23235 Office: 9th and Main Sts Richmond VA 23218

BRIEVE, FREDERICK JAY, univ. adminstr.; b. Holland, Mich., Aug. 17, 1928; s. Frank and Alice (Gebben) B.; A.B., Hope Coll., 1950; M.A., Mich. State U., 1956, Ed.D., 1963; m. Joyce Elane Baker, Aug. 11, 1950; children—Tom, Betsy. Tchr., Grand Ledge, Mich., 1950-53; high sch. prin., North Muskegon, Mich., 1955-60; supt. schs., Muskegon, Mich., 1960-63; adminstr. Mich. State U., 1963-64; adminstr. Dept. State, 1964-65; v.p. Kettering Found., Dayton, O., 1966-68; dept. chmn. U. Houston Sch. Adminstrn., 1968-70; asso. supt. schs., Dallas, 1970-71; head div. adminstrn. and ednl. services Va. Tech. U., Blacksburg, 1971—. Served with USNR, 1953-55. Mem. N.E.A. (life), Am., Tex. assns. sch. adminstrs., Am. Soc. Curriculum Devel., Council Ednl. Facilities Planners, Phi Delta Kappa. Elk. Home: 116 Canterbury Ct Blacksburg VA 24060

BRIGGLE, ANTHONY NOEL, splty. store exec.; b. Dallas, Nov. 30, 1937; s. William James and Virginia (Aechternacht) B.; B.A., So. Meth. U., 1959; m. Evelyn Carroll Cary, June 29, 1963; children—Evelyn Cary-Elisa, Georgie Fonda Schneider. Dir. pub. relations and spl. events Neiman-Marcus Co., Dallas, 1965—; asst. to v.p. sales promotion Tex. United Fund, 1963-65. Corr., Archtl. Digest, 1971. Chmn. men's div. TACA, 1970; v.p. Dallas Symphony Orch. Guild, 1971—; mem. adv. com. Jr. Players Guild, 1969—; mem. steering com. film festival So. Meth. U. Sch. Fine Arts, 1971—. Bd. dirs. Theatre Three, Dallas Civic Ballet Soc., Irish Georgian Soc. Mem. Pub. Relations Soc. Am., So. Meth. U. Alumni Assn., Kappa Alpha. Clubs: Mustang, Terpsichorean (Dallas). Home: 5453 Emerson St Dallas TX 75209 Office: Main and Ervay Sts Dallas TX 75201

BRIGGS, BRUCE BURRY, lawyer; b. Mars Hill, N.C., June 20, 1937; s. Clarence W. and Eula (Burry) B.; A.A., Mars Hill Coll., 1958; J.D., Wake Forest U., 1962; student Western Caroline U., 1958-59; m. Jean Elizabeth Miller, Nov. 26, 1967; 1 dau., Elizabeth Ashley. Admitted to N.C. bar, 1962; practiced in Asheville, N.C., 1962-69; mem. firm Riddle & Briggs, 1963-69; now individual practice law; atty., Madison County, 1968-69; asst. U.S. atty., Asheville, 1969-72. Mem. N.C. Senate, 1966-69; chmn. Madison County Republican Com., 1964-66; 11th dist. congl. chmn., 1966—; mem. N.C. Rep. Exec. and Central Coms., 1964-69; vice chmn. Young Rep. Club, 1966. Bd. advisers Western Carolina U. Served with AUS, 1962. Mem. Am. Trial Lawyers Assn., N.C., Buncombe County, Madison County, Fed. bar assns., Am. Judicature Assn., Phi Alpha Delta. Baptist (vice chmn. deacons). Lion. Home: 135 Mountainview Dr Mars Hill NC 28754 Office: Main St PO Box 81 Mars Hill NC 28754

BRIGGS, DALE JEROME, lawyer; b. Sand Springs, Okla., Feb. 4, 1926; s. Fred Gerome and Willie (Wood) B.; LL.B., U. Tulsa, 1950; student Central Mo. State Tchrs. Coll., 1944-45; m. Dorothy Jean Cardwell, Aug. 1, 1945; children—William Dale (dec.), Patricia, Judith Lynn, Robert Steven. Admitted to Okla. bar, 1950, since practiced in Tulsa; mem. firm Berringer and Briggs, Tulsa, 1950—; judge Ct. of Common Pleas, Tulsa County, Okla., 1955-59. Mem. Okla. Ho. of Reps., 1950-52; pres., bd. dirs. Okla. for Constl. Rep. and Citizens for Constl. Reapportionment, 1954-62; pres. Tulsa Council, Camp Fire Girls, 1962-64. Served with USNR, 1944-46. Mem. Am., Okla. (dir.; pres. 1969) trial lawyers assns., Am., Okla., Tulsa County bar assns., Am. Judicature Soc., Delta Theta Phi. Republican. Mason. Club: The Summit. Home: 5928 S 72d E Av Tulsa OK 74145 Office: 4th Nat Bank Bldg Tulsa OK 74119

BRIGGS, JOHN LUTHER, U.S. atty.; b. Gainesville, Fla., Mar. 20, 1919; s. John Luther and Ada (Edwards) B.; A.B., U. Fla., 1947, LL.B., 1950; postgrad. Sch. Govt. George Washington U., 1947; m. Charlotte Eskridge, June 9, 1942. Pilot Eastern Air Lines; practiced law, Gainesville; then state prosecutor, Fla., asst. U.S. atty.; U.S. dist. atty. for middle Fla., Jacksonville, 1969—. Pres. Jacksonville Improved Living of Meth. Ch., Inc., 1970—. Served with USNR, World War II, Korea. Mem. Am., Fed., Fla., Duval County bar assns., Am. Judicature Soc., Am. Arbitration Assn., Jax Legal Aid Soc. (past pres), Navy League (pres. Jacksonville council 1971-72). Home: 6080 Wateredge St Jacksonville FL 32211 Office: 409 Post Office Bldg Jacksonville FL 32201

BRIGGS, THOMAS, educator; b. N.Y.C., May 24, 1933; s. James Elmer and Carlotta (Welles) B.; B.S., Yale, 1954; Ph.D., U. Pa., 1960; m. Muriel Jacqueline Murphy, Aug. 31, 1955; children—Thomas W., Mary C., Jacqueline M. USPHS postdoctoral research fellow Guy's Hosp. Med. Sch., London, Eng., 1960-62; research asso. Sch. Medicine, Yale, 1962-67; asst. prof. biochemistry Sch. Medicine, U. Okla., 1967-70, asso. prof., 1970—. Mem. A.A.A.S., Am. Chem. Soc., Biochem. Soc. (Britain), N.Y., Okla. acads sci., Oklahoma City Astronomy Club (pres. 1971—), Sigma Xi (treas. U. Okla. Med. Center club). Contbr. articles in field to profl. jours. Home: 10603 Drury Lane Oklahoma City OK 73116

BRIGGS, WILLIAM A(DOLPHUS), architect; b. Asheville, N.C., Jan. 8, 1915; s. Henry Harrison and Attica (Lillian) B.; B.F.A. in Architecture, Yale, 1939; m. Elouise Ball McPherson, Dec. 24, 1949; children— Anthony Sanford, William Adolphus, Henry Harrison III, Edwin Gerald, Lillian Rebecca, Marella Mac. Designer, Warfield & Keeble, architects-engrs., Nashville, 1939-41; supr. methods engring. Remington Arms, Bridgeport, Conn., 1941-42; design asst. Henry Dreyfus, indsl. designer, N.Y.C., 1942-43; prin. Edwin A. Keeble Assos., architects, Nashville, 1945-52; prop. William A. Briggs, architect, Nashville, also Richmond, Va., 1952—; pres. Briggs Cons., Inc., Nashville, Washington, 1952—; design cons. to Carneal & Johnston, also Ballou & Justice, architects-engrs., 1956-61. Served as ensign USNR, 1943-44. Recipient citation for devel. spl. ordnance equipment U.S. Navy, 1944. Mem. A.I.A. (past pres. Richmond sect., mem. nat. com. auditorium and theatre architecture arts and recreation 1961—), U.S. Inst. for Theatre Tech. (bd. dirs. 1964—), Am. Ednl. Theatre Assn., Soc. Archtl. Historians, Am. Inst. Physics, Acoustical Soc. Am., Am. Soc. C.E. Episcopalian. Club: Rotunda, 2300. Contbr. articles to profl. jours. Patentee in field. Research on civic and cultural facilities. Home: 3014 Seminary Av Richmond VA 23227

BRIGHT, CORNELIUS EDISON, dentist; b. Jacksonville, Fla., Mar. 19, 1930; s. Sylvester R. and Lucille (Boyer) B.; B.S., Fla. A. and M. U., 1951; D.D.S., Howard U., 1960; m. Alma L. Lewallen, Dec. 6, 1954; children—Cornelia D., Mark A., Kim L. Asst. prof. oral surgery Howard U., Washington, 1960— practice dentistry, specializing in surgery, Washington, 1962—. Served with USAF, 1951-55. Mem. Am. Dental Assn., Dist. Dental Soc., Maimonides, Robert T. Freeman dental socs. Omicron Kappa Upsilon, N.A.A.C.P. Democrat. Baptist. Mason. Home: 205 Hermlegh Rd Silver Springs MD 20902 Office: 4629 9th St NW Washington DC 20011

BRIGHT, EDGAR ALLEN GORDON, banker; b. New Orleans, May 15, 1895; s. Edgar H. and Ella (Mehle) B.; grad. Westminster Sch., 1913; Ph.B., Sheffield Sci. Sch., Yale, 1916; m. Ethel Fox, Nov. 29, 1927; children—Edgar A.G., Jane (Mrs. Maunsel Hickey). Partner, Tullis, Craig & Bright, cotton mchts., New Orleans, 1923-56; ltd. partner Merrill Lynch, Pierce, Fenner & Smith, N.Y.C., 1957-59; chmn. bd. Standard Mortgage Corp., New Orleans, 1964—; dir. Maison Blanche, New Orleans, 1921—, Royal St. Louis, Inc., New Orleans, 1957—, Internat. Trade Mart, 1966—, Internat. House, New Orleans, 1966-69; pres. Vermillion Irrigation, New Orleans, 1959—, New Orleans Cotton Exchange, 1948-50; pres. Acadia Vermillion Rice Irrigation, 1970—, Information Council Am., 1964—. Pres. United Fund Greater New Orleans, 1960-61, treas. Community Chest, 1965—; bd. commrs. Port New Orleans, 1952-58, pres., 1956-57. Bd. dirs. Flint Goodridge Hosp., 1958—; pres. Cottage Sch. Deaf Children, 1958-70. Served to 1st lt. with U.S. Army, 1917-19, to lt. col. with AUS, 1942-45; PTO. Named Rex King of Carnival, New Orleans, 1956; recipient Loving Cup, Times-Picayune, 1966. Mem. Tennis Patrons Assn. Greater New Orleans (pres. 1960-64), Yale Alumni Assn. La. (pres. 1924-28, 47-54), St. Elmo Soc., Delta Phi. Episcopalian. Home: 421 Audubon St New Orleans LA 70118 Office: Baronne Bldg New Orleans LA 70112

BRIGHT, EDMOND SHARP, printing co. exec.; b. Birmingham, Ala., Oct. 4, 1929; s. Ernest Dewitt and Katheryn (Faughender) B.; student Botti Sch. Art., 1949; m. Beth Ingram, Mar. 24, 1956; 1 son, James Edmond. Comml. artist Moore Bus. Forms, Dallas, 1953-54, asst. adv. mgr. 1954-55, mgr. sales promotion and advt., 1955—. Dir. Lake Cities State Bank, Lake Dallas, Tex., 1971. Sec., City of Hickory Creek, Tex., 1966-69, city commr., 1969-72, mayor, 1972. Mem. Denton C. of C. (dir. 1967-68, chmn. pub. relations div. 1971). Mason (32 deg.). Home: Route 3 Box 75 Denton TX 76201 Office: PO Box 1369 Denton TX 76201

BRIGHT, HAROLD FREDERICK, univ. adminstr.; b. Smethport, Pa., Aug. 6, 1913; s. Stanley and Florence K. (Dunn) B.; A.B., Lake Forest Coll., 1937; M.S., U. Rochester, 1944; Ph.D., U. Tex., 1952; m. Elizabeth Korhumel, Mar. 23, 1938; children—Stanley Joseph, Beverly Ann (Mrs. Stephen M. White). Chmn. dept. math. San Angelo (Tex.) Coll., 1941-43, registrar, dir. guidance, 1945-49; asst. prof. math. Denison U., 1943-44, U. Rochester, 1944-45; asso. dir. research Am. Assn. Jr. Colls., 1949-52; specialist operations research and synthesis Gen. Electric Co., 1957-58; dep. dir. Human Resources Office, George Washington U., 1952-56, chmn. dept. statistics, 1958-64, dir. Computer Center, 1963-65, asso. dean faculties, 1964-66, v.p. acad. affairs, 1966—, provost, 1969—; cons. in field, 1956—. Mem. A.A.A.S., Am. Soc. Quality Control, Am. Statis. Assn., Am. Psychol. Assn., Inst. Math. Statistics, Math. Assn. Am., Royal Statis. Soc., Assn. Instl. Research, Sigma Xi, Sigma Pi Sigma. Republican. Episcoalian. Club: Cosmos (Washington). Home: 314 Branch Circle SE Vienna VA 22180 Office: George Washington U Washington DC 20006

BRIGHT, SAM RAMON, oil co. exec.; b. Fulbright, Tex., Nov. 2, 1904; s. John Ramon and Mary Elizabeth (Anderson) B.; B.A., Eastern Tex. State U., 1930; postgrad. Tyler Comml. Coll., 1937; m. Mary Pauline Hambrick, Nov. 29, 1933; children—Same Ramon, Bob, John. Prin., Red River Sch., Rugby, Tex., 1925-30; tchr. indsl. arts, Tyler, Tex., 1931-37; accountant Fair Oil Co., Tyler, Tex., 1938-45, exec. v.p., co-owner, 1945—; dir. Ind. Am. Ins. Co., Willowbrook Estates; gen. partner Bright Investments Ltd., 1969—. Bd. dirs. E. Tex. Hosp. Assn., 1949-58, Stewart Blood Bank, 1949-60, Fair Found., 1960—. Mason (32 deg., Shriner). Home: 1920 S College St Tyler TX 75701 Office: 729 Fair Bldg Tyler TX 75701

BRIGHT, THOMAS, oceanographer West Flower Coral Reef Ocean Research Center, U. Tex. Med. Br., Galveston. Research in acoustical behavior of coral reef fish. Office: West Flower Coral Reef Ocean Research Center University of Tex Medical Branch Galveston TX 77550*

BRIGHTMIRE, PAUL WILLIAM, judge; b. Washington, Mo., June 12, 1924; s. Quinton C. and Alvena (Wehr) B.; B.A., U. Tulsa, 1949, LL.B., 1951; m. Lorene E. Edwards, Nov. 7, 1952; children—Deborah Sue, William Paul, John Edward, Christiana Ann, Thomas Edward. Admitted to Okla. bar, 1951, since practiced in Tulsa; now judge Okla. Ct. Appeals, presiding judge, 1971—. Served with USNR, 1943-46. Mem. Am., Okla., Tulsa County (exec. com.) bar assns., Am. (state committeeman) Okla. (pres.), Tulsa (pres.) trial lawyers assns., Tulsa C. of C., Kappa Sigma. Democrat. Episcopalian. Mason (32 deg., Shriner). Editor: The Tulsa Lawyer. Home: 4041 S Birmingham Tulsa OK 74105 Office: 402 Center Bldg Tulsa OK 74127

BRIGHTWELL, JUANITA SUMMER (MRS. LOUIE BRIGHTWELL), librarian; b. Sylvester, Ga., Jan. 4, 1918; d. Robert Beauregard and Lottie (Davis) Sumner; tchrs. certificate in piano Kate Land Sch. Mus., 1935; normal diploma Ga. Southwestern Coll., Americus, Ga., 1936; B.S. in Edn., Woman's Coll. Ga., 1938; M.Librarianship, Emory U., 1965; m. Louie Brightwell, June 30, 1938; 1 dau., Claire (Mrs. Charles W. Shaeffer, Jr.). Tchr. Weston (Ga.) High Sch., 1937-38; tchr. English, also librarian Smithville (Ga.) High Sch., 1941-42, Americus High Sch., 1942-43; operator Brightwell's Nursery, Americus, 1946-52; asst. librarian Lake Blackshear Regional Library (formerly Americus Carnegie Library), 1952-55, dir. library services in Sumter County, 1962—, Crisp County, 1964—, Schley County and Dooly County, 1970—; tchr. New Era Elementary Sch., Americus, 1955-56; tchr. English, also library asst. Americus High Sch., 1956-62. Vol. worker Camp Fire Girls, Americus, 1944-45; vol. chmn. Sumter County Tb Assn., 1952. Tchr. Merit scholar program Ga. Dept. Edn., 1962-65. Mem. Am., Southeastern, Ga. (children's and young people's div. v.p. 1963-65, chmn. pub. library sect. 1969-71) library assns., Ga. Library Assts. Assn., Am. Assn. U. Women, D.A.R., Am. Camellia Soc., Azalea Garden Club (pres. 1955), S.W. Ga. Camellia Soc., Federated Garden Clubs Ga. (del. 1951-52), Woman's Coll. Ga. Alumnae Assn. (dist. dir. 1965-67), U.D.C., Bus. and Profl. Woman's Club (pres. 1968-69), Ga. Fedn. Bus. and Profl. Women's Clubs, Inc. (chmn. Nike Samothrace com.), Alpha Chi Omega (named Woman of Year 1968). Delta Kappa Gamma. Baptist (tchr. Sunday sch.). Home: 1307 Hancock Dr Americus GA 31709 Office: 111 S Jackson St Americus GA 31709

BRIL, JACQUES L., criminologist; b. N.Y.C., Sept. 17, 1906; s. Isaac L. and Masha (Ravid) B.; ed. Western Mil. Acad., Alton, Ill., Flint (Mich.) Jr. Coll., U. Mich., Washington and Lee Coll.; m. Ethel Wittcoff, June 7, 1936 (died 1962); children—Ira Lawrence, Marsha Susan. Began as criminologist, 1929; established firm of Jacques L. Bril, criminology consultants and investigators, N.Y.C., 1931; cons. to dist. attys. Kings County and Westchester County, N.Y., Somerset County, N.J., Atty. Gen., State of N.J., Police Dept., City of Yonkers; collaborated with Father Summers, prof. psychology, Fordham U., in development of pathometer (lie detector), 1936; authority in field of scientific detection of deception; invented Brilograf and devised technique known as Bril deception test; inventor of listening-in and recording devices; installed lie detection lab., N.J. State Hosp., Trenton; sec.-treas. 2170 Broadway Corp.; dir. Blue Bell Holdings and Rolling Gardens Corp., Benjamin Franklin Hotel, Smithtown Spa., B & B Farms, Inc. Spl. dep. commr. pub. safety, Yonkers, N.Y.; dep. chief police, Smithtown, L.I.; spl. dep. sheriff Dade County Florida. Mem. nat. bd. Am. Orgn. Rehab. through Tng. Fedn., also pres. Greater Miami chpt. Mem. Nat. Sheriffs Assn., Am. Inst. Criminal Law and Criminology, Internat. Assn. for Identification (life), Am. Radio Relay League, Nat. Aero. Assn., U.S. Civil Air Patrol, Internat. Assn. Chiefs of Police (life), N.Y. State Assn. Chiefs of Police, N.G. Assn. U.S., Vets. Assn., Inc., 22d Regiment Ofcrs. Assn., Internat. Assn. Lions Clubs. First lt. comdg. officer communication sect. New York Guard, Capt. 22d Regimental Intelligence officer; maj.-monitoring officer C.A.P.; lt. col., dir. communications N.E. region U.S. for Auliliary USAF. Address: 222 W 77th St New York City NY Box 4322 Miami Beach FL

BRILEY, CLIFTON BEVERLY, mayor; b. Nashville, Jan. 11, 1914; s. Clifton W. and Willie (Vaughan) B.; student Vanderbilt Sch. Engring., 1930; LL.B., Cumberland U., 1932; m. Dorothy Gordon, July 3, 1934; children—Clifton Beverly, Martha Diane (Mrs. P.R. Easterling). Admitted Tenn. bar, 1932, practiced in Nashville, 1932-43, 45-50; judge Davidson County, Tenn., 1950-62; mayor Met. Nashville and Davidson County, 1962—. Pres., Nat. Assn. Counties, 1962-63, Tenn. County Services Assn., 1955—; pres. Tenn. Municipal League, 1966—; mem. joint com. Am. Assn. Hwy. Commrs.-Nat. League Cities-Fed. Hosp. Council, 1963—; chmn. com. law enforcement Nat. League Cities; chmn. Urban County Congress, 1959; mem. human relations com. U.S. Conf. Mayors, 1964—; lectr. on govtl. structure. Vice pres. Middle Tenn. council Boy Scouts Am., 1956—. Mem. Tenn. Democratic Com., 1948-52. Served with USNR, 1943-45; PTO. Mem. Tenn., Nashville bar assns., Pi Kappa Alpha. Mason (Shriner). Club: Blue Grass Country (Hendersonville, Tenn.). Contbr. articles on govt. to various publs. Home: 1406 Windingway Rd Nashville TN 37216 Office: Metropolitan Courthouse Nashville TN 37201

BRILEY, GEORGE CLIFTON, JR., contracting co. exec.; b. Haynesville, La., Nov. 13, 1925; s. George Clifton and Estelle (Cloutier) B.; B.S. magna cum laude in Elec. Engring., La. Poly. Inst., 1949; m. Phyllis Lucreta Kindig, Dec. 2, 1950; children—John Clifton, Melissa Jane. With York Corp. (Pa.), 1949-60, br. mgr., 1956-57, regional mgr., 1958-60; field sales mgr. Frick Co., Waynesboro, Pa., 1960-61; v.p., br. mgr. Lewis Refrigeration Co., Houston, 1961—, dir. Served with AUS, 1943-46. Registered profl. engr. Tex., La., Miss., Ala., Ga. Mem. Nat., Tex., socs. profl. engrs., Am. Inst. Chem. Engrs., Phi Kappa Phi, Kappa Alpha, Omicron Delta Kappa. Rotarian. Home: 13334 Trail Hollow Houston TX 77024 Office: 12311 Amelia St Houston TX 77045

BRILL, DAVID H., JR., lawyer; b. Chgo., 1927; Ph.B., U. Chgo., 1945; M.A., U. Wis., 1949; J.D., Harvard, 1952; postgrad. Nat. U. Nuevo Leon Law Sch., Monterrey, Mexico. Admitted to Mexico bar; mem. firm Goodrich, Dalton, Little & Riquelme, Mexico D.F., Mexico. Address: Paseo de la Reforma 355 Mexico DF Mexico*

BRIMMER, ANDREW FELTON, educator, govt. ofcl.; b. Newellton, La., Sept. 13, 1926; s. Andrew and Vellar (Davis) B.; B.A., U. Wash., 1950, M.A., 1951; postgrad. (Fulbright fellow) U. Bombay (India), 1951-52; Ph.D., Harvard, 1957; LL.D., Neb. Wesleyan U., 1968, Marquette U., 1968, L. I. U., 1969, Oberlin Coll., 1969, Tufts U. 1970, Colgate U., 1970, Atlanta U., 1970, Middlebury Coll., 1971, U. Notre Dame, 1971, Bishop Coll., 1971, Upsala Coll., East Orange, N.J., 1972; D.C.L., U. Miami, 1971; D. Social Scis., Boston Coll., 1971; m. Doris Millicent Scott, July 18, 1953; 1 dau., Esther Diane. Economist, Fed. Res. Bank, N.Y.C., 1955-58; asst. prof. Mich. State U., 1958-61, Wharton Sch. Finance and Commerce, U. Pa., 1961-66; dep. asst. sec. Dept. Commerce, Washington, 1963-65, asst. sec. for econ. affairs, 1965-66; mem. Fed. Res. Bd., 1966—. Mem. Fed. Res. Central Banking Mission to Sudan, 1957; cons. SEC, 1962-63. Trustee Tuskegee Inst., Salk Inst., Negro Student Fund, Washington; bd. overseers Harvard; adv. com. Grad. Sch. Bus., Atlanta U. Served with AUS, 1945-46. Named Govt. Man of Year, Nat. Bus. League, 1963; recipient Arthur S. Flemming award, 1966; Ruswurm award, 1966; Capital Press Club award, 1966; Golden Plate award Am. Acad. Achievement, 1967; Nat. Honoree award Beta Gamma Sigma, 1971; Alumnus Summa Laude Dignatus award U. Wash., 1972. Fellow Am. Acad. Arts and Scis.; mem. Council on Fgn. Relations, Assn. for Study Negro Life and History (pres. 1970—), Mem. Am. Econ. Assn., Am. Finance Assn. Author: Survey of Mutual Funds Investors. 1963; Life Insurance Companies in Capital Market, 1962. Contbr. articles to profl. jours. Office: Board of Governors Federal Reserve System 20th and Washington DC 20551

BRINKLEY, DAVID, news commentator; b. Wilmington, N.C., July 10, 1920; s. William Graham and Mary (West) B.; m. Ann Fischer, Oct. 11, 1946; children—Alan, Joel, John. Reporter Wilmington (N.C.) Star-News, 1938-41; reporter, bur. mgr. United Press Assns., various so. cities, 1941-43; news writer, broadcaster radio and TV, NBC, Washington, 1943—. Office: NBC News 4001 Nebraska Av NW Washington DC 20016

BRINKLEY, JACK THOMAS, congressman, lawyer; b. Faceville, Ga., Dec. 22, 1930; s. Lonnie Elester and Pauline (Spearman) B.; student Young Harris Coll., 1947-49, Okla A. and M., 1952; LL.B. cum laude, U. Ga., 1959; m. Alma Lois Kite, May 29, 1955; children—Jack Thomas, Fred Alen II. Admitted to Ga. bar, 1958; asso. mem. firm Young, Hollis and Moseley, 1959-61; partner Coffin and Brinkley, 1961-66; part-time tchr. Columbus Coll., 1964; mem. Ga. Ho. of Reps., 1965-66; mem. 90th-92d congresses from 3d Ga. Dist., mem. armed service com. Pres. Reese Rd. P.T.A., 1963-64. Chmn. fund raising and Ga. state chmn. Nat. Found., 1966. Judge adv. South Ga. Dist. Civitan Internat., 1964-65. Served to 1st lt., pilot, USAF, 1951-56. Mem. Am., Ga., Columbus bar assns., Am. Legion, Blue Key, Phi Alpha Delta. Democrat. Baptist (supt. Sunday Sch. 1962-64). Mason. Home: 4108 Appalachian Way Columbus GA 31907 Office: Cannon Bldg Washington DC 20515

BRINKLEY, RONALD EUGENE, state ofcl.; b. Columbus, Ga., July 5, 1911; B.S., Murray State U., 1934; M.A., George Peabody Coll., 1946; m. 2 children. Tchr., Clinton (ky.) High Sch., 1935-37, Dupont High Sch., Davidson County, Tenn., 1938-39, Cumberland High Sch., 1940-43; prin. Bellevue High Sch., 1943-46, Dupont High Sch., 1946-49; state supr. Mid-Tenn. State U., 1949-55; dir. spl. edn. Tenn. Dept. Edn., Nashville, 1955-59, exec. asst. to commr., 1959-63, dep. commr., 1963—. Mem. nat. adv. edn. council Appalachian Regional Commn. Mem. Nat., Tenn. (state coordinator) assns. secondary sch. prins., Tenn. Edn. Assn., Tenn. Prin. Studies Council (exec. sec.), Council Chief State Sch. Ofcls. (nat. planning com.). Home: Lake Ct Nashville TN 37214 Office: 100-C Cordell Hull Bldg Nashville TN 37219*

BRINKLEY, WILLIAM LAMBRETH, JR., ednl. adminstr.; b. Richmond, Va., Apr. 3, 1923; s. William L. and Elizabeth (Payne) B.; A.B., Duke, 1944; M.Personnel Service, U. Colo., 1954. Asst. to sec. Duke, 1944-46, field sec. admissions, 1946-48, asst. dir. admissions, 1948-51, asst. registrar, asso. registrar, 1951-61, then dir. under-grad. admissions; dir. admissions Johns Hopkins; v.p. for student affairs Coll. of Charleston (S.C.); 1970—. Served with AUS, 1941. Mem. Assn. Coll. Admissions Counselors, Nat. Assn. Student Personnel Adminstrs., Am. Assn. Collegiate Registrars and Admissions Officers (chmn. com. nominations and elections), Nat. Trust Historic Preservation, Preservation Soc. Charleston, Alliance Francaise, Pi Kappa Phi (nat. sec.), Omicron Delta Kappa. Democrat. Methodist. Lion. Clubs: ToBac (Durham); John Hopkins (Balt.). Home: 24 Bull St Apt B Charleston SC 29401

BRINTON, EDGAR HARRY, librarian; b. Kansas City, Mo., July 5, 1916; s. Edgar Parrish and Juanita Irene (Swarner) B.; A.B., U. Denver, 1938; M.S., Columbia, 1957; m. Jane O. Dallimore, Apr. 23, 1944 (dec. Aug. 1967); 1 son, William David; m. 2d, Ann Furlong Marron, June 12, 1971. Govt. documents librarian Okla. A. and M. Coll., 1938-39, U. Kansas City (Mo.), summers 1939, 40; librarian Topeka High Sch., 1939-40; catalogue and mgr. traveling libraries Mo. Library Commn., 1940-41; seccessively chief order dept., chief extension dept., acting librarian, adminstrv. asst. Kansas City (Mo.) Pub. Library, 1941-59; dir. Jacksonville (Fla.) Pub. Library, 1959—; cons. in field, 1960—. Mem. Am. (council 1948-52), Mo. (pres. 1957-58), Fla. (pres. 1964-65) library assns., Jacksonville Area C. of C. Clubs: University, Jacksonville Civitan. Contbr. profl. jours. Editor Mo. Library Assn. Quar., 1955-57. Home: 1721 Dogwood Pl Jacksonville FL 32210 Office: 122 N Ocean St Jacksonville FL 32202

BRINTON, ETHEL, educator; b. St. John's, Newfoundland, Can., July 3, 1910; B.A., London (Eng.) U., 1932; M.A., Radcliffe Coll., 1946; postgrad. Nat. Autonomous U. Mexico. Tchr., Friary Sch., Lichfield, Eng., 1933-35, Bishop Spencer Coll., St. John's, 1935-44; lectr. English and French, Meml. Univ. Coll., St. John's, 1944-47, asso. prof., 1947-53; now supr. English studies Colegio Reina Maria, Mexico, D.F., Mexico. Translator: The Lean Lands (Agustin Yanez), 1968. Research on Mexican novels and plays of 20th century. Address: Insurgentes 1657-401 Mexico 20 DF Mexico*

BRISCOE, JOHN ERASTUS, JR., lawyer; b. Between, Ga., Oct. 4, 1922; s. John Erastus and Myrtle (Edwards) B.; student U. Ga., 1946-48; LL.B., Emory U., 1952; m. Dorothy Dyal, Mar. 22, 1953; 1 son, Jack Dyal. Admitted to Ga. bar, 1952; practiced in Monroe, Ga., 1952—; mem. firms Briscoe & Ridgway, 1960-64, Briscoe & Blasingame, 1965-67, Briscoe & Austin, 1968—; partner Phillips & Briscoe Drug Store, Monroe, 1959—, Monroe Office Supply & Equipment Co., 1957—. Mem. Ga. Ho. of Reps., 1947-50. Served with USAAF, 1942-46. Ga. (bd. govs. 1966-68), Western Circuit (pres. 1960), Walton County (pres. 1964) bar assns. Rotarian (pres. 1965-66). Home: Route 3 Monroe GA 30655 Office: 100 Lumpkin St Monroe GA 30655

BRISKY, MARY OWEN, city ofcl.; b. Anniston, Ala., May 19, 1930; d. Ozie Whitton and Melinda Everlina (Welchel) Owen; grad. high sch. div.; 1 son, James Elic. Asst. to city clk. City of Anniston, 1956-62, dep. city clk., 1962-66, city clk., 1966—. Recipient Municipal Accounting award Ala. Soc. C.P.A.'s, 1963. Baptist. Home: 1520 E 10th St Anniston AL 36201 Office: PO Box 670 Anniston AL 36201

BRISTER, COMMODORE WEBSTER, educator; b. Pineville, La., Jan. 15, 1926; s. C. W. and Elaine (Holmes) B.; B.A., La. Coll., 1947; postgrad. (fellow) La. State U., 1948-49, Tex. Christian U., 1961-62; B.D., New Orleans Bapt. Theol. Sem., 1952; Th.D., Southwestern Bapt. Theol. Sem., 1957; postgrad. Union Sem., N.Y.C., 1962, 67, (Am. Assn. Theol. Schs. fellow), Princeton Sem., 1962-63; m. Gloria Virginia Nugent, Mar. 28, 1946; 1 son, Mark Allen. Ordained to ministry Baptist Ch., 1949; pastor Haltom Rd. Bapt. Ch., Ft. Worth, 1954-57; prof. pastoral theology Southwestern Bapt. Theol. Sem., Ft. Worth, 1957—; post-doctoral research fellow in psychiatry U. Tex. Southwestern Med. Sch., Dallas, 1969-70. Guest prof. pastoral care Inst. Religion, Houston, 1961; guest lectr. pastoral counseling Internat. Bapt. Theol. Sem., Cali, Colombia, 1966; guest lectr. Round-the-World Study Tour, 1968. Bd. dirs. Ft. Worth Easter Seal Soc., 1969-72. Pres. So. Bapt. Conf. on Counseling and Guidance, 1967-68; supr. Pastoral Care Center Tex. Christian U., 1969-72. Served with U.S. Maritime Service, 1943-45. Named Man of Month, Pastoral Psychology mag., June 1971. Mem. Assn. for Profl. Edn. for Ministry, Supr. Assn. Clin. Pastoral Edn. Author: Introduction to Pastoral Care, 1959, Pastoral Care in the Church, 1964, People Who Care, 1967; Dealing With Doubt, 1970; It's Tough Growing Up, 1971. Contbg. author: Southwestern Sermons, 1960; Everday, Five Minutes with God, 1969; When Trouble Comes, 1969; Toward Creative Urban Strategy, 1970; Contemporary Trends in Christian Thought, 1972. Guest editor Pastoral Psychology, June 1971. Contbr. articles to religious publs. Home: 3533 Wooten Dr Fort Worth TX 76133

BRISTOW, WALTER JAMES, JR., lawyer, state senator; b. Columbia, S.C., Oct. 14, 1924; s. Walter James and Caroline (Melton) B.; student Va. Mil. Inst., 1941-43; A.B., U. N.C., 1947; LL.B. cum laude, U. S.C., 1949; LL.M., Harvard, 1950; m. Katherine Stewart Mullins, Sept. 12, 1952; children—Katherine Mullins, Walter James III. Admitted to S.C. bar, 1950; practiced in Columbia, S.C.; mem. firm Marchant, Bristow & Bates, 1953—; mem. S.C. Ho. of Reps., 1956-58; mem. S.C. Senate, 1958—. Nat. asso. Boys Clubs of Am., 1958—; past council commr. Central S.C. council Boy Scouts of Am.; past pres. Carolina Carillon; trustee Elvira Wright Fund for Crippled Children. Served with AUS, 1943-45. Mem. Alpha Tau Omega, Wig and Robe, Pi Gamma Mu. Democrat. Presbyn. (deacon). Elks. Home: 4149 W Buchanan Dr Columbia SC 29206 Office: 1306 Main St Columbia SC 29201

BRITO MORENO, MANUEL, lawyer; b. Mexico D.F., Mexico, Nov. 6, 1934; student Nat. Autonomous U. Mexico Law Sch. Admitted to Mexican bar, 1960; mem. firm Brito Foucher y Brito Moreno, Mexico D.F. Mem. Bar Assn. Mexico, Mexican Acad. Space Law. Author: The Value of Human Life in Mexican Law, 1961. Office: Avenida San Juan de Letran 11 Mexico 1 DF Mexico*

BRITT, CHESTER OLEN, elec. engr.; b. Hughes Springs, Tex., July 2, 1920; s. Beverly A. and Ida Emma (Martin) B.; student Texarkana Jr. Coll., 1938-40; B.S., U. Tex., 1949, M.S., 1951; Ph.D., 1962; m. Patricia Ashworth, Jan. 4, 1946. Research engr. Elec. Engring. Research Lab., Austin, Tex., 1951-56, systems devel. specialist, 1956-61; systems devel. specialist U. Tex. at Austin, 1961-62, research sci. dept. chemistry, 1962—. Served with USAAF, 1941-46. Decorated D.F.C., Air Medal with oak leaf clusters. Registered profl. elec. engr., Tex. Mem. I.E.E.E. (sr.), A.A.A.S., Am. Phys. Soc. Home: 2708 Rae Dell Av Austin TX 78704

BRITT, CLAUDE HENRY, JR., educator; b. St. Pauls, N.C., Sept. 18, 1929; s. Claude Henry and Tera (Godwin) B.; B.A., Wake Forest Coll., 1951; M.A., U. Ala., 1953; Ph.D., Northwestern U., 1966. Tchr. Spanish and history A. L. Brown High Sch., Kannapolis, N.C. 1955-56; asst. prof. Spanish, Gardner-Webb Coll., 1956-57; instr.

French, Stetson U., 1959-60; asst. prof. Spanish, Mercer U., 1960-62; asst. prof. Spanish, Ga. So. Coll., Statesboro, 1963-67, asso. prof., 1967—. Served with U.S. Army, 1953-55. Mem. Am. Assn. Tchrs. Spanish and Portuguese, Modern Lang. Assn., South Atlantic Modern Lang. Assn., Am. Assn. U. Profs., Sigma Delta Pi, Sigma Pi Alpha. Address: PO Box 1836 Ga So Coll Statesboro GA 30458

BRITT, DAVID M., judge Ct. Appeals, Raleigh, N.C. Office: Justice Bldg 1 W Morgan St Raleigh NC 27601*

BRITT, ELIZABETH LETITIA SMITH, corp. exec.; b. Medon, Tenn.; d. Samuel Edward and Rosalee (Kinney) Smith; student Union U., 1927-29; Norton Bus. Coll., 1942. Cemeterian-sec. Forest Park Cemetery, Inc., Shreveport, La., 1942—, sec.-treas., 1957—, dir., 1957—. Mem. Nat. Secs. Assn., Internat. Platform Assn., Zonta (mgr. Shreveport Antique Show). Baptist. Home: 4024 Maryland Av Shreveport LA 71106 Office: PO Box 1764 Shreveport LA 71102

BRITT, HARRY MAX, JR., geologist; b. Amarillo, Tex., Feb. 6, 1918; s. Harry Max and Kate Ann (Dykeman) B.; B.S., U. Tex. at El Paso, 1941; m. Alice Wanita Walker, June 22, 1940; children—Harry Wayne, Elizabeth Ann, Robert Max. With Sinclair-Prairie Oil Co., Tex. and Okla., 1941-42; with Diamond Shamrock Oil and Gas Corp., Amarillo, Tex., 1946—, chief geologist, 1954-63, v.p. charge geology, 1963—. Served with USMCR, 1942-46. Mem. Am. Assn. Petroleum Geologists, Soc. Econ. Paleontologists and Mineralogists, Sigma Gamma Epsilon. Home: 5017 Tawney St Amarillo TX 79106 Office: Box 631 Amarillo TX 79105

BRITT, LOIS EDNA, microbiologist; b. Atlanta, Nov. 9, 1937; d. Terrell Stephen and Julia Ruth (Jump) Britt; B.S., Ga. Coll., Milledgeville, 1960. Microbiologist, Nat. Communicable Disease Center, Atlanta, 1960—. Mem. Am. Assn. Microbiologists, Sci. Research Soc. Am., Am. Inst. Biol. Scis., A.A.A.S., Ga. Pub. Health Assn. Club: Belvedere Civic (Decatur, Ga.). Home: 1597 Stanford Way Decatur GA 30032 Office: 1600 Clifton Rd Atlanta GA 30333

BRITTAIN, JACK OLIVER, lawyer; b. Greenwood, La., Sept. 24, 1928; s. Clarence L. and Irene (Humphries) B.; B.S., La. Poly. Inst., 1949; LL.D., La. State U., 1957; m. Ann Marie Williams, Nov. 25, 1955; children—Jack Oliver, Marguerite Ann, Rebecca Ann, Lala Beth, Eliza Ann, John A., Mary Jane Ann. Land man Magnolia Petroleum Co., Midland Tex., 1953-54; admitted to La. bar, 1957; practiced in Natchitoches, 1957—; mem. firm Brittain, Carver & Williams. Owner, Crown Colony Antiques, Crown Colony Canines; dir. Pak-A-Sak, Inc., Grand Ecore Preservation, Inc., CBS Mobile Homes, Inc., Evans-Brittain, Inc. Bd. dirs. Natchitoches Youth Assn., Inc. Served to maj. AUS, 1951-53. Named Outstanding Man Natchitoches Parish, 1959; recipient Distinguished Service award Jr. C. of C., 1958. Mem. Natchitoches Parish C. of C. (pres. 1961), U.S. Jr. C. of C. (nat. dir. 1962). Am., La., Natchitoches Parish bar assns., Am. Legion, Omicron Delta Kappa, Lambda Chi Alpha, Phi Delta Phi. Democrat. Methodist (bd. stewards; chmn. adminstrv. bd. 1969). Mason, Rotarian. Home: 919 Parkway Dr Natchitoches LA 71457 Office: 111-113 E 5th St St Natchitoches LA 71457

BRITTAIN, JOHN ORIN, bus. exec.; b. South Pittsburgh, Tenn., June 12, 1902; s. Reuben E. and Martha (Jenkins) B.; A.B., U. Okla., 1926; m. Mary Elizabeth Hill, Dec. 27, 1928; 1 dau., Sally Adair (Mrs. Robert C. Saunders). Pres. Brittain Brothers, 1942—, chmn. bd. dirs., 1942—; dir. City Nat. Bank and Trust Co. Mem. Nat. Automotive Parts Assn. (dir.), Nat., Oklahoma City chambers commerce, Alpha Tau Omega, Alpha Kappa Psi. Republican. Mem. Christian Ch. Clubs: Oklahoma City Men's Dinner, Oklahoma City Golf and Country, Beacon. Home: 1708 Randel Rd Oklahoma City OK 73116 Office: 700 S Western Av Oklahoma City OK 73125

BRITTEN, MILTON REESE, editor; b. Wilkes-Barre, Pa., Dec. 17, 1924; s. Isaac Milton and Marguerite (Reese) B.; B.A. with honors, Yale, 1949; m. Virginia Butler, Nov. 11, 1951; children—Ann George, Jonathan B., Martha, Anthony. Reporter, Memphis Press-Scimitar, 1949-56. Washington corr. Memphis Press-Scimitar, also Knoxville News-Sentinel, 1956-63; night editor Scripps-Howard Newspaper Alliance, Washington, 1963-66, asst. mng. editor, 1966—. Served with AUS, 1942-45; ETO. Recipient Christopher award 1953. Mem. Phi Beta Kappa. Author: (with Andrew Tully) The Foreign Aid Story: Where Did Your Money Go, 1964. Home: 10000 Belhaven Rd Bethesda MD Office: 1013 13th St Washington DC

BRITTON, JAMES JUDSON, assn. ofcl.; b. Montgomery, Ala., July 23, 1913; s. William Brown and Ruth (Abbott) B.; LL.B., Jones Law U., U. Ala., 1936; m. Dorothy Bennett, Feb. 4, 1939; children—Karen (Mrs. John B. Johnson), Nancy A. Salesman and treas. Interstate Oil Co., Montgomery, 1943-50; dir. Ala. Petroleum Council, 1950-66; exec. v.p. Ala. State C. of C., 1966—. Chmn. Ala. Cancer Crusade, 1965. Bd. dirs. Ala. Council on Econ. Edn. Served with AUS, 1943-47, 51-52. Mem. The 13, Newcomen Soc., Ala. Hist. Soc., Ala. Export Council, C. of C. Execs. Assn. Ala., Nat. Council C. of C., U.S. C. of C. (mem. natural resources com.), Pi Kappa Alpha, U. Ala. Alumni Assn. Clubs: Country (Montgomery); Internat. (Mobile); Downtown (Birmingham). Episcopalian. Rotarian. Home: 1222 Augusta St Montgomery AL 36111 Office: PO Box 76 Montgomery AL 36101

BROACH, BILLY GENE, electronics engr.; b. Wadley, Ala., Mar. 24, 1939; s. Willie Felton and Emma Jean (Kilgore) B.; B.E.E. (Lee Moody scholar), Auburn U., 1961; postgrad. U. Ala., 1970; m. Paula Nan Clapp, Dec. 21, 1958; children—Jeffrey David, Timothy Michael. Elec. engr. Chrysler Corp., Huntsville, Ala., 1962-64, Heat Tech., Inc., 1964-66; pres. Huntsville Investors, Inc., rental property devel., 1967—; pres. Engrs. Unltd., Inc., nat. engring. placement firm, 1965—; pres. Broach Labs., Inc., med. instrumentation devel., 1963—; electronics engr. U.S. Army Missile Command, Redstone Arsenal, 1968—. Campaign mgr. Rep. candidate for sheriff of Madison County, Ala. Presbyn. Club: Sertoma (Huntsville, Ala.). Patentee in field. Home: 3610 Pulaski Pike St Huntsville AL 35810 Office: US Army Missile Command AMSMI RCR Redstone Arsenal AL 35808

BROADHEAD, SAMUEL L, JR., electronic engr.; b. Clanton, Ala., Jan. 26, 1916; s. Samuel L. and Roberta (Culp) B.; ed. U. Chgo., U. Ia.; m. Opie Merritt, Mar. 23, 1940. Civilian radar instr. U.S. Army. World War II; electronic engr. Communications Co., Coral Gables, Fla., 1946-47, Eastern Air Lines, 1947-51, Wilcox Elec. Co., Kansas City, Mo., 1951-52, Collins Radio Co., Cedar Rapids, 1952-65; sr. staff engr. SCI Electronics, Huntsville, Ala., 1965—. Sr. mem. I.E.E.E. Contbr. articles in field of advanced avionics equipment. Patentee in field. Home: 9800 Wallwood Rd SE Huntsville AL 35803 Office: 8620 Memorial Pkwy SW Huntsville AL 35802

BROADHURST, THOMAS FREDERICK, JR., chem. co. exec.; b. Middletown, Conn., Jan. 28, 1929; s. Thomas Frederick and Florence Amelia (Packenham) B.; B.S., Phila. Coll. Textiles and Sci., 1953; m. Jean Margaret Byrne, Feb. 6, 1954; children—Thomas Frederick III, Pamela Jean, Nancy Lynn, Jeffrey Dean, Timothy David. Asst. finisher trainee Joseph Bancroft & Sons, 1955-58; v.p. Tech. Sales, Ringgold, Ga., 1958-68 exec. v.p., 1970—; pres. Borders Motor Co., 1968—. Served with AUS, 1953-55. Mem. Am. Assn. Textile Chemists and Colorists. Club: Sertoma (Chattanooga, Tenn.). Home: 5809 Northshore Dr Hixson TN 37343 Office: Indsl Blvd Ringgold GA 30736

BROADY, ROBERT ALEXANDER, physician; b. Forest Hill, Ind., June 5, 1903; s. William Cowan and Nancy Katharine (Hartman) B.; B.A., Maryville Coll., 1925; M.D., U. Pa., 1930; postgrad. Coll. Chinese Studies, Peiping, 1932-33; m. Ellen Elizabeth Cox, June 14, 1930; children—Robert (dec.), William S., John Cox (dec.), JoAnn, Joe, Barbara. Intern, Presbyn. Hosp., Phila., 1930-32; missionary doctor, China, 1932-37; dir. hosp., Hunan, China, 1934-37; practice medicine, specializing in family practice, Sevierville, Tenn., 1938—; operator Broady Hosp., 1940-65; mem. staff Sevier County Hosp., 1965—. Owner dairy farm, Sevierville, 1943-69. Mem. city council, Sevierville, 1958-62, vice mayor, 1960-62. Named Sevierville Man of Year, Lions 1970. Mem. Am. Physicians and Surgeons Assn., A.M.A., Tenn., Sevier County (pres. 1956-57) med. assns. Presbyn. (elder 1960-69). Rotarian (pres. club 1972-73). Home: 223 Bruce St Sevierville TN 37862 Office: 217 Bruce St Sevierville TN 37862

BROCK, DEWEY CLIFTON, JR., librarian; b. Clemson, S.C., Sept. 13, 1930; s. Dewey Clifton and Graqe (England) B.; B.S., Clemson U., 1951; M.A., U. Mich., 1957; M.A. in Polit. Sci., Fla. State U., 1959; m. Eunice Lee Miller, Sept. 3, 1951; children—Clifton Michael, Douglas Martin, Melinda Kellner. Asst. social sci. librarian Fla. State U., Tallahassee, 1957-59; chief bus. adminstrn. and social sci. div. U. N.C. Library, Chapel Hill, 1959-66, asso. librarian, 1966—; lectr. Sch. Library Sci., U. N.C., 1962-66; vis. lectr. U. Ill., 1966. Served with USNR, 1951-55. Mem. A.L.A., Am. Polit. Sci. Assn. Author: Americans for Democratic Action; Its Role in National Politics, 1962; The Literature of Political Science; A Guide for Students, Librarians, and Teachers, 1969. Home: 316 Burlage Circle Chapel Hill NC 27541 Office: 117 Wilson Library U NC Chapel Hill NC 27515

BROCK, FRANK EDGAR, diversified Industry exec.; b. Houston, Jan. 7, 1932; s. Robert Frank and Alma (Sealock) B.; B.B.A., U. Tex., 1955; m. Rebecca Ann Morgan, Feb. 28, 1953; children—Randal Eugene, Lynne Anne. Accountant Pan American Petroleum Corp., Ft. Worth, 1955-64; chief accountant Loma Products div. Vistran Corp., mfg. fabricated household plastic goods, Ft. Worth, 1964-65, controller, 1965-68; sec., treas., controller Universal Sheet Metal Co., Ft. Worth, 1968-70; v.p. adminstrn., sec-treas. Broyles & Broyles, Inc., mech. contract constrn., 1970—, dir., 1970—; sec.-treas., dir. Universal Performance, Universal Fabrication, Mechanical Contracting Services, Inc.; v.p., Universal Insulation Co., Inc. Active children programs YMCA. Sponsoring com. Tex. Christian U. Research Found. Served to 1st lt. USAF, 1957-5?. Mem. Nat. Assn. Accountants, Arnold Air Soc. Clubs: Colonial Country (Ft. Worth); DeCordva Bend Estates Country (Granbury, Tex.). Home: 2316 Lynn Haven St Fort Worth TX 76103 Office: Box 11067 305 W Arlington St Fort Worth TX 76110

BROCK, GLEN PORTER, ry. ofcl.; b. Alden, Ia., Nov. 22, 1896; s. Loren Ellsworth and Mabel L. (Porter) B.; student Bus. Coll., Indpls.; B.Sc., U. Ill., 1922; m. Esther Goodwin, May 27, 1922; children—Paul Warrington, Glen Porter. Caller clk. Ill. Central R.R., Palestine, 1912-15; v.p., gen. mgr. of merged Gulf, Mobile & No. R.R. Co., Mobile and Ohio R.R. and Alton R.R. (now Gulf, Mobile and Ohio R.R. Co.), 1940-47; now chmn. exec. com., pres. Gulf, Mobile & Ohio R.R. Co.; pres., dir. New Orleans Gt. No. Ry. Co., G M & O Land Co.; v.p., dir. Joliet Union Depot Co.; dir. Gulf Transport Co., Mchts. Nat. Bank; alternate dir. Kansas City Terminal Ry. Co. Chmn. bd. trustees United Fund Mobile County Inc.; pres. United Fund, 1958-59; trustee Mobile Heart Assn.; bd. dirs. Mobile Assn. Blind, Mobile chpt. A.R.C.; mem. adv. com. to bd. dirs. Mobile Mental Health Center. Served in U.S. Army, 1918. Mem. Am. Legion, Pi Kappa Phi. Methodist. Mason (Shriner), Rotarian. Clubs: Lakewood Golf, Athelstan, Mobile Country, Isle Dauphin. Home: 2008 Dauphin St Mobile AL 36606 Office: 104 St Francis St Mobile AL 36602

BROCK, OTIS JEROME, ednl. adminstr.; b. Montzuma, Ga., Oct. 17, 1933; s. Odice and Ruby (Haugabook) B.; B.S., Savannah State Coll., 1956; M.A., N.Y. U., 1964, postgrad., 1965-66; m. Annette Kennedy, Dec. 22, 1962; children—Donna Lynne, Otis Jerome. Tchr., coach Johnson High Sch., Savannah, Ga., 1958-66, asst. prin., 1966-70; prin. A.E. Beach Sr. High Sch., 1970—. Part-time instr. Savannah State Coll., 1967-70. Mem. merit badge council Coastal Empire council Boy Scouts Am., 1961-72; mem. Thunderbolt Improvement Assn., Savannah, 1968—. Served with AUS, 1956-58. Mem. N.E.A. Ga., Chatham assns. educators, Alpha Phi Alpha. Democrat. Baptist. Club: The Wolves (Savannah, Ga.). Home: 3114 Whatley Av Savannah GA 31404 Office: 30001 Hopkins St Savannah GA 31405

BROCK, WALTER E., judge; b., 1918; ed. U. N.C. Admitted to N.C. bar, 1948; judge Ct. Appeals, Raleigh, N.C. Home: 204 Walden Rd Raleigh NC 27609 Office: 1 W Morgan St Raleigh NC 27601*

BROCK, WILLIAM EMERSON, III, senator; b. Chattanooga, Nov. 23, 1930; s. William Emerson and Myra (Krusei) B.; grad. McCallie Sch., 1949; B.S., Washington and Lee U., 1953; m. Laura Handly, Jan. 11, 1957; children—William Emerson IV, Oscar Handly, Laura (Mrs. Hutcheson), John Kruesi. With Brock Candy Co., Chattanooga, 1956-63; mem. 88th-91st Congresses from 3d Tenn. dist., mem. com. on banking and currency, mem. joint econ. com.; U.S. senator from Tenn., 1970—, mem. Banking, Housing and Urban Affairs Com., Com. on Govt. Operations. Served as lt. (j.g.) USNR, 1953-56; lt. Res. Mem. Sigma Alpha Epsilon. Presbyn. Home: Dogwood Dr Lookout Mountain TN 37350 Office: 304 Senate Office Bldg Washington DC 20515

BROCKENBROUGH, ELEANOR S., asst. dir. Mus. of Confederacy, Richmond, Va. Office: 120 E Clay St Richmond VA 23219*

BROCKENBROUGH, HENRY WATKINS, banker; b. Richmond, Va., Aug. 28, 1923; s. Benjamin Willard and Kathleen Reading (Watkins) B.; B.A. cum laude, Hampden-Sydney Coll., 1944; LL.B., U. Va., 1948; grad. Stonier Grad. Sch. Banking, Rutgers U., 1957; m. Mary Lane Williams, Oct. 30, 1948; children—Henry Watkins, Rebecca Lane, John Reading, Willson Williams. Admitted to Va. bar, 1949; with United Va. Bank, Richmond, 1948—; v.p., trust officer, 1963-67, sr. v.p., trust officer, 1967—. Past pres. Estate Planning Council Richmond. Vice pres., bd. dirs. St. Giles Endowment Fund. Served to lt. (j.g.) USNR, 1943-46. Mem. Richmond, Va. chambers commerce, Navy League, Lambda Chi Alpha, Delta Theta Phi. Presbyn. (elder, past chmn. bd. deacons). Club: Richmond Downtown. Home: 802 Horsepen Rd Richmond VA 23229 Office: 900 E Main St Richmond VA 23214

BROCKMAN, EDWARD WILSON, JR., lawyer; b. Pine Bluff, Ark., July 2, 1921; s. Edward Wilson and Mildred (Westmoreland) B.; student Washington and Lee U., 1938-40; B.A., U. Ark., 1942, LL.B., 1948. Admitted to Ark. bar, 1948, since practiced in Pine Bluff; pros. atty. Jefferson County, 1957-64. Mem. Ark. Gen. Assembly, 1947-55. Served with AUS, 1942-46. Mem. Am., Ark. bar assns. Presbyn. Mason (Shriner). Home: 1300 W 17th St Pine Bluff AR 71601 Office: Simmons Bldg Pine Bluff AR 71601

BROCKMAN, THOMAS, concert pianist, educator; b. Greer, S.C., Jan. 12, 1922; s. W. Thomas and Bernice (Wood) B.; student Curtis Inst. Music, 1937-40; B.S., Juilliard Sch., 1948; pupil of Edwin Fischer, Robert Casadesus, Nadia Boulanger (Europe), 1952-53. Concert pianist, European tours, 1953, 55, 56, 59; appearances with major symphony orchs. U.S.; vis. lectr. U. Ia., Iowa City, 1961; artist, lectr. So. Meth. U., 1961-62; asso. prof. piano Rollins Coll., Winter Park, Fla., 1962—. Served from pvt. to 1st lt. AUS, 1942-46. Mem. Pi Kappa Lambda (chpt. pres. 1967-69). Episcopalian. Home: 271 Virginia Dr Winter Park FL 32789

BROCKWAY, ALLAN REITZ, pub. co. editor; b. Hutchinson, Kan., Mar. 22, 1932; s. Horace Austin and Esther Jane (Reitz) B.; B.A., Hendrix Coll., 1954; B.D., So. Meth. U., 1957; M.A., U. Chgo., 1963; m. Martha Lou King, Aug. 28, 1956; children—Paul, Scot, Dan, Benjamin. Ordained to ministry Methodist Ch., 1957; campus minister West Tex. State U., Canyon, 1957-59; editor Christian Faith and Life Community, Austin, Tex., 1959-61; asst. editor The Kiwanis Mag., Chgo., 1962-63; editor Concern, Gen. Bd. Christian Social Concerns, Washington, 1963-68, editor Engage, 1968—. Bd. dirs. Big Bros. of the Nat. Capital Area, chmn. pub. relations com. 1970-71. Danforth Campus Ministry grantee, 1961, 63. Mem. Northwest Tex. Ann. Conf. United Meth. Ch., Internat. Platform Assn. Author: The Secular Saint, 1968, Uncertain Men and Certain Change, 1970. Home: 3 Park Valley Rd Silver Spring MD 20910 Office: 100 Maryland Av NE Washington DC 20002

BRODBECK, EDWARD JAMES, marketing research exec.; b. Swanton, O., July 5, 1933; s. Ernest and Oral (Myers) B.; B.S., Bowling Green State U., 1958; postgrad. La. State U., 1959-64; m. Elisa J. Portela Lavastida, Aug. 16, 1938; children—Ana Maria, Susana Elisa, Jennifer Cristina. Field marketing Dun & Bradstreet, Inc., Toledo, 1958; market research A. C. Nielsen Co., Chgo., 1958-59; market-sales analyst Copolymer Rubber & Chem. Corp., Baton Rouge, 1959-61, customer service, 1961-63, marketing research analyst, 1963-68, market devel. mgr., 1968-70, mgr. marketing research and planning, 1971—. Neighborhood group leader Republican party, 1966, 68, 70. Served with AUS, 1953-55. Mem. Am. Marketing Assn., Chem. Marketing Research Assn., Am. Chem. Soc., European Assn. Indsl. Marketing Research. Methodist Home: 7005 Whitlow Dr Baton Rouge LA 70808 Office: PO Box 2591 Baton Rouge LA 70821

BRODE, MARVIN JAY, lawyer, former state legislator; b. Memphis, Aug. 26, 1931; s. Howard M. and Erneice J. (Jacob) B.; B.A., Vanderbilt U., 1953, LL.B., 1954; m. Freda Cohn, June 24, 1965; children— William Howard, Robert Mark. Admitted to Tenn. bar, 1955; mem. firm Brode and Fisher, Memphis, 1958-65, Brode & Dunlap, 1965-70, Brode & Smith, 1970—; spl. judge City Ct., Memphis, 1957-63; Mem. Pres.'s Nat. Traffic Adv. Com., 1963-64; mem. Tenn. Art Commn., 1965-72; mem. Mayor's Community Action Com., 1965; hon. col. on staff Tenn. gov., 1967—. Del. So. Regional Edn. Conf., 1964, 1965, 1966. Mem. Tenn. Ho. Reps., 1962-65; asst. city atty. City of Memphis, 1965-68; mem. Shelby County Democratic Exec. Com., 1966—. Bd. dirs. West Tenn. chpt. Arthritis and Rheumatism Found. Mem. Am., Shelby County, Memphis bar assns., Bar Assn. Tenn., Memphis Arts Council, Phi Alpha Delta. Jewish religion (dir. Temple Brotherhood). Mason (32 deg., Shriner). Co-editor: Memphis Municipal Code. Home: 2944 Tishomingo Lane Memphis TN 38111 Office: 100 N Main Memphis TN 38103

BRODIE, RALPH GRAY, lawyer; b. Marshall, Ark., Mar. 24, 1940; s. Frank Theodore and Hazel (Gray) B.; B.S. in Indsl. Engring., U. Ark., 1963, LL.B., J.D., 1966. Admitted to Ark. bar, 1966; law clk. for Chief Justice Carleton Harris, Ark. Supreme Ct., 1966-67; asst. atty. gen. State of Ark., Little Rock, 1967-69; financial planner also house counsel Diversified Financial Services Internat., 1969—. Served with AUS, 1963-64; capt. Res. ret. Mem. Am., Ark., Pulaski County bar assns., Little Rock Jr. C. of C. (v.p. 1968-69). Democrat. Baptist. Home: 6714 Greenwood Rd Little Rock AR 72207 Office: 1540 Worthen Bank Little Rock AR 72201

BROEMSER, GARY MILTON, govt. ofc.; b. San Jose, Cal., Apr. 27, 1938; s. Milton A. and Leora (Grill) B.; B.S. with great distinction, Stanford U., 1960, M.S. (Alfred P. Sloan fellow), 1966, Ph.D. (Ford. Found. fellow, Herbert Hoover fellow), 1968, M.B.A., 1968. Systems analyst Office Asst. Sec. Def., Washington, 1968-71; sr. policy planner Office Asst. Sec. Transp. for Policy, Washington, 1971—. Asst. professorial lectr. mgmt. George Washington U., 1970. Served to lt. (j.g.), USNR, 1960-63. Mem. Phi Beta Kappa, Tau Beta Pi. Home: 324 8th St SE Washington DC 20003 Office: 400 7th St SW Washington DC 20590

BROGAN, R. THOMAS, advt. agy. exec. Vice pres. McCann-Erickson, Inc., Houston. Office: 800 Bell St Houston TX 77002*

BROGAN, THOMAS MARCUM, banker; b. Wilhoit, Ky., July 22, 1934; s. James Howard and Mary (Evans) B.; student U. Ky., 1955-56; B.S., Lincoln Meml. U., 1958; banking degree, La. State U., 1968; m. Wilma Jean Miracle, June 16, 1956; children—Teresa Ann, Timothy Scott. Investigator, Retail Credit Co., Louisville, also operator sub-office, Columbia, Ky., 1959-63; with Comml. Bank, Middlesboro, 1963—, exec. v.p., 1970—; asst. sec., treas. Comml. Securities Corp., 1967—. Mem. Middlesboro 4-H Council, 1970—. Served with USNR, 1952-55. Mem. Middlesboro C. of C. (bd. dirs. 1970—). Baptist (deacon 1963—, supt. Sunday sch. 1968—, finance com. 1968—). Rotarian (bd. dirs., v.p. 1968—). Home: 10th and Lothbury Sts Middlesboro KY 40965 Office: 1918 Cumberland AV Middlesboro KY 40965

BROMBERG, ALAN ROBERT, lawyer, educator, author; b. Dallas, Nov. 24, 1928; s. Alfred L. and Juanita (Kramer) B.; A.B., Harvard, 1949; J.D., Yale, 1952; m. Anne Ruggles, July 26, 1959. Admitted to Tex. bar, 1952, U.S. Tax Ct. bar, 1959; asso. firm Carrington, Gowan, Johnson, Bromberg and Leeds, Dallas, 1952-56; atty. and cons., 1956—; part-time lectr. Law Sch., So. Methodist U., Dallas, 1955-56, vis. asst. prof. law, 1956-57, asst. prof. law, 1957-58, asso. prof., 1958-62, prof. law, 1962—, chmn. law curriculum com., 1961—, trustee retirement plan, 1967-70, faculty rep. bd. trustees, 1969-70, mem. exec. com. faculty senate, 1968-70, mem. presdl. search group, 1971—; faculty adviser Southwestern Law Jour., 1958-65; sr. fellow Yale Law Faculty, 1966-67; vis. prof. Stanford Law Sch., 1972-73. Counsel Internat. Data Systems, Inc., 1961-65, sec., dir. 1963-65; mem. Tex. Legislative Council Bus. and Commerce Code Adv. Com., 1966-67. Sec., mem. bd. dirs. Community Arts Fund, 1963—; gen. atty. Dallas Mus. Contemporary Arts, 1956-63. Bd. dirs. Dallas Theater Center, 1955—, sec., 1957-66, finance com., 1957-65, mem. exec. com., 1957-70. Served as cpl. M.I., AUS, 1952-54. Mem. Am. Bar Assn. (mem. com. partnerships; mem. com. fed. regulation of securities), Dallas Bar Assn. (chmn. com. on uniform partnership act 1959-61), State Bar Tex. (mem. com. on corporate law revision 1957—, mem. com. on securities and investment banking 1957—, chmn. 1965-69, mem. com. on information of corp. banking and bus. law sect. 1961-69, mem. council of sect. 1963-69, vice chmn. 1965-67, chmn. 1967-68, reporter com. on revision of penal code 1967-70), Am. Law Inst., Southwestern Legal Found., Am., Assn. U. Profs. (exec. com. So. Methodist U. chpt. 1962-63; chmn. acad. freedom and tenure com. 1968-70, 71-—), Assn. Am. Law Schs. (mem. coms.), Nat. Tax Assn. Author: (with Byron D. Sher) Cases and Materials on Texas Partnerships, 1958, supplemented 1960; Supplementary Materials on Texas Corporations, 1959, rev. 1965, 71; Partnership Primer—Problems and Planning, 1961; Materials on Corporate Securities and Finance—A Growing Company's Search for Funds, 1962, rev. 1965; Securities Law-Fraud-Sec Rule 10b-5, Vol. I, 1967, Vol. II, 1970, supplements pub. annually; Crane and Bromberg on Partnership, 1968; numerous articles and revs. to law and bar jours. Adv. editor Rev. Securities Regulation, 1969-—. Lectr. numerous bar meetings, insts. Home: 3701 Stratford Dallas TX 75205

BROMBERG, HENRI LOUIE, JR., lawyer; b. Dallas, Jan. 15, 1911; A.B., U. Tex., 1932; J.D., Northwestern U., 1935. Admitted to Tex. bar, 1935; mem. firm Johnson, Bromberg, Leeds & Riggs, Dallas. Served to lt. col. AUS, 1942-46. Mem. Am., Dallas bar assns., State Bar Tex. Address: 4842 Brookview St Dallas TX 75220*

BROMBERG, MRS. HENRI L., JR., civic worker; ed. Sophie Neucomb Coll.; m. Henri L. Bromberg, Jr.; 1 son. Mem. sch. bd. Dallas Ind. Sch. Dist.; bd. dirs. Dallas Child Guidance Clinic, Services for the Blind; mem. Met. Opera Southwestern Hospitality Bd.; active Dallas Symphony, Dallas Pub. Library. Address: 4842 Brookview Dr Dallas TX 75220

BRONSON, WILLIAM H(OWARD), publisher, lawyer, radio-TV exec.; b. Dadeville, Ala., July 10, 1912; s. George A. and Meige (Berkstresser) B.; student Ala. Poly. Inst., 1929-30; B.A., U. Ala., 1933; postgrad. Harvard, 1933-34; J.D., La. State U., 1938; m. Lillian Francez, July 9, 1935; children—William H., Susan Francez (Mrs. E.S. Croft III). Admitted to La. bar, 1938, practiced in Shreveport, 1938-40; with law firm Tucker, Bronson & Martin, 1940-52; pres., pub., dir. Shreveport Times; pres., dir. Monroe (La.) News Star, Monroe Morning World, radio stas. KWKH, Shreveport, Radio Broadcasting, Inc., Shreveport, Tri State Broadcasting System, Inc., Shreveport; pres. Newspaper Prodn. Co. (agts. Shreveport Times, Shreveport Jour.), 1952; chmn. bd., dir. Ark. TV Co., Inc. (TV sta. KTHV, Little Rock), 1952-—; dir., mem. exec. com. of bd. Kansas City So. Ry.; dir., mem. exec. com. Kansas City So. Industries, Inc., La. & Ark. Ry., dir. Shreveport Engraving Co.; mem., vice chmn. La. Coordinating Council for Higher Edn., 1969-—; exec. com., dir., organizer Council Better La., 1962-—; pres. bd. trustees Southfield Sch., 1949-50. Trustee S. W. Research Inst., San Antonio, La. Council Econ. Edn., Pub. Affairs Research Council La., Shreveport Obs., 1963-—; bd. dirs. La. State Fair Assn. Mem. Nat. Planning Assn. (nat. council), Am., La. State, Shreveport, Fed. Communications bar assns., Shreveport C. of C. (dir.; 1st v.p. 1959), Newcomen Soc., Am. Judicature Soc., Sigma Delta Chi. Episcopalian (former vestryman). Clubs: Shreveport (dir.), Shreveport Country (pres. 1958); Boston (New Orleans); Press (Dallas). Home: 6024 E Ridge Dr Shreveport LA 71106 Office: care Shreveport Times 222 Lake St Shreveport LA 71130

BRONZ, GEORGE, lawyer; b. N.Y.C., July 7, 1910; B.S., Coll. City N.Y., 1939; LL.B., Columbia U., 1932. Research asst. Columbia Law Sch., 1930-33; admitted to N.Y. State bar, 1933, D.C. bar, 1953; atty. NRA, 1933-35, Office of Solicitor, Dept. Agr., 1935-39; chief legal adviser Office Bituminous Coal Consumers' Counsel, 1939-43; spl. asst. to gen. counsel for internat. finance and trade Treasury Dept., 1943-54; practiced in Washington; also counsel Sharretts, Paley, Carter & Blauvelt, Washington. Mem. U.S. delegation to Havana Conf. on Trade and Employment, 1947-48, sessions of contracting parties to GATT, 1948-52; lectr. law Harvard Law Sch., 1954. Mem. Am., Fed. bar assns., Bar Assn. D.C., Phi Beta Kappa. Editor: Columbia Law Rev., 1930-32. Contbr. articles to legal jours. Office: 888 17th St NW Washington DC 20006*

BROOKE, GEORGE MERCER, JR., educator; b. Tokyo, Japan, Oct. 21, 1914 (parents Am. citizens); s. George Mercer and Isabel (Tilton) B.; B.A., Va. Mil. Inst., 1936; M.A., Wash. and Lee U., 1942; Ph.D., U. N.C., 1955; m. Frances Fleming Bailey, June 13, 1942; children— George Mercer III, Marion Bailey (Mrs. John Robert Philpott, Jr.). Spl. agt. Md. Casualty Co., Newark, 1937-41; instr. history Va. Mil. Inst., Lexington, 1942-43, asst prof., 1948-55, asso. prof., 1955-58, prof. history, 1958-—, head dept. history, 1965-70; instr. Washington and Lee U., 1946-47, 70. Fulbright research scholar Keio U., Tokyo, 1962-63; Fulbright lectr. Am. history, Nat. Taiwan U., Taipei, 1963. Pres. Stonewall Jackson Area Council Boy Scouts Am., 1964-67, exec. bd., 1958-—. Bd. dirs. United Fund, 1965-—. Served with AUS, 1943-46. Recipient Silver Beaver award, Boy Scouts Am., 1967. Mem. Am., Rockbridge (pres. 1960-62) hist. socs., Assn. Asian Studies, Internat. House of Japan, Soc. of the Cin., Phi Beta Kappa, Kappa Alpha. Episcopalian (lay dep. to the gen. convention 1969). Author: Collected Documents of Japanese Mission to America, Vol. V, 1961. Contbr. Ency. Brit. Home: 405 Jackson Av Lexington VA 24450

BROOKER, FRANCIS MILTON, chem. co. exec.; b. Utica, Ill., May 7, 1915; s. Claud W. and Lucy (Munro) B.; B.S., Monmouth Coll., 1938; M.S., Washington U., St. Louis, 1940; m. Geneva Morton, Oct. 31, 1942; children—Linda (Mrs. David M. Welch), Francis Allen, Gail Ellen. Chief chemist B. T. Fooks Mfg. Co., Camden, Ark., 1940-42; v.p., dir. research, devel., quality control Grapette Co., Inc., Camden, 1946-—. Served to 1st lt. AUS, 1942-46. Mem. Soc. Soft Drink Technologists, Inst. Food Technologists. Presbyn. (deacon, elder). Rotarian. Home: 1033 Westwood St Camden AR 71701 Office: 157 Grinstead St Camden AR 71701

BROOKINGS, HENRY NASON KINNEY, petroleum geologist; b. San Francisco, May 25, 1917; s. Walter DuBois and Marian (Kinney) B.; grad. Phillips Exeter Acad., 1935; A.B., Princeton, 1939; m. Frances Ellis Winter, Nov. 18, 1944; children—Deborah DuBois, Henry Nason Kinney, David Winter, Jeffrey Baker. Sr. geologist Phillips Petroleum Co., El Dorado, Ark., Oklahoma City, Shreveport, La., 1939-53; ind. cons. geologist, Shreveport, 1953-58; partner, geologist Brookings, Moffatt & Waddle, oil and gas cons., Shreveport, 1958-—. Swimming meet coordinator Am. Amateur Union. Served with USNR, 1941-45. Mem. Certified Petroleum Geologists Am., Assn. Petroleum Geologists, Shreveport Geol. Soc., Res. Officers Assn., Ret. Officers Assn., Am. Legion, V.F.W. Democrat. Methodist. Club: North Shreveport Swimming (pres. 1956-62). Home: 3701 Eddy Pl Shreveport LA 71107 Office: Ray P Oden Bldg Shreveport LA 71101

BROOKS, A. GORDON, dir. div. tchrs. edn. Va. Dept. Edn. Office: State Dept of Education Richmond VA 23216*

BROOKS, CYRUS LEE, city ofcl.; b. nr. Monroe, N.C., Jan. 19, 1933; s. Judge Ellis and Hennrietta Drucella (Griffin) B.; A.B., U. N.C., 1955; postgrad. U. Alaska, 1959-60; M. Govtl. Adminstrn., U. Pa., 1962; m. Madria Sue Cumby, June 6, 1953; 1 son, Cyrus Lee II. Adminstrv. asst. to city mgr., Charlotte, N.C., 1961-62; city mgr. Town of Mooresville, 1963-66, City of Morganton, N.C., 1966-—. Chmn. Regional Solid Waste Commn., Morganton, 1971-72. Served to 1st lt. USAF, 1955-60. Mem. Am. Soc. Pub. Adminstrn., Internat. City Mgmt. Assn., Pub. Personnel Assn. Baptist (ordained deacon). Elk, Rotarian (bd. dirs. 1968-69, 72-73). Club: Catawba Valley Executive (Hickory, N.C.). Home: 109 Creekside Dr Morganton NC 28655 Office: PO Drawer 430 Morganton NC 28655

BROOKS, DANIEL LEE, ednl. adminstr.; b. St. Louis, Feb. 6, 1930; s. Robert Lee and Alma (Meredith) B.; B.S., Lincoln U., 1952; postgrad. U. Houston, 1962-63, Harvard U. Inst. Ednl. Mgmt., 1971; m. Joan Burns, Aug. 22, 1953; children—Sheryll, Dandrea. Roving insp. U.S. Ordnance, St. Louis, 1952-53; asst. bus. mgr. Prairie View (Tex.) A. and M. Coll., 1953-64; pres., gen. mgr. Tyler Barber Coll., Inc., N.Y., Ill., Tenn., Tex. locations, 1964-68, dir., 1969-— bus. mgr. Jarvis Christian Coll., Hawkins, Tex., 1968-—. Dist. finance chmn. East Tex. area Boy Scouts Am., 1965. Sloan Found grantee, 1971, Ford Found. grantee, 1971. Mem. Nat., So. assns. coll. and univ. bus. officers., Nat. Assn. Ednl. Buyers, Nat. Assn. Accountants, Omega Psi Phi. Democrat. Baptist. Home: 1722 Northridge St Tyler TX 75701 Office: Drawer G Hawkins TX 75765

BROOKS, DAVID PALMER, clergyman, religious assn. editor; b. nr. Shelby, N.C., Feb. 15, 1915; s. George Ezell and Aquilla (Scruggs) B.; student Gardner Webb Jr. Coll., 1933-35; B.A. cum laude, Wake Forest U., 1939; M.S.T., So. Baptist Theol. Sem., 1942; postgrad. Vanderbilt Div. Sch., 1968-69; m. Susan Fannie Bost, May 27, 1943; children—Susan (Mrs. James Pike) Rebekah, Jane, Polly. Ordained to ministry Baptist Ch., 1939; pastor Salem Bapt. Ch., Elizabeth City, N.C., 1943-46; dist. supt. Chowan Bapt. Assn., Elizabeth City, 1946-48; asso. state Sunday sch. dept. N.C. Bapt. Convention, Raleigh, 1948-60; adult editor Sunday Sch. Bd., So. Bapt. Conv., Nashville, 1960-—, editor young adult Bible study and advanced Bible study, 1969-—. Mem. Nashville Bapt. Assn. (chmn. Christian life com. 1968-70) mem. mission com. 1970-71), Nat. Council Chs. (com. uniform series 1960-68, sec. editors section religious edn. assn. 1962-63), Delta Kappa Alpha. Author: The Bible: How To Understand and Teach It, 1968. Contbr. articles to religious publs. Home: 2712 Western Hills Nashville TN 37214 Office: 127 9th Av Nashville TN 37203

BROOKS, DAVID WILLIAM, farmer coop. exec.; b. Royston, Ga., Sept. 11, 1901; s. David William and Letty Jane (Tabor) B.; B.S. in Agr., U. Ga., 1922, M.S., 1923; LL.D., Emory U., 1964; m. Ruth McMurray, Aug. 7, 1930; children—David William, Nancy Ruth. Tchr. agronomy div. U. Ga., 1922-25; field supr. Ga. Cotton Growers Cooperative Assn., 1925-33; gen. mgr. Cotton Producers Assn. (name now Gold Kist Inc.), Atlanta, 1933-68, chmn. bd., 1968-—; pres. Cotton States Life & Health Ins. Co., 1955-59, chmn bd., 1959-—; chmn bd., pres. Cotton States Mut. Ins. Co.; dir. internat. adv. bd. Citizens & So. Nat. Bank, Atlanta; dir. Georgia So. & Fla. Ry. Co. Dir. Am. Cotton Coop. Assn., Atlanta 1940-71; Nat. Council Farmers Coops., Washington, 1938-68, mem. exec. com. 1944-68, pres. 1951-52. Mem. Textiles Industry Adv. Com. of Army-Navy Munitions Bd., 1947-51; industry adv. Internat. Cotton Adv. Com., Washington 1950; mem. nat. adv. bd. Moblzn. Policy, 1951-52; mem. Nat. Agrl. Adv. Commn., 1953-56; mem. Benson's Cotton Export Adv. Com., 1953-56, chmn., 1953; mem. nat. cotton adv. com. U.S. Dept. Agr., 1947-50, 61-63; dir. Found. for Am. Agr., 1960-—; dir. Agr. Mission, Inc., 1959-67; mem Pres. Johnson's Nat. Agrl. Adv. Commn., 1964, Pres.'s Nat. Adv. Commn. on Rural Poverty, 1966-67. Pres. Ga. Coop. Council (Athens, Ga.), 1940-47. Trustee Found. for World Literacy, 1959-64, Wesleyan Coll., Macon, Ga., 1965-—; trustee Am. Inst. Cooperation, Washington, 1944-69, vice chmn. 1951-52; trustee Emory U., Reinhardt Coll., Waleska, Ga.; chmn. Emory U. Com. of One Hundred, 1958-—; bd. govs. Agrl. Hall of Fame, 1958-—, Nat. Council Chs., 1960-—. Selected Man of Year in Agr. for Ga. by Progressive Farmer, 1950, Man of Year in Agr. in the South, 1966. Mem. N.Y. Cotton Exchange (adv. com. 1948-69), Nat. Cotton Council (adv. com., v.p. 1958-69), Nat. Peanut Council (dir. 1959-61), Farmers Chem. Assn. (chmn. bd. 1960-69, dir.), Alpha Zeta, Phi Kappa Phi. Methodist. (steward). Mason, Kiwanian. Home: 2374 Dellwood Dr PO Box 2210 Atlanta GA 30301

BROOKS, ELSTON HARWOOD, newspaper columnist; b. Kansas City, Mo., Feb. 18, 1930; s. Amos Elston and Dorthy Miller (Gale) B.; student nights Tex. Christian U., 1957-58; m. Mary Lee O'Brien, Sept. 5, 1953; 1 son, David Bryan. Reporter, Ft. Worth Press, 1947-48; amusements editor Ft. Worth Star-Telegram, 1948-—, columnist The Elston Brooks Column, 1949-—. Star radio program Ballads by Brooks, stas. KXOL, WBAP, Ft. Worth, 1947-50, The Elston Brooks Show, sta. WBAP, 1965-—. Served with AUS, 1950-52. Recipient numerous awards for reporting from A.P., Sigma Delta Chi, State Headliners, Big Story award. Mem. Sigma Delta Chi. Home: 1951 Shelman Trail Fort Worth TX 76112 Office: Star-Telegram Ft Worth TX 76112

BROOKS, GEORGE DANIEL, ins. exec.; b. Martin, Tenn., Oct. 13, 1907; s. George Martin and Mayme (Mathis) B.; student Vanderbilt U., 1924-48; m. Julia Evans Clements, Apr. 23, 1929; children—Frances Moore (Mrs. Michael Corzine), Julia Clements (Mrs. Clarke T. Reed). Employed Caldwell & Co., investment bankers, Nashville, 1928-30, Third Nat. Bank, Nashville, 1930-31; joined Nat. Life & Accident Ins. Co., Nashville, 1931, mgr. investment dept., 1939-—, v.p., 1950-59, treas., 1953-59, financial v.p., 1959-63, sr. v.p., chmn. finance com., 1963-64, exec. v.p. 1964-65, pres., 1965-67, chmn. bd., chief exec. officer, 1967-—, also dir.; chmn. bd. WSM, Inc., NLT Corp.; trustee U.S. Trust Co. N.Y.; adv. dir. Ralston Purina Co.; mem. trust bd. 3d Nat. Bank, Nashville; dir. 1st Tenn. Nat. Corp., Memphis. Financial advisor of Old Woman's Home, Nashville; mem. adv. com. Jr. League, Nashville. Served as lt. comdr. USNR, active duty 1942-45. Decorated Commendation medal (Navy). Mem. Mortgage Bankers Assn. Am. (gov.), Life Ins. Assn. Am. (dir.), Vanderbilt U. Alumni Assn. (past pres.), Sigma Nu. Ind. Democrat. Presbyn. Clubs: Cumberland, Belle Meade Country (Nashville); National Golf (Augusts, Ga.); The Links (N.Y.C.). Home: 113 Clarendon Av Nashville TN 37205 Office: Nat Life Center Nashville TN 37203

BROOKS, GEORGE WILLIAM, educator; b. Macon, Ga., June 7, 1918; s. John William and Lois (Henderson) B.; B.S., Ind. U., 1941; M.S., 1942, Ed.D., 1955; LL.B., LaSalle Extension U., 1947; m. Fannie E. Crafton, May 25, 1945; 1 son, George W. (dec.). Inst. Voorhees Jr. Coll., 1942-43; asst. prof. social studies Prairie View A. and M. Coll. of Tex., 1943-53; prof. social studies and edn. S.C. State Coll., Orangeburg, 1955-59, chmn. dept. social studies, 1959-60, dean Sch. Grad. Studies, 1960-—. Mem council on coop. coll. projects TVA, 1963-—. Mem. Am. Assn. Sch Adminstrs., N.E.A., Nat. Council for Social Studies, S.C. Psychol. Assn., Palmetto Edn. Assn. (parliamentarian ho. of dels. 1959-—), Kappa Alpha Psi, Phi Delta Kappa, Phi Alpha Theta. Mason (Shriner). Home: State Coll Orangeburg SC 29115

BROOKS, HARLEY CALVIN, JR., librarian; b. Harrogate, Tenn., Apr. 6, 1933; s. Harley Calvin and Nelia (Sulfridge) B.; B.A., Lincoln Meml. U., 1951; M.A. (Tenn. Library Assn. scholar), George Peabody Coll., 1957; postgrad. U. N.M., 1959-61, (LaVerne Noyes fellow) U. Chgo., 1961-62; m. Barbara Anne Collier, Aug. 21, 1959; children—Amy Catherine, Emily Collier, Harley Calvin III. Meter record clk. Dayton Power & Light Co. (O.), 1951-53; tchr. Pruden (Tenn.) High Sch., 1955-56; librarian Hiwassee Jr. Coll., Madisonville, Tenn., 1957-59; cataloger U. N.M. Library, 1959-61; circulation librarian U. Chgo., 1962-64; head circulation dept. Ohio State U. Libraries, 1964-68; librarian George Peabody Coll., Nashville, 1968-—, lectr., 1968-—. Chmn. Peabody Coll. United Givers Fund Drive, 1969. Served with AUS, 1953-55. Mem. Am., Southeastern, Tenn. library assns. Baptist (deacon 1971-—). Mem. editorial adv. bd. Peabody Jour. Edn., 1968-—. Home: 4405 Farriswood Dr Nashville TN 37204

BROOKS, HARRY WALKER, farm exec.; b. Princeton, W. Va., Oct. 8, 1916; s. Yemmons Walker and Eula (Lankford) B.; student U. Tenn., 1935-37;; m. Betsy Chambers, Nov. 29, 1939; children—Randall W., Margaret Jane, Becky Leigh. With Brook Haven Farm Inc., Knoxville, Tenn., 1970-—, chmn. bd., 1970-—; parnter Brooks Payne Co., 1955-—; pres., founder Plasti Line, Inc., 1944-64. Mem. U. Tenn. Athletic Bd., 1972-—; mem. U. Tenn. Devel. Council; chmn. Easter Seal Soc. Crippled Children and Adults, Knoxville, 1961-62. Trustee, Tenn. Wesleyan Coll.; mem. Com. One Hundred, Emory U., 1961-69; bd. dirs. Knoxville YMCA. Recipient H.M. Holderness award Conn. Mut. Life Ins. Co., 1939, award Am. Inst. Indsl. Engrs. and Soc. Advancement Mgmt., 1967, award Boy Scouts Am., 1959, award Knoxville YMCA 1970. Mem. Knoxville C. of C. (pres. 1960-61), Knoxville Layman's Assn., Young Pres.'s Orgn. Methodist. Rotarian. Clubs: University of Tennessee Faculty, University of Tennessee Presidents, Cherokee Country, Bays Mountain Country, Knoxville City. Home and office: Route 3 Brook Haven Farms Seymour TN 37865

BROOKS, HENRY LUESING, judge; b. Louisville, Dec. 9, 1905; s. Horace G. and Amelia (Luesing) B.; A.B., U. Wis., 1927; J.D., U. Louisville, 1929; m. Christine Clarke, Oct. 29, 1930; children—Henry Luesing, Peggy C. (Mrs. Robert B. Beale, III), Tommy C. Admitted to Ky. bar, 1928; engaged in practice of law, Louisville, 1929-54; judge Jefferson Circuit Ct., 1946-48; faculty Jefferson Sch. Law, 1948-52; U.S. dist. judge, Louisville, 1954-69; judge U.S. Ct. of Appeals, 6th circuit, Louisville, 1969-—. Mem. Ky. Bd. Bar Commrs., 1950-54. Served as lt. USNR, 1943-46. Mem. Sigma Chi, Phi Delta Phi. Mason (32 deg., Shriner). Home: Prospect KY 40059 Office: Fed Bldg Louisville KY 40202

BROOKS, HENRY PHELPS, JR., banker; b. Balt., Jan. 12, 1918; s. Henry Phelps and Evaline Clapp (Boggs) B.; student The Citadel, 1934-37, La. State U., 1941-43; m. Lillian Verne Smith, Jan. 1, 1941; children— Lillian F. (Mrs. Forrest C. Wilkerson), Henry Phelps III. With Farrell-Birmingham Co., Buffalo, N.Y., 1937, Life Ins. Co. of Va., Greenville, S.C., 1938-38; Rock Hill Printing & Finishing Co. (S.C.), 1940, Comml. Bank, Chester, S.C., 1941-46; asst. cashier The Peoples Nat. Bank of Chester, 1946-51, dir., 1948-—, v.p., 1951-59, pres., trust officer, 1959-—; dir. Charlotte br. Fed. Reserve Bank, Spratt Savs. & Loan Assn., Chester, Investors Nat. Life Ins. Co., Columbia, S.C. Pres. Chester County Bd. Commerce and Devel., 1960-61; pres. Chester area United Fund, 1963-64. Chmn. bd. dirs. The Children's Bur. S.C., 1965-67. Mem. S.C. Bankers Assn. (pres. 1968-69), Ind. Bankers S.C. (pres. 1964-65). Rotarian (pres. 1948-49). Home: 157 Walnut St Chester SC 29706 Office: 120 Church St Chester SC 29706

BROOKS, JACK, congressman; b. Dec. 18, 1922; s. Edward Chachere and Grace Marie (Pipes) B.; m. Charlotte Collins; children—Jack Edward, Katherine Inez. Admitted to Tex. bar, 1949; mem. Tex. Legislature, 1946-50; mem. 83d-92d Congresses from 9th Tex. dist. Col. USMCR. Home: 1029 East Dr Beaumont TX 77706 Office: House Office Bldg Washington DC 20515

BROOKS, JERRY CLAUDE, food co. exec.; b. College Park, Ga., Apr. 23, 1936; s. John Bennett and Mattie Mae (Timms) B.; B.S., Ga. Inst. Tech., 1958; m. Peggy Sue Thornton, Feb. 26, 1961; children—Apryll Denise, Jerry Claude, Susan Vereen. Safety engr. Cotton Producers Assn., Atlanta, Ga., 1959-64, dir. safety and loss control, 1964-70; dir. corporate protection Gold Kist, Inc., Atlanta, 1970-—. Instr., Ga. Safety Inst., Athens, Ga., 1971-—. Bd. dirs. Greater Lithonia (Ga.) Homeowners Assn., Ga. Soc. Prevention of Blindness. Served with AUS, 1958-59. Mem. Am. Soc. Safety Engrs. (chpt. pres. 1968-69), Nat. Safety Council (gen. chmn. fertilizer sect. 1969-70), So. Safety Conf. (v.p. bus. and industry 1968-—), Am. Soc. Indsl. Security. Mason. Club: Exchange (pres. 1969-70) (Lithonia, Ga.). Home: 6411 Evans Mill Way Lithonia GA 30058 Office: 3348 Peachtree Rd Atlanta GA 30326

BROOKS, LEONARD, supt. schs.; b. Ashland, Ala., Oct. 9, 1924; s. Joseph A. and Ara (Green) B.; B.S., Auburn U., 1948, M.S., 1961; m. Willie M. Milley, Dec. 17, 1947; children—Leonard D., Tammie Luan. Tchr. various schs., 1949-61; ins. agt., Ashland, Ala., 1961-65; supt. edn. Clay County, Ashland, 1961-—, supt. schs., 1965-—. Served with AUS, 1942-46. Mem. Jr. C. of C. (pres. 1956-57). Mason, Rotarian (pres. 1966-67, dir.). Home: Route 3 Ashland AL 36251 Office: PO Box 216 Ashland AL 36251

BROOKS, MARION JACKSON, physician; b. Fort Worth, Feb. 15, 1920; s. Roy Edwin and Eula Mae (Jackson) Brooks; B.S., Prairie View A. and M. Coll., 1940; M.D., Howard U., 1951; m. Marie Louise Norris, Dec. 25, 1945; children—Marian (Mrs. William C. Bryant), Carol Eleanor, Roy Charles, Clarence Jackson, Marie Anne. Intern, Freedmen's Hosp., Washington, 1951-52; gen. practice medicine, Fort Worth, 1952-—; mem. staff St. Joseph Hosp., Harris Hosp., All Saints Hosp.; dir. Great Liberty Life Ins. Co., Dallas. Pres. Neighborhood Action, Inc., 1967-68; chmn. Sickle Cell Anemia Assn. Tex., 1971-—; active Fort Worth Symphony Assn., Community Action Agy., Fort Worth Tarrant County, Tex. Mem. Fort Worth City Park and Recreation Bd., 1963-67. Bd. dirs. Tarrant County Precinct Workers Council. Served to 1st lt. AUS, 1942-47; ETO. Mem. Tex. Council Voters (dir. 1961-—), Alpha Phi Alpha. Methodist (trustee 1963-—). Mason (Shriner). Home: 2451 Evans Av Fort Worth TX 76104 Office: 2200 Evans Av Fort Worth TX 76104

BROOKS, PAUL ALLISON, supt. schs.; b. Joy, Tex., Mar. 31, 1918; s. Isham A. and Alma E. (Hargrove) B.; B.S., North Tex. State U., 1942, M.B.A., 1949, Ed.D., 1957; m. Rhoda A. Brooks, May 18, 1940; children— Gary, Sandra, Joe M. Supt. schs., Stoneburg, Tex., 1948-53, Cedar Hill, Tex., 1953-—. Served with AUS, 1943-46. Mem. N.E.A., Am., Tex. assns. sch. adminstrs., Tex. Tchrs. Assn., Dallas County Sch. Adminstrs. (pres. 1957-58), Cedar Hill C. of C. (dir. 1962-65, 68-71). Mason. Lion. Home: 425 Lee St Cedar Hill TX 75104 Office: 333 S Hwy 67 Cedar Hill TX 75104

BROOKS, RICHARD BOYNTON, coll. dean; b. Springfield, Mass., Nov. 17, 1908; s. Walter C. and Beulah (Boynton) B.; B. Phys. Edn., Springfield (Mass.) Coll., 1930; M.A., U. Pa., 1942; Ed.D., U. Va., 1959; m. Virginia Rose Dove, Feb. 17, 1944; children—Carter D., Leila Kay (Mrs. William J. Odie). Instr. psychology Colby Coll., Waterville, Me., 1946-47; dir. counseling Coll. William and Mary, Williamsburg, Va., 1947-57, dean Sch. Edn., 1968-—; mem. faculty Longwood Coll., Farmville, Va., 1957-—, prof. edn., 1962-64, dean coll., 1964-68. Served to capt. AUS, 1942-46. Mem. Am. Psychol. Assn., Va. Edn. Assn. Conglist. Home: 11331b Mount Vernon Williamsburg VA 23185

BROOKS, TANYA WIDRIN (MRS. WALTER BOOTH BROOKS, III), writer, pub. relations exec., civic worker; b. San Francisco; d. Mark and Ellen (Foote) Widrin; student U. So. Cal., 1941, U. Hawaii, 1944; m. Walter Booth Brooks III, Sept. 27, 1953; children—Laurelle Sheedy, Walter Booth IV. Writer soc. column Chgo. Sun-Times, 1961-66; columnist Chgo. Am., 1958-61; editor Palm Beach (Fla.) Illustrated, weekly paper, 1959-61; weekly column Be My Guest, Guide of Palm Beach, 1956-62; writer Ft. Lauderdale News, 1962, staff corr., 1962-—; Palm Beach pub. relations rep. KLM Royal Dutch Airlines, 1964-66; contbr. articles to Social Spectator, Diplomat, Palm Beach Life, 1955-66; star Life in Palm Beaches, sta. WEAT-TV, 1958-62; soc. editor Social Pictorial mag., 1962-67, Status mag., 1965-67; owner, mgr. Palm Beach Candid, 1955-65, Portraits Unlimited, Palm Beach, 1961-65, Tanya Brooks, Pub. Relations, Palm Beach, 1955-—; owner Galerie Montemartre, 1965-69, Palm Beach Flea Market, 1965-69, Tanya Brooks Mini-Galerie at Palm Beach and Los Angeles, 1967-—. Mem. Women's Air Raid Def., 7th Air Force, Hawaii, 1943-45; active benefits, Palm Beach, Palm Beach Round Table; pres. Stars and Bars, U.S., Hawaii, France and Monaco, 1953-55. Recipient awards Am. Women's Vol. Services, 1942, A.R.C., 1957, 58, 59. Home: 248 Via Marila St Palm Beach FL 33480 Office: 325 Worth Av Palm Beach FL 33480

BROOM, PERRY MORRIS, educator; b. Effingham, Ill., Aug. 7, 1908; s. Charles A. and Lillian (Cohea) B.; B.S., Sam Houston State Coll., 1936; M.Ed., U. Tex., 1938; D.Ed. (Univ. fellow), 1942; M.B.A., East Tex. State Coll., 1953; m. Inez Miller, 1947 (div. 1950); 1 dau., Brenda Karen. Tchr. pub. schs., Hebbronville, Tex., 1936-37; prin. high sch., San Diego, Tex., 1937-40; instr. U. Tex., 1945-46, 50-51; asso. prof. Howard Coll., 1946-47; prof. edn. Franklin Coll., 1947-49; asso. prof. bus. administrn. East Tex. State Coll., 1951-60, prof. bus. adminstrn., 1960-—. Served to lt., USNR, 1942-45; PTO, Phillipines. Mem. N.E.A., Am. Statis. Assn., Tex. State Tchrs. Assn., Am. Inst. Mgmt., C. of C., Phi Alpha Theta, Alpha Chi, Phi Delta Kappa, Sigma Iota Epsilon, Delta Sigma Pi, Kappa Delta Pi, Pi Gamma Mu, Pi Omega Pi, Kappa Phi Kappa, Psi Chi. Baptist. Rotarian. Author: Simplified Business Statistics, 1955. Editor: (with M. Decherd) Commerce Curriculum Bull., Tex. Dept. Edn., 1938. Home: 1806 Culver St Commerce TX 75765

BROOM, ROBERT EARL, city ofcl.; b. Decatur, Ill., Dec. 4, 1937; s. Virgil M. and Marion M. (Mowry) B.; student U. Ill., 1955-56; B.S., Millikin U., 1960; m. Ruth Ann Polley, Mar. 23, 1962; children—Laura Sue, Leesa Ann. Accountant, Berry Constrn. Co., Decatur, Ill., 1959-60; prodn. supr. Permacel Mfg. Co., Decatur, Ill., 1960-61; accountant Turnbull & Schusselle, C.P.A.'s, 1962, Ill. Power Co., Decatur, 1962-63; chief accounting and data processing City of Decatur, Ill., 1963-69; finance dir. City of Ocala, Fla., 1969-—. Served with USAF, 1961-62. Mem. Data Processing Mgmt. Assn., Municipal Finance Officers Assn. U.S. and Can., Ocala and Marion County C. of C., Chi Eta Rho. Lutheran (financial sec.). Lion. Home: 4328 NE 12th St Ocala FL 32670 Office: PO Box 1270 Ocala FL 32670

BROOME, DOUGLAS RALPH, JR., electronics co. exec.; b. Columbia, S.C., Nov. 30, 1936; s. Douglas Ralph and Olive (Odom) B.; B.S. in Elec. Engring., The Citadel, 1959; m. Shirly Ruth Blizzard, Dec. 28, 1956 (dec. Apr. 1969); children—Douglas R. III, Morris L.; m. 2d, Janice Rose Laski, Oct. 4, 1969; children—David T. Laski, Pamela J. Laski. Communications engr. NASA, 1959-61, with Apollo Spacecraft Program Office, Houston, 1961-—, chief project engr. Apollo Block II; Command and Service Modules, 1965-67, chief project engr. Apollo Block I and II Command and Service Modules, 1967-68, asst. chief CSM project engring. div., 1968-70; asst. program mgr. lunar surface elec. properties expt. program Raytheon Co., Sudbury, Mass., 1970-72; v.p. DRB Systems, Columbia, S.C., 1972-—. Served to 2d lt. AUS, 1959-60, Mem. Mensa, I.E.E.E. (subgroups on tech. mgmt., information systems), Nat. Rifle Assn., The Citadel Alumni Club. Baptist. Office: DRB Systems 2501 N Main St Columbia SC 29206

BROOME, EDWARD FRANKLIN, city ofcl.; b. Blythewood, S.C., June 6, 1907; s. Charles Fletcher and Johnnie Sarah (Wooten) B.; student S.C. State Fire Coll., 1935-36, Fla. State Fire Coll., 1951; m. Ruby Taylor, July 9, 1927; children—Edward H., Sarah Martha (Mrs. Robert Kerr), Charles F. Fire engr., Columbia, S.C., 1940-42, fire capt., 1942-45, bn. chief, 1945-49, 2d asst. chief, 1949-57, 1st asst. chief, 1957-62, fire chief, 1962-—. Recipient Appreciation award Jr. C. of C., 1964; named Fireman of the Year, Columbia C. of C., 1969; Letter of Commendation for working fire prevention Pres. Nixon, 1972; award for services rendered State of S.C., 1972. Mem. Internat., Southeastern assns. fire chiefs, Internat. Fire Service Tng. Assn. (mem. exec. bd. 1954-—), S.C. State Firemen's Assn. (pres. 1962), S.C. State Fire Chief's Assn. (pres. 1967). Methodist (supt. Sunday Sch. 1942-48). Mason (Shriner), Lion. Club: Civitan (Columbia). Home: 4808 Barber St Columbia SC 29203 Office: 1001 Senate St Columbia SC 29201

BROSMAN, PAUL WILLIAM, educator; b. Macon, Ga., Sept. 16, 1927; s. Paul William and Katherine (Lewis) B.; B.A., Tulane U., 1949, M.A., 1950; Ph.D. U. N.C., 1956; m. Margaret Cuneo, June 8, 1950 (dec.); m. 2d, Catharine Savage, Aug. 21, 1970; 1 dau., Katherine E. Asst. prof. fgn. langs. North Tex. State U., 1956-57, asso. prof., 1957-58; asst. prof. fgn. langs. La. State U., 1958-62, asso. prof., 1962-65; asso. prof. comparative linguistics Tulane U., New Orleans, 1965-66, prof., 1966-—. Served to lt. USMCR, 1950-52. Mem. Linguistic Soc. Am., Internat. Linguistic Assn., Societas Linguistica Europaea, Am. Oriental Soc., Phi Beta Kappa, Omicron Delta, Kappa, Sigma Chi. Home: 7834 Willow St New Orleans LA 70118

BROSS, JOHN ADAMS, govt. ofcl.; b. Chgo., Jan. 17, 1911; s. Mason and Isabel Foster (Adams) B.; student Chgo. Latin Sch., Groton Sch.; A.B., Harvard, 1933, LL.B., 1936; m. Priscilla Prince, June 1936; children—Wendy, John, Justine; m. 2d, Joanne Bass, Oct. 28, 1947; 1 son, Peter F. Admitted to N.Y. State bar, 1938; practiced in N.Y.C., 1936-42; asso. Parker & Duryee, N.Y.C., 1936-49, mem. firm, 1942-49; asst. gen. counsel U.S. High Commr. to Germany, 1949-51; U.S. govt. cons. fgn. affairs, 1951-57, 60-63; spl. adviser, coordinator Am. embassy, Bonn, Germany, 1957-60; dep. to dir. Central Intelligence for Nat. Intelligence Programs Evaluation, 1963-—. Staff mem. task force on nat. mil. establishment Hoover Commn., 1948. Served from 2d lt. to col., USAAF, 1942-46. Decorated Legion of Merit, Bronze Star; Order Brit. Empire; King Christian X Medal of Liberty. Mem. Assn. Bar City N.Y. (chmn. com. state legislation 1946-49), Council on Fgn. Relations N.Y. Clubs: River, Harvard (N.Y.C.). Home: 4501 Crest Lane McLean VA 22101

BROTTON, WILLIAM GLEASON, wood preserving co. exec.; b. Eufaula, Okla., Jan. 29, 1922; s. Thomas Edwin and Rowena (Gleason) B.; student Okla. A. and M. Coll., 1939-41; m. Elizabeth Moran, May, 22, 1943; children—William Danile, Sally Ann, Rebecca Jane. Lumber insp. Halsey Hardwood Co., Edenton, N.C., 1947-49; ind. lumber buyer Eastern N.C., 1949-52; pres. Milwork Lumber, Inc., Scotland Neck, N.C., 1952-64; pres. Carolina Wood Preserving Co., Scotland Neck, 1960-—, also dir. Served with USMCR, 1942-43, USNR, 1943-45. Decorated Air medal. Mem. Soc. Wood Preservers Am., N.C. (pres. 1967) Wood Preservers assns., V.F.W., Am. Legion, Scotland Neck Bus. Bur. Deomcrat. Baptist. Club: Scotfield Country (Scotland Neck). Home: 814 Church St Scotland Neck NC 27874 Office: E 17th St Scotland Neck NC 27874

BROUILLETTE, BILL, motel exec.; b. New York Mills, N.Y., June 22, 1930; s. Everett Andrew and Delores Margaret (Martin) B.; grad. high sch.; m. Mary Ruth Freeman, Dec. 12, 1965; children—Bill, Roy Andrew, Brandee Rene. Chef, Madison Co., Rome, N.Y., 1950-55; salesman Continental Baking Co., Utica, N.Y., 1955-59; motel mgr. Helmsley Spear Hospitality Cons. Div., N.Y.C., 1959-70; v.p., gen. mgr. Sheraton Motor Inn, Fort Myers, Fla., 1970-—; v.p. Pate Industries, Fort Myers, 1971-—; v.p. Am. Motor Inns, 1969-—. Cons. motel multiple property supervision. Mem. Tex. Tourist Council, 1970. Served with USMCR, 1948-50. Named mgr. year Helmsley Spear Hospitality Cons. Div., 1969-70. Mem. Fla. Hotel Motel Assn., Hotel Sales Mgrs. Assn., C. of C. (tourist com. 1961-63), Nat. Def. Transp. Assn., Bons Vi Vant, Sales and Marketing Exec. Elk. Clubs: El Antonio Country, Business and Professional Mens, University (San Antonio). Home: 2337 Kent Av Fort Myers FL 33901 Office: 8900 S Tamiami Trail Fort Myers FL 33901

BROURMAN, JACQUES, orch. condr.; b. Pitts.; student (scholar) Carnegie Inst. Tech., Juilliard Sch. Music. Former asst. condr. New Orleans Symphony, condr. Boise (Ida.) Symphony; condr. Charlotte (N.C.) Symphony Orch., 1967-—. Founder, Sun Valley Music Camp, Sugar Mountain Music Camp, Banner Elk, N.C., 1972; made tour of Japan conducting all major orchs., 1971. Home: 3048 Rustic Lane Charlotte NC 28210 Office: 827 East Blvd Charlotte NC 28203*

BROUSSARD, ERNIE PAUL, city ofcl.; b. Kaplan, La., Jan. 23, 1925; s. Paulite and Edmay (Clostio) B.; B.S., U. Southwestern La., 1948; student LaSalle Inst., 1949-50; m. Sylvia Audrey Sellers, Dec. 23, 1945; children—Susan (Mrs. C. Julius Meaux), Rebecca (Mrs. John Keith Lamm), Ernie Paul II, Virginia, Catherine, Scott, Kevin. Asst. mgr. dist. office Central La. Electric Co., Ville Platte, 1948-50; office mgr. M & L Constrn. Co., Kaplan, La., 1950-51; owner Estherwood Ins. Agy. (La.), 1951-—; mayor, Estherwood, 1954-—; dir. Kaplan State Bank (La.); sec.-treas., dir. Broussard Rice Mill, Inc., 1963-—, Midway Rice Drier, Inc., 1966-—, Morse Rice Drier, Inc. (La.), 1961-—, Broussard Farms, Inc., 1964-—. Pres., P.T.A. Estherwood, 1958-59; dir. civil def., Estherwood, 1954-—. Bd. dirs. Am. Legion Hosp., Crowley, 1950-—; bd. mgrs. People to People Goodwill Tour Europe and USSR, 1971. Served with USNR, 1943-46; CBI, PTO. Mem. La. Municipal Assn. (v.p. 1971), Greater Crowley C. of C., Am. Legion (bd. dirs. 1950-—), Roman Catholic. K.C. (4 deg.), Lion. Home and office: PO Box 8 Estherwood LA 70534

BROUSSARD, JAY R., state ofcl.; b. New Iberia, La., Dec. 22, 1920; ed. La. State U., U. Southwestern La.; m. Emma Joan Landry; 3 children. Dir. La. Art Commn., Baton Rouge, 1947-—; also painter; works exhibited Corcoran Gallery Art, Washington, Pa. Acad. Design, Butler Art Museum, Youngstown, O., Denver Art Mus., High Mus. Art, Atlanta, Isaac Delgado, others. Served with USAAF, World War II. Mem. Am. Assn. Museums, Am. Fedn. Arts, Nat. Trust Historic Preservation, Mus. Modern Art N.Y., La. Crafts Council, Baton Rouge Art League (hon.), La. Art and Artists Guild (hon.), La Watercolor Soc. (hon.), Gulf State Camera Clubs (hon.). Address: la Art Commn Old State Capitol Baton Rouge LA 70801

BROUSSARD, JOEL EARL, JR., dentist; b. Houston, July 29, 1938; s. Joel Earl and Hazel Virginia (Brisbois) B.; B.S., U. Tex., 1961, D.D.S., 1967; M.S. in Orthodontics, U. Tenn., 1969; m. Anita Louise McFarland, Sept. 4, 1959; children—Anissa Lynn, Joel Evan. Research chemist Pitts. Plate Glass, Corpus Christi, Tex., 1961-63; gen. practice dentistry, Memphis, 1967-69; gen. practice orthodontics, Austin, 1969-—. Mem. Am. Dental Assn., Am. Assn. Orthodontists, Southwest Soc. Orthodontists, Omicron Kappa Upsilon, Delta Sigma Delta. Baptist. Rotarian. Home: 4603 Arapahoe Trail Austin TX 78745 Office: 4407 Manchaca Rd Austin TX 78745

BROUSSARD, SEXTON EDDIE, dentist; b. Lafayette, La., Nov. 16, 1926; s. Eddie and Elodie Mae (Broussard) B.; A.A., Lamar Jr. Coll., 1948; B.S., U. Houston, 1950; D.D.S., U. Tex., 1954; m. Marcelette Sandidge, Sept. 2, 1949. Pvt. practice dentistry, Houston, 1954-69, Rusk, Tex., 1969-—; dental cons. Rusk St. Hosp., 1969-72, staff dentist, 1972-—. Chmn. bd. dirs. Northshore YMCA, Houston, 1963. Served with AUS, 1944-46. Mem. Am., Tex. dental assns., E. Tex. Dist. Dental Soc., Tex. Assn. Instl. and Pub. Health Dentists. Clubs: Bayshore Rod, Reel and Gun (v.p. 1956-60), Sportsman of Texas (dir.). Home: Rekiaw TX 75785 Office: 203 E 7th St Rusk TX 75785

BROUSSARD, THADDEUS ARLINGTON, architect; b. Baton Rouge, July 4, 1918; s. Allen Benjamin and Adelia (Stephens) B.; B.S., La. State U., 1941; m. Lillian Ann Champagne, Nov. 19, 1941; children—Ann Elizabeth, Thad Stephens. Pvt. archtl. practice, Baton Rouge, 1948-—. Served to maj. with AUS, 1941-46. Mem. A.I.A., Am. Registered Architects, Nat. Council Archtl. Registration Bds. Democrat. Roman Catholic. Lion (pres. 1962-63). Prin. works include Scotlandville Sr. High Sch., Baton Rouge, McKinley Sr. High Sch., Baton Rouge, Dramatic and Fine Arts Bldg. at So. U., Baton Rouge. Home: 4644 Whitehaven St Baton Rouge LA 70808 Office: 1157 Laurel St Baton Rouge LA 70821

BROWER, JOHN HAROLD, educator; b. Augusta, Me., June 8,, 1940; s. Auburn E. and Lurana C. (Van Doren) B.; B.S., U. Me., 1962; M.S., U. Mass., 1964, Ph.D., 1965; m. Moonyean A. Smallidge, Sept. 1960; children—Ian T., Brook D. Vis. research asso. Brookhaven Nat. Lab., Upton, N.Y., 1961-65; research entomologist Agrl. Research Sta., U.S. Agr. Dept., Savannah, Ga., 1965-—; asst. prof. entomology U. Ga., Athens, 1971-72; prof. biology Armstrong State Coll., Savannah, 1965-72. Winner Me. Westinghouse Sci. Talent Search, 1958. Mem. Entomol. Soc. Am., Canadian, Ga. entomol. socs., Ecol. Soc. Am., Radiation Research Soc. Club: Savannah Stamp. Home: 3 Althea Pky Savannah GA 31405 Office: PO Box 5125 Savannah GA 31403

BROWER, WALTER JORDAN, physician; b. Birmingham, Ala., Feb. 5, 1921; s. Walter Scott and Elizabeth (Jordan) B.; B.A., U. Ala., 1942; M.D., Duke, 1947; m. Miriam Timmons, Jan. 20, 1949; children—William Jordan, Carl Timmons, Caroline Elizabeth, Franklin Perry. Rotating intern at Jefferson-Hillman Hosp., 1947-48, resident in radiology, 1948-51; instr. radiology Med. Coll. Ala., 1948-51; pvt. practice radiology, Birmingham, Ala., 1955-—; dir. dept. radiology VA Hosp., 1956-57; cons. radiologist Cullman, Shelby Meml., Blount Meml., Chilton hosps.; also clin. asst. prof. Med. Coll. Ala., 1957-—. Served from pvt. to pfc. Med. Dept., AUS, 1944-46; from lt. to capt. M.C., USAF, 1951-55. Mem. Am. Coll. Radiology (chpt. pres. 1969-70; councillor 1971-—), Radiol. Soc. of N.Am., So. Radiol. Conf. (charter), Am., So. med. assns., Ala., Jefferson County med. socs., Ala. Cattleman's Assn., Nat. Skeet Shooting Assn. (life), Arlington Hist. Assn., So. Commemorative Soc., Sons Confederate Vets., Soc. War 1812, Nat. Rifle Assn., Delta Kappa Epsilon, Alpha Kappa Kappa. Presbyn. Mason (Shriner). Club: Relay House (charter). Home: Hayden Route 2 Bangor AL 35079 Office: 1025 S 18th St Birmingham AL 35205

BROWN, AARON CLIFTON, lawyer, chancellor; b. Murray, Ky., Oct. 16, 1911; s. Ed and Minnie (Cotham) B.; student U. Tenn., 1931-32; LL.B., Cumberland U., 1936; m. Viria Alice Bell, Mar. 11, 1939; children—Aaron Clifton, Gerald Bell. Admitted to Tenn. bar, 1936; since practiced in Paris, Tenn.; master chancery ct. 1946-52; mayor, Paris, 1955-59; founder firm Brown, Brown & Guinn, 1965-—; chancellor 8th chancery Div. Tenn., 1968-—. Pres., Tenn. Constl. Conv., 1965; chmn. Draft Bd. Henry County, 1946-—. Mem. Tenn. Senate, 1966-68. Served with USNR, 1964-66. Mem. Bar Assn. Tenn., Am., Paris-Henry County bar assns., Am. Judicature Soc., Am. Trial Lawyers Assn., V.F.W. Methodist. Lion (Paris pres. 1957). Home: 1212 Chickasaw St Paris TN 38242 Office: 302 Commercial Bank Bldg Paris TN 38242

BROWN, ALBERT, scientist; b. Scranton, Pa., Feb. 3, 1919; s. Albert and Annie (Smyser) B.; B.A., Wesleyan U., 1940; M.A., Columbia, 1950; student Harvard, 1940-41; m. Dolores A. Dahl, Sept. 21, 1956; 1 son, Michael. Research asst., lectr. Columbia U., N.Y.C., 1947-50; mem. tech. staff Bell Telephone Labs., N.Y.C., 1951-59; dep. dir. research and devel. FAA, Washington, 1959-64; mgr. transp. and urban affairs dept. Planning Research Corp., Washington, 1966-71; dir. TCR Service, Inc., 1971-—, R.S.A. Internat. Ltd., 1972-—. Cons., Govt. of Israel, Dir. U.S. Bur. of Budget. Served to lt. comdr. USNR, 1941-46. Mem. Operations Research Soc. Am. (chmn. transp. sci. sect. 1972-73), Am. Phys. Soc., Sigma Xi. Home: 3023 Normanstone Terrace NW Washington DC 20008

BROWN, ALEX SMITH, JR., indsl. engr.; b. Tennille, Ga., Nov. 23, 1922; s. Alex Smith and Lillian (Daley) B.; B.S., The Citadel, 1947; grad. exec. program U. N.C. Sch. Bus. Adminstrn., 1971; m. Nancy Cockman, Dec. 4, 1965; 1 dau., Ellen Daley. Indsl. engr. Dan River Mills, Danville, Va., 1947-49; field engr. Am. Asso. Cons., 1949-56, chief engr., 1956-58, v.p., chief engr., dir., 1958-60; chief indsl. engr. Burlington Industries, Inc. Greensboro, N.C., 1960-—. Trustee Davison Sch., Atlanta. Served to capt. AUS, 1943-46. Mem. Soc. for Advancement of Mgmt. (past pres., v.p.), Am. Inst. Indsl. Engrs., Assn. Citadel Men (dir. 1969-70). Republican. Baptist. Club: Greensboro Country. Home: 2307 Danbury Rd Greensboro NC 27408 Office: 3330 W Friendly Av Greensboro NC 27402

BROWN, ALGIE DEE, lawyer; b. Waldo, Ark., Mar. 8, 1910; s. John Spence and Lodie (Bryan) B.; A.B., Centenary Coll., 1934; student Tex. U., 1932, La. State U. Law Sch., 1935-36; m. Hazel Turner, Dec. 27, 1947; children—Bryan Turner, Curtis Seibert. Admitted to La. bar, 1937, since practiced in Shreveport; mem. firm Brown & Dormer. Mem. La. Ho. of Reps., 1948-72; mem. Shreveport Democratic Exec. Com., 1939-—. Served as lt. USNR, 1943-46. Mem. Am., La., Shreveport bar assn., Am. Judicature Soc., Am. Legion, V.F.W. Baptist (bd. dirs.). Elk. Home: 331 McCormick Pl Shreveport LA 71104 Office: Lane Bldg Shreveport LA 71101

BROWN, ARTHUR EDWARD, physician; b. Dallas, Oct. 24, 1905; s. James Edward and Sarah (Foster) B.; B.S., Birmingham So. Coll., 1927; M.D., Northwestern U., 1931; m. Dorothy Parson, Aug. 15, 1931. Pvt. practice medicine, Columbus, Miss., 1934-42, 46-—. Pres. Columbus Community Chest, 1956-57; pres. Miss. div. Am. Cancer Soc., 1970-71. Served with USNR, 1942-46. Fellow A.C.S.; mem. Miss. State Med. Assn. (pres. 1971-72), Southeastern Surg. Congress. Club: Columbus Country (pres. 1950-52). Home: 1115 7th St N Columbus MS 39701 Office: 824 2d Av N Columbus MS 39701

BROWN, AUGUSTUS BART, geologist, rancher; b. Cocoanut Grove, Fla., Apr. 3, 1914; s. Jamot and Margaret Bart (Berger) B.; B.S., Yale, 1937; m. Jenilee Knight, July 14, 1938; children—Bart Berger, Jennifer Knight Alexander. Field geologist Hudnall & Pirtle, Tyler, Tex., 1937-38; geologist Mudge Oil Co., Dallas, 1938-40, chief geologist, 1940-42; mng. partner Hudnall, Pirtle & Brown, Dallas and San Antonio, 1946-54; engaged in petroleum exploration & investment, also ranching, Dallas, 1954-—; asso. Bass & Vessels, Bass, Vessels & Brown, McAllen Tex. and Denver, 1954-57; asso. Wood Bros. & Langham, Wood Bros., Mission, Tex., 1957-68; v.p. Berger Land Co., Denver, 1968-—; dir. Millican Oil Co., Tyler, Tex. Served to lt. USNR, 1942-46. Mem. Am. Assn. Petroleum Geologists, Am. Inst. Mining, Metall. and Petroleum Engrs., Dallas Geol. Soc. Clubs: Dallas Petroleum, Northwood. Home: 8801 Briarwood Lane Dallas TX 75209 Office: 8801 Briarwood Lane Dallas TX 75209

BROWN, BALLEY, U.S. judge; b., 1917; A.B., U. Mich.; LL.B. Harvard. Admitted to bar, 1941; now chief U.S. judge Western Dist. Tenn. Mem. Am. Bar Assn. Address: US District Court Memphis TN 38103

BROWN, BOLAR AUSTIN, accountant, ret. judge; b. Lampasas, Tex., Feb. 10, 1905; s. John Anderson and Mary (Dignan) B.; corr. course in accounting LaSalle Extension U., 1931-35; m. Georganna True, June 5, 1928; children—Bolar Austin, Richard True, Vonnabeth, Doris Ann, Mary Nell. Bookkeeper R. E. Stubbs, hardware and implements, Blanco, Tex., 1924-25, Cage Hardware & Implement Co., also credit mgr., 1926-34; clk. Kleberg County, Tex., 1935-52, county judge, 1953-70; dir. Citizens Standard Life Ins. Co., Kingsville First Savs. and Loan Assn. Mem., treas. Kingsville Salvation Army Service Unit. Mem. Nat. Assn. County Ofcls., Tex., S. Tex. (past pres.) assns. county judges commrs. Democrat. Methodist. Club: Kingsville Country. Home: Box 1602 Kingsville TX 78363 Office: E Kleberg Av Kingsville TX 78363

BROWN, BRADFORD ELLSWORTH, ecologist, educator; b. Worcester, Mass., Apr. 1, 1938; s. Horace E. and Josephine (Piper) B.; student Harvard, 1955-56; B.S., Cornell U., 1960; M.S., Auburn U., 1962; Ph.D., Okla. State U., 1969; m. Barbara Jean Moalli, Sept. 7, 1957; children—Jeffery Paul, Gregory Wayne, Douglas Bradford. Asst. in fish culture Auburn U., Ala., 1960-61; fisheries bio-statistician U.S. Bur. Comml. Fisheries Biol. Lab., Woods Hole, Mass., 1962-65; asst. prof. zoology Okla. State U., Stillwater, 1965-—, asst. leader Okla. Coop. Fishery Unit, U.S. Bur. Sport Fisheries and Wildlife, 1965-—. Mem. Okla. state adv. com. U.S. Commn. on Civil Rights, 1967-—. Served with AUS, 1956. Mem. Am. Fisheries Soc., Okla. Acad. Sci. (sect. vice chmn. 1969-70), Am. Assn. U. Profs., Am. Civil Liberties Union, N.A.A.C.P. Conglist. Home: 717 S Willis St Stillwater OK 74074

BROWN, BRADFORD S(TEARNS), statis. cons.; b. Newton, Mass., Jan. 16, 1931; s. John Fiske and Dorothy (Dudley) B.; A.B., Harvard, 1953; M.S., U. Ill., 1954; children—Rachel Elizabeth, Abigail Cathryn, Oliver Fiske. Asso. service engr. E. I. duPont de Nemours & Co., Niagara Falls, N.Y., 1956-59, statistician, Newark, 1959-63, sr. statistician, Newark, Del. and Old Hickory, Tenn., 1963-68, cons., Old Hickory, 1968-—. Pres., Fairfield Crest Civic Assn., Newark, Del., 1964. Democratic committeeman, Newark, Del., 1963-66. Served with AUS, 1954-56. Mem. Am. Statis. Assn., Am. Soc. Quality Control (local chmn. 1971-72), Mensa. Unitarian-Universalist. Home: 300 Kate St H-24 PO Box 232 Madison TN 37115 Office: ESD Computer Group DuPont Co Old Hickory TN 37138

BROWN, CALVIN ANDERSON, JR., physician; b. Athens, Ga., Sept. 13, 1931; s. Calvin Anderson and Ruth (Haynes) B.; B.S., Morehouse Coll., 1952; M.D., Meharry Med. Coll., 1958; m. Joy San Walker, Dec. 31, 1953; children—Joi Sanne, Sanna Gai. Intern, Hubbard Hosp., Nashville, 1958-59; pvt. practice medicine, specializing in family practice, Atlanta, 1959—; dir. Atlanta Southside Comprehensive Health Center, 1968; med. dir. Pineview Convalescent Center, Atlanta, 1968—; mem. staff Holy Family Hosp., Atlanta, Hughes Spalding Hosp., Atlanta; chief staff Martin Luther King, Jr. Nursing Center, Atlanta, 1971; chief physician Fulton County Jails, Atlanta, 1971; asst. prof. dept. preventive medicine Med. Sch., Emory U., 1968-69. Mem. task force on cardio-vascular disease, hypertension and diabetes Ga. Regional Med. Program, 1971. Pres. Nat. Alumni Assn. Morehouse Coll., 1962—; trustee Morehouse Coll. Served with AUS, 1952-54. Mem. Atlanta Med. Assn. (pres. 1968), Alpha Phi Alpha. Baptist (trustee 1969—). Home: 2947 Oldknow Dr NW Atlanta GA 30318 Office: 1475 Pryor Rd SW Atlanta GA 30315

BROWN, C(LAUDE) HAROLD, lawyer; b. Mendenhall, Miss., July 28, 1931; s. Claude S. and Mildred (Bush) B.; B.B.A., Vanderbilt U., 1957; LL.B., U. Tex., 1960; m. Carol Wynn, June 14, 1957; children—Tracey Gwen, Terry Lynne, Allison Anne, Harold Allen. Admitted to Tex. bar, 1960; partner firm Wynn, Irby, Brown, McConnico & Mack, Ft. Worth, 1960—. Dir. Clardy Mfg. Co., Ft. Worth, Kinro Industries, Inc., Ft. Worth. Bd. dirs. A.J. and Jessie Duncan Found., Ft. Worth, Edna Gladney Home, Ft. Worth. Served with AUS, 1953-55. Mem. State Bar Tex., Am., Ft. Worth-Tarrant County (pres. 1962) bar assns., Alpha Tau Omega, Phi Delta Phi. Republican. Mem. Disciples of Christ (bd. dirs.). Mason (Shriner), Rotarian. Clubs: Fort Worth Vanderbilt (pres. 1966), American Brittany (dir.). Home: 3470 Sageerest Terrace Fort Worth TX 76109 Office: 1300 Schick Bldg Fort Worth TX 76102

BROWN, CLAUDE LAMAR, physician; b. Mobile, Ala., Mar. 12, 1923; s. Claude Lamar and Pauline (Johanna) B.; B.S., Tulane U., 1943, M.D., 1945; m. Vernice Brown, Aug. 16, 1968; children—(by previous marriage) Claude Lamar III, Paul William, Christianna Lori. Intern City Hosp., Mobile, Ala., 1945-46; resident psychiatry Menninger Found. Sch. Psychiatry, Topeka, 1948-51; practice medicine, specializing in psychiatry, Mobile, 1951—; mem. staff Mobile Infirmary, Providence, Gen. Drs. hosps., Mobile. Cons., USPHS, 1951, Ala. Rehab. and Crippled Children Service, 1951—; chmn. Ala. State Mental Health Bd., 1967-69. Served to lt. (j.g.) M.C., USNR, 1946-48. Diplomate psychiatry Am. Bd. Psychiatry and Neurology. Fellow Am., So. psychiat. assns.; mem. A.M.A., Ala. State, So., Pan Am. med. assns., Ala. Acad. Psychiatry and Neurology, Mobile County Med. Soc. (pres. 1962). Rotarian. Home: 4951 Winslow Dr Mobile AL 36608 Office: 176 Louiselle St Mobile AL 36607

BROWN, CONNELL JEAN, educator; b. Everton, Ark., Mar. 6, 1924; s. Clarence Jackson and Winnie Dee (Trammel) B.; Student Ark. Poly Coll., 1941; B.S.A., U. Ark., 1948; M.S., Okla State U., 1950, Ph.D., 1956; m. Erma Dexter Taylor, May 19, 1946; children—Craig J., Mark A. Graduate asst. Okla. State U., Stillwater, 1948-50, 53-54; asst. prof. dept. animal sci. U. Ark., Fayetteville, 1950-53, 54-57, asso. prof., 1957-62; prof., 1962—. Cons. on ranch mgmt. and breeding problems; judge beef cattle, state, dist. regional fairs. Served with USAAF, 1943-46. Fellow A.A.A.S.; mem. Am. Soc. Animal Sci., Genetics Soc. Am., Ark. Angus Assn. (bd. dirs. 1965—), Alpha Zeta, Sigma Xi, Gamma Sigma Delta. Methodist (bd. stewards 1967-60, trustee 1972—, supt. Sunday sch. 1965-70). Kiwanian (bd. dirs. 1969—). Contbr. articles in profl. jours. Home: 1616 Wedington St Fayetteville AR 72701

BROWN, CONRAD NAGEL, mfg. co. exec.; b. Bartlesville, Okla., Mar. 28, 1934; s. Conrad Nagel and Leiah Lucille (Lawless) B.; student Okla. State U., 1952-53; B.S., U. Kan., 1958; m. Angelica Velilla Robertin, June 12, 1959; children—Conrad Nagel III, Ana Melisa, David. Pvt. archtl. practice, Tulsa, 1962-63, Guayama, P.R., 1968-70; with Phillips Petroleum Co., Bartlesville, 1963-68; gen. mgr. Modular Bldg. Systems Corp., Salinas, P.R., 1971—; pres. Brown Assos., Inc., designers, Guayama, 1969—. Served to lt. (j.g.) USNR, 1958-62. Mem. A.I.A. Clubs: Aquirre Country, Nautico de Guayama (dir.). Address: Box 1046 Guayama PR 00654

BROWN, DONALD ATHERTON, distbr.; b. Medford, Mass., Dec. 15, 1905; s. Edward Newton and Mabel (Atherton) B.; B.S., Bowdoin Coll., 1927; m. Adele Sadler, Mar. 12, 1927; children—Cynthia (Mrs. John H. Gillmore), Judith (Mrs. Gene B. Fechner), David G. Asst. sec. Stone & Webster Service Corp., Boston, 1928-30; statistician Baton Rouge Electric Co., 1930-38, ins. dir. 1938-42; asst. supt. Royal-Eagle-Globe Indemnity Co., N.Y.C., 1942-44; field mgr. Standard Research Cons., N.Y.C., 1944-49; v.p., sec. treas. dir. Gen. Telephone System, N.E. Cos., Johnstown, N.Y., 1949-62; sec., treas. Gen. Telephone of Fla., Tampa, 1962-70, ret.; distbr. Amway, 1971—. Former vice chmn. dir. Johnstown (N.Y.) chpt. A.R.C., 1956-62; adv. bd. Fulton County Salvation Army; trustee Johnstown Meml. Day Assn. Mem. Ind. Telephone Pioneer Assn., Am. Soc. Corp. Secs., Am. Soc. Ins. Mgmt., Beta Theta Pi. Presbyn. (past trustee, elder). Mason. Kiwanian. Club: Sunshine Pioneer. Home: 207 S West Shore Blvd Tampa FL 33609

BROWN, DOROTHY LAVINIA, physician; b. Phila., Jan. 7, 1919; d. Frank Brown and Emma Brown Bates, foster parents Samuel Wesley and Lola Redmon; B.A., Bennett Coll., Greensboro, N.C., 1941; M.D., Meharry Med. Coll., Nashville, 1948; 1 adopted dau., Lola Denise. Intern Harlem Hosp., N.Y.C., 1948-49; surg. residency Hubbard Hosp., Nashville, 1949-54; clin. prof. surgery Meharry Med. Coll.; chief surgery Riverside Hosp.; attending surgeon George Hubbard, Gen., Nashville hosps. Mem. Tenn. Ho. Reps. Trustee Bennett Coll. Fellow A.C.S.; mem. A.M.A., Am. Assn. U. Profs., Nat. Council Negro Women, Nashville Acad. Medicine, R. F. Boyd Med. Soc., Nat. Med. Assn., Assn. Am. Med. Colls., Negro Bus. and Profl. Women's Clubs, Internat. Platform Assn., N.A.A.C.P., Delta Sigma Theta, Kappa Delta Pi. Home: 3109 Centennial Blvd Nashville TN 37209

BROWN, DUANE HOUGHTON, financial exec.; b. Washington, Sept. 14, 1933; s. Frank Stern, Jr. and Ella (Ayers) B.; A.A., Mars Hill Coll., 1952; B.S., U. Richmond, 1954; m. Barbara Kimes Smith, Jan. 25, 1958; children—Kimberly Ann, Lynn Houghton. Sr. accountant Price Waterhouse & Co., Washington, 1957-63, A. M. Pullen & Co., Washington, 1963-64; financial asst. to exec. v.p. Barber & Ross Co., Washington, 1964-65; bus. mgr. Washington Ednl. TV Assn., Washington, 1965-68; asst. controller Leasco Systems & Research Corp., 1968-69; adminstrv. mgr. Peat, Marwick, Mitchell & Co., Washington, 1969-70; mem. treas. staff IMF, Washington, 1970—. Cons. Washington Journalism Center, Translation Cons. Ltd., Arlington, Va. Mem. City of Alexandria Adv. Tax Commn., 1967-68; mem. Alexandria Adv. Planning Commn., 1969-72. Republican candidate city councilman, Alexandria, Va., 1967. Bd. dirs. Alexandria Hosp., Children and Youth Confs. Served with AUS, 1954-57. Mem. Am., D.C. insts. C.P.A.'s, Nat. Assn. Accountants. Baptist (deacon). Mason. Home: 2906 Cameron Mills Rd Alexandria VA 22302 Office: 19th and H Sts NW Washington DC 20431

BROWN, DUDLEY EARL, JR., physician; b. Berryville, Va., Apr. 10, 1928; s. Dudley Earl and Rose Lee (Costello) B.; B.A., Washington and Lee U., 1949; M.D., Med. Coll. Va., 1953; m. Lelia Adrienne Motley, June 22, 1953; children—Jane, David, Kevin. Intern Naval Hosp., Portsmouth, Va., 1953-54, resident neuropsychiatry, 1957-60; chief neuropsychiat. unit Marine Corps Recruit Depot, Parris Island, S.C., 1960-65, U.S. Naval Hosp., Beaufort, S.C., 1960-64; dir. tng. Neuropsychiat. Treatment and Tng. Center, Naval Hosp., Phila., 1964-65, asst. chief, 1964-65, chief, 1965-70; head neuropsychiatry br. Bur. Medicine and Surgery, Dept. of Navy, Washington, 1970—; asst. prof. clin. psychiatry U. Pa.; dir. intern tng. Naval Hosp., Phila. Active Boy Scouts Am. Fellow Am., Pa. psychiat. assns., A.C.P., Am. Coll. Psychiatrists, Washington Psychiat. Soc.; mem. A.M.A., Phila. Psychiat. Soc., Aerospace Med. Assn., Assn. Mil. Surgeons U.S., Alpha Epsilon Delta. Baptist. Home: 2415 Black Cap Lane Reston VA 22070 Office: Bur Medicine and Surgery Dept of Navy Washington DC 20390

BROWN, EDGAR ALLAN, lawyer, state senator; b. nr. Aiken, S.C., July 11, 1888; s. Augustus Abraham and Elizabeth (Howard) B.; student Graniteville Acad., 1902-06; LL.B. (hon.), Clemson U., 1955; L.H.D., Med. U. S.C., 1964; LL.D., U.S.C., 1972;; m. Annie Love Sitgreaves, Dec. 30, 1913; 1 dau., Emily McBurney (Mrs. Richard M. Jeffries, Jr.). Ct. reporter 2d S.C. Circuit, 1908-18; admitted to S.C. bar 1910; sr. mem. Brown, Jefferies & Boulware, Barnwell, S.C.; dir. Bankers Trust of S.C. Mem., past chmn. bd. mgrs. Council of State Govts.; chmn., gen. counsel Clark's Hill Authority of S.C.; mem. State Budget and Control Bd. Del.-at-large Nat. Dem. Conv., N.Y.C., 1924, Phila., 1948, Chgo., 1952, 56, 68, Los Angeles, 1960, Atlantic City, 1964; candidate for U.S. Senate, 1926, 38; mem. nat. exec. com. Dem. Party of S.C., 1953-70; chmn. county Dem. exec. com., mem. state Dem. exec. com., 1914—; mem. Ho. of Reps., S.C., 1921-26; mem. S.C. Senate, 1929—, pres. pro tem, also chmn. senate finance com., 1942—. Life mem., pres. bd. trustees Clemson Coll. Mem. Am., S.C. (former pres.) bar assns., Carolina Motor Club (former chmn. bd.). Methodist (trustee). Mason (Shriner). Home: Main St Barnwell SC 29812 Office: Bankers Trust Bldg Barnwell SC 29812

BROWN, EDGAR WILLIAM, JR., banker, industrialist; b. Orange, Tex., Feb. 10, 1894; s. Edgar William and Carrie (Lutcher) B.; ed. pvt. schs.; m. Gladys Slade, July 23, 1915 (dec. Sept. 1959); children—Edgar William III, John S., L. Slade, Charles E.; m. 2d, Helen Elizabeth Smith, Nov. 20, 1960. With Lutcher & Moore Cypress Lumber Co., Ltd. (La.), 1917—, pres., 1946-64, chmn. bd., 1964—, also dir.; chmn. bd., pres. v.p., dir. Dibert, Stark & Brown Cypress Lumber Co., Donner, La., 1920-38, liquidator, 1938—; pres., dir. Higman Towing Co., Orange, 1922-59, Levingston Shipbldg. Co., Orange, 1933-46; v.p., dir. Vinton Petroleum Co., Orange, 1925-67; chmn. bd., pres., v.p.; dir. Brown Paper Mill Co., Inc., Monroe, La., 1922-55; chmn. bd., pres., dir. Orange Nat. Bank, 1928-64; organizer, chmn. bd., dir. County Nat. Bank, Orange, 1959—; chmn. bd., dir. Gulfport Shipbldg. Co., Port Arthur, Tex., 1963-70. Chmn., sec., purchasing agt., commr. Orange Wharf and Dock Commn., 1928-47; founder, bd. dirs. Orange Indsl. Devel. Com., 1946-52; mem. adv. bd., dir. Houston Livestock Show and Rodeo; chmn. bd., pres., gen. chmn., dir. Bill Williams Charity Capon Dinner Assn.; councilor Tex. A. and M. U. Research Found.; chmn., life mem. bd. dirs. Orange County chpt. A.R.C.; life mem. Orange County Meml. Hosp. Trustee Linden Fund com. Meth. Homes for Older People, Orange; mem. Intracoastal Canal Assn. La. and Tex. Methodist (trustee, trustor Slade Meml. Found.). Home: Linden-Pinehurst Ranch Orange TX 77630 Office: County Nat Bank Bldg PO Box 400 Orange TX 77630

BROWN, EDWIN RANDOLPH, editor, trade assn. exec.; b. Page, W.Va., Jan. 21, 1917; s. Chilton Eustace and Effie (Hill) B.; A.B., Marshall U., 1941; m. Helen Lucile Gravis, Apr. 9, 1944; children—Edwin Randolph, Sarah Lou, Elizabeth Gravis. Reporter, editor Huntington (W.Va.), Pub. Co., 1938-41; reporter, radio news editor, copy editor WORZ, also Orlando (Fla.) Sentinel, 1946-49; mng. editor Orlando Star, 1949-53; exec. sec. Central Fla. chpt. Asso. Gen. Contractors, Orlando, 1954—; free-lance writer, editor, 1954—; pub. Fla. Ind. Automobile Dealers Assn. Jours., Orlando, 1960—; exec. sec. Fla. Ind. Automobile Dealers Assn., Orlando, 1960—. Bd. dirs. Fla. Tb and Respiratory Disease Assn., 1949—; pres. Orange County Tb Assn., 1965; trustee Central Fla. Tb and Respiratory Disease, Assn., 1966—. Served with USAAF, 1942-45. Mem. Fla. Soc. Assn. Execs., Alpha Psi Omega. Democrat. Episcopalian. Home: 22 E Vanderbilt St Orlando FL 32804

BROWN, FREDERICK RAYMOND, govt. ofcl.; b. Peoria, Ill., Feb. 15, 1912; s. Lyman Harrison and Mary Ann (Weber) B.; B.S. in Civil Engring., U. Ill., 1934; m. Louise Ferry, June 10, 1936; children—Sandra (Mrs. Thomas N. Swilley), Frederick Raymond, Roger Alan. Chief hydrodynamics br. Waterways Expt. Sta., Vicksburg, Miss., 1934-61, chief nuclear effects div., 1961-63, asst. tech. dir., 1963-69, tech. dir., 1969—. Chmn., Vicksburg City Planning Commn., 1963—. Recipient Meritorious Civilian Service award Dept. Army, 1947, 69. Registered profl. engr., Miss. Mem. Am. Soc. C.E., Nat. Soc. Profl. Engrs., Soc. Am. Mil. Engrs. Rotarian. Home: 105 Stonewall Rd Vicksburg MS 39180 Office: PO Box 631 Vicksburg MS 39180

BROWN, GEORGE BOYLSTON, educator; M.A. in Musicology, Eastman Sch. Music, U. Rochester, 1935. Prof. music Southwestern La. U. Address: Dept Music Southwestern La U Lafayette LA 70501*

BROWN, GEORGE RUFUS, engr.; b. Belton, Tex., May 12, 1898; s. Riney Louis and Lucy Wilson (King) B.; student Rice Inst., Houston, 1918-20; M.E., Colo. Sch. Mines, 1922; LL.B. (hon.), Southwestern U., 1958; m. Alice Pratt, Nov. 25, 1925; children—Nancy Nelson (Mrs. Alfred Walter Negley), Alice Maconda (Mrs. Ralph Sturges O'Connor), Isabel Anne Wilson. Formerly chmn bd. Tex. Eastern Transmission Corp., Houston, now dir.; with Brown & Root, Inc., Houston, 1924—, exec. v.p., 1930-63, pres., 1963-65, chmn. bd., 1965—; dir. La. Land & Exploration Corp., Internat. Tel. & Tel. Corp., Halliburton Co., Southland Paper Co., Inc., First City Nat. Bank. Ret. chmn. bd. trustees Rice U. Episcopalian. Home: 3363 Inwood Dr Houston TX 75201 Office: PO Box 3 Houston TX 75201

BROWN, GERALD, lawyer; b. Piggott, Ark., Aug. 19, 1920; B.A., U. Ark., 1949, J.D., 1951. Admitted to Ark. bar, 1951; now mem. firm Kirsch, Cathey, Brown and Goodwin, Paragould, Ark. Mem. Statue Revision Commn., State of Ark. Mem. Greene-Clay County (pres. 1961), Northeast Ark., Ark., Am. bar assns. Address: 206 W Emerson St Paragould AR 72450*

BROWN, HARLAN CRAIG, librarian; b. Cleve., Jan. 26, 1906; s. Edgar Dwight and Harriet J. (Weakley) B.; A.B., U. Minn., 1930, B.S., 1931; A.M., U. Mich., 1935; m. Helen Abel, June 16, 1936. Asst. librarian S.D. State Coll., 1931-34; gen. service asst. U. Mich. Library, 1935-36; circulation librarian N.C. State Coll., 1936-39, librarian State Coll. Agr. and Engring., 1939-64; asso. dir. D. H. Hill Library, N.C. State U. at Raleigh, 1964-71, dir. emeritus, 1971—. Served to capt. AUS, 1942-46. Mem. S.D. (v.p. 1933-34), N.C. (v.p. 1946-48, pres. 1949-51). Southeastern, Am. library assns., Phi Kappa Phi. Democrat. Unitarian. Home: 3217 Merriman Av Raleigh NC 27607

BROWN, HENRY, chem. co. exec.; b. Charleston, S.C., Jan. 25, 1909; s. Charles and Clara (Rashbaum) B.; student U. N.C., 1928-30; m. Juanita Beatrice Burnstein, July 14, 1946; children—Henry Stephen, Charles Roger. Asst. store mgr. Furchgott's Dept. Store, Charleston, 1930-36; asst. store mgr. Kline's Dept. Store, Atlanta, 1936-41; state sales mgr. Am. Beauty Products Co., Richmond, Va., 1946-47; mgr., partner Va. Jewelry Store, Richmond, 1947-49; sr. v.p. sales Momar, Inc., Atlanta, 1949—, also dir. Bd. dirs. YMCA, 1957; founder, bd. dirs. Atlanta chpt. Muscular Dystrophy Assn., nat. v.p., 1953-63. Served with AUS, 1942-46; ETO. Decorated Bronze Star medal. Named Salesman of Year, Momar, Inc., 1966; recipient Sales Exec. Trophy, 1972, Exec. Sales award of Quarter Century, 1972. Mem. Res. Officers Assn., Ret. Officers Assn., Northside Bus. Assn. (dir. 1971, pres. 1972-73). Clubs: Sertoma (v.p. 1957), Standard, Fort McPherson Officers (Atlanta). Home: 4407 Jett Rd NW Atlanta GA 30327 Office: 1830 Ellsworth Dr NW Atlanta GA 30318

BROWN, HENRY S, labor union exec.; b. Pitts., Oct. 24, 1920; s. Stanley J. and Sophie B.; student San Antonio Coll., 1951, St. Mary's U., 1952, trade union program Harvard, 1956; m. Sophie E. Wegman, Sept. 30, 1939; children—Henry S., Gerald A., Sophie Eileen (Mrs. McCoy). With Nu-Way Plumbing Co., 1944-46, Shafer Plumbing Co., 1944-46; bus. agt. Plumbers and Pipefitters Local 142, San Antonio, Tex., 1946-53, 59-61; legislative dir., edn. dir. Tex. State Fedn. Labor, 1953-59; pres. Tex. AFL-CIO, Austin, 1961—; v.p. pub. relations Am. Income Life Ins. Co. Mem. labor mgmt. panel U.S. Govt. Fed. Mediation and Conciliation Service, 1965-68; mem. Nat. Adv. Commn. on Vocational and Tech. Edn., 1969; Tex. labor rep. U.S. Treasury Dept. Bond Sales Program; mem. Tex. Occupational Safety Adv. Com., 1967-69. Served with AUS. Mem. Harvard Alumni Assn., 2d Div. Assn. Home: 1411 Sunshine Dr San Antonio TX 78228 Office: PO Box 208 Waco TX 76703

BROWN, HOYT WILLIAM, JR., engring. co. exec.; b. Brunswick, Ga., Apr. 8, 1923; s. Hoyt William and Frances Rebecca (Symons) B.; B.S. U. S. Mcht. Marine Acad., 1949; B.S. in Mech. Engring., U. Wis. 1949; m. Sylvia Joyce Dickerson, Oct. 26, 1963; children—Kim (Mrs. Mark F. Shogren), Hoyt W., III, Terry D., Kelly Lee, Stacey Lynn. With Combustion div. Combustion Engring., Inc., New Orleans, 1949—, dist. mgr. 1959—. Served with USNR, 1943-46. Registered profl. engr., La., Ala. Mem. Am. Soc. M.E. (chpt. v.p. Ala., Miss. 1959), Nat. Soc. Profl. Engrs., La. Engring. Soc. (state dir. 1969, pres. 1972—). Home: 3759 Pin Oak St New Orleans LA 70114 Office: 505 John Hancock Bldg New Orleans LA 70130

BROWN, HYDER JOSEPH, JR., architect; b. Hillsboro, Tex., Oct. 16, 1925; s. Hyder Joseph and Rosalie (Wilkinson) B.; B.Arch., U. Tex., 1951. Cons. sch. architecture Tex. Edn. Agy., Austin, 1951-57; with Paderewski, Dean & Assos., architects, San Diego, 1957-62; architect partner Livingstone & Brown, La Jolla, Cal., 1962-67; project architect firm Jessen Assos., Inc. Architects and Planners, Austin, Tex., 1967—. Mem. adv. bd. Austin (Tex.) Pre-Sch. Hearing Center, 1955-56; mem. Council Ednl. Facility Planning, 1954—; mem. Planning and Zoning Commn., West Lake Hills, Tex., 1971-72, chmn., 1972—. Trustee Woodall-Bowden Trusts 1 and 2; patron Laguna Gloria Art Museum, Austin. Served with USNR, 1943-46. Mem. Tex. Soc. Architects, A.I.A. (chpt. chmn. commn. on edn. and research 1966; chmn. chpt. activities 1971; chpt. chmn. pub. service commn. 1972—; recipient outstanding service award San Diego chpt. 1962; corporate mem.). Episcopalian (lay reader). Contbr. to profl. jours. Prin. works include schs., pub. housing, residences, instns., apts., comml. bldgs. Home: 311-A Westlake Dr Austin TX 78746 Office: 401 W 29th St Austin TX 78705

BROWN, ISAAC DALE, physician; b. Mosheim, Tenn., Jan. 26, 1915; s. Walter C. and Matilda (Hartman) B.; B.A., B.S., Carson-Newman Coll., 1937; M.D., U. Tenn., 1941; m. Kathryn Jones, June 14, 1942; children—Gale Ann (Mrs. Lynn Baumgartner), Dale. Intern, Nashville Gen. Hosp., 1942; practice medicine, Mosheim, 1943—; mem. staff Greeneville, Laughlin, Takoma hosps. Mem. Am. Acad. Family Physicians, A.M.A., World, So., Tenn., Greene County (pres. 1944-52) med. assns. Republican. Mason (32 deg., Shriner). Address: Box 38 Mosheim TN 37818

BROWN, J. MARSHALL, Democratic nat. committeeman; b. 1924; m. Ellen McInniss; 1 child. Pres. Marshall Brown Ins. Agy., Inc. Democratic nat. committeeman La.; mem. La. legislature, 1952-60; campaign mgr., chmn. finance com. gov. John J. McKeithen; pres. La. bd. edn., 1962—; La. campaign mgr. Lyndon Johnson, 1964. Mem. Pres.'s Club, Nat. Capital Dem. Club. Clubs: Plimson (New Orleans). Home: 225 Baronne St New Orleans LA 70112 Office: State Capitol Baton Rouge LA 70804*

BROWN, JAMES DOUGLAS, lawyer; b. Ozark, Ala., Feb. 14, 1912; s. W. A. and Pearl (Hicks) B.; student Southwestern U., 1929, Auburn U., 1930-32; LL.B., U. Ala., 1935; postgrad. Georgetown U., 1936; m. Kathryne Parker, Nov. 1, 1944; children—Kathryne (dec.), Patricia, Clementine. Admitted to Ala. State bar, 1935, practiced in Athens, 1936-38, Ozark, 1938—; pres., dir. Ozark Broadcasting Corp., 1953—; dir. Comml. Bank of Ozark; pres., owner Douglas Brown Ins. Agy., Inc., owner Brown Real Estate Co.; pres. Brown Devel. Co., Enterprise, Ala.; owner Donnell Blvd. Shopping Center, Daleville, Ala.; dir. Enterprise Motel Co., Inc. Chmn. Ala. Adv. Com. on Civil Rights, 1959-60, Dale County Hosp. Assn., Dale County Mental Retardation Bd. Mem. Ala. Senate, 1942-46; mayor of Ozark, 1948-60, 64-68. Bd. dirs. Army Aviation Museum Assn.; bd. dirs., sec. Oakview Manor. Served from pvt. to sgt. USAAF, 1943-44. Recipient Most Outstanding Alumnus award U. Ala. Law Sch., 1971. Mem. Am., Ala. bar assns., ICC Practitioners, Law Sci. Acad., Am. Judicature Soc., Kappa Alpha, Phi Alpha Delta. Democrat. Presbyn. (deacon). Mason (Shriner), Rotarian. Clubs: Ozark Country; Dothan Country; Olympia Spa. Home: 737 E Broad St Ozark AL 36360 Office: 35 S Court Sq Ozark AL 36360

BROWN, JAMES WINSOR, banker; b. Ford City, Pa., May 24, 1929; s. Winsor William and Almira (Callen) B.; B.B.A., U. Pitts., 1951, postgrad., 1952-58; postgrad. Stonier Grad. Sch. of Banking, Rutgers U., 1968; m. Gertrude Colwell, Feb. 3, 1951; children—Alan, Susan, David, Leanne. Asst. cashier, mgr. credit dept. Pitts. Nat. Bank, 1951-59; v.p. comml. loans Dania Bank, (Fla.), 1959-67; v.p. comml. loans Coral Ridge Nat. Bank, Ft. Lauderdale, 1967; exec. v.p., cashier Guaranty First Nat. Bank, 1967-71; pres. S.E. Bank of Deerfield Beach, Fla., 1971—. Mem. Robert Morris Assos. Kiwanian. Club: Lighthouse Point (Fla.) Yacht and Tennis. Home: 1331 S E 14th Ct Deerfield Beach FL 33441 Office: 1007 South Federal Hwy Deerfield Beach FL 33441

BROWN, JEAN WILLIAM, advt., pub. relations agy. exec.; b. San Antonio, June 29, 1928; s. Frank William and Gladys (Irvine) B.; B.J., U. Tex., 1949; m. Beth Conner Reineman, Jan. 29, 1949; children—Blake Conner, Borden Matthew. Copywriter, Wilkinson, Schiwetz & Tips, Inc., 1950-54, merged McCann Erickson, Inc., 1954; account exec. Foote, Cone & Belding, 1955; account exec. Rives, Dyke and Co., Inc., Houston, 1956-60, v.p., 1960-67, dir., 1961—, pres., 1967—, chief exec. officer, 1970—. Served with USAF, 1951-53. Mem. Houston C. of C., Alpha Delta Sigma. Clubs: Houston,

Lakeside Country. Home: 106 Beavertail Point Houston TX 77024 Office: 2503 Robinhood Blvd Houston TX 77005

BROWN, JESSE GLENN, hosp. adminstr.; b. Marshall County, Ala., July 15, 1930; s. John Henry and Mary Ethel (Womack) B.; A.A., Snead Coll., 1959; student Jacksonville State U., 1960-62; grad. sch. Community and Allied Health Resources U. Ala., 1972; m. Eloise Strickland, Apr. 19, 1953; children—Jesse Glenn, Terry Lynn. Mgr. jewelry store, 1953-55; adminstrv. asst. U.S. Army Res., Decatur, Ala., 1955-57, bus. mgr. Boaz (Ala.)-Albertville, 1957-62; adminstr. Arab (Ala.) Hosp., 1962—. Chmn. fund raising United Givers Fund, Arab, 1966-67, pres., 1968-69; publicity chmn. Marshall County chpt. A.R.C., 1968-69, chpt. bd. dirs., 1966—; mem. adv. com. home health services Ala. Dept. Health, 1969—. Served with AUS, 1948-53. Mem. Ala. Hosp. Assn. (chmn. personnel practices com. 1968-70; chmn. profl. standards and services com. 1971), Northeast Ala. Hosp. Council (pres. 1966-67), Res. Officers Assn., Airborne Assn., Am. Coll. Hosp. Adminstrs., Ala. Assn. Hosp. Execs. Baptist (deacon, supt. Sunday sch. 1965-68). Mason. Home: 403 6th St Arab AL 35016 Office: 200 S Main St Arab AL 35016

BROWN, JOHN CALVIN, banker; b. Goree, Tex., Nov. 30, 1930; s. Harvey Alexander and Annie Lee (West) Brown; student U. Tex., 1948, Tex. Wesleyan Coll., 1955-58; grad. Nat. Mortgage Sch., Ohio State U., 1967; m. Nelda Jo Hinkle, Apr. 22, 1950; children—Donna Ruth, Lindsey Paul. With Ft. Worth Nat. Bank, 1950-52, 54—, asst. cashier, 1962-64, mgr. real estate and mortgage loan dept., 1964—, asst. v.p., 1964-66, v.p., 1966, mem. bank discount com., 1966—. Faculty mem. Southwestern Grad. Sch. Banking, 1967-69. Bd. dirs. West Side br. Ft. Worth YMCA; treas., bd. dirs. Tarrant County chpt. A.R.C. Served with AUS, 1952-54. Mem. Nat. Assn. Homebuilders (dir. Ft. Worth chpt. 1970-71), Tex. Bankers Assn. (mortgage finance com. 1969), Tex., Ft. Worth mortgage bankers assns. Baptist (minister music 1959—). Clubs: Petroleum, Ridglea Country (Ft. Worth). Home: 4116 Winding Way Fort Worth TX 76116 Office: 700 Main St Fort Worth TX 76101

BROWN, J(OHN) CARTER, art museum ofcl.; b. Providence, Oct. 8, 1934; s. John Nicholas and Anne (Kinsolving) B.; student Groton Sch., 1946-51, Stowe (Eng.) Sch., 1951-52; A.B. summa cum laude, Harvard, 1956, M.B.A., 1958; student Munich (Germany) U., 1958, pupil Bernard Berenson, Florence, Italy, 1958-59, mus. tng. course, Ecole du Louvre, Paris, France, 1959, Netherlands Inst. Art History, 1960; M.A., Inst. Fine Arts, N.Y.U., 1962; m. Constance Mellon Byers, 1971. Asst. to dir. Nat. Gallery Art, Washington, 1961-63, asst. dir., 1964-68, dir., 1969—, also chmn. commn. fine arts. Mem. Citizens Stamp Adv. Com., 1961—. Nat. Portrait Gallery Commn.; treas. White House Hist. Assn.; mem. mus. adv. panel Nat. Endowment for the Arts; mem. Com. Preservation White House, Fed. Council Arts and Humanities; mem. adv. com. Mus. Computer Network, adv. council Nat. Soc. Arts and Letters. Trustee Hope Found., Inst. Fine Arts N.Y.U., Nat. Trust Historic Preservation, John F. Kennedy Center Performing Arts; trustee Am. Fedn. Arts, also chmn. exhbn. com., 1966—; mem. assos. John Carter Brown Library; mem. vis. com's. library, fine arts dept. Harvard; bd. advisers to pres. U.S. Naval War Coll., Newport, R.I.; bd. Overseers Boston Symphony. Recipient Gold Medal Nat. Arts Club, 1972. Mem. Phi Beta Kappa. Episcopalian. Clubs: N.Y. Yacht, Cruising Am., Century (N.Y.C.); Harvard, Fed. City (Washington); Ida Lewis Yacht (Newport). Author-dir. films: The American Vision, 1965. Office: Nat Gallery of Art Washington DC 20565

BROWN, JOHN DANIEL, educator; b. Cabarrus County, N.C., Jan. 27, 1934; s. Robert Hall and Cordelia Cox (Ritchie) B.; B.A., Lenior-Rhyne Coll., 1956; B.D., Lutheran Theol. Sem., 1959; Th.M., Princeton Sem., 1960; Ph.D., Drew U., 1970; m. Betty Waddill Murchison, June 7, 1957; children—Karen Cox, Evelyn Christian. Ordained to ministry Lutheran Ch., 1959; served in Thomasville, N.C., 1960-62; instr. religion and philosophy Upsala Coll., East Orange, N.J., 1963-65; instr. religion Converse Coll., Spartanburg, S.C., 1965-67; asst. prof. philosophy and religion Catawba Coll., Salisbury, N.C., 1967-70, asso. prof., 1970—; vis. lectr. religion, mem. grad. faculty Wake Forest U., 1969-70. Democratic precinct capt., 1968-72; treas. Rowan Citizens for McCarthy, 1968. Mem. Lutheran Ch. in Am. Fellowship, Am. Acad. Religion, N.C. Tchrs. Religion, Am. Assn. U. Profs., Soc. for Sci. Study of Religion, Alpha Tau Kappa, Iota Epsilon Omega, Pi Kappa Delta, Kappa Chi, Gamma Beta Chi. Democrat. Lutheran. Home: 1514 W Colonial Dr Salisbury NC 28144 Office: Catawba Coll Salisbury NC 28144

BROWN, JOHN HALLUM, physician; b. Aledo, Tex., Sept. 11, 1938; s. John Allen and Margaret Martin (Hallum) B.; B.A., North Tex. State U., 1960; M.D., U. Tex. Southwestern Med. Sch., 1965; m. Eva Gay Nix, Aug. 27, 1960; children—Ray Hallum, Rhonda Gay. Intern St. Paul Hosp., Dallas, 1965-66; pvt. practice medicine, specializing in family practice, Dallas, 1968—; physician Southwest Clinic Assn., Dallas, 1968—, Lanier-Brown Clinic, Dallas, 1971—; mem. staffs St. Paul Hosp., Dallas, Med. Arts Hosp., Dallas. Inst. phys. diagnosis U. Texas Southwestern Med. Students, St. Paul Hosp., 1969-70. Webelos leader, mem. planning com. Circle Ten council Boy Scouts Am., 1970-71; mem. com. for coordinated vocational-academic edn. Dallas Ind. Sch. Dist., 1969-71. Served with USNR, 1966-68. Diplomate Am. Bd. Family Practice. Mem. Dallas County Med. Soc., Tex. Med. Assn., A.M.A., Am., Tex. acads. family practice, Phi Rho Sigma. Baptist. Home: 3221 Woodwind Lane Dallas TX 75229 Office: Lanier-Brown Clinic 9502 Webbs Chapel Dallas TX 75220

BROWN, JOHN NICHOLAS, museum cons. Chmn. adv. bd. Nat. Armed Forces Museum, Smithsonian Instn., Washington. Address: Nat Armed Forces Museum Adv Bd Smithsonian Instn Washington DC 20560*

BROWN, JOHN ROBERT, judge; b. Funk, Neb., Dec. 10, 1909; s. E. E. and Elvira (Carney) B.; A.B., U. Neb., 1930, LL.D. (hon.), 1965; J.D., U. Mich., 1932, LL.D., 1959; m. Mary Lou Murray, May 30, 1936; 1 son, John R. Admitted to Tex. bar, 1932, practiced in Houston and Galveston, mem. Royston & Rayzor, 1932-55; chief judge 5th Circuit, U.S. Ct. Appeals, Houston. Chmn. Harris County Republican Com., Tex., 1953-55. Served from lt. to maj. Transp. Corps, USAAF, 1942-46. Mem. Am., Tex., Houston bar assns., Am. Judicature Soc., Am. Law Inst., Maritime Law Assn. U.S., Assn. ICC Practitioners, Order of Coif, Phi Delta Phi, Sigma Chi. Presbyn. (elder). Clubs: Houston, Houston Country; Boston (New Orleans). Home: 3209 Ella Lee Lane Houston TX 77019 Office: US Court House Houston TX 77002

BROWN, JOHN YOUNG, JR., bus. exec.; b. Lexington, Ky., 1933; LL.B., U. Ky., 1960. Chmn. bd. exec. officer Ky. Fried Chicken Corp.; dir. Third Nat. Bank, Nashville; dir., mem. exec. com. Heublein, Inc. Chmn. Nat. Democratic Young Leadership council. Home: 5811 Orion Rd Louisville KY 40222 Office: PO Box 13331 Louisville KY 40213

BROWN, KATHERINE TSANOFF (MRS. H. FLETCHER BROWN), educator Mem. faculty art dept. Rice U., Houston. Recipient George R. Brown award superior teaching, 1970, also George R. Brown prize excellence in teaching. Address: Dept Art Rice U Houston TX 77001*

BROWN, KENNETH HAROLD, appliance mfg. exec.; b. Cleveland, Tenn., May 31, 1914; s. Grover Cleveland and Lizzie (Harrison) B.; student Tulane U., 1933-35, McKenzie Bus. Coll., 1935-36; m. Miriam Palmer Ash, June 5, 1935; children—Kenneth Harrison, Rachel Burwell. Treas., Brown Stove Works, Inc., Cleveland, 1942-43, sec.-treas., 1943-61, exec. v.p., 1961-63, pres., 1963—; pres. Brown Realty Corp., Cleveland, 1956—; dir. Cleveland Nat. Bank, 1972—. Pres. Jr. Achievement Bradley County, Inc., 1967-68; pres. Cleveland Asso. Industries, 1970-72; pres. Cleveland Community Chest, 1959-60; pres. Tri-States Assn. for Cripples, 1958-59; mem. U. Tenn. Devel. Council, 1971—; mem. exec. bd. Cherokee council Boy Scouts Am. Mem. Cleveland Sch. Bd., 1950-61, chmn., 1957-59. Bd. dirs. Hosp. for Crippled Adults, Memphis, 1958-61; trustee Cleveland Day Sch., 1964—, treas., 1968—. Mem. Inst. Appliance Mfrs. (trustee 1945-53, Gas Appliance Mfrs. Assn. (dir. 1970-72), Alpha Tau Omega. Republican. Presbyn. (chmn. bd. deacons 1959-63). Rotarian (past dist. gov.), Elk (past exalted ruler). Clubs: Cleveland Golf and Country; Atlanta Athletic. Home: Annandale Park Cleveland TN 37311 Office: Carolina and 15th Sts Cleveland TN 37311

BROWN, KERMIT EARL, educator; b. Haskell, Tex., Nov. 2, 1923; B.S. in Mech. Engring., B.S. in Petroleum Engring., Tex. A. and M. Coll., 1948; M.S., U. Tex., 1959, Ph.D., 1962; m. 1945; 3 children. Petroleum engr. Stanolind Oil & Gas Co., 1948-51; gas life engr. Garrett Oil Tolls, Inc., 1951-55; asst. prof. petroleum engring. U. Tex., 1955-64, asso. prof., from 1964; now prof. petroleum engring., v.p. for research Tulsa U.; cons. in field. Served with USAAF, 1942-46. Address: 5429 E 65th Pl Tulsa OK 74135*

BROWN, LEON, architect, educator; b. Blackville, S.C., Sept. 25, 1907; s. Isador and Sadie (Cohen) B.; student Cornell U., 1924-25; B.S. in Architecture, Ga. Inst. Tech., 1929; M.Arch., U. Pa., 1933; m. Marguerite Kahn, Aug. 30, 1944; 1 son, Warren Lee. Designer-draftsman R.B. Okie, Phila., 1929-31; jr. partner Thalheimer & Weitz, Phila., 1933-42; propr. Leon Brown, architect, Washington, 1946-50; partner Brown & Wright, architects, Washington, 1950—; prof. architecture Howard U., 1947-72. Mem. Washington Bldg. Congress, 1958—; chmn. D.C. Bd. Appeals and Rev., Licenses and Insp., 1956-60; dir. Washington Planning and Housing Assn., 1958-69; mem. urban renewal planning com. Washington Urban League, 1960-64; nat. panel arbitrators Am. Arbitration Assn., 1959—; sec. D.C. Bd. Registration Architects, 1964-67, pres., 1967-69. Treas. D.C. Com. Job Opportunities, 1956-60; co-chmn. D.C. Nat. Conf. Christians and Jews, 1966—, nat. bd. dirs., 1967, chmn. bd. Washington chpt. 1968, 72; pres. Forest Hills Citizens Assn., 1965-68. Mem. com. planning and housing Democratic Central Com., 1963-65. Bd. dirs. Northwest Settlement House, 1952-69. Served to capt. C.E., AUS, 1942-46. Recipient Meritorious Pub. Service award D.C., 1960, 69, award residential architecture Washington Evening Star, 1957; award Washington Bd. Trade, 1962; Commendation Meritorious Service, Mil. Dist. Washington, 1946. Fellow A.I.A. (pres. Washington met. chpt. 1956-58, Coll. of Fellows); mem. Assn. Coll. Sch. Architecture, Zeta Beta Tau. Jewish religion. Club: Cosmos (Washington). Author: (with others) R. Brognard Okie, Architect of Philadelphia, 1955; also articles. Home: 4158 Linnean Av NW Washington DC 20008 Office: 1640 Wisconsin Av NW Washington DC 20007

BROWN, LEROY JOHN HENRY, architect; b. Charleston, S.C., Dec. 14, 1912; s. John Henry and Elisa (Robinson) B.; B.S., A and M Coll., Orangeburg, S.C., 1936; B.S. in Architecture and Mech. Art, Howard U., 1944; M.A., Catholic U., Washington, 1955; m. Angela Mae Denton, Jan. 22, 1951. Instr. architecture Va. State U., Petersburg, 1941-42; prof. architecture Howard U., Washington, 1945—; owner, head archtl. firm Leroy J.H. Brown, Washington, 1950—. Pres. Bloomingdale Civic Assn., Washington, 1961—; mem. Citizens Zoning Com. for D.C., 1965-70; mem. com. on archtl. tech. Washington Tech. Inst., 1969—. Bd. dirs. Nat. Tech. Assn. Ednl. Fund. Recipient Pub. Service award D.C., 1968. Mem. A.I.A., Constrn. Specifications Inst., Omega Psi Phi, Tau Sigma Delta. Editor: Nat. Tech. Assn. Jour., 1965—. Important works include Alabama Av. Elementary Sch. Home: 22 Bryant St NW Washington DC 20001 Office: 3310 Georgia Av NW Washington DC 20010

BROWN, LESTER M., nutritionist; b. Paris, France, Apr. 9, 1888; s. Nathan N. and Frances Brown; student Sorbonne Coll. (Paris); B.A., N.Y.U.; m. 2 sons; m. 2d, Berthe Brown, June 9, 1958. Successively mfrs. exporter rep. Yohan Maria Farina, Am. Don Zukein; now founder, dir. House of Better Nutrition, Avon Park, Fla.; formerly nat. and internat. distbr. Neo-Life Co. Am., San Lorenzo, Cal. Pub. relation chmn. Am. Maimonides Acad. Arts and Sci. Founder, dir. Avon Park Art Gallery. Recipient certificate of merit for distinguished service to commerce and industry. Mem. Nat. Dietary Foods Assn., Nat. Fedn. Ind. Bus., Natural Food Assos., Vegetarian Hygiene Soc., Am. Assn. Ret. Persons and Tchrs. (chpt. founder), UN Assn. U.S.A., Internat. Platform Assn., Avon Park C. of C. Home: 933-A W Main St Avon Park FL 33825 Office: 933 W Main St Avon Park FL 33825

BROWN, LYLE, justice Ark. Supreme Ct.; b., 1908; A.B., Henderson State Tchrs. Coll.; M.A., So. Meth. U. Admitted to Ark. bar, 1935; now asso. justice Ark. Supreme Ct., Little Rock. Office: Ark Supreme Ct Little Rock AR 72201

BROWN, LYNDON LORAND, sch. exec.; b. Dallas, Jan. 12, 1926; s. Bert P. and Lorine (Dearing) B.; B.B.A., U. Tex., 1949; m. Doris Faye Henderson, Mar. 21, 1947; children—Sherry, Kathleen. Pres., Brown Schs., Austin, Tex., 1951-65, chmn. bd. dirs., 1965—. Pres., Brown Found. for Exceptional Children. Served with USNR, 1943-45. Fellow Am. Assn. Mental Deficiency, Am. Orthopsychiat. Assn.; mem. Am. Mgmt. Assn. (adv. council secondary sch. prins. and heads, adv. council coll. and univ. presidents), Nat., Tex. social welfare assns., Council for Exceptional Children (life), Presidents Assn., Am. Assn. Children's Residential Centers, Am. Assn. Sch. Adminstrs., Phi Delta Kappa. Home: 4006 Knollwood Dr Austin TX 78731

BROWN, MARCUS GORDON, educator; b. Miami, Fla., Mar. 14, 1908; s. David Chappel and Lula (Bell) B.; A.B., Washington Missionary Coll., 1927; M.A., Emory U., 1936; Docteur es Lettres, U. Dijon (France), 1939; Doctor en Filosofia y Letras, U. Madrid (Spain), 1940. Tchr. fgn. lngs. high sch., Jacksonville, Fla., 1927-30, Boys' High Sch., Atlanta, 1930-36; instr. English and French, U. Fla., 1936-38; asst. prof. fgn. langs. Ga. Inst. Tech., Atlanta, 1940-42, asso. prof., 1942-43, prof., 1943-50; specialist U.S. Office Edn., 1944-46; cultural attache Am. embassy, Bogota, Colombia, 1950-52, Rio de Janeiro, Brazil, 1952-54; asst. chancellor Univ. System Ga., Atlanta, 1954-57; fgn. lang. coordinator Ga. State Dept. Edn., Atlanta, 1957-62; asso. prof. Romance langs. Memphis State U., 1963-67, prof., 1967-71, prof. modern langs., 1971—. Recipient Anchieta medal Municipality of Rio de Janeiro, Brazil, 1954; medals for excellence in French lang. and llt. French Govt., 1936. Mem. Sociedad Bolivariana de Colombia, Am. Assn. Tchrs. Spanish and Portuguese, Am. Assn. Tchrs. French, Am. Assn. Tchrs. Italian, Am. Assn. Tchrs. German, Am. Assn. U. Profs., Modern Lang. Assn. Am., South Central Modern Lang. Assn., Tenn. Edn. Assn., Tenn. Philol. Assn. Author: Les Idees Politiques et Religieuses de Stendhal, 1939; La Vida y Las Novelas de Emilia Pardo Bazan, 1940; (with J. Russell) Bibliography for the Teaching of English to Foreigners, 1947. Office: Dept Fgn Langs Memphis State U Memphis TN 38111

BROWN, OTIS, state ofcl.; b. Brunswick, Va., Sept. 11, 1934; s. George Washington and Ruth (Lafoon) B.; B.A., U. Richmond, 1956; M.S., Fla. State U., 1959; m. Frances Young, Mar. 20, 1957; children— Jeffrey Alan, Susan Leigh. Asst. field sec. League of Va. Countles, Charlottesville, Va., 1959-62; asst. county exec., county exec. County of Albemarle, Va., 1962-66; dir. Va. Dept. Welfare and Instns., Richmond, Va., 1966-72; sec. human affairs Va. Gov's. Cabinet, 1972—. Served to capt. AUS. Club: Sertoma. Home: 3303 Archdale Rd Richmond VA 23235 Office: 429 S Belvidere St Richmond VA 23220

BROWN, PAUL, lawyer; b. Billings, Okla., Apr. 13, 1904; LL.B., U. Okla., 1927. Admitted to Okla. bar, 1927; now mem. firm Brown, Berity &Brown, Oklahoma City. Mem. Oklahoma County, Okla. bar assns., Phi Delta Phi. Address: Brown Verity & Brown 22220 First Nat Bldg Oklahoma City OK 73102*

BROWN, PAUL BRUCE, govt. ofcl.; b. nr. Greenwood, Miss., Aug. 12, 1909; s. William Page and Carrie Isabel (Bruce) B.; B.S., Miss. State Coll., 1932; M.S., U. Ill., 1947, Ph.D. (fellow), 1951; m. Mary Eunice Fulmer, Jan. 3, 1937; Agt., Boys 4-H Club, Miss. Agrl. Extension Service, DeSoto, Tate, and Tunica Counties, 1934-43; asst. prof. animal sci. U. Ark., 1947-49; asso. prof. animal sci. La. State U., 1951-66; dir. research coordinating unit div. vocational edn. La. Dept. Edn., Baton Rouge, 1966—. Served with AUS, 1943-46, 61-62; now lt. col. Res. ret. Mem. Am. Soc. Animal Sci., Am. Vocational Edn. Research Assn., Am., La. vocational assns., Am. Legion (comdr. 1963-64), Sigma Xi, Alpha Zeta, Gamma Sigma Delta, Methodist. Mason, Rotarian (pres. Baton Rouge 1969-70). Contbr. articles to profl. pubs. Home: 432 Stanford Av Baton Rouge LA 70808 Office: PO Box 44064 Baton Rouge LA 70804

BROWN, PHYLLIS GENEVIEVE, ret. editor; b. Richmond, Va., July 5, 1906; d. Allison Morris and Belle Coleman (Longest) Brown; student U. Chgo., 1949; B.S., Richmond Profl. Inst., 1957; M.H., U. Richmond, 1970. Sec., Tabb, Brockenbrough & Ragland, Agts., Richmond, 1925-28, Charles E. Frosst & Co., Richmond, 1928-40, office mgr., 1940-44; mem. staff Va. Edn. Assn., Richmond, Va., 1944-72, asst. to editor, 1948-54, asst. editor Va. Jour. of Edn., 1954-69, editor, 1969-72. Recipient award Va. Press Women, 1966, 68, 70, Nat. Fedn. Press Women award, 1969. Mem. Nat. Assn. State Edn. Editors (sec.-treas. 1962-64), Ednl. Press Assn. Am. (regional dir. 1962-63), Internat. Soc. Christian Endeavor (v.p. 1954-56, 67-71, exec. com. 1956-61, 65—), World Christian Endeavor Council, Va. Press Women, Va. Edn. Assn., N.E.A. (life), Va. Christian Endeavor Union (pres. 1933-35, 43), Va. Council Adminstrv. Women in Edn., Am. Assn. U. Women, Alpha Delta Kappa. Mem. Disciples of Christ Ch. (chmn. bd. 1970—). Club: Quota (pres. 1960-62, 71-72, dist. sec.-treas. 1959). Home: 4311 Stuart Av Richmond VA 23221

BROWN, RAY STEPHEN, constrn. co. exec.; b. Roanoke, Va., July 7, 1942; s. Ray Calvin and Willie Edna (Lawhorn) B.; A.A., Roanoke Tech. Inst., 1964; B.S., Va. Poly. Inst., 1968; m. Ann Graves Cundiff, June 26, 1965; 1 dau., Stephanie Rae. Mgr., Drapers Meadow Apts., Blacksburg, Va., 1964-68; sec.-treas. W. E. Cundiff Co., Inc., Vinton, Va., 1968—, Hollins Hardware Co., Inc., 1968—, v.p. Bowles-Cundiff, Inc., Vero Beach, Fla., 1971—. Mem. Local Selective Service Bd., 1972. Mem. Roanoke County Democratic Com., 1969-72. Bd. dirs. Roanoke Valley Apt. Council, 1970; bd. dirs., v.p. Vinton (Va.) Dogwood Festival. Mem. Roanoke Valley Homebuilders Assn., Southampton Homeowners Assn., Inc. (dir. 1970), Vinton Jr. C. of C. Methodist. Mason (Shriner), Moose, Lion. Club: Vico Investment (Vinton, Va.). Home: 714 Dillon Dr Vinton VA 24179 Office: 118 S Pollard St Vinton VA 24179

BROWN, RAYMOND JOSEPH, financial service co. exec.; b. Burlington, Vt., May 10, 1923; s. John Francis and Elizabeth (Lovejoy) B.; student U.S. Govt. Insts., U. Vienna, 1947-48, 53-54; m. Judith Laszlo, May 20, 1948; children—Gloria C., Raymond P., Michael S., Leslie Ann. Spl. agt. fgn. service U.S. Dept. Army, 1945-50, CIA, 1950-53 Dept. state, 1953-58; with Washington (D.C.) Planning Corp., 1958-60; exec. v.p., gen. sales mgr. Registered Funds, Inc., Charlotte, N.C., 1960-65; sr. v.p. Financial Service Corp., Atlanta, Ga., 1965-71; pres. B & S Financial Services, Inc., Charlotte, 1971—. Served with AUS, 1942-46. Mem. Internat. Assn. Financial Planners. Club: Carmel Country (Charlotte, N.C.). Contbr. articles to profl. pubs. Home: 2330 Thornridge Rd Charlotte NC 28211 Office: 4108 Park Rd Charlotte NC 28209

BROWN, RICHARD CHRISTOPHER, physician; b. Gainesville, Fla., Jan. 16, 1932; s. Joseph Pell and Mildred (Smith) B.; A.B., Western Res. U., 1953; M.D., U. Fla., 1962; M.P.H., U. Cal. at Berkeley, 1967; m. Linda Jeanne Dickinson, July 2, 1960; children—Douglas Randolph, Jennifer Anne. Intern, Virginia Mason Hosp., Seattle, 1962-63; resident VA Hosp., Portland, Ore., 1964-66; practice medicine specializing in geriatrics and gen. medicine, Clearwater, Fla., 1968—; mem. staff Morton Plant Hosp., Clearwater. Epidemiology cons. USPHS for Navajo Indian Reservation, 1967-68; instr. dept. preventive medicine U. Okla. Med. Center, 1967-68. Served with AUS, 1954-56. Mem. Am. Pub. Health Assn., Fla. Med. Assn., Fla. Soc. Preventive Medicine (sec.-treas. 1971-72), Delta Tau Delta. Home: 415 Jasmine Way Clearwater FL 33516 Office: 1014 W Bay Dr Largo FL 33540

BROWN, RICHARD F., publisher Austin American and Statesman. Office: 308 Guadalupe St Austin TX 78767*

BROWN, ROBERT O., bus. exec., b. 1908; m. With Halliburton Co., Dallas, 1932—, v.p., gen. counsel, 1954-69, sr. v.p., gen. counsel, sec., 1969—. Office: 3211 Southland Center Dallas TX 75210*

BROWN, ROBERT STOREY, educator; b. Bay City, Tex., Sept. 4, 1927; s. Samuel Lafayette and Margaret (Butler) B.; B.S. in Chemistry, U. Tex., 1952, M.Ed. in Ednl. Adminstrn., 1960, Ph.D. (Univ. fellow, doctoral fellow), 1967; m. Eleanor Michael McLernon, Dec. 22, 1951; children—Robert Storey, George McLernon, Eleanor Rutledge, Ann Rhoads. Tchr. sci. and math. San Antonio Pub. Schs., 1952-55; tchr. physics Alamo Hieghts (Tex.) Pub. Schs., 1955-59; dir. adult edn. program, Alamo Heights, 1957-59; dir. research San Angelo (Tex.) Pub. Schs., 1959-63; asst. prof. U. Fla., 1965-66; dir. research, exec. officer Inter-Am. Ednl. Center, San Antonio, 1966-68; asso. prof. Okla. State U., dir. research and student teaching Coll. Edn., Stillwater, 1968—. Proposal devel. and evaluation cons. to pub. schs. of Fla., Tex. and Okla., 1965—. Served with USNR, 1946-48. Mem. Am. Assn. U. Profs., N.E.A. (life), Am. Ednl. Research Assn., Nat. Soc. for Study Edn., Okla. Edn. Assn., Phi Delta Kappa (life). Contbg. author: Instructional Leadership Training Materials, 1964. Home: 702 N Grandview St Stillwater OK 74074

BROWN, ROBERT THOMAS, textile co. exec.; b. Paterson, N.J., July 16, 1929; s. Robert Power and Elizabeth (Nino) B.; B.S., Phila. Textile Inst., 1951; m. Helen Patricia Wilson, Apr. 11, 1953; children—Robert, Thomas, Patricia, Mary, Barbara, Margaret, Joan. Asst. supt. weaving Hill-Brown, Clifton, N.J., 1951-53; mfg. supt. Celanese Corp., Narrows, Va., 1953-67; with Cone Mills Corp., Greensboro, N.C. and Whitmire, S.C., 1967—, asst. to dir. consumer product mfg., 1967, staff asst. to pres., 1968, gen. mgr. Cone Knits Plant, 1969—. Bd. dirs. Newberry County United Fund. Mem. Am. Assn. Textile Tech. Roman Catholic. K.C. Home: 2105 Woodland Way Newberry SC 29108 Office: PO Box 31 Whitmire SC 29178

BROWN, ROBERT WOODROW, newspaper editor; b. Covington County, Miss., Jan. 3, 1912; s. Emmett Lige and Alma Louise (Garner) B.; grad. high sch.; Nieman fellow Harvard, 1951-52; m. Sarah Elizabeth Wood, Feb. 6, 1936; 1 dau., Barbara. Reporter, Hattiesburg (Miss.) American, 1930-32; mng. editor Greenville (Miss.) Delta Star, 1936-38; staff corr. United Press, New Orleans, 1938; reporter, city editor Times-Picayune and New Orleans States, 1938-42; asst. city editor Washington Daily News, 1942-43; news supr. NBC, 1943-45; exec. editor Internat. News Service, 1945-47; news editor ABC, 1947-48; editor Columbus (Ga.) Ledger, 1948-57; information officer fgn. service USIA, New Delhi, India, 1957-58; asso. editor The St. Petersburg (Fla.) Times, 1958-63; mag. editor Delta Democrat-Times, Greenville, Miss., 1963; editor Rock Hill (S.C.) Evening Herald, 1964-68; mng. editor Augusta (Ga.) Chronicle, 1968—; lectr. Am. press freedom, India and Iceland, 1954. Recipient Pulitzer prize for disinterested meritorious pub. service, 1955. Mem. Am. Soc. Newspaper Editors, So. Assn. Nieman Fellows, Inc., Sigma Delta Chi. Methodist. Author articles Parade mag., Editor and Pub. mag., others. Office: Augusta Chronicle Augusta GA 30902

BROWN, RODGERS N., food chain exec.; b. Columbia, Tenn., Jan. 3, 1911; s. William Albert and Bessie Belle Brown; grad. Inst. Mgmt., Northwestern U.; m. Mary Elizabeth Cook, Apr. 1, 1934; children—Mary Elizabeth (Mrs. James B. Green), Patricia Diane (Mrs. Louis P. Mattis), Deborah Cook. With Kroger Co., 1928-57, v.p., dir. subsidiary Wesco Foods Co., 1951-57; pres., dir. Mohican Co., 1957-59; v.p., dir. Nat. Food Stores La., Inc., 1961—; v.p. Nat. Tea Co., 1965—, regional v.p., 1967-69. Active local Community Chest, 1950, 59, 60, 64. Home: 45 Farnham Pl Metairie LA 70005

BROWN, ROGER HENRY, hwy. constrn. co. exec.; b. Helena, Ga., Nov. 22, 1921; s. William Sloan and Daisy (Blann) B.; B.C.E., Ga. Inst. Tech., 1952; m. Carolyn Moore, June 22, 1952; 1 son, Roger Henry. Hwy. constrn. engr. Ga. Hwy. Dept., 1952-62; pres. Southeastern Hwy. Constrn. Co., Gainesville, Ga., 1962—. Vice chmn. Hall County Devel. Authority, 1971; mem. exec. bd. Boy Scouts Am., 1971. Served with USNR, 1942-45. Registered profl. engr., Ga. Fellow Am. Soc. C.E.; mem. Nat. Soc. Profl. Engrs., Ga. Hwy. Contractors Assn. (pres.), Atlanta C. of C. (dir.), Nat. Alumni Ga. Inst. Tech. (trustee), V.F.W., Am. Legion, Sigma Nu. Episcopalian. Elk. Club: Chattahooches Country (pres.). Home: 3501 Edgewood Circle Gainesville GA 30501

BROWN, S. SPENCER NEVILLE, banker; b. Meridian, Miss., Dec. 29, 1920; s. Stanton and Maria F. (Neville) B.; B.B.A., Baylor U., 1942; m. Margaret Cannon Boyce, Mar. 31, 1951; children—Spencer, Jr., Margaret, Maria Stanton, Stanton Boyce. With Exporters & Traders Compress &Warehouse Co., Waco, Tex., 1946—, pres., chief exec. officer, 1959—; chmn. bd., chief exec. officer First Nat. Bank, Temple, Tex., 1970—; chmn. bd., chief exec. officer Superior Tech Mark, Dallas, 1967—; pres. Nat. Diversified, Waco, Tex., 1947—; dir. Citizens Nat. Bank, Waco, Rogers Delinted Cottonseed Co., Waco. Pres. United Fund, 1963-64; gen. chmn. Providence Hosp. Drive, Waco, 1964-65. Trustee Episcopal Theol. Sem. Southwest, 1954, Woodberry Forest Sch., 1961-67; mem. exec. com. bd. trustees Kings Daus. Hosp., 1970—. Memphis. Served with AUS. 1942-46. Mem. Nat. Cotton Compress and Cotton Warehouse Assn. (pres. 1960-61, dir. 1953-70), Waco C. of C. (dir. 1952-54, 69-71), Waco Library Assn. Episcopalian (sr. warden 1953). Rotarian (pres. 1970-71). Author: Christian Answers to Teenage Sex Questions, 1970. Home: 2620 MacArthur Dr Waco TX 76708 Office: PO Drawer 1339 Waco TX 76703

BROWN, SAMUEL LOVITT, economist; b. Topeka, Feb. 8, 1915; s. Ira William and Ruth (Lovitt) B.; Ph.B., Rockhurst Coll., 1936; M.A., Georgetown U., 1939, Ph.D., 1951; m. Martha Murray, June 15, 1946; children— Michael, Christopher, Stephen, Timothy. Instr., Coll. Arts and Scis. Georgetown U., 1947-50, asst. prof., 1950-51, lectr., 1962—; economist Chrysler Corp., Detroit, 1951-57; sr. staff mem. Council Econ. Advisers, Exec. Office President, Washington, 1957-61; sr. econ. statistician Bur. Census, 1961-64; asst. chief research div. Research and Statistics CAB, Washington, 1964-71, dir. office of plans, 1971—. Mem. Am. Statis. Assn. (past mem. council), Am. Econ. Assn. Roman Catholic. K.C. (4 deg.). Author: Price Variation in New Houses, 1964; The Demand for Air Travel, 1968. Home: 1525 44th St Washington DC 20007 Office: 1825 Connecticut Av Washington DC 20428

BROWN, SARAH COLE(MRS. STERLING F. BROWN), librarian; b. Conway, Ark.; d. Russell T. and Mary (Craig) Cole; B.A., Hendrix Coll., 1934; B.S. in Library Sci., U. Ill., 1939; m. Sterling F. Brown, Oct. 25, 1941 (dec. Sept. 1970); 1 son, Sterling Russell. Asst. librarian Ala. Coll., 1939-41, Air Corps Tactical Sch., 1941-43; cataloger, asso. librarian U. Ala. Med. Center, 1949-55, librarian, 1955—, now dir. Lister Hill Library Health Scis. Chmn. liaison com. Nat. Library Medicine-Med. Library Assn. Mem. Med. Library Assn. (dir.), Spl. Libraries Assn., Am. Assn. Med. Colls., Am. Assn. Dental Schs., (chmn. sect. learning resources 1970-71), Am. Assn. History Medicine, Am. Acad. Dental History, Am., Ala. (pres. 1969-70) library assns. Home: 2100 Mountain View Dr Birmingham AL 35216 Office: Lister Hill Library of Health Scis U Ala Univ Station Birmingham AL 35294

BROWN, SCOTT NEWTON, real estate, ins. cons.; b. Chattanooga, May 3, 1909; s. C. Victor and Catherine (Colburn) B.; student Davidson Coll., 1926-28; B.S. in Commerce, U. Tenn., 1930; student Am. Inst. Banking, 1931; spl. courses Am. Inst. Real Estate Appraisers, 1947, 68; grad. Law Sch., LaSalle Extension U.; m. Margaret Frierson Williamson, Dec. 2, 1939; children—Scott Newton, George W. Clk., Provident Life & Accident Ins. Co., 1930-31, Hamilton Nat. Bank, 1931-32; with Peerless Woolen Mills, 1932-33; property mgr. C. V. Brown & Bro., 1933-39; pres. Real Estate Mgmt., Inc., 1939-62, 1st Trust Co., 1950-62, Chattanooga Realty Co., 1940-62, Signal Properties, Inc., 1961—, Scott N. Brown Co. Real estate commr. State of Tenn., 1959-62. Vice chmn. City Planning Commn., 1940-42; dir. Chattanooga Safety Council, 1950-51; commr. Walden's Ridge Utility Dist., 1948-53, Chattanooga-Hamilton County Hist. Commn., 1953. Mem. Am. Finance Assn., Nat. Assn. Real Estate Appraisers, Nat. Apt. Assn., Chattanooga Bd. Realtors (pres. 1948, 62), Chattanooga C. of C. (pres. 1958), Insurors of Chattanooga (pres. 1949), Delta Sigma Pi, Pi Kappa Phi. Presbyn. Lion (past sec. Chattanooga). Home: 332 Beck Av Chattanooga TN 37405 Office: James Bldg Chattanooga TN 37402

BROWN, STANLEY WINFORD, dentist; b. Madison, Mo., Nov. 11, 1913; s. Arthur Merritt and Callie Braxton (Gritton) B.; student Central Coll., Fayette, Mo., 1929-30; D.D.S., Washington U., 1934; postgrad. U.S. Naval Dental Sch., 1950, Mayo Found., 1945; m. Dorus Louise Moser, July 14, 1935 (div. Dec. 1968); children—David Arthur, Stanley Mason. Pvt. practice dentistry, Jefferson City, Mo., 1934-36; Jacksonville Beaches, Fla., 1959-68, Sarasota, 1968-69, Jacksonville, 1969—. Mem. Neptune Beach (Fla.) Zoning Bd. Appeals, 1967. Served to capt. USNR, 1936-59. Recipient Alumni award Washington U. Dental Sch., 1934. Mem. Navy League, Omicron Kappa Upsilon, Delta Sigma Delta. Episcopalian. Mason. Clubs: Ponte Vedra (Fla.); Selva Marina (Atlantic Beach, Fla.). Home: 1606 El Prado Rd Jacksonville FL 32216 Office: 3263 Southside Blvd Jacksonville FL 32216

BROWN, STEPHEN PHILLIP, lawyer, state legislator; b. Birmingham, Ala., June 29, 1941; s. William Pearsall and Milledge (Anderson) B.; student Auburn U., 1959-63; J.D., Mercer U., 1967; m. Dorothy Louise Ogden, Sept. 6, 1967; children—Katherine Tolmie, Phillip Ogden. Admitted to Ga. bar, 1967; atty. chief counsel's office Internal Revenue Service, N.Y.C., 1967-69; mem. law firm Mullis, Brown and Reynolds, Macon, Ga., 1969-72, Hall & Bloch, Macon, 1972—. Mem. Ga., Ho. of Reps., 1971—. Mem. Am. Judicature Soc., Phi Delta Theta, Phi Delta Phi. Home: 2972 Woodhaven Circle Macon GA 31204 Office: 1400 GA Power Bldg Macon GA 31201

BROWN, V. JEAN, educator, pharmacist; b. Laclede, Mo., Dec. 22, 1902; d. James Henry and Dovie (Trippeer) Brown; Ph.G., U. Kan., 1923; B.A., U. Okla., 1928, M.S., 1947; postgrad. Purdue U., 1951. Pharmacist, Mo. Meth. Hosp., St. Joseph, 1924-28, Bethany Hosp., Kansas City, Kan., 1930-33, Browns Pharmacy, Laclede, 1934-43; instr. U. Okla. Coll. Pharmacy, Norman, 1946-47, asst. prof., 1949-61, asso. prof., 1961-69, prof., 1969—; asst. prof. Coll. Pharmacy, Med. Coll., Charleston, S.C., 1947-48; asso. prof. U. Miss. Coll. Pharmacy, Oxford, summers 1958, 59. Dist. dir. Gosselin Prescription Survey, Ray A. Gosselin Co., 1965-66, KETA-TV programs, 1960, 61, 65. Named prof. of Month award Drug Topics mag., 1960; recipient Lederle Faculty award, 1972. Walgreen fellow, 1967. Mem. Am. Assn. U. Women (br. pres. 1954-56), Am. Assn. Colls. of Pharmacy, Acad. Pharm. Scis. of Am. Pharm. Assn. (sect. chmn. 1965), Okla. Pharm. Assn., Okla. Edn. Assn., Mortar Bd., Sigma Xi, Lambda Kappa Sigma, Sigma Iota Pi, Delta Kappa Gamma, Gamma Phi Beta, Alpha Lambda Delta, Rho Chi. Methodist. Contbr. to Husa's Pharm. Dispensing, 1959, 66, 7th edit. entitled Dispensing of Medication, 1971. Contbr. articles to profl. jours. Home: 1357 Tarman Circle Norman OK 73069

BROWN, VIRGINIA MAE, govt. ofcl.; b. Pliny, W.Va., Nov. 13, 1923; d. Felix M. and Hester (Crandall) Brown; A.B., W.Va. U., 1945, LL.B., 1947, J.D., 1947; m. James Vernon Brown, Apr. 8, 1955; children—Victoria Anne, Pamela Kaye. Admitted to W.Va. bar, 1947; law clk. atty. gen., W.Va., 1947-49; exec. sec. W.Va. Jud. Council, 1949-52; asst. atty. gen. W.Va., 1952-61; counsel to Gov., W.Va., 1961; commnr. ins. W.Va., 1961-62; mem. W.Va. Pub. Service Commn., 1962-64; mem. ICC, 1964—, chmn., 1969. 9733 Lookout Pl Gaithersburg MD 20760 Home: 9733 Lookout Pl Gaithersburg MD 20760 Office: Interstate Commerce Commn 12th and Constitution Av Washington DC 20423

BROWN, WALTER L., lawyer; b. Precott, Ark., Oct. 23, 1893; LL.B., George Washington U., 1920. Admitted to Ark. bar, 1921; pros. atty. 13th Jud. dist. Ark., 1920; now mem. firm Brown, Compton & Prewett, El Dorado, Ark. Mem. Ark. Oil and Gas Commn., 1937-39. Chmn. Union County (Ark.) Democratic central com., 1938-50, mem. Ark. Dem. central com., 1939-40. Mem. Union County (pres. 1942-43), Ark., Am. bar assns. Address: 423 N Washington Av El Dorado AR 71730*

BROWN, WALTER RALPH, assn. exec.; b. Reidsville, N.C., 1901; ed. U. N.C., Northwestern U. Phys. edn. instr. YMCA, Greensboro, N.C., 1922; asst. mgr. Reensoboro C. of C., 1930-35; mgr. Albany (Ga.) C. of C., 1935-39, exec. sec., 1946-52, exec. v.p., 1956—; mgr. Savannah (Ga.) C. of C., 1939-42; gen. indsl. agt. Central of Savannah and Savannah & Atlanta Rys., N.Y.C., 1952-56. Organizer, bd. dirs. Community Chest, Albany; bd. dirs. YMCA, S.W. Area Ga. Planning and Devel. Commn. Served with AUS, 1942-46. Recipient distinguished service award Am. C. of C. Execs., So. Assn. C. of C. Execs., Nat. award Civic Leaders Am., 1968; named Boss of Year jr. C. of C., 1965, Man of Year Woodmen of the World, 1965, numerous others. Kiwanian (chmn. state conv. com.), Rotarian. Address: Box 308 116 W Oglethorpe Av Albany GA 31705

BROWN, WILLARD RICHARD, lawyer, banker; b. Scipio, Utah, July 25, 1909; s. George Ernest and Susan (Yates) B.; A.B., U. Utah, 1934; LL.B., Columbia, 1937; m. Mary Scull Jacoby, Nov. 24, 1948; children—Bowman, Barton, James Ralph, John Scull, Katharine Creevey. Admitted to N.Y. bar, 1938, Fla. bar, 1950; asso. Shearman & Sterling, N.Y.C., 1939-44; trust officer Chem. Bank & Trust Co., N.Y.C., 1944-50; v.p., sr. trust officer, First Nat. Bank, Miami, Fla., 1950-61; partner, Shutts & Bowen, attys., Miami, 1961—; dir. Westchester Nat. Bank, Miami, Midway Nat. Bank of Dade County. Pres., S.E. Fla. Estate Planning Council, 1959-60; guest lectr. U. Miami Law Sch. Enrollment rep. Columbia U., South Fla. Trustee J. D. Shatford Meml. Trust Assn., Halifax, N.S., Can. Mem. Am., Fla., bar assns., Bar City N.Y., Corporate Fiduciaries Assn. (pres. S.E. Fla. 1957), Fla. Bankers Assn. (past chmn. trust div., founder, trustee, instr. trust tng. sch., mem. legislative com. trust div.), Kappa Sigma, Phi Alpha Delta. Episcopalian. Kiwanian. Clubs: Church, The Pilgrims (N.Y.C.); Rivera Country, Century (Coral Gables, Fla); Naples (Fla.) Yacht. Contbr. articles to law jours. Home: 3720 Harlano St Coral Gables FL 33134 Office: First Nat Bank Bldg Miami FL 33131

BROWN, WILLIAM ARTHUR, JR., physician; b. Wildsville, La., July 17, 1930; s. William Arthur and Eula (Martin) B.; B.S., Miss. Coll., 1953; M.D., U. Miss., 1957; m. Margaret Imogene Oglesby, Aug. 19, 1954. Intern Ark. Baptist Hosp., Little Rock, 1957-58; practice gen. medicine, Mathiston, Miss., 1958—; owner Mathison Clinic, 1968—; mem. staff Houston (Miss.) Hosp. Founding pres. bd. Vadalia (La.) Furniture Mart, Inc., 1969—; partner Furniture Mart, Mathiston, 1970—. Mem. profl. sect. Am. Diabetes Assn. Mem. North Central (pres. 1970-71), Miss., Am. med. assns., Miss., Am. acads. family practice, Am. Geriatrics Soc., Am. Inst. Hypnosis, Alpha Kappa Kappa. Baptist. Mason. Contbr. profl. jours. Home: Church St Mathiston MS 39752 Office: Box 211 Mathiston Clinic Mathiston MS 39752

BROWN, WILLIAM ERNEST, univ. dean; b. Benton Harbor, Mich., Aug. 29, 1922; s. William Ernest and Gertrude (Elliot) B.; D.D.S., U. Mich., 1945, M.S., 1947; m. Theo Nesbitt McDonold, Oct. 21, 1944 (dec. July 16, 1969); children—Judith (Mrs. David Allen Smith), Wendy (Mrs. Robert Kerschbaum, Jr.), Terrence Nesbitt; m. 2d, Eula Mae Ditmore, Sept. 11, 1970. Pvt. practice dentistry, specializing in pedodontics, Ann Arbor, Mich., 1947-61; instr. pedodontics U. Mich., 1947-61, asso. dir. W. K. Kellogg Found. Inst. Grad. and Postgrad. Dentistry, 1961-69; dean Sch. Dentistry, U. Okla., Oklahoma City, 1969—. Cons. Council on Dental Edn., 1967—; mem. Dental Health Research and Edn. Adv. Com. USPHS, 1966-71; mem. dental edn. review com. NIH, 1971-75. Mem. Human Relations Commn., Ann Arbor, Mich., 1960-66, chmn., 1965-66; chmn. U. Mich. Senate Adv. Com. on Univ. Affairs, 1966-67. Recipient Gies Editorial award, 1965, 67. Diplomate Am. Bd. Pedodontics (chmn. examining bd. 1964-65). Mem. Am. Acad. Pedontics, (pres. 1963-64), Am. Soc. Dentistry for Children (pres. 1959-60), Am. Coll. Dentists (pres. 1971-72), Am., Mich. (pres. 1968-69) dental assns. Rotarian. Editor Jour. Mich. State Dental Assn., 1959-67, U. Mich. Dental Alumni Bull., 1966-69. Home: 3117 W Wilshire Blvd Oklahoma City OK 73116

BROWN, WILLIAM PERRY, SR., investment banker; b. New Orleans, Apr. 19, 1899; s. William Perry and Marguerite (Braughn) B.; student Tulane U., 1919; m. Yvonne Elder, June 20, 1923 (dec. June 1966); children— William Perry, Henry Elder, Yvonne Marguerite (Mrs. John Marshall Collier). With Shepard & Gluck, 1919-22, H.W. Fitzpatrick & Co., 1923-26, Perry Brown & Co., 1927-32, Woolfolk, Huggins & Shober, 1933-35, Newman Harris & Co., 1935-39; partner Newman, Brown & Co., 1940-66; sr. partner Kohlmeyer & Co., 1966—, (all New Orleans). Mem. faculty Loyola U. of South, New Orleans, 1932-33, Chmn., U.S. Treas. War and Savs. Bond Program, 1941—. Recipient Patriotic Service 25 yr. award U.S. Treasury, 1966, Patriotic Service award, 1971-72. Mem. Nat. (pres. 1943-44), New Orleans (past pres.) security traders assns., New Orleans Bond Club (dir.), La. Securities Assn. (v.p. 1966-72), Investment Bankers Assn. Am., Internat. House, New Orleans, Pass Christian chambers of commerce, Gulf Yachting Assn. (commodore 1970-71), Miss. Coast Yachting Assn. (past pres.), Municipal Forum N.Y., Delta Kappa Epsilon. Clubs: City of Baton Rouge; Plimsoll (New Orleans); Ponte Verdra of Fla.; Pass Christian (Miss.) Yacht (past commorore, vice commodore 1965—). Home: The Carol 2100 St Charles Av New Orleans LA 70130 Office: 147 Carondelet St New Orleans LA 70150

BROWN, WILLIAM RUSSELL, lawyer; b. Holly Springs, Miss., July 5, 1914; s. Horace Brightberry and Aileen (Blackburn) B.; B.B.A., LL.B., U. Tex., 1937; m. Ruth Cunningham, Apr. 19, 1941; children—Betsy (Mrs. Thomas M. Smith III), Virginia, Russell. Admitted to Tex. bar, 1937, since practiced in Houston; asso. firm Baker, Botts, Andrews & Wharton (now Baker & Botts), 1937—, partner, 1948—; gen. counsel, dir. Houston Lighting & Power Co. Served as lt. USNR, 1943-45. Decorated Bronze Star. Mem. Am., Tex., Houston bar assns. Democrat. Episcopalian. Clubs: Houston, Houston Country. Home: 5816 Bayou Glen Rd Houston TX 77027 Office: 29th Floor 1 Shell Plaza Houston TX 77002

BROWN, WINTHROP GILMAN, govt. ofcl.; b. Seal Harbor, Me., July 12, 1907; s. William Adams and Helen Gilman (Noyes) B.; ed. St. Paul's Sch., Concord, N.H.; B.A., Yale, 1929, LL.B., 1932; m. Peggy Ann Bell, Dec. 28, 1946; children—Winthrop, Julia, Anne. Clk., Platt, Taylor and Walker, N.Y.C., 1932-38; mem. firm Bleakley, Platt & Walker, 1938-41; in office of gen. counsel Lend Lease Adminstrn., Washington, 1941; exec. officer Harriman Mission, Am. embassy, London, 1941-43; with U.S. Lend-Lease Mission to India, 1943; exec. officer Mission for Econ. Affairs, Am. embassy, London, 1943-45, acting chief, Mar. 1945; chief Div. comml. Policy, Dept. State, Washington, 1945-48; acting dir. Office Internat. Trade Policy, 1947-48, dir., 1948-50; dir. Office Internat. Materials Policy, 1950-52; dep. to minister for econ. affairs Am. Embassy, London, Eng., 1952-55, minister, econ. affairs, dir. U.S. operations mission, 1955-57; minister-counsellor, dep. chief of mission Am. embassy, New Delhi, India, 1957-60; U.S. ambassador to Laos, 1960-62; comdt. for fgn. affairs Nat. War Coll., Washington, 1962-64; U.S. ambassador to Korea, 1964-67; spl. asst. to sec. of state, 1967-68, dep. asst. sec. for East Asian and Pacific affairs, 1967-72. Recipient Pres.'s Medal for Distinguished Fed. Civilian Service, 1963; Meritorious Honor award Dept. State, 1956, Superior Honor award, 1952, Distinguished Honor award, 1962. Mem. Soc. of Scroll and Key, Zeta Psi. Club: Chevy Chase (Washington). Home: 2435 Tracy Pl NW Washington DC 20008

BROWNELL, JAMES HENRY, mgmt. cons.; b. Burlington, Vt., Dec. 3, 1937; s. Allan Thomas and Elizabeth (Emery) B.; B.S., Norwich U., 1959; m. Martha Merselis, Jan. 21, 1967. Civil engr. State of Vt., 1959-63; civil engr. Paul Hardeman, Cape Kennedy, Fla., 1963-65; mgmt. cons. Meridian Engrs., Columbia, Md., 1965-68; v.p. Griffith Services, Charlotte, N.C., 1968; mgmt. cons. DBA Systems, Indialantic, Fla., 1969—. Served with C.E., AUS, 1960-63. Registered profl. engr., Vt. Mem. Am. Inst. Indsl. Engrs., Am. Soc. C.E., Soc. Am. Mil. Engrs., Soc. Advancement Mgmt., Nat. Soc. Profl. Engrs., Fla. Engrs. Soc. Club: Florida Norwich University Alumni (v.p. Clearwater, Fla.). Home: Route 1 Box 186 Melbourne Beach FL 32951 Office: 325 Fifth Av Indialantic FL 32901

BROWNHILL, JAMES EUGENE, chem. co. exec.; b. Kansas City, Kan., May 22, 1932; s. Earl Francis and Violet Marie (Coulson) B.; student U. Tex., 1951-53; B.S., U. Houston, 1958; m. Bettie Ann Lazalier, July 25, 1959; children—Cynthia Lynn, James Steven. Acting dist. engr. Gulf Oil Corp., 1955-56; v.p. Cron Chem. Corp., Houston, 1958—; partner Brownhill Sales Co. Chmn. licensing com. Houston Pest Control Operators. Served to capt. USAF, 1956-58. Mem. Houston Soc. Paint Tech., Houston Paint, Varnish and Lacquer Assn. Home: 1403 Anvil St Houston TX 77090 Office: 6015 Murphy St Houston TX 77033

BROWNING, BERNARD S., business counseling co. exec.; b. Browning, Mo., Nov. 7, 1923; s. John Howard and Alma Elaine (Lawrence) B.; student N.E. Mo. State Tchrs. Coll., 1939-41, Georgetown U., 1942, U. Richmond, 1943; M.B.A., Harvard, 1947; postgrad. N.Y.U., 1947-50; m. Adeline Townsend Rogers, Aug. 6, 1955; children— Frances Elaine, Virginia Diane, John Scott, Lawrence Rogers. Dir. customer relations Frederick Research Corp., Bethesda, Md., 1954-56; ind. bus. cons., Bethesda, 1956-62; pres. Gen. Bus. Services, Inc., Washington, 1962—. Lectr. money and banking Fisher Sch., Boston, 1947-58; lectr. marketing Am. U., Washington, 1955-56. Bd. govs. Boston Coll. Center for Small Bus.; trustee Boy's Club Washington. Served with USN, 1944-54; now rear adm. Supply Corps, Res. Mem. President's Assn., Internat. Franchise Assn. (dir. 1971—), Navy Supply Corps Sch. Alumni Assn. (dir. 1971—). Clubs: Army-Navy Country (Arlington, Va.); Lakewood Country (Rockville, Md.). Home: 9825 Belhaven Rd Bethesda MD 20034 Office: 7401 Wisconsin Av Washington DC 20014

BROWNING, CHARLES BENTON, educator; b. Houston, Sept. 16, 1931; s. Earl William and Emma (Sumerlin) B.; B.S., Tex. Technol. Coll., 1955; M.S., Kan. State U., 1956, Ph.D., 1958; m. Magda Luest, Jan. 14, 1956; children—Susan, Charles Benton, Steven, Karen, Heidi, Gary. Research fellow Kan. State U., 1955-58; asst. prof. Miss. State U., 1958-60, asso. prof., 1960-64, prof., 1964-66; chmn. dairy sci. dept. U. Fla., Gainesville, 1966-69, prof., 1966—, dean Coll. Agr. 1969—, also dean resident instrn. Inst. Food and Agrl. Scis. Mem. Am. Dairy Sci. Assn., Am. Soc. Animal Sci., Sigma Xi, Alpha Zeta, Gamma Sigma Delta. Kiwanian. Contbr. articles to profl. jours. Home: 5610 NW 4th Pl Gainesville FL 32601

BROWNING, ROBERT COOPER, cons. engr.; b. Balt., Oct. 31, 1919; s. Romanus Getty and Bertha (Cooper) B.; B.C.E., N.C. State Coll., 1941; m. Mary Frances Gerling, May 9, 1942; children—Robert Cooper, Lawrence Michael, Ann Frances. Field engr., v.p. Loftis Co., contractors and cons. U.S. mil. bases, 1940-41; engr. J. E. Sirrine, cons. engrs., 1941; civilian san. engr. U.S. Navy, Camp Lejeune, N.C., 1941-42; cons. mech. and elec. engr. Wm. C. Olsen, cons. engr., 1946-50; cons. engr. in pvt. practice, Raleigh, N.C., 1950—; dir. engring. Mid Atlantic Mgmt. Assos., Ltd., 1972—; v.p., dir. engring. Med. Environment Corp. Am., 1972—; mech. and elec. engring. cons. Chmn. cons. engring. Profl. Engrs. N.C., 1962, bd. dirs. Central Carolina chpt., 1962-63, state dir., 1963-66, pres., 1969—; sec., treas. Tarheel sect. Illuminating Engr. Soc., 1963; lt. comdr., edn. officer U.S. Power Squadron, Raleigh, 1963-65; comdr. Raleigh Power Squadron, 1965-66; chmn. bd. review Boy Scouts Am., 1963-66. Served as lt. and capt. C.E., AUS, 1942-45; ETO. Registered profl. engr., Md., D.C., Va., N.C., S.C., Ga., Tenn., Tex., Miss. Mem. N.C. Soc. Engrs., Profl. Engrs. N.C., Internat. Assn. Structural and Bridge Engrs., Am. Soc. Heating, Refrigeration and Air-Conditioning Engrs., Am. Radio Relay League, Royal Soc. Health (London), Triangle Internat. Trade Assn. (pres. 1972-73), N.C. Assn. Professions (bd. dirs. 1970-73). Author article. Home: 829 Bryan St Raleigh NC 27605 Office: 510 St Marys St Raleigh NC 27605

BROWNLEE, THOMAS MARSHALL, C. of C. exec.; b. Omaha, Oct. 11, 1926; s. John Templeton and Reed (Marshall) B.; B.S. in Bus. Adminstrn., U. Neb., 1950; m. Olive Ann Gettman, Sept. 13, 1950; children—Linda Sue, Thomas John, Curtis Marshall, Reed Ann. Asst. mgr. Daytona Beach (Fla.) C. of C., 1950, Tampa (Fla.) C. of C., 1952-53; exec. mgr. Tallahassee C. of C., 1953-58; exec. v.p. Greater Columbia (S.C.) C. of C., 1959-63, Winston-Salem (N.C.) C. of C., 1963-64, Orlando Area (Fla.) C. of C., 1964—. Dir. Lock Haven Art Center, Fairview Park Bd. Central Fla. Fair. Bd dirs. Chamber Inst., U. Ga. Served with USNR, 1944-46; as 1st lt. AUS, 1951-52. Mem. Am. (pres. 1966-68, bd. dirs. So. Assn.), S.C. and Fla. (pres.) chambers commerce execs. assns. Presbyn. (deacon). Rotarian. Clubs: Country of Orlando; University; Citrus; Cypress Creek. Contbr. articles profl. jours. Home: 1101 W Princeton Orlando FL 32802 Office: PO Box 1913 Orlando FL 32802

BROWNLEE, WILLIAM JESS, motor transp. co. exec.; b. Guthrie, Okla., Jan. 12, 1909; s. William Franklin and Mable (Kelley) B.; grad. high sch.; m. Virgie Lee Woodward, Aug. 12, 1929 (div. 1945); m. 2d, Gladys M. Mitchell, Sept. 17, 1945; children—Betty Jo (Mrs. Thomas B. Schnaubert), William Wesley. Pumper, Davon Oil Co., Oklahoma City, 1932-40; line driver Willingham Motor Lines, San Antonio, 1945-49; div. mgr. Gulf Southwestern Motor Transp. Co., Houston, 1952-55; v.p. operations Southwestern Motor Transp., San Antonio, 1958-72. Served with USNR, 1943-45. Mem. San Antonio Ind. Motor Carriers Assn., Nat. Defense Transp. Assn., San Antonio Transp. Club, Hermans Sons Tex. Home: 2343 Roosevelt St San Antonio TX 78210 Office: 406 E Cevallos St San Antonio TX 78204 Died Jan. 13, 1972

BROYHILL, JAMES EDGAR, furniture mfr., mem. Republican Nat. Com.; b. Wilkes County, N.C., May 5, 1892; s. Isaac and Margaret (Parsons) B.; student Appalachian Tng. Sch., Boone, N.C., 1913-17; m. Satie L. Hunt, June 21, 1921; children—Allene (Mrs. William E. Stevens, Jr.), Paul, James T., Bettie (Mrs. Willard Gortner). Joined Lenoir Furniture Corp., 1919; organized Lenoir Chair Co., 1926; exec. head Broyhill Furniture Factories, Lenoir Furniture Corp., Lenoir Veneer Co., Nat. Veneer Co., Harper Furniture Co., Lenoir Furniture Forwarding Co., Lenoir, N.C., Lenoir Chair Co. 2, Newton, N.C., Lenoir Chair Co. 3, Whitmel, N.C., Lenoir Chair Co. 5, Taylorsville, N.C., Conover Furniture Co. (N.C.), Otis L. Broyhill Furniture Co., Marion, N.C.; dir. Wachovia Bank & Trust Co., Charlotte, N.C., C. & N.-W. Ry.; mem. adv. bd. Am. Mut. Liability Ins. Co., Charlotte. Bd. govs. Am. Furniture Mart, Chgo. Mem. Rep. Nat. Com., 1948—; del. Rep. Nat. Conv., 6 times. Trustee Wake Forest Coll., Southeastern Bapt. Theol. Sem.; bd. dirs. Caldwell Meml. Hosp., Lenoir. Served with U.S. Army, World War I. Recipient Man of Year plaque by bd. govs. Am. Furniture Mart, Chgo., 1946; Free Enterprise award, 1961. Pres. So. Furniture Mfrs. Assn., 1943-46. Baptist. Mason (Shriner), K.P. Clubs: Charlotte Country, Charlotte City, Quail Hollow (Charlotte); Sedgefield (N.C.) Country; Boone (N.C.) Golf; Biltmore Forest (N.C.) Country; Cedar Rock Golf (Lenoir, N.C.); Blowing Rock (N.C.) Golf; Lenoir (N.C.) Golf, Lenoir Country. Home: Wilkesboro Rd Lenoir NC 28645 Office: 215 Oak St Lenoir NC 28645

BROYHILL, JAMES THOMAS, congressman; b. Lenoir, N.C., Aug. 19, 1927; s. James Edgar and Satie (Hunt) B.; B.S., U. N.C., 1950; m. Louise Robbins, June 2, 1951; children—Marilyn L., James Edgar II, Philip R. Mem. 88th-92d Congresses, 10th dist. N.C. Recipient Young Man of Year award City of Lenoir, 1957. Republican. Baptist (Sunday sch. tchr.). Mason (Shriner). Office 2448 Rayburn House Office Bldg Washington DC 20515 Home: Lenoir NC 28645

BROYHILL, JOEL THOMAS, congressman; b. Hopewell, Va., Nov. 4, 1919; s. Marvin Talmage and Nellie Magdalene (Brewer) B.; student Fork Union (Va.) Mil. Acad., George Washington U., 1939-41; m. Jane Marshall Bragg, May 17, 1942; children—Nancy, Jane-Anne, Jeanne Marie. Mem. 83d-92d U.S. Congresses from 10th Dist. Va. Chmn. planning commn., mem. sch. bd. constrn. adv. council, fiscal affairs adv. council, bd. trustees community fund council Arlington County; finance chmn. Arlington-Fairfax Heart Assn., 1951-52; bd. dirs. Arlington County Hosp. Fund Dr., 1951, Cancer Fund Dr.; mem. disaster com. A.R.C. Mem. County Republican Exec. Com., 1949-53, Va. State Rep. Finance Com., 1952—. Trustee Fork Union Mil. Acad. Served as capt. 106th Inf. AUS, World War II. Mem. Va. State, Arlington County (pres., bd. dirs.) chambers commerce, Nat. Assn. Home Builders, Home Builders Assn. Met. Wash., Wash. Bldg. Congress, No. Va. Home Builders Assn., Washington Bd. Trade, Alexandria-Arlington Fairfax Real Estate Bd. (past sec.), Am. Legion, Res. Officers Assn. U.S., Vets. Fgn. Wars, 40 and 8, D.A.V., Kappa Alpha Alumni Assn. Republican. Lutheran (ch. council). Mason (K.T., Shriner), Tall Cedars of Lebanon, Moose, Eagles. Clubs: Optimist (bd. dirs., p.p., sec.), Republican (pres. Arlington County 1950-51). Home: 4845 Old Dominion Drive Arlington VA 22207

BROYLES, FARRELL RUDOLPH, banker; b. Madison County, Ind., Feb. 26, 1932; s. Rudolph Farrell and Daisey Madge (Adams) B.; grad. Sch. Consumer Banking, U. Va., 1966; m. Alice Rosalyn Darter, Aug. 5, 1951 (div. Dec. 1970); children—Gregory Farrell, Jeanette Lynn. Apprentice, Del. Printing & Lithograph Co., Muncie, Ind., 1951-52; sales mgr. Goff Jewelry, Ft. Myers, Fla., 1952; with First Nat. Bank, Ft. Myers, 1953—, sr. v.p., dir., 1969—. Treas., United Fund Lee County, 1950. Mem. Am. Inst. Banking, Lee County Credit Assn., Fla. Bankers Assn. (installment credit com. 1971-72). Elk. Club: Civitan (Ft. Myers). Home: 2120 Hanson St Fort Myers FL 33901 Office: PO Box 130 Fort Myers FL 33902

BROYLES, JOHN FRANKLIN, football coach; b. Decatur, Ga., Dec. 26, 1924; s. O. T. Broyles; student Ga. Inst. Tech.; m. Barbara Day, May 1945; children—Jack, Hank, Dan, Tommy, Betsy and Linda (twins). Football coach U. Mo., Columbia, 1957-58; now head football coach U. Ark., Fayetteville. Active Boy Scouts Am., Fayetteville. Served with USNR. Mem. Football Coaches Assn. Home: 1525 Hope St Fayetteville AR 72701

BROYLES, THOMAS NATHANIEL, ednl. adminstr.; b. nr. Leon, Va., May 5, 1914; s. Robert L. and Martha Ellen (Clore) B.; B.S., Va. Poly. Inst., 1936; postgrad. U. Va., 1955-58; m. Jennie Belle Abernathy, Sept. 11, 1936; children—Greta Sue (Mrs. James L. Hammer, Jr.), Joanne (Mrs. Stan W. Biggers), Thomas Nathaniel. Tchr. vocational agr. pub. schs., Prospect Hill, N.C., 1936-37, Nokesville, Va., 1937-38, Madison, Va., 1956-58; owner, operator farm, Reva, Va., 1944—; tng. officer VA, Charlottesville, Va., 1947-55; asst. mgr. No. Piedmont Electric Coop., Culpeper, Va., 1958-61, mgr., 1961-67; dir. Piedmont Vocational Sch., Culpeper, 1967—; pres. Brookside Farms, Inc., Reva, 1970—. Mem. Madison County Com. on Standards Quality for Pub. Schs., Va., 1971—; chmn. Vocational and Indsl. Tchrs. No. Va. area, 1970-71; mem. Madison County Regional Control Bd., 1960-67; mem. Madison County Sch. Bd., 1959-67. Served to capt. AUS, 1941-44. Mem. Am., Va. vocational edn. assns., Va. Edn. Assn., Assn. Local Adminstrs., Adult Edn. Assn., Vocational and Indsl. Clubs Am. Baptist (trustee 1948—, gen. sec. Sunday Sch. 1964—). Lion (pres. 1952-53), Kiwanian (pres. Culpeper 1964, dist. lt. gov. 1970-71). Home: Route 1 Box 50 Reva VA 22735 Office: PO Box 855 Culpeper VA 22701

BRUCCOLI, MATTHEW JOSEPH, educator; b. N.Y.C., Aug. 21, 1931; s. Joseph M. and Mary (Gervasi) B.; A.B., Yale, 1953 M.A., U. Va., 1956, Ph.D., 1961; m. Arlyn Firkins, Oct. 5, 1957; children—Mary, Joseph Matthew, Josephine, Arlyn. Instr. English U. Va., 1958-59; asst. prof. Ohio State U., 1961-64, asso. prof., 1965, prof., 1965-69; prof. English, U. S.C., 1969—; dir. Center Editions Am. Authors, Modern Lang. Assn., 1969—; cons. So. Ill. U. Press, 1965—, U. Pitts. Press, 1966—; founding partner Bruccoli-Clark Publishers. Guggenheim fellow, 1971. Club: Groller. Editor: Bruccoli-Clark Books, Fitzgerald Newsletter, 1958-68, Fitzgerald/Hemingway Annual, 1969—. Author: Composition of Tender is the Night, 1962; Ernest Hemingway, Cub Reporter, 1970; Ernest Hemingway's Apprenticeship, 1971; F. Scott Fitzgerald in His Own Time, 1971; As Ever, Scott Fitz, 1972; Kenneth Millar/Ross Macdonald, 1971; John O'Hara: A Checklist, 1972. F. Scott Fitzgerald: A Descriptive Bibliography, 1972. Home: 31 Heathwood Circle Columbia SC 29205

BRUCE, CLEMONT HUGHES, geologist; b. nr. Central City, Ky., Sept. 5, 1921; s. Ezra Clemont and Nancy (Woodson) B.; B.S., U. Ky., 1948, M.S., 1949; m. Bettie J. Kemp, June 11, 1949; children—Donna Lynette, Byron Hughes. Geologist, Mobil Oil Corp., Mt. Vernon, Ill., 1949-53, Dallas, 1953-55, sr. exploration geologist, Jackson, Miss., 1955-65, asso. exploration geologist, Corpus Christi, Tex., 1965-68, geol. specialist, 1968—. Served with USAAF, 1942-45. Mem. Am. Assn. Petroleum Geologists, Geol. Soc. Am., Corpus Christi Geol. Soc., Sigma Xi, Sigma Gamma Epsilon. Baptist (deacon). Contbr. articles to profl. jours. Home: 442 Ashland Dr Corpus Christi TX 78412 Office: Box 2448 Corpus Christi TX 78403

BRUCE, ELMER IVAN, physician; b. Center, Tex., Aug. 20, 1917; s. E. Ivan and Eddie (Sanders) B.; A.A., U. Cal. at Los Angeles, 1938 M.D., U. Tex., 1942; m. Reba Lami, June 8, 1946; children—Patricia, Elizabeth, Barry. Intern, U. Wis. Gen. Hosp., Madison, 1942-43; resident U. Tex. Med. Br. Hosp., Galveston, 1946-49; now mem. staff; practice medicine, specializing in psychiatry, Galveston, 1946—; instr. U. Tex. Med. Br., 1949, asst. prof., 1949-54, asso. prof., 1954-65, prof., 1965—. Served to lt. M.C., USNR, 1944-46. Fellow Am. Psychiat. Assn., A.A.A.S., Am. Coll. Psychiatrists; mem. Am., Tex., Galveston County med. assns., Am. Assn. U. Profs., Central Neuropsychiat. Assn., Phi Rho Sigma. Episcopalian. Clubs: Doctors, Galveston Artillery. Contbr. articles to profl. jours. Home: 1901 Carter Lane La Marque TX 77568 Office: 1014 Texas Av Galveston TX 77550

BRUCE, IMON ELBA, coll. pres.; b. Blevins, Ark., Dec. 9, 1910; s. Jewell Joseph and Ada Lee (Wortham) B.; B.A., Henderson State Tchrs. Coll., 1932; M.S., La. State U., 1937; D.Ed., Ind. U., 1952; m. Catherine Coles, Dec. 24, 1938; children—Catherine Jane, Carolyn Louise, Elizabeth Ann. Tchr. math. and sci. Hope (Ark.) High Sch., 1932-33; tchr. math and sci. Fordyce (Ark.) High Sch., 1933-36; supt. schs., Fordyce, 1937-49; teaching fellow math. La. State U., 1936-37; dir. student teaching Ark. State Tchrs. Coll., Conway, 1949-53; supt. schs., Hot Springs, Ark., 1953-59; pres. So. State Coll., Magnolia, Ark., 1959—; summer vis. lectr. Ind. U., 1955, U. Ark., 1956, 57, U. N.M., 1958. Bd. dirs. So. Extrusions, Inc. Bd. dirs. South Ark. Indsl. Devel. Council. Mem. Nat., Ark. edn. assns., Am., Ark. (past pres.) assns. sch. adminstrs., Am. Ednl. Research Assn., Magnolia C. of C. (past pres.). Phi Delta Kappa. Methodist (steward). Rotarian. Home: So State Coll Magnolia AR 71753

BRUCE, JOHN IRVIN, JR., parasitologist; b. Ellicott City, Md., Aug. 1, 1929; s. John Irvin and Mary (Simms) B.; B.S., Morgan State Coll., 1953; postgrad. Columbia, N.Y.U., 1953-54, U. Md., 1957-58; M.S., Howard U., 1965, Ph.D., 1968; m. Alease L. Sully, Sept. 2, 1967. Jr. chemist Met. Hosp., N.Y.C., 1953-54; research asst. Columbia, 1954-55; med. research technician dept. med. zoology Walter Reed Army Inst. Research, Washington, 1955-59, parasitologist, 1959—, now chief schistosomiasis research unit. Served with USNR, 1946-49. Mem. Am. Inst. Biol. Sci., Am. Soc. Parasitologists, Wildlife Disease Assn., A.A.A.S., Helminthological Soc. Washington, N.Y. Acad. Sci., Am. Soc. Tropical Medicine and Hygiene, Sigma Xi, Beta Kappa Chi. Office: Walter Reed Army Inst Research Dept Med Zoology Washington DC 20012

BRUCE, MABEL LORAINE, educator; b. Winterset, Ia., Apr. 5, 1903; d. Robert William and Nellie S. (Osgood) Bruce; A.B., West Tex. State U., 1926; M.A., U. No. Colo., 1936, Ed.D., 1941. Tchr. rural schs., Potter County, Tex., 1921-23, Amarillo (Tex.) Ind. Sch. Dist., 1923-25; tchr. math. and Latin, Canadian (Tex.) High Sch., 1926-28; tchr. math. Hearne (Tex.) High Sch., 1928-35; research fellow Western Reserve U., 1936-37; tchr. math. and physics Pampa (Tex.) High Sch., 1937-46; prof. math. Amarillo Coll., 1946-70. Mem. Am. Assn. U. Women (treas. 1951-55, 59-60, parliamentarian 1955-57), Nat. Council Tchrs. of Math., Tex. State Tchrs. Assn., Alpha Chi, Kappa Delta Pi, Pi Lambda Theta, Delta Kappa Gamma. Baptist. Mem. Order Eastern Star. Author various articles pub. in profl. jours. Home: 907 Louisiana St Amarillo TX 79106

BRUCKMAN, THOMAS RICHARD, banker; b. Altoona, Pa., June 6, 1936; s. Jack Richard and Geraldine (Hoover) B.; B.S., Fla. State U., 1958; J.D., Stetson U., 1964. Vice pres., trust Investment officer 1st Nat. Bank, Clearwater, Fla., 1964-70; v.p., sr. trust officer Pinellas Central Bank and Trust Co., Largo, Fla., 1970—, also dir. Chmn. bd. dirs. Play Parc Sch. for Retarded Children, 1968—, Largo Recreation Complex & Park Devel., 1968—; bd. govs. Suncoast Sci. Center, St. Petersburg, Fla., 1971—; trustee Suncoast Hosp., 1971—. Served with USNR, 1958-61. Mem. Am., Fla. bar assns., Kappa Sigma (dist grand master Fla., 1967-71), Phi Delta Phi, Phi Eta Sigma, Clearwater Jaycees (dir. 1967). Club: Sertoma (pres. 1967-68, dist. gov. 1968-70, internat. dir. 1970-72, internat. v.p. 1972—). Home: 908 S Highland Av Clearwater FL 33516 Office: Pinellas Shopping Center Largo FL 33540

BRUHN, JOHN GLYNDON, educator; b. Norfolk, Neb., Apr. 27, 1934; s. John Franz and Margaret (Treiber) B.; B.A., U. Neb., 1956, M.A., 1958 Ph.D., Yale, 1961. Sociologist Grace New Haven Hosp., New Haven, 1960-61, Dept. Psychol. Medicine, Edinburgh, Scotland, 1961-62; instr. med. sociology, dept. psychiatry U. Okla. Med. Center, Oklahoma City, 1962-64, asst. prof. preventive medicine and pub. health, 1964-67, asso. prof., 1967-69, prof., chmn. dept. human ecology, 1969-72; asso. dean community affairs, prof. preventive medicine and community health U. Tex. Med. Br., Galveston, 1972—. Cons., Am. Soc. Anesthesiologists. Served with AUS, 1957-58. Recipient Career Devel. award Nat. Heart Inst., 1968-69. Fulbright fellow, 1961-62. Fellow Am. Sociol. Assn., Am. Pub. Health Assn., Am. Heart Assn., Royal Soc. Health; mem. Assn. Am. Med. Colls., Am. Psychosomatic Soc., N.Y. Acad. Sci., Okla. Health and Welfare Assn., Assn. Tchrs. Preventive Medicine, Am. Assn. U. Profs., Southwestern Sociol. Assn., Sigma Xi, Alpha Kappa Delta Home: Apt D-3 1726 Broadway Galveston TX 77550

BRUMBY, PAUL BINGHAM, physician; b. Goodman, Miss., Sept. 28, 1902; s. Walter Eldridge and Mattie Theodora (Alexander) B.; M.D., U. Tex., 1929; postgrad. N.Y. Polyclinic, 1935, Harvard, 1939; m. Linda Fay Patton, June 25, 1935; children—Paul Bingham, Linda (Mrs. James Donald Holder). Intern, Shreveport (La.) Charity Hosp., 1929-30; pvt. practice gen. medicine, Lexington, Miss., 1930—; chief of staff Holmes County Community Hosp., Lexington, 1946—. Bd. dirs. Miss. Found. for Med. Care., 1970—. Served with AUS, 1943-46. Decorated Bronze Star medal. Mem. North Central Miss. Med. Soc. (pres. 1954), Miss. Acad. Family Practice (v.p. 1958), Miss. State Med. Assn. (pres. 1971; trustee 1971). Presbyn. (elder 1966—). Mason (32 deg., Shriner), Rotarian. Home: 102 Westwood Av Lexington MS 39095 Office: 102 N Carrollton St Lexington MS 39095

BRUMBY, SEWELL MARION, librarian; b. Cedartown, Ga., May 20, 1911; s. Charles Rush and Annie Lee (Sewell) B.; B.S., U.S. Mil. Acad., 1932 M.S., Columbia, 1961; J.D., U. Ga., 1964; m. Mary Kent Hart, Sept. 28, 1935; children—Marianne Curran, Mira Lee Sewell, Sewell Robeson Brainerd. Commd. 2d lt. U.S. Army, 1932, advanced through grades to col., 1954; assult bn. comdr. 4th Inf. div. D-Day, Normandy; comdr. Camp Fuji, Japan, 1954; sec. U.S.-Japan Joint Com., 1955-57; ret., 1960; law librarian U. Ga., Athens, 1961—. Mem. Am. Assn. Law Libraries. Home: 350 Glenwood Dr Athens GA 30601 Office: Law Library U Ga Athens GA 30601

BRUNER, QUINTON DOSSIE, r.r. exec.; b. Dothan, Ala., June 28, 1921; s. Charlie Crozier and Annie Mae (Williams) B.; m. Mary Ellen Slusher, June 23, 1946; children—Charles Stephen, Martha (Mrs. Wayne Burdette), Mary Quinn. Sec. to auditor-treas. Atlantic & St. Andrews Bay Ry. Co., Dothan, 1939-40, sec. to asst. gen. mgr., 1940-42, sec. to pres. and gen. mgr., 1945-46, comml. agt., 1946-60, gen. agt., 1960-63, asst. gen. freight agt., 1963-68, traffic mgr., 1968-72, chief traffic officer, asst. sec., 1972—. Sec. chpt. A.R.C., 1967-68. Bd. dirs. United Fund. Served with USAAF, World War II; PTO. Mem. Assn. U.S. Army, So. Freight Assn. (mem. exec. com. 1968—), So. Ports Fgn. Freight Com. (gen. com. 1968—), C. of C. (dir. 1961-63), Com. 100. Baptist (deacon 1958—). Kiwanian (pres. 1957). Editor, The Bay Liner, 1963-69. Home: 207 Sequoyah Dr Dothan AL 36301 Office: 514 E Main St Dothan AL 36301

BRUNER, RUTH AVALINA, educator; b. Chickasha, Okla., Nov. 12, 1912; d. Peter N. and Cora (May) Bruner; B.S., Memphis State U., 1934; M.A., Northwestern U., 1946, Ph.D., 1959, La. State U. Tchr., Whitehaven (Tenn.) High Sch., 1937-40; sec. to Commr. Finance, City of Memphis, 1934-36; exec. sec. to asst. to pres. Todd-Houston Shipbldg. Corp., Houston, 1941-44; asst. prof. Northwestern State Coll., Natchitoches, La., 1946-56, asso. prof., 1956-59, prof., 1960-64; prof., head dept. office adminstrn. Northeast La. U., Monroe, 1964—. Communications cons. State Farm Ins., Monroe, La., 1971—, Internat. Tel. & Tel., Monroe, 1970—. Named Distinguished Tchr. of Year, Northeast La. U., 1972. Mem. Am. Assn. U. Women, Am. Assn. U. Profs., Nat. So., La. bus. edn. assns., Am. Bus. Women's Assn., Delta Kappa Gamma, Delta Pi Epsilon, Phi Kappa Psi (chpt. pres. 1962-63). Contbr. articles to bus. edn. jours. Home: 307 Paula Dr Monroe LA 71201

BRUNER, WILLIAM WALLACE, banker; b. Orangeburg, S.C., Nov. 6, 1920; s. Robert Raysor and Bessie (Livingston) R. children—William W., Thomas W., James L. Accountant, J. W. Hunt & Co., C.P.A.'s, Columbia, S.C., 1945-48; with First Nat. Bank S.C., Columbia, 1948—, sr. v.p., 1961-64, pres., 1964—, also dir.; dir. Palmetto State Life Ins. Co., Columbia, Columbia Coca-Cola Bottling Co. S.C. Treas., United Fund Columbia, 1958-59, bd. dirs., 1956-58, chmn. large firms div., 1965, bd. dirs. treas., 1956-57; chmn. chpt. A.R.C., 1958-60, nat. fund vice chmn., 1960-61, bd. visitors Columbia Coll.; vice chmn. bd. trustees Spartanburg (S.C.) Jr. Coll.; trustee Benedict Coll., Columbia. Treas. S.C. Soc. Crippled Children and Adults, 1967-70, v.p., 1970-71. Served to lt. comdr. USNR, 1941-45, C.P.A., S.C. Mem. Am. Inst. C.P.A.'s, S.C. Assn. C.P.A.'s, Columbia C. of C. (treas. 1961, v.p. 1962), Urban League Columbia (treas., dir.), Am. (adv. com. on fed. legislation 1966-71), S.C. (v.p. 1967-68, pres. 1970-71) bankers assns., Phi Beta Kappa, Beta Gamma Sigma, Sigma Nu. Methodist. Office: 1208 Washington St Columbia SC 29202

BRUNGARDT, ADOLPH JOHN, dentist; b. Morland, Kan., Jan. 20, 1909; s. John M. and Catherine (Bach) B.; student St. Benedict's Coll., 1929-31; D.D.S., Creighton U., 1935; m. Mildred Cates, May 27, 1940; children—Maurice Philip, Adolphine (Mrs. Richard D. Shaw), James M., Joseph A., Charles E., Mary Ann. Pvt. practice dentistry, Lindsay, Okla., 1935—. Vice pres. Garvin County Library Bd., 1969-72; mem. Lindsay Indsl. Found. Mem. Am., Okla., South Central Dist. dental assns., C. of C. Democrat. Roman Catholic (mem. ch. com. 1950-53). Rotarian (past pres.). Home: 210 Willians St Maysville OK 73057 Office: 2 W Chickasaw St Lindsay OK 73052

BRUNI, MICHAEL ARISTIA, pub. co. exec.; b. Phenix City, Ala., Oct. 13, 1921; s. Michael Aristia and Ethel J. (Kenney) B.; student Truman & Smith Bus. Coll., 1948-50; m. Ann Pekor, July 18, 1943; children—Michael Aristia, Barbara (Mrs. Ralph Fackler), Christopher S., Alan P. Asst. gen. mgr. Pekor Iron Works, 1946-51; gen. mgr. Columbus Rock Co., 1951-58; asst. to sales and mfg. coordinator Bickerstaff Clay Products, 1959-61; bus. mgr. Ledger-Enquirer Newspapers, Columbus, Ga., 1961—; dir. Columbus Cablevision, Inc. Chmn. com. mgmt. Armed Services YMCA, 1970-71. Served with M.C., AUS, 1942-46. Mem. Newspaper Purchasing Agts. Assn., Am. Legion, Assn. U.S. Army. K.C., Rotarian. Club: Mr. & Mrs. (Columbus, Ga.). Home: 3349 Flint Dr Columbus GA 31907 Office: 17 W 12th St Columbus GA 31902

BRUNINGA, WILLIAM HENRY, restaurant exec.; b. Peoria, Ill., Oct. 4, 1927; s. William John (dec.) and Helen Arlouine (Loucks) B.; student DePauw U., 1947-48; B.S., U. Ill., 1950; m. Beverly Anne Ward, July 5, 1952; children—John, Stephen, Susan. Accounting supr. Maule Industries, Inc., Miami, Fla., 1952-59; controller Velda Dairies, Miami, 1959-62, Burger King Corp., Miami, 1963-66;

operator Burger King Restaurant, Des Moines, 1967-68; sec., treas. Shoney's Big Boy Enterprises, Nashville, 1969—. Adviser Jr. Achievement, 1957-59, 1964. Served with USAAF, 1945-47. Episcopalian. Home: 2140 Timberwood Dr Nashville TN 37215 Office: 1727 Elm Hill Pike Nashville TN 37210

BRUNINI, EDMUND LAWRENCE, lawyer; b. Vicksburg, Miss., May 8, 1911; s. John and Blanche (Stein) B.; B.A., Georgetown U., 1931; LL.B., U. Miss., 1934; m. Mary Elizabeth Hickman, Sept. 19, 1935; children—Mary Bea, Tessie, Edmund Lawrence. Admitted to Miss. bar, 1934; practice in Jackson, 1945—; partner firm Brunini, Everett, Grantham & Quin, 1938—. Dir. First Nat. Bank Vicksburg, 1954-58, First Miss. Corp., 1958—, First Nat. Bank Jackson, 1961—, First Capitol Corp. Pub. mem. Legislative Resources Com. Miss., 1957-58. Bd. dirs. Miss Safety Council, 1958, Miss. A. and I. Bd., 1952-56, 68-72; mem. adminstrv. bd. Mercy Hosp., 1956-58. Col., aide-de-camp staff gov. Miss., 1952-56. Decorated knight Order St. Gregory, 1951; 1st class order Stella Della Solidaniete (Italy). Fellow Am. Coll. Trial Lawyers; mem. Am., Miss. (v.p. 1938), Hinds County bar assns., Am. Judicature Soc., Vicksburg C. of C. (pres. 1941), Mid Continent Oil and Gas Assn. (pres. Miss-Ala. div. 1954-55), Ind. Petroleum Assn. Am., Newcomen Soc. Am., Jackson C. of C. (pres. 1971—). K.C. Clubs: Jackson Country (pres. 1966), Capitol City Petroleum (pres. 1967) (Jackson); Vicksburg Country. Home: 41 North Hill Pkwy Jackson MS 39206 Office: First Nat Bank Bldg Jackson MS 39205

BRUNINI, JOSEPH BERNARD, bishop; b. Vicksburg, Miss., July 24, 1909; s. John and Blanche (Stein) B.; A.B., Georgetown U., 1930, LL.D., 1957; S.T.D., North Am. Coll., Rome, 1933; J.C.D., Cath. U., Washington, 1937. Ordained priest Roman Catholic Ch., 1933; rector Cathedral, Natchez, Miss., 1943-44; chancellor Natchez Diocese, 1941-49; pastor St. Peter's Co-Cathedral, Jackson, Miss., 1949-62; vicar gen. of Diocese, 1951-66, aux. bishop Natchez-Jackson Diocese, 1957-66, apostolic adminstr., 1966-67, bishop, 1967—. Recipient John Carroll award Georgetown U. Mem. Cath. Hosp. Assn. U.S. and Can. (past pres.), Fed. Hosp. Council, Am. Hosp. Assn. (trustee). K.C. (4 deg.). Home: 123 N West St Jackson MS 39201 Office: Box 2248 Jackson MS 39205

BRUNSON, DONALD LYONS, dentist; b. Houston, June 13, 1922; s. Howard Edward and Ouida (Lyons) B.; B.B.A., U. Tex. at Austin, 1944, D.D.S., 1950; m. Elayne Hope Duke, Aug. 18, 1942; 1 dau., Cassandra (Mrs. John D. Shearer). Gen. practice dentistry, Baytown, Tex., 1950—; dir. Citizens Nat. Bank & Trust Co. Mem. Tex. Bd. Dental Examiners. Chmn. Baytown Civil Service Commn. East Harris County campaign chmn. for Gov. Preston Smith, 1968. Trustee San Jacinto Meth. Hosp. Served with Dental Corps, USAF, 1953-55. Fellow Internat. Coll. Dentists; mem. Baytown Dental Study Club (pres. 1971-72), Am., Tex. dental assns., Houston Dist. Dental Soc., U. Tex. Ex-Students Assn. (life), Am. Acad. Gen. Dentistry, Baytown C. of C. (dir.), Psi Omega, Delta Chi. Methodist (adminstrv. bd., trustee). Club: Baytown Rotary (v.p. 1962). Home: 1803 Southwood Dr Baytown TX 77520 Office: 1105 E James St Baytown TX 77520

BRUNSON, JOEL GARRETT, physician, educator; b. Greenville, S.C., Apr. 22, 1923; s. James Edwin and Leila (Ballenger) B.; student Furman U., 1940-43, Miss. State Coll., 1943; M.D., U. Buffalo, 1950. Intern, U. Ala. Med. Center, 1950-51; resident pathology U. Minn. Hosps., 1951-55; Am. Cancer Soc. fellow U. Minn., 1951-55, instr., pathology Med. Sch., 1955-57, sr. research fellow USPHS, also asst. prof. pathology, 1957-59; prof. pathology, chmn. dept. U. Miss. Med. Center, Jackson, 1959—; cons. VA Hosp., Jackson; cons. pathology to a study sect. USPHS; mem. VA Instl. Research Programs Evaluation Com. Served with AUS, 1943-46. Diplomate Nat. Bd. Med. Examiners, Am. Bd. Pathology. Mem. Am. Assn. Pathologists and Bacteriologists, Internat. Acad. Pathology, Am. Soc. Exptl. Pathology, Am. Nuclear Soc., A.A.A.S., Soc. Research Reticuloendothelial System, Nat. Assn. Standard Med. Vocabulary, N.Y. Acad. Scis., Miss. Assn. Pathologists, Am. Heart Assn., Am. Assn. U. Profs., Am. Soc. Nephrology, Am. Assn. Pathology (dept. chmn., sec.-treas. 1967-70, v.p. 1971, pres. 1972), Cryobiology Soc., Sigma Xi, Nu Sigma Nu. Co-editor: Concepts of Disease, 1971. Contbr. articles med. jours. Mem. editorial bd. Am. Jour. Pathology. Home: RFD 2 Terry MS 39170 Office: Univ Med Center Jackson MS 39216

BRUNSON, JOHN SOLES, lawyer; b. Houston, Tex., Jan. 8, 1934; s. Nathan Bryant and Jonnie E. (Sanders) B.; B.B.A., Baylor U., 1956, LL.B., J.D., 1958; m. Joan Erwin, Dec. 26, 1953; children—Wilson Mark, Dana Ruth. Admitted to Tex. bar, 1958; asso. Dillingham & Schleider, 1958-63; partner Brunson & Brill and predecessor firms, 1964-69; v.p., gen. counsel Contran Corp., 1969-70, partner law firm Baker, Heard & Brunson, Houston, 1970-72; dir. Ward Cut-Rate Drug Co., McNair Trucklease Inc. Mem. Tex. Dem. Exec. Com., 1968—. Mem. Pres. Council, Houston Baptist Coll., 1966—. Mem. State Bar Tex., Houston, Am. bar assns. Club: Houston. Home: 10307 Greentree St Houston TX 77042 Office: 1440 One Allen Center Houston TX 77002

BRUNSON, PIERCE BUTLER, sch. adminstr.; b. Macon, Ga., Sept. 7, 1917; s. Zack A. and Hattie (Jackson) B.; student Albany State Coll. 1934-35; B.A., Morris Brown Coll. 1938; M.A., Atlanta U. 1955, postgrad. 1962-64; m. Brunetta F. Jacobs, June 19, 1946; children—Frank Bernard, Yolande Iris. Tchr., Austell (Ga.) Elementary Sch., 1938-39; ins. salesman Pilgrim Health and Life Ins. Co., Waycross, Ga., 1939-41; tchr. social sci. Hudson High Sch., Macon, Ga., 1947-49; tchr. social sci. Ballard-Hudson Sr. High Sch., 1949-65, chmn. dept. social sci., 1958-65; prin. Maude C. Pye Elementary Sch., 1965—. Bd. dirs. Macon Tchrs. Fed. Credit Union, 1966-68. Served as 1st lt. Transp. Corps, AUS, 1941-45; now capt. Res. ret. Mem. N.E.A., Ga. Assn. Educators, Ga. Elementary Prins. Assn., Bibb Elementary Prins. Assn. (v.p. 1971-72), Omega Psi Phi. Baptist (deacon 1968—). Home: 1994 Vining Circle Macon GA 31204 Office: 855 Anthony Rd Macon GA 31204

BRUNTON, JOHN GEORGE, steel co. exec.; b. San Diego, Oct. 17, 1912; s. George and Agnes McKellar (Rankin) B.; B.S., U. Cal. at Berkeley, 1934; m. Vera M. Ukeneskey, June 12, 1936; children—Nancy (Mrs. Robert H. Cox, Jr.), Robert C. Sales mgr. Pennsalt Chems. Co., 1939-49; v.p. Kolker Chem. Corp., 1949-63; mgr. crop protection chems. USS Agri-Chems. div. U.S. Steel Corp., Atlanta, 1963—. Agrl. chem. industry adviser WPB, War Food Adminstrn., 1943-46. Club: Country (Atlanta). Home: 545 Riverside Pkwy NW Atlanta GA 30328 Office: 30 Pryor St SW Atlanta GA 30301

BRUSILOW, ANSHEL, conductor; b. Phila., Aug. 14, 1928; s. Leon and Dora (Epstein) B.; grad. Curtis Inst. Music, 1943; Artist's diploma, Phila. Mus. Acad., 1947; m. Marilyn Rae Dow, Dec. 23, 1951; children—David, Jennie, Melinda. Concertmaster, asst. condr. New Orleans Symphony, 1954-55; asso. concertmaster Cleve. Orch., 1955-59; concertmaster Phila. Orch., 1959-66. Founder, condr. Phila. Chamber Orch., 1961-65, Chamber Symphony Phila., 1966-68; condr., music dir. Dallas Symphony Orch., 1971—; host TV program Portraits in Music, Sta. WRCV, 1961-63. Bd dirs. Ednl. TV Council. Named Outstanding Young Man of Year, Phila. C. of C., 1963. Office: care Dallas Symphony Orchestra Dallas TX 75205

BRUSTAD, WESLEY OTTO, state ofcl.; b. Fergus Falls, Minn., Aug. 16, 1943; s. Otto Waldemar and Doris Mina (Holoien) B.; B.A. cum laude (NSF scholar, Alcoa scholar), U. Wash., 1964, M.A., 1970; m. Karla Kay Stratford, Dec. 23, 1970; children (by previous marriage)—Robert Wesley, Jason Michael. Adviser, publicity dir. U. Wash., 1969-70; communications coordinator Friends of Youth (social agy.), Seattle, 1970; asst. dir. Ohio Arts Council, Columbus, 1970-71; exec. dir. S.C. Arts Commn., Columbia, 1971—. Cons. various theatre projects, art forms. Served with USAF, 1965-69. Mem. Am. Theatre Assn., numerous assns. arts Presbyn. Designed and conceived theatrical concept spatial theatre.‡

BRUTON, EMMA QUINTILLA GEER (MRS. JAMES DEWITT BRUTON, JR.), civic worker; b. Walton, Ky., Dec. 16, 1907; d. James Arthur and Celia Exular (Wooten) Geer; student pub. schs.; m. James DeWitt Bruton, Jr., June 11, 1932. Bookkeeper, stenographer mfg. firm, Tampa, Fla., 1927-29; clerical worker Standard Oil of Ky., 1929-31; bookkeeper, stenographer Plant City (Fla.) Courier, Wayne Thomas, Pub., 1932-34, Wayne Thomas, Real Estate and Bond Broker, 1934-41; legal stenographer, 1943-44. Mem. Fla. State Library Adv. Council, 1969—; bd. dirs., exec. com. Hillsborough County Tb and Health Assn., 1960—, v.p., 1964-66, life mem., 1967; rep. bd. dirs. Fla. Tb and Health Assn., Jacksonville, 1964; bd. Plant City Library, 1959—, chmn., 1959-67; chmn. County Adv. Library Com. 1961—; mem. Fla. State Library Bd., 1961-63, chmn., 1962-63; mem. Fla. Library and Hist. Commn., 1963-69, chmn., 1967-68; mem. Fla. Library Study Commn., 1970—. Mem. Am., Fla., Hillsborough County library assns., Am., Fla. (v.p. 1961-63) library trustee assns., Am. Assn. State Libraries, Hillsborough County Friends of Library (dir. 1960—, pres. 1967-68), Fla. Audubon Soc. (life), Nature Conservancy, Mus. Sci. and Natural History, Brandon (Fla.) friends of library, Ruskin Library Assn., Tampa Execs. Club, Aux. to Bar Assn. of Tampa and Hillsborough County. Democrat. Methodist. Clubs: Plant City Golf and Country, Plant City Garden (v.p. 1966-68), Women's (Plant City); Tampa Bird. Home: 910 Roux St Plant City FL 33566

BRUTON, JAMES DE WITT, JR., judge; b. Magazine, Ark., Feb. 2, 1908; s. James David and Pattie Lee (Bruton) B.; LL.B., U. Fla., 1931, J.D., 1967; m. Quintilla Geer, June 11, 1932. Admitted to Fla. bar, 1931, since practiced at Plant City; asst. criminal court solicitor, Tampa, 1934-37; elected to Fla. Ho. of Reps., 1935-36; municipal judge, Plant City, 1937-57; corp. and civil lawyer, 1931-61; former probate judge Hillsborough County, Fla.; now circuit judge, Tampa. Dir. Tampa Abstract & Title Ins. Co., Hillsboro Bank, Plant City. Mem. Fla. Bd. Law Examiners, Tampa Mental Health Assn., Tampa A.R.C., Inter-Profl. Family Council, Suicide Prevention Center of Hillsborough Co.; establisher, owner Bruton's Audubon Acres Bird Sanctuary, Plant City. Fellow Am. Bar Found.; mem. Fla. Municipal Judges Assn. (pres. 1956-57), Com. of 100, C. of C. Plant City (bd. dirs.), Plant City Civic Music Assn. (pres.), Jr. C. of C. (pres. 1940), U. Fla. Alumni Assn. (v.p.), Fla. (gov. 1949-50; chmn. bd. editors Jour., 1950-52; chmn. com. Am. citizenship 1952-53; chmn. com. on world peace through law 1959-61), Am. (ho. of dels. 1951-58), Tampa bar assns., Am. Coll. Probate Counsel (jud. fellow), County Judges Assn. Fla. (v.p.), Am. Judicature Soc. (dir.), Audubon Soc., Fla Cattle Assn., Tampa Humane Soc. (life), Selden Soc. London, Am. Ornithologists Union (life), Fla. Hist. Soc. (life mem., dir.), Chi Phi. Democrat. Methodist. Elk. Clubs: Kiwanis (past lt. gov.; dir. Plant City), Plant City Golf and Country; Tampa Executives (pres. 1951-52, dir.), Tampa Bird. Home: 910 Roux St Plant City FL 33566 Office: County Courthouse Tampa FL 33602

BRUTON, THOMAS WADE, state govt. ofcl.; b. Capelie, N.C., Sept. 10, 1902; s. David Dudley and Susan Eleanor (Wade) B.; A.B., Va. Mil. Inst., 1925; student Duke Law Sch., 1925-27; m. Marion Sheppard Piatt, Feb. 1, 1928 (dec. Feb. 11, 1960); m. 2d, Elizabeth Nelms Flournoy, Dec. 1964. Admitted to N.C. bar, 1927; practice law, 1927-29; mem. N.C. Ho. of Reps. from Montgomery County, 1929-31; practice law, 1931-33; asst. atty. gen. N.C., 1933-60, atty. gen., 1960—. Served to lt. col. AUS, World War II; mem. N.C. N.G., 1947—, col., 1955. Decorated Bronze Star medal, N.C. Distinguished Service medal N.C. N.G. Med. N.C. Bar Assn., Order of Coif, Kappa Sigma. Democrat. Methodist. Home: 5005 North Hills Dr Raleigh NC Office: Justice Bldg PO Box 629 Raleigh NC

BRUUN, KNUD IVAN, gas lift equipment co. exec.; b. Denmark, Dec. 22, 1903; s. Ernst and Kirstine (Jappe) B.; grad. Steam and Diesel Engring.-Tech. Sch., Copenhagen, 1924; m. Ferine Honeycutt, Dec. 30, 1949; children—Lance K., Marla S.; came to U.S., 1926; naturalized, 1937. Founder, dir. Turbolite Co., Houston, 1933—, Turbo Generators and Bug Fans, 1967—, McMurry Oil Tools, Inc., 1957—; dir. Telex Corp. Served with Danish Navy, 1924-25. Republican. Lutheran. Club: Lakeside Country (Houston). Home: 546 Stoneleigh St Houston TX 77024 Office: 1017 Hickory St Houston TX 77007

BRYAN, ALBERT VICKERS, judge; b. Alexandria, Va., July 23, 1899; s. Albert and Marion (Beach) B.; LL.B., U. Va., 1921; m. Marie Gasson, Dec. 1, 1923; children—Albert Vickers, Henry G. U.S. dist. judge, 1947-61, U.S. circuit judge, 1961—. Bd. visitors U. Va., 1956, rector, 1960-64. Mem. Am., Va. bar assns., Am. Law Inst., Phi Beta Kappa, Omicron Delta Kappa, Phi Kappa Sigma, Phi Delta Phi. Home: 2826 King St Alexandria VA 22302 Office: Fed Bldg Alexandria VA 22314

BRYAN, BART EBERT, assn. exec.; b. Johnstown, Pa., May 5, 1894; s. Bart and Carrie (Ebert) B.; student U. Mass., 1913-14, Cornell U., 1914-15; m. Marie Elizabeth Genung, Mar. 28, 1921; children—John B., William Joseph. Directory publisher, Asbury Park, N.J. 1923-24; salesman display advt. St. Petersburg (Fla.) Times, 1927-34, advt. mgr., 1934-44, pub. relation dir., 1944-59; pub. St. Petersburg Visitors News, 1944-46; pres. St. Petersburg Motor Club (A.A.A.), 1960-65, treas., 1965-70, dir., 1947—. Pres. St. Petersburg Inter Civic Council, 1942; chief fire watcher Civilian Def., 1943; treas. St. Petersburg Civic Music Assn., 1962-69; life mem. bd. Pinellas Area council Boy Scouts Am. Served with AEF, 1917-19. Recipient Mr. Citizen award, 1958; Silver citation First Fed. Savs. & Loan Assn., 1958. Mem. Am. Legion, V.F.W., Pinellas County Com. 100. Episcopalian (sec. vestry 1960-62). Clubs: St. Petersburg Yacht, Advertising (life mem.) (St. Petersburg). Editor: You Can Sell Newspaper Advertising, 1941. Address: 2616 48th St S St Petersburg FL 33711

BRYAN, DAVID TENNANT, newspaper pub.; b. Richmond, Va., Aug. 3, 1906; s. John Stewart and Anne Eliza (Tennant) B.; student U. Va., 1925-28; m. Mary Harkness Davidson, May 11, 1932. Chmn. bd., dir. Media Gen., Inc.; pub. Richmond Times-Dispatch and Richmond News Leader; dir. Asso. Press, So. Ry. Co. Vice chmn., trustee Richmond Meml. Hosp.; trustee Virginia Union U., Episcopal High Sch.; bd. overseers Hoover Instn. War, Revolution, Peace. Active USNR, 1942-46. Recipient Thomas Jefferson award for pub. service Richmond chpt. Pub. Relations Soc. Am., 1965. Mem. Am. (pres. 1958-60), So. newspaper pubs. assns., Soc. of Cincinnati, S.A.R., S.R., Va. Hist. Soc. (mem. exec. com.), Soc. Colonial Wars, Sigma Delta Chi. Clubs: Commonwealth, Country of Va. (Richmond); Farmington Country (Charlottesville); St. Anthony, Union (N.Y.C.); National Press, Alfalfa (Washington); Bohemian (San Francisco). Home: Ampthill Rd Richmond VA 23226 Office: 333 E Grace St Richmond VA 23226

BRYAN, H. CARLTON, govt. ofcl. Regional dir. NLRB, Birmigham, Ala. Address: 2026 2d Av North Birmingham AL 35203*

BRYAN, JACK YEAMAN, author, photographer, ret. fgn. service officer; b. Peoria, Ill., Sept. 24, 1907; s. James Yeaman and Regina (Gibson) B.; student U. Chgo., 1925-27; fellow philosophy, Duke, 1933-35; B.A. with high distinction, U. Ariz., 1932, M.A., 1933; Ph.D., U. Ia., 1939; m. Margaret Gardner, June 21, 1934 children—Joel Yeaman, Guy Kelsey, Donna Gardner (Mrs. Robert Warren Welch), Kirsten Stuart. Research analyst Fed. Emergency Relief Adminstrn., Washington, 1935-36; from instr. English to prof., chmn. dept. journalism, U. Md., 1936-48; pub. relations adviser OCD, 1942-43; dir. pub. information Welfare Fedn. Cleve., 1943-45; pub. information officer UNRRA, 1945-46; cultural attache Am. embassy, Manila, Philippines, 1948-51; chief program planning Internat. Exchange Service, Dept. State, 1951-53; pub. affairs officer USIS, Bombay, India, 1953-54, Bangalore, India, 1954-55; cultural affairs officer Am. embassy, Cairo, Egypt, 1956, Tehran, Iran, 1956-58; cultural attache, chief cultural affairs officer Am. embassy, Karachi, Pakistan, 1958-63; chief personnel officer for Africa, USIA, 1964-65; officer in charge Project AIM, U.S. Dept. State, Washington, 1965-67; chief cultural affairs adviser USIA, 1968; lectr. creative photography U. Cal. at Riverside, 1968—. Chmn. publs. bd. U. Md., 1946-48; chmn. bd. dirs. U.S. Ednl. Found. in Philippines, 1949-51, U.S. Ednl. Found. in Pakistan, 1958-63; exec. dir. Iran-Am. Soc. in Tehran, 1956-58; founder, exec. dir. Pakistan-Am. Cultural Center, 1959-60, 62, 63. Recipient ann. prize for best fiction Tex. Inst. Letters, 1964, Summerfield Roberts award, 1964. Mem. Tex. Inst. Letters, Tex. Hist. Assn., Am. Mus. Natural History, Am. Soc. Mag. Photographers, Am. Acad. Polit. and Social Scis., Am. Fgn. Service Assn., Phi Delta Theta, Kappa Alpha Mu, Pi Delta Epsilon. Club: Faculty (U. Cal. at Riverside). Author: (novel) Come to the Bower, 1963. Contbr. short stories, articles and photographs to various mags., anthologies, textbooks, including Sunset book on Mexico, 1972. One-man exhibit of photos of Asia touring U.S. colls. and univs.; one-man photo exhibits in India, Pakistan, Washington. Home: 3594 Ramona Dr Riverside CA 92506 also 4107 Van Buren St University Park MD

BRYAN, LYMAN LOWELL, assn. exec.; b. Newcastle, Okla., Dec. 8, 1924; s. Albert Roy and Florence (Bowlan) B.; B.A. in Journalism (Kayser scholar 1948), U. Okla., 1948; m. Alice Louise Modlin, Dec. 31, 1944; children—Lowell, Lisa, Laurel, Layne. Asst. dir. pub. relations Pan American Petroleum Co., Texas City, Tex., 1949-50; dir. information Independent Petroleum Assn. Am., Washington, 1951-54; mgr. community relations Chrysler Corp., Detroit, 1954-56; dir. Washington div. Am. Inst. C.P.A.'s, Washington, 1957—, also Washington editor Jour. of Accountancy, 1957—; guest lectr. U. Okla., Mich. State U., Southeastern U. Participant White House Conf. Bus. Editors, 1962; mem. U.S. Savs. Bonds nat. orgn. com. Treasury Dept.; del. ann. meetings U.S. C. of C., 1959-65; mem. U.S. C. of C.'s Assn. Council on Pensions. Bd. dirs. Arlington (Va.) Better Sports Club, 1963-67; mem. Com. County Expenditures, Arlington County; mem. Arlington Youth Found. Served with USAAF, 1943-45. Recipient Patriotic Civilian Service award U.S. Army Audit Agy., 1963. Mem. A.A.A.S. (mem. publs. com.), Fed. Govt. Accountants Assn., Am. Soc. Pub. Adminstrn. (mem. pub. relations com.), Am. Soc. Assn. Execs., Am. Acad. Polit. and Social Sci., Am. Judicature Soc., U. Okla. Journalism Sch. Alumni Assn. (regional v.p. Washington), Sigma Delta Chi (bd. dirs.). Baptist. Clubs: Nat. Press, University (Washington). Contbr. numerous articles to nat. farm, bus., accounting mags. Home: 2900 N Greencastle St Arlington VA 22207 Office: NADA Bldg 20th and K Sts Washington DC 20006

BRYAN, MIRIAM GERTRUDE MAY (MRS. JAMES E. BRYAN), educator; b. P.E.I., Can., Feb. 1, 1908 (parents Am. citizens); d. George William and Emma (Lawless) May; B.S. in Edn., Bridgewater (Mass.) State Coll., 1929; postgrad. Boston U., 1929-30, Yale, 1935-36, U. Cal. at Los Angeles, 1937, U. Colo., 1938; M.A., N.Y.U., 1940; m. James E. Bryan, Oct. 31, 1941. Tchr., Howard High Sch., West Bridgewater, Mass., 1929-35, Hamden (Conn.) High Sch., 1935-36, East Haven (Conn.) High Sch., 1936-40, Hastings on Hudson (N.Y.) High Sch., 1941-43; head adv. service Coop. Test Service, N.Y.C., 1943-45, adminstrv. asst., 1945-46, editor, 1947-48; editor-in-chief Coop. Test div. and nat. tchr. exams. Ednl. Testing Service, N.Y.C., 1948-49; asst. editor Silver Burdett Co., N.Y.C., 1949-55; test specialist Psychol. Corp., N.Y.C., 1955-56; asst. prof. edn. Rutgers U., New Brunswick, N.J., 1958-60, co-adjutant staff mem., 1956-58; sr. asso. in test devel. Ednl. Testing Service, Princeton, N.J., 1960-61, asso. dir. test devel., 1961-67, sr. editor and asso. dir. Coop. Test Div., 1967-68, cons. elementary and secondary sch. testing program, 1968-72, asso. dir. Atlanta office, 1972—. Test editor, cons. Ia. testing programs State U. Ia., Iowa City, 1950-56; test cons. ednl. div. Reader's Digest Services, Inc. 1955-58; research cons. N.Y. State Dept. Edn., 1962-68; cons. U. N.H., WNH-TV, 1966-67, 70-71; lectr. Mich. State U., summer 1970. Sec., West Bridgewater Republican Town Com., 1934-35. Mem. Am. Ednl. Research Assn., Internat. Reading Assn., Nat. Council on Measurements in Edn., N.E.A., Am. Assn. U. Profs., Am. Assn. U. Women, N.Y.U., Bridgewater State Coll. (Nicholas Tillinghast award 1970) alumni assns., Nat. Council Tchrs. English, Am. Personnel and Guidance Assn., USPHS Wives, Kappa Delta Pi, Pi Lambda Theta (pres. Rho chpt. 1957-58, editor nat. publs. 1961-64, 71—, chmn. nat. fellowship awards com. 1961-64, cons. 1964-65, nat. pres. 1965-69, cons. 1969). Editorial asso., contbr. 4th Mental Measurments Yearbook, 1952-53, 5th, 1957-59, 6th, 1964, 7th, 1972. Contbr. numerous articles to profl. publs. Author various tests. Home: 4978 Vernon Springs Dr Atlanta GA 30338 Office: Educational Testing Service 17 Executive Park Dr. NE Atlanta GA 30329

BRYAN, RICHARD WALKER, educator; b. Dalton, Ga., Nov. 10, 1892; s. William Edward and Alice (Lyle) B.; Ph.B., Emory U., 1916; M.S., N.Y.U., 1924, Ph.D., 1949; student Ga. Inst. Tech., 1920-21, Columbia, summers 1921, 38; m. Ellen L. Fenstermacher, Sept. 28, 1927; 1 son, Richard Walker. Asso. prof. Auburn (Ala.) U., 1934-35; head dept. bus. adminstrn. U. Tampa, Fla., 1935-40; head dept. commerce U. Bridgeport, Conn., 1940-46, Catawba Coll., Salisbury, N.C., 1946-47; prof. econs. and finance La. Polytech. Inst. (now La. Tech. U.), Ruston, 1947-58; head div. bus. adminstrn. Athens (Ala.) Coll., 1958-67, prof. econs. and finance, 1969—; prof. econs. and bus. adminstrn. Martin Coll., Pulaski, Tenn., 1967-69. Mem. Am. Legion, Delta Sigma Pi, Eta Mu Pi, Delta Pi Epsilon, Delta Mu Delta. Democrat. Methodist. Mason. Home: 206 N Madison St Athens AL 35611

BRYAN, ROSS HENRY, cons. structural engr.; b. nr. Ellsworth, Kan., Apr. 16, 1910; s. James E. and Jenny (Henry) B.; U. Kan., 1933; m. Josephine Kandt, May 30, 1936 (dec. 1968); 1 dau., Penelope (Mrs. Gerald W. Kriegel); m. 2d, Irene Hodgden Simpson, July 25, 1969. Bridge designer Kan. Hwy. Dept., Topeka, 1933-40; structural designer Panama Canal Dept., Office Engr. Div., 1940-43; structural engr. Marr & Holman, Architects, Nashville, 1946-49;

partner Bryan & Dozier, Cons. Engrs., Nashville, 1949-—; pres. Ross H. Bryan Inc., Cons. Engrs., Nashville, 1952-—. Bd. dirs. Salvation Army. Served to lt. USNR, 1943-46. Fellow Am. Soc. C.E.; mem. Nat. Soc. Profl. Engrs., Am. Concrete Inst., Prestressed Concrete Inst., Cons. Engrs. Council, Am. Inst. Cons. Engrs., Sigma Chi, Theta Tau. Kiwanian. (pres. 1968). Home: Harbor Island Old Hickory TN 37138 Office: 3d Nat Bank Bldg Nashville TN 37219

BRYANT, A(LTON) BYRNES, JR., savs. and loan exec.; b. Graniteville, S.C., Oct. 23, 1929; s. Alton B. and Roxie (Duffie) B.; B.S., U. S.C., 1955; postgrad. U.S.C., 1955, Grad. Sch. Savs. and Loan, Ind. U., 1967-69; m. Anna May Marcella, Oct. 1, 1950; children—Michael Byrnes, Karen Sue. Asst. v.p., asst. treas., loan officer Home Fed. Savs. & Loan, 1955-61; asst. v.p. Security Fed. Savs. & Loan, Columbia, S.C., 1961-63; sr. v.p. Home Fed. Savs. & Loan Assn., Columbia, 1963-—. Mem. Richland County Rural Recreation Commn.; mem. finance com. Columbia Sch. Bd. Pres. Columbia Savs. and Loan League, 1969; county chmn. S.C. Savs. and Loan League Legislative Com., 1969, circuit chmn., 1970, county chmn., 1971. Bd. dirs. United Community Services. Served with USN, 1948-52. Mem. Columbia C. of C., S.C. C. of C., Am. Savs. and Loan Inst., Assn. U.S. Army, Alpha Kappa Psi. Clubs: Forest Lake Country, Sertoma, Palmetto. Home: 187 Arcadia Springs Circle Columbia SC 29206 Office: 1500 Hampton St Columbia SC 29201

BRYANT, BEAUFORD H., educator; b. Chatham, Va., June 8, 1923; s. B. Dudley and Nannie M. (Bolling) B.; B.A., Johnson Bible Coll., 1943; B.D., Phillips U., 1946, M.A., 1944; M.Th., Princeton Theol. Sem., 1948; Ph.D., U. Edinburgh (Scotland), 1957; m. Dorothy Jane Larson, July 11, 1965; children—Susan, John Paul. Prof. Bible, Phillips U., 1945-56; prof. Bible, Milligan Coll. (Tenn.), 1956-65, prof. N.T., Emmanuel Sch. Religion, 1965-—; Welsheimer lectr., Johnson Bible Coll., 1963; alumni lectr. Ky. Christian Coll., 1971. Mem. Christian Ch. Address: Box 222 Milligan College TN 37682

BRYANT, CELIA MAE SMALL, educator; b. Porum, Okla., Aug. 11, 1913; d. George Milton and Elsie (Sigmon) Small; Mus.B. in Piano, U. Okla., 1947, Mus.M., 1948; pvt. study Frank Mannheimer; m. William Cullen Bryant III, Oct. 3, 1932 (div. May 1945); children—Ann (Mrs. Robert L. Trent), Mary Carol (Mrs. Robert Fritchof Hansen), Culleen (Mrs. Ronald George Tobin). Mem. faculty U. Okla., Norman, 1948-—, prof. music, 1967-—; vis. prof. Interlochen Music Acad., 1972. Appeared as pianist numerous recitals; music adjudicator, clinician; mem. Okla. Commn. Tchr. Edn. and Profl. Standards, 1962-63. Mem. exec. bd. Camp Fire Girls, Norman, 1950-54; bd. dirs. Nat. Music Council, 1971-—. Named one of Nine Outstanding Music Educators in Nation, Mu Phi Epsilon, 1962. Mem. Music Tchrs. Nat. Assn. (div. pres. 1956-58, nat. pres. 1969-—), Am. Music Scholarship Assn. (adv. bd. 1972-—), Okla. Music Tchrs. Assn. (pres. 1962-66), U. Okla. Tchr. Edn. Council (chmn. 1958-62), Okla. Coll. Tchrs. Assn. (sec.-treas. 1963-64), Alpha Chi Omega Alumnae Assn. (state pres. 1950-51), Pi Kappa Lambda (chpt. pres. 1965-67). Club: Mac Dowell Allied Arts Club (treas., pres. 1962-66). Editor piano pedagogy dept. Clavier Mag., 1962-—, writer series Music Lesson, 1963-—. Contbr. articles to publs. Home: 614 E Okmulgee St Norman OK 73069

BRYANT, CHALMERS, mayor; b. Dozier, Ala., Oct. 18, 1922; s. James L. and Bertha (Colvin) B.; B.S., Auburn U., 1945; postgrad. U. Ga., 1947, 48; m. Edith Telintelo, Jan. 26, 1951; children—Marilyn H. (Mrs. Stephen Wright), Kim Alan, Keith Evan, Bruce Thomas. Sales rep. Creamery Package Mfg. Co., Atlanta, 1948-54; with Covington Creamery, Inc., Andalusia, Ala., 1954-68, mgr., 1954-68, treas., 1954-68 mayor, Andalusia, 1968-—. Dir. Ala. Electric Coop., Andalusia; owner Carl's Pit Barbecue, Andalusia, 1969-—. Chmn. Covington County Blood Program A.R.C., 1961-68; capt. Andalusia Rescue Squad, 1965-68. Served with AUS, 1945-46. Named Andalusia Man of Year, Andalusia Kiwanis Club, 1966. Mem. Andalusia Mchts. Assn. (pres. 1960), Andalusia C. of C. (v.p. 1966-67). Mem. Ch. of Christ (deacon). Rotarian (pres. Andalusia club 1965-66). Home: 301 3d Av Andalusia AL 36420 Office: PO Box 292 Andalusia AL 36420

BRYANT, CYRIL ERIC, JR., ch. assn. adminstr.; b. Booneville, Ark., Aug. 8, 1917; s. Cyril Eric and Ruth Elizabeth (Best) B.; student Ouachita Coll., 1934-36; A.B., Baylor U., 1939; postgrad. So. Bapt. Theol. Sem., 1942-43; Litt.D., Ouachita Bapt. U., 1971; m. Flossie Juanita Wells, Apr. 29, 1943; children—James Edwin, Mary Elizabeth. Dir. news Baylor U., 1939-42, dir. pub. relations, 1949-57; editor Ark. Baptist News Mag., 1943-47; dir. publicity So. Bapt. Conv., 1947-49; dir. pubs. Bapt. World Alliance, Washington, 1957-71, asso. sec., 1971-—. Mem. Asso. Ch. Press, Religious Pub. Relations Council. Am. Bible Soc. (adv. council 1965-—), Sigma Delta Chi. Club: Nat. Press. Author: Operation Brother's Brother, 1968. Editor Bapt. World, 1957-—. Contbr. articles to profl. jours. Home: 1628 16th St NW Washington DC 20009 Office: 1628 16th St NW Washington DC 20009

BRYANT, DOUGLAS ARMOUR, motel exec.; b. Worcester, Mass., July 8, 1932; s. Alvin Vincent and Frances Mae (Armour) B.; B.A., Hampden-Sydney Coll., 1955; m. Mary Jane Evans, Nov. 19, 1960; children— Richard, Robin, Barbara. Mgr., Chamberlayne Motel, Richmond, Va., 1958-61, Maplewood Motel, Greensboro, N.C., 1961-64, mgr. Howard Johnson's Motor Lodge, Raleigh, N.C., 1964-—; licensee, v.p., sec. Quality Motel Palace, New Bern, N.C., 1969-—; v.p., sec. 2 Howard Johnsons Motor Lodges, Raleigh and Southern Pines, N.C., 1964-—, El Rancho Motel, Durham, N.C., 1961-—. Served with AUS, 1956-58. Mem. N.C. Motel Assn. (bd. dirs. 1965-—, treas. 1965-67), N.C. Innkeepers Assn., Sigma Chi, Eta Sigma Phi. Democrat. Episcopalian. Elk. Home: 2211 Whitman St Raleigh NC 27609 Office: 2715 N Boulevard St Raleigh NC 27604

BRYANT, GEORGE BADGER, III, newspaper editor; b. Washington, Dec. 7, 1938; s. George Badger and Elsie Freeman (Spenny) B.; A.B. in Journalism, U. N.C.; m. Mardge Etta Lupton, July 22, 1961; 1 son, George Badger IV. Reporter U.P.I., 1960; sports editor Daily Reflector, Greenville, N.C., 1961-63; reporter Virginian-Pilot, Norfolk, Va., 1963-68, city editor, 1968-—. Mem. U.S. Power Squadron, Virginia Beach, Va. Home: 2320 Dodd Dr Virginia Beach VA 23454 Office: 150 W Brambleton Av Norfolk VA 23501

BRYANT, KELLY, state ofcl.; b. Hope, Ark., Aug. 28, 1908; s. C.C. and Annie (Nelson) B.; B.S., U. Ark., 1934; m. Elizabeth Sutton; 1 dau., Elizabeth Ann. Editor, pub. Hope Jour.; printing clk. State of Ark., to 1963; sec. state Ark., Little Rock, 1963-—. Mem. Ark. Sheriff's Assn., Nat. Assn. Secs. State (treas., v.p.). Methodist (bd. stewards). Rotarian. Club: Little Rock. Home: 1405 S Main St Hope AR 71801 Office: State Capitol Little Rock AR 72201

BRYANT, M. HOWARD, educator; b. nr. Ft. Payne, Ala., Aug. 5, 1915; s. Edward Henry and Priscilla (Horton) B.; student Jacksonville State Coll., 1935-36; B.S., U. Ala., 1938; M.A., U. Va., 1949, Ed.D., 1957; m. Margueritte Neeta Posey, Nov. 8, 1941; children—M. Howard, Margaret Elizabeth. High sch. tchr. math., history, Lafayette, Ga., 1938-39, Talledega County, Ala., 1939-41; high sch. prin. Waynesboro (Va.) High Sch., 1947-49; asst. supt. schs., Danville, Va., 1949-54; dir. student aid and placement U. Va., 1954-59, also tchr. edn. courses, 1954-59, dir. urban affairs and community services Sch. Gen. Studies, prof. edn., 1970-—; regional rep. coll. and univ. assistance U.S. Office Edn., Dept. Health, Edn. and Welfare, Region III, D.C., Ky., N.C., Md., Va., W.Va., P.R., V.I., 1959-66, dir. higher edn., 1966-70. Served to lt. comdr. USNR, 1941-47; PTO. Mem. Va. Edn. Assn. (pres. Dist. D, dir.), So. Coll. Placement Officers Assn. (treas., dir.), N.E.A., Coll. Personnel Assn., Am. Assn. Higher Edn., Nat. Univ. Extension Assn., Phi Delta Kappa. Author various monographs in edn. Home: 2025 Spottswood Rd Charlottesville VA 22903

BRYANT, MILTON FLETCHER, physician; b. Blakely, Ga., Aug. 11, 1925; s. Milton F. and Beulah (Williams) B.; B.S., Mercer U., 1944; M.D., U. Mich., 1948, M.S., 1953; m. Avalon Woodruff, Dec. 12, 1947; children— Suzanne, Jonathan, Douglas. Practice medicine specializing in vascular surgery, Atlanta, 1957-—; mem. staffs Ga. Bapt., Piedmont hosps., Atlanta; research asso. Ferst Research Lab., Piedmont Hosp., 1960-—; instr. surgery U. Mich., 1953, Emory U., Atlanta, 1955-57. Served with USNR, 1943-45; to capt. M.C., AUS, 1953-55. Recipient Gold Medal awards Southeastern Surg. Congress, 1962, 65. Mem. Fulton County Med. Soc., Med. Assn. Ga., A.M.A., Internat. Cardiovascular Soc., Pan-Pacific Surg. Assn., Southeastern Surg. Congress (Gold medal awards 1962, 65), Frederick A. Coller Surg. Soc., Soc. Vascular Surgery. Contbr. articles to publs. Discoverer method preventing sloughs produced by norepinephrine, new method prevention thrombosis in small arteries. Home: 3569 Dumbarton Rd NW Atlanta GA 30327 Office: 1938 Peachtree Rd NW Atlanta GA 30309

BRYANT, PAUL WILLIAM, football coach, athletic dir.; b. Kingsland, Ark., Sept. 11, 1913; s. Wilson Monroe and Ida (Kilgore) B.; B.S., U. Ala., 1939; m. Mary Harmon Black, Aug. 3, 1934; children—Mae Martin (Mrs. John Tyson), Paul William. Asst. football coach U. Ala., 1936-40, Vanderbilt U., 1940-41; head football coach, athletic dir. U. Md., 1945, U. Ky., 1946-53, Tex. A. and M. U., 1954-57, U. Ala. at University, 1958-—; head coach Bowl Games, 1947-—. Pres. Bear Bryant Volkswagen, Tuscaloosa; v.p., dir. R.L. Zeiglers, Inc., dir. Olympia Mills of Tuscaloosa, First Nat. Bank, Cotton States Life Ins. Co. (both Tuscaloosa, Ala.). Active YMCA, United Fund, Heart Fund; chmn. fund drive Bryce Hosp. Chapel. Trustee Pop Warner Hall of Fame. Served from lt. (j.g.) to lt. comdr. USNR, 1941-45. Recipient numerous athletic awards; charter mem. Ala. Sports Hall of Fame; named to Ark. Hall of Fame, 1965; named Coach of Year, S.W. Conf., 1956, S.E. Conf., 1961, 64, 71; named Ky. col., Ark. traveler, adm. Tex. Navy; Paul Bryant Hall athletic dorm U. Ala. named in his honor; Bryce Hosp. Chapel re-named Bryant-Jordan chapel. Mem. Am. Football Coaches Assn. trustee (Coach of Yr. award 1961, 71), Assn. Am. (dir.), Boat Owners Council Am. (dir.), Omicron Delta Kappa, Sigma Nu. Methodist. Rotarian. Clubs: A. Jasons (U. Ala.). Author: Building a Championship Football Team, 1960. Home: 77 High Forest Tuscaloosa AL 35401 Office: U Ala Box K University AL 35486

BRYANT, RICHARD E., scientist. Research scientist leukocytic phagocytosis Vanderbilt Sch. Medicine, Nashville. Home: 2036 Priest Rd Nashville TN 37215 Office: Vanderbilt Sch Medicine 21st Av S Nashville TN 37203*

BRYANT, RICHARD MILES, clin. psychologist; b. Princeton, Ill., June 6, 1932; s. Miles William and Amanda (Kaar) B.; B.A., Washington U. (St. Louis), 1954; Ph.D., U. Tex., 1958; student U. Ia., 1954-55; m. Patricia Ruth Patton, Aug. 20, 1955; children—Richard Miles, William Patton, Melissa Ruth. Chief clin. psychology sect. Mental Hygiene Consultation Service, Ft. Leonard Wood, Mo., 1958-60; supr. psychol. services Juvenile Residential Treatment Program, State Hosp., Fulton, Mo., 1960-63; asst. prof. part-time Lincoln U., Jefferson City, Mo., 1960-63; spl. lectr. Wm. Woods Coll., Fulton, Mo., 1960-63; sr. clin. psychologist Children's Med. Center, Tulsa, 1963-64, dir. psychol. services, 1964-—; pvt. practice clin. psychology, Tulsa, 1964-—. Past chmn. Okla. State Bd. Examiners of Psychologists. Diplomate Am. Bd. Profl. Psychology. Mem. Am., Midwestern, Southwestern, Okla. (sec.-treas. 1969-71, pres. elect 1971-72) psychol. assns., Am. Soc. Clin. Hypnosis, A.A.A.S., Sigma Xi, Kappa Alpha, Tulsa Psychol. Assn. (past pres.). Home: 3922 E 59th St Tulsa OK 74135 Office: 4818 S Lewis Av Tulsa OK 74105

BRYANT, ROBERT PARKER, food co. exec.; b. S.I., N.Y., May 13, 1922; s. Thomas Vincent and Rosanna (McRoberts) B.; B.S., Cornell U., 1947; m. Barbara Carlson, Nov. 13, 1953; children—Elizabeth, Robert, Christine, Catherine, Martha. Food mgr. Pa. R.R. Dining Car System, 1952-56; cons. Booz Allen & Hamilton, N.Y.C., 1956-58; v.p. Frank G. Shattuck Co., N.Y.C. 1958-66; v.p. restaurant div. Marriott Corp., Washington, 1966-70, group v.p., 1970-—, corporate v.p., 1971-—. Cons. U. Pa. Hosp., 1954. lectr. Pa. State U., 1955, Farleigh Dickinson U., 1954. Panel mem. White House Conf. on Food, Nutrition and Health, 1969; chmn. Mental Health Week, Albany, N.Y., 1950; sustaining membership chmn. Morris County (N.J.) council Boy Scouts Am., 1964; mem. Bd. Edn., Chatham, N.J., 1965-66; mem. adhoc com. D.C. Minimum Wage Bd., 1971-—. Bd. dirs. YMCA Met. Washington, 1968-—, Crippled Childrens' Home. Served to 1st lt. AUS, 1942-46. Recipient Bronze medal Boy Scouts Am., 1964; decorated Army Commendation medal, Order Long Leaf Pine N.C. Mem. Nat. Restaurant Assn., Cornell Soc. Hotelmen, Ye Hosts Hon. Soc., Phi Delta Theta. Clubs: University (Washington); Touchdown (N.Y.C.). Home: 5602 Newington Rd Washington DC 20016 Office: 5161 River Rd Washington DC 20016

BRYANT, TED, newspaper editor; b. Ala., July 17, 1939; s. Will Frank and Lola (Brewer) B.; grad. U. Ala., 1958, Samford U., 1959; m. Frances Burch, Oct. 25, 1969; 1 son, Greg Sims. Reporter, The Dotham (Ala.) Eagle, 1957-59; editor The Miss. Farmer, Jackson, 1959-60; reporter Birmingham (Ala.) Post-Herald, 1960-66, city editor, 1967-—. Office: Birmingham Post-Herald 200 N 4th Av Birmingham AL 35202

BRYANT, THOMAS FLOYD, JR., physician; b. Wellington, Tex., July 17, 1937; s. Thomas Floyd and Tiny Willie (Glasgow) B.; B.A., N. Tex. State U., 1959; M.D., U. Tex., 1963; m. Beryl U. Dickens, Aug. 15, 1970;children (by previous marriage)Thomas Floyd III, Enid Tina. Intern, St. Joseph Hosp., Ft. Worth, 1963-64; resident U. Tex. Med. Br. Hosps., 1966-68; resident in pediatric anesthesiology Children's Hosp., Los Angeles, 1968-69; practice medicine, specializing in anesthesiology, Galveston, Tex., 1969-—; mem. staffs U. Tex. Med. Br. Hosps., John Sealy Hosp.; asst. prof. anesthesiology U. Tex. Med. Br., Galveston, 1971-—. Served with AUS, 1964-66. Diplomate Am. Bd. Anesthesiology. Fellow Am. Coll. Anesthesiologists; affiliate fellow Am. Acad. Pediatrics; mem. A.M.A., Am., Atlantic (hon.), Tex. socs. anesthesiologists, Gulf Coast Anesthesia Soc., Tex., Galveston County med. socs. Home: 1220 Market St Galveston TX 77550 Office: 800 Mechanic St Galveston TX 77550

BRYANT, WILLIAM ALTON, educator, univ. adminstr.; b. Sanford, Miss., Oct. 24, 1907; s. Willis Allen and Zetta (Knapp) B.; A.B., U. Miss., 1929, M.A., 1939; Ph.D., Vanderbilt U., 1941; m. Willie Hume Branham, Dec. 21, 1931; children—William Alton, Alfred Hume, David Leland, Mary Elizabeth. Tchr., Seminary (Miss.) High Sch., 1930-31; instr. Branham and Hughes Mil. Acad., Spring Hill, Tenn., 1931-32, Battle Ground Acad., Franklin, 1932-36, University (Miss.) High Sch., 1936-39; teaching fellow Vanderbilt U., 1939-41; asst. prof. English, U. Miss., 1941-45, asso. prof., 1945-46, prof. English, 1946-—, acting dir. and dir. summer session, 1942-47, acting registrar, 1944-45, instl. adviser for vets., 1945-46, chmn. dept. English, 1947-54, asst. to chancellor, 1952-53, acting dean univ., 1953-54, provost, 1954-60, vice chancellor, 1960-—. Mem. N.E.A., Modern Lang. Assn. Am., So. Lit. Festival Assn. (pres. 1948-49), Scribblers, Omicron Delta Kappa. Democrat. Presbyn. Author: Conceptions of America and Americans by the English Romantic Poets: 1790-1850 (Vanderbilt Univ. Summaries of Theses), 1945. Address: Box 128 University MS 38677

BRYANT, WILLIAM ARTHUR, physician; b. Pensacola, Fla., Sept. 1, 1919; s. James Edward and Nora (Donaldson) B.; B.S., Madison Coll., 1942; M.D., Loma Linda U., 1947; m. Vesta Elnora Dunn, June 22, 1941; children—Rodney Craig, Gary Barton, Nancy Ellen. Intern, Nashville Gen. Hosp., 1946-47; resident Madison (Tenn.) Hosp., 1947-48; practice gen. medicine, Woodbury, Tenn., 1950-—; mem. staff Good Samaritan Hosp., Woodbury. Med. examiner Cannon County, Tenn., 1965-—; dir. Peoples Bank, Woodbury. Bd. dirs., v.p. Found. for Rehab. of Emotionally Handicapped; mem. exec. bd. Middle Tenn. council Boy Scouts Am. Served to capt. M.C., AUS, 1948-50. Mem. Am., Tenn., So., Woodbury (pres. 1956-57) med. assns., Am. Acad. Gen. Practice, Rutherford County and Staved River Acad. Medicine (sec.-treas. 1972-—). Mem. Seventh-day Adventist Ch. (elder). Lion (past pres.). Home: Hollis Creek Rd Woodbury TN 37190 Office: 301 Main St Woodbury TN 37190

BRYANT, WILLIAM B., U.S. dist. judge; b. Wetumpka, Ala., Sept 18, 1911; s. Benson and Alberta Bryant; A.B., Howard U., 1932, LL.B., 1936; m. Astaire A. Gonzalez, Aug. 25, 1934; children—Astaire, William B. Asst. U.S. atty. for D.C., 1951-54; partner firm Houston, Bryant & Gardner, 1954-65; U.S. dist judge for D.C., 1965-—; prof. law Howard U. Sch. Law, 1965-—. Served with AUS, 1943-47. Mem. Am. Bar Assn. Home: 3725 17th St NE Washington DC 20018 Office: US Court House Washington DC 20001

BRYDON, NATHANIEL COLEMAN, ins. co. exec.; b. Morgantown, W.Va., Dec. 12, 1910; s. George MacLaren and Nathalie Page (Coleman) B.; B.S., U. Va., 1933; m. Grace Langhorne Slater, June 26, 1937; children— Nathaniel Coleman, Jr., George MacLaren III, Sally Slater. Clk. actuarial dept. Life Ins. Co. Va., Richmond, 1936-40, clk. underwriting dept., 1940-46; dept. head VA Ins. Service, 1946-51; mgr. actuarial and underwriting depts. Richmond (Va.) Life Ins. Co., 1952-56; actuary Fidelity Bankers Life Ins. Co., Richmond, 1956-62, v.p. operations, 1962-—. Bd. dirs. Jr. Achievement Richmond. Served with USNR, 1942-45; lt. comdr. Res. ret. Mem. Middle Atlantic Actuarial Club. Episcopalian (vestryman 1949-50, 56-58). Club: Bull and Bear (Richmond). Home: 7405 Three Chopt Rd Richmond VA 23226 Office: 9th and Main Sts Richmond VA 23219

BRYLES, HORACE LESLIE, personnel exec.; b. nr. Beebe, Ark., Apr. 16, 1933; s. William Horace and Kathryn (Golden) B.; B.S. with honors, U. Ark., 1958; m. Joann Pitts, Sept. 12, 1959; children—Leslie Ann, William David. Employment interviewer Daisy-Heddon Co., Rogers, Ark., 1958-59, asst. dir. personnel, 1959-66, dir. personnel, 1966-—. Mem. Ark. Gov.'s Adv. Council on Vocational and Tech. Edn., 1969-71; mem. Menninger Found., 1971-72. Councilman, Rogers, 1962-69. Served with USAF, 1951-55. Mem. No. Ark. Personnel Assn. (chpt. pres. 1969), Am. Soc. Personnel Adminstrn., Rogers C. of C. (dir. 1969-70, treas. 1970-71). Republican. Elk, Lion (v.p. 1971). Home: 1412 Dogwood St Rogers AR 72756 Office: Box 220 Rogers AR 72756

BRYMER, ROBERT LEWIS, advt. exec.; b. Muskogee, Okla., Mar. 7, 1932; s. Winston Edward and Lois Ross (Nash) B.; B.A., U. Colo., 1954; postgrad. U. Chgo., 1958, Northwestern U., 1957; m. Natalie Ruth Snell, June 26, 1954; children—Kathleen, Robert, Charles, William. With Young & Rubicam Advt., Chgo., 1954; dir. marketing services Borg-Warner Internat. Corp., 1956-59; account exec., v.p., dir. Zimmer, McClaskey, Lewis Inc., Louisville, 1959-—. Served with USAF, 1954-56. Decorated Commendation Medal. Mem. Ky. Indsl. Advt. Assn. (pres. 1972-73). Club: Pendennis (Louisville). Home: 525 Country Lane Louisville KY 40207 Office: 1469 S 4th St Louisville KY 40208

BRYSON, JAMES MARION, city ofcl.; b. Owings, S.C., Oct. 25, 1922; s. James Marion and Nannie (Cox) B.; B.S. in Civil Engring., U. S.C., 1943; m. Helen Wallace Bobo, Nov. 8, 1947; children—Martha (Mrs. William H. Rhodes), Sara Bobo. County engr., Laurens County, S.C., 1949-55; bldg. ofcl. City of Spartanburg (S.C.), 1955-58, dir. pub. works and urban renewal, 1958-—. Served with USAAF, 1943-46. Recipient award of excellence for community service Spartanburg Council of Architects, 1968. Mem. Am. Pub. Works Assn., Nat. Assn. Housing and Redevel. Ofcls. (pres. Carolinas council 1969-70), award for program contbg. most to city-wide housing improvement Southeastern regional council 1965. Presbyn. (elder 1966-—). Home: 409 Crestview Dr Spartanburg SC 29301 Office: PO Box 1749 Spartanburg SC 29301

BUBIER, ROBERT HARVEY, city ofcl.; b. Hartford, Conn., June 12, 1927; s. Sylvester Breed and Ruth (Harvey) B.; A.B. in Journalism, U. Miami, 1951; m. Rosemary Theresa Brogan, July 26, 1951; children—Debra Ruth, Michelle. Personnel technician City of Ft. Lauderdale (Fla.), 1956-59, acting dir. recreation, also asst. city mgr., 1961-62, city mgr., 1963-—. Dir. Civil Def., Ft. Lauderdale, 1964-—. Bd. dirs. United Fund, YMCA, Swimming Hall of Fame, A.R.C., Broward County Jr. Achievement. Served with USNR, 1943-46, USAF, 1951-53, 61-62. Recipient Good Govt. award Ft. Lauderdale Jr. C. of C., 1967. Mem. Internat. City Mgrs. Assn., Fla. (dir.), Broward County (pres.) leagues of municipalities, Florida City and County Mgmt. Assn. (pres.), Air Force Assn. (v.p. Gold Coast chpt.), Am. Legion, Sigma Delta Chi, Simga Chi. Episcopalian (vestryman). Rotarian. Elk. Home: 300 Lido Dr Fort Lauderdale FL 33301 Office: 100 N Andrews Av Fort Lauderdale FL 33302

BUCHANAN, ARCHIBALD C., judge; b. Tazewell, Va., Jan. 7, 1890; s. A. Beauregard and Nannie E. (Chapman) B.; A.B., Hampden Sydney Coll., Va., 1910, L.L.D., 1969; LL.B., Washington and Lee U., 1914, LL.D., 1949; m. Ollie McCall, Dec. 18, 1915; children—Sara (Mrs. Herbert Silvers, dec.), Archibald C. Admitted to Va. bar, 1914; gen. practice state and fed. courts, 1915-27; mem. law partnership Chapman, Peery & Buchanan, Tazewell, Va.; judge 22d Jud. Circuit of Va., 1927-46; justice Supreme Ct. of Appeals of Va., 1946-69; mayor, Tazewell, Va., 1917-21; commr. of accounts Tazewell Co., 1919-27; mem. Jud. Council of Va., 1928-32; chmn. com. of judges to fix salaries of trial justices of Va. and their clks., 1942-46; com. of Judiciary Va. State Bar, 1941-46. Recipient Algernon Sydney Sullivan Medallion, 1950. Trustee Hampden-Sydney Coll., 1928-68, Mary Baldwin Coll., Staunton, Va., 1948-62. Mem. Am., Va. bar assns., Va. Hist. Soc., Pi Kappa Alpha, Phi Delta Phi, Phi Beta Kappa. Democrat.

Presbyn. (elder). Rotarian. Clubs: Tazewell County Country, Commonwealth. Home: Tazewell VA 24651

BUCHANAN, EMMETT LASCAR, JR., sales exec.; b. Detroit, Feb. 1, 1920; s. Emmett Lascar and Lillian (Kreekun) B.; student U. Mo., 1938-39; m. Betty Jean Pounders, June 30, 1951; children—Shirley Jean, Nancy Joyce. Salesman Bankers Life Ins. Co., John Hancock Ins. Co., Proctor & Gamble, 1940-42; salesman Health-Mor, Chgo., 1942-45; with Cooper U.S.A., Chgo. 1946-—, salesman, regional mgr. So. region, 1946-—. Served with AUS, 1942-45; PTO. Mem. Entomology Soc. Am., Tex. Producers Vet. Supplies (v.p. 1960). Methodist. Club: San Antonio Golf Assn. Home: 102 W Rampart St San Antonio TX 78216 Office: 3310 Quebec Dallas TX 75427 also 1909 Clifton St Chicago IL 60614

BUCHANAN, GERALD, librarian; b. Forrest County, Miss., July 26, 1937; s. W. L. and Melba (Griffith) B.; B.A., William Carey Coll., 1957; M.S., U. So. Miss., 1965; m. Dottie Renick, May 16, 1960; children— Kay, Donna, Cynthia. English tchr. Okolona (Miss.) Pub. Schs., 1957-59, Perkinston (Miss.) Jr. Coll., 1959-62; asst. librarian Perkinston Jr. Coll., 1962-65; librarian Perkinston campus Mississippi Gulf Coast Jr. Coll., 1965-—. Mem. Am., Southeastern, Miss. library assns., Miss. Edn. Assn. Baptist. Home: PO Box 71 Perkinston MS 39573

BUCHANAN, HERSHEL, furniture mfg. co. exec.; b. Morristown, Tenn., July 31, 1918; s. James and Jane (Howard) B.; student U. Tenn., 1953; m. Mary Gertrude Horner, Sept. 30, 1939; children—Stephen Clay, Frances Sue, John Paul, Wanda Janelle. Supr. shipping Interwoven Stocking Co., Morristown, Tenn., 1940-43; gen. mill overseer Belding Heminway Co., Morristown, 1946-61; purchasing agt. Forest Products Corp., Morristown, 1961-—. Served with AUS, 1943-45. Mem. V.F.W., Am. Legion. Woodman World, Mason (Shriner). Republican. Baptist. Home: Rt 6 Morristown TN 37814 Office: 1010 Cherokee Dr Morristown TN 37814

BUCHANAN, JAMES JUNKIN, educator; b. Pitts., Mar. 7, 1925; s. John Grier and Charity (Packer) B.; A.B., Princeton, 1946, Ph.D., 1954; M.B.A., Harvard, 1948; m. Joanne Harriett Cherrington, Mar. 31, 1951; children—Susan Grier, Edison Cherrington, Constance Packer, James Junkin, Charles Sturm. Mem. staff investment adv. dept. 1st Boston Corp., N.Y.C., Pitts., 1948-51; instr. classics Princeton, 1953-56, asst. prof., 1956-60; chmn. depts. Latin and Greek, So. Meth. U., 1960-62, dean Coll. Arts and Scis., 1962-63; chmn. dept. classics Trinity U., San Antonio, 1963-64; prof. classical langs. Tulane U., New Orleans, 1964-—. Treas., U. League Nursery Sch., Princeton, 1957-59. Bd. mgrs. Am. Sch. Classical Studies, Athens, Greece. Served with USNR, 1942-43. Mem. classical Assn. Midwest and S., Classical Assn. Eng., Am. Philol. Assn., Archaeol. Inst. Am., Princeton Alumni Council (exec. council), Phi Beta Kappa. Democrat. Presbyn. Clubs: Essex (New Orleans); Princeton (N.Y.C.). Author: Boethius: Consolation of Philosophy, 1957, Theorika, 1962, Zosimus: Historia Nova, 1967. Contbr. to Ency. Americana, various jours. Home: 1542 Calhoun St New Orleans LA 70118

BUCHANAN, JAMES MCGILL, JR., economist, educator; b. Murfreesboro, Tenn., Oct. 2, 1919; s. James McGill and Lila (Scott) B.; B.S., Middle Tenn. State Coll., 1940; M.A., U. Tenn., 1941; Ph.D., U. Chgo., 1948; m. Anne Bakke, Oct. 5, 1945. Prof. econs. U. Tenn., 1950-51; prof. econs. Fla. State U., 1951-54, prof., chmn. dept., 1954-56; prof. econs., U. Va., 1956-62, Paul G. McIntyre prof. econs., 1962-68, chmn. dept., 1956-62; prof. econs. U. Cal. Los Angeles, 1968-69; prof. econs. Va. Polytech. Inst., 1969-—; dir. Center for Pub. Choice, 1969-— Fulbright research scholar, Italy, 1955-56; Ford Faculty research fellow, 1959-60; Fulbright vis. prof. Cambridge U., 1961-62. Served as lt. USNR, 1941-46. Decorated Bronze Star medal. Mem. Am. (exec. com. 1966-69, v.p. 1971), So. (pres. 1963) econ. assns., Royal Econ. Soc. Author: (with C.L. Allen and M.R. Colberg) Prices, Income and Public Policy, 1954; Public Principles of Public Debt, 1958; The Public Finances, 1960; Fiscal Theory and Political Economy, 1960; The Calculus of Consent (with G. Tullock), 1962; Public Finance in Democratic Process, 1966 The Demand and Supply of Public Goods, 1968; Cost and Choice, 1969; (with N. Devletoglor) Academia in Anarchy, 1970; (with R. Tollison) Theory of Public Choice, 1972. Contbr. profl. jours. Home: 504 South Gate Dr Blacksburg VA 24060

BUCHANAN, JOHN HALL, JR., congressman; b. Paris, Tenn., Mar. 19, 1928; s. John Hall and Ruby (Lowrey) B.; A.B., Howard Coll., 1949; grad. student U. Va., 1950-51; Th.B., So. Bapt. Theol. Sem., 1957; LL.D., Samford U., 1967; m. 2d, Elizabeth Moore, May 9, 1961; children—Elizabeth Jakes, Lynn Lowrey. Ordained to ministry Baptist Ch., 1952; pastor in Glasgow, Va., 1952-53, Hartsville, Tenn., 1955-56, Birmingham, Ala., 1957-62; minister edn. Southside Bapt. Ch., Birmingham, 1953-54; speaker, lectr. in Ala., also interim and supply pastor, 1962-64; mem. 90th-92d Congress, 6th Dist. Ala. Chmn. Jefferson County Republican Com., 1964-—; pres. Rep. Workshops Ala., 1963-64; mem. exec. com., dir. finance Ala. Rep. Com., 1963-64. Served with USNR, 1945-46. Mem. Pi Kappa Alpha. Mason, Kiwanian. Home: 4320 Overlook Rd Birmingham AL 35213 Office: Longworth House Office Bldg Washington DC 20515

BUCHANAN, JOHN O., civil engr.; b. Asheville, N.C., Oct. 11, 1921; s. Corsey C. and Lillian (Barker) B.; B.S., The Citadel, 1943; M.S., U. Mo., 1961; m. Helen M. Foote, Dec. 21, 1947; 1 son, Charles O. Commd. 2d lt. C.E., U.S. Army, 1943, advanced through grades to lt. col., 1960; chief Tokyo Dist., 1955-56, chief master planning sect. Hdqrs. 4th Army, dep. dist. engr. Alaska, 1956-66; ret., 1966; sr. constrn. supt. Dow Chem. Co., Stade, Germany, 1966-—. Leader, Blue Ridge council Boy Scouts Am., 1967-68; active San Antonio Little Theater, 1963-64; asst. tech. dir. Anchorage Little Theater, 1965-66. Registered profl. engr., Tex. Mem. Soc. Am. Mil. Engrs., Nat. Soc. Profl. Engrs., Nat. Sojourners, Heros of '76, Chi Epsilon. Mason (Shriner). Home: 126 Clover Lake Jackson TX 77566 Office: Dow Chemical Gmbh Werk Stade 2161 Butzfleth Germany

BUCHANAN, LILIAN BARKER, librarian; b. Charleston, W.Va., Sept. 24, 1896; d. John Quenton and Mamie Deborah (Keeney) Barker; B.S., Western Carolina Coll., 1934; M.S., Columbia, 1938; m. Corsey Candler Buchanan, May 10, 1920; 1 son, John Osborne. Head primary dept. Sylva (N.C.) Collegiate Inst., 1919-21; tchr. English, Sylva High Sch., 1926-27; librarian Western Carolina Coll., 1930-—. Founder, Pub. Library, Sylva, N.C., 1928. Edna M. Sanderson fellowship Columbia Library Sch., 1942-43. Mem. N.C. Library Assn. (chmn. coll. and univ. library div. 1957). Club: Twentieth Century of Sylva (1st pres. 1925-27). A founder Smoky Mountain Nat. Park. Home: Dillsboro NC 28725

BUCHANAN, PATRICK JOSEPH, govt. ofcl.; b. Washington, Nov. 2, 1938; s. William Baldwin and Catherine E. (Crum) B.; A.B. in English, Georgetown U., 1961; M.S. in Journalism, Columbia, 1962; m. Shelley Ann Scarney, May, 1971. Editorial writer St. Louis Globe Democrat, 1962-64, asst. editorial editor, 1964-66; exec. asst. to Richard M. Nixon, 1966-69; spl. asst. to Pres. Nixon, 1969-—. Mem. President's Commn. White House Fellowships. Home: 2500 Virginia Av NW Washington DC 20037 Office: The White House Washington DC 20500

BUCHANAN, WILLIAM W., govt. ofcl. Chmn. U.S. Hist. Documents Inst., Inc., Washington. Address: US Historical Documents Inst Inc 1647 Wisconsin Av NW Washington DC 20007*

BUCHER, DONALD ROY, hosp. adminstr.; b. St. Louis, Nov. 17, 1927; s. George Henry and Leonora Frances (Arms) B.; B.S., St. Louis U., 1949; m. Patricia Lakebrink, May 18, 1958; children—Amy, Anna. Accounting dept. mgr. Butler Bros.-City Products Corp., St. Louis and Kansas City, Mo., 1953-63; internal auditor Consumers Coop. Assn., Kansas City, Mo., 1963-65; controller Baugh Wiley Smith Hosp., Decatur, Ala., 1965-68, adminstr., 1968-—. Active Morgan County chpt. Nat. Cystic Fibrosis Research. Served with USNR, 1944-46, AUS, 1951-53. Mem. Ala. Hosp. Execs., Ala. Hosp. Financial Mgmt. Assn. (dir. 1969-70). Club: St. Louis University Alumni (St. Louis). Home: 1208 Noble St SW Decatur AL 35601 Office: 222 Gordon Dr SE Decatur AL 35601

BUCHHOLZ, ALBERT EDWARD, dentist; b. Pigeon, Mich., Apr. 27, 1916; s. Herman and Anna (Schuette) B.; B.S., Mich. State U., 1939; D.D.S., U. Mich., 1943; m. Margaret Olivia Petersen, June 19, 1943; children— William Arthur, Robert Alan, Mark Steven. Pvt. practice dentistry, St. Louis, Mich., 1946-54, Ft. Lauderdale, Fla., 1954-—. Chmn., United Fund, 1948, 49; coach Little League Baseball and Football, 1958-66. Served to capt. Dental Corps, AUS, 1943-46; ETO. Mem. Broward County Dental Soc., Exec. Assn. Ft. Lauderdale (bd. dirs. 1964-65), Am. Legion, Broward County U. Mich. Alumni Assn. (pres. 1971-72), Tri County Dental Soc. (pres. 1947-48), Delta Sigma Delta. Republican. Presbyn. (deacon 1962-65). Mason, Rotarian. Clubs: Tennis, Touchdown (Ft. Lauderdale, Fla.). Home: 2549 Middle River Dr Fort Lauderdale FL 33305 Office: 852 NE 20th Av Fort Lauderdale FL 33304

BUCHHOLZ, DONALD ALDEN, stock brokerage co. exec.; b. LaPorte, Tex., Mar. 10, 1929; s. Fred T. and Chrystine (McCombs) B.; B.B.A., North Tex., U., 1952; m. Ruth Vernon, May 17, 1958; children—Robert, Chrystine Louise. Accountant, staff auditor Peat Marwick Mitchell, Dallas, 1952-54; asst. sec.-treas, chief accountant ICT Discount Corp., 1954-56; comptroller Eppler-Guerin & Turner, Inc., 1956-59; partner Cheshier-Buchholz, pub. accountants, 1959-60; comptroller, sec. Parker Ford, Inc., stock brokers, Dallas, 1960-63, also dir., 1962-63; v.p. Weber Hall, Cobb & Caudle, Inc., Dallas, 1963-72, also sec., dir.; v.p., partner MidSouthwest Securities, Inc., Dallas, 1972-—; dir. Tucker Electronics Co., Garland Bank & Trust (Tex.), Gainsworth Devel. Co., Hedgfan Petroleum Co. Tchr., N.Y. Inst. Finance. Bd. govs. N.Y. Stock Exchange, 1969-72; mem. Bd. Trade City Chgo., 1963-72, Midwest Stock Exchange, 1963-72. Trustee Garland Ind. Sch. Dist., 1971-—. Served with USAAF, 1946-49. C.P.A., Tex. Mem. Dallas Security Dealers Assn. (sec. 1961). Baptist. Kiwanian (Garland v.p. 1959, pres. 1968). Home: 3627 Glenbrook Ct Garland TX 75041 Office: Mercantile Bank Bldg Dallas TX 75201

BUCHMAN, PAUL SIDNEY, lawyer, govt. ofcl.; b. Tampa, Fla., June 5, 1923; s. Julius M. and Lillian (Neuwirth) B.; LL.B., U. Fla., 1948; m. Beryle Solomon, Feb. 7, 1950; children—Julius Miles, Kenneth William. Admitted to Fla. bar, 1948; pvt. practice law, Plant City, Fla., 1948-—; city atty. Plant City, 1949-—; atty., exec. dir. Plant City Housing Authority, 1956-—; atty., exec. dir. Plant City Urban Renewal Agy., 1961-—. Chmn. Fla. Conf. of City Attys., 1960; pres. Ridge League of Municipalities, 1958. Served from pvt. to cpl. AUS, 1943-45, ETO. Decorated Purple Heart; recipient Distinguished Service award U.S. Jr. C. of C., 1961. Mem. Am. Judicature Soc., Nat. Inst. Municipal Law Officers, Fla. Bar (chmn. local govt. com. 1972-—), Fla. Assn. Housing and Redevel. Ofcls. (pres. 1968), Fla. Blue Key, Am. Legion, 40 and 8, Phi Alpha Delta, Pi Lambda Phi. Mason. Club: Lions. Home: 1010 N Knight St Plant City FL 33566 Office: 212 N Collins St Plant City FL 33566

BUCHWALD, ART, columnist; b. Mt. Vernon, N.Y., Oct. 20, 1925; s. Joseph and Helen (Kleinberger) B.; student U. So. Cal., 1945-48; m. Anne McGarry, Oct. 11, 1952; children—Joel, Conchita Mathilde, Jennifer. Syndicated columnist, newspapers throughout world; columnist N.Y. Herald Tribune, 1948-—. Served with USMCR, 1942-45. Club: Anglo-American Press (Paris); National Press (Washington). Author: Paris After Dark, 1950; Art Buchwald's Paris, 1954; The Brave Coward, 1957; A Gift From the Boys; More Caviar; Un Cadeau Pur Le Patronn (Prix de la Bonne Humeur, 1958); Don't Forget to Write, 1960; Art Buchwald's Secret List to Paris, 1961; How Much is That in Dollars, 1961; Is It Safe to Drink the Water, 1962; I Chose Capital Punishment, 1963; And Then I Told the President, 1965; Son of the Great Society, 1966; Have I Ever Lied To You, 1968. Home: 4327 Hawthorne St NW Washington DC 20020 Office: 1750 Pennsylvania Av NW Washington DC 20006

BUCK, LUCIUS A(DOLPHUS), lawyer; b. Abingdon, Va., July 3, 1905; s. E. C. and Mary (Lee) B.; student Emory and Henry Coll., Emory, Va., 1923-24; J.D., U. Va., 1929; m. Margaret Winters, Mar. 29, 1935; 1 son, David Mason V. Admitted to Va. bar, 1928, Fla. bar, 1929, N.Y. bar, 1940; practice law, West Palm Beach, Fla., 1929-34; spl. asst. to U.S. Atty. Gen., 1934-38; sr. tax asso. Davis, Polk Wardwell Sunderland & Kiendl, N.Y.C., 1938-42, 45-48; pvt. practice, Jacksonville, Fla., 1948-—; sr. partner Buck, Drew & Glocker, 1954-—; pres., dir. Sky-Tige, Inc., Chattanooga. Chmn. com. fiscal policies govt. Fla., 1955; chmn. Jacksonville Expressway Authority 1955-60. Bd. dirs. Cathedral Found., Inc., Jacksonville; trustee Frank Lubbock Miller Ednl. Found., Jacksonville Episcopal High Sch., 1966-—; founding mem., dir. gen. So. Acad. Letters, Arts and Scis., 1971-—. Served as capt. and maj. AUS, 1942-45; ETO, PTO, MTO. Decorated Bronze Star. Mem. Am., Jacksonville bar assns., Fla. Bar (chmn. tax. sect. 1955-56), Order of Coif, Raven Soc., Phi Alpha Delta, Theta Chi. Episcopalian (sr. warden 1960-61, chmn. parish day sch. div. Diocese of Fla. 1959-62, chmn. bd. regents parish and diocesan schs. Diocese Fla. 1962-67, mem. restructure commn. 1971-72). Clubs: University, River (Jacksonville, Fla.). Home: 326 Ocean Blvd Atlantic Beach FL 32003 Office: Fla Title Bldg Jacksonville FL 32202

BUCKBERG, ALBERT, economist; b. Bklyn., Aug. 25, 1922; s. Isidor Paul and Anna (Litwack) B.; B.A., George Washington U., 1947; M.A., U. Mich., 1954, Ph.D., 1960; m. Gloria Bean, Feb. 26, 1967; 1 dau., Elaine Karen. Indsl. relations analyst WSB, Washington, 1951-52; instr. econs. dept. U. Mich., 1955-57; instr., asst. prof. Ia. State U., 1957-62; economist Bur. Budget, Exec. Office of Pres., Washington, 1962-66; economist Joint Com. Internal Revenue Taxation, U.S. Congress, Washington, 1966-—; mem. review and evaluation team, tax adminstrn. assistance program AID and Internal Revenue Service, 1966; staff dir. spl. com. on social scis. NSF, 1968. Served with AUS, 1943-46. Decorated Bronze Star medal. Home: 5906 Maiden Lane Bethesda MD 20034 Office: Longworth House Office Bldg Washington DC 20515

BUCKLEW (WILLIAM) HENRY, editor, publisher; b. Maxie, Miss., Apr. 10, 1925; s. Henry and Eunice (Clark) B.; student Jones County Jr. Coll., 1942-43, Tex. State Tchrs. Coll., 1945-—; B.A., Miss. Coll., 1957; LL.B., Jackson Sch. Law, 1962; m. Euna Fern Varner, Aug. 21, 1945; children—Cheryl Darlene, Twyla Renae. Editor, pub., owner So. Bapt. News, Laurel, Miss., 1945-—. Mayor, Laurel, Miss., 1965-66; active Gov. Wallace presdl. campaign, 1964. Founder, bd. dirs. Magnolia Boys Town. Served with AUS, 1943-45. Mem. V.F.W. (Miss. Distinguished Citizen award 1960, Humanitarian award 1962, Lit. Achievement award 1963, nat. chaplain 1962-64), Am. Legion, Dixie Golf Assn. (founder, pres. 1961-62), 40 and 8. Baptist. Woodman of World, Moose, Lion. Club: Laurel Sports (past pres.). Author: Your Daily Dozen Spiritial Vitamins, 1963. Home: 753 8th Av Laurel MS 39440 Office: PO Box 608 Front & 7th St Laurel MS 39440

BUCKLEY, EMERSON, music dir., condr.; b. N.Y.C., Apr. 14, 1916; s. Wendell and Minnie (Buckley) B.; B.A., Columbia, 1936; L.H.D., U. Denver, 1959; m. Mary Henderson, May 27, 1948; children—Robert Allen, Richard Edward. Music dir. Columbia Grand Opera, 1936-38, Palm Beach (Fla.) Symphony and Chorus, 1938-41, N.Y.C., Symphony, 1941-42, San Carlo Opera, 1943-45, WOR-MBS, N.Y.C., 1945-54, Marquis de Cuevas Ballet, 1950, Mendelssohn Glee Club, N.Y.C., 1954-63, P.R. Opera Festival, 1954-58, Symphony of the Air, also Empire State Mus. Festival, 1955, Tagarazuka Dance Theatre, also Greek Theatre, Los Angeles, 1958, Chautauqua Festival, N.Y., 1960, Temple U. Music Festival and Inst., 1970; music dir. Miami (Fla.) Opera Guild, 1950-—, Central City (Colo.) Opera, 1956-—, Ft. Lauderdale (Fla.) Symphony, 1963-—, Seattle Opera, 1964-—; condr. N.Y.C. Opera, 1955-—, New Orleans, Balt., Cin., Duluth (Minn.) operas, 1970-72. Guest appearances with various orchs., including Toronto (Ont., Can.) Philharmonic, Mpls. Symphony, Miami Symphony; mem. faculty U. Denver, 1956, Columbia, 1957-58, Manhattan Sch. Music, 1958-—; dir. world premiers of Am. operas including The Ballad of Baby Doe, 1956, Gallantry, 1958, He Who Gets Slapped, 1959, The Crucible, 1961, Gentlemen Be Seated, 1963, Lady from Colorado, 1964; recordings for M-G-M, columbia, Composers Records Inc., Heliodor. Recipient Fox prize Columbia Coll., 1936; Alice M. Ditson Conductor's award, 1964; Colo. Ambassadors Sash, 1965; Gold Chair award Central City Opera, 1965; Am. Patriot award state of Fla., 1971; decorated Chevalier des Arts et Lettres (France). Mem. Nat. Assn. Am. Composers and Condrs. Mason (Shriner). Home: 2271 NE 61st Ct Imperial Point Fort Lauderdale FL 33308 Office: 450 E Las Olas Blvd Fort Lauderdale FL 33301

BUCKLEY, ERNEST LYNN, civil engr.; b. Lemmon, S.D., Feb. 17, 1924; s. Norman Claude and Eva Myrtle (Smith) B.; B.S., S.D. State U., 1947; M.S., Kan. State U., 1949; Ph.D., U. Tex. at Arlington, 1972; m. Betty Bob Diltz, Aug. 17, 1946; children—Betty Lynn, Patick Joe, Michael Jay, Norman Lee. Instr., Kan. State U., Manhattan, 1948-49; v.p. E.E. Cloer, Gen. Contractor, Fort Worth, 1956; project design engr. Gen Dynamics Co., Fort Worth, 1956-67, tech. administrv. supr., 1967-70; coordinator constrn. mgmt. Tex. Christian U., Fort Worth, 1962-70; research asso. U. Tex. at Arlington, 1970-—. Bd. dirs. Council Sci. Socs., Fort Worth-Dallas. Served with USAAF, 1942-45, to lt. col., 1949-56; ETO. Decorated D.F.C., Air medal with nine oak leaf clusters. Registered profl. engr., Tex. Mem. Am. Soc. C.E. (pres.), Tex. Soc. Profl. Engrs. (chpt. pres.), C. of C. Author: Residential Construction Management, 1959; Construction Planning and Estimating, 1964 (workbook). Contbr. articles to profl. jours. Home: 3108 Santa Fe Trail Fort Worth TX 76116 Office: Office Dean Engring Univ Tex Arlington TX 76010

BUCKLEY, J. PAUL, civil engr.; b. Utica, N.Y., June 10, 1909; s. John M. and Katherine (McDonald) B.; B.C.E., U. Mich., 1932, M.C.E., 1933; m. Lucille E. Blaess, Apr. 15, 1931; 1 son, James Edmund. Asst. civil engr. City of Detroit, 1933; with Mich. Hwy. Dept., Lansing, 1934-42, project engr., 1934-37, statis. engr., 1938-39, asst. dir. planning and traffic div., 1939-42; cons. Cal. Legislature, 1946; engr., dir. Mich. Road Fedn., Lansing, 1947; chief engr. Automotive Safety Found., Washington, 1948-69; dir. tech. services div. Hwy. Users Fedn., Washington, 1970-—. Served to maj. AUS, 1943-45. Fellow Am. Soc. Civil Engrs.; mem. Inst. Traffic Engrs., Mich. Engring. Soc., Nat. Assn. County Engrs. Club: University. Home: 305 Ellsworth Dr Silver Spring MD 20910 Office: 1776 Massachusetts Av NW Washington DC 20036

BUCKLEY, WILLIAM EDWARD, JR., banker; b. Wadsworth, O., Mar. 28, 1925; s. William Edward and Alice Marie (Rickard) B.; B.A., Ohio Wesleyan U., 1945; LL.B., U. Va., 1951; grad. Stonier Grad. Sch. Banking, Rutgers U., 1962; m. Barbara Roberts Beach, Dec. 29, 1951; children— Deborah Beach, Judith Ann. Adminstrv. asst. Union Trust Co. of Md., Balt., 1951-52; with Mchts. Nat. Bank of Mobile (Ala.), 1952-—, trust officer, 1964-—, v.p., 1969-—. Instr., Am. Inst. Banking, 1962-—. Sec. exec. com. Mobile County Republican Com., 1968-—. Bd. dirs. Friends of Mobile Library. Served with AUS, 1945-46. Mem. Ala. (asso.) Mobile (asso.) bar assns., Ala. Bankers Assn. (sec.-treas. trust div. 1962-71, pres. 1972-73), Mobile Estate Planning Council, Mobile Area C. of C., Farrah Law Soc., Sigma Phi Epsilon, Sigma Nu Phi. Rotarian. Home: 5955 Shenandoah Rd N Mobile AL 36608 Office: PO Drawer 2527 Mobile AL 36622

BUCKNER, CHARLES AMICK, JR., real estate exec.; b. Siler City, N.C., Mar. 6, 1927; s. Charlie Amick and Olive Blanch (Riddle) B.; student N.C. State Coll., 1944-47; m. Sheila H. Losey, Sept. 14, 1968; children—Kathryn Elaine, Charles Amick III. Asst. city engr. City of Ashboro (N.C.), 1947-49; city mgr. City of Eau Gallie (Fla.), 1955-57; pres. Buckner Realty & Surveying, Inc., Eau Gallie, 1957-—. County surveyor Brevard County, 1967; mem. Eau Gallie Planning Bd., 1957-68, Melbourne Planning Bd., 1968-—. Served with USNR, 1944-45. Mem. N.C. Soc. Surveyors. Baptist (treas. 1971-—). Mason (32 deg.). Home: 915 Sunset Dr Eau Gallie FL 32935 Office: 1386 Cypress Av Eau Gallie FL 32935

BUCKNER, EDWIN ERROLL, physician; b. St. Louis, Apr. 5, 1928; s. E. Erroll and June (Rausch) B.; M.D., Tulane U., 1953; m. Aurora Sanguily, Dec. 20, 1951; children—Edwin Erroll, Judith Janet, Stephen Kelly. Intern, Confederate Meml. Med. Center, 1953-54; resident E. A. Conway Meml. Hosp., 1954-55; practice medicine, specializing in family practice, Longview, Tex., 1955-—; mem. staff Good Shepherd Hosp., Longview. First violinist Longview Symphony, 1968-—; rancher. Served with USNR, 1946-48. Home: 1702 Huntington St Longview TX 75601 Office: 1603 Judson Rd Longview TX 75601

BUDD, JAMES ARTHUR, banker; b. Mena, Ark., July 31, 1935; s. James David and Berdean (Evans) B.; B.S., Oklahoma City U., 1959, postgrad. Sch. Law, 1959-60; postgrad. U. Miami, 1962-64; m. Nelva Jean Ward, Aug. 8, 1953; 1 dau., Sharon Kay. Mem. sales staff U.S. Gypsum Co., Oklahoma City, 1959-60; mgmt. trainee Travelers Life Ins. Co., Miami, 1960-62; with mortgage dept. Equitable Life Insurance Soc., Miami, 1962-63; v.p. 1st Nat. Bank Miami, 1964-72; dir. 1st Nat. Beach Bank, Jacksonville Beach, Fla.; pres. S.E. 1st Nat. Beach Bank, Jacksonville, 1972-—. Mem. Greater Miami C. of C., Mortgage Bankers Assn. Miami, Mortgage Bankers Assn. Fla., Am. Soc. Appraisers, Am. Bankers Assn. Home: 1125 Bella Vista Av Coral Gables FL 33156 Office: 100 S Biscayne Blvd Miami FL 33101

BUDD, MILLIE, newspaper editor Radio-TV editor Houston Post. Office: 2410 Polk Av Houston TX 77001*

BUDSLICK, PAUL, motel exec.; b. Peoria, Ill., Sept. 18, 1918; s. John and Mary (Starkey) B.; student U. Ill., 1939-40; m. Mary Louis, Apr. 22, 1950; children—Paul L., Kathy. Chmn. bd. Drake-Best Western Motel, Nashville, 1950-72; pres. Drake Inns. Am., Nashville, 1950-—, A.B.C. Motels, Inc., January, Tenn., 1969-72, King Bee Food, Inc., Nashville, 1969-72; gov. Best Western Motels for Western Tenn., 1971-72. Recipient Distinguished Service award Assn. Travel and Industry Tenn., 1968. Mem. Tenn. Hotel-Motel Assn. (pres. 1957-59, sec., treas. 1968-71), Am. Hotel Motel Assn. (Tenn. del. 1971-72), C. of C. Roman Catholic. Elk, K.C. Clubs: Optimist, Brentwood Country (Nashville). Home: 216 Wilsonia St Nashville TN 37205 Office: 420 Murfreesboro Rd Nashville TN 37210

BUEHLER, JOE, mfg. co. exec.; b. Schenectady, May 28, 1928; s. Arthur G. and Eileen M (Sullivan) B.; B.B.A., Sienna Coll., 1953; m. Shirley E. Sinsig, Nov. 21, 1953; children—Katherine, Susan, Mark. Chief cost accountant Nat. Automotive Fibers Corp., Cohoes, N.Y., 1953-58; asst. controller Barclay Home Products, Cohoes, 1958-60; treas. Thermo Dynamics Inc., subsidiary Foster Refrigerator Co., Hudson, N.Y., 1960-67; controller Launch Support div. Bendix Corp., Titusville, Fla., 1967-—. Served with USAAF, 1945-48. Mem. Fed. Gov. Accountants Assn. (chpt. dir. 1970-73), Nat. Assn. Accountants, U.S. Volleyball Assn. Home: 205 York Dr Cocoa FL 32922 Office: 5225 S Washington Ave Titusville FL 32780

BUEHRING, E. FRED, business exec.; b. McGregor, Tex.; ed. So. Meth. U. Vice chmn., dir., pres. Greenville div. Electrosystems, Inc., Greenville, Tex.; dir. 1st Greenville Nat. Bank. Mason. Office: PO Box 1056 Greenville TX 75401

BUENGER, DANIEL LEE, banker; b. Shiner, Tex., Feb. 1, 1925; s. Lee Edward and Mary Augustine (Engbrock) B.; grad. high sch.; m. Alma Marie Zahn, Sept. 29, 1947; children—Sandra, Daniel Lee, Thomas, Ann. With Security Bank & Trust Co., Wharton, Tex., 1948-—, cashier, 1960-71, v.p., 1971-—, also dir. Treas. Wharton (Tex.) Little League, 1962-64, E. Wharton County (Tex.) March of Dimes, 1964-69, Wharton P.T.A. Assn., 1967-69; pres. E. Wharton County (Tex.) United Fund, 1970. Bd. dirs. E. Wharton County chpt. A.R.C. Served with AUS, 1945-46. Democrat. Roman Catholic (dir. 1965-71). K.C., Lion. Home: PO Box 604 Wharton TX 77488 Office: PO Box 1150 Wharton TX 77488

BUFFUM, CHARLES EMERY, oil prodn. co. exec.; b. Toulon, Ill., June 14, 1910; s. Roy Luman and Bessie (Packer) B.; B.S., Cal. Inst. Tech., 1931, M.S., 1932; m. Marjorie Elizabeth Hall, Dec. 24, 1933; children—Robert S., Terrill E., Barbara E. (Mrs. Edward C. Colarossi), J. Bradley. Asst. test engr. Consol. Steel Corp., Maywood, Cal., 1933-34; computer Western Geophys. Co., Los Angeles, 1934-35, party chief in charge of seismological field party, 1935-38; seismograph party chief Amoco Prodn. Co., Tulsa, 1938-41, research engr., 1941-44, tech. group supr., 1944-46, supr. design constrn. and tech. service sect., 1946-49, research group supr., 1949-50, research sect. supr., 1950-52, supt. lab. services, 1953-—. Mem. Soc. Exploration Geophysicists, I.E.E.E. Home: 1530 S Yorktown Pl Tulsa OK 74104 Office: PO Box 591 Tulsa OK 74102

BUFFUM, ELIZABETH WHITNEY (MRS. WHITNEY BUFFUM), club woman; b. Pitts.; d. Frederick Delano and Helen (Kerruish) Buffum; A.B., Vassar Coll., 1936; m. John Erwin Beaumont II, June 22, 1940 (div. 1954); children—John Erwin III, Peter Whitney; m. 2d, Theodore Jack Vaitses, Dec. 3, 1955 (div. 1967). Mem. adv. bd. Am. Real Property Fedn., 1955-57, Surety Trust Co., Wakefield, Mass., 1963-64. Bd. dirs. Melrose chpt. A.R.C., 1960-64, Melrose chpt. YMCA, 1961-65. Mem. D.A.R. (past chpt. dir.), Miami Jr. League, Buffum Family Assn. (asst. historian 1959-63), New Eng. Hist. and Geneal. Soc., Bostonian Soc. Episcopalian. Clubs: Surf, Vassar (Miami, Fla.). Home: PO Box 6156 Surfside FL 33154

BUFKIN, ERNEST RALPH, banker; b. Atlanta, Nov. 27, 1931; s. Ernest Ralph and Chrystene Mercer (Cox) B.; B.S., U. Md., 1955; m. Allie Jean Meadows, July 24, 1971; children—Ernest Ralph, Mark L., Kathryn A., Angela D., James E. Staff accountant Ernst & Ernst, C.P.A.'s, Atlanta, 1955-57; partner DeLoach & Bufkin, C.P.A.'s, Brunswick, Ga., 1957-63; pres. St. Simons State Bank, St. Simons Island, Ga., 1963-—, also dir.; dir. Golden Isles Aviation, Inc. Bd. dirs. Boys Club Glynn, Inc., Salvation Army, United Community Fund, Coastal Hwy. Commn., Ft. Frederica Found., Brunswick Coll. Found., St. Simons Library Bd., Okefenokee Area council Boy Scouts Am. Served as lt. Supply Corps, USNR. C.P.A., Ga. Mem. Ind., Am., Ga. bankers assns., Ga. Soc. C.P.A.'s, Coastal Ga. Hist. Soc. (dir. 1969-—), Navy League (dir. 1967-—), St. Simons C. of C. (dir. 1964-—). Rotarian. Home: 317 Broadway St St Simons Island GA 31522 Office: Box 818 St Simons Island GA 31522

BUFORD, FREDERICK SEYMOUR, architect; b. Dallas, Oct. 10, 1909; s. Frederick Seymour and Bennie (Meadows) B.; B.S., Tex. A. and M. Coll., 1931; m. Merlene Mamie Vaughn, Oct. 26, 1935; children—John Frederic, George Meadows, Harriet Frances (Mrs. Zivko Ristevski). Supt., J. Floyd Malcom Co., gen. contractors, Abilene, Tex., 1933-36; owner Fred Buford & Co., Architects-Engrs., Abilene, 1936-40; specification writer Wyatt C. Hedrick Co., Architects-Engrs., N.Y.C., 1940-43, office mgr., Dallas, 1946-48; partner Buford & Feinberg, Architects-Engrs., Dallas, 1948-54; owner Fred Buford &Assos., Architects-Engrs., Dallas, 1954-—. Mem. adv. com. Coll. Architecture, Tex. A. and M. U.; mem. adv. com. to bd. dirs. Christian Schs., Inc., Dallas. Served to capt. USMCR, 1944-45; PTO. Recipient Meritorious Civilian award Chief, Bur. Yards and Docks, Navy Dept., 1942. Mem. A.I.A., Tex. Soc. Architects, Nat., Tex. socs. profl. engrs., Engrs. Club of Dallas (chmn. bd. 1965). Clubs: City, Brook Hollow Golf (Dallas); Canyon Creek Country (Richardson, Tex.). Important archtl. works include Central Tex. Coll. Campus, Killeen, Richardson, J.J. Pearce, Lloyd V. Berkner and Lake Highlands high schs., Richardson, Kimball High Sch. and Loos Stadium and Field House, Dallas, Waples Meth. Ch., Denison, Houston County Hosp., Crockett. Home: 4801 N Lindhurst Av Dallas TX 75229 Office: 1505 Federal St Dallas TX 75201

BUFORD, THOMAS CARNES, farmer; b. Memphis, Dec. 8, 1919; s. Thomas Carnes and Lillian Lee (Sturdivant) B.; student U. Miss., 1937-39; B.S., Washington and Lee U., 1941; M.B.A., Harvard, 1943; m. Ada Gwin Pryor, July 16, 1955; children—Lillian Lee, Gwin Pryor, Sarah Gil, Donna Mills. Partner Buford Plantations, Glendora, Miss., 1946-59, owner, 1959-—; chmn. bd. Bell Mfg. Co., Inverness, Miss.; dir. Shrimp Boats, Inc., Macon, Ga. Chmn. Tallahatchie County (Miss.) Agrl. Stblzn. and Conservation Com., 1969-72. Mem. County Republican Exec. Com., 1960-72. Served to capt. Transp. Corps, AUS, 1943-46. Mem. Phi Delta Theta. Episcopalian. (jr. warden 1969-72). Clubs: Beulah Island Hunting (pres. 1962-—) (Deshea County, Ark.); Nippisis Salmon (Quebec, Can.); Memphis Country, Memphis University (Memphis). Home: Buford Hall Glendora MS 38928 Office: Route 1 Glendora MS 38928

BUGG, JAMES LUCKIN, JR., univ. adminstr.; b. Farmville, Va., July 25, 1920; s. James Luckin and Clair (Woodruff) B.; A.B., Hampden-Sydney Coll., 1941; M.A., U. Va., 1942, Ph.D., 1950; m. Anne Barrington Hunter, June 26, 1956; children—Anne Barrington; James Luckin III. Instr. history George Washington U., summer 1948; mem. faculty U. Mo., 1949-69, prof. history Columbia, 1960-63, chmn. dept., 1959-62, dean of faculty at St. Louis, 1963-65, chancellor, 1965-69; pres. Old Dominion U., Norfolk, Va., 1969-—. Mem. nat. commn. Coll. work Episcopal Ch., 1964-70; mem. adv. com. Mo. Commn. Higher Edn., 1963-69, Southeastern Va. Med. Sch.; mem. adv. council Va. Council for Higher Edn. mem. region XI selection com. Woodrow Wilson Scholarship Found., 1959-69; bd. dirs. Central Midwestern Regional Edn. Labs., 1966-69, Louis Higher Edn. Coordinating Council, 1963-69, Norfolk Symphony Soc. Served with USAAF, 1942-46. Mem. Am., So. hist. assns., Orgn. Am. Historians, Phi Beta Kappa, Omicron Delta Kappa, Lambda Chi Alpha. Kiwanian. Author articles. Editor: Jacksonian Democracy; Myth or Reality, 1962. Home: 5000 Edgewater Dr Norfolk VA 23508

BUGGS, JOHN ALLEN, govt. ofcl.; b. Bruswick, Ga., Nov. 20, 1915; s. John Wesley and Leonora (Clark) B.; A.B., Dillard U., 1939; M.A. in Sociology, Fisk U., 1941; D.Hum., Chapman Coll., 1972; m. Mary Gale Brown, Feb. 28, 1943; children—Zara Gale, Diane Dorinda. Dir. Fessenden Acad., Ocala, Fla., 1942-51; dep. probation officer, Los Angeles County, 1952-54; exec. sec. Los Angeles County Commn. Human Relations, Los Angeles, 1954-63, exec. dir., 1963-67; dep. dir. Model Cities Adminstrn., U.S. Dept. Housing and Urban Devel., 1967-69; v.p. Nat. Urban Coalition, 1969-71; dep. staff dir. U.S. Commn. Civil Rights, Washington, 1971-72, staff dir., 1972-—. Bd. dirs. Vols. for Internat. Tech. Assistance, 1972-—. Mem. Nat. Assn. Intergroup Relations Ofcls. (dir. 1963-—, nat. pres. 1966-67), N.A.A.C.P. (sec. Fla. conf. 1945-49), Nat. Legal Aid and Defenders Assn. (exec. com. 1968-71), Episcopal Soc. Cultural and Racial Unity (dir. 1960-64), Am. Arbitration Assn. (dir.), Alpha Phi Alpha. Episcopalian. Home: 2805 Village Lane Wheaton MD 20906 Office: 1121 Vermont Av NW Washington DC

BUIE, EUGENE CLOY, govt. ofcl.; b. Stamford, Tex., Jan. 24, 1912; s. John Cloy and Pearl Eugenia (Hamm) C.; B.S. in Agrl. Engring., Tex. A. and M. U., 1933; M.S., U. Mich., 1964; m. Lucile Stocks, Mar. 31, 1934; children—Eugene Cloy, Judith Ann, Johnny Merle Price. Asst. prof. Tex. Tech Coll., Lubbock, 1934-35; asst. regional engr. Soil Conservation Service, U.S. Dept. Agr., Amarillo, Tex., 1935-41, zone engr., Ft. Worth, 1946-53, asst. watershed planning specialist, 1954-56, watershed planning specialist, Spartanburg, S.C., 1956-63; asst. dir. Watershed Planning div., Washington, 1963-65, dir. River Basins div., 1965-70, asst. dep. adminstr., 1970-—. Served with AUS, 1941-46. Recipient Superior Service award U.S. Dept. Agr. 1962. Registered profl. engr., Tex. Mem. Am. Soc. Agrl. Engrs., Soil Conservation Soc. Am. Baptist. Home: 9005 Stratford Lane Alexandria VA 22308 Office: Soil Conservation Service Washington DC 20250

BUIE, TALMADGE NEWTON, city ofcl.; b. Mertens, Tex., Sept. 26, 1937; s. E. Newton and Sally Juanita (White) B.; B.B.A., Arlington (Tex.) State Coll., 1963; m. Jaylon Mantooth, Mar. 30, 1962; children—James Talmadge, Jennifer Lyn, Carolyn Ann. Purchasing agt. City of Arlington, 1962-65, water and tax revenue mgr., 1968-69; sales rep. IBM, 1965-67; buyer Bell Helicopter Co., Ft. Worth, 1967-68; dir. finance City of Hurst (Tex.), 1969-—. Sect. chmn., Mid-Cities Govts., 1963. Served with AUS, 1959-60. Kiwanian (dir. 1970). Home: 604 Tumbleweed Trail Hurst TX 76053 Office: 1505 Precinct line Rd Hurst TX 76053

BULBER, FRANCIS GERARD, educator; b. New Orleans, Mar. 7, 1909; s. Eugene W. and Mathilda (Noullet) B.; Mus.B., La. State U., 1935, Mus.M., 1937, B.A., 1941; postgrad. Northwestern U., summer 1935; Ph.D., George Peabody Coll., 1948; m. Mayola Desporte, Feb.2, 1930 (dec. Jan. 1954); 1 dau., Mary Frances (Mrs. John Vallie Reed); m. 2d, Patricia Cavell, May 31, 1960; children—Patricia Cecile, Gerard Sean, Colette Marie. Head dept. music Pearl River Coll., Poplarville, Miss., 1937-38; dir. community music project La. State U., Baton Rouge, 1938-40; prof. music, head dept. music, McNeese State Coll., Lake Charles, La., 1940-52, dean fine arts, 1952-56, academic dean coll., 1956-62, dir. grad. studies, 1961-62, dean fine arts, 1962-—. Condr., Lake Charles Civic Symphony Orch., 1938-43, Lake Charles Messiah Chorus, 1940-—. Pres. La. Coll. Conf., 1955-56; bd. dirs. Community Concerts Assn., 1942-—. Mem. La. Music Educators Assn. (dir.), La. Tchrs. Assn., Music Educators Nat. Conf., La. Music Tchrs. Assn., Music Tchrs. Nat. Assn., Phi Kappa Phi, Phi Mu Alpha, Phi Delta Kappa. K.C. Club: Lions. Author: Teacher Activities of the Vocal School Music Program, 1948; articles pub. in profl. jours. Home: 819 Azalea St Lake Charles LA 70601

BULL, FRANK JAMES, architect; b. Chattanooga, June 25, 1922; s. Louis H. and Augusta (Clausius) B.; B.S., Ga. Inst. Tech., 1948, B. Arch., 1949; m. Betty Frances Graham, May 7, 1949; 1 son, Birney O'Brian. Pilot, Pan Am. Airways, 1942-46; architect Aeck Assos., 1949-57; partner Bull & Kenney, Architects, Atlanta, 1957-—. Vice chmn. bd. dirs., mem. exec. com. Galloway Schs., Inc., 1969-—; pres. Atlanta Spring, Inc., 1967-—. Trustee Holy Innocents Parish Day Sch., 1961-66; bd. dirs. Architects and Engrs. Inst., Atlanta, 1965-67. Mem. A.I.A. (dir. Ga. assn. 1972-—), Beta Theta Pi, Omicron Delta Kappa, Tau Beta Pi, Phi Eta Sigma, Phi Kappa Phi. Club: Cherokee Town and Country (Atlanta). Works include Sanctuary bldg. Holy Innocents Episcopal Ch., Atlanta; Speech Sch. and Clinic, Atlanta Speech Sch.; Hummel Hall, Episcopal High Sch.; Alexandria, Va. Contbr. articles to profl. jours. Home: 4723 Jett Rd NW Atlanta GA 30327 Office: 1261 Spring St NW Atlanta GA 30309

BULLARD, EDGAR EARL, instrument co. exec.; b. El Campo, Tex., Mar. 2, 1933; s. Clifton and Helen (Amman) B.; student Tulsa Tech. Coll., 1957-59; m. Josiane Desbarbieux, July 13, 1957; children—Christine, Jill. Party mgr. Teledyne Co., 1956-68; v.p. Houston Atlas, Inc., 1968-—. Served with AUS, 1953-55. Club: Fort Bend Country (Richmond, Tex.). Home: 1011 Blue Willow St Houston TX 77042 Office: 9441 Baythorne St Houston TX 77041

BULLARD, JOHN MOORE, clergyman, educator; b. Winston-Salem, N.C., May 6, 1932; s. Hoke Vogler and May E. (Moore) B.; B.A., U. N.C., 1953, M.A., 1955; B.D., Yale, 1957, Ph.D., 1962. Instr., Yale Div. Sch., 1958-61; asst. prof. religion Wofford Coll., Spartanburg, S.C., 1961-65, chmn. dept. religion, 1962-—, asso. prof., 1965-70, Albert C. Outler prof. religion, 1970-—; minister music Hamden Plains Meth. Ch., New Haven, 1955-61, Central United Meth. Ch., Spartanburg, 1961-72, Bethel United Meth. Ch., 1972-—; ordained elder Meth. Ch., 1962. Vis. prof. Bibl. lit. U. N.C., Chapel Hill, 1966, 67. Mem. Am. Guild Organists (chpt. dean 1965-67), Am. Acad. Religion, Soc. Bibl. Lit. (pres. So. sect. 1967-68), Hymn Soc. Am., Am. Schs. Oriental Research, Am. Assn. U. Profs., Am. Oriental Soc., Inst. for Mediterranean Studies, Phi Mu Alpha. Home: 2123 Selwyn Av Charlotte NC 28207 Office: Main Hall Wofford Coll Spartanburg SC 29301

BULLARD, ROGER AUBREY, educator; b. Memphis, Aug. 1, 1937; s. Roger Maurice and Mable (Bennett) B.; B.A., Union U., 1958; M.A., U. Ky., 1959; B.D., Southeastern Bapt. Theol. Sem., 1962; Ph.D., Vanderbilt U., 1965; m. Carol Louise Hawthorne, May 21, 1961; children— Kenneth Maurice, Floyd Andrew. Mem. faculty Atlantic Christian Coll., Wilson, N.C., 1965-—, prof. religion and philosophy, 1968-—. Corr. mem. Inst. for Antiquity and Christianity of Claremont, Cal., 1966-—. Recipient awards for summer study Am. Council Learned Socs., 1967, Nat. Found. Humanities, 1968. Mem. Soc. Bibl. Lit., Am. Acad. Religion, Am. Assn. U. Profs., So. Bapt. Hist. Soc., Am. Bible Soc. (mem. today's English version translations com. 1967-—). Democrat. Baptist. Author: The Hypostasis of the Archons. 1970. Abstractor New Testament Abstracts, 1966-69. Office: Atlantic Christian Coll Wilson NC 27893

BULLEN, ADELAIDE KENDALL (MRS. RIPLEY PIERCE BULLEN), anthropologist; b. Worcester, Mass., Jan. 12, 1908; d. Oliver Sawyer and Grace (Marble) Kendall, III; A.B. cum laude, Radcliffe Coll., 1943; grad. study Harvard, 1943-48, 50; m. Ripley Pierce Bullen, July 25, 1929; children—Dana Ripley II, Pierce Kendall. Research anthropologist Health Center, Radcliffe Coll., 1943-44, Fatigue Lab., Harvard Grad. Sch. Bus. Adminstrn., 1944-46; civilian cons. in anthropology U.S. War Dept., 1946; anthropologist dept. anthropology, Peabody Mus., Harvard U., 1946-48, Fla. State Mus., 1949-—. Fellow Am. Anthrop. Assn., A.A.A.S., Royal Anthrop. Inst., London, Soc. Applied Anthropology; mem. Am. Assn. Phys. Anthropologists, Am. Psychosomatic Soc., Am. Acad. Social and Polit. Sci., Soc. Research in Child Devel., World Fedn. for Mental Health, Sigma Xi. Clubs: Gainesville Garden, Gainesville Golf and Country, University Women's, Gainesville Woman's. Author: New Answers to the Fatigue Problem, 1956; also articles in field. Contbg. editor anthropology Handbook of Latin Am. Studies, Library of Congress, 1969-71. Home: 2720 SW 8th Dr Gainesville FL 32601 Office: Fla State Mus Univ Fla Gainesville FL 32601

BULLER, RALPH LELAND, physician; b. Waka, Tex., June 30, 1930; s. David Edward and Sarah (Kroeker) B.; student Grace Bible Inst., 1947-48; B.A., Phillips U., 1952; M.D., Okla. U., 1956; m. Lorraine Lohrenz, May 29, 1952; children—Brenda, Nathan, Kevin, Stephanie. Intern, Hillcrest Hosp., Tulsa, 1956-57; gen. practice resident Lafayette Charity Hosp., Lafayette, La., 1959-60; practice gen. medicine, Hydro, Okla., 1960-—; chief of staff Weatherford (Okla.) Hosp., 1963, 67. Mem. Caddo County Bd. Health, 1963-—. Trustee Okla. Rural Med. Edn. Scholarship Fund; bd. dirs. Okla. Bible Acad., Meno. Served with USAF, 1957-59. Named Doctor of the Day, Okla. Legislature, 1969. Mem. Custer County Med. Assn. (pres. 1966). Mennonite (deacon gen. conf. 1967-—). Lion. Home: 584 Broadway Hydro OK 73048 Office: 579 Broadway Hydro OK 73048

BULLOCK, CHARLES SPENCER, JR., govt. ofcl.; b. Kansas City, Mo., Dec. 10, 1914; s. Charles Spencer and Maud (Pook) B.; A.A., Kansas City N.E. Jr. Coll., 1933; A.B., William Jewell Coll., 1940; M.A., Vanderbilt U., 1942; m. Eleanor Alice Davis, Aug. 2, 1941; children—Charles Spencer III, Robert Davis. Asso. prof. Mo. State Coll., 1946; sr. statistician Tenn. Dept. Employment Security, 1946-48; regional employemnt analyst U.S. Bur. Labor Statistics, Atlanta, 1949-60, asst. regional dir., 1960-71, dep. regional dir., 1971-—; dir. Peachtree Fed. Credit Union. Served with AUS, 1943-46; CBI. Mem. Am. Statis. Assn. (chpt. pres. 1965), Atlanta Assn. Fed. Execs. (pres. 1971). Episcopalian (vestryman). Home: 4471 Cain Circle Tucker GA 30084 Office: 1371 Peachtree St NE Atlanta GA 30309

BULLOCK, JOSEPH PHILLIP, chem. co. exec.; b. Boston, Sept. 30, 1929; s. William John and Rose Ann (Boitano) B.; certificate indsl. chemistry Franklin Tech. Inst., 1950; Asso. Sci. in Chemistry, Lincoln Tech. Inst., 1956; B.B.A. in Sci. and Mgmt., Northeastern U., 1958, M.B.A., 1960; m. Helen Patricia Oakes, Sept. 26, 1948; children—Patricia (Mrs. Walter E. Farnsworth), Paula (Mrs. Richard D. Anderson), Joseph Steven, Eric Paul, Robin Eileen. Prodn. supr. Myerson Tooth Corp., Cambridge, Mass., 1950-52; prodn. supr. Am. Biltrite Rubber Co., Chelsea, Mass., 1952; chemist, prodn. supr. Carters Ink Co., Cambridge, 1952-58; chemist Boston Woven Hose & Rubber Co., Cambridge, 1958-60; sr. research chemist Naugatuck Chem. Co. (Conn.), 1960-61; tech. sales service UBS Chem. Co., Cambridge, 1961-63; tech. sales chem. div. Goodyear Corp., Boston, 1963-67; gen. sales mgr. Copolymer Rubber & Chem. Co., Baton Rouge, 1967-—. Served with AUS, 1946-48. Mem. Am. Chem. Soc., V.F.W. Home: 12461 Parkwood Av Baton Rouge LA 70815 Office: Box 2591 Baton Rouge LA 70821

BULLOCK, UBER SIDNEY, oil co. exec.; b. Harmon, La., Sept. 3, 1923; s. Uber Sidney and Ella (Loving) B.; grad. high sch.; m. Wanda Lewis, Apr. 23, 1943; children—Ella Dean (Mrs. Mickey Chambliss), Jackie Sue (Mrs. Bill Braswell). Field foreman Pan Am. Petroleum Corp., 1947-52; gen. supt. Brinsmere Oil Co., 1952-54; prodn. supt. Bogle Oil Co., Denver City, Tex., 1954-—; owner Wasson Rental Tool, 1956-59; founder, pres. Mercury Oil Service, Denver City, 1958-—; owner Savoy Oil Co., 1962-—. Mem. Denver City Zoning Com., 1964-70. Mem. devel. bd. Lubbock Christian Coll., 1964-67. Served with USAAF, 1943-46. Mem. Ch. of Christ. Mason, Lion, Rotarian. Home: 1410 Mustang Av Denver City TX 79323 Office: 1214 N Main Denver City TX 79323

BULTMAN, FRITZ, painter, sculptor; b. New Orleans, Apr. 4, 1919; s. Anthony F. and Pauline (Angele) B.; student New Orleans Arts and Crafts Sch., Munich (Germany) Prep. Sch., New Bauhaus, Chgo., Hans Hofmann Sch. Fine Arts, N.Y.C.; m. Jeanne Lawson, Dec. 24, 1943; children—Anthony Frederick IV, Johann. Tchr., Grad. Art Sch., Hunter Coll., 1959-63, Sch. Edn., Pratt Inst., 1958-59, 62-63; cons., artist-in-residence in fine arts Provincetown Fine Arts Workshop, Provincetown, Mass., 1968-69; exhbns. include Hugo Gallery, N.Y.C., 1947-50, Kootz Gallery, N.Y.C., 1951-53; one-man shows include Stable Gallery, N.Y.C., 1958, Martha Jackson Gallery, N.Y.C., 1959, Delgado Mus., New Orleans, 1959, Mayer Gallery, N.Y.C., 1960, Stadler Gallery, Paris, France, 1960-63, Tibor de Nagy Gallery, N.Y.C., 1963-65, Arts Club, Chgo., 1965. Vice pres. Bultman Mortuary Co., New Orleans, 1954-—. Mem. Tougaloo (Miss.) Coll. Art Com. Italian Govt. scholar, 1950-51; Fulbright fellow in France, 1964-65; recipient Sculpture award Am. Show, Art Inst. Chgo., 1964. Home: 176 E 95th St New York City NY 10028 Office: 3338 St Charles Av New Orleans LA

BUMGARDNER, DAVID WEBSTER, JR., mortician, state ofcl.; b. Belmont, N.C., Nov. 2, 1921; s. David Webster and Winnifred (Ballard) B.; student Belmont Abbey Jr. Coll., 1938-40, Gupton-Jones Coll. Mortuary Sci., 1941-42; m. Sara Margaret Jones, Aug. 14, 1948; children—Sharon Inez, Sandra Jo. Pres., treas. Bumgardner Funeral Home, Inc., Belmont, 1948-—. Mem. N.C. Ho. of Reps., 1967, 69, 71. Dir. Belmont Savs. and Loan Assn., N. State Gen. Ins. div. N.W. Security Life Ins. Co.; pres. Conf. Funeral Service Examining Bds. of U.S., 1955-56. Mem. adv. bd. Sacred Heart Coll., Belmont. Served with AUS, 1943-45. Named Man of Year Belmont C. of C., 1967. Fellow Dallas Inst. Mortuary Sci. Kiwanian (div. lt. gov. 1966). Home: 209 Peachtree St Belmont NC 28012 Office: P O Box 904 Belmont NC 28012

BUMPERS, DALE, state ofcl.; b. Charleston, Ark., 1925; grad. U. Ark., 1952; LL.B., Northwestern U.; m.; 3 children. Gov., Ark., 1971-—. Served with USMC, World War II. Office: State Capitol Little Rock AR 72201

BUNCE, JAMES FREDRICK, agrl. extension agt.; b. Cumberland County, N.C., Nov. 21, 1922; s. Empie Lee and Maggie Lee (Ellis) B.; A.A., Presbyn. Jr. Coll., 1943; B.S., N.C. State U., 1949, M.Ed., 1969; m. Alice Marie Parker, Aug. 6, 1950; 1 dau., Laura Kathryn. Clk. typist Civil Service, Fort Bragg, N.C., 1941-42; tchr. vocational agr. Onslow County Pub. Schs., Jacksonville, N.C., 1949-56; agr. extension agt. N.C. Agrl. Extension Service, Duplin County, Kenansville, N.C., 1956-68; county extension chmn. Carteret County, Beaufort, N.C., 1968—. Served with AUS, 1943-46; PTO. Mem. N.E.A., N.C. Tchrs. Assn. (v.p. agrl. edn. div. 1953), Nat. (Distinguished Service award 1972); N.C., assns. county agrl. agts. Baptist (deacon 1961—). Mason, Rotarian, Lion (pres. 1959). Home: 207 Vine St Beaufort NC 28516 Office: Courthouse Annex Beaufort NC 28516

BUNCE, WILLIAM DEAN, govt. ofcl.; b. Fayetteville, N.C., June 6, 1933; s. Purdue Frankle and Ethel Mae (Jackson) B.; student N.C. State Coll., 1959; m. Joanne Buie McGill, Aug. 12, 1956; children—Hilda Joanne, Amy Elizabeth, William Dean II, Alexander McGill. With N.C. Hwy. Commn., 1956—, field engr., Dunn, 1956-57, Fayette ville, 1959-64, div. staff engr., Fayetteville, 1964-69, asst. resident engr., Lumberton, N.C., 1969—. Tchr., N.C. Hwy. Commn., 1970—; designer various subdivs. N.C., 1960-71. Civil def. officer 5 N.C. counties, 1963—. Served with AUS, 1956-58. Mem. N.C. Soc. Engrs. (dir.), Cape Fear Engr. Club (sec.-treas.), N.C. Hwy. Assn. (sec.-treas.). Presbyn. (Sunday sch. supt. 1966-70, deacon, 1966, 70, 71—). Clubs: Ruritan (sec.-treas.), Green Valley Country (Fayetteville). Home: 5400 Jarvis St Fayetteville NC 28304 Office: 209 E 6th St Lumberton NC 28358

BUNCH, CHARLES, physician, ret. naval officer; b. Raleigh, N.C., Jan. 30, 1905; s. Charlie Christopher and Mattie (Hamer) B.; student U. N.C., 1924-27; M.D., Med. Coll. S.C., 1931; B.S. with honors, N.C. State Coll., 1958; m. Dell Cahoon, Mar. 5th, 1955; children—Mary Elizabeth, Linda Ann. Intern Central Dispensary and Emergency Hosp., Washington, 1932-33; resident Childrens Hosp., Phila., 1934, N.Y. Polyclinic Hosp., 1934-35; commd. lt. (j.g.) USNR, 1933, advanced through grades to capt., 1955; practice medicine, specializing in gen. surgery, Charlotte, N.C., 1935-40, 46-49; surg. staff U.S. Naval Hosp., Parris Island, S.C., 1942; sr. med. officer U.S. Naval Air Sta., Antigua, B.W.I., 1942-43, Repair Facility, San Juan, P.R., 1943-44; staff Bainbridge (Md.) Naval Tng. Sta., 1944; head surg. team USS McCracken, 1944-66; asst. chief of surgery Naval Hosp., Charleston, S.C., 1949-52; surg. staff Naval Hosp., Yokosuka, Japan, 1952; mem. USN Adv. Group, sr. med. officer, fleet activities, Sasabo, Japan, 1952-53, Pusan, Korea, 1953; sr. med. officer naval recruiting, Raleigh, N.C., 1953-57; sr. med. officer U.S. Naval Shipyard, Portsmouth, Va., 1958-61; med. officer U.S. Naval Propellant Plant, Indian Head, Md., 1961-62; asst. dist. med. officer 5th Naval Dist., Portsmouth, 1962-66, ret., 1966; mem. staff U.S. Naval Hosp., Portsmouth; mem. active surg. staffs Mercy Hosp., 1935-39, Presbyn. Hosp., 1935-39, Good Samaritan Hosp., 1935-59 (all Charlotte), now mem. hon. surg. staffs; chief surg. service, med. dir. Warren Gen. Hosp., Warrenton, N.C.; local surgeon Seaboard Coast Line R.R. Fellow A.C.S.; mem. A.M.A., Med. Soc. State N.C. (ho. of dels.), Royal Soc. Health (London, Eng.), Warren County Med. Soc. (sec.), Internat. Coll. Surgeons, Seaboard Med. Assn., So. Med. Assn., Am. Acad. Occupational Medicine, Am. Assn. Ry. Surgeons, Am. Soc. Abdominal Surgeons (mem. edn. faculty), Am., N.C. pub. health assns. Episcopalian (vestryman). Mason (32 deg., Shriner, K.T., past master), Elk, Moose, Rotarian (dir.). Clubs: Midtown (charter) (Portsmouth, Va.); Red Fez (Charlotte); City (Raleigh, N.C.); Warrenton Country, Recreation (charter mem.) (Warrenton, N.C.). Contbr. to profl. jours. Home: 105 Halifax St Warrenton NC 27589 Office: Warren Gen Hosp Warrenton NC 27589

BUNDY, STEPHEN ANDREW, textile co. exec.; b. Jamestown, N.C., Oct. 17, 1917; s. Oscar Mayfield and Nettie Lisa (Johnson) B.; B.S., N.C. State U., 1941; grad. Exec. Mgmt. Course, Sch. Bus. Adminstrn. U. Va., 1968; m. Alice Baskerville Ligon, Dec. 6, 1941; children— Stephen Andrew, Henry Ligon. Supr. quality control Burlington Hosiery Co., 1946-53, plant mgr., 1953-61, v.p. new product devel., 1961-69; pres., chief exec. officer Morganton Hosiery Mills, Inc. div. Dan River, Inc., Morganton, N.C., 1969—. Chmn. indsl. div. United Fund for Burke County, 1971; chmn. Roan County (Tenn.), March of Dimes, 1948-53; chmn. county Smoky Mountain council, Boy Scouts Am., 1955-61. Trustee, Western Piedmont Community Coll., 1969-71; bd. dirs. MHD Found., 1969-71. Served with USAAF, 1941-45. Mem. Sigma Nu, Phi Psi. Rotarian. Home: 519 Riverside Dr Morganton NC 28655 Office: 101 Lenoir St Morganton NC 28655

BUNGE, CARL CRAIG, real estate broker; b. Tebetts, Mo., Mar. 11, 1933; s. Oscar Carl and Susanna Vivian (Cannell) B.; B.S., U. Mo., 1955; m. Phyllis Sue Proctor, Dec. 24, 1955; children—Craig, Cheryl. Self-employed real estate and mortgage brokerage bus., Fort Walton Beach, Fla., 1963—; dir. First City Bank, 1969—; pres. The Bunge Corp. Capt., Okaloosa County United Fund, 1969-71. Vice pres. bd. dirs. Fort Walton Beach Bd. Realtors, 1964—; bd. dirs. Salvation Army, 1968-70, Boys' Club, 1968-70, Jr. Achievement, 1967-69. Served with USAF, 1955-63. Mem. C. of C. (v.p. 1969-70), Kappa Alpha. Mason (32 deg., Shriner), Kiwanian (pres. 1968). Home: 560 Mooney Rd Fort Walton Beach FL 32548 Office: 200 Eglin Pkwy Fort Walton Beach FL 32548

BUNN, JOHN ROBERT, geologist, oil operator; b. Ardmore, Okla., June 17, 1900; s. Clinton Orin and Mattie (Pulliam) B.; B.S., U. Okla., 1923; m. Wilma Whatley, Apr. 11, 1925; children—Jeree (Mrs. J. L. Barnett), Jack. Petroleum engr. U.S. Bur. Mines, U.S. Geol. Survey, 1923-25; cons. geologist, 1925-33; drilling contractor Continental Oil Co. Mexico, 1933-38; oil and gas explorations; U.S.; 1938—; owner Bunn Hydraulic Rig Co., Tyler, Tex., 1950-72. Served with U.S. Army, 1918. Mem. Am. Assn. Petroleum Geologists, Am. Geophys. Union, Ind. Petroleum Assn. Am., Sigma Gamma Epsilon, Kappa Sigma. Mason, Rotarian. Writer geol. and engrng. reports for state surveys Okla., Colo., Tex. Patentee in field, including 1st successful hydraulic drilling rig. Address: 325 W 4th St Tyler TX 75701

BUNN, JULIAN WILBUR, JR., steel fabrication exec.; b. Raleigh, N.C., Mar 21, 1918; s. Julian Wilbur and Maude (Davis) B.; b.s., N.C. State U., 1941; m. Martha Ware Britt, June 1, 1946; children—Julian Wilbur III, John Britt, Thomas Ware. With advance engrng. sect. Gen. Electric Co., Lynn, Mass., 1941-46; v.p., gen. mgr. Gen. Equipment Co., Raleigh, N.C., 1946-53; v.p., prodn. mgr. Aerotron Corp., Raleigh, 1953-56 prodn.-devel. engr. Aeroglide Corp., Raleigh, 1956-60, v.p. engring., 1960—, also dir. Mem. Profl. Engrs. N.C. Club: Civitan (dir.). Home: 3005 Granville Dr Raleigh NC 27609 Office: 7100 Hillsborough Rd Raleigh NC 27602

BUNN, WALLACE RAIKES, telephone co. exec.; b. Durham, N.C., Oct. 26, 1922; s. Wallace Raikes and Mary (Beck) B.; grad. pub. high sch.; m. Margaret P. Seegers, Dec. 19, 1942; children—Rodney D., Russell E. With So. Bell Tel. & Tel. Co., various locations, 1941—, v.p., gen. mgr. Tenn., Nashville, 1965-69, v.p. operations, Birmingham, Ala., 1969—, also dir. Mem. engrng. mgmt. adv. council Vanderbilt U., 1967-69. Bd. dirs. United Givers Fund, Nashville, 1967-69, Middle Tenn. council Boy Scouts Am., 1966-69, YMCA, 1965-68, Urban League, 1969, Opportunities Industrialization Center, 1969, St. Thomas Hosp., 1966-69, Salvation Army, 1966-68, Jr. Achievement, 1965-69 (all Nashville), Birmingham Boys' Club; trustee Baptist Med. Centers, Birmingham, So. Baptist Theol. Sem., Louisville. Served with USCGR, 1943-46. Named Young Man Year, Hattiesburg (Miss.) Jr. C. of C., 1958. Baptist. Rotarian (pres. Hattiesburg 1958). Clubs: Downtown, Relay House, The Club, Birmingham Country (Birmingham). Home: 4016 Old Leeds Lane Birmingham AL 35213 Office: PO Box 771 Birmingham AL 35201

BUNNELLE, ROBERT ELLSWORTH, newspaper pub.; b. Urbana, O., Aug. 21, 1903; s. Elmer Ellsworth and Olivemay (Colbert) B.; student Wittenberg Coll., 1921-23, Northwestern U., 1924; m. Margaret Elizabeth Harrison, Oct. 30, 1926 (dec.); m. 2d, Frances McKay Peace, August 23, 1962. Reporter Lynchburg (Va.) News, Asheville (N.C.) Times, also mng. editor Bristol (Va.) Bull., 1925-31; with A.P., 1931-54, beginning as editor, Atlanta, successively chief of bur., mng. exec., London, Eng., chief bur., Can., 1931-49, gen. exec., N.Y.C., 1949-54; pub. Asheville Citizen-Times, 1954—, pres., 1958—; dir. 1st Union Nat. Bank of N.C.; v.p., dir. Multimedia, Inc. Mem. 6th Dist. Adv. Council Naval Affairs; mem. N.C. Hwy. Commn., 1957-61; pres. Greater Asheville Council, Council, 1962-64. Trustee Meml. Mission Hosp., 1968-69. Mem. N.C. Press Assn. (pres. 1962-63), Am. Corrs. Assn. (pres. London 1943-44), Parliamentary Press Gallery Assn. (dir. 1950-51). Asheville C. of C. (pres. 1967), Phi Kappa Psi. Clubs: Biltmore Forest Country, Mountain City (pres. 1959), City (Asheville); Sphinx. (Raleigh); Nat. Press (Washington); Overseas Press (N.Y.C.); Greenville (S.C.) Country; Southern Cross (Little Cayman Island, N.W.I.). Home: Lower Waverly Plantation Pawleys Island SC 29585 Office: 14 O'Henry Av Asheville NC 28801

BUNTING, J(AMES) WHITNEY, coll. pres.; b. Phila., Nov. 23, 1913; s. George Miller Lewis and Helen Elizabeth (Whitney) B.; B.S., U. Pa., 1934, M.A., 1936, M.B.A., 1937, Ph.D., 1946; student U. Louisville, 1938-39; m. Mildred Eleanor Griscom, Oct. 14, 1939; 1 dau., Helen Whitney. Economist Pa. Planning Bd., Harrisburg, 1934-35; gen freight agt. Preston (Md.) Trucking Co., 1935-36; instr. econs., marketing finance Jr. Coll. Commerce, New Haven, 1937-39, coll. dean, 1949-50; asst. prof. bus. adminstrn. Hanover (Ind.) Coll., 1939-42, also dir. pub. relations; prof. applied econs. Hobart Coll., Geneva, N.Y., 1945-49, asso. and acting dean, 1946-48. dir. indsl. community program, 1947-48; asst. treas. Market Basket Corp., Geneva, 1948-49; prof. econs., chmn. dept. U. Ga., Atlanta, 1950-51, prof. econs., Athens, 1951-52, dir. bur. bus. research, 1951-52; exec. v.p. Oglethorpe U., 1952, pres., 1953-55; prof. finance N.Y. U., 1957-60; cons. higher edn. and research Gen. Electric Co., 1955-62; dean Coll. Bus. Adminstrn., U. Ga., 1962-68; pres Ga. Coll., Milledgeville, 1968—; cons. utility costs Ga. Pub. Service Commn. Economist WpB, Washington, 1942. Pres. Citizen's Com. for Rye Pub. Schs. Served as lt. Supply Corps, USNR, 1942-45. Life fellow Internat. Inst. Arts and Letters; mem. Nat. Invest in Am. Com. (bd. govs., eastern regional chmn., mem. exec. com., pres.), Am. Assn. State Colls. and Univs. (chmn. pub. affairs com. 1970—), Am. Econ. Assn., Am. Geog. Soc., Am. Marketing Assn., Am. Acad. Polit. and Social Sci., Nat. Sales Execs., So. Econ. Soc., Gamma Omicron Tau, Delta Sigma Pi, Delta Chi. Rotarian. Clubs: Milledgeville (Ga.) Country; Advertising (N.Y.C). Author: Effective Retail Selling, 1953; Ethics for Modern Business Practice, 1953; Higher Education, A Twenty Year Look Ahead, 1957; Your Share in America's Prosperity, 1960. Author, editor: Bus. Leaders in People's Capitalism, 1959. Editor of Atlanta Economic Review, 1950-51, Georgia Business, 1951-52; contbg. econs. editor Elec. South, 1952-70. Contbr. articles profl. jours. Home: The Mansion Milledgeville GA 31061 Office: Georgia Coll Milledgeville GA 31061

BUNTING, JOHN JAMES, physician; b. Sunbury, Pa., Nov. 7, 1913; s. James Henry and Doroa (Smith) B.; B.S., Lafayette Coll., 1934; M.D., U. Md., 1938; postgrad. U. Pa., 1945-46; m. Katharyne Denton, Sept. 28, 1941; children—Beverly Sue (Mrs. Robert Austin Moor), John James, William D. Intern, resident U. Hosp., Balt., 1938-40; resident Jersey City Med. Center, 1940-41; practice medicine, specializing in internal medicine, Houston, 1946—; mem. staff Meml. Hosp., Methodist Hosp., St. Luke's Episcopal Hosp., Hermann Hosp., Jefferson Davis Hosp., St. Joseph Hosp., Diagnostic Hosp., Rosewood Hosp., Twelve Oaks Hosp., Ben Taub Hosp.; founder, original sr. partner Montrose Diagnostic Center, Houston, 1953—; asso. prof. clin. medicine Baylor Med. Sch., 1947—; asso. in. medicine U. Tex., 1957—. Pres. Post Grad. Med. Assembly S. Tex. Adv. com. Civil Def., 1949-51. Served from 1st lt. to maj. USAAF, 1942-45. Diplomate Am. Bd. Internal Medicine. Fellow Am. Coll. Angiology, A.C.P., Am. Coll. Chest Physicians; mem. A.M.A., Am. Heart Assn., Am. Diabetes Assn., A.A.A.S., Am. Geriatrics Soc., NY. Acad. Sci., Tex. Acad. Internal Medicine, So. Med. Assn. Episcopalian. Asso. editor Medical Record and Annals. Contbr. articles to profl. jours. and articles on space medicine. Home: 5621 Lynbrook Dr Houston TX 77027 also Lazy-B Ranch Booth TX 7742 Office: 6436 Fannin Houston TX 77006

BUNUEL, LUIS, film dir.; b., 1900. Films include: Un Chien Andalou, 1929; L'Age d'Or, 1930; Land without Bread, 1936; Los Olvidados, 1950; The Adventures of Robinson Crusoe, 1953; The Criminal Life of Archibald de la Cruz, 1955; La Mort en ce Jardin (Evil Eden), 1956; Nazarin, 1958; Le Fievre monte a El Pao, La Jeune Fille, 1959; The Republic of Sin, 1960; The Young One, 1960; Viridiana, 1961 (prize Cannes Festival); Island of Shame, 1961; El Angel Exterminador, 1962. Address: Ultramar Films Remorna 503 Mexico City Mexico

BURBANK, LINDSEY DONALD, dentist; b. Humboldt, Tenn., Oct. 9, 1928; s. Collins Edward and Ruby Myrtle (Lindsey) B.; student Freed-Hardeman Coll., 1946-47, Union U., 1947-48; D.D.S., U. Tenn., 1951, postgrad. pedodontics, 1951; m. Linda Sue Gooch, May 26, 1953; children— Lindsey Donald, John Mark, Leanne, Laurie Susan. Pvt. practice of dentistry, Harrisburg, Ark., 1955-61, Leesburg, Fla., 1962—. Mem. Gov.'s Quarter Horse Breeding Industry Adv. Bd., 1972—. Hon. bd. dirs. Christian Home and Bible Sch., 1964—. Served with Dental Corps, AUS, 1953-55. Mem. Am. Quarter Horse Assn., Central Fla. Speed Horse Assn. (pres. 1971—), Am. Quarter Horse Racing Owners Assn. (dir. 1971—), Fla. Quarter Horse Assn., Fla. Thoroughbred Breeders Assn. Rotarian. Home: Route 1 Box 49-G Leesburg FL 32748 Office: 607 W Dixie Av Leesburg FL 32748

BURCH, DEAN, govt. ofcl.; b. Enid, Okla., Dec. 20, 1927; s. Bert Alexander and Leola (Atkisson) B.; LL.B., U. Ariz., 1953; m. Patricia Meeks, July 7, 1961; children—Shelly, Dean, Dianne. Admitted to Ariz. bar, 1953; asst. atty. gen., Ariz., 1953-54; adminstrv. asst. to Sen. Barry Goldwater, 1955-59; mem. firm Dunseath, Stubbs & Burch, Tucson, 1959-69; chmn. FCC, Washington 1969—. Dep. dir. Goldwater for President Com., 1963-64; chmn. Rep. Nat. Com., 1964-65; mgr. Goldwater for Senate Campaign, 1968. Mem. Ariz. Bd. Regents, 1969. Served with AUS, 1946-48; lt. col. Res. Mem. Phi Delta Theta, Blue Key. Office: Federal Communications Commission 1919 M St Washington DC 20554

BURCH, GEORGE WILEY, computer co. exec.; b. Tsingtao, China, Sept. 12, 1937; s. Cecil Ray and Esther (Respess) B.; B.S., U.S. Air Force Acad., 1959; postgrad. (NSF fellow) Johns Hopkins U., 1966-69; m. Susan Lynn Weller, Nov. 26, 1960; children—Melissa Caitlin, Elena Kirsten, William Linnaeus. Mathematician, Center for Naval Analysis, Washington, 1963-68; pres. Computer Cartography, Inc., Silver Spring, Md., 1968—, also dir. Lectr. John Hopkins, 1967—; cons. math. urban environments. Served with USAF, 1955-63. Mem. Operations Research Soc. Am (sr., edn. com. 1968—). Founder Jour. Differential Games, 1967, editor, 1968. Home: Apt 105 2853 Ontario Rd NW Washington DC 20009 Office: 1111 Bonifant St Silver Spring MD 20910

BURCH, LOREN WILLIAM, educator, news editor, clergyman; b. Epsilon, Mich., Jan. 9, 1907; s. Henry Alonzo and Emma (Odebrecht) B.; B.A., Kalamazoo Coll., 1927; B.D., Colgate-Rochester Div. Sch., 1932; M.A., Cornell U., 1941; m. Mary Etta Anspach 1931 (dec.); children—Phyllis (Mrs. Pernell O. Nix, dec.), Byron H., Marilyn (Mrs. John R. Swan), Loren William, James O.; m. 2d, Olive May Reed Holder, June 5, 1971; stepchildren—Jerry Holder, Raymond Holder. Ordained to ministry Bapt. Ch., 1927; pastor Manitou Beach (Mich.) Bapt. Ch., 1927-29, student pastor Riga (N.Y.) Congl. Ch., 1930-32, West Groton (N.Y.) Congl. Ch., 1932-36, New Haven (N.Y.) Congl. Ch., 1936-43, United Community Ch., Castile, N.Y., 1946-48; asso. pastor United Ch. Christ, Mascoutah, Ill., 1965-66; instr. sociology, German, history Piedmont Coll., Demorest, Ga., 1966-69; pastor Demorest Federated Ch., 1966-69, St. Paul United Ch. Christ, Marshall, 1970-72; news editor Southeast News, Tulsa, 1972—. Served to maj., chaplain USAF, 1943-46, 48-65. Recipient Freedom's Found. award, George Washington medal, 1961; Air Force Commendation medal, 1965. Kiwanian, Rotarian (dir. internat. relations 1965-66), Mason (32 deg., Shriner). Author: Little Lessons from Mighty Men, 1967; A Tale of Sixty Years, 1969. Home: 7406 E Third St Tulsa OK 74112

BURCH, RICHARD JACKMOND, dentist; b. Porter, Okla., Mar. 27, 1908; s. Horace Waldo and Frank Virginia (Goldsborough) B.; student Okla. State U., 1925-26; D.D.S., Washington U., 1931; m. Agnes Ruth Simpson, June 15, 1934; children—Agnes Ann, Sara Virginia, Jane Lee. Pvt. practice dentistry, Eufaula, Okla., 1931-39; commd. 1st lt. USAF, 1939, advanced through grades to col., 1953; chief med. cons. oral and maxillo-facial surgery Far East Air Forces, Korean Campaign, 1951-53; chmn. dept. oral surgery Lackland AFB Hosp., 1953-60; adminstr. U. Ky. Med. Center, Lexington, 1962—. Active Big Bros. Alderman, mem. city council, chmn. and dir. water, fire, police depts., Eufaula, 1936-39. Decorated Bronze Star medal. Diplomate Am. Bd. Oral Surgery. Fellow Am. Coll. Dentists; mem. Omicron Kappa Upsilon, Pi Kappa Alpha, Xi Psi Phi. Lion. Editorial bd. Jour. Oral Surgery, 1959-61. Home: 622 Tateswood Dr Lexington KY 40502 Office: 800 Rose St Lexington KY 40506

BURCHAM, JOHN B., govt. ofcl. Mem. Washington Suburban Transit Commn. Address: 6921 Nashville Rd Lanham MD 20801*

BURCHAM, RALPH JACK, civil engr.; b. Ft. Scott, Kan., Feb. 13, 1931; s. Ralph and Ruby (Hays) B.; student Ft. Scott Kan. Jr. Coll., 1949-51; B.S., U. Ark., 1957; m. Gwendolyn Francaes Parker, Apr. 19, 1955. Stress analyst Boeing Airplane Co., Wichita, Kan., 1957-59; sr. resident engr. Ark. Hwy. Dept., Little Rock, 1959-63; owner Ralph J. Burcham, cons. engrs., Little Rock, 1963-70; pres. Found. Explorations, Inc., Little Rock, 1965-70; partner Assos. Engrs. & Land Surveyors, Little Rock, Ark., 1967-70; engr. Granite Mountain Quarries, Sweet Home, Ark., 1970—. Served to capt. AUS, 1951-53. Decorated Bronze Star medal. Mem. Central Ark., Am., Ark. socs. profl. engrs., Ark. Kennel Club (dir. 1966-70), German Shepherd Dog Club Little Rock (pres. 1972). Baptist. Home: 3924 Base Line Rd Little Rock AR 72209 Office: Shamburger Lane Sweet Home AR 72206

BURCHFIELD, CLETUS, state ofcl. Sec. Okla. Bd. Edn. Address: Okla Dept Pub Instrn State Capitol Bldg Oklahoma City OK 73105*

BURCHFIELD, HARRY PHINEAS, JR., research inst. adminstr.; b. Pitts., Dec. 22, 1915; s. Harry Phineas and Florence Faye (Fearl) B.; A.B., Columbia, 1938, M.A., 1938, Ph.D., 1956; m. Eleanor Emerett Storrs, Nov. 29, 1963; children—Sarah Storrs, Benjamin Hyde. Research scientist Uniroyal Corp., Naugatuck, Conn., 1940-50, dir. plantations research dept., Indonesia, 1951-52; asso. dir. Boyce Thompson Inst. for Plant Research, Yonkers, N.Y., 1952-61; inst. scientist, mgr. S.W. Research Inst., San Antonio, 1961-65; chief pesticides research lab. USPHS, Perrine, Fla., 1965-67; sci. dir. Gulf South Research Inst., New Iberia, La., 1967—; adj. prof. chemistry U. Southwestern La., 1967—. Trustee Gulf Univs. Research Consortium, 1971—; mem. Carcinogenesis Panel of Secs., Health Edn. and Welfare Commn. on Pesticides, 1969; mem. nat. tech. adv. com. pesticides Environmental Protection Agy., 1971-72, project reviewer research grants, 1972; cons. carcinogenesis Nat. Cancer Inst., 1965-67; treas. The Acadiana Internat. Relations Assos., 1972—. Recipient award Chgo. Rubber Group, 1946. Environmental Protection Agy. grantee 1969. Mem. Am. Chem. Soc., Soc. Toxicology, Am. Inst. Biol. Scis., A.A.A.S., Am. Phytopath. Soc., N.Y. Acad. Scis. Author: (with Eleanor E. Storrs) Biochemical Applications of Gas Chromatography, 1962; (with D.E. Johnson and Eleanor Storrs) Guide to the Analysis of Pesticide Residues, 1965. Contbr. articles to profl. jours. Home: 303 Duperier Av New Iberia LA 70560 Office: PO Box 1177 New Iberia LA 70560

BURDETSKY, BEN, govt. ofcl.; b. Phila., July 15, 1928; s. Morris and Rebecca (Singer) B.; B.S. in Edn., Temple U., 1950, M.S. in Psychology, 1958; Ph.D. in Bus. Adminstrn., Am. U., 1968; m. Irene Lusky, Feb. 9, 1958; children—June, Andrew, Marjorie, Matthew, Abbe. Tchr. pub. schs., Phila., 1954-55; with U.S. Bur. Employment Security, 1955-61; chief data systems Dept. Labor, Washington, 1961-66; dir. administrv. mgmt. Bur. Labor Statistics, 1966-67; acting commr., 1968-69, dep. commr., 1967—; part-time tchr. grad. program Sch. Bus. Adminstrn., Am. U., 1963-71, George Washington U., 1971—. Served with USAF, 1950-54. Mem. Indsl. Relations Research Assn., Am. Statis. Assn., Internat. Assn. Personnel in Employment Security. Home: 4619 N Dittmar Rd Arlington VA 22207 Office: 441 G St NW Washington DC 20212

BURDICK, EVERETTE MARSHALL, cons. chemist; b. Champaign, Ill., Aug. 9, 1913; s. Pearl Oscar and Margaret Alice (Hyde) B.; B.S. cum laude, U. Miami, 1935; M.S., Purdue U., 1937, Ph.D., 1943; m. Lois Aline Enyart, Nov. 13, 1937. Research chemist U.S. Dept. Agr., Northern Regional Research Lab., Peoria, Ill., 1941-45, U.S. Fruit & Vegetable Products Lab., Weslaco, Tex., 1945-46; dir. research Texsum Citrus Exchange, Weslaco, 1946-52; tech. cons. Rio Farms, Inc., Edcouch, Tex., 1949-52; tech. dir. Am. Chlorophyll, 1952-53; dir. labs. Am. Chlorophyll div. Strong- Cobb & Co., 1953; v.p., dir. research Strong Cobb & Co., Inc., 1953-54; pres. Am. Papain & Chem. Co., Inc., 1954-57; cons. Florida Citrus Mutual, 1957-58, Wallerstein Labs., Baxter Labs., Arbee Biochem. Corp., Resources Research, 1959-64; dir. research and devel. True Taste Corp., 1961-63. Fellow Am. Inst. Chemists (chmn. Fla. sect. 1962-63), A.A.A.S.; mem. Chem. Soc., Fla. Hort. Soc., Inst. Food Technologists, N.Y. Acad Scis., Sigma Xi, Phi Lambda Upsilon.

Methodist. Mason. Co-author: Modern Chemical Processes, vols. I and IV; Fruit and Vegetable Juice Production. Contbr. to profl. jours. Patentee in field. Home: 4821 Ronda St Coral Gables FL 33146 Office: Coral Gables FL 33146

BURDICK, LARRY GENE, supt. schs.; b. Mooreland, Okla., Aug. 28, 1932; s. James Wilbur and Dorothy Dane (Wheeler) B.; B.S., Okla. State U., 1954, M.S., 1962, Ed.D., 1967; postgrad. U. Okla., 1962-63; m. Betty Lou Meyer, Sept. 6, 1953; children—Karen Ann, Kevin Lee, Keith Alan. Tchr. math., coach Garber (Okla.) Pub. Schs., 1956-61, high sch. prin., 1961-62, supt. schs., 1962-66; dir. tchr. edn. Phillips U., Enid, Okla., 1967-68; supt. schs. Pryor (Okla.) Pub. Schs., 1968—. Bd. dirs. Pryor United Fund. Served with USAAF, 1954-56. Mem. N.E.A., Am., Okla. (v.p. 1971-72, pres. elect 1972-73) assns. sch. adminstrs., Assn. Sch. Bus. Ofcls. Okla., Okla. Edn. Assn., Okla. Pub. Sch. Research Council (pres. 1969-70), Pryor C. of C. (dir. 1969-71). Methodist (bd. edn. Okla. Conf. 1968—). Rotarian. Home: 1008 SE 14th St Pryor OK 74361 Office: 521 SE 1st St Pryor OK 74361

BURDON, ARTHUR PEMBERTON, physician; b. St. Louis, Nov. 23, 1924; s. Kenneth L. and Estelle (Pemberton) B.; B.S., Tulane U., 1945, M.D., 1947; m. Jane Talmage, June 14, 1947;children—Paula, Lois, Susan, John. Intern, USPHS Hosp,, S.I., N.Y., 1947-48; resident psychiatry Harvard Med. Sch., 1948-49, research group psychotherapy, 1959-60; chief psychiatry Mt. Auburn Hosp., Cambridge, Mass., 1959-60; practice medicine, specializing in psychiatry, and psychoanalysis, New Orleans, 1960—; asso. prof. psychiatry La. State U. Med. Sch., 1960-71, prof., 1971—; v.p. Mgmt. & Personnel Services, Inc. Bd. dirs. La. Assn. Mental Health. Served with AUS, 1944-47, USPHS, 1947-48, 51-53. Fellow Am. Group Psychotherapy Assn., Am., So. psychiat. assns. Presbyn. (elder). Contbr. articles profl. jours. Home: 382 Broadway New Orleans LA 70118 Office: 3720 Prytania St New Orleans LA 70115

BURFORD, ROGER LEWIS, educator; b. Independence, Miss., Jan. 19, 1930; s. Roger W. and Christene (Lewis) B.; B,B,A., U. Miss., 1956 M.A., 1957; Ph.D., Ind. U., 1961; m. Bettye Jane Marshall, Nov. 25, 1948; children—Pamela Denise, Roger Marshall. Lectr. econs., statistics Ind. U., 1959-60; mem. faculty Ga. State Coll., 1960-63 mem. faculty La. State U., Baton Rouge, 1963—, dir. div. bus. research, 1969—. Vice pres. Econ. and Indsl. Research, Inc., Baton Rouge, 1967—. Ford Found. Predoctoral fellow, 1957-59, Fulbright fellow, 1968-69. Mem. Am., So. econ. assns., Econometric Soc., Am. Statis. Assn., Western Regional Sci. Assn. Author: Introduction to Finite Probability, 1967; Statistics-A Computer Approach, 1968; Basic Statistics for Business and Economics-A Computer Oriented Text, 1970. Home: 590 Castle Kirk Av Baton Rouge LA 70808

BURFORD, SELWYN OILVER, oil co. exec.; b. Santa Anna, Tex., Sept. 16, 1899; s. William Baxter and Effie (Oliver) B.; B.A. in Geology, U. Tex. at Austin, 1927, M.A., 1928; m. Myrle Louise Walker, Nov. 23, 1927; children—Marylouise, Patsy (Mrs. William Roy Samuel), Robert Oliver. Geologist, Henry L. Doherty Oil Co., Coahvila, Mexico, 1925; Instr. geology U. Tex., 1927-29; with Humble Oil Co. various Gulf Coast locations, 1929-64, research geologist, Houston, 1940-41, sr. geologist, Tyler, Tex., 1941-64; pres. Somyrol, Inc., Tyler, 1964—. Mgr., trustee Burford Found., 1965—. Served with U.S. Army, 1918. Mem. Am. Assn. Petroleum Geologists, East Tex. Geol. Soc., Internat. Platform Assn., Sigma Gamma Epsilon, Acacia. Mem. Christian Ch. Address: Rural Route 2 Box 531 Tyler TX 75701

BURGER, ROBERT MERCER, physicist; b. Frederick, Md., Feb. 14, 1927; s. William Leslie and Grace Allene (Mercer) B.; B.S., Coll. William and Mary, 1949; Sc.M, Brown U., 1955, Ph.D., 1955; m. Marian Elizabeth Abbott, Sept. 10, 1949; children—Sharon A., Lisa A., Robert M. Physicist, Dept. Def., Washington, 1955-59; fellow engr. Westinghouse Elec. Co., Balt., 1959-62; dir. Solid State Lab., Research Triangle Inst., N.C., 1962-67, dir. engring and environmental sci. div., 1967-71, chief scientist, 1971—. Research asso. physics U. Md., College Park, 1957-59; adj. asso. prof. elec. engring. Duke, Durham, N.C., 1962-69. Served with USNR, 1945-46. Recipient Bauch and Lamb Sci. award, 1944. Mem. Am. Phys. Soc., I.E.E.E., A.A.A.S., Am. Ordnance Assn., Sigma Xi. Republican. Presbyn. Editor: (with R.P. Donovan) Fundamentals of Silicon Integrated Device Technology, vol. 1, 1967 vol. 2, 1968. Home: 1506 Rosedale Ave Durham NC 27707 Office: PO Box 12194 Research Triangle Park NC 27709

BURGER, WARREN E(ARL), chief justice of U.S.; b. St. Paul, 1907; s. Charles Joseph and Katharine (Schnittger) B.; student U. Minn., 1925-27; LL.B. magna cum laude, St. Paul Coll. Law (now Mitchell Coll. Law), 1931; m. Elvera Stromberg, Nov. 8, 1933; children—Wade Allan, Margaret Elizabeth. Admitted to Minn. bar, 1931; partner Faricy, Burger, Moore & Costello (and predecessor firms), 1935-53; faculty Mitchell Coll. Law, 1931-48; asst. atty. gen. U.S., 1953-56; judge U.S. Ct. Appeals, Washington, 1956-69; chief justice U.S., 1969—. Office: Supreme Court US Washington DC 20543

BURGESS, ARTHUR HARRY, accountant; b. Sharon, S.C., Oct. 25, 1903; s. Arthur Calhoun and Mary (Love) B.; student Furman U., 1921-23; m. Sara Elizabeth Doll, Nov. 30, 1933; children—Sara Elizabeth (Mrs. John Sidney Frazer), Arthur Harry. Public accountant, Hickory, N.C., 1928—; dir. Maxwell Royal Chair Co., Mem. adv. bd. trustees Queens Coll. C.P.A., N.C. Mem. Am. Inst. C.P.A.'s N.C. Assn. C.P.A.'s. Presbyn. Rotarian. Clubs: Catawba (Newton, N.C.); Lake Hickory Country (Hickory). Home: 322 3d Av NE Hickory NC 28601 Office: First Security Bldg Hickory NC 28601

BURGESS, BRYAN ELIJAH, ednl. adminstr.; b. Sparta, Tenn., Oct. 27, 1937; s. Elijah Bryan and Pauline (Pennington) B.; B.S., Tenn. Tech. U., 1960; M.S., U. Tenn. 1965, postgrad., 1971; m. Katherine Kirby, June 10, 1961 (div. Dec. 1971); children—Belinda, Susan, Paula. Design engr. Hayes Internat. Co., Huntsville, Ala., 1960-61, 63-64; systems analyst Brown Engring. Co., Huntsville, 1964-67; v.p. Nashville, Speedways, Inc., 1968-70; dir. research Motlow State Community Coll., Tullahoma, Tenn. 1970—. Served to capt. AUS, 1961-63. Registered profl. engr., Tenn. Mem. Nat., Tenn. soc. profl. engrs., Tenn. Edn. Assn., Tullahoma Jr. C. of C., Nashville Amateur Boxing Assn. (dir. 1969-71). Kiwanian. Home: 706 Stone Blvd Tullahoma TN 37388

BURGESS, CHESTER FRANCIS, educator; b. Brockton, Mass., Oct. 30, 1922; s. Chester Francis and Mary Ann (Cronin) B.; B.A., Yale, 1945; M.A., U. Notre Dame, 1961, Ph.D., 1962; m. Betty Lou Reigan, Sept. 1, 1945; children—Chester F. III, Deborah Ann. Instr. English, Yale, 1946-48; mgr. retail automobile agy., Rifle, Colo., 1948-60; instr. English, U. Notre Dame, 1960-62, pub. relations asst., 1961; asst. prof. English, Va. Mil. Inst., Lexington, 1962-63, prof., 1967—. Reporter, A.P., 1939-40. Served to capt., USMCR, 1943-46, 51-52. Ford Found. fellow, 1965-66; Folger Library fellow, 1968; Am. Council Learned Socs. fellow, 1971; Am. Philos Soc. grantee, 1963, 64, 65, 68. Mem. Modern Lang. Assn. Am., Phi Beta Kappa. Author: The Letters of John Gay, 1966; Gay's Beggar's Opera and Companion Pieces, 1966; also articles. Home: 305 Letcher Av Lexington VA 24450

BURGESS, JAMES ALFRED, dentist; b. Pecola, Okla., Apr. 13, 1931; s. James Alfred and Jewell Louise (Farrar) B.; A.A., Fort Smith Jr. Coll., 1951; student U. Ark., 1954-56; D.D.S., U. Kansas City, 1959; m. Myra J. Spearman, May 27, 1951; children—Rozanne, James Alfred III, Dane Alan, Suzanne. Pvt. practice of dentistry, Greenwood, Ark., 1959—. Chmn. Greenwood Housing Authority, 1968-71; chmn. Sebastian County Housing Corp., 1971—. Bd. dirs. Sebastian County Fair, 1962-71; adv. bd. Westark Jr. Coll., 1970-71. Served with USNR, 1951-54. Mem. C. of C. (pres. 1966-67), Ft. Smith, Ark. dental socs., Am. Dental Assn., South Sebastian County Indsl. and Devel. Assn. (sec. 1969-71). Lion. Club: Greenwood Round-up (pres. 1963). Home: Greenwood AR 72936 Office: PO Box 478 Greenwood AR 72936

BURGESS, JAMES ROWLAND, JR., coll. pres.; b. Ashburn, Ga., Feb. 17, 1907; s. James Rowland and Aurena (Evans) B.; diploma Young Harris Coll., 1927; A.B., Emory U., 1931; M.Ed., Duke, 1936; LL.D., La Grange Coll., 1960; m. Martha Elizabeth Stallings, Aug. 13, 1932; children—James Rowland III, Martha S. (Mrs. James Monroe Thorn). Prin., Oak Grove Sch., 1927-28, Cataula (Ga.) High Sch., 1928-30, Pitts (Ga.) Consol. Sch., 1931-36; supt. Vienna (Ga.) Pub. Schs., 1936-41; prin. Blue Ridge (Ga.) Dist Schs., 1941-43; supt. Baxley (Ga.) Pub. Schs., 1943-44; pres. Reinhardt Coll., Waleska, Ga., 1944—. Mem. bd. edn. N. Ga. Conf., United Meth. Ch., 1956-66, del. gen. Conf., 1960, alternat. del., 1972, del. Jurisdictional Conf., 1952, 56, 60, 64, 68, 72. Mem. Ga. Assn. Jr. Colls. (past pres.), Nat. Assn. Meth. Colls. (past pres. jr. coll. sect.), Ga. Assn. Colls. (pres. 1965), Ga. Hort. Soc. (dir. 1966-68, v.p. 1971—), Pvt. Colls. and Univs. Ga. (exec. com. 1968—), Ga. Conservancy (trustee 1968-70), P.T.A. (hon. life), Kappa Phi Kappa, Kappa Delta Pi, Pi Kappa Delta, Phi Theta Kappa. Lion (pres. Canton 1962). Home: Reinhardt Coll Waleska GA 30183

BURGESS, JOHN FREDERICK, JR., ednl. adminstr.; b. Washington, Jan. 23, 1932; s. John Frederick and Thelma (Gray) B.; A.A., St. Petersburg Jr. Coll., 1956; B.S., Fla. State U., 1958, M.S., 1960, Ed.D., 1966; m Betty Margaret Cleveland, Sept. 12, 1959; children—John, Donald. Instr., dept. marketing Fla. State U., Tallahassee, 1959, research asst., tchr, Sch. Bus., 1960-62; asst. study dir. Fla. Devel. Commn., Tallahassee, 1959-60; chmn. bus. econs. dept., dir. Community Services, Columbus Coll., Ga., 1962-66, dir. community services continuing edn., 1966—. Served with AUS, 1952-54. Mem. Ga. Adult Edn. Council, Assn. Continuing Edn., Pub. Service Adminstrs. Club: Exchange (past pres.). Home: 4749 Shanandoah Dr Columbus GA 31907

BURGESS, LEONARD RANDOLPH, educator; b. Washington, Mar. 8, 1919; s. W. Randolph and May (Ayres) B.; B.A., Brown U., 1942; M.B.A., Harvard, 1947; Ph.D., Columbia, 1961; m. Virginia Frost, May 26, 1946. Chief statistician W. Va. Pulp & Paper Co., N.Y.C., 1947-52; sr. staff asso. Nat. Indsl. Conf. Bd., N.Y.C., 1952-57; lectr., instr. Coll. City N.Y., 1958-59; asst. prof. North Tex. State U., 1961-64; asso. prof. Tex A. and M. U., College Station, 1964-68, prof., 1968—. Staff asst. Brazos County Community Action Com., 1966-72, Brazos Valley Community Action Program, 1972—. Chmn., Hastings-on-Hudson (N.Y.) Citizens for Eisenhower, 1952. Trustee Hudson Guild Neighborhood House, N.Y.C., 1953-61. Served with AUS, 1941-45; lt. col. Res. Decorated Purple Heart. Mem. Acad. Polit. Sci., Am. Econ. Assn., Am. Statis. Assn., Indsl. Relations Research Assn., Southwestern Social Sci. Assn. (membership com. 1969-71, ad hoc com. status of women 1971—) Acad. Mgmt. (mem. program com. orgn. devel. div. 1971—), Delta Upsilon. Author: Top Executive Pay Package, 1963; Wage and Salary Administration in a Dynamic Economy, 1968. Contbr. articles to profl. jours. Home: 404 Timber St College Station TX 77840

BURGESS, OLIVER TAYLOR, hairstylist, cosmetologist; b. Dendron, Va.; Aug. 29, 1918; s. Herman Oliver and Virginia (Trueheart) B.; student Kirby's Beauty Sch., Norfolk, Va., 1948, Robert Fiance Hair Design Inst., N.Y.C., 1949; m. Ida Madjestic Chester, Dec. 17, 1941; 1 son, Oliver Taylor. Owner beauty salon, Wakefield, Va., 1948-50; owner beauty salons, Norfolk, 1950—, as owner Taylor Burgess Hairstyling Salons, Inc., 1962—; guest stylist John H. Breck Co., in U.S. and Europe, 1957—; pres., chmn. bd., dir. Polychem, Inc. Bd. dirs. Girl's Club of Norfolk. Cons. com. cosmetology Norfolk Tech. Vocational Center, Norfolk. Served as cpl. 116th Inf., AUS, 1941-45; ETO. Decorated Purle Heart, Bronze Star. Mem. Nat. (hair fashion com.), Norfolk hairdressers assns., Internat. Platform Assn., Intercoiffure U.S., Va. Hairdressers and Cosmetologists Assn. (pres. 1965-66), Va. Allied Council Cosmetology (charter mem.), Norfolk C. of C., Wards Corner Bus. Men's Assn. Baptist (trustee). Mason (Shriner), Lion. Club: Lafayette Yacht (Norfolk, Va.). Home: 6435 Newport Av Norfolk VA 23505 Office: 7500 Granby St Wards Corner Norfolk VA 23505

BURGESS, THOMAS JAY, city ofcl.; b. Harrisburg, Ill., July 2, 1940; s. John Edward and Leah Mae (Stonemetz) B.; B.A., U. Ill., 1962; M. Pub. Adminstrn., U. Kan., 1967; m. Leslie Louise Marks, Sept. 21, 1963; children—Jennifer Jaye, Galen John. Adminstrv. asst. to city mgr. City of Champaign (Ill.), 1965, City of Boulder (Colo.), 1966-68; asst. city mgr. City of Ft. Collins (Colo.), 1968-70; city mgr. City of Winchester (Ky.), 1970—. Served with AUS, 1963-65. Mem. Internat., Ky. (sec.-treas. 1971-72) city mgmt. assns., Am. Soc. Pub. Adminstrn., Theta Delta Chi. Elk, Rotarian. Home: 26 Millwood Dr Winchester KY 40391 Office: 30 Wall St Winchester KY 40391

BURGESS, WILBUR HARLIN, writer; b. Monmouth, Ill., Aug. 15, 1914; s. Charles Oliver and Lura (Harlin) B.; student Monmouth Coll., 1929-33; m. Suzanne Marie McLean, Dec. 29, 1940; children—Lysbeth (Mrs. John A. Chuck), Duncan H. Commd. capt. U.S. Army, 1940, advanced through grades to col.; staff comd. coll., 1953. Artillery sch. faculty, 1953-56, 59-60; adviser Korean Army, 1956-57, ret., 1960; tech. writer Franklin Co.-Phila., Ft. Sill, Okla., 1962-64; course materials writer U.S. Civil Service, Ft. Sill, 1964—. Pres. Inst. Gt. Plains. Decorated Army Commendation medal with oak leaf cluster. Mem. Nat. Trust for Historic Preservation, Smithsonian Assos., Internat. Council Museums, Am. Assn. Museums, Lawton C. of C. Home: 210 Mimosa Lane Lawton OK 73501

BURGET, CARL EDWARD, banker; b. Chandler, Okla., June 26, 1921; s. Everett Edward and Stella Lee (Hutchinson) B.; student Tonkawa Jr. Coll., 1939, Central State U., 1946-47; J.D., U. Okla., 1949; m. Mary Sue McMinimy, Nov. 25, 1946; 1 son, Mark Edward. Commd. capt. U.S. Air Force, 1947, advanced through grades to col., 1963; asst. staff judge adv. Lowry AFB, Denver, 1949-52, Hdqrs. USAFE, Wiesbaden, Germany, 1952-55, Hdqrs. Continental Mil. Air Transport Service, San Antonio, 1955-58; staff judge adv. Hdqrs. 30th Air Div., Detroit, 1958-59; asst. staff judge adv. and staff judge adv. Hdqrs. 30th Air Div., Madison, Wis., 1959-63; staff judge adv. 3320th Tech. Tng. Center, Amarillo, Tex., 1963-65; ret., 1965; admitted to Tex. bar, U.S. Supreme Ct. bar; sr. v.p., trust officer Am. Nat. Bank, Amarillo, 1965—. Pres., Amarillo Day Nursery, 1968. Bd. dirs. Amarillo Theater Co. Mem. Am., Tex. bankers assns., Bank Marketing Assn., V.F.W., Okla. Bar Assn., Amarillo C. of C., Phi Delta Phi. Mason (32 deg.). Clubs: Amarillo Country, Amarillo; Touchdown (Norman, Okla.). Home: 3806 Lynette St Amarillo TX 79109 Office: PO Box 231 120 W 7th St Amarillo TX 79101

BURGHER, EDMON, electric co. exec.; b. Clay City, Ky., June 11, 1896; s. John Everett and Denannie (McKinney) B.; grad. Mich. State Auto Sch., 1920; m. Ethel Delcinia Johnson, Oct. 10, 1921; children—Edmon, Lorraine, (Mrs. Max Ervin). Asst. editor Clay City Times, 1910-25; shop foreman Cynthiana (Ky.) Democrat, 1925-33; postmaster, Clay City, 1938-39; ry. postal clk. 1939-41; ry. clk., U.S. Postal Service, 1946-59; pub. Clay City Times, 1959-64; dir. Powell County Bank, Stanton, Ky., 1959-65, Clark Rural Electric Coop. Corp., Winchester, Ky., 1962—; charter mem. Estill Fed. Savs. & Loan Assn., Irvine, Ky. Alternate del. Nat. Democratic Conv., 1960; mayor, Clay City, 1959-61. Served with USMCR, 1917-19, USAF, 1941-44, U.S. Mcht. Marines, 1945-46. Mem. S.A.R., Am. Legion (comdr. 1961), 40 and 80, Vets. World War I, Ky. Am. Legion Press Assn. (pres. 1965). Baptist. Mason, Lion. Home: Clay City KY 70312

BURGIN, WILLIAM GARNER, JR., lawyer, state senator; b. Rock Hill, S.C., Aug. 3, 1924; s. William Garner and Susie Will (Gunter) B.; B.A., U. Miss., 1947, LL.B., 1947; m. Catherine Williams; children—Helen, William Garner III, Lilian S., Robert Melville. Admitted to Miss. bar, 1947, since practiced in Columbus, Miss. Dir. Nat. Bank of Commerce, Columbus, Miss., Columbus Hotel Co., Inc., Columbus Television Cable Corp. Mem. Miss. Senate, 25th dist., 1952-60, chmn. finance com., 1956-60; mem. Miss. Commn. of Budget and Accounting, 1956-60, 64—, Miss. Sovereignty Commn., 1956-60; trustee Pub. Employees Retirement System, 1956-60; mem. Miss. Senate, 10th dist., 1964—, chmn. senate appropriations com., 1964—; mem. Lowndes County Sch. Bd., 1949-54; mem. Miss. Medicaid Commn., 1969—; mem. Lowndes County Democratic Exec. Com., 1949—. sec., 1949-56, 59—. Baptist. Mason, Lion (pres. 1950-51). Home: 421 E Gaywood Av Columbus MS 39701 Office: 518 2d St N Columbus MS 39701

BURHANS, ROBERT DUANE, mus. dir.; b. Kalamazoo, Mar. 9, 1916; s. Leon Duane and Hazel (Brodie) B.; B.A., Mich. State U., 1938; LL.G. Smithdeal-Massey Coll. of Law, 1949; m. Janet Roy Nunnally, Mar. 20, 1943. Reporter Lansing State Jour., 1937-38, Richmond (Va.) News Leader, 1946-47; commd. 2d lt. U.S. Army, 1937, served various assignments until 1946, recalled to active duty as col. 1948, served in Dept. of Army, also Army Attache; ret., 1961; dir. Kenmore, Fredericksburg, Va., 1963—. Decorated Bronze Star medal with oak leaf cluster (U.S.); Cross of Liberation (Norway). Mem. Nat. Inst. Social Scis., Nat. Trust, Internat. Council Museums, Va. State Bar. Democrat. Episcopalian. Author: The First Special Service Force: A War History of the North Americans, 1942-44, 1947; History and Heraldry of 80th Division, 1960. Contbr. articles to profl. jours. Home: 1111 Princess Anne St Fredericksburg VA 22401 Office: 1201 Washington Av Fredericksburg VA 22401

BURKE, ART, sports editor. Sports editor New Orleans States-Item. Office: 3800 Howard Av New Orleans LA 70140*

BURKE, DENZER, dentist; b. Atlanta, Sept. 22, 1933; s. Dennis and Sarah (White) B.; B.S., U. Mich., 1956 D.D.S., Howard U., 1959, Practice dentistry, Texarkana, Tex., 1963—. Vice chmn. Tex. State Adv. Com. to U.S. Commn. on Civil Rights, 1968—; sec. exec. com. Bowie County Econ. Advancement Corp., 1964-68. Bd. dirs. Texarkana Community Chest, Bowie Orgn. Loyal Democrats, Texarkana Spl. Edn. Kindergarten and Sch. Served with USNR, 1959-63. Mem. Am., Nat., Texarkana dental assns., Texarkana Orgn., Kappa Alpha Psi (chpt. sec.-treas. 1967—). Presbyn. Home: 25 S Robison Rd Texarkana TX 75501 Office: 523 W 3d St Texarkana TX 75501

BURKE, FRANK GERARD, govt. ofcl.; b. Bklyn., Apr. 22, 1927; s. James Francis and Eleanor Josephine (Thomas) B.; student U. Alaska, 1952-55; M.A., U. Chgo., 1959, Ph.D., 1969; m. Hildegard Waltraud Arndt, Aug. 1, 1959; children—Margaret, Catherine, Christina, Thomas, Elisabeth. Asst. curator archives and manuscripts U. Chgo., 1962-64; head Preparation sect. Manuscript div. Library Congress, Washington, 1964-67; information retrieval specialist Nat. Archives and Record Service, Gen. Services Adminstrn., 1967-68, dir. ednl. programs, 1968—; cons. archival automation State of Me., 1968, 70. Served with USNR, 1945-46. Mem. Am. Hist. Assn., Soc. Am. Archivists (chmn. subcom. automation). Contbr. articles to profl. jours. Home: 3401 Charleson St Annandale VA 22003 Office: National Archives 8th and Pennsylvania Av NW Washington DC 20408

BURKE, FRANK WELSH, mayor; b. Louisville, June 1, 1920; s. Joseph M. and Ann (Welsh) B.; student U, So. Cal., 1938-39; Ph.B., Xavier U., 1942; LL.B., U. Louisville, 1948; m. Evalyne Hackett, Apr. 6, 1943; children—Lynn (Mrs. Dennis Clare), JoAnn (Mrs. George Schuhmann), Lucy, Frank Welsh. Admitted to Ky. bar, 1948, since practiced in Louisville; asst. city atty., Louisville, 1950-51; dir. pub. safety, Louisville, 1952; exec. asst. to mayor of Louisville, 1952-53; mem. U.S. Ho. of Reps. from Ky., 1958-62; mayor of Louisville, 1969—. Mem. Ky. Ho. of Reps., 1957; del. Democratic Nat. Conv., 1968. Served to lst lt. AUS, 1942-45. Mem. Ky., Louisville bar assns., Am. Legion, V.F.W., Phi Alpha Delta, Alpha Sigma Nu. Phi Kappa Psi. Roman Catholic. K.C. Home: 1234 Eastern Pkwy Louisville KY 40204 Office: City Hall Louisville KY 40202

BURKE, GERARD PATRICK, lawyer, govt. ofcl.; b. Darby, Pa., Apr. 3, 1930; s. Patrick J. and Mary E. (Breslin) B.; A.B., Holy Cross Coll., 1952; J.D., Georgetown U., 1958; postgrad. Inst. Comparative Law, U. Paris, 1960-61; m. Ann M. Burke, Nov. 12, 1955; children—Gerard Patrick, Maura Anne, Christine. Admitted to D.C. bar, 1958; cryptologist Nat. Security Agy., Washington, 1957-70, exec. asst. to dir., 1965-69; exec. sec. Pres.'s Fgn. Intelligence Adv. Bd., 1970—. Served to lt. USNR, 1952-57. Recipient Exceptional Civilian Service award Nat. Security Agy., 1969; William A. Jump Meritorious award for pub. adminstrn., 1966, 67. Mem. D.C., Fed. bar assns., Phi Delta Phi. Home: 1117 Spotswood Dr Silver Springs MD 20904 Office: The White House Washington DC 20500

BURKE, HENRY FRANCIS, physician; b. Lynn, Mass., Feb. 22, 1925; s. James Michael and Mary (Thomas) B.; student Harvard, 1942-44; M.D., Boston U., 1948; m. Dorothy Jane Egan, Sept. 6, 1949; children—Henry, Patricia, James, Jane, Michael, Maureen. Intern, Beverly (Mass.) Hosp., 1948-49; resident VA Hosp., Boston and West Roxbury, Mass., 1951-54; practice medicine, specializing in internal medicine, Lynn, Mass., 1954, 55, St. Johnsbury, Vt., 1957-58; teaching fellow medicine Tufts U., Boston, 1953-54; staff physician U. Fla., Gainesville, 1956-57; asst. chief med. service and chief cardiology sect. VA Hosp., Providence, R.I., 1958-65; chief med. service VA Hosp., Bay Pines, Fla., 1965—. Mem. med. sci. com. R.I. Arthritis and Rheumatism Found. Served to lt. M.C., USNR, 1949-51. Diplomate Am. Bd. Internal Medicine; mem. A.C.P., A.M.A., Am. Heart Assn., Mass., Vt. med. socs. Home: 8083 Stimie Av N St Petersburg FL 33710 Office: VA Hosp Bay Pines FL 33504

BURKE, J. HERBERT, congressman; b. Chgo., Jan. 14, 1913; s. Joseph Patrick and Catherine (Lobert) B.; student Northwestern U., 1934-35; A.A., Central YMCA Coll., 1936; J.D., Kent Coll. Law, 1940; L.H.D. (hon.), Drake Coll., 1967, Fort Lauderdale U., 1970; LL.D., Chgo. Coll. Law, 1969; m. Evelyn Rose Krumtinger, Sept. 4, 1946; children—Michele Kathleen, Kelly Ann. Admitted to Ill. bar, 1940, Fla. bar, 1949, U.S. Supreme Ct. bar, 1949; practiced in Chgo., 1940-49, Hollywood, Fla., 1949—; asso. firm Pam, Hurd & Reichmann, 1940-49; sr. partner Burke & McMorrough, 1957-59, Burke & Hoffman, 1959—; mem. 90th-92d Congresses, 10th Dist. Fla., mem. fgn. affairs com. Chmn. March of Dimes South Broward County, 1955, Broward County Heart Fund, 1957-58; mem. S.E. adv. bd. Small Bus. Adminstrn., 1956-60; adviser Nat. Rivers and Harbors Congress, 1958. Mem. Broward County Commn., 1952-66, chmn., 1956-58, dean, 1958-64; Republican state committeeman, 1954-59; del. Rep. Nat. Conv., 1968, also mem. platform com.; mem. nat. exec. com. Rep. Congl. Com. Served to capt. inf. AUS, 1942-45; ETO. Decorated Purple Heart, Bronze Star medal; recipient Outstanding Service medal Nat. Heart Assn., 1957; Good Govt. award Hollywood Jr. C. of C., 1963; Outstanding Citizenship award Hollywood Civitan Club, 1964; Distinguished Service award Ams. for Constl. Action, 1967, 68, 69, 70, 71; Watchdog of Treasury award Nat. Assn. Businessmen, 1967, 68, 69, 70, 71; service to Israel award Zionist Orgn. Am., 1969; citation for meritorious service Nat. Assn. Ret. Civil Employees, 1971 Mem. Am. Legion (past post comdr.), Amvets (life, citation 1969), 40 and 8, V.F.W., D.A.V., Hollywood C. of C., Phi Delta Phi. Roman Catholic. Eagle, Elk, Moose, Kiwanian. Home: 1218 Hollywood Blvd Hollywood FL 33022 Office: Longworth Bldg US Ho of Reps Washington DC 20515

BURKE, JACK DALE, univ. adminstr.; b. Weiser, Ida., Feb. 6, 1929; s. Earl Edward and Almia Etta (Burns) B.; B.A., U. Ore., 1953; B.D., Fuller Theol. Sem., 1957, M.S., 1962; Ph.D., U. So. Cal., 1968; m. Darlys Ann Cowan, Jan. 29, 1955; children—Linda, David. Tchr., Azusa (Cal.) Unified Sch. Dist., 1957-62; dir. Office Internat. Services, U. Pa., Phila., 1963-66; dir. Internat. Student Office, U. Houston, 1968—. Educare fellow U. So. Cal., 1966-68. Mem. Am. Psychol. Assn., Nat. Assn. Student Personnel Adminstrs., Nat. Assn. Fgn. Student Affairs (mem. exec. com. community sect. 1966-71). Am. Personnel Guidance Assn. Home: 13714 Perthshire St Houston TX 77024

BURKE, JOHN WOOLFOLK, JR., lawyer, assn. exec.; b. Washington, Sept. 19, 1915; s. John Woolfolk and Elizabeth Mayo (Atkinson) B.; A.B., Princeton, 1937; LL.B., U.Va., 1941; m. Agnes Alexander Spencer, June 14, 1941; children—John Woolfolk III, Elizabeth Gordon, Agnes Alexander Spencer. Pvt. practice law, 1941; dir. personnel and indsl. relations Capital Airlines, 1946-57; v.p., asst. to chmn. bd. Civil Air Transport, 1957-59; exec. dir. Bus. Council, Washington, 1959—; mem. br. adv. bd. Am. Security & Trust Co. Trustee Gunston Sch. Served from ensign to lt. comdr., USNR, World War II. Mem. Phi Delta Phi. Episcopalian (vestryman). Clubs: Chevy Chase (Md.); Metropolitan (Washington). Home: 5014 Glenbrook Rd Washington DC 20016 Office: 888 17th St Washington DC 20006

BURKE, SAM FRANCIS, ednl. assn. exec.; b. Hampton, Va., Nov. 5, 1903; s. Walter H. and Ava (Cunningham) B.; student Coll. William and Mary, 1921-22, 24, U.S. Naval Acad., 1922-23; A.B., U. S.C., 1925, A.M., 1927; m. Lucy Mae Bragg, Aug. 31, 1930; 1 son, Samuel Francis. Coach, Albany (Ga.) High Sch., 1927-31; prin., coach Greensboro High Sch., 1931-39; prin. Robert E. Lee Inst., Thomaston, Ga., 1939-41; supt. Thomaston Pub. Schs., 1941-46; 1st exec. sec. Ga. High Sch. Assn., Thomaston, 1946—. Cons. atletic, internat. athletic relations U.S. Dept. State, 1965-72; chmn. Nat. High Sch. Football Rules Com., 1949—. Chmn., (Ga.) Bd. Tax Assessors, 1966—, Thomaston and Upson County Planning Commn., 1962—; mem. Chattoochee Area Planning Commn., 1967—. Recipient Spl. Distinguished award S.C. Ofcls. Assn., 1965; Distinguished Service award Nat. Athletic Coaches Assn., 1967; Tiffany award YMCA, 1967; spl. citation Nat. Fedn. State High Sch. Assns., 1972. Mem. Nat. Fedn. State High Sch. Athletic Assn. (pres. 1954-55, 61-71, mem. exec. com. 1944—), Ga. Sch. Bd. Assn., Ga. Athletic Coaches Assn., Omicron Delta Kappa. Mason (32 deg., Shriner), Kiwanian (div. lt. gov. 1950). Home: Trice Cemetery Rd Thomaston GA 30286 Office: 151 S Bethel St Thomaston GA 30286

BURKE, THOMAS ROBERT, economist; b. Trenton, N.J., Dec. 20, 1938; s. John Thomas and Mary Cecilia (Ryan) B.; A.B. (scholar), LaSalle Coll., 1960; A.M. (Nat. Def. Edn. Act fellow), Boston Coll., 1962, postgrad., 1963; m. Sharon Lee Bucs, Aug. 18, 1962; children—Rosemary Alane, Brendan Thomas, Heather Mary. Lectr., LaSalle Coll., Phila., 1962; lectr. dept. econs. Augusta (Ga.) Coll., 1964-65, U. Ga., Augusta, 1964-65, Georgetown U., Washington, 1965-68; sr. systems economist Avco Econ. Systems Corp., Washington, 1968-70; lectr. No. Va. Coll., Annandale, 1970—; cons. Office Sec., Asst. Sec. for Planning and Evaluation, Dept. Health, Edn. and Welfare, Washington, 1970-71, sr. staff economist Office Adminstrn., asst. adminstr. planning and evaluation, Social and Rehab. Service, 1971-72; sr. staff economist Office Price Policy Exec. Office of Pres., 1972; spl. asst. to exec. dir. Com. on Health Services Industry, Exec. Office of Pres., 1972—. Mem. exec. bd. Arlingtonians for Better Community, 1970; chmn. No. Va. Community Service Com., 1969-70. Served with AUS, 1963-65. Recipient Outstanding Service award City Trenton, N.J., 1958. Mem. Am. Econ. Assn., Am. Statis. Assn., Econometric Soc., Nat. Economists Club, Royal Econ. Soc., Friendly Sons St. Patrick, Washington Statis. Soc., Alpha Epsilon. Republican. Roman Catholic. Elk. Club: University (Boston Coll., Chestnut Hill, Mass.). Home: 1947 N Vermont St Arlington VA 22207 Room 5308 2025 M St NW Washington DC 20507

BURKE, WALKER DARIN, lawyer; b. Glenville, Ga., Nov. 16, 1920; s. Hardy Walker and Eva (Starling) B.; LL.B., U. Ga., 1949, J.D., 1959; m. Doris Ruby Cox, Apr. 16, 1944; children—Ralph Walker, Edward Neadom, Tommie Richard, James Stanley. Admitted to Ga. bar, 1949, Ga. Supreme Ct. bar, 1950, Fed. Ct. bars, 1960; practice law, Jessup, Ga., 1949-58, Warner Robins, Ga., 1958—; U.S. postmaster, Jesup, 1954-58. Vice pres. United Finance and Devel. Co., Warner Robbins, 1963—; also dir. Judge, City Ct. Warner Robins, 1965-66; county atty., Houston County, 1963, 64, 69-71. Mem. Ga. Democratic exec. com., 1962-66. Served from pvt. to capt., AUS, 1942-46; ETO; 1951-52. Mem. Ga. gov.'s staff, 1962-66. Recipient 50 Year Humanitarian award Jesup and Ga. jr. chambers commerce, 1970. Mem. Jesup and Wayne County Bar Assn. (pres. 1954), Houston County Assn. (pres. 1962, 67). Baptist. Mason, Elk, Moose. Home: 117 Briardale Av Warner Robins GA 31093 Office: 1606 Watson Blvd Warner Robins GA 31093

BURKES, MARSHALL R., govt. ofcl.; b. Lindsay, Okla., Mar. 27, 1934; s. Charley McClelland and Lou Marie (Park) B.; B.S., Okla. State U., 1956; M.S., Purdue U., 1960; Ph.D., Ohio State U., 1962; m. Audrey Louise Turner, Aug. 31, 1963. Mgr., Burkes Ranch, 1953-56; economist agrl. finance First Western Bank and Trust Co., San Francisco, 1962-65; bus. analyst Berkeley Bank for Coops. (Cal.), 1965-69; asst. adminstr. Farmers Home Adminstrn., U.S. Dept. Agr., Washington, 1969-72; dep. dir. finance Fed. Home Loan Banks, Washington, 1972—. Cons. in farm and ranch budgets, cash flows, marketing, land use, land acquisition, 1965—; faculty Am. Inst. Banking, 1964-69, U. Cal. at Berkeley Extension, 1965-69. Active Boy Scouts Am., Shriner's Crippled Children's Hosp. Served with AUS, 1956-58. Mem. Am. Agrl. Econ. Assn., Am. Marketing Assn., Am. Soc. Farm Mgrs. and Rural Appraisers, Alpha Gamma Rho, Alpha Zeta. Contbr. articles to tech. jours. Home: 3910 Parsons Rd Chevy Chase MD 20015 Office: Fed Home Loan Banks 101 Indiana Av Washington DC 20252

BURKETT, DAVID WARREN, journalist, author; b. nr. McKinney, Tex., Sept. 30, 1929; s. Samuel Warner and Martha (Smith) B.; B.J., U. Tex., 1951, M.S., 1966; fellow, Columbia, 1960-61; m. Gay Allene Lancaster, Aug. 21, 1953; children—Karl, Patricia. Reporter Milw. Jour., 1951-52, San Angelo (Tex.) Standard Times, 1952-54; mng. editor Lamesa (Tex.) Reporter, 1954-56; Sunday editor Abilene (Tex.) Reporter-News, 1955-59; reporting fellow U. Tex., 1959-60, Columbia U., 1960-62; sci. editor Houston Chronicle, 1962-65; editor Sci.-Tech., McGraw-Hill World News Washington Bur., Washington, 1956—; asso. journalism Columbia U., 1961-62; acting dir. Sloan-Rockefeller Sci. Writing Program, 1961-62. Mem. Nat. Assn. Sci. Writers, Nat. Press Club, A.A.A.S., Aviation-Space Writers Assn., Sigma Delta Chi. Baptist. Author: Writing Science News for the Mass Media, 1966. Home: 5715 N 26th St Arlington VA 22207 Office: Nat Press Bldg Washington DC 20004

BURKETT, HELEN ROSE (MRS. CHARLES WILLIAM BURKETT, JR.), co. exec.; b. Cleve., Dec. 22, 1903; d. Frederick Holland and Mary Chloe (Upson) Rose; B.A., Holyoke Coll., 1925; m. Charles William Burkett, Jr., Feb. 12, 1927; children—Charles William III, Diana Rose (Mrs. Hugh Cleland Brewer, Jr.), Helen Upson (Mrs. Gilbert H. Stevens). Sec., treas. Burkett Assos., Miami, Fla., 1951—. Chmn. communications Dept. Nat. Def., Harrison, N.Y., 1941-45, chief block leader service, 1943-45; mem. Harrison War Council, 1941-45, Service Corps A.R.C., 1945-47. Mem. Harrison Republican Town Com., 1946-47; mem. Dade County Rep. Exec. Com., Fla., 1956-58. Mem. D.A.R. (Fla. chmn. radio and TV 1954-56, rec. sec. 1958-60, regent Biscayne chpt. 1956-58, regents' council, Miami (1956-60), Children Am. Revolution (sr. pres. Golden Sands soc. 1960-63, 70—, state v.p. 1972), Colonial Dames XVII Century (Fla. sec. 1957-59, treas. 1959-61, librarian gen. 1959-61, state 1st v.p. 1961-63, state pres. 1963-65, nat. curator gen. 1965-67, nat. pres.-gen. 1967-69, hon. life pres.-gen. 1969—), Colonial Dames Am. (chpt. scholarship com. 1959-61, dir. 1969-71), Cleve. Apt. Owners Assn., Nat. Assn. Parliamentarians, Daus. Am. Colonists (chpt. v.p. 1961-64), Women Descs. Ancient and Honorable Arty. Co., Daus. of 1812 (chpt. v.p. 1961-63), N.Y. Geneal. and Biog. Soc., N.E. Hist. and Geneal. Soc., Nat. Geneal. Soc., Ams. Royal Descent, Magna Charta Dames Fla. (corr. sec. 1960—). Clubs: Westchester Country (Rye, N.Y.); Greenwich (Conn.) Country; La Gorce Country, Surf, Indian Creek Country, Bath (Miami Beach, Fla.). Home: 5800 N Bay Rd Miami Beach FL 33140 Office: 8080 NE 2d Av Miami FL 33138

BURKETT, JESSE ELVIN, univ. ofcl.; b. nr. Noble, Okla., Oct. 8, 1915; s. James Marcus and Sarah Ann (McLean) B.; B.S., U. Okla., 1947, Ed.M., 1950, Ed.D., 1958; m. Wanda Lucille Stufflebean, June 3, 1939; children—James Ronald, Mark Edward. Tchr. elementary schs., Cleveland County, Okla., 1936-45; dir. Okla. Sch. of Air, U. Okla., Norman, 1947-57, asst. dir. broadcasting services, 1954-57, extension specialist in charge research, 1957-61, coordinator liberal studies, 1961-64, asst. dean Coll. Continuing Edn., 1964-68, asst. v.p. univ. projects, 1968-71, asst. v.p. continuing edn. and pub. service, 1971—. Coordinator Okla. com. White House Conf. Children and Youth, 1960; cons. to Okla. Gov's and Legislative Council Joint Com. on Higher Edn., 1961. Served with AUS, 1945-46. Recipient Jour. award Am. Soc. Tchr. Devel., 1963. Mem. N.E.A., Okla. Edn. Assn., Am. Ednl. Research Assn., Nat. History Edn. Soc., Phi Delta Kappa, Kappa Delta Pi. Author: (with Paul G. Ruggiers) Bachelor of Liberal Studies: Development of a Curriculum at the University of Oklahoma, 1965. Editor: Okla. Parent Tchr., 1963-68. Contbr. articles to profl. publs. Home: 1519 Hollywood St Norman OK 73069

BURKETT, THOMAS WILLIAM, wholesale-retail owner; b. Huntsville, Ala., July 18, 1923; s. Alva Wallace and Wanda Stone (Bobo) B.; B.S., Auburn U., 1948; m. Margaret Ann Wall, Dec. 20, 1947 children—Leslie Ann, David Wallace, Jean Ann. With U.S. Civil Service, Redstone Arsenal, Huntsville, Ala., 1941-42; asst. foreman Allis-Chalmers Mfg. Co., Gadsden, 1948-49; engr. Thiokol Corp., Huntsville, 1949-52, Marshall, Tex., 1952-56; partner Book Shop, Huntsville, 1956-59; founder Burkett Inc., Huntsville, 1959, v.p., 1959—, also dir.; established Burkett Sch. Supply Co., Huntsville, 1959, gen. mgr., 1959—. Tchr. adult edn., Huntsville, 1949-51. Mem. com. mgmt. central br. YMCA, Huntsville, 1966—. Pres. Huntsville Youth Orch., 1969-70. Served with AUS, 1943-46. Mem. Nat. Audio-Visual Assn., Nat. Sch. Supply and Equipment Assn., Ala. Sch. Distbrs. Assn. (sec. 1968-69, treas. 1969-70, pres. 1970-71) Nat. Assn. Wholesalers, Auburn Alumni Assn., Am. Book Sellers Assn., Am. Ordnance Assn., Am. Legion, V.F.W., Huntsville-Madison County C. of C., Sigma Nu. Club: Whitesburg Boat and Yacht (vice commodore 1970-71). Home: 2302 Big Cove Rd SE Huntsville AL 35801 Office: 304 Governors Dr SW Huntsville AL 35801

BURKETT, WILLIAM R., U.S. dist. atty. U.S. dist. atty. for western Okla. Office: 4916 NW 35th St Oklahoma City OK 73122*

BURKHALTER, DAVID A., city ofcl.; grad. Bethel Coll.; m. Nell Burkhalter; 1 dau. Diane. Formerly with TVA; city mgr., Elizabethton, Tenn., Johnson City, Tenn., Springfield, Mo.; now city mgr., Charlotte, N.C. Served with USN. Mem. N.C., Internat., (pres. 1970) city mgmt. assns. Presbyn. Rotarian. Address: Offices City Mgr City Hall Charlotte NC 28202*

BURKHART, KENT, broadcasting exec. Pres. radio div. stas. W2XI-W2XI-FM, Atlanta. Office: 2970 Peachtree St NW Atlanta GA 30305*

BURKS, BARNARD DEWITT, entomologist; b. Las Vegas, N.M., Nov. 12, 1909; s. John Kyrle and Emily Gardner (DeWitt) B.; B.A., U. Ill., 1933, M.A., 1934, Ph.D., 1937; m. Frances Kellie O'Neill, Oct. 1, 1966. Entomologist, Ill. Natural History Survey, Urbana, 1937-42, 46-49; entomologist U.S. Dept. Agr., Washington, 1949—, head hymenoptera sect. Systematic Entomology Lab., 1965—. Served from 1st lt. to maj. Signal Corps, AUS, 1942-46. Fellow Entomol. Soc. Am.; mem. Am. Entomol. Soc., Entomol. Soc. Washington, Sigma Xi, Phi Beta Kappa. Club: Cosmos (Washington). Home: 9703 Saxony Rd Silver Spring MD 20910 Office: Natural History Bldg Washington DC 20560

BURKS, MACK SKAGGS, mfg. exec.; b. Dallas, May 14, 1924; s. Joseph Cooper and Grace (Skaggs) B.; student U. Okla., 1942-43;; m. Peggy Crosswhite, Sept. 14, 1946; children—Cynthia, Susan, Carol. Sec.-treas. Connolly's Inc., 1947-52; partner Burks & Smartt, 1952-56; pres. Burks, Inc., 1956-61; account exec. Glenn Advt., Inc., 1962-64; v.p., sec.-treas. Keystone Industries, 1965-67; v.p. marketing Harter Concrete Products Inc., 1967— (all Oklahoma City); pres. Heritage Concrete Products, Inc., 1971—; dir. Ims, Inc. Chmn., Okla. Plan and Resources Bd., 1959-63, mem. bd., 1963-65; mem. Okla. Lakes Redevel. Authority, 1961-63; chmn. pub. relations Govs. Com. on Pub. Safety, 1962-63; mem. Oklahoma City Community Council. Bd. dirs. Traveler's Aid Soc., 1964-65, 72—, v.p., 1965, treas., 1967. Served with USNR, 1943-46. Mem. Nat. Concrete Masonry Assn. (chmn. marketing com.), C. of C. (vice chmn. tourist and conv. div.), Phi Gamma Delta. Methodist. Home: 1712 Guilford Lane Oklahoma City OK 73120 Office: 1628 W Main St Oklahoma City OK 73106

BURLAGE, DONALD WILLIAM, electronics engr.; b. St. Louis, Oct. 12, 1939; s. William Harvey and Helen Dorothea (Francis) B.; B.S. in E.E. (St. Joseph Minerals Co. scholar), U. Mo., 1961; M.S. in E.E., U. Ala., 1968, M.A., 1969, Ph.D., 1972; m. Wynona Heath, Sept. 5, 1964. Systems engr. Westinghouse Electric Corp., Lima, O., 1961-62; research engr. Boeing Co., Huntsville, Ala., 1965; sr. staff engr. Sperry Rand Corp., Huntsville, 1965-67; research asso. U. Ala., Tuscaloosa, 1967-72, instr., 1968-70; electronics engr. U.S. Army, Redstone Arsenal, Huntsville, 1972—. Served as lt. AUS, 1962-65. Registered profl. engr., Ala. Mem. I.E.E.E., Eta Kappa Nu, Kappa Kappa Psi, Pi Mu Epsilon, Sigma Xi. Home: 823 Tannahill Dr SE Huntsville AL 35803 Office: US Army Redstone Arsenal AL 35809

BURLESON, OMAR, congressman; b. Anson, Tex., Mar. 19, 1906; s. Joseph and Bettie (Couch) B.; student Abilene (Tex.) Christian Coll., 1924-26, Hardin-Simmons U., 1926-27, Cumberland U., 1927-29; LL.D. Hardin-Simmons U., 1967;; m. Ruth DeWeese, Apr. 21, 1929. County atty., Jones County, Tex., 1931-35, county judge, 1935-41; spl. agent, F.B.I., 1940-41; sec. Congressman Sam Russell, 1941-42; gen. counsel Nat. Capitol Housing Authority, Washington, Jan.-Dec. 1942; mem. 80th to 92d U.S. Congresses from 17th Tex. Dist. Served as lt. comdr., U.S. Navy, 1942-46; PTO. Pres. Tex. Welfare Assn., 1936-38; pres. County Judges and Commrs. Assn. of Tex. Mem. Lions Internat.; dist. gov. Lions Clubs, 1937-38. Democrat. Mem. Church of Christ. Mason. Home: Anson TX 79501 Office: Rayburn House Office Bldg Washington DC 20515

BURLING, EDWARD, JR., lawyer; b. Chgo., Feb. 5, 1908; Ph.B., Yale, 1929; LL.B., Harvard, 1932. Admitted to D.C. bar, 1934; now mem. firm Covington & Burling, Washington. Home: 2320 Wyoming Av NW Washington DC 20008 Office: Covington & Burling 888 16th St Washington DC 20006*

BURLINGAME, JAMES MONTGOMERY, lawyer; b. Great Falls, Mont., Dec. 25, 1926; s. James Montgomery and Eloise (Corbin) B.; B.A., Tulane U., 1949, J.D., 1950; m. Joella Claire Blache, June 15, 1950; children—James Montgomery IV, Ann Blache, John Marshall. Admitted to La. bar, 1950, U.S. Supreme Ct bar, 1961 practiced in Washington, 1950; partner Jones, Walker, Waechter, Poitevent, Carrere and Denegre, New Orleans, 1953—. Served to ensign U.S. Maritime Service, 1945-46; to capt. AUS, 1950-52. Trustee, St. Martin's Protestant Episcopal Sch., 1968—. Mem. Am., Fed., La. (chmn. mineral sect. 1971-72), New Orleans bar assns., Am. Judicature Soc., Beta Theta Pi. Episcopalian. Club: Petroleum, New Orleans Country, Pickwick, Stratford, International House (New Orleans). Home: 433 Iona St Metairie LA 70005 Office: 225 Barone St New Orleans LA 70112

BURN, HARRY THOMAS, lawyer, banker, orgn. ofcl.; b. Niota, Tenn., Nov. 12, 1895; s. James LaFayette and Febb King (Ensminger) B.; studied law with lawyers, 1919-23; m. Ellen Folsom Cottrell, Feb. 14, 1937; 1 son, Harry Thomas. Admitted to Tenn. bar, 1923; practice in Rockwood, 1923-27, Sweetwater, 1927-50; pres., chmn. 1st Nat. Bank & Trust Co., Rockwood, 1950—; sr. v.p. Belted Galloway Soc., Inc., 1967—. Mem. S.A.R., 1931, treas. gen., 1962-64, pres. gen., 1964-65, Minute Man award, 1962. Mem. Tenn. Ho. of Reps. from McMinn County, 1919-23, Tenn. Senate from 7th Dist., 1949-53; mem. Tenn. Planning Commn., 1952—; del. Tenn. Constl. Conv., 1953, 59, 65, 71. Mem. Am., Tenn. bar assns. Republican. Presbyn. Clubs: Burns (Atlanta); Civitan (pres. Rockwood 1960-61). Home: RFD 1 Niota TN 37826

BURNETT, CAREY CORLEY, civil engr.; b. Montgomery, Ala., Nov. 28, 1915; s. James Leonard and Louise (Davie) B.; student U. Fla., 1934-35; B.S., U. Ga., 1938; postgrad. Ala. Poly. Inst., 1939-40;; m. Mary Elizabeth Parker, July 5, 1946; children—Mary Kay, Carey Parker. City engr., Newman, Ga., 1940-42, 45-46; city engr., asst. city mgr., Thomasville, Ga., 1946-47; city engr., acting city mgr. City of Valdosta, Ga., 1947-51; chief design engr. J.E. Greiner Co. on USMC Supply Center Project, 1951-54; city mgr. Albany, Ga., 1954-61, chmn. elec. bd., 1954-61; city mgr. Columbia, S.C., 1961-70; v.p. environmental and municipal engring. Wilbur Smith and Assos., cons. engrs. and planners, Columbia, 1970—. Dir. Flint River Valley Devel. Assn. Chmn. plumbing code com. So. Bldg. Code Congress; mem. health bd., Albany-Doughtery County, Albany Community Council; bd. dirs. United Community Services, chmn. pub. employees div. United Fund Dr.; mem. Columbia Central City Devel. Com.; exec. com. Congaree Nav. Study Com.; adv. com. Richland Tech. Edn. Center, 1968—. Recipient Certificate Merit for Leadership, Am. City mag., 1964, 68. Served with USAAF, 1942-45; PTO. Registered profl. engr., Fla., Ga., S.C. Mem. Nat. Soc. Profl. Engrs., Internat. v.p. Southeastern region 1968-70), S.C. (state pres. 1968-69), Ga. (state pres. 1958-59) city mgrs. assns., Am. Pub. Works Assn., Nat. Planning Assn., Greater Columbia C. of C. (indsl. devel. commn.), S.C. Soc. Engrs. (regional dir.), Nat. Soc. Municipal Engrs., Nat. Soc. San. Engrs. Presbyn. Contbr. articles profl. jour. and Am. City mag. Home: 3333 Devereaux Rd Columbia SC 29205

BURNETT, COLLINS WALTER, educator; b. Anderson, Ind., Mar. 28, 1914; s. Charles and Bertha (Liget) B.; A.B., Ball State U., 1935 M.A., Ohio State U., 1940, Ph.D., 1948; m. Bernice Kathryn Kaufman, May 10, 1941; children—Arlita (Mrs. Robert W. Smith), Michael Collins. Asso. prof. Fresno State Coll., 1946-50; asst. dean Coll. Edn., prof. psychology Ohio State U., 1950-63; prof. higher edn., 1963-68; prof. higher edn. U. Ky., Lexington, 1968—. Cons., Morris Harvey Coll., Alice Lloyd Coll., U. Americas. Served to comdr. USNR, 1944-46. Recipient Distinguished Alumni Service award Ball State U., 1966. Mem. Am. Psychol. Assn., Am. Personnel and Guidance Assn., Student Personnel Assn. for Tchr. Edn. (pres. 1957-58), Am. Edn. Research Assn. Author: Introduction to Teaching, 1963, The Community Junior College: An Annotated Bibliography with Chapter Introductions, 1968. Home: 947 Edgewater Dr Lexington KY 40502

BURNETT, TRAVIS ELMON, pipeline co. exec.; b. Gap, Tex., Mar. 4, 1918; s. Thomas E. and Carolinee (Lee) B.; B.B.A. cum laude, Baylor U., 1947; LL.B., S. Tex. Coll., 1960; m. Yvonne O. Thompson, Apr. 26, 1941; children—Iravonne (Mrs. James E. Crain), Donna Sue (Mrs. David Peck), Leanne. Accountant, Humble Oil & Refining Co., Katy, Tex., 1947-49, right of way and claims agt., Houston, 1949-56, mgr. right of way and claims dept., 1956-60, atty. law dept., 1960-65; asso. gen. counsel Humble Pipe Line Co., Houston, 1965—; corp. sec. Dixie Pipeline Co., Houston, 1965—, v.p., dir., 1972—; admitted to Tex. bar, 1960. Democratic precinct committeeman, Houston, 1956-61; del. county and Tex. State Dem. convs., 1964-68. Served to 2d lt. USAAF, 1942-46. Mem. Delta Sigma Phi, Delta Theta Phi. Home: 10310 Cliffwood St Houston TX 77035 Office: PO Box 2220 Houston TX 77001

BURNETTE, ELMER WIGGINS, JR., dentist; b. Odessa, Fla., Dec. 14, 1920; s. Elmer Wiggins and Mary (Pettigrew) Burnette; student Fla. So. Coll., 1937-38; B.A., Emory U., 1943, D.D.S., 1945; certificate U. Tex., 1960; m. Rebecca Anne Benton, Apr. 2, 1941; children—Patricia (Mrs. James Redfield), Dianne (Mrs. Melvin Starr, Jr.), Susan (Mrs. Gregory Nebel), Edith (Mrs. Thomas L. Bergeron, Jr.). Intern, Fla. State Hosp., 1945-46; pvt. practice dentistry, Clearwater, Fla., 1946-50; commd. capt. U.S. Air Force, 1951, advanced through grades to col., 1966; base dental surgeon Goodfellow AFB, Tex., 1954-59; resident periodontics Lackland AFB, Tex., 1960-61, staff dept. periodontics, 1961-66, dir. tng., 1964-66; periodontist, Ramstein, Germany, 1966-68, base dental surgeon, 1968-69; chmn. dept. periodontics Andrews AFB, Washington, 1969-70, dir. dental services, dir. intern and resident tng., dental surgeon Hdqrs. Command, 1970—. Spl. cons. periodontics Surgeon Gen. U.S. Air Force, 1969-72. Diplomate Am. Bd. Periodontology. Fellow Am. Coll. Dentists; mem. Am. Dental Assn., Am. Acad. Periodontology, Southwestern Soc. Periodontists, Greater Washington Soc. Periodontology, West German Armed Forces Dental Soc. (life), Lambda Chi Alpha. Mason. Club: Exchange (pres. 1948-49) (Clearwater, Fla.). Home: 1320-1 Vandenberg Dr Andrews AFB Washington DC 20331 Office: Box 2037 Andrews AFB Washington DC 20331

BURNETTE, JOHN QUINCY, banker; b. Charlotte, N.C., June 22, 1924; s. John Quincy and Mary (Kiker) B.; student La. State U., 1961-65; m. Allie Burch, July 4, 1943; children—Diane (Mrs. Edward M. Gouge), Marie B. (Mrs. Robert Olen Deal). Vice pres., govtl. service officer N.C. Nat. Bank, Charlotte, 1946—. Treas., Men's Democrat Club, 1970-71. Bd. dirs. Caroline Carrousel, Piedmont Better Bus. Bur. Served to lt. col. AUS, 1943-45. Mem. Charlotte C. of C. Baptist. Lion. Home: 1101 Burtonwood Circle Charlotte NC 28212 Office: PO Box 120 Charlotte NC 28212

BURNETTE, VAN TYLE, veterinarian; b. Noma, Fla., June 24, 1924; s. James B. and Irene (Counts) B.; D.V.M., Auburn U., 1955; B.S.A., U. Fla., 1956; m. Jimmie Nell Galloway, Aug. 17, 1947; 1 dau., Vanessa Lynn. Gen. practice vet. medicine, Fayetteville, N.C., 1956-57; small animal practice, Winter Haven, 1958—. Council commr. Boy Scouts of Am.; first aid instr. A.R.C. instr. markmanship Boys Clubs. Bd. dirs. Salvation Army. Served as sgt. U.S.M.C., 1943-46, as capt. Vet. Corps, AUS, 1955-60; PTO; mem. Civil Air Patrol, USCG Aux. Mem. World Small Animal Vet. Assn., Am., Fla. vet. med. assns., Royal Soc. Health, Assn. Mil. Surgeons, Am. Legion, V.F.W., Nat. Rifle Assn., U.S. Animal Health Assn., Nat. Assn. Retarded Children, Marine Corps League, A.A.A.S., Internat. Platform Assn., Am. Pub. Health Assn., Am. Soc. Animal Sci., Am. Soc. Veterinary Allergist and Immunologist, Res. Officers Assn., Assn. U.S. Army, Marine Corps League, Mil. Order Devil Dogs, Am. Inst. Biol. Scis., Mil. Order of Carabao, Army and Navy Union, Alpha Zeta, Alpha Phi Omega, Alpha Beta Alpha, Phi Kappa Phi, Omicron Delta Kappa, Alpha Psi. Phi Sigma, Gamma Sigma Delta. Lion (pres. Auburndale 1966-67). Home: Pearce Rd Winter Haven FL 33880 Office: 3161 Havendale Blvd Winter Haven FL 33880

BURNEY, GRADY JACKSON, JR., banker; b. Aberdeen, N.C., Apr. 28, 1927; s. Grady Jackson and Valeria (Medford) B.; B.A., U. N.C., 1950; m. Mary Anne Moore, Feb. 4, 1956; children—Susan Anne, Michael Jackson. Promotion mgr. WSJS, Winston Salem, N.C., 1950-52; sales promotion to research mgr. Jefferson Standard Broadcasting Co., Charlotte, N.C., 1952-63; research dir. C. of C., Charlotte, N.C., 1963; dir. marketing research N.C. Nat. Bank, Charlotte, N.C., 1964—, v.p., 1964—. Lectr. U. N.C. at Charlotte. Pres., Mecklenburg Citizens for Better Libraries, 1969-70; chmn. research adv. com. TV Bur. Advt.; chmn. citizens adv. com. WTVI (Pub. TV); key person Charlotte Census Track, U.S. Dept. Commerce. Mem. Am. Marketing Assn., Am. Statis. Assn., Am. Mgmt. Assn., Nat. Indsl. Conf. Bd., Charlotte C. of C. (chmn. research com.), Bank Marketing Assn. (chmn. govt. data adv. commn.), Methodist. Club: Advertising (pres.) (Charlotte). Home: 6150 Deveron Dr Charlotte NC 28211 Office: PO Box 120 Charlotte NC 28201

BURNHAM, ROBERT CHESTER, physician; b. Waterbury, Conn., July 5, 1915; A.B., Yale, 1936, M.D., N.Y. Med. Coll., 1941; m. Donna Cecelia Boyd, May 31, 1942; children—Jeffrey Boyd, Roger Morris, Timothy Donald Eugene, Janet Christina. Intern St. Elizabeth's Hosp., Washington, 1941-42, psychiat. trainee, USN, 1942-43; psychiat. trainee Washington (D.C.) Sch. Psychiatry, 1947-51; psychoanalytic trainee Washington (D.C.) Psychoanalytic Inst., 1947-53, tng. analyst, 1958—; dir. Arlington County Guidance Center, Arlington, Va., 1948-50; practice of medicine, specializing in psychiatry, psychoanalysis, Arlington, Va., 1948—; mem. staffs Fairfax Hosp., Falls Church, Va., George Washington U. Hosp., Washington. Asso. clin. prof. psychiatry Georgetown U. Coll. Medicine, Washington, 1960—. Mem. Law Enforcement Adv. Commn., Falls Church, 1969—. Served to lt. comdr. M.C., USN, 1942-47. Fellow Am. Psychiat. Assn., Am. Acad. Psychoanalysis; mem. Washington Psychoanalytic Soc. (pres. 1965-67), Am. Psychoanalytic Assn., A.M.A., A.A.A.S. Home: 207 E Columbia St Falls Church VA 22046 Office: 333 S Glebe Rd Arlington VA 22204

BURNS, ARTHUR F., economist, govt. ofcl., educator; b. Stanislau, Austria, Apr. 27, 1904; s. Nathan and Sarah (Juran) B.; A.B., Columbia, 1925, A.M., 1925, Ph.D., 1934, LL.D., 1970; LL.D., Lehigh U., 1952, Brown U., 1956, Dartmouth Coll., 1956, Oberlin Coll., 1956, Wesleyan U., 1958, Swarthmore Coll., 1958, L.I. U., 1960, U. Chgo., 1960, Rikkyo U., Tokyo, 1965, Fordham U., 1969, N.Y. U., 1970, U. Cal., 1970; D.Sc., U. Pa., 1958, U. Rochester, 1963; L.H.D., Rutgers U., 1955, Pepperdine Coll., 1970; D. Econ., Chung-ang U., Korea, 1970; D.Phil., Hebrew U., Israel, 1970; m. Helen Bernstein, Jan. 25, 1930; children—David, Joseph. Instr. econs. Rutgers U., 1927-30, asst. prof., 1930-33, asso. prof., 1933-43, prof., 1943-44; asst. statistics Columbia, 1926, Gilder fellow, 1926-27, vis. prof., 1941-44, prof., 1944-59, John Bates Clark prof., 1959-69; research asso. Nat. Bur. Econ. Research, 1930-31, mem. research staff, 1933-69, dir. research, 1945-53, pres., 1957-67, chmn., 1967-68, hon. chmn., 1968—; counselor to Pres. U.S., 1969-70; chmn. bd. govs. Fed. Res. System, Washington, 1970—. Millar lectr. Fordham U., 1957; Murray lectr. State U. Ia., 1964; Fairless lectr. Carnegie Inst. Tech., 1965; Moskowitz lectr. N.Y. U., 1967; vis. prof. econs. Stanford U., spring 1968; trustee 20th Century Fund. Served chief statistician Ry. Emergency Bd., 1941; cons. various govtl. agencies and depts. Chmn. Pres.'s Council Econ. Advisers, 1953-56; chmn. Adv. Bd. on Econ. Growth and Stability, 1953-56; chmn. Cabinet Com. on Small Bus., 1956; mem. Pres.' Adv. Com. on Labor-Mgmt. Policy 1961-66; mem. Gov.'s Com. on Minimum Wage, 1964. Mem. research adv. bd. Rutgers U., 1947-61; adv. bd. Indsl. Coll. Armed Forces, 1958-64; bd. mgrs. Swarthmore Coll., 1959-62; trustee Tax Found., Inc., 1962-68, Freedom House, 1966-68; mem. U.S. Adv. Council on Social Security Financing, 1957-58, N.Y. Temp. State Commn. on Econ. Expansion, 1959-60. Recipient Alexander Hamilton medal Columbia U., 1969; Distinguished Pub. Service award Tax Found., 1969; Mugungwha decoration Korean govt., 1970. Fellow Am. Statis. Assn., Econometric Soc., Am. Acad. Arts and Scis.; mem. Pilgrims Soc., Am. Philos. Soc., Council Fgn. Relations, Am. Econ. Assn. (pres. 1959, distinguished fellow), Acad. Polit. Sci. (pres. 1961-68), Institut de Sci. Economique Appliquee (corr.), Phi Beta Kappa. Clubs: Cosmos (Washington); Men's Faculty (Columbia U.), Century Assn. Author: Production Trends in the U.S. since 1870, 1934; Economic Research and the Keynesian Thinking of Our Times, 1946; Frontiers of Economic Knowledge, 1954; Prosperity Without Inflation. 1957; (with W.C. Mitchell) Measuring Business Cycles, 1946; The Management of Prosperity, 1966; (with P.A. Samuelson) Full Employment, Guideposts and Economic Stability, 1967; (with Jacob Javits, Charles Hitch) The Defense Sector and the American Economy, 1968; The Business Cycle in a Changing World, 1969. Home: 2510 Virginia Av NW Washington DC 20037 Office: Federal Reserve Bldg Washington DC 20551

BURNS, DANIEL HOBART, mgmt. cons.; b. Atlanta, Jan. 26, 1928; s. Hobart H. and Florence (Kuhn) B.; B.A., U. Ala., 1946-49; grad. Aid Command and Staff Coll., 1969, Air War Coll., 1972; m. Ann Grimsley, Jan. 15, 1949; children—Eric Grimsley, Daniel Hobart, Barbara Bennett, Arlene Chester. Account exec. radio sta. WCOS, Columbia, S.C., 1949-51; sales mgr. sta. WIS, Columbia, 1951-57; ins. agt. Aetna Life Ins. Co., Columbia, 1957-60; self-employed as mgmt. cons. and broker, Columbia, 1960—; pres., dir. Nat. Search, Inc., 1966—; Indsl. Surveys, Inc., 1968; pres. Internat. Communications Resources Found. Guest lectr. U. S.C.; asst. project dir. statewide law enforcement edn. through TV, 1966-68; cons. govts. of Israel, Greece and Fed. Republic Germany, 1967; cons. S.C. Ednl. TV Network, 1966—; cons. sales mgmt., market analysis. Pres., Schneider Sch. P.T.A., 1963-66; supr. registration City of Columbia, 1962-69; dist commr., scoutmaster Boy Scouts Am.; treas., bd. dirs. Columbia (S.C.) council USO, bd. dirs. nat. council; bd. dirs. Columbia Travelers Aid Soc; Nat. Travelers Aid Assn., Richland County chpt. Nat. Found.; pres., bd. dirs. Internat. Communications Resources Found., 1968. Pres. ward 15 Republican com. Served with USAAF, 1943-46, to lt. col. USAFR. Mem. S.C. Football Ofcls. Assn., Nat. Sales Execs. Assn., Columbia Real Estate Bd., Air Force Assn., Am. Y-Flyer Yacht Racing Assn., Soc. Real Estate Appraisers, Am. Mgmt. Assn., Nat., Assn. Ednl. Broadcasters, Am. Soc. Personnel Adminstrn., Soc. Advancement Adminstrn., Am. Soc. Real Estate Appraisers, Nat. Assn. Securities Dealers, Soc. Am. Archivists, Internat. Platform Assn., Am. Legion, Columbia C. of C., Columbia Advt. Club, Columbia Marketing and Execs. Club, North Am. Yacht Racing Union, Sigma Phi Epsilon. Episcopalian (lay reader, brotherhood pres.). Mason (32 deg., Shriner). Lion. Clubs: Charleston (S.C.) Yacht; Forest Lake Country, Columbia Squash Racquets (Columbia, S.C.) Yachting of Am.; Wateree Gun; Caprician. Home: 2504 Canterbury Rd Columbia SC 29204 Office: PO Box 866 Columbia SC 29202

BURNS, EDWARD CLYDE, JR., physician; b. Greenville, S.C., Nov. 20, 1923; s. Edward Clyde and Etta Victoria (Green) B.; B.A., Emory U., 1944, M.D., 1946; m. Sally Louise Horne, Oct. 20, 1945; children—Barbara (Mrs. James Prather), Edward Clyde III, Carol Anne (Mrs. Melvin Horne), Alan, Bruce Mallory. Intern, Univ. Hosp., Augusta, Ga., 1946-47, resident, 1949-51; resident Percy Jones Gen. Hosp., Battle Creek, Mich., 1947-49, Royal Infirmary, Edinburgh, Scotland, 1950-51; pvt. practice medicine, specializing in radiology, Lake Wales, Fla., 1951—; dir. dept. radiology Lake Wales Hosp., 1951—, Polk Gen. Hosp., Bartow, Fla., 1951—, Bartow Meml. Hosp., 1951—, Winter Haven (Fla.) Hosp., 1955—, Heart of Fla. Hosp., Haines City, 1965—, Morrow Meml. Hosp., Auburndale, Fla., 1966—, Walker Meml. Hosp., Avon Park, Fla., 1962—, Highlands Gen. Hosp., Sebring, Fla., 1965—; pres. Drs. Burns and Assos., 1963—. Organizer, dir. 1st Nat. Bank, Lake Wales, 1960—. Served as capt. M.C., AUS, 1947-49. Diplomate Am. Bd. Radiology. Mem. Fla., Polk County (pres. 1966-67) med. assns., A.M.A., Am. Coll. Radiology. Baptist. Home: 960 Lakeshore Blvd Lake Wales FL 33853 Office: Lake Wales Hosp Lake Wales FL 33853 also Winter Haven Hosp Winter Haven FL 33880

BURNS, GROVER PRESTON, physicist; b. nr. Hurricane, W.Va., Apr. 25, 1918; s. Joshua Alexander and Virgie (Meadows) B.; A.B., Marshall U., 1937; M.S., W.Va. U., 1941; student Duke, 1939-40, U. Md., 1946; m. Julie Belle Foster, Nov. 4, 1941; children—Julia Corinne, Grover Preston. Tchr. high sch., W.Va., 1937-40; fellow W.Va., U., 1940-41; instr. physics U. Conn., 1941-42; asst. prof. Miss State Coll., 1942-44, acting head physics dept., 1944-45; asst. prof. physics Tex. Tech. Coll., 1946; asso. prof. math. Marshall U., 1946-47; research physicist Naval Research Lab., Washington, 1947-48; asst. prof., chmn. physics dept. Mary Washington Coll., 1948-68, asso. prof., chmn., 1968-69; quality control supr. Am. Viscose div. FMC Corp., 1950-67; pres. Burns Enterprises, Inc., Fredericksburg, Va., 1958—; mathematician U.S. Naval Weapons Lab., 1967—. Served with AUS, 1945-46. Mem. Am. Phys. Soc., Am. Soc. for Quality Control, Am. Assn. Physics Tchrs., Fed. Profl. Assn., Brit. Computer Soc., Internat. Orgn. Vacuum Sci. and Tech. Author various articles pub. in profl. jours. Patentee in field of thermometers, conductivity testers, star finders. Research in fields of superconductivity, synthetic div., thermoelectricity, numerical integration, exterior ballistics. Home: 600 Virginia St Fredericksburg VA 22401 Office: U S Naval Weapons Lab Dahlgren VA 22448

BURNS, HENRY KNOX, III, brick co. exec.; b. Macon, Ga., Apr. 2, 1941; s. Henry Knox and Anne (Holmes) B.; student Ga. Inst. Tech., 1959-64; m. Katharine Miller, Aug. 24, 1962; children—Henry Knox IV, Stuart, Hubert. Foreman, Burns Brick Co., Macon, Ga., 1964-69, plant mgr., 1969—, also dir., asst. sec., 1971—. Mem. Am. Ceramics Soc. Presbyn. (deacon 1970—). Elk. Home: 1830 Redwood Dr Macon GA 31201 Office: 711 10th St Macon GA 31208

BURNS, HOWARD DEWITT, aerospace engr.; b. Buhl, Ala., Dec. 11, 1921; s. Howard and Edna (Eaton) B.; B.S. in E.E., U. Ala., 1946, LL.B., 1950; m. Marcella Holland, June 15, 1957; children—Howard DeWitt, Katherine Joyce. Jr. engr. Ala. Power Co., 1947-48; Redstone project mgr. indsl. div. Army Ballistic Missile Agy., Redstone Arsenal, Ala., 1959-60, dep. dir. test, evaluation and firing lab., 1960-62; chief Systems Integration and Evaluation Office, Systems Engring., Office Manned Space Flight, 1962-63; chief Saturn V Test Mgmt. Office, Indsl. Operations, Marshall Space Flight Center, Huntsville, Ala., 1963-70, chief vehicle devel. devel. office Space Shuttle Task Team, 1970—. Served with USAAF, 1944-45. Registered profl. engr., Ala. Mem. Ala. State Bar, Theta Tau. Methodist. Home: Rural Route 10 Box 61 Athens AL 35611 Office: Huntsville AL 35812

BURNS, JIMMY CLAY, physician; b. Brownwood, Tex., July 16, 1935; B.S. (Julia Ball Lee fellow), Tex. A. and M. U., 1957; M.D., Baylor U., 1960; m. Patsy Ann Cowan, Aug. 13, 1956; children—Clay Brooks, Ty Rolland, Kaylynn, Guy Akin. Asst. circulation mgr. Sweetwater Reporter, 1950-53; clk., timekeeper Santa Fe R.R., 1953-56; radioisotope technician Methodist Hosp., Houston, 1956-60; intern Jefferson Davis Hosp., Houston, 1960-61; practice medicine, specializing in family practice, West Columbia, Tex., 1963—; owner Pecan Oaks Farm, West Columbia, 1968—; mem. staff Sweeny, Bay City, Deaton hosps.; chief of staff Sweeny Community Hosp., 1968-70. Dir. First Capitol Bank, West Columbia; cons. Columbia Brazoria Sch. Dist.; health officer City of West Columbia. Active Boy Scouts Am. Served with USNR, 1961-63. Named Outstanding Young Man of Am., U.S. Jaycees, 1967. Mem. West Columbia C. of C., A.M.A., Am., Tex. acads. family practice, Tex. Med. Assn., Brazoria County Med. Soc., Southwestern Cattleman, Am. Internat. Charolais Breeders, Phi Eta Sigma, Phi Kappa Phi. Rotarian. Home: Farm Rd 2852 West Columbia TX 77486 Office: Columbia Clinic 503 Dance Dr West Columbia TX 77486

BURNS, JOHN GLASGOW, elec. engr., patent agt.; b. Narberth, Pa., Mar. 3, 1919; s. Arthur Wellwood and Effie (MacNiven) B.; B.S. in Elec. Engring., Va. Poly. Inst., 1941; grad. student U. Miami, 1963-64; m. Mary Sydnor Tait, Aug. 14, 1942; 1 son, John Glasgow. Student engr. Gen. Electric Co., Schenectady, 1941-42; elec. engr. Bur. Ships, Navy Dept., Washington, 1942-46; asst. patent examiner U.S. Patent Office, Washington, 1946-55; patent agt., Miami, Fla., 1955—; field engr. Fla. Power & Light Co., Miami, 1955-61, engr., 1961—. Mem. So. Fla. Corrosion Coordinating Com., sec., 1963-64, 65, program chmn. Fla. Gen. Conf. Corrosion, 1965; com. mem. Fla. Gen. Conf. and Corrosion Short Course, 1958-64, chmn. program com., 1962, visual aids com., 1964. Asst. cub master Boy Scouts Am., Alexandria, Va., 1954, mem. cub pack com. South Miami, 1955. Recipient awards for orchids. Mem. Nat. Assn. Corrosion Engrs. (sec.-treas. Miami sect. 1958, 62, chmn. Miami sect. 1963), Am. Assn. Registered Patent Attys. and Agts., Nat. Geog. Soc., So. Fla. Orchid Soc., Golden Triangle, Am. Orchid Soc., Fla. Orchid Assn., Fla. Patent Law Assn. Democrat. Presbyn. (deacon 1962, 63, 65). Club: South Dade Amateur Orchid. Exhibited in Internat. Orchid Show, 1957-60, Ft. Lauderdale Orchid Show, 1959. Home: 1036 Sorolla Av Coral Gables FL 33134 Office: 4200 W Flagler St PO Box 3100 Miami FL 33101

BURNS, KENNETH HAROLD, lawyer; b. Rockford, Ill., July 6, 1929; s. Harry Harold and Gladys (Rasmussen) B.; student U. Ill., 1947-51; B.S., Trinity U., 1954; J.D., St. Mary's U., 1958; m. Laura Mae Howe, Mar. 28, 1951; children—Coni Jo, Pamela Sue, Lori Lynn. Admitted to Tex. bar, 1958, U.S. Supreme Ct. bar, 1962, D.C. bar, 1968; asst. to dir. traffic ct. program Am. Bar Assn., Chgo., 1958-59; asst. atty. gen. Tex., Austin, 1959-60; adminstrv. asst. to U.S. rep., Athens, Tex., Washington, 1960-61; practice law, Dallas, 1961-62; spl. asst. to adminstr. U.S. Maritime Adminstrn., Washington, 1962-65, dir. congl. and legal matters, spl. asst. to chmn. Fed. Maritime Commn. and Solicitor, Washington, 1965-70; practice law, Houston, Washington, 1970—. Pres., Gustafson P.T.A., 1958-59. Bd. dirs. Arthritis and Rheumatism Assn.; trustee Nat. Multiple Sclerosis Soc. Served with USNR, 1948-51, USAF, 1951-55. Named Hon. Citzen Tenn., Gov. of Tenn., 1958; adm. Tex. Navy, 1960; Ky. col., 1965. Mem. Nat., Fed. (bd. govs. 1969), Am. bar assns., Am. Legion, Delta Theta Phi (spl. asst. to the nat. chancellor), Pi Kappa Delta, Kappa Pi Sigma, Alpha Phi Omega. Methodist. Mason. Club: Texas Breakfast (pres.1968) (Washington). Contbr. articles to profl. jours. Home: 450 Wilchester Blvd Houston TX 77024 Office: Main Bldg Houston TX 77002 also 2000 L St NW Washington DC 20036

BURNS, SALLY GIPE (MRS. LEONARD O. BURNS), bus. exec.; b. Moody, Tex., Jan. 17, 1925; d. William Franklin and Velma (Meador) Gipe; student Draughn Bus. Sch., 1942; m. Leonard Odell Burns, Nov. 15, 1942; children—James Odell, Alton Jay. Office mgr. Garland (Tex.) Daily News, 1952-54; with Eastern Hills Country Club, Garland, 1955—, office mgr., 1955-61, gen. mgr., 1961—. Pres. Altrusa Club Garland, 1967-68, P.T.A., 1965 (hon. life mem. 1966). Precinct chmn. Democratic Party, 1966. Named Altrusa Woman of Yr., 1971. Mem. Garland Fedn. Womans Clubs (sec.), Nat. Club Mgrs. Assn., Dallas-Fort Worth Club mgrs., Am. Bus. Women. Baptist. Home: 1621 Apache Dr Garland TX 75040 Office: Country Club Rd Garland TX 75040

BURNSIDE, HAMILTON STANLEY NATHANIEL, life underwriter; b. Nassau, New Providence, Bahamas, Nov. 22, 1899; s. Herbert Nathaniel and Caroline (Poitier) B.; student Cambridge U.; m. Mary Elizabeth Haynes, July 6, 1940; 1 dau., Florence Caroline (Mrs. Mays). Baggage and checking room Fla. East Coast R.R., 1922-25; also part-time sales Afro-Am. Life Ins. Co., 1922-25; agt., asst. mgr., mgr., agy. asst. Nat. Benefit Life Ins. Co., 1925-33; organized Columbia Life Ins. Co., 1933-35; field supr., mgr. Pilgrim Health & Life Ins. Co., 1935-45, mgr., 1954-69, cons., 1969—; mgr., supr. Guaranty Life Ins. Co., 1945-50; mgr. Mammoth Life Ins. Co., 1951-54. Divisional chmn. Cherokee div. N.E. Ga. Boy Scouts Am., 1942-69; chmn. bd. mgmt. Samuel F. Harris YMCA, Athens 1956-69, chmn. emeritus, 1969—; chmn. co-chmn. campaigns A.R.C., Community Services, and others. Served as cpl. Royal British Army, 1916-19. Recipient Silver Beaver Award Boy Scouts Am., 1950. Episcopalian. Home: 191 Chicamauga Av SW Atlanta GA 30314 Office: 181 W Washington St Athens GA 30601

BURR, HELEN GUNDERSON (MRS. HORACE BURR), educator; b. Iowa City, Dec. 30, 1918; d. George Byron and Grace (Farrell) Gunderson; B.A., Stanford, 1937; M.A., U. So. Cal., 1940; Ph.D., Columbia, 1949; post-doctoral study U. So. Cal., summer 1950, U. Mich., summer 1952; m. Horace Burr, July 24, 1954; 1 son, David Stanford. Speech pathologist, N.Y.C. and Los Angeles, 1944-50; asst. prof., dir. speech clinic State U. N.Y., 1950-50; asst. prof. U. Va., Charlottesville, 1953-60, asso. prof. speech pathology and audiology, 1961-66, prof., 1966—, dir. speech and hearing center, 1961—, chmn. dept. speech pathology and audiology, 1962—. Mem. coordinating com. on crippled children's services Va. Council on Health and Med. Care. Bd. dirs. Va. Hearing and Speech Found., Va. Soc. Crippled Children and Adults. Fellow Am. Speech and Hearing Assn., N.Y. Acad. Arts and Scis., Speech and Hearing Assn. Va. (pres. 1960, editor jour. 1961—); mem. Am. Assn. U. Women, English Speaking Union, Albemarle Hist. Assn., Albemarle Art Assn., A.A.A.S., Am. Assn. U. Profs., Linguistic Soc. Am., Speech Assn. Am., Internat. Soc. for Gen. Semantics, Delta Delta Delta, Pi Lambda Theta, Kappa Delta Pi, Delta Kappa Gamma (pres. 1972—). Editor: The Aphasic Adult, 1965. Home: Carrsgrove Stribling Av Charlottesville VA 22903

BURR, SAMUEL ENGLE, JR., educator, historian; b. Bordentown, N.J., Dec. 6, 1897; s. Samuel Engle and Elizabeth (Thompson) B.; Litt.B., Rutgers U., 1919; M.A., U. Wis., 1925, Columbia, 1927; Ed.D., U. Cin., 1936; m. Alice Elizabeth Gratz, June 28, 1924; children—Evelyn (Mrs. Eugene Dorr Biddle) (dec.), Samuel Engle III. Supt. schs., New Castle, Del., 1934-39, Rye Neck, N.Y., Mamaroneck, N.Y., 1939-42; dir. Am. U. Inst. World Affairs, Washington, 1949-59, prof. edn., 1947-68, dean summer sessions, 1963-65, prof. emeritus, 1968—; vis. prof. history Weatherford (Tex.) Coll., 1969-72; mng. dir. Burr Pubs., Ltd., Ft. Worth and Linden, 1968—. Mem. textbook selection com. U.S. Air Force Inst., Washington, 1955-59; dir. Skyland Community Corp., Linden, Va. Served to 2d lt. U.S. Army, 1918, to lt. col. inf., AUS, 1942-47. Decorated Purple Heart; recipient awards from various fgn. countries. Mem. Fed. Schoolmen's Club (pres. 1967-68), New Edn. Fellowship (pres. chpt. 1960—), S. Atlantic Philosophy Edn. Aaron Burr Assn. (pres. gen. 1946—), Nat. Hist. Soc., Tex. Hist. Assn., 14th Air Force Assn., Phi Kappa Phi, Kappa Phi Kappa, Phi Delta Kappa, Kappa Delta Pi, Phi Theta Kappa. Republican. Episcopalian. Rotarian (hon.). Author: Napoleon's Dossier on Aaron Burr, 1969; An Introduction to Progressive Education, 1937; Small Town Merchant, 1957; Colonel Aaron Burr: The American Phoenix, 1963; Colonel Aaron Burr: The

Misunderstood Man, 1967; The Burr-Hamilton Duel & Related Matters, 1971. Home and Office: Tremont Inca Rd Linden VA 22642

BURRELL, MARTIN OMAR, physicist; b. Atlanta, Mar. 24, 1925; s. Henry G. and Ethel (Woodring) B.; A.B., Emory U., 1950, M.A., 1951; m. Jennie B. Tallman, July 18, 1946; children—Alvin Jerome, Alice Estelle, Eric Omar. Tng. officer U.S. Air Force, Macon, Ga., 1951-55, mathematician, operations research team, Macon, 1955-57; nuclear analyst, asso. scientist Lockheed Ga. Co., Marietta Ga., 1957-61; mathematician, supervisory physicist NASA, Huntsville, Ala., 1961-70, chief radiation physics br. Space Scis. Lab., Marshall Space Flight Center, 1970—. Served with AUS, 1943-46. Mem. Am. Nuclear Soc. Democrat. Episcopalian. Mason. Club: Huntsville Chess (sec. 1965-67). Research in radiation shielding in both nuclear and space radiations. Contbr. articles in field to profl. jours. Home: Route 4 Rainbow Dr Madison AL 35758 Office: Marshall Space Flight Center Huntsville AL 35812

BURRIS, ALFRED LLOYD, dentist; b. Healdton, Okla., Aug. 9, 1916; s. Frank Milton and Mamie (Johnson) B.; B.S., Central State U., Edmond, Okla.; postgrad. Okla. State U., 1940, 41; D.D.S., Baylor U., 1947; m. Vesper Elaine Jacobs, Nov. 3, 1939. Tchr. high schs., jr. coll., Garvin and Cherokee counties, Okla., 1939-41; instr. radio operating Scott Field, Belleville, Ill., 1941-42; gen. practice dentistry, Gainesville, Tex., 1947—; mem. staff Gainesville Meml. Hosp. Served with USAAF, 1942-44, Dental Corps AUS, 1960-61. Mem. Acad. Gen. Practice, Am., Tex. dental assns., 4th Dist. Dental Soc. (pres. 1955-56), Delta Sigma Delta. Kiwanian. Mason (32 deg.). Home: 502 S Chestnut Gainesville TX 76240 Office: 110 1/2 S Dixon Gainesville TX 70240

BURRUS, GEORGE JOSEPH, III, govt. ofcl.; b. Columbus, Ga., July 17, 1914; s. George J. and Effie May (Pierce) B.; B.S. in M.E., Auburn U., 1937; m. Mary J. Leonard, Dec. 14, 1962. Test engr. B-47 and C-130 aircraft Lockheed Aircraft Co., Marietta, Ga., 1952-57; field test engr. Thor Missile, Douglas Aircraft, Cape Canaveral, Fla., 1957-58; sr. field test engr. missile nose cones Avco, Cape Canaveral, 1958-63; engring. project mgr. mobile service structure NASA, Kennedy Space Center, 1963—. Pres. G.J. Burrus Co., Cocoa Beach, Fla., 1959—; owner Burrus Bldg., 1959—, Cocoa Beach Shopping Center, 1963-68. Charter mem. Melbourne (Fla.) Municipal Band, 1964—. Served to maj. USAAF, 1942-46; now lt. col. Res. ret. Mem. Melbourne C. of C. (mem. mil. affairs com.), Air Force Assn. (state v.p. 1964-67, pres. Cape Canaveral chpt. 1971—), NASA Athletic and Recreation Soc. (sec. 1967-69), Alpha Tau Omega. Baptist. Club: Patrick AFB Officers. Home: 707 N Palm Av Indialantic FL 32901 Office: John F Kennedy Space Center FL 32899

BURRUS, JOHN NEWELL, educator; b. Gilmer, Tex., Jan. 23, 1920; s. Herman Clifford and Beulah (Blalack) B.; A.B., U. Miss., 1942; M.A., La. State U., 1944, Ph.D., 1950; postgrad. U. Minn., 1945-47, Vanderbilt U., 1948. Grad. fellow La. State U. 1942-44, 48-49, research asso., 1949-50; teaching fellow U. Minn., 1945-47; faculty U. Miss., 1943-45, Vanderbilt U., 1947-48, U. Fla., 1950-51; faculty, chmn. dept. sociology U. So. Miss., Hattiesburg, 1951-70, prof., 1957-70, Distinguished U. prof., 1970—, mem. Council U. Honors Program, 1959-67. Active A.R.C. Mem. Am. Sociol. Assn., So. (nomination com. 1966-68, sect. chmn. 1968, mem. exec. com. 1955-58), Rural sociol. socs., Sigma Chi, Alpha Kappa Delta, Pi Gamma Mu, Phi Kappa Phi. Kiwanian. Author: Life Opportunities: Differential Mortality in Mississippi, 1951; (with C.A. McMahan, R.H. Bradford) Manual to Accompany the Sociology of Urban Life, 1952; (with H.A. Pedersen, M.B. King) Mississippi Life Tables, 1954; Mississippi's People, 1950; (with others) Social Problems, 1955. Mem. editorial bd. So. Quar., 1962-70, chmn., 1967-68. Contbr. articles, book revs. to profl. publs. Home: 213 Arlington Loop Hattiesburg MS 39401

BURSON, JOHN HENRY, III, educator; b. Carrollton, Ga., July 30, 1934; s. John Henry and Clara (Miles) B.; B.Chem. Engring., Ga. Inst. Tech., 1956, M.S. in Metallurgy, 1963, Ph.D. in Chem. Engring., 1964; m. Barbara Anne Vaughn, Dec. 18, 1955; children—Susan Elaine, Sandra Anne, John Henry IV, Thomas Edward. Chief chemist Testworth Labs., 1956-59; mem. faculty Ga. Inst. Tech., Atlanta, 1959—, sr. research engr., 1964—, asso. prof. chem. engring., 1969—. Served with AUS, 1957. Recipient Research award Sigma Xi, 1964. Registered profl. engr., Ga., Cal., Pa. Mem. Am. Chem. Soc., Nat. Soc. Profl. Engrs., Am. Inst. Chem. Engrs. (chpt. chmn. 1970-72), Res. Officers Assn. (chpt. sec.-treas. 1970—), Fine Particle Soc. (nat. pres. 1969-70), Ga. Football Ofcls. Assn. (v.p. 1971-72), Sigma Xi. Contbr. articles to publs. Home: 1198 Citadel Dr NE Atlanta GA 30324

BURSON, WILLIAM HOMER, state ofcl.; b. Thomaston, Ga., July 31, 1928; s. Jobie B. and Mildred L. (Pitts) B.; A.B.J. magna cum laude, U. Ga., 1948; m. Lila LaVerne Womble, July 28, 1951; children—Forrest, Leigh, Louise. Circulation mgr., reporter Thomaston (Ga.) Times, 1943-44, news editor and editorial columnist, 1944-45; copy desk and reporter Athens (Ga.) Banner-Herald, 1945; staff writer, dept. pub. relations U. of Ga., 1945, asst. dir., 1946, dir., 1946-48; became staff corr. United Press Assn., 1948, war corr., 1950, assigned to Korea, Miss. mgr., 1952-53; aide and press sec. gov. Ga., 1953-54; exec. sec. to atty. gen. Ga., 1955-56; press sec., editorial asst. to Sen. Herman Talmadge, 1956, exec. aide, press sec., 1957-62; asst. to comptroller. Ga., 1963; aide to Gov. Ga., 1963; state dir. probation, 1963-65; asst. to regional dir. U.S. P.O. Dept., 1965-67; dir. Ga. Dept. Family and Children Services, 1967-70; treas. State of Ga., 1971—. Cited 17 Inf. Regt. for bravery in reporting under heavy fire. Recipient Speaker of Year award Emory U.; Citizenship award Civitan Club. Mem. Phi Beta Kappa, Phi Kappa Phi, Omicron Delta Kappa, Sphinx, Sigma Delta Chi, Phi Eta Sigma, Alpha Phi Omega, Lambda Chi Alpha, Blue Key. Baptist. Home: 3004-1 Buford Hwy NE Atlanta GA 30329 Office: State Capitol Atlanta GA 30334

BURT, ALVIN VICTOR, JR., newspaperman; b. Carlton, Ga., Sept. 11, 1927; s. Alvin Victor and Mabel (Sorrow) B.; B.A. in Edn., U. Fla., 1949; m. Gloria White. With U.P., 1949-50, Atlanta Jour., 1950-51, Jacksonville (Fla.) Jour., 1951-55; with Miami (Fla.) Herald, 1955-66, Latin Am. editor, 1962-66, assigned Washington, 1962; editor Hartwell (Ga.) Sun, 1966-67; editorial writer Miami Herald, 1967—. Recipient Ernie Pyle award for newspaper writing, 1961; State award A.P. for feature writing, 1964; citation Fla. Legislature, 1965; Scripps-Howard award for best interviews in nation, 1966. Mem. Sigma Delta Chi. Co-author: Papa Doc, 1969. Home: 10701 SW 69th Av Miami FL 33156 Office: Miami Herald Miami FL 33101

BURT, GEORGE DOLE WADLEY, newspaperman; b. Bolingbroke, Ga., Oct. 1, 1909; s. William Giroud and Sarah Lois (Wadley) B.; ed. Woodbury Forest, Va., and Lanier High Sch., Macon, Ga.; student Ga. Sch. Tech., 1926-27; m. Gwyneth Margaret Miller. Reporter, Macon Telegraph, 1928-36; writer and editor Asso. Press, 1936-38; editor Macon (Ga.) Evening News, exec. editor Macon Telegraph, 1938-40; staff Courier-Journal and Louisville Times, Louisville, Ky., 1940—, chief editorial writer, 1948-56; editorial page editor The Louisville Times, 1956—. Served to capt. AUS, World War II. Mem. Am. Soc. Newspaper Editors, Nat. Conf. Editorial Writers, Inter-Am. Press Assn. Democrat. Home: Prospect KY 40059 Office: Louisville Times Louisville KY

BURTON, ANNIE UNA, mfg. co. exec.; b. Thorton, R.I., Oct. 9, 1889; d. Joseph Godber and Annie (Severn) Burton; B.A., Randolph Macon Woman's Coll., 1912. Tchr. schs., Lynchburg, Va., 1912-16; sec., treas. Lynchburg Hosiery Mills, 1916-67, now trustee, mem. bd. Mem. Am. Assn. U. Women, Bus. and Profl. Women's Club. Club: Lynchburg Art (treas.). Home: 3819 Fort Av Lynchburg VA 24502

BURTON, GEORGE AUBREY, JR, accountant, city ofcl.; b. Texarkana, Ark., June 21, 1925; s. George Aubrey and Theo (Simmons) B.; B.S., Centenary Coll. La., 1951m. Joan Cunningham, July 31, 1947; children—George Aubrey III, Sandra. Sr. accountant Opferkuch & McGuirt, Shreveport, La., 1950-53; partner Opferkuch, McGuirt, Watts & West, Shreveport, La., 1953-54; accountant G. A. Burton, Jr., Shreveport, La., 1954-66; partner Burton & Penn, Shreveport, 1966—; commr. finance City of Shreveport, 1971—. Instr., Centenary Coll., 1957-59. Mem. Shreveport Housing Rehab. Bd., 1956-57; mem. Caddo Sch. Bd. Com. for Rapid Learners, 1957-59; mem. citizens adv. com. Caddo Police Jury, 1967-68. Mem. Republican State Central Com., 1964—, sec., 1972—; mem. Caddo Parish Rep. Exec. Com., 1954—, chmn., 1960—. Mem. La. Jaycees. Home: 4423 Creswell Rd Shreveport LA 71106 Office: 1234 Texas Av Shreveport LA 71101

BURTON, GEORGE WASHINGTON, educator; b. Brosville, Va., July 4, 1908; s. John William and Annie (Harvey) B.; B.S., U. Va., 1929, M.A., 1942; m. Sarah Dudley, Mar. 24, 1945; children—Sarah Elizabeth, Brown Dudley. Tchr. high sch., Henry County, Va., 1930-32, prin., 1932-42; supt. schs., Clarke County, Va., 1946-66; state dir. secondary edn. Dept. Edn., Richmond, Va., 1966-68, asst. state supt. for instrn., Richmond, 1968-72, asst. state supt. adminstrv. field services, 1972—. Served with AUS, 1942-46. Mem. Am., Va. assns. sch. adminstrs., Va. Edn. Assn., C. of C. (pres. 1957-58). Lion (pres. 1960-61). Home: 2000 Riverside Dr Richmond VA 23225 Office: State Dept Edn Richmond VA 23216

BURTON, JAMES ROBERT, electronics co. exec.; b. Weirgate, Tex., June 1, 1928; s. James G. and Marjorie (Roberts) B.; B.S., U. Tex., 1950; m. Maebelle Freeman, Mar. 19, 1949; children—Charlotte Ann, James Donald, Russell Lynn. Planning rep. IBM Corp., White Plains, N.Y., 1950-59; mgr. product marketing Tex. Instruments, Houston, 1959-63; self employed as cons. Houston, 1963-66; v.p., gen. mgr. computer div. Geospace Corp., 1966-67; v.p. component and systems tech. group Sterling Electronics Corp., Houston, 1967-69; chmn., pres. Houston Scientific, 1969—. Served to lt. USNR, 1952-55. Mem. I.E.E.E., Data Processing Mgmt. Assn. Home: 449 Hollow Dr Houston TX 77024 Office: 4202 Directors Row Houston TX 77018

BURTON, JOSEPH JOHN, advt. exec.; b. Greensboro, N.C., Mar. 9, 1919; s. Hilary Goode and Sarah (Harriss) B.; student Guilford Coll., 1936-38; B.S. in Commerce, U. N.C., 1940; m. Virginia Garrison Williams, Feb. 5, 1944; children—Joseph John Jr., Robert Dalrymple. Asst. to pres., gen. advt. mgr. Colonial Stores Inc., Atlanta, 1949-59; v.p. firm Liller Neal Battle, Atlanta, 1959-65; pres. Burton-Campbell Inc., Atlanta, 1965—. Publicity chmn. Am. Heart Assn., Atlanta, 1969—. Bd. dirs. Goodwill Industries, Atlanta, St. Jude's House, Atlanta. Served with USNR, 1940-45. Mem. Phi Beta Kappa, Beta Gamma Sigma, Alpha Delta Sigma. Democrat. Episcopalian. Contbr. poetry mags. Home: 2879 Normandy Dr NW Atlanta GA 30305 Office: 1800 Peachtree Rd NW Atlanta GA 30305

BURTON, ROBERT COOPER, chem. co. exec.; b. Memphis, Aug. 17, 1909; s. Madison Theodore and Lula (Cooper) B.; B.S., U. Tenn., 1930; D.Sc. (hon.), Emory & Henry Coll., 1965; m. Anna Beatrice Johnson, Oct. 5, 1929. With Tenn. Eastman Co., Kingsport, Tenn., 1930—, sr. v.p., 1969—; vice chmn. Eastman Chem. Products, Inc., 1969-72, Tex. Eastman Co., 1969—; asst. gen. mgr. Eastman Chems. div. Eastman Kodak Co., 1972—; v.p. Carolina Eastman Co., 1966—; pres. Holston Def. Corp., 1966—. Dir. First Nat. Bank of Sullivan County, 1969—. Bd. dirs. Kingsport Community Chest, 1954—, Holston Valley Community Hosp., 1964—; mem. devel. council U. Tenn., 1969—. Mem. Kingsport C. of C., Am. Chem. Soc., Am. Inst. Chem. Engrs., Am. Ordnance Assn., Tau Beta Pi, Alpha Chi Sigma. Republican. Methodist. Club: Ridgefields Country (Kingsport, Tenn.). Home: 3600 Orebank Rd Kingsport TN 37664 Office: Eastman Rd Kingsport TN 37662

BURTON, UVA MARIE LOFTIS (MRS. J. B. BURTON), lawyer, realtor; b. Mena, Ark., Nov. 21, 1911; d. Charles Lemuel and Brooke Corene (Wimberly) Loftis; student Tulane U., 1929-30; LL.B., So. Meth. U., 1942; m. Hal Erwin, Oct. 24, 1942 (dec. Mar. 1953); children—William Hal, Judith Marie; m. 2d, Jesse Byron Burton, July 25, 1959 (dec. Jan. 1962). Family caseworker United Charities, Dallas, 1930-33; personnel and legal worker Atlantic Refining Co., Dallas, 1933-43; admitted to Tex. bar, 1942; lawyer, Houston, 1956—; asso. realtor Saffold Realty Co., Houston, 1965. Parliamentarian, Lynn Park Civic Club, Houston, 1963—. Mem. State Bar Tex., Houston Bd. Realtors, Tex. Real Estate Assn., Nat. Assn. Real Estate Bds., Women's Assn., Alpha Omicron Pi, Kappa Beta Pi. Episcopalian. Home: 4019 Sul Ross St Houston TX 77027 Office: 1314 Texas Av Houston TX 77002

BURWELL, CLAYTON L., lawyer; b. Charlotte, N.C. Oct. 29, 1910; B.S., U. of the South, 1932; B.A. in Jurisprudence (Rhodes scholar), Oxford (Eng.) U., 1935; LL.B., U. N.C., 1936. Admitted to N.C. bar, 1941, U.S. Supreme Ct. bar, 1942; gen. counsel, v.p. Resort Airlines, 1945-48; spl. asst. to sec. navy, 1948-50; gen. counsel Ind. Airlines Assn., 1958-59, pres., 1959-61; now mem. firm Burwell, Hansen & McCandless, Washington. Mem. U.S. Travel Service adv. com., 1962. Served with USNR, 1941-45. Mem. Naval Res. Assn. (nat. pres. 1953), Va., Am. bar assns., Bar Assn. D.C. Home: 1348 Lynnbrook St Dr Arlington VA 22201 Office: Burwell Hansen & McCandless 700 Federal Bar Bldg West Washington DC 20006

BUSBEE, CYRIL B., supt. edn. S.C.; b. Wagener, S.C., Dec. 17, 1908; s. William J. and Minnie (Toole) B.; B.S., U. S.C., 1928, M.A., 1938, LL.D., 1969; grad. student Coll. William and Mary, 1941, Columbia U., 1955; LL.D., Wofford Coll., 1970; m. Thelma Ecord, July 20, 1929; children—Carolyn (Mrs. Robert Carpenter), Cyril B. Supt., Windsor Sch., Aiken County, S.C., 1930-35, Baron DeKalb Sch., Kershaw County, S.C., 1935-43, Brookland-Cayce (S.C.) Schs., 1943-67; supt. edn. S.C., 1967—. Dir. Citizens and So. Nat. Bank, Columbia, S.C., 1960—. Mem. steering com. Edn. Commn. States. Served with USNR, 1943-46. Mem. Nat. Council Chief State Sch. Officers (chmn. policy com.), S.C. Edn. Assn. (pres. 1965-66), W. Columbia-Cayce C. of C. (pres. 1962). Democrat. Methodist (ofcl. bd., trustee). Lion (pres. Cayce-W. Columbia 1959), Kiwanian (pres. Camden 1940). Home: 900 Naples Av Cayce SC 29033 Office: Rutledge Bldg Columbia SC 29201

BUSBEE, ELIZABETH DIVERS (MRS. CHARLES MANLY BUSBEE), county ofcl.; b. Roanoke, Va., May 15, 1912; d. Alfred and Mary Bessie (Ramsey) Divers; student Martha Washington Coll., 1928, Milligan (Tenn.) Coll., 1928-29; B.S., Radford (Va.) Coll., 1934; postgrad. U. N.C., 1944-45, U. Va., 1945-46, Coll. William and Mary, 1966; m. Charles M. Busbee, July 3, 1957. Instr., coach West Jefferson (N.C.) High Sch., 1935-37, Gretna (Va.) High Sch., 1937-38; social worker Franklin County Dept. Pub. Welfare, Rocky Mount, Va., 1938-42, supt., 1942—. Bd. dirs. S.W. Soc. for Crippled Children, 1944-50; treas. Franklin County chpt. Nat. Found. for Infantile Parlysis, 1938—; pres. Va. League Local Welfare Execs., 1956-58; rep. from 5th Congl. Dist. Va. on League Local Welfare Execs., 1950-54, 63-65. Organizer, Woman's Club Rocky Mount, 1945, pres., 1950-52, 71-73, organizer Jr. Woman's Club, 1949; pres. U.D.C., 1956—. Home: 114 Taliaferro Av Rocky Mount VA 24151 Office: Franklin County Dept Pub Welfare Rocky Mount VA 24151

BUSC, ROBERTO, univ. ofcl. Pres. U. P.R. Council of Higher Edn. Office: Av Gandara Rio Piedras PR 00928*

BUSH, ALBERT ERNEST, assn. exec.; b. Cedar Falls, Ia., May 19, 1931; s. Ernest M. and Mary (Jackle) B.; student Open Bible Coll., 1954, Midland Coll., 1954, Drake U., 1955-57; B.A., Tulsa U., 1963; m. Marilyn Ruth Huffman, Jan. 30, 1953; children—Carol Marie, Marta Lynn. Dept. mgr. Oral Roberts Assn., Inc., Tulsa, 1957-60, asst. operations mgr., 1960-63, operations mgr., 1963-66, exec. v.p., 1966-69, pres., 1969—, bd. regents Oral Roberts U., 1969—; pres. Traco Advt., Inc., Tulsa, 1966—; dir. Boulder Bank & Trust Co., Tulsa, Mentor Corp. Bd. dirs. YMCA, Arts Council Tulsa, Tulsa Housing Authority, University Village, Inc.; mem. advt. bd. Jr. League, Tulsa. Mem. Am. Mgmt. Assn., Young Pres. Orgn., Direct Mail Advt. Assn. Tulsa C. of C. (div. planning group). Republican. Presbyn. Kiwanian. Clubs: Tulsa, Summit, Southern Hills Country. Home: 2660 E 75th St Tulsa OK 74136 Office: 7777 S Lewis Av Tulsa OK 74136

BUSH, DOROTHY VREDENBURGH, sec. Dem. Nat. Com.; Baldwyn, Miss., Dec. 8, 1916; d. Will Lee and Lany (Holland) McElroy; student George Washington U., summer 1935; B.S. Miss. State Coll. for Women, 1937; m. Peter Vredenburgh, 3d, Dec. 27, 1940 (dec.); stepson, Peter (dec.) m. 2d, John W. Bush, Jan. 13, 1962. Sec. to dir. ins. bus. Tenn. Coal, Iron & R.R. Co., subsidiary U.S. Steel, Birmingham, Ala., 1937-40. Nat. committeewoman Ala. Young Democrats, 1941-50; asst. sec. conv. Young Dems. Am., 1941, v.p., 1943-48; co-chmn. Jackson Day dinners of Ala., 1944; sec. Dem. Nat. Com., 1944— (1st woman to hold this position), acting pres. Young Dems. Am., 1944; sec. Dem. Nat. Convs. 1944—. Life mem. Ark. Traveler, Beta Sigma Phi. Baptist. Clubs: Maskers (Miss. State Coll. for Women), Jane Jefferson (life), Nat. Fedn. Bus. and Profl. Women's. Home: 4201 Cathedral Av NW Washington DC 20016 Office: Democratic Natl Com Washington DC 20037

BUSH, EUNICE CARROLL, ins. co. exec.; b. Merryville, La., Jan. 7, 1907; d. Guy and Jennie (Hargrove) Carroll; student La. State Coll., 1924; m. Harry F. Bush, Nov. 6, 1933 (dec. July 1951); 1 son, Robert A. Seals. With Mut. Life Ins. Co. of N.Y., Baton Rouge, 1931—, successively dist. mgr., supervisory asst., asst. mgr., Baton Rouge, 1938-58, tng. asst. home office, N.Y.C., 1958, mgr., 1958-1964, life underwriter, 1964—. Pres. bd. dirs. YWCA, Baton Rouge, 1951-52, mem. adv. bd., 1962-63; mem. adv. bd. Baton Rouge Gen. Hosp., 1952-57; bd. dirs. Community Chest and United Givers of Baton Rouge, 1954-55. C.L.U. Mem. Nat. Assn. Life Underwriters (trustee 1950, vice chmn. com. on assns. 1962-63), Baton Rouge Life Underwriters Assn. (pres. 1942-43), Beta Gamma Sigma (hon.). Club: Quota (charter, past pres. Baton Rouge, lt. gov. 21st Dist.) Home: 9544 Goodwood Blvd Baton Rouge LA 70806 Office: Republic Towers Bldg 5700 Florida Blvd Baton Rouge LA 70806

BUSH, JOHN J., ret. govt. ofcl., cattle farmer; b. Weiser, Ida., Mar. 26, 1914; s. Clarence and Amelia (Fennell) B.; student Sacramento Jr. Coll., also McClellan U., 1950-51; m. Rosa C. Leoni, Nov. 21, 1935 (dec. Apr. 1965); children—Jan Clarence, Jon Leland, Jens Eric, Marcella Emelia (Mrs. Dale B. Smith); m. 2d, Alma T. Hinton, Feb. 1966. Jr. engr. Bush Constrn. Co., Rupert, Ia., 1935-37, engr., 1937-39, partner, 1939-41; with aircraft maintenance field McClellan Field AFB, Sacramento, 1941-56, shop worker, mgmt. analyst, indsl. engr., prodn. supr., prodn. specialist; dep. dir. maintenance engring. Brookley AFB, Ala., 1956-66; dep. chief F-102/106 SSM, Kelly AFB, Tex., 1966-68, dep. chief elec. equip. div., 1968-70, chief materiel services div., 1970-72; cattle farmer, Richton, Miss., 1972—. Mem. exec. bd., chmn. camp devel. com. Mobile area council of Boy Scouts Am. Bd. dirs. Mobile County (Ala.) chpt. A.R.C. Recipient Silver Beaver award Boy Scouts Am.; Meritorious Service award U.S. Air Force. Registered Profl. Engr., Cal. Mem. Soc. Am. Mil. Engrs. (past pres.), Cal. Soc. Profl. Engrs. (past dir. Cal.), Soc. Indsl. Engrs., Am. Soc. Metals, Am. Mgmt. Assn., Pub., Gulf Coast personnel assns. Santa Gertrudis Breeders Assn. Mason (Shriner). Clubs: Kelly Management; Canyon Creek Country. Mobile Yacht; Laurel Country. Address: Pine Branch Farm Route 4 Box 4 Richton MS 39476

BUSH, NORMAN, statistician; b. N.Y.C., Dec. 10, 1929; s. Louis and Ida (Trembola) B.; B.A., Coll. City N.Y., 1951, M.B.A., 1952, Ph.D., N.C. State Coll., 1962; m. Audrey Blumberg, Dec. 28, 1952; children—Stewart A., I. Jeffrey, Ellen G. Statistician U.S. Army Chem. Corps, 1954-56, RCA Service Co., Patrick AFB, Fla., 1956-58, Instrument Corp. Fla., Melbourne, 1962-63; dir. tech. staff D. Brown Assos., Melbourne, 1963-64; prin. engr. Pan Am. World Airlines, Patrick AFB, 1964-72, Ensco, Cocoa Beach, Fla., 1972—. Instr. Fla. Inst. Tech., Melbourne, 1964-67; asst. prof. genesys U. Fla., Cape Canaveral, 1967—. Served with AUS, 1952-54. Mem. Am. Statis. Assn., Inst. Transp. Sci., Technometrics, Operations Research Soc. Am. Contbr. articles to profl. jours. Home: 1127 Seminole Dr Indian Harbour Beach FL 32937 Office: 1980 N Atlantic Av Cocoa Beach FL 32931

BUSH, PETER BIRDSALL, newspaper exec.; b. Milw., Oct. 1, 1924; s. Fred Randall and Marie (Donner) B.; grad. Advanced Mgmt. Program, Harvard, 1960; S. M., Syracuse U., 1958; m. Mary Ann Kumler, May 5, 1945; children—Carol Lynnlee, Marc Randall. Advt. dir. Norfolk (Va.)-Portsmouth Newspapers, Inc., 1960-64; v.p., gen. mgr. Greensboro (N.C.) Daily News and Rec., now pres. Served as aviator USNR, World War II. Mem. Newspaper Advt. Execs. Assn. (v.p. Va. 1964), Am. Newspaper Pubs. Assn., Greensboro C. of C., Greensboro Better Bus. Bur., Greensboro Advt. Club, Sales and Marketing Execs. Norfolk-Portsmouth (pres. 1964-65). Rotarian. Author: Newspaper Advertising Ethics, 1964; Newspaper Advertising Effectiveness Studies, 1963. Home: 4121 Dogwood Dr Greensboro NC 27410 Office: 200 N Davie St Greensboro NC

BUSH, STUART ALAN, cattle farmer; b. New Milford, Conn., Aug. 24, 1936; s. Raymond M. and Evelyn C. (Storm) B.; student U. Colo., 1954-55; B.A., M.E., U. Denver, 1957; m. Sharon M. Kissinger, Sept. 9, 1956; children—Christopher Alan, Caryn Lee. Various positions G. L. Martin Co., Denver, 1956-58; final acceptance insp. Beech Aircraft Corp., Boulder, Colo., 1958-59; asst. mech. engring. dept. U. Denver, 1960-61; welding technician Dow Chem. Co., Golden, Colo., 1961-66, engr. research and devel., 1966-71; co-owner, operator Squire B Farms, Berryville, Ark., 1971—. Mgr., Nat. Little League Baseball Team, 1965—. Mem. Am. Welding Soc., Am. Metals Soc., Am. Ordnance Assn., Ark. Cattlemen's Assn., Am., Ark., 4-State angus assns., Am. Nat. Cattlemen's Assn., Anti-theft Assn. Patentee in field. Address: Route 2 Box 268 Berryville AR 72616

BUSH, WILLIAM EDWARD, civil engr.; b. Jackson, Tenn., Dec. 6, 1924; s. Cecil Warren and Chrystabel (Herrick) B.; student Memphis State U., 1942-43, Miss. Coll., 1943-44; B.S., U. Tenn., 1949; m. Gladys E. Parker, Sept. 17, 1953; children—Nancy C., William Scott. Hydraulic engr. U.S. Corps of Engrs., Vicksburg, Miss., 1949-50, constrn. engr., Memphis, 1952-53; hydraulic engr. Soil Conservation Service, U.S. Dept. Agr., Memphis, 1953-62, soil conservationist, 1962-72, urban engring. specialist, 1972—. Cons., Water Resource Devel. Served with USNR, 1943-46; served with AUS, 1950-52. Recipient Achievement award, 1962, Writers award, 1970, Spl. Achievement award Soil Conservation Service, U.S. Dept. Agr., 1971. Registered profl. engr., Tenn. Mem. Am. Soc. C.E. Methodist. Contbr. profl. jours. Home: 2462 Inverary Dr Memphis TN 38138 Office: 5119 Summer Av Memphis TN 38122

BUSHNELL, DAVID SHERMAN, assn. exec.; b. Whittier, Cal., Jan. 7, 1927; s. David Sherman and Lillian (Dudley) B.; Ph.B., U. Chgo., 1947, M.A., 1950; postgrad. (Research fellow) U. Wash., 1951-53; m. Alice Mencher, Aug. 14, 1965; children—Beckie Lynn, Kimberlie Anne, Karin Jo. Asst. study dir. U. Mich. Survey Research Center, 1953-55; mgmt. communications cons., corporate staff IBM Corp., N.Y.C., 1955-61; research sociologist Stanford Research Inst., Menlo Park, Cal., 1961-64; research dir. U.S. Office Edn., 1964-69; advance study fellow Battelle Meml. Inst., Washington, 1969-70; research dir. Am. Assn. Jr. Colls., Washington, 1970-72; sr. research scientist Human Resources Research Orgn., Arlington, Va., 1972—. Cons. local, state depts. edn., pvt. industry; vis. lectr. U. Washington Sch. Bus. Adminstrn., summer 1955, vis. prof. Ohio State U. Grad. Sch. Edn., 1970. Chmn. UN Week, Rochester, Minn., 1957; chmn. edn. com., bd. dirs. Rochester Art Center, 1957-61; pres. Rochester Personnel Assn.; mem. adv. bd. New Masters Coll., Antioch Coll. Served with USNR, 1945-46. Fellow Am. Sociol. Soc.; mem. Am. Ednl. Research Assn., Am. Psychol. Assn., Am. Vocational Assn., A.A.A.S. Author: Planned Change in Education; Organizing for Change: New Priorities for Community Colleges. Editorial bd. Jour. Human Resources, 1966-71. Home: 9620 Hawick Lane Kensington MD 20795 Office: 300 N Washington St Arlington VA 22314

BUSO, ROBERTO, educator Pres. U. P.R. Council Higher Edn. Home: Av Gandara Rio Piedras PR

BUSQUETS, CARMEN TERESA PESQUERA (MRS. JAIME BUSQUETS), home economist; b. Ponce, P.R., May 21, 1920; d. Enrique Pesquera Pascual and Carmen Umpierre Carmona; B.S., U.P.R., 1941; M.S., Cornell U., 1955, Ph.D., 1961; m. Jaime Busquets, Aug. 18, 1945; children—Jaime Enrique, Eduardo Hiram, Carmen Teresa. Home mgmt. supr. Farm Security Adminstrn., 1942-45; home demonstration agt. Agrl. Extension Service, 1949-54; home mgmt. specialist, asso. prof. sci. Coop. Extension Service, Coll. Agr., U. P.R., Rio Piedras, 1955—; home economist Orgn. Am. States ICA, Costa Rica, 1962-64. Pres. Gov's. Com. Consumer Affairs, 1970-71; mem. Pres. Council Consumer Affairs, 1970-72. Recipient award Phi Kappa Phi, 1971. Mem. Home Econs. Assn., Phi Kappa Phi, Epsilon Sigma Phi, Gamma Sigma Gamma, Pi Lambda Theta. Home: 3-10 Madrid Torrimar Guaynabo PR 00657 Office: Box AR Rio Piedras PR 00929

BUSSARD, RICHARD, newspaper editor. City editor Jacksonville (Fla.) Journal. Office: One Riverside Av Jacksonville FL 32201*

BUSSE, EWALD WILLIAM, psychiatrist; b. St. Louis, Aug. 18, 1917; s. Frederick Ewald and Emily Louise (Stroh) B.; A.B., Westminister Coll., 1938; M.D., Washington U., 1942; D.Sc., Westminster Coll. 1960;; m. Ortrude Helen Schnaedelbach, July 18, 1941; children— Ortrude Susan (Mrs. White), Barbara Ann, Ewald Richard, Deborah Emily. Intern, resident in neurology St. Louis City Hosp., 1942-43; asst. neurology Washington U., 1942-43; chief resident Colo. Psychopathic Hosp., 1946-48; chief electroencephalography U. Colo. Med. Center, 1946-53, instr. U. Colo., 1946-47, asst. prof., 1947, asso. prof., 1948-50, prof., head psychosomatic medicine, 1950-53; didactic psychoanalysis, 1948-50; prof. Duke University Sch. Medicine and Hosp., 1953-66. J. P. Gibbons prof. psychiatry 1966—, chmn. dept. psychiatry, 1953—, dir. Center for Study of Aging and Human Devel., 1957-70; cons. neuropsychiatry VA, AUS, USAF, USPHS. Served as maj. AUS, 1943-46, chief electroencephalography, asst. chief neuropsychiat. service. Recipient Edward Allen award Am. Geriatrics Soc., 1967; Strecker award Inst. Pa. Hosp., 1967; Robert Kleemeier research award, Gerontol. Soc., 1968; Modern Medicine award 1972. Diplomate Am. Bd. Psychiatry and Neurology (dir., sec.-treas. 1961-69). Fellow A.C.P. (William C. Menninger award 1971), Am. Psychiat. Assn. (v.p. 1966-67; pres. 1971-72), Am. Coll. Psychiatrists, Gerontol. Soc. (mem. council, pres. 1967); mem. Assn. Research in Mental and Nervous Diseases, Am. Psychopath. Assn., N.C. Neuropsychiat. Assn., Am. Geriatrics Soc., Am. Psychosomatic Soc., Am. Orthopsychiat. Assn., Eastern, Central electroencephalographic socs., A.M.A., So. Electronencephalographic Assn., Am. Assn. Chmn. Depts. Psychiatry (pres. elect 1972-73), So. Psychiat. Assn., Sigma Xi, Phi Delta Theta, Phi Beta Pi, Omicron Delta Kappa. Mason, Rotarian (pres. Durham club 1972-73). Contbr. sci. articles profl. publs. Home: 1132 Woodburn Rd Durham NC 27705 Office: Duke U Med Center Durham NC 27710

BUSSEY, THOMAS PATRICK, state justice; b. Parksville, S.C., May 7, 1905; s. John Morgan and Lillie Mobley (Connor) B.; LL.B., U. S.C., 1927; m. Louise McKelvey Florence, Dec. 6, 1931; 1 dau., Patricia B. Wheeler; stepson, Quinton Florence Jr. Admitted to S.C. bar, 1927, and practiced in Charleston until 1958; judge 9th Jud. Circuit S.C., 1958-61; asso. justice Supreme Ct. S.C., 1961—. Mem. Am. Bar Assn. Episcopalian. Mason. Home: 8 Broughton Rd The Crescent Charleston SC 29407 Office: Charleston County Ct House PO Box 326 Charleston SC 29401

BUSTAMANTE, MIGUEL E., pub. health adminstr.; b. Oaxaca, Mexico, May 2, 1898; s. Manuel and Luz (Vasconcelos) B.; student Inst. Sci. and Art. Oaxaca, 1914-19; M.D., Nat. U. of Mexico, 1925; D.P.H., Johns Hopkins, 1928; m. Alice Mary Connolly, Oct. 6, 1928; children—Miguel Enrique, Nancy Jane, Mary Elizabeth, Charles Joseph. Intern. Gen. Hosp., Mexico City, 1924-25; fellow Rockefeller Found., 1926-28; chief health unit Veracruz, 1930; asst. chief Fed. Health Service Republic of Mexico, 1931, chief, 1932-35; prof. med. sch. Nat. U. of Mexico since 1931, chief Mexican States welfare services, 1938; sci. investigator Inst. de Salubridad Enfermedades Tropicales, 1939; dir. Inst. Pub. Health and Tropical Diseases, 1942-43, 1946-47; sec.-gen. Pan-Am. San. Bur., Washington, 1947-56; dir. dept. med. sociology and preventive medicine Med. Sch. Nat. U. Mexico, 1956-58; gen. dir. health services Secretaria de Salubridad y Asistencia, Mexico, 1958-59, undersec. of health, 1959-64; sec. gen. Nat. Health Council, 1965—. Health del. in Ixtlahuaca, 1935. Pres. exec. bd. UNICEF, 1962-63. Mem. Mexican Nat. Commns. for drafting Sanitary Code, 1934, 65, 72, pub. health laws for Coordination of fed., state, and municipal services; mem. study groups for nat. health program, 1934-35, 1945-46; mem. spl. Yellow Fever Studies, 1942-43, Spotted Fever Commn., 1943-47. Spl. lectr. tropical med., U.S. univs., 1942-43; hon. prof. faculty of med., Haiti, 1943. Decorated Dr. Eduardo Liceaga medal for spl. pub. health service, Mexico, 1946; Finlay Order, Cuba. Hon. mem. Soc. of Parasitology and Tropical Med., Caracas, 1947, Am. Acad. of Tropical Medicine; mem. Am. Pub. Health Assn., Soc. Mexicana de Pediatria, Soc. Medica Veracruzana, Am. Soc. Tropical Med., Soc. Mexicana de Hist. Natural, Acad. Nacional de Med. de Mexico (pres. 1962). Author med. reports. Contbr. articles on pub. health adminstrn. and tropical diseases. Home: Viena 22 Coyoacan Mexico City 21 Mexico Office: Paseo de la Reforma 445 Mexico City Mexico

BUSTOS, JAVIER, banker. Vice pres. Banco Nacional de Mexico, Mexico City. Address: Isabel La Catolica 44 Banco Nacional de Mexico Mexico 1 DF Mexico*

BUSWELL, ARTHUR WILCOX, physician, surgeon; b. Oklahoma City, Jan. 6, 1926; s. Albert Currier and Enid May (Scott) B.; B.Sc., U. Okla., 1950, M.D., 1952; m. Loleta JoAnn Sherrill, June 11, 1950; children—Arthur Lee, Robert Joseph, Barbara JoAnn, Brian A., Gayla, Richard; m. 2d, Jane Marie Fuksa, Mar. 1, 1969. Intern, Fitzsimons Army Hosp. Aurora, Colo., 1952-53; surg. resident Wesley Hosp., Oklahoma City, 1954-55; pvt. practice medicine and surgery, Hennessey, Okla., 1955-63; dep. surgeon, Fort Wainwright and Yukon Command, 1963-65; chief staff Kingfisher, (Okla.) Community Hosp., 1956-57; supt. health Kingfisher County, 1960-61; chief profl. services Bassett Army Hosp., 1963-65; div. surgeon 1st Armored Div., Ft. Hood, Tex., 1965-67, 1st Inf. Div., 1967-68; med. project officer U.S. Army Combat Devels. Command, Experimentation Command, Ft. Ord. Cal., 1968-72, also chief human factors div. and chief experimentation div. of experimentation command; assigned to med. dept. activities, Ft. Sill, Okla., 1972—. Served with AUS, 1944-46, 1st lt. 1952-54, maj. to col., 1961—. Decorated Legion of Merit, Soldier's medal, Bronze Star for Valor with one oak leaf cluster, Air medal with 3 oak leaf clusters, Army Commendation medal; Gallantry cross with palm, Honor medal 1st class (both Vietnam). Fellow Royal Soc. Health. Mem. Am., Okla. State (mem. ho. dels), Aerospace, Army Aviation (charter) med. assns. Garfield-Kingfisher County Med. Soc. Home: Route 5 Kingfisher OK 73750 also US Army Med Dept Activities Ft Sill OK 73503

BUTCHER, ROBERT KIMBERLIN, advt. exec.; b. Harrodsburg, Ind., Feb. 9, 1910; s. Ralph E. and Hattie (Kimberlin) B.; student Okla. A. and M. Coll., 1927-29; m. Joanna Van Smith, May 10, 1936; children—Phillip Hurxthal, John Kimberlin. Pres., Robert K. Butcher & Assos., Inc., Shreveport, La., 1952—. Mem. Pub. Relations Soc. Am., Am. Assn. Advt. Agys., Nat. Press Club, Am. Gas Assn., So. Gas Assn. Democrat. Episcopalian. Home: 921 Unadilla St Shreveport LA 71106 Office: PO Box 1 Slattery Bldg Shreveport LA 71161

BUTLER, ALGERNEN LEE, U.S. judge; b. Clinton, N.C., Aug. 2, 1905; s. George Edwin and Eva Boykin (Lee) B.; student Trinity Coll., U.N.C. (asso. editor Law Rev. 1927-28); m. Josephine Lydia Broadwell, June 5, 1935; children—Eva Josephine (Mrs. Louise B. Daniel, Jr.), Algernon Lee, George Edwin. Admitted to N.C. bar, 1928; gen. practice, Clinton, 1928-59; county atty. Sampson County, 1938-51; U.S. dist. judge Eastern Dist. N.C., 1959—, now chief judge. Mem. N.C. Gen. Assembly, Sampson County, 1931; organizer, 1st chmn. Young Republican Clubs N.C., 1932-34; del. Rep. Nat. Conv., 1936, 40, 48; mem. Rep. Exec. Com. N.C., 1942-59, asst. chmn., 1946-50. Mem. Am., N.C., Sixth Dist. (pres. 1953), Sampson County (pres. 1958) bar assns., Sigma Nu. Episcopalian (vestryman). Rotarian (pres. Clinton 1935). Home: 403 Butler Dr Clinton NC 28328 Office: Post Office Bldg W Main St Clinton NC 28328

BUTLER, BRUCE, JR., surgeon; b. Pitts., Aug. 4, 1929; s. Bruce and Elizabeth (Truitt) B.; B.S., Franklin and Marshall Coll., 1951; M.D., George Washington U., 1955; m. Mary Eleanor Osborn, Apr. 15, 1954; children—Judy Ann, Bruce Alan, Lawrence Todd, Daniel Leonard, James Steele, Mary Beth. Intern, orthopaedic resident Walter Reed Gen. Hosp., 1955-60, hand surgery residency, 1961, chief hand surgery, asst. chief orthopaedic surgery, 1964-67; asst. chief orthopaedic surgery Madigan Gen. Hosp., Tacoma, 1962-64; chief, hand surgery D.C. Gen. Hosp., 1967—; asso. prof. orthopaedic soc. Howard U., Washington, 1967—; cons. orthopaedic surgery VA Hosp., Washington, 1965—, USPHS, washington, Surgeon Gen. U.S. Army, Kimbrough Army Hosp., Ft. Meade, Md.; attending surgeon hand surgery Arlington County Crippled Children's Clinic. Served with M.C., AUS, 1955-67. Diplomate Am. Bd. Orthopaedic Surgery. Fellow A.C.S.; mem. Am. Acad. Orthopaedic Surgeons, Am. Soc. for Surgery of Hand, Assn. Mil. Surgeons. Contbr. articles to profl. jours. Home: 2625 E Meridith Dr Vienna VA 22180 Office: 5021 Seminary Rd Alexandria VA 22311

BUTLER, HERBERT HARRISS, govt. ofcl.; b. Ada, O., Oct. 11, 1906; s. Herbert R. and Orienne (Harriss) B.; A.B., Washington Lee U., 1928; postgrad. Johns Hopkins, 1931-32; m. Vera E. Buck, Dec. 31, 1932; children—Herbert H., Jon T. Mgr. brs. C & P Telephone Co., Washington, Balt., 1928-41; pres., gen. mgr. Ill. Telephone Co., Bloomington, 1946-53; v.p., gen. mgr. Commonwealth Telephone Co., Dallas, Pa., 1954-61; sec., dir. govt. relations U.S. Ind. Telephone Assn., Washington, 1962-72; spl. asst. to Congressman Lawrence J. Hogan 5th dist. Md., 1972—. Served with AUS, 1941-45. Decorated Legion Merit. Mem. Ind. Telephone Pioneer Assn. (sec. 1964-72), Phi Beta Kappa, Delta Upsilon. Rotarian. Home: 1612 22d St S Arlington VA 22202 Office: 1027 Longworth House Office Bldg Washington DC 20515

BUTLER, JACK BANKS, banker; b. Corsicana, Tex., May 5, 1940; s. Clark Earl and Hatcher Floy (Banks) B.; B.A., Baylor U., 1962; postgrad. So. Meth. U., 1969; m. Sandra Kay Styles, Apr. 17, 1966; children— Brian Samuel, Kevin Matthew. Adminstrv. asst. Southwestern Life Ins. Co., Dallas, 1962-66; area life spl. agt. Floyd West & Co., Dallas, 1966-67; asst. cashier State Nat. Bank, Corsicana, Tex., 1967-69, v.p., 1969; v.p. Huntsville (Tex.) Nat. Bank, 1969—. Drive chmn. Heart Fund, 1968, Huntsville United Fund, 1971. Bd. dirs. Community Concert Bd., 1969. Named Jaycee of the Year, 1968. Mem. Am. Quarterhorse Assn. (life), Houston Livestock Show and Rodeo (life), Bank Marketing Assn., Huntsville C. of C. (1st v.p. 1971). Baptist (ordained deacon 1969—). Mason (Shriner), Kiwanian. Home: 228 Willowbend Huntsville TX 77340 Office: PO Box 272 Huntsville TX 77340

BUTLER, JACK LAWRENCE, newspaper editor; b. Seymour, Tex., Oct. 21, 1917; s. Wash Cain and Margaret (Lawrence) B.; B.J., U. Tex., 1939; m. Mary Louise Ford, Oct. 26, 1940; children—Lawrence Ford, Helen Lynn (Mrs. David Hays). Mng. editor Tyler (Tex.) Morning Telegraph, 1940, Gladewater (Tex.) Tribune, 1940-41; news editor Austin (Tex.) Tribune, 1942-43; with Ft. Worth Star-Telegram, 1943—, city editor, 1951-54, news editor, 1954-58, asst. mng. editor, 1958-63, editor, 1963—. Bd. dirs. Tex. Christian U. Research Found.; trustee So. Meth. U., 1972—. Served with USNR, 1944-45. Mem. Am. Soc. Newspaper Editors, Sigma Delta Chi (pres. Tex. Assn. 1956). Home: 1613 Scenery Hill Rd Fort Worth TX 76103 Office: 400 W 7th St Fort Worth TX 76102

BUTLER, JESSE WILLARD, lawyer; b. Telico Plains, Tenn., June 15, 1924; s. William M. and Clara R. (Payne) B.; J.D., U. Tenn., 1950; m. Betty M. Butler. Admitted to Tenn. bar, 1950; head legal drafting dept. Roane-Anderson Co., 1951-52; gen. practice law, 1953—; partner Greene & Butler, 1955—; municipal judge City of Knoxville, 1966—; sec. Cherokee Aviation Aircraft Co. Bd. dirs. Knoxville Area Council on Alcoholism, Municipal Court Com. on Alcohol, Gideon, M. Jellinek Center. Served with A.C., AUS, 1943-45. Decorated D.F.C., Air medal with three oak leaf clusters. Mem. N. Am. Judges Assn., Knox County Humane Soc., Tenn. Knoxville bar assns. Methodist. Home: 2338 Island Home Av Knoxville TN 37920 Office: 3601 Chapman Hwy Knoxville TN 37920

BUTLER, MANLEY CALDWELL, state ofcl., lawyer; b. Roanoke, Va., June 2, 1925; A.B., U. Richmond (Va.), 1948; J.D., U. Va., 1950; m. June Nolde. Chmn. Roanoke City Rep. party, 1960-61; mem. Va. Ho. of Dels., 1962-72, minority leader, 1966-72. Mem. Va. State Bar, Am., Roanoke bar assns., Raven Soc., Order of the Coif, Phi Beta Kappa, Tau Kappa Alpha, Omicron Delta Kappa, Phi Gamma Delta. Episcopalian (vestryman). Home: 845 Orchard Rd SW Roanoke VA 24014 Office: PO Box 2887 Roanoke VA 24001

BUTLER, MARION TYUS, univ. adminstr.; b. Carrollton, Ga., Oct. 3, 1914; s. John Marion and Mary Emma (Tyus) B.; A.B. in Journalism, U. Ga., 1935; M.A., La. State U., 1939, postgrad. U. Wis., 1941; m. Laurie Engenia Walker Reade, Sept. 7, 1946; children—Marion Tyus, Thomas W.; 1 step-son, William W. Reade. Asso. editor Calhoun (Ga.) Times, 1936, Cedartown (Ga.) Standard, 1937; prof. journalism U. Ga., Athens, 1939—, dir. alumni relations, 1956—. Served with AUS, 1943-46; lt. col. Res., ret. Mem. Blue Key, Sphinx, Gridiron, Phi Kappa Phi, Omicron Delta Kappa, Phi Delta Theta, Phi Gamma Mu, Sigma Delta Chi. Editor: Ga. Local Govt. Jour., 1955-58, Ga. Alumni Rec., 1946-56. Home: 108 Inverness Rd Athens GA 30601

BUTLER, MARY LOUISE, ret. educator; b. Goldsboro, N.C.; d. Alman Holmes and Gatsey Louise (Stanton) Butler; A.B., E. Carolina U., 1940; M.Edn. in History, U. N.C. at Chapel Hill, 1961; postgrad. Columbia, 1950, U. Ga., 1965. Tchr. pub. schs., Burlington, 1941-44, Greensboro, 1944-46, Charlotte, 1946-71 (all N.C.). Mem. N.C. Fedn. Music Clubs (sec.-treas. So. dist. 1963-67), Charlotte Music Club (chmn. scholarship com. 1957-63, scholarship loan com. 1958-64), D.A.R., Nat., N.C. edn. assns., Nat., N.C., Charlotte depts. of classroom tchrs., Nat., N.C. councils for social studies, Mecklenburg Hist. Assn. (charter mem.). Mem. M.E. Ch. Author: A Butler Family History: William Butler, John W. Butler of Sampson County, North Carolina and Their Descendants, 1972. Commenting cons. Critical Incidents in Teaching (Carsini and Howard), 1964. Home: 1121 Mrytle Av Charlotte NC 28203

BUTLER, MAURICE EARL, banker; b. Mpls., Nov. 21, 1917; s. Earl I. and Clara (Tvedt) B.; B.S., U. N.D., 1940, LL.B., 1950; postgrad. Ill. Bankers Assn., 1952, Northwestern U. Trust Sch., 1952, Hanover Trust Sch., 1957; m. Edith F. Sewright, Jan. 22, 1942; children—Stuart Lee, Sindra Lea. Trust officer First Nat. Bank, Rochester, Minn., 1950-56; with Tex. Nat. Bank Commerce (name changed to Tex. Commerce Bank Nat. Assn. 1970), Houston, 1956—, trust officer, 1956—, v.p., 1966-69, sr. v.p., 1969—. Pres. Florence Crittenton Services, Houston, 1971-72; mem. agt. operations com. United Fund, Houston, 1971; trustee United Fund, Houston. Served to capt. USAAF, 1940-46. Mem. Phi Alpha Delta, Delta Tau Delta. Episcopalian (chmn. finance com. 1970—). Mason. Club: Houston. Home: 346 Tamerlaine St Houston TX 77024 Office: 712 Main St Houston TX 77002

BUTLER, PHILANDER L., ins. co. exec.; b. Bessemer, Ala., Nov. 26, 1922; s. Herbert C. and Lillian (Kelley) B.; student Miles Coll., Talledega Coll.; LL.B., Howard U., 1948; m. Barbara Dixon. Vice pres., sec., gen. counsel Booker T. Washington Ins. Co., Birmingham, Ala., 1950—. Prof. law Booker T. Washington Bus. Coll. Bd. dirs. Travelers Aid of Birmingham, Birmingham Health and Tb Assn., Birmingham Urban League. Served with AUS, 1943. Mem. Nat., Ala., Birmingham bar assns., Alpha Pi Alpha. Mason. Home: 214 11th Av N Birmingham AL 35204 Office: 1527 5th Av N Birmingham AL 35202

BUTLER, RICHARD COLBURN, banker, lawyer; b. Little Rock, Jan. 1, 1910; s. Colburn and Edna (Clok) B.; student Little Rock Jr. Coll., 1929; A.B., U. Ark., 1931; m. Gertrude Remmel, Mar. 7, 1936; 1 son, Richard Colburn III. Admitted to Ark. bar, 1933, also U.S. Supreme Ct.; gen. practice law, Little Rock, 1933-63; partner firm House, Holmes, Butler & Jewell, 1941-63; chmn. Comml. Nat. Bank Little Rock, 1963—; pres., dir. Ark. Nat. Stockyards Co., 1958—; v.p., dir. Peoples Savs. & Loan Assn. Little Rock; dir. Rock Island Lines, Ark. Power & Light Co., Coca Cola Bottling Co. Ark. Pres. bd. trustees Little Rock U., 1961-63; nat. asso. for Ark., Boys Clubs Am., 1964—. Trustee Hendrix Coll., Conway, Ark. Served to maj. USAAF, 1942-46; CBI. Decorated Bronze Star. Mem. Am., Ark. bar assns., Am. Judicature Soc., Assn. Res. City Bankers, Am. Iris Soc. (life, regional v.p. 1960-61), Little Rock C. of C. (pres. 1952). Methodist (chmn. trustees). Clubs: Little Rock Country, Little Rock. Home: 36 River Ridge Rd Little Rock AR 72207 Office: 200 Main St Little Rock AR 72203

BUTLER, ROBERT NEIL, psychiatrist; b. N.Y.C., Jan. 21, 1927; s. Fred and Easter (Dikeman) B.; B.A., Columbia, 1949, M.D., 1953; m. Diane McLaughlin, Sept. 2, 1950; children—Ann Christine, Carole Melissa, Cynthia Lee. Intern St. Lukes Hosp., N.Y.C., 1953-54; resident U. Cal. Langley Porter Clinic, 1954-55, Nat. Inst. Mental Health, 1955-56; research psychiatrist Nat. Inst. Mental Health, USPHS, 1955-62; founder geriatric unit Chestnut Lodge, 1958, adminstr., 1958-59; research psychiatrist Washington (D.C.) Sch. Psychiatry, 1962—. Mem. faculty George Washington U. Med. Sch., Washington, 1962—, Howard U. Sch. Medicine; cons. Nat. Inst. Mental Health, 1967—, U.S. Senate Spl. Com. on Aging. Sec. Nat. Ballet of Washington, 1962—, trustee, 1962—; chmn. D.C. Adv. Commn. on Aging, 1969—; bd. dirs. Nat. Council on Aging. Served with U.S. Maritime Service, 1945-47. Fellow Am. Psychiat. Assn., Am. Geriatrics Soc.; mem. Group for Advancement Psychiatry (chmn.), Gerontol. Soc. Club: Cosmos (Washington). Author: (with others) Human Aging, 1963. Mem. editorial bd. Jour. Geriatric Psychiatry Aging and Human Devel. Contbr. articles to publs. Address: 3815 Huntington St NW Washington DC 20015

BUTLER, WENDELL HARDING, dentist; b. Carthage, Tex., Oct. 12, 1924; s. Thomas Butler and Inez (Black) B.; student Prairie View Coll., 1941-44; D.D.S., Howard U., 1949; m. Susie Sparrow, June 18, 1949; children—Wanda Marie, Karen Diane, Carol Diane, Susan Jean. Instr. Howard U., Washington, 1950-51; pvt. practice dentistry, Roanoke, Va., 1953—. Dir., sec., treas. Northwest Roanoke Corp., 1965—. Bd. dirs. Hunton YMCA. Commr. Roanoke Redevel. and Housing Authority, 1968-70; mem. Roanoke City Sch. Bd. 1970—. Roanoke City Democratic committeeman, 1970—; mem. Va. Dem. Central Com., 1972—. Served to capt. USAF, 1951-53. Mem. Am. Dental Assn., Omega Psi Phi. Mason. Home: 2118 Andrews Rd Roanoke VA 24017 Office: 721 11th St NW Roanoke VA 24017

BUTLER, WENDELL (PACE), state ofcl.; b. Sulphur Well, Ky., Dec. 18, 1912; s. Henry and Pearl (Pace) B.; A.B., Western Ky. State Coll., 1936; M.A., U. Ky., 1950, postgrad., 1951; m. Edna Ford, Jan. 15, 1947; children—Rendell and Kendell (twins), Wendell Ford. Tchr. pub. schs., Metcalfe County, Ky., 1931-36, supt. schs., 1938-42; supt. pub. instrn., Ky. Dept. Edn., 1952-55, 60-63; commr. agr. Commonwealth of Ky., 1964-67, 72-—, supt. pub. instrn., 1968-71. Pres., mgr. School Service Co., Frankfort, Ky. 1956-59. Mem. Ky. State Senate, 1947-51, mem. com. on edn., 1950. Served with USNR, World War II. Mem. Nat., Ky. edn. assns., Farm Bur., Am. Legion, Vets. Fgn. Wars, Phi Delta Kappa, Kappa Delta Pi. Methodist. Mason. Home: 121 Crittendon Rd Frankford KY 40601 Office: State Dept Agr Frankfort KY 40601

BUTT, HOWARD EDWARD, supermarket exec.; b. Memphis, Apr. 9, 1895; s. Charles C. and Florence (Thornton) Butt; student pub. schs.; m. Mary Elizabeth Holdsworth, Dec. 5, 1924; children—Howard Edward, Charles C., Margaret Eleanor (Mrs. William H. Crook). Chmn. bd. H. E. Butt Grocery Co., Corpus Christi, Tex., 1920-—; operator H.E.B. Food Stores, Tex., 1920-—. Baptist. Mason (33 deg.). Home: 3700 Ocean Dr Corpus Christi TX 78411 Office: 807 N Broadway Corpus Christi TX 78408

BUTT, LILLIAN STUART, educator; b. nr. Abingdon, Va., Nov. 25, 1901; d. Charles Henry and Josephine (Bailey) Butt; student Martha Washington Coll., 1919-20, Va. Intermont Coll., 1920-21; B.S., U. Va., 1929, M.S., 1936; summer study U. Wash., 1939. Tchr., Abingdon, Va., 1921-36, Charlottesville, Va., 1936-68, supervising tchr. dept. edn. U. Va., 1950-68; now ret.; chmn. social studies dept. Lane High Sch., 1953-64. Sponsor Jr. Red Cross, 1940-59; mem. youth in govt. com. Va. dist. YMCA. Recipient Valley Forge Classroom Tchrs. medal, 1959; Jeweled Tri-Hi-Y pin, 1951, YMCA plaque for service to youth, 1956, 66. Mem. Am. Assn. U. Women, D.A.R., U.D.C., Washington County, Albermarle hist. socs., Va. Charlottesville (pres. 1955-57) edn. assns., Va. Council for Social Studies (exec. bd. mem.), English-Speaking Union, Johnston Meml. Hosp. Aux., Wesleyan Service Guild, Nat. Retired Tchrs. Assn., Delta Kappa Gamma. Democrat. Methodist. Club: Booklovers. Home: 363 Bradley St Abingdon VA

BUTT, THOMAS FRANKLIN, judge; b. Eureka Springs, Ark., Mar. 26, 1917; s. Festus O. and Esther (Cox) B.; J.D., U. Ark., 1938; m. Cecilia King, Apr. 25, 1942; children—Thomas King, Martin Andrew, William Jackson II. Admitted to Ark. bar, 1938, U.S. Supreme Ct. bar, 1955, Ct. Mil. Appeals, 1968; practiced in Eureka Springs, 1938, Fayetteville, 1939-40, 46-50; title examiner land dept. Carter Oil Co., Mattoon, Ill., 1938-39; prof. law U. Ark., 1939-40; area rent dir., atty. OPA, Fayetteville, 1946-49; chancery and probate judge, Fayetteville, 1951-—. Pres. Ark. Jud. Council, 1956-57; mem. West Ark. Area council Boy Scouts Am., 1955-56. Served with AUS, 1940-46; brig. gen. Res. Mem. Am., Ark., Washington County bar assns., Res. Officers Assn., Mil. Govt. Assn., Judge Advocate Gen. Assn., C. of C. Methodist. Mason. Club: Fayetteville Country. Home: 1004 Rebecca St Fayetteville AR 72701 Office: Court House Fayetteville AR 72701

BUTTERFIELD, ALEXANDER PORTER, ret. air force officer, govt. ofcl.; b. Pensacola, Fla., Apr. 6, 1926; s. Horace Bushnell and Susan A. (Alexander) B.; B.S., U. Md., 1956; M.S., George Washington U., 1967; m. Charlotte Mary Maguire, Sept. 9, 1949; children—Leslie Carter (dec.), Alexander Porter, Susan Carter, Elisabeth Gordon. Commd. 2d lt. USAF, 1949, advanced through grades to col., 1966; fighter pilot, mem. Skyblazers, U.S. jet aerobatic team, Europe, 1949-53; aide to comdr. 4th Allied Tactical Air Force NATO, 1954-55; operations officer interceptor squadron, 1955-56; instr. U.S. Air Force Acad., 1957-59; sr. aide to comdr.-in-chief USAF Pacific, 1959-62; comdr. jet fighter squadron, S.E. Asia, 1963-64; policy planner USAF hdqrs., 1964-65; mil. asst. to spl. asst. sec. of def., 1965-66; sr. mil. rep. for U.S., also rep. for comdr.-in-chief Pacific Forces, Australia, 1967-69; ret., 1969; dep. asst. to President Richard M. Nixon, 1969-—. Decorated Legion of Merit, D.F.C., Bronze Star medal, Air medal with 3 oak leaf clusters, Air Force Commendation medals. Mem. Acad. Polit. Sci., Sigma Nu. Republican. Author articles in field. Home: 7416 Admiral Dr Alexandria VA 22307 Office: The White House Washington DC 20500

BUTTERWORTH, WILLIAM EDMUND, III, author; b. Newark, Nov. 10, 1929; s. William Edmund and Gladys (Schnable) B.; m. Emma Josefa Macalik, July 14, 1950; children—Patricia Olga (Mrs. John A. Hood), William Edmund IV, John Scholefield II. Author: Comfort Me With Love, 1959; Hot Seat, 1960; No French Leave, 1960; Where We Go From Here, 1961; The Love Go Round, 1962; The Loved and The Lost, 1962; Heartbreak Ridge, 1962; Courtmartial, 1962; Hell on Wheels, 1963; The Girl in the Black Bikini, 1963; The Wonders of Astronomy, 1964; Once More With Passion, 1964; Le Falot, 1964; Article 92, Murder-Rape, 1965; The Wonders of Rockets and Missiles, 1965; Doing What Comes Naturally, 1965; L'il Wildcat, 1965; Warrior's Way, 1965; Fast Green Car, 1966; Tiger Rookie, 1966; Make War in Madness, 1966; Stock Car Racer, 1966, Soldiers on Horseback, 1966; The Image Makers, 1967; Helicopter Pilot, 1967; Road Racer, 1967; Bryans' Dog, 1967; Hunger for Racing, 1967; Air Evac, 1967; Fastest Funny Car., 1967; Grand Prix Racing, 1968; Orders to Vietnam, 1968; Maverick on the Mound, 1968; Redline 7100, 1969; Stop and Search, 1969; Up to the Quarterdeck, 1969; The Wheel of a Fast Car, 1969; Racing to Glory, 1969; Stars and Planets, 1969; Grand Prix Driver, 1969; Susan and Her Classic Convertible, 1970; Yankee Boy, 1970; Marty and the Micro-Midgets, 1970; Fast and Smart, 1971; Moving West on 122, 1971; The 12-Cylinder Screamer, 1971; Crazy to Race, 1971; Drag Race Driver, 1971; My Father's Quite a Guy, 1971; Return to Racing, 1971; Wheels and Pistons, 1971; The High Wind, 1971; Flying Army, 1971; Gestern Wir Ich Noch Allein, 1971; Racing Mechanic, 1971; The Sex Traveller, 1971; Flat Out, 1971; Long Ride on a Cycle, 1972; Team Racer, 1972; Dateline: Talladega, 1972; the Race Driver, 1972; the Narc, 1972; Sky Jacked, 1972. Home: PO Drawer Al Fairhope AL 36532 Office: care Paul R Reynolds Inc 599 Fifth Av New York City NY 10017

BUTTON, ROBERT YOUNG, state govt. ofcl.; b. Culpeper, Va., Nov. 2, 1899; s. John Young and Margaret Agnes (Duncan) B.; LL.B., U. Va., 1922; m. Kathleen Mary Antoinette Cheape, Aug. 20, 1931; children— Kathleen Margaret (Mrs. L. H. Ginn), Robert Young. Admitted to Va. bar, 1922; practice in Culpeper, 1922-61, 70-—; atty. gen. Va., 1962-70; Dir. Mut. Fire Ins. Co. Loudoun, Mchts. Grocery Co. Culpeper, 2d Nat. Bank Culpeper, Central Hardware Co. Mem. Va. Commns. Pub. Edn., 1954, 59, Potomac River Commn., 1958, Va. Bd. Edn., 1945-60, Va. Parole Bd., 1942-45. Mem. Va. Senate from 27th Dist., 1946-61. Trustee Jamestown Corp. Fellow Am. Coll. Trial Lawyers, Am. Judicature Soc., Va. State Bar (council 1950-56). Am., Va., Richmond City bar assns. Democrat. Baptist. Mason. Rotarian. Club: Commonwealth (Richmond). Home: Culpeper VA 22701 Office: 139 W Davis St Culpeper VA 22701

BUTTON, WILLIAM GARLAND, utility co. exec.; b. McKinney, Tex., Dec. 1, 1918; s. Augusta Garland and Verba (Jessee) B.; B.S., E. Tex. State U., 1938; postgrad. U. Tex., 1939, 42; m. Margaret Miller, June 1, 1942; children—Betty Jo, Robert and William (twins). Tchr. adminstrn. Lindale (Tex.) High Sch., 1938-41; head dept. bus. adminstrn., sr. counselor Gladewater (Tex.) High Sch., 1941-44; plant accountant Tex. Telephone Co., Sherman, Tex., 1944-45; clk.-asst. v.p. Tex. Power & Light Co., Dallas, 1945-54, Taylor dist. mgr., 1954-55, So. div. mgr., Waco, 1955-61, Eastern div. mgr., Tyler, 1961-64, dir. indsl. devel., Dallas, 1964-66, gen. mgr. operations, Dallas, 1966-67, v.p. in charge operations, 1967-—. Chmn. bd. regents E. Tex. State U. Mem. Taylor C. of C., Inter-Univ. Council Dallas, S.A.R., Council Governing Bds. State U. Lambda Chi Alpha. Episcopalian (vestryman, sr. warden). Mason (Shriner). Rotarian. Home: 2121 Abshire Lane Dallas TX 75228 Office: 1511 Bryan St Dallas TX 75222.

BUTTS, JAMES ALLEN, physician; b. Gainesville, Ga., July 6, 1936; s. Hubert L. and Mary Louise (Starr) B.; M.D., Emory U., 1960, postgrad., 1960-61; m. Wynelle Lowery, Sept. 3, 1960; children—James Allen, Lawrence Eugene, Katherine Louise. Resident physician Atlanta VA Hosp., 1963-65; splty. tng. internal medicine Emory U. and Atlanta VA Hosps., 1963-65; fellow hematology and oncology Emory U. Hosp., Atlanta, 1965-66; practice medicine, specializing in internal medicine and hematology, Gainesville, Ga., 1966-—; mem. staff Hall County Hosp., Gainesville, chief med. service, 1971-—. Served with USPHS, 1961-63. Diplomate Am. Bd. Internal Medicine. Mem. A.M.A., A.C.P. (asso. mem.), Am. Soc. Hematology, Am. Heart Assn., Med. Assn. Ga. Home: 1732 Valley Rd Gainesville GA 30501 Office: 1114 Vine St Gainesville GA 30501

BUTTS, JOSEPH GRIZZARD, lawyer; b. Roanoke Rapids, N.C., Mar. 11, 1912; s. Joseph G. and Cecil (Feild) B.; J.D., George Washington U., 1938; m. Ruth Harrison, Dec. 28, 1935; children—Joseph Allan, Richard Everard, Ruth Ann (Mrs. Michael Cornwell). Admitted to D.C. bar, 1939; chief clk. com. elections U.S. Ho. of Reps., 1937-39; adminstrv. asst. to U.S. Congressman John H. Kerr, 1939-44; asso. atty. Gall, Lane & Powell, Washington, 1944-59; counsel Am. Enterprise Inst. Pub. Policy Research, Washington, 1959-—, dir. legislative analysis, 1961-—, sec., 1962-—. Mem. Am. Bar Assn., Bar Assn. D.C., Fed. Bar Assn. Author: (with Thomas F. Johnson, James R. Morris) Renewing America's Cities, 1962. Contbr. articles to profl. jours. Home: 3001 Veazey Terrace NW Washington DC 20008 Office: 1150 17th St NW Washington DC 20036

BUTTS, ULYS RENEAU, engr.; b. Miami, Ariz., Sept. 12, 1918; s. Ulysses Reneau and Zula Beatrice (Jones) B.; student Kilgore (Tex.) Jr. Coll., 1937-39, U. Ark., 1939-40, B.S. in Mech. Engring., U. Houston, 1950; m. Evelyn Glenora Turner, Feb. 19, 1955; 1 son, Richard Alan. Mech. engr. Ellington AFB, 1951-54; mech. engr. pub. works dept. U.S. Naval Air Sta., Corpus Christi, Tex. 1954-55; engring. div. dir., 1955-—. Partner, Turner's Tall Fashions. Mem. Nat., Tex. socs. profl. engrs., Soc. Am. Mil. Engrs. Methodist. Home: 526 Catalina Pl Corpus Christi TX 78411 Office: US Naval Air Station Corpus Christi TX 78419

BUTZNER, JOHN DECKER, JR., U.S. circuit judge; b. Scranton, Pa., Oct. 2, 1917; s. John Decker and Bess Mary (Robison) B.; B.A., U. Scranton 1939; LL.B., U. Va., 1941; m. Viola Eleanor Peterson, May 25, 1946; 1 son, John Decker III. Admitted to Va. bar, 1941; practiced in Fredericksburg, 1941-58; judge 15th and 39th Jud. Circuit of Va., 1958-62; U.S. dist. judge Eastern Dist. Va., 1962-67; U.S. circuit judge 4th Circuit, 1967-—. Served with USAAF, 1942-45. Home: 5507 Dorchester Rd Richmond VA 23225 Office: PO Box 2188 Richmond VA 23217

BUXBAUM, MARTIN, poet; b. Richmond, Va., June 27, 1912; s. David and Sadie (McGuffin) Noll; student Columbia Tech. Coll., 1934-38; m. Alice Lee Lyons, Sept. 4, 1938; children—Joan (Mrs. Robert Galope), Alice (Mrs. Daniel Dick), Rosemary (Mrs. Samuel D. Redding), Roberta (Mrs. Daniel Walker), Martha (Mrs. Thomas Newpher), Kathleen, Martin, William. Editor, Hechinger Co., Washington, 1933-38; timekeeper Diamond Constrn. Co., Washington, 1938-39; free lance writer, photographer, 1939-41; editor mags. Engring. and Research Corp., Riverdale, Md., 1941-45, So. Dairies, Inc., Washington, 1945-53; became editor Table Talk, Marriott Corp., Washington, 1953, also dir. communications. Recipient George Washington Medal of Honor, 1964, 71; named Poet of Year, State of Md., 1967; Syracuse U. established Martin Buxbaum Manuscript Collection, 1960; Lizette Woodward Reese Poetry award Md. Poetry Soc., 1969; named Ky. col., 1971. Mem. Internat. Platform Assn., Fraternal Order Police, Md. Poetry Soc. Author: (poetry) Rivers of Thought, 1958, The Underside of Heaven, 1963; Table Talk for Family Fun, 1964; The Unsung, 1964, vol. II, 1965; The Unbroken Circle, 1964; Whispers in the Wind, 1966; Around Our House, 1968; Once Upon a Dream (poetry), 1970. Home: 7819 Custer Rd Bethesda MD 20014 Office: 5161 River Rd Washington DC 20016

BUYCK, FRANCES REEDY, civic leader; b. Columbia, S.C., Apr. 27, 1938; d. Francis Crittendon and Rose (Stroman) Reedy; B.A., Converse Coll., 1960; M.B.A., U. S.C., 1962; m. William O. Buyck, Aug. 30, 1967; 1 dau., Rose Reedy. Mgr. gen. office First Nat. Bank of S.C., Columbia, 1962-64, personnel asst., 1964-66; office mgr., tchr. Wade Hampton Acad., Orangeburg, S.C., 1967-68; dean Sch. Bus., Orangeburg-Calhoun Tech. Edn. Center, 1968-70; dir. Bank of Clarendon, Manning. Chmn. Orangeburg March of Dimes, 1972; mem. Orangeburg Jr. Service League, 1970-—, mem. exec. bd., 1972-—; chmn. S.C. Rose Festival Rose Show, 1972, Exhibited group art shows in Manning, Summerton, Columbia, Greenville and Spartanburg, S.C. Mem. D.A.R., Am. Legion Aux. (girl's state counsellor 1961, 71, bus. mgr. 1972), Converse Coll. Alumnae Assn. (pres. Orangeburg 1967), Am. Assn. U. Women, Garden Club S.C. (treas. 1969-71, rec. sec. 1971-73). Clubs: Mid-Carolina Gun (sec-treas. 1968-69); Orangeburg Garden (pres. 1972). Address: 1035 Middleton St Orangeburg SC 29115

BUZZELL, DONALD ALAN, assn. exec.; b. Englewood, N.J., Jan. 25, 1927; s. Dow Alan and Grace Helen (Blomquist) B.; B.S. in Engring., George Washington U., 1949; m. Betty Mae Smith, June 21, 1945; children—Donald, Dow Stephen, Kathy Elizabeth. Design engr. U.S. Army Corps Engrs., Seattle, 1949-51, research project engr., Ft. Belvoir, Va., 1951-53; div. mgr. Asso. Gen. Contractors, Washington, 1953-61; exec. dir. Cons. Engrs. Council, Washington, 1961-—. Served with USNR, 1943-45. Registered profl. engr., Va. Mem. Soc. Am. Mil. Engrs., Am. Soc. C.E., Am. Pub. Works Assn., Am. Soc. Assn. Execs. (key award 1968). Home: 507 N Livingston St Arlington VA 22203 Office: 1155 15th St NW Washington DC 20005

BYBEE, WILLIAM CECIL, accountant; b. Idabel, Okla., Aug. 11, 1933; s. William J.B. and Mary Lula (Watts) B.; student Tex. Wesleyan Coll., 1950-51, San Antonio Coll., 1955-56; B.B.A., Tex. Technol. Coll., 1958; m. Helen Joyce Hollowell, Nov. 6, 1954; children—Luretta, Laura Sue. With Price Waterhouse & Co., Houston, 1958-65, sr. accountant, 1962-65; controller Granite Constrn. Co., Houston, 1965-66; partner Grimland & Bybee, C.P.A.'s, Midland, Tex., 1966-68, Main Lafrentz & Co., Midland, 1968-—. Pres. W. Tex. chpt. Arthritis Found., 1971-72. Bd. dirs. Midland County United Fund, 1971-—, treas., 1972. Served with AUS, 1953-55. C.P.A., Tex. Mem. Am. Inst. C.P.A.'s, Tex. Soc. C.P.A.'s, Midland C. of C. (treas. 1972, dir. 1972-—), Permian Basin Chpt. C.P.A.'s (profl. devel. dir. 1968-69). Methodist (steward, mem. finance commn. 1966-68). Rotarian (treas. 1969-70, dir.). Home: 3302 Camarie St Midland TX 79701 Office: Wilkinson-Foster Bldg Midland TX 79701

BYCK, MARY HELEN, mem. Democratic Nat. Com.; b. Louisville, June 28, 1907; d. Cyrus Lincoln and Alice Belle (Goldsmith) Adler; A.B. Vassar Coll., 1928; L.H.D., Catherine Spalding Coll., Louisville, 1961; m. Dann C. Byck, June 27, 1931 (dec. 1960); children—Lucy (Mrs. Jack Shapero), Betty (Mrs. Stephen N. Goodman), Dann C. Pres. Bych Bros. & Co., 1942-45, 60-64, chmn. bd., chief exec. officer, 1964-—. Mem. Ky. Democratic Central Com., 1964-—; Dem. mem. Conv. Center Bd., 1962-—; mem. Dem. Nat. Com. for Ky., 1964-—; chmn. primary and gubernatorial race Jefferson County, spring and fall, 1963, senate and presdl. race, 1964, woman's chmn. campaigns spring and fall, 1965; mem. Ky. Woman's Adv. Com., gubernatorial race, 1963; mem. adv. com. City/County Dem Com., 1962-—. Mem. exec. com. Louisville Central Area, 1962-—, Gov. Ky. Commn. Human Rights, 1959-—; mem. Coordinating Com. Jefferson County and Louisville Schs., 1964-—. Pres. Louisville Orch., 1949-56, life mem., 1956-—; bd. overseers U. Louisville, 1960-—; bd. counselors Catherine Spalding Coll., 1961-—; exec. bd. com. Louisville Fund, 1956-—; disbursing com. Louisville found., 1959-—. Recipient Citizen Laureate award Younger Women's Club Louisville, 1963; Blanche C. Ottenheimer award Jewish Community Center, 1964; Giovanni Martini award Bellarmine Coll., 1966; Citizen of Yr. award Advt. Club, 1967; award for outstanding contbn. to community in politics, edn. and culture Nat. Conf. Christians and Jews, 1967. Home: 332 Penruth Av Louisville KY 40207 Office: 532 S 4th St Louisville KY 40202

BYERS, HORACE ROBERT, meteorologist; b. Seattle, Mar. 12, 1906; s. Charles Hopkins and Harriet (Ensminger) B.; A.B., U. Cal., 1929 S.M., Mass. Inst. Tech., 1932, Sc.D., 1935; m. Frances Isabel Clark, Oct. 6, 1927; 1 dau., Henrietta Louise (Mrs. T.W. Billhorn). With Scripps Instn. Oceanography, 1932-33; instr. meteorology Transcontinental & Western Air Inc., Kansas City, Mo., 1932-34; meteorologist U.S. Weather Bur., Washington, 1935-40; asso. prof. meteorology U. Chgo., 1940-44, prof., 1944-65, chmn. dept. meteorology, 1948-60; dean Coll. Geoscis., Tex. A. and M. U., College Station, 1965-68, acad. v.p., 1968-71, Distinguished prof. meteorology, 1965-—; dir. Thunderstorm Project, 1945-49; cons. U.S. Weather Bur., 1954-62. Chmn. dir. Gulf Universities Research Corp., 1965-71. Mem. subcom. on meteorol. problems NACA, 1948-59; trustee U. Corp. for Atmospheric Research, 1960-69, chmn. bd. trustees, 1962-64. Recipient Robert M. Losey award Inst. Aero. Scis., 1941; award of merit Chgo. Tech. Socs. Council 1959. Fellow Am. Geophys. Union, Am. Meteorol. Soc. (pres. 1952-53, Charles F. Brooks award 1960, Award of Recognition 1972); mem. A.A.A.S., Mt. Washington Obs. Assn., Am. Geog. Soc., Nat. Acad. Sci. (chmn. sect. geophysics 1966-69), Internat. Assn. Meteorology, Internat. Geophys. Union (pres. 1960-63), Sigma Xi, Phi Kappa Phi. Clubs: Warwick (Houston); Briarcrest Country (Bryan); Cosmos (Washington). Author: Synoptic and aeronautical meteorology, 1937; General Meteorology, 1944; (with R. R. Braham, Jr.) The Thunderstorm, 1950; Elements of Cloud Physics, 1965; also articles. Home: 305 Brookside Dr Bryan TX 77801 Office: Tex A & M U College Station TX 77843

BYKOSKI, LOUIS MARION, social scientist; b. Cleve., Feb. 7, 1928; s. Stanley and Theresa (Sladewski) B.; B.S., Ohio State U., 1954, M.B.A., 1955; Ph.D., Western Res. U., 1965; m. Janet Elizabeth Davis, Oct. 15, 1955; children—Mark, Karen. Trainee employee relations program Gen. Electric Co., Ft. Wayne, Ind., Conneaut, O. and Schenectady, 1955-58, specialist personnel practices Knolls Atomic Power Lab., Schenectady, 1958-59, specialist personnel, orgn. and procedures, 1959-60; mgr. econ. planning program Spindletop Research Inc., Lexington, Ky., 1965-—. Adj. lectr. U. Ky. at Lexington, 1969. Served with USNR, 1946-48. Nat. Bank Cleve. Scholarship grantee, 1963-64. Mem. Assn. Am. Geographers, Am. Econ. Assn., Indsl. Relations Research Assn., Nat. Acad. Econs. and Polit. Sci., A.A.A.S., Soc. Internat. Devel., Gamma Theta Upsilon, Alpha Delta Sigma, Omicron Delta Epsilon, Beta Gamma Sigma, Pi Sigma Alpha. Home: 505 Holly Hill Dr Lexington KY 40503 Office: Iron Works Pike Lexington KY 40507

BYNUM, RALEIGH WESLEY, optometrist; b. Jacksonville, Fla., May 27, 1936; s. John Thomas and Corene (Brown) B.; student Fla. A. and M. U., 1954-56, Roosevelt U., 1956; B.S., Ill. Coll. Optometry, 1959, D.Optometry, 1960; postgrad. Trenton State Coll., 1963-64, U. Vienna Med. Sch., Austria, 1966; m. Thelmetia Yvette Argrett, Aug. 10, 1963; children—Raleigh Wesley, Zerrick Argrett, Monjya Felisha. Optometrist with Dr. Lee Mandel, 1960-62; private practice optometry, Charlotte, N.C., 1967-—. Vision cons. U.S. Mil. Induction Center, Charlotte, 1967-—; vision cons. Concentrated Employment Program, Charlotte, 1968-—, Fla. Steel Corp., Charlotte, 1969-—. Bd. dirs., pres. Bethlehem Center, Charlotte. Served to capt. AUS, 1962-67. Fellow Am. Acad. Optometry; mem. Mecklenburg County Assn. Optometrists, Nat. Optometric Assn. (editor newsletter), N.C. State Optometric Soc., Charlotte C. of C. (law enforcement com.), Am. Optometric Assn. (dir. minority recruitment So. region), Alpha Phi Omega (advisor to J.C. Smith U. chpt. 1968-—). Democrat. Baptist (pres. men's brotherhood 1968-—). Mason. Club: Toastmasters International (pres. Bavarian chpt. 1966-67). Home: 1323 Squirrel Hill Rd Charlotte NC 28213 Office: 2301 Keller Av Charlotte NC 28216

BYNUM, RAYMOND TAPLEY, band dir., educator; b. Springdale, Ark., Aug. 14, 1906; s. William Arthur and Clara (Davis)B.; A.B., Hardin Simmons U., 1926, Mus.B., 1931; student, U. Mexico, 1926; Mus.D., Oklahoma City U., 1960; m. Mary Catherine Adamson, June 8, 1934; children—Ann, Raymond, William, Mary Sue. Dr. instrumental music Abilene City Schs., 1926-46; dir. band, prof. instrumental music McMurry Coll., 1946-72, prof. emeritus, 1972-—; concert tour of Europe, 1955, Mexico City, Mexico, 1964; clinician numerous band festivals; contest judge numerous band contests. McMurry Coll. Band Hall renamed Bynum Band Hall, 1972. Mem. Tex. Music Educators' Assn. (past pres.), Am., Tex. (past pres., Tex. Bandmaster of the Year, 1967-68) bandmasters assns., Pi Beta Mu. Presbyn (elder). Mason (Shriner), Rotarian (hon., past pres.). Contbr. numerous articles mus. jours. Home: 1501 N 14th St Abilene TX 79601

BYNUM, ROBERT EUGENE, social worker; b. Wilburton, Okla., May 23, 1930; s. Turner Coleman and Clara (Boggs) B.; B.S., Oklahoma City U., 1955 M.S.W., U. Okla., 1957; m. Frances Ruth Pace, July 29, 1950; children—Genece Jo, Donna Sue. Psychiat. social worker-supr. Central State Mental Hosp., Norman, Okla., 1957-62; coordinator USPHS Nursing Home Project in Okla., 1962-65; social work cons. Okla. Dept. Health Regional Guidance Center, McAlester, Okla., 1965-67; social work cons. Okla. Dept. Health, Oklahoma City, 1967-—. Rep. from Okla., Leadership Tng. Program for Social Workers in Mental Health Field. Served with C.E., AUS, 1950-52. Mem. Acad. Certified Social Workers, Nat. Assn. Social Workers, Okla. Health and Welfare Assn. (mem. exec. bd.), Am., Okla. (pres.) pub. health assns. Home: 607 Jean-Marie Dr

Norman OK 73069 Office: 3400 N Eastern St Oklahoma City OK 73105

BYNUM, WILLIAM TURNER, physician; b. Oklahoma City, Okla., Sept. 2, 1910; s. Ernest Taylor and Maude (Shattuck) B.; B.S., U. Okla., 1932; M.B., Northwestern U., 1934, M.D., 1935; m. Pauline Green, Sept. 18, 1970; children—Turner Edward, Lincoln James. Intern, Oklahoma City Gen. Hosp., 1934, St. Anthony Hosp., 1934-35; fellow in internal medicine Cleve. Clinic Found., 1935-37; practice medicine, specializing in internal medicine and gastroenterology, Chickasha, Okla., 1937-43, Oklahoma City, 1946—; chief medicine Mercy Hosp., Oklahoma City, 1956-66; mem. attending staff Baptist, Mercy, St. Anthony hosps., Oklahoma City; cons. internal medicine Oklahoma City VA Hosp.; asso. prof. internal medicine Okla. U. Med. Sch., 1950-72. Chmn. Okla. State Alcoholism Com., 1961-68; pres. Oklahoma City Council on Alcoholism, 1962-69. Served to lt. comdr., M.C., USNR, 1943-46; PTO. NIH grantee, 1962-63. Diplomate Am. Bd. Internal Medicine. Fellow A.C.P., Am. Gastroenterology Assn. Episcopalian (mem. vestry 1952-55). Home: 6436 Brandywine Lane Oklahoma City OK 73116 Office: 510 NW 12th St Oklahoma City OK 73103

BYRD, BENJAMIN FRANKLIN, JR., surgeon, educator; b. Nashville, May 18, 1918; s. Benjamin Franklin and Ida (Brister) B.; A.B., Vanderbilt U., 1938, M.D., 1941; m. Allison Caldwell, Feb. 6, 1950; children—Benjamin Franklin III, Barney Duncan, Damon Winston, Andrew Wayne, Evelyn Brister, John W. Thomas. Intern Nashville Gen. Hosp., 1941-42, asst. resident, 1942; asst. resident Vanderbilt U. Hosp., 1945-47, resident, 1947-48; practice medicine specializing in surgery, Nashville, 1948—; chief surgery St. Thomas Hosp.; mem. staff Baptist Hosp., VA Regional Hosp.; instr. surgery Vanderbilt U., Nashville, 1947-59, asso. clin. prof. surgery, 1958-63, clin. prof. surgery, 1963—; asso. clin. prof. surgery Meharry Med. Coll., Nashville, 1951-69, prof. clin. surgery, 1969—. Pres., Tenn. div. Am. Cancer Soc., 1963—, nat. bd. dirs., 1965—, nat. exec. com., 1970—; pres., mem. exec. bd. Tenn. Bot. Gardens and Fine Arts Center; pres. M.B.A. Fathers Club. Bd. trustees Sr. Citizens; bd. dirs. Children's Museum. Served to lt. col. MC, AUS, 1941-45. Decorated Bronze Star with oak leaf cluster, Silver Star, Purple Heart. Fellow A.C.S. (chmn. commn. on cancer); mem. Am. Surg. Assn., So. Surg. Assn., Am. Thyroid Assn., Nashville Surg. Soc. (pres. 1962—), James Ewing Soc., Tenn. (mem. council), So. (mem. council) med. assns., Southeastern Surg. Congress (mem. council, pres. 1968-69), Nashville C. of C. (mem. health and hosp. coms. bd. govs., v.p. 1970), Nashville Exchange Club (pres. 1963—), Sigma Xi. Home: 400 Ellendale Dr Nashville TN 37205 Office: 2122 W End Av Nashville TN 31203

BYRD, CHESTER LAMAR, air cargo equipment co. exec.; b. Oklahoma City, Okla., Oct. 4, 1936; s. Hubert Joe and Lottie Owana (Thompson) B.; B.S. in M.E., U. Okla., 1958; m. Sandra Puryear, Aug. 15, 1957; children—Rebecca Shell, Matthew Lamar, Wesley Allen. Maintenance engr. Union Carbide Chems., Texas City, Tex., 1961-63; sr. engr. Am. Airlines, Tulsa, 1963-66; with Brownline div. Tripair Industries, Los Angeles, 1966-67; sr. engr. Am. Airlines, Tulsa, 1967-69; v.p. prodn. and engring. Air Cargo Equipment Corp., Tulsa, 1969—. Served with AUS, 1959-61. Rotarian. Patentee plastic cargo container, crane guidance system, container ship loading. Home: 6778 S 71st St E Av Tulsa OK 74133 Office: 5555 S Garnett Rd Tulsa OK 74145

BYRD, CONLEY F., judge; b. Poughkeepsie, Ark., Jan. 14, 1925; s. Robert Lee and Artie (Barnes) B.; LL.M., U. Ark., 1950; m. Frances Hardin, Sept. 4, 1949; children—Conley, Susan, J. Paul. Asst. atty. Ark. Dept. Revenue, 1952; reporter Supreme Ct., 1954-60; law clk. judge U.S. Dist. Ct., 1963-65; formerly practice law, asso. William R. Butler and Omar Greene, Little Rock; now asso. justice Supreme Ct., Little Rock. Served with USNR. Home: PO Box 61 Redfield AR 72132 Office: Justice Bldg Little Rock AR 72201

BYRD, DAVID QUITMAN, clergyman; b. Brookhaven, Miss., June 14, 1922; s. David Quitman and Maude (May) B.; B.A., Miss. Coll., Clinton, 1943; B.D., So. Bapt. Theol. Sem., Louisville, 1946, Th.M., 1947, Th.D., 1949; m. Floriene Williams, June 24, 1945; children—John Timothy, Rebecca Elizabeth, Laura Beth. Ordained to ministry Bapt. Ch., 1943; minister Bapt. chs., Harrodsburg, Ky., 1943-46, Waddy, Ky., 1947-49, Meridian, Miss., 1949-53, Jackson, Tenn., 1953—. Pres., Tenn. Bapt. Conv.; bd. dirs. YMCA, Boys Club Am.; trustee, bd. dirs. Jackson Mental Health Council; trustee Union U., Jackson, Annuity Bd. So. Bapt. Conv.; bd. govs. Jackson Coliseum. Recipient City Maker award Jackson C. of C., 1969. Home: 50 Maryland Dr Jackson TN 38301 Office: 259 W Deaderick St Jackson TN 38301

BYRD, DOROTHY FAY, educator; b. Brownwood, Tex., Dec. 23, 1927; d. Earl D. and Fay (Alexander) Byrd; B.A. in Econs., Tex. Woman's U., 1949, M.A. in Econs., 1966; student U. Colo., Hardin-Simmons U., Eastern N.M. U., Colo. State Coll.; Ph.D., N. Tex. State U. Tchr. pub. schs., Hobbs, N.M., 1949-50, Andrews, Tex., 1950-57; real estate broker, Andrews, 1954-57; city sec., tax assessor-collector City of Andrews, 1957-66; teaching fellow Coll. Bus. Adminstrn., N. Tex. State U., Denton, 1967, 69-70, research asst. div. mgmt., 1969, research asso. Univ. Center Community Services, 1968-69, projects coordinator, 1968-70; dir. Univ. Center Community Services, N. Tex. State U., 1970—; pvt. bus. cons. govtl. systems. State del. White House Conf. on Aging, 1971. Mem. Tex. Assn. Community Services and Continuing Edn. (sec., dir.), Am. Assn. U. Women (dir. Andrews 1958-62, v.p. 1958-60; pres. 1964-65), Andrews Classroom Tchrs. Assn. (founding pres. 1955), Bus. and Profl. Women's Clubs, Assn. City Clks. and Secs. Tex. (sec.-treas. 1960-63, v.p. 1963-64, pres. 1964-65), Am. Acad. Polit. and Social Sci., Tex. Assn. Assessing Officers (dir. 1961-63), Am. Soc. Pub. Adminstrn., Sigma Iota Epsilon, Pi Sigma Alpha. Contbr. articles profl. jours. Editor: Municipal Matrix. Episcopalian. Home: 1824 Ruddell Denton TX 76201 Office: 1510 Maple St Denton TX 76201

BYRD, GRETCHEN THOMSON (MRS. HARRY FLOOD BYRD, JR.), wife Senator of Va.; b. New Orleans, Dec. 27, 1917; d. Paul J. and Gretchen (Bigelow) Thomson; m. Harry Flood Byrd, Jr. (U.S. senator from Va.), Aug. 9, 1941; children—Harry Flood III, Thomas Thomson, Beverley Bigelow (Mrs. George Greenhalgh III). Home: 411 Tennyson Av Winchester VA 22601

BYRD, HAL CLIFFORD, textile co. exec.; b. Bunnlevel, N.C., Aug. 25, 1918; s. James Caleb and Melinda Anne (Hobbs) B.; B.S., N.C. State U., 1940; m. Martha Lisabeth Harris, Mar. 17, 1943; children—Hal C., Martha Lisabeth, Melinda Anne. Sales engr. trainee Saco Lowell Shops, Biddeford, Me., 1940; partner Byrd & Vermont, Real Estate & Ins. Co., Spartanburg, S.C., 1946-48; vice pres. purchasing agt. Deering Milliken Service Corp., Spartanburg, S.C., 1948—. Vice chmn. Spartanburg County Devel. Commn., 1960—. Chmn. S.C. Republican Finance Com., 1966-69, 70-72; mem. Nat. Rep. Finance Com. Trustee, Spartanburg Day Sch. Served to maj. AUS, 1940-45. Mem. Phi Kappa Tau, Phi Psi, Spartanburg C. of C. (dir. 1969—), S.C. C. of C. (dir. 1964-69). Clubs: Piedmont, Spartanburg Country, Cotillion and Beaux Arts. Home: 1009 Glendalyn Circle Spartanburg SC 29302, Office: PO Box 1926 Iron Ore Rd Spartanburg SC 29301

BYRD, HARRY FLOOD, JR., newspaper editor, U.S. senator; b. Winchester, Va., Dec. 20,, 1914; s. Harry F. and Anne Douglas (Beverley) B.; student Va. Mil. Inst., 1931-33, U. Va., 1933-35; numerous hon. degrees; m. Gretchen B. Thomson, August 9, 1941; children—Harry Flood III, Thomas Thomson, Beverley Bigelow (Mrs. G. P. Greenhalgh IV). Editor Winchester (Va.) Evening Star, 1935—; pub. Harrisonburg (Va.) Daily News-Record, 1937—; pres., dir. Rockingham Pub. Co., 1946—; dir. H. F. Byrd, Inc., 1948—; dir. Asso. Press, 1950-59, 61-66, v.p., mem. exec. com.; mem. U.S. Senate from Va., 1965—; mem. Va. Senate, 1947-65, author state automatic tax reduction law. Mem. State Democratic Central Com., 1940-66. Served as lt. comdr. USNR, 1942-46, exec. officer Patrol bombing squadron, Pacific. Recipient Honor Medal Freedoms Found. Mem. V.F.W., Am. Legion. Clubs: Rotary (pres. Winchester 1940-41); Nat. Press, Army-Navy (Washington). Home: 411 Tennyson Av Winchester VA 22601 Office: Senate Office Bldg Washington DC 20510

BYRD, JOHN QUILLIAN, county ofcl.; b. Waycross, Ga., Dec. 28, 1920; s. Thomas Jefferson and Fannilu (Arrington) B.; grad. high sch.; m. Ira Kathleen Kincaid, Oct. 22, 1949; 1 son, Thomas Kincaid. Teller Comml. State Bank, Hamlet, N.C., 1939-42; accountant G.C. Lundin Co., Laurinburg, 1947-55, Paul H. Livingston, C.P.A., Laurinburg, 1955-62; county mgr. Scotland County (N.C.), Laurinburg, 1962—. Served with AUS, 1942-46. Recipient Outstanding Pres. award Optimist Club, 1964, 65. Mem. Am. Legion, V.F.W. Presbyn. Clubs: Laurinburg Optimist (pres. 1964), Scotch Meadows Country. Home: 113 Franklin Av Westwood Laurinburg NC 28352 Office: 212 Biggs St Laurinburg NC 28352

BYRD, VEDA ENGLAND WOMACK (MRS. JUSTIN S. BYRD), ednl. adminstr.; b. Ramsey, Ill., Oct. 16, 1911; d. Andrew and Edith Cline (Augustine) England; B.A., U. Tampa, 1949; M.A., U. Fla., 1952; m. Tornie Womack, May 2, 1934 (div. June 1945); m. 2d, Justin S. Byrd, Dec. 22, 1945 (dec. 1971). Tchr. elementary sch., Ill., 1930-45, Tampa, Fla., 1945-50; tchr. Bayside Sch. Physically Handicapped, Tampa, 1950-55; prin. Henderson Sch. for Educable and Elementary, Tampa, 1955-57, LaVoy Sch. Trainable Mentally Retarded, Tampa, 1957—; mem. staff MacDonald Tng. Center. Vice pres. Hillsborough Assn. Retarded Children, 1964-65. Mem. Gov.'s State Adv. Council on Mental Retardation, 1967-72, Recipient Dr. Tom Dooley humanitarian award St. Patrick's Day Assn., 1962; citation MacDonald Tng. Center, 1966. Mem. Fla. Council Exceptional Edn. (past pres.), Tampa Bay Area Chpt. Exceptional Children (past pres.), Am. Assn. U. Women, Hillsborough County Assn. Adminstrs. and Suprs. (treas.), Hillsborough Assn. Retarded Children (dir.), Nat., Fla., Tampa elementary prins. councils, Alpha Delta Kappa. Home: 113 Cedar Av Tampa FL 33606 Office: 4410 Main St Tamp FL 33607

BYRD, WILLIAM HUGH, JR., supt. schs.; b. Chireno, Tex., Oct. 6, 1921; s. William Hugh and Lola (Shippey) B.; B.S., Stephen F. Austin State Tchrs Coll., 1943; M.Ed., Stephen F. Austin State Coll., 1952; m. Dell Glazener, June 1, 1941; children—Mary (Mrs. Ken O'Grady), Anne. Band dir. Lufkin (Tex.) Ind. Sch. Dist., 1943-55, jr. high prin., 1955-61, asst. supt. schs., 1961-63; supt. schs. Mt. Pleasant (Tex.) Ind. Sch. Dist., 1963-66, Duncanville (Tex.) Ind. Sch. Dist., 1966—. Bd. dirs. A.R.C. Served with AUS, World War II. Mem. Nat. P.T.A. (life), Am., Tex. assns. sch. adminstrs., Tex. Tchrs. Assn., Duncanville C. of C., Phi Beta Mu, Phi Delta Kappa. Methodist. (steward 1963-71). Mason (32 deg., Shriner), Lion (past pres.). Home: 502 Alexander St Duncanville TX 75116

BYRNE, JOHN FRANCIS, mental health adminstr., educator; b. Northampton, Mass., Nov. 11, 1924; s. John Charles and Margaret (Costello) B.; A.B. cum laude U. Mass., 1950; Ph.D., U. Tenn., 1956; m. Maxine A. McCormack, Aug. 21, 1948; children—Steven, Timothy, Thomas, Marianne, Erin. Instr. Marquette U., Milw., 1956-57; chief psychologist Mental Health Center, Oak Ridge, Tenn., 1957-64, dir., 1964—. Mem. faculty U. Tenn., Knoxville, 1963—, prof. psychology, 1967—. Served with AUS, 1943-46. Diplomate in clin. psychology Am. Bd. Examinors. Mem. Am., Tenn. psychol. assns., Tenn. Bd. Examiners in Psychology, Sigma Xi, Phi Kappa Phi. Home: 133 N Seneca Rd Oak Ridge TN 37830 Office: 240 W Tyrone Rd Oak Ridge TN 37830

BYRNE, ROBERT LEE, educator; b. East Liverpool, O., Feb. 22, 1931; s. Robert L. and Noal (Parsons) B.; B.S., Ohio U., 1952; M.A., Kent State U., 1957; Ed.D., George Peabody Coll., 1962; m. Shirley M. Smith, Sept. 9, 1951; children—Robert L. III, Susan Ann, Colleen Anne. Tchr., Madison Sch., Hamilton, O., 1952-56, Lakeview Sch., Lorain, O., 1956-59; coordinator remedial reading Child Study Center, George Peabody Coll., 1959-60; instr. speed reading U. Tenn., 1960; dir. Reading Clinic, U. Mass., 1960-65; dir. Reading Center, Eastern Ky. U., Richmond, 1965—, dir. undergrad. research tng. program, 1967; vis. prof. Appalachian State Coll., 1964-65, Kent State U., 1970-71. Cons. Asso. Cons., Inc. Mem. Am. Edn. Research Assn., Internat. Reading Assn. (Ky. pres. 1969-70), Nat. Reading Conf., Am. Assn. U. Profs., Kappa Delta Pi, Phi Delta Kappa. Mason. Author: Remedial Reading, 1968; Dictionary Skills, vol. I, vol. II, 1967. Home: 110 Westwood Dr Richmond KY 40475

BYRNES, JAMES BERNARD, mus. dir.; b. N.Y.C., Feb. 19, 1917; s. Patrick J. A. and Janet E. (Geiger) B.; student Nat. Acad. Design, 1936-38, Am. Artist Sch., 1938-40, Art Students League, 1940-42, U. Perugia (Italy), 1951, Istituto Meschini, Rome, 1952; m. Barbara A. Cecil, June 10, 1946; 1 son, Ronald L. Art tchr. mus. activity program N.Y.C. Bd. Edn., 1936-40; indsl. designer Michael Saphier Assos., N.Y.C., 1940-42; docent Los Angeles County Mus., 1946-47, asso. curator modern contemporary art, 1947-48, curator, asst. to dir., 1948-53; dir. Colo. Springs Fine Arts Center, 1954-55; asso. dir. N.C. Mus. Art, 1956-58, acting dir., 1958-60; dir., 1960-62; dir. New Orleans Mus. of Art, 1962—. Vis. lectr. U. Fla., fall 1961, Newcomb Coll., Tulane U., spring 1963; art cons. Decorated Knight Order Leopold II (Belgium). Mem. Western (sec.-treas. 1955), S.E. (council) assns. art mus. dirs., Am. Soc. Aesthetics, Am. Assn. Museums, Am. Fedn. Arts, American Institute of Designers (hon.). Author: Masterpieces of Art, W. R. Valentiner Memorial, 1959; Tobacco and Smoking in Art, 1960; Fates de la Palette, 1963: Edgar Degas, His Family and Friends in New Orleans, 1965; Odyssey of an Art Collector, 1966; Arts of Ancient and Modern Latin America, 1968; also numerous mus. catalogs. Home: 1243 Bourbon St New Orleans LA 70116 Office: New Orleans Mus of Art City Park New Orleans LA 70119

BYRNSIDE, OSCAR JEHU, JR., assn. exec.; b. Huntington, W.Va., June 2, 1935; s. Oscar Jehu and Eula (Bayliss) B.; B.S., Concord Coll., 1960; M.S., Va. Poly. Inst. and State U., 1961; Ph.D., Ohio State U., 1968; m. Patricia Ann Oxley, Aug. 1, 1954; children—Barbara Ann, Brenda Gail, Bethany Lynne. Tchr. bus. Kanawha County (W.Va.) Schs., 1960; coordinator vocational office tng. Danville (Va.) Pub. Schs., 1961-63; asst. prof. bus. edn., dir. data processing center Longwood Coll., Farmville, Va., 1963-65; state dir. bus., office and distributive edn. W.Va. Bd. Edn., 1965-66; cons., research asso. program evaluation Center for Research and Leadership Devel. in Vocational and Tech. Edn., Ohio State U., 1966-68; exec. dir. Nat. Bus. Edn. Assn., Washington, 1968—, also Future Bus. Leaders Am. Vis. prof. Va. Poly. Inst. and State U., Catholic U. Am.; cons. Ednl. Testing Service, Princeton, N.J.; bus. edn. equipment cons. for edn. projects World Bank; mgmt. cons. to bus. and industry. Served with USMCR, 1953-56. Recipient award Acad. Faculty of Vocational and Tech. Edn., Ohio State U., 1970. Mem. N.E.A., Am. Vocational Assn., Nat. Bus. Edn. Assn., Am. Assn. Sch. Adminstrs., Nat. Assn. Secondary Sch. Prins., Assn. Supervision Curriculum Devel., Internat. Soc. Bus. Edn., Blue Key (bd. dirs.), Phi Kappa Phi, Phi Delta Kappa, Pi Omega Pi, Delta Pi Epsilon, Kappa Delta Pi. Editor: Bus. Edn. Forum, 1968—. Home: 8208 Donset Dr Springfield VA 22152 Office: 1201 16th St NW Washington DC 20036

BYRUM, ALBERT GASKINS, JR., orthodontist; b. Edenton, N.C., Apr. 22, 1937; s. Albert G. and Ruth (Pruden) B.; B.S., U. N.C., 1959, D.D.S., 1963; M.S., Fairleigh Dickinson U., 1970; m. Patricia Beams, Aug. 23, 1958; children—Elizabeth Holt, Martha Ruth, Albert G. III. Pvt. practice dentistry, Martinsville, Va., 1966-70; pvt. practice orthodontics, 1970—. Served to capt. USAF, 1963-66. Mem. Va., Patrick Henry (sec. 1970) dental socs., Am. Assn. Orthodontists, Zeta Psi, Delta Sigma Delta. Club: Chatmoss Country. Author: Evaluation of Anterior-Posterior and Vertical Skeletal Change Vs. Dental Change in Rapid Palatal Expansion Cases as studied by Latoral Cephalograms, 1970. Home: 906 Hunting Ridge Rd Martinsville VA 24112 Office: Box 3271 Martinsville VA 24112

BYRUM, WOODROW ROBERT, educator; b. Phoebus, Va., Jan. 24, 1914; s. Robert L. and Mattie A. (Clark) B.; student William and Mary Coll., 1933-34; B.S., Med. Coll. Va., 1937; Ph.D., Ohio State U., 1947; m. Mary Cecelia Collier, Apr. 11, 1939; children—Linda Susan (Mrs. David W. Naumann), Nancy Lou (Mrs. Hill Gresham Morgan Jr.), Beverly Ann. Pharmacist Richmond, Va., 1937-41; asst. prof. U. Ga., Athens, 1945-46, Ohio State U., 1946-47; asso. prof. pharmacology U. Ariz., Tucson, 1948-50, U. Ga., 1950-52, dir., dean Sch. of Pharmacy, Samford U., Birmingham, Ala., 1952—. Mem. Am., Ala. pharm. assns., Birmingham Retail Druggists Assn., Soc. Ala. Hosp. Pharmacists, Am. Soc. Pharmacognosy, Am. Inst. History of Pharmacy, Am. Assn. Colls. Pharmacy, Omicron Delta Kappa, Rho Chi, Kappa Psi, Sigma Xi. Rotarian. Contbr. articles in field to profl. jours. Home: 2204 Lester Lane Birmingham AL 35226

BYWATERS, JERRY, artist, educator; b. Paris, Tex., 1906; s. Porter A. and Hattie (Williamson) B.; B.A., So. Meth. U., 1927; student Art Students League, N.Y.C., 1927; studied in Mexico, Europe; m. Mary McLarry, Nov. 3, 1930; children—Jerry, Dick. Prof. art So. Meth. U., 1936—, head art dept., 1965-67; dir. Pollack Galleries, 1965-71; dir. Dallas Museum of Fine Arts, 1943-64; works exhibited Met. Mus., San Francisco Mus., others; painter, printmaker, lectr. art, 1930—; art critic Dallas News, 1933-39; art editor Southwest Review, Dallas, 1950-60. Home: 3625 Amherst Dallas TX Office: Southern Methodist U. Dallas TX

CABALLERO, EMILIO, educator; b. Newark, July 4, 1919; s. Juan and Magdalena Caballero; A.A., Amarillo Coll., 1940; B.A., W. Tex. State U., 1942; M.A., Columbia, 1949, Ph.D (Agnes Russell Center fellow), 1955; m. Mary Elizabeth Ready, Dec. 31, 1941; children—Lou Ann (Mrs. Gary L. Shell), Charles Thomas. With W. Tex. State U., Canyon, 1949—, prof., head dept., 1955—; spl. art cons. Amarillo pub. schs., 1947-49; executed mosaic mural Midland (Tex.) Pub. Library, 1959; executed enamel on copper mural Municipal Bldg., Amarillo, 1966, mobile, enamel copper mural Bank of Southwest, Midland, 1967; represented in pvt., pub. permanent collections. Served with Inf., AUS, 1942-46; ETO, PTO. Recipient Excellence in Teaching award W. Tex. State U., 1972. Fellow Royal Soc. Art Gt. Britain; mem. Tex. Tchrs. Assn., Llano Estacado Heritage (charter), Am. Watercolor Soc., Soc. Archtl. Historians, Lubbock Art Assn., Tex. Fine Arts Assn., Am. Art Therapy Assn., Phi Delta Kappa Tex. Assn. Sch. Adminstrs., Tex. Assn. Coll. Tchrs. Home: Box 96 West Tex Sta Canyon TX 79015

CABANISS, CHARLES DAVIS, lawyer; b. Birmingham, Ala., Feb. 5, 1927; s. Walter Marcus and Inez (Eaton) C.; B.A. in Liberal Arts, Tex. A. and M. Coll., 1950; J.D., U. Tex., 1955; m. Mary Kathryn Landers, July 29, 1961; children—Kevin Charles, Kristin. Admitted to Tex. bar, 1955; asst. to Tex. legislator, Austin, 1955; news reporter The Garland (Tex.) Daily News, 1955; asst. dist. atty., Dallas County, 1955-58, asst. atty. gen. Tex., Austin, 1959-60; practiced in Dallas and Garland, 1960-62; editor Tex. Mesquiter, Mesquite, 1960-62; asst. U.S. atty. No. Dist. of Tex., 1962—. Bd. dirs. N. Tex. Municipal Water Dist.; bd. dirs. Delta Theta Phi Ednl. Found., sec.-treas., 1960-61; alternate mem. Dallas-Ft. Worth Fed. Exec. Bd.; del. Nat. Jr. Bar Conf., 1960-61; adv. bd. Garland Parks and Recreation Dept. Served to 1st lt. AUS, 1945-47; 50-52. Decorated Bronze Star, Purple Heart. Mem. Am., Tex., Travis County, Dallas, Fed. (v.p. 5th circuit 1967-69, pres. Dallas 1970-71) bar assns., Dallas (pres. 1958), Austin (bd. dirs. 1959-60) jr. bar assns., Dallas Fed. Bus. Assn. (dir. 1968-71), Austin Alumni (senate dean 1959-60), Dallas Alumni Senate, Delta Theta Phi, Phi Kappa Phi, Phi Eta Sigma, Sigma Delta Chi. Democrat. Clubs: Kiwanis (pres. 1957-58, chmn. div. officers council 1958), Texas A. and M. (local pres. 1957-58) (Garland). Home: 9611 Trailview Dr Dallas TX 75238 Office: 16 G 28 US Courthouse Dallas TX 75202

CABBAGE, JOHN TAYLOR, petrochem. co. exec.; b. Tuskahoma, Okla., Dec. 16, 1916; s. John E. and Eva (Taylor) C,; B.S. in Chem. Engring., Okla. State U., 1939; m. Opal Sudheimer, Oct. 4, 1941; children—Mary Lynn, John Philip. With Phillips Petroleum Co., 1941—, supervising process engr., 1948-54, project engr., Bartlesville, Okla., 1955-66, tech. supt. plant, Guayama, P.R., 1966-70, mgr. project devel., 1970—. Registered profl. engr., Okla. Mem. Nat. Assn. Profl. Engrs. Baptist. Patentee in field. Home: 6 Cautino Guayama PR 00654 Office: GPO 4129 San Juan PR 00936

CABELL, EARLE, congressman, dairy products, food co. exec.; b. nr. Dallas, Oct. 27, 1906; s. Ben E. and Sadie (Pearre) C.; student Tex. A. and M. Coll., So. Meth. U.; m. Elizabeth Holder, Feb. 22, 1932; children—Elizabeth Lee (Mrs. Pulley), Earl, Jr. With Cabell's, Inc., 1932—, successively sec. treas., exec. v.p., 1932-52, pres., 1952—, chmn. bd., 1961—; chmn. Cabell Dairies, Dallas; mem. 89th to 92d congresses from 5th dist. Tex. Pres. Dallas Crime Commn., 1954-56. Dir. Jr. Achievement; circle ten. Boy Scouts Am. Mem. Gov.'s Econ. Adv. Commn., 1954-56; sec., mem. exec. com. Tex. Law Enforcement Found.; mem. adv. bd. Tex. Indsl. Comm. Mayor City of Dallas, 1961-64. Served from capt. to col., Tex. State Guard, 1941-46. Mem. Southwestern Law Enforcement Inst. (exec. com.), E. Tex. C. of C. (past dir.), Dallas Sales Execs. Club (past pres.). Dairy Products Inst. Tex. (past pres.), Texas Mfrs. Assn. (past pres.). Dallas Salesmanship Club, Dallas C. of C. Clubs: Dallas Country, Dallas Athletic (past dir.), McKinney Lake (past pres.), City. Home: 3701 Turtle Creek Blvd Dallas TX 75219 Office: 1110 Commerce St Dallas TX 75202

CABELL, ROYAL EUBANK, JR., lawyer; b. Richmond, Va., June 25, 1923; s. Royal Eubank and Lillian Hoge (Lorraine) C.; B.A., Hampden-Sydney Coll., 1943; LL.B., U. Va., 1948; m. Kathleen Shirley Buchanan, Oct. 30, 1948; children—Royal E. III, Charles Lorraine, Kathleen. Admitted to Va. bar, 1948; mem. law firm Moncure & Cabell (formerly Cabell & Cabell), Richmond, 1948—. Dir., C.F. Sauer Co., Richmond, C & T Refinery, Inc., Richmond,

Dean Foods Co., Richmond, Owens, Minor & Bodeker, Inc., Richmond, Powers & Anderson, Inc., Richmond; pres. Dominion Leaf Tobacco Co., Inc., Richmond; chmn. bd. Commonwealth Tobacco Co., Inc., Kenbridge, Va.; pres. Sarawak Co. (1959) Sinderhian Berhad, Sarawak, Malaysia, Marks Surg. Supplies, Inc., Augusta, Ga., Va. Hauling Co., Richmond. Pres., Richmond Symphony, 1957—. Chmn. 3d Dist. Republican Com., 1956; Rep. candidate for Congress, 1956; mem. Henrico County Rep. Com., 1956—. Trustee, sec. William H., John G., Emma Scott Found., 1956; trustee Collegiate Schs., Richmond Meml. Hosp., Hanover Presbytery, Hampden-Sydney Coll.; bd. dirs. Richmond Cerebral Palsy Center. Served to lt. (j.g.) USNR, 1943-46. Mem. Am., Richmond bar assns., Va. State Bar Assn., Am. Judicature Soc., Va., Richmond chambers commerce, English Speaking Union (pres. Richmond br. 1968-70). Presbyn. (mem. joint com. Ref. Ch. in Am. and Presbyn. Ch. U.S. 1962-69). Kiwanian. Clubs: Commonwealth, Country of Virginia, Downtown (pres. 1957-58) (Richmond). Home: 510 Sleepy Hollow Rd Richmond VA 23229 Office: 921 Ross Bldg Richmond VA 23211

CABIBI, CHARLES EDMOND, lawyer, notary public; b. New Orleans, Nov. 26, 1914; s. Frank and Alice (Driscoll) C.; J.D., Loyola U., 1936; m. Dorothy McWaters, May 28, 1937; 1 son, Charles Edmond. Admitted to La. bar, 1937; practiced in La., 1937—; asst. city atty., New Orleans, 1946-60; pres. Cabibi Title Ins. Agy., Inc., 1971—; sec., L. F. Gaubert & Co., Inc., Marine Indsl. Cable Corp., Michoud Indsl. Complex, Carmel Devel. Corp. Atty., New Orleans R.R. Terminal Bd., 1950-60; bd. advisers Bank New Orleans and Trust Co.; notary pub. First Homestead & Savs. Assn., 1966—. Bd. dirs., chmn. bd., pres. St. Bernard Gen. Hosp. Mem. Am. Judicature Soc., Am., La., New Orleans bar assns. K.C. Clubs: Optimist, Young Men's Business (New Orleans). Office: Richards Bldg New Orleans LA 70112

CABLE, RHEA WATSON (MRS. JOHN L. CABLE), pianist, composer; b. Lima, O., Sept. 1; d. Albert C. and Alice May (Mankopf) Watson; student Chgo. Mus. Coll., 1906, also pvt. mus. tng.; m. John L. Cable, Dec. 9, 1910; children—Alice Mary (Mrs. Samuel P. Hayes), Davis W. Tchr., mus. coach, Lima, also Washington; founder, dir. Bach Choir, Lima. Mem. Nat. Children Am. Revolution (past v.p.), Nat. League Am. Pen Women (past v.p. Washington), D.A.R., Lima Friends Music. Clubs: Arts, Washington. Address: 117 N Washington Dr Sarasota FL 33577

CACE, JOHN STEPHAN, JR., restaurant exec.; b. New Orleans, Jan. 8, 1917; s. John and Anastasia (Evasovich) C.; student La. State U., 1933-35; m. Valerie Savony, Nov. 30, 1939; children—John Stephan III, Gerard C., Daniel G. Owner Johnny Cace's Seafood and Steak House, Longview, Tex., 1949—; dir. Longview Bank & Trust Co. Bd. dirs. United Fund. Served with USAAF, 1942-46. Named Restaurateur of Year State, Tex. Restaurant Assn., 1968, Man of the Month East Tex. C. of C., May 1967; recipient Silver Beaver award Boy Scouts of Am., 1968. Mem. Tex. Restaurant Assn. (pres. 1966-67), Longview C. of C. (pres. 1967-68), East Tex. C. of C. Roman Catholic. K.C. (4 deg.). Clubs: Pinecrest Country, Cherokee Country, Civitan (v.p. 1969) Columbus (dir. 1964-71) (Longview). Home: 13 Normandy Circle Longview TX 75601 Office: 1501 E Marshall St Longview TX 75601

CACERES, CESAR AUGUSTO, physician, scientist; b. Honduras, Apr. 9, 1927; s. Julian R. and Mariana (Culotta) C.; B.S., Georgetown U., 1949, M.D., 1953. Research, George Washington U., 1956-60, asso. prof. medicine, 1964-69, prof., chmn. dept. clin. engring., med. center, 1969—; chief med. systems devel. lab. USPHS, Washington, 1960-69. Mem. Assn. Computing Machinery, Am. Fedn. Clin. Research, Am. Pub. Health Assn., N.Y. Acad. Sci., Fed. Profl. Assn. (v.p.), Soc. Advanced Med. Systems (pres. 1969-70), Assn. Advancement Med. Instrumentation (pres. 1971-72). Author: Electronic and Computer Assisted Studies of Bio-Medical Problems, 1964; BioMedical Telemetry, 1965; The Innocent Murmur, 1966; Diagnostic Computers, 1968; Clinical Electrocardiography and Computers, 1970. Contbr. articles to profl. jours. Home: 2500 Virginia Av NW Washington DC 20037 Office: 1759 Q St NW Washington DC 20009

CADDY, MICHAEL DOUGLAS, lawyer; b. Long Beach, Cal., Mar. 23, 1938; s. Frank Edward and Tabitha (Miles) C.; B.S. in Fgn. Service, Georgetown U., 1960; J.D., N.Y. U., 1966. Admitted to D.C. bar, 1970; exec. dir. Com. on Pub. Affairs, McGraw-Edison Co., N.Y.C., 1960-61; asst. to lt. gov. N.Y., 1962-65; asst. to exec. v.p. Nat. Assn. Mfrs., N.Y.C., 1966-67; Washington liaison Gen. Foods Corp., 1968-70; practice law as mem. firm Gall, Lane, Powell & Kilcullen, Washington, 1970—. Republican County committeeman, N.Y.C., 1965-66; Trustee Robert Schuchman Meml. Found., N.Y.C. Scholar, Intercollegiate Studies Inst., 1957-59. Mem. Am., D.C. bar assns., Am. Judicature Soc., Am. Econ. Assn., Am. Acad. Polit. and Social Sci. Clubs: Union League (N.Y.C.); Georgetown, Capitol Hill, Nat. Economists, (Washington). Home: 2121 P St NW Washington DC 20037 Office: 1250 Connecticut Av NW Washington DC 20036

CADENHEAD, ALFRED PAUL, lawyer; b. LaGrange, Ga., Oct. 14, 1926; s. Roy E. and Omie (Bishop) C.; jr. coll. certificate W. Ga. Coll., 1944; LL.B., Emory U., 1949; m. Sara Davenport, Oct. 14, 1945; children— Steven Paul, David James. Admitted to Ga. bar, 1949; with firm Nall, Miller and Cadenhead and predecessors, Atlanta, 1949—, partner, 1954—; dir. various corps. Pres., Atlanta Legal Aid Soc., 1957, Met. Atlanta Mental Health Assn., 1964-65, Ga. Assn. for Mental Health, 1968. Served with AUS, 1944-46. Mem. Atlanta Bar Assn. (spl. pros. 1958-60, pres. 1970-71). Presbyn. (elder 1954—, commr. to gen. assembly 1966). Home: 6305 Riverside Dr NW Atlanta GA 30328 Office: 1500 Equitable Bldg Atlanta GA 30303

CADLE, DEAN, educator; b. Middlesboro, Ky., Jan. 16, 1920; s. David Bert and Dora (Brooks) C.; B.A., Berea Coll., 1947; postgrad. Columbia, 1946, Stanford, 1947-49, U. Kan., 1949, U. Tenn., 1951; M.A., U. Ia., 1950; M.S. in Library Sci., U. Ky., 1957; m. Jo Lee Dannel, May 28, 1952. Lit. tchr. Union Coll., Barbourville, Ky., 1950-53, Detroit Inst. Tech., 1954-55; librarian Frankfort (Ky.) Dept. Libraries, 1957-59, U. Ky., 1959-60, U. Ky. Southeast Community Coll., Cumberland, 1960-66; asso. prof., asst. librarian U. N.C., Asheville, 1966—. Winner nat. short story contest sponsored by Tomorrow mag. and Creative Age Press, 1947; Wallace Stegner Creative Writing fellow Stanford, 1947-48; short stories listed on honor roll and distinctive lists of Best Am. Short Stories anns. Mem. N.C., Southeastern library assns. Editor: High Cost of Writing, 1965, Gambit, 1950-53; faculty adviser Images, 1966—. Contbr. fiction and criticism to various mags. and jours. including Yale Rev., S.W. Rev., Tomorrow, Carolina Quar., N.M. Quar., to anthologies Stanford Short Stories, 1949, Deep Summer, 1963. Home: 30 Valle Vista Dr Asheville NC 28804

CADWALLADER, LEWIS WESTON, electric utility exec.; b. Balt., July 25, 1908; s. Edgar C. and Helen V. (King) C.; student evenings Johns Hopkins Sch. Engring., 1927-32, George Washington U. Sch. Engring., 1937-38; m. Gretchen A. Bergner, July 18, 1936; 1 son, Lewis Edgar. With Balt. Gas & Electric Co., 1927-33; with Potomac Electric Power Co., Washington, 1933—, charge power plant engring. and operation, 1948-57, v.p., 1957—. Named Engr. of Year, Washington Soc. Engrs., 1964. Registered profl. engr., Md., Va., D.C. Fellow Am. Soc. M.E.; mem. Nat. Soc. Profl. Engrs. Lutheran. Mason (32 deg., Shriner). Contbr. numerous articles on thermal pollution of rivers to profl. publs. Home: Route 3 Box 71 Turkey Foot Rd Gaithersburg MD 20760 Office: 1900 Pennsylvania Av NW Washington DC 20006

CAFFERY, PATRICK THOMSON, congressman; b. Franklin, La., July 6, 1932; s. Ralph Earl and Letitia (Decuir) C.; B.A., U. Southwestern La., 1955 J.D., La. State U., 1956; m. Anne Bercegeay, Jan. 30, 1954; children—Patrick Thomson, Kevin, Michael St. M. Partner firm Helen, Simon & Caffery, 1957, Caffery, Duhe & Davis, 1965-69; asst. dist. atty. 16th Jud. Dist. La., 1958-62; mem. 91st-92d Congresses, 3d Dist. La. Past pres. Iberia Parish United Givers Fund; mem. exec. bd. Evangeline area council Boy Scouts Am., past dist. commr. Bd. dirs. Iberia Crippled Children's Assn. Mem. La. Ho. of Reps., 1964-68. Rotarian (past pres.). Asso. mng. editor La. Law Rev., 1955-56. Home: 116 Hacker St New Iberia LA 70560 Office: Cannon Office Bldg Washington DC 20515

CAFFEY, GUY HAMILTON, JR., banker; b. Montgomery, Ala., Feb. 16, 1926; s. Guy Hamilton and Mamie Susan (Barber) C.; B.S., Samford U., 1951; grad. Stonier Sch. Banking, New Brunswick, N.J., 1963; m. Marjorie Sue Courtney, Dec. 26, 1948; children—Guy Hamilton, III, William Courtney, Mamie Susan. With Birmingham Trust Nat. Bank, 1951—, v.p., 1957-64, supr. brs., 1964-66, sr. v.p., 1966-69, pres., 1969—, also dir. Instr., Am. Inst. Banking, 1961-64; lectr. Banking Sch. South, Baton Rouge, 1965-67. Jefferson County chmn. Ala. Heart Fund, 1964; chmn. outlying div. United Appeal, 1965, chmn. met. div., 1968. Mem. Vestavia Hills Planning and Zoning Bd. Mem. met. bd. YMCA; bd. dirs. Warrior Tombigbee Devel. Assn., Nat. Council Br. Banks, Operation New Birmingham. Served with USAAF, 1944-46. Named Outstanding Young Banker of Year, Ala. Bankers Assn., 1961; recipient Distinguished Alumni award Samford U., 1967. Mem. Am. Bankers Assn. (mem. installment credit com.). Rotarian. Clubs: Relay House, Vestavia County, Country of Birmingham, The Club (Birmingham). Home: 1245 Graylynn Dr Birmingham AL 35216 Office: 112-118 N 20th St Birmingham AL 35202

CAFFEY, HORACE ROUSE, educator, agrl. researcher; b. Grenada, Miss., Mar. 24, 1929; s. Clarence Horace and Anna Belle (James) C.; B.S., Miss. State U., 1951, M.S., 1955; Ph.D., La. State U., 1959; m. Jane Claire Hall, May 31, 1954; children—Brenda Diane, Jerry Wayne, Belle Renee, Rex Hall. Agronomist Miss. Rice Growers Assn., Cleveland, Miss., 1955-57; asso. agronomist Delta Br. Expt. Sta., Miss. Agrl. Expt. Sta., Stoneville, 1958-62; asso. agronomy dept. La. State U., Baton Rouge, 1957-58, prof. agronomy, supt. rice sta., Crowley, 1962-70; asso. dir. La. Agrl. Expt. Sta., Baton Rouge, 1970—. Cons. rice prodn., marketing to various govts., govt. agys. Bd. dirs. Internat. Rice Festival. Served to 1st lt. AUS, 1951-54. Mem. C. of C. (dir.), Blue Key, Omicron Delta Kappa, Alpha Zeta, Beta Beta Beta, Gamma Sigma Delta, Phi Kappa Phi. Rotarian (pres. 1965-66). Address: La Agrl Experiment Sta PO Drawer E La State U Baton Rouge LA 70803

CAFFEY, JOHN WILLIAM, JR., physician; b. Greensboro, N.C., Sept. 29, 1927; s. John William and Pattie (Brawley) C.; A.B., Duke, 1949, M.D., 1953;; m. Clotiel F. Moody, Jan. 13, 1964; children—Katie Jean, John William III; 1 step-son, Daniel Claude McMillan. Intern, N.C. Meml. Hosp., Chapel Hill, 1953-54, resident surgery, 1954-56, resident anesthesia, 1956-58; practice medicine, specializing in anesthesiology, Jacksonville, Fla., 1958—; mem. staff Bapt. Meml., St. Vincents, Hope Haven, DuVal, St. Lukes, Riverside, Beaches hosps., Meml. Hosp. Jacksonville. Served with AUS, 1944-46. Diplomate Nat. Bd. Med. Examiners; Am. Bd. Anesthesologists. Fellow Am. Coll. Anesthesiologists; mem. A.M.A., So., Fla., Duval county med. assns., Am., Fla. socs. anesthesiologists, Internat. Research Soc. Anesthesia. Republican. Presbyn. (deacon). Home: 6224 Kellow Dr Jacksonville FL 32216 Office: 1453 Louisa St Jacksonville FL 32207

CAFFREY, WILLIAM DANIEL, lawyer; b. Morehead City, N.C., Nov. 5, 1928; s. Daniel F. and Audrey (Phillips) C.; B.S., Ind. State U., 1950; M.A., George Washington U., 1954; postgrad. U. N.C., 1954; J.D., Duke, 1958; m. Ona Faye Willis, June 3, 1952; children—William Daniel, Russell Howard. Tchr., guidance counsellor, asst. prin. Aycock Jr. High Sch., Greensboro, N.C., 1950-54; prin. David Caldwell Sch., 1954-55; admitted to N.C. bar, 1958; mem. firm Jordan, Wright, Nichols, Caffrey & Hill, and predecessor, 1958—; instr. Greensboro div. Guildford Coll., 1959—; adj. prof. law (civil trial practice and ins.) Duke Sch. Law, 1969-71. State chmn. Def. Research Inst.; chmn. United Forces for Edn.; past pres. Joyner Sch. P.T.A. Trustee Greensboro Served with USAAF, 1946-48. Mem. Am., N.C., Greensboro bar Coll. and Meth. Children's Home. assns., Am. Judicature Soc., Internat. Assn. Ins. Counsel, Duke Law Alumni Assn. (past nat. pres.), Am. Acad. Polit. and Social Sci., Acad. Polit. Sci., Order of Coif, Blue Key, Phi Delta Phi, Pi Gamma Mu, Kappa Delta Pi. Democrat. Methodist (chmn. council of ministries). Elk. Home: 2902 Round Hill Rd Greensboro NC 27408 Office: 500 W Friendly Av Bldg Greensboro NC 27402

CAGLE, WESLEY JACKSON, agrl. engr.; b. Turkey, Tex., June 12, 1930; s. Robert Nathan and Clara (Land) C.; certificate of proficiency, U. Okla., 1951; B.S. in Agrl. Engring., Tex. Tech. U., 1958; m. Sammie Pittman, Aug. 31, 1958; children—Wesley M., Bradley A. Sr. design engr. Massey Ferguson, Detroit, 1959-62; engr. Burch Plow Works, Evansville, Ind., 1962-63; project engr. J.I. Case Co., Rockford, Ill., 1963-67; chief engr. John Blue Co., Huntsville, Ala., 1967—. Served with USAF, 1951-53. Mem. Am. Soc. Agrl. Engrs. Mason. Patentee in field. Home: 9003 Shereton Rd Huntsville AL 35802 Office: PO Box 1607 Huntsville AL 35807

CAHILL, CARL HENRY, ins. co. exec.; b. Louisville, Ky., Dec. 18, 1931; s. Carl F. and Rosa (Eskridge) C.; m. Rachel Sue Whiteley, Mar. 2, 1951; children—Stephen Craig, Susan Gayle, Gregory Scott, David Carl. Regional dir. Okla. Belknap Hardware & Mfg. Co., 1953-60; div. mgr. also asst. state mgr. Nat. Investors Life Ins. Co., 1960-63; state mgr. Investors Equity Life Ins. Co., Hawaii, 1963-65; exec. v.p., dir., 1965-67; exec. v.p., dir. Investors Equity of the West, 1964-67; pres. Hark Corp., Honolulu, 1965-68; exec. v.p., dir. Great Atlantic Life Ins. Co., Orlando, Fla., 1967—; pres., chmn. bd. Southland Equity Corp., 1970—; regional v.p., dir. Nat. Investors Life Ins. Co. Ala., Nat. Investors Life Ins. Co. Ga.; eastern regional mgr. Nat. Investors Life Ins. Co. Ark.; founder, chmn. bd., pres. SEC Life Ins. Co., 1971—. Bd. dirs., treas. Mental Health Assn. Fla. Mem. Orlando, Winter Park chambers commerce, Internat. Platform Assn. Club: Sales and Marketing Execs. (Honolulu). Baptist (deacon). Home: 2920 Cove Trail Maitland FL 32751 Office: Suite 224 5600 Diplomat Circle Orlando FL 32810

CAHILL, CARL JAMES, constrn. co. exec.; b. Lamar, Colo., Feb. 1, 1921; s. Alva Sheridan and Violet Grace (Mosley) C.; student pub. schs., Topeka; m. Wanda B. Rape, Aug. 12, 1942; children—Carl James, Diana (Mrs. Richard G. Stanley). Owner, Carl J. Cahill, Inc., dirt contractor, Sonora, Tex., 1946—; owner, operator ranches, Sonora, 1958—. Served with USNR, 1943-45. Mem. Sonora C. of C. (pres. 1958), West Tex C. of C. Methodist. Mason, Lion. Clubs: Sonora Golf, Tarantella Dance, Fling Ding (Sonora). Home: E 2d St Sonora TX 76950 Office: PO Box 1154 Sonora TX 76950

CAHILL, KEVIN EDWIN, cons. geologist; b. Iowa City, Ia., Dec. 13, 1933; s. William E. and Marie (Mackey) C. B.A., U. Ia., 1955, M.S., 1962; m. Verna Joan Westendorf, Nov. 12, 1955; 1 dau., Corinne M. Geologist, Texaco, Inc., Shreveport, La., 1962-66; dist. geologist Placid Oil Co., Jackson, Miss., 1966-69; v.p., chief geologist Southeastern Exploration Co., Jackson, 1969-72; cons. geologist, 1972—. Served as 1st lt. USAF, 1956-59. Mem. Miss. Geol. Soc. (pres. 1969-70), Am. Assn. Petroleum Geologists, Am. Inst. Profl. Geologists. Home: 1115 Winnrose St Jackson MS 39211 Office: 1290 Petroleum Bldg Jackson MS 39201

CAHN, EDGAR S., lawyer, b. 1935; B.A., Swarthmore Coll.; LL.B., Yale, M.A., 1957, Ph.D., 1960; m. Jean Cahn. Admitted to D.C. bar, 1963; dir. Citizens Advocate Center, co-dean Antioch Sch. of Law, Washington. Home: 5500 39th St NW Washington DC 20015 Office: 1145 19th St NW Washington DC 20036

CAHN, JEAN CAMPER, lawyer; b. Balt., May 26, 1935; d. John Emory-Toussaint and Florine (Thompson) Camper; B.A., Swathmore Coll., 1957; postgrad. Newnham Coll., Cambridge, 1958-59; LL.B., Yale, 1961; m. Edgar S. Cahn, Mar. 22, 1957; children—Jonathan, Reuben. Admitted to D.C. bar, since practiced in Washington; founder, co-dean Antioch Sch. of Law, Washington; prof. law Howard U.; faculty, lectr. Yale Law Sch.; founder, mem. nat. adv. bd. Office Econ. Opportunity Nat. Legal Services Program; internat. atty., adviser on African affairs U.S. Dept. State; asso. counsel land acquisition div. New Haven Redevel.; Dixwell neighborhood atty. Neighborhood Services Program, Community Progress, Inc.; dir. community orgn. staff Harlem Park Renewal Area, Balt. Urban Renewal and Housing Agy.; cons. Ford Found., Neumeyer Found.; chmn. Navajo Nation; bd. dirs. Southeastern Pa. Transp. Authority, Nat. Inst. for Consumer Justice; lectr. Expt. in Internat. Living, 1966-69. Mem. ad hoc adv. com. Center for Urban Edn.; mem. adv. bd. Reginald Heber Smith Fellowship Program; bd. dirs. Martin Luther King Center for Advanced Study Medicine; chmn. bd. dirs. Inst. for Polit. Service to Soc.; mem. adv. council Urban Affairs Found. Recipient award City Council D.C., Sigma Gamma Rho award. Nat. John Hay Whitney fellow, Benneke scholar, Yale Law Sch. fellow, Md. State scholar. Mem. Nat., Am., Washington, Conn. bar assns., Yale Alumni Assn. (mem. exec. com.), Black Am. Law Students Assn. (nat. bd.). Author: Red Tape, 1968. Contbr. articles profl. jours. Home: 5500 39th St NW Washington DC 20015 Office: 1145 19th St NW Washington DC 20036

CAHN, ROBERT, journalist, govt. ofcl.; b. Seattle, Mar. 9, 1917; s. Adolph and Edna (May) Cahen; B.A., U. Wash., 1939; m. Patricia Lovelady, Dec. 8, 1951. Reporter, Seattle Star, 1939-41, Pasadena (Cal.) Star-News, 1946-48; corr. Life mag., 1948-51; corr., sr. editor Collier's mag., 1951-56; free-lance mag. writer, 1957-61, 70—; Midwest bur. chief Sat. Eve. Post, 1962; White House reporter USIA, 1963-64; staff corr. Christian Sci. Monitor, 1965-70; mem. Pres.'s Council on Environmental Quality, Washington, 1970—. Served with AUS, 1942-46; ETO. Decorated Bronze Star; recipient Conservation Service award U.S. Dept. Interior, 1968; Pulitzer prize in journalism for nat. reporting, 1969. Mem. Sigma Delta Chi. Christian Scientist. Author: (with Perle Mesta) Perle, My Story, 1960. Home: 3416 O St NW Washington DC 20007 Office: Executive Office of the President 722 Jackson Pl NW Washington DC 20006

CAHOON, ROY C., govt. ofcl. Exec. dir. Joint Commn. on the Coinage, Washington. Office: Main Treasury Dept Bldg Washington DC 20020*

CAILLEAU, RELDA MARIE, biochemist; b. San Francisco, Feb. 1, 1909; d. Armand Michael and Rose (Adler) Cailleau; A.B., U. Cal. at Berkeley, 1930, M.A., 1932; D.Sc., U. Paris (France), 1937. French Nat. Research fellow Pasteur Inst., Paris, 1937-40; asst. microbiologist vitamin assays U. Cal. at Berkeley, 1941-43; asso. nutritionist, home economist U.S. Dept. Agr., Washington, 1943-46; charge de recherche Nat. Center Sci. Research, French Ministry Edn., 1947-49; jr. asst. research biochemist U. Cal. at Berkeley, 1950-53, asst. research biochemist tissue culture, 1953-55; research asso. oncology, asst. research biochemist Cancer Research Inst., U. Cal. Med. Sch. at San Francisco, 1955-59, asso. research biochemist, 1959-70; research asso. dept. medicine M.D. Anderson Hosp. Tumor Inst., Houston, 1970—. Mem. Tissue Culture Assn., Soc. Exptl. Biology and Medicine, N.Y. Acad. Scis., Assn. de Microbiologistes de la Langue Francaise, Internat. Soc. Cell Biology, Sigma Xi, Iota Sigma Pi. Home: 7232 Staffordshire St Houston TX 77025 Office: M D Anderson Hospital Tumor Institute Dept of Medicine Houston TX 77025

CAILLOUET, LOUIS ABEL, bishop; b. Thibodaux, La., Aug 2, 1900; s. Louis Phillip and Marie Adele (Lagarde) C.; M.A., St. Mary's Sem., Balt., 1921; student U. Propaganda Fide, Rome, 1921-25; S.T.L. Ordained priest Roman Catholic Ch., 1925, consecrated bishop, 1947; now aux. bishop Archdiocese of New Orleans. Home: 1342 Moss St New Orleans LA 70119

CAIN, DONALD EZELL, lawyer, judge; b. San Marcos, Tex., Oct. 8, 1921; s. Erie Montclair and Betty (Howell) C.; Asso. Sci., Arlington State Coll., 1941; B.B.A., U. Tex., 1943, LL.B., 1948;; m. Betty Anne Culberson, June 14, 1952; children—David, Dale, Donald Ezell, Randolph C. With contracts dept. Convair div. Gen. Dynamics Corp., 1948-50; admitted to Tex. bar, 1948; asso. Rogers & Thompson, Pampa, 1951-52, Curtis Douglass, 1952-53; pvt. practice, Pampa, 1954—; county atty. Gray County, 1955-69, judge, 1969-71, county judge, 1971—. Bd. dirs. United Fund, 1956-60; pres. Adobe Walls council Boy Scouts Am. 1957-60. Served from ensign to lt. USNR, 1943-46, lt. 1950-51. Recipient Silver Beaver award Boy Scouts Am., 1958. Mem. Am., Gray County (pres. 1968) bar assns., State Bar Tex., C. of C. (dir. 1959-60), Am. Judicature Soc., Phi Alpha Delta. Democrat. Baptist. Rotarian (pres. 1958-59). Home: 1826 Williston St Pampa TX 79065 Office: Court House PO Box 2160 Pampa TX 79065

CAIN, HERMAN WILTON, gas co. exec.; b. Lufkin, Tex., Nov. 4, 1922; s. Herman Curtis and Blanche (Zuber) C.; B.S. in Chem. Engring., U. Tex. at Austin, 1948, postgrad. Columbia, 1953-54; m. Jessie Lee Roark, Sept. 6, 1944; children—Allan R., Mary Lee, Carol Ann. Trainee, A. O. Smith Corp., Houston, 1948-51, br. mgr., New Orleans, 1951-53, sales engr., N.Y., 1953-56; analyst Tex. Eastern Transmission Corp., Shreveport, La., 1956-58; asst. to pres. Trunkline Gas Co., Houston, 1958-66; v.p. Panhandle Eastern Pipe Line Co. and Trunkline Gas Co., Houston, 1966—. Mem. Houston Planning Commn. Bd. dirs. council Boy Scouts Am.; trustee Houston Mus. Natural Sci. Served to capt. USAAF, 1942-45. Decorated Air medal with 7 oak leaf clusters (Army), D.F.C. with 2 oak leaf clusters. Registered profl. engr., Tex., La. Mem. Am., Ind. natural gas assns., Am. Petroleum Inst., Am. Inst. Chem. Engrs., Tex. Mfrs. Assn., Am. Mgmt. Assn., A.I.M., Soc. Advancement Mgmt., S. Tex. C. of C. (dir.). Home: 107 Willowend Dr Houston TX 77024 Office: 3000 Bissonnet Av Houston TX 77001

CAIN, JAMES BYERS, bus. exec.; b. Uniontown, Pa., June 25, 1922; s. John Smith and Margaret Eleanor (Byers) C.; grad. Schreiner Inst., 1940; B.B.A., So. Meth. U., 1942; m. Lillian Kilgore, Apr. 28, 1944; children—Margaret Elaine, John Charles. Pres., Austin Flying Service (Tex.), 1946-47; owner Aero-Tel Airport, Austin, 1947-51; owner Athens Laundry and Laundromatic Enterprises (Tex.), 1951-60; pres. Tex. Wholesale Supply Co., Athens, 1960-65; sec., treas., dir. Henderson County Savs. and Loan Assn., Athens, 1965—; dir. 1st Nat. Bank, Athens. Chmn., City Indsl. Team, 1963—; pres. Athens Indsl. Found., 1965—, Athens Cemetery Assn., 1968—. Trustee Athens Municipal Water Authority, Athens City Commn., Athens Ind. Sch. Dist., Lakewood Pvt. Sch.; bd. dirs. Schlesinger Home Nursing Service. Served with USNR, 1941-46. Recipient Achievement award Kiwanis Club, 1964, Athens Salesman award Athens Jr. C. of C., 1969; various indsl. devel. citations. Mem. Athens (pres., recipient Community Leadership award 1971), E. Tex. (dir.) chambers commerce, Kappa Alpha. Presbyn. Mason (Shriner). Home: 1012 E Tyler Athens TX 75751 Office: PO Box 29 Athens TX 75751

CAIN, JOSEPH ALEXANDER, artist, educator; b. Henderson, Tenn., May 27, 1920; s. Thomas Watson and Rose Annas (Wimberly) C.; B.A., U. Cal. at Berkeley, 1947, M.A., 1948; m. Mabel Louise Barton, Aug. 21, 1945; 1 dau., Jonizo. One-man shows Centennial Mus., Corpus Christi, Tex., 1950, Tex. Coll. Arts and Industries, 1952. Art Center, Richmond, Cal., 1951, Little Theater, Corpus Christi, 1956, Victoria, Tex., 1957, Southwestern U., Georgetown, Tex., 1961, Incarnate Word Coll., San Antonio, 1961, Ligoa Duncan Gallery, N.Y.C., 1963, U. Corpus Christi, 1967, San Diego State Coll., 1969, Tex. U., N.M. State U., 1969, Tex. Christian U., 1969, Baylor U., 1970, others; exhibited in group shows at Grand Central Galleries, Petite Gallerie, N.Y.C., Los Angeles County Museum, other museums and galleries; tchr. art Corpus Christi High Sch. and W. B. Ray High Sch., 1948-66, Del Mar Coll. Extended Day Sch., 1950—, art editor Corpus Christi Caller-Times, 1955—; asst. prof. art Del Mar Coll., 1966-67, asso. prof., 1970-72, prof., 1972—, chmn. dept. art, 1967—; represented in permanent collections D.D. Feldman Collection Contemporary Tex. Art, Michael M. Engel, M. Grumbacher, Inc., Seton Hall U., Del Mar Coll., Goliad Library Rosenberg Gallery, Tex. Instruments, Dallas, Witte Mus., San Antonio, others; executed mosaic murals Spohn Hosp., Buccaneer Bowl, 1961. Mem. Corpus Christi Municipal Art Council, 1967-69, 72—; juror Competitive Art Show, Hemisfair, 1968, Spring Juried Art Show, Tex. Fine Arts Assn., 1968. Served to capt. USMCR, 1942-46, 50-52; col. Res. Recipient numerous awards in nat. regional, local exhbns., including Sarah Goode award Nat. Soc. Painters in Casein, 1963, Prix de Paris citation, 1963, M. Grumbacher award, 1965, Wall St. Transcript award, 1970; Cal Nat. Watercolor Soc. purchase prize, 1969. Fellow Royal Soc. Arts London; mem. S. Tex. Art League (pres. 1961—), Tex. Watercolor Soc. (regional dir. 1958—), 3d v.p. 1963-64), Nat. Soc. Painters Casein, Tex. Fine Arts Assn. (regional dir. 1957—), Sarasota (Fla.), Miss. art assns., Ala., Cal. watercolor socs., Internat. Platform Assn., Western Artist's Assn., N.E.A., Tex. Classroom Tchrs. Assn., Corpus Christi Municipal Art Council (chmn. 1972-73), Men-of-art-guild. Home: 402 Troy Dr Corpus Christi TX 78412

CAIN, LEONARD FRANCIS, ednl. adminstr.; b. Pottstown, Pa., Jan. 29, 1922; s. Leonard F. and Catherine E. (McEvoy) C,; A.B., St. Joseph's Coll, 1943; M.A., Cath. U. Am., 1947, Ph.D., 1966; postgrad. Georgetown U., 1943. U. Wis., 1948-49; m. Mary T. Townsend, Mar. 10, 1944; children—Michael, Sheila, Patrick, Eileen, Teresa, Kevin, Christopher, Monica, Brendan, Anthony, Deirdre. Mem. faculty Cath. U. Am., Washington, 1949—, dean Coll. Arts and Scis., 1966—. Bd. dirs. nat. capital region Nat. Conf. Christians and Jews, 1965—; chmn. Family Life Movement, Archdiocese of Washington, 1965-67. Served with AUS, 1943-46. Mem. Am. Assn. U. Profs., Am. Conf. Acad. Deans, Am. Econ. Assn., Am. Polit. Sci. Assn., Indsl. Relations Research Assn., Econ. and Social Research Inst. (Dublin), Pi Gamma Mu, Alpha Sigma Nu, Delta Epsilon Sigma. Democrat. Roman Catholic. Home: 1026 Newton St NE Washington DC 20017

CALATAYUD, JUAN BAUTISTA, physician; b. Valencia, Spain, May 17, 1928; s. Aqustin and Carmen (Llobat) C.; M.D., U. Valencia (Spain), 1952; m. Helen T. Lupton, July 2, 1960; children—Mary Carmen, Juan Cesar. Intern, Alexian Bros. Hosp., Elizabeth, N.J., 1955; resident St. Pauls Hosp., Dallas, 1956-57; fellow in medicine George Washington U. Hosp., Washington, 1957-60, asst. prof. medicine, 1962-69, asso. prof. medicine, 1969-70; asso. dir. med. edn. Doctors Hosp., Washington, 1970—; research asst. U. Montreal (Que., Can.), 1960; fellow medicine Montreal Gen. Hosp., 1961; house physician Deborah Hosp., Browns Mills, N.J., 1961-62; practice medicine specializing in cardiology, Washington, 1962—; cons. VA Center, Martinsburg, W.Va., 1965—. Mem. Am., Washington heart assns., Am. Fedn. Clin. Research (v.p. 1966-67, pres. 1967-68), Am. Coll. Angiology, D.C. Med. Soc., A.A.A.S., Pan Am. Med. Assn., Peruvian Cardiac Soc. (hon.), Peruvian Angiology Soc. (hon.). Contbr. articles in field to profl. jours. Home: 6217 Cheryl Dr Falls Church VA 22044 Office: 1801 I St NW Washington DC 20006

CALAWAY, PAUL KENNETH, educator; b. Bethesda, Ark., Mar. 31, 1910; s. William Lawrence and Ada (McSpadden) C.; A.B., Ark. Coll., 1931; M.S., Ga. Tech. Inst., 1933; Ph.D., U. Tex., 1938; m. Josephine Fant, Feb. 11, 1945; children—Paul Kenneth, Josephine F., Elizabeth M. Grad. asst. chemistry Ga. Tech. Inst., 1931-33, instr., 1933-35, 38-42, asst. prof., 1942-44, asso. prof., 1944-47, prof., dir. dept. chemistry, 1947-54, dir. exptl. sta., 1954-57; prof. chemistry Tex. A. and M. U., 1957—, head dept., 1957-64. Mem. Am. Chem. Soc., Sigma Xi. Home: 1201 Ashburn St College Station TX 77840

CALCOTE, CLARENCE EDGAR, orthodontist; b. Tupelo, Miss., Jan. 10, 1930; s. Clarence I. and Mary (Edgar) C.; B.S. in Chemistry, Davidson Coll., 1951; D.D.S., U.N.C., 1955, M.S. in Orthodontics, 1958; m. Frances Traver Dudley, Mar. 19, 1955; children—Frank Edgar, Robert Dudley, Thomas Daniel, Catherine Elizabeth. Individual practice orthodontics, Charleston, S.C., 1958—. Pres. Alfa Corp., Bravo Leasing Co.; sec. Delta Ltd.; sec., dir. Fine Arts Broadcasting Corp.; dir. Urban Builders Inc. Served as capt. USAF, 1955-57. Diplomate Am. Bd. Orthodontists. Mem. U.N.C. Orthodontic Alumni Assn. (pres. 1963-64), S.C. Orthodontic Soc. (past pres.), Charleston Dental Soc. (past pres.), Nat. Flying Dentists Assn. (past pres.). Delta Sigma Delta, Pi Kappa Phi. Presbyn. (elder). Club: Sertoma (Charleston). Home: 673 N Shore Rd Charleston SC 29407 Office: 163 Rutledge Av Charleston SC 29403

CALDWELL, BETTYE (MCDONALD), psychologist, educator; b. Smithville, Tex., Dec. 24, 1924; d. Thomas Milton and Juanita (Mayes) McDonald; A.B., Baylor U., 1945; M.A., State U. Ia., 1947; Ph.D., Washington U., 1951; m. Fred Thomas Caldwell, Jr., 1947; children—Paul Frederick and Elizabeth Lanier (twins). Asst. in med. psychology Washington U. Sch. Medicine, 1947-50, instr. 1950-53, dir. child evaluation clinic, 1956-58; research asso., dept. pediatrics, Upstate Med. Center, Syracuse, N.Y., 1959-69, dir. Children's Center, 1966-69; asst. prof. psychology Northwestern U., 1953-55; Dual prof. child devel. and edn. Syracuse U., 1966-69; prof. edn. U. Ark., Little Rock, 1969—, dir. Center for Early Devel. and Edn., 1969—. Fellow Am. Psychol. Assn., Am. Orthopsychiat. Assn.; mem. Soc. Research in Child Devel., Nat. Assn. for Edn. Young Children, Assn. for Childhood Edn. Internat., N.E.A. Editor: Child Devel., 1968-71; co-editor Rev. Child Devel. Research. Home: 187 Pleasant Valley Dr Little Rock AR 72207 Office: 814 Sherman St Little Rock AR 72202

CALDWELL, CHARLES KENNETH, dentist; b. Chickamauga, Ga., Jan. 20, 1940; s. John Richard and Ruth Ellen (Scurlock) C.; B.S., U. Tenn., 1961, D.D.S., 1964; m. Janet Blunt, Nov. 11, 1966; children—Anne Nibbi, Kimberly Ellen. Pvt. practice dentistry, Reidsville, N.C., 1968—. Served with AUS, 1966-68. Mem. Xi Psi Phi. Kiwanian. Home: 2208 Cypress Dr Reidsville NC 27320 Office: 602 S Main St Reidsville NC 27320

CALDWELL, CLAUD REID, lawyer; b. Augusta, Ga., Sept. 18, 1909; s. John Mars and Ethel (Bennett) C.; student Acad. Richmond County, 1922-26; m. Josephine F. Clarke, June 30, 1940; children—Claud R., Kathryn C., James W. Admitted to Ga. bar, 1932, practiced in Augusta, 1934—; judge Municipal Ct., City of Augusta, 1948-49. Pres., Richmond County Independent Party, 1950-51. Dir. Augusta chpt. A.R.C., YMCA; chmn. Augusta council Boy Scouts Am., 1949-50. Served with AUS, 1941-45; ETO. Recipient Distinguished Pistol Marksman award U.S. Army, 1965. Mem. Am., Ga. bar assns., Nat. Rifle Assn. Am. (dir.), Ga. Sport Shooting Assn. (dir., past pres.). Presbyn. (deacon). Mason. Home: 343 Hemlock Hill Rd Augusta GA 30904 Office: Southern Finance Bldg Augusta GA 30902

CALDWELL, DONALD HARRISON, hosp. adminstr.; b. Matthews, N.C., Feb. 27, 1930; s. John McCamie and Mary Ella (Shannon) C.; A.A., Charlotte Coll., 1950; B.S., U. N.C., 1952; M.B.A., Emory U., 1961; m. Mary Josephine Snyder, Jan. 19, 1957; children—Donald Harrison, Stephen Alexander, Jeffrey Shannon. Asst. cashier Bank of Matthews, 1954-56; payroll auditor Travelers Ins. Co., Charlotte, N.C., New Orleans, 1956-59; adminstrv. asst. Anderson Meml. Hosp. (S.C.), 1961, asst. adminstr., 1961-63; adminstr. Stephens County Hosp., Toccoa, Ga., 1963—. Served with AUS, 1952-54. Mem. Am. Coll. Hosp. Adminstrs., Am., Ga. hosp. assns., N.E. Ga. Hosp. Council, Ga. State Bd. Nursing Home Adminstrs., C. of C. Presbyn. (deacon 1955-72). Rotarian. Office: Falls Rd Toccoa GA 30577

CALDWELL, ERSKINE, writer; b. White Oak, Ga., Dec. 17, 1903; s. Ira Sylvester and Caroline Preston (Bell) C.; student Erskine Coll., 1920, 21, U. Va. 1922, 25, 26, U. Pa., 1924; m. Helen Lannigan, Mar. 3, 1925; children—Erskine Preston, Dabney Withers, Janet; m. 2d, Margaret Bourke-White, Feb. 27, 1939; m. 3d, June Johnson, Dec. 21, 1942; 1 son, Jay Erskine; m. 4th, Virginia Moffett Fletcher, Jan. 1, 1957. Newspaper writer, 1925; successively cotton picker, stage hand, profl. football player, book reviewer, lecturer, editor; motion picture screen writer in Hollywood, Cal., 1933-34, 42-43; correspondent in Mexico, Spain and Czechoslovakia in 1938 and 39, in China, Mongolia and Turkestan in 1940; editor American Folkways, 1940-55; war corr. in Russia for Life mag., PM, CBS, 1941. Recipient Yale Review 1,000 dollar award for fiction, 1933. Mem. Authors League Am., Nat. Inst. Arts and Letters, P.E.N., Euphemian Lit. Soc., Raven Soc. Club: Overseas press (N.Y.C.); Phoenix (Ariz.) press; Press (San Francisco). Author: The Bastard, 1929; Poor Fool, 1930; American Earth, 1931; Tobacco Road, 1932; God's Little Acre, 1933; We Are The Living, 1933; Journeyman, 1935; Kneel to the Rising Sun, 1935; Some American People, 1935; You Have Seen Their Faces (with Margaret Bourke-White), 1937; Southways, 1938; North of the Danube (with Margaret Bourke-White), 1939; Trouble in July, 1940; Jackpot, 1940; Say Is This the U.S.A. (with Margaret Bourke-White), 1941; All-Out on the Road to Smolensk, 1942; Moscow Under Fire, 1942; All Night Long, 1942; Georgia Boy, 1943; Stories, 1944; Tragic Ground, 1944; A House in the Uplands, 1946; The Sure Hand of God, 1947; This Very Earth, 1948; Place Called Estherville, 1949; Episode in Palmetto, 1950; Call It Experience, 1951; The Courting of Susie Brown, 1952; A Lamp for Nightfall, 1952; The Complete Stories of Erskine Caldwell, 1953; Love and Money, 1954; Gretta, 1955; Erskine Caldwell's Gulf Coast Stories, 1956; Certain Women, 1957; Molly Cottontail, 1958; The Sacrilege of Alan Kent, 1958; Claudelle Inglish, 1959; When You Think of Me, 1959; Jenny by Nature, 1961; Close to Home, 1962; The Last Night of Summer, 1963; Around About America, 1964; In Search of Bisco, 1965; The Deer at Our House, 1966; In The Shadow of The Steeple, 1966; Writing in America, 1966; Miss Mamma Aimee, 1967; Deep South, 1968; Summertime Island, 1968; The Weather Shelter, 1969; The Earnshaw Neighborhood, 1971. Contbr. to mags. Home: PO Box 820 Dunedin FL 33528 Office: care McIntosh & Otis Inc 28 E 41st St New York City NY 10017

CALDWELL, FREDERICK CLAY, farm equipment mfg. exec.; b. Corpus Christi, June 29, 1921; s. Edward Lasater and Mabel (Beckner) C.; student pub. schs., Corpus Christi, Tex.; m. Jean Lindberg, Nov. 13, 1943; children—Karen Jean (Mrs. George Acuff), Janet Ann. Partner, Caldwell Cypress Cistern Co., Corpus Christi, 1945-48; partner E. L. Caldwell & Sons, Corpus Christi, 1948-60; pres. E. L. Caldwell & Sons, Inc., Corpus Christi, 1960—; v.p. Caldwell Bros. Export Corp., Corpus Christi, 1953—; dir. Corpus Christi Bank & Trust Co. Bd. dirs., exec. com. Better Bus. Bur. Served from 2d lt. to maj. AUS, 1942-46. Decorated Bronze Star medal, Purple Heart with oak leaf cluster. Mem. Regional Export Expansion Council, Farm Equipment Mfrs. Assn. (dir. 1968-69), U.S. C. of C., Corpus Christi C. of C. (dir., mem. exec. com. 1968-69). Clubs: Port Aransas Rod & Reel (past pres.), Corpus Christi Yacht, Corpus Christi Country, Corpus Christi Gun. Patentee in field. Home: 5022 Cape Romaine Corpus Christi TX 78412 Office: 3204 Agnes St Corpus Christi TX 78403

CALDWELL, GEORGE HOWARD, librarian; b. Holton, Kan., Sept. 29, 1926; s. Lewis Harold and Lucile Bessie (Howard) C.; B.A., (Summerfield scholar), U. Kan., 1948; M.A. (Lehman fellow), Harvard, 1950; postgrad. Wichita U., 1951-53; M.S. in L.S., Columbia, 1955; m. Marcia Edith Sweetman, Jan. 6, 1952. Writer tng. dept. Boeing Aircraft Co., Wichita, Kan., 1951-54; intern trainee, bibliographer, asst. head European exchange sect. Library of Congress, Washington, 1955-57, head pub. reference sect., 1966—; head govt. documents sect., head reference dept. U. Kan. Library, Lawrence, 1957-66. Instr., U.S. Dept. Agr. Grad. Sch., Washington, 1967-69. Pres., Lawrence League for Practice Democracy, Lawrence, Kan., 1963-65; chmn. Fair Housing Coordinating Com., Lawrence, 1965-66; 2d v.p. Kan. Adv. Council on Civil Rights, 1965-66. Grantee, Harvard Grad. Sch. Bus. Adminstrn., 1962. Mem. A.L.A., D.C. Library Assn., Phi Beta Kappa, Omicron Delta Kappa. Conglist. Contbr. articles to profl. jours. Home: 10010 Frederick Av Kensington MD 20795 Office: General Reference and Bibliography Div Library of Congress Washington DC 20540

CALDWELL, HAROLD LEROY, petroleum engr.; b. Pawnee, Okla., Aug. 14, 1925; s. Harold Ralph and Eula P. (Buckner) C.; B.S. in Petroleum Engring., U. Tulsa, 1951; m. Patricia T. Poorman, December 24, 1948; children—Michael Alan, and Douglas Owen. Exploitation engineer Sunray Oil Co., 1951-55; chief engr. Keener Oil Co., Tulsa, 1955-59, gen. supt. prodn., 1959-62; cons. engr., 1962-63; drilling engr. Fenix & Scisson, Inc., Tulsa, 1963-65; gen. prodn. supt. K.W.B. Oil Property Mgmt., Inc., 1965—; engr. Williams Bros. Engring. Co., 1967—. With AUS, 1943-46. Registered profl. engr., Okla. Mem. Am. Inst. Mining Engrs., Am. Petroleum Inst., Okla. State Profl. Engrs. Republican. Mem. Reorganized Ch. of Jesus Christ of Latter-day Saints. Home: 5129 S Richmond Tulsa OK 74135 Office: Resource Sciences Center Tulsa OK 74103

CALDWELL, HOWARD EUGENE, investment counselor; b. Jacksonville, Fla., Mar. 16, 1924; s. Howard Eugene and Marye Elsie (Manning) C.; B.B.A. with high distinction, Emory U., 1948; m. Martha Norton, July 25, 1970; 1 son, Orman Norton. Security analyst Trust Co. Ga., Atlanta, 1948-53; security analyst Montag & Caldwell, Inc., investment counsel, 1953-56, partner, 1956-68, pres., 1968—; adv. dir. Mercantile Nat. Bank of Atlanta; sr. v.p., dir. Alpha Fund, Alpha Research, 1968—. Served with AUS, 1942-45. Decorated Purple Heart. Mem. Financial Analysts Fedn., Inst. Chartered Financial Analysts, Investment Counsel Assn. Am. (bd. govs. 1971). Methodist. Kiwanian. Home: 77 E Addrews Dr NW Atlanta GA 30305 Office: 2901 First National Bank Bldg Atlanta GA 30303

CALDWELL, JAMES, broadcasting exec. Vice pres., sta. mgr. WAVE, Louisville. Office: 725 S Floyd St Louisville KY 40203*

CALDWELL, JAMES ELAM, JR., city ofcl.; b. Charlotte, N.C., June 7, 1938; s. James Elam and Sara (Barber) C.; A.B., U. N.C., Chapel Hill, 1960, postgrad., 1964-66; m. Iris Rilla Bailey, June 3, 1962. Accountant Fed. Res. Bank, Charlotte, 1961-64; asst. town mgr. Town of Chapel Hill, 1965-67; city mgr. City of Clinton (N.C.), 1967—. Mem. N.C. City and County Mgmt. Assn. (sec., treas. 1972). Episcopalian (vestryman, del. conv. 1972). Kiwanian (pres. 1969, div. lt. gov. 1971-72). Home: 123 Doris Av Clinton NC 28328 Office: City Hall Clinton NC 28328

CALDWELL, JAMES NEELY, III, assn. exec.; b. Rock Hill, S.C., Nov. 26, 1926; s. James Neely and Ruby (Graham) C.; A.B., U.S.C., 1948, LL.B., 1950. Admitted to S.C. bar, 1950; atty. Nat. Inst. Municipal Law Ofcls., Washington, 1951; trial atty. U.S. Dept. Justice, Washington, 1951-55; atty. civil service com., judiciary com. U.S. Senate P.O., 1955-57; legal counsel, asst. dir. Municipal Assn. S.C., 1957-60, exec. dir. 1960—. Bd. dirs. YMCA, Columbia, S.C., 1959-61; pres. bd. dirs. Columbia Symphony Orch., 1972-73. Served with AUS, 1945-47. Mem. Fed., S.C., Richland County bar assns., Nat. League Cities, Phi Kappa Sigma, Phi Delta Phi, Omicron Delta Kappa, Kappa Sigma Kappa. Presbyn. (elder, deacon). Kiwanian. Home: 819 Albion Rd Columbia SC 29205 Office: PO Box 306 Columbia SC 29202

CALDWELL, JERRY, educator; b. Tallassee, Ala., May 1, 1938; s. Obie Eric and Cora (Powell) C.; B.S., Auburn U., 1960, M.S., 1962; Ph.D., Tex. A. and M. U., 1969; m. Etharee Faye McFarland, Apr. 7, 1962; children—Janet Marie, Eric Vernon, Lester Wade. Asst. prof. animal sci. Tex. A. and M. U., 1968-69, 70—; NIH fellow U. Cal. at Davis, 1969-70; vis. prof. George Peabody Coll., 1970. Served with USAF, 1962-65. Mem. Am. Soc. Animal Sci., Alpha Zeta, Sigma Xi, Gamma Sigma Delta. Kiwanian. Home: 1600 Laura Lane College Station TX 77840 Office: Animal Sci Dept Tex A and M U College Station TX 77843

CALDWELL, JOHN TYLER, univ. adminstr.; b. Yazoo City, Miss., Dec. 19, 1911; s. Joseph Redford and Lilley (Tyler) C.; B.S., Miss. State Coll., 1932; A.M., Duke, 1936, LL.D., 1965; Ph.D. (Julius Rosenwald fellow), Princeton, 1939; postgrad. U. Wis., summer 1938; postgrad. Columbia U. (Naval Sch. Mil. Govt.), 1943, M.A., 1945; LL.D., Coll. of Ozarks, 1955, Wake Forest Coll., 1960, U. Md., 1970; m. Catherine Wadsworth Zeek, May 16, 1947 (dec. 1961); children—Alice, Andrew, Charles, Helen; m. 2d, Carol Schroeder Erskine, June 29, 1963; children—Melanie and Carol Erskine. Tchr. social scis., band dir. Holmes, Jr. Coll., Goodman, Miss., 1932-36; jr. economist U.S. Resettlement Adminstrn., State Coll., Miss., and Little Rock, Ark., 1936-37; asst. econ., land use planning, Bur. Agrl. Econs., U.S. Dept. Agr., Vicksburg, Miss., summer, 1939; instr. polit. sci. Vanderbilt U., 1939-42, asst. prof., 1942-46, asso. prof., 1946-47; pres. Ala. Coll., Montevallo, 1947-52; pres. U. Ark., 1952-59; chancellor N.C. State U., 1959—. Mem. U.S. nat. commn. UNESCO, 1968-70; bd. dirs. Overseas Devel. Council, 1969—. Trustee Ednl. Testing Service, 1957-60, 1965-69, 70—, chmn., 1966-67, 68-69. Bd. visitors Air U., Maxwell AFB, 1970—, chmn., 1972-73. Served to lt. comdr. USN, 1942-46, Decorated Bronze Star medal. Ofcl. mem. for Ala. bd. control So. Regional Edn., 1948-52. Mem. Am., So. (rec. sec. 1942) polit. sci. assns., Am. Soc. Pub. Adminstrn., Nat. Assn. State Univs. and Land Grant Colls. (chmn. exec. com. 1963, pres. 1962, chmn. internat. affairs com. 1966-69), Am. Council Edn. (commn. internat. edn. 1966-69, chmn. 1967-69), Blue Key, Omicron Delta Kappa, Kappa Phi Kappa, Pi Kappa Alpha. Democrat. Christian Scientist. Rotarian. Home: 1903 Hillsborough St Raleigh NC 27607

CALDWELL, MILLARD F., JR., judge; b. Knoxville, Tenn., Feb. 6, 1897; s. Millard Fillmore and Martha Jane (Clapp) C.; student Carson and Newman Coll., 1913-14, U. of Miss., 1917-18, U. Va., 1919-22; LL.D., Rollins Coll., U. Fla., Fla. So. U., Fla. State U.; m. Mary Rebecca Harwood, Feb. 14, 1925; children—Millard Fillmore III (dec.), Sally. Purkins McCord, Susan B. Admitted to Tenn. bar 1922, Fla. bar, 1925; served as pros. atty. and county atty., Santa Rosa County, Fla., and city atty., Milton; elected to Fla. State Legislature, 1928 and 1930; mem. 73d to 76th Congresses (1933-41), 3d Fla. Dist.; voluntarily retired from Congress to resume practice of law at Milton and Tallahassee, Fla.; elected gov. of Florida for term 1945-49; Fed. Civil Def. adminstrator 1950-52; justice Florida Supreme Court 1962—, chief justice, 1967—. Del. Interparliamentary Union. Chmn. Nat. Govs. Conf., 1946-47; pres. Council of State Govts., 1946-48; chmn. bd. of control S. Regional Edn., 1947-50; chmn. Fla. Commn. Constl. Govt., 1957-66. Served as pvt. and 2d lt., F.A., U.S. Army, World War I. Mem. Am. Judicature Soc., Newcomen Soc., Huguenot Soc., S.A.R., Alpha Kappa Psi, Blue Key, Kappa Sigma, Phi Alpha Delta. Democrat. Home: Harwood Plantation Old Bainbridge Rd Tallahassee FL 32301 Office: Supreme Court Bldg Tallahassee FL 32302

CALDWELL, NATHAN GREEN, reporter; b. St. Charles, Mo., July 16, 1912; s. Albert Green and Sara (Jetton) C.; student Southwestern Coll., 1933, Cumberland U., 1934; Nieman fellow Harvard, 1940; m. Camilla Frances Jonston, Nov. 16, 1936; 1 son, John Sam. Polit. writer Nashville Tennessean, 1934-56, econs. and regional resource devel. reporter, 1956—. Co-recipient Pulitzer prize for nat. affairs reporting, 1961. Rosenwald fellow, 1947. Author: The Cotton Picker Moves People, 1947; The Strange Romance of John L. Lewis and Cyrus Eaton, 1961. Home: 1216 Eastdale Av Nashville TN 37206 Office: 1100 Broad St Nashville TN 37203

CALDWELL, SHIRLING SAM, state ofcl.; b. East Point, Ga., Jan. 22, 1929; s. Paul Favor and Minnie (Baker) C.; student North Ga. Coll., 1948-50; A.B., U. Ga., 1952; m. Jeanette Josephine Nemie, July 17, 1952; children—Josette Tina, Valerie Jean, Rachael Angela, Patrick Shirling, Victor. Pub. relations pvt. industry and govt., 1956-62; personnel dir. Ga. Hwy. Dept., Atlanta, 1962-66; commr. labor State of Ga., Atlanta, 1966—. Mem. Ga. Democratic Exec. Com. Bd. dirs. Model Cities Project Atlanta, People to People. Served with USMCR, 1946-48; with AUS, 1952-54. Mem. Farm Bur., V.F.W., Am. Legion, Woodmen of World, Sigma Delta Chi. Baptist. Elk. Home: 2703 Hawaii Ct Decatur GA 30033 Office: State Labor Bldg Atlanta Ga 30334

CALFEE, DONALD P., editor. City editor Fla. Times-Union. Office: 1 Riverside Av Jacksonville FL 32201*

CALFEE, WILLIAM NOWARD, sculptor, painter; b. Washington, Feb. 7, 1909; s. Lee Price and Carrie L. (Whitehead) C.; studied sculpture Beaux Arts, Paris, also Cranbrook Acad., Mich.; m. Gertrude H. Dunn, 1951; children—Adriana, Richard, Judy, Helme, William, Alan Edward. Instr. spl. skills div. Resettlement Adminstrn., Cumberland Homesteads, Tenn., 1935; executed murals, sculptures, fine arts sect. procurement div. U.S. Treasury Dept., 1936-41; psychotherapy worker St. Elizabeth's Hosp., Washington, 1942-43; works exhibited most museums; one-man show painting Wehye Gallery, N.Y.C., sculpture Graham Gallery, Balt. Mus., Corcoran Gallery, Philbrook Art Mus., Tulsa; rep. in Root Collection, Phillips Gallery, Corcoran Gallery. Tchr. mural technique Centre d'Art, Port au Prince, Haiti, 1949; guest asso. prof. painting U. Cal. at Berkeley, 1951; chmn. dept. painting and sculpture Am. U., Washington until 1954, now artist in residence; initiated Watkins Meml. Collection, Watkins Gallery; executed altar, font, candle sticks St. Augustine's Chapel, Washington, 1968. Home: 4817 Potomac Av NW Washington DC 20007

CALHOUN, CALVIN LEE, educator; b. Atlanta, Jan. 7, 1927; s. Robert and Mary (Huff) C.; B.S., Morehouse Coll., 1948; M.S., Atlanta U., 1950; M.D., Meharry Med. Coll., 1960; m. Evelyn Greene, Feb. 14, 1948; 1 son, Calvin Lee. Instr. biology Morehouse Coll., 1950-51; faculty Meharry Med. Coll., Nashville, 1951—, asso. prof. neurology, 1966—, asso. prof. anatomy, 1969—, dir. div. neurology, 1966—, chmn. dept. anatomy, 1968—. Served with AUS, 1948. USPHS spl. fellow, 1965-66. Mem. Am. Acad. Neurology, Am. Assn. Anatomists, Christian Med. Soc., Urban League, Beta Kappa Chi, Alpha Omega Alpha. Baptist (deacon 1968). Home: 4217 King's Ct Nashville TN 37218

CALHOUN, EVELYN WILLIAMS, social worker; b. Tyler, Tex., Sept. 12, 1921; d. James Stanley and Norma (Skelton) Williams; B.A., Baylor U., 1941; M.S.W., Worden Sch. Social Work, 1960; postgrad. U. Chgo., 1955-56; m. William Benjamin Calhoun, Jr., Mar. 15, 1942 (div. Mar. 1949); children—William Bejamin III, Anne Stanley (Mrs. Donald Elliot Loyd). Field worker Tex. Dept. Pub. Welfare, Tyler, 1953-55; field placement Salvation Army Family Service, Chgo., 1955-56; child welfare worker Tyler-Smith County Child Welfare Unit, 1957-59; field placement Tex. Inst. Rehab. and Research, Houston, 1959-60, med. social worker, 1960-64; research social worker pre-natal research project, dept. obstetrics, gynecology U. Tex. Med. Br. at Galveston, 1964-66, supr. social service, dept. obstetrics, gynecology, 1966—, cons. satellite clinics, 1967—, cons. family planning program, 1969—; field instr. U. Houston Grad. Sch. Social Work, 1968—. Bd. dirs. Galveston County Community Action Council, 1966-68. Mem. Tex. Social Welfare Assn., Nat. Assn. Social Workers (chmn. research council San Jacinto chpt. 1963-64, chmn. Galveston br. 1964-67, sec. 1967-68, group leader so. regional inst. 1966, Tex. del. 1969—, alternate del. Tex. state council 1967), Acad. Certified Social Workers, Am. Assn. U. Women, Order De Moley, Delta Alpha Pi. Episcopalian. Toastmistress. Home: 802 Ball St Galveston TX 77550

CALHOUN, JOHN C., JR., coll. adminstr.; dean; b. Betula, Pa., Mar. 21, 1917; s. John C. and Martha (Rowe) C.; B.S. in Petroleum and Natural Gas Engring.,Pa. State U., 1937, M.S., 1941, Ph.D., 1946; m. Ruth Elizabeth Huston, June 10, 1941; children—John, Emily, Mary Beth, Ruth Ellen. Research asst., instr. Pa. State U., 1937-46, prof. petroleum and natural gas engring., head dept., 1950-55; asso. prof., then prof., then chmn. Sch. Petroleum Engring. U. Okla., 1946-50, 50, chmn. Sch. Petroleum Engring., 1948-50; dir. Am. Petroleum Inst. dean Sch. Engring., A. and M. Coll. Tex., 1955-57; dir. Tex. Engring. Expt. Sta., Tex. Engring. Extension Service, 1955-57, v.p. engring., Tex. A. and M. Coll. system, 1957-59. vice chancellor for engring., 1959-60, for devel., 1960-63, v.p. programs, 1967-71; asst., also sci. adviser to sec. of Interior, Washington, 1963-65; distinguished prof. petroleum engring., Tex. A. and M. U., 1965—, distinguished dir. office sea grant programs, 1968—; dean geoscis., 1969-71, v.p. acad. affairs, 1971—. Acting dir. Office Water Resources Research, 1964; cons. petroleum engr., research cons.; mem. Fed. Council for Sci. and Tech., 1963-65; chmn. com. on oceanography Nat. Acad. Scis., 1967-70, chmn. ocean sci. affairs bd., 1970—; mem. Environmental Pollution Panel, Pres.' Sci. Adv. Com., 1964-66; chmn. com. on marine resources program devel. Dept. Interior, 1966, chmn. spl. study group on sonic boom in relation to man, 1967-68, chmn. marine affairs action group, 1970; mem. Presdl. Task Force on Oceanography, 1969; chmn. Pres.' Santa Barbara Oil Spill Panel and Panel on Union Oil Lease, 1969; Vice chmn. Engring. Coll. Research Council, 1959-62. Chmn. Coll. Station United Fund, 1961. Trustee U. Corp. for Atmospheric Research, 1959—, chmn. bd., 1968-71; trustee Tex. A. and M. Research Found.; bd. dirs. EDUCOM, 1966-69; exec. dir., pres. Gulf Univs. Research Corp., 1966-69. Mem. A.A.A.S., Am. Inst. Mining, Metall. and Petroleum Engrs., Am. Soc. Oceanography, Sigma Xi, Tau Beta Pi, Sigma Gamma Epsilon, Phi Kappa Phi, Tau Kappa Epsilon. Presbyn. Club: Cosmos. Author: Fundamentals of Reservoir Engineering, 1953. Contbr. to profl. jours. Home: 1106 Ashburn St College Station TX 77840

CALHOUN, MILBURN EUGENE, pub. co. exec., physician; b. West Monroe, La., Jan. 15, 1930; s. Darrell Lavelle and Mary (Crowell) C.; student N.E. La. State U., 1947-49; B.S., La. State U., 1951, M.D., 1955; m. Nancy Kathryn Harris, July 14, 1956; children—Kathleen Elizabeth, David Harris. Intern Charity Hosp. La., New Orleans, 1955-56; practice medicine, specializing in gen. practice, Buras, La., 1956-57, 59-65, Marrero, La., 1965—; mem. staff West Jefferson Gen. Hosp., Marrero; clin. instr. Med. Sch., La. State U., New Orleans, 1970—, Tulane U. Med. Sch., New Orleans, 1971—; founder, owner Bayou Books, Gretna, La., 1961—; pub., pres. Pelican Pub. Co., Inc., Gretna, 1970—; sec., dir. Nicholson Baehr Calhoun, M.D.'s, Ltd., Marrero, 1971—. Served with USAF, 1957-59. Diplomate Am. Bd. Family Practice. Mem. Assn. Am. Pubs., Am. Booksellers Assn., Am. Acad. Family Practice, A.M.A., La. Med. Soc. (com. on hwy. safety; hist. com.), La. Hist. Soc. Baptist. Pub., book rev. editor La. Hist. Quar., 1971—. Mailing address: 2600 Gallinghouse St New Orleans LA 70114 Office: 829 Barataria Blvd Marrero LA 70072 also 630 Burmaster St Gretna LA 70058

CALHOUN, WANDA JUNE, librarian; b. Mayfield, Ky., Jan. 23, 1932; d. Thomas Lewis and Lucile (Hamlet) Calhoun; B.S., Murray State Coll., 1953; M.A. in L.S., U. Mich., 1955, postgrad., 1956-58; postgrad. U. Minn., 1960. Divisional librarian U. Mich., 1955-58; head librarian Heidelberg Coll., 1958-63, Fla. Presbyn. Coll., St. Petersburg, 1963—. Vis. specialist in library services United Bd. for Christian Higher Edn. in Asia, 1965-66, 71; library cons. United Bd. Sch., P.I., Hong Kong, Taiwan, Korea. Mem. Am. Assn. U. Women (chpt. v.p. 1962-63), Am., Fla. library assns., Am. Assn. U. Profs. Presbyn. Office: Fla Presbyn Coll St Petersburg FL 33733

CALHOUN, WILLIAM MCCALL, physician; b. Arlington, Ga., Sept. 13, 1932; s. William Wright and Mary Maude (Taylor) C.; B.S., N.Ga. Coll., 1952; postgrad. U. Mich., 1953, U. Ga., 1953-54; M.D., Med. Coll. Ga., 1958; m. JoAnn LeSueur, Oct. 10, 1961; children—William McCall, Anne, Mary Clay, Virginia. Intern, U.S. Naval Hosp., Phila., 1958-59; gen. practice medicine and surgery, Buena Vista, Ga., 1961—; mem. staff, sec. med. staff, chief med. and pediatric services Marion Meml. Hosp., Buena Vista, Ga. Served with USNR, 1958-61. Hon. mem. Ala. Senate, 1971—; mem. gov's. staff Ala., 1971—. Mem. Am. Acad. Gen. Practice, A.M.A., Med. Assn. Ga., So. Med. Assn., Alpha Kappa Kappa, Sigma Alpha Epsilon. Mason (Shriner). Club: Tri County Country (Buena Vista). Home: Walton Woods Rd Buena Vista GA 31803 Office: E Court Square Buena Vista GA 31803

CALIFANO, JOSEPH ANTHONY, JR., lawyer; b. Bklyn., May 15, 1931; s. Joseph Anthony and Katherine (Gill) C.; A.B., Holy Cross Coll., 1952; LL.B., Harvard, 1955; m. Gertrude Zawacki, July 4, 1955; children— Mark Gerard, Joseph Anthony III, Claudia Frances. Admitted to N.Y. State bar, 1955, D.C. bar; with firm Dewey, Ballantine, Bushby, Palmer & Wood, N.Y.C., 1958-61; spl. asst. to gen. counsel Dept. Def., 1961-62; spl. asst. to sec. army, 1962-63; gen. counsel Dept. Army, 1963-64; spl. asst. to sec. and dep. sec. def., 1964-65; spl. asst. to Pres. U.S., 1965-69; partner Arnold & Porter, Washington, 1969-71; mem. firm Williams, Connolly & Califano, Washington, 1971—. Served to lt. USNR, 1955-58. Recipient Distinguished Civilian Service award Dept. Army, 1964, Dept. Def., 1968; Man of Year award Justinian Soc. Lawyers, 1966; One of Ten Young Outstanding Men Am., U.S. Jr. C. of C., 1966. Mem. Am., Fed. bar assns., Am. Judicature Soc. Democrat. Author: The Student Revolution: A Global Confrontation, 1969. Home: 3551 Springland Lane Washington DC Office: 1000 Hill Bldg Washington DC 20006

CALKIN, CARLETON I., assn. exec. Acting dir. St. Augustine (Fla.) Hist. Preservation Com. Office: Box 1987 St. Augustine FL 32904*

CALKINS, GARY NATHAN, lawyer; b. N.Y.C., Mar. 1, 1911; s. Gary Nathan and Helen R. (Williston) C.; student Ecole Internationale, Geneva, Switzerland, 1926-27, Storm King Sch., 1927-29; A.B., Columbia, 1933; LL.B., Harvard, 1936; m. Susannah Eby, Nov. 19, 1949; children—Helen, Margaret, Sarah, Abigail. Admitted to N.Y. bar, 1936, D.C. bar, 1955; asso. Beekman & Bogue, N.Y.C., 1936-41; staff Civil Aeros. Bd., 1941-56, chief internat. and rules div., 1947-56; partner Galland, Kharasch & Calkins, Washington, 1956-62; partner Galland, Kharasch, Calkins & Lippmann, 1962-69, Galland, Kharasch, Calkins, & Brown, Washington and N.Y.C., 1970—. Mem. U.S. del. legal com. Internat. Civil Aviation Orgn., 1947-55, delegation chmn. 1st, 3d, 5th, 9th and 10th meetings; chmn. U.S. delegation Internat. Diplomatic Conf. for Revision of Warsaw Conv., The Hague, 1955; chmn. legal div. U.S. Air Coordinating Com., 1955-56. Served as lt. USNR, 1943-45. Mem. Am., D.C. bar assns., Soc. Quiet Birdmen. Clubs: Internat., Nat. Aviation, Internat. Aviation (Washington). Asso. editor United States and Canadian Aviation Reports, 1956; asso. editor Jour. Air Law and Commerce, 1956-58, editor-in-chief, 1958-63. Author profl. papers. Home: 6504 Dearborn Dr Falls Church VA 22044 Office: Canal Sq 1054 31st St Washington DC 20007 also 40 Wall St New York City NY 10022

CALKINS, JOHN THIERS, lawyer; b. Elmira, N.Y., May 14, 1925; s. John Thiers and Laura (Westervelt) C,; A.B,, Syracuse U,, 1949 postgrad. U. London, summer 1951; J.D., Georgetown U., 1957; m. Patricia Painton, Dec. 27, 1952; children—Sharon, Carolyn. Admitted to D.C. bar, 1958. Asst. to rep. J.C. Davies, Washington, 1949-51; account exec. Mellor Advt. Agy., Elmira, N.Y., 1952; asst. to Rep. Sterling Cole, Washington, 1953-58; exec. asst. to Rep. Howard W. Robison, Washington, 1958-70; exec. dir. Nat. Republican Congl. Com., Washington, 1970—; dir. Elmira Data Processing Co. Inc., 1964—. Chmn. Syracuse U. Alumni Giving Program, Washington, 1964. Chmn. com. spl. assts. Nat. Rep. Congl. Com., 1962-69. Trustee, Nat. Rowing Found., 1970—. Served with AUS, World War II. Congl. staff fellow Am. Polit. Sci. Assn., Inst. Internat. Studies, Geneva, Switzerland, 1965. Mem. D.C. Bar Assn., Psi Upsilon. Episcopalian. Clubs: Elmira City, Capitol Hill (Washington). Home: 2329 California St NW Washington DC 20008 Office: Congressional Hotel Washington DC 20003

CALL, EVERETT RALPH, assn. exec.; b. Manchester, N.H., June 17, 1922; s. Ralph Harvey and Erna (Schricker) C.; B.S. in Exec. Bus. Adminstrn., Georgetown U., 1949; m. Rosalind Warner Kain, Mar. 23, 1945; children—M. Christine, Jocelyn G., Phyllis A. Asst. to sec. U.S. Ind. Telephone Assn., Washington, 1946-49; statistician Inst. Shortening and Edible Oils Inc., Washington, 1950-55; dir. mgmt. information Nat. Paint and Coatings Assn., Washington, 1955—; pres. Call Marketing Services, Washington, 1959—. Pres. Civic Assn., Fairfax, Va., 1953-54. Served with USMC, 1942-46. Mem. Washington Soc. Assn. Execs. (recipient Outstanding Contbrs. award 1966, v.p. 1969-70, pres. 1970-71), Color Marketing Group (dir. 1962—). Unitarian (trustee). Home: 2608 N Pocomoke St Arlington VA 22207 Office: 1500 Rhode Island Av NW Washington DC 20005

CALLAHAN, GEORGE MICHAEL, govt. ofcl.; b. Kansas, Ala., Sept. 10, 1925; s. George W. and Hazel (Tesney) C.; B.B.A,. U. Miami, 1955; m. Josephine Jeannette Meyer, June 23, 1946; children—Carol (Mrs. John E. Balkcom), George Jr., Joseph, Suzanne. Agt. Internal Revenue Service, Miami, Fla., 1949-58; accountant SEC, Atlanta, 1958-68, chief accountant, 1968—. C.P.A., Fla. Home: 2370 Nesbitt Dr NE Atlanta GA 30319 Office: SEC 1371 Peachtree St NE Atlanta GA 30309

CALLAHAN, RALPH WILSON, newspaper exec.; b. Anniston, Ala., Apr. 18, 1906; s. Joseph Abner and Bertha (Roberts) C.; student Howard Coll. (now Samford U.), 1925-27; m. Ida Bell Price, June 25, 1938; children—Evelyn Roberts (Mrs. Louis Amis), Ralph Wilson. With Anniston Star, 1927—, retail and nat. advt. mgr., 1940-45, bus. mgr., 1945-60, exec. v.p., gen. mgr. Consol. Pub. Co., 1960-69, pres., 1969—; pres. Piedmont Pub. Co., Anniston, 1963—, Cast, Inc., Talladega, Ala., 1965—, Lake Louise Co., Anniston, 1964—; exec. v.p. Calhoun Pub. Co., Jacksonville, 1964—, Talladega Pub. Co., 1964—; treas. Anniston Devel. Co., 1961—. Sec. Anniston Bd. Edn., 1946-50; mem. exec. com. Choccolocco council Boy Scouts Am., 1955—, nat. rep., 1960—. Bd. dirs. United Givers Fund, pres. 1954, Calhoun County (Ala.) Infantile Paralysis Bd. (pres. 1958), Anniston Acad. Recipient Certificate of Achievement. Chem. Corps Tng. Command, AUS, 1960, Certificate of Appreciation, U.S. Dept. Army, 1966; Silver Beaver award Boy Scouts Am., 1966. Mem. So. Inst. Mgmt., Ala. Press Assn. (pres. 1965, chmn. bd. 1966—), So. Newspaper Pubs. Assn. (pres. 1969-70), Newcomen Soc., Anniston C. of C. (pres. 1962-63, chmn. bd. advt., chmn. mil. affairs com. 1965-66, dir.), Sigma Delta Chi, Pi Kappa Alpha. Methodist (ofcl. bd.). Kiwanian (pres. Anniston 1951). Clubs: Anniston Country; Mountain Brook Country, The Club (Birmingham, Ala.); Five-W (Ohatchee, Ala.). Home: 336 Mountain Manors Anniston AL 36201 Office: 216 W 10th St Anniston AL 36201

CALLAHAN, VINCENT FRANCIS, JR., publisher, state legislator; b. Washington, Oct. 30, 1931; s. Vincent Francis and Anita (Hawkins) C.; B.S. in Fgn. Service, Georgetown U., 1957; m. Dorothy Helen Budge, Aug. 27, 1960; children—Vincent Francis III, Elizabeth Lauren, Anita Marie, Cynthia Helen, Robert Bruce, Became partner Callahan Publs., 1957, now pres., editor numerous publs., 1957—; past pres. Ind. Newsletters Assn., Washington; mem. Va. Ho. of Dels., 1968—. Candidate for lt. gov. Va., 1965; state finance chmn. Rep. Party of Va., 1966-68. Served with USMC, 1950-53; as lt. USCGR, 1959-63. Mem. U.S. Naval Inst., Am. Inst. Aero. and Astronautics, Am. Ordnance Assn. Republican. Roman Catholic. Clubs: National Press; Kiwanis (past pres.) (McLean, Va.); Bull and Bear (Richmond, Va.). Author eight books including; Missile Contracts Guide, 1958; Space Guide, 1959; Underwater Defense Handbook, 1963; Military Research Handbook, 1963. Home: 6220 Nelway Dr McLean VA 22101 Office: 1427 Center St McLean VA 22101

CALLAHAN, WALTER STEWART, microbiologist; b. N.Y.C., July 28, 1920; s. Walter Joseph and Rose (Tierney) C.; student N.Y. State U., 1939-41; A.B., Hofstra U., 1949; M.S., U. Mich., 1951, Ph.D., 1955. Chief bacteriology lab. Univ. Hosp., Ann Arbor, Mich., 1955-63; instr. bacteriology U. Mich., 1956-63, research asso. tumor immunology, 1954-61; chief div. bacteriology, virology D.C. Dept. Pub. Health, Washington, 1963-70, acting chief bur. labs., 1970—; part-time lectr. Bethesda Naval Hosp. Served with AUS, 1942-46. F. G. Novy fellow, 1953. Diplomate Am. Acad. Microbiologists. Mem. Am. Soc. Microbiology, A.A.A.S., Sigma Xi. Contbr. numerous articles to sci. jours. Home: 3422 R St NW Washington DC 20007 Office: 300 Indiana Av Washington DC 20001

CALLAN, PATRICK JOSEPH, tourist attraction exec.; b. Washington, Mar. 2, 1937; s. John Lawrence and Rose Elizabeth (Goodwin) C.; B.S. in Advt., U. Fla., 1965; m. Judith Lorene Clark, July 27, 1963; children—Patricia Lee, Patrick Clark. Dir. pub. relations and advt. Fla. Cypress Gardens, 1962—. Pub. relations cons., 1962—. Mem. Winter Haven (Fla.) Promotions Com., 1969—. Mem. campaign staff Senator Edward Gurney, 1968. Recipient Fla. Gov.'s award for tourism, 1966. Mem. Pub. Relations Soc. Am., Fla. Pub. Relations Assn. Home: Box 10 Cypress Gardens FL 33880 Office: Box 1 Cypress Gardens FL 33880

CALLAWAY, EDWIN BROWN, editor; b. Americus, Ga., Apr. 28, 1910; s. Timothy Furlow and Lula (Brown) C.; student Mercer U., 1929-31; m. Bettina Silva, Dec. 14, 1940; children—Bette (Mrs. Donald Cohen), Edwin Brown. With various newspapers, Ga., Ala., Fla., 1937-59; editor Panama City (Fla.) News-Herald, 1960-67; Beaches editor Jacksonville (Fla.) Jour., 1967—. Mem. Sigma Delta Chi, Phi Delta Theta. Episcopalian. Home: 345 1st St Atlantic Beach FL 32003 Office: 1 Riverside Av Jacksonville FL 32207

CALLAWAY, HOWARD H., bus. exec., Republican nat. committeeman; b. LaGrange, Ga., Apr. 2, 1927; s. Cason Jewell and Virginia (Hand) C.; student Ga. Inst. Tech., 1945; ed. U.S. Mil. Acad., 1945-49; m. Elizabeth Walton; children—Elizabeth Walton, Virginia Hand, Howard Hollis, Edward Cason, Ralph Walton. Pres. Callaway Gardens, Pine Mountain, Ga., 1953-72; pres. Interfinancial, Inc., Atlanta, 1972—; chmn. finance com. Gardens Services, Inc., Pine Mountain. Mem. Adv. Commn. on Intergovernmental Relations, Washington; civilian aide to U.S. Sec. of Army. Mem. 89th congress from 3d Ga. dist.; Republican nominee gov. Ga., 1966; now Ga. mem. Rep. Nat. Com. Mem. bd. regents univ. system Ga., 1953-64; bd. dirs. Nat. 4-H Service Com.; chmn. trustees Freedoms Found, Valley Forge, Pa.; trustee Ida Cason Callaway Found. Served to 1st lt. AUS, 1949-52. Decorated Combat Infantryman badge, Korean Service medal with 3 bronze stars, Republic of Korea badge, UN Service medal. Episcopalian. Office: 230 Houston St NW Atlanta GA 30327

CALLAWAY, KATHERINE, educator; b. Baconton, Ga.; d. Eugene and Kate (Watson) Callaway; B.C.S., U. Ga., 1950, also postgrad. pub. sch. tchr. Sparta (Ga.) schs., 1947-48, Trion City (Ga.) schs., 1948-50, Atlanta pub. schs., 1950—. Recipient first place award Kazanjian Found., 1967; Valley Forge Tchrs. award. Mem. U.D.C. (treas. 1964-67), Nat., Ga., Atlanta (sec. 1966-67) edn. assns., Ga. Assn. for Childhood Edn. (v.p. 1964-67), Alpha Delta Kappa (charter). Methodist (steward, mem. ofcl. bd. 1967-68). Chief architect in compiling A Handbook for Atlanta Teachers, 1966. Home: 680 Carriage Dr Atlanta GA 30328 Office: Arlington Schs Fairburn Rd SW Atlanta GA 30331

CALLAWAY, PAUL SMITH, organist; b. Atlanta, Ill., Aug. 16, 1909; s. Ralph Vernon and Mattie (Cubbage) C.; student Westminster Coll., Fulton, Mo., 1927-29, Mus.D. (hon.), 1959; Mus.D. (hon.), Washington Coll., Chestertown, Md., 1967. Organist, choirmaster St. Thomas Chapel, N.Y., 1930-35, St. Mark's Ch., Grand Rapids, Mich., 1935-39, Washington Cathedral, 1939—; condr. Cathedral Choral Soc., Washington, 1942—; mem. faculty Peabody Conservatory, Balt., 1953-57, Coll. Ch. Musicians, Washington, 1962-69. Berkshire Music Center, Tanglewood, Mass., 1965-67, Blossom Music Center, 1968; condr. Opera Soc. Washington, 1956—, Lake George Opera Festival, 1967—. Served AUS, 1942-46. Fellow Am. Guild Organists; mem. Lit. Soc. Wash. Episcopalian. Clubs: Cosmos, City Tavern Assn. (Washington); St. Wilfred (N.Y.C.). Composer: An Hymne of Heavenley Love, 1935; The Office of the Holy Communion, 1945; Hark The Glad Sound, 1946; O Saving Victim, 1947. Home: 2230 Decatur Pl NW Washington DC 20008 Office: Washington Cathedral Mount St Alban Washington DC 20016

CALLAWAY, WILLIAM CHOTEAU, banker; b. Oakland, Miss.; May 4, 1914; s. Gilbert Evans and Bell (Duke) C.; student Miss. State U., 1931-33, George Washington U., 1934-36; m. Ann J. Monteith, May 18, 1947; 1 son, William Chouteau, 1 step-dau., Patricia Ann (Mrs. Jake Gibbs). With U.S. Dept. Interior, Washington, 1936-38, Dist. Govt. Washington, 1938-41; with Bank of Oakland (Miss.). 1951—, successively bookkeeper, cashier, exec. v.p., 1951-59, pres., 1959—. Mem. council Town of Oakland, 1957-61, mayor, 1965—. Served with AUS, 1941-45; vet. adviser VA, 1946-51. Mem. Am. Legion, V.F.W. Presbyn. (elder). Rotarian. Office: Bank of Oakland Oakland MS 38948

CALLENDER, MARTHA V. LINDER (MRS. RICHARD ERVIN CALLENDER), club woman, genealogist, artist; b. Prairie Dell, Bell County. Texas; d. Franklin Trimmier and Adeline (Hunter) Linder; student Baylor Coll., 1914-16; grad. Sam Houston State Tchrs. Coll., Huntsville, Tex., 1916; m. Richmond Ervin Callender, July 9, 1919; children—Catherine V. (Mrs. Merrill Smith), Richard Ervin (dec. 1963). Tchr. pub. schs., Rosenberg, Tex., 1917-18; sec. Gulf Oil Co., Houston 1918-19; exec. sec. Fed. Farm Loan Assn., Lockhart, Tex., 1925-30. Recipient various awards for artwork. Corr. sec. A. and M. Garden Club, 1968—; mem. A. and M. Mother's Club, A. and M. Social Club, Extension Service Club, Arts and Crafts Group. Mem. Tex. Hist. Soc., Tex. Fine Arts Assns., D.A.R. (chpt. corr. sec. 1952-54, librarian 1948-50; nat. vice chmn. scholarships com. 1960-62, Tex. chmn. geneal. records com. 1952-58, chpt. registrar 1950-52, 60-62, chpt. regent 1965-67), Daus. Am. Colonists (Tex. chmn. colonial and geneal. records 1957-59, regent Louis Guion chpt. 1961-63, Tex. parliamentarian 1959-61, state registrar 1963-65, chmn. our colonial heritage com. 1965-67, 2d vice regent chpt.

1967—), U.D.C. (pres. L.S. Ross chpt. 1961-63, chpt. registrar 1963-65 dist. chmn. 1964-66), Children Am. Colonists (nat. chaplain, sr. adv. council 1964-66, v.p. So. sect. 1971—), Brazos County Bar Assn. Aux., United Daus. 1812 (state chmn. 1971—), Tex. State Geneal. Soc., Linder Family Assn. (1st pres.), Brazos Valley Art Assn. Clubs: Bryane College Station Art (charter); Wednesday Bridge. Home: 209 Lee Av College Station TX 77840

CALLIHAM, EDITH MADELIN ETHEREDGE (MRS. GEORGE NOLLON CALLIHAM,JR.), banker; b. Ridgeville, S.C., Jan. 4, 1928; d. John Beckwith and Exie (Singletary) Etheredge; grad. high sch.; m. George Nollon Calliham, Jr., Nov. 25, 1946; children—George Nollon III, Robert L. With S.C. Nat. Bank, Naval Base, S.C., 1944-49, supr. transit and bookkeeping dept. 1947-49; with 1st Nat. Bank of S.C., Charleston, 1952—, mgr. Air Base Facility, 1955-68, asst. cashier, 1961—, mgr. Air Base and Naval Base Facilities, 1961-68, asst. v.p., 1968—, operation and mgr. credit card dept., Charleston office, 1968—. Active P.T.A., Community Civic Club. Mem. Nat. Assn. Bank Women (past chmn. S.C. group), S.C. Bankers Assn. (exec. council women's div. 1971—), Altrusa Internat. (pres. Greater Charleston 1964-66), C. of C. Methodist (sec. jr. dept. ch. sch. 1962-64). Home: 1609 Holton Pl Charlestowne Estates Charleston SC 29407 Office: 1st National Bank of SC PO Box 959 Charleston SC 29402

CALLIHAN, E. L., educator; b. Lockhart, Tex., Dec. 6, 1903; s. Jefferson Davis and Elizabeth (Horner) C.; B.J., U. of Tex., 1929; M.S.J., Northwestern U., 1939; m. Lillian Edwards, Nov. 28, 1928. Free lance writer, editor and reporter Tex. newspapers, 1923-30; sports editor. Sherman (Tex.) Daily Democrat, 1930-32; publicity writer, Austin Coll., 1931-32; publicity dir., instr. journalism, Ft. Worth (Tex.) Pub. Schs., 1933-40; prof. journalism, Drake U., 1940-45; prof. journalism, univ. news bur. dir., Baylor U., 1945-46; chmn. dept. journalism, So. Methodist U., 1946—. Mem. Assn. for Edn. in Journalism, Southwestern Journalism Congress, Am. Soc. Journalism Sch. Adminstrs., Sigma Delta Chi, Key Club, Kappa Tau Alpha (nat. pres). Author: Grammer for Journalists, 1957, rev. edit., 1969. Co-author: Exercises and Tests for Journalists, 1970; Instructor's Manual of Corrected Exercises, 1970. Editor: Drake Creative Awards anthologies, 1940-45. Contbr. publs. in field. Home: Rancho Poquito Rt 2 Mesquite TX 75149 Office: Southern Methodist U Dallas TX 75222

CALLIS, JAMES TAYLOR, physician; b. Ridgely, Tenn., June 14, 1929; s. Carmel Wilkins and Azelia (Bradshaw) C.; B.A., Vanderbilt U., 1951; M.D., U. Tenn., 1954; m. Barbara J. Watson, Feb. 26, 1971; children—(by previous marriage) Cathy Ann, Sandra Rae, James Miles, Charles Bradshaw. Intern, Hillcrest Med. Center, Tulsa, 1954-55; practice medicine specializing in gen. and medicine and pediatrics, Crossville (Tenn.) Med. Group Profl. Assn., 1954—, chmn. bd., 1971—; mem. staff Cumberland Med. Center Hosp., chief medicine 1970—, chmn. lab. com., 1968—; med. examiner Cumberland County, 1960—; dir. Lake Tansi Village Resort, Crossville, Holiday Hills Devel., Crossville; county chmn. A.R.C., 1963—, adviser Bloodmobile; med. dir. Civil Def., Cumberland County, Tenn., 1962; active East Tenn. Heart Assn.; active Smokey Mountain council Boy Scouts Am. Commr. water, Lantana Dist., Crossville, 1966—. Served to lt. M.C., USNR, 1956-58; now lt. col. Army Res. Recipient citation of merit Tenn. N.G., 1970. Mem. A.A.A.S., Am. Acad. Gen. Practice, Am., Tenn. (legislative pub. affairs com. 1961-65) med. assns., Am. Assn. Physicians and Surgeons, Cumberland City Med. Soc. (sec. 1961-64), C. of C., Alpha Tau Omega, Phi Chi. Democrat. Methodist (ofcl. bd. 1962-64). Mason (32 deg. Shriner), Lion. Home: Route 5 Box 190 Lake Tansi Village Crossville TN 28555 Office: 208 Lantana Rd Crossville TN 38555

CALLISON, CAROLINE HOLLINGSWORTH, physician; b. Charleston, S.C., Aug. 20, 1914; d. Henry Grady and Ethel (Jagar) Callison; B.S., Coker Coll., 1936; M.D., Med. Coll. S.C., 1939; M.P.H., Columbia, 1947. Intern, Crawford W. Long Meml. Hosp., 1939-41; health officer Washington Coosa, Clarke, St. Clair counties, Ala., 1941-45, McCormick and Greenwood counties, S.C., 1945-46; asst. health officer Charleston County, S.C., 1947-48; county health officer Marlboro, Chesterfield, Abberville, McCormick counties, S.C., 1948-52; dept. state health officer Queen Anne's County, Md., 1952-61; health dir. Sampson and Bladen counties, N.C., 1961—. Mem. Am. Coll. Preventive Medicine, Am. Assn. Pub. Health Physicians, N.C. Med. Assn., A.M.A., Am., N.C. pub. health assns., Sampson County Med. Soc. Episcopalian. Home: 406 Parker Dr Clinton NC 28328 Office: County Health Dept Clinton NC 28328

CALLOWAY, WILLIAM LEVI, realtor; b. Atlanta, June 16, 1908; s. Henry C. and Americus Ann (Moon) C.; B.S., Tuskegee Inst., 1933; postgrad. Atlanta U., 1941-42; m. Lillian V. Strong, Aug. 13, 1934; 1 dau., Delores. Tchr. math. Booker T. Washington High Sch., 1933-42; partner Alexander-Calloway Real Estate Co. and Ins., 1942-60; owner Calloway Realty Co., Atlanta, 1960—; founder, v.p. Consol. Mortgage & Investment Co. Vice chmn. bd. dirs. Econ. Opportunity Atlanta; bd. dirs. Central Atlanta Progress, Inc., Atlanta Community Council; trustee Nat. Council YMCA's. Recipient Outstanding Achievement award Omega Psi Phi, 1959; W.D. Morrison award for meritorious service in field of real estate, 1970; YMCA Bd. Dirs. award, 1967; Outstanding Service award Empire Real Estate Bd., 1965; award Nat. Assn. Real Estate Brokers, 1971; Econ. Opportunity Atlanta award and YMCAs of Met. Atlanta award, 1968-69. Kiwanian. Clubs: Resurgens, Atlanta Guardsmen's, Graduate. Home: 2948 Keats Dr SW Atlanta GA 30311 Office: 193 Auburn Av NE Atlanta GA 30303

CALMAN, EDWIN CHARLES, JR., editor, pub.; b. Bonne Terre, Mo., Aug. 21, 1928; s. Edwin C. and Ethel (Radle) C.; student U.S. Mil. Acad., 1946-47, U. N.C., 1948, U. Ky., 1949; B.S., Western State U., Bowling Green, Ky., 1951; m. Patsy J. McGaw, Aug. 20, 1950; children—Linda Kay, Keary, Karol, Kristy. With Sturgis (Ky.) News, 1953—, mng. editor, 1962-67, pub., 1968—. Served with AUS, 1945-49, to capt. USAF, 1951-53; now lt. col. USAF Res. Decorated Bronze Star medal. Mem. Ky., Western Ky. (pres. 1967) press assns., Am. Legion (dist. comdr. 1956, state dir. publicity 1957). Kiwanian (pres. 1964). Home: 1124 Washington St Sturgis KY 42459 Office: Box 218 Sturgis KY 42459

CALVERLEY, JOHN ROBERT, physician, educator; b. Hot Springs, Ark., Jan 14, 1932; s. John A. and Della (O'Neill) C.; B.S., U. Ore., 1953, M.D., 1955; m. Alice Mae Feller, Dec. 27, 1953; children—Mark, David. Intern U. Ia., Iowa City, 1955-56, resident in neurology, 1956; resident internal medicine Mayo Found., Rochester, Minn., 1957, neurology resident, 1957-59; mem. faculty div. neurology, med. br. U. Tex., Galveston, 1964—, asso. prof., 1966-70, prof., 1970—, chief div. neurology, 1967—. Cons. neurology U.S. Air Force, 1965—. Served to capt. USAF, 1957-64. Diplomate neurology Am. Bd. Psychiatry and Neurology, 1962. Mem. A.M.A., Tex. Med. Assn., Am. Acad. Neurology, Am. Neurol. Assn., Am. Epilepsy Soc., Assn. Research Nervous and Mental Diseases, Sigma Xi. Home: 39 Colony Park Circle Galveston TX 77550 Office: 915 Strand St Galveston TX 77550

CALVERT, DELBERT WILLIAM, corp. exec.; b. Bosworth, Mo., Jan. 29, 1927; s. William McKinley and Ruby (Berrier) C.; B.S. in Civil Engring., U. Mo., 1952; m. Mary Lee Brown, Feb. 10, 1947 (div. Mar. 1971); children—Gary D., Daniel L.; m. 2d, Melva A. Allen, Sept. 4, 1971; stepchildren—Holly Hurst, Allen Hurst. With Phillips Petroleum Co., Bartlesville, Okla., 1952-63, supr. econ. devel., supply and transp. div., 1956-60, asst. mgr. transp. div., 1960-61, mgr. automotive div.-supply and transp. div., 1961-63; asst. to v.p. Eastern Transmission Corp., Houston, 1963-65; mgr. diversification dept. No. Natural Gas Co., Omaha, 1965-68; pres. Williams Bros. Pipe Line Co., Tulsa, 1968-71; exec. v.p. Williams Cos., Tulsa, 1971—, also dir.; dir. Suburban Cos., Pomona, Cal., Edgcomb Steel Co., Phila., Williams Energy Co., Tulsa, Willchemco., Inc., Tulsa, Sci. Assistance Co., Los Angeles. Mem. exec. bd. Indian Nations council Boy Scouts Am., 1969—. Chmn. bd. dirs. Devel. Fund U. Mo.; bd. dirs. Goodwill Industries Tulsa, Ark. Basin Devel. Assn., Inc. Served with AUS, 1945-47. Mem. Okla. Petroleum Council (dir. 1968), Am. Petroluem Inst. (mem. gen. com. div. transp. 1971), Transp. Assn. Am. (mem. pipe line panel 1969), Tau Beta Pi, Chi Epsilon, Pi Mu Epsilon. Republican. Clubs: Oak Country, University, Southern Hills Country (Tulsa). Home: 7277 S Pittsburg St Tulsa OK 74105 Office: 825 Nat Bank Tulsa Bldg Tulsa OK 74103

CALVERT, FLOYD OLAN, educator; b. Mountain View, Okla., Aug. 23, 1925; s. Jesse Roy and Jewel (Bourns) C.; B.S., U. Okla., 1950, M.S., 1958, Engring. D., 1969; postgrad. U. Cal. at Berkeley, 1960-61, U. Ariz., 1963-64; m. Dorothy Jean Carnes, Nov. 25, 1947; children—Sherry Lynn, Hallie Ann, Paula Joyce, Cary Mark, Wendy Jean. Instr., asst. prof. mech. engring. U. Okla., Norman, 1956-60, asso. prof. Sch. Architecture, 1969—; asst. prof. Cal. State Poly. Coll., Pomona, 1961-62; asst. prof., asso. prof. mech. engring. U. N.M., 1962-67; mech. engr. Internat. Paper Co., Corp. Engrs., Bechtol Corp., 1950-56. Served to 2d lt. C.E., AUS, 1945-47. NSF Sci. Faculty fellow, 1960-61, 63-64. Registered profl. engr., Okla. Mem. Am. Soc. M.E., Am. Soc. Heating, Refrigeration and Air Conditioning Engrs., Am. Soc. Engring. Edn., Pi Tau Sigma, Tau Beta Pi. Baptist (deacon). Home: 731 Nancy Lynn St Norman OK 73069 Office: 180 W Brooks St Norman OK 73069

CALVERT, GORDON LEE, lawyer; b. Wardensville, W. Va., Sept. 2, 1921; s. Aaron Lee and Ada (Brill) C.; A.B. with distinction, George Washington U., 1943, J.D. with distinction, 1945; m. Margaret Frances James, June 9, 1945; children—Gordon Rodney, Roger Lee, Walter Randolph. Admitted to D.C. bar, 1946; asso. firm Covington and Burling, 1945-46; mem. staff Investment Bankers Assn. Am., Washington, 1946-71, municipal dir., asst. gen. counsel, 1955-66, exec. dir., gen. counsel, 1966-71; exec. v.p. gen. counsel Securities Industry Assn., Washington, 1972—. Mem. adv. com. Harvard Law Sch. Study of State Securities Regulation, 1954-55. Active Boy Scouts Am. Mem. Am. Bar Assn., Am. Soc. Assn. Exec., Order of the Coif, Pi Kappa Alpha, Phi Delta Phi, Omicron Delta Kappa, Pi Gamma Mu. Clubs: Metropolitan. Columbia (Washington). Author: Fundamentals of Municipal Bonds, 1959, 63, State Pension Funds-Digest of Authorized Investments and Actual Investments, 1960, 64. Home: 6712 Michaels Dr Bethesda MD 20034 Office: 425 13th St NW Washington DC 20004

CALVERT, ROBERT S., state ofcl.; b. Tex., Apr. 27, 1892; s. Cleon H. and Sallie (Neff) C.; student Howard Payne Coll., 1909; m. Josie Moody, Mar. 24, 1920; 1 dau., Josephine (Mrs. Leonard Baker). Asst cashier 1st Nat. Bank Sweetwater (Tex.), 1917-30; statistician for state comptroller Tex., Austin, 1930-44, chief clk., 1944-49; state comptroller State of Tex., Austin, 1949—. Bd. dirs. Fedn. Tax Adminstrs. Served with U.S. Army, World War I. Named Man of Year, Howard Payne Coll., 1957. Mem. Am. Legion, V.F.W., S.A.R., Sons Confederacy, Nat. Assn. State Auditors, Comptrollers and Treasurers, Nat. Tax Assn., Austin C. of C. Mem. Christian Ch. Mason, Lion. Home: 2115 Enfield Rd Austin TX 78703 Office: State Capitol Austin TX 78711

CALVERT, ROBERT W(ILBURN), judge; b. nr. Pulaski, Tenn., Feb. 22, 1905; s. Porter and Maud (Richardson) C.; LL.B., U. Tex., 1931; m. Frances Freeland, June 6, 1933 (div. 1958); children—Carolyn, James Porter; m. 2d, Corinne Lundgren, Jan. 26, 1962. Admitted to Tex. bar, 1931, practiced Hillsboro, 1931-50, with Morrow & Calvert, 1934-50; dist. atty. Hill County, 1943-47; asso. justice Supreme Ct. Tex., 1950-61, chief justice, 1961—. Mem. Tex. Ho. of Reps., 1933-39, speaker, 1937-39. Chmn. Dem. State Exec. Com., 1946-48. Home: 1411 W 29th St Austin TX 78702 Office: Supreme Ct Austin TX 78711

CALVIN, LARRY O., zoo adminstr. married; 1 son. Formerly curator Dallas Zoo, now dir. Mem. Am. Assn. Zool. Parks and Aquariums, Nat. Recreation and Park Assn. Kiwanian. Home: 1507 Oak Glen Trail Dallas TX 75232 Office: Clarendon Dr Dallas TX 75023*

CAMERON, BENJAMIN FRANKLIN, JR., orgn. exec.; b. Meridian, Miss., Nov. 4, 1920; s. Benjamin Franklin and Polly (Paine) C.; B.S., U. South, 1942; M.S. in Engring., U. Cin., 1944, Sc.D., 1948; m. Ruth Anders, Dec. 21, 1942; children—Douglas Winston, Robert Boatner, Elizabeth Anne. Research asst. Cin. Milling Machine Co., 1942-44, 44-48; research chemist, 1948-49; asst. prof. chemistry U. South, Sewanee, Tenn., 1949-51, dir. admissions, 1951-59; trustee Coll. Entrance Exam. Bd., N.Y.C., 1958-59, So. regional dir., Sewanee, 1959-63, v.p., 1964-70; pres. Outdoor Enterprises, Inc., 1970—; bd. dirs. So. Edn. Reporting Service. Cons. in edn. Ford Found., 1964-65; research cons. Carlisle Chem. Co., Norwood, O., 1949-50. Chmn. Sewanee Community Chest, 1950-51, 63-64; pres. Sewanee Civic Assn., 1951-52, Sewanee P.T.A., 1959-60. Served to lt. (j.g.) USNR, 1944-46; PTO. Mem. Am. Chem. Soc., A.A.A.S., Am. Assn. Collegiate Registrars and Admissions Officers, Assn. Coll. Admissions Counselors (exec. bd. 1958-59), So. Coll. Scholarship Group (chmn. 1956-59), Blue Key, Sigma Xi, Alpha Chi Sigma, Omicron Delta Kappa, Kappa Alpha. Democrat. Episcopalian. Contbr. numerous articles on student financial aid to profl. publs. Home: Sewanee TN 37375 Office: Outdoor Enterprises Inc Sewanee TN 37375

CAMERON, CURTIS ALFRED, rancher; b. Fredericksburg, Tex., Apr. 27, 1939; s. Alfred Louis and Helen Alma Mathilda (Dittmar) C.; B.B.A., S.W. Tex. State Coll., 1961; m. Mary Katharine Redman, Apr. 8, 1967; children—Catharine Helen, Cyrena Christine. Self employed rancher, Gillespie, Llano and Kimble counties, Tex., 1961—. Dir. Fredericksburg Nat. Bank. Pres. Gillespie County Fair Assn., 1964-65, now bd. dirs., futurity chmn. Served with USAF, 1961-67. Recipient Appreciation award Gillespie County Fair Assn., 1965. Mem. Tex. Sheep and Goat Raisers Assn., Fredericksburg Ex-Students Assn. (dir. 1971—), Am. Quarter Horse Assn., Farm Bur. Lutheran. Home: Route 1 Box 252 Fredericksburg TX 78624 Office: 155 E Main St Fredericksburg TX 78624

CAMERON, DONALD FIELD, JR., retail trade exec.; b. Knoxville, Tenn., Feb. 11, 1916; s. Donald Field and Katherine Mae (Knight) C.; student U. Tenn., 1934-37; m. Elizabeth Rutelia McCampbell, Nov. 29, 1942; children—Virginia Susan (Mrs. Elbert Allen Springer, Jr.), Donald Field III. With Miller's Inc., retail trade, Knoxville, 1937, v.p., 1959—, merchandising mgr., 1961—; dir. Talcor, Inc., Jefferson City, Tenn. Pres., Cancer Soc., Knoxville, 1957-58; bd. dirs. United Fund, 1958-62. Served with Armed Forces, 1941-46, 50-52. Mem. Nat. Retail Mchts. Assn. (dir. 1958-64, 68-71. Mem. Christian Ch. (trustee 1969—, deacon 1953—, chmn. ch. bd. 1960-66). Clubs: Holston Hills Country, Fort Loudoun Yacht. Home: 5110 E Sunset Rd Knoxville TN 37914 Office: 600 Henley St Knoxville TN 37902

CAMERON, EDMUND MCCULLOUGH, educator. Athletic dir. Duke U., Durham, N.C. Address: Duke U Durham NC 27706*

CAMERON, EDMUND MCCULLOUGH, JR., soft drink co. exec.; b. Durham, N.C., Feb. 20, 1939; s. Edmund McCullough and Mary (Toms) C.; grad Choate Sch., 1957; B.A., Duke, 1962; m. Marguerite Walker Hines, June 6, 1960; children—Edmund McCullough III, Marguerite Hines. Mgr. time payment direct loans Waohovia Bank & Trust Co., 1962-66, mgr. mortgage loans, 1966—; sec.-treas., gen. mgr. Harvey C. Hines Co., Coca-Cola Bottling Co., Kinston, N.C., 1966—; sec.-treas. Kinston Holding & Investment Co. Elk, Rotarian. Home: 1902 Cambridge Dr Kinston NC 28501 Office: Box 337 Kinston NC 28501

CAMERON, LINUAL, ret. univ. exec.; b. Denton, Ark., Oct. 7, 1905; s. Jason W. and Minnie (East) C.; B.A., Ark. State U., 1937; M.A., U. Ark., 1948; postgrad. U. Omaha, 1954; m. Inez Garner, Mar. 26, 1937; children—Kay, Robert L., Suzi. Tchr. pub. schs., 1929-37; supr. Lawrence County Schs., 1937-51; v.p. finance Ark. State U., State U., 1951-71. Chmn., County Library Bd., 1945-48. Named Man of Year Lawrence County, 1937. Mem. N.E.A. (life), Ark. Edn. Assn. (life), So. Assn. Coll. Bus. Officers (pres.), Nat. Assn. Ednl. Buyers, Schoolmasters Club (past pres.), Phi Delta Kappa, Delta Kappa Pi. Methodist. Rotarian. Home: 1905 Eldridge St Jonesboro AR 72401

CAMFIELD, DOROTHEA JORDAN (MRS. ARTHUR G. CAMFIELD), club woman; b. Bklyn., Oct. 13, 1917; d. Stroud and Virgie (Marshburn) Jordan; student Coll. of William and Mary, 1935-36; m. Arthur Gray Camfield, Oct. 13, 1938; children—Clarissa, Valerie, Stroud, Gray. Pres. Miami Jr. Woman's Club, 1946, hon. mem., 1951—, now sr. adv.; pres. Coral Way Elementary Sch. P.T.A., 1954, 66-68; founding mem. Women's Aux. Nat. Propeller Club, 1955, hon. mem., 1957—; founding mem. woman's div. Miami C. of C., 1950, Bayshore Woman's Club, Cancer Cytology Clinic Women's Aux., Miami, 1955; mem. Miami Women's Mil. Affairs Com., Miami Children's Theater, Miami Woman's Club, Miami Com. Am. Security, Miami chpt. Inventors Council, Dade County Cleanup Council, Civil Defense Council Dade County, Dade County Pollution Bd., Fla. Council Clean Air; chmn. Air Conservation Com. Dade County; mem. Interagy. Council for Smoking and Health, Health Planning Council Dade County, Third Army Adv. Com., Miami Hospitality Com., Dade County U.S.O. Com., Dade County YWCA Bd., White Adv. Council Negro Youth Council, Dade County Council Girl Scouts U.S.A., Dade County Grand Jury Assn., Dade County Fedn. Women's Clubs (conservation chmn.); dir. at large Fla. Tb and Respiratory Disease Assn., D.A.R. (conservation chmn. Everglades chpt.), Internat. Platform Assn., Dade County P.T.A. Council, Alianza Interamericana, Miami Day Nursery Bd., Florence Crittendon Home Soc., Viscayans, Woman's Democratic Club Dade County, Psi Psi Psi, Gamma Phi Beta Alumnae; area chmn. Community Chest, 1946-47; dir., sec. Dade-Monroe Tb and Respiratory Disease Assn.; fund raising chmn. Dade County United Fund, 1959; pres. Children's Home Soc. Aux.; life mem. Fla. PTA; mem. U.D.C.; pres. Shenandoah Jr. High Sch. Concerned Parents, 1971-73; pres. Children's Home Soc. S.E. Fla. Aux., 1971-73; mem. com. services to older children Children's Home Soc. Fla. Sec., treas. Dade County Young Democrats, 1949-52; v.p. 4th dist. Young Dems. Clubs Fla., 1951-52. Chmn. dist. 11 Jr. Women's Clubs, 1947-48; mem. Jr. Mus. Guild, Poinciana Festival Com.; co-chmn. Y-Teens; bd. dirs. Miami Jr. Women's Club. Recipient citations Gen. Fedn. Women's Clubs, 1946, Dept. Navy, 1942, Office Pres. U.S., 1948, Miami C. of C., 1949-51, Country of Ecuador, 1949, Miami Jr. Woman's Club, 1951, Country of France, 1954, U.S. State Dept., 1953, Dade County Dist. 11th Jud. Circuit Ct., 1956, Fed. Civil Def. Adminstrn., 1956. Home: 1730 Nocatee Dr Miami FL 33133

CAMILLETTI, PAUL CARMEN, lawyer; b. Wheeling, W.Va., Oct. 25, 1932; s. D. Paul and Nell E. (DiBacco) C.; (B.S., Mt. St. Mary's Coll., 1954; LL.B., W. Va. U., 1957; m. Margaret E. Rocks; children—Paul, Michael, David, Stephen, Joseph, Mark, Christopher, Pamela, Catherine. Admitted to W. Va. bar, 1957; practiced in Wheeling, 1957-69; U.S. atty., No. Dist. W. Va., Wheeling, 1969—. Lectr. Wheeling Coll., 1964—. Mem. Am., W. Va., Ohio County bar assns., W. Va. State Bar. Roman Catholic. Elk, K.C. Home: 22 Bae Mar Place Wheeling WV 26003 Office: 243 Fed Bldg Wheeling WV 26003

CAMINITA, LUDWIG, JR., govt. ofcl.; b. Pitts., Feb. 22, 1910; s. Ludwig and Amelia (Fontanella) C.; B.S., George Washington U., 1934, M.A., 1937; m. Margaret Rosalie Hicks, Aug. 13, 1967. Press, radio writer U.S. Fish and Wildlife Service, 1938-42; information specialist to dir. pub. relations Petroleum Adminstrn. for War, 1942-45; partner Sessions & Caminita, 1946-64; spl. asst. to commr. Community Facilities Adminstrn., Housing and Home Finance Agy., 1964-66; spl. asst. to the asst. sec. Dept. Housing & Urban Devel., Washington, 1966-68; mgmt. analysis officer Office Dep. Asst. Postmaster Gen., U.S. Postal Service, 1968-70, Office Sr. Asst. Postmaster Gen. for Employee and Labor Relations, 1971—; adj. prof. dept. communications Am. U., Washington, 1950-68; adj. prof. dept. journalism U. Md., 1968—. Mem. pub. relations adv. com. A.R.C., 1952-70. Pres. bd. trustees Sandy Spring (Md.) Friends Sch., 1965-70. Mem. Pub. Relations Soc. Am. (accredited). Mem. Soc. of Friends (clk. Sandy Spring Friends Meeting 1967-70). Home: Box 68 Sandy Spring MD 20860 Office: 12 Pennsylvania Av NW US Postal Service Washington DC 20260

CAMINO, RICHARD, civil engr.; b. N.Y.C., Nov. 15, 1931; s. Antonio and Carmen (Carlo) C.; B.S., U. P.R., 1954; M. Civil Engring., U. City N.Y., 1961; postgrad. U. Fla., 1963; m. Ivette Gaztambide, June 4, 1955; children—Richard F., Darlene, Lisette. Structural designer Robins Engrs., N.Y.C., 1957-59; asst. civil engr. N.Y.C. Housing Authority, 1959-61; civil engr. Tippetts-Abbott-McCarthy-Stratton, San Juan, P.R., 1961-63, Sarriera-Sifontes & Assos., San Juan, 1963-64; partner Feheley-Bartolemei-Camino, Hato Rey, P.R., 1965—. Served with AUS, 1955-57. Recipient award P.R. Jr. C. of C., 1969. Mem. Am. Soc. C.E., Am. Concrete Inst., Coll. Engrs., Architects and Surveyors P.R., P.R. Soc. Civil Engrs., San Juan Jr. C. of C. (pres. 1968), Puerto Rico Jr. C. of C. (pres. 1971). Home: 106 Rimac St Rio Piedras Heights Rio Piedras PR 00926 Office: Box 498 Hato Rey PR 00919

CAMP, CLIFTON DURRETT, JR., newspaper exec.; b. Trenton, Ky., Aug. 2, 1927; s. Clifton Durrett and Virginia (McElwain) C.; B.S., U. Ky., 1950; m. Jane Peters, June 9, 1950; children—Daniel Durrett, Thomas Clifton, Pamela Jane, Emily Ann. Accountant, Sheldon, Curry, Canning & Wells, St. Petersburg, Fla., 1950-54; asst. controller Times Pub. Co., St. Petersburg, 1954-57, controller, 1957-71, treas., 1960—, v.p., 1967—, sec., 1969—, dir., 1962—; treas. Congl. Quar., Inc., 1962—, sec., 1969—. Treas., Poynter Fund, 1962—. Adv. bd. St. Petersburg Salvation Army, 1970—; mem. Com. of 100 of Pinellas County. Served with USNR, 1945-46. Mem. Inst. Newspaper Controllers and Finance Officers, Am. Mgmt. Assn., Nat. Assn. Accountants, St. Petersburg C. of C. Methodist. Clubs: Yacht, Lakewood Country (St. Petersburg, Fla.). Home: 2411 Sunrise Dr SE St Petersburg FL 33705 Office: 490 1st Av S St Petersburg FL 33731

CAMP, EDWARD FRANKLIN, JR., football coach; b. Trenton, Ky., Dec. 23, 1905; s. Edward Frank and Matie (White) C.; B.S., Transylvania Coll., 1930; postgrad. U. Ill., 1931; M.A., Columbia, 1941; m. Emelyn McCord, Aug. 1931 (dec. 1934); m. 2d, Nancy Elmore, Mar. 10, 1946; children—Marilyn Sue (Mrs. Thomas S. Ramey), Jeanne Carol (Mrs. Donald Blackburn), Linda Marie, Joyce Deane. Coach pub. schs., Hodgenville, Ky., 1930-35, Glasgow, Ky., 1935-42, Henderson, Ky., 1943-46; football coach, asst. athletic dir., prof. U. Louisville, 1946—. Chmn. Ky. Easter Seal campaign, 1966-68. Bd. dirs. Red Shield Boys Club. Mem. Am. Football Coaches Assn. (trustee). Rotarian. Home: 2501 Napoleon Blvd Louisville KY 40205 Office: U louisville Louisville KY 40208

CAMP, JOHN CLAYTON, lawyer; b. Arab, Ala., Sept. 23, 1923; s. Roy H. and Alice (Cox) C.; student Birmingham So. Coll., 1940-42, U. Ala., 1943, Auburn U., 1944; LL.B., La. State U., 1948; m. Frances Spencer, Nov. 3, 1944; children—Elizabeth Ann, Martha Lynn, Charles Henry, John Clayton II. Admitted to La. bar, 1948; asso. firm Thompson, Lawes & Cavanaugh, Lake Charles, 1948-55; partner firm Camp, Carmouche, Palmer, Carwile & Barsh, Lake Charles, 1955—. Dir. Land & Royalty Owners La. Chmn., Calcasieu Indsl. Devel. Bd., 1963-64; committeeman La. Bd. Edn.; adv. com. La. Law Inst. Served with USAAF, 1943-46. Fellow Internat. Acad. Law and Sci.; mem. Am. Arbitration Assn., Am., Fed., La. bar assns., Fgn. Relations Assn. New Orleans, Gulf Area Devel. Com., Houston Estate and Financial Forum, Am. Mgmt. Assn., La. Civil Service League (dir. 1970—), La. Forestry Assn., Miss. Valley World Trade Council, La.-Miss. Export Expansion Council, La. Intercoastal Seaway Assn. (dir. 1970—), Internat. Trade Mart New Orleans, U.S. (internat. com. 1972), La. (dir. 1971), Greater Lake Charles (pres. 1971, dir.) chambers commerce, Internat. Platform Assn. Clubs: Plimsoll, Internat. House (New Orleans); Propeller. Home: 224 W Spring St Lake Charles LA 70601 Office: PO Drawer 2001 Lake Charles LA 70601

CAMP, JOHN N. HAPPY, congressman; b. Enid, Okla., May 11, 1908; s. John Rowland and Minnie Catherine (Newbold) C.; ed. Phillips U., Enid; m. Vera Juanita Overman, Nov. 26, 1930; children—Patricia (Mrs. Roy G. Rainey), Kay (Mrs. Dan Dillingham), John N. III, Steven Richard. Mem. Okla. Legislature; chmn. Okla. Bd. Pub. Affairs; mem. 91st-92d congresses, 6th Dist. Okla. Pres. Great Salt Plains Plaines council Boy Scouts Am.; legislative supt. Okla. Girls State; area dir. Okla. Northwest. Bd. dirs. Miss Okla. Pageant; mem. grad. sem. council Phillips U.; mem. gov. com. Christian Ch. Found. Recipient Silver Beaver award Boy Scouts Am.; Master Farmers certificate Future Farmers Am. Hon. mem. 4-H Clubs Okla.; mem. Okla. C. of C. (bd. dirs.), Hist. Soc. Mem. Disciples of Christ Ch. (charter). Mason (32 deg., Shriner, Jester). Office: House Office Bldg Washington DC 20515

CAMP, LAWRENCE H., business exec.; b. Brunswick, Va., 1915; ed. Ferrum Jr. Coll., Va. Mech. Inst. With Carter Bros., Inc., 1936-44; staff accountant Leach, Calkins & Scott, 1944-49, partner, 1949-61; with Chesapeake Corp. Va., 1961—, controller, 1961-63, treas., 1963-66, v.p. finance and treas., 1966-68, sr. v.p. and treas., 1968, exec. v.p., treas. and chief exec. officer, 1968-69, pres. and chief exec. officer, 1969—, also dir.; treas., dir. Balt. Box Co., Binghamton Container Co., Greenlife Products Co., Miller Container Corp., Scranton Corrugated Box Co., So. Corrugated Box Corp., David Weber Co. Address: Chesapeake Corp Va West Point VA 23181

CAMP, RICHARD JOSEPH, govt. ofcl.; b. Antwerp, O., Sept. 17, 1920; s. Dallas A. and Clara (Lucas) C.; B.S., Bowling Green State U., 1942; M.S., State U. Ia., 1951; m. Ruth E. Williamson, Jan. 26, 1945; children—Richard Michael, Kathryn Louise. Instr. State U. Ia., 1949-52; operations analyst SAC, Omaha, 1952-64; mgr. operations research USAF, Washington, 1964—. Served with USNR, 1942-49. Mem. Operation Research Soc. Am., Sigma Xi, Kappa Delta Pi, Kappa Mu Epsilon. Home: 9218 Volunteer Dr Alexandria VA 22309 Office: USAF Washington DC 20005

CAMP, RICHARD OLLIE, petroleum co. exec., banker; b. Phil Campbell, Ala., Jan. 8, 1913; s. Loyd Amos and Carrie (Riddle) C.; student Florence State U., 1937; B.S., Auburn U., 1941; m. Fay Self, Dec. 20, 1938. Tchr., prin. pub. schs., Morgan County, Ala., 1934-41; sr. prodn. dispatcher Bechtel-McCone Corp., Birmingham, Ala., 1941-45; tng. coordinator for vets. VA, 1945-52; oil jobber Shell Oil Co., Hartselle, Ala., 1952-72; chmn. bd. Am. Bank & Trust Co., Hartselle. Mem. N. Central Ala. Planning Com., 1965—; chmn. Morgan County fund drs. United Fund, 1955—, A.R.C., 1954—; adviser League Women Voters Ala., 1965—. Recipient Outstanding Service award Kiwanis, Hartselle, 1956, Ala. Petroleum Council, 1962. Mem. Ala. Jobber Assn., Morgan County Petroleum Council (chmn.), Hartselle Aviation Assn. (v.p. 1964-65). Democrat. Baptist. Mason. K.P. Home: 302 Pearl St Hartselle AL 35640 Office: 323 S Railroad St Hartselle AL 35640

CAMP, THOMAS EDWARD, librarian; b. Haynesville, La., July 12, 1929; s. Charles W. and Annie Laura (Brazzell) C.; B.A., Centenary Coll. La., 1950; postgrad. Div. Sch. Vanderbilt U., 1950-51; M.S., La. State U., 1953; m. Elizabeth Anne Sowar, Sept. 4, 1952; children—Anne Winifred, Thomas David. Asst. in binding dept. La. State U. Library, 1951-53; circulation librarian Bridwell Library, Perkins Sch. of Theology, So. Meth. U., Dallas, 1955-57; librarian Sch. Theology U. of South, Sewanee, Tenn., 1957—. Mem. credit com. Sewanee Credit Union. Served with AUS, 1953-55. Mem. Franklin County Assn. for Retarded Children and Adults (pres. 1971-72), Am. Guild Organists, Am. Theol. Library Assn. (exec. sec. 1965-67), Kappa Alpha, Omicron Delta Kappa, Phi Kappa Phi, Beta Phi Mu. Author: (with E.V. Aldrich) Using Theological Books and Libraries, 1963. Contbr. articles in field to profl. jours. Home: Carruthers Rd Sewanee TN 37375

CAMP, THOMAS LEE, judge; b. Fairburn, Ga., Mar. 9, 1905; s. Thomas Wiley and Lula (Duggan) C.; A.B., Oglethorpe U., 1925; LL.B., George Washington U., 1931; m. Gladys Palmer Hobgood, June 15, 1927; children—Gladys (Mrs. John Gordon Hiles), Sara Ann (Mrs. Julian Wilson Swann). Admitted Ga. bar, 1933; clk., Atlanta and Lowry Nat. Bank (now 1st Nat. Bank Atlanta), and high sch. tchr., 1925-27; sec. to congressman, clk., Civil Service Com. U.S. Ho. Reps., 1927-44; pvt. practice law, Atlanta; commr. Fulton County (Ga.), 1947-56; judge Civil Ct. Fulton County, 1957-66, chief judge, 1966—. Bd. trustees Oglethorpe U. Mem. Am., Ga. bar assns. Methodist (chmn. ofcl. bd. 1958-59). Mason (Shriner). Clubs: Lawyers, Kiwanis, Atlanta Athletic City and Country, Ansley Golf. Home: 169 Robin Hood Rd NE Atlanta GA 30309 Office: Civil Ct Bldg Atlanta GA 30303

CAMP, WILLIAM BACON, govt. ofcl.; b. Greenville, Tex., Nov. 25, 1913; s. William Hille and Marguerite (Bacon) C.; student Tex. Mil. Coll., 1932, Baylor U., 1933; m. Lida Eileen Conner, Nov. 23, 1947. With Office Comptroller of Currency, 1937—, asst. chief Nat. Bank Examiner, 1961, 1st dep. comptroller, 1963-67, comptroller of currency, 1967—; mem. faculty Stonier Sch. Banking, Rutgers U., 1962—. Mem. Christian Ch. Rotarian. Home: 1397 Canterbury Way Rockville MD 20854 Office: Main Treasury Bldg Washington DC 20220

CAMPBELL, AGNES KNIGHT (MRS. JOHN FRANKLIN CAMPBELL), social agy. exec.; b. Boom, Tenn.; d George Allen and Nora (Clark) Knight; B.S., Tenn. Tech. U., 1934; postgrad. Vanderbilt U., 1935, U. Chgo. Sch. Social Service Adminstrn., 1942, 46; M.S., U. Tenn. Sch. Social Work, 1953; m. John Franklin Campbell, June 20, 1942. Regional dir. Tenn. Dept. Pub. Welfare, Nashville, 1942-55; social worker Youth Service, Child and Family Service, Knoxville, Tenn., 1955-58; exec. dir. Knoxville Travelers Aid Soc., 1958—. Bd. dirs. Knoxville Legal Aid Soc., planning council United Community Services Greater Knoxville. Mem. Nat. Assn. Social Workers (pres. 1951-53, sec. 1966-68), Tenn. Conf. of Social Work (state sec. 1955), Nat. Travelers Aid Assn., Profl. Execs. Knoxville (pres. 1967-68). Club: Social Service of Knoxville. Author script: Some of Those We Help, 1962; play: Trouble Away From Home, 1964. Home: 6515 Sherwood Dr Knoxville TN 37919 Office: 100 Magnolia Av Knoxville TN 37917

CAMPBELL, ARCHIBALD ALGERNON, lawyer, state legislator; b. Wytheville, Va., July 23, 1921; s. P. Fitzgerald and Mary (Austin) C.; B.S., Va. Mil. Inst., 1943; LL.B., U. Va., 1949; m. Eloise Richberg, Feb. 19, 1950; children—Donald Richberg, Marenda Ann, Florence Weed. Admitted to Va. bar, 1948; temporary foreign service officer Amfoge II, Greece, 1946; partner Campbell & Campbell, attys., Wytheville, Va., 1949—; mem. Va. Ho. Dels., 1966—; adv. bd. First Nat. Exchange Bank Va., Wytheville; dir., treas. Tourists, Inc., Wytheville, 1960—. Mem. exec. com. Va. State Tb. Assn., 1958-63; sec. Smyth-Wythe Joint Airport Commn., 1958-69; chmn. Wythe County Economy Commn., 1962-63. Served with USMCR, 1943-46. Decorated D.F.C. Mem. Am., Va. State (v.p. 1962-63) bar assns., Southwest Va. Horsemen's Assn. Democrat. Presbyn. Rotarian (local pres. 1958-59). Home: Pine Ridge Wytheville VA 24382 Office: 210 W Main St Wytheville VA 24382

CAMPBELL, BEATRICE BERNICE, educator; b. Collins, Miss., Dec. 10, 1916; A.A., Jones County Jr. Coll., 1936; B.S., U. So. Miss., 1938; M.S., Miss. State U., 1948. Vocational home econs. tchr. Puckett (Miss.) High Sch., 1938-40, Dexter High Sch., Tylertown, Miss., 1940, Black Jack High Sch., Batesville, Miss., 1942, Tylertown High Sch., 1942-44, Clara (Miss.) High Sch., 1945; tchr. vocational home econs., dean attendance center Leland (Miss.) Consol. High Sch. 1946—. Mem. Miss. Future Homemakers Am. (dist. supr. 1948—), Miss. (pres. 1959), Am. vocational assns., Miss. (pres. 1966-68, councilor 1969), Am. home econs. assn., N.E.A., Miss. Edn. Assn., LeLand Tchrs. Assn., Dept. Classroom Tchrs. Assn., Delta Kappa Gamma (chpt. pres. 1960-62), C. of C. Democrat. Methodist. Home: 408 4th St St Leland MS 38756

CAMPBELL, BILLY GAY, physician; b. Moran, Tex., Sept. 5, 1924; s. William Gay and Tressie Belle (Cadenhead) C.; B.A., Baylor U., 1949; M.D., U. Tex., 1954; children—Richard, Ann, Carol, David. Intern, Robert B. Green Hosp., San Antonio, 1954-55; gen. practice medicine, San Antonio, 1955-68; mem. active staff Bapt. Meml. Hosp.; mem. courtesy staff Nix Hosp., Santa Rosa Med. Center, St. Benedicts Hosp.; dir. student health S.W. Tex. State U., 1968—; acting med. dir. Gary Job Corps, 1971. Cons., Salvation Army Hosp., San Antonio, 1957-68, Planned Parenthood, San Marcos, Tex., 1968-71; team physician Somerset High Sch., 1960-65, S.W. Tex. State U., 1968-71. Trustee Bexar County United Physician Fund, 1965-68. Served with USMCR, 1942-46; PTO. Mem. A.M.A., Bapt. Tex. Med. Assn., Osteon, Alpha Kappa Kappa, Beta Beta Beta. Home: PO Box 1290 San Marcos TX 78666 also Old YMCA Rd Wimberley TX 78676

CAMPBELL, BOBBY JACK, educator; b. Fort Worth, Oct. 12, 1929; s. Jack Bryan and Opal (Lamberth) C.; B.A., Tex. Christian U., 1951, M.A., 1953; Ph.D., U. N.C., 1960; m. Frances Carol Alexander, Aug. 24, 1957; children—Carol S., John W. Asst. dir. automotive crash injury research project Cornell U., 1960-63, head accident research br., aero. lab., 1963-66; dir. hwy. safety research center U. N.C., Chapel Hill, 1966—, asso. prof. psychology, 1969—. Vice pres. research Nat. Safety Council, 1967—; chmn. tech. com. U.S.A. Standards Inst., 1967; mem. N.C. Gov.'s Spl. Adv. Com. Hwy. Safety, 1967—. Served with AUS, 1948-49. Recipient Met. Life Ins. Co. award for research in accident prevention, 1960, 71. Mem. Am. Psychol. Assn. Author: Driver Improvement: The Point System, 1958. Contbr. article to ency., chpts. to books, articles to sci. publs. Mem. editorial bd. Jour. of Safety Research, 1969—, Jour. Accident Analysis and Prevention, 1969—, Behavioral Research in Traffic Safety, 1969—. Home: 502 Belmont St Chapel Hill NC 27514

CAMPBELL, CHARLES BOYLE, JR., city ofcl.; b. College Station, Tex., Nov. 13, 1922; s. Charles Boyle and Margaret (Boulware) C.; B.B.A., Tulane U., 1943; B.S., Tex. A. and M. U., 1948; m. Katherine Love Harrison, July 1, 1950; children—Ann Hamilton, Margaret Womack, Charles Brice. Asst. prof. naval sci. and tactics Tex. U., 1945-46; landscape architect Lambert Landscape Co., Dallas, 1948-49; mgr. R. Lacy Nursery Co., Longview, Tex., 1949-51; asst. mgr. Tex. Nursery Co., Sherman, 1951-54; dir. parks and recreation City of Midland, Tex., 1954-62, City of Ft. Worth, 1962—. Served with USNR, 1943-46; PTO. Mem. Am. Park and Recreation Soc. (dir.), Tex. Municipal Park and Recreation Assn. (pres. 1972), Tex. Turfgrass Assn. (past pres.), Phi Delta Theta. Developer 1st municipal zoo, Midland, 1954-62, Dennis the Menace playground, Midland, 1960. Home: 3600 Westcliff Rd N Fort Worth TX 76109 Office: 1000 Throckmorton St Fort Worth TX 76102

CAMPBELL, CHARLES CLINTON, ins. exec.; b. Bolivar, Tenn., Aug. 2, 1923; s. Charles Ray and Tommie (Clinton) C.; grad. high sch.; m. Johnsye Craft, Apr. 22, 1950; children—Theresa Lee, Charles Lamar, Philip Wayne, Pamela Louise. Clk., Comml. Nat. Bank, Little Rock, 1941; finance clk. U.S. Engrs., Little Rock, 1941-42; spl. agt. W.M. Apple & Co., Little Rock, 1946-56; exec. v.p. Rebsamen & Assos., Inc., Little Rock, 1956—. Vice pres. Optimist Internat., 1966-67, pres. elect, 1969-70, pres., 1970-71; bd. dirs. Optimist Internat. Found. Bd. dirs. Presbyn. Village, Little Rock Boys Club. Served to comdr. USNR, 1942-46. Decorated Air medal with 2 oak leaf clusters. Mem. Ark. Assn. Ins. Agts. (mem. exec. com. 1964-68), So. Agts. Conf. (chmn. casualty com. 1967-69). Presbyn. (elder, deacon). Clubs: Pleasant Valley Country, Little Rock, Capital, Top of the Rock. Home: 7215 I St Little Rock AR 72207 Office: Tower Bldg Little Rock AR 72201

CAMPBELL, CLARENCE L., state ofcl.; b. Indpls., Sept. 24, 1921; s. Clarence L. and Louise (Altvater) C.; student Fla. So. Coll., 1939-41; D.V.M., Ohio State U., 1945; m. Dorothy Marguerite Watford, June 10, 1950. Pvt. practice vet. medicine, Kewanee, Ill., 1945; field veterinarian Fla. Livestock San. Bd., 1945-48; asst. veterinarian State of Fla., 1948-52, acting state veterinarian, 1953; sec. Fla. Livestock Bd., 1961; dir. div. animal industry Fla. Dept. Agr., 1961-69; state veterinarian, dir. div. animal industry Fla. Dept. Agr. and Consumer Services, Tallahassee, 1969—. Recipient Man of Year award Progressive Farmer Mag., 1963; award for meritouious service, 1962. Mem. U.S., So. (pres. 1966-67) animal health assns., Am. (chmn. com. on council on pub. health and regulatory vet. medicine 1962, recipient Certificate of Service 1959-61), Fla. vet. med. assns., Nat. Assembly State Veterinarians, Am. Assn. Equine Practitioners, Arabian Horse Assn. Fla., Alpha Psi, Gamma Sigma Delta. Office: Div Animal Industry Fla Dept Agriculture and Consumer Services Room 328 Mayo Bldg Tallahassee FL 32304

CAMPBELL, EDWARD GROSS, govt. ofcl.; b. New Cumberland, Pa., May 20, 1912; s. John and Hannah Criswell (Gross) C.; A.B., Princeton, 1933; M.A., Columbia, 1934, Ph.D., 1938; m. Frances Watson James, Oct. 16, 1941; 1 son, John. With Nat. Archives, Gen. Services Adminstrn., Washington, 1938—, dir. Region 3, 1958-67, asst. archivist, 1967—. Served with AUS, 1943. Mem. Soc. Am. Archivists. Home: 1715 N Huntington St Arlington VA 22205 Office: Nat Archives Bldg 9th St and Pennsylvania Av NW Washington DC 20408

CAMPBELL, ELIZABETH P. (MRS. EDMUND D. CAMPBELL), educator, assn. exec.; b. Clemmons, N.C., Dec. 4, 1902; d. John Kenneth and Bessie (Whittington) Pfohl; A.B., Salem Coll., 1923; M.A., Tchrs. Coll., Columbia, 1924; postgrad. U. Pa., 1927-28, U. Mich., 1932; m. Edmund Douglas Campbell, June 16, 1936; children—Edmund Douglas, Virginia B. (Mrs. Everett W. Holt), Benjamin Pfohl, Henry Donald. Instr. English, Salem Acad. and Coll., Winston-Salem, N.C., 1924-27; dean of women Moravian Coll. for Women, Bethlehem, Pa., 1927-28; dean Mary Baldwin Coll., Staunton, Va., 1929-36. Mem. Arlington County Bd. Edn., 1947-55, 59-63; v.p. Washington Met. Area YWCA; pres. Greater Washington Ednl. TV Assn., 1957—; adv. com. George Mason Coll., U. Va., 1964—. Regional chmn. Va. Mental Retardation Planning Council; bd. dirs. Arlington YMCA. Pres. 10th Va. dist. Women's Democratic Club, 1956-57. Trustee, Salem (N.C.) Coll., 1969—. Recipient Algernon Sydney Sullivan award, 1936; award and citation Washington chpt. Pub. Relations Soc. Am., 1960; McCall's Golden Mike award Am. Women in Radio and TV, 1962; Distinguished Alumna award Salem Coll., 1972; named Woman of Yr., Marymount Coll., 1967. Mem. Am. Assn. U. Women, Arlington Council Ch. Women (pres. 1959), Delta Kappa Gamma. Quota (hon.). Home: 2912 N Glebe Rd Arlington VA Office: 2600 4th St NW Washington DC 20001

CAMPBELL, ELLIS, JR., govt. ofcl. U.S. dist. dir. Internal Revenue Service. Address: 1600 Patterson St Dallas TX 75201*

CAMPBELL, GEORGE SUMMERS, cons. engr.; b. Chattanooga, Tenn., Mar. 29, 1911; s. George Eugene and Winona Isabelle (Hinshaw) C.; B.S., U. Tenn., 1933; m. Irma Lee Carson; children—Nancy, George. Sales engr. Tenn. Elec. Power Co., 1935-37; sales engr. John Bouchard and Sons, contractors, 1938-40; owner George S. Campbell, cons. engr., 1940-41, 1946-50; pres. Campbell Industries, Inc., 1951-55; pres. George S. Campbell and Assos., Inc., cons. engrs., 1956—. Served to lt. USNR, 1942-46. Registered profl. engr., Ala., Ga., Tenn., Va. Mem. Cons. Engrs. Council (pres. chpt. 1967—), Nat. Soc. Profl. Engrs., Am. Soc. Heating, Refrigeration and Air-Conditioning Engrs., Illuminating Engrs. Soc., Am. Soc. M.E., Am. Soc. Plumbing Engrs., Chattanooga C. of C. (com. chmn. 1967). Episcopalian. Rotarian. Club: Civitan (pres. 1951). Home: Cravens Terrace Route 4 Chattanooga TN 37409 Office: 701 E 4th St Chattanooga TN 37403

CAMPBELL, GEORGE THOMAS, social worker; b. Dodge City, Kan., July 1, 1922; s. Ralph W. and Matilda (Waller) C.; B.A., U. Kan., 1950, M.S.W., 1952; m. Pearl Marie Clothier, July 26, 1948 children—Stephen Thomas, Paul Jeffrey. Caseworker, United Jewish Social Services, 1952-54; clin. social worker Vets. Hosp., Kansas City, Mo., 1954-59; dir. social service Christ's Haven for Children, Keller, Tex., 1959-61; supt. Maude Carpenter Children's Home, Wichita, Kan., 1961-63; exec. dir. Christian Homes of Abilene (Tex.), Inc., 1963-69; cons. for instns. Tex. Dept. Public Welfare, Austin, 1969—. Served with USNR, 1940-44. Mem. Nat. Assn. Social Workers, Child Welfare League Am., Tex. Assn. Social Welfare, Acad. Certified Social Workers, Tex. Assn. for Services to Children. Home: 1711 Vista Lane Austin TX 78703 Office: John H Reagan Bldg Austin TX 78701

CAMPBELL, GUY DOUGLAS, physician; b. Lauderdale, Miss., Oct. 15, 1915; s. Walter H. and Anna Adele (Nicholson) C.; B.S., U. Miss., 1946; M.D., Harvard, 1949; m. Margaret Mary Ford, May 20, 1950; 1 son, Guy Douglas. Intern, Charity Hosp., New Orleans, 1949-50; resident internal medicine Miss. State Sanatorium, 1950-51, VA Hosp., New Orleans, 1953-55; practice medicine, specializing in internal medicine, Jackson, Miss., 1955—; mem. staff VA Hosp., Univ. Hosp.; mem. faculty U. Miss. Sch. Medicine, Jackson, 1956—, asso. prof. medicine, 1967—; chief pulmonary disease sect. VA Hosp., Jackson, 1960—; coordinator Miss. Regional Med. Program, 1966-71. Pres. Miss. TB Assn., 1966-68. Bd. dirs. Nat. TB and Respiratory Diseases Assn., 1972—. Diplomate Am. Bd. Internal Medicine, and subsplty. bd. pulmonary diseases. Fellow Am. Coll. Chest Physicians (gov.), A.C.P. (gov.); mem. Am. Thoracic Soc., Sigma Xi, Omicron Delta Kappa, Kappa Sigma. Methodist. Mailing Address: 2015 Cherokee Dr Jackson MS 39211 Office: VA Hosp Jackson MS 39216

CAMPBELL, HENRY ARVILLE, JR., coll. adminstr.; b. Cosmos, Wash., Aug. 27, 1925; s. Henry Arville and Viva Ethel (Blair) C.; A.B., U. Ky., 1949; M.A., N.M. State U., 1957, Ed.S., 1961; postgrad. Syracuse U.; Ph.D., U. Tex., 1963; m. Nancy Elizabeth Belew, Jan. 4, 1965; children—Micca Lauren, Jan Rebecca, Sheryl Robin. Tchr. high schs., Lancaster, Ky., 1949-51, Cumberland, Ky., 1951-54, Benham, Ky., 1954-55; tchr., chmn. math. dept. Alamogordo (N.M.) High Sch., 1955-63; pres. Crowder Coll., Neosho, Mo., 1963-64, dir.; Alamogordo Community Coll., 1957-63; dir. Prestonsburg (Ky.) Community Coll., 1963—; acting dir. Hazard Community Coll., 1967-68. Served with AUS, 1943-45. Mem. N.E.A., S.W. N.M. (chmn. math., sci. sect.), Ky., Eastern Ky. edn. assns., Am. Math. Assn., Nat. Council Math. Tchrs., N.M. Acad. Sci., Floyd County Hall of Fame, Order of Red, Red Rose. Democrat. Methodist. Lion, Kiwanian (dir.), Rotarian. Home: PO Box 589 Prestonsburg KY 41653 Office: PO Box 110 Prestonburg KY 41653

CAMPBELL, HUGH BROWN, judge; b. Waynesville, N.C., Mar. 14, 1907; s. Wilburn Camrock and Stella (Brown) C.; A.B., Amherst Coll., 1929; J.D., U. N.C., 1932; m. Thelma Welles, Dec. 2, 1933; children—Hugh Brown, Thelma Elizabeth, Wilburn Welles. Admitted to N.C. bar, 1932, pvt. practice, Goldsboro, 1932-34, Charlotte, 1934-55; mem. Campbell, Craighill, Rendleman & Kennedy, 1952-55; judge N.C. Superior Ct., 1955-67, N.C. Ct. Appeals, 1967—; city atty., Charlotte, 1941-45. Mem. airport adv. com., 1945-61. Mem. St. Peters Hosp. Found. Mem. Am., N.C. bar assns. Democrat. Episcopalian. Kiwanian. Home: 1626 Queens Rd Charlotte NC 28207 Office: NC Ct Appeals Ruffin Bldg Box 888 Raleigh NC 27602

CAMPBELL, INEZ GIBSON, editor, publisher; b. Tyler, Tex., Feb. 24, 1914; d. Robert N. and Beatrice (Martin) Gibson; student E. Tex. State Tchrs. Coll., 1929-32; m. Jack W. Campbell, July 12, 1935;

children— Melinda Lee, Melissa Ann. Supr. mail opening dept. Montgomery Ward, 1935-41; supr. recap dept. N.Am. Aviation, Inc., 1942-45; sec., aviation dept. mgr. Ft. Worth C. of C., 1946-47; sec. claims dept. Comml. Standard Ins. Co., Ft. Worth, 1947-49; owner Campbell Secretarial Service, Ft. Worth, 1952-—; prodn., circulation mgr. Trade Jour., Bicycle Jour., 1954-—; editor Ft. Worther Mag., 1956-64, editor and pub., 1964-67; editor, Pub. Key-Ft. Worth Mag., 1967-—; editor Lawn Equipment Jour., 1959-—; Yardware nat. trade publ. Dir. Nat. Visitor Mag. Group, Inc., Chgo., 1962-68. Publicity chmn. Ft. Worth chpt. Internat. Good Neighbor Council, 1963-64; rec. sec. Provarsu Study Club, Ft. Worth, 1963-64. Mem. Ft. Worth C. of C. (mem. conv. and tourist com.). Clubs: Press of Ft. Worth, The Ft. Worth, Woman's Club Ft. Worth, Ridglea Country, Casa Del Sol (dir.) (Ft. Worth). Home: 4020 White Settlement Rd Fort Worth TX 76107 Office: 3339 W Freeway PO Box 1570 Fort Worth TX 76107

CAMPBELL, JAMES DAVID, dentist; b. Memphis, Sept. 22, 1941; s. Jesse Dethaniel and Esther (Grubbs) C.; student Memphis State U., 1959-63; D.D.S., U. Tenn., 1966; m. Marjorie Sue Thrash, July 7, 1961; children—Shanna Leigh, James David. Practice gen. dentistry, Panama City, Fla., 1968-—. Mem. adv. bd. dental assts. program. Gulf Coast Community Coll., Panama City, 1970-—. Served with Dental Corps, USAF, 1966-68. Named Jaycee of Month, Panama City, 1969. Mem. U.S. Jr. C. of C., Panama City-Bay County C. of C., Am., Fla. dental assns., Bay County Dental Soc. (pres.), Am. Acad. Gen. Practice, Nat. Geographic Soc., Psi Omega. Methodist. Mason (32 deg., Shriner), Elk. Home: 827 Brandeis Av Panama City FL 32401 Office: Panama City FL 32401

CAMPBELL, JAMES HENRY, city ofcl.; b. Cushing, Tex., Feb. 2, 1924; s. Jim and Ottie (Studdard) C.; student Stephen F. Austin State Tchrs. Coll., Nacogdoches, 1941-42, 46-48; m. Nellie Fae Gewin, June 25, 1947; children—James Ross, Gary Martin, Michael Robert, Brian Keith, Joel Dewayn. Gen. clk., dist. office mgr. United Gas Corp., Nacogdoches, Lufkin and Beaumont, Tex., 1948-64; city mgr. City of Liberty, Tex., 1964-—; dir. Tex.-La. Electric Coop., Sam Dam Electric Coop. Sec., bd. dirs. S.E. Tex. Resource Conservation and Devel.; bd. dirs. Municipal Adv. Council on Power for S.W. Served with cav., AUS, 1943-46 CBI. Mem. Liberty C. of C. (dir.). Home: 130 Hillside St Liberty TX 77575 Office: 1829 Sam Houston St Liberty TX 77575

CAMPBELL, JAMES VERNON, state ofcl.; b. Austin, Tex., Feb. 1, 1922; s. Harry and Anna Bell (Thomason) C.; B.S., U. Tex., 1951; m. Catherine Elizabeth Margos, Aug. 10, 1946; children—Patricia Ann, Wesley Howard, James Gregory. Engr., Humble Oil & Refining Co., Baytown, Tex., 1951-56; dir. plant maintenance Tex. Dept. Mental Health and Mental Retardation, Austin, 1956-—; mem. Tex. Boiler Adv. Bd., 1962-—. Served with USNR, 1942-46; PTO. Registered profl. engr., Tex. Mem. Nat., Tex. socs. profl. engrs., Pi Tau Sigma, Tau Beta Pi. Presbyn. (deacon). Home: 3101 Oakmont Blvd Austin TX 78703 Office: Box 12668 Capitol Sta 909 W 45th St Austin TX 78711

CAMPBELL, JAMES WHITE, JR., accountant; b. Plano, Tex., July 16, 1911; s. James White and Julia (Coldwell) C.; B.S. in Commerce, So. Meth. U., 1932; m. Vera Beth Bramblitt, Nov. 23, 1938; children—James Wade, Paul Carson. Various positions, 1932-38; agt. Internal Revenue Service, Wichita, Kan., 1939-40; with Standard Brands Inc., 1940-45, Southwest dist. accountant, 1944-45; pub. accountant, 1945-50; partner Campbell & White, Dallas, 1950-71. Mem. Spl. Dallas County Grand Jury Ins. Frauds, 1957. Bd. dirs. Big Springs Cemetery Mgmt. Assn., Dallas, 1947-—, treas., 1947-—. C.P.A., Tex. Mem. Tex. Soc. C.P.A.'s (mem. sub-com. accounting prins. 1967-—). Presbyn. (mem. com. nat. missions 1965-—). Home: 1005 N Plano Rd Richardson TX 75074 Office: 3777 First Nat Bank Bldg Dallas TX 75202

CAMPBELL, JOHN CLINE, chem. engr.; b. Kline, Colo., Feb. 5, 1922; s. Charles and Elizabeth (Cline) C.; B.S., U. Mo., 1948; m. Barbara Elaine Bivona, July 23, 1950; children—Sarah Jeanne, Jay Graham. Research engr. Texaco, Inc., Port Arthur, Tex., 1948-54; cooling tower sales coordinator Hudson Engring. Corp., Houston, 1954-64; sr. process engr. The Lummus Co., Houston, 1964-65, El Paso Products Co., Odessa, Tex., 1965-67; v.p. engring. Ceramic Cooling Tower Co., Ft. Worth, 1967-—. Served with USNR, 1944-47. Mem. Am. Soc. M.E., Cooling Tower Inst., Tau Beta Pi. Contbr. articles on heat transfer to profl. jours. Home: 725 Bedford Ct W Hurst TX 76053 Office: 2821 W 7th St Fort Worth TX 76101

CAMPBELL, JOHN ROBERT, ednl. adminstr.; b. Dalton, O., Aug. 6, 1927; s. Daniel Cavitt and Alice (Pinnock) C.; B.A., Sterling Coll., 1949; Ph.D., U. Kan., 1952; m. Margaret Eloise Treaster, June 8, 1948; children—Barry, Lynn, Brian, Daniel. Instr. Washington U., St. Louis, 1954-64; chmn. div. natural sci., prof. chemistry, asst. acad. dean Tarkio (Mo.) Coll., 1964-68; v.p. acad. affairs Midwestern U., Wichita Falls, Tex., 1968-—. Research specialist Monsanto Co., St. Louis, 1952-64; mem. comm. on ednl. relations Assn. Tex. Colls. and Univs., 1969-—. Mem. Citizens Adv. Com., Wichita Falls, 1968-—, Commn. on Human Relations, Wichita Falls, 1969-—. Mem. Am. Assn. Higher Edn., Am., So. confs. and acad. deans, Tex. Assn. Acad. Deans, Am. Chem. Soc., Sigma Xi, Phi Lambda Upsilon. Republican. Presbyn. Patentee in field. Home: 2401 Dartmouth St Wichita Falls TX 76308

CAMPBELL, JOHN WESLEY, aluminum co. exec.; b. Goodlettsville, Tenn., Jan. 13, 1916; s. John W. and Hattie (Benson) C.; B.S. in Accounting, U. Tenn., 1936; m. Cecile Mattox, Oct. 17, 1937; children—John Wesley, William M., Jane E. Clk. TVA, Knoxville, Tenn., 1936-37; with Internal Revenue Service, 1937-47; with Tenn. Products & Chem. Corp., Nashville, 1947-59, sec.-treas., 1948-59; with Natcor Co., Nashville, 1959-—, pres., 1967-—. C.P.A., Tenn. Mem. Am. Inst. C.P.A.'s, Tenn. Soc. C.P.A.'s. Methodist (mem. ofcl. bd. 1950-—). Home: 6305 Wildwood Valley Dr Route 2 Brentwood TN 37027 Office: 2963 Foster Creighton Dr Nashville TN 37204

CAMPBELL, JOSEPH EDWARD, dentist; b. Wilmington, N.C., Mar. 7, 1923; s. Cornell and Lulua (Harris) C.; B.S., N.C. Central U., 1950; D.D.S., Howard U., 1955; m. Dorothy Gwendolyn Wilson, Aug. 27, 1955; children—Joseph Edward, Kenneth B., Cynthia V. With Del. Dept. Pub. Health, Dover, 1955; pvt. practice dentistry, Durham, N.C., 1955-—; dentist Durham Pub. Health Dept., 1955-57; mem. cons. staff Lincoln Hosp. Mem. med. and dental adv. com. Durham County Hosp. Commn.; adv. com. on dental edn. N.C. Bd. Edn., N.C. Bd. Higher Edn., 1969-—. Bd. dirs. Office Econ. Opportunity Antipoverty Program for Children, Mt. Gilead Bapt. Ch. Day Care Center, Delta Dental Plans Assn. N.C. Served with USNR, 1944-46. Mem. Nat. (past state v.p.), Am., N.C., Old North (past pres.), Alexander Hunter (past program chmn.) dental socs., Durham Acad. Medicine (past pres.), Durham Mchts. Assn., Omega Psi Phi (sec.), Chi Delta Mu (sec.-treas.). Democrat. Baptist (trustee). Mailing Address: 905 Jerome Rd Durham NC 27707

CAMPBELL, JUNE COLLYER PETERS (MRS. LEROY M. CAMPBELL), social worker; b. Pitts., June 18, 1929; d. Nathaniel R. and Cleo (Minor) Peters; B.A., Howard U., 1951, M.S.W., 1964; M.A., Am. U., 1959; m. Leroy M. Campbell, Aug. 22, 1952; 1 dau., Sharon. With Prince George's County Dept. Social Services, Hyattsville, Md., 1957-—, caseworker, 1957-64, supr., 1964-66, asst. dir., 1967-70, dir. Bur. Services to Families and Children, 1970-—. Mem. task force treatment of emotionally disturbed youth Md. Gov.'s Conf. Crime and Delinquency, 1968-—. Mem. Nat. Assn. Social Workers, Am. Pub. Welfare Assn., Alpha Kappa Alpha. Home: 8019 16th St NW Washington DC 20012 Office: Prince Georges County Dept Social Services 6525 Belcrest Rd Hyattsville MD 20782

CAMPBELL, LEROY MILLER, architect; b. N.Y.C., July 5, 1927; s. Allan and Roma Gwendolyn (Miller) C.; B.Arch., Howard U., 1951; m. June Collyer Peters, Aug. 22, 1952; 1 dau., Sharon June. Draftsman, Alexander Richter, Kensington, Md., 1952; draftsman, job capt. Hilyard R. Robinson, Washington, 1952-56; job capt. Mcleod Ferrara, Washington, 1956-59; job capt., designer John Hans Graham, Washington, 1959-63; job capt. Cohen Haft, Silver Spring, Md., 1963-66; partner Sulton Campbell Assos., Washington, 1966-—. Bd. dirs. Neighbors, Inc., Washington Planning Workshop, 1970-—, Met. Washington Planning and Housing Assos., 1970-—. Served to cpl. USAAF, 1945-46. Mem. A.I.A., Nat. Tech. Assn., Alpha Phi Alpha. Democrat. Episcopalian. Home: 8019 16th St NW Washington DC 20012 Office: 7600 Georgia Av NW Washington DC 20012

CAMPBELL, LESLIE DUNLOP, JR., lawyer; b. Hanover, Va., Jan. 26, 1925; s. Leslie D. and Norine (Dickson) C.; student Randolph-Macon Coll., 1946-48; LL.B., U. Richmond, 1951; m. Eleanor Dickson, July 18, 1959 children—Sarah Payne, Mary Scott, Leslie D. III, Virginia Wells. Admitted to Va. bar, 1951; sr. partner Campbell, Ellis & Campbell, Ashland, 1956-70, Campbell & Campbell, 1970-—; Commonwealth atty. for Hanover County,Va., 1955-63; mem. Va. Senate, 1963-—. Dir., Hanover Nat. Bank, Ashland. Substitute judge Hanover County ct., 1954-55; Hanover appeals agt., Selective Service Bd. Hanover County, 1954-71; mem. Air Pollution Commn., Commn. on Constl. Govt.; mem. exec. bd. Robert E. Lee council Boy Scouts Am., 1966-—; chmn. legislative commn. YMCA, Model Gen. Assembly Com.; mem. Va. Traffic Safety Study Com., 1966-—. Bd. dirs. Greenlawn Memory Gardens, Inc. Served with USNR, 1944-46. Mem. Va. State Bar Assn., 15th Jud. Circuit Bar Assn., Jamestowne Soc., Soc. Cin., Am. Legion. Episcopalian. Kiwanian, Lion. Clubs: Ruritan Montpelier; Fishing Bay Yacht (Deltaville). Home: Lochland Route 1 Doswell VA 23047 Office: 113 Hanover Av Ashland VA 23005

CAMPBELL, MARY GRACE WILLIAMS (MRS. WALTER ROBERT CAMPBELL, JR.), business exec.; b. New Bern, N.C., Nov. 5, 1928; d. Leon Franklin and Sadie (Scurlock) Williams; student E. Carolina Coll., 1946-47; m. Walter Robert Campbell, Jr., July 8, 1949; children—Walter Robert III, Mary Lynn, Douglas Alan. With Barbour Boat Works, Inc., New Bern, 1947-—, asst. sec.-treas., 1954-63, supr. office personnel, 1961-—, sec.-treas., 1964-—, also dir.; sec.-treas. Barbour Boats, Inc., 1962; sec.-treas., dir. Marine Trading Corp., New Bern, 1953-—; sec., dir. Williams Oil Co., Inc., New Bern, 1955-—. Pres., Brinson Meml. Sch. P.T.A., 1959-61; tchr. Sunday Sch. class Riverdale Meth. Ch., New Bern, 1960-—, mem. ofcl. bd., 1952-—; sub-dist. leader Woman's Soc. Christian Service Meth. Ch. 1964-68. Mem. Pi Omega Pi. Club: New Bern Golf and Country. Home: Route 4 Box 26 New Bern NC 28560 Office: PO Box 1069 New Bern NC 28561

CAMPBELL, MCCOY CLEMPSON, III, banker; b. Spring Hill, Tenn., Apr. 5, 1918; s. McCoy Clempson and Annie (Woodard) C.; B.A., Vanderbilt U., 1940; postgrad. Stonier Grad. Sch. Banking, Rutgers U. 1955-57; m. Josephine McHenry, Dec. 2, 1944; children—Lucinda (Mrs. John N. Peabody), Laura Ann. Mgr. personnel RFC custody depts. Fed. Res. Bank Atlanta, Nashville, 1940-50; v.p., dir. personnel First Nat. Bank Atlanta, 1950-68; v.p. personnel adminstrn. Am. Nat. Bank & Trust Co., Chattanooga, 1968-71, sr. v.p. personnel adminstrn., 1971-—. Lectr. Stonier Grad. Sch. Banking, Rutgers U., 1959-62, 69-—, Colo. Sch. Banking, U. Colo., Boulder, 1970, Sch. Bank Adminstrn., U. Wis., Madison, 1971-—. Chmn. adv. com., bd. dirs. So. Coll. Placement Assn., 1965-68; bd. dirs. YMCA, Chattanooga. Served to 1st lt. F.A., AUS, 1942-46. Mem. Am. Inst. Banking, Am. Bankers Assn. (lectr. personnel adminstrn. 1964-—), Ga. Personnel and Guidance Assn. (past pres.), Bank Adminstrn. Inst. (dir.), Greater Chattanooga C. of C. (gen. chmn. Career Opportunities Day 1970), Kappa Alpha Alumni Assn. Presbyn. Club: Lookout Moutain (Tenn.) Fairyland. Cons. editor: The Bankers Handbook, 1966. Home: 308 Henry Lane Lookout Moutain TN 37350 Office: PO Box 1638 Chattanooga TN 37401

CAMPBELL, N., acting chancellor U. Tenn., Martin. Office: U Tennessee Martin TN 38237*

CAMPBELL, O.H., co-op. exec.; b., 1917; B.S., U. Ky. Farmer, Henderson, Ky.; formerly v.p., past pres. So. States Co-op., Inc., Richmond, Va., now only dir. Office: So States Bldg Richmond VA 23219

CAMPBELL, ROBERT CLYDE, corp. rep.; b. Honea Path, S.C., May 18, 1903; s. John James and Leona (Elgin) C.; B.A., Furman U., 1926; M.A., George Peabody Coll., 1929; student U. N.C., 1930; m. Priscilla Augusta Dillard, May 2, 1931; 1 dau., Priscilla Ann. Tchr., prin. Norway (S.C.) High Sch., 1926-29; supt. pub. schs., Richburg, S.C., 1929-43, Bethune, S.C., 1943-45, Pageland, S.C., 1945-68; supt. Chesterfield County Sch. Dist., 1968-71; rep. Greater Carolinas Corp., Columbia, S.C., 1972-—. Mem. N.E.A., Am. Assn. Sch. Adminstrs., Pageland C. of C., S.C. Ret. Educators Assn. Baptist. Mason, Lion. Home: PO Box 307 Pageland SC 29728

CAMPBELL, STEPHEN ROY, physician; b. New Orleans, Feb. 5, 1904; s. Stephen Frank and Mary Alice (Healy) C.; student Chenet's Inst., 1922-25; B.S., Tulane U., 1929, M.D., 1931; m. Marie McDowell Pilkington, Oct. 21, 1933; children—Marie (Mrs. Henry J. Legendre, Jr.), Judith (Mrs. Kennette C. Cranor), Stephenie (Mrs. William O. Jeansonne), Kathleen, Claire (Mrs. Joseph R. Gendron). Intern Charity Hosp., New Orleans, 1931-33; practice medicine Vacherie, La., 1933-—. Active pub. health services, 1933-50; examining physician St. James Parish, SSS, 1942-50. Recipient Selective Service medal U.S. Congress, World War II. Mem. A.M.A., La., Tri-Parish med. socs. Address: Box 106 Route 2 Vacherie LA 70090

CAMPBELL, STEWART NELSON, contract gas compression co. exec.; b. Benton, Ark., Mar. 21, 1931; s. J.J. and Mildred (Trantham) C.; B.S., U. Tex., 1953; m. Rose Ann Nikolich, Nov. 13, 1955; children—Sherri, Carrie. Engr., Cooper-Bessemer, Houston, 1953-66; co-founder Prodn. Operators, Inc., Houston, 1961, officer, 1961-—; dir. Unicapital Corp., Atlanta. Hughes Tool scholar, 1952. Mem. Tau Beta Pi, Pi Tau Sigma. Clubs: Coronado (Houston), Houston Racquet. Home: 414 Thamer Lane Houston TX 77035 Office: Box 36528 Houston TX 77036

CAMPBELL, WILLIAM DABNEY, ins. co. exec.; b. Waxahachie, Tex., Dec. 19, 1909; s. Lee Robert and Minnie Evelyn (Sims) C.; B.S., So. Meth. U., 1932; m. Mary Ethel Gannon, Nov. 7, 1941; children—William, Patricia, Priscilla, Gannon. Br. mgr. Motors Ins. Corp., Abilene, Tex., 1936-40; mgr. auto dept. Republic Ins. Co., Dallas, 1940-47; pres., dir. Comco Ins. Co., Amarillo, Tex., 1948-—; dir. Western Nat. Life Ins. Co., Amarillo; v.p. Southwestern Ins. Co., Amarillo, 1948-—. Bd. dirs. YMCA, Amarillo, 1965-70. Served to 1st lt. AUS, 1943-46. Mem. C. of C. Methodist. Home: 2601 Hawthorne St Amarillo TX 79109 Office: 205 E 10th St Amarillo TX 79105

CAMPBELL, WILLIAM P., mus. curator. Acting chief curator Nat. Gallery of Art, Washington. Office: National Gallery of Art Constitution at 6th St Washington DC 20565*

CAMPFIELD, WILLIAM LOUIS, govt. ofcl.; b. Tuskegee Inst., Ala., Jan. 5, 1912; s. Charles Gary and Isabella (Kent) C.; B.C.S., N.Y.U., 1933; M.B.A., U. Minn., 1937; Ph.D., U. Ill., 1951 Chief accountant Johnson Smith U., Charlotte, N.C., 1938-41; supervisory accountant Ford Motor Co., Richmond, Cal., Kaiser Co., Richmond, 1941-44; pvt. practice pub. accounting, San Francisco, 1945-49; dir. staff mgmt. U.S. Army Audit Agy., San Francisco, Washington, 1952-65 asso. dir. U.S. Gen. Accounting Office, Washington, 1966-—; vis. prof. accountancy Ohio State U., 1964, U. Mo., 1968, U. Ill., 1969, Columbia, 1970, U. Cal., 1971. Mem. profl. adv. bd. dept. accountancy Sch. Bus. Adminstrn., U. Ill. Recipient Meritorious Civilian Service award Dept. Army, 1962. Mem. Am. Inst. C.P.A.'s, Am. Accounting Assn., Nat. Assn. Accountants, Fed. Govt. Accountants Assn., Beta Alpha Psi. Author: (with others) Readings in Auditing, 1960; Professional Auditing Standards, 1963. Contbr. articles profl. jours. Home: 9061 Manchester Rd Silver Spring MD 20901 Office: US Gen Accounting Office Washington DC 20548

CAMPIOLI, MARIO ETTORE, architect; b. Parma, Italy, Sept. 3, 1910; s. Marcello and Genevieve (Pesci) C.; student Columbia, 1930; B.A., N.Y.U., 1937; postgrad. Beaux Arts Inst. Design. 1933-36;; m. Margaret Giordano, May 29, 1933; children—Genevieve (Mrs. Irwin W. Kemp), Elizabeth (Mrs. J. R. Lovewell), Margaret (Mrs. Wesley W. Dement), Carl Michael. Asso., Dwight James Baum, architect, N.Y.C., 1928-39; prodn. mgr. Eggers & Higgins, architects, N.Y.C., 1940-49; dir. architecture Colonial Williamsburg, Inc., 1949-57; asso. Alfred Easton Poor, architect, N.Y.C., 1957-59; asst. and/or acting architect of U.S. Capitol, 1959-—. Mem. bd. archtl. cons. Old Georgetown act. Washington Commn. Fine Arts, 1965-70; trustee, bd. cons. U.S. Capitol Hist. Soc., 1966-—. Recipient Water Color award, Morse prize N.Y.U., 1931; medal in design Soc. Beaux Arts Architects, 1935; Michelangelo award in architecture Sons Columbus, 1970; Nat. Capital award for profl. achievement in architecture D.C. Council Engring. and Archtl. Socs., 1972. Registered architect, N.Y., N.J., Va. Mem. A.I.A., Soc. Archtl. Historians, Am. Registered Architects (hon., Spl. Service award 1968), Nat. Sculpture Soc. (allied Profl. mem.), Producers' council (hon.). Home: 1136 Basil Rd McLean VA 22101 Office: US Capitol Washington DC 20515

CAMPO, HENRY ANDREW, geol. cons.; b. Mystic, Conn., July 1, 1912; s Eugene and Teresa (Cercina) C.; B.A., Cornell Coll., 1937; postgrad. U. Tulsa, 1940-41; m. Jo Ann Ross, June 30, 1951; children—Henry Andrew, Terri Jo, Kathi Margaret. Geologist, Atlantic Richfield Co., Okla., Tex. and La., 1937-70; geol. cons., Oklahoma City, 1970-—. Precinct sect. leader Houston Com., 1969-70; area coordinator Republican Com., Oklahoma City, 1972-—. Treas., Meml. Glen Pool Club, 1967-69. Served from pvt. to 1st lt., C.E., AUS, 1942-45. Mem. Am. Assn. Petroleum Geologists, Oklahoma City Geol. Soc. Roman Catholic. Home: 2937 Chaucer Dr Oklahoma City OK 73120 Office: 302 Cravens Bldg Oklahoma City OK 73102

CANAAN, GERSHON, architect; b. Berlin, Germany, Jan. 19, 1917; s. Ernst and Hedwig (Davidson) Kortner; B.A., Technion (Haifa, Israel), 1938; M.A., U. Tex., 1952, B.A. in City Planning, 1954; m. Doris Smith, May 23, 1954; 1 son, Robert Ernst. Apprentice Erick Mendelsohn, Israel, 1937, Frank Lloyd Wright, U.S.A., 1947; instr. archtl. design U. Tex., 1950-51; prin. architecture and planning. Dallas, 1958-—. Spl. archtl. adviser U.S. Pub. Housing Authority, 1962-65, nat. design cons., 1965-68. Consul of Fed. Republic of Germany. Initiator Ann. Celebration of German Day in Tex., 1963-—, Presdl. proclamation Von Steuben Day, 1964; mem. welcoming com. for German Chancellor Erhard at LBJ Ranch; mem. of Am. Council on Germany; chmn. Tex. German Day Council, 1963-—; founder, pres. Dallas Goethe Center, 1964-71. Served to capt. Garrison Engr., Royal Engrs., Brit. Army, 1942-45; served as field comdr. and staff officer Israel Def. Army, 1948. Recipient Presdl. Citation, 1964; Medal of Merit, German Inst. Fgn. Relations, 1967; Officers Cross of Order of Merit, Germany, 1968; medal Americanism, D.A.R., 1968; named Ambassador of Goodwill, Gov. of Tex., 1965; hon. citizen of Tex., Ft. Worth, Dallas, San Antonio, Fredericksburg, Houston; Israel's Fighter and Statehood medals, 1969; Israel's Volunteerism medal, 1969; Resolution of Merit, Selfhelp, Inc., Dallas, 1971; Honor plaque City of Frankfort, Germany, 1972; Plaque of Distinction, Dallas Goethe Center, 1971; Gold medal Tex. German Day Council, 1972. Mem. A.I.A. (asso.), Dallas Consular Corps, C. of C. (mem. world trade com.), Internat. Trade Assn., Tex. Soc. Architects. Author: Rebuilding the Land of Israel, 1954; Design of Memorials, 1960; Shopping Centers/Office Buildings and Residents. Home: 4700 St. Johns Dr Dallas TX 75205 Office: Simons Bldg Dallas TX 75201

CANADY, GEORGE MASABEAN, JR., constrn. co. exec.; b. Charleston, S.C., Oct. 18, 1919; s. George Masabean and Artha Marie (Stephens) C.; B.S., The Citadel, 1947; m. Evelyn Elizabeth Koenig, Nov. 24, 1940; children—Lynda Rae, George Masabean III, Brian Lee. Trainee, Canady Constrn. Co., Charleston, 1940-41, v.p., 1947-61, pres., 1961-—, also chmn. bd. Chmn. Gen. Contractors Licensing Bd. Charleston County, 1968-—. Bd. dirs. Carolina Nursing Center. Served to capt. USAAF, 1941-45; lt. col. Res. ret. Mem. Asso. Gen. Contractors Am., Sigma Phi Sigma. Methodist (trustee). Mason (32 deg.). Club: Square and Level (pres.) (Charleston). Home: 706 Shamrock Lane Charleston SC 29407 Office: Box 932 Charleston SC 29402

CANADY, HELEN JEFFERS DEIMAN (MRS. PAUL J. CANADY), social worker; b. Chgo.; d. Harry C. and Katharine (Jeffers) Deiman; B.A., Grinnell Coll., 1932; M.A., U. Denver, 1933; postgrad. N.Y. Sch. Social Work, 1937; m. Paul J. Canady, Apr. 28, 1933; children—Peter Deiman, Katharine Jeffers (Mrs. Robert Harrison Owen). Jefferson County supr. Ala. State Bd. Childrens Welfare, Birmingham, 1933-34; adoption social worker N.J. Childrens Home Soc., Trenton, 1934-39; dir. Princeton (N.J.) Family Agy., 1939-41; med. social worker Tidewater Retarded Children Agy., Norfolk, Va., 1958-61; psychiat. social worker, med. social worker Bur. Alcohol Studies and Rehab., Va. State Health Dept., Norfolk, 1961-—. Bd. dirs. Florence Crittendon Home, Trenton, Internat. House, Trenton. Mem. Nat. Assn. Social Workers, Acad. Certified Social Workers. Home: 1143 Lexan Av Norfolk VA 23508 Office: 401 Colley Av Norfolk VA 23507

CANALES, LUIS LOPEZ, artist; b. Mexico, D.F., Nov. 14, 1928; s. Luis Cosio and Elvira Zalazar (Canales) Lopez; student Plastic Arts Nat. Sch., St. Charles, 1947-50, Inba Sculpture and Painting Sch., 1963-65; m. Puerto Alvarez Concepcion, June 16, 1951 children—Lopez Puerto, Laura, Alma, Luis, Hugo, Eduardo, Adrian. Exhibited in group shows at Mexican Art Inst., 1964, Mexican-N.Am. Cultural Relations Inst., 1965, Guanajuato U., 1965, Chapultepec Gallery, 1966, Santo Domingo, Oaxaca, Mexico, 1966, Taxco, Bellas Arts Sch., 1966, Mexican Art Inst. Individual Expn., 1967, Festival Internat. Arts, 1968, Mexican Art Inst., 1968; interior decorator, designer furniture. Recipient hon. mention Ann. Expn. Painting and Sculpture Sch., 1963, Water Color Painters award Mexican Art Inst., 1965; Painters award Mexican Art Inst., 1966; Acquisition award Water Color Mus., 1969; Golden medal Water-Color Mexican Soc., 1970. Mem. Mexican Watercolor Soc. Home: 101 depto 2 Florida Mexico D F 14 Mexico Office: 141 Puebla Mexico D F Mexico

CANALS, CESAR S., civil engr.; b. Ponce, P.R., Dec. 20, 1902; B.C.E., Mass. Inst. Tech., 1926. Test foreman Pub. Service Electric Corp., Irvington, N.J., 1926-27; asst. engr. P.R. Govt. Irrigation Service, 1927-28; resident engr. Manati River bridge constrn. P.R. Dept. Interior, 1928-29; with Frederick Snare Corp., contracting engrs., N.Y.C., 1929-65, ASST. resident engr. constrn. projects, Malpaso, Peru, 1929-31, N.Y.C., 1931-32, Cartagena, Colombia, 1932-34, asst. supt., resident engr. Peruvian Naval Arsenal, Callao, 1937-39, project mgr. harbor and terminal constrn. Govt. of Peru, Matarani, 1939-41, asst. project mgr., resident engr. constrn. facilities U.S. Navy, Balboa, C.Z., Cristobal, C.Z., 1942-45, mgr. office P.R., 1946-56, Colombia, 1956-57, Venezuela, 1957-58, project mgr. in charge of field investigations, surveys, preliminary layouts, designs, N.Y.C., 1959-65; partner C.S. Canals-Sargent Webster Crenshaw & Folley, asso. architects, engrs., planners, Santruce, P.R., 1965-67; prin. Cesar S. Canals Assos., cons. engrs., architects, planners, Santurce, P.R., 1967—; v.p. Buck, Seifert & Jost S.A., cons. engrs., Santurce, 1967—. Exec. dir. P.R. Ports Authority. Fellow Am. Soc. C.E.; mem. Coll. Engrs. P.R., M.I.T. Club of P.R. (v.p., dir. 1948-53), Soc. Engrs. P.R., Inter-Am. Assn. San. Engring., Inter-Am. Planning Soc., Planning Soc. P.R. Clubs: Berwind Country, Bankers of P.R., Buchanan Golf, U.S. Propeller (pres. 1949, dir. 1949-52) (San Juan). Address: PO Box 13931 Santurce PR 00908

CANAN, HOWARD VOORHEIS, cons. engr., author; b. Omaha, Aug. 6, 1894; s. Clarence John and E. Lizette (Voorheis) C.; B.S., U.S. Mil. Acad., 1918; postgrad. U.S. Army Engring. Sch., 1921, Command and Gen. Staff Coll., 1939, Naval War Coll., 1942. Commd. 2d lt. U.S. Army, 1918, advanced through grades to col.; with C.E., 1921-28; asst. prof. mil. sci. and tactics Colo. Sch. Mines, Golden, 1928-32; asst. dist. engr. Duluth, 1932-34; dist. engr. U.S. Lake Survey, 1934-36; gen. staff M.I. Div. War Dept., 1939-41; G-2 sec. GHQ, 1941-42; duty with Amphibious Corps and Force, Pacific Fleet, 1942-43; asst. to engr. ETO, 1943-46; dist. engr. Nashville, 1946-49; engr. 2d Army, Ft. Meade, Md., 1949-52; engring. insp. gen., 1952-53; asst. chief engrs. for real estate, 1953-54; ret., 1954; cons. practice, 1954-56; cons. civil engr. Melpar, Inc., Alexandria, 1956-60; cons. engr., 1960—. Trustee Patriotic Edn., Inc. Decorated Legion of Merit, Bronze Star (U.S.); Croix Guerre (France). Fellow Am. Soc. C.E., Am. Geog. Soc.; mem. Mil. Inst., Society Am. Mil. Engrs., S.A.R., Civil War Round Table. Clubs: Cosmos, Army and Navy. Contbr. articles to profl. and hist. jours. Home: Apt 522 1200 S Washington St Alexandria VA 22314

CANCIENNE, EMILE ADOLPH, entomologist; b. Napoleonville, La., Jan. 15, 1920; s. John Eno and Rita Ann (Adolph) C.; B.S. in Agr., La. State U., 1942, M.S. in Entomology, 1968; m. Mildred Ione Rushing, Feb. 5, 1949; children—David, Cynthia, Susan, William, Charles, Marilyn. Survey entomologist S.E. region Bur. Entomology, U.S. Dept. Agr., 1946-47; plant entomologist La. State Dept. Agr., Baton Rouge, 1947-56, state entomologist, 1956-60; extension entomologist La. State U., Baton Rouge, 1961—. Served with USNR, 1942-46. Mem. Nat., La. agrl. applicators assns., Entomol. Soc. Am., La. Entomol. Soc., Gamma Sigma Delta. Roman Catholic. K.C. Home: 208 Bellewood Dr Baton Rouge LA 70806 Office: Knapp Hall La State Univ Baton Rouge LA 70803

CANCIO, HIRAM RAFAEL, judge, educator, govt. ofcl.; b. San Sebastian, P.R., Aug. 26, 1920; s. Miguel Cancio-Cores and Camelia Vilella-Malaret; B.A., U. P.R., 1942, LL.B., 1948; m. Carlota Alfaro Bou, Aug. 11, 1951; children—Camelia, Hiram Rafael, Rosa Matilde. Psychometrist VA, 1946-48; trial examiner P.R. Labor Relations Bd., San Juan, 1948, asst. chmn., head legal div., 1949-52; chmn. wages and hours coms. under Fair Labor Standards Act, U.S. Dept. Labor, 1952-58; dir. Labor Relations Inst., U. P.R., San Juan, 1952-55, dean adminstrn., 1955-58; atty. gen. Commonwealth P.R., San Juan, 1959-66; chief dist. judge, San Juan, 1966—. Prof. labor relations and labor law U. P.R., 1952—. Served with AUS, 1944-46. Recipient Merit award P.R. Bar Assn., 1960. Mem. Am. Judicature Soc., P.R. Bar Assn., Am. Soc. Pub. Adminstrn., Pub. Personnel Assn., Phi Sigma Alpha. Roman Catholic. Author: Labor Management Arbitration in Puerto Rico, 1954; Workers Education in Labor Relations Institutes, 1954. Home: 566 Ramon Gandia St San Juan PR 00918 Office: PO and Ct House Bldg San Juan PR 00904

CANDELA, FELIX, architect; b. Madrid, Spain, Jan. 27, 1910; s. Felix Candela Magro and Julia Outerino Echeverria; Architect, Escuela Superior de Aqguitectura de Madrid, 1935; m. Eladia Martin, May 3, 1940 (dec. Sept. 5, 1963); children—Antonia, Manolita, Teresa and Pilar (twins). Practice architecture in Mexico City, also Acapulco; builder reinforced concrete shells, 1951—, important works include Church La Virgen Milagrosa, Mexico City; pres. Cubiertas Ala S.A., 1950—; prof. structures Escuela Nacional de Arquitectura, Universidad Nacional Autonoma de Mexico; Charles Eliot Norton prof. poetry Harvard, 1961-62. Served as capt., C.E., Republican Army, Spanish Civil War. Recipient Gold medal Instn. Structl. Engrs., London, 1961; Price Auguste Parret, Internat. Union Architects, 1961. Mem. Internat. Assn. Shell Structures (hon.), Sociedad Venezolana de Arquitectos (hon.), Sociedad de Arquitectos Colombianos, Sociedad de Arquitectos Mexicanos, Am. Concrete Inst., Internat. Assn. Bridge and Structural Engring., Institut Techinique du Batiment et Des Travaus Publics, A.I.A. (hon.), Royal Inst. Brit. Architects (hon.). Home: Juarez 14 Tlacopac Mexico 20 DF Mexico Office: Ramon Guzman 123 Mexico 4 DF Mexico

CANDER, LEON, physician, educator; b. Phila., Oct. 7, 1926; s. Joseph Harry and Anna (Glick) C.; M.D., Temple U., 1951; m. Geraldine Piontkowski, Dec. 11, 1954; children—Alan Drew, Harris Scott. Intern Einstein Med. Center, Phila., 1951-52; resident Beth Israel Hosp., Boston, 1956-58; practice medicine specializing in internal medicine (chest diseases), Boston, 1958-60, Phila., 1960-66, San Antonio, 1966—; fellow in physiology U. Pa., 1952-54, instr., 1954-55, asso., 1955-56; asst. in medicine Harvard, 1957-58; sr. instr. Tufts U., 1958-60; asst. prof. Hanemann Med. Coll., Phila., 1960-63, asso. prof. medicine, 1963-66; prof., chmn. dept. prof., chmn. dept. physiology and internal medicine South Tex. Med. Sch., San Antonio, 1966—; cons. chest diseases VA Hosp., Phila., 1962-66. Served with USNR, 1945-46. Markle scholar, 1961-66; NRC fellow, 1955-56. Fellow A.C.P.; mem. Am. Physiol. Soc., Am. Thoracic Soc., Am. Fedn. Clin. Research. Home: 201 Towne Vue Pl San Antonio TX 78213 Office: 7703 Floyd Curl Dr San Antonio TX 78229

CANDLER, JOHN SLAUGHTER, II, lawyer; b. Atlanta, Nov. 30, 1908; s. Asa Warren and Harriet Lee (West) C.; A.B. magna cum laude, U. Ga., 1929; J.D., Emory U., 1931; m. Dorothy Bruce Warthen, June 13, 1933; children— Dorothy Warthen (Mrs. Joseph W. Hamilton, Jr.), John Slaughter. Admitted Ga. bar, 1931, partner Candler, Cox & Andrews and other law firms, 1931—; pres., chmn. bd., dir. So. Toy & Novelty Co., 1940—; v.p., gen. counsel, dir. Palmer, Inc., 1939—; sec., dir. Leon Propane, Inc., Peachtree Realty & Ins. Co., Weatherly Corp., Propane Gas Service, Inc., D. M. Weatherly Co.; dir. P. D. Christian Co., Sungas, Inc., Equipment Sales Co., Christian and Rose Constrn. Corp.; dep. asst. atty. gen. State of Ga., 1951-68. Mem. Greater Atlanta Council USO, 1969—. Trustee Ga. Student Ednl. Fund; trustee Kappa Alpha Scholarship Fund, pres., 1970-72. Served from capt. to col. AUS, 1941-46. Decorated Commendation Ribbon. Fellow Am. Coll. Probate Counsel (Ga. state chmn. 1965-68, regent 1968—), Internat. Acad. Law and Sci.; mem. Tax Inst. Am. (adv. council 1969—), Am. Judicature Soc., State Bar Ga. (chmn. sect. on fiduciary law 1964-65), Am., Atlanta bar assns., Internat. Platform Assn., Atlanta Estate Planning Council (pres. 1963-64), Lawyers Club Atlanta, Am. Legion (post comdr. 1949-50), Res. Officers Assn. (state pres. 1946, nat. exec. com. 1947), Mil Order World Wars, English-Speaking Union, Phi Beta Kappa, Phi Kappa Phi, Phi Delta Phi, Kappa Alpha, Sigma Delta Chi. Democrat. Episcopalian (vestryman 1953-56, sr. warden, 1955, cathedral trustee 1957-67, Lay reader 1971—). Mason, Kiwanian (v.p. 1950, dir. 1948-50, 1958-59; trustee Northside Atlanta Found. 1959—, chmn. 1959—). Home: 413 Manor Ridge Dr NW Atlanta GA 30305 Office: 2400 Gas Light Tower Atlanta GA 30303

CANFIELD, EARL RODNEY, dentist; b. Toledo, O., Dec. 19, 1916; s. Howard Stowe and Alice (Wynn) C.; A.B., Emory U., 1938, D.D.S., 1942; m. Evelyn Louise Flowers, Dec. 26, 1940; children—Merilyn Canfield (Mrs. J. Arthur Mozley), Earl Rodney. Practice gen. dentistry, Atlanta, 1942, 52, 70—, College Park, Ga., 1967, 69; partner College Park Supply Co., 1951-71, sec., treas., 1955-71; pres. Herff Jones Co., Indpls., 1968. Mem. Arts Festival, Atlanta, 1965—. Served to maj. Dental Corps, AUS, 1942-46, USAAF, 1951-54; Korea, CBI. Decorated Bronze Star medal. Fellow Am. Coll. Dentists, Internat. Coll. Dentists; mem. Am., Ga. dental assns., No. Dist. (mem. exec. council), 5th Dist., Chgo. dental socs., Fedn. Dentaire Internationale (life), Am. Analgesia Soc., Atlanta Civil War Round Table, Am. Legion, V.F.W., Sigma Pi. Mason (32 degree, Shriner), Elk. Clubs: Cherokee Town and Country, Commerce (Atlanta). Home: 6 Montclair Dr Atlanta GA 30309 Office: 305 Buckhead Av Atlanta GA 30305

CANFIELD, EDWARD FRANCIS, lawyer; b. Phila., Apr. 7, 1922; s. Frank James and Eunice C. (Sullivan) C.; B.A., St. Joseph's Coll., 1943; LL.B., U. Pa., 1949; m. Janet Powell Trotter, Jan. 12, 1952; children— Andrew Trotter, Janet Powell. Admitted to Pa. bar, 1949; practice in Phila., 1949-51; with RCA, 1953-60, marketing mgr. def. electronics products, 1957-60; with Philco-Ford Corp., 1960-69, corp. dir. marketing, 1961-63, v.p. govt. planning and marketing, 1964-67, v.p. marketing, electronics group, 1967-69; pres. Leisure Time Industries, Inc., 1969-71; practice law, Washington, 1971—. Served as officer USNR, 1942-46, 51-53. Mem. Phila. Bar Assn., I.E.E.E., Armed Forces Communications and Electronics Assn., Electronics Industries Assn. Clubs: Congressional Country, International. Home: 9600 Weathered Oak Ct Bethesda MD 20034 Office: 1200 18th St NW Washington DC 20006

CANN, KENNETH THOMAS, educator; b. N.Y.C., Apr. 29, 1926; s. Kenneth Wilkins and Gladys (Harpell) C.; B.S., Georgetown U., 1950; M.A., Ind. U., 1960, Ph.D. (Midwest Universities Consortium grantee 1964-65), 1967; m. Maria Nilda de Carvelho Jordao, Jan. 21, 1962. Appraiser VA, Washington, 1950-56; real property officer FHA, Indpls., 1956-59; teaching asst. Ind. U., 1960-63, lectr., 1965-66, asst. prof., 1967-68; asso. prof. Western Ky. U., 1968-70, prof., head dept. econ., 1970—; instr. U. Wis., 1963-65. Served with AUS, 1944-46. Mem. Am., So., Midwest econ. assns., Soc. for Internat. Devel. Home: 1017 Ridgecrest Dr Bowling Green KY 42101 Office: Dept Economics Western KY U Bowling Green KY 42101

CANN, WILLIAM DERWOOD, JR., paper co. exec.; b. Monroe, La., Sept. 12, 1919; s. William Derwood and Lodi (DeSeay) C.; student La. State U., 1938-42; m. Arabella Ochiltree Bancroft, Nov. 6, 1954; children—Vada Speed, Arabella Bancroft; 1 step-son, Thomas C. Nash. Served as maj. U.S. Army, 1942-45, ETO; master parachutist; advanced through grades to lt. col., 1956; mem. joint U.S. mission to Turkey, 1951-54; head mil. dept. N.E. La. State Coll., 1954-56; resigned, 1956; with Bancroft Paper Industries, West Monroe, La., 1956—, exec. v.p., 1965—, also dir.; exec. v.p. Bancroft Bay, Inc.; treas. Bancroft Paper Co., Monroe, La.; dir. Bancroft Bag Factory, West Monroe. Mem. Monroe City Sch. Bd.; gen. campaign mgr. United Givers Fund, 1970. Bd. dirs. State of La. Bd. Commerce and Industry, YMCA, A.R.C., Soc. Crippled Children. Decorated Bronze Star and cluster, Purple Heart and cluster. Mem. Mil. Order of World Wars, Kappa Alpha. Episcopalian (vestry 1962-65). Democrat. Club: Bayou DeSiard Country (bd. dirs. 1969-71). Home: 3704 Deborah Dr Monroe LA 71291 Office: PO Box 307 West Monroe LA 71291

CANNON, CARROLL CONWAY, lawyer; b. St. Louis, July 22, 1909; s. Thomas D. and Marguerite (Carroll) C.; student Washington U., 1926-28; LL.B., City Coll. Law, 1933; m. Helen Harrelson, Nov. 2, 1940; children—Carroll C., Cathlyn II., Helen M. Abstracter Title Ins. Corp., St. Louis, 1928-33; atty. Fed. Land Bank St. Louis, 1933-38; practice law, St. Louis, 1938-41; spl. agt. FBI, 1942-46; practice of law Forrest City, Ark., 1946—; pres. St. Francis County Abstract Co. Pres. St. Louis Jr. C. of C., 1942; dir., mem. exec. com. Forrest City C. of C., 1947-51. Mem. Am., Ark., St. Francis County (pres. 1963) bar assns., Ark. Land Title Assn. (pres. 1951-52). Lion (pres.). Home: 2917 E Broadway Forrest City AR 72335 Office: 112 S Izard Forrest City AR 72335

CANNON, GARLAND HAMPTON, educator; b. Ft. Worth, Dec. 5, 1924; s. G. H. and Myrtle (Goss) C.; B.A. in English, U. Tex., 1947, Ph.D. in English, 1954; M.A. in English, Stanford, 1952; m. Sally Patricia Richardson, Feb. 14, 1947; children—Margaret, Elizabeth, Jennifer, William. Instr. English, Allen Acad., Bryan, Tex., 1947-48; teaching fellow Stanford, 1948-49; instr. English, U. Hawaii, 1949-52, U. Tex., 1952-54, U. Mich., 1954-55; asst. prof. speech U. Cal. at Berkeley, 1955-56; acad. dir. Am. U. Lang. Center, Bangkok, Thailand, 1956-57; asst. prof. English, U. Fla., 1957-58; asst. prof. linguistics Tchrs. Coll., Columbia, 1959-62; asso. prof. Northeastern Ill. State Coll., Chgo., 1962-63; asso. prof. English, Queens Coll. City U. N.Y., 1963-66; asso. prof. Tex. A & M U., College Station, 1966-68, prof. English, 1968—; cons. in bilingualism, U.S. Office Edn., 1968—. Prof. linguistics U. P.R., 1958-59, Canadian Linguistic Assn., 1964; dir. English lang. program Columbia's Afghanistan project, 1960-62; vis. prof. English, U. Wash., summer 1967, vis.prof. humanities U. Mich., 1970-71. Served with USMCR, World War II. Grantee, Am. Philos. Soc., Eng., 1964, 66. Mem. Linguistic Soc. Am., Internat. Linguistic Assn., Am. Dialect Soc., Conf. Coll. Composition and Communication, Nat. Council Tchrs. English, Modern Lang. Assn. Am., Phi Kappa Phi. Author: Sir William Jones, Orientalist, 1952; Oriental Jones: A Biography, 1964; The Letters of Sir William Jones, 1970; A History of the English Language, 1972; also articles in field. Office: Coll Liberal Arts Tex A & M U 805 Hawthorn College Station TX 77840

CANNON, HUGH, lawyer; b. Albemarle, N.C., Oct. 11, 1931; s. Hubert Napoleon and Nettie (Harris) C.; A.B., Davidson Coll., 1953; B.A. (Rhodes scholar) Oxford U., 1955, M.A., 1960; LL.B., Harvard, 1958; m. Jessie Mercer, Jan. 26, 1956; children—John Stuart, Marshall, Martha Janet. Admitted to N.C. bar, 1958; mem. staff U. N.C. Inst. Govt., Chapel Hill, 1959; atty. Sanford, Phillips, McCoy & Weaver, Fayetteville, 1960; asst. to Gov. of N.C., Raleigh, 1961; dir. adminstrn. State of N.C., 1962-65, state budget officer, 1963; mem. firm Sanford, Cannon, Adams & McCullough, Raleigh, 1965—. Parliamentarian N.E.A., 1965—; lectr. N.S. State U., Raleigh, part-time, 1965, 66. State dir. N.C. Emergency Resources Planning Com., 1962-65; pres. Friends of Coll., Raleigh, 1963. Alternate del. Nat. Democratic Conv., 1964. Bd. dirs. Grow, Inc., Raleigh, U. N.C.; trustee Davidson Coll. Mem. Phi Beta Kappa, Omicron Delta Kappa, Phi Gamma Delta. Democrat. Methodist. Home: 163 Pasquotank Dr Raleigh NC 27609 Office: Br Bank Bldg Box 389 Raleigh NC 27602

CANNON, JOE A., elementary sch. prin.; b. nr. Blakely, Ga., Oct. 19, 1927; s. Dewey D. and Gatsie Mae (Sheffield) C.; grad. Abraham Baldwin Coll., 1948; B.S., U. Ga., 1950, M.A., 1962; Specialist degree Auburn U., 1968; m. Lois Strickland, July 16, 1950; children—Dewey, James, Billy. Vocational agr. tchr., Plains, Ga., 1950, Richland, Ga., 1950-54; feed salesman H.L. Moore Co., 1954-55; vocational agr. tchr., Jakin, Ga., 1955-59; prin. Jakin High Sch., 1960-62, Early County Elementary Sch., Blakely, 1963—. Served with AUS, 1946-48. Mem. N.E.A., Ga., Early County edn. assns., Nat., Ga. assns. elementary sch. prins. Club: Blakely Lions (v.p. 1970). Home: Route 5 Blakely GA 31723 Office: 649 Howell St Blakely GA 31723

CANNON, WILLIAM JOHN, educator; b. Glamorgan, S. Wales, U.K., Sept. 16, 1908; s. Frederick John Harold and Elsie (Keturah) C.; student Stanborough Coll., Watford, Eng., 1927-31, Oxford U., 1931; F.L.C. Th., London Coll., 1946; M.A., Potomac U., 1954; Ph.D., Am. U., 1959; m. Dorothy Olive Tasker, Aug. 19, 1931 (dec. Sept. 1969); 1 dau., Ruth Olivia (Mrs. Gerald J. Gelford); m. 2d, Lois Lowry, Apr. 1, 1971; children—Beverly (Mrs. Lvoders), Barbara (Mrs. Orr), Susan (Mrs. Christenson), Shelley, Malcolm, Warren. Asst. prof., counsellor Theol. Seminary, Andrews U., Berrier Springs, Mich., 1956-60; acting chmn. social sci. Columbia Union Coll., Takoma Park, Md., 1960-61, chmn. behavioral sci., 1961-70, prof. psychology, 1964-70, dir. guidance, 1962-67; asso. sec. dept. edn. Gen. Conf. Seventh Day Adventist Ch. Counseling psychologist Cedarcroft Sanitarium and Hosp., Takoma Park, Md., 1960-62, Oaklea Hall, Washington Sanitarium and Hosp., Takoma Park, Md., 1954—. Home: 1705 Ritchie Rd Washington DC 20028

CANNON, WILLIAM RAGSDALE, bishop; b. Dalton, Ga., Apr. 5, 1916; s. William Ragsdale and Emma (McAfee) C.; A.B., U. Ga., 1937; B.D., Yale U., 1940, Ph.D., 1942; D.D., Asbury Coll., 1950; LL.D., Temple U., 1955; L.H.D., Emory U., 1969. Dean, Candler Sch. Theology, Emory U., Atlanta, 1953-68; resident bishop Raleigh (N.C.) area United Methodist Ch., 1968—. Chmn. Am. sect. World Methodist Council; chmn. dept. ministry United Methodist Bd. Edn. Trustee, Emory U., Duke U., Asbury Coll. Author: A Faith for These Times, 1944; The Christian Church, 1945; The Theology of John Wesley, 1946; Our Protestant Faith, 1949; Our Faith in Love, 1949; The Redeemer, 1950; The History of Christianity in the Middle Ages, 1960; The Journeys after St. Paul, 1963. Home: 2301 Beechridge Rd Raleigh NC 27605 Office: Methodist Bldg 1307 Glenwood Av Raleigh NC 27605

CANO ABASCAL, JUAN JOSE, Spanish diplomat; b. Madrid, Spain, Dec. 4, 1919; s. Juan Jose Cano Abascal; ed. U. Madrid; m. Hannia Maria Rodriguez Tamara, 1950. Successively with commn. to pres. Nicaragua; sec. Spanish embassy, San Jose, Costa Rica, Amman, Jordan; charge d'affaires of Spain, Teheran, Iran; consul gen. of Spain, Galveston, Tex., now New Orleans. Decorated Red Cross of Mil. Merit, Medal of War, knight comdr. Order Civil Merit, knight Order of Isabel la Catolica, knight comdr. Star of Jordania, knight Imperial Crown of Iran. Office: 2 Canal St New Orleans LA 70130

CANON, ROBERT ATKINSON, govt. ofcl.; b. Fremont, Ia., June 4, 1905; s. Harry English and Laura (Hedge) C.; grad. Lake Forest (Ill.) Acad., 1923; grad., Walton Sch. Commerce, 1924-25; m. Elizabeth Murphy, Nov. 21, 1933 (dec. June 1969); children—Bradley, Warren, Elizabeth. With Stone and Webster Securities Corp., Chgo., 1923-44; co-mgr. Graham, Parsons & Co., Chgo., 1944-47; self employed, 1947-64; dep. tax assessor Broward County, Fla., 1965-67; congl. dist. aide 10th Congl. dist., Ft. Lauderdale, Fla., 1967-69; mem. governmental efficiency study com., 1969-70; mgr. spl. projects Port Everglades Authority (Fla.), 1969—. Broward commr. Fla. Inland Nav. Dist., 1964-69. State committeeman Republican Com. Broward County, 1964-66, acting county chmn., 1966—; vice chmn. Rep. Exec. Com. of Broward County, 1970—. Mem. Allendale Assn. (sec., dir. 1941-47). Home: 1012 Harrison St Hollywood FL 33020 Office: Port Everglades Authority Port Everglades FL 33316

CANO PALACIOS, JOSE INES, Mexican diplomat. Consul gen. from Mexico, San Antonio. Address: 127 Navarro San Antonio TX 78205*

CANTER, DONALD LYNN, banker; b. Morristown, Tenn., Nov. 8, 1936; s. Cecil Franklin and Mary (Talley) C.; grad. high sch.; m. Sue Carolyn Stout, June 8, 1957; children—David Lynn, Angela Carol. Teller, Hamilton Nat. Bank, Morristown, 1955-59; asst. nat. bank examiner U.S. Comptroller of Currency, 1960-63; cashier Cumberland County Bank, Crossville, Tenn., 1965-67, exec. v.p., dir., 1967—; pres. 1st Nat. Bank of Loudon (Tenn.), 1967—, also dir.; dir. Hamilton Nat. Bankshares, Chattanooga. Vice chmn. Crossville Planning Commn., 1964-67; chmn. Loudon Housing Authority, 1969—; v.p. Ft. Loudon Indsl. Devel. Co., Inc., 1968—; dir. Com. of 100, 1968—; mem. Loudon County Bond Bd., 1970—. Served with AUS, 1959. Mem. C. of C. Baptist. Rotarian. Composer The Battle Song, 1970. Home: Butler Dr Loudon TN 37774 Office: PO Drawer A Loudon TN 37774

CANTEY, JAMES WILLIS, banker; b. Columbia, S.C., Mar. 3, 1917; s. J. M. and Elizabeth (Childs) C.; B.A., U. S.C., 1938; m. Nancy Moorer, Apr. 19, 1941; children—James Willis, Joseph Moorer, John Childs. With Columbia Outdoor Advt., Inc. 1945—, pres., 1947—, also dir.; with Citizens & So. Nat. Bank S.C., Charleston, 1958—, pres., 1960-71, chmn. bd., 1971—, also dir.; pres., dir. State Investment Co., Inc., Columbia, 1950—; dir. Charlotte br. Fed. Res. Bd., 1967—, State Record Co., 1962—; dir. Liberty Life Ins. Co. Mem. S.C. Ports Authority, 1956-65, chmn., 1963-65. Served with inf. AUS, Wordl War II; ret. as col., 1955. Decorated Silver Star with 2 oak leaf clusters, Bronze Star with 3 oak leaf clusters, Legion of Merit, Purple Heart; Croix de Guerre (France). Mem. Sigma Alpha Epsilon,

Beta Gamma Sigma, Omicron Delta Kappa, Kappa Sigma Kappa. Episcopalian. Kiwanian. Home: 1400 Westminster Dr Columbia SC 29204 Office: PO Box 727 Columbia SC 29202

CANTOW, EDWARD FRANCIS, physician; b. Balt., Jan. 17, 1936; s. Edward Henry and Cecilia (Hart) C.; B.S., Manhattan Coll., 1957; M.D., Georgetown U., 1961; m. Theresa Scala, July 11, 1959; children—Christine Marie, Loretta Ellen, Claire Denise, Diana Jacqueline, Edward Francis Jr. Commd. ensign, U.S. Navy, 1961, advanced through grades to comdr., 1971; intern U.S. Naval Hosp., Portsmouth, Va., 1961-62, resident, 1963-66, mem. staff internal medicine, 1967-68, asst. dir. hematology service, 1970-72; resigned, 1972; mem. staff internal medicine, hematologist Naval Hosp., Camp Pendleton, Cal., 1968-69; fellow in hematology Naval Hosp., Phila., 1969-71; pvt. practice medicine, specializing in hematology and oncology, Portsmouth, 1972—; cons. hematology USPHS Hosp., Norfolk, Va. Fellow A.C.P.; mem. Bur. Medicine and Surgery Grants for Clin. Investigation in Hematology, Am. Soc. Hematology, A.M.A., Am. Fedn. Clin. Research, Am. Bd. Med. Examiners, Phi Chi. Roman Catholic (dir. youth activities 1969-70, dir. tchrs. 1969-70). Home: 2904 Duke of York Dr Chesapeake VA 23321 Office: 3315 County St Portsmouth VA 23707

CANTRELL, DOROTHY DEAN, educator; b. nr. Milan, Tenn., May 26, 1934; d. George W. and Lura Eddie (Oliver) C.; A.B., Lambuth Coll., 1956; M.A., George Peabody Coll. Tchrs., 1961; Ph.D., U. Tenn., 1970. Tchr. Milan (Tenn.) City Sch., 1955-58, Nurnburg, Germany, 1959, John H. Poly. High Sch., Los Angeles, 1960, John F. Regan Sch., Houston, 1961-63; instr. Berry Coll., 1962-64, asst. prof., 1965—, also chmn. dept. English and speech. Co-chmn. publicity com. Rome (Ga.) Symphony Guild, 1965-67. Mem. Am. Assn. U. Women (pres. Rome br. 1965-67, edn. chmn. 1967-68), S. Atlantic Modern Lang. Assn., Nat., Ga. councils tchrs. English, Sigma Tau Delta, Iota Tau Delta, Delta Kappa Gamma (pres. Iota chpt. 1972-74). Baptist. Democrat. Home: Box J Berry College Mount Berry GA 30149

CANTRELL, FRANK WILLIAM, business cons.; b. Poplar Bluff, Mo., Oct. 11, 1902; s. William Ambrose and Josephine (Catern) C.; student S.E. Mo. State Coll., 1918-21; m. Julia Peironnet Albert, Sept. 4, 1925; children—Frank Peironnet, Julie. With Western Electric Co., 1921-23; various editorial positions Ark. Gazette, Little Rock, 1924-44; exec. v.p. Ark. C. of C., Little Rock, 1945-68, Asso. Industries Ark., Inc., Little Rock, 1948-68. Industry mem. S.W. Regional Wage Stblzn. Bd., Dallas, 1950-52; chmn. Conf. So. Indsl. Assn., 1959-60, Nat. Indsl. Council, 1963; mem. adv. council Ark. Employment Security Div., 1962—. Mem. Ark. Constl. Conv., 1969-70. Mem. Beta Gamma Sigma. Presbyn. Clubs: Top of Rock, Little Rock, Little Rock Country. Address: 15 Beverly Pl Little Rock AR 72207

CANTRELL, FRED HILTON, univ. dean; b. Chattanooga, Oct. 11, 1918; s. Fred H. and Anna Cicelia (Hilton) C.; B.S. in Bus. Adminstrn., U. Fla., 1940; grad. U.S. Army Command and Gen. Staff Coll., 1951, U.S. Army War Coll., 1958; m. Roberta Clarkson Rhyne, Dec. 31, 1946; children—Heyward M., Fred Hilton, Helen Clarkson. Commd. 2d. lt. U.S. Army, 1940, advanced through grades to col.; bn. comdr., ETO, PTO, World War II; instr. U.S. Mil. Acad.; various assignments in Washington; brigade comdr., Korea; course dir. Army War Coll.; ret., 1963; v.p. Tung Oil Products, Inc., Gainesville, Fla., 1963-66; v.p. research and marketing 1st Nat. Bank of Gainesville, 1966-68, now dir.; dean univ. relations and devel. U. Fla., Gainesville, 1968—, exec. dir. U. Fla. Found., Inc., 1968—; dir. Guaranty Fed. Savs. of Gainesville. Past pres., campaign chmn. United Fund; chmn. Com. of 100; v.p. Alachua County chpt. Am. Cancer Soc. Bd. dirs. Boy's Club, Salvation Army. Decorated Legion of Merit, Silver Star, Bronze Star with oak leaf cluster. Mem. Am. Alumni Council, Am. Coll. Pub. Relations Assn., Gainesville Area C. of C. (dir.). Episcopalian (vestryman). Kiwanian (dir.). Club: Gainesville Golf and Country (pres. 1970). Home: 6420 SW 35th Way Gainesville FL 32601

CANTRELL, ROY HERBERT, coll. pres.; b. Kansas City, Mo., Nov. 4, 1904; s. Herbert H. and Mable (Munch) C.; student Pasadena Coll., 1921-22; Asbury Coll., 1922-25; A.B., U. Ky., 1925-26; student Bibl. Sem., 1926-27; A.M., N.Y.U., 1928; B.D., Asbury Sem., 1927; D.D., Northwest Nazarene Coll., 1944; D.R.E., Southwestern Baptist Sem., 1955; m. Evelyn Mikkelson, June 19, 1929. Ordained to ministry Ch. of Nazarene, 1927; prof. Eastern Nazarene Coll., Wollaston, Mass., 1927-29, dean of men, 1928-29; pastor Ch. of the Nazarene, Syracuse, N.Y., 1929-34, Binghamton, N.Y., 1934-39; dist. supt. Ch. of Nazarene, Ont. Dist., Toronto, 1939-42, Minn. Dist., St. Paul, 1941-46, Kan. Dist., Wichita, 1946-47; pres. Bethany-Peniel Coll., Bethany, Okla., 1947—. Mem. gen. bd. and mem. dept. edn. ch. schs. Ch. of Nazarene. Dir. Community Nat. Bank; trustee Okla. County Utility Service Authority. Trustee Eastern Nazarene Coll., 1930-41, Northwestern Nazarene Coll., 1942-46, Sem. of Kansas City, Mo., 1944-47, Bethany Hosp. Kiwanian. Co-author: Exploring Christian Faith. Home: 4300 N College Av Bethany OK 73008

CANTRELL, WILLIAM ALLEN, educator; b. Everton, Ark., Nov. 6, 1920; s. William E. and Vida (Vinson) C.; B.S., McMurry Coll., 1940; M.D., U. Tex., 1943; m. Joyce LaRee Hobbs, Jan. 17, 1945; children—Mary Elizabeth, William Robert. Rotating intern U.S. Naval Hosp., Corona, Cal., 1943-44; resident neuropsychiatry U. Tex. Med. Br. Hosps., 1947-49; asst. prof. neuropsychiatry U. Tex. Med. Br., 1949-54; practice medicine, specializing in psychiatry, Houston, 1951-63; prof. psychiatry Baylor Coll. Medicine, Houston, 1963—. Chief psychiatry service Meth. Hosp., Houston, 1966—; mem. med. adv. com. Tex. Bd. Mental Health and Mental Retardation, 1965—, chmn., 1965-69; bd. dirs. Tex. Assn. Mental Health, 1965—. Served to lt. M.C., USNR, 1944-47. Fellow Am. Psychiat. Assn. (br. pres. 1958-59), Am. Coll. Psychiatrists; mem. A.M.A., Tex. Med. Assn., Tex. (v.p. 1958-59), Central neuropsychiat. assns., Houston Psychiat. Soc. (pres. 1956). Home: 5018 Loch Lomond St Houston TX 77035

CAPE, CHARLES ALBERT, physician, educator; b. Grand Forks, N.D., Apr. 27, 1933; s. Thomas Wilson and Julia (Porter) C.; B.S., U. N.D., 1955, B.A., 1956, B.S. in Medicine, 1957; M.D., Wake Forest Coll., 1959; m. Gloria Joyce Torgerson, Dec. 18, 1955; children—Cheryl Ann, Connie, Barbara Lee, Richard Charles, Catherine Joyce. Intern U. Ia., Iowa City, 1959-60, resident neurology, 1960-63, research neurologist, 1963-64, instr. dept. neurology, 1964-65; asst. prof. neurology U. Tenn., Memphis, 1965-69, asso. prof., 1969—; practice of medicine specializing in neurology, Iowa City, 1963-65, Memphis, 1965—; mem. staffs City of Memphis, Baptist, Methodist hosps. (all Memphis). Mem. A.M.A., Am. Acad. Neurology. Contbr. articles to publs. Home: 724 Center Dr Memphis TN 38128 Office: Suite 101 B 20 S Dudley St Memphis TN 38103

CAPEL, ARRON LEON, banker; b. Troy, N.C., Feb. 22, 1900; s. Arron W. E. and Nancy (Smitherman) C.; student N.C. State U., 1917-18, Shenandoah Valley Collegiate Inst., 1918, U. N.C., 1919-21; m. Clara May Smith, Aug. 25, 1928; children—Arron Leon, Jr., Jesse Smith, Arron William Eligah II, Blanche Neilson. Prin., A. Leon Capel, until 1957, inc., 1957, pres., 1957—; pres. Bank of Montgomery, Troy, N.C., 1940-60, chmn. bd., 1960—. Finance commr., chmn. exec. bds., City of Troy, 1948-65; treas. Montgomery Meml. Hosp., Troy, 1948-65. Home: 205 E Main St Troy NC 27371 Office: 831 Main St Troy NC 27371

CAPERS, CHARLOTTE, state ofcl.; b. Columbia, Tenn.; d. Walter B. and Louise (Woldridge) Capers; student Millsaps Coll., 1930-32, U. Colo., 1932; B.A., U. Miss., 1934. With Miss. Dept. Archives and History, 1938—, successively sec., research and editorial assist., asst. dir., 1938-55, dir., 1955-69, dir. spl. projects, 1969—; asst. editor Jour. Miss. History, 1942-43, asso. editor, 1943-55, editor-in-chief, 1956-69; columnist Jackson Daily News, 1944-55, State Times, 1955, Dixie Roto Mag., 1957; book revs. N.Y. Times Book Rev., various hist. jours. Chmn. Miss. Hist. Commn. Fellow Soc. Am Archivists; mem. Jr. League Jackson, Miss. State Hist. Soc. (sec.-treas.), Am., So. hist. assns., Am. Assn. Museums. Episcopalian. Editor: (with William D. McCain) Papers of the Washington County Historical Society, 1954; editorial dir. Mississippi in the Confederacy, 1961; mem. adv. editorial bd. Jefferson Davis Papers, Rice U.; publs. com. Mississippi as a Province, Territory and State (J.F.H. Claiborne), 1964; contbg. editor The Delta Review, 1966-70. Home: 4020 Berkley Dr Jackson MS 39211 Office: Box 571 Jackson MS 39205

CAPERS, THOMAS STACY, JR., advt. agy. exec.; b. Savannah, Ga., July 28, 1913; s. Thomas Stacy and Ann Keene (Hedges) C.; B.A., Princeton, 1937; postgrad. U. Pa., 1938; M.A., U. Wis., 1964; m. Virginia Woodcock, Jan. 17, 1942; children—Candace (Mrs. James Finnigan), Carol. Commd. 1st lt. U.S. Army, 1941, advanced through grades to col., 1945; dir. personnel U.S. Mil. Acad., West Point, N.Y., 1958-62; dir. pub. affairs UN, Republic Korea, 1964-66; advt. mgr. U.S. Army, 1966-68; ret., 1968; pres. Capers Assos., Satellite Beach, Fla., 1968—. Cons. Internat. Transactional Analysis Assn., 1971—, Am. Inst. Plant Engrs., 1969-71; cons., mgmt. staff Trans World Air Lines, Kennedy Space Center, 1968-71. Chief finance div. Brevard County United Fund, 1970; v.p. pub. relations com. Penninsula Civic Opera, 1967. Bd. dirs. U.S. Savs. Bond Campaign, Kennedy Space Center. Decorated Legion of Merit (2); recipient citation Editors and Pubs. Assn. Republic Korea, 1966. Mem. Pub. Relations Soc. Am., Internat. Pub. Relations Com., Am. Inst. Plant Engrs. Mason. Club: Princeton (Richmond, Va.). Editor Korean edit. Stars and Stripes, 1964-66, Profl. Jour. for Career Counseling, 1966-68. Home: 440 Glenwood Av Satellite Beach FL 32927

CAPERTON, LUCIEN MARSHALL, bank exec.; b. Lawrenceburg, Tenn., Nov. 3, 1910; s. William Carrell and Sarah Leona (Dalton) C.; student Vanderbilt U., 1928-29; B.S. in Civil Engring., Va. Mil. Inst., 1929-33; m. Mary Elizabeth McMann, June 12, 1933; children—Beth (Mrs. Thomas Donald Rayfield), Jane (Mrs. Joe Gleaves), Melinda (Mrs. Donald Crews). Owner Caperton Ins. Agy., Lawrenceburg, 1933—, Caperton Chevrolet Co., Lawrenceburg, 1949-55; dir. Murray Ohio Mfg. Co., Nashville and Lawrenceburg, Tenn., 1958—; with 1st Nat. Bank, Lawrenceburg, 1954—, dir., 1954—, pres., 1954-69, chmn. bd., 1969—; v.p., dir. Bank Loretto (Tenn.), 1956—. Pres. Tenn. Fedn. Young Republicans, 1940-46. Served to maj. AUS, 1942-45. Mem. Lawrenceburg C. of C. (pres. 1952), Am. Legion (comdr. 1946-47), Phi Kappa Sigma. Republican. Mason (Shriner), Lion (pres. 1935). Home: 205 Caperton Av Lawrenceburg TN 38464 Office: 116 Pulaski St Lawrenceburg TN 38464

CAPLAN, FRED HARRY, state justice; b. Clarksburg, W.Va., Dec. 3, 1914; s. Henry A. and Hannah (Siegelman) C.; A.B., W.Va. U., 1939; LL.B., U. Richmond, 1941; m. Miriam Kessler, Nov. 12, 1941; 1 dau., Betty Lee. Admitted to W.Va. bar, 1941; practice in Clarksburg, 1946-53; asst. atty. gen. W.Va., 1953-61; chmn. Pub. Service Commn. W.Va., 1961-62; judge Supreme Ct. Appeals W. Va., 1962—, chief justice, 1970—. Mem. W.Va. Legislature from Harrison County, 1949-53. Served with AUS, 1941-46; PTO. Mem. Am., W.Va., Harrison County bar assns., W.Va. State Bar, W.Va. Jud. Assn., U. Richmond Law Sch. Assn. (past pres.). Democrat. Jewish religion. Mem. B'nai B'rith. Home: 4218 Noyes Av SE Charleston WV 25304 Office: Supreme Court Appeals Charleston WV 25301

CAPO, BERNARDO GUILLERMO, agrl. cons.; b. Guayama, P.R., Dec. 28, 1908; s. Rafael E. and Dolores (Capo) C.; B.S., U.P.R., 1929; M.S., Cornell U., 1941, Ph.D., 1942; m. Juanita de Choudens, Jan. 4, 1930; children—Ada Teresa (Mrs. Jaime A. Colley), Carlota. Fertilizer chemist dept. agr., P.R., 1929-36; soil chemist agrl. expt. sta. U.P.R., 1936-42, acting head soils dept., 1942-43, biometrician, 1943-44, biometrician and head dept. agronomy and horticulture, 1944-48, asst. dir., 1948-50, asso. dir., 1951-64; project mgr. UN Spl. Fund agrl. research sta., Damascus, Syria, 1964-66; agrl. cons., P.R., 1966—; agrl. research cons. Land Authority P.R., 1967—. Recipient award Gamma Sigma Delta, 1965. Mem. Coll. Chemists P.R., Internat. Soc. Sugarcane Technologists, Am. Statis. Assn., Inst. Math. Statistics, Soc. Agrl. Scis. P.R., Statis. Soc. P.R., Assn. Agrl. Cons. (pres. 1967-69). Contbr. articles profl. jours. Address: 1749 Santa Praxedes Rio Piedras PR 00926

CAPP, THERON EARL, city govt. ofcl.; b. Rockwall, Tex., Oct. 26, 1912; s. Michael Acie and Mabel (Davis) C.; student Chillicothe (Mo.) Coll., 1930; m. Stella Tarver, Apr. 23, 1946. Accountant Borden Milk Co., Oklahoma City, 1937-42; accountant C.C. Wilson, C.P.A., Vaughn & Fortner, C.P.A.'s, Duncan, Okla., 1946-50, Internal Revenue Service, 1954, C.P. Carter Constrn. Co., Duncan, 1950-54, 55-58; city clk., treas. City of Duncan, Okla., 1958—, also treas., sec., trustee City Duncan Pension System for Pub. Employees. Receiver, trustee for royalty owner group oil and gas lease, 1950-54. Served with M.C., AUS, 1942-43. Mem. Okla. Municipal Clks. and Treas. Assn. (pres. 1959-60), Internat. Inst. Municipal Clks., C. of C., Duncan Hist. Soc. Kiwanian, Mason (32 deg., Shriner). Author: Studies in Municipal Finances—with particular reference to Oklahoma and Duncan, 1968. Patentee bookkeeping device. Home: 2012 Park Dr Duncan OK 73533 Office: PO Box 969 City Hall Duncan OK 73533

CAPPAERT, F.L., modular home mfg. co. exec.; b. Clare, Mich., 1919; grad. Alma Coll.; m. Marilynn Cappaert; 2 sons, 3 daus. From laborer to gen. mgr. Alma Trailer Plant; with home mfg. co., Vicksburg, Miss., 1947-53; founder Magnolia Homes Mfg. Corp., Vicksburg, 1953-66; chmn. bd., pres. Guerdon Industries (merger Magnolia Homes Mfg. Co. and Guerdon Industries), 1966—. Office: P O Box 1259 Louisville KY 40201

CAPPS, CLIFTON ROWLAND, mfrs. rep.; b. nr. Middleburg, N.C., Dec. 17, 1893; s. Lewis Boyd and Mary Ida (Dowling) C.; student N.C. State U., 1942-43; m. Lida Jane Roberts, Nov. 12, 1930. Clk., bookkeeper Aberdeen Hardware Co. (N.C.), 1910-12; with Lee Hardware Co., Sanford, N.C., 1912-19; mgr. Capps Hardware Co., Sanford, 1919-26; with Shapleigh Hardware, St. Louis, 1927-28, Simmons Hardware Co., Atlanta, 1924-31; operator produce warehouse, Sanford, 1932-33; salesman, buyer Carolina Hardware, Raleigh, N.C., 1934-46; prin. Clifton R. Capps Co., mfrs. reps., Cary, N.C., 1946—; dir. Council Tool Co., Wananish, N.C. Methodist (bd. stewards 1944-48). Mason. Home and office: 401 N Academy St Cary NC 27511

CAPPS, RANDALL, educator; b. Peytonsburg, Ky., Oct. 23, 1936; s. Mitchell T. and Robbie (Hoffman) C.; B.A., Ky. Wesleyan Coll., 1957; M.A., Western Ky. U., 1961; Ed.D., U. Va., 1970; m. Joan Gray, Aug. 19, 1961; 1 dau. Jill Robbie. Tchr. Owensboro pub. schs., 1957-58, Lawrenceburg High Sch., 1958-59, Bardstown High Sch., 1959-62; mem. faculty Western Ky. U., Bowling Green, 1962—, dir. speech activities, 1962—, acting head dept. speech and theatre, 1968-70, asso. prof., head dept., 1970—. Bd. dirs. Wesley Found., Bowling Green. Mem. Speech Assn. Am., Ky. (pres. 1966-67), So. speech assns., Am. Forensic Assn., Bardstown Classroom Tchrs. Assn. (pres. 1961-62), Ky. Oratorical Assn. (exec.sec. 1963—, pres. 1969—), Sigma Nu, Kappa Delta Pi. Phi Delta Kappa (pres. 1968—). Methodist. Rotarian. Home: 1915 Kay Av Bowling Green KY 42101

CAPSAS, CLEON WADE, educator; b. Birmingham, Ala., Oct. 2, 1925; s. George Alexander and Veva (Perry) C.; A.B., George Peabody Coll., 1948; M.A., U. N.M., 1959, Ph. D., 1964; m. Rita Ann Nourot, Oct. 24, 1958 children—George Alexander, Alexander Wade. Pres., Acoma Adjustment Co., Albuquerque, 1954-57; instr. U. N.M., 1958-62; asst. prof. Appalachian State U., 1962-63; cons. U.S. Peace Corps, 1961-62; dir. Tng. Center, U. N.M., 1963-64; asso. prof. langs. U. Tex. at El Paso, 1964-65; dir. field investigations Tex. Tech. NDEA Summer Lang. Inst., Argentine, 1964; asso. prof. langs. U. Kan. at Lawrence, 1965-68; now chmn. dept. modern langs. U. So. Fla.; co-dir. U. Kan. Summer Session, Mexico, 1966; Cons. Nat. U. N.M., 1966-67, 69-72. Served with USNR, 1943-47, 50-54, asst. naval attache, Rio de Janeiro, Brazil, 1952-54 (comdr. Res.). Mem. Am. Assn. Tchrs. of Spanish and Portuguese, Modern Lang. Assn. Am. Author: (with A.R. Lopes, M.A. Rodriguez) The Spanish Verb 3d edit., 1969; (with Gina Cantoni Harvey and others) The Italian Verb, 1967; (with Ralf R. Nicolai and others) The German Verb, 1968. Contbr. Funk & Wagnalls New Internat. Yearbook, 1960-66; collaborator articles in Mexican mags. Office: U So Fla Dept Modern Langs Tampa FL 33620

CARBAUGH, HARRY ALBERT, indsl. engr.; b. Tionesta, Pa., July 25, 1923; s. Curtis Custer and Eva May (Whitman) C.; student Gen. Elec. Co. Night Sch., 1941-44, Pa. State Coll. Extension, 1951; m. Mary Helen Stanley, Dec. 12, 1948; children—Barbara (Mrs. Jimmy Downs), Lawrence, Ronald, Gary, David, Terry, Cindy. Apprentice tool maker Gen. Elec. Co., Erie, Pa., 1941-44, tool maker, 1946-50, tool and process planner, foreman, quality control engr., advanced mfg. engr., Louisville, 1950-68, specialist methods and planning, supr., Greenville, S.C., 1968—. Mem. Pa. State Police, 1949-52. Served with AUS, 1944-46; ETO. Decorated Bronze Star medal with oak leaf cluster, Combat Inf. badge. Registered profl. engr., Ky. Republican. Lutheran (v.p. council). Mason, Elk. Home: 240 Greenbrier Dr Simpsonville SC 29681 Office: Box 648 Greenville SC 29602

CARBAUGH, HARRY CLARKE, mem. Republican Nat. Com.; b. Tasso, Tenn., May 11, 1895; s. Harvey Francis and Bertha (Fletcher) C.; student U. Chattanooga, 1914-16; m. Alyce Katherine Huffaker, Dec. 10, 1917; 1 dau., Betty Carolyn (Mrs. Richard Fancher). Partner Carbaugh & Co., Chattanooga, 1918-20; gen. mgr. Tenn. Egg Co., 1920-, v.p., 1920-27, pres., 1927-63; pres. Scenic City Investment Corp.; dir. Hamilton Nat. Bank, Interstate Life & Accident Ins. Co., Interstate Fire Ins. Co. Chmn. City-Wide Eastern Sunrise Service, 1947-55; exec. com., pres. Community Chest, 1946-47; exec. com. United Fund, 1959-69. Vice chmn. for So. states Nat. Republican Finance Com., 1960-63; mem. Rep. Nat. Com. for Tenn., 1961—; chmn. Tenn. Rep. Finance Com., 1944-62; del. Rep. Nat. Conv., 1948-68. Vice chmn. bd. trustees U. Chattanooga, 1950-69; bd. dirs. YMCA. Served from 2d lt. to 1st lt. inf. U.S. Army, 1916-19. Mem. U.S. (dir. 1959-65), Chattanooga (pres. 1941, dir. 1940) chambers commerce, Inst. Am. Poultry Industries (dir., exec. com. 1958), Nat. Butter and Egg Assn. (pres. 1947-48), Sigma Chi. Baptist (deacon). Rotarian (pres. 1943-44). Clubs: Executive (pres. 1943-44); Fairyland, Mountain City (Chattanooga). Home: 219 W Brow Oval Lookout Mountain TN 37350 Office: Maclellan Bldg Chattanooga TN 37402

CARDELLI, GIOVANNI GUIDO CARLO, architect, producer; b. London, Eng., Oct. 2, 1910; s. Giovanni and Ruth (Lamson) C.; M.A. Scis. Politiques, Lycee Jansen, Paris, France, 1928; m. Jacqueline Stewart, Nov. 22, 1931; children—Diane (Mrs. Lawrence O. Houghon), Gioia. Came to U.S., 1933. naturalized, 1941. Naval architect, designer, Chgo., N.Y.C., Southampton, N.Y., Westport, Conn., 1932-64; resident naval architect Rybovich & Sons Boat Works Inc., West Palm Beach, Fla., 1964-70; exec. v.p. John H. Witman Interiors, Palm Beach, 1970-72; dir. interior design Outcalt Environment, Stuart, Fla., 1972—; asst. to pres. Chgo. Opera Co., 1938-40; gen. mgr. Opera Theater, Chgo., 1940-49; producer Rape of Lucretia, Chgo., N.Y.C., 1948-49; gen. mgrs. Dallas Symphony, 1949-52. Clubs: River, New York Yacht (N.Y.C.); Seawanhaka Yacht (Center Island, N.Y.), Arts Club (Chgo.); Westhampton Yacht, Delray Beach Yacht; Coral Harbor Yacht (Nassau); Sag Harbor Yacht (Long Island). Translator operas, 1939-54. Home: 166 Beacon Lane Jupiter FL 33458 Office: 736 Colorado Av Stuart FL 33494

CARDER, CLARENCE ALLISON, univ. adminstr.; b. Johnson City, Tenn., Dec. 12, 1913; s. Mace Herbert and Nana Elizabeth (Butler) C.; A.B., Tusculum Coll., 1938; Th.M., So. Bapt. Theol. Sem., 1943; Ed.D., U. Tenn., 1955; m. Alma Trivett, July 28, 1967. Tchr. elementary schs. Tenn., 1935-37; tchr. English McDonald High Sch., Greene County, 1938-40; associational field worker Holston Assn. Baptists, Johnson City, Tenn., 1943; minister of music and religious edn. First Bapt. Ch., Elizabethton, 1944-46; instr. Bible and psychology Baylor U., 1946-47; chmn. dept. edn. and psychology, dir. audio-visual edn. E. Tenn. State Coll., Johnson City, 1947-57; dir. elementary edn. Brevard County Schs., Titusville, Fla., 1957-58; prof. edn., dir. placement Appalachian State Tchrs. Coll., Boone, N.C., 1958-60; asso. prof. edn., psychology Carson-Newman Coll., Jefferson City, Tenn. 1960, prof. and chmn. dept. edn. and psychology, until 1967; dean of student personnel services Lincoln Meml. U., 1967-69, acad. dean, 1969-71; dir. guidance and counseling Piedmont Coll., Demorest, Ga., 1971-72, acad. dean, 1972—. Mem. Am. Guild Organists (hon. pres. E. Tenn. chpt.), E. Tenn. (hon. chmn. audio-visual sect.), Tenn. (hon. chmn. audio-visual sect.), Fla., Brevard edn. assns., N.E.A., Tenn. Acad. Sci., Am. Assn. U. Profs., Internat. Council Exceptional Children, Fla. Council Elementary Edn., Tenn (v.p.), E. Tenn. (pres.) student teaching assns., Phi Delta Kappa, Lambda Chi Alpha, Phi Mu Alpha Sinfonia, Alpha Psi Omega, Kappa Delta Pi, Psi Chi. Mason, Kiwanian. Author: A Study of Teacher Education in Southern Baptist Colleges and Universities, 1955. Home: Summit Av Cornelia GA 30531 Office: Dept Psychology Piedmont Coll Demorest GA 30535

CARDINAL, PAUL J(OSEPH), pharm. and mgmt. con., writer; b. Paterson, N.J. Mar. 2, 1904; s. Alphonse A. and Mary M. (Froehlich) C.; student Stevens Prep. Sch., Hoboken; B.S. in Engring. and Bus. Adminstrn., Mass. Inst. Tech., 1924; m. Lorene F. Lapham, June 26, 1929; children—Lorene M. (Mrs. Walter Welsh), Joan R. (Mrs. Donald MacMurray), Paul Joseph, John, Richard, Anne (Mrs. Arthur O'Connell, Jr.), Carolyn (Mrs. C. Roy Walker, Jr.), Alan. Employed Hoffmann-LaRoche, Inc., Nutley, N.J., 1924-63, successively advt. asst., advt. mgr., office mgr., mgr. hosp. dept., co-dir. sales staff, mgr. bulk vitamin div., v.p. charge vitamin div., v.p. charge indsl. relations,

1958-63; cons. in relations Inst. Human Nutrition, Columbia, N.Y.C., 1963-71. Vice pres. Nat. Vitamin Found., 1958, treas., 1959-71; bd. dirs. N.Y. Bd. Trade, 1959-62; exec. com. Drug, Chem. and Allied Trades Assn., 1956-63, treas., 1961-62, v.p., 1962-63; vol. Internat. Exec. Service Corps. Recipient Coronat medal St. Edwards U., 1963. Mem. Am. Pub. Health Assn., Pharm. Advt. Club (life), N.A.M., Phi Kappa Theta, Pi Delta Epsilon. Clubs: Mass. Inst. Tech. (Fla.). Home: 707 Port Side Dr Naples FL 33940

CARDINALE, ANTHONY, govt. ofcl.; b. Washington, Jan. 7, 1930; s. Antonio and Mary (Straccomore) C.; B.A., Wilson Tchrs. Coll., 1952; M.A., George Washington U., 1958, Ed.D., 1966; m. Patricia Wilson, Mar. 1, 1951; children—Michael, Deborah, Anthony. Asst. dir. Navy Dependents Schs. Dept. Def., Washington, 1957-59, dir., 1958-63; asst. dir. Dependents Schs. Div. Dept. Def., 1963-65, dir., 1965—; tchr. U. Va. extension. Bd dirs. St. Coletta Sch. Mentally Retarded, Arlington, Va. Served with USMC, 1952-54. Mem. Nat. Soc. Study Edn., N.E.A., Am. Assn. Sch. Adminstrs., Phi Delta Kappa, Phi Sigma Pi. K.C. (3 deg.). Home: 4408 Braeburn Dr Fairfax VA 22030 Office: Pentagon Washington DC 20301

CARDONE, JOHN ELMO, investment co. exec.; b. Madisonville, La., Dec. 15, 1927; s. Joseph Salvador and Eunice Elizabeth (Stein) C.; B.S., La. State U., 1948, postgrad., 1951-52; m. Mary Magdalene Niel, Apr. 23, 1950; children—Gwendolyn Ann, John Elmo, Jay Anthony, Mary Ann. Chemist, Mathieson Chem. Co., Lake Charles, La., 1948-49, process engr., 1950-60, plant supt., 1961-62; co-founder Cesco, Inc., indsl. service and proprietary chem. co., Maplewood, La., 1962, v.p., 1962-71, operational mgr., 1967-69, mgr. engring and product line devel., 1967-71, mgr. fgn. operations, 1969-71, also dir.; self employed Cardone Enterprises, 1971—; dir. Cosmopolitan Life Ins. Co., Lake Charles, La. Mem. Am. Chem. Soc., Maintenance Engr. Inst., Am. Inst. Chem. Engrs., Nat. Assn. Corrosion Engrs. Democrat. Roman Catholic. K.C. (grand knight 1960), Lion. Home: 1236 Bayouwood Dr Lake Charles LA 70601 Office: PO Box 0118 Lake Charles LA 70601

CARDWELL, HORACE MILTON, hosp. adminstr.; b. Oklahoma City, Feb. 3, 1919; s. Horace M. and Lona (Bridges) C.; B.S. in Econs., Tex. A. and M. Coll., 1941; m. 2d, Billie Jo Cardwell; children (by previous marriage)—Barbara Ann, Beverly Kay, Horace Milton III. Asst. adminstr. Herman Hosp., Houston, 1946-48; adminstr. Meml. Hosp., Lufkin, Tex., 1948—. Chmn. Hosp.-Ins.-Physicians Joint Adv. Com. Tex., 1954—; mem. Tex. Commn. Patient Care, 1957-61; pres. State Bd. Vocational Nurse Examiners, 1962-68; dir. Med. Information, 1968—; bd. dirs. Blue Cross Tex., 1962—. Chmn. Lufkin United Fund, 1961; med. adv. com. State Dept. Pub. Welfare, 1968-70. Served AUS, 1941-46; ETO, PTO. Fellow Am. Coll. Hosp. Adminstrs.; mem. Am. (ho. dels. 1956-68, mem. council govt. relations 1966—, mem. council on adminstrv. practice 1957-61, trustee 1968-71), Tex. (pres. 1956-57, chmn. council govt. relations 1958—, chmn. bldg. com. 1965—, Earl M. Collier award 1970) hosp. assns., Tex. Assn. Hosp. Accountants (pres. 1953-54), C. of C. Rotarian (local pres. 1969-70). Address: PO Box 1447 Lufkin TX 75902

CAREY, MARK OLIVER, JR., dentist; b. New Orleans, Aug. 10, 1915; s. Mark Oliver and Mary (Schroeder) C.; D.D.S., Loyola U. South, 1938; m. Mona Eugenin Drez, Oct. 11, 1939; children—Mary Clo, Karen Ann, Mark Oliver III. Pvt. practice dentistry, New Orleans, 1938-63, Gretna, La., 1963—. Mem. com. Boy Scouts Am., 1966-69, com. chmn., 1969—. Served with AUS, 1940-46, 1950-52. Mem. Southeast Acad. Prosthetics, Am., La., New Orleans dental assns., Am. Acad. Implant Dentistry. Mason. Kiwanian. Home: 4922 St Bernard Av New Orleans LA 70114 Office: 36 West Bank Expressway Gretna LA 70053

CARGILLE, CHARLES MORELL, endocrinologist; b. Newark, July 6, 1934; s. Ralph Phillips and Esther Anna (Malmsten) C.; student U. Aberdeen (Scotland), 1954-55; B.A., Bucknell U., 1956; postgrad. (Josiah Macy Jr. Found. scholar 1957, 58), Johns Hopkins U., 1956-59, M.D., 1961; postgrad. Am. U., student U. Djakarta, Indonesia, 1959-60; m. Francis Custis Johnson, June 11, 1961; children—James Royal, Christopher Allen, Johnathan Morell, David Lee. Intern obsetrics and gynecology Barnes Hosp., St. Louis; resident in internal medicine Mountainside Hosp., 1962-63, 64-65, Seton Hall Coll. Medicine-Hersey City Med. Center, Jersey City, 1963-64; NIH research fellow in endocrinology N.J. Coll. Medicine, Jersey City, 1965-66; sr. investigator, attending physician Nat. Cancer Inst. NIH, 1966-70, Nat. Inst. Child Health and Human Devel. NIH, 1970-72; dep. dir. div. metabolic and endocrine drug products Office Sci. Evaluation Bur. Drugs FDA, Rockville, Md., 1972—. Mem. radiation com. NIH, 1967-69; mem. radioimmunoassay task force Nat. Pituitary Agy., Balt., 1967-69; rep. for Nat. Cancer Inst. Assembly, Scientists in Interassembly Council Assemblies Scientists NIH, 1970; mem. com. on sci. and human values Nat. Inst. Allergy and Metabolic Diseases NIH, 1971. Bd. dirs. Cargille Sons Inc., Little Falls, N.J., 1959—, R.P. Cargille Labs., Inc., Little Falls, 1965—, Cargille Sci., Inc., Little Falls, 1965—. Fellow Royal Soc. Health, Am. Acad. Reproductive Medicine; mem. A.M.A., Johns Hopkins Med. and Surg. Assn., Am. Fedn. for Clin. Research, Endocrine Soc., Internat. Soc. Endocrinology, Am. Fertility Soc., Soc. for Study Reprodn., Am. Pub. Health Assn., Am. Assn. for Automotive Medicine, Physicians for Automotive Safety, Population Assn. Am., Ecol. Soc. Am., Soc. for Exptl. Biology and Medicine, N.Y. Acad. Scis., Eugenics Soc. (Gt. Britain), Soc. for Study Fertiligy (Gt. Britain), Am. Soc. Animal Sci., Human Ecol. Soc., Population Reference Bur., Am. Assn. for World Health, Soc. for Sci. Study Sex, Eta Kappa Nu (motor vehicle safety group). Baptist. Contbr. numerous articles in field to sci. jours. Reviewer Jour. Clin. Endocrinology and Metabolism, 1968—, Pediatric Research: An Internat. Jour. Human Developmental Biology, 1969, Endocrinology, 1970, Jour. Lab. and Clin. Medicine, 1971. Home: 2307 McAuliffe Dr Rockville MD 20851 Office: 5600 Fishers Lane Rockville MD 20851

CARIDAKIS, GEORGE, Marine Corps officer; b. Syracuse, N.Y., Nov. 24, 1927; s. Frank and Frances (Psaltides) C.; student Colgate U., 1945-46; B.S., U. Neb., 1963; M.A., Washington U., St. Louis, 1966; Ph.D., Am. U., 1972; m. Minnie Margaret Coston, Mar. 25, 1950; children—Frank, Thomas, George, Constance. Joined U.S. Marine Corps, 1946; commd. 2d lt., 1948, advanced through grades to col., 1969; infantry officer, aerial observer, research and devel. officer; chief air observer 1st Marine Div., 1957-59; dir. surface and amphibious programs Office Naval Research, 1966-68; chief operational plans Mil. Assistance Comd., Vietnam, 1968-69; dir. Office of Manpower Utilization, 1969—. Instr., Marine Corps Edn. Center, Command and Staff Coll., 1961-62, Basic Sch., 1951-52. Decorated Bronze Star medal with combat V, Legion of Merit with combat V. Mem. Marine Corps Assn., U.S. Naval Inst., Am. Ordnance Assn., Operations Research Soc., Mil. Operations Research Soc. Home: 8917 Glenbrook Rd Fairfax VA 22030 Office: Hdqrs USMC Washington DC 20380

CARLAN, CHARLES HAMPTON, civil engr.; b. DeFuniak Springs, Fla., July 21, 1937; s. Loy and Eleanor (Flow) C.; B.C.E., Auburn (Ala.) U., 1960; m. Sandra Edwards, Apr. 12, 1958; children—David Loy, Larry Edward. Profl. baseball player Milw. Braves, 1959-60; trainee, project engr., maintenance engr. Fla. State Rd. Dept., 1960-65; supt. City of Pensacola, Fla., 1965-68, city engr., 1969-70; staff dir. transp. com. Fla. Senate, Tallahassee, 1971-72; dir. profl. devel. Barrett, Daffin & Figg, Engrs., Architects & Planners, 1972—; pres. Carlan Constrn. Co., Inc. Chmn. employees exec. com. City of Pensacola, 1968-70. Mem. Fla. Engring. Soc. (past sec. N.W. Fla. chpt.), Pensacola Jr. C. of C. (dir.). Methodist. Lion. Home: 4007 Roscrea Dr Tallahassee FL 32303 Office: 3100 Capital Circle NE Tallahassee FL 32303

CARLETON, R. E., supt. schs.; b. Pauls Valley, Okla., Aug. 14, 1914; s. Robert Edward and Ethel (Edwards) C.; B.S., E. Central State Coll., 1937, M.A., Okla. U., 1943, postgrad. summers 1955, 58, 60, 62, 64, 66; postgrad. Colo. U., 1948; m. Emma Lou Frost, Oct. 16, 1942; children—David Frost, Mary Janet, Susan Louise. Tchr. high sch., Purcell, Okla., 1937-40, Waurika, Okla., 1940-41, Pauls Valley (Okla.) high sch., 1941-45; prin. Pauls Valley High Sch., 1945-55, supt., 1955—; mem. Okla. Curriculum Improvement Commn., 1960—, exec. com. Okla. Commn. Ednl. Adminstrn., 1964-68; mem. profl. standards bd. Okla. Dept. Edn.; bd. dirs. Mid-Continent Ednl. Lab., Kansas City, Mo., 1964—; mem. So. Okla. Devel. Assn., 1964—; mem. Okla. Bd. Edn., 1970—. Mem. Okla. Edn. Assn. (mem. exec. com 1965—, mem. policies commn. 1966—), Okla. Assn. Sch. Adminstrs. (pres. 1967—), Pauls Valley C. of C. (bd. dirs. 1955—). Democrat. Presbyn. Kiwanian (editor Ki-Notes, Tex., Okla. Dist. 1960). Home: 908 S Walnut St Pauls Valley OK 73075

CARLETON, R. V., ret. airline exec.; b. nr. Elk City, Okla., Sept. 4, 1905; s. Virgil Francis and Olga M. (Smallwood) C.; student Okla. U., 1927-29; m. Alice Ruth Calmes, July 22, 1928; 1 dau., Rosemary Leigh. With Curtiss-Wright Flying Service. Portland, Me., 1929-31; airline capt. Braniff Airways, 1931-42, chief pilot, 1942-45, dir. flight operations, 1945-52, operations mgr., 1952-54, v.p. operations, 1954-61, became sr. v.p., 1961, exec. v.p., asst. to chmn. bd., until 1970 also dir., 1956-70, also mem. exec. com., ret., 1970. Pres. Air Transport Assn. Operators Conf., 1960. Bd. Dirs. Blakley-Braniff Found., 1954-64. Mem. Internat. Air Transport Assn. (tech. com. chmn. 1961). Presbyn. Clubs: Northwood Country; Dallas Salesmanship. Home: 4314 Willow Grove Rd Dallas TX 75220

CARLIN, JAMES BOYCE, educator; b. Paducah, Ky., June 19, 1932; s. Lois W. and Flora (Newton) C.; A.A., Paducah Jr. Coll., 1952; student Union U., 1952-53; A.B., Murray State U., 1954; M.A., George Peabody Coll., 1957; Ed.D., U. Miss., 1969; m. Hellon L. Upchurch, June 22, 1968. Tchr., Hendron Elementary Sch., Paducah, Ky., 1954-63, head tchr., 1962-63; asst. prof. edn. Middle Tenn. State U., 1964-67; supr. reading Meridian (Miss.) Pub. Sch. System, 1967-68; asst. prof. edn. U. Miss., 1968-69; asso. prof. edn. Murray (Ky.) State U., 1969—. Reading cons., coordinator, S., Midwest, 1964—. Mem. Internat. Reading Assn., Nat. Soc. Study Edn., N.E.A., Ky. Edn. Assn., Murray State U. Edn. Assn., Nat. Council Tchrs. English, Kappa Delta Pi (Zeta Eta chpt. pres. summer 1964), Phi Delta Kappa. Democrat. Baptist. Rotarian. Home: 1102 Doran Rd Murray KY 42071

CARLINER, DAVID, lawyer; b. Washington, Aug. 12, 1918; ed. Am. U., U. Va.; LL.B., Nat. U., 1941. Admitted to Va. bar, 1940, D.C. bar, 1946, U.S. Supreme Ct. bar, 1953; practice in Washington. Mem. Am., Internat. (immigration and nationality com. 1954-56, 69—) bar assns., Va. State Bar, Am. Civil Liberties Union, Am. Soc. Internat. Law, World Peace Through Law Center. Office: 932 Pennsylvania Bldg 425 13th St NW Washington DC 20004*

CARLISLE, BRAD, editor. City editor Nashville Banner. Office: 1100 Broadway Nashville TN 37203*

CARLISLE, CHARLES HENRY, coll. adminstr.; b. Newberry, S.C., Sept. 15, 1924; s. Hubert Toland and Ora (Askins) C.; B.S., Newberry Coll., 1944, LL.D., 1972; M.A., U. S.C., 1947; postgrad. U. Omaha, 1959; m. Jean Kennedy Todd, June 1, 1950; children—Lucille Askins, Charles Todd, Catherine Kennedy. Prin., Williston-Elko High Sch., Williston, S.C., 1944-46; asst. prof. history Erskine Coll., Due West, S.C., 1947-54, bus. mgr., 1954-66, v.p. for bus. and finance, 1966—. Mem. Abbeville County Devel. Bd. Trustee, sec. bd. trustees Erskine Coll. Mem. S.C. Hist. Assn. (sec.-treas. 1949-54), So. Assn. Coll. and Univ. Bus. Officers. Presbyn. (elder, moderator 1972-73). Rotarian (pres. 1972). Home: Box 185 Due West SC 29639

CARLISLE, LAWRENCE GREELEY, mfg. co. exec.; b. Louisville, Apr. 25, 1901; s. Horace G. and Blanche (Burkhart) C.; student U. Ky. extension, 1942; m. Elsie Nau, June 25, 1924; 1 son, Norman G. Engr. Am. Elevator Co., Louisville, 1920-32; chief elevator insp. City of Louisville, 1933-37; chief engr. Murphy Elevator Co., Louisville, 1937-46, exec. v.p., dir., 1945—; co-founder, Murphy Mfg. Co., Louisville, 1951—, pres., 1970—; also dir.; v.p., dir. Murphy Machine & Tool Co., Louisville, 1953—. Optimist. Home: 1509 Vivian Lane Louisville KY 40205 Office: 600 Bergman St Louisville KY 40203

CARLISLE, ROBERT MERRILL, economist; b. Notasuiga, Ala., May 24, 1927; s. Robert Lee and Sarah Lula (Bentley) C.; student Millsaps Coll., 1945, Tulane U., 1945-46; B.S., Auburn U., 1949; M.S., Purdue U., 1951; postgrad. U. Cal. at San Diego, 1957-61. Instr. econs. and bus. Memphis State U., 1954-55; sr. operations research analyst Lockheed Aircraft Co., Marietta, Ga., 1955-57; sr. research engr. Gen. Dynamics-CONVAIR, San Diego, 1957-59; mem. profl. staff Gen. Elec. Co., Santa Barbara, Cal., 1959-63; sr. tech. staff Aerospace Corp., Los Angeles, 1963-65; sr. staff engr. Bendix Systems Div., Ann Arbor, Mich., 1965-67; sr. research economist, dir. Dikewood Inst., Alburquerque, 1967-69; dir. program evaluation and adminstrn. Pub. Broadcasting Environment Center, Corp. for Pub. Broadcasting, Washington, 1970-71; mgr. cost and financial systems analysis Teledyne Brown Engring. Co., Huntsville, Ala., 1971—; pres. Telephone Answering Service, Inc., Ann Arbor, 1966-67; instr. econs. Ga. State Coll., 1956. Treas., Point Loma (Cal.) Democratic Club, 1959. Served with USNR, 1945-47. Mem. Am. Econ. Assn., Inst. Mgmt. Scis., Operations Research Soc. Am., Am. Inst. Aeros. and Astronautics, Am. Astronautical Soc., Alpha Gamma Rho, Tau Kappa Alpha, Alpha Zeta, Kappa Delta Pi. Unitarian. Moose. Home: 6313 B2 Madison Pike AL 35806

CARLO, ALPHONSE PHILIP, educator, violinist; b. New Haven, Conn., Aug. 14, 1913; s. Lawrence and Jennie (Petocchi) C.; student Yale Music Sch., 1927-29, Juilliard Music Sch., 1930-35, Nat. Orchestral Assn., 1936-40; m. Katherine Braun, Aug. 3, 1942. Mem. faculty So. Meth. U., 1942-44; mem. faculty Rollins Coll., Winter Park, Fla., 1944—, prof. violin, 1944—. Concertmaster Fla. Symphony Orch., 1949—, Bach Festival of Winter Park (Fla.), 1944—; asso. condr. Fla. Youth Symphony, 1955—; mem. World Symphony Orch., 1971—; adjudicator Fla. State Music Tchrs. Convs., 1960—. Recipient William Freeman Blackman Medal of Honor for distinguished service Rollins Coll., 1972. Mem. Pi Kappa Lambda. Home: 2001 Dundee Dr Winter Park FL 32789

CARLOCK, HENRY ARTHUR, educator; b. Alexandria, O., Sept. 30, 1905; s. Frank H. and Elizabeth (Kimpton) C.; B.S., Denison Coll., 1928; M.S., Ohio State U., 1931; postgrad. (White fellow, U. fellow) Cornell U., 1934-36; m. Mary McCaffrey, Aug. 1, 1936; 1 son, Henry Arthur. Research asst. physics Union Coll., Schnectady, 1931-32; TV engr. Gen. Electric Co., Schenectady, 1936-38; prof. physics Miss. Coll., Clinton, 1938-41, 46—; prof. advanced electronic engring. Cook's Inst. Electronics Engring., 1969—; prof. La. Coll., Pineville, 1945-46. Cons. applied physics and ultrasonics, 1948—. Radiol. officer Miss. Civil Def. Counsel. Served to lt. col., Signal Corps, AUS, 1941-45. Mem. Am. Assn. Physics Tchrs., Am. Meteorol. Soc., Miss. Acad. Sci., Sigma Xi, Sigma Pi Sigma. Baptist. Clubs: Lions (gov. dist.), American Commons (Clinton). Home: 508 W College St Clinton MS 39056

CARLOSS, HARRY WORTHINGTON, utility co. exec.; b. Gracey, Christian County, Ky., Apr. 11, 1908; s. Harry Dabney and Anna Pearl (Tuggle) C.; B.S. in Mech. Engring., U. Ky., 1931; m. Rebecca Long, Dec. 21, 1935; children—Rebecca Anne (Mrs. Thomas Page), James D., Harry Worthington. With Ky. Utilities Co., Lexington, 1931—, comml. service adviser, 1935-40, indsl. engr., 1940-48, mgr. indsl. engring. and service, 1948-50, asst. dir. customer service, 1955-53, dir. customer service, 1953-56. dir. bus. devel., 1959-66, asst. v.p., 1966-67, v.p., 1967—. Pres., Ky. Council for Comml. and Area Devel., 1964-65; mem. Indsl. Devel. Com., 1949—; dir. Asso. Industries Ky., 1968—. Mem. Ky. Hist. Events Com., 1970—. Bd. dirs. Florence Crittendon Home, Lexington, Salvation Army. Registered profl. engr., Ky. Mem. Ky. Soc. Profl. Engrs., Edison Electric Inst. (chmn. area devel. com. 1961-62, mem. exec. com. marketing div.), U.S. (mem. constrn. and comml. devel. com. 1963-65, co-chmn. Ky. clean-up and beautification, 1965—), Ky. (regional v.p. 1963—), Lexington-Fayette County (dir. 1964-65) chambers commerce, Electric Heating Assn., Newcomen Soc. N. Am. Club: Optimist (pres. 1961-62) (Lexington). Home: 205 Albany Rd Lexington KY 40503 Office: 120 S Limestone St Lexington KY 40507

CARLSON, GORDON, state ofcl.; s.; Carl John and Laura Mathilda (Carlson) C.; student U. Tex., 1926-28; m. Mary Nell Fredrickson, Sept. 7, 1949; 1 son, John Gordon. Asst. dir. Tex. Motor Vehicle Div., Austin, 1926-53; owner, cons. Motor Vehicle Cons. Service, Austin, 1953-54; chief of staff services Tex. Water Devel. Bd.; owner, operator Carlson Trailer Village, Point Comfort, Tex., 1955-57, owner, 1957-63. Mem. City Council, Manor, Tex., 1965-67; mayor, Manor, Tex., 1967-71. Vice chmn. exec. com. Austin-Travis County Regional Planning Commn., 1967-70. Democrat. Baptist. Lion. Home: PO Drawer J Manor TX 78653 Office: PO Box 13087 Capitol Station Austin TX 78711

CARLSON, HARVE JAMES, scientist; b. Jerome, Ida., June 10, 1911; s. Casper Julius C.; B.S., U. Wash., 1934, postgrad., 1934-35; postgrad. U. Cal., 1936; M.P.H., U. Mich., 1941, D.P.H., 1943; m. Priscilla Church, Aug. 28, 1937; children—Ann (Mrs. John H. Shahan), James H., Robert. Lab. technician Ida. State Dept. Health, 1936-39, asst. bacteriologist, 1939-40; research asso. U. Mich., 1941-42, instr. bacteriology, 1942-43; asst. prof. pediatric research Western Res. U., 1946-51; biologist Office Naval Research, Cal., 1951-56; sci. liaison officer, London, Eng., 1956-58; then head microbiologist Office Naval Research, Washington; program dir. Facilities and Spl. Programs NSF, Washington, 1959-60, dep. asst. dir. for biol. and med. scis., 1960-61, div. dir. for biol. and med. scis., 1961—. Chmn. Interagy. Coordinating Com. for Internat. Biol. Program. Ex officio mem. bd. regents Nat. Library Medicine. Served with USNR, 1944-46. Polio Found. grantee, 1941, 42, 43, Gen. Electric, 1947, 48, 49. Mem. Sigma Xi, Phi Sigma, Delta Omega, Kappa Phi Kappa. Club: Cosmos (Washington). Home: 5510 Hoover St Bethesda MD 20034 Office: 1800 G St NW Washington DC 20550

CARLSON, HOWARD LINN, dentist; b. Barnesville, Minn., July 15, 1919; s. Albert Amandus and Lillie Alfreda (Linn) C.; student Ia. State Coll., 1937-41; D.D.S., U. Minn., 1950; m. Sonia Etoile Carloss, Mar. 25, 1945; children—Paul Howard, Candace Linn. Pvt. practice dentistry, Red Wing, Minn., 1953-54, Spartanburg, S.C., 1954—. Bd. dirs., dhmn. bd. Spartanburg Speech and Hearing Clinic, 1966-68; bd. dirs., chmn. bd. Charles Lea Rehab. Center. Served with F.A., AUS, 1941-46, Dental Corps, 1950-53. Mem. Am. (5th dist. del. 1971-72), S.C. (pres. 1971-72) dental assns., Am. Soc. Preventive Dentistry, S.E. Acad. Prosthodontics, S.C. Acad. Practice Adminstrn., Piedmont Dist. Dental Soc. (pres. 1963-64). Rotarian. Home: 2094 E Main St Spartanburg SC 29302 Office: 2086 E Main St Spartanburg SC 29302

CARLSON, J(OHN) PHILIP, lawyer; b. Shickley, Neb., Apr. 16, 1915; s. Christopher Theodore and Klara (Blomquist) C.; student Luther Coll., Wahoo, Neb., 1931-33; A.B., Neb. State Tchrs. Coll. 1935; M.A., Columbia U., 1967; J.D., Georgetown U., 1951; m. Maryjo Suverkrup, Oct. 14, 1950. Tchr., coach high sch., Bristow, Neb., Carroll, Neb., Ashland, Neb., 1935-42; vets. relations adviser OPA, Washington, 1946-47; tng. specialist Dept. Navy, Washington, 1947-56; minority counsel Com. on Govt. Operations, Ho. of Reps., Washington, 1956—; admitted to D.C. bar, 1952, U.S. Supreme Ct. bar, 1957, U.S. Ct. Mil. Appeals bar, 1970; Am. Polit. Sci. Assn. congl. staff fellow Columbia U., 1964-65, 66-67. Served from aviation cadet to capt. USAAF, 1942-45; lt. col. USAF Res. ret. Decorated D.F.C., Air Medal with oak leaf cluster. Mem. Am. Econ. Assn., Am., Fed. bar assns. Republican. Lutheran. Clubs: Nat. Lawyers, Capitol Hill, National Economists, George Town (Washington). Home: 7110 Marlan Dr Alexandria VA 22307 Office: House of Reps Washington DC 20515

CARLSON, JOHN SWINK, lawyer, petroleum co. exec.; b. Ft. Collins, Colo., June 16, 1911; s. George A. and Rosa (Alps) C.; A.B., U. Colo., 1932; LL.B., Harvard, 1936; m. Sara A. Mott, June 22, 1940; children—John Swink, Lucie Pamela, Ann Brockenbrough, Virginia Charles, Thomas George (dec.). Admitted to Okla. bar, 1937; legal staff Shell Oil Co., 1936-37, Turman Oil Co., 1937-38; legal asso. Yancey & Spillers, Tulsa, 1938-39; legal counselor Chapman, Barnard & McFarlin, oil, cattle and investments, Tulsa, 1939-42; gen. counsel Seismograph Service Corp., Tulsa, 1942-49; practice law, Tulsa, 1949-51; gen. counsel Okla. Natural Gas Co., 1951-61; sr. partner Carlson, Lupardus, Matthews, Holliman & Huffman, Tulsa, 1951-61; head legal firm John S. Carlson, Tulsa, 1961—. Sec., gen. counsel, dir. Century Geophys. Corp., 1951-71, sr. v.p., 1957-71; sec., dir., gen. counsel Hayward-Wolff Research Corp., 1951; v.p., sec., dir., gen. counsel Exploration Cons., Inc., 1951, Canadian Geophys. Measurements, Ltd., 1954, Venezuela Geophys. Measurements, S.A., 1957, 66; pres., dir., gen. counsel Petroleum Research Corp., 1957-66; chmn. bd., gen. counsel Community Merchandisers, Inc., 1959; pres., dir., gen. counsel Western Petroleum Co., Inc., 1960; v.p., sec., dir., gen. counsel Enterprises & Businesses, Inc., 1960-65; sec., dir. Western Hemisphere Trade & Credit Corp., 1960, v.p., 1961; sec., dir. Hemisphere Constrn. Co., 1960, v.p., 1961; v.p., sec., dir., gen. counsel Jameson Corp., 1961, pres., chmn. bd. T'Oil, Inc., 1962-65; pres., dir. Oil Enterprises Inc., 1965—. Mem. Am., Okla., Okla. Jr. (pres. 1943-44), Tulsa County bar assns., Am. Soc. Internat. Law, Phi Beta Kappa, Delta Sigma Rho. Clubs: Tulsa, Harvard (pres. 1949-50) (Tulsa). Editor: Compendium of Laws Relating to Problems of Men in the Armed Forces, 1943. Contbr. sect. to report on 34th Nat. Fgn. Trade Council. Office: 15 W 6th St Tulsa OK 74119

CARLSON, MAURICE IRWIN, educator, editor; b. Fulton, Ky., July 26, 1914; s. Peter Arvid and Della Elizabeth (Irwin) C.; B.A. with honors, Southwestern Coll., Memphis, 1936; M.A., Vanderbilt U., 1937; postgrad., Brown U., La. State U., 1938-39; m. Martha Elizabeth Deniger, Jan. 13, 1939; children—Martha Ann, Martha Elizabeth (Mrs. Michael Wayne Crain). Agt., br. mgr. Acacia Mut. Life Ins. Co., Memphis, New Orleans, field supr., Washington, 1941-47; mgr. N.Tex. dept. Reliance Life Ins. Co. Pitts., Dallas, then supt. agys., Pitts., 1947-51; v.p. Universal Life and Accident Ins. Co., Dallas, 1951-59; with Life Ins. Co. N.Am., Tex., 1959; pres., dir. Reliance Life and Accident Ins. Co. Am., Dallas, 1959-65; mem. English and Greek faculties U. Tex., Arlington, 1966—, editor Arlington Quar., 1967—. Guest lectr. So. Meth. U., U. Tex., Arlington; a founder weekly newspaper Hudkins Jour. (now Dallas County Jour.), 1962. Gen. chmn. Dallas County Cancer Crusade, 1954, Dallas County chpt. Nat. Kidney Disease Found., 1960; organizer Greater Dallas Citizens Com. for Old-Time Celebration Am. Ind. Day, 1961, chmn. adv. bd., 1961-67; chmn. adv. bd. Operation LIFT, 1962-65; pres. Dads' Club So. Meth. U., 1963-64. Chmn., Dallas County Republican Exec. Com., 1958-60; co-founder Dallas Charter League, 1961, exec. com., 1961-65, pres., 1965. Bd. dirs. Dallas Council on World Affairs, Dallas UN Assn. U.S. C.L.U. Mem. Dallas Forum, Tex. Bur. Econ. Understanding (pres. 1971). Author: Aubrey Beardsley: A Study in Decadence, 1937; book reviewer Dallas Times-Herald, 1950—. Home: 3520 Centenary Dr Dallas TX 75225 Office: Box 366 Univ Station U Tex at Arlington Arlington TX 76010

CARLSON, NORMAN A., govt. ofcl.; b. Ia. Correctional officer Ia. State Penitentiary, Fort Madison, 1956; parole officer U.S. Penitentiary, Leavenworth, Kan., 1957; casework supr. Fed. Youth Center, Ashland, Ky., 1958-59; project dir. Community Treatment Centers, 1961-65; asst. supr. div. institutional services Fed. Bur. Prisons, 1960, exec. asst., 1966-70, dir., 1970—. Home: 8702 Piccadilly Pl Springfield VA 22151*

CARLSON, ROBERT KENNETH, mfg. exec.; b. Chgo., July 7, 1928; s. Axel Frederick and Ester (Johnson) C.; Ph.B., Northwestern U., 1955; m. Marjorie Gwyne Norman, Dec. 3, 1954; children—Kevin Patrick, Kimberley Georgianne. Chemist, Great Lakes Carbon Research Center, Morton Grove, Ill., 1949-57; research chemist, project leader Borg Warner Research Center, Des Plaines, Ill., 1957-59; sr. materials engr., head materials scis. LTV Research Center, Dallas, 1959-64; v.p. Poco Graphite, Inc., Decatur, Tex., 1964—, also dir. Served with AUS, 1950-52. Fellow Am. Inst. Chemists; mem. Am. Chem. Soc., Research Soc. Am., Sigma Xi. Patentee in field. Home: Route 3 Box 32AA Decatur TX 76234 Office: PO Box 2121 Decatur TX 76234

CARLTON, CHARLES THADDEUS, judge; b. Ft. Pierce, Fla., Nov. 7, 1935; s. Thaddeus Hudson Carlton and June (Pinson) Carlton Vest; B.A., U. Fla., 1957; J.D., Stetson U., 1963; m. Ida May Peacock, Oct. 7, 1967; children—Charles Thaddeus II, Kelley, Marshall Hudson. Admitted to Fla. bar, 1963; asso. Carlton & McCain, Ft. Pierce, 1963-65; partner Carlton, McCain, Carlton & Brennan, Ft. Pierce, 1965-67; partner Carlton, Brennan & McAllen, Ft. Pierce, Fla., 1967-70; asst. city atty., Ft. Pierce, 1965-69; state atty. 19th Jud. Circuit, 1967-70; circuit judge 20th Jud. Circuit, Punta Gorda, Fla., 1970—. Owner, operator citrus groves, cattle ranches, St. Lucie, Glades, Hendry counties, Fla.; pres. Legal Services, Inc., Ft. Pierce, 1966-67. First v.p. United Fund, 1966-67. Served to 1st. lt. USMCR, 1957-60. Mem. U. Fla. Alumni Assn. (pres. 1964), Stetsen Lawyers Assn., U.S. Dist. Atty.'s Assn., Fla. Pros. Atty.'s Assn., Fla. Circuit Judges Conf., U.S. Trial Judges Assn., Am., Fla. bar assns., Fla. Acad. Trial Lawyers, Am. Trial Lawyers Assn., Airplane Owners and Pilots Assn., Cattlemen's Assn. Elk. Club: Pelican Yacht (Ft. Pierce). Home: PO Box 235 Carlton Ranch Moore Haven FL 33471 Office: Circuit Judges Office Charlotte County Ct House Punta Gorda FL 33471

CARLTON, EMORY LINWOOD, lawyer, state ofcl.; b. nr. Tappahannock, Va., July 15, 1906; s. Ellis Mortimer and Ruby Evans (Lumpkin) C.; B.B.A., U. Richmond, 1929, J.D., 1933; m. Nan Page Trent June 28, 1941; 1 dau., Betty Page (Mrs. Henry John Schroeder, Jr.). Admitted to Va. bar, 1933; practice law Tappahannock, 1933—; state's atty. bar Essex County, Va., 1936-42, 45-64; dir. Bank Essex, Tappahannock, 1954—. Served to lt. comdr. USN, 1942-45. Mem. Am., Va. bar assns., Commonwealth Attys. Assn. (pres. 1963), Nat. Dist. Attys. Assn. (v.p. 1962-63), Soc. Cincinnati, Jamestowne Soc. (gov. 1971-72), Kappa Sigma. Democrat. Baptist (chmn. bd. deacons). Mason. Home: Box 605 Tappahannock VA 22560 Office: E 407 Prince St Tappahannock VA 22560

CARLTON, THOMAS ARLIS, educator; b. Vivian, La., May 3, 1927; s. Thomas Arlis and Tinie (Hart) C.; B.S., Tex. A. and M. U., 1950, M.S., 1955; Ph.D., U. Tex., 1962; m. Betty Bliss Ballerstedt, June 12, 1950; children—Terry, Thomas Arlis III, Stanley, Charlotte. Engr., Tex. Hwy. Dept., 1950-53; asst. prof. Lamar U., Beaumont, Tex., 1953-56; asst. prof. U. Tex., 1956-59; asso. prof. Miss. State U., 1959-61; prof. civil engring; U. Ala., Tuscaloosa, 1962—; partner T.L. Douglas Assos., civil engrs., Birmingham, Ala., 1969—. Mem. County bd. FHA, Tuscaloosa, 1970-71. Served with AUS, 1945-47. Mem. Am. Soc. C.E. Mason (Shriner). Home: Route 1 Box 414 Tuscaloosa AL 35001

CARLTON, THOMAS CLARENCE, oral surgeon; b. Birmingham, Ala., Feb. 7, 1938; s. George Skelton and Rose (Park) C.; student Duke, 1956-60; D.M.D., U. Ala., 1964; m. Lois Elizabeth Bloodgood, June 10, 1967; children—Thomas C., Kathryn Howell. Intern oral surgery Jackson Meml. Hosp., Miami, Fla., 1967-68, resident, 1968-69; resident Georgetown U., 1970; practice oral surgery, Fort Lauderdale, Fla., 1970—; mem. staff Broward Gen. Hosp., Fort Lauderdale, Plantation (Fla.) Hosp., Holy Cross Hosp., Fort Lauderdale, Beach Hosp., Fort Lauderdale. Served to lt. USNR, 1964-67. Mem. Am., Borward County dental assns., Fla., Atlantic Coast Dist. dental socs., Fla. Soc. Oral Surgeons, Jr. C. of C., Psi Omega, Pi Kappa Alpha. Home: 2115 NE 67th St Fort Lauderdale FL 33308 Office: 906 NE 26th Av Fort Lauderdale FL 33304

CARLTON, VASSAR BENJAMIN, judge; b. Island Grove, Fla., Nov. 13, 1912; s. Benjamin F. and Zeffie (Ergle) C.; student U. Fla., 1931; LL.D, Stetson U., 1937; m. Grace Ramer, Sept. 23, 1959; children—Mary Carol (Mrs. Buddy Crisafulli), Martha (Mrs. Bryan Fulmer), Barbara, Pamela. Admitted to Fla. bar, 1937; county judge Brevard County, Titusville, Fla., 1941-54, circuit judge 9th jud. circut ct., 1954-69; justice Supreme Ct., Tallahassee, 1969—. Mem. Jr. C. of C. (pres. 1939). Baptist. Mason (32 deg., Shriner). Elk, Kiwanian. Home: 1103 Gardenia Dr Tallahassee FL 32303 Office: Supreme Ct Bldg Tallahassee FL 32304

CARLUCCI, FRANK CHARLES, III, govt. ofcl.; b. Scranton, Pa., Oct. 18, 1930; s. Frank Charles Jr. and Roxanne (Bacon) C.; A.B., Princeton, 1952; postgrad. Sch. Bus. Adminstrn., Harvard, 1956; m. Jean Phyllis Anthony, July 10, 1954; children—Karen, Frank. With Jantzen Co., Portland, Ore., 1955-56; fgn. ser. officer Dept. State, 1956, vice consul, econ. officer, Johannesburg, S. Africa, 1957-59, second sec., polit. officer, Kanshasa, Congo, 1960-62, officer in charge Congolese polit. affairs, 1962-64, consul gen., Zanzibar, 1964-65, counselor for polit. affairs, Rio de Janeiro, Brazil, 1965-69; asst. dir. for ops, Office Econ. Opportunity, Washington, 1969-70, dir., 1971; asso. dir. Office Mgmt. and Budget, 1971—. Served as lt. (j.g.) USNR, 1952-54. Recipient Superior Service award Dept. State 1962, Superior Honor award, 1966-69. Home: 3624 Brandywine St NW Washington DC 20008 Office: 1200 19th St NW Washington DC 20506

CARMAN, GEORGE HENRY, physician, educator; b. Albany, N.Y., Sept. 23, 1928; s. Simon Peter and Mary (Whish) C.; B.A., Cornell U., 1948, M.D., 1951. Intern, Barnes Hosp., St. Louis, 1951-52, asst. resident, 1952-53; asst. resident medicine Salt Lake County Gen. Hosp., Salt Lake City, 1955-56; chief resident VA Hosp., Salt Lake City, 1956-57; fellow cardio-vascular diseases U. Utah Coll. Medicine, 1957-60; pvt. practice Dallas, 1960—; clin. instr. internal medicine U. Tex. Southwestern Med. Sch., Dallas, 1960-66, clin. asst. prof. internal medicine, 1966-69, clin. asso. prof., 1969—; asst. attending physician Baylor U. Med. Center; attending physician Presbyn. Hosp., Gaston Episcopal Hosp., Dallas. Mem. med. adv. bd. Parkland Meml. Hosp. Served to 1st lt. M.C., AUS, 1953-55. Diplomate in cardiovascular disease Am. Bd. Internal Medicine. Fellow A.C.P. (asso.); mem. A.A.A.S., Am. Fedn. Clin. Research A.M.A., Tex. Acad. Internal Medicine, Am. (fellow council clin. cardiology), Tex. (dir.), Dallas (dir., pres.-elect) heart assns., Dallas Acad. Internal Medicine, Confrerie de Chaine des Rotisseurs (chevalier), Phi Beta Kappa, Alpha Omega Alpha. Episcopalian. Clubs: Dallas Internist, Dallas Gun. Home: 6211 W Northwest Hwy Dallas TX 75225 Office: 3710 Swiss Av Dallas TX 75204

CARMICHAEL, HARRY ST. GEORGE TUCKER, JR., ret. cons. engr.; b. Hagerstown, Md., July 13, 1907; s. Harry St. George Tucker and Anna Lowry (Hetzel) C.; B.S. in Civil Engring., Va. Mil. Inst., 1927, C.E., 1932; M.B.A., Harvard, 1929; m. Margaret Lyle MacCorkle, May 12, 1934 (dec. Nov. 1968); children—Margaret Lyle (Mrs. William Woolums), Harry St. George Tucker III; m. 2d, Alberta M. Barnes, Feb. 28, 1971. Instr. Va. Mil. Inst., 1930-33; state engr. PWA, Ky., also regional engr., Atlanta, 1933-39; sr. engr. ERTC, Ft. Belvoir, Va., 1939-40; chief engr., Ft. Campbell, Ky., 1941-42; dir. planning and 1st asst. chief engr. Ky. Dept. Hwys., 1944-46; chief engr. U.S. Army, Philippines, Greece, 1946-48; chief engr. Wilson, Bell & Watkins, Ft. Campbell, Ky., 1940-43, chief constrn. engr., 1949-62; v.p. Watkins and Assos Inc., Cons. Engrs., Lexington, Ky., 1962-63, exec. v.p., 1964-65, pres., 1966-67, chmn. bd., 1968-70. Registered profl. engr., Ky., Va. Fellow Am. Soc. Civil Engrs.; mem. Ky., Nat. socs. profl. engrs., Am. Inst. Cons. Engrs., Am. Road Builders Assn., Ky. C. of C. (dir. 1968-71), Va. Mil. Inst. Alumni Assn. (nat. pres. 1957-59, dir., 1952-71), Kappa Alpha. Episcopalian. Home: 101 S Hanover St Apt 7-A Lexington KY 40502 101 S Hanover St Apt 7-A Lexington KY 40502

CARMICHAEL, HENRY NEWMAN, JR., retail chain store exec.; b. Knoxville, Tenn., Apr. 29, 1918; s. Henry Newman and Geraldine (Hale) C.; B.A., U. Tenn., 1938; M.B.A., Harvard, 1940; m. Katherine Miles Eastin, Dec. 28, 1943; 1 dau., Jeannine Eastin (Mrs. Douglas Joseph McKamey). Mgmt. trainee Stokely Van-Camp, Inc., Indpls., 1946, Fowler Bros., Knoxville, Tenn., 1946-47; with Ira A. Watson Co., Knoxville, 1947—, sec., 1948-62, treas., 1964-65, adminstrv. v.p., 1959—, dir., 1948—; pres., corp. dir. Appalachian Distbg. Corp., Knoxville, 1962—. Chmn. Knox County chpt. United Fund, 1949. Served from 2d. lt. to lt. col. USAAF, 1941-46. Mem. Nat., Tenn. (dir. 1970—) retail mchts. assns., U.S. C. of C., S.A.R., Mil. Order World Wars, Mil. Ret. Officers Assn., Sigma Alpha Epsilon. Baptist. Clubs: Cherokee Country, Mens Cotillion. Home: 865 Cherokee Blvd Knoxville TN 37919 Office: 3550 Pleasant Ridge Rd Knoxville TN 37921

CARMICHAEL, JACK CHARLES, engr.; b. Dodd City, Tex., Oct. 11, 1918; s. Horace Henry and Edna (Gay) C.; B.S., U. Tex., 1942; M.S., Johns Hopkins, 1947; m. Doris Eloise Heuschkel, Mar. 14, 1942; children— Cynthia (Mrs. William H. Oliver III), Richard Charles, Lawrence Jack. Commd. 2d lt. USAF, 1942, advanced through grades to col., 1967; sr. san., indsl. hygiene engr. Hdqrs. USAF, Washington, 1950-54, chief med. facilities div., 1958-64; chief engring. br., chief enviromental health lab. br. hdqrs., Air Material Command, Dayton, O., 1954-58; chief of staff Aerospace Med. Div., San Antonio, 1964-65; asst. med. facilities planning Office Sec. Def., Washington, 1965-67; ret., 1967; asst. prof. dept. preventive medicine, asst. to dean Ohio State U. Coll. Medicine, Columbus, 1967-70; dir. Tex. Health Data Inst., Gov.'s Office, 1970-71; mgr. health and resources div. Office of Gov., Austin, Tex., 1971—. Cons. environmental engring., med. facilities planning, 1967—. Decorated Legion of Merit with 2 oak leaf clusters. Registered profl. engr., Tex. Diplomate Am. Acad. Enviromental Engrs. Mem. Fed. Conf. Environmental Engrs. (pres. 1957-58), Aerospace Med. Assn., Am. Conf. Govtl. Indsl. Hygienists. Mason (Shriner). Home: 7214 W Rim Dr Austin TX 78731

CARMICHAEL, JAMES VINSON, bus. exec.; b. nr. Smyrna, Ga., Oct. 2, 1910; s. John Vinson and Emma Mae (Nolan) C.; LL.B., Emory U., 1933; m. Frances Elizabeth McDonald, June 3, 1938; children—Mary Emma, James Vinson, Frances Elizabeth. Admitted to Ga. bar, 1933, practiced Marietta, 1933-44; exec. dir. state revenue commn., 1943; mem. commn. to redraft state constn.; gen. mgr., v.p. Bell Aircraft Corp., Marietta, 1944-46; asst. to pres. Scripto, Inc., 1946, pres., 1947-64, chmn. bd., 1964—; v.p., gen. mgr. Ga. div. Lockheed Aircraft Corp., Marietta, 1951-52, now dir.; dir. Scripto Pens, Ltd., London, Trust Co. of Ga., Southern Co., Ga. Internat. Life Ins. Co.; of counsel Smith, Currie & Hamrock, Atlanta. Former nat. vice chmn. A.R.C. Trustee Com. Econ. Devel., Interdenominational Theol. Center; adv. com. bus. programs Brookings Instn.; grad. mem. The Bus. Council; former chmn. bd. trustees Boys Estate, Ga.; mem. Ga. Sci. and Tech. Commn., Ga. Nuclear Adv. Commn.; trustee, exec. com. Emory U.; regent U. System of Ga.; vice chmn. Atlanta Sch. Art; trustee Atlanta Arts Alliance. Mem. Ga. Legislature, 1936-40; candidate for gov. of Ga., 1946. Decorated Order St. John of Jerusalem (England); recipient Presdl. Citation of Merit; Distinguished Service award Woman's Coll. Ga., 1964; Ga. Medal for Distinguished Pub. Service, 1964. Mem. Atlanta Art Assn. (past pres.), Atlanta Music/Festival Assn. (v.p.), Atlanta Symphony Guild (past pres.), Nat. Fountain Pen and Mech. Pencil Mfrs. Assn. (past pres), Am., Ga., Atlanta bar assns., Alpha Kappa Psi, Sigma Pi, Phi Alpha Delta, Omicron Delta Kappa. Presbyn. Kiwanian (past gov. Ga. dist.). Clubs: Capital City (past pres.), Piedmont Driving (Atlanta); Buck's (London, Eng.); Marietta Country; Century Assn. (N.Y.C.). Home: 1031 Cherokee St Marietta GA 30060 Office: Scripto Inc PO Box 4847 Atlanta GA 30302

CARMICHAEL, JOSEPH PLEDGER, editor, educator; b. Temple, Ga., July 27, 1917; s. Charles Rufus and Mae (Edmondson) C.; student W. Ga. Coll., 1935-37; A.B. in Journalism, U. Ga., 1940, M.S. in Agr., 1953; m. Stella Cornelia Daniel, Sept. 1, 1946. Reporter Carroll Free Press, Carrollton, Ga., 1937-38, 40; news editor Carroll County Times, Carrollton, 1941; mng. editor Carroll Pub. Co., 1941-42; asst. extension editor U. Ga. Coll. Agr., Athens, 1942-43, acting editor, 1943-46, asso. editor, 1946-56, editor, 1956—, chmn. div. agrl. information, 1962—, prof. agrl. extension, 1963—; editorial columnist Athens (Ga.) Banner-Herald, 1967—. Mem. exec. com. Ga. Livestock Expn., 1965-68; hon. dir. Nat. Farm-City Com., 1969-70. Recipient Golden Anniversary medallion, Fed. Land Banks, 1967. Hon. mem. Master 4-H Club, Ga.; mem. Am. Assn. Agrl. Coll. Editors (pres. 1968-69, dir. 1969-70), Fanny Farmers (pres. 1966—), Atlanta C. of C. (Farmers club), Sigma Delta Chi, Phi Kappa Phi, Epsilon Sigma Phi, Mu Zeta Alpha, Zeta Sigma Phi. Baptist (sec. bd. deacons 1963-68). Contbr. articles to mags., profl. publs. Home: 200 Plum Nelly Rd Athens GA 30601

CARMICHAEL, LEONARD, assn. exec.; b. Germantown, Phila., Nov.9, 1898; s. Thomas Harrison and Emily Henrietta (Leonard) C.; grad. Germantown Friends Sch., 1917; B.S. summa cum laude, Tufts Coll., 1921, Sc.D., 1937; Ph.D. (Sheldon traveling fellow), Harvard, 1924, LL.D., 1952; grad. study U. Berlin, 1924; LL.D., Boston U., 1938, Colgate U., 1938, Northeastern U., 1941, R.I. State Coll., 1942, St. Lawrence U., 1943, Boston Coll., 1951, Amherst Coll., 1954, U. Mass.; 1954; Litt.D., Portia, 1939, Clark U., 1953; L.H.D., U. Me., 1949; D.Sc., Brown U., 1952, George Washington U., 1956, Tulane U., 1958; D.C.L., Dickinson Coll., 1955; LL.D., Fairleigh Dickinson U., 1959; D. Sc., Lowell Inst. Tech., 1955, Drexel Inst. Tech., 1959; Sc.D., Trinity Coll., 1960, Worcester Poly. Inst., 1964; m. Pearl Kidston, June 30, 1932; one dau., Martha (Mrs. S. Parker Oliphant). Instr. biology Tufts Coll., part-time 1923-24; instr. psychology Princeton, 1924-26, asst. prof., 1926-27; asso. prof. psychology Brown U., 1927-28, prof., 1928-36, dir psychol. lab., 1927-36, dir. lab. sensory physiology, 1934-36; chmn. dept. psychology, dean faculty arts and sci. U. Rochester, 1936-38; pres. Tufts U., also dir. lab. sensory psychology and physiology, 1938-52; sec. (the seventh) Smithsonian Instn., 1953-64; now v.p. for research and exploration, chmn. mus. com. Nat. Geog. Soc.; lectr. Harvard, summers 1927-31; vis. prof. exptl. psychology Clark U., 1931-32; vis. prof. psychology Harvard, 1935; vis. prof. Radcliffe Coll., 1935, U. Wash., 1940; lectr. Naval War Coll. to 1953; Arthur D. Little lectr. Mass. Inst. Tech., 1953; Herbert S. Langfeld lectr. Princeton, 1967. Dir. Nat. Roster Sci. and Specialized Personnel, 1940-44; mem. sci. com. Nat. Resources Planning Bd., 1941-43; chmn. com. sci. research personnel War Manpower Commn., 1941-43; chmn. anthropology and psychology div. NRC 1941-45; mem. applied psychology panel OSRD, 1942-45; mem. adminstr.'s spl. com. on vocational rehab., edn. and tng. problems VA, 1945-52; dir. human resources NSRB, 1948; chmn. com. N.E. Comprehensive Econ. Survey, 1950-54; mem. com. on human resources Research and Devel. Bd., 1952-53, mem. Naval Research Adv. Com., 1947-52; mem. Internat. Union Sci. Psychology, 1948-52; vice chmn. Harvard Found. Advanced Study and Research, 1951-54, 58-64; mem. com. research Ednl. Testing Service, 1952-57; bd. sci. dirs., trustee Roscoe B. Jackson Meml. Lab., 1952—. Hon. trustee Brookings Instn.; dir. Research Corp. (N.Y.); trustee Sci. Service, 1955-72, pres. bd., 1955-57, pres. emeritus, 1972—; mem. NACA, 1952-58, vice chmn., 1956-58; chmn. U.S. delegation Internat. Conf., The Hague, signer for U.S., Treaty for Protection Cultural Property in Time of War, 1954. Trustee Tufts U., George Washington U., Textile Mus., Nat. Trust Historic Preservation; dir. White House Hist. Assn. Mem. bd. sci. dirs. Yerkes Labs. Primate Biology, 1942-69, chmn., 1942-60; sci. adv. bd. Tulane Delta Regional Primate Research Center, 1964—; chmn. selections com. Time Capsule, N.Y. World's Fair; mem. Army Sci. Adv. Panel, 1956-62, cons., 1963—. Decorated knight comdr. Order of Alfonso the Wise (Spain); knight comdr. cross with star Order of Merit of Fed. Republic of Germany; comdr. Order of Dannebrog (Denmark); commendatore dell'Ordine Al Merito della Republica Italiana (Italy); Hartley Pub. Welfare medal Nat. Acad. Scis., 1972. Fellow Royal Soc. Arts, Am. Acad. Arts and Scis., A.A.A.S.; mem. Am. Philos. Soc. (pres. 1970—), Nat. Acad. Sci. (chmn. sect. psychology 1950-53), NRC, Soc. Exptl. Psychologists. Soc. Research in Child Devel., Internat. Primatological Soc. (pres. 1964-68), Nat. Geog. Soc. (trustee), Am. Psychol. Assn. (pres. 1939-40), Soc. Exptl. Biology and Medicine, Internat. Union Biol. Scis. (pres sect. exptl. psychology and animal behavior 1961-69), Soc. of the Cin., S.A.R., Am. Legion, Newcomen Soc., Lit. Soc. Phi Beta Kappa, Sigma Xi; hon. mem. Ergonomics Research Soc. Eng., Soc. Francaise de Psychologie. Episcopalian. Clubs: St. Botolph (Boston); Century Assn. (N.Y.C.); Princeton, Alfalfa, Metropolitan, Chevy Chase, Cosmos (Washington). Co-author books, 1925—, including Elements of Human Psychology. Editor, contbg. author: Manual of Child Psychology, 3d edit., 1970. Co-editor: The Selection of Military Manpower, 1952; Basic Psychology, 1957. Asso. editor Jour. Genetic Psychology, Genetic Psychology Monographs, Brit. Jour. Ednl. Psychology. Editor Houghton Mifflin Co. series of books on psychology. Contbr. psychol. jours. Home: 4520 Hoban Rd NW Washington DC 20007 Office: Nat Geog Soc 17th and M Sts NW Washington DC 20036

CARMICHAEL, STOKELY, civil rights worker; b. N.Y.C., circa, 1941; grad. Howard U.; m. Miriam Makeba, Apr. 1968. Former field sec. Student Non-Violent Coordinating Com. for Ala., later nat. chmn., until 1967, later field comdr.; organized Lowndes County Freedom Orgn.; continued Meredith March through Miss., 1966; originator term Black Power; now living in Guinea.*

CARMICHAEL, WILLIAM GREGORY, author; b. Birmingham, Ala., Mar. 27, 1922; s. Robert Edward and Annie (Noyes) C.; B.A., U. Ala., 1943; B.S., Princeton, 1945; masso-therapist, Johns-Hopkins, 1969. Graphics designer; pres. Three B's, Ltd., Great Falls, Va., 1964—; researcher, speech writer White House during adminstrns. Truman, Eisenhower, Johnson, Nixon. Dir. pub. relations, and advt. Nat. Symphony Orch., 1949-53; dir. vol. radio, speech program A.R.C., 1959-61. Mem. Pub. Relations Soc. Am. Clubs: National Press, Arts (bd. govs.), 1925 F St. (all Washington). Author: Spaniel in the Lion's Den, 1947; Chatillion in Mexico, 1948; A Din of Antiquity, 1967; Alligators in the Bath Tub, 1969; Incredible Collectors, Weird Antiques and Odd Hobbies, 1971. Home: 8818 Jeffery Rd Great Falls VA 22066 Office: Box 1 Great Falls VA 22066

CARMODY, ARTHUR RODERICK, JR., lawyer; b. Shreveport, La., Feb. 19, 1928; s. Arthur R. and Caroline (Gaughan) C.; B.S., Fordham U., 1949; LL.B., La. State U., 1952; m. Renee Aubry, Jan. 26, 1952; children—Helen Bragg, Renee, Arthur Roderick III, Patrick, Timothy, Mary, Virginia, Joseph. Admitted to La. bar, 1952; mem. firm Wilkinson, Woods, Carmody & Peatross, Shreveport, 1952—. Dir. Kansas City So. Transport Co., Kansas City, Shreveport and Gulf Terminal Co., Shreveport Cable TV Co., Inc., Shreveport Braves Baseball Club. Chmn. Met. Shreveport Zoning Bd. Appeals, 1959—; bd. dirs. Caddo Democratic Assn., Shreveport, 1966—. Trustee Jesuit High Sch., Shreveport, Schumpert Meml. Hosp., Shreveport; bd. dirs. La. State U. Found., Baton Rouge, Agnew Day Sch., Shreveport, Ridgewood Montessori Sch., Shreveport. Mem. Am. La., Shreveport bar assns., Am. Judicature Soc., Nat. Assn. R.R. Trial Counsel, Shreveport C. of C. (bd. dirs. 1967—), Soc. Hosp. Council, Phi Delta Phi, Kappa Alpha. Roman Catholic. Clubs: Touchdown, Petroleum (Shreveport); Pierremont Oaks Tennis. Home: 255 Forest St Shreveport LA 71104 Office: Beck Bldg Shreveport LA 71102

CARNAHAN, ROBERT GORDON, psychiatrist; b. Louisville, Nov. 18, 1913; s. Robert and Ida May (Holman) C.; student Vanderbilt U., 1931-33; M.D., U. Tenn., 1936; m. Sara Elisabeth Alexander, Sept. 8, 1938. Intern Yonkers (N.Y.) Gen., 1937; practice gen. medicine, San Antonio, Tex., 1938-44; resident psychiatry Colo. Psychiat. Hosp., Denver, 1944-48; ednl. dir. Ingleside Hosp., Hastings, Neb., 1949;

mem. staff Ark. State Hosp., Little Rock, 1949-—, sect. chief, 1966-—; clin. prof. psychiatry U. Ark., 1966-—. Bd. dirs. Pulaski County Assn. Crippled. Fellow Am. Psychiat. Assn.; mem. A.M.A., Mid-Continent, Ark. psychiat. assns. Home: 4313 W Markham St Little Rock AR 72201

CARNES, DONA COULTER, civic worker; b. Bryan, Tex., 1878; d. John William and Nannie (Robinson) Coulter; student Kidd-Key Coll., Sherman, Tex.; m. Malcolm Carnes, Apr. 24, 1901 (dec.). Editor social column Bryan Daily Eagle, 1901-30; world traveler, lectr. on travels before local and out-of-town clubs. With mother and brother, W. J. Coulter, made gift to First Methodist Ch. of Bryan of 0,000 as a Coulter Meml.; also presented to City of Bryan an air field known as Coulter Field, used to train men in the Air Service, World War II; now used as tng. field for pilots; presented stained glass meml. window to A. and M. Meth. Ch., College Sta., Tex.; parade-size silk Tex. flag to Allen Mil. Acad.; antique English mirror to Women's Club Bldg. Life mem. Tex. Woman's Press Assn. (past pres.); charter mem. Brazos County chpt, A.R.C., Bryan Assembly No. 135 social order of Beauceant; charter mem., life mem., sec., Bryan Cemetery Assn., 1925-—. Life mem. Woman's Soc. Christian Service, First Meth. Ch., Bryan. Mem. Nat. Soc. Arts and Letters, Nat. Fedn. Press Women, Inc. (life mem., regional v.p. 1942; Dona Coulter Carnes Workshop named for her), D.A.R. (hon. regent William Scott chpt., div. vice chmn. spl. gifts D.A.R. House), Brazos Aviation Assn. (hon.), Order Eastern Star (charter, life mem., past worthy matron), Authors and Composers Assn., Nat. Editorial Assn., C. of C., Bus. and Profl. Womens Clubs, Am. Legion Aux., U.D.C., Delta Kappa Gamma. Home: 502 E 26th St Bryan TX 77801

CARNES, MRS. JACK, Democratic nat. committeewoman. Mem. Dem. Nat. Com. from Ark., 1944-—; del. Dem. Nat. Conv., 1944-—. Trustee, mem. state bd. Crippled Children's Found. Mem. Bus. and Profl. Women's Club. Clubs: Camden Country, Little Rock Country. Address: 308 Washington St NW Camden AR 71701*

CARNES, JAMES ROBERT, trade assn. exec.; b. Acworth, Ga., Oct. 23, 1909; s. James Erwin and Fannie (McDowell) C.; B.S., Ga. Inst. Tech., 1930; J.D., Emory U., 1936; postgrad. George Washington U., 1962-63; m. Virginia Richmond, Aug. 20, 1940; 1 son, Thomas Peter. Operating mgr. B.F. Goodrich Co., Johnson City, Tenn., 1930-33; admitted to Ga. bar, 1935; practiced in Columbus, 1936-41, 46; commd. ensign USN, 1946, advanced through grades to capt., 1954; asst. judge adv. gen. Navy, 1959-61; ret., 1961; dir. govt. relations Mfg. Chemists Assn., Washington, 1962-67, sec.-treas., 1967-—, v.p., 1972-—. Decorated Bronze Star medal. Mem. Am. Soc. Assn. Execs., Alpha Tau Omega, Phi Delta Phi. Democrat. Conglist. Clubs: Army and Navy, Army Navy Country (Washington); Chemists (N.Y.C.). Home: 5702 Overlea Rd Washington DC 20016 Office: 1825 Connecticut Av NW Washington DC 20009

CARNETT, JOHN WILLIAM, librarian; b. Somerset, Ky., Dec. 13, 1913; s. James E. and Icy (McGahan) C.; B.A., E. Tex. Bapt. Coll., 1952; M.S., E. Tex. State U., 1967; m. Eunice Ashby, June 24, 1935; children— John Ashby, Judith Anne. Ordained to ministry Baptist Ch., 1947; pastor East End Bapt. Ch., Henderson, Tex., 1953-65; spl. edn. tchr., Longview, Tex., 1965-67; dir. library Kilgore Coll. (Tex.), 1967-—. Mem. Am., Tex. library assns., Tex. State Tchrs. Assn., Tex. Jr. Coll. Assn. Home: 1308 Ash Lane Kilgore TX 75662

CARNEVALE, REYNOLDS ALFONSO, dentist; b. Newark, Dec. 18, 1923; s. Victor Nicholas and Margaret (Belfi) C.; B.S., U. N.C. at Raleigh, 1950; D.D.S., U. N.C. at Chapel Hill, 1961, M.S. in Periodontics, 1968; m. Myrtle Lee Debnam, Aug. 28, 1948; children—Victor Nicholas, Patricia Lee. Analytical chemist E.I. duPont de Nemours, Kinston, N.C., 1952-57; dentist, Goldsboro, N.C., 1961-66; practice dentistry, specializing in periodontics, Fayetteville, N.C., 1968-—. Asst. prof. periodontics U. N.C., Chapel Hill, 1971-—. Pres., Cumberland County Cancer Soc., 1971-72. Served with AUS, 1942-45. Mem. Am. Dental Assn., N.C. Dental Soc., Cumberland County Dental Soc., Periodontal Study Club. Research in gingival healing after surgery, 1966-68. Home: Iron Gate Golf Club Fayetteville NC 28304 Office: 3419 B Melrose Rd Fayetteville NC 28304

CARNEY, FREEMAN HARDIN, assn. exec.; b. nr. Waco, Tex., June 27, 1910; s. Charles Hardin and Betty (Butler) C.; A.B., Baylor U., 1933; spl. courses Southwestern C. of C. Inst., Mich. State U.; m. Avis Lee McGinnis, June 19, 1938; 1 son, Jack F. Asst. mgr. Waco (Tex.) C. of C., 1938-42; mgr. Denison (Tex.) C. of C., 1946-57; exec. v.p. Tyler (Tex.) C. of C., 1957-—. Served as capt. USAAF, 1942-46. Certified C. of C. exec. Mem. C. of C. Mgrs. Assn. E. Tex. (pres. 1956), Tex. C. of C. Mgrs. Assn. (pres. 1962), So. Assn. C. of C. Execs. (dir.) Am. C. of C. Execs., Tex. Indsl. Devel. Council (dir.), Tyler Petroleum Club. Methodist. Mason (Shriner), Rotarian. Club: Willowbrook Country (Tyler). Home: 1426 Westfield St Tyler TX 75701 Office: 301 N Broadway Tyler TX 75701

CARNEY, ROBERT BOSTWICK, ret. naval officer; b. Vallejo, Cal., Mar. 26, 1895; s. Robert Emmett and Bertha V.H. (Bostwick) C.; B.S., U.S. Naval Acad., 1916; LL.D. (hon.). Commd. ensign USN, 1916, advanced through grades to adm., 1950; chief staff to Adm. W.F. Halsey, Jr., Comdr. S. Pacific Force (later Comdr. 3d Fleet in Central Pacific), 1943-44; dep. chief naval operations (logistics), until 1950; comdr. 2d Fleet, East Coast U.S., 1950; comdr. in chief U.S. Naval Forces, Eastern Atlantic and Mediterranean, hdqrs. London, Eng., 1950-51; comdr. in chief Allied Forces So. Europe, 1951-53; comdr. Allied Naval Forces So. Europe, 1952-53; apptd. chief naval operations USN, 1953. Chmn. bd. Bath Iron Works Corp., Bell Intercontinental Corp.; asso. Vandeburg-Linkletter Assos.; mgmt. cons., mem. bd. Logetronics; cons. Westinghouse Electric Corp.; dir. Nation-Wide Securities Co., Inc., Dividend Shares, Inc., VEK Assos. Mem. acad. adv. bd. U.S. Naval Acad.; served on mil. adv. com. Gaither Study Group. Chmn. bd. Naval Hist. Found., Truxton-Decatur Mus. Decorated Bronze Star medal, D.S.M. with 3 gold stars, Navy Cross, Legion Merit, also fgn. decorations. Mem. U.S. Naval Inst. (twice pres.), Nat. Security Indsl. Assn. (hon. life), Am. Ordnance Assn. (Gold Medal life mem.), Naval Acad. Alumni Assn. (pres.). Clubs: Chevy Chase, Army and Navy, Alfalfa, Alibi (Washington); Brook (N.Y.C.). Home: Washington DC Office: care Truxtun-Decatur Museum 1610 H St NW Washington DC 20006

CARNEY, ROBERT WILLIAM, educator; b. Sidman, Pa., Oct. 3, 1923; s. Morgan R. and Olive (Smay) C.; B.S., Kent State U., 1949; M.S., Cornell U., 1952, Ph.D., 1956; m. Beverly B. Cook, Dec. 27, 1947; children—Kevin Douglas, Cheryl Sandra. Asst. prof. mgmt. U. Louisville, 1952-55; asso. prof., dir. center bus. and industry Kalamazoo Coll., 1955-57; dir. indsl. relations dept. Nat. Waterlift Co., Kalamazoo, 1955-57; asso. prof. mgmt., dir. Sea Island Advanced Mgmt. Program, Emory U., 1957-60; asso. prof. indsl. mgmt., dir. mgmt. dynamics course Ga. Tech. U., 1960-—, prof., 1965-—; cons. in field. Bd. dirs. Briarcliff Woods Civic Assn., Atlanta, 1961-66. Served with USAAF, 1943-46. Mem. Am. Soc. Personnel Adminstr. (dir. 1960-62), Am. Soc. Tng. and Devel. (dir. 1958-63), Indsl. Relations Research Assn., Acad. Mgmt. Contbr. articles profl. jours.; speaker on mgmt. topics. Home: 2055 Chrysler Dr NE Atlanta GA 30329

CARNLEY, SAMUEL FLEETWOOD, judge; b. Elba, Ala., Nov. 13, 1918; s. Jefferson A. and Mary (Ray) C.; B.A., U. Ala., 1939, LL.B., 1941; m. Mary Magdalene Talbot, Mar. 21, 1939 children—Nancy Hart (Mrs. Paul Clifford Morrow), Mary Oliver (Mrs. Donald Hubert Brown), Terry David, Samuel Fleetwood II, Melanie. Admitted to Ala. bar, 1941; practice law, Elba, 1941-44, 46, 53-—; dir. indsl. relations State Ala., Montgomery, 1947-50; judge 12th Jud. Circuit Ala., Elba, Troy, 1950-52, Inferior Ct. Coffee County, Ala., 1969-—. Mem. Interstate Conf. Employment Security Agys., 1947-50, mem. exec. com., dist. pres., 1948; mem. Elba Bd. Edn., 1953-58; pageant dir., master ceremonies Elba Centennial, 1953; mem. exec. com. Elba P.T.A., 1960-63, pres., 1966-68; chpt. chmn. A.R.C., 1966-68; program chmn. Elba Halloween Carnival, 1960-63; pres. Elba Little Theater, 1964-65; moderator Coffee County Bapt. Assn., 1967-68; mem. Ala. Bapt. Commn. on Higher Edn., 1967-—. Trustee Judson Coll., 1960-—, v.p., 1964-69, acting pres., 1969-—. Served with AUS, 1944-45. Recipient Algernon Sidney Sullivan award Judson Coll., 1970. Mem. Am. Judicature Soc., Am., Coffee County (past pres.) bar assns., Ala. State Bar, Elba C. of C., Pi Kappa Phi (past pres.). Democrat. Baptist (chmn. bd. deacons, Sunday sch. tchr., trustee state pres. brotherhood). Club: Elba Country. Home: 416 W Collier St Elba AL 36323 Office: 463 Carnley Av Elba AL 36323

CARO, PAUL WILEY, research psychologist; b. Pensacola, Fla., Sept. 30, 1931; s. Paul W. and Doris (Hatton) C.; State U., 1955, M.A., 1956; Ph.D., U. Tenn., 1961; m. Mary Elizabeth Davis, Aug. 6, 1955; children—Philip Davis, Victoria Doris. Training psychologist Mead Corp., Chillicothe, O., 1961-62; with Human Resources Research Orgn., Fort Rucker, Ala., 1958-60, 63-—, sr. staff scientist aviation div., 1969-—. Sr. asso. Applied Psychology Assos., Dothan, 1965-70; pvt. practice psychology, 1970-—; cons. sch. systems industry U.S. Air Force. Served with USAF, 1951-54. Mem. Am., Southeastern, Ala. psychol. assns., Assn. Aviation Psychologists, Am. Helicopter Soc. (sect. v.p. 1967-71), Civil Air Patrol, Sigma Xi. Presbyn. (elder). Designer synthetic flight training systems and behavior control programs. Contbr. articles to profl. publs. Home: 1105 Evergreen Av Dothan AL 36301 Office: Human Resources Research Orgn Div No 6 PO Box 428 Fort Rucker AL 36360

CAROW, RAYMOND EDWARD, TV exec.; b. Bklyn., Dec. 13, 1922; s. Edward and Jennie (Altenburg) C.; B.A., Hofstra U., 1950, postgrad., 1950-51; m. Elsie Frost Carow, Aug. 16, 1969; children—Kathleen J., Karen C. (Mrs. James B. Hall), Kurt, Cassandra. Prodn. mgr. WEAR-TV, Pensacola, Fla., 1953-55; mgr. WCTV, Tallahassee, 1955-57; gen. mgr. WALB-TV, Albany, Ga., 1957-—; v.p. Gray Communications Systems, Inc., Albany, 1967-—, also dir. Pres. Dougherty County Mental Health Assn., 1966. Asst. chmn. Ga. Democratic Com., 1966-—. Served to lt. comdr. USNR, 1942-46, 50-53. Named Broadcaster of Year of Ga. Ga. Assn. Broadcasters, 1965. Mem. Ga. Assn. Broadcasters (pres. 1964-65), U.S. Navy League, Albany C. of C. Home: 2702 Doublegate Rd Albany GA 31705 Office: Gray Communications Systems Inc. PO Box 408 Albany GA 31701

CARPENTER, ALLAN LEE, traffic engr.; b. Huntington, W.Va., Mar. 10, 1931; s. Cecil Clayton and Leola Belle (Klopp) C.; B.S., U. Ill., 1952; m. Eudell Denton Jones, May 23, 1961; 1 dau., Lee Ella. With So. Ry. System, 1950-59, track supr., 1956-59; instrument man C.J. Fuller cons. engrs., Inc., Lexington, Ky., 1959-61; pvt. practice civil engring., Lexington, 1961; jr. engr. C. & O. Ry., Richmond, Va., 1961-62; asst. engr. Norfolk & Portsmouth Beltline R.R. Co. (Va.), 1962-69; traffic engr. City of Chesapeake, Va., 1969-—. Tchr. Tidewater Community Coll., Portsmouth, part-time 1970-—. Served with AUS, 1954-56. Mem. Nat., Va. socs. profl. engrs., Va. Assn. Surveyors, Va. Assn. Traffic Engrs. Club: Exchange (past dist. bd. dirs.). Home: 336 E McGinnis Circle Norfolk VA 23502 Office: 1202 20th St Chesapeake VA 23324

CARPENTER, BENJAMIN HOWARD, life ins. exec., cattle rancher; b. Dallas, Mar. 10, 1924; s. John William and Flossie (Gardner) C.; B.B.A., U. Tex., 1948; m. Betty Dupree, June 18, 1948; children—Laura Lucinda, John William, III, Elizabeth Carolyn, Barbara Dupree, Ellen Belle Gardner. Chmn. bd., chmn. exec. and investment coms. Southland Life Ins. Co.; pres. The Crockett Co., Beeftex Cattle Co., Nat. Real Estate Devel. Corp., Trinity Valley Cattle Co.; dir. Texas Power and Light Co., Nat. Finance Credit Corp., Republic Nat. Bank of Dallas, Community Gen. Stores, Inc., Kroger Co. Chmn. Livestock San. Commn. of Tex., 1951-57. Dir., 1st pres. Trinity River Authority; bd. dirs. Dallas Agrl. Club; v.p., bd. dirs. Trinity Improvement Assn. Served as 1st lt. AUS, 1943-46. Decorated Silver Star. Mem. Tex. Livestock Marketing Assn. (dir.), Tex. Beef Council (dir.), Am. Brahman Breeders Assn. (dir.), Tex. and Southwestern Cattle Raisers Assn. (dir.), Phi Eta Sigma, Sigma Alpha Epsilon. Home: Box 99 Route 6 Dallas TX 75220 Office: Southland Center Dallas TX 75201

CARPENTER, CHARLES JEROULD, constrn. co. exec.; b. Norfolk, Va., Mar. 20, 1932; s. Charles Clinton and Phyllis (Stamp) C.; grad. Woodberry Forest Sch., 1950; B.S., Mass. Inst. Tech., 1954; m. Nancy Stephens Norfleet, Jan. 23, 1960; children—Margaret Courtney, Charles Clinton II. Jr. estimator, field engr. Carpenter Constrn. Co., Inc., Virginia Beach, Va., 1956-63, v.p., gen. exec., 1963-—. Jr. dir. Norfolk Central YMCA, 1962-65, pres., 1965, dir., 1966-68; capt. Va. Beach Rescue Squad, 1968, life mem., 1970; officer, dir. Cavalier Park-Bay Colony Community League, 1964-—, pres., 1967. Mem. ednl. council Mass. Inst. Tech., 1958-—; bd. dirs. Gen. Hosp. Virginia Beach, 1968-—. Served from 2d lt. to 1st lt. C.E., AUS, 1954-56. Mem. Delta Kappa Epsilon. Episcopalian. Home: 1105 Brandon Rd Virginia Beach VA 23451 Office: PO Box 953 Virginia Beach VA 23451

CARPENTER, CLAUDE S., govt. ofcl.; b. Robbinsville, N.C., Feb. 13, 1920; s. Herbert Ferdinand and Mamie (Greene) C.; B.S. cum laude, Western Carolina U., 1940; M.B.A., U. Chgo., 1951; postgrad. U. Mo., 1959-63; m. Elona Weber, Aug. 29, 1946; children—Linda L., Wendy M. (Mrs. Donald M. Paulson, Jr.), John H., Claudia A. Pilot, Pan-Am. Grace Airways, Lima, Peru, 1946-47; commd. 2d lt. USAAF, 1942, advanced through grades to col. USAF, 1968; prin. researcher for sec. def., 1966; prin. staff mem. President's Blue Ribbon Def. Panel, 1969-70; ret., 1970; spl. asst. for emergency planning Regional Fed. Hwy. Adminstr., Balt., 1971-—; cons. Output System Corp., Arlington, Va. Decorated Bronze Star medal, Air medal, Commendation medal. Mem. Am. Econ. Assn., Nat. Def. Transp. Assn., Beta Gamma Sigma, Alpha Pi Zeta. Club: Fort Myer (Va.) Officers. Home: 1609 8th Pl McLean VA 22101 Office: Fed Hwy Adminstrn Fed Bldg 31 Hopkins Plaza Baltimore MD 21201

CARPENTER, DAVID LOWE, lawyer; b. Ossining, N.Y., Apr. 27, 1928; s. Samuel Emlin and Evelyn (Barringer) C.; LL.B., U. Va., 1953; m. Clarissa L. Nash, Dec. 26, 1967; children—Ashby Lynn, Frederica. Admitted to Va. bar, 1952, D.C. bar, V.I. bar; asst. commonwealth atty., Arlington County Govt., Arlington, Va., 1953-55; gen. practice law, Arlington, 1953-67; partner firm Ryland, Winston & Carpenter, Arlington, 1955-65. gen. asst. atty. gen. V.I., 1967-71. With David L. Carpenter & Assos., real estate developers, 1960-—. Served with AUS, 1946-47. Mem. Arlington County State Bar, Va. State Bar, Am. Bar Assn., Am. Trial Lawyers Assn. Home: 9101 Cathedral Av Washington DC 20036 also Estate Bolongo Bay St Thomas VI 00801Office: 1140 Connecticut Av NW Washington DC 20036

CARPENTER, HOWARD RALPH, educator; b. Natural Bridge, N.Y., Oct. 11, 1919; s. Clinton Charles and Sophie (Chaffee) C.; Mus.B., U. Ala., 1947; B.S., U. N.Y., 1942; Mus.M., U. Rochester, 1948, Ph.D., 1953; m. Milton Jean Carter, July 15, 1942; 1 son, John Howard. Head dept. music, tchr. music history U. Richmond, Va., 1948-51; prof. music Western Ky. U., Bowling Green, 1953-65, head dept. music, 1965-—. Violinist, Rochester Philharmonic Orch., 1947-48, Nashville Symphony, 1953-65. Served with USAAF, 1942-46. Home: 1730 Chestnut St Bowling Green KY 42101

CARPENTER, LONNIE CLOY, social welfare adminstr.; b. Panhandle, Tex., May 31, 1921; s. Lonnie Calvert and Lela (Toler) C.; B.A., McMurry Coll., 1941; B.D., So. Meth. U., 1944; M.S., Columbia, 1949; M.B.A., U. Louisville, 1972; m. Leonore Melnicoff, Aug. 18, 1946 (div.); children—Dean Kenneth, Sherry Linda. Adminstrv. asst. to med. dir. N.J. State Hosp., Trenton, 1945-48; cons. div. child care Fedn. Protestant Welfare Agys., N.Y.C., 1949-51; exec. dir. Children's Center, Greenville, S.C., 1951-55; asst. supt. Louisville and Jefferson County Children's Home, 1955-59, supt., 1959-67; dir. staff devel. and tng. Community Action Commn., Louisville, 1967-—. Mem. Am. Soc. for Pub. Adminstrn., Nat. Assn. Social Workers, Acad. Certified Social Workers, Am. Soc. Tng. and Devel., Nat. Assn. Community Devel. Unitarian-Universalist. Home: 3621 A Brownsboro Rd Louisville KY 40207 Office: 617 W Jefferson St Louisville KY 40202

CARPENTER, RONALD, state edn. ofcl.; b. Reed, Okla., Oct. 24, 1910; B.S., Southwestern State Coll., Okla., 1937; M.A., Western State Coll., 1949; m. 1933; 2 children. Tchr. sci. Reed Pub. Schs., 1932-37; prin. high sch. City View Pub. Schs., 1937-41; supr. high sch. White Flat Pub. Schs., 1941-53, Duke Pub. Schs., 1953-62; dir. tchr. edn. and certification Okla. Dept. Edn., Oklahoma City, 1962-—. Exec. sec. Okla. Tchr. Edn. and Profl. Stardards Commn., 1964-69; sec.-treas. Nat. Assn. State Dirs. Tchr. Edn. and Certification, 1969-70; exec. sec. Okla. Profl. Standards Bd., 1969-70. Mem. N.E.A., Okla. Edn. Assn., Okla. Adminstrs. Assn. Address: 2801 SW 78th Oklahoma City OK 73159

CARPENTER, SAMUEL EMLEN, III, real estate exec.; b. Ossining, N.Y., Nov. 29, 1925; s. Samuel Emlen and Evelyn (Wallace) C.; student Emory Henry U., 1943-44; B.S., U. Va., 1948; m. Lois Ann Waterbury, June 18, 1949; children—Perry Newbold, Brien Waterbury. Asst. to sales mgr. Liquid Carbonic Corp., N.Y.C., 1948-51; sales rep. Owens Corning Fiberglas, Washington, 1951-55, Toledo, 1955-57; mgr. ceiling materials div., v.p. A.W. Lee Co., Rosslyn, Va., 1957-63; v.p. Carpenter Investments, Washington, 1963-70; dir. spl. projects Dept. Housing and Urban Affairs, Washington, 1970-—; pres. Carpenter Assos., Washington, 1970-—. Cons. U.S. Navy Family Housing Program, Found. for Coop. Housing, Stamford, Conn., Diversified Communities Newport Beach, Cal. Republican chmn. Fairfax County, Va., 1966-68, state chmn. for Va., 1968-70; mem. Rep. Nat. Com., 1968-70. Served with USNR, 1943-46. Recipient Outstanding Achievement award Owens Corning Fiberglas Sales Club, 1955. Mem. Bldg. Owners and Mgrs. Assn., Washington Bldg. Congress, McLean (Va.) Citizens Assn. (dir. 1959-61), Madeira Sch. Fathers Assn. (pres. 1969-70). Home: 976 Saigon Rd McLean VA 22101 Office: 1612 K St NW Washington DC 20006

CARPENTER, STEPHEN HILLIARD, apparel mfg. co. exec.; b. Rockmart, Ga., Nov. 15, 1941; s. Hilliard Newton and Opal Mattie (Brown) C.; Asso. Sci. Mgmt. Tech., So. Tech. Inst., 1961, Asso. Sci. Mgmt. Option, 1961; m. Peggy Sue Love, June 1, 1963; children—Carol, Russell, Lori, Amy. With C.W. Henson Garment Co., Monroe, Ga., 1961-70, plant mgr., 1966-67, v.p. mfg., 1967-70; dir. mfg. Carwood Mfg. Co., Athens, Tenn., 1970-—. Mem. Monroe Jr. C. of C. (sec.-treas. 1961-62). Mem. Christian Ch. (chmn. bd. 1969-—). Home: Route 2 Englewood TN 37329 Office: Carwood Mfg Co PO Box 866 Athens TN 37303

CARPENTER, THOMAS EARL, publishing co. exec.; b. Nashville, Dec. 1, 1925; s. Charles Hugo and Ethel Powers (Wilson) C.; student Carson Newman Coll., Jefferson City, Tenn., 1944-45, Duke, 1945-46; B.S., George Peabody Coll., 1947, M.A., 1948; m. Mildred Ann Reynolds, Dec. 18, 1946; children—Mary Stephanie, Thomas Earl, Emily Reynolds, Laurale. Tchr. math. Springfield (Tenn.) High Sch., 1948-52; gen. mgr. Reynolds Co., Nashville, 1952-58; with Abingdon Press, Nashville and N.Y.C., 1958-61, 63-70, mgr., 1963-70; v.p. Methodist Pub. House, Nashville, 1970-—. Trustee Martin Coll., Pulaski, Tenn. Mem. Protestant Ch.-Owned Pubs. Assn., Religious Pubs. Group, Assn. Am. Meth. Socs., Coop. Publn. Assn. (officer 1970-—), Nashville Met. C. of C., Phi Delta Kappa. Meth. (exec. com., chmn. com. membership materials, 1963-—; chmn. ofcl. bd. 1963-69). Home: 512 Alta Loma Dr Goodlettsville TN 37072 Office: 201 8th Av S Nashville TN 37203

CARPENTER, THOMAS GLENN, univ. pres.; b. Atlanta, Feb. 27, 1926; s. Walker Glenn and Loreta (Jackson) C.; student Ga. Inst. Tech., 1943-45; B.S., Memphis State U., 1949; M.A., Baylor U., 1950; Ph.D., U. Fla., 1963; m. Oneida Pruette, Oct. 30, 1948; children—Debra, Thomas Glenn. Gen. mgr. Laundry & Cleaning Co., Memphis, 1950-54; instr. econs. U. Fla., Gainesville, 1957-59, asst. dir. housing, 1959-64; dir. auxs. Fla. Atlantic U., Boca Raton, 1964; bus. mgr. U. West Fla., Pensacola, 1965, dean adminstrv. affairs, 1965-67, v.p. for adminstrv. affairs, 1967-69; pres. U. North Fla., Jacksonville, 1969-—. Dir. Barnett Bank of Regency, Channel 7. Bd. dirs. Jacksonville Symphony Assn. Served with USNR, 1944-46. Mem. Jacksonville C. of C. (gov.), Beta Gamma Sigma, Phi Delta Theta. Presbyn. (former deacon). Rotarian. Home: 7647 Hollyridge Rd Jacksonville FL 32216 Office: 8057 Arlington Expressway PO Box 17074 Jacksonville FL 32211

CARPENTER, WILLIAM M., diversified co. exec.; b. Burlington, Wis., Aug. 9, 1925; s. William and Olive (Eppers) C.; B.A., U. Wis., 1948; m. Elaine H. Jacobson, Aug. 17, 1945; children—William Scott, Deborah Elaine, Robert Todd. Asst. dir. pub. relations Kohler Co. (Wis.), 1949-56; pub. relations dir. Trane Co., LaCrosse, Wis., 1956-58; v.p., dir. Klau-Van Pietersom-Dunlap, Milw., Wis., 1959-62; dir. pub. relations Walker Mfg., Racine, Wis., 1962-67, dir. pub. relations, advt., sales promotion, 1967-69, v.p., 1969; v.p. Tenneco Inc., Houston, 1970-—. Bd. dirs. Houston Kidney Found. Served with AUS, 1943-45. Mem. Pub. Relations Soc. Am., Pub. Relations Soc. Houston, Assn. Nat. Advertisers, Nat. Investor Relations Inst. Home: 11918 Churchill Ct Houston TX 77024 Office: PO Box 2511 Houston TX 77001

CARPENTER, WOODROW WILSON, ceramic engr.; b. West Union, Ill., Sept. 11, 1915; s. Marion E. and Margaretta (Fawver) C.; B.S. in Ceramic Engring. U. Ill., 1939; m. Fay D. Turner (div.); 1 dau., Gay M. (Mrs. Glenn E. Caldwell); m. 2d, Irmgard K. Toberg, Sept. 3, 1960. Research engr. Ingram Richardson Inc., Frankfort, Ind., 1939-42, sales engr., 1946-54; dir. research Barrows Corp., Cin., 1954-58; pres. Ceramic Coating Co., Newport, Ky., 1958-—; pres.

Florence Enameling Co. Inc. (Ala.), 1965—. Served to lt. col. AUS, 1942-46; PTO. Patentee in field. Home: 5494 Cannas St Cincinnati OH 45238 Office: PO Box 370 Banklick Rd Newport KY 41072

CARPER, JULIAN F., labor union ofcl. Pres., Va. AFL-CIO. Office: 3315 W Broad St Richmond VA 23230

CARPER, WILLIAM HUDSON, city mgr.; b. Roanoke, Va., Oct. 6, 1911; B.S., Roanoke Coll., 1936; B.S. in Civil Engring., Va. Poly. Inst., 1938; m. Mary Alice Carper; 2 daus., 1 son. Formerly engr. Town of Salem, Va., apprentice draftsman Va. Bridge & Iron Co., city engr. City of Fredericksburg, Va.; town mgr. Town of Culpeper, Va., 1940-43; city mgr. City of Clifton Forge, 1943-45, City of Harrisonburg, 1946-47, City of Burlington, N.C., 1947-50, City of Raleigh, 1950—; planning cons. Va. Planning Bd., 1945-46. Mem. N.C. Recreation Commn. Bd. dirs. United Fund, Raleigh, 3 terms, Wake Community Council, Inc. Recipient Silver Beaver award Boy Scouts Am.; Boss of Year award Jr. C. of C., 1968. Mem. Internat., N.C. (past pres.) city mgrs. assns., C. of C. (bd. dirs. 1967-68, exec. com.), Sigma Chi, Tau Beta Pi. Methodist (steward). Kiwanian (dir. Raleigh 1 yr., Kiwanian of Year, 1965). Home: 2117 Cowpen Dr Raleigh NC 27608 Office: Municipal Bldg Raleigh NC 27601

CARR, BINION HAROLD, elec. constrn. supply co. exec.; b. Hubbard, Tex., July 14, 1924; s. Ira Lindon and Hester (Vandyke) C.; grad. pub. high sch.; m. Patsy Barton, Apr. 20, 1950; children—Binion Harold, Thomas David, Timothy Daniel. Supt., Lloyd Thomas Co., Wichita Falls, Tex., 1955-63; pres. Carr Elec. Constrn. Co., Wichita Falls, 1963—, Indsl. Elec. Supply Co., Wichita Falls, 1962—. Served with USMCR, 1942-45; PTO. Mem. troop com. N. Tex. Area council Boy Scouts Am., 1965—. Served with USMCR, 1942-45; PTO. Mem. Ch. Christ (deacon). Co-inventor oil well tester, 1964. Home: 1528 Celia St Wichita Falls TX 76302 Office: 8503 Jacksboro St Wichita Falls TX 76307

CARR, CHARLES ALBERT, tobacco co. exec.; b. Greenville, N.C., Aug. 23, 1907; s. Charles S. and Pattie (Skinner) C.; B.S. in Commerce, U. N.C., 1929; m. Sarah P. Badham, Oct. 22, 1938; children—Sarah Paxton, Charles Albert, Henrietta Skinner. Supr. purchases E. B. Ficklen Tobacco Co., Greenville, 1929-33, 34-38, dir.; mgr. Pacific Leaf Tobacco Co., Shanghai, China, 1933-34; supr. purchases Dibrell Bros., Inc., Danville, Va., 1938-42, v.p., 1943-58, pres., 1959-68, chmn. bd., 1968—, also dir.; pres. Am. Interiors, Danville, 1969—; dir. Am. Nat. Bank, Danville. Bd. dirs. Danville Meml. Hosp., Danville YMCA; chmn. bd. trustees St. Paul's Coll., Lawrenceville, Va. Mem. Soc. of Cincinnati. Episcopalian (past sr. warden). Club: Danville Golf (Va.) Home: 115 Linden Dr Danville VA 24541 Office: Dibrell Bros 512 Bridge St Danville VA 24541

CARR, DUANE, surgeon; b. Ann Arbor, Mich., Feb. 5, 1902 s. Lauren Duane and Mabel E. (Mills) C.; student U. Ariz., 1921-22, U. Colo., 1922-23; B.A., U. Mich., 1924; M.D., Harvard, 1929; m. Louise Everett Dearing Neill, Feb. 12, 1930; children—Elizabeth (Mrs. W.W. Sprague, Jr.), Diana (Mrs. Hal Bailey, Jr.). Intern, resident N.Y. State Sanatorium for Incipient Tb, Ray Brook, 1929; resident surgery Boston City Hosp., 1930-31; resident thoracic surgery U. Mich. Hosp., 1931-34; practice medicine, specializing in thoracic surgery, Memphis, 1934—; mem. staff City of Memphis Hosps., 1935—; mem. staff Bapt. Meml. Hosp., 1934—, chief of staff, 1950, chief of surg. staff, 1938, pres. of staff, 1959; cons. staffs Meth., St. Joseph's, LeBonheur Children's, West Tenn. Tb hosps. Mem. faculty U. Tenn., 1934—, prof. surgery, 1949—. Past mem. Mayor's Fact-Finding Slum Clearance Com. Bd. dirs. Shelby United Neighbors. Mem. Bd. Thoracic Surgery, 1963-69. Diplomate Am. Bd. Surgery. Fellow A.C.S., Am. Coll. Chest Physicians (pres. So. sect. 1949); mem. Am. Assn. for Thoracic Surgery (sr.), Soc. Thoracic Surgeons (founders group), Memphis and Shelby County Med. Soc. (past pres.), So. Tb Conf. (past pres.), So. Surg. Assn. (sr.), A.M.A., Tenn. Med. Assn., Am., Memphis (past pres.) thoracic socs., So. Med. Assn. (life), Memphis Surg. Soc., So. Thoracic Surg. Assn. (past pres.), So. Trudeau Soc. (past pres.), Memphis and Shelby County Tb Assn. (past pres.), Phi Delta Theta, Alpha Kappa Kappa. Episcopalian (past sr. warden). Club: Memphis Country. Contbr. articles to profl. jours. Home: 475 N Highland St Memphis TN 38122 Office: 20 S Dudley St Memphis TN 38103

CARR, EVA RUTH SHIELDS (MRS. H. HARRIS CARR), educator; b. Magnolia, Ala., Apr. 24,, 1929; d. Samuel Lowry and Lillian (Taylor) Shields; B.S., Livingston State Tchrs. Coll., 1949; M.S., Auburn U., 1960, Ed.D., 1969; m. Harris Carr, Aug. 26, 1957; children—Richard Marvin, Lillian Marie. Tchr., Sweet Water (Ala.) High Sch., 1949-50; sec. Supt. Edn., Selma, Ala., 1950-52; sec. to real estate officer 1st Nat. Bank, Montgomery, Ala., 1953-55; tchr. Robert E. Lee High Sch., Montgomery, 1955-57, chmn. bus. dept., 1957-64; state supr. bus. and office edn., Ala. Dept. Edn., Montgomery, 1964—. Mem. Nat., So. (editor 1966-67), Ala. (pres. 1966) bus. edn. assns., Soc. of Golden Key, Am., Ala. vocational assns., Ala. Edn. Assn., Nat. Assn. State Suprs. Bus. and Office Edn. Contbr. articles to profl. jours. Home: 2715 Green Oaks Dr Montgomery AL 36107

CARR, GERALD PAUL, astronaut; b. Denver, Aug. 22, 1932; s. Thomas Ernest and Freda (Wright) C.; B. Mech. Engring., U. So. Cal., 1954; B.S. in Aero. Engring., U.S. Naval Postgrad. Sch., 1961; M.S. in Aero. Engring., Princeton, 1962; m. JoAnn Ruth Petrie, June 20, 1954; children—Jennifer, Jamee, Jeffrey, John, Jessica, Joshua. Commd. 2d lt. USMC, 1954, advanced through grades to lt. col., 1969; jet fighter pilot U.S., Mediterranean, Far East, 1956-65; astronaut NASA, Houston, 1966—, comdr. 3d Skylab Manned Mission. Mem. Marine Corps. Assn., Tau Kappa Epsilon. Presbyn. Office: Code CB NASA MSC Houston TX 77058

CARR, HAROLD N(OFLET), airlines exec.; b. Kansas City, Kan., Mar. 14, 1921; s. Noflet B. and Mildred (Addison) C.; B.S., Tex. A. and M. U., 1943; postgrad. Am. U., 1944-46; m. Mary Elizabeth Smith, Aug. 5, 1944; children—Steven Addison, Hal Douglas, James Taylor, Scott Noflet. Asst. dir. route devel. Trans World Airlines, Inc., 1943-47; exec. v.p. Wis. Central Airlines, Inc., 1947-51; mem. firm McKinsey & Co., 1951-54; pres., dir. North Central Airlines, Inc., 1954-67, chmn. bd., pres., 1967-69, chmn. bd., chief exec. officer, 1969—; professorial lectr. mgmt. engring. Am. U., 1952-62; dir. Detection Scis., Inc., 1st Internat. Corp., Stange Co. Councilor Tex. A. and M. Research Found. Bd. nominations Nat. Aviation Hall Fame. Bd. dirs. Minn. Safety Council, Airline Indsl. Relations Conf., Assn. Local Transp. Airlines. Served with AUS, 1942-43. Mem. World Bus. Council, Smithsonian Assos., Minn. Execs. Orgn., A.I.M. (pres.'s council), Tex. A. and M. Former Students Assn., Nat. Aero. Assn. (Washington), Am. Assn. Airport Execs., Nat. Def. Transp. Assn., Air Transp. Assn. (dir.), Am. Econ. Assn., Mpls., St. Paul chambers commerce, Stearman Alumnus Club, Pine Beach Peninsula Assn. Episcopalian. Clubs: Nat. Aviation, Nat. Aero (Washington); Wings (N.Y.C.); Briarcrest Country (Bryan); Racquet (Miami); Midway Civic (Mpls./St. Paul); Gull Lake Yacht (Brainerd, Minn.); Minneapolis. Home: 3505 Parkway Terrace Bryan TX 77801 Office: 7500 Northliner Dr Minneapolis MN 55450

CARR, HORACE MIXON, agr. extension dir.; b. Enterprise, Ala., Dec. 3, 1923; s. John Bunion and Lola Elizabeth (Browning) C.; B.S., Auburn U., 1950; m. Gloria Anne Weaver, Oct. 9, 1948 (dec. June 1968); children—Helen (Mrs. Eddie Joe Comerford), Joe Anne, Horace Mixon, William John, Carolyn. Asst. county agrl. agt. Calhoun County, Blountstown, Fla., 1951; county agrl. agt. Liberty County, Bristol, Fla., 1951-54; county extension dir. Bay County, Panama City, Fla., 1954—. Served with 4th Armored Div., AUS, 1944-46. Decorated Purple Heart, Combat Inf. Badge. Mem. Fla. Assn. County Agrl. Agts. (pres. 1970-71), Fla. County Agts. Assn., Nat. Assn. County Agrl. Agts., Fla. Cattlemen's Assn., Fla. Farm Bur., Am. Legion, Bay County Fair Assn., Auburn Alumni Assn., Lambda Chi Alpha. Democrat. Methodist. Kiwanian (lt. gov. 1969), Mason. Home: 119 S MacArthur St Panama City FL 32401 Office: 301 McKenzie Av Panama City FL 32401

CARR, HOWARD ERNEST, ins. agy. exec.; b. Johnson City, Tenn., Oct. 4, 1908; s. William Alexander and Gertrude (Feathers) C.; B.S., E. Tenn. State U., 1929; M.Ed., Duke, 1935; postgrad. U. N.C., 1938-39; m. Thelma Northcutt, June 11, 1937; 1 son, Howard Ernest. Supt., Washington Coll. (Tenn.), 1929-35; ednl. advisor U.S. Office Edn., Ft. Oglethorpe, Ga., 1935-37; prin. Greensboro (N.C.) city schs., 1937-42; dir. activities First Presbyn. Ch., Greensboro, 1946-47; with Jefferson Standard Life Ins. Co., Greensboro, 1947—, spl. rep., 1947-54, supr. agy. Greensboro, 1964, mgr., 1964-67; pres. Everett's Lake Corp. Chmn. Guilford County Bd. Edn., 1950—; vice chmn. N.C. Gov's Com. Edn., 1956-60; N.C. rep. White House Conf. Edn., 1955. Mem. adv. com. Greensboro div. Guilford Coll., 1958—; head Guilford County Cancer Drive, 1956, bd. dirs Cancer Soc., 1956—; v.p. N.C. State Sch. Bds. Assn., 1959-61; bd. dirs. Greensboro Jr. Mus., 1956-62, Sternberger Found. Served to lt. with USNR, 1942-46, asst. head motion picture dept., Washington; to capt., 1951-54, as head motion picture dept; ret. as capt., 1968. Recipient Nat. Quality award, Nat. Assn. Life Underwriters, 1948—; named Boss of the Year, Lou-Celin chpt. Am. Bus. Woman's Assn., 1967. Mem. Nat., N.C. (pres. 1964-65; Man of Year award 1969), Greensboro (pres. 1956-57) assns. life underwriters, N.C. Leaders Club, Greensboro C. of C. (chmn. edn. com. 1960-62). Presbyn. (elder). Mason (32 deg.), Kiwanian (pres. Greensboro 1951). Author: History of Higher Education in East Tennessee, 1935. Home: 3927 Madison Av Greensboro NC 27410 Office: 301 Battleground Av Greensboro NC 27401

CARR, JOE CORDELL, sec. state Tenn.; b. Cookeville, Tenn., June 20, 1907; s. Sidney Forrest and Laura (Burton) C.; student pub. schs., Nashville; m. Mary Oliver Hart, Sept. 12, 1934; children— Carolyn (Mrs. George N. Welch III), Joe Cordell. Bill clk. Tenn. Ho. of Reps., 1929-33, asst. chief clk., 1933-37, reading clk., 1937-39, chief clk., 1939-41, 53-55; sec. state State of Tenn., Nashville, 1941-45, 47-49, 57—. Pres. Tenn. Bapt. Brotherhood. Organizer, sec. Young Democratic Clubs of Tenn., 1933, pres., 1934; sec. Young Dem. Clubs Am., 1937, pres. 1941. Trustee Belmont Coll. Served with AUS, 1944-45. Mem. Am. Legion, 40 and 8, Soc. Amateur Chefs. Baptist (deacon). Mason (33 deg., Shriner, Jester), Elk. Clubs: Cumberland, Richland Country, Exchange (pres. 1954). Home: 3508 Hampton Av Nashville TN 37203 Office: State Capitol Nashville TN 37203

CARR, JOHN HIRAM, engring. co. exec.; b. Columbus, Ga., Apr. 4, 1914; s. William Manassas and Mary (McClellan) C.; B.S. in Elec. Engring., Ga. Inst. Tech., 1934; m. Frances Elizabeth Smith, June 8, 1946; children—Carmen Elizabeth (Mrs. Glenn Herbert Meyer), John Hiram, Marie Malinda. Exec. v.p. Sumter Motor Co., Wildwood, Fla., 1935-37; constrn. v.p. Carrier Corp., N.Y.C., Phila., Atlanta, 1937-42; partner G.V. Carr & Co., Columbus, Ga., 1946—; v.p. McClellan Home Furnishings, Inc., Columbus. Served to lt. comdr. USNR, 1942-46. Registered profl. engr., Ga. Mem. Nat., Ga. socs. profl. engrs. Methodist (steward). Home: 4616 Buena Vista Rd Columbus GA 31907 Office: 2627 Schaul St Columbus GA 31906

CARR, JOSEPH A., JR., curator, planetarium exec.; b. Mpls., Sept. 26, 1920; s. Joseph A. and Vesta N. (Lindsey) C.; B.S., Gemol. Inst. Am., 1950; M.S., U. Minn., 1953; m. Anita R. Gibson, Mar. 12, 1943; 1dau., Janine. Jeweler, Bemidji, Minn., 1947-53; curator, instr. dept. astronomy U. Minn., Mpls., 1953-60; curator, demonstrations lectr. dept. physics and phys. sci. U. S. Fla., Tampa, 1960-64, curator, dir. planetarium, 1964—, instr. dept. astronomy and phys. sci., 1964—; prof. astronomy Fla. Inst. for Continuing U. Studies, 1964, St. Leo Coll., 1965; cons, Tampa Mus. Sci. and Natural History; mem. solar eclipse expdn., El Cameron, Mexico, 1970. Served with Signal Corps, AUS, 1942-45. Mem. Am. Assn. U. Profs., Am. Inst. Physics, Am. Assn. Physics Tchrs., Fla. Acad. Sci., Am. Astronomy League, Am. Astron. Soc., Sigma Pi Sigma. Mason (K.T.). Home: 3402 Riverview Dr Tampa FL 33604 Office: 4202 N Fowler St Tampa FL 33620

CARR, LAWRENCE EDWARD, JR., lawyer; b. Colorado Springs, Colo., Aug. 10, 1923; s. Lawrence Edward and Lelah R. (Rubert) C.; B.S., U. Notre Dame, 1948, LL.B., 1949; LL.M., George Washington U., 1954; m. Agnes Isabel Dyer, Dec. 26, 1946; children—Mary Lee, James Patrick, Lawrence Edward III, Eileen Louise, Thomas Vincent. Admitted to Colo. bar, 1949, D.C. bar, 1952, Md. bar, 1961; with Travelers Ins. Co., 1949-51; practiced in Washington, 1952—; sr. partner firm Carr, Bonner, O'Connell, Kaplan, Thompson & Diuguid, 1960—. Pres., Capital Investment Co. of Washington, 1962—. Served with USMCR, 1943-46, 51-52; col. Res. Mem. Am. Bar Assn., Bar Assn. D.C. (dir. 1969-71). Home: 9616 Culver St Kensington MD 20795 Office: 1001 Connecticut Av NW Washington DC 20036

CARR, WESLEY ALLEN, dentist, oral surgeon; b. Truckee, Cal., June 2, 1913; s. Arthur and Ella (Podd) C.; A.A., Sacramento Jr. Coll., 1935; postgrad. U. Mo., 1936-37; B.S., U. Ga., 1938; D.D.S., Atlanta So. Dental Sch., 1942; m. Elizabeth Pauline Moss, July 1, 1938; children—Wesley Allen, Paula Karen. Practice dentistry, Royston, Ga., 1946-52, Augusta, Ga., 1952—; chief dental staff Univ. Hosp. Augusta, 1954—; mem. staff St. Joseph Hosp.; asso. prof. Med. Coll. Ga. Sch. Dentistry, 1968—. Cons. U.S. Army, VA Hosp., Grace Wood State Hosp., Talmadge Meml. Hosp.; mem. adv. bd. Radiation Center, Augusta, 1971—. Mem. Ga. Bd. Health, 1964-72, regional Bd. Health, 1972—. Served with USNR, 1942-46; PTO. Fellow Royal Soc. Health, Am. Coll. Dentists, Internat. Coll. Dentists, Ga. Dental Assn. (hon.; pres. 1964); mem. Am., Ga. socs. oral surgeons, Eastern Dist. Dental Soc. (dentist of year 1965), Am. Dental Assn., Internat. Assn. Oral Surgeons, (pres. Eastern dist.), Ga. Acad. Dental Practice. Elk, Kiwanian. Clubs: West Lake Country (Augusta), Augusta Country. Home: 708 Aumond Rd Augusta GA 30904 Office: 1105 Druid Park Av Augusta GA 30904

CARRASGUILLO, QUINONES ERNESTO, Puerto Rican senator; b. Yabucoa, P.R., Nov. 7, 1901; s. Pablo and Juanita (Quinones) C.; Tchr.'s Diploma; m. Conchita Lopez Lopez, Apr. 8, 1933; children—Ernesto Luis, Connie Margarita. Tchr., Dept. Edn., Yabucoa, 1921-40; mayor, Yabucoa, 1940-48; mem. Wage Minimum Bd., P.R., 1942-44; mem. P.R. Ho. of Reps., 1936-40; mem. P.R. Senate, 1948—. Pres., Popular Party, Yabucoa, 1938-66. Mem. P.R. Tchrs. Assn. Democrat. Roman Catholic. Address: Degetau St Yabucoa PR 00767*

CARRAWAY, HOWARD ERNEST, telephone exec.; b. Olanta, S.C., Oct. 22, 1917; s. Simeon Carlyle and Blanche (Ivy) C.; A.B., Furman U., 1940; m. Avis Cecelia Norman, Jan. 17, 1942 (dec. July 1970); children—Cathleen (Mrs. Duane T. Farmer), Nancy Ann, John MacDonald; m. 2d, Barbara Begg Heilman, July 17, 1971; 1 stepson, Donald Keith Heilman. Mng. editor Florence (S.C.) Star, 1940-41; reporter Florence Morning News, 1946; owner, editor Pageland (S.C.) Jour., 1946-59; staff writer-columnist Ft. Pierce (Fla.) News-Tribune, 1959-63; pres. Pageland Printing Co., 1953-59, Times Pub. Co. Timmonsville, S.C., 1957-58; pres. Ft. Pierce Press., 1959-63; adminstrv. aide Fla. Pub. Service Commn., Tallahassee, 1963-67, adminstrv. sec., dir. adminstrv. services, 1967-70, asst. exec. dir., 1970-72; exec. dir. Fla. Telephone Assn., Tallahassee, 1972—. Mem. Chesterfield (S.C.) County Welfare Bd., 1957-59. Served with USNR, 1941-46, 51-53. Kiwanian (dir. 1968-70, v.p. 1970-71, pres. elect 1971-72). Home: 2116 Spence Av Tallahassee FL 32303 Office: Suite 103 1030 East Lafayette St Tallahassee FL 32301

CARRELL, HILMA BARTLETT, educator, counselor; b. Lamesa, Tex., May 11, 1911; d. Homer T. and Lois Irma (Hill) Bartlett; B.A., Tex. Tech. Coll., 1932; M.A.; Tex. Coll. Arts and Industries, 1951; postgrad. Pan Am. Coll., summer 1952, Tex. U. Extension, 1951-53, S.W. Tex. U. Extension, 1962, U. Utah, 1963, U. Wyo., 1962, 63; Ed. D., 1968; m. Sawnie Morgan Carrell, May 25, 1934; 1 dau., Sawndra D'Aun (Mrs. Wallis Franklin Altom). Tchr. Dimmitt (Tex.) High Sch., 1932-49, Mercedes (Tex.) High Sch., 1949-51, Weslaco (Tex.) High Sch., 1951-58; counselor Kerrville (Tex.) Tivy High Sch., 1958-60; Kendall County coop. counselor Comfort (Tex.) High Sch. and Boerne (Tex.) High Sch., 1960-63; counselor Boerne High Sch., 1963-69; dir. counseling center Amarillo (Tex.) Coll., 1969—. Mem. Am. (life), Tex., Wyo., S. Tex. personnel and guidance assns., Nat. Assn. Women Deans and Counselors, Tex. Tchrs. Assn., Tex. Jr. Coll. Assn., Internat. Educators Assn., Am. Sch. Counselor Assn., Delta Kappa Gamma. Home: Box 51 Dimmitt TX 79027 Office: Amarillo Coll Amarillo TX 79105

CARRERA, ANA ESTRADA (MRS. GUILLERMO M. CARRERA), physician, pathologist; b. Rio Piedras, P.R., Apr. 16, 1921; d. Manuel and Josefina (Marquez) Estrada; student Stanford, 1945, Newcomb Coll., 1945-47; M.D., Tulane U., 1951; m. Guillermo M. Carrera, Sept. 5, 1945; children—Guillermo F., Carlos J. Am. Cancer Soc. research fellow Tulane U., New Orleans, 1951-53, research asso., instr. medicine, 1957-62, asso. prof. medicine, 1968—; clin. pathologist Ochsner Clinic, Ochsner Found. Hosp., New Orleans, 1958—, active staff clin. pathologist, 1961—. Mem. Am., Pan Am. med. assns., Am. Med. Women Assn., Coll. Am. Pathologists, Am. Soc. Clin. Pathologists, Am. Soc. Hematology, Alpha Omega Alpha, Sigma Xi. Contbr. articles to med. jours. Home: 3118 Jena St New Orleans LA 70125 Office: 1514 Jefferson Hwy New Orleans LA 70121

CARRERA, GUILLERMO MANUEL, pathologist; b. Vieques, P.R., Jan. 3, 1913; s. Guillermo and Carlota (Benitez) C.; B.S., U. P.R., 1933, M.D., Tulane U., 1937; m. Ana Luisa Estrada, Sept. 5, 1945; children—Guillermo Federico, Carlos Jose. Intern, San Juan city hosps., 1937-39; resident surgery Univ. Hosp., San Juan, 1939-40, resident pathologist, 1940-45; instr. pathology and tropical medicine Tulane U. Sch. Medicine, New Orleans, 1945-48, asst. prof., 1948-52, asso. prof., 1952-54; head dept. pathology Ochsner Clinic and Ochsner Found. Hosp., New Orleans, 1954—. Mem. A.M.A., A.A.A.S., Soc. Exptl. Biology and Medicine, Am. Soc. Exptl. Pathology, Am. Soc. Clin. Pathology, Coll. Am. Pathologists, Am. Assn. Pathologists and Bacteriologists, So. Med. Assn., Sigma Xi. Home: 3118 Jena St New Orleans LA 70125 Office: 1516 Jefferson Hwy New Orleans LA 70121

CARRERE, CHARLES SCOTT, lawyer; b.Dublin, Ga., Sept. 26, 1937; B.A., U. Ga., 1959; LL.B., Stetson U., 1961. Admitted to Fla. bar, 1961, Ga. bar, 1960; law clk. to U.S. Dist. Judge, Orlando, 1962-63; asst. U.S. atty., Middle Dist. Fla., 1963-66, chief trial atty., 1965-66, spl. asst. to U.S. atty., 1966-67; partner firm Harrison, Greene, Mann, Davenport, Rowe, and Stanton, St. Petersburg, 1970—. Served with inf. AUS. Mem. Am., Fla., St. Petersburg bar assns., Stetson Lawyers Assn. (dir. 1968), Phi Beta Kappa, Phi Delta Phi. Office: First Federal Bldg St Petersburg FL 33701

CARRICO, HARRY LEE, state justice; b. Va., Sept. 4, 1916; s. William Temple and Nellie Nadalia (Willett) C.; jr. certificate, George Washington U., 1938, LL.B., 1942; m. Betty Lou Peck, May 18, 1940; 1 dau., Lucretia Ann. Admitted to Va. bar, 1941; with firm Rust & Rust, Fairfax, 1941-43; trial justice Fairfax County, Va., 1943-51; pvt. practice, Fairfax, 1951-56; judge 16th Jud. Circuit Va., 1956-61; asso. justice Supreme Ct. Appeals Va., 1961—. Served to ensign USNR, 1945-46. Mem. Phi Delta Phi. Episcopalian. Home: 2634 Hunker Mill Rd Oakton VA 22124 Office: Courthouse Fairfax VA 23219 also Supreme Ct Bldg Richmond VA 23219

CARRIER, GLASS BOWLING, JR., banker; b. Lexington, Ky., Sept. 2, 1931; s. Glass Bowling and Margaret (Sexton) C.; B.S., U. N.C., 1953; m. Dorothy Kay Olsen, June 15, 1957; children—Catherine Anne, David Bowling. Supr., Allstate Ins. Co., Charlotte, N.C., 1956-61, div. supr., St. Petersburg, Fla., 1961-62; sr. v.p., investment div. head First Union Nat. Bank, Charlotte, 1962—. Bd. dirs. N.C. Municipal Council. Served with USNR, 1953-56. Presbyn. (elder 1966—). Home: 3635 Severn Av Charlotte NC 28210 Office: 1 Jefferson First Union Plaza Charlotte NC 28201

CARRIER, LEONARD SAMUEL, educator; b. New Rochelle, N.Y., May 23, 1934; s. Samuel Joseph and Anna Rauha (Vuokko) C.; B.A. magna cum laude, U. Miami, 1956, M.A., 1958; Ph.D. (Stanford Wilson fellow), 1967; m. Claire Lorette Arnold, Feb. 2, 1957; children—Erica Claire, Samuel Glenwood. Teaching asst. philosophy Stanford U., Palo Alto, Cal., 1962-65; lectr. philosophy Macquarie U., Sydney, Australia, 1966-68; research grantee, asst. prof. philosophy U. S. Fla., 1969-71; asso. prof. philosophy U. Miami (Fla.), 1971—. Served to lt. USAF, 1958-61. Mem. Am. Philos. Assn., So. Soc. Philosophy and Psychology, Sigma Alpha Epsilon, Phi Kappa Phi. Democrat. Home: 6050 Moss Ranch Rd Miami FL 33156

CARRIER, RONALD EDWIN, coll. pres.; b. Bluff City, Tenn., Aug. 18, 1932; s. James Murphy and Melissa (Miller) C.; B.S., E. Tenn. State U., 1955; M.S., U. Ill., 1957, Ph.D. (Earheart fellow), 1960; m. Edith Marie Johnson, Sept. 7, 1955; children—Michael Lavon, Linda Lois, Jennine Maria. Asso. prof. econs. U. Miss., 1960-63; dir. Bur. Bus. and Econ. Research, Memphis State U., 1963-66, provost, prof. econs., 1966-69, v.p. acad. affairs, 1969-71; pres. Madison Coll., Harrisburg, Va., 1971—. Dir. Leader Fed. Savings & Loan Assn., Rockingham Nat. Bank; cons. Harland Bartholomew & Assos. Trustee Madison Coll. Found. Recipient Distinguished Service award Jr. C. of C., 1965, Ben Franklin award Memphis Printing Industry, 1966. Mem. Am., So. econ. assns., Am. Mgmt. Assn., Va. Edn. Assn., Omicron Delta Gamma, Sigma Phi Epsilon, Beta Gamma Sigma, Omicron Delta Kappa. Methodist. Rotarian. Contbr. articles, monographs to profl. lit. Home: Hillcrest Madison Coll Harrisonburg VA 22801

CARRILLO, MANUEL, amateur photographer; b. Mexico City, Mexico, Jan. 17, 1906; s. Lauro and Guadalupe (Palacios) C.; m. Consuelo Cadena, Feb. 19, 1951; 1 son by previous marriage, Manuel. Gen. agt. I.C. R.R. in Mexico City; amateur photographer; seventy exhibits in U.S., Europe, Central and S.Am. under titles Mi Pueblo and The Inseparables. Recipient 1st prize black and white photography Sat. Rev., 1967. Mem. Liga Defensora de los Animales S.A., Soc. Protectora de los Animales S Am., Traffic Club Mexico City. Lion. Address: Bolivar No 21 Mexico City Mexico

CARRILLO SANCHEZ, JOSE LUIS, entomologist; b. Mexico City, Mexico, June 23, 1934; s. Gilberto Carrillo and Mercedes Sanchez; Ing. Agron., Escuela Nacional de Agricultura, 1957; M.S., Ore. State U., 1962; Ph.D., U. Cal. at Berkeley, 1966; m. Maria Teresa Aguado, July 26, 1958; children—Jose Luis, Maria Teresa, Lourdes, Jaime. Investigator, Office of Spl. Studies, Mexico, 1958-60; investigator Nat. Inst. Agrl. Research, Mexico, 1962-63, head biol. control of insects sect., 1967—; instr. Nat. Sch. Agr. and Postgrad. Coll. Mem. Sociedad Mexicana de Entomologia, Ingenieros Agronomos Parasitologos A.C., Entomol. Soc. Am., Internat. Orgn. for Biol. Control. Contbr. articles field biology, ecology and control of insects to Mexican and Am. jours. Home: 13 Cebadales Mexico 22 DF Mexico Office: Dept Entomologia INIA APDO Postal 6-882 Mexico 6 DF Mexico

CARRINGTON, ENNIS BUFORD, educator; b. Diana, Tex., Jan. 8, 1908; s. Joseph Travis and Florence (Wilson) C.; B.S., E. Tex. State U., 1935; M.Ed., U. Tex., 1940; m. Claudia Mae Dill, May 27, 1939; children— Rosanne (Mrs. Vernon O. Root), Sue (Mrs. James King), Martha Nell, Joe. Prin. rural schs., Harrison and Upshur Counties, Tex., 1927-36; tchr. social studies, math. White Oak (Tex.) High Sch., 1936-42; prin. White Oak Elementary Sch., 1942-58; supr. schs., White Oak, Tex., 1958—. Pres. White Oak Community Fund, 1960—; bd. dirs. A.R.C., Longview Tex., 1958—, Gregg County Tb Assn., Longview, 1956—, East Tex. Area Council Boy Scouts Am., 1944—, recipient Silver Beaver award, 1949. Mem. N.E.A. (life mem.), Tex. State Tchrs. Assn., Am. Assn. Sch. Adminstrs. Baptist. Lion. Home: Box 8 White Oak TX 75693

CARRINGTON, PAUL, lawyer; b. Mexico, Mo., Sept. 24, 1894; s. William Thomas and Mary (Holloway) C.; A.B., U. Mo., 1914; LL.B., Harvard, 1917; m. Frances DeWitt, Nov. 5, 1921; children—Frances (Lee), Paul DeWitt. Admitted to Tex. bar, 1919, since in practice civil law, Dallas; sr. mem. firm Carrington, Coleman, Sloman, Johnson and Blumenthal, attys. Chmn. N. Tex. Com. Econ. Devel., 1943-46, Alien Enemy Hearing Bd. of N. Tex., 1942-45; pres. Greater Dallas Planning Council, 1948-53; chmn. bd. Dallas Council on World Affairs, 1953-54; trustee Southwestern Legal Found., 1949—; v.p. Dallas Boy Scouts Am., nat. councilor, 1945-64; pres. Dallas YMCA, 1946-49. Served as 2d lt., instr. primary flying U.S. Army, 1918-19. Fellow Am. Bar Found. (chmn. 1965-66); mem. Am. Bar Endowment (dir. 1964-70), State Bar Tex. (chmn. revising corp. laws Tex. 1949-56, 1st chmn. sect. corp., banking and bus. law 1954, pres. 1960-61), Am. (mem. Ho. of Dels. 1958-70, chmn. sect. corp., banking and bus. law 1955-56, chmn. com. on lawyer referral service 1959-63), Dallas (pres. 1940) bar assns., U.S., Dallas (pres. 1940-42), E. Tex. (pres. 1950-51) chambers commerce, Am. Soc. Internat. Law (exec. council 1961-67), Am. Arbitration Assn. (dir. 1935—), Am. Law Inst., Am. Judicature Soc. (dir. 1960-63), Harvard Law Sch. Assn. (pres. 1959-61, nat. council 1953—), S.A.R. Democrat. Mem. Christian Ch. (elder). Mason (32 deg.). Clubs: Dallas Country, Petroleum (Dallas); Harvard (N.Y.C.); Metropolitan (Washington). Home: 6315 Lupton Dallas TX 75225 Office: One Main Pl Dallas TX 75250

CARRION-SERNA, ASENSIO, ednl. adminstr.; b. Cartagena, Spain, Nov. 20, 1932; s. Asensio Carrion-Aviles and Pilar Serna-Gabaldon; student Nat. U. Mexico, 1950-52; C.P.A., Monterry Technol. Inst., 1956; M.B.A., Tex. Christian U., 1957; postgrad. Cornell U., 1959-62; m. Idalia Martinez, Apr. 17, 1969; 1 son, Asensio. Jr. accountant Despacho Freyssinier Morin, 1952, jr. auditor, 1955-56, sr. auditor, controller, 1956-57; prof. accounting Monterrey Technol. Inst. (Mexico), 1957-59, 1962-64, head dept. accounting, 1964-68, asso. dean Sch. Bus., 1968-70, asso. dean, dir. grad. program in bus., 1970—; cons. finance, accounting, mgmt.; guest prof. Mexican, Colombian Univs. Mem. Am. Finance Assn., Am. Econ. Assn., Am. Accounting Assn., Nat. Assn. Accountants, Western Finance Assn., Inst. Mexicano de Contadores Publicos, Instituto de Contadores Publicos de N.L., Assn. de Ejecutives de Finanzes, Inst. Mgmt. Scis. Roman Catholic. Home: 132 A Ote Missouri Garza Garcia NL Mexico Office: ITESM Sucursal de Correos J Monterrey NL Mexico

CARRITHERS, PAUL NORMAN, realtor; b. Hindman, Ky., Apr. 16, 1923; s. Oliver Roy and Leah (Wiseman) C.; student, N.C. State Coll., Raleigh, 1940-41, Coll. William and Mary, 1949—; m. Marie Brown, July 20, 1944; children—Faye Jeanette, Kaye Louise, Gaye Elizabeth. Realtor Fidelity Real Estate Service, Newport News, Va., 1947—, mgr., 1950—; a founder 1st Peninsula Bank & Trust Co. of Hampton (Va.), 1970. Chmn. adv. bd. Salvation Army, 1965-68; bd. pres. Peninsula Family Counseling Agy., Newport News, 1956-60. Served with USAAF, 1944-46. Mem. Nat. Assn. Real Estate Bds., Nat. Inst. Real Estate Brokers, Va. Assn. Realtors, Newport News-Hampton Bd. Realtors, Peninsula C. of C. Mason. Clubs: Newport News Kiwanis. Home: 898 Cloverleaf Lane Newport News VA 23601 Office: 99 28th St Newport News VA 23607

CARROCCIO, CHARLES SALVATORE, dentist; b. N.Y.C., Nov. 25, 1920; s. Anthony and Josephine (Morello) C.; B.S. in Biology, Catholic U. Am., 1941; D.D.S., Georgetown U., 1944; m. Margaret Murray Brennan, Dec. 2, 1944; children—A. Thomas, Cristina (Mrs. Walter James Sears III), Charles, Maria, Margaret, Michelle, Andrea, Paul, Peter, John. Practice gen. dentistry, Washington, 1946—, Bethesda, Md., 1955—; mem. staff Providence Hosp., Washington, 1960—; instr. operative dentistry Sch. Dentistry, Georgetown U., 1946—. Cubmaster, Bethesda, 1954-56, pack chmn., 1956-57. Served with AUS, 1944-46. Mem. Am. Dental Assn., D.C. Dental Soc. (exec. com.), Pierre Fauchard Acad., Catholic U. Alumni Assn. (gov., past pres.), Xi Psi Phi. Roman Catholic (mem. parish council). K.C. Home: 5501 Albia Rd Bethesda MD 20014 Office: 2025 Eye St Washington DC 20016

CARROLL, CHARLES A., judge; b., 1898; B.A., Villa Maria Coll., 1924; LL.B., Harvard. Judge, 3d Appellate Dist. Ct. Fla., Miami. Home: 4100 Malafa Miami FL 33133 Office: 1350 NW 12th Miami FL 33133*

CARROLL, COLEMAN FRANCIS, archbishop; b. Pitts., Feb. 9, 1905; s. William J. and B. Margaret (Hogan) C.; B.A., Duquesne U., 1926; L.S.T., St. Vincent's Sem., Latrobe, Pa., 1930; J.C.D., Catholic U. Am., 1942. Ordained priest Roman Catholic Ch. 1930 asst. pastor Resurrection, St. Scholastica, St. Basil, Holy Cross, 1930-49; pastor St. Maurice Parish, Pitts., 1949-51, Sacred Heart Ch., East End, Pitts., 1951-58; became 1st Bishop, Miami, Fla., 1958; now archbishop Miami Beach, Fla.; domestic prelate, Rt. Rev. Msgr., 1952; aux. biship of Pitts., 1953-58. Address: 6301 Biscayne Blvd Miami FL 33138

CARROLL, DEWITT EDWARD, public relations co. exec.; b. Gastonia, N.C., Oct. 4, 1914; s. Wiley Tot and Constance (Hege) C.; student U. N.C., 1932-36; m. Marguerite Elizabeth Bishop, Apr. 8, 1943; 1 dau., Betsy Bishop (Mrs. Robert F. Alexander, Jr.). With U.P.I., 1936; with Raleigh (N.C.) Times, 1936-40, city editor, 1939-40; asst. city editor Greensboro Record, 1951-52; asst. city editor Greensboro Daily News, 1952-53; exec. sec. Piedmont Asso. Industries, 1953-60; v.p., sec. John Harden Assos., Greensboro, 1960-72; owner DeWitt Carroll/Pub. Relations, 1972—. Cons. bus. letter and report writing, speech writing, pub. relations, co. publs., 1955—. Exec. committeeman, pub. relations chmn. Carolinas United, 1966-67; mem. budget com., Greensboro United Fund, 1953-54; mem. adv. bd. Greensboro div. Guilford Coll., 1954-64, Guilford Tech. Inst., 1956-60. Served to capt. USAAF, 1942-45, USAF, 1950-52; Korea. Mem. Pub. Relations Soc. Am. (pres. N.C. chpt. 1969), Platform Assos. Episcopalian (vestryman, lay reader 1969-70). Home: 1503 Seminole Dr Greensboro NC 27408 Office: 1503 Seminole Dr Greensboro NC 27420

CARROLL, DONALD K(INGERY), judge; b. Hartington, Neb., April 16, 1909; s. Charles Eden and Blanche Elsie (Kingery) C.; A.B., Harvard, 1930; student U. Miami, 1931-33; J.D., U. Fla., 1935. Asst. to editor Nat. Mag., Boston, 1930-31; admitted to Fla. bar, 1935, and since practiced in Jacksonville; mem. Milam, McIlvaine, Carroll & Wattles, Jacksonville, 1938-57, ret.; judge Dist. Ct. of Appeal, 1st Dist. Fla., 1957—; asst. atty. gen. Fla., 1941. Dir. Crime Commn. of Greater Jacksonville, 1952—; pres. Civic Round Table, 1950-51; pres. Fla. Citizenship Clearing House, 1957—. Served as capt. Judge Adv. Gen. Dept., AUS, 1942-46, ETO. Mem. Am. (exec. council, jr. bar conf. 1940-42; ho. of dels. 1952-56), Jacksonville (treas. 1938-40; sec. 1946-48; pres. 1949) bar assns., Fla. Bar (pres. 1955-56), Am. Judicature Soc. (dir.), Am. Legion (state comdr., 1950-51), Jr. C. of C. (pres. 1942), Phi Kappa Phi. Democrat. Methodist. Mason (32 deg., Shriner), Elk. Club: Torch. Author, editor: Handbook for Judges, 1961. Office: Supreme Ct Bldg Box 87 Tallahassee FL 32302

CARROLL, EDWARD JOSEPH, psychoanalyst; b. Pitts., Feb. 24, 1910; s. Edward Joseph and Stella (Bonner) C.; B.S., U. Pitts., 1933, M.D., 1934; m. Mildred Clark, Aug. 10, 1935; 1 son, Clark E. Intern St. Francis Hosp., Pitts., 1934-35, resident, 1935-37; individual practice pschoanalysis, Pitts., 1946-65, Miami, Fla., 1965—; dir. Craig House Children, Pitts., 1955-64; tng. analyst Phila. Psychoanalytic Inst., 1956-65, Psychoanalytic Inst., Pitts., 1962-65; clin. asso. prof. psychiatry U. Pitts., 1950-65; clin. asso. prof. psychiatry U. Miami, 1965-69, clin. prof., 1969—. Mem. Pa. Adv. Council Mental Health, 1960-65, chmn., 1963-65 mem. Pa. Bd. Pub. Welfare, 1963-65. Served with M.C., AUS, 1940-46. Mem. Am., Pitts., Fla. psychoanalytic socs. Address: 8201 Ponce de Leon Rd Miami FL 33143

CARROLL, FRANK ANDREW, JR., physician; b. Scranton, Pa., May 21, 1924; s. Frank Andrew and Evangeline (Farrell) C.; B.S., U. Scranton, 1947; M.D., Jefferson Med. Coll., 1951; m. Suzanne Teres Clarke, July 9, 1949; children—Suzanne, Drew, Ellen, Megan, David, Gail. Intern, Scranton State Gen. Hosp., 1951-52; gen. practice medicine, Alexandria, Va., 1952—; dir. No. Va. Doctors Hosp. Corp., Circle Terrace Hosp. Corp., Alexandria; chief dept. family practice No. Va. Doctors Hosp., 1962—. Served with AUS, 1943-45. Decorated Purple Heart, Bronze Star. Fellow Am. Acad. Family Practice; mem. No. Va. Acad. Gen. Practice (pres. 1966-67), Va. Acad. Gen. Practice (dir. 1965-68), So., Va., Alexandria med. socs. Roman Catholic. Clubs: Belle Haven Country (Alexandria, Va.), Scranton Country (Scranton, Pa.). Home: 3505 Sterling Av Alexandria VA 22304 Office: 1707 Osage St Alexandria VA 22302

CARROLL, GEORGE JOSEPH, physician; b. Gardner, Mass., Oct. 14, 1917; s. George J. and Kathryn (O'Hearn) C.; A.B., Clark U., 1939; M.D., George Washington U., 1944. Intern, Worcester (Mass.) City Hosp., 1944-45; resident Doctors Hosp., 1945-46, Sibley Hosp., 1948-49, VA Hosp., 1949-50, all Washington; asst. pathologist DC Gen. Hosp., 1950-51, pathologist, 1951-52; practice medicine, specializing in pathology, Suffolk and Franklin, Va., 1952—; pathologist Louise Obili Meml. Hosp., Suffolk, Southampton Meml. Hosp., Franklin, Greensville Meml. Hosp., Emporia, Va., all 1952—; instr. pathology Med. Sch., Georgetown U., Washington, 1950-52; instr. clin. micrology Am. U., Washington, 1950-51; asso. clin. prof. pathology Med. Coll. Va., Richmond, 1968—; clin. prof. pathology Health Sci. Center, Va. Commonwealth U., Richmond, 1970—. Mem. Va. Bd. Med. Examiners, 1967—, sec., treas., 1970—. Bd. dirs. Va. div. Am. Cancer Soc., 1955-62, Va. Med. Service Assn., 1960-71. Diplomate Am. Bd. Pathology. Fellow Am. Soc. Clin. Pathologists (chmn. bd. censors 1970-71, dir.), Coll. Am. Pathologists, A.C.P.; mem. Am. Assn. Blood Banks, Va. Soc. Pathology (sec., treas. 1954-68, mem. council), Va. Med. Soc. (mem. ho. of dels. 1960-68), So. Med. Assn. (councillor from Va. 1965-70, chmn. council 1969-70, 1st v.p. 1971-72), 4th Dist. Med. Soc. Va. (pres. 1968), Internat. Acad. Pathology, A.M.A., George Washington, D.C. (asso.), Seaboard (past pres.) med. socs., Am. Soc. Clin. Pharmacy and Therapeutics, Washington Pathol. Assn., Soc. Nuclear Medicine. Rotarian. Home: 219 Northbrook Av Suffolk VA 23434 Office: Louise Obici Meml Hosp Suffolk VA 23434

CARROLL, HAZEL HORN, educator; b. Dallas; d. Albert Curtis and Mintie R. (Pittman) Horn; B.A., So. Meth. U., 1930; M.Ed., Tex. Wesleyan Coll., 1952; m. Timothy Carroll, Aug. 6, 1944. Tchr. high sch. Carrollton (Tex.) Ind. Sch. Dist., 1930-32; elementary tchr. Highland Park Ind. Sch. Dist., Dallas, 1934-44, D.C. schs., Washington, 1944-45; asst. prof. edn., asst. dir. Reading Clinic, So. Meth. U., 1950—; cons. on reading. Mem. Tex. Assn. for Improvement of Reading (pres. 1965, dir. 1962—), Nat. Reading Conf. (sec., dir.), Internat. Reading Assn. (coordinator radio and TV prodn. 1971—), Alpha Delta Pi, Mortar Bd. (past pres.) Baptist. Author: Play Like series (plays for young children), 1969. Contbr. articles to profl. jours. Home: 4717 Cherokee Trail Dallas TX 75209

CARROLL, JOHN ELLSWORTH, JR., banker; b. Bedford, O., Nov. 22, 1930; s. John Ellsworth and Margaret Helen (Allen) C.; B.S. in Banking and Finance, U. Fla., 1957; m. Alma Pauline Smith, June 5, 1952; children— Paula Eileen, John Ellsworth 3d, William Raymond, Mary Lou. With 1st Nat. Bank of Kissimmee (Fla.), 1949-50, 1954—, v.p., 1961—. Bd. dirs. United Appeal of Osceola County, 1965—, pres., 1971—; bd. dirs. Med. Center of Kissimmee. Served with USN, 1950-54; Korea. Mem. S.A.R., Am. Legion, V.F.W., Delta Tau Delta. Clubs: Silver Spurs Riding, Tohopekaliga Yacht (Kissimee). Mason, Elk, Rotarian. Home: Kings Hwy Kissimmee FL 32741 Office: 8 Broadway Kissimmee FL 32641

CARROLL, JULIAN MORTON, lawyer, state ofcl.; b. Paducah, Ky., Apr. 16, 1931; s. Elvie B. and Eva (Heady) C.; A.A., Paducah Jr. Coll., 1952; A.B., U. Ky., 1954, LL.B., 1956; m. Charlann Harting, July 22, 1951; children—Kenneth Morton, Iva Patrice, Bradley Harting. Admitted to Ky. bar, 1956; mem. Ky. Ho. of Reps., 1962-72, speaker of ho., 1968-72; lt. gov. of Ky., 1971—. Trustee Paducah (Ky.) Jr. Coll. Mem. Am., Ky., Paducah bar assns., Phi Delta. Club: Optimist. Home: Route 1 West Paducah KY 42086 Office: 621 Broadway Paducah KY 42001

CARROLL, PAUL, broadcaster; b. N.Y.C., July 22, 1933; s. Tom. and Grace (Morin) C.; B.A. in Telecommunication, U. So. Cal., 1960; m. Jean Hawes, June 4, 1955; children—Jamie Leigh, Timothy. Reporter, San Francisco Chronicle, 1964-65; advt.-promotion dir. radio sta. KNEW, San Francisco and Oakland, Cal., 1965-68, radio sta. KGO (ABC), San Francisco, 1968-70; gen. mgr., v.p. Rand Broadcasting, Tampa, Fla., 1970—. Served with USAF, 1956-60. Mem. San Francisco Press Club, Tampa C. of C., Fla. Broadcasting Assn. Author: A Year in August, 1971. Home: 11311 N 22d St Tampa FL 33612 Office: 512 N Florida Av Tampa FL 33401

CARROLL, RICHARD LYNN, govt.ofcl.; b. Laurel, Md., Oct. 1, 1932; s. Thomas Fenton and Hester Elizabeth (Doss) C.; B.A., George Washington U., 1960, M.A., 1962, Ph.D. (Gilbert H. Grosvenor teaching fellow 1962-64), 1966; m. Ruth Gail Hodges, Sept. 14, 1957; children— Alena Leticia, Park Kim. Cartographer supr. Army Map Service Dept. of Army, Washington, 1951-57; pub. health adviser D.C. Pub. Health Dept., 1966; spl. asst. Dept. Housing and Urban Devel., Washington, 1967-68; dir. policy and planning Am. Revolution Bicentennial Commn., Washington, 1969-70, dept. exec. dir., 1971—. Served with USNR, 1952-54. Ford Found. travel grantee, India, 1964-65. Home: 4720 20th Pl North Arlington VA 22207 Office: 736 Jackson Pl NW Washington DC 20276

CARROLL, ROBERT CLINTON, JR., elec. engr.; b. Florence, S.C., June 11, 1930; s. Robert Clinton and Harriet (Holland) C.; B.S., Clemson U., 1953; m. Helen White, Aug. 29, 1954; children—Robert F., Helen Haynsworth. Sr. elec. engr. Broad River Elec. Coop, Gaffney, S.C., 1956-57; extension engr. Clemson U., 1957-58; engr. Horry Elec. Coop, Conway, S.C., 1958-60; mgr. bd. pub. works Water Power & Sewer Utility, Gaffney, 1960-65; elec. engr. Harwood Beebe Co., Cons. Engrs., Spartanburg, S.C., 1965—, dirs., 1971—; pres. Dixie Ltd. Inc. Served with AUS, 1953-55. Mem. Spartanburg Soc. Profl. Engrs. (pres. 1968-69), S.C. Pollution Control Assn. (pres. 1965-66), Am. Water Works Assn., I.E.E.E. Rotarian. Home: Route 7 Box 149 Hillside Dr Gaffney SC 29340 Office: 2000 E Main St Spartanburg SC 29302

CARROLL, THOMAS WATSON, ret. supt. schs.; b. Clayton, Ala., Oct. 5, 1906; s. William M. and Annie (Adams) C.; Diploma, Troy State U., 1930; B.S., U. Ala., 1936, M.A., 1938; postgrad. U. Cin., 1940-53; m. Vivian Weaver, June 10, 1950; children—Thomas Watson, David Arthur, Andrew Brian. Tchr. elementary sch. Henry County, Ala., 1924-25; prin., tchr. pub. schs. Houston County, Ala., 1925-26; tchr. elementary and high sch. coach, prin. jr. high sch. Covington County, Ala., 1926-42; asst. prin. Red Level (Ala.) High Sch., 1947-51; asst. supt. schs., Andalusia, Ala., 1951-53; supt. Covington County (Ala.) Schs., 1953-72. Mem. Covington County Mental Health Assn., 1958—, pres., 1964-65; mem. South Central Ala. Mental Health Center, 1968—, chmn. exec. com., 1970—; mem. Covington County Interagy. Council, 1970—. Served with AUS, 1942-47; to maj. USAF, 1965. Mem. N.E.A., Ala., Covington County edn. assns., Dept. Rural Edn., Dept. Suprs. and Dirs. Instrn., Am. Assn. Sch. Adminstrs., Ala. and Covington County Farm Bur., Phi Delta Kappa, Kappa Delta Pi. Democrat. Baptist (deacon 1962). Mason, Rotarian (pres. 1967-68); mem. Order Eastern Star. Home: 507 Sanford Rd Andalusia AL 36420

CARROLL, (JOHN) WALLACE, journalist; b. Milw., Dec. 15, 1906; s. John Francis and Josephine (Meyer) C.; B.Litt., Marquette U., 1928, LL.D., 1972; LL.D., Duke, 1968; m. Margaret Sawyer, May 25, 1938; children—Margaret, John, Rosamond, Patricia. With United Press, 1928-1941; London, 1929-31, Paris, 1931-34, Geneva, 1934-38; corr. Spanish Civil War, 1938; diplomatic corr., London, 1938; mgr. of bur., London, 1939; covered England's first 2 years of war; Russian front, 1941. With U.S. Office of War Information 1942-45; dir. London office: 1942-44; deputy dir. Overseas Br. (for Europe), 1944-45; exec. news editor Winston-Salem Jour. and Sentinel, 1949-55, editor, pub., 1963—; Washington news editor N.Y. Times, 1955-63. Cons. to Dept. State Dept. Army, Psychol. Strategy Bd., 1947-52, Mass. Inst. Tech. 1952-54, U. N.C. 1952-54; lectr. Nat. War Coll., Air War U., other services instns. Mem. Am. Revolution Bicentennial Commn., 1968-69; mem. adv. bd. Pulitzer Prizes, 1969—. Trustee N.C. Sch. Arts. Winner Nat. Headliners Club award for outstanding dispatches on war in Russia, 1942. Author: We're in This With Russia, 1942; Persuade or Perish, 1948. Home: 852 Wellington Rd Winston-Salem NC 27102 Office: Journal and Sentinal Winston-Salem NC 27102

CARROON, LAMAR EVAN, engr.; b. University Park, N.M., Sept. 28, 1922; s. William Evan and Florence Ruth (Brownlee) C.; B.S., N.M. State U., 1943; m. Barbara Carter Paddock, Jan. 19, 1947; children—Robert Evan, Barbara Ann, Jean Carter. With U.S. Geol. Survey, 1946—, dist. engr., Montgomery, Ala., 1959-61, Tuscaloosa, Ala., 1961-64, regional staff engr., Denver, 1964-68, dist. chief water resources div., Jackson, Miss., 1968—. Guest lectr. Pan. Am. Health Orgn., Bridgetown, Barbados, 1967. Registered profl. engr., N.M., Ala., Colo., Miss. Fellow Am. Soc. C.E. (sec.-treas. sect. 1958-59), Miss. Soc. Profl. Engrs., Assn. Fed. Adminstrs. (sec.-treas. 1961), Fed. Exec. Assn., Am. Geophys. Union, Internat. Assn. Scientific Hydrology. Presbyn. (ruling elder 1954-68). Club: Jackson Yacht. Contbr. articles to profl. pubs. Home: 5818 N Dale St Jackson MS 39211 Office: 430 Bounds St Jackson MS 39206

CARROZZA, VINCENT ADOLPH, realtor; b. N.Y.C., Jan. 15, 1925; s. Rocco and Barbara (DeLuca) C.; A.B., Columbia, 1949; m. Anne Reeves, Jan. 21, 1954; children—Fay, Lynn, Robert. Exec. v.p. Dallas Tex. Corp., 1960-69; pres. Center City, Inc., Dallas, 1969—, North Am., Inc., Dallas, Tex., 1969—. Cons., Selective Am. Realty Fund, 1969—, Raymond D. Nasher Realty Interests, 1969-70. Mem. exec. com. Dallas Central Bus. Dist. Assn., 1970—; mem. central area sub-com. Dallas City Planning Commn., 1970—. Trustee Dallas Mus. Fine Arts; bd. dirs. Theater Three, Dallas Theater Center, Columbia Coll. Council. Served with AUS, 1943-45. Recipient Richard H. Fox Meml. prize Columbia, 1949. Clubs: City (Dallas); Woodvale Fishing (Mineola, Tex.). Home: 7301 Turtle Creek Blvd Dallas TX 72525 Office: Kirby Bldg Dallas TX 72501

CARRUTH, HUGH B., elec. engr.; b. Nashville, Ark., Nov. 10, 1907; s. Hugh Bernard and Effie (Clendenin) C.; student Henderson Brown Coll., 1925; B.S., U. Ark., 1929; m. Lois Dodson, June 14, 1935 children—Hugh Bernard III, Joseph T., John Michael. Elec. engr. Commonwealth Co., Chgo., 1929-30; city engr. Nashville, Ark., 1930-41; elec. engr., Southwestern Electric Power Co., Dequeen, Ark., 1945—. Served to maj. C.E., AUS, 1941-45; ETO; lt. col. Res. ret. Decorated Bronze Star. Recipient Silver Beaver award Boy Scouts Am. Registered profl. engr., Ark. Mem. I.E.E.E. (sr.), DeQueen C. of C. (bd. dirs. 1964-67). Methodist (bd. stewards, tchr.). Home: 509 Heynecker Av Dequeen AR 71832 Office: PO Box 271 Dequeen AR 71832

CARRUTH, IRBY BREWSTER, supt. schs.; b. Comanche, Tex., July 6, 1900; s. Robert Edwin and Cora Mae (Brewster) C.; B.A., West Tex. State Coll., Canyon, 1927; M.A., U. Chgo., 1931; postgrad. U. Tex., Columbia, Stanford; LL.D., Tex. Christian U., 1957; m. Tip Bradford, Aug. 25, 1924; children—Robert Bruce, Stanley Bradford. Classroom tchr., prin., supt., Canyon, Tex., 1927-38; supt. schs.,

Bonham, Tex., 1938-44, Waco, Tex., 1944-50, Austin, Tex., 1950-71. Bd. mgrs. Tex. Congress Parents and Tchrs., 1954-57; bd. dirs. Aerospace Edn. Council of Air Force Assn., 1960-63; bd. dirs. Joint Council on Econ. Edn.; past mem. Com. on Nat. Def. and Guidance Counseling Program. Mem.-at-large Nat. council Boy Scouts Am., 1957-63; mem. exec. bd. Goodwill Industries, Inc., Austin, 1960—; past mem. bd. Tex. Safety Assn., YMCA, Salvation Army, local council Boy Scouts Am. Mem. Waco Park Commn., Austin Library Commn. Mem. Am. Assn. Sch. Adminstrs. (pres. 1962-63, mem. 1956 Yearbook commn.), Tex. Assn. Sch. Adminstrs. (past pres.), Austin C. of C. (past dir.), N.E.A., Tex. Tchrs. Assn., Phi Delta Kappa. Mem. Disciples of Christ. Rotarian (pres. Austin 1958-59). Home: 5 Niles Rd Austin TX 78703

CARRUTH, THOMAS PAIGE, ednl. adminstr.; b. Vernon, Tex., Mar. 17, 1931; s. Otho Thomas and Florine (Robinson) C.; student Tex. A. and M. U., 1948-49; B.S., West Tex. State U., 1952, M.Ed., 1955; Ed.D., Tex. Tech. U., 1958; m. Norma Lee Durrett, Aug. 15, 1952; children—Alan Wayne, Geraldine Louise, Joe Keith, Thomas Paige, Melissa. Social studies tchr. Kermit (Tex.) Ind. Sch. Dist., 1955-58; teaching fellow Tex. Tech. U., 1958-59; asst. dean men West Tex. State U., 1959-63, dean student life, 1963-70, v.p. student affairs, 1970—. Pres. Randall County chpt. Am. Cancer Soc., 1965-66, mem. pub. edn. com. Tex. div., 1971-72; mem. com. Llano Estacado council Boy Scouts Am., 1963-66. Served with AUS, 1952-54. Decorated many service medals. Mem. Tex. Assn. Student Personnel Adminstrs. (pres. 1965-66), Southwestern Assn. Student Personnel Adminstrs. (exec. com. 1964-65, 1967—), Panhandle Sch. Leaders Assn. (pres. 1965-66), Canyon C. of C. (dir. 1962-65), Phi Delta Kappa (pres. Gamma Xi chpt. 1962-63). Methodist (lay leader 1965-67). Rotarian (pres. 1964-65, dist. gov. 1971-72). Home: Box 277 West Tex Sta Canyon TX 79015

CARRUTHERS, EWING, ins. agt.; b. Memphis, Mar. 14, 1917; s. Ewing and Willie Emore (Vandegrift) C.; B.A. Southwestern Coll., Memphis, 1939; m. Mary Jane Ogden, Apr. 12, 1952; children—Jan, Ewing III, Cage, Tracy. Agt., Mass. Mut. Life Ins. Co., Memphis, 1939—. Speaker, cons. life ins. at various ednl. instn. seminars. Mem. Shelby County Human Relations Commn., 1968-71, v.p., 1970-71; chmn. French Camp (Miss.) Project, 1951. Mem. Civil Service Bd., City of Memphis, 1969—. Bd. dirs. Arts Appreciation, Memphis. Served to lt. (j.g.) USNR, 1942-46; now lt. Res. ret. C.L.U. Mem. Million Dollar Round Table (life mem.; mem. found ad hoc com. 1970-71), Nat. Assn. Life Underwriters (mem. fed. law and legislation com. 1959-71), Assn. for Advanced Life Underwriting (pres. 1966-67), chmn. long-range planning com. 1971—), Memphis Life Underwriters Assn. (pres. 1955-56), Estate Planning Council Memphis. Republican. Episcopalian (v.p. Episcopalian Laymen of Tenn. 1964-65, mem. vestry 1966-69). Clubs: University, Tennessee (Memphis). Author: A Way of Life, 1969. Contbr. articles to profl. jours. Home: 4134 Kriter Lane Memphis TN 38117 Office: 100 N Main St Memphis TN 38103

CARSON, CHRIS JOHN, architect; b. San Antonio, May 4, 1933; s. John and Sophie (Couloheras) C.; B.Arch., Tex. A. and M. U., 1956. Partner Ford, Powell & Carson, Architects. Registered architect, Tex. Home: 1408 Wiltshire San Antonio TX 78209 Office: 528 King William St San Antonio TX 78204

CARSON, DALE, city ofcl; grad. Ohio State U., 1949; m. Doris N. Carson; children—Dale, Chris, Cynthia. Formerly with FBI; sheriff, Jacksonville, Fla., 1958—. Lectr. polit. sci. various colls. and univs. Mem. Fla. Police Standards Council; mem. Fla. Gov.'s Council on Criminal Justice. Mem. Nat., Fla. (past pres.), sheriffs assns., Internat. Assn. Chiefs of Police. Home: 3875 Rosalind Pl Jacksonville FL 32205 Office: Duval County Courthouse Jacksonville FL 32202*

CARSON, EDWARD FLOYD, ednl. adminstr.; b. Valley View, Tex., June 24, 1916; s. Thomas Augusta and Eva Lou (Fryer) C.; Asso. Sci., N. Tex. Agrl. Coll., 1937; B.S., Tex. A. and M. U., 1939; M.Ed., N. Tex. State U., 1966; m. Regina Jane Mitchell, June 28, 1959; children—Evalyn Dean, Mitchell Edward, Jane Grace. High sch. vocational agr. tchr. Southmayd (Tex.) High Sch., 1939-43; coordinator, Cooke County Vets. Vocational Sch., 1946-61; Cooke County sch. supt., Gainesville, Tex., 1963—. Treas. Nor-Tex Fed. Credit Union, Gainesville, 1966—; fiscal officer Nor-Tex. Edn. Coop., 1968—. Served with USAAF, 1943-46; PTO. Decorated Bronze Star (3). Named Outstanding Conservation Farmer Upper Elm Red Soil Conservation Dist., 1956. Mem. Am., Tex. assns. sch. adminstrs., Tex. State Tchrs. Assn., Tex. County Supts. Assn., Manpower Adminstrv. Programs Assn. Tex., Tex. Farm Bur., V.F.W., Gainesville C. of C. (mem. edn. com. 1970—). Mason, Kiwanian. Club: Cooke County A. and M. (pres. 1971—) (Gainesville). Home: Route 1 Box 87A Valley View TX 76272 Office: 100 California St Gainesville TX 76240

CARSON, LEON HALDEN, JR., coll. football coach; b. Brackenridge, Pa., Apr. 28, 1931; s. Leon Halden and Margaret (Bricker) C.; B.A., U. N.C., 1952, postgrad., 1955-56; m. Doris Jean Hetrick, June 15, 1957; children—Dana Lynn, Clifford Scott. Head coach Scottdale (Pa.) High Sch., 1955-57; asst. football coach U. N.C., Chapel Hill, 1957-64, U. S.C., 1965; football coach Ga. Inst. Tech., Atlanta, 1966—. Bd. dirs. Leukemia Found. Served with USMCR, 1952-54. Mem. Phi Delta Theta. Kiwanian. Home: 3484 Embry Circle Chamblee GA 30341 Office: Ga Inst Tech Atlanta GA 30332

CARSON, RICHARD LAFAYETTE, lawyer; b. nr. Knoxville, Tenn., Sept. 22, 1912; s. Thomas Callaway and Fannie (Cox) C.; LL.B., U. Tenn., 1935; m. Ruth Elisabeth Brown, Oct. 31, 1942; 1 son, Bruce Alexander. Admitted to Tenn. bar, 1935; since practiced in Knoxville; mem. firm Hodges, Doughty & Carson, 1959—; trial atty. City of Knoxville, 1946-52. Chmn. bd. Royal Crown Bottling Co., Knoxville, Smoky Mountains Beverage Co.; dir. Tenn Mill and Mine Supply Co., Callaway Bldg. Products, Inc., Knoxville Parkrite, Inc., Knox Allright, Inc. Served as capt. AUS, 1942-45. Decorated Purple Heart. Fellow Am. Coll. Trial Lawyers; mem. Am., Tenn., Knoxville (pres. 1950-51) bar assns., S.R. (pres. 1950), Am. Judicature Soc., Phi Gamma Delta, Scarabbean. Presbyn. (deacon). Clubs: City, Cherokee Country. Home: Route 1 Westland Dr Concord TN 37720 Office: Hamilton Nat Bank Bldg Knoxville TN 37901

CARSON, RUBY BARRETT, concert pianist, composer; b. Cowan, Ind.; d. George T. and Mary (Robe) Barrett; B.S., Ind. State U., 1927; postgrad. Columbia U., Julliard Sch. Music; studied piano with Emil Liebling, voice with Orville Harrold, tenor Met. Opera Co.; m. C.C. Carson, Feb. 21, 1914 (dec.); 1 son, Robe Barrett. Instr., Muncie Conservatory Music, Ball State Tchrs. Coll., 1910-16, Ind. State Tchrs. Coll., Terre Haute, 1916; dean Miami Beach (Fla.) Coll. Music., 1930—; composer, pianist; composer Allegro Brilliante, pub. by Boston Music Co., 1947, Nocturne in G. 1949, Prayer for Peace, 1951. Honored with presentation of compositions and story of life and accomplishments, radio program Indiana Presents, Ind. U. Sta. WIRE, Indpls., 1945; named Fla. composer of Year, Fla. Fedn. Music Clubs, 1951; featured in column Music Educator of Note, by N.Y. Mus. Courier, 1929; named Fla. Woman of Distinction, 1969. Mem. Nat. League Am. Penwomen (chmn. music dept. Miami br.), Phi Gamma Mu. Mem. Christian Ch. Home: 1710 W 23'D St Sunset Island Three Miami Beach FL 33140

CARSON, RUBY LEACH, journalist; b. Joplin, Mo., June 9, 1894; d. John Milton and Minnie (Robinson) Leach; A.B., U. Miami; M.A., U. Fla.; m. James Milton Carson, Jan. 3, 1926 (dec.); children—Carol (Mrs. Thomas A. Stanford), Jackson C. Reporter, Miami (Fla.) Metropolis (now Miami News), 1916-22; v.p. S. Dade Pub. Co., Homestead, Fla., 1923-27; instr. Fla. history U. Miami, 1939-41; co-founder Homestead (Fla.) Leader, 1923; free lance writer, 1924—. Mem. Hist. Assn. So. Fla. (dir.), Fla. Hist. Soc. (past dir.), Nat. League Am. Penwomen, Sigma Alpha Iota (patroness). Author: Fabulous Florida, 1942; Fla. story for Children of the U.S.A., 1946; (with others) The East Coast of Florida, 1961; (with C.W. Tebcau) Florida from Indian Trail to Space Age, 2 vols., 1965 also articles in hist. jours. Home: 3373 SW 7th St Miami FL 33135

CARSWELL, ELBA WILSON, journalist; b. nr. Bonifay, Fla., Jan. 4, 1916; s. John Robert and Victoria (Judah) C.; A.B., La. Poly. Inst., 1946; m. Mabel Bagley, Apr. 5, 1947 (dec. Jan. 1953); children—Carol, David Clements; m. 2d, Catherine Powell, Apr. 4, 1958; 1 dau., Catherine Melody. Exec. sec. Santa Rosa County C. of C., also asso. editor The Milton (Fla.) Gazette, 1946; asst. dir. publicity, asst. prof. journalism La. Poly. Inst., Ruston, 1947-49; editor The Milton Gazette, 1949-53, Graceville News, Graceville, Fla., Washington County News, Chipley, Fla., 1953-61; staff writer Pensacola News Jour.; editor, co-founder The Tri-County Gazette, Jay, Fla., 1951-53; staff writer Pensacola News-Jour., Chipley, 1961—; pres. Central Office Supply and Pub. Co., Bonifay, Fla., 1963-71. Mem. N.W. Fla. Regional Housing Authority, Citizens' Tax Council; chmn. Washington County Rural Area Devel. Council, 1961-66; chmn. Fla. adv. com. Farmers Home Adminstrn.; mem. regional adv. com. Fla. Dept. Recreation and Parks, 1972—; adv. com. on pub. relations Fla. State Welfare Bd., 1960-71; chmn. Fla. Bd. Parks and Historic Memls., 1966—; chmn. Washington County Hist. Commn., 1965-66; bd. dirs. Children's Home Soc. Florida. Mayor, Chipley, Fla. 1963-67; chmn. Washington County Democratic Com., 1958-62. Adv. bd. Washington-Holmes Area Vocational-Tech. Sch., Chipley, Fla. Recipient Florida Forestry editorial award, 1956, 57, 58, Fla. State U. editorial award, 1958, Fla. Gov.'s Festival of Fla. Products award, weekly newspaper div., 1958; Fla. Press Assn. editorial oscar, 1959; Fla. Outdoor Writers award, 1960; Fla. Outstanding Conservationist award Soil Conservation Soc. Am.; Fla. Man of Yr. for Agr., Fla. Assn. Agrl. Agts., 1966, Gov.'s appreciation award outstanding contbns. to State of Fla., 1969. Served with AUS, 1942-45. Mem. Fla. Municipal Judges Assn., Washington County C. of C. (pres. 1961—), Fla. Hist. Soc., Washington County League Municipalities (pres. 1967), V.F.W., Am. Legion, Alpha Lambda Tau, Sigma Tau Delta. Tau Kappa Epsilon. Democrat. Methodist. Mason, Kiwanian (Chipley pres. 1960). Author: Among These Hills, 1968; Holmes Valley, 1969; also numerous hist. articles. Home: Dekle St at Forest Av Chipley FL 32428 Office: PO Box 584 Chipley FL 32428

CARSWELL, T.N., loans, investments, income tax service, tax cons.; b. Homerville, Ga., Oct. 22, 1887; s. Andrew J. and Martha (Smith) C.; grad. Ga. Normal Coll. and Bus. Inst., 1908 A.B. magna cum laude, Simmons Coll., 1915; m. Byrdie P. Townley, Aug. 1921; 1 dau., Peggy A. (Mrs. William Peacock, Jr.). Tchr. bus. adminstrn. and comml. law; bus. mgr. and registrar, Simmons Coll.; treas. Western Produce Co.; mgr. Abilene C. of C. and W. Tex. Fair; organizer and pres. mgr. Merchants Paper Co.; owner Carswell Agy. and Carswell Travel Service. Adv. bd. Tex. Centennial. Served U.S.N.R.F., World War I; maj. Tex. Def. Guard, organized, commanded 10th Battalion. Chmn. Taylor Co. Vol. Parole Bd. Trustee Hardin-Simmons U.; trustee, co-founder Hendrick Meml. Hosp. Mem. Am. Legion (former dept. vice comdr.), Nat. Assn. Tax Cons., Tex. Cotton Coop. Assn. (state adv. bd.; organizer 7th dist.), Am. Cotton Coop. Assn. (nat. adv. bd.). Democrat (former mem., Taylor County exec. com.). Baptist (deacon). Mason (K.T., Shriner). Clubs: Abilene Country (charter), Lions (past dep. dist. gov.; instituted crippled children's work, local club). Speaker on moral, social and patriotic subjects. Home: 1501 Ambler Av Abilene TX 79601 Office: 1334 Pine St PO Box 2178 Abilene TX 79604

CARTER, AMON, JR., publisher; b. Ft. Worth, Dec. 23, 1919; s. Amon G. and Nenetta (Burton) C.; B.B.A., U. Tex., 1941. With Carter Pubs., 1936—, pres., 1952—; pres. pub. Ft. Worth Star-Telegram; dir. Am. Airlines, Inc. 1957—. Served as capt. AUS, 1941-45; prisoner of war, Germany, 1943-45. Decorated Purple Heart, Bronze Star. Mem. Kappa Sigma. Club: Exchange. Home: 29 Valley Ridge Rd Fort Worth TX 76107 Office: Star-Telegram Fort Worth TX 76102

CARTER, BARBARA L., banker. Br. v.p. Annadale office Woodlawn Nat. Bank. Office: care Woodlawn National Bank Woodlawn VA 24381*

CARTER, BETTY LOU (MRS. CHARLES E. CARTER), educator; b. Collierville, Tenn., July 6, 1907; d. Claude Marcellus and Eloise (Neville) Ballard; B.A. magna cum laude Lambuth Coll., 1928; M.A., La. State U., 1935; m. Charles E. Carter, Sept. 6, 1930; 1 son, Charles Ballard. Tchr. French, Medina (Tenn.) High Sch., 1928-29; tchr. English, Pope (Miss.) High Sch., 1929-30; instr. French, Belhaven Coll., Jackson, Miss., 1940; instr. English, Southwestern Coll., Memphis, 1943-44; tchr. English, St. Mary's Episcopal Sch., Memphis, 1944-45; prof. French, Texarkana (Tex.) Coll., 1953-70. Bd. dirs. local chpt. A.R.C., 1950; mem. Community Service Council, 1949-50; active Heart Fund, 1957-60. Trustee Texarkana Coll. Named Tchr. of Year, Texarkana Coll., 1962; R.E. Womack award Lambuth Coll., 1969. Mem. Am. Assn. Tchrs. French, Modern Lang. Assn., S. Central Modern Lang. Assn., Coll. English Assn., Am. Assn. U. Women, Am. Assn. U Profs., Tex. Tchrs. Assn., Tex. Jr. Coll. Tchrs., P.E.O. (pres. chpt. 1960-61, 67-68), Delta Kappa Gamma. Methodist. Home: 2801 Stillwell Dr Texarkana TX

CARTER, BETTY WERLEIN (MRS. HODDING CARTER), journalist; b. New Orleans; d. Philip and Elizabeth (Thomas) Werlein; B.A., Newcomb Coll., 1931; m. Hodding Carter, Oct. 14, 1931; children—Hodding III, Philip Dutartre Carter. Newspaper reporter Daily Courier, Hammond, La., 1932-36, Delta Star, Greenville, Miss., 1936-38; reporter Delta Democrat-Times, 1938-40, 45-72, pub., 1972—; researcher O.W.I., 1942-45; freelance writer. Mem. So. dist. Marshall Scholarship Com., 1961-69; mem. corp. U.S. Com. for UNICEF. Named Woman of the Year, Beta Sigma Phi, 1947. Episcopalian. Author: (with husband) So Great a Good, A History of the Episcopal Church in Louisiana, 1805-1955, 1955, Doomed Road of Empire, 1962. Home: Feliciana Greenville MS 38701 Office: Box 1018 Greenville MS 38701

CARTER, BRUCE GILBERT, coll. pres.; b. Elgin, Tex., July 29, 1904; s. Jefferson Lee and Emma (Condron) C.; B.A., Okla. Bapt U., 1928, LL.D. (hon.), 1951; M.A., U. Okla., 1932, Ed.D., 1950; m. Mary Nola Funderburk, July 4, 1929; children—Robert Bruce, Marilyn (Mrs. Jerry Owen), John Carroll. Tchr. Wewoka (Okla.) High Sch., 1929-38; postmaster, Wewoka, 1938-39; adminstr. Nat. Youth Adminstrn., Okla., 1940-43; pres. Northeastern Okla. A. and M. Coll., Miami, 1943-69; spl. adviser to Gov. of Okla., 1971-72; pres. Okla. Coll. Liberal Arts at Chickasha, 1972—. Okla. chmn. March of Dimes, 1952-60, Mental Health Assn., 1961-65; chmn. Okla. Ednl. TV Authority, 1968-69; exec. dir. Higher Edn. Alumni Council, Okla., 1969-71. Bd. dirs. Bapt. Found. Okla., Okla. Bapt. U. Mem. Miami C. of C. (pres. 1953), Council N. Central Jr. Colls. (pres. 1968—). Baptist (mem. exec. com. conv.). Home: Okla Coll Liberal Arts Chickasha OK 73019

CARTER, CHARLES HERSCHEL, physician; b. Castleberry, Ala., June 18, 1917; s. Joel and Fay (Menchien) C.; B.A., U. Ala., 1938; M.D., U. Tenn., 1940; m. Mary Dickson, Oct. 9, 1942; children—Nancy, David. Intern John Gaston Hosp., Memphis, 1941; resident U. Tenn. Teaching Hosp., 1941-43; practice medicine specializing in pediatrics, Memphis, 1943-51; med. dir. Sunland Tng. Center, Gainesville, 1951-60; med. and research dir. Sunland Hosp., Orlando, Fla., 1960—. Mem. Gov.'s Adv. Com. Mental Retardation, 1961—. Bd. dirs. Luther Rice Sem., Jacksonville, Fla., Edgewood Boys' Ranch, Orlando, Fla., Kradie-Kare, Maitland, Fla. Recipient various awards for outstanding service to mentally retarded. Fellow Am. Acad. Mental Retardation; mem. Am. Acad. Gen. Practice Am. Assn. Mental Deficiency, Am. Pediatric Asnn., A.M.A., So. Med., Christian Med. Soc. Baptist. Editor: Medical Aspects of Mental Retardation, 1965. Author: Handbook of Mental Retardation Syndromes, 2d edit., 1970. Contbr. articles to publs. Address: Box 3513 Sunland Hosp Orlando FL 32802

CARTER, CHARLES HILL, JR., county ofcl.; b. Charles City, Va., Aug. 16, 1919; s. Charles Hill and Emily (Harrison) C.; B.S. in Gen. Agr., Va. Polytech. Inst., 1943; m. Helle M. Klingemann, Aug. 4, 1960; children—Charles Hill, Robert Randolph, Harriet Emily. Owner, Shirley Plantation, Charles City, 1957—; bd. suprs. Charles City County, 1953—, chmn., 1960-72. Mem. Charles City Planning Commn., 1955-72; chmn. County Democratic Com., 1961—. Served with AUS, 1943, Episcopalian (sr. warden 1966, 69). Home: Shirley Plantation Box 57 Route 2 Charles City VA 23030

CARTER, FLETCHER FAIRWICK, educator; b. Bagdad, Fla., Feb. 12, 1930; s. Ollie Martin and Florence (Owens) C.; B.A., U. Fla., 1953; M.A., Appalachian State Tchrs. Coll., 1960; Ph.D. (Kellogg fellow 1963), Fla. State U., 1965; m. Edith Houston, Apr. 2, 1961. Tchr Santa Rosa County (Fla.) pub. schs., 1957-61; registrar Mitchell Coll., Statesville, N.C., 1963-64; instr. Fla. State U., 1964-65; asso. prof. edn. Radford (Va.) Coll., 1965-67, prof. edn., 1968—, asst. to dean div. edn., 1967-69, dir. instl. research, 1969—; instr. Appalachian State U., summer, 1961; ednl. cons. Va. high schs., 1965—. Served to 1st lt. with AUS, 1953-55. Mem. Pi Gamma Mu, Phi Delta Kappa (sec. 1969-70). Episcopalian. Mason. Home: PO Box 638 Radford Coll Radford VA 24141

CARTER, FRANCES TUNNELL (MRS. JOHN T. CARTER), educator; b. Springville, Miss., May 21, 1922; d. David Atmond and Mary Annie (McCutcheon) Tunnell; A.A., Wood Jr. Coll., 1942; student Blue Moutain Coll., 1942; B.S., U. So. Miss., 1946; M.S., U. Tenn., 1948; Ed.D., U. Ill., 1954; postgrad. Ursuline Coll., 1961, Dayton U., 1963, Fla. State U., 1970; m. John T. Carter, Mar. 16, 1946; children—John Wayne, Frankye Nell. Elementary sch. tchr. Thaxton (Miss.) Sch., 1942-43, Cumberland (Miss.) Elementary Sch., 1943-44, home econs. Randolph (Miss.) High Sch., 1944-45, Maben (Miss.) High Sch., 1946-47, Wood Jr. Coll., 1948; head dept. home econs. East Central Jr. Coll., 1948-49; Clarke Meml. Coll., 1950-56; mem. faculty Samford U., Birmingham, Ala., 1956—, asst. prof., 1956-57, asso. prof., 1957-63, prof., 1963—. Vis. prof. Hong Kong Bapt. Coll., 1965-66; dir., also cons. workshops for tchrs., summers, 1962—. Mem. Gov.'s Com. on Status of Women, 1964-68, adv. bd. Nat. Dairy Council Greater Birmingham, 1966—; organizer, former leader troop Girl Scouts U.S.A., 1963—. Recipient Spl. Service award A.R.C., 1962. Mem. Internat. Council on Edn. for Teaching, P.T.A., Nat. Assn. for Edn. Young Children, Civil Air Patrol (maj.), Assn. for Childhood Edn. (adviser Samford U. br. 1963—, state 1st v.p. 1968-70, pres. 1970-72), Nat. Soc. D.A.R., Internat. Council Women, Ala. Writers Conclave, Internat. Reading Assn., Ala. Poetry Soc., Soc., Ala. assns. children under six, Nat. League Am. Penwomen (pres. Birmingham br. 1968), Ala. Assn. Tchr. Educators, Kappa Delta Epsilon (nat. v.p. 1966-70), Alpha Delta Kappa, Kappa Delta Pi (co-sponsor 1970—), Kappa Omicron Phi. Baptist. Author: Sammy in the Country, 1960; Teachers Guide for Mission Books, 1969; 'Tween-age Ambassadors, 1970; (with others) Sharing Times Seven, 1971. Contbr. profl. jours. Home: 2561 Rocky Ridge Rd Birmingham AL 35243

CARTER, FRANK, real estate devel. and marketing co. exec.; b. Atlanta, July 21, 1925; s. Frank and Mary (Stewart) C.; B.S., Washington and Lee U., 1949; m. Jane Munnerlyn, June 25, 1949; children— Frank, Benjamin Munnerlyn, Wilson Munnerlyn, Jane Stewart. Salesman, Draper-Owens Co., Atlanta, 1952-58; pres. Pope & Carter Co., Atlanta, 1958-71, Crow, Carter & Assos., Atlanta, 1971—; dir. Alpha Fund, Inc. Trustee, treas. Lovett Sch.; trustee United Appeal; past mem. bd. visitors Emory U. Mem. Atlanta Real Estate Bd. (past officer, dir.; Realtor of Year 1966), Atlanta C. of C. (pres. 1969), Washington and Lee U. Alumni Assn. (past pres. Atlanta chpt.). Presbyn. (chmn. bd. deacons 1971). Clubs: Piedmont Driving (past dir.), Commerce, Capital (Atlanta). Home: 3800 Northside Dr NW Atlanta GA 30305 Office: 1100 Spring St NW Atlanta GA 30309

CARTER, HARRY NELSON, univ. adminstr.; b. Haileyville, Okla., Mar. 7, 1912; s. Ed and Cora (Baldwin) C.; B.S., Northeastern Okla. State Coll., 1940; M.S., U. Colo., 1950; grad. study U. Tulsa, U. Colo.; m. Bonnie Jackson, Oct. 27, 1939. Tchr. pub. schs., Ark. and Okla., 1936-41; instr. math. Spartan Sch. Aeros., 1941-45; instr. math. U. Tulsa, 1945-46, asst. prof., 1946-53, asso. prof., 1953-61, prof. 1961—, asst. dean of engring., 1958-59, acting dean, 1959-60, men's counselor, 1960-62, dean of students, 1962-70, coordinator student services, 1970—. Mem. Am. Soc. Engring. Edn., Am. Math. Soc., Okla. Acad. Sci., N.Y. Acad. Scis., Math. Assn. of Am., Am. Assn. U. Profs., A.A.A.S., Nat. Assn. Student Personnel Adminstrs., Omicron Delta Kappa, Kappa Mu Epsilon, Phi Eta Sigma, Alpha Phi Omega, Lambda Chi Alpha. Methodist. Club: University (Tulsa). Contbr. math. jours. Home: 3739 S Fulton Av Tulsa OK 74135

CARTER, HENRY ZAC, shipyards exec.; b. Troy, Ala., Mar. 4, 1907; s. Cada Sanders and Lucy L. (Kelly) C.; B.S., U. Ala., 1931; LL.B., Georgetown U., 1939; m. Myrtle E. Mooneyham, June 1, 1932; children—Henrietta Sue (Mrs. Jack C. Watson), Henry Zac, Stephanie Ellen (Mrs. John Borders). Gen. auditor U.S. Maritime Commn., 1940-47; with Avondale Shipyards, Inc., New Orleans, 1947—, pres., 1961-72, chmn. bd., 1972—, also dir.; exec. asst. chmn. bd. Ogden Corp., 1972—; dir. La. and So. Life Ins. Co., 1962—, Whitney Nat. Bank, So. Ry. Active local Girl Scouts, United Fund. Named Maritime Man of Year in La., 1962; recipient New Orleans Press Club award, 1964; named Man of Year in La., Sales Execs. C. of C., 1966. Mem. New Orleans C. of C. (pres. 1969). Clubs: Propeller, Internat. House, Marine, Petroleum, Indsl. Mgmt. (New Orleans). Home: 28 Audubon Pl New Orleans LA 70118 Office: Suite 1815 1010 Common St New Orleans LA 70112

CARTER, HERBERT EDMUND, educator, chemist; b. Mooresville, Ind., Sept. 25, 1910; s. George Benjamin and Edna (Pidgeon) C.; A.B., DePauw U., 1930, Sc.D., 1952; A.M., U. Ill., 1931,

Ph.D., 1934; m. Elizabeth Winifred DeWees, Aug. 30, 1933; children—Anne Winsett, Jean Elizabeth. Instr. chemistry U. Ill., 1933-35, asso., 1935-37, asst. prof. 1937-43, asso. prof. 1943-45, prof., 1945—, acting dean grad. coll., 1963-64, head dept. chemistry and chem. engring., 1954-67, vice chancellor for acad. affairs, 1967-71; coordinator interdisciplinary programs U. Ariz., 1971—. Mem. Pres.'s Com. on Nat. Medal of Sci., 1963-66; mem. nat. sci. bd. NSF, 1964—, chmn., 1970—. Awarded Rector Scholarship, Rector Fellowship, DePauw U.; Eli Lilly & Co. ann. award (, 000 and bronze medal to bio-chemist under 35 years of age showing promise in research), 1943; Am. Oil Chemist's Soc. award in lipid chemistry, 1966. Mem. exec. com. div. chemistry and chem. tech. NRC, 1949-55, 57-58. Mem. Am. Chem. Soc. (dir., asso. editor Bio-Chemistry 1961—; recipient William H. Nichols medal N.Y. sect., also Spencer award Kansas City sect. 1969), Am. Inst. Nutrition (sec. 1945-47), Am. Soc. Biol. Chemists (editorial bd. 1951-60, editorial com. 1963-66, pres. 1956-57), Nat. Acad. Scis. (chmn. sect. biochemistry 1963-66, mem. council 1966—), Sigma Xi, Phi Beta Kappa, Phi Eta Sigma, Blue Key, Lambda Chi Alpha, Gamma Alpha, Alpha Chi Sigma. Democrat. Presbyn. Mem. editorial bd. Bio Chem. Preparations, editor-in-chief, Vol. I. Contbr. tech. publs. Home: 2401 Cerrada de Promesa Tucson AZ 85718 Office: National Science Bd 1800 G St NW Washington DC 20550 also 512c Adminstrn Bldg Uhiv Ariz Tucson AZ 85721

CARTER, HERBERT FRANKLIN, clergyman, ch. exec.; b. Clinton, N.C., June 20, 1933; s. Arby Herring and Betty (Lockerman) C.; student Holmes Theol. Sem., 1952-53; B.Sacred Lit., William Carter Coll., 1955, B.A., 1962; m. Mary Elizabeth Key, Nov. 20, 1955; children—James Arby, Herbert Randal. Ordained to ministry Bapt. Ch., 1954; pastor, Dunn, N.C., 1955-59; gen. supt. Pentecostal Free Will Bapt. Ch., Inc., Dunn, 1959—, editor Messenger, 1959—, dir. world mission, 1970—; acting acad. dean William Carter Coll., Goldsboro, N.C., 1963—, bd. dirs., 1959—. Vice chmn., sec., local chpt. coordinator Pentecostal Fellowship N.Am., editor News; radio speaker Hour of Blessing, Sta. WTAB, Tabor City, WCKB, Dunn, 1963—, WXRI, Norfolk, Va. Bd. adminstrn. Beulah Heights Coll. and Inst., Atlanta, 1963—. Named Alumnus of Yr., William Carter Coll., 1961. Mem. Woodmen of World. Kiwanian. Home: Route 4 Dunn NC 28334 Office: PO Box 966 Dunn NC 28334

CARTER, HODDING, editor, pub. author; b. Hammond, La., Feb. 3, 1907; s. William Hodding and Irma (Dutartre) C.; B.A., Bowdoin Coll., 1927; grad. student journalism Columbia, 1927-28, Tulane U., 1928-29, Harvard, 1939; M.A. (hon.), Harvard, 1947; Litt.D., Bowdoin Coll., 1947; L.H.D., Washington U., 1954, Protestant Episcopal Theol. Sem., 1965; D.Humanities (hon.), Coe Coll., Allegheny Coll.; m. Betty Werlein, Oct. 14, 1931; children—William Hodding III, Philip Dutartre. Teaching fellow Tulane U., 1928-29; reporter New Orleans Item-Tribune, 1929; night bur. mgr., United Press, New Orleans, 1930; mgr. A.P. Bur., Jackson Miss., 1931-32; started Daily Courier, Hammond, La., editor, pub. 1932-36; started Delta Star, Greenville, Miss., editor, pub., 1936-38; editor, pub. Delta Democrat-Times, Greenville, 1939—; newspaper editor PM, 1939; co-owner Radio Sta. WDDT, Greenville, 1956; civilian aide to sec. army, 1952—; writer in residence Tulane U., 1962-69. Trustee George Peabody Coll. for Tchrs., 1952-65; bd. overseers Bowdoin Coll.; mem. Nat. Citizens Council Better Schs.; bd. visitors Tulane U., 1953—; mem. Pulitzer Prize Adv. Bd. Joined N.G., 1938; pub. Dixie, 31st div. paper, Camp Blanding, Fla., 1940; Army Bur. of Pub. Relations, Washington, D.C., 1940-41; editor Stars and Stripes, Yank. Middle East edits., Cairo, Egypt; ret. as maj., 1945. Recipient War Dept. citation, 1946; Nieman fellowship for newspapermen, Harvard, 1939, Guggenheim fellowship, 1945, Pulitzer prize, 1946. So. Literary Award, 1945; fellow Sigma Delta Chi, 1954; Nat. Citation Journalistic Merit, William A. White Found., 1961; Bowdoin prize, 1963; 1st Fed. award of Miss., 1968; Journalism award Columbia, 1971. Mem. Am. Soc. Newspaper Editors. Author: Civilian Defense of the United States (with Col. R. Ernest Dupuy), Lower Mississippi, 1942; The Winds of Fear, 1945; Flood Crest, 1947; Southern Legacy, 1950; Gulf Coast Country (with Anthony Ragusin), 1951; Where Main Street Meets the River, 1953, Robert E. Lee and The Road of Honor, 1954, Marquis De Lafayette, Bright Sword for Freedom, The Angry Scar, So Great a Good; (with Mrs. Hodding Carter) Doomed Road of Empire, 1962; First Person Rural, 1963; The Ballad of Catfoot Grimes and Other Verses, 1964; So the Heffners Left McComb, 1965; The Commandos of World War II, 1966; Their Words Were Bullets, Man and the River: The Mississippi, 1970. Contbr. to mags. Home: Feliciana Farm Greenville MS 38701 Office: Delta Democrat-Times Greenville MS 38701 Died Apr. 4, 1972

CARTER, HOMER MUNROE, SR., ret. textile co. exec.; b. Van Zant Co., Tex., Dec. 16, 1901; s. Jesse O. and Mary E. (Barber) C.; B.S., Ga. Sch. Tech., 1923; m. Mary Jane McGinnis, June 30, 1925; 1 son, Homer Munroe. Joined Pepperell Mfg. Co., 1925, gen. mgr. Ala. div., 1931-59, exec. v.p., 1959-61, pres., 1961-66, dir., 1952-65; pres. West Point-Pepperell, Inc., 1965-68, vice chmn., 1968-69, dir., 1965-71; dir. Farmers Nat. Bank, Opelika, Ala. Mem. Phi Delta Theta, Phi Kappa Phi. Meth. Clubs: Union League (N.Y.C.); Capital City (Atlanta). Home: 2637 Peachtree Rd NE Atlanta GA 30305

CARTER, HUGH (SEVIER), sociol. cons., writer; b. San Antonio, Apr. 5, 1895; s. David W. and Cornelia (Keith) C.; A.B., Southwestern U., 1916; M.A., U. Minn., 1922; Ph.D., Columbia, 1927; m. Isabel Gordon, June 22, 1925; children—Eleanor Jean (Mrs. Charles W. Brome), Janet C. (Mrs. Frank Hannigan). Prin. high sch., Hearne, Tex., 1916-17; instr. sociology U. Pa., 1924-29, asst. prof., 1929-45; chief gen. research Immigration and Naturalization Service, U.S. Dept. Justice, 1945-52; chief marriage and divorce statistics Nat. Center Statistics, U.S. Dept. Health, Edn., Welfare, 1952-65; vis. prof. sociology Purdue U., 1965; adj. prof. sociology Am. U., 1966; sociol. cons. and writer, Washington, 1966—. Statistician Com. Cost Med. Care, 1929-30; research analyst U.S. Housing Authority, 1939-40; mem. Del Internat. Union for Study of Popul, Vienna, Austria, 1959, London, Eng., 1969; mem. Nat. Council on Family Relations, Internat. Sci. Commn. on Family. Served to 2d lt. U.S. Army, 1917-18. Recipient Stuart A. Rice award, 1970. Mem. Am. Sociol. Assn. (council 1953-56, com. on govt. statistics), A.A.A.S. Am. Statis. Assn., Population Assn. Am. (sec.-treas. 1953-56, v.p. 1958), D.C. Sociol. Soc. (pres. 1953). Club: Cosmos (Washington). Author: Social Theories of L. T. Hobhouse, 1927, 2d edit., 1968; (with Paul C. Glick) Marriage and Divorce: A Social and Economic Study, 1970. Contbr. articles to profl. jours. Address: 2039 New Hampshire Av NW Washington DC 20009

CARTER, JAMES DAVID, historian; b. Evant, Tex., Jan. 27, 1907; s. David Henry and Sudie Lena (Longmire) C.; student John Tarleton Agrl. Coll., 1922-25; B.S., North Tex State Tchrs. Coll., 1931, M.A. (History fellow), 1950; Ph.D., U. Tex., 1954; m. Lowell Lona Burney, June 30, 1927; children—Jeanell (Mrs. Alfred Edward Faubion), Carolyn (Mrs. Edward Louis Malcolm), Roaslie (Mrs. Joel Douglas Ward). Adminstr. pub. schs. Tex., 1926-36; owner Carter Ranch, nr. Lampasas, Tex., 1936-49; instr. North Tex. State Coll., 1950-51; asso. prof. U. Tex., 1952-55; historian, editor Grand Masonic Lodge of Tex., Waco, 1956-63; historian Supreme Council 33 deg. So. Jurisdiction U.S.A., Washington, 1963—. Sec. bd. radio sta. KBGO, Waco, Tex. Bd. dirs. Scottish Rite Found. Tex. Served as lt. U.S. Army, 1925-27. Recipient Legion of Honor, Order of DeMolay, 1963; Grand Cross of Color, Order of Rainbow for Girls, 1955; named Ky. col. Commonwealth of Ky., 1971; Research grantee Grand Lodge of Tex., 1953-54. Fellow Tex. Hist. Assn., Philalethes Soc., Tex. Lodge of Research; mem. Soc. Blue Friars (sec.-gen. 1970). Mem. Christian Ch. Mason (33 deg.), Lion. Club: Commercial. Author: Masonry in Texas, 1955; Education and Masonry in Texas, 2 vols., 1963; History of the Supreme Council, 2 vols., 1967. Editor: Transactions Texas Lodge of Research, 1961; First Century of Scottish Rite Masonry in Texas, 1967; Texas Grand Lodge Mag., 1955-63. Home: 10621 Stone Canyon Dallas TX 75230 Office: PO Box 15197 Dallas TX 75201

CARTER, JAMES EARL, JR., govt. of Ga.; b. Plains, Ga., Oct. 1, 1924; s. James Earl and Lillian (Gordy) C.; student Ga. Southwestern U., 1941-42, Ga. Inst. Tech., 1942-43; B.S., U.S. Naval Acad., 1947; postgrad. Union Coll., 1952; m. Rosalynn Smith, July 7, 1946; children—John William, James Earl III, Donnel Jeffrey, Amy Lynn. Peanut farmer, warehouseman, 1953—; gov. State of Ga. (Atlanta), 1971—. Mem. Ga. Senate, 1962-66. Served with U.S. Navy, 1947-53. Home: 1 Woodland Dr Plains GA 31780 Office: Governors Office State Capitol Atlanta GA 30334

CARTER, JAMES EDWARD, JR., dentist, assn. ofcl.; b. Augusta, Ga., July 1, 1906; s. James Edward and Emma (Barnett) C.; D.D.S., Howard U., 1930; postgrad. Haines Normal and Indsl. Inst., 1920-24; m. Marjorie Butler, Jan. 7, 1928; 1 son, James Edward III. Pvt. practice dentistry, Augusta, 1930—. Mem. Nat. Council YMCA, 1958-64, 67-69; chmn. 9th St. YMCA, Augusta, 1950-57; active United Coll. Fund, Cancer Dr., United Chest Fund, Boy Scouts Am. Del. Republican Nat. Conv., 1960. Bd. dirs. Augusta-Richmond County Library. Recipient Achievement award in pub. service Upsilon Sigma chpt. Omega Psi Phi, 1949; award of merit Georgia Dental Soc., 1961. Fellow Am. Coll. Dentists; mem. Nat. (past pres.; mem. exec. bd. 1940-52), Am., Ga., (pres. 1940-41) dental assns., Stoney-Med. and Dental Soc. (pres. 1961-63), Acad. Gen. Dentistry, John A. Andrew Clin. Soc. (pres. dental sect. 1947), Omega Psi Phi (past basilius Psi Omega chpt. 1936-37, treas. 7th dist. 1943—; recipient achievement award human relations Psi Omega chpt. 1963), Sigma Pi Phi. Republican. Baptist (chmn. bd. trustees 1937; deacon 1961—). Club: Frontiers (Augusta, Ga.). Home: 2347 Fitten St Augusta GA 30904 Office: 1141 12th St Augusta GA 30901

CARTER, JAMES JOHNSTON, lawyer; b. Samson, Ala., Apr. 13, 1913; s. Castilla L. and Mary Ann (Smith) C.; LL.B., Jones Law Sch., 1934, grad. law study, U. Mich., 1940, U. Va., 1941; m. Eva Jane Edwards, Sept. 6, 1947; children—Harold M., David E. (stepsons), James M., Kathy Jane. Admitted to Ala. bar, 1934; atty. Montgomery County Probate Ct., 1935-38; law clk., sec. U.S. Circuit Judge Leon McCord, Montgomery, Ala. and New Orleans, 1938-47; mem. firm Hill, Hill, Stovall, Carter & Franco, Montgomery, 1947—; apptd. spl. judge 15th Jud. Circuit Ala., 1949, 51, 55, 60; pres. Jones Law Sch. 1963-72. Served from pvt. to 1st lt. AUS, 1943-46; spl. agt. criminal investigation div. S.W. Pacific, and pros. officer legal sect. H.Q. Supreme Comdr. for Allied Powers, Tokyo, Japan, 1945-46. Recipient Distinguished Service award U.S. Jr. C. of C. 1937. Mem. (hon.) Circuit Conf. U.S. Circuit and Dist. Judges, 5th Circuit. Fellow Am. Bar Found.; mem. Jud. Conf. Ala., Am., Ala. State Bar (bd. bar examiners 1969—, pres. 1962-63), Montgomery County (pres. 1957), Tenn. (hon.) bar assns., Ala. Law Inst. (mem. council 1970—), Sigma Delta Kappa. Presbyn. (moderator E. Ala. Presbytery). Clubs: Country, Beauvoir. Home: 2602 Wildwood Dr Montgomery AL 36111 Office: Hill Bldg PO Box 116 Montgomery AL 36101

CARTER, JOHN BOYD, JR., investment banker, oil operator; b. Ft. Worth, Oct. 19, 1924; s. John Boyd and Enlie (Corder) C.; student Kemper Mil. Sch., 1941-43, U. Tex., 1943-46, Babson Inst., 1946-47; m. Susie Ann Browne, Feb. 9, 1946 (div. Dec. 1968); children—Catherine Browne, John Mason; m. 2d, Winifred Trimble Runnels, Feb. 23, 1970. Mortgage loan supr. Am. General Investment Corp., 1947; ind. oil operator, 1948-49; sec., treas. Tex. Fund, Inc., 1949-52, mem. investment adv. bd., 1951—; pres. Tex. Fund Research and Mgmt. Assos., 1950-52; ind. oil operator and financial cons., 1952-58; southwestern rep. Lehman Bros., 1959-65, gen. partner, 1965—, mng. dir., 1970—; chmn. exec. com. Capital Nat. Bank; dir. Marine Service Corp.; dir. Am. Marine Corp., Hill and Hill Truck Lines, Inc., Austral Oil Co., Inc., Sea Drilling Corp. Trustee Houston Mus. Fine Arts, Baylor Coll. Medicine; bd. dirs. Houston Symphony Soc. Mem. Ind. Petroleum Assn. Am., Tex. Ind. Producers and Royalty Owners Assn., Sigma Alpha Epsilon. Clubs: Houston Country, St. Charles Hunting, Coronado; River (N.Y.C.). Home: 3682 Willowick Dr Houston TX 77019 Office: 1 Allen Center Houston TX 77002

CARTER, JOHN THOMAS, educator; b. Mantee, Miss., Dec. 16, 1921; s. John Franklin and Mattie (George) C.; student Clarke Meml. Coll., 1940-42; B.S., Miss. State U., 1947; M.S., U. Tenn., 1948; Ed.D., U. Ill., 1954; postgrad. U. Dayton, 1961; m. Frances Larraine Tunnell, Mar. 16, 1946; children—John Wayne, Frankye Nell. Prin. elementary sch., Maben, Miss., 1946-47; supr. on-farm tng. VA, Maben, 1947; prof. agr. Wood Jr. Coll., 1948; prof. Clarke Meml. Coll., 1948-56; prof., dir. student teaching, dir. workshops tchrs. Samford U., 1956—; vis. prof. Hong Kong Bapt. Coll., 1965-66; cons. psychologist, lectr. Stockham Valve and Fitting Co., Thomas Foundries, Birmingham, Ala., 1962, 64—; cons. in field; mem. Ala. Commn. Tchr. Edn. and Profl. Standards, 1963-64, 70-71; dean juvenile lit. Ala. Writers Conclave, 1969; Ala. adviser Student N.E.A., 1963-64. Served with AUS, 1943-45. Decorated Bronze Arrowhead. Mem. Ala. Assn. Student Tching. (pres. 1964-65), Ala. Civil Air Patrol (dir. aerospace edn. 1968—), N.Y., Ala. acads. sci., Nat. Assn. Coll. Tchrs. Edn., Internat. Council Tchr. Edn., Nat. Aerospace Edn. Assn. (nat. bd. dirs.), Phi Delta Kappa, Kappa Phi Kappa. Republican. Baptist. Author: Mike and His Four-Star Goal, 1960; East is West, 1966; Witness in Israel, 1969; Sharing Times Seven, 1971. Contbr. column Guidelines for Daily Living, Ambassador Life; articles mags. Home: 2561 Rocky Ridge Rd Birmingham AL 35243 Office: 800 Lakeshore Dr Birmingham AL 35209

CARTER, JOSEPH EMERSON, engring. firm exec.; b. Birmingham, Ala., Oct. 28, 1920; s. Joseph Emerson and Mildred (Rumph) C.; B.Engring. with honors, Johns Hopkins U., 1950; student U. Ala., 1945, postgrad., 1956, 57; m. Beth Miller, Nov. 24, 1945; children—Joseph Emerson, Beth Ann, Mary Ellen. Structural engr. Harbert Constrn. Corp., Birmingham, Ala., 1957-58; with Rust Engring. Co., Birmingham, 1954-57, 58—, v.p., chief engr., 1968—. Served to capt. USAAF, 1941-45, USAF, 1951-53. Decorated Silver Star, Air medal with two oak leaf clusters. Registered profl. engr., Ala., Okla., Fla., Cal., Wash. Mem. Am. Soc. C.E., Nat. Soc. Profl. Engrs., Am. Inst. Chem. Engrs., Tech. Assn. Pulp and Paper Industry. Home: 3501 Westbury Pl Birmingham AL 35223 Office: PO Box 101 Birmingham AL 35202

CARTER, LAMORE JOSEPH, ednl. adminstr.; b. Carthage, Tex., Apr. 18, 1925; s. Peter and Nancy (Fite) C.; student Wiley Coll., 1946-47; A.B., Fisk U. 1950; M.S., U. Wis., 1952; Ph.D., State U. Ia., 1958; postgrad. U. Chgo., summer 1954, U. Tex., summer 1966, Columbia, summer 1967, Emory U. summer 1970; m. Lena Mae Jones, Aug. 18, 1957; children—Greta Lisa, Kris-Lana. Tchr. Union High Sch., Gallatin, Tenn., 1950-51; asso. prof. edn. and psychology, dir. spl. edn. center Grambling Coll. (La.), 1958-61, asso. dean of coll., 1971—, prof. edn. and psychology, dir. spl. edn. center, 1961-66, adminstr. Instl. Research, 1966-69; dean of faculties Tex. So. U., Houston, 1970-71; research asst. State U. Ia., 1956-58; licensed to practice psychology La. 1965—. Dir. Grambling Motel Internat. Cons. Social Security Adminstrn. Bd. Hearings and Appeals, 1965—, U.S. Office Edn., 1967—, Peace Corps, 1970-72, Commn. Colls., So. Assn. Colls. and Schs., 1970—. Served with AUS, 1943-46. Decorated Bronze Service Star medal; Distinguished prof. psychology Morehouse Coll., Atlanta, 1970; Nat. Edn. Research fellow U.S. Office Edn., 1969-70. Diplomate Am. Bd. Profl. Psychology. Mem. Am. Assn. U. Profs. (chpt. pres. 1960-63), Am., Southwestern, La. psychol. assns., Nat. Council Univ. Research Adminstrs., Assn. for Instl. Research, Am. Ednl. Research Assn., Assn. for Higher Edn., Nat. Soc. for Study Edn., Am. Assn. on Mental Deficiency, N.Y. Acad. Sci., La. Assn. Mental Health, N.E.A., Council Exceptional Children, Internat. Platform Assn., Phi Beta Sigma, Phi Delta Kappa. Democrat. Methodist. Mason (32 deg.). Contbr. articles in field to profl. jours., monographs, books. Home: 110 Richmond Dr Grambling LA 71245

CARTER, LAURIE MAE (MRS. CARSON CARTER), educator; b. Meridian, Miss., Oct. 23, 1903; d. Calvin Columbus and Flossye Bell (Hodges) Clay; B.S., Miss. So. Coll., 1934; M.A., George Peabody Coll., 1940, Ed.S., 1957; summer study U. Wis., 1950-51, Am. U., 1947; Columbia, 1957; doctoral study Peabody Coll., 1958-59; summer study Moreno Inst., 1959, 60, certificate of tng. in psychodrama, group psychotherapy and sociometry, dir. psychodrama, group psychotherapy in edn., 1961; m. Carson A. Carter, June 23, 1925. Tchr. Oakland Heights Elementary Sch., Meridian, Miss., 1922-34, prin., 1934—; instr. Miss. So. Coll., summer, 1941, 50, Copiah Lincoln Jr. Coll. summer, 1944; counselor Meridian Pub. Schs., 1962-64; asso. dean students Doane Coll., Crete Neb., 1964-65; pvt. personal and ednl. counselor, Meridian, Miss., 1965—; lectr. edn. and mental health. Sec. bd. dirs. Lauderdale County Cancer Assn.; bd. dirs. Miss. Mental Health Assn., 1963-65. Mem. Miss. Edn. Assn. (pres. 1948, dir. profl. relations 5th congl. dist. 1938-62, dir. 1960-64), Am. Assn. U. Women (area rep. legislative com. 1967-71, area rep. Meridian br.) N.E.A., Meridian Bus. and Profl. Women's Club (pres. 1962-63; chmn. personal devel. com. 1967-68, 71-72, chmn. program. com., named one of 12 outstanding bus. women 1971, chmn. young career woman's com. 1972-73), Meridian League Women Voters (pres. 1963-64), Internat. Platform Assn., Miss., Lauderdale County mental health assns., Miss. Women's Cabinet of Pub. Affairs (pres. 1948-49), Nat., Miss., Meridian ret. tchrs. assns., Delta Kappa Gamma (chmn. research com. 1968-69). Club: Literary Corner. Author articles in field. Home: 3211 24th Av Meridian MS 39301

CARTER, LEVONNE RAILEY, dentist; b. Tompkinsville, Ky., May 19, 1925; s. Earl Railey and Ovy Gladys (Pickerell) C.; B.S., Western Ky. State U., 1951; D.M.D., U. Louisville, 1955; m. Hazel Idell Miller, Feb. 7, 1947; children—Vondell, Barry. Intern, Fla. State Hosp., 1955-56; gen. practice dentistry, Ft. Lauderdale, Fla., 1956—. Mem. exec. council Henry, Glades and Broward County Tb Assn., 1970—, trustee, 1971—. Served with USNR, 1943-46. Decorated Purple Heart. Mem. Ft. Lauderdale C. of C., Am., Fla., Atlantic Coast, Broward County (pres. elect) dental assns. Baptist (deacon). Kiwanian. Club: Metropolitan Dinner (Ft. Lauderdale). Home: 181 Nurmi Dr Fort Lauderdale FL 33301 Office: 305 S Andrews Av Fort Lauderdale FL 33301

CARTER, MILTON PEARSON, educator; b. Philadelphia, Miss., Dec. 3, 1910; s. Jessie Martin and Minnie (Crews) C.; A.A., E. Central Jr. Coll., 1935; B.S., Miss. State Coll., 1938; M.Ed., Miss. State U., 1951; m. Mildred Elizabeth Thetford, Feb. 25, 1939; children—Cynthia E. (Mrs. Joe E. Turner), Ronald Pearson. Tchr. vocational agr. Whiffield High Sch., Ovett, Miss., 1938-42, Jones County Agrl. High Sch., Ellisville, Miss., 1942-50; head agr. dept. Jones County Jr. Coll., Ellisville, Miss., 1951-63; dir. vocational-tech. edn. Jones County Jr. Coll., 1964—. Chmn. Long-Range Planning Com., Ellisville, Miss., 1957-69; mem. Jones County Long-Range Planning Com.; mem. Miss. Ancillary Manpower Tng. Com., 1972, Miss. Manpower Devel. Adv. Com. Law Enforcement Edn., 1972. Mem. Jones County Democratic Exec. Com., 1956-68, Ellisville Democratic Exec. Com., 1961-69. Chmn. bd. dirs. S.E. Miss. Indsl. Devel. Council, 1968-70. Bd. dirs. So. Miss. Planning and Devel. Dist. Mem. Miss. Jr. Coll. Agr. Tchrs. Assn. (pres. 1958-60), Jones County Tchrs. Assn. (pres. 1958-59), C. of C. (past pres.). Baptist. Mason, Rotarian (past pres.). Home: 1204 Augusta Rd Ellisville MS 39437

CARTER, NATHANIEL ONIS, judge; b. Vidalia, Ga., Feb. 15, 1926; s. Nathaniel Onis and Juel Judith (Darby) C.; student Princeton, 1945, Howard Coll., 1945, U. S.C., 1945-48; LL.B., Mercer U., 1949; m. Jeanne Marie Cone, Dec. 22, 1946; children—Gale (Mrs. Charles Goldenberg), Brenda J., Natalie Michelle. Admitted to Ga. bar, 1949, Middle Jud. bar, 1949; practice law, Vidalia, 1949—; judge Recorder's Ct., City of Vidalia 1951—. Dir. 1st Nat. Bank & Trust Co., Vidalia, United Communications, Inc., Vidalia; pres., dir. Beverage Discount, Inc., Vidalia, 1970—. Served with USNR, 1943-46; PTO. Elk, Moose. Club: Vidalia Country. Home: 101 Darby Circle Vidalia GA 30474 Office: 800 E 1st St Vidalia GA 30474

CARTER, OLIVER MARTIN, JR., steel co. exec.; b. Murfreesboro, Ark., Sept. 30, 1920; s. Ollie Martin and Florence Lesta (Owens) C.; A.A., U. Fla., B.S. with honors, U. Fla., 1942; m. Irene Elizabeth Brosius, Oct. 22, 1949; children—Irene B., Oliver Martin III, Robert B. Product specialist Armco Steel Corp., Houston, 1946-49, Southwestern div. engr., 1949-54, sales mgr., Memphis, 1954-68, S.W. region sales mgr., Houston, 1968—; dir. Hagan Mfg. Co., Memphis. Served to maj. C.E., AUS, 1942-46. Fellow Am. Soc. C.E. (dist. council pres. 1963-64, sect. pres. 1961-62), Tau Beta Pi, Sigma Tau. Mason; mem. Order Eastern Star. Clubs: Petroleum, Lakeside Country (Houston). Home: 12410 Broken Bough St Houston TX 77024 Office: 1455 W Loop St S Houston TX 77027

CARTER, OTHA BURNETTE, supt. schs.; b. Gordo, Ala., Nov. 28, 1907; s. Earnest Atlas and Cora Bell (Free) C.; B.S., Auburn U., 1929; M.A., U. Ala., 1941; m. Sara Flewellen, Aug. 23, 1936; children—Sarah S. (Mrs. Carl Parrish), Otha Burnette, Louise F., Mary E. Coach, Louisville High Sch., 1929-34; tchr., Eufaula (Ala.) High Sch., 1934-41, prin., 1941-44, supt., 1944—. Mem. State Retirement Bd. Mem. Ala. Edn. Assn. (pres. 1965-66), Pi Kappa Phi. Baptist (chmn. bd. deacons 1935-71). Kiwanian. Club: Eufaula Country. Home: 343 N Randolph Av Eufaula AL 36027 Office: PO Box 270 Eufaula AL 36027

CARTER, ROBERT LEON, physician; b. Meansville, Ga., Aug. 14, 1895; s. Robert Reid and Hattie Julia (Aldredge) C.; student U. Ga., 1912-13; M.D., Emory U., 1917; postgrad. U. Paris, 1919; m. Christine Lowe, Dec. 17, 1938; children—Evangeline (Mrs. Raymond C. Carter), Robert C. Intern, Riverside Hosp., N.Y.C., 1917; resident surgeon Ga. Bapt. Hosp., 1919-20; gen. practice medicine, Thomaston, Ga., 1920-67; mem. staff Upson County Hosp., Thomaston. Served with M.C., AUS, 1917-19. Mem. A.M.A., Ga. Med. Assn., Upson Med. Soc., Upson Hist. Soc. (pres. 1969-72), Thomaston C. of C. Democrat. Methodist. Kiwanian. Mason. Author weekly column Thomaston Times, 1968—. Home: 700 Andrews Dr Thomaston GA 30286

CARTER, ROBERT LEON, foundry exec.; b. Memphis, June 26, 1926; s. Harry Edward and Dollie Inez (Shearon) C.; B.S., Memphis State U., 1957; m. Dorothy Adrion, Feb. 16, 1966. Staff accountant Seidman & Seidman, C.P.A.'s, Memphis, 1957-62; controller Weis Butane Gas Cos., West Memphis, Ark., 1962-66; controller Kast Metals Corp., and Hica Corp., Shreveport, La., 1966-69, sec.-treas., 1969—, dir., 1969—. Active Jr. Achievement. Trustee, Mc Chesney, Miller, Dimond Trusts, Shreveport, La. Served with USAF, 1950-54. Mem. Am. Inst. C.P.A.'s, Tenn., Memphis socs. C.P.A.'s, Steel Founder Soc., Nat. Assn. Accountants, Shreveport C. of C., Delta Sigma Pi. Baptist. Mason. Clubs: East Ridge Country, Metropolitan Dinner, Little Theater (Shreveport). Home: 9523 Hollyoak St Shreveport LA 71108 Office: PO Box 6611M Shreveport LA 71106

CARTER, ROLAND WHITE, mineral co. exec.; b. South Bend, Ind., Nov. 22, 1919; s. Roy Gee and Hazel (White) C.; student Purdue U. 1937-38; B.S. with distinction, U. Mich., 1941, postgrad., 1940-41; m. Helen Sue Smith, Feb. 20, 1954; 1 dau., Suzy Jean; children (by previous marriage)—Thomas M., William M., Stephen W. Party chief Seismograph Service Corp., Tulsa, 1941-48; geophysicist Union Producing Co., Shreveport, 1948-63, mgr. producing property acquisition, 1965-68; corporate planning asso. United Gas Corp., Shreveport, 1963-65; vice pres. exploration Freeport Oil Co. div. Freeport Minerals Co., New Orleans, 1968—. Mem. Soc. Exploration Geophysicists (Silver certificate 1969), Am. Assn. Petroleum Geologists, Soc. Petroleum Engrs., Phi Beta Kappa, Sigma Xi. Home: 6710 Canal Blvd New Orleans LA 70124 Office: PO Box 52349 New Orleans LA 70150

CARTER, ROY R., JR., banker; b. Fayetteville, Tenn., Nov. 13, 1915; s. Roy R. and Fannie Neil (Lamb) C.; student Marion County Bus. Sch., 1936; m. Marian Chase Woodfin, Nov. 24, 1937; children—Margaret (Mrs. C. Kenneth Adams), Katherine (Mrs. Rod. P. Whittington). With First Nat. Bank, South Pittsburg, Tenn., 1936—, pres., 1963—; dir. B.C.W. Realty Co.; sr. partner Carter & Wilson Ins. Agy.; dir. Hamilton Bancshares, Inc., Chattanooga. Finance commr. South Pittsburg, 1956-57; chmn. South Pittsburg Planning Commn., 1964-68. Bd. dirs. Marion County Tb Assn.; trustee South Pittsburg Meml. Hosp., Wonder Cave. Mem. C. of C. (pres. 1966-67). Democrat. Methodist (trustee). Clubs: Sequatchie Valley Golf and Country. Lion. Editorial bd. Golfdom, 1968-69. Home: 701 Magnolia Ave South Pittsburg TN 37380 Office: 406 Cedar Av South Pittsburg TN 37380

CARTER, SYLVIA JOAN WARNER (MRS. ALBERT J. CARTER), home economist; b. Dallas, June 30, 1929; d. Steven S. and Mildred (Mason) Warner; B.S., La. State U., 1951; m. Albert J. Carter, Mar. 24, 1951; children—A. Jay, Melody B. Dietary aide St. Patrick's Hosp., Lake Charles, La., 1961; home economist Gulf States Utilities Co., Lake Charles, 1962-66; instr. in Sch. food service Sowela Tech. Inst., Lake Charles, 1967-68; asst. home demonstration agt. Calcasieu parish, 1968—. Dir. Glamorama—Something for Every Woman, KPLC-TV, Lake Charles, 1955-66. Mem. Lake Charles Jr. League, 1965—. Mem. Am., La. home econs. assns., La. Home Economists in Bus., Lake Charles Home Economists in Homemaking, Am. Assn. U. Women, A.I.A. Aux., Young Men's Bus. Club Aux. (past pres.), Lake Charles Chi Omega Alumnae Assn. Home: 4304 Sarver St Lake Charles LA 70601

CARTER, THOMAS D., sch. adminstr.; b. Oglesby, Tex., Sept. 7, 1931; s. O. Dan and Margrette (Baker) C.; student Tex. A. and I. Coll., 1948-49, Sam Houston State Coll., 1949-51, Tenn. Poly. Inst., 1951; B.A., Baylor U., 1956; M. Ed., U. Tex. at Austin, 1959, Ph.D., 1966; m. Jo Ann Respess, Aug. 31, 1952; children—Tommy Dan, Sheree. Tchr. English David Crockett High Sch., Conroe, Tex., 1956-58; intern prin. William B. Travis High Sch., Austin, 1959 tchr. English Brazosport High Sch., Freeport, Tex., 1959-60; supr., counselor pub. schs., Gonzales County, Tex., 1960-61; curriculum coordinator, Beeville, Tex., 1961-64; intern supt. schs., League City, Tex., 1965; teaching asst. U. Tex. at Austin, 1965-66; asst. supt. Alamo Heights Ind. Sch. Dist., San Antonio, 1966-71; dep. supt. research and devel. Goose Creek Consol. Sch. Dist., Baytown, Tex., 1971-72; supt. Eanes Ind. Sch. Dist., Austin, Tex., 1972—. Dir. Bee County (Tex.) Assn. Retarded Children, 1961-63; v.p. Council Exceptional Children, Corpus Christi, 1962-63; mem. planning com. Bee County Jr. Coll., 1963. Served with USAF, 1951-54. Mem. N.E.A. (membership chmn. 1962-63), Tex. Elementary Prins. and Suprs. Assn. (membership chmn. 1961-63), Tex. Assn. Instructional Suprs., So. Assn. Colls. and Schs. (chmn. program studies 1962-69), Phi Delta Kappa. Methodist (mem. bd.). Kiwanian (sec. 1961-63), Rotarian (chmn. crippled children com. 1968-69). Contbr. articles profl. jours. Home: 101-C Blue Ridge Terrace Austin TX 78746

CARTER, THOMAS SMITH, JR., bus. exec.; b. Dallas, June 6, 1921; s. Thomas Smith and Mattie L. (Dowell) C.; B.S. in Civil Engring., So. Meth. U., 1944; m. Janet R. Hostetter, July 3, 1946; children—Janet Diane, Susan Jean, Charles T., Carol Ruth. With M.-K.-T. R.R., 1941-44, 46-66, successively asst. engr., St. Louis, asst. dist. engr., Franklin, Mo., dist. engr., Parsons, Kan., asst. chief engr., St. Louis, chief engr., St. Louis and Dallas, 1946-61, v.p. operations, Dallas, 1961-66; v.p. Kansas City So. Ry. Co., La. & Ark. Ry. Co., Shreveport, La., from 1966; now with Servitron Inc., Shreveport. Served with C.E., AUS, 1944-46. Registered profl. engr., Ark., La., Mo., Kan., Okla., Tex. Fellow Am. Soc. C.E.; mem. Am. Ry. Engring. Assn., Nat. Soc. Profl. Engrs., Alpha Tau Omega, Chi Epsilon. Presbyn. Club: Shreveport Country. Home: 8614 W Wilderness Way Shreveport LA 71106 Office: 4601 Blanchard Rd Shreveport LA 71107

CARTER, TIM LEE, physician, congressman; b. Tompkinsville, Ky., Sept. 2, 1910; s. James Clark and Idru (Tucker) C.; A.B., Western Ky. University, 1934; M.D., U. Tenn., 1937; m. Kathleen Bradshaw, Nov. 13, 1931; 1 son, Billy Starr. Gen. practice medicine, Tompkinsville, 1937—; mem. 89th to 92d Congress, 5th Ky. Dist., mem. interstate and fgn. commerce com. Dir. Deposit Bank of Monroe County, Tompkinsville. Mem. staff Monroe County War Meml. Hosp. Mem. Pres.'s Commn. on Marihuana and Drug Abuse. Served to capt., inf. AUS, World War II. Decorated Combat Med. Badge, Bronze Star. Mem. Am., Ky. med. assns., Am., Ky. acads. gen. practice, Am. Legion, V.F.W., Alpha Omega Alpha. Republican. Mason (32 deg., Shriner). Home: 701 N Main St Tompkinsville KY 42167 Office: Longworth Office Bldg Washington DC 20515

CARTER, VERNON LEE, JR., govt. ofcl.; b. Wadley, Ala., Oct. 6, 1934; s. Vernon Lee and Mary Ruth (Moon) C.; D.V.M., Auburn U., 1958; M.S., Ohio State U., 1966; m. Elizabeth Mary Kohring, Sept. 4, 1965. Vet. clinician Aeromed. Research Lab., Holloman AFB, N.M., 1960-64; toxicologist Aerospace Med. Research Lab., Wright-Patterson AFB, O., 1966-70; chief toxicology sect. NASA Manned Spacecraft Center, Houston, 1970—. Served to lt. col. USAF, 1958—. Decorated Air Force Commendation medal. Diplomate Am. Bd. Vet. Toxicology. Fellow Am. Coll. Vet. Toxicology; mem. Am. Vet. Med. Assn., Soc. Toxicology, Omega Tau Sigma, Phi Kappa Phi. Home: 1511 Davon Lane Houston TX 77058 Office: NASA MSC DB5 Houston TX 77058

CARTER, WATT, state ofcl.; b. Sarepta, Miss., Jan. 25, 1911; s. John Wesley and Luna (Phillips) C.; B.S., Miss State U., 1938; m. Katie Will Edmondson, Aug. 13, 1939; children—Joe Jon, Phillip Conner. Tchr., Sarepta, 1934, prin., tchr., 1935-36; agr. tchr. Montpelier (Miss.) High Sch., 1938; tchr. agr. Vardaman (Miss.) High Sch., 1939-58, prin., 1959-63; dir. vocational tng. Miss. State Penitentiary, 1964-67; Miss. land commr., Jackson, 1968—. Mason. Home: 109 Old Canton Hill Dr Jackson MS 39211 Office: State Office Bldg Jackson MS 39205

CARTER, WILBUR LEE, JR., ins. co. exec.; b. Greensboro, N.C., Jan. 23, 1922; s. Wilbur Lee and Marie Estelle (Cranford) C.; B.S., Davidson Coll., 1943; m. Martha Virginia Sauvain, Dec. 16, 1943; children—Judith Marie, Carolyn (Mrs. David E. Yawars), Wilbur Lee III. Vice pres. So. Life Ins. Co., Greensboro, 1946-64, pres., 1964—; dir. Jefferson Standard Life Ins. Co., Greensboro, Jefferson-Pilot Corp., Greensboro, N.C. Nat. Bank, NCNB Corp. Mem. United Community Services for Greater Greensboro, 1962—. Bd. dirs. Wesley Long Community Hosp., L. Richardson Hosp., Excellence Fund of U. N.C. at Greensboro, N.C. Ins. Edn. Found. Served as capt. AUS, 1943-46; ETO. C.L.U. Mem. Greensboro Investors, Inc. (Pres.), Greensboro Cotillion, Greensboro Sports Council, Greensboro Life Underwriters. Presbyn. (elder). Clubs: Greensboro Country; Country of North Carolina (Pinehurst); Sedgefield Hunt (joint master 1963—) (Greensboro). Home: 1012 Country Club Dr Greensboro NC 27408 Office: 330 S Green St Greensboro NC 27402

CARTER, WILLIAM DOUGLAS, geologist; b. Keene, N.H., Apr. 24, 1926; s. William Ambrose and Laura (Tuckerman) C.; A.B., Dartmouth, 1949; postgrad. Johns Hopkins, 1951; m. Mary Shannon, Sept. 10, 1950; children—Cindy Jean, Judy Lynn, Katherine Ann, William Douglas. With U.S. Geol. Survey, Alaska, summers 1948-50; project geologist Colo. Plateau Uranium, Grand Junction, 1951-57; copper deposit geologist, trainer Chilean geologists U.S. A.I.D., Chile, 1957-62, Silica deposits Appalachian Region, 1962-65, commodity geologist Washington, 1965; chief mineral and land resources working group Earth Resources Observation Systems Program, U.S. Dept. of Interior, 1965-72, asst. mgr. applications research, 1972—. Served with USAAF, 1944-45. Fellow Geol. Soc. Am.; mem Am. Assn. Petroleum Geologists, Soc. Econ. Geology, Am Soc. Photogrammetry, Geol. Soc. Washington (sec. 1969). Home: 2404 Paddock Lane Reston VA 22070 Office: US Geol Survey Washington DC 20242

CARTER, WILLIAM EUGENE, editor; b. Jonesville, Va., Nov. 16, 1905; s. Joel Miles and Mary (Cass) Carter; student Emory and Henry Coll., 1923-26, U. Chattanooga, 1932-33; m. Delphia Tabb, Nov. 30, 1964; children by previous marriage—Penelope (Mrs. Lee R. Ross), Mary Patrica. Prin., Rocky Point (N.C.) Sch., 1926-30; tchr. Chattanooga city schs., 1930-40; copy editor Chattanooga Times, 1940-43, news editor, 1943-61, Sunday editor, 1961—. Bd. dirs. Chattanooga Opera Assn., 1964-68, Chattanooga Symphony, 1957-67. Mem. Chattanooga Newspaper Guild (pres. 1965-67). Episcopalian. Club: Rivermont Golf and Country (Chattanooga). Home: Continental Apts Chattanooga TN 37405 Office: 117 E 10th St Chattanooga TN 37401

CARTER, WILLIAM HEDDING, III, newspaper editor; b. New Orleans, Apr. 7, 1935; s. William Hedding and Betty Brunhilde (Werlein) C.; student Phillips Exeter Acad., 1949-51; B.A. summa cum laude, Princeton U., 1957; postgrad. (Nieman fellow) Harvard U., 1965-66; m. Margaret Ainsworth Wolfe, June 21, 1957; children—Catherine Ainsworth, Elizabeth Fearn, William Hedding IV, Margaret Lorraine. Reporter, Delta Democrat-Times, Greenville, Miss., 1959-62, mng. editor, 1962-65, editor, asso. pub., 1965—; dir. Civic Communications Corp., Jackson, Miss. Juror, Pulitzer Prize Awards Com., 1971, 72. Mem. exec. com. So. Regional Council; mem. Miss. adv. com. U.S. Commn. on Civil Rights. Mem. rules reform commn. Nat. Democratic Com.; co-chmn. Young Dems. of Miss., 1965-68; co-chmn. Loyalist Dems. delegation Nat. Dem. Conv., 1968; mem. bd. Voter Edn. Projects. Bd. dirs. Mary Holmes Coll., Miss. Action for Progress, Inst. of Politics, New Orleans, Robert F. Kennedy Meml.; trustee 20th Century Fund, N.Y.C. Served to 2d lt. USMCR, 1957-59. Recipient Urban Service award Office Econ. Opportunity, 1967, Appley Youth Leadership award Am. Mgmt. Assn., 1968, Silver Em award U. Miss., 1968. Mem. Miss. Press Assn., Miss. Council on Human Relations (R.F. Kennedy award), Am. Council Young Polit. Leaders (dir.), Atlantic Assn. Young Polit. Leaders (exec. com.), Atlantic Council (dir.), Com. for Pub. Justice. L.Q.C. Lamar Soc. (dir.), Sigma Delta Chi (award for editorial writing 1961). Episcopalian. Author: The South Strikes Back, 1959; contbr. to We Dissent, 1963, Race and the News Media, 1967. Home: 1203 Kirk Circle Greenville MS 38701 Office: Delta Democrat-Times North Broadway Extended Greenville MS 38701

CARTER, WILMOTH ANNETTE, educator; b. Reidsville, N.C.; d. W. Percy and Margaret (Milner) Carter; A.B., Shaw U., 1937; M.A., Atlanta U., 1942; Ph.D., U. Chgo., 1959. Chmn. dept. sociology So. Univ. in New Orleans, 1963-64; research asso. race relations U. Mich., 1964-65, Tuskegee Inst., 1965-66; mem. faculty Shaw U., Raleigh, N.C., 1950-63, 66—, prof. sociology, 1959—, ednl. devel. officer, 1971—. Rosenwald fellow, 1947-48; Danforth fellow, 1957-59. Mem. Am. Assn. U. Profs., Am. Assn. U. Women, Am. Civil Liberties Union, Am., So. sociol. assns., Voters League, Alpha Kappa Delta. Author: Urban Negro in the South, 1961; New Negro of the South, 1967; Shaw's Universe: A Monument to Educational Innovation, 1971. Home: 1400 E Davie St Raleigh NC 27610

CARTWRIGHT, JOHN DOUGLAS, banker; b. Greeneville, Tenn., Sept. 13, 1909; s. Oatho A. and Bertha L. (Solomon) C.; student Perry Bus. Coll., 1933-34, Tusculum Coll., Greeneville, evenings 1953-58, Am. Inst. Banking, 1959-60, E. Tenn. State U., 1969; m. Nell M. Luttrell, Aug. 31, 1930. With 1st Nat. Bank, Greeneville, 1929—, head bookkeeper, 1934-37, asst. cashier, 1937-46, auditor, 1946-48, cashier, 1948-59, v.p., cashier, 1959-62, v.p., asst. trust officer, 1962-68, sr. v.p., trust officer, 1968—, also dir. Scoutmaster Sequoia council Boy Scouts Am., 1936-42, neighborhood commr., 1947-48. Served with AUS, 1943-45; ETO. Decorated Bronze Star medal; named Exchangite of Year, Greeneville, 1971. Mem. V.F.W., Am. Legion, Bankers Inst. (dir. Holston chpt.). Methodist (past mem. ofcl. bd., supt. ch. sch.). Elk, (trustee 1953), Mason (Shriner). Club: Exchange (pres. Greeneville 1948). Home: 303 Hermitage Dr Greeneville TN 37743 Office: 109 Main St Greeneville TN 37743

CARTWRIGHT, OSCAR LING, museum curator; b. Sharpsville, Pa., Apr. 12, 1900; s. William Robert and Lydia Blanche (McDowell) C.; B.S., Allegheny Coll., 1923; M.Sc., Ohio State U., 1925; m. Sara Marie Richbourg, Dec. 18, 1928. Research entomologist S.C. Agr. Expt. Sta., 1925-45, 47; sanitarian USPHS, 1945-46; asso. curator div. insects U.S. Nat. Mus., Smithsonian Instn., 1948-63, curator coleoptera, dept. entomology, 1963-70, emeritus entomologist, 1970—; spl. taxonomic research in Scarabaeidae; field studies in Costa Rica, 1951, El Salvador, 1958, Tex., 1951, Ariz., 1956, Fla., 1959, Andros, Bahamas, 1966. Recipient Smithsonian Service award, 1954; NSF grant, 1963. Fellow Entomol. Soc. Am.; mem. Entomol. Soc. Washington, Assn. Tropical Biology, Biol. Soc. Washington, Soc. Systematic Zoologists, A.A.A.S., Sigma Xi, Alpha Chi Rho, Phi Beta Phi, Gamma Alpha. Club: Cosmos (Washington). Author numerous reports and articles. Home: 2110 Greenwich St Falls Church VA 22043 Office: Dept Entomology US Nat Mus Washington DC 20560

CARUBBI, ANGELO JOSEPH, JR., lawyer; b. Galveston, Tex., Jan. 1, 1932; s. Angelo Joseph and Madeline (La Barbera) C.; Ph.B. in Commerce, U. Notre Dame, 1952 LL.B., U. Tex., 1968 children—Kathy, Richard, Thomas, Kelly, Amy. Admitted to Tex. bar, 1957; asso. Gordon, Gordon & Buzzard, Pampa, 1958-60; sr. partner Carubbi, Warner & Jeter, Pampa, 1960-66; corp. ct. judge City of Pampa, 1960-62; exec. asst. to Atty. Gen. of Tex., 1966-68; asso. Dyche, Wheat, Thornton & Wright, Houston, 1969-70; partner Dyche, Wright, Sullivan, Bailey & King, 1971—. Corporate sec. H & C Inc., Houston, 1969—. Bd. dirs. Gonzales Warm Springs Found., Gonzales, Tex., Tex. Jr. C. of C. Found., Grand Prairie Tex. Served with AUS, 1962-64. Recipient Distinguished Service award Pampa Jr. C. of C., 1966, named Outstanding Young Man in Community, 1966. Mem. Houston Bar Assn., State Bar of Tex., Tex. Jr. C. of C. (pres. 1965-66). U.S. Jr. C. of C. (legal counsel 1967-68), Phi Alpha Delta, Phi Kappa Theta. K.C. Home: 2128 Sul Ross Houston TX 77006 Office: Mellie Esperson Bldg Houston TX 77002

CARUTHERS, PRESTON C., constrn. co. exec.; b. Covington, Okla.; ed. George Washington U. Pres. constrn. firm in No. Va.; dir. 1st Va. Bank. Former mem. Arlington (Va.) Planning Commn.; former chmn. Arlington County Sch. Bd; mem. Va. Bd. Edn., 1970—, pres., 1971—. Mem. Arlington C. of C. (past pres.). Address: care Virginia Board of Education 9th St Office Bldg Richmond VA 23216*

CARVER, JOHN ALFRED, JR., govt. ofcl.; b. Preston, Ida., Apr. 24, 1918; s. John Alfred and La Verne (Olson) C.; A.B., Brigham Young U., 1939; LL.B., Georgetown U., 1947; m. Ruth Patricia O'Connor, June 7, 1942; children—John A. III, Craig, Candace Elaine. With various depts. U.S. Govt., 1940-47; admitted to Ida. and D.C. bars, 1946; asst. atty. gen. Ida., 1947-48; practice of law, Boise, 1948-56; administrv. asst. to U.S. Senator Church, 1957-61; asst. sec. interior pub. land mgmt., 1961-64, under sec. of interior, 1964-66; commr. Fed. Power Commn., 1966—. Served with USAAF, 1943-46. Mem. Am., Fed., Ida., D.C. bar assns. Home: 4421 25th St N Arlington VA 22207 Office: GAO Bldg 441 G St NW Washington DC 20426

CARWILE, ATWOOD SMITH, banker; b. Gladys, Va., Sept. 27, 1925; s. Walter Ray and Mary Lucile (Smith) C.; grad. high sch.; M. Josephine Elaine Church, Apr. 5, 1947; children—Timothy C., William A. With Campbell County Bank, Rustburg, Va., 1946-63, asst. cashier, 1948-54, cashier, 1954-60, v.p., 1960-63; v.p. Fidelity Nat. Bank, Lynchburg, Va., 1963-70, sr. v.p., 1970—. Mem. Campbell County Redistricting Commn., 1967. Mem. Campbell County Sch. Bd., 1968—. Served with USNR, 1944-46. Methodist (chmn. bd. 1967-69). Mason, Lion. Club: Falling River Country (Appomattox, Va.). Home: Route 1 Box 61 Rustburg VA 22488 Office: 901 Main St Lynchburg VA 24505

CASA, VICTORIO, soccer player; b., 1944; m. 2 children. Profl. soccer player since age 16; mem. San Lorenzo (Argentina) soccer team in 1965 when lost right arm in freak shooting, returned to playing 22 days later; mem. Washington Whips club, 1968, Washington Darts, 1971—. Address: care Washington Darts 4832 MacArthur Blvd NW Washington DC 20007

CASADA, JAMES HUBERT, agrl. engr.; b. Pulaski, Ky., Sept. 24, 1931; s. Lewis Walter and Laura Gertrude (Vaught) C.; B.S., U. Ky., 1960, M.S., 1966; m. Emma Jean Simpson, Sept. 18, 1955; children—Rhonda Sue, Mark Edwin, Alan Thomas. Instr., U. Ky., Lexington, 1960-61, research specialist, 1967—; agrl. research engr. tobacco investigations Agrl. Research Service, Dept. Agr., Lexington, 1961-67. Served with USAF, 1953-57. Registered profl. engr., Ky. Mem. Am. Soc. Agrl. Engrs., Ky. Sect. Agrl. Engrs., Sigma Xi, Alpha Zeta. Baptist (deacon). Home: 3473 Dixiana Dr Lexington KY 40502

CASADAY, THOMAS CALVIN, county ofcl.; b. Milstead, Ala., Feb. 3, 1925; s. Clifton F. and Gussie L. (Davis) C.; B.S., Auburn U., 1949, M.S., 1960; postgrad. U. Ark., 1953, Colo. State U., 1967; m. Vernie D. Miller, Nov. 22, 1958; children—Tommy, Warren. Asst. county agt., Rockford, Ala., 1949-55; asst. county agt. farm and home devel., Enterprise, Ala., 1955-61; specialist Rural Resource Devel., Ozark, Ala., 1961-63; county extension chmn. Coffee County, Enterprise, 1963—. Bd. dirs. Coffee County 4-H Found. Served with AUS, 1943-46. Winner state, regional and nat. news writing program sponsored by Nat. County Agts. Assn. Presbyn. (elder). Lion (dir. Enterprise club, 1966-67, zone chmn. 1968-69, cabinet sec. dist. 34-G, 1970-71, dist. gov. dist. 34-G 1971-72). Home: 103 Bay St Enterprise AL 36330 Office: Courthouse Enterprise AL 36330

CASE, GEORGE MILTON, state legislator; b. Canton, Miss., July 5, 1934; s. Willie and Mamie (Smith) C.; B.A., U. Miss., 1955, LL.B., 1956. Admitted to Miss. bar, 1956; partner Case & Montgomery, Canton, Miss., 1956—; mem. Miss. Ho. of Reps., 1960-64, 64-68, 68—; atty. towns Ridgeland, 1960, 65, Miss., Madison County sch. dist.,1959—. Trustee Madison County Library Commn., 1965—; mem. Miss. Medicaid Commn. Served to 1st lt.with AUS, 1957-59. Mem. Omicron Delta Kappa, Phi Delta Phi. Mason (Shriner), Elk, K.P., Lion. Home: Green Acres Subdivision Canton MS 39046 Office: 232 W Pearce St Canton MS 39046

CASE, W(ARD) R(OLAND), JR., corp. exec.; b. Jamestown, Tenn., Oct. 31, 1918; s. Ward Roland and Mollie (Albertson) C.; LL.B., Cumberland U., Lebanon, Tenn., 1940; m. Sarah Helen Whitefield, July 26, 1940; children—Ward Roland III, John Howard. Title examiner, Tenn. Valley Authority, Paris, Tenn., 1941-42; admitted to Tenn. bar, 1940, pvt. practice, Jamestown, Tenn., 1945-57; legal counsel Magnet Cove Barium Corp., Houston, 1957-65, sec., 1959-65; v.p. internat. dept., 1965-66; exec. v.p. Dresser Magcobar div. Dresser Industries, Inc., Houston, 1966-69, v.p. planning and adminstrn. Petroleum and Minerals Group, 1969—. Chmn. bd. Union Bank, Jamestown, Tenn., 1949-59. Served with AUS, 1942-45. Mem. Bar Assn. Tenn., Am. Bar Assn. Republican. Mem. Ch. of Christ. Mason (Shriner). Home: 5014 Carew St Houston TX 77035 Office: 3133 Buffalo Speedway Houston TX 77005

CASEY, ALBERT E(UGENE), pathologist; b. N.Y.C., Mar. 13, 1903; s. Eugene Joseph and Anna Alma (Powell) C.; A.B., Spring Hill Coll., 1922 M.D., St. Louis U., 1927; m. Bourdon Eason Veazey, Apr. 19, 1928; children—Anna Elizabeth (Mrs. Clement Fisher Kent, Jr.), Bourdon Irene (Mrs. Charles Lee Payne), Albert Eugene; m. 2d, Joanne Gunn, Nov. 8, 1952; 1 son, Paul Travis. Intern St. Louis U. Hosp., 1926-27; asst. anatomy St. Louis U., 1924-27, asso. prof. pathology, 1936-38; asst. and asso. in pathology and bacteriology Rockefeller Inst., 1927-34; asso. prof. pathology U. Va., 1934-36; sr. asst. prof. pathology and bacteriology La. State U., 1938-42; sr. vis. pathologist Charity Hosp. of La., New Orleans, 1938-42; pathologist, dir. labs. Birmingham Bapt. Hosps., 1942-72, pres. staff 1956, chmn. exec. com., 1958; prof. pathology U.Ala., 1953—, dir. Meml. Inst. of Pathology, 1961—; cons. pathologist Childrens Hosp., pres. staff,

1947; cons. pathologist Univ. Hosp., VA Hosp., Longview Hosp., Hillcrest Hosp., Peoples Hosp., Salvation Army, Eye Found., Jefferson County San., So. Research Inst.; field epidemiologist Nat. Found. Infantile Paralysis, 1941-42, 45-50. Bd. dirs. Blue Cross, Blue Shield of Ala., 1957-60. Diplomate Am. Bd. Pathology. Mem. Coll. Am. Pathologists (chmn. S.E. regional com. 1954-57), Ala. Assn. Pathologists (pres. 1947), Soc. Exptl. Biology and Medicine (council 1941-43), Am. Soc. Clin. Pathology, (counselor 1947-50), Am. Soc. Exptl. Pathology, Am. Inst. Chemists, Internat. Acad. Pathology, Internat. Cancer Congress, Am. Soc. Phys. Anthropology, Am. Assn. Anatomists, Am. Assn. Cancer Research, N.Y. Acad. Sci., A.A.A.S., Am. Assn. Blood Banks (Ala. rep. 1959-67), Am. Assn. Pathology and Bacteriology, Am. Pub. Health Assn., Am., So. (chmn. sect. pathology 1955-56) med. assns., Miss. Geneal. and Hist. Soc. (hon.), Am. Irish Hist. Soc. (v.p., life member), Sigma Xi, Phi Beta Pi, Alpha Omega Alpha. Democrat. Baptist. Mason (32 deg.). Clubs: Clinical, The Club, Vestavia Country, Exchange (Birmingham). Author: (with others) Amite County, Miss. History, 4 vols. 1948, 52, 57, 68; Slieve Lougher and Upper Blackwater in Ireland, 15 vols., 1954, 58, 59, 60, 62, 63, 64, 65, 66, 67, 68, 70, 72; Encyclopedia of Pathologists Southern U.S.A., 1963; Host Reaction and Cancer, 1962; articles on cancer, blood, virus diseases, med. edn., anthropology in profl. jours. Editor Jefferson County Med. Soc. Bull., 1956-59. Home: 2011 Southwood Rd Birmingham AL 35216 Office: Dept Path U Ala Birmingham AL 35205

CASEY, BEVERLY ALLEN, JR., hotel exec.; b. N.Y.C., Jan. 5, 1934; s. Beverly Allen and Jennie Lynn (Toye) C.; student Auburn U., 1952-54, U. Chattanooga, 1954-55; m. Emma Berry Patten, Apr. 20, 1963; children—Lynn Patten, Elizabeth Patten. Partner, Caldwell-Casey Ins. Co., Chattanooga, 1958-70; pres. Town House Properties, Inc., Chattanooga, 1963—, also dir. Mem. allocations com. United Fund, 1971, Indsl. Com. of 100, 1971. Bd. dirs. Chattanooga YMCA, 1967-70. Named Jaycee of Year Chattanooga Jaycees, 1957. Mem. Tenn. Hotel and Motel Assn. (1st v.p. 1970-71), Jr. C. of C. (past state v.p.), Chattanooga Conv. and Visitors Bur. (dir. 1971), Chattanooga C. of C. Episcopalian. Clubs: Lookout Mountain (Tenn.) Fairyland; Parliament (Chattanooga). Mailing Address: 831 Georgia Av Chattanooga TN 37402 Home: 113 W Fleetwood Dr Lookout Mountain TN 37350

CASEY, JOHN JOSEPH, airlines exec.; b. Boston, Oct. 3, 1918; s. John Joseph and Norine (Doyle) C.; S.B., Mass. Inst. Tech., 1940; postgrad. Cornell U., 1942; m. Mary June Reipe, Apr. 21, 1945; children—John Joseph III, David Vaughan, Janet Marjorie, Mary June. Stress engr. Curtiss-Wright Corp., Buffalo, 1940-42; mgr. air cargo engring. Am. Airlines, St. Joseph, Mo., 1946-47, service engr., N.Y.C., 1947-49, asst. v.p. maintenance, 1950-56; v.p. R. Dixon Speas Assos., aviation cons., Manhasset, N.Y., 1956-62; sr. v.p. operations, dir. Seaboard World Airlines, N.Y.C., 1962-68; exec. v.p., dir. Braniff Internat., Dallas, 1968—. Mem. exec. bd., v.p. Circle 10 council Boy Scouts Am., commr. Nassau County council. Served with USAAF, 1942-46. Mem. Am. Inst. Aero. and Astronautics, Soc. Automotive Engrs., Mass. Inst. Tech. Alumni Assn. (bd. govs., v.p. N.Y.C. 1959), Air Force Assn. Clubs: Wings (N.Y.C.); Manhasset Bay Yacht (Port Washington, N.Y.); Northwood, Dallas Corinthian Yacht (Dallas). Home: 6837 Meadowcreek Dr Dallas TX 75240 Office: Braniff Internat Exchange Park Dallas TX 75235

CASEY, OFFA LUNSFORD, lawyer; b. Mobile, Ala., Apr. 22, 1912; s. Benjamin Dudley and Ethel Lou (Shivers) C.; student Jones County Jr. Coll., 1929-30; B.A., U. Miss., 1935, J.D., 1936; m. Muriel Elizabeth Terry, Nov. 21, 1936; children—Thomas Lunsford, Michael Reynolds. Admitted to Miss. bar, 1936; pvt. practice, Laurel, 1936-38, 46-48; atty. lands div. Dept. Justice, Washington, 1938-40; asst. to gen. counsel Adminstr. of Export Control, Washington, 1940-42; judge City Ct., Laurel, 1947-48; asst. U.S. Dist. Atty., So. Dist. Miss., 1949; judge county and youth cts., Laurel, 1951-55; circuit ct. judge 18th dist., Laurel, 1955-70; mem. firm Maxey, Clark & Casey, 1971—. Pres. Miss. Assn. Crime and Delinquency, 1953-55; chmn. Easter Seal Soc., Jones County, 1959-61. Served from 2d lt. to lt. col. AUS, 1942-46, PTO; now col. Res. ret. Mem. Am., Jones County bar assns., Miss. State Bar (jud. adminstrn. com. chmn. 1969-70, commr. 1971-72), Miss. Circuit Judges Assn. (chmn. 1969-70), Jones County Bapt. Assn. (moderator 1957-58), Pi Kappa Phi, Phi Alpha Delta. Democrat. Baptist. Mason, K.P., Rotarian (pres. 1967-68). Home: 1006 Broadway Laurel MS 39440 Office: PO Box 185 Laurel MS 39440

CASEY, ROBERT RANDOLPH, congressman; b. Joplin, Mo., July 27, 1915; s. Samuel R. and Mabel (Caywood) C.; student U. Houston, also S. Tex. Coll. Law, 1934-40; m. Hazel M. Brann, Aug. 13, 1935; children—Hazel Mary, Robert Randolph, Catherine, Bonnie, Michael, Shawn, Bridget, Eileen, Timothy, Kevin Casey. Admitted to Tex.bar, 1940 practice in Alvin, 1941-43, Houston, 1947-51; asst. dist. atty. Harris County, 1943-47; county judge, 1951-58; mem. 86th-91st 92d Congresses, 22d Dist. Tex. Mem. Tex. Legislature, 1949-50. Club: Houston Yacht. Home: 2256 Dryden St Houston TX 77025 also 5406 Albia Rd Washington DC 20016 Office: Rayburn Office Bldg Washington DC 20515

CASEY, SAM HOWARD, oil co. exec.; b. Mt. Vernon, Ill., July 12, 1917; s. Howard Zadok and Edna Bertha (Hestwood) C.; student U. Ill., 1935-36, Millikin U., 1936-38; m. Imogene McCraw, July 23, 1939; children—Carolyn Sue, Linda Kay, Frances Ann, Jo Alice. Crude purchasing rep. Standard Oil Co. of Ohio, 1942-48 gen. mgr. Supply and transp. Standard Oil (Ind.) affiliates, 1948-57; with Commonwealth Oil Refining Co., Inc., N.Y.C., 1957—, exec. v.p., 1958-60, pres., chief exec. officer, 1960—; dir. Banco Credito y Ahorro Ponceno. Bd. dirs. Presbyn. Hosp., Salvation Army, Navy League P.R. Council, Fedn. YMCA P.R. Trustee, devel. fund chmn. Inter Am. U. P.R. Mem. Am. Petroleum Inst., Nat. Petroleum Refiners Assn. (dir.). Home: Laguna Terrace Condominium San Juan PR 00936 Office: GPO Box 4065 San Juan PR 00936

CASEY, SAM RUSSEL, JR., scientist; b. Joplin, Mo., July 14, 1912; s. Sam Russel and Maybelle Edith (Caywood) C.; B.A. in Civil Engring., Houston Engring. Coll., 1935; postgrad. U. Houston, 1941, Harvard, 1942-43; m. Marjorie Lou Vedder, Oct. 14, 1939; children—Jane (Mrs. August B. Seiler), Patrick Vedder. Engr., Shell Pipe Line Co., 1935-36; geol. draftsman Speed Oil Co., 1936-39; chief geologist Woodley Petroleum Co., 1939-50; cons. earth scientist, 1950-68; mgr. marine scis. and ocean engring., cons. earth scientist Bovay Engrs., Inc., Houston, 1968—; pres. Union of Tex. Oil Co., 1950-56. Cons. Project Mohole, NSF, 1964-67. Served to capt. C.E., AUS, 1942-49. Recipient commendation Com. on Oceanography, State of Tex. Ho. of Reps., 1971. Mem. Permanent Internat. Assn. Nav. Congresses, Am. Assn. Petroleum Geologists, Soc. Ind. Profl. Earth Scientists, Marine Tech. Soc. Episcopalian. Author: Precept for Benthic Exploration, 1968. Patentee in field. Home: 2233 Troon Rd Houston TX 77019 Office: 5009 Caroline St Houston TX 77004

CASEY, STEPHEN HUNTLEY, ins. agy. exec.; b. Anderson, S.C., Feb. 20, 1939; s. David Gordon and Lucy Marguerite (Leverett) C.; A.B., Duke, 1960; M.B.A., So. Meth. U., 1968; m. Terry Pearlstone, Jan. 31, 1961; children—Karen Elizabeth, Stephen Huntley. Partner, Pearlstone-Casey Agy., Inc., Dallas, 1964-70, pres., 1970—; dir. Main St. Nat. Bank, Dallas. Pres. 500, Inc., 1971-72. Bd. dirs. Dallas Civic Opera Guild, 1968-69, Dallas Civic Opera, 1972-73, Dallas Arts Found., Inc., 1972-73, U.S.A. Film Festival, 1972-73. Served with USNR, 1960-64. Mem. Nat., Tex., Dallas assns. life underwriters, Chartered Life Underwriters (dir. Dallas chpt. 1971-72, sec.-treas. 1972-73), Dallas Assn. Ins. Agts., Dallas Estate Council, Million Dollar Roundtable, Tex. Leaders Roundtable, Dallas Jr. C. of C. (dir. 1967), Dallas Duke U. Alumni Assn. (pres. 1971-72). Club: City. Home: 4211 Arcady St Dallas TX 75205 Office: 1015 Elm St Dallas TX 75202

CASEY, WARREN VALE, educator, ednl. adminstr.; b. Pitts., Aug. 31, 1916; s. William Sherman and Bertha Ester (Vale) C.; B.S. in Edn., Ohio State U., 1939, M.A., 1947, Ph.D., 1960; postgrad. U. Minn., 1961; m. Martha Elizabeth Greene, Dec. 26, 1939; children—Thomas Warren, Daniel Theodore. Art supr. Worthington (O.) Schs., 1939-42; art dir. Columbus (O.) Sch. for Girls, 1946-48; dir. children's classes Columbus Art Gallery, 1947-48; prof. art Ball State U., 1948-64; dean coll. fine arts, chmn. dept. art Tex. Woman's U., Denton, 1964-70, prof. art history, 1970—. Served with USNR, 1943-45. Mem. Am. Assn. U. Profs., Coll. Arts, Nat. Art Edn. Assn., Internat. Council Fine Arts Deans, Denton Men's Forum, Tex. Assn. Coll. Tchrs. Kiwanian. Executed bronze head of Socrates, Butler U., Pittinger Meml. portrait bronze, Wagoner Meml. bronze (both Ball State U.).

CASEY, WILLIS R., athletic dir. Dir. athletics N.C. State U., Raleigh. Office: Athletic Dept NC State U Raleigh NC 27607*

CASGRAIN, ARDOIN EDMOND, govt. ofcl.; b. Winchester, Mass., Feb. 23, 1897; s. Louis Amedee and Zelia (Goddu) C.; student, U.S. Mil. Acad., 1918-20, Brown U., 1928-30, Northwestern U., summer 1934, in Edn., Harvard, 1938, in Pub. Administrn., Am. U., 1941; m. Mildred Chaloner Davis, Feb. 21, 1934; children—Norman Williams, Charlotte Ardoin, Louise Amedee (Mrs. James H. Noyes Jr.). Asst. sec. Providence (R.I.) C. of C., 1928-30; sec. Watertown (Mass.) C. of C., 1931-35; adult edn. dir. fed. works program Community Service, Boston 1935-36; regional adviser so. states U.S. Office Edn., 1937-39; regional information rep. U.S. Housing Authority, Washington, 1939-41; regional rent dir. OPA, N.Y.C., 1941-42, regional homes use dir., 1943; civilian moblzn. adviser Office Civil Def., Washington, 1944; chief UN Relief and Rehab., Washington, 1945-46; exec. dir. Nat. Com. Atomic Information, Washington, 1947; chief community relations Dept. Army, Washington, 1948-49, dep. dir. community services adj. gen. office, 1950-53, adminstrv. officer, mgmt. analyst, 1954-65; program adviser adminstrn. aging Dept. Health, Edn. and Welfare, 1966-67; asst. dir., cons. community services Sr. Aides Program Dept. Labor, Washington, 1968—; mem. cons. panel Volt Service Corp., Washington, 1969—; lectr. Simmons Sch. Social Work, Boston, 1934, N.Y. Sch. Social Work, 1943. Mem. bd. Nat. Council Sr. Citizens, Washington, 1969; spl. adviser govt. employee groups, 1967-69; cons. older Am. problems various nat. orgns.; cons. Inst. Lifetime Learning. Served with U.S. Army, World War I. Recipient Meritorious Civilian Employee award Dept. Army, 1966, Mem. Am. Legion, Assos. Grad. U.S. Mil. Acad., Am. Assn. Retired Persons (pres. Nat. Capital chpt. 1971-72). Address: 4000 Cathedral Av NW Washington DC 20016

CASGRAIN, CHARLOTTE ARDOIN, educator; b. Washington, Apr. 24, 1940; d. Ardoin Edmund and Mildred C. (Davis) Casgrain; A.B., Pembroke Coll. in Brown U., 1962; M.S., U. Bridgeport, 1966; postgrad. Universite de Poiters, Universite de Aix Marseille. Asst. to dir., head counsellor tng. program Les Chalets Francaise, Deer Isle, Me., 1958—; French specialist Greenwich (Conn.) Bd. Edn., 1962—. Recipient Danforth Found. citizenship award, 1955; Lucy Brownback award in French, 1955; French Govt. award for excellence in French, 1956; Fulbright award for travel-study in France, 1964; Alliance Francaise de N.Y. scholarship for study in France, 1969-70. Mem. Am. Assn. Tchrs. French, Nat., Conn., Greenwich edn. assns., Assn. for Childhood Edn. Internat., Am. Assn. U. Women, Conn. Tchrs. of Lang., Pembroke Coll. Alumnae, Georgetown Visitation Alumnae. Home: 4000 Cathedral Av NW Apt 11B Washington DC 20016 Office: Pres du Port Stonington ME 04681

CASH, CLAYBOURNE ALLISON, chem., oil and gas co. exec.; b. McLean, Tex., Oct. 31, 1914; s. Claybourne Jeremiah and Lavada (Phillips) C.; student Tex. Technol. U., 1933-35; m. Juanita Ball, Sept. 13, 1936; 1 dau., Elaine (Mrs. C.D. Culver). With Shamrock Oil and Gas Corp., Amarillo, Tex., 1935-67, v.p., asst. to pres., 1955-57, exec. v.p., 1957-60, pres., 1960-67; dir., 1956-67; pres. Diamond Shamrock Oil & Gas Co., 1967-69, chmn., 1969-71; exec. v.p. Diamond Shamrock Corp., 1967-71, vice chmn. bd., 1971, pres., 1971—, also dir.; dir. Terra Chems. Internat., 1st Nat. Bank Amarillo; chmn., Gas Supply Com. Mem. Am. Petroleum Inst. (dir., mem. natural gas com.), Tex. Mid-Continent Oil and Gas Assn. (dir.), Ind. Petroleum Assn. Am., Newcomen Soc. N.Am., Am. Chem. Soc. Methodist. Mason. Clubs: Amarillo, Amarillo Country; Citadel (Austin); Dallas Petroleum; Houston, Houston Petroleum; Union (Cleve). Home: 2028 Austin St Amarillo TX 79109

CASH, JOHNNY, singer, composer; b. Kingsland, Ark., Feb. 26, 1932; s. Ray and Carrie (Rivers) C.; grad. high sch.; m. June Carter, Mar. 1, 1968; 1 son, John Carter; children by previous marriage—Rosanne, Kathleen, Cindy, Tara. Rec. artist with Sun Records, 1955-58, Columbia Records, 1958—; researched and recorded documentary album, True West, for Columbia, 1965; pres. South Wind Music, 1970-N.C.; motion pictures Five Minutes Live, A Gunfight, 1970; soundtracks for motion pictures I Walk the Line, Little Fuass and Big Halsy; star of Johnny Cash Show, ABC-TV, 1969—; owner House of Cash, Inc., pub. Song of Cash, Inc.; guest appearances numerous TV programs. Served with USAF 1950-54. Recipient Citation for USO shows in Far East, Def. Dept. Composer over 200 songs including: I Walk the Line, I Still Miss Someone, Don't Take Your Guns to Town. Address: PO Box 508 Hendersonville TN 37075

CASHEN, HENRY CHRISTOPHER, II, lawyer, govt. ofcl.; b. Detroit, June 25, 1939; s. Raymond and Catherine C.; grad. Cheshire Acad., 1957; A.B. in Classics with honors, Brown U., 1961; postgrad. U. Mich., 1963; m. Leslie Renchard, June 28, 1967; 1 son, Raymond Cashen II. Admitted to Mich. bar; mem. firm Dickinson, Wright, McKean and Cudlip, Detroit, 1964-69; dep. asst. to Pres. Nixon, Washington, 1969—. Mem. University Club, Barristers Soc., Psi Upsilon, Phi Delta Phi. Republican. Roman Catholic. Clubs: Country Club (Detroit), Metropolitan. Home: 1231 33rd St NW Washington DC 20007 Office: The White House Pennsylvania Av Washington DC 20500

CASHMAN, JOHN MARVIN, engr.; b. Stephensport, Ky., Sept. 7, 1926; s. Alpha Byron and Nellie (Bacbee) C.; B.S. in Elec. Engring., U. Ky., 1949; m. Edna Lucille Stevens, Aug. 28, 1948; 1 dau., Carol Ann. Staff adjustor Motors Ins. Corp., Flint, Mich., Louisville, Bowling Green, Ky., 1949-53; claims investigator Horton Adjustment Co., Bowling Green, 1953-54; engr. Detrex Chem. Industries, Inc., Bowling Green, 1954—, supr. repetitive equipment engring. and engring. standards, 1965—, supr. engring. proposals Indsl. Equipment Div., 1960-64; part-time instr. electronics Western Ky. U., 1970—; co-owner Ky. Belle Riverboat Restaurant, 1968—. Exec. mem. Ky. beautification com. Ky. Dept. Conservation, Frankfort, 1961—; mem. Gov.'s Citizens Com. for Tourist and Travel Devel. and Hwy.; chmn. bd. elec. examiners City of Bowling Green, 1970—. Bd. dirs. Bowling Green Girls Club. Served with USNR, 1945-46. Registered profl. engr., Ky. Mem. Nat., Ky. (past Ky. registration chmn., past pres. Mammoth Cave chpt.) socs. profl. engrs., Ky. Jr. C. of C. (past state chmn. Ky. community devel. Explore Ky. com.), Ky. Restaurant Assn. (chpt. v.p. 1970-71), Am. Legion. Democrat. Baptist. Club: Optimist (former pres. Bowling Green). Home: 1601 Nutwood Av Bowling Green KY 42101 Office: Emmett Dr Bowling Green KY 42101

CASILLAS, LUIS REY, economist; b. Mexico City, Mar. 30, 1941; s. Luis R. and Rosario Celis (Salazar) C.; came to U.S., 1961; student U. Cal. at Berkeley, 1961-64; B.S. in Fgn. Service, Georgetown U., 1966, Ph.D. summa cum laude, 1971; M.P.A., Inst. Econs., Oslo, 1967; postgrad. Kings Coll., Cambridge, Eng., 1967, Mass. Inst. Tech., 1968. Area economist Brazil, Paraguay, Peru, Bolivia, Inter-Am. Devel. Bank, Washington, 1968-70, fiscal economist Office of Pres. Inter-Am. Devel. Bank, 1971, econ. adviser to pres., 1972—. Econ. cons.on energy devel., Washington; lectr. Georgetown U.; sec., econ. adviser Gov. State of Puebla, Mexico, 1966; Inter-Am. Devel. Bank rep. to Alliance for Progress, 1969, to Internat. Conf. on Taxation, Panama City, 1971, Mexico City, 1972, to Internat. Conf. on Econometrics, U. Pa., 1972. OAS fellow, 1966-68, Norwegian Govt. fellow, 1967. Mem. Am. Econ. Assn., Royal Econ. Soc., Inter-Am. Statis. Inst., Philosophy of Sci. Assn. Author: Topics in Economic Theory and Econometrics, 1972. Home: 4977 Battery Lane Bethesda MD 20014 Office: 808 17th St NW Washington DC 20577

CASNER, STANLEY WAYNE, JR., physician; b. Marfa, Tex., Aug. 14, 1927; s. Stanley Wayne and Kathryn (Sheen) C.; student Tex. Tech. U., 1948-50; M.D., U. Tex., 1958; m. Lucille Fay McGee, Apr. 18, 1957; children—John Wayne, Barbara Fay, Peggy Gayle. Intern, Meth. Hosp., Houston, 1958-59; resident in surgery John Sealy Hosp., U. Tex. Med. br., Galveston, 1959-63; practice medicine, specializing in family practice, Austin, Tex., 1968—; mem. staff Brackenridge Hosp., Holy Cross Hosp., St. Davids Hosp., Seton Hosp. (all Austin); team physician U. Tex. Student Health Center and Athletic, 1961-66; dir. Casner Research Labs., Austin, Tex., 1967—. Served with USAAF, 1944-46. Fellow Am. Coll. Family Practice; mem. A.M.A., Am. Diabetes Assn., Tex. Med. Assn., Travis County Med. Soc., Theta Kappa Psi. Baptist. Kiwanian. Home: 4016 Rustling Oaks St Austin TX 78766 Office: 4019 Spicewood Springs Rd Austin TX 78766

CASON, DICK KENDALL, physician; b. Beaumont, Tex., June 27, 1922; s. Dick Kendall and Maurine (Mills) C.; B.A., Rice U., 1945; M.D., U. Tex., 1945; m. Maxine Skocdopole, Apr. 4, 1946; children—Dick Mills, Alma Christine. Intern Kings County Hosp. Bklyn., 1945-46; med. resident Meth. Hosp., Dallas, 1948-49; gen. practice medicine, Hillsboro, Tex., 1949—; staff mem. Grant-Buie Hosp. Charter mem. Am. Bd. Family Practice. Pres. Hillsboro Indsl. Devel. Found., 1955-60; mem. regional adv. com. Dallas Civic Opera Co., 1960—. Served from 1st lt. to capt., AUS, 1946-48. Mem. Hill County Med. Soc. (pres. 1951), Tex. Med. Assn. (councilor 12th dist.), Am. Acad. Gen. Practice, N.Y. Acad. Sci., Am. Assn. Ry. Surgeons, Cotton Bowl Assn., C. of C., Hill County Soc. Crippled Children. Presbyn. (elder). Clubs: Hillsboro Country, Rotary (pres. Hillsboro 1955). Author articles profl. jours. Home: 1303 Park Dr Hillsboro TX 76645 Office: 150 Circle Dr Hillsboro TX 76645

CASON, JAMES LEE, educator; b. Shongalou, La., Feb. 22, 1922; s. James Kyle and Amy (Lee) C.; B.S., La. Tech. U., 1948; M.S., Mich. State U., 1950; Ph.D., N.C. State U., 1956; m. Georgia Jewel Spivey, Mar. 16, 1946; children—Benjamin Kyle, James Lee Jr. Asst. prof. dairying La. Tech. U., 1948; instr. dairying U. Ark., 1950-53, asst. prof., 1953-54; asst. prof. dairying Rutgers U., 1956-59; asso. prof. dairying U. Md., 1959-67, prof., 1967-70; prof. animal sci., head dept. agr. Northeast La. U., Monroe, 1970—. Served with USNR, 1942-46. Mem. Am. Dairy Sci. Assn., Am. Soc. Animal Sci., Biometric Soc., Md. Dairy Shrine, Eastern Guernsey Breeders Assn., La. Teachers Assn., Nat. Assn. Colls. and Tchrs., Demeter, Sigma Xi, Epsilon Sigma Phi. Kiwanian. Home: 214 Country Club Rd Monroe LA 71201 Office: Dept Agr Northeast La U Monroe LA 71201

CASON, M. LOUISE, physician; b. Lakeland, Fla., Mar. 26, 1923; d. L. Oscar and Mossie (Turner) Cason; B.S., Fla. State U., 1945; M.D., U. Chgo., 1950. Intern in pediatrics Duke U. Hosp., 1950-51; resident pediatrics Jewish Hosp. of Bklyn., 1951-53; practice medicine specializing in pediatrics, Miami, 1953—; clin. asso. prof. pediatrics U. Miami Sch. of Medicine, 1961—; chief dept. pediatrics Variety Children's Hosp., 1958—; attending pediatrician Jackson Meml. Hosp., Variety Children's Hosp.; cons. pediatrician to Children's Service Bur., Cath. Welfare Bur. Diplomate Am. Bd. Pediatrics. Fellow Am. Acad. Pediatrics. Mem. Am., So., Fla., Dade County med. assns., Miami Pediatric Soc., Fla. Pediatric Soc. Episcopalian. Office: 3041 Grand Av Miami FL 33133

CASON, THOMAS EDWARD, JR., sales co. exec.; b. Plain Dealing, La., June 22, 1921; s. Tom E. and Nettie (Bounds) C.; student So. State Coll., Magnolia, Ark., 1938-40; B.S., La. State U., 1942; m. Alma Dean Lester, Nov. 5, 1942; children—Cheryl Ann (Mrs. Doug Wallace), Gwendolyn, Tommy, Randall. Tchr. high sch., Lutcher, La., 1942-43; tchr. Bradley (Ark.) High Sch., 1946-66; project instr. Ark. Dept. Edn., 1966-68; owner Cason Distbrs., Batesville, Ark., 1968—; regional dir. Pennyrich Corp., Batesville, 1968—; pres. Pennyrich Distbrs. Assn., 1971—; gen. distbr. Holiday Magic Cosmetics, Batesville, 1965—. Civil def. dir., Bradley, 1958-66. Alderman, Bradley, 1948-50, 54-56. Served with AUS, 1943-46 ETO. Mem. Ark. Press Assn., N.E.A., Ark. Vocational Agr. Tchrs. Assn., Batesville C. of C., Little Rock Better Bus. Bur., Alpha Tau Alpha. Methodist (tchr., lay leader). Rotarian. Editor Bradley Pioneer, 1960-66. Home: 315 Craig St Batesville AR 72501 Office: 310 College St Batesville AR 72501

CASO Y ANDRADE, ALFONSO, scientist; b. Mexico City, Mexico, Feb. 1, 1896; s. Antonio and Maria (Andrade) C.; U. Mexico, 1929; doctor honoris causa U. Nat. Mexico, U. Merida, U. Morelia, U. N.M., U. Cal. at Los Angeles; m. Maria Lombardo, Aug. 21, 1922; children—Beatriz (wife of Carlos Solorzano), Andres, Alejandro Eugenia; m. 2d, Aida Lombardo. Prof. faculty philosophy and letters, 1918-40, Escuela de Layes, 1919-29; dir. Escuela Nacional Preparatoria, 1928; head dept. archeology Museo Nacional, 1930-33, dir., 1933-34; dir. explorations, Monte Alban, Oaxaca, 1931-44; dir. higher learning and sci. investigation, 1944; rector U. Nacional Mexico, 1944-45; sec. nat. properties and adminstrv. inspection, 1946-48; dir. Inst. Nacional Indigenista, Revista Estudios Antropologicos. Recipient First medal Viking Fund for Archaeology, 1952. Fellow Royal Anthrop. Inst. Great Britain and Ireland (hon.); mem. Nat. Acad. Scis. Antonio Alzate (pres.); Nat. Coll., Soc. Geography and Statistics, N.Y., Washington acads. sci., Archaeol. Inst. Am. (hon.), Am. Philos. Soc., Royal Anthrop. Inst. (hon.), Soc. Am. Paris (hon.), Brit. Acad. (hon.), Am. Anthrop. Assn., Soc. Geography and History Guatemala, Am. Assn. Tchrs. Spanish, Deutsche Gesellschaft fur Volkerkunde. Author numerous books including Urnas de Ooxaca, 1950; The People of the Sun, 1952; Codex

Bodley, 1960; Codex Selden, 1964. Dir., founder Boletin Bibliog. de Antropologia Am. Home: Avenue Central 234 Tlacopac Sn Angel Mexico 20 DF Mexico Office: Instituto Nacional Indigenista Av Revolucion 1279 Mexico City 20 Mexico

CASPER, THOMAS PATRICK, supt. schs.; b. Louisville, Feb. 7, 1931; s. Burke and Sara (Husson) C.; Ph.B., Pontifical Gregorian U., Rome, Italy, 1953, licentiate sacred theology, 1957; Ph.D. in Edn., St. Louis U., 1964. Ordained priest Roman Cath. Ch., 1956; asst. supt. Cath. schs., Louisville, 1957-67, supt. schs., 1967—; asso. pastor Cathedral Ch., Louisville, 1957-62, 64—, St. Clement Ch., Louisville, 1963-64; mem. edn. dept. Catherine Spalding Coll., 1963-65. Mem. Community Action Commn., 1967-69; dir. Jr. Great Books Program, 1958-67. Trustee Library Bd. Mem. Nat. Cath. Edn. Assn., Louisville C. of C. (Health and Welfare Council). Home: 443 S 5th St Louisville KY 40202 Office: 435 S 5th St Louisville KY 40202

CASSATA, JOHN T., clergyman. Ordained priest Roman Catholic Ch., 1932; apptd. bishop of Bida, aux. bishop of Dallas-Fort Worth, 1968; bishop of Fort Worth, 1969—. Address: 1206 Throckmorton St Fort Worth TX 76102*

CASSEDY, MARSHALL ROYAL, lawyer; b. Short Hills, N.J., July 28, 1928; s. Pierce A. and Callene (Thomas) C.; B.A., Hobart Coll., 1951; LL.B., Coll. Law Duke, 1956; m. Donna Louise Anderson, July 5, 1952; children—Marshall, Thomas A., Kristine C., Melissa H. Admitted to Fla. bar, 1956; asso. firm Turnbull & Senterfitt, Orlando, Fla., 1956-58; staff counsel The Florida Bar, Tallahassee, 1958-61, exec. dir., 1961—. Treas. Tallahassee YMCA, 1966-68. Served to lt. col. USMCR, 1951-53. Mem. Am. Bar Assn. (ho. of dels. 1971-72), Am. Judicature Soc., Fla. Bar, Am. Soc. Assn. Execs. Episcopalian. Home: 707 Live Oak Plantation Rd Tallahassee FL 32303 Office: The Florida Bar Tallahassee FL 32304

CASSELL, CHARLES IRVIN, architect, educator; b. Washington, Aug. 5, 1924; s. Albert Irvin and Martha Ann (Mason) C.; student Cornell U., 1942-44; grad. Rensselaer Poly Inst., 1951; div.; children—Norma Elaine, Kathryn Annette. Asso. with Albert I. Cassell, architect, 1951-69; architect Bur. Yards and Docks, VA and GSA, 1951-68; pvt. practice as architect, part-time 1957—; dir. tech. services Reconstrn. and Devel. Corp., 1969-70; prof. Fed. City Coll., Washington, 1970—; architect-in-residence Urban Law Inst., 1971-72; founder, exec. dir. D.C. Council Black Architects, 1972—; lectr. colls. and univs.; cons. urban problems. Mem. D.C. Bd. Edn., 1970—; vice chmn. Emergency Com. Transp. Crisis. Pres. D.C. Sch. Action Council, also editor, pub. newsletter; co-chmn. D.C. Statehood Party. Candidate U.S. Ho. Reps., 1972. Served with USAAF, 1942-44. Mem. A.I.A., Alpha Phi Alpha. Home: 1845 Summit Pl NW Washington DC 20009 Office: 1145 19th St NW Washington DC 20036

CASSELL, RICHARD SAMUEL DAVID, real estate, oil investments; b. N.Y.C., June 30, 1938; s. Marvin and Junia (Schonwald) C.; B.A., Cornell U., 1960. Gen. mgr. Schonwald & Cassell, Oklahoma City, 1963-64; pres. Richard S. D. Cassell Co., Oklahoma City, 1964—. Chmn. Oklahoma City area Cornell U. Alumni Secondary Schs. Com.; treas. Class 1960 Cornell U., 1970—. Capt. AUS Res., 1967—. Mem. Oklahoma City Bd. Realtors, Nat. Inst. Real Estate Brokers, Internat. Real Estate Fedn., Okla. Zool. Soc., Oklahoma City C. of C., Oklahoma City Assn. Bldg. Owners and Mgrs., Mil. Police Assn., 89ers. Mason (Shriner). Clubs: City Athletic (N.Y.), Oklahoma City Press (dir.), Beacon. Home: 2753 Clermont Pl Oklahoma City OK 73116 Office: 415 N Broadway Oklahoma City OK 73102

CASSELL, ROBERT BERNARD, editor; b. Chattanooga, Feb. 16, 1918; s. Samuel and Katherine (Lesser) C.; B.A., U. Chattanooga, 1937; M.A., Vanderbilt U., 1938; m. Vylva Irene Holland, May 27, 1943; 1 son, Robert Holland. Supr. Hist. Records Survey, Nashville, 1938-42; indsl. economist Tenn. Planning Commn., Nashville, 1946-53; dir. research Tenn. Indsl. and Agrl. Devel. Commn., Nashville, 1953-60; editor Ga. Devel. News, Ga. Inst. Tech., 1960—. Served with AUS, 1942-46. Fellow Am. Indsl. Devel. Council (pres. 1971-72); mem. So. Indsl. Devel. Council (pres. 1968). Contbr. articles to profl. lit. Home: 2694 Briarcliff Rd N E Atlanta GA 30329 Office: 1132 W Peachtree St N W Atlanta GA 30309

CASSENS, FRANK PAUL, educator; b. New Orleans, July 12, 1918; s. Frank Paul and Agnes (Humphries) C.; B.A., Tulane U., 1938, M.S., 1942; Ph.D., La. State U., 1966; m. Dorothy I. Galightly, June 25, 1942; children—Cordell Paul, Denise Maria. Personnel technician Adj. Gen. Office, War Dept., 1942-48; counselor Ohio State U., Columbus, 1945-48; indsl. psychologist Lago Oil & Transport Co. Ltd., Aruba, Netherlands West Indies, 1948-55, Humble Oil & Refining Co. Ltd., Baton Rouge, 1955-68; asso. prof. behavioral sci. Grad. Sch. Bus. Adminstrn., Tulane U., New Orleans, 1968—; mgmt. cons., 1966—. Pres., East Baton Rouge Mental Health Assn., 1967-68. Diplomate Indsl. Psychology; Am. Bd. Profl. Psychology. Fellow A.A.A.S.; mem. Nat. Vocational Guidance Assn., Am. Psychol. Assn., Southeastern, La. psychol. assns., Inter. Am. Psychology Assn., Indsl. Relations Research Assn. Home: 5301 Haring Ct Metairie LA 70002 Office: Tulane U St Charles Av New Orleans LA 70118

CASSIBRY, FRED JAMES, judge; b. D'Lo, Miss., Sept. 26, 1918; s. Reginald E. and Lelia (Garner) C.; B.A., Tulane U., 1941, LL.B., 1943; m. Lorraine E. Patterson, Dec. 21, 1940; 1 dau., Elizabeth. Admitted to La. bar, 1944; engaged in practice law, New Orleans, 1947-60; mem. firms Cassibry & Zengel, 1946-47, Dymond &Cassibry, 1950-55, Cassibry, Jackson & Hess, 1955-60, judge Civil Dist. Ct., Parish of Orleans, 1960-66; U.S. dist. judge Eastern Dist. La., 1966—. Mem. com. on jud. ethics La. Supreme Ct., 1965-66. Mem. city council New Orleans, 1954-61; bd. commrs. New Orleans City Park, 1962-68. Del. Democratic Nat. Conv., 1956. Served from ensign to lt. (j.g.) USNR, 1944-46. Mem. Am. Judicature Soc., Am., La., New Orleans bar assns., La. Dist. Judges Assn. (pres. 1965), Am. Legion, Tulane U. Alumni Assn. (exec. com. 1962-65). Home: 400 Royal St New Orleans LA 70130 Office: Wildlife and Fisheries Bldg 400 Royal St New Orleans LA 70130

CASSIDY, JUANITA NEWTON HARRIS (MRS. LEWIS C. CASSIDY), lawyer; b. Newtonville, S.C.; d. Giles Preston and Jessie Lee (Moore) Newton; student Wingate Coll., 1913-15, Ph.D. (hon.), 1960; student Duke, 1915-16; J.D., George Washington Nat. U., 1941; m. Everett Grant Harris, Apr. 14, 1918 (dea.); children—Everett G., Charles Giles, Newton Nolen (dec.); m. 2d, Lewis C. Cassidy, July 8, 1943 (dec. Feb. 1949). Admitted to Mont. bar, 1941, Fed. bar; atty. and counsellor Supreme Ct. of Mont., 1941-62, of U.S., 1952—. Gray Lady, A.R.C., 1952—. Recipient Certificate Alumni Achievement, Wingate Coll., 1960. Mem. Gold Star Wives Am. (nat. parliamentarian), U.D.C. (chpt. historian, state historian), D.A.R., Am. Legion Aux., Mont. la., state socs., Va., D.C. hist. socs., Nat. Soc. Magna Charta Dames, Eng. Speaking Union, U.S. Capitol Hist. Soc. (hon. life), George Washington U. Club (charter), Newton Reunion Assn., Daus. 1812 (asso.), Smithsonian Instn. (asso.), Sovereign Colonial Soc. Ams. Royal Descent, Colonial Order of Crown, Internat. Platform Assn., Daus. Brit. Empire U.S.A., Mont. Bar Assn., Sigma Chi Mothers Club, Gen. Fedn. Woman's Clubs, Villages Citizens Assn., Kappa Beta Pi (life). Mem. Order Eastern Star. Clubs: Woman's (co-chmn., chaplain) (Lyon Village); Fort Meyer Officers (Arlington); Naval Officers (Bethesda, Md.). Home: 3137 Key Blvd Arlington VA 22201

CASSIDY, ROBERT GORDON, elec. engr.; b. West Baden, Ind., Mar. 15, 1917; s. Elza and Alta (Wininger) C.; B.S. in Elec. Engring., Rose Polytech. Inst., 1950; m. Lilah Beryl Pinnick, Jan. 31, 1946; children—Daniel G., Marcia G., Mary D., Christine M. Various positions including auto mechanic, store clk., 1934-42; elec. engr. Hill AFB, Utah, 1951-53; elec. engr. U.S.Army C.E., 1953—, chief, elec. sect. engring. div., Jacksonville Fla., 1967—. Served with AUS, 1942-45. Registered profl. engr., Fla., Ind. Methodist. Home: 5514 Norde Dr Jacksonville FL 32210 Office: 400 W Bay St Jacksonville FL 32201

CASSITY, LLOYD, dairy co. exec.; b. nr. Ashland, Ky., Aug. 10, 1918; s. Ted E. and Elizabeth (McGuire) C.; A.B., Morehead (Ky.) State U., 1941; m. Hazel Helmintoller, Oct. 14, 1939; 1 dau., Lynn Diane. Tchr., Boyd County High Sch., Ashland, Ky., 1941; accountant Stone & Webster Engring. Corp., Oak Ridge, 1942-43; gen. mgr. automobile agys., Morehead and Ashland, Ky., 1946-49; v.p. Johnson's Dairy, Ashland, 1949-68, pres., 1968—; dir. Birch Distbr., Home Fed. Savs. & Loan Assn., Am. Bus. Mens Life Ins. Co., Louisville, Ashland Indsl. Corp. Pres. Ky. Joint Alumni Council, Boyd County Community Chest. Mem. Ashland Urban Renewal Authority. Bd. regents Morehead State U. Served with AUS, 1943-46. Mem. Ky. Dairy Products Assn. (v.p.), Assn. Dairy Food Mfrs. (dir.), Ashland area C. of C. (v.p.), Morehead State U. alumni assn. (past pres.). Democrat. Mem. Christian Ch. Mason (Shriner), Kiwanian, Club: Bellefonte Country (Ashland). Home: 636 Amanda Dr Ashland KY 41101 Office: 2516 Carter Av Ashland KY 41101

CASSO, RAUL, III, warehouse exec.; b. Laredo, Tex., Apr. 7, 1931; s. Raul, Jr. and Enriqueta (Garcia) C.; student Tex. A. and M. U., 1949-51; B.B.A., St. Mary's U., 1953; m. Eugenia Majalca, June 30, 1956; children—Eugenia, Raul IV, Roberto, Adriana, Guillermo. With Casso, Guerra & Co., 1956-66; exec. co-owner Internat. Bonded Warehouses, Inc., Laredo, 1967—; co-owner Brownsville Internat. Bonded, Inc., Andy's Customs Bond Warehouses, Inc., Border Bonded Warehouses, Inc.; pres., co-owner Pearl Beer Distbg. Co., Laredo. Pres. Laredo Jr. C. of C., 1960-61; dir. Laredo C. of C., 1962-64; chmn. internat. relations Tex. Jr. C. of C., 1962, childrens home chmn., 1963-64, dir. to 1966. Mem. Laredo City Planning and Zoning Commn., 1964—. Bd. dirs. Sacred Heart Childrens Home, United Fund, 1961. Served to 1st lt., arty., AUS, 1954-56. Recipient Tall Tex. award, 1964, various Key Man awards; named Jaycee of Year, 1958, Outstanding Young Man of Am., 1965. Mem. Tex. Wholesale Beer Distbrs. Kiwanian, Elk. Home: 1920 O'Kane St Laredo TX 78040 Office: 2001 Scott St Laredo TX 78040

CASTANEDA, CARLOS M., journalist. Editor, El Nuevo Dia. Address: CP 164 Ponce PR 00731*

CASTEEL, WYNNE MARCUS, JR., lawyer; b. Binghamton, N.Y., Jan. 22, 1933; s. Wynne Marcus and Mona (Carnahan) C.; grad., U. Mo., 1950-54; LL.B, Stetson Coll. of Law. 1956-58; m. Sandra Lee Smith, July 31, 1954; children—Cathleen Lee, Mark Wynne, Russell Edmund. Admitted to Fla. bar. 1958; practiced in Ft. Lauderdale, Fla., 1958—; mem. firm Cabot, Scott, Wonkstern & Casteel; asso. municipal judge Fort Lauderdale, 1961, 68—, municipal judge, 1961-63. Served with AUS, 1954-56. Mem. Am., Broward County bar assns., Fla. Bar, Acad. Fla. Trial Lawyers, Phi Delta Theta. Republican. Baptist. Clubs: Touchdown, Elks. Home: 829 Ponce De Leon Dr Fort Lauderdale FL 33301 Office: 2190 SE 17th St Fort Lauderdale FL 37316

CASTILLO LOPEZ, ENRIQUE ALBERTO, civil engr.; b. Quebradillas, P.R., Dec. 15, 1902; s.Juan E. and Maria (Lopez) C.; student pub. schs. of P.R.; m. Julia San Miguel, Oct. 4, 1921; children—Enrique, Fernando, Jose Roberto; m. 2d, Maria Luisa Blanco, Mar. 18, 1933; children—Ernesto, Eduardo, Elsa. Pub. works insp. Govt. of P.R., 1924-26; asst. engr. Loiza Sugar Co., 1926-28; asst. chief engr. Fajardo Sugar Co., 1928-34; owner Enrique A. Castillo, Engr., 1934-41; became pres. Enrique A. Castillo, Inc., 1951, chmn bd. 1964—; pres. Fine-Wood Mfrs., Inc., 1944—; chmn bd. Caribe Millwork Corp., Ferreteros del Caribe, Inc. Royal Swedish consul for P.R., 1952-68. dean Consular Corps, 1965-67. Recipient Distinguished Services award P.R. Mfrs. Assn., 1962; named Knight Order Vassa First Class (Sweden), 1962. Mem. Mfrs. Assn. P.R. (pres. 1956-59), Nat. Geog. Soc. Coll. Engrs., Architects and Surveyor P.R., Sales Exec. Club, Am. Scandinavian Found., hon. mem. Internat. Found. Eloy Alfaro of Panama, Internat. Platform Assn. Roman Catholic. Clubs: Lions (San Juan); Yaucano; Rotary (pres. Villa Capara 1951). Home: Sagrado Corazon St 465 Santurce PR 00915

CASTLE, HENRY GRADY, JR., architect; b. Abilene, Tex. Oct. 4, 1923; s. Henry Grady and Mary (Gist) C.; B.Arch., U. Tex., 1951 children—Mina Johanna (Mrs. Dosier), Susan Reida (Mrs. von Rosenberg), Diane Castle. Asst. dir., regional architect properties and facilities Am. Airlines, Inc., N.Y., 1955, Dallas, 1955-57, Los Angeles, 1957-59; architect Page Southerland Page, A.I.A., 1960-64, Golemon & Rolfe, A.I.A., Houston, 1965-69, Lloyd, Morgan & Jones, architects, Houston, 1969-70; staff architect Walter W. Scarborough, Architect, Houston, 1970—. Served to 1st lt. USAAF, 1942-46, as lt. col. USAF, 1951-53, Korea; col. Res. Decorated Air medal with 3 oak leaf clusters, Air Force Commendation medal. Mem. A.I.A., Constrn. Specifications Inst., Tex. Fine Arts Assn., Tex. Soc. Architects, Soc. Am. Mil. Engrs., Air Force Assns., Sphinx Archtl. Soc., Res. Officers Assn., Tex. Ex-Student Assn. Home: 513 S Post Oak Lane Houston TX 77027 Office: 3100 W Alabama St Houston TX 77006

CASTLEBERRY, VIVIAN LOU ANDERSON (MRS. CURTIS WALES CASTLEBERRY), newspaper editor; b. Lindale, Tex., Apr. 8, 1922; d. William Clarence and Jessie Lee (Henderson) Anderson; B.S., So. Meth. U., 1944; m. Curtis Wales Castleberry, May 4, 1946; children—Carol Janet (Mrs. Michael Lynn Tate), Chanda Elaine (Mrs. George Philip Robertson), Keeta Shawn, Kimberley Diana, Catherine Ann. Editorial asst. Petroleum Engr. Pub. Co., 1944-45; editorial asst. Cousins Pub. Co., 1945-46; womens editor Tex. A. and M. Bull., 1948-51; home editor Dallas Times Herald, 1954-56, womens editor, 1957—. Cons. Mgmt. Seminar for Women Execs., 1963—. Mem. women's group Dallas Council World Affairs, 1964—, Dallas Internat. Cultural and Social Circle, 1965—. Bd. dirs. Women for Change, 1971—. Recipient awards for womens news reporting U.P.I., 1963, 65; Outstanding Woman award So. Meth. U., 1970; award Southwestern Journalism Forum, 1971. Mem. Dallas Press Club. Home: 11311 Buchanan St Dallas TX 75228 Office: 1101 Pacific Av Dallas TX 75202

CASTLES, F.A., supt. schs. Supt. of Canal Zone Schs. Address: Division of Schools Balboa Heights Canal Zone*

CASTORO, WILLIAM MICHAEL, indsl. exec.; b. N.Y.C., June 25, 1930; s. John M. and Helen (Wells) C.; student U. Buffalo, 1953-55, U. Okla. 1964; m. Viviane Hogberg, Sept. 1, 1956; children—Lisa Marie, Paula Ann. Consular affairs Am. Fgn. Service, Dept. State, 1951-53; exec. dir. Pinella Industry Council, Pinellas County, Fla., 1961—; dir. Pinellas Mfrs. Assn. Served with USAAF, 1947-50. Home: 8275 132d St N Seminole FL 33540 Office: PO Box 13000 St Petersburg FL 33733

CATALINO, ANTHONY, social worker; b. Reggio, Italy, July 13, 1916; s. Rocco and Angeline (Gallo) C.; B.S., U. Rochester, 1948; M.S.W., U. Buffalo, 1950; postgrad. U. Cal. at Berkeley, 1960; m. Isabell M. Small, Jan. 6, 1942; children—Suzanne, Raymond. Came to U.S., 1919, naturalized, 1935. Social worker youth parole Indsl. and Agrl. Sch., Industry, N.Y., 1950-58; dir. cottage program Highland Tng. Sch., 1958; dir. social services New Hampton Tng. Sch., 1959-60; asst. supt. Tng. Inst. Central Ohio, Columbus, 1960-62, supt., 1963-67; cons. child detention care N.Y. State, 1962-63; dir. Youth Devel. Center, Phila., 1967; dir. bur. children's instns. Pa. Dept. Pub. Welfare, Harrisburg, 1967-70; supt. Fla. Sch. for Girls, Ocala, 1970—. Field instr. St. Paul's Sch. Social Work, Ottawa, Ont., Can., 1958, Buffalo Sch. Social Work, 1958; vis. lectr. Franklin U., 1966, Ohio State U., 1966, Pa. State U., 1969. Served with F.A., AUS, 1941-45. Mem. Nat. Assn. Social Workers, Acad. Certified Social Workers, Nat. Assn. Tng. Schs. and Juvenile Agys. (gov.). Contbr. articles on social work to profl. publs. Address: Fla Sch for Girls Ocala FL 32670

CATER, KATHARINE C., educator; b. Macon, Ga., Sept. 1, 1914; d. Thomas J. and Maybelle (Moore) Cater; A.B. magna cum laude, Limestone Coll., 1935, Litt.D. (hon.), 1958; M.A., Mercer U., 1938; M.S., Syracuse U., 1942, postgrad., 1945-46. Tchr., Boiling Springs High Sch., Spartanburg, S.C., 1935-37; instr. English and French, Limestone Coll., Gaffney, S.C., 1937-40; dir. student personnel Furman U., Greenville, S.C., 1942-45; dean of women Auburn U., Ala., 1946—. Bd. dirs. Auburn Community Chest, 1955-57. Mem. Ala. Assn. Women Deans and Advisers (pres. 1947-49), Ala. Edn. Assn., Ala. Guidance Assn. (v.p. 1954-56, treas. 1957-58), Am. Coll. Personnel Assn., Am. Personnel and Guidance Assn., Am. Assn. U. Women (div. pres. 1954-56), Nat. Assn. Women Deans and Counselors, Assn. Coll. and Univ. Concert Mgrs. (mem. exec. bd. 1963-66), So. Coll. Personnel Assn., Garden Ala. (life), Kappa Delta Pi, Alpha Lambda Delta (nat. pres. 1970—), Delta Kappa Gamma (chpt. v.p. 1960-62), Phi Kappa Phi (chpt. pres. 1963-64), Mortar Bd., League Women Voters (state dir. 1965-69), P.E.O. Democrat. Baptist. Clubs: Saugahatchee Country, Alabama Federation Womens, Auburn Campus, Auburn Faculty, Auburn Women, Auburn Study. Home: Social Center Auburn U Auburn AL 36830

CATES, AUBREY MARION, JR., judge; b. Oklahoma City, Mar. 5, 1909; s. Aubrey Marion and Laura (Watkins) C.; B.A., U. Louisville, 1930; B.A. Jur. (Rhodes scholar) Oxford (Eng.) U., 1933; M.A., 1963; m. Dorothy May Bear, May 8, 1939; children—Dorothy Ellen (Mrs. Rex Dee Adams), Aubrey Marion III, Laura Compton (Mrs. Michael H. Luckett). Admitted Ky. bar, 1933, Ala. bar, 1937; practiced in Louisville, 1932-33; counsel Pub. Works Adminstrn., Washington, Louisville, Montgomery, Ala., Austin, Tex., Lincoln, Neb., San Francisco, 1933-40, Maritime Commn., 1940-42; asst. gen. counsel War Shipping Adminstrn., Washington, 1942; practiced in Montgomery, 1942-56; mem. law firm Bear & Cates, 1942-43, Cates & Huddleston, 1950-56; judge Ala. Ct. Appeals, Montgomery, 1956-69; asso. judge Ala. Ct. Criminal Appeals, Montgomery, 1969-72, presiding judge, 1972—. Instr. econs. labor relations, real estate U. Ala. Montgomery Center, 1948-56. Pres., Montgomery Tb and Health Assn., 1952. Served from lt. (j.g.) to lt., USNR, 1943-46. Mem. Ala. State Bar, Am. Bar Assn., Am. Soc. for Legal History, Inst. Jud. Adminstrn., Selden Soc. (London). Democrat. Presbyn. Home: 1946 Ridge Av Montgomery AL 36106 Office: Jud Bldg Montgomery AL 36101

CATES, WALTER THRUSTON, comml. orgn. exec.; b. Burlington, N.C., Apr 28, 1913; s. Claud Holt and Ella Lee (Cheek) C.; student U. N.C., 1931-32. Southeastern Inst. for C. of C. Execs., 1942-47; m. Martha Fonville, June 12, 1932; children—George E., Jeanie (Mrs. Rodney O. Siggelkow). Sales mgr. Alamance Motors, Burlington, 1932-41; mgr. Burlington C. of C., 1941-44; Macon (Ga.) C. of C., 1945-52; exec. v.p. Ga. C. of C., Atlanta, 1952—; pres. Empress Hosiery Corp., Atlanta, 1943—; instr., pres. dean of faculty S.E. Inst. Comml. Orgns. Execs., U. N.C., 1951-59. Mem. State Economy Study Commn., Ga. Employment Security Adv. Bd.; mem. Regional Export Expansion Council, Gov.'s European Trade Mission, 1962. Mem. Selective Service Bd., 1941-45; mem. adv. bd. Salvation Army, 1961—. Mem. Am. C. of C. Execs., Sigma Phi Epsilon. Baptist. Elk, Mason, Kiwanian. Home: 2045 Springlake Dr NW Atlanta GA 30305 Office: Commerce Bldg Atlanta GA 30303

CATHEY, GERALD MASON, univ. dean; b. Gastonia, N.C., Feb. 9, 1935; s. Lester Mason and Mary Louise (Johnston) C.; B.S., Davidson Coll., 1957; D.D.S., U. N.C., 1961; M.S., U. Wash., 1966; m. Shirley Maria Barrett, Dec. 20, 1958; children—Kristin Linne, Bart Page. Instr., U. N.C. Sch. Dentistry, Chapel Hill, 1961-62, asst. prof., 1962-67, asso. prof., 1967—, asst. dean, 1970—. Cons. Residency Tng. Programs, U.S. Army, 1966—. Recipient Richard F. Hunt, Jr. Meml. award Loblolly Study Club, 1969-70. Diplomate Am. Bd. Endodontics. Mem. Am. Assn. Endodontists, Am. Assn. Dental Schs., Am. Dental Assn., N.C. Dental Soc., Omicron Kappa Upsilon. Home: Route 3 Old Lystra Rd Chapel Hill NC 27514

CATHEY, GRADY HILLMAN, supt. schs.; b. El Dorado, Ark., Aug. 8, 1929; s. Grady Hillman and Lula (Dunn) C.; B.S., So. State Coll., 1954; M.Ed., E. Tex. State U., 1963; postgrad. U. Ark., 1970; m. Lulamae Black, Dec. 22, 1955; children—Mark Ray and Kelley Jaye (twins). Head football coach pub. schs., Gurdon, Ark., 1955-63; prin. high sch., Waldo, Ark., 1963-65, Hope, Ark., 1965-67; supt. schs., Blevins, Ark., 1967-69, Rison, Ark., 1969—. Served with AUS, 1947-49, 51. Home: 704 Main St Rison AR 71665 Office: Box 307 Risen AR 71665

CATHEY, JAMES LEROY, city ofcl.; b. Arcadia, La., Apr. 30, 1919; s. John Leroy and Clotile (Brice) C.; student Centenary Coll., Shreveport, La., evenings 1939, 42; m. Dorothy Louise Williams, July 7, 1941; children—Sharon (Mrs. Robert Durwood Thorn), Karen (Mrs. Frederick Lee Green), Kathe (Mrs. Donald Lee Townsend). Safety insp. Camp Polk (La.) Fire Dept., 1940; fireman, Camp Livingstone, La., 1941, La. Ordnance Plant, 1942; mcht. dept., furniture and grocery stores, Bossier City, La., 1946-49; policeman Bossier City Police Dept., 1949-53, chief of police, 1953-70; asst. to mayor Bossier City, 1965—, adminstr., coordinating agt., 1970—. Instr., La. Law Enforcement Inst., Bossier City, 1966; dep. sheriff Bossier Parish, 1963—; 1st juvenile officer Bossier City and Parish, 1950-53. Chmn., Bossier City March of Dimes, 1951-52, Muscular Dystrophy, Bossier, 1968—, Bossier Parish chpt. A.R.C., 1967—; chmn. Bossier Parish Heart Fund, 1970—, bd. dirs. state com., 1971; co-chmn. Barksdale AFB Domes-Action Com., 1970-71. Mem. Bossier City Central Democratic Com., 1948-52. Bd. dirs. N.W. La. Fed. Law Enforcement Adv. Com., Family Counseling and Children's Service of Bossier and Caddo Parish, Home Health Services Bossier Parish. Served with USAAF, 1943-46; lt. col. USAF Res. Named Most Courteous Policeman Optimist Club, 1950; recipient Young Man of Year award Bossier Jr. C. of C., 1953; James Cathey

Appreciation Day city of Bossier, 1968. Mem. Am. Legion (comdr. 1952-53), C. of C. (charter mem., dir. 1951-54, 70-71), V.F.W., La. Peace Officers Assn. (dir., past pres.), La. Municipal Police Assn. (dir. 1953—), La. Chiefs of Police (dir. 1953—). Methodist (ofcl. bd. 1947—, trustee 1967—). Lion (pres. Bossier City 1953-54), Mason (Shriner). Home: 317 Yarbrough St Bossier City LA 71010 Office: 708 Barksdale Blvd Bossier City LA 71010

CATHEY, MAURICE, lawyer; b. Paragould, Ark., June 23, 1910; J.D., Washington U., 1931. Admitted to Mo. bar, 1931, Ark. bar, 1933, also U.S. Dist. Cts.; mem. firm Kirsch, Cathey, Brown & Goodwin, Paragould; dep. pros. atty. Greene County, Ark., 1935-36. Mem. Am., Greene County, Northeast Ark., Ark. (chmn. jurisprudence and law reform com.; chmn. probate law com. 1950-51, mem. exec. com. 1962-67, v.p. 1966, pres. 1967), Delta Theta Phi. Office: 206 W Emerson St Paragould AR 72450*

CATHEY, RODNEY DEAN, ednl. adminstr.; b. Childress, Tex., Jan. 30, 1924; s. James E. and Gertrude (Land) C.; B.A., Hardin-Simmons U., 1948, M.A., 1950; Ed.D., U. Tex., 1962; m. Martha Carolyn Brown, Aug. 24, 1948; children—Blake, Christine, Deana, Ross. Prin. Sudan (Tex.) Elem. Sch., 1949; prin. Sanderson (Tex.) High Sch., 1949-51; prin. Winters (Tex.) High Sch., 1952-60; asst. supt. schs., Pharr, Tex., 1961; supt. schs., Bay City, Tex., 1963-69; supt. schs., McAllen, Tex., 1969—. Served with AUS, 1943-46. Mem. Tex. Assn. Sch. Adminstrs. (mem. exec. com. 1967-69), Brazos-Colo. Adminstrs. Assn. (pres. 1967-69), Nat. Assn. Sch. Adminstrs., N.E.A., Tex. State Tchrs. Assn., Phi Delta Kappa (pres. Rio Grande Valley chpt. 1970-71). Lion. Home: 625 E Dallas St McAllen TX 78501 Office: 110 S 10th St McAllen TX 78501

CATLETT, LEON BIDEZ, lawyer; b. Dardanelle, Ark., Mar. 26, 1909; s. Samuel Graham and Alix (Bidez) C.; LL.B., U. Ark., 1932; m. Sally Cooper, Mar. 12, 1936. Admitted to Ark. bar, 1932. Sec. Ark. state com. Democratic party, 1959-63, chmn., 1963-68. Vice chmn. bd. trustees U. Ark., 1960-70. Served with AUS, 1944-45. Mem. Am. Coll. Trial Lawyers, Am. Ark., Pulaski County, Fed. bar assns., Am. Judicature Soc., Am. Coll. Probate Counsel, Am. Legion, Phi Alpha Delta, Kappa Alpha. Presbyn. (elder). Mason (Shriner). Clubs: Little Rock Country, Little Rock, Capitol, North Hills Country. Home: 324 Midland Av Little Rock AR 72203 Office: Pyramid Life Bldg Little Rock AR 72201

CATON, IRMA JEANNE, educator; b. Newport, Tenn.; d. Benjamin Dickerson and Bernice (Easterly) Caton; B.S., E. Tenn. State U., 1946; M.S., U. Tenn., 1949, Ed.D., 1962. Tchr. pub. schs. Marion, Va., 1946-47, Newport, Tenn., 1947-48, Parrottsville, Tenn., 1949-50; asso. prof. phys. edn. Concord Coll., Athens, W.Va., 1950-60; instr. U. Tenn., Knoxville, 1961-62; asso. prof. phys. edn. N. Tex. State U., Denton, 1962-65, prof., chmn. women's div. dept. health, phys. edn. and recreation, 1965—. Mem. Gov.'s Phys. Fitness Commn., 1971—. Mem. Am., Tex. assns. health, phys. edn. and recreation, N.E.A., Am. Assn. U. Women, Am. Assn. U. Profs., Tex. Assn. Coll. Tchrs., Pi Lambda Theta, Beta Sigma Phi, Kappa Delta Alumni Assn., Delta Psi Kappa. Mem. Christian Ch. Contbr. to profl. jours. Home: 1003 Eagle Dr Denton TX 76201

CATRON, GAIL MARLENE SATTERFIELD (MRS. GILBERT WAYNE CATRON), counselor; b. Knoxville, Tenn., May 1, 1943; d. Jess Willard and Grace (Varner) Satterfield; B.A., Emory and Henry Coll., 1965; M.S., Radford Coll., 1967; m. Gilbert Wayne Catron, Aug. 30, 1964; 1 son, Christopher Wayne. Tchr., Fort Chiswell High Sch., 1965-66, counselor, 1966-67; psychol. counselor Blue Ridge Job Corps, Marion, Va., 1967—. Pres., Wythe County Mental Health Assn., 1966-68; mem. Wytheville Jr. Woman's Club; sec. Wythe County chpt. A.R.C., 1967—. Mem. Am., S.W. (pres. 1968-69), Va. (chmn. study commn. disadvantaged children 1969-70) personnel and guidance assns., Am. Assn. U. Women. Home: 450 W Ridge St Wytheville VA 24382 Office: Box 425 Marion VA 24354

CATUCCI, HENRY GABRIEL, telecommunication co. exec.; b. Washington, Jan. 29, 1916; s. Ernesto and Francesca (Trozini) C.; LL.B., Cath. U., 1940; m. Margaret J. Halden, Apr. 6, 1947. Regional mgr. Western Union Cables, Washington, 1947-58; exec. dir. Western Union Telegraph Co., N.Y.C., 1959-64; v.p. Western Union Internat., Inc., Washington, 1964—; dir. several corps. Bd. dirs. Villa Rosa Home for Aged, Mitchelville, Md. Recipient Order of Merit, St. Penford (Spain), 1960. Mem. Armed Forces Communications and Electronic Assn. K.C. Clubs: Nat. Press, University, Columbia Country. Home: 3001 Veazey Terrace NW Washington DC 20008 Office: 2100 M St NW Washington DC 20037

CAUBLE, FLORENCE HORKAN, mem. Republican Nat. Com.; b. Moultrie, Ga., July 4, 1929; d. George Arthur and Martha (Olliff) Horkan; A.B., Wesleyan Coll., Macon, Ga., 1950; m. John A. Cauble, Oct. 14, 1950; children—Sally, Susan, David. Tchr., Dekalb County, Ga., 1950-51. Pres. Cherokee Fedn. Republican Women, 1960-64; vice chmn. Rep. Party Cherokee County, 1962-64; treas. Ga. Fedn. Rep. Women, 1965-68; women's activities dir. Congl. campaign, 1964; mem. Rep. Nat. Com. for Ga., 1968—; mem. Ga. Rep. Com., 1966-67, 68—, mem. exec. com., 1968—. Named Outstanding Rep. Woman in Ga., 1966. Methodist. Home: Route 6 Box 51 Sunset Dr Canton GA 30114

CAUDILL, ESTILL LEFTRAGE, JR., surgeon, utility exec.; b. Narrows, Va., Aug. 21, 1916; s. Estill Leftrage and Flora (Weatherly) C.; student U. Tenn., E. Tenn. State U., Va. Polytech. Inst., 1934-37; M.D., Med. Coll. Va., 1941; m. Lucy Denny Bolton, Nov. 25,1939; children—Estill L. III, Anne (Mrs. Clifton Reginald Lewis, Jr.), Lucy (Mrs. John Newby Austin, Jr.). Intern, Baroness Erlanger Hosp., Chattanooga, 1941-42; individual practice gen. surgery, Elizabethton, Tenn., 1946-66; med. dir. Beaunit Corp. div. El Paso Natural Gas, Elizabethton, 1966—. Dir., Elizabethton Security Fed. Savs. and Loan Assn., Citizens Bank; med. examiner Carter County, 1961—. Mem. Tenn. Bd. Med. Examiners, 1964—; mem. Carter County Bd. Health, 1946—. A founder Appalachian Regional Center for Healing Arts, 1968, bd. dirs.; sec.-treas. Elizabethton Airport Commn., 1972—. Served with M.C., AUS, 1942-46, USPHS, 1960—. Decorated Bronze Star medal, Combat Med. badge. Past Pres. Tenn. Acad. Gen. Practice, 1960. Mem. Tenn. Med. Assn. (bd. trustees 1963-66), Am. Soc. Abdominal Surgeons, A.M.A., Phi Gamma Delta, Theta Kappa Psi. Rotarian (pres. 1950), Mason (32 deg.). Home: PO Box 551 Elizabethton TN 37643 Office: Beaunit Fibers Elizabethton TN 37643

CAUDILL, JOHN, agriculturist; b. Blackey, Ky., May 28, 1927; s. George Matt and Dora Alice (Fields) C.; B.S. in Agr., U. Ky., 1953, M.S., 1962, postgrad. in econ. resource devel., 1968; m. Alma Florence Lane, June 11, 1949; children—Aaron Mark, John Maurice. Asst. county agrl. extension agt. U.S. Dept. Agr., Whitley and Perry Counties, Ky., 1953, county agrl. extension agt., Owsley and Wolfe Counties, Ky., 1954-66, area extension resource devel. specialist, Quicksand Area, 1967-68, county extension agt. for agr., Wolfe County, Ky., 1969—. Bd. dirs. vol. fire depts., Hazel Green and Campton, Ky., 1968—. Served with AUS, 1945-47. Recipient award Ky. Div. Natural Resources, 1968, Ky. Service to Agr. citation, 1971, Distinguished Service award Nat. Assn. County Agrl. Agts., 1971. Mem. Nat. Assn. County Agrl. Agts., Community Devel. Soc., Epsilon Sigma Phi. Kiwanian (pres. Wolfe County 1965, dir. 1965—). Instrumental in mobilizing and organizing local leaders to bring improvements to area, including new electronics plant, pub. library, city water and sewer systems, 2 vol. fire depts., other. Home: PO Box 163 Hazel Green KY 41332 Office: PO Box 146 Campton KY 41301

CAUFFIEL, PAUL WENDELL, educator; b. Johnstown, Pa., Dec. 10, 1923; s. Paul Wendell and Adelene Lucille (Williams) C.; B.A. in Psychology, Pa. State U., 1948, M.S. in Clin. Psychology, 1950, Ed.D. in Counseling and Guidance, 1952; m. A. Lorayne Tarr, Nov. 22, 1950. Research analyst Pa. Employment Service, Harrisburg, 1950; appraiser and guidance center clinician Pa. State U., University Park, 1948-50, grad. asst., 1950-52; asst. prof. psychology Mt. Union Coll., Alliance, O., 1952-54; asso. prof. psychology, dean students, chmn. div. human relations Henderson State Tchrs. Coll., Arkadelphia, Ark., 1954-56; dir. student personnel Key West (Fla.) High Sch., 1956-57; asso. prof. psychology, dir. Counseling Center, So. State Coll., Magnolia, Ark., 1957-59; coordinator guidance services, dir. Nat. Def. Edn. Act Guidance Research Project, Sarasota (Fla.) Bd. Pub. Instrn., 1959-62; cons. test dept. Harcourt, Brace & World, Inc., Atlanta, 1962-65; head dept. psychology and edn. Broward Jr. Coll., Ft. Lauderdale, Fla., 1965—, also chmn. div. social scis. Gen. clin. counselor, sch. psychologist, counselor trainer, 1950—. Served inf. AUS, World War II; PTO. Decorated Purple Heart. Mem. Am., Fla. psychol. assns., Am. Personnel and Guidance Assn., Nat. Vocational Guidance Assn., Nat. Assn. Guild Suprs. and Counsel Trainers, Am. School Counselors Assn., Am. Coll. Personnel Assn., Am. Radio Relay League, Am. Edn. Research Assn., Fla. Assn. Deans and Counselors, Phi Delta Kappa, Pi Gamma Mu, Iota Alpha Delta, Psi Chi, Sigma Chi. Home: 2418 Marathon Lane Fort Lauderdale FL 33312

CAULEY, JOHN ROWAN, newspaper corr.; b. Rushville, Ind., Apr. 25, 1908; s. Thomas S. and Mary Ann (Kelly) C.; student Rockhurst Coll., Kansas City, Mo., 1926-28, L.H.D., 1968; B.J., U. Mo., 1932. Pub. weekly newspaper The Summit News, Kansas City, Mo., 1933-36; mem. staff Kansas City (Mo.) Star, 1936—, news editor, 1954, fgn. affairs editor Washington bur., 1957-64, chief bur., 1964—. Recipient Pro-Meritis award Rockhurst Coll., 1960. Mem. A.P. Mng. Editors Assn. (bd. dirs. 1952-54). White House Corr. Assn., John Carroll Soc., Mo. Acad. Squires, Sigma Delta Chi. Roman Catholic (usher). Clubs: Kansas City Press (pres. 1950); Nat. Press (bd. govs.), Gridiron (Washington). Home: 1727 Massachusetts Av NW Washington DC 20036 Office: 1750 Pennsylvania Av NW Washington DC 20006

CAUSEY, JAMES BENJAMIN, physician; b. Furman, S.C., Sept. 22, 1938; s. Malcolm Lander and Martha Ann (Jenkins) C.; B.A., Emory U., 1960; M.D., Med. Coll. S.C., 1964; m. Julia Peeples, Aug. 20, 1960; children—James Benjamin, Charles Allen, Rebecca P. Intern, Med. Coll. S.C., Charleston, 1964-65, asst. resident medicine, 1967-68; gen. practice medicine, Hampton, S.C., 1968-69; family practice medicine Family Med. Center, Estill, S.C., 1969—; mem. staff Hampton Gen. Hosp., Varnville, S.C. Med. adviser Hampton County March of Dimes, 1970—. Mem. pub. safety com. advisory Low County Regional Planning Council, 1970—. Bd. dirs. Patrick Henry Acad., Estill. Served to capt., M.C., AUS, 1966-68. Decorated Bronze Star. Mem. Am. Acad. Gen. Practice, Am. Legion, Am. Heart Assn., Sigma Chi. Republican. Episcopalian (sr. warden 1971—). Home: PO Box 336 Estill SC 29918 Office: 60 3d St E Estill SC 29918

CAUSEY, JAMES CAMPBELL, JR., city mgr.; b. Suffolk, Va., Apr. 23, 1902; s. James C. and Marguerite (Crump) C.; B.S., Va. Mil. Inst., 1924; m. Margaret Urquhart Jordan, June 9, 1928; children—James Campbell III, Margaret (Mrs. Bedford Horton Brown). Transitman Bd. Commrs. Everglades Drainage Dist., State Fla., West Palm Beach, 1924-25; asst. engr. Moore Haven (Fla.) Engring. Co., Moore Haven, Fla., 1925-26; engr. Wallis Engring. Co., Tallahassee, 1926; timber surveys Surry Lumber Co., Sedley, Va., 1926-27; engr. R. G. Lassiter & Co., 1927; bridge insp. The Virginian Ry. Co., 1927-32; city engr. City of Suffolk, Va., 1932-42, city mgr., 1942-46, 55—; sr. engr. Myron Sturgeon Engrs., Norfolk, 1946-53; partner Causey & Weeks, Engrs., 1953-55; dir. A. B. Miner Co. Bd. dirs. Louise Obici Meml. Hosp. Registered civil engr., Va. Mem. Am. Soc. C. E., City Mgrs. Assn., Soc. Am. Mil. Engrs., Nat., Va. fox hunters assns. Episcopalian. Rotarian. Home: 883 Carolina Rd Suffolk VA 23434 Office: City Mgr Municipal Bldg Market St Suffolk VA 23434

CAUSEY, NELL B. (MRS. DAVID CAUSEY), zoologist; b. Trenton, Tenn., Dec. 8, 1910; d. Harvey M. and Nettie (Hester) Bevel; B.S., Coll. of Ozarks, 1931; M.A., U. Ark., 1937; Ph.D., Duke, 1940; m. David Causey, Aug. 2, 1938. Tchr. high sch., Alma, Van Buren, Ark., 1931-36; biologist Marine Lab., Duke, 1944; instr. zoology U. Ark., 1943, 45-48; ind. investigator, 1948-64; asst. prof. zoology La. State U., 1964-66, asso. prof. zoology, 1966-71, prof., 1971—. Mem. Nat. Speleological Soc., Soc. Study Evolution, Soc. Systematic Zoology, Phi Beta Kappa, Sigma Xi. Author numerous articles profl. jours. Editor: Proc. of La. Acad. Scis., 1965—. Research in taxonomy of the Diplopoda. Home: 1110 Magnolia Woods Dr Baton Route LA 70808

CAUSEY, WILLIAM WATKINS, clergyman; b. Greenville, Miss., May 17, 1931; s. John Davis and Ruby (McCarley) C.; B.A., Miss. Coll., 1952, D.D., 1968; B.D., So. Bapt. Theol. Sem., 1955; m. Charlotte Rose, Jan. 24, 1954; children—William Watkins, Carol Carley. Ordained to ministry Bapt. Ch., 1951; pastor Hopewell Bapt. Ch., rural Ky., 1952-55; asso. pastor Parkway Bapt. Ch., Jackson, Miss., 1955-57; pastor Poplar Springs Dr. Bapt. Ch., Meridian, Miss., 1957-63, Parkway Bapt. Ch., Jackson, 1963—. Instr. Old Testament, Sem. Extension Service, 1958; chaplain Miss. Jr. C. of C., 1967—. Trustee, Miss. Bapt. Hosp., Miss. Bapt. Sem.; bd. dirs. Met. YMCA, Boys Club. Nominee for Outstanding Young Man of Year Jr. C. of C., Meridian, Miss., 1961, Jackson, Miss., 1966. Club: Civitan (Jackson). Contbr. articles to religious publs., Zondervan Pastor's Ann. Home: 930 Arbor Vista Blvd Jackson MS 39209 Office: Box 10564 Jackson MS 39209

CAUTHEN, IRBY BRUCE, JR., univ. dean; b. Rock Hill, S.C., Aug. 24, 1919; s. Irby Bruce and Ruth (Kimbrell) C.; B.A. Furman U., 1940; M.A., U. Va., 1942, Ph.D., 1951; m. Elizabeth Bagby Greear, Aug. 28, 1954; children—Irby Bruce III, James Noah Greear. Asst. prof. English, Hollins Coll., 1951-54; mem. faculty U. Va., 1954—, prof. English, 1964—, asso. dean, 1958-62, dean coll., 1962—, chmn. Peters Rushton Seminars, 1958-61, 68—, asso. dir. summer sessions, 1958-72. Chmn. regional selection com. Woodrow Wilson Fellowship Found., 1961—; exec. com. United Givers Fund, 1966—. Trustee Belfield Sch., 1963-70. Served to lst lt. AUS, 1942-46; N. Africa, Italy. Decorated Bronze Star. Mem. Bibliog. Soc. U. Va. (v.p. 1961—), Modern Lang. Assn., Shakespeare Assn., Am. Assn. U. Profs., Va. Assn. Summer Sch. Deans (chmn. 1967-68), Phi Beta Kappa (Va. pres. 1969-71), Omicron Delta Kappa. Democrat. Presbyn. Clubs: Colonnade, Farmington, Boar's Head (Charlottesville). Editor: Norton and Sackville's Gorboduc: Two Mementoes from the Poe-Ingram Collection. Contbg. editor Beaumont and Fletcher Canon. Contbr. profl. jours. Home: 1824 Winston Rd Charlottesville VA 22903

CAVANAH, FRANCES, author; b. Princeton, Ind., Sept. 26, 1899; d. Rufus Oscar and Luella (Neale) Cavanah; A.B., DePauw U., 1920. Editorial staff Child Life Mag., Rand McNally & Co., Chgo., 1923-29, asso. editor, 1930-38; contbg. writer Western Printing Co., Row, Peterson & Co., Evanston, Ill., 1939-42; biography editor 1947 revision World Book Ency., Field Enterprises, Chgo., 1943-46, anthology editor 1949 revision Childcraft, 1947-48; dir. biography Real People series Row, Peterson & Co., 1948-52; free lance author, 1953—. Recipient Headliner award Theta Sigma Phi, 1942; citation for Meritorious Achievement DePauw U., 1952. Mem. Soc. Midland Authors, Am. Newspaper Women's Club, Washington Children's Book Guild, Mortar Bd., Nat. Hist. Soc., Delta Delta Delta, Theta Sigma Phi. Democrat. Author numerous books, including Our Country's Story, 1945; We Came to America, 1954; Abe Lincoln Gets His Chance (recipient Ind. U. Writers Conf. citation for Most Distinguished Children's book by Hoosier author 1960), 1959; Adventure in Courage, the Story of Theodore Roosevelt, 1961; Meet the Presidents, 1962; Triumphant Adventure, the Story of Franklin D. Roosevelt, 1964; Our Country's Freedom, 1966; Holiday Roundup, 1968; Freedom Ency., American Liberties in the Making, 1968; Jenny Lind's America (Christian Herald Family Bookshelf selection), 1969; Jenny Lind and Her Listening Cat, 1970; When Americans Came to New Orleans, 1970; We Wanted to Be Free, 1971; contbr. to sch. readers. anthologies (several books recorded for the blind, transcribed into braille). Home: 5100 Fillmore Av Alexandria VA 22311

CAVENDER, JACK EDMOND, architect; b. Atlanta, Oct. 12, 1929; s. Jewel Edmond and Dallie Lou (McGiboney) C.; B.S. in Architecture, Ga. Inst. Tech., 1957; m. Bobbie Garrett, July 27, 1951 (dec. Dec. 1969); children—Jackie, Jenny, David; m. 2d, Celeta Estes, Feb. 12, 1971. Architect, East Point, Ga., 1960-61; asso. Shugart & Cavender, Atlanta, 1961-63; architect, Decatur, Ga., 1963-71; prin. Cavender Assos., East Point, 1971—. Vice pres. Summit Investment Co., Inc., East Point, 1966—. Mem. A.I.A. Kiwanian. Prin. archtl. works include 1st Alliance Ch., S.W. Christian Ch., Emmanuel Luth. Ch., W.D. Luckie Masonic Lodge, Bottle Hill Masonic Lodge (all Atlanta), Gulf Disney Facility, Walt Disney World, Fla. Home: 3000 Continental Colony Pkwy SW Atlanta GA 30331 Office: 1677 Dorsey Av East Point GA 30044

CAVERT, TILLMAN, JR., paper co. exec.; b. Nashville, July 31, 1916; s. Tillman and Florence (Peterson) C.; LL.B., Cumberland U., 1937; m. Ellen Josephine McGehee, Oct. 19, 1940; children—Tillman III, Ray Rives (Mrs. Richard Martin), Ellen Peterson (Mrs. James Gilbert, Jr.), Grace Haynes. Admitted to Tenn. bar, 1937; practiced in Nashville, Tenn., 1937-40; with Calcasieu Paper Co., Inc., Jacksonville, Fla., 1945—, pres., chmn. bd., 1964—; pres., chmn. bd. Ironkraft Bag Co. (formerly So. Maid Paper Co.), Jacksonville, 1964—; v.p., dir. Unijax, Inc., Jacksonville; dir. Am. Nat. Bank, Jacksonville, Fla. Mem. Tenn. Ho. of Reps., 1939. Bd. dirs. Ray Sutton McGehee Found. Served to 1st lt. AUS, 1940-42; served to capt. USAAF, 1942-45. Mem. Paper Bag Inst. Am. (v.p. 1968-69, pres., mem. exec. com. 1970), Sigma Alpha Epsilon. Mem. Ch. of Christ. Mason (32 deg.). Clubs: San Jose Country, Hidden Hills Country, University, River. Home: 942 Maple Lane Jacksonville FL 32207 Office: 808 W Bay St Jacksonville FL 32203

CAVILEER, CURTIS MONROE, food mfg. co. exec.; b. Phila., May 26, 1918; s. Curtis Monroe and Evea (Haggerty) C.; student Goodyear Indsl. U., 1941; m. Justina C. Coe, June 7, 1939; children—Carol L., Mikele D., David C. Sales mgr. Lutz & Schramm, Inc., Pitts., 1950-57, gen. mgr., exec. v.p., dir., Ayden, N.C., 1959—; field mgr. Clark Candy Co., Pitts., 1957-58; dir. Planters Nat. Bank. Chmn., United Fund, Ayden, 1963. Bd. dirs. Carolinas United, 1963, Pitt County United Fund, 1962-64. Served with AUS, 1945-46. Mem. Pickle Packers Internat. (dir.), U.S., Ayden (pres. 1964) chambers commerce, Am. Legion, N.C. Pickle Producers Assn. (dir. 1966, pres. 1967-68, sec., treas. 1971-72), N.C. Hort. Council (commn. 1970-72), Mid-East Devel. Council (commn. 1969-72). Mem. Disciples of Christ Ch. Mason (32 deg.), Rotarian (pres. Ayden, dist. dir.). Home: Pine Forest Dr Ayden NC 28513 Office: 904 S Lee St Ayden NC 28513

CAVINESS, VERNE STRUDWICK, physician; b. Hillsborough, N.C., Feb. 9, 1895; s. Newby and Nora (Cummings) C.; A.B., Trinity Coll., 1915; student U. N.C., 1916-19; M.D., Jefferson Med. Coll., 1921; postgrad. McGill U., 1936; m. Alice Webb, Oct. 14, 1933; children—Verne Strudwick Jr., Elizabeth (Mrs. George E. Levings III), Alice (Mrs. Richard Hardy). Intern Jefferson Med. Coll., 1921-22, resident, 1922-23; pvt. practice medicine, specializing in internal medicine and cardiology, cardiology, Raleigh, N.C., 1923—; chief cardiovascular medicine, Rex Hosp., Raleigh, 1937-65; med. dir. Occidental Life Ins. Co., Raleigh, 1926-52; asso. prof. clin. medicine U. N.C., 1952-65, prof. emeritus, 1965—; cons. Physician Methodist Home for Children, Raleigh, 1923—. Pres. Travelers Aid, 1928-29; pres. Raleigh Salvation Army, 1938-39; pres. Broughton High Sch P.T.A., 1951-52; pres. Daniels Jr. High Sch. P.T.A., 1960-61. Served with U.S. Army, 1918. Fellow A.C.P.; mem. Am., Raleigh (past pres., dir.) heart assns., Am., N.C., Wake County med. assns., Raleigh Acad. Medicine, Am. Diabetes Assn. Democrat. Methodist. Mason (Shriner). Home: 913 Vance St Raleigh NC 27608 Office: 109 N Boylan Av Raleigh NC 27603

CAWELTI, GORDON LOU, supt. schs.; b. Reinbeck, Ia., Dec. 5, 1929; s. Clarence and Grace (Olthoff) C.; B.A., State Coll. Ia., 1951; M.A., Colo. State Coll., 1954; Ph.D., U. Ia., 1962; postgrad. U. Chgo., 1968-69; m. Diana Janssen, Dec. 16, 1961; 1 dau., Kimberly Ann. Tchr. sci. Lytton (Ia.) High Sch., 1954-56, prin., 1956-58; prin. Spirit Lake (Ia.) High Sch., 1958-60; asst. prin. Univ. High Sch., Iowa City, 1961-62; exec. sec. North Central Assn., Chgo., 1962-69; supt. schs., Tulsa, 1969—; vis. lectr. U. Kan., summer 1964, U. Colo., summer 1965, U. Ill., summer 1966. Mem. def. adv. com. Armed Forces Edn., Dept. Def., Washington, 1963-66; insp. mil. schs. Am. Dependents Schs. Com., 1963, 65, 68. Mem. adv. bd. St. John's Hosp., Tulsa; bd. dirs. Nat. Conf. Christians and Jews, Thomas Gilcrease Inst., Tulsa; trustee Holland Hall Sch., Tulsa, Joint Council Econ. Edn., N.Y.C. Served with AUS, 1951-53. Mem. Am. Assn. Sch. Adminstrs. (mem. program commn. Nat. Acad. Sch. Execs. 1970). Rotarian. Editorial bd. Nation's Schs., 1965—. Contbr. articles to profl. jours. Home: 6753 S 73d East Av Tulsa OK 74133 Office: PO Box 45208 Tulsa OK 74145

CAWTHON, ELENORA ALBRECHT (MRS. JOHN ARDIS CAWTHON), coll. administr.; b. nr. Victoria, Tex., Dec. 6, 1917; d. Otto H. and Lillie (Lassmann) Albrecht; A.A., Victoria Jr. Coll., 1936; B.S.; U. Tex., 1938, M.S., 1939, Ed.D., 1948; m. John Ardis Cawthon, May 30, 1948; 1 dau., Elisabeth Albrecht. Tchr. pub. schs., Bandera, Tex., 1938-40, Woodsboro, Tex., 1940-46; asst. depts. govt., elementary edn., curriculum and instrn. U. Tex., Austin, 1936-38, summers 1943-46, 46-48; dir. tchr. edn. Ark. Polytech. Coll., Russellville, 1948-54; dir. dept. placement and service La. Polytech. Inst., Ruston, 1955—, sec. faculty senate, 1966-67, senate mem., 1967-68. Trustee Coll. Placement Council Found., 1967-68; chmn. visitation teams Coll. Placement Services, Inc., 1967-68; bd. dirs. Bus.

and Profl. Womens Found., 1956-57; scholarship com. Delta Kappa Gamma Soc., Epsilon State Orgn., 1961—. Mem. Bus. and Profl. Womens Club (pres. Ark. fedn. 1954-55), La. Fedn. Womens Clubs, Coll. Placement Council, (v.p. editorial 1967-68, pres. 1972—), S.W. Placement Assn. (pres. 1959-61), La. Council Coll. Placement Officers (pres. 1967-68), La. Tchrs. Assn., Am. Personnel and Guidance Assn., Am. Coll. Personnel Assn., Am. Assn. U. Women, Delta Kappa Gamma, Pi Sigma Alpha, Pi Lambda Theta, Alpha Tau Delta, Phi Kappa Phi. Club: Pierian. Contbr., articles to profl. jours. Home: 815 Wilaford St Ruston LA 71270

CAWTHON, JOHN ARDIS, educator; b. Koran, La., Mar. 16, 1907; s. James Alexander and Maggie Mae (Dance) C.; B.A., La. Poly. Inst., 1934; M.A., La. State U., 1937; Ed.D., U. Tex., 1948; m. Elenora Albrecht, May 30, 1948; 1 dau., Elisabeth Albrecht. Tchr., Sarepta High Sch., 1934-39; supr. Demonstration Sch., La. Poly. Inst. at Ruston, 1940-41, vis. prof., 1948, head secondary edn. dept., 1954—; supr. Demonstration Sch., La. State Normal Coll., 1941-42, 46; grad. teaching asst. U. Tex., 1946-48; chmn. edn. dept. Ark. Poly. Inst., 1948-54. Served to capt. AUS, 1942-45. Mem. Nat. Edn.Assn., Assn. Supervision and Curriculum Devel., Assn. Student Teaching, La. Tchrs. Assn., La., N. La., Darlington (S.C.) hist. assns. Phi Kappa Phi, Phi Delta Kappa, Sigma Tau Delta, Omicron Delta Kappa. Author: The Inevitable Guest-Life and Letters of Jemima Darby, 1965. Contbr. articles to profl. jours. Home: 815 Wilaford St Ruston LA 71270 Office: PO Box 6245 Tech Sta Ruston LA 71270

CAWTHON, WOODSON ARTHUR, C. of C. exec.; b. Roxton, Tex., Oct. 5, 1918; s. William Arthur and Lura (Denton) C.; A.A., Paris Jr. Coll., 1937; B.S., Tex. A. and M. U., 1940; m. Merle Nance, July 4, 1942; children—Ann, Wesley Arthur. Mgr. W.A. Cawthon Wholesale Petroleum Co., Paris, Tex., 1946-54; owner, mgr. Cawthon's, Paris, 1955-67; mgr. Silsbee (Tex.) C. of C., 1967—. Mem. Paris (Tex.) City Council, 1959-61; mayor, Paris, Tex., 1961-63. Served to maj. AUS, 1942-46. Mem. Ch. Christ (deacon 1948-60, elder 1960-67). Lion (pres. 1971—). Home: Route 1 Box 406 Silsbee TX 77656 Office: 270 Hwy 96 South Silsbee TX 77656

CAYCE, EDGAR EVANS, elec. engr.; b. Selma, Ala., Feb. 9, 1918; s. Edgar and Gertrude Salter (Evans) C.; B.S. in E.E., Duke, 1939; m. Kathryn Anderson Bane, June 13, 1942; children—Edgar Evans, Janet Gail. With Va. Electric & Power Co., Norfolk, 1940—, engr. dist. planning dept., 1955—. Vice pres. Edgar Cayce Found., 1960—. Trustee Atlantic U. Served to capt. AUS, 1941-45. Registered profl. engr., Va. Mem. Assn. for Research and Enlightenment (trustee 1960—). Presbyn. Author: Edgar Cayce on Atlantis, 1968; (with Hugh Lynn Cayce) The Outer Limits of Edgar Cayce's Power, 1971. Home: 1565 Michigan Av Virginia Beach VA 23453 Office: 2700 Cromwell Rd Norfolk VA 23510

CAYCE, LEE FARRAR, physician; b. Nashville, Tenn., Jan. 12, 1915; s. John Smith and Martha (Farrar) C.; B.A., Vanderbilt U., 1936; M.D., Washington U., St. Louis, 1940; m. Mary Baker Gregory, Dec. 30, 1937; children—Mary Farrar (Mrs. Alfred George Nicols), Patricia Lee (Mrs. Lucien Caldwell Simpson). Intern Nashville Gen. Hosp., 1940-41, resident 1941-43; practice medicine specializing in otolaryngology and ophthalmology, Nashville, 1945—; chmn. dept. ophthalmology Mid-State Bapt. Hosp., Nashville, 1965—, mem. med. adv. com., 1965—; mem. staffs St. Thomas, Park View hosps. Bd. and hon. mem. Bill Wilkerson Hearing and Speech Center, Nashville. Served to capt. AUS, 1943-46. Mem. Tenn. State, Nashville med. socs., Nashville Acad. Ophthalmology and Otolaryngology, Contact Lens Assn. of Ophthalmology, Am. Assn. Ophthalmology, Pan Am. Assn. Ophthalmology, Royal Soc. Health. Mem. Ch. of Christ. Clubs: Nashville, Civitan. Home: 915 Robertson Academy Rd Nashville TN 37220 Office: Mid-State Med Bldg Nashville TN 37203

CAYWOOD, DELMORE THOMAS, JR., traffic engr.; b. Bowling Green, Ky., July 13, 1934; s. Delmore Thomas and Emma (Blewett) C.; student U. Louisville, 1956-59; student Northwestern U., 1970. Engring. lab. technician Gen. Electric Co., Louisville, Ky., 1956-59; traffic engr. Ky. Dept. Hwys., Frankfort, 1964—. Served with USAF, 1951-55. Registered profl. engr., Ky. Mem. Ky. Assn. Hwy. Engrs., Inst. Traffic Engrs. Democrat. Mem. Christian Ch. Elk, Lion. Home: 110 E Campbell St Frankfort KY 40601 Office: State Office Bldg Frankfort KY 40601

CAZAN, MATTHEW JOHN, educator; b. Beclean, Romania, Mar. 10, 1912; s. John and Marie (Sipos) C; student U. Bucharest Law Sch., Youngstown Coll., Georgetown U. Sch. Fgn. Service; m. Sylvia Marie Buday, July 14, 1935; 1 son, Matthew John George. Lectr. Georgetown U., 1942-44; spl. lectr. Indsl. Coll. of the Armed Forces, 1947; asso. in Romanian Georgetown U. Inst. Langs. and Linguistics, 1949—, lectr. polit. sci. and econs. Sch. Fgn. Service, 1943-57; lectr. The Inst. Fgn. Service Officer Preparation, 1953—; lectr. polit. sci. George Washington U., 1963—; spl. employee U.S. Dept. of Justice, 1947-60, 63—; internat. claims analyst fgn. claims settlement commn., 1960-63. Chmn. Lobarca youth guidance com. Va. Gov.'s Conf. Youth. Mem. Am. Assn. U. Profs., Am. Polit. Sci. Assn., Am. Soc. Internat. Law, Conf. Democratic Theory, Pi Gamma Mu. Home: 6369 Lakeview Dr Lake Barcroft Estates Falls Church VA 22041 Office: George Washington U Washington DC also Dept Justice Washington DC

CAZAN, SYLVIA MARIE BUDAY (MRS. MATTHEW JOHN CAZAN), realtor; b. Youngstown, O., Nov. 17, 1915; d. John J. and Sylvia (Grama) Buday; student U. Bucharest, (Romania), 1933-35, Youngstown Coll., 1936-38, Georgetown U. Inst. Langs. and Linguistics, 1950; m. Matthew John Cazan, July 14, 1935; 1 son, Matthew John G. Adminstrv. asst. statistics U.S. Dept. Def., 1941-52; spl. employee Dept. Justice, 1956-58; mgr. James L. Dixon & Co. Realtors, Falls Church, Va., 1959-70; Va. sub div. mgr. Lewis & Silverman, Inc., 1970—. Mem. Bd. Examiners Georgetown U., 1950. Bd dirs. Magnolia Internat. Debutante Ball. Recipient Commendation and Meritorious award Dept. Justice, 1958. Mem. Gen. Fedn. Women's Clubs (pres. 1955-56), Interscholastic Debating Soc., Washington, No. Va. real estate bds. Mem. Romanian Orthodox Ch. Home: 6369 Lakeview Dr Lake Barcroft Estates Falls Church VA 22041 Office: 8401 Connecticut Av Chevy Chase MD 20015

CECIL, ANDREW R., educator; b. Warsaw, Poland, May 11, 1911; s. Ignace and Celina (Rockover) C.; LL.B., U. Warsaw, 1930, LL.M., 1932, LL.D., 1935; LL.D., Lambuth Coll., 1965; m. Katherine Sand, 1935; 1 dau., Christine R. (Mrs. T. Alex Eastus). Came to U.S., 1949, naturalized, 1955. Prof., Universidad Nacional Mayor de San Marcos, Peru, 1945-49; head econs. dept. Lambuth Coll., Jackson, Tenn., 1949-51; dean Sch. Bus. Adminstrn., McMurry Coll., Abilene, Tex., 1951-58; exec. v.p., ednl. dir. Southwestern Legal Found., Dallas, 1958-72, pres., 1972—, also trustee. Trustee, Nat. Meth. Found. Christian Higher Edn. Mem. Assn. Continuing Legal Edn. Administrs. Methodist. Rotarian. Author, contbr. articles profl. jours. Home: 3221 Villanova St Dallas TX 75225 Office: 3315 Daniels St Dallas TX 75205

CECIL, SAM KENNETT, distillery exec.; b. Bardstown, Ky., Oct. 26, 1918; s. Francis Lavielle and Mary Elizabeth (Thompson) C.; student U. Louisville, 1939-40, 46-48, Bellarmine Coll., 1960-64; m. Mary Bernadine Greenwell, Oct. 30, 1940; children—Bernardine (Mrs. Joe Robert Strange), Beverly (Mrs. William K. Roberts), Francis Lavielle, Anthony Gerst, Sam Kennett III. Chemist, T.W. Samuels Distillery, Deatsville, Ky., 1937-41, Heaven Hill Distilleries, Bardstown, 1945-52; quality control supr. Dant Distillery, Gethsemane, Ky., 1952-54; prodn. mgr., v.p. Star Hill Distillery, Loretto, Ky., 1954—, also dir. Vice pres. P.T.A., Bardstown, 1963-64, pres., 1964-65, 70-71. Served with AUS, 1941-46;PTO. Decorated Bronze Star medal. Mem. Nat. Assn. Power Engrs. (sec. local chpt. 1963-64, pres. 1964-65). Democrat. Roman Catholic. Club: Old Kentucky Home Country (Bardstown). Home: Route 1 Box 206 Bardstown KY 40004 Office: Star Hill Farm Loretto KY 40037

CEDERVALL, ANTON ARNOLD, architect; b. Peking, China, Mar. 29, 1923; s. Anton Adolf and Sara Margareta (Elmgren) C.; student North Park Jr. Coll., 1941-42, Harvard, 1943-44; B.A., U. Mich., 1949, postgrad., 1949-50; m. Georgiana Gale Clark, Jan. 6, 1945; children—John, Edward, Jari, Sharon, Lisa, Sara; m. 2d, Brenda O. Burns, Feb. 5, 1972. Architect, various archtl. firms, 1960-68; partner, Eugene Lawrence, Assos., Architects, Palm Beach, Fla., 1968-69; pvt. practice as architect, Riviera Beach, Tequesta, Fla., 1969—; dir., cons. architect Modular Industries, Inc., Indiantown, Fla. Mem. planning and zoning bd., Longboat Key, Fla., 1958-59, Palm Beach Shores, Fla., 1969-70; bldg. ofcl., Juno Beach, Fla., 1966-68. Served with AUS, 1943-48, 51-56. Mem. A.I.A., Fla. Assn. Architects, Jupiter-Requesta C. of C. (chmn. com. 1970—). Episcopalian. Kiwanian, Rotarian (pres. 1972). Prin. archtl. works include Overseas Service Corp. Bldg., West Palm Beach, Fla., St. Maurice Cath. Ch., Hollywood, Fla. Home: 115 Country Club Dr Tequesta FL 33458 Office: 535 E Indiantown Rd Jupiter FL 33458

CELLA, FRANCIS RAYMOND, economist; b. Harrison, N.J., July 16, 1909; s. Frank L. and Kathryn (Hanlon) C.; A.B., Wesleyan Coll., 1933; A.M., U. Ky., 1937; m. Mildred Russell, Dec. 11, 1944; 1 son, Charles Ronald. Statistican Ky. Agrl. Expt. Sta., 1935-37; research dir. Ky. Unemployment Compensation Commn., 1937-42; dir. bur. bus. research, prof. econs. U. Okla., 1946-68; dir. research Bus. Research, Inc., 1968—, prof. bus. statistics, 1946—, economist Washita Valley Improvement Assn., 1953-56; cons. USAF, 1954-56; mgmt. research cons. Okla. Restaurant Assn., 1966—. Faculty Co-ordinator Com. for Econ. Devel., 1951-57; mem. Gov.'s Council Coal Industry, 1964—; mem. Gov.'s Gen. Adv. Com., 1964-66; pres. Assn. Univ. Bur. Bus. and Econ. Research, 1962-64. Served as capt. USAAF, 1942-46, lt. col. USAF, Res. ret. Mem. Am. Statis. Assn., Operations Research Soc. Am., Inst. for Mgmt. Scis., Econometric Soc., S.W. Social Sci. Assn., S.W. Shippers Assn., Beta Gamma Sigma Episcopalian. Author brochures, articles. Editor: Okla. Bus. Bull., 1946-68. Home: 719 Hoover St Norman OK 73069

CEPAS, KOSTAS V(YTAUTAS), educator; b. Griskabudis, Lithuania, 1911; s. Motiejus and Marija (Jablonskyte) C.; LL.M., State U. Lithuania, 1933, D. Law, 1937, Dr. Juris Habilis, 1938; postgrad. U. Zurich (Switzerland), 1934-35, U. Grenoble (France), 1935, U. Vienna (Austria), 1935, U. Paris (France), 1936, U. Bern (Switzerland), 1938; m. Manomaityte Lidija, June 26, 1937; children—Vilija (Mrs. Charles Reagan), Gintaras. Came to U.S., 1949, naturalized, 1955. Cons. Council Codification Laws, Lithuania, 1938-39; asst. prof. law State U. Lithuania, 1939-44; dean, asso. prof. law Unrra Baltic U., Hamburg, Germany, 1946-48; tchr. French J. Burke High Sch., Boston, 1962; instr. J. C. Smith U., Charlotte, N.C., 1963-64, asst. prof. German and history, 1964-65, asso. prof., 1965-66; asso. prof. German and Latin Elon Coll., 1966—, chmn. dept. langs., 1971—. Mem. Internat. Bur. Displaced Persons Div. Boy Scout Movement, 1947-49, spl. nat. commr. Boy Scouts Am., 1950. Mem. Am. Assn. Tchrs. German, Am. Assn. U. Profs. Author: Tutelage of Adults, 1939; Condition of Woman in Contemporary Society, 1939. Home: 210 Summerbell Av Elon College NC 27244

CEPEDA, LOPEZHERMOSA, RODOLFO, lawyer; b., 1937; grad. summa cum laude Nat. U. Mexico; internat. program in taxation Harvard U. Law Sch., 1962. Admitted to bar, Mexico, 1962; mem. firm Bufete Cepeda Villareal, Mexico City; prof. law Nat. U. Mexico, 1963—. Mem. Inter-Am. Bar Assn. Office: Bufete Cepeda Villareal Amberes 38-M Mexico City 6 Mexico*

CEPEDA, V. ONESIMO, lawyer; b. Monterrey, Mexico, June 5, 1905; student U. Nuevo Leon; Licenciado in Law, Nat. U. Mexico, 1926; student Faculte de Droit U. Paris, 1926-27; J.D., Northwestern U., 1928. Admitted to bar, Mexico, 1926; with legal dept. Am. Smelting & Refining Co., N.Y.C., 1928-30; practice law, Mexico, 1931-50; gen. counsel Mexico, 1950-62; v.p., gen. counsel Compania Menera Asarco, S.A., 1963-65; v.p., gen. counsel Asarco Mexicana, S.A., 1965-70, adviser to pres., 1970-71; prof. civil law Nat. U. Mexico, 1937-55. Mem. council Mexican Mining Chamber, 1950-71; mem., sec. Nat. Banking Commn., 1951-71; v.p. coal mines com. ILO, 1953, 59, pres., 1964, del., Dusseldorf, 1953, Geneva, 1959, 64; mem. com. on legislature and fiscal matters Confedn. Indsl. Chambers Mexico, 1960—, also former mem. bd. dirs. and exec. com.; arbitrator Mexican sect. Inter-Am. Com. on Comml. Arbitration. Mem. Barra Mexicana (pres. 1967-69, hon. life pres. 1971—), Intern-Am. (mem. council), Internat. (mem. council, chmn. com. real property, sect. bus. law) bar assns. Address: Ortiz, Ramos & Inman Morelos 98-303 Mexico City Mexico*

CEPEDA LOPEZHERMOSA, ANTONIO, lawyer, 1938; grad. summa cum laude Nat. U. Mexico; LL.M., Harvard, 1964; M.B.A., Northwestern U., 1964. Admitted to bar, Mexico, 1963; mem. firm Bufete Cepeda Villareal, Mexico City. Office: Amberes 38-M Mexico City 6 Mexico*

CERGNUL, EMIL ANTHONY, elec. wire and cable mfg. co. exec.; b. Buckner, Ill., July 10, 1926; s. John and Dolly (Maragni) C.; grad. pub. schs.; m. Jean Bond, Sept. 14, 1946; children—Barbara (Mrs. John Moranvill), Dolly (Mrs. Joe Hader), Emil Anthony, Jr., John. Machine operator Gen. Cable Corp., Memphis, Tenn., 1949-50, shift dept. mgr., 1950-51, dept. mgr., 1951-53, div. supt., St. Louis, 1953-57, plant supt., Memphis, 1957-58, plant mgr., 1958—. Served with USNR, 1943-46. Roman Catholic. Moose. Home: 5755 Buxbriar St Memphis TN 38117 Office: 1278 Orgill St Memphis TN 38106

CERNAN, EUGENE A., astronaut; b. Chgo., Mar. 14, 1934; s. Andrew C. Cernan; B.S. in Elec. Engring., Purdue U., 1956; postgrad. student U.S. Naval Postgrad. Sch., Monterey, Cal.; m. Barbara Jean Atchley; 1 dau., Teresa Dawn. Joined U.S. Navy, 1956, advanced through grades to lt.; former mem. attack squadrons 126, 113, Miramar (Cal.) Naval Air Sta.; now astronaut with Manned Spacecraft Center, NASA. Mem. Tau Beta Pi. Address: care Manned Spacecraft Center NASA Houston TX 77001*

CERVERA, NICHOLAS JOSEPH, lawyer; b. N.Y.C., Sept. 25, 1940; s. Joseph J. and Rose (Romano) C.; B.S., Troy State U., 1963; J.D., Cumberland Sch. Law, Samford U., 1966; m. Patricia Ann Summer, June 2, 1967; children—Richard David, Michael James. Econ. researcher Eastern Air Lines, Inc., N.Y.C., 1964-65; prof. law Troy State U., Ala., 1966—; admitted to Ala. bar, 1966; practiced in Troy, 1966— mem. firm Cervera and Folmar, 1966—. Pres., Fonceco, Inc., 1967—; treas. Lakewood, Inc., 1968—. Mem. Am. Bus. Law Assn., Pike County Bar Assn. (pres. 1967—), Am. Assn. U. Profs., Phi Alpha Delta, Tau Kappa Epsilon. Mason (Shriner). Club: Lions. Home: 106 Lakeview Circle Troy AL 36081 Office: Box 325 Troy AL 36081

CESSAC, FREDDY RAY, dentist; b. Nederland, Tex., Apr. 15, 1933; s. Dupree Joseph and Bethel (Bonnette) C.; student Baylor U., 1950-51; B.S., Lamar Tech. Inst., 1954; postgrad. U. Tex., 1956-58, D.D.S., 1960, M.S., 1968; m. Theta Dell Morgan, Sept. 3, 1955; children—Philip Joseph, Dane Urshel. Individual practice dentistry, Pearland, Tex., 1962-66; individual practice pedodontics, Webster, Tex., 1968—. Served with AUS, 1954-56. Mem. Am. Soc. Denistry Children, 9th Dist. Dental Soc., Am. Dental Soc., Pearland C. of C. (pres. 1964-65), Xi Psi Phi. Methodist (trustee). Lion. Home: 3302 Nottingham St Pearland TX 77581 Office: 812 NASA Webster TX 77598

CETINER, AYHAN, educator; b. Iskenderun, Turkey, Sept. 2, 1938; s. Mehmet Yusuf and Naciye (Mustafa) C.; came to U.S., 1961; B.S. in C.E., Robert Coll., Istanbul, Turkey, 1961; M.C.E., U. Va., 1964, D.Sc., 1966; m. Tukel Hantal, Dec. 18, 1967; children— Suzan, Aygen. Asso. prof. civil engring. Tex. A. and M. U., College Station, 1966—. Registered profl. engr., Tex. Mem. Am. Soc. C.E., Am. Soc. Engring. Edn., Tex. Soc. Profl. Engrs., Sigma Xi, Chi Epsilon. Home: 1209 Boswell St College Station TX 77840

CHABLE, E(UGENE) ROBERT, clergyman; b. Cleve., June 7, 1920; s. Eugene Ray and Marion Margaret (Skym) C.; B.B.A., Cleve. State U., 1944; M.Div., Colgate Rochester Div. Sch., 1946; M.A., U. Rochester, 1948; Ph.D., Columbia, 1955; postgrad. Union Theol. Sem., 1951-54, Princeton, 1952; m. Marion Hayes Boynton, Oct. 26, 1946. With Elizabeth Jones Studios, Cleve., summer 1938, Gage Gallery, part-time 1939-40, Fed. Res. Bank, 1940-41, Crane Co., 1941-44; ordained to ministry Bapt. Ch., 1946; asso. minister Brighton Presbyn. Ch., Rochester, N.Y., 1944-45; minister 1st Bapt. Ch., Palmyra, N.Y., 1945-51; interim minister Wyckoff (N.J.) Reformed Ch., 1951-53; asso. minister Park Av. Meth. Ch., N.Y.C., 1954; dir. student personnel, dean of men, asso. prof. history Hillsdale Coll., 1954-57; dean of student personnel, acting registrar, prof. philosophy and religion Rio Grande Coll., 1957-59; incorporator, mem. exec. com. New Coll., Inc., Sarasota, Fla., 1959-62; v.p., bus. rep. Venice-Nokomis Bank, Venice, Fla., 1959-63; minister Venice United Ch. of Christ, 1963—. First v.p. Fla. Migrant Ministry, 1967-68. Asso. mem. Fla. Soc. for Prevention of Blindness, 1964—; mem. Am. Mus. Natural History; v.p. Sarasota County Community Health and Welfare Council. Bd. dirs. S. Sarasota County Retarded Children's Assn., 1961-63, Venice-Nokomis Art Assn., 1961-63; bd. dirs. Venice Little Theatre, 1962-65, treas., 1963-64, 64-66; bd. dirs. Family Service Assn., Sarasota County, 1963-65; trustee New Coll., Sarasota, Fla.; mem. S. Sarasota County Meml. Hosp. Assn., chmn. nominating com. 1962. Mem. Venice Area Ministerial Assn. (pres. 1967-69), Soc. Bibl. Lit. and Exegesis Am. Council of Learned Socs., W. Central Assn. Fla. Conf. United Ch. of Christ, Wilderness Soc., Audubon Soc., Nat. Geog. Soc., Delta Sigma Phi. Rotarian, Mason (33 deg., K.T., Shriner); mem. Order DeMolay. Club: Venice (Fla.) Yacht. Contbr. articles to profl. jours. Home: 104 Alba St W Venice FL 33595 Office: PO Drawer 998 Venice FL 33595

CHABON, STEVE, ret. army officer, elec. co. exec.; b. Gilberton, Pa., Mar. 4, 1931; s. Onufer and Anna (Bobiak) C.; B.A. in Govt. and Politics, U. Md., 1968; m. Roberta Jean McGuire, Oct. 30, 1954; children—Stephen J., Gregory M. With Johns-Manville Corp., 1950; served with USNR, 1949-50; joined USAF, 1950, resigned as master sgt., 1962; commd. lt. U.S. Army, 1962, advanced through grades to maj., 1968; stationed in Korea, 1962-63, Vietnam, 1968-69; mil. asst. to spl. asst. Office Sec. of Def., Washington, 1965-67; exec. asst. to asst. sec. Office Asst. Sec. of Army, 1969-71; dir. adminstrn. Def. Systems Mgmt. Sch., 1971; mem. profl. staff Gen. Electric Corp. (Tempo), Washington, 1972—. Decorated Legion of Merit, Meritorious Service medal, Joint Service Commendation medal. Composer: Rhapsody in Notes, 1953; also ballads. Home: 6026 Haverhill Ct West Springfield VA 22152 Office: 777 14th St NW Washington DC 20005

CHACKO, GEORGE KUTTICKAL, operations researcher; b. Trivandrum, India, July 1, 1930; s. Geevarghese Kuttickal and Thankamma (Mathew) C.; certificate advanced tng. Indian Statis. Inst., Calcutta, India, 1951; B. Commerce Calcutta U., 1952; M.A., Madras U., Tambaram, India, 1950 Ph.D., New Sch. Social Research, 1959; m. Yo Yee, Aug. 10, 1957; children—Rajah Yee, Ashia Yo. Came to U.S., 1953. Asst. editor Indian Finance, Calcutta, 1951-53; comml. corr. Times of India, Calcutta, 1953; asso. test devel. math. Ednl. Testing Service, Princeton, N.J., 1955-57; dir. marketing mgmt. research Royal Metal Mfg. Co., N.Y.C., 1958-60; operations research cons. RAND Corp., Santa Monica, Cal., 1961-62; mgr. operations research dept. Hughes Semicondr. div. Newport Beach, Cal., 1960-61 operations research cons. Union Carbide Corp., N.Y.C., 1962-63; staff mem. Research Analysis Corp., McLean, Va., 1963-65; staff mem. MITRE Corp., Arlington, 1965-67; sr. staff scientist TRW Systems Group, Washington, 1967-70; asst. prof. U. Cal. at Los Angeles, 1960-61; instr. U.S. Dept. Agr. Grad. Sch., 1965-67, asst. professorial lectr. George Washington U., Washington, 1965-68; professorial lectr. Am. U., Washington, 1967-70, adj. prof., 1970—; vis. prof. systems mgmt. U. So. Cal., 1970-71, prof., 1971—. Cons. Inst. for Creative Studies, Washington, UN Pub. Adminstrn. Div., N.Y., Milcom Systems Corp., Rockville, Md., Aries Corp., McLean, Va., York U., Toronto, Can., Canadian Internat. Devel. Agy., U.S. Dept. Def., Indsl. Coll. Armed Forces, So. Ry. System. Sec.-treas. Am. Com. Friends of Serampore, N.Y.C., 1959-63, treas., 1963-65; youth cons. World Council Chs. Trustee Washington Operations Research Council, 1967-69. Fellow A.A.A.S., Am. Astron. Soc. (nat. v.p. publs. 1969-71, dir. 1972—, rep. to A.A.A.S. 1968—); mem. Operations Research Soc. Am. (nat. vice-chmn. health applications sect. 1966-68, mem. sect. council 1971—, mem. nat. com. meetings 1966-67, mem. nominations com. 1972—, chmn. arrangements nat. meeting 1970), Econometric Soc., Am. Econ. Assn., World Future Soc. Presbyn. (mem. nat. council 1969-71). Kiwanian (chmn. support chs. com. 1965-66, chmn. internat. relations com., 1966-77, chmn. boys and girls com. 1967, 68, past 1st v.p.; dist. chmn. agr. and conservation com. 1967, dist. chmn. spl. communications 1969-70, div. chmn. newsletter 1968-70, div. chmn. internat. relations 1971—). Author: India-Toward an Understanding, 1959; International Trade Aspects of Indian Burlap-An Econometric Study, 1961; Today's Information for Tomorrow's Products, an Operations Research Approach, 1966; Studies for Public Men, 1968; Applied Statistics in Decision-Making, 1971; Computer-Aided Decision-Making, 1972; Decision Design for Def. and Devel., 1972. Translator: Mar Thoma Syrian Liturgy, 1956; Mar Thoma Syrian Church-Order of Holy Matrimony, 1957. Editor: Reducing the Cost of Space Transportation, 1969; The Recognition of Systems in Health Services, 1969; Systems Approach to Environmental Pollution, 1972; Alternative Approaches to the National Delivery of Health Care, 1972; co-editor: Planning Challenges of the 70's in the Public Domain, 1971. Editor: Washington Operations Research Council Newsletter, 1967-68;

Operations Research Soc. Health Applications Section Newsletter, 1966-—; acting mng. editor Jour. Astronautical Scis., 1969-70, mng. editor, 1971-—; editor Kiwanis Newsletter, Capitol dist., div. 1, 1968-70, Am. Astron. Soc. jour., 1968-70. Contbr. articles to profl. jours. Home: 6809 Barr Rd Washington DC 20016 Office: USC Office 4301 Columbia Pike Arlington VA 22204

CHADICK, T. C., civil ct. judge; b. Winnsboro, Tex., Sept. 21, 1910; s. Walter Martin and Carrie (Mars) C.; LL.B., Cumberland U., 1933; m. Doris Adlyne Scruggs, Apr. 14, 1941; children—Mary Susan, Nancy Doris. Admitted to Tex. bar, 1933; pvt. law practice, 1934-40; county atty., Wood County, Tex., 1939-40; state senator, 1941-49; dist. judge, Quitman, Tex., 1949-56; chief justice Ct. of Civil Appeals, Texarkana, Tex., 1956-—. Mem. Tex. Constl. Revision Commn. Pres. Tex. Civil Judicial Council, 1961-64. Democrat. Meth. Mason (Shriner). Home: 4017 Potomac St Texarkana TX 75501 Office: Texas City Hall Texarkana TX 75501

CHADWICK, CHARLES WILLIAM, veterinarian; b. Jackson, Miss., Mar. 8, 1912; s. Hudson and Anne Louise (Eley) C.; student Hinds Jr. Coll., 1933; D.V.M., Tex. A. and M. Coll., 1938; m. Evelyn Elizabeth Clark, June 14, 1938; children—Charles Eley, Martha Ann, Evelyn Elizabeth, William Lyon, Hudson Barnett, Clara Gene. With U.S. Bur. Animal Industry, Jacksonville, Fla., 1938-42; practice vet. medicine, Jackson, Miss., 1946-—. Cons., veterinarian Union Stock Yards, Jackson, 1946-—. Vice pres. S.W. Jackson Improvement Assn.; mem. Jackson Pub. Schs. Survey Com., 1961; parent council Wilkins Sch., 1963-—. Trustee Forest Hill Sch., 1955; bd. dirs. YMCA. Served as officer Vet. Corps, AUS, World War II. Col. Gov.s Staff, State of Miss., 1960-—. Mem. Am., Miss. Vet. Medicine assns., Miss., Cattlemen's Assn., Farm Bur., Tex. A. and M. Former Student's Assn., Sons Confederate Vets. Methodist. Mason (Shriner). Contbr. cartoons, articles vet. publs. Home: 1426 Raymond Rd Jackson MS 39204

CHADWICK, GEORGE GILBERT, electronics exec.; b. Lawrence, Mass., Mar. 20, 1933; s. Gilbert Roy and Rita Blanche (Simmers) C.; B.S., U. N.H., 1955; m. Mary Ann Newman, Feb. 14, 1959; children—George A., Caroline A. Sr. engr. Melpar, Inc., Falls Church, Va., 1956-58; electronics dir. antenna lab. Aero Geo Astro Corp., Alexandria, Va., 1958-60; electronics sr. v.p. engring. Radiation Systems, Inc., McLean, Va., 1960-—. Mem. electronics tech. adv. bd. No. Va. Community Coll., 1967-—, chmn., 1969-70. Mem. Profl. Group Antennas and Propagation (nat. chmn. 1968-69), I.E.E.E. Patentee in field. Home: 8905 Burbank Dr Annandale VA 22003 Office: 1755 Old Meadow Rd McLean VA 22101

CHADWICK, JAMES CARROLL, clergyman; b. Carthage, Tex., Jan. 10, 1915; s. William Sandy and Martha Beulah (Ingram) C.; A.A., Marshall Coll., 1935; B.A., Baylor U., 1937; B.Th., Southwestern Theol. Sem., 1940; D.D., E. Tex. Bapt. Coll., 1953; m. Marieta Todd, Feb. 22, 1942; children—Daniel David, Martha Lou, Carleta Louise. Ordained to ministry Bapt. Ch., 1934; student pastor, 1933-40; pastor 1st Bapt. Ch., Leonard, Tex., 1940-42, Center, Tex., 1942-—. Dir. Gt. Commonwealth Life Ins. Co., Dallas, First Home Credit, Jacksonville, Logos Corp., Ft. Worth, Treasure Chest Bookstores, Dallas. Rep., Home Mission Bd. Dept. Evangelism, Alaska, 1954; participant, Bapt. World Alliance meeting, Rio de Janeiro, Brazil, 1960; preacher, Europe, Africa, Asia, Holy Land, 1962; participant New Life Movement, Japan, Hong Kong, 1963. Dir., v.p., chmn. religious awards East Tex. council Boy Scouts Am. Sec., Tex., So. U. Bd. Regents, Houston, 1955-—; trustee E. Tex. Bapt. Coll., Valley Bapt. Acad., Pineywoods Bapt. Encampment; life mem. East Texas Coll. Bd. Mem. So. Bapt. Conv. (state missions commn., mem. exec. bd. 1954-62, annuity bd. 1962-—, nomination bd.), Bapt. Gen. Conv. Tex. (chmn. exec. bd. 1963-65, pres. conv. 1965-67, chmn. state missions commn.). Home: 210 Pecan St Center TX 75935 Office: Cora at Pecan St Center TX 75935

CHAET, ALFRED BERNARD, marine physiologist, coll. adminstr.; b. Boston, June 7, 1927; s. Joseph and Viola (Ellis) C.; B.S., U. Mass., 1949, M.S., 1951; Ph.D., U. Pa., 1953; postgrad. Oak Ridge Inst. Nuclear Studies, 1961; m. Shirley Rice, Sept. 2, 1950; children—Douglas Lee, Mark Steven, Judi Elise. Sci. investigator Marine Biol. Lab., Woods Hole, Mass., 1949, 51-53, 55-63; instr. zoology U. Me., Orono, 1953-56; asst. prof. physiology Boston U., 1956-58; prof. biology Am. U., Washington, 1958-66; NIH fellow Scripps Inst. of Oceanography, U. Cal. at San Diego, LaJolla, 1964-66; provost, prof. biology, dean for scis. U. W. Fla., Pensalcola, 1966-—. Active sci. workshops, panels. Served with AUS, 1944-46. Recipient numerous research grants. Mem. Am. Zoology Soc., Am. Soc. Oceanography, Am. Physiol. Soc., Marine Biol. Lab. Soc., Soc. Cell Biology, Soc. Gen. Physiology, Biophysics Soc., A.A.A.S., Am. Inst. Biol. Sci., Sigma Xi, Beta Beta Beta, Phi Kappa Phi. Contbr. articles in field to profl. jours. Office: U W Fla Pensacola FL 32505

CHAFFE, LEWIS KENNETH, tobacco co. exec.; b. Buckfastleigh, Devon, Eng., Oct. 20, 1913; s. William James and Ada (Bowerman) C.; grad H. Ffoulks Lynch Accounting Corr. Coll. (Eng.), 1934; m. Violet Catherine Moseley, Aug. 26, 1939; 1 son, Roger Lewis. Came to U.S., 1951. Auditor, Tax asso. Binder Hamlyn & Co., London, Eng., 1935-46; tax accountant British-Am. Tobacco Co. Ltd., London, 1946-50; finance cons. Brown & Williamson Tobacco Corp., Louisville, 1951-59; with Export Leaf Tobacco Co., Richmond, Va., 1959-—, treas., dir., 1967-—, v.p. finance, adminstrn., 1969-—; asst. sec. British-Am. Tobacco Co., 1962-—. Air raid warden, London, 1939-45. Fellow Inst. Chartered Accountants (Eng.); mem. Nat. Assn. Accountants. Episcopalian. Club: Salisbury Country (Richmond). Home: 2214 McRae St Richmond VA 23235 Office: 1601 W Leigh St Richmond VA 23261

CHAFFIN, CHARLES HUBERT, JR., ins. agt.; b. Macon, Ga., Aug. 18, 1933; s. Charles Hubert and Jesse (Wasdin) C.; student Mercer U., 1955-56; m. Bonny Gayle Register, Mar. 15, 1956; 1 dau., Melinda Lori. Spl. agt. Ins. Co. of N. Am., 1957-65; v.p. broker The Wightman Agy., Inc., 1965-69; ins. agt. Murphy, Taylor & Ellis, Inc., Macon, Ga., 1969; ins. agt., asst. v.p. Fickling & Walker Agy., Inc., Macon, 1969-—. Served with AUS, 1952-55. Mem. Soc. Chartered Property and Casualty Underwriters. Presbyn. Home: 3065 Stuart Dr Macon GA 31204 Office: 577 Mulberry St PO Box 779 Macon GA 31202

CHAFIN, JAMES L., mining co. exec.; b. Port Arthur, Tex., Apr. 25, 1922; s. James L. and Mary Josephine (Oney) C.; B.S., Southwestern U., 1948; m. Emma Dell Matherne, Apr. 17, 1952; children—Mary Susan, Debra Ann, James L., III, Peggy Lynn. Vice-pres. sales L.A. Mud Co., Inc., Houma, La., 1963-—. Served with USMCR, 1942-46. Mem. Am. Petroleum Inst. (pres. 1964-65). Presbyn. (deacon 1970-71, elder 1971-—). Elk. Club: Ellendale Country (Houma). Home: 409 Mire St Houma LA 70360 Office: Box 1187 Foot of Palm Av Houma LA 70360

CHAFIN, ROBERT NEIL, C. of C. exec.; b. Winston-Salem, N.C., Oct. 16, 1936; s. William Cornelius and Annie (Futrell) C.; student Duke U., 1955-57; A.B., Wake Forest U., 1960; m. Emily Mae Councilman, Dec. 20, 1958; children—Christopher Neil, Emily Elizabeth. Sales mgr. J. S. Sargent & Co., Burlington, N.C., 1960-61; tchr. Bartlett-Yancey High Sch., Yanceyville, N.C., 1961-64; dist. exec. Boy Scouts Am., Burlington and Reidsville, N.C., 1964-67; exec. v.p. Reidsville (N.C.) C. of C., 1967-69; exec. v.p. Rocky Mount (N.C.) C. of C., 1969-—. Chmn. dist. leadership tng. East Carolina council Boy Scouts Am., 1970-—. Mem. N.C. Assn. C. of C. execs. (dir. 1968-69, sec. 1970-71, sec.-treas. 1971-72, v.p. 1972-—), So. Assn. C. of C. Execs., Am. C. of C. Execs., Kappa Sigma. Baptist (deacon 1968-69). Kiwanian. Home: 3128 Ridgecrest Dr Rocky Mount NC 27801 Office: 317 S Franklin St Rocky Mount NC 27801

CHAFIN, WILLIAM VERNON, JR., assn. exec.; b. Waycross, Ga., Dec. 4, 1936; s. William Vernon and Sara (Whitaker) C.; A.B., U. Ga., 1958; m. Kaye Beth Cleveland, June 21, 1958; children—Sally, Mary Kaye, Will. Bus. office supr. So. Bell Tel. Co., Atlanta, Savannah and Albany, Ga., 1961-63; agt. Aetna Life Ins. Co., Albany, Ga., 1963-64; asst. mgr. Albany (Ga.) C. of C., 1964-68; exec. v.p. Columbia-Mt. Pleasant C. of C., Columbia, Tenn., 1968-—. Served with AUS, 1959-61. Mem. Am. C. of C. Execs., So. Assn. C. of C. Execs., Tenn. C. of C. Execs., So., Tenn. indsl. devel. councils. Methodist (sec. adminstrv. bd. 1970-71, tchr. ch. sch. 1969-—). Kiwanian. Home: 1110 Sunnyside Dr Columbia TN 38401 Office: 308 W 7th St Columbia TN 38401

CHAIKIN, GERALD, indsl. engr.; b. N.Y.C., Apr. 5, 1934; s. Jack and Leah (Schultz) C.; student Hunter Coll., 1951-53; B.S., Purdue U., 1956; m. Clarice Mary Barrett, June 27, 1957; children—Jamine Jean, Stewart Phillip. Product engr. Sperry Gyroscope Co., Great Neck, N.Y., 1956-57; gen. engr. human factors U.S. Army Human Engring. Labs., Aberdeen Proving Ground, Md., 1959-60; gen. engr. human factors U.S. Army Missile Command, Redstone Arsenal, Ala., 1960-—. Served with AUS, 1957-59. Registered profl. engr., Ala. Mem. Human Factors Soc. (chpt. pres. 1968), Assn. U.S. Army, Air Force Assn., Am. Ordnance Assn. Home: 906 Four Mile Post Rd Huntsville AL 35802 Office: AMSMI-RLH US Army Missile Command Redstone Arsenal AL 35809

CHAKALES, HAROLD HARRY, physician; b. Bklyn., June 11, 1934; s. Harry John and Venus (Trakas) C.; B.S., Wake Forest Coll., 1955, M.D., Bowman Gray Sch., 1958; m. Linda Carol Haskett, Sept. 25, 1965; children—Harry John II, Carrie Glenn. Rotating intern Jefferson Davis Hosp., Houston, 1958-59; resident Baylor U. Coll., Houston, 1959-61, U. Ark. Med. Center, Little Rock, 1961-63; practice medicine, specializing in orthopedic surgery, Little Rock, 1963-—; staff orthopedist VA Hosp., Little Rock; instr. orthopedic surgery U. Ark. Med. Center, 1963-65, asst. prof., 1965-69, clin. asst. prof. orthopedics, 1969-—. Diplomate Am. Bd. Orthopedic Surgery. Fellow A.C.S.; mem. A.M.A., Pulaski County, So. med. assns., Ark. Orthopedic Assn., Am. Acad. Orthopedic Surgery. Home: 11119 Eden Lane Little Rock AR 72207 Office: 405 N University St Little Rock AR 72209

CHALFANT, JOSEPH SHAW, packaging exec.; b. Richmond, Ind., Apr. 12, 1936; s. Ray King and Margaret (Shaw) C.; B.S., Ind. U., 1958; postgrad. U. Louisville Sch. Law, 1959-62; m. Harriet Vaughan Strange, June 6, 1959; children—Martin Joseph, Matthew Christopher. Sales, Colgate-Palmolive Co., 1958, merchandising rep., 1959-61; sales mgr. Mid-Continent Carton Corp., Louisville, 1961-63, pres., 1963-—; dir. for mfg. Ky. Fried Chicken Corp. Active March of Dimes. Served with AUS, 1958-59. Mem. Sigma Alpha Epsilon, Alpha Delta Sigma. Republican. Methodist. Clubs: Ad, Rotary. Home: Trimingham Rd New Albany IN 47150 Office: 3025 W Madison Louisville KY 40211

CHALKER, ROY FLETCHER, editor, pub.; b. Swainsboro, Ga., Sept. 12, 1915; s. Gozie Fletcher and Isla (Brown) C.; student John Marshall Law Sch., 1955-56; m. Mae Evelyn Gisson, July 21, 1944; children—Roy Fletcher, Philip C. Founder, editor The Ga. Guide, Gibson, 1936-42; owner, editor The True Citizen, Waynesboro, Ga., 1945-—; co-owner, radio sta. WBRO, Waynesboro, 1954-55. Mayor, Gibson, 1936; mayor, Waynesboro, 1954-55; state dir. parks, 1955-56; chmn. State Hwy. Dept., 1957-58; chmn. Rural Rds. Authority, 1957-58; chmn. State Bridge Bldg. Authority, 1957-58. Served with SUNR, 1941-44. Mem. Ga. Press Assn. (pres. 1953-54, dir. 1951-52), Sigma Delta Chi. Democrat. Baptist. Mason, Rotarian. Home: 514 Forest Dr Waynesboro GA 30830 Office: 202 E 6th St Waynesboro GA 30830

CHALLINOR, DAVID, museum ofcl.; b. N.Y.C., July 11, 1920; s. David and Merecedes (Crimmins) C.; B.A., Harvard, 1943; M.F., Yale, 1959, Ph.D., 1966; m. Joan Ridder, Nov. 22, 1952; children—Julia M., Mary E., Sarah L., D. Thompson. With Offerman-Anderson, Clayton &Co., Houston, 1947-51; cotton farmer, Culberson County (Tex.), 1951-53; asst. sec. First Mortgage Co. Houston, 1953-57; research asst. Conn. Agr. Expt. Sta., New Haven, 1959-60; dep. dir. Yale Peabody Mus., New Haven, 1960-65, acting dir., 1965-66; spl. asst. in tropical biology Smithsonian Instn., Washington, 1966-67, dep. dir. Office Internat. Activities, 1967-68, dir., 1968-70, asst. sec. (sci.) Smithsonian Instn., 1971-—. Am. adminstrv. sec. Charles Darwin Found., 1971-—; mem. biol.-agr. com. Nat. Acad. Scis., 1971-—. Trustee Manhattanville Coll. Served with USNR, 1943-46. Fellow A.A.A.S.; mem. Sigma Xi. Contbr. articles to sci. jours. Home: 3117 Hawthorne St NW Washington DC 20008 Office: 114 Smithsonian Institution Washington DC 20560

CHAMBERLAIN, JEROME VIZE, dist. judge; b. Dallas, Jan. 29, 1923; s. Jerome DeVize and Lois (Sellers) C.; B.S. in Journalism, So. Meth. U., 1950, LL.B., 1950; m. Greta Beck, Sept. 8, 1962; children—Jamey Anne, Nancy Lois. Admitted to Tex. bar, 1950; with Mobil Oil Corp., Dallas, 1950-55; gen. counsel Stanray Mining Co., Grand Junction, Colo., 1955-57; asst. criminal dist. atty., Dallas, 1957-61; mem. firm Chamberlain and Schwille, Dallas, 1961-64; judge corp. ct., Dallas, 1964-68, judge criminal dist. ct., Dallas, 1968-—. Served with AUS, 1942-46. Mem. Am., Dallas bar assns., State Bar Tex., Dallas County Criminal Bar (pres. 1964), Tex. Assn. Municipal Judges, N.Am. Judges Assn., Phi Alpha Delta. Clubs: Dallas Athletic, King's Club (Dallas). Office: Criminal Dist Ct New County Courthouse Dallas TX 75202

CHAMBERLIN, GARWOOD, printing exec.; b. Evanston, Ill., May 29, 1920; s. Richard and Elizabeth (Garwood) C.; B.S., U. Md., 1942; m. Sarah Ann Bemis, Dec. 22, 1959; children—Garwood Bemis, Sarah Hepworth. Vice pres. Merkle Press, Inc., Washington, 1946-67, Publishers Co., Inc., Washington, 1967-71; pres. Kaufmann/Graphics, Inc., 1971-—. Served with AUS, 1942-45. Mem. Printing Industry of Washington (pres. 1955-56), Beta Alpha Psi. Home: 5404 Burling Rd Bethesda MD 20014 Office: 1110 Okie St NE Washington DC 20002

CHAMBERLIN, JAMES ALLEN, surgeon; b. Houston Nov 19, 1911; s. Willis West and Eva (Allen) C.; B.A. Rice U., 1936; M.D., Tulane U., 1942; m. Caryl Jean Wirth, Mar. 21, 1942; 1 dau., Caryl Jayne. Fellow obstetrics and gynecology Ochsner Clinic, New Orleans, 1942-43; asst. surg. resident Meml. Cancer Center, N.Y.C., 1943-44, surg. fellow, 1946-48, sr. surg. resident, 1948-49; surg. intern Jersey City Med. Center, 1944-45, house surgeon, 1945-46; chief surg. resident, chief of residents Roper Hosp., Charleston, S.C., 1945-46; asso. surgeon, acting chief clinics, head div. head and neck surgery M.D. Anderson Hosp., Houston, 1949-50; practice medicine specializing in surgery of head and neck, Houston, 1950-— teaching asst. obstetrics and gynecology Tulane U., 1942-43; teaching fellow surgery Med. Coll. S.C., 1945-46; asso. prof. surgery U. Tex. Postgrad. Sch. Medicine 1949-50; clin. asso. prof. Baylor U. Coll. Medicine, Houston 1950-—; attending surgeon Hermann, St. Joseph's Med. Arts, Heights, Twelve Oaks, Sharpstown, VA, Ben Taub Gen. hosps., Houston; cons. head and neck surgery St. Luke's Episcopal Tex. Children's hosps., Houston; courtesy staff Meml. Hosp. Houston; asso. surgeon Meth. Hosp., Houston. Dir. Med. Center Nat. Bank, Buffalo Savs. & Loan Assn. Fellow A.C.S; mem. Harris County Med. Soc. Am. Tex. (mem. com. on atomic energy and nuclear medicine 1955-67), med. assns., Am. Radium Soc., James Ewing Soc., Tex. Surg. Soc., Am. Thyroid Assn., Soc. Nuclear Medicine (pres. Southwestern chpt. 1963-64). Club: Doctors (bd. govs.) (Houston). Author: Lectures on Gynecological Pathology, 1943. Contbr. articles to med. jours. Home: 6260 Burgoyne St Houston TX 77027 Office: Hermann Profl Bldg Houston TX 77025

CHAMBERS, CHARLES MCKAY, ednl. cons.; b. Hampton, Va., June 22, 1941; s. Charles MacKay and Ruth Elinore (Wallach) C.; B.S., U. Ala., 1962, M.S. (Nat. Def. Edn. Act fellow), 1963, Ph.D. in Physics, 1964; postgrad. math. (NSF fellow), Harvard, 1964-65; m. Barbara Mae Fromm, June 9, 1962; children—Charles Catherine, Christina. Aerospace engr. NASA, 1962-63; research asso. U. Ala. Research Inst., 1963-64, asso. prof. math. univ., 1965-69; research fellow Harvard, 1964-65; asso. dean George Washington U., 1969-72; officer Univ. Assos., Inc., Washington, 1969-—, also dir.; dist. mgr. Life Ins. Co. Am.; cons. U.S. Congress, NSF, U.S. Office Edn., Salk Inst., Office Equal Opportunity; lectr. in field. Recipient Tau Beta Pi award, Am. Legion citizenship award. NSF research grantee, NASA grantee. Mem. N.Y. Acad. Sci., Am. Math. Assn., A.A.A.S., Am. Assn. Physics Tchrs., Internat. Platform Assn., Phi Beta Kappa, Sigma Xi, Pi Mu Epsilon, Sigma Pi Sigma. Contbr. articles to profl. jours. Home: 4220 Dandridge Terrace Alexandria VA 22309 Office: 485 L'Enfant Plaza West Suite 2100 Washington DC 20024

CHAMBERS, FRANKLIN DELANO, bus. exec.; b. Lawrenceburg, Tenn., Nov. 8, 1932; s. Carl C. and Leona Mae (Morgan) C.; student Middle Tenn. State U., 1951-53; B.S. in Indsl. Engring., U. Tenn., 1963; M.B.A., U. Louisville, 1966; m. Helen L. Stewart, Dec. 31, 1955; children—Sandra, Jeffrey W. Indsl. engr. Am. Air Filter, Louisville, 1963-66; with Trane Co., Clarksville, Tenn., 1966-68; v.p., gen. mgr. Universal Wire Container Corp., Clarksville, 1968-69; v.p., gen. mgr. mfg. div. Convenient Industries Am., Louisville, 1969-71; pres. Munday Modular Homes Mfg. Co., Inc., Madisonville, Ky., 1971-—. Served with USAF, 1955-60. Mem. Nat. Home Builders Assn., Alpha Pi Mu. Republican. Mem. Ch. of Christ. Home: 150 Carlisle Dr Madisonville KY 42431 Office: Hwy 41A Madisonville KY 42431

CHAMBERS, HENRY CARROLL, concrete co. exec.; b Beaufort, S.C. July 23, 1928; s. Carroll Jones and Virginia (Pollitzer) C.; B.C.E., Clemson U., 1949; m. Elizabeth Lee Brewer, July 8, 1950; children—Henry Carroll (dec.) Julia Dargan, Roscoe William, Joseph Brewer, Elizabeth Carroll. Constrn. supt. engr. Cecil's Inc. Spartanburg, S.C., 1950; mgr., partner Burton Block Co. Inc., Beaufort, 1952-59, v.p., 1959-65, pres., 1966-—; pres. Chambers-Cleckley, Inc., asphalt paving, Burton Block & Concrete Co., Inc., Beaufort Concrete Co., Deerfield Sand & Mining Co., Inc. Deerfield Sand & Mining Co. of Branchville, S.C., S. Atlantic Leasing Corp; treas., dir. Palmetto State Savs. & Loan Assn. Chmn., Beaufort County Devel. Bd., 1958-63; pres., campaign chmn. Beaufort County United Fund, 1960-63, Campaign chmn., 1969-70; chmn. bd. visitors Clemson U., 1971; mem. exec. com. Coastal Cardina council Boy Scouts Am., 1959-—, v.p., 1964-68, pres., 1968, mem. nat. council, 1964-68, scoutmaster, 1953-61. Mayor, City of Beaufort, 1970-—. Trustee, pres. Beaufort Acad. Served with AUS, 1950-52. Named Beaufort Young Man of Year, 1961; recipient Silver Beaver award Boy Scouts Am., 1968, Silver Antelope award, 1968. Mem. Am. Concrete Inst., S.C. Concrete Masonry Assn. (pres. 1965-66), Soc. Am. Mil. Engrs., Nat. Soujourner. Presbyn. (ruling elder). Mason (32 deg.), Rotarian (dir. Beaufort). Club: Sertoma (past pres.) (Beaufort, S.C.) Home: 2609 Fripp St Beaufort SC 29902 Office: Hwy 21 Burton SC 29904

CHAMBERS, JAMES FLOYD, JR., newspaperman; b. Houston, May 13, 1913; s. James Floyd and Elizabeth (Troutman) C.; student Terrill Prep. Sch. for Boys, 1932; m. Elizabeth Valerie Moore, Jan. 4, 1935; children—James Floyd III, Elizabeth Valerie. Copy boy, reporter Dallas Dispatch (later Dallas Dispatch-Jour.), 1934-35, telegraph editor, 1935-36, asst. sports editor, 1936-38, asst. city editor 1938-39, city editor, 1940-41; pub. relations dir. Dallas C. of C., 1941-42, North Am. Aviation, 1942-44; exec. news editor Dallas Times Herald, 1945, mng. editor, 1946-—, dir., 1952-—, v.p., gen. mgr., 1952-60, pres., 1960-—, also pub.; dir. Times Herald Printing Co.; covered atom bomb test at Bikini, 1946; ghost writer for several nat. sports figures, including Byron Nelson and Doak Walker. Mem. Sigma Delta Chi. Methodist (steward). Clubs: Brook Hollow, City, Dallas Country (Dallas). Home: 5319 Castlewood St Dallas TX 75229 Office: Dallas Times Herald 1101 Pacific Av Dallas TX 75202

CHAMBERS, JOHN ED, banker; b. Danville, Ark., Mar. 17, 1917; s.John E. and Lydia (Littlejohn) C.; A.B. U. Ark. 1939, LL.B., 1940; postgrad. Grad. Sch. Banking of the South, summers 1953-56.; m. Patricia Sloan, Feb., 1941; children—Eugenia Carol (Mrs. Jerral W. Jones), John Ed III, Patricia Dian (Mrs. William R. Meeks), Catherine Sloan. Admitted to Ark. bar 1940; practiced in Danville, 1940-43; ct. reporter, Danville, 1940-43; pres. Danville State Bank, 1946-—; mayor of Danville, 1940-43, 56-60. Dir. Empire Life Ins. Co. of Am. Chmn. Yell County Soil Conservation Dist. 1940-—; chmn. conservation and devel. project Ark. River Valley Resources, 1966-—; exec. council ARVAC, Inc. area v.p. Ark. Assn. Soil Conservation Dist., 1952-57, pres. 1957-59, state treas., 1967-—; Chmn. Yell County Devel. Council, 1962-—; mem. Yell County Hosp. Bd. Trustee Ark. Polytechnic Coll. Served from ensign to lt. USNR, World War II 1943-46. Recipient Boss of Yr. award Ark. Jaycees, 1971. Mem. Am. (exec. council 1967-69), Ark. (mem. exec. council, mem. advt. and promotion com.) bankers assns., Ark. Library Assn., U. Ark. Alumni Assn. (alumni bd. 1964-—, pres. 1969-70). Democrat. Methodist. Lion (past pres.). Address: Danville AR 72833

CHAMBERS, JULIUS LEVONNE, lawyer; b. Montgomery County, N.C., Oct. 6, 1936; B.A., N.C. Central U., 1958; M.A., U. Mich., 1959; LL.B., U. N.C., 1962; M.L., Columbia, 1963. Admitted to N.C. bar, 1962, now practicing in Charlotte. Mem. Am., N.C. bar assns., N.C. State Bar, Order Golden Fleece, Order Coif. Home: 3208 Dawnshire Av Charlotte NC 28216 Office: 237 W Trade Charlotte NC 28202*

CHANCE, DONALD PAUL, surgeon; b. Hagan, Va., Feb. 28, 1916; s. David Preston and Berneice (Parkey) C.; student Tenn. Wesleyan Coll., 1932-34; B.S., U. Tenn., M.S., 1938; M.D., U. Va., 1943; m. Marie Elizabeth Garley, Sept. 10, 1952; children—Elizabeth Anne, Margaret Rose, Donald Paul II. Teaching fellow zoology in comparative anatomy U. Tenn., 1936-68; prof. zoology Tenn. Wesleyan Coll., 1938-39; intern dept. surgery U. Va. Hosp., 1943, asst. resident surgery, 1946-47; fellow in surgery, first asst. in surgery, asst. surgeon Mayo Found. and Mayo Clinic, 1948-54; head sect. thoracic surgery, asso. dept. surgery Foss Clinic, Geisinger Hosp., Danville, Pa., 1954-58; attending surgeon Holston Valley Community Hosp., Kingsport, Tenn., 1958—. Served with USNR, 1944-46. Diplomate Am. Bd. Surgery. Fellow A.C.S., Southeastern Surg. Assn.; mem. Raven Soc., Pi Kappa Alpha, Alpha Omega Alpha, Omicron Delta Kappa. Republican. Presbyn. Moose, Eagle. Home: Route 12 Hemlock Park Kingsport TN 37663 Office: 613 Watauga St Kingsport TN 37660

CHANDLER, ALBERT BENJAMIN, lawyer, former gov. of Ky.; b. Corydon, Ky. July 14, 1898; s. Joseph and Callie (Sanders) C.; A.B., Transylvania Coll. 1921, LL.D., 1936; student Harvard, 1921-22; LL.B. U. Ky., 1924, LL.D., 1937; m. Mildred Watkins, Nov. 12, 1925; children—Marcella (Mrs. Thomas D. Miller), Mildred (Mrs. James J. Lewis), Albert Benjamin, Joseph Daniel. Began law practice Versailles, Kentucky, 1924; apptd. master commr. Circuit Ct., Woodford County 1928; elected mem. Ky. Senate, Ky., 22d Ky. Dist., 1929; lt. gov. of Ky., 1931-35; gov. of Ky., 1935-39, 55-59; resigned 1939, and apptd. U.S. senator to fill vacancy caused by death of Marvell Mills Logan; elected, 1940, to fill remainder of term to 1943, re-elected for 1942; high commr. baseball, 1945-51; pres. Internat. Baseball Congress, Wichita; commr. Continental Profl. Football League, 1965—; v.p., dir. First Flight Golf Co., Chattanooga; dir. Coastal States Life Ins. Co. Ga., United Bank & Trust Co., Versailles. Receiver for Inter-Southern Life Ins. Co., Louisville, 1932; an organizer Ky. Home Life Ins. Co., Louisville, 1932. Served with U.S. Army, 1918; capt. (Reserves) Judge Advocate Gen.'s Dept. (ret.). One of five Senators designated by U.S. Senate to visit world battle fronts in 1943, at which time they made first landplane flight ever made across Indian Ocean from Ceylon to Australia. Chmn. Woodford County Dem. Exec. Com. Trustee Ty Cobb Found.; chmn. bd. trustees U. Ky., 1935-39, 55-59, trustee, 1968—; chmn. Transylvania Coll. Bd. Trustees and Fund Raising Com; trustee Transylvania Coll. Democratic Nat. Committeeman for Ky. Named Kentuckian of Year, Ky. Press Assn. and Ky. Broadcasters Assn.; recipient Bishop's medal Episcopal Ch., 1959; Cross of Mil. Service, U.D.C., 1959; 50th Anniversary commemorative medallion Am. Legion of Ky.; named to Newspaper Hall of Fame, Internat. Newspaper Circulation Mgrs. Assn., 1967. Mem. Am. Legion, Forty and Eight, Pi Kappa Alpha. Episcopalian. Mason (32 deg., K.T., Shriner). Clubs: Ky. Mountain (hon.), Lexington Country, Idle Hour Country (Lexington). Football coach Centre Coll., Danville, Ky., 1922-27. One of 1st 10 named to Ky. Sports Hall of Fame 1957. Home: Versailles KY 40383

CHANDLER, ISAAC, JR., county agt.; b. Havana, Fla., Oct. 9, 1922; s. Isaac and Lillie (McGriff) C.; B.S., Fla. A. and M. Coll., 1952; m. Gene Elizabeth Hopkins, Aug. 12, 1961; children—Marcia Elizabeth, Isaac Eugene. Farmer, Havana, Fla., 1946-48; county agrl. agt. Hamilton County, Fla., 1952-63, asst. county agt., 1963-69, county extension agr. agt., 1969—. Served with AUS, 1942-45. Mem. Am. Legion. Methodist (sec.-treas. 1970-71). Mason. Home: PO Box 101 Jasper FL 32052 Office: PO Drawer K Jasper FL 32052

CHANDLER, STEPHEN S., ret. judge; b. Blount County, Tenn., Sept. 13, 1899; s. Stephen Sanders and Evelyn Amelia (Johnson) C.; student, U. Tenn. 1917-18, J.D., U. Kans. 1922; m. Margaret Patterson, 1922 (dec.); children—Frances Patterson (Mrs. Sim K. Sims), Stephen Sanders III, Frank Patterson. Pvt. law practice, Oklahoma City, 1922-43; U.S. Dist. judge for Western Dist. of Okla., 1943— chief judge, 1956-69. Recipient Hatton Summers award in 1961. Mem. Am. Bar Assn. (sec. jud. adminstrn. 1960), other bar and other legal assns., Sigma Alpha Epsilon, Phi Delta Phi, Order of Coif. Democrat. Methodist. Mason (Shriner), Rotarian (pres. Oklahoma City Club 1940-41). Clubs: Oklahoma City Golf, Lotus, Petroleum. Home: Oklahoma City OK 73102 Office: US Court House Oklahoma City OK 73101

CHANDLER, THOMAS WALTER, JR., librarian; b. Carrollton, Ga., Nov 12, 1924; s. Thomas Walter and Florence (Pope) C.; student W. Ga. Coll., 1942-43, 46-47; B.A., Emory U., 1949, M.Library Sci., 1951. With Ga. State Coll., 1951-61, beginning as book order librarian, 1951-57, head acquisitions dept., 1957-61; head librarian Oglethorpe U., Atlanta, 1961—. Served AUS, 1943-45. Decorated Purple Heart. Mem. Ga. Library Assn. Democrat

CHANDLER, WALLACE LEE, tobacco co. exec.; b. South Boston, Va., Oct. 18, 1926; s. Joseph Beale and Esma (Clement) C.; A.B., Elon Coll., 1949; LL.B., Smithdeal Coll. Law, 1953; m. Virginia Juanita Hodnett, Feb. 25, 1950; children—Elizabeth Hardy, Brenda Lee, Jacqueline Blair. Admitted to Va. bar, 1954; with tax dept. Universal Leaf Tobacco Co., Inc., Richmond, Va., 1949-53, asst. sec., 1953-63, sec. gen. counsel, 1963-69, adminstrv. v.p., mem. exec. com., 1969—, dir., 1966—. Trustee Madison Coll., Elon Coll. Served with AUS, 1944-46. Mem. Am., Va., Richmond bar assns., Elon Coll. Alumni Assn. (past dir.), Alpha Phi Delta. Republican. Baptist. Clubs: Country of Virginia, Commonwealth, Willow Oaks Country (past officer, dir.). Home: 2 Raven Rock Rd Richmond VA 23229 Office: Hamilton at Broad St Richmond VA 23230

CHANDLER, WAYNE A., sports publicity exec.; b. Richmond, Ind.; A.B., Ind.; U., 1950; m. Viola Eschliman; children—Justin, Abigail. Formerly newspaperman, Ohio, Fla.; joined Houston Sports Assn., 1963, asst. publicity dir. Houston Astrodome, 3 years, publicity dir. Astroworld, 2 years, now publicity dir. Houston Astros baseball team and Astrodome, 1970—. Office: Houston Astros Houston TX 77001*

CHANDLER, WILLIAM C., lawyer; b. Cambridge, Eng., July 26, 1895; A.B., Harvard, 1919, LL.B., 1922. Admitted to N.Y. bar, 1923; corp. counsel, N.Y.C., 1938-42. Formerly mem. Lawyers for Johnson-Humphrey. Fellow Am. Coll. Trial Lawyers. Home: 1530 Peabody Av Memphis TN 38104*

CHANDLER, WILLIAM JAMES, state ofcl.; b. Charlotte, N.C., June 9, 1908; s. George Wallace and Emily (Crosbie) C.; B.A., U. N.C., 1931, M.A., 1932;; m. Helen Kuck, June 16, 1934; 1 son, William James. Head dept. English Oak Ridge (N.C.) Mil. Inst., 1932-44, dean prin., 1947-65, supt., 1965-67, bd. dirs., 1950-67; instr. U. N.C., 1945-47; state supr. English, Dept. Pub. Instrn., State of N.C., Raleigh, 1967—. Pres., Guilford County Sch. Bd. Assn., 1955-56. Served with USNR, 1944-46. Mem. N.C. Coll. Conf., N.C. Collegiate Registrars, So. Assn. Colls. and Secondary Schs. (administrv. council, 1958—, chmn. central reviewing com., 1960—, chmn. N.C. com. 1966), Delta Sigma Pi, Chi Tau. Democrat. Home: 3102 Ruffin St Raleigh NC 27607 Office: Edn Bldg Raleigh NC 27602

CHANDLER, WINSTON GRIGGS, transp. corp. exec.; b.Clinton, Ark., Oct. 9, 1919; s. Lester W. and Mattie (Griggs) C.; student Coll. Ozarks, 1940; LL.B., Ark Law Sch., 1951; m. Ouida G. Hunnicutt, Sept. 16, 1942; children—Winston Griggs, Michael Lee, Jeffrey Scott. Owner Chandler 5 and 10, Clinton, Ark., 1946-48; safety insp. Ark. Pub. Service Commn., Little Rock, 1949-53; chmn. bd. Chandler Trailer Convoy, Inc., Little Rock, 1953—, dir., 1963-67; v.p. Razorback Realty; dir. Safety Boom, Inc. Mem. Ark. Athletic Commn., 1954-56; formerly chmn. Sch. Bd., Pulaski County; mem., chmn. Ark. State History Commn., Little Rock, 1957-67. Mem. pres. devel. council Harding Coll., Searcy, Ark. Served to maj. USAAF, 1941-45. Mem. Am. Legion, Ark. Pioneers, Air Force Assn. (charter), Ark. Truck and Bus. Assn., Tenn. Walking Horse Assn., Internat. Platform Assn. Democrat. Mem. Ch. of Christ (deacon). Lion. Home: 545 Valley Club Circle Little Rock AR 72207 Office: 8828 N Benton Hwy Little Rock AR 72204

CHANDLER, WYETH, city ofcl. Former mem. Memphis City Council, 4 years; mayor Memphis, 1972—. Office: City Hall Memphis TN 38103*

CHANEY, BOBBY LEE, supt. schs.; b. Graham, Ky., Sept. 5, 1934; s. Volla T. and Hazel D. (Matheney) C.; B.S., Murray State U., 1961, M.A., 1963; postgrad. Eastern Ky. State U., 1969; m. Drue Malone, Nov. 22, 1956; children—Leesa Drue, Terrea Jean, Robert Eric. Tchr., coach Christian County Schs., 1954, Calloway County Schs., 1956-60, Muhl County Schs., 1955; tchr., prin. Webster County Schs., 1961-66, supt., 1969—; high sch. prin., Harrodsburg, Ky., 1966-69. Mem. Am., Ky. assns. sch. adminstrs., Kappa Delta Pi. Methodist. Lion. Home: Dixon KY 42409

CHANEY, J. D., ednl. adminstr.; b. Roby, Tex., Sept. 13, 1925; s. Arthur and Thelma (Widener) C.; B.S., Tex. A. and M. U., 1949, M.E., 1952; m. Lona Faye Stewart, Feb. 28, 1947; children—Jack Dennis, Pamela Loraine, Karen Ruth, Nancy Faith. Tchr., Caddo Parish Schs., La., 1949-50; tchr., bus. mgr. A. and M. Consol. Schs., College Station, Tex., 1950-62; prin. Navasota (Tex.) Ind. Sch. Dist., 1962-65; supt. Avalon (Tex.) Ind. Sch. Dist., 1965-68, Wylie (Tex.) Ind. Sch. Dist., 1968—. Served with USAF, 1944-45. Decorated Air medal. Mem. Tex., Am. assns. sch. adminstrs., Tex. State Tchrs. Assn., N.E.A. Mason. Lion (pres. 1968-69). Mailing Address: 404 Briarwood St Wylie TX 75098 Office: Supt's Office Wylie Ind Sch Dist Wylie TX 75098

CHANEY, WILL WILSON, oil co. exec.; b. Ameagle, W.Va., Feb. 9, 1922; s. John F. and Parlee (Farley) C.; student Draughon's Bus. Sch., Tulsa, 1946; m. Anna Mae Trout, July 8, 1945; children—James, William, Michael, Richard. Purchasing agt. Western Supply Co., Tulsa, 1946-63; mgr. Mylon C. Jacobs Supply Co., Tulsa, 1963—. Served with AUS, 1942-45. Decorated Purple Heart with 2 oak leaf clusters, Bronze Star with 2 oak leaf clusters. Mem. Purchasing Mgmt. Assn. (dir. Tulsa 1968), Transp. Club. Elk. Home: 3816 E 55th St Tulsa OK 74135 Office: PO Box 2366 Tulsa OK 74101

CHANG, JEFFREY P., educator; b. Changteh, Hunan, China; came to U.S., naturalized; grad. Nat. Central U. China; M.S., U. Ill., 1946, also Ph.D. Acting chief, sect. exptl. pathology U. Tex. M.D. Anderson Hosp., Houston, until 1964, prof. biology, also mem. faculty Grad. Sch. Biol. Scis., 1964-71; prof. cellular biology U. Tex. Med. Br., Galveston, 1971—. Formerly cons. NIH, USAF Sch. Aerospace Medicine, Brooks AFB, Tex.; chmn. Symposium Preparative Histochemistry, 1st Internat. Congress Histochemistry and Cyto Chemistry, Paris, session chmn., Japan, 1972; vis. prof., lectr. Vanderbilt U., U. Kan. Sch. Medicine, U. Taiwan, Chin Hwa U., Med. Coll. of Dept. Defense, Republic of China, others. Contbr. articles to profl pubis. Developer open-top cryostat; research tumors, electron microscopy, histochemistry, contraception. Office: U Tex Med Sch Sealy and Smith Bldg Galveston TX 77550*

CHAPEL, STEPHEN W., economist; b. Jackson, Wyo., Sept. 28, 1942; s. Dan L. and Helen (Lambert) C.; B.S., U. Wyo., 1966, M.S., 1968; m. Mary Ann Wilson, July 19, 1966; children—Robyn Michele, Kelly Marie. Commd. 2d lt. U.S. Air Force, 1968, advanced through grades to capt., 1971; econometrician Hdqrs. U.S. Air Force, Washington, 1968-71; operations research analyst Office of Asst. Sec. Defense, Washington, 1971—; instr. No. Va. Community Coll., 1970—. Mem. Am. Econ. Assn., Sigma Chi. Home: 37 Canterbury Sq Alexandria VA 22304 Office: 2d277 The Pentagon Washington DC 20301

CHAPLIN, ROBERT ROGERS, JR., physician; b. Emporia, Va., Jan. 4, 1936; s. Robert Rogers and Gertrude Mae (Michael) C.; B.S., Hampden Sydney Coll., 1958; M.D., Med. Coll. Va., 1962; m. Judith Falconer Preddy, Mar. 7, 1969; 1 son, Robert Rogers III. Intern, Stuart Circle Hosp., Richmond, Va., 1962-63, house physician, 1965-68, now mem. staff; gen. practice medicine, Richmond, 1968—; mem. staff Johnston-Willis Hosp., Grace Hosp., St. Luke's Hosp., St. Elizabeth Hosp., all Richmond. Served as capt. USAF, 1963-65. Mem. Richmond Acad. Medicine, Med. Soc. Va., Va. Acad. Family Practice. Episcopalian. Mason. Home: 2720 Kenbury Rd Richmond VA 23225 Office: 7111 Jahnke Rd Richmond VA 23225

CHAPMAN, ALVAH HERMAN, JR., newspaper exec.; b. Columbus, Ga., Mar. 21, 1921; s. Alvah Herman and Wyline (Page) C.; B.S., The Citadel, 1942; m. Betty Bateman, Mar. 22, 1943; children—Dale Page (Mrs. Dennis L. Webb), Chris Ann. Bus. mgr. Columbus Ledger, 1945-53; v.p., gen. mgr. St. Petersburg (Fla.) Times, 1953-57; pres., pub. Morning News and Evening Press, Savannah, Ga., 1957-60; pres. Savannah News-Press, Inc., 1957-60; exec. Knight Newspapers, Miami, Fla., 1960—, exec. com., exec. v.p. Knight Newspapers, Inc., 1967—; v.p., gen. mgr. The Miami Herald, 1962-69, pres., 1969—; lectr. Am. Press Insts., Columbia. Served from 2d lt. to maj., USAAF, World War II. Decorated D.F.C. with 2 oak leaf clusters, Air medal with 5 clusters (U.S.); Croix de Guerre; named one of five outstanding young men in Ga., 1951; Outstanding Young Man, Columbus Jr. C. of C., 1952; Dade County's Outstanding Citizen of 1968-69. Mem. Am., So. newspapers pubs. assns. Methodist. Kiwanian. Home: 4255 Lake Rd Miami FL 33137 Office: Miami Herald Miami FL 33101

CHAPMAN, CECIL CAREY, cons. hydraulic and san. engr.; b. White Pond, S.C., July 18, 1908; s. Carl McNeil and Myra (Scott) C.; B.S. in Civil Engring., U.S.C., 1931; m. Gertrude Rowe, Sept. 30, 1933. Insp., S.C. Hwy. Dept., 1931-32; chief draftsman U.S. Forest Service, 1933-34; engr. S.C. Geod. Survey, 1934-35; engr. U.S. Soil Conservation Service, 1935-41, drainage and irrigation engr., 1946-48, hydraulic engr. flood control, 1948-51; design engr. U.S.C.E., 1941-42; asso. Walter E. Rowe, municipal engring., 1935-41; partner Rowe & Chapman, designing and cons. engrs., Williston, S.C., 1951-53; co-partner Chapman Engring. Co., design and cons. engrs., Williston, 1953—. Served with USNR, 1943-45; PTO. Registered profl. engr., S.C., Ga., N.C., Fla. Diplomate Am. San. Engrs. Intersoc. Bd. Mem. Am. Soc. C.E., Nat. Soc. Profl. Engrs., Am. Concrete Inst., Am. Water Works Assn., Am. Soc. for Testing and Materials, Water Pollution Control Fedn., S.C. Water and Pollution Control Assn., S.C. Soc. Cons. Engrs., Cons. Engrs. Council, Am. Iris Soc., Am. Legion. Home: 312 W Main St Williston SC 29853 Office: PO Box 218 Williston SC 29853

CHAPMAN, CHARLES HICKERSON, JR., mem. Republican Nat. Com., former constrn. co. exec.; b. Dothan, Ala., Apr. 17, 1920; s. Charles Hickerson and Florrie (Malone) C.; B.S., Washington and Lee U., 1941; m. Martha Farmer, Dec. 30, 1943; children—Charles Hickerson III, Davis F., Florrie Lou. Pres. Chapman Constrn. Co., Dothan, 1946—; chmn. bd. Malone Industries, Inc.; dir. First Nat. Bank Dothan, Dothan Oil Mill Co. Chmn. Houston County Heart Fund, 1965. Mem. Rep. Nat. Committeeman for Ala., 1964—. Served to lt. USNR, 1942-45. Mem. Dothan C. of C. (dir., past chmn. indsl. com., govtl. affairs com.). Home: Enterprise Hwy Dotham AL 36301 Office: PO Drawer 220 Dothan AL 36301

CHAPMAN, JAMES EMORY, educator; b. Atlanta, Mar. 15, 1917; s. Lindsey F. and Lourah (Elder) C.; B.C.S., Ga. State Coll., 1948; M.S., Ga. Inst. Tech., 1950; Ph.D., U. Ala., 1956; student Emory U., U. Tex., U. Fla., Harvard; m. Betty Jean Gaston, Sept. 2, 1950; children—James Emory, Carl Gregory, Candace, Joyce. With Western Electric Co., Atlanta, 1937-41; accounting clk. Gulf Oil Corp., Atlanta, 1941-42; mem. faculty Ga. State Coll., Atlanta, 1950—, prof. mgmt., 1958—. Ednl. dir. Atlanta chpt. Am. Inst. Banking, 1966—; pres. Fidelity Investment Club, Inc. Atlanta, 1966-68; instr. for govtl. and pvt. orgns. Bd. dirs. Atlanta Tb Assn., 1959—, Atlanta Camp Fire Girls, 1971—. Served to 1st lt. AUS, 1942-45. Mem. Acad. Mgmt., So. Case Writers Assn., So. Mgmt. Assn., Alpha Kappa Psi, Beta Gamma Sigma, Pi Kappa Phi. Methodist. Mem. bd. editors So. Jour. Bus., 1965-70. Author monograph. Contbr. sects. to books, articles to pubis. Home: 950 Richmond Hill Dr SE Marietta GA 30060

CHAPMAN, JOE NORWIN, judge, financial exec.; b. Hopkins County, Tex., May 18, 1908; s. B.F. and Dama (McCullough) C.; B.S., East Tex. U., 1931; postgrad. Tex. U., 1932-33; LL.B., Cumberland U., 1934, J.D., 1969; m. Idell Jones, Aug. 7, 1937; children—Joe N., James L. Admitted to Tex. bar, 1934, D.C. bar, 1946; asst. state's atty., Hopkins County, Tex., 1935-41; atty. FTC, Washington, 1941-42, 46-50; gen. practice law, Sulphur Springs, Tex., 1950-65; dist. trial judge 8th dist. Tex., Sulphur Springs, 1965-72. Pres., dir., Cattlemen's Investment Corp., Sulphur Springs, 1956-66; chmn. bd. Peoples Nat. Bank of Sulphur Springs, 1963-72. Mem. Tex. Ho. of Reps. 1953-65; mem. Tex. Civil Jud. Council, 1959-67. Chmn., Hopkins County A.R.C., 1953-54. Served to lt. comdr. USNR, 1942-46. Named hon. life mem. E. Tex. delegation of Tex. Legislature, 1965. Mem. Hopkins County C. of C. (dir.), State Bar of Tex. (exec. com. jud. sect. 1970-71), Tex., N.E. Tex., Hopkins County bar assns., Am. Legion, D.A.V. Methodist (ofcl. bd.). Mason (Shriner). Home: 729 Church St Sulphur Springs TX 75482 Office: PO Box 233 Chapman Bldg 210 Church St Sulphur Springs TX 75482

CHAPMAN, JOEL ALVIN, supt. schs.; b. Anderson, S.C., Apr. 14, 1918; s. Joseph Wilhite and Eliza Eugenia (Hall) C.; B.A., Presbyn. Coll., 1939; M.A., Columbia, 1949; m. Carolyn Woods Embry, Jan. 26, 1942; 1 dau., Diana (Mrs. Richard John Monsour). Prin., Chambliss Jr. High Sch., Americus, Ga., 1939-40, Taylors (S.C.) Elementary Sch., 1940-41, Leland (Miss.) High Sch., 1946-51; Supt. Port Gibson (Miss.) Pub. Schs., 1953-65, Bolivar County Sch. Dist., Shelby, Miss., 1965—. Bd. dirs. Little Theatre Groups. Served to col. AUS, 1941-45, 51-53. Mem. Am. Assn. Sch. Adminstrs., Miss. Assn. Sch. Supts., Miss. State Guidance Council, Miss. Lang. Tchrs. (pres. 1950-51). Mason, Rotarian, Lion. Home: 119 Lauderdale St Shelby MS 38774 Office: Box 28 Shelby MS 38774

CHAPMAN, JOHN STEWART, educator; b. Sweetwater, Tex., Jan. 30, 1908; s. Alfred Alexander and Ollie (Johnson) C.; B.A., So. Meth. U., 1927, B.S., 1927, M.A., 1928; M.D., U. Tex., 1932; m. Marianne Ryan, Nov. 12, 1932; 1 dau., Carolyn (Mrs. Frederick D. Hamilton). Pvt. practice medicine, Dallas, 1943-52; with U. Tex. Southwestern Med. Sch. at Dallas, 1952—, asst. dean postgrad. edn., 1952—, asst. dean for sponsored research, 1972—, prof. internal medicine, 1952—; dir. lab. investigation East Tex. State Chest Hosp.; cons. VA Hosp., Dallas; VA Hosp., Temple, Tex.; med. adv. Dept. Health, Edn. and Welfare, Social Security Adminstrn. Mem. Gov.'s Adv. Bd. for Tb; mem. adv. com. U.N. Conf. on Internat. Environment, 1971—. Mem. A.M.A. (chmn. council on environmental and pub. health 1969-72). Editor publ. Archives of Environmental Health, A.M.A., 1971. Home: 3606 Lovers Lane Dallas TX 75225 Office: 5323 Harry Hines Blvd Dallas TX 76235

CHAPMAN, JOSEPH F., III, lawyer, state ofcl.; b. Brewton, Ala., Aug. 4, 1938; s. Joseph F., Jr. and Gladys (Alford) C.; ed. U. Fla.; m. Jeannette Elizabeth Byers, July 26, 1964; children—Mary Marie Elizabeth, Joseph F. IV, Kristian Byers. Fomer atty. Fla. Gov's Office; former gen. counsel Fla. Rd. Bd.; mem. Fla. Ho. of Reps.; now state atty. Dist. 9. Chmn., Pub. Safety Com. Mem. Fla. Bar Assn., Blue Key, Sigma Chi. Baptist. Address: 408 Magnolia Av Panama City FL 32401*

CHAPMAN, LEONARD F., JR., marine corps officer. Comdt., U.S. Marine Corps, Washington. Office: 8th and I Sts SE Washington DC 20003*

CHAPMAN, MARGARET LOUISE, librarian; b. New Bern, N.C., Apr. 6, 1916; d. Kena King and Louise (Lane) Chapman; A.B., Greensboro Coll., 1938; B.S. in L.S., U.N.C., 1945; M.A., 1956. Librarian, New Bern Pub. Library, 1940-43, Barbour Boat Works, New Bern, 1943-44; asst. in cataloging U. N.C. Library, 1945, cataloger, 1947-51; alumni recorder U. N.C. Alumni Office, 1945-47; cataloger Fla. State U. Library, 1951-54; cataloger, asst. law librarian U. N.C. Law Library, 1954-56; head bibliography room U. Fla. Library, 1956-58; librarian P.K. Yonge Library of Fla. History, U. Fla., 1958-62; spl. collections librarian U. South Fla., Tampa, 1962-71; dir. library Queens Coll., Charlotte, N.C., 1971—. Dir. Hillsborough County Hist. Commn., 1963-71. Mem. Southeastern, Fla. (pres., 1965-66) library assns., Fla. Hist. Soc. (dir. 1960-62, exec. sec. 1962-70, v.p. 1970—), Am. Assn. for State and Local History, Tampa Hist. Soc., Phi Alpha Theta. Democrat. Methodist. Editor: Florida Breezes (Ellen Call Long), 1962. Reviewer adult books Fla. Libraries, 1969-71. Home: 201 N Canterbury Rd Charlotte NC 28211 Office: Everett Library Queens Coll Charlotte NC 28207

CHAPMAN, MARY LUCILE, educator; b. Louisa, Ky., Dec. 13, 1901; d. Napoleon Bonaparte and Ida Belle (Porter) Chapman; A.B., U. Ky., 1929; A.M., 1937; Ph.D., 1945. Tchr. pub. schs. Ashland, Ky., 1921-40, supr., 1940-56; asst. prof., history Marshall Coll., Huntington, W.Va., 1946-48; asso. prof. history E. Tenn. State Coll., Johnson City. 1948-55; prof. social studies Jr. Coll., 1955-57; prof. history Ashland Center U. Ky., 1957-59; head dept. history Piedmont Coll., Demorest, Ga., 1959-62; asso. prof. history Jacksonville (Ala.) State U., 1962-65, prof., 1965—, chmn. div. social studies, 1959-62. Mem. Nat. Council Social Studies, Am., So., Ala. hist. assns., Nat., Ga. hist. socs., Am. Assn. U. Women (pres. Anniston br. 1967-69, mem. Ala. div. bd.), Internat. Fedn. U. Women, Am. Assn. U. Profs., Calhoun County Hist. Assn., Orgn. of Am. Historians, Atlantic Council of U.S., Nat., Ala. edn. assns., Acad. Polit. Sci., So. Polit. Sci. Assn., Coalition for Better Schs. in Ala., Ala. Woman's Civil Def. Orgn., Polit. Sci. Soc., Council So. Life and Work, Internat. Platform Assn., Am. Acad. Polit. and Social Sci., U.D.C., Kappa Delta Pi. Democrat. Methodist. Club: Jacksonville State College Faculty. Home: 703 12th Av Jacksonville AL 36265

CHAPMAN, PHILIP KENYON, physicist, astronaut; b. Melbourne, Australia, Mar. 5, 1935; s. Colin Robison and Phyllis (Kenyon) C., came to U.S., 1961, naturalized, 1967; B.Sc. in Physics, Sydney (Australia) U., 1956; S.M. in Aero. and Astronautics, Mass. Inst. Tech., 1964, Sc.D. in Instrumentation, 1967; m. Pamela Gatenby, Dec. 4, 1959; children—Peter Hume, Kristen de Querilleau.

Electronic engr. Philips Electric Indsl. Pty. Ltd., Sydney, 1956-57; auroral physicist Australian Nat. Antarctic Research Expdn., Mawson, 1958-59; electro-optical engr. Canadian Aviation Electronics Ltd., Montreal, 1960; staff physicist Exptl. Astronomy Lab., Mass. Inst. Tech., 1961-67, research asso., 1967—; scientist-astronaut NASA, 1967—; electro-optical cons., 1963-67. Recipient British Polar medal. Mem. A.A.A.S., Brit. Interplanetary Soc., Am. Astron. Soc. (sr.), Am. Inst. Aero. and Astronautics, Australian Nat. Antarctic Research Expdns. Club. Office: Code CB NASA Manned Spacecraft Center Houston TX 77058

CHAPMAN, RICHARD FRANKLIN, lawyer; b. nr. Ovilla, Tex., Dec. 19, 1903; s. Sumner Franklin and Lillian (Hill) C.; B.A., Trinity U., 1926; LL.B., U. Tex., 1929; m. Hazel Irene Stevens, July 15, 1931; children—Richard A., Steven F. Admitted to Tex. bar, 1929, since practiced in Waxahachie; atty., dir., exec. com. Citizens Nat. Bank, Waxahachie, 1940—; pres., atty., dir., incorporator Waxahachie Fed. Savs. and Loan Assn., 1934—; atty., dir. CBB Investment Corp., Waxahachie, 1968—. Mem. exec. bd. Circle Ten council Boy Scouts Am., Dallas, 1960—, mem. nat. council from Dallas, 1960—. Asst. dist. atty., 1930; city atty., Waxahachie, 1931-40; mem. City Council, 1941. Bd. dirs. U.P. Homes for Children, 1960—, sec., 1963—; incorporator, trustee, sec. Waxahachie Found., Inc. Named Outstanding Citizen Waxahachie C. of C., 1970. Mem. Waxahachie C. of C. (pres., dir.), State Bar Found. Tex. (charter), State Bar Tex., Am. Bar Assn., Ellis County Bar Assn. (past pres.), Trinity U. Alumni Assn. (nat. pres., dir.). Democrat. Club: Chaparral (Dallas). Home: 1604 Alexander Waxahachie TX 75165 Office: PO Box 641 Waxahachie TX 75165

CHAPMAN, RICHARD LEROY, polit. scientist; b. Yankton, S.D., Feb. 4, 1932; s. Raymond Young and Vera (Trimble) C.; B.S., S.D. State U., 1954; postgrad. Cambridge U., 1954-55; M.P.A., Syracuse U., 1958, Ph.D., 1967; m. Marilyn Jean Nicholson, Aug. 14, 1955; children—Catherine Ruth, Robert Matthew, Michael David, Stephen Raymond, Amy Jean. Mgmt. asst. Office Sec. Def., 1958-59; asst. dir. research S.D. Legislative Research Council, Pierre, 1959-60; budget examiner U.S. Bur. Budget, Washington, 1960-61; adminstrv. officer, project mgr. Adv. Research Projects Agy., Dept. Def., Washington, 1961-63; staff asst. Office Dir., NIH, Washington, 1965-66, exec. sec. Grants Assos. Program 1967-68; mem. profl. staff Govt. Operations Com., U.S. Ho. of Reps., Washington, 1966-67; sr. research asso Nat. Acad. Pub. Adminstrn., Washington, 1968—. Served with inf., AUS, 1955-57. Rotary Found. fellow, 1954-55, Syracuse U. fellow, 1957, 63, Brookings Instn. fellow, 1964. Mem. Royal Inst. Pub. Adminstrn., Am. Soc. Pub. Adminstrn., So. Polit. Sci. Assn., A.A.A.S., Phi Kappa Phi, Pi Kappa Delta. Republican. Methodist. Mason. Home: 8204 Chivalry Rd Annandale VA 22003 Office: 1225 Connecticut Av NW Washington DC 20036

CHAPMAN, SAMUEL GREELEY, educator; b. Atlanta, Sept. 29, 1929; s. Calvin C. and Jane (Greeley) C.; A.B., U. Cal. at Berkeley, 1951, M.A., 1959; m. Patricia Hepfer, June 19, 1949; children—Lynn Randall, Deborah Jane. Officer, Police Dept., Berkeley, Cal., 1950-56; police cons. Pub. Adminstrn. Service, Chgo., 1956-63; police chief Multnomah County, Portland, Ore., 1963-66; asst. dir. Nat. Crime Commn., Washington, 1966-67; prof. dept. polit. sci. U. Okla., Norman, 1967—, chmn. athletic council, 1971-72. Author: The Police Heritage in England and America, 1962; Police Patrol Readings, 1964, rev. edit., 1970. Home: 2421 Hollywood St Norman OK 73069

CHAPMAN, STEVEN FRANKLIN, lawyer; b. Waxahachie, Tex., May 8, 1940; s. Richard Franklin and Hazel (Stevens) C.; B.B.A., So. Meth. U., 1962, LL.B., 1965; m. Hilda Harbin, June 12, 1964; children—Jim, Jill. Admitted to Tex. bar, 1965; since practiced in Waxahachie, Tex., 1965—; mem. firm Chapman and Chapman, 1967—; city atty., Waxahachie, 1969—, Midlothian, Tex., 1970—. Judge, City Corp. Ct., Waxahachie, Tex., 1967-69. Bd. dirs. Ellis County Hist. Mus. and Art Gallery, pres., 1972; bd. dirs. Community Chest and United Fund, 1967-69, pres., 1968-69. Mem. Am., Ellis County (pres. 1970-71) bar assns., State Bar of Tex. Presbyn. (pres. bd. trustees 1972). Rotarian (pres. 1969-70). Home: 419 Bird Lane Waxahachie TX 75165 Office: Citizens Nat Bank Bldg Waxahachie TX 75165

CHAPMAN, WILLIAM FRED, JR., coll. dean; b. Belton, S.C., Apr. 13, 1931; s. William Fred and Iver (Cooper) C.; B.S., Clemson U., 1957, M.S., 1958; Ph.D., U. Fla., 1963; m. Nancy Jean Bryant, June 10, 1955; children—William Anthony, Nancy Jean. Asst. prof. Clemson U., 1957-59, prof., 1965-66; marketing economist Econ. Research Service, U.S. Dept. Agr., U. Fla., Gainesville, 1959-64; prof., head dept. econs. and bus. adminstrn. Presbyn. Coll., Clinton, S.C., 1964-65, 66-69, acad. dean, prof., 1969—. Cons., Clemson U., 1964-65, 66-67, U.S. Dept. Interior, 1966-67, U.S. Dept. Agr., 1964-65, 65-66. Served from pvt. to 1st lt. AUS, 1951-53. Decorated Combat Infantry badge, Purple Heart, Silver Star. Mem. Am., So. econs. assns., Am. Farm Econs. Assn., Am. Assn. U. Profs., Am. Statis. Assn., Alpha Zeta, Gamma Sigma Delta. Contbr. monographs, bulls. to profl. jours. Home: Huntington Rd Clinton SC 29325

CHAPPELEAR, JOHN WILLIS, JR., architect; b. High Point, N.C., Feb. 3, 1929; s. John Willis and Floyce Lee (Goodson) C.; student N.C. State Coll., 1945-48; m. Betty Jean Hooker, Aug. 24, 1948; children—John III, Donald Eugene, Karen Lynn, Jean Marie. Designer, Eric G. Flannagan, Henderson, N.C., 1949-52, Frantz & Addkison, Roanoke, Va., 1953-59; designer, asso. Randolph Frantz & Assos., Roanoke, 1959-64; partner Frantz & Chappelear, Roanoke, 1965—. Apptd. by gov. to Va. Art Commn., 1970; pres. Downtown Roanoke, Inc., 1965; chmn. Roanoke Bd. Zoning Appeals, 1964—; pres. Central Roanoke Devel. Found., 1968—. Registered profl. architect, N.C., Va. Mem. A.I.A. (pres.-elect Va. chpt. 1971). Prin. archtl. works include Roanoke Civic Center, Hollins Coll. (Va.) Sci. Bldg., Va. Western Community Coll., Madison Jr. High Sch., Roanoke, Melrose Towers Apts., Roanoke. Home: 2535 Robin Hood Rd Roanoke VA 24014 Office: 606 State and City Bldg Roanoke VA 24011

CHAPPELL, BUFORD SOUTER, physician; b. Bookman, S.C., July 28, 1914; s. Oscar and Belva (Leuer) C.; M.D., Med. Coll. S.C., 1938; m. Mary Marjorie Cooper, Nov. 8, 1940; children—Buford Souter, Mary (Mrs. Charles F. Mills), Richard F., Pamela A. Intern, St. Francis Infirmary, Charleston, S.C., 1937-38, U. Kan. Hosp., Kansas City, 1938-39; asst. resident urology U. Va., 1945-46, resident urology, 1947; sr. resident urology VA Hosp., Columbia, 1948-49, cons. urology, 1949—; practice medicine, specializing in urology Columbia, 1949—; chief urology service Columbia (S.C.) Hosp., 1950-60; active urology staff Providence Hosp., Columbia, Bapt. Hosp. Served from capt. to lt. col. M.C., AUS, 1942-46. Fellow Internat. Coll. Surgeons; mem. A.M.A., So. Med. Assn., Am. Urol. Assn. Home: 1373 Kathwood Rd Columbia SC 29206 Office: 2011 Hampton St Columbia SC 29204

CHAPPELL, FRED, author; b. Canton, N.C., May 28, 1936; s. James Taylor and Anne (Davis) C.; B.A., Duke, 1961; m. Susan Nichols, Aug. 2, 1959; 1 son, Heath. Gen. mgr. Brown Supply Co., Candler, N.C., 1957-59; credit mgr. Candler Furniture Co., 1959-60; proofreader Duke U. Press, Durham, N.C., 1961. Woodrow Wilson fellow, Nat. Def. Edn. Act fellow. Mem. Southeastern Renaissance Assn. Author: It Is Time, Lord, 1963; The Inkling and Dagon. Former editor The Archive; former contbg. editor Skyhook. Contbr. to Holiday, little mags. Address: care English Dept U of NC at Greensboro Greensboro NC 27412*

CHAPPELL, THOMAS WARREN, agrl. engr.; b. Newport News, Va., July 18, 1943; s. Richard Jennings and Edith (Brown) C.; B.S., Va. Poly. Inst. and State U., 1965, M.S., 1967; m. Margaret Louise White, Oct. 14, 1967; children—David, Michael, Wallace. Research agrl. engr. Forest Service, U.S. Dept. Agr., Auburn, Ala., 1967—. Mem. Am. Soc. Agrl. Engrs., Forest Products Research Soc., Sigma Xi, Alpha Epsilon, Gamma Sigma Delta. Home: 1212 Old Mill Rd Auburn AL 36830 Office: USDA Forest Service Agrl Engring Bldg Auburn U Auburn AL 36830

CHAPPELL, WILLIAM VENROE, JR., congressman, lawyer; b. Kendrick, Fla., Feb. 3, 1922; s. William Venroe and Laura (Kemp) C.; B.A., U. Fla., 1947, LL.B., 1949; m. Marguerite Gushall, Mar. 22, 1944; children—Judith Jane (Mrs. Taylor), Deborah Kay (Mrs. Bond), William Venroe III, Christopher Clyde. Admitted to Fla. bar, 1949; pvt. practice law, Ocala, 1949—, now mem. firm Sturgis, Chappell & Welsch; County pros. atty., Marion County, Ocala, 1950-54; mem. Fla. Ho. of Reps., 1954-64, 67-69, speaker, 1961-63; mem. 91st Congress from 4th Fla. dist. Served to capt. USNR, 1943—. Mem. Am. Bar Assn., Fla. Bar, Acad. Fla. Trial Lawyers. Democrat. Methodist. Mason, Lion, Elk, Moose. Home: 1910 SE 12th St Ocala FL 32670 Office: 221 E Silver Springs Blvd Ocala FL 32670

CHARDON, FERNANDO, Puerto Rican govt. ofcl.; b. Ponce, P.R., Sept. 5, 1907; s. Carlos Felix and Isabel (Palacios-Pelletier) C.; B.S.A., Cornell U.; LL.D., Interam. U. P.R.; m. Carmin Guyar Gatell, Aug. 1931; children—Diana Maria (Mrs. Rengel), Carmen Isabel (Mrs. Ortiz), Fernando Luis, Marissa. Asst. agronomist for research in sugar cane and tobacco U. P.R., 1928-39; chief sect. agrl. rehab. div. P.R. Reconstrn. Adminstrn., 1937; field mgr. Constancia Sugar Mill, Toa Baja, P.R., 1939-41; dir. appraisal div. P.R. Land Authority, 1946-47; v.p. in charge operations and colonies Eastern Sugar Assn., Fajardo Eastern Sugar Assn., 1947-61; sec.-treas. P.R. Sugar Producers Assn., 1962—; now sec. of state, P.R. Served to lt. col. AUS, 1941-46; PTO. Mem. Internat. Soc. Sugar Cane Technologists (sec. gen.), P.R. Technologists Assn. Mem. New Progressive Party. Roman Catholic. Address: Calle Fortaleza 54 Apartado 3271 San Juan PR 00904*

CHARLES, GEORGE JAMES, lawyer; b. Toronto, Ont., Can.; s. James E. and Despina C.; came to U.S., 1934, naturalized 1940; B.A. with honors, U. Pa., 1950; J.D. with honors, George Washington U., 1952; m. Helen Clara Chigges, June 20, 1947; children—James George, Deborah, Mary Elizabeth, Constance. Admitted to D.C. bar, 1953, Md. bar, 1958, U.S. Supreme Ct. bar, 1960; press and information officer Royal Greek Embassy, 1950-57; pvt. practice law, Washington, 1953—. Press aide to King and Queen of Greece on royal tour of U.S., 1953. Pres. bd. trustees St. Sophia Cathedral, Washington, 1963-68, mem. exec. com. Archdiocesan Council Greek Orthodox Archdiocese N. and S. Am.; chmn. Met. Washington Council Greek Orthodox Chs., 1963—; mem. Order St. Andrew, Eucemenical Patriarchate Eastern Orthodox Ch.; mem. gen. bd. Nat. Council Chs. of Christ, U.S.A., 1969—. Served as maj. USAAF, World War II, Africa, Italy, Germany; lt. col. USAF Res. ret. Decorated Bronze Star. Mem. Am. Bar Assn., Bar Assn. D.C., Phi Delta Phi. Clubs: Nat. Lawyers; Bethesda Country. Home: 7604 Carter Ct Bethesda MD 20034 Office 1250 Connecticut Av NW Washington DC 20036

CHARLESWORTH, ARTHUR RIGGS, clergyman, educator; b. South Fork, Pa., Sept. 23, 1911; s. Thomas and Cora Crina (Riggs) C.; B.A. with honors, U. Pitts., 1933; B.D., M.Div., Theol. Sch., Drew U., Ph.D., 1946; m. Martha Jean Hamilton, July 11, 1935; children—Lois Jean, James Hamilton, Arthur Thomas. Ordained to ministry United Methodist Ch., 1938; minister, then sr. minister Bryan Meml. United Meth. Ch., Miami, Fla., 1959-63; head religion and philosophy Bethune-Cookman Coll., Daytona Beach, Fla., 1963—, also pres. faculty assn. Participant seminar Near Eastern Civilizations, Holy Land and Greece, summer 1968, seminar The Living God, Oxford U., Eng., summer 1969, seminar Profs. to Africa, summer 1970; mem. summer inst. Inst. on Theology, Princeton Theol. Sem., 1971. Mem. Am. Assn. U. Profs. (pres. 1967), N.E.A., Drew U. Alumni Assn. (pres. Fla. chpt. 1967-70), Am. Acad. Religion, Soc. Bibl. Lit., Am. Sch. Oriental Research. Rotarian. Home: 1231 Florence Ct Holly Hill FL 32017 Office: Box 303 Bethune-Cookman Coll Daytona Beach FL 32015

CHARTERIS, LESLIE, author; b. Singapore, May 12, 1907; student Cambridge U., 1926; studied art in Paris; m. Pauline Schishkin, 1931 (div. 1937); 1 dau., Patricia Ann; m. 2d, Barbara Meyer, 1938 (div.); m. 3d, Elizabeth Bryant Borst, 1943 (div.); m. 4th, Audrey Long, 1952. Naturalized U.S. citizen, 1946. Fellow Royal Soc. Arts; mem. Mensa. Clubs: Royal Nassau Sailing, Yacht de Cannes, Savage. Author numerous books from Meet the Tiger, 1928, to Saint to the Rescue, 1959; Trust the Saint, 1962; The Saint in the Sun, 1963; Vendetta for the Saint, 1964; The Saint on TV, 1968; The Saint Returns, 1968; The Saint & The Fiction Makers.; The Saint & The People Importers, 1971; The Saint in Pursuit, 1971. Editor The Saint Detective Mag. Contbr. numerous mags.; also written several motion picture plays. Office: Box 2614 Palm Beach FL 33480

CHARYK, JOSEPH VINCENT, bus. exec.; b. Canmore, Alta., Can., Sept. 9, 1920; s. John and Anna (Dorosh) C.; B.Sc. in Engring. Physics, U. Alta., 1942, LL.D. (hon.), 1964; M.S., Cal. Inst. Tech., 1943, Ph.D., 1946; m. Edwina Elizabeth Rhodes, Aug. 18, 1945; children—William R., Joseph J., Christopher E., Diane E. Came to U.S., 1942, naturalized, 1948. Sect. chief Jet Propulsion Lab., Cal. Inst. Tech., 1945-46, instr. aero., 1945-46; asst. prof. aero. Princeton, 1946-49, asso. prof., 1949-55; dir. aerophysics and chemistry lab. missile systems div. Lockheed Aircraft Corp., 1955-56; dir. aero. lab. Aeronutronic Systems, Inc., subsidiary Ford Motor Co., 1956-58, gen. mgr. space tech. div., 1958-59; dir. Sanders Assos., Inc. Cons. Sci. Adv. Bd. USAAF, 1957-58, mem., 1958-59; asst. Sec. Research and Devel., U.S. Air Force, 1959; under sec. Air Force, 1960-63; pres., dir. Communications Satellite Corp., 1963—. Tech. adv. panel aero. Dept. Def., 1956-58; mem. subcom. fluid mechanics NACA, 1957-58. Fellow Am. Inst. Aeros. and Astronautics; mem. Internat. Acad. Astronautics, Conf. Bd., Newcomen Soc. N.Am., Nat. Inst. Social Scis., Internat. Broadcast Inst., Sigma Xi. Clubs: 1925 F Street, Federal City, Congressional Country, Chevy Chase, Nat. Space (bd. govs.). Asso. editor, gen. editor High Speed Aerodynamics and Jet Propulsion (12 vols.), 1954-58. Contbr. articles tech. jours. Home: 5126 Tilden St NW Washington DC 20016

CHASE, FRANK REYNOLDS, librarian; b. Chgo., June 9, 1915; s. Frank Maxwell and Ethel R. (Drummond) C.; B.A., U. Ill., 1942; B.L.S., Columbia, 1947; m. Anne Margaret Cameron, Aug. 18, 1962. Head reference librarian Bradley U., Peoria, Ill., 1947-52; asst. reference librarian Peoria Pub. Library, 1952-59; asst. sci. librarian Morris Library, So. Ill. U., Carbondale, 1959-65; head reference librarian John Grant Crabbe Library, Eastern Ky. U., Richmond, 1965—. Served with AUS, 1942-43. Mem. A.L.A., Ky. Library Assn., Alpha Phi Omega (adviser 1949-65). Home: Box 30-A Route 2 Richmond KY 40475

CHASE, LORING DUBOIS, clergyman; b. Greenfield, Mass., July 13, 1916; s. Loring Bertie and Edith (MacLaury) C.; A.B., Middlebury Coll., 1937; B.D., Yale, 1941; m. Helene Giannina Cosenza, Aug. 17, 1939; children—Christopher L., David M. Ordained to ministry Congl. Ch., 1941; minister Ledyard (Conn.) Congl. Ch., 1939-44; minister-at-large Conn. Conf. Congl. Chs., 1944-47; minister New Canaan (Conn.) Congl. Ch., 1947-64, Westmoreland Congl. Ch., Washington, 1964—. Dir. office of communication United Ch. Christ, 1965—; pres. United Ch. Bd. for World Ministries, 1969—; sec. Commn. to Prepare a Statement of Faith United Ch. Christ, 1957-59. Author: Words of Faith, 1968; The Church, Community of Response and Mission, 1969. Home: 5107 Dalecarlia Dr Washington DC 20016 Office: 1 Westmoreland Circle Washington DC 20016

CHASE, THOMAS GEORGE, lawyer; b. Memphis, Sept. 28, 1911; s. James P. and Fanny (George) C.; B.S., U. Ark., 1934, LL.B., 1936; student U. Mich., 1934-35; m. Ellender Stribling, Oct. 23, 1941; children—Thomas George, Davis S., James Phipps III. Admitted to Ark. bar, 1936, Tenn. bar, 1937, Tex. bar, 1956; pvt. practice, Memphis, 1936-41; pres. Chase Beverage Co., Waco, Tex., 1945-56; partner Naman, Howell, Smith & Chase, 1956—; dir. Southwest Beverages, Inc.; chmn. bd. Hacienda Valle de Viento, S.A., San Jose, Costa Rica; owner Runnymede Land & Cattle Co. Pres. Friends Waco Pub. Library, Inc., 1967; bd. commrs. Waco-McLennan County Library. Chmn. exec. com. McLennan County Rep. Com., 1954. Bd. dirs. Friends Waco Pub. Library, Waco Legal Aid Clinic. Served from ensign to lt. USNR, 1942-45. Fellow Tex. Bar Found.; mem. Am., Waco-McLennan County (dir. 1962—, pres. 1965) bar assns., State Bar Tex., Assn. Ins. Attys., Internat. Assn. Ins. Counsel, Tex. Assn. Def. Counsel (dir. 1969—). Episcopalian (sr. warden 1954). Clubs: City (Waco); Rotary, Ridgewood Country, Ridgewood Yacht. Home: 3524 Carondolet Dr Waco TX 76710 Office: First Nat Bldg Waco TX 76701

CHASTAIN, JAMES ROY, civil engr.; b. Charkston, Ga., June 26, 1923; s. Johnson Elijah and Lucille (Mullins) C.; B.C.E., U. Fla., 1954; m. Ramona Martin, Aug. 8, 1948; children—James Roy, Charles Randall, Edward Lee. Cons. engr., land surveyor Lakeland Engring. Assos., Inc. (Fla.), 1954—; sec.-treas. Chastain Groves, Inc., 1960-72. Dist. chmn. Thunderbird council Boy Scouts Am., 1970; chmn. Engring. Coll., U. Fla. Alumni-Faculty Com., 1970-71. Served with USNR, 1942-46. Fellow Fla. Engring. Soc.; mem. Am. Soc. C.E., Am. Congress Land Surveyors, Nat. Soc. Profl. Engrs., Am. Water Works Assn. Rotarian. Club: Toastmasters (Lakeland, Fla.). Home: 610 Glendale St Lakeland FL 33803 Office: 3114 S Florida Av Lakeland FL 33802

CHASTAIN, WALTER RALPH, JR., banker; b. Columbia, S.C., Mar. 26, 1939; s. Walter Ralph and Maitland Pearl (Mitchell) C.; B.A., U. South, 1961; M.B.A., U. S.C., 1963; m. Nell Williams Stevenson, Dec. 6, 1969. Asst. cashier Citizens and So. Nat. Bank, Charleston, S.C., 1965-66, bond officer, 1966-68, asst. v.p., mgr. bond dept., 1968-69, v.p., mgr. bond dept., 1969—. Instr. U. S.C., 1963, Fla. State U., 1966-71, Bapt. Coll. Charleston, 1967-71, Am. Inst. Banking, 1963-71, Bank Adminstrn. Inst., U. Wis., 1971—. Treas. Charleston County Heart Assn., 1965-71; mem. investment com. S.C. Heart Assn., 1971. Served with S.C. N.G., 1963-69. Recipient Service award S.C. Heart Assn., 1969. Mem. Nat. Assn. Accountants, Bank Adminstrn. Inst., Huguenot Soc. Va., S.A.R., S.C. Bankers Assn. (mem. investment com. 1971). Episcopalian. Clubs: Carolina Yacht (Charleston); Spring Valley Country (Columbia). Home: 37 N Adgers Wharf Charleston SC 29401 Office: 46 Broad St Charleston SC 29401

CHASTEEN, JOSEPH WILEY, JR., property devel. co. exec.; b. Huntsville, Ala., Dec. 9, 1921; s. Joseph Wiley and Ola Lee (Brown) C.; A.B., William Jewell Coll., 1950; postgrad. U. Pa., 1952-55; Drexel Inst. Tech., 1956; M.B.A., Rollins Coll., 1962; m. Mae Lyndal Miller, Oct. 31, 1941; children—Joseph Wiley III, David A. Tchr., Central Tech. Inst., Kansas City, Mo., 1946-50; engr. RCA, Camden, N.J., 1951-56; group engr. Martin Co., Balt., 1956-57; asst. mng. engring. Martin Marietta Corp., Orlando, Fla., 1957-63, engring. mgr., 1963-67, tech. mgr., 1967-69; advance projects mgr. Emerson Electric Co., St. Louis, 1969-70; pres. PWC Assos., Inc., Orlando, 1970—. Chmn., Pine Hills Area Round Table, 1963-64; pres. Robinswood Civic Assn. 1963-65; commr. Pine Hills Fire Dist., 1964-65, Orange County (Fla.) Local Study Group. Bd. dirs. Robinswood Recreation Park, Orlando. Served with USNR, 1944-46, 50-51. Asso. fellow Am. Inst. Aero. and Astronautics; mem. I.E.E.E. (sr.), Am. Ordance Assn., Am. Mgmt. Assn., Sigma Pi Sigma, Kappa Mu Epsilon. Contbr. articles to profl. jours. Home: 6108 Hudson St Orlando FL 32808 Office: PO Box 15606 Orlando FL 32808

CHATHAM, WALTER ALBERT, printing exec.; b. Houston, Nov. 11, 1913; s. William Lewis and Lillie Mae (Schnauburt) C.; B.B.A., S. Tex. Coll., 1938; student U. Houston, 1948; m. Barbara Jane Paulson, Feb. 18, 1938; 1 son, Stephen Walter. With accounting dept. Tex. Pipe Line Co., Houston, 1935-46; mgr. Chatham & Sterling Printers, Houston, 1946-65; partner, owner Chatham Printers, Houston, 1965—. Sec.-treas. Masonic Bldg. Assn. Houston, Mason. Home: 5630 Ella Lee Lane Houston TX 77027 Office: 5521 Clinton Dr Houston TX 77020

CHATTIN, CHESTER COLES, judge; b. Winchester, Tenn., Nov. 2, 1907; s. Edward Walter, and Ellen (Shadow) C.; B.S., U. South, 1929; LL.B., Cumberland U., 1930; m. Mary Kiningham, May 15, 1935; 1 dau., Mary Kay. Admitted to Tenn. bar, 1930; practiced law, Winchester, 1930-47; asst. dist. atty. Gen. 18th Jud. Circuit, Winchester, Tenn., 1935-37, 39-47; dist. atty. Gen. 18th Jud. Circuit, Winchester, Tenn., 1947-58; circuit judge, 1958-62; judge Ct. Appeals Tenn., Winchester, 1962-64, Supreme Ct. Tenn., Winchester, 1964—; dir. rep. Franklin County, Tenn., 1941-43; dir. Farmers Nat. Bank, Winchester. Served with USNR, 1945. Mem. Tenn. Bar Assn., Tenn. Jud. Conf., Franklin County C. of C., Franklin County Hist. Soc., Am. Legion, Phi Gamma Delta. Episcopalian. Mason (Shriner). Club: Franklin County Country. Home: 801 S Jefferson St Winchester TN 37398 Office: 107 1st Av SW Winchester TN 37398

CHAUVIN, ROBERT SILAS, coll. dean; b. West Beekmantown, N.Y., Nov. 20, 1920; s.Silas Nelson and Marie (Woodley) C.; B.S., State U. Coll. N.Y., 1943; M.Ed., U. Houston, 1947; M.A., Columbia, Ed.D., 1950; m. Della Faye Freeman, May 16, 1947; children—Robert Silas, Randall Freeman. Prof. geography, geology Stetson U., DeLand, Fla. 1960, dean sciences, 1968-69, dean Coll. Liberal Arts, 1969—; vis. asst. prof. geography Columbia U., 1954; vis. prof. geography-geology Neb. State Coll., Kearney, 1957. Mem. Govs. Bd. on Resource-Use, State of Fla., 1958—. Served with AUS, 1943-46. Mem. Assn. Am. Georgraphers, U.S. Naval Inst., Lambda Chi Alpha, Gamma Theta Upsilon. Democrat. Baptist. Home: 851 E Minnesota Av DeLand FL 32720

CHAVES-GARCIA, CARLOS FRANCISCO, dentist; b. Isabela, P.R., Nov. 2, 1937; s. Francisco Chaves and Martina Garcia; B.S., U. P.R., 1959, D.M.D., 1963; m. Celida Nieves Maldonado, Dec. 27, 1962; children—Aixa Odette, Elga Enid, Carlos Omar. Practice dentistry, Barbosa Isabela, P.R., 1963—, P.R. Health Dept., Isabela, 1965—. Pres. Gallitos de Isabela, Inc., 1967-68, Cooperative Credito Isabela, 1968-69; v.p. Cooperativa Consumo Isabela, 1970-71. Mem. P.R. Dental Assn., Omicron Kappa Upsilon, Xi, Psi Phi. Mem. Popular Party. Roman Catholic. Lion. Home: Rural Route 2Bo Coto Isabela PR 00662 Office: Barbosa 8 Isabela PR 00662

CHAVEZ, CARLOS, conductor, composer; b. Mexico, June 13, 1899. Former head Dept. of Fine Arts of Mexico, past dir. Nat. Conservatory, Mexico; founder Symphony Orch. of Mexico City, 1928, and since condr.; has been guest condr. of many major orchs. U. S.; Charles Eliot Norton prof. poetry Harvard, 1958-59. Decorated many fgn. govts. Hon. mem. Am. Acad. Arts and Scis., Nat. Inst. Arts and Letters. Composer Sinfonia Antigona, Sinfonia India, music for ballet symphony, H.P. (the initials standing for Horse Power), 4th Symphony, Romantica, 1959, Soli Number 1 for Wind Quartet, and many other leading works. Author: Toward a New Music, 1937; Musical Thought, 1960. Address: Av Pirineos 775 Lomas de Chapulltepec Mexico City 10 Mexico

CHAVEZ, IGNACIO, physician; b., 1897; ed. Nat. U. of Mexico hon. degrees univs. Paris, Montpellier, Lyon, Mexico, Sao Paulo, Oxford, Bologna, Praga, others. Clin. prof. Nat. U. of Mexico, 1923-50, dir. Faculty Medicine, 1933-34, prof. cardiology Sch. Grads., 1946-61, rector Nat. U., 1961-66. Founder, dir. Nat. Inst. Cardiology of Mexico; founder, mem. Colegio Nacional. Hon. rector U. Michoacan; hon. prof. univs. Guadalajara, Guatemala, San Salvador, Rio de Janeiro, others. Recipient Palmes Academiques. Decorated Legion of Honor, Order Pub. Health (France); comdr. Order Finlay (Cuba); Order Quetzal (Guatemala); Order Cruzeiro do Sul (Brazil); Medal of Civil Merit, (Mexico); Order Nassau (Holland); Merito (Italy); Polonia Restituta; Roi Leopoid (Belgium); recipient Scientific prize of Mexico. Mem. Inter-Am. Soc. Cardiology (hon. pres.), Acads. Medicine of Mexico, N.Y., Buenos Aires, France, Rome, others. Author books. Address: Paseo de la Reforma 1310 Lomas City 10 Mexico Office: Avenida Nuevo Leon 78 Mexico City 11 Mexico

CHEATHAM, FRANK SELLARS, JR., judge; b. Savannah, Ga., Jan. 11, 1924; s. Frank S. and Margaret (Caldwell) C.; student Armstrong Coll., 1942-44; A.B., U. Ga., 1946, LL.B., 1948. Admitted to Ga. bar, 1948; gen. practice, Savannah, 1948-72; judge Superior Ct., Eastern Jud. Dist. Ga., 1972—. Dir. First Bank of Savannah, 1968-72. Mem. Ga. Ho. of Reps., 1953-60, chmn. appropriations com., 1959-60; mem. Gov's Commn. on Jud. Selection, 1963-67. Pres. YMCA Bd., 1964-68. Trustee Candler Gen. Hosp. Named Outstanding Young Man in Ga., Ga. Jr. C. of C., 1951. Mem. Savannah Bar Assn. (pres. 1966), Blue Key, Sigma Alpha Epsilon, Phi Delta Phi, Omicron Delta Kappa. Kiwanian (pres. Savannah 1969). Home: 4622 Cumberland Savannah GA 31405 Office: 214 County Court House Savannah GA 31401

CHEATUM, ELMER PHILIP, biologist, educator; b. Langdon, Kan., July 19, 1901; s. Jasper W. and Grace (Wright) C.; A.B., Southwestern Coll., 1924; M.S., Kan. State U., 1925; Ph.D., U. Mich., 1933; m. Edith Deck, Aug. 8, 1925; children—Don, Dan. Asst. prof. So. Meth. U., Dallas, 1925-31, asso. prof. biology, 1933-41, prof. biology, 1941—, chmn. biology dept., 1955-64; instr. zoology U. Mich., 1931-33. Mem. Tex. Acad. Sci. (pres. 1941-42), Phi Kappa Phi, Sigma Xi. Contbr. articles in aquatic biology, ecology of gastropods, and Pleistocene paleoecology to profl. jours. Home: 3304 Centenary St Dallas TX 75225

CHEEK, CHARLES WALL, investment co. exec.; b. Lexington, N.C., Mar. 20, 1921; s. John Merritt and Maud (Wall) C.; B.S., Wake Forest U., 1941; m. Betty Green Johnson, Dec. 28, 1944; children—Mary Charles (Mrs. Charles Torrence Armstrong), Catherine, Alexander. Prodn. mgr. Cheek-Holton Co., Durham, N.C., 1946-50; trust officer Fidelity Bank, Durham, 1952-56; vice-pres. Wachovia Bank, Durham, 1956-60; v.p. First Nat. Bank of S.C., Charleston, 1960-63; pres. Piedmont Financial Co., Greensboro, N.C., 1963—, also dir.; dir., chmn. Piedmont Adv. Corp.; v.p., dir. Richardson Corp.; dir. Piedmont Mgmt. Co.; dir. Reinsurance Corp. of N.Y. Pres. Charleston Civic Ballet, 1962; pres. Greensboro Civic Ballet, 1965. Pres., bd. dirs. United Arts Council, 1968; mem. exec. bd. Gen. Greene council Boy Scouts Am., 1970; bd. visitors U. N.C. Bus. Sch.; trustee Wake Forest U., Smith Richardson Found. Served to capt. USNR, 1950-52. Clubs: Greensboro Country, Carolina Yacht. Home: 804 Sunset Dr Greensboro NC 27408 Office: PO Box W-1 Greensboro NC 27402

CHEEK, GEORGE CURTIN, trade assn. exec.; b. Seattle, Jan. 23, 1931; s. George C. and Evelyn (Kinvig) A.; B.S., Gonzaga U., 1954; postgrad. Harvard, 1957; m. Nancy May Powers, June 13, 1953; children— Allison, David, Jennifer, Sarah. Reporter, editor The Spokesman Rev., Spokane, 1951-59; writer, pub. relations mgr. information services Am. Plywood Assn., Tacoma, 1959-68; account supr. Cole &Weber, Seattle, 1968-69; dir. plans and programs Nat. Forest Products Assn., Washington, 1969-70; exec. v.p. Am. Forest Inst., Washington, 1970—. Pres. Tacoma Municipal League, 1968-69. Chmn. bd. advisers St. Patrick's and Aquinas Acad., Tacoma, 1967-68. Mem. Arctic Inst., Wilderness Soc., Pub. Relations Soc. Am., Am. Soc. Assn. Execs. Home: 2522 Lakevale Dr Vienna VA 22180 Office: 1619 Massachusetts Av NW Washington DC 20036

CHEEK, JAMES EDWARD, univ. pres.; b. Roanoke Rapids, N.C., Dec. 4, 1932; s. King Virgil and LeeElla (Williams) C.; B.A., Shaw U., 1955, D.H., 1970; B.D., Colgate Rochester Div. Sch., 1958; Ph.D., Drew U., 1962, LL.D., 1971; L.H.D., Trinity Coll., 1970; LL.D. (hon.), A. and T. State U., 1971, Del. State U., 1972; Ed.D. (hon.), Providence Coll., 1972; Dr. honoris causa, L'Univ. d'Etat d'Haiti, 1972; m. Celestine Juanita Williams, June 14, 1953; children—James Edward, Janet Elizabeth. Teaching asst. hist. theology Drew Theol. Sch., 1959-60; instr. Western history Union Jr. Coll., Cranford, N.J., 1959-60; vis. instr. Christian history Upsala Coll., E. Orange, N.J., summer 1960; asst. prof. N.T. and hist. theology Sch. Religion, Va. Union U., Richmond, 1961-63; pres. Shaw U., 1963-69, Howard U., Washington, 1969—. Dir. First Nat. Bank Washington. Mem. Pres.'s Commn. on Campus Unrest, 1970; spl. cons. to Pres. U.S. on black colls and univs., 1970; mem. com. internat. edn. Coll. Entrance Exam. Bd.; mem. nat. adv. council Peace Corps; mem. Mayor's Econ. Devel. Com. Trustee, Colgate Rochester Div. Sch., Internat. Council for Ednl. Devel.; bd. dirs. Nat. Assn. for Equal Opportunity in Higher Edn. Nat. Council Educating the Disadvantaged, Fund for Advancement Theol. Edn., Ednl. Policy Center, Nat. Lab. for Higher Edn., Internat. African C. of C., People United to Save Humanity; trustee Fund for Edn. in World Order, VITA, Drew U., Bd. Fgn. Scholarships, Middle States Assn. Colls. and Secondary Schs., U. Miami, Inst. Internat. Edn.; bd. advisers Nat. Coordinating Council Drug Abuse Edn. and Information, Am. Hosp. Assn. Nat. Adv. Com. Health, Student Nat. Med. Assn., Assn. Integration Mgmt., African Free Sch., Minority Advt. and Journalism Inst.; mem. policy council Common Cause; mem. pres.'s devel. council Wilberforce U.; mem. Nat. Adv. Council Independent Found.; mem. adv. com. Woodrow Wilson Internat. Center Scholars; mem. nat. council U.S. Peoples Fund for UN; mem. nat. adv. com. Nat. Assn. Black Adult Educators. Served with USAF, 1950-51. Colgate Rochester Grad. fellow, 1958; Lily Found. fellow, 1958, 59; Rockefeller Doctoral fellow, 1960. Mem. Soc. Bibl. Lit. and Exegesis, Am. Soc. Ch. History, Nat. Assn. Bibl. Instrs., Am. Assn. U. Profs., Am. Acad. Religion, Religious Research Assn., Am. Assn. Higher Edn. (mem. bd.), Am. Assn. of Colls. for Tchr. Edn. (mem. bd.), Am. Mgmt. Assn., Alpha Kappa Delta, Alpha Phi Alpha. Bd. editors Jour. Black Studies. Home: 8035 16th St NW Washington DC 20012 Office: Howard U Washington DC 20001

CHEELEY, JOSEPH ELBERT, JR., lawyer, judge; b. Buford, Ga., Nov. 4, 1928; s. Joseph Elbert and Willie (Westbrook) C.; J.D., U. Ga., 1950; m. Selma M. Medlock, July 13, 1952; children—Joseph Elbert III, Robert D., Susan, John, James. Admitted to Ga. bar, 1950; since practiced Buford, Ga.; state judge Gwinnett County, 1958—. Vice pres., dir., gen. counsel Buford Comml. Bank. Mem. Lake Lanier Islands Devel. Authority. Solicitor, Gwinnett County, 1954-58. Bd. trustees Gainesville Coll. Served to capt. USAF, 1952-53. Decorated Bronze Star medal; named One of Five Outstanding Young Men Ga., 1963, Outstanding Young Man of Gwinnett County, 1963, One of Nation's Outstanding Young Men, 1964. Mem. Gwinnett Bar Assn. (pres. 1961-62), Gridiron, C. of C. (dir.), Phi Alpha Delta, Omicron Delta Kappa. Democrat. Methodist (chmn. ofcl. bd.). Kiwanian (lt. gov. 1957-58). Home: 105 Shadburn Ferry Rd Buford GA 30518 Office: Buford Comml Bank Bldg Buford GA 30518

CHEEVERS, FRANK STANLEY, hosp. adminstr.; b. Kovno, Lithuania, Aug. 19, 1920; s. Joseph and Veronica (Adam) C.; came to U.S., 1923, naturalized, 1943; student Wayne State U., 1936-41; m. Hollie C. Brownd, Nov. 14, 1943; children—Hollie Jeanne, Brian Frank. Frozen foods mgr. Quaker Dairies, Detroit, 1936-37; machinist, tool maker Barkley-Gro Aircraft Corp., Detroit, 1937-38, Garwood Industries, Detroit, 1938-42; housing mgr. Moore County (Tex.) Housing Authority, 1946-48; adminstr., Meml. Hosp., Dumas, Tex., 1948—; dir. North Plains Savings & Loan Corp. Fund raising chmn. Llano Estacado area council Boy Scouts Am., 1956; com. mem. Tex. Gov.'s Regional Health Planning Council, 1969—. Mem. Dumas Indsl. Devel. Bd., 1967-71; mem. Parks and Recreational Bd., Dumas, Tex., 1956-71. Bd. dirs. Little League Baseball Assn., Dumas, Tex., 1969-70; trustee Amarillo council Girl Scouts. Served with AUS, 1942-45; ETO. Mem. Tex. Hosp. Assn., Panhandle Tex. Area Hosp. Council (past v.p.), Dumas C. of C. (dir. 1962-63). Democrat. Baptist. Rotarian. Home: 219 Morton Av Dumas TX 79029 Office: 224 E 2d St Dumas TX 79029

CHEGIN, LEE JOSEPH, civil engr.; b. Donora, Pa., Mar. 4, 1929; s. George Julius and Irene Helen (Szabo) C.; B.S., Va. Mil. Inst., 1950; M.S., Ohio State U., 1962; m. Betty Lee Lodek, Dec. 18, 1954; children—Catherine, John, Thomas. Commd. 2d lt. U.S. Army, 1950, advanced through grades to lt. col., 1971; combat engr., Korea; constrn. engr., France; mem. faculty U.S. Army Engr. Sch.; chief constrn. and inspection, Taiwan; br. comdr., Ft. Devens, Mass.; chief mapping, charting and geodesy, Vietnam; personnel exec. office Chief Engrs., Washington; ret., 1971; supr. plans and specifications City Water Bd., San Antonio, 1971—. Decorated Bronze Star medal with oak leaf cluster. Registered profl. engr., Ala. Mem. Am. Soc. C.E., Soc. Am. Mil. Engrs. Home: 4006 Oakhaven San Antonio TX 78217 Office: 1001 E Market San Antonio TX 78298

CHEN, JOHN HSUEH MING, educator; b. Shanghai, China, June 24, 1931; s. Yi-Fun and Sun-tse Chen; M.S., Va. Poly. Inst., 1957; M.S. in L.S., Columbia, 1962; M.A., N.Y. U., 1964; Ed.D., Pa. State U., 1968; m. Susan B. Dick, Jan. 12, 1968; children—Dean and Paul (twins), Alicia, Cassandra. Dir. instructional materials center State U. N.Y., 1962-65; dir. library, prof. edn. W.Va. Inst. Tech., Montgomery, 1965-66; dir. library, prof. edn. and library sci. Lynchburg (Va.) Coll., 1966-68; dir. libraries, prof. library sci., Wis. State U., Stevens Point, 1968-70; chmn. dept. library sci., prof. library sci. U. So. Miss., Hattiesburg, 1970—. Vis. prof. Va. Commonwealth U., Richmond, 1968. Named Hon. Citizen of State W.Va., 1968. Mem. A.L.A., Am. Soc. Information Sci., Am. Assn. U. Profs., Assn. Edn. Communications and Tech., Internat. Council Edn., Assn. Am. Library Schs., Phi Delta Kappa, Alpha Phi Omega. Rotarian. Home: Box 223 So Sta Hattiesburg MS 39401

CHEN, WAYNE H., educator; b. Soochow, China, Dec. 13, 1922; s. Ting Li and Yung-Chin (Hu) C.; came to U.S., 1947, naturalized, 1957; B.S. in Elec. Engring., Nat. Chiao Tung U., 1944; M.S., U. Wash., 1949, Ph.D., 1952; m. Dorothy Teh Hou, June 7, 1957; children— Avis Shirley and Benjamin Timothy (twins). Electronic engr. cyclotron project Applied Physics Lab., U. Wash., 1949-50, asso. math., 1950-52; mem. faculty U. Fla., 1952—, prof. elec. engring., 1957—, chmn. dept., 1965—; vis. prof. Nat. Chiao Tung U., also Nat. Taiwan U., spring, 1964; vis. scientist Nat. Acad. Scis. to USSR, 1967; mem. tech. staff Bell Telephone Labs., summers 1953, 54, cons., 1955-60; mem. tech. staff Hughes Aircraft Co., summer 1962. Served to lt. col. Chinese Army, 1942-47. Recipient Fla. Blue Key Outstanding Faculty award, 1960; Outstanding Publn. award Chia Hsin Cement Co. Cultural Fund, Taiwan, 1964, Tchr. Scholarship award U. Fla., 1971. Fellow I.E.E.E.; mem. Am. Assn. U. Profs., Am. Soc. Engring. Edn., Elect. Engring. Dept. Heads Assn. (nat. chmn. 1969-70, region III chmn. 1971-73), Sigma Xi (pres. U. Fla. chpt. 1967-68), Sigma Tau, Eta Kappa Nu, Tau Beta Pi. Rotarian. Author: The Analysis of Linear Systems, 1963; Linear Network Design and Synthesis, 1964. Patentee in field. Home: 2065 NW 19th Lane Gainesville FL 32601

CHENAULT, B(ERTIE) J(EAN), pub. accountant; b. Mart, Tex., Apr. 21, 1927; s. Davis Oscar and Bertie (Mills) C.; B.B.A., Baylor U., 1950; m. Helen Louise Hancock, Mar. 8, 1947; children—Robert Louis, Catherine Ann. Jr. staff accountant Burns B. DuBois, Waco, Tex., 1947-49, Harry Wrench, 1949; semi-sr. staff accountant F. G. Masquelette &Co., Houston, 1949-51, Henslee & Hopson, 1951-52, John E. Doyle, San Antonio, 1952-53; sr. staff accountant Peat, Marwick, Mitchell & Co., Dallas, 1953-54, Payne Harrison & Co., 1954-55, F.W. LaFrentz & Co., 1955-56; internal auditor, controller Bush Enterprises, 1956-57; staff accountant supr. Lybrand, Ross Bros. & Montgomery, 1957-63; v.p., treas. Annuity Bd., So. Bapt. Conv., Dallas, 1963—. Crusader, Am. Cancer Soc. Served with USNR, 1945-46. C.P.A., Tex. Mem. Am. Inst. C.P.A.'s, Tex. Soc. C.P.A.'s. Baptist (deacon). Home: 10456 Coleridge St Dallas TX 75218 Office: N Akard Bldg Dallas TX 75201

CHENERY, PETER JASPERSEN, govt. ofcl.; b. Chgo., May 26, 1919; s. William Ludlow and Dai (Smith) C.; B.S., Harvard, 1940; m. Faeth Rider-Hall, Nov. 22, 1941; children—Peter Taylor, Gilbert Rider, Mary Faeth. Research asst. Mass. Inst. Tech., Cambridge, 1940-42; asst. product engr., engr. sect. head Sperry Gyroscope Co., Great Neck, N.Y., 1942-44, 46-54; dir. research and devel. Wright Machinery Co., Div. Sperry-Rand Corp., Durham, N.C., 1954-63; dir. N.C. Bd. of Sci. & Tech., Research Triangle Park, N.C., 1963—; chmn. bd. Faeth Co., Kansas City, Mo., 1967—. Bd. dirs. Better Health Found., Durham, N.C., 1960-65, pres., 1963-64. Served with USNR, 1944-46. Mem. I.E.E.E., A.A.A.S., Am. Soc. Information Scis. Clubs: Kiwanis, Harvard (pres. 1960-61, 65-66, 67-69) (Durham, N.C.). Home: 50 Beverly Dr Durham NC 27707 Office: Box 12235 Research Triangle Park NC 27709

CHENEY, REYNOLDS SMITH, lawyer; b. Jackson, Miss., Oct. 17, 1910; s. William Newton and Emma Laura (Wilson) C.; A.B., Millsaps Coll., Jackson, Miss., 1931; LL.B., Jackson Sch. of Law, 1932; m. Winifred Tunstall Green, Oct. 25, 1934; children—Reynolds Smith, William Garner, Winifred Calhoon. Admitted to Miss. bar, 1931, since practiced Jackson, mem. firm Green, Cheney, Jones & Hughes. Dir., Miss. Cottonseed Products Co., Mchts. Co., Engle Acoustic and Tile, Inc. Organizer, trustee St. Andrews Episcopal Sch., 1947-56, 60-70. Fellow Am. Coll. of Probate Counsel; mem. Am. Acad. Polit. and Social Sci., Am. Newcomen Soc., Jackson Symphony Orch. Assn., Family Service Assn. (dir., pres. 1958), Am., Miss., Hinds County bar assns., Estate Planning Council Miss., Am. Judicature Soc., Omicron Delta Kappa, Kappa Alpha (sr. councilor, nat. v.p.). Episcopalian (dep. to gen. conv. 1958, 61, 64, 67, 69, 70, vice chancellor 1947-66, chancellor 1966—, standing com. Diocese Miss. 1948-66). Club: Capitol City Petroleum (Jackson). Home: 1407 Riverside Dr Jackson MS 39202 Office: Electric Bldg Jackson MS 39201

CHENG, TSUNG O., educator; b. Shanghai, China, Mar. 30, 1925; s. Keith S. and Fanny (Wang) C.; B.S., St. John's U. (China), 1945; M.D., U. Pa., 1950, M.S., 1956; m. Marie Ellen Roe, June 18, 1955; children—Mark Dudley, Yvonne Joyce. Came to U.S., 1950, naturalized, 1960. Intern, St. Barnabas Hosp., Newark, 1950-51; resident Cook County Hosp., Chgo., 1952-55; fellow in cardiovascular disease George Washington U. Sch. Medicine, Dist. of Columbia Gen. Hosp., Washington, 1955-56; instr. cardiology Mass. Gen. Hosp., Boston, 1956-57; fellow cardiorespiratory physiology Johns Hopkins U. Sch. Medicine and Hosp., Balt., 1957-59; acad. medicine, specializing in cardiology, Washington, 1970—; asst. prof. medicine U. State N.Y., 1959-70; asso. prof. medicine George Washington U. Sch. Medicine, 1970-72, prof. medicine, 1972—; chief cardiology D.C. Gen. Hosp., Washington, 1971-72; asso. dir. div. cardiology, dir. cardiac catheterization lab. George Washington U. Med. Center, Washington, 1972—; asst. physician Cardiac Clinic, Johns Hopkins Hosp., Balt., 1957-59, mem. staff cardiac catheterization lab., 1957-59; dir. cardiopulmonary lab. Bklyn. Hosp., 1959-66, co-chief Pediatric Cardiac Clinic, 1959-66, chief Adolescent Cardiac Clinic, 1961-66, attending physician Adult Cardiac Clinic, 1959-66; chief pediatric cardiac clinic Cumberland Hosp., Bklyn., 1963-66; asst. chief cardiology VA Hosp., Bklyn., 1966-69, chief Cardiovascular Lab., 1966-70; asst. vis. physician Kings County Hosp. Med. Center, Bklyn., 1964-70; attending physician Univ. Hosp., State U. N.Y., 1967-70; chief cardiology VA Hosp., Bklyn., 1969-70; co-chief cardiology George Washington U. Med. div. D.C. Gen. Hosp., 1970-71. Diplomate Nat. Bd. Med. Examiners. Fellow A.C.P., Am. Coll. Chest Physicians, Am. Coll. Cardiology, Am. Heart Assn., Council Clin. Cardiology; mem. Am. Fedn. Clin. Research, Am. Heart Assn., Washington Heart Assn., A.A.A.S., D.C. Med. Soc., A.M.A. Contbr. numerous articles to sci., med. jours. Home: 7508 Cayuga Av Bethesda MD 20034 Office: George Washington Univ Med Center 2150 Pennsylvania Av NW Washington DC 20037

CHENG, TUNG CHAO, architect; b. Chao-An, Kwangtung, China, June 17, 1931; s. See Min and Min (Yuen) C.; B.S., Taiwan Coll. Engring., 1953; M.S., Va. Poly. Inst., 1957; m. Jeanne Yu-Fang Yin, July 4, 1959; children—Andrew Y., Ann C. Came to U.S., 1955, naturalized, 1968. Designer, Kwan, Chu & Yang, architects and engrs., Taipei, Taiwan, 1954-55; teaching asst. dept. architecture Va. Poly. Inst., 1955-56; designer, King & King, architects, Syracuse, N.Y., 1956; jr. architect Hayes, Seay, Mattern & Mattern, architects and engrs., Roanoke, Va., 1956-57; designer Saunders, Pearson & Partners, Alexandria, Va., 1957-63, job capt., 1958-63, project mgr., chief designer, 1963-69, project architect, 1969-71, co-chmn. archtl. design and planning, 1969—, asso., 1963-71; partner Saunders, Pearson, Appleton and Partners, 1972—. Cons. architect Chao-I Constrn. Co., Taiwan, 1954-60. Chmn. com. on outdoor phys. edn. facilities Hollin Meadows Elementary Sch. P.T.A., 1970. Recipient 1st prize Archtl. Bldg. Competition, Taiwan Coll. of Eng., 1952; 2d prize Pres. Hall Competition, Kaohsiung, Taiwan, 1953. Mem. A.I.A., Hollin Hills Civic Assn. (dir. at large 1969), Fairfax County C. of C., Phi Kappa Phi, Tau Sigma Delta. Club: Hollin Meadows Swim and Tennis (dir. 1970-72) (Va.). Prin. archtl. works include Jefferson Bldg., Alexandria, Va., 1963, Fountains Apts., Alexandria, 1966, Seminary Plaza Bldg., Alexandria, 1968, Va. Poly. Inst. Forest and Wildlife Bldg., Blacksburg, Va., 1970, Kings Park br. Fairfax County Pub. Library, Fairfax, Va., 1971; U.S. Army Res. Center, Ft. Belvoir, Va., 1972. Home: 7511 Range Rd Alexandria VA 22306 Office: Seminary Plaza Bldg Alexandria VA 22304

CHENNAULT, ANNA CHAN (MRS. CLAIRE LEE CHENNAULT), journalist, author, lectr.; b. Peiping, China, June 23, 1925; d. Sam Y.W. and Bessie (Jeong) Chan; B.A. in Journalism, Ling Nan U., Hong Kong, 1944; Litt. D., Chungang U., Seoul, Korea, 1967; LL.D., Lincoln U., 1970; H.H.D., Manahath Ednl. Center, 1970; m. Claire Lee Chennault, Dec. 21, 1947 (dec.); children—Claire Anna, Cynthia Louise. Came to U.S. 1948, naturalized, 1950. War corr. Central News Agy., 1944-48; feature writer Hsing Ming Daily News, Shanghai, China, 1946-49; pub. relations officer Civil Air Transport, Taipei, 1947-57, editor Civil Air Transport Bull., Taiwan, 1946-57; U.S. corr. Hsin Sheng Daily News, Washington, 1958—. Lectr., 1950—; fashion designer, 1952—; Chinese sect. chief machine translation research Georgetown U., Washington, 1958-63; with Voice of Am., Washington, 1963-66; spl. corr. to Washington Central News Agy., 1965—; v.p. internat. affairs The Flying Tiger Line, Inc.; dir. D.C. Nat. Bank. Pres. Gen. Claire L. Chennault Found., Chinese Refugee Relief; Mem. U.S. nat. commn. UNESCO; membership adviser Nation's Capital chpt. Air Force Assn.; adviser Radio Free Asia, Nat. League Families Am. Prisoners and Missing in S.E. Asia. Mem. finance com. D.C. Republican Com.; chmn. nat. women's finance com. Republican Campaign, 1967-68; chmn. nat. adv. com. Women for Nixon, 1967-68; del. platform com. Rep. Nat. Conv., 1972; co-chmn. Finance Com. to Re-Elect the Pres., 1972; co-chmn. Republican Heritage Groups Council, 1972; mem. spl. com. Transpo '72, also chmn. sec.'s com. for spl. activities; chmn. U.S. Citizens in Asia for Nixon, 1972; spl. asst. to chmn. Asian-Pacific Council of Amchams. Mem. Pres.'s adv. com. on arts John F. Kennedy Center for Performing Arts; trustee Center for Study of Presidency; mem. exec. com. Am. Acad. Achievement, Dallas; bd. visitors Civil Air Patrol. Decorated Order of Lafayette; recipient Freedom award Free China Relief Assn., 1966; Golden Plate award Am. Acad. of Achievement, 1967. Mem. Free China Writers Assn., Nat. League Am. Pen Women, Flying Tigers Assn., 14th Air Force Assn. (chmn. awards). Republican. Clubs: U.S. Air Force Wives, Capitol Hill, International, F Street, Am. Newspaper Women's (Washington). Author 15 books in Chinese, 1948—; Thousand Springs, 1962; Dictionary of New Simplified Chinese Characters, Telegraphic Code Chinese-English Dictionary, 1963; Chennault and the Flying Tigers, 1963. Translator: Way of a Fighter, 1955. Home: 2510 Virginia Av NW Washington DC 20037 Office: Investment Bldg Washington DC 20005

CHERASKIN, EMANUEL, educator; b. Phila., June 9, 1916; s. Herman and Celia (Homes) C.; A.B., U. Ala., 1939, M.A., 1941, D.M.D., 1952; M.D., U. Cin., 1943; m. Carol Elizabeth Elwood, Sept. 23, 1944; 1 dau., Lisa. Intern, Hartford (Conn.) Municipal Hosp., 1943-44; resident St. Mary's Hosp. Evansville, Ind., 1946-47; gen. practice medicine, Moundville, Ala., 1947-48; instr. anatomy U. Ala. Med. Center, 1948-50, asst. prof. physiology, 1950-52, asso. prof., chmn. dept. oral medicine, 1952-56, prof., chmn. div. oral surgery, 1956-62, prof., chmn. dept. oral medicine, 1962—. Served to capt. M.C., AUS, 1944-46. Recipient Samuel Charles Miller Meml. Lectr. award Am. Acad. Dental Medicine, 1964. Mem. A.M.A., Am. Dental Assn., Am. Acad. Dental Medicine. Author: (with W.M. Ringsdorf Jr. and J.W. Clark) Diet and Disease, 1968, Diet and the Periodontal Patient, 1970; (with W.M. Ringsdorf Jr.) New Hope for Incurable Diseases, 1971. L. Langley, R. Sleeper) Dynamic Anatomy and Physiology, 1958. Home: 2435 Monte Vista Dr Vestavia Hills AL 35216 Office: Univ Ala Univ Sta Birmingham AL 35294

CHERNER, BENNETT LEE, govt. ofcl.; b. Bessemer, Ala., Nov. 5, 1936; s. Jacob and Muriel (Weiss) C.; student U. Pa., 1954-56; B.S., Samford U., 1961; m. Barbara Lorraine Finkelstein, Jan. 24, 1969; children—Stacey, Jason, Rebecca. Pres. Jefferson Furniture Co. div. Cherner Enterprises, Inc., Bessemer, Ala., 1957—; mem. Ala. House of Reps., 1966—. Chmn. Bessemer Aviation Com., 1965-72. Mem. Ala. Furniture Assn. (dir.), Bessemer C. of C., Bessemer Jaycees (past pres.). Jewish religion. Mason (Shriner), Lion. Home: 613 Melody Lane Bessemer AL 35020 Office: PO Box 669 Bessemer AL 35020

CHERRY, JAMES DILLON, bus. mgr.; b. Williamston, N.C., June 17, 1928; s. James Russell and Euzelia (Harris) C.; B.S., East Carolina U., 1958; spl. course U. Neb., 1971; m. Louise Wynne Simmons, Nov. 28, 1958; 1 son, Brad; stepchildren—John E. Simmons, Betty L. Simmons. Instr. Walter Williams High Sch., 1958-59; with quotations dept. Carolina Biol. Supply Co., Burlington, N.C., 1959-65; instr., dept. head Tech. Inst. Alamance, Burlington, 1965-67, bus. mgr., 1967—. Served with AUS, 1950-52. Mem. Am., N.C. vocational assns., Schoolmasters Club, East Carolina Alumni (pres. local chpt. 1969-70), Pi Omega Pi. Presbyn. (ruling elder, asso. v.p. presbytery). Club: Ruritan (Bear Grass, N.C.). Home: 309 Burlington St Gibsonville NC 27249 Office: 411 Camp Rd Burlington NC 27244

CHERRY, JIM DAVID, supt. schs.; b. Edison, Ga., Jan 1, 1911; s. Drew Fred and Nannie Iver (McKinnon) C.; B.S., Ga. So. Coll., 1936; M.A., U. N.C., 1939; postgrad. U. Ga., 1947-49, Emory U., 1949; m. Virginia Brown, June 4, 1939; children—Lynn, Jim David, Vicki (Mrs. Robert Fowler), Sally (Mrs. Jack Ferguson). Tchr., sci. coach Douglas (Ga.) High Sch., 1937-39; dir. guidance Waycross (Ga.) High Sch., 1939-42; dir. guidance and curriculum Albany (Ga.) High Sch., 1942-43; state sch. supr. Ga. Dept. Edn., 1946-47; supt. schs., DeKalb County (Ga.), 1949—. Mem. DeKalb Bd. Health, 1949—. Bd. dirs. Fulton-Rockdale-DeKalb chpt. Nat. Found., 1949—, sec., 1954; bd. dirs. Ga. unit Am. Cancer Soc., past pres. DeKalb unit; bd. dirs. YMCA, Ga. So. Found. Served with USNR, 1943-46; PTO. Recipient award for patriotic service U.S. Treasury, 1957, Award of Merit, and Minute Man award, 1966, Freedom Found. award, 1958. Mem. N.E.A., Am. Assn. Sch. Adminstrs., Am. Legion, Ga. Ednl. Assn. (pres. 1951), Ga. Assn. Educators, DeKalb C. of C., Baptist. Elk, Rotarian. Home: 2142 E Lake Rd NE Atlanta GA 30307 Office: 556 N McDonough St Decatur GA 30030

CHERRY, PHILIP, fgn. service officer; b. Phila., Aug. 14, 1931; s. Harry and Betty (Tull) C.; B.S., Temple U., 1956; certificate Hague (The Netherlands) Acad. Internat. Law, 1958; LL.B., U. Pa., 1959; m. Barbara Ronelda Clay, June 3, 1961; children—William Clay, John Bradford, Bettina Marguerite, James Douglas. Fgn. service officer U.S. Dept. State, Rhodesia, 1962-64, Zanzibar, 1964, Kenya, 1964-67, Mauritius, 1969, New Delhi, India, 1971—; asst. statistics Temple U., 1955-56. Served with USNR, 1949-53. Mem. Hague Acad., Temple U. alumni assns. Clubs: Hare Law Club (U. Pa.); New Delhi Golf; Parklands, Kenya, Salisbury, Rhodesia, Chelmsford, New Delhi Sports Clubs. Home: 9422 Locust Hill Rd Bethesda MD 20014 Office: Dept of State Washington DC 20521

CHESNUT, CORRIE LEE HANKINSON (MRS. J. HARVEY CHESNUT), club woman; b. Sylvania, Ga., July 23, 1906; d. Minus McElmurray and Martha (Humphries) Hankinson; B.A., Brenau Coll., 1924; spl. courses U. Ga., Piedmont Coll.; m. J. Harvey Chesnut. Asst. prin. jr. high sch., Millhaven, Ga., 1924-37; supr. pub. sch. art, Sylvania, Ga., 1937-43; temp clk. mailing dept. Post Office, Savannah, Ga., 1943-44; chief clk. tax assessors office, City of Savannah, 1944-60. Pres. Women's Soc. of Christian Service, Sylvania, 1940-42; pres. Bus. and Profl. Women's Club, Savannah, 1955-57, pres. Ga. Fedn., 1957-59, treas. Savannah Fedn. Women's Clubs, 1956-59; sec. Active Citizens for Edn., 1957-58; pres. Sagamore Hills Garden Clubs Council, 1962-63, Ladies Aux. Mounted Patrol of Shriners, 1966-68, N. Met. Bus. Women's Club, Atlanta, 1967-68. Trustee Rosebud McCormick Found. Mem. Women's Div. C. of C., N. DeKalb Bus. and Profl. Women's Club, Lamps, Delta Zeta. Methodist. Clubs: Atlanta China Painters (treas. 1969-71); La Vista Woman's (pres. 1963-65), Garden Gate Garden (pres. 1963-64) (Atlanta). Editor: Georgiana, 1959-61. Home: 1459 Council Bluff Dr NE Atlanta GA 30329

CHESNUT, LAWRENCE JAMES, clergyman, educator, author, broadcaster; b. Westplains, Mo., Dec. 6, 1908; s. Jim Jackson and Ida Louisa (Luna) C.; student Sherwin Cody Sch. English, Wyo., 1931-33, Central State Tchrs. Coll., Edmond, Okla., 1935-36; B.Th., Berean Bible Coll., Elk City, 1946; m. Jessie Mae Hill, Dec. 10, 1927; children—Daniel Lawrence, Samuel Joseph. With Ohio Oil Co. of Okla., 1927-36; ordained to ministry Ch. of God, 1931; pastor Capitol Hill Ch. of God, Oklahoma City, 1938—. Radio broadcaster, 1945—; TV broadcaster, 1955—; extension tchr. Anderson (Ind.) Coll. and Theol. Sem., 1938—; speaker to ministerial convs., camp meetings. youth convs.; leader religious dept. Nat. Radio Conv. Am., Norman, Okla., 1954; various nat., state positions in Ch. of God, including nat. Day-man rep., mem. nat. steering com., pres. 15 years, sec.-treas. 6 years of Bd. Ch. Extension of Ch. of God of Okla., pres. Campgrounds Assn., 12 years, pres. State Youth conv., 12 years, now ofcl. mem. Campgrounds Assn., mem. state program com. Ch. of God Okla. Past mem. Oklahoma City Police Reform Com.; spl. asst. to dist. judge working with problem children. Bd. dirs. Central Okla. Camp Meeting Assn. Decorated for outstanding ability in radio broadcasting. Author: True Bible Tongues, Their Proper Place and Use in the Church, 1948; The Battle of Armageddon-What, Where and When, 1949; Divine Physical Healing for You, 1949; Twentieth Chapter of Revelation Explained, 1954; The Sabbath, Mosaic and Christian, 1959. Contbr. numerous articles to profl. jours. Home: 3121 S Harvey Av Oklahoma City OK 73109 Office: 3120 S Harvey Av Oklahoma City OK 73109

CHESNUT, RALPH CARL, petroleum refining co. owner; b. West Planes, Mo., Dec. 28, 1909; s. James Jackson and Ida (Luna) C.; grad. pub. schs.; m. Ruby May Taylor, Oct. 11, 1930. Gang pusher Marathon Oil Co., Bristow, Okla., 1929-32, Deep Rock Oil Co., Bristow, 1932-36; prodn. foreman Barnsdall Oil Co., Odessa, Tex., 1936-39; prodn. mgr. Brodrick & Calvert, Odessa, 1939; prodn. foreman Phillips Petroleum Co., Odessa, 1940-55; owner Chesnut Well Service, Odessa, 1955—; pres. Posture Magic Cushion Co., Rosenberg, Tex., 1967—. Foreman, Ector County Petty Jury, 1958-62; mem. Ector County Sheriff's Posse, 1961—; life mem. Odessa Meteorite Mus.; mem. Permian Playhouse, Odessa, Tex., 1967—. Bd. dirs. Otto's Boys Club of Odessa, 1957-63. Mem. Am. Petroleum Inst. Moose. Clubs: Odessa Basin Lions, Odessa Country. Home: 3008 N Century Av Odessa TX 79760 Office: PO Box 1491 Odessa TX 79760

CHESNUTT, NELSON PHELPS, natural gas utility exec.; b. Henrietta, Tex., May 15, 1911; s. Robert Cleveland and Cora (Gragg) C.; B.S. in Mech. Engring., U. Okla., 1935; grad. Advanced Mgmt. Program, Harvard, 1964; m. Mary Gertrude Schreck, Nov. 26, 1936; children—Robert P., Mary Patricia (Mrs. Richard A. Strother). With So. Union Gas Co., Dallas, 1935—, chief engr., 1948-60, v.p., operating mgr., 1960—. Served from 1st lt. to lt. col., AUS, 1941-46. Decorated Bronze Star. Registered profl. engr., Colo., N.M., Ariz., Tex. Mem. Am. (service award), So. (service award) gas assns., Dallas Engrs. Club, Dallas Petroleum Club. Mason (32 1/2 deg.). Home: 6653 Gaston Av Dallas TX 75214 Office: Fidelity Union Tower Dallas TX 75201

CHESSER, VICTOR LEON, dentist; b. Bessemer, Ala., Jan. 21, 1931; s. Ophus Charles and Mabel (Griffith) C.; student Livingston State Coll., 1949-51; A.B., Birmingham So. Coll., 1954; D.M.D., U. Ala., 1958; student N.Y.U., 1962; m. Jacqueline Ruth Cogbill, May 11, 1956; children—Karl Eric, Mark Victor. Lab. asst. Birmingham So. Coll., 1952-53; first aid man, ambulance driver Lloyd Noland Hosp., Fairfield, Ala., 1952-54, part-time, 1954-58; dentist USPHS, N.Y. State Dept. Health, 1962-63; profl. edn. radiol. health dental X-ray program Central Radiation Health Lab., Rockville, Md., 1963-69; ret., 1969. Served with USNR, 1958-62. Mem. Phi Eta Sigma. Presbyn. Prin. author: Physical Survey Manual, 1964, rev. edn., 1967. Home: 5036 Pleasant Hill Rd SE Bessemer AL 35020

CHESSHIR, JANE SUZANNE LOYD (MRS. JAMES WILLIAM CHESSHIR), civic leader; b. Little Rock, May 7, 1937; d. Dale Claude and Frances (Pearson) Loyd; student Lindenwood Coll. for Women, 1955-56; student U. Ark., 1957-58; m. James William Chesshire, June 7, 1959; children—Deborah Jane, James William, Bryan Loyd. Sec., Hosp. Aux. Clark County, Arkadelphia, Ark., 1964-65, pres., 1965-66; pres. Clark County Cancer Drive, Ark., 1965-66, chmn. meml. fund, 1966-67; mem. D.A.R., Arkadelphia, 1965—, historian, 1966-68, librarian, 1968—, state chmn. jr. membership, 1969—, named outstanding Jr. Mem., 1969, mem. Mine Creek Chpt., 1970—, vice regent chpt., 1970-74, state organizing sec., 1972-74; sr. soc. pres. Children Am. Revolution, state registrar sr., 1968-69; mem. Internat. Platform Assn., 1969—. Recipient Appreciation certificate Am. Cancer Soc., Ark., 1965. Mem. Beta Sigma Phi (pres. 1968-69). Home: 522 N 3d St Nashville AR 71852

CHEVALIER, DOUGLAS, news photographer; b. Moutier, Switzerland, Aug. 21, 1919; s. Henry G. and Rachel (Jeanmaire) C.; came to U.S., 1923, naturalized, 1928; student Syracuse U., 1937-38, Kenyon Coll., 1947-49; B.A., George Washington U., 1951; m. Helen Werner, Dec. 23, 1950; children—Kimberly Ann, Michael Douglas, Tracy Rose. Reporter with Mansfield (O.) News-Jours., 1949-50; reporter-photographer Neenah (Wis.) News-Record, 1950-51; Washington photographer Washington Post, 1952—. Recipient 1st prize photography competition, White House Photographers, 1954, 3d pl., 1953, 56, 69; two 2d prizes White House competition, 1960; two 1st prizes photographic competition Wash. Newspaper Guild, 1960. Mem. U.S. Senate Press Photographers Gallery (sec.-treas.), White House News Photographers Assn. (sec. 1960-61), Nat. Press Photographers Assn., Washington Newspaper Guild. Home: 7325 Blair Rd NW Washington DC 20012 Office: Washington Post 1515 L St NW Washington DC 20005

CHEVALIER, ROBERT BURRIS, cardiologist, educator; b. Indpls., Nov. 25, 1927; s. Arthur Burris and Martha (Whetstine) C.; B.A., DePauw U., 1950; M.D., Med. Coll. Va., 1955; m. Barbara Evans, Dec. 30, 1950; children—Karen, Timothy, Jeffrey, Victoria, Robert, Holly. Intern, Meth. Hosp., Indpls., 1955-56, resident, 1956-59; fellow in cardiology Sch. Medicine, Ind. U., 1959-60; instr. dept. medicine Ind. U., Indpls., 1960-63, asst. prof., 1963-65; research asso. Krannert Inst. Cardiology, Indpls., 1960-63, sr. research asso., 1963-65; practice medicine, specializing in cardiology, Indpls., 1965-71; asso. prof. medicine U. Ala. Sch. Medicine, Birmingham, 1971—, also dir. ambulatory services, 1971—. Pres. Washington Twp. (Ind.) Sch. Planning Com., 1964-65. Adv. bd. Vols. of Am., Ind., 1960-65. Served as sgt. AUS, 1946-47. Nat. Heart Inst. trainee, 1959-60; Nat. Heart Inst. grantee, 1962-63, Ind. Heart Assn. grantee, 1960-64, A.M.A.-Tobacco Research Found. grantee, 1963-65. Diplomate Am. Bd. Internal Medicine. Fellow A.C.P., Am. Coll. Cardiology, Am. Coll. Chest Physicians; mem. Am., Ind. (pres. 1969-71), Ala. (exec. com. 1971—) heart assns., Am. Fedn. Clin. Research, Central Ind. DePauw Alumni Assn. (pres. 1962-63), Phi Chi, Alpha Tau Omega. Republican. Episcopalian (vestryman 1969-71). Clubs: University of Indianapolis; Mountain Brook (Ala.) Swim and Tennis. Research and publs. on cardiopulmonary response to exercise, effects of smoking on cardiopulmonary responses. Home: 4424 Fredericksburg Dr Birmingham AL 35213 Office: 619 S 19th St Birmingham AL 35233

CHEVES, HARRY LANGDON, JR., physician; b. Birmingham, Ala., Oct. 17, 1924; s. Harry Langdon and Myrtle (Churchill) C.; A.B., Mercer U., 1949; M.D., Med. Coll. Ga., 1953; m. Lois Rebecca Corry, Dec. 25, 1949; children—Rebecca Churchill, Harry Langdon III; m. 2d, Mary Agnes Moon. Intern Univ. Hosp., Augusta, Ga., 1953-54; practice medicine, East Point, Ga.; mem. staff S. Fulton Hosp. Served with USAAF, 1942-46. Fellow Internat., Am. colls. angiology; mem. A.M.A., So. Med. Assn., Am. Acad. Gen. Practice, Atlanta Med. Soc., Am. Geriatric Soc., Med. Assn. Ga., Ga. Heart Assn., Phi Delta Theta. Clubs: Lions, Am. Antique Automobile. Home: 333 Plantation Circle Riverdale GA 30274 Office: 2726 Felton Dr East Point GA 30344

CHICHESTER, JOHN D., real estate cons.; b. Birmingham, Ala.; s. John D. and Minnie Mae (Jolly) C.; student Gulf Coast Mil. Acad., 1913-14, U. Ala. Law Sch., 1915-16; m. Mattie Eugenia Ormond, Nov. 20, 1916; 1 son. Real estate cons., appraiser, Birmingham, 1925—; lectr. real estate. Mem. Ala. Ho. of Reps. 2 terms; real estate commr. State Ala. Mem. Ala. Real Estate Assn. (past pres.), Birmingham Real Estate Bd. (past pres.), Am. Inst. Real Estate Appraisers (pres. Ala. chpt., dir.), Nat. Assn. Real Estate Bds. (past v.p.), Omicron Delta Kappa, Phi Kappa Sigma. Club: Relay House. Home: 2057 S 20th Av Birmingham AL 35205 Office: Jefferson Fed Bldg Birmingham AL 35203

CHICK, JOHN BRADLEY, real estate appraiser, broker; b. Titusville, Pa., Feb. 8, 1900; s. Maxwell Benedict and Rose (Bradley) C.; A.B., Princeton, 1922; m. Alice Irene Sutton, Apr. 17, 1928 (deceased October 1965); children—John Bradley, William Maxwell, Cynthia Ann (Mrs. Nolan Bruce Pitsinger); m. 2d, Helen Hine Benson, Mar. 4, 1967. Real estate sales Clark T. Chambers, Inc., N.Y.C., 1922-23; pres. Maxwell B. Chick Co., Titusville, Pa., 1923-38, owner, 1938-41; self-employed, 1941-43, 46-51; served as lt. col. U.S. Air Force, 1951-60, chief installations div., Paris (France) office 1958-60; real estate appraisals and sales, Ft. Lauderdale, Fla., 1960-63, 65—; exec. dir. Redevel. Authority, Titusville, Pa., 1963-66. Served from lt. to comdr., USNR, 1943-46. Mem. Am. Inst. Real Estate Appraisers, Navy League, Air Force Assn., Ret. Officers Assn. Presbyn. Mason, Rotarian. Club: Princeton (N.Y. and Ft. Lauderdale, Fla.); Nassau (Princeton, N.J.) Home: 2840 N Ocean Blvd Fort Lauderdale FL 33308 Office: care Wm H West 2425 E Commercial Blvd Fort Lauderdale FL 33308

CHICK, NICHOLAS, physician; b. Brackenridge, Pa., Jan. 30, 1913; s. Achille and Olga (Mattioli) C.; B.S., Loyola, Chgo., 1937; B.M, Chgo. Med. Sch., 1942, M.D., 1943; m. June N. Rotert, Aug. 6, 1943; 1 dau., Janis Paige. Intern St. Francis Hosp., Grand Island, Neb., 1940-43, Camp Claiborne Sta. Hosp., Alexandria, La., 1943-45; resident Camp Chaffee Hosp., Ft. Smith, Ark., 1945-46; practice medicine specializing in surgery, Arapahoe, Neb., 1947-50, North Platte, Neb., 1950-66, Amarillo, Tex., 1966-71, Bonham, Tex., 1971—; staff mem. St. Mary Hosp., North Platte, mem. exec. bd., 1953-55, 61-63, sec. staff, 1953, pres. staff, 1955; staff mem. Meml. Hosp., North Platte, sec. staff, 1963, v.p. staff, 1964, pres. staff, 1965-66; staff internal medicine and dermatology, VA Hosp., Amarillo, 1966-70, acting chief med. service, acting chief dermatology, 1969-70; chief radiology, chief lab., chief of staff VA Center, Bonham, 1971—. 4-H leader, 1955-67. Mem. North Platte Bd. Edn., 1954-66, sec., 1955, 58, pres., 1956, 58; mem. Lincoln County Fair Bd., 1960-66, pres., 1963-66. Served with M.C., AUS, 1943-46. Fellow Am. Geriatrics Soc., Am. Soc. Abdominal Surgeons; mem. A.M.A., Neb. Med. Assn., Lincoln County Med. Soc. (past sec., pres.), Lincoln County Wildlife Assn. (past pres.), Am., Neb., Buffalo Bill quarterhorse assns. Address: VA Center Bonham TX 75418

CHIEPALICH, RIA JANE CLINKSCALES (MRS. JOHN B. CHIEPALICH), educator; b. Anderson, S.C., 1918; d. Julian Edgar and Mary (Gilreath) Clinkscales; A.B., Brenau Coll., 1940; postgrad, Mass. Inst. Tech., 1943-44; M.A., U. Ala., 1947; m. John Barbich Chiepalich, May 14, 1949; children—Maria Jane, Mary Violet, Helen Patricia, Emma Alice. Instr., Hinds Jr. Coll., Raymond, Miss., 1942-43, Shaw, Miss. and Lee High Sch., Montgomery, 1956-57, U. Ala., Tuscaloosa, 1946-49, Huntington Coll., Montgomery, 1960-61; asst. prof. math. Jacksonville (Ala.) State U., 1961—. Pres., Jacksonville High Sch. P.T.A., 1967-68; active Girl Scouts U.S.A. Served as aerologist, lt. (j.g.) WAVES, 1943-46, Mem. Nat. Council Tchrs. Math., Am. Math. Assn., Ala. Edn. Assn., Sigma Xi, Phi Mu Chi Beta (sponsor 1962-68), Phi Mu, Pi Mu Epsilon, Phi Beta Sigma. Baptist. Clubs: Jacksonville Garden (pres. 1968-70); Calhoun County Rock and Mineral (pres. 1970—). Home: 606 6th St Jacksonville AL 36265

CHIERI, PERICLE ADRIANO C., educator, mech. and aero, engr., naval architect; b. Mokanshan, Chekiang, China, Sept. 6, 1905; s. Virginio and Luisa (Fabbri) C.; Dr. Engring., U. Genova, Italy, 1927; M.E., U. Naples, Italy, 1927; Dr. Aero. Engring., U. Rome, 1928; m. Helen Etheredge, Aug. 1, 1938. Naturalized Am. citizen, 1952. Naval architect. mech. engr. research and exptl. divs., sub-marines and internal combustion engines, Italian Navy, Spezia, Italy, 1929-31; naval architect, marine supt. Navigazione Libera Triestina Shipping Corp., Libera Lines, Trieste, Italy, 1931-32, Genova, Italy, 1933-35; aero. engr., tech. adviser Chinese Govt. commn. aero. affairs, Nat. Govt. Republic of China, Nanchang and Loyang, 1935-37; engring. exec., dir. aircraft materials test lab., supt. factory's tech. vocational instrn., SINAW Nat. Aircraft Works, Nanchang, Kiangsl, China, 1937-39; aero. engr. FIAT aircraft factory, Turin, Italy, 1939; aero. engr. and tech. sec. Office: Air Attache, Italian Embassy, Washington, 1939-41; prof. aero. engring. Tri-State Coll., Angola, Ind., 1942; aero. engr., helicopter design Aero. Products, Inc., Detroit, 1943-44; sr. aero. engr. ERCO Engring. & Research Corp., Riverdale, Md., 1944-46; asso. prof. mech. engring. U. Toledo, 1946-47; asso. prof. mech. engring., faculty grad. div. Newark (N.J.) Coll. Engring., 1947-52; prof., head dept. mech. engring. U. Southwestern La., Lafayette, La., 1952—; research engr., adv. devel. sect., aviation gas turbine div., Westinghouse Electric Corp., So. Philadelphia, Pa., 1953. Instr. Water Safety A.R.C. Nat. Aquatic Schs., summers 1958-67. Bd. dirs. Lafayette Parish chpt. A.R.C. Registered profl. engr., Italy, N.J., La., S.C.; chartered engr., U.K. Asso. fellow Am. Inst. Aeronautics and Astronautics; fellow Royal Instn. Naval Architects London; mem. Soc. Naval Architects and Marine Engrs., A.A.A.S., Am. Assn. U. Profs., Am. Soc. Engring. Edn., Am. Soc. M.E., Soc. Automotive Engrs., Instrument Soc. Am., Soc. Exptl. Stress Analysis, Nat. Soc. Profl. Engrs., N.Y. Acad. Scis., La. Engring. Soc., La. Tchrs. Assn., A.A.H.P.E.R., La. Acad. Scis., Commodore Longfellow Soc., Phi Kappa Phi. Pi Tau Sigma. Home: 142 Oak Crest Dr Lafayette LA 70501

CHIESA, CARMEN (DE PEREZ), author; b. Yabuoca, P.R., June 1, 1914; d. Pedro Chiesa and Damiana (Nieves) C.; B.S., Pa. State Coll., 1939; M.A., Columbia U., 1946, postgrad., 1946-47; postgrad., U. P.R., 1950-60; m. Juan Perez Cruz, June 25, 1939; children—Dra. Ivette, Marta, Janet. Tchr. pub. schs., P.R., 1936-56; instr. U. P.R., 1958-59; faculty Ursuline Coll., New Orleans, 1947-48; prin. schs. P.R., 1940-43; 1948-49; vocational guidance counsellor Central High Sch., Santruce, P.R., 1948-49. Mem. Damas Auxiliares de Rio Piedras, Agrupacion de Maestros Retiradosde de R.P., Asociacion de Maestros, Pa. State Alumni Assn., Soc. de. Autores Puertorriquenos, Union de Mujeres Americanas, Graduadas de la U. P.R. Author: Enjoy Puerto Rico, 1961: (short story) Principe, 1963; (essay) Proyecciones del Modernismo, 1964: (novel) La Telarana, 1971. Address: Flamboyanes 208 Hyde Park Rio Piedras PR 00927

CHILD, ROBERT DANVERS, rancher; b. El Dorado, Ark., Sept. 21, 1927; s. Thomas Harold and Sarah (Wallace) C.; B.S., U. Ark., 1950, M.S., 1966; m. Wanda Gay Daniel, May 3, 1951; children—Lisa Gay, Robert Danvers, Jr. Research and teaching asst. U. Ark., 1962-65; div. mgr. Carlisle div. Winrock Farms, Carlisle, Ark., 1965-67, operations mgr., Morrilton, Ark., 1967-69, gen. mgr., 1969—. Served with USNR, 1944-46. Mem. Nat. Livestock and Meat Bd. (dir.), Am. Nat. Cattlemen's Assn. (regional v.p.), Santa Gertrudis Breeders Internat. (mem. exec. com.), Ark. Cattlemen's Assn. (past pres.), Alpha Zeta, Gama Sigma Delta. Contbr. articles to farm jours. Address: Route 3 Morrilton AR 72110

CHILDERS, WYON DALE, state legislator; b. Fla., Nov. 25, 1933; s. Neil R. and Myrtle R. (Smith) C.; B.S., Fla. State U., 1955; m. Ruth A. Johnson, Dec. 21, 1953; children—Gail, Jeanna, Karen, Marvel. Tchr., Santa Rosa County Schs., 1956; pres., gen. mgr. A & E Stores, Pensacola, Fla., 1957; mem. Fla. Senate. Mem. Fla. Council on Crime and Delinquency. Mem. Farm Bur., Am. Pharm. Assn. Baptist. Lion. Home: 5900 Chicago Av Pensacola FL 32506 Office: Box 3327 Pensacola FL 32506*

CHILDRESS, JAMES WALTER, hosp. adminstr.; b. Lake Charles, La., Feb. 24, 1930; s. Mack Z. and Elizabeth (Carruthers) C.; student U. Corpus Christi, 1951-54; m. Joyce Marvine Shoemaker, Nov. 24, 1960; children—Shari Lea, Michael Wayne, James Kevin. Asst. bus. mgr. Meth. Hosp., Dallas, 1962-64; financial counselor Med. Center Hosp., Odessa, Tex., 1964-66; adminstr. Meml. Hosp., Seminole,

Tex., 1966-67, Gladewater (Tex.) Municipal Hosp., 1967—. Bd. dirs. United Cancer Fund, 1966-67; chmn. United Heart Fund, 1967-68. Served with USNR, 1947-50. Mem. Tex. Hosp. Assn., Tex. Assn. Hosp. Accountants, Hosp. Financial Mgmt. Assn. (dir. 1967-68, 1st v.p. 1967-70). Home: 1020 Chevy Chase St Gladewater TX 75647 Office: 300 W Upshur St Gladewater TX 75647

CHILDRESS, WILLARD JOPLING, city ofcl.; b. Rankin, Tex., Feb. 28, 1926; s. Calbert C. and Polly Katheryn (Hickox) C.; student Sul Ross State Tchrs. Coll., 1943-44, 46-49; m. Bessie Stingley, Apr. 30, 1950. Fire fighter Odessa (Tex.) Fire Dept., 1948-50, capt., 1950-56, asst. chief, 1956-58, dep. chief, 1958-62, fire chief, 1962—. Instr., Tex. Firemen's Tng. Sch., Tex. A. and M. U., 1952—. Pres., Odessa area chpt. Muscular Dystrophy Assn., 1966-68. Served with USNR, 1944-46; PTO. Decorated Bronze Star with oak leaf cluster. Named Boss of Year, Odessa Jaycees, 1964. Mem. Tex. Fire Chiefs Assn. (sec.-treas. 1965-71), Odessa Bowling Assn. Eagle. Home: 1304 N Kelly Odessa TX 79760 Office: 210 N Lincoln Odessa TX 79760

CHILDS, CLIFTON EDWARD, banker; b. Fairfield, Tex., Feb. 26, 1899; s. Lonnie and Ruby (Newman) C.; student Nell B. Lynn Bus. Sch., 1917-18; m. Corin Watson, June 26, 1926; children—Clifton Edward, Carolyn Ann (Mrs. James Daniel Hudson, Jr.). With Fairfield State Bank, 1917-41, 44—, pres., 1941-65, chmn. bd., chief exec. officer, 1965—; sec.-treas. Mexia Prodn. Credit Assn. (Tex.), 1941-44. Mem. Freestone County Sch. Bd., 1937-38; mem. City Council, Fairfield, 1939-40, mayor, 1941; pres. Freestone County Hosp., 1946-47, Freestone County Fair Assn., 1948-49. Mem. East Tex. C. of C. (dir. 1958-59), Fairfield C. of C. (pres. 1948-50, 56-57). Baptist (chmn. bd. deacons 1926—). Mason, Rotarian (pres. Fairfield 1947-48). Club: Freestone County Recreational. Home: 201 W Commerce St Fairfield TX 75840 Office: 200 E Commerce St Fairfield TX 75840

CHILDS, H(ENRY) PRENTISS, broadcasting co. exec.; b. Iowa City, June 9, 1927; s. Marquis W. and Lue (Prentiss) C.; student Mass. Inst. Tech., 1944-45; B.A., Yale, 1949; postgrad. Columbia, 1962-63; m. Nancy Jane Craze, Jan. 24, 1960; children—Catherine Clenn, Christina Prentiss, Marquis Bradley. Asst. producer CBS News, 1956-60, producer, 1960—; produced Lamp Unto My Feet, 1960-62, Face The Nation, 1963—. Bd. dirs. Orizon Inst. Served with USNR, 1945-46. Home: 5045 Reno Rd NW Washington DC 20008 Office: 2020 M St NW Washington DC 20036

CHILDS, JAMES BENNETT, librarian; b. Van Buren, Mo., June 2, 1896; s. Trall Bennett and Mary (Michener) C.; A.B., U. Ill., 1918, B.L.S., 1921; m. Eleanor Atala Pirkner, Nov. 20, 1927; children—James Bennett Jr., Herbert A., Robert F., Daniel B., Rudolph W., Philip D., Richard P. Cataloger John Crerar Library, Chgo., 1921-25; chief Documents div. Library of Congress, Washington, 1925-29, 34-43, chief catalog div., 1929-34, chief documents officer, 1943-54, specialist govt. document bibliography, 1954-67, hon. cons. govt. document bibliography, 1967—. Mem. A.L.A., Library Assn. U.K., Bibl. Soc. Am., Am. Polit. Sci. Assn., Am. Econ. Assn., Phi Beta Kappa. Clubs: Cliff Dwellers, Cosmos. Author: Entry for Government Publications, 1941; German Democratic Republic Official Publications, 1960-61; German Federal Republic Official Publications, 1958; Government Document Bibliography in the U.S. and Elsewhere; Guide to the Official Publications of Other American Republics, 1945-48; Memorias of the Republics of Central America and of the Antilles, 1932; Spanish Government Publications after July 17, 1936, 1965-69. Home: 1221 Newton St NE Washington DC 20017 Office: Library of Congress Washington DC 20540

CHILDS, MARQUIS WILLIAM, journalist; b. Clinton, Ia., Mar. 17, 1903; s. William Henry and Lilian Malissa (Marquis) C.; A.B., U. Wis., 1923; A.M., U. Ia., 1925; LL.D., Upsala Coll., 1943; Litt. D., U. Wis., 1966, U. Ia., 1968; m. Lue Prentiss, Aug. 26, 1926 (dec.); children—Prentiss, Malissa (Mrs. Elliott); m. 2d, Jane Neylan McBaine. With United Press, 1923, 25-26, St. Louis Post-Dispatch, 1926-44, spl. corr., 1954-62, chief Washington corr., 1962-69, contbg. editor, 1969—. Columnist, United Feature Syndicate, 1944-54; made 3 mos. tour battlefronts, 1945; lectr. Columbia U. Sch. Mexico 1950. Decorated Order of North Star (Sweden); recipient Sigma Delta Chi award for best Washington corr., 1944; award for journalism U. Mo.; Pulitzer prize for commentary, 1970. Mem. Kappa Sigma, Sigma Delta Chi. Clubs: Overseas Writers (pres. 1943-45); Century (N.Y.C.); Washington Press, Gridiron (pres. 1957), Metropolitan, Cosmos (Washington). Author: Sweden—The Middle Way, 1936; They Hate Roosevelt, 1936; Washington Calling, 1937; This Is Democracy, 1938; This Is Your War, 1942; I Write From Washington, 1942; The Cabin, 1944. Edited and wrote Evaluation for New Edition of Brooks Adams' America's Economic Supremacy, 1947; The Farmer Takes a Hand, 1952; Ethics in Business Society with Douglass Cater), 1954; The Ragged Edge, 1955; Eisenhower. Captive Hero, 1958; The Peacemakers, 1961; A Taint of Innocence, 1967. Co-editor: Walter Lippmann and His Times, 1959. Home: 3554 Edmunds St NW Washington DC 20007 Office: 1028 Connecticut Av Washington DC 20036

CHILES, LAWTON, U.S. senator; b. Lakeland, Fla., Apr. 3, 1930; B.S., U. Fla., 1952, LL.B., 1955; m. Rhea Grafton; children—Tandy, Lawton III, Edward G., Rhea Gay. Admitted to Fla. bar, practiced in Lakeland; mem. Fla. Ho. of Reps., 1958-66; mem. Fla. Senate, 1966-70; U.S. Senator from Fla., 1971—. Served with AUS; Korea. Democrat. Home: 221 E Lime St Lakeland FL 33801 also 3807 N Woodstock St Arlington VA 22207

CHILTON, STUART, educator; b. Marlin, Tex., May 27, 1927; s. Albert H. and Ethel L. (Stuart) C.; B.A., Baylor U., 1950; M.A., Hardin-Simmons U., 1954; Ed.D., North Tex. State U., 1964; m. Anna Dickie Negy, Dec. 27, 1951; 1 son, Brad. Tchr. pub. schs., Falfurrias and Abilene, Tex., 1950-53; dir. pub. information Tarleton State Coll., Stephenville, Tex., 1954-57, registrar, dean students, 1957-64, dean student personnel services, 1964-66; prof. ednl. adminstrn. East Tex. State U., Commerce, 1966—. Cons. pub. schs., ednl. service centers. Chmn., Commerce United Fund, 1970. Served with USNR, 1945-46. Postdoctoral study Nat. Acad. Sch. Execs., 1969-70. Mem. Stepenville C. of C. (dir. 1963-66), Am. Assn. Sch. Adminstrs., Phi Delta Kappa (pres. local chpt. 1971-72). Methodist (mem. adminstrv. bd. 1967). Lion (1st v.p. Stephenville club 1965-66), Mason. Editor: Selected Readings in Educational Administration, 1970. Contbr. articles to profl. jours. Home: 3007 Tanglewood Dr Commerce TX 75428

CHILTON, WILLIAM RANSDELL, banker; b. Ottoman, Va., Jan. 16, 1911; s. William Collin and Kathrine Elizabeth (Kamps) C.; B.S., Va. Mil. Inst., 1931; m. Catherine R. Barham, Jan. 21, 1947; 1 stepson, C. Barham Peirce. Tchr. pub. schs., Lancaster County, Va., 1931-36; dir., asst. mgr. Kilmarnock Fish Products, Inc. (Va.), 1933-41; pres., owner Chilton Fuels, Inc., Kilmarnock, Va., 1938-64; v.p. Peoples Oil Co., Inc., Warsaw, Va., 1956—; pres. Bank Lancaster, Kilmarnock, Va. 1967—; chmn. bd. Sylvia Motor Co., Burgess, Va., 1971—; dir. Tidewater Telephone Co., Warsaw, Va. Mem. Va. Hwy. Commn., 1962-68; mem. No. Neck Regional Planning and Econ. Devel. Com., 1960-70. Bd. dirs. Community Library, Kilmarnock, Found. Historic Christ Ch., Inc., Irvington, Va., Mary Ball Meml. Mus. and Library, Lancaster, Va. Served to lt. comdr. USNR, 1942-46. Mem. Va. State C. of C. (dir. 1969—). Episcopalian (vestryman 1969—). Clubs: Indian Creek Yacht and Country (pres. 1961-63) (Kilmarnock); Commonwealth (Richmond, Va.); Chesapeake (Irvington). Home: Box 142 Lancaster VA 22503 Office: Box 75 Kilmarnock VA 22482

CHIPLEY, ALFRED SANGSTER, govt. ofcl.; b. Uniontown, Pa., Oct. 24, 1912; s. Edmund Lee and Grace (Noble) C.; B.S. in M.E., U. Fla., 1936; m. Willie Josephine Page, July 7, 1937; children—Jo Ann (Mrs. William P. Blair, Jr.), Richard Lee, Carol Grace (Mrs. David M. Mastro), Robert Page. Research engr. Burgess Battery Co., Madison, Wis., Chgo., 1936-42; chief research engr. Burgess-Menning Co., Libertyville, Ill., 1945-51; poultry farmer, Bokeelia, Fla., 1951-62; vector control specialist USPHS, Fla., 1963-68, also state project officer, Ala.; dir. div. solid waste and vector control Ala. Dept. Pub. Health, Montgomery, 1968—. Served from 2d lt. to maj. Ordnance Corps, AUS, 1942-46; ETO. Registered profl. engr., Ill., Ala. Mem. Am. Mosquito Control Assn., Ala. Sanitarians Assn., Am. Pub. Health Assn., Sigma Tau. Patentee in air velocity, air distbn., air cleaning, radiant heating and cooling, and engine exhaust and intake silencing devices. Home: 3728 Princeton Rd Montgomery AL 36111 Office: Dept Health State Office Bldg Montgomery AL 36104

CHIPMAN, DONALD J., newspaper co. exec. Pres., gen. mgr. Winston-Salem Journal Sentinel. Office: 416-20 N Marshall St Winston-Salem NC 27201*

CHIPPS, HENRY DAVIS, physician, educator; b. Smithland, Ky., Aug. 30, 1909; s. Henry Duley and Gene (Davis) C.; student U. Va., 1926-28; B.S., U. Ala., 1930; M.D., U. Louisville, 1934; m. Frances Sydnor deButts, Nov. 7, 1937; children—Mary Elizabeth (Mrs. Mark Dent-Broklehurst), Genie Davis. Intern, Lloyd Nolan Hosp., Birmingham, Ala., 1934-35; resident Meth. Hosp., Indpls., 1937-39, Royal Victoria Hosp., Montreal, Can., 1939-41; practice medicine, specializing in pathology, Lexington, Ky., 1954—; mem. staff Bapt. Hosp., Lexington; instr. pathology McGill U. Med. Sch., Montreal, 1939-41; asso. prof. pathology U. Wash. Sch. Medicine, Seattle, 1947-52; dir. pathology Ochsner Found. Hosp., New Orleans, 1952-54; prof. clin. pathology U. Ky. Sch. Medicine, Lexington, 1960—. Bd. dirs. Ky. div. Am. Cancer Soc., 1960—, pres. Ky. div., 1970; bd. dirs. Order Lafayette, 1962—. Served to col. M.C., AUS, 1942-46. Fellow Coll. Am. Pathologists (founding mem.); mem. Am. Assn. Pathologists and Bacteriologists, Ky. Hist. Soc., Civil War Round Table, The Lexington Club, Sigma Xi, Phi Chi, Phi Delta Theta. Home: 101 S Hanover St Lexington KY 40502 Office: 1740 S Limestone St Lexington KY 40503

CHISHOLM, ARTHUR GORDON, med. book distbg. co. exec.; b. New Orleans, July 22, 1911; s. Arthur Caspar and Annie (Thomas) C.; student Loyola U., New Orleans, 1943-44; m. Andrea Francis, Oct. 8, 1931; children—Arthur Gordon, Carol Ann, Andrea (Mrs. John J. Kuglar). With J.A. Majors Co., New Orleans, 1926—, chief clk., 1943-47, mgr. Atlanta office, 1948-56, v.p., 1956—. Mem. Atlanta C. of C., Atlanta Hist. Soc., Clan Chisholm Soc. Home: 1905 Sandgate Circle College Park GA 30349 Office: 139 Forrest Av NE Atlanta GA 30303

CHISHOLM, DAVID HUGH, librarian; b. Philadelphia, Miss., Mar. 23, 1922; s. Robert Benjamin and Fanny Ellen (Randoll) C.; A.A., East Central Jr. Coll., 1946; B.B.A., U. Miss., 1948, B.A., 1948; B.S. in L.S., La. State U., 1952; postgrad. U. Tex., 1952-62. Field asst. CCC, Wash. and Ore., 1941; clk. Civil Service, Washington, 1942, 48-49; tchr. English and comml. subjects La. State U., 1952, sec. to Grad. Sch. Library Sci., summer 1952; reference librarian U. Tex., 1952-54, acquisitions librarian, 1954—. Served with USNR, 1942-45. Decorated D.S.M. Mem. A.L.A. Home: 1802 Lavaca St Austin TX 78701 Office: 1801 Main Bldg Library U Tex Austin TX 78712

CHISHOLM, LESLIE LEE, JR., physician, surgeon; b. Cairo, Ill., Feb. 6, 1931; s. Leslie Lee and Lila (Cates) C.; B.S., U. Neb., 1953, M.D., 1960; m. Phyllis June Segar, Aug, 13, 1953; children—Leslie Lee III, Douglas Scott, Philip Kent. Intern, Tampa Gen. Hosp., 1961; eye resident U. Louisville Gen. Hosp., 1961-64; civil service med. project officer Wright Patterson AFB, Dayton, O., 1967; practice medicine specializing in ophthalmology, Tampa, Fla., 1964—; teaching staff Tampa Gen. Hosp., vice chief sect. on ophthalmology, 1967, chief sect. ophthalmology, 1968-70; mem. attending staff St. Joseph, U. Community, Centro Astruiano hosps. Pres., Doctor's Optical Co., Inc. Bd. dirs. Fla. Council for Blind. Served with USAF, 1954-56. Diplomate Am. Bd. Ophthalmology. Mem. A.M.A., Am. Assn. Ophthalmologists, Contact Lens Assn. Ophthalmologists, Assn. Am. Physicians and Surgeons, So., Fla., Hillsborough County med. assns. Republican. Home: 10913 Carrollwood Dr Tampa FL 33618 Office: 5206 N Armenia Av Tampa FL 33603

CHISM, OLIN, editor. Music editor Dallas Times Herald. Office: 1101 Pacific Av Dallas TX 75202*

CHISMAN, THOMAS PESCUD, broadcasting co. exec.; b. Hampton, Va., Dec. 8, 1921; s. Samuel Reade and Mary Lee (Cannon), C.; B.A., U. Va., 1943; m. Martha Pamela Merritt, Oct, 2, 1943; children—Thomas Pescud IV, Martha Pamela, Lila Elizabeth, Anne Meriwether Michie. Mgr., Chisman Fuel Co., Hampton, 1946-47; pres., gen. mgr. Peninsula Broadcasting Corp., Hampton, 1947— pres. PBK Ltd., Peninsula Cable Corp., Multra-Guard, Inc., Multra-Guard of Va.; dir. Va. Nat. Bank. Mem. Peninsula Port and Indsl. Authority, 1956-65; chmn. Peninsula Stadium Authority, 1963-64; mem. Hampton Rds. Area Cooperation Com., 1961-65; mem. Adv. Com. on Naval Affairs, 1959-65; chmn. Old Hampton Redevel. Com. 1963-65; chmn. Citizens Adv. Com. for Community Improvement, 1964-65. Trustee Old Dominion U. Found.; bd. visitors Old Dominion U.; bd. dirs. Va. Peninsula Symphony Orch. Served to lt. (j.g.) USNR, 1943-46, to capt. AUS, 1947-52. Mem. Va. Assn. Broadcasters (dir. 1955-63, pres. 1960-61), Nat. Assn. Broadcasters, Radio and Television Execs. Assn. N.Y., ABC Affiliates Assn. (chmn. bd. govs. 1962-64), Am. Legion, Peninsula C. of C. (dir. 1953-64). Episcopalian. Clubs: Huntington (chmn. bd.); Harbor; James River Country. Hampton Roads German; Broadcasters (Washington). Home: 2300 Chesapeake Av Hampton VA 23361 Office: 1930 E Pembroke Av Hampton VA 23363

CHITTY, ARTHUR BENJAMIN, JR., univ. adminstr.; b. Jacksonville, Fla., June 15, 1914; s. Arthur Benjamin and Hazel Talitha (Brown) C.; student U. Fla., summer 1934; A.B., U. of South, 1935; M.A., Tulane U., 1952; L.H.D., Canaan Coll., 1970; m. Mary Elizabeth Nickinson, June 16, 1946; children—Arthur Benjamin III, John Abercrombie Merritt, Em Turner, Nathan Harsh Brown. Vice pres. Chitty & Co., Jacksonville, Fla., 1937-41, chmn. bd. dirs., 1963-67, dir. pub. relations U. of South, 1946-65, 70—, historiographer, 1955—, exec. dir. Asso. Alumni 1946-65; pres. Assn. of Episcopal Colls., N.Y.C., 1965-70, sec., dir., 1971—. Pres., Sewanee Civic Assn., 1948-49; mem. Tenn. Bishop and Council, 1956-65; nat. convenor Episcopal historiographers, 1961-66, 71—; nat. council Brotherhood St. Andrew, mem. exec. com., 1966—, v.p., 1968; Am. coordinator Oxford Scholar Program, Keble Coll., Eng. 1970—. Bd. dirs. Living Ch. Found., Ch. Hist. Soc.; trustee St. Augustine's Coll.; trustee, sec. bd. St. Andrew's Sch. Served with USNR, 1942-45. Mem. N.Y. Acad. Scis., St. Georg's Soc., English-Speaking Union (pres. local chpt. 1972—), Phi Beta Kappa (pres. 1963-64), Pi Gamma Mu, Phi Alpha Theta, Sigma Upsilon, Sigma Nu, (pres. Ednl. Found. 1969—). Episcopalian. Clubs: Century Assn., Church (N.Y.C.). Author: Reconstruction at Sewanee, 1954. Contbr. Articles to profl. jours. Editor: Sewanee News, 1946-65; Historiographical Newsletter, 1962-67; Franklin County (Tenn.) Historian, 1965-69. Editor: (with Elizabeth N. Chitty) Ely: Too Black, Too White, 1970. Home: Sewanee TN 37375 Office: care U of South Sewanee TN 37375

CHITWOOD, JERRY DAVID, dentist; b. Eufaula, Okla., Dec. 2, 1931; s. Dave and Edith (Painter) C.; student W. Tex. State U., 1950-51, Frank Phillips Jr. Coll., 1955, N. Tex. U., 1955-56, Baylor U., 1956-60; m. Dorothy Louise Drake, Aug. 20, 1957; children—Michael David, Jeri Jean. Private practice dentistry, Dallas 1960—. Dir. White Rock Nat. Bank, Dallas. Served with USNR, 1951-55. Mem. Am., Tex. dental assns., Am. Quarter Horse Assn., Palomino Horse Breeders Am., Kappa Alpha. Episcopalian. Club: Northlake Exchange (pres. 1964). Home: 9665 Broken Bow Rd Dallas TX 75238 Office: 8535 Ferndale Rd Dallas TX 75238

CHIU, KUN-YOUNG, cons. engr.; b. Taipei, Taiwan, Formosa, June 23, 1937; s. Jiun and Luan Yin (Lin) C.; B.S., Nat. Taiwan U., 1960; M.S., U. Fla., 1964; 1 dau., Michelle Karen. Came to U.S., 1963. Asst. mgr. Yun-long Engring. Co. Inc., Taipei, Taiwan, 1956-60; research and teaching asst. Nat. Taiwan U., Taipei, 1961-63; research asst. U. Fla., Gainesville, 1963-64; structural engr. Wm. T. Mathis & Assos., Jacksonville, Fla., 1964-67, resident engr., Valdosta, Ga., 1967-70; prin. Kun-young Chiu & Assos., cons. engrs., Valdosta, 1970—; v.p. Jacksonville Engring. & Testing Co., 1970—. Registered profl. engr., Fla., Ga., Ky., S.C. Mem. Am. Soc. C.E., Am. Concrete Inst., Chinese Inst. Civil Engring., Nat. Soc. Profl. Engrs. Contbr. articles in field to profl. jours. Address: 109 E Adair St Valdosta GA 31601

CHIU, WEN JUNG, physician; b. Taiwan, Formosa, May 6, 1924; s. Yi Pau and Chuan Hau (Chen) C.; M.D., Nat. Taiwan U., 1947; m. So-Khim Tan, Dec. 14, 1953; children—Mark, Peter, James. Came to U.S., 1952, naturalized, 1969. Intern, 1st Mil. Forces Gen. Hosp., Taipei, Taiwan, 1947-48; resident in anesthesiology Peter Bent Brigham Hosp., Boston, 1953, Boston Children's Hosp., 1954, Boston Lying-in Hosp., 1954; resident U. Tex., M.D. Anderson Hosp. and Tumor Inst., Houston, 1954-57, asso. anesthesiologist, asst. prof., 1965—; anesthesiologist E. Tex. Tb Hosp., Tyler, 1957-61; asst. prof. U. Tex. Med. Sch., Houston, 1971—. Fellow Am. Coll. Anesthesiologists; mem. Internat. Anesthesia Research Soc., Am. Soc. Anesthesiologists, A.M.A., Tex. Med. Assn., Harris County Med. Soc., Doctors' Club Houston. Presbyn. Home: 5034 Glenmeadow St Houston TX 77035 Office: 6723 Bertner Dr Houston TX 77025

CHOKISKI, EARL L., city ofcl.; b. San Antonio, Apr. 22, 1920; s. Charles Steven and Gertrude (Benfer) C.; student Harvard; m. Claire Edith Steffens, July 21, 1949. With El Paso (Tex.) Police Dept., 1946—, now chief of police. Served with Armed Forces, 1939-45. Decorated Bronze Star. Mem. Tex. Police Assn., Internat. Assn. Chiefs Police, First Cav. Assn. Mason (32 deg.). Home: 3620 Comstock Ct El Paso TX 79904 Office: 500 E San Antonio El Paso TX 79901

CHOMMIE, JOHN CAMPBELL, educator; b. Thief River Falls, Minn., Sept. 5, 1914; s. Hans O. and Florence (Campbell) C.; student U. Minn., 1932-33, 35-36, U. N.D., 1934-35; LL.B., St. Paul Coll. Law, 1941, B.S.L., 1942; LL.M., U. So. Cal., 1952; LL.M., N.Y. U., 1956, J.S.D., 1960; m. June K. Ray, July 5, 1947; children— Barbara (Mrs. Lloyd Tosse), Frances (Mrs. Phillip Knox), Johanna, Karen, John, Catherine. Traffic mgr. Navjo Ordance Depot, 1942-43; prof. law S.W. U., Los Angeles, 1948-53, Dickinson Sch. Law, 1953-56; research asso. Harvard Law Sch., 1957-58; prof. law U. Miami, Coral Gables, Fla., 1956—, dir. tax program, Law Sch., 1965—; vis. prof. La. State U., 1965. Mem. Fla. Citizens Com. for Promotion of Humanities, 1971. Served with U.S. Mcht. Marine, 1944-45. Mem. Am. Trial Lawyers Assn., Minn., Interamerican bar assns., Am. Assn. U. Profs., Dade County Bar Assn. (asso.). Author: (with George Eder) Taxation in Columbia, 1964; Federal Income Taxation, 1968; The Internal Revenue Service, 1970. Editor, contbr. El Derecho de Los Estados Unidos, 3 vols., 1963. Home: 9225 SW 63d St Miami FL 33143 Office: Sch Law U Miami Coral Gables FL 33134

CHORLEY, GEORGE HAROLD, sch. adminstr.; b. Sledge, Miss., Oct. 6, 1922; s. George Harvey and Annie L. (Jones) C.; B.S., Delta State Coll., 1950; M.A., Memphis State U., 1961; postgrad. Ark. State U., 1960-61; m. Catherine L. Snipes, May 3, 1946; 1 son, George Harold. Tchr., Helena and West Helena (Ark.) Pub. Schs., 1950-60, prin., 1960-61, dir. instrn., 1961-68, supt. schs., 1968—. Served with inf. AUS, 1941-45; PTO. Mem. Ark. Edn. Assn., Am., Ark. assns. sch. adminstrs. Rotarian. Home: 339 S 8th St West Helena AR 72390 Office: 216 Biscoe St Helena AR 72342

CHRISMAN, JOHN DOUGLAS, educator; b. Berea, Ky., Jan. 13, 1921; s. Robert Henry and Laura (Coyle) C.; B.S., Juilliard Sch. Music, 1948, M.S., 1949; private study piano Rio Nardi, Florence, Italy; m. Dorothy Currier, May 31, 1952; children—Martha Carol, Richard Lawrence, Charles David, James William, John Robert. Mem. faculty Berea (Ky.) Coll., 1949—, asso. prof. music, 1964-69, prof., 1969—, chmn. music dept., 1959-60, 68-69. Adjudicator piano contests, festivals, Ky., Ohio, Tenn., W.Va., Ill. Served with AUS, 1942-45; ETO. Recipient Charles Ward Seabury award for excellence in teaching Berea Coll., 1969. Mem. Music Tchrs. Nat. Assn. (exec. bd. 1958-63, mem. nat. certification bd. 1971—, mem. exec. bd. So. div. 1971—), Ky. Assn. Coll. Music Depts. (sec.-treas. 1972—), Ky. Music Tchrs. Assn. (pres. 1958-62, chmn. tchr. certification bd. 1964-69), Phi Kappa Phi (pres. Berea Coll. chpt. 1966-68). Home: 103 Lorraine Ct Berea KY 40403

CHRISTEN, ALBERT, state ofcl. Commr., Dept. Finance, State of Ky. Office: New Capitol Annex Frankfort KY 40601*

CHRISTENBERRY, HERBERT WILLIAM, ret. U.S. judge; b. New Orleans, Dec. 11, 1897; s. Herbert Aden and Anna (Schmitt) C.; student Soule Coll., New Orleans; LL.B., Loyola U., 1924; student N.Y. U., 1927; m. Anna Born, Aug. 5, 1924; children—Carolyn Ann, Herbert William. Practiced law, 1924-38; asst. atty., Bd. Comrs. of Port of New Orleans, 1933-35; dep. commr. La. Debt Moratorium Commn., 1935; asst. dist. atty., Parish of Orleans, 1935-37; asst. U.S. atty., Eastern Dist. La., 1937-42, U.S. atty. 1942-47; became U.S. dist. judge, New Orleans, 1947, dist. chief judge, 1949-67; instr. Loyola U. of South Sch. Law. Mem. Fed., Am., La., New Orleans bar assns. Democrat. Office: 400 Royal St New Orleans LA 70130

CHRISTENSEN, BENT AKSEL, educator; b. Copenhagen, Denmark, Mar. 22, 1928; s. Aksel M. and Dagmar S. (Anderson) C.; Filosofikum, U. Copenhagen, 1948; M.S. in Civil Engring., Tech. U. Denmark, 1951; certificate (Fulbright scholar 1955, Alfred P. Sloane fellow 1955), Mass. Inst. Tech., 1955; Ph.D., U. Miami, 1961; m. Annikki Hilja Hannula, Dec. 28, 1958; children—Kim, Eva. Prof. civil engring. U. Fla., Gainesville, 1965—, head hydraulics div., 1965—, prof. coastal and oceanographic engring., 1970—. Hydraulic engring. cons. Europe, Middle East, U.S.A., Can., 1955—. Recipient award for excellence in teaching Tau Beta Pi/Sigma Tau, 1969; Scandinavian Am. Found. fellow, 1959; NATO fellow, 1960, Mem. Internat. Assn. Hydraulic Research, Am. Soc. C.E., Am. Water Resources Assn., Am. Soc. Engring. Edn., Sigma Tau, Tau Beta Pi. Home: 111 NW 29th St Gainesville FL 32601

CHRISTENSEN, CARLO MOLLER, Danish diplomat; b. Copenhagen, Denmark, Dec. 22, 1903; s. Hans and Lucia (Jensen) C.; L.H.D., Dana Coll., 1966; m. Elizabeth Futtrup, Nov. 1, 1925; 1 dau., Inge Futtrup. Farmer, gardener, free lance writer, chief Danish-Am. Press Service, Copenhagen, 1936-42, asst. Ministry Fgn. Affairs, Copenhagen, 1942-45, consul, cultural counselor Royal Danish Embassy, Washington 1945—; dean cultural and ednl. officers Embassies, Washington, 1956—. Mem. Danish Resistance Movement, 1940-45. Decorated knight Order Dannebrog 1st class; recipient citation for brave conduct in Danish Resistance Movement, Gen. Eisenhower, 1945, Howard U. award, Internat. Cultural Relations award, 1952; Isaiah award for human relations Am. Jewish Com., 1968. Mem. Danish Authors Soc., Am. Scandinavian Found. N.Y. Club: Cosmos (Washington). Author: Collection of Poems: Oest og vest, 1928; Collection of poems: Eventyret kaldte, 1932; History of Occupation: Under Jorden i Borgergade, 1945; History About the First Danes in New York: De foerste Danske i New York, 1953; History from the Virgin Islands: Peter von Scholten, 1955. Home: 2122 Massachusetts Av NW Washington DC 20008 Office: 3200 Whitehaven St NW Washington DC 20008

CHRISTENSEN, DAVID LEE, aerospace and bus. cons.; b. Birmingham, Ala., Apr. 7, 1932; s. Arne Scove and Susie (Harvey) C.; student U. Ala., 1955-57; m. Doris Margaret Baker, Mar. 19, 1949; children— David Lee, Erik Lane. Design engr. Hayes Internat., Birmingham, Ala., 1955; cons. engr. Cons. & Designers, Inc., Redstone Arsenal, Ala., 1956-60; aerospace cons., 1960—; to Arthur D. Little, Inc., 1969—; pres. TEC Prodns., Inc., Huntsville, Ala., 1960-63; now pres. Interserve Corp. Bd. dirs. Sci. and Tech. Edn. Center. Served with U.S. Army, 1953-55. Mem. Am. Inst. Aeros. and Astronautics, Soc. Tech. Writers and Pubs., Rocket City Astron. Soc., Aviation Space Writers Assn., Huntsville C. of C. (pub. relations com.). Co-author: Twenty Centuries of Space Travel, Dividends from Space, Stations in Space, Rendezvous at Reutte. Asst. editor Space Jour., 1957-60. Chmn. lit. com. Ala. Space Sci. Exhibit; research asso. U. Ala. Research Inst. on History of Saturn Rocket Project. Home: 11015 Vivian Dr Huntsville AL 35810 Office: PO Box 3180 Huntsville AL 35810

CHRISTENSEN, RAYMOND LYLE, educator; b. Winterset, Ia., July 16, 1920; s. Harry N. and Leta (Bush) C.; B.Ed., Colo. State U., 1964; student Internat. Corr. Schs.; M.S. in Edn., So. Ill. U., 1965, postgrad., 1966-67; m. Fern E. Breakenridge, Feb. 24, 1944; children— Raymond Lyle, Christena S. Asst. plant supt. Northwestern Ill. Gas & Electric Co., Savanna, 1953-55; elec. engr. Electric Energy Inc., Joppa, 1955-59; instr. So. Ill. U., Carbondale, 1959-66; mem. faculty Northwestern State U., Natchitoches, La., 1966—, asst. prof. elec. engring. tech., 1966—, dir. elec. div., 1966—. Cons. sch. surveys, tech. edn. Served with USNR, 1942-45. Recipient Outstanding Service award Natchitoches Lion's Club, 1968. Mem. I.E.E.E., Am. Vocational Assn., Am. Tech. Edn. Assn., La. Tchrs. Assn., Am. Assn. U. Profs. (chpt. 1st v.p. 1967-69, treas. chpt. 1971-72, sec.-treas. state conf. 1970-72), Am. Legion, Phi Delta Kappa (1st v.p. chpt. 1969-70, pres. 1970-71), Iota Lambda Sigma (chmn. grand council 1972). Methodist (men's club pres. 1964-66, 68-72, pres. Open Door Sunday sch. class). Lion (treas. 1968-70, 3d v.p. 1971-72, 2d v.p. 1972—). Home: 1017 Oma St Natchitoches LA 71457

CHRISTENSON, VICTOR JUNIOR, univ. adminstr.; b. Jackson, Minn., May 12, 1924; s. Victor Edwin and Mina Maurine (Thornburg) C.; B.A., Buena Vista Coll., 1949; M.Ed., Mont. State U., 1956; Ed.D., U. Neb., 1967; m. Inez Mildred Johnson, Oct. 28, 1924; children—Bruce Martin, Brett Junior. High sch. tchr., Cleghorn, Ia., 1949-52; high sch. prin., Sutherland, Ia., 1954-58; supt. schs., Royal, Ia., 1958-63; exec. sec., dir. Neb. Council Ednl. TV, Inc., Lincoln, Neb., 1963-67; supt. schs., Oskaloosa, Ia., 1967-69; head dept. sch. adminstrn. Western Ky. U., Bowling Green, Ky., 1969—; owner Sporting Goods Store, 1960-65. Cons. Ednl. TV, 1963-65; Served with AUS, 1943-46, 52-54. Decorated Bronze Star medal. Mem. N.E.A., Nat. Council Profs. Ednl. Adminstrn., Am., Ky. assns. sch. adminstrs., Ky. Edn. Assn., Ky. Assn. Sch. Bus. Ofcls. Elk. Home: 1316 Willow Lane Bowling Green KY 42101

CHRISTERSON, ROBERT KELLY, coll. adminstr.; b. nr. Springfield, Ky., May 10, 1924; s. Garnett Phillip and Mattie (Goode) C.; m. Alberta Jones, Mar. 22, 1947; children—Garnett Kelly, Marcus Allen, Sandra Gail. Bookkeeper, First Nat. Bank, Springfield, Ky., 1946-58; asst. cashier First and Peoples Bank, Springfield, 1959-63, asst. v.p., 1964-66; controller Campbellsville (Ky.) Coll., 1967-69, bus. mgr., 1970—. Treas., Taylor County Park Bd. Served with AUS, 1944-47. Baptist. Mason. Home: Route 2 Campbellsville KY 42718 Office: Campbellsville Coll Campbellsville KY 42718

CHRISTIAN, DELOS HORACE, life ins. co. exec.; b. Scarville, Ia., June 15, 1920; s. Gilbert Frank and Tena (Drugsvold) C.; B.A., U. Ia., 1942; student N.Y. U., 1942; U. Richmond, 1957; m. Veloa D. Montgomery, Oct. 3, 1942; children—Ken Arden, Rose Ann, Dale Allen, Cheryl Lynn. Mathematician, Equitable Life Assurance Soc., 1946-52; with Life Ins. Co. Va., Richmond, 1952—, asst. to pres., 1961-63, sr. v.p., 1963-64, 1st v.p., 1964-65; exec. v.p., 1965—, also dir.; pres., dir. 1st Funds of Va.; exec. v.p., dir. Richmond Corp.; mem. Richmond bd. First & Mchts. Bank; dir. Leatherby Ins. Co., 1st Va. Mgmt. & Research Corp., Equivest, Systems Engring. Corp. Served to maj. USAAF, 1942-46. Decorated Air medal. Fellow Soc. Actuaries; mem. Mid Atlantic Actuarial Club (pres. 1959), Phi Beta Kappa. Presbyn. (elder). Home: 802 Coleridge Lane Richmond VA 23229 Office: 914 Capitol St Richmond VA 23219

CHRISTIAN, FLOYD THOMAS, state ofcl.; b. Bessemer, Ala., Dec. 18, 1914; s. Henry Clayton and Mabel Blanche (Jones) C.; A.B. in Edn., U. Fla., 1937, M.A. in Sch. Adminstrn. and Supervision, 1949; m. Margaret Littlejohn, Aug. 27, 1938; children—Zera Ellen (Mrs. Claud Leiby). Floyd Thomas, Robert Rick. Tchr., athletic dir., head coach Clearwater (Fla.) High Sch., also Ft. Myers (Fla.) High Sch., 1937-41; adminstr. charge Fla. Dept. Vets. Affairs, 1946-48; supt. schs. Pinellas County, Fla. (St. Petersburg), 1948-65; state supt. pub. instrn. State Fla., 1965—. Chmn. bd. Central Plaza Bank & Trust Co., St. Petersburg, 1960-65. Mem. Pinellas County Juvenile Welfare Bd., Pinellas County License Bd., Fla. Children's Com.; cons. ednl. TV, Internat. Trade Fair, Turin, Italy, 1961. Bd. regents State of Fla., 1965. Recipient Good Govt. award St. Petersburg Jr. C. of C., 1957. Mem. Fla. Assn. County Supts. (past pres.), Fla. (past pres.), Nat. (life) edn. assns., Am. Assn. Sch. Adminstrs., Fla. Ednl. TV Commn., Fla. W. Coast Ednl. TV. Mason, Rotarian. Home: 2609 Lotus Dr Tallahassee FL 32303 Office: State Dept Edn The Capitol Tallahassee FL 32304

CHRISTIAN, GEORGE LLOYD, JR., newspaper editor; b. Houston, May 29, 1927; s. George Lloyd and Hazel Margaret (Singleton) C.; B.S. in Journalism, U. Houston; m. Mary Frances Blount, Sept. 22, 1956; children— Stephen Scott, Karen Elizabeth, Devin Alan. With Houston Post, 1949—, successively reporter, film critic, drama critic, mag. editor, now asst. mng. editor. Free-lance writer. Served with AUS, 1945-46. Home: 1108 Danbury Rd Houston TX 77055 Office: 4747 Southwest Freeway Houston TX 77001

CHRISTIAN, JOHN KENTON, publisher; b. Pana, Ill., Nov. 6, 1927; s. Ben Ross and Ruth (Stevenson) C.; student Westminster Coll., 1945, Colo. Coll., 1948, Emerson Coll., 1949; B.S., Boston U., 1951; student Am. U., 1954-55; m. Marjorie Adair Pollock, Nov. 28, 1958; children—Jefrey, Dwane, Kevin. Relief editor, rep., columnist St. Louis Daily Record, 1950-51; reporter Commerce Clearing House, Washington, 1952; with U.S. News and World Report, 1953-68, regional sales mgr., Los Angeles, 1960-63, marketing mgr., Washington, 1964-68; pub. Nation's Cities Mag., Washington, 1968—; dir. pub. affairs Nat. League of Cities and U.S. Conf. Mayor's, Washington, 1971—. Served with USAAF, 1945-48. Mem. Nat. Press. Club, Am. Marketing Assn., Assn. Indsl. Advertisers, Delta Tau Delta. Presbyn. Home: 5217 Wapakoneta Rd Washington DC 20016 Office: 1612 K St NW Washington DC 20006

CHRISTIAN, JOSEPH ROY, banker; b. Tenaha, Tex., June 20, 1927; s. Joe Richard and Irene Elizabeth (Brown) C.; student Tex. Technol. Coll., 1944, N.M. A. and M. Coll., 1944-45; B.S. in Petroleum Engring., La. State U., 1949; m. Mary Delores Dooley, Nov. 16, 1951; children—Randall Allen, Marc Richard. Petroleum engr., div. prodn. geologist Shell Oil Co., Hobbs, N.M. and Odessa, Tex., 1949-57; petroleum engr. DeGolyer & MacNaughton, Dallas, 1957-59; area engr., chief engr. Stekoll Petroleum Corp., Dallas, 1959-61; sr. engr. Colo. Interstate Gas Co., Colorado Springs, 1961-62; petroleum engr. R.F. Kravis Assos., Tulsa, 1962-63; v.p. Oliver & West, Inc., Dallas, 1963-65; v.p., trust officer First Nat. Bank in Dallas, 1965—. Group chmn. Dallas County United Fund, 1970, 71. Served with AUS, 1945-47. Mem. Toastmasters Internat. (pres. White Rock club 1971—), Am. Inst. M.E., Soc. Petroleum Engrs., Ind. Petroleum Assn. Am., Mid-Continental Oil and Gas Assn., Tex. Mid-Continental Oil and Gas Assn., Am. Assn. Petroleum Landmen, West Tex. Geol. Soc., Internat. Oil Scouts Assn., Petroleum Engrs. Club of Dallas (program com. 1971-72), Engrs. Club of Dallas. Home: 9923 Miller Rd No 1163 Dallas TX 75238 Office: PO Box 6031 Dallas TX 75222

CHRISTIAN, RAYMOND L., supt. schs. Supt. Birmingham (Ala.) City Schs. Office: PO Drawer 10007 Birmingham AL 35202

CHRISTIANSEN, KENNETH ALEXANDER, educator, TV exec.; b. Sansarc, S.D., July 20, 1913; s. S. A. and Laurena (Jensen) C.; B.E., Moorehead State Tchrs. Coll., 1938; M.A., U. Denver, 1939; Ed.D., U. Mo., 1949; m. Olive Aulie, May 30, 1943; children—Gary Allen, Kim Bruce. Tchr. rural sch., Minn., 1931-33; faculty Hutchinson (Kan.) Jr. Coll., 1938-39, Stephens Coll., Columbia, Mo., 1946-53, Ind. State Tchrs. Coll., Terre Haute, 1945-46, U. S.D., 1939-44; project dir. ednl. TV, So. Regional Edn. Bd., 1953-56; program mgr., asst. to pres. Nat. Ednl. TV, Ann Arbor, Mich., 1956-59; prof. communications, chmn. dept. broadcasting, dir. TV, U. Fla., Gainesville, 1959—; TV project dir. Govt. India, New Delhi, 1960-65; adviser closed circuit project U. Sao Paulo, 1965; Am. specialist Dept. State, Korea, Philippines, Indonesia, Singapore, Thailand, summer 1969. Recipient Kiwanis citation for services as lt. gov., 1968. Mem. Nat. Assn. Ednl. Broadcasters, Assn. for Profl. Broadcasting Edn., Phi Delta Kappa, Sigma Delta Chi. Kiwanian. Home: 11129 NW 12th Pl Gainesville FL 32601 Office: Stadium Bldg U Fla Gainesville FL 32601

CHRISTIANSON, HERBERT B., dermatologist, educator; b. Sheldon, Wis., 1915; M.D., Marquette U., 1939; M.D. in Dermatology and Syphilology, U. Minn., 1956. Intern Milw. County Hosp., 1938-39; fellow dermatology and syphilology Mayo Clinic and Found., 1953-56, 1st asst. dermatology and syphilology, 1955-56; head sect. dermatology Ochsner Found. Hosp., New Orleans; later chief Dermatology Dept., Ochsner Clinic, New Orleans; practice medicine specializing in dermatology, New Orleans; sr. vis. physician Charity Hosp.; asst. prof. dermatology Tulane U., New Orleans, 1957-64, clin. asso. prof., 1964-69, clin. prof., 1969—. Served to maj. M.C., AUS, 1940-46. Mem. Am. Dermatol. Assn., A.M.A., Am. Acad. Dermatology, Soc. Investigative Dermatology, Soc. Internat. Tropical Dermatology, N. Am. Clin. Dermatol. Soc. Office: 1514 Jefferson Hwy New Orleans LA 70121

CHRISTIE, DUDLEY BENJAMIN, supt. schs.; b. Parrott, Ga., Jan. 13, 1918; s. Dudley Whaley and Mary (Kirksey) C.; B.S., U. Ga., 1942, M.S., 1943, 6 yr. certificate U. Ga., 1963; m. Hazel Mixon, Aug. 21, 1943; children—Dudley Benjamin, Hugh Allen. Tchr., coach high sch., Ludowici, Ga., 1937-40; prin., coach Washington (Ga.) High Sch., 1943-44; prin. Fitzgerald (Ga.) High Sch., 1944-48; supt. city schs., Eastman, Ga., 1948-51; prin. Griffin (Ga.) High Sch., 1951—; supt. Griffin-Spalding County Schs., 1967—. Mem. Ga. Improvement Council; merit counsellor Flint River council Boy Scouts of Am., 1951-64; v.p. Boys Club, Griffin; treas. Flint River Regional Library, 1967— mem. Spalding County Bd. Health, 1967. Bd. dirs. State YMCA, 1965, Central West Dist. YMCA, 1966-68; mem. bd. Southeastern Regional Lab. Served with USMC, 1936-37. John Hay fellow U. Ore., 1964. Mem. N.E.A., Ga., Dodge County (past pres.) edn. assns., Am., Ga. assns. sch. adminstrs., Ga. Congress Parents and Tchrs., Nat., Ga. (past pres.) prins. assns., So. Assn. Colls. and Schs. (mem. Ga. com.), Ga. Assn. Sch. Supts. (pres. 1972-73), Ga. Tchr. Edn. Council, Middle Ga. Coll., Ga. Tchrs. Coll. alumni assns., Sigma Nu. Baptist (deacon). Kiwanian (v.p. 1959), Elk. Club: Griffin Country. Home: 621 Forest Av Griffin GA 30223 Office: PO Box 622 Griffin GA 30223

CHRISTMAN, JON DAVID, printing co. exec.; b. Dayton, O., Aug. 15, 1936; s. James E. and Minnie S. (Humphrey) C.; B.A., Wittenberg Coll., 1958; m. Carol Ann Weaver, July 6, 1956; children—Scott, Jennifer, Jeffrey, Tamera, Teresa, Jill. Personnel mgr. McCall Printing Co., 1959-61, dir. customer service, 1961-69; pres. Foote & Davies, Doraville, Ga., 1969—; v.p., dir. McCall Printing Co. Chmn. indsl. com. United Appeal, Dayton, O., 1968. Mem. DeKalb C. of C. (dir. 1970-71, v.p. 1972), Pi Kappa Alpha. Republican. Lutheran. Mason. Clubs: Commerce, Athletic (Atlanta). Home: 5384 Pheasant Run Stone Mountain GA 30083 Office: 3101 McCall Dr Doraville GA 30340

CHRISTMAS, JOSEPH THEODORE, physician; b. Vienna, Ga., Jan. 9, 1923; s. George B. and Edye Mae (Sangster) C.; student Ga. Southwestern Coll., 1939-41; B.S. in Agr., U. Ga., 1943, postgrad., 1949-50; M.D., Med. Coll. Ga., 1954; m. Lucy Farris Smith, Apr. 7, 1944; children—Karen Sue, Timothy Lane. Tchr. vocational agr. Americus (Ga.) High Sch., 1943-44; county agrl. extension agt., Lanier County, Ga., 1946-49; intern Macon Hosp., 1954-55; gen. practice medicine, Vienna, Ga., 1955—; mem. staff Dooly Med. Center, Vienna, Crisp County Hosp., Cordele, Ga. Chmn., Dooly County Bd. Edn., 1959-69. Bd. dirs. Ga. Med. Care Found. Served with USNR, 1944-45; PTO. Mem. Ga. Acad. Gen. Practice (dir. 1969—), Med. Assn. Ga. (dist. councilor 1968—), Flint Med. Soc., Am., Ga. Holstein-Fresian assns., Alpha Omega Alpha. Baptist (deacon 1966-69). Lion. Address: PO Box 247 Vienna GA 31092

CHRISTOPHER, WILFORD SCOTT, assn. exec.; b. Enid, Okla., Feb. 8, 1916; s. W. Scott and Mary Elizabeth (Heaton) C.; B.A., Phillips U., 1938; M.A., U. Ia., 1941; m. Marjorie Lois Lester, Dec. 30, 1941; 1 son, Scott Douglas. Asst. prof. speech Phillips U., 1939, asso. prof. sociology, 1940-42; pub. relations dir. Miami (Fla.) C. of C., 1946-51; gen. mgr. Greater Tampa C. of C., 1951-64, exec. v.p. 1964—. Chmn. Nat. Adv. Council Urban Devel., 1959-60; mem. adv. council U. Tampa, 1966-69; mem. tech.- occupation adv. com. Hillsborough Jr. Coll., 1969—, chmn. advanced mgmt. curriculum com., 1958-59; mem. Adv. Group on Continuing Edn. for Urban Leadership, 1967-68. Bd. dirs. Tampa Philharmonic Orch. Assn., Tampa Oral Sch. for Deaf. Trustee U. South Fla. Found., 1959-65; trustee Berkeley Prep. Sch., 1963, v.p., 1965—. Mem. Fla. C. of C. Execs. Assn. (pres. 1954), Southeastern Inst. C. of C. Execs. (pres. 1956), So. Assn. C. of C. Execs. (pres.-elect 1971), Inst. Orgn. Mgmt. (bd. regents), Am. C. of C. Execs. (sec.-treas., v.p. 1960, pres. 1961-62, chmn. nat. panel on exec. certification 1966). Clubs: Tampa Exchange (pres. 1955), Executive (past pres.), University (dir.), Tampa Yacht and Country; Ye Mystic Kreme of Gasparilla. Contbr. to Chamber of Commerce Administration. Home: 10701 Carrollwood Dr Tampa FL 33618 Office: 801 E John F Kennedy Blvd Tampa FL 33601

CHRISTOPHERSON, MERRETH EUGENE, sales co. exec.; b. Canton, S.D., Apr. 5, 1926; s. Ole C. and Annie Sabina (Swanson) C.; B.S., S.D. State U., 1947; M.S., Kan. State U., 1951; m. Marian Kathryn Schaeffer, Nov. 23, 1946; children—Mary Pamela, Paige Ann, Janet Kay. Athletic dir., coach, tchr., South Sioux City, Neb., 1947-55; ins. rep., mgr. N.Y. Life Ins. Co., Mankato, Minn., 1955-63; v.p., marketing mgr. Kayot, Inc., Mankato, 1963-69; pres. C & S Sales Co., Inc., Easley, S.C., 1969—. Councilman, Mankato, 1962-64; mem. exec. com. Blue Earth County, Minn., 1964-69. Served with USNR, 1943-45. Mem. Boating Industry Assn. (mem. govt. relations com. 1965—), Am. Legion, Am. Marketing Assn., Phi Kappa Phi, Phi Epsilon Kappa. Republican. Presbyn. (elder, trustee, deacon). Mason, Rotarian (dir. Easley 1970). Club: Pickens (S.C.) County Country. Home: Old Stagecoach Rd Easley SC 29640 Office: 149 Cumberland Av Easley SC 29640

CHRISTOPHERSON, WILLIAM MARTIN, educator, physician; b. Salt Lake City, July 2, 1916; s. George Walter and Myrtle (Jack) C.; student U. Utah, 1938; M.D., U. Louisville, 1942; m. Kathryn Donley, July 24, 1943; 1 son, George Walter II. Intern, Akron (O.) City Hosp., 1942-43, resident, 1946-48; resident U. Louisville Hosp., 1948-49; fellow pathology Meml. Hosp., N.Y.C., 1949-50; faculty U. Louisville Grad. Sch., 1950—, prof. pathology, chmn. dept., 1956—; spl. cons. Nat. Cancer Inst., bur. state service USPHS, adv. com. cancer control program, 1963-67; cons. Louisville VA Hosp. Pres. Ky. div., mem. at large bd. dirs., mem. exec. com. Am. Cancer Soc.; temporary adviser WHO. Served to capt. AUS, 1943-46. Mem. N.Y. Acad. Sci., Am. Soc. Cytology (pres. 1966-67), Am. Soc. Cancer Edn. (past pres.), Soc. Exptl. Pathology, Internat. Acad. Pathology (pres. 1971-72), Assn. Pathologists and Bacteriologists, Am. Soc. Clin. Pathology, Sigma Xi, Alpha Omega Alpha. Mem. editorial bd. Yearbook of Cancer, Am. Jour. Clin. Pathology, Acta Cytologica, Cancer. Home: 2211 Cherokee Pkwy Louisville KY 40204

CHRISTY, GEORGE WASHINGTON, city ofcl.; b. Pottstown, Pa., Feb. 22, 1889; s. John and Ida Christy; student pub. schs.; m. Beth Donaldson, Nov. 10, 1940; 1 son, George W. Builder movie theatres, 1907; circus owner, Springville, N.Y., 1908; owner Heber Bros. Circus, 1919-25, Lee Bros. Circus and Tex. Ranch Wild West, 1925, Christy Bros. Circus, 1920-30; operated indoor circus unit, 1930-44. Mayor, South Houston Tex., 1949—. Mem. State Hwy. Planning Commn. on Transp. Served with U.S. Army, 1918. Mem. Am. Judicature Soc. Rotarian (charter pres. 1950), Lion. Address: 5922 Shady River Houston TX 77027

CHRISTY, RALPH LAWRENCE, JR., physician, navy officer; b. Kansas City, Mo., Oct. 2, 1913; s. Ralph Lawrence and Louise (Rodgers) C.; A.B., U. Colo., 1936; M.D., U. Colo., 1940; m. Mary Lou Sweet, Mar. 17, 1941; children—Ralph Lawrence III, Charles W., James G., Daniel M.m. 2d, A. Louise Meyer, July 28, 1966. Intern, Colo. Gen. Hosp., 1940-41, resident, 1941-42; commd. lt. (j.g.) M.C., USN, 1942, advanced through grades to capt., 1955; sr. med. officer U.S.S. F.D. Roosevelt, 1952-54; dir. aviation medicine operations div. Bur. Medicine and Office Chief Naval Operations, 1954-58; trainee U.S. Naval Hosp., Bethesda, Md., 1958-61; head neuropsychiatry br. Bur. Medicine, Navy Dept., Washington, 1961-68, spl. asst. for med. dept. spl. projects, profl. div., 1968—. Cons. NASA, U.S. surgeon gen. Dept. Def. rep. Nat. Adv. Mental Health Council, 1962—. Decorated Legion of Merit, Navy Commendation medal. Recipient William Porter lecture award Assn. Mil. Surgeons, 1963. Diplomate Am. Bd. Preventive Medicine. Fellow Am. Psychiat. Assn. (mem. com. govtl. services 1962-67), Am. Coll. Preventive Medicine, Aerospace Med. Assn. (Louis H. Bauer Founders award 1972, Eric Liljencrantz award 1964, pres. space medicine br. 1966-67, pres. 1970); mem. Internat. Acad. Aviation and Space Medicine, A.M.A. (com. on aerospace medicine 1963—), Soc. Cons. Surgeon Gens. Armed Forces, Group for Advancement Psychotherapy, Phi Rho Sigma, Alpha Sigma Phi. Contbr. articles to publs. Home: 5826 Conway Rd Bethesda MD 20034 Office: 23d and E Sts Washington DC 20390

CHU, TSING-KANG, Taiwan diplomat; b. Kiangsu, July 28, 1918; B.A., Nat. S.W. Assn. U., 1943; postgrad. U. Ottawa (Can.); m. Jean Liu; 2 sons. Vice consul to consul of Taiwan, Vancouver, B.C., Can., 1948-56; chief, 1st sec. Dept. Am. Affairs, Ministry Fgn. Affairs, 1956-60; 1st sec. Chinese Republic embassy, Washington, 1960-64; consul. Chinese Republic embassy, Ottawa, 1964-66; consul gen., Houston, 1966—. Address: 4063 Drummond St Houston TX

CHU, WEN-HWA, aero. engr.; b. Shanghai, China, Jan. 3, 1926; s. King C. N. and Z. S. (Yang) C.; B.S., Nat. Central U., 1947; M.S., U. Wash., 1950; Ph.D., Johns Hopkins U., 1963; m. Leo-Nore Sotomayor, Oct. 3, 1959; 1 son, Kayne M.C. Came to U.S., 1948, naturalized, 1964. Research asst. U. Md., 1953-55; research fellow U. Minn., 1955-56; research engr. S.W. Research Inst., San Antonio, 1958-60, sr. research engr., 1960-71, staff scientist, 1971—. Mem. Am. Inst. Aero. and Astronautics, Research Soc. Am., Am. Soc. M.E., Soc. Indsl. and Applied Math., Sigma Xi. Home: 3611 Crossette St San Antonio TX 78228 Office: 8500 Culebra Rd San Antonio TX 78284

CHUCHEK, FRANK CHARLES, ednl. adminstr.; b. Johnstown, Pa., Jan. 21, 1911; s. Frank and Theresa (Benchina) C.; B.S., Shippensburg State Coll., 1940; Ed.M., U. Pitts., 1947; student Duke, 1947, U. Va., 1954, 1957; m. Norma Eloise Case, Dec. 14, 1946; children—Norma Jeanne (Mrs. Lester Dupuy Sears), Joanne Marie (Mrs. Danny J. Blue); stepson—Franklin Case Weightman. Tchr., Chase City (Va.) High Sch., 1940-42; prin. Chase City Schs., 1942-55; prin. Bluestone High Sch., Skipwith, Va., 1955-59; prin. Sayre Area Jr. High Sch., 1959-61; prin. Appomattox (Va.) High Sch., 1961-70; prin.

Appomattox County High Sch., 1970—. Bd. dirs. Appomattox unit Am. Cancer Soc., Am. Heart Assn. Mem. Va., Nat. edn. assns., Nat. Assn. Secondary Sch. Prins., Va. Soc. Secondary Sch. Prins., Phi Sigma Pi. Democrat. Baptist (tchr. Sunday sch. 1947-69). Home: Rt 1 Box 38 Appomattox VA 24522 Office: PO Box 637 Appomattox VA 24522

CHUCULATE, RICHARD WOODROW, social worker; b. Sallisaw, Okla., Apr. 16, 1913; s. Isaac and Nellie (Christie) C.; B.A., U. Chgo., 1942; M.S.W., U. Okla., 1957; m. Ada Maxine Breuninger, Nov. 18, 1938; children—Richard William, Max James. Asst. community worker Bur. Indian Affairs, Rosebud, S.D., 1936-42, edn. field agt., Harlem, Mont., 1942-43; timekeeper Engring. Labs., Inc., Tulsa, 1943-44; caseworker Dept. Pub. Welfare, Sallisaw, 1944-52, dist. child welfare supr., 1957-72, social service rep., 1967-72; project dir. Cherokee social work Sch. Social Work, U. Okla., Norman, 1972—; community worker Cherokee Indian Found., Bartlesville, Okla., 1952-55. Mem. exec. com. Cherokee Nation of Okla., 1958—; Indian adv. com. mem. Bd. Nat. Missions of U.P. Ch. Am., 1962—; chmn. Sequoyah County March of Dimes.; mem. Sequoyah County Selective Service Bd.; trustee Sequoyah County Devel. Found. Mem. Nat. Assn. Social Workers Presbyn. (elder). Mason; mem. Order Eastern Star. Home: 419 Poplar Pl Sallisaw OK 74955

CHUN, MELVIN ERNEST, elec. engr.; b. Houston, July 18, 1911; s. William A. and Eva (Gammon) C.; B.S. in Elec. Engring., Rice Inst., 1933, E.E. (M.S.), 1934. Engr., Gen. Electric Co., Bridgeport, Conn., 1934-36; elec. engr. Lane-Wells Co., Los Angeles, 1936-42, U. Cal., Div. War Research, San Diego, 1942-46, U. Cal. Radiation Lab., Berkeley, 1946-52; head elec. engring. dept. S.W. Research Inst., San Antonio, 1952-54; engr. tech. oilfield services Halliburton Oil Well Cementing Co., Houston, 1954-58; head tech. information services Tex. Instruments, Inc., Dallas, 1958-62, mem. tech. staff, 1962-66; adminstrv. asst. engring. dept. Geo Space Corp., Houston, 1966-67; tech. staff space sci. dept. Rice U., Houston, 1967—. Registered elec. engr., Cal., Tex. Sr. mem. I.E.E.E.; mem. Acoustical Soc. Am. Home: 1907 Albans Rd Houston TX 77005

CHURCH, ARCHER EDWARD, JR., naval officer; b. Bradford, Pa., Apr. 23, 1929; s. Archer Edward and Berta Marie (Unger) C.; B.S., U.S. Naval Acad., 1951; B.Civil Engring., Rensselaer Poly. Inst., 1955; M.S., Princeton, 1962; m. Marie Lucy Ciampitti, June 27, 1970. Commd. ensign U.S. Navy, Civil Engr. Corps, 1951, advanced through grades to comdr., 1965; asst. dir. engring. Navy facilities, Southeastern U.S., 1962-63; asst. pub. works officer Pensacola Naval Air Sta., 1963-65; constrn. program mgr. mil. assistance, Vietnam, 1965-66; asst. dist. civil engr., 4th Naval Dist., 1966-67; chief civil engr. U.S. facilities, Antarctica, 1967-70; spl. asst. for contracts Naval Ship Systems Command Hdqrs., Washington, 1970—. Decorated Bronze Star medal, Air medal. Registered profl. engr., Ala. Mem. Am. Soc. C.E., Soc. Am. Mil. Engrs., Tau Beta Pi, Chi Epsilon. Episcopalian. Author: (with G. Breese et al) The Impact of Large Installations on Nearby Areas, 1965. Home: 332 M St S W Washington DC 20024 Office: NAVSHIPSYSCOM HQ Code 70C Washington DC 20360

CHURCH, JOHN TRAMMELL, chain store exec.; b. Raleigh, N.C., Sept. 22, 1917; s. Charles Randolph and Lela (Johnson) C.; student Catawba Coll., 1936-38 B.S., U. N,C., 1942; m. Emma Thomas Rose, Dec. 31, 1943; children—John Trammell, Elizabeth Howard. With Rose's Stores, Inc., Henderson, N.C., 1945—, successively trainee, asst. buyer, 1945-48, asst. sec., dir., 1948—, buyer, 1949-57, v.p., sec., 1954-61, mdse. mgr., 1957-61, now sr. v.p., sec.; mem. exec. com., dir. Paul H. Rose Corp., Norfolk, Va.; dir. Peoples Bank & Trust Co., Henderson, also Rocky Mount, N.C. Mem. exec. bd., past pres. Occoneechee Council, Boy Scouts Am., 1955-69; past chmn. Kerr Lake Devel. Reservoir Commn., 1967. Mem. Tax Study Commn. N.C., State Art Mus. Bldg. Commn.; mem. dist. Morehead Scholarship Selection Com. City councilman, Henderson, N.C., 1965-66; chmn. N.C. Democratic Exec. Com.; mem. N.C. Ho. of Reps., 1967-69, N.C. Senate, 1971—. Past trustee Boys Home of N.C., Lake Waccamaw; trustee Vance County Tech. Inst., Peace Coll., U. N.C.; sec. bd. trustees Maria Parham Hosp., Henderson, N.C.; vice chmn. bd. trustees Louisburg Coll., N.C.; past mem. adv. bd. Salvation Army; bd. dirs. U. N.C. Bus. Found., Chapel Hill; trustee U. N.C., also mem. legislative services commn., chmn. utilities study commn., mem. exec. residence bldg. commn.; mem. exec. com. N.C. Citizens Assn. Served to capt. USMRCR, 1942-45. Decorated Air medal (10), D.F.C. (3); recipient Silver Beaver award Boy Scouts Am. Mem. N.C. Mchts. Assn. (past pres.), Am. Retail Fedn. (v.p. 1965—), C. of C., Am. Legion, 40 and 8, Newcomen Soc. N.C. Methodist (trustee). Mason (Shriner). Clubs: Elks, Rotary (past pres.), Henderson Henderson Country (past pres.). Home: 420 Woodland Rd Henderson NC 27536

CHURCH, RANDOLPH W., state ofcl. Librarian, State of Va., Richmond. Office: Va State Library Capitol St Richmond VA 23219*

CHURCH, ROBERTA, govt. ofcl.; d.; Robert R. and Sara (Johnson) Church; A.B., Northwestern U., 1935, M.A., 1937 Social worker Family and Child Welfare div. Chgo. Welfare Adminstrn., 1940-43, adoption div. Ill. Children's Home and Aid Soc., Chgo., 1943-53; cons. for minority groups U.S. Dept. Labor, 1953-61; cons. Rehab. Services Adminstrn., U.S. Dept. Health, Edn. and Welfare, 1961—. Mem. Pres.'s Nat. Adv. Council on Adult Edn., 1970—; mem. Rep. State Exec. Com. Tenn., 1952-53. Recipient Certificate of Merit, Alpha Phi Alpha, 1956. Mem. Nat. Assn. Social Workers, Delta Sigma Theta. Republican. Episcopalian. Home: 1629 Columbia Rd NW Washington DC 20009 Office: US Dept Health Edn and Welfare Washington DC 20201

CHURCHILL, DARRELL OLIVER, oil co. exec.; b. Pipestone, Minn., Jan. 6, 1917; s. Ernest L.M. and Parthenia (Patterson) C.; LL.B. cum laude, U. Omaha, 1938; J.D., U. Neb. at Omaha, 1969; m. Velma Caroline Bell, Nov. 6, 1949; children—John O., James E. Admitted to Neb. bar, 1938, Cal. bar, 1950; stenographer legal and claims dept. Woodmen of World Life Ins. Soc., 1934-37, Interstate Transit Lines, Omaha, 1937-38; sec. to gen. claim agt. Union Pacific R.R. Co., Omaha, 1938-39, sec. to gen. atty., 1939-40, sec. to Western gen. counsel, 1940-41, sec. to pres., 1941-42, 46-49, asst. spl. counsel, 1949-56, gen. atty., Los Angeles, 1956-58, asst. to v.p. oil dept., 1958-61, asst. to chief exec. officer natural resources div., 1961-66, asst. sec., 1965—, gen. mgr. mineral lands and contracts natural resources div., 1966-71; v.p. land and leasing Champlin Petroleum Co., Ft. Worth, 1971—; dir. Uinta Devel. Co.; sec. Calnev Pipe Line Co., 1967-70, 71—, Union Pacific Resources Ltd., Calgary, Alta., Can., 1968—; asst. sec. Union Pacific Resources Corp., 1969—. Exec. asst. to rubber dir. WPB, Washington, 1942-43. Served with AUS, 1943-36; PTO. Mem. Rocky Moutain Oil and Gas Assn. (dir., mem. exec. com. 1971—, vice chmn. pub. lands com. 1969-71, chmn. pub. lands com. 1971—), Western Oil and Gas Assn. (mem. pub. lands com., 1968-70), Am. Ft. Worth, Denver, Los Angeles assns. petroleum landsmen, Cal., Neb. bar assns. Clubs: Ridglea Country Petroleum (Ft. Worth); Hacienda Golf (La Habra, Cal.). Home: 3937 Van Denman Dr Fort Worth TX 76116 Office: 5301 Camp Bowie Blvd Fort Worth TX 76107

CICIO, ANTHONY LEE, lawyer; b. Birmingham, Ala., July 8, 1926; s. Joseph and Rosa Tom (Burello) C.; B.S., Samford U., 1951; student U. Ala., 1952; LL.B., Birmingham Sch. Law, 1955; m. Yvonne Antonio, Nov. 4, 1959; children—Valerie, Anthony Lee, Mark. Admitted to Ala. bar, 1956; individual practice law, Birmingham, 1959—; partner firm Cicio & Winston. Mem. Democratic Com., Birmingham, 1960—. Served with USAAF, 1944-46. Mem. Birmingham, Ala., Am. bar assns., Am. Trial Lawyers Assn., Pi Kappa Alpha, Sigma Delta Kappa. Roman Catholic. Clubs: Roma Country, The Club (Birmingham). Home: 3128 N Woodridge Rd Birmingham AL 35223 Office: 1316 2121 Bldg Birmingham AL 35203

CIMIJOTTI, LEW F., architect; b. Mason City, Ia., May 18, 1931; s. Leo M. and Mary E. (Pedelty) C.; A.A., Mason City Jr. Coll., 1951; B.S., Ia. State U., 1958; m. Patricia J. Kennedy, Sept. 17, 1956; children—Mark Trenton, Bruce Trenton, Laura Denise (dec.). Practice architecture, Chgo., 1960-65, Fairborn, O., 1965-68; with Dept. Housing and Urban Devel., 1968—. Prodn. mgr. Space Jour. mag., Huntsville, Ala., 1958. Served with AUS, 1956-58. Recipient Lincoln Arc Welding Found. award, 1958. Mem. Ill. Soc. Architects, Am. Registered Architects, A.I.A., Toastmasters Internat. Home: 963 Parkridge Circle W Jacksonville FL 32211

CIRE, GEOEGE E., dist. judge; b., 1922; B.S., St. Edwards U., 1948; LL.B., U. Tex. Dist. judge Harris County, Tex. Office: Civil Courts Bldg Houston TX 77002*

CIRLOT, FELIX WILLIAM, city ofcl.; b. Moss Point, Miss., Sept. 17, 1903; s. Joseph Mitchell and Madora (Smith) C.; student pub. schs., Moss Point. With L.N. Dantzler Lumber Co., Inc., Moss Point, 1919-38, asst. auditor, 1934-38; project auditor C.E., Keesler Field Air Force Tech. Sch., Biloxi, Miss., 1941-42; mcht. Exclusive Women's Wear, Moss Point, 1955-70; mayor City of Moss Point, 1947-50, city clk., 1965—; practice pub. accounting, Moss Point and Pascagoula, Miss., 1938-40, 51-55. Pres., Griffin Cemetery Assn., 1947-55, sec.-treas., 1957—, trustee, 1969—; charter mem. Moss Point Philharmonic Soc., 1922—; active Little Theatre Coop. Concerts. Del. to city, county, state and nat. Democratic convs., 1952. Trustee Moss Point Civic League. Mem. Pascagoula-Moss Point C. of C. (pres. 1949-50), V.F.W. (post comdr. 1966-67). Methodist (ch. sch. supt. steward 1934-40). Elk. Mailing Address: PO Box 504 Moss Point MS 39563

CLACCIO, PHILIP C., city ofcl. Dist. councilman, New Orleans. Office: 7341 Spring Lake New Orleans LA 70126*

CLAGETT, BRICE MCADOO, lawyer; b. Washington, July 6, 1933; s. Brice and Sarah Fleming (McAdoo) C.; A.B. summa cum laude, Princeton, 1954; postgrad. (Rotary Internat. fellow), U. Allahabad, India, 1954-55; J.D. magna cum laude, Harvard, 1958; m. Virginia Lawrence Parker, Sept. 18, 1965; children—John Fitzhugh de Treville, Ann Calvert Brooke. Research asst. in history Princeton, 1952-53; tutor in history St. Albans Sch., 1956, 57, freshmen advisers and teaching fellow, 1957-58; admitted to D.C. bar, 1958; asso. firm Covington & Burling, Washington, 1958-67, partner, 1967—. Juridical counsellor Cambodian delegation to Internat. Ct. of Justice, 1960-62. Trustee Md. Hist. Trust. Decorated comdr. Royal Order of Cambodia; recipient Bishop Satterlee medal, 1950, Lawrence Hutton prize in history, 1954. Mem. Internat. Law Assn., Washington Inst. Fgn. Affairs, Am. Soc. Internat. Law, Sons Confederate Vets., Bar Assn. D.C., Soc. Cincinnati Md., Am. Bar Assn., Phi Beta Kappa. Episcopalian. Clubs: Princeton, Metropolitan (Washington); Harvard (N.Y.). Bd. editors Harvard Law Rev., 1956-58; contbr. articles to legal and hist. jours. Home: Holly Hill Friendship MD 20758 Office: 888 16th St NW Washington DC 20006

CLAGETT, CHARLES THOMAS, JR., coal co. exec.; b. Washington, Nov. 19, 1914; s. Charles Thomas and Mary Elizabeth (Lutz) C.; B.A., St. Johns Coll., 1939; m. Nancy Leiter, Feb. 22, 1941; children—Juliette Nancy (Mrs. Leslie McLennan), Charles Thomas III. With Chesapeake & Potomac Telephone Co., Washington, 1939-41; with Airways Engring. Consultants, Washington, 1945-47; sec.-treas. Laurel Harness Racing Assn., Laurel, Md., 1947-50; exec. v.p., chmn. exec. com. Zeigler Coal & Coke Co., Chgo., 1947—; dir. Bituminous Coal Research Corp.; adv. bd. brs. Riggs Nat. Bank; exec. com. adv. bd. Park Rd., Dupont Circle, Northwest Universal brs. Riggs Bank. Chmn., D.C. Republican Dinner Com., 1969. Mem. long-range planning com., chmn. bldg. and grounds com., trustee Wash. Hosp. Center; bd. dirs. Internat. Eye Found. Mem. S.A.R., Soc. Cin., Navy League, Nat. Rifle Assn., Def. Orientation Conv. Assn. Episcopalian (vestryman, mem. dept. finance Washington Diocese 1967-71). Mason (32 1/2 deg.). Clubs: Newport Country, Newport Reading Room; Seawanhaka Corinthian Yacht (L.I.); Metropolitan, Chevy Chase, Burning Tree (Washington). Home: 2700 Virginia Av NW Washington DC 20037 Office: Ring Bldg Washington DC 20036

CLAIBORNE, JACK, editor. City editor Charlotte (N.C.) Observer. Office: 600 S Tyron St Charlotte NC 28201*

CLAIBORNE, RANDOLPH ROYALL, JR., ret. bishop; b. Farmville, Va., Nov. 7, 1906; s. Randolph Royall and Mary Thomas (Clark) C.; B.A., U. Va., 1928; B.D., Va. Theol. Sem., 1931, D.D., 1950; D.D. (hon.), U. of South, 1949; m. Clara Virginia Kinney Stribling, 1955. Ordained to ministry P.E. Ch., 1931, rector St. James Ch., Macon, Ga., 1931-38; also priest-in-charge St. Andrews Ch., Fort Valley, Ga.; rector Ch. of Nativity, Huntsville, Ala., 1938-49; consecrated suffragan bishop P.E. Ch. Diocese Ala., 1949-53; bishop P.E. Ch. Diocese of Atlanta, 1953-72. Home: 2324 Waterton Ct Dunwoody GA 30338

CLAIN-STEFANELLI, VLADIMIR, museum curator; b. Czernowitz, Austria, Jan. 2, 1914; s. Wilhelm Klein and Theodora Stefanelli; M.A., U. Carol II, 1936, Ph.D., 1938; m. Elvira Eliza Olinescu, Dec. 29, 1938; 1 son, Alexander. Came to U.S., 1951, naturalized, 1956. Librarian, Seminar for South-East European History, 1932-37; asst. Seminar Greek and Roman Epigraphy, in charge coin collections Carol II U., Cernauti-Czernowitz, 1936-38; asst. in temporary charge excavations at Mangalia, 1936-37; museum asst. Museul Regele Carol II, 1937-38; charge Greek Coin Corpus, Prussian Acad. Scis., 1939; cons. coins and medals, firms in Rome and N.Y.C., 1949-56; curator div. numismatics U.S. Nat. Mus., Smithsonian Instn., 1956—. Adviser on status gold coins Dept. Treasury. Recipient Prix de Rome, 1939-40. Fellow Am. Numis. Soc., Royal Numis. Soc. (London); mem. Am. Numis. Assn. (hon. life mem., curator), Internat. Bank Note Soc., Washington, Md., N.Y., Ga. numis. socs., Archeol. Inst. Am. (gov., past pres. Washington), Internat. Inst. Conservation Historic and Artistic Works, Bavarian, Austrian, French numis. socs. Author: History of the National Numismatic Collections, 1968. Contbr. papers on numismatics to tech. lit. Home: 2608 N Nelson St Arlington VA 22207 Office: Smithsonian Institution Washington DC 20560

CLAIRE, WILLIAM FRANCIS, editor; b. Northampton, Mass., Oct. 4, 1935; s. William Cahill and Vena Marie (Lasonde) C.; B.A., Columbia, 1958. Legislative asst. U.S. Rep. Silvio O. Conte, 1961-63; dir. govt. relations Am. Paper Inst., 1963-68; exec. dir. World Federalists U.S.A., 1968-71; dir. Washington office State U. N.Y., 1971—; editor, pub. Voyages, 1967—. Trustee, Internat. Devel. Corp., 1968-69; exec. bd. Coalition on Nat. Priorities, 1968-69. Chmn. Columbia Students for Stevenson, 1956; state coordinator Humphrey-Muskie U.S. presdl. campaign, 1968. Served with AUS, 1958-59. Recipient Ernie Pyle award Pacific Stars and Stripes, 1959; Editors award Nat. Found. Arts and Humanities, 1970. Mem. Friends of Kennedy Center, Friends of Folger Library. Clubs: National Press, International (Washington). Contbr. articles, poems, essays and revs. tech. lit. Home: 2710 Macomb St NW Washington DC 20008 Office: State Univ New York Island Av NW Washington DC 20036

CLANCY, THOMAS HANLEY, clergyman, educator; b. Helena, Ark., Aug. 8, 1923; s. Thomas Hornor and Ruth (Lewis) C.; A.B., Spring Hill Coll., 1949; M.A., Fordham U., 1950, S.T.L., Facultes S.J. Louvain, Belgium, 1956; Ph.D., U. London, 1960. Ordained priest, Roman Catholic Ch., 1955; instr. Spring Hill Coll., 1950-52; instr. Loyola U. of New Orleans, 1960-64, asst. prof., 1964-66, asso. prof., 1966—, chmn. dept. history, polit. sci., 1966-68, v.p. acad. affairs, 1968-70; asso. editor America mag., 1970-71; provincial superior New Orleans province Soc. Jesus, 1971—. Bd. dirs. Urban League of Greater New Orlenas, 1964-65, Loyola U., 1968—, Inst. Politics, 1969—. Mem. Nat. Student Assn. (faculty adv. to So. project 1961-65), Am., So. polit. sci. assns., Hist. Soc. London, Catholic Record Soc. Democrat. Author: Papist Pamphleteers, 1964. Contbr. articles in field to hist. jours., New Catholic Encyclopedia. Home: 6301 Stratford Pl New Orleans LA 70114

CLAPP, ALLEN LINVILLE, utilities engr.; b. Raleigh, N.C., Oct. 8, 1943; s. Byron Siler and Alene (Linville) C.; B.S., N.C. State U., 1967; m. Anne Stuart Calvert, Dec. 18, 1966. Asst. engr. Booth-Jones & Assos. Inc., Raleigh, N.C., 1964-67; elec. engr., asst. research U.S. Army, Picatinny Arsenal, Dover, N.J., 1967-69; cons. engr. Booth-Jones & Assos., Raleigh, 1969-71; utilities engr. N.C. Utilities Commn., Raleigh, 1971—; pvt. cons. practice, Raleigh, 1971—. Served with AUS, 1967-69. Registered profl. engr., N.J., N.C. Mem. Nat. Soc. Profl. Engrs., Profl. Engrs. N.C., Constrn. Specifications Inst. Home: 1321 Hathaway Rd Raleigh NC 27608 Office: Box 991 Raleigh NC 27602

CLAPP, VANCE CURTIS, educator; b. Hitchita, Okla., Jan. 13, 1915; s. Horace William and Pearl (Boyd) C.; B.A., U. Denver, 1950, M.A., 1951, Ed.D., 1953; postgrad. U. Cal. at Berkeley, 1958, Ind. U. (Ford Found. fellow), 1963, U. So. Cal., 1964; m. Bertha May Germany, Dec. 24, 1938. Accountant, Baker, Hanna & Blake Co., Oklahoma City, 1937-41, Swift & Co., 1941-42; examiner-insp. Santa Barbara Def.-Rental Area, Santa Barbara and Ventura, Cal., 1946-48; tchr., counselor, Central High Sch., Pueblo, Colo., 1953-55; prof. bus., Ore. State Coll., Corvallis, 1955-59, Wayland Coll., Plainsview, Tex., 1959—. Cons. in human relations and personal adjustment, 1955—; pres. Colo Distributing Co., Denver, 1953-55; pres. High Plains Products, Plainview, Tex., 1959-67. Served with USNR, 1942-46. Mem. Am. Accounting Assn., Assn. to Advance Ethical Hypnosis, Am. Personnel and Guidance Assn., Phi Beta Lambda, Beta Alpha Psi. Baptist. Lion. Research in causes and treatment alcoholism, 1959—. Home: 711 Portland St Plainview TX 79072

CLAPPER, THOMAS WAYNE, chem. co. exec.; b. Middleboro, Pa., Oct. 15, 1915; s. Thomas H. and Magdalene Ann (Sterrett) C.; student Gannon Coll., 1933-35; B.S., St. Vincent Coll., 1937; M.S., Pa. State U., 1940, Ph.D., 1942; m. Anne M. Anderson, Aug. 2, 1941; children—Thomas H., Robert A., Andrea M. Research chemist Calco Chem. div. Am. Cyanamid Corp., Bound Brook, N.J., 1940-44, asst. chief chemist pharm. div., 1944-45, chief chemist, 1945-48, prodn. mgr., 1948-50, prodn. mgr., 1950-51, tech. dir. Atomic Energy div., Idaho Falls, Ida., 1951-52, gen. supt., 1952-53, asst. gen. mgr., 1953-54; plant mgr. Calera Mining Co., Chem. Constrn. Corp., cobalt refinery, Garfield, Utah, 1954-56; mgr. research Am. Potash and Chem. Corp., Henderson, Neb., 1956-63, dir. research, Whittier, Cal., 1963-68; dir. research Kerr-McGee Corp., Oklahoma City, 1968—. Mem. Am. Chem. Soc., Indsl. Research Inst., Electrochem. Soc., Sigma Xi, Alpha Chi Sigma. Elk. Patentee in field. Contbr. articles to profl. pubs. Home: 12104 Camelot Place Oklahoma City OK 73120 Office: Kerr McGee Technical Center PO Box 25861 Oklahoma City OK 73125

CLARE, MICHAEL JAMES, lawyer; b. Louisville, Dec. 22, 1920; s. James John and Hannah (Guider) C.; student Morehead State Coll., 1946; LL.B., U. Ky., 1950; m. Mary Helen French, June 13, 1953 (dec. Jan. 1968); children—Michael, Mary Helen, Teresa Lynn, James Gregory, Cynthia Anne, Brian Edward, Stephen Thomas. Admitted to Ky. bar, 1950; trial atty., office chief counsel Internal Revenue Service, U.S. Treasury Dept., Cin., Cleve., 1951-54; practiced in Louisville, 1954—; instr. bus. law Bellarmine Coll., 1955-59. Mem. Jefferson County (Ky.) Registration and Purgation Bd., 1956-60, chmn., 1961-69. Served with AUS, 1943-46. Decorated Bronze Star medal with oak leaf cluster. Mem. Am., Fed. (pres. Louisville 1961-62), Ky., Louisville bar assns., Am. Legion, Phi Alpha Delta. Roman Catholic. Lion, K.C. Home: 33 Hill Rd Louisville KY 40204 Office: Ky Home Life Bldg Louisville KY 40202

CLARK, ALBERT EDWIN, newspaperman; b. Chatham County, N.C., May 12, 1915; s. Walter B. and Mary Hughes (Burns) C.; student Campbell Coll., Buie's Creek, N.C., 1935-37, U. N.C., 1939-40; m. Naomi Ruth Rouse, Aug. 22, 1942; children—Albert E., George B., Carolyn (dec.). Reporter, Daily News, Greensboro, N.C., 1940-45. The Evening Sun, 1945; reporter Wall Street Jour., Washington bur. chief, 1953-60; exec. asst. U.S. News and Report, 1960-66, adminstrv. editor, 1966—. Mem. pres.'s council advisers Campbell Coll., 1968—. Mem. Sigma Delta Chi. Home: 6535 Copa Ct Falls Church VA 22044 Office: 2300 N St NW Washington DC 20037

CLARK, ALBERT HATCHER, educator; b. Americus, Ga., Feb. 9, 1931; s. George Amos and Maida (Hatcher) C.; B.B.A., U. Ga., 1952, M.B.A., 1956; Ph.D., U. Pa., 1961; m. Edith Lloyd, Sept. 7, 1957; children—Cynthia Anne, Kathryn Jean, Constance Lynn. Instr. econs. Clemson U., S.C., 1956; dir. exams Am. Coll. Life Underwriters, Phila., 1959-61; prof. finance Ga. State U., Atlanta, 1961—. Served to 1st lt. USAF, 1952-54, Ford Found. fellow, 1957-59; S.S. Huebner Found. fellow, 1959. Home: 2822 Foster Ridge Dr NE Atlanta GA 30345 Office: 33 Gilmer St SE Atlanta GA 30303

CLARK, ARTHUR BARNETT, JR., judge; b. Indianola, Miss., Oct. 19, 1920; s. Arthur B. and Ada (Neill) C.; B.A., U. Miss., 1942; postgrad. U. Ala., 1945; LL.B., Harvard, 1948; m. Dollie Hughes, June 16, 1943; 1 son, Arthur Barnett III. Admitted to Miss. bar, 1948; mem. firm Neill, Clark & Townsend, Indianola, 1948-58; judge 4th Circuit Ct. Dist. of Miss., Indianola, 1959—. Bd. dirs. Delta area council Boy Scouts Am. Served to 1st lt., inf., AUS, 1942-45; ETO. Decorated Purple Heart with 2 oak leaf clusters. Mem. Am., Miss., Sunflower County (past pres.) bar assns., Am. Legion, Vets. Fgn. Wars. Democrat. Presbyn. Rotarian (past pres. Indianola). Home: W Augusta St Indianola MS 38751 Office: Courthouse Indianola MS 38751

CLARK, ARTHUR WATTS, life ins. co. exec.; b. Seattle, Nov. 28, 1922; s. Irving Marshall and Nell Snowden (Watts) C.; A.B., U. N.C., 1943; M.A., U. Cal. at Berkeley, 1948; postgrad. U. N.C., 1960; m. Mary Dick Cannon, Nov. 21, 1942; children—Arthur Watts, Claiborne Marshall, Johnston Jewell. With Home Security Life Ins. Co., Durham, N.C., 1948—, dir. planning, 1952-59, v.p., 1959-64, exec. v.p., 1964-67, pres., 1967—, chmn. finance com., 1965—, also dir.; dir., chmn. bd. Home Security Broadcasting Co. Chmn. vis. council dept. geology and geography U. N.C., 1959-60. Chmn. Durham Sch. Study Com., 1959-60; treas., mem. exec. com. Research Triangle Regional Planning Commn., 1959-67; mem. N.C. Health Ins. Adv. Bd., 1966-70. Bd. dirs. N.C. Ins. Ednl. Found. Served to brig. gen. USAF, 1942-46, 50-52. Mem. Nat. Assn. Flight Instrs., Durham C. of C. (v.p. 1968-69). Pres. Assn., Am. Mgmt. Assn., Phi Beta Kappa, Sigma Xi. Presbyn. (elder 1964-69, 72—). Home: 3540 Rugby Rd Durham NC 27707 Office: Box 61 Durham NC 27702

CLARK, BILLY CURTIS, author; b. Catlettsburg, Ky., Dec. 29, 1928; s. Mason E. and Bertha (Hewlett) C.; A.B., U. Ky., 1966; m. Ruth Ann Bocock, July 15, 1956; children—Billy Curtis, Melissa Beth. Lectr. colls., univs., 1958—; tchr. creative writing, writer-in-residence U. Ky., Somerset Community Coll., 1968—. Served in 1st Cavalry, AUS, 1949-52; PTO. Commd. Ky. col., 1959. U.Ky. Writing fellow, 1963-67. Republican. Baptist. Author: (short stories) A Heap of Hills, 1953; (novel) Trail of the Hunter's Horn (selected Collier-McMillan Classics 1963), 1957; (novel) Song of the River (Friends of Am. Writers award as 1 of 3 best books pub. in Southwest 1957), 1957; (novel) Mooneyed Hound, 1958; (novel) River Boy, 1959; (autobiography) A Long Row to Hoe (selected Time Mag. best reading list 1960), 1960; (novel) Useless Dog, 1961; (novel) Goodbye Kate (movie rights sold to Walt Disney 1963), 1964; (novel) The Champion of Sourwood Mountain, 1966; The Illiterate Spider and Other Stories, 1968. Contbr. short stories, poems, articles to nat. mags. Home: Rt 2 Box 281 Somerset KY 42501

CLARK, CHARLES FRANKLIN, supt. schs.; b. Van Lear, Ky., Jan. 1, 1913; s. John Brown and Campbell (Chadwick) C.; B.A., U. Ky., 1938, M.A., 1952; m. Annis Conley, Dec. 29, 1938; children—Jon Darrol, Michael Chadwick. Tchr. English and social studies, 1938-42; prin. Garrett (Ky.) High Sch., 1946-60; supt. Floyd County (Ky.) Schs., 1960—. Ednl. co-chmn. Appalachian Regional Hosp. Assn.; mem. Floyd County Library Bd. Mem. N.E.A., Nat., Ky. assns. schs. adminstrs., Ky. Edn. Assn., Floyd County Tchrs. Assn. Home: Garrett KY 41630 Office: care Supt of Schs Prestonsburg KY 41653

CLARK, CHARLES M(ARVIN), psychologist; b. Johnstown, O., Nov. 25, 1927; s. Floyd Monroe and Josephine (Willard) C.; B.A., U. Akron, 1951, M.A., 1956; Ph.D., Ohio State U., 1960; m. Mary Jane Koury, Nov. 22, 1951; children—Cheryl L., Mark C., Christopher S. Coordinator child study and guidance Pub. Schs., Marion, O., 1955-58; instr., counseling psychologist Ohio State U., Columbus, 1958-60; asst. prof. U. Tex., 1960-65; asso. prof. Cal. State Coll. at Hayward, Cal., 1965-67; dir. psychology and assessment Corpus Christi (Tex.) Ind. Sch. Dist., 1967-72; pvt. practice psychology, 1972—. Cons. prof. U. Corpus Christi, 1970; dir. Inst. Child Devel., 1970. Served with AUS, 1951-52. Diplomate in sch. pscyhology Am. Bd. Profl. Psychology. Mem. Am. Psychol. Assn., Am. Personnel and Guidance Assn., Am. Group Psychotherapy Assn., Am. Ednl. Research Assn., A.A.A.S., Tex. Psychol. Assn. (pres. div. sch. psychology 1970), Phi Delta Theta, Phi Delta Kappa. Episcopalian. Mason. Home: 710 Burkshire Corpus Christi TX 78412 Office: 1202 Third St Corpus Christi TX 78404

CLARK, DENNIS ALLEN, mining engr.; b. Chgo., June 5, 1940; s. Joseph Patrick and Theresa Cathryn (Prester) C.; B.S., U. Mo., 1963. Mine engr. ASARCO, Tucson, 1965-67; cons. engr. Rock Mechanics, Louisville, 1967-70; asst. to v.p. operations USNR Mining & Minerals, Inc., Louisville, 1970—; cons. drilling and blast design. Served to 1st lt. C.E., AUS. Registered profl. engr., Ky. Mem. Am. Soc. Mining Engrs. Home: 1040 Cherokee St Louisville KY 40204 Office: 3825 Bardstown Rd Louisville KY 40218

CLARK, DOUGLAS ALAN, educator; b. Bklyn., Aug. 26, 1917; s. George Harold and Jessie (Weekes) C.; B.S., Wheaton (Ill.) Coll., 1940; M.Div., Eastern Bapt. Theol. Sem. 1943; M.A., U. Ill., 1957; postgrad. Tex. Tech. Coll., 1963-64; m. Ruth Porter Campbell, Sept. 16, 1944; children—Jonathan Alden, Stephen Alan, Stanley Andrew. Ordained to ministry Bapt. Ch., 1943; pastor, Romney, W.Va., 1944-46, Back Bay, Va., 1946-48, Morris, N.Y., 1948-52, Hoopeston, Ill., 1952-56; asst. prof. sociology Wayland Coll., 1958-65; chmn. dept. sociology Okla. Bapt. U., Shawnee, 1966—, Lectr. summers Acadia U., Wolfville, N.S., Can., 1963, Western Carolina U., 1964; vis. prof. U. Sask. (Can.), Saskatoon, summers 1970, 71, exchange lectr. Western Australian Inst. Tech., South Bentley, 1972. Pres., Hale County (Tex.) Social Welfare Assn., 1963; dir. Tex. Social Welfare Assn., 1963, Salvation Army, Plainview, Tex., 1963-65. Mem. Am. Sociol. Assn., Nat. Council Family Relations, Canadian Sociol. and Anthrop. Assn., Am. Assn. U. Profs. Home: 4207 Blaine Rd Shawnee OK 74801

CLARK, EARL MORROW, headmaster; b. Hamlet, N.C., May 5, 1915; s. Robert Page and Roberta (Morrow) C.; student Presbyterian Jr. Coll., 1932-34; B.S., Davidson Coll, 1936; M.A., Columbia U., 1946; m. Edwina Nelson Hussey, July 31, 1945; children—Gaire Lee, Earl M. Tchr. Gulf Coast Mil. Acad., Gulfport Miss., 1936-37, Riverside Mil. Acad., Gainesville, Ga., 1937-42, Adm. Farragut Acad., St. Petersburg, Fla., 1946-48, headmaster, 1948—. Served with AUS, 1942-45. Former mem. Fla. Commn. So. Assn. Colleges and Schs. Office: 5th Av Nat Park St St Petersburg FL 33710

CLARK, EDITH MONTCALM, ret. librarian; b. Salisbury, N.C., Aug. 7, 1910; d. Byron Currie and Edith (Oldham) Clark; A.B. in L.S., U. N.C., 1930; student Catawba Coll., summer 1933. Asst., Charlotte (N.C.) Pub. Library, 1930-31; tchr., librarian Cannon High Sch., Kannapolis, N.C., 1931-32, city schs., Salisbury, 1932-36; dir. Rowan Pub. Library, Salisbury, 1936-72; instr. sch. library sci. Catawba Coll., summer 1936. Past bd. dirs. Salisbury chpt. Nat. Conf. Christians and Jews; sec. Historic Salisbury Found. Mem. Am., N.C. (sec. pub. library sect. 1947), Southeastern library assns., N.C. Symphony Soc. Presbyn. (mem. permanent com. hist. affairs N.C. synod). Home: 120 N Craige St Salisbury NC 28144

CLARK, EDWARD EASTERS, JR., mortgage banker; b. Lampasas, Tex., April 5, 1908; s Edward E. and Mable (Shaw) C.; B.A., Trinity U., 1929; hon. degree So. Meth. U.; m. Mary Belt Clark, Jan. 16, 1932; children—Edward E. III, Mary Ann, William Daniel. S.W. regional investment supr. Kansas City Life Ins. Co., Dallas, 1931—. Trustee Waxahachie Ind. Sch. Dist., 1949-55, pres., 1954-55. Trustee United Presbyn. Homes Children and Aged; exec. com., treas. bd. trustees U.P. Homes, Mem. Mortgage Bankers Assn. Am., Tex. Mortgage Bankers Assn., Tex. Agrl. Workers Assn., C. of C., Tex. Real Estate Assn., Am. Inst. Real Estate Appraisers, Pi Kappa Delta, Phi Gamma Mu. Episcopalian (vestryman), Mason. Clubs: Waxahachie Country, Rotary (dir.). Home: Route 1 Waxahachie TX 75165 Office: 608 N St Paul St Dallas TX 75201

CLARK, EMORY EUGENE, ins. agy. exec.; b. Opelika, Ala., Jan. 24, 1931; s. Bunk Henry and Dorothy (Bolt) C.; grad. pub. schs.; m. Jean F. Reed, Sept. 30, 1951; children—Steven E., Michael E. With Mgrs. Life Ins. Co., 1956—, agt., supr., Los Angeles, 1956-60, mgr. Hawaii br., 1960-65, Pitts. br., 1965-68, Houston br., 1968—. Served with AUS, 1950-56. Mem. Houston Life Underwriters Assn., Houston Gen. Agts. and Mgrs. Assn., Houston C. of C. Home: 11719 Flintwood Dr Houston TX 77024 Office: 2100 Travis St Houston TX 77002

CLARK, EUGENIE, zoologist; b. N.Y.C., May 4, 1922; B.A., Hunter Coll, 1942; M.S., N.Y.U., 1946, Ph.D. (Pacific Sci. Bd. fellow 1949), 1950; m. Roy Umaki, 1942; m. 2d, Ilias Konstantinu, 1949; 4 children; m. 3d, Chandler Brossard, 1967; m. 4th, Igor Klatzo, 1969. Research asst. ichthyology Scripps Instn. Oceanography, 1946-47; with N.Y. Zool. Soc., 1947-48; research animal behavior Am. Mus. Nat. History, N.Y.C., 1948-49, research asso., 1950-54; instr. Hunter Coll., 1954; exec. dir. Cape Haze Marine Lab., Sarasota, Fla., 1955-67; asso. prof. biology College City N.Y., 1966-67; now asso. prof. zoology U. Md.; spl. research reproductive behavior fishes, morphology and taxonomy plectognath fishes, isolating mechanisms poecillid fishes. Fellow AEC, 1950; Fulbright scholar, Egypt, 1951; Saxton fellow, 1952; Breadloaf Writer's fellow; recipient Alumnae award Hunter Coll. Mem. Am. Soc. Icthyology and Herpetology, Soc. Women Geographers. Author: Lady with a Spear, 1953; Lady and the Sharks, 1969. Home: Bethesda MD 20034 also Sarasota FL 33578

CLARK, FLOYD EVERETT, coll. adminstr., clergyman; b. McTaggart, Sask., Can., Apr. 23, 1916; s. Edward Everett and Bonnie (Cave) C., came to U.S., 1937, naturalized, 1953; A.B., Johnson Bible Coll., 1941, D.D., 1968; B.D., Butler Sch. Religion, 1944; m. Lillian A. Frazier, July 2, 1941; 1 dau., Betty Ann. Prof., Greek and New Testament, Johnson Bible Coll., Kimberlin Heights, Tenn., 1944—, dean of men, 1945—, acad. dean, 1962-67, 68—, acting exec. v.p., 1967-68, mem. council of 70, 1972—; ordained to ministry Christian Ch., 1938; student minister Christian chs., Gap Creek, 1938-39, Bernard St., Knoxville, 1940-41 (all Tenn.), Buck Creek Chapel, Indpls., 41-44; minister 1st Christian Ch., Maryville, Tenn., 1944-59, Thorn Grove Christian Ch., Strawberry Plains, Tenn., 1960-63, Meadowbrook Christian Ch., Maryville, 1963-66, Forest Av. Christian Ch., Knoxville, 1966—. Mem. council advisers Internat. Christian U., 1972—. Chmn. French Christian Mission, 1956—; bd. dirs. Christian Mission to S. Korea, 1965—, Sunny Hills Children's Home, Kimberlin Heights, 1962—. Address: Johnson Bible Coll Kimberlin Heights TN 37920

CLARK, FRANKLIN JACOB, JR., architect; b. Anderson, S.C., Dec. 7, 1937; s. Franklin Jacob and Corrie Elizabeth (Watson) C.; B.Arch., Clemson U., 1962; m. Beverly Thornton Bowie, Nov. 19, 1960; 1 son, Franklin Jacob III. Designer A.G. Odell, Jr., & Assos., 1966, Ledbetter & Earle Architects, 1966-67; dir., asso. architect, v.p. Odell Assos., Inc., Charlotte, N.C., 1967—; works include Burlington Corporate Hdqrs. Bldg., Greensboro, N.C., N.C. Blue Cross and Blue Shield Hdqrs. Mem. Mint. Mus. Art. Served to lt., USAF, 1962-66. Registered architect, S.C., N.C., Tenn.; certified Nat. Council Archtl. Registration Bds. Mem. A.I.A., N.C. Soc. Preservation of Antiquities, Charlotte C. of C. Presbyn. (elder). Club: Charlotte City. Home: 1100 Queens Rd Charlotte NC 28207 Office: 102 W Trade St Charlotte NC 28202

CLARK, HARRY MCDONOUGH, ednl. adminstr.; b. Mobile, Ala., Dec. 18, 1937; s. Harry Patrick and Margaret Ellen (McDonough) C.; student Tulane U., 1955-58; B.S., Auburn U., 1960; M.A., U. Ala., 1962; Ed.D., Columbia, 1967; m. Clara Mildred Ball, July 21, 1962; children—Connolly Lightfoot, Erin McDonough. Teaching fellow U. Ala., 1961; instr. art U. So. Miss., 1962-64; asso. fellow ednl. adminstrn. Columbia Tchrs. Coll., 1964-67; asst. prof. ednl. adminstrn. U. So. Ala., 1968-69; asso. prof. ednl. adminstrn. U. S.C., 1969-70; asso. prof. ednl. adminstr. U. So. Miss., Biloxi, 1970—; adminstrv. dir. Coastal Med. Center, Biloxi, 1971—; pres. Mgmt. Approach Planning; sec.-treas. R.W. Bell Cos., Inc. Acting headmaster Gulf Day Sch., Ocean Springs, Miss., 1971-72; compliance insp. VA, 1971—. Bd. dirs. Gulf Day Sch., Ocean Springs. Mem. Council Ednl. Facilities Planners, Am. Assn. U. Profs., Am. Assn. Sch. Adminstrs., Southeastern Sch. Bus. Ofcls., Med. Group Mgmt. Assn., Phi Delta Kappa, Kappa Pi. Republican. Club: St. Andrews Country (Ocean Springs); Broadwater Country (Biloxi). Author: Methods for Computing School Building Capacity, 1967. Home: 306 Lovers Lane Ocean Springs MS 39564 Office: Box 4080 Biloxi MS 39531

CLARK, HOWARD DAVID, physician; b. Richton, Miss., Jan. 22, 1927; s. Leonard M. and Dicie (Culpepper) C.; M.D., Tulane U., 1955. Rotating intern U. Med. Center, Jackson, Miss., 1955-56; gen. practice medicine, Morton, Miss., 1956—; chief staff Scott County Hosp., Morton. Served to 2d lt. AUS, 1944-46. Diplomate Am. Bd. Family Practice. Mem. A.M.A., Am. Assn. Physicians and Surgeons, Am. Assn. Ry. Surgeons. Home: 841 4th St Morton MS 39117 Office: 221 2d St Morton MS 39117

CLARK, JACK CROWLEY, physician; b. Whitleyville, Tenn., Feb. 24, 1936; s. Cordell Hull and Clio Elizabeth (Cassetty) C.; student Vanderbilt U., 1954-57; M.D., U. Tenn., 1961; m. Janet Sue Chailland, June 21, 1959; children—Jack Crowley, Christopher David, Julie Elizabeth. Intern, Nashville Gen. Hosp., 1961-62; gen. practice medicine, Lafayette, Tenn., 1962-71; resident in radiology U. Tenn., 1972—; mem. staff Smith-Chitwood Hosp., Lafayette, 1962-71. Med. dir. Cordell Hull Econ. Opportunity Corp., Lafayette, 1967-71; dir. Citizens Bank, Lafayette, Tenn. Mem. Gov's. Adv. Bd. on Mental Retardation, 1969—. Mem. City Council, Lafayette, 1964-68; mem. Macon County Election Commn., 1968-70. Bd. dirs. Macon County Cancer Soc.; trustee Tenn. Mental Health Dept. Mem. Am. Acad. Gen. practice, So., Tenn. med. assns., Memphis, Shelby County roentgen socs., Phi Chi, Pi Kappa Alpha. Democrat. Methodist. Home: 1349 Hickory Ridge Cove Memphis TN 38116 Office: U Tenn Dept Radiology 865 Jefferson St Memphis TN 38103

CLARK, JAMES ANDREW, JR., pediatrician; b. Ruleville, Miss., Dec. 18, 1911; s. James Andrew and Virginia (Miller) C.; student Sunflower Jr. Coll., 1933; B.S., U. Miss., 1936; M.D., U. Tenn., 1938; m. Margaret Ellen Smith, June 5, 1946 (dec. Feb. 1971); children—James Andrew III, Mary Charlotte, John Arthur, Margaret Ellen. Intern, John Gaston Hosp., Memphis, 1938-40; house physician Good Samaritan Hosp., West Palm Beach, Fla., 1940-41; resident pediatrics U. Tenn., 1953-54; gen. practice medicine, Ruleville, Miss., 1946-52; practice medicine specializing in pediatrics, Memphis, 1955—; mem. staffs LeBonheur Children's, Bapt. Meml., Meth., St. Joseph hosps. Served from 1st lt. to maj. M.C., AUS, 1941-46. Mem. Am. Legion, V.F.W., D.A.V., Disabled Officers Assn., Ret. Officers Assn., Mil. Order World Wars. Home: 4149 Poplar Av Memphis TN 38117 Office: 4515 Poplar Av Memphis TN 38117

CLARK, JAMES ANTHONY, author, petroleum historian and biographer; b. Abita Springs, La., Sept. 7, 1907; s. Edward Arlie and Laura (Page) C.; student Lamar Tech. Coll., 1928; m. Estelle Walton, Apr. 8, 1934. Partner James A. Clark Co., 1953-63, pres., 1963—; pres. Clark Book Co. Trustee Houston Mus. Natural Sci.; founding mem., pres., dir. Energy Research and Edn. Found.; columnist Energy News. Served with AUS, 1941-46; PTO. Decorated Bronze Star Medal. Mem. Houston Horse Show Assn. (v.p.), Authors Guild. Roman Catholic. Clubs: Nat. Press, Headliners, Press of Houston. Author: (with Michel T. Halbouty) Spindletop, 1952; (with Weldon Hart) The Tactful Texan, 1958; Three Stars for the Colonel, 1954; The Chronological History of the Petroleum and Natural Gas Industries, 1963; (with Nathan Broch) A Biography of Robert Alonzo Welch, 1963; Founders of Oil Industry, 1967; A Geography of Oil, 1959; Marrs McLean, A Biography, 1969; (with Michel T. Halbouty) The Last Boom, 1972; An Oilman's Oilman, 1972. Home: 2171 University Blvd Houston TX 77025 Office: Houston Club Bldg Houston TX 77002

CLARK, JOE RICHARD, oil co. exec.; b. Burleson, Tex., Feb. 26, 1927; s. Hugh Milton and Mary (Baker) C.; B.M.E., Tex. A. and M. U., 1948; m. Betty Nan White, Aug. 21, 1948; children—James Rod, Carolyn Louise, Joseph Breen. Dist. reservoir engr. Stanolind Oil & Gas Co., Lubbock, Tex., 1948-55; div. reservoir engr. TXL Oil Corp., Midland, Tex., 1955-62; div. sec. reservoir engr. Texaco Inc., Midland, 1962-63; ind. cons. engr. Midland, 1963-64; v.p. prodn. Tex. Pacific Oil Co., Dallas, 1964—. Served to 1st lt. AUS, 1951-53. Mem. Am. Petroleum Inst., Am. Inst. Mining and Metal. Engrs., Tex.-Mid Continent Oil and Gas Assn., N.M. Oil and Gas Assn., Nat., Tex. socs. profl. engrs. Mason. Club: Dallas Petroleum. Home: 3605 Colgate St Dallas TX 75225 Office: 1700 One Main Pl Dallas TX 75250

CLARK, JOHN CONRAD, internat. banker; b. N.Y.C., Feb. 19, 1913; s. John C. and Marie (Sparnect) C.; student N.Y.U., 1930-33; m. Lillian Fischer, Dec. 17, 1949; 1 son, Roger Scott. Municipal bond trader Shields & Co., N.Y.C., 1935-40; pres. John C. Clark & Co., Inc., N.Y.C., 1946-47; asst. mgr. bond dept. Chase Manhattan Bank, N.Y.C., 1947-51; mgr. pub. finance, sr. v.p., mgr. bond dept. Wachovia Bank & Trust Co., Winston-Salem, N.C., 1952-69; bd. dirs. Export-Import Bank of U.S., Washington, 1969—. Vice chmn. bd. N.C. Municipal Council, 1961-67; sec. N.C. Securities Adv. Com. to Banks in N.C., 1962—. Served to lt. col. AUS, 1941-46; ETO. Recipient certificate of award, comptroller of currency, 1963. Mem. Investment Bankers Assn. Am. Contbg. author: The Bankers Handbook. 1966. Home: 4141 River St Arlington VA 22207 Office: Export-Import Bank of US 811 Vermont Av NW Washington DC 20571

CLARK, JOHN MARTIN, JR., research engr.; b. San Antonio, Oct. 5, 1916; s. John Martin and Dorothy (Hilgers) C.; B.S. in Mech. Engring., Rice Inst.; Tech., 1940, M.S., Mass. Inst. Tech., 1941; m. Mary Frances Dittmar, Aug. 23, 1941; children—Anne, Marsha (Mrs. Ed Page), John Martin III. Powerplant designer, test engr. Douglas Aircraft, Santa Monica, Cal., 1941-47; pres. John Clark Industries, San Marcos, Tex., 1947-55; sr. research engr. Southwest Research Inst., San Antonio, 1955-58, dir. dept. automotive research, 1958—. Mem. Soc. Automotive Engrs., Am. Soc. M.E., Sci. Research Soc. Am. Republican. Episcopalian. Contbr. articles to profl. jours. Patentee in field. Home: 707 Lake Placid Dr Sequin TX 78155 Office: 8500 Culebra Rd San Antonio TX 78206

CLARK, JOHN RAY, state legislator; b. Hancock, Md., June 9, 1924; s. John N. and Della M. (Alderton) C.; A.B., Transylvania Coll., 1947; M.A., U. Ky., 1949; m. Geneva Rolfe, Nov., 18, 1962; children—John (dec.), Douglas, Robert, James, Sandra, Edward, Randall. Formerly tchr., mem. Fla. Ho. of Reps. 1966—. Bd. dirs. Polk County (Fla.) Juvenile Home. Served with AUS, 1940-45. Mem. Am. Legion, Pi Kappa Alpha. Democrat. Elk, Moose. Home: 515 Queens Loop Lakeland FL 33803 Office: 417 Arcade Bldg Lakeland FL 33801

CLARK, JOHN RUSSELL, airplane mfg. co. exec.; b. Rockport, Mass., Sept. 21, 1908; s. John Franklin and Florence (Ellis) C.; B.S. in Aero. Engring., Mass. Inst. Tech., 1929; m. Dorothy Virginia Auger, July 30, 1930; children—John Russell, Mary A. (Mrs. Richard Ryder, Jr.), Dorothy A. (Mrs. Allan E. Kemp). Aircraft design engr. N.Am. Aviation Co., 1933-35; chief project engr. Sikorsky VS-300 helicopter United Aircraft Corp., 1935-40, Corsair fighter airplane, chief design Chance Vought div. of corp., 1940-45, transonic aircraft XF7U-1, XF-6U-1 of div., 1946-48, asst. chief engr. aircraft and missiles, exptl. mfg. and flight test of div., 1949-52; asst. chief engr., chief designer supersonic Crusader airplane Chance Vought Corp., 1952-57, chief engr. aircraft, 1957-58, dir. engring. aircraft and missiles, 1958-60, gen. mgr. astronautics div. producing Scout space vehicle, also v.p. corp., 1961-64; gen. mgr. Vought aero. div., also corporate v.p. LTV Aerospace Corp., 1964—, sr. v.p., tech., 1969—. Chmn. Mass. Inst. Tech. Ednl. Council, Dallas, 1956-67, hon. sec. inst., 1958—. Mem. subcom. high speed aerodynamics NACA, 1954-58; mem. USAF Sci. Adv. Bd., 1967—. Fellow Am. Inst. Aero. and Astronautics (guided missile council 1961—); mem. Am. Astronautical Soc., Am. Rocket Soc., Soc. Automotive Engrs. (tech. bd.), U.S. Air Force Assn., U.S. Army Assn., Navy League (life). Clubs: Mass. Inst. Tech. (pres. 1958-66) Royal Oaks Country (Dallas); Mass. Inst. Tech. (N.Y.C.). Home: 6615 Norway Rd Dallas TX 75230 Office: PO Box 5003 Dallas TX 75222

CLARK, LAMAR SHAFFER, clergyman; b. Durant, Okla., Dec. 19, 1911; s. Alexander Marion and Donna Marie (Hilton) C.; student Lon Morris Jr. Coll, 1931-32, B.A., U. Southwestern La., 1934; student Perkins Sch. Theology, So. Meth. U., 1935-37, B.D., 1944; D.D. (hon.) Southwestern U., 1966; m. Lenora Fay Newbern, Apr. 26, 1936; children—Donna Dean (Mrs. Gerge H. Hutcherson), Jan Carolyn (Mrs. George M. Atkinson). Ordained to ministry Methodist Ch., as deacon, 1939, elder, 1941; pastor Meth. chs., Bellville, 1937-41, Pleasant Retreat, Tyler, 1941-42, Frankston, 1945-47, Glenwood Ch., 1947-50, St. John's Ch., Richmond, 1950-56, 1st Ch., Jasper, 1956-61, 1st Ch., Texarkana, 1961-64 (all Tex.); exec. sec. Tex. Annual Conf. United Meth. Ch., 1964-70; pastor Grace United Meth. Ch., Baytown, 1970-72, First United Meth. Ch., La Marque, 1972—. Chmn. United Meth. Communications Council of Tex., 1968-70; del. World Meth. Conf., London, 1966, Denver, 1971; mem. World Meth. Council, 1971—; trustee, sec. bd. trustees Mt. Sequoyah United Meth. Assembly, Fayetteville, Ark.; chmn. bd. trustees Tex. Ann. Conf. United Meth. Ch., 6 years, vice chmn. bd. edn., 8 years. Trustee Lydia Patterson Inst., El Paso, Tex., San Jacinto Meth. Hosp., Baytown, Tex., Happy Harbor Home for Older People, La Porte, Tex. Served as chaplain AUS, 1942-46. Decorated Bronze Star, Purple Heart. Mason (32 deg.). Rotarian (pres. Jasper 1958). Home: 10 Perthius Dr La Marque TX 77568 Office: First United Meth Ch Scott and Howell Sts La Marque TX 77568

CLARK, MRS. MEREDITH PLIER, mem. Republican Nat. Com.; b. Oconto Falls, Wis., Jan. 14, 1927; d. Arnold W. and Herasa (Boyce) Plier; B.A. in Psychology, Lawrence U., 1948; postgrad. N.Y. Sch. Social Work, 1949; m. Philip Cannady Clark, June 24, 1950; children—James William, Meriweather Kaye. Head stock dept. Saks Fifth Av., N.Y.C., 1948-49; psychiat. social worker Bklyn. State Hosp., 1949-50; clk. U.S. Govt., 1951-53; clk.-typist V.I. Telephone Co., St. Croix, 1956, V.I. law firm, 1956-57. Treas. St. Croix br. Rep. Party V.I., 1963-65; mem. Rep. Territorial Com. V.I., 1964—, sec., 1964-68; charter mem. V.I. League Women Voters, 1969; mem. task force V.I. Comprehensive Health Planning Council, 1969, V.I. Inauguration Com. for Pres. Nixon, 1969; V.I. publicity chmn. 17th Ann. Rep. Women's Conf., 1969; mem. Rep. Nat. Com. for V.I., 1968—; adviser inaugural com. 1st elected Gov. V.I., 1971. Mem. Nat. Fedn. Bus. and Profl. Women's Club, St. Croix Arts Council, St. Croix Diving Assn., Kappa Delta (pres. Lawrence U. chpt. 1946-47). Methodist. Clubs: St. Croix Tennis; Capitol Hill. Home: Estate the Sight P O Box 788 Christiansted St Croix VI 00820

CLARK, MILDRED N., securities co. exec.; m. Joel H. Clark, 1954 (dec. Feb. 1968). Stockbroker Clark & Clark Securities, Inc., Dallas, 1953-67, pres., 1967-70, v.p., 1970—; mem. Midwest Stock Exchange, 1968. Office: 1010 Fidelity Union Tower Dallas TX 75201

CLARK, ROBERT EARL, JR., assn. exec.; b. Louisville, Miss., Mar. 1, 1934; s. Robert Earl and Charlie Mae (Garriques) C.; student Miss. State U., 1952-54; B.S., U.S. Mil. Acad., 1958; student Rensselear Poly. Inst., 1964; m. Sylvia Duck, July 19, 1958; children—George Robert, Camille. Commd. 2d lt. U.S. Army, advanced through grades to maj., 1970; resigned, 1970; mgr. Clark Ranch, Louisville, 1970—, Louisville-Winston County C. of C., 1970—. Decorated Commendation medal, Bronze Star. Mem. Am. Legion (post comdr.), Louisville Businessmen's Club. Methodist (sec. adminstrv. bd., mem. council ministries). Rotarian (dir. Louisville). Home: Box 373 Louisville MS 39339 Office: Box 551 Louisville MS 39339

CLARK, ROBERT EMMETT, JR., plastic bearing mfg. co. exec.; b. San Fernando, Cal., Mar. 2, 1906; s. Robert Emmett and Alice Leslie (Barnett) C.; student U.S. Naval Acad., 1925-26, U. Cal. at Berkeley, 1932-34, U. Cal. Los Angeles Extension, 1934-37; m. Mary Elizabeth Farmer, July 26, 1947; children—Robert, Alice Katherine (Mrs. David Cyril Johnson), Michael, Colleen (Mrs. Richard Olan Stegall), Thomas, Owen, Mary Ellen, Kevin. Trainee, Gen. Petroleum Corp. div. Mobil Oil Corp., Casper, Wyo., 1937-39; founder, owner Graflube Bearing Co., Long Beach, Cal., 1939-49; v.p. sales Eastman Oilwell Survey Co., Denver, 1949-51; sales and product devel. engr. Master Lubricants Co., Los Angeles, 1953-57; founder, pres., chief exec. officer Lubrication Engring. and Mfg. Co., Inc., Midland, Tex., 1957—. Dir. polit. action com. Big Four A.F.L.-C.I.O., Long Beach, Cal., 1946-49; asst. chmn. indsl. div. United Fund, Houston, 1950-51. Mem. finance com. Democrat party, Los Angeles, 1946-48. Served with USMCR to lt. col., 1942-45. Roman Catholic. K.C., Elk. Patentee oil-less, self-lubricated plastic bearing. Developed spray on dry bearing, plastic pillow block, combination mill and underreamer. Home: 2202 Chisholm Dr Duncan OK 73533 Office: 1011 S Big Spring St Midland TX 79701

CLARK, ROBERT PHILLIPS, newspaper editor; b. Randolph, Vt. Dec. 3, 1921; s. James S. and Gladys M. (Phillips) C.; A.B., Tufts U., 1942; M.A., U. Mo., 1948; Nieman fellow, Harvard, 1960-61; m. Jeanne Orr Rice, Dec. 14, 1949; children—Patricia Orr, Elizabeth Phillips. Reporter, Owensboro (Ky.) Messenger & Inquirer, 1948-49; reporter, sci. writer Courier-Jour., Louisville, 1949-62, Washington corr., 1958; mng. editor Louisville Times, 1962-71; exec. editor Courier-Jour. and Louisville Times, 1971—. Sec. bd. trustees Louisville Presbyn. Theol. Sem. Served to capt. AUS, World War II. Decorated Bronze Star, Purple Heart. Mem. Am. Soc. Newspaper Editors, A.P. Mng. Editors Assn. (dir.), Sigma Delta Chi, Delta Tau Delta, Democrat. Presbyn. Home: 5811 Brittany Valley Rd Louisville KY 40222 Office: 525 W Broadway Louisville KY 40202

CLARK, ROSS BERT, milk marketing exec.; b. Janesville, Wis., June 16, 1907; s. David Bert and Ina (Gibson) C.; student Purdue U., 1927-30, B.S., 1938; m. Pauline Frances Wilkinson, Aug. 16, 1930 (dec.); 1 son, Ross B. II. Milk sanitarian Indpls. Bd. Health, 1938-40, Ind. State Bd. of Health, 1940-43; milk marketing specialist Mid-South Milk Producers Assn., Memphis, 1943-53, mgr., 1953-69; mgr. Mid-South div. Milk Producers Inc. region Asso. Milk Producers, Inc., 1969—; dir. Memphis Dairy Council, 1953—, pres. bd. 1962-64, 68-69; bd. dirs. Nat. Dairy Council, Chgo., 1967-70; exec. bd. Asso. Dairymen, Kansas City, Mo., 1965-69. Mem. Nat. Milk Producers Fedn. (dir. 1968—), Am. Dairy Sci. Assn.; Phi Gamma Delta. Episcopalian. Clubs: Summit, University, Rotary. Home: 198 Windover Rd Memphis TN 38111 Office: 1319 Heistan Pl Memphis TN 38104

CLARK, STEPHEN PATRICK, city ofcl.; b. Florence, Kan., Nov. 19, 1923; s. Stephen Peter and Gertrude (Fisher) C.; grad., U. Miami, (Fla.); m. Faye Knowles, June 8, 1947; children—Peter, James, Theresa, John, Cecile, Paul. Vice pres. Clark Constrn. Co., Miami; dir. Airline and Travel Agy. Sch., U.S. Internat., Inc. Mem. bd. commrs. City of Miami, 1967-67; mayor, Miami, 1967—. Mem. Interam. Center Authority; mem. adminstrv. bd. Biscayne Coll. Bd. dirs. Jr. Achievement Greater Miami. Served with USAF. Mem. Am. Legion. Democrat. K.C., Moose, Elk. Home: 3051 NW 4th St Miami FL 33125 Office: 3500 Pan American Dr Miami FL 33133

CLARK, TALMADGE, hosp. adminstr.; b. Sumrall, Miss., July 10, 1912; s. Robert C. and Lula (Davis) C.; certificate Jones Jr. Coll., 1930; m. Vondee Davis, May 30, 1939. Parnter, Hemeter Co., Seminary, Miss., 1936-47, Davis-Clark Supply Co., Sumrall, 1947-60, C & D Milling Co., Sumrall, 1960-64; adminstr. Covington County Hosp., Collins, Miss., 1964-69, Aberdeen-Monroe County Hosp., Aberdeen, Miss., 1969—. Mayor, Town of Sumrall, 1951-64. Served as sgt. AUS, 1943-46. Mem. Am. Acad. Med. Adminstrs., Am. Hosp. Financial Mgmt. Assn., Am., Miss. hosp. assns., V.F.W., Am. Legion, East Miss. Council. Lion (pres. 1950-51). Clubs: Sportsmans (Sumrall); Exchange (Aberdeen). Home: 104 Burnett St Aberdeen MS 39730 Office: PO Box 290 Aberdeen MS 39730

CLARK, THOMAS ALEXANDER, librarian; b. Iuka, Miss., Mar. 12, 1936; s. Ezekiel Candler and Arvis (Fancher) C.; student N.E. Miss. Jr. Coll., 1954-56; B.S., U. So. Miss., 1958; M.L.S., U. Miss., 1966. Librarian, Belmont (Miss.) High Sch., 1958-66, Valdosta (Ga.) State Coll., 1966—. Active Valdosta Lowndes YMCA. Mem. Valdosta Lowndes Mental Health Assn., Ga., Southeastern library assns. Methodist. Mason. Club: Civitan (pres. 1960-61) (Belmont, Miss.). Home: 1709 N Ashley St Valdosta GA 31601

CLARK, TURNER, librarian; b. McKenzie, Tenn., Mar. 9, 1913; s. Walter Clifford and Claudia (Selesnia) C.; B.A., Bethel Coll., 1939; B.S. in L.S., Peabody Library Sch., 1940, postgrad., 1951. Library asst. Bethel Coll., McKenzie, Tenn., 1938-40; library asst. edn. and extension depts. Newark Pub. Library, 1940-42; dir. Shelby Co. Libraries, 1946-60; asst. dir. Memphis Pub. Library, 1960—. Served with M.C., AUS, 1942-45. Mem. A.L.A., Southeastern (exec. bd.), Tenn. (past pres., past treas.) library assns. Methodist. Home: 207 S Barksdale Memphis TN 38104 Office: 258 S McLean Memphis TN 38104

CLARK, VERNON RAY, petroleum engr.; b. McPherson, Kan., May 5, 1932; s. Martin Joel and Laura (Wann) C.; student McPherson Coll., 1955-56; B.S., Kan. State U., 1959; m. Donna Marlene Alexander, May 5, 1955; children—Kyanna Kay, Kevin Ray, Keith Warren, Kayla Ann. Asso. engr. Nortronics Inc., Hawthorne, Cal., 1959-61; design engr. Gen. Dynamics Astronautics, Salina, Kan., 1961-62; sr. engr. Chrysler Space Div., Huntsville, Ala., 1962-65; project engr. Applied Automation, Bartlesville, Okla., 1965—. Served with AUS, 1953-55. Registered profl. engr., Ala. Mem. Bartlesville Bible Ch. (deacon 1970—). Research, devel. latest state-of-the art computerized process control systems. Patentee in field. Home: 3308 Nowata Rd Bartlesville OK 74003 Office: 215 RB2 PRC Pawhuska Rd Bartlesville OK 74003

CLARK, WILLIAM ALBERT, banker; b. Corpus Christi, Tex., Aug. 16, 1939; s. George R. and Juanita (Bright) C.; B.A., Stanford, 1961; M.B.A., Harvard, 1963; m. Margaret Lasater, Nov. 6, 1965; children—Kittie Kampmann, William Albert. Data processing salesman IBM Corp., Corpus Christi, Tex., 1963-64; asst. to pres. Storm Drilling Co., Corpus Christi, 1964-66; v.p. Corpus Christi State Nat. Bank, 1966—; dir. Comanche Life Ins. Co., vice pres., bd. dirs. Bayshore Found.; bd. dirs. S. Tex. Art Found., YMCA. Mem. Corpus Christi Tennis Assn. (dir. 1969-72), Theta Delta Chi. Republican. Presbyn. Home: 3333 Floyd St Corpus Christi TX 78411 Office: 502 N Water St Corpus Christi TX 78403

CLARK, WILLIAM BURTON, chain variety store exec.; b. Blountstown, Fla., Dec. 4, 1917; s. Charles Dennis and Margaret (Messer) C.; student U. Ala., 1937-38, N. Fla. Jr. Coll., 1958-62; m. Eunice Otelia Priest, July 9, 1939; children—Rosemary Otelia (Mrs. William Charles Stiefel), William Burton IV, Margaret Irel (Mrs. John MacDonell Lester), Elizabeth Rosalie (Mrs. Harry Gerald Rotter). Store mgr. Van H. Priest Co., Madison, Fla., 1940-45, mdse. supt.; 1946-65, v.p., dir., 1965—. Mem. exec. com. Boy Scouts Am., 1958-61; mem. Govs. Exec. Com., 1949-52; pres. N. Fla. Jr. Coll. Artist Series, 1966-68. Trustee N. Fla. Jr. Coll. Found.; chmn. bd. trustees Madison Country Hosp.; bd. dirs. So. Scholarships and Research Found. Mem. Delta Kappa Epsilon. Democrat. Baptist (deacon). Mason (Shriner), Rotarian. Home: 204 Lake St Madison FL 32340 Office: 201 Lake Shore Dr Madison FL 32304

CLARK, WILLIAM FLOYD, devel. co. exec.; b. Palestine, Tex., Sept. 18, 1915; s. William S. and Virginia L. (Everett) C.; LL.B., S. Tex. Sch. Law, 1937; m. Edith Epley, May 28, 1938; children—Steve, Denny, Jana, Jill, Bill. Sales mgr. Western Auto Supply Co., 1937-44, field personnel mgr., 1945-46, div. mgr., 1946-69; partner Clark Devel. Co., Houston, 1960—; dir. First Nat. Indemnity Corp., First Nat. Indemnity Corp. Investors, Inc., Consol. Bankers Life Ins. Co., Pinemont Bank. Councilman, City of Spring Valley, Tex., 1956-57. Trustee Brazos Presbyn. Homes, Inc. Mem. Spring Br.-Meml. C. of C. (pres. 1965). Presbyn. (elder). Mason (Shriner). Home: 11526 Wendover St Houston TX 77024 Office: 8337 Long Point Rd PO Box 55126 Houston TX 77055

CLARK, WILLIAM KENLEY, marina owner; b. Portsmouth, Va., Dec. 16, 1920; s. Kenley Jesse and Ruth (Thomasson) C.; B.S., Tex. A. and M U., 1942; M.A., U. Tex., 1949, Ph.D., 1952; m. to Barbara Jean Hosterman, Sept. 7, 1949; children—Maribeth, Christine Ruth. Instructor in zoology, Fla. State U., 1949-50; INSTR. IN BIOLOGY, U. Richmond (Va.), 1951-52; prof., head biology dept. Sam Houston State Coll., 1952-67; v.p. Brenau Coll. Gainesville, Ga., 1967-68, pres., 1968-70; pres. Holiday Harbor Marine Devel. Corp., Pensacola, Fla., 1970—. Bd. dirs. Gonzales Warm Springs Found., 1957-58. Pres. Walker County (Tex.) United Fund 1957. Served with AUS, 1942-46. Mem. Ecol. Soc. Am., Am. Soc. Mammalogists, Soc. for Study Evolution, Sigma Xi (pres.). Presbyn. Kiwanian (dist. dir. Circle K 1967). Home: Rt 1 Box 995 B Pensacola FL 32507

CLARK, WILLIAM LOREN, aircraft co. exec.; b. Poplar Bluff, Mo., Sept. 20, 1923; s. William Everett and Elizabeth Lillian (Vawter) C.; B.A., Yale, 1949, J.D., 1952; m. Alice Manley, June 4, 1951; children—Madia, Margaret, Amy, Ann. Asso., Chadbourne, Parke, Whiteside & Wolff, N.Y.C., 1952-55; asst. gen. counsel N.Am. Aviation, Los Angeles, 1955-60, corp. dir. contracts, 1960-67; v.p. contracts N.Am. Rockwell, Los Angeles, 1967-69, staff v.p., Washington, 1969—. Mem. bd. advisors Commn. on Govt. Procurement, 1970—, Fed. Contracts Report, Bur. Nat. Affairs. Bd. dirs. Montessori Schs., Los Angeles, 1966-69; mem. mgmt. bd. Central YMCA, Washington, 1971—. Served with AUS, 1943-46. Mem. Am., Fed. bar assns., Nat. Security Indsl. Assn. (dir. 1969—, trustee 1969—), A.I.A. (chmn. procurement and finance com. 1968-70), Am. Inst. Aeros. and Astronautics. Episcopalian. Clubs: Yale, George Town (Washington); Kenwood Country (Bethesda, Md.). Home: 5965 Searl Terrace Washington DC 20016 Office: 1629 K St NW Washington DC 20006

CLARK, WILLIAM MOORE, lawyer; b. Monroe, La., Feb. 25, 1921; s. William Edward and Iris (Moore) C.; B.A., Vanderbilt U., 1942; LL.B., Yale, 1948; m. Elizabeth Gardner Hall, Apr. 21, 1945; children—William Moore, Elizabeth Gardner Hall. Admitted to Ark. bar, 1948; practiced in Little Rock, 1948—; partner House, Holmes & Jewell, 1955-71. Served to lt. USNR, 1942-46. Mem. Phi Beta Kappa. Episcopalian. Home: 18 Edgehill St Little Rock AR 72207 Office: Worthan Bank Bldg Center St Little Rock AR 72201

CLARK, ZONA GALE, city ofcl.; b. Gould, Okla., Nov. 9, 1925; s. William Thomas and Mary Elizabeth (Smith) C.; student fire service tng. Okla. State U., 1953—; m. Betty Jo Harmon, Apr. 2, 1949; children— Stanley Terril, Archie Wayne, Dennis Keith. With Norman (Okla.) Fire Dept., 1951—, chief, 1967—. Served AUS, 1945-46; PTO. Mem. Internat. Assn. Fire Chiefs, Okla. Fire Chief Assn., Met. Area Fire Chiefs, Okla. State Firefighter's Assn. Moose (gov. 1970). Club: Noble (Okla.) Takedown (pres. 1969). Home: Route 2 Box 86 Norman OK 73069 Office: 400 E Main St Norman OK 73069

CLARKE, CLIFFORD MONTREVILLE, indsl. assn. exec.; b. Ludowici, Ga., July 20, 1925; s. Clifford Montreville and Lella Bertrue (Hightower) C.; A.B. in Polit. Sci., Emory U. 1951. Radio engr. and announcer WSAV, Savannah, 1941-43; pub. relations dir. Dept. Ga., Am. Legion, 1945-47; instr. Armstrong Coll., Savannah, 1947-48; asst. supt. Savannah Park and Tree Commn., 1951; instr., then supr. tng. dept. Lockheed Aircraft Corp., Marietta, Ga., 1951-52, mgr. employee services dept., 1952-53; exec. v.p. Asso. Industries Ga., 1953-68; pres. Ga. Bus. and Industry Assn., 1968—; mem. Am. Soc. Execs., 1955—, bd. dirs., 1958-67, mem. exec. com., 1960-67, treas., 1962-64, sr. v.p., 1964-65, pres., 1965-66; pres. Ga. Soc. Assn. Execs., 1958-60; chmn. state group Nat. Indsl. Council, 1970-72. Mem. Ga. Urban and Tech. Assistance Adv. Council, 1965-70, Ga. Intergovtl. Relations Commn., 1966; mem. Ga. Ednl. Improvement Council, 1964-69, chmn., 1967-69, vice chmn., 1970-71; mem. Forward Ga. Commn., 1969-72; vice chmn. Ga. Commn. for Nat. Bicentennial Celebration, 1969—; chmn. Chartered Assn. Exec. Chartering Bd., 1969-71; bd. dirs. Atlanta Conv. Bur., 1968-71; exec. com. Conf. State Mfrs. Assns., 1969-72; Ga. del. to Bicentennial Council 13 Original States, 1971—, chmn., 1972—; chmn. Gov.'s Commn. Student Financial Aid, 1972—. Mem. policy com. Grad. Sch. Bus., U. Ga., 1966-71; adv. bd. Ga. Vocational Rehab., 1964-70; dirs. Arthritis Found. Ga., 1965-71; Atlanta Community Services to Blind, Coop. Services for Blind, 1964-71, Atlanta Sch. Art. Served with inf. AUS, World War II. Decorated Purple Heart with 2oak leaf clusters; hon. consul Mexico, 1970—. Mem. Am. Soc. Assn. Execs. (trustee Found.), Chartered Assn. Execs. (trustee). Home: 1115 Beechhaven Rd NE Atlanta GA 30324 Office: 181 Washington St SW Atlanta GA 30303

CLARKE, EUGENE SINGLETON, accountant; b. Hollandale, Miss., June 15, 1933; s. Eugene Singleton and Georgia (Wicks) C.; B.S. in Accounting, Miss. State U., 1955; m. Grace Ellen Oakes, June 19, 1955; children—Eugene Singleton, David Estill. Staff accountant Dick D. Quin & Co., Jackson, Miss., 1957-60; staff accountant Peat, Marwick, Mitchell & Co., Jackson, 1960-62; partner firm Moody & Clarke, C.P.A.'s, Hollandale, Greenville and Leland, Miss., 1962-67; individual practice as C.P.A., Hollandale, 1968—. Dir. Hollandale Indsl. Found., 1964—; sec.-treas. Washington County Devel. Commn.; treas. Hollandale Minority Devel. Corp. Scoutmaster, Boy Scouts Am., Hollandale, 1962—, Trustee, Hollandale Consol. Sch. Dist. Served to 1st lt. USAF, 1955-57, Mem. Am. Inst. C.P.A.'s (treas.), Miss. Soc. C.P.A.'s (past pres. Miss. Delta chpt.), Hollandale C. of C. (past pres.), Sigma Alpha Epsilon. Methodist. Rotarian (past pres. Hollandale). Clubs: Sharkey Country, Highland. Home: Treadway Circle Hollandale MS 38748 Office: Bank of Hollandale Bldg Hollandale MS 38748

CLARKE, HARVEY EDEN, electronic engr.; b. Birmingham, Ala., July 26, 1924; s. Fredrick William and Helen (Scott) C.; B.E.E., Ala. Poly. Inst., 1952; m. Iva M. Williams, Feb. 9, 1947; children—Linda Eden (Mrs. John Martin Willcox), James Harvey. Electronic technician Civil Service Commn., U.S. Air Force, Brookley AFB, 1946-49, electronic engr., 1954-62; instr., field engr. Westinghouse Elec. Corp., Balt. and Jacksonville, Fla., 1952-54; electronic engr. U.S. Corps Engrs., Mobile, Ala., 1962—. Served with USNR, 1943-46. Registered profl. engr. Ala. Mem. Nat. Assn. Govt. Engrs. Baptist (deacon 1964—, Sunday sch. tchr. 1955-67, dir. adult No. 6 dept. 1969—). Mason. Home: 507 Newport Dr W Mobile AL 36609 Office: Corps Engrs Mobile Dist Office Box 2288 Mobile AL 36628

CLARKE, JACK WELLS, developer, realtor; b. Abingdon, Va., June 26, 1914; s. James Sydnor and Ottie B. (Wells) C.; A.B., Williams Coll., 1935; postgrad. N.Y.U., 1935-37; m. Dorothy Irelan, Mar. 24, 1938. Bond analyst, statistician, N.Y.C., 1935-37; with Lion Oil Co., 1938-51, successively asst., mgr. budget and statis. dept., asst. to pres., asst. to chmn. bd., dir. pub. relations; dir. pub. relations Tex. Eastern Transmission Corp., 1951-55; exec. v.p. Freestate Indsl. Devel. Co., 1955-56, pres. dir., 1956-68; dir. Currey Sanders Aircraft Co., Inc. Mem. Shreveport-Bossier Found., Urban Land Inst., Am. Indsl. Devel. Council, Internat. Council Shopping Centers, Nat. Rivers and Harbors Congress, Shreveport Com. 100. Mem. La. State Democratic Central Com.; dir. Caddo Parish Dem. Assn.; vice chmn. Caddo Parish Dem. Exec. Com. Served from ensign to lt. USNR, 1942-45. Mem. Navy League, Res. Officers Assn., Pub. Affairs Research Council La., Nat. Assn. Real Estate Bds., Shreveport C. of C., Shreveport-Bossier Bd. Realtors, Phi Delta Theta. Episcopalian. Clubs: Shreveport, Shreveport Country. Home: 708 Azalea Dr Shreveport LA 71106 Office: Box 7776 Shreveport LA 71107

CLARKE, JAY, newspaper editor; b. Jacksonville, Fla., Oct. 6, 1927; s. Charles Williamson and Gabrielle (Creusot) C.; A.B., U. Miami, Coral Gables, Fla., 1950; m. Patricia Hughes, Nov. 2, 1963; children—Anne Patrice, Dougan, Paul. Mng. editor Trilane Publs., N.Y.C., 1951-52; copy editor Fairchild Publs., N.Y.C., 1952-55; Sunday editor The Miami (Fla.) Herald, 1955—. Served with AUS, 1946-48. Mem. Soc. Am. Travel Writers (dir.), Sigma Delta Chi, Omicron Delta Kappa, Sigma Alpha Epsilon. Episcopalian. Contbr. to mags. and newspapers. Home: 1001 Sunset Dr Coral Gables FL 33143 Office: 1 Herald Plaza Miami FL 33101

CLARKE, LEE BEN, II, hosp. adminstr.; b. Atlanta, Dec. 18, 1931; s. Maurice Lee Ben and Frances Myrinie (Scruggs) C.; student U. Ga., 1950-53; B.B.A., Ga. State U., 1957, certificate in hosp. adminstrn., 1958; m. India Katherine Harvey, Dec. 12, 1953; children—Lee Ben III, Frances Lynn, Harrell Harvey. Adminstrv. resident Macon Hosp., 1957-58, bus. office mgr., 1958; asst. adminstr. City-County Hosp., LaGrange, Ga., 1958-60; adminstr. Humphreys Meml. Hosp., Fernandina Beach, Fla., 1960-66, Glades Gen. Hosp., Belle Glade, Fla., 1966—. Mem. Palm Beach County Health Planning Council, Glades Pub. Health Adv. Bd. dirs. Palm Beach County Mental Health Center, 1967-71. Served with AUS, 1953-55. Mem. Am., Fla. (trustee 1964-65) hosp. assns., E. Central Fla. Hosp. Council, Palm Beach County Soc. Hosp. Adminstrn., N.E. Fla. Hosp. Council (pres. 1964-65), Pi Epsilon Rho. Presbyn. (deacon, elder 1963-66). Elk, Lion. Home: 1125 1/2 S Main St Belle Glade FL 33430 Office: 1201 S Main St Belle Glade FL 33430

CLARKE, LEWIS JAMES, landscape architect; b. Carlton Notts., Eng., Mar. 10, 1927; s. Roland and May (Pringle) C.; Dip. Arch. Sch. Architecture, 1950; Dip. L.D., Kings Coll., U. Durham, 1951; M.W.A., Harvard, 1952; m. Abbie Pearl Swinson, Nov. 24, 1954; children—Lewis Nigel, Jennifer Kay, Rachel May, Liza Elaine. Came to U.S., 1951. Prin. Lewis Clarke Assos., landscape architecture and site planning, Raleigh, 1952—; prof. Sch. Design N.C. State U., Raleigh, 1952-68, acting head dept. landscape architecture, 1967-68, dir. Futures, Inc. Mem. Planning Commn. Raleigh, 1967-69. Recipient Fulbright grant, Smith Mundt award; Distinguished Tchr. award, 1961, 67. Mem. N.C. Arts Council, Am. Soc. Landscape Architects; Royal Inst. British Architects, British Inst. Landscape Architects. Home: 3215 Darien Dr Raleigh NC 27607 Office: 2230 Hillsborough St Raleigh NC 27607 also Suite 230 550 Interstate Pkwy N Atlanta GA 30339

CLARKE, LYNN BENJAMIN, univ. adminstr.; b. N.Y.C., Aug. 2, 1926; s. Lynn Banks and Mary Louise (Farrell) C.; B.A., Princeton, 1947; m. Mildred Kate Stine, Dec. 18, 1950; children—Lynn Bernard, Stephen Dawson, Edward Joseph. Mem. editorial, promotion and advt. sales staffs Time Inc., N.Y.C., 1947-53, Chgo., 1953-57; pres. Russell Clarke, Inc., St. Petersburg, Fla., 1957-65; dir. pub. relations U. Miami, Coral Gables, Fla., 1966—. Exec. dir. Ind. Colls. and Univs. Fla., 1962-65. Served to lt. USNR, 1944-46, 49-51. Mem. Pub. Relations Soc. Am. (pres. S. Fla. chpt. 1969-71, nat. vice chmn. Southeast dist. 1972), Am. Coll. Pub. Relations Assn., Children Am. Revolution, Coral Gables C. of C. (dir. 1969-71), Fla. Presbyn. Coll. Charter Alumni Assn., Alpha Kappa Psi. Democrat. Roman Catholic. Club: Charter (Princeton, N.J.). Home: 9450 Palmetto Club Lane E Miami FL 33157 Office: PO Box 8105 U Miami Coral Gables FL 33124

CLARKE, MORRIS ANDREW, ednl. adminstr.; b. Columbus, Ga., Nov. 2, 1918; s. George and Annie Lee (Morris) C.; A.B. Morris Brown Coll., 1939; vocational certificate Savannah State Coll., 1949-50; M.A., N.Y.U., 1956; postgrad. Atlanta U., 1955, 69, U. Okla., 1957, Auburn U., 1970-71, U. Ga., 1971; m. Anne Victoria Greer, Jan. 4, 1942; children—Morris Otis, George Allen, Betty (Mrs. Clifton Tinsley). Tchr. Thomaston Jr. High Sch., 1939-40, Talbatton High Sch., 1940-43; prin. Eddy High Sch., 1943-46, Stephens Lee High Sch., Ashville, N.C., 1947, tchr., head coach Carver High Sch., Milledgeville, Ga., 1946-47; supr., prin., coach Carver High Sch., Douglas, Ga., 1947-50; prin., coach Radcliff Elementary Sch., 1950-69; prin., Marshall Jr. High Sch., Columbus, Ga., 1969—. Mem. Mayor's Adv. Com.; active Boy Scouts Am., Jr. Police League, YMCA. Vice-chmn. Met. Govt.; mem. Democratic Exec. Com. Ga.,

1966-72. Recipient Merit award Nat. Found., 1969, Golden Anniversary award Ga. Tchr. Edn. Assn., 1968, Outstanding Leadership award State Prins. Council, 1968, Man of Year Trophy, Dept. Elementary Sch. Prins. 1969. Mem. N.E.A., Assn., Sch. Bus. Ofcls., Nat. Assn. Secondary Sch. Administrs., Internat. Platform Assn., N.A.A.C.P., Assn. U.S. Army Dept. Elementary Sch. Prins. (state pres. 1967-70), Nat. Com. Educators for Human Rights, Ga., Muscogee assns. educators, Urban League, Muscogee County Fed. Credit Union, C. of C. (mem. com. on children and youth 1971-73), Phi Beta Sigma, Epsilon Delta Chi. Mason. Clubs: Path Seekers, Modernistic (Columbus). Home: 1483 Brazil Av Columbus GA 31903 Office: 800 Tent Av Columbus GA 31901

CLARKSON, ALLEN B., clergyman; b. Columbia, S.C.; B.A., U. S.C. Rector, Ch. of Good Shepherd, Augusta, Ga. Dep. to 6 gen. convs. Episcopal Ch.; pres. standing com. Diocese Ga.; mem. council Province Sewanee; mem. council Assn. Episcopal Schs. Home: 2347 Walton Way Augusta GA 30904

CLARKSON, LAWRENCE WILLIAM, aircraft co. exec.; b. Grove City, Pa., Apr. 29, 1938; s. Harold William and Jean Henrietta (Jaxtheimer) C.; A.B., DePauw U., 1960; J.D., U. Fla., 1962; m. Barbara Louise Stevenson, Aug. 20, 1960; children—Michael, Elizabeth, Jennifer. Admitted to Fla. bar, 1963; mem. firm, Caldwell, Pacetti, Barrow, Palm Beach, Fla., 1965-67; dept. counsel Pratt &Whitney, Fla. Research and Devel. Center, West Palm Beach, 1967-69, mgr. contract adminstrn., 1969—. Musical dir. North County Choral Soc., 1968—. Mgr., Leroy Collins campaign U.S. Senate, Palm Beach County, 1968; mem. Palm Beach County Democratic Exec. Com., 1967-68; town counsel, Town of Haverhill, Fla., 1968—, pres. town counsel, 1971—, judge, 1970—. Bd. dirs. Palm Beach County Goodwill Industries, 1966-68, Palm Beach County chpt. Am. Cancer Soc. Served to capt. USAF, 1962-66. Mem. Am. Bar Assn., Fla. Bar, Am. Judicature Soc., Phi Delta Phi, Delta Chi, Phi Mu Alpha. Episcopalian. Club: LaCoquille (Palm Beach, Fla.). Home: 5070 Ponderosa Lane West Palm Beach FL 33406 Office: Box 2691 Beeline Hwy West Palm Beach FL 33402

CLARKSON, MARK H., educator; b. Lafayette County, Mo., Sept. 27, 1917; s. Julius A. and Frances (Anderson) C.; B.S. in Aero. Engring., U. Minn., 1939; M.S., U. Tex., 1948, Ph.D., 1953; m. Florence Johnston, Mar. 14, 1941; children—David, Michael, Linda. With Douglas Aircraft Co., 1939-41, Consol. Vultee Co., 1942-45; research engr., research mathematician Def. Research Lab., U. Tex., 1945-53; supr. theoretical aerodynamics Chance Vought Aircraft Corp., 1953-59, supr. aerophysics, 1959-61; prof. aerospace engring., chmn. dept. U. Fla., 1961—; mem. part-time grad. faculty So. Meth. U., 1954-59; cons. to industry, 1961—. Asso. fellow Am. Inst. Aero. and Astronautics; mem. Am. Soc. Engring. Edn. (chmn. aerospace div. 1968), Sigma Xi. Contbr. profl. jours. Home: 2400 NW 18th Pl Gainesville FL 32601

CLARKSTON, N. HEYWARD, JR., lawyer; b. Columbia, S.C., Feb. 14, 1911; B.S., U. S.C., 1933, LL.B., 1935. Admitted to S.C. bar, 1937; mem. firm Clarkson & McCants, Columbia. Sec. Bd. Commrs. on Grievances and Discipline, 1964-68. Served with USNR, 1942-46. Mem. Am., S.C., Richland County (pres. 1960) bar assns., Am. Judicature Soc., Phi Peta Kappa, Omicron Delta Kappa. Office: Palmetto State Life Bldg Columbia SC 29211*

CLAUDE, INIS LOTHAIR, JR, educator, polit. scientist; b. Yellville, Ark., Sept. 3, 1922; s. Inis Lothair and Parilla Jane (Pledger) C.; B.A. with high honors, Hendrix Coll., 1942; M.A., Harvard, 1947, Ph.D. (Chase prize 1949), 1949; m. Marie Stapleton, Aug. 1, 1943; children—Susan, Robert Burr, Cathy. Instr., then asst. prof. govt. Harvard, 1949-56; asso. prof. polit sci. U. Del., 1956-57; asso. prof. polit. sci. U. Mich., 1957-60, prof. 1960-68; Edward R. Stettinius Jr. prof. govt. and fgn. affairs U. Va., 1968—, mem. Center Advanced Study, U. Va., 1968-71; vis. research scholar Carnegie Endowment Internat. Peace, 1960-61; faculty chmn. course internat. relations Inst. Social Studies, The Hague, 1964-65. Mem. exec com. Center Research Conflict Resolution, 1959-63; chmn. com. internat. orgn. Social Sci. Research Council, 1962-69; mem. research group UN financial problems Brookings Instn., 1962-63; occasional lectr. Nat., Army and Navy war colls., Air Command and Staff Coll., Fgn. Service Inst., Fed. Exec. Inst., UN Fgn. Service Tng. Seminar; cons. Dept. State, 1962-71; mem. adv. com. fgn. relations Dept. State, 1968—, chmn., 1971-72. Served with AUS, 1942-46. Faculty fellow Fund Advancement Edn., 1951-52; Rockefeller research grantee, 1958-59; Horace H. Rackham Grad. Sch. research grantee, 1963; Guggenheim fellow, 1964-65; Fulbright research grantee, 1964-65; Distinguished Alumnus award Hendrix Coll., 1968. Mem. Am. (Woodrow Wilson Found. award 1963), Internat. (rapporteur gen. internat. orgn. 1964), So. (mem. exec. council 1970) polit. sci. assns. Am. Soc. Internat. Law, Am. Assn. U. Profs. Author: National Minorities: An International Problem, 1955; Swords Into Plowshares: The Problems and Progress of International Organization, 4th edit., 1971; Power and International Relations, 1962; The Changing United Nations, 1967. Bd. editors Internat. Orgn., 1960—; chmn. bd. editors Jour. Conflict Resolution, 1961-63; cons. editor internat. affairs Random House, Inc., 1962—. Home: 103 Melissa Pl Charlottesville VA 22901

CLAUSELL, BERNYCE HALL (MRS. JAMES AARON CLAUSELL), educator; b. nr. Thomasson, Ga., Nov. 19, 1916; d. Nathan and Eva (Hall) Hall; A.A. Wash. Jr. Coll., 1954; B.S., Fla. A. and M. U., 1956, M.S. in Edn., 1961; m. James Aaron Clausell, Sept. 1, 1945; children—Mary Bernyce, Aaronetta Eva. Sec., Fraternal Council of Negro Chs., Washington, 1942-45, Fla. A. and M., Tallahassee, 1956; tchr. Griffin Jr. High Sch., Tallahassee, 1956-62, chmn. elementary dept., 1962-65, English tchr., asst. chmn. English dept., 1966-67; tchr. intermediate dept. Pineview Elementary Sch., Tallahassee, 1967-69; tchr. sci. Bellevue Middle Sch., 1969—. Pres., Bapt. ministers' wives council of Tallahassee, 1964-68; active Girl Scouts U.S.A., 1964-68. Named Woman Citizen of Year, Fla. A and M U., 1963; recipient Distinguished Service award Art Cultural and Civic Guild of N.Y., 1965. Mem. Nat. Assn. Coll. Women (founder, pres. Tallahassee br. 1957-60, Woman of Year 1959), Nat. Assn. Negro Bus. and Profl. Women (founder pres. Tallahassee club 1959-66, Sojourner Truth award 1962), Nat., Fla., Leon County edn. assns., Nat. Assn. Tchrs. English, Assn. Supervision and Curriculum Devel., Fla. Missionary and Ednl. Conv. (bd. dirs. 1958—). Kappa Delta Pi, Alpha Kappa Mu. Baptist (co-founder Calvary Bapt. Ch. 1958, dir. music and youth activities 1958—, dean of dist. Sunday Sch. Congress 1967—). Author: Today In Paradise, 1966. Home: 1028 Joe Louis St Tallahassee FL 32304

CLAUTICE, WILLIAM EDWARD, aerospace engr.; b. Balt., Jan. 12, 1918; s. Edward P. and Edith (Adams) C.; B.S. in Mech. Engring., Johns Hopkins, 1943, postgrad. metallurgy, 1948-51; m. Lois Orma Russell, Aug. 2, 1958; children—Paula E., William Edward, John R. Laurie E., Russell L., Richard B. Ronald B. Metall. engr. Westinghouse Electric Corp., Pitts., 1946-47; mech. engr. C.E., U.S. Army, Balt. dist., 1947-48; metall. engr. Bur. Ships, Navy Dept., Washington, 1948-62; aerospace engr., structural materials tech. staff, design engring. NASA, Kennedy Space Center, Fla., 1962—. Bd. dirs. Community Assn., Severna Park, Md., 1961-62. Served to lt. with USNR, 1943-46. Registered profl. engr., Ala. Mem. Canaveral Council Tech. Socs., Am. Inst. Aero. and Astronautical Engrs., Am. Soc. Metals, Am. Welding Soc. (chmn. Central Fla. sect. 1966-67), Am. Soc. M.E.s. Home: 68 Westview Lane Cocoa Beach FL 32931 Office: Design Engineering DD-MDD-1 Kennedy Space Center FL 32899

CLAY, EDWIN SAMUEL, III, librarian; b. Richmond, Va., July 16, 1945; s. Edwin Samuel and Margaret Rose (Inge) C.; B.A., Randolph Macon Coll., 1966; M.S. (Library fellow), U. N.C., 1967; m. Linda Beatrice Nall, Sept. 1, 1967. Library dir. Va. Wesleyan Coll., 1967-70; dir. Dept. Pub. Libraries, City of Virginia Beach, Va., 1970—. Pres. Tidewater Literacy Council, 1971—; v.p. Planned Parenthood, Virginia Beach 1970—; active Va. Museum Fine Arts. Trustee Virginia Beach Arts Center. Mem. Am., Va. library assns., Am. Civil Liberties Union (dir. Va. 1969-71). Jewish religion. Home: 4760 Haygood Circle Virginia Beach VA 23455 Office: Muncipal Center Virginia Beach VA 23456

CLAY, HARRIS AUBREY, chem. engr.; b. Hartley, Tex., Dec. 28, 1911; s. John David and Alberta (Harris) C.; B.S., U. Tulsa, 1933; Ch.E., Columbia, 1939; m. Violette Frances Mills, June 19, 1948. Pilot plant operator Phillips Petroleum Co., Burbank, Okla., 1939-42, resident supr. Burbank pilot plants, 1942-44, process design engr., Bartlesville, Okla., 1944-45, process engring. supr. Philtex Plant, Phillips, Tex., 1946-56, tech. adviser to pilot plant mgr., Bartlesville, 1957-61, chem. engring. asso., 1961—; chmn. tech. com. Fractionation Research, Inc., 1966—. Mem. Am. Inst. Chem. Engrs., Am. Chem. Soc., Electrochem. Soc. Presbyn. Elk. Contbr. articles to profl. jours. Patentee in field. Home: 1723 Church Ct Bartlesville OK 74003 Office: 125 Research Bldg 3 Phillips Petroleum Co Bartlesville OK 74003

CLAY, JAMES HORACE BEVERLEY, forestry exec.; b. Crewe, Va., Feb. 13, 1924; s. Charles Richard and Augusta (Redford) C.; student U. Richmond, 1946-47, U. Rochester, 1943; m. Phyllis Laughlin, Oct. 26, 1963; children—Vivian, Adrian. Press sec. to congressman, Washington, 1958-60; staff mem. Senate Republican Policy Com., Washington, 1960-61; legislative asst. Senator John Tower, Washington, 1961-63; free lance polit. writer, 1963-66; founder, pres. Washington Nat. Press, Inc., 1967-70; pres. Pub. Affairs Book Club, Inc., 1968-70; co-founder with Orville L. Freeman, pres. U.S. Tree Farms System, Inc., Washington, 1970—. Served with USAAF, 1943-45, with USAF, 1952-53. Mem. Am. Polit. Sci. Assn. Republican. Episcopalian. Clubs: Capitol Hill, Kenwood Golf and Country. Author: Hoffa, 1965. Home: 5210 Dorset Av Chevy Chase MD 20015 Office: 955 L'Enfant Plaza SW Washington DC 20024

CLAY, JAMES LLOYD, lawyer, bus. exec.; b. Paintsville, Ky., Oct. 20, 1911; s. J. Lloyd and Grace (VanHoose) C.; A.B., U. Ky., 1937. LL.B., 1940; m. Dorothy Davis, 1932 (div. 1953); children—Robert L., James L., William Wade; m. 2d, Della Richmond Callahan, Apr. 12, 1968. Admitted to Ky. bar, 1940, and since in practice of law at Lexington; tchr. and prin. Johnson County and Paintsville City Schs., 1931-37; asst. adj. gen. of Ky., 1946-47; engaged in individual practice law. Dir., sec., treas. J.H. Warrington Co., Inc.; pres. Perma Glaze of Ky., Perma Cement of Ky., Gale Builders, Glazon Industries, Inc., P & L Constrn. Co., Days Inns Ky., Inc.; sec. Johnson Electronics Co. Past mem. Lexington-Fayette County Planning and Zoning Commn. Mem. Fayette County Rep. Exec. Com. (past chmn.), Woodford Rep. Exec. Com., Citizens for Eisenhower (past dist. chmn.). Served as lt. comdr. USCG Res., 1942-45. Mem. Am. Ky., Fayette County bar assns., Am. Legion (past state exec. com., past post comdr.), Jr. C. of C. (past dir.), U. Ky. Law Coll. Alumni Assn. (past pres.), V.F.W., Disabled Am. Vets., Phi Delta Phi. Methodist. Mason (Shriner). Clubs: Kiwanis, Ky. Mountain (past v.p.), Pyramid; Tates Creek County Thoroughbred of America. Home: 40 Glenhaven Dr Route 4 Versailles KY 40383 Office: 1634 N Broadway Lexington KY 40504

CLAY, PAUL EUGENE, mech. engr.; b. Texarkana, Tex., Dec. 16, 1933; s. Paul Eugene and Ruth (Elmer) C.; B.S. in Mech. Engring., U. Ark., 1960; M.S. in Mech. Engring., La. Poly. Inst., 1965; postgrad. La. State U., 1968—; m. Mary Elizabeth Brown, June 11, 1955; children—Paul Eugene III, Charlotte Elizabeth, Mitchell Brown. Engr., AMF Beaird Inc., Shreveport, La., 1960-62, sr. engr., 1963-66, product engr., 1967-69, asst. mgr. Maxim Silencer div., 1969-70, mgr. engring., 1970-72, dir. engring., 1972—. Served with USMCR, 1955-58. Registered profl. engr., Ark. Mem. Am. Soc. M.E. Republican. Methodist. Contbr. articles to profl. jours. Patentee in field. Home: 1047 Southfield Rd Shreveport LA 71106 Office: 601 Benton Kelly Rd Shreveport LA 71106

CLAY, ROSS COLLINS, educator; b. Conehatta, Miss., Dec. 15, 1908; s. George Walker and Ida (Hambrick) C.; B.S., Jackson State Coll., 1934; M.A., Fisk U., 1940; Mus. M., Northwestern U., 1953; postgrad. Ind. U., 1961-62; m. Lillie James, 1940 (dec.); 1 son, Ross Collins; m. 2d, Ollie D. Billingslea, Aug. 7, 1955. Dir. music Easom High Sch., Corinth, Miss., 1934-36, Ark. Bapt. Coll., Little Rock, 1936-38, Geeter High Sch., Whiteheaven, Tenn., 1940-43, Friendship Jr. Coll., Rock Hill, S.C., 1945-46, Philander Smith Coll., Little Rock, 1946-48, Lane Coll., Jackson, Tenn., 1948-53; def. worker, Detroit, 1943-45; dir. music edn. Jackson (Miss.) State Coll., 1953—; church pianist, organist. Mem. Miss. Tchrs. Assn., Nat. Assn. Negro Musicians, N.E.A., Am. Assn. U. Profs., Music Educators Nat. Conf. Baptist. Mason. Club: Harmonia (Jackson, Miss.). Home: 1750 Topp St Jackson MS 39204

CLAY, WATSON, state ct. ofcl.; b. Pitts., Jan. 17, 1908; s. Francis Warfield and Jane Swigert (Watson) C.; A.B., U. Mich., 1930, LL.B., 1932; m. Virginia Murphey Alexander, Sept. 26, 1936; children—Sallie (Mrs. James Forrest Thompson), Jane (Mrs. Clay Wyatt, Jr.). Admitted to Ky. bar, 1934; mem. firm Trabue, Doolan, Helm & Helm, Louisville, 1933-42; chief price atty. OPA, Louisville, 1942-43; partner firm Ogden, Galphin, Tarrant & Street, Louisville, 1946-47; commr. Ky. Ct. Appeals, Frankfort, 1947-71. Served with USNR, 1943-46. Mem. Am., Ky. State (Outstanding Service award 1971), Louisville bar assns., Am. Judicature Soc., Phi Delta Theta. Republican. Presbyn. Club: Frankfort Country. Author: Kentucky Practice: Rules of Civil Procedure, 1963. Editor: Kentucky Wills and Trust Manual, 1967-71. Home: 518 Logan St Frankfort KY 40601 Office: New Capitol Bldg Frankfort KY 40601

CLAY, WILLIAM CALDWELL, JR., lawyer, corp. exec.; b. Mt. Sterling, Ky., Dec. 28, 1915; s. William Caldwell and Kathryn (Greene) C.; A.B., Dartmouth, 1937 LL.B., Yale, 1940; m. Esther Briggs, Apr. 13, 1946; children—Jeanette Dobbs, Sally Sue, Kathryn Caldwell. Admitted to Ky. bar, 1939, since practiced in Mt. Sterling; with Anti-trust div. Dept. Justice 1938-40; counsel pub. relations Burley Auction Warehouse Assn., 1946-56; chmn. bd. Exchange Bank of Ky., Clay Tobacco Co.; pres. Capital Broadcasting Co., Delaware-Marysville Broadcasting Service, Inc., The Cola Corp.; sec., dir. Cowden Mfg. Co., Montgomery Nat. Bank, Hwy. Concrete Pipe, Inc. Mem. bd. curators, mem. exec. com. Transylvania Coll. Mem. Am., Ky. bar assns., C. of C., Sigma Alpha Epsilon. Mem. Christian Church. Odd Fellow, Mason, Rotarian. Author: Farmers Tax Manual, 1943; Farmers Tax Manual Account Book, 1943; Tobacco Fire and Casualty Insurance Survey, 1953. Contbr. to trade publs. Office: 50 Broadway Mount Sterling KY 40353

CLAYPOOLE, WILLIAM HENRY, orthodontist; b. Mt. Holly, N.J., June 29, 1940; s. William Hilliard and Eleanor (Broome) C.; B. A., Pfeiffer Coll., 1963; D.M.D., U. Pa., 1969; M.S., U. N.C., 1972; m. Kathryn Sue Phillips, Sept. 21, 1961; children—Deborah Jean, W. Christopher. Orthodontist, post-doctoral research fellow Nat. Inst. Health, Durham, N.C., 1969—. Mem. Am. Assn. Orthodontists, Am. Dental Soc., Am. Cleft Palate Assn., N.C. Dental Soc., Am. Assn. Dentistry for Children, Matthew H. Cryer Honor Soc. (pres. 1969), Omicron Kappa Upsilon. Home: 2918 Friendship Rd Durham NC 27705 Office: 3333 Chapel Hill Blvd Durham NC 27707

CLAYTON, CHARLES PRENTICE, city planner; b. Savannah, Mo., Apr. 30, 1911; s. William Prentice and Blanche (Vail) C.; B.S. in Landscape Architecture, Ia. State Coll., 1938; m. Elinor Hale, Sept. 3, 1935; children—Charles Harrison, Elinor Ann (Mrs. Joe L. Clark), Thomas Hale. Landscape foreman Nat. Park Service, Devil's Den State Park, Fayetteville, Ark., 1933-36; landscape architect regional office Resettlement Administrn., Little Rock, 1936-37; landscape designer; field supt. Maurice Shamburger, landscape contractor, Tyler, Tex., 1938-39; asso. with Ruth London, Houston, 1939-41; landscape architect U. Ark.; pvt. practice in Mpls., summers 1941-43; site planner Skidmore, Owings & Merrill, Oak Ridge, 1943-44; prin. planning technician Ala. Planning Bd., Birmingham, 1944-47; town planner FHA, land planning sect., Southeastern states, 1947-50, chief land planning cons., 1950-51; mgr. Southeastern office Harland Bartholomew & Assos., 1951—, partner, 1961—. Fellow Am. Soc. Landscape Architects; mem. Am. Inst. Planners, Am. Soc. Planning Ofcls., Am. Planning and Civic Assn., Ga. Engring. Soc., Tau Sigma Delta, Alpha Zeta. Presbyn. (elder). Home: 479 S Woodland Dr Marietta GA 30060 Office: 1700 Commerce Dr Atlanta GA 30318

CLAYTON, CURTIS ABBITT, hosp. adminstr.; b. Portsmouth, Va., July 25, 1927; s. Graham W. and Charlotte (Williamson) C.; B.S., Va. Inst. Tech., 1952; M.H.A., Med. Coll. Va., 1954; m. Betty Cook, June 17, 1952; children—Debra Rea, Mark W. Asst. supt. Md. Gen. Hosp., Balt., 1954-55; hosp. specialist Kendall Co., Chgo., 1955-59; asst. dir. U. Va. Hosp., Charlottesville, 1959-64; adminstr. Circle Terrace Hosp., Alexandria, Va., 1964—; chmn., mgr. engring. for hosps. State of Va., 1969. Bd. dirs. Fairfax Nursing Home. Served with AUS, 1945-47. Fellow Am. Coll. Hosp. Adminstrs.; mem. Alumni Assn. Med. Coll. Va. Sch. Hosp. Adminstrn. (past pres.). Methodist (lay leader 1968—). Rotarian. Home: 2427 Central Av Alexandria VA 22302 Office: 904 Circle Terrace Dr Alexandria VA 22302

CLAYTON, JOE EDWARD, govt. ofcl.; b. Tillar, Ark., Sept. 17, 1932; s. Dewey Theodore and Ruby (Price) C.; student Ark. A. and M., 1950-52; B.S., U. Ark., 1959; M.S., Clemson U., 1960; m. Myrtle Biggs, June 21, 1952; children—Sharon Kay, Judy Lynn, Janet Marie, Carol Jean. Project engr. Allis-Chalmers Mfg. Co., Independence, Mo., 1959; research agrl. engr. U.S. Dept. Agr., Stoneville, Miss., 1960-64, Belle Glade, Fla., 1965—. Served with S.C., AUS, 1954-56. Mem. Am. Soc. Agrl. Engrs. (chmn. Fla. 1970), Tau Beta Pi, Gamma Sigma Delta, Pi Me Epsilon, Kappa Sigma Kappa. Methodist (vice chmn. ofcl. bd.). Club: Civitan (Belle Glade). Contbr. to profl. jours. Home: 1002 SE 3d St Belle Glade FL 33430 Office: Everglades Exptl Sta Box 758 Belle Glade FL 33430

CLAYTON, SAMUEL EDGAR, chem. co. exec.; b. Lawn, Tex., Feb. 22, 1921; s. William Edward and Ellen Mae (Martin) C.; student Coe Coll., 1943; m. Edna Earl Winter, Apr. 27, 1940; 1 dau., Patricia Earl (Mrs Lawrence H. Woods). Owner Clayton Chem. Co., Abilene, Tex., 1948—. Served with USAAF, 1942-46. Baptist. Home: 1802 Glen Haven Abilene TX 79603 Office: 128 Graham St Box 2173 Abilene TX 79604

CLAYTOR, WILLIAM GRAHAM, JR., lawyer, railroad exec.; b. Roanoke, Va., Mar. 14, 1912; s. William Graham and Gertrude Harris (Boatwright) C.; grad. Riverdale Country Sch., 1930; B.A., U. Va., 1933; LL.B. summa cum laude, Harvard, 1936; m. Frances Murray Hammond, Aug. 14, 1948; children—Frances Murray, William Graham III. Admitted to N.Y. bar, 1937, D.C. bar, 1938; law clk. to U.S. Judge Learned Hand, 1936-37, Mr. Justice Brandeis, 1937-38; asso. firm Covington & Burling, Washington, 1938-47, partner, 1947-67; v.p. law So. Ry. Co., 1963-67, pres., dir., 1967—; chief exec. officer, dir. other companies comprising So. Ry. System; dir. Fla. East Coast Ry. Co., Richmond, Fredericksburg & Potomac R.R.Co., Richmond-Washington Co., J.P. Morgan & Co., Inc., Morgan Guaranty Trust Co. N.Y., Penn Va. Corp., Phila. Dir. Assn. Am. Railroads. Trustee Episcopal Home Children, Washington, 1960-65, v.p., 1960-63; bd. govs. Beauvoir Sch., Washington, 1958-61, St. Albans Sch., Washington, 1961-67. Served to lt. comdr. USNR, 1941-46. Mem. Am. Bar Assn. Am. Law Inst., Am. Judicature Soc. Democrat. Episcopalian. Clubs: Metropolitan, City Tavern Assn. (bd. govs. 1961-64) (Washington); Chevy Chase (Md.); Gibson Island (Md.); Shenandoah (Roanoke). Pres. Harvard Law Rev., 1935-36. Home: PO Box 1808 Washington DC 20013 Office: So Ry Bldg 920 15th St NW Washington DC 20005

CLEAR, JAMES ARTHUR, JR., city ofcl.; b. Petersburg, Va., June 1, 1916; s. James Arthur and Catherine B. (Hammond) C.; student in surveying Internat. Corr. Schs., 1940; student Engring. Sch., Ft. Belvoir, Va., 1943; student in municipal pub. works U. Tenn., 1956; m. Hazel Marsh, Apr. 21, 1935; 1 dau., Catherine Jane. Instrument man survey party Tenn. Hwy. Dept., Knoxville, 1938-40; surveyor Am. Bemberg Corp., Elizabethton, Tenn., 1940-41; cartographer U.S. Coast and Geodetic Survey, Washington, 1941-43; asst. city mgr., dir. pub. works City of Elizabethton, 1946—. Pres., United Fund, 1963-64, campaign dir., 1964-65; pres. Boys Club, 1964-65; chmn. Carter County, Nat. Found. March of Dimes, 1966-67. Served with AUS, 1943-46; PTO. Named Outstanding Citizen of Carter County, V.F.W., 1968; recipient Honor award Carter County C. of C., 1963; Outstanding Community Service award Elizabethton Jr. C. of C., 1964; Outstanding Citizenship award United Fund, 1964, 65. Mem. Elizabethton C. of C. (pres. 1963-64), Am. (nat. dir. 1969—), Tenn. (pres. 1969-70) pub. works assns., Tenn. Municipal League, Tenn. Water and Waste-Water Assn., Am. Legion, V.F.W., Y's Men. Methodist (chmn. bd. stewards 1966-67). Club: Civitan (Elizabethton). Home: 505 Carter Blvd Elizabethton TN 37643 Office: Municipal Bldg Elizabethton TN 37643

CLEGG, GILES CONNELL, JR., lawyer; b. San Angelo, Tex., Apr. 1, 1929; s. Giles Connell and Eula (Griggs) C.; B.S., Tex. A. and M. U., 1951; LL.B., So. Meth. U., 1960; M. Nancy Moore, July 25, 1953; children— Stephen, Karen, Richard; m. Lynaveta Bates, Dec. 30, 1967. With Tex. Eastern Transmission Corp., 1953-55, Tex. Instruments, Inc., 1955-61; admitted to Tex. bar, 1960, since practiced in Dallas. Served to lt. USAF, 1951-53. Mem. I.E.E.E., Am. Patent Law Assn., Am. Bar Assn., State Bar Tex., Dallas-Ft. Worth Patent Assn. Home: Route 3 Roanoke TX 76262 Office: 1950 One Main Pl Dallas TX 75250

CLEGG, LEONARD BRUCE, food co. exec.; b. Milw., July 31, 1928; s. Gilbert and Nina (Oatman) C.; B.B.A., U. Wis., 1950, M.B.A., 1951; m. Gretchen Joy Zentner, Dec. 10, 1955; children—David Bruce, Julie Ann, Laura Lynn. With Red Dot Foods, Inc., Madison, Wis., 1951-61, dir. tng., 1957-58, dir. personnel, 1958-61; with Frito-Lay, Inc., Detroit and Dallas, 1961—, mgr. labor relations, Dallas,

1964-69, v.p. labor relations, 1969—. Lectr. supervisory tng. extension div. U. Wis., Madison, 1969. Troop chmn. Circle Ten council Boy Scouts Am., 1969—. Served with AUS, 1951-53. Mem. Am. (workshop chmn.), Tex. (mem. Tex. labor relations com.) mfrs. assns. Methodist. (chmn. council on ministries). Kiwanian. Club: Brookhaven Country (Dallas). Home: 4927 Forest Bend Rd Dallas TX 75234 Office: Box 35034 Dallas TX 75235

CLEGG, RUBY FRANCES, educator; b. Rotan, Tex., Aug. 10, 1939; d. Joseph Frank and Narcissia (Poteet) Clegg; B.S., Bethany Nazarene Coll., 1962; M.S., Okla. State U., 1964, postgrad., 1966-70. Research asst. Bethany Nazarene Coll., 1959-62; NSF Academic Yr. Inst., Okla. State U., Stillwater 1962-63, teaching asst. dept. zoology, 1963-64, teaching asst. dept. physiology, 1966-67, NIH fellow dept. physiology, 1967-70; instr. biology Southwestern State Coll., Weatherford, Okla., 1964-66; research asso. dept. obstetrics and gynecology Vanderbilt U. Sch. Medicine, Nashville, 1970-71; asso. prof. sci. Western Tex. Coll., Snyder, 1971—. Mem. Am. Soc. Zoologists, Soc. for Study of Reprodn. (charter), A.A.A.S., Am. Assn. U. Profs., Southwestern Assn. Naturalists, Tex. Tchrs. Assn., Tex. Jr. Coll. Tchrs Assn. Contbr. articles to profl. jours. Home: Box 863 407 N Garfield St Rotan TX 79546 Office: Dept of Science Western Texas College Snyder TX 79549

CLEGG, WARREN E., tile co. exec.; b. Monroe, Ga., Apr. 30, 1925; s. Joel and Lena (Moon) C.; B.B.A., U. Ga., 1950; m. Evelyn Whitley, Nov. 23, 1950; children—Laura, Elizabeth. Asst. personnel analyst Union Bag & Paper Co., Savannah, Ga., 1950-52; personnel mgr. Steel Products Co., Savannah, 1952-56; employment, tng. supr. Chamet, Inc., Chattanooga, 1956-58; chief employee relations Thiokol Chem. Corp., Huntsville, Ala., 1958; dir. personnel Sikes Corp. (formerly Fla. Tile Industries, Inc.), Lakeland, 1958-60, v.p. indsl. relations, 1960—. Mem. adv. bd. Salvation Army, Lakeland, 1964—. Bd. dirs. Lakeland Indsl. Bd., 1963-65, Lakeland Civil Service Bd., 1968—. Served to lt. AUS, 1943-46. Mem. So. Indsl. Relations Conf. Bd. Democrat. Episcopalian. Elk, Kiwanian. Home: 2208 Coventry Av Lakeland FL 33803 Office: 608 Prospect St Lakeland FL 33802

CLEGHORN, REESE, newspaper editor; b. Lyerly, Ga., Apr. 9, 1930; s. John Storey and Nona Martin (Reese) C.; B.A., Emory U., 1950; M.A., Columbia U., 1956; m. Gwendolyn Michael, Dec. 28, 1954; children—Nona Elizabeth, John Michael. Asso. editor The Atlanta Jour., 1964-69; writer residence So. Regional Council, 1969-71; editor of editorial pages The Charlotte (N.C.) Observer, 1971—. Served with USAF, 1951-52. Author: (with Pat Watters) Climbing Jacob's Ladder, 1967. Office: The Charlotte Observer 600 S Tryon St Charlotte NC 28201

CLEMENT, WALTER STONE, railroad exec.; b. Roanoke, Va., Sept. 12, 1912; s. Allen W. and Berta L. (Bousman) C.; ed. Washington and Lee U., Boston Coll.; m. Jane Henderson, Nov. 15, 1940; children—Zack, Tiffany. With N. & W. Ry., 1935—, asst. roadmaster, 1947-50, roadmaster, 1950-54, asst. trainmaster, 1954-55, trainmaster, 1955-57, supt., 1957, asst. gen. supt., 1957-59, gen. supt., Roanoke, Va., 1959-60, resident v.p., Norfolk, Va., 1960-64, v.p. lake region, Cleve., 1964-66, v.p. Western region, St. Louis, 1966-69, v.p. Washington, 1969-71, v.p. pub. affairs, Roanoke, 1971—. Served to capt. C.E., AUS, 1942-46. Mem. Ohio C. of C. (dir.). Democrat. Baptist Clubs: Burning Tree (Washington); Roanoke Country. Office: 8 N Jefferson St Roanoke VA 24011

CLEMENTS, ABRAHAM WALLER, state ofcl.; b. nr. Morganfield, Ky., Dec. 9, 1916; s. Baldwin Johnson and Margaret Elizabeth (Kagey) C.; grad. high sch.; m. Lena Ray Sosh, Nov. 25, 1939; 1 dau., Bonnie Lou (Mrs. DeMotte Little). With Ky. Dept. Hwys., 1934—, chief constrn. engr., 1963-66, dist. engr., Madisonville, 1966—. Served with USNR, 1942-45. Registered profl. engr., Ky. Mason (Shriner), Kiwanian. Home: 24 Valley Dr Madisonville KY 42431 Office: P O Drawer D Madisonville KY 42431

CLEMENTS, CHARLES RUNCIE, JR., ins. exec.; b. Nashville, Oct. 8, 1910; s. Charles Runcie and Frances (Moore) C.; B.A., Vanderbilt U., 1932; m. Valeria Hughes, June 22, 1932; children—Betty (Mrs. James H. Armistead, Jr.), Charles Runcie III. With Nat. Life and Accident Ins. Co., Nashville, 1932—, pres., 1967—, also dir.; Radio Sta. WSM. Mem. adv. bd. St. Thomas Hosp., Salvation Army. Served with USNR, 1943-45. Mem. Life Insurers Conf. (exec. com.), C. of C. (past gov.), Kappa Alpha. Roman Catholic. Clubs: Belle Meade Country; Cumberland. Home: 114 Clarendon Av Nashville TN 37205 Office: Nat Bldg Nashville TN 37219

CLEMENTS, JOHN J.A., public relations exec.; b. Walnut, Kan.; s. George Hanson and Emma Catharine (Mills) C.; m. Stasia Mayer, July 29, 1949. With Hearst Corp., N.Y.C., 1924—, pub. relations dir., 1939-68; formerly owner, pub. Hunterdon Newspapers, Inc.; editor Am. Mercury, 1953-56. Clubs: Advertising, New York Athletic (N.Y.C.); Nat. Press (Washington); Coppper Hill Golf; Overseas Press. Home: 2500 NE 48th Lane Fort Lauderdale FL 33308

CLEMENTS, OMER RANDOLPH, petro-chem. mfg. co. exec.; b. Ida, La., Aug. 14, 1925; s. Quilla Zedoic and LaVada (Slay) C.; B.S., La. Poly. Inst., 1950; m. Lovenia Holder, Dec. 22, 1950; 1 son, Terence Christopher. Plant engr. Southwest Gas Producing Co., 1950-51; with Western Co., Midland, Tex., 1951-52, Henderson Engring. Co., Shreveport, La., 1952-53, El Paso Natural Gas Co., 1953-61, operations mgr., 1963-65; with El Paso Products Co., Odessa, 1961—, v.p., gen. mgr., mfg. operations, 1968—. Bd. regents Odessa Coll. Served with AUS, 1943-45. Registered profl. engr., Tex., Mem. Am. Inst. Chem. Engrs., Nat., Tex. socs. profl. engrs., Tex. Mfrs. Assn. (bd. dirs.), W. Tex. (bd. dirs.), Odessa (bd. dirs.) chambers commerce. Home: 2927 Kirkwood St Odessa TX 79760 Office: PO Box 3986 Odessa TX 79760

CLEMENTS, REXFORD SCOTT, banker; b. Hartford, Conn., Aug. 30, 1936; s. Rolf Victor and Eleanor Benedict (Baldwin) C.; B.A. in Econs., Dickinson Coll., 1959; M.A. in Econs., Trinity Coll., 1968; postgrad. Stonier Grad. Sch. Banking, Rutgers U., 1972—; m. Arline Florence Bishop, Aug. 17, 1962; children—Kate Baldwin, Amy Elizabeth, Rebecca Lee, Sarah Lynn. Asst. cashier Hartford Nat. Bank and Trust Co. (Conn.), 1963-68; v.p. Atlantic Nat. Bank of Jacksonville (Fla.), 1968—; v.p. Atlantic Bancorp., 1972—. Instr., Am. Inst. Banking, 1968—. Treas., United Negro Coll. Fund, 1971—; subcom. chmn. budget com. United Fund, 1970—; active Big Bros. of Jacksonville, 1970—. Mem. Republican Town Com., Windsor, Conn., 1967-68. Served with USNR, 1959-62. Mem. Greater Jacksonville C. of C. (mem. state and local govt. com. 1970—), Financial Analysts of Jacksonville, Municipal Forum of Washington, Am. Inst. Banking. Unitarian. Clubs: San Jose Country, University (Jacksonville). Home: 7375 San Pedro Rd Jacksonville FL 32217 Office: West Bay Sta Jacksonville FL 32203

CLEMENTS, ZEKE, musician; b. Dora, Ala., Sept. 6, 1911; s. Andrew Jackson and Viola (Peters) C.; student pub. schs.; m. Helen E. Dalton, May 21, 1944; 1 dau., Sally R. Star of Grand Ole Opry, Nashville; writer numerous songs including Just a Little Lovin, Smoke on the Water, Why Should I Cry, Live and Learn, Somebody's Been Beatin' My Time, Me and My Big Mouth, I Love the Name of Jesus. Mem. Song Writers Hall Fame. Address: PO Box 35 Nashville TN 37202

CLEMMONS, ROBERT STARR, minister, educator, author; b. New London, O., Oct. 21, 1910 ; s. William E. and Tella (Tissot) C.; B.A., Ohio Wesleyan U., 1933; B.D., Union Theol. Sem., 1936; S.T.M., Oberlin Coll., 1951; postgrad. Vanderbilt U., George Peabody Coll., U. Pitts., Columbia; m. Beatrice Marian Winter, Aug. 27, 1936; children— Lynne Marie (Mrs. Judson Henry Morris, Jr.), David Robert. Ordained to ministry Methodist Ch., 1934; mem. staff Ch. of All Nations, N.Y.C., 1934-36; minister, Brecksville, O., 1936; dir. Wesley Found., State U., Kent, O., 1940-45; mem. staff young adult work Gen. Bd. Edn. United Meth. Ch., Nashville, 1945-57, dir. Council of Adult Work, 1957-67, asst. to gen. sec. program design and coordination, 1967—. Lectr. Emory U., Iliff Sch. Theology, Scarritt Coll.; field work cons. Vanderbilt U. Divinity Sch.; mem. nat. family life com. United Meth. Ch., 1956-68, mem. nat. curriculum com., 1945-68, mem. interagy. staff planning com., 1968—. Mem. Am. Acad. Religion, Adult Edn. Assn., Am. Acad. Arts and Scis., World Futurist Soc. Methodist. Author: Dynamics of Christian Adult Education, 1957; Young Adults in the Church, 1959; Adult Education in the Methodist Church, 1961; Education for Churchmanship, 1966. Home: 2019 Overhill Dr Nashville TN 37215 Office: PO Box 871 1001 19th Av S Nashville TN 37203

CLEMMONS, SLATON, lawyer; b. Rome, Ga., July 19, 1909; s. Thomas Edmondson and Annie Ross (Slaton) C.; student Davidson Coll., 1926-27; LL.B., U. Ga., 1929; postgrad. U. Pa., 1929-30; m. Starr Reynolds Quigg, 1939 (div. 1957); children—Diana Edmondson, Byard Quigg, Thomas Slaton; m. 2d, Frances Mansell Crowder, Nov. 1965. Admitted to Ga. bar, 1929; practiced in Rome, 1930-35, 46-54; spl. atty. U.S. Dept. Justice, 1935-37, 42-46; spl. atty. gen. Ga., 1938-39; spl. asst. to atty. gen. U.S., 1940-41; asst. U.S. atty. No. dist. Ga., 1954-62; 1st asst. U.S. atty., 1962-70, ret., 1970. Served as lt. (j.g.) USNR, 1942. Fellow Internat. Acad. Law and Sci.; mem. Am., Ga., Rome (past pres.) bar assns., Am. Judicature Soc., Am. Acad. Polit. and Social Sci., Am. Legion, Mil. Order World Wars, Phi Delta Phi, Sigma Alpha Epsilon. Democrat. Presbyn. Mason. Clubs: Coosa Country, Nine O'clock Cotillion (Rome, Ga.). Home: 412 E 3d Av Rome GA 30161

CLENDENING, JOHN ALBERT, palynologist; b. Martinsburg, W.Va., Mar. 6, 1932; s. Charles Brady and F.D. Myrtle (Remsburg) C.; student Shepherd Coll., 1954-56; B.S., W.Va. U., 1958, M.S., 1960, Ph.D., 1970; m. Cleo Dorothy Bond, Sept. 26, 1954; children—Kyra Lynn, Rebecca Lea, Shawna Ruth. Coal geologist-palynologist W.Va. Geol. Survey, Morgantown, 1960-68; palynologist Pan Am. Petroleum Corp., Ft. Worth, 1968-71, Amoco Prodn. Co., Houston, 1971—. Served with inf., U.S. Army, 1951-54. Decorated Purple Heart. Fellow Geol. Soc. Am.; mem. Bot. Soc. Am., W.Va. Acad. Sci. Methodist. Mason (K.T.). Author: (with W.H. Gillespie) West Virginia Geology, Archeology and Pedology, 1964; (with Gillespie & Latimer) Plant Fossils of West Virginia, 1966; Sporological Evidence on the Geological Age of the Dunkard Strata in the Appalachian Basin, 1970. Contbr. articles profl. jours. Home: 1018 Tulip Tree Lane Houston TX 77090 Office: Box 3092 Houston TX 77001

CLENDINEN, JAMES AUGUSTUS, newspaper editor; b. Eufaula, Ala., Dec. 1, 1910; s. Thomas A. and Katherine (Powell) C.; student U. Fla., 1929-30; m. Barbara Harrison, May 22, 1943; children—James Dudley, Melissa Louise. Reporter Clearwater (Fla.) Eve. Sun, 1930-34, mng. editor, 1934-35; reporter Tampa Morning Tribune, 1935-42, state news editor, 1946-49, asso. editor, 1949-58, editor, 1958—. Bd. dirs. U. So. Fla. Found.; mem. Pulitzer prize jury, 1967-68. Served as tech. sgt. USAF, 1942-45. Recipient first prize for editorial writing Fla. Daily Newspaper Assn., 1955, 57, 58, 60, 64; Editorial Writing Distinguished Service award Sigma Delta Chi, 1961; Editorial Writing award Fla. Edn. Assn., 1963; Consistently Outstanding Editorial Page award Nat. Headliners Club, 1964; Freedoms Found. award, 1961, 62; Editorial Writing award Fla. Press Assn., 1966, 1967, 69; Pub. Service award Fla. Bar Assn., 1965. Nieman Travelling fellow to study conditions in Spain, 1957. Mem. Nat. Conf. Editorial Writers (pres. 1966), Fla. Soc. Editors (founder and first pres.), Am. Soc. Newspaper Editors, Sigma Delta Chi, Phi Kappa Tau. Episcopalian. Mem. Ye Mystic Krewe of Gasparilla. Clubs: University, Exchange, Tampa Yacht and Country. Home: 3000 Schiller Av Tampa FL 33609 Office: 505 E Kennedy Blvd Tampa FL 33602

CLERICO, LOUIS RICHARD, interior designer; b. Yonkers, N.Y., Mar. 30, 1918; s. Ludovico Michael and Mary Lucia (Esposito) C.; grad. Newark Fine and Indsl. Arts Sch., 1935; student Art Students League, 1945-46, N.Y.U., 1946-49; m. Antoinette Francis Oliveri, June 6, 1952; children—Louis, Candace, Melodi, Valerie. Owner, Louis R. Clerico Assos., N.Y.C., 1948-62; pres., chief designer Louis R. Clerico, Miami, 1962-69; sr. partner I.D. Assos., Miami, 1969-70; v.p. charge design Louis R. Clerico Assos., Inc., Miami, 1970—. Cons. for design and color Jo Gresite Ceramic Tile Corp., Milan, Italy, 1961-63. Mem. Fla. Gov's. Council, 1967-70. Served to 1st lt. AUS, 1940-45. Recipient 1st prize for package design Art Dirs. Club Greater Miami, 1953, award for outstanding design achievements Euster Merchandise Mart, 1970, Interior Design award Miami Mdse. Mart, 1969. Mem. Am. Inst. Interior Designers, Indsl. Designers Soc. Am. (chmn. S.W. chpt. 1965). Designers and Decorators Guild (pres. 1962-63), Miami Design Assn. (v.p. design 1967-68), Nat. Home Builders Assn., Ret. Officers Assn. Clubs: Country (Coral Gables, Fla.); Jockey (Miami); Delray Beach (Fla.), Sky Lake (North Miami, Fla.); Inverrary Racquet (Ft. Lauderdale, Fla.). Co-author, illustrator Never Unarmed, 1944. Home: 235 NE 122d St Miami FL 33161 Office: 54 NE 54th St Miami FL 33137

CLEVELAND, CONRAD PIERCE, JR., banker; b. Spartanburg, S.C., Sept. 6, 1914; s. Conrad P. and Louise (Williams) C.; B.S., The Citadel, 1935. Realtor, 1946-48; organizing dir. Piedmont Nat. Bank, 1947-63, v.p., mgr. Main St. br., 1953-63; v.p. Main St. office S.C. Nat. Bank, Spartanburg, 1963-65, v.p. charge Montgomery bldg. office, 1965—; owner Clevedale Farms. Past pres. Spartanburg Music Found.; active Boy Scouts Am., formerly dist. commr. Spartanburg; adv. com. Third Army. Served from 1st lt. to lt. col. AUS, 1940-46; col. Res. Recipient Silver Beaver, Distinguished Eagle Scout awards Boy Scouts Am. Mem. Assn. Citadel Men (past pres., life mem.). Assn. U.S. Army, Res. Officers Assn. Episcopalian (sr. warden, layreader, vestryman; sec. Upper S.C. Diocese Found.). Clubs: Country, Piedmont (Spartanburg). Home: Clevedale Farms Spartanburg SC 29301 Office: South Carolina National Bank Spartanburg SC 29301

CLEVEN, CATHERINE LOUISE SEWARD (MRS. EDMUND H. CLEVEN), author; b. Dayton, O.; d. Edmund Garfield and Elizabeth (Smith) Seward; B.A., U. Ill., 1927; m. Edmund H. Cleven, Oct. 18, 1930. Mem. Nat. League Am. Penwomen (v.p. Ft. Lauderdale, Fla. br. 1968-70), Women's Nat. Book Assn., Mystery Writers Am., Inc., Soc. Midland Authors, Chgo. Children's Reading Round Table. Author: Secret of the King's Field, 1952; Flight Angel, 1961; Pirate Dog, 1962; John Hancock, 1963; Black Hawk, Young Sauk Warrior, 1966. Home: 1545 SE 14th St Deerfield Beach FL 33441

CLIFF, EDWARD P., forestry cons.; b. Heber City, Utah, Sept. 3, 1909; s. Edward Parley and Geneva Rachel (Bergener) C.; B.S., Utah State U., 1931, D. Sc. (hon.), 1965; m. Kathryn Mitchell, Apr. 2, 1931; children—Carolyn, Jane. With U.S. Forest Service, 1931-72, as jr. range examiner Wenatchee Nat. Forest, Wash., 1931-34, range examiner in charge wildlife mgmt. Pacific N.W. Region, Portland, Ore., 1934-39, supr. Siskiyou Nat. Forest, Grants Pass, Ore., 1939-41, Fremont Nat. Forest, Lakeview, Ore., 1942-44, asst. chief div. range mgmt., Washington, 1944-46, asst. regional forest charge div. range and wildlife mgmt. Intermountain Region, Ogden, Utah, 1946-49, regional forester Rocky Mountain Region, Denver, 1950-52, asst. chief charge nat. forest adminstrn., Washington, 1952-62, chief Forest Service, 1962-72; forestry cons., 1972—. Mem. U.S. Bd. Geog. Names, 1952-67, chmn., 1962-65; alternate mem. Adv. Council on Historic Preservation, 1967-72; chmn. N. Am. Forestry Commn., 1964-65, 71-72. Recipient Distinguished Service award Utah State U., 1958; Dept. Agr., 1962; career service award Nat. Civil Service League, 1968. Mem. Soc. Am. Foresters, Wildlife Soc. (charter), Am. Soc. Range Mgmt. (charter), Am. Forestry Assn., Wilderness Soc. Mem. Church of Jesus Christ of Latter-Day Saints. Mason. Clubs: Cosmos (Washington); Boone and Crockett. Author: Range Plant Handbook (with W.A. Dayton and others), 1937; articles govt. publs. Home: 221 N Royal St Alexandria VA 22314

CLIFFORD, ALAN FRANK, educator; b. Natick, Mass., June 8, 1919; s. Arthur Woodbury and Elva (Buck) C.; A.B., Harvard, 1941; M.S., U. Del., 1947, Ph.D., 1949; m. Shirley Catherine Mittlemen, Aug. 20, 1949; children—Abbie Louise, Philip Alan. Chemist, Kankakee Ordnance Works, Joliet, Ill., 1941-43; chemist, Manhattan project U. Chgo., Clinton Labs, Oak Ridge Tenn., Hanford Engring. works, Richland, Wash., 1943-45; chemist DuPont Expt. Sta., Wilmington, Del., 1945-46; instr. U. Del., Newark, 1947-49; asst. prof. Ill. Inst. Tech., Chgo., 1949-51; asst. prof. Purdue U., Lafayette, Ind., 1953-58, asso. prof., 1958-66; prof., head dept. chemistry Va. Poly. Inst., Blacksburg, Va., 1966—. Guggenheim fellow, Cambridge (Eng.) U., 1951-53. Mem. Am. Chem. Soc., Chem. Soc. London, Faraday Soc., N.Y. Acad. Sci., A.A.A.S., Alpha Chi Sigma. Author: Inorganic Chemistry of Qualitative Analysis, 1961 (Italian transl. 1970); Chemistry in Nonaqueous Ionizing Solvents, Vol I, Part 1, Inorganic Chemistry in Liquid Hydrogen Fluoride, 1971. Contbr. articles to profl. jours. Home: 860 Hutcheson Lane Blacksburg VA 24060 Office: Dept Chemistry Va Poly Inst Blacksburg VA 24061

CLIFFORD, CLYDE WOODS, broadcasting exec.; b. Shelbyville, Tenn., Aug. 23, 1937; s. Buford A. and Dora (Scales) C.; B.S., Middle Tenn. State Coll., 1961; m. Peggey Ann Elam, July 22, 1956; children— Majoria Leigh, Anjanette. Sr. accountant Price Waterhouse & Co., Nashville, 1961-65; v.p., treas. LIN Broadcasting Corp., Nashville, 1965—; pres. Al Hirt Sandwich Saloons, Inc., 1966. Served with AUS, 1956-59. C.P.A., Tenn. Mem. Am. Inst. C.P.A.'s, Tenn. Soc. C.P.A.'s. Home: 920 Tyne Blvd Nashville TN 37220 Office: Elliston Pl Nashville TN 37203

CLIFFORD, PAUL INGRAHAM, psychologist, assn. exec.; b. Martinsburg, W.Va., Jan. 22, 1914; s. J. Paul and Mabel (Douglass) C.; B.S., State Tchrs. Coll., Shippensburg, Pa., 1938; A.M., Atlanta U., 1948; Ph.D., U. Chgo., 1953; m. Elizabeth Edith Sterrs, Jan. 21, 1950. Civilian administrv. asst. USAAF, 1941-46; prof. chemistry Paine Coll., Augusta, Ga., 1947-48; instr. in edn. Atlanta U., 1948-51, asst. prof., 1952-54, asso. prof., 1954-57, prof., 1957-68, registrar, 1954-66, dir. admissions, 1954-66, dir. summer sch., 1957-68; staff psychologist Am. Mgmt. Psychologists, Inc., 1966—, v.p., dir., 1969—, nat. dir. profl. services, 1971—. Cons. U.S. Office Edn., 1961—; vis. prof. edn. U. Cal. at Berkeley, 1968-69; cons. psychologist various indsl. orgns. Dir. So. Fellowships Fund; trustee Zale Found., Dallas. Licensed psychologist, Ga., Ill. Fellow A.A.A.S., Ga. Psychol. Assn.; mem. Am., Southeastern psychol. assns., Soc. for Psychol. Study Social Issues, Nat. Soc. Study Edn., Am. Assn. U. Profs., Assn. for Higher Edn., N.E.A., Am. Ednl. Research Assn., Am. Personnel and Guidance Assn., Nat. Vocational Guidance Assn., Nat. Assn. Guidance Suprs., Assn. Counselor Edn. and Supervision, Nat. Council on Measurement in Edn., Am. Acad. Polit. and Social Scis., N.Y. Acad. Scis., Phi Delta Kappa, Omega Psi Phi. Episcopalian. Author monograph, articles for ednl. and psychol. jours. Home: 859 Woodmere Dr NW Atlanta GA 30318 Office: Lennox Towers Atlanta GA 30326 also Borg-Warner Bldg Chicago IL 60604

CLIFTON, BLOIS JACKSON, ednl. adminstr.; b. Hollins, Ala., June 25, 1934; s. Stonewall Jackson and Ellie (Johnson) C.; B.S., Ala. Christian Coll., 1956; m. Mary Lucille Bowles, Apr. 10, 1959; children—Stephen Gregg, Lana La'Shawn. Bursar, Ala. Christian Coll., Montgomery, 1956-69, comptroller, dir. bus. affairs 1969—. Bd. dirs. Ala. Christian Sch. Religion. Mem. Church of Christ (deacon 1971). Home: 3201 N Colonial Dr Montgomery AL 36111 Office: 5345 Atlanta Hwy Montgomery AL 36109

CLIFTON, CHARLES LAMAR, assn. exec.; b. Albany, Ga., Apr. 18, 1929; s. Charles Bruce and Sally (Hopkins) C.; student N. Ga. Coll., 1946-48; A.B., U. Ga., 1950, M.Ed., 1955; postgrad. U. Fla., 1953-54; m. Mary Evelyn Butler, May 23, 1953; children—Charles Lamar, Cary Evelyn, Dodd Butler. Pub. relations Genesco, Nashville, 1950-51; tchr., coach Albany High Sch., 1955; sales rep. Met. Life Ins. Co., Albany, 1956-57; asst. mgr. Albany C. of C., 1957-59; exec. mgr. Columbia (S.C.) C. of C., 1959-67; gen. mgr. WIS Radio div. Cosmos Broadcasting Corp., 1967-69; dist. mgr. C. of C. U.S., Atlanta, 1969—; dir. Cosmos Broadcasting Corp., State Bank & Trust Co. of S.C. Vis. instr. U. S.C., 1962. Bd. dirs. Richland Tech. Edn. Center, Columbia Better Bus. Bur.; mem. Columbia City Planning Comm.; mem. Richland County Adv. Com. Hosps. and Edn.; pres. Brennan Sch. P.T.A.; chmn. United Fund Drive. Served with AUS, 1951-53. Decorated Bronze Star medal. Mem. Am. C. of C. Execs., Demosthenian Literary Soc. (pres. 1950), S.C., (edn. com.), So. C. of C. execs., Am., So. indsl. devel. councils, Nat., S.C. assns. broadcasters, Scabbard and Blade, Phi Kappa Phi, Sigma Delta Chi, Phi Delta Kappa. Baptist (deacon; chmn. planning and survey com.). Kiwanian (dir.). Home: 1706 Marbury Lane Albany GA 31705 Office: 3376 Peachtree Rd NE Atlanta GA 30326

CLIFTON, DREW SPENCER, judge; b. Meridian, Miss., Nov. 26, 1909; s. Sid Spencer and Frances (Whitlock) C.; student Tex. Christian U., 1929-31, Columbia, 1931, Cumberland U., 1935-36; LL.B., Jefferson U., 1938; m. Mildren Inez Jones, July 3, 1938. Asst. mng. dir., mng. dir., Panther Boys Club, Ft. Worth, 1929-32; agt. N.M. Rural Rehab. Corp., 1934-35; admitted to Tex. bar, 1936; practicing lawyer, Dallas, 1936-38, Ft. Worth, 1938-42, 45; asst. dist. atty., Tarrant Co., 1944; judge County Ct. 1946—; judge adv., dir. Vets. Meml., Inc.; lectr. Rep. Mid.-Century White House Conf. Children and Youth, Tex., 1950. Trustee Greenwood Cemetery Perpetual Fund; dir. Tarrant County Mental Health Assn.; director Fort Worth Rehab. Farm, Ft. Worth-Tarrant County Employment Handicapped. Served from pvt. to warrant officer (j.g.), U.S. Army, 1942-44. Mem. State Bar Tex. (exec. com. jud. sect.), Ft. Worth, Am. bar assns., Am. Judicature Soc., Am. Authors and Composers Assn., Council Social Agencies (mem. bd. and exec. com.), Ft. Worth C. of C., Am. Vets.

World War II, Disabled Veterans Am., Tex. Judiciary Conf., Am. Legion (nat. child welfare com.; Tex. child welfare com.), V.F.W., Forty and Eight. Democrat. Baptist. Mason (K.T., Shriner). Clubs: Tex. Gridiron, Kiwanis (v.p.). Home: 5208 Byers Av Fort Worth TX 76107 Office: Tarrant County Courthouse Fort Worth TX 76101

CLIFTON, EMBROSE WILLIAM, advt. exec.; b. Savannah, Ga., Dec. 16, 1931; s. Edward William and Alberta (Simpson) C.; student Armstrong State Coll., 1956-57; m. JoAnne Colley, Mar. 1, 1952; children— Edward William, Christopher Dean, Terri, Laura. With Savannah (Ga.) Newspaper, 1957-66, asst. class mgr. classified advt. sales dept., 1957-60, nat. advt. mgr., 1960-63, retail advt. mgr., 1963-66; advt. mgr. Today Newspaper, Cocoa Beach, Fla., 1966; asst. dir. bus. devel. Fla. Times-Union/Jacksonville Jour., 1966-67, nat. advt. mgr., 1967-68, retail advt. mgr., 1968-72, advt. dir., 1969—. Adviser Explorer post N. Fla. council Boy Scouts Am., 1970-72. Served with USAF, 1951-55. Mem. Internat. Newspaper Advt. Execs., Fla. Newspaper Advt. Execs. (state sec. 1971-72), Jacksonville Advt. Fedn. (pres. 1972-73), Sales Marketing Execs. Jacksonville, C. of C. Mem. Ch. of Jesus Christ of Latter-day Saints. Rotarian. Clubs: Sertoma, University, Deerwood Country (Jacksonville); Ponte Vedre (Fla.) Country. Home: 5060 Somersby Rd Jacksonville FL 32217 Office: 1 Riverside Av Jacksonville FL 32201

CLIFTON, H. P., city mgr. City mgr., Abilene, Tex. Office: City Hall Abilene TX 79604*

CLIFTON, JOSEPH WENDEL, ret. govt. ofcl.; b. Brunswick, Neb., July 30, 1913; s. Kem A. and Pauline (Hoscheit) C.; student Neb U., 1930-31; m. Helen Mach, Oct. 4, 1941. Tchr., Boyd County (Neb.) rural schs., 1931-34; clk., field supr. Boyd County A.A.A., U.S. Dept. Agr., 1934-36; farmer, Boyd County, 1937-38; supr. Neb. Office Prodn. and Marketing Adminstrn., 1938-42, 46-48; adminstrv. officer Fed. Crop Ins. Corp., Washington, 1949-51; staff asst. Prodn. and Marketing Adminstrn., Dept. Agr., Washington, 1951-57, dep. dir. aerial photography div. Agrl. Stblzn. and Conservation Service, Washington, 1957-61, dir., 1961-69, asso. dir. program performance div., 1969-72, coordinator aerial photog. work, 1968-72; chmn. earth resources survey com. Dept. Agr., 1971-72. Served with AUS, 1942-45; ETO. Decorated Purple Heart, Bronze Star; recipient Certificate Merit, Dept. Agr., 1962, 64, 66, 67, 68, 69, 70, 71, 72. Mem. Am. Soc. Photogrammetry, Orgn. Profl. Employees Dept. Agr. Democrat. Mason (Shriner). Home: 1301 Elsinore Av McLean VA 22101 Office: US Dept Agr 14th and Independence Washington DC 20250

CLIFTON, NOEL SAMUEL, state bar ofcl.; b. Danville, Va., Dec. 11, 1929; s. Noel Samuel and Lessie Adele (Megginson) C.; B.S. in Commerce with honors, U. Va., 1952; LL.B., George Washington U., 1959; m. Barbara Hyams, June 1, 1969. Admitted to Va. bar, 1960, practiced in Alexandria until 1962; dir. econs. dept. Am. Bar Assn., Chgo., 1963-66; asst. dir. Va. State Bar, Richmond, 1967-69, exec. dir., 1969—. Served as lt. USNR, 1952-56; Korea. Mem. Delta Theta Phi, Phi Eta Sigma. Home: 4903 Sulky Dr Richmond VA 23228 Office: Virginia State Bar Imperial Bldg Richmond VA 23219

CLIFTON, ROBERT WENDELL, metal finishing co. exec.; b. Middletown, O., Aug. 19, 1921; s. Everett and Mary (Armitage) C.; grad. Middletown High Sch., 1941; m. Agnes Marie Robinette, June 7, 1942; children—Robert James, Susalee, Cathy Jo. Pres., Valley Plating Co., Richmond, Va., 1958—; pres. Richmond Galvanizing Co., Richmond, 1962—. Served with USAAF, 1942-46. Home: Ingleside Farm Box 296 Mechanicsville VA 23111 Office: 920 E Laburnum Av Richmond VA 23222

CLINE, FRANCIS XAVIER, JR., orthopedic surgeon; b. Monroe, La., Mar. 16, 1927; s. Francis X. and Josephine (La Baume) C.; student N.E. State Coll., 1944-46; diploma La. Tech. Inst., 1947; M.D., La. State U., 1951; postgrad. Tulane U., 1957-58; m. children—Colleen, Francis Xavier III, Catherine. Intern, Touro Infirmary, New Orleans, 1951-52; resident orthopedic surgery Confederate Meml. Med. Center, Shreveport, La., 1957-60; gen. practice medicine, Delhi, La., 1955-57; practice orthopedic surgery, Monroe, La., 1960—; vis. staff St. Francis Hosp.; vice chief staff Glenwood Hosp., 1968; cons. E.A. Conway Meml. Hosp.; cons. handicapped children's service La. Bd. Health; med. adviser Social Security Adminstrn.; vice pres. Doctors Bldg., Monroe. Served to capt. with USAF, 1953-55. Fellow A.C.S. (mem. La. com. on trauma 1966—), Am. Acad. Orthopedic Surgeons; mem. A.M.A., So. Med. Assn., La. Orthopedic Assn., Ouachita Paris Med. Soc. (v.p. 1968-69), U.S. Power Squadron (comdr.), La. Farm Bur., Monroe C. of C. Episcopalian. Clubs: Bayou De Siard Country, D'Arbonne Yacht (commodore 1968-70). Home: 3418 Westminster St Monroe LA 71201 Office: 313 Wood St Monroe LA 71201

CLINE, FRANK RAY, investments; b. Greenville, S.C.; s. Hunley and Lila (Ballew) Cline; m. Betty Virginia Smith, June 20, 1948; 1 dau., Deborah Anne. Asst. mgr. J. C. Penney Co., 1951-56; div. mgr. Waddell & Reed, Inc. Dir. Cumberland County United Fund, 1958-59; gen. campaign chmn. United Services Fund for Fayetteville. Ft. Bragg, Pope Field, 1965-66. Mem. 3d Army Adv. Bd., 1957-58. Served as staff sgt. AUS, 1942-46. Mem. Internat. Platform Assn., Assn. U.S. Army. Methodist (steward). Clubs: Lions (past pres.), Executives (dir., past pres.) (Fayetteville). Home: 2518 Dartmouth Dr Fayetteville NC 28304 Office: First Union Nat Bank Bldg Fayetteville NC 28301

CLINE, MARJORIE ANN, editor; b. Washington, Mar. 9, 1920; d. Sheldon Scott and Mary Marjorie (Brigham) C.; student Strayer's Bus. Coll., 1939-40, George Washington U., 1943-44, Dunbarton Coll., 1945-46. Secretarial worker Nat. Wildlife Fedn., WPA, 1941-43; with Evening Star Newspaper Co., Washington, 1943—, asst. women's editor, 1961—, also society editor. Home: 9823 Old Georgetown Rd Bethesda MD 20014 Office: 225 Virginia Av SE Washington DC 20003

CLINE, PAUL CHARLES, educator; b. Clarksburg, W.Va., Dec. 26, 1933; s. Kemper Price and Irene (Neff) C.; A.A., Potomac State Coll., 1953; A.B., W.Va. U., 1955, J.D., 1957, M.A., 1961; Ph.D., Am. U., 1968; m. Diane Chilcote, Aug. 10, 1958; children—Alice J., Camille N. Admitted to W. Va. bar, 1957; practiced in Huntington, 1959-60; asst. prof. polit. sci. Madison Coll., Harrisonburg, Va., 1961-68, asso. prof., 1968-70, coordinator fed. grants and programs, 1966-67, exec. asst. to pres., 1967-69, head dept. polit. sci. and geography, 1969-71, prof. polit. sci., 1970—. Chmn. Harrisburg City Planning Commn., 1971—; mem. Harrisonburg City Council, 1972—. Precinct chmn., 1966—. Served with AUS, 1957-59. Mem. Am. Polit. Sci. Assn., Shenandoah Valley Folklore Soc., W. Va. State Bar, Phi Alpha Delta, Phi Alpha Theta, Phi Sigma Alpha, Pi Sigma Mu. Home: 221 Dixie Av Harrisonburg VA 22801

CLINKSCALES, MAYLON BAXTER, judge; b. Starr, S.C., Mar. 9, 1921; s. Milton Baxter and Karon (Traynham) C.; A.B., U. Ga., 1940; LL.B., U. Va., 1942; m. Vans Randall Brinson, Oct. 5, 1949; children—Maylon Baxter, Floride Randall, Milton Brinson. Admitted to Ga. bar, 1946; practiced in Gainesville, Ga., 1946-51, Commerce, Ga., 1951—; partner Clinkscales and Whelchel, Gainesville; judge Superior Ct. Ga., 1956-61. Owner Cli-Pet Ice Co., 1942—; agt. Standard Oil Co., 1947—; owner Cli-Pet Ins. Co., 1948—, S. Pacific Motel, Panama City. Bd. dirs. Ga. Soc. for Crippled Children, 1956—. Served with inf. AUS, World War II. Mem. Am. Legion, Gridiron Secret Soc., 40 and 8. Baptist (founder, tchr. young men's Sunday sch. class). Mason (Shriner), Elk. Clubs: Athens (Ga.) Country, Athens Touchdown; Capital City (Atlanta). Home: 214 Washington Av Commerce GA 30529 Office: N Broad St PO Box 36 Commerce GA 30529

CLODY, HARRY WILLIAM, ins. cons.; b. S.I., N.Y., Mar. 28, 1917; s. Harry William and Marie J. (Allen) C.; student N.Y.U., 1934-35; grad. exec. program U. N.C., 1960; m. Marcia Hope Fisher, Aug. 11, 1941; 1 son, William F.M. With group ins. dept. Equitable Life Assurance Soc., N.Y.C., 1934-46; group service mgr. Pilot Life Ins. Co., Greensboro, N.C., 1946-48; mgr. group div. State Capital Life Ins. Co., Raleigh, N.C., 1948, v.p., 1949-70; v.p. Durham Life Ins. Co., 1970; exec. v.p. Mid-South Ins. Co., 1970-71; owner, cons. Carolina Ins. Advisors, 1971—; chmn. bd. So. Roofing & Metal Co., Raleigh; v.p., dir. Soramco Corp. Bd. dirs. Raleigh Lions Clinic for Blind. Served from pvt. to staff sgt. USAAF, 1942-46. Mem. Acad. Polit. Sci., Internat. Platform Assn., Assn. U.S. Army, Am. Legion, Newcomen Soc., N.C. Fraternal Congress (past pres., dir.), Am. Acad. Consultants, Life Office Mgmt. Assn. (group ins. adminstrn. com.), Ins. Accounting and Statis. Assn. (research com., group ins. com.). Lion (pres., dir., zone chmn., dep. dist. gov.), K.C. (past state dep.). Clubs: Raleigh Sales and Marketing Executives (dir.), Raleigh Country. Home: 2805 Churchill Rd Raleigh NC 27607 Office: Box 2416 Raleigh NC 27602

CLOER, CARROLL MARTIN, textile engr.; b. Patterson, N.C., Jan. 29, 1926; s. Carl Elisha and Nannie (Holder) C.; B.S., N.C. State Coll., 1950; grad. Air War Coll., 1970, Indsl. Coll. Armed Forces, 1971; m. Rachel Tuttle, Oct. 2, 1954. Overseer, Hudson (N.C.) Mfg. Co., 1950-52; head quality control Rhodhiss (N.C.) Mills, Burlington Industries, 1952-61; supt. quality control polyester plant Beaunit Fibers, Elizabethton, Tenn., 1961-68; asst. prof., head textile dept. Danville Community Coll., 1968-69; mfg. supt. Arista Mills, Winston-Salem, N.C., 1969-70, Virginia Mills, Swepsonville, N.C., 1970-71; quality control mgr. Firestone Textiles, Gastonia, N.C., 1971—; treas. Burkwell Investors, Rhodhiss, 1960—. Staff officer Tenn. Dept. Civil Def., 1967—. Served with USAAF, 1944-45; now maj. USAF Res. Decorated Air Medal with three oak leaf clusters. Mem. Am. Soc. for Testing and Materials, Am. Soc. Quality Control, Soc. Aerospace and Material Engrs., Am. Assn. Textile Technologists, Am. Mgmt. Assn., V.F.W., Air Force Assn., Res. Officers Assn., Sigma Tau Sigma. Home: 1279-D Carriage House Lane Gastonia NC 28052 Office: Firestone Textiles Gastonia NC 28052

CLOER, JOHN WINFRED, lawyer; b. Springdale, Ark., Sept. 25, 1908; s. John William and Hettie (Lowe) C.; LL.B., U. Ark., 1933; m. Isabel Aileen Long, Oct. 17, 1935; children—Barbara Joan (Mrs. James David Hash), James Richard, Linda Sue (Mrs. Ernest Cate). Admitted to Ark. bar, 1933, since practiced in Springdale. Fruit farmer, 1946-65. Mem. Ark. Ho. of Reps. from Washington County, 1937-43; mem. Ark. Senate, 1943-55. Mem. Christian Ch. (elder). Home: 704 Maria St Springdale AR 72764 Office: 103 E Emma Av Springdale AR 72764

CLONTZ, LUTHER HALL, physician; b. Morganton, N.C., Mar. 19, 1932; s. Vester Herman and Annie Ophelia (Butler) C.; M.D., U. N.C., 1957; m. Fannie Ruth Cagle, Sept. 9, 1954; children—Geoffrey, Deborah, Dana. Intern, U.S. Navy Hosp., Charleston, S.C., 1957-58; pvt. practice medicine, Morganton, N.C., 1960-63; dir. Alcoholism and Drug Program, Broughton Hosp., 1963-66; asst. supt. med. services Western Carolina Center, Morganton, 1966—. Fund-raising chmn. Cerebral Palsy Burke County, 1960-61. Served with USNR, 1957-60. Mem. Phi Beta Kappa. Democrat. Baptist. Home: 408 W Union St Morganton NC 28655 Office: Western Carolina Center Morganton NC 28655

CLOSE, HUGH WILLIAM, textile mfg. exec.; b. Phila., Nov. 18, 1919; s. Hugh William and Marian Lucy (Crandall) C.; student Mercersburg Acad. (Pa.), 1937-38; B.S., U. Pa., 1942; LL.D. (hon.), U. S.C., 1967; m. Anne Kingsley Springs, Nov. 23, 1946; children—Lillian Crandall (Mrs. Erskine B. Bowles), Frances Allison, Leroy Springs, Patricia, Elliott Springs, Hugh William, Derick Springsteen, Katherine Anne Close. With Springs Mills, Inc., N.Y.C., 1946—, beginning as mem. sales staff, Fort Mill, S.C., successively apprentice Springs Cotton Mills, asst. supt., asst. mgr. Fort Mill plant, gen. supt. card and spinning, asst. gen. mgr., asst. to pres., v.p., 1946-59, pres., dir. Springs Mills, Inc., Fort Mill S.C., 1959-69; chmn. bd., 1969—; pres., dir. Lancaster Trust Co., Ft. Mill Trust Co., Bank of Lancaster, Kanawha Ins. Co., Lancaster & Chester R.R., Leroy Springs & Co.; dir. The Springs Co., Carolina & Northwestern Ry. Co. Pres., dir. Elliott White Springs Found., Inc.; bd. dirs. Elliott White Springs Meml. Hosp., Lancaster, S.C.; bd. dirs. U. S.C. Devel. Commr. for 5th congl. dist. Dept. Parks, Recreation and Tourism, State of S.C., 1967—; mem. adv. council J.E. Sirrine Found. Served as pvt. AUS, 1942; ensign to lt. (s.g.) USNR, 1942-46. Named Textile Man of Year, N.Y. Bd. Trade, 1963. Mem. Am. Textile Mfrs. Inst. (dir., pres. 1972-73), S.C. Textile Mfrs. Assn. (ex-officio mem. bd.), Newcomen Soc. N.Am., Phi Gamma Delta, Beta Gamma Sigma. Episcopalian. Club: Lions (Fort Mill). Home: Fort Mill SC 29715 Office: Springs Mills Inc Fort Mill SC 29715

CLOUD, JAMES WAYLAND, govt. ofcl.; b. Okmulgee, Okla., Oct. 18, 1924; s. Frank Wayland and Louise M. (Beck) C.; B.S., Okla. A. and M. Coll., 1949; m. Billie R. Johnson, Oct. 2, 1949; children—James Wayland, Susan D., Pamela L., Lisa C. Engr., Okla. Hwy. Dept., Oklahoma City, 1949-51; constrn. engr. Black Constrn. Co., Oklahoma City, 1951-52; paving engr. Portland Cement Assn., Okla., 1952-65; chief engr. sect., civil engr. airports dist. office FAA, Bethany, Okla., 1965—. Sec. Town of Village Okla. Traffic and Safety Commn., 1954-58. Mem. Indian Terr. Possee. Served with inf. AUS, World War II. Decorated Purple Heart, Bronze Star medal, Combat Inf. badge. Registered profl. engr., Okla., Tex., La. Mem. Midwest City C. of C. (hon.), Chi Epsilon. Mason (32 deg., K.T.). Contbr. articles to profl. jours. Home: 11204 Greystone St Oklahoma City OK 73120 Office: FAA Bldg Wiley Post Airport Bethany OK 73008

CLOUD, RUSSELL WALKER, textile co. exec.; b. Albemarle, N.C., May 24, 1932; s. Jesse Walker and Etta Ramelle (Russell) C.; student Davidson Coll., 1950, Elon Coll., 1951; student U. N.C., 1951-53; m. Isabel N. Blackburn, Mar. 21, 1953; children—Judy, Kathryn, Jeanne, Ruth, Carol. With Jackson & Jackson, Inc., Tryon, N.C., 1960—, sec., asst. treas., 1961-68, v.p., 1968-70, pres., treas., 1970—; dir. Northwestern Bank, Tryon, 1971—. Served with AUS, 1953-55. Club: Tryon Country. Home: Wilderness Rd Tryon NC 28782 Office: 240 Pacolet St Tryon NC 28782

CLOWDIS, CHARLES WILBURN, JR., mgmt. cons.; b. Lafayette, Ga., Sept. 5, 1944; s. Charles Wilburn and Margaret Mae (Robinson) C.; A.A., Young Harris Coll., 1964; B.B.A., U. Ga., 1966. Exec. trainee Gulf & Western Industries, Houston, 1966-67; exec. asst. Provident Life & Accident Ins. Co., Chattanooga, 1967-68, with PLA Securities subsidiary, 1968, asst. sec., 1968-69, sec.-treas., 1970-71; sr. partner Charles W. Clowdis Jr. & Assos., Lafayette, 1972—; sec., dir. Actuarial Services of Mich., Inc., Grand Rapids, Mich., 1970—; sr. partner Aviation Assos., Lafayette, Ga., 1970—. Mem. Lafayette C. of C. (charter), Young Harris Alumni Assn. (dir. 1969—), Nat. Assn. Pub. Accountants, Internat. Assn. Financial Counsellors, Am. Marketing Assn. Democrat. Elk. Home: PO Box 592 301 Sequoia Lane Lafayette GA 30728 Office: 202 W Cherokee St Lafayette GA 30728

CLUM, DENNIS PATRICK, city ofcl.; b. Poughkeepsie, N.Y., May 1, 1925; s. Frederick J. and Margaret M. (Murphy) C.; B.A., Union Coll., Schenectady, 1947; LL.B., Fordham U., 1951; m. Dorothy M. Diederichs, Oct. 14, 1953; children—Dennis Patrick, Robert, Laura. Sr. v.p., trust officer, dir. Miami Beach, First Nat. Bank (Fla.), 1954-71; sr. v.p., dir. United Bancshares of Fla., Inc., 1965-71; exec. v.p., trust officer First State Bank of Miami (Fla.), 1972; now dir. Crime Commn., Miami. Pres. Estate Planning Council Dade County; bd. dirs. Miami Heart Inst., Variety Childrens Hosp., Dade Found., Com. of 100 Miami Beach; mem. adminstrv. bd. Biscayne Coll.; mem. devel. fund bd. Barry Coll.; co-chmn. endowment fund com. U. Miami. Served to lt. USNR, 1943-46, 51-54. Mem. Miami Shores C. of C., Corporate Fiduciaries Assn. Kiwanian. Clubs: Surf, La Gorce, Miami Shores Country, Rod and Reel, Miami, Palm Bay, Racquet, Standard, Jockey, Army and Navy, Bal Harbor. Home: 898 NE 95th St Miami Shores FL 33138 Office: 8017 NE 2d Av Miami FL 33138

CLYBURN, THOMAS MILBURN, scientist; b. Lancaster, S.C., Mar. 15, 1906; s. Lewis Marcellus and Elizabeth (Belk) C.; B.S., Clemson Coll., 1929; postgrad. Ia. State U., 1937-38; m. Bess Edith Plyler, June 3, 1933; 1 son, Thomas Milburn. Coop. agt. agrl. research Clemson Coast Sta., U.S. Dept. Agr., S.C., 1930-37, asst. county agt., Greenwood, S.C., 1938-46; asso. animal husbandry Clemson Coast Sta., Summerville, 1946-51; asst. prof. animal sci. U. Ga., Ga. State Prison Farm, Reidsville, 1951—. Instr. Clemson Coll., 1938. Served to maj. USAAF, 1942-46. Mem. Am. Soc. Animal Sci., Alpha Zeta. Methodist (supt. Sunday Sch. 1949-50). Mason, Lion, Rotarian. Club: Exchange (Greenwood, S.C.). Home: Star Route 22D Reidsville GA 30453

COATES, JESSE, educator; b. Baton Rouge, Mar. 12, 1908; s. Charles Edward and Ollie (Maurin) C.; B.S., La. State U., 1928; student Mass. Inst. Tech., 1930-31; M.S., U. Mich., 1932, Ph.D., 1936; m. Judith Mills Williams, Apr. 16, 1938; children—Judith Mills, Jesse, Victor Maurin (dec.). Chemist, treating engr. Nat. Lumber and Creosoting Co., 1928; chemist Internat. Paper Co., 1928-29, Meeker Sugar Refinery, 1930-31, Punta Alegre Sugar Co., 1931; chem. engr. Tex. Pacific Coal & Oil Co., 1932-33, United Gas Pub. Service, 1933-36; asst. prof. chem. engring., La. State U., 1936-42, asso. prof., 1942-47, prof., 1947-69, Alumni prof. chem. engring., 1969—, chmn. dept. 1955-67; cons. chem. engr.; mem. La. Bd. Registration Profl. Engrs. Active Boy Scouts Am. Recipient Technol. Accomplishment medal La. Engring. Soc., 1958, Charles E. Coates meml. award Am. Chem. Soc.-Am. Inst. Chem. Engrs., 1958; named Man of Month, Chem. Engring. Mag., 1958, distinguished service certificate Nat. Council Engring. Examiners, 1969. Fellow Am. Inst. Chemists; mem. Am. Chem. Soc., La. Acad. Sci., Am. Inst. Chem. Engrs., Am. Soc. Engring. Edn., Sigma Xi, Phi Kappa Phi, Alpha Chi Sigma, Phi Lambda Upsilon, Kappa Alpha, Omicron Delta Kappa. Episcopalian (past vestryman). Author various articles in La. State U. Engring. Expt. News, Chem. Eng. mag., other publs. Home: 2320 Terrace Av Baton Rouge LA 70806

COATES, JOE ROY, city ofcl.; b. Swannanoa, N.C., Sept. 8, 1929; s. Albert Coburn and Emma Josephine (Creaseman) C.; student U. Miami, 1953; B.S., Fla. State U., 1956, postgrad., 1956-58; m. Frances Diane Kearns, Sept. 19, 1959; children—Thomas Frederic, Mary Louise, Michael Alexander, Joseph Andrew. Intern city mgr., adminstrv. asst. City of Sarasota, Fla., 1956-58; grad. fellow Fla. State U., 1958; grad. asst. Fla. Indsl. Commn., Tallahassee, 1958-59; supr. safety tng. and edn., adminstrv. asst. City of Sarasota, 1959-61; city mgr. City of Dade City, Fla., 1961-62; dir. taxation and revenue City of Zanesville, O., 1963-67; asst. city mgr., dir. finance City of Melbourne, Fla., 1967-68; dir. adminstrn. and finance City of Pensacola, Fla., 1968—; grad. asst. Bur. Govtl. Research & Service, Fla. State U., 1958. Served with USCG, 1948-52. Recipient Undergrad. grant Selby Found., Sarasota, 1956. Mem. Internat. City Mgrs. Assn., Am. Soc. Safety Engrs., Municipal Finance Officers Assn., Nat. Safety Council (Fla. rep. for pub. employees 1959-60), Am. Soc. for Pub. Adminstrn. (pres. Fla. chpt. 1954-56), Nat. Rifle Assn., U.S. Navy League. Home: 321 Dolphin St Gulf Breeze FL 32561 Office: P O Box 1471 Pensacola FL 32501

COATS, JOHN ROBERT, JR., orthodontist; b. Beaumont, Tex., Aug. 4, 1937; s. John Robert and Hilda (Buchanan) C.; B.S., Lamar State Coll. Tech., 1960; D.D.S., U. Tex., 1964, M.S., 1968; m. Alice Lynn Danforth, Feb. 13, 1965; children—John Daniel, Jennifer Lynn. Pvt. practice orthodontics, Austin, Tex., 1968—. Served to capt., USAF, 1964-66. Mem. Am., Tex. dental assns., Am. Assn. Orthodontics, Tex. Orthodontic Assn., Austin Dist. Dental Soc., U. Tex. Alumni Orthodontic Assn. Club: Town Lake Breakfast (Austin). Home: 4204 Gnarl Dr Austin TX 78731 Office: 4004 Marathon Blvd Austin TX 78756

COATS, WENDELL JOHN, army officer; b. Sterling, Colo., July 28, 1915; s. Elbert W. and Hannah Grace (Castleberry) C.; B.S., U.S. Mil. Acad., 1940; M.A., U. Wis., 1949; Ph.D., Georgetown U., 1963; grad. Command and Gen. Staff Coll., 1952, Army War Coll., 1956; m. Benny Lee Smith, Feb. 11, 1946; children—Wendell J., Nathan Ben, Wilson C. Commd. 2d lt. U.S. Army, 1940, advanced through grades to maj. gen., 1967; comdg. officer 39th F.A. bn., Sicily, Italy, France, Germany, 1940-45; sec. gen. staff U.S. Army Hdqrs., Europe, Heidelberg, Germany, 1954-55; exec. officer 1st Cav. Div., Korea, 1960-61; exec. officer internat. security affairs. Office Sec. Def., Washington, 1963-64; dep. dir. logistics U.S. European Command, Paris, 1965-66; chief information Dept. Army, Washington, 1967-68; comdg. gen. 2d Armored Div., Fort Hood, Tex., 1969-71; chief staff U.S. Readiness Command, MacDill AFB, Fla., 1972—. Decorated D.S.M., Silver Star, Legion of Merit with 2 oak leaf clusters, Bronze Star medal. Center for Internat. Affairs fellow, Harvard, 1961-62. Mem. Assn. U.S. Army, Am. Polit. Sci. Assn., Pi Sigma Alpha. Author: Armed Force as Power: The Theory of War Reconsidered, 1966. Home: 402 Staff Loop MacDill AFB FL 33621 Office: Headquarters US Readiness Command MacDill AFB FL 33608

COATS, WILLIAM EDWARD, supt. schs.; b. Coal Hill, Ark., Nov. 25, 1933; s. Earl and Xenya (Meyers) C.; A.A., Ft. Smith Jr. Coll., 1953; B.S., Coll. Ozarks, 1957; M.Ed., U. Ark., 1961, postgrad., 1966; m. Jimmy Lue Coffee, Sept. 3, 1955; children—Thomas, Karen. Tchr., Ft. Smith (Ark.) Pub. Schs., 1959-61; supt., Hartman (Ark.) Pub. Schs., 1961-63, Smackover (Ark.) Pub. Schs., 1963-66, Batesville (Ark.) Pub. Schs., 1966—. Served with USAF, 1954-59. Mem. N.E.A., Am. Assn. Sch. Adminstrs., Ark. Sch. Adminstrs. Assn., Ark. Edn. Assn., Phi Delta Kappa. Democrat. Presbyn. (deacon 1968-69). Mason, Lion, Rotarian. Club: Optimist (Batesville). Home: 385 17th St Batesville AR 72501 Office: 507 7th St Batesville AR 72501

COBB, DAN, newspaper editor; m. Stella Morris; 1 son, David Childs. Formerly city editor Birmingham News, also Houston Chronicle; now news editor Houston Chronicle. Home: 10423 Green Willow Dr Houston TX 77035 Office: 512-20 Travis St Houston TX 77002

COBB, GEORGE HAMILTON, research exec.; b. St. Louis, Aug. 16, 1911; s. George H. and Julia L. (Middleton) C.; student Okla. State U., 1929-30, U. Neb., 1934; B.S., U. Kan., 1939; m. Esther Victoria Preston, Nov. 30, 1957; 1 dau., Carolyn Rozella Palamar. Petroleum engr. Kerr-McGee Corp., Oklahoma City 1939-41, prodn. supt., 1942-47, prodn. mgr. 1948-53, asst. to pres., 1953-56, v.p. exploration, 1959-60, v.p. minerals div., 1960-63, v.p. exploration-research, 1964-67, sr. v.p., chmn. operating com., 1967-71, exec. v.p., 1971—; v.p., dir. Community Nat. Bank of Warr Acres, Oklahoma City. Registered profl. engr., Okla., Tex. Mem. Am. Inst. M.E., Am. Petroleum Inst., Am. Assn. Petroleum Geologists, N.M., Colo. mining assns. Home: 1506 Buttram Rd Oklahoma City OK 73120 Office: Kerr-McGee Bldg Oklahoma City OK 73102

COBB, HOWELL, lawyer; b. Atlanta, Dec. 7, 1922; s. Howell and Dorothy (Hart) C.; student St. John's Coll., 1940-42; LL.B., U. Va., 1948; m. Torrance Chalmers, 1943 (dec. 1963); children—Catherine Louise, Howell III, Mary Ann; m. 2d, Amelie Suberbielle, July 3, 1965; children—Caroline, Thomas Hart. Admitted to Ga. bar, 1948, Tex. bar, 1949; asso. firm Kelley & Ryan, also Fountain, Cox & Gaines, Houston, 1949-54; partner Orgain, Bell & Tucker, Beaumont, 1955—. Pres., Beaumont Art Mus., 1967-69. Served with USMCR, World War II. Decorated Air Medal with gold star. Mem. Am., Jefferson County, Houston bar assns., State Bar Tex., Internat. Assn. Ins. Counsel, Tex. Assn. Def. Counsel. Republican. Episcopalian. Clubs: Beaumont, Beaumont Country. Home: 1385 Thomas Rd Beaumont TX 77706 Office: Beaumont Savings Bldg Beaumont TX 77701

COBB, J. C., polit. party ofcl.; b. Iowa Park, Tex.; ed. N. Tex. State U.; B.S. in Pharmacy, Capitol Coll. Pharmacy; m. Rheba Cobb; 1 son, Larry. Pharmacist; in retail drug bus. Mayor, Tishomingo, Okla., 1950-54; sec. State Bd. Pharmacy, 1951-62; chmn. rules com. Okla. Dem. State Convs.; del. Dem. Nat. Conv., 1964, 68; Democratic nat. committeeman, Okla., 1968—. Mem. Nat. Assn. Retail Druggists (Past pres.). Presbyn. Mason (Shriner), Rotarian (pres.). Address: 215 W Main St Tishomingo OK 73460*

COBB, JAMES HARREL, educator; b. Bloomfield, Ind., Nov. 13, 1906; s. John and Margaret (Harrel) C.; A.B., Ind. State U., 1927, postgrad., 1928-29; M.A., Ind. U., 1930; B.D., Garrett Theol. Sem., 1942; postgrad. U. Utah, 1935-39, U. Chgo., 1942-46, Hebrew Union Coll., 1953-54 Tchr., Princeton (Ind.) High Sch., 1927-28; instr. English, Ind. State U., 1929-30, Mont. State U., 1930-32; supr., state curriculum specialist Adult Edn., Salt Lake City, 1932-39; asso. prof. English dept. Kan. Wesleyan U., 1946-47; asst. prof. Central Coll., 1947-48; asst. prof. Bible and religion U. Toledo, 1948-50; vis. asso. Greek and Hebrew, Vanderbilt U. Div. Sch., 1951-52; prof. Yankton Coll. Sch. of Theology, 1954-60; asst. prof. dept. English, speech S.E. Community Coll., U. Ky., 1960-63, U. Ky. at Lexington, 1963—. Mem. Am. Acad. Religion, Nat. Assn. Profs. Hebrew, Am. Philos. Assn., Ky. English Assn., Pi Kappa Delta, Kappa Delta Pi, Lambda Iota Tau, Phi Delta Kappa. Republican. Jewish religion. Author: Principles and Concepts of Tanak (Old Testament), 1972; (corr. courses) The Literature of the New Testament, 1972. Home: 242 S Limestone St Lexington KY 40508

COBB, JERRIE M., aviation/aerospace cons.; b. Norman, Okla., Mar. 5, 1931; d. William Harvey and Helena Butler (Stone) Cobb. Profl. pilot, 1949—; chief pilot South American Fleetway, Inc.; mem. adv. com. FAA, 1964-69; now aviation/aerospace cons. in pvt. practice, also missionary jungle pilot in South Am. Founder, Jerrie Cobb Found. Named 1 of 9 women selected in the 100 most important in U.S., 1962; first woman to pass astronaut tests, 1960; recipient Gold Wings, Fedn. Aeronautique Internationale; named Woman of Yr. in Aviation, Women's Nat. Aero. Assn.; hon. pilot Colombian Air Force, 1964. Mem. Am. Inst. Aeronautics and Astronautics, Am. Astronautical Soc., Aerospace Medicine Assn., Nat. Aero. Assn., 99's (Amelia Earhart Gold medal), Nat. Pilots Assn. (Pilot of Year 1959), Women's Nat. Aero. Assn. Club: Whirlygirls. Author: (with Jane Rieker) Woman Into Space: The Jerrie Cobb Story, 1963. Home: 4057 Malaga St Miami FL 33133

COBB, JOE BAILEY, govt. ofcl.; b. Tishomingo, Okla., Nov. 17, 1909; s. John Knox and Margaret (Howell) C.; ed. pub. schs.; ed. Chillicothe Bus. Coll.; m. Otherine Pansy Standifer, Nov. 28, 1941; children—Donna Kay (Mrs. Tommy Holt), Sara. County commr., 1930-37; senator Okla. Senate, Oklahoma City, 1942-54, 1958-64; state auditor State of Okla., Oklahoma City, 1967—. Democrat. Home: 733 S W 40th St Oklahoma City OK 73109 Office: 310 State Capitol Bldg Oklahoma City OK 73105

COBB, JOE HACKLER, civil engr.; b. nr. Brownsville, Tenn., Mar. 6, 1927; s. Paul Hackler and Zina Maie (Proctor) C.; B.S., U. Tenn., 1965; m. Myrtle Louise Wilson, Sept. 20, 1969. Rodman, instrument man Tenn. Hwy. Dept., Covington, 1958-62; jr. engr. Brown Engring. Co., aerospace, Huntsville, Ala., 1965-67; structural engr. Brighton Engring. Co., cons. engrs., Nashville, Tenn. and Frankfort, Ky., 1967-69; prin. civil engr. Met. Dept. Pub. Works, Nashville, 1969—. Registered profl. engr., Tenn., Ky. Mem. Am. Soc. C. E., Nat. Soc. Profl. Engrs., Am. Pub. Works Assn., Tau Beta Pi. Baptist. Home: 2929 Berry Hill Dr Nashville TN 37204 Office: 720 S 5th St Nashville TN 37206

COBB, THOMAS TRACY, lawyer; b. Washington, Nov. 13, 1916; s. William M. and Bessie (Coghill) C.; LL.B., John B. Stetson U., 1939; m. Jane Carter Campbell, Mar. 15, 1941; children—Jane Tracy (Mrs. Jerry M. Trammell), Thomas Carter, Charlotte Susan (Mrs. Thomas Clayton), Jennifer Jerome. Admitted to Fla. bar, 1939; trustee Lawyer's Title Guaranty Fund, Orlando, Fla., 1949-51; city atty., Daytona Beach, Fla., 1953-55; gen. counsel Fla. State Road Bd., 1961-65; mem. Fla. Bd. Bar Examiners, 1969—, chmn., 1972-73; gen. counsel, dir., sec. News-Jour. Corp., Daytona Beach, 1961—. Served with USNR, 1944-45. Mem. Volusia County, Am. bar assns., Fla. Bar, Am. Judicature Soc. Presbyn. (elder). Kiwanian. Home: 58 S Beach St Ormond Beach FL 32074 Office: 444 N Beach St Daytona Beach FL 32015

COBB, WILLIAM HERVEY, paving contractor; b. Vaughan, N.C., Aug. 13, 1916; s. Herman Bryan and Mamie Lee (Fishel) C.; student U. N.C., 1935-36, Wake Forest U., 1943-44; m. Eloise Teacue, July 25, 1947; children—William Hervey III, Bryan, Robert F. Sec., treas. Barrus Constrn. Co., Kinston, N.C., 1937—. Served with AUS, World War II. Elk. Club: Kinston (N.C.) Country. Home: 1204 West Rd Kinston NC 28501 Office: New Bern Hwy Kinston NC 28501

COBBS, JAMES HAROLD, petroleum engr.; b. Bristow, Okla., Aug. 25, 1928; s. Harold M. and Ella (Rouintree) C.; B.S., U. Okla., 1949, postgrad., 1949-51; postgrad. U. Tulsa, 1955-67; m. Charlotte Marie Fisher, Aug. 16, 1953; children—James Harold, David C., Gregory L., Matthew L. Grad. asst. U. Okla., 1949-51; asso. engr. Tidewater Oil Co., Midland, Tex., 1951-52, reservoir engr., Houston, 1952-55, div. reservoir engr., Tulsa, 1955-59; pvt. practice petroleum engring., Tulsa, 1959-63, 69—; sr. engr. Fenix & Scisson, Inc., Tulsa, 1963-69. Committeeman, asst. scoutmaster Indian Nations council Boy Scouts Am., 1962—; instr. first aid A.R.C., 1969—. Precinct chmn. Republican party, 1961-62. Fellow A.A.A.S.; mem. Soc. Petroleum Engrs., Nat., Okla. socs. profl. engrs., Sigma Phi Epsilon. Mem. Christian Ch. (elder, chmn. bd. 1971-72). Patentee in field. Home: 5144 S New Haven St Tulsa OK 74135 Office: 5200 S Yale St Tulsa OK 74135

COBIAN, RAFAEL RAMOS, theatre exec.; b. Patillas, P.R., Mar. 19, 1904; s. Jose R. and Josepha Cobian; B.S. in Pharmacy, U. P.R., 1926; m. Juliette Coronel, Feb. 14, 1966; children—(by previous marriages) Rafael, Ruddy, Ronard, Randolph. Pres., Cobian Theatres, San Juan, P.R., 1940—, United Theatres, San Juan, 1953—, Cobian Met. Circuit, Inc., 1952—, Commonwealth Theaters P.R., Inc., San Juan, 1954—; chmn. bd., chief exec. officer Cinecom Corp., N.Y.C. Adviser, World U. Del., Democratic Convs., 1956, 60, 64. Served as capt. Spl. Services, AUS, 1941-43. Named one of Ten Leading Businessmen of P.R., 1966. Mem. A.I.M. (pres.'s council), Soc. Press, Radio and TV, Nat. Assn. Theatre Owners (mem. bd.), Casino de P.R. Elk, Lion. Clubs: Exchange, Bankers of San Juan; Presidential (Palm Springs, Cal.); N.Y. Athletic; Variety Internat. (life). Home: Penthouse Condominio San Luis San Juan PR 00609 Office: Banco Popular Center Bldg Hato Rey PR 00919

COBURN, RICHARD WELDON, oil co. exec.; b. N.Y.C., Mar. 24, 1920; s. Richard Alan and Helen (Denning) C.; student Hofstra Coll., 1937-39; B.S., Tulsa U., 1943; m. Mary Jean Holm, Aug. 31, 1943; children—Gayle Coburn (Mrs. Frank Eby), Sharon Ann. Asst. dist. supt. Atlantic Refining Co., Enid, Okla., 1946-52; chief engr., asst. to v.p. Champlin Refining Co., Tulsa, 1952-57; v.p. operations Stiles Engring. Co., Tulsa, 1957-63; pres. dir. Petrop Internat., Inc., Tulsa, 1963-69; pres., dir. King Oil Co., Tulsa, 1969—. Served to lt. (j.g.) USNR, 1942-46. Mem. Am. Inst. Mining, Metall. and Petroleum Engrs., Soc. Petroleum Engrs., Am. Petroleum Inst. Contbr. articles profl. jours. Home: 2121 E 34th Tulsa OK 74105 Office: 35 E 18th St Tulsa OK 74119

COCA-MIR, RAFAEL, physician; b. San Juan, P.R., Aug. 15, 1922; s. Luis and Maria (Mir) Coca-Hernandez; M.D. cum laude, Syracuse U., 1945; m. Maria Lopategui, Apr. 19, 1968; children—Elsa, Eugenio, Pablo. Intern, Presbyn. Hosp., San Juan, 1945-46; resident George Washington U. Hosp., 1948-50, Johns Hopkins Hosp. and U. Cal. Hosp., 1952-54; asso. prof. internal medicine and cardiology U. P.R. Med. Sch., 1954-60; practice medicine specializing in internal medicine and cardiology, Santurce, P.R., 1961—; mem. staff San Juan hosps.; cons. medicine San Juan VA Hosp., 1956-70, Personnel Office, Govt. P.R., 1960—. Served to capt. M.C., AUS, 1941-45, 50-52. Mem. A.C.P., P.R. Med. Assn. (pres. credit coop. 1968—), Syracuse Alumni P.R. (pres. 1954—), Alpha Omega Alpha. Club: Pan Am. Gun (Bayamon, P.R.). Home: 501 Safrado Corazon St Santurce PR 00918 Office: 115 Parque St Santurce PR 00914

COCHRAN, JEAN DOROTHY, librarian; b. Irwin, Pa., July 12, 1910; d. Ira Lee and Luella (Farmer) Cochran; A.B., Guilford Coll., 1932; B.S. in L.S., U. N.C., 1941. Tchr. pub. sch., Kernersville, N.C., 1933-41; asst. librarian Davidson County Pub. Library, Lexington, N.C., 1941-43; cataloger U. Ga. Library, Athens, 1943-44; head librarian Carnegie Pub. Library, Sumter, S.C., 1945-48; dir. Augusta (Ga.) Pub. Library, 1949—. Co-organizer, 1st pres. C.S.R.A. Library Assn.; library bldg. cons.; mem. library adv. com. pub. library bldg. constrn. Ga. Dept. Edn., 1964—. Bd. dirs. local YWCA, 1954-58, Augusta Players, 1957-58, Sr. Citizens Council, 1967-72, Augusta Art Assn. Recipient Community Service award Credit Women's Assn., 1962; named Boss of Year, Fairways chpt. Nat. Secs. Assn., 1962. Mem. A.L.A. (mem. council 1969-71, friends of library com. 1954-58; coordinating com. 1962-63, pub. library assn. standards com. 1969-72), S.E. (chmn. pub. library sect. 1962-64), Ga. (v.p. 1957-59, pres. 1967-69; chmn. pub. library sect. 1963-65; chmn. intellectual freedom com. 1961-63, chmn. statistics com. 1961-63) library assns., Am. Assn. U. Women, Augusta Opera Assn., Augusta Mus., Historic Augusta, League Women Voters, Ga. Ornith. Soc., Friends Augusta Library, Richmond County Hist. Soc. Presbyn. Clubs: Bird (Augusta), Augusta Music. Contbr. library periodicals. Home: 2515 Parkway Dr Augusta GA 30904 Office: 902 Green St Augusta GA 30902

COCHRAN, KENDALL PINNEY, educator; b. Newton, Kan., Dec. 12, 1924; s. William Walter and Enid (Pinney) C.; B.A., U. Tex., 1949, M.A., 1950; Ph.D., Ohio State U., 1955; m. Lois Eyvonne Adams, Aug. 14, 1949; m. 2d, Beverly Ray Bradbury, July 11, 1969. Instr. econs. Ohio State U., 1953-55, asst. prof., 1955-57; asso. prof. econs. North Tex. State U., 1957-59, prof., 1959—, chmn. dept., 1969—; dir. NSF Econs. Inst., 1964—. Dir. Denton County Credit Union, 1961—. Mem. Am., Southwestern (pres. 1965) econ. assns., Assn. Evolutionary Econs. (exec. com. 1964), Tex. Assn. Coll. Tchrs., Am. Assn. U. Profs. (nat. council 1967-70). Democrat. Asso. editor of Southwestern Social Sci. Quar., 1962-64; asso. editor of Southwestern Jour. Social Edn., 1970—. Editorial bd. North Tex. Bus. Studies, 1961—. Home: 1911 Whippoorwill St Denton TX 76201

COCHRAN, LEWIS W., univ. ofcl., physicist; b. Perryville, Ky., Oct. 12, 1915; s. Ernest Beeler and Mayme (Martin) C; B.S., Morehead State Coll., 1936; M.S., U. Ky., 1939, Ph.D., 1952; m. Carolyn Wilson, Nov. 20, 1940; children—Sue Carol, Philip. Instr. physics Morehead (Ky.) State Coll., 1939-40, 41, asst. prof., 1946 instr. physics Cumberland U., 1941 radio engr. Lexington Signal Depot, 1942; faculty U. Ky., 1946—, prof. physics, 1957—, acting head dept., 1956-58, asso. dean Grad. Sch., 1963-65, provost, 1965-70, acting dean Grad. Sch., 1966-67, dean Grad. Sch., v.p. univ. research, 1967-70, v.p. for acad. affairs, 1970—; research physicist Oak Ridge Nat. Lab., summers 1949, 50, 53, 59-60; spl. research low energy nuclear physics, gaseous electronics, neuron physics. Served to maj. AUS, 1942-46. Mem. Am. Phys. Soc., Am. Assn. Physics Tchrs., Health Physics Soc., Sigma Xi, Sigma Pi Sigma, Omicron Delta Kappa, Presbyn. (elder). Home: 1581 Beacon Hill Rd Lexington KY 40506

COCHRAN, MCKENDREE THOMAS, JR., dairy co. exec.; b. Altus, Okla., May 24, 1918; s. McKendree Thomas and Ray (Wheeler) C.; Asso. B.A., Kemper Mil. Sch., 1937; B.A., U. Okla., 1939; m. Mary Delores Coleman, June 22, 1940; children—Mary Chris (Mrs. Alexander Pryor Murray), McKendree Thomas, III, William Chesley, James Coleman. Asst. to pres. Eskimo Pie Corp., Bloomfield, N.J., 1940-52; gen. mgr. ice cream div. DCA Food Industries, N.Y.C., 1952-57; v.p., gen. mgr. dairies div. Southland Corp., Dallas, 1957—. Served to lt. USNR, 1943-46. Mem. Nat. Dairy Council (dir.), Dairy Products Inst. Tex. (pres. 1966-67), Internat. Assn. Ice Cream Mfrs. (dir. 1968—), So. Assn. Dairy Food Mfrs. (pres. 1971-72), Dallas Sales Exec. Club, Kappa Alpha. Presbyn. Club: Northwood Country (Dallas). Home: 6440 Northport Dr Dallas TX 75230 Office: 2828 N Haskell St Dallas TX 75230

COCHRAN, WENDELL ALBERT, editor; b. Carthage, Mo., Nov. 29, 1929; s. Wendell Albert and Lillian (Largent) C.; A.B., U. Mo., 1953, A.M. in Geology, 1956, B.J., 1960; m. Elizabeth Groves, Nov. 9, 1963. Geologist U.S. Geol. Survey, Sacramento, 1956-58; copy editor Kansas City (Mo.) Star, 1960-63; editor Geotimes Mag. Am. Geol. Inst., Washington, 1963—. Mem. Am. Geophys. Union, Washington Geol. Soc., Gamma Alpha. Home: 3519 Raymond St Chevy Chase MD 20015 Office: 2201 M St NW Washington DC 20037

COCKE, DUNCAN M., hist. restoration ofcl. Sr. v.p. Colonial Williamsburg. Address: Goodwib Bldg Williamsburg VA 23185*

COCKERHAM, SARAH FRANCES WHITE (MRS JOHN W. COCKERHAM), librarian; b. Brownwood, Tex., Nov. 8 1930; d. Todd Rector and Edith (Lloyd) White; B.J., U. Mo., 1951; tchrs. certificate Tex. Womans U., 1956; librarians certificate Sam Houston State Tchrs. Coll., 1962; m. John W. Cockerham, Dec. 1, 1956. Soc. editor Gainesville (Tex.) Daily Register, 1951; tchr. journalism Winters (Tex.) High Sch., 1952, Iraan (Tex.) High Sch., 1953-54, Port Neches (Tex.)-Groves High Sch., 1955-60; librarian Groves (Tex.) Jr. High Sch., 1961—. Mem. Tex. Library Assn., Classroom Tchrs. Assn., Tex. Tchrs. Assn., Alpha Delta Pi, Theta Sigma Phi, Beta Sigma Phi. Democrat. Methodist. Home: 1025 Montrose Dr Port Neches TX 77651 Office: Cleveland Av Groves TX 77619

COCKRELL, ANGUS HARDEE, JR., accountant; b. Floresville, Tex., Jan. 17, 1911; s. Angus Hardee and Vera (Cocke) C.; student Tex. A. and M. Coll.; m. Vivian Smith, Dec. 25, 1933; children—Barbara Ann, Joan. C.P.A., San Antonio, 1933—; mem. firm George, Thrift & Cockrell, 1941-64; partner Ernst && Ernst, 1964—. Mem. pub. safety com. U.S. Jr. C. of C., 1944-46. Mem. Tex. State Bd. Pub. Accountancy. Bd. mgrs. San Antonio City-County Hosp.; vice chmn. bd. commrs. San Antonio Urban Renewal Agy. Mem. Tex. (chmn. pub. safety com., recipient distinguished service award), San Antonio (past pres.) jr. chambers commerce, C. of C. (v.p. 1966). Mem. Christian Ch. Clubs: San Antonio (past pres.), Oak Hills Country, St. Anthony. Home: 7500 Callaghan Rd San Antonio TX 78229 Office: Tower Life Bldg San Antonio TX 78205

COCKRILL, EDITH HERRING, lawyer, judge; b. Covington, Tenn., Mar. 11, 1914; d. Lucian and Martha (McLennan) Cockrill; student So. Meth. U., 1936-37; A.B., U. Tenn., 1936, LL.B., 1940. Admitted to Tenn. bar, 1940; govt. atty. 1943-44; pvt. practice law Washington, 1944-49; juvenile ct. judge, Washington, 1949-57. Trustee United Community Services D.C.; dir. Soc. for Prevention of Blindness D.C., D.C. Rehab. Service White House Conf., 1950; hearing examiner ICC, 1960-72, adminstrv. law judge, 1972—; pres. Eade Enterprises, Inc., radio-TV producers. Mem. Nat. Council Juvenile Court Judges (treas. 1952-54, exec. com. 1953-55), Profl. Panhellenic Assn. D.C., Fed. Women's Bar Assns., Fed. Trial Examiners Conf., Mortar Board, Washington Heart Assn., D.C. Crippled Children's Soc., YWCA, Kappa Delta, Phi Kappa Phi, Phi Delta Delta. Presbyn. Clubs: Altrusa, Am. Newspaper; Farmington Country. Home: 3016 Tilden St Washington DC 20008 Office: ICC Washington DC 20423

COCKRILL, JOHN LONG, diversified corp. exec.; b. Quincy, Ill., Aug. 6, 1920; s. Lowell E. and Anna Josephine (Lillard) C.; B.A., State U. Ia., 1941; J.D., 1942; m. Ellen Schocke, Aug. 22, 1942; children—Joanne (Mrs. Paul K. Vetterick), John. Admitted to Ia. bar, 1942, Ill. bar, 1945; with Wilson & Co., Inc. Chgo., 1943-67, v.p. law, tax, real estate and ins., indsl. relation, casualty and med. and retirement and group ins. divs., 1950-63, v.p. plant operating, engring., quality control, indsl. relations, casualty and med. retirement and group ins. divs., 1963-65, named exec. v.p. adminstrn., 1965; v.p. adminstrn. Ling Temco-Vought, Inc., Dallas, 1967-69; chmn. bd., pres., chief exec. officer Altec Corp., Inc., Dallas, 1969—; chmn. bd. Tamar Electronics, Inc., 1969—, Allied Radio Corp., 1969-70; dir. LTV Corp., Staco, Inc. Regional exec. Nat. Alliance Businessmen, 1968; mem. Southwestern regional manpower adv. council U.S. Dept. Labor, 1969-71; mem. Adv. Council for Tech.-Vocational Edn. in Tex., 1969—. Mem. Delta Chi. Presbyn. Mason. Clubs: Midlothian Country; Preston Trails Golf; Lancer's. Home: 5832 Lupton Dr Dallas TX 75225 Office: PO Box 30385 Dallas TX 75230

CODY, MARTHA JANE BALLARD (MRS. WILLIAM JOSEPH CODY), ret. educator; b. Washington, June 25, 1897; d. Thomas Victor and Ada E. (Janney) Ballard; student Ala. Coll., 1914-16; B.S., U. Ala., 1918; M.S., U. Chgo., 1935; postgrad. U. Fla.,; m. William Joseph Cody, Dec. 16, 1954. Tchr. English, art in pub. schs., Ala., Fla., 1918-30; dept. head fine arts and home arts State Tchrs Coll., Troy, Ala., 1931-51; arts and crafts supr. Southeastern Area A.R.C., Keesler Field, Ft. Jackson, 1944-46; asst. prof. U. Fla. Coll. Edn., Gainesville, 1951-57. Dir. Boys' Clubs Am., 1956—, sec. bd., 1965—, chmn. arts and crafts, library, 1962— mem. Safety Council, 1958— (all Gainesville). Bd. dirs. Sante Fe Library, Gainesville. Mem. Ala. Tchrs. Art (pres. 1941), Nat. League Am. Pen Women (pres. Gainesville chpt. 1961-63, rec. sec. 1963-65, sec. 1965-67), Internat. Platform Assn., Zeta Tau Alpha, Delta Kappa Gamma (v.p. Ala. 1941, sec. Delta chpt. 1965-67), Kappa Delta Pi, Pi Lambda Theta (charter). Episcopalian (mem. St. Patrick's woman's club 1957—, St. Margaret's Circle, Holy Trinity Ch. 1951, Women of Ch. 1951—). Research on family life of Ala. tenant farmer, devel. of curriculum for Korean schs. Home: 1831 NE 7th Terrace Gainsville FL 32601

COE, MIRIAM, writer, librarian; b. Liverpool, Eng., July1, 1902; d. David Avrom and Shaynah Froma (Lippsman) Cohen; honors diploma, Oulton Coll.; diploma, Skerry's Coll.; student Liverpool U., Liverpool City Sch. Art, U. Rochester (N.Y.), Columbia U., N.Y. Sch. Theatre, Carnegie Hall Studios, Sch. Chinese Brushwork, L.I. U., George Peabody Coll. for Tchrs., Utah, Fla., La. State univs. Sec., J. Ogden Co., Shipbrokers, Eng., 1916-19; tchr. violin, 1924-29; article writer Liverpool Express, 1928; lectr. on psychology of music Sta. WHAM, Stromberg Carlson Telephone Co., Hotel Sagamore, Rochester; comml. artist, N.Y.C.; coach in English lang.; librarian, Baton Rouge; exhibitor paintings, N.Y., La. Recipient various awards and prizes. Mem. A.L.A. (coll. and research div.), La., Southwestern library assns., Round Table for Blind, Am. Assn. Polit. and Social Scis., Am. Social. Assn., Am. Judicature Soc., Am. Pub. Health Assn., Am. Soc. Photogrammetry, Liverpool Psychol. Assn. (asso.), Alumni Palmer Grad. Sch. L.S. Coll. and Research Libraries, Baton Rouge Arts and Crafts Guild, Am. Assn. Museums, La. Library Assn., La. Water-color Soc., La. Art and Artists Guild, Am. Dickens League (hon.), Mystery Club, Alpha Beta Alpha. Author: Librarians Manual; Careers in Art, Poems, Juveniles; Dictionary of Terms Related to Photogrammetry. Editor: Anthology of World Literature, A Sociological Cyclopedia; Pitirim Sorokin: An Introduction to his Work. Developed original color system for teaching typewriting; inventor spectrum color system for teaching music; inventor type-face, adjuncts for mechanism in constructing typewriters. Home: Apt 29 839 Azalea Baton Rouge LA 70802 Office: Box 18184 La State U Baton Rouge LA 70803

COE, RICHARD LIVINGSTON, drama and film critic; b. N.Y.C., Nov. 8, 1916; s. Elmer James Secor and Lillie Isabel (Mustgrave) C.; student George Washington U., 1934-38; m. Christine Sadler, May 4, 1946. Radio editor, asst. drama-film critic Washington Post, 1938-42, drama editor and critic, 1946-69, drama critic, 1969—; theater and film commentator NBC-WRC-TV, 1969—; spl. U.S. corr. Reynolds

News, London, Eng., Egyptian Gazette, Cairo, Egypt. Guest lectr. Am. U., Cairo, Egypt; drama panel ANTA; staff of President's Progrm for Cultural Exchange. Served as staff sgt. AUS, 1942-46; columnist, editor Middle East edit. Stars and Stripes. Recipient pub. service award Newspaper Guild, 1949; achievement award Gen. Fedn. Women's Clubs, 1957; award Washington Bd. Trade, 1957, D.C. Theater, 1957; Critic of Year award Directors Guild Am., 1963. Mem. Am. Newspaper Guild. Clubs: National Press, Variety (Washington); Overseas Press (N.Y.C.); The Players. Home: 2713 Dumbarton Av NW Washington DC 20007 Office: 1515 L St NW Washington DC 20005

COE, ROBERT MILTON, educator; b. Saltville, Va., Aug. 28, 1931; s. Thomas Edward and Annie Blackwell (Virginia) C.; B.S. in Music Edn., Appalachian State U., 1952; M.A., Eastern Ky. U., 1953; Ed.D., Colo. State Coll., 1961; postgrad. Eastman Sch. Music, 1965, 67, Mozartzum, Salzburg, Austria, summer 1971; m. Kathryn Louise Simmons, Aug. 30, 1959; children—Holly Elizabeth, April Suzanna. Band dir. Suwannee High Sch., Live Oak, Fla., 1955-56; teaching fellow Colo. State Coll., Greeley, 1956-58; organist First Congl. Ch., Greeley, 1958-63; mem. faculty W. Ga. Coll., Carrollton, 1963—, head dept. fine arts, 1963—, prof. music, 1963—. Organist, choir dir. various chs.; performer in piano, organ recitals; adjudicator, clinician, Colo., Neb., Ga., Kan.; asst. prof. music Hastings (Neb.) Coll., 1959-63. Pres. W.Ga. Mutual Concert Assn., 1966-68. Bd. mem. fine arts com. W.Ga. Regional Library, Carrollton, 1967—. Served with AUS, 1953-55. Recipient scholarship Eastern Ky. U., 1953. Mem. Music Tchrs. Nat. Assn., Music Educators Nat. Conf., Am. Assn. U. Profs., Coll. Music Soc., Nat. Assn. Schs. Music, Phi Delta Kappa. Episcopalian (vestryman 1964-67). Kiwanian. Home: E Club Dr Carrollton GA 30117

COERPER, MILO GEORGE, lawyer; b. Milw., May 8, 1925; s. Milo Wilson and Rose (Schubert) C.; B.S., U.S. Naval Acad., 1946; LL.B., U. Mich., 1954; M.A., Georgetown U., 1957; Ph.D., 1960; m. Lois Hicks Coerper, Apr. 11, 1953; children—Milo Wilson, Allison Lee, Lois Paddock. Admitted to D.C. bar, 1954; asso. firm Wilmer & Broun, Washington, 1954-60, firm Coudert Brothers, 1961-63, partner, 1964—. Trustee Sheridan Sch., vice chmn., 1972—; trustee House of Mercy, pres., 1970—. Served to ensign USN, 1946-49, to lt., 1951-53. Mem. Bar Assn. D.C., Assn. Bar City N.Y., Am. Bar Assn., Am. Soc. Internat. Law. Internat. Law Assn., Am. Law Inst. Clubs: Union League (N.Y.C.); Metropolitan, Army and Navy. Nat. Lawyers, Chevy Chase; Potomac Racquet (pres. 1971—). Contbr. articles to profl. jours. Home: 7315 Brookville Rd Chevy Chase MD 20015 Office: 1 Farragut Square S Washington DC 20006

COFER, VERNON LONSDALE, JR., physician; b. Norfolk, Va., Apr. 9, 1924; s. Vernon Lonsdale and Nancy Carola (Ross) C.; student Coll. William and Mary, 1942-44; M.D. with honors, Med. Coll. Va., 1948; m. Judith Ball Wysong, July 1, 1950; children—Thomas L., James S. Intern, Wis. Gen. Hosp., Madison 1948-49; resident internal medicine Kansas City Gen. Hosp., 1950-51; fellow, 1st asst. in internal medicine Mayo Clinic, 1951-53; practice medicine, specializing in internal medicine and hematology, Norfolk, Va., 1954—; dir. dept. medicine DePaul Hosp., 1964-69, dir. hematology clinic, 1955-69; pres. med. staff, 1970-71; attending staff, teaching faculty Norfolk Gen. Hosp., 1954—. Served to capt. Med. Corp. AUS, 1948-50. Mem. Am., So. med. assns., Va. Med. Soc., Norfolk County Med. Soc. (exec. com.), Am. Soc. Internal Medicine, A.C.P. (life mem.). Clubs: Norfolk Yacht and Country, Izaak Walton, Tidewater Anglers' (Norfolk); Cape Hatteras (N.C.) Billfish; Ocean Reef (Key Largo, Fla.). Home: 5326 Edgewater Dr Norfolk VA 23508 Office: 421 Wainwright Bldg Norfolk VA 23510

COFFEY, JOHN WALTER, dentist; b. Shawnee, Okla., May 9, 1939; s. Thomas Ray and Edna May (Poindexter) C.; student U. Okla., 1957-61; D.D.S., Baylor U., 1965; m. Joy Diane Arrington, Aug. 6, 1960; children—Dana Catherine, Jennifer Diane, Anne Elizabeth, Emilie Lyn. Practice dentistry, Stillwater, Okla., 1968—; mem. staff, cons. Stillwater Municipal Hosp. Active YMCA memberships drs.; mem. budget com. United Fund, 1969—. Served to capt., USAF, 1965-68. Mem. Am. Soc. Preventive Dentistry, Am. Soc. Dentistry for Children (sec.-treas. Okla. unit 1971—), Acad. Gen. Dentistry (charter mem. Okla.), Am., Okla. (del.) dental assns., Stillwater, Ponca City dental study clubs, Sigma Nu. Republican. Presbyn. Home: 220 Ridge Rd Stillwater OK 74074 Office: 823 S Pine Stillwater OK 74074

COFFIELD, CONRAD EUGENE, lawyer; b. Hot Springs, S.D., Nov. 26, 1930; s. Eugene M. and Alice (Hotvet) C.; student S.D. Sch. Mines and Tech., 1948-49; B.B.A., Washington U., St. Louis, 1952; LL.B., U. Tex., 1959; m. Maggie Lee Murphey, Aug. 1, 1953; children— Conrad Eugene, Michael, Megan, Edward, Philip. Admitted to Tex., N.M. Bars, 1959; practiced in Roswell, N.M., 1959-66, Midland, Tex., 1966—; mem. firm Hervey, Dow & Hinkel, 1959-64; gen. partner Hinkle, Bondurant, Cox & Eaton, Roswell, 1964-66, resident partner, Midland, 1966—; dir., counsel Grammer-Murphey, Inc., Midland. Mem. N.M. Republican party orgn., 1959-66, Midland County Rep. party orgn., 1966—; 1st v.p. Midland County Rep. Men's Club, 1971—. Served with USCGR, 1952-56. Mem. Am., Tex., N.M., Midland County bar assns., N.M. Oil and Gas Assn. Episcopalian (vestryman). Kiwanian (Man of Year 1969). Clubs: Midland Petroleum, Midland Country, Torero, Cotillion. Home: 2813 W Dengar St Midland TX 79701 Office: Midland Tower Midland TX 79701

COFFMAN, BEN, state ofcl. Asst. supr. rehab. services bur. State of Ky., Frankfort. Office: Rehabilitation Services State Dept of Education Frankfort KY 40601*

COFFMAN, CHARLIE QUINN, educator; b. Lula, Miss., Feb. 20, 1923; s. Tulus Jackson and Addie (Mick) C.; B.S., Delta State Coll., Cleveland, Miss., 1948; M.A. (scholar), U. So. Miss., Hattiesburg, 1951; D.Ed. (scholar), U. Miss., 1964; m. J'Nell Posey, Aug. 23, 1947; children—Deborah (Mrs. Gerald Juzwiak), Marilyn Mick. Athletic dir. Tunica (Miss.) High Sch., 1948-50; prin. Shelby (Miss.) High Sch., 1951-53; supt. schs., Arcola, Miss., 1953-56; asst. supt. schs., Cleveland, 1957-60, Hinds County (Miss.) schs., 1961-67; dir. lay renewal United Methodist Ch., 1967-69; asso. dir. for planning in higher edn. State of Miss., 1969—; tchr. grad. studies ednl. adminstrn. U. Miss., 1964—; coordinator Title I Higher Edn. Act for Miss., 1969—. Asso. lay leader, chmn. conf. program council, conf. leadership devel. United Meth. Ch.; dir., charter mem. Jackson (Miss.) Contact Telephone Ministry; tng. officer Explorer Scout leaders. Bd. dirs. local A.R.C., Delta State Coll. Found. Served with USMC, 1941-45. Decorated Purple Heart. Mem. Am. Assn. Sch. Adminstrs., Assn. Instl. Research, Phi Delta Kappa. Mason, Lion. Club: Brookwood Country (Jackson). Author: Ministry of the Laity Training Program, 1968; Growing Together in Small Groups, 1968. Home: Route 1 Box 37AA Jackson MS 39212 Office: PO Box 2336 Jackson MS 39205

COFFMAN, JERRY LYNN, archtl. engr.; b. Terrell, Tex., Sept. 28, 1933; s. Harry C. and Norma Onieta (Rainey) C.; B.S., U. Houston, 1957; m. Glenn Horton, Apr. 9, 1960; children—Charles Horton, Kelly Lynn. With SI P, Inc., engring. and constrn., Houston, 1953—, v.p., 1960—, also dir.; exec. v.p. Acadian Engring. Co., Baton Rouge, 1964—. Bd. dirs. Broadcasters Trust, S.I.P. Charitable Found. Mem. Houston Engring. and Sci. Soc. (pres. 1971-72, bd. dirs. 1970-72), Employers Council of Houston (bd. dirs. 1968-72). Editor: Slide Rule monthly pub. Houston Engring. and Sci. Soc., 1971—. Home: 1318 North Blvd Houston TX 77006 Office: PO Box 26266 Houston TX 77032

COFFMAN, JOHN HARRISON, ins. co. exec.; b. Thrall, Tex., Sept. 1, 1920; s. John Harrison and Jessie (Lawrence); student Central City Comml. Coll., 1937-38; m. Rose Mary Angelo, Dec. 10, 1939; children— Janean (Mrs. James Carey), Rosanne (Mrs. Olle J. Lorehn), John Harrison III, Stephen Anthony. Salesman, Prudential Ins. Co. Am., Waco, Tex., 1948-50; agy. mgr., agy. officer Tex. Life Ins. Co., Waco, 1950-57; sr. officer, agy. v.p. Lincoln Liberty Life Ins. Co. (Neb.)., 1957-68; exec. v.p., dir. United Fidelity Life Ins. Co., Dallas, 1968—; v.p., dir. United Fidelity Investments Inc. Served with USAAF, 1944-45. Decorated Air Medal with 6 oak leaf clusters. Mem. Mktg. Vice-Pres.'s of Am. (chmn. 1971—), V.F.W. (post comdr. 1948-50), Sales and Mktg. Execs. of Dallas. K.C. (grand knight 1949-50, dist. dep. 1950-52). Club: Serra of Metropolitan Dallas (trustee 1971—). Home: 6819 Midcrest St Dallas TX 75240 Office: 1025 Elm St Dallas TX 75202

COFFMAN, MOODY LEE, physicist, educator; b. Abilene, Tex., July 25, 1925; s. Jesse Lee and Mattie (Moody) C.; student Southwestern U., Georgetown, Tex., 1943-44, Notre Dame U., 1944; B.A., Abilene Christian Coll., 1947; M.A., M.S., U. Okla., 1949; Ph.D., Tex. A. and M. U., 1954; m. Marjorie Vern Echols, Mar. 30, 1947; children—Kenneth Lynn, Donald Wayne, Paul Edward, Sharon Kay. Instr. physics E. Tex. State U., 1949-51, Tex. A. and M. Coll., 1951-54; sr. nuclear engr., Convair, Ft. Worth Div., Gen. Dynamics Corp., 1954-55; asso. prof. physics, head dept., Abilene (Tex.) Christian Coll., 1955-60; sr. physicist, missiles and space systems dept.; Hamilton Standard div. United Aircraft Corp., Conn., 1960-61; prof. physics, head dept., Okla. City U., 1961-68; prof. physics Central State U., Edmond, Okla., 1968—. Cons. on aircraft nuclear propulsion project to Convair div., Gen. Dynamics, Ft. Worth, Tex., 1955-57; dir., v.p. research, Acoustic Controls, Inc., Abilene, Tex., 1961—; cons. various aircraft and oil industries; dir. Republic Airlines, Inc., Oklahoma City. Dir., Thinking for Industry, Oklahoma City, 1965—; mem. Nat. adv. council Christian Coll. of S.W., Dallas. Served to lt. comdr. USNR, 1943-46. Fellow Tex. Acad. Sci.; mem. Am. Phys. Soc., Am. Math. Soc., Am. Assn. Physics Tchrs. (founding pres. Ark., Okla., Kan. sect., 1963), Am. Geophys. Union, Okla. Acad. Sci. (sec. 1968-71), Sigma Xi. Mem. Ch. of Christ (deacon). Contbr. to books and profl. jours. Patentee in field. Home: 3612 N Ann Arbor Av Oklahoma City OK 73122 Office: Dept Physics Central State U Edmond OK 73034 also 1832 NW 17th St Oklahoma City OK 73106

COFFMAN, PENELOPE DALTON (MRS. ALDINE J. COFFMAN, JR.), lawyer; b. Pulaski, Va., Apr. 16, 1938; d. Gomez and Hazel (Davis) Dalton; A.B., Randolph-Macon Womans Coll., 1958; J.D., Coll. William and Mary, 1966; m. Aldine J. Coffman, Jr., Mar. 27, 1965. Research chemist, research biologist Arthur D. Little, Inc., Cambridge, Mass., 1958-63; admitted to Va. bar, 1966; law clk. Asso. Justice C. Vernon Spratley, Va. Supreme Ct. Appeals, Hampton, Va., 1966-67; practiced in Norfolk, Va., 1967-68, Virginia Beach, Va., 1968—; mem. firm Coffman, Perry and Etheridge, 1971—; asst. commonwealth atty. for City Virginia Beach, 1971—. Mem. Va. Adv. Council on Ednl. TV, 1971—. Mem. Va. State, Virginia Beach bar assns., Nat. Assn. Women Lawyers, William and Mary Alumni Assn., William and Mary Soc., Randolph-Macon Womans Coll. Alumni Assn., Zeta Tau Alpha. Home: 2861 River Rd Virginia Beach VA 23454 Office: 4999 Cleveland St Virginia Beach VA 23462

COGAN, MICHAEL AARON, physician; b. Holyoke, Mass., Dec. 3, 1908; s. Benjamin William and Sarah (Dyrdack) C.; A.B., Dartmouth Coll., 1930; M.D., Vanderbilt U., 1936; m. Betty Solin (dec. 1962); children—James M., Michael L., Jane, Judy, Robin, Darcy, Amy; m. 2d, Carol Otzelberger. Intern, Mercy Hosp., Springfield, Mass., 1936-37; resident Grasslands Hosp., Valhalla, N.Y.., 1937-38; practice medicine, specializing in internal medicine and cardiology, Springfield, Mass., 1945-56, Miami Beach, Fla., 1956-57, North Miami, Fla., 1959—; pres. staff Springfield Municipal Hosp., 1951-53; sr. staff North Miami Gen. Hosp., Miami Heart Inst., N. Shore Hosp., Miami. Bd. dirs. Heart Assn. Western Mass., 1952-56, Civic League Miami Beach, 1958-62. Served with AUS, 1941-45. Diplomate Am. Bd. Internal Medicine. Fellow A.C.P., Am. Coll. Cardiology, Am. Coll. Chest Physicians; mem. Am. Soc. Internal Medicine, Am. Heart Assn., A.M.A., Mass. Fla., Dade County med. assns. Mason, Elk. Office: 12302 NE 6th Av North Miami FL 33161

COGBILL, T.C., JR., state ofcl. Mem. Ark. Bd. Edn. Address: care State Board of Education Bldg Little Rock AR 72203*

COGGESHALL, KENNETH MORRISON, pub. relations exec.; b. St. Louis, June 27, 1920; s. Kenneth McCandless and Eva Louise (Morrison) C.; B.A. in Journalism, B.A. in English, U. Mo., 1948; certificate in pub. relations Washington U., 1951; m. Corinne Beard, May 23, 1942; children—Diane (Mrs. Ralph Conlin), David Knight. Asst. pub. relations dir. McDonnell Aircraft Corp., 1949-53; dir. pub. relations Bank Bldg. Corp., St. Louis, 1953-58; cons. pub. affairs, Washington, 1958—. Dir. 1st Internat. Trauma Symposium, 1970; mem. Pub. Relations Soc. Task Force on Environment, 1970—. Served with AC, AUS, 1942-46. Recipient Silver Anvil award Pub. Relations Soc. Am., 1961; Pub. Service citation Am. Pub. Relations Assn. Mem. Pub. Relations Soc. Am. (chmn. eligibility com. Nat. Capital chpt. 1967). Am. Helicopter Soc., Helicopter Assn. Am. Home: 8212 Carrleigh Pkwy Springfield VA 22152 Office: 400 Maryland Av SW Washington DC 20202

COGGESHALL, LOWELL THELWELL, physician, educator; b. Saratoga, Ind., May 7, 1901; A.B., Ind. U., 1922, A.M., 1923, M.D., 1928, LL.D., 1947; L.H.D., Jefferson Med. Coll., 1956, Lake Forest Coll., 1961; Sc.D., Chgo. Med. Sch., 1962, Albany Med. Coll., 1964; m. 1930; 3 children. Mem. staff Rockefeller Found., 1924-26, 35-41; instr. anatomy Ind. U. Sch. Medicine, 1926-27; instr. medicine U. Chgo., 1931-33, asst. prof., 1933-35, chmn. dept. medicine, from 1947, v.p., from 1960, dean div. biol. scis., 1947-60, now ret.; prof. epidemiology U. Mich. Sch. Pub. Health, 1941-43, chmn. dept. tropical diseases, 1943; Del., WHO, 1959. Trustee Rockefeller Found., Josiah Macy, Jr. Found., Crerar Library, Mus. Sci. and Industry, LaRabida Sanitarium. Served to capt. M.C., USNR, 1944-46. Recipient Gorgas medal, 1945; Jesuit Centennial citation, 1957; Founders Day award Loyola U., 1961; Abraham Flexner award, 1963; James D. Bruce Meml. award, 1971. Mem. Nat. Acad., A.A.A.S., Soc. Clin. Investigation, Soc. Tropical Medicine and Hygiene (v.p. 1957), A.C.P., Am. Pub. Health Assn., Am. Cancer Soc. (pres. 1958), Am. Philos. Soc., Assn. Am. Med. Colls. (pres. 1958). Home: Foley AL 36535

COGGESHALL, ROBERT WALDEN, cons.; b. Darlington, S.C., Sept. 11, 1912; s. Robert Werner and Beulah (Walden) C.; B.S., U. S.C., 1932; M.A., George Washington U., 1964; postgrad. Am. U., 1964-69; m. Ellie Mason Thomas, Sept. 3, 1934; children—Peter Collin V, John Pennington. Administrv. analyst Home Owners Loan Corp., Washington, 1934-41; budget analyst Fed. Works Agy., 1941-43; asst. dep. adminstr. for rent control OPA, 1943-46; chief systems and procedures Bur. Reclamation, 1946-53; editor Postal Manual, Office Postmaster Gen., 1954; chief mgmt. analysis Bur. Indian Affairs, 1954-57; chief div. mgmt. sci. Office of Sec., Dept. Interior, Washington, 1957-68; research fellow Brookings Instn., 1968-69; faculty U.S. Dept. Agr. Grad. Sch., 1959-65. Mem. Am. Soc. Pub. Adminstrn., A.A.A.S., Alpha Tau Omega. Episcopalian. Author: Administrative Functions of the Fish and Wildlife Service, 1958; Coordination of Federal Oceanography, 1963. Home: Ballentine SC 29002

COGGINS, WADE THOMAS, assn. exec.; b. New Market, N.C., Dec. 12, 1924; s. Charles Lee and Laura Jean (Hinshaw) C.; B.S., Nyack Missionary Coll., 1955; M.A., U. Md., 1965; m. Jane Marguerite Wells, Aug. 18, 1945; 1 son, Robert Charles. Ordained to ministry Christian and Missionary Alliance Ch., 1947; minister, Norwoodville Ch., Des Moines, 1945-47; missionary, tchr. Christian and Missionary Alliance, Columbia, 1948-55; minister Alliance Ch., Knoxville, Tenn., 1956-58; asso. exec. sec. Evang. Fgn. Missions Assn., Washington, 1958—. Mem. Alumni Assn. Nyack Missionary Coll. (v.p. 1966-67). Mem. Christian and Missionary Alliance Ch. (elder 1959—). Editor: (with Clyde W. Taylor) Protestant Missions in Latin America, 1961; (with Clyde W. Taylor) Mobilizing for Saturation Evangelism, 1970. Editor, Missionary News Service, 1958—. Home: 4913 Bangor Dr Kensington MD 20795 Office: 1405 G St NW Washington DC 20005

COHEN, DANIEL MORRIS, biologist; b. Chgo., July 6, 1930; s. Leonard U. and Myrtle (Gertz) C.; A.B., Stanford U., 1952, M.A., 1953, Ph.D., 1958; m. Anne Carolyn Constant, Nov. 4, 1955; children—Carolyn A., Cynthia S. Acting instr. biol. scis. Stanford U., 1956-57; asst. prof. biol. scis, U. Fla., 1958; ichthyologist Ichthological Lab. U.S. Fish and Wildlife Service, 1958-62, lab. dir., 1962—, now dir. systematics lab. Nat. Marine Fisheries Service; research asso. Smithsonian Instn. Mem. Am. Soc. Ichthyology and Herpetology, A.A.A.S., Biol. Soc. Washington (pres. 1971), Soc. Study Evolution, Soc. Systematic Zoology. Contbr. articles in field to profl. jours. Home: 6803 Florida St Chevy Chase MD 20015 Office: Systematics Lab National Marine Fisheries Service US National Museum Washington DC 20560

COHEN, DAVID, legislative rep.; b. Phila., Oct. 10, 1936; s. Joseph and Gertrude (Schwalb) C.; A.B., Temple U., 1957; m. Carla Furstenberg, Sept. 7, 1958; children—Aaron, Eve. Dir. contacts and research Upholsterers Internat. Union, Phila., 1959-63; legislative rep. Americans For Democratic Action, Washington, 1963-67, bd. dirs., 1956-59, chmn. nat. exec. com., 1969-71, nat. vice chmn., 1971—; legislative rep. Indsl. Union Dept. AFL-CIO, Washington, 1967-68; legislative rep. Com. for Community Affairs, Washington, 1968-71; dir. field orgn. Common Cause, Washington, 1971—; lectr. polit. sci. Coe Coll., 1964—. Mem. Humphrey Campaign Task Force on Housing and Consumer Affairs, 1968—. Recipient Civil Rights award Phila. Fellowship Commn., 1961. Mem. Am. Newspaper Guild. Home: 1322 Holly St NW Washington DC 20012 Office: Common Cause 2100 M St NW Washington DC 20037

COHEN, EUGENE ERWIN, univ. adminstr.; b. Johnstown, Pa., Nov. 1, 1917; s. LeRoy S. and Ann (Aronson) C.; B.B.A., U. Miami, 1941; M.B.A., 1951; postgrad. Wayne State U., 1944-45, U. N.C., 1951-52; m. Lee Woodard Edmundson, Dec. 31, 1944; children—William Palmer, Margaret Gene, Ann Woodard. Asst. auditor, Embry Riddle Co., Miami, Fla., 1940-41; faculty U. Miami, 1945—, asso. prof. accounting, 1954-67, prof., 1967—, treas., 1957—, v.p., treas., 1958-72, v.p. financial affairs, 1972—, also treas. Internat. Research Found.; v.p., dir. Dormitory Housing Assn., Inc. Dir. Garrett & Co., N.Y.C.; mem. adv. bd. Am. Bankers Ins. Co. Fla. Cons., NSF, NIH; mem. com. taxation Am. Council Edn.; cons. editor Coll. and U. Bus., 1959—. Vice pres. Nat. Childrens Cardiac Hosp.; asso. mem. Orange Bowl Com.; dir. Greater Miami Indsl. Commn.; mem. Miami Mayor's Spl. Adv. Com. on Interama. Bd. dirs. Goodwill Industries, Miami, Family Service of Miami. Served with AUS, 1941-45. Mem. So. Assn. Coll. and U. Bus. Officers (pres. 1963), Financial Execs. Inst. (pres. Fla. chpt. 1963). Nat. Assn. Coll. and U. Bus. Officers, Am. Mgmt. Assn., Coll. and U. Personnel Assn., Coll. and U. Housing Officers Assn., Nat. Assn. Accountants, Newcomen Soc., Dade County C. of C., Omicron Delta Kappa, Phi Mu Alpha, Alpha Phi Omega, Alpha Kappa Psi. Methodist. Mason. Clubs: Miami University Yacht; El Centro de las Americas, Miami; Kings Bay Yacht. Home: 6700 SW 117th St Miami FL 33156 Office: Ashe Adminstrn Bldg U Miami Coral Gables FL 33124

COHEN, H(ERMANN) E(DMOND), ret. textile co. exec., civic worker; b. Ukraine, Oct. 10, 1889; s. Edell and Sarah (Rosenstein) C.; Came to U.S., 1892, naturalized citizen; extension student Mechanics Inst. Va., 1909-10, U. Va., 1912; m. Claire Rosenberg, Apr. 6, 1921 (dec. Apr. 1960). Formerly textile selling agt.; pres. Priestly Knitting Co., 1948; owner Chester Knit Goods Co., Charlotte, N.C., 1948-72. Mem. adv. com. So. Sch. for Workers, 1940-55; mem. adv. com. League for Mut. Aid, 1959—; charter mem. Am. Civil Liberties Union, Charlotte-Mecklenburg Council on Human Relations, Charlotte-Mecklenberg Symposium on World Affairs; mem. Central Com. for Conscientious Objectors; mem. internat. com. Thomas Paine Found., 1958—, organizer Charlotte chpt. Thomas Paine Soc., 1963. Recipient awards Nat. Conf. Christians and Jews, 1958, 63. Mem. Internat. Platform Assn., C. of C. Jewish religion (mem. temple adult edn. com., pres. Men's Club): Unitarian; mem. Community Ch. Mason (Shriner). Elk (chaplain). Clubs: Executives, Toastmasters (Charlotte). Former mem., editorial bd., cofounder The Carolina Israelite. Home: 301 W 10th St Charlotte NC 28202

COHEN, HYMAN JACOB, lawyer; b. Boston, July 27, 1905; s. Benjamin L. and Kate (Bazol) C.; B.S., Tufts U., 1928; LL.B., Harvard, 1931; m. Ann Rosen, Nov. 1940; children—Amy Rose (Mrs. Mark P. Scher), Judith F. (Mrs. David. C. Wilson), Kate B. (Mrs. Cohen Schachter). Admitted to D.C. bar, 1947, Va. bar, 1948; pvt. practice law, 1931-42; field worker U.S.O., 1942-43; atty. U.S. Govt., 1943-47; pvt. practice law, Washington, Va., 1947—; print collector, exhibiting D.C., Md. and Va. Mem. adv. bd. Independence Fed. Savs. & Loan Assn. Mem. min. standards housing bd. Arlington County Youth Commn., 1960—; mem. nat. council U.S.O. 1959—; mem. dist. adv. council Small Bus. Adminstrn.; mem. region 3 archives adv. council Gen. Services Adminstrn.; mem. Arlington County Hist. Commn., World Peace Through Law Center, Arlington County Bicentennial Commn., Arlington History Commn.; mem. adv. com. N.E. region Nat. Park Service. Trustee United Jewish Appeal, Greater Washington Jewish Community Found.; bd. regents James Monroe Law Office-Mus. and Meml. Library; bd. dirs. Touro Synagogue-Nat. Historic Shrine. Mem. Am., Va. bar assns., Bar Assn. D.C., Am. Trial Lawyers Assn. (asso. editor), Am. Forestry Assn., Nat. Trust for Historic Preservation, Nature Conservancy (life), UN Assn. U.S.A., Wilderness Soc., Jewish Hist. Assn. Greater Washington (pres.), Am. Jewish (exec. council), U.S. Capitol hist. socs., Pi Lambda Phi. Mem. Washington Hebrew Congregation (dir.). Mason. Club: Torch. Home: 5300 36th St N Arlington VA 22207 Office: 910 17th St NW Washington DC 20006

COHEN, JERRY S., lawyer. Chief counsel, staff dir. Senate Antitrust and Monopoly Subcom. Author: (with Morton Mintz) America, Inc.: Who Owns and Operates the United States, 1972. Address: 3110 Rodman NW Washington DC 20008*

COHEN, MARSHALL HERBERT, govt. ofcl., free-lance photographer; b. Providence, Sept. 23, 1932; s. Samuel H. and Lucille (Seigal) C.; B.A., Brown U., 1954; M.A., Georgetown U., 1966; postgrad. Am. U., Boston U. Economist, Europe and Soviet Union br. U.S. Dept. Agr., 1963—; free lance photographer. Bd. dirs. govt. div. United Jewish Appeal. Recipient Blue Ribbon Nat. award for contbns. to fgn. agr., 1970. Mem. Am. Scandinavian Found., Am. Assn. Agrl. Economists, Am. Econ. Assn. Clubs: Brown, Georgetown (Washington). Author: Agricultural Economy and Trade of Denmark, 1968; Summary of Projections of Long Range Supply and Demand for Agricultural Products in Denmark, 1970; The Agricultural Situation in Western Europe, 1971. Contbr. articles profl. jours. Home: 2725 39th St NW Washington DC 20007 Office: ERS/FRAD 500 12th St SW Washington DC 20250

COHEN, MICHAEL LEROY, optometrist; b. Cumberland, Md., Feb. 17, 1939; s. Harry Earl and Lee (Markowitz) C.; A.A., U. Fla., 1959; student U. Md., 1959-60, Am. U., 1960; O.D., Pa. State Coll. Optometry, 1964; m. Sherry S. Shapiro, June 23, 1963; children—Bruce Evan, Flint Gregory. Practice optometry, Alexandria, Va., 1964—. Pres., AMDAS Corp., Alexandria, 1968—, Am. Med.-Dental Assts. Schs., Arlington, Va., 1967—; cons. Obrig Labs., Sarasota, Fla., 1968—; mem. Nat. Eye Research Found. Mem. Alexandria Crime Commn., 1966—. Bd. dirs. Alexandria Boy's Club, 1965-66, pres. adv. bd., 1968—; bd. dirs. Mental Health Assn., City Alexandria Pub. Schs. Health Professions Career Bd. Mem. Am., Va. optometric assns., Alexandria Bd. of Trade, Urban League, Jr. C. of C. (v.p. 1965-66). Inventor poly-lens clear corneal contact lens. Home: 4542 LaSalle Av Alexandria VA 22041 Office: 3509 S Jefferson St Bailey's Crossroads VA 22041

COHEN, ROBERT ABRAHAM, physician; b. Chgo., Nov. 13, 1909; s. Ezra Harry and Catherine (Kurzon) C.; B.S., U. Chgo., 1930, Ph.D., 1935, M.D., 1935; m. Mabel Jean Blake, Mar. 21, 1933; children—Donald Edward, Margery Jean. Intern, Michael Reese Hosp., Chgo., 1936-37; resident Johns Hopkins, Sheppard-Pratt hosps., 1937-41; pvt. practice, Washington, 1946-48; clin. dir. Chestnut Lodge, Rockville, Md., 1948-53; dir. div. clin. and behavioral research Nat. Insts. Mental Health, Bethesda, Md., 1953—, also dep. dir. mental health intramural research programs. Bd. dirs. Founds. Fund for Research chmn. bd., 1962-63; trustee William Alanson White Psychiatric Found. Served from lt. (j.g.) to comdr. M.C., USNR, 1941-46. Recipient Distinguished Service award Dept. Health, Edn. and Welfare. Fellow Am. Psychiatric Assn.; mem. Am. Psychoanalytical Assn., Washington Psychoanalytic Soc. (pres. 1951-53), Washington Psychiatric Soc. (pres. 1958-59), Washington Psychoanalytic Inst. (chmn. edn. com. 1953-58, dir. 1959-63), Washington Acad. Medicine. Home: 4514 Dorset Av Chevy Chase MD 20015 Office: 9000 Wisconsin Av Bethesda MD 20014

COHEN, STANLEY LEON, accountant; b. N.Y.C., Apr. 27, 1925; s. Max and Edna (Goldberg) C.; B.B.A., Coll. City N.Y., 1947; postgrad. Oxford U., 1945, Cornell U., Ithaca, N.Y., 1944-45, N.Y. U., 1947-48, Hofstra Coll., 1954; m. Sonia Auerbach, Sept. 1, 1946; children—Matthew, Debra, Cara, Jana. Partner, Sidney G. Spero & Co., N.Y.C., 1948-57; prin., sr. partner Stanley L. Cohen & Co., C.P.A.'s, and predecessor co., North Miami Beach, Fla., 1962—; pres. Matra Assos., Inc.; dir., chmn. trust adv. com. Pan Am. Bank Dade County; dir. P.E.C. Corp., Am. Community Systems, Inc., Pub. Service Commn. North Miami Beach, 1958-62; vice chmn. Dade County Water and Sewer Bd., 1964-67. Served with inf. AUS, 1943-46; ETO. Decorated Purple Heart, Bronze Star medal, Combat Inf. Badge. Mem. Am. Inst. C.P.A.'s, Fla. (com. on ecology), N.Y. insts. C.P.A.'s. Author: Auditing for Home Builders, 1957; Cost of Money-Water Utilities, 1966; Bankruptcy and the C.P.A., 1965; Ecology and the C.P.A., 1972. Home: 20130 NE 21st Ct North Miami Beach FL 33162 Office: 633 NE 167th St North Miami Beach FL 33162

COHEN, TED ELLIS, pub. relations exec.; b. N.Y.C., Aug. 13, 1922; s. Irving and Gertrude (Cantor) C.; student U.S. Naval Acad., 1942-45; m. Carolyn Bloom, June 1944 (div. Sept. 1960); children—Constance Diane, James David, Ellen Jane. Partner, DiLido Hotel, Miami Beach, Fla., 1950-53; real estate salesman J.A. Cantor Assos., Miami, 1952-53; real estate broker Ted Cohen, Realtor, Miami Beach, 1953-56; pres. Ted Cohen Assos., Pub. Relations, Miami Beach, 1956—. Exec. dir. Fla. Fashion Council, 1965-68. Mem. Mayor's Safety Com., Miami Beach, 1955-70, chmn. 1959-61; pres. Pres.'s Council, 1964-65; chmn. S. Fla. council Boy Scouts Am., 1960. Democratic committeeman, 1962-70, state Dem. committeeman, 1971—; pres. Young Dems., 1959-61; chmn. Dade County Dem. Exec. Com., 1971—. Served with USNR, 1942-45. Named Outstanding Young Man Miami Beach 1959, Outstanding Citizen Fla., 1961 (both Jaycees). Elk (exalted ruler 1971-72). Clubs: Civic League (pres. 1967-68), Civitan (pres. 1959-60). Home: 5 Island Av Miami Beach FL 33139 Office: 1 Lincoln Rd Miami Beach FL 33139

COHN, ISIDORE, JR., surgeon, educator; b. New Orleans, Sept. 25, 1921; s. Isidore and Elsie (Waldhorn) C.; M.D., U. Pa., 1945, M.Med.Sci. in Surgery, 1952, D.M.S. in Surgery, 1955; m. Jacqueline Heymann, July 4, 1944 (div. Aug. 27, 1971); children—Ian Jeffrey, Lauren Kerry. Intern, Grad. Hosp. U. Pa., 1945-46, resident in surgery, 1949-52; fellow dept. surg. research U. Pa., 1947-48; vis. surgeon Charity Hosp., New Orleans, 1952-62, sr. vis. surgeon, 1962—; surgeon-in-chief La State U. Service, Charity Hosp., 1962—; cons. surgeon VA Hosp, Touro Infirmary (both New Orleans); instr. surgery La. State U. Sch. Medicine, New Orleans, 1952-53, asst. prof., 1953-56, asso. prof. 1956-59, prof., 1959—, chmn. dept. surgery, 1962—. Mem. surg. research rev. com. VA, Washington. Served to capt. M.C., AUS, 1946-47. Diplomate Am. Bd. Surgery. Fellow A.C.S.; mem. A.M.A., Soc. Exptl. Biology and Medicine, Am., So., La. (2d v.p. 1966, 1st v.p. 1967, pres. 1968) surg. assns., So. Med. Assn., La., Orleans Parish med. socs., Internat., New Orleans (v.p. 1966, pres. 1967) surg. socs., Soc. Univ. Surgeons, Southeastern Surg. Congress (chmn. forum on progress in surgery 1967-69, councillor for La. 1967—, 2d v.p. 1965, 1st v.p. 1969, pres. 1972), Surg. Biology Club II, Assn. Acad. Surgery, Allen O Whipple, James D. Rives surg. socs., Am. Gastroenterol. Assn., Bockus Soc. Gastroenterology, So. Soc. Clin. Research, Soc. Surgery Alimentary Tract (trustee 1969—), Am. Soc. Microbiologists, N.Y. Acad. Scis., Soc. Surg. Chmn., Am. Assn. Cancer Research, Collegium Internationale Chirurgiae Digestivae, Am. Cancer Soc. (vice chmn. clin. investigation adv. com. 1969, chmn. clin. investigation adv. com. 1969—), Sigma Xi. Mem. editorial bd. Am. Surgeon, Review of Surgery, Am. Jour. Surgery, Surgery Digest. Home: 510 Iona St Metairie LA 70005 Office: Louisiana State Univ School of Medicine New Orleans LA 70112

COHN, SAMUEL MAURICE, govt. ofcl.; b. Phila., Nov. 11, 1915; s. Herman and Bessie (Weisberg) C.; B.A., U. Pa., 1936, postgrad., 1936, 38-40; m. Alma R. Cantor, Oct. 2, 1948; children—Anne L., Richard D. Research asst. Wharton Sch. Finance, U. Pa., 1938-39, 41-42; research asst., relocation dir. Phila. Housing Authority, 1939-40; econ. analyst Office War Moblzn. and Reconversion, Washington, 1946-47; fiscal economist Bur. of Budget, Washington, 1947-52, chief economist, 1953-55, chief fiscal analysis, 1956-60, dep. asst. dir. for budget rev., 1961-65; asst. dir. Office Mgmt. and Budget, Exec. Office Pres., 1966—. Served with AUS, 1942-45. Recipient Exceptional Ser. award Bur. of Budget, 1962; Career Ser. award Nat Civil Ser. League, 1968, President's award for distinguished fed. civilian ser., 1971. Mem. Am. Econ. Assn., Am. Statis. Assn., Am. Soc. Pub. Adminstrn., Econometric Soc. Contbr. articles to profl. publs. Home: 3400 Rose Lane Falls Church VA 22042 Office: Exec Office Bldg Washington DC 20503

COINER, RICHARD TIDE, JR., aviation cons., ret. air force officer; b. Washington, Sept. 2, 1910; s. Richard T. and Emily (Hall) C.; B.S., U.S. Mil. Acad., 1932; m. Helen Lanier Nix, Feb. 22, 1936; children—Richard Tide III, Beverly Nix, William Lanier. Commd. 2d lt. U.S. Army, 1932, advanced through grades to maj. gen. USAF, 1952; exec. to asst. sec. of war for air, 1941-43; comd. 397th Bomber Group, ETO, 1943-45; RAF Staff Coll., 1946; Hdqrs. U.S. Air Force Europe, 1946-49; div. mil. application AEC, 1949-51; dep. comdr., field command Armed Forces Spl. Weapons Project, 1951-54; asst. dep. chief of staff Operations for Atomic Energy, Hdqrs. USAF, 1954-58, asst. chief staff, Air and Spl. Operations, SHAPE, 1958-61; comdr. Headquarters Ninth Air Force, 1961-63; dir. transp. Hdqrs. USAF, 1963-66; aviation cons., 1966—. Vice pres., dir. Nix Profl. Bldg. Corp., Nix Hosp. Corp. Episcopalian. Clubs: Argyle, San Antonio Country (San Antonio); Army and Navy (Washington). Home: 140 Patterson Av San Antonio TX 78209

COINTMENT, JOSEPH DELMA, dental surgeon; b. Plaquemine, La., Dec. 2, 1902; s. Joseph Delma and Elfie (McCabe) C.; ed. Loyola U., New Orleans, La. State Dental Sch.; m. Althea Schwing, Apr. 22, 1936; children— Joseph Delma III, Janie, Althea Schwing. Asso. dentist Rhodes J. Spedale Gen. Hosp., Plaquemine, 1960-72, dental surgeon, 1972—. Chmn., A.R.C. Chmn., Plaquemine Recreation Commn. Former bd. dirs. Plaquemine Acad.; bd. dirs. Rhodes J. Spedale Gen. Hosp. Served to capt. Dental Corps, USAAF, 1942-45. Recipient Plaque for Citizen of Year, Amvets, 1949, Citizenship award Cancer Crusade, 1968. Mem. Am., La., 6th Dist. (pres. 1939) dental assns., Am. Legion, Amvets, C. of C. (pres. 1949). Rotarian (past program chmn., pres. 1961—), Lion (pres. 1947), Elk. Clubs: Country (Baton Rouge); Riverdale Golf (Donaldson, La.); Westside Golf (Brusly, La.). Home: 906 Eden St Plaquemine LA 70764 Office: 406 Eden St Plaquemine LA 70764

COIT, ROBERT DANIEL, lawyer; b. Enterprise, Miss., Mar. 31, 1930; s. Robert Edwin and Faye (Armstrong) C.; student Meridian Jr. Coll., 1947-49; B.S., Miss. State Coll., 1952; LL.B., U. Miss., 1956; m. Elna Faye Haden, Aug. 2, 1959; children—Lauren Faye, Linda Ann, Nancy, Edwin. Admitted Miss. bar. 1956; since practiced in Meridian, Miss.; mem. firm Huff & Williams, 1956-62; gen. practice, Meridian, 1962—. Mem. Selective Service Bd. Incorporator, pres. Lamar Sch. Found. Served to lt. AUS, 1952-54. Col. on Gov.'s Staff, 1972—. Mem. Am., Miss. State, Lauderdale County bar assns., Miss. Forestry Assn., Phi Alpha Delta, S.C.V., Miss. Pvt. Sch. Assn. (dir.), Am. Legion, Am. Right of Way Assn., Miss. Claims Assn. Presbyn. Mason. Home: 2305 36th Av Meridian MS 39301 Office: Lamar Bldg Meridian MS 39301

COKE, C(HAUNCEY) EUGENE, textile scientist; b. Toronto, Ont., Can., July 27, 1905; s. Chauncey Eugene and Edith May (Redman) C.; B.Sc., U. Manitoba, 1927, M.Sc., 1929; M.A., U. Toronto, 1930; Ph.D., U. Leeds, Eng., 1938; m. Sally B. Tolmie, June 12, 1941. In charge research Courtaulds (Can.) Ltd., Cornwall, Ont., 1939-42; dir. research and devel. Guaranty Dyeing & Finishing Co., St. Catharines, Ont., 1946-48; mgr. indsl. yarn sales and devel. Courtaulds (Can.) Ltd., Montreal, 1948-54, mgr. devel. dept., 1954-59; dir. research and devel. Hart-Fibres Co., 1959-62, also mem. exec. com.; tech. dir. textile chem. dept. Drew Chem. Corp., Boonton, N.J., 1962-63; mgr. new products fibers div. Am. Cyanamid Co., Bound Brook, 1963-70; pres. Coke & Assos. Cons., 1970—. Served from 2d lt. to maj. RCAF, 1942-46. Recipient bronze medal Canadian Assn. Textile Colourists and Chemists, 1963. Fellow Soc. Dyers and Colourists (Gt. Britain), Royal Inst. Chemistry (Gt. Britain), Textile Inst. (Gt. Britain), Chem. Inst. Can., A.A.A.S., N.J. Acad. Sci.; mem. Am. Assn. Textile Tech. (past pres; Bronze medal 1971), Canadian Assn. Textile Colourists and Chemists (past pres.), Inst. Textile Sci. (Can.) (cofounder, past pres.), N.Y. Acad. Scis., Fiber Soc., Internat. Platform Assn. Club: The Chemist's. Author articles in field. Office: Ormond Beach FL 32074

COKER, DARBY TRIMBLE, lawyer, realtor; b. East Point, Ga., July 6, 1915; s. William Henry and Emma (Ledford) C.; J.D., Woodrow Wilson Coll. Law, 1942; A.B., Williams Coll., 1970; Ph.D., Neotarian Coll. Philosophy, 1970; m. Athalia Chappell, Nov. 12, 1938; children—Darby Trimble Jr., Stanley C. Admitted to Ga. bar, 1942; practice law, real estate and appraisal, East Point, 1942—; dir. Citizens & So. Bank, East Point, 1960—. Served with Armed Forces, World War II. Mem. Am. Soc. Appraisers (sr.), Soc. Real Estate Appraisers. Mason (Shriner). Kiwanian. Home: 3116 Boulder Way East Point GA 30344 Office: Brogdon Bldg 1783 Washington Av P O Box 90337 East Point GA 30344

COKER, HOMER, educator; b. Turbeville, S.C., Feb. 14, 1923; s. Clarence Epps and Laura Jane (Dennis) C.; B.S., Clemson U., 1948; M.Ed., U. S.C., 1953, Ph.D., 1968; m. Mary Alice Adams, June 30, 1944; children—Thomas A., Michael D. Coach, prin., supt. schs. Stephen (S.C.) High Sch., 1948-56; area supt., asst. supt., coordinator fed. programs Aiken County, S.C., 1964-67; asso. prof. edn. W. Ga. Coll., Carrollton, 1968—; v.p. Innovations, Inc. Served with USNR, 1943-46. Kellogg fellow, 1955-56. Mem. N.E.A., A. Assn. Sch. Adminstrs., Am. Ednl. Research Assn., S.C. Edn. Assn., Ga. Assn. Retarded Children, Ga. Mental Health Assn. (editor newsletter), So. Regional Council Ednl. Adminstrn. (sec.-treas. 1970—), W. Ga. Ednl. Devel. Program (exec. dir. 1968— editor newsletter), Am. Legion. Mason (Shriner), Rotarian. Club: Ruritan (St. Stephen, S.C.). Home: 306 Tanner St Carrollton GA 30117

COLAY, HARRY BRADFORD, lawyer; b. Cleveland, Ark., May 31, 1908; s. John Henry and Mabel (Bradford) C.; B.A., U. Ark., 1932; postgrad. Ark. Law Sch., 1933-35; m. Ruth Marie Aday, Oct. 28, 1933; 1 dau., Mabel Jo. High sch. prin. Conway County (Ark.) schs., 1932-33; admitted to Ark. bar, 1935; with firm E. A. Williams, Morrilton, Ark., 1935-36; 1st lt. Res. Officers Corps, Civilian Conservation Corps, Cal., Wash., Ida., 1936-38; practiced law in Magnolia, Ark., 1938—; with firm Davis & Colay, 1939-44; mem. Ark. Ho. of Reps., 1946-57, 59-70, mem. legislative council 1949-51, chmn. Ark. com. on higher edn., 1951-53, mem. legislative joint audit com., 1963-70, chmn. house judiciary com., 1963. Chmn. Columbia County Devel. Authority, 1963—. Mem. Nat., Ark. trial lawyers assns., Nat. Soc. State Legislators (pres. 1965-66, chmn. past president's adv. com.), Am., Ark., Columbia County (sec.-treas. 1957—), 13th Jud. Dist. (sec.) bar assns., Assn. Interstate Commerce Practitioners, Am. Judicature Soc., Am. Legion, C. of C., Ark. Hist. Assn. Democrat. Baptist. Mason (32 deg., K.T., Shriner) K.P. Club: Magnolia Country. Died Mar. 30, 1972. Home: Magnolia AR

COLBATH, WALTER NEWELL, JR., lawyer; b. Evanston, Ill., Aug. 21, 1934; s. Walter N. and Vesta (Swenson) C.; B.S. in Marketing, Ind. U., 1956; LL.B., U. Miami, 1965 children—Walter N. III, Jeffrey J., Stephanie L. Salesman, Kaiser Aluminum, Cleve., 1958-60; sec.-treas. Colbath Steel Service, Riviera Beach, Fla., 1960-62; admitted to Fla. bar, 1965; pub. defender 15th Jud. Circuit Fla., 1966—; partner Campbell, Colbath, Kapner & Bratten, West Palm Beach, 1967—. Dir. O'Donnell's Drape & Carpet Div., Inc., Pami, Inc. (both Lake Park, Fla.), Carnaby St. East Ltd., Inc., Jupiter, Fla., Fla. Coin Collectors., Inc., West Palm Beach. Bd. dirs. Vis. Nurses Assn., Comprehensive Community Mental Health Center, Mental Health Assn. Palm Beach County, YMCA (all West Palm Beach). Served with USNR, 1950-52, AUS, 1956-58. Named Most Outstanding Graduating Sr. U. Miami, 1965. Mem. Am. Trial Lawyers Assn., Fla. Acad. Trial Lawyers, Am. Palm Beach County bar assns., Fla. Pub. Defenders Assn. (pres. elect). Republican. Home: 501 Gulf Rd North Palm Beach FL 33403 Office: Harvey Bldg West Palm Beach FL 33401

COLBENSON, PAUL DAHLE, trade assn. exec.; b. Rushford, Minn., Mar. 20, 1920; s. Henry Carl and Clara (Dahle) C.; student Winona State Tchrs. Coll., 1938-40; U. Fla., 1947; B.S., U. Tenn., 1950; m. Thelma Peters, Apr. 16, 1943; children—Peter D., Peggy Jane (Mrs. James B. Brown). Instr., U. Tenn., 1947-50; appraiser engr. U.S. Dept. Agr., Knoxville, Tenn., 1950-54; engr. Douglas Fir and Am. Plywood Assn., Tacoma, Wash., 1954-56, field rep., Birmingham, Ala., 1956-57, Clearwater, Fla., 1957-63, regional mgr., Atlanta, 1963—. Served to lt. comdr. USNR, 1941-46. Decorated Air medal with one star. Mem. Am. Soc. Agrl. Engrs., Phi Kappa Phi, Alpha Zeta. Home: 1710 Timothy Dr SW Atlanta GA 30311 Office: PO Box 90550 Atlanta GA 30344

COLBY, WILLIAM EGAN, govt. ofcl.; b. St. Paul, Jan. 4, 1920; s. Elbridge and Margaret (Egan) C.; B.A., Princeton, 1940; LL.B., Columbia U. Law Sch., 1947; m. Barbara Heinzen, Sept. 15, 1945; children— Jonathan, Catherine, Carl, Paul, Christine. Admitted to N.Y. State bar, 1947; atty. Donovan Leisure Newton & Irvine, N.Y.C., 1947-49, Nat. Labor Relations Bd., Washington, 1949-50; attache Am. embassy, Stockholm, Sweden, 1951-53, Am. embassy, Rome, Italy, 1953-58; 1st sec. Am. embassy, Saigon, Vietnam, 1959-62; chief Far East div. CIA, Washington, 1962-67, exec. dir., 1972—; ambassador, dir. Civil Operations and Rural Devel. Support, Saigon, 1968-71. Served to maj. AUS, 1941-45. Decorated Silver Star, Bronze Star; St. Olafs medal (Norway); Croix de Guerre (France). Mentioned in Despatches (Brit.). Mem. Phi Beta Kappa. Roman Catholic. Clubs: Cosmos (Washington); Special Forces (London, Eng.); Linge Klubben (Oslo, Norway); France Combattant (Paris, France). Home: 5317 Briley Pl Washington DC 20016 Office: CIA Washington DC 20505

COLE, BENJAMIN RICHASON, newspaperman; b. Indpls., July 10, 1916; s. Almon Theodore and Maude (Richason) C.; student Butler U., 1934-35, Ind. State Tchrs. Coll., 1938, Am. Press Inst. of Columbia, 1948; m. Alice Louise Porteous, Sept. 11, 1937; children—Alan Andrew, Amy (Mrs. George E. Martin, Jr.), Benjamin Richason. Reporter, Terre Haute Tribune-Star Pub. Co., 1938-40, Terre Haute Star, 1940-44; with Indpls. Star, 1944—, statehouse reporter, 1945-48, asst. city editor, 1948, city editor, 1948-49, Washington corr., 1949—; corr. Arizona Republic, Phoenix, 1955—. Mem. Sigma Delta Chi. Presbyn. Mason. Clubs: Gridiron, National Press (Washington); Press (Indpls.) Home: 6529 Beverly Av McLean VA 22101 Office: Nat Press Bldg Washington DC 20004

COLE, FRANK W., petroleum cons.; b. Connerville, Okla., Aug. 14, 1925; s. Fred W. and Velma (Ingram) C.; B.S., U. Okla., 1948, M.S., 1949; m. Martha Barton, Feb. 7, 1968; 1 son, Frank Warren. Petroleum engr. Humble Oil & Refining Co., Houston, 1949-51, 53-55; asso. prof. petroleum engring. U. Okla., 1955-63; pres. Frank W. Cole Engring. Co., Dallas, 1963—, Continental Energy Corp., Dallas. Served with USNR, 1943-46, 51-53. Author: (with A.W. McCray) Oil Well Drilling Technology, 1959; Reservoir Engineering Manual, 1961; Well Spacing in the Areth Reservoir, 1962; Basic Principles of Reservoir Engineering, 1963; (with P.L. Moore) Drilling Operations Manual, 1964. Contbr. papers to tech. lit. Home: 5710 Forest Lane Dallas TX 75230 Office: Meadows Bldg Dallas TX 75206

COLE, GEORGE LEE, supt. schs.; b. Spearsville, La., July 11, 1910; s. George Lee and Isadora (Waldrop) C.; B.S., La. State U., 1940; M.S., Ark. U., 1953; m. Clyta Holloway, Jan. 10, 1933; 1 son, Herbert Larry. Prin elementary sch., Cross Roads, La., 1933-39; tchr. agr. pub. schs., Downsville, La., 1940-46; prin. high sch., Spearsville, La., 1946-57; supr. high sch., Union Parish, La., 1957-69; supt. Union Parish Schs., Farmerville, La., 1969—. Chmn. constrn. Spearsville Drug Co. Chmn. bd. dirs. Office Equal Opportunity Mayor, City of Spearsville, 1969—. Chmn. bd. dirs. constrn. of Bernice (La.) Clinic and Hosp. Mem. La. Sch. Adminstrs. Assn., La. Tchrs. Assn. Baptist. Home: Box 45 Spearsville LA 71277 Office: Box 308 Farmerville LA 71241

COLE, HARPER LEROY, JR., coll. administr.; b. Pasadena, Cal., Dec. 5, 1921; s. Harper Leroy and Maidie Belle (McBride) C.; A.B., Bethany Nazarene Coll., 1965; M.A., U. Okla. 1970; m. Pearl Mae Cook, Aug. 2, 1942; children—Stephen Leroy, Myrla Dawn (Mrs. Carl Ray Cook). Ordained to ministry Nazarene Ch., 1945; minister Christian edn. Ch. of Nazarene, Bethany, Okla., 1945-48, Kansas City, Mo., 1949-51, Oklahoma City, 1953-56; asst. to gen. treas. Ch. of Nazarene, Kansas City, Mo., 1951-53, 56-66; administrv. asst., asst. prof. bus. Bethany Nazarene Coll., 1966—, dir. data processing, 1966—. Mem. Soc. for Advancement Mgmt., Nat. Assn. Accountants, Acad. of Mgmt., Am. Mgmt. Assn., Okla. Edn. Assn. Kiwanian. Home: 3117 N Mueller St Bethany OK 73008

COLE, HENRY CAMPBELL, sch. supt.; b. Fayetteville, N.C., Jan. 19, 1932; s. Roland Jennings and Eva (Kale) C.; A.A., Campbell Coll., 1956; B.A., Wake Forest U., 1958; M.A., East Carolina U., 1961; grad. Advanced Ednl. Adminstrn. Program, U. N.C., 1967; Ed.D., Duke, 1971; m. Nadine Grimes Cole Oct. 29, 1950; children—Alicia Lynn, Andrew Campbell. Tchr. Winston-Salem/Forsyth Pub. Schs., Winston Salem, N.C., 1958-59; tchr. Goldsboro (N.C.) City Schs., 1959-60, adminstrv. asst., 1960-62; asst. supt. Alamance County Schs., Graham, N.C., 1962-67; supt. Wilson (N.C.) County Schs., 1967—. Adj. prof. edn. Atlantic Christian Coll., Wilson, 1967—. Mem. Wilson County Bd. Health, 1967—, Alcohol Bd. Control, 1967—; chmn. edn. div. United Fund, 1968. Served with AUS, 1953-55. Inst. for Devel. Ednl. Advancement Kettering Found. fellow, 1970. Mem. Am. Assn. Sch. Adminstrs., N.E.A., N.C. Assn. Educators (mem. com. 1961), Kappa Delta Phi. Democrat. Baptist (chmn. personnel com. 1963—, tchr. Sunday Sch.). Rotarian. Home: 1109 Parkside Dr Wilson NC 27893 Office: 112 W Nash St Wilson NC 27893

COLE, HERSCHEL EUGENE, lawyer; b. Dallas, Ga., May 23, 1905; s. Jesse T. and Pearl (Cole) C.; LL.B., Atlanta Law Sch., 1925; LL.D., Cleveland-Marshall Law Sch., 1954; m. Rose B. Dumas, Jan.

14, 1930; 1 dau., Barbara Ann. Admitted to Ga. bar, 1925; practice of law, Atlanta, 1925-—; instr. Atlanta Law Sch., 1934-55, sec., 1937-53, dean, 1958-—; judge traffic div. Municipal Ct., Atlanta, 1959-—. Vice pres., dir. Kings Mountain Mica Co. (N.C.); dir. English Mica Co. (Spruce Pine, N.C.). Mem. Ga., Atlanta bar assns., Sigma Delta Kappa. Baptist. Mason. Home: 831 Crestridge Dr NE Atlanta GA 30306 Office: Rhodes Haverty Bldg Atlanta GA 30303

COLE, HOUSTON, univ. pres.; b. Fort Payne, Ala., Nov. 24, 1902; s. John and Pollyana (Cash) C.; B.S., M.S., U. Ala., 1927, LL.D., 1948; postgrad. U. Chgo., Columbia U.; m. Leone Pruett, Sept. 14, 1904; 1 dau., Beth. Supt., Guntersville (Ala.) schs., 1925-33; supt. Tuscaloosa County (Ala) schs., 1934-39, prof. edn., U. Ala., 1939-41; state dir. Civilian Def., Ala., 1941-42, OPA, 1942; pres. Jacksonville (Ala.) State Coll., 1942-—. Dir. First Nat. Bank Jacksonville, Nat. Educators Life Ins. Co., Ft. Worth. Established High Sch. Civil Def. councils, foreruner of Victory Corps; Boy Scouts leader; pub. speaker. Named Man of Yr. in Calhoun County, Anniston Star, 1966; recipient certificate of appreciation Anniston C. of C., 1966. Mem. Phi Beta Kappa, Kappa Delta Pi, Phi Delta Kappa. Democrat. Methodist. Rotarian (Ala. dist. gov. 1938). Contbr. articles to mags. Address: Jacksonville AL 36545

COLE, JOHN, state ofcl. Vice chmn. Ark. Bd. Edn. Office: care State Board of Education Education Bldg Little Rock AR 72203*

COLE, LUTHER FRANCIS, judge; b. Alexandria, La., Oct. 25, 1925; s. Clem and Catherine (Wiley) C.; student La. Poly. Inst., 1943-44; J.D., La. State U., 1950; grad. Nat. Coll. State Trial Judges; m. Juanita Barton, Mar. 9, 1945; children—Frances Jeannette, Jeffrey Martin, Christopher Warren. Admitted to La. bar, 1950; mem. firm Cole & Mengis, Baton Rouge, 1950-66; dist. judge 19th Jud. Dist., 1966-—. Mem. La. Ho. of Reps., 1964-66. Served to lt. (j.g.) USNR, 1943-46. Mem. La. Law Inst., Jud. Council La. Supreme Ct., Judiciary Commn. La., Am., La., Baton Rouge (pres. 1966) bar assns., Am. Judicature Soc., La. Dist. Judges Assn. (pres. 1972). Baptist. Club: Exchange (past pres.). Home: 9525 Donna Dr Baton Rouge LA 70815 Office: Court House Bldg Baton Rouge LA 70801

COLE, NOMAN MONROE, JR., nuclear engr.; b. Parris Island, S.C., Mar. 10, 1933; s. Noman Monroe and Bessie (Owens) C.; B.M.E., U. Fla., 1955; grad. AEC Nuclear Engring. and Physics Grad. Sch., Bettis Lab., 1957; m. Janet Audrey Nelson, Mar. 1, 1958; children—Keith Noman, Nelson Owens. Project mgr. AEC Natural Circulation Reactor Devel. Project, U.S. Navy, 1960-66; asst. dept. dir. Howard Research div. Control Data Corp., Washington, 1966-67; sr. engr. MPR Assos., Inc., Washington, 1967-—. Treas. Gunston Hall Sch., 1966-67; pres. Mason Neckand and Hallowing Point Civic Assn., 1963-70. Chmn. Va. State Water Control Bd., 1970-—. Served to lt. USNR, 1956-60. Mem. Phi Delta Theta. Methodist. Home: 5917 River Dr Lorton VA 22079 Office: 1140 Connecticut Av NW Washington DC 20036

COLE, ROBERT JOBE, dentist; b. Galesburg, Ill., Feb. 21, 1924; s. Glen R. and Marian Vinnie (Robinson) C.; B.S., U. Ia., 1945, D.D.S., 1946; m. Kathrn Ann O'Brien, June 17, 1944; children—Brian Robert, Jo Anne. Pvt. practice dentistry, St. Petersburg Beach, Fla., 1948-—. Mem. adv. com. Dental Hygiene Sch., St. Petersburg Jr. Coll., 1964-69, lectr., 1966-—; mem. adv. com. DentalSch., U. Fla., Gainesville, 1966-—. Chmn. fluoridation com. City of St. Petersburg, 1952-58; coach Little League, 1958-62; active Boy Scouts Am. Served to lt. (j.g.) USNR, 1946-48. Recipient Distinguished Service award Jr. C. of C., 1959. Fellow Am. Coll. Dentists; mem. Am. (del.), Fla. dental assns., West Coast (pres. 1968), Pinellas County (pres. 1959) dental socs., Beta Theta Pi, Delta Sigma Delta. Methodist (dir. 1958-71). Kiwanian. Club: Lakewood Country (St. Petersburg). Home: 690 Boca Ciega Isle N St Petersburg FL 33706 Office: 511 76 Av St Petersburg Beach FL 33706

COLE, SAMUEL JENNINGS, sch. supt.; b. Elizabethtown, N.C., Mar. 21, 1930; s. Roland Jennings and Eva (Quale) C.; diploma, Louisburg (N.C.) Jr. Coll., 1950; A.B., High Point (N.C.) Coll., 1952; postgrad. U. N.C., 1954-55; M.A., East Carolina U., 1957; m. Martha Ann Lewis, Aug. 3, 1952; children—Sharon, Nancy, Tracy, Samuel II. Supt., Fremont (N.C.) City Schs., 1958-62; asst. supt. Gov. Morehead Sch., Raleigh, N.C., 1962-67, supt., 1968-—. Served with M.C. AUS, 1952-54. Rotarian. Home and Office: 301 Ashe Av Raleigh NC 27606

COLE, THOMAS EDWARD, lawyer, judge; b. Knoxville, Tenn., May 14, 1920; s. Vernon Edward and Katherine (Ellis) C.; B.S., U. Tenn., 1946, J.D., 1948; m. Mary Jean Bell, May 26, 1943; children—Thomas Marshall, Robert Armistead, William Edward. Admitted to Tenn. State bar, 1947; engaged in practice law, Knoxville, 1948-51, 53-61; judge 2d Circuit Ct., Knox County, Tenn., 1961-—. Commr. of elections, Knox County, 1958-61; pres. Tenn. Jud. Conf., 1971-72. Served with AUS, 1942-45; as 1st lt. Judge Adv. Gen.'s Corps, AUS, 1951-53. Mem. Order of Coif, Phi Delta Phi, Delta Tau Delta. Democrat. Lutheran. Home: 201 Geneva Rd Knoxville TN 37919 Office: Knox County Court House Knoxville TN 37902

COLEMAN, CARL DUBOIS, lawyer; b. Danville, Va., June 19, 1910; s. Charles Cornelious and Vetie (Brown) C.; A.B., Howard U., 1931, LL.B., 1935; m. Pearl Elfreda Goodlow, June 8, 1943. Admitted to D.C. bar, 1936; practice law, Washington, 1936-50; asst. corp. counsel, 1950-62; spl. asst. Bd. Commrs., 1962-67; spl. asst. to Mayor, 1967-68 (all Washington); chmn. D.C. Bd. Parole, 1968-—. Mem. Montgomery County (Md.) Human Relations Comm., 1961-65; chmn. non-discrimination com. Health and Welfare Council, 1969. Served with AUS, 1943-45. Mem. Nat., Fed., Washington, D.C. bar assns., Kappa Alpha Psi. Conglist. Home: 2 Elwyn Ct Silver Spring MD 20910 Office: 614 H St NW Washington DC 20001

COLEMAN, FRANK CARTER, physician, med. lab. adminstr.; b. Jackson, Miss., May 14, 1915; s. Francis Marion and Emma (Carter) C.; B.A., Miss. Coll., 1935; M.D., Tulane U., 1941; m. Ruth Yvonne Ellzey, Sept. 2, 1937; children—Nancy Ruth (Mrs. James Lujan), Stephen Carter, John Timothy, Jeanne Laurie. Intern, Touro Infirmary, New Orleans, 1941-42, resident in pathology, 1942-45, asst. dir. pathology, 1945; practice medicine, specializing in pathology, Des Moines, 1946-64, Tampa, Fla., 1964-—; dir. labs. Mercy Hosp., Des Moines, 1945-64, Patterson Coleman Labs., Tampa, Fla., 1964-—; dir. dept. pathology Centro Asturiano Hosp., Tampa, Fla., 1964-—, Citrus Meml. Hosp., Inverness, Fla., 1964-—, Hillsborough County Hosp., Tampa, 1964-—, Jackson Meml. Hosp., Dade City, 1965-—, Wood Meml. Hosp., Arcadia, 1971-—, Hardee Meml. Hosp., Wauchula, Fla., 1970-—, Centro Espanol Hosp., Tampa, 1967-—, N. Orange Meml. Hosp., Apopka, 1967-—, Community Hosp., New Port Richey, 1971-—, Tarpon Springs (Fla.) Gen. Hosp., 1967-—, West Pasco Hosp., New Port Richey, 1966-—, G. Pierce Wood Meml. Hosp., Arcadia, 1971-—; resident asst. in pathology Sch. Medicine Tulane U., 1942-44, instr. pathology, 1944-45; asst. clin. prof. dept. pathology Coll. Medicine U. Neb., 1951-—; cons. Tampa Gen. Hosp., 1964-—, dept. pathology residency program St. Joseph's Hosp., Tampa, 1967-—; med. dir. S.W. Fla. Blood Bank, 1971-—. Mem. Pres.'s Com. Health Services Industry, 1971-—, Gov.'s Community Hosp. Edn. Council, 1971-—. Vice pres. Gulf Coast Symphony, 1970-72. Bd. dirs. Blue Shield of Fla., 1967-70; bd. dirs. Am. Med. Polit. Action Com., 1960-69, chmn., 1965-67. Recipient award of merit Ia. Med. Soc., 1957; Sci. Products Found. award for outstanding service to pathology and medicine, 1965. Diplomate Am. Bd. Pathology (trustee 1964-—). Fellow Am. Soc. Clin. Pathologists, Coll. Am. Pathologists (bd. govs. 1953-58, pres. 1960-61, mem. nat. legislative com. 1966-—, chmn. legislative com. 1971-—), A.C.P., Am. Coll. Chest Physicians; mem. A.M.A. (chmn. council legislative activities 1963-64, vice chmn. council health manpower 1971-—), Fla. Med. Assn. (chmn. com. on blood 1969-—), Hillsborough County Med. Soc. (chmn. membership com. 1966-67, 69, mem. exec. council 1967-—, chmn. pub. service com. 1970-—, del. to Fla. Med. Assn.), Am. Assn. Pathologists and Bacteriologists, Am. Assn. Blood Banks (pres. 1968-69, dir.), N.Y. Acad. Scis., Fla. Soc. Pathologists (chmn. ins. com. 1966-—, chmn. com. contractual and profl. ethics 1968-—), Soc. Nuclear Medicine, Am. Therapeutic Soc., A.A.A.S., Am. Soc. Cytology, Fla. Assn. Blood Banks (pres. 1970-—), Internat. Acad. Pathologists, Am. Pub. Health Assn., Tampa C. of C. (chmn. air pollution task force 1971-—, chmn. med. sch. com. 1966-67, chmn. health com. 1969-—), Theta Kappa Psi, Alpha Omega Alpha. Presbyn. (elder). Rotarian. Clubs: Krewe of Venus, University, Carrollwood Golf and Country. Contbr. articles to profl. jours. Contbg. editor Recent Advances in Clinical Pathology, 1971. Home: Route 2 Box 737 Lutz FL 33549 Office: Suite 23 4600 N Habana Av Tampa FL 33614

COLEMAN, GORDON KENNETH ANDREW, educator; b. Bismarck, N.D., Dec. 1, 1934; s. Floyd Milo and Leah (Teske) C.; student Bismarck Jr. Coll., 1953-54; N.D. Agri. Coll., 1954-56; B.S., N.D. State U., 1964; M.S., 1966; postgrad. U. Minn., 1968-69, Tex. A. and M. U., 1969-71; m. Ruth Virginia Hintsala; children—Joni Yvonne Lee, Gordon Kenneth Andrew II. Engr., Western Electric Co., Chgo., 1956-57, asso. engr., 1961-62, 1963; tchr. math. Emmetsburg (Ia.) Jr. Coll. and High Sch., 1965-66; instr. polit. sci. No. Mich. (Marquette) U., 1966-68; teaching asst. U. Minn., 1968-69; instr. Tex. A. and M. U., 1969-71, lectr., 1971-—. Served with AUS, 1957-61. Mem. Am. Fedn. Musicians, Am. Assn. U. Profs., Am. Polit. Sci. Assn., Am. Soc. Pub. Adminstrn., Math. Assn. Am., Amvets, Clowns of Am. Methodist. Mason (Shriner, organizer, chmn., pres. Brazos Shrine Clowns). Home: 3721 Atlas El Paso TX 79904 Office: Texas A and M Univ Dept Polit Sci College Station TX 77843

COLEMAN, JAMES PLEMON, judge; b. Ackerman, Miss., Jan. 9, 1914; s. Thomas A. and Jennie Essie (Worrell) C.; student U. Miss., 1932-35; LL.B., George Washington U., 1939, LL.D., 1960; m. Margaret Janet-Dennis, May 2, 1937; 1 son, Thomas Allen. Sec. to Rep. Aaron Lane Ford, Washington, 1935-39; admitted to Miss. bar. 1937, since practiced in Ackerman; dist. atty. 5th circuit Ct., Dist. of Miss., 1940-46, circuit judge, 1946-50; commr. Supreme Ct. of Miss., Sept. 1, to Oct. 23, 1950; atty. gen., Miss., 1950-56; gov. Miss., 1956-60; mem. Miss. Ho. Reps. from Choctaw County, 1960-65; judge U.S. Ct. Appeals 5th Circuit, 1965-—. Publisher Choctaw Plaindealer, weekly, 1949-56. Trustee Miss. Coll., 1952-56. Democrat (presdl. elector 1944). Baptist. Mason (Shriner), Rotarian. Home: Ackerman MS 39735 Office: 115 E Quinn Av Ackerman MS 39735

COLEMAN, JAMES SAMUEL, JR., justice; b. Mobile, Ala., June 8, 1906; s. James Samuel and Mary Belle (Peteet) C.; student Marion Inst., Ala.; grad. U.S. Naval Acad., 1927; student U. Ala., Law Sch.; m. Eleanor Ruth Montgomery, Sept. 17, 1933 (dec. Oct. 1959); 1 son. James Samuel III; m. 2d, Mary Ruth (Morgan) Hobbs, Feb. 20, 1965. Admitted to Ala. bar, 1934, practiced in Eutaw, 1934-57; asso. justice Supreme Ct. of Ala., 1957-—. Mem. Ala. Senate, 1946-50, 54-56. Served as lt. comdr. USNR, 1942-45. Mem. V.F.W., Am. Legion. Presbyn. (elder). Lion (1st pres. Eutaw; pres. Montgomery 1965). Home: 2803 Woodley Rd Montgomery AL 36111 Office: PO Box 218 Montgomery AL 36101

COLEMAN, JOHN DEE, veterinarian; b. Dozier, Tex., Oct. 2, 1932; s. Jay Dee and Paralee (Brock) C.; D.V.M., Tex. A. and M. U., 1956; M.S., Auburn U., 1964; m. Sandra Burden, Aug. 26, 1954; children—Carol, Susan, Scott. Vet. ednl. cons. Tex. A. and M. U., 1956-60; post veterinarian, Ft. Rucker, Ala., 1960-62; NIH fellow Auburn U., 1962-64; sr. research scientist Abbott Labs., North Chicago, Ill., 1964-68; pvt. practice veterinary medicine, McLean, Tex., 1968-70; asso. prof. feedlot cattle disease research Tex. A. and M. U., Bushland, 1970-—. Served with AUS., 1960-62. Mem. Am., Tex. vet. med. assns., Am. Assn. Vet. Nutritionists, Am. Soc. Animal Sci., Plains Nutrition Council. Club: Rotary of Mymensingh (East Pakistan). Home: 520 12th Av Canyon TX 79015 Office: TAES-USDA Research Center Bushland TX 79012

COLEMAN, MARION LESLIE, ins. co. exec.; b. Mobile, Ala., Mar. 20, 1925; s. Luther Woodward and Carrie (Lockler) Coleman; student pub. schs.; m. Joyce Kelley, Aug. 29, 1944; children—Connie, Woodward L. and Franklin M. (twins). Agt., Life Ins. Co. of Ga., Mobile, 1946-53, staff mgr., Texarkana, Ark., 1953-55, dist. mgr., El Dorado, Ark., 1955-56, Hattlesburg, Miss., 1957-60, Meridian, Miss., 1957-60, Meridian, Miss., 1960-64; v.p., agy. dir. Nat. Preferred Life Ins. Co., Atlanta, 1964-65; v.p. tng. Found. Life Ins. Co., Atlanta, 1965-67; v.p., dir. agys. Tenn. Nat. Life Ins. Co., Nashville, 1967-—, also dir.; v.p. Kelley Blakeley Land Co., Inc., Mobile, Ala.; owner Meridian Sportarama, Inc. Yamaha Sports World, Mel co Ltd., Fashion Tailors (all Meridian). Served with USNR, 1943-46. Mem. Life Underwriters Assn., Sales and Marketing Execs. Club, Civitan Club (pres. Meridian). Home: 2100 23d Av Meridian MS 39301 Office: Citizen National Bank Bldg Meridian MS 39301

COLEMAN, ROBERT BOISSEAU, JR., lawyer; b. Birmingham, Ala., Mar. 15, 1916; s. Robert Boisseau and Jessie (Wheeler) C.; B.S., N.C. State U., 1939; postgrad. Mass. Inst. Tech., 1940; LL.B., Birmingham Sch. Law, 1952; m. Ann Alderson, Mar. 16, 1956; children—Clayton L. Campbell, Claire Campbell Lindberg, Mary Virginia, Robert Boisseau III, Barbara Anne, Caroline. Metall. engr. Am. Cast Iron Pipe Co., Birmingham, 1940-41; acid plant supr. E.I. duPont de Nemours & Co., Inc., Kankakee Ordnance Plant, 1941-42, metall. engr. Kings Mills Ordnance Plant, 1942-43, chem. engr. ammonia dept., Charleston, W.Va., 1943-44; tech. asst. to plant mgr. Indsl. Rayon Co., Covington, 1944-48; research engr. So. Research Co., Birmingham, 1948-50, So. Cement Co., Birmingham, 1948-53; admitted to Ala. bar, 1952; Okla. bar, 1953; patent atty. Phillips Petroleum Co., Bartlesville Okla., 1953-59; real estate, ins. broker Alderson Coleman Agy., Ada, Okla., 1959-64; supr. patents and trademarks Continental Oil Co., Ponca City, Okla., 1964-—; partner Coleman Bros. Investments; dir. Investors Security. Past pres. Ada Boys Club. Registered profl. engr., Ala., Okla. Mem. Am. Inst. Chem. Engrs., Am. Chem. Soc., Nat. Soc. Profl. Engrs., Am. Patent Layers Assn. (past com. chmn.), Am., Okla., Pontotoc County (past sec.-treas.) bar assns. Episcopalian. Mason, Rotarian. Home: 2513 Mockingbird Lane Ponca City OK 74601 Office: 1000 S Pine St Ponca City OK 74601

COLEMAN, RUSSELL, assn. exec.; b. Montpelier, Miss., Dec. 23, 1913; s. Oscar Willis and Alice (Marshall) C.; B.S., Miss. State Coll., 1936; M.S., 1937; Ph.D., U. Wis., 1941; m. Laura Elizabeth Burrous, Aug. 18, 1937; children—Peggy (Mrs. Robert H. Best, Jr.), Susan (Mrs. Garry Blunt), Russell Clayton. Grad. asst. Miss. Agr. Expt. Sta., 1936-37, asst. agronomist, 1937-39, asst. dir., 1946, dir., 1947-48; grad. asst. U. Wis., 1939-40; asso. prof. soils Miss. State Coll., 1940-45; pres. Nat. Fertilizer Assn., 1948-55, exec. v.p. Nat. Plant Food Inst., 1955-60; pres. Sulphur Inst., Washington, 1960-—. Mem. fertilizer industry adv. panel FAO, 1963-—. Trustee, Am. Freedom from Hunger Found. Fellow Am. Soc. Agronomy; mem. Soil Sci. Soc. Am., Alpha Zeta. Presbyn. Clubs: Cosmos, University (Washington); Columbia Country (Chevy Chase, Md.). Contbr. numerous articles to tech. jours. Home: 3806 Woodbine St Chevy Chase MD 20015 Office: Sulphur Inst 1725 K St NW Washington DC 20006

COLEMAN, WILLIAM CLIFTON, constrn. co. exec.; b. Sandy, Tex., Jan. 28, 1932; s. Ralph R. and Vina (Puryear) C.; student pub. schs.; m. Anita Joyce Winters, Nov. 25, 1952; children—Clifton Winters, David Franklin, Shelton Keith. Supt., M.C. Winters Co., Johnson City, Tex., 1956-59, gen. supt., 1959-61, v.p., 1961-—; pres. W. C. Coleman, Inc., 1965-—; partner C P & W Cattle Co. Served with AUS, 1953-55. Democrat. Baptist. Mason. Home: Hwy 281 Johnson City TX 78636 Office: Box 37 Johnson City TX 78636

COLEMAN, WILLIAM OWEN, electric utility co. exec.; b. Stillwater, Okla., June 21, 1923; s. Lester L. and Juanita Mae (Geller) C.; student Okla. State U., 1941-43, postgrad. mgmt., 1955-57; B.S. in Elec. Engring., U. Okla., 1947; postgrad. mgmt. Ga. Inst. Tech., 1968; m. Mary Jane Goff, July 16, 1955. Elec. engr. Okla. Gas and Electric Co., Oklahoma City and Ardmore, Okla., 1947-56, area engr., 1956-60, Oklahoma City, dist. supt., 1960-63, div. line supr., asst. div. supt., Shawnee, 1963-66, div. supt. Shawnee, 1966-67, div. mgr. central div., Sapulpa, Okla., 1967-69, v.p., div. mgr., Ark. div., Fort Smith, Ark., 1969-—. Dir. Fort Smith United Fund, 1970-—; pres., 1971; mem. Ark. Indsl. Council Bd. dirs. Jr. Achievement Fort Smith. Registered profl. engr., Okla. Sr. mem. I.E.E.E.; mem. Nat. Soc. Profl. Engrs., U. Okla. Assn., Ark. (dir. 1970-—), Fort Smith (v.p. 1972) chambers commerce, Soc. Indsl. Developers Ark., Sigma Alpha Epsilon. Episcopalian. Mason (32 deg.), Lion. Clubs: Town, Hardscrabble Country (Ft. Smith). Home: 3126 S 32d St Fort Smith AR 72901 Office: 311 Lexington Av Fort Smith AR 72901

COLES, WILLIAM SWANEY, banker; b. Nashville, July 12, 1936; s. John William and Margaret Jackson (Swaney) C.; B.S., Bowling Green Coll., 1958; postgrad. U. Ala., 1971-72; m. Trula Faye Dailey, Aug. 5, 1962; 1 son, John William II. Asst. cashier, br. mgr. Commerce Union Bank, Nashville, 1958-62; asst. v.p. First Peoples Bank, Johnson City, Tenn., 1962-63; v.p., personnel dir. State Nat. Bank, Decatur, Ala., 1963-—. Pres., Ala. United Cerebral Palsy Assn., 1969-70, Southeastern regional v.p., 1971-72. Served with Tenn. Air Nat. Guard, 1954-62. Mem. Am. Inst. Banking (chmn. Southeastern regional sch. relations com. 1964, pres. Decatur chpt. 1970, Ala. Bankers Assn. (group chmn. jr. sect. 1967, named outstanding chmn. in state 1967). Clubs: Decatur Country, Decatur Toastmasters (pres. 1972). Home: 1807 Woodmont Dr SE Decatur AL 35601 Office: 251 Johnston St SE Box 1487 Decatur AL 35601

COLEY, PAUL A(NDREW), sch. adminstr.; b. Montrose, Ga., Sept. 23, 1923; s. Talmadge D. and Eula F. (Coley) C.; B.S., U. Ga., 1950; M.E., 1953; m. Vida Messer, Dec. 2, 1945; 1 son, Andrew Paul. Sci. tchr. Marianna High Sch., Monticello, Fla., 1950-53, supervising prin., 1954-70; prin. Godby High Sch., 1970-—. Served with USAAF, 1942-45. Mem. Fla. High Sch. Activities Assn., Fla. Edn. Assn., Am. Legion. Methodist (dist. lay leader Tallahassee conf.). Rotarian, Lion. Home: 909 San Luis Rd Tallahassee FL 32304

COLINS, CHRISTOPHER, social worker; b. Lynn, Mass., Sept. 3, 1925; s. James and Pota (Scipitari) Kolinites; B.A., U. Mass.; M.S.W., U. Pa., 1950, postgrad., 1955-56; m. Christine Maynard, Aug. 3, 1953. Social worker VA Regional Office, Roanoke, Va., 1952-56; dir. social services Embreeville (Pa.) State Hosp., 1956-60; program adminstr. Piedmont Mental Health Complex, Concord, N.C., 1960-70; clin. social worker Lenoir County Mental Health Clinic, Kinston, N.C., 1970-—. Mental health cons. various community resources. Served with USAAF, 1943-46. Recipient certificate for dedicated service Pa. Mental Health Assn., 1960. Methodist (chmn. social concerns com.). Home: 310 Sherwood Pl Kinston NC 28501 Office: 111 S McElwean St Kinston NC 28501

COLLETT, TOD ROBINSON, III, computer co. exec.; b. Dallas, Sept. 8, 1940; s. Tod Robinson and Willie May (Cooke) C.; B.B.A., Tex. Tech. U., 1962, M.B.A., 1963; m. Suzanne Dinon Wigginton, Dec. 22, 1962; children—Tod Randall, Shelley. With IBM Corp., 1963-67; exec. v.p. Data Automation Co., 1967-68, now dir.; pres., chief exec. officer Carterfone Communications Corp., 1968-71; pres. Terminal Equipment Exchange, Dallas, 1971-—, also dir.; dir. Carterfone Corp., Morsbach Data Products. Teaching fellow Tex. Tech. U., 1962-63. Active YMCA, Boy Scouts Am. Mem. Phi Delta Theta. Republican. Methodist. Home: 437 Crestover Circle Richardson TX 75080 Office: 2860 Walnut Hill Lane Dallas TX 75229

COLLIER, CALVIN JEFFERSON, JR., tool co. exec.; b. Cedar Valley, Tex., Aug. 20, 1923; s. Calvin Jefferson and Bathsheba Mary (Milam) C.; B.B.A., U. Tex., 1949; m. Doris Elaine Fritts, Oct. 20, 1945; 1 dau., Tracy Diane. Staff accountant Haskins & Sells, C.P.A.'s, Houston, 1949-54; adminstrv. asst. to v.p. and treas. Hughes Tool Co., Houston, 1954-60, asst. sec., 1960-72, sec., 1972-—, asst. treas., 1960-63, v.p., treas., 1963-—, also dir.; dir. Hughes Tool Co. Ltd., Hughes Tool Co. Australia Ltd., Hughes de Mexico, S.Am. de C. V., Hughes Tool Co. de Mexico, S.Am. de C.V., Hughes Air Corp., Hughes Sports Network, Inc., The Sands, Inc., Sands Country Club, Inc., Hotel Properties, Inc., Desert Inn Improvement Co., Harolds Club, Inc. Served with USAAF, 1943-46. Decorated D.F.C., Air medal with two oak leaf clusters. C.P.A., Tex. Mem. Am. Inst. C.P.A.'s, Tex. Soc. C.P.A.'s, Beta Alpha Psi. Home: 8119 DeLeon Dr Houston TX 77017 Office: Humbel Bldg Houston TX 77002

COLLIER, COURTLAND ALDEN, civil engr.; b. Buffalo, July 29, 1925; s. Leo Robert and Marcheniel Overton (Bass) C.; B.E. in Civil Engring., Yale, 1949; grad. Canadian Summer Inst. Linguistics, Cavenport, Sask., 1955; M.E., U. Fla., 1963; m. Albertine Elizabeth Taylor, Aug. 8, 1946 (div. Feb. 1963); children—Deborah Elizabeth, Nathan Stafford, Dennis Brainerd; m. 2d, Marian Fryer Legate, Feb. 22, 1971; stepchildren—Alexis Arthur, Amy Alice, Michael Fryer, Becky Marie. Jr. civil engr. Cal. Div. Hwys., 1950-51; office engr. Western Contracting Corp., 1951; asst. city engr. Dodge City, Kan., 1951-52; asso. resident engr. Tex. Hwy. Dept., Pharr, 1952-55; instr. mechanics div. Coll. Engring., Lehigh U., 1955-56; field engr. Raymond Conc. Pile Co., Havana, Cuba, 1956-57; design engr. Lummus Co., Edmonton, Alberta and Maracaibo, Venezuela, 1957-59; design engr. D.E. Britt & Assos., Ft. Lauderdale, Fla., 1960-61; cons. engr., asst. prof. Coll. Engring., U. Fla., 1961-—; v.p. C.A.V. Inversiones Zulianas, Maracaibo. Mem. Gainesville (Fla.) City Commn., 1967-—; chmn. Pub. Works Commn. Gainesville, 1967-—, chmn. pub. safety commn., 1971-—. Mem. Am. Soc. C.E. (pres. Gainesville br. 1966-67), Fla. Engring. Soc., Am. Assn. Cost Engrs., Am. Arbitration Assn. Club: Exchange (2d v.p.) (Gainesville, Fla.). Home: 2809 SW 1 Way Gainesville FL 32601

COLLIER, DURWARD REED, dentist; b. Weir, Miss., Jan 5, 1932; s. George Hester and Eva Mae (Braswell) Collier; B.S., Miss. State U., 1955; D.D.S., U. Tenn., 1957; M.P.H., U. Mich., 1958; m. Doris Jeanette Morrow, June 8, 1950; children—Lisa Kay, Cheryl Lynn, Gina Laura, Paul Reed. Dir. div. dental Health, Ark. State Bd. Health, 1958-59; practice dentistry, Brandon, Miss., 1959-60; regional dental officer Tenn. Dept. Pub. Health, 1960-67; asst. chief, div. dental health, Ill. Dept. Pub. Health, chief Bur. Spl. Projects and Research Dental Div., 1967-68; dir. div. dental health services Tenn. Dept. Pub. Health, Nashville, 1968—. Diplomate Am. Bd. Dental Pub. Health. Fellow Am. Pub. Health Assn. (mem. governing council 1969-71); mem. Am. Dental Assn., Am. Assn. Pub. Health Dentists (sec.-treas. 1970—), Tenn. Pub. Health Assn. (sec.-treas. 1971—; chmn. elect, chmn. dental section 1971—), Pierre Fauchard Acad. Mason (32 deg.). Baptist (deacon). Contbr. articles to profl. pubs. Home: 2442 Rychen Dr Nashville TN 37217 Office: 310 Capitol Towers Nashville TN 37219

COLLIER, EVERETT DOLTON, newspaper exec.; b. Long Beach, Miss., Feb. 26, 1914; s. Thomas Lee and Elizabeth Naomi (Cruthirds) C.; B.A., Rice Inst., 1937; m. Mary Margaret Chisholm, Mar. 26, 1950; 1 son, Ervin Cornell. Mem. staff Houston Chronicle, 1934—, polit. editor, 1946-52; editorial writer, 1952-57, asst. editor, 1957-59, mng. editor, 1959-65, editor, v.p., dir., 1965—; dir. Houston Chronicle Pub. Co., Fairbanks State Bank. Mem. editorial adv. bd. Rice U. Bd. dirs. Tex. Water Found., Salvation Army, Houston Fat Stock Show Assn.; mem. bd., v.p. Mus. Med. Sci. Mem. Rice U. Alumni Assn. (pres. 1963). Methodist (ofcl. bd.). Home: 4622 Ingersoll Av Houston TX 77027 Office: Houston Chronicle 801 Texas Av Houston TX 77002

COLLIER, GAYLAN JANE, educator; b. Fluvanna, Tex., July 23, 1924; d. Ben Vivian and Narcis (Smith) Collier; B.A., Abilene Christian Coll., 1946; M.A., U. Ia., 1949; Ph.D., U. Denver, 1957. Instr. speech and drama Woman's Coll. U., N.C., 1947-48; asst. prof. Greensboro (N.C.) Coll., 1949-50; asst. prof., then asso. prof., dir. theatre Abilene Christian Coll., 1950-60; asso. prof. Ida. State U., 1960-63, summers 1958, 59; asso. prof. speech and drama Sam Houston State Coll., Huntsville, Tex., 1963-65, prof. drama, 1965-67; prof. theatre arts Tex. Christian U., Ft. Worth, 1967—; dir. Pkwy. Playhouse, Burnsville, N.C., summer 1951; guest dir. U. Denver, summer 1962; dir. Scott Theatre Actors' Repertory Co., summers 1968,69. Mem. Am. Ednl. Theatre Assn., Southwestern Theatre Conf. (past v.p. Rocky Mountain Theatre conf. 1962-63), Children's Theatre Conf. (past dir., editor region 4, adminstrv. asst. to dir. 1965-67). Center for Research in Frontier Theatre, Zeta Phi Eta. Author: Assignments in Acting, 1966. Contbr. articles to profl. jours. Home: 2725 Lubbock Av Fort Worth TX 76109

COLLIER, HENRY MORGAN, JR., physician, surgeon; b. Savannah, Ga., Aug. 7, 1916; s. Henry M. and Annie B. (Gilliard) C.; A.B. cum laude, Savannah State Coll., 1935; M.D. Meharry Med. Coll., Nashville, 1942; m. Mozella B. Gaither, June 22, 1943; children—Vincent Louis, Roberle E., Henry M. III. Resident Kate Bitting Reynolds Meml. Hosp., Winston-Salem, N.C., 1942-43; practice medicine, Savannah, 1943-52, 55—; treas., chief staff Charity Hosp., 1959-64; asso. staff St. Josephs Hosp., Warren A. Candler Hosp.; pres. bd. dirs. William A. Harris Hosp. and Nursing Home; active staff Meml. Hosp. of Chatham County, Ga., Ga. Infirmary, Savannah. Treas. Seaside Devel. Corp., Hilton Head, S.C.; owner, operator Collier Meml. Beach, Hilton Head. Mem. Savannah Port Authority, 1970—, Savannah Devel. Authority, 1971—. Vice pres. Coastal Empire council Boy Scouts Am., 1972—. Trustee W. Broad St. YMCA; past pres. Savannah chpt. Nat. Guardsmens, Inc. Served to capt. USAF, Force, 1952-55. Recipient Silver Beaver award Boy Scouts Am., 1970. Fellow Am. Soc. Abdominal Surgeons; mem. A.M.A., Ga. Med. Soc., Med. Assn. Ga., Nat., Ga. (pres. 1961-62) med. assns., South Atlantic Med. Soc. (past pres.), Mid Town C. of C. of Savannah (pres. 1956-69), N.A.A.C.P., Alpha Phi Alpha. Democrat. Eqiscopalian. Club: Hub Business and Professional Men's (pres. 1961-62). Home: 1827 Mills B Lane Blvd Savannah GA 31405 Office: Collier Profl Bldg 900 W Broad St Savannah GA 31401

COLLIER, O. E. (BOB), security co. exec.; b. Chilton, Tex., July 28, 1920; s. Oscar E. and Ida Mae (Collins) C.; student Oklahoma City U., 1947; B.A., So. Meth U., 1955; m. Charlotte Elizabeth Michael, Apr. 3, 1947; 1 son, Robert Michael. Auditor, Rep. Nat. Bank, Dallas, 1951-53, Westinghouse Co., 1954-59; v.p., comptroller Schneider, Bernet & Hickman, Inc., Dallas, 1960—. Served with AUS, 1939-44. Mem. Dallas Security Dealers Assn. (organizer, charter pres.), Dallas Security Dealers Comptrollers Assn. (sec.-treas. 1967-68). Baptist (deacon 1953—). Mason. Home: 606 Misty Glen Dallas TX 75232 Office: First Nat Bank Bldg Dallas TX 75202

COLLIER, ROBERT ARTHUR, lawyer, oil co. exec.; b. Wichita Falls, Tex., Apr. 3, 1917; s. Robert Heber and Lulu (Cross) C.; LL.B., U. Tex., 1940; m. Jeanne Claybrook, Sept. 19, 1942; children—Claybrook, Deborah Leigh. Admitted to Tex. bar 1940, D.C. bar, 1954; partner Collier, Shannon, Rill & Edwards, and predecessor firm Washington, 1956—. Chmn. bd. Macmillan Ring-Free Oil Co., N.Y.C., 1963—. Mem. Pres.'s Com. on Mental Retardation; mem. nat. adv. com. Jobs for Vets. Home: 6202 Fort Hunt Rd Alexandria VA 22307 Office: 1625 Eye St NW Washington DC 20006

COLLIER, SHELLEY HALE, JR., banker; b. Mercedes, Tex., July 1, 1928; s. Shelley Hale and Marguerite (Feike) C.; B.B.A., U. Tex., 1950; postgrad. La. State U., 1960-63; m. Caryl Ann Hunt, Nov. 11, 1958; children— Michael Melinda, Shelley Hale III, Susan Gail, Kay Caryl. Asst. cashier First Nat. Bank, Mercedes, 1951-54, cashier, 1954-57, v.p., 1957-60, pres., 1960-71, also dir.; pres., dir. Valley Nat. Bank, McAllen, Tex., 1971—; dir. First Nat. Bank, LaFeria, Tex., J & C Royalty Corp., B & P Bridge Co., Mid-Valley Community Motor Hotel Devel. Co., Mid-Valley Industries, Inc. Bd. regents Pan Am. Coll., Edinburg, Tex., 1961-65; bd. dirs., sec. Rio Grande Valley Pollution Control Authority. Mem. Tex. (mem. exec. council 1969-71), Rio Grande Valley (pres.) bankers assns., Mercedes C. of C. Rotarian. Home: 1520 Ulex St McAllen TX 78501 Office: 2400 N 10th St McAllen TX 78501

COLLIER, VIRGINIA ROLLWAGE, music patroness, assn. exec.; b. Forrest City, Ark., July 5; d. Otto Benjamin and Virginia (Anderson) Rollwage; student Lenox Hall, St. Louis, Nat. Coll. Edn., Evanston, Ill., Columbia, George Washington U.; m. John Francis Collier (div. 1937). Tchr. math. Comstock Sch. for Girls, N.Y.C., 2 years; econ. analyst and internat. economist U.S. Dept. Commerce, Washington, 1943-53. Pres. Motion Picture and TV Council D.C., 1952—. Chmn. Embassy of Iran Benefit Ball for Blind, 1965; judge U.S. Navy Band Ann., 1970. Mem. Dept. State com. Partner in Alliance. Mem. Nat. Assn. Am. Composers and Condrs. (award for outstanding service to Am. music 1953, founder D.C. chpt. 1950, pres.), Nat. League Am. Pen Women (gen. chmn. nat. biennial conv. 1960), U.D.C. (chmn. Confederate meml. com. 1963, 64; bd. trustees Confederate Meml. Hall; pres. Stonewall Jackson chpt. 1967-68), Nat. Soc. Arts and Letters (nat. 1st v.p. 1964-66; gen. chmn. nat. 20th anniversary; gen. chmn. ann. chpt. benefit 1967-68), Nat. Fedn. Women's Clubs (chmn. dept. pub. affairs 1970-72, chmn. dept. performing arts 1972—), D.C. Soc. Dames Ct. Honor (state treas. 1971—), Pan Am. Liaison Com. Women's Orgn. Club: Washington. Author govtl. publs.; columnist Box Office Weekly mag., 1961—. Home: 5112 Connecticut Av NW Washington DC 20008

COLLIER, WILLIAM MARION, state ofcl.; b. Colorado City, Tex., Dec. 11, 1908; s. William M. and Rebecca (Gore) C.; B.S., Tex. A. and M. U., 1931; m. Mable Leona Bowlin, June 12, 1943; children—William M. III, Caroline Jane (Mrs. John M. Pinson). Archtl. practice, Abiline, Tex., 1941-60; chief, health facilities constrn. sect. Tex. State Dept. of Health, Austin, 1960—. Mem. adv. council Mental Health Dept., 1968—. Mem. Tex. Soc. Architects, A.I.A. Home: 2803 Greenlawn Pkwy Austin TX 78757 Office: 1100 W 49th St Austin TX 78756

COLLIGAN, FRANCIS JAMES, internat. relations cons.; b. San Francisco, Dec. 27, 1908; s. Dr. Francis Joseph and Mary Helen (Barrett) C.; A.B., U. San Francisco, 1929; A.M., U. Cal., 1933; Ph.D., 1941; student Latin Am. Inst., Am. Council Learned Socs., 1941; Prof. (hon.), Sch. Letters and Edn., Nat. U. Ecuador, 1944; m. Margaret Clara Haxton, Aug. 1, 1933; 1 son, Francis Sherwin. Jr. Employee Bank of Am., 1929; jr. underwriter State Compensation Ins. Fund, 1930; instr. to asst. prof. U. San Francisco, 1931-35; organizer and dir. library services City Coll. San Francisco, 1935-40, chmn. dept. English and speech, 1941; cultural relations attache U.S. Embassy, Quito, Ecuador, 1942-44; sect. chief Div. Cultural Cooperation Dept. of State, 1944-45, asst. chief Div. Exchange of Persons, 1946, chief Div., 1947-52; dep. dir. Internat. Ednl. Exchange Service, also exec. sec. U.S. Bd. Fgn. Scholarships, 1948-57; dir. Cultural Planning and Coordination Staff, 1958-60; dir. Edn. and Cultural Plans and Devel. Staff, 1960-62; dir. Edn. and Cultural Policy Rev. Staff, 1962-70, sr. policy adviser ednl. and cultural affairs, 1970-71; exec. dir. Inter-Agy. Council on Internat. Ednl. and Cultural Affairs, 1964-70; vis. Rockefeller Public Service fellow Princeton, fall 1956; U.S. rep. Ad Hoc Com. on Cultural Policy, SEATO, 1958; U.S. rep. Commn. on L.S. Rowe Fund, Orgn. Am. States, 1948-50; U.S. mem. com. experts UNESCO, Paris, 1960, 62; mem. Anglo-Am. Conf. on English, Eng., 1965; adviser U.S. del. Inter-Am. Cultural Council, Mexico, 1951 P.R., 1959, Inter Am. Conf., Caracas, 1954; adviser U.S. delegation Geneva Meeting of Fgn. Ministers, 1955. Mem. Adv. council Inst. Langs. and Linguistics Georgetown U.; cons. internat. commn. Am. Council on Edn., 1966-70. Recipient Rockefeller Pub. Service award, 1955; Superior Honor award State Dept., 1966, 71; Distinguished Service award Bd. Fgn. Scholarships, 1971. Mem. Modern Lang. Assn., Internat. Platform Assn., Am. Fgn. Service Assn., Soc. Internat. Devel., Am. Acad. Polit. and Social Sci., Internat. St. Assn.; hon. mem. Grupo Am. Sociedad Juridico-Literaria (Ecuador), Nat. Assn. U. Men Finland. Roman Catholic. Clubs: Bethesda (Md.) Country; Commonwealth (San Francisco); Cosmos, Internat. (Washington). Co-author Fundamentals of Public Speaking, 1935; (with Walter Johnson) The Fulbright Program, A History, 1965; articles on cultural relations. Home: 5200 Oakland Rd Chevy Chase MD 20015

COLLIGNON, ARTHUR P., safety cons.; b. Cin., Dec. 9, 1889; s. John F. and Elizabeth (Bidner) C.; C.E., U. Cin., 1915; Aero. Engr., Mass. Inst. Tech., 1918; B.S., N.Y.U., 1923; m. Marion Tourison, July 10, 1924 (dec.); m. 2d, Charlotte Field, Jan. 16, 1954. Eastern mgr. Brunhoff Mfg. Co., merchandising mgr. nat. advt. N.Y. Eve. Jour.; asst. agt. N.Y. dist. Standard Brands, Inc.; pres. mgr. Putnam County Reporter; asst. state safety cons. N.Y. State F. W.A.; former dist. engring mgr. Am. Mut. Liability Ins. Co., ret. 1955; now engaged as safety cons. Chmn. com. vehicle sect., mem. operating com. Greater N.Y. Safety Council; vice chmn. marine ins. safety com. N.Y. Shipping Assn. Mem. Safety Execs. Club N.Y., Am. Soc. Safety Engrs., Am. Legion, Army Athletic Assn., Vets. of Safety, Naples Moorings Assn., Nat. Audobon Soc., Canopus Civic Assn., Inc. (pres.), Naples Civic Assn., Delta Tau Delta. Presbyn. Mason (32 deg.). Clubs: Country (Naples, Fla.); Square (Putnam Valley). Author engring. articles for co. mag. Address: 3400 Gulf Shore Blvd Naples FL 33940

COLLINGS, CHARLES KENNETH, educator; b. Princeton, Mo., Apr. 18, 1905; s. Charles Henry and Virgie (Staley) C.; B.S., U. Mo., 1927; M.A., 1932; D.D.S., Baylor U., 1949; m. Helen Marie Fenimore, Oct. 30, 1926; children—Shirley Marie (Mrs. Gene Towry), Helen June (Mrs. Dave Adams). Biology tchr. secondary schs., 1927-31, 33-44; instr. zoology U. Mo., 1931-33; asst. prof. anatomy and physiology Baylor U. Coll. Dentistry, Dallas, 1944-49, asso. prof., 1949-51, prof., chmn. dept. periodontology, 1951—. Cons. William Beaumont Gen. Hosp., El Paso, USPHS Hosp., Fort Worth, Brooke Gen. Hosp., Fort Sam Houston, VA Hosp., Dallas, Reynolds Army Hosp., Fort Sill, Okla. Named Piper Prof., Tex., Minnie Stevens Piper Fund, 1962. Diplomate Am. Bd. Periodontology. Fellow Am. Coll. Dentists; mem. Am., Tex., Korean (hon.) dental assns., A.A.A.S., Am. Acad. Periodontology, S.W. Soc. Exptl. Biology and Medicine, Southwestern Soc. Periodontists, Internat. Assn. Dental Research, Am. Assn. U. Profs., Korean Acad. Periodontology (hon.), Turkish Periodontology Assn. (hon.), Sigma Xi, Omicron Kappa Upsilon, Phi Delta Kappa. Editor: Baylor Dental Jour., 1955-60, Dallas Dental Soc. News, 1962-63; adv. com. Tex. Dental Jour., 1958-62, chmn., 1962. Contbr. articles to profl. jours. Home: 2020 W Five Mile Pkwy Dallas TX 75224 Office: 800 Hall St Dallas TX 75226

COLLINS, BOYD WINSTON, supr. sch.; b. Glenville, W.Va., Jan. 21, 1923; s. Boyd Creed and Dovie (Sommerville) C.; A.B., Glenville State Coll., 1948; M.A., W.Va. U., 1949; postgrad. U. Va., 1953-70; m. Betty Jo Simon, June 25, 1949; children—Anita Beth, Stephen Boyd. Tchr., prin. elementary sch. Warren County (Va.) Sch. Bd., 1949-52; tchr., prin. Fairfax County Sch. Bd., Springfield, Va., 1952-69, supr. area 2, 1969—. Served with USNR, 1944-46. Mem. Nat., Va., Fairfax edn. assns., Fairfax County Elementary Prins. Assn. Methodist. Mason. Home: 7109 Lavender Lane Springfield VA 22150

COLLINS, CARR P., JR., ins. co. exec.; b. Dallas, Feb. 9, 1918; s. Carr P. and Ruth (Woodall) C.; B.S., So. Meth. U., 1939; grad. bus. study Harvard, 1939-40; LL.D., Howard Payne Coll.; m. Calvert Keoun, Dec. 24, 1941; children—Carr P. III, Richard Howell, Christy Calvert; m. 2d, Yvvonne Deakins, Jan. 1, 1968; children—Mark Bond, Brad Bond. Vice pres., dir. Fidelity Union Life Ins. Co., 1949-70, pres., 1970—; pres. S.W. Bank & Trust Co., 1955-56, Investment Trust Co., 1949—. Arbitrator, N.Y. Stock Exchange Panels Arbitrators, 1957—; mem. U.S. Trade Mission to Pakistan, 1960. Italian vice-consul for Dallas, 1962-71. Adv. bd. Italian-U.S. Center Jud. Studies, 1965. Served to maj. USAAF, 1940-45; PTO. Decorated Air medal, Purple Heart, Knight-officer Order of Merit (Italy); recipient Freedom medal Douglas MacArthur Acad. Freedom, 1965. C.L.U. Fellow Am. Soc. Psychical Research; mem. Phi Delta Theta, Alpha Kappa Psi. Episcopalian. Mason (32 degree, Shriner). Clubs: Idlewild, Terps, Dallas Country, Petroleum. Home: 4801 St Johns Dr Dallas TX 75205 Office: Fidelity Union Life Bldg Dallas TX 75201

COLLINS, CLARENCE TILLMAN, educator; b. Greenup, Ky., May 20, 1933; s. John Tillman and Marie (Stevens) C.; B.S., Eastern Ky. State U., 1957; Materials Handling Engr., Detroit Indsl. Tech., 1959; postgrad. U. Mich., 1959, Mich. State U., 1960-63; M. Engring., U. Ky., 1967, postgrad., 1969-71; m. Ruby Dean Holbrook, July 3, 1954; children—Toni Dee, John Tillman II. Tchr., Ottawa Hills High Sch., Grand Rapids, Mich., 1957; asst. to mgr. Rapids Standard Co., Inc., 1958, field engr., 1959, asst. mgr. engring. dept., 1960; tchr. indsl. engring. Mich. State U., 1959-60; tchr. tech. writing Grand Rapids Jr. Coll., 1961-62; mgr. Westdale Co., Inc., 1961-62; tchr. Kenowa Hills High Sch., 1962-63; chmn. dept. English Wolfe County High Sch., 1967-68; instr. English and philosophy Lees Jr. Coll., Jackson, Ky., 1968-69, chmn. dept. humanities, asso. prof. English and philosophy, 1969—, dir. devel., 1970-71. Corp. mgr. Rapistan Carolinas, Charlotte, 1963. Mem. adv. staff Govt. Housing, 1969-71; ednl. cons. So. Consortium of 14 Colls. on Ednl. Media and Philosophy of Edn., 1969-71. Bd. dirs. Career Opportunities Program. Served with USNR, 1950-53. Mem. Nat. Reading Assn., N.E.A., Nat. Assn. Material Handling Engrs., Am. Assn. U. and Coll. Profs., Am. Assn. Jr. Colls., Nat. Assn. Tchrs. English, Ky. Edn. Assn. Methodist. Lion. Club: Wolfe County Fish and Game (pres. 1970-71) (Campton, Ky.). Author: First Aid to Composition, 1968; Easy Street, 1969; To Each His Own, 1971; Strange Lady, 1972. Home: Collinswood Pine Ridge KY 41360 Office: 601 Jefferson St Jackson KY 41339

COLLINS, CLYDE, state ofcl.; b. Cotter, Ark., Oct. 4, 1924; s. Sneed Claude and Pearl (Noe) C.; B.S., Ark. Tech. Coll., 1951; M.S., U. Ark., 1952; M.A., U. Ala., 1966; m. Thomasine Du Laney, May 22, 1949; children—Ronald Thomas, Deborah Ann. Coach, tchr. biol. gen. scis. Cotter High Sch., 1951-52; prin., coach Crane (Mo.) High Sch., 1952-57; became dean, dir. admissions Reinhardt Coll., Waleska, Ga., 1957, also tchr. health and phys. edn., dir. intra-murals; now asst. state program supr. Office Rehab., Ga. Dept. Edn., Atlanta. Del., Ga. Democratic Conv., 1961. Served with USNR, World War II. Mem. Nat. Intra-Mural Assn., Nat. Rehab. Assn., Ga. Edn. Assn., Am. Assn. Collegiate Registrars and Admission Officers. Baptist (deacon). Kiwanian (chmn. Circle K 1960—). Home: 2410 Lavista Rd NE Atlanta GA 30354 Office: State Office Bldg Atlanta GA 30334

COLLINS, DAVID ARTHUR, univ. ofcl.; b. Greenville, S.C., July 4, 1927; s. Ernest Fleming and Lula (Weeks) C.; student Am. U., 1947-48; B.A., Presbyn. Coll., 1954; M.A., Memphis State U., 1962; postgrad. U. Tenn., 1964-66; m. Anna Kay Maples, July 31, 1957; children—Debra Ann, David Arthur. Field sec., adminstrv. asst., asst. exec. sec. Pi Kappa Alpha, Memphis, 1954-61; asst. dean student affairs Auburn (Ala.) U., 1962-64; asst. dean students Memphis State U., 1964-69, dean student activities, 1969-71, asst. v.p. for student affairs, 1971—. Exec. sec. So. Univ. Student Gov't. Assn., 1967-70. Served with USNR, 1945-46. Mem. Tenn. Edn. Assn., So. Coll. Personnel Assn., So. Deans Assn., Assn. for Coordination Univ. Religious Affairs, Blue Key, Pi Kappa Alpha, Omicron Delta Kappa, Phi Delta Kappa. Presbyn. (deacon). Home: 1591 Page Cove Memphis TN 38117

COLLINS, DAVID BROWNING, clergyman; b. Hot Springs, Ark., Dec. 18, 1922; s. Charles Frederick and Agnes Elizabeth (George) C.; B.A., U. of South, 1943, B.D., 1948, S.T.M., 1962; diploma St. Augustine's Coll., Canterbury, Eng., 1961; m. Maryon Virginia Moise, Oct. 14, 1945; children—Melissa (Mrs. Mark Sterling), Christopher B., Matthew B., Geoffrey C. Ordained to ministry Episcopal Ch.; rector St. Andrew's Ch., Marianna, Ark., 1948-53; chaplain, asso. prof. religion U. of South, Sawanee, Tenn., 1953-66; dean Cathedral of St. Philip, Atlanta, 1966—. Vice pres. Christian Council Met. Atlanta, 1968-70; dep. Episcopal Gen. Conv., 1967, 69, 70. Bd. dirs. Episcopal Radio-TV Found., Atlanta Opportunities Industrialization Center, Atlanta. Served as lt. (j.g.) USNR, 1943-46. Mem. Blue Key, Phi Beta Kappa, Omicron Delta Kappa, Kappa Sigma. Contbr. articles to religious publs. Home: 2799 Andrews Dr NW Atlanta GA 30305 Office: 2744 Peachtree Rd NW Atlanta GA 30305

COLLINS, DONALD LAMAR, lawyer; b. Gadsden, Ala., Sept. 8, 1929; s. Luther Thomas and Mattie (Scarborough) C.; student U. Ala., 1948-49; B.S., Jacksonville State U., 1952; J.D., U. Ala., 1957; m. Hannah Case Snellgrove, Aug. 30, 1952; children—Henry Clay, Cynthia Case, Donald Lamar, Hannah Case. Admitted to Ala. bar, 1957; U.S. Supreme ct. bar; law clk. Supreme Ct. Ala., 1957-58; asso. law firm Martin & Blakey, Birmingham, Ala., 1958, Deramus, Johnston, Barton, Proctor and Swedlaw, 1958-62, partner, 1962-70; partner firm Collins and Hamilton, 1970—. Mem. Ala. Ho. of Reps., 1963-67; Republican candidate for atty. gen. of Ala., 1966; Ala. coordinator for Nixon-Agnew, 1968. Served to maj., USMCR. Mem. Ala. State Bar, Am., Birmingham bar assns., Am. Judicature Soc., Am. Legion, V.F.W., Phi Alpha Delta, Omicron Delta Kappa. Episcopalian. Rotarian. Asso. editor Ala. Law Rev. 1957. Home: 29 Ridge Dr Birmingham AL 35213 Office: City Federal Bldg Birmingham AL 35203

COLLINS, EDWARD MATTHEW, research and devel. exec.; b. Houston, July 2, 1917; s. Dennis Michael and Lucy Agnes (Edwards) C.; B.S., U. Md., 1953; M.A. in Govt., Georgetown U., 1956, Ph.D., 1966; m. Mary Elizabeth Richter, Mar. 30, 1940; children—Edward Matthew (dec.), Mary Elizabeth, Colin Patrick, Dennis Michael. Commd. 2d lt. USAAF, 1943, transferred to USAF, 1947, advanced through grades to col., 1959; pilot, operations officer, squadron comdr., World War II; chief mil. applications div. AF Intelligence Center, 1958-60; chief spl. adv. group ACS/Intelligence, Hdqrs., 1960-62; chief plans and policy J-2, U.S. European Command, 1963-66; ret., 1967; mgr. research and devel. and studies areas IBM Corp., Gaithersburg, Md., 1967—. Decorated Legion of Merit. Mem. Am. Acad. Arts and Scis., Am. Acad. Polit. and Social Sci., Am. Polit. Sci. Assn., Gold Key, Pi Sigma Alpha. Author, editor: War, Politics and Power, 1962. Home: 12278 Greenleaf Av Potomac MD 20854 Office: 18100 Frederick Pike Gaithersburg MD 20760

COLLINS, ELSON K., lawyer; mem. Democratic Nat. Com.; b. nr. Laurel, Miss., Dec. 17, 1911; s. William Thomas and Susanna (Cooley) C.; student Jones County Jr. Coll., Miss State U., Cumberland U.; m. Grace Easterling, Aug. 19, 1932; children—Peggy R. (Mrs. Joseph S. Gatlin), Sylvia (Mrs. J. Hood Garber). Admitted to Miss. bar, 1941; sr. partner Collins & Tew, attys., Laurel, 1959—; pros. atty. Jones County, 1948-52; mem. Miss. Senate, 1960-72, chmn. judiciary com., 1961-72. Del. Nat. Democratic Conv., 1960; mem. Dem. Nat. Com., 1963—. Adv. bd. U.S. Office of Housing Expediter, 1949. Served with AUS, 1943-46. Decorated Bronze Star medal. Recipient citation and regional award in mineral conservation Miss. Wildlife Assn., 1964. Mem. Am. Trial Lawyers Assn. (asso. editor Law Jour.), Am., Miss. (commr. 1960, certificate of merit 1962), Jones County (past pres.) bar assns., V.F.W. (chmn. So. conf. 1951-52, nat. chief staff 1963-64), Miss. State U., Cumberland U. alumni assns. Presbyn. Mason (Shriner). Clubs: Laurel Country. Home: Waynesboro Dr Laurel MS 39440 Office: PO Box 732 Laurel MS 39441

COLLINS, GALEN FRANKLIN, pharm. chemist; b. Winona Lake, Ind., Dec 29, 1927; s. Harry Franklin and Elsie (Bahney) C.; B.S., Purdue U., 1949, M.S., 1952, Ph.D., 1954; m. Ann Elizabeth Averitt, Sept. 30, 1956; children—Galen Robert, Amalia Lynn, Scott Franklin, Daniel Chancelor. Grad. asst. Purdue U., 1949-52, research fellow, 1952-53; pharm. chemist Miles Labs., Inc., Elkart, Ind., 1953-58, asst. to dir. Miles-Ames pharm. research lab., 1958-59, sr. research scientist, sect. head Ames Products, 1959-60; sect. chief Norwich Products Devel., Norwick Pharmacal Co. (N.Y.), 1960-63; mgr. research div. S.E. Massengill Co., Bristol, Tenn., 1963-67, dir. research, 1967-71; v.p. research and devel. Dade div. Am. Hosp. Supply Corp., Miami, Fla., 1971-—. Bd. dirs. Bristol unit Am. Heart Assn., 1967-71, pres., 1969-71. Fellow A.A.A.S., Am. Inst. Chemists; mem. A.I.M., Am. Chem. Soc., Am. Pharm. Assn., Acad. of Pharm. Scis., Multiple Sclerosis Soc., Sigma Xi, Rho Chi, Phi Lambda Upsilon. Presbyn. Elk. Patentee in field. Home: 10800 SW 69th Av Miami FL 33156 Office: PO Box 672 Miami FL 33152

COLLINS, GENEVIEVE (MRS. FRANK COLLINS, JR.), organist, choir dir.; b. Meeker, La., July 12, 1912; d. Claude E. and Bessie (Hamberlin) Cox; Mus. B., La. State U., 1933; Mus.M., 1934; pvt. study with Louis Vierne, Paris, 1935; m. Frank Collins, Jr., June 7, 1933; 1 son, James F. C. Organist, choirmaster Temple B'nai Israel, Baton Rouge, 1935-67, 68-—; organist First Meth. Ch., 1943-45; organist, choirmaster Trinity Episcopal Ch., 1949-—; recitalist; mem. faculty Hardtner Choir Camp, 1956-62; tchr. piano, 1944-58. Mem. music commn. Episcopal Diocese La. Mem. Am. Guild Organists (dean La. chpt. 1945-47; 50-51, 59-61, state chmn. 1966-—, sub-dean, program chmn. Baton Rouge chpt. 1972), Past Presidents Assn. Baton Rouge (pres. 1952), Baton Rouge Piano Tchrs. Assn. (pres. 1951), Pan-Hellenic Assn. Baton Rouge (pres. 1939), Alpha Chi Omega (pres. alumnae club 1938), Sigma Alpha Iota. Episcopalian. Home: 406 Delgado Dr Baton Rouge LA 70808 Office: 3552 Morning Glory Av Baton Rouge LA 70808

COLLINS, HAROLD RAY, supt. schs.; b. Hartford, Ala., Mar. 14, 1919; s. Francis Alex and Vestie (Kinsaul) C.; B.S., Troy State Coll., 1946; M.A., U. Ala., 1953, Ed.D., 1966; m. Ruth Bassett, Mar. 1, 1941; children—Harold Ray, Gene Bassett. Prin. Zion Chapel Sch., Jack, Ala., 1944-48, Goshen (Ala.) High Sch., 1948-66; supt. Pike County Schs., 1966-70, Mobile County (Ala.) Pub. Schs., 1970-—. Mem. Ala. State Textbook Commn.; mem. Ala. Jr. Coll. Selection Com. Mem. Nat., Ala. assns. secondary sch. prins., Am., Ala. assns. sch. adminstrs., N.E.A., Ala. Edn. Assn., Nat. Assn. Sch. Bds., Ala. Assn. Elementary Sch. Prins, Kappa Phi Kappa, Kappa Phi Delta. Baptist. Rotarian. Club: Civitan (Mobile). Home: 3251 Rivere du Chien Dr Mobile AL 36606 Office: PO Box 1327 Mobile AL 36601

COLLINS, HUBERT ARTHUR, grocery store exec.; b. Chesnee, S.C., May 1, 1904; s. John Joseph and Mary (Kimbrell) C.; A.A., Mars Hill Jr. Coll., 1922; student Atlanta So. Dental Coll., 1922-25; m. Mary Louise Lever, Aug. 2, 1931; children—Patsy Ann (Mrs. Roy Lee Cartee), Mary Jo (Mrs. Horace Leslie Miller), Carol Louise (Mrs. Robert Link Larson). Formerly asst. rural mail carrier; then co-owner grocery store, Chesnee, S.C., owner, 1951-66. Loan committeeman, dir. Chesnee State Bank. Mem. bd. Spartanburg County Mental Health Assn. Baptist. Clubs: Elloree Hunting, Chesnee Country, Fripp Island Golf, Cherokee National Golf and Recreation. Home: 115 N Alabama Av Chesnee SC 29323

COLLINS, JAMES ALTON, editor; b. Pecos, Tex., Nov. 24, 1934; s. Harlin Alton and Ada Belle (Hayes) C.; B.A., Tex. A. and M. U., 1956; candidate M.A., U. Tex., 1964; m. Jerry LaVerne Ratliff, Apr. 29, 1963; 1 dau., Christina Carmen. Reporter, Pecos (Tex.) Enterprise, 1956; tchr., coach Barstow (Tex.) Ind. Schs., 1956-59; reporter Wichita Falls (Tex.) Times, 1959-60, Roswell (N.M.) Daily Record, 1960-61, Pecos (Tex.) Daily News, 1961; reporter U.P.I., Albuquerque, 1962; reporter, photographer New Mexican, Santa Fe, 1962-63, sports editor, 1964; editor N.M. Farm and Ranch Mag., 1964-65; staff writer The Pipeliner, El Paso Natural Gas Co. (Tex.), 1965-68, editor, 1968-—. Served with AUS, 1957. Mem. Internat. Assn. Bus. Communicators. Democrat. Home: 9925 Bourbon St El Paso TX 79924 Office: Box 1492 El Paso TX 79978

COLLINS, JAMES MITCHELL, congressman; b. Hallsville, Tex., Apr. 29, 1916; s. Carr P. and Ruth (Woodall) C.; B.S.C., So. Meth. U., 1937; M.B.A., Northwestern U., 1938, Harvard, 1943; C.L.U., 1940; m. Dorothy Dann, Sept. 16, 1942; children—Michael James, Dorothy Colville (Mrs. David R. Weaver), Nancy Miles. Pres. Consol. Industries, Inc., 1954-65, Internat. Industries, Inc., 1954-65, Fidelity Union Life Ins. Co., 1954-65; mem. 90th-92d Congress 3d Dist. Tex. Active local Greater Dallas Planning Council, Salvation Army, Dallas Council World Affairs, Served to capt. C.E., AUS, World War II. Mem. Am. Legion, V.F.W., Phi Delta Theta. Republican. Baptist. Home: 1525 Hardrock Rd Irving TX 75060 Office: Longworth Office Bldg Washington DC 20515

COLLINS, JAMES SPENCER, petroleum co. exec.; b. Dallas, Jan. 10, 1922; s. Robert Oron and Hallie Rhea (Jowell) C.; B.S., Tex. Coll. Mines, 1947; postgrad. Harvard Bus. Sch., 1964; m. Mary White, Apr. 15, 1944; children—Gregory Newton, Kelly Anne. Geologist, Union Oil Co., Corpus Christi, Tex., 1947-50; geologist York & Harper, Midland, Tex., 1950-52; div. geologist Tenneco Oil Co., Houston, 1952-57, exploration mgr., 1957-59, v.p., 1959-—. Chmn. oil industry sect. United Fund, 1969. Served with USMCR, 1942-46. Mem. Am. Assn. Petroleum Geologists, Soc. Exploration Geophysicists, Am. Assn. Petroleum Landmen. Club: Houston. Home: 3815 Olympia St Houston TX 77019 Office: Box 2511 Tenneco Bldg Houston TX 77001

COLLINS, JASON HAYDEL, physician; b. New Orleans, Aug. 13, 1918; s. Charles and Amelie (Haydel) C.; B.S., Tulane U., 1938, M.D., 1941; m. Marie Elaine White, June 30, 1949; children—Denise Adele, Marie Elaine, Janine Ann, Jason Haydel, Lynette Joan, Charles Louis. Intern, Wis. Gen. Hosp., 1941-42; resident Ochsner Clinic, New Orleans, 1946-48; practice medicine, specializing in obstetrics and gynecology, New Orleans, 1946-—; prof. clin. obstetrics and gynecology, Tulane U., 1959-71, prof., acting chmn. dept. obstetrics and gynecology Sch. Medicine, 1971-72, C. Jeff Miller prof., chmn., 1972-—; dir. med. edn. So. Bapt. Hosp., New Orleans; sr. cons. obstetrics and gynecology USPHS Hosp., New Orleans; cons. Mercy Hosp., Touro Infirmary. Served with AUS, 1942-45; PTO. Mem. Am. Gynecol. Soc., A.C.S., Am. Coll. Obstetrics and Gynocology, Am. Assn. Obstetrics and Gynocology, Am. Gynecol. Club, Delta Kappa Epsilon. Club: Boston (New Orleans). Home: 366 Walnut St New Orleans LA 70118 Office: 1430 Tulane Av New Orleans LA 70112

COLLINS, JOHN FOSTER, mech. engr.; b. Fontana, N.C., Apr. 24, 1934; s. Henry Salem and Anna Elizabeth (Helmick) C.; student Apprentice Sch. Hydraulic Designer, 1958; B.S. in M.E., Va. Poly. Inst., 1961; m. Hazel Jennette Walker, June 22, 1957; children—Kimberly, Gregory. Sr. designer Newport News Shipbldg. & Dry Dock Co., 1952-63; engring. supr. Space div. Chrysler Corp., 1963-69, Omark Industries, Zebulon, N.C., 1969-—. Bd. dirs. Zebulon (N.C.) Library. Registered profl. engr., Fla., N.C. Mem. Am. Soc. M.E., Nat. Soc. Profl. Engrs., Pi Tau Sigma, Tau Beta Pi, Pi Delta Epsilon, Omicron Delta Kappa. Mason, Lion. Home: PO Box 694 Zebulon NC 27597 Office: PO Box 946 Zebulon NC 27597

COLLINS, JOHN P., football exec. Exec. v.p. Houston Oilers. Office: 6910 Fannin Houston TX 77025*

COLLINS, LESTER ALBERTSON, landscape architect; b. Moorestown, N.J., Apr. 19, 1914; s. Lester and Anne (Albertson) C.; grad. Choate Sch., Wallingford, Conn., 1933; A.B., Harvard 1938, M.L.A., 1942; m. Petronella le Roux, July 8, 1947; children—Abigail Anne, Lester Adrian, Oliver Michael. Chmn. dept. landscape architecture, Harvard, 1950-53; prin. Collins, Simonds and Simonds landscape architects and planners, Washington, Pitts., 1955-—. Mem. Am. the Beautiful Fund of Natural Area Council, Washington; mem. Joint Com. on Nat. Capital, Washington; mem. Hubbard Ednl. Trust, Boston; pres. Innisfree Found., Millbrook, N.Y., 1960-—. Fullbright scholar, 1953-54. Fellow Am. Soc. Landscape Architects. Mem. Soc. of Friends (with Am. Field Service 1942-45). Clubs: Harvard (Boston); Cosmos (Washington); Century Assn. Address: 1619 33d St NW Washington DC 20007

COLLINS, MARVIN BOBBY, retail grocery exec.; b. Tarpon Springs, Fla., Mar. 17, 1929; s. Marvin Bartow and Elsie Idella (Hughes) C.; student pub. schs.; m. Mary Marie Mock, June 20, 1948; children—Mark Ryan, Marcia Ann. Mgr. meat dept. Winn Dixie Food Stores, Inc., Tallahassee, 1947-55, Melbourne, Fla., 1955-58; owner pres. Minit Saver Food Stores, Inc., Melbourne, Fla., 1958-66; v.p. Certified Grocers of Fla., Ocala, 1963-64, dir., 1963-66; vice pres., dir. Minit Ranch, Inc., Melbourne, Fla., 1965-—; pres. Quik Way Food Stores, Inc., Anderson, S.C., 1966-—; pres. Quik Way of Carolina, Inc., 1967-—; dir., pres. Asso. Grocers Inc. of S.C., 1968-—; chmn. Travelers Petroleum, Inc.; partner Lease Way Enterprises. Dir. Salvation Army Adv. Bd., Anderson. Served with AUS, 1952-54. Mem. Retail Grocers Assn. of Fla. (dir. until 1966), Nat. Assn. Convenience Stores (dir.), C. of C. (sec., dir. 1962-66). Baptist. Mason (32 deg., Shriner). Home: 221 Timberlake Rd Anderson SC 29621 Office: 1007 N Fant St Anderson SC 29621

COLLINS, MICHAEL, museum dir.; b. Rome, Italy, Oct. 31, 1930 (parents Am. citizens); s. James L. Collins; B.S., U.S. Mil. Acad., 1952; m. Patricia Mary Finnegan, 1957; children—Kathleen, Ann Stewart, Michael Lawton. Commd. 2d lt. USAF, advanced through grades to col.; formerly exptl. test pilot Air Force Flight Test Center, Edwards AFB, Cal.; formerly astronaut with Manned Spacecraft Center, NASA, pilot Gemini X, nation's 3d space walker, mem. 1st lunar landing crew, 1969; asst. sec. state for pub. affairs, Washington, 1970-71; dir. Nat. Air and Space Mus., Smithsonian Instn., Washington, 1971-—. Mem. Soc. Exptl. Test Pilots. Office: National Air and Space Museum Smithsonian Instn Washington DC 20560

COLLINS, MORRIS WILLIAM HOLLOWELL, JR., educator; b. Athens, Ga., Aug. 13, 1917; s. Morris W.H. and Eula (Thomas) C.; A.B., U. Ga., 1939, M.A., 1940; postgrad. U. Wis., 1940-41; Ph.D., Harvard, 1953; m. Maysie Sloan Lyons, Dec. 23, 1947; children—Susan S., Morris H., John G., Margaret S. Faculty, U. Ga., 1946-47, 50-—, prof. polit. sci., 1962-—, dir. bur. pub. adminstrn., 1952-54, asso. dir. Ga. center continuing edn., 1954-57, asso. dir. U. Ga. Study, 1956-58, dir. inst. govt., 1957-—; teaching fellow, tutor Harvard, 1948-50. Staff dir. Gov.'s Commn. on Economy and Reorgn. of Ga. State Govt., 1959; gen. staff cons. tax research council Ga. C. of C., 1960-61; exec. dir. Gov.'s Commn. for Efficiency and Improvement in Govt., 1963-66; mem. Sec.'s Com. on Fed. State Health Relationships, Dept. Health, Edn. and Welfare, 1966-67; tech. adviser Citizens Com. on Ga. Gen. Assembly, 1969-71; mem. 3-man observation team vis. European continuing edn. acads. Ford Found.-Internat. City Mgmt. Assn., 1971. Chmn. task force on precinct worker tng. Democratic Nat. Com., 1956-60; mem. adv. com. polit. orgn., 1956-60; chmn. Profs. for Johnson-Humphrey, Ga., 1964. Vice chmn. bd. visitors U.S. Army Mil. Police Sch.; bd. dirs. Nat. Tng. and Devel. Service for State and Local Govt. Served from 2d lt. to maj. Inf., AUS, 1941-45; PTO. Named Ga. Citizen of Year, Assn. County Commrs. Ga., 1962; recipient Profl. Devel. award Ga. Municipal Assn., 1972. Mem. Am. (past mem. council), So. (past mem. exec. council, membership chmn. 1960-—) polit. sci. assns., Nat. Adv. Council, Nat. Civil Service League, Conf. on Pub. Service, Am. Soc. Pub. Adminstrn. (council 1967-70), Conf. U. Burs. Govt. Research (chmn. 1967-69), Nat. Acad. Pub. Adminstrn., Nat. Assn. Schs. Pub. Affairs and Adminstrn. (pres. 1972-—), So. Pub. Adminstrn. Research Council, Am. Assn. U. Profs., Ga. Edn. Assn., Res. Officers Assn. Democrat. Presbyn. Author: (with A.J. Brumbaugh) Final Report, The University of Georgia Study, 1958. Editor: Instructor's Manual, Democratic Precinct Worker's Course, 1956, rev., 1959; (chart) Organization of the State Government of Georgia, 1962, rev., 1964, 70; State Policies Conducive to the Growth of the Pledmont Crescent, 1968; also papers in field of edn. Home: 220 Meadowview Rd Athens GA 30601

COLLINS, MURIEL MORSE (MRS. DENIS AUGUSTUS COLLINS), journalist; b. Bklyn., Apr. 15, 1912; d. Frederick and Henrietta (Grasser) Morse; grad. high sch; m. Denis Augustus Collins, Nov. 15, 1952. Dept. head Uniform Printing & Supply Co., Bklyn., 1935-45; sec., bookkeeper Borough Press, Inc., N.Y.C., 1945-52; pvt. sec. to service mgr. Atlantic Service Co., 1952-57; asst. sec., asst treas., confidential sec. to pres. Shaker Mus. Found., Inc., Old Chatham, N.Y., 1957-68; sec. Port Charlotte (Fla) C. of C., 1969-70; reporter Sarasota Jour., 1970-—. Mem. Old Chatham Improvement Assn., 1952-69; chaplain Old Chatham Grange, 1962-69; charter mem. v.p. Tri-Village Fire Aux., 1963-64, pres., 1965-68; sec. Charlotte County Pageant Assn., Inc. Mem. Nat Fedn. Bus. and Profl. Women's Clubs (charter pres. Chatham club 1968), Port Charlotte Bus. and Profl. Women's Club (2d v.p. 1971), Am. Assn. Ret. Persons, Animal Welfare League Charlotte County, Port Charlotte Civic Assn. Clubs: Empire State (Charlotte County, Fla.); Alan Devoe Bird. Home and office: 250 NE Gibraltar Dr Port Charlotte FL 33950

COLLINS, STANLEY NEWCOMB, JR., airline pilot, state legislator; b. Alexandria, Va., Jan. 30, 1937; s. Stanley Newcomb and Mary Elsie (Bloxom) C.; B.S., U. Md., 1962; M.Ed., Coll. William and Mary, 1965; m. Joyce Diane Pratt, July 18, 1958; children—Kendra Ann, Andrew, Daniel, Katie Louise. Tchr. Richmond (Va.) Pub. Schs., 1962-64; pilot Delta Air Lines, Atlanta, 1965-—; dir. Cheatham Chem. Co., Atlanta. Mem. Ga. Ho. of Reps., 1969-70, 71-72. Served with USMC, 1956-60; maj. Res. Mem. Airline Pilots Assn., Res. Officers Assn., Marine Corps Res. Officers Assn. (sec., treas. Atlanta chpt. 1970-71), Iota Lambda Sigma.

COLLINS, THOMAS O., JR., lawyer. Exec. dir. La. Bar Assn., New Orleans. Office: Supreme Court Bldg New Orleans LA 70112*

COLLISON, KODER MACKLIN, govt. ofcl.; b. Phila., Jan 25, 1910; s. Harry Benjamin and Lula Mae (Macklin) C.; grad. Mercersburg Acad., 1929; student U. Va., 1929-30, U. Pa., 1942-43, Rutgers U., 1943-44; m. Sibyl Joan Rhoades, Sept. 24, 1943; children—Judith Dunning, Kathryn Macklin. System indsl. rep. Pa. R.R., Phila., 1941-48, indsl. agt., Indls., 1949-52; dir. Springfield (O.) Devel. Council, 1953-57; dir. bus. and indsl. Expansion Dayton (O.) C. of C., 1957-59; dir., cabinet officer det. indsl. and econ. devel. State of Ohio, Columbus, 1959-62; dep. commr. W.Va. Dept. Commerce, 1963, commr., 1963-65; state devel. specialist Appalachian Regional Commn., U.S. Govt., 1965-—. Mem. Am. Indsl. Devel. Council, Nat. Indsl. Zoning Com.,Urban Land Inst., Assn. State Planning and Devel. Agys. (exec. com. 1960-62), W. Va. Hist. Soc., W. Va. Indsl. Devel. Assn. Author numerous articles on econ. devel. and plant location factors for various publs.; contbr. ency. Home: 2401 Calvert St NW Washington DC 20008

COLMER, WILLIAM MEYERS, congressman; b. Moss Point, Miss., Feb. 11, 1890; s. Henry and Anna S. (Meyers) C.; student Millsaps Coll., Jackson, Miss., 1910-14; m. Ruth Miner, Sept. 17, 1917; children— William Meyers, James Henry Thomas Warren. Began as sch. teacher, 1914; admitted to Miss. bar, 1917; county atty. Jackson County, 1921-27; dist. atty., 2d Dist. of Miss., 1928-33; mem. 73d to 87th Congresses from 6th Miss. Dist., 88th-91st Congresses from 5th Miss. Dist., chmn. com. on postwar policy and planning for 78th and 79th Congresses, chmn. com. on rules 90th-92d Congresses. Pvt. U.S. Army, 1918, discharged as regtl. sergt. maj., 1919. Mem. Am. Legion, 40 Hommes and 8 Chevaux, Pi Kappa Alpha. Democrat. Methodist. Mason (33 deg.), Elk, Woodman, Rotarian. Home: 2017 East Beach Pascagoula MS 39567 Office: Rayburn House Office Bldg Washington DC 20515

COLODNY, EDWIN IRVING, airline exec.; b. Burlington, Vt., June 7, 1926; s. Meyer and Lena (Yett) C.; A.B., U. Rochester, 1948; LL.B., Harvard, 1951; m. Nancy Dessoff, Dec. 11, 1965; children—Elizabeth, Mark, David. Admitted to N.Y. bar, 1951, D.C. bar, 1958; with Office Gen. Counsel, Gen. Services Adminstrn., 1951-52; with CAB, 1954-57; with Allegheny Airlines, Inc., 1957-—, exec. v.p. legal affairs and marketing services, 1969-—; sec., treas., dir. Washington Airways, Inc. Served to 1st lt. AUS, 1952-54. Recipient James D. McGill Meml. award U. Rochester. Mem. Am. Bar Assn. Home: 6135 Nevada Av Chevy Chase MD 20015 Office: Hangar 12 Washington Nat Airport Washington DC 20001

COLOMB, C(HARLES) EARL, realtor, bldg. co. exec.; b. New Orleans, July 19, 1911; s. Frederick J. and Josephine (Bauer) C.; student pub. schs.; m. Mary Williams, July 3, 1929; children—C. Earl, Sylvia (Mrs. Ferdinand VonBehren III), Carl Edward, Shirley M.Pres., Chalmette Bldgs. & Supply Co. (La.), 1945-—, Chalmette Vista, Inc., 1945-—, Vista Village II, 1959-—; owner C. Earl Colomb, realtor, Chalmette, 1930-—. Bd. dirs. New Orleans Tidwater Devel. Com. Mem. Nat. Assn. Real Estate Bds., Nat. Assn. Home Builders, Urban Land Inst., Bur. Govtl. Research, Pub. Affairs Research Council, C. of C. (past pres.). Rotarian (dist. gov.). Home: 41 E Carmack Dr Chalmette LA 70043 Office: 50 Madison Av Chalmette LA 70043

COLON, ANGEL ALBERTO, educator; b. Rio Piedras, P.R., Nov. 5, 1915; s. Isidoro A. and Josefina (Olivieri) C.; B.S., La. State U., 1937, M.S., 1939; D.Sc., Carnegie Inst. Tech., 1943; M.D., U. Madrid (Spain), 1962; m. Madeline Terry, Sept. 15, 1938; children—Madeline L., David A. Instr. chemistry U. Rio Pedras (P.R.), 1937-39, asst. prof., 1939-43, asso. prof., 1943-46, prof. chemistry, 1946; asst. prof. medicine in charge biochem. research Med. Sch., Hato Rey, P.R., 1963-67, asst. clin. prof. medicine, 1967-—; research chemist Merck & Co., Rahway, N.J., 1946-50; supr. research Econ. Devel. Adminstrn., Hato Rey, 1950-56, asst. dir. research, 1951-58; dir Inst. Health Labs., Dept. Health P.R., Hato Rey, 1967-—; asst. sec. for environmental health and consumer protection Dept. Health P.R., 1969-71; dean student affairs U. P.R. Med. Scis. Campus, 1971-—; clin. pathologist P.R. Cancer Hosp., Rio Piedras, 1967-—. Exec. sec. Gov.'s Com. on Pollution; mem. Adv. Council on Air Pollution Control. Fellow Am. Heart Assn., Am. Inst. Chemists, A.A.A.S.; mem. Colegio Quimicos de P.R. (pres. 1953-65), Am. Chem. Soc. (local chpt. pres. 1954), P.R. Med. Assn., Am. Pub. Health Assn., Asociacion de Salud Publica de P.R., Academia Puertorriquena de Artes y Ciencias, Assn. Food and Drug Ofcls. U.S., Sigma Xi, Alpha Chi Sigma, Phi Lambda Upsilon, Phi Kappa Phi. Rotarian (pres. 1945). Roman Catholic. Home: 1817 Miosotis St Rio Piedras PR 00927 Office: GPO Box 5067 San Juan PR 00936

COLONEY, WAYNE HERNDON, civil engr.; b. Bradenton, Fla., Mar. 15, 1925; s. Herndon Percival and Mary Adore (Cramer) C.; B.C.E. summa cum laude, Ga. Inst. Tech., 1950; m. Anne Elizabeth Benedict, June 21, 1950; 1 dau., Mary Adore. Project engr. Fla. Rd. Dept., Tallahassee, 1950-55; hwy. engr. Gibbs & Hill, Inc., Guatemala, 1955-57, project engr., Tampa, Fla., 1957-59; prject engr. J.E. Greiner Co., Tampa, 1959-62, asso., 1962-63; partner Barrett, Daffin & Coloney, Tallahasse, 1963-70; pres. Wayne H. Coloney Co., Inc., Tallahassee, 1970-—. Dir. Internat. Enterprises, Inc. Pres. United Fund. Bd. dirs. Springtime Tallahassee, Fla. Heritage Found. Served with AUS, 1943-46. Registered profl. engr. and land surveyor, Fla., Ga., Nat. Council Engring. Examiners. Fellow Am. Soc. C.E.; mem. Nat. Soc. Profl. Engrs., Fla. Engring. Soc. (sr.), C. of C., Anak, Phi Kappa Phi, Omicron Delta Kappa, Sigma Alha Epsilon, Tau Beta Pi. Patentee. Office: PO Drawer 3966 Tallahassee FL 32303

COLSKY, JACOB, physician; b. Memphis, Dec. 5, 1921; s. Abraham Samuel and Jennie (Shefsky) C.; student Memphis State Coll., 1938-40; M.D., U. Tenn., 1944; m. Irene Vivian Belen, July 26, 1953; children—Liane Caryl, Arthur Spencer, Andrew Evan. Intern, Jackson Meml. Hosp., Miami, Fla., 1944-45; fellow dept. preventive medicine Johns Hopkins Med. Sch., 1947-50, instr. dept. preventive medicine, 1950-51; asst. chief clin. research unit Nat. Cancer Inst., Balt., 1951-52; asst. physician, out-patients Johns Hopkins Hosp., Balt., 1947-52; asso. dir. medicine Maimonides Hosp., Bklyn., 1952-57; asso. attending physician Kings County Hosp. Med. Center, 1955-57; instr. medicine State U. N.Y. Coll. Medicine, N.Y.C., 1952-54, asst. prof. medicine, 1954-55, asso. prof. 1955-57; pvt. practice medicine, specializing in internal medicine and med. oncology, Miami, Fla., 1957-—; mem. staffs Cedars of Lebanon, Jackson Meml. hosps., Miami; cons. Bapt., Mount Sinai, VA hosps., Miami; asso. prof. medicine U. Miami Sch. Medicine, 1957-—; dir. med. oncology sect. dept. medicine U. Miami and Jackson Meml. Hosp., 1960-70; sr. investigator Eastern Coop. Oncology Group, 1960-—. mem. exec. com. 1971-—; pres. Med. Oncology and Chemotherapy Found. Miami, Inc., 1970-—. Bd. dirs. Papanicolaou Cancer Research Inst., 1969-72. Served to capt. M.C., AUS, 1945-47. Diplomate Am. Bd. Internal Medicine. Fellow Bklyn. Soc. Internal Medicine, N.Y. Acad. Medicine, A.C.P.; mem. N.Y. Acad. Sci., A.A.A.S., Am. Fedn. Clin. Research, Am. Assn. Cancer Research, Am. Geriatrics Soc., Leukemia Soc. (state bd. dirs. 1970-72), Am. Cancer Soc. (county bd. dirs. 1968-72), Am. Soc. Clin. Oncology (founding mem.). Contbr. numerous articles to profl. jours. Home: 8220 S W 52d Av Miami FL 33143 Office: 1150 NW 14th St Miami FL 33136

COLSON, CHARLES WENDELL, lawyer; b. Boston, Oct. 16, 1931; s. Wendell Ball and Inez (Ducrow) C.; A.B., Brown U., 1953; J.D., George Washington U., 1959; m. Nancy Billings, June 3, 1953; children—Wendell Ball II, Christian B., Emily Ann; m. 2d, Patricia Ann Hughes, Apr. 4, 1964. Admitted to D.C. bar, 1961, since practiced in Washington; admitted to Va. bar, 1959, Mass. bar, 1964; asst. to asst. sec. Navy, 1955-56; adminstrv. asst. Senator Leverett Saltonstall U.S. Senate, 1956-61; sr. partner Gadsby & Hannah, 1961-69; spl. counsel to Pres. U.S., 1969-—. Campaign mgr. Saltonstall campaign, 1960. Served to captain USMCR, Korean Conflict. Recipient Outstanding Young Man of Boston award Jr. C. of C., 1960. Mem. Order of Coif, Beta Theta Pi. Republican. Episcopalian. Club: Capital Hill. Home: 1350 Ballantrae Lane McLean VA 22101 Office: The White House Washington DC 20500

COLSON, JOSEPH V., govt. ofcl. Exec. dir. Gulf States Marine Fisheries, New Orleans. Office: Wildlife and Fisheries Bldg 400 Royal St New Orleans LA 70130*

COLTEN, ARTHUR THOMAS, city ofcl.; b. Detroit, Oct. 21, 1922; s. Arthur and Judith (Gaines) C.; student Tex. A. and M. U., 1943-44, Washington and Lee U., 1944-45; B.S. in Pub. Adminstrn., DePauw U., 1947; m. Jane Kimmel, June 21, 1947; children—Connie, Craig, Lee. Bus. mgr. Bogalusa (La.) Daily News, 1948-55; pub., owner Minden (La.) Press & Herald, 1956-65; exec. dir. Minden (La.) C. of C., 1965-66; mayor City of Minden, 1967—. Pres., La. Municipal Assn., 1972—. Mem. Republican Central Com., chmn. Webster County Rep. Com. Served with AUS, 1943-46. Named Minden Man of Year, 1967. Mem. La. Press Assn. (pres. 1964-65), Minden C. of C. (pres. 1964-65), Nat. Editorial Assn. (state chmn. 1965-66), Delta Upsilon, Sigma Delta Chi, Pi Sigma Alpha. Presbyn. (chmn. ch. bd. deacons 1964-65). Clubs: Lions (v.p. 1962-63), Minden Exchange (pres. 1963), Rotary (v.p. 1954-55). Home: 1202 Drake Dr Minden LA 71055 Office: City Hall 520 Broadway St Minden LA 71055

COLTHARP, LELAND HOMER, JR., lawyer; b. Maringouin, La., Mar. 8, 1926; s. Leland Homer and Una Mae (Lefeaux) C.; student McNeese State Coll., 1946-47; LL.B., La. State U., 1950; m. Barbara Anne Bennett, Aug. 16, 1947; children—Karen L., Debra J., Pamela A. Admitted to La. bar, 1950; practice law, La., 1950-51; asst. U.S. atty. Western Dist. La., 1951-53; partner LeCompte, Hall & Coltharp, DeRidder, La., 1953-60, Hall & Coltharp, DeRidder, 1960—; asst. dist. atty. 30th Dist. of La., 1955-64; city atty. City of DeRidder, 1960-70; gen. counsel So. Casualty Ins. Co. Mem. Beauregard Parish Pub. Library, 1964—, pres., 1968—; mem. Library Devel. Com. La., 1968—, chmn., 1970—; mem. La. State Adv. Council on Libraries, 1971—. Trustee Beauregard Meml. Bapt. Hosp., 1954-66, chmn. bd., 1958-59. Served with USNR, 1944-46. Mem. Am., La. bar assns., S.W. La. Def. Counsel Assn. (pres. 1967-68), Am., La. library trustee assns. Methodist (trustee). Club: Lions (DeRidder). Home: 605 S Division St DeRidder LA 70634 Office: 205 W 2d St DeRidder LA 70634

COLVIN, DONALD WOODSON, supt. schs.; b. Germantown, Ky., Sept. 19, 1922; s. Noah Richard and Stella Ann (Peddicord) C.; B.S., Eastern Ky. U., 1948, M.A., 1949; m. Rosalyn Bay, June 10, 1946; children—Ted L., Rhonda G. Tchr., Western Hills Sch., 1949-50, prin., 1950-63; supt. Bracken County (Ky.) Schs., 1963—; dir. Bank Germantown. Served with F.A., AUS, 1943-46. Recipient Leadership award Eastern State U., 1967. Mem. Am., Ky. assns. sch. adminstrs., N.E.A., Ky. Edn. Assn. Home: Route 1 Foster KY 41043 Office: Bracken County Schs Brooksville KY 41004

COLVIN, OTIS HERBERT, JR., educator; b. El Dorado, Ark., Mar. 18, 1923; s. Otis Herbert and Irene (Hammons) C.; B.A., Baylor U., 1944, M.B., 1948; Mus.M., U. Colo., 1950; Ph.D., U. Rochester (N.Y.), 1957; m. Mary Ila Ullom, June 18, 1948; children—Carol Kay, Mary Edith, Susan Elizabeth. Instr. music Tex. Technol. Coll., 1950-55; chmn. piano dept. Baylor U., Waco, Tex., 1957-62, chmn. dept. theory and composition, 1962—; teaching asst. Eastman Sch. Music, Rochester, 1955-57. Served USNR, 1944-46; PTO. Mem. Music Tchrs. Nat. Assn., Am. Guild Organists (dean Waco chpt. 1958-60), Phi Mu Alpha. Baptist. Mason (32 deg.); Kiwanian. Editor choral compositions. Composer: Organ Voluntaries Based on Early American Hymn Tunes, Short Pieces Organ, For Sunday (6 organ pieces based on modal melodies). Contbr. to profl. publs. Home: 9121 Pin Oak Dr Waco TX 76710

COMBEST, EARL EDGAR, ins. co. exec.; b. Paducah, Tex., Feb. 5, 1899; s. Obe Jasper and Mollie (Meeks) C.; student Tyler Comml. Coll., 1917-18, Tex. Christian U., 1918-20; m. Erna Williams, June 3, 1937. Gen. ins. bus., 1921-35; v.p., exec. com., dir. Gt. Am. Res. Ins. Co., Dallas, 1935—; exec. v.p., treas. Home Mortgage &Investment Co., Dallas, 1935—; v.p., dir., mem. exec. com. Gt. Am. Fire & Casualty Co., Dallas. Trustee Tex. Christian U., Ft. Worth. Served with U.S. Army, 1918. Mem. Nat., Tex., Dallas assns. life underwriters, Am., Tex. life convs., Dallas Ins. Club. Mason (32 deg., Shriner). Club: Lake Wood Country. Home: 6644 Avalon St Dallas TX 75214 Office: 2020 Live Oak Dallas TX 75221

COMBS, ARTHUR WRIGHT, educator; b. Newark, June 3, 1912; s. Arthur W. and Charlotte (Vyse) C.; B.Sc.Ed., Ohio State U., 1935, M. A., 1941, Ph.D., 1945; m. Mildred Janet Mitchell, Sept. 23, 1934; children—Carol Andrea (Mrs. Jeremy G. Hole), Peter Arthur. Tchr., sch. psychologist pub. schs., Alliance, O., 1935-41; teaching asst. Ohio State U., 1941-43; asst. prof. psychology, head U. Counseling Service, dir. clin. tng. Syracuse U., 1943-54; prof. edn. U. Fla., 1954—, dir. Center for Humanistic Edn., 1972—, chmn. dept. founds. in edn., 1967-69. Cons. pub. schs., colls., industry. Recipient John Dewey award, 1967. Diplomate in clin. psychology, Am. Bd. Examiners in Profl. Psychology. Fellow Am. Psychol. Assn., Soc. Psychol. Study of Social Issues; mem. N.E.A., Assn. for Supervision and Curriculum Devel. (pres. 1967), Fla. Assn. Sch. Psychologists (pres. 1967), Phi Delta Kappa, Sigma Xi. Author: (with D. Snygg) Individual Behavior, 1959; The Professional Education of Teachers, 1965; Florida Studies in the Helping Professions, 1969; (with D. Avila and W. Purkey) Helping Relationships: Basic Concepts for the Helping Professions, 1972, Helping Relationships Sourcebook, 1972. Contbr. profl. jours. Home: 2904 SW 2d Court Gainesville FL 32601

COMBS, BENNETT ALBERT, advt. exec., bus. film producer; b. Oklahoma City, Apr. 1, 1941; s. William Grady and Ina (Shultz) C.; B.A., U. Ark., 1964; postgrad. Columbia, 1964-65; m. Judy Martha Edwards, Nov. 29, 1968; children—(by previous marriage) Kathryn Ann Pryor, Jefferson Pryor. Nat. field rep. Am. Cancer Soc., N.Y.C., 1964-66; promotion dir. KTHV, Little Rock, 1966-67; pub. affairs dir. KATV, Little Rock, 1967-69; pub. relations dir., editor Briggs Assos., Little Rock, 1969; v.p., creative dir. Carroll & Assos., Little Rock, 1970—. Pub. relations bd. Am. Cancer Soc., 1967-68. Mem. Ark. Advt. Fedn. Home: 5 Blue Ridge Circle Little Rock AR 72207 Office: National Old Line Bldg Little Rock AR 72201

COMBS, BERT THOMAS, judge, former mem. Dem. Nat. Com., former gov. Ky.; b. Manchester, Ky., Aug. 13, 1911; s. Stephen Gibson and Martha (Jones) C.; student Cumberland Coll., 1919-31; L.L.B., U. Ky., 1937; m. Mabel Hall, June 15, 1937; children—Lois Ann, Thomas George. Admitted to Ky. bar, 1937; law practice, 1938-41, 46-51; city atty., Prestonsburg, Ky., 1950; commonwealth atty. 31st Jud. Dist. of Ky., 1950-51; judge Ct. Appeals of Ky. 1951-55; gov. Ky., 1959-64; now judge U.S. Ct. of Appeals, Louisville. Former mem. Democratic Nat. Com. Served as capt., judge adv. gen. dept., AUS, 1941-46; assisted in investigation and prosecution Japanese war criminals, P.I., 1945-46. Decorated Bronze Star medal; Medal of Merit (P.I.). Mem. Jr. Bar Assn. Ky. (pres. 1946-47), Am. Bar Assn., Order of Coif, Phi Delta Phi. Home: Prestonsburg KY 41653

COMBS, CLARENCE H., dentist; b. Beattyville, Ky., Mar. 10, 1919; s. Joseph Oscar and Maude M. (Congleton) C.; tchrs. certificate, Eastern Ky. State Coll., 1941; B.S., U. Ky., 1947; D.M.D., U. Louisville, 1951; m. Maxine Land, Feb. 29, 1964; children—Clarence H., Gene Alan, Brian Keith. Gen. practice dentistry, Beattyville, Ky., 1951—; pub. health dentist Lee County Pub. Healty Dept., part-time 1951—. Mem. Lee County Bd. Health, 19——. Scoutmaster Eastern Tng. Sch. br. Richmond (Ky.) council Boy Scouts Am., 1941-42. Served with USNR, 1943-45. Decorated Purple Heart. Mem. Blue Grass Dental Soc. (pres. 1970-71), Am. Legion, Psi Omega. Democrat. Mem. Christian Ch. Kiwanian. Address: Box 387 Beattyville KY 41311

COMBS, HOMER CARROLL, ednl. adminstr.; b. Rosalia, Wash., July 31, 1907; s. Henry Clay and Leanna (Caddell) C.; A.B., Georgetown Coll., 1929; M.A., Northwestern U., 1933, Ph.D., 1939; m. Jean Cozzens, Apr. 1952 (dec. Apr. 1970); 1 son, Paul L. Mem. faculty Northwestern U., 1935-45, Washington U., 1946-52, Kan. State U., 1952-61, Manatee Jr. Coll., 1961-67; mem. faculty Fla. Tech. U., 1968—, asst. dean Coll. Humanities and Fine Arts, 1969—. Episcopalian. Author: A Concordance to the English Poems of John Donne, 1940, A Book of the Essay, 1950. Contbr. articles, poems to profl. pubs. Home: 249 Spartan Dr Maitland FL 32751 Office: PO Box 25000 Orlando FL 32816

COMBS, JERRY WALKER, JR., govt. ofcl.; b. Monticello, Ga., Mar. 7, 1913; s. Jerry Walker and Myrtle (Mobley) C.; B.A., Presbyn. Coll., 1934; M.A., U. Tenn., 1948; Ph.D., Columbia, 1954; m. Eve Decker, Aug. 26, 1944; children—Margaret Browning, Elizabeth Walker. Tchr. pub. schs., Atlanta, 1934-47; asst. prof. sociology Emory U., 1951-53; analytical statistician manpower div. Human Resources Research Inst., Maxwell Field AFB, 1953-56, Air Force Personnel and Tng. Research Center, Lackland AFB, 1956-57; chief European br., fgn. demographic analysis div. U.S. Bur. Census, Washington, 1957-69; chief behavioral scis. br. Center for Population Research, Nat. Inst. Child Health and Human Devel., NIH, Bethesda, Md., 1969—. Mem. planning commn. City of Alexandria, Va., 1963-71; mem. No. Va. Regional Planning and Econ. Devel. Commn., 1964-70. Served to maj. AUS, 1942-46. Fellow Am. Sociol. Assn., A.A.A.S.; mem. Population Assn. Am., Internat. Union for Sci. Study of Population, So. Sociol. Soc., Blue Key, Phi Kappa Phi. Home: 4711 Richmarr Pl Alexandria VA 22304 Office: Center for Population Research NIH Bethesda MD 20014

COMBS, JOSEPH FRANKLIN, author, columnist; b. Center, Tex., Nov. 23, 1892; s. Frank and Annie Mae (Beck) C.; student Tex. A. and M. Coll., 1917; m. Addie Laura Brittain, Sept. 8, 1912; children—Talmage Franklin, Doris Addie Mae (Mrs. Aubrey Bedford), Thomas Buchanan, Jo Ruth (Mrs. Travis Price). Rural sch. tchr. Shelby County, Tex., 1910-17; agrl. agt. Tex. A. and M. Coll. Extension Service, Montgomery County, Tex., 1917-27; county agrl. agt., Beaumont, Tex., 1927-55; farm editor Beaumont Enterprise, 1955-58; farm columnist Beaumont Enterprise, 1958—. Adminstr., New Deal Agrl. Acts, Jefferson County, Tex., 1933-38; operator German Prisoner of War Farm Labor Camp, Jefferson County, 1944-45; pres. Montgomery County Fair, 1923-27. Bd. dirs. Houston Fair and Exposition, 1923. Bd. dirs. Camp Fire Girls. Served with Tex. State Guard, 1941-47; mem. Res. Mem. Am. Mus. Natural History, Nat. Geog. Soc., Tex. Guard Assn., Coastal Cattleman's Assn. (sec. Jefferson County 1934-54), Tex. and Southwestern Cattle Raisers Assn. (dir. Ft. Worth 1948-55), C. of C. Baptist. Mason. Author: Growing Pastures In The South, 1936; Farm Corner, Nature Stories, 1963; Legends of the Pineys, 1965; Gunsmoke in the Redlands, 1968; Kudjo Quatterman, 1972. Discoverer grass species. Home: 5635 Duff Av Beaumont TX 77706

COMBS, KATHRYN FLORENCE REED (MRS EUGENE HURST COMBS), civic worker; b. Logan, W. Va., Dec. 6, 1918; d. John Edward and Lottie (McRae) Reed; student Longwood Coll., 1937-39; B.S., W.Va.U., 1941; m. Eugene Hurst Combs, Oct. 4, 1942. Home economist Ky. Power Co., Hazard, 1941-44; asst. mgr. Grand-vue Drive-in Theatre, Hazard, 1949-57; sec.-treas. Meadowbrook Terrace Inc., Hazard, 1967-68. Mem. adv. council 4H Clubs, 1946-52; pres. Perry Assn. for Retarded Children, 1958-63; chmn. community facilities Perry County Devel. Assn., 1963—; mem. exec. com. Clean-up and Beautification Dept. Natural Resources, 1963—; mem. adv. bd. Appalachian Regional Hosp., Hazard, 1963-68; pres. Perry County Garden Club, 1948-50, 67-69, Ladies Assn. Hazard Golf Club, 1948, Garden Club Ky., Inc., 1963-65, Hazard Urban Homemakers Club, 1968, Woman's Soc. Christian Service, 1970-72; S. Atlantic regional dir. Nat. Council State Garden Clubs, 1965-67; bd. dirs. Perry County A.R.C., 1960-64, Perry County Homemakers, 1968. Recipient Beautification and Conservation Merit award Ky. Dept. Natural Resources, 1964, 65, 66; named Woman of Year, Bus. and Profl. Woman's Club, 1963; Girl of Yr., Beta Sigma Phi, 1969; Ky. Col. Mem. Ky. Conservation Soc., Ky. Ornithol. Soc., Pi Beta Phi, Beta Sigma Phi. Republican. Methodist. Home: Meadowbrook Farm Hazard KY 41701

COMBS, PAT (WILLIAM MALONE), city ofcl.; b. Haskell, Okla., June 4, 1908; s. William Eli and Burla (Malone) C.; student U. Ark., 1925-26; m. Frances Harsha, Sept. 2, 1928; 1 son, Bill; m. 2d, Peggy Avis Dugan, Sept. 28, 1963. Teller, Exchange Nat. Bank Tulsa, 1926-34; salesman P. Lorillard Co., Muskogee, Okla., 1934-37; utility clk. Nat. Bank Tulsa, 1937-41; flight instr. Tulsa Aviation, 1941-44; owner, operator Skymerchants Flying Service, Tulsa, 1945-54; contract pilot Union Oil Co. Cal., Tulsa, 1950-55; mgr. airports Tulsa Airport Authority, 1955—. Mgr., Tulsa Municipal Airport Trust, 1967-71, Tulsa Airports Improvement Trust, 1967-71. Bd. dirs. Travelers Aid Soc. Tulsa. Served with USAAF, 1944-45. Mem. Airport Operators Council Internat. (dir. 1962-67, pres. 1965-66), Quiet Birdmen, Sigma Phi Epsilon. Mason. Home: 2815 N Sheridan Rd Tulsa OK 74151 Office: Box 51286 Terminal Bldg Tulsa Internat Airport Tulsa OK 74151

COMBS, PAUL NAPIER, charitable soc. exec.; b. Hazard, Ky., Jan. 5, 1919; s. Emanuel and Mollie (Napier) C.; student Hazard Jr. C. Coll., 1936-37, Georgetown Coll., 1939-40; A.B., U. Ky., 1947; m. Lottie Louise Herald, Apr. 8, 1951; children—Nancy, Rebecca. Writer, Ky. Hwy. Dept., Frankfort, 1947; promotion mgr., news dir. Radio Station WKIC, Hazard, 1948-49; news editor Hazard Herald, 1949; dep. commr. Dept. Indsl. Relations, Commonwealth of Ky., 1950-53, acting commr., 1953-55, deputy commr., 1955-56; field rep. Ky. Soc. for Crippled Children, Louisville, 1956-57, pub. relations dir., 1957—. Mem. Ky. Ho. of Reps., 1950. Served with Armed Forces, 1942-45. Mem. Pub. Relations Soc. Am., Ky. Press Assn., Nat. Easter Seal Exec. Assn., Combs Family Assn. (dir. 1963—), U. Ky. Alumni Assn., Advt. Club of Louisville. Democrat. Presbyn. Mason. Home: 9510 Aylesbury Dr Louisville KY 40222 Office: 233 E Broadway Louisville KY 40202

COMBS, ROBERT HEARIN, utilities exec.; b. El Dorado, Ark., Feb. 11, 1923; s. John Hearin and Estelle (Hammons) C.; student U. Ark., 1940-43, 47, U. Okla., 1958, Okla. State U., 1959, U. Tex., 1961; m. Toni Louise Rogers, June 12, 1945; children—Gary L., William Bryce. Sales mgr. Ark.-La. Gas Co., 1947-56; dist. sales mgr. Okla. Natural Gas Co., Tulsa, 1956-63; dir. sales, promotion Am. Gas Assn., N.Y.C., 1963-65; v.p. marketing Western Ky. Gas Co., Owensboro, 1965—. Pres., Audobon council Boy Scouts Am., 1969-71. Bd. dirs., trustee Ky. Ind. Coll. Fund.; bd. dirs. Owensboro United Fund. Served to maj. USAF, 1943-47, 51-52. Recipient Gas Industries Hall of Flame award, 1959, Silver Beaver award Boy Scouts Am., 1971; named Boss of Year, Am. Bus. Womens Assn., 1968. Mem. Tulsa Exec. Assn. (past pres.), Am., So. (sect. chmn.), Ky. (past pres.) gas assns., Sales and Marketing Exec. Internat., Tulsa (life), Ky., Owensboro chambers commerce. Baptist. Mason (32 deg., Shriner), Rotarian, Kiwanian (past pres.). Home: 2169 N Stratford Dr Owensboro KY 42301 Office: 311 W 7th St Owensboro KY 42301

COMBS, ROBERT LEE, JR., dentist; b. Seguin, Tex., July 5, 1906; s. Robert Lee and Matilda Brahan (Jefferson) C.; D.D.S., U. Tex., 1929; m. Alice Morrell, Mar. 18, 1958; children by previous marriage—Betty Lee (Mrs. Lloyd deLatour), Robert Lee III, John Laurin, Henrietta (Mrs. William Hughes), Michael Thomas. Practice dentistry, Seguin, 1929-42; commd. lt. USN, 1942, advanced through grades to capt., 1955; sr. dental officer Submarine Tender USS Griffin, World War II, Destroyer Tender USS Prairie, Korea, Taiwan, 1963-65; ret., 1967. Naval rep., dir. Pensacola Art Center, 1958-60. Mem. Am. Dental Assn., Tex. Dental Soc., First Families Va., S.A.R., Psi Omega. Episcopalian. Elk. Clubs: Pensacola Country, Pensacola Yacht; Golden Isles Sportfishing (Brunswick, Ga.). Home: 234 S Coconut Lane Palm Island Miami Beach FL 33139

COMER, DONALD, JR., textile mill exec.; b. Birmingham, Ala., May 18, 1913; s. Donald and Gertrude (Miller) C.; grad. U. N.C.; m. Isabel Anderson, Oct. 29, 1936; children—Donald, Isabel Anderson. With Avondale Textile Mills, Sylacauga, Ala., 1932—, exec. v.p. textiles, 1954-70, pres., treas., 1970—, also mem. exec. com., dir.; with Cowikee Mills, Eufaula, Ala., 1943—, pres., treas., 1956-67, chmn. bd., 1967—; dir. First Nat. Bank Birmingham, First Fed. Savs. and Loan Assn., Sylacauga, Home Fed. Savs. & Loan, Birmingham, Am. Mut. Liability Ins. Co., Boston; mem. adv. bd. Chem. Bank N.Y. Trust Co. Bd. dirs. Ala. Aero. Bd.; trustee So. Research Inst., Birmingham, Birmingham Symphony Assn.; pres. bd. trustees Choccolocco council Boy Scouts Am.; bd. govs. Ala. Assn. Independent Colls. and Univs.; trustee Cowikee Edn. and Charitable Found., Avondale Ednl. and Charitable Found. Mem. Am. Textile Mfrs. Inst. (v.p., bd. dirs.), Nat. Assn. Mfrs. (bd. dirs.), So. Indsl. Relations Conf. (bd. dirs.), Asso. Industries Ala. (bd. dirs.), Ala. Textile Mfrs. Assn., Newcomen Soc., Phi Psi. Clubs: Birmingham Country, Downtown, Mountain Brook Country Relay, the Club (Birmingham); Coosa Valley Country (Sylacauga, Ala.); Union League, Weavers (N.Y.C.). Home: Comer Hill Sylacauga AL 35150 Office: Avondale Av Sylacauga AL 35150

COMISKEY, JAMES AUGUST, U.S. dist. judge; b. New Orleans, Oct. 16, 1926; s. James Edward and Laura (Arceneaux) C.; B.A., Loyola U., New Orleans, 1948, LL.B., 1951; m. Blanche Catherine Mouledoux, Aug. 20, 1952; children—Margaret, Marian, James, Laura, Michelle, Jeanne, Eileen, Paula, Louise, Elizabeth, Catherine. Admitted to La. bar, 1951; partner firm Comiskey & Schaff, New Orleans, 1951-67; U.S. judge Eastern Dist. La. 1967—. Past dir. Bank of La., Bank of South, Fidelity Bank and Trust Co. Councilman-at-large, New Orleans, also pres. council, 1961-62; del. La. Dem. nat. convs., 1956, 60, 64; candidate for mayor New Orleans, 1962. Past mem. men's adv. bd. Sara Mayo Hosp.; bd. dirs. New Orleans Floral Trail, Greater New Orleans Police Found.; adv. dir. Vols. Am. Served with inf. AUS, 1944-46. Mem. Am., La., New Orleans, Fed., Criminal Cts. bar assns., St. Thomas More Catholic Lawyers Assn. K.C. Home: 1100 City Park Av New Orleans LA 70119 Office: 400 Royal St New Orleans LA 70130

COMM, EDWARD DANIEL, mgmt. and civil engring. cons.; b. Fargo, N.D., Jan. 10, 1912; s. Otto Ben and Emily (Riebhoff) C.; B.S., N.D. State U., 1933; grad. U.S. Army War Coll., 1953. Practice civil engring., N.D., 1933-40; commd. 1st lt. C.E., U.S. Army, 1940, advanced through grades to col., 1944, ret., 1967; served N. Africa, Italy, France, Germany, 1942-45; exec. asst. to Q.M. Gen. and dir. logistics, Washington, 1946-52; asst. chief of staff logistics, France, 1953-56; engr. U.S. Army Engr. Dist., Louisville, 1956-58; mem. Joint Chiefs Staff, Washington, 1958-60; comdg. officer Advanced Individual Tng. Regiment, Ft. Leonard Wood, Mo., 1960-62; spl. asst. to dep. chief staff for logistics Dept. Army, Washington, 1962-67; cons. to Dept. Def., Washington, 1967-69. Mem. directorate Presdl. Task Force on Structure SSS, 1967. Decorated D.S.M., Legion of Merit with two oak leaf clusters, Bronze Star, Army Commendation medal, officer Order Brit. Empire; Legion of Honor, Croix de Guerre (France) comdr. Crown of Italy Medahla de Guerra (Brazil). Fellow Am. Soc. C.E.; mem. Soc. Am. Mil Engrs., Amateur Trapshooting Assn., Phi Kappa Phi, Tau Beta Pi. Clubs: Army and Navy (Washington); Army-Navy Country (Arlington, Va.). Address: 1111 Army Navy Dr Arlington VA 22202

COMOLA, JAMES PAUL, water resource devel. cons.; b. Leland, Miss., Nov. 16, 1931; s. Wilson and Freda (Saba) C.; student Hinds Jr. Coll., 1950; B.A., Millsaps Coll., 1957; profl. social worker Fla. State U., 1958; postgrad. U. Miss., 1959-62; m. Mary Jacqueline Petermann, May 27, 1956; children—James Paul, Jon Ronald. Asst. buyer Kennington's, 1954-57; dir. Miss. Dept. Pub. Welfare, Yazoo County, 1957-59; tech. liasion Commn. Small Watersheds, U.S. Ho. of Reps., 1959-60; exec. v.p. Miss. Rivers and Harbors Assn., 1960-62; asst. gen. mgr. Trinity Improvement Assn., Arlington, Tex., 1962-66, gen. mgr., 1967-70; cons., 1970—. Mem. Bedford City Council, Tex., 1963-65, chmn. mid-cities adv. council, 1963-66. Served with USNR, 1950-54. Recipient award Rivers and Harbors Assn. Miss., 1962; Appreciation award Bedford Council Good Govt., Bedford, 1966. Mem. Miss. Valley Assn. (dir.), Tex. Water Conservation Assn., Nat. Rivers and Harbors Congress (dir.), Nat. Waterways Conf., Water Resources Asso., Internat. Navigational Congress, Gulf Intracoastal Canal Assn. Lion (dir. Bedford). Editor Trinity Valley Progress, 1963-67. Contbr. articles to profl. jours. Home and office: 1301 Cliffwood Rd Euless TX 76039

COMPTON, CLEON, govt. ofcl.; b. Weches, Tex., Sept. 3, 1934; s. Thad Lee and Monnie Levica (Boykin) C.; student Massey Bus. Coll., 1958-60, North Tex. State U., Tex. A. and M. Coll.; m. Anna F. Saxton, June 25, 1956; children—Brenda, Karlene, Dempsey, Mike. Treas., tax assessor City of Nacogdoches, Tex., 1960-63, sec.-treas., 1960-68, adminstrv. asst., sec.-treas., 1968—. Del. county and state Democratic Conv., 1965. Served with USNR, 1953-57. Decorated UN medal; named Outstanding Jaycee, 1964; awarded senatorship in Jr. C. of C. Internat., 1971, life time fellow, 1971. Mem. Nacogdoches Jaycees (sec.-treas. 1963, dir. 1964, pres. 1965). Home: 1320 Virginia St Nacogdoches TX 75961 Office: PO Box 1301 Nacogdoches TX 75961

COMPTON, RAYMOND J., govt. ofcl. Regional dir. Nat. Labor Relations Bd., Hato Rey, P.R. Office: 255 Ponce De Leon Av Hato Rey PR 00919*

COMPTON, ROBERT CURRAN, lawyer; b. El Dorado, Ark., Mar. 27, 1929; s. Thomas J. and Virginia (Knox) C.; B.A., Hendrix Coll., Conway, Ark., 1949; LL.B., U. Ark., 1952; m. Margaret Tyler Villee, Apr. 7, 1951; children—Robert Curran, Cathleen Villee, Walter Knox. Served with FBI, Washington and Pitts., 1952-54; admitted to Ark. bar, 1952; practiced in El Dorado, 1954—; partner Brown, Compton & Prewett and predecessors, 1957—. Chmn., Cancer Drive, 1956. Candidate for Gov. Ark., 1970. Bd. dirs. Salvation Army. Mem. Am., Ark. (mem. exec. com.), Union County (past pres.) bar assns., El Dorado C. of C., Trial Lawyers Assn., Blue Key, Kappa Sigma.

Democrat. Presbyn. (trustee). Mason (Shriner). Rotarian. Club: El Dorado Golf and Country (past pres.). Home: 2504 Forestlawn Dr El Dorado AR 71730 Office: 423 N Washington St El Dorado AR 71730

COMPTON, SUSAN LANELL, librarian; b. Batesville, Ark., Aug. 20, 1917; d. Thomas Smith and Susan (Whitlow) Compton; B.S. in Edn., Ark. State Tchrs. Coll., 1939; B.S. in L.S., Peabody Coll. Tchrs., 1948. Asst. cataloger U. Ark. Gen. Library, Fayetteville, 1948-49; head catalog dept. Ark. Library Commn., Little Rock, 1949—. Free lance writer. Mem. Nat. League Am. Pen Women, Ark. Choral Soc., Am. Assn. U. Women, Ark. Hist. Assn., Ark. Fedn. Women's Clubs. Christadelphian. Author: Beauty Transient & Other Poems, 1969. Contbr. to Collier's Ency., 1971. Home: 4911 Lee Av Little Rock AR 72205 Office: 506 1/2 Center St Little Rock AR 72201

CONAGHAN, BRIAN FRANCIS, state legislator; b. Tonkawa, Okla., Feb. 8, 1927; s. Billy Frank and Letha (Siler) C.; grad. No. Okla. Jr. Coll., 1948; B.S. in History, U. Okla., 1951; m. Dorothy Dell Miller, June 10, 1951; children—Joseph Lee, Charles Alan, Roger Lloyd. Owner, Contractors' Bit Service, Tonkawa, 1956—; mem. Okla. Ho. of Reps., 1963—. Active No. Okla. Jr. Coll. Alumni Trust Fund. Pres., Kay County Young Republicans, 1957. Served with AUS, 1944-47. Mem. Am. Legion, Tonkawa C. of C., Acacia, Oklahoma Ct. Chevaliers. Republican. Baptist. Mason (32 deg.); mem. Order Eastern Star, Order DeMolay; Elk. Home: 904 E Grand St Tonkawa OK 74653 Office: Box 402 Tonkawa OK 74653

CONANT, RALPH WENDELL, educator; b. Hope, Me., Sept. 7, 1926; s. Earle Raymond and Margaret (Long) C.; B.A., U. Vt., 1949; M.A., U. Chgo., 1954; Ph.D., 1959; m. F. Audrey Karl, Aug. 27, 1950; children— Beverlie Elaine, Lisa Audrey, Jonathan Arnold. Instr. dept. polit. sci. Mich. State U., 1956-57; staff asso. Nat. Municipal League, N.Y.C., 1957-59; dir. civic affairs research Muskegon, Mich., 1959; exec. dir. Citizens for Mich., Detroit, 1959-60; asst. prof. U. Denver, 1960-62; asst. to dir. Joint Center for Urban Studies, Mass. Inst. Tech., and Harvard U., 1962-66; asso. dir. Lemberg Center for Study of Violence, Brandeis U., Waltham, Mass., asso. prof. dept. politics, 1967-70; prof. urban studies Rice U., Houston, 1970—; dir. Inst. Urban Studies, U. Houston, 1970—; pres. S.W. Center for Urban Research, Houston, 1970—; lectr. Boston Coll. Sch. Social Work, 1963; dir. Intergovtl. Relations Project New Eng. Econ. Research Found., 1966; cons., dir. Conn. Legislative Commn. on Met. Govt., 1966-67. Mem. Democratic Town Com., Weston, Mass. Served with USAAF, 1944-45, AUS, 1951-53. Unitarian-Universalist Ch. (dir. service com. 1967—, chmn. prudential com. 1967—. Author: The Public Library and the City, 1965; The Politics of Community Health, 1968; The Prospects for Revolution, 1971. Home: 11841 Bayhurst Dr Houston TX 77024

CONCEPCION, CARLOS VICTOR, dentist; b. Santa Clara, Cuba, July 28, 1933; s. Jose M. De La and Maria Zoila (Garcia) C.; B.S., Instituto de Santa Clara, 1951; D.D.S., U. Havana, 1956; D.M.D., U. Pitts., 1967; postgrad. U. Miami, 1965; m. Teresita Machado Concepcion, Sept. 8, 1956; children—Carlos Francisco, Jorge Luis, Eduardo Gerardo. Came to U.S., 1962, naturalized, 1968. Dental student Municipal Pub. Health, Cuba, 1955-56; oral surgeon Santa Clara Clinic, 1956-62; dentist, oral surgeon Marta Abreu Central Clinic, 1956-62; pvt. practice dentistry, 1956-62; dental officer Avon Park Correctional Institution, Fla. Div. of Correction, 1967-68; pvt. practice dentistry, Miami, Fla., 1968—. Tech. instr. crown and bridge U. Havana, 1955-56. Mem. Cuban, Santa Clara, Am., Fla. dental assns., Cuban Soc. Dentistry for Children, Pan Am. Council Dentistry for Children, Pa. Acad. Gen. Dentistry, Cuban Dental Assn. in Exile, East Coast Dist. Dental Soc., Miami Dental Soc. Cuban Soc. Orthodontics, Cuban Soc. Oral Surgeons, Delta Sigma Delta. Episcopalian (sr. warden 1969—). Rotarian. Clubs: American (Miami), Miami Tennis. Home: 14401 Cedar Ct Miami Lakes FL 33014 Office: 705 Huntington Bldg 168 S E 1st St Miami FL 33131

CONDOM, JAIME ERNESTO, hosp. adminstr., physician; b. Mariel, Cuba, Feb. 27, 1932; s. Jaime Simeon and Maria Matilde (Valera) C.; B.S., U. Havana, 1957; M.D., U. Madrid, 1962; m. Mirtha Esther Sanchez, Nov. 30, 1952; 1 dau., Marie Elizabeth. Came to U.S., 1960, naturalized, 1966. Intern, Mobile Gen. Hosp., 1962-63; staff physician Searcy State Hosp., Mt. Vernon, Ala., 1963-68, acting clin. dir., 1968-69, clin. dir., 1969-70, acting supt., clin. dir., 1970, supt., 1970—. Mem. Assn. Med. Supts. Mental Hosps., Med. Assn. State Ala., Mobile County Med. Soc., Gulf Coast Soc. Neurology, Psychiatry, Neurosurgery and Psychology. Address: Searcy Hosp PO Box 23 Mount Vernon AL 36560

CONDON, JOHN EARL, govt. ofcl., engr.; b. Mt. Vernon, O., Apr. 17, 1928; s. John Robert and Alice (Wysner) C.; B.S., U. Dayton, 1951; M.S., Ohio State U., 1956; D.S., George Washington U., 1967; m. Dolores Rose Peterson, Nov.8, 1952; children—Susan Eileen, John Patrick, Margaret Ellen, Mary Lynn, Michael Robert. Statistician USAF Air Material Command, Wright-Patterson AFB, O., 1953-55, 57-59; operations research analyst Ohio State U., 1956; sr. research specialist Nat. Cash Register Co., Dayton, O., 1960-61; asst. chief quality control USAF Logistics Command, Wright-Patterson AFB, 1961-62; dir. reliability and quality assurance NASA, Washington, 1962—; vis. lectr. U. Dayton, 1968, George Washington U., 1966-67; vis. gen. chmn. Symposium Reliability, 1970. Served with USMC, 1951-53. Fellow Am. Soc. Quality Control; mem. Internat. Assn. Statistics. Home: 4906 Bristow Dr Annandale VA 22003 Office: 600 Independence Av SW Washington DC 20546

CONDON, LESTER P(ATRICK), corp. exec.; b. Mt. Vernon, N.Y., Oct. 13, 1922; s. Lester P. and Eileen V. (Malone) C.; B.S., Providence Coll., 1943; student Georgetown Law Sch., 1947-51; m. Vera Crossley, Apr. 21, 1946; children—Thomas J., John K., Leslie Patricia, Marietta, Lisa Ann. Spl. agt. FBI, 1947-51; asst. chief security OPS, 1951-53; dir. investigation U.S. Ho. of Reps. Com. on Govt. Operations, 1953-54; spl. asst. to adminstr. HHFA, 1954-55, dir. compliance div., 1955-60; dep. commr. FHA, 1960-61, asst. commr. audit and exam. FHA, 1961-62; insp. gen. U.S. Dept Agr., 1962-69; asst. sec. for adminstrn. Dept. Housing and Urban Devel., Washington, 1969-72; exec. v.p., dir. Fed. Nat. Mortgage Assn., Washington, 1972—. Sec., treas., dir. Nat. Center for Housing Mgmt. Served to lt. (j.g.) USNR, World War II. Decorated Purple Heart. Recipient Distinguished Service awards HHFA, also Dept. Housing and Urban Devel.; Personal Achievement award Providence Coll. Alumni Assn., 1972. Mem. Soc. Former Spl. Agts. FBI, Inst. Internal Auditors, Phi Delta Phi. Roman Catholic. Club: Springfield Golf and Country. Home: 1306 Janneys Lane Alexandria VA 22302 Office: Federal National Mortgage Assn 1133 15th St NW Washington DC 20005

CONDON, RICHARD BERNARD, ins. co. exec., state ofcl.; b. Omaha, Sept. 23, 1914; s. Roy Bernard and Mary Josephine (Sheehy) C.; grad. Creighton U., 1932-36; m. Nadine Evelyn Wrabetz, May 15, 1937; children— Linda (Mrs. Glen Donaldson), Kathi (Mrs. Michael Wade), Michele, Judith (Mrs. John Dostal), Mary N., Richard Bernard. With Mut. of Omaha Ins. Co., Omaha, 1936-44, asso. mgr. Ky. agy., 1944-50, gen. agt., 1950—; pres., gen. agt. R.B. Condon Agys., Inc., Louisville, 1950—. Chmn. bd. Ky. Bd. Edn., 1969—; pres. Ky. Derby Festival Com., 1963, chmn. bd., 1964-65; bd. overseers Bellarmine-Ursuline Colls., 1959-69; trustee Louisville Free Pub. Library, 1963-71. Roman Catholic. Clubs: Pendennis, Big Springs Country (Louisville); Delray Beach (Fla.). Home: 503 Altagate Rd Louisville KY 40206 Office: 1126 Commonwealth Bldg Louisville KY 40202

CONE, CEASER, textile mfr.; b. N.Y.C., Jan. 30, 1908; s. Ceaser and Jeanette (Siegel) C.; A.B., U. N.C., 1928; M.B.A., Harvard, 1930; m. Martha Abercrombie, Nov. 19, 1938; children—Ceaser III, Martha, Lawrence. With Cone Mills Corp., 1930—, treas., dir., 1945-56, pres., dir., 1956-65, chmn. bd., 1965—, now bd. dirs. Pres. Greensboro United Fund, 1965, Moses H. Cone Meml. Hosp., 1971—; pres., bd. dirs. N.C. United Community Services, 1970. Mem. Am. Textile Mfrs. Inst. (dir. 1956-59, 61-64, 70—), Greensboro C. of C. (pres. 1955). Rotarian. Home: 506 Cornwallis Dr Greensboro NC 27408 Office: Cone Mills Corp Greensboro NC 27405

CONE, WICE EARL, state ofcl.; b. Montgomery, Ala., Feb. 8, 1925; s. Wice C. and Florence Inez (Farmer) C.; C.E., Internat. Corr. Schs., 1966; m. Hazel Padgett, Jan. 17, 1948; children—Carolyn Hazel, Nancy Ann. With Ala. Conservation Dept., 1946-48; with Ala. Hwy. Dept., 1948—, asst. secondary road engr., Montgomery, 1963—. Served with USNR, 1943-46. Mem. Nat. Soc. Profl. Engrs., Ala. Soc. Profl. Land Surveyors (charter). Home: Route 1 Box 264 A Montgomery AL 36105 Office: Ala Hwy Dept 11 Union St Montgomery AL 36104

CONGER, CLEMENT ELLIS, fgn. service officer; b. Rockingham, Va., Oct. 15, 1912; s. Clement E. and Hallie (Ramsay) C.; grad. Strayer Coll., 1932; student George Washington U., 1933-34; grad Adj. Gen. Officer Candidate Sch., Ft. Washington, Md., 1943; m. Lianne Hopkins, May 29, 1948; children—William Ramsay, Jay Alden, Shelley Louise. Asst. finance examiner PWA, 1933-34; officer mgr., corr. Chgo. Tribune, Washington, 1934-41; office mgr. U.S. Rubber Co., Washington, 1941-42, pub. relations asst., N.Y.C., 1946-47; staff asst., asst. exec. dir. asst. sec. state for occupied areas Dept. State, 1947-49, staff asst., asst. exec. dir. Bur. German Affairs, 1949-54; asst. chief protocol, 1955-57, dep. chief protocol, 1958-61; spl. asst. to dir. and exec. sec. U.S. Arms Control and Disarmament Agy., Dept. State, Washington. 1962-69: dep. chief protocol, 1969-70; protocol asst. to chmn. Nixon-Agnew Inaugural, 1968-69; chmn. fine arts com. Dept. State, 1961—; White House curator, 1970—; White House alternate rep. Pres.'s Adv. Council Hist. Preservation Producer color motion picture travel films, lectr. U.S. Trustee Mus. Fine Arts, Richmond, Va., Lee-Jackson Found., U.S. Capitol Hist. Assn.;v.p., mem. bd. Historic Alexandria Found.; chmn. Alexandria (Va.) Hist. Restoration and Preservation Commn., 1968—; mem. Gov.'s Mansion Com., Richmond, Va.; mem. Adv. Hist. Com. on Supreme Ct.; mem. Americana Com. for Nat. Archives. Served from 2d lt. to maj. AUS, 1942-46; asst. sec. combined civil affairs com. Combined Chiefs staff. Episcopalian. Clubs: Metropolitan, Chevy Chase, City Tavern (Washington). Contbr. articles, illustration to various publs. Home: 320 Mansion Dr Alexandria VA 22302 Office: The White House Washington DC 20500 also Dept of State Washington DC 20520

CONGER, GEORGE D(REW), physician, surgeon; b. Tifton, Ga., Oct. 25, 1897; s. Ero and Missouri (Roberts) C.; student Abraham Baldwin Coll., 1912-16, U. Ga., 1916-20, Emory U., 1920-22; M.D., U. Tenn., 1925; m. Annie Laurie Thomas, Dec. 22, 1920; children—Helen (Mrs. Dayton), Anne (Mrs. Cooper), George D., Mary (Mrs. Johnson), Laurie (Mrs. Cauthen), Martha P. (Mrs. Hotham), Merle (Mrs. Ekberg), and Thomas. Intern, Oakville Meml. Hosp., 1925-26; private practice, Miami, Florida, 1926—; founder, pres. Conger Life Ins. Co., 1945—; chmn., capital Nat. Bank of Miami (Fla.). Served in World War I. Mem. A.M.A., So. Med. Assn., Fla., Dade County med. socs., Miami Underwriters Assn., Allapattah Businessmen's Assn. Baptist. Mason (Shriner), K.P. (grand chancellor Domain of Fla. 1957-58), Woodman, Eastern Star. Clubs: Miami Acacia, Exchange. Home: 1051 NW 18th Av Miami FL 33125 Office: 5050 Biscayne Blvd Miami FL 33142

CONGER, STEPHEN HALSEY, lumber co. exec.; b. Asheville, N.C., July 14, 1927; s. Allen Ford and Margery (Evans) C.; B.S., U. Ga., 1949; m. Marian Lansdell Meiere, June 29, 1951; children—Susan deCamp, Stephen Halsey, Robert Cody Lansdell, Marian Lansdell Meiere. Forester, Coastal Lumber Co., Lake City, S.C., 1950-51; asst. sales mgr. Commonwealth Lumber Co., Murphy, N.C., 1951-52; sales Ga. Pacific Corp., Augusta, 1952-54; pres. Coastal Sales Co., Weldon, N.C., 1954-68, Pioneer Lumber Corp., Dailey, W.Va., 1961-70; exec. v.p. Coastal Lumber Co., Weldon N.C., 1969—; dir. Dubarco Lumber Co., Havana, Fla. Caro-Craft, Inc., Sharpsburg, N.C. Chmn. Halifax County Republican Party, 1960-65; mem. exec. com. N.C. Rep. Party, 1963-65; treas. American Party, N.C., 1969-71, mem. exec. com. of central com., 1969-71, mem. nat. com., 1969-71. Served with C.E., AUS, 1945-46. mem. Soc. Am. Foresters, Nat Forest Products Assn., (dir.), So Cypress Mfrs. Assn. (v.p., treas.), S.A.R., Holland Soc. N.Y., Sigma Alpha Epsilon. Baptist. Club: Chockoyotte Country. Office: Box 231 Weldon NC 27890

CONGER, THOMAS DECKMAN, architect; b. Dallas, Aug. 7, 1927; s. Thomas Doris and Margaret Bell (Deckman) C.; B.Arch., U. Tex., 1953; m. Pauline Djerf, July 29, 1950; children—Natalie, Norman, Nathan. With archtl. firm Bennett & Crittenden, Dallas, 1953-55, Tatum & Quade, Dallas, 1955-58; with 8th Naval Dist., New Orleans, 1958-59; with Bur. Yards & Docks, Washington, 1959-61; with NASA, Langley Field, and Houston, Tex., 1961—. Mem. A.I.A., Tex. Soc. Architects, Constrn. Specifications Inst., U. Tex. Alumni Assn., Phi Kappa Tau. Club: Officers (Ellington AFB). Home: 322 Ravenhead St Houston TX 77034 Office: Engineering Division Manned Spacecraft Center Nat Aeros and Space Adminstrn Houston TX 77034

CONIGLIO, JOHN GIGLIO, educator; b. Tampa, Fla., July 21, 1919; s. Giuseppe and Maria (Giglio) C.; B.S., Furman U., 1940; Ph.D., Vanderbilt U., 1949; m. Carmen Moreno, Dec. 27, 1942; children—John William, Robert Freeman, David Martin. Tchr. Kershaw (S.C.) High Sch., 1940-41; supr. Ala. Ordnance Works, Childersburg, 1942, chemist, 1943; chemist, supr. Tenn. Eastman Corp., Oak Ridge, Tenn., 1944-45; asst. prof. Vanderbilt U., Nashville, 1952-55, asso. prof., 1955-61, prof. dept. biochemistry, 1961—. Mem. Am. Soc. Biol. Chemists, Am. Oil Chemists Soc., Am. Inst. Nutrition, Sigma Xi. Contbr. articles in field to sci jours. Home: 202 Lauderdale Rd Nashville TN 37205

CONN, FREDERICK JAMES, JR., pub. co. exec.; b. Lynchburg, Va., Feb. 20, 1908; s. Charles Richard and Bessie E. (Stemple) C.; B.A., U. Ky., 1929; m. Blanche Montgomery, Jan. 31, 1936; children—Frederick James III, Cathy. Advt. salesman Sherman (Tex.) Democrat, 1926-36; advt. mgr. Marshall (Tex.) News Messenger, 1936-40; v.p. Denison (Tex.) Herald, 1940-44, publisher, 1944-64; publisher San Angelo (Tex.) Standard Times, 1964—. Mem. Presdl. Adv. Bd. Water Pollution Control, 1972—. Head restoration com. Eisenhower Birthplace, Denison, 1952-62; pres. Denison Camp Fire Girls, 1957; chmn. indsl. devel. coms., Denison, 1946-60, San Angelo, 1965, 68; v.p. Denison Library, 1945-64; chmn. Miss. Wool of Am. Pageant, San Angelo, 1965; chmn. Denison Meml. Hosp. 1960-64; chmn. Houston Harte Found., Angelo State U., 1971; mem. Upper Colorado River Authority Bd., 1966—; pres. San Angelo Entertainment Assn., 1969. Named Most Valuable Citizen, San Angelo C. of C., 1970. Mem. Sigma Delta Chi. Rotarian (pres. 1955). Clubs: San Angelo Tex Country, River. Home: 1525 Paseo de Vaco San Angelo TX 76901 Office: 28 W Harris St San Angelo TX 76901

CONNALLY, BEN C., judge; b. Marlin, Tex., Dec. 28, 1909; s. Tom and Louise (Clarkson) C.; A.B., U. Tex., 1930 LL.B., 1933; LL.M., Harvard, 1934; m. Sarah Nell Allen, Sept. 27, 1937; children—Tom, Louise. Admitted to bar, Tex., 1933; practiced as mem. firm Sewell, Taylor, Morris & Connally, Houston, 1934-42, Butler & Binion, 1945-49; U.S. dist. judge So. Dist. of Tex., 1949—, now chief judge. Served with AUS, 1942-45. Mem. Am., Houston bar assns., State Bar Tex., Am. Legion, Houston C. of C. Democrat. Methodist. Home: 244 Hedwig Rd Houston TX 77057 Office: Post Office Bldg Houston TX

CONNALLY, JOHN BOWDEN, past sec. treasury; b. Floresville, Tex., Feb. 27, 1917; s. John Bowden and Lela (Wright) C.; LL.B., U. Tex.; m. Idanell Brill, Dec. 21, 1940; children—John Bowden III, Sharon (Mrs. Robert Ammann), Mark. Admitted to Tex. bar, 1938; pres., gen. mgr. radio sta. KVET, Austin, Tex., 1946-49; adminstrv. asst. to Senator Lyndon B. Johnson, 1949; mem. firm Powell, Wirtz & Rauhut, Austin, 1949-52; atty. for Sid. W. Richardson & Perry R. Bass, ind. oil operators, Ft. Worth, 1952-61; sec. of the navy, 1961; gov. of Tex., 1963-69; partner Vinson, Elkins, Searls & Connally, Houston, 1969-71; sec. treasury, 1970-72. Recipient Distinguished Alumnus award U. Tex. Ex-Student Assn., 1961. Democrat.

CONNAR, RICHARD GRIGSBY, surgeon; b. Zanesville, O., Jan. 11, 1920; s. Virgil Norwood and Anna Margaret (Grigsby) C.; B.A., Duke, 1941, M.D., 1944; m. Elizabeth Dickens, May 18, 1946; children—Cathleen, Elizabeth Ann, Richard Grigsby. Intern, Duke Hosp., Durham, 1944-45, resident in internal medicine, 1945-46, resident in gen. and thoracic surgery Duke U. Sch. Medicine, 1948-53, asst. prof. surgery, 1953-55; practice medicine specializing in thoracic and cardiovascular surgery, Tampa, 1955—; cons. throacic and cardiovascular surgery Fla. Crippled Children's Commn., MacDill AFB Hosp., S.W. Fla. Tb Sanitarium; chmn. med. adv. bd. Hillsborough County Hosp. and Welfare Bd., 1962-64; mem. Fla. Tb Bd., 1964—. Bd. dirs. Fla. (award 1967), Hillsborough County (award 1960) heart assns., U.S. Fla. Found.; chmn. Duke U. Nat. Council, 1970-71. Served as capt. with USAAF, 1946-48. Fellow A.C.S. (bd. govs. 1970—, pres. Fla. chpt. 1967—); mem. A.M.A. Cho. of dels. 1971—), Fla., Hillsborough County (pres. 1970-71) med. assns., So. Surg. Assn., Am. Assn. Thoracic Surgery, So. Thoracic Surg. Assn., Fla. Thoracic Soc. (pres. 1971-72), Soc. Thoracic Surgeons, Duke U. Alumni Assn. (v.p. 1971-72), Phi Beta Kappa, Alpha Omega Alpha. Clubs: University, Tampa Yacht and Country; Ye Mystic Krewe of Gosparilla; Palma Ceia Golf and Country. Contbr. articles in field to profl. jours. Home: 3305 Jean Circle Tampa FL 33609 Office: 1 Davis Blvd Tampa FL 33606

CONNELL, EDWARD PEACOCK, lawyer; b. Memphis, Apr. 8, 1936; s. Charles Willis and Georgia (Peacock) C.; student Tulane U., 1954-55; B.B.A., U. Miss. 1958; LL.B., 1961; postgrad. N.Y.U., 1962; m. Eva B., Nov. 23, 1968. Admitted to Miss. bar, 1961; since practiced in Clarksdale; mem. Holcomb, Connell & Fleming, and predecessor firm, 1961—; municipal judge, Clarksdale, 1961-68; adj. prof. law U. Miss., 1963—. Mem. Miss. Jr. Bar (pres. 1966-67), Am., Miss (2d v.p. 1967-68) bar assns., Young Lawyers Conf. (exec. council 1966-68). Rotarian (pres. 1967-68). Home: 111 Cypress Av Clarksdale MS 38614 Office: 152 Delta Av Clarksdale MS 38614

CONNELL, WESSIE GERTRUDE, librarian; b. Cairo, Ga., 1915; d. John H. and Gertrude (Pearce) Connell; grad. high sch. Librarian, dir. Cairo (Ga.) Pub. Library, 1939-64; librarian, dir. Roddenbery Meml. Library, Cairo, 1964—. Pres. Wesleyan Service Guild Meth. Ch., 1960-61; co-organizer County Hist. Soc., Book Clubs and social groups. Recipient John Cotton Dana Publicity awards, 1948, 49, 58, 59, Library Pub. Relations Council award, 1950, Merit award Garden Club Ga., 1961; named Citizen of Year, Kiwanis Club Cairo, 1948, Top Flight Woman Ga., Bus. and Profl. Womens Club, 1952, Woman of Year, Mens Clubs, 1959; hon. life mem. Womens Soc. Christian Service. Mem. Am., Southeastern, Ga. library assns., Library Pub. Relations Council, Ga. Adult Edn. Council, Ga. Hist. Soc., Nat. Geneal. Assn., Ga. Writers Assn., Nat. Wildlife Fedn., Delta Kappa Gamma. Methodist. Clubs: Cairo Book, Camellia Garden. Contbr. chpt. The Wonderful World of Books, 1952, Public Relations for Libraries, 1972. Contbr. articles to profl. jours. Address: 410 N Broad St Cairo GA 31728

CONNELLY, TRULYN GENE, architect; b. Iowa City, Ia., Mar. 29, 1930; s. Clifford and Waneta Myrtle (Zager) C.; B.Arch., Ia. State U., 1952; m. Katherine Jean Nesbit, Jan. 19, 1957; children—Steven Nesbit, Daniel Clifford, Todd Andrew, Matthew Wilson. With Leo A. Daly Co., architects and engrs., Seattle, 1956-59, Walker and Walker, architects, Shreveport, La., 1959-62; pvt. practice architecture, Magnolia, Ark., 1962-63; dir. Cromwell, Neyland, Truemper, Millett, and Gatchell, architects and engrs., El Dorado, 1963—. Mem. S. Ark. Devel. Council, 1963—. Mem. Magnolia City (Ark.) Planning Commn., 1964—. Bd. dirs. Magnolia Boys Club, Magnolia Arts Council. Served to lt. comdr. USNR. Mem. A.I.A., C. of C., Tau Sigma Delta, Theta Delta Chi. Presbyn. (chmn. bd. deacons 1963-70, elder 1971—). Mason, Rotarian (dir. 1968—). Clubs: El Dorado Country, Magnolia Country. Home: 100 Lawton Circle Magnolia AR 71753 Office: 107 N Jackson St El Dorado AR 71730

CONNER, DOYLE E., farmer, state ofcl.; b. Starke, Fla., Dec. 17, 1928; s. Leon and Ruby (Clemons) C.; B.S. in Agr., U. Fla., 1952; m. Johnnie Bennett, June 28, 1953; children—Doyle E., Kimberly Ann, John Bryant. Engaged in gen. farming and ins. bus.; commr. agr. State of Fla., Tallahassee, 1961—. Nat. pres. Future Farmers Am., 1948-49; mem. Nat. Food for Peace Com. Former mem., speaker Fla. Ho. of Reps. Named One of 5 Outstanding Men, Fla. Jr. C. of C., 1950, Outstanding farmer, Bradford County Jr. C. of C., 1958, one of 10 Outstanding Young Men, U.S. Jr. C. of C., 1961; numerous other awards. Mem. Nat. (pres. 1970-71), So. assns. state depts. agr., Fla. Farm Bur., Fla. Cattlemens Assn., Fla. C. of C., U. Fla. Alumni Assn. (pres. 1970-71), Fla. Blue Key, Alpha Gamma Rho. Baptist. Mason (Shriner), Elk. Home: 2902 Woodside Dr Tallahassee FL 32303 Office: Capitol Bldg Tallahassee FL 32304

CONNER, EUGENE HAYWARD, anesthesiologist; b. Balt., Dec. 2, 1921; s. James Moses and Mary (Fader) C.; M.D., U. Md., 1945; m. Mary Lou Brown, Sept. 7, 1946; children—Janice, Jeffrey, Marcia, Melissa. Intern, Univ. Hosp., Balt., 1945-46; resident Univ. Hosp., Balt., 1947-49, Hosp. Univ. Pa., Phila., 1949-50; practice medicine specializing in anesthesiology, Phila., 1950-57, Louisville, 1957—; mem. staffs Louisville Gen., Meth.-Evang. hosps.; asst. prof. anesthesiology U. Pa. Sch. Medicine, 1951-57; mem. faculty U. Louisville, 1957-71, prof. anesthesiology, chmn. dept., 1957-71. Served with USAAF, 1946-47. Mem. Am. Soc. Anesthesiologists, Assn. U. Anesthetists, Assn. for History Medicine, Alpha Omega Alpha. Home: 5704 Apache Rd Louisville KY 40207

CONNER, JAMES THOMAS, JR., entomologist; b. Ripley, Miss., Dec. 9, 1916; s. James Thomas and Golden (Arnold) C.; B.S., Miss. State U., 1938; m. Gladys Mae Bentley, Oct. 14, 1939; children—James Thomas III, Bentley E. Tobacco insect research U.S. Dept. Agr. Bur. Entomology and Plant Quarantine, 1938-42; entomologist N.C. Agr. Extension Service, 1945-49; v.p. Taylor Chem. Co., Aberdeen, N.C., 1949-57; pres. Champion Chem. Co., Canton, Miss., 1957-67; v.p. Riverside Chem. Co., Canton, 1967-69; entomologist Nat. Agrl. Chems. Assn., Washington, 1969-71; Washington rep. Chemagro div. Baychem Corp., 1971—. Mem. regional adv. com. Regional Med. Program, 1965-69. Mem. exec. com. Andrew Jackson council Boy Scouts Am.; mem. governing bd. Pearl River Valley Water Supply Dist. Served with AUS, 1942-45. Decorated Bronze Star medal, Silver Star medal. Mem. A.A.A.S., Entomol. Soc. Am., Elisha Mitchell Sci. Soc., Miss. Entomol. Soc., N.C. Entomological Soc., Am. Soc. Agronomy, Miss. Econ. Council (past dir.), Canton C. of C. (past pres., dir.). Baptist. Mason (Shriner), Lion, Elk, Rotarian. Home: 469 E Peace St Canton MS 39046 Office: 1140 Connecticut Av NW Washington DC 20036

CONNER, JOHN DAVIS, lawyer; b. Seminary Hill, Tex., Feb. 24, 1911; s. Walter Thomas and Blanche Ethel (Horne) C.; A.B., Baylor U., 1933; LL.B., George Washington U., 1938; m. Carolyn Rose Hyatt, Nov. 17, 1934; children—Rose Mary, Jenny Lu, John Davis, Walter Thomas. Admitted to D.C. bar, 1938, since practiced in Washington; mem. firm Sellers, Conner & Cuneo, Washington. Served as lt. (s.g.) USNR, 1943-46. Fellow Am. Bar Found.; Am. (chmn. com. econs. law practice), D.C. (chmn. administrv. law 1956-57, dir. 1957-58) bar assns., Am. Judicature Soc. (dir. 1967). Baptist. Clubs: Metropolitan, University (Washington); Belle Haven Country (Alexandria, Va.). Author: Compilation of Economic Poisons Laws and Regulations; Manual of Chemical Products Liability; Product Liability Trends; Lawyers Handbook, others. Home: 506 W Braddock Rd Alexandria VA 22302 Office: 1625 K St Washington DC

CONNER, NED FELL, hosp. adminstr.; b. Bethlehem, Pa., June 6, 1915; s. Max Bowman and Mayda (Schmidt) C.; student Pa. Sch. Phys. Therapy, 1937, Moravian Coll., 1940, Miss. So. U., 1951; m. Desiree Pamela Palmer, Oct. 7, 1944; children—Cheryl, Peter, Christopher, Daniel, David. Commd. 2d lt. U.S. Air Force, 1942, advanced through grades to col., 1966—; mem. med. adminstrn. office U.S. Army, India and Burma, 1941-45; hosp. adminstr. Keesler AFB, Miss., 1946-51, Parks AFB, Cal., 1951-53, Burderop, Eng., 1953-56, Barksdale AFB, La., 1956-61; chief med. financial programming 2d Air Force, Shreveport, La., 1961-63; dir. med. adminstrv. service 3d Air Force, Eng., 1963-66; chief med. constrn. programming, Washington, 1966-67; hosp. adminstr. Homestead AFB, Fla., 1967—. Mem. Am. Coll. Hosp. Adminstrs., Am. Acad. Med. Adminstrn., Royal Soc. Health (Eng.) Northwest La. Hosp. Council (pres. 1961), Fla., South Fla. hosp. assns. Home: 8480 SW 143d St Miami FL 33158 Office: US Air Force Hosp Homestead AFB FL 33030

CONNOR, SEYMOUR VAUGHAN, educator; historian; b. Paris, Tex., Mar. 4, 1923; s. Aikin Beard and Gladys (Vaughan) C.; B.A., U. Tex., 1948, M.A., 1949, Ph.D., 1952; 1 son, Charles Seymour. Archivist, W. Tex. State U., 1952-53, Tex. State Library, 1953-55; prof. history, dir. S.W. collection Tex. Tech. U., Lubbock, 1955-63, prof. history, editor, 1965—. Served with AUS, 1943-45; ETO. Fellow Tex. Hist. Assn. (mem. exec. council 1957—, pres. 1967-68); mem. Panhandle-Plains Hist. Soc. (editor Rev. 1954-59; life mem.), W. Tex. Hist. Assn. (exec. council 1960-63), W. Tex. Mus. Assn. (exec. council 1956-62), Western Hist. Assn., Am. Assn. State and Local History, Orgn. Am. Historians, Phi Kappa Tau, Phi Kappa Psi, Phi Alpha Theta. Author: Preliminary Guide to Texas Archives, 1956; Peters Colony of Texas, 1959; A Biggers Chronicle, 1961; Adventure in Glory, 1965; Texas: A History, 1971; (with Odie Faulk) North America Divided, 1971; (with W.C. Pool) Texas, the 28th state, 1971. Editor: Texas Treasury Papers (3 vols.), 1955; The West Is for Us, 1957; Builders of the Southwest, 1959; Saga of Texas (6 vols.), 1965; Dear America, 1971. Contbr. articles to profl. jours. Home: 3503 45th St Lubbock TX 79413

CONOMOS, WILLIAM G., newspaper pub.; b. Blairsville, Pa., Apr. 29, 1931; s. Van H. and Grace (Hoover) C.; student Orlando (Fla.) Jr. Coll., Rollins Coll., Winter Park, Fla.; m. Dorothy Bradford McGuffin, Mar. 17, 1956; stepchildren—Bradford, Amelia, Joanna Silliman; children—Andrew, Christopher. Pres., pub. editor Orlando Sentinel & Star, Orlando. Home: 1223 Ensenada St Orlando FL 32807 Office: 633 N Orange Av Orlando FL 32801

CONOVER, FRED JOE, chief of police; b. Ft. Cobb, Okla., Dec. 15, 1930; s. Joseph Boone and Elva Alberta (Churchill) C.; ed. pub. and police schs.; m. Nancy Carolyn Lowe, Apr. 28, 1951; children—Steve, Ronnie, Patricia. With LTV, 1949-50, 52-54; with Grand Prairie (Tex.) Police Dept., 1954—, chief of police, 1961—. Dir. Dallas Area Organized Crime Task Force, 1970—; mem. N. Central Tex. Crime Information Center Policy Bd., Dallas County Criminal Justice Council, 1971-72; dir. N. Central Tex. Regional Police Acad.; dep. dir. Grand Prairie Civil Def., 1961—. Mem. adv. com. to police sci. program El Centro Coll., 1969-70; bd. dirs. YMCA. Served with USMC, 1948-52. Named Outstanding Young Man of Year, Grand Prairie Jr. C. of C., 1961. Mem. Internat. Assn. Chiefs Police, Tex. Police Assn., Tex., N. Tex. (pres. 1965-66) chiefs of police assns., Nat. Police Officers of Am., Sheriff's Assn. Tex., N. Tex. Teletype Assn., Grand Prairie C. of C. (dir., life mem.). Mem. Christian Ch. Rotarian (dir. Grand Prairie club 1964). Home: Route 2 Box 323K Grand Prairie TX 75050 Office: 317 W Main St Grand Prairie TX 75050

CONRAD, C. CARSON, govt. ofcl. Exec. dir. Pres.'s Council on Phys. Fitness and Sports. Office: 7th and D St SW Washington DC 20202*

CONRAD, CHARLES, JR., astronaut; b. Phila., June 2, 1930; s. Charles and Frances V. (Sargent) C.; B.S. in Aero. Engring., Princeton, 1953, M.A. (hon.), 1966; LL.D., Lincoln-Wesleyan U., 1970; D.Sc. (hon.), Kings Coll., 1971; m. Jane DuBose, June 17, 1953; children—Peter, Thomas, Andrew, Christopher. Commd. U.S. Navy, 1953, advanced through grades to lt. comdr., 1964; project test pilot, armaments test div. Navy Dept., 1959-60; flight instr., performance engr. U.S. Naval Test Pilot Sch., 1960-61; flight instr. for F4H, Naval Air Sta., Miramar, Cal., 1961-62; safety flight officer Fighter Squadron, 96, 1963; astronaut Manned Spacecraft Center, NASA, Houston, 1964—, now chief Skylab operations; pilot Gemini V, 1965; comdg. pilot Gemini XI, 1966; spacecraft comdr. Apollo XII, 1969. Recipient Distinguished Service medal, 2 Exceptional Service medals (all NASA); D.S.M., D.F.C. with oak leaf cluster (Navy); various other awards. Asso. fellow Am. Inst. Aero. and Astronautics; mem. Soc. Exptl. Test Pilots. Home: 102 Whispering Oaks Seabrook TX 77586 Office: Manned Spacecraft Center NASA Houston TX 77058

CONRAD, EDWARD VICTOR, producer trade shows; b. Elizabeth, N.J., July 7, 1910; s. Edward and Maryanna (Muznerowska) C.; A.B., U. N.C., 1933; postgrad. Mercer Beasley Sch. Law, 1934; m. Pamela Robertson, Jan. 3, 1945 (dec.); children—Penelope (Mrs. Leslie Alexander Clements), Edward Charles; m 2d, Catherine Portwood Stanley, Apr. 22, 1966. Sales rep. Minn. Mining & Mfg. Co., N.Y.C., 1935-41; sales mgr. Sullivan-Waldron, Seattle, 1947; pres. Aidmore Products, Orange, N.J., 1948, Ballard-Conrad Labs., Orange, 1949-52; merchandising exec. Young & Rubicam Advt., N.Y.C., 1953-55; sales mgr. Hubley Mfg. Co., Atlanta, 1956-62; pres. So. Expn. Mgmt. Co., Atlanta, 1962—; dir. Semco, Inc.; partner, cons. Parker, DeLacey, Cronk & Partners, mgmt. cons., London, Eng. Served to lt. comdr. USNR, 1942-46; ETO. Decorated Crois de Guerre (France). Mem. Marine Trade Assn. Atlanta, Southeastern Toy Travelers (past pres.), Lambda Chi Alpha. Founder, Atlanta Boat Show, So. Camping Show, Atlanta Toy Shows, Macon Boat and Sportsman Show, Atlanta Internat. Sports Car Show. Home: 6910 Castelton Dr NW Atlanta GA 30328 Office: 6065 Roswell Rd NE Atlanta GA 30328

CONRAD, EMMETT J., surgeon, city ofcl.; b. Baton Rouge, Oct. 6, 1923; s. John Hamilton and Flora M. (Paulfrey) C.; ed. So. U., Stanford; M.D., Meharry Med. Coll., 1948; m. Eleanor E. Nelson; 1 dau., Cecilia. Intern St. Louis City Hosp. System, 1948-49; cancer research fellow City Hosp. St. Louis, resident surgery, 1951-55; practice medicine, specializing in surgery, Dallas, 1955—; mem. active staff St. Paul Hosp., Dallas. Vice pres. Dallas Bd. Edn., 1969—. Mem. Goals for Dallas Conf.; mem. legislative and health com. Community Council Greater Dallas; chmn. State Adv. Com. Career Edn.; mem. Senate Com. Urban Edn. Fellow Nat. Inst. Urban Affairs; mem. A.M.A., Tex. Med. Assn., Dallas County Med. Soc., A.R.C., Am. Cancer Soc., Woodlawn Assn., Am. Legion. Democrat. Methodist. Mason. Home: 2003 Lanark St Dallas TX 75203

CONRAD, JOSEPH EDWARD, financial cons.; b. Middletown, O., Oct. 26, 1922; s. Clarence Johann and Marie (Smith) C.; student U. Cin., 1941, 46-48; B.S., Ohio State U., 1951; postgrad. Northwestern U., 1964; m. Jean Ann Tatgenhorst, Aug. 25, 1949; children—Jill Allison, Susan Lynn, Clayton Reid. With Armco Steel Corp., Middletown, O., 1942, 46-49; br. store mgr. Union Co., Columbus, O., 1949-52; applications engr. Indsl. Nucleonics, Columbus, 1952; field sec. Ohio State U. Alumni Assn., Columbus, 1952-55; dir. regions and spl. gifts Mass. Inst. Tech., 1955-59; v.p. for devel. Stephens Coll., 1959-63; dir. alumni programs Northwestern U., 1963-66; asso. campaign dir. U. Chgo., 1966-68; dean planning and devel. Episcopal High Sch., Jacksonville, Fla., 1968-70; exec. v.p. Sheldrick-Conrad Assos., Inc., Jacksonville, 1969—; pres. Fla. First Corp., Jacksonville, 1969—. Bd. dirs. Fla. Edn. Found. Served with USAAF, 1942-45. Mem. Ye Mystic Revellers, Phi Delta Theta, Chi Epsilon, Republican. Episcopalian. Rotarian. Clubs: Florida Yacht, River (Jacksonville). Contbr. articles to profl. jours. Home: 4810 Arapahoe Av Jacksonville FL 32210 Office: 1424 Barnett Bank Bldg Jacksonville FL 32202

CONRAD, THEODORE CHARLES, accountant, lawyer; b. Anderson, Ind., July 29, 1903; s. Charles William and Lydia (Lukens) C.; A.B., DePauw U., 1925; J.D., Harvard, 1933; postgrad. bus. adminstrn. Northwestern U., 1936-39; m. Mary Emma Gilby, Mar. 30, 1935; children—Mary Jo (Mrs. James L. Cresimore), Theodore Charles, Carolyn Jame (Mrs. Vann O. Trapp), Jeanne Minette (Mrs. Louis A. Trosch), Virginia Dianne (Mrs. Gene Draper), Doris Ellen. Admitted to Ill. bar, 1934, N.C. bar, 1953; pvt. practice law, Chgo., 1934-40; mgr. tax dept. Baumann Finney & Co., Chgo., 1940-44; supr. tax dept firm Ernst & Ernst, Boston, 1944-49; mgr. tax dept. George G. Scott & Co., Charlotte, N.C., 1950-52; sr. partner Conrad, Hoey, East & Co., Charlotte and Spartanburg, S.C., 1952—; dir. De Lacy Wyman & Co., Charlotte, N.C. Republican candidate for state auditor, 1968. C.P.A., Ill., Mass., Ky., N.C., S.C. Mem. N.C. Assn. C.P.A.'s (pres. Charlotte chpt. 1956-57), Am. Inst. C.P.A.'s, Nat. Assn. Accountants (nat. dir., v.p. 1963-64). Baptist. Mason (Shriner); Kiwanian. Clubs: Charlotte Execs., Charlotte City, Harvard Charlotte. Home: 4615 Walker Rd Charlotte NC 28211 Office: 301 N Caswell Rd Charlotte NC 28204

CONRAD, TROY LAVERNE, petroleum co. exec.; b. Frederick, Okla., Jan. 8, 1932; s. Harold Raymond and Mary Ruth (Harwood) C.; B.S., U. Okla., 1958; m. Gloria Darlene Knox, June 20, 1954; children—Mark R., Kirk W., Beth Ann. Petroleum engr. Felmont Oil Corp., Owensboro, Ky., 1958-60; dist. petroleum engr. Ashland Oil & Refining Co., Monroe, La., 1960-65; prodn. supt. Grigsby Oil & Gas Co., Shreveport, 1965—. Served with USAF, 1951-53. Mem. Am. Inst. Mech. Engring. (chpt. dir. 1971—). Elk. Club: Petroleum (Shreveport). Home: 340 Carroll St Shreveport LA 71105 Office: 1108 Commercial National Bank Bldg Shreveport LA 71101

CONREY, KENNETH KERWIN, city ofcl.; b. Cheyenne, Wyo., Aug. 25, 1924; s. John Wesley and Mable (Kerwin) C.; B.A., U. Denver, 1950; postgrad., mgmt. seminar, U. Chgo., 1963; m. Donna Jean Sapp, Sept. 18, 1944; children—Megganey Sue, James Todd, Calvin Frank. IBM operator and various other positions, Union Pacific R.R., N. Platte, Neb., 1942-59, treas. Union Pacific employee credit union, 1953-57; sec.-treas. Local 609, Am. Fedn. Musicians, N. Platte, Neb., 1950-59; city clk., N. Platte, 1957-59; adminstrv. asst. to city mgr., Borger, Tex., 1959-60; city mgr., Spearman, Tex., 1960-65, Weatherford, Tex., 1965-68; city clk., Pensacola, Fla., 1968-72; dir. finance, Pensacola, 1972—. Served with USAF, 1943-45; ETO. Decorated Air medal with three clusters. Mem. Fla. City Mgrs. Assn. (asso.), Internat. City Mgrs. Assn., Fla. Municipal Finance Officers Assn. Presbyn. (elder). Lion (pres. 1962-63). Home: 3790 Tom Lane Dr Pensacola FL 32504 Office: City Hall PO Box 1471 Pensacola FL 32502

CONROY, DAVID JEROME, lawyer; b. New Orleans, Dec. 27, 1929; s. George E. and Lilyon (Bowling) C.; B.A., Tulane U., 1950, J.D., 1952; m. Ann Kathryn Gunderson, May 15, 1954; children—Kathryn Ann, David Michael, Elizabeth Helen, Mary Daire, Peter George Edward, Patrick Frank. Admitted to La. bar, 1952; partner firm Milling, Seal, Benson, Woodward & Hillyer, New Orleans, 1956—; sec. Jahncke Service Inc., New Orleans, 1961-69, Pub. Grain Elevator New Orleans, 1964—; sec., dir. C.B. Fox Co., New Orleans, 1965—. Bd. dirs. New Orleans Speech and Hearing Center, 1968—, pres., 1970—; bd. dirs. Greater New Orleans Tourist and Conv. Commn., 1971—, Louise S. McGehee Sch., 1970—. Served with AUS, 1952-54. Mem. Am., La. (chmn. sect. corp. law 1968-69, mem. ho. of dels. 1970-71), New Orleans bar assns., Internat. House, St. Thomas More Cath. Lawyers Assn. (bd. govs. 1969—), La. Hist. Soc. (exec. council 1971—). Roman Catholic. Clubs: Pickwick, New Orleans Country, Plimsoll, Essex. Home: 437 Dorrington Dr Metairie LA 70005 Office: Whitney Bldg New Orleans LA 70130

CONSTABLE, STUART, architect, landscape architect; b. Columbus, O., Sept. 9, 1900; s. Thomas Gibson and Francis M. (Whisner) C.; B.S., Ohio State U., 1922; M.Landscape Architecture, Harvard, 1927; m. Margaret Joyce Cottingham, Sept. 9, 1922; children—John Stuart (killed in action 1944), Thomas Gibson II. Pvt. practice, St. Petersburg, Fla., Stamford, Conn., 1924-35; chief designer dept. parks City N.Y., 1936-55, exec. officer, 1955-60; acting commr. N.Y.C. Planning Commn., 1950-60, N.Y.C. Art Commn., 1949-55; v.p. operations N.Y. World's Fair 1964-65 Corp., 1960-66; pres C & T Enterprises, Ft. Lauderdale, Fla., 1966—; cons. 1st hdqrs. UN, Jones Beach State Pkwy. Authority and N.Y. State Power Authority, also James Found. of St. James, Mo., Dorado, P.R. Winner Bklyn. War Meml. Competition, 1945. Mem. Am. Soc. Testing Materials, Ohio Soc. N.Y., Alpha Gamma Rho. Clubs: Brook, Surf, Wrightsville Beach, North Carolina; Cape Fear Country (Wilmington, N.C.). Home: The Meed Route 1 Box 3 Hampstead NC 38443 Office: PO Box 381 Pompano Beach FL 33061

CONSTANGY, FRANK A., lawyer; b. Atlanta, Feb. 23, 1911; A.B., U. Ga., LLB., 1930. Admitted to Ga. bar, 1930; mem. firm Constangy & Prowell, Atlanta; lectr. Woodrow Wilson Coll. Law, 1931-35, 41-43. Industry mem., chmn. industry mems. Regional War Labor Bd. and Wage Stblzn. Bd., 1944-46; mem. bd. rev. Ga. Employment Security Agy., 1944—, chmn. 1950—. Mem. Am. (chmn. labor relations law sect. 1967-68, ho. of dels. 1969-70), Atlanta bar assns., State Bar Ga., Omicron Delta Kappa. Office: Constangy & Powell 230 Peachtree St NW Atlanta GA 30303*

CONSTANT, CLINTON, chem. engr.; b. Nelson, B.C., Can., Mar. 20, 1912; s. Vasile and Annie (Hunt) C.; B.Sc. with honors, U. Alberta, 1935, postgrad., 1935-36; Ph.D., Western Res. U., 1939; m. Mary E. Dunlap, Apr. 21, 1950. Came to U.S., 1936, naturalized, 1942. Development engr. Harshaw Chem. Co., Cleve., 1936-38, mfg. foreman, 1938-43, sr. engr. semi-works dept., 1948-50; supt. hydrofluoric acid dept. Nyotex Chems., Inc., Houston, 1943-47, chief devel. engr., 1947-48; mgr. engring. Ferro Chem. Co., Bedford, O., 1950-52; tech. asst. mfg. dept. Armour Agrl. Chem. Co. (formerly Armour Fertilizer Works), Bartow, Fla., 1952-61, mgr. research and devel. div., 1961-63, mgr. spl. projects, research div. (co. name changed to USS Agri-Chems. 1968), 1963-65, project mgr., 1965-70; chem. adviser Robert & Co. Assos., Atlanta, 1970—. Fellow A.A.A.S., Am. Inst. Chemists; mem. Am. Inst. Chem. Engrs., Am. Chem. Soc., Am. Inst. Aeronautics and Astronautics, Am. Astron. Soc., Astron. Soc. Pacific, Royal Astron. Soc. Can., Am. Water Works Assn., Ga. Water and Pollution Control Assn. Author tech. reports, sci. fiction. Home: PO Box 1221 Atlanta GA 30301 Office: Robert and Co Assos 96 Poplar St Atlanta GA 30303

CONSTANT, ELMER EDWARD, banker; b. Mammoth Cave, Ky., Dec. 2, 1902; s. Elige Wilson and Sally (Caswell) C.; ed. Western Ky. State U.; m. Pauline Barks, Oct. 1, 1934; children—J. Wayne, Maxine (Mrs. Ralph Kessinger), Grace (Mrs. R. W. Evette). Cashier, dir. Brownsville Deposit Bank, 1928-33; agt. Internal Revenue Service, 1933-40; self-employed as pub. accountant, 1940-70; pres. Farmers' Nat. Bank, Scottsville, Ky., 1971—, also dir. Democrat. Baptist. Mason, Elk, Rotarian. Home: N Court St Scottsville KY 42164 Office: N Court St Scottsville KY 42164

CONSTANTIN, JAMES ALFORD, educator; b. Tulsa, June 15, 1922; s. Jules Joseph and Nelle (Alford) C.; B.B.A., U. Tex., 1943, M.B.A., 1944, Ph.D., 1950; m. Wanda Anita Moyer, May 18, 1941; children—Nina Katherine (Mrs. Robert Dean Beaird), James Alford, Jr., Jules Joseph II, Anne Louise (Mrs. Michael Gordon Keown). Instr., U. Tex., 1946-47; asst. prof., asso. prof., asst. dir. Bur. Bus. Research, U. Ala., Tuscaloosa, 1947-52; asso. prof. U. Wash., 1952-53; prof. marketing and transp. U. Okla., Norman, 1953-69, David Ross Boyd prof. marketing and transp., 1969—. Served with USAAF, 1942-43. Mem. Am. Econ. Assn., Transp. Research Forum, Am. Soc. Traffic and Transp., S.W. Social Sci. Assn. Author: (with W.J. Hudson) Motor Transportation, 1958, Principle of Logistics Management, 1966; (with W.N. Peach) World Resources and Industries, 1972. Home: 929 W Lindsey St Norman OK 73069

CONSTANTINE, EDWIN B., govt. ofcl.; b. Fredericksburg, Va., Sept. 17, 1928; s. Edwin B. and Mary (Buchanan) C.; B.C.E., N.C. State U., 1952; m. Ruth L. Golding, June 15, 1950; children—Edwin G., Douglas K., Russell T., Joyce E. and Janice G. (twins). Asso. C. Fred Duel & Assos., pub. relations, St. Petersburg, Fla., 1958-62; cons. engr. Russell & Axon of Daytona Beach (Fla.), 1960-62; chief traffic engr. N.C. Hwy. Dept., 1962-63; owner-developer Aquia Park, Stafford, Va., 1963-68; dir. planning U.S. Marine Corps, Quantico, Va., 1968—. Served with AUS, 1941-47. Mem. Va. Camp Ground Owners Assn. (pres. 1965-66, chpt. dir. 1965-66). Mason. Home: P O Box 207 Stafford VA 22554 Office: PWO - MCB Quantico VA 22134

CONSTANTINE, OLEINICK PAVLOVITCH, neuropsychiatrist; b. Ostrog, Ukraine, Oct. 22, 1908; s. Pavel Ivanovich and Thekla (Doschuk) Oleinik; student Polish Tchrs. Sch., 1924-26; B.S., Eastern U., 1931; B.A., Columbia Bible Coll., 1932; M.A., U.S.C., 1932; M.D., Baylor Coll., 1937; m. Ethelwyn G. Brown, Dec. 23, 1935; children—Paula Joy (Mrs. Ted L. Edwards, Jr.), Paul D. Came to U.S., 1926, naturalized, 1937. Intern, Baylor U. Hosp., Dallas, 1937-38; asst. physician Tex. San Antonio State Hosp., 1938-39; resident Kings Park State Hosp., N.Y., 1941-43; psychiatrist VA Hosp., Canandaigua, N.Y., 1943-49, chief continued treatment service, 1946-49; psychiatrist VA Hosp., Waco, Tex., 1949—, chief combined treatment service, 1949-56; neurologist Columbia Presbyn. Med. Center, N.Y.C., 1942-44. Served to major M.C., AUS, 1944-46. Diplomate Am. Bd. Psychiatry and Neurology. Fellow Am. Psychiat. Assn., A.M.A., Royal Soc. Health; mem. Tex. Med. Assn. Presbyn.-Baptist. Mason. Home: 3825 Austin Av Waco TX 76710

CONSTANTINIDES, CONSTANTINE (DINOS) DEMETRIOS, composer, violinist, educator; b. Ioannina, Greece, May 10, 1929; s. Demetrios Constantine and Magdaleni (Papastergiou) C.; diploma in violin Greek Conservatory, 1950, in theory, 1957; diploma in violin (Found. of Greece scholar) Juilliard Sch. Music, 1960; M.Music, Ind. U., 1965; Ph.D. in Composition, Mich. State U., 1968; m. Judith Rose Hursh, July 1, 1962; children—Lenna Rose, John Demetrios. Came to U.S., 1957, naturalized, 1967. First violin Athens (Greece) State Orch., 1952-57, 61-63, also 1st violin Radio Symphony Orch.; 1st violin Indpls. Symphony Orch., 1963-65; asso. prof. violin, composition and theory La. State U., Baton Rouge, 1966—, dir. prep. dept. for strings, 1971—. Concertmaster Baton Rouge Symphony, 1966—, Baton Rouge Civic Ballet, 1967—, Beaumont (Tex.) Civic Opera, 1967—; mem. Festival Arts Trio, La. State U., 1966—; tchr., coach La. State U. Extension Div., 1966. Co-founder, co-chmn. New Times, orgn. promoting performance contemporary music, Baton Rouge, 1971—. Grad. Research grantee La. State U., 1970; Distinguished Faculty fellow La. State U. Found., 1971-72. Mem. Am. Assn. U. Profs., Am. Musicological Soc., Coll. Music Soc., Music Educators Nat. Conf., Music Tchrs. Nat Assn. (teaching award So. div. 1970), Am. String Tchrs. Assn., Am. Fedn. Musicians, Webern Soc., Phi Kappa Phi, Phi Mu Alpha, Pi Kappa Lambda. Mem. Greek Orthodox Ch. Composer: Symphony No. 1, 1966; Woodwin Quartet, 1966; Trio, 1967; String Quartet, 1966; Triple Concerto, 1967; Composition for String Orch., 1968; Twentieth Century Studies for Two Violins, 1970; Study for Brass, 1970; Sonata for Viola and Piano, 1971; Designs for Strings, 1971; Kaleidoscope for Voice, Violin, Cello, Piano and 2Slide Projectors, 1972; Exploding Parallels for Instrumental Ensemble, Reader and Audience, 1972. Home: 947 Daventry Dr Baton Rouge LA 70808

CONTE, NICHOLAS FERDINAND, physician; b. Scranton, Pa., Dec. 6, 1918; s. Matthew Arthur and Mary Ann (Jordan) C.; B.S., U. Scranton, 1941; M.D., U. Pa., 1944; m. Virginia Mae Bertolett, Sept. 22, 1944; children—Norman Richard, Claude V. (dec.), Frederic Arthur. Intern, Phila. Gen. Hosp., 1944-45; resident VA Hosp., Aspinwall, Pa., 1948-50; commd. capt. U.S. Army, 1950, advanced through grades to col., 1968; asst. chief Med. Service, U.S. Army

Hosp., Ft. Carson, Colo., 1956-61; chief med. service 121 Evacuation Hosp., Korea, 1961-62; fellow basic scis. Walter Reed Inst. Research, 1960-61; fellow endocrinology U. Cal. Sch. Medicine, San Francisco, 1962-63; asst. chief, then chief dept. medicine, Valley Forge Gen. Hosp., Phoenixville, Pa., 1963-67; med. cons. to surgeon gen. U.S. Army, Vietnam, 1967-68; co-dir. U.S. Army Med. Research Lab., Ft. Knox, Ky., 1969-72; chief med. cons. Office Surgeon Gen., Washington, 1972—. Asst. clin. prof. medicine Woman's Med. Coll., Phila., 1964-67. Served to capt. M.C., AUS, 1945-47. Decorated Legion of Merit. Diplomate Am. Bd. Internal Medicine. Fellow A.C.P.; mem. A.M.A., N.Y. Acad. Scis., Am. Assn. Blood Banks. Republican. Contbr. articles to profl. pubs. Home: 4100 Tidewater Ct Alexandria VA 22309

CONTNEY, JOHN JOSEPH, assn. exec.; b. Milw., Oct. 15, 1932; s. Francis Anthony and Rose (Nowicki) C.; B.S., Marquette U., 1956, M.B.A., 1965; m. Dawn Georgette Wintz, Sept. 7, 1963; children—Wade Anthony, Ross Joseph. Asst. to v.p. Boston Store, Milw., 1950-56; v.p., sales mgr. Records Unlimited, Inc., Milw., 1956-60; v.p., sales mgr. Columbia S.E., Miami, Fla., 1960-63; asst. to pres. Color Corp., Tampa, Fla., 1964-65; mgr. marketing Linen Supply Assn. Am., Miami Beach, Fla., 1965—; speaker before various groups. Served with AUS, 1954-56. Mem. Am. Marketing Assn., Am. Pub. Health Assn. (mem. environmental control com.), Alpha Delta Sigma. Contbr. articles profl. jours. Home: 705 NE 94th St Miami Shores FL 33138 Office: 975 Arthur Godfrey Rd Miami Beach FL 33140

CONVERSE, J. GERARD, physician; b. Boston, Sept. 21, 1918; s. Frederick F.B. and Rosita (McVey) C.; B.A. cum laude, Boston Coll., 1940; M.D. cum laude, Tufts Med. Sch., 1943; m. Gwendolyn Stone Connor, Sept. 26, 1964; children by previous marriage—Sharon Ann, Geoffrey Michael. Intern, U.S. Naval Hosp., Chelsea, Mass., 1944; resident Boston City Hosp., 1947-48, VA Hosp., W. Roxbury, 1948-49, Children's Med. Center, Boston, 1949; instr. anesthesiology Albany (N.Y.) Med. Coll., 1949-50, asst. prof., 1950-52, prof., chmn. dept., 1952-56; prof., chmn. dept. anesthesiology U. Miami (Fla.) Sch. Medicine, 1956-62, clin. prof., 1963—; dir. dept. anesthesiology Albany Hosp., 1952-56, Jackson Meml. Hosp., Miami, 1956-62; attending anesthesiologist Winter Haven (Fla.) Hosp., 1962—. Cons. VA Hosp., Albany, 1950-56, Coral Gables, Fla., 1956-62; asso. examiner Am. Bd. Anesthesiologists, 1955—. Hon. mem. Fla. Sheriff's Assn., 1963—. Served to lt. with M.C., USN, 1944-47. Decorated Bronze Star medal. Fellow Boston Med. Library. Mem. Am., Fla., So. med. assns., Am. (dir. 8th dist.), Fla. (pres. 1966, dir. 1961—) socs. anesthesiologists, Am. Heart Assn., Assn. U. Anesthetists, Internat. Anesthesiologists Research Soc., A.A.A.S., Am. Conservative Union, Alpha Omega Alpha. Clubs: Faculty (U. Miami); Capitol Hill (Washington); Lake Region Yacht and Country. Contbr. articles to profl. jours. Home: W Lake Hamilton Drive Winter Haven FL 33880 Office: Med Arcade Bldg 1st St N Winter Haven FL 33880

CONWAY, ADRIAN PAUL, assn. exec.; b. Phila., June 7, 1924; s. Paul and Isabel (Schlack) C.; B.A., U. Bridgeport, 1949; m. Carlene Mae Woods, Jan. 3, 1950 (dec.); m. 2d, Susan Ellen Bowling, Apr. 17, 1971; children—Damond L., David Lindon, Brenda Lee Brooks. News reporter, city desk rewrite Bridgeport (Conn.) Telegram, 1946-50; news dir. Radio Sta. WNLK, Norwalk, 1950-52; publicity mgr. Conn. Blue Cross, New Haven, 1952-53; dir. pub. relations Conn. Med. Service, New Haven, 1953-56; publicity mgr. Plumbing Fixture Mfrs. Assn., Washington, 1956-59; asst. account exec. Carl Byoir & Assos., N.Y.C., 1959-64, account exec., 1964-65, v.p., account exec., 1965-70; dir. pub. relations and promotion Gas Appliance Mfrs. Assn., Arlington, Va., 1970—. Served with USAAF, 1942-45. Recipient citation for alumni accomplishment U. Bridgeport, 1964. Mem. Pub. Relations Soc. Am. (accredited). Home: 8300 Tobin Rd Annandale VA 22003 Office: 1901 N Fort Myer Dr Arlington VA 22209

CONWAY, FRENCH HOGE, lawyer; b. Danville, Va., June 11, 1918; s. Lysander Broadus and Mildred (Hoge) C.; B.S., U. Va., 1942, LL.B., 1946; m. Louise Throckmorton, Feb. 3, 1961; children—French Hoge, William Chenery, Helen (Mrs. W.C. Brann), Donna (Mrs. W.B. Salmon). Admitted to Va. bar, 1942, since practiced in Danville; mem. firm Clement, Conway & Winston, 1950-60. Dir., Danville Industries (Va.). Sec. Danville Elect. Bd., 1969—. Served with USNR, 1942-46. Mem. Am., Va., Danville bar assns., Ret. Officers Assn., Boat Owners Assn. U.S. Kiwanian, Mason. Club: Danville Golf. Home: 912 Main St Danville VA 24541 Office: 515 Lynn St Danville VA 24541

CONWAY, MACK HOWARD, JR., profl. assn. exec.; b. Jacksonville, Fla., Aug. 20, 1926; s. Mack Howard and Roberta (Arnold) C.; student Va. Comml. Coll., 1946-48; m. Agnes Mae Powell, Sept. 17, 1948; children— Mack Howard III, Richard, Patricia, Christine. Accounting mgr. Gen. Motors Acceptance Corp., Roanoke, Va., 1948-54; bus. mgr. Paul H. Pusey, Inc., Richmond, Va., 1954-56; treas., gen. mgr. Nick Allen Motors, Inc., Newport News, Va., 1956-60; pres. Conway Ford Sales, Inc., Blackstone, Va., 1960-65; exec. v.p. Housing and Builders Assn., Hampton, Va., 1965—. Pres., Newport News Homeownership Assn., 1970—; mem. citizens adv. com. to City Council, Newport News; pub. Guide to Peninsula Living, Newport News, 1969—. Served with USNR and USMCR, 1943-46. Recipient awards Nat. Assn. Home Builders, 1965, 69, 70, 71. Mem. Am. Legion (post comdr. 1969-70). Mason. Moose. Home: 8 Meadow Dr Newport VA 23606 Office: 2607 W Mercury Blvd Hampton VA 23366

CONWAY, MARTHA BELL, ednl. adminstr.; b. Raleigh, N.C., July 24, 1917; d. Elijah James and Cora (Henderson) Conway; student William and Mary Coll., 1932-35; LL.B., U. Richmond, 1939. Admitted to Va. bar, 1940, since practiced in Richmond; commr. chancery Hanover Co. Circuit Court, 1943-51; real estate broker, 1951-55; sec. of Commonwealth of Va., 1952-70; adminstr. grants and contracts Med. Coll. Va., Health Scis. Div., Va. Commonwealth U., Richmond, 1970—. Dist. counsel OPS, 1951-52. Mem. bd. Family and Children's Service Soc. Registered patent atty., Va. Mem. Am. Assn. U. Women. Democrat. Methodist. Author: Compacts of Virginia, 1963; also profl. publs. Home: 2500 Grove Av Richmond VA 23220 Office: Med Coll Va Health Scis Div Va Commonwealth U Richmond VA 23220

CONWAY, ROBERT NELSON, govt. ofcl.; b. Rochester, N.Y., Nov. 15, 1917; s. Reginald J. and Anne (Nelson) C.; B.Aero. Engring., Rensselaer Polytech. Inst., 1939; m. Janet Grant Alling, May 25, 1940; children— Bruce A., Michael A., David L. Aero. engr. NASA Langley Research Center, Hampton, Va., 1939-47, asst. budget officer, 1947-61, budget officer, 1961-68, dep. asst. dir. resources, 1968-71, asst. dir. adminstrn., 1971—. Committeeman, Boy Scouts Am., Hampton, Va., 1951-61; dir. Peninsula Community Services Planning Council, Newport News, Va., 1965-67. Mem. Pennisula Engrs. Club. Episcopalian. Club: Hampton Yacht (commodore 1967). Home: 39 Hampton Roads Av Hampton VA 23361 Office: Langley Research Center Hampton VA 23365

CONWAY, WILLIAM RAYFORD, state legislator; b. Green Cove Springs, Gla., July 25, 1911; s. James Franklin and Idella Jane (Minton) C.; B.S. in Bus. Adminstrn., U. Fla., 1936; m. Dianne Anger, Feb. 4, 1950; children—William Rayford, Robert Fisher, James Marvin, Julia Ann, John Charles. Pres., Fla. Liquified Gas Assn., 1950; mem. Fla. Ho. of Reps., 1966—. Chmn., Cancer Crusade, 1965. Served from lt. (j.g.) to lt. comdr. USNR, 1942-45; PTO. Decorated Bronze Star. Mem. U. Fla. Nat. Alumni Assn. (pres. 1963), Pi Kappa Phi. Episcopalian. Mason (Shriner), Kiwanian (local pres. 1953). Club: University. Address: 734 John Anderson Dr Ormond Beach FL 32074*

CONWELL, JOSEPH THOMAS, lawyer; b. Oakman, Ala., Nov. 9, 1914; s. Joe D. and Elma Pettus (Wells) C.; student Transylvania Coll., 1934-45; B.A., U. Ala., 1937, LL.B., 1940; m. Winifred Maxwell, June 25, 1946; 1 son, Joseph Thomas. Admitted to Ala. bar, 1940; pvt. practice law, Jasper, Ala., 1940-42, Birmingham, Ala., 1946-48, Huntsville, Ala., 1955—; atty. ICC, Atlanta, 1948-49; claim and ins. investigator, San Francisco, 1949-54. Pres., Madison County Citizens Council, 1965-66; mem. Huntsville Indsl. Expansion Com. Served with AUS, World War II, lt. col. Ala. State Militia. Mem. Am., Ala., Huntsville-Madison County bar assns., Ala. Trial Lawyers Assn., Am. Judicature Soc., Farrah Law Soc., Civitan Club, Am. Legion. Democrat. Episcopalian. Mem. Woodmen of World. Home: 7118 Chadwell Rd SW Huntsville AL 35802 Office: Conwell Legal Bldg 607 Madison St Huntsville AL 35801

COOK, BUREN EUGENE, agriculturist; b. Colquitt, Ga., Mar. 10, 1917; s. Booley C. and Ethel D. (Donley) C.; grad. high sch.; m. Vera E. Grogan, Sept. 24, 1938; 1 son, Buren E. With B.C. Cook & Sons, Inc., Haines City, Fla., 1931—, sec., sales mgr., 1970—. Bd. dirs. Brotherhood of Ridge Bapt. Assn. Mem. Polk County Farm Bur. (v.p., dir. 1971), Fla. Aberdeen-Angus Assn. (past dir.), C. of C., Fla. Citrus Commn. (mem. citrus juice extractor com.), Future Farmers Am. (life hon.). Farm Bur. (chmn. citrus com.). Baptist (chmn. bd. deacons 1965-66). Kiwanian (pres. 1969, chmn. agr. and conservation com. 1970-72). Home: Lake Elsie Dr Haines City FL 33844 Office: 413 N 12th St Haines City FL 33844

COOK, CHARLIE HYRAM, civil engr.; b. Greenville, Ala., Sept. 4, 1923; s. William Claude and Mary (Rainee) C.; B.S. in Civil Engring., U. Ala., 1950; m. Mary Catherine Dunn, Jan. 6, 1946; children—James Charles, Kathryn Marie. Civil engr. Ala. Hwy. Dept., Montgomery, 1950-52, bridge design engr., 1954—, now chief bridge design engr.; civil engr. E. I. duPont de Nemours Co., Aiken, S.C., 1952-54. Served with USNR, 1942-45. Mem. Am. Soc. C.E., Am. Soc. Profl. Engrs. Baptist. Mason (32 deg., Shriner). Home: 1879 Robison Hill Rd Montgomery AL 36106 Office: Ala Hwy Dept Montgomery AL 36106

COOK, CLARENCE RICHARD, city ofcl.; b.Houston, Oct. 11, 1927; s. John Thomas and Mary Jane (Mills) C.; grad. Aldine High Sch.; m. Mary Belle Bennett, Oct. ll, 1944; 1 son, Richard Carlton. Engaged in bus., Houston, 1945-50; chauffeur Houston Fire Dept., 1950-53, jr. capt., 1953-56, sr. capt., 1956-58, dist. chief, 1958-64, dep. dist. chief, 1964-67, asst. fire chief, 1967-68, fire chief, 1968—. Office: 410 Bagby Houston TX 77002

COOK, CLARENCE SHARP, physicist; b. St. Louis Crossing, Ind., Aug. 18, 1918; s. Clarence C. and Musa (Sharp) C.; B.A. in mathematics and physics, DePauw U., 1940; M.A. in physics, Ind. U., 1942, Ph.D. in physics, 1948; m. Marian N. Waring, June 19, 1943; children—Sherma Louise, Wayne W. Teaching asst. physics dept. Ind. U., 1940-42, research asst. 1946-48; asst. prof. physics, Washington U., 1948-53; head nuclear radiation br. USN Radiolog. Def. Lab., San Francisco, 1953-60, head nucleonics division, 1960-61, 65-66, physics cons. to scientific dir., 1962-65, head radiation physics div., 1966-69; lectr. U. Santa Clara, 1969-70; prof. physics dept. U. Tex., El Paso, 1970—, chmn. dept., 1970-72. Mem. bd. of Civil Service Examiners for Scientists, Engrs., Pasadena, Cal., 1955-58, chmn., 1957-58; mem. profl. council for scientists and engrs. Civil Service Commission, 1967-69; bd. dirs., exec. bd. El Paso Cancer Treatment Radiation Center, 1971—; bd. dirs. El Paso Pub. TV Found., 1972—. Fulbright research scholar at Aarhus University, Denmark, for year 1961-62. Served from second lieutenant to captain United States Army, 1943-46. Fellow Am. Physics Soc., Cal. Acad. Scis.; mem. Am. Assn. Physics Tchrs., Am. Geophys. Union, Phi Beta Kappa, Sigma Xi. Author: Modern Atomic and Nuclear Physics, 1961; Structure of Atomic Nuclei, 1964. Address: Box 204 U Tex El Paso TX 79968

COOK, CLAUDE KARON, composer, pianist, organist, educator; b. Wallburg, N.C., Apr. 20, 1922; s. Charles Isom and Cora (Taylor) C.; A.B., Guilford Coll., 1944; postgrad. Julliard Sch. Music, 1946; M.A., Columbia, 1947, postgrad., 1961-69; Fontainebleau, 1951, Paris Conservatory, 1951-52, Clarkson Coll. Tech., 1944-45, U. Pitts., 1945. Tchr., Wake Forest Coll., 1947-52; mem. Bapt. Fgn. Mission Bd., 1952-58; minister music Centenary Meth. Ch., Richmond, Va., 1955-61; with choral publs. dept. VAMS E.C. Schirmer, 1961-63; minister music, dir. Handbell Chorus, 1961-62; asst. prof. music Guilford Coll., Greensboro, N.C., 1962—. Served with AUS, 1942-46. Mem. Fontainebleau Alumni Assn., Kappa Delta Pi. Composer: The Babe in Bethlehem's Manger Lay, 1961; The Oceans Limit I Have Never Seen, 1962; Fantasie on Greensleeves, Choral, 1963. Home: PO Box 8454 Greensboro NC 27410 also Ye Olde Compayne Mille Route 1 Climax NC 27233

COOK, DARLUS COLLON, city ofcl.; b. Damascus, Ark., Apr. 23, 1929; s. Calvin O. and Lizzie V. (Lutton) C.; diploma Hampton Roads Bus. Coll., 1956; m. Claudelle Irene Garrison, Jan. 31, 1959; children— Andy Bernard, Rena Delores, Warren Clifford. Office mgr. various automobile dealerships, Newport News, Va., 1956-61; auditor City of Newport News, Va., 1961-66; auditor City of Hampton, Va., 1966-69, dir. finance, 1969—. Served with AUS, 1946-53. Mem. Inst. Internal Auditors (treas. Tidewater chpt. 1969-70, v.p. 1970-71, pres. 1971—), Nat. Municipal Finance Officers Assn., Am. Legion. Home: 5 Clark Rd Hampton VA 23364 Office: 30 N King St City Hall Bldg Hampton VA 23369

COOK, DAVID RAY, mech. engr.; b. Tulsa, June 19, 1936; s. Artie Wrothal and Nellie Mae (Miller) C.; B.S. in M.E., Okla. State U., 1959; M.S. in Systems Mgmt., Fla. Inst. Tech., 1969, M.S. in Contract, 1970; student Internat. Corr. Schs., 1963, 70; m. Benetta Borne, May 26, 1959; children—Kathryn, Karlene, Kristine. Design engr. Douglas Aircraft Co., Santa Monica, Cal., 1959-60; sr. design engr. Convair, Omaha, 1960-62; design engr. Boeing Co., Huntsville, Ala., 1962-65; sect. supr. Launch Support div. Bendix Corp., Kennedy Space Center, Fla., 1965-69, dept. mgr., 1969—; instr. mgmt. Bay State Coll., Titusville, Fla., 1971, Rollins Coll., 1971—. Vol. counselor Brevard County (Fla.) Econ. Devel. Commn., 1971—. Mem. Brevard Symphony Orch. Recipient Citizenship award Am. Legion, Broken Arrow, Okla., 1954. Registered profl. engr., Ala. Mem. Am. Mgmt. Assn., Am. Soc. M.E. (chmn. program 1971—), Soc. Automotive Engrs. (mem. space transp. com. 1972), Nat. Soc. Profl. Engrs. Methodist (mem. finance com.). Toastmaster. Home: 2932 E Carriage Dr Titusville FL 32780 Office: Bendix Corp BEN 4300 PO Box 21086 Kennedy Space Center FL 32815

COOK, EDWARD SMITH, JR., educator; b. Atlanta, Feb. 14, 1920; s. Edward Smith and Willie May (Carter) C.; B.S. in Elec. Engring., Ga. Inst. Tech., 1941; M.Ed., Emory U., 1951; Ed.D., U. Ga., 1953; m. Mary Helen Wright, Aug. 21, 1948; children—Edward Spencer, Leslie Ann. High sch. tchr., Atlanta, 1947-52; prin. S.M. Inma Sch., Atlanta, 1952-56; area supt. Atlanta Pub. Schs., 1956-65, asst. supt., 1965—. Active various community drives. Served from 2d lt. to lt. col., AUS, 1941-46; now col. Res. Fellow A.A.A.S.; mem. Am. Ednl. Research Assn., Ga. Assn. Sch. Bus. Ofcls. (past pres.), Atlanta Prins. Club (pres. 1953-54), Kappa Phi Kappa, Phi Delta Kappa, Psi Chi. Methodist. Mason. Club: Civitan (gov. Ga. dist. N.; v.p. 1968-70) (Atlanta). Home: 4715 Towanda Circle College Park GA 30337 Office: 224 Central Av SW Atlanta GA 30303

COOK, EDWARD WILLINGHAM, bldg. products mfr., commodity mcht.; b. Memphis, June 19, 1922; s. Everett Richard and Phoebe (Willingham) C.; grad. Hotchkiss Sch., 1940; A.B., Yale, 1944; m. Nancy Barber, Apr. 29, 1947; children—Edward Willingham, Everett Richard II, Barbara Moore. Pres., Cook Industries, Inc., Memphis, N.Y.C., Chgo., Fresno, Cal., Los Angeles, Kansas City, Osaka, Tokyo, Japan, Hong Kong, Rotterdam, Paris, 1952—, Cook Y Cia, de Mexico, S.A., 1952—; dir. S.L.-S.F. Ry., 1st Nat. Bank of Memphis, United Foods, Memphis. Mem. Cotton Adv. Commn., 1964-68. Chmn. Memphis-Shelby County Airport Authority, 1968—. Mem. Shelby County Quar. Ct. Served to maj. USAAF, 1943-45; MTO. Decorated D.F.C., Bronze Star, Air medal with six oak leaf clusters. Mem. Am. Cotton Shippers Assn. (pres. 1966-67). Democrat. Episcopalian. Clubs: Memphis Country, Memphis Hunt and Polo; Links (N.Y.C.); Boston (New Orleans); Everglades (Palm Beach, Fla.). Office: 2185 Democrat Rd Memphis TN 38116

COOK, GEORGE THOMAS, newspaper editor; b. Indpls., Apr. 12, 1921; s. James Merkle and Mary Audra (Harp) C.; A.B. in Journalism, U. Ala., 1949; m. Mary Frances Berry, May 3, 1952; children—Frances Ellen, Christopher Alan. Reporter, Birmingham (Ala.) Post-Herald, 1949-63, state editor, 1963-65, city editor, 1965-66, mng. editor, 1966—. Served with AUS, 1940-46. Methodist. Home: 1905 Helen Circle Birmingham AL 35226 Office: 2200 4th Av N Birmingham AL 35202

COOK, H. K., banker; b. Mooreland, Okla., Jan. 22, 1933; s. William C. and Mary B. (Egbert) C.; student Cameron Jr. Coll., Lawton, Okla., 1952; student Trinity U., San Antonio, 1953-55; grad. Southwestern Grad. Sch. Banking, So. Meth. U., 1969; m. June B. Toepperwein, July 31, 1954; children—Darrell and Cheryl (twins), Pamela, Bradley. Profl. football player, Can., 1956-57; with SIC Finance Loan, San Antonio, 1957-63, br. mgr., Ponca City, Okla., 1963-65; v.p. loans and pub. relations, dir. Bank of Commerce, Tonkawa, Okla., 1965-68; v.p. Community Nat. Bank, Oklahoma City, 1968—. Pres., Tonkawa Safety Council, 1968; mem. Community Council No. Okla. Coll. and city of Tonkawa, 1968. Bd. dirs. United Fund, Tonkawa, 1966-68, pres., 1966; bd. dirs., treas. Tonkawa Youth Recreation, 1966-68. Mem. City Council, Tonkawa, 1967, mayor, 1968. Mem. Okla. Bankers Assn. (vice chmn. pub. relations and marketing com. 1971—). Lutheran. Elk. Home: 4202 N Barr Oklahoma City OK 73122 Office: 5800 N W 39th St Oklahoma City OK 73122

COOK, HENRY MORGAN, JR., physician; b. Belton, Tex., June 23, 1922; s. Henry Morgan and Maude Hazel (Gaeckler) C.; B.S., U. Neb., 1945, M.D., 1945; m. Nancy Leontine Gill, July 7, 1947; children—Carol Ann (Mrs. Truman Harris), Henry Morgan III, William, James. Commd. 2d lt. U.S. Army, 1942, advanced through grades to col., 1968; ret., 1972; intern Kings Daus. Hosp., Temple, Tex., 1945-46; resident internal medicine Brooke Gen. Hosp., San Antonio, Tex., 1949-52; resident pulmonary diseases Fitzsimons Gen. Hosp., Denver, 1952-53; chief med. service U.S. Army Hosp., Okinawa, 1953-56; resident allergy U. Va. Hosp., 1957-58, chief outpatient service Letterman Gen. Hosp., San Francisco, 1958-62; chief med. service U.S. Army Hosp., Ft. Carson, Colo., 1962-63; chief med. adv. div. MAAG, Taiwan, 1963-67; med. rep. U.S. Army Standardization Group, Ottawa, Ont., Can., 1967-70; chief profl. services, chief dept. medicine Womack Army Hosp., Ft. Bragg, N.C., 1970-72; dir. med. service San Antonio Chest Hosp., 1972—. Diplomate Am. Bd. Internal Medicine. Mem. A.M.A., A.C.P., Assn. Mil. Surgeons. Home and office: PO Box 23340 Hilland Hills Station San Antonio TX 78223

COOK, JAY DEARDORFF, JR., educator; b.Chester, Pa., Apr. 26, 1921; s. Jay Deardorff and Margaretta (Nelson) C.; B.A., Washington and Lee U., 1943; M.B.A., Wharton Sch., U. Pa., 1948; Ph.D., Ohio State U., 1956; m. Florence Levis Garrett, Dec. 28, 1946; children—Jay D. III, Richard Garrett. Instr., Denison U., 1948-50, asst. prof., 1950-53; asst. prof. Washington and Lee U., Lexington, Va., 1953-56, asso. prof., 1956-62, prof. accounting, 1962—, head dept. accounting, 1960—. Pres., dir. Lexington-Rockbridge Mental Health Assn., 1963; dir. Lexington-Rockbridge Mental Health Clinic, 1967—. Served to capt. USMCR, 1943-46. Decorated D.F.C., Air medal with oak leaf cluster. Mem. Am. Accounting Assn., Am. Econ. Assn., Va. Soc. C.P.A.'s (asso.). Home: 905 Sunset Dr Lexington VA 24450

COOK, JIM, state govt. ofcl. Commr. charities and corrections State of Okla. Office: Capitol Bldg Oklahoma City OK 73105*

COOK, KENNETH GRAHAM, research psychologist; b. Phila., Aug. 21, 1931; s. Joseph and Anna (Graham) C.; B.S., Pa. State U., 1954, M.S., 1955; Ph.D., Am. U., 1967; m. Jane Davis, Dec. 17, 1955; children— Kenneth Graham, Sara Ann. Residence hall counselor Pa. State U., University Park, Pa., 1954-55; personnel asst. Chrysler Corp., Detroit, 1955; survey asst., personnel mgmt. br. The Adjutant General's Office, U.S. Army, Washington, 1956-57, statistical research asso., personnel research br. 1957-59; research asso. Century Research Corp., Arlington, 1959—, v.p., 1961—, dir., 1962—. Served with AUS, 1955-57. Mem. Am., Eastern, D.C. psychol. assns., Human Factors Soc., A.A.A.S., Phi Beta Kappa, Kappa Phi Kappa, Phi Kappa Phi, Phi Eta Sigma, Psi Chi. Contbr. articles in field to profl. jours. Home: 6542 35th Rd N Arlington VA 22213 Office: 4113 Lee Hwy Arlington VA 22207

COOK, LELAND BLANCHARD, civil engr.; b. Tupelo, Miss., June 7, 1920; s. Thomas Blanchard and Verlie Rebecca (Christian) C.; B.S., Miss. State U., 1942; m. Mary Agnes Livingston, Sept. 30, 1942; children— Mary Lee (wife of Dr. John Paul Bryson), Rebecca Caye, Stephen Roy. With Ingalls Shipbldg. Corp., Pascagoula, Miss., 1942-44; cons. engr., Tupelo, 1946-60; partner Cook Coggin Engrs., Inc., Tupelo, 1960—; pres. Found. Services, Inc.; v.p. Planning Consultants, Inc., Jim Johnson & Assos. Architects. Mem. Miss. Bd. Registration for Profl. Engrs.; mem. engring. adv. com. Miss. State U. Served as lt. USNR, 1944-46. Mem. Cons. Engrs. Council Miss. (past pres.), Miss. Soc. Profl. Engrs., Am. Soc. C.E. (dir. Miss. sect.), Miss. Profl. Engrs. Pvt. Practice (past pres.). Baptist. Home: 1006 Jackson St Tupelo MS 38801 Office: 703 Crossover St Tupelo MS 38801

COOK, MARLOW WEBSTER, U.S. senator; b. Akron, N.Y., July 27, 1926; s. Floyd Truman and Mary Lee (Webster) C; LL.B. U. Louisville, 1950; m. Nancy Elizabeth Remmers, Nov. 22, 1947;

children—Christine, Caroline, Nancy, Mary Louise, Marlow Webster. Admitted to Ky. bar, 1950; mem. firm Hotell and Stephenson, Louisville, 1952-61; judge Jefferson County, 1961-65, 66-68; mem. U.S. Senate from Ky., 1969—. Mem. Ky. Ho. of Reps., 1958-61. Served with USNR, 1944-46. Home: 4000 River St North Arlington VA 22207 Office: Old Senate Office Bldg Washington DC 20510

COOK, WENDELL HOLMES, physician; b. Philadelphia, Miss., July 4, 1912; s. Thomas Michael and Emma Frances (Rea) C.; B.S., Millsaps Coll., 1934; M.D., Tulane U., 1938; m. Jane Elizabeth Peneguy, June 14, 1938; children—Wendell Holmes, James Michael, John Patrick. Intern, So. Bapt. Hosp., New Orleans, 1938-39; physician, Civilian Conservation Corps, Ft. Oglethorpe, Ga., 1939-40; resident physician Huey P. Long Hosp., Pineville, La., 1940; attending surgeon Civilian Conservation Corps, Ft. Oglethorpe, Ga., 1940-42; gen. practice medicine, Gulfport, Miss., 1942, Meridian, Miss., 1946—; div. surgeon 31st Inf. Div., 1947-67; supt. Matty Hersee Hosp., Meridian, 1948-60; pres. med. staff St. Joseph's Hosp., Meridian, 1966-67. Served to capt. M.C., AUS, 1942-46; ETO; lt. col. M.C., 1951-52; Korea; brig. gen. N.G. ret. Decorated Bronze Star, Magnolia Cross. Mem. A.M.A., So., Miss. med. assns., Pi Kappa Alpha, Theta Kappa Psi. Home: 1829 43d St Meridian MS 39301 Office: 1209 21st Av Meridian MS 39301

COOKE, DORSEY MCKINLEY, ednl. adminstr.; b. Cleveland, Va., Jan. 11, 1910; s. Morgan and Nannie (Street) C.; B.S., Mary Washington Coll., 1935; M.A., E. Tenn. State U., 1960; postgrad. U. Va., 1969-71; m. Nola Mae Smith, Jan. 1, 1937; children—Dwayne, Sue (Mrs. Glen Osborne). Tchr., prin. Russell County (Va.) Schs., 1932-43; operator farm, 1944-47; prin. Valley Inst. High Sch., Washington County, Va., 1948-57; supr. schs. Washington County Schs., Abingdon, Va., 1958-64, dir. instrn., 1965—. Adv. council Speech and Hearing Clinic, Mt. Rogers Planning Commn., Washington County Easter Seal Campaign. Mem. Washington County Edn. Assn. (numerous coms. 1960—), Phi Delta Kappa. Baptist (deacons, usher, tchr. Bible, pres. adult dept.). Home: Route 1 Box 425 Bristol VA 24201 Office: Sch Bd Office Drawer G Abingdon VA 24210

COOKE, HEREWARD LESTER, JR., museum curator; b. Princeton, N.J., Feb. 16, 1916; s. Hereward Lester and Olive (McCallum) C.; student Harrow Sch., Eng., 1929-34; B.A., Oxford U., 1937; student Yale Sch. Fine Arts, 1939-41; M.F.A., Princeton, 1949, Ph.D., 1956; student the Sorbonne, U. Paris, France, 1952-53; m. Elizabeth Miles, Nov. 11, 1942. Free lance artist, 1937-42; instr., artist-in-residence, Princeton, 1946-51; museum curator Nat. Gallery Art, Washington, 1955-62, curator painting, 1962—. U.S. Army combat artist, S. Vietnam, 1967. Served with USAAF, 1942-46. Decorated Air medal, Bronze Star medal; Order Merit, Italy; recipient Fulbright award, France, 1951-52; Prix-de-Rome, 1952-54. Author: Roman Drawings at Windsor, 1961; La Galeria Nacional de Washington, 1965; Painting Lessons from the Great Masters, 1967; National Gallery of Art, 1969; Eyewitness to Space, 1971. Home: 808 Swink's Mill Rd McLean VA 20212 808 Swink's Mill Rd McLean VA 20212 Office: Nat Gallery Art Washington DC 20565

COOKE, JAMES L., educator; B.S., Tex. Tech. U.; M.S., U. Tex.; Ph.D., Northwestern U. Prof. elec. engring. Lamar U., Beaumont, Tex. Registered profl. engr. Home: 6235 Westgate Dr Beaumont TX 77706*

COOKE, JOHN WARREN, state legislator; b. Mathews, Va., Feb. 28, 1915; ed. Va. Mil. Inst.; m. Anne Brown Rawn. Newspaper publisher, pres. Tidewater Newspapers, Inc.; dir. Tidewater Telephone Co.; mem., speaker Va. Ho. of Reps. Democrat. Episcopalian. Office: State Capitol Richmond VA 23219

COOKE, MAXWELL ELWOOD, automobile agy. exec.; b. Gardner, Mass., June 10, 1931; s. Maxwell Edward and Edith Vincent (Gridley) C.; A.B., Duke, 1958; m. Vivien Anne Ridener, Oct. 14, 1952; children—Maxwell Edward, Courtney Crittendon, Ashleigh Elizabeth. Vice pres., gen. mgr. Cooke Cadillac Co., Sarasota, Fla., 1958—. Pres., Asolo Opera Guild, Sarasota, 1968—; v.p. Asolo State Theater of Fla., Sarasota, 1970-72. Bd. dirs. Fla. West Coast Symphony, Sarasota. Served with USN, 1952-56. Mem. Sarasota County Auto Dealers Assn. (pres. 1970-71). Clubs: Field, University (Sarasota); Forest Lakes Country. Home: Med-Court Acres 3425 W Forest Lake Circle Sarasota FL 33580 Office: 2200 Bee Ridge Rd Sarasota FL 33578

COOKE, WILLIAM CECIL, banker; b. Winston-Salem, N.C., Dec. 4, 1927; s. Millard Vance and Flora (Blevins) C.; B.A., Appalachian State Tchrs. Coll., 1952; m. Barbara Jean Rucker, July 11, 1953; children— Cela Dawn, Rucker Van. Exec. trainee McLean Trucking Co., Winston-Salem, 1953-55; territory mgr. Security Life and Trust Co., Chattanooga, 1955-58; sales mgr. Dixie Ohio Express Co., Chattanooga, 1958-65; exec. v.p. Fayetteville 1st Fed. Savs. and Loan Co. (Tenn.), 1965-70; pres. Lincoln County Bank, Fayetteville, 1970—. Mem. Middle Tenn. exec. bd. Boy Scouts Am., 1965—, vice chmn. Davey Crockett dist., 1969—, recipient Long Rifle award, 1969, Silver Beaver award, 1970; mem. Lincoln County Library Com., 1970—. Magistrate, Lincoln County Quar. Ct., 1970—; mem. Lincoln County Budget Com., 1970, Lincoln County Planning Commn., 1971—. Served with USNR, 1946-48. Elk. Club: Fayetteville Golf and Country. Home: Route 1 Old Mulberry Rd Fayetteville TN 37334 Office: 302 E College St Fayetteville TN 37334

COOKENBOO, JOHN B., utility exec.; b. Wharton, Tex., 1910; grad. S. Tex. Coll., 1943. Exec. v.p., dir. Houston Natural Gas Corp.; exec. v.p., dir. Houston Pipe Line Co., Houston Natural Gas Products Co., H.N.G. Petrochems., Valley Gas Transmission, Inc., Valley Pipe Lines, Inc., Liquid Carbonic Corp. Home: 250 Chimney B Rock Rd Houston TX 77024 Office: Houston Natural Gas Bldg Houston TX 77002

COOKSEY, JAMES ALLEN, sales exec.; b. Greenville, S.C., Mar. 23, 1913; s. Oscar Allen and Ollie (Hood) C.; ed. pub., bus. and indsl. tng. schs.; m. Blanche Wilbanks, Sept. 7, 1934; 1 dau., Sheila (Mrs. James Carter Blandford). Sales mgr. Coca-Cola Bottling Co., Greenville, 1928—. Campaign dir. March of Dimes, 1971. Mem. Sales Marketing Execs. Internat. (pres. 1966-67). Baptist (deacon). Mason; mem. Woodmen of World. Club: Greenville Civitan (treas. 1969). Home: 137 Scarlett St Greenville SC 29607 Office: 516 Buncombe St Greenville SC 29602

COOKSEY, WILLIAM TRAVIS, bus. exec.; b. Phenix City, Ala., Mar. 20, 1915; s. Samuel Hill and Verna (Brodnax) C.; student pub. schs.; m. Mildred Alice Jenkins, May 16, 1936. Accounting dept. Tom Huston Peanut Co., Columbus, Ga., 1931-39; salesman Liley Ames Corp., Columbus, O., 1939-40; chief clk. supply Q.M.C., Ft. Benning, Ga., 1940-44; gen. mgr. Blue Springs Farms-Cason J. Callaway, Hamilton, Ga., 1944-60; sec. Ida Cason Callaway Found., Pine Mountain, Ga., 1951—, treas., 1960—, exec. sec., 1964—. Instl. rep. Boy Scouts. Bd. dirs. Harris County Mental Health Assn.; bd. dirs., chmn. water safety com. Harris County chpt. A.R.C.; bd. dirs., past pres. Ga. Lions Lighthouse Found; sec.-treas., trustee Pine Mountain Clinic; bd. dirs. Peach Bowl, Inc. Mem. U.S. Hwy. 27 of Ga. (dir., past pres.). Methodist (steward, chmn. ofcl. bd.). Mason (K.T.). Lion (past pres., zone chmn., dep. dist. gov.). Home: Blue Springs Rd Hamilton GA 31811 Office: Pine Mountain GA 31822

COOLEY, DAVID WILLIAM, assn. exec.; b. Hendersonville, N.C., Feb. 6, 1929; s. Arthur Guilford and Reina (McNee) C.; m. Diane Clair Miller, Oct. 24, 1953; children—Ann, David Jr., John, Philip, Matthew. Chief exec. officer Greer C. of C. (S.C.), 1951-52, Hendersonville (N.C.) C. of C., 1952-58, Greenville (S.C.) C. of C., 1958-64; chief exec. officer Jacksonville (Fla.) C. of C., 1964-68; now chief exec. officer Memphis Area C. of C. Served with USMCR, 1948-50. Episcopalian. Mason (Shriner). Home: 219 Cherokee Dr Memphis TN 38111 Office: Chamber of Commerce PO Box 224 Memphis TN 38101

COOLEY, DENTON, surgeon, educator; b. Houston, Aug. 22, 1920; s. Ralph C. and Mary (Fraley) C.; B.A., U. Tex., 1941; M.D., Johns Hopkins, 1944; m. Louise Goldsborough Thomas, Jan. 15, 1949; children—Mary, Susan, Louise, Florence, Helen. Asso. prof. surgery Baylor U. Coll. Medicine, Houston, 1954-62, prof. surgery, 1962—; chief cardiovascular service St. Luke's Hosp., Tex. Children's Hosp. Dir. Southwestern Savs. Assn., Bank of Tex. Trustee St. Stephens Episcopal Sch., Austin, Tex. Served as capt. M.C., AUS, 1946-48. Named one of Ten outstanding Young Men in U.S., by U.S. Jr. C. of C., 1955; decorated Condecoracion Al Merito (Republic Ecuador); recipient Grande Medaille, U. Ghent, Belgium, 1963, Humanitarian award Variety Clubs Internat., 1963, Coronet medal St. Edwards U., 1963; Kappa Sigma Man Yr., 1964; Distinguished Citizen award Rotary Club Houston, 1965. Diplomate Am. Bd. Surgery, Am. Bd. Thoracic Surgery (mem. bd. 1965—). Fellow A.C.S. (gov. 1965-68); mem. Soc. Thoracic Surgeons, Thoracic Soc., So. Med. Assn., Am. Assn. Thoracic Surgery, Soc. U. Surgeons, Am. Coll. Cardiology, Am. Coll. Chest Physicians, Am., Pan-Pacific, Western surg. assns., Tex. Acad. Sci., Soc. for Clin. Surgery, Internat. Cardiovascular Soc., Soc. for Vascular Surgery, Western So. surg. assns., Halsted Soc., Tex. Surg. Soc., Internat. Soc. Surgery. Home: 3014 Del Monte Dr Houston TX 77019

COOLEY, JOSEPH BERNARD, physician; b. Atlanta, July 1, 1920; s. Lewis Robert and Pallie Clementine (Hudgins) C.; A.B., Emory U., 1942; M.D., Med. Coll. Ga., 1945; m. Mary Elizabeth Longley, Oct. 11, 1946; children—William Robert, Joseph Howell, John Cline, Stephen Lewis. Intern, Crawford W. Long Meml. Hosp., Atlanta, 1945-46, now mem staff; gen. practice medicine, Lithonia, Ga., 1949-52, Atlanta, 1952—; mem. staff DeKalb Gen. Hosp., Decatur, Ga. Served with M.C., AUS, 1942-48. Mem. John Birch Soc. (chpt. leader 1968—), Theta Kappa Psi. Baptist. Home: 5127 Stratmor Ct Stone Mountain GA 30083 Office: 572 Fayetteville Rd SE Atlanta GA 30316

COOLEY, MCWHORTER STEPHENS, accountant; b. nr. Homer, Ga., Jan. 11, 1907; s. William Pledger and Lilly (Rogers) C.; B.S.C., U. Ga., 1928, M.S.C., 1929; m. Thelma Jane Leathers, Aug. 30, 1930; children—Janey Mae, William Leon. Instr. accounting U. Ga., 1929-30; acct. Richardson, Jackson & Davis, C.P.A.'s, Atlanta, 1930-38; self-employed as C.P.A., Athens, Ga., 1938—; dir. So. Mut. Ins. Co. C.P.A., Ga. Mem. Am. Inst. Accountants, Ga. Soc. C.P.A.'s, Alpha Kappa Psi, Beta Gamma Sigma, Phi Kappa Phi. Home: 435 Hampton Ct Athens GA 30601 Office: Southern Mutual Bldg Athens GA 30601

COOLIDGE, WARREN H., lawyer; b. Plattsburg, N.Y., July 30, 1930; s. Victor A. and Laura (Cook) C.; A.A., Campbell Coll., 1957; A.B., U. N.C., 1958, LL.B., 1961; m. Nancy Harnish, Mar. 19, 1951. Admitted to N.C. bar, 1961; practiced in Fayetteville, N.C.; instr. N.C. State U., 1962; city solicitor, Fayetteville, 1965-69; U.S. atty. Eastern Dist. N.C., 1969—. Exec. sec. N.C. Republican Party, 1960; Cumberland County Rep. chmn., 1961, 7th dist. chmn., 1962-63. Served with AUS, 1947-55. Mem. Am., N.C., 7th Dist., Cumberland County bar assns., Campbell Coll. Alumni Assn. (county pres. 1965-66). Mason (32 deg., Shriner, K.T.), Rotarian. Home: 224 Woodcrest Rd Fayetteville NC 28305 Office: PO Bldg Raleigh NC 27602

COONEY, JOHN THOMAS, optical mfg. co. exec.; b. Mpls., Apr. 17, 1921; s. John Thomas and Helen (Bork) C.; B.B.A., U. Minn., 1943; grad. Advanced Mgmt. Course, Harvard, 1971; m. Margaret Frances Bonner, Oct. 30, 1948; children—Mary, John Thomas Jr., Patricia, David, Stephen, Michael, Thomas. Public relations officer M & O Paper Co., Mpls., 1946-49; territory mgr. Univis, Inc., Fort Lauderdale, Fla., 1949-52, regional sales mgr., 1952-57, product mgr., 1957-59, gen. sales mgr., 1959-61, v.p. marketing 1961-68, group v.p., 1968-71, exec. v.p., 1971—; dir. Bank Commerce, Ft. Lauderdale.Bd. dirs., v.p. Boys Club Broward County. Trustee Marymount Coll., Boca Raton. Served to maj. AUS, 1943-46. Decorated Silver Star, Bronze Star, Legion of Honor, Crown of Leopold. Mem. Am. Mgmt. Assn. (planning council), Ft. Lauderdale C. of C., Sales and Marketing Execs. (past pres., dir.), Beta Theta Pi. Roman Catholic. Clubs: Serra; Coral Ridge Country. Home: 22 Minnetonka Rd Fort Lauderdale FL 33310 Office: Univis Inc Vision Park Fort Lauderdale FL 33310

COONS, HERBERT, JR., state ofcl. Exec. sec. Fla. Bd. Architecture. Address: 725 S Bronough St Tallahassee FL 32304*

COONS, THOMAS ELMER, milling co. exec.; b. Mt.Sterling, Ky., Dec. 7, 1903; s. John Thomas and Lucy (Duff) C.; B.S. in Commerce, U. Ky., 1926; m. Louise Atkins, July 12, 1929. Farmer, Mt. Sterling, 1926—; field supr. FCA, St. Louis, 1934-42; assn. supr. farm credit Prodn. Credit Corp., Louisville, 1942-45; owner, operator Monarch Milling Co., Mt. Sterling, Ky., 1945—; pres., chmn. bd. dirs. Central Ky. Prodn. Credit Assn., Lexington, 1960—; dir. Exchange Bank Ky., Mt. Sterling. Mem. Montgomery County Agrl. Council, 1968—. Mem. Phi Kappa Tau. Democrat. Mem. Christian Ch. (deacon 1944—; trustee 1950—). Home: 195 Antwerp Av Mount Sterling KY 40353 Office: 101 S Maysville St Mount Sterling KY 40353

COOPER, AGNES PEARSON (MRS. DAVID ACRON COOPER), educator; b. Bonner Springs, Kan., Oct. 18, 1910; d. James P. and May B. (Luther) Pearson; B.S., Kan. State Tchrs. Coll., 1932; M.S., U. Denver, 1938; postgrad. Harvard, 1939, 40; m. David Acron Cooper, Oct. 15, 1941; 1 son, David Acron. Tchr. high schs., Kan., Mo., 1929-37; tchr. Wyandotte High Sch., Kansas City, Kan., 1937-39; instr. secretarial sci. Alfred U., 1939-41; instr. U. Tenn., 1941-42; dir. edn. and placement Knoxville (Tenn.) Bus. Coll., 1942-48; dir. edn., treas. Cooper Inst., Inc., Knoxville, 1948—. Mem. Knox County adv. com. Tenn. Welfare Dept., Knoxville, 1955—, chmn. 1959; mem. E. Tenn. Community Improvement Central Com., 1952—, pres., 1968; hostess spl. luncheons Tenn. Valley Agrl. and Indsl. Fair, 1956—. Mem. nat. bd. Woman's Med. Coll. of Pa. Mem. E. Tenn. Edn. Assn. (chmn. bus. sect. 1958, sec. 1957), Nat. Office Mgrs. Assn., Am. Assn. U. Women, Am. Bus. Women's Assn., Better Bus. Bur. Baptist. Club: Quota (gov. 23d dist. 1956-57, gov. 8th dist. 1949-51, trustee ednl. revolving fund Knoxville 1962-63, internat. pres. 1965-66). Home: 720 N 5th Av NE Knoxville TN 37917

COOPER, BENJAMIN F., coll. dean; b. Warsaw, N.C., Nov. 22, 1924; s. Ben F. and Macy (Jones) C.; A.B., U. N.C., 1947, B.S., 1950, M.S., 1951, Ph.D., 1956; m. Hazel May Strickland, Sept. 17, 1947; children—Ben F., Caran S., Cana S. Asst. prof. U. N.C., 1956-57; asso. prof. Ore. State U., 1957-61, U. Ga., 1961-65, prof., 1965-66; dean Coll. Pharmacy Allied Health Professions, N.E. La. State U., Monroe, La., 1966—; cons. USPHS, NSF. Served with USNR, 1944-46, 51-53. Mem. Am., La. pharm. assns., Sigma Xi, Rho Chi, Phi Delta Chi, Pi Kappa Alpha. Mason, Elk, Lion. Clubs: Toastmasters (pres.), Rotary. Home: 3813 Forsythe Av Monroe LA 71201 Office: Northeast La State Univ Coll of Pharmacy and Allied Health Professions Monroe LA 71201

COOPER, CHARLES BRADFORD, broadcasting co. exec.; b. Augusta, Ga., Dec. 6, 1943; s. J.W. and A.A. C.; A.A., Miami-Dade Jr. Coll., B.B.A., Miss. Coll. Formerly exec. trainee Sears Roebuck & Co., Coral Gables, Fla.; adminstrv. asst. Eastern Air Lines, Miami, Fla.; then announcer radio sta. WJDX, Jackson, Miss., now gen. mgr. Office: WJDX P O Box 2171 Jackson MS 39205

COOPER, CHARLES DEWEY, educator; b. Whittier, N.C., Jan. 11, 1924; B.S., Berry Coll., 1940; M.A., Duke, 1948, Ph.D., 1950; m. Corrie Willie Johnson, Dec. 21, 1946; children—Norma Louise, Virginia Claire, Edward Howell. Asst. prof. physics U. Ga. at Athens, 1950-55, asso. prof., 1955-61, prof., 1961—; research fellow Harvard, 1954-55. Cons. Oak Ridge Nat. Lab., 1968—. Served to lt USNR, 1944-46. Fellow A.A.A.S.; mem. Am. Inst. Physics (regional counselor 1967-70), Am. Phys. Soc., Am. Assn. U. Profs., Sigma Xi. Home: Route 3 Athens GA 30601

COOPER, CLEMENT THEODORE, lawyer; b. Miami, Fla., Oct. 26, 1930; s. Benjamin Leon and Louise (Bethel) C.; A.B., Lincoln U. of Mo., 1952; postgrad. Boston U., 1954-55; J.D., Howard U., 1958; postgrad. U. Cal. at San Francisco, 1971; m. Nannie Coles; children—Stephanie L., Bridgette L., Patricia E., Karen G. Admitted to Mich., D.C. bars, 1960, Supreme Ct. bar, 1963; gen. practice Washington, 1960—; pres., gen. counsel Bayshore Resources Co., Inc. Mem. D.C. Pub. Welfare Adv. Council, 1966-68. Served with AUS, 1952-54. Mem. U.S., D.C. chambers commerce, Bar Assn. D.C., Am., Nat., Washington bar assns., Am. Civil Liberties Union, Am. Judicature Soc., Alpha Phi Alpha. Author: The Sealed Verdict, 1964. Home: 728 Dahlia St NW Washington DC 20012 Office: 918 F St NW Washington DC 20004

COOPER, CURTIS VICTOR, health services adminstr.; b. Savannah, Ga., Sept. 22, 1932; s. Joshua and Clara (Baxley) C.; B.S., Savannah State Coll., 1955; m. Constance Y. Hartwell, Apr. 8, 1956; children—Curtis, Constance. Debit mgr. Guaranty Life Ins. Co., 1955-57; salesman, rent agt. Toomer Realty Co., 1957-59; research technician Stored-Product Insects Lab., 1959-71; program developer for comprehensive health center Econ. Opportunity Authority for Savannah, Chatham Area, Inc., 1971—. Mem. Community Vascular Council, County Mosquito Control Commn.; treas. Butler Sch. P.T.A. Bd. dirs. Hodge Meml. Day Care Center, Inner City Developers, Inc., Savannah br. N.A.A.C.P.; mem. curriculum adv. com. Savannah Area Tech. Trade Sch. Recipient Man of Year award Savannah State Coll., 1955; Alpha Man of Year award, 1964; Tompkins Future Farmers of Am. award, 1967; named Prince Hall Mason of Year for community service, 1969. Mem. Ga. Entomology Soc., Entomol. Soc. Am., Alpha Phi Alpha. Baptist (deacon). Mason. Contbr. articles profl. jours. Home: 910 Googe St Savannah GA 31401 Office: 21 W Park Av Savannah GA 31401

COOPER, DAVID ACRON, coll. pres., public accountant, tax cons.; b. Charlotte, N.C., October 16, 1910; s. David P. and Roberta (Lewis) C.; B.S., U. Tenn., 1931, M.S., 1934; A.M., Columbia, 1938; grad. student Harvard, 1939, Washington & Jefferson Coll., 1943, Am. U., Biarritz, France, 1945; m. Agnes Pearson, Oct. 15, 1941; 1 son, David A. Tchr. Knoxville (Tenn.) High Sch, 1931-34; spl. cons. bus. edn. Southwestern Pub. Co., Cin., 1935-39; personnel dir. S. H. George & Sons, Knoxville, 1941-48; owner, mgr. Dapco Sales & Services, 1949—; pres. Cooper Inst., Inc., 1948—; instr. Am. U., Biarritz, France, 1945; asso. prof. bus. Knoxville Coll., 1967—. Treas. Mental Health Clinic; mem. Com. on Teaching Bible in Pub. Schs. Sec. Bd. Edn. Served as tech. sgt. U.S. Army, ETO, 1943-45. Mem. Am. Mgmt. Assn., Nat. Assn. Accountants, Internat. Platforms Assn., C. of C., Baptist. Clubs: Kiwanis, North Knoxville Business Men's. Home: 720 N 5th Av Knoxville TN 37917

COOPER, EARL DANA, govt. engr.; b. Washington, Apr. 16, 1926; s. Dana Cockrill and Mildred (Schultz) C.; student Hampden Sydney Coll., 1944; B.E.E., George Washington U., 1948; postgrad. U. Md., 1949-51; m. Elaine LaDona Tibben, Apr. 16, 1949; children—Denise Kay, Karl Dennis. Elec. engr. Bur. Ships, Washington, 1948-55; guided missile design engr. and ordance engr. Navy Bur. of Ordnance, 1955-59; aerospace engr. Bur. Naval Weapons, 1959-62, tech. dir. air launched weapon systems 1962-66, tech. dir. advanced systems Naval Air Systems Command, Washington, 1966—; cons. to exec. com. Aircraft Armament div., Am. Ordnance Assn. Served with USNR, 1944-45. Mem. Assn. Naval Engrs. and Scis. (past sec.), Am. Ordnance Assn., I.E.E.E., Am. Inst. Aeros. and Astronautics. Lutheran. Home: 8265 The Midway Annandale VA 22003 Office: Code AIR-03P Washington DC 20360

COOPER, HARRY EZEKIEL, educator; b. Kansas City, Mo., Dec. 10, 1897; s. Ezekiel and Helen (Moore) C.; Mus.B., Horner Inst. Fine Arts, 1920; Mus.D., Bush Conservatory, 1923; A.B., Ottawa U., 1937; m. Agnes Bickford, Nov. 18, 1926; children—Robert Ezekiel, Alice Caroline (Mrs. Theo Robert Potter). Supt. music Liberty (Mo.) Schs., 1917-19; prof. music, chmn. dept. William Jewell Coll., 1919-28; dean music Ottawa U., 1928-37; chmn. dept. music, prof. music Meredith Coll., 1937—. Organist, choirmaster Kansas City (Mo.) Chs., 1911-37, Christ Ch., Raleigh, N.C., 1937-47, 1st Bapt. Ch., 1948—; organist N.C. Symphony Orch., 1949. Condr., Raleigh Oratorio Soc., 1940-48. Fellow Am. Guild Organists; mem. N.C. Music Tchrs. Assn. (pres. 1943-44), Raleigh Chamber Music Guild (pres. 1942-43). Writer musical articles, various songs, others. Home: 3 Henderson St Raleigh NC 27607

COOPER, ISABEL HOFFMANN (MRS. MILTON H. COOPER), real estate asso.; b. Pitts.; d. Alvin Anthony and Fannie (McCormick) Hoffmann; student voice diction and piano, pvt. tutors, 1914-35; student voice Cin. Conservatory Music, 1921; student God's Bible Coll., 1920, Missionary Tng. Inst., 1922, (Organ scholar) Pa. Coll. for Women (now Chatham Coll.), 1924; m. Milton H. Cooper, Sept. 15, 1928 (dec. July 1946); children—Paul Milton, Ethel (Mrs. Henry William Kurtz, Jr.), Ruth (Mrs. James Huber). Profl. soprano soloist radio stas. KDKA, 1926-28, also 1/2 hour program WCAE, summer 1928; numerous concert appearances include Boston Symphony Orch., harpist, 1927, Little Symphony Orch., 1939, also soprano soloist Christ Meth. Ch., 1940-46, First Presbyn. Ch., 1946-53 (all Pitts.); with YMCA, 1926-28, Maison Frederick Sch. Beauty Culture, 1938, Labor Standards Assn., 1939-42, USO, 1942-46 (all Pitts.); sec. to v.p. Hickman, Williams & Co., 1947-50; controlled materials sec. Dravo Corp., 1950-52 (both Pitts.); asst. to dir. Pitts. Found., 1952-67; sec.-bookkeeper Pitcairn-Crabbe Found., also sec. to cons. Howard Heinz Endowment, 1952-67 (both Pitts.);

adminstr. theater parties Pitts. Playhouse; adminstrv. exec. World Center Liturgical Studies, Inc., Boynton, Fla., 1969; adminstrv. asst. Frank Martens and Asso., Ft. Lauderdale, Fla., 1970; asso. Westdale Co. Realty, Plantation, Fla., 1972-—. Corr. sec., mem. exec. com., chmn. promotions com. Opera Workshop, Chatham Coll., 1959-—, judge competitive auditions of singers, 1963-—. Mem. Hist. Soc. Western Pa., Chatham Coll. Alumnae Assn. Episcopalian. Club: Women's City (music com. 1962-64) (Pitts.). Address: Village Green Apts 4200 NW 3d Ct Plantation FL 33313

COOPER, JEROME MAURICE, architect; b. Memphis, Jan. 24, 1930; s. Samuel and Bessie (Phillips) C.; B.S., Ga. Inst. Tech., 1952, B. Arch., 1955; postgrad. Universita di Roma, Rome, Italy, 1956-57; m. Jean Kanter Cooper, Dec. 29, 1957; children—David Franklin, Samuel Randolph, Beth Lauren. Draftsman Willner & Millkey, Atlanta, 1955-56; Fulbright fellow Rome, Italy, 1956-57; designer Abreu & Robeson, Atlanta, 1957-59, Heery & Heery, Atlanta 1959-60; pres. Cooper, Salzman & Carry, 1960-—. Served to lt. (j.g.) USNR, 1952-54. Mem. A.I.A. (v.p., pres. elect N. Ga. chpt.). Prin. archtl. works include: Classroom-Arts bldg. W. Ga. Coll., Briarcliff Village Shopping Center, Atlanta, Chateau-Fleur-di-Lis Restaurant, Atlanta, Sheraton Emory Inn, Riverbend Apts., Macon Youth Devel. Center, Landmark Office Bldg., Westlake Mall Shopping Center, also elementary schs. Home: 1070 Judith Way NE Atlanta GA 30324 Office: 836 W Peachtree St NW Atlanta GA 30308

COOPER, JOHN ROBERT, educator; b. Greenville, S.C., June 1, 1934; s. John R. Roy and Edith (Mills) C.; B.S., Clemson U., 1955, M.S., 1957; Ph.D., U. Va., 1967; m. Jo Poole, Nov. 27, 1959. Research asst. Clemson U., 1955-57; instr. and asst. prof. econs. Coll. Charleston, 1957-60; instr. econs. U. Va., 1960-63; asso. economist Fed. Res. Bank of Atlanta, 1963-64; asso. prof. econs. Winthrop Coll., Rock Hill, S.C., 1964-69, prof., 1969-—, dir. instl. research, 1967-70, dir. acad. planning and instnl. research, 1970-72, v.p. adminstrn. and planning, 1972-—. Served with AUS, 1957. Mem. So. Econ. Assn., Public Choice Soc., Omicron Delta Kappa, Omicron Delta Epsilon. Rotarian. Episcopalian. Home: Rt 1 Box 363 Rock Hill SC 29730

COOPER, JOHN SHERMAN, U.S. senator; b. Somerset, Ky., Aug. 23, 1901; s. John Sherman and Helen (Tartar) C.; A.B., Yale, 1923; student law Harvard, 1923-26; LL.D., U. Ky., Centre Coll., Georgetown (Ky.) Coll., Berea (Ky.) Coll., Eastern Ky. State Coll.; L.H.D., Lincoln Meml. U., Harrogate, Tenn.; D.C.L., Nasson Coll., Springdale, Me.; LL.D., Yale, U. Pitts.; m. Lorraine Rowan Shevlin, Mar. 17, 1955. Mem. lower house Ky. legislature, 1928-30; judge, Pulaski County, Ky., 1930-38; circuit judge 28th Jud. Dist., Ky., 1946-52; senator from Ky., 1946-48, 52-54, 57-—, mem. com. fgn. relations, pub. works, rules and adminstrn., select com. standards and conduct; U.S. ambassador to India, 1955; mem. law firm Gardner, Morrison & Rogers, Washington, 1949-51. Assisted in reorgn. German jud. system, Bavaria, after World War II hostilities ceased. Adviser to sec. of state, London and Brussels meetings Council of Ministers, NATO, 1950; U.S. del. Gen. Assembly UN, 1948, 68, alternate del., 1950, 51; congl. adviser U.S. delegates UNESCO Conf., 1958. Chmn. Nat. Lincoln Sesquicentennial Commn.; mem. Nat. Monument Commn., Pres.'s Commn. to Investigate Assassination Pres. Kennedy; mem. adv. com. of Inst. Politics, Harvard U. Mem. bd. trustees U. Ky., 1935-46. Georgetown Coll., Centre Coll.; mem. Yale U. Council. Served from pvt. to capt. AUS, 1942-46; ETO. Decorated Bronze Star Medal. Mem. Am., Ky. bar assns., Am. Legion. V.F.W., Beta Theta Pi. Republican. Baptist. Rotarian. Home: 2900 N St NW Washington DC 20007 Office: Senate Office Bldg Washington DC 20510

COOPER, LENOX GORE, ins. and real estate broker; b. Wilmington, N.C., Feb. 8, 1901; s. William Bryant and Ada (Gore) C.; student The Citadel, 1917-19; A.B., U. N.C., 1921; postgrad. Harvard, 1921-22; m. Mary Benthall Hardin, Apr. 27, 1935; children— Lenox Gore, Mary Hardin (Mrs. Ralph L. Falls, Jr.). Teller, Comml. Nat. Bank, 1922; ins., real estate broker, Wilmington, N.C., 1923-—; pres. Wilmington Bd. Underwriters, 1936-37; mem. Wilmington Bd. Realtors, v.p., 1960, pres., 1970; mem. New Hanover County Airport Authority, 1946-47, New Hanover Airport Commn., 1970-—. Mem. adv. bd. Salvation Army. Bd. govs. U. N.C.; founding trustee Meth. Coll., Fayetteville, N.C. Served from lt. to lt. comdr. USNR, 1942-45. Mem. Wilmington C. of C. (past pres.), N.C. Assn. Ins. Agts. (past bd. dirs.), Huguenot Soc. S.C., S.A.R., Am. Legion, V.F.W., Pi Kappa Alpha. Democrat. Methodist (trustee). Rotarian (pres. 1938-39). Clubs: Execs. (past pres.), Carolina Yacht (past commodore), Cape Fear (past pres.), Cape Fear Country, Surf (Wrightsville Beach, N.C.). Home: 1413 Country Club Rd Wilmington NC 28401 Office: 209 Princess St Wilmington NC 28401

COOPER, L(EROY) GORDON, JR., aerospace cons.; b. Shawnee, Okla., Mar. 6, 1927; s. Leroy Gordon and Hattie Lee (Herd) C.; student U. Hawaii, 1946-49, European extension U. Md., 1951-53; B.S. in Aero. Engring., Air Force Inst. Tech., 1956; grad. Exptl. Test Pilot Sch., USAF, 1957; m. Susan T. Taylor, May 6, 1972; children by previous marriage—Camala Keoki, Janita Lee. Commd. USAF, 1949, advanced through grades to col., 1965; jet fighter pilot, 1950-54; pilot exptl. flight test engring., 1957-59; became astronaut with Project Mercury, NASA, 1959; made 22 orbit flight in Faith 7, May 1963; made 122 Orbit flight in Gemini V, 1965; now mgmt. and engring. cons. to aviation and aerospace industries and airlines Gordon Cooper Consultants, Inc., Opalocka, Fla. Mem. Am. Inst. Aero. and Astronautics. Home: 5055 Collins Av Miami Beach FL 33140 Office: Bldg 147 Opalocka Airport Opalocka FL 33054

COOPER, MILES ROBERT, physician; b. Elizabeth City, N.C., Oct. 21, 1933; s. Miles Watson and Lucy Esther (Olds) C.; B.S., N.C. State U., 1955; M.D. (William Neal Reynolds scholar 1958-62), Bowman Gray Sch. Medicine, Wake Forest U., 1962; m. Myra Jean Batten, May 5, 1956; children—Michael Robert, Timothy Allen. Intern, U. Va. Hosp., 1962-63; asst. resident, chief resident, fellow N.C. Bapt. Hosp., 1963-66, asst. prof. medicine, 1966-70; asso. prof. medicine Bowman Gray Sch. Medicine, 1971-—; practice medicine, specializing in internal medicine, Winston-Salem, N.C., 1968-—. Served from 1st lt. arty. to capt. M.C., U.S. Army, 1956-58. Diplomate Am. Bd. Internal Medicine. Mem. Am. Soc. Hematology, Am. Soc. Oncology, Sigma Xi, Phi Eta Sigma, Phi Kappa Phi, Alpha Zeta. Home: 330 Staffordshire Rd Winston Salem NC 27104 Office: Bowman Gray Sch Medicine Winston Salem NC 27103

COOPER, RICHARD HOLCOMB, judge; b. Birmingham, Ala., Aug. 30, 1920; s. William Gerald and Ethel (Cobb) C.; A.B., Fla. So. Coll., 1940, LL.D., 1965; J.D., Stetson U., 1948; m. Bess Constantine Blanton, June 15, 1941; children—Bess Ann (Mrs. Robert L. Castlen), Sharon Lorraine (Mrs. J. Roger Efird), Thomas Richard. Admitted to Fla. bar. 1949; practiced in Orlando, 1949-67; prosecutor Orange County Criminal Ct. Record, 1953-59, judge, 1959-66; circuit judge 9th Jud. Circuit, Orlando, 1966-—; moderator Moral Issues of Our Times, weekly panel program WFTV, 1962-67. Served to col. AUS, 1942. Recipient First prize for Law Day address Am. Bar Assn., 1968. Mem. Fla. So. Coll. Nat. Alumni Assn. (past pres.), V.F.W. (state chmn. N.C. and res. activities), Res. Officers Assn., Am. Legion, Fraternal Order Police Assn. Methodist. Lion, Elk. Home: 80 Loudon Ct Maitland FL 32751 Office: Orange County Court House Orlando FL 32802

COOPER, ROBERT GILBERT, librarian; b. St. Louis, Feb. 24, 1930; s. Robert Kehr and Irma Emilie (Wagner) C.; B.S. in Edn., Union Coll., 1952; M.S. in L.S., U. So. Cal., 1966; m. Vivian Bernice Rabun, Aug. 9, 1953; children—Teresa Lynette, Stanley Wayne. Tchr., Tex. Conf. Seventh-day Adventists, Ft. Worth, 1952-62; librarian Loma Linda U., 1962-67, Findley Meml. Library, Southwestern Union Coll., Keene, Tex., 1967-—. Mem. A.L.A., Tex. Library Assn. Mailing Address: Findley Meml Library Southwestern Union Coll Keene TX 76059 Home: 408 N College Dr Keene TX 76059

COOPER, SELDON AMZI, civil engr.; b. Dixon, Miss.,Sept. 26, 1913; s. John Jessie and Carry Lucinda (Thomas) C.; B.C.E., Miss. State Coll., 1935; m. Monta Glee Allman, Sept. 11, 1940. Asst. engr. Gulf, Mobile & No. R.R. (Name later changed to Gulf, Mobile & Ohio R.R. Co.), 1935-37, asst. supr., 1937-38, asst. engr., 1938-41, resident engr., 1941-57, chief engr., 1957-—. Mem. Am. Ry. Engring. Assn. (dir. 1968-71). Democrat. Methodist. Office: 104 St Francis St Mobile AL 36624

COOPER, TIM ERVIN, JR., physician; b. Jackson, Miss., Dec. 23, 1933; s. Tim Ervin and Virginia (McAlpin) C.; B.S., Davidson Coll., 1955; M.D., Duke, 1959; m. Susan Rees, Sept. 9, 1961; children—Tim Ervin III, Rees Mahone. Rotating intern Charity Hosp., New Orleans, 1959-60; gen. practice medicine, Baton Rouge, 1960-62; resident internal medicine Henry Ford Hosp., Detroit, 1964-67; practice medicine, specializing in pulmonary diseases Whiteside/Cooper, Providence Med. Center, Charlotte, N.C., 1967-—; mem. staff Meml. Hosp., Presbyn. Hosp., Charlotte; med. faculty U. N.C., 1967-—. Mem. exec. com. Tb Assn., 1970-72. Bd. dirs., Am. Heart Assn. Served to capt. M.C., U.S. Army, 1962-64. Diplomate Am. Bd. Internal Medicine. Mem. A.M.A., N.C. Soc. Internal Medicine, Mecklenberg County Med. Soc. Club: Carmel Country (Charlotte). Home: 118 Sardis View Rd Charlotte NC 28211 Office: 1850 E 3d St Charlotte NC 28204

COOPER, WALTER GERALD, lawyer; b. Atlanta, Mar. 22, 1904; s. Walter G. and Belle (Bacon) C.; A.B., U. Ga., 1924; student Harvard Law Sch., 1925-27; LL.B. Emory U., 1929. Admitted to Ga. bar, 1929; regional atty. NLRB, 10th Region, 1936, litigation atty., 1937; chief enforcement atty. Southeastern states for OPA, Atlanta, 1942; mem. firm Tye, Cooper & Bill, 1952-55, McFarland & Cooper, Atlanta, 1955-64; mem. law firm Poole, Pearce, Cooper & Smith, and predecessor firm, Atlanta, 1964-—; mem. law faculty at Emory U., 1932-64. Served as lt. USNR, World War II. Mem. Am., Ga., Atlanta bar assns., Res. Officers Assn., Atlanta Lawyers Club (past v.p. and sec.), Phi Beta Kappa, Phi Delta Phi. Mason, Democrat, Baptist. Clubs: Ansley Golf, Optimist. Author articles Ga. Bar Assn. Jour. Home: 200 Montgomery Ferry Dr NE Atlanta GA 30309 Office: Nat Bank of Ga Bldg Atlanta GA 30303

COOPER, WILLIAM FRAZIER, educator; b. Louisville, Feb. 14, 1932; s. William Lowrey and Catherine (Tomlinson) C.; B.A., Baylor U., 1954, M.A., 1959; B.D., So. Bapt. Theol. Sem., 1958; Ph.D., Ind. U., 1967; m. Thelma Lou Smith, Dec. 24, 1959; children—Richard Lowrey, Jonathan Bagby, Dorisanne. Asst. prof. philosophy Lycoming Coll., Williamsport, Pa., 1964-65; asst. prof. philosophy Baylor U., Waco, Tex., 1965-68, asso. prof., 1968-71, prof., 1971-—. Sec. S.W. Alliance for Latin Am., 1969-70, v.p., 1970-—, also bd. dirs. Fulbright grantee for travel to Argentina, 1962-63. Mem. Am. Philos. Assn., Southwestern Council Latin Am. Studies, Southwestern Philos. Soc., Am. Assn. U. Profs. Translator: Theory of Man, 1964, Homenaje a Romero, 1964. Home: 204 Guittard St Waco TX 76706

COOTS, WILLIAM NORVELL, physician; b. Richmond, Va., Oct. 11, 1905; s. William R. and Juanita C. (Harris) C.; B.S., Va. Union U., 1930; M.D., Meharry Med. Coll., 1936; postgrad. Cook County Postgrad. Sch., Chgo., 1944; m. Theresa O. Palmer, June 28, 1955; children— William Norvell (dec.), Norvell Vandervall. Intern, Providence Hosp., Balt., 1936, Kansas City Gen. Hosp., 1937; practice medicine, specializing in gen. practice, Tulsa, 1937-—; chief staff Moton Meml. Hosp., 1948-53, vice chief staff, 1959-64. Bd. mgmt. Carver Youth Center, 1948-49; treas., founder Tulsa Urban League, 1953; sponsor, pres. Coots Apts., Inc., 1949-55. Recipient plaque Greenwood C. of C., 1970. Fellow Am. Geriatrics Soc.; mem. A.M.A., Okla. Med. Assn., Alpha Phi Alpha. Democrat. Baptist. Mason. Home: 512 E Mohawk Blvd Tulsa OK 74106 Office: 2623 N Peoria St Tulsa OK 74106

COOVER, HARRY WESLEY, JR., chem. co. exec.; b. Newark, Dela., Mar. 6, 1918; s. Harry Wesley and Anna (Rohm) C.; B.S., Hobart Coll., 1941; M.S., Cornell U., 1943; Ph.D., 1944; m. Muriel Zumbach, Sept. 17, 1941; children—Harry Wesley III, Stephen R., Melinda R. Research chemist Eastman Kodak Co., Rochester, N.Y., 1944-49; sr. research chemist Tenn. Eastman Co., mfr. plastics, chemicals, fibers, Kingsport, 1949-54, research asso., 1954-63, div. head, 1963-65, dir. research, 1965-70, v.p., 1970-—. Recipient So. Chemist award Memphis sect. Am. Chem. Soc., 1960. Mem. A.A.A.S., Am. Chem. Soc., Am. Ordnance Assn., Am. Assn. Textile Tech., N.Y. Acad. Sci., Sigma Xi, Epsilon Pi Sigma, Phi Kappa Phi. Patentee in field. Contbr. articles to profl. pubs. Home: 1335 Linville St Kingsport TN 37660 Office: Tennessee Eastman Company PO Box 511 Kingsport TN 37662

COPE, LAWRENCE LYNDON, editor; b. N.Y.C., Oct. 5, 1918; s. Oliver Franklin and Gladys Edith (Willes) C.; B.A., Fla. So. Coll., 1940; postgrad. Northwestern U., 1941-42, Loyola U., New Orleans, 1953, U. Ill. at Urbana, 1957, U. Chgo., 1964; m. Dorothea Anne Herrick, June 25, 1944; children—Patricia (Mrs. Theodore T. Tackett), Laurence B. Asst. advt. mgr. Greenwich (Conn.) Times, 1945-47; mgr. sales promotion Nat. Circulation Co., N.Y.C., 1947-52; field editor H.L. Peace Publs., New Orleans, 1952-53; mgr. promotion Simmons-Boardman Pub. Co., N.Y.C., 1953-56; mgr. devel. Am. Chem. Soc., Washington, 1956-65; editor Guild Guide, Guild Prescription Opticians of Am., Washington, 1966-—; cons. publs., Washington, 1965-—. Coordinator Community Chest, New Orleans, 1952. Served to lt. comdr., USNR, 1941-45. Recipient Lloyd F. Wood Meml. award Mail Advt. Club, Washington, 1970. Mem. Am. Med. Writers Assn., Direct Mail Advt. Assn. (chmn. com. 1963-66). Roman Catholic. Clubs: National Press, Advertising, Mail Advertising (dir. 1959-62) (Washington). Editor, The Eye Physician, 1967-69; asso. editor Volta Rev., 1968-70. Home: 5407 Newington Rd Washington DC 20016 Office: Guild Guide Opticians Assn of Am 1250 Connecticut Av Washington DC 20036

COPE, LOUIS THOMAS, mfr. chem. process equipment; b. Nashville, Jan. 14, 1930; s. Bedford D. and Mary (Grubbs) C.; student Nashville Tech. Coll., 1948-50; m. Hester Twilo Adams, Jan. 18, 1946; children—Louis Thomas, Cherrie Gail, Connie Joan, Lindsey Nannette. With Olin Mathieson Chem. Co., 1949-53, 55-69, tech. sales rep., 1959-62, sales engr., Chattanooga, 1962-64 mgr. Coz Equipment div., Atlanta, 1964-69; millwright Atlas Powder Co., Tyner, Tenn., 1953-55; pres. Tomco Equipment Co., Atlanta, 1969-—. Served with USCG, 1947-48. Mem. Aircraft Owners and Pilots Assn. Club: Churchill Downs Civic (bd. dirs. 1965-—) (Decatur, Ga.). Patentee in field. Home: 3713 Greentree Farms Dr Decatur GA 30034 Office: 800 Confederate Av SE Atlanta GA 30312

COPELAND, DELBERT HENRY, librarian; b. Philadelphia, Miss., Dec. 3, 1928; s. Linard G. and Effie A. (Cumberland) C.; A.A., East Central Jr. Coll., Decatur, Miss., 1948; B.S., Miss. So. Coll., 1950, M.A., 1954; postgrad. U. Fla., 1955-56, U. Miss., 1958, U. So. Miss., 1957; m. Julia Ann Bivins, Aug. 22, 1958; 1 son, Delbert Mark. Tchr., Goodhope (Miss.) High Sch., 1950-51, Bratt (Fla.) Jr. High Sch., 1952-55; tchr., librarian Leesburg (Fla.) High Sch., 1955-64; dir. library services Lake-Sumter Community Coll., Leesburg, 1964-—. Mem. Fla. Textbook Adoption Com. in Lit., 1958-—; sec. adv. bd. Leesburg Pub. Library, 1958-60. Served with AUS, 1951-52. Mem. Fla. Library Assn., Fla. Assn. Community Colls., Democrat. Methodist (ofcl. bd. stewards). Mason. Home: 907 North Shore Dr Leesburg FL 32748

COPELAND, EMILY AMERICA, educator, librarian; b. Tifton, Ga.; d. Jerry and America (Vaughn) Copeland; A.B., Spelman Coll., 1937; B.S. in L.S. (Carnegie grantee) Atlanta U., 1942; M.S., Columbia, 1948, postgrad., 1959-60; postgrad. N.Y. U., 1949-50, U. S.C., 1969. Tchr., Tift County Indsl. High Sch., Tifton, 1937-38; librarian Finley High Sch., Chester, S.C., 1938-41; library asst. Atlanta U. Library, summers 1938-40, 42; head librarian Gammon Theol. Sem., Atlanta, 1942-44; acquisitions librarian Atlanta U., 1944-46; reference, sch. work sst. N.Y. Pub. Library, N.Y.C., 1945-46; head dept. library sci. S.C. State Coll., 1946-51; prof., chmn. dept. library service Fla. A. and M. U., Tallahassee, 1951-—; pres., founder Black Research Information Coordinating Service, Inc., 1972-—. Recipient certificate of merit Spelman Coll., 1968. Mem. S.C. Library Devel. Com., 1947-51, S.C. Library Edn. Planning Com., 1948-51; mem. Fla. com. Columbia Campaign Fund, 1967-69. Mem. Am. (mem. nat. planning com. 1956-62, E.P. Dutton McRae award com. 1971, mem. right to read com. pub. library div. 1972-—, minority recruitment cons. 1972), Southeastern, Fla. (pres. 1953-56) library assns. Marquis Biog. Library Soc. Author: A Handbook for the Guidance of Students in School Library Intership, 1964. Contbr. articles to profl. jours., World Book Ency., Black Librarian in Am. Home: 614 Howard Av Tallahassee FL 32304 also 1212 Peachtree St Tifton GA Office: Box 245 Fla A and M U Tallahassee FL 32307

COPELAND, H., life ins. co. exec.; b. Waverly, Va., Aug. 30, 1929; s. S. E. and Katherine (Harrell) C.; B.S., Richmond Profl. Inst., 1953; postgrad. Va. Poly. Inst., 1954-55; m. Mary Louise Lozier, June 21, 1953; children—Edward H., David Lozier, Paul W. Distributive edn. coordinator Hopewell Sch. System, 1953-57; career agt. Fidelity Bankers Life Ins. Co., 1957-60, career agy. mgr., Petersburg, Va., 1960-62, adminstrv. asst. home office agy. dept., Richmond, Va., 1962-64, tng. dir., 1964, 2d v.p., tng. dir., brokerage liaison officer, 1965-66, v.p. career agys., 1967-—. Mem. Mid-Atlantic Tng. Dirs. Assn. (mem. tng. and communications com. 1965-68), Richmond Assn. Life Underwriters, Petersburg/Hopewell Life Underwriters Assn. (v.p. 1961). Presbyn. Kiwanian. Club: Bull and Bear. Home: 8821 Michaux Lane Richmond VA 23229 Office: 9th and Main Sts Richmond VA 23219

COPELAND, HARRY ELBERT, JR., pub. relations and advt. counselor; b. Houston, June 16, 1931; s. Harry Elbert and Laura Elisabeth (Robertson) C.; B.J., U. Tex., 1952; m. Ann Bryan, Sept. 15, 1955; children—Elaine Suzette, Douglas Carter. Pub. relations and advt. counsel Hal Copeland Co., Dallas, 1957-—. Mem. Pub. Relations Soc. Am. (pres. North Tex. chpt. 1965), Dallas C. of C. (communications com. 1971-—), Phi Delta Theta, Alpha Delta Sigma. Presbyn. Rotarian (pub. relations chmn. 1971-72). Club: Press (Dallas). Home: 2800 McFarlin Blvd Dallas TX 75205 Office: 4228 N Central Expressway Dallas TX 75206

COPELAND, JAMES WILLIAM, superior ct. judge; b. Woodland, N.C., June 16, 1914; s. Luther Clifton and Nora (Benthall) C.; A.B. Guilford Coll., 1934; J.D., U. N.C., 1937; m. Nancy Hall Sawyer, Oct. 11, 1941; children—Emily, James William, Buxton. Admitted to N.C. bar, 1936; pvt. practice law, Woodland, 1937-42, Murfreesboro, 1946-61; dir. Farmers Bank, Murfreesboro. Mayor, Woodland, 1938-42, Murfreesboro, 1947-50; mem. N.C. Senate, 1951, 53, 57, 59, chmn. judiciary com., 1957, mem. adv. budget commn., 1957-61, chmn. appropriations com., 1959, legislative counsel to gov. 1961 session; spl. judge Superior Ct., 1961-—. Delegate Dem. National Conv., 1956. Served as lt. USNR, 1942-45. Mem. Am. Legion, Am. (del. trial judges conf. 1969-—), N.C. bar assns., V.F.W. Mason (Shriner). Home: 407 E High St Murfreesboro NC 27855

COPELAND, JOSEPH J., coll. pres.; b. Ferris, Tex., May 22, 1914; s. Henry Hillard and Cora Lemmar (Richardson) C.; B.A., Trinity U., San Antonio, Tex.; 1936, D.D., 1950; B.D., McCormick Theol. Sem.; 1939; LL.D., Maryville (Tenn.) Coll., 1960; m. Glenda Lee Mullendore, May 30, 1938; children—Joseph Kirk, Karen Lee (Mrs. Meldrum Gray III). Ordained to ministry Presbyn. Ch., 1939; pastor in Okla., 1939-41, Tex., 1942-52, Tenn., 1952-61; pres. Maryville Coll., 1961-—, also mem. bd. dirs. Moderator weekly TV series, sta. WBIR, Knoxville, 1956-—. Mem. bd. Christian edn. United Presbyn. Ch. U.S.A., 1950-65, mem. div. radio and TV, 1957-65, moderator Synod Mid-South, 1959-60, also chmn. com. higher edn., 1945-55, chmn. Westminster Found., 1952-66; chmn. counseling com. ch. and soc. United Presbyn. Ch. U.S.A., 1961-65; mem. commn. on Delta ministry Nat. Council Chs. Christ U.S.A., 1964-—. Mem. Presbyn. Coll. Union (pres. 1969), Tenn. Coll. Assn. (pres. 1970-71), Affiliated Ind. Colls. Tenn., So. Assn. Colls. and Schs. Kiwanian. Contbr. articles to mags. Home: Maryville Coll Maryville TN 37801

COPELAND, KENNETH WILFORD, clergyman; b. Bexar, Ark., Apr. 3, 1912; s. John Wesley and Nancy Elizabeth (Hively) C.; student Westminster Coll., Tehuacana, Tex., 1930-32, East Tex. State Tchrs. Coll., 1933-34; B.A., So. Meth. U., 1938; student Garrett Bibl. Inst., 1947; D.D. (hon.), Southwest U., Georgetown Tex., 1951; S.T.D. (hon.), Neb. Wesleyan U., 1961; LL.D., So. Meth. U., 1964; m. Catherine Andrews, October 5, 1933; children—Patricia Ann (Mrs. James Wilbur Ard, Jr.), Martha Sue (Mrs. Preston Hastings Dial, Jr.). Ordained to ministry Methodist Ch., 1931; pastor, Corsicana, Tex., 1929-32, Cooper, Tex., 1932-34, Dallas, 1934-38; pres. Tex. Conf. Meth. Protestant Ch., 1938-39; pastor, Wichita Falls, Tex., 1939-40, Haskell, Tex., 1940-44, First Ch., Stillwater, Okla., 1944-49, Travis Park Ch., San Antonio, 1949-60; became bishop Neb. area Meth. Ch., 1960, now bishop Houston area. Alt. del. uniting conf. M.E. Ch., Meth. Protestant Ch., Meth. Episcopal Ch. South, 1939; mem. jurisdictional confs., 1940, 48, 52, 56, 60, gen. confs., 1952, 56, 60; v.p. Gen. Bd. Missions, pres. joint commn. on edn. and cultivation; mem. Gen. Bd. Christian Social Concerns. Trustee Alaska Meth. U., So. Meth. O., Neb. Wesleyan U., St. Paul Sch. Theology Methodist. Mason (K.T., Shriner), Lion. Author: A Primer of Beliefs for Methodist Laymen, 1959. Office: 5215 Main Houston TX 75250

COPELAND, PAUL WILLIAM, journalist; b. Columbus, O., Aug. 12, 1917; s. Paul Walter and Helen Marie (Kanmacher) C.; student Ohio State U., 1933-34, Franklin U., 1934-35; m. Annita Auteri, Jan. 28, 1949; children—Robert, Judith, Mary, Constance. Radio, TV dir. Byer & Bowman Advt. Agy., Columbus, O., 1936-45, 49-50; pub.

relations dir. Hallmark Motion Pictures, Hollywood, Cal., 1950-51; columnist Sarasota (Fla.) Jour., 1951—; columnist McCall's, mag., 1969-70. Served with AUS, 1945-49; PTO. Author: The File on Charlie, 1968. Home: 5720 Antilles Dr Sarasota FL 33581 Office: Sarasota Journal Box 1719 Sarasota FL 33578

COPELAND, ROGER PRENTICE, sch. supt.; b. Philadelphia, Miss., Sept. 22, 1926; s. Linard Gaston and Effie Aurilla (Cumberland) C.; B.S., U. So. Miss., 1951, M.A., 1954; postgrad., 1970; m. Dorothy Ree Irons, Oct. 21, 1945; children—Roger Lynn, Rex Byron. Coach Neshoha County Schs., Philadelphia, 1951-61; prin. Neshohe County High Sch., Philadelphia, 1961-65, supt., 1965—. Bd. edn. East Central Jr. Coll., 1965. Served with AUS, 1945-46, 1950-51. Mem. Miss. Tchrs. Assn., Miss. Assn. Sch. Adminstrn., Miss. Sch. Supts. Assn., Nat. Assn. Sch. Adminstrs. Rotarian (dir. 1971), Mason. Home: Route 2 Philadelphia MS 39350 Office: Ct House Philadelphia MS 39350

COPLEY, WAVERLY EMMETT, supt. schs.; b. Lynchburg, Va., Apr. 23, 1931; s. Horace Otis and Nell Hardy (Hurt) C.; B.A., Randolph-Macon Coll., 1953, M.A., Longwood Coll., 1963 (both Coll. William and Mary); m. Mary Anne Hammer, Apr. 16, 1960; 1 dau., Anne Simmons. Athletic dir., coach Amelia County (Va.) Pub. Schs., 1955-62, supt., 1967—; prin. Amelia High Sch., 1962-67. Scoutmaster Piedmont council Boy Scouts Am., 1955-57. Served with AUS, 1953-55. Mem. Am. Assn. Sch. Adminstrs., P.T.A., Va. Edn. Assn. Methodist (tchr. men's Bible class). Home: PO Box 65 Amelia VA 23002 Office: PO Box 276 Amelia VA 23002

COPP, JAMES HARRIS, sociologist, educator; b. Thief River Falls, Minn., Apr. 28, 1925; s. Vivian Emory and Irene (Sorenson) C.; B.A. magna cum laude, U. Minn., 1949, M.A., 1951; Ph.D., U. Wis., 1954; m Veronica Fliegel, Sept. 12, 1953; children—Christine Ann, John Frederick, Karen Amalia, Sarah Catherine, Martha Alice. Research project leader Wis. 4-H Club Office, Madison, 1953-54; asst. prof. rural sociology Kan. State U., Manhattan, 1954-55, U. Wis., Madison, 1955-56; asst. prof., asso. prof., prof. rural sociology Pa. State U., University Park, 1956-67; chief human resources br. Econ. Devel. Div., Econ. Research Service, U.S. Dept. Agr., Washington, 1967-72; prof., head dept. sociology, asso. head dept. agrl. econs. and rural sociology Tex. A. and M. U., College Station, 1972—. Book review editor Rural Sociology, 1966-72. Mem. Am. Sociol. Assn., Rural Sociol. Soc. (v.p. 1967, pres. 1971), A.A.A.S., D.C. Sociol. Soc. Home: 1101 Pershing Dr College Station TX 77840

COPPAGE, WILLIAM THOMAS, state ofcl.; b. nr. Front Royal, Va., May 1, 1929; s. Alvin T. and Emma (Eastham) C.; B.A., U. Richmond, 1951; M.A., U. Va., 1962; M.S. in Rehab. Counseling, Richmond Profl. Inst., 1968; m. Beverly Manning, May 30, 1959; children—Linda Beth, William Thomas, John Robert. Area supr. Bus. Enterprises For Blind, 1951-55, asst. workshop supt., 1955-61; asst. dir. State Agy. for Blind, Richmond, Va., 1961-64, dir., 1964—. Instr., Va. Commonwealth U. Mem. adv. council Sch. Community Services, Dept. Rehab. Counseling; mem. Gov.'s Overall Adv. Com. on Needs Handicapped Children, 1964—, chmn., 1967-71; service adv. com. Am. Found. for Blind, 1969—. Bd. dirs. Nat. Council Workshops for Blind. Recipient certificate of award for service as mem. Va. Mental Health Study Commn., Gov. Va., 1965; certificate of recognition Va. Rehab. Assn., 1969, R.N. Anderson award, 1971. Mem. Am. Soc. Quality Control, Nat. Rehab. Assn., Am., Va. (dir.) assns. workers for blind. Nat. Council State Agys. for Blind (pres. 1968-69), Council State Adminstrs. Vocational Rehab., Internat. Platform Assn., Va. Soc. Prevention of Blindness (dir., treas. 1971-72), Lambda Chi Alpha. Lion. Home: 8000 Moorfield Rd Richmond VA 23229 Office: 3003 Parkwood Av Richmond VA 23221

COPPEDGE, DONALD LEROY, newspaper pub.; b. Hollywood, Cal., May 29, 1931; s. Charles M. and Loraine (Fultz) C.; B.A., N. Tex. State U., 1956; m. Bettye Suzanne Crawford, Jan. 12, 1952; children—Dana (dec.), D'on, Denise, Derek. Wire editor Denton (Tex.) Record-Chronicle, 1956; state editor San Angelo (Tex.) Standard-Times, 1956-58; editor Brownwood (Tex.) Bull., 1958-62; press aide Gov. John Connally, Fort Worth and Austin, 1962, dist. coordinator, 1962—; co-pub. Waxahachie (Tex.) Daily Light, 1962—; v.p., dir. Craco, Inc.; v.p., part owner Stephenville (Tex.) Daily Empire. Mem. Waxahachie Park Bd., 1966—, chmn., 1971-72; mem. Waxahachi Charter Commn., 1969; founding dir. Ellis County Hist. Mus. and Art Gallery, 1967—; bd. dirs. Community Chest, 1962-65, Brazos River Authority, 1967-73; mng. dir. Waxahachie Family Welfare Fund.; dir. Trails Dist., Boy Scouts of Am., 1966—, dist. chmn. Bluebonnet dist. 1969-71; bd. dirs. Waxahachie YMCA, Camp Grady Spruce, Dallas. Served with AUS, 1953-55. Named Outstanding Young Man, Waxahachie, 1964. Mem. Tex. Press Assn. (dir. 1963—, pres. 1972—), N. and E. Tex. Press Assn. (dir. 1964—, president 1969), C. of C. (dir. 1964-67, pres., 1968). Episcopalian (vestryman, 1963—). Home: 307 Monticello St Waxahachie TX 75165 Office: PO Box 354 Waxahachie TX 75165

COPPEDGE, WAYLAND THOMAS, JR., bus. exec.; b. Jacksonville, Fla., July 8, 1919; s. Wayland Thomas and Carlie Margaret (Tuttle) C.; B.S., Tulane U., 1940; M.D., Tulane U., 1943; m. Lauren Shields MacFarlane, Mar. 31, 1969; children—Mary Margaret, Wayland Thomas III. Intern, U.S. Naval Hosp., Oakland, Cal., 1943-44, resident surgery, 1945-46; resident surgery St. Luke's Hosp., Jacksonville, 1946-47; fellow anesthesiology Ochsner Clinic, New Orleans, 1947-49; pvt. practice medicine, specializing in anesthesiology, Jacksonville, 1949-56; v.p. Fla. Towing Corp., marine towing, 1956-71; pres. Fla. Towing Co., Inc., 1971—, White Stack Towing Corp., Charleston, S.C., 1962—; pres., owner Thor Chevrolet, Jacksonville Beach, Fla., 1958—; dir. San Jose Barnett Bank, Jacksonville. Served with M.C., USNR, 1940-46. Diplomate Am. Bd. Anesthesiology. Mem. Soc. Naval Architects and Marine Engrs., Sigma Alpha Epsilon, Nu Sigma Nu. Clubs: Propeller, Hidden Hills Country (founder and builder) (Jacksonville); Whitehall (N.Y.C.); Bay Hill (Orlando, Fla.). Home: 197 San Juan Dr Ponte Vedra Beach FL 32082 Office: 1935 E Beaver St Jacksonville FL 32201

COPPIN, JOHN STEPHENS, artist, portrait painter; b. Mitchell, Ont., Can., Sept. 13, 1904; s. Thomas Pascoe and Maude (Levette) C.; stu., Stratford Collegiate Inst., 1918-21, Wicker Art Sch., 1923-27, study trip, Europe, 1938; m. Sidni Lovelace, Feb. 7, 1948; 1 son, Torry John. Art dir. Mich. Motor News, 1930-60; art instruction, 1928; free lance artist and illustrator, 1928—; portrait painter. Recipient Scarab gold medals, 1941, 1944, 1946; Detroit Inst. Arts popular prize, 1933, 1939, 1946, 1950. Carl F. Clark award, 1953. Murals in Mich. Bar Assn. Bldg., Lansing, Detroit Central High Sch., Detroit Gas Co., Adam Strohm Hall, Detroit Pub. Library; works in Detroit Inst. Arts, Nat. Historic Mus., Frederiksborg, Denmark. Portraits include Edgar A. Guest, Alvan McCauley, Mrs. Alfred Glancey, George Romney, Dr. Henry Vaughan, George W. Stark; ex-governors Wagoner, Kelly and Sigler; Henry Ford, Paul Paray, Alec Guinness, Mennen G. Williams, Wm. S. Knudsen, James M. Roche and others; numerous commissioned portraits of prominent persons; hist. paintings Mich. State U. Fellow Internat. Inst. Arts and Letters; mem. Am. Fedn. Artists, Mich. Acad. Sci., Arts and Letters, Sarasota, Longboat Key art assns., Ringling Mus. Assn. Clubs: Prismatic (hon. pres.), Scarab (past pres.), Detroit Press, Acanthus, St. Dunstan's Guild, Cranbrook (past pres.) (Detroit); Sarasota Yacht. Selected works of John S. Coppin, 1948. Home: 226 Golden Gate Point Sarasota FL 33577 Office: 1750 Benjamin Franklin Dr Sarasota FL 33577summer: Beachcliff Bayfield Ontario Canada

COPPINGER, WALTER CLESTON, accountant; b. nr. McMinnville, Tenn., May 1, 1923; s. Walter Edgar and Rebecca (Barker) C.; student Northwestern U., 1945; B.S., Tenn. Tech. U., 1947; m. Jennie Finchum, June 15, 1946; children—Becky Elaine, Steve Cleston. Pub. accountant Walter C. Coppinger, C.P.A.'s, Rockwood, Tenn., 1947-50, 52—. Served with USNR, 1943-46, with AUS, 1950-52. Mem. Tenn. Assn. Pub. Accountants (pres. 1960-61). Club: Civitan. Home: 429 E. Baldwin Av Rockwood TN 37854 Office: 305 W Rockwood St Rockwood TN 37854

COPPINGER, WALTER T., govt. ofcl. Dist. dir. Internal Revenue Service. Office: 2121 8th Av N Birmingham AL 35203*

CORBETT, LESLIE WILLIAM, banker; b. Britton, Okla., Aug. 6, 1915; s. Leland M. and Laura M. (Leslie) C.; student Central State U., 1933-34, Am. Inst. Banking, 1936-38; m. Opal Jane McWilliams, Apr. 6, 1957. With First Nat. Bank, Edmond, Okla., 1935-41; asst. nat. bank examiner, 1946-51; with Okla. Nat. Bank, Duncan, 1951—, pres., 1968—. Pres., Duncan Community Chest, 1957. Served with USNR, 1941-46. Mem. C. of C. (dir. 1961-65, v.p., 1964-65). Elk, Rotarian (pres. 1962-63). Home: 1001 Oakview Dr Duncan OK 73533 Office: Box 1508 Duncan OK 73533

CORBIN, WELDON ROGER, county ofcl.; b. Gainesville, Tex., Oct. 24, 1937; s. Bailey and Thelma A. (Atteberry) C.; B.S. in Animal Sci., Tex. Tech. U., 1961; M.S., E. Tex. State U., 1967; m. Melveene Gibson, Aug. 31, 1956; children—Sheri Kay, Mason Gene. Instr. vocational agr., Callisburg, Tex., 1961-65; Ellis County agrl. agt. Tex. A. and M.U.; Waxahachie, 1965—. Show coordinator Ellis County Purebred Livestock Show, 1967—. Bd. dirs. Community Chest United Fund. Mem. Texas County Agrl. Agts. Assn., Tex. Tech. U. Alumni (pres.), Tex. A. and M. Extension, Alpha Zeta. Baptist (men's dir.). Lion (dir. 1970). Club: National Block & Bridle (Lubbock, Tex.). Home: 113 Pensacola Waxahachie TX 75165 Office: Courthouse Waxahachie TX 75165

CORBITT, DUVON CLOUGH, educator; b. nr. Pearson, Ga., July 4, 1901; s. Martin S. and Minnie Frazier (Faircloth) C.; student Meridian Coll., 1918-20; A.B., Asbury Coll., 1923; M.A., Emory U., 1926; Ph.D., U. N.C., 1938; m. Roberta Day, June 3, 1924; 1 son, Duvon Clough. Head dept. English, Candler Coll., Havana, Cuba, 1927-29, 31-43, 45-46; chmn. history dept. Columbia (S.C.) Coll., 1943-45; mem. faculty Asbury Coll., Wilmore, Ky., 1946—, prof., chmn. social studies div., 1946—. Vis. prof. Fla. State U., Ohio State U., 1944, U. Omaha, 1945; lectr. Nat Def. Edn. Act Lang. Inst., Vanderbilt U., 1963. Recipient Marti Centenniel medal Cuba, 1955; decorated officer Carlos J. Finlay Order Merit (Cuba); Ky. Col. Mem. Latin Am. Studies Assn., Am., East Tenn., So. hist. assns., Sociedad Cubana de la Historia de la Medecina. Republican. Author: The Chinese in Cuba, 1944; A Study of the Chinese in Cuba 1847-1947, 1971. Contbr. to Latin America: A Guide to Historical Literature; also numerous articles, book revs. to profl. lit. Research in history of Cuba and the Caribbean. Home: 205 E Morrison St Wilmore KY 40390

CORBOY, MICHAEL ROBERT, marketing co. exec.; b. Chgo., Aug. 1, 1930; s. William J. and Eileen (Dunne) C.; B.S. in Elec. Engring., U.S. Naval Acad., 1953. With Tex. Instruments, Inc., Dallas, 1957-68, successively sales engr., dist. mgr., midwest and central region mgr. U.S., field sales mgr., European marketing mgr. Semicondr.-Component div., Geneva, Switzerland, corporate mgr. investor relations, Dallas, 1966-68; gen. partner New Bus. Resources—Venture Capital Partnership, Dallas, 1968-72; pres. Trans World Marketing, Inc., Dallas, 1972—; v.p. finance dir. Medicus Corp. Active Dallas County United Fund, operating fund campaign U. Dallas. Trustee Jesuit Coll. Prep. Sch., Dallas. Served with USN, 1953-57. Clubs: Las Colinas Country; N.Y. Athletic; Onex Golf (Geneva, Switzerland). Home: 3883 Turtle Creek Blvd Dallas TX 75219 Office: 2539 Cedar Springs Rd Dallas TX 75201

CORCORAN, HOWARD FRANCIS, U.S. judge; b. Pawtucket, R.I., Jan. 25, 1906 S. Thomas Patrick and Mary Josephine (O'Keefe) C.; grad. Phillips Exeter Acad., 1924; A.B., Princeton, 1928; LL.B., Harvard, 1931; m. Esther Pierce, May 31, 1952. Admitted to N.Y. bar, 1935, D.C. bar, 1956; with Dept. Agr., 1933-34, TVA, 1934-35; legal asso. SEC, 1935-38; asst. Office U.S. Atty. for So. Dist. of N.Y., 1938-43; U.S. atty. So. Dist. N.Y., 1943; partner firm Corcoran, Kostelanetz & Gladstone, N.Y.C., 1946-54, Corcoran, Foley, Youngman & Rowe, Washington, 1954-65; U.S. dist. judge for D.C., Washington, 1965—. Served to lt. col. AUS, 1943-45. Decorated Bronze Star, Croix de Guerre with star (France). Mem. Am., Fed., N.Y. State, N.Y. County bar assns., Bar Assn. of D.C., Assn. Bar City N.Y., Phi Delta Phi. Roman Catholic. Clubs: Princeton, Harvard, Army-Navy, Congressional Country, University (Washington). Home: 9004 Congressional Ct Potomac MD 20854 Office: US Courthouse Washington DC 20001

CORCORAN, JOHN JOSEPH, govt. ofcl.; b. N.Y.C., Aug. 12, 1920; s. John Joseph and Ellen Frances (Fitzgerald) C.; B.S., Georgetown U. Sch. Fgn. Ser., 1948; J.D., Law Center, 1951; m. Evelyn Dynan Madden, Apr. 29, 1943; children—Patricia (Mrs. David Lee Holt), Joanne, John, Maureen, Mary. Admitted to D.C. bar, 1952; legal cons. Am. Legion Nat. Rehab. Com., Washington, 1951-56, dir., 1958-67; atty. adviser Nat. Security Agy., Ft. Meade, Md., 1957; asst. to gen. counsel VA, Washington, 1967-69, gen. counsel, 1969—. Served with USAAF, 1942-45. Decorated D.F.C., Air medal with 3 clusters. Mem. Am., Fed bar assns., Am. Legion, Phi Alpha Delta. Club: Army Navy (Washington). Home: 9513 Cable Dr Kensington MD 20795 Office: 810 Vermont Av NW Washington DC 20420

CORCORAN, LISTON A., city ofcl., ins. exec.; b. Russell County, Ala.; student bus. coll., Birmingham; m. Maurine Walker, 1 son. With Rating Bur. Workmen's Compensation, 10 years; later v.p. of ins. co., 25 years; established (with sone) own ins. agy., Birmingham, circa 1960; mem. Birmingham City Council. Fomer mem., pres. Birmingham Bd. Edn. Past chmn. Northeast br., bd. mrs. Met. YMCA; pres. bd. dirs. East End Meml. Hosp. Baptist (past chmn. bd. deacons). Mason (Shriner), K.P., Lion (former local pres.). Address: care City Council City Hall 710 N 20th Birmingham AL 35203*

CORDELL, ARLING LYNDON, supt. schs.; b. Colbert, Okla., Sept. 30, 1907; s. Arling Lyndon and Lela Lucille (Hill) C.; B.S., Southeastern State Coll., 1941; M.S., North Tex. State U., 1950, then postgrad.; m. Clara Dean Summerhill, June 26, 1941; children—Jimmy Lyndon, Billy John. Prin. high sch., Colbert, Okla., 1930-46; supt. pub. schs., Colbert, 1947-57, Gordon, Tex., 1957-59, Wheeler, Tex., 1959-68, Clarendon, Tex., 1968—. Recipient Fellowship in Americanism, Abilene Christian Coll., 1962-63. Mem. C. of C. (pres. 1965), Phi Delta Kappa. Kiwanian (dir. 1959-68), Lion (pres. 1971), Mason. Home: 707 Bond St Clarendon TX 79226 Office: 700 4th St Clarendon TX 79226

CORDELL, DEWITT BYNUM CROMER (MRS. ALFRED ROBERT CORDELL), civic worker; b. Winston-Salem, N.C., Feb. 27, 1930; d. Clarence Franklin and Grace (Bynum) Cromer; A.B., Duke, 1950; postgrad. U. Buffalo, 1956-57; m. Alfred Robert Cordell, June 4, 1955; children—Alfred Robert, Franklin Cromer, Carl DeWitt, Mark Bynum. Pres., Winston-Salem Jr. League, 1963-64; dir. region XIII Assn. Jr. Leagues Am., 1965-67, 2d v.p., 1967-68; treas., 1st v.p., pres., bd. dirs. YWCA, 1962-68; pres., v.p., bd. dirs. Forsyth-Stokes County Med. Aux., 1967-69; asst. sec., pres., bd. dirs. Nature-Sci. Center, 1965-72; v.p. Civic Music Assn., 1964-68; pres. Amos Cottage Guild, 1969-70; mem. bd. United Fund, 1968-72; bd. dirs. Experiment in Self Reliance, 1969-70, v.p., 1970—; mem. exec. com. N.C. Council on Crime and Delinquency, 1969-70, 1st v.p., 1970—; v.p. Regional Health Planning Council, 1971-72; sec. Forsyth Health Planning Council, 1970-71, v.p., 1971-72; mem. Mayor's Com. on Historic Preservation Winston, 1971—. Bd. dirs. Forsyth County Heart Assn., (pres. 1969-70), Amos Cottage. Mem. Winston-Salem Symphony Guild, Bowman Gray Guild, Alpha Delta Pi. Home: 349 Arbor Rd Winston-Salem NC 27104

CORDER, WILLIAM NEWTON, supt. schs.; b. Ballinger, Tex., May 16, 1915; s. Noah William and Lora (Tennison) C.; A.A., Victoria Jr. Coll., 1936; B.S., S.W. Tex. State Tchrs. Coll., 1938, M.A., 1948; m. Audrey Blanche Spellmann, June 11, 1940; children—William David, Michael Spellmann and John Tennison (twins), Carolyn. Prin., tchr. Shiller-Hood Elementary Sch., Victoria County, Tex., 1934-35; tchr., coach Moulton (Tex.) High Sch., 1938-39; prin., tchr., coach Shiner (Tex.) High Sch., 1939-40; tchr., coach Lyford (Tex.) High Sch., 1940-42; chmn. bus. adminstrn., dir. athletics, dean of men, dir. cafeteria services Tex. Luth Coll., Sequin, 1942-49; prin. Robstown (Tex.) High Sch., 1949-67; supt. schs., Robstown, 1967—; mem. Tex. Commn. Preparation Sch. Adminstrs., 1970—. State coordinator secondary study State of Tex., 1964; mem. state com. So. Assn. Colls. and Schs., 1962-67; mem. secondary commn., 1965-68; mem. state bd. examiners tchr. edn. Tex. Edn. Agy., 1963—; chmn. joint com. Region II Ednl. Media Center. Scoutmaster, Alamo and Gulf Coast councils Boy Scouts Am., 1942-62, mem. exec. bd. Gulf Coast council, 1949—, nat. jamboree leader, 1957, 60; chmn. gen. solicitations United Fund, 1958; area chmn. Tex. Pub. Schs. Week, 1956—. Named Father of Yr., Guadalupe County, 1949; recipient Silver Beaver award Boy Scouts Am., 1959; Ancient and Beneficient Order of Red, Red Rose, 1964. Mem. Nat. (nat. adv. council 1964), Tex. (pres. 1964) assns, secondary sch. prins., N.E.A., Am. Assn. Sch. Adminstrs., Tex. Tchrs. Assn. (mem. exec. bd. dist 3, 1954-60), C. of C. (dir.). Methodist (chmn. commn. on edn. 1964—). Mason, Lion (past pres.). Home: 200 E Lingustrum Office: 801 N. First St., Robstown, Tex., 78380

CORDOVA, JORGE LUIS, govt. ofcl.; b. Manati, P.R., Apr. 20, 1907; B.A., Catholic U. Am., 1928; LL.B., Harvard, 1931; m. Dora Rodriguez children—Jorge Luis, Elvira (Mrs. Gonzalez), Irene, (Mrs. Subira), Fernando. Admitted to P.R. bar, 1931, practiced in San Juan, 1931-40, 46-68; judge Superior Ct. of P.R.; asso. justice Supreme Ct. of P.R., 1940-46; resident commr. P.R., 1969—. Mem. Fed., P.R. bar assns. Mem. New Progressive Party. Roman Catholic. Office: Longworth House Office Bldg Washington DC 20013

CORE, JESSE ROZELL, III, pub. relations counsel; b. Pine Bluff, Ark., Dec. 11, 1920; s. Jesse Rozell and Adelaide Newton (MacCammon) C.; student U. Ark., 1938-39, So. Meth. U., 1940, 50, U.S. Fgn. Service Inst., 1951; m. Marilou Ruggles, Mar. 31, 1950; children— Philip MacCammon, Marguerite Montague, Mason Mosby. Asst. editor Scene mag., Dallas, 1946; reporter Dallas Morning News, 1949-50, New Orleans Item, 1948; staff corr. UP, New Orleans, 1947; vice consul. press information officer U.S. Fgn. Service, Madras, India, 1950-53; dir. pub. relations Internat. Trade Mart, New Orleans, 1955-63; pres. Jesse Core and Co., pub. relations advt., 1963-67; exec. v.p. Scott Wilson & Assocs., pub. relations, advt., New Orleans, 1967-68; pres. Jesse Core & Assos., New Orleans, 1968—. Served maj. USAF, 1941-46; now lt. col. Res. Decorated D.F.C., Air medal with 6 oak leaf clusters (Army) (U.S.); Croix de Guerre avec palme, La Medale d'Afrique de Nord pour Tunisie (France). Mem. S.R., S.A.R., Soc. 1812, Royal St. George Soc., U.S. Fgn. Service Assn., Dallas, New Orleans press clubs, Pub. Relations Soc. Am., Advt. Fedn. Am., Am. Fighter Pilots Assn., Pershing Rifles (hon. col.). Sigma Alpha Epsilon. Democrat. Episcopalian. Club: Pendennis (New Orleans). Home: 4429 St Charles Av New Orleans LA 70115 Office: Gateway Bldg 124 Camp St New Orleans LA 70130

CORIDEN, GUY EDWARD, govt. ofcl.; b. Syracuse, N.Y., May 31, 1921; s. Guy Edward and Lucy (Lamb) C.; B.S., Ind. U. 1942; M.A., Marquette U., 1950, Fletcher Sch. Law and Diplomacy, 1951; m. Mary Louise Winbigler, Apr. 21, 1956. Security analyst Paul H. Davis & Co., Chgo., 1946-48; reins. underwriter AMRICO, Chgo., 1948-49; adminstrv. positions with U.S. Govt., 1951-60; staff adminstr. President's Commn. Nat. Goals, 1960-61; dir. Office European Programs, Bur. Ednl. and Cultural Affairs, State Dept., 1962—. Mem. nat. adv. com. Wayne State U. Urban Affairs Inst., 1968—; treas. N.W. council Big Bros. Nat. Capital Area, 1967—. Served with AUS, 1942-45; ETO. Decorated Bronze Star. K.C. Club: Lakewood Country (Rockville, Md.). Home: 2204 Wyoming Av NW Washington DC 20008 Office: Dept of State Washington DC 20520

CORK, ROBERT LANDER, lawyer; b. Central, S.C., Oct. 27, 1927; s. James Walter and Emma Lila (Mitchell) C.; A.B. in Law, U. Ga., 1951, LL.B., 1953; m. Anne McNeill Ward, Oct. 11, 1952; children—Mary Leah, Robert Lander, Travis Walter, Patrick Carlyle. Admitted to Ga. bar, 1951, Fla. bar, 1958; partner Cork & Gaines, Athens, Ga., 1951-53; gen. practice, Valdosta, Va., 1953—; gen. counsel Warrior Land & Cattle Co. S. Ga., 1961—; local counsel, agt. Louisville Title Ins. Co., 1962—. Atty., City of Dasher (Ga.), 1967—, Sch. Bd. of Ga. Christian Sch., 1967—; pros. atty. for Ga., So. Jud. Circuit, 1970-71. Council adviser Boy Scouts Am. Vice chmn. Valdosta and Lowndes County sect. Ga. Goldwater for Pres. drive, 1964; mem. exec. com. American Party of Ga. Served with 101st Airborne Inf. Div., AUS, 1945-46, Q.M.C., 1955. Mem. Am. So. Circuit, Valdosta bar assns., State Bar Ga., The Fla. Bar, Am. Judicature Soc., Citizens Councils Am. (mem. nat. bd. 1969), S.A.R., Am. Legion (mem. nat. law and order com. 1968-69, judge adv. 8th Congl. dist.). Methodist (trustee, chmn. bd. stewards). Mason (Shriner, K.T.), Lion (pres. 1971-72, chmn. S. Ga. Eye Bank com. 1964). Home: Sunnyside Frances Lake RFD Lake Park GA 31636 Office: 505 N Patterson St Valdosta GA 31601

CORLEW, JAMES BLAKE, mech. engr.; b. Charlotte, Tenn., Dec. 27, 1916; s. Blake L. and Myrtle (Loggins) C.; B.S., Tenn. Tech. U., 1938; m. Margaret Long, Nov. 25, 1951; 1 dau., Marjorie Anne. Civil service examiner Phila. Navy Yard, 1940-41; design draftsman Newport News Shipbldg. (Va.), 1941-45; application engr. Worthington Corp., Holyoke, Mass., 1945-47; owner, pres. Corlew Engring. Co., Chattanooga, 1947—. Mem. Tenn. Soc. Profl. Engrs., Am. Soc. Heating, Refrigeration and Air Conditioning Engrs. Home: 702 N Crest Rd Chattanooga TN 37406 Office: 2910 Dodson Av Chattanooga TN 37406

CORLISS, CARLTON JONATHAN, railway historian; b. Crystal, Me., Apr. 20, 1888; s. John Segee and Mary (Bell) C.; student Ricker Classical Inst., 1904-05; m. Loretta Billings, Dec. 8, 1913; 1 dau., Marion Virginia (Mrs. Kendall C. Beavers, Jr.). With motive power dept. Boston & Maine R.R., Boston, 1905-06; ticket seller Boston Terminal Co., 1907-08; copyist land and tax dept. Erie R.R., N.Y., 1908; various positions including chief clk. to chief constructing engr. Fla. East Coast Ry., Ky West Extension, 1909-14; computer, draftsman, asst. engr., chief clk. to valuation engr. I.C. R.R., 1916-24, asso. editor I.C. mag., 1925-34, exec. dept., asst. in pub. relations, 1934-36, historian exec. dept., 1947-49; mgr. pub. sect. Assn. of Am. Railroads, Pub. Relations Dept., 1937-47, mgr. pub. sect., 1950-58. Mem. Railroad Pub. Relations Assn., Am. Ry. Mag. Editors Assn., Columbia, U.S. Capitol hist. socs., Lincoln Group of D.C. (past pres.), Fla., Tallahassee hist. socs., Lincoln Sesquicentennial Commn. (hon.), Manuscript Soc. Author: Main Line of Mid-America, 1950; Trails to Rails, 1934; Am. Railroads: Their Growth and Development, 1955; The Am. Railroad Industry, 1955; also booklets, and numerous articles on railroads; cons. on railroads Am. Coll. Dictionary. Home: 2218 Thomasville Rd Tallahassee FL 32303

CORLISS, JACK ARTHUR, librarian; b. Brookings, S.D., May 6, 1933; s. Fred Arthur and Annie (Boulton) C.; M.A., Baylor U., 1961; m. Barbara Ann Mann, Aug. 29, 1961. Grad. library asst. Baylor U. 1960-61; young adult librarian Waco Pub. Library, 1961-65; dir. libraries Arlington (Tex.) Pub. Library, 1965—. Served to capt. USAF, 1953-60. Mem. Am., Tex. (mem. council 1970), Tarrant Regional (pres. 1966, 67, 71) library assns. Rotarian. Club: Civitan (pres. 1969) (Arlington, Tex.). Home: PO Box 1165 Arlington TX 76010 Office: 106 W Main St Arlington TX 76010

CORMAN, WILLIAM FRANKLIN, telephone co. exec.; b. Louisville, Mar. 26, 1916; s. Minor and Willye (Bright Pierce) C.; B.B.A., U. Ore., 1937; M.B.A., Harvard, 1939; m. Gladys Juliette Temple, June 19, 1952; children—Jim, Myna, Julie, Page. Bookkeeper Collierville Telephone Co. (Tenn.), 1939-41; mgr. Southland Telephone Co., Atmore, Ala., 1945—. Pres., Atmore United Fund, 1958; chmn. Atmore Indsl. Devel. Bd., 1965—. Mem. Escambia County Republican Exec. Com., 1967. Served to lt. col. USAAF, 1941-46. Decorated Bronze Star. Named Man of Year, Ala.-Miss. Ind. Telephone Assn., 1966, Nat. Tel. Coop. Assn., 1968. Mem. Ala.-Miss. Ind. Telephone Assn. (pres. 1954), Orgn. Protection and Advancement Small Telephone Cos. (pres. 1963-65), Nat. R.E.A. Telephone Assn. (dir.), U.S. Ind. Telephone Assn. (dir.), Atmore C. of C. (pres. 1947, 61), Ala. Safety Council (dir.), I.E.E.E. Presbyn. (elder). Club: Atmore Lions (pres. 1955). Author: Cost Studies, a Tool for Management, 1963; The Misunderstood Half Billion Dollars, Independent Toll Revenue, 1967; The Pricing of Telephone Service, 1971. Contbg. editor Telephone Engr. and Magmt., 1949—. Home: 800 1st Av Atmore AL 36502 Office: 201 S Pensacola Av Atmore AL 36502

CORMIER, RICHARD, orch. condr.; b. Orange, Mass., May 10, 1929; s. Ernest A. and Doris Hunt (Deane) C.; B.Mus., New Eng. Conservatory Music, 1951; M.A., Columbia U. Tchrs. Coll., 1955, Ed.D., 1964. Mem. Birmingham (Ala.) Symphony Orch., 1951, Kansas City (Mo.) Philharmonic Orch., 1955-62, Santa Fe Opera Orch., Summers 1957, 58; music dir., condr. Charlotte (N.C.) Symphony Orch., also Charlotte Symphony Youth Orch., 1963-67; dir. instrumental music Park Coll., Parkville, Mo., 1956-63, asso. prof., chmn. music dept., 1961-63; music dir., condr. Chattanooga Symphony and Youth Orch., 1967—; music dir. Oak Ridge Civic Music Assn. Symphony and Chorus, 1968—; instr. conducting and brass instruments Tchrs. Coll., Columbia U., summers 1964-67. Condr. Cormier Chamber Orch., Kansas City, Mo., 1956-63; Youth Symphony Orch., Kansas City, 1959-61, St. Joseph (Mo.) Symphony Orch., 1959-63. Served with USMCR, 1952-53, Res., 1953-58. Mem. Pi Kappa Lambda, Phi Mu Alpha Sinfonia. Home: 1209 Peter Pan Lookout Mountain TN 37350 Office: 730 Cherry St Chattanooga TN 37402

CORNELL, CORWIN DAVID, ednl. adminstr.; b. Des Moines, Feb. 5, 1924; s. Corwin S. and Margaret (Hardie) C.; student U. Kan., 1943-44; B.A., State U. Ia., 1947, M.A., 1949, postgrad., 1949-50, 55; postgrad. U. Cal. at Los Angeles, 1959-60; m. Ruth Marian Reininga, Sept. 7, 1946 (div. 1965); children—Barbara Jean, Corwin Bruce, Phillip Craig, Stewart David; m. 2d, Jean S. Harkness, Nov. 4, 1966. Civilian chief, instr. tng. br. Plans and Operations Office, Adj. Gen.'s Sch., Ft. Harrison, Ind., 1952-54; instr. speech Pomona Coll., Claremont, Cal., 1954-56; staff asst. to mgr. indsl. relations Gen. Dynamics/Pomona, (Cal.), 1956-57, asst. to pres., 1957-64; asst. v.p. Newhall Land & Farming Co., Valencia, Cal., 1964-65; dir. pub. affairs Cal. Land Co., Valencia 1964-65; dir. devel. and planning Scripps Coll., Claremont, Cal., 1965-69; dir. officer agy. liaison, office v.p. for ednl. devel. and research U. Ia., Iowa City, 1969-71; v.p. finance and devel. Davidson (N.C.) Coll., 1971—. Dir. Community Properties, Inc., 1971—, Piedmont Bank's Trust Co., Davidson. Cons. communication field, 1955—; lectr. indsl. communication Cal. Inst. Tech., Pasadena, 1958, 59, 61, 67; lectr. organizational communication Claremont Men's Coll., 1956-57, 59-69; lectr. exec. communication U. Ida., Moscow, 1960—. Nat. council Old Gold Devel. Fund, State U. Ia. Found. 1962-69; community leader 4-H Club, LaVerne, Cal., 1962-64; chmn. Archtl. Commn., Claremont, 1962-64. Bd. dirs. Pomona Valley United Fund, 1958-61, Claremont chpt. A.R.C., 1960-63; trustee Pomona Valley Community Hosp., 1964-65, Mercy Hosp., Iowa City, 1970-71. Served with AUS, 1942-46; ETO; 1950-52. Recipient George Washington Honor medal, 1968. Mem. Speech Assn. Am., State Hist. Soc. Ia. (life), Pub. Relations Soc. Am., State U. Ia. Alumni Assn. (pres. 1968-69, life), Am. Bus. Com. Assn., Am. Coll. Pub. Relations Assn., Am. Assn. Higher Edn., Phi Beta Kappa, Omicron Delta Kappa, Delta Sigma Rho. Episcopalian. Home: 544 Concord Rd Davidson NC 28036

CORNELY, PAUL BERTAU, educator, physician; b. Guadeloupe, French W. Indies, Mar. 9, 1906; s. Eleodore and Adrienne (Mellon) C.; came to U.S., 1921, naturalized, 1934; A.B., U. Mich., 1928, M.D., 1931, D. Pub. Health, 1934, D. Sc. (hon.), 1968; m. Mae Stewart, June 23, 1934; 1 son, Paul Bertau. Intern Lincoln Hosp., Durham, N.C., 1931-32; faculty Howard U. Coll. Medicine, 1934—, chief div. phys. medicine and rehab., 1959-64, prof. preventive medicine, 1947-70, head dept. preventive medicine and pub. health, 1955—; med. dir. Freedman's Hosp., Washington, 1947-58, chief div. phys. medicine and rehab., 1959-64; asst. to exec. med. officer, welfare and retirement fund United Mine Workers Am., 1971-72; cons. Health and Welfare Council Nat. Capital Area, 1957—; cons. AID, 1960—. Mem. Pres.'s Commn. on Population Growth and Future of Am., 1970-72. Bd. dirs. Physicians Forum, 1947—, pres., 1960-61; pres. Community-Group Health Found. Recipient Sesquicentennial award U. Mich., 1967. Diplomate Am. Bd. Preventive Medicine and Pub. Health. Fellow Am. Coll. Preventive Medicine; mem. Med. Soc. D.C. (Community Service award 1964), Am. Cancer Soc. (v.p. 1962-63), Am. Pub. Health Assn. (exec. com. 1964-71, pres. 1969-70, chmn. exec. bd. 1970-71), D.C. Pub. Health Assn. (pres. 1963-65). Home: 1338 Geranium St NW Washington DC 20012

CORNETT, JACK BURKE, cons. engr.; b. Beggs, Okla., Mar. 15, 1920; s. John B. and Floy Lee (Jeffries) C.; B.S. in Civil Engring., U. Okla., 1948, M.C.E., 1964; m. Margie Lou Anderson, Dec. 25, 1946; children—Sandra Kay (Mrs. Richard A. Sands), Susan Carol, Robert Anderson. Structural engr. C.E., U.S. Army, Tulsa, 1948-50; with W.R. Holway & Assos., Tulsa, 1950-52, Wood & Craig Engrs., 1952-54, self-employed, 1954-56; partner Cornett-Wood & Assos., Tulsa, 1956-59; v.p. Holway Engrs. Inc., Tulsa, 1959—; dir., sec. Testing Engrs. Inc., Tulsa, 1968—; v.p. Long-Holway Engrs., Inc., Oklahoma City, 1971—. Served with USAAF, 1941-45; ETO. Decorated D.F.C. Registered profl. engr., Ark., Kans., Okla., Tex. Fellow Am. Soc. C.E.; mem. Cons. Engrs. Council Okla. (pres. 1969-70), cons. Engrs. Council U.S. (chmn. domestic bus. devel. com. 1972—), Water Pollution Control Fedn. (nat. dir. 1968-71), Am. Water Works Assn., Nat. Soc. Profl. Engrs., Am. Petroleum Inst., Sigma Xi. Home: 5370 E 26th Pl Tulsa OK 74114 Office: 1850 S Boulder St Tulsa OK 74119

CORNISH, EDWARD SEYMOUR, editor; b. N.Y.C., Aug. 31, 1927; s. George Anthony and Elizabeth Furniss (McLeod) C.; diplome d'etudes U. Paris (France), 1948; A.B., Harvard, 1950; m. Sally Woodhull, Oct. 12, 1957; children—George Anthony, Jefferson Richard Woodhull, Blake McLeod. Copy boy, cub reporter Evening Star, Washington, 1950-51; staff corr. U.P. Assn., Richmond, Va., 1951-52, Raleigh, N.C., 1952-53, London, Eng., 1953-54, Paris, 1954-55, Rome, Italy, 1956; staff writer Nat. Geog. Soc., 1957-69; founder, pres., World Future Soc., Washington, 1966, creator, editor The Futurist jour., 1966, editor World Future Soc. Bull., 1968—. Cons. to other govts., bus., ednl. orgns. Mem. A.A.A.S. Editorial cons. Nat. Goals Research Staff, 1970, White House report Toward Balanced Growth, 1970. Home: 5501 Lincoln St Bethesda MD 20034 Office: World Future Soc PO Box 19285 20th St Sta Washington DC 20036

CORREA M., ANTONIO, lawyer; b. Aguascalientes, Mexico, 1901; ed. Escuela Libre de Derecho. Admitted to bar, Mexico, 1924; mem. firm Basham Ringe &Correa. Office: Calle de Liverpool 123 Mexico City 6 Mexico*

CORREA M., ENRIQUE, lawyer; b. Aguascalientes, Mexico, 1903; ed. Escuela Libre de Derecho. Admitted to bar, Mexico, 1925; mem. firm Basham, Ringe & Correa. Office: Calle de Liverpool 123 Mexico City 6 Mexico*

CORRELL, WARD FORREST, shopping center exec.; b. Delta, Ky., Jan. 7, 1928; s. Charlie and Clora Alice (Hammonds) C.; grad. high sch.; m. Regina Tarter, Mar. 27, 1953; children—Rebekah, Kirk, Jesse, Vincent, Susan, Christa, Melinda. Transmission tester Chrysler Corp., Detroit, 1948; farmer, Somerset, Ky., 1949-50, 52-54; partner Sci. Hill Stockyards, Science Hill, Ky., 1955-60; partner Correll Auto Sales, Somerset, 1956—; pres. Tradewinds Shopping Center, Somerset, 1966—. Fund raising chmn. for Pulaski County, Lake Cumberland 4-H Center, 1967—. Served with AUS, 1950-52. Baptist (Sunday sch. tchr. 1953-71). Home: Box 44 Route 2 Somerset KY 42501 Office: Tradewinds Shopping Center Somerset KY 42501

CORRICK, JAMES ADAM, JR., educator; b. Parsons, W.V., Sept. 21, 1913; s. James Adam and Nelle (Felton) C.; student Davis-Elkins Coll., 1930-32; B.S., U. Ten., 1935, Ph.D., 1968; M.S., W.Va. U., 1939; m. Harriet Moore Perry, Aug. 13, 1937 children—James Adam III, Harriet Perri. Agrl. agt. Agrl. Extension Service, W.Va. U., Morgantown, 1935-42; commd. 2d lt. U.S. Navy, advanced through grades to capt., 1960; exec. officer Naval Air Sta., Astoria, Ore., 1944-46; dir. food engring. and sci. div. Navy Research and Devel. Facility, Bayonne, N.J., 1950-53; dir. catalog div. ept. Navy, Washington, 1955-58; dir. mgmt. planning Def. Indsl. Supply Center, Phila., 1959-61; dir. publs. and information div. Dept. Navy, 1961-63; asst. prof. Inst. Agr., U. Tenn., Knoxville, 1968—. Mem. U.S. Naval Inst., Am. Soc. Mil. Engrs., Inst. Food Tech., Am. Soc. Animal Sci., Sigma Xi, Phi Kappa Phi, Alpha Zeta, Epsilon Sigma Phi, Epsilon Phi Epsilon. Mason, Rotarian. Home: 2116 Lake Av Knoxville TN 37916

CORSO, LEE, coach. Football coach U. Louisville. Office: Athletic Dept Univ Louisville Louisville KY 40208*

CORSON, LOUIS DAMARIN, educator; b. Portsmouth, O., July 30, 1915; s. Louis Damarin and Ada Russell (Moore) C.; A.B., W.Va. U., 1937, M.A., 1942; Ed.D., Stanford, 1951; m. Joan Adelaide Stifel, June 17, 1947; children—Linda Diane, John Adelaide. Teaching fellow dept. history W.Va. U., 1946, faculty resident men's residence halls, 1946-48; dean of men, prof. Fla. State U., 1953-55; dean of men U. Ala., 1955-57, dir. of Retired Profs. Registry, 1957-62; cons. Assn. Am. Colls., 1963-64; adminstr. Coll. Church Musicians, Washington Cathedral, 1963-67. Capt., USAAF, 1942-46, USAF, 1951-52; dir. air crew ground tng. night fighter tng. group, dir. instr. tng. sch. Mem. Am. Personnel and Guidance Assn., Am. Assn. U. Profs., Assn. Higher Edn., N.E.A., Nat. Assn. Student Personnel Administrs. (exec. com. 1955-56), Am. Acad. Polit. and Social Sci., Am. Hist. Assn., Company Mil. Collectors and Historians, Am. Numis. Assn., A.A.A.S., Mountain, Sphinx, Kappa Kappa Psi, Alpha Phi Omega, Alpha Epsilon Delta, Phi Kappa Psi (dir. frat. edn. 1946-48, dir. scholarship, 1958-61, v.p. 1960-62, pres. 1962-64), Phi Delta Kappa, Phi Eta Sigma, Phi Alpha Theta. Episcopalian. Clubs: Cosmos, University (Washington); Fort Henry (Wheeling, W. Va.); Annapolis (Md.) Yacht. Home: RFD 6 720 N Holly Dr Annapolis MD 21401

CORWIN, WILLIAM, physician; b. Boston, Oct. 28, 1908; M.D., Tufts Coll., 1932; m. Frances M. Wetherell (dec.)m. 2d, Joyce S. Newman, 1965. Intern Wesson Meml. Hosp., Springfield, Mass., 1932-33; physician Met. State Hosp., Waltham, Mass., 1933-37, asst. supt., 1937-42; research fellow Harvard, 1937-46; practice medicine, specializing in psychiatry, Springfield, Mass., 1946-54, Miami, Fla., 1954—; mem. staff Jackson Meml. Hosp., Miami; instr. psychiatry Boston U., 1937-46, Tufts Coll., 1941-46; clin. asso. prof. psychiatry U. Miami, 1955-70, clin. prof., 1970—. Dir. Pan Am. Bank, Coral Gables. Past mem. State Fla. Adv. Com. on Mental Health; agy. operations com. United Fund. Bd. dirs. Family and Childrens Services Miami, United Health Found. Served to lt. col. M.C., USAAF, 1942-46. Diplomate Am. Bd. Psychiatry and Neurology. Fellow Am. Psychiat. Assn. (life); mem. A.M.A., Fla. Psychiat. Soc. (councillor). Cons. editor: Indsl. Medicine and Surgery. Contbr. articles on physiology of schizophrenia to profl. publs. Home: 3929 Granada Blvd Coral Gables FL 33134 Office: Dupont Plaza Center Miami FL 33131

CORWIN, WILLIAM MOORE, farm coop. exec.; b. Port Huron, Mich., July 13, 1912; s. William Henry and Columbia Camdelia (Moore) C.; A.B., W.Va. U., 1932; m. Mary Rose Kimmell, Nov. 20, 1940; 1 dau., Cathryn Ann (Mrs. William Anthony Meyer). Reporter, Clarksburg (W.Va.) Exponent, 1933-34; asst. in pub. relations dept., editor co. mag. Monongahela Power Co., Fairmont, W. Va., 1934-44; dir. publs. So. States Coop., 1944-48, dir. information publs. service, 1947—. Active Richmond area Tb Assn. Mem. Nat. Council Farmer Coops. (chmn. pub. relations com. 1957-58, 69-70), Nat. Coop. Editorial Assn. (pres. 1963), Nat. Coop. Advt. Council (pres. 1964-65), Advt. Relations Council (dir. 1962-64), Richmond Pub. Relations Assn. (pres. 1951-52), Richmond Advt. Club (dir. 1964-67), Richmond (chmn. agrl. com. 1963-65), Va. chambers commerce, Phi Kappa Tau, Kappa Tau Alpha. Democrat. Methodist. Home: 5106 Riverside Dr Richmond VA 23225 Office: 7th and Main Sts Richmond VA 23219

COSBY, HARRY, JR., physician; b. Memphis, Apr. 6, 1923; s. Harry and Mary (Johnson) C.; student Memphis State U., 1940-42; M.D., U. Tenn., 1945; m. Mary Elizabeth Richardson, Dec. 16, 1944; children—Walter Nathan, Harry Thomas. Intern, John Gaston Hosp., Memphis, 1945-46; practice gen. medicine, Iuka, Miss., 1947—; mem. staff Tishomingo County Hosp., Iuka, Miss.; Project dir. N.E. Miss. Multiphasic Testing Unit, 1970—. Mem. planning com. Memphis Regional Med. Program, 1971-72, county adv. bd. Head Start, 1968—, Miss. Comprehensive Planning Med. Agy., 1970—; cons. preventive medicine dept. U. Tenn., 1971—. Served with AUS, 1946-47. Mem. Am., N.E. Miss., Miss. med. assns., So. Med. Soc., Soc. for Advanced Med. Systems. Established first rural, doctor-oriented preventive med. testing unit, 1970. Home: Hwy 25 N Iuka MS 38852 Office: 309 N Main St Iuka MS 38852

COSBY, JOSEPH HATHAWAY, clergyman, sch. pres.; b. Hampton, Va., June 2, 1902; s. Joseph Hugh and Harriett Edmonds (Hathaway) C.; student Fork Union Mil. Acad., 1918-21; Th.B., So. Bapt. Theor. Sem., 1926; A.B., U. Richmond, 1929, LL.D. (hon.), 1959; M.A., U. Va., 1937; m. Helen Frances Eubank, Sept. 17, 1924; 1 dau., Jayne Hathaway. Ordained to ministry Bapt. Ch., 1928; pastor, Danville, Va., 1929-30, Irvington, 1930-35, Crozet, 1935-37, Lexington, 1937-42, Richmond, 1946-51; pres. Hargrave Mil. Acad., Chatham, Va., 1951—. Moderator Augusta Bapt. Assn., 1942; recording sec., chmn. exec. com., mem. Va. Bapt. Bd. Missions and Edn., 1946-51; pres. Richmond Bapt. Ministers Conf., 1949-50. Chmn. A.R.C. (Lancaster and Rockbridge cos.). Mem. bd. trustees Golden Gate Bapt. Theol. Sem., Berkeley, Cal. Served as maj., combat chaplain U.S. Army, World War II. Decorated 6 battle stars. Mem. So. Assn. Colls. and Schs. (chmn. Va. com.; com. policies and functions), Nat. Study Secondary Sch. Evaluation, So. Assn. Independent Schs. (past pres.), Assn. NDCC Schs. (past pres.), Phi Beta Kappa, Omicron Delta Kappa. Lion (charter pres. Lexington 1941). Address: Hargrave Mil Acad Chatham VA 24531

COSBY, WALTER THOMAS, constrn. co. exec.; b. Athens, Ala., Apr. 24, 1939; s. Laken and Maudie Beatrice (Garrison) C.; student Alcorn A. and M. Coll., 1957; m. Phyllis Eusebin White, July 8, 1957; children— Karen Elyce, Gale, Walter Thomas, William Jamal. Vice pres. Laken Cosby Concrete Constrn. Co., Louisville, 1958-65; pres. Cosby-Wilson Corp., Louisville, 1966—; dir. Village Pup Furnishings, Crese Corp., Novotey Industries, Nepco. Campaign mgr. Luther J. Wilson for U.S. Congress, 1970. Bd. dirs. Cosby-Wilson Found. Served with AUS, 1961-63. Mem. Negro. Bus. League, Gen. and Specialty Contractors Assn. Home: 620 S 42d St Louisville KY 40211 Office: 2809 Damesnil St Louisville KY 40311

COSSAR, GEORGE PAYNE, lawyer, state legislator; b. Webb, Miss., Aug. 26, 1907; m. children—John, Bill, George Payne. Lawyer, mem. Miss. Ho. of Reps., 1944-48, 52—. Mem. So. Regional Edn. Bd.; exec. com. Council of State Govts.; exec. com. Nat. Conf. State Legislative Leaders. Mem. Omicron Delta Kappa, Phi Alpha Delta, Sigma Nu. Methodist. Mason (Shriner), Rotarian. Home: Box 50 Charleston MS 38921 Office: Mississippi House of Reps Jackson MS 39201

COSTELLO, DONALD PAUL, zoologist; b. Detroit, Sept. 27, 1909; s. Thomas William and Frances Lydia (Hering) C.; A.B., Coll. City Detroit, 1930; Ph.D., U. Pa., 1934; m. Helen Mar Miller, June 20, 1936; children—Robert Charles, George Alfred. Instr. in zoology U. Pa., 1930-34; Nat. Research fellow Hopkins Marine Sta. of Stanford U., 1934-35; Rockefeller fellow and research asso. Stanford, 1941-42; asst. prof. zoology U. N.C., 1935-40, asso. prof., 1940-43, prof. zoology, 1943-49, Kenan prof. zoology, 1949—, chmn. dept. zoology 1947-57, mem. adminstrv. bd. of grad. sch., 1948-53, mem. Univ. Research Council since 1949; mem. exec. com. (vice chmn. 1949) and adv. council N.C. Inst. of Fisheries Research, 1948-53, chmn. exec. com., 1953-57; mem. embryology course staff Marine Biol. Lab., Woods Hole, Mass., summers 1939-46, mem. exec. com., 1951-53, dir. embryology course, summers 1946-50, trustee of lab., 1946-54, trustee, 1955—, exec. com., 1955-58. Mem. morphology and genetics study sect. NIH, Bethesda, Md., 1956-58, cell biology study sect., 1958-60, 63-66, chmn. cell biology study sect. B, 1966-67. Fellow A.A.A.S., N.Y. Acad. Scis., Inst. Internat. d'Embryologie; mem. Internat., Am. socs. cell biology, Am. Soc. Zoologists, Am. Soc. Naturalists (treas. 1948-50), NSF (div. com. Biology), Sigma Xi. Editorial bd. Biol. Bull., 1947-51, mng. editor, 1951-68; editorial bd. Jour. Morphology, 1950-52, Growth, 1953-63. Author articles, reports, revs. in research of exptl. embryology and exptl. cytology. Home: 507 Monroe Street Chapel Hill NC 27514

COSTON, HAROLD PRESTWOOD, hosp. adminstr.; b. Winston-Salem, N.C., Aug. 30, 1926; s. Fred E. and Lula Gertrude (Prestwood) C.; B.S., Wake Forest Coll., 1946; M.P.H., Johns Hopkins, 1952; m. Vivian Landis Johnson, Oct. 18, 1949; children—Carolyn (Mrs. Terry Leap), Deborah, Pamelia. Adminstr. Levering Hosp., Hannibal, Mo., 1960-66; asso. prof. hosp. adminstrn. U. N.C. Sch. Medicine at Chapel Hill, 1966-68; adminstrv. dir. N.C. Meml. Hosp., U. N.C. at Chapel Hill, 1968—; vis. lectr. Washington U. Sch. Hosp. Adminstrn., St. Louis. Pres. P.T.A., Rawls County, Mo.; chmn. bldg. fund YMCA, Hannibal; mem. St. Louis Commn. Hosps. and Homes. NIH Gen. Clin. Research Center grantee Bethesda, Md.; Bur. Health Services, Dept. Health, Edn. and Welfare grantee, Washington. Mem. Am. Coll. Hosp. Adminstrn. (fellowship award 1965), Am. Hosp. Assn., Am. Pub. Health Assn., Assn. Am. Med. Colls., N.C. Hosp. Assn. Methodist. Rotarian. Club: Men's Garden. Author pamphlets, booklets in field. Home: 2125 N Lake Shore Dr Chapel Hill NC 27514 Office: Room 111 N C Meml Hosp Chapel Hill NC 27514

COSTON, WILLIS DAN, chem. co. exec.; b. Scranton, Pa., Apr. 29, 1928; s. Willis Windsor and Esther W. (Williams) C.; B.A., Dickinson Coll., 1959; postgrad. Va. Poly. Inst., 1962-63, Mass. Inst. Tech., 1969; m. Sally Louise Specker, Sept. 10, 1960; children— Kimberly, Stacey. Personnel rep. Celanese Fibers Co., Pearisburg, Va., 1961-63, personnel supr., 1964-65; supr. personnel adminstrn. Celanese Chem. Co., Bay City, Tex., 1965-66, mgr. personnel, N.Y.C., 1966-68, mgr. indsl. relations Tech. Center, Corpus Christi, Tex., 1968—. Lectr. Va. Poly. Inst., 1963-64, Ga. Inst. Tech., 1963, Rider Coll., 1968, Dickinson Coll., 1962. Bd. dirs. Coastal Bend Cerebral Palsy. Scoutmaster Gulf Coast council Boy Scouts Am., 1971-72; chmn. blood drive A.R.C., 1962, 63, 64; chmn. drive United Fund, 1965-71. Served to 1st lt. Inf. AUS, 1960. Mem. Am. Mgmt. Assn., South Atlantic Council Indsl. Editors, Corpus Christi Personnel Assn., Corpus Christi C. of C. (mem. indsl. com. 1971). Moose. Club: Pharaoh Valley Country (Corpus Christi, Tex.). Home: 4309 Key West St Corpus Christi TX 78411 Office: PO Box 9077 Corpus Christi TX 78408

COTEY, HADDON EUGENE, clergyman; b. Alexandria, La., Apr. 30, 1927; s. Haddon Spurgeon and Eloise (Cordill) C.; B.A., Union U., 1949; B.D., So. Bapt. Theol. Sem., 1952, Th.D., 1957; m. Jean Lipsey, June 6, 1952; children—Sara Elizabeth, David Eugene, Stephen Ray,

James Cavin. Ordained to ministry Bapt. Ch., 1948; pastor 1st Bapt. Ch., Oxford, Ala., 1957-60, 1st Bapt. Ch., Murfreesboro, Tenn., 1961—. Pres. exec. bd. Tenn. Bapt. Conv., 1969; mem. hist. commn. So. Bapt. Conv.; mem. arrangements com. Tenn. Bapt. Conv. Mem. Rutherford County Job Opportunity Com.; chmn. Murfreesboro chpt. A.R.C., 1965-67; chmn. profl. div. United Givers Fund, Murfreesboro, 1965-66. Trustee Nashville Bapt. Hosp., 1965-71, Belmont Coll., Nashville. Served with USNR, 1945-46. Mem. Soc. Bibl. Lit. Democrat. Rotarian. Contbr. to Teaching Adult Life and Work Lessons, 1970—. Home: 1607 Grigg St Murfreesboro TN 37130 Office: 200 E Main St Murfreesboro TN 37130

COTHEN, GRADY COULTER, sem. pres.; b. Poplarville, Miss., Aug. 2, 1920; s. Joseph Herbert and Mamie (Coulter) C.; B.A., Miss. Coll., 1941, D.D., 1965; D.D., Cal. Baptist Coll., 1964; M.C.T., New Orleans Bapt. Theol. Sem., 1944; LLD., William Jewel Coll., 1971; m. Martha Elizabeth Major, June 11, 1941; children—Grady Coulter, Carol Lorraine (Mrs. Don C. McChesney). Ordained to ministry Bapt. Ch., 1939; pastor in Chattanooga, 1946-48, Oklahoma City, 1948-59, Birmingham, Ala., 1959-61; exec. sec-treas. So. Bapt. Gen. Conv. Cal., 1961-66; pres. Okla. Bapt. U., 1966-70, trustee, 1955-59; pres. New Orleans Bapt. Theol. Sem., 1970—. Mem. fgn. mission bd. So. Bapt. Conv., 1949-55, 1st v.p., 1963; exec. com. Bapt. World Alliance. Exec. com. Okla. Health Scis. Found.; mem. Okla. bd. Oklahoma City Symphony, 1966-70; chmn. edn. com. Okla. Edn. Commn., 1969-70. Trustee New Orleans Bapt. Theol. Sem. Served as chaplain USNR, 1944-46. Mem. Am. Assn. Ind. Coll. and Univ. Pres., Am. Acad. Polit. and Social Scis., Am. Assn. Higher Edn., Am. Acad. Religion, Omicron Delta Kappa, Pi Kappa Delta. Democrat. Rotarian. Author: God of the Beginnings, 1955. Home: 4111 Seminary Pl New Orleans LA 70126

COTHRAN, SAMUEL ALEXANDER, newspaper editor; b. Laurens, S.C., Dec. 13, 1915; s. Frank Harrison and Blanche (Clardy) C.; student Davidson Coll., 1938; B.A. cum laude, U. S.C., 1939; m. Nona Owens Crane, Apr. 8, 1942; children—Samuel Alexander, THomas Crane, Frank Chiles. Reporter, Index-Jour., Greenwood, S.C., 1939; reporter News and Courier, Charleston, S.C., 1939-41, asst. city editor 1947-51, city editor, 1951-58, mng. editor, 1958-68; pres., editor Aiken (S.C.) Standard, 1968—; pres. Aiken Communications, Inc., S.C. A.P., 1964; v.p. Aiken Cablevision, Inc. Served from 2d lt. to lt. col. Inf., AUS, 1942-45; ETO. Mem. Phi Delta Theta. Presbyn. (elder). Rotarian. Clubs: Carolina Yacht, Country of Charleston; Palmetto Golf. Home: 553 Sumter St SE Aiken SC 29801 Office: PO Box 456 124 Rutland Dr Aiken SC 29801

COTNER, NORMAN ANDREW, physician; b. Booneville, Ark., Mar. 28, 1927; s. Harrison H. and Myrtle E. (Rothwell) C.; B.S., Okla. A. and M. U., 1950, postgrad., 1951-54; M.D., U. Okla., 1958; m. Ruth Anna Giem, Dec. 22, 1949; children—Mark, Paul, Jeffrey, Sarah, Martha. Intern, Mercy Hosp., Oklahoma City, 1958-59; gen. practice medicine, Grove, Okla., 1959—; pres. Grove Med. Center, Inc., 1963—; chief staff Grove Gen. Hosp. Dir. State Bank Grove, Glassmaster Plastics. Chmn. Airport Authority, 1964-68; chmn. Grove Airport Bd., 1969—; chmn. Grove Indsl. Devel. Authority, 1968—. Chmn. town bd. trustees, 1962. Served with USN, 1944-48; PTO. Recipient Seabees Nat. Meml. Scholarship Fund award, 1971. Mem. Am. Acad. Gen. Practice, A.M.A., Okla., Delaware County med. assns., Tri-County Med. Soc. (pres. 1961-62), Okla. Rural Med. Assn. (mem. scholarship bd. 1970-71), Okla. Med. Alumni Assn., Phi Chi. Democrat. Elk. Home: 1211 Carolyn Dr Grove OK 74344 Office: PO Box 370 Grove OK 74344

COTNOIR, RAYMOND EUGENE, ins. co. exec.; b. Lowell, Vt., Oct. 12, 1934; s. Antoine Hercules and Rose Elda (Girouard) C.; student Tex. A. and M. U., 1953; B.A., So. Meth. U., 1965; m. Sybil Ann Fain, Sept. 13, 1957; children—Caryn Renee, Charon Nicole, Julie Michelle. With U.S. Fidelity & Guaranty Co., Dallas, 1956—, underwriter, 1958-68, asst. supt., 1968-70, supt., 1970—. Gen. chmn. Cotton Bowl Invitational Intercollegiate Basketball Tournament, 1970, adv. com. mem., 1971. Served with Tex. Air N.G., 1957-69. Mem. Surety Underwriters Assn. Dallas (pres. 1970), St. Augustine Home and Sch. Assn. (pres. 1969-71), Pi Kappa Alpha. K.C. Club: Mustang. Home: 1524 Brockham Circle Dallas TX 75217 Office: Mercantile Bank Bldg Dallas TX 75201

COTTER, VINCENT P., sporting goods co. exec.; b., 1927; B.S. in Bus. Adminstrn., Northeastern U., 1952, M.B.A., 1965. Office mgr. Wilson Sporting Goods Co., Chgo., 1953-65; adminstrv. asst. to treas., asst. treas., Wilson & Co., Inc., Chgo., 1965-68, treas., 1968-69, v.p., treas., 1969—. Home: 8016 Lakehurst Dr Oklahoma City OK 73120 Office: 4545 N Lincoln Blvd Oklahoma City OK 73105

COTTINGHAM, FRANK DINWIDDIE, clergyman; b. Cheraw, S.C., Sept. 14, 1904; s. Theodore Smith and Minnie Leila (Sherrill) C.; student Charleston Coll., 1920-21; m. Mary De Spears, July 20, 1945; children—Minnie Ruth, Theodore Joseph, Part-owner T. S. Cottingham & Son tire shop, Florence, S.C., until 1945; ordained to ministry Assembly of God Ch., 1942; pastor, Dexter, Ga., 1945-47, Charleston Heights, 1947-53, Charleston, 1956-62; pastor Bethel Temple, Charleston, 1962—; partner (with wife) Cottingham Musical Home, Charleston Heights, S.C., 1947—, Cottingham Counseling Service, Charleston Heights, 1967—. Mem. Gen. Council Assembly of God, S.C. Dist. Council Assembly of God, Charleston, N. Charleston ministerial unions. Address: 208 Chestnut St Charleston Heights SC 29405

COTTON, HYRAM COULTER, county ofcl.; b. Rockdale, Tex., Feb. 12, 1911; s. James C. and Docia (Curry) C.; student pub. schs.; m. Ruth Elizabeth Griffin, Apr. 9, 1934; 1 son, Hyram C. With Humble Oil & Refining Co., New London, Wink, Denver City, Tex. and Hobbs, N.M., 1932-45; owner, operator Denver City Electric Co., 1945-51. Mayor, Denver City, Tex., 1948-49, councilman, 1950-51; county commr., Yoakum County, Tex., 1951—; mem. Denver City Sch. Bd., 1946-52, Denver City Fire Dept., 1945—. Dir. League Vis. Nurses Sch. for Nurses, Yoakum County Hosp. Mem. County Judges and Commrs. Assn. Democrat. Baptist. Mason (32 deg.; past master), mem. Order Eastern Star, Odd Fellow. Home: 521 W 7th St Denver City TX 79323 Office: 700 W Cedar Denver City TX 79323

COTTON, RICHARD GENE, baking co. exec.; b. Alexandria, La., Jan. 18, 1935; s. William F. and Genevieve Winifred (Hathorn) C.; B.S., La. State U., 1957; m. Nancy Wilson, Aug. 9, 1958; children—Richard, William, Tracy. With Cotton Bros. Baking Co., Inc., Alexandria, La., 1957—, gen. mgr., 1963-66, v.p., 1966-67, pres., 1967—; chmn. bd. Data Route, Inc., Dallas; dir. W. E. Long Co., Chgo. Bd. dirs. Rapides United Givers, Alexandria. Served with U.S.N.G., 1951-65. Mem. Young Pres. Orgn., C. of C. (bd. dirs. 1964-65, 67-68), Kappa Sigma. Mason (Shriner), Kiwanian. Home: 4511 Willowick Blvd Alexandria LA 71301 Office: PO Box 5405 Alexandria LA 71301

COTTON, WILLIAM FREDERICK, bakery exec.; b. Corley, Ark., Oct. 23, 1897; s. John Thomas and Emily (Peters) C.; student U. Ark., 1921-22; m. May Compton, Dec. 9, 1969; children—William Frederick, Richard Gene. Chmn., Cotton Bros. Baking Co., Cotton Baking Co., Cotton's, Inc., Cotton's Holsum Bakers, Cotton's Ouchita Bakery, Alexandria, La., 1965—; dir. Guaranty Bank & Trust Co. Finance adviser, Alexandria, 1946—. Dir., mem. exec. com. Rapides Parish Sch. Bd., 1963—. Served with USNR, World War II. Democrat. Baptist. Mason (Shriner), Lion. Clubs: Baton Rouge Country; Alexandria Country; Shreveport (La.). Home: 1516 City Park Blvd Alexandria LA 71301 Office: 3400 McArthur St Alexandria LA 71301

COUCH, DONALD PETER, diversified bus. exec.; b. New Orleans, Mar. 20, 1940; s. Harvey Crowley, Jr. and Beatrice (Kearney) C.; B.A., Notre Dame U., 1962; m. Susan Kay Watkins, June 6, 1962; children—Laura Kay, Cynthia Marie, Donald Peter. Trainee, First Nat. Bank, Magnolia, Ark., 1963-64, also dir.; trainee Union Nat. Bank, Little Rock, 1964-68, v.p., dir., 1968, pres., co-chmn. bd., 1968-70; pres. Internat. Properties, Inc., Circle Realty Co., 3C's, Inc., Little Rock, 1970—. Bd. dirs. Pulaski County chpt. A.R.C.; mem. exec. bd. Quapaw Area council Boy Scouts Am. Mem. Little Rock C. of C. Clubs: Little Rock Country, Pleasant Valley Country Top of the Rock (all Little Rock), Little Rock. Home: 453 Valley Club Circle Little Rock AR 72207 Office: Tanglewood Office Center Little Rock AR 72207

COUCH, HOUSTON BROWN, educator; b. Estill Springs, Tenn., July 1, 1924; s. Charles Emmett and Grace (Watson) C.; B.S. in Agriculture, Tenn. Technol. U., 1950; Ph.D. in Plant Pathology, U. Cal. at Davis, 1954; m. Billie Spencer, Oct. 3, 1945; children—Charles, Jonathan, James, Betty, Wayne. Asst. prof. plant pathology Pa. State U., State College, 1954-60, asso. prof. plant pathology, 1960-65; prof. plant pathology, head dept. plant pathology and physiology Va. Poly. Inst. and State U., Blacksburg, 1965—. Collaborator U.S. Dept. Agr. Regional Pasture Research Lab., State College, Pa., 1960-65; cons. to agrl. chem. industries, 1958-72. Served with AUS, 1943-45. Decorated Purple Heart. Mem. Mid-Atlantic Food Processors Assn. (mem. com. 1966-72), Am. Phytopathol. Soc. (div. pres. 1964-65), Am. Soc. Agronomy, Soil Sci. Soc. Am., Am. Soc. Plant Physiologists, Eastern Ecology Root Disease Conf. (chmn. exec. com., program com. 1968), Sigma Xi. Mem. Ch. of Christ. Author: Diseases of Turfgrasses, 1962. Home: 605 Landsdowne St SE Blacksburg VA 24060

COUCH, JAMES HOUSTON, educator; b. Easley, S.C., June 5, 1919; s. A. Waverly and Gertrude (Foster) C.; B.S., Clemson U., 1941, M.S., 1952; grad. Inst. for Materials Handling Tchrs., Northwestern U., 1969; grad. Materials Handling Inst., Purdue U., 1972; m. Sarah Crenshaw, Jan. 11, 1942; children—James F., Dorothy C. (Mrs. Gerald Stafford). Asso. prof. indsl. engring. Clemson (S.C.) U., 1941-68, prof. indsl. engring., 1956-68, asso. prof. engring. services, 1969—. Research engr. Lockheed Aircraft Corp., part time, Lockheed-Ga. Co., part-time 1955-69. Bd. dirs. Foundry Edn. Found., Cleve. Mem. Am. Welding Soc. (Meritorious award 1964, Adams Meml. membership award 1965), Am. Soc. for Metals, Am. Foundrymen's Soc. Author: Manufacturing Processes and Materials, 1967; Engineering Manufacturing Processes, 1960. Home: 408 College Av Clemson SC 29631

COUCH, JOE, apparel mfg. co. exec.; b. Little Rock, Apr. 2, 1941; s. Lonnie and Mimi (Beal) C.; B.S. in Adminstrn., U. Ark., 1964; m. Natalie Sue Noland, June 6, 1964. Writer mens fashions Titches Dept. Store, 1964-67; copy chief Dreyfuss Dept. Store, 1967-68; dir. advt. Haggar Slacks, Dallas, 1968—, editor Haggar Highlights, 1968—. Served with AUS, 1968. Mem. Dallas Jr. C. of C. (bd. dirs.). Club: Press of Dallas. Home: 7078 Town North Dallas TX 75209 Office: Haggar Co 6113 Lemmon Av Dallas TX 75209

COUCH, RILEY CARLTON, JR., farmer, rancher; b. Haskell, Tex., Jan. 3, 1919; s. Riley C. and Ada (Baker) C.; B.S. in Agr., Tex. A. and M. U., 1941; postgrad. Command and Gen. Staff Coll., 1967; m. Jerrene Couch, Sept. 4, 1943; children—Jerre Sue (Mrs. W.R. Moore, III), Riley III. Owner, operator farm and ranch, Haskell County, Tex., 1947—; dir. Haskell County Warehouse and Compress, Inc., Haskell, Haskell Nat. Bank. Field supr. Haskell County Agrl. Stblzn. and Conservation Service, 1960—. Pres., Haskell Civic Center, 1971—, Homecoming Assn., 1971—. Vice pres., dir. Municipal Water Authority, North Central Tex., 1967—. Served with AUS, 1941-46. Decorated Bronze Star medal. Mem. Farm Bur., Farmers Union, Am. Legion, Res. Officers Assn. Baptist. Rotarian (past pres.). Home and office: Box 771 Haskell TX 79521

COUCH, WILSON PAUL, physician; b. Louisville, Feb. 17, 1929; s. Joseph M. and Flora Freda (Thom) C.; A.B., Snead Jr. Coll., 1948; B.S., Tulane U., 1953, M.D., 1956; m. Merle Louise Kepler, Jan. 26, 1952; children—David K., Stephen W., Wilson Paul II. Intern, William Beaumont Army Hosp., El Paso, Tex., 1956-57; post-grad. tng. LaLee Kemp Charity Hosp., 1957; gen. practice medicine, Paradis, La., 1957—; mem. med. staff St. Anne's Hosp., Raceland, La., St. Charles Hosp., Luling, La. Mem. St. Charles Parish Bd. Health, 1962—; mem. Council Med. Staffs, 1971; asst. coroner St. Charles Parish, 1967—. Mem. St. Charles Parish Bd. Drainage, 1965-71. Served with USMC, 1946-48, 50-51, as capt. M.C., AUS, 1956-57. Diplomate Am. Bd. Family Practice. Fellow Am. Geriatric Soc.; mem. Am. Acad. Gen. Practice (pres. 2d dist. 1968-70), La., Tri-Parish med. socs., Am., La. acads. family practice, Tulane Alumni Assn., Am., La. heart assns., Assn. Mil. Surgeons, Phi Kappa Sigma, Theta Kappa Psi. Home: Route 1 Luling LA 70070 Office: Box 3498 Paradis Medical Clinic Paradis LA 70080

COUGHLAN, JOHN WALKER, accountant; b. Calgary, Alta., Can., July 30, 1927; s. John Bernard and Etta (Walker) C.; B.A., U. Alta., 1948, B.Com., 1949; M.A., U. Western Ont., 1952; Ph.D., Johns Hopkins, 1955; m. Betty June Boyd; children—Victoria Ruth, Brian Walker, John Anthony. Budget accountant Interprovincial Pipeline Co., Edmonton, Alta., 1949-50; financial analyst Olin-Mathieson Chem. Corp., Balt., Md., 1953-54; chmn. dept. accounting George Washington U., 1963-67; pub. accountant, Washington, 1958—; pres. C.P.A. Sch. Washington, Inc.; dir. Compudemics, Inc. Served to capt. Canadian Army, 1948-49, 54-55. Recipient Research award Crane & Co., 1967. Canadian Officers Tng. Corps Meml. fellow, 1950-51, Canadian Social Sci. Research fellow. Mem. Am. Assn. U. Profs., Soc. for Advancement Mgmt. (past v.p. Washington chpt.). Author: Guide to Contemporary Theory of Accounts, 1964. Contbr. articles to profl. jours.Home: 3819 Lee St Fairfax City VA 22030 Office: 1601 Connecticut Av NW Washington DC 20036

COUGHLIN, ROBERT LAWRENCE, economist; b. Portland, Ore., June 26, 1928; s. William Henry and Cecelia Ottllie (Freund) C.; B.S., U. Ore., 1951; M.A., Stanford, 1952; m. L. Merle Doney, Jan. 26, 1954; children—Arthur, James, Donald. Portfolio analyst J. Henry Helser & Co., investment mgmt., Portland, 1953-57; security analyst First Cascade Corp., securities dealer, Portland, 1958-62; economist N.W. regional office Fed. Water Quality Adminstrn., Portland, 1962-66, chief planning br., 1964-66; sr. economist Environmental Protection Adminstrn., Washington, 1966—. Served with USMCR, 1945-46. Mem. Am. Econ. Assn., Am. Acad. Polit. Sci., Am. Acad. Polit. and Social Sci. Home: 1223 Massachusetts Av SE Washington DC 20003 Office: Environmental Protection Adminstrn 4th and M St NW Washington DC 20024

COULTER, BAILEY MARTIN, JR., mech. engr.; b. North Little Rock, Ark., Oct. 22, 1936; s. Bailey M. and Canzadie (Box) C.; student Ark. State Tchrs. Coll., 1959; B.S. in Mech. Engring., U. Ark., 1962; m. Anita Jean Mitchell, Dec. 23, 1960; children—Laura Lynn, Shelly Diane, Bailey Martin III. Mech. engr. Pratt & Whitney Aircraft Co., West Palm Beach, Fla., 1962-64; systems engr. Chrysler Corp. space div., Huntsville, Ala., 1964-66; mech. engr. The Boeing Co., Cocoa Beach, Fla., 1966-69; engr. nuclear div. Union Carbide, Oak Ridge, 1969—. Served with USAF, 1954-58. Registered profl. engr., Fla. Mem. Am. Soc. M.E.s., Nat. Soc. Profl. Engrs., Fla. Engring. Soc. Pub. Fluid Mechanics Abstracts, 1971—. Address: RR 2 Powell TN 37849

COULTER, BORDEN MCKEE, JR., indsl. engr.; b. Casper, Wyo., Feb 9, 1917; s. Borden McKee and Josephine Helen (Grother) C.; B.S., U. Cal. at Los Angeles, 1939, M.B.A., 1947; m. Emily Sawtelle, Aug. 23, 1950; children—Borden, Terry Lynn, Leigh, Richard. Research analyst Australian Nat. R.R., 1939-40; indsl. engr. Lockheed Aircraft, 1940-47, staff indsl. engr., 1948-50; with div. indsl. engring. U.S. Steel Corp., 1947; mgr. prodn. control Bakewell Products, 1947; supr. orgn. and procedures Norris Thermador Corp., 1950-53; gen. mgr. Roed Engring. Assos., 1943—; prin., v.p., dir. The Emerson Cons., Inc., mgmt. cons., N.Y.C., 1954—. Mem. Am. Inst. Indsl. Engrs. (pres. Los Angeles), System and Procedures Assn. (program chmn.), Am. Mgmt. Assn., Nat. Assn. Foremen, Am. Inst. Plant Engrs., Nat. Assn. Accountants Am., Newcomen Soc., U.S. Naval Inst., Navy League U.S., Am. Forestry Assn., Inst. Mgmt. Consultants, Houston Petroleum Club, Blue Key, Kappa Kappa Psi, Alpha Kappa Psi, Tau Kappa Alpha, Phi Gamma Delta. Home: 2112 Amberly Ct Houston TX 77042

COULTER, WILLIAM WALLACE, JR., physician; b. Hensley, Ark., Jan. 16, 1916; s. William Wallace and Sue Virginia (Tilton) C.; B.S., Agrl. and Mech. Coll. Tex., 1936; M.D., La. State U., 1940; m. Martha Lilly Harper, Feb. 18, 1944; children—Martha Lee, Carol (Mrs. Joseph L. Pritchett III), Augusta (Mrs. Robert G. Szabo). Intern, Jefferson Davis Hosp., Houston, 1940-41; practice medicine, Kerrville, Tex., 1941-44; instr. medicine Baylor U. Coll. Medicine, 1944-45; resident Tex. State Sanatorium, 1945-46; practice medicine, McAllen, Tex., 1946-49; clin. asso. prof. medicine La. State U. Coll. Medicine, 1967-72, instr., 1949-50; resident pathology Jefferson-Davis Hosp., Houston, 1949; practice medicine, specializing in internal medicine, Lafayette, La., 1960—; mem. staffs Lafayette Charity Hosp., Our Lady of Lourdes Hosp., Lafayette Gen. Hosp.; med. dir. Lafayette Charity Hosp. Tb Annex, 1957-60. Diplomate Am. Bd. Internal Medicine, Am. Bd. Pulmonary Diseases. Fellow Am. Coll. Chest Physicians, A.C.P.; mem. Am. Assn. Tb Physicians, La. Thoracic Soc. (pres. 1959-60), A.M.A., La., Lafayette Parish (sec.-treas. 1960-61) med. assns., La. Tb Assn. (pres. 1960-62), S.A.R., Alpha Kappa Kappa. Roman Catholic. Clubs: Oakbourne Country, Town House (Lafayette). Home: 1000 W Bayou Pkwy Lafayette LA 70501 Office: 1229 Coolidge Lafayette LA 70501

COUNTESS, ROBERT HARVEY, educator; b. Memphis, Aug. 26, 1937; s. Parks Lowry and Kathleen Gladys (Casey) C.; A.B., Bob Jones U., 1961, M.A., 1963, Ph.D., 1966; M.A., U. Ga., 1968; postgrad. U. Ark., 1961, Westminster Theol. Sem., 1964-65; m. Patricia Ann Davis, Aug. 5, 1961; children—Timothy Daniel, Stephen Paul. Instr., John Knox Jr. Coll., Wilmington, Del., 1965; instr. Bible, philosophy, Greek, chmn. fgn. lang. dept. Covenant Coll., Lookout Mountain, Tenn., 1966-68; asst. adminstr. U. Tenn., Nashville, 1969; asst. prof. philosophy Tenn. State U., Nashville, 1969—. Pastor, Reformed Presbyn. Ch. Nashville, 1968-69. Served with AUS, 1955-58. Recipient fellowship U. Ga., 1967-68. Mem. Am. Assn. U. Profs., Evangelical Theol. Soc., Soc. Bibl. Lit. and Exegesis, Am. Acad. Religion. Presbyn. (vice-moderator So. Presbytery 1968). Contbr. articles to profl. jours. Home: 433 Wilclay Dr Nashville TN 37209

COUNTS, GURDON WRIGHT, JR., physician; b. Prosperity, S.C., Nov. 12, 1933; s. Gurdon Wright and Violet Marjorie (Epting) C.; B.S., Newberry Coll., 1955; M.D., Med. Coll. S.C., 1959; m. Elizabeth Mae Rickenbacker, Dec. 20, 1959; children—Gurdon Wright III, Karl F., Walter E., Philip J., Anthony J. Intern, Greenville (S.C.) Gen. Hosp., 1960, resident, 1961-62; practice medicine, specializing in family practice, Prosperity, S.C., 1961, Batesburg-Leesville, S.C., 1964—; mem. staff Lexington County Hosp. Served with USAF, 1962-64. Named Batesburg-Leesville Young Man of the Year, Jr. C. of C., 1967. Mem. A.M.A., S.C., Ridge med. socs., Batesburg-Leesville C. of C. (dir. 1965-69, pres. 1967-68, state dir. 1968-71). Lutheran (mem. ch. council 1965-68, 70—). Home: 501 E Church St Leesville SC 29070 Office: E Columbia Av Batesburg SC 29006

COURSEN, RICHARD DENNISON, assn. exec., govt. cons.; b. Newark, Dec. 2, 1917; s. H. Preston and Ruth (Dennison) C.; grad. Phillips Andover Acad., 1936; B.A., Yale, 1940; m. Helen Wilson Stevens, July 18, 1942; children—Timothy S., Christopher D.; m. 2d, Carolyn Hinman Yeaw, May 22, 1971. Advt. product mgr. Pillsbury Mills, Inc., 1945-48; account exec. Campbell-Mithun, 1948-49; dir. marketing Northrup, King & Co., 1949-54; dir. edn., editor Council Agrl. and Chemurgic Research, 1954-57; v.p., dir. Cornwell, Inc., 1954-57; dir. Malayan Tin Bur., Washington, 1957—; pres. Coursen & Co., govt. consultants, Washington, 1970—. Served from pvt. to capt. cav. AUS, 1940-45. Decorated Bronze Star. Republican. Episcopalian. Clubs: Burning Tree, Chevy Chase, 1925 F Street, Capitol Hill, Yale (past pres.). Home: 5053 Loughboro Rd NW Washington DC 20016 Office: 2000 K St NW Washington DC 20006 also 1101 17th St NW Washington DC 20036

COURSHON, ARTHUR HOWARD, lawyer, savs. and loan exec.; b. Chgo., Feb. 21, 1921; s. Aaron H. and Beatrice (Pollak) C; B.A., U. Fla., 1942; LL.B., U. Miami, Coral Gables, Fla., 1947; m. Carol Biel, Feb. 20, 1943; children—Barbara, Deanne. Admitted to Fla. bar, 1947; asso. firm Goldstein & Klein, Miami Beach, Fla., 1947-48; partner firm Courshon & Courshon, Miami Beach, 1948—; organizer, chmn. bd. dirs. Washington Fed. Savs and Loan Assn., Miami Beach, 1952—, Washington Security Co., Miami, Fla., 1956—; trustee, treas., organizer First Mortgage Investors, Miami Beach, 1961—. Cons. savs. and loan system in Chile, ICA, 1958—, housing finance com., 1960—; cons. housing loans to Latin Am., 1960—, Devel. Loan Fund, Inter-Am. Devel. Bank, 1961—; cons. Govt. of Peru, 1960—; mem. U.S. Govt. task force Fed. Home Loan Bank, 1961-62; housing finance cons. Latin Am. Affairs Subcom, Senate Fgn. Relations Com., 1960—; housing finance com. U.S. Operations Mission, Santiago, Chile, 1958—. Mem. Miami Beach Civic League, Miami Beach Planning Com., 1949-51. Chmn. Miami Beach financial com. Democratic Nat. Com., 1960; mem. Fla. Kennedy-Johnson Campaign Com., 1960. Served with USAAF, 1942-46. Recipient citation for establishment savs. and loan system in Chile, ICA, 1960, Housing and Home Finance Agy., 1961. Mem. Am., Dade County bar assns., Fla. Bar, U.S. Savs. and Loan Inst., Nat. League Insured Savs. Assns. (exec. com., chmn. Fed. regulations com.), U.S. Savs. and Loan League (atty.'s com.), Internat. Union Bldg. Socs. and Savs. Assn., Am. Legion, Miami Beach C. of C., Nu Beta Epsilon, Pi Lambda Phi. Democrat. Jewish religion. Home: 1620 Daytonta Rd Miami Beach FL 33141 Office: 1701 Meridian Av Miami Beach FL 33139

COURSHON, JACK ROBERT, lawyer, banker; b. Evanston, Ill., Oct. 6, 1924; s. Aaron Hyman and Beatrice (Pollak) C.; student U. Fla., 1941-43; J.D., U. Miami, 1948; m. Dolores Bloom, Mar. 10, 1946; children— Denise (Mrs. Ronald Lavan), William, Bonnie, Alison. Admitted to Fla. bar, 1948; partner firm Courshon & Courshon, 1948-—; co-founder, dir. Washington Fed. Savs. and Loan Assn., Miami Beach, 1952-—, Jefferson Nat. Bank, Miami Beach, 1963-—; organizer, mng. trustee, sec. 1st Mortgage Investors, Boston, 1961-—; organizer, chmn. bd. 1st Mortgage Adv. Corp., Miami Beach, 1961-—, 1st Realty Investment Corp., Miami Beach, 1968-—, Median Mortgage Adv. Corp., Miami Beach, 1970-—; organizer, chmn. trustees, mng. trustee Median Mortgage Investors, Boston, 1970-—; co-founder, vice chmn. bd. Jefferson Bancorp, Inc., 1970-—. Active various community drs. Trustee Greater Miami Philharmonic Soc.; bd. dirs. Miami Beach Symphony; bd. govs. Nat. Assn. Real Estate Investment Funds, 1962-—. Served from 2d lt. to 1st lt. USAAF, 1944-46; PTO. Decorated Air Medal. Mem. Am., Fla., Miami Beach, Dade County bar assns. Democrat. Jewish religion. Clubs: Ocean Reef (Key Largo, Fla.); Jockey (Miami). Home: 1440 W 23d St Sunset Island 3 Miami Beach FL 33140 Office: 801 41st St Miami Beach FL 33140

COURTNEY, ALBERT KENNETH, physician; b. Wills Point, Tex., Feb. 5, 1929; s. Albert and Lottie Ethel (Miracle) C.; B.A., U. Tex., 1953, M.D., 1963; m. Eleanor Kay Dunks, July 1, 1961; children—Steven Paul, Deborah Kay, David Allen, Philip Edward. Intern, U. N.M. Hosp., 1963-64; gen. practice resident Monterrey County Hosp., Salinas, Cal., 1964-66; gen. practice medicine, Midland, Tex., 1967-—; mem. med. staff Midland Meml., Parkview hosps., Midland. Served to lt. (j.g.) USNR, 1954-57. Mem. Am. Acad. Gen. Practice, Assn. Am. Physicians and Surgeons, So. Tex. (mem. com. on pvt. practice 1970-71), Midland County med. assns., Phi Beta Pi. Republican. Baptist (deacon 1966-—). Mason. Clubs: Antique Automobile, Permian Basin Rifle and Pistol (Midland). Home: 1601 W College St Midland TX 79701 Office: 210 N C St Midland TX 79701

COURTNEY, J(OHN) CAL(HOUN), investment and found. exec.; b. Aiken, S.C., Apr. 12, 1916; S. James Edwin and Alice (Guy) C.; B.S. in Civil Engring., George Washington U., 1939, M.S. in Mgmt. Engring., 1948; m. Zoleta Meachum, Jan. 19, 1947; children—John Calhoun IV, Winfree Meachum, Zoleta Guy. Staff asst. White House, Washington, 1948-52; indsl. cons. Tex. Power & Light Co., Dallas, 1952-57; pres. Tex. Investment & Mgmt. Co., Dallas, 1959-—, Sam Rayburn Found., Dallas, 1962-—; pres. Greater Laredo Devel. Found., Laredo, Tex., 1968-—; dir. Ga.-Fla. Oil & Refining Co., Jacksonville, Internat. Projects & Devel. Co., Dallas, Continental Sulphur & Phosphate Co., Dallas, Graham Land & Devel. Co., Dallas, Bank Tex., Hounston; exec. v.p. Nat. Conv. Corp., Dallas, 1956. Chmn., Vets. Com. for Eisenhower-Nixon, 1956; ind. candidate for U.S. Senate from Tex., 1957. Trustee, Hosp. of S.W.; bd. dirs. Tex. Found. for Higher Edn. Served to col. USAAF, 1946. Named Outstanding Citizen Mil. Order Equalizers, 1957; recipient Distinguished Service award V.F.W., 1962. Mem. Am. Polit. Sci. Assn., V.F.W., Am. Mgmt. Assn., Am.-Mexican Assn. (pres.). Methodist Clubs: Brookhaven Country (Dallas); Willowbrook Country (Tyler, Tex.); Army-Navy. Contbg. editor Commodity Year Book, 1948. Home: 7210 S Jan Mar Dr Dallas TX 75230 Office: Praetorian Bldg 1607 Main St Dallas TX 75201

COUSINS, RUTH HUBBARD, assn. exec., editor; b. Waleska, Ga.; d. Charles T. and Mary (Boston) Hubbard; student Duke; A.B., George Washington U., 1958, M.A., 1963; m. James F. Cousins, Mar. 1, 1941 (dec. Sept. 1959); children—Carol Tracy, Joan Hubbard. Exec. dir., treas., editor nat. publ. Psi Chi, 1958-—. Mem. Am., D.C. psychol. assns., Am. Assn. U. Women, Great Books Club, Internat. Council Psychologists, Assn. Coll. Honor Socs. (council), Am., Wash. socs. assn. execs., Soc. Tech. Writers and Pubs., World Future Soc., Phi Delta Gamma, Psi Chi (nat. council), A.A.A.S., Eastern, Mid-western, Rocky Mountain, Southeastern, Southwestern, Western psychol. assns. Club: Potomac Women's. Co-author New Form of Analogies Test. Home: 1711 Massachusetts Av NW Washington DC 20036 Office: 1200 17th St NW Washington DC 20036

COUSINS, THOMAS G., diversified bus. exec.; ed. U. Ga.; m. Ann Draghon; children—Jane Caroline, Lillian, Thomas G. Chmn. bd., chief exec. officer Cousins Properties Inc., Atlanta, subsidiaries 1st Am. Investment Corp., Investment Mortgage Co., Retail Planning Corp., Southeastern Land Fund, Inc., Investment Adv. Co.; prin. owner Atlanta Hawks, 1968-—; mem. Atlanta bd. Citizens and So. Nat. Bank. Mem. exec. com. Central Atlanta Progress, Inc. Trustee Atlanta Arts Alliance, Rockefeller U. Presbyn. (chmn. bd. deacons). Club: Commerce of Atlanta (dir.). Office: Atlanta Hawks 148 Cain NE Atlanta GA 30303*

COVEY, CYCLONE, educator; b. Guthrie, Okla., May 21, 1922; s. Cyclone Davis and Lola Effie (Best) C.; B.A., Stanford, 1944, Ph.D., 1949; postgrad. U. Chgo., 1944-45, U. Okla., 1945-46, Harvard, 1953-54; m. Bonnie Mae Bagby Hansen, June 12, 1949; children—Christopher Cyclone, Mark Nicholas, Julie Kristiana, Jonathan Baldridge, Timothy Nathaniel. Grad. asst. history Stanford, 1946; instr. history and humanities Reed Coll., Portland, Ore., 1947-50; instr. humanities and music Okla. A. and M. Coll. Stillwater, 1950-51; prof. govt., history and fgn. langs. McKendree Coll., Lebanon, Ill., 1951-53, 54-56; faculty fellow Harvard, Cambridge, Mass., 1953-54; vis. asst. prof. Am. studies Amherst (Mass.) Coll., 1956-57; asst. prof. music, humanities and hist. research Okla. State U., Stillwater, 1957-60, asso. prof., 1960-65, prof., 1965-68; prof. history Wake Forest U., Winston-Salem, N.C., 1968-—, dir. Wake Forest in Venice, 1972. Ford postdoctoral fellow, 1953, Okla. State U. Research Found. grants, 1958-68. Democrat. Author: The Wow Boys, 1957; The American Pilgrimage, 1960; Cabeza de Vaca's Adventures in the Unknown Interior of America, 1961; A Cyclical Return to the Timeless Three-Clock Revolution, 1966; The Gentle Radical, 1966. Home: 4071 Tangle Lane Winston Salem NC 27106

COVINGTON, CECIL LYONS, electronics co. exec.; b. Dallas, Nov. 21, 1911; s. William Roper and Mary Eliza (Lyons) C.; A.B. cum laude, Baylor U., 1933; LL.B., Nat. U., 1939, M.P.L., S.J.D., 1940; m. Phyllis Ruth McIntyre, Feb. 17, 1943; 1 son, Mark Roper. Adminstrv. asst. PWA Washington, 1933-40; clk. to Senator Tom Connally of Tex., 1940-41; spl. asst. on contracts OSRD, 1941-43; spl. asst. to dir. tng., facilities service VA, in charge review contracts negotiated with all schs. and colls. Ark., La., Okla., Miss., Kan., Tex., Mo., 1946-53; contract adminstr. Texas Instruments, Inc., 1953-56, controller apparatus div., 1956-58, mgr. govt. contracts adminstrn., 1958-61, mgr. govt. contracts and banking relations, 1962-63, mgr. govt. relations, 1964-66, adminstrv. asst. to chmn. bd., 1967, contracts mgr. govt. products div., 1968, mgr. govt. relations equipment group, 1969-—. Served as lt. USNR, 1944-46. Mem. Financial Execs. Inst. (govt. procurement policy com.), Nat. Security Indsl. Assn. (chmn. procurement adv. com.), N.A.M. (nat. def. com.), Electronic Industries Assn. (govt. procurement relations dept.), Sigma Tau Delta, Beta Pi Theta, Sigma Nu Phi. Presbyn. Clubs: Corinthian Sailing, Glen Lakes Country. Home: 9531 Windy Hill Rd Dallas TX 75238 Office: 13500 North Central Expressway Dallas TX 75222

COVINGTON, GEORGE ARMFIELD, ret. profl. assn. exec.; b. Jamestown, N.C., Feb. 2, 1905; s. Charlie Chesley and Jenevieve (Armfield) C.; student U. N.C., 1924-26; LL.D., High Point Coll., 1971; m. Susan Everitt, May 23, 1934. With Carolina Warehouse, Greensobro, N.C., 1927-28, Clover Brand Dairies, Greensboro, 1929; with tax dept. City of Greensboro, 1929-32; asst. mgr., sec. Lindale Dairy, High Point, N.C., 1933-52; Mayor City of High Point, 1953-57; exec. v.p. High Point C. of C., 1958-71; dir. 1st Fed. Savings and Loan Assn. Bd. dirs. Guilford Tech. Inst., Evergreens Nursing Home, House of Prayer for Alcoholics; chmn. Guilford County Health Dept., 1948-53, U.S. C. of C. Regional Inst., 1965. Mem. N.C. C. of C. Execs. (pres. 1961). Presbyn. (elder 1959-—). Mason, Lion (pres. 1953). Home: 1408 Wendover Dr High Point NC 27262

COVINGTON, J. HARRY, lawyer; b. Easton, Md., Mar. 7, 1909; A.B., Princeton, 1931; LL.B., U. Pa., 1938. Admitted to D.C. bar, 1938; mem. firm Covington & Burling, Washington. Home: 2320 Wyoming Av Washington DC 20008 Office: 888 16th St Washington DC 20006*

COVINGTON, JAMES O., engr. Project engr. Flowers Garden Ocean Research Center, U. Tex. Med. Br. Office: U of Tex Medical Branch Galveston TX 77550*

COVINGTON, ROBERT NEWMAN, educator; b. Evansville, Ind., Sept. 9, 1936; s. George M. and Roberta (Newman) C.; B.A., Yale U. 1958; J.D., Vanderbilt U., 1961; m. Paula Anne Haltox, July 29, 1972. Admitted to Tenn. bar, 1961; asst. prof. Vanderbilt U. Sch. Law, Nashville, 1961-64, asso. prof., 1964-69, professor, 1969-—; consultant Tenn. State Law Library Commn., 1965-—;chairman Southern Law Review Conf., 1963-64; mem. Labor Law Group Trust, 1969-—. Pres. Henry County (Tenn.) Young Democrats Club, 1959. Mem. Am., Tenn. bar assns., Am. Judicature Soc., Order of Coif, Phi Beta Kappa, Phi Delta Phi. Democrat. Episcopalian. Club: University (pres. 1968-70) (Nashville). Author: Problems in Professional Responsibility: Insurance, 1966; co-editor: (with Thomas G. Roady Jr.) Essays in Procedure and Evidence, 1961 (with others) Cases and Materials on Legal Methods, 1969; (with A. Caghan) Social Legislation, 1971; (with J. Jones and A. Cagham) Discrimination in Employment, 1971. Contbr. articles in field to legal jours. Home: 907 Estes Rd Nashville TN 37215

COWAN, CLIFFORD WILBERT, educator; b. Ellwood City, Pa., July 2, 1931; s. Joseph L. and Velma (Wood) C.; B.E.E., Ga. Inst. Tech., 1958, M.S. in Elec. Engring., 1970; m. Nancy Patricia Smith, July 23, 1954; children—David C., Gary S. Instr. elec. tech., 1958-62; aircraft research engr. Lockheed Ga. Co., Marietta, 1962-64; asst. prof. elec. tech. So. Tech. Inst., Marietta, 1964-69, asso. prof. elec. engring. tech., 1969-—. Cons. NSF/AID India Program, summers, 1968, 69, also various cos. Served with AUS, 1955-56. Registered profl. engr., Ga. Mem. Analog Computer Ednl. Soc., Am. Soc. Engring. Edn. Home: 2167 Sun Valley Dr Marietta GA 30060

COWAN, ELIZABETH HANES (MRS. JAMES A. COWAN), artist, craftsman; b. Atlanta; d. Samuel Bartow and Mary (Moore) Hanes; student Randolph-Macon Women's Coll., 1933-34; grad. Edgewood Park Jr. Coll., 1935; m. James A. Cowan, May 30, 1935 (dec. Oct. 1967). Designer, craftsman felt accessories, N.Y.C., 1935-42; ceramic objects, jewelry, N.Y.C., Washington, 1942-—; writer How To articles for mags., newspapers, 1948-—; burlap designer clothes Burlap Council, Asso. Jute Mills India, Tintex, 1950-55; burlap promotion, clothes Pakistan Consulate, Embassy, Chandler Mfg. Co., N.Y.C., 1955-56; indsl. display designs, N.Y.C., 1959-—; producer fashion shows McCall Needlework Clinic, N.Y.C., 1959-65, dir. clinic, 1970; fashion cons. Sadge's Splty. Shop, Brunswick, Ga., 1971-—; one-man show Left Bank Gallery, 1968; exhibited Met. Mus., 1942, 57th St. Galleries, 1939-42, Keramic Soc., 1935-—, Pen and Brush, 1948-—, Palette Art, N.Y.C., 1950; craft chmn. Washington Sq. Outdoor Art Exhibit, 1959-66, dir, 1964-66. Vol. worker Greenwich Village Fresh Air Fund, 1960-68, chmn., 1964-67. Mem. Nat. Home Fashions League, Pen and Brush (pres., past treas., v.p.), Keramic Soc. (pres.), Am. Artists Profl. League (treas. 1965-66), Catherine Lorilard Wolfe Art Club, Glynn Art Assn. Home and studio: Sea Island GA 31561

COWAN, JOEL HARVEY, real estate exec.; b. Marietta, Ga., June 23, 1936; s. Charles A. and Bernice (Kemp) C.; B.S., Ga. Inst. Tech., 1958; m. R. Geraldine Matthews, Dec. 21, 1957; children—Joel H., Mark Kemp, Jennifer Matthews. Pres. Phipps Land Co., Atlanta, 1968-—; chmn. Phipps-Harrington Corp., Atlanta, Fayette State Bank, Peachtree City, Ga., Bessemer Devel. Corp., Atlanta; dir. Interstate Gen. Corp., San Juan, P.R., Nat. Bank Ga., Atlanta. Kiwanian Home: Pebble Point Peachtree City GA 30214 Office: One Northside 75 Atlanta GA 30303

COWAN, RICHARD SUMMER, sci. adminstr.; b. Crawfordsville, Ind., Jan. 23, 1921; s. Walter Harrison and Eura B. (Walker) C.; A.B., Wabash Coll. 1942; M.S., U. Hawaii, 1948; Ph.D., Columbia, 1952; m. Mary Frances Minnich, June 28, 1941; children—Richard A., Diedra Anne, Charles Ian. Teaching asst. U. Hawaii, 1946-48; tech. asst. N.Y. Bot. Garden, N.Y.C., 1948-52, asst. curator, 1952-57; asso. curator Smithsonian Instn., Washington, 1957-62, asst. dir. Mus. Natural History, 1962-65, dir., 1965-—; sec. nat. com. XI Internat. Bot. Congress; mem. nat. com. Internat. Biol. Program. Served with USNR, 1943-45. NSF fellow, 1952-53. Mem. Am. Inst. Biol. Scis., A.A.A.S., Am. Soc. Plant Taxonomists, Internat. Assn. Plant Taxonomy. Methodist. Contbr. articles profl. jours. Home: 4409 Tonquil Pl Beltsville MD 20705 Office: Smithsonian Instn Washington DC 20560

COWAN, WALTER G., newspaper editor. Editor, New Orleans States-Item. Address: 3800 Howard Av New Orleans LA 70140*

COWAND, JOHN WESLEY, JR., paper co. exec.; b. Windsor, N.C., July 4, 1935; s. John Wesley and Iva Burnice (Parker) C.; B.S., N.C. State U., 1957; m. Joyce Claire Hubbard, Oct. 25, 1959; children—John Wesley III, Mary Claire. Chem. engr. Humble Oil Co., Baytown, Tex., 1957-58; chem. engr. Riegel Paper Corp., Riegelwood, N.C., 1958-63, customer service supr., 1963-65, tech. dir., 1965-—. Bd. dirs. Cape Fear Area council Boy Scouts Am., finance chmn. 1971-72. Served with AUS, 1959. Mem. T.A.P.P.I. (sect. chmn. 1972-73), Am. Inst. Chem. Engrs., Wilmington Engrs. Club, Nat. Rifle Assn., Nat. Skeet Shooting Assn. Democrat. Baptist (finance chmn. 1971-72, deacon 1972-—). Rotarian (bd. dirs. 1971-—). Club: Buccaneer Gun (Wilmington, N.C.). Home: 426 Wayne Dr Wilmington NC 28401 Office: Riegelwood NC 28456

COWARD, WORTH MONROE, dentist; b. Greensboro, N.C., Aug. 29, 1918; s. Walter Monroe and Mary Louvella (York) C.; student Columbia, 1945, Newberry Coll., 1946-47; D.D.S., Emory U., 1952; m. Rachel Lou Dollar, May 25, 1946; children—Gregory Monroe, Susan Worth. Pvt. practice dentistry, Greensboro, 1952-—. Served to capt. USAF, 1943-45. Decorated Air Medal. Elk. Club: Green Valley Country (Greensboro). Home: 2002 Cheltenham Ct Greensboro NC 27407 Office: 2320 Battleground Av Greensboro NC 27408

COWART, DAVID GEORGE, ednl. adminstr.; b. Ludowici, Ga., Jan. 18, 1940; s. William Madison and Alta Mae (Bacon) C.; B.S., Ga. So. Coll., 1961, M.Ed., 1966; postgrad. U. Ga., summer 1962, Valdosta State Coll., 1971; m. Carole Biddy, Dec. 17, 1960; children—Leisha, Michael. Tchr. math, sci. Swainsboro (Ga.) High Sch., 1961-62; prin. Brookfield (Ga.) Jr. High Sch., 1962-63, Monroe County Elementary Sch., Forsyth, Ga., 1963-68, Carver Elementary Sch., Milledgeville, Ga., 1968-71; dir. Elementary Secondary Edn. Act project PRIDE, Waycross, Ga., 1971-—. Named Outstanding Young Educator, Monroe County Jaycees, 1968, by Milledgeville Jaycees, 1969; recipient Humanitarian Service in Edn. award Baha'i Faith, 1970. Mem. N.E.A., Ga., Waycross assns. educators, Ga. Dept. Elementary Sch. Prins., Council Exceptional Children, Phi Delta Kappa. Home: 1706 Camellia Dr Waycross GA 31501 Office: 1492 Bailey St Waycross GA 31501

COWART, GRIGGSBY THOMAS, physician; b. Atlanta, Aug. 19, 1919; s. Griggsby Thomas and Gilley Pearl (Johnson) C.; A.B., Emory U., 1941, M.D., 1944; m. Anne Henderson, Mar. 4, 1944; children—Dorothy Anne, Griggsby Thomas. Intern, Emory U. Hosp., Atlanta, 1944-45, asst. resident surgery, 1945-46; resident urology Lawson VA Hosp., Chamblee, Ga., 1948-51; chief of urology Atlanta VA Hosp., 1951-54, cons., 1954-—; individual practice medicine, specializing in urology, Atlanta, 1954-—; clin. asst. prof. surgery Emory U. Sch. Medicine, 1964-—. Dir. So. Fed. Savs. and Loan Assn., Atlanta. Served to capt. M.C., AUS, 1946-48. Diplomate Am. Bd. Urology. Fellow A.C.S.; mem. A.M.A., So. Med. Assn., Am., Southeastern, Ga. Urol. assns., Phi Beta Kappa, Sigma Nu. Contbr. articles to profl. jours. Home: 18 Blackland Rd NW Atlanta GA 30342 Office: 384 Peachtree St Atlanta GA 30308

COWDEN, BURNEY BEAUCHAMP, county ofcl.; b. Oklahoma City, Oct. 21, 1914; s. Albert Buckner and Maude (Beauchamp) C.; B.S. in Civil Engring., U. Fla., 1940; M.S. in San. Engring., Harvard, 1951; m. Nancy Iva Barber, July 27, 1940; children—John Burney, Cynthia Lynne. Jr. san. engr. Fla. Bd. Health, Jacksonville, 1940-42, asst. san. engr., 1946; san. engr. Polk County Health Dept., Winter Haven, Fla., 1946-—, dir. sanitation, 1948-—. Served from ensign to lt. USNR, 1942-46; lt. comdr. Res. ret. Registered profl. engr., Fla. Diplomate Am. Acad. San. Engrs. Fellow Fla. Engring. Soc. (past chpt. pres.; state dir.); mem. Nat. Soc. Profl. Engrs., Am. Water Works Assn., Fedn. Pollution Control Assns., Fla. Pub. Health Assn. Democrat. Baptist (deacon, trustee). Home: 929 Terrace Dr Eagle Lake FL 33839 Office: Av D and 3d St NW Winter Haven FL 33880

COWELL, RICHARD COX, constrn. co. exec.; b. Pitts., June 13; s. Thomas Richard and Margaret Elizabeth (Cox) C.; grad. St. Paul's Sch., 1945; B.S., Harvard, 1952; m. Melissa Tomlinson; 1 son, Richard Cox. Pres., dir. Cowell Corp., Lake Worth, Fla., 1968-—; chmn. exec. com. Compo Industries; pres., dir. West Indies Caribbean Devel. Ltd., Minerals & Industries, Inc.; dir. Internat. Investors, Inc. Served with USMC, 1945-46. Mem. Small Bus. Adminstrs. (past mem. nat. bd. field advisers). Clubs: Bath and Tennis, Everglades (Palm Beach, Fla.); River, Racquet (N.Y.C.); Corviglia (St. Moritz, Switzerland). Home: 1600 S Ocean Blvd Palm Beach FL 33480 Office: 2545 Lake Worth Rd Lake Worth FL 33460

COWEN, RICHARD K., govt. ofcl. Spl. asst. to Pres. U.S. Office: The White House Washington DC 20500*

COWEN, ROBERT H., lawyer; b. Williamston, N.C., Jan. 16, 1915; s. Henry Herbert and Jenette (Mobley) C.; LL.B., Wake Forest Coll., 1942; m. Sue Henderson, August 6, 1953; children—Robert H., Susan Carol, Sarah Cantrell. Admitted to N.C. bar, 1942, and since practiced in Williamston; atty. U.S. Dept. Labor, Richmond, 1945-46; counsel to com. on mcht. marine and fisheries U.S. House of Representatives; U.S. atty. Eastern District N.C., 1961-69; counsel to joint com. on printing U.S. Senate, 1969-— Mayor, Williamston, N.C., 1947-57; mem. N.C. Senate, 1957-58. Dir. N.C. League Municipalities. Served with USNR, World War II. Mem. Am., N.C. bar assns., Jr. C. of C., Am. Legion. Baptist. Clubs: Rotary, Roanoke Country. Home: 103 Woodlawn Dr Williamston NC

COWEN, WILSON, judge; b. nr. Clifton, Tex., Dec. 20, 1905; s. John Rentz and Florence Juno (McFadden) C.; LL.B., U. Tex., 1928; m. Florence Elizabeth Walker, Apr. 18, 1930; children—W. Walker, John E. Admitted to Tex. bar, 1928; pvt. practice Dalhart, 1928-34; county judge Dallam County, 1935-38; dir. for Tex., Farm Security Adminstrn., 1938-40, regional dir. 1940-42; commr. U.S. Ct. Claims, 1942-43, 45-59, chief commr., 1959-64; chief judge, 1964-—; asst. adminstr. War Food Adminstrn., 1943-45; spl. asst. to sec. agr., 1945. Past chmn., past trustee Landon Sch. for Boys, Bethesda. Mem. State Bar Tex., Am., Fed. bar assns., Order of Coif, Delta Theta Phi. Presbyn. Mason, Clubs: Cosmos, Nat. Lawyers (Washington). Home: 2500 Virginia Av Washington DC 20037 Office: US Court Claims Washington DC 20005

COWGILL, LOGAN O., govt. ofcl.; b. Wabash, Ind., Feb. 24, 1919; s. Logan O. and Norene (delCamp) C.; A.B., Ind. U., 1939; postgrad. George Washington U., 1942, Am. U., 1947-48; m. Martha Anne O'Brien, Sept. 3, 1949. Ordnance engr. U.S. Army, Washington, 1943-46, librarian C.E., 1949-55, chief Library br. Office Chief Engrs., Dept. Army, 1955-59, chief Sci. and Tech. Information div., 1964-67, project mgr. tech. library improvement studies, 1965-67; bibliographer Hispanic Found. Library Congress, 1946-48; asst. mgr. Water Resources Sci. Information Center, Dept. Interior, Washington, 1967-—. Chmn. adv. com. acquisitions Brookings Instn. Survey Fed. Libraries, 1961-62. Friend, Harvard Coll. Library, Princeton U. Library. U.S. Civil Service Commn. Adminstrv. intern, 1947. Mem. Am. Documentation Inst., Bibliog. Soc. Am., Spl. Libraries Assn. (pres. Washington chpt., past chmn. mil. librarians div.), Permanent Internat. Assn. Nav. Congresses, Bibliog. Soc. U. Va. Club: Grolier (N.Y.C.). Home: 26 6th St SE Washington DC 20003 Office: Dept Interior Washington DC 20240

COWLES, MILLY, educator; b. Ramer, Ala., May 29, 1932; d. Russell Fail and Sara (Mills) Cowles; B.S., Troy State U., 1952; M.A., U. Ala., 1958; Ph.D. (grad. fellow), 1962. Tchr. pub. schs., Montgomery, 1952-59; asst. then asso. prof. Grad. Sch. Edn., Rutgers U., 1962-66; asso. prof. U. Ga., 1966-67; prof. early childhood devel. and edn. Sch. Edn., U. S.C., Columbia, 1967-—. Cons. So. Edn. Found., Atlanta, Ga. Inst. Higher Edn. U. Ga., also numerous sch. systems throughout Northeast and South; chief cons., dir. career opportunities program Williamsburg County (S.C.) Pub. Schs., 1968-—. Pres. bd. dirs. 2d Reformed Ch. Nursery Sch., New Brunswick, N.J., 1963-66. Mem. Am. Ednl. Research Assn., Soc. for Research Child Devel., A.A.A.S., Am. Assn. U. Profs., Nat. Council Tchrs. English, Internat. Reading Assn., Nat. Assn. for Edn. Young Children, N.E.A. (mem. parent involvement com. elementary, kindergarten and nursery educators dept. 1972-—), Assn. for Supervision and Curriculum Devel. (mem. council on early childhood edn. 1969-71), Am. Psychol. Assn., N.Y. Acad. Sci., Kappa Delta Pi (chpt. treas. 1964-66), Delta Kappa Gamma. Editor, contbg. author: Perspectives in the Education of Disadvantaged Children, 1967; also articles. Home: 301 N Stonehedge Columbia SC 29210

COWLEY, LEONARD MERWYN, real estate appraiser, cons.; b. Bladen, Neb., Mar. 16, 1899; s. Charles Wesley and Flora (Cramer) C.; A.B., U. Neb., 1922; postgrad. So. Meth. U., 1947-49, U. So., Cal., 1939; m. Irene Leona Holston, Aug. 13, 1922; 1 dau., Barbara Lou (Mrs. C. Russell Smith, Jr.). Vice pres. Cowley, Higgins & Delph Investment Co., Phoenix, 1927-38; owner Cowley & Co., 1937-40; mgr. Appraisal Assos., Dallas, 1952-55; mng. partner Leonard M. Cowley & Assos., Dallas, 1955—; pres. Appraisal Library, Inc., 1959—; real estate cons. Oak Lawn United Methodist Ch. Adj. gen Ariz., 1929. Sec. Ariz. Republican Central Com., county chmn. Rep. County Com., 1932. Served to col. C.E., AUS, 1940-47. Decorated Legion of Merit. Mem. Am. Inst. Real Estate Appraisers (charter pres. N. Tex. chpt.), Am. Soc. Appraisers (past chpt. pres., regional gov.), Farm and Ranch Mgrs. and Appraisers, Retreads (past comdr. Tex. dept., past nat. vice comdr.), Sigma Delta Chi, Phi Sigma Kappa. Mason (Shriner). Clubs: Dallas Press. Contbr. articles profl. jours. Home: 6305 Lange Circle Dallas TX 75214 Office: 6162 E Mockingbird Lane Dallas TX 75214

COWLEY, LUIS M., hosp. supt., psychiatrist; b. Havana, Cuba, June 22, 1921; s. Luis M. and Guillermina (Morales) C.; M.D., Havana U., 1944; m. Yolanda M. Perez, Aug. 29, 1948; children—Ana, Margarita, Luis, Maria, Yolanda, Felipe. Came to U.S., 1960, naturalized, 1967. Student house officer Havana (Cuba) U. Hosp., 1940-44, intern, 1944-45; resident psychiatry San Juan de Dios Psychiat. Sanatorium, Havana, 1945-47, psychiatrist, vice dir., 1947-49, psychiatrist, 1949-60; psychiatrist, clin. dir. Perez Vento Psychiat. Sanitorium, Havana, 1957-60; asso. psychiatry Havana U. Hosp., 1946-50; instr. adjoined prof. clin. therapeutics Havana U. Sch. Medicine, 1946-50; clin. dir. Elizabeths Hosp., Washington, 1947; staff physician charge intensive treatment Terrell (Tex.) State Hosp., 1961, staff physician, supr. psychiat. residency tng. and white female acute treatment program, 1961-62, clin. dir., 1963-64, supt., 1967—; psychiat. resident Parkland Meml. Hosp., Dallas, 1962-63; clin. prof. psychiatry U. Tex. Southwestern Med. Sch., 1965—. Recipient ann. award Tex. Assn. Mental Health, 1967; hon. mem. Psychology Club, East Tex. State U., 1969. Fellow Am. Psychiat. Assn.; mem. Pan Am., Am., Tex. med. assns., Kaufman County Med. Soc., Tex., Dallas neuropsychiat. assns., Guild Catholic Psychiatrists, N.Y. Acad. Scis. Address: PO Box 70 Terrell TX 75160

COWLING, HERFORD TYNES, photographic engr., movie producer, explorer, ret. air force officer; b. Nansemond County, Va., Aug. 20, 1890; s. John Phillips and Caroline Weaver (Tynes) C.; student George Washington U., 1912-13; m. Virginia Hardin, Jan. 14, 1927. Chief photographer U.S. Reclamation Service, 1909-16; traveled extensively in U.S., Canada and Mexico, 1913-16; headed cinematographic expdn., 1917, to Formosa. Philippines, Indo-China, Siam, Malay States, Indonetia, Australia, Tasmania, China, Japan, New Zealand and South Sea Islands, producing Paramount—Burton Holmes Travel Films; produced motion pictures of Europe, 1919, including France, Belgium, Germany, Austria, Switzerland, Czechoslovakia, Italy, also Algeria, Tunisia, Tangier, Morocco, Sicily, Spain, Egypt, Palestine, Turkey, Cuba and Mexico, 1921-23; expdns. to Brit. East Africa, Uganda, Belgian Congo and The Sudan, filming big game hunting, 1922; India, Kashmir, Tibet, Burma, Sumatra, Malaysia, 1924; China war corr. Fox News Movietone Films, produced motion picture of coronation of Maharaja of Kashmir, 1926; tech. dir. teaching films dept. Eastman Kodak Co., 1927-32; ofcl. photographer Century of Progress, Chgo., 1933; supr. motion picture prodn. Emergency Conservation Works in Nat. Parks, 1934; tech. dir. div. motion pictures and sound rec. U.S. Nat. Archives, Washington, 1935-37; tech. asst. to adminstr. Nat. Unemployment Census, Washington, 1937; sr. administrv. asst. Dept. Commerce, 1938-40, then chief photog. services U.S. Dept. Labor. Served with USAAF, 1941-46, USAF, 1946-50; col. USAF ret. Fellow Royal Photog. Soc. (Gt. Britain); mem. Fed. Photog. Soc. (pres. 1915-16, hon. mem.), Biol. Photographic Assn., Am. Soc. Cinematographers, Soc. Motion Pictures Engrs., S.A.R. Mason (Shriner). Clubs: Explorers (fellow) (N.Y.C.); Army-Navy Country, Army and Navy (Washington). Home: 808 S Ode St Arlington VA 22204

COWPER, ALBERT WALLACE, superior ct. judge; b. Kinston, N.C., July 14, 1911; s. George Vernon and Rosabel (Rountree) C.; LL.B., U. N.C., 1935; m. Virginia Bland Lee, Apr. 10, 1943; children—Richard Green, Lee Fitzgerald. Admitted to N.C. bar, 1934; individual practice law, Kinston, 1935-41, 60—; spl. agt. FBI, 1941-45; Judge Recorder's Ct., Kinston, 1946-56, Superior Ct., 1960—. Pres., N.C. Conf. Superior Ct. Judges, 1970. Served with AUS, 1945-46. Home: 604 Edwards Av Kinston NC 28501 Office: Lenoir County Superior Courthouse Kinston NC 28501

COX, ALBERT EDWARD, ins. exec.; b. Chatham, Va., Aug. 21, 1910; s. Albert Henry and Anna (Jackson) C.; student William and Mary Coll., 1927-29, U. Va., 1929-30; m. Glenn Jones; children—Albert Jones, Anna Glenn, Sally Ruth. Pres. Cox & Goodridge, Inc., Danville, Va., 1940—; ins. agt., Danville, 1934-40; owner South Side Gen. Agy., Danville, 1951—; mem. Danville bd. Va. Nat. Bank. Chmn. ins. adv. com. City of Danville. Chmn. bd. trustees Anderson Student Aid Fund. Co-chmn. War Fund of Pittsylvania County, Va., 1944-45, citation for service. Mem. Va. Gov.'s Redistricting Commn., 1961. Del. Dem. Nat. Conv., 1960. Mem. Va. Assn. Ins. Agts. (pres. 1954-55). Va., Danville chambers commerce, Nat. Assn. Ins. Agts. (state bd. dirs.), Kappa Alpha. Baptist. Mason, Rotarian (pres. 1956-57). Clubs: Danville Golf (pres. 1963); Commonwealth (Richmond, Va.). Fire Insurance Field (award Agent of Year 1951). Home: 491 Hawthorne Dr Danville VA 24541 Office: 128 S Market St Danville VA 24541

COX, CALVIN KENNEDY, newspaperman; b. Greenwood, Miss., Dec. 19, 1918; s. Robert Kennedy and Katherine (Durham) C.; B.B.A., U. Georgia, Atlanta, 1955; m. Dorothy Davis, May 3, 1940; children—Carolyn K., Eugenia, Carey. Various positions Greenwood Commonwealth, 1932-43; from copy editor to news editor Atlanta Constn., 1945-71; Sunday editor Atlanta Jour.-Constn., 1971—. Served with C.E., AUS, 1943-45. Club: Atlanta Press (pres. 1966, 67). Home: 1076 Forrest Blvd Decatur GA 30030 Office: Atlanta Jour-Constn Atlanta GA 30302

COX, CARL THOMAS, ednl. adminstr.; b. Bridgeton, N.C., Jan. 12, 1925; s. Henry Albert and Emily Alice (Miller) C.; B.S., East Carolina Coll., 1949; postgrad. Atlantic Christian Coll., 1960-63; M.A., East Carolina U., 1967; m. Scottie Winstead, Nov. 23, 1950; children—Scott Lee, Carla Sue. Office mgr. utility dept. T.A. Loving & Co., constrn., Goldsboro, N.C., 1949-58; office mgr. Carolina Plywood Dist. and Patelos Door Corp., Wilson, N.C., 1959-63; instr. Wayne Community Coll., Goldsboro, 1963-65; bus. mgr., 1965—. Mem. N.C. accreditation com. Dept. Community Colls., 1967-72. Served with USNR, 1943-46. Mem. Nat., N.C. edn. assns., Community Coll. Bus. Ofcls. Mem. Christian Ch. (chmn. bd. 1965-67). Mason (Shriner), Elk. Club: Goldsboro Country. Home: 709 Pittman St Goldsboro NC 27530 Office: PO Box 1878 Goldsboro NC 27530

COX, ERNEST HAYNES, educator, univ. adminstr.; b. Ashland City, Tenn., Aug. 17, 1907; s. Eugene Alexander and Clara M. (Haynes) C.; B.A., Carson-Newman Coll., 1927; M.A., U. Tenn., 1930; Ph.D., U. N.C., 1936; m. Annie Belle Smith, Aug. 28, 1936; children—Mary Margaret (Mrs. Charles Overbey), Clara Jean (Mrs. Maurice Todd). Prin. pub. sch., Waynesville, N.C., 1927-29; supt. schs., Elizabethton, Tenn., 1930-32; asso. prof. English, Mary Hardin-Baylor Coll., 1936-38; dean Blue Mountain Coll., 1938-47; prof. English and logic, counselor U. Fla., 1947-62, asst. dean Univ. Coll., 1962-65, prof. English, asst. dean Coll. Arts and Scis., 1965—. Democrat. Baptist. Rotarian. Home: 2159 NW 9th Av Gainesville FL 32601 2159 NW 9th Av Gainesville FL 32601

COX, GAYLORD HAINES, design engr.; b. Jacksonville, Ore., Mar. 26, 1906; s. Alva Carl and Emma Mildred (Haines) C.; B.A., U. Ore., 1931; m. 2d, Edith Rogers, 1968; children (by previous marriage)—Dennis, Phillip, Rosemary Louise. Pvt. engring. practice, Portland, Ore., 1931-35; gen. engr. Crosby Chem. Co., DeRidder, La., 1945-49; design engr. Cit-Con Oil Corp., Lake Charles, La., 1949-65; mem. W.H. Woodward & G.H. Cox, Architects and Cons. Engrs., 1951—, prin., 1965—; dir. Mid-South Financial Corporation. Adviser Boy Scouts. Capt., U.S. Army, 1935-45. Mem. Nat. Assn. Corrosion Engrs., I.E.E.E., La. Engring. Soc., Am. Legion (chmn., mem. commn. Americanism, mem. nat. com. constitution and bylaws), Nat. Rifle Assn., Nat. Soc. Profl. Engrs., Air Craft Owners and Pilots Assn. Methodist. Home: 1362 W Jefferson St Lake Charles LA 70601 Office: 714 Hodges St Lake Charles LA 70601

COX, HAROLD WAYNE, architect, poet; b. nr. Munfordville, Ky., Nov. 20, 1935; s. William T. and Mable (Cook) C.; student U. Louisville, 1955, U. La. Sch. Urban Planning, 1970, Bellarmine Coll., 1970-71; m. Barbara Ann Decker, July 2, 1955 (div. 1971); children—Harold Wayne, Steven Lee; m. 2d, Barbara T. Hunter, Nov. 26, 1971. Mem. design team Villa West low-cost housing devel. McCulloch & Bickel Architects, Louisville, 1964-65; capt. classroom bldg. project Oberwarth Assos., Frankfort, Ky., 1966; project architect, head specification writer firm Hartstern, Schnell Architects, Louisville, Ky., 1971—; prin. Cox & Assos., architects, 1972—; cons. non-profit orgns. for mulitfamily housing devels.; pres. C & H Prodns., pub., Louisville. Served with AUS, 1957-60. Decorated Medal Commendation. Mem. Constrn. Specifications Inst. (nat. pub. relations com., pres. chpt. 1971); corporate mem. A.I.A. Contbr. articles profl. jours. Home: 1815 Gardiner Lane Louisville KY 40205 Office: 3707 Bardstown Rd Louisville KY 40218 also C & H Prodns PO Box 2151 Louisville KY 40201

COX, HERMAN GHRAME, JR., architect; b. Ft. Worth, Tex., Aug. 16, 1907; s. Herman Ghrame and Agnes (Kerfoot) C.; B.S., Tex. A. and M. U., 1929; m. Harriett Elizabeth Copeland, June 18, 1932; children—Mary Lynn (Mrs. Phillip Crow), Carol Lee (Mrs. Glenn Cope), Herman Ghrame III. Architect, engr. Am. Airways, Dallas, 1929-33, airport engr. State of Tex., 1934; architect, engr., Ft. Worth, 1935-40, 1946—. Mem. Zoning Bd. Adjustment, 1946-61, chmn., 1951-60; mem. Ft. Worth Planning Commn., 1962-67; mem. Animal Control Authority, 1953-61; chmn. Central Bus. Dist. Redevel. Com. Town Hall, 1964. Served to lt. col. AUS, 1940-45. Fellow A.I.A.; (chpt. pres. 1954); mem. Tex. Soc. Architects (dir. 1951-53), Nat. Soc. Profl. Engrs., Nat. Council Archtl. Registration Bds., Tau Beta Pi. Clubs: Kiwanis (v.p. 1956), Ft. Worth River Crest Country, Ft. Worth Boat. Author: Your Dachshund, 1966. Home: 430 Ridgewood Rd Ft Worth TX 76107 Office: 415 Neil P Anderson Bldg Ft Worth TX 76102

COX, JACK, investment co. exec.; b. Breckenridge, Tex., Aug. 20, 1921; s. Richard M. and Louella (Cargill) C.; B.S. in Govt., N. Tex. U., 1947; m. Joyce Smyrl, Oct. 15, 1942; children—Jack, Callan Sue. Owner, Jack Cox Motors, Breckenridge, 1949-53; asst. to pres. So. Minerals Corp., Corpus Christi, Tex., 1953-56; exec. v.p. Freedom in Action, Houston, 1956-58; partner Pico Drilling Co., Breckenridge, 1958-63; exec. v.p. South Padre Investment Corp., Austin, Tex., 1964-65; v.p., gen. mgr. Sandlin Mortgage Corp., Austin, 1966—, Sandlin and Co., 1966—; lectr., writer on U.S.-Latin Am. relations. Mem. Tex. Commn. on Higher Edn., 1955-61. Mem. Tex. Ho. Reps., 1947-53; Rep. leader, Breckenridge, Tex. Served USNR, 1940-45. Recipient Valley Forge Freedom Found. awards, 1958, 59, 61. Mem. Am. Legion, V.F.W., Tex. Farm Bur. Mem. Christian Ch. Club: Forty Acres (pres. 1966). Author: And The Pursuit of Happiness, 1962. Home: 3815 Hillbrook Austin TX 78759 Office: 308 W 15th St Austin TX 78701

COX, JACK FRANK WELLS, oil producer, real estate resort exec.; b. Kingwood, W.Va., May 20, 1914; s. Frank Wells and Helen (Berry) C.; B.S. in Petroleum Engring., Stanford, 1932-36; m. Marilyn Edna Hawbaker, Oct. 18, 1952; children—Lynne, John, Berry. Pres., Cox Drilling Co., Owensboro, Ky., 1938—, Bahama Reef Devel. Co., Freeport, Grand Bahama, 1962-67, Royal Oak Resort, Titusville, Fla., 1962—. Served to lt. comdr. USNR, 1941-46. Mem. Delta Kappa Epsilon. Episcopalian. Elk. Home: 1114 SE 12th Terrace Deerfield Beach FL 33441 Office: Country Club Dr Titusville FL 32780

COX, JACKSON BARCUS, utilities exec.; b. Mexico, D.F., Mexico, Sept. 10, 1910 (parents Am. citizens); s. Jackson Berry and Julia (Barcus) C.; A.B., U. Tex., 1933; m. Beatrice Deborah Von Zuben, Nov. 24, 1941; children—Julia (Mrs. Stuart Howard Lee), Deborah (Mrs. John Andrew Styrsky). Editor U. Tex. Student Publs., 1932-33; reporter, sports editor Austin (Tex.) Daily Dispatch, 1934-35; asst. to welfare officer Civilian Conservation Corps, Ft. Worth, 1935-37; clk. accounting Community Pub. Service Co., Ft. Worth, 1937-42, asst. sales mgr., 1946-66, mgr. advt., 1956-66, dir. advt. and pub. relations, 1966—, editor Communicator, 1966—. Served from pvt. to capt. AUS, 1942-46. Mem. Pub. Utilities Advt. Assn., W. Tex. Press Assn. Methodist. Clubs: Fort Worth Press, Advertising (Ft. Worth). Home: 3608 Wedgway Dr Ft Worth TX 76133 Office: Community Pub Service Co 501 W 6th St Ft Worth TX 76102

COX, JAMES EDWIN, retail stores exec.; b. Ollie, Ia., Nov. 18, 1918; m. Lora Dell Kennedy, Dec. 6, 1945; children—Susanne, Cynthia, Stephen. Treas., TG & Y Stores Co., Oklahoma City. C.P.A. Address: PO Box 25967 Oklahoma City OK 73125

COX, JAMES M(IDDLETON), JR., publisher; b. Dayton, O., June 27, 1903; s. James Middleton and Mary Simpson (Harding) C.; student Culver Mil. Acad., 1917-20, Cheshire (Conn.) Acad., 1922-24; Ph.B., Yale, 1928; m. Helen Rumsey, Nov. 21, 1930. Joined Dayton Daily News, 1929, gen. mgr., 1931-38, asst. pub., 1938-39, asst. pub. and v.p., 1939-49, dir., pres., 1949-56; pres. dir. Dayton Journal-Herald, 1948-56; vice chmn., pres. Dayton Newspapers, Inc., 1957-58, chmn., pres., 1958—; established Radio Sta. WHIO, Dayton, 1934; pres., dir. Miami Valley Broadcasting Corp., Dayton, 1949-58, chmn. bd., pres., 1958—; chmn. bd. Atlanta Newspapers, Inc., 1957—; v.p. Springfield (O.) Daily News and Sun, 1938-54; pres., dir. Springfield Newspapers Inc., 1954-58, chmn. bd., pres., 1958—; chmn. bd. Carolina Broadcasting Co., 1959—; pres. Miami (Fla.) Daily News, 1957—; v.p., dir. Radio Sta. WIOD, Miami, 1947-56; v.p. Biscayne TV Corp., Miami, 1956—; pub. Miami News, Miami. Active Community Chest, A.R.C., Salvation Army. Mem. asso. bd. lay trustees U. Dayton. Served as lt. comdr. Naval A.S., USNR, 1942-45. Episcopalian. Home: 4358 N Bay Rd Miami Beach FL 33139 Office: care The Miami News Miami FL 33132

COX, JANSON LAVERN, museologist; b. Laurens, S.C., Jan. 18, 1941; s. Harold Elias and Elizabeth (Winnies) C.; B.S., in Math., The Citadel, 1963; M.A., N.Y. State U. Coll. at Oneonta, 1966; m. Cleta Vale Higgins, July 8, 1967. Acting dir. Citadel Mus., Charleston, S.C., 1963-65; dir. Oneida Hist. Soc., Utica, N.Y., 1966-68; chief historian div. parks and recreation S.C. Dept. Parks, Recreation and Tourism, Columbia, 1968—. Cons. N.Y. State Council on the Arts, 1966-68; asso. faculty Utica Coll., Syracuse U., 1966-68; guest lectr. Mohawk Valley Community Coll., 1968. Mem. Am. Assn. Museums, Internat. Inst. Conservation (London), Am. Assn. for State and Local History. Home: 5917 Corley St Columbia SC 29210 Office: PO Box 1358 Columbia SC 29202

COX, JAY CARROLL, lawyer, state senator; b. Washington, May 16, 1936; s. Marvin Hill and Mary (Rountree) C.; A.B., U. Ga., 1959, LL.B., 1961. Admitted to Ga. bar, 1961; atty. U.S. Dept. Justice, Washington, 1962-64; practiced in Swainsboro, Ga., 1965—; mem. Ga. Senate, 1967—. Mem. Ga. Bar Assn. Club: Exchange (Swainsboro). Home: PO Box 633 Twin City GA 30401 Office: PO Box 37 Swainsboro GA 30471

COX, LOEL DENE, agrl. exec.; b. Sidney, Tex., Apr. 12, 1926; s. Ottie Scott and Gladys (McCarty) C.; A.S., John Tarleton Agrl. Coll., 1946; B.S., Tex. A. and M. U., 1948; m. Sara Lou McCarrol, Feb. 26, 1949; 1 son, Lowell Dean. Instr. agr. San Angelo Coll., 1948-50; instr. Comanche County Vocational Sch., 1951-52; salesman Moorman Mfg. Co., Comanche, Tex., 1952, dist. mgr., San Antonio, Tex., 1952-53, state sales mgr., Comanche, 1953—, profl. feed counsellor, 1971—; dir. Comanche Nat. Bank, 1965—. Served with USNR, 1944-46. Decorated Purple Heart; recipient Lone Star Farmer degree Tex. Future Farmers Am. Home: 203 Williams Dr Comanche TX 76442 Office: 203 Williams Dr Comanche TX 76442

COX, MORT SEBRING, banker; b. North Little Rock, Ark., Oct. 14, 1914; s. Reginald P. and Clara (Taylor) C.; student Henderson State Coll., 1948-51, Am. U., 1951-53; m. Freda Springstead, June 8, 1940; children—Carolyn Louise (Mrs. Bryan Layne Mashburn), Mary Elizabeth Henry (Mrs. Richard Lee Henry), Claudia Irene. Adminstrv. officer USPHS, 1937-53; exec. v.p. Hot Springs (Ark) C. of C., 1953-64; v.p. Ark. Bank & Trust Co., Hot Springs, 1964—. Chmn. Hot Springs Advt. Commn., 1965-69. Sec., Garland County Indsl. Devel. Corp., 1957-71. Mem. Hot Springs City Council, 1971-72. Served from 1st lt. to capt. AUS, 1941-46. Decorated Bronze Star Medal. Mem. Pub. Relations Soc. Am. (chpt. pres. 1970), Nat. Guard Assn. Ark. (past pres.). Home: 106 Brentwood Dr Hot Springs AR 71901 Office: Broadway Square Hot Springs AR 71901

COX, OTIS BENNS, pub. co. exec.; b. Butler, Ga., July 10, 1925; s. Otis Edward and Ruby Eugenia (Cox) C.; student Ga. Inst. Tech., 1942; m. Elizabeth Deloria Tidd, July 30, 1948; children—Matthew Edward, Mary Ann. Prodn. mgr. The Democrat, Tallahassee, 1966-68; gen. mgr. The Times, Thomasville, N.C., also prodn. mgr. The Enterprise, High Point, N.C., 1968-71; prodn. dir. Knight Pub. Co., Charlotte, N.C., 1971—. Bd. dirs. Lively Tech. Inst., Tallahassee, 1967. Served with USNR, 1943-46. Club: Southern Furniture (High Point, N.C.). Home: 217 Woodrow St High Point NC 27262 Office: 600 S Tryon St Charlotte NC 28201

COX, PAUL JEFFERSON, textile mill exec.; b. Wilcoe, W. Va., Aug. 9, 1934; s. Andrew Jackson and Emma (Presley) C.; B.S., Ohio State U., 1960, M.A. (William Green Meml. fellow), 1961; m. Pearl Louise Cheek, Aug. 9, 1952; children—Pamela Gwyn, Paula Jeanine. Mgr. labor relations Whirlpool Corp., St. Joseph, Mich., 1961-64; mgr. flight contracts Eastern Airlines, Miami, 1964-65; mfg. mgr. Collins & Aikman Corp., Albemarle, N.C., 1965—. Trustee Marion (N.C.) Gen. Hosp., 1970-71. Served with USNR, 1952-56. Mem. Albemarle Jr. C. of C. (pres. 1967-68), Am. Bus. Club (v.p. 1968-69), Am. Econ. Assn., McDowell County C. of C. (bd. dirs.). Methodist. Lion. Home: 900 Honeysuckle Lane Albemarle NC 28001 Office: Box 580 Albemarle NC 28001

COX, RAYMOND EDWARD, supt. schs.; b. Whitefield, Okla., Jan. 31, 1908; s. Allen Barney and Elizabeth (Duke) C.; B.A., Eastern State Coll., 1936; student Southeastern State Coll.; M.S., Okla. State U., 1940; D.Ed., Okla. U., 1958; m. Eva Juanita McIntosh, Sept. 11, 1932; children—Barbara Jean (Mrs. James Beymer), Larry Ray, James Edward. Elem. prin. Bowers, Okla., 1929-33, Gowen, Okla., 1933-36; prin. high sch., Panola, Okla., 1936-38; supt. schs., Panola, 1938-47, Wilburton, Okla., 1947-61, Henryetta, Okla., 1961—. Active Boy Scouts; bd. dirs. TB Assn. Served with USNR, 1945-46. Mem. Henryetta C. of C., Nat., Okla. (bd. dirs.) edn. assns., Okla. Assn. Sch. Adminstrs., Am Assn. Sch. Adminstrn., Okmulgee County Tchrs. Assn. (past pres.), Kappa Delta Pi, Pi Delta Kappa. Mason (Shriner), Lion. Home: 1007 N 5th Henryetta OK 74437 Office: Box 130 Henryetta OK 74437

COX, VERNON LOUIS, cabinet mfr.; b. Apex, N.C., Jan. 23, 1930; s. Zennie Exum and Annie (Dixon) C.; grad. high sch.; m. Montez Ann Hobbs, July 19, 1952; children—Marian Ann, Gail Lucretia, Ted Louis (dec.). Owner, operator Apex Cabinet Co. (N.C.), 1954—. Mem. Apex C. of C. Baptist (deacon 1963-66). Home: PO Box 141 Town Pond Rd Apex NC 27502 Office: PO Box 141 Apex NC 27502

COX, WILLIAM CARL, ednl. adminstr.; b. Walterboro, S.C., Sept. 2, 1929; s. Joseph Carl and Claudine Ellen (Jenkins) C.; A.B., U. Ga., 1950; M.Ed., Ga. So. Coll., 1962, Edn. Specialist, 1964; m. Eugenia Louise Barrs, Aug. 17, 1958; 1 dau., Amanda Ellen. Tchr., Bradwell Inst., Hinesville, Ga., 1954-60, counselor, 1960-68, prin., 1968—. Mayor, Allenhurst, Ga., 1964—. Mem. Liberty County (Ga.) Health Adv. Bd. Served with AUS, 1951-53. Mem. Liberty County Hist. Soc. (pres. 1967-69). Presbyn. (clk. session 1966—). Clubs: Cherokee Country (Hinesville). Home: Providence Hall Allenhurst GA 31310 Office: P O Box 558 Bradwell Inst Hinesville GA 31313

COX, WILLIAM HAROLD, U.S. dist. judge; b. Indianola, Miss., June 23, 1901; s. Adam Charles and Lillie Emma (Ray) C.; B.S., LL.B., U. Miss., 1924; m. Edwina Berry, June 30, 1927; children—William Harold, Joanne (Mrs. Paul Bellenger, Jr.). Admitted to Miss. bar, 1924, and practiced in Jackson until 1961; U.S. dist. judge So. Dist. Misc., 1961—, chief judge, 1962-71. Mem. Miss. Bd. Bar Admissions, 1932-36. Chmn. Hinds County Democratic Exec. Com., 1950-61; presdl. elector, 1952. Home: 133 Woodland Circle Jackson MS 39216 Office: US Post Office Bldg Jackson MS 39205

COX, WILLIS RAYMOND, accountant; b. Marietta, Ga., Oct. 27, 1912; s. Raymond H. and Emma (Smith) C.; B.C.S., Ga. State Coll., 1946; postgrad. Northeastern U., 1946, Centenary Coll., 1950-58; m. Madge Snow, Oct. 12, 1946; children—Madge Irene, Carey Francis. Examiner accounts Fed. Power Commn., Washington, 1939-48; supr. accounting Tex. Eastern Transmission Corp., Shreveport, La., 1948-66, mgr. accounting, 1966-68, mgr. systems, 1968—; sec.-treas. Trans-World Life Ins. Co. Served with USAAF, 1942-45. C.P.A., La. Mem. Am. Inst. C.P.A.'s, La. Soc. C.P.A.'s, Am. Gas Assn., Am. Petroleum Inst. Baptist (deacon). Home: 4704 Carolyn Lane Shreveport LA 71105 Office: PO Box 1612 Shreveport LA 71105

COXE, MRS. THOMAS CHATTERTON (EMILY BADHAM COXE), civic worker; b. Edenton, N.C., May 3, 1910; d. Richard Paxton and Emily Wood (Fagan) Badham; grad. St. Mary's Jr. Coll., 1929; m. Thomas Chatterton Coxe, Jr., Nov. 6, 1929; children—Thomas Chatterton III, Emily Wood (Mrs. William Alfred Winburn III), Patricia Barringer (Mrs. Marshall Taylor Ware), Charlotte Victoria (Mrs. Charles E. Commander, III), Richard Badham. Mem. state bd. dirs. S.C. div. Am. Cancer Soc.; mem. area bd. dirs. Tb Assn.; mem. adv. bd. Palmetto Outdoor Hist. Drama Assn. Mem. bd. visitors St. Mary's Jr. Coll. Mem. Nat. Soc. Colonial Dames Am., Internat. Platform Assn., Darlington County Hist. Soc. Episcopalian. Author: (with Frances Warfield) Mother of the Maid, 1960. Home: Skufful Farm Darlington SC 29532

COY, CHARLES R., lawyer; b. Madison County, Ky., Jan 12, 1926; grad. Eastern Ky. U.; LL.B., U. Ky., 1951; m. Gay Alley; children—Russell Gay, Reba Jane. Admitted to Ky. bar, 1951, U.S. Supreme Ct. bar, 1960; mem. firm Coy and Coy, Richmond, Ky.; commonwealth's atty. 25th Jud. Dist., 1969. Mem. Madison County, Ky. State (bd. govs. 1964-66, pres. 1967-68), Am. (ho. of dels. 1967-69) bar assns., Internat. Assn. Ins. Counsel, Am. Judicature Soc. (dir. 1968—). Office: 212 N 2d St Richmond KY 40475

COZART, REED, lawyer; b. nr. Normangee, Tex., Apr.8, 1904; s. William H. and Anna (Reed) C.; A.B., U. Tex., 1926, J.D., 1929; postgrad. St. Mary's U., 1937-38, William and Mary Coll., 1939; m. Ruth Mae Bourn, July 17, 1931; 1 son, William Reed. Tchr., Tivy High Sch., Kerrville, Tex., 1924-25; admitted to Tex. bar, 1929; asso. firm Morriss & Morriss, San Antonio, 1929-32; chief U.S. probation officer, San Antonio, 1932-40; asst. supt. classification Bur. Prisons, Washington, 1940-41; warden Fed. Correctional Instn., Texarkana, Tex., 1941-42, Seagoville, Tex., 1945-52; La Tuna, Tex., 1956-57; asst. warden U.S. Prison, Leavenworth, Kan., 1942-45; dir. corrections, Baton Rouge, 1952-55; U.S. pardon atty. Dept. Justice, Washington, 1955-68; program dir., project dir. Am. Correctional Assn. project Am. U., 1968—; spl. asst. atty. gen. U.S.; cons. Bd. dirs. Asso. Community Rehab. Enterprises, Valley Forge, Pa. and Washington. Active United Givers Fund drives, YMCA, boys clubs; mem. Nat. Council Crime and Delinquency. Bd. advisers Am. U. Mem. Internat. Platform Assn., Tex. Probation Assn. (pres.), Tex. Social Welfare Assn. (dir.), Council of Chs. (pres. Alexandria; dir. Nat. Capital area), Welfare Council Dallas, Fed. Execs. Assn. (Dallas pres.), Am. Correctional Assn. (dir.), Nat. Conf. Social Work, Am., Tex. bar assns., Tex. State Soc., U. Tex. Ex-students Assn. (local pres., council), Osborne Assn. (dir.), Pi Sigma Alpha. Democrat. Presbyn. (elder, deacon, commr. to gen. assembly). Mason (32 deg.), Rotarian (v.p., dir.). Club: International Relations (U. Tex.). Contbr. articles to profl. and popular publs. Home: 808 Chalfonte Dr Alexandria VA 22305

COZBY, JOE BLANTON, profl. assn. exec.; b. Robert Lee, Tex., Apr. 30, 1918; s. Leonard Drew and Cossie Lee (Turner) C.; student John Tarleton Coll., 1937-38, Tex. U., 1938-40; grad. Southwestern Inst., 1950; m. Nona Denney, May 15, 1959; children—Rosalind (Mrs. Gary Ray Huckabey), Donna (Mrs. James Edwards), Karen (Mrs. Albert Linker), Judi (Mrs. Clayton Pulley), Linda (Mrs. Ricky Ray). Mgr., Odessa C. of C. (Tex.), 1947; bus. mgr. Odessa Chuck Wagon Gang, 1947-56; owner Alamo Directory Co., pub. city directory, Alamagordo, N.M., 1957-65, Uptown Cleaners and Laundry, 1959-64; mgr. Monahans (Tex.) C. of C., 1969—. Sec., Monahans Indsl. Found. Served with AUS, 1940-44. Decorated Purple Heart. Home: 1203 E 9th St Monahans TX 79756 Office: 4th and Dwight Sts Monahans TX 79756

CRABILL, DONALD E., govt. ofcl. Chief natural resources program Office Mgmt. and Budget, Washington. *

CRADDOCK, GEORGE BARKSDALE, physician; b. Lynchburg, Va., Oct. 24, 1908; s. Abram Poindexter and Ella Elizabeth (Goodwin) C.; A.B., Washington and Lee U., 1930; M.D., Jefferson Med. Coll., 1935; m. Mary Spencer Jack, Feb. 1, 1941; children—George Barksdale, Theodore Jack, Alice Ashley. Rotating intern Phila. Gen. Hosp., 1935-37, resident pathology, 1937-38; asst. resident medicine Med. Coll. Va., 1938-39, resident, 1939-40; practice medicine, specializing in internal medicine, Lynchburg, 1940-42, 46—. Mem. alumni bd. dirs. Washington and Lee U. Served to maj. M.C., AUS, 1942-46. Diplomate Am. Bd. Internal Medicine. Fellow A.C.P.; mem. Lynchburg Acad. Medicine (past pres.), Va. Soc. Internal Medicine (past pres.), Va. Bd. Med. Examiners, Sigma Alpha Epsilon. Episcopalian. Club: Boonsboro Country. Home: 1500 Langhorne Rd Lynchburg VA 24503 Office: 620 Court St Lynchburg VA 24503

CRADDOCK, THOMAS ELMORE, utility exec.; b. Seymour, Tex. Dec. 13, 1893; s. E. L. and Susan (Birdsell) C.; student high sch.; engring. dept. U. Tex., 1911-13; m. Marie Knoerr, Apr. 12, 1919. Engaged in business for self; city mgr., 1929-47; pres. Nat. Rural Electric Coops. Assn., 1947-48, now sec.-treas., mgr. rural electrification project; sec.-treas. Brazos River Power Coop.; dir. Farmers Nat. Bank, Vice pres. N.W. Tex. council Boy Scouts Am., Bd. regents Mid-Western U. Vice chmn. Region IX Tex. Edn. Service Center. Served as sgt., 1st class, Q.M.C. Finance Div., 13 mos. during World War I. Named Man of Year in Tex. Agr., 1972. Mem. N.W. Tex. Water Works Assn., C. of C., Am. Legion. Democrat. Mem. Christian Ch. Clubs: Lions, Golf and Country. Address: Box 672 Seymour TX 76380

CRAFT, HARVEY MILTON, educator; b. Hattiesburg, Miss., Nov. 22, 1925; s. Harvey Moses and Irene (Collins) C.; B.A., U. So. Miss., 1945, M.A., 1956; M.A., U. Ala., 1948; Ph.D., Tulane U., 1964; m. Mary Beth Stoner, Aug. 28, 1946; children—Susan, Cynthia, John, Stephen. Instr. English, U. So. Miss., Hattiesburg, 1955-57, asst. prof., dir. freshman English, 1959-61; asst. prof. English Delta State Coll., Cleveland, 1957-58; mem. faculty Tulane U., New Orleans, 1961-69, asst. prof., dir. freshman and sophomore English, 1963-66, asst. dean coll. arts and scis., 1966-67, head dept. English, 1967-69; dean instrn. Miss. State Coll. Women, Columbus, 1969—. Served to 1st lt. AUS, 1951-53. Mem. Modern Lang. Assn., Nat. Council Tchrs. English (affiliate pres. 1966-67), Sigma Nu, Phi Delta Kappa, Kappa Delta Pi, Omicron Delta Kappa. Democrat. Episcopalian. Home: 301 Forrest Blvd Columbus MS 39701

CRAFT, JOHN RICHARD, mus. dir.; b. Uniontown, Pa., June 15, 1909; s. Samuel Colvin and Ella Kate (Litman) C.; grad. Phillips Acad., Andover, Mass., 1929; student Yale, 1929-30, U. Paris, France, 1936-38; Am. Sch. Classical Studies, Athens, Greece, 1937-38, 39; M.A., Johns Hopkins U., Ph.D., 1940; m. Marjorie Hinman Magraw, Oct. 30, 1931; 1 son, Christopher Hinman. Dir. Washington County Mus. Fine Arts, Hagerstown, Md. 1940-50, Columbia (S.C.) Mus. Art, 1950—; pres. Southeastern Mus. Conf., 1952-55; chmn. So. Art Mus. Dirs. Assn., 1956; pres. Yale Club of Central S.C., 1963-64. Mem. Am. Assn. Museums, Am. Inst. Interior Designers. Home: 712 Kipling Dr Columbia SC 29205 Office: Senate and Bull Sts Columbia SC 29201

CRAFT, RANDAL ROBERT, realtor; b. Ellisville, Miss., July 13, 1918; s. Tilden Bayard and Annie Laurie (Vining) C.; student Miss. State U., 1935-37; m. Elizabeth Ann Nelson, Feb. 3, 1940; children—Randal Robert, Ann Elizabeth. With Belzoni Provision Co. (Miss.), 1937-42; partner, sales mgr. Craft Co., Jackson, Miss., 1946-49; real estate salesman Reid-McGee & Co., Jackson, Miss., 1949-51; owner Craft Hosiery Co., Dallas, 1952-54; v.p. in charge sales Craft Co., Dallas, Jackson, 1954-64; owner Randal Craft, Realtor, Jackson, 1964—; pres. Craft Builders, Inc., Jackson, 1969—; dir. Multiple Listing Service, Inc., Jackson, pres., 1967; dir. All Points Relocation Service, Atlanta. Pres., Hinds County Heart Assn., 1968-69. Served with USAAF, 1942-45, served to capt. USAF, 1951-52. Mem. Nat. Inst. Real Estate Brokers (mem. governing council 1972—), Jackson Bd. Realtors (dir., sec.-treas. 1966-68), Miss. Assn. Realtor Bds. (sec.-treas. 1968), Nat. Inst. Farm and Land Brokers, C. of C., Rho Epsilon (dist. dir. 1969-71). Baptist (deacon). Clubs: Knife and Fork (v.p. 1969-70), Civitan (pres. 1969-70). Home: 2310 Twin Lakes Circle Jackson MS 39211 Office: 4554 Office Park Dr Jackson MS 39216

CRAGO, H. CARMAN, II, glass co. exec.; b. Wheeling, W.Va., Aug. 23, 1921; s. Homer C. and Ethel (Kittle) C.; A.B., W.Va. U., 1943; postgrad. U. Pitts., 1950-51; m. Sarah Kathleen Carter, Aug. 4, 1945; children—David Hughes, John Carman. Adminstrv. asst. Hazel-Atlas Glass Co., Wheeling, W.Va., 1944-49, product mgr. beverage containers, 1950-55; dist. sales mgr. Glass div. Continental Can Co., Cleve., 1955-56, Clin. 1957-60. Midwest area mgr., Chgo., 1961-64; regional mgr. Knox Glass, Inc., Palestine, Tex., 1964-69; mgr. S.W. region Glass Containers Corp., Dallas, 1969-70; nat. sales mgr. Obear-Nester Glass, 1971—. Served to lt. (j.g.) USNR. 1943-44. Mem. Nat. Assn. Bus. Econs., Phi Delta Theta Alumni Assn. Presbyn. (elder). Mason. Club: Meadowbrook Country (Palestine, Tex.). Home: 7606 Chattington Dr Dallas TX 75240 Office: 2000 Broadway East St Louis IL 62205

CRAIG, A. H., state legislator. Mem. Fla. Ho. of Reps., chmn. com. natural resources. Address: 20 Granada St St Augustine FL 32084*

CRAIG, BEN T., textile co. exec., b. 1933; B.S. in Econs., Davidson Coll., 1954. With Wachovia Bank & Trust Co., 1954-61, br. bank mgr., 1956-60, asst. v.p., mem. corr. bank dept., 1960-61; asst. to pres. Nat. Bank S.C., 1961-63; exec. v.p. Bank Lancaster, 1963-67; asst. treas. Springs Mills, Inc., Fort Mills, S.C., 1967-68, treas., 1968—. Office: Springs Mills Inc Fort Mills SC 29715*

CRAIG, CLIFTON MORTON, state ofcl.; b. Durham, N.C., Aug. 4, 1918; s. Clifton M. and Hester (Billings) C.; B.S. in Commerce, U. N.C., 1939; M.B.A., George Washington U., 1953; m. Gertrude Iredale, July 24, 1950; children—Clifton M., Jr., Karen Dale. Commd. 2d lt USMC, 1940, advanced through grades to col.; communication officer stationed at Iceland, S. Pacific, 1940-45; supply and logistics officer, 1945-62; mgmt. analyst office Sec. Def., Washington; ret., 1962; indsl. dir. Durham (N.C.) C. of C., 1962-65; asst. commr. N.C. Dept. Pub. Welfare, Raleigh, 1965-66, commr., 1966—. Mem. N.C. Inter-Agy. Council, 1966—; chmn. Eugenics Bd., 1966—. Bd. dirs. N.C. Juvenile Corrections, N.C. Med. Care Commn. Recipient Distinguished Service award N.C. Assn. Homes for Aging, 1967. Mem. Am. Pub. Welfare Assn., N.C. Council Social Services. Methodist. Home: 5706 Deblyn Av Raleigh NC 27609 Office: Edn Bldg Corner Salisbury and Edenton Sts Raleigh NC 27602

CRAIG, CONWAY C., newspaper pub.; b. Glen Cove, Tex., Aug. 31, 1901; s. James William and Florence Ellen (Smith) C.; B.A., Hardin-Simmons U., 1925; m. Gaynelle Porter, Mar. 21, 1926. With Abilene (Tex.) Reporter, 1926-27, Corpus Christi (Tex.) Times, 1928-29, Southwestern Engraving Co., San Antonio, 1929-30; sales rep. Mills Engraving Co., later Southwestern Engraving Co., 1929-30; with Corpus Christi Caller and Times, 1930-62, pub., 1939-62, pres., 1945-62; pub. Express Pub. Co., San Antonio, 1962—, also chmn. bd. A founder United Fund Corpus Christi, 1954; pres. bd. govs. United Community Services Corpus Christi, 1961; organizer Corpus Christi Art Found., 1940, permanent v.p. charge ways and means, 1940—; an organizer Downtown Businessmen's Assn., Corpus Christi, 1954; chmn. non-Jewish div. Jewish Social Service Fedn., San Antonio, 1963; pres. Corpus Christi Symphony Soc., 1956. Bd. govs. Southwest Research Inst.; bd. dirs. San Antonio Livestock Exposition, Tex. Good Roads Assn., Fiesta San Antonio Commn. Mem. San Antonio C. of C. (pres. 1964). Home: Knight Robin Dr San Antonio TX 78209 Office: PO Box 2171 San Antonio TX 78205

CRAIG, FLOYD ALLEN, religious assn. exec.; b. Oklahoma City, Okla., Feb. 25, 1933; s. Floyd Marion and Bonnie (Mitchell) C.; A.B., Okla. Bapt. U., 1955; B.D., Southwestern Bapt. Theol. Sem., 1960; postgrad. U. Mo., 1961, U. Chgo., 1964; m. Alice Anne Bolt, Feb. 19, 1956; children—Paul, Suzanne. Ordained to ministry So. Baptist Ch., 1951; pastor chs., Okla. and Tex., 1953-60; asst. dir. pub. relations Southwestern Bapt. Theol. Sem., Fort Worth, 1960-62; dir. communications Bapt. Gen. Conv. of Okla., 1962-67; dir. photog. coverage World Congress on Evangelism, Berlin, 1966; dir. pub. relations Christian Life Commn. of the So. Bapt. Conv., Nashville, Tenn., 1967—. Communications and pub. relations cons. to chs., and religion and non-profit agys., 1965—. Pub. relations com. Nashville Urban League, 1970—. Recipient Hinkhouse award Religious Pub. Relations Council, 1968, 70; numerous awards from profl. pub. relations and photog. socs. Mem. So. Bapt. Pub. Relations Assn. (pres. 1968), Nat. Religious Pub. Relations Council, Lord's Day Alliance (bd. dirs. 1969-72), Pub. Relations Soc. Am., Okla. City Press Club. Baptist (dir. Sunday sch. dept. 1969—). Author: Christian Communicators Handbook, 1969. Contbr. articles to profl. pubs. Produced several hundred original cover photographs for religious mags., newspapers and record jackets. Home: 223 Haverford Dr Nashville TN 37219 Office: 460 James Robertson Pkwy Nashville TN 37219

CRAIG, HORACE, newspaper editor. City editor Fort Worth Star-Telegram. Office: 400 W 7th St Fort Worth TX 76101*

CRAIG, HUBERT MAXTON, JR., machine co. exec.; b. nr. Stanley, N.C., Jan. 16, 1931; s. Hubert Maxton and Beulah Edna (Rimmer) C.; B.S., Wake Forest U., 1952; m. Constance Virginia Rollins, Aug. 23, 1952; children—Susan Anne, Hubert Maxton III, Mary Cynthia, David Rimmer. Office mgr. to pres. Gaston County Dyeing Machine Co., Stanley, 1952—; pres. H.M. Craig Metal & Supply Co., 1960—, Craig Realty & Devel. Co., 1955—; dir. Citizens Nat. Bank of Gastonia, N.C. Mem. Gaston Bd. Realtors. Candidate for Gaston County Commr., 1962; alternate del. Republican Nat. Conv., 1964, 68; mem. N.C. Ho. of Reps. from 41st Dist., 1966-68. Bd. dirs. Gaston County Center for Handicapped Children, Gaston chpt. A.R.C., Gaston County Heart Fund; trustee Gardner-Webb Coll. Recipient Citizens citation for ednl. and civic leadership Gardner-Webb Coll., 1970. Mem. Am. Textile Machinery Assn., N.A.M., Gaston C. of C., Delta Sigma Pi. Baptist (deacon). Lion. Home: Wheeler St Stanley NC 28164 Office: 200 S Main St Stanley NC 28164

CRAIG, JAMES B., editor. Editor, American Forests. Office: 919 17th St NW Washington DC 20006*

CRAIG, JAMES CONOVER, life ins. exec.; b.Jacksonville, Fla., Dec. 2, 1908; s. Marion Bookman and Elizabeth (Stork) C.; student U. Fla., 1926-29; m. Julia Bryan, Dec. 28, 1932; children—Julia Oliver (Mrs. Richard Brooke, Jr.), Cynthia Bryan (Mrs. John McKey, Jr.). Mem. editorial staff Fla. Times-Union, Jacksonville, 1929-57; dir. pub. relations Ind. Life & Accident Ins. Co., Jacksonville, 1957—, v.p., 1958—; v.p. Herald Life Ins. Co. Pres., Duval County chpt. Mental Health Assn., 1962. Mem. Pub. Relations Soc. Am., Fla. Pub. Relations Assn., Life Advertisers Assn., S.A.R. (chpt. pres. 1950), Fla. (pres. 1970-72), Jacksonville (pres. 1958-59) hist. socs., English Speaking Union (br. pres. 1965), Jacksonville C. of C., So. Hist. Assn., Com. of 100, Ye Mystic Revellers. Episcopalian. Clubs: Timuquana Country; University; Ponte Vedra; Fla. Yacht; River. Contbr. numerous articles profl. jours. Home: 4201 Yacht Club Rd Jacksonville FL 32210 Office: 233 W Duval St Jacksonville FL 32201

CRAIG, JAMES PATRICK, librarian; b. Gould, Ark., Dec. 10, 1942; s. Hubert Eldridge and Mary Lorean (Dean) C.; B.S.E. in Edn. and Music, Ark. A. and M. Coll., 1963; M.A. in L.S., North Tex. State U., 1970; postgrad. State Coll. Ark., U. Ark. Tchr. English, Linwood Sch., Moscow, Ark., 1963; dir. libraries Gould pub. schs., 1964-70; circulation librarian U. Ark., Gould, 1970—. Sponsor, Nat. Guild Piano Tchrs. Mem. Am. Coll. Organists, Nat. Ark. Sch. Librarian Assn., N.E.A., Ark. Edn. Assn., A.L.A. Mem. Christian Ch. Lion. Home: PO Box 378 Gould AR 71643

CRAIG, JAMES WILLIAM, forestry supply co. exec.; b. Pope, Miss., Sept. 30, 1912; s. John William and Annie Laurie (Craig) C.; B.S. in Forestry, Purdue U., 1936; M.S., N.Y. State Coll. Forestry, 1938; m. Dorabel Moore, Dec. 14, 1941; children—Mary Elizabeth, Annie Laurie, John Moore. Watershed forester, Rochester, N.Y., 1938-41; asst. chief forest fire control, Miss., 1946-47, chief, 1947-48; cons. forester, merchandiser forestry supplies, 1948-52; Miss. State forester, 1952-56; mgr. cons. div. Forestry Suppliers, Inc., Jackson, Miss., 1956, gen. mgr., 1956-69, pres., 1956—. Served from 1st lt. to lt. col. AUS, 1941-45; ETO. Mem. Soc. Am. Foresters (vice chmn. Gulf States sect. 1949, chmn. 1958), Forest Products Research Soc. (chmn. 1954), Miss. Forestry Assn. (pres. 1963, dir. 1952—). Methodist (treas.) Rotarian. Home: 5420 Red Fox Rd Jackson MS 39211 Office: 205 W Rankin St Jackson MS 39204

CRAIG, JOE BILLY, dentist; Cherryville, N.C., July 25, 1931; s. Henry Marshall and Vergie (Ross) C.; A.B., Fla. So. Coll., 1954; B.S., U. N.C., 1956, D.D.S., 1961; m. Nancy Margaret Heafner, Mar. 2, 1951; children—Debra Joan, Joseph Marshall, William Allen. Ednl. cons. Fla. So. Coll., 1954-55; chemist Liggit-Meyers Tobacco Co., Durham, N.C., 1956; practice dentistry, Charlotte, N.C., 1961—; chief cons., dir. tech. staff Charlotte Police Dept.; mem. teaching staff Meml. Hosp. Mem. Disaster Team Western N.C. Served with USAF, 1951-55, USPHS Res., 1960—. Mem. Am. Dental Assn., N.C. Police Exec. Assn., N.C. Assn. Dentistry for Children, N.C. C. of C. Baptist. Mason (Shriner). Club: Optimist (past pres. Charlotte). Home: 2224 Ramblewood Lane Charlotte NC 28210 Office: 4300 Park Rd Charlotte NC 28209

CRAIG, LOUIS ELWOOD, chem. co. exec.; b. Clifton Hill, Mo., Dec. 10, 1921; s. Clyde Allen and Elsie (Metcalf) C.; A.B., Central Coll., 1943; Ph.D. in Organic Chemistry, U. Rochester, 1948; m. Lorene Virginia Higgins, July 17, 1943; children—James Allen, David Andrew, Margaret Louise, Barbara Jean. Chemist Am. Cyanamid Co., Stamford, Conn., 1943-46; research fellow U. Rochester, 1946-48; research chemist Gen. Aniline Film Corp., Easton, Pa., 1948-54; dir. research John Deere Chem. Co., Tulsa, 1954-59, dir. research and tech. service, 1959-61, dir. marketing services, 1961-65; mgr. market research and devel. Kerr-McGee Chem. Corp., Oklahoma City, 1965-67, Western area marketing mgr., 1967-68, v.p. mfg., 1968-70, v.p. chem. mfg. div., 1972—; v.p. information services Kerr-McGee Corp., Oklahoma City, 1970-72. Mem. Am. Chem. Soc. (past chmn. Tulsa sect.), A.A.A.S., Am. Mgmt. Assn. Contbr. articles profl. jours. Patentee. Home: 4921 NW 32d St Oklahoma City OK 73122 Office: Kerr McGee Center Oklahoma City OK 73102

CRAIG, NANCY RYAN (MRS. WILLIAM JOSEPH CRAIG), physician; b. Norman, Okla., June 24, 1924; d. Henry Grady and Anna (Butler) Ryan; B.S., U. Okla., 1946; M.D., U. Okla., 1949; m. William Joseph Craig, Apr. 25, 1946; children—John Joseph, Christopher Patrick, Mary Elizabeth, Kathleen Frances. Intern, U. Okla. Hosps., 1949-50; residency anesthesiology, 1955-57, dir. health service, 1951-53; mil. dependent in Alaska, 1953-54; pvt. practice anesthesiology, 1957—; mem. staffs St. Anthony, Presbyn., Baptist Meml., Mercy, Oklahoma City Gen., U. Okla. hosps.; asst. attending anesthesiologist Mt. Sinai Hosp., N.Y.C., 1968; asso. clin. prof. U. Okla. Hosp. Mem. Okla. Art Center, Oklahoma City Symphony Soc., Diplomate Am. Bd. Anesthesiology. Mem. Am., So., Okla., Oklahoma County med. assns., Am., Okla. socs. anesthesiologists, Internat. Anesthesia Research Soc., Oklahoma City Clin. Soc., N.Y. Acad. Scis., Phi Beta Kappa, Alpha Lambda Delta, Alpha Epsilon Delta, Phi Sigma, Alpha Epsilon Iota. Republican. Roman Catholic. Club: Oklahoma Medical Faculty. Home: 525 NW 39th St Oklahoma City OK 73118 Office: 525 NW 11th St Oklahoma City OK 73103

CRAIG, PAUL C., exec., editor. Vice pres., editor in chief Steck-Vaughn Co., Austin, Tex. Office: Box 2028 Austin TX 78767*

CRAIG, PETER STEBBINS, lawyer; b. Bklyn., Sept. 30, 1928; s. Clarence Tucker and Rena (Stebbins) C.; B.A. Oberlin Coll., 1950; LL.B., Yale, 1953; m. Lois Achor, June 9, 1950 (div. Oct. 1969); children— Stephen, Carolyn, Jennifer; m. 2d, Sally Love Banks, Feb. 14, 1970; 1 dau., Katherine. Spl. asst. Ho. of Reps. Judiciary Com., Washington, 1951-52; admitted to D.C. bar, 1953; practiced in Washington, 1953-63; commerce counsel So. Ry. Co., Washington, 1964-67; asst. gen. counsel, litigation Dept. of Transportation, Washington, 1967-69; gen. atty. So. Ry. Co., Washington, 1969—. Urban transp. planning cons., 1960-67, 69—. Trustee, Com. of 100 on the Fed. City, 1965—. Mem. Am., D.C. bar assns. Quaker. Home: 3406 Macomb St NW Washington DC 20016 Office: So Ry Bldg McPherson Sq Washington DC 20013

CRAIG, THOMAS E., accountant; b. Moulton, Ala., Sept. 25, 1915; s. R. Clyde and Lassie (Fretwell) C.; student pub. schs. of Leon County, Tallahassee. Partner Partner Pentland & Cowles, C.P.A.'s, Tampa, Fla., 1952-63. Cowles, Craig, Silverman & Wooten, C.P.A.'s, Tampa, 1963—. Served with USAAF, World War II. C.P.A., Fla. Mem. Am. Inst. C.P.A.'s, Fla. Inst. C.P.A.'s. Club: Propellor. Home: 212 S Church Tampa FL 33609 Office: 1st Nat Bank Bldg Tampa FL 33602

CRAIG, WALTER, television, radio cons,; b. St. Louis, Dec. 5, 1900; s. Frank E. and May (Goodrich) C.; student Westminster Coll., Fulton, Mo., 1918; m. Margaret Guthrie Gray, Sept. 13, 1946; 1 dau., Patricia Anne. Vaudeville actor, Keith and Orpheum Circuits, 1920-22; juvenile leads musical comedy, Broadway and road, 1923-29; dir. programs World Broadcasting System, N.Y.C., 1930-32; ind. radio prodn., 1933-38; radio dir. Street & Finney, Inc., N.Y.C., 1939-40; dir. programs radio sta. WMCA, N.Y.C., 1940-42; radio dir. Benton & Bowles, Inc., 1943-45, v.p. in charge radio, 1945-47, v.p. in charge radio and TV, 1948-53; v.p. advt. dir. Pharms. Inc., 1953-54;

partner Norman, Craig & Kummel, Inc., 1955-60, TV cons., 1960—; pres. First Fla. Funding Corp., Sarasota, Fla., 1961-67; creative dir. Hansen-Rubensohn-McCann-Erickson, Sydney, Australia, 1967-69; dir. Guaranteed Weather, Inc. Mem. Sarasota C. of C. Am. Assn. of Advt. Agys. (chmn. radio and TV prodn. com., 1948-53), Assn. Nat. Advertisers, Dramatists Guild, Author's League, Clubs: Sarasota Yacht; Athletic (N.Y.C.); Australian International (Sydney). Lectr. on TV N.Y.U., 1947-59. Home: 175 Morningside Dr Lido Shores Sarasota FL 33577 Office: Citizens Bank Bldg Sarasota FL 33578

CRAIGE, BRANCH, JR., physician; b. El Paso, Tex., Feb. 6, 1915; s. Branch and Else (Kohlberg) C.; student Tex. Coll. Mines and Arts, U. Tex., 1931-32; A.B., U. N.C., 1935; M.D., Harvard, 1939; m. Jean Mohler McCracken, Aug. 18, 1945; children—Betty Jean, Mary Josephine (Mrs. Bruce B. Johnson), Branch Criage III. Intern, New Haven Hosp., 1940-41, resident, 1941-43; practice medicine specializing in internal medicine, El Paso, 1946—; mem. staffs Hotel Dieu, El Paso, Providence Meml. Hosp., El Paso, Southwestern Gen. Hosp., El Paso, Sun Tower Hosp., El Paso, St. Joseph's Hosp., El Paso; dir., pres., Med. Center Corp., 1956-58, 61-63, 68-71, pres., 1963; cons. William Beaumont Gen. Hosp., 1947—; pres. Kohlberg Corp., 1951—; pres. El Paso County Bd. Health, 1950-51. Served with AUS, 1943-46. Diplomate Am. Bd. Internal Medicine. Fellow A.C.P.; mem. Am., So., Tex. med. assns., El Paso County Med. Soc., Tex. Soc. Internal Medicine, Alpha Omega Alpha, Sigma Nu. Club: Coronado Country. Contbr. articles to profl. pubs. Home: 2432 Savannah Av El Paso TX 79930 Office: 5B 1501 Arizona Av El Paso TX 79902

CRAIGHEAD, GORDON FULTON, JR., hotel exec.; b. Pitts., Apr. 2, 1925; s. Gordon Fulton and Gladys (McKinnon) C.; student Carnegie Inst. Tech., 1943, U. Rochester, 1943-44; B.S., B.Mgmt. Engring., Rensselaer Polytech. Inst., 1947; B.S. in Hotel Adminstrn., Cornell U., 1949; m. Eugenia Anne Garard, Sept. 10, 1951; children—Eugenia Anne, Barbara Evans, Cameron Garard. Steward, Madison Hotel, Atlantic City, N.J., 1949-50; asst. mgr. Hidden Valley Inn, Somerset, Pa., 1950; mgr. Langwell Hotel, Elmira, N.Y.., 1951; resident mgr. The Inn, Ponte Vedra Beach, Fla., 1952; asst. mgr. Cloister Hotel, Sea Island, Ga., 1952-57; restaurant mgr. Marshall Field & Co., Chgo., 1957-60; asst. dir. Presbyn.-St. Lukes Hosp., Chgo., 1960-66; v.p. Sea Pines Co., Hilton Head Island, S.C., 1966—. Mem. Council on Hotel, Restaurant and Instl. Edn., 1969—. Served to lt. (j.g.) USNR, 1943-46. Mem. Hilton Head Island (dir., pres. 1969-70), Beaufort County (dir.) chambers commerce, S.C. Innkeepers Assn., So. Innkeepers, Am. Hotel & Motel Assn., Nat. Restaurant Assn., Hotel Sales Mgrs. Assn., Cornell Soc. Hotelmen (regional v.p. 1970). Republican. Clubs: Oglethorp, Chatham (Savannah, Ga.); Indian Hill (Winnetka, Ill.); Plantation, Hilton Head Golf (Hilton Head Island). Home: Beach Lagoon Rd Hilton Head Island SC 29928 Office: Sea Pines Co Hilton Head Island SC 29928

CRAIN, CHARLES ROBERT, educator; b. Wichita, Kan., Mar. 13, 1938; s. William Kenneth and Rosemary (May) C.; Mus. B., Phillips U., Enid, Okla., 1959; Mus.M., Ind. U., 1961; performer's diploma, Vienna (Austria) Acad. Mus., 1960; m. Sally Lucile Bonham, Sept. 10, 1960; children—Barry Dewynne, Brooke Elise. Choir and orch. dir. Brainerd High Sch., Chattanooga, 1961-65; founder, condr. Chattanooga Youth Symphony Orch., 1963-65; brass instrument instr. U. Chattanooga, 1962-65; asst. prof. music Tenn. Tech. U., Cookeville, 1965—; prin. French horn Chattanooga Symphony Orch., 1963-65, Chattanooga Opera Orch., 1963-67, Memphis Symphony Orch., 1966—. Mem. Internat. Brass Quintet; faculty artist and condr. Sewanee Summer Music Center (Tenn.), 1965-67. Fulbright fellow to Vienna, Austria, 1959-60; named Outstanding Young Male Tchr. of Year, Chattanooga Jr. C. of C., 1965. Mem. Music Educators Nat. Conf., N.E.A., Tenn. Edn. Assn., Nat. Assn. Coll. Wind and Percussion Instrs., Am. Choral Dirs. Assn., Tenn. Music Educators Assn. (state bd. control), Phi Mu Alpha. Contbr. articles profl. jours. Home: 925 Briarwood Dr Cookeville TN 38501

CRAIN, DARRELL CLAYTON, JR., physician; b. Washington, Mar. 29, 1910; s. Darrell Clayton and Annie (Rau) C.; M.D., George Washington U., 1932; m. Louise Moore, July 12, 1934; children—Barbara (Mrs. Mark Rollinson), Anne (Mrs. Richard Fitzgerald), Darrell Clayton III. Intern, Central Dispensary and Emergency Hosp., Washington, 1932-33, resident, 1933-34; med. officer Walter Reed Gen. Hosp., Washington, 1934-37; practice medicine, specializing in Reumatic diseases, Washington, 1937-42, 45—; mem. staff Georgetown U. Hosp., Drs. Hosp.; cons. Surgeon Gen. U.S. Army, Surgeon Gen. USPHS; clin. prof. medicine Georgetown U., 1969—. Mem. med. adv. bd. Vis. Nurses Soc., Washington, 1960—. Bd. dirs. Westminster Found., Annapolis, Md., Arthritis Rehab. Center. Served to maj. M.C., AUS, 1942-45. Diplomate Am. Bd. Internal Medicine. Fellow A.C.P.; mem. Med. Soc. D.C. (pres. 1965), A.M.A., Am. Soc. Internal Medicine, Am. Rheumatism Assn., Rheumatism Soc. D.C. (pres. 1946-48; sec.-treas. 1948-52), Am. Therapeutic Soc., Am. Congress Phys. Medicine and Rehab., So. Med. Assn., A.A.A.S., N.Y. Acad. Sci., Pan-Am., Internat. med. socs., Washington Acad. Medicine, Am. Med. Authors, Arthritis and Rheumatism Assn. Met. Washington (pres. 1948-52, dir., adv. bd. 1948-72), Assn. Oldest Inhabitants D.C. Contbr. numerous articles to Crain, Darrell Clayton, Jr., profl. jours. Home: 6422 Garnett Dr Kenwood Chevy Chase MD 20015 Office: 1234 19th St NW Washington DC 20036

CRAIN, HAROLD STARK, civil engr.; b. Elkhart, Ind., Nov. 7, 1899; s. George M. and Harriett (Stark) C.; B.S., Purdue U., 1922; m. Nelle R. Snyder, Sept. 1926 (dec. May 1955); children—Mary Helen (Mrs. Laurence D. Savadove), Harold Stark, Elizabeth T. (dec.); m. 2d, Virginia Ruth Floyd, May 26, 1956. Estimator, supt. Am. Crain & Co., Chgo., 1922-26; v.p., mgr. Frost Constrn. Co., Tampa, Fla., 1927-29; estimator, supt. McMillan & Shelton, Enid, Okla., 1929-31; v.p., gen. mgr. William Muirhead Constrn. Co., Durham, N.C., 1932-41, 42-46; project mgr. Triangle Constrn. Corp., Army Cantonment, Camp Butner, N.C., 1941-42; pres. Crain & Denbo Inc., Piedmont Housing & Constrn. Co., Thrift Investment Co. (all Durham), 1946—; v.p. Durham Excavating Co., 1946—. Project mgr. Def. Housing, Portsmouth, Va., 1939-40; chmn. N.C. Licensing Bd. for Contractors, 1950-51. Pres., Constrn. Edn. Found. N.C., 1959—; pres. Watts Hosp., Durham, 1962-68. Served with S.A.T.C., 1918. Recipient Spl. Recognition award Friends of Watts Hosp., 1969. Mem. Durham Contractors Assn. (pres. 1962), N.C. Soc. Engrs. (pres. 1955-56), Assn. Gen Contractors Am. (br. pres. 1951), S.A.R., U.S. Power Squadron (comdr. Durham 1970; Outstanding Comdr.'s award dist. 27, 1971), Purdue Alumni Assn., Sigma Phi Epsilon. Mason. Lion (past pres. Durham). Home: 10th St W and Yacht Dr Long Beach NC 28461 Office: Highland and Britania Sts Durham NC 27702

CRAIN, JOSEPH, chief of police; b. N.Y.C., Aug. 19, 1915; s. Ike and Rose Marie (Strikoff) C.; grad. high sch.; m. Helen Louise Smith, Sept. 7, 1951; 1 son, Thomas Michael. With oil heat co., N.Y.C., 1935-37; self-employed Ace Trucking Co., N.Y.C., 1937-42; with police dept. City of Hot Springs, Ark., 1947—, chief of police, 1969—. Served with AUS, 1942-47. Mem. Internat. Chiefs of Police Assn., Ark. Municipal Assn., Ark. Chiefs of Police Assn. Baptist. Mason, Elk. Home: 133 Mount View St Hot Springs AR 71901 Office: Office of City Clerk City Hall Hot Springs AR 71901

CRAMER, GEORGE HALLOCK, electronics co. exec.; b. St. Louis, Apr. 9, 1927; s. George Hallock and Pearl (Patterson) C.; B.S. in Elec. Engring. with honors (physics scholar), So. Meth. U., 1949; M.S. in Elec. Engring., Stevens Inst. Tech., 1952; m. Patsy Rhea Thrasher, Oct. 10, 1949; children—Georgia Sue, Scott Patrick, George Hallock. Research microwave engr. RCA, 1949-52; sr. microphysics engr. Convair, 1952-54; corporate dir. electronics Ling Temco Vought, Dallas, 1954-69; founded Resalab, Inc., Dallas, 1969, pres., 1969—; dir. 1st State Bank of Dennison (Tex.), Metrocom, Dallas, Town North Plaza, Dallas. Cons. to various cos.; industry rep. for U.S. govt. to Internat. Standardization Com., 1970. Asst. scoutmaster Boy Scouts Am., Dallas, 1968. Served with USNR, 1945-46. Registered profl. engr., Tex. Mem. I.E.E.E., Old Crows (pres. Dallas 1970), Alpha Tau Omega, Eta Kappa Nu, Kappa Mu Epsilon, Delta Phi Alpha, Sigma Tau. Research in magnetron tuning and electronic reconnaissance systems. Home: 4248 Armstrong Parkway Dallas TX 75205 Office: Town North Plaza Dallas TX 75234

CRAMER, JOHN SCOTT, banker; b. Charlotte, N.C., Dec. 10, 1930; s. Stuart Warren, Jr. and Julia (Scott) C.; A.B., U.N.C., 1953; m. Nancy Arnott, Aug. 9, 1952; children—Julia Baxter, Alice Arnott. With Wachovia Bank & Trust Co., 1955—, asst. v.p., Charlotte, 1958-61, v.p., 1961-64, sr. v.p., bd. mgrs. Charlotte office, 1964-71, exec. v.p., head banking div., Winston-Salem, N.C., 1971—; v.p., dir. John M. Scott & Co.; dir. Am. Credit Corp., Shadowline, Inc. Bd. visitors Davidson Coll.; bd. dirs. N.C. Episcopal Ch. Found., Inc.; bd. advisers Wingate Coll. Served to 1st lt. USAF, 1953-55. Named one of Charlotte's Ten Outstanding Young Men, Jr. C. of C., 1964. Mem. Winston-Salem C. of C. Clubs: Charlotte Country; Linville Golf; Old Town Club (Winston-Salem). Home: 2700 Reynolds Dr Winston-Salem NC 27104 Office: PO Box 3099 Winston-Salem NC 27102

CRAMER, WILLIAM CATO, lawyer, former congressman; b. Denver, Aug. 4, 1922; s. Walter Bruce and Doreen Emma (Walters) C.; student St. Petersburg Jr. Coll., 1941-43; A.B., U. N.C., 1946; LL.B., Harvard, 1948; J.D. (hon.), U. Tampa, 1957; m. Alice Janet Jones, Dec. 7, 1951; children—William C., Mark Clifton, Allyn Walter. Admitted to Fla. bar, 1948, Mass. bar, 1948; practice of law, 1948-65; partner Ramseur, Bradham, Lyle, Skipper & Cramer, St. Petersburg; mem. Fla. Legislature, 1950-52, minority leader, 1951; county atty. Pinellas Co., Fla., 1953-54; mem. 84th-91st Congresses, 8th Fla. dist. Republican nat. committeeman, Fla., 1964—; vice chmn. Fla. delegation Rep. Nat. Convs., 1956-60, chmn. host com. Rep. Nat. Conv., 1968; vice chmn. Republican Congl. Campaign Com., vice chmn. Rept. Conf., also Rep. policy com. Served as lt. (j.g.) USNR, World War II. Mem. Am., Mass., Fla., St. Petersburg bar assns., V.F.W., Am. Legion, Phi Beta Kappa, Phi Alpha Phi (hon.), Alpha. Methodist. Mason (Shriner). Clubs: Grotto, Kiwanis (St. Petersburg). Home: 1200 Monterey Blvd St Petersburg FL Office: Federal Bldg 144 1st Av S St Petersburg FL 33701

CRAMER, WILLIAM FRED, indsl. products co. exec.; b. Oak Park, Ill., Aug. 9, 1923; s. Alfred William and Flora Marie (Contios) C.; student Baylor U., 1946-47; B.S., U. Tex., 1950; postgrad. Tex. Christian U., 1951-52; m. Nancy E. Ward, Nov. 18, 1943; children—William Fred, Kenneth A. With Chance Vought Aircraft, Dallas, 1950-62, chief indsl. engring., 1960-62; with Ling Temco Vought, 1962—, v.p., gen. mgr. indsl. products div., 1968—. Bd dirs. YMCA, Grand Prairie, Tex., 1963-65. Served with AUS, 1940-45. Mem. Air Force Assn., Am. Astronitical Soc. Optimist (pres. 1960-62). Home: 10757 Bushire Dr Dallas TX 75229 Office: 2345 W Mockingbird Lane Dallas TX 75235

CRAMMER, PHILIP, plastics engr.; b. Chester, N.J., June 16, 1917; s. William H. and Mabel (Apgar) C.; student Newark Coll. Engring., 1937-39, Rutgers U., 1950-53; m. Mary E.L. Knickel, Dec. 25, 1942; children—David Charles, John Richard, Mark Andrew. Methods engr. Diehl Mfg. div. Singer Co., Somerville, N.J., 1946-51, mfg. mgr. plastics div., 1960-63, mgr. plastics div., motor products div., Anderson, S.C., 1963-64, plastics process engr., 1964-72, plastics tech. coordinator, 1972—. Plastics instr. Tri-County Tech. Edn. Center, Pendleton, S.C., 1965—. Exec. v.p. Morris and Orange Presbytery Council of Presbyn. Men, 1961-63, mem. Nat. Council, 1962-63, adult class leader, 1966—. Served with USNR, 1944-46. Mem. Soc. Plastics Engr. (pres., dir. Va.-Carolinas sect.). Republican. Presbyn. (elder). Elk. Contbr. articles to profl. jours Home: 517 Timber Lane Anderson SC 29621 Office: Box 1110 Anderson SC 29621

CRANE, FORREST BENNETT, city ofcl.; b. Fairmont, W.Va., Nov. 7, 1912; s. Clyde Forrest and Sadie (Bennett) C.; A.B., Fairmont State Coll., 1933; m. Bettye Allison, Nov. 5, 1945; 1 dau., Carolyn Allison. Sports, city mng. editor Fairmont (W.Va.) Times, 1932-37; publicity specialist Monongahela Power Co., 1937-42; publicity dir. W.Va. U., 1942-51; publicity advt. dir. City Fort Lauderdale, Fla., 1951—. Served to lt. USNR, 1943-46. Home: 1207 Cordova Rd Fort Lauderdale FL 33316 Office: City Hall 100 N Andrews Av Fort Lauderdale FL 33302

CRANE, FRANK, state ofcl.; b. Waxhaw, N.C., Aug. 18, 1907; s. James Thomas and Emma (Lathan) C.; A.B., U. N.C., 1931, postgrad., summers 1932-34; m. Mary Browning Cromer, Nov. 27, 1963. Tchr., coach, Welcome, N.C., 1931-34; safety dir. N.C. Indsl. Commn., 1934-39; factory safety insp. N.C. Dept. Labor, Raleigh, 1939-54; dir. N.C. Counciliation Service, Raleigh, 1941-54; commr. labor State of N.C., Raleigh, 1954—. Mem. Soc. Safety Engrs., Vets. of Safety. Democrat. Methodist. Home: 2608 Hazelwood Dr Raleigh NC 27608 Office: Labor Bldg PO Box 1151 Raleigh NC 27602

CRANE, GARRY MITCHELL, govt. ofc.; b. Newton, Ia., July 23, 1940; s. Paul T. and Norma (Mitchell) C.; B.A., U. Chgo., 1962, postgrad., 1962-63; Ph.D., George Washington U., 1971; m. Kathryn Ann Kadane, June 13, 1965; children—Daniel Kadane, Paul Kadane. Cost analyst Center for Naval Analyses, Arlington, Va., 1963-65; economist Operations Research, Inc., Silver Spring, Md., 1965-66; economist tech. analysis div. Nat. Bur. Standards, Dept. Commerce, 1968—. Mem. Am., So. econ. assns., Omicron Delta Epsilon. Home: 3907 Isbell St Silver Spring MD 20906 Office: Nat Bur Standards Washington DC 20234

CRANE, KENT B., govt. ofcl.; grad. with honors, Dartmouth, 1957; married; two children. Assigned Am. embassy, Djakarta, Indonesia, 1960-62; with U.S. Dept. State, Washington, 1963-64; served in Zanzibar, 1964-65, Accra, Ghana, 1965-67; sr. research asso. fgn. affairs and sec. task force on conduct of fgn. relations Rep. Nat. Com., 1967-68; spl. asst. to U.S. Senator George Murphy, 1968-69; asst. for nat. security affairs Office of Vice Pres., Washington, 1969-71; asst. dir. for East Asia and Pacific, USIA, Washington, 1972—. Office: 1750 Pennsylvania Av Washington DC 20547

CRANE, WILLIAM HARRY, public accountant; b. Montgomery, Ala., Mar. 21, 1925; s. Harold Curtis and Alvira (Landon) C.; student Clemson Coll., 1943, Duke, 1946-47; B.S., M.S., U. Ala., 1950; m. Joanna Breedlove, Sept. 1970; children—(by previous marriage) Dorothy Jean (Mrs. Alan Adams), Lucy Anne (Mrs. Duane Newby), Mary Elizabeth (Mrs. Clifford Hornady), Suzanne Victoria. Partner, Crane, Jackson & Thornton, C.P.A.'s, Montgomery, 1953-64 Crane & Crane, C.P.A.'s, Montgomery, 1964-67; pres. William H. Crane & Co., C.P.A.'s, Montgomery, 1967—. Budget dir., exec. com. United Appeal, Montgomery, 1962-64. Bd. dirs. Montgomery chpt. A.R.C. Served with AUS, 1943-45. Decorated Bronze Star medal, Silver Star medal; named Ky. col. Mem. Ala. Soc. C.P.A.'s (chmn. council 1964-65), Am. Inst. C.P.A.'s, Montgomery Assn. C.P.A.'s (pres. 1961-62), Delta Sigma Pi. Rotarian (dist. gov. 1969-70). Home: 3300 Drexel Rd Montgomery AL 36106 Office: 200 S Hull St Montgomery AL 36104

CRANFILL, HENRY LEE, JR., supt. schs.; b. Clairette, Tex., Nov. 25, 1917; s. Henry Lee and Mary Frances (Sowell) C.; B.A., Baylor U., 1946, M.S., 1950; m. Irma Geraldine King, Apr. 4, 1938; children—Carol, John, Charles. Supt. schs., Alexander, Tex., 1948-50, China Spring, Tex., 1950-52, Oglesby, Tex., 1952-56, La Vega, Waco, Tex., 1964—. Served with USAAF, 1943-46. Mem. Am., Tex. assns. sch. adminstrs. Mason. Home: 4511 Concord St Waco TX 76705 Office: 3100 Bellmead Dr Waco TX 76705

CRANFORD, HENRY CLAY, JR., health ins. co. exec.; b. Monroe County, Ala., Sept. 20, 1920; s. Henry Clay and Minnie Idelia (Barton) C.; student U. N.C., 1940-45; m. Lois Adele Ribelin, Nov. 8, 1943; children— Susan Carole, Kathryn Gail. Reporter, Durham (N.C.) Sun, 1940-41; exec. dir. N.C. Good Health Assn., 1946-49; dir. pub. relations Hosp. Care Assn., Durham, 1949-68; v.p. N.C. Blue Cross and Blue Shield, Durham, 1968—. Campaign chmn. Durham (N.C.) United Fund, 1968, pres., 1969; chmn. N.C. Com. Patient Care, 1963-64; pres. Family Counseling Service and Better Health Found., Durham, 1965-66. Served with USMCR, 1942-45. Mem. Pub. Relations Soc. Am., N.C. Health Council (v.p.), Durham C. of C. (pres. 1972). Baptist. Rotarian. Home: 8 Chantilly Pl Durham NC 27707 Office: 800 S Duke St Durham NC 27702

CRANFORD, WAYNE, advt. exec.; b. Bald Knob, Ark., Jan. 1, 1933; s. Benjamin Franklin and Rachel (Jacobs) C.; B.S.E., Ark. State Tchrs. Coll., 1953; m. Frances Jane Anderson, Sept. 15, 1962; children—Jay Wayne, Anderson Ross. Instr. Bald Knob (Ark.) High Sch., 1953-55; reporter Ark. Democrat, Little Rock, 1955-56; dir. pub. relations Little Rock C. of C., 1956-57; account exec. The Hockersmith Agy., Little Rock, 1957-61; pres. Cranford/Johnson/Hunt & Assos., Inc., Little Rock, 1961—; dir. Better Bus. Bur. of Pulaski County, River Devel. Corp. Bd. dirs. A.R.C., state fund chmn., 1966-67; bd. dirs. Ark. State Festival of Arts, Pulaski County chpt. Nat. Found., Presbyn. Found Synod Ark.-Okla., 1969, Capital City 150th Anniversary, 1971, Ark. Orch. Soc.; trustee Ark. Arts Center. Named one of Ark.'s Outstanding Young Men, Ark. Jr. C. of C., 1969. Mem. Am. Assn. Advt. Agys. (bd. govs. S.W. council 1967-71, chmn. 1970-71), Ark., Little Rock (dir.) chambers commerce, Pub. Utilities Adv. Assn., Ark. Press Assn., Bank Marketing Assn., Ark. Hall Fame, Pub. Relations Soc. Am., Fifty for the Future, Phi Sigma Epsilon. Presbyn. Clubs: Capital (dir. 1971-72), Razorback, Country of Little Rock. Home: 1917 N Spruce Little Rock AR 72207 Office: First National Bank Bldg Little Rock AR 72201

CRANK, JAMES ELDON, hosp. adminstr.; b. Puxico, Mo., Aug. 22, 1925; s. John C. and Luda (Harty) C.; B.S. in Edn., S.E. Mo. State Coll., 1950; M.P.H., U. N.C., 1952; m. Vera Emma Rau, May 18, 1949; children—Kyla Rau, Kimberly Ann, James Floyd. Field rep. Ga. Tb Assn., Atlanta, 1949-51; asst. to dir. local health services Ga. Dept. Health, Atlanta, 1952-54; with U. Ala. Hosp., Birmingham, 1954-65, asso. gen. dir., 1963-65; adminstr. Meth. Hosp., Inc., Birmingham, 1965-69; hosp. dir., prof. health care adminstrn. U. Ark. Med. Center, Little Rock, 1969—. Clin. asso. prof. Med. Coll. Ala., Birmingham, 1965-69; hosp. cons. Ariz. Med. Sch. Study, 1961—; adj. asso. prof., preceptor U. Ala. Sch. Community and Allied Health Resources, 1970—; mem. Ark. Commn. Renal Disease, 1971—. Founder, Health Careers Council Ala., 1964, pres., 1964-69; chmn. Joint Am. Hosp. Assn.-Nat. Health Council Com. on Health Careers Councils, 1968-70. Fellow Am. Coll. Hosp. Adminstrs., Am. Pub. Health Assn.; mem. Am. Assn. Med. Colls. (mem. council teaching hosps. 1969—). Presbyn. (trustee). Home: 50 Nob View Circle Little Rock AR 72205 Office: U Ark Med Center Little Rock AR 72201

CRASILNECK, HAROLD BERNARD, clin. psychologist; b. San Antonio, Apr. 4, 1921; s. John N. and Kate (Wolfson) C.; B.A., Trinity U., 1947; M.A., U. Tex., 1949; Ph.D., U. Houston, 1954; m. Sherry Gold Knopf, Jan. 18, 1959; children—Robert Ingram Knopf, Suzy Carol, Candace Elizabeth (Mrs. Philip Eugene Rosen), Jonathan, John, Robert. Asst. prof. psychology Trinity U., 1948-51; instr. psychology U. Houston, 1951-52; lectr. psychology So. Meth. U., 1952-53; asst. prof. psychiatry Southwestern Med. Sch., U. Tex., 1954-60; clin. psychologist Dallas Neurol. Clinic, 1960-61; pvt. practice clin. psychology, Dallas, 1961—. Served with USMCR, 1942-45. Diplomate Am. Bd. Examiners Psychol. Hypnosis (sec., treas. 1959-62). Fellow Am. Soc. for Clin. Hypnosis (Merit award for outstanding dissertation 1958, Ben Raginsky award, 1965, Morton Prince award 1968, certificate merit best clin. paper 1969, 71, Roy M. Dorcus award 1971), Soc. for Clin. and Exptl. Hypnosis (pres. 1963-65); mem. Am., Tex., Dallas (pres. 1959-60) psychol. assns., Ecuatoriana de Medicina (hon. pres. 1972), Sigma Xi, Phi Kappa Phi. Contbr. articles to various publs. Home: 5635 Yolanda Circle Dallas TX 75229 Office: 712 N Washington St Dallas TX 75246

CRAVEN, AVERY CLARENCE, retail co. exec.; b. Thomasville, N.C., Feb. 1, 1896; s. Charles and Elizabeth (Welborn) C.; student Oak Ridge Mil. Inst., 1916-17; m. Frances Josephine Smith, Apr. 20, 1921; 1 dau., Francella (Mrs. Robert Kenyon Kerr). Auditor, Belk Dept. Stores, Charlotte, N.C., 1920-26, sec.-treas., Mooresville, N.C., 1926-51; exec. v.p. Belk, Mooresville, 1952—, Belk, Union, S.C., Belk-Harry Co., Salisbury, N.C., 1952—, Belk Dept. Store, Statesville, N.C., 1962—; dir. Citizens Savs. and Loan, Mooresville, 1st Nat. Bank Mooresville. Mem. mgmt. action com. Belk Stores Services, Inc., Charlotte, N.C., 1962—. Chmn. bd. Lowrance Hosp., Inc., Mooresville, 1959-62; bd. dirs. Tri-County Mental Health Complex. Served with U.S. Army, 1917-18. Named Mcht. of Year, Mooresville Mchts. Assn., 1969. Mem. C. of C., Mooresville Mchts. Assn., Soc. Descs. Knights of Most Noble Order of Garter. Elk, Kiwanian (pres. 1933). Mailing Address: PO Box 330 Mooresville NC 28115 Home: Route 1 Box 25 Mooresville NC 28115

CRAVEN, FRANK EDWARD, govt. ofcl.; b. Oswego, N.Y., Aug. 29, 1926; s. Frank Ray and Rose (LeBlanc) C.; B.S., Forestry U. Ga., 1951; m. Mildred Morgan, Nov. 11, 1950; children—Karen Rose, Valerie Diane. Forest ranger Butts County, Ga., 1950-51; asst. dist. forester Ga. Forestry Commn., McRae, 1951-52, dist. forester, Rome, 1955-57, chief forest edn., Macon, 1957—. Pres. Middle Ga. Profl. Agr. Workers Council, 1960. Served with AUS, 1945-46. Named Outstanding Ga. Forester, Ga. Sportsman Fedn., 1970; recipient Nat. Forest Fire Prevention award U.S. Forest Service, 1972; col. Gov.'s Staff. Mem. Soc. Am. Foresters (editor newsletter 1959-60, past pres. Ga. chpt.), Soil Conservation Soc. Am. (past pres. Ga. chpt.), Ga. Peace Officers Assn., Xi Sigma Pi. Kiwanian (past pres., dist. lt. gov.). Editor Ga. Forestry mag. Home: 1542 Westminster Dr Macon GA 31204 Office: Box 819 Macon GA 31202

CRAVEN, JAMES BRAXTON, JR., judge; b. Lenoir, N.C., Apr. 3, 1918; s. James Braxton and Katherine Simmons (Covington) C.; A.B., Duke, 1939, student Law Sch., 1946; LL.B., Harvard, 1942; m. Jean Bible, Aug. 15, 1952; children—James Braxton III, Stephen K., Elizabeth Bible. Admitted to N.C. bar, 1946; solicitor Burke County Criminal Ct., 1947; asst. U.S. atty., Charlotte-Asheville, 1948-52; became judge Superior Ct. of North Carolina, 1956; U.S. dist. judge Western Dist. N.C. 1961-66; U.S. circuit judge 4th Circuit Ct. Appeals, 1966-—. Vis. prof. constl. law U.N.C., Chapel Hill, 1967, Fed. Cts., U. Tex., Austin, 1968; lectr. constl. law U. N.C. Law Sch., summer 1970. Del. Southeastern Jurisdictional Conf. Meth. Ch., 1960, Gen. Conf. Meth. Ch., 1964. Trustee Duke U. Served from ensign to lt. USNR, 1942-46. Mem. Am., N.C. (v.p. 1959-60), Burke County bar assns., Am. Judicature Soc., Am. Law Inst. Order of Coif, Phi Beta Kappa, Omicron Delta Kappa. Address: PO Drawer 491 Asheville NC 28802

CRAVEN, WILLIAM HERBERT, JR., educator; b. Bamberg, S.C., Nov. 1, 1929; s. William Herbert and Marion (Easterling) C.; B.S., Clemson U., 1950; postgrad. U. Wis., 1956; m. Lois Anita Kearse, July 21, 1951; children— William Herbert III, Pamela Ann. Agronomist, Epting Distbn. Co., Leesville, S.C., 1950-52; asst. county agt. Clemson U. Extension service, Edgefield, S.C., 1953-56, county agt., Saluda, S.C., 1956-71; county agt. Ga. Extension Service, Waynesboro, Ga., 1971-—. Weekly newspaper columnist 5 area newspapers, 1956-—. Sec. Ridge Farmers Mut., Ridge Spring, S.C., 1965-71, Ridge Mut. Ginnery, 1961-71. Dist. chmn. Central S.C. council Boy Scouts Am., 1964. Sec., Saluda County Aeros. Commn., 1967-71. Served to 1st lt., AUS, 1952-53. Recipient Silver Beaver award Boy Scouts Am., 1969; named Coop. Man of Year S.C., 1967. Methodist. Lion (dist. gov. 1969-70). Home: PO Box 112 Waynesboro GA 30830

CRAVER, WILLIAM EVERETT, JR., finance, mfg., real estate, shipping exec.; b. Columbus, Ga., Aug. 14, 1922; s. William Everett and Myrtle (Ivey) C.; student George Washington U., 1940-43; B.S., U.S. Mcht. Marine Acad., 1945; m. Jane Honour McDonald, Oct. 19, 1946; children—Virginia St. Clair (Mrs. Joseph C. Good, Jr.), Ellen Lloyd, Jane Honour, William Everett III. Administrv. asst. OPM, WPB, Washington, 1940-43; founder, partner Bradham-Craver Co., 1946-49; founder, owner, partner Craver and Co., pub. accountants, Charleston, S.C., 1948-58; founder, pres. So. Gen. Corp. (formerly Craver Industries, Inc.), Charleston, 1949-—, also dir.; founder, pres. Carolina Gen. Corp., Charleston, 1952-—; founder, pres. Coastal Investors, Inc., 1955-56, Beautyguard Mfg. Corp., 1962-67, Craver Indsl. Park, Inc., 1963-67, Leasemasters, 1968-—; founder, pres. Universal Financial Corp., 1962-—, also dir. Vice chmn. Charleston Cancer Crusade, 1965; mem. Charleston County Aviation Authority, 1970-—, chmn., 1971-—; chmn. parents adv. council Converse Coll., 1972-—. Served to lt. USNR, 1945-46; PTO, ETO. Recipient Outstanding Bus. Achievement award U.S. Mcht. Marine Acad. Alumni, 1960, Meritorious Alumni award, 1970. Mem. Am. Soc. Metals, Hibernian Soc., Navy League (pres. Charleston council 1971-—), Greater Charleston C. of C., U.S. Mcht. Marine Acad. Alumni Assn. (chpt. charter pres. 1964-65, S. Atlantic regional gov. 1965-71, life mem.), S.C. Hist. Soc., Preservation Soc. Charleston, Pi Kappa Alpha. Democrat. Presbyn. (deacon). Clubs: Metropolitan (N.Y.C.); Piedmont (Spartanburg, S.C.); Charleston Country, Albemarle (pres. 1965-66), Sertoma (past dir., life mem.), Propeller (Charleston). Patentee metal forming equipment and device field. Home: 82 Tradd St Charleston SC 29401 also Sullivan's Island SC Office: PO Box 1014 Charleston SC 29402

CRAWFORD, BENNY ROSS, JR. (HANK), jazz musician; b. Memphis, Dec. 21, 1934; student music theory, composition Tenn. State U. Baritone saxophonist Ray Charles band, 1958-59, alto saxophonist, 1958-63, mus. dir., 1961-63, tours Europe, 1961, 62, 63; formed own band, 1963, appearance Monterey Jazz Festival, 1964; also pianist. Composer: The Peeper; Stony Lonesome; Dig These Blues. Numerous recordings Atlantic label. Address: 2426 Hunter Av Memphis TN 38108*

CRAWFORD, CARL LEROY, physician; b. Grinnell, Ia., Oct. 26, 1928; s. William Lester and Eva Wilma (Flanigan) C.; B.S., U. N.M., 1953; M.D. (fellow), Med. Coll. Ga., 1965; m. Joe Ann Simmons, Nov. 22, 1959; 1 dau., Constance S. Tchr. sci. high sch., Ia., 1953-56; profl. service rep. Geigy Pharm., Macon, Ga., 1957-61; intern Macon (Ga.) Hosp., 1965-66; gen. practice medicine, Americus, Ga., 1966-68, Warner Robins, Ga., 1968-—; mem. med. staff Americus and Sumter County Hosp., 1966-68, Houston County Hosp., Warner Robins, 1968-—; med. dir. Plains (Ga.) Convalescent Home, 1966-67; coll. physician Ga. Southwestern Coll., 1967; med. dir. Hallmark Nursing Home, Warner Robins, 1968-—. Profl. v.p. Houston County chpt. Am. Cancer Soc., 1969-—; pres. Houston County Assn. Exceptional Children, 1971-—. Bd. dirs. A.R.C., chmn. Houston County Bloodmobile program; bd. dirs. Warner Robins chpt. Houston County United Givers Fund, Salvation Army. Served with AUS, 1946-49. Recipient Citizen of Yr. award Warner Robins Jaycees, 1971. Mem. A.M.A., Am., Ga. acads. gen. practice, Am. Heart Assn., So. Med. Assn., Med. Assn. Ga., 3d Dist. Med. Soc. (sec.-treas. 1967-69), Air Force Assn. (life), Franklin Mint Collectors Soc., Med. Coll. Ga. Alumni Assn., Alpha Kappa Kappa. Republican. Episcopalian. Rotarian. Club: Houston Lake Country (Perrry, Ga.). Home: 105 Granada Terrace Warner Robins GA 31093 Office: 124 Hospital Dr Warner Robins GA 31093

CRAWFORD, CHARLES LEE, dentist; b. Bethlehem, Ky., Aug. 23, 1901; s. Charles Lee and Caroline Monfort (Claxon) C.; student Henderson Brown Coll., 1919-23; D.D.S., Tulane U., 1927; m. Madeleine Madrara Stier, Aug. 4, 1966. Practice dentistry, specializing in dental surgery and radiology, New Orleans, 1927-—. Home: 916 Leontine St New Orleans LA 70115 Office: 3732 Canal St New Orleans LA 70119

CRAWFORD, EDWIN MCNEILL, ednl. adminstr.; b. Montgomery, Ala., May 14, 1929; s. William H. and Mary (Thomas) C.; B.S., Auburn U., 1951; m. Mary Jean Barrett, Mar. 5, 1955; children—Ellen McNeill, Edwin Barrett, Graham Thomas. Reporter, Decatur (Ala.) Daily, 1951; editor Auburn (Ala.) U. Alumnews, 1952, Montgomery Examiner, 1953-54; account exec. Sparrow Advt. Agy., Birmingham, 1954-58; exec. asso. So. Regional Edn. Bd., Atlanta, 1958-62; dir. univ. relations Auburn U., 1962-66; asso. dir., dir. Office Instl. Research, Nat. Assn. State Univs. and Land-Grant Colls., Washington, 1966-70; v.p. for pub. affairs U. Va., Charlottesville, 1970-—. Asso. dir. NSF Regional Sci. Seminar, U. Fla., 1961. Mem. Ala. Civil War Centennial Commn., 1962-64. Del., Democratic Nat. Conv. from 9th Dist. Ala., 1956; mem. Jefferson County Dem. Exec. Com., 1958. Recipient Silver Anvil awards Pub. Relations Soc. Am., 1962, 64. Mem. Am. Coll. Pub. Relations Assn. (certificate of exceptional achievement 1963, trustee 1971-—), Edn. Writers Assn., Mid-South St. Andrews Soc., Omicron Delta Kappa, Sigma Nu. Presbyn. Home: 68 Tanglewood Rd Charlottesville VA 22901

CRAWFORD, FELIX CONKLING, dentist; b. Midland, Tex. Jan. 11, 1938; s. Marshall Holloway and Lela Mary (Heard) C.; student Tex. Technol. Coll. 1956-59; D.D.S., U. Tex., 1963; m. Roberta Jeanne Craze, July 22, 1961; children—Christin Kay, Boyd William. Pvt. practice dentistry, Plainview, Tex., 1965-—. Chmn. Hale County Health Bd., 1972. Served with Dental Corps, AUS, 1963-65. Mem. Am., Tex. dental assns., S. Plains Dist. Dental Soc. (v.p., 1972), Psi Omega, Sigma Alpha Epsilon. Rotarian (pres. 1970). Clubs: Knife and Fork (pres. 1967), Plainview Country (bd. dirs. 1969-72), Toastmasters (pres. 1968) (Plainview). Home: 1409 Canyon St Plainview TX 79072 Office: 2615 W 24th St Plainview TX 79072

CRAWFORD, FRANKLIN D., chmn. U.S. Hist. Documents Inst., Inc., Washington. Office: 1647 Wisconsin Av NW Washington DC 20007*

CRAWFORD, GRADY LELAND, judge; b. Palatka, Fla., Mar 22, 1915; s. Grady Leland and Emma (Creekman) C.; LL.B, John B. Stetson U., 1939; m. Alleyne Carolyn Foster, May 8, 1942; 1 dau., Lee Carolyn. Admitted to Fla. bar, 1939; asso. Shutts, Bowen, Simmons, Prevatt and Julian, 1939-42, partner, 1949-51; circuit judge 11th Judicial Circuit Fla. 1951-—. Chmn. Fla. State Conf. Circuit Judges, 1971-—. Chmn. Gov.'s Com. on Seminole Indian Affairs, 1959-60. Served from ensign to lt. comdr. USN, 1942-46. Mem Am., Fla., Dade County bar assns., Navy League, Am. Legion. Democrat. Episcopalian. Mason (33 deg.), Kiwanian (pres. 1959). Home: 7911 SW 58th St Miami FL 33143 Office: Court House Miami FL 33130

CRAWFORD, J. M., hosp. adminstr.; b. Waynesville, N.C., Feb. 7, 1931; s. Jerry Morris and Pearl (Davis) C.; B.S., Western Carolina U., 1953; student Duke U., 1968-69; m. Susie J. Stamey, June 9, 1952; children—Susan Leigh, Gregory Morris. Bus. mgr., asst. adminstr. Haywood County Hosp., Waynesville, 1953-67; adminstr. Angel Community Hosp., Franklin, N.C., 1967-—. Bd. dirs., mem. exec. com. State of Franklin Health Council. Mem. Am. Coll. Hosp. Adminstrs., N.C. Hosp. Assn. (chmn. Dist. I 1971-72). Democrat. Baptist. Home: Childress Rd Franklin NC 28734 Office: Riverview St Franklin NC 28734

CRAWFORD, JOE EARL, railroad exec.; b. nr. Bertram, Tex., May 14, 1933; s. Ralph Albert and Rena Vesta (Rowney) C.; student Dunham Sch. of Accounting, 1955; m. Geneva Henry, July 27, 1956; children— Joel Scott, Victor Dale, James Barton. With Georgetown R.R. Co. (Tex.), 1962-—, v.p. operations, 1965-—; v.p. Eureka Terminal Co., Houston, 1965-—. Campaign chmn. Heart Fund, 1971; pres. Indsl. Corp. Georgetown, 1970-71. Mem. Georgetown City Council, 1970-—; mayor, Georgetown, 1972-—. Served with USN, 1951-55. Mem. Georgetown C. of C. (pres. 1968). Mem. Ch. of Christ. Mason (32 deg.), Rotarian. Club: Georgetown Country. Home: 1804 Louise St Georgetown TX 78626 Office: 310 Austin Av Georgetown TX 78626

CRAWFORD, JOHN MILTON, JR., assn. exec.; b. Tyler, Tex., Jan. 7, 1939; s. John Milton and Winifred (Robinson) C.; B.B.A., U. Tex, 1961; m. Carolyn Tyson DeVault, Aug. 29, 1963. Field rep. U. Tex. Ex-Students Assn., 1961-62; asst. promotional dir. S.W. Republic Corp. 1965; exec. dir. Tex. Nursing Home Assn., 1965-69 (all Austin, Tex.); exec. v.p. Screen Printing Assn. Internat., Falls Church, Va., 1969-—; guest lectr. univs., 1966-67. Loan exec. United Fund, 1965; mem. exec. com. printing and pub. sect. Nat. Safety Council; mem. McLean Hamlet Citizens Assn. Democratic precinct worker, 1966-67. Mem. governing bd. McLean Community Center. Served with Intelligence Corps, AUS, 1962-65. Recipient SPOKE Jaycee award, 1961; Sparkplug Jaycee award, 1970, 71. Mem. McLean Jr. C. of C. (pres. 1971), Tex. Soc. Washington, Am., Washington socs. assn. execs., Internat. Platform Assn., Am. Coll. Nursing Home Adminstrs., Soc. Assn. Mgrs. (charter mem.), Meeting Planners Inst. (charter mem.), Postal Commerative Soc., Graphic Arts Assn. Execs., Cowboy Hall of Fame, U. Tex. Ex-students Assn., Delta Sigma Pi. Baptist. Editor: Caring, 1965-69, Spotlights, 1961-62, 65-66, Highlights, 1965. Contbr. articles newspapers, mags. in U.S. Home: 1318 Macbeth St McLean VA 22101 Office: 150 S Washington St Falls Church VA 22046

CRAWFORD, LESTER MILLS, JR., ednl. adminstr.; b. Demopolis, Ala., Mar. 13, 1938; s. Lester Mills and Susan Doris (Mitchell) C.; D.V.M., Auburn U., 1963; Ph.D., U. Ga., 1969; m. Catherine Walker, July 27, 1963; children—Catherine Leigh, Mary Stuart. Intern, Dr. J. P. Carney, Meridian, Miss., 1963; asso. veterinarian in group practice, Birmingham, Ala., 1963-64; regional tech. dir. S.E. region Am. Cyanamid Co., Atlanta, Ga., 1964-66; instr. pharmacology Coll. Vet. Medicine, U. Ga., Athens, 1966-68, asst. dean, 1968-70, asso. dean, 1970-—. Lectr. Council on Gerontology, U. System of Ga., 1968-—. Pres. Cedar Creek Civic Assn., Athens, Ga., 1971-72; chmn. Ga.-S.C. Vet. Conv., 1969. Mem. Am., Ga. vet. med. assns., History of Sci. Soc., Am. Soc. Animal Sci., Ga. Acad. Sci., A.A.A.S., Phi Kappa Phi, Sigma Xi, Phi Zeta, Omicron Delta Kappa, Jr. C. of C. Methodist (chmn. council on ministries 1971-72). Club: University of Georgia Faculty (bd. dirs. 1971-—). Contbr. articles to profl. pubs. Home: 260 Cedar Creek Dr Athens GA 30601

CRAWFORD, MARTIN, educator; b. Lake City, Tenn., Mar. 10, 1934; s. Guy and Hedwig Rosa (Walther) C.; B.S., U. Tenn., 1954, M.S., 1958; Ph.D. (U.S. Rubber Co. fellow), Ga. Inst. Tech., 1963; m. Carolyn Miree Johnson, Mar. 16, 1968; 1 son, Thomas McLendon. Instr. mech. engring. U. Tenn. at Knoxville, 1955-56; asst. prof. mech. engring. Va. Poly. Inst. at Blacksburg, 1956-58, asso. prof. mech. engring., 1962-64, 65-68; asso. prof. mech. engring. U. Ala. at Birmingham, 1968-70, prof. mech. engring., 1970-—. NSF sci.-faculty fellow U. Minn., 1964-65. Mem. A.A.A.S., Am. Soc. M.E., Am. Soc. Engring. Edn., Sigma Xi (award 1963), Phi Kappa Phi, Pi Tau Sigma, Tau Beta Pi. Home: 1405 Miami Dr Birmingham AL 35214

CRAWFORD, OLIVER RAY, paper co. exec.; b. Amarillo, Tex., July 19, 1925; s. George Gordon and Bell Elizabeth (Allston) C.; student Wash. State Coll., 1943-44, S. Tex. Sch. Law, 1953-55; m. Margaret Ann Barker, Jan. 1, 1946; children—Lynda Ann, Carolyn Rae, Richard Alan. Div. mgr. Phillips Petroleum Co., Midland, Tex., 1947-52; mgr. tax and tile dept. Houston Oil Co. Tex., 1952-56; asst. to gen. mgr. Southwestern Settlement and Devel. Co., Jasper, Tex., 1956-59; gen. mgr. Southwestern Timber Co., 1956-—; v.p. Eastex, Inc., 1956-—; v.p., treas. Jasper Timber Co., Newton Timber Co., Bleakwood Timber Co., San Augustine Timber Co., 1960-—; dir. First State Bank, Jasper. Mem. Tex. Liquor Control Bd., 1965-69. Pres. So. Forest Research Inst., 1963-—; adv. com. Tex. Forest Service, 1957-—; dir. Tex. forest industries com. Am. Forest Products Industries. Pres. Jasper Youth Baseball Assn., 1958-—. Bd. dirs. A.R.C., Operation Orphans, Inc., Tex. Law Enforcement Found.; mem. century council Tex. A. and M. U.; trustee Southwest Research Inst.; v.p., bd. dirs. Tex. chpts. Leukemia Soc. Am. Served as fighter pilot USAAF, 1943-45; brevet maj. gen. U.S. Air N.G. Named Man of Month, East Tex. C. of C., 1961; recipient hon. Lone Star Farmer degree Tex. Assn. Future Farmers; Forest Mgmt. award Nat. Lumber Mfrs. Assn.; Mr. East Texas award, operating dirs. of Tyler County Dogwood Festival, 1967. Hon. life mem. Jasper Youth Baseball, Nat. Congress P.T.A., Future Farmers Am.; mem. Am. Pulpwood Assn. (dir.), Tex. Forestry Assn. (dir., pres. 1970-71), Sportsman's Clubs Tex. (v.p., mem. exec. com.), Jasper C. of C. (pres. 1964), Def. Orientation Conf. Assn. Presbyn. Home: 971 Ogden St Jasper TX 75951 Office: 229 N Bowie St Jasper TX 75951

CRAWFORD, RICHARD GEORGE, newspaper editor; b. Sequim, Wash., Aug. 15, 1911; s. George E. and Julia T. (Fritz) C.; student Western Inst. Accounting, 1931-32. Adj. Gen.'s Sch., 1942; m. Olive O. Ericksen, Aug. 5, 1933; children—James Richard, Lawrence Robert. Joined U.S. Army, 1931; advanced through grades to lt. col., 1953; with 3d Inf. Div., II Corps, 5th Army, 1942-45; adj. gen. officer, 1945-49; adj. gen. Engring. Center, Ft. Belvoir, Va., 1949-52; sec. joint staff Alaskan Command, 1952-54; exec. officer; adj. gen. sect. Ft. Jackson, 1954-57; ret., 1957; founder Cape Coral (Fla.) Breeze Newspaper, 1961, mng. pub., 1966-—. Treas., dir. Citizens Mut. of Cape Coral, Inc., 1965-—; dir. Cape Coral Bank. Bd. dirs. Lee County Assn. Retarded Children, 1962-67, Lee County Cancer Soc., 1961-68. Decorated Bronze Star medal. Mem. Cape Coral C. of C. (pres. 1968). Home: 5363 Nautilus Dr Cape Coral FL 33904 Office: 1620 SE 47th Terrace Cape Coral FL 33904

CRAWFORD, VERNON D'ORSAY, educator; b. Amherst, N.S., Can., Feb. 13, 1919; s. Roy David and Lydia (Edgett) C.; B.A., Mount Allison U., Sackville, N.B., 1939; M.Sc., Dalhousie U., Halifax, N.S., 1943; Ph.D., U. Va., 1949; m. Helen Dell Avison, May 15, 1943; children—Lynn Kathleen (Mrs. David Hood), Dell Marie (Mrs. Ronald Byrd). Came to U.S., 1947; naturalized 1953. Physicist, Naval Research Establishment of Can., Halifax, N.S., 1943-45; lectr. Dalhousie U., 1944-47; asso. prof. physics Ga. Inst. Tech., Atlanta, 1949-55, prof., 1955-64, dir. sch. physics, 1964-68, dean gen. coll., 1968-69, acting pres., 1969, v.p. acad. affairs, 1969-—. Bd. dirs. Atlanta chpt. Leukemia Soc. Am., Inc. 1967-—. Mem. Sigma Xi, Phi Kappa Phi, Sigma Pi Sigma, Omicron Delta Kappa, Phi Kappa Sigma. Home: 1526 Walthall Ct NW Atlanta GA 30318

CRAWFORD, WILLIAM FRANKLIN, banker; b. Brookhaven, Miss., July 31, 1929; s. William F. and Lena (Moreton) C.; B.S., U. So. Miss., 1951, M.A., 1952, postgrad., 1953; m. Anne S. Jordan, Oct. 15, 1955; 1 son, Robert Michael. Asst. cashier, dir. State Bank & Trust Co., Brookhaven, 1954-58, asst. v.p., 1958-60, v.p., 1960-65, vice chmn. bd., 1965, chmn. bd., 1966-—. Treas., Brookhaven Beautiful; mem. adv. bd. Copiah-Lincoln Vocational Tech. Sch. Treas., bd. dirs. Brookhaven Music Assn.; bd. dirs. S.W. Miss. Devel. Dist. Chmn. bd. dirs. Miss. Sch. Banking, 1971. Mem. Am., Miss. bankers assns., Newcomen Soc. N.Am., Lincoln County C. of C. (pres.), Phi Delta Kappa, Kappa Delta Pi. Presbyn. Kiwanian. Club: Brookhaven Country. Home: 613 S Jackson St Brookhaven MS 39601 Office: PO Drawer 319 Brookhaven MS 39601

CRAYTON, JENKINS STREET, banker; b. Charleston, S.C., July 29, 1928; s. Maxwell Sloan and Juanita Jenkins (Street) C.; B.S. cum laude, Coll. Charleston, 1949; m. Betty Jane Goldsmith, Oct. 29, 1960; children—Jenkins Street, William G. With Citizens & So. Nat. Bank of S.C., Charleston, 1953-—, pres. computer subsidiary, 1968-69, sr. operations officer, v.p., 1969-—. Instr. Am. Inst. Banking, 1961, 69, 70, 71. Chmn. budget com. Charleston United Fund, 1966. Served with AUS, 1950-52. Mem. Alpha Tau Omega, Sigma Alpha Phi. Rotarian. Home: 4801 Devereaux Rd Columbia SC 29205 Office: 1801 Main St Columbia SC 29202

CREAGER, CHARLES EDWIN, mgmt. cons., economist; b. Hagerstown, Md., Oct. 20, 1925; s. Edwin and Mary Editn (Bloyer) C.; B.S., U. Balt., 1950, J.D., 1972; M.B.A., Am. U., Washington, 1959; m. Alice Eleanor Hollenbach, Oct. 9, 1948 (div. 1970); children—Charles Edwin, Karen Elaine and Roger Thomas (twins); m. 2d, Dolores Constance Yanuk, 1970. Traffic rep. Charlton Bros. Transp. Co., Inc., Balt., 1946-49; transp. cons., 1950-—. Gen. freight agt. Novick Transfer Co., Inc., Balt., 1949-58, So. div. sales mgr., Winchester, Va., 1958-59, gen. traffic mgr., 1960-62, v.p. traffic, 1962-64; dir. sales Halls Motor Transport, Sunbury, 1959-60; v.p. traffic Nat. Transport Co., Inc., Bridgeport, Conn., 1964-65, cons., 1965-—; partner Germelman, Alt & Creager, 1966-68; owner Charles E. Creager & Assos., Silver Spring, Md., 1968-—. Asst. prof., dir. transp. insts. Am. U., 1965-67. Served with USAAF, 1943-46. Bd. dirs. Middle Atlantic Conf., Washington, 1963-67. Mem. Eastern Shipper-Motor Carrier Council (pres. 1964-65, chmn. exec. com. 1965-66), Shenandoah Traffic Club, traffic clubs N.Y., Balt., Nat. Shipper Motor Carrier Conf. (exec. com. 1964-65), Assn. ICC Practitioners, Episcopalian. Elk. Club Winchester Golf and Country. Home: 816 Easley St Silver Spring MD 20910 Office: Suite 523 816 Easley St Silver Spring MD 20910

CREECH, DANTEN DAYLE, coll. pres.; b. Seiling, Okla., Aug. 1, 1917; s. Jesse Blaine and Frankie (Jacobs) C.; student John Brown U., 1933-35; B.S., Southwestern State Coll., Weatherford, Okla., 1938; M.S., Okla. State U., 1949; Ed.D., U. Okla., 1966; m. Dorothy Aline Buss, June 5, 1947; children—Cynthia Jan, James Robert, Dan. Tchr., Royal High Sch., 1938-40, Mutual High Sch., 1940-42; prin. Sharon High Sch., 1946-47; supt. Fargo Pub. Schs., 1947-50, Arnett Pub. Schs., 1950-57, Velma-Alma Pub. Schs., 1957-60, Pryor Pub. Schs., 1960-68 (all Okla.); supt. pub. instrn. State of Okla., Oklahoma City, 1968-70; pres. Northeastern Okla. A. and M. Coll., Miami, 1970-—. Served with USNR, 1942-46. Mem. Am., Okla assns. sch. adminstrs., Am., Okla. assns. jr. colls., Okla. Edn. Assn., Miami C. of C. Methodist. Rotarian. Home: 821 4th St NE Miami OK 74354

CREECH, GLENWOOD LEWIS, educator, univ. administr.; b. Middleburg, Ky., Dec. 31, 1920; s. Chester B. and Tennie (Estes) C.; B.S. in Agr. U. Ky., 1941, M.S. in Agrl. Edn., 1950; Ph.D., U. Wis., 1957; m. Martha J. Brooks, Apr. 4, 1942; children—Carolyn Ann (Mrs. Gordon Zaloom), Walton Brooks. Tchr. vocational agr. Stanford (Ky). High Sch., 1946-49; asso. prof. Nat. Agrl. Extension Center for Advanced Study, also dept. agrl. and extension edn., U. Wis., 1957-59; research specialist Coll. Edn., 1951-64; U. Ky., Lexington, asso. agrl. editor Coll. Agr., 1954-56, v.p. univ. relations, also prof. agrl. extension, 1965-—. Vis. prof. summer sch. Cornell U., 1958; dir. div. agr. W.K. Kellogg Found., Battle Creek, Mich., 1959-65; cons. Comm. on Rural-Devel., AID, U.S. Dept. of State, 1961-—, U.S. Dept. of Agr., 1957-—. Mem. U. Ky. Research Found. Bd. dirs. Lexington United Community Fund, 1968-71, Living Arts and Sci, Center, Inc., Lexington. Served with USAAF, 1941-46. Mem. Am. Coll. Pub. Relations Assn. (rep. U. Ky. 1965-—), Nat. Assn. State Univs. and Land Grant Colls., U. Ky. Athletics assn., (ex-officio bd. dirs. 1967-—), U. Ky. Alumni Assn. (ex-officio bd. dirs. 1965-—, Distinguished Service award 1970), Greater Lexington C. of C. (bd. dirs. 1966-69), Newcomen Soc. N.Am., Phi Delta Kappa. Home: Apt 2 3051 Kirklevington Dr Lexington KY 40502

CREEKMORE, J. HOWARD, bus. exec. Pres. Houston Endowment Inc., publishers of Houston Chronicle. Office: care Houston Chronicle 512-20 Travis St Houston TX 77002*

CREEL, LUIS J., JR., lawyer; b. Mexico City, Mexico, Oct. 21, 1942; B.S., Colegio Franco Ingles, Mexico City, 1960; student Loyola Coll., Montreal, Que., Can.; Licenciate in Law, Escuela Libre de Derecho, Mexico City, 1965; O.P.A.L., Princeton, 1966; LL.M., Harvard, 1967. Admitted to bar, Mexico, 1967; asso. firm Creel &Ogarrio, Mexico City; prof. pvt. internat. law Universidad Iberoamericana, 1967-69. Mem. Barra Mexicana, Colegio de Abogados, Inter-Am. Bar Assn. Office: Creel & Ogarrio Paseo de la Reforma 156 Mexico City 6 Mexico*

CREIGHTON, WILLIAM FORMAN, bishop; b. Phila., July 23, 1909; s. Frank Whittington and Maud R. (Hawk) C.; B.A., U. Pa., 1931, S.T.B., Phila. Div. Sch., 1934, D.D., 1957; D.D., Va. Theol. Sem., 1959; L.H.D., Rikkyo U. (Tokyo, Japan), 1964; m. Marie-Louise Forrest, June 2, 1934; children—William Wendel, Michael Whittington, Maxwell Forrest. Ordained deacon Episcopal Ch., priest, 1934; vicar, St. Mark's, Oakes, N.D., 1937-37; rector St. Clements Ch., St. Paul, 1937-43, St. Johns Ch., Bethesda, Md., 1946-59; bishop co-adjutor Diocese of Washington, 1959-62, bishop of Washington, 1962-—. Trustee Phila. Div. Sch., 1961-—, Va. Theol. Sem., 1962-—; chmn. bd. trustees Ch. Pension Fund. Served as chaplain USNR, 1943-46. Home: Mount St Alban Washington DC 20016 Office: Episcopal Ch House Mt Saint Alban Washington DC 20016

CRELLIN, DAVID ALEXANDER, pub. relations exec.; b. St. Clair Shores, Mich., Apr. 1, 1926; s. Charles G. and Kathleen M. (Carroll) C.; student Mich. State U., 1946-47, Wayne State U., 1947-50; m. Patricia J. Guzinski, May 18, 1964; children—Timothy M., Charles E., Wendy P., Michelle L., David Alexander, Heather K. Gen. reporter Detroit Times, 1947-51; sect. supr. sales operation Ford Motor Co., Dearborn, Mich., 1951-56, staff rep. pub. relations office, 1956-64, southwest pub. relations mgr., 1964-67; exec. v.p., partner Thomas J. Tierney & Assos., Inc., Dallas, 1967-70; pres. Glenn Pub. Relations, Dallas, 1970-—. Served with AUS, 1944-46. Mem. Press Club (bd. dirs. 1968), Pub. Relations Soc. Am. (bd. dirs. N. Tex. chpt. 1967-70). Home: 7261 Ashington St Dallas TX 75225 Office: Republic Bank Tower Dallas TX 75201

CREMEENS, CARLTON, TV journalist; b. Imboden, Ark., Jan 6, 1922; s. Arvil W. and Viola (Blansett) C.; student Little Rock U., 1951, 52, 53, N.W. Sch. Radio and TV, Hollywood, Cal., 1955; m. Helen Evelyn Johnson, Jan. 9, 1946; children—John Carlton, Paula Yvonne. Reporter, news dir. radio stas. KTHV, KTHS, Little Rock, 1955-60; news dir. sta. WAFB-TV, Baton Rouge, La., 1960-—; free lance writer on social issues for radio, TV sta. U.S., Can., 1957-—. Served with USNR, 1939-45. Contbr. fiction, articles to lit. mags., also to The Cosmos Reader, Handbook of Short Story Writing. Home: 1212 Country Club Dr Baton Rouge LA 70806 Office: 844 Government St Baton Rouge LA 70806

CRENSHAW, GORDON LEE, tobacco co. exec.; b. Richmond Va., Jan. 19, 1922; s. Walter and Hattie (Ready) C.; B.A. in Econ., U. Va., 1943; m. Deubre Anne Roper, May 12, 1945; children—Clarke Hutchins, Gordon Lee. With Universal Leaf Tobacco Co., 1946-—, v.p., 1958-65, pres., 1965-—, chief exec. officer, 1966-—, also dir.; dir. Life Ins. Co. Va., Va. Indsl. Devel. Corp., State Planters Bank of Commerce and Trusts. Bd. dirs. Richmond Boys Club Am., Nat. Tobacco Festival; bd. govs. Richmond Home for Boys. Served to lt. USNR, 1943-46. Mem. Tobacco Assn. U.S. (bd. govs., past pres.). Episcopalian. Home: 111 Windsor Way Richmond VA 23221 Office: 201 S 3d St Richmond VA 23219

CRENSHAW, JOHN THOMAS, physician; b. Maysville, Ga., Sept. 2, 1933; s. Howard and Annie Elizabeth (Morris) C.; B.S., U. Ga., 1960; M.D., Med. Coll. Ga., 1964; m. Frances Hallie Goodyear, June 15, 1964; children—Hallie Alisa, Elizabeth Ann. Intern, Spartanburg (S.C.) Gen. Hosp., 1964-65; gen. practice medicine, St. Marys, Ga., 1965-66, Clayton, 1967-—; mem. staff Rabun County Hosp., Clayton, Ga., Ridgecrest Med. Center, Clayton. Served with USNR, 1952-56. Mem. A.M.A., Ga., Rabun County (sec. 1971) med. socs. Clubs: Kingwood Country (Clayton). Home: PO Box 885 Clayton GA 30525 Office: P O Box 746 Clayton GA 30525

CRENSHAW, JOSEPH WILLIAM, state ofcl.; b. Millington, Tenn., Nov. 7, 1914; s. Ura and Helen (Anderson) C.; B.S., Memphis State U., 1935; M.A., Columbia, 1947, Ed.D., 1953; m. Mary E. Carmignani, Dec. 29, 1951; children—William Donald, Helen Camille. Asst. prin. Bolton High Sch., Arlington, Tenn., 1935-42; dean students, prof. edn. Pratt Inst., 1946-57; dean students, prof. edn. Jersey City State Coll., 1957-61; asst. dir. instructional services Fla. Dept. Edn., 1961-65, asst. commr. edn., 1965-—; dir. Southeastern Ednl. Lab., Atlanta, 1969-—. Vis. prof. Western Carolina U., summers 1963-70; cons. in field. Vice pres. Tallahassee Little Theater, 1966-67. Served with AUS, 1942-45; ETO. Mem. Am. (dir. 1965-69), Fla. (pres. 1970-71, v.p. 1971-72) assns. supervisions curriculum devel., Am. Psychol. Assn., Future Farmers Am. (hon.), Phi Delta Kappa, Kappa Delta Pi, Alpha Phi Omega. Democrat. Author: Student Administration of Activity Funds, 1954. Contbr. articles to profl. jours. Home: 2314 W Indian Head Dr Tallahassee FL 32301 Office: Knott Bldg Tallahassee FL 32304

CRESSE, JACK R., broadcasting exec. Vice pres., gen. mgr. KVOO, Tulsa. Office: 37th and Peoria Sts Tulsa OK 74105*

CRESSE, JOSEPH PARKER, state ofcl.; b. Cutler, Ind., Oct. 7, 1928; s. Bruce Dudley and Lela Mariam (Fisher) C.; B.A., U. Fla., 1950; m. Susie Marlene Heflin, June 11, 1955; children—Elaine, Kay. Jr. auditor Price Waterhouse & Co., N.Y.C., 1953-54; auditor State of Fla., Tallahassee, 1954-55; internal auditor, controller State Tb Bd., Tallahassee, 1955-60; budget examiner Budget Commn., State of Fla., Tallahassee, 1960-64, asst. budget dir., 1964-69, chief Bur. Budgeting, Dept. Adminstrn., 1969-71, asst. dir. planning and budgeting Dept. Adminstrn., 1971-—. Served with Adj. Gen. Corps, AUS, 1950-52. Mem. Nat. Assn. State Budget Officers, Beta Alpha Psi. Presbyn. Toastmaster (pres. 1964). Club: Killearn Golf and Country (Tallahassee). Home: 2917 Woodside Dr Tallahassee FL 32303 Office: Dept Adminstrn The Capitol Tallahassee FL 32304

CRETINI, EUGENE JOSEPH, JR., state ofcl.; b. New Orleans, Jan. 24, 1928; s. Eugene Joseph and Ernet (Elliott) C.; B.A. in Advt., La. State U., 1952; m. Blanche Vignes Myers, Jan. 30, 1960; 1 child, Julia. Picture editor mil. yearbooks Army & Navy Pub. Co., Baton Rouge, 1952-54; asst. dir. advt., promotion La. Dept. Commerce and Industry, Baton Rouge, 1954-56, dir. advt., promotion, 1965-—, editor La. Horizons, 1966-—; account exec. Ed Reed Orgn., Baton Rouge, 1956-64. Served with UNSR 1946-50. Home: 732 Leeward Dr Baton Rouge LA 70808 Office: La Dept Commerce and Industry PO Box 44185 Baton Rouge LA 70804

CREWS, MALCOLM KNIGHT, city ofcl.; b. Arcadia, Fla., Apr. 2, 1923; s. Chester Arthur and Florence Hortenze (Meliza) C.; student S.Fla. Jr. Coll., 1968-69; m. Betty G. Lanier, Apr. 16, 1955; children—Dennis Mark, Keith Knight. Asst. operations clk. Lodwick Aviation Mil. Acad., 1941-44; asst. sec.-treas. Avon Park Citrus Growers Assn. (Fla.), 1944-51; city clk., treas., tax collector city of Avon Park, 1951-55, city clk., treas., 1967-—; gen. mgr. Wells Better Homes Co., Avon Park, 1955-60; sec.-treas. Wells Motor Co., Avon Park, 1960-67; appraiser, dir. 1st Fed. Savs. and Loan Assn. Hardee County, Wauchula, Fla., 1960-—. Mem. Chrysler Corp. Accountants Inst. (life), Fla. Assn. Realtors, Fla. Municipal Finance Officers Assn., Fla. Assn. Assessing Officers, Fla. Pollution Control Assn., Avon Park C. of C. (past pres.). Baptist (treas., deacon, Sunday sch. tchr.). Lion. Home: 421 E State St Avon Park FL 33825 Office: City Hall Avon Park FL 33825

CREWSON, THOMAS STEWART, municipal ct. judge; b. Sand Springs, Okla., Oct. 13, 1933; s. Ura B. and Corinne (McIlhattan) C.; B.A., Okla. State U., 1956; J.D., U. Tulsa, 1962; postgrad. U. Denver, 1964, Northwestern U., 1966; m. Ella Wyatt Davis, Nov. 22, 1961. Jr. engr. tng. program, in land dept. Cities Service Oil Co., Bartlesville, Okla., 1957-59; admitted to Okla. bar, 1962; with firm Swift & Loving, Sand Springs, Okla., 1962; asst. county atty., Tulsa, Okla., 1962-65; with trust dept. First Nat. Bank, Colorado Springs, 1965-66; asst. dist. atty., Tulsa, 1966-69; municipal judge City of Tulsa, 1969-—. Mem. Tulsa Area Safety Council, 1964-—, Mayor's Safety Coordinating Com., 1969-70; active Community Chest, Pub. Health Assn. Served with inf., AUS, 1967. Mem. Am., Okla., Fed., Tulsa County bar assns., Am. Judicature Soc., Phi Alpha Delta, Kappa Sigma. Home: 304 E 29th Pl Tulsa OK 74114 Office: Civic Center Plaza Tulsa OK 74103

CRIDLIN, JOSEPH NELSON, judge; b. Jonesville, Va., Apr. 13, 1913; s. George P. and Sallie (Smith) C.; A.B., B.C.L., Coll. of William and Mary, 1935; m. Fay Fuller, June 12, 1946; children—George F., Josephine. Admitted to Virginia bar; practiced law in Jonesville, 1935-60; judge 24th Jud. Circuit of Va., 1961-—. Served as 2d lt. AUS, 1942-46. Mem. Am. Legion, 40 and 8. Methodist (bd. stewards). Mason, Lion. Home: Jonesville VA 24263

CRIPPEN, ROBERT LAUREL, astronaut; b. Beaumont, Tex., Sept. 11, 1937; s. Herbert W. and Ruth (Andress) C.; B.S. in Aerospace Engring., U. Tex., 1960; m. Virginia E. Hill, Sept. 8, 1959; children—Ellen M., Susan L., Linda R. Commd. ensign USN, 1960, advanced through grades to lt. comdr., 1969; completed naval aviation tng., 1962; attack pilot in U.S.S. Independence, 1962-65; student USAF Test Pilot Sch., Edwards AFB, Cal., 1965; mem. flight crew USAF Manned Orbiting Lab., 1966-69; astronaut NASA Manned Spacecraft Center, Houston, 1969-—. Office: Astronuat Office NASA Manned Spacecraft Center Houston TX 77058

CRISCILLIS, PAUL ADRIAN, postmaster; b. Caudill, Ky., Sept. 16, 1922; s. George Calvin and Margaret (Franklin) C.; student Cumberland Jr. Coll., 1939-41, U. Ky., 1941-43; B.S. in Phys. Sci., U. Chgo., 1944; m. Anne Elizabeth Bohannon, Dec. 9, 1945; children—Paul Adrian, Jr., Arthur Lee. Supr. logging operations Vestal Lumber &Mfg. Co., Knoxville, Tenn., 1946-47; bookkeeper, supt. sales Bobo & Denham Coal Co., Williamsburg, Ky., 1947-54; postmaster, Williamsburg, 1954-—. Dir. Farmers Nat. Bank, Williamsburg. Active youth groups. Served with USAF, 1943-46. Named Hon. Col. Ky. State Police, 1959, Ky. Col., 1966. Mem. Nat. Assn. Postmasters U.S. (chpt. pres. 1965), Am. Legion. Club: Optimist (pres. 1963) (Williamsburg, Ky.). Home: 291 S 3d St Williamsburg KY 40769 Office: US Post Office Williamsburg KY 40769

CRISMON, LEO TAYLOR, librarian; b. Iberia, Mo., Feb. 24, 1906; s. Frederick Pinkney and Sarah Elizabeth (Shelton) C.; A.B., William Jewell Coll., Liberty, Mo., 1930; Th.M., So. Bapt. Theol. Sem., Louisville, 1933, Ph.D., 1935; M.S. in L.S., Columbia, 1956; m. Viola Fowler, May 31, 1931; children—Leola Jo (Mrs. William M. Waller), Frederick William. Asst. librarian, asso. librarian, acting librarian So. Bapt. Theol. Sem., 1937-51, librarian, 1951-71; ret., 1971; library cons. libraries of sems. Fgn. Mission Bd., So. Bapt. Conv. in S.E. Asia, 1971-—. Mem. Am. Theol. Library Assn. Club: Filson (Louisville). Home: 404 Pleasantview Av Louisville KY 40206

CRISSMAN, WALTER EDGAR, superior ct. judge; b. nr. Siloam, N.C., Dec. 11, 1902; s. Charles Edgar and Ollie (Huff) C.; A.B., U. N.C., 1926, grad. law sch., 1928; m. Wilma Planzer, Apr. 6, 1935; children— Walter Edgar Jr., Kathryn Jane. Admitted to N.C. bar, 1929; individual practice law, High Point, N.C., 1929-55; asst. atty., High Point, 1938-44, pros. atty. municipal ct., High Point, 1945-46; judge superior ct. 18th Jud. Dist. N.C., 1955-—; dir. Carson's Inc., Crestwood Furniture Co., Davidson Electric Wholesale Supply Inc., Piedmont Electric Repair Co., Central Stone Works Inc. Chmn. High Point Democratic Exec. Com., 1933-43; mem. N.C. Ho. of Reps., 1945, 47, 49, 51, 53. Trustee Children's Home, Lexington, N.C., Wake Forest U., 1959-67. Mem. N.C. Bar Assn. (v.p. 1968-69), Conf. Superior Ct. Judges (pres. 1968-69), Chi Psi. Baptist (trustee, deacon, past state pres. brotherhood). Kiwanian, Mason. Home: 1310 Longcreek Dr High Point NC 27260 Office: City-County Bldg S Hamilton St High Point NC 27260

CRIST, ALLAN GILBERT, editor; b. Harrisburg, Pa., Dec. 14, 1908; s. Charles West and Mabel (Weand) C.; grad. high sch.; m. Violet Mary Stuart, June 1, 1931 (dec. Apr. 24, 1945); children—Larry Stuart, Diane (Mrs. James Prichard); m. 2d, Margaret Jean Zimmerman, Nov. 26, 1953; children—Lucinda, Ann, Laura. Reporter The Patriot, Harrisburg, 1926-29, U.P., Harrisburg, Buffalo, 1929-30, N.Y.C., Harrisburg, 1931, Brit. United Press, Ltd., Toronto, Ont., Can., 1930-31, A.P., Phila., Harrisburg, 1931-36, Harrisburg, 1937-40, 45-46, Phila. Inquirer, 1937, Pa. Dept. Mil. Affairs, 1946; editor Nat. Guardsman, Nat. Guard Assn. U.S., Washington, 1947-—. Served with AUS, 1941-45. Home: 705 Woodside Pkwy Silver Spring MD 20910 Office: Nat Guardsman Nat Guard Assn U S 1 Massachusetts Av NW Washington DC 20001

CRISWELL, VIVIAN SAM, educator, agrl. cons.; b. Purcell, Okla., Aug. 20, 1907; s. John Jefferson and Henretta Ellen (McDonald) C.; student E. Central State Coll., Ada, Okla., 1931-32; B.S., Okla. State U., 1941, M.S., 1964; m. Nora Celesta Boyd, Dec. 26, 1935; children—Joyce (Mrs. Harold Wayne Burton), Patricia (Mrs. Stephen K. Kim), Beverly. Tchr., prin. Gerty (Okla.) Sch., 1932-36, Ladd Sch., Purcell, Okla., 1936-39; adminstrv. officer Agrl. Adjustment Agy., Idabel, Okla., 1942-44; county extension dir. Okla. State U., Stigler, Eufaula, Idabel, and McAlester, 1944-71; agrl. cons. 1st Nat. Bank and Trust Co., McAlester, 1972-—. Chmn., McAlester Model Cities Adv. Com., 1968-—, McAlester Safety Council, 1960-—. Recipient Distinguished Service award Nat. Assn. County Agrl. Agts., 1955, Community Service award McAlester Kiwanis Club, 1970. Mem. Okla. Assn. County Extension Agts. (pres. 1967-68), Alpha Zeta. Presbyn. (trustee, deacon, elder, 1941-71, supt. Sunday sch. 1954-71). Mason (32 deg.), Lion (pres. 1962-63, dep. dist. gov. 1965-66). Author overall econ. devel. program for Pittsburg County (Okla.) Home: 1401 E Miami McAlester OK 74501 Office: 1st Nat Bank and Trust Co. P.O. Box 948 McAlester OK 74501

CRISWELL, W.A., clergyman; b. Eldorado, Okla., Dec. 19, 1909; s. Wallie Amos and Anna (Currie) C.; A.B., Baylor U., 1931; D.D., 1945; Th.M., So. Bapt. Theol. Sem., Louisville, 1934, Ph.D., 1937; m. Betty Harris, Feb. 14, 1935; 1 dau., Mabel Ann. Ordained to ministry First Bapt. Ch., Amarillo, Tex., 1927; pastor First Bapt. Ch., Chickasha, Okla., 1937-41, Muskogee, Okla., 1941-44, Dallas, 1944-—. Dir. Relief and Annuity Bd. Southern Bapt. Conv., conv. pres., 1968-70; mem. exec. bd., Tex. Bapt. Conv. Trustee So. Bapt. Theol. Sem., Louisville, Baylor U., Waco. Tex. Author: The Gospel According to Moses, 1950; These Issues We Must Face, 1953; Did Man Just Happen, 1956; Five Great Questions of The Bible, 1958; (with others) Passport to the World, 1951; Five Great Affirmations of the Bible, 1959; Expository Notes on Gospel of Matthew, 1961; Expository Sermons on the Revelations, 1962; The Bible in Today's World 1965; The Holy Spirit in Today's World 1966; In Defense of the Faith, 1967; Expository Sermons on Daniel, 1968; Why I Preach that the Bible Is Literally True, 1969; Preaching at the Palace, 1969; Look Up Brother, 1970. Home: 5901 Swiss Av Dallas TX 75214 Office: First Bapt Ch Dallas TX 75221

CRITCHFIELD, RICHARD PATRICK, journalist; b. Mpls., Mar. 23, 1931; s. Ralph James and Ann (Williams) C.; B.A., U. Wash., 1953; M.S., Columbia, 1957; student Leopold Fraenzens U., Innsbruck, Austria, 1958, U. Vienna (Austria), 1958-59, Northwestern U., 1960. Reporter, Cedar Valley Daily Times, Vinton, Ia., 1955-56; Washington corr. Salt Lake City Deseret News, also other papers Munroe News Bur., Washington, 1957-58; acting asst. prof. U. Nagpur (India), 1960-62; Asian corr. Washington Star, 1963-68, White House corr., Washington, 1968-69, spl. projects writer, 1971-72. Vice pres. Internat. Relations Club, Nagpur, 1961-62. Served with AUS, 1953-55; Korea. Recipient travel award Alicia Patterson Fund, 1969-71; Ford Found. grantee, 1972-—. Mem. Cercle Sportif Saigonnais, Phi Kappa Psi. Clubs: Overseas Press (award best daily reporting Viet Nam 1965) (N.Y.C.); Nat. Press (Washington). Author: The Indian Reporter's Guide, 1962; The Long Charade: Political Subversion in the Vietnam War, 1968; also articles. Editor, illustrator: Lore and Legend of Nepal, 1962. Home: Bannockburn Farm Blake Lane Oakton VA 22124 Office: Evening Star 2d and Virginia Sts Washington DC 20003

CRITES, SHERMAN EDWIN, communications co. exec.; b. Chadron, Neb., Jan. 12, 1918; s. Frederick A. and Marion (Hart) C.; student Neb. State Coll., 1934-37; B.S., Mass. Inst. Tech., 1941; M.S., N.Y. U., 1947; m. Florence Virginia Stiles, Dec. 22, 1940; children—Sherman Edwin, Patricia L., James F. Various engring. positions Pan Am. World Airways, N.Y.C., 1941-47, asst. prof. A. and M. Coll. of Tex., 1947-49, asso. prof. 1949-50; product planning engr. aircraft gas turbine div. Gen. Electric Co., Lynn, Mass., 1950-52, mgr. new product planning, Evendale, O., 1952-55, from mgr. product planning to mgr. marketing, small aircraft engine dept., Lynn, 1955-60; v.p., gen. mgr. transmission products dept. ITT Kellogg, Raleigh, N.C., 1960-62; pres., chief exec. officer Aero Electronics, Inc. (now Aerotron, Inc.), Raleigh, 1962-65, pres., chmn. bd., 1965-71; pres. C.H. Electronics, Inc., Raleigh, 1971-—, also dir. Mem. Gov.'s Tech. Utilization Adv. Bd. for State of N.C. various community drives. Bd. dirs. United Fund Wake County; adv. bd. N.C. Vet. Research Found. Mem. Am. Horse Show Assn. Clubs: Carolina Country, Sphinx; United Hunt Racing. Home: Pine Hall Farm 5300 Castlebrook Dr Raleigh NC 27604 Office: PO Box 14042 Raleigh NC 27610

CRITTENDEN, JOHN, editor. Sports editor Miami (Fla.). News. Office: 1 Herald Plaza Miami FL 33101*

CRITTENDON, WILLIAM D., editor. Polit. sci. and sci. editor U. S.C. Press. Office: Univ of SC Press Columbia SC 29208*

CROCKER, ROWELL THOMAS, lawyer; b. Bruce, Miss., Feb. 20, 1898; s. George Campbell and Catherine (Chrestman) C.; M.A., Baylor U., 1949 Admitted to Miss. bar, 1920, D.C. bar, 1950, Supreme Ct. U.S., 1944; mem. law firm Evans & Crocker, Calhoun City, Miss., 1920-28; head dept. history Clarke Meml. Coll., Newton, Miss., 1930-34; mem. law firm Horne & Crocker, Jackson, Miss., 1936-37; pvt. law practice and legal and hist. research Tex. and S.W. U.S., 1937-—. Mem. Miss. Ho. of Reps., 1920-24. Mem. Am. Bar Assn., Am. Judicature Soc. Home: Box 1163 Jackson MS 39205

CROCKER, WILLIAM HENRY, anthropologist; b. San Francisco, Aug. 20, 1924; s. William Willard and Ruth Mary (Hobart) C.; B.A., Yale, 1950; M.A., Stanford, 1953; Ph.D., U. Wis., 1962; m. Elizabeth Roma Dillon Smyth, Apr. 11, 1969; 1 son, Myles Hobart; step-children—Granha, Michael, Tara, Hugh, Philip. Asso. curator dept. anthropology Mus. Natural History, Smithsonian Instn., Washington, 1962-—. Former Provident Securities Co., San Franciso 1965-69; tchr., cons. George Washington U., Washington, from 1965; pres. Internat. Student House, Washington, 1971-74. Trustee Mary A. Crocker Trust, San Francisco. Served with AUS, 1943-46. Fellow Am. Anthrop. Assn. Clubs: Cosmos (Washington); Pacific Union, Bohemian (San Francisco). Home: 3333 P St NW Washington DC 20007 Office: Dept Anthropology Smithsonian Instn Washington DC 20560

CROCKETT, GIBSON MILTON, editorial cartoonist, artist; b. Washington, Sept. 18, 1912; s. Hal Gibson and Gertrude (Lentz) C.; student pub. schs.; m. Florence Elizabeth Crockett, July 4, 1937; children—David (dec.), Gary Abbott (dec.), Sandra Lea. Apprentice, Washington Evening Star, 1933-34, successively artist, gen. cartoonist, ct. sketching, 1942-47, sport cartoonist, editorial cartoonist, 1948-—; art dir. Am. Pub. Co., Washington, 1944-—; portrait painter; exhibited one man shows, George Washington U. Library, Evening Star; group shows Smithsonian Inst., Arts Club (all Washington), Rockville (Md.) Civic Center, Silver Spring (Md.) Gallery, Am. Watercolor Soc., N.Y. Bd. trustees Am. Art League. Mem. Washington Landscape Club (pres. 1961-62). Club: Manor Country (Norbeck, Md.). Home: 4713 Great Oak Rd Rockville MD 20853 Office: 225 Virginia Av SE Washington DC 20003

CROLEY, JAMES EVERETT, JR., dentist; b. Corbin, Ky., May 14, 1924; s. James Everett and Huldah (Schormann) C.; student Cumberland Coll., 1941-43, Berea Coll., 1943-45; D.D.S., U. Mo., 1947; m. Anna Lou House, June 8, 1947; children—James Everett III, Jennifer Lou. Pvt. practice dentistry, Middlesboro, Ky., 1947-50, Pineville, Ky., 1953-—. Mayor, City of Pineville, 1958-62. Mem. adv. com. Ky. Tourist and Travel Commn., 1960-64, Union Coll. Environmental Ednl. Center, 1970-—, Ky. Med. Assistance Program, 1972-—. Trustee Cumberland Coll.; bd. dirs. outdoor drama Book of Job. Served with USNR, 1943-45, 51-53. Named Outstanding Young Man, Ky., 1957. Mem. Am., Ky. State dental assns., Southeastern Dist. Dental Soc. (pres. 1954-55, 1968-69). Republican. Baptist. Home: 145 Horseshoe Dr Pineville KY 40977 Office: Flocoe Drug Bldg Pineville KY 40977

CROMARTIE, JOHN LLOYD, poultry exec.; b. Gainesville, Ga., June 10, 1905; s. Jefferson and Mary Magadline (Richardson); ed. pub. schs.; m. Frances Williard Hubbs, Dec. 22, 1935; children—Margaret Lee (Mrs. Robert L. Walls), John Lloyd, Sarah Huske. With Ga. Hwy. Dept., 1923-29; bookkeeper, salesman, sales mgr., gen. mgr., v.p. wholesale feed, grocery and bldg. material co., Gainesville, 1929-50; founder, head John L. Cromartie Co., Gainesville, 1950-—; founder Twin Oaks Hatchery, Inc., Gainesville, 1950, pres., dir., 1954-—; pres., dir. Helen Feed Store, Inc. (Ga.),1954-—, C.W.T. Farms, Inc., 1958-—; v.p., dir. Lanier Feed Mills, Inc., 1958-—; sec., dir. Lanier Sales Co., Inc., 1962-—, Orbit Egg Co., Inc., 1964-—; dir. Mar-Jac Poultry Co., Inc. Commr., City Gainesville, 1960-65, mayor pro tem, 1963-64, mayor, 1965-70. Scoutmaster, N.E. Ga. council Boy Scouts Am., 1935-40, troop committeeman, treas. exec. com., 1935-72; mem. Upper Chattahoochee Devel. Commn., 1965-—; mem. community devel. com. Nat. League Cities, 1964-—; mem. Ga. Mountains Planning-Devel. Commn., 1964-—, Gainesville-Hall County Econ. Opportunity Orgn., 1965-—; mem. Hall County Library Bd., 1964-—. Trustee Joint Municipal Employees Retirement System. Recipient Silver Beaver award Boy Scouts Am., 1961. Mem. United Comml.

Travelers, Ga. Poultry Producers' (pres. 1965), Ga. Poultry Fedn. (dir.), Ga. Municipal Assn. (pres. 1966-67, exec. bd., dir.), Gainesville-Hall County C. of C., Ga. Feed Dealers Assn. (sec.-treas. 1960-61). Methodist (ofcl. bd. 1963-65). Lion, Elk. Club: Chattahoochee Country. Home: 1171 Dixon Circle NW Gainesville GA 30501 Office: PO Box 1396 Gainesville GA 30501

CROMER, DAVID ANDREWS, supt. schs.; b. Tryon, N.C., Nov. 24, 1922; s. John S. and Ruth (Farr) C.; A.B., Wofford Coll., 1944; M.A., Columbia, 1954. Instr., Carlisle Mil. Sch., Bamberg, S.C., 1944-49; tchr. Tryon High Sch., 1950; prin. Stearns Sch., Columbus, 1951-55, Alamance Sch., Greensboro, 1956-59; supt. Polk County Schs., Columbus, 1959— (all N.C.). Treas. N.C. State Theatre; trustee Patterson Sch.; v.p. Tryon Little Theatre; bd. dirs. Vagabond Sch. Drama; mem. bd. vis. Brevard Music Center. Served with AUS, 1943. Mem. Am. Assn. Sch. Adminstrs., N.E.A., Am. Guild Organists, Tryon Concert Assn. (pres.), N.C., Polk County edn. assns., Lambda Chi Alpha. Episcopalian. Clubs: Men's (past pres.), Kiwanis. Home: Box 428 Tryon NC 28782 Office: Box 697 Columbus NC 28722

CRONIN, RALPH MARVIN, operating co. exec.; b. Dayton, O., Dec. 13, 1907; s. Aaron J. and Esther (Levit) C.; B.Sc., Ohio State U., 1929; Ph.D., U. Mich., 1942; m. Ruthlouise Sachs, Jan. 13, 1939. With Keller Crescent Co., Evansville, Ind., 1930-39, 47-69, v.p., 1955-69; with Jam Handy Orgn., Detroit, 1940-41; dir., v.p. Nat. Industries, Inc., Louisville, 1964—; v.p., dir. Found. Life Ins. Co., Atlanta, 1964-66; v.p. Lasalle Nat. Ins. Co. Chgo., 1965-69; dir. Computer Research Inc., Pitts., Gen. Nursing Homes, Inc. Pres., Nat. Conf. Christians and Jews, Louisville, 1969—, nat. trustee, 1971—. Trustee Old Ky. Home council Boy Scouts Am. Served to lt. with USNR, 1942-46. Recipient Distinguished Selling award, Nat. Sales Execs., 1964. Mem. Sales Execs. (pres. 1960-61), Am. Marketing Assn. (dir., named Man of Yr. 1972), Navy League (pres. Louisville, nat. trustee), Civil War Roundtable. Club: Jefferson. Home: 2352 Village Dr Louisville KY 40205 Office: 510 W Broadway Louisville KY 40201

CRONIN, WALTER FRANCIS, govt. ofcl.; b. Oneida, N.Y., Aug. 16, 1917; s. Frank T. and Rose E. (Lanz) C.; A.B., Hamilton Coll., 1938; A.M., Fletcher Sch. Law and Diplomacy, 1939; postgrad. Sch.Advanced Internat. Studies, 1946; Ph.D., Harvard, 1950; m. Ardith Lakin, Sept. 13, 1947; children—Jefferson Shaw, Gregory Lanz. With Oneida Ltd., 1939-40, Gen. Electric Co., 1940-41; with U.S. Dept. of State, 1949-67, prof. Fgn. Service Inst., 1962-67; chief historian U.S. Dept. Transp., Washington, 1967—. Served to capt. AUS, 1942-46. Mem. Am. Polit. Sci. Assn., Am. Hist. Assn., Phi Beta Kappa, Delta Sigma Rho. Home: 607 Poplar Dr Falls Church VA 20046 Office: US Dept Transp Washington 20590

CRONVICH, ALWYNN JOSEPH, lawyer, sheriff; b. New Orleans, Apr. 16, 1921; s. James A. and Mary Louise (Lester) C.; B.B.A., Tulane U., 1940, J.D., 1948; m. Berenice Hautau, June 30, 1948; children—Fred Lester, Alwynn Lee, Karen Ann. Accountant, supr. pub. funds State of La., 1941-42; admitted to La. bar, 1948; practice law, New Orleans, 1948-62, Metairie, La., 1962—; mem. firms Cronvich, Ciaccio, Wambsgans & Perry, 1962-68, Cronvich & Wambsgans, 1969—. Sheriff of Jefferson Parish (La.), 1964—; bd. dirs. Met. Bank of Jefferson, Metairie. Mem. La. Commn. on Law Enforcement; pres. Met. Law Enforcement Commn. Mem. adv. bd. Christ in Christmas com. Our Lady of the Rivers and Madonna Manor, 1964—. Bd. mem. Columbian Found., Inc., New Orleans. 1959—, legal counsel, 1959—. Served to lt. comdr. USNR, 1942-46. Recipient awards including Outstanding Lawman of Year award Kiwanis Club, 1968, Service to law enforcement award Met. Crime Commn., 1967, Am. Legion award, 1971. Mem. Am., La. State (ho. of dels. 1963-66), Jefferson Parish bar assns., Am. Trial Lawyers Assn., Nat. (state dir.), La. (chmn. various coms.) sheriff's assns., Blue Key. Democrat. Roman Catholic (trustee). K.C. Kiwanian. Home: 10024 Hyde Pl New Orleans LA 70123 Office: 3300 Metairie Rd Metairie LA 70001 also New Courthouse Bldg Gretna LA 70053

CROOK, ROBERT LACEY, state senator, lawyer; b. Bolton, Miss., Apr. 22, 1929; s. Walter Barber and Louise (Lacey) C.; student U. Miss., 1952-53; LL.B., Jackson Sch. Law, 1965; m. Brigita Vija Nerings, Sept. 20, 1953; children—Robert Lacey II, Hubert William. Operator, Ruleville (Miss.) Dry Cleaners, 1953-60; Miss. dir. Civil Def., Jackson, 1960-64; admitted to Miss. bar, 1965, since practiced firm R.L. Crook, Ruleville; mem. Miss. Senate, 1964—. Mem. adv. bd. St. Dominic Hosp., Jackson, Miss. Served with USMC, 1949-51. Mem. State Civil Def. Dirs. Assn. (nat. v.p. 1962-63), Miss. Bar Assn., Am. Legion, S.C.V., Order Stars and Bars. Democrat. Home: 3615 Crane Jackson MS 39216 also Ruleville MS 38771 Office: 118 N Ruby Av Ruleville MS 38771

CROOM, WILLIAM STERLING, physician; b. Morrilton, Ark., July 3, 1925; s. Adlai Stevenson and Margaret Price (Harris) C.; student Phillips U., 1943, Harding Coll., 1943, Abilene Christian Coll., 1943-44; M.D., U. Okla., 1948; m. Karen Ausburn, June 3, 1968; children—William Sterling, Brad Franklin, Christian. Intern, U. Ind. Med. Center, Indpls., 1948-49; resident internal medicine U. Okla. Hosp., 1949-52; pvt. practice internal medicine, Oklahoma City, 1952-53, Lubbock, Tex., 1953—; mem. staff Methodist, St. Mary's hosps., (both Lubbock); courtesy staff W. Tex. Hosp., Lubbock; clinical asst. internal medicine U. Okla. Hosps., 1952-53; asso. clin. prof. medicine Tex. Technol. U., 1972—. Served to lt. USNR, 1954-56. Diplomate Am. Bd. Internal Medicine. Fellow. Am. Coll. Chest Physicians; mem. A.C.P., Tex. Acad. Internal Medicine, Am. Heart Assn., Tex. Med. Assn., Phi Chi. Republican. Mem. Ch. of Christ. Club: Lubbock Country. Home: 6219 Kenosha Dr Lubbock TX 79413 Office: 3801 19th St Lubbock TX 79410

CROSBY, HAROLD BRYAN, univ. pres.; b. Jacksonville, Fla., Sept. 21, 1918; s. Arthur Francis and Marie (Long) C.; student Northwestern U., 1934-35, 36-37; LL.B., U. Fla., 1948; m. Margaret Frances Dutton, Apr. 18, 1939; children—Susan Frances, Anne Bryan. With Atlantic Coast R.R. Co., 1937-41; res. prof. law U. Fla. Coll. Law, 1948; admitted to Fla. bar, 1948; pvt. practice, Kissimmee and Pensacola, 1948-55; circuit judge 1st Jud. Circuit Fla., 1955-60; prof. law U. Fla., 1960-64, asst. dean Coll. Law, 1961-62, dean univ. relations and devel., 1962-64; pres. U. W. Fla., Pensacola, 1964—. Dir. Fla. Trial Judges Seminar, 1960-61, 64; Southeastern dir. Joint Com. Effective Adminstrn. Justice, 1961-62; dir. S.E. Seminar State Trial Judges, 1962; mem. Nat. Conf. Commrs. Uniform State Laws, 1962-64; cons. Fla. Constl. Adv. Commn., 1956-57; Fla. commr. to promote uniformity legislation, 1962-64; mem. com. standard jury instructions Supreme Ct. Fla., 1962-64; mem. commn. on colls. So. Assn. Colls. and Schs., 1970—; pres. Assn. Upper Level Colls. and Univs., 1970—; mem. exec. com. Fla. Assn. Colls. and Univs., 1970—. Chmn. W. Fla. Natural Resources Council. Trustee U. Fla. Law Rev., 1961, U. Fla. Law Center Assn., 1961; bd. dirs. U. Fla. Center, 1962-64. Served to maj. USAAF, 1942-45, USAF, 1951-53. Mem. Fla. Bar (bd. govs. 1950-52, pres. jr. bar sect. 1951-52), Am. Bar Assn. (Fla. chmn. jr. bar sect. 1951), Order of Coif, Theta Xi, Phi Alpha Delta, Fla. Blue Key, Phi Kappa Phi. Methodist (trustee, past ofcl. bd.). Contbr. articles legal jours. Home: 30 Rockwood Rd River Gardens Pensacola FL 32504

CROSBY, HENRY EDWARD, dentist; b. Ridgeland, S.C., Apr. 12, 1940; s. Henry Edward and Dale (Theus) C.; B.S., U. S.C., 1962; D.M.D., U. Ala., 1966; m. Patricia McCollum, July 6, 1963; children—Shelly, Moss, Chris. Practice dentistry, Georgetown, S.C., 1968—; mem. staff Georgetown County Hosp. Served to capt. USAF, 1966-68. Mem. Georgetown Mental Health Assn., Jr. C. of C. (parliamentarian 1970-71, trustee Danny Dawson Meml. Fund). Methodist (lay leader 1971, adminstrv. bd. 1970-71). Mailing Address: 419 Wood St Georgetown SC 29440 Home: Box 499A Allston St Georgetown SC 29440 Office: 419 Wood St Georgetown SC 29440

CROSS, BILLY BENSON, supr. schs.; b. Lebanon, Va., Dec. 25, 1935; s. Floyd Gilmen and Bessie Lee (Price) C.; B.S., Va. Poly. Inst., 1958; M.S., E. Tenn. State U., 1966; m. Clara Ruth Caudill, Oct. 10, 1957; children—Billy G., Diane Rebecca, Vicki Sue. Tchr. chemistry Lebanon High Sch., 1958-65, asst. prin., 1965-68; gen. supr. Russell County Schs., Lebanon, 1968—, chmn. sci. dept., 1966—; farmer raising dairy cattle, Lebanon 1959—; operator, owner West and East Lebanon Laudromatts, 1962—, retail gasoline sta., Lebanon, 1965—, beauty salons, 1968—, bldg. contracting and real estate, 1970—. Bd. dirs. Boy Scouts Am., Lebanon. Named Russell County Bus. Man of Year, Lebanon Jaycees, 1966. Mem. Nat., Va., Russell County (treas. 1967) edn. assns., Russell County Tchr. Assn. (treas. 1968—), Lebanon Jr. C. of C. (sec. 1966), Phi Delta Kappa, Methodist (supr. Sunday sch. 1969-71). Woodsman. Home: Box 576 Lebanon VA 24266

CROSS, CHARLES BRINSON, JR., lawyer; b. Portsmouth, Va., Mar. 10, 1914; s. Charles Brinson and Ethel (Maywood) C.; student William and Mary Coll., 1930-32; J.D., Washington and Lee U., 1936; m. Eleanor Royce Phillips, Apr. 19, 1944; children—Martha Eleanor, Charlotte Marie. Admitted to Va. bar, 1936; law practice in Portsmouth, Norfolk, South Norfolk and Norfolk County, 1936-61; comm. in chancery Circuit Ct., Chesapeake, Va., 1949, Portsmouth, 1950-53, Norfolk, 1956-61, Corp. Ct., South Norfolk, 1953-56; clk. Circuit Ct., County of Norfolk, 1961-63, City of Chesapeake, Va., 1963—. Mem. Va. Ho. of Reps., 1956-61; mem. Va. Commn. Constnl. Govt., 1959-63. Mem. Democratic State Central Com., 1964-66. Chpt. chmn. Portsmouth A.R.C., 1950-51; bd. visitors Old Dominion U., 1962-68. Bd. dirs. Va. State Library, Tidewater Community Coll. Served to lt. comdr. USNR, 1941-45. Recipient Outstanding Civic Achievement award Chesapeake C. of C., 1966; First Citizen award Jr. C. of C., 1970. Mem. Va., Norfolk-Portsmouth, Chesapeake bar assns., So., Va. hist. socs., Norfolk County Hist. Soc. of Chesapeake, Co. of Mil. Historians, Chesapeake C. of C. (v.p.), Kappa Alpha, Phi Delta Phi. Democrat. Methodist. Mason (32 deg., Shriner), Kiwanian (pres. Portsmouth 1942, Chesapeake 1966). Club: Churchland Ruritan (pres. 1962). Author: The County Court 1637-1904, Norfolk County, Virginia; The Chesapeake-A Biography of a Ship (Am. Assn. State and Local History certificate of commendation 1969); Memoirs of Helen Calvert Maxwell Read, 1970. Co-author: Glencoe Diary, 1968. Home: 320 Kemp Lane Chesapeake VA 23325 Office: Civic Center PO Box 15205 Chesapeake VA 23322

CROSS, DONALD MELVIN, state legislator; b. Meridian, Miss., Aug. 14, 1935; s. Will Joe and Eula (Todd) C.; B.S., Miss. Coll., 1957; m. Frances L. Abernathy, June 11, 1961; children—Julianne, Donald Joseph. Mem. Miss. Ho. of Reps., 1966—. Served with AUS, 1958-60. Mem. Miss. Marine Resource Council, Am. Legion, Miss. C. of C., Jr. C. of C., Am. Soc. M.E., V.F.W. Home: 3 Grandview Dr Vicksburg MS 39180

CROSS, GEORGE LYNN, educator, banker; b. Woonsocket, S.D., May 12, 1905; s. George William and Jemima (Dawson) C.; B.S., S.D. State Coll., 1926, M.S., 1927, D.Sc. (hon.), 1960; Ph.D., U. Chgo, 1929; LL.D., Oberlin Coll., 1960; m. Cleo Sikkink, Oct. 26, 1926; children—Mary-Lynn, George W., Braden Riehl. Instr., head dept. botany U. S.D., 1930-34; prof. botany U. Okla., 1934-38, head dept. botany, 1939-42, acting dean, Grad. Coll., 1942-44; acting dir., Research Inst., 1942-44, pres. of univ., 1944-68, pres. emeritus, prof. botany and microbiology, 1968—; chmn. bd. Fed. Home Loan Bank of Topeka, 1960-68, Am. Exchange Bank, & Trust Co., Norman, Okla.; dir. Friendly Nat. Bank, Central Nat. Bank, Oklahoma City, Midland Mortgages Investors Trust, Santa Ana, Cal. Pub. panel 8th Dist. War Labor Bd., 1942. Trustee Assn. Sci. and Industry; exec. council U. Okla. Research Inst.; research com. Okla. Med. Research Found.; mem. bd. dirs., pres. Okla. Health Scis. Found., 1968—; pres. Okla. Presbyn. Found., Inc., 1969—; mem. bd. dirs. Okla. Association Mental Health, 1969—; director Thomas Gilcrease Inst. Am. History and Art, Okla. Cowboy Hall of Fame. Harry S. Truman Library, Inc. Elector N.Y.U. Hall of Fame, 1951; elected Okla. Hall of Fame, 1951; recipient citation for promotion religious and racial understanding in Okla., Am. Conf. Christians and Jews, 1st annual human relations award, Southwestern regional Anti-Defamation League of B'nai B'rith Found. Fellow A.A.A.S.; mem. Nat. Assn. State Univ. Profs. (pres. 1959-60), Am. Assn. Univ Profs., Nat. Farm Chemurgic Council, Torrey Bot. Club, Bot. Soc. Am., N.E.A., Okla. Acad. Sci., Nat. Geog. Soc., Am. Soc. Naturalists, Nat. Planning Assn. (nat. council), Okla. Hist. Soc., C. of C.,Newcomen Soc., Sigma Xi, Phi Sigma, Phi Beta Kappa, Alpha Phi Omega, Omicron Delta Kappa. Presbyn. Club: Men's Dinner (pres. 1960) (Oklahoma City). Home: 812 Mockingbird Lane Norman OK 73069

CROSS, GUSTAV CARLSON, auditor; b. Jacksonville, Fla., Sept. 14, 1934; s. Fred Edgar and Margaret Elizabeth (Philips) C.; B.S., U. Fla., 1956; student Rollins Coll., 1969-71; m. Helen Louise Gurnther, Oct. 27, 1956; children—Margaret, Gustav, Paul, Michael. Treas. Electron Machine Corp., Umatilla, Fla., 1961—. Served to sgt. AUS Intelligence Corp., 1956-61. Presbyn. Home: Route 1 Box 360 Altouna FL 32702 Office: 1500 W Ocala Av Umatilla FL 32784

CROSS, JOSEPH RUSSELL, ednl. adminstr.; b. Cross, S.C., Feb. 24, 1914; s. Joseph Pressley and Addie Lea (Russell) C.; A.B., Wofford Coll., 1935; M.Ed., U.S.C., 1950; m. Julia Harrington Rogers, Aug. 23, 1941; children—Gertrude Celeste (Mrs. Wiggins Ellison Singletary), Julia Harrington (Mrs. Warren Shuler Lambert), Elizabeth Rogers (Mrs. William Spencer Hutto), Joseph Russell. Suppt. Cross (S.C.) area schs., 1946-71; asst. supt. for pupil affairs Berkely County Sch. Dist., Moncks Corner, S.C., 1971—. Extension instr. U. S.C., 1969—. Chmn., Berkeley County Hist. Comnn., 1968—. Pres., Cross Democratic Club, 1960-70; del. Democratic County Conv., 1946—, Dem. State Conv., 1966. Trustee Berkeley County Library. Served with AUS, 1941-46. Named Hon. State Farmer, Future Farmers of Am. Mem. Berkeley County Edn. Assn. (pres.), Huguenot Soc. S.C. (chmn. research com.), N.E.A. (life), Am. Assn. Sch. Adminstrs., S.C. Hist. Soc., Am. Legion, 40 and 8, Blue Key. Rotarian. Contbr. articles on early Berkeley County history to hist. jours. Home: Cherokee Path Cross SC 29436 Office: County Office Bldg. Main St Moncks Corner SC 29461

CROSS, LAURA ELIZABETH, lawyer; b. Lathrop, Mo.; d. Pross T. and Nina (Peel) Cross; A.B., Lindenwood Coll., 1923; B.Litt., Columbia Sch. Journalism, 1925; J.D., George Washington U., 1939. Bibliog. research Library of Congress, Washington, 1931-42; admitted to D.C. bar, 1940; atty. office chief of engrs. U.S. Army, 1942—. Mem. Fed. Bar Assn., Bar Assn. D.C., Kappa Beta Pi, Theta Sigma Phi. Home: Wisconsin Av Washington DC 20007 Office: Chief of Engrs Forrestal Bldg Washington DC 20013

CROSS, PRICE RANDOLPH, ins. exec.; b. Santa Fe, Sept. 5, 1899; s. George H. and Frances Randolph (Bartlett) C.; student pub. schs., N.M., pvt. studies; m. Julia Quarterman, July 22, 1920; children—George Randolph, Margaret Marianne (Mrs. William J. Turner). Legislative messenger, exec. sec. to N.M. govs. McDonald, DeBaca, Larrazolo and Lindsey, 1915-21; asso. C.A. Bishop & Co., ins. and investments, Santa Fe, 1922-25; asst. to mng. v.p. Occidental Life Ins. Co., Albuquerque, also Raleigh, N.C., 1926, agy. sec., 1927-28, dir. agys., 1929-35; agy. dir. So. Life Ins. Co. Ga., 1936-41; asst. to pres. State Mut. Ins. Co., Rome, Ga., 1942-43, sec., 1944-57, v.p., sec., 1958, exec. v.p., sec., 1958—. Organizer, 1st sec. N.M. Assns. Ins. Agts., 1922-25, mem. Com. of Three to codify N.M. ins. laws, 1922-23; organizer, 1st sec. Ins. Fedn. N.C., 1929-30, pres., 1931-32, mem. com. to draft 1st N.C workmen's compensation act. Mem. Internat., Ga. assns. health and accident underwriters, Health Ins. Council N.Y. (Ga. com.), Asso. Industry of Ga., Nat. Assn. Life Cos. (agy. com.), N.M. Hist. Soc. (life), S.A.R. Republican. Episcopalian. Club: Callier Springs Country (Rome). Contbr. articles to trade and profl. jours. Home: 112 Dartmouth Av Avondale Estates GA 30002 Office: State Mut. Bldg 1600 block Martha Berry Blvd Rome GA 30161

CROSSLAND, EDWARD JOHN, seismograph co. exec.; b. Okmulgee, Okla., Jan. 17, 1927; s. Samuel Hess and Iva (Jones) C.; B.S., U. Tulsa, 1954; m. Joyce Gardner, Dec. 28, 1963; children—Joy Lorraine, Iva Lynn, Lisa Pauline. Engr., Philco Corp., Phila., 1950-51; research engr. Seismograph Service Corp., Tulsa, 1951-56, mgr. new product devel., 1957-59, engring. mgr. voting machine div., 1959-65, nat. marketing mgr. voting products, 1966-68, exec. engring. cons. P.E.D./Seiscor Div., 1969—. Mem. Okla. State Bd. Registration for Profl. Engrs., 1962-67, chmn., 1966-67. Trustee Tulsa State Fair Bd., 1956-57. Served with USAAF, 1945-49. Registered profl. engr., Okla. Mem. Nat., Okla. socs. profl. engrs. Patentee in field. Home: 4636 E 59th St Tulsa OK 74135 Office: 6200 E 41st St PO Box 1590 Tulsa OK 74102

CROSSMAN, MORTON, dentist; b. Ansonia, Conn., Oct. 31, 1906; s. Murray Alquin and Lulu (Kaminer) C.; student N.Y.U., 1924-25; D.D.S., U. Pa., 1929; m. Estelle Olderman, Dec. 24, 1936; children—William, Allan, Sandra. Practice gen. dentistry, Hamden and New Haven, Conn., 1930-48; real estate broker, Fla., 1950-52; pvt. practice dentistry, Hollywood, Fla., 1953-67; ret., 1967; v.p., dir. Wallingford Properties. (Conn.); dental columnist, 1968-70. Served as capt. Dental Corps, AUS, 1941-45; PTO. Mem. Am. Dental Assn., Fla., Conn., Broward County, North Dade dental socs., Am. Numis. Assn. Jewish religion. Mason. Contbr. articles profl. jours. Home: 1316 Washington St Hollywood FL 33020

CROSSWELL, CAROL MCCORMICK, lawyer; b. Buffalo, Dec. 21, 1925; d. Albert L.L. and Helen (McDowell) McCormick; student Radcliffe Coll., LL.B. cum laude, U. Buffalo, 1947; postgrad. Columbia, 1960, Harvard, 1961; m. William J. Crosswell (dec. 1947); m. 2d, Gilbert Wheatland Smith, Feb. 2, 1952 (div. Feb. 1969); children—Carol, Linda. Admitted to N.Y. bar, 1948, Washington bar, 1953, Fla. bar, 1967; mem. legal staff UN, 1947-51; mem. U.S. Govt. Psychol. Strategy Bd., 1951-53; U.S. del. Inter Am. Council Jurists, Santiago, Chile, 1960; practiced in N.Y.C., 1950—, Palm Beach, Fla., 1967—; mem. firm Weidon and Crosswell, 1950-66. Mem. Fla. Marine Commn., 1968—. Bd. dirs. Jr. League, Millard Fillmore Hosp., Buffalo, Save the Children Fedn., Gebbie Found. Mem. Soc. Women Geographers, Fellows of Harvard. Clubs: Indian Harbor Yacht (Greenwich, Conn.); Buffalo Country; N.Y. Skating; Palm Beach Yacht, Sail Fish (Palm Beach, Fla.); Royal Canadian Yacht (Toronto, Ont.); Trident Yacht (Ont.). Author: Protection of International Personnel, 1956; Financing Foreign Investment, 1962; International Business Techniques, 1962. Home: 1204 N Ocean Blvd Palm Beach FL 33480 also Cherrycroft Burt NY Office: 60 E 42d St New York City NY 10017

CROSSWHITE, WILLIAM EUGENE, lawyer; b. Bristol, Va., Apr. 26, 1933; s. Lawrence F. and Juanita (Thomas) C.; A.B., Catawba Coll., 1956; J.D., Wake Forest U., 1961; m. Jessie Neil Sowers, June 2, 1956; children—Joseph Neil, Robert Neil, Rebecca Neil. Admitted to N.C. bar, 1961; mem. law firm Sowers, Avery & Crosswhite, Statesville, N.C., 1961—; solicitor Statesville Records Ct., 1962-70. Served with AUS, 1956-58. Mem. N.C., 22d Jud. Dist. (v.p. 1971-72), Iredell County (pres. 1970-71) bar assns., Am. Assn. Trial Lawyers, N.C. Acad. Trial Lawyers, Phi Alpha Delta, Sigma Pi Alpha. Presbyn. Elk, Lion. Home: 564 Stoneybrook Rd Statesville NC 28677 Office: First Savs and Loan Bldg Statesville NC 28677

CROTTS, MARCUS BOWMAN, mech. engr.; b. Winston-Salem, N.C., Aug. 6, 1931; s. Marcus James and Daphne (Bowman) C.; B.S., N.C. State U., 1953; B.A., Wake Forest U., 1954; M.S., U. Ill., 1956; m. Margo Jackson, May 12, 1955; children—Van, Laura. Mech. engr. Duke Power Co., Winston-Salem, 1947-49, Babcock & Wilcox Co., Canton, O., 1950-51, Western-Electric Co., Winston-Salem, 1954-55; partner Crotts & Saunders Engring., Inc., Winston-Salem, 1956—. Dir. Electronic Data Control. Class pres. N.C. State U.; dist. commr. Boy Scouts Am. Served to lt. USAF, 1954-56. Registered profl. engr., N.C., S.C., Va. Mem. Am. Soc. M.E. (past nat. v.p., mem. council), Am. Soc. Mfg. Engrs. (past regional chmn., nat. chmn. membership com.), Nat. Soc. Profl. Engrs., Numerical Control Soc., Profl. Engrs. N.C. (dir.), N.C. Soc. Engrs. (dir.), Alumni Assn. N.C. State U. (dir.), Phi Kappa Phi, Tau Beta Pi, Theta Tau, Pi Tau Sigma. Mem. United Ch. Christ (deacon, elder, trustee). Rotarian (dir. Stratford club). Club: Engineers (pres.). Home: 10 Gomar Lane Winston-Salem NC 27106 Office: PO Box 1 4000 Silas Creek Pkwy Winston-Salem NC 27102

CROUCH, (NORA) JOSEPHINE, librarian; b. Hereford, Tex.; d. Joseph Evvy and Nora (Betts) Crouch; B.S., Ga. Coll., 1942; M.L.S., George Peabody Coll., 1950 Librarian, Boy's High Sch., Rome, Ga., 1942-44, Parker High Sch., Greenville, S.C., 1944-46; library supr. Bartow (Fla.) Sch. System, 1946-47; librarian high sch. Aiken, S.C., 1950-53; chief librarian Aiken County Pub. Library, 1954-58; dir. Aiken-Bamberg-Barnwell-Edgefield Regional Library, Aiken, 1958—. Appointed dir. to establish 1st S.C. Regional Demonstration Library, 1958—; library rep. 2d to 9th S.C. Governor's Conf. Bus., Industry, Edn. and Agr., 1960-68; mem. S.C. Gov.'s Conf. Pub. Libraries, 1965; mem. S.C. Gov's Conf. State-wide Traffic Safety, 1961-63; mem. spl. com. S.C. Progress, 1962. Sec. Dibble Meml. Library Bd., 1963—, S.C. Council Common Good, 1968-69, 69-70. Mem. A.L.A., Southeastern, S.C. (chmn. pub. library sect. 1956-58, mem. exec. bd. 1956-58, 64-70, mem. state exec. com. 1965-69, pres. 1966, 67; A.L.A. fed. relations coordinator 1963-65), Central Savannah River Area library assns., Am. Assn. U. Women (mem. state bd. 1957-58, br. bd. 1958—; state div. parliamentarian 1965-67; exec. bd. 1964-67; br. pres. 1966-67), Council for Common Good (sec. 1968-70). Aiken County Hist. Soc. Club: Pilot. Contbr. to profl. publs. Home: 823 Fermata Pl SW Aiken SC 29801 Office: 504 Richland Av W Aiken SC 29801

CROUCH, THOMAS HENRY, air force med. officer; b. Douglas, Ariz., Aug. 26, 1915; s. Aziel Guy and Jewell (Coggin) C.; student U. Ariz., 1933-34; M.D., Tulane U., 1939; m. Alfred Kemp King, June 14, 1939; children—Thomas Jeffrey, James Alfred, Mary Lynn (Mrs. William E. Spangler). Intern, City County Hosp., El Paso, Tex., 1939-40; commd. 1st. lt., M.C., U.S. Army, 1940, advanced through grades to maj. gen. M.C., U.S. Air Force, 1969; assigned PTO, World War II, orthopaedic surg. tng. Fitzsimons Gen. Hosp., Denver, 1947-50; chief surg. service Clark AFB, Philippines, 1950-52; hosp. comdr. Westover AFB, Mass., 1952-55. Wiesbaden, Germany, 1955-59, Carswell AFB, Ft. Worth, 1959-61; surgeon 2d Air Force, Barksdale AFB, La., 1961-62; dep. dir., then dir. med. staff and edn. Hdqrs. USAF, 1962-65; comdr. Wilford Hall USAF Hosp., Lackland AFB, Tex., 1965-68; dir. profl. services Surgeon Gen. Hdqrs. USAF, 1968-70; dep. surgeon gen. USAF, 1970-72; ret., 1972; cons. orthopaedic surgeon gen. USAF, 1955—; clin. asso. prof. orthopaedic surgery U. Tex. Med. Sch., San Antonio. Decorated D.S.M., Legion of Merit with oak leaf cluster, Air Force Commendation medal with oak leaf cluster. Diplomate Am. Bd. Orthopaedic Surgeons, Am. Bd. Preventive Medicine. Fellow A.C.S. (gov.), Am. Acad. Orthopaedic Surgeons, Am. Coll. Preventive Medicine, Aerospace Med. Assn.; mem. Soc. Air Force Clin. Surgeons (pres. 1963), Inst. Fed. Hosp. Adminstrs. (pres. 1964), Am., Tex. med. assns., Air Force Assn., San Antonio Surg. Soc., Soc. USAF Flight Surgeons, Loyal Order Boar, Sophos, Kappa Sigma, Alpha Kappa Kappa. Episcopalian. Mason (32 deg.), Rotarian. Contbr. profl. jours. Home: 5001 River Hill Washington DC 20016 Office: Surgeon Gen Hdqrs USAF Washington DC 20314

CROUT, JAMES MCBRIDE, supt. schs.; b. Gilbert, S.C., June 12, 1916; s. Earle Julian and Effie Estelle (Smith) C.; B.A., Wofford Coll., 1937; M.Ed., U. S.C., 1947; m. Gladys Lorene Keisler, June 19, 1937; children—Kathryn Anne (Mrs. John C. Shelley, Jr.), Linda Jean. Classroom tchr., Irmo, S.C., 1937-39; supt. schs., Ward, S.C., 1939-44; high sch. prin., Batesburg-Leesville, S.C., 1944-46, dist. supt., 1946—. Mem. S.C. Adv. Council on Tchr. Edn., 1971—; mem. Com. of Forty to Study Tchr. Certification and Tchr. Pay in S.C., 1968—. Mem. budget and admissions com. Met. United Fund, Columbia, S.C., 1963—, trustee, 1969—. Served with USNR, 1945. Mem. N.E.A., S.C. (pres. 1969-70), Lexington County edn. assns., S.C. Assn. Sch. Supts. (pres. 1964-65), S.C. Assn. Sch. Adminstrs. (pres. 1964-65), Eastern Conf. Sch. Adminstrs. (chmn. 1963-64). Lion (sec. 1950—). Methodist (lay speaker). Home: 102 Schoolhouse Lane Batesburg SC 29006

CROW, BOBBY JOE, banker; b. Alvarado, Tex., Dec. 13, 1929; s. Oliver S. and Oma (Smith) C.; student N. Tex. State U., 1947-48, Tex. Christian U., 1954-56; m. Betty Louise Bryant, Apr. 1, 1956; children—James Gregory, Carol Annette, Lisa Gayle. With First Nat. Bank, Ft. Worth, 1948—, v.p., sr. trust officer, 1960—. Bd. dirs. Wesley Found., Tex. Christian U., All-Church Home for Children, Tarrant County chpt. Easter Seal Soc. Served with USAF, 1951-54. Mem. Am. Inst. Banking. Methodist. Clubs: Civitan (v.p., dir.), Colonial Country. Home: 229 Hallbrook Dr Fort Worth TX 76134 Office: 1 Burnet Plaza Fort Worth TX 76102

CROW, JAMES SYLVESTER, banker; b. Mobile, Ala., June 23, 1915; s. James S. and Elizabeth (Jackson) C.; student U. Ala., 1946-48; grad. Rutgers Sch. Banking, 1959; m. Helen De Blanc, Apr. 20, 1945; children—Michele Marie (Mrs. John Z. Higg, III), Denise Anne (Mrs. Walter C. Andrews, Jr.), Marcia Lynn, Deborah Jane. Clk. First Nat. Bank Mobile, 1932-41, 45-48, mgr. bond dept., 1949-50, asst. cashier, 1951, asst. v.p., 1952; sales mgr. Hendrix & Mayes Investment Bankers, Birmingham, Ala., 1952-53; asst. cashier First Nat. Bank Birmingham, 1954-55, asst. v.p., 1955-56, v.p., 1957-60, sr. v.p., 1961-66, exec. v.p., 1966-67; v.p. finance So. Ry. Co., Washington, 1967-70; exec. v.p. First Nat. Bank Mobile, 1970-71, pres., 1971—; dir. several railroads, 1st Nat. Bank Mobile, Ala. Dry Dock & Shipbldg. Co. Lectr. Sch. Banking S. La. State U., 1962-67. State chmn. Am. Cancer Soc., 1971. Trustee So. Research Inst. Birmingham. Mem. Ala. Security Dealers Assn. (pres. 1955), Ala. Bankers Assn. (v.p. 1966-67), Newcomen Soc. N. Am. Episcopalian. Clubs: Country, Downtown (Birmingham); Athelstan, Country, Lakewood, Internat., Isle Dauphine (Mobile). Home: 217 Berwyn Dr Mobile AL 36608 Office: PO Box 1467 Mobile AL 36601

CROW, JOHN ORIEN, govt. ofcl.; b. Salem, Mo., Sept. 7, 1912; s. Charles Drake and Lucy (Murray) C.; grad. Haskell Inst., Lawrence, Kan., 1933; m. Juanita James, July 21, 1934 (div. 1956); 1 dau., Emily (Mrs. James G. Gilbert); m. 2d, Bernese Bonga, Nov. 23, 1957. With Bur. Indian Affairs, Dept. Interior, successively supt. Truxton Canon Agy., Ariz., Mescalero Agy., N.M., Fort Apache Agy., Ariz., Unitah and Ouray Agy., Utah, 1942-57, dep. asst. commr., 1957-59, chief branch of realty, 1959-60, acting commr., 1961, dep. commr., 1961-66, asso. dir. Bur. Land Mgmt., Washington, 1966-71; dep. commr. Indian affairs Bur. Indian Affairs, Dept. Interior, 1971—. Recipient Outstanding Fed. Career Service award Nat. Civil Service League, 1964. Mason. (32 deg.). Home: 2386 N Edgewood Arlington VA 22207 Office: Bureau of Indian Affairs Dept Interior Washington DC 20242

CROW, NEIL EDWARD, physician; b. Belton, Tex., July 12, 1926; s. Floyd Charles and Mary (Martin) C.; student Henderson Coll., 1943-44, Tex. Christian U., 1944-45; B.S., U. Tex., 1946; M.D., U. Ark., 1951; m. Mary Katherine Claxton, Sept. 11, 1948; children—Neil E., Katherine Lee. Intern, U. Ark. Med. Center, 1951-52, splty. tng. in radiology, 1953-56, asst. clin. prof. radiology, 1960—; gen. practice medicine, Hope, Ark., 1952-53; radiologist Holt-Krock Clinic and Sparks Meml. Hosp., Fort Smith, Ark., 1960—; cons. USPHS, U.S. Army and USAF Surgeon Gen., Fort Chaffee, Ark. Served to lt. (j.g.) USNR, 1944-47; to lt. col. USAF, 1953-60; now col. M.C. Res. Diplomate Am. Bd. Radiology. Mem. Am. Coll. Radiology, A.M.A., Ark. Med. Soc., Air Force Assn., Am. Fedn. Clin. Research, Alpha Omega Alpha. Phi Chi. Democrat. Presbyn. Contbr. articles to profl. jours. Home: 19 Berry Hill Rd Fort Smith AR 72901 Office: 1500 Dodson Av Fort Smith AR 72901

CROW, WILLIAM CECIL, govt. ofcl.; b. Oneonta, Ala., Oct. 4, 1904; s. Mandeville McAlpin and Flora Jane (Brice) C.; A.B., Maryville Coll., 1924; A.M., U. Chgo., 1929; LL.D., Maryville College, 1969; m. Mary Lucille Johnson, July 5, 1935; 1 son, William Cecil. Asst. prof. econs., Ala. Poly. Inst., 1930-35; with U.S. Dept. Agr., 1935—, successively with Bur. Agrl. Econs., 1935-42, War Food Adminstrn. and Prodn. and Marketing Adminstrn., 1942-53, dir. transp. and facilities research div., and liaison with state dept. agr. Agrl. Marketing Service, 1953-63, dir. transp. and facilities research div. Agrl. Research Service, 1963—. Mem. Arlington (Va.) Com. of 100; chmn. Arlington County Pub. Utilities Commn. Trustee Presbytery of Washington. Decorated Chevalier de l'Ordre du Merite Agricole (France); recipient Achievement award Nat. Assn. Produce Market Mgrs., Superior Service award U.S. Dept. Agr., citation Greater Phila. Movement; named Ky. Col. Hon. mem. Am. Warehouseman's Assn., Nat. Assn. Produce Market Mgrs.; mem. Am. Farm Econs. Assn., A.A.A.S. Presbyn. Club: Springfield Golf and Country. Author many publs. Home: 1258 N Buchanan St Arlington VA 22205 Office: US Dept Agr Washington DC 20025

CROWDER, CHARLIE CLEMONS, JR., services corp. exec.; b. Danville, Va., July 26, 1940; s. Charlie Clemons and Avis Louise (Griffith) C.; B.S., Va. Mil. Inst., 1962; m. Carolyn Marie Willis, June 16, 1962; children—Coni, Christin, Catherine. Commd. 2d lt., U.S. Army, 1962, advanced through grades to capt., 1965; combat engr. unit comdr., Ft. Meade, Md., 1962-64; post engr., Aschaffenburg, Germany, 1964-66; comdr. Port Constrn. Co., Ft. Belvoir, Va. and Qui Nhou, Vietnam, post engr., Tobyhanna (Pa.) Army Depot, 1968; ret., 1968; dir. pub. works City of Danville, 1969-72; mgr. store engring. Asso. Service Corp., Danville, Va., 1972—. Decorated Bronze Star (U.S.), Order of Merit 2d Class (Vietnam). Mem. Am. Pub. Works Assn. Baptist (deacon). Mason. Home: 116 Huntington Pl Danville VA 24541 Office: Asso Services Corp Danville VA 24541

CROWDER, HENDERSON MATTHIAS, educator, chemist; b. Hanford, Cal., Nov. 30, 1909; s. Louis Marvin and Sarah (Amen) C.; student Madison Coll., 1936-38; B.S., U. Fla., 1947, M.S., 1953; m. Sophia Augusta Masterson, Apr. 11, 1954. Research asst. U. Tenn. AEC program, Oak Ridge, 1952-55; lab. technician animal husbandry dept. U. Tenn., 1957-60, asst. chemist, 1960-67, asst. prof., 1967—. Served with AUS, 1942-45. Mem. Am. Soc. Animal Prodn., Am. Feed Control Ofcls., Am. Assn. U. Profs., Tenn. Edn. Assn., So. Appalachian Mineral Soc., Am. Soc. Animal Sci. Seventh Day Adventist. Club: University of Tennessee Faculty. Contbr. articles profl. jours. Home: 5001 Shannon Lane Knoxville TN 37918 Office: Dept Animal Husbandry U Tenn Knoxville TN 37916

CROWDER, JACK ANDREW, trade assn. exec.; b. Charleston, W.Va., Jan. 2, 1927; s. John Amos and Helen (Gallagher) C.; B.A. magna cum laude, Washington and Lee U., 1948, LL.B. cum laude, 1950; m. Barbara Grace Ochtman, Nov. 4, 1950; children—Mary C., Jack Andrew, Marjorie H., Barbara E., Patricia F., James T. Admitted to District of Columbia Bar, 1950; gen. practice law, Washington, 1950-65; exec. v.p., counsel Nat. Assn. Wool Mfrs., Washington, 1965-67, pres., 1967-71; gen. counsel Am. Textile Mfrs. Inst., Washington, 1971—. Mem. Pres.'s Labor-Mgmt. Textile Adv. Com.; mem. U.S. delegation Internat. Wool Textile Orgn. Cons. Nat. Council Catholic Men. Served with AUS, 1945-46. Mem. Am. Bar Assn., Phi Beta Kappa, Omicron Delta Kappa, Sigma Alpha Epsilon. Roman Catholic. Home: 3607 Bent Branch Ct Falls Church VA 22041 Office: 1150 17th St NW Washington DC 20036

CROWDER, WILLIAM LEE, engring. exec.; b. Arkansas City, Kan., Apr. 14, 1930; s. Ralph and Josephine (Burba) C.; B.S., Okla. A. and M. Coll., 1957; m. Nancy M. Pitts, July 8, 1972. Engr., dept. chief, asst. mgr. indsl. engring. Western Electric Co., N.C., Okla., N.J., 1957-67; corporate mgr. indsl. engring. Allis Chalmers Co., West Allis, Wis., 1967; mgr. indsl. engring. Martin Marietta Corp., Orlando, Fla., 1967—. Bd. dirs. Maitland Woods Assn. Served with USAF, 1951-54. Registered profl. engr., Okla. Mem. Nat. Soc. Profl. Engrs. (past sect. chmn.), Fla. Engring. Soc., Am. Inst. Indsl. Engrs. (pres. Central Fla. chpt.). Contbr. articles to profl. jours. Home: 2100 S Conway St Orlando FL 32806 Office: PO Box 5837 Orlando FL 32805

CROWE, ELLENIA AUGUSTA BATES, artist, author; b. Dardanelle, Ark.; d. James Fillmore and Alice (Putnam) Bates; student Columbia, 1946; m.. Theopholis Waldon Crowe; children—Blonnie Dell (Mrs. Eugene Lambert), Adrian Bates, Rodney Page Thomas, Doris Ellenia (Mrs. Shannon Townley). Sales, Macy's, N.Y.C., 1946; one-man shows Little Rock Fine Arts Bldg., Old South Restaurant; exhibited in group shows at Philbrook, Tulsa, U. Ark., Ark. Arts Center, Verdigris Valley, Independence, Kan., Fort Smith Arts Center. Mem. Ark. Art Center, D.A.R. (treas.), Friends of Library, League Women Voters, Fort Smith Asso. Artists, Ark. Letos, Phi Sigma Alpha. Methodist. Author: volume of poetry, 1954; (novel) Hilda's Miracle, 1955; Days of Passion, Nights of Love, 1964. Home: 718 N 16th St Fort Smith AR 72903

CROWE, GUTHRIE FERGUSON, judge; b. La Grange, Ky., July 24, 1910; s. Robert Thomas and Fannie Florence (Eastes) C.; student Ky. Mil. Inst., 1926-27, U. Ky., 1928-29, U. Louisville, 1930-32; LL.B., Cumberland U., 1933; m. Sue Eliza Vance, Jan. 18, 1939; 1 dau., Betty Gwyn. Admitted to Ky. bar, 1933; practiced law, La Grange, 1933-42, 46-52; judge La Grange, 1938-42; U.S. dist. judge Canal Zone, 1952—. Elected state rep. 53d Dist. Ky., 1942; commr. Ky. State Police 1948-52. Bd. dirs., chmn. bd. mgmt. YMCA; chmn. C.Z. Red Cross, Scouts Am., A.R.C. (C.Z.). Served as lt. comdr. USNR, 1942-45; comdr. Res. ret. Decorated Bronze Star, Navy and Marine Corps medal, Sec. Navy Citation. Pres. Ky. Assn. Theater Owners, 1945-52. Mem. Fed. (pres. C.Z. 1964), C.Z. bar assns., Am. Legion (dept. comdr. Ky. 1948-49), V.F.W., Phi Delta Theta, Sigma Delta Kappa. Democrat. Methodist. Home: Balboa Heights CZ Office: Box 2006 Balboa Heights CZ

CROWE, WILLIAM EUGENE, lawyer; b. Braymer, Mo., May 6, 1893; s. Thomas William and Laura (Penny) C.; A.B., Central Coll., 1916; LL.B., U. Mo., 1921; m. Hilda Anita Kindt, June 17, 1933. Admitted to Okla. bar, practiced in Enid, Okla., 1921—; judge Spl. Sessions Ct., Enid, 1959-69. Mem. Am., Okla. (pres. 1947)bar assns., Acacia, Order of Coif, Delta Sigma Rho. Home: 1931 Live Oak Enid OK 73701 Office: Broadway Tower Enid OK 73701

CROWELL, JOSEPH GEORGE, dentist; b. Hoquiam, Wash., Apr. 9, 1918; s. Ernest Benjmian and Georgia Ann (Sorrells) C.; student Brevard Coll., 1939-40, Western Carolina U., 1940-42; D.D.S., Emory U., 1945; m. Buris Lenora Franks, Oct. 17, 1942; children—Dianne (Mrs. Thomas Hilton House), Wanda (Mrs. George Michael White), Joseph Robert. Dentist, Fifth Av. Clinic, Hendersonville, N.C., 1946—. Bd. dirs. Pardee Margret R. Meml. Hosp., Hendersonville. Served with USAF, 1955-57. Mem. Henderson County Dental Soc. (pres. 1963-64). Democrat. Methodist (bd. dirs. 1970—). Rotarian (pres. 1961-62), Elk. Clubs: Beacon (Hendersonville), Hendersonville Country. Mailing Address: 724 Fifth Av Hendersonville NC 28739 Home: 16 Lake Dr Hendersonville NC 28739 Office: 724 Fifth Av Hendersonville NC 28739

CROWELL, WAYNE ALLEN, veterinarian; b. Sterling, Colo., Nov. 25, 1940; s. Carl L. and Lorraine E. (Rambow) C.; B.S., Colo. State U., 1963, D.V.M., 1964; postgrad. U. Neb., 1962, Ind. State U., 1969; m. Mary Linn Scott, Apr. 27, 1962; children—Chery Linn, George Scott. Pvt. practice vet. medicine, Glasgow, Ky. and Colorado Springs, Colo., 1964-66; research veterinarian Comml. Solvents Corp., Terre Haute, Ind., 1968-70; research asso. Coll. Vet. Medicine, U. Ga., Athens, 1970—. Served with AUS, 1966-68. Decorated Army Commendation medal. NSF Research grantee 1962, Colo. State U. Alumni award of Merit, 1963. Mem. Am. Vet. Med. Assn., Indsl. Veterinarians Assn., Am. Legion, Am. Contract Bridge League, Alpha Gamma Rho (pres.), Phi Zeta, Beta Beta Beta. Republican. Presbyn. Mason. Home: 120 Richard Way Athens GA 30601

CROWN, DAVID ALLAN, govt. ofcl.; b. Long Beach, N.Y., Sept. 13, 1928; s. John and Florence (Coe) C.; B.S., Union Coll., 1948; M. Criminology, U. Cal., 1960, D. Criminology, 1969; m. Maria Braml, Feb. 13, 1954; children—Ingrid, Eric. Spl. agt. CIC, 1951-53; asst. dir. San Francisco Identification Lab., U.S. Postal Inspection Service, 1957-67; dir. Questioned Document Lab., Records Analysis Group, Dept. Army, Washington, 1967—. Lectr. Chabot Coll., Hayward, Cal., 1966-67; professorial lectr. Am. U., Washington, 1971. Mem. Am. Acad. Forensic Scis. (exec. com. 1970—, chmn. questioned document sect. 1969-70), Am. Soc. Questioned Document Examiners (chmn. accreditation com. 1969-70), Am. Soc. Testing and Materials (chmn. questioned document com. 1970-71), Forensic Sci. Found. (bd. dirs. 1971—), Am. Coll. Document Examiners (bd. dirs. 1970—). Author: The Forensic Examination of Paints and Pigments, 1968. Contbr. articles to profl. pubs. Editorial bd. Jour. Forensic Sciences, 1971—. Home: 3103 Jessie Court Fairfax VA 22030 Office: Pentagon Bldg Washington DC 20310

CROWSON, DAVID LAMAR, dentist; b. Randolph, Miss., Aug. 9, 1917; s. Quinton Throne and Priscilla Estelle (Lamar) C.; B.S., Miss. State U., 1939; D.D.S., Loyola U. of South, New Orleans, 1950.; m. Lillian Catherine Rankin, Feb. 17, 1955; children—Cathie Clair, Neville Rankin. Practice dentistry, Calhoun City, Miss., 1950-51, Petal, Miss., 1951—. Served with AUS, 1942-46. Mem. Am., Miss. dental assns., Forrest County Dental Soc. (pres. 1956). Kiwanian (pres. 1957), Elk. Patentee teeth cleaning system. Home: Hillcrest Loop Petal MS 39465 Office: 108 N Main St Petal MS 39465

CRUDUP, JACK MELTON, rubber products co. exec.; b. McAlester, Okla., Jan. 28, 1925; s. Herbert E. and Katharine E. (Elliott) C.; B.S., U. Tulsa, 1950; m. Dorothy Lewis, Dec. 7, 1945; children—Susan Kay (Mrs. Larry Dilliard), Roger E., Steven E. With U.S. Rubber Co., Tulsa, 1950-60; sales mgr. Acushnet Co., Fort Worth, 1961-71; gen. mgr. Polymer Products Co., Grand Prairie, Tex., 1971—. Served with inf. AUS, 1943-45. Decorated Purple Heart (2). Mem. Sigma Phi Epsilon. Home: 1001 Whispering Oak Ct Arlington TX 76012 Office: PO Box 1107 Grand Prairie TX 75050

CRUM, WALLACE ELLIOTT, banking exec.; b. Orangeburg, S.C., Nov. 26, 1910; s. William Wallace and Rebecca Collier (Elliott) C.; B.S., in Elec. Engring., U. S.C., 1932, B.S. in Civil Engring., 1937; m. Mary Lou Funderburk, Sept. 16, 1939; children—Mary Lou (Mrs. John Asbil Cloyd), Collier (Mrs. John Robert Turnbull), Wallis Elliott. Bridge design engr. S.C. Hwy. Dept., 1933-42, mgr. bridge design group, 1946-56, chief bridge engr. design, 1956—; pres., chmn. bd. E.C. Bldg. & Investment Corp., Columbia, S.C., 1963—. Hon. mem. spl. choir Westminster Abbey, London, Eng., 1968—. Served as lt. comdr. USNR, 1942-46. Mem. Am., Southeastern (chmn. bridge com. 1958—) assns. state hwy. ofcls., Am. Soc. C.E., S.C. Soc. Engrs., Internat. Assn. Bridge and Structural Engrs. (chmn. bridge com. design 1968—), English Speaking Union (br. pres. 1971—, dir. 1968-71). Episcopalian. Clubs: Columbia Ball Debutant, Kiwanis (chmn. tennis com. 1959—), Corsair, Arrow, Forest Lake Country. Address: 2710 Canterbury Rd Columbia SC 29204

CRUMBLEY, D. LARRY, educator; b. Kannapolis, N.C., Jan. 18, 1941; B.S. cum laude, Pfeiffer Coll., 1963; M.S., La. State U., 1965, Ph.D. (Ford Found. fellow 1966-67; Humble Oil Co. fellow 1966-67), 1967; m. 2 children. Mgmt. intern Tip-Top Hosier Mill, Asheville, N.C., 1962; research asst. La. State U., 1963-64, 65, teaching asst., 1965-66; staff accountant Seidman & Seidman, 1967; asst. prof. Pa. State U., 1967-69; faculty resident Arthur Andersen & Co., 1969-70; asso. prof. accounting U. Fla., Gainesville, 1970—. C.P.A., N.C. Mem. Am. Inst. C.P.A.s, Fla. Inst. C.P.A.s, Nat. Tax Assn., Am. Accounting Assn., Numismatic Lit. Guild (life), Phi Kappa Phi, Beta Gamma Sigma, Beta Alpha Psi. Co-author newspaper column The Reluctant Taxpayer, 1971-72. Book rev. editor Fla. Certified Pub. Accountant; regional editor Estate Tax Pub. Co., 1971-72. Contbr. monthly column to Numismatic Scrapbook Mag., numerous articles to profl. jours. Home: 5013 N W 18th Pl Gainesville FL 32601

CRUMBLEY, GEORGE PIERCE, JR., advt. exec.; b. Atlanta, June 15, 1923; s. George Pierce and Mary (Hicks) C.; A.B., Emory U., 1949; m. Sarah Carolyn Hardy, July 4, 1944; children—Thomas McMahan, Cheryl Marie. Sales mgr. WSB-TV, Atlanta, 1948-57; southeastern mgr. Headley-Reed Radio-TV Reps., 1957-59, CBS Radio, 1959-62; pres. Crumbley, Robertson, Riley Advt., Inc., 1962—. Chmn. DeKalb County Cancer Crusade, 1965-67. Bd. dirs. Met. Atlanta Better Bus. Bur., Met. Atlanta Assn. for Blind; trustee Found. Visually Handicapped Children; exec. dir. Peach Bowl, Inc. Served with USAAF, 1942-46. Mem. Atlanta Advt. Club (dir.), Alpha Delta Sigma, Sigma Delta Chi. Methodist. Mason, Lion (life dir. Lighthouse for Blind; pres., dist. pub. relations chmn., dist. gov.). Clubs: Druid Hills Country, East Lake Country. Home: 873 Castle Falls Dr NE Atlanta GA 30329 Office: 20 Marietta St NW Atlanta GA 30303

CRUME, PAUL, columnist; b., 1912. Columnist, Dallas Morning News. Author (essays): A Texan at Bay, 1961. Address: Dallas Morning News Communications Center Dallas TX 75222*

CRUME, RONALD GLENN, dentist; b. Covington, Ky., Sept. 19, 1935; s. Thomas Clinton and Helen Madiline (Craddock) C.; U. Ky., 1954-57, Austin Peay Coll., 1959-60, Thomas Moore Coll., 1961; D.M.D., U. Louisville, 1966; m. Barbara Ann Denham, June 12, 1954; children—Lou Ann, Ronald Glenn. Practice dentistry, Florence, Ky., 1966—. Cons., Boone County (Ky.) Bd. Health, 1969—, Woodspoint Extended Care Home, 1970—. Magistrate, Boone County, 1970—. Trustee Ohio, Ky., Ind. Regional Planning Authority. Served with AUS, 1959-61. Named Ky. col., 1971, Tenn. Squire, 1970; Outstanding Young Man of Year, Boone County Jr. C. of C., 1969. Mem. Boone County Jr. C. of C., Boone County Businessmen's Assn., Phi Delta, Psi Omega. Democrat. Baptist. Home: 7544 Dogwood St Florence KY 41042 Office: 8315 US 42 Florence KY 41042

CRUMPACKER, RALPH, trucking co. exec.; b. Frazier, Ark., Jan. 11, 1915; s. Dave Barry and Perna (Welch) C.; grad. high sch.; m. Mozelle Knoll, May 28, 1940; children—David Eugene, Carol Ann, Donald Paul (dec.). With Jones Truck Lines, Inc., Springdale, Ark., 1933—, operations mgr., 1958-65, v.p. charge operations, 1965-68, exec. v.p., 1968—. Bd. dirs. Springdale United Fund. Mem. Springdale C. of C. Baptist (ordained deacon 1955, chmn. deacon bds., treas.). Mason (32 deg.), Kiwanian. Home: 1113 N West End St Springdale AR 72764 Office: 610 E Emma Av Springdale AR 72764

CRUMPLER, HARRY ABNER, judge; b. Magnolia, Ark., Oct. 4, 1914; s. Samuel Abner and Kathleen (Warnock) C.; student So. State Coll., Magnolia, 1933-34; LL.B., U. Ark., 1939; m. Laura Hays, July 22, 1950; children—Kathleen W., Harry A., Laura Ann. Admitted to Ark. bar, 1939; city atty., Magnolia, 1940-42; dep. pros. atty. Columbia County, Ark., 1946-48; pros. atty. 13th Jud. Circuit, 1949-52; pvt. practice law, Magnolia, 1953-64; circuit judge 13th Jud. Circuit, 1st Div., Magnolia, 1965—. Mem. Constl. Revision Study Commn. of Ark., 1967-68. Served with AUS, 1942-45. Named Ky. col. Mem. Ark., 13th Dist. (v.p. 1950-52), Columbia County (pres. 1956-58) bar assns., Kappa Sigma. Home: RFD 1 Box 67E Magnolia AR 71753 Office: 114 E Calhoun St Magnolia AR 71753

CRUMPLER, ROBERT, editor. City editor Louisville Times. Office: 525 W Broadway Louisville KY 40202*

CRUMPTON, JOHN LAYMAN, ins. exec.; b. Roxboro, N.C., Oct. 8, 1895; s. Robert Wilmot and Rosa (Pleasants) C.; B.Ph., Elon Coll., 1917, LL.D., 1969; m. Beatrice Pretto Browne, Sept. 25, 1926. Tchr. English, Winston-Salem (N.C.) High Sch., 1917-18; spl. sales dir. Pilot Life Ins. Co., 1918-22; sales dir. Western Carolina, Pacific Mut. Co., 1922-30; salesman, mgr. Sun Life Co. of Can., 1930-46; mgr. for N.C. of Profl. Group div. Continental Ins. Cos. N.Y., 1946-70; chmn. bd. J.L. and U.S. Crumpton, Inc., Durham, N.C., 1970—. Bd. dirs. Durham (N.C.) Community Fund, 1944-50, pres., 1944; active Durham YMCA, pres., 1946-47; N.C. campaign mgr. War Fund Drive, 1946; trustee, chmn. devel. com. for bd. trustees, mem. exec. com. Elon Coll., chmn. steering com. E 4 fund campaign, 1968—. Recipient award from gov. N.C. for successful War Fund Dr., 1946; Alumnus of Year, Elon Coll. Gen. Alumni Assn., 1966; award for service as chmn. beautification and improvement com. City of Durham, 1961. Mem. Underwriters' Assn. (pres. Winston-Salem 1924-25, Durham 1940-41), Nat. Forensic League (hon. life), S.A.R. Democrat. Mem. Congl. Christian Ch. (chmn. bd. trustees; chmn. bldg. com. 1961-65). Mason, Rotarian (v.p. Durham chpt. 1945-46, Rotary award 1960). Address: PO Drawer 1767 Durham NC 27702

CRUTCHFIELD, CHARLES H., broadcasting exec.; b. Hope, Ark., July 27, 1912; student Wofford Coll., 1929-30, Mgmt. Devel. Seminar Harvard, 1959; m. 2 children. Announcer, program dir. radio stas., N.C. and S.C., 1929-33; announcer radio sta. WBT, Charlotte, N.C., 1933-35, program dir., 1935-45, acting gen. mgr., 1945, now pres. WVT-AM-FM, WBTV Jefferson Prodns.; gen. mgr. Jefferson Standard Broadcasting Co., Charlotte, 1945—, v.p., 1947-52, exec. v.p., 1952-63, pres., 1963—, also dir. Pres. Charlotte Better Bus. Bur., 1950-51; chmn. publicity com. Charlotte YMCA Bldg. Fund, 1956; mem. gifts com. Queens Coll. Centennial Fund, 1957, 58; mem. gen. crusade com. Billy Graham Crusade, 1958; mem. N.C. Gov.'s com. Traffic Safety Council, 1954-55, radio-TV chmn. com. pub. sch. amendment, 1956; mem. nat. radio com. Brotherhood week Nat. Conf. Christians and Jews, 1955; vice chmn. N.C. Radio Free Europe Fund, 1963; mem. Charlotte Jr. League Opera com., 1965-67; mem. Charlotte Bicentennial Com., 200, 1966-68; mem. exec. com. Converse Coll. Ednl. Conf., 1966-67; mem. N.C. council Nat. Council Crime and Delinquency, 1968-71. Dir. Young Ams. for Freedom, 1968. Bd. dirs. A.R.C., 1950-54, Mecklenburg County (N.C.) Tb and Health Assn., 1952-53, Charlotte Arts Fund, 1958-59, Jr. Achievement, Charlotte, 1957-59, Carolinas United, 1956-57; bd. advisers Belmont Abbey Coll., Belmont, N.C., 1957-58; charter mem. bd. Sch. Journalism Found., U. N.C. at Chapel Hill, 1954-59. Recipient Broadcast Preceptor award San Francisco State Coll., 1967, Internal Revenue Service award, 1967, Silver medal Charlotte Advt. Club, 1968, Book of Golden Deeds award Charlotte Exchange Club, 1969; named Man of Year Charlotte Bar Assn., 1968. Mem. Nat. Assn. Broadcasters (mem. research com. 1962—), Charlotte Choral Soc., Charlotte C. of C. (pres. 1971). Presbyn. Club: London Dinner (Charlotte). Address: Sta WBT L Julian Price Pl Charlotte NC 26208

CRUTCHFIELD, SAM SHAW, JR., lawyer; b. Nashville, July 15, 1934; s. Sam Shaw and Alfreda (Whitworth) C.; B.A., George Washington U., 1960, J.D., 1963; m. Sylvia Ann Dinneen, May 14, 1958; children—Catherine Anne, Firmadge Whitworth, Elizabeth Victoria. Admitted to D.C. bar, 1963; jud. law clk. Hon. Frank H. Myers, D.C. Ct. of Appeals, 1963-64; exec. dir. Va. Commn. Constl. Govt., 1964-67; asso. counsel Am. Enterprise Inst. Pub. Policy Research, Washington, 1967-70, asst. to pres., 1970—. Mem. Jud. Conf. for D.C. Circuit, 1969. Vice pres. Young Republican Club, Arlington, Va., 1968-69; mem. Arlington County Rep. Com., 1968-70; exec. dir. Young Rep. Fedn. Va., 1968-69. Trustee Del. Law Sch. Served with AUS, 1953-56. Mem. Am., D.C. (asst. editor jour. 1971—), Fed. bar assns., Am. Judicature Assn., Phi Delta Phi. Contbr. articles to profl. jours. Editor: D.C. Young Lawyer, 1968-69. Home: 1804 N Quinn St Arlington VA 22209 Office: 1150 17th St NW Washington DC 20036

CRUZ CONTRERAS, RUDOLFO, lawyer; b., 1926; B.A., U. P.R.; LL.B., U. Miami. Admitted to P.R. bar, 1952, since practiced in San Juan. Mem. Bar Assn. P.R. (past pres.). Office: P O Box 4227 San Juan PR 00905*

CRUZ HERNANDEZ, MIGUEL ANGEL, dentist; b. Mayaguez, Puerto Rico, Apr. 3, 1931; s. Miguel A. Cruz Velez and Aurea E. Hernandez; B.S., U. P.R., 1955, D.M.D., 1965; m. Margie E. Caballero, Dec. 18, 1965; children— Marisel, Magaly, Marleen. Practice dentistry Hosp. Distrito Aguadilla, Aquadilla, P.R., 1965-66, Hormigueros Hosp., Lajas, P.R., 1966—; instr. U.S. Army Res. Sch., 1969—. Served with inf. AUS, 1950-52. Recipient Lion of the Year award Lajas Lions Club, 1970-71. Mem. Am. Dental Assn., Colegio Cirujanos Dentistas, Fedn. Dental. Internat., U.S. Res. Officers Assn., Xi Psi Phi, Phi Delta Gamma. Lion (dep. gov. 1971-72). Club: Deportivo Del Oeste (Lajas, P.R.). Home: 28 Rosales St Lajas PR 00667 Office: 12 Concordia St Lajas PR 00667

CUBBAGE, THOMAS LEON, ret. petroleum co. exec.; b. Okarche, Okla., Aug. 29, 1907; s. Guy S. and Mary Catherine (Shearn) C.; B.S. in Engring., U. Okla., 1937; m. Mildred Hart, Jan. 2, 1937; children—Thomas Leon II, Nancy (Mrs. Thomas L. Oakley). With Phillips Petroleum Co., 1926-71, engr., Borger, Tex., 1930-43, asst. supt. plains butadiene plant, Borger, 1943-44, supt., 1944-51, v.p., asst. gen. mgr. Phillips Chem. Co., Bartlesville, Okla., 1951-63, v.p. chem. dept. Phillips Petroleum Co., Bartlesville, 1963-71, also dir.; v.p., dir. Phillips Films Co., Inc.; v.p., gen. mgr. Phillips Pacific Chem. Co.; v.p., dir. Am. Thermoplastics Corp., Phillips Products Co., Inc., Sealright Co., Inc., H. P. Smith Paper Co., Revonah Spinning Mills, Wall Tube & Metal Products Co., Phillips Fibers Corp.; dir. Applied Automation, Inc., Can. Western Cordage Co. Ltd. Mem. Am. Mgmt. Assn., Mfg. Chem. Assn., Sulphur Inst. (dir.), Internat. Inst. Synthetic Rubber Producers (dir.), Bartlesville C. of C. Home: 2325 Windsor Way Bartlesville OK 74003

CUDAHY, WILLIAM BREWER, banker; b. Chgo., Jan. 23, 1912; s. Edward Ignatius and Leonore (Brewer) C.; grad. Middlesex Sch., 1930; B.A. magna cum laude, Harvard, 1934; J.D., Northwestern U., 1937; m. Evelyn Wilkinson, Apr. 5, 1951; children—Joseph Michael, Victoria Fenton. Sec., dir. Callaghan & Co., Chgo., 1937-41; asst. sec. No. Trust Co., Chgo., 1945-51; v.p. Am. Nat. Bank & Trust Co., Chgo., 1951-60; sr. v.p., dir. 1st Nat. Bank in Palm Beach (Fla.), 1960—; dir. Sterling Precision Corp. (N.Y.C.). Dir. Palm Beach Civic Assn. Served as lt. USCG, 1941-45; ETO, PTO. Mem. Nat. Fedn. Financial Analysts. Republican. Episcopalian (vestryman). Clubs: Everglades (dir., sec., treas.), Bath and Tennis (dir., pres.) (Palm Beach); Coral Reef Yacht (Miami); Beverly Yacht (Marion, Mass.). Home: 159 Via Del Lago Palm Beach FL 33480 Office: 255 S County Rd Palm Beach FL 33480

CUDDINGTON, RUTH A., sch. adminstr.; b. Hickory, N.C., May 27, 1910; d. Donald E. and Elizabeth (Clark) Abee; A.B., U. S.C., 1943, M.A., 1945; postgrad. Lenoir Rhyne Coll., Radford Coll.; m. William Franklin Cuddington, Jr., Aug. 29, 1932; children—William Franklin III, Betty (Mrs. Richard O. Newman), David Abee. Tchr., Wagner (S.C.) Centralized High Sch., 1943-45, Hickory High Sch., 1944-45; prin. Cloverdale Elementary Sch., Botetourt County, Va., 1946-54; tchr. Lee Jr. High Sch., Roanoke, 1954-55; prin. Belmont Elementary Sch., Roanoke, 1955-69, Monterey Elementary Sch., Roanoke, 1969—. Active YWCA, 1955—. Bd. dirs. Crippled Children's Soc., Mental Hygiene Assn., Cerebral Palsy Assn., Roanoke Council Christians and Jews. Named Woman of Year, Roanoke, 1959. Mem. Nat. (state pres., nat. bd. mem., nat. rec. sec.), Va., councils adminstrv. women in edn., Va., Roanoke City, Botetourt County (v.p.) edn. assns. Nat., Va., Roanoke depts. elementary sch. prins, N.E.A., Am. Assn. U. Women, Internat. Platform Assn., Smithsonian Assos. Home: 233 Christian Av NE Roanoke VA 24102

CUEVAS, JOSE LUIS, artist; b. Mexico City, Mexico, Feb. 26, 1933; student Nat. Sch. Painting and Sculpture, Mexico City. One man shows, Mexico City, 1947, Pan-Am. Union, Washington, 1954, Galerie Edouard Loeb, Paris, France, 1955, Havana, Cuba, 1956, N.Y.C., 1957, 60, Caracas, Venezuela, 1958, Buenos Aires, Argentina, 1959, Sao Paulo, Brazil, 1959; represented permanent collection Museum Modern Art, others; prof. art Universidad Iberoamericana, Mexico City, 1956—; vis. prof. Phila. Museum Art Sch., 1957. Illustrator The Worlds of Kafka and Cuevas, 1959; Poems (W. McLeod Rivera), 1960. Contbr. to newspapers, mags. Address: 1766 Lanier Pl NW Washington DC also 1028 Calle del Valle Providencia Mexico DF Mexico

CUFFIC, ARTHUR WILLIAM, JR., scientist. Prof. R. L. Reagan Nat. Cancer Inst. Address: Chateai West Apt 411 9737 Mt Pisgah Rd Silver Springs MD 20903

CUITUN, LUIS LORENZO, feed co. exec.; b. Merida, Mexico, Aug. 22, 1939; s. Celestino C. and Felicitas (Yeh) C.; Ing.Agronomo, Pan Am. Agrl. Sch., 1961; B.Sc., U. Ariz., 1963, M.Sc., 1965. With CYCASA, 1961-65, technician ruminant feeds div., 1962-63, tech. supr., 1965; nutritionist AISA, 1965-66; head nutrition dept. Industrieas Avicolas S.A., Hermosillo, Sonora, Mexico, 1966—. Cons. animal nutrition. Former Rockefeller scholar, Pan Am. Agrl. Sch. scholar, ITAV scholar, BCO de Mexico scholar. Mem. Am. Soc. Animal Sci., Latin Am., Mexican (founder) socs. animal prodn. Home: 43 Dr Aguilar Hermosille Mexico Office: PO Box 1138 Hermosillo Sonora Mexico

CULBRETH, RAYWARD BILL, clergyman; b. Columbia, Ala., Dec. 17, 1921; s. Jesse A. and Ettie (Webb) C.; A.B., Howard Coll., 1944; B.D., So. Bapt. Theol. Sem., 1947, Th.M., 1948, Th.D., 1951; m. Ella Florine Eaton, June 3, 1943; children—Karen F., Randall E. Ordained to ministry Baptist Ch., 1942; pastor, Choccolocco, Ala., 1942-44, New Haven, Ky., 1945-47, Clermont, Ky., 1947-49, First Bapt. Ch., Miami, Fla., 1949-58, Miami Springs (Fla.) Bapt. Ch., 1958-61, Met. Bapt. Ch., Washington, 1961-66, Huffman Bapt. Ch., Birmingham, 1966—. Moderator Miami (Fla.) Bapt. Assn., 1957; mem. Christian life commn. So. Bapt. Conv., 1958-61, mem. Sunday Sch. Bd., 1962-66; pres. D.C. Pastor's Conf., 1966; mem. Ala. Bd. Missions, 1967-72; mem. exec. bd., chmn. evangelism com. Birmingham Bapt. Assn., 1968. Chmn. bd. Cook Springs Home for Sr. Citizens 1968-72. Recipient Freedoms Found. Valley Forge Freedom award, 1962. Address: 700 Huffman Rd Birmingham AL 35215

CULL, JOHN GUINN, JR., educator; b. Venice, Ill., Nov. 9, 1934; s. John Guinn and Geneva Mae (Crippen) C.; B.S., Tex. A. and M. U., 1959, M.Ed., 1960; Ph.D. in Psychology, Tex. Tech U., 1965; m. Linda Carol Abbott, June 29, 1957; children—David Lawrence, Dana Lorene, Rebecca Lynn. Vocational rehab. counselor Tex. Edn. Agy., San Antonio, 1961-64; dir. div. research and program devel. Va. Dept. Vocational Rehab., Richmond, 1965-66; asso. prof. rehab. Va. Commonwealth U., 1966—, dir. regional counselor tng. program; adj. prof. U. Va., 1972—. Mem. adv. council Facilities Tng. program Indsl. Edn. dept., U. Md.; cons. Rehab. Services Adminstrn. Dept. Health, Edn. and Welfare, Washington, 1968, Central Shenandoah Aging Program, Waynesboro, Va., Sarah bonwell Hudgins Regional Center, Hampton, Va., Bur. Hearings and Appeals Social Security Adminstrn., Washington. Mem. health and human resources com. Central Shenandoah Planning Commn., Staunton, Va., 1969—, mem. criminal justice com., 1971—. Bd. dirs. Valley Workshops, Inc., Waynesboro, Lurnmor Sch., Waynesboro, Dunsmore Coll., Staunton. Served to lt. USNR, 1964-65. Recipient Community Service award Peninsula Assn. Retarded Children, 1971, Community Service award S.B. Hudgins Center, 1972, Outstanding Community Achievement award, Waynesboro, Va.; named Ky. Col. Mem. Am. Correctional Assn., Am. Personnel and Guidance Assn., Am. Psychol. Assn., Council Rehab. Counselor Educators, Internat. Assn. Rehab. Facilities, Nat. Assn. Retarded Children, Nat. Rehab. Assn. Presbyn. Author: (with R.E. Hardy) Vocational Rehabilitation: Profession and Process, 1971; (with C. R. Colvin) Contemporary Field Work Practices in Rehabilitation, 1972; (with R. E. Hardy) Social and Rehabilitation Services for the Blind, 1972; Fundamentals of Criminal Behavior and Correctional Systems, 1972; Introduction to Correctional Rehabilitation, 1972. Cons. editor Charles C. Thomas Pub., 1970—. Home: 324 Stuart Av Stuarts Draft VA 24477 Office: PO Box 499-WWRC Fishersville VA 22939

CULLINAN, EDMUND P., govt. ofcl. Chief dep. clk. U.S. Supreme Ct., Washington. Address: U. S. Supreme Ct 1 1st St NW Washington DC 20543

CULLINAN, GERALD, assn. exec.; b. San Francisco, Jan. 6, 1916; s. Eustace and Katherine (Lawler) C.; B.A., Oxford U. (Eng.), 1937, M.A., 1957; m. Barbara Lynch, Jan. 2, 1943; children—Mary Patricia, Thomas. Reporter, editor San Francisco Call-Bull., 1938-43; partner Mooney & Cullinan, Dallas, 1946-53; asst. to postmaster gen., Washington, 1953-58; asst. to pres. Nat. Assn. Letter Carriers, Washington, 1959—. Mem. Inst. on Fgn. Relations (chmn. Friends Service com. 1950). Roman Catholic. Clubs: Serra Internat., National Press (Washington); Kenwood Country (Chevy Chase, Md.). Author: 4000 Years in San Antonio, 1949; A Financial Policy for the U.S. Post Office, 1955; The Post Office Department, 1967; The U.S. Postal Service, 1973. Home: 6205 Nebraska Av Washington DC 20015 Office: 100 Indiana Av Washington DC 20001

CULLINS, JOHN GRAYDON, physician; b. Junction City, Ark., Dec. 11, 1893; s. John Robert and Mary Elizabeth (Gardner) C.; Ph.B., Little Rock Coll., 1930; M.D., U. Ark., 1917; m. Alma B. Conrad, Aug. 9, 1918. Asst. attending surgeon USPHS, Little Rock, San Antonio, Ft. Worth, 1918-19, U.S. Pellagra Hosp., Spartanburg, S.C., 1919-20; neuropsychiatrist VA Hosp., Lake City, Fla., 1920-21, North Little Rock, Ark., 1921; neuropsychiatrist, roentgenologist VA Hosp., Bronx, N.Y., 1922-28, Northport, N.Y., 1928-31; clin. dir. VA Hosp., North Chicago, Ill., 1931-37, Marion, Ind., 1937-39; mgr. VA Hosp., Am. Lake, Washington, 1939-45, Knowville, Ia., 1945-47 chief neuropsychiat. service VA Hosp., Wadsworth, Kan., 1947-61; with Benton unit State Hosp., Ark., 1961-63. Served as col. M.C., AUS, 1942-47. Diplomate Am. Bd. Psychiatry and Neurology. Fellow A.M.A., Am. Psychiat. Assn.; mem. Union County Med. Soc., Ark. Med. Soc., Radiol. Soc N.A., Assn. Mil. Surgeons of U.S., Heroes of '76, Nat. Sojourners, Chi Zeta Chi, Phi Rho Sigma. Mason. Contbr. articles med. jours. Address: 1412 S Taylor St Little Rock AR 72204

CULLUM, WILLIAM ELDRIDGE, retail store exec.; b. Columbia, S.C., Oct. 24, 1921; s. Lorenzo Dow and Jessie (Mack) C.; B.S. in Bus. Adminstrn., U. S.C., 1947; m. Alpha Wilson Hammond, Apr. 8, 1947; children—William Eldridge, Robert Dow, Elizabeth Wilson. Stock boy Saxon-Cullum Shoe Co., Columbia, S.C., 1939-40, salesman, 1940-42., salesman Davison-Paxon Co., 1946, buyer men's shoes and furnishings, 1947; asst. buyer women's shoes Davison's, Atlanta, 1947-50; buyer men's, women's and children shoes Cullum's, Augusta, 1950-51, gen. store mgr. gen mdse. mgr., buyer shoes, 1951-60; mdse. mgr., buyer shoes, accessories, pres., dir. Cullum's of S.C., Columbia, 1960—; v.p., dir. Cullum's, Inc. and all subsidary cos., Augusta, 1965—. Dir. S.C. Retail Council; mem. Shoes Asso. Mem. Higher Edn. Com., Columbia, 1962-64. Served with USMC Res., 1942-46. Mem. Nat. Shoe Retailers Assn. (dir.; mem. women's shoe style com.; v.p. 1967—), Columbia C. of C., Pi Kappa Phi. Presbyn. Clubs: Lion, Sertoma; Forest Lake (Columbia, S.C.); Pinnacle (Augusta, Ga.). Home: 1680 Woodlake Dr Columbia SC 29206 Office: 1601 Main St Columbia SC 29201

CULP, DELOS POE, univ. pres.; b. Clanton, Ala. July 26, 1911; s. Joseph Daniel and Lela (Popwell) C.; student Jacksonville State Coll., 1932-34; B.S., Auburn U., 1937, M.S., 1940; Ed.D., Columbia, 1949; m. Martha Edwardine Street, Dec. 23, 1934; children—Martha Jean, James David, John Stephen. Tchr., prin. Chilton, Butler counties, Ala., 1935-42; supt. Chilton County Schs., Ala., 1942-46; supr. pub. sch. trans., asst. dir. div. adminstrn. and finance State Dept. Edn., Montgomery, Ala., 1946-51; prof. edn. Ala. Polytech. Inst., 1951-54; pres. Livingston State Coll., 1954-63; pres. Ala. Coll., Montevallo, 1963-67; pres. E. Tenn. State U., Johnson City, 1967—. Dir. First Peoples Bank. Mem. com. on studies Am. Assn. State Colls. and Univs., 1970—. Chmn. Nat. Commn. on Safety Edn., 1965—; mem. survey team for Philippine Sch. Bur. Survey, 1959-60; mem. bd. advisers Meth. Children's Home, Selma, Ala.; mem. nat. com. on exploring Boy Scouts Am., 1971—. Mem. Ala. Edn. Commn. (exec. dir. 1957-59), Ala. Edn. Assn. (chmn. policies commn. 1965—), Am. Assn. U. Profs., Ala. Acad. Sci., Am. Assn. Sch. Adminstrs., Ala. Hist. Assn., Kappa Delta Pi, Kappa Phi Kappa, Phi Delta Kappa, Phi Kappa Phi. Democrat. Methodist. Rotarian. Home: Pres's Home East Tenn State University Johnson City TN 37601

CULP, MARTHA EDWARDINE STREET (MRS. DELOS POE CULP), educator, civic worker; b. Gadsden, Ala., Nov. 4, 1915; d. Alonzo Cranford and Mattie (Miller) Street; student Jacksonville State Coll., 1932-34; B.S., Auburn U., 1940; postgrad. Columbia, 1948, Birmingham Mus.; m. Delos Poe Culp, Dec. 23, 1934; children—Martha Jean (Mrs. William McIver Flanigan), James David, John Stephen. Tchr, elementary grades, Ala. Schs., 1934-42; sec. to sch. supt. Chilton County, Ala., 1942-45; tchr. pub. kindergarten Tappan, N.Y., 1948-49; tchr. Marbury, Ala., 1950-51, Auburn, Ala., 1952-53; coll. registrar Livingston State Coll., 1957-63. Chmn., Easter Seal Soc. for Crippled Children and Adults. Pres.'s rep. to bd. Carroll Reece Mus. Soc.; mem. bd. United Fund, Johnson City Symphony Orch. Mem. D.A.R. (vice regent), U.D.C. (v.p.), Nat. League Am. Pen Women, Am. Hemerocallis Soc., Tenn. Women's Press and Authors, Watauga Valley Art League (charter), Delta Kappa Gamma, Kappa Delta Pi. Clubs: Johnson City Garden; Faculty Women's (past pres.); Monday; Music. Contbr. articles newspapers, mags. Home: Presidents Home East Tenn State University Johnson City TN 37601

CULPEPPER, FRED CARROLL, JR., engring. and constrn. co. exec.; b. Monroe, La., Nov. 16, 1918; s. Fred Carroll and Elizabeth (Schulze) C.; B.C.E., Va. Mil. Inst., 1940; m. Mary Frances Moore, June 6, 1941; children—Fred Carroll III, Carol (Mrs. J. Wayne Smith), Dorothy (Mrs. John Schween), Patricia. Project mgr. Ford, Bacon & Davis, 1941-63, mgr. bus. devel., 1963-69, exec. v.p., resident mgr., Monroe, La., 1970—, dir., 1963—; pres. Sealants Internat. Inc.; dir. Ouachita Nat. Bank, Monroe, La. Mem. council Small Bus. Adminstrn. for La., 1969-70; mem. La.-Miss. Regional Export Council Dept. Commerce, 1969-70; mem. exec. com. Jr. Achievement of Monroe, La., 1970—. Served with AUS, 1941-45. Decorated Bronze Star medal with one oak leaf cluster; Purple Heart medal with one oak leaf cluster. Mem. Nat. Soc. Profl. Engrs., La. Engring. Soc. (dir. 1970), Am. Soc. C.E. (mem. exec. com. 1970-71), Nat. Constructors Assn. Clubs: N.Y. Athletic, Harbor View, Bayou de Siard Country. Home: 3506 Loop Rd Monroe LA 71201 Office: PO Box 1762 Monroe LA 71201

CULPEPPER, GEORGE B., JR., lawyer; b. Fort Valley, Ga., Dec. 4, 1899; s. George B. and Lillian (Shepard) C.; student pub. schs.; m. Mary Elizabeth Adams, Apr. 24, 1919; children—George B. III, Mary Lillian (Mrs. Robert Lawson Harris). Admitted to Ga. bar, 1923; chief Selective System, Ga., 1918-19; ins. bus., Ft. Valley, Ga., 1920-22; mem., vice chmn. bd. trustees and chmn. investment com. Employees Retirement System of Ga., 1949-63. Mem. Govs. staff, 1948-63. Hon. v.p. Am. Sunday Sch. Union, 1958—. Mem. Ga. Gov.'s Staff, 1971—. Mem. Am. Bar Assn., Am. Judicature Soc., Nat. Railroad Trial Counsel Assn. Methodist. Mason. Kiwanian. Home: 401 Forrest Dr Ft Valley GA 31030 Office: 206 Central Av Ft Valley GA 31030

CULPEPPER, JAMES EUELL, ret. sch. adminstr.; b. nr. Statenville, Ga., Aug. 8, 1905; s. James W. and Eugenia M. (Clayton) C.; M.S., Fla. State U., 1959; m. Cuba L. Kinsey, Feb. 28, 1933; children—Luverne (Mrs. Lloyd Wheeler), Vernon, Nell (Mrs. Lavaughan Hughes), Elaine (Mrs. W. R. Henderson), Brooks, Sandy (Mrs. Yates McDade). Pub. sch. tchr., Clinch County, Ga., 1926-33, Echols County, Ga., 1933-52, Lowndes County, Ga., 1953-63; county sch. supt. Echols County, 1964-68; prin. Jennings (Fla.) Elementary Sch., 1969-71. Mem. Civil Air Patrol; v.p. Coastal Plains Area Tourism Council. Served to maj. State Guard, 1940-45. Lion. Home: Route 2 Lake Park GA 31636

CULVER, NOREEN RAGSDALE (MRS. CECIL L. CULVER), banker; b. Dexter, Tex., Sept. 5, 1905; d. K. D. and Willie (Stiles) Ragsdale; student pub. schs., Dexter; m. Cecil L. Culver, Aug. 16, 1924; 1 son, Cecil L. Bookkeeper, State Nat. Bank, Groom, Tex., 1941-46, asst. cashier, 1946-51, cashier, 1951-70, v.p., cashier, 1970—, dir., 1952—. Mem. Groom Community Exec. Club (past pres.), Groom Country Neighbors (past pres.). Mem. Order Eastern Star (past worthy matron). Home: Box 220 Groom TX 79039 Office: State Nat Bank Groom TX 79039

CUMBIE, CALVIN ARTIMUS, univ. adminstr.; b. Athens, Tex., July 19, 1922; s. Artimus and Rubie (Richardson) C.; B.A., N. Tex. State U., 1943, M.A., 1948; B.S., Tex. Christian U., 1953, M.Ed., 1951. Tchr., San Marcos Mil. Acad., 1946-47; instr. Tex. Mil. Coll., 1947-49; asst. registrar Tex. Christian U., 1949-54, registrar, 1954—. Served to lt. col. AUS, 1942; now active Res. Mem. Assn. U.S. Army, Res. Officers Assn., Am. (pres. 1972—), Tex. (pres. 1962-63), So. (pres. 1968-69) assns. collegiate registrars and admissions officers, Internat. Assn. Torch Clubs, N. Tex. State U., Tex. Christian U. (sec. (1962-63) ex-students assns., Phi Delta Kappa, Alpha Phi Omega, Pi Omega Pi, Alpha Sigma Lambda. Baptist. Rotarian. Home: 3141 Cockrell Av Fort Worth TX 76109 Office: Sadler Hall Tex Christian U Fort Worth TX 76129

CUMBO, HAROLD WALLACE, govt. ofcl.; b. Philomath, Ore., Apr. 1, 1920; s. George Wallace and Jennie T. (Hockema) C.; B.A., Walla Walla Coll., 1944; postgrad. Andrews U., 1944-45; m. Dorothy Catherine Blasko, June 17, 1951; children—Sharon Lael, Cathy Uel. With Library of Congress, Washington, 1945—, reference asst., 1945-51, head spl. study facilities, 1951-62, librarian spl. collections, 1962-67, editor Nat. Register Microform Masters, 1967—; stock broker Financial Planning Co., Hyattsville, Md., 1961-66. Mem. Nat. Microfilm Assn., D.C. library Assn. Home: 8402 11th Av Silver Spring MD 20903 Office: Library of Congress Washington DC 20540

CUMFER, DONALD ALONZO, JR., paper co. exec.; b. Oak Park, Ill., Jan. 31, 1924; s. Donald Alonzo and Ruth (Shannon) C.; B.E., Vanderbilt U., 1949; m. Winifred Eugenia Johnson, Oct. 2, 1925; children—Cynthia Dee, Neil Shannon, Shawn Johnson, Eric Michael. Mgr. Dura-Containers, Inc., Clarksville, Tenn., 1961-65; product planning and devel. mgr. Mead Packaging Co., Atlanta, 1965-68; v.p. Hamilton Mfg. Co., Richmond, Va., 1968—. Chmn., Ashland Christian Emergency Service, 1969—; chmn. Hanover County FISH, 1971—. Served with USAAF, 1942-46. Decorated D.F.C., Air medal with 1 oak leaf cluster. Mem. T.A.P.P.I., Am. Soc. for Testing and Materials. Presbyn. (chmn. bd. deacons 1971). Mason, Kiwanian. Home: 301 College St Ashland VA 23005 Office: 1901 Ellen Rd Richmond VA 23230

CUMING, GEORGE SCOTT, lawyer, gas co. exec.; b. Lakewood, O., Apr. 10, 1915; s. George Scott and Josephine (MacInnes) C.; A.B. cum laude, Western Res. U., 1937; postgrad. Harvard Law Sch., 1941-42, 45-46; J.D., Northwestern U., 1948; m. Dorothy Jane Herbst, May 12, 1943; children—Holiday (Mrs. Jason Baker Tuttle), Noelle (Mrs. John David Brock), George Scott, IV, Reid MacInnes. Auditor, Gen. Electric Co., Cleve., 1937-41; admitted Ill. bar, 1948, Mich. bar, 1950; asst. sec., asst. gen. atty. Mich.-Wis. Pipeline Co., Detroit, 1948-52, Pacific N.W. Pipeline Corp., Salt Lake City, 1955-59; tax accountant Arthur Andersen & Co., Chgo., 1952-55; asst. sec. El Paso Natural Gas Co. (Tex.), 1960-65, Rocky Mountain regional counsel, 1960-64, Washington counsel, 1964-65, gen. counsel, 1965-69, v.p., gen. counsel, 1969—, also dir. Served to lt. USNR, 1942-45. Recipient 1st Pres.'s prize for oratory Western Res. U. Mem. Am., Ill. bar assns., State Bar Mich., Delta Phi Alpha, Delta Sigma Rho, Sigma Delta Psi, Phi Delta Phi. Episcopalian. Clubs: Metropolitan, Congressional Country (Washington); University (Salt Lake City); El Paso, Coronado (El Paso). Home: 433 Borealis Lane El Paso TX 79912 Office: El Paso Natural Gas Bldg El Paso TX 79978

CUMMING, HUGH SMITH, JR., former govt. ofcl.; b. Richmond, Va., Mar. 10, 1900; s. Hugh Smith and Lucy A. (Booth) C.; student Va. Mil. Inst., Lexington, Va., 1917-20, U. Va., 1920-24; m. Winifred Burney West, Sept. 21, 1935. Mem. Va. bar; banker, London, Bombay, Singapore, Peking, 1924-27; tech. advisor U.S. State Dept., 1928; asst. to U.S. delegation Internat. Econ. Conf., London, and 7th Pan-Am. Conf., Montevideo, 1933; exec. asst. to Sec. of State, 1934, detailed to U.S. Consulate, Geneva, in connection Italo-Ethiopian affairs, 1935-36; spl. mission to Scandinavia and Netherlands, 1939; mem. exec. com. U.S Antartic Service, 1939-41; spl. mission Greenland, 1941; mem. Econ. Warfare Mission, also U.S. del. Internat. Whaling Conf., London, 1943; spl. mission to Sweden, 1943; rep. State Dept. on Anglo-Swedish-Am. Commn., and chief div. No. European Affairs, 1944; polit. liaison officer U.S. delegation UN Conf. on Internat. Orgn., San Francisco, 1945; spl. mission Iceland, 1946; counselor of Embassy, Stockholm, 1947-50; counselor of Embassy with personal rank of minister, Moscow, 1950-52; dep. sec. gen. for polit. affairs NATO, Paris, 1952-53; ambassador to Indonesia, 1953-57; spl. asst. to sec. of state, ir. Intelligence, Dept. of State, 1957-61, cons., 1961-64; mem. bd. examiners Am. Fgn. Service, 1957-62; adv. bd. Fgn. Service Inst., 1957-62; v.p. West-Wilholt Co., Stockton, Cal., 1961-63. Former mem. bd. govs. Columbia Hosp. for Women, Washington. Trustee Washington Inst. Fgn. Affairs, Meridian House Found., Washington, Family and Child Services of Washington; v.p. Overseas Mission Soc., 1963—. Chmn. adv. com. John Foster Dulles Library, Princeton; mem. adv. council Sch. Internat. Service, Am. U.; trustee Washington Cathedral; bd. dirs. Historic Georgetown, Inc.; adv. bd. Woodrow Wilson House Nat. Trust; pres., mem. bd. mgrs. Bath County Community Hosp., Hot Springs, Va. Served as 2d lt. U.S. Army, 1918. Mem. U. Va. Law Sch. Assn., Mil. Order World Wars, S.A.R., Nat. Cathedral Assn. (trustee, pres. 1962-65). Diplomatic and Consular Officers Ret. (pres.), Com. 100 for Fed. Capital, Raven Soc., Zeta Psi. Episcopalian (vestryman). Clubs: Metropolitan (past pres.), Cosmos, Alibi (Washington); Chevy Chase (Md.); Royal Swedish Yacht, Sallskopet (Stockholm). Home: 2811 O St NW Washington DC 20007 also Overlook Hot Springs VA 24445 Office: 2811 O St NW Washington DC 20007

CUMMING, JOSEPH BRYAN, lawyer; b. Augusta, Ga., Aug. 10, 1893; s. Bryan and Mary Gairdner (Smith) C.; Litt.B., Princeton U., 1915; student Harvard Law Sch., 1915-17; m. Virginia Neville Burum, Nov. 15, 1922; children—Neville Cumming Riley, Joseph Bryan, Nancy C. Connolly. Admitted to Ga. bar, 1920, since practiced in Augusta; mem. firm Cumming & Harper, now Cumming, Nixon, Yow, Waller & Capers. Dir. Ga. R.R. & Banking Co., Augusta. Mem. Gen. Assembly of Ga., 1923-24; mem. Pres.'s Adv. Council Hist. Preservation. Chmn. bd. trustees Summerville Cemetery; pres. Acad. of Richmond County, Tubman Home; trustee Clinton Anderson Hosp., Augusta Mus., Herbert Meml. Inst. Art; pres. trustees Young Men's Library Assn. Fund; chmn. Ga. Hist. Commn. Hon. ambassador of Cherokee Nation. Fellow Am. Bar Found., Am. Coll. Trial Lawyers; mem. Am., Ga. (pres. 1938-39), Augusta (pres. 1935-36). Democrat. Episcopalian. Home: 2231 Cumming Rd Augusta GA 30904 Office: Ga RR Bank Bldg Augusta GA 30902

CUMMINGS, CHARLES EDWARD, physician; b. Richmond, Va., Oct. 2, 1931; s. Thomas and Virginia (Jackson) C.; B.S., Va. Union U., 1954; M.D., Howard U., 1958; m. Mary Quash, July 28, 1953; children—Charles Edward, Kevin Antonio. Intern, D.C. Gen. Hosp., 1958-59, resident, 1959-60; practice medicine specializing in internal medicine, Richmond, 1964—; mem. staff Richmond Meml. Hosp., Retreat for Sick, Richmond; chmn. dept. medicine Richmond Community Hosp., 1968-70; dir., co-founder North Av. Med. and Profl. Center, 1971—. Served with USAF, 1950-54. Fellow Royal Soc. Health, Beta Kappa Chi, Alpha Kappa Mu, Omega Psi Phi. Home: 3007 Brook Rd Richmond VA 23227 Office: 2809 North Av Richmond VA 23222

CUMMINGS, DON GUSTAV, author; b. Dec. 5, 1921; s. John G. and Cora Belle (Strum) C.; B.A., 1946; m. Iva Florence Gibson, Sept. 22, 1943; children—Robert Lee, Barbara Kay, Debra Carolynn, Donald Lee. Actor in Gas Light, 1947, Twelfth Night, 1948; producer Ezra Walker and His Arkansas Travelers, 1941-42; Talent of Tomorrow, 1952-56; pres. Heartbreak Records, Heartbreak Music Pubs., Inc., 1960—; dir. music Williams & Hospies. Nat. promotion dir. Bapt. Lifeline Boys Ranch, Colorado Springs, 1962; bd. dirs. Mission for Needy. Mem. Delta Si Omega. Republican. Baptist. Moose. Author: Aglutination As A Control of Leukemia, 1960; Birth of Grand Ole Opry, 1964. Home: 229 Theadore Nashville TN 37214 Office: 806 16th Av S Nashville TN 37203

CUMMINGS, DONALD LAWRENCE, engr.; b. Boston, Sept. 13, 1922; s. Dennis L. and Hazel (Beaton) C.; student Tufts Coll., 1941-42, Boston Arch. Center, 1946-47; Engrs. degree with honors, Northeastern U., 1951; postgrad. Mass. Inst. Tech., 1952-53; m. Irene B. Budrick, Mar. 11, 1945; children—Pamela Gail, Cynthia, Valerie. Draftsman, John P. Heffernan, architect, 1939-40, Stone & Webster, 1940-41; architect, project engr., dir. constrn., dir. estimating dept. Metcalf & Eddy, Boston, 1946-63; asst. project engr., mgr. engring. Reston Va., Inc., 1963-66; v.p. planning, engr. Gulf Reston, Inc., 1966-72; v.p. planning, engr. Gulf Oil Real Estate Devel. Co., 1972—. Mem. bd. elevator appeals Commonwealth of Mass., 1961—; mem. com. reviewing and revising zoning ordinance County of Fairfax, Va., 1970—. Served as naval aviator USNR, 1942-46. Registered profl. engr., Mass., Conn., N.Y., Va. Mem. Boston Soc. Civil Engrs., Nat. Soc. Profl. Engrs. Contbr. numerous papers on land devel., erosion and sedimentation control, New Town devel., related fields. Home: 3700 Whispering Lane Falls Church VA 22041 Office: Reston VA

CUMMINGS, HATCH WHITFIELD, JR., physician; b. Hearne, Tex., Dec. 6, 1903; s. Hatch Whitfield and Pauline (Eckerle) C.; student U. Tex., 1921-24; M.D., Tulane U., 1928; m. Olivette Wise Nunn, June 22, 1935; stepchildren—Huberta Read Nunn (Mrs. Vernon Gerald Wright), Robert Read Nunn. Intern Grad. Hosps., U. Pa., 1928-29; preceptorship Dr. Marvin L. Graves, emeritus prof. U. Tex., Houston, 1929-33; practice medicine, specializing in internal medicine, Houston, 1933—; chief medical service Meth. Hosp., 1946-70; prof. clin. medicine Baylor U. Coll. Medicine, 1946—. Served to capt. M.C., USNR, 1942-46. Fellow A.C.P. (gov. Tex. 1963-69); mem. Tex. Acad. Medicine (past pres.), Tex. Club Internal Medicine (past pres.), Alpha Omega Alpha, Phi Gamma Delta, Nu Sigma Nu. Home: 2137 Chilton Rd Houston TX 77019 Office: 6516 Bertner Av Houston TX 77025

CUMMINGS, JILL, lawyer; b. N.Y.C., Dec. 1, 1936; A.B., Vassar Coll., 1958; student Am. U., Columbia; J.D., George Washington U., 1970. Admitted to D.C. bar, 1970; now resident asso. firm Cadwalader, Wickersham & Taft, Washington. Mem. Bar Assn. D.C. Address: Cadwalader Wickersham & Taft 1000 Connecticut Av NW Washington DC 20036

CUNNINGHAM, CARL ROBERT, music critic, educator; b. Los Angeles, Oct. 21, 1931; s. William Clement and Ruth (George) C.; Mus.B., U. Notre Dame, 1952; M.A., U. So. Cal., 1965. Instr. piano and theory Punahou Sch., Honolulu, 1960-63; lectr. music theory U. Hawaii, 1962-63; choir dir. Sacred Heart Catholic Ch., Honolulu, 1959-63; music critic San Francisco Chronicle, 1965-66; music editor Houston Post, 1966—; spl. lectr. music U. St. Thomas, Houston, 1968—, chmn. music dept., 1970—. Served with USN, 1952-56. Rockefeller Found. fellow, 1964-66. Address: 4747 Southwest Freeway Houston TX 77001

CUNNINGHAM, EMORY O., publisher; b. Kansas, Ala., Mar. 17, 1921; s. Emory O. and Belle (Kelly) C.; B.S. in Agrl. Sci., Auburn U., 1948; m. Jeanne Loftis, Dec. 21, 1951; children—James Emory, David Lee, Sara Jeanne, Mary Lou. Advt. salesman Progressive Farmer Mag., Chgo., 1948-56, asst. advt. mgr., Birmingham, Ala., 1956-60, advt. mgr., 1960-66; advt. dir. Progressive Farmer and Southern Living, 1966-67, pub., 1967—; pres. Progressive Farmer Co., 1968—; dir. Birmingham Trust Nat. Bank. Bd. dirs. Audit Bur. Circulation. Bd. govs. Internat. Ins. Seminar, Inc. Named Man of Year, Birmingham Advt. Club, 1971. Mem. Agrl. Pubs. Assn. (dir.), Mag. Pubs. Assn. (dir.), Birmingham Area C. of C. (dir.). Home: 1605 Gentilly Dr Birmingham AL 35226 Office: 821 N 19th St Birmingham AL 35202

CUNNINGHAM, FIRMAN LYTLE, ednl. adminstr.; b. McMinnville, Tenn., Oct. 3, 1919; s. James Firm and Lula Pearl (Davenport) C.; B.S., Middle Tenn. State U., 1947; M.S., U. Tenn., 1949; Ph.D., Vanderbilt U., 1962; m. Loraine Jones, Oct. 24, 1941; children—Philip Wayne, Paul Howard. Elementary sch. prin. Warren County (Tenn.) Pub. Schs., 1939-41; instr. bus. Bluefield (Va.) Coll., 1948-52; instr. econs. Middle Tenn. State U., Murfreesboro, 1952-56, asst. prof., 1956-63, asso. prof., 1963-65, prof., 1965—, dean Sch. Bus. and Econs., 1964—. Cons., U.S. Dept. Labor, 1958-64, State Farm Ins. Co., 1954-60. Bd. dirs. Tenn. Econ. Edn. Assn., 1962. Served with AUS, 1942-45. Decorated Silver Star, Bronze Star, Purple Heart. Recipient Dept. Army award, 1971. Ford Found. scholar, 1953. Mem. Am., So. econ. assns., Am. Higher Edn. Assn., Nat., Tenn. edn. assns., Am. Mgmt. Assn. Baptist (deacon 1964—). Kiwanian (dir. 1962). Home: 715 Shawnee Dr Murfreesboro TN 37130

CUNNINGHAM, FLOYD WADE, lawyer; b. Marietta, Miss.,Feb. 23, 1905; s. James Andy and Carolyn Nancy (Floyd) C.; student Millsaps Coll., 1921-24; LL.B., U. Miss., 1928; m. Estha Lee; 1 son, Larry. Admitted Miss. bar, 1928; pros. atty. Prentiss Co., Miss., 1932-36; dist. atty. First Judicial Dist. Miss., 1936-44; mem. firm Cunningham & Cunningham, Booneville, Miss., 1945—; on leave to act as prosecutor Internat. Prosecution sect. in trial of Tojo, et al. before Internat. Mil. Tribunal for the Far East, Tokyo, Japan, 1947-48. Served as capt. USAAF, 1942-45. Mem. Internat. Soc. Barristers, Am., Miss., 1st Circuit Ct. Dist. (pres. 1965-66) bar assns., Am. Judicature Soc., V.F.W. (past State dept. adv., past dist. comdr.) Am. Legion (past comdr. local post, past dist. comdr.), 40 and 8 (past grande advocate, Miss.), Miss. Assn. Hosp. Governing Bds., Kappa Sigma, Sigma Upsilon. Methodist. Mason (32 deg., Shriner), Elk, Rotarian. Home: PO Box 168 Booneville MS 38829

CUNNINGHAM, FRANK WILLIS, ret. educator; b. Lecompton, Kan., Nov. 19, 1896; s. Frederick Bartlett and Cora (Day) C.; A.B., Kan. Wesleyan U., 1921; M.S., Ft. Hays Kan. State Coll., 1936; D.Sc., Coll. of Ozarks, 1967; m. Edna Mae Kirk, June 14, 1923; children—Charlotte Edna (Mrs. John W. Daniels), Willis Charles. Tchr. pub. schs., Lebanon, Kan., 1931-37, prin., Riverton, Kan., 1937-42; faculty Northeastern Okla. A. and M. Coll., 1942-64, prof. chemistry, chmn. sci. div., 1945-64, prof. chemistry, chmn. sci. div., 1945-64; faculty Coll. of Ozarks, Clarksville, Ark., 1964-71. NSF fellow, 1957. Fellow Am. Inst. Chemists; mem. Am. Chem. Soc., A.A.A.S., Am. Assn. U. Profs., N.E.A., Am. Legion. Methodist. Mason, Rotarian (pres. 1962-63, 70-71). Research in lead and zinc in N.E. Okla. area. Author chemistry manual. Home: 502 Park Miami OK 74354

CUNNINGHAM, JACQUELYN MARIE, librarian; b. Glouster, O., Aug. 16, 1926; d. Raymond Linscott and Wilhelmine (Grothaus) Cunningham; B.A., Westhampton Coll., U. Richmond, 1949; M.A., George Peabody Coll. Tchrs., 1958. Tchr., Garden High Sch., Oakwood, Va., 1949-51; librarian, Powhatan (Va.) High Sch., 1951-55, Waterloo (Md.) Jr. High Sch., 1955-56; asst. librarian Norview Jr. High Sch., Norfolk, Va., 1956-58; children's librarian Belmont br. Richmond (Va.) Pub. Library, 1958-60; asst. librarian Tuckahoe Jr. High Sch., Richmond, 1960-62; librarian Henrico High Sch., Richmond, 1962—; mem. adj. faculty Va. Commonwealth U., 1969—. Mem. N.E.A., Va., Henrico edn. assns., Va. Library Assn. (chmn. sch. libraries sect. 1964-65), Am. Assn. U. Women, Children's Book Council Richmond, Wesleyan Service Guild (local pres. 1963-65, Richmond dist. sec. 1965-68), Bus. and Profl. Women's Clubs, Order Eastern Star, Alpha Delta Kappa Methodist. Home: 4902 Laurie Lane Richmond VA 23223 Office: 302 Azalea Av Richmond VA 23227

CUNNINGHAM, JAMES ALLEN, supt. schs.; b. Shamrock, Tex., July 1, 1927; s. Thomas Riley and Cordelia Lillian (Glazner) C.; B.S., Tex. Technol. U., 1950, M.Ed., 1959, postgrad., 1963—; m. Ethyl Faye Neeley, June 2, 1951; children—Allen Ray (dec.), Mark Thomas. Tchr., Whiteface (Tex.) Ind. Sch. Dist., 1951-62, coach, 1951-62, adminstr., 1962-68; supt. Spearman (Tex.) Ind. Sch. Dist., 1968—. Chmn. Hansford County unit A.R.C., 1969—; mem. Hansford County Library Bd. Served with AUS, 1945-47. Mem. Tex. Assn. Sch. Adminstrs. (chmn. adminstrs. sect. dist. 16 1970-71), Nat. Assn. Sch. Adminstrs., Tex. State Tchrs. Assn., N.E.A. Home: 1107 Bernice St Spearman TX 79081

CUNNINGHAM, JOSEPH CONRAD, librarian; b. Asheville, N.C., Jan. 10, 1925; s. Cornelius Carman and Bernice Anna (Fry) C.; B.A., U. Ore., 1949; B.S. in L.S., U. Cal. at Berkeley, 1950; m. Nella Mae Steussy, Oct. 20, 1970. Catalogue librarian Fresno (Cal.) State Coll. Library, 1950-51; catalogue librarian Los Angeles State Coll. Library, 1951-54; catalogue librarian U. Tex. Library, Austin, 1954—. Served with AUS, 1943-46; ETO. Mem. Am. Assn. U. Profs. Democrat. Unitarian. Home: 1904 Miles St Austin TX 78745

CUNNINGHAM, MORRIS, newspaperman; b. McMinnville, Tenn., July 27, 1917; s. Oscar Lafayette and Jessie Lee (Crawford) C.; m. Helen Henry Morris, Oct. 25, 1947; children—Diane, Morris Frank. Corr., state news editor, state capitol reporter Nashville Tennessean, 1935-43; reporter, news editor A.P., Nashville, N.Y.C., 1943-45; corr. Time, Life, Fortune mags., Nashville, 1945-53; Nashville corr. Memphis Comml. Appeal, 1945-53, Washington corr., 1953—. Adv. com. tng. tchrs. deaf Office Edn., 1962-64. Mem. White House Corrs. Assn., Sigma Delta Chi. Methodist. Clubs: Overseas Writers, Nat. Press (Washington); Kenwood Golf and Country. Home: 6002 Woodacres Dr Wood Acres Washington DC 20016 Office: 1013 13th St NW Washington DC 20005

CUNNINGHAM, RONNIE WALTER, devel. co. exec., former astronaut; b. Creston, Ia., Mar. 16, 1932; s. Walter Wilfred and Gladys Thelma (Backen) C.; B.A., U. Cal. at Los Angeles, 1960, M.A., 1961; m. Lo Ella Irby, July 8, 1956; children—Brian Keith, Kimberly Anne. Research asst. Planning Research Corp., Westwood, Cal., 1959-60; physicist Rand Corp., Santa Monica, Cal., 1960-64; astronaut NASA, Manned Spacecraft Center, Houston, 1964-71, crew mem. Apollo 7, 1968; v.p. charge operations div. Century Devel. Corp., Houston, 1971—. Founding dir. Earth Awareness Found. Served with USMC, 1951-56. Recipient Exceptional Service award NASA, Astronaut Wings, USN; Alumni Profl. Achievement award U. Cal. at Los Angeles, 1969; Spl. Trustees award Nat. Acad. Television Arts and Scis., 1969; co-recipient Haley Astronautics award Am. Inst. Aeros. and Astronautics, 1969. Asso. fellow Am. Inst. Aeros. and Astronautics; mem. Soc. Exptl. Test Pilots, Marine Air Res., Am. Geophys. Union, Sigma Xi, Sigma Pi Sigma. Club: Explorers. Office: 1 Greenway Plaza Houston TX 77046

CUNNINGHAM, THOMAS JEFFERSON, JR., physician; b. Redfield, Ark., Aug. 31, 1911; s. Thomas Jefferson and Leila Hayden (Trotter) C.; B.S., Tulane U., 1929-33; M.D., U. Ark., 1937; m. Margaret Louise Davis, Sept. 18, 1939; children—Mary M. (Mrs. Chares R. Carlot), Thomas Jefferson III, James R. Intern, Shreveport (La.) Charity Hosp., 1937-38, surg. resident, 1938-39; gen. practice medicine, Pine Bluff, Ark., 1939—; mem. staff Jefferson Hosp., Pine Bluff. Mem. A.M.A., So. Med. Assn., Ark., Jefferson County med. socs., Am. Coll. Family Practice. Mason (Shriner). Home: 1316 W 29th St Pine Bluff AR 71601 Office: 300 W 6th St Pine Bluff AR 71601

CUNNINGHAM, THOMAS SIDNEY, educator; b. Rocky, Okla., Feb. 21, 1915; s. James Newt and Clara (Payton) C.; B.S. Okla. State U., 1942, M.S., 1944, Ed.D., 1966; m. Doris Vivian Mathis, June 8, 1940 children— TeLoris Ann, DeVonna Lee. Plant scientist Bur. Plant Industry, Woodward, 1942-44; county agrl. agt., hollis Okla. 1945-51; mgr. Farmers Coop. Cotton Gin and Grain Elevator, Hollis, 1951; supt. Sandy Land Research Sta., Mangum, Okla. 1952-58; extension agronomist Okla. State U., Stillwater, 1959-62, extension family life specialist, 1963—. Mem. exec. com. Okla. Gov.'s Com. on Children and Youth, 1968—; adv. mem. to spl. unit on aging Okla. Dept. Instns. and Social and Rehab. Services. Founding bd. mem. Westview Boys Home, Hollis, 1957-59; asso. bd. mem. Okla. Christian Coll., Oklahoma City, 1954-66. Mem. Nat., Okla. (pres. 1967-68) councils family relations, Nat., Okla. home econs. assns., Okla. Council Family Planning (exec. com. 1967—), Okla. Health and Welfare Assn. (dir., v.p. 1967), Sigma Xi, Phi Eta Sigma, Epsilon Sigma Phi, Alpha Zeta. Mem. Ch. of Christ (elder 1965—). Home: 908 Knapp St Stillwater OK 74074

CUNNINGHAM, WALTER CLIEVE, ednl. adminstr.; b. Clarksville, Tex., Sept. 26, 1905; s. George Washington and Lillie (Townsend) C.; B.A., Tex. Inst. Tech., 1930, M.A., 1939; student Southeastern State Coll., 1927-28; m. Ruth Lee Garrett, Apr. 5, 1930; children—Walter Lee, Sandra Sue (Mrs. Phillip Wayne Rollins). Formerly coach McCarty, Tex., Sparenberg, Tex., Whiteflat, Tex.; supt. schs., Benjamin, Tex., 1936-42, Munday, Tex., 1942-46, Muleshoe, Tex., 1946-49, Mineral Wells, Tex., 1952-71, Galena Park, Tex., 1956—. Mem. Gov.'s Com. for Spl. Edn., 1953-54. Mem. Harris County (pres. 1953-54), Tex. State (mem. exec. com. 1966-72) Sch. Adminstrs. Mason, Rotarian. Home: 2222 8th St Galena Park TX 77547 Office: 202 North Loop Houston TX 77008

CUNNINGHAM, WARREN PEEK, JR., dist. judge; b. Hampton, Va., Jan. 20, 1915; s. Warren Peek and Anne (Ponton) C.; LL.B. U. Tex. 1937, B.A., 1938; LL.M, Harvard 1939; m. Ellen Benner, Nov. 20, 1942; children—Marianne, Tom Alan, Warren Peek III. Admitted to Tex. bar, 1937 spl. atty. anti-trust div. U.S. Dept. Justice, 1939-42; asst. mgr. regional office VA, Houston, 1946-47; pvt. practice law, Houston, 1947-63; dist. judge 164th Dist. Ct. Harris County, Houston, 1963—. Dir. officer Cunningham Bearing Co. Bd. dirs. Sam Houston Area council Boy Scouts Am., Houston and Harris County Community Council; trustee United Fund, Houston. Served to lt. commdr. USNR, 1942-45. Mem. Am., Houston bar assns., State Bar Tex. Home: 405 Timberwild St Houston TX 77024 Office: Civil Courts Bldg Houston TX 77002

CURBO, ROBERT STUART ACREE, educator, accountant; b. Mineral Wells, Miss., Dec. 27, 1932; s. Homer F. and Leah (Acree) C.; B.B.A., U. Miss., 1957, M.B.A., 1958; m. Dorothy Jean Lanier, Dec. 20, 1956; children— Pamela Jean, John Robert. Accountant, Lawrence W. Curbo, Bahalia, Miss., 1958-65, Curbo & Curbo, Olive Branch, Miss., 1965-69, Robert S. Curbo, Olive Branch, 1969—; asso. prof. accounting, Memphis State U., 1961—; asso. dir. Bank of Olive Branch. Cons. in field. Served with AUS, 1953-55. Baptist. Mem. Miss. Soc. C.P.A.'s, Beta Alpha Psi, Alpha Tau Omega, Delta Sigma Pi. Clubs: Accounting (Memphis); Olive Branch Country (sec. 1966-69). Home: PO Box 445 Olive Branch MS 38654 Office: Sch Bus Memphis State U Memphis TN 38111

CURL, H. JOSEPH, hosp. adminstr.; b. Hinckley, Minn., Jan. 6, 1929; B.S. in Commerce (Joseph L. Shaughnessy scholar), St. Louis U., 1950; M.B.A. (USPHS grantee), U. Chgo., 1967; m. 3 children. Personnel dir. Mercy Hosp., Bay City, Mich., 1950-51; mem. staff hosp. supply div., Am. Hosp. Supply Co., 1955-60, S.W. regional mgr., 1960-64; hosp. sales mgr. Am. Seating Co., Dallas, 1964-65; hosp. cons. John Gompper & Assos., 1965-67; asst. dir. Loyola U. Hosp., Chgo., 1967-68, acting dir., Maywood, Ill., 1968, asso. dir., 1969-70; adminstr. Georgetown U. Hosp., Washington, 1970—; mem. faculty Coll. DuPage, 1968-70; asst. prof. community medicine and internat. health Georgetown U., 1970—; preceptor, adj. asst. prof. George Washington U., 1970—; adj. asst. prof. Grad. Program Hosp. Adminstrn. U. Ala., 1970—; adv. cons. Pan Am. Health Orgn., 1971—. Chmn. Inst. Quality Health Care D.C. Dept. Human Resources. Dir. local P.T.A. Mem. Am. Coll. Hosp. Adminstrs., D.C. Hosp. Assn. (pres. elect 1972), Tri-State Hosp. Assn. (trustee), Met. Hosp. Assn. Nat. Capital Area (mem. negotiating com.). Address: Georgetown U Hosp 3800 Reservoir Rd NW Washington DC 20007

CURLEE, JOHN EDWARD MARTIN, banker; b. Beeville, Tex., May 31, 1942; s. Wiley Edward Curlee and Mary Elizabeth Martin; student Victoria Coll., 1960-62, U. Tex., 1962-64; m. Mary Ann Alstrin, June 8, 1963; with First Nat. Bank, Goliad, Tex., 1964—, v.p., loan officer, dir., 1968—; dir. Goliad Royalty Co., 1966—, sec.-treas., 1967—. Mem. Tex. Banking Assn., Am. Inst. Banking, Tex. Cattle Raisers Assn., Tex. Ex-students Assn., C. of C., Farm Bur. Democrat. Episcopalian. Rotarian. Home: 308 Davis Av Goliad TX 77963 Office: 222 S Market St Goliad TX 77963

CURRAN, CHARLES EDWARD, educator, clergyman; b. Rochester, N.Y., Mar. 30, 1934; s. John Francis and Gertrude Louise (Beisner) C.; B.A., St. Bernard's Sem. and Coll., 1955; Ph.D., Pontifical Gregorian U., Rome, Italy, 1961; Ph.D., Pontifical Lateran U., Rome, Italy, 1961. Ordained priest Roman Cath. Ch., 1958; prof. moral theology St. Bernard's Sem., Rochester, N.Y., 1961-65; prof. theology Cath. U. Am., Washington, 1965—. Fellow Kennedy Center Bio-ethics, 1972; faculty fellow grantee Am. Assn. Theol. Schs., 1971-72. Mem. Cath. Theol. Soc. Am. (pres. 1969-70), Am. Soc. Christian Ethics (pres. 1971-72), Coll. Theology Soc. (past pres.) Am. Assn. U. Profs. Author: Christian Morality Today, 1966; A New Look at Christian Morality, 1968; Contemporary Problems in Moral Theology, 1970; Catholic Moral Theology in Dialogue, 1972; (with others) Dissent in and for the Church, 1969, The Responsbility of Dissent: The Church and Academic Freedom, 1969. Editor: Absolutes in Moral Theology, 1968; Contraception: Authority and Dissent, 1969, Shared Responsibility in the Local Church, 1970. Contbr. articles to profl. jours. Address: Caldwell Hall Catholic University Washington DC 20017

CURRENT-GARCIA, EUGENE, educator; b. New Orleans, July 8, 1908; s. Joseph R. and Bertha (Ehrhardt) Current Garcia; A.B., Tulane U., 1930, M.A., 1932; A.M., Harvard, 1942, Ph.D., 1947; postgrad. (Ford Found. fellow), Princeton U., 1953-54; m. Alva Adele Garrett, June 18, 1935; children—William J., Alison (Mrs. Raymond F. Heyd), Adele (Mrs. Lewis F. Mayson II). Instr. English, U. Neb., Lincoln, 1936-39, La. State U., Baton Rouge, 1944-47; asst. prof. English Auburn (Ala.) U., 1947-50, asso. prof., 1950-54, prof., 1955—; Fulbright lectr. Am. Lit., Greece, 1956-58. Mem. South Atlantic Modern Lang. Assn., So. Humanities Conf., Ala. Hist. Assn., Phi Beta Kappa, Phi Kappa Phi, Omicron Delta Kappa. Author: O. Henry, 1962. Author and editor: American Short Stories, 1952; What is the Short Story, 1962; Realism & Romanticism in Fiction, 1964; Short Stores of the Western World. Co-editor: Southern Humanities Rev., 1967—. Home: 510 E Samford Av Auburn AL 36830

CURRERI, PETER A., physician; b. Phila., 1923; M.D., Temple, 1948. Intern, St. Luke's Hosp., Phila., 1948-49, resident surgery, 1949-50; resident obstetrics and gynecology Abington (Pa.) Meml. Hosp., 1950-53; practice medicine, specializing in obstetrics and gynecology, 1953—; asso. surgeon, obstetrician and gynecologist Abington Meml. Hosp.; former asso. attending surgeon Holy Redeemer Hosp., Meadowbrook, Pa.; chief obstetrician and gynecologist Knud-Hansen Meml. Hosp., St. Thomas, V.I. Served to capt. USAF, 1953-55. Diplomate Am. Bd. Obstetrics and Gynecology. Mem. A.M.A., V.I. Med. Assn. (pres. 1970). Office: Knud-Hansen Meml Hosp St Thomas VI 00801

CURREY, CECIL BARR, educator; b. Clarks, Neb., Nov. 29, 1932; s. Chalmers Cecil and Edith Estelle (Barr) C.; A.B., Fort Hays (Kan.) State Coll., 1957, M.Sc., 1958; Ph.D., U. Kan., 1965; m. Laura Gene Hewett, Aug. 14, 1952; children—Samuel Bowman, Anne Estelle, Laura Alise. Ordained to ministry Conglist. Ch., 1957; chaplain N.G., 1965—; asst. prof. history Neb. Wesleyan U., Lincoln, 1964-67; asso. prof. history U. South Fla., Tampa., 1967-71, prof., 1971—. Cons. on new grad. programs in history. Served with AUS, 1953-55. Recipient grants S & H Lectureship Program, Sperry & Hutchins Found., 1966, 67. Mem. Am. Assn. U. Profs., Am. History Assn., Orgn. Am. Historians, Conf. on Faith and History, Mil. Chaplains Assn., Fla. Coll. Conf. Tchrs. History (exec. council 1968-69), Phi Delta Kappa, Phi Kappa Phi, Phi Alpha Theta. Republican. Author: Road to Revolution, Ben Franklin in England, 1965-75, 1968; Code number 72: Ben Franklin and the American Revolution, 1775-1785, 1972. Contbr. articles to profl. jours. Home: Route 2 Box 690 Lutz FL 33549

CURRIE, F.A., judge; b. Vancouver, B.C., Oct. 17, 1907; s. George Graham and Lulu Marion (Angevine) C. (parents Am. citizens); LL.B., U. Fla., 1932, J.D. (hon.), 1967; m. Reese Tumlin Vermilya, Aug. 15, 1958. Admitted to Fla. bar, 1932; practiced in West Palm Beach, Fla., 1932-51; judge Small Claims-Magistrate Ct., Palm Beach County, Fla., 1951—. Municipal judge, West Palm Beach, Fla., 1943-46; mem. Fla. Childrens Commn., 1949-52. Served with AUS, 1942-43. Mem. Fla., Palm Beach County bar assns., Sigma Chi. Democrat. Episcopalian. Mason, Elk, Kiwanian. Home: 200 Rugby Rd West Palm Beach FL 33405 Office: Palm Beach County Ct House West Palm Beach FL 33401

CURRIE, JOHN STUART, psychologist; b. McBee, S.C., Oct. 6, 1938; s. William Margret and Lona (Cruse) C.; student Mercer U., 1957-59; B.A. Fla. State U., 1961; M.A., U. Fla., 1962, Ph.D., 1965; m. Beverly Jo Unick, Sept. 2, 1962; children—William Kennedy, Donya Lynn. Clin. psychologist Macon-Bibb County Health Dept., 1965-68; pvt. practice psychology, Atlanta, 1968—. Mem. staff Atlanta Psychiat. Clinic; cons. Ga. Depts. Family and Children Services, Children's Homes; asst. prof. Ga. Inst. Tech., 1968; mem. Collegium Musicum, Emory U., 1968-70. Mem. Am. Acad. Psychotherapists, Ga. Psychol. Assn., (treas. 1969—), Assn. Aviation Psychologists, Am. Psychol. Assn., Aircraft Owners and Pilots Assn., Am. Psychology-Law Soc. Club: Druid Hillbillies Square Dance. Home: 1615 Berkeley Lane NE Atlanta GA 30329 Office: 6363 Roswell Rd Atlanta GA 30328

CURRIE, ROYCE ALEXANDER, mfg. exec.; b. Anniston, Ala., July 14, 1929; s. Royce Alexander and Cora Lee (Morrison) C.; B.S. in Mech. Engring., Auburn U., 1953; m. Martha Ann Hughes, Aug. 22, 1952. Supervisory engr. U.S. Steel Corp., Birmingham, Ala., 1953-65; engring. mgr. Steel City div. Midland-Ross Corp., Athens, Tenn., 1965-68; chief mfg. engr., mfg. engring. mgr. Gabriel div. Maremont Corp., Pulaski, Tenn., 1968—. Served as sgt. U.S. Army, 1946-49. Registered profl. engr., Tenn., Ala. Mem. Am. Soc. M.E., Tenn. Soc. Profl. Engrs., Giles County C. of C. Methodist. Home: Route 6 Pulaski TN 38478 Office: Maremont Corp PO Box 617 Pulaski TN 38478

CURRY, DONALD CHARLES, pub. relations exec.; b. Utica, N.Y., Dec. 27, 1929; s. Donald Caryl and Emily Grace (Pettis) C.; A.B., Hamilton Coll., 1952; M.A., Johns Hopkins, 1954; postgrad. George Washington U., 1957-59. Fgn. service officer USIA, 1954; nat. def. analyst Legislative Reference Service, 1957; editor N.E.A., 1957-58; information dir. Middle East Inst., 1958-60; account exec. Bozell & Jacobs, 1960-67; v.p., dir. Washington office Underwood, Jordan Assos., 1967—. Served with AUS, 1954-56. Mem. Pub. Relations Soc. Am., Middle East Inst., Am. Legion. Clubs: Nat. Press, Nat. Capital Democratic, Capitol Hill (Washington). Home: 5166 34th St NW Washington DC 20008 Office: National Press Bldg Washington DC 20004

CURRY, JOHN WILLIAN, food wholesale co. exec.; b. Tampa, Fla., Oct. 18, 1921; s. Allen Benjamin and Vashti (Hewett) C.; B.Bus.Sci., Tampa Coll., 1950; m. Mildred Luella Spindler, May 8, 1942; children—John Allen, David Christian, Donald William. Instr. accounting Tampa Coll., 1950-51; accountant Winn-Dixie Supermarkets, Tampa, 1951-53, div. controller, Louisville, 1953-61; v.p. Gafford Brokerage Co., Louisville, 1962-63; dir. systems and procedures Stevens Supermarkets, Miami, 1963-64; with Hill Bros., Inc., Miami, 1964—, operations mgr., 1968-70, v.p., sec., 1968—, also dir. Served with USN, 1941-47; PTO. Mem. Phi Theta Pi. Rotarian. Home: 6245 W 10th Av Hialeah FL 33012 Office: 3475 NW 60th St Miami FL 33152

CURRY, LANDON, geologist; b. Ft. Worth, Mar. 24, 1927; s. Arthur Ray and Miriam Marguerite (Lewis) C.; B.S., U. Tex., 1950; m. Connie Cacciola, Aug. 16, 1952; children—Landon, Frankie Anne. Geophysicist, N.Am. Geophys. Co., Houston, 1946-48; geophysicist So. Geophys. Corp., Ft. Worth, 1950; geologist Sunray Oil Corp., San Antonio, 1950-53; geologist Heep Oil Corp. & Conroe Drilling Co., Corpus Christi, Tex., 1953-55; partner Easley & Curry petroleum geologists, Corpus Christi, 1955—. Mem. Geol. Soc. Am., Am. Inst. Profl. Geologists, Am. Assn. Petroleum Geologists, Corpus Christi Geol. Soc., S. Tex. Art League, Tex. Fine Arts Assn. Home: 318 Cape Aron Dr Corpus Christi TX 78412 Office: 920 Vaughn Plaza Corpus Christi TX 78403

CURRY, RICHARD EARL, newspaper editor; b. Waxahachie, Tex., Sept. 21, 1933; s. O.T. Cooper and Annie Mabel (Walters) C.; B.J., U. Tex., 1954; m. Para Lee Cain, Oct. 6, 1956; children—David Lee, Richard Tillman, Charles Frederick, Rebecca. Staff Dallas Times Herald, 1956—, oil editor, 1959-63, financial editor, 1963—. Mem. regional export expansion council U.S. Dept. Commerce, 1964—. Served with AUS, 1954-56. Recipient Headliner's Club of Austin award, 1962, 68, 69, 70; A.P. and U.P.I. awards. Mem. Soc. Am. Bus. News Writers, Dallas C. of C. (mem. world trade com. 1964—), Sigma Delta Chi. Home: 1934 Dancliff Dr Dallas TX 75224 Office: Dallas Times Herald Dallas TX 75202

CURRY, ROBERT H., state ofcl.; b. Plain Dealing, La. Exec. Ark. La. Gas Co.; mem. La. Bd. Edn., 1942—. Former pres. Norwela council Boy Scouts Am. Mem. Shreveport C. of C. (past pres.). Presbyn. (elder). Lion. Clubs: Shreveport Country, Shreveport; Palmetto Country; Petroleum. Address: State Bd Edn Box 44064 Baton Rouge LA 70804

CURTIN, WILLIAM JOSEPH, lawyer; b. Auburn, N.Y., Mar. 9, 1931; s. W. Joseph and Edith (Murray) C.; B.S., Georgetown U., 1953, J.D., 1956, LL.M., 1957; m. Helen Bragg White, Aug. 3, 1956; children— Helen Bragg, Caroline Goddard, William Joseph III, Christopher Newport. Admitted to D.C. bar, 1956; asso. firm Morgan, Lewis & Bockius, Washington, 1960-64, partner, 1965—. Pub. mem. Adminstrv. Conf. U.S., 1968-72. Recipient Outstanding Service award Am. Arbitration Assn., 1966. Mem. Am. Bar Assn. (chmn. spl. com. to study nat. strikes in transp. industries), Bar Assn. D.C. (mem. labor law com. 1960—, chmn. 1969-70). Editor-in-chief Negotiated Employee Benefit Plans Service. Contbr. law jour. Home: 5206 Dorset Av Chevy Chase MD 20016 Office: 1140 Connecticut Av NW Washington DC 20036

CURTIS, CHAUNCIE CAROLINE (MRS. HOWARD CROSBY CURTIS), club woman; b. Laurel Hill, Tenn., Aug. 14, 1895; d. Thomas Jefferson and Mattie (McDonald) Smith; R.N., Peabody Coll.; m. Howard Crosby Curtis, Oct. 14, 1912 (dec.); children—Howard Jefferson, Caroline Lark. Fellow Inst. Am. Genealogy; mem. English-Speaking Union, Dames Ct. Honor, Daus. Am. Colonists, D.A.R., U.D.C. Episcopalian. Clubs: Capitol Speakers, Welcome to Washington (chmn. internat. luncheon div. Washington), Country. Home: 4600 Connecticut Av Washington DC 20008 also 140 E 63rd St New York City NY 10021

CURTIS, DON TEEL, oral surgeon; b. Amarillo, Tex., Aug. 29, 1937; s. Stephen Teel and Zallee (Williams) C.; student U. Colo., 1955-56, U. Tex., 1956-58; grad. Baylor U. Coll. Dentistry, 1962;; m. Suzanne Stokes, June 16, 1961; children—Margaret Anne, Stephen Teel, II, Sara Catharine. Resident, Parkland Meml. Hosp. Dallas, 1962-65; exchange resident Queen Victoria Hosp., East Grinstead, Eng., 1965; pvt. practice oral surgery, Amarillo, Tex., 1965—. Clin. instr. Baylor U. Coll. Dentistry, 1962-65; chief dental sect. N.W. Tex. Hosp., Amarillo, 1969—; mem. task force on cancer Regional Med. Program Tex., 1970—. Bd. dirs. Potter Randall Unit Am. Cancer Soc., Amarillo, 1966—, dir. at large Tex. div., 1969—; bd. dirs. Amarillo Health Sci. Mus.; bd. dirs. Amarillo Little Theater, 1969—, pres., 1972; bd. dirs. Kilgore Childrens Psychiat. Hosp. and Center, 1969—, pres., 1972. Diplomate Am. Bd. Oral Surgery. Mem. Potter, Randall, Panhandle dist. dental socs., Am., Tex. dental assns., S.W. Soc. Oral Surgery, Am. Soc. Oral Surgeons. Presbyn. (deacon 1971). Office: 1901 Medi-Park Amarillo TX 79106

CURTIS, JAMES ROBERT, lawyer; b. Ft. Worth, Oct. 4, 1905; s. Charles Robert and Betty (Lacy) C.; B.A., Tex. Christian U., 1927, B.E., 1928; M.A., So. Meth. U., 1929; LL.B., Cumberland U., 1930; diploma Grad. Sch. of Banking, Rutgers U., 1945; J.D., Samford U., 1969; m. Sarah DeRue Armstrong, June 30, 1935; children—Elizabeth DeRue, James Robert. Admitted to Tex. bar, 1930; practice of law 1930—; city judge Longview, Tex., 1933-35; sec., mgr. First Fed. Savs. and Loan Assn., 1934, dir., 1935—, v.p., 1955-72, pres., 1972—; pres. Voice of Longview Radio Sta. KFRO (established 1935, 1000 watts,) 1934—, Workmen's Oil Co., 1933—, Nat. Security Ins. Co., 1947-63, Courtesy Life Ins. Co., 1955-57, Trans. Security Investment Co., 1955-60; owner Etex Sales Co., 1940-42; v.p., dir. Rogers Nat. Bank, Jefferson, Tex., 1942-50; pres. First Internat. Co., 1966-67; dir. Gillespie Paint Co., Longview; dir. 1st Nat. Bank, Longview. Pres., Jr. C. of C., 1935, E. Tex. Girl Scouts, 1950-52; dist. dir. Am. Cancer Soc., 1957-58; dir. Longview Salvation Army, 1957—, chmn. bd., 1958; bd. dirs. E. Tex. area council Boy Scouts Am., 1956—, dist. chmn., 1959-63, council v.p., 1965—, recipient Silver Beaver, 1966; mem. Tex. Blind Commn., 1959-65, chmn., 1963-65; bd. devel. So. Meth. U., 1966—; (dir. 1964-66), pres. Curtis Found., 1945—. Hon. col. Tex. N.G. Diploma Life Ins. Mgmt. Assn., 1951. Mem. Am. Inst. Mgmt. (charter mem. pres. council), Tex. Broadcasters Assn., Nat. Assn. Broadcasters (bd. dirs. 1964-66), Am., Tex. bar assns., Fed. Communications Bar, Colonial Order Crown, C. of C. (v.p. 1955-56), Radio Pioneers, Sovereign Colonial Soc., Am. Royal Descent, Am. Radio Relay League, Oil Belt Assn. Life Underwriters (v.p. 1954-56), S.R., Tex. Ind. Producers and Royalty Owners Assn. (exec. com. 1957-58), S.A.R., Magna Charta Barons, Sigma Alpha Epsilon, Mem. Christian Ch. Mason. Clubs: Knife and Fork (pres. 1948, 59-60). Lions (pres. 1952, dist. gov. 1954-55; v.p. Tex. Lions Crippled Children Camp 1957-66), Pinecrest Country. Home: 2118 E Marshall Av Longview TX 75601 Office: Curtis Bldg Box 792 Longview TX 75601

CURTIS, MARILYN S. (MRS. JON E. CURTIS), pharmacist, flight instr.; b. Astoria, L.I., N.Y., Aug. 25, 1934; d. Bernard P. and DeRetta (Williamson) Smith; B.S., U. Tex., 1955; m. Charles Stoneberg, June 28, 1958 (dec. Apr. 1968); m. 2d, Jon E. Curtis, Mar. 28, 1969. Pharmacist, Med. Arts Pharmacy, San Antonio, 1955-56, Northside Drug, San Antonio, 1956-58, Jones Apothecary, Houston, 1958-68, Madings Drugs, 1968-69, Phillips Pharmacy, 1968-70, Gloyer's Pharmacy, 1969—, Fed-Mart Pharmacy, Pasadena, Tex., 1970-72. Flight instr. Barstow Aviation, Houston, 1962, free lance, 1962-64, Consol. Aero, Houston, 1967-68; participant Powder Puff Derby, 1960, Internat. Air Race, 1962, All Women's Internat. Air Race, 1964, other races; mem. 1st Women's Nat. Pylon Racing Team, 1967-71. Mem. Tex. State Aviation Assn. (sec.-treas. 1962-64), Petticoat Pilots (pres. 1964-65), 99's (pres. Houston 1966-68), Aircraft Owners and Pilots Assn., Nat. Assn. Flight Instrs., Animal Behavior Soc. Home: 25414 Friar Lake Lane Spring TX 77373 Office: 1010 W Main St Tomball TX 77375

CURTIS, MARY GERVASE BARNETT (MRS. BUFORD C. CURTIS), publisher, genealogist; b. Little Rock, June 8, 1924; d. Edgar Wheeler and Nellie (O'Neal) Barnett; grad. high sch.; m. Buford C. Curtis, Sept. 19, 1943; children—Mary Michele (Mrs. William Boyd Hill), Buford C., Robert Thornton Higgins, Eura Melisa, Sidney Watson, Katherine Victoria. Editor, South Fort Worthian, weekly, 1954-56, Strickland & Allied Families Query & Answer Exchange, quar., 1958—; owner Arrow Printing Co., Ft. Worth, 1953—; founder, pres. Am. Reference Publishers, Inc., 1967—; owner Geneal. and Hist. Book Lists, 1972—; publisher, owner Mag. of Bibliographie's, 1972—; dir. Ft. Belknap Archives, Inc., 1971— Chmn. ramp com. Tarrant County of Tex. Hist. Survey Com., 1959-66. Mem. Tex. (charter mem., rec. sec. 1960—), Ft. Worth (charter mem., chmn. publicity 1959-60) geneal. socs., Tex., Cath. (pres. Ft. Worth 1959—), Tarrant County (dir. 1962—, rec. sec. 1962-63) hist. socs., Cath. Daus. Am. Home: 3812 Lafayette Ft Worth TX 76107 Office: 2921 Morton St Ft Worth TX 76107

CURTIS, RALPH FRANKLIN, JR., life ins. co. exec.; b. Carmichaels, Pa., Feb. 5, 1929; s. Daniel Ralph and Retha (Dugan) C.; B.S., Waynesburg Coll., 1951; m. Margaret Rizer, July 3, 1954; children—Linda Joyce, Thomas David, Steven Douglas. Agt., Fidelity Union Life Ins. Co., Houston, 1955-56, gen. agt., Pasadena, Tex., 1956-59, div. mgr., Dallas, 1959-60, regional v.p., Dallas, 1960-64; v.p., agy. dir. Western Security Life Ins. Co., Oklahoma City, 1965-69, also Gulf Atlantic Life Ins. Co. (both cos. merged with Gulf Atlantic Surviving Co. 1971); v.p. marketing Gulf Atlantic Surviving Co., Dallas, 1971—. Bd. dirs. Cub Scouts of Am., 1965-67, N. Side All Sports Program, 1965-67. Served with USAF, 1951-56. Mem. Sales and Exec. Club. Presbyn. Club: Prestonwood Golf and Country. Home: 6562 Briarmeade Dr Dallas TX 75240 Office: 3417 Gillespie Dallas TX 75221

CURTIS, WILLIAM DWIGHT, orthodontist; b. Columbia, Mo., June 14, 1905; s. Winterton Conway and Marion (Hitchcock) C.; A.B., U. Mo., 1930; D.D.S., Washington U., 1935; m. Elizabeth Ilda Poulter, July 3, 1931; children—Marion, Elizabeth Anne, Caroline, Constance. Intern Forsyth Dental Infirmary for Children, Boston, 1935-36, New Haven Hosp., 1936-38; mem. staff Childrens Hosp., Washington, 1942—. Diplomate Am. Bd. Orthodontics. Fellow Am. Coll. Dentists; mem. Am. Dental Assn., Am. Assn. Orthodontists, D.C. Dental Soc. (v.p. 1947-48), So. Soc. Orthodontists (v.p. 1954-55), Washington Dental Club (pres. 1960). Lion (pres. 1945-46). Home: 5408 Moorland Lane Bethesda MD 20014 Office: 1726 I St NW Washington DC 20006

CUSH, JOSEPH WILBUR, dentist; b. Natchitoches, La., Aug. 22, 1929; s. Samuel and Angeline Marie (Catanese) C.; student Centenary Coll., 1946-48; D.D.S., Loyola U. of So., 1953; m. Beverly Jean Burch, Aug. 21, 1954; children—Joseph Wilbur, Derrie Anne, Gregory Samuel, Bryan Stephan, Angela Marie. Intern oral surgery Charity Hosp., New Orleans, 1953-54; resident oral surgery Confederate Meml. Med. Center, Shreveport, La., 1956-58; pvt. practice oral surgery, Shreveport, 1958—; mem. staffs La. State Sch. Medicine Post Grad. Dept. Pres. N.W. La. Cancer Soc., 1970. Served with USAF, 1954-56. Fellow Acad. Internat. Dentistry; mem. Am. Dental Soc. of Anesthesiology, Am., La., 4th Dist. (pres. 1965) dental assns., Pierre Fauchard Acad., C. of C., Delta Sigma Delta, Am. Legion. Roman Catholic. K.C., Rotarian. Clubs: Serra, Pierremont Oaks Tennis, East Ridge Country. Home: 307 Deborah St Shreveport LA 71106 Office: 3304 Youree Dr Shreveport LA 71105

CUSHMAN, ROBERT EVERTON, Marine Corps officer; b. St. Paul, Dec. 24, 1914; s. Robert Everton and Jennie Line (Cumley) C.; B.S., U. S. Naval Acad., 1935; m. Audrey Boyce, Jan. 17, 1940; children—Roberta Lind (Mrs. Bernard J. Cauley), Robert Everton III. Commd. 2d lt. U.S. Marine Corps, 1935, advanced through grades to gen., 1972; asst. to v.p. U.S. for nat. security affairs, 1957-61; asst. chief of staff Marine Corps, 1962-64; comdt. gen. Marine Corps Base, Camp Pendleton, Cal., 1964-67; comdr. gen. III Marine Amphibious Force, Vietnam 1967-1969; dep. dir. CIA, 1969-71; comdt. Marine Corps, Washington, 1972—. Decorated Navy Cross, D.S.M. with gold star, Legion of Merit with combat V, Bronze Star medal with combat V; also decorations Argentina, Vietnam, Korea. Home: CMC House Marine Barracks 8th and I Sts S E Washington DC 20390 Office: Hdqrs U S Marine Corps Washington DC 20380

CUSHWA, BETTY L., hotel exec. Sec., asst. v.p. Marriott Corp., Washington. Home: 4805 Montgomery Av Washington DC 20016 Office: 5161 River Rd NW Washington DC*

CUSTER, DOROTHY ELIZABETH MASSIE (MRS. LYLE EDGAR CUSTER), FAULCONER), educator, state ofcl.; b. Amherst, Va., Apr. 15, 1922; d. William Joseph and Winnie (Coleman) Massie; A.B., Lynchburg Coll., 1948; M.Ed., U. Va., 1953, Ed.D., 1971; m. Edward Perkins Faulconer, Apr. 9, 1942 (dec. July 1967); m. 2d, Lyle Edgar Custer, May 1, 1971. Tchr., Amherst County (Va.) Schs., 1943-45, elementary supr., 1953-55; prin. Clifford (Va.) Elementary Sch., 1945-47; tchr. Amherst High Sch., 1948-52, Garland Rodes Sch., Lynchburg, 1952-53; gen. and high sch. supr. Buckingham County Schs., Buckingham, Va., 1955-60; dir. Sweet Briar Coll. Nursery Sch., instr. edn. Sweet Briar Coll., 1960-65, dir. reading improvement program, 1962-65; instr. U. Va. Sch. Gen. Studies, 1963-65; asst. supr. elementary edn. Va. Dept. Edn., Richmond, 1965—. Mem. Am. Assn. U. Profs., Am. Assn. U.

Women (br. chmn. 1964-65), N.E.A., Va. Edn. Assn., Assn. Supervision and Curriculum Devel. (area chmn. 1958-59), Assn. Childhood Edn. Internat., Va. Assn. Early Childhood Edn., Nat. Assn. Edn. Young Children, Nat. Council Tchrs. English, D.A.R. (chmn. chpt. edn. com. 1964-65), Kappa Delta Pi, Delta Kappa Gamma (chmn. chpt. profl. affairs com. 1966-68). Mem. Order Eastern Star (past worthy matron). Home: 3117 Windsorview Dr Richmond VA 23225 Office: 14th and E Grace St Richmond VA 23216

CUTTS, ERNEST A(LLEN), newspaperman; b. Augusta, Ga., Nov. 27,, 1912; s. Allen Sherrod and Mary (Moorman) C.; student Acad. Richmond County, Jr. Coll. of Augusta, U. S.C., 1933-35; m. Susan Maner Dotterer, May 2, 1942; children—Susan Dotterer, Mary Allen (Mrs. James A. Gardner), Anna Maner (Mrs. Harold J. Burns). Reporter Augusta Herald, 1937-40; reporter News and Courier, Charleston, 1940-42, sports editor 1943; reporter Charleston Evening Post, 1944, city editor, 1945-—, news editor, 1953, mng. editor, 1954-—. Pulitzer Prize juror, 1972. Hon. asso. curator zoology Charleston Mus., 1956-—, trustee, 1959-68. Past pres. S.C. News Council. Mem. A.P. Mng. Editors Assn. (dir. 1964-69, exec. com., treas. 1971, charter mem. regents), S.C. Press Assn. (exec. com.), Charleston Natural History Soc. (pres. 1967-68), Wilson Ornithol. Soc., Carolina Bird Club, Sigma Delta Chi (S.C. chpt. v.p.). Club: Country of Charleston (dir. 1970-—). Asso. editor Chat mag., 1954-70. Home: 1466 S Edgewater Dr Charleston SC 29407 Office: 134 Columbus St Charleston SC 29402

CYLKE, FRANK KURT, librarian; b. New Haven, Feb. 13, 1932; s. Frank Anton and Helen Mary (Callahan) C.; B.A., U. Conn., 1954; M.L.S., Pratt Inst., 1957; postgrad. Fairfield U., 1959, Am. U., 1968-69; m. Mary Elizabeth Zembroski, Dec. 28, 1962; children—Frank Kurt, Mary Amanda. Librarian Graham-Eckes Sch., Palm Beach, Fla., 1957-58; reference librarian Bridgeport (Conn.) Pub. Library, 1958-62; head pub. services New Haven Pub. Library, 1962-65; asst. librarian Providence Pub. Library, 1965-68; chief library and information scis. research program U.S. Office Edn., 1968-69; exec. sec. Fed. Library Com. Library Congress, Washington, 1970-—. Instr. U. R.I. Grad. Library Sch., 1967-68. Exec. sec. panel on edn. and tng. Com. on Sci. and Tech. Information; chmn. librarians tech. com. Met. Washington Council Govts., 1970-71; sec. U.S. Book Exchange, 1972-—; sec.-treas. Joint Venture Pub. Activity, 1970-—. Mem. East Greenwich (R.I.) Free Library Corp., 1967-—; adv. bd. Ednl. Resources Information Center/Clearinghouse on Library and Information Sci., 1970-72. U.S. Office Edn. grantee to develop a survey fed. libraries, 1972. Mem. A.A.A.S., Am., D.C., Mass., New Eng. library assns., Am. Soc. for Information Sci., Internat. Fedn. for Documentation, Pvt. Libraries Assn., Spl. Libraries Assn., Lewes Hist. Soc. Roman Catholic. Clubs: Branford Yacht; Dinghy Cruising Assn. Editor: Captains Shelf, 1964-66, FLC Newsletter, 1970-—. Home: 6210 12th St N Arlington VA 22205 Office: Library of Congress Washington DC 20540

CYPHERT, FREDERICK RALPH, univ. adminstr.; b. Brookville, Pa., Jan. 4, 1928; s. Ralph Leroy and Bessanna (Nail) C.; B.S., Clarion State Coll., 1949; M.A., Syracuse U., 1950; Ed.D., U. Pitts., 1957; m. Lois Florence Grosz, June 1, 1957; children—Stacey Todd, Holly Susan. Tchr., curriculum coordinator pub. schs., Penn Hills, Pa., 1950-56; asst. prof. Ball State U., Muncie, Ind., 1956-57; dir. instrn. pub. schs., Torrance, Cal., 1957-59; prof. Ohio State U., Columbus, 1959-65, asso. dean Coll. Edn., 1965-68; dean Sch. Edn., U. Va., Charlottesville, 1968-—. Served with USAAF, 1946-47. Recipient Distinguished Alumni award Clarion State Coll., 1967. Mem. Ohio Council on Tchr. Edn. (pres. 1966-68), Assn. Supervision and Curriculum Devel., Am. Ednl. Research Assn., Am. Assn. Colls. for Tchr. Edn., Am. Assn. Sch. Adminstrs., Phi Delta Kappa, Phi Sigma Pi, Pi Gamma Mu. Author: Teaching in America, 1962; Teaching in the American Secondary School, 1964; An Analysis and Projection of Research in Teacher Education, 1965; A Taxonomy of Teacher Classroom Behavior, 1966. Contbr. articles to profl. jours. Home: 2411 Brook Rd Charlottesville VA 22901

CYR, LOUIE MCGOWEN, lawyer; b. Jeanerette, La., May 12, 1913; s. Paul N. and Mary (McGowen) C.; b.a., southwestern La. Inst., 1936; LL.B., La. State U., 1940; m. Mary Elizabeth Junot, Aug. 19, 1942; children—Patricia Jean, Paul N. Admitted to La. bar, 1940; practiced in New Iberia, 1940-—. pres. Iberia Savings & Loan Assn., New Iberia, 1967-—, dir., 1952-—; dir. La. Land and Royalty Owners Assn., 1964-—. Chmn. Iberia Crippled Children's Assn., 1942-62; v.p. La. Sugar Cane Festival and Fair Assn., 1946; pres. Iberia Municipal Concert Assn., 1947; pres. Community Chest, 1954; mem. Park and Recreation Commn., 1951-—, chmn., 1964-—; city judge, 1943-46 (all New Iberia). Recipient Distinguished Service award, New Iberia Jr. C. of C., 1947; citation La. Recreation and Parks Assn., 1963. Mem. Am., La. State, Iberia Parish (pres. 1950-51) bar assns., Am. Judicature Soc., New Iberia Jr. C. of C. (pres. 1946), C. of C. (bd. dirs. 1947-49, 51-55), Iberia Parish Rod and Gun Club (pres. 1954-56). Kiwanian (pres. New Iberia 1947, lt. gov. Div. 1957). Home: 409 Loreauville Rd New Iberia LA 70560 Office: 301 Julia St New Iberia LA 70560

CYRUS, JOHN HOLMAN, state ofcl.; b. Louisburg, N.C., Aug. 14, 1920; s. John Henry and Bettie (Hicks) C.; B.S. in Agrl. Edn., N.C. State U., 1948; m. Billie Marie Watkins, Feb. 11, 1950; children—John Michael and Gary Holman (twins). Tchr. vocational agr. Moncure (N.C.) High Sch., instr. Vets. Farm Tng. Program, 1946-49; specialist tobacco marketing N.C. Dept. Agr., Raleigh, 1949-65, dir. tobacco marketing sect., 1966-—, pub. ann. N.C. Tobacco Report, 1949-—. Adv., cons. Industry-Wide Flue-Cured Marketing Com., 1967-—; bd. dirs. Nat. Tobacco Growers Information Com., 1966-—; bd. dirs., exec. com. Nat. Tobacco Tax Council, since 1966-—. Mem. Democratic Precinct Election Com., 1969-—. Bd. dirs. Nat. Tobacco and Cotton Mus. Served with USAAF, 1942-45; ETO. Decorated Air medal with three oak leaf clusters; named Tarheel of Week, Raleigh (N.C.) News and Observer, 1968; recipient commendation N.C. Grange, 1971. Mem. Kappa Phi Kappa, Alpha Gamma Rho. Baptist (deacon, chmn. bd., tchr. Sunday sch.). Clubs: Farm Hands, North Carolina State University Alumni (Raleigh). Editor: The Tobacco Story, 1966. Contbr. articles newspapers and profl. jours. Home: 113 Clarendon Crescent Raleigh NC 27610 Office: N C Dept Agr PO Box 27647 Raleigh NC 27611

DABBS, JACK AUTREY, educator; b. Mercury, Tex., Jan. 31, 1914; s. John Franklin and Florence (Boyd) D.; B.A., U. Tex., 1935, M.A., 1936, Ph.D., 1950; m. Anna Viola Johnson, May 25, 1940; 1 dau., Danielle Elizabeth. Tchr., Tex. Wesleyan Acad., Austin, 1935-36, Lockhart (Tex.) High Sch., 1937-38; instr. St. Edward's U., Austin, Tex., 1938-40, 1948-50; asst. prof. Tex. A. and M. U., College Station, 1950-54, asso. prof., 1954-59, prof. modern langs., 1959-—. Dir. Am. Lang. Inst., Baghdad, Iraq, 1957-58. Served with inf., mil. govt. AUS, 1940-48. Mem. Modern Lang. Assn., Linguistic Soc. Am., Am. Name Soc. Author: History of Discovery and Exploration of Chinese Turkestan, 1962; The French Army in Mexico, 1963. Home: 1011 Edgewood St Bryan TX 77801 Office: Tex A and M U College Station TX 77843

DABBS, MIRIAM ADAIR (MRS. CHESTER NORWOOD DABBS), journalist, artist; b. Rialto, Cal., May 6, 1908; d. Watts McIntosh and Betty (Pearson) Adair; B.A., Miss. Sate Coll. for Women, 1930; m. Chester Norwood Dabbs, Dec. 24, 1933; 1 son, Willis Norwood. English instr., Jones County Jr. Coll., Ellisville, Miss., 1933-34; instr. Am. history Northwest Jr. Coll., Senatobia, Miss., 1935-36; soc. editor Clarksdale (Miss.) Daily Register, 1942-47; feature writer, corr. Clarion-Ledger, Jackson, Miss., 1964-—; corr. Jackson Daily News, 1968-—; Press-Scimitar, Memphis, 1969-—. Exhibited one-man shows Galeries Raymond Duncan, Paris, France, 1970, 71, Ligoa Duncan Gallery, N.Y.C., 1971, also regional exhbns.; works represented in pvt. and museum collections; lectr. in field, 1972. Chmn., Missionary Soc. Bapt. Ch., 1952-53; mem. Clarksdale Beautification Commn., chmn., 1952-54, 56-63, sec., 1955, 68. Recipient Beautification Merit award, Miss. C. of C. community program at Clarksdale, 1961; Prix de Paris for painting Bridge to Sunrise, 1970. Mem. Nat. League Am. Pen Women (award; editor Pen Drifts, 1957), Ulster-Scot Hist. Soc. (Belfast, Ireland), D.A.R. Clubs: Clarksdale Woman's (past pres.), Town and Country Garden (Clarksdale, Miss.). Author: Idyls of the Delta: Coahoma, 1948; The Passing Storm; Sepaled Horns; Sonnets From India, 1962. Contbr. articles on founding families of Miss. to tech. lit. Research in genealogy. Home: 321 Maple St Clarksdale MS 38614 Office: Clarion Ledger Jackson MS 39205

DABNEY, HOVEY SLAYTON, banker; b. Charlottesville, Va., Sept. 18, 1923; s. Wythe and Mabel (Williams) D.; LL.B., U. Va., 1949; m. Patricia Ann Schmidt, Feb. 14, 1948; children—Hovey Slayton, Ann Williams, Jill Godsell. With Nat. Bank and Trust Co., Charlottesville, 1949-—, asst. cashier, 1951-56, v.p., 1956-62, exec. v.p., 1962-64, pres., 1964-—, also dir.; dir. Inland Service, Charlottesville. Pres. Charlottesville Parking Center Inc.; commr. Va. Pub. Sch. Authority. Bd. govs. St. Anne's Belfield, Inc., 1967-—, chmn., 1968-—; bd. dirs. Blue Cross Va., Charlottesville chpt. Am. Cancer Soc., Charlottesville chpt. Va. Student Aid Found. Served with USAAF, World War II; ETO. Decorated Air medal with oak leaf clusters, Purple Heart; named Outstanding Young Man of Year, Charlottesville, Albemarle, 1957. Mem. Va. Bankers Assn. (past pres.), Am. Bankers Assn. (bd. dirs.), U.S. C. of C., Newcomen Soc., Theta Chi. Club: Farmington Country (v.p., dir.) (Charlottesville). Home: 2117 Morris Rd Charlottesville VA 22903 Office: 123 E Main St Charlottesville VA 22902

DABNEY, JOHN CORNELIUS, real estate appraiser; b. Atlanta, Nov. 2, 1918; s. John Cornelius and Edna (Blackmon) D.; B.A., Emory U., 1940; M.S., U. Tenn., 1943; m. Eleanor Sargent Hoyt, June 25, 1947; children—John Cornelius, Russell Hoyt, Ann Marie. Dir. phys. edn. and recreation Norris (Tenn.) Sch., 1943-45; asst. dir. Fritz Orr Club Camp Sch., Atlanta, 1945-46; sec., v.p., pres., chmn. bd. W. R. Hoyt & Co., insurers and realtors, Atlanta, 1946-—; owner Dabney & Assos., real estate appraisers and consultants, 1954-—. Mem. Am. Soc. Real Estate Counselors, Am. Inst. Real Estate Appraisers, Soc. Real Estate Appraisers (internat. v.p. 1965), Atlanta Real Estate Bd., C. of C., Lambda Chi Alpha, Phi Delta Kappa, Rho Epsilon (hon.). Presbyn. Rotarian. Club: Atlanta Athletic. Home: 3927 Parian Ridge Rd NW Atlanta GA 30327 Office: Equitable Bldg 100 Peachtree St NW Atlanta GA 30303

DABNEY, ROBERT LEWIS, JR., lawyer, rancher; b. Houston, May 7, 1931; s. Robert Lewis and Christe (Storey) D.; student Woodberry Forest Sch., 1946- 49; B.A., U. Va., 1953; LL.B., U. Tex., 1956; m. Susan Nina Schmutte, Jan. 26, 1966; children—Robert Lewis III, James Storey, John Nelson. Admitted to Tex. bar, 1956; staff atty. Gulf Oil Corp., 1956-64; partner Austin, Dabney, Northop & Garwood, Houston, 1964-—. Active Boy Scouts Am. Trustee Houston Kidney Found.; past regional v.p. Nat. Kidney Found. Served to maj. with AUS, 1957-65. Mem. State Bar of Tex., Houston Bar Assn., St. Anthony Hall, Delta Psi, Delta Theta Phi. Episcopalian. Home: 3215 Ella Lee Lane Houston TX 77019 Office: Chamber of Commerce Bldg Houston TX 77002

DABROWSKI, MIREK JAN, assn. exec.; b. Buffalo, July 26, 1922; s. Boleslaw Joseph and Martha (Sulecki) D.; B.A., U. Buffalo, 1947, postgrad., 1950-51; postgrad. Yale, 1943-44, William and Mary Coll., 1953-54, U. Md., 1965-68; m. Frances Elizabeth Shirley, Sept. 17, 1949; children—Kristina Anne, Jana Elizabeth, Martha Lynn, Mira Carol, Mirek Jan III, Halina, Stefan Michael, Peter Alexander. News dir. WGMS Radio Sta., Washington, 1954-58; producer USIA Voice Am., 1958-60; mgr. pub. relations Bea Constrn. Co., 1960-61; sec. nat. fire safety com., nat. inter-chamber fire safety contest com., asst. mgr. ins. dept. U.S. C. of C., 1961-64; cons. pub. relations, speech communication, Washington, 1964-71; exec. dir. Tobacconists Assn. Am., 1969-—. Lectr. speech George Washington U., 1956-66. Pub. relations dir. Republican party Montgomery County, 1962-66; capt. United Givers Fund team, 1967-68; press asst. Citizens for Nixon, 1968; spl. asst. press accreditation Inaugural Com., 1969. Dir. Montgomery Players, Bethesda, Md., 1961-62. Served with AUS, 1943-46, 51-53; lt. col. Res. Decorated Bronze Star medal. Recipient Am. Legion Scholastic award, 1940. Mem. Polish-Am. Arts Assn. Washington (dir.), Pub. Relations Soc. Am., Nat. Press Club, Internat. Platform Assn., Speech Assn. Am., Internat. Communications Soc., Am. Soc. Assn. Execs., Bisonhead. Roman Catholic. Author: A Shorter Work Week, 1962; Look Forward to Your Retirement, 1963. Editor: Fire Prevention and Community Development, 1963; Analysis of Workmen's Compensation Laws, 1963; Annapolis Report, 1963-66; Montgomery County Humane Soc. newsletter Smoke Rings. Home: 4500 Leland St Chevy Chase MD 20015 Office: 1725 K St NW Washington DC 20006

DAGLEY, FRANK ALLEN, cons. engr.; b. Charlotte, N.C., Mar. 12, 1940; s. Ray Harrison and Elizabeth Alice (Graham) D.; B.C.E., Auburn U., 1964; m. Catherine Mary Slaughter, Dec. 21, 1963; 1 dau., Valerie Annette. Asst. engr. Atlantic Coast Line R.R., Florence, S.C., 1964-65, cons. engr., Hensley-Schmidt, Inc., Marietta, Ga., 1965-67, Palmer & Baker Engrs., Inc., Mobile, Ala., 1967-—. Registered profl. engr., Ala. Presbyn. Home: 5538 Nassau Dr Mobile AL 36608 Office: 1050 Government St Mobile AL 36604

DAHL, EDWARD, economist; b. Buffalo, Mar. 15, 1900; s. Edward George and Augusta (Sommer) D.; B.A., Yale, 1923; m. Clemence Eirene Liesching, Oct. 11, 1932; children—Georgia Hermione (Mrs. Clare A. Schmutz), Edward Carle. Asst. mgr. Socony Vacuum Corp., Calcutta, India, also Colombo, Ceylon, 1927-33; mgr. Dodge & Seymour, Ltd., Rangoon, Burma, 1933-36, asst. to v.p., N.Y.C., 1936-40; mgr. export office Reynolds Metals Corp., Richmond, Va., 1940-41; supr. Va. Dept. Edn., Richmond, 1941-42; internat. economist Dept. State, Washington, 1947-50, 1952-70, pub-affairs officer, 1952-62, chief fgn. reporting staff, 1962-70; cons. South Asia, 1970-—; comml. attache Am. embassy, Karachi, Pakistan, 1950-52. Served with U.S. Army, World War I, 1918; to lt. comdr. USNR, 1942-46. Mem. Internat. Council for Christian Leadership (chmn. exec. com. Internat. Luncheon Group 1954-—), Ret. Officers Assn., Nat., Md. ret. officers assns., English-Speaking Union, Lambda Chi Alpha. Clubs: University, Dacor, Yale (Washington). Home: The Spruces 7800 Old Chester Rd Bethesda MD 20034

DAHL, ELMER VERNON, physician, educator; b. Colby, Kan., Apr.17, 1921; s. Henry S. and Marie A. (Berg) D.; B.S., U. So. Cal., 1943, M.D., 1952; m. Josephine M. Townzen, June 14, 1944; children—Linette, Jonathan, Hans, Elizabeth, Andrew. Intern Walter Reed Hosp., Washington, 1952-53; instr. and fellow in pathology Duke, Durham, N.C., 1953-54, Mayo Found., Rochester, Minn., 1954-59; commd. 1st lt., USAF, 1952; advanced through grades to col., 1966; chief pathology br. Sch. Aerospace Medicine, San Antonio, 1959-61, cons., 1961-68; comdr. Epidemiological Lab., San Antonio, 1961-68; comdr. Epidemiological Flight, Manila, P.I., 1968-69; research asso. prof. pathology U. Tex. Med. Br., Galveston, 1969-—; cons. lab. medicine to Surgeon Gen. U.S. Air Force, 1961-65; spl. cons. pathology to 6571st Aeromed. Research Lab., Holloman AFB, N.M., 1964-68. Recipient Research award Mayo Alumni Assn., 1958. Diplomate Am. Bd. Pathology. Fellow Coll. Am. Pathologists; mem. Am. Soc. Exptl. Pathology, Am. Soc. Tropical Medicine and Hygiene, A.M.A., Sigma Xi. Home: 124 Tuna Galveston TX 77550

DAHL, ORVILLE JEROME, tire co. exec.; b. Chgo., Jan. 10, 1917; s. Harold P. and Rachel A. (Ibsen) D.; B.S., U. Wis., 1941; m. Roma W. Wenger, Feb. 21, 1942; children—Barbara (Mrs. Charles F. Struck), Mary (Mrs. Thomas W. Winton). Chemist, Pitts. Plate Glass Co., Milw., 1941-42; chemist B.F. Goodrich Co., Akron, Los Angeles, The Netherlands, 1942-53, tech. mgr., Miami, Okla., 1953-—. Home: 1223 N Elm St Miami OK 74354 Office: 1000 Goodrich Blvd Miami OK 74354

DAHLGREN, JOHN ONSGARD, lawyer; b. Missoula, Mont., Sept. 7, 1913; s. John and Geneva (Newhouse) D.; B.A., George Washington U., 1936; J.D., Georgetown U., 1939 children—John Robert, Robin Reed. Admitted to D.C. bar, 1939, Md. bar, 1956; chief counsel requisition div. Bd. Econ. Warfare, Washington, 1941-42; partner law firm Dahlgren, Darragh and Close, 1946-—; Pres. Internat. Humanities, Inc. Served from ensign to lt. comdr. USNR, 1941-46; comdr. Res. ret. Mem. Am., Inter-Am. (sec. gen 1967-—), Fed. bar assns., Am. Soc. Internat. Law, Am. Judicature Soc., Bar Assn. D.C. Lutheran. Clubs: University, Internat. Home: 5300 Westbard Av Bethesda MD 20016 Office: 1000 Connecticut Av NW Washington DC 20036

DAIGLE, LOUIS JOHN, agriculturist; b. East Millinocket, Me., Apr. 3, 1916; s. Amedie and Modeste (DesRosier) D.; B.S.A., U. Fla., 1948, M.A. in Agr., 1949; m. Margarida C. Cavalcanti, May 10, 1945; children—Eugene, Maria (Mrs. Daniel Joseph Lessard), Martha. Instr. horticulture Mary Karl Vocational Sch., Daytona Beach, Fla., 1949-54; plant insp. Fla. Plant Bd., Miami, 1954-59; agriculturist Fla. Cooperative Extension Ser., Miami, 1960-—. Host TV shows Tropical Gardener, Miami, 1962-68, Growing Things, Miami, 1968-—; instr. gardening Miami-Homestead, 1960-—. Served with USN, 1941-47. Recipient Fla. Citizen commendation Doyle Conner, 1969, County Conservation award Fla. Wildlife Fedn., 1969. Mem. Dale Carnegie Club Internat. (pres. 1953-54), Fla. Assn. County Agr. Agrs. (dir. 1970-71). Home: 3011 NW 158th St Opalocka FL 33054 Office: 2690 NW 7th Av Miami FL 33127

DAIGRE, P. A., museum curator. Curator exhibits Museum Natural Scis La. State U., Baton Rouge. Address: La State U Museum Natural Scis Baton Rouge LA 70803*

DAILEY, GEORGE CURTIS, dentist; b. Newcastle, Pa., Oct. 29, 1941; s. George William and Ann Stuart (Miller) D.; D.D.S., Ohio State U., 1966; certificate in Orthodontics, U. Ala., 1971; m. Marianne L. Barker, June 27, 1964; children—Suzanne Renee, Curtis William. Dental intern Brooke Army Med. Center, San Antonio, 1966-67; resident in orthodontics U. Ala., 1969-71; practice dentistry, specializing in orthodontics, Hampton, Va., 1971-—. Served to capt. AUS, 1966-69. Mem. Am., Va. dental assns., Am. Assn. Orthodontists, So. Soc., Orthodontists, Va. Peninsula Dental Soc., Tidewater Orthodontic Soc., Omicron Kappa Upsilon, Delta Sigma Delta. Home: 216 Shifting Log Hampton VA 23369 Office: 1610 B Aberdeen Rd Hampton VA 23366

DAILEY, MARTEL JENNINGS, physician; b. Powellsville, N.C., Oct. 6, 1925; s. Louis Ellsworth and Mary Elizabeth (Owens) D.; B.A., U. Va., 1947; M.D., Med. Coll. Va., 1951; m. Olive Thomas Trader, June 10, 1950 (div. Aug. 1970); children—Charles, Jean, Olivia, John. Intern, Norfolk (Va.) Gen. Hosp., 1951-52; gen. practice medicine, Reedville, Va., 1952-63, Williamston, N.C., 1963-—; mem. staff Bertie County Hosp., Windsor, N.C., 1963-71; Martin Gen. Hosp., Williamston, 1963-71 officer in charge USPHS, Reedville, 1955-63; med. dir. Martin County Health Dept., Williamston, 1970-71; clinician Planned Parenthood Clinic, Martin County, 1966-71. Chmn. Martin County Red Cross, 1963-69. Mem. Bertie County Med. Soc. (sec., 1965-—), Alpha Omega Alpha, Alpha Chi Sigma. Baptist. Club: Roanoke Country. Research in fetal and neonatal hepatitis. Home: Williamston By Pass Williamston NC 27892 Office: Smithwick St Williamston NC 27892

DAILEY, THOMAS MILLS, JR., gas co. exec.; b. Austin, Tex., Oct. 16, 1913; s. Thomas Mills and Renee E. (Tinney) D.; B.B.A., U. Tex., 1934, postgrad., 1935-36; postgrad. Houston Law Sch., 1937-38; m. Inez Fleming, Sept. 30, 1944; children—Thomas Mills, William Anson. Petroleum economist, Humble Oil, Houston, Tex., 1946-55; mgr. coporate planning and research Tidewater Oil Co., Los Angeles, 1955-64; v.p. West Fla. Natural Gas Co., Panama City, 1964-—; also dir. Served to lt. USNR, 1944-46. Mem. Am. Petroleum Inst., Fla. Natural Gas Assn. Episcopalian. Clubs: Bay West Country, Signal Hill Country, St. Andrews Bay Yacht. Home: 405 Bayshore Dr Panama City FL32401 Office: PO Box 1460 Panama City FL 32401

D'AIUTO, LEONARD N., lawyer; b. Dover, O., Feb. 19, 1932; s. Nick L. and Theresa (Minadeo) D'A.; student Kent State U., 1950-52; J.D. with honors, U. Fla., 1960; m. Rose Marie Preisel, Dec. 26, 1953. Admitted to Fla. bar, 1960; labor adminstr. Eastern Airlines, Miami, Fla., 1960-61; with firm Langbein and Burdick, West Palm Beach, Fla., 1961-62; mem. firm Howell, Kirby, Montgomery and Sands, Jacksonville, 1962-64; mng. partner firm Howell, Kirby, Montgomery and D'Aiuto, Cocoa, 1964-68; pres. profl. assos. Howell, Kirby, Montgomery, D'Aiuto, Dean & Hallowes, Jacksonville, Orlando, Cocoa, Ft. Lauderdale, West Palm Beach, 1968-—. Served as aviator USNR, 1952-65; comdr. Res. Rotarian (pres. Cocoa 1968-69). Home: 1024 Fairlawn Dr Rockledge FL 32955 Office: 1150 Hartford Bldg 200 E Robinson St Orlando FL

DALE, GROVER CLEVELAND, physician; b. nr. Seven Springs, N.C., Apr. 7, 1897; s. Curtis James and Julia (Thompson) D.; A.B., U. N.C., 1920; M.D., U. Pa., 1925; m. Sarah Maud Eason, May 18, 1929. Intern St. Joseph's Hosp., Lancaster, Pa., 1925-26; practice medicine, specializing in proctology, Goldsboro, N.C., 1926-—; electrocardiologist Wayne Meml. Hosp., Goldsboro, 1936-—; med. dir. Wayne County Sanitorium, 1940-53. Served as seaman 2d class USN, 1918-19. Fellow A.C.P.; mem. N.C., Fourth Dist., Wayne County (pres. 1939) med. socs., A.M.A. Democrat. Presbyn. Mason (32 deg.). Contbr. articles med. jours. Home: 307 S Pine View Av Goldsboro NC 27530 Office: Wachovia Bldg Goldsboro NC 27530

DALE, JAMES C., JR., lawyer; b. Dec. 14, 1906; M.A., Vanderbilt U., 1928. Admitted to Tenn. bar, 1931; clk., master Chancery Ct., 1939-46; now mem. firm Bailey, Ewing, Dale & Conner, Nashville. Mem. Nashville, Tenn., Am. bar assns., Phi Beta Kappa. Office: Nashville Bank & Trust Bldg Nashville TN 37201*

DALE, STONEWALL HANNA, telephone co. exec.; b. New Orleans, Mar. 18, 1929; s. Joseph W. and Ella Virginia (Hanna) D.; B.A., La. State U., 1956; m. Feb. 19, 1955; children—Terri Lee, Stonewall Hanna, Jodi Lynn. With South Central Bell Telephone Co., various locations, 1957—, div. pub. relations mgr., 1964-70, La. pub. relations mgr., New Orleans, 1970—. Mem. Met. Area Com., 1965—, Regiona Nine Sci. Fair, 1965—, Pete Fountain's Half Fast Walking Club, Carnival Orgn., 1969—; pub. relations com. United Fund Greater New Orleans, 1969-71. Mem. La. State U. Alumni Assn. (past pres.), Press Club New Orleans (sec. 1965—), Pub. Relations Soc. Am. (pres. 1971), Advt. Club New Orleans (dir., 1965—), La. Press Assn., La. Assn. Broadcasters, New Orleans Area C. of C. (council, 1965—), Sigma Delta Phi. Roman Catholic. Clubs: Gridiron (New Orleans); Colonial Country (Hanrahan, La.). Home: 3444 Edenborn St Apt 5 Metairie LA 70002 Office: 1215 Prytania St New Orleans LA 70140

D'ALEMBERTE, TALBOT, state legislator; b. Tallahassee, June 1, 1933; s. Dan W. and Eleanor (Whitfield) D'A.; B.A., U. of the South, 1955; postgrad. (Rotary Found. fellow) U. London (Eng.), 1958-59; LL.B. with honors, U. Fla., 1962; m. Linda Sears, July 12, 1968. Admitted to Fla. bar; mem. Fla. Ho. of Reps., 1966—, chmn. community affairs com. Served with USNR, 1955-58. Mem. John Marshall, Am., Dade County bar assns., Dade County Young Lawyers (pres. 1966-67), Blue Key, Order Coif, Alpha Tau Omega, Omicron Delta Kappa. Democrat. Episcopalian. Home: 7741 S W 51st Av Miami FL 33143 Office: 1414 First Nat Bank Bldg Miami FL 33133*

D'ALESSANDRO, EDWARD ANTHONY, library adminstr.; b. Cleve., Mar. 11, 1913; s. Rocco M. and Isabella (Romanelli) D'A.; B.A. magna cum laude, John Carroll U., 1937; B.S. in L.S. (William Howard Brett scholar), Western Res. U., 1938; m. Grace Martha Musche, Nov. 29, 1947; children—Edward R., Paul A. With Cleve. Pub. Library, 1927-70, jr. asst. librarian sociology div. main library, 1938-41, asst. br. librarian Euclid-100 br., 1941-42, br. librarian Woodland br., 1942-43, Fleet br., 1946-49, Eastman br., 1949-51, head book repair dept. 1951-54, asst. head main library, 1954-56, bus. mgr., 1956-59, asst. dir., 1959-66, dep. dir., 1966-69, dir., 1969-70; spl. asst. for planning mgmt. reference dept. Library of Congress, Washington, 1970—. Mem. personnel com., trustee Cleve. U. Settlement, 1948-51; mem. Citizen's League Cleve., 1963-70; mem. Fairfax Police Youth Club, 1970—. Served with USAAF, 1943-45, AUS, 1945-46. Mem. A.L.A. (past mem. library equipment com.), John Carroll U., Western Res. alumni assns., D.C. Library Assn., Library of Congress Profl. Assn., Library of Congress Welfare and Recreation Assn. Lutheran. Home: Apt 19 9930 Fairfax Sq Fairfax VA 22030 Office: Library of Congress Washington DC 20540

D'ALESSIO, EDWARD RONALD, educator; b. Orange, N.J., May 20, 1932; s. Gerard and Angela (Picariello) D'A.; B.A., Seton Hall U., 1954; M.S., Fordham U., 1955, Ph.D., 1967; postgrad. Harvard, 1967; m. Rose Mary Racanelli, Aug. 12, 1956; children—Judith A., Edward P., John G., Teresanne R. Lectr. in edn. Fordham U., N.Y.C., 1956-58; tchr. Orange (N.J.) Pub. Schs., 1957-58; asst. prof. edn. Seton Hall U., South Orange, 1958-67, asst. to dean grad. studies, 1962-63, asst. dean Sch. Edn., 1963-67, asso. prof. edn., 1967; coordinator govtl. programs div. elementary and secondary edn. U.S. Cath. Conf., Washington, 1967-70, dir., 1970—. Cons., lectr.; dir. workshop in govtl. programs for nonpub. sch. adminstrs., 1969, 70; mem. nat. adv. com. Nat. Sch. Food Service Finance Project, 1969-71; non-voting commr. Edn. Commn. U.S., 1969—. Mem. United Community Corp., Newark, 1966. Mem. Am. Assn. Sch. Adminstrs., Am. Assn. U. Profs., Higher Edn. Group Washington, Nat. Cath. Ednl. Assn., N.E.A., Am. Assn. for Higher Edn., Nat. Soc. for Study Edn., N.J. Edn. Assn. Contbr. articles to profl. publs. Home: 4204 Laurel Rd Alexandria VA 22309 Office: 1312 Massachusetts Av NW Washington DC 20005

DALEY, ROGER A., newspaper exec. Pres. Knoxville News-Sentinel Co. Office: 294 W Church St Knoxville TN 37901*

DALEY, WILLIAM THOMAS, educator; b. San Jose, Ill., Oct. 10, 1923; s. Thomas John and Ella Christine (Schlitt) D.; student St. Mary's Coll., 1941-43; A.B., Cath. U. Am., 1950, M.A., 1951; m. Winifred Elizabeth Marty, Apr. 19, 1949; children—Christine Margaret, Robert Joseph, Sharon Ann, Maureen Jane, Kathryn Marie. Mem. faculty Cath. U. Am., Washington, 1951—, instr. speech pathology, audiology, 1951-56, asst. prof., 1956-63, dir. speech and hearing clinic, 1963—. Cons. speech pathology, audiology Hosp. for Sick Children, Washington, 1966—; mem. adv. panel Council Adult Stutterers 1965—. Pres., mem. bd. dirs. Campus Sch., Washington, 1968-69. Served with AUS, 1943-46. Mem. Am., D.C. (pres. 1962-64) speech and hearing assns. Editor: Speech and Language Therapy with the Brain-Damaged Child, 1962; Speech and Language Therapy with the Cerebral Palsi Child, 1964; co-editor Speech Therapy, 1961. Home: 1012 Taussig Pl NE Washington DC 20017 Office: Speech Hearing Clinic Cath U Am Washington DC 20017

DALLAS, SHERMAN FORBES, educator; b. Buffalo, May 22, 1919; s. Sherman LeFurge and Mabel (Forbes) D.; B.A., Ohio No. U., 1949; M.A., Ind. U., 1951, Ph.D., 1955; m. Betty Lou Sears, May 11, 1945; children— Barbara (Mrs. T. Allan Wilson), George Sherman. Asst. prof. econs. Ga. Tech. Inst., Atlanta, 1952-54; lectr. Ind. U., Bloomington, 1954-55; asst. prof. econs. Ind. State Tchrs. Coll., Terre Haute, 1955-57, asso. prof., 1957-58; commr. Fed. Mediation and Conciliation Service, Detroit, 1958-59; asso. prof. econs. Coll. Indsl. Mgmt., Ga. Tech. U., 1959-61, prof., 1961—, acting dir., 1960-61, asso. dir., 1963-65, dir., 1965-69, dean, 1969—; internat. adv. bd. Citizens and So. Nat. Bank, Atlanta; dir. Ellijay Telephone Co., (Ga.). Impartial umpire Canton Mills, Texile Workers Union, 1964-71, Atlanta Housing Authority, bldg. service employees, 1965-71; arbitrator Am. Arbitration Assn., Fed. Mediation and Conciliation Service panels, 1959—; cons. Hertz Corp., Reynolds Metal Co., George C. Marshall Space Flight Center, John F. Kennedy Space Flight Center, Jacksonville (Fla.) Naval Air Station, Communicable Disease Center, Def. Contract Adminstrn. Service, Birmingham, Atlanta, Nuclear Assurance Corp., Atlanta, Navy Yard, Charleston, S.C. Served to 2d lt. AUS, 1942-45. Mem. Indsl. Relations Research Assn., Am. Econ. Assn., Omicron Delta Kappa, Phi Kappa Phi, Beta Gamma Sigma, Alpha Kappa Psi. Methodist. Rotarian. Home: 3325 Valley Rd NW Atlanta GA 30305

DALLMAN, GLENN ROBERT, library dir.; b. Oconomowoc, Wis., July 31, 1927; s. Henry William and Alma (Baehler) D.; B.A. magna cum laude, Northland Coll., 1950; M.Ed., U. Wis. at Milw., 1954; M.S. in Library Sci., Western Res. U., 1962; m. Charlotte Marie Frank, June 26, 1954; children—Jeffry Paul, Jaclyn Marie. Tchr. Trinity High Sch., Fort Lauderdale, Fla., 1950-51; tchr., prin. Lutheran Tchrs. Tng. Coll., Ibakachi, Nigeria, 1951-57; tchr., librarian Concordia Coll., Portland, Ore., 1957-58; tchr. Luth. High Sch., Cleve., 1959-61; librarian Cleveland Heights (O.) Pub. Library, 1961-62; dir. library Indian River Community Coll., Fort Pierce, Fla., 1962-66, St. Petersburg Jr. Coll., Clearwater, Fla., 1966—. Served with USNR, 1945-46. Mem. A.L.A., Southeastern, Fla., St. Lucie County (dir., pres., 1965-66) library assns., Fla. Assn. Community Colls. Home: 1740 Harmony Dr Clearwater FL 33516 Office: 2465 Drew St Clearwater FL 33515

DALMAU, EDUARD MARTINEZ, bishop; b. Havana, Cuba, June 29, 1893; s. Cecil Martinez and Sophie Dalmau; ed. philosophy and theology, Rome, Italy, 1908-16. Ordained priest Roman Catholic Ch.; prof. history and canon law, Rome, 1917-26; bishop of Cienfuegos, Cuba, 1933-61; titular bishop, Euzi, West Palm Beach, Fla., 1961—. Decorated officer Legion of Honor; great cross Carolos M. Cespeo (Cuba). Address: 208 Evernia St West Palm Beach FL 33401

DALQUEST, WALTER W., educator; b. Seattle, Sept. 11, 1917; s. Neils Walter and Florence (Woelber) D.; B.S., U. Wash., 1940, M.S., 1941; Ph.D., La. State U., 1951; m. Peggy Burgner, Aug. 8, 1940; 1 dau., Linda Lee. Research asso. U. Kan., 1945-49; teaching fellow La. State U., 1949-51; prof. biology Midwestern U., Wichita Falls, Tex., 1951—. Author: Mammals of Washington, 1948, Mammals of the Mexican State of San Luis Potosi, 1953. Home: Route 3 Box 248A Wichita Falls TX 76308

DALRYMPLE, DAVID EDWARD, physician; b. Elkhart, Ind., Nov. 10, 1936; s. Thurlow Edward and Irene Guinevere (Northrop) D.; A.B., DePauw U., 1958; M.S., Purdue U., 1960; postgrad. Ind. U., 1960-61; M.D., U. Chgo., 1965; m. Carol Mae Anderson, Aug. 2, 1959; children— David Northrop, Brian Anderson. Intern State U. Ia., 1965-66, resident, 1966-68; NIH fellow Washington U. Sch. Medicine, St. Louis, 1968-69; practice medicine specializing in internal medicine, Atlanta, 1971—. Vis. clin. instr. Med. Coll. Ga., Augusta, 1969-70. Chmn. med. com. drug abuse Sandy Springs (Atlanta), Ga. Served with AUS, 1969-71; med. officer Specialized Treatment Center, Ft. Gordon. Recipient Resident award U. Ia., Iowa City, 1965. Diplomate Am. Bd. Med. Examiners. Mem. Am. Fedn. for Clin. Research, Fulton County Med. Soc., A.M.A., U.S. Handball Assn., Atlanta, Ga. med. assns., Diabetes Assn. Atlanta, Ga. Thoracic Soc., Sigma Xi, Alpha Tau Omega. Episcopalian. Club: Flying. Contbr. articles to profl. jours. Home: 5515 Whitewood Ct Dunwoody GA 30338 Office: 6500 Vernon Woods Dr Atlanta GA 30328

DALTON, ALVIN RAY, banker; b. Plainview, Tex., Nov. 28, 1932; s. Bernice A. and Clarice (Harlin) D.; student Tenn. Poly. Inst., 1951; courses Am. Inst. Banking; m. Barbara Ann Bowers, Nov. 27, 1953; children—Terry Ray, Kathryne Sheree. With 1st Nat. Bank of Fort Worth, 1955—, v.p. data processing, 1968—. Active Boy Scouts Am., Civil Air Patrol. Served with USAF, 1951-55. Mem. Data Processing Mgrs. Assn. (past chpt. pres., individual performance award), Am. Inst. Banking, Nat. Rifle Assn. Baptist. Home: 6328 Friar Ct Fort Worth TX 76119 Office: 1 Burnett Plaza Fort Worth TX 76101

DALTON, CHARLES CHESTER, physicist; b. Powersburg, Ky., Feb. 19, 1923; s. Charlie Elvis and Lucy Amy (Rector) D.; B.S. in Physics, U. Ky., 1949, postgrad., 1950-51; M.A. in Math., U. Ala., 1957, postgrad., 1958; m. Charlotte Kurschat, Dec. 31, 1952; children—Karla Winifred, Eric Charles. Research optical and illumination engr. Corning Glass Works (N.Y.), 1949-50; optics physicist Evans Signal Lab., Belmar, N.J., 1951-54; gen. physicist Armament Center, Elgin AFB, Fla., 1954-55; supv. physicist Redstone (Ala.) Arsenal Ordnance Missile Labs., 1955-59; flight systems physicist Army Ballistic Missile Agy., 1959-60; aerospace engr. NASA Marshall Space Flight Center, Huntsville, Ala., 1960—. Recipient Superior Performance award Army Ballistic Missile Agy., 1960. Mem. A.A.A.S., Sci. Research Soc. Am., N.Y Acad. Scis., Nat. Geog. Soc. Contbr. articles in field to profl. jours.; also tech. reports. Home: 8012 Camille Dr SE Huntsville AL 35802 Office: NASA Marshall Space Flight Center Huntsville AL 35812

DALTON, DONALD H., lawyer; b. Stitzer, Wis.; s. Charles Christian and Alvina (Rose) D.; student U.S. Naval Acad., 1925-29, Columbia U., 1930; B.S., U. Chgo., 1931; postgrad. Yale, 1934-35; J.D., Georgetown U., 1947; m. Virginia Brady, Sept. 20, 1931; 1 dau., Sylvia (Mrs. Howard R. Searight); m. 2d, Irene Martin, Sept. 16, 1939; children—Doris J. (Mrs. John R. Harper), Donald H., Diane I. Reporter Washington Post, 1945; admitted D.C. bar, 1947, Ill. bar, 1947, Md. bar, 1952; pvt. practice law, Washington, Ill., Md.; prof. pub. bar, relations Southeastern U., 1949-58. Bd. dirs. Aid Bur., D.C.; trustee Legal Aid Soc. D.C. Served with USNR, World War II. Recipient certificate of pub. relations achievement Am. Pub. Relations Assn., 1957; Distinguished Alumni award Columbia U. Club, Washington, 1968. Mem. Am. (chmn. pub. relations com. gen. practice sect.), Fed., D.C. (1st v.p., dir.), Md. (mem. pub. relations com.), Chgo. bar assns., Am. Arbitration Assn. (adv. com. to pub. relations com.), English-Speaking Union, Am. Legion, Res. Officers Naval Service (pres.), Judge Advocates Gen. Assn. (dir.), 40 and 8, The Counsellors, U.S. Capitol, Montgomery County hist. socs., U. Chgo. Alumni Assn., U.S. Naval Acad. Alumni Assn., Lincoln Group D.C. (pres. 1971—), Newcomen Soc., S.A.R., Mil. Order Fgn. Wars, Civil War Round Table, Delta Theta Phi. Mason. Clubs: Columbia U. (pres. Washington 1960-71); Elks, Army and Navy Country, Yale, Army and Navy. Home: 8603 Springdell Pl Chevy Chase MD 20015 Office: Fed Bar Bldg W 1819 H St NW Washington DC 20006

DALTON, HAROLD EUGENE, supt. schs.; b. Anson, Tex., Oct. 9, 1924; s. Scott and Ruby M. (Kirkland) D.; B.S., W. Tex. State U., 1949, M.S., 1954; m. Mary Lucille Hanna, Aug. 3, 1947; children—Deborah Denise, Mark Wellington. Tchr., coach Stinnett (Tex.) Ind. Sch. Dist., 1950-52, prin. high sch., 1952-60, supt., 1960—. Active A.R.C., Hutchinson County Cancer Soc. Served with USMCR, 1943-45. Decorated Air medals (3). Mem. North Canadian River Supts. (chmn. 1969-71), Tex. Assn. Sch. Adminstrs. (dist. pres. 1966-67), Tex. State Tchrs. Assn. (county pres. 1959-60), C. of C. Mason, Lion, Kiwanian. Address: Drawer Y Stinnett TX 79083

DALTON, JESS N., lawyer. Mem. firm Goodrich, Dalton, Little & Riquelme, Mexico City, Mexico. Address: Paseo de la Reforma 355 Mexico DF Mexico*

DALTON, JOHN NICHOLS, lawyer; b. Emporia, Va., July 11, 1931; s. Ted R. and Mary (Turner) D.; A.B., William and Mary Coll., 1953; LL.B., U. Va., 1957; m. Edwina Jeanette Panzer, Feb. 18, 1956; children— Katherine Scott, Ted Ernest, John Nichols, Mary Helen. Admitted to Va. bar, 1957; partner Dalton, Turk & Stone, Radford, Va., 1957—. Mem. adv. bd. First & Mchts. Nat. Bank, Radford, 1965—; v.p., dir. Meredith & Tate, Pulaski, Va., 1961—; dir. Sutton Devel. Corp., Radford. Pres., Young Republican Fedn. Va., 1960; treas. Va. Rep. Com., 1960, gen. counsel, 1961—. Mem. Va. Ho. of Dels., 1966—. Served to 1st lt. AUS, 1954-56. Mem. Am. Legion, Sigma Alpha Epsilon. Mason (Shriner, 32 deg.), Moose, Odd Fellow. Home: 411 4th St Radford VA 24141 Office: Norwood St Radford VA 24141

DALTON, TED, U.S. dist. judge; b. Carroll County, Va., July 3, 1901; s. Currell and Lodaska Vernon (Martin) D.; A.B., Coll. William and Mary, 1924, LL.B., 1926, LL.D., 1972; LL.D., Milligan Coll., 1966; m. Mary Turner, Jan. 4, 1932; 1 son, John N. Admitted to Va. bar, 1923; atty. Commonwealth of Va., Radford, 1928-36; mem. Va. Senate, 1944-59; U.S. dist. judge Western Dist. Va., 1959-61, chief U.S. dist. judge, Roanoke, Va., 1962—. Mem. Republican Nat. Com. for Va., 1952-59; Rep. candidate for gov. of Va., 1953, 57; mem. Va. Constl. Revision Commn., 1970. Mem. Am., Va. (v.p. 1944), Montgomery-Radford-Floyd (pres. 1948-49) bar assns., Order of Coif, Phi Beta Kappa, Alpha Kappa Psi, Omicron Delta Kappa, Phi Delta Phi, Sigma Nu. Club: Flat Hat. Address: Radford VA 24141

DALVIT, LEWIS, condr. Condr. Jackson (Miss.) Symphony Orch. Address: Box 4584 Jackson MS 39216*

DALY, JAMES JOSEPH, pub. co. exec.; b. Jersey City, June 11, 1916; s. Bernard B. and Anna (Leiner) D.; student St. Peters Coll.; m. Catherine Mary Adams, June 26, 1937; children—Ann, Catherine. Classified advt. mgr. N.Y. Sun, 1946-49, World-Telegram Sun, 1950-55; classified advt. mgr. Washington Post, 1955-60, bus. mgr., 1960-65, v.p., gen. mgr., 1965-72. Chmn., v.p. Tenafly (N.J.) Community Chest, 1955; mem. budget com. Washington Health and Welfare Council, 1961-64; hon. asso. C. W. Post Coll., 1966; past bd. dirs. United Givers Fund. Served with AUS, 1943-45. Mem. Washington Advt. Club, Washington Bd. Trade (dir.), Am. Newspaper Pubs. Assn., John Carroll Soc., Silurians. Rotarian. Clubs: Columbia Country, Nat. Country; Boca Raton. Home: 5340 Falmouth Rd Spring Hill Washington DC 20016

DALY, JOHN WILLIAM, govt. ofcl.; b. Portland, Ore., June 8, 1933; s. John Ellis and Hilda (Mussel) D.; B.S., Ore. State U., 1954, M.A. (NSF fellow), 1955; Ph.D., Stanford, 1958; m. Sarah Stone, Aug. 22, 1956 (div. Sept. 1960); children—Kathryn Ann, Shannon Elizabeth. With USPHS, 1958-60; biochemist, instr. grad. program NIH, Bethesda, Md., 1960—. Mem. A.A.A.S., Am. Chem. Soc., Am. Soc. Pharmacology and Exptl. Therapeutics, Sigma Xi. Contbr. numerous articles profl. jours. Home: 3410 17th St NW Washington DC 20010 Office: NIH Bethesda MD 20014

DALY, REX FELTON, economist; b. Panguitch, Utah, Mar. 4, 1915; d. John H. and Leone (Little) D.; B.S., Utah State U., 1938; M.S., U. Md., 1939; Ph.D., U. Ill., 1951; m. Gloria A. Yeager, Aug. 26, 1963; children—Patricia, Thomas, Dana. Prof. U. So. Utah, 1940-42; with U.S. Dept. Agr., 1942-43, 46—, dir. econ. and statis. analysis div., 1969—; economist U.S. AID Mission, Pakistan, 1958-60. Cons. FAO, 1971—, OECD, 1971—. Pres. P.T.A., 1955—. Served with USNR, 1943-46. Recipient Superior Service award U.S. Dept. Agr., 1956. Mem. Am. Agr. Econ. Assn., Am. Econ. Assn., Am. Statis. Assn., Nat. Economists, Citizen's Assn. (pres. 1954—), Phi Kappa Phi, Alpha Zeta. Editor Agrl. Econ. Jour., 1961-65. Home: 3838 Columbia Pike Arlington VA 22204 Office: 500 12th St SW Washington DC 20250

DALY, ROBERT PATRICK, financial cons.; b. Bklyn., Feb. 13, 1910; s. William James and Sarah Alice (Dunn) D.; student St. Charles Coll., 1923-28, Spring Hill Coll., 1928-31, U. Vienna, 1966, U. Miami, 1968; m. Doreen Marion Coutts, Sept. 30, 1949; children—Patricia, Paris, Marion, Gaelan. Owner, Daly Pub. Relations, Miami, Fla., 1945—, Eagle Advt., Miami, 1962—, Audio Services of Miami, 1966—; dir. marketing, advt. and promotion Gramco, Nassau, Bahamas, 1966-67; founder U.S.A. Mgmt. Co. Fla., Miami, 1968 (merged with U.S. Mgmt. Co. Fla. 1969), pres., 1968-69. Charter organizer, mem. adv. bd. mgrs. Nat. Bank of Hialeah (Fla.), 1964-65. Dir. Md. governship campaign for Spiro T. Agnew, 1966. Mem. Am. Pub. Relations Assn. (charter, chpt. pres. 1955-60), Internat. Platform Assn., Pub. Relations Soc. Am. (del. 1967-68). Nat. columnist various legal newspapers, 1964-67. Home: 7440 SW 69th Terrace Miami FL 33143 Office: 201 SW 13th St Miami FL 33131

DAME, LAWRENCE, author, art critic; b. Portland, Me., July 2, 1898; s. Edward Lawrence and Katherine (Gunn) D.; ed. Harvard, Ecole des Hautes Etudes Sociales (Paris), U. Grenoble, U. Toulouse (France), Instituto de Burgos (Spain), Boston U.; m. Rachel Wells, Sept. 25, 1958. Editorial staffs, 1919-39; explored Yucatan and Quintana Roo, 1940-41; relief worker. Unitarian Service Com., Portugal 1941; art editor and spl. writer Boston Herald-Traveler, 1940-48; staff critic Art Digest London, 1950-53; with Turkish Times, Istanbul, il Mattino d'Italia Centrale, Florence, and Rome Daily Am., 1952-53; asso. editor Nantucket (Mass.) Inquirer and Mirror, 1953-54; art, books and theatre editor Sarasota (Fla.) Herald-Tribune, 1954-61; with Social Pictorial, Palm Beach, Fla., 1961—; dir. Harvard News Office, 1943-45, 1946-47. Served arty., France, 1917-18. Decorated by French and Portuguese govts. for war work, 1941. Mem. S.A.R., Soc. Colonial Wars, Wine and Food Soc. of Boston (gov.). Wine and Food Soc. Palm Beach (pres.), Harvard Musical Assn., Sarasota Literary Forum (pres.). Clubs: Vet. Motor Car of Am., Rolls-Royce Owners, Overseas Press (N.Y.C.); Harvard (Palm Beach); Pacific. Wharf Rat (Nantucket Island, Mass.). Author: New England Comes Back, 1940. Yucatan, 1941; Mava Mission, 1967; Backabush Jamaica; co-author: Boston Murders, 1948. Contbr. articles to mags. Cycling and Wine authority. Home: Horse Guards Plantation Maidstone PO Jamaica WI Office: PO Box 2392 Palm Beach FL 33480

DAMERON, THOMAS BARKER, JR., orthopaedic surgeon; b. Rocky Mount, N.C, June 1, 1924; s. Thomas Barker and Isa (Sills) D.; student The Citadel, 1941-42, U. N.C., 1942-44, Duke, 1947; M.D., U. Cal., 1945; m. Nancy Jane Henry, Aug. 26, 1949; children—Thomas Barker III, David Henry, Christopher Buxton Williams, Nancy Van Vleet, Rebecca Jane. Intern, Baylor U. Hosp., 1947-48; surg. house staff Grady Meml. Hosp., 1948-49; resident orthopaedic surgery Johns Hopkins Hosp., Balt., 1949-54; practice medicine, specializing in orthopaedic surgery, Raleigh, N.C., 1954—; mem. staff Rex Hosp., Wake Meml. Hosp.; clin. asso. prof. surgery (orthopedics) U. N.C. Sch. Medicine; adj. prof. poultry sci. N.C. State U. Mem. regional com. Morehead scholarships U. N.C.; bd. dirs. Raleigh United Fund; accreditation com. N.C. Crippled Children's Services. Served with USNR, 1943-45, 59-61. Diplomate Am. Bd. Orthopaedic Surgery. Mem. Am. Acad. Orthopaedic Surgery, Assn. Bone and Joint Surgeons, N.C. (past pres.), Am. (exec. com.), Piedmont orthopaedic assns., Am., So. councilor, mem. exec. com.), N.C., Wake County (pres.) med. socs., N.Y. Acad. Sci. Methodist (ofcl. bd.). Asso. editor Clin. Orthopaedics and Related Research. Contbr. articles profl. jours. Home: 414 Scotland St Raleigh NC 27609 Office: 600 Wade Av Raleigh NC 27605

DAMIAN, RAYMOND TRAIAN, parasitologist; b. Phila., Aug. 11, 1934; s. Romulus and Christina (Pepici) D.; B.S., U. Akron, 1956; M.S., Fla. State U., 1958, Ph.D., 1962; m. Anna Jean Clifton, Aug. 31, 1957; children—Jane Camille, David Clifton, Leah Dawn. Research asso. Fla. State U., Tallahassee, 1962-63; asst. prof. biology Emory U., Atlanta, 1963-67; immunologist Southwest Found. for Research and Edn., San Antonio, 1967-69, asso. found. scientist, 1969—. Mem. Am. Soc. Parasitologists, A.A.A.S., Am. Soc. Tropical Medicine and Hygiene, Southwest Assn. Parasitologists, Am. Assn. U. Profs., Sigma Xi. Conglist. (deacon). Contbr. sci. articles to profl. jours. Home:

10606 Tioga Dr San Antonio TX 78230 Office: 7480 W Commerce St San Antonio TX 78284

DAMOURS, LEON WILLIAMS, water devel. adviser; b. Brighton, Colo., Apr. 19, 1911; s. Leon Albert and Elizabeth Lillian (Williams) D.; B.S. in C.E., Colo. State U., 1933; m. Kathryn Francis Burch, May 23, 1937; children—Carolyn (Mrs. Harold T. Commons, Jr.), Stephen L. Surveyor, Bur. Pub. Rds., Yellowstone Park, Wyo., 1934-36; engr. Bur. Reclamation, Denver, 1936-51, chief fgn. relations, Washington, 1951-65; Mekong liaison officer AID, Dept. State, Bangkok, Thailand, 1965-67, dep. dir. East Asia Engring. Agy., Washington, 1967-69; water devel. adviser to govt. Internat. Bank for Reconstrn. and Devel., Maseru, Lesotho, 1971—. Served to maj. AUS, 1941-46. Fellow Am. Soc. C.E.; mem. Internat. Commn. Large Dams, Internat. Commn. Irrigation and Drainage. Baptist. Home: 5130 28th St North Arlington VA 22207 Office: Ministry of Works PO Box 20 Maseru Lesotho Africa

DANAHY, PAUL W., state legislator. Mem. Fla. Ho. of Reps. Address: 1210 First Nat Bank Bldg Tampa FL 33602*

DANBURG, DWIGHT STERLING, physician, hosp. adminstr.; b. Miller, S.D., July 3, 1914; s. Daverne and Mary (Nicholas) D.; student S.D. State Coll., 1932, Dakota Wesleyan U., 1933-35; B.S. in Medicine, U. S.D., 1937; M.D., U. Louisville, 1939; m. Hildegard New, June 11, 1939; children—Dwight S., Mary Kay (Mrs. Milton Watts). Intern, Providence Hosp., Seattle, 1939-40; resident Firland's Sanitorium, Seattle, 1940-41; asst. med. dir. Boeing Aircraft Co., Seattle, 1942-44; staff physician Uncas-on-Thames Sanitorium, Norwich, Conn., 1945-49; supt., med. dir. Greenwell Springs (La.) Tb Hosp., 1949—. Cons., La. State U. Sch. Social Welfare, Baton Rouge Regional Chest Clinic, La. Dept. Health. Bd. dirs. Audubon council Girl Scouts U.S.A. Mem. La. (adv. panel La. Dept. Pub. Welfare), East Baton Rouge med. socs., Am. Coll. Chest Physicians (past pres.), Am., La. thoracic socs., A.M.A., So. Med. Assn. Lutheran (pres. exec. bd., mem. sub-com. on social welfare Div. Missions So. Dist. Mo. Synod 1964—). Office: Greenwell Springs Tb Hospital Greenwell Springs GA 70739

DANDRIDGE, WILLIAM SHELTON, orthopedic surgeon; b. Atoka, Okla., May 21, 1914; s. Theodore Oscar and Estelle (Shelton) D.; B.A., U. Okla., 1935; M.D., U. Ark., 1939; M.S., Baylor U., 1950; m. Pearl Sessions, Feb. 3, 1941; 1 dau., Diana Dawn. Intern St. Paul's Hosp., Dallas, 1939-40; surgical residence Med. Arts Hosp., Dallas, 1940; commd. 1st lt. USAF, advanced through grades to lt. col., 1950; chief reconditioning service and reconstructive surgery Ashburn Gen. Hosp., McKinney, Tex., 1945-46; neurosurgical resident Brooke Army Med. Center, San Antonio, 1946-47; orthopedic surgical resident, 1947-50; chief orthopedic service and gen. surgery Fransis E. Warren AFB Cheyenne, Wyo., Travis AFB, Susan, Cal., 1950-51; chief orthopedic service and gen. surgery Shepherd AFB, 1951-52; comdg. officer, chief orthopedic service, chief gen. surgery Craig AFB Hosp., Selma, Ala., 1952-53; pvt. practice medicine, specializing in orthopedic surgery Muskogee, Okla., 1954-69; orthopedic cons., active staff mem. St. Mary's Hosp., Enid, Okla.; active staff mem. Bass Meml. Bapt. Hosp., Enid, Okla. Exec. mem. Eastern Okla. council Boy Scouts Am. Fellow A.C.S., Internat. Coll. Surgeons; mem. Am. Fracture Assn., Nat. Found. (adviser 1958-61), N.Y. Acad. Sci., Okla. State, Pan-Am., So., Aerospace med assns., A.M.A., Garfield County Med. Soc., S.W. Surg. Congress, Am. Rheumatology Soc., Democrat. Methodist. Mason (32 deg., K.T. Shriner, Jester), Lion. Club: Oakwood Country. Contbr. profl. jours. Home: 2502 Wildwood Dr Enid OK 73701 Office: 330 S 5th St Enid OK 23701

DANIEL, ARTHUR RATCLIFFE, JR., engring. co. exec.; b. Blackstone, Va., Aug. 19, 1932; s. Arthur Ratcliffe and Susie (Waller) D.; B.S.C.E., Va. Poly. Inst., 1954; m. Eva Delorous Foster, May 18, 1952; children— Sherri Delorous, Arthur Ratcliffe III. Div. traffic engr. Ohio Dept. Hwys., Marietta, 1955-59 area traffic engr. N.C. Hwy. Commn., Raleigh, 1959-64; dir. Louisville-Jefferson County (Ky.) Dept. Traffic Engring., 1964-69; pres. Sherridan Engring. Inc., Louisville, Ky., 1966—. Chmn. engring. com. Citizens Traffic Commn., Marietta, 1956-59; mem. Ky. Gov.'s Efficiency Task Force, 1967. Registered profl. engr., Ind., Ky., N.C., Ohio, Tenn., W. Va. Mem. Inst. Traffic Engrs. (gen. chmn. 1967 ann. meeting So. sect.), Ohio Soc. Profl. Engrs. (sec.-treas. Muskingum Valley chpt. 1958-59), Ky., Nat. socs. profl. engrs. Elk. Clubs: Plantation Country, Jeffersonville-Elks Country. Author: Urban Transportation in Louisville, Kentucky, 1966. Home: 3511 Forest Brook Dr Louisville KY 40207 Office: 120 Village Louisville KY 40243

DANIEL, AUBREY MARSHALL, III, lawyer; b. Monks Corner, S.C., May 16, 1941; s. Aubrey Marshall, Jr. and Laura Francis (Morris) D.; grad. Woodberry Forest Sch., 1959; B.A., U. Va., 1963; LL.B., U. Richmond, 1966; m. Shirley Virginia Hanbury, June 19, 1965; children—Laura Elizabeth, Ann Meade. Admitted to Va. bar, 1966, D.C. bar, 1971; mem. firms Minor, Thompson, Savage, Richmond, Va., 1966-67, Williams, Connolly & Califano, Washington, 1971—. Served to capt. AUS, 1967-71. Decorated Army Commendation medal; recipient Outstanding Service award Nat. Dist. Attys. Assn., 1971; Elliott-Black award Am. Ethical Union, 1972. Mem. Am., Va., D.C. bar assns., Am., Va. trial lawyers assns., Phi Delta Phi, Delta Phi. Home: 6744 N 27th St Arlington VA 22213 Office: Williams Connolly & Califano 839 17th NW Washington DC 20006

DANIEL, CLAUDE PIPPO, dentist; b. Franklinton, La., Feb. 27, 1916; s. Chester Pippo and Elizabeth Van Dora (Simmons) D.; student La. State U., 1935-36; D.D.S., Loyola U., 1940; postgrad. Northwestern U., 1949, Washington U., 1951, U. Ala., 1954; m. Erephile Margaret Gremillion, June 22, 1940; children—Claudia (Mrs. John Atkins Melton), Janis (Mrs. Joseph Albert Roman), Anne (Mrs. Greg Herman Briese), Claude Pippo. Pvt. practice dentistry, Bogalusa, La., 1950—, Slidell, La., 1952—; mem. staff Charity Hosp. chief orthodontics Bogalusa Community Med. Center, 1955—. Pres. Crippled Children Bogalusa, 1960-72; active United Fund. Served to 1st lt. USAAF, 1941-45. Decorated Bronze Star medal. Mem. Acad. Internat. Dentistry, Am. Dental Soc., Kells Hon. Orthological Soc., Am., So. socs. orthodontics, La., New Orleans orthodontics socs., Am. Legion, V.F.W., D.A.V., Bogalusa C. of C., Psi Omega. Democrat. K.C., Rotarian. Home: 1532 Founders Dr Bogalusa LA 70427 Office: 315 Memphis St Bogalusa LA 70427

DANIEL, COLDWELL, III, economist, educator; b. New Orleans, Aug. 30, 1926; s. Coldwell and Josephine (Weick) D.; B.B.A., Tulane U., 1949; M.B.A., Ind. U., 1950; Ph.D., U. Va., 1959; postgrad. U. Chgo., 1964-65; m. Joan Nellie Haddad, Dec. 19, 1959; children—Anne Alexis, Coldwell IV. Research co-ordinator So. Cal. Research Council, and instr. econs. Pomona Coll., 1956-57; prof. econs., chmn. dept. U. So. Miss., 1958-65, acting dir. bur. econ. and bus. research, 1963-65, chmn. bd. editors So. Quar., 1962-65; prof. econs. U. Houston, 1965-70, Memphis State U., 1970—. NSF sci. faculty fellow, 1964-65; Fulbright vis. prof. econs. Dacca U. Pakistan, 1961-62; project dir. NASA, Miss. Test Facility Econ. Impact Study, 1963; lectr., conferee So. Bell Tel. & Tel. Co., 1961, 63; conferee Am. Tel. & Tel. Co., 1966, So. Central Bell. Tel. & Tel. Co., 1972. Mem. La.-Miss. Regional Export Expansion Council, 1963-65; mem. com. on Miss. Economy, State of Miss., 1960. Served as 1st lt. AUS, 1951-53. Mem. Am., So., Pakistan econ. assns., S.W. Social Sci. Assn., Raven Soc., Beta Gamma Sigma, Pi Gamma Mu, Pi Kappa Pi, Delta Sigma Pi, Pi Sigma Epsilon, Delta Sigma Phi, Omicron Delta Epsilon, Omicron Delta Kappa. Lion. Author: Mathematical Models in Microeconomics. Asso. editor for econs. Social Sci. Quar., 1968—. Contbr. articles to profl. jours. Home: 1776 Carr St Memphis TN 38104

DANIEL, EDWARD IRWIN, II, food co. exec.; b. St. Francisville, La., Dec. 17, 1918; s. Robert Harrison and May (Young) D.; B.S., La. State U., 1940; m. Thelma Percy Walker, Apr. 21, 1941; children—Beryl Gene (Mrs. William L. Lott, Jr.), Edward Irwin, III. With Princeville Canning Co. (merger Joan of Arc Co. 1969), St. Francisville, 1940—, raw product mgr., 1940-45, plant mgr., 1945-70, v.p. So. operations, 1970—; dir. Bank Commerce & Trust Co., St. Francisville, La., Fed. Land Bank Assn., Baton Rouge. Mem. exec. com. Pub. Affairs Research Council, 1960-71; bd. dirs. West Faliciana Parish Hosp., 1967-70. Mem. La. Sweet Potato Assn. (pres.), La. Sweet Potato Adv. Commn. Democrat. Methodist (chmn. bd. stewards 1960-71). Clubs: Civic (pres. 1962-63) (St. Francisville); City (Baton Rouge). Home: Box 27 St Francisville LA 70775 Office: Drawer 490 St Francisville LA 70775

DANIEL, HARBEN, broadcasting exec. Pres. WSAV, Savannah, Ga. Office: 1430 E Victory Dr Savannah GA 31404*

DANIEL, HAROLD TURNER, sch. supt.; b. Locust Grove, Ga., May 26, 1916; s. Emmett Benjamin and Willie (Mae) D.; A.B., U. Ga., 1937, M.Ed., 1948, postgrad., 1963, Specialist in Edn., 1971; m. Mary Rowan, Mar. 3, 1940; children—Harold Turner, Evelyn Claire, Randolph. Tchr., Spalding County Bd. Edn., 1938-39; prin. Butts County Bd. Edn., 1941-42; prin. Pike County Bd. Edn., 1942-44; supt. Pike County Schs., Zebulon, Ga., 1945-72. Bd. dirs. Flint River Regional Library. Mem. N.E.A., Ga. Edn. Assn., Ga. Assn. County Sch. Supts. (pres.). Methodist. Mason, Lion. Address: Zebulon GA 30295

DANIEL, HARRY, bank exec.; b. Old Fort, N.C., Apr. 25, 1904; s. Robert L. and Lidie (Finch) D.; B.A., Wofford Coll., 1926; m. Mariana Camak, Aug. 18, 1940; 1 dau., Anna Louise. Note clk. First Nat. Bank, Spartanburg, S.C., 1926-32; with payroll dept. Pacific Mills, Lyman, S.C., 1932-36; asst. cashier Bank Greer (S.C.), 1936-49, cashier, 1949-55, v.p., 1955-65, exec. v.p., 1965-66, pres., 1966—, dir., 1953—. Trustee, Spartanburg (S.C.) Jr. Coll., 1966—, Greenville (S.C.) Gen. Hosp. System, 1967—. Lay del. S.C. Ann. United Meth. Conf., 1972; mem. Emory U. Com. 100, Candler Sch. theol., 1971-73. Named Boss of the Year, Greer Jr. C. of C., 1967, Citizen of the Year, Greer Kiwanis Club, 1967. Mem. S.C. Bankers Assn. (exec. council 1971-73). Methodist (chmn. bd. trustees 1965—). Kiwanian (pres. 1940, lt. gov. Carolina dist. 1942). Home: 201 W Arlington Av Greer SC 29651 Office: 116 Trade St Greer SC 29651

DANIEL, HOMER FRANK, architect; b. Miami, Apr. 15, 1931; s. James Frank and Margaret Melanie (Peeples) D.; student Miss. So. U., 1950-51; student in archtl. engring. U. Miami, 1963-65; m. Anne O'Neil Moody, Mar. 24, 1955; children—Lynn, Michael, Lori. Designer, Gerald Pitt, Miami, 1956-60; draftsman Penney-Dekonshin, Miami, 1961-62, Carson B. Wright, Miami, 1962-65; architect, Miami, 1966—; v.p. Clive-Dan Corp., Fla. Land Holding Co., Bear Rock Mountain Co., N.C. Land Devel. Co. Served with USAF, 1950-54; ETO. Mem. A.I.A. Elk. Home: 13325 SW 83d Ct Miami FL 33156 Office: 8960 SW 87th Ct Miami FL 33156

DANIEL, JAMES MARTIN, state med. adminstr.; b. Greenville, N.C., Sept. 4, 1915; s. James Martin and Ellen L. (Garrett) D.; A.B., Duke, 1936, course in hosp. adminstrn., 1938; m. Virginia Elizabeth Skinner, Nov. 9, 1940; children—James Martin III, Elizabeth S. Asst. sec.-treas. Hosp. Care Assn., Durham, N.C., 1938-40; asst. supt. James Walker Meml. Hosp., Wilmington, 1940-43; adminstr. Rockingham Meml. Hosp., Harrisonburg, Va., 1943-46; supt. Columbia Hosp. of Richland County, Columbia, S.C., 1946-70; asst. coordinator S.C. Regional Med. Program, Columbia, 1970—. Dir. S.C. Blue Cross, 1949-71. Chmn., bd. dirs. Richland County Area council Boy Scouts Am.; bd. dirs. A.R.C., Harrisonburg, Richland County Crippled Children's Assn., Va.-Carolina's Hosp. Conf., 1948-60; mem. hosp. adv. council S.C. Bd. Health, 1947-71, chmn., 1965-68, chmn. licensing com., 1947-65; bd. dirs., pres. Hosp. Data Center S.C., Inc., 1968-70. Fellow Am. Coll. Hosp. Adminstrs. (adminstrv. chmn., mem. membership div. bd. credentials); mem. Am. (ho. dels. 1950-60, trustee 1960-63; del. at large ho. dels. 1968-72), S.C. (pres. 1948, trustee, past treas.) hosp. assns. Episcopalian. Clubs: Rotary, Civitan (past v.p.), Lions (past pres.); Forest Lake Country. Home: 213 Pinebrook Rd Columbia SC 29206 Office: 2414 Bull St Suite 317 Columbia SC 29202

DANIEL, JOE H., lawyer; b. Daniel's Landing, Tenn., Oct. 17, 1917; J.D., U. Miss., 1940. Admitted to Miss. bar, 1940; now mem. firm Daniel, Coker, Horton, Bell and Dukes, Jackson, Miss. Fellow Am. Coll. Trial Lawyers; mem. Hinds County (pres. 1958-59), Am. bar assns., Miss. State Bar, Miss. Def. Lawyers Assn., Fedn. Ins. Counsel, Phi Delta Phi. Author: Comments on Mississippis Counterclaim Statute, 1953. Address: 405 Tombigbee St at South Congress Jackson MS 39205*

DANIEL, JOSEPH CALDWELL, seed and fertilizer co. exec.; b. Mullins, S.C., Dec. 17, 1923; s. William Henry and Eva (Bell) D.; student The Citadel, 1941-43; m. Catherine Timmons, June 17, 1947; children—Roberta Timmons, Mary Catherine. With W.H. Daniel Supply Co., dealer fertilizer, seed, coal, Mullins, S.C., 1947—, sec., 1950—; partner Daniel Warehouse, tobacco warehouse, 1947—, Brick Warehouse, 1952—; for Tobacco Auction System, 1960—; dir. Davis Nat. Bank. Trustee, Mullins Hosp.; bd. visitors Vardell Hall Prep. Sch. Served with AUS, 1943-46. Mem. Mullins C. of C. (dir. 1965-67). Baptist (chmn. deacons 1961-64). Home: 1321 Sandy Bluff Rd Mullins SC 29574 Office: South Park St Mullins SC 29574

DANIEL, KATHRYN BARCHARD (KATHRYN BARCHARD DANIEL), educator; b. Foley, Ala., Jan. 9, 1931; d. Frank Vernon and Myrtle (Morris) Barchard; B.S., U. Ala., 1952, M.A., 1961, Ph.D., 1963; m. James L. Daniel, 1954 (div. 1958); 1 dau., Pamela Kathryn. Tchr. pub. schs. Baldwin County, Foley, Ala., 1952-60; asst. prof. ednl. psychology Monmouth Coll., West Long Branch, N.J., 1963-64; asso. prof. ednl. psychology Newark State Coll., Union, N.J., 1964-66; asso. prof. U. S.C., Columbia, 1966-69, prof., chmn. com. ednl. psychology, 1969—. Cons., Regional Ednl. Lab., pub. schs. N.C., S.C., Va., N.J., 1963-68; evaluation cons. pilot kindergarten program S.C. Dept. Edn., 1970—, early childhood edn. program Williamsburg County (S.C.) Sch. Dist., 1970—. Nat. Def. Edn. Act fellow, 1960-63. Mem. Am. Psychol. Assn., Am. Personnel and Guidance Assn., Am. Ednl. Research Assn., Assn. Supervision and Curriculum Devel., Soc. Research Child Devel., Am. Assn. U. Profs., Assn. Student Tchrs., A.A.A.S. Contbr. articles to profl. jours. Home: 301 N Stonehedge Dr Columbia SC 29210

DANIEL, KENNETH RULE, iron and steel mfg. co. exec.; b. Milford, Conn., Oct. 13, 1913; s. Cullen Coleman and Margaret Estelle (Elliott) D.; B.S., U. Ala., 1936, Profl. degree in Mech. Engring., 1957; m. Virginia Moody Simpson, June 11, 1938; children—Kenneth Rule, Cullen Coleman, Robert Tennent Simpson, William Francis McKemie. With Am. Cast Iron Pipe Co., Birmingham, Ala., 1936—, chief engr., 1948-55, v.p. engring., 1955-59, v.p. engring. and purchases, 1959-61, exec. v.p., 1961-63, pres., 1963—, also dir., dir. various subsidiaries; dir. Seaboard Coast Line R.R., Exchange Security Bank, 1st Ala. Bancshares. Mem. Ala. Bd. of Registration for Profl. Engrs. and Land Surveyors, 1967—; mem. regional adv. council Nat. Indsl. Conf. Bd., 1967—, Ala. Export Council, 1966-69. Bd. dirs. Community Chest, Jr. Achievement, Birmingham Urban League, 1968-70, Birmingham Centennial Corp., warrior-Tombigbee Devel. Assn.; gen. co-chmn. United Appeal, 1964, chmn. indsl. div., 1958; chmn. Radio Free Europe, Birmingham, 1966; mem. Jefferson County Judicial Commn., 1967—; mem. Ala. Commn. on Higher Edn., 1970-71; mem. adv. council home and hosp. Salvation Army, chmn. adv. bd., 1968-69. Trustee Foundry Ednl. Found. (pres. 1964-65); trustee, mem. exec. com. So. Research Inst.; trustee, v.p. Birmingham Symphony Assn.; bd. dirs. Carraway Meth. Hosp.; bd. visitors Berry Coll., Mt. Berry, Ga. Served to lt. col. AUS, 1941-46; ETO. Decorated Bronze Star, Legion of Merit; Croix de Guerre (France); recipient Gold Knight of Mgmt. award Nat. Mgmt. Assn., 1965, William Booth award Salvation Army, 1967; named Engr. of Year, Birmingham Engring. Council, 1967. Registered profl. engr. Ala. Fellow Am. Soc. M.E. (chmn. Birmingham sect. 1950-51); mem. N.A.M. (dir. 1967-70), Asso. Industries Ala. (dir.), Birmingham Area C. of C. (pres. 1969), Assn. Iron and Steel Engrs. (chmn. Birmingham sect. 1954, nat. dir. 1955), Am. Ordnance Assn. (pres. Birmingham post 1964), Am. Foundrymen's Soc., Am. Soc. for Engring. Edn., Engring. Soc. Birmingham, Newcomen Soc. N.Am., Sigma Alpha Epsilon, Theta Tau, Tau Beta Pi. Methodist (past chmn. bd. stewards). Kiwanian. Clubs: Birmingham Country, The Club, Mountain Brook, Downtown, Relay House, Vestavia Country (Birmingham); Indian Hills Country (Tuscaloosa, Ala.); N.Y. Athletic (N.Y.C.). Home: 3212 Brookwood Rd Birmingham AL 35223 Office: PO Box 2727 Birmingham AL 35202

DANIEL, LOIS H., librarian; b. Columbia, Tenn., May 12, 1911; d. David and Mahalah (Lloyd) Daniel; B.S., Tenn. Agrl. and Indsl. State U., 1933; B.S. in L.S., Hampton Inst., 1937; A.M., U. Chgo., 1945. Tchr. math., history Central High Sch., Alamo, Tenn., 1933-34; asst. librarian Tenn. Agrl. and Indsl. State U., 1934-36, head cataloging dept., instr. library sci., 1937-44, head librarian Martha M. Brown Meml. Library, also head library service dept., prof. library sci., 1945—. Mem. adv. com. Hadley Park bd. Nashville Pub. Library. Mem. A.L.A., Am. Assn. Sch. Librarians, Assn. Coll. Reference Librarians, Alpha Kappa Mu, Alpha Kappa Alpha (regional dir.). Club: Library of Nashville (vice chmn.). Office: Tennessee Agricultural and Industrial State U Nashville TN 37203

DANIEL, PRICE, judge; b. Dayton, Tex., Oct. 10, 1910; s. Marion Price and Nannie (Partlow) D.; A.B., Baylor U., 1931, LL.B., 1932, LL.D., 1951; m. Jean Houston Baldwin, June 28, 1940; children—Price, Jean, Houston, John. Reporter, Ft. Worth Star Telegram, 1926-27, Waco News Tribune, 1929-31; admitted to Tex. bar, 1932, and practiced law, Liberty, Tex., 1932-43; speaker Tex. Ho. of Reps., 1943; atty. gen. Tex., 1946-53; U.S. senator from Tex., 1953-56; gov. State of Tex., 1957-63; practice of law, Austin, Tex., 1963-70; asso. justice Tex. Supreme Ct., 1971—; co-pub. Liberty Vindicator and Anahuac Progress, 1939—. Chmn. So. Govs. Conf., Interstate Oil Compact Commn.; dir. Office Emergency Planning, Presdl. asst. fed.-state relations; mem. Adv. Commn. Inter-Govtl. Relations, Washington; mem. Nat. Security Council; mem. sr. emergency planning com. NATO; chmn. U.S. sect. U.S.-Mex Com. on Emergency Planning for Mut. Assistance in Case of Disaster, Washington, 1967-69. Mem. State Dem. Exec. Com., 1939-41; mem. speakers' bur. Dem. nat. campaigns, 1932, 36, 40. Trustee Baylor U., Waco, Tex., Baylor Med. Sch., Houston. Served with AUS, 1943-46; with Security Intelligence Corps, 1 yr.; PTO; disch. rank capt. Mem. Am. Soc. Internat. Law, Internat. Law Assn. Am. Bar Assn., State Bar Tex., Liberty C. of C. (pres. 1939-41), Sigma Delta Chi, Pi Kappa Delta. Mason (Shriner), Elk, Woodman, Rotarian. Author: Texas Publication Laws, 1951; Texas Election Laws, 1952. Author treaties on Tex. Ownership of Submerged Lands and The Annexation Agreement between Texas and the U.S. Editor: Lariat (daily newspaper) and Round-up (yearbook), Baylor U., 1931-32. Home: Liberty TX 77575 Office: Supreme Ct Tex Capitol Sta Austin TX 78711

DANIEL, ROBERT RAY, state ofcl.; b. Woodbury, Tenn., July 23, 1923; s. James Mitchell and Hattie (Cope) D.; B.S., Middle Tenn. State U., 1947, M.A., 1954; postgrad. Columbia, 1955; m. Lillian Nelms, Nov. 24, 1949; children—Kenny Maurice, Melody Rae. Band and choral dir. McMinnville (Tenn.) Central High Sch., 1948-50; band and choral dir., tchr. art Lakeland (Fla.) High Sch., 1951-56; music supr. McMinnville City High Sch., 1956-64; supr. instrn. music and art Tenn. Dept. Edn., Nashville, 1964—. Adviser to Tenn. Arts Commn., 1968—; mem. research com. Nat. Council of State Suprs. Music, 1964—; U.S. rep. as weaver Internat. Soc. Edn. Through Art, N.Y.C., 1969. Served with AUS, 1943-46. Mem. Nat. Council State Arts Dirs. (dir.), Music Educators Nat. Conf. Home: PO Box 492 McMinnville TN 37110 Office: Cordell Hull Bldg Nashville TN 37219

DANIEL, ROLLIN AUGUSTUS, JR., surgeon; b. Union Point, Ga., June 14, 1908; s. Rollin Augustus and Mary (Frazer) D.; B.A., Vanderbilt U., 1930, M.D., 1933; m. Ann Kelley, Jan. 15, 1939; children—Ann, Rollin Augustus III. Intern, Vanderbilt U. Hosp., Nashville, 1933-34, resident, 1934-38; asst. resident surgeon Barnes Hosp., St. Louis, 1934-35; asst. prof. surgery Vanderbilt U. Sch. Medicine, 1941-47, asso. prof. surgery, 1947-51, prof. surgery, 1951-54, prof. clin. surgery, 1954—; chief surg. service St. Thomas Hosp., 1962-66, 70—; cons. thoracic surgery VA Hosp., Nashville, 1946—. Diplomate Am. Bd. Surgery, Am. Bd. Thoracic Surgery (chmn. 1966-67, sec.-treas. 1968—). Fellow A.C.S.; mem. Middle Tenn. Heart Assn. (past pres.), Vanderbilt U. Alumni Assn. (bd. dirs.), Am. Surg. Assn., Soc. Clin. Surgery, So. Surg. Assn., Am. Assn. Thoracic Surgery, Am., So., Tenn. med. assns., Nashville Surg. Soc., Nashville Acad. Medicine. Baptist. Club: Belle Meade Country (Nashville). Home: 618 Lynwood Blvd Nashville TN 37205 Office: 2000 Hayes St Nashville TN 37203

DANIEL, WILBUR CLARENCE, U.S. congressman; b. Chatham, Va., May 12, 1914; m. Ruby McGregor. Formerly asst. to pres. Dan River Mills, Inc.; mem. Va. Ho. of Dels., 1960-68; mem. 91st-92d congresses 5th Va. Dist. Vice pres., dir. Security Bank & Trust Co., Danville, Va.; dir. Fred W. Richardson Security Storage. Mem. Va. Commn. on Constl. Govt., Govt. Com. on Employment; pres. People to People Com. Trustee Averett Coll., Danville, Va.; bd. visitors U.S. Naval Acad. Served with USNR. Decorated Star Italian Solidarity, Croix de Merit. Mem. Am. Legion (past. nat. comdr.), Va. State C. of C., Omicron Delta Kappa. Baptist. Mason, Elk, Kiwanian. Club: Danville Golf. Address: Post Office Bldg Danville VA 24541 also 357 N St SW Washington DC 20024

DANIELS, FRANK A(RTHUR), newspaper exec.; b. Raleigh, N.C., June 8, 1904; s. Josephus and Addie Worth (Bagley) D. A.B., U. N.C., 1927; m. Ruth Aunspaugh, Nov. 20, 1929; children—Frank Arthur, Patricia Woronoff. With mech., circulation and advt. depts. News and Observer, Raleigh, N.C., 1927-32, treas., 1932-56, gen. mgr., 1942-68, pres., 1956-70, chmn. bd., 1970—; pub. News & Observer, Raleigh Times; mem. Raleigh bd. N.C. Nat. Bank. Chmn. N.C. Bd. Pub. Welfare, 1948-56; mem. N.C. Tax Study Commn., 1956-57. Bd. dirs. Research Triangle Inst. Mem. Am. (treas.), So. (pres. 1951-52) newspaper pubs. assns., Delta Kappa Epsilon. Presbyn. Clubs: Carolina Country, Sphinx (Raleigh). Home: 1515 Glenwood Av Raleigh NC 27608 Office: News and Observer Raleigh Times 215 S McDowell St Raleigh NC 27601

DANIELS, G. GOINGS, clergyman. Rec. sec. Nat. Bapt. Conv. Am. Address: 1215 Church St Georgetown SC 29440*

DANIELS, JACK BOBBIE, sch. supt.; b. Hallettsville, Tex., Dec. 14, 1930; s. Ernest S. and Roxie (Moore) D.; B.S., N. Tex. State U., 1952, M.Ed., 1958; postgrad. Coll. So. Utah, fall 1969; m. Betty Endres, Jan. 3, 1955; children—Jack Bobbie, Lyndon S., Debra Ann. Tchr., prin. elementary sch. McMullen County Sch. System, 1957-61; mem. adminstrv. staff N. Tex. State U., Denton, 1962-63; asst. bus. mgr. Victoria (Tex.) Ind. Sch. Dist., 1963-66; bus. mgr. Bay City (Tex.) Ind. Sch. Dist., 1966-67; asst. adminstr. fed. programs Yoakum (Tex.) Ind. Sch. Dist., 1967-68; supt. schs. Normangee (Tex.) Ind. Sch. Dist., 1968-69, Warren (Tex.) Ind. Sch. Dist., 1969—. Cons. wage and hour law Tex. Tech. U., Lubbock, 1967, local taxation and sch. desegregation Tex. A. and M. U., 1969. Served with AUS, 1952-54. Named Hon. Senator Tex., 1967, Outstanding Educator Am., 1970. Mem. Am. Assn. Sch. Adminstrs., N.E.A., Assn. Sch. Bus. Ofcls. U.S. and Can., Tex. Tchrs. Assn., Tex. Assn. Sch. Bd. Ofcls., C. of C., Phi Delta Kappa. Presbyn. (deacon). Lion. Author: (with J.A. Anderson) Bond Issue, Techniques Used in Promoting School Bond Elections, 1966. Mem. editorial bd. Tex. Sch. Bus. Mag., 1967-68. Home: PO Box 262 Warren TX 77664 Office: PO Box 68 Warren TX 77664

DANIELS, JONATHAN (WORTH), editor, author; b. Raleigh, N.C., Apr. 26, 1902; s. Josephus and Addie Worth (Bagley) D.; A.B., U. N.C., 1921, M.A., 1922; student Columbia U. Law Sch., 1922-23; m. Elizabeth Bridgers, Sept. 5, 1923 (dec. Dec. 1929); 1 dau., Elizabeth Bridgers (Mrs. C. B. Squire); m. 2d, Lucy Billing Cathcart, Apr. 30, 1932; children—Lucy (Mrs. Thomas P. Inman), Adelaide (Mrs. B. J. Key), Cleves (Mrs. Cleves Daniels Rich). Reporter Louisville Times, then reporter Raleigh (N.C.) News and Observer, Washington corr., 1925-27, editor, 1933-42, 48-70, editor emeritus, 1970—; asst. dir., Office Civilian Def., 1942; adminstrv. asst. to Pres., 1943-45; press sec. to Pres., 1945; U.S. mem. UN sub-com. Prevention of Discrimination and Protection of Minorities, 1947-53; mem. pub. adminstrv. bd. ECA and Mut. Security Agcy., 1948-53; mem. Fed. Hosp. Council, 1949-53; editorial staff, Fortune mag., N.Y.C., 1930, 31-32; contbr. weekly page A Native at Large, to the Nation, 1941-42. Democratic nat. committeeman N.C., 1949-52. Bd. dirs. Vassar Coll., 1942-48. Guggenheim fellow, 1930-31. Mem. Delta Kappa Epsilon. Democrat. Episcopalian. Clubs: Carolina Country; National Press (Washington). Author: Clash of Angels (novel), 1930; A Southerner Discovers the South, 1938; A Southerner Discovers New England, 1940; Tar Heels: A Portrait of North Carolina, 1941; Frontier on the Potomac, 1946; The Man of Independence, 1950; The End of Innocence, 1954; The Forest is the Future, 1957; Prince of Carpetbaggars, 1958; Mosby, Gray Ghost of the Confederacy, 1959; Stonewall Jackson, 1959; Robert E. Lee, 1960; The Devil's Backbone; The Story of the Natchez Trace, 1962; They Will be Heard, 1965; The Time Between the Wars, 1966; Washington Quadrille, 1968; Ordeal of Ambition— Jefferson, Hamilton, Burr, 1970; The Randolphs of Virginia, 1972. Contbr. articles and revs. mags. Home: Box 191 Raleigh NC 27602 also Calibogue Cay Hilton Head Island SC 29928 Office: News and Observer Raleigh NC 27602

DANIELS, ROBERTSON BALFOUR, cons., editor; b. Princeton, N.J., Aug. 6, 1900; s. Winthrop More and Joan (Robertson) D.; grad. Gilman Sch., 1918; A.B. with high honors, Princeton, 1922; LL.B., Yale, 1925, Ph.D., 1934, J.D., 1971; m. Lola Burran, June 3, 1936; children— Penelope (Mrs. Daniel Pearson) David Winthrop. Admitted to N.Y. bar, 1926; practiced in N.Y.C., 1926-29; asso. Hornblower, Miller & Garrison, 1925-26, Larking, Rathbone & Perry, 1927-29; instr. English, U. Tenn., 1935, Edinburg Coll., Tex., 1935-37; asso. prof. English, Kan. State Tchrs. Coll. at Pittsburg, 1937-39; mem. faculty U. Houston, 1939-70, prof. English, 1947-70, dean Coll. Arts and Scis., 1950-58, Grad. Sch., 1958-59; writer's cons., editor, Houston, 1970—. Served with U.S. Army, 1918, USAAF, 1942-45. Mem. Modern Lang. Assn. Am., South Central Modern Lang Assn. (editor Bull. 1966-68), Mil. Order World Wars (past comdr. Tex.), Phi Delta Phi, Phi Kappa Phi. Clubs: Cosmos (Washington); Briar, MacGregor Park and Civic (past pres.) (Houston); Princeton (N.Y.C.); Nassau (Princeton, N.J.). Author: Some Seventeenth-Century Worties, 1940, 71; To the Dark Covert, 1947. Contbr. articles profl. jours. Home and office: 20 N Wynden St Houston TX 77027

DANIELS, STANLEY LEE, architect; b. Washington, Apr. 28, 1937; s. Morris Joseph and Rose (Bomel) D.; student Emory U., 1954-56; B.S., B.Arch., Ga. Inst. Tech., 1960; certificate with honors Ecoles d'Art Americaines, Fontainebleau, France, 1961. Designer, draftsman various archtl. firms, 1960-66; v.p.-treas. Jova Daniels Busby, architects, Atlanta, 1966—. Chmn. architects and engrs. div. United Appeal, 1970; pres. Uptowne Neighborhood Assn. Trustee, Architects Found. N. Ga. Recipient certificate of service A.I.A., 1964, award of Honor for design excellence A.I.A., 1966, 70. Mem. A.I.A. (v.p. 1969, chmn. com. social responsibility 1970, 71, chmn. regional conv. com. 1966, 67, 68), Atlanta Arts Assn., Constrn. Specifications Inst. Greater Atlanta Arts Council (dir. 1965—, pres Leadership Atlanta), Ga. Inst. Tech., Emory U., Fontainbleau alumni assns., Ga. Archtl. and Engring. Soc., Atlanta, Atlanta Jr. chambers commerce, Tau Epsilon Phi. Mem. B'nai B'rith. Clubs: Commerce, Atlanta Press (hon.). Home: 843 Mentelle Dr NE Atlanta GA 30308 Office: 1175 Peachtree St NE Atlanta GA 30309

DANNAHOWER, WILLIAM ROY, dentist; b. Ft. Pierce, Fla., July 10, 1927; s. Franklin Roy and Ruth Merry (Landis) D.; A.B., U. Mo., Kansas City, 1950, D.D.S., 1953; m. Lucia Ann Sevier, June 23, 1950; children— William D., James L., Steven B., Linda A. Asst. prof. diagnosis and roentgenology U. Mo., Kansas City, 1953-56; individual practice dentistry, Ft. Pierce, Fla., 1956—. Chmn., Govt. Study Commn., 1970—; mem. Fla. Bd. Dentistry, 1971—. Mem. Ft. Pierce City Commn., 1962-64, mayor, 1964-66. Served with AUS, 1945-46. Recipient Distinguished Service award Ft. Pierce Jr. C. of C., 1960, Good Govt. award, 1966; Recognition plaque USPHS, 1966; Silver Beaver award Boy Scouts Am., 1971. Mem. Fla. Dental Assn. (chmn. state fluoridation com. 1962—), Am. Dental Assn., Delta Sigma Delta. Democrat. Presbyn. Elk, Kiwanian. Home: 809 S Indian River Dr Fort Pierce FLA 33450 Office: 1205 Delaware Av Fort Pierce FL 33450

DANNE, HERBERT JOHN, mfg. co. exec.; b. Kingfisher, Okla., Mar. 11, 1926; s. John L. and Helen Irene (Thompson) D.; B.S., Okla. State U., 1950; m. Helen Marie Baird, Aug. 21, 1948; children—John G., William A., Susan M., Carol J., Karen L., James R., Lynn A. Sales engr. Standard Magnesium Corp., Tulsa, 1950-51; sales and design engr. Western Supply Co., Tulsa, 1951-58; v.p. sales and engring. Indsl. Fabricating Co. div. Bendix-Fram, Tulsa, 1958-63, exec. v.p., 1963-70; chmn. bd., pres. Thermic, Inc., 1971—. Pres., Bishop Kelly Found., 1971-72. Served with USNR, 1944-46. Mem. Am. Inst. Chem. Engrs., Tubular Exchanger Mfrs. Assn. (past pres.), Phi Kappa Theta. Republican. Roman Catholic. K.C. Clubs: University, Harvard. Mailing Address: 5823 E 57th St Tulsa OK 74135

DANNEBAUM, JOSEPH BOWMAN, cons. engr.; b. Houston, Sept. 15, 1898; s. Henry Joseph and Sadie (Bowman) D.; student Tex. A. and M. Coll., 1920; m. Janice Denny, Apr. 10, 1929; 1 son, James D. Asst. engr. Humble Oil & Refining Co., Goose Creek, Tex., 1919; party chief Humble Pipe Line Co., Houston, 1919; asst. engr. Crown Oil & Refining Co., Pasadena, Tex., 1919-20; engr. James Stewart & Co., Houston, 1920, Tellepsen Constrn. Co., 1922; constrn. engr. Am. Constrn. Co., Houston, 1923-24; owner J. B. Dannenbaum, Inc., Houston, 1924-33; city chief water works engr., Houston, 1933-35; mgr., pres. San Jacinto Constrn. Co., 1935-38; plant and prodn. engr. Water Dept., Houston, 1938-40; asst. chief engr. Helland & Drought, Camp Wallace, Tex., 1940-41; office engr. Hubbard, Knutson-Mitchell, San Jacinto Ordnance Depot, Houston, 1941; chief civil engr. Monsanto Chem. Co., Texas City, 1941, Arthur G. McKee & Co., Sheffield Steel Co., Houston, 1942; chief purchasing engr. J. F. Pritchard Co., Sweeney and Houston, 1942, USN sponsored addition to Todd-Galveston Dry Docks, Galveston, 1943; office engr. San Jacinto River Water Div., City Houston, 1943-45; pvt. practice cons. engr., Houston, 1945—; chmn. bd. Dannenbaum Engring. Corp. Registered profl. engr., Tex., La. Fellow Am. Soc. C.E.; mem. Tex. (pres. 1956), Nat. socs. profl. engrs., Am. Pub. Works Assn., Water Pollution Control Fedn., Am. Water Works Assn., Newcomen Soc., C. of C., Chi Epsilon. Episcopalian. Club: Briar. Home: 5622 Lynbrook Dr Houston TX 77027 Office: 3915 Essex Lane Houston TX 77027

DANNELLEY, RONALD JACK, real estate exec., city ofcl.; b. Hebbronville, Tex., Oct. 2, 1935; s. Jack and Geraldine (Winburn) D.; B.A., S.W. Tex. State U., 1957; student U.S. Army Survey Sch., 1958; m. Linda Crofford, Apr. 6, 1963; children—Ronald Jack, Kenneth Dale. Chief dispatcher, ct. clk. City of San Marcos (Tex.), 1954, identification officer, ct. clk., 1963; relocation officer Urban Renewal Agy., City of San Marcos, 1963-66; comml. sales rep. Balcones Real Estate Co., San Marcos, 1966—. Mem. City Council, San Marcos, 1968—; mayor-pro-tem, San Marcos, 1969—. Mem. Tex. Democratic Exec. Com., 1969. Served with AUS, 1964. Mem. Tex. Real Estate Assn., Hays County Bd. Realtors, Bldg. Ofcl. Assn. Tex., Nat. Chrysanthenum Soc., San Marcos Shrine Assn. (pres. 1965), Sigma Nu. Methodist. Mason; mem. Order Eastern Star. Kiwanian (dir.). Home: 304 Lamer Av San Marcos TX 78666 Office: City Hall San Marcos TX 78666

DANNELY, ED, state ofcl. Mem. Ala. Bd. Edn., Montgomery. Address: Dept Edn State Ala Montgomery AL 36104*

DANNENBAUM, JAMES DENNY, cons. engr.; b. Houston, July 22, 1939; s. Joseph B. and Janice (Denny) D.; B.S., U. Tex., 1962; m. Shirley Kay McKinley, Dec. 21, 1963; 1 dau., Kay Elizabeth. Pres., Dannenbaum Engring. Corp. Houston, 1962—; adv. dir. Transport Life Ins. Co.; dir. Bank Harris County N.A.; Tex. Nat. Life Ins. Co.; co-chmn. Southwestern Bank. Mem. Harris County Hist. Survey Com.; mem. Houston Adv. Com. Rapid Transit; mem. Tex. Adv. Com. Intergovtl. Relations; mem. exec. com. Houston chpt. March of Dimes, Tex. Urban Devel. Commn., The Houston Com. Trustee, Tex. Air and Water Resources Found.; exec. bd. Sam Houston area council Boy Scouts Am.; mem. exec. com. Soc. for Performing Arts, Houston; bd. dirs. Tex. Bill of Rights Found.; devel. council Houston Museum Natural Sci.; bd. dirs. Tex. Beta Student Aid Fund, Coastal Indsl. Water Authority, Arts and Scis. Found. U. Tex., Tanglewood Homes Assn. Named Outstanding Young Engr., Sam Houston chpt. Tex. Soc. Profl. Engrs., 1967; Outstanding Young Man, Jr. C. of C., Houston, 1969; One of 5 Outstanding Young Texans, Texas Jaycees, 1970. Mem. Houston C. of C., Friar Soc., Nat., Tex. (chmn. engrs. council state affairs) socs. profl. engrs., Am. Soc. C.E., Am. Indsl. Hygienists Assn., Engrs. Council Houston, Newcomen Soc., Beta Theta Pi, Tau Beta Pi, Chi Epsilon, Phi Eta Sigma. Episcopalian. Clubs: Lakeside Country, Plaza. Home: 5324 Holly Springs Houston TX 77027 Office: PO Box 22292 Houston TX 77027

DANTI, AUGUST GABRIEL, educator, pharmacist; b. New Eagle, Pa., Jan. 26, 1923; s. Tony and Lucy (Vecchioli) D.; B.S. in Pharmacy, U. Pitts., 1950, M.S., 1952; Ph.D., Ohio State U., 1955; m. Tina Clare Dipaola, July 17, 1950; 1 son, Guy Charles. Lectr., U. Pitts., 1950-52, instr. pharmacy, 1952-53; pharmacist Thrift Drugs, Pitts., Monesson, Pa., 1950-53; asst. pharmacy Ohio State U., 1953-54; pharmacist Cunningham Drugs, Detroit, 1956-59; asst. prof. pharmacy Wayne State U., 1956-59; asso. prof. pharmacy N.E. La. U., Monroe, 1959-64, prof. pharmacy, 1964—, head dept. allied health scis., 1968-71; pharmacist Walgreen Drugs, Monroe, 1964—. Pres., Ouachita Parish Heart Council, Monroe, 1963-65, v.p., 1961-63; mem. La. Adv. Council for Drug Edn., N.E. La. Alcoholism Adv. Bd., N.E. La. Health Planning Council, Ouachita Parish Mental Health Assn.; v.p. N.E. La. Alcohol and Drug Abuse Council, 1971; active Boy Scouts Am., Arthritis Found., United Givers. Bd. dirs. La. Heart Assn. Served with A.A.A., AUS, 1943-45; PTO. Decorated Bronze Star. Recipient Lederle Lab. Pharmacy Faculty award, 1962; Service Recognition awards, Kappa Psi-Gamma Mu, 1965, Am. Heart Assn., 1965, 66, 67, 69, 70; Citizenship award Ouachita Parish Med. Soc. and Monroe Jr. C. of C., 1963; Distinguished Tchrs. award N.E. La. U., 1969; A.H. Robins Bowl, Hygeia, 1970; Distinguished Alumnus award U. Pitts., 1969. Mem. Am., La. (pres. 1968-69, sec. 5th dist. La. 1961-63, pres. 5th dist. 1963-64) pharm. assns., Acad. Pharm. Sci., Ouachita Parish Mental Health Assn. La. (v.p. 1972—), Am. Assns. Coll. Pharmacy (Service Recognition awards 1965-66, vice chmn. conf. tchrs. 1966-67, chmn. 1967-68, sec. pharm. tchrs. sect. 1962-65, chmn. 1965-66, mem. exec. com. 1967-68), A.A.A.S., N. La. Soc. Hosp. Pharmacists, Am. Coll. Apothecaries, Assn. Schs. Allied Health Professions, Am. Legion (Service Recognition award 1972), La. Acad. Scis., Holy Name Soc., Sigma Xi, Rho Chi, Phi Lambda Upsilon, Kappa Psi (grand regent 1969-72), Omicron Delta Kappa. Roman Catholic. K.C., Kiwanian. Home: 2211 Ann St Monroe LA 71201

DANZEY, J. EUGENE, broadcasting exec.; b. Fla., Dec. 8, 1933; m.; 2 children. With sales dept. radio sta. WTMP, Tampa, Fla., 1963-68, sales mgr., 1968-70, gen. sta. mgr., 1970—. Mem. St. Petersburg's Ad Club (dir.). Address: Radio Sta WTMP 8508 Grapefruit Av Tampa FL 33619*

DA PONTE, JOHN JOSEPH, JR., govt. ofcl.; b. Briston, R.I., May 12, 1933; s. John J. and Mary Elizabeth (Ferris) DaP.; A.B., Providence Coll., 1955; J.D., Boston U., 1962; LL.M., Georgetown U., 1966; m. Gunilla K. Tornhagen, Apr. 18, 1971. Admitted to Mass. bar, 1962, D.C. bar, 1964; atty.-adviser Office Gen. Counsel, U.S. Treasury Dept., Washington, 1962-67; atty-adviser, exec. sec. Bur. Internal Commerce and Fgn. Trade Zones Bd., Dept. Commerce, 1968—. Served to 1st lt. AUS, 1955-59. Recipient Am. Jurisprudence prize for paper on internat. law problems, 1966. Mem. Mass., Fed. bar assns., Am. Soc. Internat. Law. Editorial bd. Boston U. Law Rev., 1960-62. Home: 5334 42 Pl NW Washington DC 20015 Office: Dept Commerce 14th and Constitution Av NW Washington DC 20230

DAPPRICH, JOHN WILLIAM, interior designer; b. Dearborn, Mich., Mar. 6, 1937; s. Elton and Ellen (Ketchum) D.; student Easter U., 1956-57; diploma Kendall Sch. Design, 1962. Interior designer Burdines Dept. Stores, Miami, Fla., 1963-64, Jordan Marsh Dept. Store, Miami, 1964-66; interior designer Waldo Perez Interiors, Coconut Grove, Fla., 1967-68; owner Dapprich Interiors, Coconut Grove, 1968-70; dir. interior design Deltona Corp., Miami, 1970—. Served with AUS, 1957-59. Mem. Am. Inst. Designers. Interior designer pent-house Joe Garagiola, Marco Island, 1970, also interior designer for Jack Paar, Key Biscayne, 1972, Henry Kissinger, Key Biscayne, 1972, Gene Sarazen, Marco Island, 1972. Home: 3927 Douglas Rd Coconut Grove FL 33133 Office: 3250 SW 3d Av Miami FL 33133

DARBY, LLOYD HUBERT, III, dentist; b. Metter, Ga., June 18, 1937; s. Lloyd Hubert, Jr. and Carolyn Adamson (Hale) D.; student Medill Sch. Journalism, Northwestern U., 1956-57; B.A., Emory U., 1959, D.D.S., 1964; postgrad. U. Ga., 1959-60; m. Loretta Wilkes, Aug. 16, 1958; children—Carolyn Leslie, Jennifer Wilkes, Pamela Elaine. Individual practice dentistry, Vidalia, Ga., 1966—. Chmn., Toombs County Republican party, 1969—; vice chmn. 1st Congl. Dist. Ga. Rep. Com., 1970—. Served to lt., Dental Corps USNR, 1964-66. Recipient Am. Coll. Dentists Essay award, Emory U., 1964, Block Drug Co. Essay award Emory U. Mem. Am., Ga. dental assns., Central Dist. Dental Soc., Acad. Gen. Dentistry, Phi Delta Theta, Psi Omega. Home: 202 W 9th St Vidalia GA 30474 Office: 308 Jackson St Vidalia GA 30474

DARBY, MICHAEL RUCKER, furnace mfg. co. exec.; b. Dallas, Nov. 24, 1945; s. Joseph Jasper, Jr. and Frances Adah (Rucker) D.; A.B., Dartmouth, 1967; M.A., U. Chgo., 1968, Ph.D., 1970; m. Emily Ann Loutrel, June 19, 1965; 1 dau., Margaret Loutrel. Vice pres., economist Paragon Industries, Inc., Dallas, 1961—, dir., 1964—; asst. prof. econs. Ohio State U., 1970—. Woodrow Wilson fellow, 1967-68, NSF Grad. fellow, 1967-69, Fed. Deposit Ins. Corp. Grad. fellow, 1969-70. Mem. Am. Econ. Assn., Econometric Soc., Am. Statis. Assn., Phi Beta Kappa, Omicron Delta Epsilon. Episcopalian. Club: Hyannis Port Yacht (Hyannis Port, Mass.). Contbr. articles to profl. jours. Home: 3937 Purdue St Dallas TX 75225 also 6166 Northgate Rd Columbus OH 43229 Office: PO Box 10133 Dallas TX 75207 also 1775 S College Rd Columbus OH 43210

DARBY, WILLIAM THOMAS, lawyer; b. nr. Vidalia, Ga., May 12, 1914; s. Lloyd H. and Embelle (Dickens) D.; student Mercer U., 1930-31; grad. Brewton-Parker Jr. Coll., 1932; LL.B., Atlanta Law Sch., 1935; grad. So. Bus. U., 1935; m. Gladys Wood, Dec. 8, 1940; children—William T., Robert Wood. Admitted to Ga. bar, 1935; city atty. Vidalia, 1947-48, county atty., 1951-52; solicitor county, 1953-57; county judge, 1961—; county juvenile judge, Vidalia, 1963-70; dir., sec., gen. counsel Rosebud Mfg. Co. div. Athlone Industries, Vidalia; pres., gen. counsel Aimwell Enterprises, Inc.; dir., gen. counsel Darby Banking Co., Inc., Darco, Inc., Piggly Wiggly So., Inc., Shuman Saveway; div. counsel Belle Interiors, Inc. Gen. counsel Vidalia Devel. Authority. Active Boy Scouts. Served with USNR, 1944-45. Mem. Am. Judiciary Soc., Am. Trial Lawyers Assn., Am., Ga. bar assns., State Bar of Ga., Vidalia C. of C. Rotarian (pres. club), Mason (Shriner), Lions. Elk. Home: 1007 Center Dr Vidalia GA 30474 Office: PO Box 648 Vidalia GA 30474

DARDEN, FRED HUBERT, JR., sch. supt.; b. Pensacola, Fla., Nov. 16, 1929; s. Fred Hubert and Mertie (Bowman) D.; B.S. in Zoology, North Ga. Coll., 1950; M.Ed., U. Va., 1959; postgrad. Ga. State U., 1970; m. Elizabeth Pearce, Sept. 2, 1951; children—Fred, Nancy, David. Tchr. Blakely (Ga.) High Sch., 1953-54; prin. Cuthbert (Ga.) Elementary Sch., 1956-57; tchr. Randolph County High Sch., Cuthbert, 1957-60, prin., 1960-68; supt. schs. Randolph County, Cuthbert, 1968—. Sec. treas. Randolph County Bd. Health, 1968—. Served with inf., AUS, 1951-53; Korea. Methodist (chmn. adminstrv. bd.). Rotarian. Home: 323 Highland Av Cuthbert GA 31740 Office: Courthouse Cuthbert GA 31740

DARDEN, NORMAN DELMAS, cotton mcht.; b. Goodwater, Ala., May 31, 1911; s. John Austin and Vashti Olise (Sellers) D.; student Howard Coll., 1928-29; m. Ila Maurine Maddux, June 6, 1936; children—Norman, Winston Alan. With W.E. Walker & Co., cotton mchts., Albertville, Ala., 1929-52; founder, owner, now partner Darden Cotton Co., Albertville, 1952—; pres. Claybrooke Warehouse Co., Albertville, 1960—. First pres. Albertville United Givers Fund, 1960; mem. adv. bd. Snead Jr. Coll., Boaz, Ala., 1968—; dir. Marshall County Gas Dist., 1968—, pres., 1971—. Mayor, Albertville, 1968—. Bd. dirs. Mountain Valley Council on Arts. Served with AUS, World War II. Named Man of Year Albertville C. of C., 1968. Mem. Atlantic Cotton Assn. (past dir.), Am. Cotton Shippers Assn., Ala. League of Municipalities (dir. 1969, 70, mem. exec. bd. 1972). Baptist (mem. state exec. bd. 1967—). Lion (pres. 1949-50, dist. gov. 1959-60). Club: Albertville Country. Home: 105 E Alabama Av Albertville AL 35950 Office: 105 McDonald Av Albertville AL 35950

DARDEN, WILLIAM ALLEN, civil engr., govt. ofcl.; b. Nashville, Mar. 29, 1910; s. William Allen and Kathryn Belle (Edwards) D.; student Vanderbilt U., 1930-31; B.S., Ga. Inst. Tech., 1935; grad. Army Command and Staff Coll., 1952; M.S., George Washington U., 1970; m. Mary Elizabeth Ransom, Jan. 7, 1939; children—Kathryn, Michael, Cynthia, Richard. Civil engr. C.E., Nashville, 1935-42; commd. lt. U.S. Army, 1942, advanced through ranks to col., 1959, ret., 1965; area engr., Nashville, Atlanta, Wright Field engring. dists., 1942-43; engr. brigade staff officer, New Guinea, Philippines, Okinawa, 1944-45; asst. corps engr., Korea, 1946; post engr., squadron comdr., March Field, 1947-48; mil. adviser, air engr. Mil. Mission to Greece, 1948-51; asst. dist. engr., Tullahoma, 1952-55; attache Am. embassy, New Delhi, 1956-59; bn. comdr., Ft. Dix, N.J., 1959-60; mem. staff Dept. Army, Washington, 1960-62; comdr. Army sect. Joint Mil. Mission to India, 1962-63; chief operations inspections Dept. Army Insp. Gen., 1963-65; spl. asst. to U.S. Army Dist. Engr., Nashville, 1966-71, exec. asst., 1971—. Dist. chmn. camping and activities Coffee Dist. council Boy Scouts Am., 1953-55, chmn. pack com., 1964-65. Decorated Legion of Merit, Bronze Star with oak leaf cluster; Royal Order of George I (Greece); Philippine Liberation medal. Registered profl. engr., Tenn. Fellow Am. Soc. C.E.; mem. Nat., Tenn. socs. profl. engrs., Soc. Am. Mil. Engrs. (post pres. 1954), Engrs. Assn. Nashville (bd. dirs. 1970-72), Soc. Am. Value Engrs., Middle Tenn. Fed. Exec. Assn., Internat. Assn. Nav. Congresses, Am. Mgmt. Assn., Assn. U.S. Army, Phi Kappa Sigma. Republican. Episcopalian. Club: Brentwood Country, Propeller (Nashville). Home: 1300 Old Hickory Blvd Brentwood TN 37027 Office: Federal Office Bldg Nashville TN 37203

DARITY, MARTIN JOSEPH, govt. ofcl.; b. nr. Macon, Ga., July 25, 1928; s. Freeman A. and Irma (Nobles) D.; student U. Ga., 1952-54, LaSalle U., 1954-56; m. Elizabeth Ann Green, Nov. 27, 1947; 1 dau., Katie Elizabeth. Sales rep. Campbell Soup Co., Columbus, Ga., 1947-57; sales mgr. R.C. Cola Co., Columbus, 1958-59; account exec. Radio Sta. WRBL, Columbus, 1959-61; mgr. Radio Sta. WULA, Eufaula, Ala., 1961-64; dir. promotions WRBL-TV, Columbus, 1964-67; dir. Bur. Pub. and Information, State of Ala., Montgomery, 1967-70; state-city coordinator U.S. Travel Service, U.S. Dept. Commerce, Washington, 1970—. Mem. Gov.'s Cabinet, 1967-70, Gov.'s Council on Youth Opportunity, 1969—; commr. Ala. Ednl. TV Commn. Bd. dirs. Ala. Hist. Commn., 1968; v.p., treas. Lurleen Wallace Courage Crusade, 1968; treas. So. Travel Dirs. Council, 1969; sec. ex-officio Ala. Sesquicentennial Commn., 1969. Mem. Montgomery Advt. Club (dir. 1968—). Home: 3342 Vaughn Rd Montgomery AL 36106 US Commerce Bldg US Dept of Commerce Washington DC 20006

DARK, DELPHOS JOSIAH, govt. ofcl.; b. nr. Silver City, N.C., June 12, 1912; s. Josiah Samuel and Mary Emma (Burns) D.; student Campbell Coll., 1930-32; B.S., Wake Forest U., 1934; m. Louise Holt Cole, June 15, 1946. Tchr. pub. schs., Franklin County, N.C., 1934-42; prin. Epson High Sch., Henderson, N.C., 1942-45; with N.C. Bd. Edn., Raleigh, 1945—, transp. asst., 1952-67, dir. div. transp., 1967—. Mem. N.C. Pupil Transp. Assn., N.C. Assn. Educators, Am. Assn. Sch. Adminstrs., Nat. Assn. Dirs. Pupil Transp. Services, Nat. Pupil Transp. Conf. (exec. com., 1970-73), Southeastern States Pupil Transp Conf. (pres. 1971-72). Democrat. Methodist (mem. adminstrv. bd.). Mason. Home: 2412 Oxford Rd Raleigh NC 27608 Office: Div Transportation State Dept Education Raleigh NC 27602

DARLAND, DWIGHT DAVID, edn. assn. exec.; b. Coleridge, Neb., Aug. 11, 1917; s. Floyd Lambert and Hazel Maude (Roland) D.; B.S., Neb. State Tchrs. Coll., 1939; M.A., U. Wyo., 1942; Ed.D., Columbia, 1947; m. Elinore M. Fritz, Dec. 28, 1940; children—David Floyd and Dallas Leland (twins). Tchr. sci., prin. high sch., Newcastle, Wyo., 1939-42; supt. schs. Teton County, Jackson, Wyo., 1942-45; instr. psychology Newark State Tchrs. Coll., 1945; tchr. sci. Birch-Wathen Sch., N.Y.C., 1946-47; asst. dir. community services U. Wyo., Laramie, 1947-48; dean students, prof. edn., chmn. grad. com. Pacific U., Forest Grove, Ore., 1948-53; ednl. cons. Am. Osteo Assn., Chgo., 1953-56; dir. profl. services Ore. Edn. Assn., Portland, 1956-59; asso. exec. sec. div. instructional and profl. devel. (formerly Nat. Commn. on Tchr. Edn. and Profl. Standards), N.E.A., Washington, 1959—, editor Jour. Tchr. Edn., 1962—. Professorial lectr. tchr. edn. George Washington U., 1959—; program specialist Ford Found., Colombia, Venezuela, 1963-64; cons. on tchr. edn. AID Mission to East Africa, 1966; cons. to bd. trustees State Colls. Md., 1966-68; coordinator Antioch-Putney Grad. Sch. Edn., Washington, 1967-68. Mem. governing bd. Futures for Children, Washington. Mem. N.E.A. (life), Am. Assn. Sch. Adminstrs., Am. Assn. U. Profs., Higher Edn. Assn. Washington, Wilderness Soc., Assn. for Student Teaching, Assn. for Supervision and Curriculum Devel., Phi Delta Kappa, Lambda Delta Lambda, Kappa Delta Pi. Club: City (Portland). Contbr. articles to profl. publs., also chpts. to books. Home: 341 O St SW Washington DC 20024 Office: 1201 16th St NW Washington DC 20036

DARLING, JOSEPH WARREN, army officer, govt. ofcl.; b. Chestnut Hill, Phila., May 5, 1908; s. Joseph Robinson and Charlotte (Kelsey) D.; student U. Madrid, Spain, 1926; S.B., Harvard, 1931; M.B.A., U. Pa., 1934; student Temple Law Sch., Phila., 1935-37, student George Washington U., 1941-43, LL.B., 1954, LL.M., 1959; m. Helene Manley, May 29, 1943; children—Mary Beal, Albert Beal, Venie Helene McNab. Bank examiner Commonwealth Pa., 1935-37; financial coordinator Socony Vacuum Oil Co., Hamburg, The Hague, N.Y.C., Caracas, Venezuela, 1937-42; served as officer U.S. Army, 1942—, now col. Ordance Corps and Res.; administrv. exec. officer Office Chief Ordnance, Washington, 1942-44; with econs. div. Office Mil. Govt., Eng., France, Germany, also acting chief control and inspection sect. Western zones Germany, 1944-48, dep. chief, acting chief econs. br., Berlin, assisting in policy and procedures Berlin airlift, policy advisor concerning Berlin Trade Assn., C. of C., industry and handycraft, 1948-50; U.S. land observer Dept. State, providing information to H.I.C.O.G. on devels. Land Nordrhein-Westfalen, Brit. Zone, Germany, rep. U.S. in zone, assisting Brit. by advice, cons. reports to obtain uniformity in adminstrn. Germany, responsible to U.S. High Commr., 1950-51; chief European br. Fgn. div. NPA, Washington, 1951-55; cons. Office Sec. Def. for Internat. Security Affairs, 1955-56; dep. dir. investment devel. div. Bur. Fgn. Commerce, Dept. Commerce, 1956-57; fgn. investment adviser Econ. and Financial Mission to Govt. Chile, Santiago, 1957-58; with investment div. Small Bus. Adminstrn., 1959-62; dir. Office Fgn. Econ. Affairs, Office Sec. Def., Washington, 1962—; pres., chmn. D & D Ventures Corp., Washington; pres., dir. Chestnut Hill Investment Corp., Phila.; dir. Darling Investment Corp.; financial adviser A. W. Kelsey and C. C. Washburn estates. Mem. Washington Bd. Trade. Chmn. disaster com. Wissahickon area E. Pa. chpt. A.R.C.; mem. zoning com. Springfield Twp. Civic Assn. Bd. dirs. Thomas A. Roberts Sch., Montgomery County (Pa.) Citizens Council; trustee Israel Washburn Home, Livermore Falls, Me. Mem. Am., Fed., Inter-Am. (mem. mil. justice com.) bar assns., Bar Assn. D.C. (com. relationships with internat. bar assns., del.), Washington Soc. Investment Analysts, C. of C., Res. Officers Assn. (past pres. chpt.), Soc. Internat. Devel. (com. law devel.), Washington Fgn. Law Soc. (dir.), Greater Phila. and South Jersey Council, Phila. Assn. Profl. Consultants, S.A.R. Episcopalian (treas. 1965—). Mason. Clubs: Chevy Chase (Md.); Harvard, Cricket, Penn (Phila.); Harvard (Boston); American (London); Sporting Club de France (Paris); Am. Yacht, American (Berlin); University, Harvard, International, University, National Lawyers, National Sojourners (Washington). Home: 423 New Jersey Av SE Washington DC 20003 Office: Office Sec of Def Pentagon Washington DC 20025

DARRACOTT, HALVOR THOMAS, govt. ofcl.; b. Wichita Falls, Tex., Aug. 21, 1910; s. Charles William and Allie Mae (Moore) D.; B.S. in Math., Drury Coll., 1933; M.S. in Physics, U. Ark., 1939; m. Margaret Jane Mitchell, May 24, 1940; children—Hattiejane, William Michael, James Patrick. Instr. physics, math. Fayetteville (Ark.) High Sch., 1939-41; instr. math. U. Va. adult classes, Washington, 1951-54; exec. engr. Adler Electronics, New Rochelle, N.Y., 1962-63; prin. tech. forecaster Hdqrs., U.S. Army Materiel Command, Washington, 1964—, also chief Technol. Forecasting div. Advanced Materiel Concepts Agy., Washington; lectr. tech. forecasting seminar, Harvard, 1967. Dir. Welfare Council, Atlantic City, 1959-62. Served from 2d lt. to col. Signal Corps, AUS, 1941-62. Fellow Washington Acad. Scis.; mem I.E.E.E. (sr.), Am. Phys. Soc., Am. Math. Soc., A.A.A.S., Armed Forces Communications Electronics Assn., Soc. Information Display, World Future Soc., Assn. U.S. Army, Ret. Officers Assn., Lambda Chi Alpha, Sigma Pi Sigma. Mason (32 deg., Shriner), Kiwanian. Home: 3325 Mansfield Rd Falls Church VA 22041 Office: US Army AMXAM-TF Army Materiel Command Washington DC 20315

DARRAH, WILLIAM LEE, lawyer, oil co. exec.; b. Cody, Wyo., Feb. 8, 1911; s. Hudson W. and Kathleen (Talmadge) D.; A.B., U. Neb., 1931, LL.B., 1933, J.D., 1969; m. Inga Margit Sundheim, Oct. 24, 1943; children—Gary Spencer, Richard William. Admitted to Neb. bar, 1933, Tex. bar, 1934; asso. firm Madden, Adkins, Pipkin & Keffer, 1935-39; atty. Amarillo Oil Co. (Tex.), 1939—, v.p., 1949—. Mem. exec. bd. Llano Estacado council Fais dist. chmn. Boy Scouts Am., 1966-67; bd. dirs. Potter County (Tex.) chpt. A.R.C., 1949-50. Mem. State Bar Tex., Am., Amarillo (sec.-treas. 1936) bar assns., Fed. Power Bar Assn., Ind. Natural Gas Assn., Toastmasters, Chi Phi, Phi Delta Phi. Presbyn. Mason, Kiwanian (past dir.). Home: 1115 La Paloma St Amarillo TX 79106 Office: PO Box 151 Amarillo TX 79105

DARROUGH, PAUL G., lawyer; b. Oklahoma City, 1892; student Epworth U.; A.B., U. Okla., 1913, LL.B., 1915. Admitted to Okla. bar, 1914; referee bankruptcy, Oklahoma City, 1930-61; mem. firm Darrough & Darrough, Oklahoma City. Mem. Oklahoma County, Okla., Am. bar assns., Mineral Lawyers Group, Oklahoma City Title Lawyers Group, Order Coif, Phi Beta Kappa, Phi Delta Phi. Address: Darrough & Darrough 100 Park Av Bldg Oklahoma City OK 73102*

DARROW, SUSAN HORNSTEIN, ednl. adminstr.; b. Orlando, Fla., Dec. 25, 1941; d. Louis Albert and Mildred (Bruce) Hornstein; A.B., Wheaton Coll., 1963; postgrad. Fla. State U., 1963; M.S. in Edn., No. Ill. U., 1967. Tchr. English, Apopka, Fla., 1964; with WMFE-TV, Orlando, 1965; residence hall dir. Wheaton (Ill.) Coll., 1965-67, asst. dean students, 1967-68; asso. dean students Gordon Coll., Wenham, Mass., 1968-71; counselor Valencia Community Coll., Orlando, Fla., 1971—. Mem. Nat. Assn. Student Personnel Adminstrs., Nat. Assn. Women Deans and Counselors, Am. Personnel and Guidance Assn., Christian Women Deans. Home: 2858 N Pine Hills Rd Orlando FL 32808 Office: Box 3028 Orlando FL 32808

DARSEY, JOSEPH FREDERICK, clothing mfg. exec.; b. Amsterdam, Ga., Apr. 11, 1926; s. Charles H. and Mettie (Connell) D.; B.Indsl. Engring., Ga. Inst. Tech., 1949; m. Parkerlyn Florence, Dec. 27, 1952; children—Laurie, Joseph, Steven, Jonathan. Mgmt. trainee Stockham Valves & Fittings Co., Birmingham, Ala., 1948-49; engr. Jaco Pants, Inc., Ashburn, Ga., 1950, plant mgr., 1951-53; v.p., gen. mgr. Anniston (Ala.) Sportswear Corp., 1954-59; founder, pres., gen. mgr. Darsey Mfg. Co., Tallapoosa, Ga., 1960—; pres. Darsey Clothing Co., Inc., East Point, Ga. Dir. W. Ga. Bank of Tallapoosa. Mem. exec. bd. Atlanta area council Boy Scouts Am. Mem. adv. bd. Shorter Coll., Rome, Ga. Named Man of Yr., City of Tallapoosa, 1969. Served with AUS, 1944-46. Mem. Am. Inst. Mgmt., Am. Apparel Mfrs. Assn., Ga. Inst. Tech. Alumni Assn. (trustee), Tau Beta Pi, Alpha Tau Omega. Presbyn. (elder). Home: Box 187 Tallapoosa GA 30176 Office: Darsey Mfg Co Box 187 Stoffel Dr Tallapoosa GA 30176

DARSIE, RICHARD FLOYD, JR., govt. ofcl.; b. Scottdale, Pa., Jan. 28, 1915; s. Richard Floyd and Helen (Colvin) D.; B.A., Bethany Coll., 1937; M.S., U. Pitts., 1941; Ph.D., Cornell U., 1949; m. Lucinda Alton Sherrick, Apr. 6, 1948; children—Janet (Mrs. George L. Gattoni), Richard Floyd III. Instr. biology Franklin and Marshall Coll., Lancaster, Pa., 1949-50; asso. prof. entomology U. Del., 1950-62; malaria specialist AID, State Dept., Kathmandu, Nepal, 1962-67; instr. entomology USPHS, Malaria Eradication Tng., Philippines, 1967-71; chief vectorborne disease tng. unit Center Disease Control, Atlanta, 1971—. Served with USAAF, 1941-45. Mem. Entomol. Soc. Am., Entomol. Soc. Washington, Am. Mosquito Control Assn., Am. Soc. Tropical Medicine and Hygiene, Philippine Soc. Entomologists, Indian Soc. Malaria and other Communicable Diseases, Sigma Xi, Sigma Nu. Author: Manual of Malaria Entomology, 1969. Home: 2648 Hawthorne Dr NE Atlanta GA 30345 Office: Center Disease Control Atlanta GA 30333

DART, STEPHEN PLAUCHE, lawyer; b. New Orleans, Sept. 21, 1924; s. Benjamin Wall and Clarabel (Cromwell) D.; B.B.A., Tulane U., 1946; B.S. in Elec. Engring., La. State U., 1951, LL.B., 1951, J.D., 1970; m. Elisabeth Ann Kilbourne, Feb. 3, 1951; children—James K., Ann Holcombe. Admitted to La. bar, 1951; practice law, New Orleans, 1952-53, St. Francisville, La., 1951-52, 1953—; sr. v.p. Bank of Commerce & Trust Co., St. Francisville, La., also dir., 1964—. Mem. adv. com. La. Law Inst. Com. of Continuous Revision of Code Civil Procedures, 1962—; lectr. trust estates, 1962-63. Mem. Democratic State Central Com., 1958—; chmn. West Feliciana Parish Dem. Exec. Com., 1968—. Served as lt. (j.g.) USNR, 1941-46. Mem. Am., La. bar assns., Am. Judicature Soc., Delta Kappa Epsilon, Phi Delta Phi. Clubs: Boston, New Orleans City; Baton Rouge. Address: Box 489 St Francisville LA 70775

DARTER, OSCAR HADDON, educator; b. Church Hill, Tenn., Sept. 9, 1891; s. Henderson and Betty M. (Derrick) D.; A.B., Okla. State Tchrs. Coll., 1922; student U. Okla., 1917; A. M., Columbia U., 1926; Ed.D., George Washington U., 1948; m. Lela Mae Deere, Dec. 29, 1920. Prin. pub. schs., Okla., 1915-25; supt. schs., Johnston County, Okla., 1920-22; instr. State Tchrs. Coll., Ada, Okla., summers 1922-25, prof. social sci., chmn. dept., 1926-44; prof. history, chmn. dept. Mary Washington Coll., U. Va., 1944—; tchr. E. Carolina State Coll., Greenville, summers, 1950, 52. Mem. So. Conf. for Human Welfare Nat. Council on Social Studies, Nat. Com. on Atomic Information, Danforth Found. Fellow, Com. on Interracial Relations, George Peabody Coll., 1934, Carnegie Inst. on Internat. Law, U. of Mich.,1935, European seminar in modern hist., Columbia, summer 1932. Mem. Va. Social Sci. Assn., Am. Acad. Polit. and Social Sci., Am. Assn. U. Profs., Pi Gamma Mu, Phi Delta Kappa. Mason, Rotarian. Author: Colonial Fredericksburg and Neighborhood in Perspective; The History of the Fredericksburg Baptist Church; The Darter-Tarter Family History. Co-author: The History of Marlborough, Va. Home: 1313 Sunken Rd Fredericksburg VA 22401 Office: Mary Washington Coll of U Va Charlottesville VA 22904

DARTER, VERNON WEBSTER, univ. adminstr.; b. Hiltons, Va., Feb. 6, 1904; s. Ernest D. and Margaret Pearl (Howard) D.; A.B., King Coll., 1926; B.S., U. Tenn., 1930; M.P.A., Harvard, 1952, D.P.A., 1955; m. Ida Sue Taylor, Oct. 6, 1930. Prin., Sullivan County (Tenn.) Elementary Sch., 1926-27; tchr. Church Hill High Sch., Hawkins County, Tenn., 1927-28; dir. milk sanitation Bur. Health, Knoxville, Tenn., 1930-35; asst. county agt. U. Tenn., Johnson County, 1935-42, county agt., 1942-43; dep. dir. food and agr. Office Mil. Govt., Bavaria, 1946-49; chief agrl. prodn. and distbn. br. Office High Commr., Frankfort, Germany, 1949-51; Eastern rep. Fund for Adult Edn., 1953-54; prof., leader extension tng. and studies Coll. Agr., U. Tenn., Knoxville, 1954-57, dir. Agrl. Extension Service, 1957-68, dean, 1968—. Bd. dirs. Tenn. chpt. Am. Cancer Soc. Served to capt. AUS, 1943-46. Named Man of Yr. in Service to Tenn. Agr., Progressive Farmer mag., 1971. Mem. Am. Agrl. Econs. Assn., Assn. Land-Grant Colls. and State Univs., Phi Kappa Phi, Alpha Zeta, Gamma Sigma Delta. Presbyn. (elder). Kiwanian. Home: 2300 Lakemoor Dr Knoxville TN 37920 Office: Agrl Extension Service PO Box 1071 Knoxville TN 37901

D'ASSARO, CHARLES PHILIP, hosp. adminstr.; b. Bklyn., May 4, 1929; s. Vincent and Rose (Travagliante) D' A.; B.S., N.Y. U., 1956; m. Bella DiLeone, June 5, 1954; children—Vincent M., Charles A., Lisa R. Staff accountant Phagan, Tillison, & Tremble, N.Y.C., 1953-54; sr. staff accountant J. Edward MacDermott & Co., N.Y.C., 1954-65; asst. adminstr. Daytona Beach Gen. Hosp., Holly Hill, Fla., 1965-67; asst. adminstr., treas. Ormond Beach (Fla.) Osteo. Hosp., 1967—. Mem. audit com. United Fund of East Volusia County, 1966-68; treas. Cub Scout Pack, Daytona Beach, 1968, Dr. John S. Hull Meml. Fund, Ormond Beach, 1969. C.P.A., N.Y., Fla. Mem. Nat. Assn. Accountants (chpt. treas. 1968, 69), Am. Coll. Osteo. Hosp. Adminstrs., Hosp. Financial Mgmt. Assn., Am. Inst. C.P.A.'s, N.Y. State Soc. C.P.A.'s, Fla. Inst. C.P.A.'s. Home: 3020 Stanford Av Daytona Beach FL 32018 Office: 264 S Atlantic Av Ormond Beach FL 32074

DASTUGUE, FERNAND JOSEPH, JR., physician; b. New Orleans, Apr. 26, 1922; s. Fernand Joseph and Frances Eliza (Brownson) D.; B.S., Tulane U., 1941, M.D., 1944; m. Shirley Louise Labbe, Dec. 10, 1955; children—Patrice L., Suzanne M., Michele C. Intern Chairty Hosp., New Orleans, 1944-45; asst. dept. anatomy Tulane U., 1946-47; resident internal medicine Charity Hosp., 1947-50; staff physician VA Center, Biloxi, Miss., 1950-60, Ochsner Clinic, New Orleans, 1960—; sec. staff Ochsner Found. Hosp., 1966-69. Served to comdr., USNR, 1945-46, 52-54. Diplomate Am. Bd. Internal Medicine. Mem. A.C.P. (asso.), A.M.A., So. Med. Assn., Orleans Parish Med. Soc., New Orleans Acad. Internal Medicine, Cath. Physicians Guild, Pub. Affairs Research Council La., Phi Beta Kappa, Omicron Delta Kappa, Alpha Omega Alpha. Democrat. Roman Catholic. Clubs: Timberlane Country, Empire, New Orleans Opera (New Orleans). Home: 35 Colony Rd Gretna LA 70053 Office: 1514 Jefferson Hwy New Orleans LA 70121

DATH, ROBERT J., govt. ofcl. Dist. dir. U.S. Internal Revenue Service, Louisville. Address: Internal Revenue Dist Office Post Office Bldg Louisville KY 40202

DATTA, PADMA RAG, chemist; b. Jorhat, Assam, India, Feb. 27, 1927; s. Parasu Ram and Budhi Prava (Das) D.; M.S., U. Mass., 1950; Ph.D., W.Va., U., 1956; m. Lois-ellin Greene, Dec. 21, 1951; children—Tane Mohan, Eric Raman. Came to U.S., 1948, naturalized, 1959. Research fellow FELS Research Inst., Temple Med. Sch., Phila., 1956-57; sr. research fellow Agr. Research Service, U.S. Dept. Agr., Phila., 1957-60; research chemist Rohm & Haas Co., Bristol, Pa., 1960-63, FDA, Washington, 1963-71; chemist Environmental Protection Agy., Washington, 1971—. Research cons. dept. biochemistry George Washington U. Sch. Medicine, Washington, 1965—. Fellow Am. Inst. Chemists; mem. Fedn. Am. Socs. for Exptl. Biology and Medicine, A.A.A.S., Am. Chem. Soc., Coblentz Soc., N.Y. Acad. Scis., World Future Soc., Internat. Soc. Tech. Assessment, Internat. Platform Assn., Sigma Xi. Contbr. articles to profl. jours. Home: 8514 Whittier Blvd Bethesda MD 20034 Office: 401 M St SW Washington DC 20460

DAUBENSPECK, WAYNE MARTEL, clergyman; b. Selinsgrove, Pa., Nov. 25, 1904; s. Lloyd Mosheim and Della Almeda (Burns) D.; A.B., Susquehanna U., 1927; grad. Susquehanna Theol. Sem., 1930; m. Ethel Mason, July 15, 1931; children—Richard Edward, Ruth Elizabeth (Mrs. G. Kieth Kistler), Henry Mason. Ordained to ministry Luth. Ch., 1930; minister ch., Oshkosh, Neb., 1930-35; chaplain Neb. Dist. CCC, 1936-38, U.S. Penal System (Northeastern and Ft. Leavenworth), 1938-40; Luth. service pastor Japan and Korea, 1954-63; pastor St. David's Ch., Kannapolis, N.C. 1964-70; ret., 1970. Served as chaplain AUS, 1940-54, commd. 1st. lt., 1935; col. Res. ret. Decorated Bronze Star medal. Mem. V.F.W. (chaplain N.C. dept.). Mason (32 deg.). Home: 208 W 22d St Kannapolis NC 28081

DAUGHERTY, FREDERICK ALVIN, judge; b. Oklahoma City, Aug. 18, 1914; s. Charles L. and Felicia A. (Mitchell) D.; LL.B., Cumberland U., 1934; postgrad. Oklahoma City U., 1934-35, U. Okla., 1936-37; m. Marjorie E. Green, Mar. 15, 1947 (dec. Feb. 1964); m. 2d, Betsy F. Amis, Dec. 15, 1965. Admitted to Okla. bar, 1937; practiced in Oklahoma City, 1937-40; mem. firm Ames, Ames & Daugherty, Oklahoma City, 1946-50, Ames, Daugherty, Bynum & Black, Oklahoma City, 1952-55; judge dist. ct. 7th Jud. Dist. Okla., 1955-61; U.S. dist. judge Western, Eastern, No. dists. Okla., Oklahoma City, 1961—. Mem. profl. adv. com. Okla. County Assn. Mental Health, 1964-70; mem. exec. com. Oklahoma City Council on Alcholism, 1964—, Okla. Med. Research Found., 1966-69. Nat. bd. govs. A.R.C., 1963-69, 3d vice chmn., 1968-69, nat. fund vice chmn. Okla., 1956-58; trustee United Fund Greater Oklahoma City, v.p., 1960, pres., 1961; bd. dirs. Community Council Oklahoma City and County, pres., 1967-69. Served with AUS, 1940-45; PTO; 1951-52; Korea; served to maj. gen Okla. N.G., 1934-64. Decorated Legion of Merit with two oak leaf clusters, Bronze Star with oak leaf cluster, UN Distinguished Service medal; recipient Okla. Distinguished Service medal, recipient award to mankind Oklahoma City Sertoma Club, 1962, Outstanding Citizen award Oklahoma City Jr. C. of C., 1965; named to Okla. Hall of Fame, 1969. Mem. Okla., Am., Fed. bar assns., Am. Bar Found., Oklahoma City C. of C. (dir. 1960-61, 66-70, 72—), N.G. Assn. U.S. (Distinguished Service medal 1965), 45th Inf. Div. Assn., Amvets, Am. Legion, Assn. U.S. Army (Okla. pres. 1962-65, dir. 1964-70), Okla. N.G. Assn. (pres. 1947), V.F.W., Mil. Order World Wars (chpt. comdr. 1968-69), Sigma Alpha Epsilon, Phi Delta Phi. Episcopalian. Kiwanian (pres. Oklahoma City 1957), Mason (32 deg., Shriner, Jester). Club: Oklahoma City Men's Dinner (exec. com. 1963-65, pres. 1966-69). Home: 1800 Coventry Lane Oklahoma City OK 73120 Office: US Courthouse Oklahoma City OK 73102

DAUGHERTY, HARRY HAMPTON, bldg. material co. exec.; b. Jacksonville, Fla., Aug. 28, 1934; s. Harry Lyle and Frances (Parker) D.; B.S., U. Fla., 1959; m. Marjorie Dorsey, Sept. 1, 1956; children—Patricia, Vicki, Sandra, Harry. Sales rep. U.S. Gypsum Co., Gainesville, Fla., 1959-63; pres. State Plastering Co., Gainesville, 1963—, State Contractor Spltys., Gainesville, 1964—; dir. Comml. Bank, Gainesville, also dir. various real estate and devel. corps. Served with USNR, 1953-55. Recipient Grantland Rice award U. Fla. Coll. Advt., 1958, Home Builders award Gainesville Home Builders Assn., 1969. Mem. C. of C., Internat. Assn. Wall and Ceiling Contractors, Home Builders Assn., Sigma Nu. Methodist. Lion. Club: Quarterback (Gainesville). Home: 4611 N W 17th Pl Gainesville FL 32601 Office: 3038 N Waldo Rd Gainesville FL 32601

DAUGHERTY, MARSHALL HARRISON, educator; b. Macon, Ga., Sept. 6, 1915; s. Harrison and Susie (Hopkins) D.; student Mercer U., 1932-33, Yale U. Sch. Fine Arts, 1933-37, Cranbrook Acad. Art, 1937-38; m. Gertrude Baker, Sept. 6, 1940; children—Carla Sue (Mrs. Davis McAuley), Deryl Ann (Mrs. L. Keitt Dantzler). Instr. sculpture Wesleyan Sch. Fine Arts, Macon, Ga., 1940-45; chmn. art dept. Mercer U., Macon, 1945—; exhibited portrait and garden sculpture N.Y., New Haven, Houston, Atlanta, Detroit; represented in pvt. collections and instns. Pres. Ocmulgee Monument Aux. Corp., Macon, 1961-64. Carnegie grantee, 1946, 47; Yaddo fellow Yaddo Corp., Saratoga Springs, N.Y., 1939. Mem. Assn. Ga. Artists (pres. 1944), Macon Art Assn. (pres. 1948), So. Assn. Sculptors (v.p. 1964-67). Originator cineform. Important works include John Wesley Monument, Savannah, Ga. Home: 1831 Upper River Rd Macon GA 31201

DAUSSMAN, GROVER FREDERICK, elec. engr.; b. Newburgh, Ind., May 6, 1919; s. Grover Cleveland and Madeline (Springer) D.; student U. Cin., 1936-38, Carnegie Inst. Tech., 1944-45; George Washington U., 1948-56; B.S. in Elec. Engring., U. Ala., 1963; postgraduate study University Ala., 1963-64, Indsl. College Armed Forces, 1955, 63; m. Ella Margaret Kilian, Dec. 27, 1941;

children—Cynthia Louise (Mrs. Kenneth E. Quinn), Judith Ann, Margaret Elizabeth. Coop. engr. Sunbeam Elec. Mfg. Co., Evansville, Ind., 1936-38; engr. draftsman Phila. Navy Yard, 1941-42; elec. engring. supr. shipbldg. USN, Neville Island, Pa., 1942-45; engr. Pearl Harbor Navy Yard, 1945-48; with Bur. Ships, USN, Washington, 1948-56; with Guidance and Control Tech. Liaison, Army Ballistic Missile Agy., Huntsville, Ala., 1956-58, chief program coordination Guidance and Control Lab., 1958-60; chief program coordination Astrionics Lab., Marshall Space Flight Center, Huntsville, 1960-62, staff asst. for advanced research and tech. Astrionics Lab., 1962-70; engring. cons., 1970-71; project dir. fallout shelter surveys Mil. Dept. Tenn., 1971—. Recipient certificate Hon. Service, USN, 1945; Performance Award certificate U.S. Army, 1960. Registered profl. engr., Ala., Va., D.C. Mem. U. Ala. Alumni Assn., Ala. (Engr. of Yr. award 1968, pres. chpt. 1966-67, state dir. 1962-65, 68-71), Nat. socs. profl. engrs., I.E.E.E. (sr. mem., sect. chmn. N.Ala. sect. 1961-62, engring. mgmt. chpt. chmn. 1964-65, mem. adminstrv. com. engring. mgmt. group 1966—, sec. group 1969-71, Engr. of Yr. award 1969, research com. 1965-67, dir. S.E. region, mem. nat. bd. dirs. 1972-73), A.A.A.S., Am. Ordnance Assn. (chpt. dir. Tenn. Valley), Am. Inst. Aeros. and Astronautics, Am. Soc. Naval Engrs., Missile, Space and Range Pioneers, U.S. Naval Inst., Assn. U.S. Army, Internat. Platform Assn., Huntsville Assn. Tech. Socs. (sec. 1969-71, v.p., dir.). Democrat. Mem. United Ch. of Christ (sec. ch. council 1965-66, vice moderator Ala-Tenn. Assn. 1965-68, bd. dirs. S.E. conv. 1965-66). Home: 1910 Colice Rd SE Huntsville AL 35801 also Apt E10 420 Elysian Fields Rd Nashville TN 37211 Office: Mil Dept Tenn Div Civil Def Emergency Operations Center Sideo Dr Nashville TN 37204

DAVALOS, EDUARDO, Ecuadorian diplomat; b. Quito, Ecuador, Sept. 11, 1914; s. Ignacio and Maria (Pareja) D.; ed. U. Quinto, U. Rome (Italy); m. Fanny Liscano, May 14, 1949; children—Eduardo, Liliana. With diplomatic corps, Ecuador, 1945—, now consul gen. from Ecuador to U.S., New Orleans. Recipient decorations from Colombia, Chile, Ecuador. Office: Office of Ecuadorian Consul Gen Internat Trade Mart New Orleans LA 70130

DAVENPORT, FOUNTAIN ST. CLAIR, electronic engr.; b. Harmony, N.C., Jan. 16, 1914; s. Dennis F. and Margaret E. (Winfield) D.; B.S., U. Miami, 1950; postgrad. U. Miami, U. Balt., Johns Hopkins, U. Fla., Rollins Coll., Brevard Engring. Coll., 1952-64; M.S., Fla. Inst. Tech., 1970; m. Jane Helena Hermann, June 11, 1948; 1 dau., Sylvia Jane. Engr., Bendix Aviation Corp., Towson, Md., 1951-53; project engr. Vitro Labs., Eglin AFB, Fla., 1953-55; engr. A, RCA Missile Test Project, Patrick AFB, Fla., 1955-60; spur. radar engring., guided missiles range div., Pan Am. World Airways, Inc., Patrick AFB, Fla. 1960-65, sr. systems engr. Aerospace Services Div., 1965—. Cons. N.R.C, Churchill Research Range, Man., Can., 1966-67; faculty Fla. Inst. Tech., 1958-60, 62-63, mem. edn. com., 64. Served with USN, 1934-37; with USNR, 1942-45. Life mem. Friends Melbourne Library; patron Indian River Players. Mem. Fla. Engring. Soc. (sr.), Nat. Soc. Profl. Engrs., A.A.A.S. Mason (32 deg.). Home: 2110 Shannon Av Indialantic FL 32901 Office: Mail Unit 706 Pan Am World Airways Inc Patrick AFB FL 32925

DAVENPORT, GUY MATTISON, JR., educator, author; b. Anderson, S.C., Nov. 23, 1927; s. Guy Mattison and Marie (Fant) D.; B.A., Duke, 1948; B.Litt. (Rhodes scholar), Oxford U., 1950; Ph.D., Harvard, 1960. Instr., Washington U., 1952-54; asst. prof. Haverford Coll., 1960-63; prof. English, U. Ky., Lexington, 1963—; contbr. Nat. Rev., 1960—. Served with airborne corps, AUS, 1950-52. Recipient Anne Flexner award, 1948; Blumenthal-Leviston prize, 1967. Author: The Intelligence of Louis Agassiz, 1963; Carmina Archilochi, 1964; Sappho; Poems and Fragments, 1965; Flowers and Leaves, 1965; Ezra's Bowmen of Shu, 1965; Cydonia Florentia, 1965; The Iliad: A Handbook, 1966; The Odyssey: A Handbook, 1966. Home: 621 Sayre Av Lexington KY 40508

DAVENPORT, WILLIAM HAROLD, mathematician; b. Jackson, Tenn., Dec. 21, 1935; s. John Heron and Mary (Troutt) D.; B.S. in Engring. Physics, U. Tenn., 1962; M.S. in Math, Tex. A. & M. U., 1966; Ph.D. in Math., U. Ala., 1971; m. Mary Janice Johnson, Mar. 18, 1960; children—Mark Edson, Amber Yvette. Aerospace tech. NASA Manned Spacecraft Center, Houston, 1962-64; research mathematician Brown Engring. Co., Huntsville, Ala., 1966-67; teaching fellow, instr. math. U. Ala., 1967-71; mathematician U.S. Army Missile Command, Huntsville, 1971—. Served with USN, 1954-58. Mem. Am. Math. Soc., Sigma Pi Sigma, Phi Kappa Phi, Pi Mu Epsilon. Home: 3120 Teton Circle Huntsville AL 35810 Office: AMSMI-REO Bldg 5400 US Army Missile Command Redstone Arsenal AL 35809

DAVID, EDWARD EMIL, JR., Presdl. adviser; b. Wilmington, N.C., Jan. 25, 1925; s. Edward Emil and Beatrice (Liebman) D.; B.E.E., Ga. Inst. Tech., 1945; S.M., Mass. Inst. Tech., 1947, Sc.D., 1950; m. Ann Hirshberg, Dec. 23, 1950; 1 dau., Nancy. With Bell Telephone Labs., Murray Hill, N.J., 1950-70, supr. acoustics research, 1954-56, head dept. visual and acoustics research, 1956-58, asst. dir., 1958, dir., 1958-62, dir. computing and information research center, 1963-65, exec. dir. research Communications Systems div., 1965-70, sci. adviser to Pres. Nixon, 1970—, also dir. Office Sci. and Tech., Washington; prof. elec. engring. Stevens Inst. Tech., Hoboken, N.J., 1966—. Mem. Postmaster Gen.'s Adv. Council, 1966-68; mem. nat. adv. com. on edn. deaf Dept. Health, Edn. and Welfare, 1966-69; cons. Dept. Def., 1964-70, Office Sci. and Tech., 1968-70; mem. vis. coms. Carnegie-Mellon U., 1965-70, Mass. Inst. Tech., 1965-68, U. Rochester, 1966-70, Princeton, 1967-70, Ga. Inst. Tech., 1970. Bd. dirs., v.p. Summit (N.J.) Speech Sch., 1967-70. Served to lt. (j.g.) USNR, 1943-46. Named Outstanding Young Engr. of Year, Eta Kappa Nu, 1954; recipient George W. McCarty award Ga. Inst. Tech., 1958; named Outstanding Young Man of Year, Summit Jr. C. of C., 1959. Fellow I.E.E.E. (ednl. activities bd. 1968-69, nominations and appointments com. 1968-69, dir. 1967-69), Accoustical Soc. Am., Audio Engring. Soc., Am. Acad. Arts and Scis.; mem. Nat. Acad. Engring. (council 1970—). Author: (with J. R. Pierce) Man's World of Sound, 1958; (with J.R. Pierce and W.A. Van Bergeijk) Waves and the Ear, 1960. Editor: (with J.G. Truxal) The Man-Made World, 1971. Contbr. numerous articles to profl. jours. Patentee in field. Office: The White House Washington DC 20500

DAVID, HENRY, educator, labor specialist; b. N.Y.C., Dec. 5, 1907; s. George and Esther (Silver) D.; B.A., Coll. City of N.Y., 1929; M.A., Columbia, 1930, Ph.D., 1936; m. Byrna Ball, Nov. 20, 1959; 1 son (by previous marraige), Paul Allan. Instr. hist. dept. Coll. City N.Y., 1930-38; lectr. New Sch. for Social Research, 1936-37; prof. hist. dept. Queens Coll., 1938-54; prof. grad. sch. bus. Columbia U., 1954-59; dean grad. faculty polit. and social sci. New Sch. for Social Research, prof. history, dean. grad. faculty, 1959-61, pres. sch., 1961-63; dir. research B.B.C., 1942-45, adviser on Am. affairs, 1945-47; cons. Rand Corp., 1948-55, 63—; exec. dir. Nat. Manpower Council, 1951-61, mem., 1961—; head office sci. resources planning NSF, 1964-66; exec. sec. div. behavioral scis. Nat. Acad. Scis.-NRC, 1966—; cons. editor labor Random House, Benjamin Franklin fellow Royal Soc. of Arts; mem. Am. Hist. Assn., Soc. Am. Historians, Indsl. Relations Research Assn., Acad. Polit. Sci., Phi Beta Kappa. Author: History of the Haymarket Affair, 1936, 58; (with others) History of Western Civilization, 1935; Labor Problems in America, 1940; House of Labor, 1951; America in Crisis, 1952; 11 publs. Nat. Manpower Council 1952—; Common Frontiers of the Social Sciences, 1957; Public Education in America, 1958; Manpower Policies for a Democratic Society, 1965; articles and reviews to periodicals. Co-editor: The Economic History of the United States Series, 1945—. Contbg. editor Labor and Nation, 1946-52. Home: 2206 Wyoming Av NW Washington DC 20008 Office: 2101 Constitution Av NW Washington DC 20418

DAVID, LILY MARY, economist; b. Chgo., June 22, 1914; d. Emile F. and Lily (Kramer) David; Ph.B., U. Chgo., 1935. Economist, U.S. Dept. Labor, 1939—, chief wage and indsl. relations devels., Bur. Labor Statistics, 1949-59, chief br. current wage and development Wage Trends and Spl. Research, 1959-62, chief div. wage economics, 1962-69, chief div. wage and labor standards Office Policy Devel., Office Asst. Sec. for Policy, Evaluation and Research, 1969-71; mem. econ. research com. Muskie for Pres. campaign, 1971-72. Chmn. U.S. delegation Tripartite Tech. Meeting on Hotels, Restaurants and Similar Establishments, 1965. Grey Lady, A.R.C., 1950-54, nurses aide, 1956—. Recipient Rockefeller Pub. Service award, 1959. Mem. Indsl. Relations Research Assn., Phi Beta Kappa. Author articles in field. Home: 4647 3d St S Arlington VA 22204

DAVID, NEYLON CALVIN, JR., physician; b. Searcy, Ark., Aug. 10, 1923; s. Neylon Columbus and Lottie May (Fawcett) D.; B.S., U. Ark., 1948, M.S., 1950, M.D., 1953; m. Gloria Josephine Dusek, Aug. 7, 1950; children—Gloria Vida, Cassandra Sue. Rotating intern Ark. Bapt. Hosp., 1953; surg. resident Little Rock VA Hosp., 1957-58; gen. practice medicine, Beebe, Ark., 1954-57, Brinkley, Ark., 1958—; mem. staff Mercy Hosp., Brinkley, chief staff, 1962, 66, 70. Commr., Ark. Dept. Aeros., 1969-71. Served with AUS, 1944-46. Mem. A.M.A., Am. Geriatric Soc., Am., Ark. acads. gen. practice, Mid South, Ark., Monroe County (pres. 1962, 66, 70) med. socs., Flying Physicians Assn., So. Med. Assn., Am. Legion, V.F.W. Baptist. Mason, Elk. Club: Brinkley Country. Home: W Hwy 70 Brinkley AR 72021 Office: 108 W Ash St Brinkley AR 72021

DAVIDOW, HOWARD BRUCE, aerospace co. exec.; b. Lakeland, Fla., Mar. 16, 1933; s. Samuel and Rose (Lefkowitz) D.; B.A., U. Miami, 1959; m. Vasaliki Jacqueline Voyantzis, July 5, 1959; Gen. sales mgr. E. Farnell & Co., Inc., West Palm Beach, Fla., 1958-62; pres., dir. H. M. Melard Corp., Miami, 1959—; pres. Maru Avionics, Inc., 1963-67; exec. v.p. Aero Sytems, Inc., Miami, 1967-72, also dir.; pres., dir. Aero Systems Avionic Sales Div. subsidiary, Miami, 1967—; sec., dir. Microtenna Corp., Miami, 1969. Mem. Living Inst. for Edn., Miami. Served to 1st lt. SAC, USAF, 1954-57. Home: 6705 SW 117th St Miami FL 33156 Office: 5700 NW 36th St Miami FL 33148

DAVIDSON, MRS. CHARLES (KATE S. DAVIDSON), educator; b. Emporia, Va., May 13, 1910; d. John William and Ida Florence (Hill) Saunders; student Chowan Coll., 1926-27; A.A., Louisburg Coll., 1927-28; summer student Forest Coll., 1928, 29. Longwood Coll., 1932; m. Charles Reuber Davidson, July 1, 1933; 1 dau., Katharine Saunders (Mrs. John Byers Horner). Tchr. Emporia High Sch., 1930-33, 1946-50, substitute tchr., 1950—. Gen. chmn., dir. Greenville Tb Assn.; 2d v.p. Southside area council Girl Scouts U.S.A.; dir. Southside Area Planning Bd., A.R.C.; sec. Emporia Band Boosters Club; mem. state nursing scholarship com. Tb and Respiratory Disease Assn.; pres. Greenville Meml. Hosp. Aux.; rep. dir. Va. Tb Assn.; bd. dirs. Commonwealth council (Va.) Girl Scouts, Richmond council Girl Scouts, Southside Tb and Health Assn.; rec. sec. pub. affairs Ch. Hosp. Aux. Mem. P.T.A. (asst. dist. dir. Southside area, dir. Emporia, Va.), U.D.C. (ures local chpt.; registar), Va. Hist. Soc., Butts Tavern Assn. (dir., trustee), Woman's Soc. Christian Service (promotion sec. corr.; edn. ch. pres., Dora Armstrong zone leader, pres., memb. bd. Petersburg dist.). Methodist (supt. CradleRoll, mem. bd. edn., mem. ch. adminstrv. bd., dir.). Clubs: Emporia Ladies Golf Assn. (pres.), Riparian Federated Woman's (v.p.), Woman's (past pres., parliamentarian, edn. chmn., mental health chmn.), Emporia Federated Garden, Wednesday. Home: 506 Ingleside Av Emporia VA 23847

DAVIDSON, GORDON BYRON, lawyer; b. Louisville, June 24, 1926; s. Paul Byron and Elizabeth (Franz) D.; A.B., Centre Coll., 1949; J.D., U. Louisville, 1951; LL.M., Yale, 1952; m. Geraldine B. Geiger, Dec. 21, 1948; children—Sally Burgess, Stuart Gordon. Asst. Army staff judge advocate of First Army, Govs. Island, N.Y., 1952-54; law clk. Mr. Justice Stanley Reed, Supreme Ct. of U.S., Washington, 1954; partner Wyatt. Grafton and Sloss, 1954—; lectr. U. Louisville Law Sch., 1958—. Pres. Louisville Central Area, Inc., 1971-72; mem. Louisville Commn. Fgn. Relations. Bd. dirs. Norton-Children's Hosps., Inc., Louisville Fund for Arts; trustee St. Francis Sch., Centre Coll., Louisville Theatrical Assn. Served as cadet midshipman U.S. Mcht. Marine Acad., 1944-45; 1st lt. AUS, 1952-54; Korea. Mem. Am., Ky., Louisville, Fed. bar assns., Phi Delta Theta, Omicron Delta Kappa, Phi Kappa Phi. Democrat. Presbyn. Clubs: Harmony Landing Country; Jefferson (bd. govs.), Louisville Country (bd. govs.); Tavern; Young Lawyer's; Pendennis. Home: 435 Lightfoot Rd Louisville KY 40207 Office: Marion E Taylor Bldg Louisville KY 40202

DAVIDSON, HERBERT MARC, newspaper editor; b. N.Y.C., Nov. 8, 1895; s. Julius and Rose (Scharles) D.; B.Litt., Columbia, 1918; m. Liliane Refregier, June 14, 1919; 1 son. Tippen. Reporter, Kansas City Star, 1917, Portland (Ore.) Jour., 1919, Fourth Estate, 1920, Los Angeles Examiner, 1920-21, Paris bur. Internat. News Service, 1922; rewrite, editorial writer, feature editor Chgo. Daily News, 1922-28; editor Daytona Beach (Fla.) News-Jour., 1928-62; editor, pub., 1962—; v.p. News-Journal Corp., 1928-62, pres., 1962—. Past dir. A.R.C.; pres; Daytona Beach Community Chest, 1953-54. Trustee Bethune-Cookman Coll. Mem. Fla. Pubs. Assn. (past pres.). Am. Soc. Newspaper Editors, So. Regional Council, Sigma Delta Chi. Unitarian (past pres.). Rotarian (past pres.). Home: 2 Braddock Av Daytona Beach FL 32018 Office: News-Journal Daytona Beach FL 32015

DAVIDSON, JOHN KENNETH, educator; b. Augusta, Ga., Oct. 25, 1939; s. Larcie Charles and Betty (Corley) D.; student Augusta Coll., 1956-58; B.S. Ed., U. Ga., 1961; M.A., 1963; postgrad. U. Fla., 1971—; m. Josephine Frazier, Apr. 11, 1964; children—John Kenneth, Stephen Wood. Asst. prof. dept. psychology and sociology Armstrong State Coll., Savannah, 1963-67; asst. prof. dept. sociology Augusta Coll., Augusta, Ga., 1967—; research cons. dept. obstetrics and gynecology Med. Coll. Ga., Augusta, 1969—, pediatrics, 1972—, also asso. dir. health care project, 1971—, research instr., summer 1971, research asso., summer 1972. Program coordinator Community Devel. in Process Phase II and III, Title I Higher Edn. Act of 1965, 1970; chmn. curriculum sub-com. sociology and anthropology Univ. System Ga., 1970-72; mem. Nat., Ga., Southeastern councils on family relations. Bd. dirs. Augusta Area Planned Parenthood Assn. Mem. Ga. Acad. Sci., Am. Sociol. Assn., So., Ga. sociol socs., Am. Assn. U. Profs., Augusta Coll. Alumni Soc., Law and Soc. Assn., U. Ga. Alumni Soc., Ga. Sociol. and Anthropol. Assn. (sec.-tres. 1969-71), Kappa Delta Pi, Phi Kappa Phi, Phi Theta Kappa, Alpha Kappa Delta (pres. Beta chpt. 1971-72). Episcopalian. Home: 1908 Valley Spring Rd Augusta GA 30904

DAVIDSON, NELLE CATHERINE, librarian; b. Greenville, S.C., July 7, 1908; d. Thomas Noah and Mary (Pickel) Davidson; B.S., State Tchrs. Coll., Johnson City, Tenn., 1932; B.L.S., George Peabody Coll., 1937; M.A., U. Denver (Colo.), 1958. Librarian, Washington Coll. (Tenn.) High Sch., 1933-37, Sr. High Sch., Johnson City, 1937-38, Carson-Newman Coll., 1938-44; librarian New Orleans Bapt. Theol. Sem., 1944—, now head librarian; instr. library sci. Kan. State Tchrs. Coll., summer 1941; cataloger Tulane U., summer 1946. Mem. hist. commn. So. Bapt. Conv. Mem. E. Tenn. Edn. Assn. (chmn. registration 1961), Southwestern Library Assn., A.L.A., La. Library Assn. (nominations com. 1972-73), Spl. Libraries Assn. (sec.-treas. La. chpt. 1958-59), Am. Theol. Library Assn. Baptist. Clubs: Greater New Orleans Library (pres. 1971-72), Altrusa. Home: 4075 DeMent St New Orleans LA 70126 Office: 4110 Seminary Pl New Orleans LA 70126

DAVIDSON, VANDA ARTHUR, physician, educator; b. Dubach, La., Oct. 9, 1918; s. Vanda Arthur and Flossie (Rainwater) D.; B.S., La. Poly. Inst., 1938; M.D., Tulane U., 1942; m. Earline Givens, Sept. 12, 1945; children—Vanda Lewis, Darrell Dale, Elizabeth Dianne. Intern, Charity Hosp., New Orleans, 1942-43, resident obstetrics, gynecology, 1946-49; instr. obstetrics and gynecology Tulane U., 1945-46; pvt. practice medicine specializing in obstetrics, gynecology, Dallas, 1949—; mem. staffs Baylor Med. Center, Brookhaven Gen., Bristol Gen., Presbyn., Parkland Meml. hosps. (all Dallas); clin. instr. Southwestern Med. Sch. Tex., 1950-51, asst. clin. prof., 1951—. Dir. Ling Temco Vought, 1958-70, mem. exec. com., 1951-70, mem., chmn. compensation com., 1956-70; dir. United Tech. Labs., Dallas, Electro Data Inc., Dallas. Bd. dirs. Tulane Med. Center, New Orleans. Served from 1st lt. to maj. AUS, 1943-46. Decorated Bronze Star medal, Legion of Merit. Fellow A.C.S., Internat. Coll. Surgeons, Am. Coll. Obstetrics, Gynecology; mem. A.M.A., Tex., Dallas County med. socs., Central Assn. Obstetrics and Gynecology, Tex., Dallas, Ft. Worth, Conrad and Collins (pres. 1958), N.M. (hon.) obstetrics and gynecology socs. Club: Dallas Gun, Chapparell and Lancers (Dallas). Home: 5615 Yolando Circle Dallas TX 75229 Office: 712 N Washington St Dallas TX 75246

DAVIE, JONES REEVES, agriculturist; b. Hickman, Ky., Apr. 24, 1918; s. Jones Roper and Erlinda (Saunders) D.; B.S., U. Ky., 1942, M.S., 1967; m. Susan Word, June 17, 1943; children—Faye, Alfred Reeves, Gene Roper. County agrl. agt., Carlisle County, Ky., 1946-56; county agrl. agt. Christian County, Ky., 1956—. Served with USMCR, 1942-46. Mem. Ky. Assn. County Agrl. Agts. (pres. 1967, sec. 1962, 63, 65), Am. Agrl. Econs. Assn., So. Agrl. Econs. Assn. Mem. Disciples of Christ Ch. (elder 1961—). Home: Rt 4 Hopkinsville KY 42240 Office: PO Box 522 Hopkinsville KY 42240

DAVIES, DON, govt. ofcl.; b. Mpls., Dec. 28, 1926; s. Clifford Goetz and Gladys (Herr) D.; A.B., Stanford, 1948, M.A., 1949; Ed.D., Columbia, 1956; m. Mary Joyce Liscom, Dec. 27, 1949; children—Druanne, Donna Joanne. Tchr., Beverly Hills (Cal.) High Sch., 1949-53; instr. Adelphi Coll., Garden City, N.Y., 1953-56; asst. prof., San Francisco State Coll., 1956-57; asso. prof. U. Minn., Mpls., 1957-61; exec. sec. Nat. Commn. on Tchr. Edn. Profl. Standards, 1961-68; asso. commr. U.S. Office Edn., Dept. Health, Edn. and Welfare, Washington, 1968-71, dep. commr. for devel., 1971—. Bd. dirs. John F. Kennedy Center, Peabody Coll., Nashville. Served with USNR, 1945-46. Recipient Superior superior Service award Dept. Health, Edn. and Welfare, 1970. Mem. Phi Delta Dappa, Kappa Delta Pi, Sigma Delta Pi, Alpha Delta Phi. Democrat. Contbr. numerous articles to profl. jours. chpts. to books. Home: 9904 Brixton Lane Bethesda MD 20034 Office: Dept Health Edn Welfare 400 Maryland St SW Washington DC 20202

DAVIES, EVERETT FREDERICK SAMUEL, educator; b. Freetown, Sierra Leone, July 21, 1902; s. Frederick Isaac and Elizabeth (Bright) D.; B.A., Talladega Coll., 1927, B.D., 1928; M.A., Yale U., 1930; Ed.D., Columbia U., 1946; m. Marguerite Marion Buckner, Dec. 17, 1931. Asso. prof. edn. and psychology Bishop Coll., 1932-35; asso. prof. philosophy and sociology, dir. religious activities Va. State Coll., 1936-44, prof. philosophy, 1946—. Mem. exec. com. Richmond-Petersberg Council on Human Relations, 1961-65; mem. Ettrick (Va.) Town Council, 1950—; v.p. Va. Council on Human Relations, 1962-64. Rockefeller Found. fellow, 1946. Mem. Va. Philos. Assn. (sec. 1963, v.p. 1964, pres. 1965) Am. Assn. U. Profs., Am. Philos. Assn., Inst. Religion, Philosophy of Edn. Soc., D.C. Philosophy Club, Alpha Phi Alpha. Home: 20607 3d Av Ettrick VA 23803 Office: Dept Philosophy Va State Coll Petersburg VA 23803

DAVIES, ROBERT STOCKWELL, mfg. co. exec.; b. Syracuse, N.Y., Apr. 25, 1925; s. Harry William and Ruth (Heath) D.; student Dartmouth, 1943-45; B.Arch., Syracuse U., 1951; m. Janice Hudson, Feb. 20, 1954; children—Gail Brewer, Robert Stockwell, James Hudson. Project architect Carl W. Clark, Syracuse, 1954-59; adminstr. Lockwood Green Engrs., Inc., Spartanburg, S.C., 1962-65; asst. to pres. Blackman Uhler Industries, Spartanburg, 1965-68; sec.-treas., Synalloy Corp. (formerly Blackman Uhler Industries), Spartanburg, 1968-69, v.p. adminstrn., sec., 1970—, dir., 1971—; dir. Whiting Engring. Co., Camden, S.C., Multifab, Inc., Spartanburg, Balco Realty Co., Spartanburg, Delmar Equipment Co., Spartanburg. Mem. Spartanburg Safety Council, 1968-69. Served to lt. USNR, 1943-46, 51-53. Mem. Spartanburg Council Architects, Gargoyle Soc., Phi Delta Theta. Republican. Presbyn. Home: Quailhurst Route 2 Campobello SC 29322 Office: PO Box 5627 Spartanburg SC 29301

DAVILA, CARLOS V., justice; b. Bayamon, P.R., May 2, 1914; s. Sebastian and Luisa Davila; B.A., B.L.L., U. P.R., 1938; m. Adaljisa Velez, Nov. 28, 1958; children—Maria, Adalijisa, Carlos Sebastian. Asso. justice Supreme Ct. of P.R. Address: Supreme Ct San Juan PR

DAVIS, ALBERT ROY, scientist; b. Halifax, N.S., Can., June 18, 1915; s. William Albert and Annie Agnes (Robinson) D.; grad. U. Fla., 1936. Came to U.S., 1922, naturalized, 1936. Owner, mgr. Roy Davis Research Lab., Green Cove Springs, Fla., 1938—; writer tech. papers on radiol. fallout AEC, 1945-46. Asso. prof. biomagnetic scis. Naihati (West Bengal, India) Research Center, 1964-68; cons. on bd. asso. Hon. Degree Scis., 1965—. Bd. dirs. Albert Roy Davis Aerial Phenomena Research Assn., Green Cove Springs, United Sci. Fedn., Green Cove Springs. Served under contract Air Transport Command, USAAF, Port Security div. USCG, 1942-43. Recipient acknowledgement for work introducing biomagnetic scis. to doctors and scientists in India, Prime Minister India, 1971; acknowledgment indsl. mfg. firms of Japan for work to serve humanity through sci. of bio-magnetics, 1971. Author: Biomagnetic Effects on Living Systems, 1965; Cancer and Biomagnetics; The Anatomy of Biomagnetics: Sex, Life and Ageing; Natures Library of Magnetism and Its Effects on Biological Systems; Cancer and Biomagnetic Arrest; also numerous gen. sci. courses for grade sch., high sch. and colls. Developer methods of milk products stimulation by, and control of, milk products through application of magnetic fields and energies, 1965; methods to control nitrogen in water, in ecology studies, by biomagnetic molecular magnetic stimulations, 1969. Address: 520 Magnolia Av Green Cove Springs FL 32043

DAVIS, ANDREY B., govt. ofcl. Med. historian research dept. Smithsonian Instn., Washington. Address: Smithsonian Instn Washington DC 20560*

DAVIS, ARCHIBALD KIMBROUGH, banker; b. Winston-Salem, N.C.; Jan. 22, 1911; s. Thomas W. and Frances (Conrad) D.; A.B. U. N.C., 1932; student Grad. Sch. Banking Rutgers U., 1940; m. Mary L. Haywood, May 12, 1938; children—Archibald Hilliard, Louise, Haywood, Thomas W., III. With Wachovia Bank & Trust Co., 1932—, sr. v.p. charge Winston-Salem, office, 1946—, chmn., 1956—; dir. Charlotte br. Fed. Res. Bank of Richmond, 1959-61; dir. Am. Tel. & Tel. Co., Chatham Mfg. Co., Jordan Spinning Co., Sellers Mfg. Co., Sellers Dyeing Co., So. Ry., Royal Cotton Mills, So. Ry. Co., Media Gen., Inc. Founder, 1st pres. Northwest N.C. Indsl. Devel. Assn.; mem. Nat. Commn. Productivity. Pres. Research Triangle Found., 1959—. Chmn. bd. trustees N.C. Found. Ch.-Related Colls. Mem. U.S. C. of C. (v.p. 1958-61, chmn. bd., pres., dir. 1971-72), Soc. of Cincinnati, Am. Bankers Assn. (pres. state bank div. 1956-57, nat. pres. 1965-66), Joint Council Econ. Edn., Com. Econ. Devel. (trustee), Newcomen Soc., Phi Beta Kappa. Rotarian (pres. 1958-59). Home: 2828 Forest Dr Winston-Salem NC 27104 Office: Wachovia Bank & Trust Co Winston-Salem NC 27102

DAVIS, BEN ARTHUR, JR., assn. exec.; b. Meridian, Miss., Oct. 27, 1930; s. Ben Arthur and Sarah (Combs) D.; student Meridian Jr. Coll., 1948-49, Miss. State U., 1949-50; B.S. in Forestry, Auburn U., 1955; m. Georgia Ann Coleman, Aug. 20, 1954; children—Anne Miller, Ben Arthur III. Fire prevention specialist Miss. Forestry Commn., 1955; asst. exec. sec. Miss. Forestry Assn., Jackson, 1956-57, exec. sec., 1957-58, exec. v.p., 1958—. Served with USAF, 1951-52. Mem. Pub. Relations Assn. Miss. (pres. 1961), Am., Miss. (pres. 1961) socs. assn. execs., Nat. Council Forestry Assn. Execs. (pres. 1964-65), Miss. Hwy. Users Conf. (dir.), Am. Forestry Assn. Home: 5420 Charter Oak Pl Jackson MS 39211 Office: Standard Life Bldg Jackson MS 39201

DAVIS, BEN REEVES, newspaper editor; b. Huntington, Ark., Apr. 1, 1927; s. Lester Belton and Jessie (Reeves) D.; B.A. in Journalism, U. Ala., 1949; m. Margaret Lee Rogers, Nov. 26, 1950; 1 son, Ben Reeves. Reporter, Selma (Ala.) Times-Jour., 1949-50; mng. editor Jasper (Ala.) Mountain Eagle, 1950-52; sports writer, copy editor Birmingham (Ala.) News, 1952-56; mng. editor Tuscaloosa (Ala.) News, 1956-64; exec. mng. editor Montgomery Advertiser and Ala. Jour., 1964—. Bd. dirs. Montgomery United Appeal. Served with USNR, 1945-46. Mem. A.P. Mng. Editors Assn., Ala. A.P. Assn. (pres. 1964-65), Sigma Delta Chi, Pi Kappa Phi. Methodist. Home: 1411 Bancroft Av Montgomery AL 36111 Office: 200 Washington Ave Montgomery AL 36102

DAVIS, BENJAMIN FRANKLIN, II, nursery co. exec.; b. Tahlequah, Okla., Mar. 6, 1937; s. James Edward and Virginia (Hixson) D.; student Tex. A. and M. Coll., 1955-56; B.S., Northeastern State Coll., Tahlequah, 1959; m. Phyllis Ann McMillan, Dec. 31, 1958; children—Benjamin Franklin III, Cynthia Gale, Stephanie Lynn, Jeanette Revau. Prodn. mgr. Ozark Nurseries Co., Tahlequah, 1959-63, exec. v.p., 1963—. County chmn. Young Republicans, 1963-64. Mem. Wholesale Nursery Growers Am. (dir. 1968—), Internat. Plant Propatagor's Soc., Tahlequah Jr. C. of C. (treas. 1966). Club: Redmen Promenadors Square Dance. Home: 510 Judy Lane Tahlequah OK 74464 Office: Route 2 Tahlequah OK 74464

DAVIS, BENJAMIN M., paper co. exec.; b. Oak Grove, Ala., Apr. 29, 1921; s. Howard Ellis and Marie (McMillan) D.; B.S., Auburn U., 1943; m. Anna Sherling Davis, Nov. 4, 1943; children—Anna Boulware, Benjamin McMillan, Dan Sherling. With Internat. Paper Co., Mobile, 1946—, logging engr., 1966-69, dir. logging and equipment engring., 1969—. Served to capt. AUS, 1943-46. Decorated Air medal. Mem. Am. Soc. Agrl. Econs., Soc. Am. Foresters. Home: 603 Spanish Main St Spanish Fort AL 36527 Office: Paper Mill Rd Mobile AL 36601

DAVIS, BENJAMIN OLIVER, JR., govt. ofcl.; b. Washington, Dec. 18, 1912; s. Benjamin Oliver and Sadie (Overton) D.; student Western Res. U., 1929-30, U. Chgo., 1930-32; B.S., U.S. Mil. Acad., 1936; postgrad. Air War Coll., 1950; D.Mil. Sci., Wilberforce U., 1948; D.Sc., Morgan State Coll., 1963; LL.D., Tuskegee Inst., 1963; m. Agatha Scott, June 20, 1936. Commd. 2d lt. U.S. Army, 1932; commd. maj. U.S. Air Force, 1942, advanced through grades to lt. gen., 1965; prof. mil. sci. Tuskegee Inst., 1938-41; comdr. 99th Fighter Squadron, North Africa, Sicily, 1943; comdr. 332d Fighter Group, Italy, 1943-45; comdr. 51st Fighter-Interceptor Wing. Korea, 1953; vice comdr. 13th Air Force, and comdr. Air Task Force 13, 1955-57; chief of staff 12th Air Force, 1957; dep. chief of staff for ops. Hdqrs. USAFE, Germany, 1957-61; chief of staff UN Command, Korea, 1965-67; comdr. 13th Air Force, 1967-68; dep. comdr. U.S. Strike Command, 1968-70; ret., 1970; dir. Office of Civil Aviation Security, Transp. Dept., Washington, 1970-71, asst. sec. transp. for safety and consumer affairs, 1971—. Dir. pub. safety City of Cleve., 1970. Decorated D.S.M. with two oak leaf clusters, Silver Star, D.F.C., Legion of Merit with two oak leaf clusters Air medal with five oak leaf clusters. Home: 1001 Wilson Blvd Arlington VA 22206 Office: 400 7th St S W Washington DC 20590

DAVIS, BERNARD, mus. exec. Pres. Miami (Fla.) Mus. Modern Art. Office: 2000 N Bayshore Dr Miami FL 33137*

DAVIS, BERNARD BYRD, lawyer; b. nr. Shelbyville, Ky., Feb. 17, 1912; s. John Fulton and Annie (Bailey) D.; LL.B., Washington and Lee U., 1933; m. Sarah Ware, Aug. 12, 1933. Admitted to Ky. bar, 1932, gen. practice, Shelbyville, 1933-63, Louisville, 1971—; spl. agt. FBI, 1942-45; commr. Ky. Ct. of Appeals, Frankfort, 1963-71. Chmn., Shelby County Democratic Exec. Com., 1936-40. Home: 1315 Walnut St Shelbyville KY 40065 Office: Marion & Taylor Bldg Louisville KY 40202

DAVIS, BERNARD JOSEPH, chem. co. exec.; b. Phila., Nov. 18, 1918; s. Nathaniel Robert and Sally Marie (Steene) D.; B.S., Temple U., 1941; Ph.D., U. Del., 1945; m. Agnes Ellen Darreck, Oct. 8, 1941; children—Roger, Joseph, Jeffrey, Mary Ellen, Patricia Ann. Mem. market devel. and prodn. devel. Am. Cyanamid Co., N.Y.C., 1945-50; with Shell Oil Co., N.Y.C., 1950-62; dir. research and devel. Reichold Chemicals, Inc., Gulfport, Miss., 1962—. Cons. Commerce Dept., 1969-70. Radiol. def. officer Miss., 1962—. Mem. Am. Chem. Soc. Patentee in polymers and organic chemistry. Home: 108 Hursey St Pass Christian MS 39571 Office: PO Box 1326 Gulfport MS 39501

DAVIS, BERTRAM HYLTON, educator, assn. exec.; b. Ozone Park, N.Y., Nov. 30, 1918; s. Hubert Edwin and Gladys (Greenidge) D.; grad. Phillips Acad., Andover, Mass., 1933-37; student Hamilton Coll., Clinton, N.Y., 1937-39; A.B., Columbia, 1941, M.A., 1948, Ph.D., 1956; m. Ruth Austin Benedict, Jan. 11, 1946; children—Ralph Paul, Kathryn Austin (Mrs. Person), Richard Austin. Lectr. English, Hunter Coll., 1947-48; instr., then asst. prof. English, Dickinson Coll., 1948-57; staff asso. Am. Assn. U. Profs., 1957-63, dep. gen. sec., 1963-67, gen. sec., 1967—. Served to capt. AUS, 1941-46. Mem. Modern Lang. Assn., Johnsonians, Catch Soc. Am. (exec. bd.), Am. Civil Liberties Union. Author: Johnson Before Boswell, 1960. Editor: (Sir John Hawkins) Life of Samuel Johnson LL.D., 1961. Editor bull. Am. Assn. U. Profs., 1960-65. Home: 3009 Daniel Lane NW Washington DC 20015 Office: Suite 500 1 DuPont Circle Washington DC 20036

DAVIS, CALVIN GRIER, clergyman; b. Wilmar, Ark., Sept. 15, 1906; s. Coleman Robert and Ollie (Hillard) D.; student Hendrix Coll., 1923-24; A.B., Davidson Coll., 1927; postgrad. Princeton Theol. Sem., 1928-29; B.D., Union Theol. Sem., 1931, Th. M., 1935, Th. D., 1943; D.D., Davidson Coll., 1943, Tusculum Coll., 1943; m. Rebecca McDowell, July 6,1935; children—Calvin Grier, James McDowell. Ordained to ministry Presbyn. Ch., 1931; asst. pastor Grace Covenant Ch., Richmond, Va., 1931-33; pastor Second Ch., Norfolk, 1933-38, First Ch., Asheville, N.C., 1938-59; pres. Mountain Retreat Assn., Montreat-Anderson Coll., Montreat, N.C., 1959-71. Dir. Northwestern Bank. Moderator Norfolk Presbytery, 1935, Asheville Presbytery, 1940, Synod of Appalachia, 1950; mem. bd. Annuities and Relief; bd. mgrs. Lord's Day Alliance. Trustee Montreat-Anderson Coll., Davidson Coll., King Coll., Mountain Retreat Assn. Contbg. editor Presbyn. Outlook. Home: 87 Shorewood Dr Asheville NC

DAVIS, CHARLES, broadcasting exec. Program dir. WAPI, Birmingham, Ala. Office: PO Box 1310 Birmingham AL 35201*

DAVIS, CHARLES CURTIS, supt. schs.; b. Hopewell, Va., Sept. 27, 1928; s. Curtis Reginald and Frances Lunez (McDaniel) D.; A.B., Wofford Coll., 1955; NSF scholar, Duke, 1961-64; M.A., East Carolina U., 1963; m. Rosa Moore, May 16, 1959; children—Charles Curtis, Mathieson, Patterson. Lab. work Allied Chem. Corp., Hopewell, 1945-48; tchr. pub. schs., 1955-63; prin. Williston (S.C.) Elementary Sch., also dir. Fed. projects, 1963-67; supt. schs., Estill, S.C., 1967—; tchr. field courses U. S.C. Sec.-treas. Estill Indsl. Bd., 1967-72. Served with M.C., AUS, 1948-52. Recipient Boss of Yr. award Jaycees, 1969. Mem. S.C. Assn. Sch. Supts., N.E.A., S.C. Edn. Assn., Hampton County Edn. Assn., Estill C. of C. (sec.-treas.), Am. Legion, Phi Delta Kappa. Mason. Home: 187 Lilly St N Estill SC 29918 Office: Box757 Estill SC 29918

DAVIS, CHARLES HOWARD, educator; b. Woodstown, N.J., May 7, 1929; s. Charles Toy and Agnes (Heppard) D.; A.B., Guilford Coll., 1951; M.A., Vanderbilt U., 1952, Ph.D., 1968; m. Mary Kathryn Brown, Aug. 10, 1963; children—Charles Howard. Economist, planner Tenn. Planning Commn., Nashville, 1964-66; indsl. economist Fed. Res. Bank of Dalls, 1966-68; asso. prof. econs. dept. Memphis State U., 1968—. Mem. Am., So. econ. assns. Mem. Soc. of Friends. Home: 4652 Chicasaw Memphis TN 38117

DAVIS, CHARLES MITCHELL, JR., educator; b. Washington, July 2, 1925; s. Charles Mitchell and Blanche (Scott) D.; A.B., Catholic U. Am., 1951, M.S., 1954, Ph.D., 1962; m. Senora Margaret Jessup, April 1947; children—Kathleen Lee, Theresa Sue, Rebecca Ann, Thomas Scott. Physicist Naval Ordnance Lab., White Oak, Md., 1951-62, parttime 1962-69; instr. U. Va. No. Extension, parttime 1956-62; profl. lectr. physics dept. Am. U., Washington, 1961-62, asso. prof. physics dept., from 1962, now prof. (on leave); head phys. acoustics br. Naval Research Lab., Washington, 1970—. Served with USNR, 1943-46. Mem. Am. Phys. Soc., Acoustical Soc. Am., Phi Beta Kappa, Sigma Xi. Contbr. articles to profl. jours. Home: 8458 Portland Pl McLean VA 22101 Office: Acoustics Div Naval Research Lab Washington DC 20390

DAVIS, CHARLES SHEPARD, coll. pres.; b. Mobile, Ala., Aug. 13, 1910; s. Matthew and Ruth (Shepard) D.; B.S., Ala. Poly. Inst., 1931, M.S., 1932; Ph.D., Duke, 1938; m. Mary G. Merritt, June 6, 1936; children— Mary (Mrs. Atherton), Catherine (Mrs. Antoine Vinel), Charlotte (Mrs. F. Straie Fairey, Jr.). Asso. prof. history Ala. Poly. Inst., 1941; mem. faculty Fla. State U., 1947—, asst. dean coll. arts and scis., 1949, asso. dean 1950, acting dean 1951, dean 1952, prof. history 1949-59, dean faculties, 1958-59; pres. Winthrop Coll., S.C. Coll. for Women, 1959—. Chmn. bd. Home Fed. Savs & Loan Assn., Rock Hill. Pres. S.C. Assn. Colls., 1964-65. Trustee Voorhees Coll.; bd. dirs. Regional Learning Lab. Carolinas & Va. Served as maj. C.E., AUS, 1942-45; col. USAF Res. Decorated Bronze Star Medal. Mem. Rock Hill C. of C. (pres. 1964, dir.), So. Assn. Colls. and Secondary Schs., N.E.A., Newcomen Soc. Eng., So., Hist. Assn., Council Pres.'s State Colls. and Univs. (chmn. S.C. 1962-64), Phi Beta Kappa, Phi Kappa Phi (nat. pres. 1957-62), Omicron Delta Kappa, Scabbard and Blade, Pi Kappa Alpha, Blue Key, Democrat. Episcopalian. Author: The Cotton Kingdom of Alabama, 1939. Editor: Report of Operations of the U.S. Seventh Army, 1945; Colin J. McRae: Confederate Financial Agent, 1961. Contbr. articles. Home: 601 Oakland Av Rock Hill SC 29730

DAVIS, CLIFFORD YOUNG, JR., banker; b. Memphis, Sept. 21, 1932; s. Clifford Young and W.E. (Wells)D.; B.S., U. of South, 1954; postgrad. Sch. Bank Marketing, Northwestern U., 1964; m. E. June Hargis, Aug. 7, 1955; children—Melissa Dawn, Clifford Young III. Editor So. Motor Cargo mag., Memphis, 1957-59; pub. relations rep. Fla., Inc., Miami, 1959-61; mgmt. trainee 1st Nat. Bank Memphis, 1961-62, sr. v.p., dir. marketing, 1970—. Bd. dirs. Memphis and Shelby County Health and Welfare Planning Council, 1971—. Served with USAF, 1955-56. Mem. Bank Marketing Assn. (dir. 1970), Pub. Relations Soc. Am., Memphis Advt. Fedn., Alpha Delta Sigma. Club: Colonial Country. Home: 6218 Malloch Dr Memphis TN 38117 Office: 165 Madison Av Memphis TN 38103

DAVIS, COURTLAND HARWELL, JR., neurol. surgeon; b. Alexandria, Va., Feb. 14, 1921; s. Courtland Harwell and Mary Helen (Fox) D.; A.B., George Washington U., 1941, M.D., U.Va., 1944; m. Marilyn Bauer, Sept. 14, 1942; children—Courtland Harwell III, Randon, Richard, Jean Campbell, Cameron, Marilyn. Rotating intern U.S. Marine Hosp., New Orleans, 1944-45; asst. resident neurosurgery U. Va., 1945-46; postdoctoral research fellow neuropathology NIH, Duke Med. Center, 1948-49; asst. resident neurosurgery Duke Hosp., 1950-51, resident, 1951-52; practice medicine, specializing in neurosurgery, Winston-Salem, N.C., 1952—; instr. medicine Duke Hosp., 1949-50; instr. neurosurgery Bowman Gray Sch. Medicine, 1952-55, asst. prof., 1955-59, asso. prof., 1959-67, prof., 1967—; mem. staff N.C. Bapt. Hosp., 1952—, Kate Bitting Reynolds Meml. Hosp., 1953-58, City Meml. Hosp., 1953-58; cons. VA Hosp., Salisbury, N.C., 1954—, Regional Office VA, Winston-Salem, 1954; vis. prof. neurosurgery CARE-MEDICO, Malaysia, 1966; vis. prof. neurosurgery Christian Med. Coll., Vellore, India, 1966; vis. neurosurgeon HOPE, Cartagena, Colombia, S.Am., 1967, Kingston, Jamaica, 1971. Vice chmn. Gov.'s Commn. on Mental Retardation, 1962-64, N.C. Legislative Council on Mental Retardation, 1964-71. Pres. Bowman Gray Med. Found., Goodwill Industries, Assn. for Handicapped Childrens Center; bd. dirs. Forsyth County Rehab. House, Forsyth County Sheltered Workshop. Served to capt. M.C., AUS, 1946-48. Diplomate Am. Bd. Neurol. Surgery. Fellow A.C.S.; mem. A.M.A., So., Med. Assn., Med. Soc. N.C. (past del.), Forsyth County Med. Soc., Am. Assn. Mental Deficiency, Congress Neurol. Surgeons, So. Neurol. Soc., Am. Assn. Neurol. Surgeons, Neurol. Soc. Am. (pres.), Nat. Assn. for Retarded Children, Assn. for Research in Nervous and Mental Disease, Am. Acad. Neurol. Surgeons, So. Neurol. Surgeons, Soc. Brit. Neurol. Surgeons (hon.), Alpha Omega Alpha. Presbyn. (elder). Rotarian. Home: 921 Goodwood Rd Winston Salem NC 27106 Office: 300 Hawthorne Rd Winston Salem NC 27103

DAVIS, DAVID KEITHLEY, petroleum co. exec.; b. Sayre, Okla., July 19, 1926; s. Orville Keithley and Ruth (Johnson) Wilson; student Oklahoma City U., 1943-44, 46-47; student Cameron State Coll., 1955; m. Wanda Jean Martin, July 20, 1944; children—David Michael, Derek Hamilton, D'Et Suzanne. Bombsight technician Air Service Com., Oklahoma City, 1943; computer, party chief seismograph crew Century Geophys. Corp., Tulsa, 1947-50; party chief, supr. seismograph Midwestern Geophys. Lab., Tulsa, 1950-55; supr. Exploration Surveys Inc., Dallas, 1955-58; chief geophysicist, Frankfort Oil Co. Dallas, 1958-62; exec. v.p. Longhaorn Prodn. Co., Dallas, 1962-64; exec. v.p. Exploration Surveys Inc., Dallas, 1964-71; pres. Computer Systems Corp., Dallas, 1967-71; ind. geophys. cons., exec. v.p. Natural Gas Finders Inc., Dallas, 1971—; pres. Exploration Service Co., 1967-71; owner D.K. Davis: Geoscience, Dallas, 1972—; partner Landmark Geoscience Assos., Dallas, 1972—, dir. Norandco Mining Co., Calgary, Alta., Can.; dir. Mustang Computing Co., Dallas. Served with USAAF, 1944-45. Mem. Soc. Exploration Geophysicists, Dallas Geol. Soc., Dallas Geophys. Soc., Houston Geophys. Soc., Internat. Oceanographic Found. Republican. Baptist. Mason (32 degree, Shriner). Clubs: Cowboy, Toastmasters. Home: 10850 Ridge Spring Dr Dallas TX 75218 Office: 532 Meadows Bldg Dallas TX 75206

DAVIS, DON ERWIN, coll. pres.; b. Aulne, Kan. Nov. 7, 1906; s. Charles William and Ida Belle (Pratt) D.; A.B., Southwestern Coll., 1930; B.S., Kan. State Tchrs. Coll., 1935, M.S., 1943; Ed.D., Wayne State U., 1951; m. Eva Marcille Bard, Aug. 14, 1939; 1 dau., Jacqueline Jo. Tchr. pub. schs., Protection, Kan., 1935-39; prin. pub. sch., Clements, Kan., 1939-43, Emporia, Kan., 1946-47; supt. lab. schs., dir. supervised teaching Kan. State Tchrs. Coll., 1947-49, chmn. div. tchr. edn., 1951-58; instr. Wayne State U., 1949-51, asst. prof., 1958-59, asso. prof., 1959-61, prof., chmn. dept. elementary edn., 1961-62; pres. Coll. Ozarks, 1962—. Dir. Western Ark. Devel. Assn.; mem., v.p. W. Central Ark. Econ. Devel. Dist.; mem. adv. council South Central Region Ednl. Lab; mem. Gov's Adv. Council; del. to State Constl. Conv., 1969, Ark. Health Planning Commn. Served with USNR, 1943-45. Mem. Nat., Ark. edn. assns., Internat. Platform Assn., Newcomen Soc., Johnson County C. of C. (pres.), Kappa Delta Pi, Phi Epsilon. Democrat. Presbyn. Mason, Rotarian (dist. gov. elect). Contr. profl. articles publs. Home: 603 Buchanan St Clarksville AR 72830

DAVIS, DONALD DEAN, civil engr; b. Decatur, Ill., May 28, 1928; s. Chauncey Depew and Gertie (Owen) D.; Asso. Sci, in Indsl. Elec. Engring., Arlington State Coll., 1949, student 1951-52; B.S. in Civil Engring, Tex. A. and M. U., 1954. Jr. elec. engr. Tex. Electric Service Co., Ft. Worth, 1949-51; sr. engring. asst. Tex. Hwy Dept., 1954-57; civil engr. S.W. region FAA, Ft. Worth, 1957-61, chief radar plant unit, 1961-62, chief plant engring. sect. for design and constrn. air navigational and facilities So. region, Atlanta, 1962-65, chief terminal sect., 1965-66, chief plant engring. br., 1966-69, asst. chief airway facilities div. So. region, Atlanta, 1969—. Lt. col. C.E., U.S. Army Res. Registered profl. civil engr., Tex., Ga., Miss., Ala., Tenn. Mem. Am. Soc. C.E., Am. Mgmt. Assn., Soc. Am. Mil. Engrs., Res. Officers Assn., Am. Concrete Inst., Ga. Engring. Soc., Assn. U.S. Army. Home: 2567 Headland Dr East Point GA 30344 Office: FAA PO Box 20636 Atlanta GA 30302

DAVIS, DREXEL CARTER, dentist; b. Kilsyth, Tenn., Feb. 7, 1914; s. John Calvin and Ida Bell (Drake) D.; B.S., U. Tenn., 1939, D.D.S., 1949; m. Bertha Irene McNew, June 1, 1938; children—Drexel Carter II, Stanley Paul; m. 2d, Nora Jane Townsend Hawk, Feb. 5, 1972; 1 stepdau., Kathryn Elaine Hawk. Tchr., prin. Westbourne (Tenn.) Elementary Sch., 1936-38; prin. Midway Sch., Knox County (Tenn.), 1938-39; tchr. sci. Halls High Sch., Knox County (Tenn.), 1940-43; tchr. adult edn., supr. practice tchrs. U. Tenn., 1945-46; indsl. engr. Fulton Sylphon Co., Knoxville, 1942-46; pvt. practice dentistry, Knoxville, 1950—. Active Boy Scouts Am. Recipient Distinguished Service award Kiwanis Club, 1970; named Outstanding Kiwanian, 1971. Mem. Am. Dental Assn., 2d Dist. Dental Soc., Delta Sigma Delta. Republican. Mason (32 degree), Kiwanian. Home: Route 18 Oak Ridge Hwy Knoxville TN 37921 Office: 5317 Clinton Hwy Knoxville TN 37912

DAVIS, EDWARD FREE, JR., carpet mfr.; b. Valdosta, Ga., Sept. 18, 1929; s. Edward Free and Elise (Holder) D.; B.A., Emory U., 1949, B.B.A., 1951; m. Roberta Williams, Aug. 14, 1954; children—Ellen, Angela. With Trust Co. of Ga., Atlanta, 1951-52; pres. Modern Tufting, Co., Dalton, Ga, 1954-65; pres., chmn., dir. Colony Carpets, Inc., Dalton, 1965—, Colony Spinning, Inc., Dalton, 1969—; dir. C & S Nat. Bank of Dalton, Ins. Industries, Inc., Atlanta, Williams Spltys., Inc., Dalton. Pres. Lake Francis, Dalton, 1968—. Mem. adminstrv. bd. United Meth. Ch., 1970—. Served with AUS, 1952-54. Mem. Young Pres. Orgn., Sigma Alpha Epsilon. Methodist (supt. Sunday sch. 1967—). Clubs: Dalton Golf and Country (pres. 1962-63), Exchange. Home: 751 Emmons Dr Dalton GA 30720 Office: 207 Bear Creek Rd Dalton GA 30720

DAVIS, ELMER P., govt. ofcl. Regional dir. NLRB, Fort Worth. Address: NLRB Fed Office Bldg Fort Worth TX 76102*

DAVIS, ERNEST B., state ofcl.; b. Danielsville, Ga.,Sept. 12, 1919; s. James Wylie and Lora (Burroughs) D.; B.C.S., Ga. State Coll., 1947; m. Mary Louise Walton, Jan. 10, 1946; children—Lee Nannette, Lauren Patricia. Sec.-treas. bd. health State of Ga., 1951-61, budget officer, 1962-65, state auditor, 1965—. Home: 1679 Timberland Rd Atlanta GA 30329 Office: State Capitol Bldg Atlanta GA 30334

DAVIS, FRANCES IRENE, ct. reporter; b. Lathrop, Ala., Mar. 2, 1924; d. John Everette and Samantha Texanna (O'Bryant) Davis; student pub. schs. Timekeeper, DeBardeleben Coal Corp., Holt, Ala., 1943-46; town clk., Reform, Ala., 1946-47; chief probate clk. to probate judge of Pickens County, Carrollton, 1953-59; bookkeeper D. T. Hannah Lumber Co., Gordo, 1959-61; sec. Ala. Farm Bur. Ins. Co., Carrollton, 1962; ct. reporter 24th Jud. Circuit Ala., Carrollton, 1963—. Sec.; Civic Improvement Council, Reform, 1963-66. Sec., Pickens County Democratic Exec. Com., 1963—. Mem. Bus. and Profl. Women's Club. Ala. Shorthand Reporters Assn., Wesleyan Service Guild (pres. 1958-59, v.p. 1965-66). Methodist. Mem. Order Eastern Star (sec. 1965-66, worthy matron 1955-56, 63-64). Club. Reform Homemakers (sec. 1963-66). Home: PO Box 566 Reform AL 35481 Office: PO Box 299 Carrollton AL 35447

DAVIS, F(RANK) DONALD, hosp. adminstr.; b. Mitchellville, Tenn., Aug. 14, 1934; s. Frank William Davis and Roberta (Keene) Wilson; B.S., U. Tenn., 1961; M.H.A., U. Minn., 1964; m. Mary Louise Richardson, Mar. 31, 1955; 1 dau., Tammye Lynn. Asst. storekeeper Mid-Tenn. Tb Hosp., Nashville, 1955-57, storekeeper, 1957-58, adminstrv. asst., 1958-59; design progress adminstr. engring. operations Saturn br. Boeing Co., Huntsville, Ala., 1962; adminstrv. resident U. Ala. Hosps. and Clinics, Birmingham, 1963-64; exec. v.p. Andalusia (Ala.) Hosp., Inc., 1964-71; exec. dir. Med. Center Hosp., Huntsville, 1971—. Dir. Blue-Cross-Blue Shield Ala. Hosp. cons., constrn., planning, orgn. St. Clair County Hosp., Pell City, Ala.,

1968-69; chmn. Health Careers Council, Covington County, Ala., 1968-69; faculty rep. U. Ala. Bd. dirs. United Fund, Andalusia, 1968-71, Covington County Crippled Children's Soc., 1968-71. Mem. Ala. Hosp. Assn. (chmn. pub. relations and edn. com. 1969-70), Ala. Assn. Hosp. Execs., S.E. Ala. Hosp. Council (pres. 1967-68), U. Minn. Program in Hosp. Adminstrn. Alumni Assn. (regional coordinator 1967-68), Am. Coll. Hosp. Adminstrs. Baptist. Rotarian. Home: Huntsville AL Office: 911 Big Cove Rd Huntsville 35801

DAVIS, FRANK MARVIN, entomologist; b. Greenwood, Miss., Sept. 15, 1939; s. Mallory Coleman and Josephine (Holloman) D.; B.S., Miss. State U., 1961, M.S., 1963, Ph.D., 1965; m. Carole Elizabeth L. McReynolds, Mar. 21, 1964; 1 son, Frank Marvin. Research entomologist U.S. Dept. Agr., Boll Weevil Research Lab., State College, Miss., 1965—. Tchr. insect ecology Miss. State U., 1969-71, adj. prof. entomology, 1966-71. Recipient Nat. Def. Act fellowship Miss. State U., 1963-65. Mem. Entomology Soc. Am., Miss. Entomology Assn., Gamma Sigma Delta, Sigma Alpha Epsilon. Presbyn. Club: Miss. State Tennis Boosters (State College). Home: 518 Poplar Rd Starkville MS 39759 Office: Boll Weevil Research Lab Box 5367 State College MS 39762

DAVIS, FRANK WILBUR, aero. engr.; b. Charleston, W.Va., Dec. 6, 1914; s. Madison T., Jr., and Julia (Staunton) D.; B.S. in Mech. Engring., Cal. Inst. Tech., 1936; D.Sc., W.Va. U. 1960; m. Frances Washington, Mar. 15, 1941; children—Caroline (Mrs. O. D. Calvert, Jr.), Frank Wilbur, William Brewster. With Convair div. Gen. Dynamics Corp., 1940—, successively engring. test pilot, chief aerodynamics and flight test, chief design engr., asst. chief engr., asst. to v.p. engring., chief engr., 1940-54, pres., mgr., chief engr. Ft. Worth div., 1954-70, corporate sr. v.p., 1959—, also pres. Convair Aerospace div., 1970—; dir. Canadair, Ltd. Bd. dirs. Ft. Worth YMCA, Internat. Sci. Fair. Served with USMC, 1937-40. Recipient Silver Anniversary All Am. award Sports Illustrated mag. Registered profl. engr., Cal., Tex. Fellow Am. Inst. Aero. and Astronautics, Soc. Exptl. Test Pilots (hon.); mem. Tex. (Engr. of Year award Ft. Worth sect. 1957), Nat. socs. profl. engrs., Soc. Automotive Engrs., Nat. Alliance Businessmen (met. chmn. 1968-71), Nat. Acad. Engring., S.W. Center Advanced Studies, Air Force Assn., Navy League U.S., Assn. U.S. Army, Nat. Aeros. Assn., Airpower Council. Patentee spring tab for aircraft control, ejection seat for escape from aircraft. Pioneer design of intercontinental ballistic missile. Home: 6328 Curzon St Fort Worth TX 76116 Office: Convair Aerospace Div Gen Dynamics Box 748 Fort Worth TX 76101

DAVIS, GEORGE K(ELSO), educator; b. Pitts., July 2, 1910; s. Ross Irwin and Jennie L. (Kelso) D.; B.S., Pa. State U., 1932; Ph.D., Cornell U., 1937; m. Ruthanna Wood, Jan. 25, 1936; children—Dorothy Jeanne (Mrs. Arthur C. Aikin, Jr.), Mary Ellen (Mrs. W. Edgar Benedict), Ruthanna Marie (Mrs. Donald W. Davidson), Virginia Kay (Mrs. John M. Fedison), Robert Wyatt, George William Ross. Research asst. Cornell U., Ithaca, N.Y., 1932-37; research asst. prof. chemistry Mich. State U., 1937-42; prof. nutrition and animal nutritionist U. Fla., Gainesville, 1942—, dir. nuclear scis., 1960-65, dir. biol. scis., 1965-70, dir. sponsored research, 1970—. Chmn., Internat. Biol. Program Sect. on Use and Mgmt. Biol. Resources, 1966—. Rep., U. Fla. Council Oak Ridge Asso. Univs., 1960-66; cons. Minister Agr., Costa Rica, univs. Costa Rica, Buenos Aires, San Marcos (Peru), Universidad Agraria (Peru), Sao Paulo (Brazil), FAO, UN, OEA, INTA (Argentina), U.S. Dept. Agr., Dept. Health, Edn. and Welfare, Nutrition Found., Fla. Dept. Agr.; mem. Internat. Biol. Program Com., Nat. Acad. Sci.-NRC Food and Nutrition Bd. and Com. on Animal Nutrition, 1956-71. Recipient Distinguished Faculty award U. Fla., 1960, named Faculty Lectr., 1960. Fellow A.A.A.S.; mem. Am. Chem. Soc. (sec.-treas. Fla. sect. 1955, chmn., 1958, recipient Fla. award 1956), Am. Soc. Animal Sci. (nat. v.p. 1961-62, sec. So. sect. 1962-63), Am. Inst. Nutrition (jour. mgmt. com. 1961, mem. council 1971—, recipient Borden award 1964), Am. Soc. Biol. Chemists, Soc. Exptl. Biology and Medicine, Am. Dairy Assn., Am. Nuclear Soc., Am. Inst. Biol. Sci. (chmn. Southeastern regional council for biol. satellite programs), Sao Paulo Vet. Soc. (hon.), Peruvian Veterinarian Assn. (hon.), Sigma Xi (pres. Fla. 1956-57), Blue Key (Fla. Faculty award 1958), Alpha Zeta, Phi Lambda Upsilon, Gamma Sigma Delta, Phi Eta Sigma, Phi Sigma, Gamma Sigma Epsilon. Mem. editorial bds. Jour. Nutrition, 1960-66, Jour. Animal Sci., 1959-65. Contbr. articles to textbooks, sci. jours. Research radio-active isotopes as biol. tracers, sources of ionizing radiation. Home: 2903 SW 2d Ct Gainesville FL 32601

DAVIS, GERTRUDE ELIZABETH CODDINGTON (MRS. WILLIAM L. DAVIS), librarian; b. Roanoke, Va., June 7, 1915; d. Harry Wilbur and Ruth (Todd) Coddington; student Coll. William and Mary, 1932-33; student Roanoke Coll., Berea Coll; B.A. in English Lit., Oberlin Coll., 1936; B.S. in L.S., U.N.C., 1942; postgrad. George Washington U., U. Va., Drexel Inst. Tech. Grad. Sch. L.S.; M.S., Columbia, 1969; m. William L. Davis, May 16, 1942 (dec. May 1962); children—Dorothy Scott (Mrs. Douglas S. Fiedler), William Shannon. Sec., Assn. Am. Railroads, Washington, 1936-39; children's asst. N.Y. Pub. Library, N.Y.C., 1941-42; librarian Staunton (Va.) Mil. Acad., 1955-57, Mary Baldwin Coll. Library, Staunton, 1957—. Mem. Am., Southeastern, Va. library assns., Archeol. Soc. Va., Augusta County Hist. Soc. (charter), D.A.R., Am. Assn. U. Women, Staunton Fine Arts Assn., Beta Phi Mu. Methodist. Club: Augusta Country. Home: 315 Vine St Staunton VA 24401 Office: Mary Baldwin Coll Library Staunton VA 24401

DAVIS, GORDON WILLIAM, educator; b. Galva, Ill., Oct. 7, 1910; s. William George and Beatrice (Gordon) D.; A.B., Knox Coll., 1934; M.S., Washington U., 1938. Asst. plant physiology Washington U., 1935-39; head sci. dept. Leadwood (Mo.) High Sch., 1937-39; tch. sales dir. Printograph Co., Kansas City, Mo., 1939-41; instr. sci., English, math. Morgan Park Mil. Acad., Chgo., 1941; head sci. dept. Elkader (Ia.) Jr. Coll., 1941-42; asst. prof., sci. supr. Winthrop Coll., Rock Hill, S.C., 1957-58; prof. biology and chem., chmn. sci. dept., Frederick Coll., Portsmouth, Va., 1958-59; asst. prof. chem. and math. Ferris State Coll., Big Rapids, Mich., 1959-63; asso. prof. phys. scis. Miami-Dade Jr. Coll., Miami, 1963—. Commd. capt. AUS, 1942, advanced through grades to lt. col., Res., 1953; chem. br. advisory S.C. Mil. Dist., also chem. U.S. Army Res. adviser for chem. units, Charleston, S.C., 1953-57. Mem. Mo. Acad. Sci., Res. Officers Assn., Armed Forces Chem. Soc., Nat. Honor Soc., Nat. Sci. Tchrs. Assn. (life), Am. Assn. U. Profs. (pres., founder Miami-Dade Jr. Coll. chpt. 1966—), Am. Chem. Soc., Dade County Classroom Tchrs. Assn., Am. Assn. Physics Tchrs., Am. Ordnance Assn. (life), N.E.A., Fla. Edn. Assn., Assn. for Higher Edn., Internat. Platform Assn., Fla. Acad. Sci., Sigma Xi, Phi Sigma. Club: Chemist. Home: 10545 NW 28th Av Miami FL 33147

DAVIS, GWENDOLYN LIGON (MRS. RAMON TARVER DAVIS), state ednl. adminstr.; b. Weslaco, Tex., July 21, 1922; d. Argalus Neal and Bonnie (Sheppard) Ligon; grad. Lebanon (Tenn.) High Sch., 1940; m. Ramon Tarver Davis, May 24, 1941; 1 dau., Diana Lynn (Mrs. C. C. Mason Jr.). Various secretarial positions, Lebanon, Tenn., 1941-54; commnr. personnel State of Tenn., 1967—. Mem. exec. com. So. Baptist Conv., 1961—, sec., 1965-66; mem., past pres. local ch. and Wilson County (Tenn.) Women's Missionary Union, music dir. state conv., 1966; pres. Wilson County Concert Assn., 1956-58. State committeewoman, 4th Congl. Dist., Democratic Party, 1966-70, currently mem. exec. com. Bd. dirs. YMCA. Mem. Am. Legion Aux. (past sec., pres., sec. to pres. state unit), Assn. Preservation Tenn. Antiquities, Tenn. Fedn. Women's Clubs (state music chmn., 1968—), Tenn. Fedn. Music Clubs (v.p. middle Tenn., 1958-59), Nat. Soc., Magna Charta Dames. Bapt. (past youth choir dir.). Clubs: Music (past pres.), La Coterie (past pres.) (both Lebanon). Home: Route 4 Oak Shores Lebanon TN 37087 Office: State of Tenn Dept of Personnel Cordell Hull Bldg Nashville TN 37219

DAVIS, HAL D., banker; b. Toccoa, Ga., Oct. 7, 1905; s. Jefferson and Myrtle (Yow) D.; student U. Miami, 1945-47; m. Margaret Brown Wilson, Oct. 3, 1934; children—Jefferson II (dec.), Margaret Moseley, Myra Anne. With 1st Fed. Savs. & Loan Assn. Miami, 1938—, v.p., sec., 1950-69, sr. v.p., sec., 1969—, sr. v.p., sec.-treas., 1971, dir., sr. v.p., sec.-treas., 1972—. Bd. dirs. Grand Jury Assn., Inc., 1968—. Mem. S.A.R., Hist. Assn. So. Fla., Fla. Hist. Assn. Presbyn. (elder). Clubs: Century of Coral Gables, Riviera Country of Coral Gables. Kiwanian. Home: 1420 Sopera Av Coral Gables FL 33134 Office: 100 NE 1st Av Miami FL 33132

DAVIS, HAROLD, ret. mil. systems analyst; b. Willimantic, Conn., June 12, 1917; s. Isaac and Sarah (Ronkin) D.; B.A., Bklyn. Coll., 1939; postgrad. George Washington U., 1941, Am. U., 1942-45, U. Cal. at Berkeley, 1948; m. Frances Hilda Armel, Jan. 20, 1946; children—Bruce Donald, Bret Jay. Statistician, Census Bur., Washington, 1940-44, Dept. Navy, Washington, 1944-47, Naval Ordnance Test Sta., Inyokern, Cal., 1947-50; operations analyst Hdqrs. Far E. Air Forces, Tokyo, Japan, 1954-57; chief operations analysis office Hdqrs. 4th Allied Tactical Air Force, Germany, 1957-59; sr. operations analyst Dept. Air Force, Washington, 1959-62; chief Office Research, U.S. Arms Control and Disarmament Agy., Washington, 1963-67, 67-72; chief evaluation div., region 2 AID, Vietnam, 1967. Mem. Operations Research Soc. Am., Am. Statis. Assn., Inst. Math. Statistics, Inst. Strategic Studies, A.A.A.S. Home: 10900 Childs St Silver Spring MD 20901

DAVIS, HARRY GORDON, pub. co. exec.; b. Houston, June 26, 1912; s. Harold Richard and Elsie Claire (Barrett) D.; student Houston Jr. Coll. and Houston Law Sch., 1937-38; m. Bernice Shannon Davis, Sept. 2, 1950. With circulation dept. Houston Post, 1930-34, police reporter, 1934-37; criminal investigator Harris County, 1937-39; dist. circulation mgr. Houston Post, 1939-42, 46-47; sec.-mgr. Gulf Coast Express, Inc., Houston, 1947-51; v.p., gen. mgr. Bluebonnet Express, Houston, 1950-52; part owner G.A. White Express, Houston and Dallas, 1953-57; with Houston Post, 1958—, purchasing mgr., 1962-71, dir. distbn., 1971—. Served with AUS, 1942-46. Mem. Newspaper Purchasing Mgrs. Assn., Ret. Officers Assn., Tex. Circulation Mgrs. Assn., Am. Legion, Am. Auto Assn. Democrat. Methodist. Mason (32 deg.); mem. Eastern Star. Club: Indian Shores Golf. Home: 2040 Westcreek Lane Apt 29C Houston TX 77027 Office: 4747 Southwest Freeway Houston TX 77001

DAVIS, HARTWELL, lawyer; b. Auburn, Ala., Dec. 18, 1906; s. Christopher Hartwell and Elizabeth Myrick (Dowdell) D.; student U. Fla., 1923-24; B.S., Auburn U., 1928; Woodrow Wilson Meml. scholar U. Va. Law Sch., 1929-30; LL.B., Emory U., 1931; LL.D., 1970; m. Elizabeth Mardre, Feb. 24, 1933; children—Hartwell, Letitia Dowdell (Mrs. R. Wilkins Hamill, III). Clk. Bradenton Bank & Trust Co. (Fla.), 1924-25; admitted to Ga., Ala. and Fla. bars, 1931, and since practiced at Opelika and Montgomery, Ala.; asst. U.S. atty. Middle Dist. Ala., 1932-51, U.S. atty., 1953-62; atty. City of Montgomery, 1951-53; spl. asst. atty. gen. Ala., 1964-71. Del. S. E. jurisdictional confs. Meth. Ch., 1948, 52, 56; mem. Meth. Gen. Bd. Evangelism, 1952-56; sec.-treas. Meth. Ala. Conf. Bd. Lay Activities, 1945-60. Pres. Montgomery YMCA, 1938-40, bd. dirs., 1935-57; chmn. Ct. Honor, Tuckabatchie area Boy Scouts Am., 1951-52, chmn. merit badge com., 1953; bd. dirs. Ala. Meth. Children's Home; trustee George Wheeler Meml. Scholarship Fund, 1941-71. Mem. Fed., Am., Ala., Montgomery bar assns., C. of C., Am. Judicature Soc., Am. Trial Lawyers Assn., Sigma Nu, Phi Alpha Delta, Theta Alpha Phi. Republican. Kiwanian (pres. 1938). Club: Montgomery Gun. Home: 2216 Allendale Pl Montgomery AL 36111 Office: 1st Nat Bank Bldg Montgomery AL 36104

DAVIS, MRS. HARTWELL (ELIZABETH MARDRE), educator, civic worker; b. Lumpkin, Ga.; d. Wilson Little and Sarah (Bivins) Mardre; student U. Cal. at Berkeley, 1927; B.S., Auburn U., 1929; m. Hartwell Davis, Feb. 24, 1933; children—Hartwell, Letitia Dowdell. Tchr. English, Clift High Sch., Opelika, Ala., 1929-33, Lanier High Sch., Montgomery, Ala., 1934-36, 39, Robert E. Lee High Sch., Montgomery, 1962-68, Jefferson Davis High Sch., Montgomery, 1968-69. Mem. Ala. Citizens Adv. Ednl. Council, Ala. Com. for Better Schs., Inc.; pres. Montgomery Know-Your-Schs. Com., 1951-52. Trustee Carnegie Library Assn. Mem. Montgomery County Republican Exec. Com., 1956-66, 70—; vice chmn. Rep. State Exec. Com., 1961-62; mem. Congl. Dist. and State Republican exec. coms., 1960-66; pres. Montgomery County Rep. Women, 1970-72. Mem. United Church Women (pres. Montgomery 1951-53, pres. Ala. 1955-57, mem. adminstrv. and exec. coms. gen. dept. 1957-58), D.A.R., League Women Voters (exec. bd. Montgomery 1952-54), Auburn U. Alumni Assn. (v.p. 1946-48), Kappa Delta, Phi Kappa Phi, Kappa Delta Pi. Methodist. (exec. com., sec. promotion Ala.-W. Fla. Woman's soc. 1952-58, mem. Ala.-W. Fla. Conf. Bd. Missions 1960-62). Clubs: 20th Century Literary (pres. 1944-45, 72-73), Hypatia Literary (pres. 1944-45). Panjandrum Literary (pres. 1948-49). Home: 2216 Allendale Pl Montgomery AL 36111

DAVIS, HENRY GORDON, JR., physician; b. Sylvester, Ga., Feb. 21, 1919; s. Henry Gordon and Lillie (Wingate) D.; B.S., U. Ga., 1941; student Young Harris Coll., 1939, U. Okla., 1943, Med. Coll. Ga., 1941-45; M.D., Cook County Grad. Sch. Medicine, 1955; m. Francis Marion Salisbury, Dec. 7, 1941; children—Henry Gordon III, Francis Marion, Margaret Davis, Barbara Jeanne. Intern, resident Coker Hosp., Cantonga, 1945-46, U.S. Army Hosp., 1946-48; pvt. practice medicine, Sylvester, 1948—; staff Worth County Hosp., chief staff, 1955; chmn. bd. Worth Loans, Inc; dir. Sylvester-Worth County Tobacco Co., Sylvester Banking Co., Security Bank & Trust Co., Albany, Ga. Pres. Ga. Care, Inc., S.W. Ga. Nursing Home Council; bd. dirs. Ga. Nursing Home Assn. Served from 1st lt. to capt. AUS, 1946-48. Diplomate Am. Bd. Abdominal Surgeons. Fellow Am. Geriatrics Soc.; mem. Am., So., Ga. med. assns., Am., Ga. (dir.) acads. family practice, Worth County (pres. 1953, 57, 61), 2d Dist. (pres. 1964-65) med. socs., Am. Heart Assn. Democrat. Baptist. Kiwanian (pres. 1963). Home: 305 King St Sylvester GA 31791 Office: 108 Liberty Av Sylvester GA 31791

DAVIS, HILLIS DWIGHT, librarian; b. Selma, Ala., Jan. 24, 1932; s. Jordan and Mary Emma (Wright) D.; B.S., Johnson C. Smith U., 1954; M.S., Atlanta U., 1958; m. Marian Louise Anderson, Dec. 23, 1958; children—Hillis D., Marian P. Asst. librarian, head cataloger W.Va. State Coll., Institute, 1957-65; dir. libraries Hampton (Va.) Inst., 1965-69; dir. Coop. Coll. Library Center, Atlanta, 1967—. Cons. So. Assn. Colls. and Schs., 1970-71. Served with AUS, 1955-57. Mem. Am., Ga. library assns., Omega Psi Phi. Home: 3855 Village Dr SW Atlanta GA 30331 Office: 159 Forest Av NE Atlanta GA 30303

DAVIS, HORACE GIBBS, JR., educator, journalist; b. Manchester, Ga., 1924; B.A. with high honors, U. Fla., also M.A. in Journalism; m. Marjorie Lucile Davis, 1948; children—Gregory, Jennifer. Formerly columnist Bradford County (Fla.) Telegraph, state capitol corr. Jacksonville (Fla.) Times-Union, Tallahassee; mem. faculty Sch. Journalism U. Fla., 1949—, now prof.; editorial writer Gainesville (Fla.) Sun. Recipient Pulitzer prize editorial writing, 1971. Mem. Sigma Delta Chi (faculty adviser; nat. v.p. acad. affairs), Omicron Delta Kappa (faculty adviser). Address: Sch Journalism U Florida Gainesville FL 32601 also Gainesville Sun Box 14425 Gainesville FL 32601*

DAVIS, HOWARD ECKERT, educator; b. Palmerton, Pa., Sept. 16, 1933; s. Howard Edward and Clara (Eckert) D.; A.B., Dickinson Coll., 1955; M.A., Yale, 1956, Ph.D., 1962; m. Elizabeth Holbrook Forbes, June 29, 1957; children—Lisa Jeanne, Jill Rebecca, Thomas Howard. Asso. prof. polit. sci. Randolph-Macon Coll., Ashland, Va., 1959-62, prof., chmn. dept. polit. sci., 1962-70, dean, 1970—. Lectr. Va. Commonwealth U., 1961-70, U. Richmond, 1961-64, Richmond Dept. of Police Tng. Sch., 1961—. Mem. Phi Beta Kappa, Sigma Alpha Epsilon. Home: 111 Cub's Lane Ashland VA 23005

DAVIS, HOWARD HALL, newspaper editor; b. Crandall, Fla., Sept. 4, 1915; s. Howard Hall and Beulah (Mizell) D.; student U. Ga., 1935-36; m. Kathleen Knight, June 30, 1946; 1 son, Howard Hall. Owner, editor Fernandina (Fla.) Beach News, 1937-42; owner Davis Motors, 1947-54; mgr., editor Southeast Georgian, Kingsland, 1954—. Vice pres., dir. Citizens Bank, Kingsland; profl. photographer, 1950—. Past exec. sec. Camden Community Chest. Mem. Kingsland City Council. Served with AUS, 1942-45. Mem. Kingsland C. of C. (pres. 1967-68). Methodist (steward 1938—, chmn. ofcl. bd. 1961-62). Mason, Lion (pres. 1962-63). Home: 112 E William St Kingsland GA 31548 Office: 112 S Lee St Kingsland GA 31548

DAVIS, HOWARD W., broadcasting exec. Pres. KMAC, San Antonio.Office: 509 Howard St San Antonio TX 78212*

DAVIS, J. BRATTON, govt. ofcl.; b. Hartsville, S.C., Oct. 27, 1917; s. J. Bratton and Sarah Dee (Causey) D.; B.A., U. S.C., 1938, J.D., 1940; postgrad. Harvard, 1941; m. Margaret Smyth McKissick, Dec. 3, 1954; children—Sherwood McKissick Cleveland, William Choice Cleveland, Jean McKissick. Admitted to S.C. bar, 1940, U.S. Supreme Ct. bar, practiced, Columbia, S.C., 1945-69; U.S. referee in bankruptcy State of S.C., 1969—; mem. S.C. Policy Planning and Coordination Commn. Spl. judge Ct. of Common Pleas, Lexington County (S.C.), Ct. of Gen. Sessions, Williamsburg County (S.C.), Ct. of Gen. Sessions, Greenville County (S.C.), Juvenile-Domestic Relations Ct., Richland County (S.C.). Chmn., S.C. Devel. Bd.; mem. Jud. Conf. 4th Circuit Ct. Appeals. Del. Democratic Nat. Conv., 1960, 64, S.C. Dem. Conv., 1952, 54. Bd. dirs. Byrnes Found.; trustee Ednl. Resources Found. Served to lt. (j.g.) USNR, World War II. Mem. Am., S.C. (circuit v.p.), Richland County (exec. com.) bar assns., Nat. Conf. Referees in Bankruptcy, Newcomen Soc., S.C. Hist. Soc., Kappa Alpha, Omicron Delta Kappa, Phi Delta Phi. Clubs: Forest Lake Country, Palmetto; Coral Beach and Tennis (Paget, Bermuda). Home: 6201 Eastshore Dr Columbia SC 29206 Office: US Courthouse Columbia SC 29201

DAVIS, JADA, telephone co. exec.; b. DeLeon, Tex., July 29, 1919; s. Elijah M. and Sallie Hassie (Jenkins) S.; B.J., U. Tex., 1949; m. Mary Alice Calhoun, Jan. 5, 1943; children—Jeffry Brett, Mark William. Editor, Odessa Am., 1940-41, 43-46; pub. Odessa Herald, 1946-48; editor Stephenville Empire, 1950-51; with Southwestern Bell Telephone Co., St. Louis, 1951—, gen. pub. relations mgr., 1968—. Served with AUS, 1941-43. Author: One For Hell, 1956; The Outraged Sect, 1958. Home: 7711 Broadway St San Antonio TX 78209 Office: 1010 N St Marys St San Antonio TX 78206

DAVIS, JAMES ELSWORTH, food exec.; b. Henderson, Ark., July 31, 1907; s. William M. and Ethel (Chase) D.; student U. Ida., 1925-27; H.H.D., Stetson U., 1960; LL.D., Bethune-Cookman Coll., 1964; m. Florence Novinger, Jan. 27, 1932; children—Dorothy (Mrs. Brice R. Smith, Jr.), Andrew Dano. Pres. Economy Wholesale Grocery Co., 1939-42, v.p., dir., 1925—; exec. v.p. Winn & Lovett Grocery Co., 1946-50; chmn. bd. Winn-Dixie Stores, Inc.; v.p. Economy Wholesale Distbrs., Inc.; chmn. bd., dir. Am. Heritage Life Investment Corp.; dir., v.p. Crackin's Good Bakers Inc.; pres., dir. Danov Corp.; pres. Estuary Corp., D.D.I., Inc.; v.p. Deep South Products, Astor Products, Inc.; dir. Bahamas Supermarkets, Ltd. (Nassau), Barnett First Nat. Bank, Jacksonville; chmn. bd. trustees Am. Century Mortgage Investors; v.p. Monterey Canning Co. Bd. dirs. Bolles Sch.; v.p. Winn-Dixie Stores Found.; pres. Elsworth Davis Family Found.; bd. dirs. St. Luke's Hosp. Assn., Jacksonville; trustee Bethune-Cookman Coll., Daytona Beach, Fla. Commd. capt. U.S. Army, 1943; advanced through grades to lt. col., 1945; officer charge Q.M.C. Market Center, N.Y.C., 1944-45, perishable foods, ETO, MTO, NATOUSA; released from service, 1945. Decorated Legion of Merit. Mem. Nat. Assn. Food Chains, Alpha Kappa Psi, Sigma Chi. Home: 3960 Ortega Blvd Jacksonville FL 32210 Office: Drawer B West Bay Sta Jacksonville FL 32203

DAVIS, JAMES EVANS, surgeon; b. Goldsboro, N.C., Mar. 2, 1918; s. Daniel Wilborn and Maude (Evans) D.; A.B., U. N.C., 1940; M.D., U. Pa., 1943; m. Margaret Royall, June 14, 1943; children—James Evans, Kenneth Royall, George Harrison. Intern and resident surgery New York Hosp.-Cornell U. Med. Center, N.Y.C., 1944-45, 46-51; practice of surgery in Durham, N.C., 1951-53, 54—; chief surg. service Watts Hosp.; attending staff Lincoln Hosp., Durham, Dorothea Dix Hosp., Raleigh, N.C.; asso. prof. surgery U. N.C. Med. Sch., Duke U. Med. Sch. Served as lt. comdr. USNR, 1945-46, 53-54. Diplomat Am. Bd. Surgery. Fellow A.C.S. (past pres. N.C. chpt.); mem. So. Surg. Assn., So. Soc. Clin. Surgeons, Southeastern Surg. Congress, A.M.A., So. Med. Assn., N.C. Med. Soc. (speaker ho. dels.), N.C. Surg. Assn. (past pres.), Alpha Tau Omega, Phi Chi. Episcopalian. Kiwanian. Home: 7 Beverly Dr Durham NC 27707 Office: 1200 Broad St Durham NC 27705

DAVIS, JAMES FRANKLIN, govt. ofcl.; b. Ft. Wayne, Ind., Aug. 11, 1934; s. John Forrest and Lucrece (Shoemaker) D.; B.S. in Chem. Engring. with honors, U. Ill., 1957; J.D., Georgetown U., 1963; m. Mary Karen Biddle, Dec. 29, 1957; children—John Montgomery, Mary Melinda, Jennifer Susan. Admitted to Ill. and D.C. bars, 1964; examiner U.S. Patent Office, 1961-62; patent atty. firm Wenderoth, Lind & Ponack, Washington, 1962-63; law clk. to Judge Rich, U.S. Ct. Customs and Patent Appeals, 1963-64; patent atty. firm Bair, Freeman & Molinare, Chgo., 1964-66; commr. U.S. Ct. of Claims, 1966—; instr. chemistry U.S. Naval Acad., 1959-61; adj. prof. law Georgetown U. Law Sch., 1966-68. Served with USNR, 1957-59; lt. comdr. Res. Mem. Am. Bar Assn., Am. Patent Law Assn., Phi Lambda Upsilon, Theta Chi. Home: 8000 Hampden Lane Bethesda MD 20014 Office: 717 Madison Pl Washington DC 20005

DAVIS, JAMES VERLIN, univ. dean; b. De Kalb, Ill., Dec. 14, 1935; s. Verl James and Esther Jane (Thomas) D.; B.A., Wabash Coll., 1957; M.A., Vanderbilt U., 1963; Ph.D. (Research scholar), Cornell U., 1967; m. Bessie Anita Taylor, June 10, 1961; children—Elizabeth

Lee, Jonathan James, Amy Lynn. Systems analyst Prudential Ins. Co., Chgo., 1957-58, 60-61; financial analyst Ford Motor Co., Dearborn, Mich., 1963-64; asso. dean Grad. Sch. Mgmt., Vanderbilt U., 1967—. Trustee, treas. Nashville Child Center, Inc. Served with AUS, 1958-60. Recipient Madison Saratt Prize for excellence in undergrad. teaching Vanderbilt U., 1969. Ford Found. fellow, 1964-66. Mem. Am. Econ. Assn., Am., Western, So. finance assns. Club: University (dir. 1970—) (Nashville). Home: 519 Colice Jeanne Rd Nashville TN 37221

DAVIS, JAMES WILFRED, editor, publisher; b. Knoxville, Ia., June 15, 1934; s. Wilfred W. and Ethel (Shutter) D.; student Gen. Motors Inst., Flint, Mich., 1951-52; m. Georgia Elizabeth Baggett, June 17, 1955 (div. Jan. 1968); children—Linda Diane, Robin Teresa, John Douglas; m. 2d, Sue Jenkins, Aug. 9, 1968. Mech. designer United Design Service, Arlington, Va., 1954-64; partner Eastern Pub. Co., 1964-69; owner Jim Davis Prodns., Arlington, Va., 1969—. Clubs: Nat. Potomac Yacht (gov.); Tantallon Yacht (charter mem.). Home: 1600 S Eads St Arlington VA 22202 Office: 1911 Jefferson Davis Hwy Arlington VA 22202

DAVIS, JEFFERSON, lawyer, utilities exec.; b. Indianola, Miss., July 3, 1909; s. Sidney F. and Florence L. (Heard) D.; A.B., Southwestern U., 1931; LL.B., Cumberland U., Lebanon, Tenn., 1932; m. M. Jerdone Kimbrough, Apr. 28, 1934; children—Jefferson, A. Kimbrough, M. Jerdone. Admitted to Miss. bar, 1932, Ga. bar, 1947; gen. practice law, Indianola, 1932-41; asst. atty. gen. of Miss., 1941-46; exec. asst., legal adviser to gov. of Miss., 1946-47; atty. So. Bell Tel. & Tel. Co., Atlanta, 1947-49, gen. atty., 1949-52, gen. solicitor, 1952-56, gen. counsel, 1956—, v.p., 1961—. Dir. Nat. Bank Georgia. Bd. dirs. YMCA Met. Atlanta, pres., 1964-68; v.p. So. Area Council of YMCAs, 1966—; bd. dirs. Nat. Council YMCAs; mem. adv. bd. Cumberland Sch. Law of Sanford U. Served with USNR, World War II. Mem. Am., Miss., Ga., Atlanta bar assns., Am. Law Inst., Alpha Tau Omega, Omicron Delta Kappa. Presbyn. (elder). Democrat. Mason (32 deg., K.T.). Clubs: Lawyers, Commerce, Capital City (Atlanta). Home: 3651 Rembrandt Rd NW Atlanta GA 30327 Office: Hurt Bldg Atlanta GA 30303

DAVIS, JEFFERSON LEE, judge; b. Cartersville, Ga., Aug. 28, 1912; s. William Robert and Deborrah (Hobgood) D.; student Ga. Inst. Tech., 1930-31; LL.B., Atlanta Law Sch., 1943; postgrad. Nat. Coll. State Trial Judges, U. Nev., 1969; m. Eloine Greene, Apr. 1, 1942; children—Ronald L., Jefferson Lee, Sarah Grace. Admitted to Ga. bar, 1943; practiced in Cartersville, 1943-58; judge Superior Cts. Cherokee Jud. Circuit, Cartersville, 1958—. Pres., First Ga. Financial Corp., Johnson-Davis Co.; sec. Gurvis Corp.; exec. v.p., dir. Bartow County Savs. & Loan Assn. Chmn., Cartersville Bd. Edn., 1954-57. Mem. Ga. Ho. of Reps., 1947-51; Senate, 1955-56. Mem. Ga. Bar Assn. (past bd. govs.), Demosthenian Lit. Soc., Gridiron Secret Soc. Episcopalian. Mason (Shriner), Lion. Home: Old Alabama Rd Cartersville GA 30120 Office: Savs & Loan Bldg Cartersville GA 30120

DAVIS, JESSE DUNBAR, lawyer; b. Burden, Kan., June 19, 1908; s. Jesse Bowman and Hazel (Dunbar) D.; student U. Okla., 1926-28; LL.B., U. Tulsa, 1944; m. Frances Lou Vinson, June 19, 1929; children—Sydney (Mrs. William Albert Russell, Jr.), Brett Vinson. Asst. mgr. Long-Bell Lumber Co., Muskogee, Okla., 1928-32, gen. mgr., Tulsa, 1933-48, div. mgr., Kansas City, Mo., 1949-57; admitted to Okla. bar, 1944, U.S. Supreme Ct. bar, 1950, Mo. bar, 1959, Fed. bar, 1963; v.p., dir. Tamko Asphalt Products, Inc., Joplin, Mo., 1958-59; gen. counsel Southwestern Lumberman's Assn., Kansas City, Mo., 1960-65, corporate sec., 1962-65; gen. practice law, Kansas City, Mo., Tulsa, 1960—; mgmt. cons., Tulsa, 1965—; realtor, Tulsa, Columnist, Retail Lumberman Mag., 1962-65; cons. industry Sch. Forestry, U. Mo., 1962-65; tchr. bus. law U. Mo., 1946-65; tchr. real estate law U. Tulsa, 1969—; v.p., dir., asso. editor Retail Lumberman Pub. Co., Kansas City, 1962-65. Served to lt. USNR, 1944-46. Recipient Civic award Tulsa YMCA, 1946-47. Mem. Am. Judicature Soc., Lawyers Assn. Kansas City, Tulsa Bd. Realtors (dir. 1970-71, corporate sec. 1972), Tulsa C. of C. (Civic award 1939), Res. Officers Assn. U.S., Claremore C. of C. (dir. 1972—), Am., Tulsa County, Rogers County, Kansas City bar assns., S.A.R., U.S. Navy League, Phi Delta Theta, Phi Beta Gamma. Clubs: University (charter mem.), Kiwanis (sec.-treas. Tex.-Okla. dist. 1942). Home: 3231 S Utica Av Tulsa OK 74105 Office: 3233 S Utica Av Tulsa OK 74105

DAVIS, JESSE EDWIN, JR., wood products exec.; b. Atlanta, Feb. 4, 1910; s. Jesse Edwin and Eufa (Swilling) D.; B.S., Ga. Sch. Tech., 1931; LL.B., Woodrow Wilson Coll., 1937; m. Sarah Etta Fitzpatrick, Apr. 7, 1938; children—Carolyn W. (Mrs. Edward W. Riser), Sarah K. (Mrs. M. Rick Taylor), Jesse Edwin III, Marion H. Admitted to Ga. bar, 1937; sales rep. Atlantic Steel Co., 1937-43, Tidewater Supply Co., 1943-49; v.p., treas. Thackston-Davis Supply, 1949-59; with Marwin Co., Columbia, S.C., 1959—, pres., treas., 1959—; pres., dir. Russell-Davis Devel. Corp., 1965— (all Columbia). Chmn. religious work com. Columbia YMCA, 1956—, also bd. dirs. Trustee, United Community Services. Mem. Columbia Com. of 100, Sigma Chi, Alpha Kappa Psi, Pi Delta Epsilon. Baptist (deacon). Mason (Shriner), Lion. Home: 4829 Carter Hill Rd Columbia SC 29206 Office: PO Box 9126 Atlas Rd Columbia SC 29209

DAVIS, JOE WALTER, ch. ofcl.; b. Hobart, Okla., Aug. 11, 1913; s. Lee and Willie (Stewart) D.; B.S., Southwestern U., 1935; B.C.S., Benjamin Franklin U., Washington, 1942; m. Ethel Lois Wiemers, Apr. 24, 1937; children—Edith Marie (Mrs. Alan W. Loveland), Eugene Stewart, George Edward, Mary Ellen (Mrs. Phillip H. Arnold), Elizabeth Ann. Identification officer FBI, Washington, 1937-42, spl. agt., 1942-44; auditor Southwestern U., 1944-54; treas., bus. mgr., div. television, radio and film communication Program Council, United Meth. Ch., 1954—. Past mem. bd. mgrs., bus. finance com. of broadcasting and film commn. Nat. Council Chs. Sch., bd. sec., Georgetown, Tex., 1951-54. Home: 210 Emery Dr Nashville TN 37214 Office: 1525 McGavock St Nashville TN 37203

DAVIS, JOHN EMERSON, educator; b. Detroit, Jan. 1, 1907; s. Emerson and Marion (Biegler) D.; A.B., Oberlin Coll., 1930; M.S., U. Mich., 1931; Ph.D., U. Chgo., 1936; m. Unni Dorothea Haerem, Sept. 2, 1935; 1dau., Barbara Jean. Instr. physiology Med. Coll. Va., 1935-37; instr. U. Ala., 1937-38; asst. prof. pharmacology U. Vt., 1938-42; asso. prof., prof. U. Ark., 1942-51; prof. U. Tex., Austin, 1952—. Sec. staff U. Ark. Med. Sch. Hosp., 1951. Mem. Pharmacology and Endocrinology Fellowships Rev. Panel, NIH, 1960-64. Fellow Am. Coll. Angiology, A.A.A.S., Am. Coll. Cardiology; mem. Am. Heart Assn. (council on basic scis.), Am. Physiol. Soc., Am. Soc. Pharmacology and Exptl. Therapeutics, Soc. Exptl. Biology and Medicine, N.Y. Acad. Scis., Western Pharmacology Soc. Contbr. articles to med. jours. Home: 1413 Larkwood Dr Austin TX 78723

DAVIS, JOHN GRIFFITH, assn. exec.; b. Frostburg, Md., Sept. 13, 1933; s. John Gerard and Virginia (Griffith) D.; student Frostburg State Coll., 1951-53; B.A., George Washington U., 1956; m. Mildred Eliose Ward, Apr. 8, 1956; children—Stephen Robert, Scott Richard, John William. Sports reporter Washington Post, 1954-61; pub. relations asst. Nat. Assn. Real Estate Bds., Washington, 1961-62; asst. exec. v.p. Soc. Indsl. Realtors, Washington, 1962—. Served with AUS, 1957-59. Mem. Nat. Press Club, Pub. Relations Soc. Am. Republican. Mem. United Ch. Christ (elder). Home: 7306 Statecrest Dr Annandale VA 22003 Office: 1300 Connecticut Av NW Washington DC 20036

DAVIS, JOHN STAIGE, IV, educator; b. N.Y.C., Oct. 28, 1931; s. John Staige and Camilla (Cole) D.; grad. Deerfield Acad., 1949; B.A., Yale, 1953; M.D., U. Pa., 1957; m. Frederica R. Abbott, June 22, 1956; children—Susan, John, Stewart, Frederica, Rufus. Intern Hosp. U. Pa., 1957-58; asst. resident in medicine U.Va., 1958-60, fellow rheumatology, 1960-61; mem. faculty Sch. Medicine, U. Va., Charlottesville, 1961—, asst. prof. internal medicine, 1964-67, asso. prof., 1967-72, prof., 1972—, chief div. rheumatology, 1967—, pres. clin. staff, 1970-71; vis. investigator Chair of Immunology, U. Milan (Italy), 1966-67. Mem. Charlottesville Republican Com., 1969—. Markle scholar, 1964-69; Arthritis Found. sr. investigator, 1964-69. Fellow A.C.P.; mem. A.M.A., Am. Fedn. Clin. Research, Am. Assn. Immunologists, Albemarle, Va. med. socs., Sigma Xi, Nu Sigma Nu. Clubs: Farmington Country, Colonnade (Charlottesville). Home: 325 Kent Rd Charlottesville VA 22903 Office: Sch Medicine U Va Charlottesville VA 22901

DAVIS, JOHN WILLIAM, congressman; b. Rome, Ga., Sept. 12, 1916; s. John Camp and Era (DeLay) D,; A.B., U. Ga., 1937, LL.B., 1939; m. Vivian Hawkins, Feb. 6, 1944 (dec.); children—Katherine DeLay (Mrs. Lloyd Mewbourne), John William, Mary Ellen; m. 2d, Bridget O'Sullivan Chrisman, June 26, 1971; stepchildren—Norman Chrisman, Paul Chrisman. Admitted to Ga. bar, 1939; practice in Rome, 1939-42, Summerville, 1946-55; solicitor gen. Rome Circuit, 1950-53; judge Lookout Mountain Jud. Circuit, 1950-53; judge Lookout Mountain Jud. Circuit, 1955-60; mem. 87th-92d congresses 7th Dist. Ga. Served with AUS, World War II. Democrat. Mason, Lion. Home: 100 Espy St Summerville GA 30747 Office: House Office Bldg Washington DC 10025

DAVIS, JOHN WILLIAM, educator; b. Clendenin, W.Va., July 15, 1925; s. Benjamin H. and Grace Louise (Counts) D.; A.B., W.Va. U., 1950; postgrad. Ohio State U., 1950-51, 54-55; Ph.D., Emory U., 1957; children—Nancy, Amy, Paul. Salesman, John J. Getreu & Son, Columbus, O., 1951; v.p., sales mgr. Continental Distbg. Co., Columbus, 1952-55; timekeeper N. Am. Aviation, Inc., Columbus, 1954-55; asst. prof. philosophy U. Tenn. at Knoxville, 1957-64, asso. prof., 1964-66, prof., 1966—, head dept., 1966. Bd. dirs. Found. for Creative philosophy. Served with AUS, 1945-46. Mem. Am. Philos. Assn., Am. Soc. for Value Inquiry (pres. 1970-72), So. Soc. Philosophy and Psychology (mem. council 1971-72), Sigma Chi. Club: Optimist (Knoxville). Home: 6201 Apache Trail Knoxville TN 37920

DAVIS, JOSEPH SOLOMON, coll. adminstr.; b. Macon, Ga., Apr. 8, 1938; s. Oscar Lee and Alice Mae (Lucas) D.; B.S., Tuskegee Inst., 1960, M.Ed., 1968; m. Sarah Frances Striggles, July 28, 1962; children—Joan Yvette, Oscar Wendall. Tchr., counselor Boggs Acad., Keysville, Ga., 1961-67; dir. financial aid Stillman Coll., Tuscaloosa, Ala., 1967—. Fellow Assn. Colls. and Secondary Schs., 1967. Home: 8 Oak Ridge Tuscaloosa AL 35401 Office: Stillman College Tuscaloosa AL 35401

DAVIS, JUNIUS AYERS, research psychologist; b. Raleigh, N.C., Feb. 4, 1925; s. Roy and Vivian (Johnson) D.; A.B., U. N.C., 1946; A.M. Columbia, 1950; Ph.D., 1956; m. Pegge Jill Morris, Nov. 9, 1946; children—Michael Ayers, Christopher Morris, Cynthia Jill. Control buyer Sears Roebuck, Greensboro, N.C., 1946-48; asst. dir. counseling service Princeton, 1952-54; asst. prof. psychology Emory U., 1954-57; dir. testing and guidance bd. regents Univ. Systems, Ga., 1957-58; grad. dean U. N.C., Greensboro, 1958-61; research psychologist Ednl. Testing Service, Princeton, N.J., 1961-67; dir. southeastern office Ednl. Testing Service, Durham, N.C., 1967—. Adj. prof. edn., lectr. psychology Duke, 1968—; lectr. edn. U. N.C. at Chapel Hill, 1970—. Served from ensign to lt. (j.g.), USNR, 1942-46, 48-49. Mem. Am. Psychol. Assn., Am. Personnel and Guidance Assn., Am. Ednl. Research Assn., Assn. for Instl. Research, Sigma Xi, Phi Delta Kappa, Kappa Delta Pi. Presbyn. (ruling elder 1964-67). Home: 405 Holly Lane Chapel Hill NC 27514 Office: 501 Willard St Durham NC 27701

DAVIS, LAMBERT, editor; b. Lynchburg, Va., June 1, 1905; s. Horatio Minor and Lottie Suydam (Lambert) D.; student Ga. Sch. Tech., 1921-22; A.B., U. Va., 1925, A.M., 1926; m. Isabella Winston Symmers, June 24, 1933; children—Charlotte Lambert (Mrs. Montgomery Furth), Martha Winston (Mrs. Basil King), William Minor. Mem. editorial staff Street, Smith and Doubleday, Doran and Co., 1926-28; mng. editor Va. Quar. Review, 1928-33, editor, 1933-38; N.Y. editor Bobbs-Merrill Co., 1938-40; editor Harcourt, Brace and Co., 1940-48; dir. U. N.C. Press, 1948-70; acting dir. East-West Center Press, 1971—. Exec. com. Assn. Am. U. Presses, 1954-58, pres., 1955-57; exec. com. N.C. Tercentenary Commn., 1959-61. Mem. Raven Soc., Phi Beta Kappa, Phi Kappa Sigma. Democrat. Episcopalian. Club: Colonnade. Home: Greenwood Rd Chapel Hill NC 27514

DAVIS, LAWRENCE ARNETTE, coll. pres.; b. McCrory, Ark., July 4, 1914; s. Virgil and Pawnee (Willimas) D.; A.B., Agrl., mech. and Normal Coll., Pine Bluff, Ark., 1937; A.M., U. Kan., 1941; grad. study, N.Y. U.; Ph.D., U. Ark., LL.D., Lane Coll., 1948, Morehouse Coll., 1950; m. 1936; children—Lawrence Arnette, Larnell Wilkerson, Ronald Laval; m. 2d, Rachel Lorraine Johnson, October 4, 1946; children—Sharon, Michael, Gail and Janice. Registrar and asst. to pres. of Mech. Coll. now Agrl. Tech. and Normal Coll. Pine Bluff, Ark., 1939-42, dean adminstr., 1941-43, acting pres., 1942-43, pres., 1943—. Mem. Com. on Action to Improve Conditions of Farm Laborers, etc., U. Chgo., 1946. Recipient Certificate of Merit from Chgo. Defender. Mem. Negro Land Grant Coll. Presidents Assn. (exec. com.), N.E.A., Am., Ark tchrs. assns., Nat. Council Tchrs., English Am. Assn. Sch. Adminstrs., Omega Psi Phi, Alpha Kappa Mu, Omega Psi Phi. Mason (33). Address: Agricultural and Mechanical College Pine Bluff AR 71601

DAVIS, LOUIS FREEMAN, petroleum co. exec.; b. Longview, Tex., May 5, 1914; s. Edward William and Bertha (Lee) D.; B.S. in Mech. Engring., U. Tex., 1934; postgrad. Tex. A. and M. Coll., 1935; m. Duskianne Few, Aug. 2, 1936; children—Fred Edward, Louis Freeman. With Atlantic Refining Co., 1935-66, v.p., gen. mgr. N. Am. producing dept., 1965-66; sr. v.p. N.Am. producing div. Atlantic Richfield Co., 1966-68, exec. v.p., 1968—, also dir.; pres., dir. Richfield Athabasca Petroleum Co., Hondo Oil & Gas Co.; chmn. bd., dir. Atlantic Richfield Canada, Ltd. Mem. engring. adv. bd. U. Tex. Mem. Am. Petroleum Inst., Soc. Petroleum Engrs., Mid-Continent Oil and Gas Assn., Dallas C. of C., Dallas Council World Affairs, Dallas Citizens Council. Methodist. Clubs: Petroleum, Brook Hollow, (Dallas); California (Los Angeles). Home: 7027 Desco Dr Dallas TX 75225 Office: PO Box 2819 Dallas TX 75221

DAVIS, M.J., judge. Judge Duval County (Fla.). Office: Duval County Court House Jacksonville FL 32202*

DAVIS, MARGUERITE, news editor; b. Huntington, W. Va.; d. Eugene and Marguerite (Saunders) Davis; student Lausanne Sch. Girls, Memphis, Gulf Park Coll., Gulfport, Miss., Sophie Newcomb Coll., New Orleans. Joined U.P.I., Madison, Wis., 1943, mgr. Lincoln (Neb.) bur., 1945, mgr. Chgo. radio bur., 1951, mgr. combined Chgo. radio and news depts., 1955-59, corr., Washington, 1959—. Mem. Kappa Kappa Gamma. Club: Women's Nat. Press (Washington). Home: 2475 Virginia Av NW Washington DC 20037 Office: Nat Press Bldg Washington DC 20004

DAVIS, MARK, leasing co. exec.; b. Asheville, N.C., Aug. 25, 1913; s. Jay Palm and Bessie Lee (Menius) D.; B.S., Appalachian State U., 1934; m. Rae Smith, July 4, 1938; children—Mark, Lawrence Eugene. Sec.-treas., gen. mgr. Rutherfordton (N.C.) Credit Assn., 1935; sec.-treas., gen. mgr. Statesville (N.C.) Prodn. Credit Assn., 1936-42; Statesville Nat. Farm Loan Assn., 1943-49; pres. Coast Truckways, Inc., Hickory, N.C., 1949-63; owner Mark Davis Trucking Co., 1961; comptroller DeHart Motor Lines, Inc., Conover, N.C., 1963-70; chief exec. officer, chmn. bd. Equitable Leasing Corp., Asheville, 1969—; dir. Pextile, Inc., Stoneville, N.C. Mem. Appalachian State U. Found., Boone, N.C., 1970—, gowth and devel. com. Appalachian State U., 1969—, adv. council Coll. Bus., 1970—. Mem. Hickory Regional Planning Commn., 1966—. Presbyn. (deacon). Club: Lake Hickory Country. Home: 431 9th St NW Hickory NC 28601 Office: Northwestern Bank Bldg Asheville NC 28802

DAVIS, MARK VINCENT, mfg. co. exec.; b. Wabash, Ind., Aug. 26, 1913; s. Joseph A. and Edna (Firth) D.; student U. Toledo, 1931-32; m. Josephine DeVaux Hissong, Dec. 29, 1934; children—Judy Jo (Mrs. John David Rainey), Mark Vincent Jr. Mem. staff stores dept. Libbey-Owens-Ford Glass Co., Toledo, O., 1935-43; mgr. Charles R. Baum Constrn. Co., Houston, 1946-50; operations mgr., div. mgr. Ada Oil Co., Houston, 1950-59; pres. Marand Sales Co. Inc., Houston, 1959-70, dir., 1959—; pres. Jet Mfg. Co. Inc., Houston, 1964—, also dir. Served with AUS, 1943-45; ETO. Mem. Petroleum Equipment Inst., Houston C. of C., Houston Power Squadron. Roman Catholic. K.C. Home: 12343 Rip Van Winkle Dr Houston TX 77024 Office: 5611 Clinton Dr Houston TX 77001

DAVIS, MATTIE BELLE EDWARDS, county judge; b. Ellabell, Ga., Feb. 28, 1910; d. Frank Pierce and Eddie (Morgan) Edwards; student law in law office; m. Troy Carson Davis, June 6, 1937 (dec. Aug. 1948); stepchildren—Jane (Mrs. Cordie L. Pearson, Jr.), Betsy (Mrs. James W. Clark, Jr.). Legal sec., 1927-36; admitted to Fla. bar, 1936, U.S. Supreme Ct. bar, 1950; practice with husband in Miami, 1936-48; pvt. practice, Miami, 1948-59; judge Met. Ct. Dade County, Fla., 1959—. Exec. com. Women's Conf. Nat. Safety Council, 1960—, chmn., 1968-70; bd. dirs. Nat. Safety Council, 1965-71; mem. Nat. Hwy. Safety Adv. Com., 1967-70, Gov.'s Hwy Safety Commn., 1971—; mem. registrants adv. bd. SSS. World War II; pres. Dade County Tb Assn., 1960-62; exec. com. Fla. Tb and Respiratory Disease Assn., 1960-66; pres. Haven Sch. Mentally Retarded, 1958-60, sec., 1960-69. Trustee Andrew Coll., Cuthbert, Ga. Fellow Am. Bar Found.; mem. Nat. (treas. 1961-62, corr. sec. 1962-63, v.p. 1963-64, pres. 1965-66), Fla. (pres. 1957-58) assns. women lawyers, Am. (ho. dels. 1967—), Dade County bar assns., Fla. Bar, Internat. Fedn. Women Lawyers, Miami Bus. and Profl. Women's Club (pres. 1952-54), Nat. Fedn. Bus. and Profl. Women's Clubs (dir. dist. Fla. 1956-57). Kappa Beta Pi. Democrat. Methodist (supt. Sunday sch. 1948-54, chmn. ofcl. bd. 1957-60, trustee 1952-67, ofcl. bd. 1968—). Club: Zonta. Home: 402 Como Av Coral Gables FL 33146 Office: 1351 NW 12th St Miami FL 33215

DAVIS, N. KNOWLES, public utility cons.; b. Atlanta, Feb. 20, 1904; s. Archibald H. and Susan (Topliff) D.; B.S., Ga. Inst. Tech., 1925; E.E., Cornell U., 1926; m. Jean Nutting, June 21, 1932; 1 dau., Jean (Mrs. Daniel Fort Flowers). Transmission engr. Ga. Power Co., Atlanta, 1926-32; chief engr. Ga. Pub. Service Commn., 1933-41, dir. utilities div., 1945-55; chief power allocation WPB, Washington, 1942-44; dir. rates Tenn. Gas Transmission Co., Houston, 1956-58, v.p., 1959-67, sr. v.p., asst. to pres., 1967-69; pub. utility cons., Houston, 1969—. Guest lectr. Ia. State U., 1963, 72, Am. Law Inst., 1954, 67. Bd. dirs. Epilepsy Fedn. Am. Mem. Nat., Tex. socs. profl. engrs., Am., Fed. Power, Ga. bar assns., Am., So. gas assns., Am. Judicature Soc., Chi Psi. Presbyn. Rotarian. Home: 3420 Overbrook Lane Houston TX 77027 Office: 1932 Chamber of Commerce Bldg Houston TX 77002

DAVIS, NANCY BRAWLEY HOWARD (MRS. BENJAMIN CUMMINGS DAVIS), librarian; b. Mooresville, N.C., Dec. 9, 1910; d. Henry North and Jessie Anna (Brawley) Howard; A.B. in L.S., Woman's Coll., U. N.C., 1931; m. Benjamin Cummings Davis, Mar. 29, 1936; children—Nancy Elizabeth (Mrs. Francis Michael Fennegan), John Allen. Library asst. Woman's coll. U. N.C., Greensboro, 1927-31; librarian, also tchr. Taylorsville (N.C.) City Schs., 1933-35; librarian Hugh Morson High Sch., Raleigh, N.C., 1935-36; supr. WPA Library Project, Mecklenburg and Stanley counties, N.C., 1937-38; librarian Harding High Sch., Charlotte, N.C., 1938-40, 49-55; librarian Southern Pines (N.C.) Sch., 1942-43; children's librarian Greensboro Pub. Library, 1943-44; librarian Mooresville (N.C.) High Sch., 1944-46; librarian elementary schs., Charlotte, 1947-49; tchr. Mooresville Jr. High Sch., 1955-57; librarian Iredell County Pub. Library, Statesville, N.C., 1957-59; reference, circulation librarian Davidson (N.C.) Coll. Library, 1959-60; librarian Kenly Sch., Tampa, Fla., 1960-61, John McKnitt Alexander Jr. High Sch., Huntersville, N.C., 1961—. Ednl. chmn. Iredell County Cancer Soc., Statesville, 1958-60; chmn. Mooresville Community Achievement Program, 1961-62. Bd. dirs. Mooresville Community Fund, 1958-60. Mem. Am., N.C., Charlotte-Mecklenberg library assns., N.E.A., N.C., Charlotte-Mecklenburg edn. assns., Iredell County Friends of the Library (chmn. membership com.). Democrat. Presbyn. (ch. librarian). Club: Mooresville Woman's (pres. 1958-60). Specializes in organizing and reorganizing sch. and community libraries. Home: 313 W McLelland Av Mooresville NC 28115 Office: Route 1 Huntersville NC 28078

DAVIS, NOLRA EARL, pub. health engr.; b. Rotan, Tex.,Feb. 25, 1908; s. Arlon Barton and Cora (Alves) D.; student U. Tex., 1924-27; m. Elizabeth Mary Brogger, Aug. 16, 1934; 1 son, Carl Francis. With City of San Antonio Engring. Dept., 1928-30, chemist, asst. supt. wastewater works, 1930-41; dist. engr. Tex. San. Engring. Dept., 1941-56; chief engr. water pollution control div. Tex. Health Dept., Austin, 1956—. Registered profl. engr., Tex. Mem. Tex. Water Utilities Assn., Nat., Tex. socs. profl. engrs., Tex. Pub. Health Assn., U.S.-Mexico Border Pub. Health Assn., Herman Sons of Tex. Roman Catholic. Author: (with D.F. Smallhorst) Manual for Sewage Plant Operators, 1969; Manual of Wastewater Operations, 1971. Contbr. articles to profl. jours. Home: 1707 Virginia Av Austin TX 78704 Office: 1100 W 49th St Austin TX 78756

DAVIS, OSCAR HIRSH, U.S. judge; b. N.Y.C., Feb. 27, 1914; s. Jacob and Minnie (Robison) D.; A.B., Harvard, 1934; LL.B., Columbia, 1937. Admitted to N.Y. bar, 1938; pvt. practice, N.Y.C., 1937-39; with Dept. Justice, 1939-42, 46-62; first asst. to solicitor gen., 1954-62; asso. judge U.S. Ct. Claims, 1962—. Served to capt. USAAF, 1942-46. Mem. Am., Fed., N.Y. State bar assns., Am. Law

Inst., N.Y. County Lawyers Assn. Home: 1101 3d St SW Washington DC 20024 Office: US Ct Claims Washington DC 20005

DAVIS, PAUL P., motor freight co. exec.; b. Goldsboro, N.C., Aug. 21, 1915; s. John Samuel and Mary (Porter) D.; B.S., U. N.C., 1935; m. Margaret Mebane, June 12, 1937; children—Paul Michael and Allen Mebane (twins), John Kent. With McLean Trucking Co., Winston-Salem, N.C., 1943—, v.p. sales, dir., 1948-55, pres., dir., 1955-61, pres., chmn. exec. com., dir., 1961-70, chmn. bd., chief exec. officer, dir., chmn. exec. com., 1970—; dir., mem. exec. com. Transport Mgmt. Co., Dallas, 1970—; Transport Ins. Co., Dallas; dir. N.C. Nat. Bank, Winston-Salem. Pres. So. Motor Carriers Rate Conf. Mem. Am. Trucking Assn. (v.p. at large), Am. Soc. Traffic and Transp. (founding mem.), Trucking Employers, Inc. (dir.), Traffic Club Winston-Salem. Elk. Clubs: Twin City, Oldtown Country (Winston-Salem). Home: 1055 Kent Rd Winston-Salem NC 27104 Office: PO Box 213 Winston-Salem NC 27102

DAVIS, RALPH, state ofcl.; b. Lakeland, Fla.; grad. Journalism U. Fla.; m. Lollie Phillips; children—Mrs. Tom Burt, Mrs. James L. Ferman. Formerly reporter Polk County Reporter, Lakeland Ledger, Tampa Tribune; joined banking dept. Fla. Treas.'s office, 1935-37, head Cabinet Affairs Div., 1967-70; dep. ins. commr. State of Fla., 1937-41; exec. sec. to Senator Spessard L. Holland of Fla., 1941, exec. sec., adminstrv. asst., 1949-55; exec. dir. Fla. State Rd. Dept., 1955-67; now exec. dir. Fla. Dept. Hwy. Safety and Motor Vehicles. Served with AUS, World War II. Mem. Blue Key, Sigma Delta Chi, Omicron Delta Kappa, Pi Delta Epsilon, Alpha Tau Omega. Baptist. Kiwanian. Address: Neil Kirkman Bldg Tallahassee FL 32304

DAVIS, RAYMOND MAURICE, dentist; b. Hollis, Okla., July 21, 1906; s. James Hugh and Martha (Kennedy) D.; student West Tex. State Coll., 1927-30, Okla. State U., 1930; D.D.S., Baylor U., 1937; postgrad. U. Mich., 1941-42; m. Alice Langford, Nov. 12, 1938; 1 dau., Charlotte Ovada. Dir. dental health Tarrant County Unit, Ft. Worth, 1938-40; health edn. cons., asst. dir. dental health Tex. Health Dept., Austin, 1946; practice periodontics, El Paso, 1946-53, 66—, Roswell, N.M., 1953-66. Cons. periodontics Ft. Bayard (N.M.) VA Hosp., 1951—, Walker AFB Hosp., Roswell, 1961—. Mem. El Paso Bd. Health, 1950-53. Served to maj. AUS, 1942-46. Mem. Am., N.M. dental assns., Am., Western socs. peridontists, Western Soc. Periodontology, Acad. Internat. Dentistry, Pierre Fauchard Acad. Republican. Presbyn. Rotarian. Home: 81 Sutton Pl El Paso TX Office: Coronado Tower El Paso TX

DAVIS, ROBERT AUBREY, realtor; b. San Antonio, Nov. 2, 1932; s. Gordon Edwin and Audrey (Morehead) D.; B.A., U. Tex., 1957; postgrad. U. Tex. Sch. Law, 1957, Loyola U. Sch. Law, 1959, St. Louis U. Sch. Law, 1962-63; m. Gayle Bradford, Apr. 9, 1955; children—Robert Scott, Thomas Edwin, Debra Ann, Sandra Gayle. Landman, Standard Oil Ind., 1957-63, real estate rep., mgr., 1963-65; comml., indsl. real estate broker, Tex. and La., 1965—. Served to capt., AUS, 1951-53. Mem. Baton Rouge Bd. Raltors, Nat. Assn. Real Estate Bds., Nat. Inst. Real Estate Brokers (certified comml.-investment mem.). Methodist. Home: 12243 Warwick Av Baton Rouge LA 70815 Office: IBM Bldg I-12 and Sherwood Forest Blvd Baton Rouge LA 70816

DAVIS, ROBERT G., corp. exec.; b. Dallas, 1935; LL.B., St. Mary's U., 1959. Sec., Texstar Corp., Grand Prairie, Tex.; sec. A.R.A. Mfg. Co., Grand Prairie, Rajay Industries, Inc., Long Beach, Cal., Kreck Packing Co., Dallas, Quaker Oil Corp., St. Louis, Aztec Ceramics Co., San Antonio, AMXCO, Inc., Arlington, Tex. Home: 1122 Dumont St Richardson TX 75080 Office: PO Box 685 Grand Prairie TX 75050

DAVIS, ROSS DANE, govt. ofcl; b. Bklyn., Mar. 21, 1919; s. Abraham N. and Gertrude (Ross) D.; B.A., Brown U., 1941; LL.B., Columbia, 1947; m. Margaret Gould Roos, May 30, 1958. Admitted N.Y. bar, 1948, D.C. bar, 1968, also U.S. Supreme Ct.; asso. firm Davis & Heffner, N.Y.C., 1947-51; with U.S. Govt., 1951-69, exec. adminstr., then acting adminstr. Small Bus. Adminstrn., 1965-66, adminstr. Econ. Devel. Adminstrn., 1966, asst. sec. Econ. Devel. U.S. Dept. Commerce, 1966-69; dir. Center for Program Implementation, Nat. League Cities-U.S. Conf. Mayors, 1969—. Served to capt. AUS, 1942-46; PTO. Mem. Am., Fed. bar assns. Clubs: Nat. Capital Democratic, Nat. Lawyers, City Tavern Assn. (Washington). Author articles in field. Home: 3421 N St NW Washington DC 20007 Office: 1612 K St NW Washington DC 20006

DAVIS, RUFUS CELMORE, JR., physician; b. Waurika, Okla., Jan. 17, 1920; s. Rufus Celmore and Lou Nettie (Davis) D.; B.A., Daniel Baker Coll., 1941; M.D., U. Tex., 1950; m. Barbara Maud Cooze, Sept. 24, 1944; children—Natica, Cheryl, Brian. Gen. practice medicine Pasadena, Tex., 1951—; dir. Pasadena Bayshore Hosp. Served with USNR, 1942-45. Mem. A.M.A., Tex. Med. Assn., Harris County Med. Soc., Am. Acad. Gen. Practice. Mason. Home: 1014 Austin St Pasadena TX 77502 Office: 3901 Woodlawn St Pasadena TX 77504

DAVIS, RUSSELL LEWIS, lawyer, state ofcl.; b. Rocky Mount, Va., Mar. 8, 1903; s. Beverly A. and Mary (Gravely) D.; student Augusta Mil. Acad., 1919-20; student Roanoke Coll., 1920-23, U. Va., 1926; m. Winifred Skinnell, Oct. 8, 1933; children—Emily (Mrs. C. Dean Londos), Russell L., William G., Julia W., Katherine. Admitted to Va. bar, 1926; practiced in Rocky Mount, 1926—; mem. firms Davis, Davis, Davis & Raine; mem. Va. Ho. of Dels., 1966—. Dir. Peoples Nat. Bank, Rocky Mount. Mem. Va. State Bar Assn., Pi Kappa Phi, Phi Alpha Delta. Republican. Mason, Lion. Home: 116 Taliaferro St Rocky Mount VA 24151 Office: 113 E Court St Rocky Mount VA 24151

DAVIS, SAM W., judge. Dist. judge, Harris County (Tex.). Office: Civil Cts Bldg Houston TX 77002*

DAVIS, SAM WARREN, cons. engring. firm exec.; b. Doniphan, Mo., Apr. 20, 1902; s. Daniel H. and Emily Belle (Warren) D.; B.S. in Elec. Engring., Okla. State U., 1928; m. Marion Elizabeth White, Sept. 14, 1930; children—Warren Eugene, Stanley Kent, Jerry Marshall, Rebecca Ann (Mrs. Henry Martin Gibson). With Tex. Power & Light Co., Dallas, 1928-29, Cosden Oil Co., Big Spring, Tex., 1929-30; with Southwestern Pub. Service Co., Amarillo, 1930-48, div. engr., 1940-48; self employed elec. engr., contractor Panhandle Engrs. & Contractors (inc. 1971), Amarillo, 1948-66, partner, 1965-71, chmn. bd., treas., 1971—; sec.-treas., dir. Audio-Video Corp., Amarillo, 1959—. Mem. adv. bd. Salvation Army, 1968-71; bd. dirs. Amarillo Little Theater, 1970—; mem. Tex. N.G., 1941-45. Named Outstanding Young Man of Year Amarillo Jr. C. of C., 1941. Registered profl. engr., Tex., N.M., Okla. mem. I.E.E.E. (life mem.), Tex. Soc. Profl. Engrs. (chpt. pres. 1945-46), Kappa Alpha. Presbyn. (elder). Lion (Lion of Yr. award Downtown Amarillo Club 1971, bd. dirs. 1971-72). Club: Amarillo. Contbr. articles to publs. Home: 2611 Henning St Amarillo TX 79106 Office: PO Box 9194 Amarillo TX 79105

DAVIS, SAVILLE ROGERS, journalist; b. Watertown, Mass., Apr. 5, 1909; s. Francis Woodward and Esther (Saville) D.; A.B., Williams Coll., 1930; M.B.A., Harvard, 1932; m. Anita Pawolleck de Varon, Aug. 12, 1935; 1 dau., Julie Fee (Mrs. Jewett). Reporter Christian Science Monitor, Boston and N.Y.C., 1932-39, radio news writer, broadcaster, 1934-36, State Dept. corr., Washington, 1939, Mediterranean corr., Rome, Italy and Madrid, Spain, 1939-41, asst. to editor, 1941-45, chief London (Eng.) News Bur., roving corr. European Internat. confs., 1945-47, Am. news editor, 1947-57, mng. editor, 1957-61, chief editorial writer, 1961-64, White House corr., 1965-71, chief Washington news bur., 1965—; freelance journalist, 1971—; lectr., radio TV news analyst. Trustee Wheelock Coll., chmn., 1963-65; trustee Harvard Business Sch. Alumni Assn. (pres. 1960-61), Am. Acad. Arts and Scis., Internat. Inst. for Girls in Spain (pres. 1949-70), Phi Beta Kappa. Christian Scientist. Clubs: Nat. Press, Federal City (Washington); Harvard (Boston). Home: Winter St Lincoln Center MA 01773

DAVIS, SID, news corr.; b. Youngstown, O., Nov. 13, 1927; s. Morris and Hilda (Friedman) D.; B.S., Ohio U., 1952; m. Barbara J. Flint, July 21, 1960; children—Lawrence Jay, Morse Robert. News reporter sta WJEH, Gallipolis, O., 1950-51; news dir. Sta. WKBN, Youngstown, 1952-59; White House corr. Westinghouse Broadcasting Co., Washington, 1959-68, chief of Washington news bur., 1968—; producer Dialogue on Dallas, eyewitness account Kennedy assassination, 1963. Served with USNR, 1946-48; duty in U.S.S. Toledo, U.S.S. Astoria. Named Sigma Delta Chi Outstanding Journalism Grad., Ohio U., 1952. Mem. White House Corrs. Assn. Radio, TV News Dirs. Assn., Sigma Delta Chi, Omicron Delta Kappa, Tau Kappa Alpha. Clubs: National Press, Federal City (Washington). Covered Krushchev's tour U.S., 1959, U.S. space launchings, 1960-63, Kennedy tours abroad as pres., Johnson's travels as pres. One of three reporters to witness swearing in of Pres. Johnson in Dallas, polit. reporting of major nominating convs., campaigns and elections beginning in 1960, including extensive travel with all Presdl. candidates. Home: 7103 Annan Pl Bethesda MD 20034 Office: 1625 K St NW Washington DC 20006

DAVIS, SPENCER P., sch. supt.; b. Dide, La., Feb. 5, 1926; s. John Henry and Mary (Gibson) D.; B.S., Troy State U., 1950; M.Adminstrn., Fla. State U., 1961, postgrad., 1962-63; m. Lucy Virginia Martin, Feb. 27, 1948; children—Diane, Mary Frances (Mrs. Leonard Reynolds), Spencer Penny, John Lofton. Tchr. pub. schs., Evergreen, Ala., 1950-51, Dale County, Ozark, Ala., 1951-54; tchr. pub. schs., Bainbridge, Ga., 1954-66, asst. prin., 1962-66; prin. Bainbridge Jr. High Sch., 1966-70; supt. pub. schs. Americus, Ga., 1970—, Bd. dirs. Mix Found., Americus. Served with USCGR, 1943-46. Mem. N.E.A., Ga. Edn. Assn., Nat., Ga. assns. sch. adminstrs., Christian Businessmen's Com., Jr. C. of C. Baptist (deacon). Mason. Home: 207 Shirley Rd Americus GA 31709 Office: 101 W Lamar St Americus GA 31709

DAVIS, STAFFORD WINE, coll. adminstr.; b. Buffalo, Dec. 3, 1902; s. Vernon John and Arvilla W. (Stafford) D.; student Northwestern U., Chgo., 1932-36; m. Violet Lucille Grise, June 3, 1923; 1 son, Stafford Grise. Accountant, South Bend, Ind. and Chgo., 1922-47; partner Raymond S. Blunt & Co., C.P.A.'s, Chgo., 1947-65; controller Para-Tone, Inc., LaGrange, Ill., 1965-68; finance officer Fla. Keys Community Coll., Key West, 1968—. Trustee, treas. Fla. Keys Jr. Coll. Found. C.P.A., Ill. Mem. Am. Inst. C.P.A.'s, Fla. Assn. Pub. Jr. Colls. Home: 509B Key West Towers Key West FL 33040

DAVIS, SUSAN SCOTT (MRS. GAYLORD DAVIS), civic worker; b. Kearney, Neb.; d. Thomas Jefferson and Mary Estelle (Grant) Scott; A.B., U. Neb., 1918, Neb. State Tchrs. Coll., 1919; M.A., Columbia, 1935; m. Gaylord Davis, July 4, 1925; 1 dau., Susanne (Mrs. Daniel Oliver Newberry). Dir. tng. sch., dept. kindergarten Neb. State Tchrs. Coll., 1914-16; mem. casts plays in N.Y. theatres, 1921-23. Mem. Council Juvenile Planning Group, Asheville and Buncombe County, N.C., 1956-59; sec. exec. com. Buncombe County Com. 1960 White House Conf. Children and Youth; dir. Children's Welfare League, Asheville, N.C., 1949, 52, 60, pres., 1955-57; bd. dirs. Family and Children's Service Agy., Asheville, N.C., 1948-55, Asheville Community Concerts Assn., mem. Family and Children's Services Buncombe County Planning Council, 1967—. Bd. dirs. United Social Services, 1955-60, Candelight Concerts, Inc., 1960-63, Civic Arts, Inc., 1960-68; bd. dirs. Asheville Day Nursery, 1960-62, 68—, v.p., 1963-64, pres., 1964-66. Mem. Buncombe County Republican Women's Club, 1963—; mem. Women's Nat. Rep. Club, N.Y.C., 1963—, mem. nat. council, 1963—, mem. membership com., 1969—; mem. exec. com. permanent conf. Buncombe County Planning Council, 1965-70. Mem. English-Speaking Union, Ikebana Internat., Pi Beta Phi. Republican. Christian Scientist. Clubs: Biltmore Forest Country, The DueHers (founder 1947). Home: 12 Fairway Pl Biltmore Forest Asheville NC 28803

DAVIS, THOMAS HENRY, airline exec.; b. Winston-Salem, N.C., Mar. 15, 1918; s. Egbert L. and Annie (Shore) D.; student U. Ariz., 1935-39; m. Nancy Caroline Teague, Oct. 28, 1944; children—Thomas Henry, Winifred (Mrs. Alfredo Torres Bond), George Franklin, Nancy Caroline, Juliana. Aircraft salesman Piedmont Aviaton, Inc., Winston-Salem, 1940, v.p., treas., 1941-43, pres., treas., 1943—; dir., mem. exec. com. Wachovia Corp. Mem. Urban Redevel. Commn., 1955—. Trustee Wake Forest U. Recipient Winston-Salem and N.C. Jr. C. of C. Distinguished Service award, 1954, Frank Davison trophy for outstanding service to aviation in N.C., 1949. Mem. Air Transport Assn. (dir.), Nat. Aviation Club, Soaring Soc. Am., Newcomen Soc., Winston-Salem C. of C. (past pres.), Pi Kappa Alpha. Democrat. Baptist. Rotarian. Clubs: Forsyth Country, Old Town (Winston-Salem); Wings (N.Y.C.). Home: 1190 Arbor Rd Winston-Salem NC 27104 Office: Smith Reynolds Airport Winston-Salem NC 27102

DAVIS, THOMAS NED, physician; b. Sparta, Ga., Apr. 8, 1926; s. Charles Barney and Bernice (McConnell) D.; student Ga. Inst. Tech., 1943-44. West Ga. Coll., 1946-47; A.B., Emory U., 1949; M.D., Med. Coll. Ga., 1953; m. Margaret Steele Dendy, June 11, 1949; children—Thomas Ned, Margaret Dendy, William Steele. Intern Macon (Ga.) Hosp., 1953-54; gen. practice medicine, Irwinton, Ga., 1954—. Chmn. Wilkinson County Bd. Health, 1954-61. Chmn. Wilkinson County Bd. Edn., 1967—. Served with USNR, 1943-46. Mem. A.M.A., Ga. Med. Assn., Bibb County Med. Soc., Phi Chi. Baptist. Mason, Lion. Club: Wilco Touchdown (pres. 1962, 66, 67) (Irwinton). Address: Box 156 Irwinton GA 31042

DAVIS, TRUE, banker; b. St. Joseph, Mo., Dec. 23, 1919; s. William True and Helen (Marstella) D.; student Cornell U., 1937-40; L.H.D., Tarkio Coll., 1963; m. Virginia Bruce Motter, Jan. 24, 1948 (dec. Sept. 1969); children—William True, Bruce Motter, Lance Barrow. Salesman Anchor Serum Co., So. St. Joseph, 1940-42, v.p., sales mgr., 1945-50, pres., 1950-60; pres., dir. Research Labs., Inc., 1952-60, Pet's Best Co., 1954-60; v.p., dir. Phillips Electronics & Pharm. Industries Corp., N.Y.C., 1959-63; pres., dir. Philips-Roxane, Inc., N.Y.C., 1959-63, Med. Industries, Inc., 1956-63, True Davis Founds., Inc., 1955—, Carolina Vet Supply, Inc., Charlotte, N.C., 1956-60, Wilke Labs, Inc., West Plains, Mo., Wilke Labs of Tenn., Inc., Memphis, 1956-60, Peters Serum Co., Kansas City, 1956-60, Gothic Advt., Inc., St. Joseph, Mo., 1956-60, World Health Inst., Ltd., 1958-60, Peerless Serum Co., 1956-60, Certified Labs., Inc., 1958-60, Davis Estate, Inc., Anchor Serum Co. of N.J., 1959-60, Anchor Serum Co. of Ind., 1959-60, Anchor Serum Co. of Minn., 1960-63; chmn. Thompson-Hayward Chem. Co., Kansas City, Mo., 1961-63; chmn., dir. Chemico Labs., Inc., Miami, Fla., 1960-63; U.S. ambassador to Switzerland, 1963-65; asst. sec. U.S. Treasury, 1965-68; U.S. exec. dir. Inter-Am. Devel. Bank, 1966-68; chmn. bd., dir. Nat. Bank Washington, 1968—, pres., 1970—. Dir. Laurel (Md.) Race Course, 1970—; mem. adv. bd. Washington Mut. Investors Fund, 1971—. Bd. dirs. Animal Health Inst., 1946-59, pres., 1954-56; mem. Nat. Serum Control Agy., 1947-58, chmn. 1954-55; chmn. U.S. Port Security Com., 1966-68, N.Y. Pier Com., 1966-68, Pub. Adv. Com. on Customs Adminstrn., 1966-68; mem. exec. com. United Fund, 1960; mem. Adv. Council on Naval Affairs, 1958-60; pres. Met. Washington Urban Coalition, 1971—; chmn. Met. Washington Invest-in-Am. Council, 1970-71; mem. steering, nat. coms. Corcoran Gallery Art, 1970—, spl. commn. on urban renewal D.C. City Council, 1971—, D.C. Bicentennial Commn., 1971—. Police commr., St. Joseph, 1949; mem. Democratic Nat. Finance Council, 1970—. Bd. dirs. Little League, Nat. Assn. Boys Club Am., Children's Hosp. Washington, Washington div. Am. Health Found., Agrl. Hall Fame; trustee Mo. Valley Coll., Coll. Mt. St. Vincent's, Fleming Coll. and Inst. Fgn. Affairs, Switzerland; bd. dirs. Close-Up, D.C. chpt. A.R.C., World Information Found., Nat. Capital Area council Boy Scouts Am., Research Found. Washington Hosp. Center, Meridian House Found., Washington; trustee Fed. City Council, Washington Center for Met. Studies, D.C. chpt. Am. Cancer Soc., Downtown Progress Assn. D.C., Washington Bd. Trade; adv. bd. Md. Commn. on Dope Addiction. Served to lt. USNR, 1942-45. chief test pilot Naval Air Sta., Pearl Harbor; lt. col. staff Mo. Gov., 1949-54, 60—, Ky. Gov., 1953-54. Recipient Boss of Year award St. Joseph Jr. C. of C., 1960; Exceptional Service award U.S. Treasury, 1968. Hon. fellow Consular Law Soc.; mem. N.A.M. (nuclear energy com.), N.Y. Acad. of Scis., Res. City Bankers, Washington Drama Soc. (dir.), Am. Automobile Assn. (dir. St. Joseph), Good Roads Assn. (dir. Jefferson City), Ballet Soc. (dir.), Performing Arts Soc. (dir.), Am. Royal Assn. (gov. 1960), Mo. C. of C. (dir. 1963-64), UN Assn. (dir. capital area div.), Newcomen Soc., Mo. Soc. of N.Y., Nat. Thoroughbred Breeders Assn., Am. Legion, V.F.W. (mem. nat. Americanism com., Mo. chmn. Americanism com., outstanding citizen award St. Joseph 1960, Nat. Gold Medal for Americanism 1967), Council on Fgn. Relations, Res. Officers Assn. (hon. life), Am. Soc. for Friendship with Switzerland (hon. life), Mil. Order World Wars, 40 and 8, Phi Gamma Delta Elk. Clubs: Benton (pres. 1949-50), Country (St. Joseph); Keeneland, Thoroughbred of Am. (Lexington, Ky.); Marco Polo, N.Y. Athletic, Cornell (N.Y.C.); River (Kansas City, Mo.); Minnesouri Angling (pres. Alexandria, Minn.); Metropolitan, City Tavern, F Street (Washington); Brook (N.Y.C.). Author: Americanism vs. Communism, 1962; The Partnership Between the Federal Government and American Universities in Financing Scientific Enquiry, 1967. Contbr. articles to various trade and farm publs. Home: 2860 Woodland Dr NW Washington DC 20008 Office: 619 14th St NW PO Box 1537 Washington DC 20013

DAVIS, VINCENT, educator; b. Chattanooga, May 3, 1930; B.A., Vanderbilt U., 1952; M.P.A., Woodrow Wilson Sch. Pub. and Internat. Affairs Princeton, 1959, M.A., 1960, Ph.D., 1961; m.; 3 children. Mem. faculty dept. politics, research asst. Center Internat. Studies Princeton, 1959-61; mem. faculty Dartmouth, 1961-62; mem. faculty Grad. Sch. Internat. Studies, research asso. Social Sci. Found. U. Denver, 1962-71; Patterson Chair prof. internat. studies, dir. Patterson Sch. Diplomacy and Internat. Commerce U. Ky., Lexington, 1971—; Nimitz prof. polit. Sci. U.S. Naval War Coll., 1970-71; cons., lectr. in field. Served with Armed Forces, 1952-56. Mem. Internat. Studies Assn. (exec. dir. 1964-71), Am. Polit. Sci. Assn., Am. Assn. U. Profs., A.A.A.S. Author: Postwar Defense Policy and the U.S. Navy, 1943-46, 1966; The Admirals Lobby, 1967; The Politics of Innovation, 1967; The Analysis of International Politics, 1971, also monographs, spl. reports. Editor Sage Profl. Papers in Internat. Studies. Contbr. articles to profl. jours. Address: Patterson Sch Diplomacy and Internat Commerce U Ky Lexington KY 40506

DAVIS, WADE HALL, educator; b. Fullerton, La., Sept. 17, 1920; s. John Francis and Ellen Jane (Hall) D.; B.A., N.W. La. State Coll., 1941; M.A., George Peabody Coll. Tchrs., 1948, Ed.S., 1955; m. Bunah Mae Bass, May 26, 1941; children—Janice Lynn, Sharon Gay, Wade Hall. Asst. prin. Brame Grammar Sch., Alexandria, La., 1948-50; supt. La. State Sch. Spastic Children, Alexandria, 1950—. Chmn. council spl. schs. La. Bd. Edn. Served with USNR, 1943-45. Named Outstanding Young Man of Yr., Rapides Parish Jr. C. of C., 1948. Baptist. Mason (32 deg., Shriner). Address: PO Box 4027 Alexandria LA 71301

DAVIS, WAYNE HARRY, educator; b. Morgantown, W.Va. Dec. 31, 1930; s. Hannibal Albert and Tyreeca Alizabeth (Stemple) D.; A.B., W.Va. U., 1953; M.S., U. Ill., 1955, Ph.D., 1957; m. Shirley Ann Johnson, June 21, 1958; children—Carolyn, Beverly, Daniel. Research fellow U. Minn., 1957-59; instr. biology, Middlebury (Vt.) Coll., 1959-62; prof. zoology U. Ky., Lexington, 1962—. Environmental columnist Louisville Times and Courier Jour., 1970—. Author (with Roger W. Barbour): Bats of America, 1969; Readings in Human Population Ecology, 1971. Editor Bat Research News, 1960-70. Home: 130 Jesselin St Lexington KY 40503

DAVIS, WILBUR MCLAURIN, oral surgeon; b. Orlando, Fla., Sept. 5, 1939; s. Wilbur McLaurin and Emilie May (Haneaur) D.; D.D.S., Emory U., 1964, M.S., 1967; postgrad. U. Pa., 1964-65; m. Roselyn Marie David, Aug. 1, 1964; 1 dau., Mary McLaurin. Resident oral surgery Grady Meml. Hosp., Atlanta, 1965-67; individual practice oral surgery, Orlando, Fla., 1969—. Pres. Orange County Dental Research Dental Clinic, 1971-72. Bd. dirs. Orange County br. Am. Cancer Soc. Served to lt. USNR, 1967-69. Diplomate Am. Bd. Oral Surgeons. Mem. Am., Fla. dental assns., Am., Southeastern socs. oral surgeons, Orange County Dental Soc., Sigma Chi, Psi Omega. Home: 689 Dunraven Dr Winter Park FL 32789 Office: 508 N Mills Av Orlando FL 32803

DAVIS, WILL DAVID, lawyer; b. Houston, July 18, 1929; s. David and Nita (Barnett) D.; A.A., Lamar Coll., 1950; B.B.A., Baylor U., 1954, LL.B. cum laude, 1954; m. Ann Vanice Byargeon, Dec. 17, 1954; children—Lisa Ann, Mary Lynn, Will David. Admitted to Tex. bar, 1954; pvt. practice law, Austin, 1959—; asst. atty. gen. Tex., 1954-56; chief appellate div. Office Atty. Gen. Tex., 1956, chief ins., banking and securities div., 1956-57; gen. counsel State Bd. Ins. Tex., Austin, 1957-59; partner law firm Heath, Davis & McCalla, Austin, 1959—. Mem. Tex. Election Law Study Commn., 1966; mem., v.p. Tex. Hist. Survey Com.; mem. Coordinating Bd. Univ. and Coll. System of Tex., 1968-71; pres. Tex. Council Maj. Schs., 1970—; mem. exec. com. Tex. Assn. Sch. Bds., 1971—. Del. Democratic Nat. Conv., 1964, 68; chmn. Tex. Dem. Exec. Com., 1965-68, Gov's Inaugural Com., 1965, 67, 69; Tex. Presdl. elector, 1968. Trustee, pres. Austin Ind. Sch. Dist., 1966—; trustee Baylor U.; bd. dirs. v.p. Tex. Hist. Found. Recipient Distinguished Grad. award Lamar U., 1971. Mem. Am., Travis County bar assns., State Bar Tex., Baylor Ex-Students Assn. (dir., sec.-treas., v.p. pres.), Am. Judicature Soc., Fedn. Ins. Counsel, Omicron Delta Kappa, Phi Alpha Delta. Baptist. Clubs: Headliner's Resident's, Citadel (pres.). Home: 2407 Woodmont St Austin TX 78703 Office: Perry-Brooks Bldg Austin TX 78701

DAVIS, WILLIAM BURSON, cons. engr.; b. Clarendon, Tex., Feb. 20, 1930; s. Clifford L. and Jessie (Burson) D.; B.S., U. Colo., 1952; M.S., San. Engr., Mass. Inst. Tech., 1959; Sc.D., Washington U., St. Louis, 1968; m. Sallie Ann McKinney, Dec. 28, 1950; children—Martha Mabry, Mary Luree, Sarah Young. Engr., Freese, Nichols & Endress, Cons. Engrs., Ft. Worth, 1952-55; sr. engr. Tex. Health Dept., Amarillo, 1959-61, Jefferson Chem. Co., Port Neches, Tex., 1961-63; head, environmental engring. Tex. A. and M. U., College Station, 1963-71; pres. Cons. & Research Services, Inc., Bryan, Tex., 1969-71, Davis-Langley and Assos., Bryan, 1971—. Cons. Corn Products, Inc., Bovay Engrs., Uncle Ben's Inc., Ashbrook Corp., Bush Bros., Envicon, Inc., Avco Econ. Systems, Fed. Water Pollution Control Adminstrn., du Pont, Westinghouse Corp. Mem. Nat. Soc. Profl. Engrs., Am. Soc. C.E., Water Pollution Control Fedn., A.A.A.S., Am. Inst. Chem. Engrs., Am. Chem. Soc., Am. Soc. Engring. Edn., Sigma Xi, Chi Epsilon, Phi Kappa Phi. Contbr. articles to profl. jours. Home: 400 North Av Bryan TX 77801 Office: PO Box 3596 4015 Texas Av Bryan TX 77801

DAVIS, WILLIAM GLENN, JR., orthodontist; b. High Point, N.C., June 28, 1938; s. William Glenn and Hazel (Hicks) D.; B.S., U. N.C., 1956, D.D.S., 1963, M.S., 1967; m. Ann Sherrill, July 29, 1961; children—William Glenn III, Katherine Ann, Ashlyn Lee, Carolyn Kelly. Pvt. practice orthodontics, Chapel Hill, N.C., 1967—. Lectr., U. N.C., 1967—. Served with USNR, 1963-65. Mem. Am., N.C. dental assns., Am. Assn. Orthodontists, So. Soc. Orthodontists, N.C. State Orthodontic Assn. (v.p. 1969), Phi Beta Kappa, Omicron Kappa Upsilon. Rotarian. Home: 2014 N Lakeshore Dr Chapel Hill NC 27514 Office: Med Arts Bldg W Willow Dr Chapel Hill NC 27514

DAVIS, WILLIAM PRATHER, designer; b. Waco, Tex., July 30, 1914; s. James Lee and Frances Kirkpatric (Prather) D.; grad. Hill Sch., 1933; ed. U. Tex., 1933-37; m. Rosalie Jenkins, Oct. 15, 1949; 1 son, Donald Benjamin. Farmer, rancher, Waco, 1938-66; pres., Brazos Valley Cotton Oil Co., Waco, 1942-48; pres., owner Braswell-Davis & Assos., Waco, 1946—. Pres. St. Paul's Day Sch. Bd., 1972-73. Trustee J.T. Davis Estate. Fellow Am. Inst. Interior Designers (nat. v.p. 1962-63), C. of C. (chmn. cultural relations com. 1971-72). Rotarian. Home: Lake Air Tower Waco TX 76710 Office: 701 New Rd Waco TX 76710

DAVIS, WINBORN ELTON, educator; b. Helflin, La., Aug. 26, 1917; s. John Henry and Joanna (McKinney) D.; student La. Poly. Inst., 1935-37; B.A., La. State U., 1940; M.S.W., Tulane U., 1948; m. Edith Claire Causey, Aug. 5, 1940; 1 son, David Michael. Family service supr. U.S. Dept. Agr., Thibodaux, La., 1941-42; social worker VA, Shreveport, La., 1946-47; chief div. mental health La. Dept. of Hosps., Baton Rouge, 1949-51, dir. tng. and research, 1958-61, asst. dir., 1962-63, dir., 1964; asso. prof. mental health Southeastern La. Coll., Hammond, 1952-55; dir. La. Evaluation Center for Exceptional Children, New Orleans, 1956-57; adminstr. Student Health Service, asso. prof. mgmt. La. State U., 1965-70, adminstr. dept. psychiatry Sch. Medicine, 1970-71, asst. dean for adminstrn. Sch. Medicine, 1971—; lectr. dept. psychiatry Tulane U., 1950—, adj. asso. prof. Sch. Pub. Health, 1970—; mgmt. cons., 1957—; spl. cons. U.S. Surgeon Gen., 1964-68. Mem. adv. council La. Commn. on Aging, 1963-66; mem. adv. com. Baton Rouge Family Ct., 1957-61; sec. Gov.'s Com. on Mentally Retarded, 1959-60; sec. State Adv. Com. on Edn. Handicapped, 1950-55. Chmn. adv. council Protestant Childrens Home, 1964-65; dir. Baton Rouge Guidance Center, 1952-54. Trustee La. State Employees Retirement System, 1962-66, chmn., 1964-66; bd. dirs. La. Dept. Hosps. Credit Union. Served to lt. (j.g.) USNR, 1942-45. Mem. Nat. Assn. Social Workers (charter mem., mem. cabinet div. of profl. standards), La. Conf. on Social Welfare (pres. 1961-63), La. Psychiat. Assn., New Orleans Soc. Neurology and Psychiatry (asso.), Nat. Assn. State Mental Health Program Dirs., La. Assn. Mental Health, Am. Coll. Health Assn., La. Hosp. Assn. Democrat. Baptist. Author: (with James A. Knight) Manual for Comprehensive Mental Health Clinics, 1964. Contbr. articles to profl. jours. Home: 5057 Whitehaven St Baton Rouge LA 70808

DAVISON, DENVER N., justice Okla. Supreme Ct.; b. Rich Hill, Mo., Oct. 9, 1891; s. Benjamin P. and Lottie (Jones) D.; LL.B., U. Okla., 1915; m. Barbara Wilhelm, July 29, 1917; 1 son, Denver B. (dec.). Practiced law, Coalgate, Okla., 1915-1927, Ada, Okla., 1927-37; mem. Supreme Ct. of Okla., Oklahoma City, 1937—, chief justice on two occasions. Mem. original Will Rogers Commn. Served with U.S. Army, World War I. Mem. Alpha Tau Omega, Phi Delta Phi. Elk, Mason, K.P. Home: 1806 Huntington St Oklahoma City OK 73116 Office: State Capital Bldg Oklahoma City OK 73102

DAVISON, FREDERICK CORBET, univ. pres.; b. Atlanta, Sept. 3, 1929; s. Fred C. and Gladys (Carsley) D.; D.V.M., U. Ga., 1952; Ph.D., Ia. State U., 1963; m. Dianne Castle, Sept. 3, 1952; children—Frederick, William C., Anne. Pvt. practice vet. medicine, Marietta, Ga., 1952-58; research asso. Ia. State U., Ames, 1958-59, asst. prof., 1960, asso. inst. for atomic research, 1960; asst. dir. sci. activities Am. Vet. Med. Assn., Chgo., 1963-64; dean sch. vet. medicine U. Ga., Athens, 1964-66; vice chancellor Univ. System Ga., Atlanta, 1966-67; pres. U. Ga. at Athens, 1967—; dir. Clarke Fed. Savs. & Loan Assn. Mem. rural devel. com., exec. com. 6th region Boy Scouts Am.; mem. Council of Synod of Ga. Trustee Rabun Gap-Nacoochee Sch. Mem. Am. (council on biol. and therapeutic agts.), Ga. vet. med. assns., Inst. Lab. Animal Research of Nat. Acad. Scis., Nat. Com. on Pharmacy and Vet. Medicine, Sigma Xi, Phi Kappa Phi, Sigma Alpha Epsilon, Omega Tau Sigma, Alpha Zeta, Phi Zeta, Gamma Sigma Delta. Contbr. articles to profl. jours. Home: 570 Prince Av Athens GA 30601 Office: U Ga Athens GA 30601

DAVISON, ROGER S., broadcasting exec. Sta. mgr., gen. mgr. WJBO, Baton Rouge.Office: 444 Florida St Baton Rouge LA 70821*

DAVISON, THOMAS, III, lawyer; b. Scranton, Pa., Mar. 16, 1923; s. Thomas and Ann (Kellaway) D.; A.A., Keystone Jr. Coll., 1943; A.B., Bucknell U., 1945; J.D., U. Miami, 1949; m. Virginia M. Seymour, May 23, 1952; 1 son, Thomas IV. Admitted to Fla. bar, 1949; title officer Land Title Co., Coral Gables, 1949-52; practiced law, Miami, 1952-55, Coral Gables, 1955—; mem. firm Padgett, Teasley, Niles & Davison, and predecessor firm, 1955—. Dir. Coll. Law, U. Miami Alumni. Mem. Am., Dade County, Coral Gables (pres. 1961-62) bar assns., Fla. Bar, U. Miami Alumni Assn. (dir., pres.), U. Miami Law Sch. Alumni Assn. (v.p.), Lambda Chi Alpha. Republican. Mem. Christian Ch. (elder, chmn. bd.). Mason, Kiwanian (pres. Coral Gables club). Club: Riviera Country. Home: 1436 Ancona Av Coral Gables FL 33146 Office: 2505 Ponce de Leon Blvd Coral Gables FL 33134

DAVISSON, NELSON MARE, dentist, army officer; b. Winchester, Ind., Sept. 16, 1938; s. Ray Marcus and Garnet Rebecca (Addington) D.; A.B., DePauw U., 1960; D.D.S., Ind. U., 1964; m. Patricia Ann Crossen, Aug. 24, 1963; children—George William Tennis, Lani Catherine. Commd. capt. U.S. Army, 1964, advanced through grades to maj., 1968; practice dentistry, Ft. Gordon, Ga., 1964-68, Viet-Nam, 1968-69, Fort Sam Houston, Tex., 1969-70; asst. chief crown and bridge service Walter Reed Hosp., Washington, 1971—. Decorated Bronze Star. Mem. Am. Dental Assn., V.F.W., Psi Omega. Mem. Ch. of Jesus Christ of Latter-day Saints (elder 1971—). Home: 608 Main St Dunedin FL 33528 Office: Box 158 Walter Reed Hosp Walter Reed Army Medical Center Washington DC 20012

DAVY, LEE GEORGE, mfg. exec.; b. Boulder, Colo., Nov. 16, 1908; s. George W. and Hettie (Shaub) D.; A.B., Cornell U., 1931, Ph.D., 1934; D.Sc., King Coll., 1962; m. Helen L. Pratt, June 9, 1931; children—L. Nevil, George P., Susan J. With Tenn. Eastman Co., Kingsport, 1934—, research chemist, chief chemist RDX devel. work Holston ordnance works, asst. div. supt., div. supt., gen. supt., dir. new product devel., 1934-63, exec. v.p., 1963—. Pres., Kingsport Symphony Orch. Assn. Trustee King Coll. Fellow Am. Inst. Chemists; mem. Am. Chem. Soc., A.A.A.S., Am. Inst. Chem. Engrs., Sigma Xi, Phi Kappa Phi. Presbyn. (elder). Rotarian (past pres.). Home: 1532 Belmeade Dr Kingsport TN 37664 Office: Tenn Eastman Co Kingsport TN 37662

DAWAHARE, SERUR FRANK, JR., retail trade co. exec.; b. Neon, Ky., Aug. 10, 1927; s. Serur Frank and Selma (Cury) D.; student Millersburg Mil. Sch., 1939-42, 45-46; m. Patricia Ann Hangis, Aug. 30, 1962; children—Sadie Rose Lee, Serur Frank III, Patrick (dec.), Amy Grant. Vice pres., asst. mgr. Dawahare's of Pikeville, 1946-61; v.p. Dawahare's Inc., Lexington, 1961—. Bd. dirs. Millersburg Mil. Sch., 1970—. Served with AUS, 1951. Mem. Menswear Retail Am., Mens Wear Assn. Ky., Tenn. Mens Wear Assn. Democrat. Kiwanian. Club: Wildcast Booster (Lexington). Home: 1117 The Lane Lexington KY 40504 Office: 1845 Alexandria Dr Lexington KY 40504

DAWES, CHARLES EDWARD, mfg. co. exec.; b. Peoria, Okla., Feb. 7, 1923; s. Charles Gates and Lottie (Nonkesis) D.; A.A., Joplin (Mo.) Jr. Coll., 1950; B.S., U. Ark., 1953; m. Lorraine Mercer, Apr. 16, 1948; children—Charla Rene, Kevin Lawrence. Mgr. mfg. Vickers, Inc., Joplin, 1953-57; sales engr. Sebastian Diesel Co., Joplin, 1957-59; gen. mgr. Duplex Mfg. Co., Ft. Smith, Ark., 1959—. Chief, Ottawa Indians of Okla. Pres., bd. dirs. Abilities Unlimited, Inc.; bd. dirs., mem. exec. com. Ft. Smith United Fund; mem. adv. bd. Seneca Indian Sch. Served with USAAF, 1943-46. Mem. Am. Soc. Tool and Mech. Engrs., Ft. Smith C. of C. (dir.), Personnel Assn. N.W. Ark., Western Ark. Purchasing Assn., Nat. Congress Am. Indians, Okla. Inter-Tribal Council. Republican. Presbyn. Mason. Home: 2010 Wolfe Lane Fort Smith AR 72901 Office: 1415 N 32d St Fort Smith AR 72901

DAWES, HARRY ANDERSON, cotton mill exec.; b. Eastman, Ga., Apr. 22, 1938; s. Harry Laister and Frances Pendleton (Anderson) D.; B.S., U.S.C., 1960; m. Zermah Pope Smith, July 2, 1965; children—Jonathan, Timothy. With tng. program Crain Cotton Co., Memphis, 1961; mem. tng. program Townsend Cotton Mill, Anderson, S.C., 1962-64, v.p., 1965-68, pres., 1968—; dir. 1001 Corp., Greenville, S.C. Served with AUS, 1960. Episcopalian. Clubs: Poinsett (Greenville, S.C.), Country (Greenville, S.C.); Green Valley Country (Greenville); West Carolina Sailing (Anderson). Home: 9 W Avondale Dr Greenville SC 29609 Office: 1000 Bleckley St Anderson SC 29621

DAWKINS, BEN C., JR., judge; b. Monroe, La, Aug. 6, 1911; s. Ben C. and Alice (McLeod) D.; A.B., Tulane U., 1932; LL.B., La. State U., 1934; m. Harriet White, Jan. 1, 1936; children—Cynthia, Ben C., Franklin White. Admitted to La. bar, 1934; practiced in Monroe, 1934-35, Shreveport, 1935-53; mem. firm Blanchard, Goldstein, Walker & O'Quin, 1935-53; U.S. dist. judge Western Dist. La., Shreveport, 1953—. Research fellow Southwestern Legal Found. Pres. Shreveport Recreation Council, 1941; Mem. sch. bd. Caddo Parish Sch., 1949-53, pres., 1950-52; chmn. legislative com. 5th Circuit Jud. Conf. Mem. council La. State Law Inst.; bd. dirs. Children's Service Bur., 1947-51, Child Guidance Clinic, 1952. Served as lt. comdr., air navigator USNR, 1942-45. Mem. Am., La. (gov. 1950-52), Shreveport (pres. 1949) bar assns., Jr. C. of C. (dir. 1941-42). Am. Legion, V.F.W. (post comdr. 1946-47, judge adv. La. dept. 1947-48), Delta Kappa Epsilon, Phi Delta Phi, Omicron Delta Kappa. Episcopalian (vestryman). Home: 4054 Baltimore St Shreveport LA 71106 Office: Fed Bldg Shreveport LA 71101

DAWKINS, DAVID WAYNE, dentist; b. Moscow, Tenn., Nov. 29, 1942; s. Daniel Stanton and Eleanor Mae (Harris) D.; student Memphis State U., 1960-63; D.D.S., U. Tenn., 1963-67; m. Mary Ann McGuire, June 24, 1967. Clin. dentist Tenn. Dept. Pub. Health, Chattanooga, 1967-68, asst. project dir., 1970—; individual practice dentistry, Colliersville, Tenn., 1968-69; clin. suprs. Shelby County Dept. Pub. Health, 1969-70. Asst. project dir. Incremental Dental Care Program, Tenn. Dept. Pub. Health, 1970—. Recipient award Am. Assn. Endodontists, 1967. Mem. Am., Tenn. dental assns., Am., Tenn. pub. health assns., Xi Psi Phi. Home: 1539 N Concord St Chattanooga TN 37421 Office: 6050 Lee Hwy Chattanooga TN 37421

DAWKINS, JAMES ROBERT, ret. judge; b. Truxno, La., July 3, 1901; s. James Monroe and Callie (Smith) D.; J.D., La. State U., 1928; m. Marie Elaine White, Apr. 18, 1924; children—Jean (Mrs. Eugene Preston Langford), Robert Glen. Admitted to La. bar, 1928; pvt. practice law, Monroe, La., 1928-29, Farmerville, La., 1929-53; judge 3d Dist. Ct. La., Ruston, 1953-72. Mem. 4th Ct. Appeals, New Orleans, summer 1965; mem. Judicial Council La., 1963-66. Mayor, Farmerville, 1931-35. Mem. La. Bar Assn., Phi Delta Phi, Mu Sigma Rho. Baptist (deacon 1943—). Clubs: Ruston (La.) Golf. Home: PO Box 182 Ruston LA 71270

DAWN, FREDERIC SHINYUAN, aerospace engr., govt. ofcl.; b. Wusih, Kiangsu, China, Nov. 24, 1914; s. Yung Tsien and Yufu (Yufu) D.; B.S., Kwang Hwa U., 1934; B.S. in Textile Engring., Inst. Tech., 1936, D.Sc. 1949; postgrad. Lowell Technol. Inst., 1938; M.S. in Textile Engring., U. N.C., 1939; postgrad. in plastic tech. U. Wis., 1956; D.Sc., Nat. Acad. Scis. Republic China, 1967; m. Marie Dunn, Oct. 1, 1934; children—Robert C., William S., Victoria W. Came to U.S., 1951, naturalized, 1961. Chmn. dept. textile engring. Nantung U., 1939-42, China Inst. Agr. and Textiles, 1942-43, Shanghai Inst. Tech., 1943-45, Shanghai Municipal Inst. Tech., 1946-49; v.p. China Inst. Tech., 1946-48, pres., 1948-50; v.p., dir. Standard Plastics Corp., 1940-50, China Chem. and Pharm. Co., 1941-50, China Gen. Import & Export Co., 1941-50, Kai Yuan Textile Mfg. Co., 1946-50, China Indsl. Devel. Corp., 1946-50; gen. mgr. Yih Hsing Textile Mfg. Corp., 1939-45; tech. dir. China Textile Industries, Inc., 1946-49; cons. textile and allied industries for S.E. Asian and S.Am. countries, 1951-54; lab. dir. Decar Plastic Corp., Middleton, Wis., 1956-60; sr. research engr. Aero. Systems div. U.S. Air Force, Wright-Patterson AFB, O., 1960-62; aerospace engr. Manned Spacecraft Center, NASA, Houston, 1962-64, chief materials lab., 1964-69, dir. materials research, 1969—. Mem. adv. com. Ministry Econ. Affairs, Ministry Agr. and Forestry, Ministry Edn., Ministry Industry, 1946-49; mem. Bd. Profl. Certification Exam., Yuan, 1946-49. Bd. dirs. Dawn Found., St. Luke's Hosp. Recipient various citations and award from Chinese govt. agys., NASA, also indsl. and ednl. orgns. on indsl. and ednl. devel. programs. Registered profl. engr., Tex. Fellow Am. Inst. Chemists, Am. Ordnance Assn.; mem. Am. Chem. Soc., N.Y. Acad. Scis., Am. Inst. Aeros. and Astronautics, Internat. Platform Assn., A.A.A.S., Soc. Plastics Engrs., Am. Soc. M.E., Nat. Soc. Profl. Engrs., Soc. Aerospace Materials and Processes Engrs., Phi Lambda. Methodist. Mason (32 deg., Shriner). Club: Optimist (Madison, Wis.). Contbr. numerous articles profl. jours. Patentee textiles, plastics and machinery fields. Home: 1615 Richvale Lane Houston TX 77058 Office: Manned Spacedreft Center NASA Houston TX 77058

DAWSON, AMOS COUNCIL, ednl. adminstr.; b. Jacksonville, N.C., Sept. 9, 1915; s. Amos Council and Emma (Raynor) D.; A.B., Atlantic Christian Coll., 1937; M.A., U. N.C., 1954; LL.D., Atlantic Christian Coll., 1955; m. Margaret Virginia Hilburn, July 19, 1941; children—Donna (Mrs. James Van Ness IV), Amos Council III, Linda, Pamela. Tchr. Southern Pines (N.C.) High Sch., 1937-39, prin., 1939-51; supt. schs., Southern Pines, 1951-59; exec. sec. N.C. Edn. Assn., 1959-70; exec. sec. N.C. Assn. Educators, 1970—. Dir. Horace Mann Ins. Cos.; chmn. bd. Horace Mann Mut. Ins. Co. Trustee Nat. Edn. Assn. Ins. Trust Mem. Am. Assn. Sch. Adminstrs., Horace Mann League, Nat. Assn. State Pres. and Exec. Secs., N.C. Edn. Assn. (acting pres. 1947-48, pres. 1948-49, state chmn. legislative com. 1949, 1951, 1955, 57), Nat. Council State Edn. Assns. (pres. 1968-69). Home: 2104 Barfield Ct Raleigh NC Office: NC Assn Educators Raleigh NC 27602

DAWSON, HOWARD ATHALONE, JR., judge; b. Okolona, Ark., Oct. 23, 1922; s. Howard A. and Mamie (Watson) D.; B.S. in Commerce, U. N.C., 1946; LL.B., George Washington U., 1949; m. Marianne Atherholt, Feb. 2, 1946; children—Amy, Suzanne. Admitted to D.C. bar, 1949; pvt. practice law, Washington, 1949-50; atty. Internal Revenue Service, Washington, 1950-53, asst. regional counsel, Atlanta, 1953-58, regional counsel, Atlanta, 1958-59, asst. chief counsel (adminstrn.), Washington, 1959-62; judge Tax Court of U.S., Washington, 1962—. Served with Finance Corps, USAAF, World War II; ETO. Mem. Am., Fed. bar assns. Home: 7408 Nevis Rd Bethesda MD 20034 Office: Tax Ct US Washington DC 20044

DAWSON, JACK, asso. supt. schs.; b. Bloomfield, Ky., July 11, 1906; s. Charles B. and Agnes (Allen) D.; A.B., Georgetown Coll., 1930; M.A., U. Louisville, 1948; m. Allice Scott, June 21, 1933. With Jefferson County Sch. System, Louisville, 1931—, adminstr., 1954-60, asso. supt., 1960—. Mem. adv. com. Croft Sch. Bus. Service, New London, Conn., 1966—. Bd. dirs. YMCA, 1962-70. Served with USNR, 1942-45. Mem. High Sch. Prins. Assn. (past pres.), Pi Kappa Alpha. Mason, Rotarian. Clubs: Middletown, St. Matthews. Home: 100 Bellemeade Rd Louisville KY 40222 Office: 3332 Newburg Rd Louisville KY 40218

DAWSON, JAMES PAUL, real estate co. exec.; b. Cloud Chief, Okla., Jan. 19, 1903; s. William David and Mary (Martin) D.; teaching certificate Central State Coll., 1924; m. Martha Vandivere, June 13, 1942. Tchr. Cool Br. sch., Carter County, Okla., 1921, prin. Washington High Sch., 1923-24; P.O. clk., San Diego and Atlanta, 1930-47; salesman Southwest Text Book div. Prentice Hall Inc., Dallas, 1947-51, salesman Addressograph Corp., Atlanta, 1952-54; real estate and securities sales, 1955-68; pres. Southern Planning Co., Atlanta, 1969-71; exec. v.p. Camelot of Ga., Inc., 1972—; instr. Clemson U., 1962—. Dist. Sec. Democratic Party, 1971-72. Served with USMCR, 1927, AUS, 1942-43. Mem. Christian Ch. (elder 1962—, lay minister 1964-69). Mason. Home: 2150 Beecher Rd SW Atlanta GA 30311 Office: 1670 NE Expressway NE Atlanta GA 30329

DAWSON, PETER EDWARD, physician; b. Plaquemine, La., Nov. 18, 1931; s. James Henry and Elnora (Kinchen) D.; B.S., Xavier U., 1954; M.D., Meharry Med. Coll., 1962.m. Jean Patricia Lezama, Aug. 24, 1958; children—Jonathan Paul, Patricia Elizabeth. Inter, resident family practice St. Joseph's Hosp., Syracuse, N.Y., 1962-64; practice medicine, Plaquemine, 1964—; mem. staff R.J. Syndale Gen. Hosp., Plaquemine; asst. dir. infirmary So. U., Plaquemine, 1968-71. Chmn. bd. Iberville Enterprise, Inc., Plaquemine, 1967—. Pres. N.A.A.C.P., Plaquemine, 1967—; parliamentarian Iberville Indsl. Voters League, 1966-70. Served with inf. AUS, 1954-56. Mem. A.M.A., La., East Baton Rouge med. assns., Iberville Parish Med. Soc., La. Heart Assn., Alpha Phi Alpha. Democrat. Baptist. Home: 1505 Meriam St Plaquemine LA 70764 Office: 1314 Meriam St Plaquemine LA 70764

DAWSON, RAYMOND HOWARD, ednl. adminstr.; b. Camden, Ark., Oct. 12, 1927; s. Hilary Herbert and Mildred Mae (Pye) D.; A.B. summa cum laude, Coll. Ozarks, 1949; M.A., Vanderbilt U., 1951; Ph.D., U. N.C., 1958; m. Alice Jo McKeehen, May 26, 1949; children—Alice Catherine, Carolyn Marie. Asso. prof. Presbyn. Jr. Coll., Maxton, N.C., 1951-55; instr. U. N.C., Chapel Hill, 1958-59, asst. prof., 1960-63, asso. prof., 1963-68, prof. polit. sci., 1968—, dean, Gen. Coll. and Coll. Arts and Scis., 1968-72, v.p. for academic affairs, 1972—. Mershon Post-doctoral fellow Ohio State U., 1959-60; Fulbright lectr. Kings Coll., London, 1964-65; vis. asso. prof. Columbia, N.Y.C., 1967-68. Mem. exec. com. bd. govs. Research Triangle Inst.; mem. exec. com. Am. Conf. Acad. Deans. Served with USAAF, 1945-47. Recipient Tanner award U. N.C., 1962; E. Harris Harbison prize Danforth Found., 1968. Mem. Am., So. polit. sci. assns., Inst. Strategic Studies. Author: The Decision to Aid Russia, 1941: Foreign Policy and Domestic Politics, 1959. Home: 304 Glendale Dr Chapel Hill NC 27514

DAWSON, WILLIAM JOHN, cons. engr.; b. Batesville, Ark., Feb. 12, 1925; s. Allie Raphael and Mary (Smith) D.; B.S., La. State U., 1952; m. Madge Kenny, Sept. 2, 1950; children—Donna Louise, William John, Mary Ann, David Charles. Cons. engr., pres. Dawson Engrs., Inc., Baton Rouge, 1954—. Served with USMCR, 1942-46. Mem. Am. Soc. C.E. Home: 7623 Bocage Blvd Baton Rouge LA 70809 Office: 5700 Florida Blvd Baton Rouge LA 70806

DAWSON, WILLIAM LEVI, composer, condr.; b. Anniston, Ala., Sept. 26, 1899; s. George W. and Eliza M. (Starkey) D.; student composition, orchestration Washburn Coll; Mus. B. Horner Inst. Fine Arts, Kansas City, Mo., 1925; M. Composition, Am. Conservatory Music, Chgo., 1927; Mus. D., Tuskegee Inst.; 1955; postgrad. Eastman Sch. Music; m. Cornelia D. Lampton, May 25, 1927 (dec. Aug. 1928); m. 2d, Cecile D. Nicholson, Sept. 21, 1935. Dir. music, Topeka, Kansas City, 1921-25, then 1st trombonist Chgo. Civic Symphony Orch.; dir. Tuskegee Inst. Sch. Music, Tuskegee Choir; led Tuskegee Choir at opening Radio City Music Hall, 1932-33, on many tours, in concert series NBC, CBS, ABC; guest condr. numerous state choral festivals, choral groups in Spain under auspices U.S. State Dept., 1956, Kansas City Philharmonic Orch., 1966, Nashville Symphony Orch., 1966, Talladega Choir and Mobile Symphony Orch., 1968. Winner Rodman Wanamaker contest for composition, 1930, 31; Chgo. Daily News contest for band condrs., 1929; recipient award and citation U. Pa. Glee Club, 1967; Alumni Achievement award U. Mo. at Kansas City, 1963. Composer: numerous arrangements Negro folk songs for voices, Break, Break (with orch.); Out in the Fields; Scherzo for Orch.; Negro Work Song for Orch.; Trio in A (violin, cello, piano), Sonata in A (violin and piano); Negro Folk Symphony. Address: PO Box 1052 Tuskegee Institute AL 36088

DAWSON, WILLIAM SIDNEY, JR., physician; b. West Logan, W.Va., July 2, 1932; s. William Sidney and Mary Elizabeth (Bratton) D.; B.A., Berea Coll., 1954; M.D., W.Va. U. and Med. Coll. Va., 1961; m. Sylvia Copley, Jan. 13, 1961; children—William Sidney III, John Stuart, Mary Elizabeth. Intern, Mound Park Hosp., St. Petersburg, Fla., 1961-62; gen. practice medicine, Fremont, N.C., 1962-66;

partner with E.B. Aycock, Greenville, N.C., 1966—; mem. staff Pitt County Meml. Hosp., Greenville, N.C. Charter mem. E Carolina U. Found., Greenville, 1968-69. Served with AUS, 1954-56. Mem. A.M.A., Med. Soc. N.C., Pitt County Med. Soc. Methodist. Home: 203 King George Rd Greenville NC 27834 Office: 210 W 4th St Greenville NC 27834

DAWSON, WINTER WOOD, dentist; b. Cary, Miss., Oct. 1, 1908; s. Walter Putnam and Carrie (Byerly) D.; student Miss. State U., 1926-28; D.D.S., U. Tenn., 1932; m. Helen Virginia Moore, Aug. 3, 1935; children— Thomas Winter, Helen Virginia. Gen. practice dentistry, Brooksville, Miss., 1932-38, Meridian, Miss., 1938—. Served with USNR, 1942-46. Fellow Internat. Coll. Dentists; mem. Pierre Fauchard Acad., Miss., Am. dental assns., Psi Omega, Omicron Kappa Upsilon. Methodist. Rotarian. Home: 2214 39th St Meridian MS 39301 Office: 601 22d Av Meridian MS 39301

DAY, CHARLES RICHARD, architect; b. Johnson City, Tenn., Oct. 1, 1933; s. John Harvey and Nannie (Byrd) D.; B.S., U. Cin., 1957; m. Rebecca Louise Wyatt, Dec. 28, 1968. Draftsman, Beeson & Beeson, architects, Johnson City, 1960-63; architect, partner, Abingdon, Va., 1963—. Washington County chmn. March of Dimes, 1962, Heart Fund, 1965—; mem. citizens adv. com. Va. Highlands Community Coll., 1969—. Served to lt. USAF, 1958-60. Mem. Jr. C. of C. (v.p. 1961-63). Presbyn. Rotarian (past pres.). Clubs: Washington County Sportsman's Abingdon. Prin. archtl. works include: Mchts. and Farmers Bank, Galax, Va.; addition to Johnston Meml. Hosp., Abingdon; YMCA Bldg., Bristol, Tenn.-Va. Home: 179 Hillside Dr Abingdon VA 24210 Office: Lee Hwy PO Box 650 Abingdon VA 24210

DAY, JOHN PAT, drilling co. exec.; b. Mansfield, Tex., July 19, 1907; s. John Frances and Mary Matilda (Reitz) D.; student U. Dallas, 1924-27; m. Alma Aileen Sprinkle, Apr. 11, 1934; children— Patsy, Joleen, Luke, Randolph, Rampy, Johnie. Owner, Day Drilling Co., Mansfield, 1960—; pres. Farmers Lumber Co., Mansfield, 1951-72; dir. Mansfield State Bank, 1947—. Mem. city council, Mansfield, 1966-72, mayor pro tem, 1966-71; water and sewer commr., 1966-72. Roman Catholic. Home: 204 Brown St Mansfield TX 76063 Office: 106 S Main St Mansfield TX 76063

DAY, LEROY EDWARD, govt. ofcl.; b. Doswell, Va., Jan. 2, 1925; s. Ira Eugene and Sallie (Lester) D.; B.Aero. Engring., Ga. Inst. Tech., 1946; M.S. in Engring., U. Cal. at Los Angeles, 1955; M.S. in Indsl. Mgmt., Mass. Inst. Tech., 1960; m. Mary Elizabeth Hornbuckle, May 18, 1947; children—David, Jean, Michael. Dep. head missile program dept. U. S. Naval Missile Center, 1946-62; with NASA, 1962—, mgr. space shuttle, 1969—; lectr. U. Cal. at Los Angeles, 1958-59. Local troop chmn. Boy Scouts Am., 1962. Served with U.S. Navy, 1943-48. Sloan fellow, 1959; recipient Superior Achievement award NASA, 1967, Exceptional Service medal, 1969. Mem. Research Soc. Am., Tau Beta Pi, Phi Kappa Phi. Republican. Episcopalian. Author papers in field. Home: 11709 Magruder Lane Rockville MD 20852 Office: 600 Independence Av Washington DC 20003

DAY, MELVIN SHERMAN, govt. exec.; b. Lewiston, Me., Jan. 22, 1923; s. Israel and Frances (Goldberg) D.; B.S., Bates Coll., 1943; postgrad. U. Tenn., 1953-54; m. Annette Barbara Berman, Feb. 8, 1948; children—Cynthia, Wendy, Robert. Chemist, Metal Hydrides, Inc., 1943-44, Tenn. Eastman Corp., 1944-46; sci. analyst AEC, 1946-49, asst. chief tech. information service extension, 1950-56, chief, 1956-58, dir. office of tech. information, 1958-60; dep. dir. Office of Tech. Information and ednl. program NASA, 1960-61, dir. Office Sci. and Tech. Information, 1961-67, dep. asst. adminstr. for tech. utilization, 1967-70; head Office Sci. Information, NSF, Washington, 1970-72; dep. dir. Nat. Library Medicine, Dept. Health, Edn. and Welfare, 1972—. Cons. IAEA, 1959-60, OECD, 1970; mem. documentation com. AGARDNATO, 1960-70; chmn. adv. bd. Sci. Information Exchange, 1963-68; chmn. com. on sci. and tech. information Fed. Council, 1970—; mem. adv. bd. CAS, 1965-67; mem. Com. on Intergovtl. Sci. Relations; chmn. Environmental Quality Information Panel OECD, 1970—; mem. com. libraries, documentation and archives UNESCO, 1971—; mem. panel tech. information for developing countries Nat. Acad. Scis., 1971—; mem. Fed. Library Com., 1969-72. Bd. dirs. Smithsonian Sci. Information Exchange, 1972; trustee Found. Center, 1972—. Served with AUS, 1944-46. Recipient Sustained Superior Performance award AEC, 1960; Exceptional Service medal NASA, 1970. Mem. Am. Chem. Soc., Am. Soc. Information Service, A.A.A.S., N.Y. Acad. Scis., Am. Soc. Information Sci., Spl. Libraries Assn. Clubs: Nat. Space, Nat. Aviation, Internat. (Washington). Home: 7805 Beech Tree Rd Bethesda MD 20034 Office: 8600 Rockville Pike Bethesda MD 20014

DAY, NANCY JANE, librarian; b. Pendleton, S.C., May 1, 1905; d. Robert Bolt and Kate (Eskew) Day; B.A., Furman U., 1925; B.S., Columbia, 1933; M.A. in L.S., U. Mich., 1943. Tchr. pub. schs., Winston-Salem, N.C., 1925-30; asst. librarian Reynolds High Sch., 1930-33; librarian Woman's coll. Furman U., 1933-34; asst. librarian Greenville (S.C.) Pub. Library, 1934-35. Furman U., 1935, Fla. State Coll. for Women, 1935-39; instr. library sci. Winthrop Coll., 1939-43, dir. workshop, 1947; asst. prof. Emory U., 1943-46; supr. library service S.C. Dept. Edn., 1946-72; dir. workshop Madison Coll., 1950; instr. summer session U. N.C., 1950, post session U. So. Cal., 1952; Fulbright lectr. Chulalongkorn U., Thailand, 1953-54. Mem. exec. com. Tenn. Valley Library Council for Southeastern States Coop. Survey, 1946-49. Mem. Am. (council 1949-53, bd. edn. for librarianship 1952-58), S.C. (sec. 1947), Southeastern (pres. 1954-56) library assns., Am. Assn. Sch. Librarians (pres. 1954-55), N.E.A., Am. Assn. U. Women, Delta Kappa Gamma. Baptist. Home: 3210 Duncan St Columbia SC 29205 Office: Dept of Edn Columbia SC 29201

DAY, WILLIAM EDWIN, commr. U.S. Ct. Claims; b. Washington, July 17, 1912; s. Ralph Edwin and Mary Agnes (Smith) D.; LL.B., Nat. U., 1935, LL.M., M.P.L., 1937; m. Mary Redmond, May 28, 1938. Admitted to D.C. bar, 1936; with Govt. Printing Office, 1931-37; instr. printing Coll. Engring., Carnegie Inst. Tech., P.Hs., 1937-40; pvt. practice law, Washington, 1940-41; spl. atty. antitrust div. Dept. Justice, 1941-42, spl. asst. to atty. gen. antitrust div., 1945-49; commr. U.S. Ct. Claims, 1949—. Served to lt. comdr. USCGR, 1942-45. Mem. Am., D.C. bar assns. Clubs: Army Navy Country (Arlington, Va.); Culpepper (Va.) Country. Home: 3601 N Roberts Lane Arlington VA 22207 Office: US Ct Claims 717 Madison Pl NW Washington DC 20005

DAYTON, EDWARD PHILLIP, real estate exec.; b. Dallas, June 19, 1942; s. Sidney and Betty Ruth (Margules) D.; student Am. Inst. Banking, 1966, Southwestern Grad. Sch. Banking, So. Methodist U., 1967; m. Linda Dianne Wiman, Nov. 23, 1965. Credit mgr. Preston State Bank, Dallas, 1960-63; asst. nat. bank examiner Office of Comptroller of Currency, U.S. Treasury Dept., 1963-64; v.p. Commonwealth Nat. Bank, Dallas, 1964-68, Dallas County State Bank, Carrolton, Tex., 1968-70; sales mgr. Regal Realtors, Dallas, 1970—. Instr., Am. Inst. Banking, 1964-70. City chmn. United Fund, 1971. Mem. Greater Northwest C. of C. (chmn. pub. affairs and legis. com., Tex. Assn. Realtors. Elk, Optomist (pres. 1969). Clubs: Brookhaven Country Farmers Branch, Tex. Home: 3405 Apple Valley St Dallas TX 75234 Office: 2725 Valley View St Dallas TX 75234

DEABLER, HERDIS LEROY, clin. psychologist, educator; b. Howell, Mich., Jan. 27, 1910; s. John S. and Mary (Dunkelberger) D.; A.B., N. Central Coll., 1931; Ph.D. Lucinda Bidwell Beebe fellow, Boston U., 1936; m. Oleva Gingrich, Sept. 12, 1933; children—Donna Jean (Mrs. Donna J. DuRant), JoAnn (Mrs. Frank E. Crawford), Herdis LeRoy, Mary Elizabeth (Mrs. Fredric William Corwin Jr.). Personnel dir. N. Central Coll., 1936-45, asst. prof., 1937-40, asso. prof., 1940-43, prof. psychology, 1943-45, prof., head dept., 1946-49; sr. counselor, asst. prof. psychology U. Minn., 1945-46; chief clin. psychologist VA Hosp., Gulfport, Miss., 1949-60; asst. prof. psychology, coordinator Gulf Coast Extension Center, U. Miss., Gulfport, 1951-60; area chief psychologist VA Area Med. Office, Boston, 1960-64; asso. prof. psychology State Coll. Boston, 1963-67; chief clin. psychologist VA Outpatient Clinic, Boston, 1964-67; extension asst. prof. psychology Boston U., 1966-67; chief psychology service VA Hosp., New Orleans, 1967—; clin. asso. prof. dept. neurology and psychiatry Tulane U. Sch. Medicine, New Orleans, 1967—; clin. prof. psychology La. State U., New Orleans, 1970—. Vis. lectr. psychology La. State U. Sch. Medicine, New Orleans, 1957-60; vis. prof. psychology Tulane U., 1968—. Pres., Citizens Scholarship Found., Hingham, Mass., 1965-67. Diplomate Am. Bd. Examiners in Profl. Psychology. Mem. La. Psychol. Assn. (chmn. bd. profl. affairs 1968—). Home: 6509 Center St New Orleans LA 70124 Office: 1601 Perdido St New Orleans LA 70140

DEALEY, JOSEPH MACDONALD, newspaper exec.; b. Dallas, July 18, 1919; s. Edward Musgrove and Clara (MacDonald) D.; A.B., U. Tex., 1941; m. Doris Carolyn Russell, Jan. 18, 1947; children—Joseph MacDonald, Russell Edward, Pamela Carolyn, Frances Patricia. Reporter, Dallas Morning News, 1942-50, asst. sec., 1950-55, dir. 1952—, sec., 1955-60, pres., 1960—. Pres., County chpt. A.R.C., 1961-63; vice chmn., bd. govs. A.R.C.; mem. exec. com. Community Council Greater Dallas, 1960—, pres., 1965-66; bd. dirs. Dallas Citizens Council, 1960—, pres., 1964-65; bd. dirs. Childrens' Med. Center, 1950—, pres., 1964-67; bd. dirs. Dallas Council Social Agys., 1958—; trustee Dallas Theater Center; bd. dirs. Dallas County United Fund, 1961—, mem. exec. com., 1962—, v.p., 1963-65, pres., 1967, campaign chmn., 1966-67; bd. dirs. United Community Funds and Councils Am.; bd. dirs. State Fair Tex.; mem. U. Tex. Devel. Bd. and Chancellor's Council, chmn., 1967-68. Served to lt. USAAF, 1942-46. Mem. Dallas C. of C. (dir., dir. Bur. Advt.), Am. (dir.), So. (dir.; pres. 1969) newspaper pubs. assns., Tex. Daily Newspaper Assn. (mem. exec. com., pres. 1969), Press Club Dallas, Sigma Delta Chi, Phi Delta Theta. Clubs: Dallas Country, Koon Kreek, Las Colinas Country. Home: 4332 Arcady St Dallas TX 75205 Office: Dallas Morning News Dallas TX 75222

DEAN, BOB WESLEY, mech. engr.; b. Birmingham, Ala., Aug. 6, 1924; s. Robert Leon and Gertrude (Griffith) D.; B.Mech. Engring., Auburn U., 1945; M.S. in Engring., U. Ala., 1948; m. Martha Stone Grace, July 15, 1944; children—Robert Allbritton, Elizabeth Cary, Thomas Wesley, DeForest DeSha, David Bryant. Various positions, 1948-52; mfrs. rep. F. J. Evans Engring. Co., Atlanta, 1952-57; design engr. Robert & Co., Atlanta, 1957-62; with Mallory & Evans, Inc., Scottdale, Ga., 1962—, v.p., project engr., 1965—; asso. Mech. Engring., Inc., Scottdale, Ga., 1965—. Mem. State Ga. Bd. Examiners Warm Air Heating Contractors, 1970—. Registered profl. engr., Ind., Pa., Cal., Miss., Ala., Ga., Fla., Tenn., S.C., N.C., Neb., N.Y., Va., Ky., Del., Minn. Mem. Am. Soc. Heating, Refrigeration and Air Conditioning Engrs. (chpt. pres. 1963-64). Home: 3482 Piedmont Rd NE Atlanta GA 30305 Office: 646 Kentucky St Scottdale GA 30079

DEAN, BURNETT GERALD, civil engr.; b. Goodwater, Ala., Dec. 28, 1919; s. John Owen and Lucy (Blair) B.; B.C.E., Auburn U., 1947; student N.Y.U., 1943-44; m. Vernaize Pendarvis, May 29, 1963; 1 dau., Christy Sylvia. San. engr. Palgaze & Basenberg, Birmingham, Ala., 1947-51; gen. engr. Civil Service U.S. Army, 1952-54, 1956—; supt. Shaw & Estes, Dallas, 1955; owner Burnett Engring. Co., Huntsville, Ala., 1954—. Served to capt. USAAF, 1943-46. Mem. Am. Legion, V.F.W., Chi Epsilon, Tau Beta Pi, Phi Kappa Phi. Optimist (v.p., 1970-71). Home: 1018 Gordon Dr SE Decatur AL 35601 Office: Safeguard SSC-SC PO Box 1500 Huntsville AL 35807

DEAN, CHARLES EARLE, translation editor; b. nr. Central, S.C., May 23, 1898; s. Charles Lewis and Eloise (Earle) D.; A.B., Harvard, 1921; M.A., Columbia U., 1923; Ph.D., Johns Hopkins U., 1927; m. Mildred Caroline Waters, Sept. 10, 1927; children—Robert Waters, Margaret Lewis (Mrs. Robert Morris Vogel). Tech. asst. Bell Tel. Labs., N.Y.C., 1921-24; various positions including cons. engr. Hazeltine Corp., Little Neck, N.Y., 1929-63; translation editor Scripta Pub. Corp., Washington, 1964—. Mem. Am. Civil Liberties Union, Americans for Democratic Action. Fellow I.E.E.E., Radio Club of Am.; mem. Wash. Ethical Soc. Co-editor book Principles of Color Television, 1956. Home: 115 Sherman Av Takoma Park MD 20012 Office: 1511 K St NW Washington DC 20005

DEAN, CHARLES HERMON, JR., architect; b. Brookhaven, Miss., Mar. 15, 1910; s. Charles Hermon and Clemmie Mord (Tucker) D.; B.Arch., Tulane, 1932; m. Elizabeth Nan Morgan, Sept. 5, 1939 (dec. July 1951); children—Rebecca Nan (Mrs. R. Clifton Cox), Richard Morgan, David Franklin; m.2d, Doris Jewell Bolian, Sept. 27, 1952. Draftsman Miss. Hwy. Dept., Jackson, 1937-38; dist. insp. Miss. Rating Bur., Jackson, 1938-45; with N.W. Overstreet architect, Jackson, 1945-49; prin. Charles H. Dean Architect, Jackson, 1949-50; partner Turner & Dean, Jackson, 1950-52; prin. Charles H. Dean, Jackson, 1952-58; partner Dean & Pursell (and predecessor firms), Jackson, 1958—. Mem. Miss. Econ. Council, 1954—, Jackson Symphony Orch. Assn., 1960—, Jackson Music Assn., 1960—, Miss. Art Assn., 1954—, Jackson Little Theater, 1967—; mem. Jackson Citizens Council, 1956—, pres., 1970—. Mem. central center holding bd. Miss. Bapt. Sem., 1964-69. Mem. Jackson C. of C., A.I.A. (bd. dirs., 1971), Miss. Bd. Architecture (pres. 1965-68), Constrn. Specifications Inst. (pres. 1971). Baptist (deacon). Architect Chapel of Memories Miss. State U., 1965, adminstrn. bldg. Miss. Chem Corp., Yazoo City, Miss., 1968. Home: 4058 Eastwood Pl Jackson MS 39211 Office: 4516 Office Park Dr Jackson MS 39206

DEAN, CLAY HUTCHINSON, state ofcl.; b. Moultrie, Ga., July 23, 1917; s. Clay Lehman and Chloe Fay (Hutchinson) D.; B.S. in Civil Engring., Auburn U., 1938; M.S., Harvard, 1948; postgrad. Oxford (Eng.) U., 1943, U. Ala., 1965; m. Vickie Wilkerson, July 30, 1938; children—Vickie Fay (Mrs. E. C. Missildine), Joseph Clay. Draftsman Ala. Hwy. Dept., Montgomery, 1938; sanitation officer Clay County Health Dept., Ashland, Ala., 1938-41; with Ala. Dept. Health, Montgomery, 1941—, dist. engr. sanitation bur., 1941-42, asst. san. engr. bur. sanitation, 1945-47, dir. hosp. planning div., 1948-65, dir. bur. health facilities constrn., 1966—. Mem. Ala. Adv. Council Rehab. Facilities, 1968-72, Ala. Adv. Council Sheltered Workshops, 1968-72, Gov.'s Ad Hoc Com. Comprehensive Cancer Control, 1969-72, planning com. U. Ala. Med. Center, 1968-72, Ala. Planning and Adv. Council of Developmental Disabilities Act, 1971-72, nat. com. health services data collection USPHS, 1970-72, nat. states plans adv. council, 1971-72. Active Boy Scouts Am., Montgomery. Served to 1st lt., AUS, 1942-45; ETO, maj. Res. ret. Registered profl. engr., land surveyor, Ala. Mem. Am., Ala. pub. health assns., Am. Assn. Hosp. Planning, Am. Assn. Pub. Adminstrn., Forest Farmers Assn., Res. Officers Assn., Ala. Hist. Assn., Am. Heritage Soc., Nat. Geog. Soc., Chi Epsilon, Sigma Phi Epsilon. Methodist. Club: Dixie Sailing. Home: 3143 Gilmer Av Montgomery AL 36105 Office: Ala Dept Health 501 Dexter Av Montgomery AL 36104

DEAN, DAVID PARKS, oil co. exec.; b. Detroit, Tex., July 23, 1898; s. William Alexander and Minnie (Lee) D.; student Austin Coll., 1915-16, U. Tulsa, 1916-17; B.A., Okla. U., 1920; m. Ruby Macy Boren, Mar. 12, 1953. Geologist, Waite Phillips Co., later Barnsdall Oil Co., 1921-30; partner Dean Bros., 1931-48; pres., Great Expectations Oil Corp., Fort Worth, 1948—. Trustee Reformed Theol. Sem., Jackson, Miss., 1968-71. Served as pvt. U.S. Army, World War I, to capt. AUS, World War II. Recipient 50 yr. award Am. Assn. Petroleum Geologists, 1969, Austin Coll., Sherman, Tex., 1966. Presbyn. Author: Smackover Rose, 1967, adaptation for play, 1971. Home: 2125 Park Pl Av Fort Worth TX 76110 Office: First Nat Bank Bldg Fort Worth TX 76102

DEAN, HARDY ROBINSON, city ofcl.; b. Jacksonville, Fla., Sept. 13, 1913; s. William Henry and Callie (Easterlin) D.; student pub. schs.; m. Gladys Estell Cooper, Apr. 25, 1952; children—Hardy R., Patricia Ann, Verley E., Steven C., Susan C. Agt. Liberty Nat. Life Ins. Co., Chiefland, Fla., 1939-41, staff mgr., 1941-43; agt. Life Ins. Co. of Ga., Chiefland, 1946-59; city mgr. Chiefland, 1959—; owner Suwannee Valley Cleaners, Chiefland, 1964-69. Mem. Chiefland City Commn., 1957-59, Chiefland Planning Commn., 1963-71. Bd. dirs. Chiefland Activities Inc., 1965—. Served with USNR, 1943-46. Mem. Fla. City Mgrs. Assn., Internat. City Mgmt. Assn. Club: Lions (sec. 1967-71). Home: 903 W Boundary St Chiefland FL 32626 Office: 25 N Main St Chiefland FL 32626

DEAN, JACK FREDERICK, dentist; b. Ponca City, Okla., Nov. 16, 1923; s. Herman Hilbert and Lula May (Adair) D.; student No. Okla. Jr. Coll., 1941-43; D.D.S., St. Louis U., 1946; B.S. with honors, Baylor U., 1958. Private practice gen. dentistry, Ponca City, 1949-57; pvt. practice oral surgery, Dallas, 1961—. Instr. physiology Baylor Dental Sch., 1966-72; mem. sr. attending staff Dept. Oral Surgery, U. Tex. Southwestern Med. Sch., 1966—. Served with USPHS, 1946-49. Diplomate Am. Bd. Oral Surgery. Fellow Am. Coll. Dentists; mem. Am. Dental Assn., Am., S.W. socs. oral surgery. Mason (Shriner). Home: 1631 Windchime Dallas TX 75224 Office: 223 W 10th St Dallas TX 75208

DEAN, JAMES EDWARD, state legislator, univ. ofcl.; b. Atlanta, Mar. 14, 1944; s. Steve and Dorothy (Cox) D.; student San Francisco City Coll., summer 1962; B.A., Clark Coll., 1966; certificate Fisk U., summer 1967, U. Ga., 1967; M.S.W., Atlanta U., 1968; m. Vyvyan Ardena Coleman, June 12, 1966; 1 dau., Sonya Velika. Clk., Magic Carpet, Atlanta, 1957-58; rep. Atlanta Daily World, 1957-62; mgr. edn. bd. Atlanta Inquirer Inc., 1962-65; clk. BMC Realty Co., BMC Ins. Co., 1965-66; counselor, asst. manpower dir. Office Econ. Opportunity, Atlanta, 1965-66; community relations specialist, 1968; tchr. Atlanta Bd. Edn., 1966; recreation project dir., field rep. Atlanta Urban League, 1967, dir. Lynwood Park Neighborhood Center; mem. Ga. Ho. of Reps., 1968—; now dir. alumni affairs Clark Coll., Atlanta. Mem. Nat. Com. in Support of Pub. Schs., Eastlake Civic League, Eastside Community Council; chmn. spl. interest groups and edn. com. Dekalb unit Am. Cancer Soc.; mem. Met. Mental Health Assn. Recipient Achievement award Atlanta Inquirer. Mem. Am. Acad. Social Sci., Am. Acad. Polit. Sci., Nat. Assn. Social Workers, Acad. Certified Social Workers, Internat. Platform Assn., Am. Acad. Social and Polit. Sci., Soc. Fund Raisers, Am. Alumni Council, Soc. State Legislators, Nat. Assn. Black Elected Ofcls., Alpha Kappa Delta, Alpha Phi Alpha. Home: 17 Eastlake Dr NE Atlanta GA 20217 Office: 240 Chestnut St NW Atlanta GA 30319

DEAN, JOHN EDWARD, lawyer, accountant; b. Carrie, Va., Feb. 16, 1914; s. George Paris and Mary (Breeding) D.; A.B., Emory and Henry Coll., 1934; M.B.A., U. Ga., 1948, J.D., 1950; m. Priscilla Ross, Nov. 25, 1944; children—Nancy Karen, John Edward, George Ross, Robert David. Tchr., Jenkins (Ky.) Consol. Schs., 1934-35; head social sci. dept. Beckley (W.Va.) Coll., 1936-38; pres. Logan (W.Va.) Coll., 1938-39; pub. accountant, Louisville, 1939-41; head bus. adminstrn. dept. N.M. Mil. Inst., Roswell, 1941-42, asst. prof. U. Ga., 1946-51; admitted to Ga. bar, 1951; atty. Internal Revenue Service, Washington, 1951-52, So. Garment Mfrs. Assn., Washington, 1952-53, FCC, Washington, 1954; sr. auditor, staff mgr. Army Audit Agy., Atlanta, 1954-59; asst. atty. gen. Ga., Atlanta, 1959-66; pvt. practice law, Atlanta, 1966—. Bd. dirs. Atlanta Met. Area A.R.C. Served from apprentice seaman to lt. USCGR, 1942-46. C.P.A., Tenn., Ga. Mem. Ga., Clayton County bar assns., Am. Arbitration Assn. (nat. panel arbitrators), Internat. Platform Assn., Am. Acad. Polit. and Social Sci., Am. Judicature Soc., Clayton County C. of C. (pres. 1962-65), Delta Theta Phi, Alpha Kappa Psi, Lambda Chi Alpha, Artus Club, Phi Kappa Phi. Home: Route 2 Lovejoy Hampton GA 30228

DEAN, MILES TILLMAN, personnel adminstr.; b. Birmingham, Ala., June 28, 1923; s. Claude A. and Louise (Moseley) D.; B.A., Howard Coll., 1948; M.A., Fla. State U., 1950; m. Fazil D. Starling, June 10, 1950; children—Diane Louise, Miles Patrick. Mem. faculty Fla. State U., 1949-57; chief classification and pay Fla. Merit System, 1957-59; dir. div. personnel Fla. State Bd. of Health, 1960-70; personnel officer Dept. Health and Rehabilitative Services, Tallahassee, 1970—. Served with USNR, 1943-46, 51-53. Mem. Am. Pub. Health Assn., Fla. Pub. Health Assn. (pres.), Sigma Nu, Delta Sigma Pi, Phi Delta Kappa. Presbyn. Elk. Club: Selva Marina Country. Home: 210 14th St Atlantic Beach FL 32003 Office: IBM Bldg Tallahassee FL 32304

DEAN, ROBERT BETHEL, social worker; b. El Monte, Cal., Apr. 17, 1931; s. Bethel Boneham and Eunice (Walker) D.; B.S., Stephen F. Austin Coll., 1960; M.S.W., Worden Sch. Social Service, 1964; m. Mary Frances McGee, Mar. 24, 1951; children—Susan Frances, Judith Ann, Robert Bethel, Stephen Andrew. Field worker Tex. Dept. Pub. Welfare, Waco, 1956-58, Dallas, 1960-61; caseworker, supr. Buckner Bapt. Benevolences, 1961-62; psychiat. social worker VA Hosp., Dallas, 1965—. Served with USAF, 1951-54. Mem. Nat. Assn. Social Workers. Baptist. Mason. Home: 2336 Dorrington Dr Dallas TX 75228 Office: 4500 S Lancaster Rd Dallas TX 75216

DEAN, ROBERT JACK, county agt.; b. Athens, Tex., Mar. 5, 1924; s. Charlie J. and Ruby (Browning) D.; B.S., Tex. A. and M. U., 1949, M.S., 1954; m. Eugenia Gould, Dec. 23, 1949; children—Charlie J., Sharon A. Asst. county agr. agt., Morris County, Tex., 1955-72, county agt., 1955—. Served with USAAF, World War II. Recipient Distinguished Service award Nat. County Agr. Agts. Assn., 1970. Mem. Tex. County Agts. Assn. (dir. 1969-71). Kiwanian. Home: 1966 Wildwood Dr Daingerfield TX 75638 Office: County Agts Office 1966 Wildwood Dr Daingerfield TX 75638

DEAN, ROMEO BARNES, JR., bank exec.; b. Greenville, S.C., May 19, 1928; s. Romeo Barnes and Pearl (Griffin) D.; grad. Palmetto Inst. Accountancy, 1950, Sch. Consumer Banking, U. Va., 1959, Stonier Grad. Sch. Banking, Rutgers, 1966; m. Eileen Knutson, Sept. 11, 1946; children—Claudia (Mrs. Thomas E. Chandler), Julie (Mrs. John W. Flowers), Carol. With S.C. Nat. Bank, Greenville,

1947—, v.p., city exec. officer, Sumter, S.C., 1963—. Campaign chmn. United Fund, Sumter, 1969, pres., 1971; pres. United Way S.C., 1972. Served with USAAF, 1945-47. Recipient Boss of Yr. award Sumter Jaycees, 1970; named S.C.'s United Way Man of Yr., Gov. S.C., 1970. Mem. C. of C. (pres. 1972), Am. Legion (vice comdr. 1957-58). Episcopalian. Home: 79 Paisley Park Sumter SC 29150 Office: PO Box 1678 Sumter SC 29150

DEAN, STANLEY ROCHELLE, physician; b. Stamford, Conn., Feb. 13, 1908; s. Jacob and Gerta (Rochelle) D.; B.S., U. Mich., 1930, M.D. cum laude, 1934; children—Lori (Mrs. Joel Schonfeld), Michael Louis; m. 2d, Marion Jamieson, Nov. 8, 1967. Intern, Hurley (Mass.) Hosp., Boston Psychopathic Hosp., 1934-35; resident psychiatry Taunton (Mass.) State Hosp., 1935-37; sr. physician Fairfield State Hosp., Newtown, Conn., 1937-40; practice medicine, specializing in psychiatry, Stamford, 1940-64, Miami, Fla., 1964—; clin. prof. psychiatry U. Fla. Coll. Medicine, Gainesville; chief Stamford Hosp., Psychiat. Clinic, 1934-43. Founder, v.p. Research in Schizophrenia Endowment, 1958-62. Served to capt. AUS, 1943-45. Recipient New Eng. Psychiat. Assn. prize for research, 1942; donor Stanley R. Dean award for research in psychiatry. Diplomate Am. Bd. Psychiatry. Fellow Am. Psychiat. Assn., Am. Coll. Psychiatrists, A.A.A.S., Royal Soc. Medicine (Gt. Britain); mem. Internat. Assn. Social Psychiatry (trustee), Am. Assn. Social Psychiatry (mem. exec. council), Internat. Fedn. Hygiene, Preventive Medicine and Social Medicine (mem. exec. council), Pan. Am. Med. Assn. (v.p. psychiat. sect.). Adv. bd. Transcultural Psychiat. Review. Contbr. articles to profl. jours. Address: 2121 N Bayshore Dr Miami FL 33137

DEAN, TALMAGE WHITMAN, educator, composer; b. Russellville, Tenn., Jan. 29, 1915; s. Thomas Elmo and Lucinda (Hale) D.; B.A., B.M., Hardin-Simmons U., 1940; M.Mus., Eastman Sch. Music, 1941; Ph.D., U. So. Cal., 1960; m. Frances Bama Sibley, Feb. 18, 1938; children—Linda Catherine (Mrs. Arthur Goolsbee), Diana Carol (Mrs. Curby Ligon), Katrina Frances (Mrs. Robert Fink), Thomas Sibley. Mem. faculty Hardin-Simmons U., Sch. Music, Abilene, Tex., 1941-43, 46-56, dean, 1952-56, 1967—; mem. faculty U. Tex., 1943-44; chmn. grad. studies in music Southwestern Bapt. Sem., 1956-67. Composer, arranger for Bapt. Radio and TV, 1957-63, Tex. Girls Choir, 1966-67. Served with USNR, 1944-46; Korea. Recipient Honors award in musicology U. So. Cal., 1960. Mem. Am. Musicol. Soc. (pres. Tex. chpt. 1953-54, sec.-treas. 1958-60), So. Bapt. Ch. Music Conf. (pres. 1961-63), Ft. Worth League of Composers, Phi Mu Alpha. Kiwanian. Composer: Baptist Hour Choral Series, 1957-67; The Raising of Lazarus, cantata for organ and chorus, 1961; Behold the Glory of the Lamb, oratorio for chorus and orch., 1963; Proclaim the Word, cantata for brass and chorus, 1965; Pax Vobis, contata for orch. and chorus, 1967; numerous contatas, anthems and instrumental works. Home: Route 3 Box 313 Abilene TX 79605

DEAN, THOMAS SCOTT, educator; b. Sherman, Tex., July 6, 1924; s. Lura Cecil and Lucille (Scott) D.; B.S., N. Tex. State U., 1947; M.S., Mass. Inst. Tech., 1949; postgrad. So. Meth. U., 1955-59; Ph.D., U. Tex., 1963; m. Jan Marie Dixon Irvine, June 1, 1945; children—Tamarie, Dixon Lee, Thomas Scott. Pvt. practice as architect and engr., Dallas, 1950-60; lectr., cons. So. Meth. U., Dallas, 1955-59; lectr. archtl. engring. U. Tex., Austin, 1960-64; prof. architecture Okla. State U., Stillwater, 1964—. Cons. Tex. Industries, Inc., Dallas, 1955-59. Served with C.E., AUS, 1943-44. Research fellow Latin Am. Studies Inst., 1963. Registered profl. engr., Tex., Okla.; registered architect, Tex., Okla. Mem. A.I.A., Nat. Soc. Profl. Engrs., Am. Soc. Engring. Edn., Am. Soc. C.E., Am. Soc. Heating, Refrigeration and Air conditioning Engrs. Contbr. articles to profl. jours. Home: 2002 Cresent Dr Stillwater OK 74074

DEANE, FREDERICK, JR., banker; b. Boston, Aug. 5, 1926; s. Frederick and Julia (Coolidge) D.; B.A., Harvard, 1948, M.B.A., 1951; m. Dorothy Legge, Dec. 21, 1948; children—Dorothy Porcher, Eleanor Dodds, Frederick III. Asst. to pres. Bank of Va., 1953-56, v.p., 1956-59, sr. v.p., 1959-64, exec. v.p., 1964-67, pres., 1967-69, vice chmn. bd., 1969—; exec. v.p. Va. Commonwealth Bankshares, Inc., 1963-65, pres., 1965—; dir. Mut. Insurers, Inc., Wards Co., Inc., Pres. Richmond Area Assn. for Retarded Children, 1958-62; active United Givers Fund; v.p., mem. finance com. Richmond Symphony, 1958-65. Trustee Va. Mus. Fine Arts; pres., dir. exec. com. Blue Cross of Va. Served to 1st lt. AUS, 1944-47; 1st lt., 1951-53. Mem. Young Presidents Orgn., Assn. Res. City Bankers, Richmond Soc. Financial Analysts (past pres.), Financial Analysts Fedn. Episcopalian. Clubs: Harvard of Virginia (past v.p., pres. bus. sch. sect.); Hasty Pudding Inst. 1770, Delphic (Harvard); Commonwealth; Country of Virginia; Harvard, Brook (N.Y.C.). Home: 110 W Hillcrest Av Richmond VA 23226 Office: 7 N 8th St Richmond VA 23260

DEANS, PARKER DUDLEY, atomic energy engr.; b. Coshocton, O., Jan. 27, 1916; s. Alvah Wilkins and Bessie (Joynes) D.; B.S. in Chem. Engring., Ga. Inst. Tech., 1938; m. Marie Edgeworth Killen, June 27, 1941; children—Margaret Virginia, Catherine Edgeworth. Research chemist So. Cotton Oil Co., Savannah, Ga., 1938-41; engr. E. I. duPont de Nemours & Co., Old Hickory, Tenn., 1941-42, research engr., sr. engr., Bridgeport, Conn., 1942-45, quality control supr., Old Hickory, 1945-49, research engr., statis. cons., Richmond, Va., 1949-51, quality control supt., area supt. Savannah River Plant, Aiken, S.C., 1951—. Pres., Crosland Park Civic Assn., 1952-53; commr. Aiken (S.C.) Recreation Commn., 1953-54; pres. Aiken Community Playhouse, 1962-64, 1965. Sr. mem. Am. Soc. Quality Control (chmn. Tenn. sect. 1946-47, nat. dir. 1946-48); mem. Am. Statis. Assn., Internat. Platform Assn. Episcopalian (pres. Men's Club 1954, sr. warden 1960-62). Home: 539 Highland Park Av SW Aiken SC 29801 Office: Savannah River Plant Aiken SC 29801

DEAR, HOWARD MARSHALL, banker; b. Houston, Apr. 5, 1939; s. Johnnie Maxwell and Evelyn Nell (Berry) D.; student Henderson County Jr. Coll., 1958-59, Grad. Sch. Banking Lon Morris Jr. Coll., 1959-60; B.B.A., Stephen F. Austin State Coll., 1962; m. Phyllis June Vaughan, May 26, 1961. Vice pres. First State Bank, Rusk, Tex., 1961-68; exec. v.p. First Nat. Bank, New Boston, Tex., 1968—; pres. Dear & Co., Inc., New Boston, 1970—; owner New Boston Real Estate Agy., New Boston, 1968—, New Boston Ins. Agy., 1968—. Dist. vice chmn. Caddo Area council Boy Scouts Am., 1969-71; pres. Athletic Booster Club, 1969-70. Baptist. Lion (v.p. 1969-70). Home: Imperial Apts Hwy 8 North New Boston TX 75570 Office: Box 608 New Boston TX 75570

DEARE, EARL WESLEY, JR., city ofcl.; b. Jeanerette, La., Oct. 7, 1931; s. Earl Wesley and Olive (Hebert) D.; student Internat. Inst. Municiapl Clks., 1971. Internat. Career Mgmt. Inst., 1969; m. Margaret Ann Miller, Feb. 24, 1952; children—Julie, Ricky, Kris, Mike. City clerk, treas., tax collector, Jeanerette, 1959—, personnel dir., 1965—. Served with USMCR, 1950-53. Named Outstanding Citizen, Jeanerette C. of C., 1970. Clk. of Year, Internat. Inst. Municipal Clks., 1971. Mem. Am. Legion, La. Municipal Clks. Assn. (pres. 1970-71), Jeanerette C. of C. (pres. 1970-71), Jeanerette Recreation Assn. Democrat. Roman Catholic. Home: E Side Bayou Jeanerette LA 70544 Office: Main St Jeanerette LA 70544

DEARING, HERMAN ANDREW, oil co. exec.; b. Dallas, Apr. 8, 1911; s. Willis R. and Nannie (Briggs) D.; student Tarleton State Coll., 1929-31, Tex. A. amd M. U., 1931-34; m. R. Lucille Findley, Nov..8, 1933; children—Betty Joan (Mrs. Jack V. Sears), Willis C. With Royal Petroleum Corp. and Dearing Corp., Dallas, 1932—, pres., 1965—; chmn. bd. Airscoe, Inc., Dallas; v.p. Civic Savs. & Loan Assn., Irvine, Tex., 1966—. Trustee C.C. Young Meml. Home, Dallas, 1956—. Methodist. Mason (Shriner, 32 deg.). Clubs: Dallas Petroleum, Las Colinas Country. Home: 6335 W Northwest Hwy Apt 1214 Dallas TX 75225 Office: 622 Meadows Bldg Dallas TX 75206

DEARMAN, WILBUR ELISHA, judge; b. Cuba, Ala., Oct. 9, 1908; s. John Albert and Annie (Shaw) D.; B.S., Auburn U., 1931; LL.B., Cumberland U., 1933; J.D., Samford U., 1969; m. Mary Emma Turner, Aug. 15, 1942; children—Marianne (Mrs. George D. Rainer), Jean Shaw (Mrs. Walter Mark Anderson III), Juanita (Mrs. Eladio Rubira II). Admitted to Ark. bar, 1934, Ala. bar, 1935; mem. firm Patton & Patton, Livingston, Ala., 1935—. Pres., Livingston P.T.A. Mem. Ala. Ho. of Reps., 1939-46; chmn. Sumter County Democratic Exec. Com., 1944-46; probate judge Sumter County, Ala., 1953—. Mem. Sumter County Hist. Soc. (pres.), Am., Ala. bar assns., Ala. Hist. Soc., Ala. Law Inst., Continuing Legal Edn. Ala. (exec. com.), Barristers, Blue Key, Tau Kappa Epsilon. Baptist (deacon, supt. Sunday sch.). Lion. Club: Commercial (Livingston). Home: Main and Spring Sts Livingston AL 35470 Office: Courthouse Livingston AL 35470

DEATHERAGE, WILLIAM GEIER, banker; b. Carrollton, Ky., Aug. 26, 1912; s. George William and Florence (Geier) D.; A.B., Centre Coll., 1933; m. Helen Frances Early, June 5, 1943; children—William G., Sara Jane, Julie Ann. Asst. cashier First Nat. Bank, Carrollton, Ky., 1934-37; cashier Deposit Bank, Shelbyville, 1937-40; bank examiner State of Ky., Frankfort, 1940-42; cashier Bank of Oldham County, LaGrange, 1947-50; v.p. Planters Bank & Trust Co., Hopkinsville, 1950-61, pres., 1961—; dir. Louisville br. Fed. Res. Bank St. Louis, Pennyrile Rural Electric Coop. Corp., Lincoln Income Life Ins. Co. Past bd. dirs. Hopkinsville Givers Fund; mem. Mayor's Adv. Com., 1963. Bd. dirs., Hopkinsville Servicemen's Center; bd. dirs., sec.-treas. Hopkinsville Indsl. Found.; mem. adv. bd. U.Ky., Hopkinsville Community Coll. Served to capt. AUS, 1942-46. Mem. Assn. Mil. Banks (past pres., dir.), Am. Bankers Assn. (regional v.p.), Ky. (dir.), Hopkinsville (dir.) chambers commerce, Sigma Alpha Epsilon. Democrat. Mem. Disciples of Christ Ch. Rotarian. Home: Route 2 Hopkinsville KY 42240 Office: 712 S Main St Hopkinsville KY 42240

DEATON, CHARLES MILTON, state legislator; b. Hattiesburg, Miss., Jan. 19, 1931; s. Ivan Dean and Martha (Fortenberry) D.; B.A., Millsaps Coll., 1956; LL.B., U. Miss., 1958; postgrad. George Washington U., 1952; m. Mary Dent Dickerson, Aug. 15, 1951; children—Beverly Diane, Dara Lane, Charles Milton II. Admitted to Miss. bar, 1958, since practiced in Greenwood; mem. firm Brewer, Deaton and Evans, 1963—; mem. Miss. Ho. of Reps., 1960—. Sec., Fish and Farms, Inc., 1966-67, now pres.; sec. Glass, Inc., 1965-67 (both Greenwood). City atty., Greenwood, Miss. Mem. Miss. Research and Devel. Council, 1964-72; mem. Gov.'s Program Statewide Planning for Vocational Rehab. in Miss.; chmn. Leflore County Rural Area Devel. Com.; mem. Miss. Commn. Budget and Accounting. Bd. dirs. Leflore County Sch. Handicapped Children. Served with USNR, 1951-54. Mem. Am., Miss. bar assns., Miss. Rivers and Harbors Assn. (pres. 1966-67), Kappa Sigma, Phi Delta Phi, Omicron Delta Kappa. Episcopalian. Lion (pres. 1966-67). Home: 501 E Harding St Greenwood MS 38930 Office: Drawer B Greenwood MS 38930

DEATON, HILLMAN EDWARD, safety exec.; b. Hope, Ark., July 9, 1922; s. Lewis Edward and Beartie (Tarpley) D.; student East Tex. Bapt. Coll., 1958-59, Centenary Coll., 1960-62; B.A., Bapt. Christian Coll., 1963; postgrad. Nat. Christian U., 1970-71; m. Billy Faye Johnson, Feb. 14, 1949; children—Larry, Phillip, Peggy. Bus operator Southwestern Greyhound Lines, Dallas, 1948-50; examiner motor vehicle operations Red River Arsenal, Texarkana, Tex., 1951-53; mgmt. trainee East Tex. Motor Freight Lines, 1953-57; fleet safety engr. J. B. Beard Co., Shreveport, La., 1957; dir. safety AMF Beaird, Inc., Shreveport, La., 1957—; group cons. gen. products group Am. Machine & Foundry Corp., Shreveport, La., 1966-68, corporate cons., N.Y.C., 1968—. Mem. Pres. Kennedy's Com. on Occupation Safety, 1961. Served with USAAF, 1942-46. Recipient Distinguished Service award Am. Soc. Safety Engrs., Ark.-La.-Tex. chpt., 1968. Mem. Am. Soc. Safety Engrs. (pres. Ark.-La.-Tex. chpt. 1965-66), La. Motor Transport Assn. (dir. 1961-62), Shreveport C. of C. (chmn. indsl. sect. 1968-69), Am. Indsl. Hygiene Assn. Mason. Home: 3106 Green Terrace Shreveport LA 71108 Office: PO Box 1115 Shreveport LA 71130

DE AVILA, ALEJANDRO, physician; b. Oaxaca, Mexico, Aug. 16, 1922; s. Alejandrino and Refugio (Cervantes) de Avila; student Universidad Autonoma de San Luis Potosi, 1937-41; M.D., Universidad Nacional Autonoma de Mexico, 1949; m. Alice Blomberg, Mar. 24, 1956; children—Alejandro, Mark Edward, David Michael, Elizabeth. Physician, Social Service, El Fuerte, Sinaloa, 1948-49; intern, King County Hosp. System, Seattle, 1951-52; anesthesia resident King County Hosp. System, Children's Orthopedic Hosp., Seattle, 1952-54; anesthesiologist Am. Brit. Cowdray Hosp., Mexico, 1959—, dir. inhalation therapy service, 1966—. Mem. Am. Soc. Anesthesiologists, Sociedad Mexicana de Anesthesiologia, World Fedn. Neurology, Pan Am. Med. Assn., Asociacion Mexicana de Hospitales, Phi Chi. Rotarian. Author (with Everado Ortiz) Temas Medico Quirurgicas; (with Juan Cardenas) Neurologia, 1960. Editor: Revista Mexicana de Anesthesiologia, 1959-61. Address: 810 Crater St Mexico DF Mexico

DEBAKEY, MICHAEL E(LLIS), surgeon; b. Lake Charles, La., Sept. 7, 1908; s. Shaker Morris and Raheiga (Zerba) DeB.; B.S., Tulane U., 1930, M.D., 1932, M.S., 1935; Dr. honoris causa, U. Lyon, 1961, U. Brussels, 1962, U. Ghent, 1964, U. Athens, 1964, U. Turin, 1965; L.L.D., Tulane U., 1965, Lafayette Coll., 1965, U. Cin., McNeese U., 1972; D.Sc., D'Youville Coll., 1967, U. Mich., 1967, Fla. State U., 1968, MacMurray Coll., 1971; Dr. Med. Scis., Aristotelean U. of Thessaloniki, 1971; D.Sc. honoris causa, Assumption Coll., 1971, L.I. U., 1971; Hon. Dr., Ljubljana U., 1971; M.D. honoris causa, U. Louvain; m. Diana Cooper, Oct. 15, 1936; children—Michael Maurice, Ernest Ochsner, Barry Edward, Denis Alton. Intern Charity Hosp., New Orleans, 1932-33, asst. in surg., 1933-35; asst. in surg. U. Strasbourg, 1935-36; instr. surgery Tulane U., 1937-40, asst. prof., 1940-46, asso. prof., 1946-48; prof. surgery, chmn. dept. Baylor U., Houston, 1948—, pres., chief exec. officer Coll. Medicine, 1969—, Distinguished Service prof., 1968—; pvt. practice Ochsner Clinic, New Orleans, 1946-48; sr. attending surgeon, dir. Cardiovascular Research Center, Methodist Hosp., Houston, 1967—; hon. faculty medicine U. Chile, Santiago, 1964; surgeon in chief Ben Taub Gen. Hosp., Houston; cons. staff, mem. exec. com. St. Luke's Episcopal Hosp., Houston; cons. surgery M.D. Anderson Hosp. and Tumor Inst., Tex. Children's Hosp. (both Houston); clin. prof. surg. U. Tex. Dental Br., Houston, 1971-72; distinguished prof. surgery Tex. A. and M. U., 1972—; cons. Tex. Inst. Rehab. and Research, Brooke Gen. Hosp., Ft. Sam Houston; area cons. thoracic surgery to VA, 1946—. Mem. med. adv. com. Sec. of Def., 1948-50; chmn. com. on surgery NRC, 1953, mem. exec. com., 1953; mem. task force Commn. for Reorgn. Exec. Br. Govt.; mem. Nat. Adv. Health Council, 1961-65, Nat. Adv. Council Region Med. Programs, 1965—, Civilian Health and Med. Adv. Council Office Asst. Sec. Def.; mem. med. adv. bd. Am. Hosp. of Paris, 1971—; cons. cardiovascular surgery to surgeon gen. U.S. Air Force; mem. adv. council Nat. Heart Inst. Bd. visitors Tulane U., 1970—; trustee S.W. Research Inst., 1972—. Served as col., Office of Surgeon Gen., AUS, 1942-46, surg. cons. to surgeon gen., 1946—. Decorated Legion of Merit, knight comdr. Order of Merit Italian Republic; recipient Rudolph Matas award, 1954; Hektoen Gold Medal, A.M.A.; Internat. Soc. Surgery award, 1958, 59; Distinguished Service award A.M.A., 1959; Albert Lasker award for clin. research, 1963; St. Vincent prize med. scis. U. Turin, 1965; Orden del Libertador Gen. San Martin, Argentina, 1965; Hunterian medal St. George's Hosp. Med. Sch., London, Eng., 1966; Centennial medal Albert Einstein Med. Center, 1966; P.A. Gertzin medal Internat. Med. Sci. Orgn. of Surgeons, Moscow, 1971, medallion Tex. Med. Center, 1972, Spl. Recognition award Merck Sharp & Dohme, 1971, Distinguished Citizens award Rotary Club, 1972, others. Diplomate Am. Bd. Surgery, Am. Bd. Thoracic Surgery, Nat. Bd. Med. Examiners. Fellow A.C.S., Am. Coll. Cardiology (hon.); mem. Internat Cardiovascular Soc. (pres. N.Am. chpt. 1964), Southwestern Surg. Congress (pres. 1952), Soc. Vascular Surgery (pres. 1953), A.M.A., Tex. Med. Assn. Council on med. edn. and hosps. 1971—), Am., So., Western surg. assns., Am. Assn. Thoracic Surgery (pres. 1959), Soc. Clin. Surgery, Soc. U. Surgeons, Internat. Soc. Surgery, Soc. Exptl. Biology and Medicine, Sociedad Nacional de Cirugia, Am. Acad. Achievement (gov.), A.A.A.S., Am. Assn. Cancer Research, Am. Soc. Contemporary Medicine and Surgery (pres. 1971—), Am. Trauma Soc. (founding), N.Y. Acad. Scis., World Med. Assn., Philos. Soc. Tex., Mexican Acad. Surgery, Cuban Med. Assn. in Exile (hon.), Udruzenje Kirurga Jugoslavia (hon.), Acad. Medicine of Turin (fgn. hon. asso.), Am. Geriatric Soc., Am. Heart Assn. (founding mem. council cerebrovascular disease, mem. council on thrombosis), Alpha Omega Alpha. Democrat. Episcopalian. Rotarian (hon. Houston). Clubs: Cosmos, University (Washington); Press (Houston). Author: (with Kilduffe) Blood Transfusion, 1942; (with Gilbert W. Beebe) Battle Casualties, 1952; (with Alton Ochsner) Textbook of Minor Surgery, 1955. Editor surg. vols. AUS Medical History of World War II; Year Book of General Surgery; mem. editorial bd. surg. jours.; mem. editorial adv. bd. Biomed. Materials and Artificial Organs, 1971—. Home: 5323 Cherokee St Houston TX 77005 Office: 1200 Moursund Av Houston TX 77025

DE BAUERNFEIND, JOSEPH BUFFINGTON, chem. co. exec.; b. Nelson, Neb., Nov. 7, 1916; s. Frank E. and Nell M. (Buffington) de B.; B.A., Ohio Wesleyan U., 1938; m. Marjorie Anne Skelton, Jan. 17, 1942; 1 dau., Deborah Lee. Vice-pres. S. S. Skelton Co., Cleve., 1947-52; product mgr. Glidden Co., Jacksonville, Fla., 1953-62; mgr. sales and marketing, terpene and aromatics div. Union Camp Corp., Jacksonville, 1962—. Asso. trustee Ohio Wesleyan U. Served with USNR, 1941-45. Mem. Essential Oil Assn., Phi Gamma Delta. Presbyn. (elder 1949—). Club: Timuquana Country (Jacksonville). Home: 4209 Forest Park Rd Jacksonville FL 32210 Office: PO Box 6170 Jacksonville FL 32205

DEBAYLE, LUIS MANUEL, Nicaraguan diplomat; b. Leon, Nicaragua, May 24, 1894; s. Luis H. and Casimira (Sacasa) D.; B.Scis. and Letters, Instituto Nacional de Occidente, 1912; B.S., U. Pa., 1913, M.D., 1919; M.P.H., Johns Hopkins, 1934. Intern hosps., Phila., 1919-20; asst. dean, prof. surg. chemistry Sch. Medicine, Universidad de Occidente, Leon, 1924-26; chief surgeon Hosp. San Vicente, Leon, 1925-30; first gen. dir. Dept. Health Nicaragua, created 1st pub. health law of republic, 1925; consul of Nicaragua in Balt., 1930; del. 6th Comml. Conf., Washington; minister fgn. relations, chief delegation Peace Conf., Buenos Aires, 1936; founder Primera Escuela de Visitadoras Sanitarias de Nicaragua, 1937; col. Nicaraguan N.G., also med. dir. N.G., 1937-46; founder, dir. Boletin Sanitario de Nicaragua, 1937; personal rep. of Pres. of Nicaragua to Pres. Roosevelt on spl. mission to obtain funds, 1937; various pub. health and diplomatic posts, 1938-45; del. San Francisco conf. UN, 1945; then minister fgn. relations; E.E. and chancellor of Nicaragua to Pope Pius XII, 1948; rep. to Nat. Assembly, senator, pres. Senate and Congress, 1950-55; first designate to Presidency of Republic, 1956; E.A. on spl. mission, chief delegation inauguration Pres. Mateos of Mexico, 1959; E. and P. ambassador, permanent rep. of Nicaragua to UN, 1960—; now consul gen. of Nicaragua, Miami. Pres., Compania Nacional Productora de Cemento, Managua, Compania de Productores de Leche, Managua; dir. Compania Nacional de Seguros de Nicaragua. Decorated gold sash and star Order of Jade (Nationalist China); grad. sash and star Order Vasco Nunes de Balboa (Panama); Medal of Merit (Ecuador); Medal of Honor (Mexico City); Presdl. Medal of Merit, Medal of Valor (Nicaragua); gran banda y placa Order del Aguila Azteca (Mexico); gran banda y placa Order del Servicio Distinguido (Spain); gran banda y placa Order of Chipre (Jerusalem); gran banda y placa Order del Cruzeiro do Sul (Brazil); decoration Instituto Finlay (Cuba); Rockefeller fellow. Mem. Internat. Coll. Surgeons (founder, v.p. Nicaragua chpt., recipient medal), sociedads medica de Nicaragua, de Managua, Academia de Ciencia Sinalogica de Nicaragua (pres.), Bassini Surg. Soc. Phila., Pan Am. Med. Assn. (founding mem.), Phi Kappa Delta, Nu Sigma Nu; hon. mem. Lucha Anti-Tb Centroamerioana, Lucha Anti-Venerea Centroamerican, Museo Social Argentina, U.S. Assn. Pub. Health, Assn. Mil. Surgeon U.S. (Gold cross), Pan Am. socs. N.Y., San Francisco. Lion (founder in Nicaragua, 1st regional vice gov.). Clubs: Social Terraza, Internacional (Managua); Nejapa Country; Social (Chinandega). Author numerous med. and polit. articles. Home: 3290 Riviera Dr Miami FL 33134

DE BEAUBRIEN, PHILIP FRANCIS, banker; b. Conneaut, O., Feb. 9, 1913; s. Jay William and Eileen Anne (Schubert) deB.; student pub. schs.; m. June Elizabeth Hesse, June 18, 1937; children—Philip Francis, Suzette Farie (Mrs. George L. Brown III), Hugo Hesse. Detroit mgr. Good Housekeeping mag., 1945-50; central zone mgr. Look Mag., 1950-56; pub. Detroit Times, 1956-61; v.p. Comml. Bank, Daytona Beach, Fla., 1963—. Writer financial column under pseudymon Homer Holiday, Fla. newspapers, 1963—. Pres., Halifax Cultural Found., 1965-67. Mem. Fla. Bankers Assn. (chmn. pub. edn. com. 1966-67, chmn. advt. com. 1967-69). Home: 709 Ocean Shore Blvd Ormond Beach FL 32074 Office: 120 S Ridgewood Daytona Beach FL 32014

DEBENPORT, JERALD RANDOLPH, JR., indsl. engr., mayor; b. Tyler, Tex., Jan. 10, 1928; s. Jerald Randolph and Maurinne (Teller) D.; B.S., E. Tex. State U., 1953; m.Martha Sue Allsopp, Aug. 12, 1950; children—Cliff Edmund, Don Albert. Asso. customer engr., customer engr. IBM Corp., Tyler, 1953-60, sr. customer engr., 1960—; mayor, Tyler, 1970—. Chmn. Smith County Youth Adv. Bd., 1963-65; scoutmaster Rose City council Boy Scouts Am., 1953-59. Mem. Tyler City Commn., 1969. Served with USNR, 1945-46. Republican. Baptist (deacon). Kiwanian. Patentee in field. Home: 1220 Parkdale St Tyler TX 75701 Office: 321 E Front St Tyler TX 75701

DE BESCHE, HUBERT WATHIER AUGUST, Swedish diplomat; b. Froso, Jamtlands lan, Sweden, July 7, 1911; s. Hubert W. and Ebba A. (Froberg) de B.; degree in law U. Stockholm, 1935; student U. Grenoble (France), U. Heidelberg (Germany); m. Eva Rhedin, Mar. 21, 1946; children—Caroline, Gunilla. Joined Swedish Fgn. Ministry, 1936; assigned London, Eng., 1937-40; assigned Fgn. Ministry, 1940-49, charge Commn. Trade and Commerce, 1947-49; econ. counselor embassy, Washington, 1949-53; head trade dept. Fgn. Ministry, 1953-56; dep. sec. gen. Fgn. Ministry, 1956-64; Swedish ambassador to U.S., 1964-—. Mem. steering bd. for trade OEEC, 1956-60; vice chmn. trade com. OECD, 1960-63; chmn. prep. com. European Free Trade Assn., Stockholm, 1959; chmn. Swedish trade delegation to Finland, Spain, U.K., 1954-55, to GATT, 1955-60; vice chmn. negotiations Free Trade Area, Paris, France, 1956-58; vice chmn. Swedish delegation European Free Trade Assn., 1960-63. Decorated knight comdr. Order North Star (Sweden); knight grand cross Iranian Order Homayoun; knight grand cross Portuguese Order Christ; knight grand cross Order Merito (Chile); also numerous other decorations. Home: 3900 Nebraska Av NW Washington DC 20016 Office: Watergate 600 New Hampshire Av NW Washington DC 20037

DE BLIEUX, JOSEPH DAVIS, state senator; lawyer; b. Columbia, La., Sept. 12, 1912; s. Honore Louis and Ozet (Perot) BeB.; student Ouachita Parish Jr. Coll., 1932-34; LL.B., La. State U., 1938; m. Dorothy Lepine, Apr. 22, 1946; 1 son, Paul Louis. Admitted to La. bar, 1938, U.S. Supreme Ct. bar, 1958; practiced in Baton Rouge, 1938-—; mem. firm DeBlieux Guidry & Lowe, Baton Rouge, 1959-—; mem. La. Senate, 1956-60, 64-—. Mem. Pub. Affairs Research Council, Baton Rouge, 1952-—; chmn. La. Adv. Com., U.S. Commn. on Civil Rights, 1960-—. Bd. dirs. Community Advancement, Inc., Greater Baton Rouge Mental Health Assn. Del. Democratic Nat. Conv., 1956, 64, 68; mem. La. Central Com., 1960-—. Served with AUS, 1942-45. Decorated knight St. Gregory the Great, Pope Pius XII, 1958. Mem. Am., La. Baton Rouge bar assns., Baton Rouge C. of C., Am. Legion, Amvets. Roman Catholic. Moose, K.C., Lion. Club: Serra (Baton Rouge). Home: 3755 Churchill Av Baton Rouge LA 70808 Office: PO Box 3574 Baton Rouge LA 70821

DEBORD, ROBERT EDWARD, physician; b. Marion, Va., Sept. 28, 1922; s. John Thompson and Emma (McCready) DeB.; B.S., Emory and Henry Coll., 1949; M.D., Med. Coll. Va., 1953; m. Martha Jane Porter, Feb. 6, 1954; children—Martha, Nancy, Emily, Robert, David. Intern Med. Coll. Va., 1953-54; practice medicine specializing in family practice, Williamsburg, Va., 1954-—; coll. physician Coll. William & Mary, Williamsburg, 1954-—; mem. staff Community Hosp., pres., 1969-70. Vice pres. Mill Creek Corp., Williamsburg, 1970-71; med. examiner James City County and Williamsburg, 1956-—. Bd. dirs. Jamestown Acad., Williamsburg, 1966-—. Served with AUS, 1942-46. Mem. James City County Med. Soc. (pres. 1961-62), Ruritan. Home: 202 Matoaka Ct Williamsburg VA 23185 Office: 224 Monticello Av Williamsburg VA 23185

DEBRUCQUE, WILLIAM ROBERT, dentist; b. Tulsa, Apr. 23, 1929; s. Phillip Baldwin and Ruby (Ragan) DeB.; B.S., U. Tulsa, 1958; D.D.S., Baylor U., 1957; m. Linda Sue Thompson, Sept. 23, 1955; children—Valerie Kay, Natalie Rae. Practice gen. dentistry, Dallas, 1957-—. Bd. dirs. Tex. Found. for Dental Health. Served with AUS, 1946-48, 50-52. Mem. Dallas County (bd. dirs.), Tex., Am. dental assns., Internat. Assn. Orthodontics, Psi Omega, Kappa Sigma. Republican (del. to state conv. 1970-—). Editor Dallas Dental Soc. News, 1969-70. Contbr. to profl. jours. Home: 522 Brook Valley Lane Dallas TX 75232 Office: 4323 Lemmon Av Dallas TX 75219

DEBUS, KURT HEINRICH, govt. ofcl.; b. Frankfurt-am-Main, Germany, Nov. 29, 1908; s. Heinrich P.J. and Melly (Graulich) D.; M.S. in Elec. Engring., Darmstadt Tech. U., 1936, Ph.D. in Elec. Engring., 1939; LL.D. (hon.), Rollins Coll., 1967; D.Eng., Fla. Technol. U., 1969; D.Sc., Fla. Inst. Tech., 1970; m. Irmgard Helene Brueckmann, June 30, 1937; children—Ute Irmgard, Sigrid Monika (Mrs. William R. Northcutt). Came to U.S., 1945, naturalized, 1959. Asst. prof. Darmstadt Tech. U., 1939-42; test engr., flight test dir. Peenemuende Rocket Center, 1942-45; dep. dir. guidance and control div., staff asst. to Wernher von Braun, Army Ballistic Missile Agy., U.S. Army, Huntsville, Ala., 1945-52, dir. missile firing lab., Cape Canaveral, Fla., 1952-60; dir. launch operations directorate G.C. Marshall Space Flight Center, NASA, Cape Canaveral, 1960-62, dir. Launch Operations Center, 1962-63, dir. John F. Kennedy Space Center, Fla., 1963-—. Mem. sr. mgmt. council Office Manned Space Flight, NASA. Chmn. Brevard County U.S. Savs. Bond Drives, 1962-—; chmn. Brevard-Indian River campaign Muscular Dystrophy Assn. Am., 1969-70. Recipient Exceptional Civilian Service award U.S. Army, 1959; Frank A. Scott gold medal Am. Ordnance Assn., 1964; NASA Outstanding Leadership award, 1964; Pioneer of Windrose award Order of the Diamond, 1965; AAS Space Flight award, 1968; Outstanding Achievement award U.S. Treasury Dept., 1968; Nat. Civil Service League Career award, 1969; Distinguished Service medal for Apollo 8, NASA, 1969, for Apollo 11, 1969, Apollo Achievement award, 1969; named to Nat. Space Hall of Fame, 1969; recipient Americanism medal D.A.R., 1969; decorated comdr.'s cross Order of Merit Fed. Republic of Germany, 1971. others. Mem. Hermann Oberth Geselischaft (hon., recipient Honor Ring 1971), Brit. Interplanetary Soc. (adv. bd. 1968), Am. Ordnance Assn. (life), German Soc. Rocket Tech. and Space Flight (hon.), Instrument Soc. Am. (hon.). Club: Nat. Space (gov. 1963). Home: 280 Bahama Blvd Cocoa Beach FL 32931 Office: John F Kennedy Space Center NASA Kennedy Space Center FL 32899

DE CARDONA, JORGE HIRAM, dentist; b. Aguadilla, P.R., Nov. 13, 1915; s. Francisco and Maria (Quinones) de C.; student U. P.R., 1933-34; D.D.S., Temple U., 1938; postgrad. in surgery U. P.R., 1971, in oral cancer, 1971-72;; m. Alicia Martinez Bianchi, Mar. 16, 1942; children—Alicia (Mrs. Nelson Fernandez), Hiram Arsenio, Olga Maria. Dentist, Am. Jr. Red Cross, 1938-40, Aguadilla (P.R.) Health Dept., 1940-42; pvt. practice dentistry, Aguadilla, 1938-—. Served from 1st lt. to maj., AUS, World War II. Mem. Am. Dental Assn., Colegio Cirujanos Dentistas (pres. Aguadilla dist. 1963-64), Cirujanes Dentistas de P.R., Order San Juan Bautista, Phi Eta Mu. Roman Catholic. Home: 62 Betances St Aguadilla PR 00603 Office: 62 Altos Betances St Aguadilla PR 00603

DECELL, JOHN ASHLAND, health care center exec.; b. Vicksburg, Miss., Dec. 21, 1935; s. Halbert Clayton and Frances (Chichester) DeC.; B.A., U. Miss., 1958; m. Mary Elizabeth Weir, Aug. 9, 1958; children— Katherine Elizabeth, Frances Shannon, Elizabeth Anne. Asst. v.p. Allied Mortgage Co., Memphis, 1961-64; v.p. Wallace E. Johnson, Inc., Memphis, 1964-65; pres., dir. Medicenters Am., Inc., Memphis, 1965-—. Served with USAF, 1958-61. Mem. Omicron Delta Kappa, Delta Sigma Pi, Phi Delta Theta. Clubs: Sales Executives (Memphis). Home: 3670 Shady Hollow Lane Memphis TN 38116 Office: 1331 Union Av Memphis TN 38104

DE CHABERT, ANSETTA (MRS. RALPH DE CHABERT), Democratic nat. committeewoman; b. Christiansted, St. Croix, V.I., Feb. 11, 1908; m. Ralph de Chabert (dec.); children— Ralph, Austin, Mario, Rita (Mrs. Schuster), Shirley (Mrs. Highfield). Mem. Pub. Welfare Bd., also Bd. Edn., V.I.; Dem. nat. committeewoman, V.I., 1964-—; del., mem. majority platform com. Dem. Nat. Com., 1968; finance chmn. St. Croix Dem. Com. Vice chmn. Red Cross. Mem. Charles Howard Hosp. Aux. (pres.), Bus. and Profl. Women's Club, League Women Voters, Friends of Denmark. Address: PO Box 889 Christiansted St Croix VI 00820*

DECHELLIS, LOUIS JOHN, chem. co. exec.; b. Struthers, O., Feb. 9, 1926; s. Carlo and Antoinette (Pompeo) DeC.; B.S., U. Notre Dame, 1949; m. Helen Louise Flanagan, July 3, 1954; children—Anita, Marc, Anthony, Teresa. Chief chemist Andrew Brown Co. Tex., Irving, 1950-61; area mgr. Glidden-Durkee div. SCM Corp., Dallas, 1961-68; pres. L. J. DeChellis Co., Dallas, 1968-—. Served with AUS, 1944-46, USNR, 52-54. Mem. Dallas Soc. Paint Tech., Dallas Paint Varnish and Lacquer Assn. Elk. Home: 1725 Hillcrest Dr Irving TX 75060 Office: 3200 Irving Blvd Dallas TX 75247

DECHERD, H. BEN, newspaper exec.; b. Dallas, Mar. 14, 1915; s. Henry Benjamin and Fannie (Dealey) D.; B.A., U. Tex., 1936; m. Isabelle Thomason, Dec. 17, 1938; children—Dealey (Mrs. H. David Herndon), Robert W. With A.H. Belo Corp., pub. Dallas Morning News, Tex. Suburban Dailies and Tex. Almanac; owner radio-TV stas. WFAA, TV sta. KFDM, Beaumont, Tex., 1936, 38-—, v.p., sec., 1960-64, chmn. exec. com., 1964-68, chmn. bd., 1968-—; with Balt. Sunpapers, 1937. Past pres., Family Guidance Center, Incarnation Day Sch., S.W. Sch. Printing, St. Marks Sch. Tex.; bd. dirs. Central Bus. Dist. Assn., Dallas Zool. Soc., Dallas Symphony Orch., Southwestern Legal Found., St. Mark's Sch. Tex.; trustee Dallas Hist. Soc., Tex. Research Found. Served to lt. col. inf. AUS, 1942-46. Decorated Bronze Star medal. Mem. Tex. Daily Newspaper Assn. (past pres.), Phi Beta Kappa, Phi Delta Theta. Episcopalian. Clubs: City, Dallas Country, Northwood, Petroleum, Idlewild (Dallas). Home: Apt 1A 3131 Maple Av Dallas TX 75201 Office: Dallas Morning News Dallas TX 75222

DECHOUDENS-LABOY, JOSE MIGUEL, social worker; councelor; b. Guayama, P.R., Feb. 14, 1934; s. Rafael and Felicita (Laboy) DeC.; B.S., John Carroll U., Cleve., 1957; M.S.W., Fordham U., 1959; postgrad. U. P.R., 1965-69; m. Dimna Marrero-Aulet, July 25, 1959; children— Yvonne, Lourdes. Psychiat. social worker Childrens Village, N.Y.C., 1959-61, Northside Center for Child Devel., N.Y.C., 1961-65, Family Inst. P.R., 1965-—; research interviewing Community Council Greater N.Y. Bd. dirs. Puerto Rican Family Inst.-N.Y.C., 1960-64, Legal Service P.R. Mem. Nat., P.R. (sec.) assns. social workers, Acad. Certified Social Workers. Home: JJ-13 Fiqueras Villa Andalucia Rio Piedras PR 00926 Office: 154 Los Myrtis St Hyde Park Rio Piedras PR 00928

DECK, PHILIP EUGENE, electronics engr.; b. Cin., Oct. 12, 1935; s. Elah Michael and Kathryn Lucille (DeVore) D.; B.A., Rice U., 1957, B.S. in E.E. (J. Venn Leeds scholar), 1958, M.S. (Westinghouse scholar), 1960; m. Carolyn Louise Sanders, June 10, 1958; children—Patricia Lynn, Deanna, Kathryn Marie. Staff engr. Rice U. Computer Project, Houston, 1958-60; chief engr. Osage Computer Project, U. Okla. Research Inst., Norman, 1962-64; dir. engring. Telex Computer Products, Tulsa, Okla., 1964-—. Cons. John D. Foster Co., Norman, Okla., 1962-64. Mem. indsl. technologies adv. com. Tulsa Jr. Coll., 1970-—. Served to lt. USNR, 1960-62. Mem. I.E.E.E., R Assn., Sigma Xi, Sigma Tau. Republican. Methodist. Club: Tulsa Country. Patentee in field. Home: 221 E Woodward Blvd Tulsa OK 74114 Office: 6422 E 41st St Tulsa OK 74135

DECKARD, CHARLES, financial exec.; b. nr. Bloomington, Ind., June 1, 1927; s. James Andrew and Nora (Sipes) D.; B.S., Ind. U., 1951; m. Emily Jane Dwyer, Dec. 25, 1948; children—Norita Charlene, Charles Kevin, Mark Alison. Instr. Ind. U., 1951-52; with Bendix Corp., South Bend, Ind., 1951-61, asst. to mgr. internal audit staff, 1956-61, controller Sheffield Corp., Dayton, O., 1961-66, div. controller Automotion and Measurement div. Bendix Corp., Dayton, 1966-69, Automotive Electronics div., Balt., 1969-70, Newport News, Va., 1971-—. Served with AUS, 1945-46. Methodist. Club: Four Seasons Towne (founding trustee, treas.) (Dayton). Home: 1 Digges Dr Newport News VA 23602 Office: 615 Bland Blvd Newport News VA 23602

DECKER, ALLAN FRANCIS, banker; b. Fairbury, Neb., Sept. 17, 1929; s. Oscar C. and June L. (Brunner) D.; B.S., U. Neb., 1951, LL.B., 1955; m. Teckla Ellen Stelling, Aug. 22, 1953; children—Kathy A., Robert E., William J. Spl. agt. FBI, 1956-59; trust officer S.C. Nat. Bank, Charleston, 1959-64; v.p. trust investment officer First Nat. Bank, Fort Myers, Fla., 1964-—. Mem. Estate Planning Council, Lee County, Fla., v.p., 1971-72. Mem. Lee County exec. com. Republican party, 1966-69. Served to 1st lt. AUS, 1951-53. Mem. Financial Analysts Soc. Central Fla., Neb. State Bar Assn., Soc. Former Spl. Agts FBI (pres. S.W. Fla. chpt. 1969-70), C. of C. Home: 1096 N Town and River Dr Fort Myers FL 33901 Office: PO Box 130 Fort Myers FL 33902

DECKERT, GORDON H., psychiatrist, educator; b. Freeman, S.D., 1930; M.D., Northwestern U., 1955. Intern Passavant Meml. Hosp., Chgo., 1955-56; fellow in internal medicine Mayo Clinic and Found., Rochester, Minn., 1956-57; resident in psychiatry Okla. Med. Center, 1956-62; clin. investigator in psychiatry VA Hosp., Oklahoma City, 1964-66; practice medicine specializing in psychiatry, Oklahoma City; asst. prof. psychiatry U. Okla., Norman, 1964-66, career tchr. psychiatry, 1966-68, asso. prof., 1966-—, chmn. dept. psychiatry and behavioral sci., 1969-—. Served to capt. M.C., USAF, 1957-59. Diplomate Am. Bd. Psychiatry and Neurology. Mem. A.M.A., Am. Psychiat. Assn., A.A.A.S., Am. Psychosomatic Soc., Assn. Psychophys. Study Sleep, Soc. Psychophysiol. Research, Am. Assn. U. Profs., Sigma Xi, Alpha Omega Alpha. Office: 800 NE 13th St Oklahoma City OK 73104

DECKLER, EDNA PERRY, genealogist; b. Haslet, Tex., Jan. 1, 1920; d. Guy Stockton and Mary Estill (Burgess) Perry; student U. Tex.; m. Hyman Deckler, Aug. 21, 1943; 1 dau., Joyce Patricia. Organizer, Ft. Worth Geneal. Soc., pres., editor, 1957-61; organizer Tex. State Geneal. Soc., 1960, pres., editor, 1960-—; trustee Bd. Certification Genealogists. Bd. dirs. Camp Fire Girls, Christian Women's Fellowship, P.T.A. Fellow Soc. Antiquaries Scotland; mem. Daus. Republic Tex. (pres. Van Zandt chpt.), U.S. Daus. 1812 (rec. sec. Tarrant chpt. 1960-62), Tarrant County Hist. Survey Com. (chmn.), Daus Am. Colonists (geneal. registrar Livingston chpt. 1962-64), Ft. Worth Geneal. Soc. (parliamentarian 1963), Friends Ft. Worth Pub. Library (dir.), Tex. Library Assn. (chmn. archives roundtable, lay mem.), Md. Geneal. Soc., Tex., Anne Arundel (Md.) hist socs., U.D.C., Am. Assn. State and Local History, Nat. Geneal Soc., D.A.R. (chpt. regent), Daus. Colonial Wars, A.L.A., Am. Hist. Assn., Soc. Am. Archivists (mem. oral history com. 1970), New Eng. Hist. Geneal. Soc. Editor The Geneal. Soc. Bull., 1957-61, editor Stirpes, 1961-—. Address: 2528 University Dr S Fort Worth TX 76109

DEDRICK, ROBERT LYLE, chem. engr., govt. ofcl.; b. Madison, Wis., Jan. 12, 1933; s. Calvert Lampert and Ruth (Larson) D.; B.Engring., Yale, 1956; M.S. in Engring. (Gen. Electric fellow), U. Mich., 1957; Ph.D. (NSF sci. faculty fellow 1963-64), U. Md., 1965; m. Marion Virginia Repass, Aug. 6, 1955; children—Elizabeth Ann, John Robert, David Lars. Asst. prof. George Washington U., Washington, 1959-63, asso. prof., 1965-66; acting chief chem. engring. sec. NIH, Bethesda, Md., 1966-67, chief, 1967-—; lectr. dept. chem. engring. U. Md., 1969-—. Served with USAF, 1957-59. Recipient Yale Engring. Assn. High Scholarship prize, 1956; award for sci. achievement in engring. scis. Washington Acad. Scis., 1971. Mem. Am. Inst. Chem. Engrs., Am. Chem. Soc., Am. Soc. Engring. Edn., Washington Philos. Soc., Am. Soc. Artificial Internal Organs, A.A.A.S., Sigma Xi (asso.), Tau Beta Pi, Phi Kappa Phi, Phi Lambda Upsilon, Alpha Chi Sigma. Methodist. Home: 1633 Warner Av McLean VA 22101 Office: NIH Bethesda MD 20014

DEEB, RICHARD JAMES, state senator; b. Tallahassee, Sept. 8, 1924; s. George and Mary (Shaheen) D.; B.S. in Civil Engring., U. Notre Dame, 1947; m. Catalina Panayotti, Jan. 7, 1950; children—Alex, Richard, Teresa, Thomas. Operator Dick Deeb Realtor, St. Petersburg, Fla., 1952-—; pres. Deeb Constrn. Co., Inc., St. Petersburg, 1952-—; mem. Fla. Ho. of Reps., 1963-66; mem. Fla. Senate, 1966-—, Republican floor leader, 1971-72; chmn. 15 state sub-com. on Local Govt. Fiscal Affairs, 1967-68. Rep. Fla. Legislature to Nat. Legislative Council, 1963-64, 67-68. Chmn. St. Petersburg Minimum Housing Standards Bd., 1963-64; nat. v.p. Aiding Leukemia Striken Am. Children, St. Jude Children's Hosp., 1962-63. Served with AUS, 1945-46. Recipient award for outstanding service to all Fla. Vets. AMVETS, 1967; award for outstanding service on behalf all civic orgns. Lions Internat., 1967; Distinguished Pub. Service award Fla. Assn. Realtors, 1967; Distinguished Service award Contractors and Builders Assn., 1969; award for assistance to Fla. citrus industry Fla. Citrus Mut., 1969; Distinguished Service award K.C., 1968. Mem. St. Petersburg Bd. Realtors, Contractors And Builders Assn. Pinellas County, Amvets., Am. Legion. K.C. Clubs: Exchange, Rod and Gun (St. Petersburg). Home: 5750 7th Av N St Petersburg FL 33710 Office: 5675 5th Av N St Petersburg FL 33710

DEEN, BRASWELL DRUE, JR., judge; b. McRae, Ga., Aug. 16, 1925; s. Braswell Drue and Emma Corinne (Smith) D.; LL.B., Ga. Law Sch., 1950; m. Jean Strickland Buie, June 9, 1953; children—Braswell Drue III, Sanders Buie. Admitted to Ga. bar, 1949; practiced in Alma, 1950-—; sr. mem. firm Deen & Powell, 1950-52, Deen, 1963-—; county atty. Bacon County, 1958-64; judge Ga. State Ct. Appeals, 1965-—. Mem. Ga. Ho. of Reps., 1950-58; exec. dir. Housing Authority of Alma. County chmn. fund drive A.R.C., 1953-54; past pres. Alma Devel. Council; pres. Alma Credit-Trade Bur.; chmn. bd. County Library Bd.; asst. scoutmaster Boy Scouts Am., 1951-52. Dist. chmn. Senator C.E. Sanders campaign for gov., 1962-63; Bacon County chmn. J.F. Kennedy campaign for Pres., 1960-61; 3d vice chmn. Ga. Dem. Exec. Com. Served with USMC, 1943-45. Decorated Purple Heart. Mem. Ga. Chess Assn. (state pres.), Am. Legion, V.F.W. (comdr.; dist. judge adv.), Pi Kappa Alpha, Delta Theta Phi. Methodist (bd. stewards). Lion (dep. dist. gov.). Clubs: Atlanta Athletic, Piedmont Driving, Capitol City, Atlanta County (Atlanta). Home: 4715 Kitty Hawk Pl NW Atlanta GA 30305 Office: State Jud Bldg Atlanta GA 30334

DEERE, CHARLES JOSEPH, physician; b. Lexington, Tenn., June 28, 1909; s. Joe Allen and Annie Louise (Hesse) D.; B.S., Union U., 1929, M.S., 1932, Ph.D., 1937; M.D., U. Tenn., 1939; m. Ella Ingram, Sept. 19, 1933. Teaching fellow, instr. chemistry U. Tenn., Memphis, 1929-37; intern John Gaston Hosp., Memphis, 1939-40; practice medicine, specializing in internal medicine, Memphis, 1945-—; mem. staff Bapt. Meml. Hosp., John Gaston Hosp., Meth. Hosp., St. Joseph Hosp.; instr., then asst. and asoo. prof. U. Tenn., 1946-66, clin. prof. medicine, 1966-—. Served to maj. AUS, 1941-45. Diplomate Am. Bd. Internal Medicine. Fellow A.C.P.; mem. A.M.A., Tenn. State, Memphis, Shelby County med. assns., Alpha Omega Alpha. Home: 5381 Pecan Grove Lane Memphis TN 38117 Office: 910 Madison St Memphis TN 38103

DEERIN, JAMES BENEDICT, assn. exec.; b. Orange, N.J., Sept. 4, 1915; s. James Benedict and Beatrice (Connolly) D.; student Seton Hall Prep. Sch., 1930-34. Army Command and Gen. Staff Coll., 1951; m. Lucy Lewis, Jan. 17, 1942 children—James Benedict, Margaret Lesesne, Beatrice C., Virginia W., John E. Reporter, Newark News, 1938-41, 46-52; mag. editor, pub.,N.J., 1952-54; news corr., Vietnam, 1965; exec. dir. N.G. Assn. of U.S., Washington 1958-—. Served with AUS, 1941-46; to col. U.S. Army, 1954-58. Decorated Bronze Star medal, Army Commendation medal. Mem. Nat. Pres Club. Author: Guide for Army National Guardsman, 1959. Home: 6501 Utah Av Washington DC 20015 Office: 1 Massachusetts Av NW Washington DC 20015

DEERING, FERDIE JACKSON, editor; b. Denison, Tex., Oct. 24, 1910; s. Norman Henry and Hattie (Brand) D.; student East Central State Coll., Ada, Okla., 1928-33; m. Flora Mildred Jennings, May 3, 1935; children—Cheryl Beth (Mrs. R.R. Dick Wilson), Robert Edward. Bus. mgr. East Central Jour., Ada, 1932-33; advt. salesman Denison Herald, 1933-34; night editor Ada News, 1934-37; asso. editor Farmer-Stockman, Oklahoma City, 1937-42, acting editor, 1942-43, editor, 1943-67; editor, mgr. The Farmer-Stockman Okla. Pub. Co., Oklahoma City, 1967-—, asst. sec., 1958-—, also dir.; editor Orbit Mag., Okla. Pub. Co., 1961-69; editor, mgr. RX Golf and Travel Mag., 1967-68; treas., dir. State Farm Mag. Bur., Chgo., 1968-—. Mem. Gov.'s Agri-Industry Task Force, 1967-70; past chmn. Buy Okla. Com., 1967; mem. com. Okla. 4-H and Future Farmers Am. Jr. Livestock Show, 1945-—. Bd. govs. Bapt. Meml. Hosp., Oklahoma City. Trustee S.W. Am. Livestock Found. Recipient numerous awards and plaques, including Gov.'s award for Soil Conservation, 1957, Okla. Cattlemen's Assn. award, 1960, Nat. Plant Food Assn. award for editors 1960, Freedoms Found. at Valley Forge award, 1969. Mem. Am. Agrl. Editors Assn. (past pres.), Agrl. Pubs. Assn. (dir.), Am. Assn. Agrl. Coll. Editors, Oklahoma City Press Club, Oklahoma City C. of C., Oklahoma City Farm Club (dir., past pres.), Farm Bur., Flying Farmers (hon. lifetime mem.). Baptist (deacon). Club: Men's Dinner Quail Creek Golf and Country, Sirloin of Oklahoma (past pres.) (Oklahoma City). Author: USDA, Manager of American Agriculture, 1945. Home: 3232 Whippoorwill Rd Oklahoma City OK 73120 Office: 500 N Broadway PO Box 25125 Oklahoma City OK 73125

DEERING, RONALD FRANKLIN, librarian; b. Paxton, Ill., Oct. 6, 1929; s. Minor Franklin and Grace Gilmore (Perkins) D.; B.A. summa cum laude, Georgetown Coll., 1951; B.S., So. Bapt. Theol. Sem., 1955, Th.D., 1961; M.S. in Library Sci., Columbia, 1967; m. Edith Ann Proctor, June 12, 1966; 1 son, Mark David. Ordained to ministry Bapt. Ch., 1950; instr. religion Georgetown (Ky.) Coll., 1951; pastor Blue River Bapt. Ch., Salem, Ind., 1955-58; instr. Greek, So. Bapt. Theol. Sem., Louisville, 1958-61, research librarian, 1962-67, asso. librarian, 1967-71, librarian, 1971-—. Recipient Lilly Fund grant, 1967. Mem. Am. Assn. U. Profs., Am. Acad. Religion, Soc. Bibl. Lit., Phi Alpha Theta, Sigma Tau Delta, Beta Phi Mu. Home: 3803 Layside Dr Louisville KY 40220

DEES, JAMES PARKER, clergyman; b. Greenville, N.C., Dec. 30, 1915; s. James Earl and Margaret Burgwin (Parker) D.; A.B., U. N.C., 1938, postgrad., 1938-39; B.D., Va. Theol. Sem., 1949; D.D. honoris causa, Bob Jones U., 1965; m. Margaret Lucinda Brown, Aug. 10,

1940; children—Margaret Lucinda, Eugenia Johnston. Ordained priest Protestant Episcopal Ch., 1949; priest Aurora, N.C., 1949-52, Beaufort, N.C., 1952-55, Statesville, N.C., 1955-63; resigned, 1963; founder Anglican Orthodox Ch., Statesville, 1963, consecrated bishop, 1964, metropolitan Anglican Orthodox Communion, 1969. Baritone soloist, N.Y.C. Opera Co., 1945. Pres. P.T.A., 1964-66; founder, pres. N.C. Defenders of States' Rights, Inc., 1956; mem. editorial bd. Citizen's Councils Publ., Jackson, Miss., 1959; mem. policy bd. Liberty Lobby, Washington. Bd. dirs. Fedn. Constl. Govt., New Orleans, 1957-60, Independence Found., Portland, Ind., Nat. Conservative Council, Richmond, Va. Served with inf. AUS, 1943-45: Italy. Recipient Liberty award Congress of Freedom, 1969, 70. Mem. Mayflower Soc. Home: 618 Walnut St Statesville NC 28677 Office: 323 Walnut St Statesville NC 28677

DEES, THOMAS HAROLD, real estate exec.; b. Keiser, Ark., May 7, 1940; s. William Thomas and Lucinda Evelyn (Scott) D.; B.S., Ark. State Coll., 1962; M.S., Ark. State U., 1968; m. Nellie Katherine Bowman, Mar. 26, 1963; children—Leslie DeAngela, Lucinda Michelle. Prin. schs., dir. fed. programs Keiser (Ark.) High Sch., 1963-67; prin. schs. Osceola (Ark.) Pub. Schs., 1967-68; bus. mgr., v.p. bus. affairs Ark. Coll., Batesville, 1968-70; treas. Hot Springs (Ark.) Village Property Owners Assn., 1970-71; asst. to financial v.p. Cooper Communities, Inc., Bentonville, Ark., 1971—. Chmn. Mississippi County Heart Fund, 1968. Mem. Nat. Assn. Accountants, Mississippi County Edn. Assn. (pres. 1966-67), Phi Delta Kappa, Alpha Kappa Psi. Baptist. Home: 4 Boyce Dr Bella Vista AR 72712 Office: Box 60 Bentonville AR 72712

DE ESTAVILLO, GREGORIO GOMEZ, author, translator. Address: 1607 9 Norte Puebla Puebla Mexico*

DEFALCO, LAWRENCE MICHAEL, bishop; b. McKeesport, Pa., Aug. 25, 1915; s. Rosario and Margret (Desmone) DeF.; student St. Vincent's Coll., Latrobe, Pa., 1933-35, St. John's Mission Sem., Little Rock, 1935-42; J.C.L., Gregorian U., Rome, Italy, 1955. Ordained priest Roman Catholic Ch., 1942; asst. pastor St. Patrick's, Ft. Worth, 1942-52, pastor, 1962; asst. pastor Sacred Heart Cathedral, Dallas, 1952; vice chancellor Dallas-Fort Worth Diocese, 1952-55, sec. Marriage Tribunal, 1955-62; pastor Our Lade Perpetual Help Ch., Dallas, 1956-62; bishop of Amarillo, Tex., 1963—. Address: 1800 N Spring St Amarillo TX 79107

DE FELICE, FRANK, economist; b. Boston, Dec. 20, 1932; s. Frank and Karoline (Reis) De F.; B.A. magna cum laude, Mich. State U., 1961; M.B.A., U. N.C. (Nat. Def. Edn. Act fellow 1961-64), 1963, Ph.D., 1967; m. Eleanor Elizabeth Sullivan, June 20, 1950; children—Frank, Kathleen Ann, William. Asst. prof. div. econs. and bus. adminstrn. U. N.C., Charlotte, 1966-69; asso. prof. econs. East Carolina Coll., 1965-66; asso. prof. econs., dir. Computer Center, Queens Coll., 1969-71; prof. econs. Belmont Abbey Coll., Belmont, N.C., 1971—; dir., pres., gen. mgr. Frank DeFelise & Assos., Inc. Vis. asso. prof. Davidson Coll., 1970. Chmn. adv. bd. West Charlotte High Sch., 1972—. Ford postdoctoral fellow, 1968-69. Mem. Am., So. econ. assns., Beta Gamma Sigma, Phi Kappa Phi, Alpha Kappa Psi, Tau Sigma. Contbr. articles to profl. jours. Home: 5032 Allen Rd E Charlotte NC 28213 Office: Belmont Abbey Coll Belmont NC 28012

DE FIGUEIREDO, RUI JOSE PACHECO, educator; b. Pangim, Goa, Inda, Apr. 19, 1929; S.B., Mass. Inst. Tech., 1950, S.M. in Elec. Engring., 1952; Ph.D. in Applied Math., Harvard, 1959; m. Isabel Colaco; children— Alcina, Paul, John, Rui. Teaching asst. Mass. Inst. Tech., 1950-52; devel. engr. Transistor Products, Inc., Waltham, Mass., 1952-53; vis. research fellow Ecole Normale Superieure, Paris, France, 1953; cons. Portugese AEC, 1955-59; head applied math. and physics group, 1959-62; vis. asso. prof., then asso. prof. elec. engring. Purdue U., Lafayette, Ind., 1962-64; asso. prof. elec. engring. Rice U., Houston, 1965-67, prof., 1967-68, prof. elec. engring. and math. scis., 1968—; vis. asso. prof. U. Ill. at Urbana; vis. prof. Tex. Technol. U., Lubbock, summer 1971; research mem. Math. Research Center U. Wis. at Madison, 1972-73; cons. in field. Mem. Portugese delegation Internat. Confs. Peaceful Uses Atomic Energy, Geneva, Switzerland, 1955, 58. Recipient 1st prize, Mass. Inst. Tech. br., Am. Inst. Elec. Engring., 1950. NSF grantee; NASA grantee. Mem. I.E.E.E. (mem. program com. Internat. Symposium Circuit Theory 1970; reviewer publs.), A.A.A.S., Sigma Xi, Eta Kappa Nu. Contbr. articles to profl. jours. Address: Rice U Houston TX 77001

DEFORD, WILSON ROBERT, educator; b. Hartford, Conn., June 11, 1934; s. Arthur Robert and Dorothy Mary (Parker) D.; student St. Thomas Sem., 1954; B.A., Belmont Abbey Coll., 1959; M.A., Cath. U. Am., 1968. Asso. pastor St. Paul's Roman Cath. Ch., Spartanburg, S.C., 1963-64; adminstr. St. Joseph's Ch., Chester, S.C.; dean studies Cardinal Sem., Rock Hill, S.C., 1963-65, philosophy instr., 1963-65; Roman Catholic chaplain S.C. State Hosp., Columbia, 1967-68; philosophy instr. St. Leo (Fla.) Coll., 1968—, dir. men's housing, 1970-71, dir. student orgns., 1971—. Mem. Am. Cath., Fla. philos. assns., Guild Cath. Psychiatrists. K.C. Home: 260 E Jasmine Blvd Port Richey FL 33568 Office: St Leo Coll St Leo FL 33574

DEFOREST, ELBERT MURRAY, petroleum engr.; b. Natoma, Kan., July 17, 1917; B.S., Tulsa U., 1940; m. Lois Ellen Wimmer, Sept. 25, 1942; children— Elbert Lee, Kenneth. Jr. petroleum engr. Gulf Oil Corp., 1940-41; chemist, E. I. duPont de Nemours & Co., 1941-42, devel. process engr., 1942-46; sr. process engr. Spencer Chem. Co., 1946-47, mgr. process engring., 1947-49; sr. project engr. Pan Am. Petroleum Corp., Standard Oil Co., 1949-50, supt. chem. mfg., 1950-52; mgr. new projects Frontier Chem. Co. div., Vulcan Materials Co., Birmingham, Ala., 1952-59, mgr. research and devel., 1959-67; v.p. research and devel. Vulcan Materials Chems. and Metals, 1967—. Mem. Inst. Chem. Engrs., Am. Chem. Soc., A.A.A.S., Forest Products Research, Am. Inst. Mining, Metall. and Petroleum Engrs., Am. Wood-Preserving Assn. Home: 412 S Maize Rd Wichita KS 67209 Office: PO Box 7497 Birmingham AL 35223 also PO Box 545 Wichita KS 67201

DEFOREST, JOHN DUANE, govt. economist; b. Peabody, Kan., Jan. 13, 1930; s. John Daniel and Cleo (Marsh) D.; B.S., Kan. State U., 1955, M.S., 1957; postgrad. (Cordell Hull fellow), Vanderbilt U., 1956-57; Ph.D., U. Ia., 1961; post-doctoral fellow U. Mich., 1964-65; m. Peggy Glee Stratman, June 15, 1952; children—Debra Dru, Denise Sue, Deanne. Asst. prof. econs. Denison U., Granville, O., 1959-62; program economist U.S. Aid Mission to Colombia, 1962-64; prof. econs. Parsons Coll., Fairfield, Ia., 1965-67; economist Econ. Devel. Adminstrn., U.S. Dept. Commerce. Washington, 1967-71, Office of Environmental Affairs, 1971—. Professorial lectr. bus. adminstrn. George Washington U., Washington, 1968—. Served with USMC, 1948-51. Mem. Am. Men Sci., Am. Econ. Assn., A.A.A.S., Phi Kappa Phi, Alpha Kappa Psi, Beta Theta Pi. Home: 3204 Wessynton Way Alexandria VA 22309 Office: US Dept Commerce Washington DC 20230

DE FRANK, VINCENT, condr.; ed. Juilliard Sch. Music, Ind. U. Debut as condr. radio sta. WNYC Radio Orch.; formerly mem. Detroit Symphony, St. Louis Symphony; founder Memphis Chamber Orch., 1952; founder, condr. Memphis Sinfonietta (became Memphis Symphony 1960), 1952; condr. Memphis Youth Symphony; guest condr. numerous musical group, summer music camps, clinics. Address: Box 4682 Crosstown Station Memphis TN 38104

DE GAUTIER, FELISA RINCON UDA, Democratic nat. committeewoman; b. Ceiba, P.R., Jan. 9, 1897; d. Enrique Rincon Plumey and Rita Marrero Rivera; LL.D., Marymount Coll., Milw., 1958; L.H.D., Temple U., 1960; m. Jenaro Gautier, Mar. 23, 1940. City mgr., San Juan, P.R., 1946-61, mayor, 1961-69. Founder, past pres. San Juan Xmas Festival Found. Mem. Popular Democratic Party P.R.; mem. Dem. Nat. Com. for P.R. Recipient Woman of Am. award Union Am. Women, 1954; Golden Medal Honor, Don Quijote medal, Daus. Charity medal (Spain); Jean of Arc medal (France); Golden Medal of Honor (Ecuador); Bolivar medal (Venezuela); Fed. Women's Club Am. medal; Jane Adams medal (San Juan); Nat. Order Honor and Merit (Haiti); Order Merit (Israel); Sacred Sepulchre medal (Vatican). Mem. City Mgrs. Assn., Mayor Assn., Fedn. Women's Club (coadj. founder P.R. chpt.), Mayor's Assn. P.R. (past pres.), Union Mujeres Americana (coadj. founder), Alianza Interamericana (coadj. founder). Address: Box 6607 San Juan PR 00914

DEGGES, IRA DONALD, civil engr.; b. Gulledge, Ark., Apr. 17, 1929; s. Ira Dwight and Annie (Gibbs) D.; B.S. in Civil Engring., La. Poly. Inst., 1958; m. Vonnie Faye Mayo, Apr. 15, 1960; children—James Ira, Paul Donald, Karen Elizabeth, Bruce Neal. Self-employed pulpwood producer, Hamburg, Ark., 1947-51, 53-54; project engr. La. Dept. Hwys., Monroe, Tallulah, 1958-62; with Fed. Hwy. Adminstrn., 1962—, asst. area engr., Austin, Tex., 1962-63, area engr., Oklahoma City, 1963-66, dist. engr., Little Rock, 1966-69, asst. div. engr., engring. coordinator, Nashville, 1969—. Served with AUS, 1951-53. Mem. Am. Soc. C.E., Nat. Soc. Profl. Engrs. Baptist. Home: 2662 Forest View Dr Antioch TN 37013 Office: Fed Hwy Adminstrn 4004 Hillsboro Rd Nashville TN 37215

DEGRAFFENRIEDT, FREDERICK, JR., archtl. designer; b. Moncure, N.C., Sept. 20, 1940; s. Frederick and Alfreda (Hornton) DeG.; Asso. Sci., A. and T. State U., 1964; m. Mary Madglene Winford, Oct. 3, 1965. Draftsman, Thomas P. Heritage, Architect and Engr., Greensboro, N.C., 1963; draftsman W.E. Jenkins, Architect, Greensboro, 1964-66; designer, chief draftsman Clinton E. Gravely, Architect & Assos., Greensboro, 1967—. Mem. camping com. Gen. Greene council Boy Scouts Am., 1968—. Home: 2107 Tuscaloosa St Greensboro NC 27401 Office: 500 Banner Av Greensboro NC 27401

DEGRAVELLES, CHARLES CAMILLE, Republican nat. committeeman; b. Morgan City, La., June 4, 1913; B.A., La. State U., 1936; m. Virginia Wheadon, Sept. 15, 1935; children—May Alix (Mrs. W.P. Begneaud Jr.), Elizabeth Claire (Mrs. Robert A. Cloninger), Virginia Ann (Mrs. Charles W. McBride), Charles Nations and John Wheadon (twins). Mem. staff, land dept., petroleum co., 1937-68; instr. oil and gas law U. Southwestern La., 1955-62; now mem. staff, land dept. Pan Am. Petroleum Co. Active presdl. campaigns, 1956-68; dir. La. Republican Com., 1967, chmn., 1968, 70—; del. Rep. Nat. Conv., 1968; now mem. Rep. Nat. Com. Mem. adv. bd., past pres. Salvation Army. Mem. Phi Delta Phi, Kappa Alpha Alumni. Episcopalian. Address: 409 Azalea St Lafayette LA 70501*

DE GREGORI, THOMAS ROGER, educator; b. Cleve., May 5, 1935; s. James Victor and Mary Anne (Tambascio) De G.; B.A., U. N.M., 1959; M.A., 1959; Ph.D., U. Tex., 1965; m. Gayle Sutherland, Oct. 22, 1960; children— Alice, James, Roger. Teaching asst. econs. U. Tex., Austin, 1959-62; vis. lectr. econs. U. Khartoum, Sudan, 1962-63; asst. prof. dept. humanities Case Inst. Tech., Cleve., 1963-67; asso. prof. econs. U. Houston, 1967—, chmn. dept., 1969-71. Author: Economic Development: The Cultural Context, 1969; Technology and the Economic Development of the Tropical African Frontier, 1969. Home: 2327 Goldsmith St Houston TX 77025

DEHAAN, HENRY JOHN, psychologist; b. East St. Louis, Ill., Nov. 23, 1920; s. Henry J. and Fanny (Haislip) deH.; A.B., Washington U., St. Louis, 1942, M.A., 1949; Ph.D. U. Pitts., 1960; m. Mary J. Farrell, Oct. 22, 1943. Research psychologist VA Hosp., Coatesville, Pa., 1960-62; research scientist Human Resources Research Office, George Washington U., 1962-64; research psychologist Armed Forces Radiobiology Research Inst., Naval Med. Center, Bethesda, Md., 1965-69, U.S. Army Behavior and Systems Research Lab., Arlington, Va., 1969—. Faculty, U.S. Dept. Agr. Grad. Sch., 1967—. Served with USNR, 1944-46. Mem. A.A.A.S., Am. Psychol. Assn., Animal Behavior Soc., Internat. Primatological Soc., Soc. for Neurosci., Sigma Xi. Contbr. articles to profl. lit. Home: 5403 Yorkshire St Springfield VA 22151 Office: US Army Behavior and Systems Research Lab Arlington VA 22209

DEHAVEN, ERNEST THOMAS, hosp. adminstr.; b. Hiram Twp., O., Aug. 7, 1928; s. Ernest Roy and Bertha Catherine (Thomas) DeH.; A.B., Hiram Coll., 1949; M.H.A., Med. Coll. Va., 1957; m. Barbara Ann Hoskin, Aug. 21, 1955; children—Matthew, Stephen, Catherine. Adminstr. Albert Schweitzer Meml. Hosp., Haiti, 1958-59, Jackman Meml. Hosp., Bilaspur, India, 1959-64; asst. adminstr. Lake County Meml. Hosp., Painesville, O., 1965-67; adminstr. Carroll County Meml. Hosp., Carrollton, Ky., 1967—. Served with AUS, 1953-54. Mem. Ky. Hosp. Assn. (v.p. 1969-70, trustee 1970—), Am. Coll. Hosp. Adminstrs. Mem. Christian Ch. Rotarian. Home: 119 Comanche Trail Carrollton KY 41008 Office: 309 11th St Carrollton KY 41008

DEIDESHEIMER, HAROLD JACOB, advt. exec.; b. N.Y.C., Feb. 1, 1917; s. Charles Phillip and Adeline (Erdenbrecher) D.; student pub. schs.; m. Mary Ann Moroni, Jan. 26, 1958; 1 dau., Annamaria E. Dir. printing Hazard Advt. Co., N.Y.C., 1948-53; salesman, printing cons. Reiman Conway Assos., N.Y.C., 1953-55; prodn. mgr., dir. printing and purchasing Harris & Whitebrook & Co., Miami Beach, Fla., 1955-57; prodn. mgr. C.J. LaRoche & Co., N.Y.C., 1957-58; asso. mgr. advt. prodn. controls Gen. Food Corp., White Plains, N.Y., 1959-64; adminstrv. mgr., account exec. firm Bishopric Green Fielden Advt., Miami, Fla., 1966-71; pres. Financial Plaza Advt. Co., Ft. Lauderdale, Fla., 1971—. Recipient Cronite awards Art Dirs. Club N.Y., 1952. Miami, 1956, Detroit, 1958. Address: 2230 NE 62d Ct Fort Lauderdale FL 33308

DEINZER, HARVEY THEODORE, educator; b. Monroe, Mich., Dec. 24, 1908; s. Edwin Frederick and Emily Marie (Meissner) D.; A.B., U. Mich., 1932, M.B.A., 1933, Ph.D., 1947; J.D., U. Fla., 1955; m. Margaret Emily Reed, June 18, 1934; 1 son, Robert Reed. Accountant, Ernst & Ernst, Detroit, 1933-37; with F. E. Ross & Co., Ann Arbor, Mich., 1937-38; staff cons. Pub. Adminstrn. Service, Chgo., 1938-39; fiscal analyst, bus. economist U.S. Govt., Washington, 1942-43; asso. prof. accounting U. Fla., Gainesville, 1947-49, prof., 1949—. Served to 1st lt. AUS, 1943-46. Mem. Am. Accounting Assn., Am. Econ. Assn., Order of the Coif, Beta Gamma Sigma, Phi Delta Phi. Home: 928 NW 21ST Terrace Gainesville FL 32601

DEITENBECK, WILLIAM, editor; b. LaGrange, Ill., Oct. 30, 1919; s. Max and Sarah Claire (Collins) D.; B.A., Birmingham So. Coll., 1942; m. Madelyn Ruth Downs, Mar. 9, 1948; 1 son, William. Mgr. Paramount Theatres, So. cities, 1945-56; dir. pub. relations, editor Cinderella Internat. Corp., 1957-59, Viviane Woodard Corp., 1960-62; mgr. advt. Fla. Field Report, Orlando, 1963-64, editor, 1965—, owner, 1968—. Treas. United Cerebral Palsy of Miss., 1954-56. Served with USAAF, 1942-45; PTO. Recipient Distinguished Service award Fla. Dairy Products Assn., 1971. Mem. Agribus. Inst. Fla. (bd. dirs.), Fla. Mag. Assn. (award 1970; bd. dirs, v.p.), Fla. Press Assn. Democrat. Presbyn. Home: 3000 Delaney Av Orlando FL 32806 Office: Fla Field Report 320 N Magnolia Av Orlando FL 32801

DEITZ, ROBERT EUGENE, journalist; b. Winona, W.Va., May 8, 1940; s. Merritt Singleton and Irene Elizabeth (Wilder) D.; student U. Ky., 1959-62; m. Marsha Ann Kingsley, Aug. 1, 1964; children—Marcus Wilder, Robert Addison. Reporter, Lexington (Ky.) Herald, 1962-63; polit. reporter Louisville Courier-Jour., 1963-67, asso. editor, 1970—; staff writer Nat. Observer, Silver Spring, Md., 1967-68; mgr. systems planning Louisville Courier-Jour. and Louisville Times, 1968-70; Nieman fellow, Harvard, 1971-72. Served with USMCR, 1957-61. Home: 2366 Valley Vista Rd Louisville KY 40205 Office: Louisville Courier-Journal 525 W Broadway Louisville KY 40202

DEJARNETTE, JAMES TERRY, state ofcl.; b. Bessemer, Ala., Jan. 30, 1909; s. James Terry and Daisy Laura (Marbut) deJ.; A.B., U. Ala., 1931; postgrad. Ala. Poly. Inst., 1940. Ga. State Coll., 1961-63; m. Dorothy Leona Davis, June 27, 1946; 1 dau., Ethel Terry. Chief engr. Ala. Dept Conservation, 1941-42; bus. mgr. Ga. Youth Devel. Center, Milledgeville, 1969—. Served to col C.E., U.S. Army, 1958-62. Decorated Legion of Merit. Registered profl. engr., Ga. Mem. Delta Chi. Clubs: Milledgeville Country, Milledgeville Rotary; Old Guard (Atlanta). Home: Macon Hwy Milledgeville GA 31061 Office: PO Box 1092 Milledgeville GA 31061

DEJEAN, CHARLES EDWARD, constrn. co. exec.; b. Biloxi, Miss., July 15, 1912; s. Charles and Ethel (George) DeJ.; B.A., Baylor U., 1935, postgrad., 1936-37; m. Doris Gamble, Sept. 20, 1944; children— Sandra (Mrs. Thomas L. Patterson), Jon Cherrie. Insp. Blue Bonnet Ordnance Plant, McGregor, Tex., 1942-43; asst. chief chemist Premier Oil Co.; Cotton Valley, La., 1943-45; owner Eze Orange Bottling Co., Prichard, Ala., 1945-47; soils dir. A.W. Williams Inspection Co., Mobile, Ala., 1947-53; co-owner, pres., dir. soils chemistry and asphalt depts. Dixie Labs., Inc., Mobile and Dothan, Ala. and Columbus, Ga., 1953—. Pres. Exchange Club, Prichard, 1963. Mem. Am. Chem. Soc., Am. Soc. Testing Materials, C. of C., Better Bus. Bur. Baptist (bd. deacons 1958-71). Club: Lake Forrest Country (Spanish Fort, Ala.). Home: 113 Baratara Dr Mobile AL 36611 Office: 604 Loeffler St Mobile AL 36607

DE JESUS, JOSE ANGEL, physician; b. San Juan, P.R., May 18, 1920; s. Angel R. and Rosa (Sanjuan) DeJ.; student U. P.R., 1934-36, Columbia, 1937; M.D., U. Va., 1943; postgrad. U. Pa., 1949; m. Sara Jean Kitchen, Dec. 14, 1942; children—Jose Angel, Martha Rosa (Mrs. J. M. Brennan), Sally (Mrs. P. W. Kellogg), Everett Michael. Intern, USPHS Hosp., S.I., 1944; resident fellow U. Va. Hosp., 1948-49; chief resident VA Hosp., Richmond, Va., 1950-51; practice medicine specializing in internam medicine, San Juan, P.R., 1958—; chief gastroenterology, allergy VA Hosp.; cons. gastroenterology Presbyn. Hosp., 1956—; asso. attending physician internal medicine U. P.R. Hosp.; prof. clin. medicine U. P.R. Sch. Medicine, 1959—, prof. Med. Sch. Dentistry, 1960—; med. dir. Carribean area Am. Cynamid Corp., 1959—. Served with AUS, 1944-46. Diplomate Am. Bd. Internal Medicine. Fellow A.C.P. (gov. for P.R. 1966-72); mem. Socaedas Venezolana de Gastroenterologia, P.R. Heart Assn. (dir. 1961-68), P.R. Med. Assn. (pres. 1960), P.R. Soc. Gastroenterology. Club: Caparra Country (Villa Caparra, P.R.). Editor: Proceedings of the XI Latin American Congress of Gastroenterology, 1959. Home: Box 10059 Caparra Heights Sta San Juan PR 00922 Office: 1475 Wilson Av Santurce PR 00907

DE JESUS TORO, ROBERTO, banker; b. San Juan, P.R., July 27, 1918; s. Francisco and Graciela (Toro) de Jesus; B.S. in Econs., Wharton Sch. Finance and Commerce, U. Pa., 1940; M.B.A., 1943; m. Sylvia Pou, Aug. 17, 1947; children—Roberto, Sylvia, Nestor, Ana Maria. Dir. Bur. of Budget, Govt. of P.R., 1945-51; v.p. Govt. Devel. Bank of P.R., San Juan, 1951-54; exec. v.p. Banco de Ponce (P.R.), 1954-59, pres., 1959—, also dir.; dir. Puerto Rican Cement Co. Inc., Puerto Rican and Am. Ins. Co., Ponce Hotel Corp., Union Carbide Inc. Served to sgt. AUS, 1943-45. Home: Generalife and Arrayanes La Alhambra Ponce PR 00731 Office: Banco de Ponce PO Box 4228 Ponce PR 00731

DEKIEFFER, EUGENE LUDWIG, bank exec.; b. Chgo., Mar. 4, 1912; s. Otto M. and Irene (Eulette) deK.; B.S. in Econs., Northwestern U., 1934; m. Betty Harwood, Oct. 25, 1946; 1 dau., Christine. Economist, Swift & Co., Chgo., 1934-36; So. div. sales mgr. Weber Costello Co., Chicago Heights, 1936-40; asst. mgr. Prudential Ins. Co. Am., Dallas, 1946-50; asst. v.p. First Nat. Bank Dallas, 1950-54; ins. counselor Mut. of N.Y., Dallas, 1954-61, asst. mgr., 1957-61; ins. counselor Conn. Mut. Life Ins. Co., 1961-66; v.p., trust officer Exchange Bank & Trust Co., Dallas, 1966—. Spl. guest lectr. bus. ins. Inst. Ins. Marketing, 1947-63. Bd. dirs. Dallas council U.S.O., 1961—, pres., 1967-68; dir. Dallas com. Young Life Campaign, 1967-69; trustee Tex. Coll. Osteo. Medicine, 1972—. Mem. Dallas Crime Comm., 1951-54; spl. investigator Preparedness Sub Com., U.S. Senate Mil. Affairs Com., 1951. Served as officer USNR, 1940-46; comdg. officer Air Wing 70 Naval Air Sta., Dallas, 1949-55; capt. USNR, ret., 1961. Dir. of Episcopal Collegiate Center at So. Meth. U., 1954-57. Mem. Res. Officers Assn. (nat. com. legislation 1955-56) pres. Dallas Chpt. 1967-68), Dallas Mgmt. Assn. (dir. 1960-61), Mil. Order World Wars (comdr. Dallas chpt. 1962-63), Dallas Gen. Agts. and Mgrs. Assn. (dir. 1959-60, treas. 1961), Nat. Assn. Life Underwriters, C. of C., Navy League (dir. Dallas council 1964-65, 69-70, v.p. 1970—, pres. 1972-73), Nat. Assn. Estate Planning Councils (gen. chmn. nat. conv. 1971, v.p. for S.W. 1972-73), Dallas Estate Council (officer 1969-72, pres. 1972-73), Phi Gamma Delta. Episcopalian (vestry). Club: Chaparrel. C.L.U. Home: 3132 Bryn Mawr Dr Dallas TX 75225 Office: Exchange Bank & Trust Co Dallas TX 75235

DE LA COLINA, RAFAEL, Mexican ambassador; b. Tulancingo, Hidalgo, Mexico, Sept. 20, 1898; s. Manuel and Maria (Riquelme) C.; B.S., Nat. U. Mexico, 1915, Fgn. Service Officer, 1918; m. Ruth Rosecrans, Dec. 24, 1920 (dec.); children—Ruth (Mrs. Francis W. Silk), Rafael; m. 2d, Amanda Steinmeyer, July 22, 1944. Chancellor, Mexican consulate, Phila., 1918; vice-consul, St. Louis, 1922; chief adminstrv. Consular Dept., Fgn. Office, Mexico City, 1923; consul of Mexico, Boston, 1924-25, New Orleans, 1926-27, Laredo, Tex., 1928-29, Los Angeles, 1930-31; chief consular dept., Fgn. Office, Mexico City, 1932; chief Bur. Licenses, Govt. of City of Mexico, 1933; consul-gen., San Antonio 1934-35, N.Y.C., 1936-42; minister-conselor, Mexican embassy, Washington, 1943-44, E.E. and M.P., 1944-48, charge d'affaires ad interim, 1948, A.E. and P., 1949-53; permanent rep. of Mexico to UN, 1953-59; Mexican ambassador to Can., 1959-62; Mexican ambassador to Japan, Tokyo, 1962-64, to OAS, 1965—. Mem. Mexican delegation: as del. UNRRA, Atlantic City, 1943 (elected v.p. 1st session), Montreal, Can., 1944, Interim Commn. (FAO) Washington, 1944-45, Interam.

Econ. and Financial Tech. Com., Washington, 1943-45; as alternate del., Security Council UN, N.Y.C., 1946, P.I.C.A.O. (Caribbean regional meeting), Washington, 1946; adviser, U.N.C.I.O., San Francisco, 1945; dep. sec. gen. Interam. Conf. on Problems of War and Peace, Mexico City, 1945; Mexican rep. Com. Experts, Security Council, 1946. Mexican alternate del., 1946; Mexican del. Provisional Internat. Civil Aviation Orgn., 1946, UN Gen. Assembly, N.Y.C., 1946, (alter-N.Y., 1947 2d Extraordinary Session, Lake Sucnat) Gen. Assembly, 2d Session, Lake Success, 1948; Mexican rep. (alternate) Council OAS (Consejo de la Organizacion de los Estados Americanos), Washington, 1948; Mexican del. Japanese Peace Conf., San Francisco, 1951, 2d spl. Inter Am. Conf., Rio de Janeiro, 1965; acting chief Mexican delegation, VII to XIII. Gen. Assembly UN, chief Mexican delegation spl. commn. amendments to charter OAS, Panama City, 1966; chief Mexican delegation Intelsat Conf., Washington, 1969-70, mem. arbitration panel, 1971. Decorated Order of Merit (Chile); Order Honneur et Merite (Haiti); Order of Merit Juan Pablo Duarte (Dominican Republic); Order of Vasco Nunez de Balboa (Panama); Imperial Order Rising Sun (Japan); Order of Liberator Simon Bolivar (Venezuela); Order San Carlos (Colombia). Mem. Acad. of History (Mexico), Mexican Acad. Internat. Law, Am. Soc. Internat. Law. Clubs: Internat. (Washington). Address: 2440 Massachusetts Av NW Washington DC 20008

DE LA GARZA, ELIGIO, congressman; b. Mercedes, Tex., Sept. 22, 1927; s. Dario and Elisa (Villarreal) de la G.; student Pan Am. Coll., Edinburg, Tex., 1947-48; J.D., St. Mary's U., San Antonio, 1951; m. Lucille Alamia, May 29, 1953; children—Jorge Luis, Michael Alberto, Angela Dolores. Admitted to Tex. bar, 1951; mem. Tex. Ho. of Reps. from Hidalgo County, 1953-64; mem. 89th-92d congresses 15th Dist. Tex. Served USNR, World War II, with AUS, Korea. Democrat. Home: 1812 Cummings St Mission TX 78572 also 1409 Layman St McLean VA 22101 Office: House Office Bldg Washington DC 20515

DE LA HOUSSAYE, EDWARD ANTHONY, III, judge; b. Franklin, La., May 4, 1930; s. Edward Anthony and Heloise (Fay) de la H.; B.S., La. State U., 1951; LL.B., Tulane U., 1956, J.D., 1956; grad. Nat. Coll. State Trial Judges, Reno, 1969; m. Mary Kay Oakley, Dec. 21, 1957; children—Mary Downs, Jeanne Marie, Heloise Marie, Lisette Anne, Adrienne Claire. Admitted to La. bar, 1956; practiced in Franklin, 1957-66; 1st asst. dist. atty. 16th Judicial Dist. La., 1964-66; judge 16th Judicial Dist. Ct. La., 1966—. Dist. chmn. Teche dist. Evangeline Area council Boy Scouts Am., 1963, 64, chmn. finance drive, 1965-66; chmn. finance drives A.R.C., 1959-60, March of Dimes, 1960-61. Chmn. Municipal Democratic Exec. Com., Franklin, 1961-64. Served to 1st USAF, 1951-53. Mem. Moot Ct. Bd. Tulane U. Law Sch. Mem. La. Juvenile Judges Assn. (pres. 1970-71, dir.), La. Dist. Judges Assn. (v.p., dir.), La. Soc., S.A.R. Beta Theta Pi, Phi Delta Phi. K.C. (4 deg.). Club: Belleview Golf and Country (past pres.) (Franklin). Home: 112 Oakwood Dr Franklin LA 70538 Office: St Mary Parish Court House Franklin LA 70538

DE LA HOUSSAYE, LIONEL LOUIS, oral surgeon; b. Crowley, La., Aug. 8, 1940; s. Benton Cason and Minnie Louis (Thomas) de la H.; student La. State U., 1958-61; D.D.S., Loyola U., New Orleans, 1965; m. Marie Louise Ogden, July 7, 1962; children—Lionel Louis, Jean-Paul Pelletier, Marie Louise. Pvt. dental practice, Crowley, 1965-66, Shreveport, La., 1968; resident oral surgery Confederate Meml. Med. Center, Shreveport, 1968-71; oral surgeon, Lake Charles, La., 1971—. Oral surgery missionary, Saltillo, Mexico, 1971. Col., staff Gov. John McKeithen, 1967-71. Served with AUS, 1966-68. Mem. La., 7th Dist., Calcasieu Parish, Am. dental assns., S.A.R., Kappa Sigma, Delta Sigma Delta. Lion. Home: 1308 Jefferson Dr Lake Charles LA 70601 Office: 1702 Oak Park Blvd Lake Charles LA 70601

DELAITSCH, DALE M., educator; b. Colfax, Wis., Dec. 18, 1922; B.S., U. Chgo., 1944; A.B., St. Olaf Coll., 1946; Ph.D. in Chemistry, U. Minn., 1950; m. 1945; 2 children. Asst. prof. chemistry U. Southwestern La., Lafayette, 1950-52, asso. prof., 1952-63, prof., 1963—. Served to 1st lt. USAAF, 1943-46. Mem. Am. Chem. Soc. Address: Dept Chemistry U Southwestern La Lafayette LA 70501*

DELAMERENS, SERGIO ANDRES, hematologist; b. Havana, Cuba, Feb. 4, 1928; s. Arturo A. and Dolores (deZayas) DeL.; B.S., PreUniv. Inst., Matanzas, Cuba, 1946; M.D., Havana U., 1953; M.S., U. Tenn., 1967; m. Maria Teresa Ortiz, June 22, 1957; children—Sergio, Maria Teresa, Goar. Intern, U. Hosp., Havana, 1953-54; resident in pediatrics Univ. Hosp., Havana, 1954-56, Frank Tobey Hosp., Memphis, 1961-63; practice medicine, specializing in pediatrics, Havana, 1956-60, Milw., 1965-67, Memphis, 1967—; instr. pediatrics U. Havana Med. Sch. 1956-60 asst. prof. pediatrics Marquette U., 1965-67; asst. prof. pediatrics, chief pediatric hematology U. Tenn. Med. Sch., 1967-72, asso. prof. pediatrics, chief pediatric hematology, 1972—; hematology cons. Milw. Childrens Hosp., Meth. Hosp., Bapt. Hosp., St. Joseph Hosp., LeBonheur Hosp., Memphis. Chmn. med. adv. council chpt. Memphis Hemophilia Found., 1967-69. Recipient Cabrera Saavedra award, 1956, Aballi award, 1956 Havana. Mem. So. Soc. Pediatric Research, Am. Hematology Soc., Am. Acad. Pediatrics, A.M.A., Pediatric Soc. Medellin, Bogota and Cali, Sigma Xi. Contbr. articles profl. jours. Home: 5200 Walnut Grove Rd Memphis TN 38117 Office: 860 Madison Av Memphis TN 38103

DELANEY, THOMAS CALDWELL, JR., museum exec.; b. Danville, Va., Jan. 1, 1918; s. Thomas C. and Ethel (Loving) D.; B.S., Spring Hill Coll., 1941; M.A., U. Ala., 1952; m. Lois Jean Fitzsimmons, July 20, 1960. Dean U. Mil. Sch., Mobile, Ala., 1941-56; founder, supt. Julius T. Wright Sch. for Girls, Mobile, 1956-65; mus. dir. City of Mobile, 1965—. Mem. adv. bd. Providence Sch. Nursing, 1956-59, U.S. Civil War Centennial Commn., 1958-65; rep. Mobile County Ala. First Capital Commn., 1961-65. Bd. dirs. Mobile Civic Music Assn., Mobile Symphony, Historic Mobile Preservation Soc. Recipient Ala. Penwomen award, 1962. Mem. Ala. Hist. Assn. (pres. 1962-63), Mobile Art Assn. Rotarian, Author: Deep South, 1942; Remember Mobile, 1948, 69; The Story of Mobile, 1953, 61; Madame Octavia Walton LeVert, 1961; Mary McNeil Fenollosa, 1963; The Phoenix Volunteer Fire Company of Mobile 1838-1888, 1967; The First Hundred Years, 1968; Craighead's Mobile, 1968; Confederate Mobile, 1971. Home: 8 S Ann St Mobile AL 36604 Office: 203 S Claiborne St Mobile AL 36602

DE LANY, WALTER STANLEY, ret. naval officer; b. Reading, Pa., Jan. 21, 1891; s. Irvin F. and Mary E. (Dunkle) DeL.; B.S., U.S. Naval Acad., 1912; m. Lou May Sharman; children—Kathryn (Mrs. Emerson E. Fawkes), Walter S. Commd. ensign U.S. Navy, 1912, advanced through grades to rear adm., 1942; battleship service, World War I; head Navy Recruiting Sta., Albany, N.Y., 1919-21; exec. officer destroyer Lamson, 1923-24; 1st lt. U.S.S. Oklahoma, 1927-30; with ships' movements div. Office Chief Naval Operations Navy Dept., Washington, 1930-33; navigator U.S.S. New York, 1933-35; exec. U.S. Naval Acad., Annapolis, Md., 1935-37; comdr. Destroyer Div. 7, 1938-39; chief staff, aide to comdr. cruisers, 1939-41; asst. chief staff and operations officer on staff comdr. in chief Pacific Fleet, 1941-42; comdr. cruiser New Orleans, 1942-43; asst. chief staff, to comdr. in chief U.S. Fleet, Washington, 1943-45; head operational readiness sect. Office Chief Naval Operations, 1945-46; comdt. 3d Naval Dist., N.Y.C., 1948-52; ret., 1953; dep. adminstr. Mut. Def. Assistance Control Act, Washington, 1953-61; pres. Naval Hist. Soc., 1967—. Bd. mgrs. Navy Relief Soc. Decorated 2 Legions of Merit, numerous service and theatre medals; spl. collar Order Yun Hui (China). Mem. Huguenot Soc., S.R. Club: Army and Navy (Washington). Address: 1610 H St NW Washington DC 20006

DE LA PARTE, LOUIS ANTHONY, state senator; b. Tampa, Fla., July 27, 1929; s. Louis and Dulce (Santa Cruz) de la P.; B.A., Emory U.; LL.B., U. Fla.; m. Helen C. White, Nov, 23, 1957; children—Louis David, Martha Ann. Admitted to Fla. bar; practice law, Tampa; spl. asst. atty. gen. State of Fla., 1953; asst. county solicitor, Hillsborough County, Fla., 1957-60; asst. state atty. 13th Jud. Circuit, 1960-61; mem. Fla. Senate, 1966—. Mem. Fla. Ho. of Reps., 1962-66; del. Democratic nat. conv., 1968. Served to capt. USAF, 1953-56. Recipient Allen Morris award, 1967; named Most Valuable Senator St. Petersburg (Fla.) Times, 1969, 70, Legislator of Year Fla. Assn. Retarded Children, 1968-70, Legislator of Year Fla. Vol. Health Assns., 1970. Mem. Am., Fla. bar assns., Am., Fla. trial lawyers assns., Phi Delta Phi, Eta Sigma Phi, Sigma Alpha Epsilon. Roman Catholic. Home: 8003 N Rome St Tampa FL 33604 Office: 725 E Kennedy Blvd Tampa FL 33602*

DE LA ROSA, MANUEL, ednl. adminstr.; b. Saltillo, Coahuila, Mexico, June 2, 1941; s. Manuel and Gloria (Ramirez) de la R.; B.S., U. Coahuila, Saltillo, 1958; D.D.S. (Proctor & Gamble Co. fellow), U. Nuevo Leon, Monterrey, Mexico, 1964; M.S., Baylor U., 1966; m. Lucila Garza, July 6, 1968; children—Manuel, Lucila. Chmn. Dental Research Center, U. Nuevo Leon, Monterrey, 1967—, also prof. oral pathology, gen. histology, periodontology, 1966—. Cons. San Jose Hosp., Monterrey. Mem. Internat. Assn. Dental Research, Am. Acad. Periodontology, Mexican Dental Assn., Mexican Assn. Pathology, Childrens Dental Assn., others. Home: 7422 Rosemont Rd Dallas TX 75217 Office: Av Gonzalitos 250 Sur Desp 105 Monterrey NL Mexico

DE LA SIERRA, JOSE, lawyer; b. Mexico City, Mexico, Aug. 15, 1917; student Colegio Williams, Colegio Aleman; LL.B., Nat. U. Mexico, 1934. Admitted to Mexican Republic bar, 1939; dir. Revista de Derecho y Ciencias Sociales, 1936-39; now mem. firm Hill-DeLa Sierra & Prado, Mexico City. Mem. hon. council Govt. Morelos, 1942-45, 51. Fellow Am. Coll. Probate Counsel; mem. Inter-am., Internat. bar assns., Comml. Law League Am., Barra Mexicana-Colegio de Abogados, Instituto del Amparo, Asociacion Mexicana de Agentes de la Propiedad Industrial. Author: El Divoricio y su Procedimiento, 1939. Address: Hill-De La Sierra & Prado Gante No 4 Mexico 1 D F Mexico*

DELAUGHTER, GEORGE W., automobile agy. exec.; b. Sparkman, Ark., Oct. 11, 1916; s. George W. and Mary Pearl (Cookston) DeL.; student Ouachita Bapt. Coll., 1935-38; m. Martha Jean Taylor, Apr. 28, 1946; children—Abigail (Mrs. Larry F. Pennington), Susan. Mgr., Sparkman Motor Co., 1940—; pres. DeLaughter Butane Co., Sparkman, 1946, Zero Gas Co., Inc., Arkadelphia, Ark., 1950—; sec. Quality L.P. Gas Co., Inc., Nashville, Ark., 1964-68; pres. DeLaughter Transport Co., Inc., Sparkman, 1962—; v.p., dir. Mchts. & Planters Bank, Sparkman. Mem. Ark. Liquefied Petroleum Gas Control Bd. Chmn., Sparkman Housing Authority, 1964—; mayor Sparkman, 1952-64. Past pres. Dallas County Fair Assn. Trustee Ouchita Bapt. U. Served to maj., inf. AUS, 1942-46. Decorated Bronze Star. Mem. Res. Officers Assn., Am. Legion. Democrat. Baptist. Lion. Address: PO Box 97 Sparkman AR 71763

DELAUGHTER, JERRY WILLFRED, journalist; b. nr. Brookhaven, Miss., Jan. 1, 1935; s. H. M. and Grace E. (Rials) DeL.; B.A., Miss. Coll., 1958; M.A., U. Miss., 1959; m. Mary Norman Van Zandt, Oct. 28, 1960. Sports editor The Natchez (Miss.) Democrat, 1957; sports writer The Clarion-Ledger, Jackson, Miss., 1957-58, editorial staff, 1959-63; writer, travel dept. Miss. Agrl. and Indsl. Bd., Jackson, 1964-66; chief Miss. bur. Memphis Comml. Appeal, Jackson, 1966-70; dir. Inst. of Politics in Miss., Millsaps Coll., Jackson, 1970—. Recipient Sullivan Writing Award, 1958; A.P. Newswriting award, 1963. Mem. Sigma Delta Chi, Sigma Tau Delta. Home: 1033 Auburn Dr Jackson MS 39211

DELAUNE, GARY (GLASSCOCK), TV news and sportscaster; b. Olathe, Kan., June 20, 1933; s. Norman Ira and Sudie (Abney) Glasscock; student Kan. U., 1952-53; B.A., Okla U., 1956; m. Jo Fern Taylor, Aug. 3, 1963; children—Andrea Jene, Shannon. Newsman, announcer KBIX, Muskogee, Okla., 1957; with CBS, Hollywood, Cal., 1957-59, WFAA, Dallas, 1960, KLIF, Dallas, 1961-65; sports and news announcer KRLD-TV, Dallas, 1965-66; dir. news and sports KNUZ, Houston, from 1966; now news and sportscaster sta. KENS-TV, San Antonio. Mem. editorial bd. A.P., N.Y.C.; mem. Tex. Lt. Gov.'s Com. to Study Relationship of Press and Govt. Served with 3d Armored Div., AUS, 1956-57. Recipient award for report on Nieman Marcus Fire in Dallas, U.P.I., 1964; award for best radio documentary Jack Ruby's 11th Hour, A.P., 1967. Mem. Tex. A.P. Broadcasters Assn. (pres.), Alpha Epsilon Rho. Club: Press (Houston). Featured news reporter record album The Fateful Hours. Home: 544 Ventura Dr San Antonio TX 78232 Office: Station KENS-TV San Antonio TX

DELAUP, PAUL S(IDNEY), educator; b. New Orleans, Sept. 1, 1902; B.E., Tulane U., 1923, M.S., 1925; Ph.D. in Physics, U. Chgo., 1930; m. 1934. Instr. physics Tulane U., New Orleans, 1923-25, 29-30; instr. physics and astronomy U. Chgo., 1931-32; prof. physics, head dept. U. Southwestern La., Lafayette, 1934—. Mem. Assn. Physics Tchrs., Am. Phys. Soc. Address: Dept Physics U Southwestern Louisiana Lafayette LA 70501*

DELAURA, DAVID JOSEPH, educator; b. Worcester, Mass., Nov. 19, 1930; s. Louis and Helen Adeline (Austin) DeL.; B.A., Boston Coll., 1955, M.A., 1958; Ph.D., U. Wis., 1960; m. Ann Beloate, Aug. 19, 1961; children—Michael, Catherine, William. Mem. faculty U. Tex. at Austin, 1960—, asso. prof. English, 1964-68, prof., 1968—. Guggenheim fellow, 1967-68; recipient Annual award for outstanding article in Modern Lang. Assn. publ., 1964. Mem. Modern Lang. Assn., Am. Assn. U. Profs., South-Central Modern Lang. Assn. Author: Hebrew and Hellene in Victorian England: Newman, Arnold and Pater, 1968. Editor: Apologia Pro Vita Sua (John Henry Newman), 1968. Contbr. to profl. jours. Home: 3208 Gilber St Austin TX 78703

DELAVEGA, FEDERICO, chem. engr.; b. El Paso, Tex., Sept. 1, 1931; s. Artemio and Kathryn (Matthews) de la V.; student Mass. Inst. Tech., 1949-53, Tecnologico de Monterrey, 1953-56; m. Maria Guadalupe Arizpe, Sept. 26, 1959; children—Mariam, Timmy, Alexandra. Chem. engr. Carta Blanca, Juarez, Chihuahua, Mex., 1957—, dir., 1965-71; dir. Am. Bank of Commerce, El Paso, Banco Comml., Mexicano, S.D. Pres., Juarez chpt. A.R.C. Internat. com. chmn., dir. Instituto Regional, Juarez, 1966, 69. Mem. Border Cities Assn. (pres. 1969), Juarez C. of C. (pres. 1961). Presbyn. Home: 862 Maria Arizpe Juarez Mexico Office: 606 Insurgentes St Juarez Chihuahua Mexico

DE LA VERGNE, HUGUES JULES, II, lawyer; b. New Orleans, Feb. 18, 1931; s. Charles Eduoard and Marcelle (Menard) de la V.; student U. Notre Dame, 1948-49; A.B., Tulane U., 1953, LL.B., 1957; m. Beatrice Badger, Mar. 8, 1966. Admitted to La. bar, 1957; partner de la Vergne & Meyers, New Orleans, 1957—; pres. Lake Mgmt., Inc.; v.p. Mentab, Inc. Del., Republican Nat. Conv., 1960, 64, 68, sec. Rep. State Central Com. La., 1963—; chmn. Young Rep. Fedn. La., Inc., 1959-62. Sec., treas. Bd. Commrs. Liberty Pl., 1959—. Served as lt. (j.g.) USNR, 1953-55. Mem. La., New Orleans bar assns., Soc. War of 1812, S.A.R., Delta Kappa Epsilon. Roman Catholic. Clubs: Pickwick, Stratford, Essex. Home: 4010 St Charles Av New Orleans LA 70117 Office: 611 Gravier St New Orleans LA 70130

DE LA VERGNE, JULES KRISTIAN, architect; b. New Orleans, Aug. 17, 1911; s. Hugues Jules and Marie Louise (Schmidt) de la V.; B.Arch., Notre Dame U., 1933; postgrad. Harvard, 1933-34; m. Betty Parham Felder, Oct. 27, 1936; children—Paulette (Mrs. Frank B. Stewart, Jr.), Jules Christian. Partner, Wogan, Bernard & de la Vergne, 1946-48; owner Jules K. de la Vergne & Assos., New Orleans, 1948—. Mem. Pub. Affairs Research Council La., 1962—; mem. Com. for Better La., 1964—; mem. Isaac Delgado Mus. Art Assn., 1957—. Bd. dirs. Spring Fiesta, 1963-65; mem. Met. Crime Commn., 1968; v.p., bd. dirs. Alumni Bd. U. Notre Dame. Served to lt. USNR, World War II. Mem. A.I.A., La. Architects Assn., La. Landmarks, Soc. Archtl. Historian, New Orleans C. of C., Internat. House, S.A.R., Soc. War 1812, Navy League U.S., Soc. Founders of New Orleans, France-Amerique de la Louisiane (past pres.). Clubs: Plimsoll, Serra (past pres.), Notre Dame (past pres.), Pickwick, Stratford, Pendennis, Round Table (New Orleans); Lake Shore (Slidell). Home: 5811 Hurst St New Orleans LA 70115 Office: Pere Marquette Bldg New Orleans LA 70112

DELCHAMPS, ALFRED FREDERICK, food chain store exec.; b. Mobile, Jan. 25, 1895; s. Alfred W. and Annie Marie (Theuer) D.; ed. Mobile pub. schs.; LL.D. (hon.) Huntingdon Coll., Montgomery, Ala., 1955; m. Lucile Crowell, June 19, 1930; children—Alfred Frederick, Margaret (Mrs. Edward W. Young), Lucile (Mrs. Richard T. Nelson). Partner Delchamps Grocery Co., Mobile, 1921-46; pres. Delchamps, Inc., Mobile, 1946-65, chmn. bd., 1965—; dir. First Nat. Bank Mobile. Mem. bd. edn. Mobile County Schs., 1946-58, pres., 1950-52, 56-58; sec. Indsl. Devel. Bd. Mobile, 1966—; 1st v.p. Mobile County Found. Pub. Higher Edn. 1962—. Bd. dirs. United Fund Mobile County; trustee Bellingrath-Morse Found., Mobile, 1955—; chmn. bd. Huntingdon Coll., 1948—; bd. dirs. United Funds and Council Am., 1958-64, sec. bd., 1963-64. Served with U.S. Army, 1917-19. Named Mobilian of Year, 1950. Mem. Nat. Assn. Food Chains, Super Market Inst., Mobile Area C. of C. (pres. 1960-62, bd. dirs. 1959—), Religious Heritage of Am. (dir.). Methodist (chmn. trustees). Clubs: Lions, Mobile Country, Athelstan (Mobile); International Trade; Bienville. Home: 2559 S Delwood Dr Mobile AL 36606 Office: 305-307 N Water St Mobile AL 36601

DELCO, EXALTON ALFONSO, JR., coll. dean; b. Houston, Sept. 4, 1929; s. Exalton Alfonso and Pauline (Broussard) D.; B.A., Fisk U., 1949; M.S., U. Mich., 1950; Ph.D., U. Tex., 1962; m. Wilhelmina Ruth Fitzgerald, Aug. 23, 1952; children—Deborah Diane, Exalton Alfonso III, Loretta Elmirle, Cheryl Pauline. Instr. biology Tex. So. U., Houston, 1950-54, asst. prof., 1957-60; research asst. vertebrate speciation lab. U. Tex., Austin, 1958-62; asso. prof. biology Huston-Tillotson Coll., Austin, 1960-63, prof., 1963—, Piper prof., 1967—, acad. dean coll., 1967—, dir. Upward Bound project, 1965-67. Cons. NSF, 1959—. Eagle dist. commr. Boy Scouts Am., Austin, 1965-68; bd. dirs. Central Tex. Comprehensive Health Planning Commn., 1966-68, Natural Sci. Center, Austin, 1967-68. Served with AUS, 1955-56; Germany. Fellow A.A.A.S., Tex. Acad. Sci. (vis. sci. tchr. 1960-66); mem. Travis County Grand Jury Assn., Am. Inst. Biol. Scis., Assn. Coll. Honor Socs. (council 1963-68), Am. Fisheries Soc., Am. Soc. Ichthyologists and Herpetologists (Stoye prize 1960), Am. Soc. Limnology and Oceanography, N.Y. Acad. Sci., Sigma Xi, Beta Kappa Chi (exec. sec. 1964-68, v.p. S.W. region 1964-67). Contbr. articles profl. jours. Home: 1805 Astor Pl Austin TX 78721

DELEON, EDWIN LAZARO, oral surgeon; b. Aguadilla, P.R., Jan. 20, 1937; s. Candido E. and BeLen (Sein) DeL.; B.A., Fla. State U., 1961; D.M.D., U. Louisville, 1965; m. Helen Amelia Sheppard, Sept. 9, 1960; children—Melinda Amelia, Jon Deni. Intern, Hillsborough County Dental Research Clinic, 1965-66; oral surgery resident U. Tenn. Meml. Research Center and Hosp., 1966-69; pvt. practice oral surgery, Madison, Tenn., 1969—. Served with USAF, 1954-58. Fellow Royal Soc. Health; mem. Am., Southeastern socs. oral surgeons, Am., Nashville dental assns., Psi Omega. Episcopalian. Author numerous articles in field. Office: 607 W Due West Av Madison TN 37115

DELGADO, MARIA ELENA, sculptress; b. Monclova, Coahuila, Mexico, Nov. 5, 1921; student Technol. Inst. High Studies, Monterrey, Mexico, 1946-55, U. Nuevo Leon, 1955; pupil Guillermo Castano, J. Tovar. One-man shows include Arts A.C., Monterrey, 1956, Soc. Architects, Mexico City, 1957, Regional Inst. Fine Arts, Acapulco, Mexico, 1958, Mexican Plastics, 1968, Welna Gallery, Chgo., 1968, Museum Ciudad Juarez, 1969, Escudero Gallery, 1970, Visual Arts Orgn. Am. States, Washington, 1972; works included in group exhbns., Mexica, U.S., Can., Europe; represented in permanent collections U. Nuevo Leon, Teatro Juarez, Monterrey, La Ciudadela, Monterrey; bust John F. Kennedy in brass exhibited Mexico Pavilion World's Fair, N.Y.C., 1964. Address: Alabama 90 Mexico DF Mexico*

DELGADO, PRIMITIVO, coll. dean; b. Caibarien, Cuba, Dec. 9, 1912; s. Victor Mariano and Andrea (Perez) D.; came to U.S., 1935; A.B., Carson-Newman Coll., 1941; Th.M., So. Bapt. Theol. Sem., 1944, Th.D., 1948; M.S., Radford Coll., 1971; m. Hazel Frances Martin, Oct. 20, 1944; children—Lofton Primo, Andrea Maria. Ordained to ministry Baptist Ch., 1939; minister Marion (Va.) Bapt. Ch., 1947-57; prof. religion Bluefield (Va.) Coll., 1957-58, acad. dean, dir. admissions, prof. religion and philosophy, 1958—. Bd. dirs. Bluefield chpt. A.R.C., Mercer County Mental Health Assn. Mem. Assn. Bapt. Profs. Religion, Am. Acad. Religion. Assn. Deans So. Colls. Rotarian. Address: Bluefield Coll Campus Bluefield VA 24605

DELGADO (CARRION) RAFAEL, librarian; b. Rio Piedras, P.R., Oct., 1937; B.A. in Edn., U. P.R., 1958; M.S. in L.S., 1960. Librarian I Dept. Edn., San Juan, P.R., 1958-59, librarian II, 1960-62; librarian II U. P.R. at Humacao, 1962-64, library dir., 1964-66; library dir. Gen. Library U. P.R. at Mayaguez, 1966—, dir. Gen. Archives, 1969—. P.R. exec. dir. Nat. Library Week, 1965; mem. adv. bd. Tech. Information Center P.R., 1968—. Mem. A.L.A., Sociedad de Bibliotecarios de P.R. (v.p. 1964-65), Asociacion intermaericana de Bibliotecarios, Documentalistas Agricolas. Rotarian. Address: Box 5202 College Station Mayaguez PR 00708*

DELIUS, JACK CORAM, city ofcl.; b. Smyrna, Ga., Mar. 18, 1933; s. Charles Harold and Emma (Coram) D.; B.B.A., Ga. State U., 1965; certificate N.C. State U., 1967; postgrad. U. Ga., 1968; m. Lillian Rozella Bullard, Oct. 22, 1966; 1 son, John Charles. Traffic engr. asst. City of Atlanta 1953-56, 57-61, office mgr., sec. parks com., 1961-64, gen. mgr. parks and recreation, 1964—. Cons. Vice Pres.'s Council on Summer Youth Sports and Recreation, 1968—, del White House Conf. on Natural Beauty, 1965. Bd. dirs. Arts Festival of Atlanta, Dogwood Festival of Atlanta, Community Council of Atlanta, Model Cities, Econ. Opportunity Atlanta; trustee Leisure Careers Found., Atlanta Zool. Soc. Served with AUS, 1955-56. Fellow Nat. Recreation and Park Assn.; mem. Assn. Adminstrn. Dept. Heads (pres. 1971—), Am. Assn. Zool. Parks and Aquariums (asso.), DeKalb Hist. Soc. Episcopalian. Lion, Elk. Home: 4313 Riverwood Circle Decatur GA 30032 Office: 260 Central Av SW Atlanta GA 30303

DELO, DAVID M(ARION), univ. chancellor; b. Mt. Morris, Ill., Dec. 20, 1905; s. Frank Sherman and Ina Salome (Colburn) D.; A.B., Miami (O) U., 1926, LL.D. (hon.), 1956; M.A., U. Kan., 1928; Ph.D., Harvard, 1935; postgrad. Northwestern U., 1930-31; Sc.D. (hon.), Hartwick Coll., 1954; L.H.D., Rollins Coll., Winter Park, Fla., 1968; m. Elsie Muriel Crooker, June 17, 1933; children—Diana, David Michael, Virginia Ann. Geologist, So. Crude Oil Purchasing Co., 1928-29; instr., Washington U., St. Louis, 1929-30, Northwestern U., 1930-32; chmn. dept. geology Lawrence Coll., Appleton, Wis., 1934-37; chmn. dept. geology and geography Knox Coll. 1937-46, certificated instr. civilian pilot tng. program, 1939-43; tech. aide Office Sci. Research and Devel., 1944-46; chief sci. manpower br. Research and Devel. div., Gen. Staff, Dept. Army, 1946-49; exec. dir. Am. Geol. Inst.; exec. sec. div. geology and geography NRC, 1949-52; cons. on sci. manpower Research and Devel. Command, U.S. Air Force, 1951; pres. Wagner Luth. Coll., 1952-58; pres. U. Tampa, Tampa (Fla.), 1958-71, chancellor, 1971—. Recipient grant-in-aid NRC, 1936, mem. com. tng. in geology, 1946, com. on geologic personnel, 1948. Recipient George Washington medal Freedoms Found., 1966. Pres. Fla. Assn. Colls. and Univs., 1964-65; chmn. Ind. Colls. and Univs. of Fla., 1966-68. Fellow Geol. Soc. Am.; mem. Assn. Geol. Tchrs. (pres. 1952), Phi Beta Kappa, Sigma Xi, Beta Theta Pi. Kiwanian. Club: Cosmos (Washington). Author of books, including Phacopid Trilobites of North America, 1940; Scientists in Uniform, 1948; also articles. Co-author: Years of This Land, 1943. Home: 528 W Davis Blvd Tampa FL 33606

DE LORENZI, JOHN, assn. exec.; b. Perth Amboy, N.J., Nov. 21, 1921; s. Otto and Honora (Martin) deL.; B.J., U. Mo., 1947. Reporter-editor Baytown (Tex.) Sun. 1947-48; night editor, cable editor Internat. News Service, Dallas and N.Y.C., 1948-51; account exec. Carl Byoir & Assos., N.Y.C., 1951-57; asst. pub. relations dir., asso. editor King Features Syndicate, N.Y.C., 1957-62; pub. relations dir. Am. Automobile Assn., Washington, 1963-65, mng. dir. pub. and govt. relations, 1966—. Vice-pres. Martin Estates Inc., Edison, N.J., 1969—. Mem. adminstrv. com. Nat. Hwy. Users Conf., Washington, 1966-69; chmn. pub. relations adv. com. Pres.'s Com. on Traffic Safety, 1964-66; mem. policy adv. com. Hwy. Users Fedn. for Safety and Mobility, 1970—. Served with USAAF, 1942-45. Decorated Air Medal with 2 oak leaf clusters. Mem. Internat. Platform Assn., Pub. Relations Soc. Am., Discover Am. Travel Orgns., Ark. Traveler, Sigma Delta Chi. Clubs: Nat. Aviation, Nat. Press (Washington); Overseas Press (gov. 1961-65) (N.Y.C.). Home: 1500 Massachusetts Av NW Washington DC 20005 Office: 1712 G St NW Washington DC 20006

DEL TORO TORRES, PEDRO ENRIQUE, retail co. exec.; b. Sabana Grande, P.R., Dec. 8, 1920; s. Thomas and Generosa (Torres) del Toro; B.B.A. cum laude, U. P.R., 1954, postgrad., 1961-63; m. Panchita Garcia, Mar. 9, 1945; 1 son, Pedro Enrique. Chief accountant Sharp & Dohme, Inter-Am. Corp., Santurce, P.R., 1948-53; pub. accountant, mem. auditing staff Deloitte, Plender, Haskins & Sells, San Juan, P.R., 1954-55; asst. comptroller Commonwealth Oil Refining Co., Inc., Ponce, P.R., 1955-58, asst. treas., 1958-61; comptroller Passalacqua & Cia, Inc., Santurce, 1961-64; mem. auditing staff Haskins & Sells, C.P.A.'s, 1964-67; controller Ochoa Investment Corp., Hato Rey, P.R., 1967-72, Gonzalez Padin Co., San Juan, 1972—. Pres., Credit Union of Employees Commonwealth Oil Refining Co., 1957-58; lectr. Cath. U. P.R., 1958-59. Served with AUS, 1946. C.P.A., P.R. Mem. Nat. Assn. Accountants, Am., P.R. (treas. Ponce chpt. 1959-60) insts. C.P.A.'s. Lion. Home: Apt 7-C El Dorado Condominium Ponce de Leon Av and Trigo Miramar Santurce PR 00907 Office: 3d floor Gonzalez Padin Bldg Plaza de Armas San Juan PR 00901

DELYANNIS, LEONIDAS THEODORE, structural engr.; b. Athens, Greece, Nov. 8, 1926; s. Theodore L. and Xanthi (Mamouri-Goura) D.; B.S., Greek Mil. Acad., 1947; B.S., Greek Tech. Mil. Coll., 1954; M.S., U. Ill., 1958; m. Georgia H. Alexander, Feb. 21, 1957; children— Theodore, Harry-Michael. Came to U.S., 1957, naturalized, 1963. Chief structural engr. Ben Dyer & Assos., Hyattsville, Md., 1958-60; chief bridge engr. David Volkert & Assos., Washington, 1960-70; prin. L.T. Delyannis & Assos., Arlington, Va., 1970—. Program chmn. Internat. Symposium on Concrete Bridge Design, Toronto, Ont., Can., 1967, Chgo., 1969. Mem. Nixon-Agnew Inaugural Com.; mem. Va. Republican Central Com.; chmn. Va. Rep. Nationalities Council. Registered profl. engr., Ala., Md., Va., D.C. Mem. Am. Soc. C.E.s, Nat. Soc. Profl. Engrs., Am. Concrete Inst. (com. on concrete bridge design), Soc. Am. Mil. Engrs., Pan-Arcadian Fedn. Am., Internat. Assn. for Bridge and Structural Engring. Mem. Greek Orthodox Ch. Lion. Contbr. articles to tech. publs. Home: 2350 N Taylor St Arlington VA 22207 Office: 4620 Lee Hwy Arlington VA 22207

DEMAYA, CHARLES BERTRAND, lab. exec.; b. Belem, Para, Brazil, Sept. 12, 1909; s. Charles and Lucilla M. (Pinho) D.; came to U.S., 1919, naturalized, 1929; A.B., Columbia, 1931, B.S., 1933, Chem. E., 1935; m. Janet Moore Ewart, Oct. 10, 1931 (dec. 1971); children—Kathryn E. (Mrs. William C. Armstrong), Charles C. M. Foreman hydrogenation dept. Durkee Famous Foods, Inc., 1935-36; night supt. Wecoline Products Co., Boonton, N.J., 1936; devel. engr. essential oils dept. Trubek Labs., Inc., Rutherford, N.J., 1936-37; supt. cosmetics Spl. Toiletries Corp., N.Y.C., 1937; from devel. engr. to research mgr. Gen. Foods Corp., N.Y.C. and Hoboken, N.J., 1937-54; owner, dir. Sun Tests Unltd., Sarasota, Fla., 1954—; pres. Food Products Corp., Sarasota, 1967—. Mem. A.A.A.S., Am. Assn. Textile Colorists and Chemists, Am. Chem. Soc., Inst. Food Technologists, Am. Oil Chemists Soc., Am. Assn. Candy Technologists, Am. Ordnance Assn., Electro-chem. Soc. (sec. 1933). Episcopalian. Contbr. articles to food publs.; patentee in field. Address: Box 3707 Sarasota FL 33578

DEMECS, DESIDERIO DEZSO, educator; b. Bolyk, Hungary, Nov. 8, 1923; s. Dezso and Erzsebet (Szulak) D.; Ph.D. in Econs., Universita degli Studi, Bologna, Italy, 1955, D.C.S., 1955; Ph.D. in Philosophy, State U. N.Y. at Buffalo, 1965. Came to U.S., 1956, naturalized, 1961. Asso. prof., head dept. philosophy U. Dubuque (Ia.), 1965-66; asso. prof. humanities and philosophy U. Ark. at Pine Bluff, 1967—. Mem. Am. Philos. Assn., Am. Assn. U. Profs., Internat. Phenomenological Soc., Internat. Platform Assn., Alumni Assn. State U. N.Y. at Buffalo (club leader for Central Ark.). Home: PO Box 4066 Pine Bluff AR 71601

DE MENT, IRA, U.S. atty.; b. Birmingham, Ala., Dec. 21, 1931; s. Ira and Helen Virginia (Sparks) De M.; Asso. in Sci., Marion Inst., 1951; A.B., U. Ala., 1953, J.D., 1958; m. Ruth Lester Posey, Oct. 22, 1959; 1 son, Charles Posey. Admitted to Ala. bar, 1958, U.S. Ct. Appeals for 5th Circuit, 1958, U.S. Dist. Ct. for Middle Dist. Ala., 1958, U.S. Supreme Ct. bar, 1965; law clk. to asso. justice Supreme Ct. Ala., 1958-59; asst. U.S. atty. for middle dist. of Ala., Montgomery, 1959-61, U.S. atty., 1969—; practiced in Montgomery, 1961-69; asst. atty. City of Montgomery, 1965-69; spl. asst. atty. gen. State of Ala., 1966-69. Instr. agy., criminal and constl. law Jones Law Sch., 1961-63. Served to 1st lt., inf. AUS, 1953-55; lt. col. Res. Mem. Am., Fed., Montgomery bar assns., Ala. State Bar, Am. Judicature Soc., Nat. Dist. Attys. Assn., Am., Ala. trial lawyers assns., Am. Arbitration Assn. (nat. panel arbitrators), Phi Alpha Delta, Sigma Chi. Republican. Methodist. Mason (32 deg., Shriner). Club: Montgomery Country. Home: 3437 Warrenton Rd Montgomery AL 36111 Office: Lock Drawer 197 Montgomery AL 36101

DEMENT, JACK DONOVAN, fruit co. exec.; b. Haughton, La., Sept. 14, 1924; s. Benny Alderson and Myrtie Inez (Rounsavalle) DeM; B.S., La. State U., 1948, M.S., 1949; Ph.D., Ohio State U., 1954; m. Marcia Virginia Russell, Mar. 3, 1951; children—Elise, Amy. Asst. agronomist La. State U., Baton Rouge, 1949-52; dir. soil testing Ohio State U., Columbus, 1954-55; research agronomist TVA, Florence, Ala., 1955-62; sr. agronomist Esso Research and Engring. Co., Linden, N.J., 1962-64; dir. research Standard Fruit and Steamship Co., New Orleans, 1964—. Served with AUS, 1943-46. Mem. Am. Soc. Agronomy, Alpha Zeta, Sigma Psi. Inventions in field of fertilizer mfg. Home: 157 Country Club Dr Covington LA 70433 Office: 2 Canal St New Orleans LA 70150

DEMEO, RALPH ANTHONY, constrn. exec.; b. Irvington, N.J., Aug. 11, 1925; s. Ralph John and Mildred (Rao) D.; grad. high sch.; m. Catherine Anna DeGisi, July 8, 1950; children—Ralph, Robert, Richard. Pres., dir. A.D.H., Inc., 1955—, JAR Bldg. Supplies, 1955—, ADH Devel. Corp., 1955—, ADH Systems, Inc., 1970—; sec.-treas., dir. Fairmont Steel Corp., 1970—; v.p., dir. Gulfstream Land & Devel. Corp., 1971—. Chmn. Cerebral Palsey Telethon, 1971. Trustee Bldg. Industry Advancement Fund, Miami, Fla., 1969—. Served with USNR, 1943-46; served with USMC, 1951-52. Recipient awards including Distinguished Service award for membership Nat. Assn. Home Builders, 1970, Spike award Builders Assn. South Fla., 1970, Outstanding Service award United Cerebral Palsey Assn. Miami, Inc., 1971, Civic Minded award Bd. County Commrs. Dade County, Fla., 1971. Mem. Greater Miami C. of C., Nat. Assn. Home Builders (trustee 1968-71, vice chmn. com. 1969, dir. 1970—), Fla. Home Builders Assn. (dir. 1969—, chmn. membership and spike coms.), Builders Assn. South Fla. (pres. 1971, dir. 1971). Roman Catholic. K.C. Home: 270 NW 120 St Miami FL 33054 Office: 2070 NW 141 St Opa Locka FL 33054

DEMERE, MCCARTHY, plastic surgeon; b. Memphis, Jan. 20, 1918; s. Clifton and Leona (McCarthy) DeM.; B.S. with honors in biology, Southwestern Coll., 1939; M.D., U. Tenn., 1942; LL.B., U. Memphis, 1960; m. Ruth Mary Pidgeon, May 23, 1953; children—McCarthy, Michael, Patrick, Marie. Intern, resident surgery Barnes Hosp., St. Louis, 1942-44; surgical resident St. Luke's Hospital, N.Y.C., 1946-47; fellow plastic surgery Washington U., St. Louis, 1947-50; practice medicine specializing in plastic surgery, Memphis, 1950—; mem. staff St. Joseph, Meth., LeBonheur hosps.; asso. staff Bapt. Hosp.; instr. surgery and plastic surgery U. Tennessee Medical School, 1950-62, asst. prof. surgery, 1962—; instr. law Memphis State U. Law School. Consultant USPHS Hosp., 1950- 59, 60—, U.S. Naval Hosp., 1950-59; guest lectr. plastic surgery Paris, Barcelona and Geneva, 1955; panelist Law Sch. Week, Houston, 1960. Chairman of adv. council Memphis Juvenil Ct. Campaign mgr. for Chancellor Hoffmann, Memphis, 1958; del. Democratic Nat. Conv., 1960. Bd. dirs. Memphis Boys Town, 1956—, Memphis Symphony Soc., 1958-59; founding mem., bd. dirs. Little City of Mid-South for Retarded Children, 1959; pres. Sertoma Projects, Inc., sponsoring Boys Town and Girls Club, 1958; sponsor grad. class U. Tenn. Med. Sch., 1952, 54, 55; chmn. bd. dirs. U. Interfaith Assn. Served to capt., M.C., AUS, 1944-46. Decorated Croix de Guerre (Luxembourg). Diplomate Am. Bd. Plastic Surgery, Am. Bd. Surgery. Fellow Am., Internat. colls. surgeons, Legal Sci. Inst. (founding mem.), Am. Acad. Ophthalmology and Otolaryngology, Southeastern Surg. Soc. (sr.); mem. Am., Southeastern (fouding mem., bd. dirs., pres. 1964-65) socs. plastic and reconstructive surgery, A.M.A., Am. Soc. Head and Neck Surgeons, Am., Tenn. bar assns., Am. Legion, Nat. Honor Soc. (charter), Chi Beta Phi, Kappa Alpha (pres. 1957-59), Delta Theta Phi (pres. 1958-59), Phi Chi. Clubs: University; Tenn. Sertoma (pres. Memphis 1960-61, internat. award for outstanding service 1958). Author sci. papers in field. Developed original methods total ear and eyelid reconstrn., research carcinogenesis implated polymer plastics. Home: 826 Reddoch Memphis TN 38117 Office: 1460 Madison Memphis TN 38104

DEMING, FRANK CAMMACK, civil engr.; b. Suggsville, Ala., Aug. 14, 1922; s. Lon Albert and Gertrude (Cammack) D.; B.S., U. Ala., 1948; m. Gloria A. Herndon, Apr. 15, 1950; 1 son, Herndon Cammack. With C.E., U.S. Army, Mobile, 1948—, asst. chief engring. div., 1967-68, chief design br., engring. div., 1968—. Instr. U. Ala. Extension at Mobile, 1949. Served with AUS, 1943-45; ETO. Decorated Purple Heart. Recipient Outstanding Performance ratings Army Dept. Fellow Am. Soc. C.E. (dir. Ala., 1970—), Soc. Am. Mil. Engrs. (recipient Merit award, 1970, v.p., 1971), Internat. Commn. Large Dams, Nat. Assn. Govt. Employees, S.A.R., 95th Inf. Div. Assn., 320th Engring. Bn. Assn., Chi Epsilon, Tau Beta Pi. Mason. Clubs: Isle Dauphine Country, Skyline Swim. Mailing Address: 4155 Belvedere St Mobile AL 36609

DE MONTEBELLO, GUY-PHILIPPE LANNES, museum dir.; b. Paris, France, May 16, 1936; B.A. magna cum laude, Harvard, 1961; postgrad. (Woodrow Wilson fellow) N.Y.U. Inst. Fine Arts; m. Edith Bradford Myles, June 24, 1961; children—Marc, Laure, Charles. Asso. curator European paintings Met. Mus. Art, N.Y.C., 1963-69; dir. Mus. Fine Arts, Houston, 1969—. Mem. adv. bd. Alley Theatre, Houston; mem. adv. com. Houston C. of C. Served to 2d lt. AUS, 1956-58. Mem. Am. Assn. Museums, Am. Assn. Mus. Dirs. Club: Knickerbocker (N.Y.C.). Author: Peter Paul Rubens, 1968. Contbr. articles to art bulls. Home: 3440 Wickersham St Houston TX 77027 Office: PO Box 6826 Houston TX 77005

DE MONTFORT, HAROLD, educator; b. Birmingham, Ala., Oct. 5, 1912; s. Harold R. E. and Marie (Greene) de M.; A.A., Tex. Mil. Coll., 1932; B.A., U. Chgo., 1937; M.A., U. Ala., 1958; postgrad. Harvard, Tulane U., Fla. State U., Auburn U.; M.S., U. So. Miss., 1970. Unemployment claims examiner, adminstrv. office supr., dept. mgr. employment service office, labor market analyst La. Div. Employment Security, 1945-47; tng. officer regional office VA, New Orleans, 1947-51; orgn., methods examiner Cal. Mil. Dist., U.S. Army, 1951; adminstrv. asst. Baton Rouge Engr. Depot, U.S. Army, 1951-52; adminstrv. asst. New Orleans Civil Def., 1952; individual practice, personal vocational counseling, 1953-56; grad. asst. guidance Fla. State U., 1957-58; sch. psychologist Brevard Guidance Center, Cocoa, Fla., 1958-59; grad. asst. psychology Auburn U., 1959; instr. Lyman Ward Mil. Acad., Camp Hill, Ala., 1960; asst. comdt., prof. mil. sci. Chamberlain-Hunt Acad., Port Gibson, Miss., 1961-62; dean of students, sch. psychologist Jr. U. New Orleans, 1962-63; became dean Monticello Acad., Jefferson Parish, La., 1964; col. govs. staff La. Militia, a.d.c. to gov., 1964; headmaster The Sanctuary Sch., New Orleans, 1964-65; ednl. counseling, 1966—. Mem. exec. com. New Orleans Meml. Day Assn., 1960, 63. Served with Royal Canadian Army, 1939-43, AUS, 1943-45. Decorated knight comdr. Sovereign Greek Order of St. Dennis of Zante; comdr. Nat. Order of Honor and Merit (Haiti); Royal Yugoslav Commemorative War Cross (1941-45); recipient medal for essay, Internat. Colonial and Overseas Expedition, Paris, 1931; Cross of Merit, Nat. Legion of Greek-Am. War Veterans in Am., 1966; gold medal City of Mesolongi (Greece), 1966; medal Japanese Red Cross Soc., 1967. Mem. La. State Rifle and Pistol Assn. (past pres., mem. exec. council), Am. Legion, V.F.W., Internat. Platform Assn., Mensa, Am. Personnel and Guidance Assn., Nat. Vocational Guidance Assn., Intertel, Pi Gamma Mu, Kappa Delta Pi. Club: New Orleans Shooting (pres., dir.). Home: 241 Chartres St New Orleans LA 70130

DEMPSEY, HUGH JAMES, educator; b. Ottawa, Ont., Canada, Nov. 2, 1929; s. Hugh Campbell and Cameron Bertha (Rowatt) D.; student Lisgar Collegiate, Ottawa, Can., 1942-47; M.D., U. Ottawa, 1953, B.Sc., 1956; m. Elaine Hackworth, Feb. 22, 1963; 1 son, Scott Rowatt. Resident internal medicine Ottawa Gen. Hosp., 1953-55; med. researcher Banting Inst., U. Toronto, 1956; researcher clin. hematology U. Utah, 1956-58; researcher endocrinology U. Ala., Birmingham, 1960-61, prof. medicine Sch. Medicine, 1962—. Fellow Royal Coll. Physicians, Am. Soc. Exptl. Biology, A.C.P.; mem. Am. Soc. Hematology. Author numerous research papers in various medical jours. Home: 3417 Stone Ridge Dr Birmingham AL 35243 Office: Dept of Medicine U Ala Sch of Medicine Birmingham AL 35233

DEMPSEY, PHILIP AUGUSTUS, park exec.; b. Cleve., May 31, 1925; s. Joseph Cleaveland and Mary (Harks) D.; B.A., Kent State U., 1949; m. Fion Marie Aspery, June 4, 1955; children—Michael Aspery, Patrick Joseph, Kerry Ann, James Philip, Kelly Marie. Reporter, Wooster (O.) Daily Record, 1949, Mansfield (O.) News Jour., 1949-50; copy writer Koehl, Landis, & Landan Advt. Agy., 1950-51, mgr. Cleve. Conv. Bur., 1951-61; conv. mgr. Am. Mining Congress, Washington, 1961-62; exec. v.p. Cin. Conv. and Visitors Bur., 1962-71; dir. marketing Kings Island Amusement Park, Cin., 1971—. Bd. dirs. Campbell Lodge Home for Boys. Served with USNR, 1943-46, Mem. Am. Soc. Assn. Execs., Internat. Assn. Conv. Burs., Phi Delta Theta. Roman Catholic. Rotarian. Clubs: Cincinnati; Summit Hills Country (Fort Mitchell, Ky.). Home: 1076 Emerson Rd Park Hills KY 41011 Office: PO Box 400 Kings Mills OH 45034

DEMPSEY, WILLIAM HENRY, JR., lawyer; b. New Ulm, Minn., Dec. 1, 1930; s. William H. and Myra (Seifert) D.; A.B., U. Notre Dame, 1952; LL.B., Yale, 1955; m. Mary Studer, Aug. 25, 1954; children—William Henry III, Robert J., Timothy M., Elizabeth, Thomas, Mary. Admitted to D.C. bar, 1955; law clk. to Judge Charles Fahy, U.S. Ct. Appeals, 1955-56; chief law clk. Chief Justice of U.S., Washington, 1959-60; mem. firm Shea & Gardner, Washington, 1960-72; chmn. Nat. Ry. Labor Conf., Washington, 1972—. Served as 1st lt. with Judge Adv. Gen.'s Corps. AUS, 1956-59. Mem. Yale Law Sch. Assn. Washington (pres. 1966; mem. exec. com.), Phi Alpha Delta. Roman Catholic. Home: 3311 N Glebe Rd Arlington VA 22207 Office: 1225 Connecticut Av NW Washington DC 20036

DENABURG, CHARLES ROBERT, metall. engr.; b. Birmingham, Ala., Apr. 23, 1935; s. Simon and Mary (Rosenblum) D.; B.S. in Metall. Engring., U. Ala., 1959; m. Sara Rose Lepp, Aug. 12, 1956, children—Elisa Jan, Cheryl Lyn, Danial. Mem. staff aerospace tech. and materials NASA, Marshall Space Flight Center, Ala. 1963-67, mem. staff aerospace tech. and materials failure analysis, Kennedy Space Center, Fla., 1967—. Cons. engr. structural failures and corrosion prevention. Mem. Indian Harbour Beach (Fla.) Planning and Zoning Bd. Served with AUS, 1961-62. Recipient Snoopy award Astronaut Office NASA, 1969. Registered profl. engr., Ala. Mem. Am. Soc. Metals, Nat. Assn. Corrosion Engrs. Home: 325 Eutau Court Indian Harbour Beach FL 32937 Office: Kennedy Space Center FL 32899

DENBO, BRUCE FREDERICK, editor; b. Port Arthur, Tex., May 20, 1913; s. Bruce Emerson and Ursula (Hamilton) D.; B.A., La. State U., 1936; M.A., La. State U., 1940; Litt.D., Berea Coll., 1970; m. Helen Lenora Hunt, Dec. 18, 1939; 1 dau., Geri Lynn (Mrs. John L. Greenway). Editor La. State U. Press, 1938-46, mgr., 1946-50; dir. U. Ky. Press, Lexington, 1950-69, U. Press of Ky., 1969—. Served to capt. USAAF, 1943-46. Mem. Assn. Am. U. Presses (v.p. 1965), Orgn. Am. Historians, So. Hist. Assn., S.O.R., Ky. Heritage Found., Lexington Civil War Round Table (program chmn., 1955—). Episcopalian. Rotarian (pres. 1972-73). Author: Notice by Publication in Louisiana, 1942. Home: 525 Ridge Rd Lexington KY 40503 Office: University Press Ky Lexington KY 40506

DENHAM, DICK, broadcasting exec. Program mgr. WRC, WRC-FM, Washington. Office: 4001 Nebraska Av NW Washington DC 20016*

DENHAM, GLENN WILDER, lawyer; b. Pulaski, Tenn., Sept. 6, 1918; s. Ernest Myers and Dove (Browning) D.; student Cumberland Coll., 1935-37; LL.B., U. Ky., 1946; m. Lyda Belle Culver, Dec. 1, 1949; children—Suzanne, Steven Culver, Rebecca D., David Wilder. Admitted to Ky. bar, 1941; law clk. Ky. Ct. Appeals, 1946-47; practices law, Williamsburg, Ky., 1947-51, Middlesboro, Ky., 1951—. Dir. Comml. Bank, Middlesboro. Pres. Middlesboro Indsl. Found.; trustee Appalachian Regional Hosps. Inc. Served with USNR, 1942-45. Decorated Navy Cross, Air medal. Mem. Middlesboro C. of C. (pres. 1963—), Ky. C. of C. (dir. 1969—), Ky. Bar Assn. (v.p. 1971-72, pres. elect 1972). Home: 207 Arthur Heights Middlesboro KY 40965 Office: 2121 1/2 Cumberland Av Middlesboro KY 40965

DENHOLM, DONALD HOWARD, educator; b. Elizabeth, N.J., May 31, 1920; s. William M. and Alice May (Speidel) D.; B.S., Pa. State U., 1943; M.S., Wash. U., 1952; m. Mildred Marie Bausticker, May 21, 1943; children—William E., Sheila Anne. Chief indsl. engr. Chase Bag Co., N.Y.C., 1947-60; chief planning and control Teledyne-Brown Engring., Huntsville, Ala., 1960-68; prof. indsl. engring. Auburn U., 1968—. Served to lt. USNR, 1942-46. Mem. Nat. Soc. Profl. Engrs., Am. Inst. Indsl. Engrs. (dir. chpt. programs 1968-72), Ala. Edn. Assn., Am. Soc. Engring. Edn. Club: Saugahatchee Country. Home: 1109 Felton Lane Auburn AL 36830 Office: Indsl Engring Dept Auburn U Auburn AL 36830

DENISON, MRS. FRANKLIN AUGUSTUS, shipyard exec.; b. Chgo., Feb. 25, 1915; d. Clarence Morton and Geraldine (Strickland) Winslow; student Lyons Twp. Jr. Coll., 1935; m. Franklin Augustus Denison, Dec. 27, 1947; children—Christopher Winslow, Franklin Augustus, Keneim Winslow. Sec.-treas. Broward Marine, Inc., Ft. Lauderdale, Fla., 1948—, interior decorator, designer of yacht interiors G. Winslow Denison, 1960. Mem. D.A.R. Home: 1801 SW 20th St Fort Lauderdale FL 33302 Office: 1601 SW 20th St Fort Lauderdale FL 33302

DENISON, ROBERT CARLYS, city postmaster; b. Deport, Tex., Oct. 26, 1919; s. Robert Lloyd and Tommie Rae (Norrell) D.; student Paris Jr. Coll., 1937-38; m. Betty Jo Guest, July 1, 1944; 1 son, John

Robert. Parts mgr., bookkeeper Chevrolet Agy., automobile dealership, Deport, Tex., 1949-61; postmaster, 1961—. Served with AUS, 1941-46. Mem. Nat. Assn. Postmasters U.S., Deport C. of C. (sec.-treas. 1965—), Am. Legion. Presbyn. (sec.-treas. 1957—). Mason. Address: Deport TX 75435

DENMAN, BEN P., ins. co. exec.; b. Brownwood, Tex., 1916; grad. U. Tex., 1942. Exec. v.p. Southwestern Life Ins. Co. Office: PO Box 2699 Dallas TX 75221*

DENNARD, BILLY MILLINGTON, ednl. adminstr.; b. Pineview, Ga., Feb. 2, 1934; s. Willie Thomas and Esther Armenia (Hodd) Dennard; student Middle Ga. Jr. Coll., 1952-54; B.S., Ga. So. Coll., 1956; M.Ed., U. Ga., 1969; postgrad. Mercer U., 1960, Ga. State U., 1969. Tchr., coach Cook High Sch., Adel, Ga., 1956-57, Luthersville (Ga.) Pub. Sch., 1960-61, Luthersville Elementary Sch., 1961-63; sales rep. Cities Service Oil Co., Atlanta, 1963-64; tchr. Powder Springs (Ga.) Elementary Sch., 1964-65; prin. McEachern Jr. High Sch., 1965—. Served with AUS, 1957-60. Recipient presidents award Booster Club, 1967-68. Mem. N.E.A., Nat. Assn. Secondary Sch. Prins., Ga. Prins. Assn., Ga. Assn. Educators, Cobb County Adminstrs. Assn., Cobb County Ednl. Assn., Cobb County Jr. High Prins. Assn., McEachern Parent Tchr. Student Assn.; hon. mem. Ga. Sheriffs Assn. Democrat. Baptist. Club: McEachern School Athletic Booster. Contbr. articles to profl. pubs. Home: Box 24 Pineview GA 31071 Office: McEachern Jr High School Route 1 Macland Rd Powder Springs GA 30073

DENNARD, HOYT LANE, supt. schs.; b. Gordon, Ga., Jan. 18, 1914; s. William Chandler and Alice (Johnson) D.; student Abraham Baldwin Coll., 1949-51; B.S., U. Ga., 1952, M.Ed., 1955, postgrad., 1967-68; m. Marjorie Rebecca Bozeman, Dec. 26, 1941; children—Hoyt Lane, Timothy Ray, Ina Rebecca. Farmer, Gordon, 1930-40; self employed lumber business, Gordon, 1945-49; agr. tchr. Cherokee County Bd. Edn., (Ga.), 1953-55, Wilkinson County Bd. Edn., 1955-68; supt. schs. Wilkinson County Schs., (Ga.), 1969—. Bd. dirs. Wilkinson County Health Dept., 1969-71. Served with AUS, 1940-45. Recipient citation Cherokee County bd. Edn., 1955. Mem. Wilkinson County Edn. Assn. (pres. 1956-57), Ga. Assn. Sch. Supts., Ga. Assn. Sch. Personnel Adminstrn., Ga. Sch. Bds. Assn., Wilkinson County Farm Bur. (organizer 1956, adv. 1956—), Am. Legion (com. on Americanism 1968—), Union Soc. Savannah; hon. mem. Bethesda Home for Boys. Methodist. (adminstrv. bd. 1955—). Mason. Home: Box 302 Gordon GA 31031 Office: Box 206 Irwinton GA 31042

DENNERY, PHYLLIS S. (MRS. MOISE W. DENNERY), civic worker; b. N.Y.C.; d. Harry and Frieda (Seydel) Sugarman; grad. Collegiate Inst., N.Y.C., 1937; m. Moise W. Dennery, June 7, 1941; children—Harry, Richard. Pres. WYES-TV. Exec. com. Adult Edn. Assn. La.; nat. conv. chmn. Nat. Council Jewish Women, 1959, pres. New Orleans, 1952-54; pres. Friends New Orleans Pub. Library, 1955-59; chmn. com. ways and means, teen age adviser Madison (Settlement) House, N.Y.C., 1938-40; active ARC, 1941-42; chmn. vols. United Seamen's Service, New Orleans, 1944-45; v.p. League Jewish Women, New Orleans, 1953-55; women's adv. com. Crusade for Freedom, New Orleans, 1958—; co-chmn. New Orleans Am. Jewish Com., 1958-60, bd. dirs. 1958—; chmn. budget com. Jewish Welfare Fund, 1959, chmn. women's div., 1958; exec. com. Cultural Attractions Fund, Nat. Friends Pub. Broadcasting; mem. La. Co-ordinating Council Higher Edn. Bd. dirs. Jewish Community Center, New Orleans, Anti-Defamation League, New Orleans Pub. Library, Urban League, Newman P.T.A., Jewish Fedn., Charity Hosp.; pres. Greater New Orleans Ednl. TV Found., 1966-69; trustee Nat. Citizens for Pub. TV. Mem. Touro Sisterhood, League Women Voters, Am., La. library assns. Home: 2303 Broadway New Orleans LA 70125

DENNETT, HUGH FRANCIS, educator, cons. engr.; b. Washington, Dec. 30, 1903; s. Frank Emory and Sarah Olive (Jones) D.; profl. degree in Elec. Engring., Marquette U., 1926; M.S. in Indsl. Engring., U. Ark., 1959; m. Genevieve F. Droppers, Nov. 28, 1928; children—Donald K., Roger D. Asst. engr. Mich. Electric Ry. & Mich. R.R. Co., 1926-28; cons. engr. Am. Inst. Laundering, 1928-37; pvt. practice cons. engr., mech. design, 1937-45; plant and prodn. mgr., pvt. practice, 1945-48; cons. engr., 1948-53; faculty U. Ark., Fayetteville, 1953—, asso. prof. indsl. engring., 1958—, acting head dept., 1969-70. Registered profl. engr., Wis., Ark. Mem. Am. Soc. Engring. Edn., Nat. Soc. Profl. Engrs., Am. Inst. Indsl. Engring., N.W. Ark. Safety Orgn., Alpha Pi Mu (hon.), Alpha Sigma Tau. Home: Route 9 Fayetteville AR 72701

DENNEY, GEORGE COVERT, JR., govt. ofcl.; b. Pitts., July 18, 1921; s. George Covert and Ruth (Crowthers) D.; B.S., Waynesburg Coll., 1942; LL.B., Harvard, 1948; M.A., Columbia, 1950; m. Alice McCauley, Apr. 13, 1946; children—Christopher Stock, Jill McCauley. Admitted to Mass. bar, 1948, D.C. bar, 1961; fgn. affairs officer State Dept., 1950-52; asst. gen. counsel Office Dir. Mut. Security, Exec. Office Pres., 1953-54; dep. asst. gen. counsel internat. matters Office Sec. Dept. Def., 1954-56; cons. com. fgn. relations U.S. Senate, 1956-62; dep. dir., bur. intelligence and research State Dept., 1963—. Fellow Inst. Current World Affairs, N.Y.C., 1962-63. Served to lt. USNR, 1942-46. Mem. Am. Bar Assn., Am. Soc. Internat. Law. Home: 2604 36th St NW Washington DC 20007 Office: Bur Intelligence and Research Dept State Washington DC 20234

DENNEY, JEAN STONE, state ofcl.; b. Milan, Tenn., May 27, 1918; s. John Dunlap and Mina (Stone) D.; B.A., Cumberland U., 1942; LL.B., Memphis State U., 1967; m. Wanda Hundley, Sept. 29, 1946; children— Hundley Stone, Janet Lynn, Lisa Luanne. Foreman, Wolf Creek Ordnance Plant, Proctor & Gamble Def. Corp., Milan, 1942-44; reemployment rep. U.S. Dept. Labor, 1944-45, Gibson County service officer, 1945-49; field rep. Div. Vets. Affairs, State of Tenn., 1949-60; v.p. Milan Banking Co., 1961-63; fiscal officer Tenn. Dept. Conservation, Nashville, 1963—. Dir. Milan Banking Co. Chmn. Gibson County Adv. Citizen's Com., 1963-64. Founding dir. 4H Club Am., 1962—. Served with AUS, World War II. Named Man of Year Milan C. of C., 1963; recipient G.W. Stegall trophy Am. Legion, 1960, 61, 63. Mem. Tenn. (group pres. 1963), Gibson County (pres. 1963) bankers assns., Southeast Fiscal Officers Assn., Am. Records Mgmt. Assn. (chpt. charter mem.), Am. Legion (mem. nat. rehab. commn. 1956-61, nat. com. for post activities 1960-70, service officer 1943-69), Milan C. of C. (pres. 1962-64), Sigma Alpha Epsilon. Presbyn. (Sunday sch. supt. 1960—, ruling elder). Clubs: Rotary (pres. 1962), Am. Legion Century. Home: 6825 Pennywell St Nashville TN 37205 Office: 2611 West End Av Nashville TN 37203

DENNEY, ROGER PEARSON, JR., corp. exec.; b. Columbus, O., Apr. 26, 1937; s. Roger Perle and Donna (Pearson) D.; B.Engring. Sci., Johns Hopkins, 1959, M.S., 1961; m. Barbara Spicer, Aug. 6, 1966; children—Cynthia Ellen, Tobin Spicer. Employment rep. Westinghouse Elec. Corp., Pitts., 1961-62, tng. counselor, 1962-63, mfg. planner, Balt., 1963-65; editor-in-chief publs. Am. Inst. Indsl. Engrs., N.Y.C., 1965-71, dir. publs. and information services, 1969-71; dir. adminstrn. MEDICUS Corp., Dallas, 1971—. Served to 1st lt. AUS, 1961. Registered profl. engr., Cal. Mem. Am. Inst. Indsl. Engrs. (sr.), Inst. Mgmt. Scis., Alpha Pi Mu (hon.). Home: 411 Ridgehaven Pl Richardson TX 75080 Office: 1104 Expressway Tower Dallas TX 75206

DENNIS, CHARLES EDWIN, JR., bldgs. engr.; b. Balt., Oct. 26, 1894; s. Charles Edwin and Annie (Wetzel) D.; student Balt. Poly. Inst., 1908-12; B.S. in Civil Engring., U. Wis., 1918; m. Emma Brown Griswold, Nov. 27, 1929; children—Charles Edwin III, Roy Oliver. Instr., Balt. Poly. Inst., 1912-14, 15-16; research work U.S. Forest Products Lab., Madison Wis., 1918-19; draftsman constrn. work Union Shipbldg. Co., Balt., 1919-21; asst. engr. charge telephone bldg. planning Chesapeake and Potomac Telephone Cos., Washington, 1921-29; engr. bldgs. Chesapeake and Potomac Telephone Co. Va., Richmond 1929-59; pres. Project Services, Inc., Richmond, 1959-60; chief architect's insp. for municipal housing project, Richmond, 1961-62. Mem. Telephone Pioneers Am., Triangle. Republican. Episcopalian. Home: 2409 Tusing Av Craney Island Estates Mechanicsville VA 23111

DENNIS, EDWARD FRANCIS, application engr.; b. Fernwood, Miss., Sept. 17, 1921; s. Oscar Newton and Josie (Case) D.; student Internat. Corr. Schs., 1941-42; B.S. in Elec. Engring., U. Ala., 1950; m. Mary Beatrice Kilpatrick, Oct. 11, 1941. Head plant engring. Rohm & Haas Co., Redstone Arsenal, Ala., 1950-59; chief engr., gen. mgr. Bagwell Co., 1959-65; chief operating engr. Stewart Co., Merril Co., 1965-67; chief appliance engr. Bendix-Westinghouse Refrigerator Div. (name later changed to Americold Compressor Corp.), Cullman, Ala., 1967—; partner Asso. Engrs., Montgomery, Ala., 1960-65. Served with USNR, 1943-45; PTO. Mem. I.E.E.E. (nat. com. automatic control; pres. Huntsville, Ala., sect.), Nat. Soc. Profl. Engrs., S.A.R. Methodist (tchr. sunday sch.). Lion. Principal work design of spl. equipment for rocket motor. Home: Rt 9 Box 20 Cullman AL 35035 Office: Americold Compressor Corp U S 31 North Cullman AL 35055

DENNIS, FRANK LANDT, lawyer; b. Larkspur, Cal., Sept. 26, 1907; s. Frank A. and Leila (Landt) D.; B.A., U. Okla., 1929; LL.B., Harvard, 1935; m. Katherine Wright, July 15, 1935; 1 son, Frank L. Reporter, Kansas City Star, 1928-30; night city editor Boston Herald, 1930-35; asst. mng. editor Daily Oklahoman, Oklahoma City, 1935-39; city editor, asst. mng. editor Washington Post, 1939-52; ofcl. Marshall Plan, 1952-53, USIA 1953-58; Washington rep. Am. Petroleum Inst., 1958-65; pres. Historic Figures, Inc., 1957—; dir. Vt. Marble Co. Mem. Pi Kappa Phi. Clubs: Burning Tree, Metropolitan, Nat. Lawyers, Nat. Press. Home: 2540 Massachusetts Av NW Washington DC 20008 also Pleisurely Marshall VA 22115 Office: 1001 5th St NW Washington DC 20001

DENNIS, HALBERT FLOYD, JR., lawyer, educator; b. Antioch, Cal., Apr. 17, 1928; s. Halbert Floyd and Viola (Hinton) D.; student Middle Tenn. State Coll., 1948-49; J.D., Vanderbilt U., 1958; m. Mary Elizabeth Tittsworth, Dec. 27, 1951; children—John Michael, Patricia, Patrick. Admitted to Tenn. bar, 1958; asst. dist. atty. gen. 8th Jud. Circuit, Shelbyville, Tenn., 1961—; spl. counsel Tenn. Legislative Council, 1961, 63, 65, 67; spl. atty. Tenn. Ltd. Constl. Conv., 1965; retardation programs coordinator State of Tenn., 1967-71; community programs coordinator John F. Kennedy Center for Research on Edn. and Human Devel., George Peabody Coll. for Tchrs., Nashville, 1971—, research asso. prof. spl. edn., 1971—. Chmn. Tenn. dist. Crusade Am. Cancer Soc., 1960-64; mem. Tenn. Gov.'s Com. on Aging, 1960—; project dir. Tenn. Law Revision Commn.'s Revision Tenn. Criminal Code, 1965, 66, 67. Mem. Tenn. Ho. of Reps. from 18th Dist., 1958-59. Served with USAF, 1950-55. Recipient Pub. Service award Tenn. Optometric Assn., 1972, Outstanding Service award Tenn. Assn. Retarded Children and Adults. Mem. Am. Bar Assn., Am. Assn. Mental Deficiency, Nat. Assn. Retarded Children. Baptist. Editor: Tennessee Plans for Her Retarded Citizens. Home: 3042 Boulder Park Dr Donelson TN 37214 Office: PO Box 43 Peabody College Nashville TN 37203

DENNIS, LYMAN CLARK, II, operations research co. exec.; b. Wink, Tex., Jan. 26, 1941; s. Lyman Clark and Yvonne (Huot) D.; student U. Tulsa, 1959-61; B.S. in Physics, Purdue U., 1964; M.B.A. in Operations Research, Tulane U., 1966, postgrad., 1966-69; m. Sue Haire, June 5, 1967. Systems engr. IBM, Mobile, Ala., 1965; research asst. Balintfy-Tulane Menu Planning Project, New Orleans, 1965-66, 66-68, project dir., 1968-69; operations research analyst IBM-France, Paris, 1966; pres. Mgmt. Optimization Systems, Inc., New Orleans, 1969—. Instr., Tulane U., New Orleans, 1966-68. Served with USCGR, 1958-59. Kappa Sigma scholar, 1962-63. Mem. Assn. Internationale des Etudiants en Scis. Economiques et Comml. (v.p. 1966-67), Operations Research Soc. Am., Inst. Mgmt. Scls., Soc. Advancement Food Service Research, Phi Eta Sigma, Phi Mu Epsilon, Kappa Sigma. Author monographs: (with others) Menu Planning and Scheduling by Linear Programming in Single Stage, 1971; Modified Diet Menu Planning System 1972. Home: 2926 Palmer St New Orleans LA 70118 Office: Nat Bank of Commerce Bldg New Orleans LA 70112

DENNIS, ROGER MITCHELL, ins. co. exec.; b. Hattiesburg, Miss., Mar. 10, 1939; s. Mitchell Michael and Annie Laurie (Bryant) D.; student Western Ky. State U., 1957-58; B.S., U. So. Miss., 1960; m. Merrill Flowers, Aug. 31, 1960; children—Michael Roger, Annie Laurie, Theresa Merrill. Agt., N. Am. Co. for Life, Health and Accident Ins., Tallahassee, 1960-61, Franklin Life Ins. Co., Jackson, Miss., 1962; with Coastal States Life Ins. Co., Maryville, Tenn., 1962—, v.p. sales, 1967—. Pres., Crest Enterprises, Inc., Maryville, 1969—, Fabric King Stores, Maryville, 1969—; sales v.p. Aquila Life Ins. Co. subsidiary Coastal States, Indpl., 1970—. Served with AUS, 1962. Recipient Gold Plaque award Nat. Assn. Life Cos., 1966-70. Mem. Omicron Delta Kappa, Pi Sigma Epsilon. Republican. Methodist. Home: 1018 Oak Park Av Maryville TN 37801 Office: Blount Nat. Bank Bldg Maryville TN 37801

DENNISTON, ALFRED BENJAMIN, state ofcl.; b. Mt. Pleasant, Pa., Sept. 27, 1904; s. Samuel Lowry and Elouise (Reppert) D.; B.S., U.S. Mil. Acad., 1928; M.S., U. Mich., 1934; m. Frances Reeder Wilson, Aug. 25, 1928; children—Carol D. (Mrs. George W. Campbell), Kendall D. (Mrs. Charles K. Newman). Commd. 2d lt. U.S. Army, 1928, advanced through grades to maj. gen., 1956; mem. faculty Army War Coll., 1950-53, dep. q.m. gen. 1953-58, comdg. gen. q.m. tng. command, 1958-62; ret. 1962; asst. dir. indsl. devel. Office Gov. Va., Richmond, 1962-65, co-ordinator civil def., dir. emergency planning, 1965—. Decorated Legion of Merit with 2oak leaf clusters (U.S.), Order of Orange-Nassau (Netherlands). Home: Tattoo Hill Route 2 Chesterfield VA 23832

DENNY, CHARLOTTE CURTI (MRS. ERNEST O. DENNY), educator; b. Boston; d. Harry and Olive (Drewett) Curti; diploma Central Islip State Hosp. Sch. Nursing, 1941; B.S. magna cum laude, N.Y. U., 1955; M.A., U. Ky., 1959; postgrad. Coll. City N.Y.; m. Ernest O. Denny, Feb. 16, 1941; children—Warren, Linda. Pub. health nurse Nassau County (N.Y.), 1949-52; sch. nurse, tchr. Harborfields Sch. Dist., Greenlawn, N.Y., 1954-57; coordinator practical nurses edn. Huntington (N.Y.) High Sch., 1957-58; asst. prof. Coll. Nursing, U. Ky., Lexington, 1959-66; asso. prof., chmn. dept. nursing Eastern Ky. U., Richmond, 1967—. Vice pres. Northport-Ocean Av. P.T.A., 1953; chmn. health, nutrition, mental health, exec. council 7th Congl. dist. P.T.A., Ky., 1960-63. Recipient Founder's Day certificate N.Y. U., 1956. Fellow Am. Sch. Health Assn., Am. Pub. Health Assn. (mem. ad hoc com. to study sch. health); mem. Am., Ky. (dist. pres. 1970-72) nurses assns., Royal Soc. Health, Nat. League Nursing (chmn. health and career com. Ky. 1960-62), Am. Personnel and Guidance Assn., Assn. Higher Edn., Am. Assn. U. Profs. Home: 3569 Olympia Rd Lexington KY 40502 Office: Eastern Ky U Richmond KY 40475

DENNY, J(AMES) WILLIAM, music pub.; b. Nashville, Aug. 25, 1935; s. James R. and Margaret (Osment) D.; student Vanderbilt U., 1953-57; m. June Ralls Denny, Aug. 31, 1957; children—Kevin, Steven, Jennifer. Rd. mgr. Philip Morris Country Music Show, 1957-58; pres. So. Star Investors Assos., 1960; account exec. McDonald & Alsup Advt. Agy., 1958-59; mgmt. trainee Third Nat. Bank, 1959-61; mgr. Columbia Records Rec. Studio & Columbia Records Custom Prodns., 1961-63; exec. v.p. radio stas. WJAT, Inc., Swainsboro, Ga., WRBO, Waynesboro, Ga., WSNT, Sandersville, Ga., 1963—; pres. Cedarwood Pub. Co., Inc., 1963—; Country Music Assn., 1965—; partner Hatch Show Print, 1964—; dir. Country Music Assn. Bd. dirs. Nashville Cancer Soc., 1967-69. Chmn. bd. Country Music Found., 1967. Recipient Spl. Achievement award Record World mag., 1967; named Country Music Pub. of Yr., Music Bus. mag., 1964. Mem. Nat. Acad. Rec. Arts and Scis. (bd. govs., sec. Nashville chpt. 1964—) Nashville Jr. C. of C. (bd. govs.; man of yr. award 1967), Sigma Alpha Epsilon, Alpha Phi Omega. Methodist (dir. 1967—). Home: 800 Caldwell Lane Nashville TN 37204 Office: 815 16th Av Nashville TN 37203

DENT, ALBERT WALTER, univ. pres.; b. Atlanta, Sept. 25, 1904; s. Albert and Daisy (Thomas) D.; A.B., Morehouse Coll., 1926, LL.D., 1947; LL.D., Bishop Coll., 1969, Tulane U., 1969; m. Ernestine J. Covington, June 23, 1931; children—Thomas Covington, Benjamin Albert, Walter Jess. Auditor, Atlanta Life Ins. Co., 1926; v.p. Safety Constrn. Co., Houston, Tex., 1927-28; alumni sec. Morehouse Coll., 1928-31; supt. Flint-Goodridge Hosp. of Dillard U., 1932-41; bus. mgr. Dillard U., 1935-41, pres., 1941—. U.S. del. World Health Assembly, 1948, 55, 58; cons. health adv. com. FOA, 1954. Bd. dirs. So. Regional Council, 1944—, v.p., 1952-65; bd. dirs. Nat. Orgn. Pub. Health Nursing, 1944-50, Com. for Nation's Health 1946-52; bd. dirs. Nat. Health Council, 1949—, pres., 1953-55; bd. dirs. United Negro College Fund; mem. Commn. on Health Careers, 1958—; La. adv. com. Civil Rights Commn., 1959—; bd. dirs. Nat. Med. Fellowship, Inc., 1959—; bd. assos. Chgo. Theol. Sem., 1962—; mem. Nat. Commn. Community Health Services, 1962—, Fed. Hosp. Council, 1946-50, 61—; mem. civilian adv. com. Sec. Navy; trustee Meharry Med. Coll., 1951-54; mem. com. on fellowships Ford Found., 1951-54. Fellow Am. Coll. Hosp. Adminstrs.; mem. Assn. Colls. and Secondary Schs. for Negroes (pres. 1948-49), Am. Hosp. Assn. (commn. hosp. care), U.S. Children's Bureau (commn. on Children and Youth), Nat. Planning Assn. (com. on South, exec. com. 1952—), Nat. Tb Assn. (pres. 1965-66), Nat. Student Health Assn. (pres. 1942-48), Nat. Conf. Hosp. Adminstrs. (chmn. 1936-42), Morehouse Coll. Alumni Assn. (pres. 1936-39), Omega Psi Phi (past grand basileus). Home: Dillard Univ New Orleans LA 70122

DENT, BEN, dentist; b. Nashville, Nov. 11, 1908; s. David and Rebecca (Ballon) D.; student West Tenn. State Tchrs. Coll., 1926-28; D.D.S., U. Tenn., 1932; m. Regina Rose Brandt, Oct. 24, 1933; 1 son, Amiel Joseph. Practice dentistry, Hayti, Mo., 1932-34, Memphis. 1934—; mem. cons. staff St. Joseph Hosp., LeBonheur Childrens Hosp.; lectr. operative dentistry U. Tenn., 1951-56; vis. lectr. So. Coll. Optometry, 1947-66, instr., 1966-69, adj. instr., 1969—. Bd. dirs. West Tenn. chpt. Nat. Found. Neuromuscular Diseases, 1961-65. Fellow Am. Soc. for Advancement Gen. Anesthesia (citation for outstanding achievement as lectr. 1971), Acad. Gen. Dentistry (dir. 1959-73); mem. Am., Tenn. dental assns., Memphis Dental Soc., Am. Acad. Dental Medicine, Tenn. Soc. Dentistry for children, dir. 1949, Am. Acad. for Plastics Research in Dentistry (v.p. 1961-62, pres. 1963-64, Meritorious Service award 1964), Tenn. Acad. Gen. Dentistry (pres. 1964), Pierre Fauchard Acad., Federation Dentaire Internationale, Am. Prosthodontics Soc., Southeastern Acad. Prosthodontics, Chgo. Dental Soc. (asso.), Canadian Dental Assn. (asso.), Acacia (hon.), Alpha Omega, Theta Nu Epsilon. Mason (32 deg.); mem. Order of Eastern Star. Contbr. articles to profl. jours. Home: 5442 Laurie Lane Memphis TN 38117 Office: Suite 310 1st Nat Bank Bldg 4990 Poplar Av Memphis TN 38117

DENT, FREDERICK BAILY, textile co. exec.; b. Cape May, N.J., Aug. 17, 1922; s. Magruder and Edith (Baily) D.; grad. St. Paul's Sch., 1940; B.A., Yale, 1943; m. Mildred C. Harrison, Mar. 11, 1944; children—Frederick Baily, Mildred Hutcheson, Pauline Harrison, Diana Gwynn. Magruder Harrison. Dir., Joshua L. Baily & Co., Inc., N.Y.C., 1946-47; pres. Mayfair Mills, Arcadia, S.C., 1947—, also dir.; dir. Gen. Electric Co., S.C. Nat. Bank, Crompton Co., Scott Paper Co., Mut. Life Ins. Co. N.Y. Chmn. Spartanburg County Planning and Devel. Commn., Bus. Council, 1960—. Trustee Inst. Textile Tech., Spartanburg Day Sch. Served with USNR, 1943-46. Mem. S.C. Textile Mfrs. Assn. (dir.), Am. Textile Mfrs. Inst. (dir.). Episcopalian. Home: 19 Montgomery Dr Spartanburg SC 29302 Office: Mayfair Mills Arcadia SC 29320

DENT, HARDY LEE, JR., profl. assn. exec.; b. Hale Center, Tex., Dec. 3, 1920; s. Hardy Lee and Clara (Allen) D.; student C. of C. Inst., 1957, U. Colo., 1958-59; m. Juanita Carmickle, Apr. 17, 1946; children—Hardy Lee. Mgr. Ponca Wholesale Co., Austin, 1947-50; owner Dent Service Sta., Hale Center, 1951-56; gen. mgr. Hale Center C. of C., 1956—. Exec. dir. Fed. Housing Authority, Hale Center, 1966—. Chief Hale Center Vol. Fire Dept., 1953—; sec. Community Fund Bd., Hale Center, 1968—; coordinator Disaster and Clean-up orgn. tornado disaster, 1965. Bd. dirs. Salvation Army, Hale Center. Served with AUS, 1941-46, 50-51. Recipient Service to Youth award Am. Legion, 1962, Service to Youth award 4-H Club, 1965. Mem. C. of C. Execs. Assn. West Tex., Tex. C. of C. Mgrs. Assn., Panhandle Fireman's Assn. (pres. 1967), Internat. Assn. Fire Chiefs. Lion. Baptist. Home: 407 Main St Hale Center TX 79041 Office: City Hall Main St Hale Center TX 79041

DENT, HARRY SHULER, govt. ofcl.; b. St. Matthews, S.C., Feb. 21, 1930; s. Hampton N. and Sallie (Prickett) D.; B.A., Presbyn. Coll., Clinton, S.C., 1951, LL.D., 1972; LL.B., George Washington U., 1957, LL.M., 1959; D.Polit. Sci., Baptist Coll., Charleston, S.C., 1972; m. Betty Francis, Aug. 16, 1951; children—Harry Shuler, Dolly, Virginia, John. Washington corr. several S.C. newspapers and radio stas., 1954; adminstrv. asst. to U.S. Senator Strom Thurmond, 1955-65; admitted to S.C. bar, 1957; practiced in Columbia and St. Matthews, 1965-68; chmn. S.C. Republican, Com., 1965-68; spl. counsel to Pres. Nixon, 1968—. Pres. S.C. State Soc., Washington, 1960; founder, chmn. Senate Staff Prayer Breakfast Group, 1962. Active S.C. Rep. campaigns, 1964-68. Trustee Freedoms Found., 1969. Served with AUS, 1951-53; Korea, maj. Res. Baptist (deacon, trustee). Home: 2030 Bermuda Hills Rd Columbia SC 29204 Office: The White House Washington DC 20500

DENT, THOMAS, ednl. adminstr.; b. Albany, Ga., June 12, 1925; d. Henry and Euzella (Haywood) D.; B.S., Albany State Coll., 1950; M.S., Ind. U., 1954; postgrad. Atlanta U., 1952, Fla. A. and M. U., 1955, 56, 63, U. Ga., 1966, 67; m. Ella Mae Potts, Apr. 24, 1946; children—Thomas II, Leander D., Audrey M., Brenda M., Michael A. Tchr., Edison High Sch., Calhoun County (Ga.) Bd. Edn., 1950-52; prin., tchr. Arabi (Ga.) Elementary Sch., Crisp County Bd. Edn., 1952-57; tchr. Crisp County Tng. Sch., 1957-58; prin. Cordele (Ga.) County Tng. Sch., Crisp County Bd. Edn., 1958-70, Blackshear Trail Elementary Sch., 1970—. Chmn. March of Dimes, 1958-62. Bd. dirs. Crisp County unit, Am. Cancer Soc. Served with AUS, 1943-46. Mem. N.E.A., Am. Legion, Ga. Edn. Assn., Phi Beta Sigma. Baptist (parlimentarian 1968-72). Mason. Home: 1806 11th Sts Cordele GA 31015 Office: Blackshear Rd Cordele GA 31015

DENTON, EMMA MANEY, banker; b. Hiawassee, Ga., Oct. 25, 1905; d. Milton M. and Missouri (Eller) Maney; student pvt. schs., Hiawassee, Ga.; m. James Young Denton, May 20, 1920; children—J. C., Evelyn Isabel (Mrs. William T. Groves), Ruth Elois (Mrs. Robert L. Anderson), J. William, Emma Jean (Mrs. Ray W. Anderson). Cashier, Bank of Hiawassee, Ga., 1936—, dir., 1950—. Chmn. county dr. Am. Cancer Soc., 1944-60. Mem. D.A.R., Friendship Community Club, Hiawassee Garden Club (charter mem., pres. 1960—). Baptist. Address: Hiawassee GA 30546

DENTON, JESSE CAMERON, educator; b. Tarboro, N.C., Nov. 23, 1923; s. Claude Kitchen and Ludie (Cherry) D.; B.S., Swarthmore Coll., 1948; M.S., Cal. Inst. Tech.,1949; Ph.D., Tex. A. & M. U., 1963; m. Alice Lucile Deatherage, May 1, 1948; children—Laura Anne, Thomas Cameron. Research engr. Cal. Inst. Tech. Hydrodynamics Lab., Pasadena, 1949-50; aerodynamicist Ryan Aero. Co., San Diego, 1950-51; sr. thermodynamics engr. Gen. Dynamics Corp., San Diego, 1951-58, cons., 1961-62; chmn. prof. aerospace mech. engring. dept. So. Meth. U., Dallas, 1958-68; staff asso. univ. sci. devel. sect. NSF, 1968-70, Office Interdisciplinary Research, 1970-71, program mgr. research applied to nat. need, 1971—. Research cons. Mobil Oil Co. Field Research Lab., Dallas, 1960-68, Vector Engring. Co., Dallas, 1958-59. Active Boy Scouts Am. Served with USNR, 1943-46. Recipient Chance-Vought Chair of Aeronautics, 1958-60; named Danforth Tchr., 1961-62, Sci. Faculty fellow, 1962-63. Mem. Am. Soc. Engring. Edn., Am. Soc. M.E., Am. Inst. Aero. and Astronautics, A.A.A.S., Sigma Xi, Phi Kappa Phi, Tau Beta Pi, Sigma Tau, Pi Tau Sigma. Conglist. Home: 6512 Machodoc Ct Falls Church VA 22043

DENTON, JOE DON, banker; b. Milford, Tex., Oct. 23, 1924; s. John Fletcher and Dora Mae (Varner) D.; student Hillsboro Coll., 1942, Okla. A. and M. Coll., 1948; LL.B., Baylor U., 1953; m. Genia Elouise Sansom, Aug. 26, 1950; children—Kay Ann, Genia Lynn, John Herman, Joe Don. Admitted to Tex. bar, 1953, also fed. ct. bars; practice law, Waco, Tex., 1953-60; atty., v.p., trust officer Oak Cliff Bank and Trust Co., Dallas, 1961—; dir. Champions Life Ins. Co., Dallas. Bd. dirs. Oak Cliff YMCA; trustee Methodist Hosp., Dallas. Served with USAF, 1942-48. Mem. Am., Dallas bar assns., Tex. Bar, Oak Cliff C. of C. (dir. 1966-71). Clubs: Rock Creek, Oak Cliff Country (Dallas). Home: 1578 Bar Harbor Dr Dallas TX 75232 Office: 400 S Zang Blvd Dallas TX 75208

DENTON, ROBERT M., dentist. Exec. dir. Bd. Dentistry, Fla. Dept. Profl. and Occupational Regulation. Address: 4415 Beach Blvd Jacksonville FL 32207*

DE-NUR, AMNON, investment co. exec.; b. Haifa, Israel, Nov. 16, 1926; s. Mordechai and Hanna (Bernstein) Cohen; B.A., N.Y. U., 1951, M.A., 1952; came to U.S., 1957; m. Gail Levin, Oct. 20, 1948; 1 son, Jack Boaz. Controller, adminstr. Beach Finance Co., L & L Investors Lincoln SBIC Inc., others, 1958-67; v.p., dir. Investors, Lincoln SBIC Inc., others, 1958-67; v.p., dir. Intercontinental Industries, Inc., Dallas, 1967—; pres. H. P. Townsend Mfg. Co., Cleveland Topping Machine Co., Bland Co., 1969—. Served as pilot Israeli Air Force, 1948-50. C.P.A., Fla., Tex. Mem. Fla., Am. insts. C.P.A.'s, Tex. Soc. C.P.A.'s. Mason. Home: 5045 Royal Lane Dallas TX 75229 Office: 113 Braniff Mall Dallas TX 75235

DEODATI, JOSEPH BENJAMIN, aero. engr.; b. San Antonio, Dec. 17, 1916; s. Michael N. and Lydia (Rotondi) D.; B.S., Tex. A. and M. U., 1939 M.S., Cal. Inst. Tech., 1946, Aero. Engr., 1947; m. Mildred Perkins, Mar. 2, 1944; children—Debora (Mrs. Michel Breger), Joseph Benjamin. Commd. ensign USN, 1941, advanced through grades to comdr., 1953; naval aviator, World War II; aero. engr., Pacific and Atlantic fleets, U.S.; ret., 1961; dir. research, engring. systems engring. div. Pnuemo Dynamics Corp., Bethesda, Md., 1961-63; aero. engr. advanced programs Gen. Dynamics Co., Ft. Worth, 1963—. Decorated Air medal with two gold stars. Mem. Operations Research Soc. Am., Nat. Mgmt. Assn., Navy League U.S., Air Force Assn., Am. Security Council, Cal. Inst. Tech. Alumni Assn., Sigma Xi. Home: 2512 Ridgmar Fort Worth TX 76116 Office: PO Box 748 Fort Worth TX 76101

DEPALMA, NICHOLAS, clin. psychologist; b. Naples, Italy, Aug. 30, 1913; s. Joseph and Caroline (Musto) DeP.; A.B., Harvard, 1939; M.A., Boston U., 1942; Ed.D., Calvin Coolidge U., 1955; m. Ruth A. Warren, Apr. 24, 1944; children—W. Brett, Nicholas B., Niki A. Came to U.S., 1921, naturalized, 1921. Psychologist, VA, Murfreesboro, Tenn., 1959-62; chief psychologist Met. Bordeaux Hosp., Nashville, 1957—; pvt. practice psychology, Nashville, 1957—. Tchr. U. Tenn., 1960—. Served with USAAF, 1942-45. Mem. Nat. Assn. Vocational Rehab., Am., Tenn. psychol. assns. Author: Professional Ethics: A Survey, 1955; Psychotherapy with Low Grade Morons, 1956; Rorschack Combined Location and Record Form, 1957; The 16 PF Test and Alcoholics, 1960. Home: 811 Caldwell Lane Nashville TN 37204 Office: 1619 17th Av S Nashville TN 37212

DEPILLA, A. T., horticulturist. Mem. staff U.S. Bot. Garden, Washington. Address: US Botanical Garden 1st and Canal St SW Washington DC 20024*

DEPOE, CHARLES EDWARD, educator; b. Southampton, N.Y., Sept. 18, 1927; s. Herbert Charles and Marian (Tooker) De P.; Asso. Applied Sci. in Ornamental Horticulture, L.I. Agrl. and Tech. Inst., 1952; B.S. in Zoology, B.S. in Ornamental Horticulture, N.C. State U., 1956, M.S. in Ornamental Horticulture 1958, Ph.D. in Botany, 1961; m. Marie Jessie Butto, Oct. 18, 1952. Asst. prof. biology, Northeast La. U., Monroe, 1961-65, asso. prof. 1965—. Trustee, Little Theater of Monroe, 1966-69. Served with USNR, 1945-46. Fellow, A.A.A.S. (council 1969—); mem. Assn. Acads. Sci. (sec. treas., 1969-71), La. (pres. 1972—), La. Jr. (dir. 1966-69; pres.-elect 1972), N.C. acads. sci., Am., Internat. assns. plant taxonomists, Soc. Study of Evolution, Am. Ecol. Soc., Am. Soc. Botanists, Southwestern Assn. Naturalists, Assn. So. Biologists, Sigma Xi, Tau Alpha Sigma, Alpha Zeta. Contrb. articles in field to sci. mags. Home: 100 Curve Dr Monroe LA 71201

DEPREIST, JAMES ANDERSON, condr.; b. Phila., Nov. 21, 1936; s. James Henry and Ethel (Anderson) DeP.; B.S., U. Pa., 1958, M.A., 1961; student Phila. Conservatory Music, 1959-61; m. Betty Louise Childress, Aug. 10, 1963. Music dir. Contemporary Music Guild, Phila., 1959-62; v.p. charge music Allen's Lane Art Center, Phila., Am. specialist music for State Dept., 1962-63; conductor-in-residence, Bangkok, Thailand, 1963-64; asst. condr. to Leonard Bernstein and N.Y. Philharmonic Orch., 1965-66; music dir., conductor sta. WCAU-TV, Phila., Music-Specials series, 1965, 66; music dir., summer music program Westchester County, N.Y., 1965, 66; asso. condr. Nat. Symphony, Washington, 1971—. Recipient 1st prize gold medal Dimitri Metropoulos Internat. Music Competition for Condrs., 1964. Mem. Sigma Pi Phi. Composer: (ballet scores) Vision of America, 1960, Tendrils, 1961, A Sprig of Lilac, 1964; (theme music) Eye on N.Y., series WCBS-TV, 1965; (concert) Requim, 1965.‡

DEPUY, MARY BONNAR (MRS. HENRY C. DEPUY), librarian; b. New Bedford, Mass., Aug. 19, 1917; d. James Miller and Jane (Forsyth) Bonnar; A.B. Colby Coll., 1940; B.A. in L.S., Simmons Coll., 1941; m. Henry C. DePuy, Sept. 29, 1967. Reference librarian N.Y. Pub. Library, N.Y.C., 1941-45; lit. searcher Am. Chem. Soc., N.Y.C., 1945-46; librarian Burroughs Wellcome & Co., Inc., Tuckahoe, N.Y., 1947—. Cons. H.W. Wilson Co., 1965-70. Mem. Am. Soc. Information Sci., Spl. Libraries Assn. (chmn. pharm. div. 1957-58). Home: 5918 Winthrop Dr Raleigh NC 27609 Office: Burroughs Wellcome & Co Inc 3030 Cornwallis Rd Research Triangle Park NC 27709

DERAMUS, JUDSON DAVIE, ednl. adminstr.; b. Speigner, Ala., June 22, 1896; s. William Neal and Josephine (Flinn) DeR.; B.S., U. Ala., 1917; student Pell Law Sch., Raleigh, N.C., 1923-24; m. Nina D. Jerome, Nov. 26, 1940; 1 son, Judson Davie. Admitted to N.C. bar, 1926; with VA, Raleigh, Charlotte, Fayetteville, N.C., 1923-42, mgr. N.C. regional office, Winston-Salem, 1946-66; cons. asso. Mgmt. Inst. Wake Forest U., 1966-70, dir., 1970—. Dir. Winston-Salem United Fund, 1959-65; chmn. adv. bd. Winston-Salem, Forsyth County Civil Def., 1967-69; chmn. Winston-Salem Army Adv. Com. Dir. of Winston-Salem Goodwill Industries, 1962-68, Winston-Salem Industries for Blind, 1962-68, Expt. in Self Reliance, 1967-69. Served with U.S. Army, World War I; AEF in France; served to col. AUS, World War II. Decorated Purple Heart; recipient Humanitarian Service award Winston-Salem Hadassah, 1957, V.A.s Exceptional Service award, 1958, VA'S Distinguished Career award, 1965; selected by Nat. Civil Service League as one of top ten career employees in fed. govt., 1960. Mem. Am. Legion (citation N.C. 1964), V.F.W. (citation 1965), D.A.V. (citation N.C. 1960), Res. Officers Assn. U.S., N.C. Fed. Personnel Mgmt. Council (life), Winston-Salem Fed. Council, Mil. Order World Wars, Beta Gamma Sigma (hon.). Methodist. Rotarian. Home: 2201 Buena Vista Rd Winston-Salem NC 27104

DERBES, VINCENT JOSEPH, dermatologist; b. New Orleans, 1912; M.D., Tulane U., 1934. Intern Charity Hosp., New Orleans, 1934-35, later vis. physician; resident in allergy and internal medicine Vaughan-Graham Clinic, Richmond, Va., 1940-41; instr. medicine, also med. officer Hutchinson Meml. Clinic, 1941-45; now prof. dermatology, also med. dir. Dermatology and Allergy Sect., Tulane U., New Orleans. Diplomate Am. Bd. Dermatology, Am. Bd. Internal Medicine. Fellow Am. Coll. Physicians; mem. A.M.A., Am. Coll. Allergists, Am. Acad. Allergy, Am. Fedn. Clin. Research (S.W. sect.), Allergy Forum, Am. Acad. Dermatology, Soc. Investigative Dermatology, Am. Dermatol. Assn. Office: 1430 Tulane Av New Orleans LA 70112

DERHAM, JOHN PICKENS, JR., banker; b. Green Sea, S.C., Apr. 27, 1896; s. John Pickens and Loula Jackson (McGougan) D.; B.S., Clemson U., 1917; m. Sarah Louella Ivy, Apr. 19, 1968; children by previous marriage—Mary L. (Mrs. Junius P. Roberts), Anne A. (Mrs. Gilbert Coleman). With Seaboard R.R., 1920-66, beginning as devel. agt., successively contracting freight agt., comml. agt., dist. freight agt., asst. freight traffic mgr., all Jacksonville, Fla., freight traffic mgr., asst. v.p., both Norfolk, Va., 1920-54, v.p., Richmond, Va., 1954-66; sr. v.p., dir. Barnett Bank of Winter Haven (Fla.), 1966—; sr. v.p. Barnett Bank of Cypress Gardens; v.p. Auburndale Barnett Bank. Served to 1st lt. inf., U.S. Army, 1917-19. Mem. Nat. Freight Traffic Assn. (life), Nat. Def. Transp. Assn. (life), Jacksonville Traffic Club (life, past pres.), Fla. Traffic Assn., Future Farmers Am. (hon.), Future Farmers Fla. (hon.). Mason (Shriner). Clubs: Deerwood (Jacksonville, Fla.); Lake Region Yacht and Country (Winter Haven). Home: 700 Mirror Terrace Winter Haven FL 33880 Office: 11 5th St Winter Haven FL 33880

DERIAN, PATRICIA MURPHY (MRS. PAUL S. DERIAN), Democratic nat. committeewoman; b. N.Y.C.; d. Ronald and Ruby (Haridman) Murphy; ed. Palos Verdes Coll., Millsaps Coll.; grad. U. Va. Sch. Nursing; m. Paul S. Derian, Mar. 7, 1953; children—Michael Tabore, Thomas Craig, Renee Brooke. Chmn. Women in Miss. for Humphrey-Muskie, 1968; mem. Dem. Nat. Com., 1968—; del. Dem. Nat. Conv., 1968, 72, vice chmn. rules com., 1972; mem. exec. com. So. Regional Council, Dem. Policy Council; co-chmn. Policy Council Com. on Women's Polit. Power. Bd. dirs. Miss. Council Human Relations, Operation Shoestring, Mississippians for Pub. Edn., Delta Ministry, Miss. office Children's Television Workshop; chmn. bd. dirs. Civic Communications Corp. Am. Civil Liberties Union (Miss. dir.), Gallery Guild, League of Women Voters. Address: 2349 Twin Lakes Circle Jackson MS 39211

DERIAN, PAUL SAHAK, educator; b. L.I., N.Y., July 25, 1922; s. Sahak B. and Renee (Tabore) D.; student N.Y. U., 1940-41; B.A., U. Va., 1946, M.D., 1947; m. Patricia S. Murphy, Mar. 7, 1953; children—Michael, T. Craig, Renee Brooke. Intern, St. Vincent's Hosp., N.Y.C., 1951-52; resident orthopedic surgery U. Va., Charlottesville, 1952-53; sr. resident, 1956-57; resident Alfred I. Dupont Inst., Wilmington, Del., 1954-55, Children's Hosp., Cerebral Palsy, Reisterstown, Md., 1955, Rehab. Center, Fishersville, Va., 1955; practice medicine specializing in orthopedic surgery, Pineville, W. Va., 1953-54, Marion, O., 1959; instr. orthopedic surgery Ohio State U., 1958-60, also chief orthopedic surgery F. C. Smith Clinic; asso. prof., chief orthopedic surgery U. Miss. Med. Center, Jackson, 1960-66, prof., chief orthopedic surgery, 1966—, also adj. prof. law; vis. lectr. Sch. Law, Oxford; cons. Jackson VA Hosp., 1960—, Keesler AFB, Biloxi, Miss.; adj. prof. U. Miss. Sch. Law, Oxford. Served with USNR, 1942-45. Fellow Nat. Polio Found; 1956-57. Diplomate Am. Bd. Orthopedic Surgery, also examiner; fellow Am. Acad. Orthopedic Surg., A.C.S.; mem. Am., Miss. State, So., Va., Ohio, W. Va. med. assns., Soc. Nuclear Medicine, Am. Med. Colls., Am. Assn. U. Profs., Miss. Assn. Medicine (bd. advisers), Southeastern Surg. Congress, Tri-County, Central, Hinds County med. socs., Am. Assn. Surgery of Trauma, Miss. Orthopedic Soc. (pres. 1968-69), Research Soc. Am., Nat. Rehab. Soc., Am. Arthritic and Rheumatology Soc., Am. Civil Liberties Union, Sigma Xi, Raven Soc. (U. Va.). Author: Outline Orthopaedic Surgery, 1968. Contbr. articles in field profl. jours. Home: 2349 Twin Lakes Circle Jackson MS 39211

DERRICK, CLARENCE, educator; b. New Britain, Conn., Apr. 8, 1912; s. Clarence and Eva (Reid) D.; A.B., Trinity Coll., Hartford, Conn., 1935; M.A., Western Res. U., 1945; Ph.D., U. Chgo., 1953; m. Mary Elizabeth Tyler, July 4, 1945; children—Mary T., Thomas J. Tchr., Avon (Conn.) Old Farms Sch., 1935-41, Univ. Sch., Shaker Heights, O., 1941-47; asst. dir., dept. exams. Chgo. Bd. Edn., 1948-49; supr. humanities sect. Ednl. Testing Service, Princeton, N.J., 1949-53; prof. humanities, chmn. dept. U. Fla., 1953—. Home: 818 NW 21st Terrace Gainesville FL 32601

DERRICK, GEORGE LYNN, physician; b. Columbia, S.C., Feb. 13, 1932; s. Curtis Eugene and Pearle (Derrick) D.; student U. S.C., 1954; M.D., Med. Coll. S.C., 1958; postgrad. Colby Coll., 1964, U. Miami, 1965, U. Chgo., 1966; m. Sylvia Anne Turner, June 1, 1956; children—George Lynn, Katherine Laine. Intern, Med. Center Hosp., Charleston, S.C., 1958-59; resident internal medicine Columbia Hosp., 1959-60; pvt. practice medicine, Columbia, 1960-63; resident ophthalmology Med. Coll. Hosp., Charleston, 1963-66; teaching fellow Med. Coll. S.C., 1965-66; clin. fellow Johns Hopkins, 1966; instr. ophthalmology Med. Coll. S.C., Columbia, 1966—; instr. spl. studies U. S.C., 1968—. Cons. Eye Bank, 1966—, S.C. Blind Commn.; mem. rotating surg. staff Project Hope, Ceylon, 1968-69. Served with AUS, 1950-52. Diplomate Am. Bd. Ophthalmology. Fellow Am. Acad. Ophthalmology and Otolaryngology. Club: Sertoma (Richland). Home: 4859 Forest Ridge Lane Columbia SC 29206 Office: 1520 Laurel St Columbia SC 29201

DERRICK, HOMER, banker, ins. exec.; b. Lexington, S.C., Dec. 10, 1906; s. Edwin Paris and Mayme Eva (Hughes) D.; student U. S.C., 1923-24; grad. Am. Inst. Banking, 1932; m. Mabel Ellison Beckham, Sept. 1, 1924; children—Jeanne (Mrs. James E. Morris), Betsy (Mrs. Philip S. Calvo), Homer E. Vice pres. S.C. Nat. Bank, Columbia and Greenville, 1926-50; pres. Carolina Nat. Bank, Easley and Pendleton, S.C., 1951-54; pres., chmn. bd. First Nat. Bank, Lexington, Va., 1955—; organized and 1st pres. Great Eastern Life Ins. Co., Greenville, 1954— Eastern Fire & Casualty Ins. Co., Greenville, Atlantic & Gulf States Ins. Co., Easley, S.C., partner The Sherwood Co., 1951—; pres. First Eastern Financial Corp., First Eastern Securities Corp., Lexington, Virginia; past pres. Financial Internat. Corp., Washington; past chmn. adv. council Financial Gen. Corp., Washington; dir. Appalachian Fruit Growers Coop. Assn., Raphine, Va. Episcopalian. Club: Tri-Brook Country (1st pres.). Home: Windswept Lexington VA 24450 Office: First Nat Bank 22 S Main St Lexington VA 24450

DERRICK, JOHNNY B., ednl. adminstr.; b. Gilmer, Tex., Feb. 27, 1930; s. Avery and Fessie (Jeffrey) D.; B.A., Tex. Coll., 1957; M.B.A., Tex. So. U., 1967; m. Pearlia Mae Wallace, July 18, 1953; children—Frederick D., LeNard D. Cashier, Fla. Meml. Coll., St. Augustine, 1957-65, business mgr., 1963-65; fed. loans officer Tuskegee Inst., Ala., 1965-68; dir. student financial aid Tex. Coll., Tyler, 1968—. Active Boy Scouts Am. Mem. Bi-racial com. Tyler div. Eastern Dist of Tex., 1971—; mem. Bd. of Adjustment, Tyler, Pk. Bd., Tyler. Served with AUS, 1951-53. Mem. Am. Assn. Colls. and U Bus. Adminstrn., So. Assn. Student Financial Aid Adminstrs., Tex. Assn. Student Financial Aid Adminstrs., Nat. Assn. Student Financial Aid Adminstrs., Tyler Orgn. Men (treas. 1968—), Tex. Coll. Alumni Assn. (chpt. treas. 1970—), Alpha Phi Alpha. Baptist (trustee). Home: 1602 Northridge Dr Tyler TX 75701 Office: 2404 N Grand Av Tyler TX 75701

DERRYBERRY, EVERETT, univ. pres.; b. Columbia, Tenn., Oct. 11, 1906; s. Felix Oscar and Bonnie Everett (McDonald) D.; B.A., U. Tenn., 1928; B.A. (Rhodes scholar), U. Oxford (Eng.), 1932, M.A., 1939; D.Litt., U. Chattanooga, 1965; LL.D. (hon.), Pepperdine Coll., 1967; m. Joan Pitt-Rew, Aug. 5, 1933; children—Walter Everett, June Elisabeth. Prof. English, Burritt Coll., Spencer, Tenn., 1932-33; head dept. English, U. Tenn. Jr., Coll., 1933-38; head dept. langs. and lit. Murray (Ky.) State Coll., 1938-40; pres. Tenn. Technol. U., Cookeville, 1940—. Regional dir. U.S.O. and Nat. War Fund, 1943-46. Chmn. Tenn. Edn. Legislative Com., 1943, 44, 45; adv. bd. Tenn. Congress P.T.A.; sec. Conf. on Public Instns. in So. States, 1949; mem. Tenn. Jud. Council; pres. Tenn. Water Safety Congress, 1951. Mem. Am. Assn. U. Profs. Nat. Council English Tchrs., U. Tenn. Alumni Assn. (pres. 1946), Tenn. Coll. Assn. (pres. 1945). So Assn. Colls. (commn. on higher edn.), Phi Delta Kappa, Sigma Chi, Phi Kappa Phi, Pi Kappa Delta, Omicron Delta Kappa, Kappa Delta Pi. Rotarian, Lion. Address: Tenn Technol U Cookeville TN 38501

DERRYBERRY, LARRY DALE, lawyer; b. Altus, Okla., Apr. 22, 1939; s. Willis L. and Willene F. (Woodall) D.; B.A., U. Okla., 1961, LL.B.,; m.Marcia Gale Brazil, June 6, 1963; children—Darren Bret, Dara Michelle. Admitted to Okla. bar, 1963; practiced in Altus, Okla., 1963—; mem. firm Oden and Oden, 1963-67, Oden, Oden and Derryberry, 1967-71; mem. Okla. Ho. of Reps., 1962-70, asst. majority floor leader, 1967-68, speaker pro tempore, 1969-70; atty. gen. Okla., 1971—. Mem. Am., Okla., Jackson County (pres. 1966-67) bar assns., Altus Jaycees, C. of C., Phi Delta Phi, Pi Kappa Alpha. Methodist. Democrat. Address: State Capitol Oklahoma City OK 73105

DERTHICK, LAWRENCE GRIDLEY, ret. ednl. assn. exec.; b. Hazel Green, Ky., Dec. 23, 1906; s. Henry J. and Pearl S. (Derthick) D.; A.B., Milligan Coll., 1927, LL.D., 1953; A.M., U. Tenn., 1930; student Peabody Coll., 1934, Columbia, 1939; LL.D., U. Chattanooga, 1954, Franklin Coll., 1957, Kent State U., 1958; Sc.D. Edn., U. Me., 1958; Ed.D., R.I. Coll. Edn., 1958; LL.D. (hon.), Boston U., 1959, Fairleigh Dickinson U., 1960; L.H.D. (hon.), Yeshiva U., 1959; Dr. Pub. Service (hon.), Ohio Wesleyan U., 1959; Ed.D. (hon.), Bryant Coll., 1960; m. Helda Lee Hannah, Sept. 16, 1927; children—Lawrence Gridley, Alan Wendell, Louann. Tchr. and prin. consol. schs. Greene County, Tenn., 1927-29; prin. Joint City-County High Sch., Clarksville, Tenn., 1930-35; state high sch. visitor East Tenn., prof. edn. E. Tenn. State Coll., Johnson City, 1935-39; asst. supt. charge instrn. pub. schs., Nashville, 1939-42; supt. city schs., Chattanooga, 1942-56; U.S. commr. edn. Dept. Health Edn. and Welfare, Washington, 1956-60; asst. exec. sec. profl. devel. and instructional services N.E.A., 1961-71; chief ednl. br. Office Mil. Govt. for Bavaria, 1948-49. Dir. Internat. Textbook Co. Chmn. Interdeptl. Com. on Edn. Activities in Internat. Orgns.; chmn. U.S. Office Edn. team to study schs. of Soviet Union, 1958. Mem. U.S. nat. commn. for UNESCO, 1957-60; U.S. del. 1st Regional Edn. Seminar, sponsored by South Pacific Commn., Brisbane, Australia, 1959; mem. President's Com. on Employment Physically Handicapped; mem. com. on sch. service Boy Scouts Am.; adv. com. on sch. relations Girl Scouts U.S.A.; life mem. Nat. Congress Parents and Tchrs.; bd. dirs. Foreign Study League; mem. Fulbright Bd. Fgn. Scholarships, 1957-60; Tenn. del. White House Conf. on Edn., 1955. Mem. N.E.A. (life, mem.; adviser ednl. policies commn.), Tenn. Edn. Assn., Am. Assn. Sch. Adminstrs. (mem. yearbook commn. 1948, chmn. 1953; pres. 1953-54; chmn. com. for advancement sch. adminstrn. 1955-57), Newcomen Soc., Phi Kappa Phi, Kappa Delta Pi, Phi Delta Kappa. Co-author: Be Safe and Live; contbr. numerous edn. and other publs. Office: Box 817 121 N Washington St Alexandria VA 22314

DERVELOY, THOMAS SHAFTER, state ofcl.; b. Youngsville, La., Aug. 31, 1918; B.S., U. Southwestern La., 1947; M.S., La. State U., 1957; m. 1941; 4 children. Tchr. vocational agr. Acadia Parish (La.) Sch. Bd., 1950-52; supervisory tchr. U. Southwestern La., 1951-64; tchr. Lafayette Parish (La.) Sch. Bd., 1952-64; program specialist La. Dept. Edn., 1964, coordinator manpower devel. and tng., 1964-65, dir. vocational agr., 1965-69, asst. supt. vocational edn., 1969—. Mem. La. Farm Bur., La. Tchrs. Assn., La. Agr. Tchrs. Assn., La., Am.

vocational assns., Nat. Vocational Agr. Assn., N.E.A., Soil Conservation Soc. Am., Phi Delta Kappa, Gamma Sigma Delta. Address: State Dept Edn PO Box 44064 Captiol Station Baton Rouge LA 70804*

DE SAUSSURE, RICHARD LAURENS, JR., surgeon; b. Macon, Ga., Dec. 29, 1917; s. Richard Laurens and Margaret (Hamilton) DeS.; A.B., U. Va., 1939, M.D., 1942; m. Phyllis Helen Falk, June 12, 1948; children—Alexis, Richard Laurens III, Denise. Intern, U. Va. Hosp., Charlottesville, 1942-43, resident neurosurgery, 1946-47; vol. fellow neurosurgery Cin. Gen. Hosp., 1947-48; asst. chief neurosurgery Kennedy VA Hosp., Memphis, 1949-50, chief neurosurgery, 1950; practice medicine specializing in neurosurgery, Memphis, 1950-—; clin. prof. neurosurgery U. Tenn. Coll. Medicine; chief staff Bapt. Meml. Hosp., Memphis, pres., 1966; mem. courtesy staff Meth., St. Joseph, William F. Bowld, John Gaston hosps. (all Memphis). Served from 1st lt. to maj. with M.C., AUS, 1943-46; ETO. Decorated Bronze Star medal; recipient Superior Leadership award Memphis area C. of C., 1966. Diplomate Am. Bd. Neurol. Surgery (mem. bd. 1966-—, sec. 1970-—). Mem. Tenn. Med. Assn. (speaker ho. of dels. 1969-70), Am. Assn. Neurol. Surgery (v.p. 1966), Congress Neurol. Surgeons (past pres.), A.C.S. (chmn. adv. council neurol. surgery 1964-69). Home: 4290 Heatherwood Lane Memphis TN 38117 Office: 20 S Dudley St Memphis TN 38103

DESCHLER, LEWIS, parliamentarian; b. Chillicothe, O., Mar. 3, 1905; s. Joseph Anthony and Lilian Louise (Lewis) D.; student Miami U., Oxford, O., 1922-25, LL.D., 1963; student George Washington U., 1925, LL.D., 1968; M.P.L., J.D., Nat. U., 1932, LL.D., 1947; m. Virginia A. Cole, Jan. 18, 1931; children—Lewis II, Joan Mari (Mrs. William B. Eddy). Admitted to D.C. bar, 1934, U.S. Supreme Ct. bar, 1937. Apptd. messenger at speakers table U.S. House of Reps., 1925, asst. parliamentarian, 1927, parliamentarian, 1928-—. Asst. sec. Am. Group of Interparliamentary Union Conf., London, 1930. Mem. Nat. Portrait Gallery Commn. Recipient Gov.'s award State of Ohio, 1970, 1st Ann. John W. McCormack award of excellence, 1970. Mem. Delta Tau Delta (Distinguished Service award 1964). Editor: House Rules and Manual, 1929-—. Office: Speakers Rooms House of Reps Washington DC 20515

DE SEGONZAC, ADALBERT RENE DE BARDON, journalist; b. Paris, France, July 25, 1912; s. Jean Ludovic and Daisy Mathilde (d'Erlanger) de S.; m. Marie-Madeleine duCailar, Jan. 29, 1943; children—Lionel, Catherine, Laurence-Diane, Jean-Renaud. Reporter, L'Intransigeant, 1932-33, Le Jour, Paris, 1934-35; asst. bur. chief London, Eng. for Paris-Soir, 1936-39; chief corr., London, 1945-56, chief corr. N. Am., Washington, 1956-—. Served with French Army, 1939-40; mem. Free French Air Force, 1941-44; prisoner of war in Germany. Decorated officer Legion of Honor, Croix de Guerre with 5 clusters (France); D.F.C. (Eng.). Clubs: Fed. City, Overseas Writers, Nat. Press (Washington). Author: Visa for Peking, 1956. Home: 5100 Loughboro Road NW Washington DC 20016 Office: Nat Press Bldg Washington DC 20004

DESHAZO, ELMER ANTHONY, educator; b. Winters, Tex., June 22, 1924; s. William Thomas and Dott (Jolley) DeS.; B.B.A. magna cum laude, Tex. Tech. Coll., 1953, M.A., 1954; Ph.D., Ind. U., 1957; m. Helene Ruth Schmidt, Feb. 19, 1972; 1 dau. by previous marriage, Frances Michelle. Teaching fellow Tex. Tech. Coll., 1953-54; teaching asst. Ind. U., 1954-57; instr. S.W. Tex. State U., San Marcos, 1957-58, asst. prof., 1958-63, asso. prof., 1963-68, prof. govt., 1968-—, chmn. dept., 1969-70, univ. coordinator internat. programs, 1969-—. Export asst. Internat. Milling Co., N.Y.C., 1946-49; with USNR Intelligence Program, 1957-70, officer in charge, 1962-65; mem. Equal Opportunities Commn., 1963-66; mem. Tex. Adult Probation Adv. Council, 1968-69; chmn. San Marcos Hermann Sons Corp., 1965-67. Served with USCG, 1942-46. Mem. Internat. Studies Assn. (sec.-treas. 1969-—), Gamma Theta Upsilon, Delta Sigma Pi, Phi Eta Sigma, Alha Chi, Pi Sigma Alpha, Pi Gamma Mu, Delta Tau Kappa. Kiwanian. Author: (with others) Documents and Readings in American and Texas Government, 1969. Contbr. articles to profl. jours. Home: PO Box 1245 San Marcos TX 78666

DE SHONG, ANDREW WALTER, JR., bus. exec.; b. New Boston, Tex., Sept. 26, 1908; s. Andrew Wesley and Lottie (West) Des.; student Paris Jr. Coll., 1925-26; B.S., So. Methodist U., 1929; m. Dorothy Rose, Apr. 20, 1935; children—Dorothy Margaret (Mrs. Charles T. McGregor, III), Andrew Walter, III. With editorial dept. Dallas Times 1929-36; asst. to Tex. div. mgr. N.Am. Aviation Co., Dallas, 1941-45; asst. to div. mgr. Chance Vought Aircraft div. United Aircraft Corp., 1948-53; staff Dallas C. of C., 1936-41, 45-48, 53-71, v.p., gen. mgr., 1961-71; staff exec. E. Hayes Enterprises, Dallas, 1971-—. Mem. adv. bd, Grad. Research Center S.W. Bd. dirs. State Fair Tex. Mem. So. Assn. C. of C. Execs. (pres.). Home: 5510 Nakoma St Dallas TX 75209 Office: 1507 Pacific Av Dallas TX 75201

DESKINS, JOHN ALBERT, food retailer; b. English, W.Va., Apr. 11, 1910; s. John and Julia (Mundy) D.; grad. high sch.; m. Hazel Virginia White, Mar. 16, 1931; children—James A., William W., Patricia Jean. Founder, Deskins Super Market, Inc., North Tazewell, Va., 1946, pres., 1946-—; pres. Richmond Dry Cleaners; dir. Bank of War. Mem. W.Va. Assn. Retail Grocers (dir.). Mason (Shriner), Odd Fellow. Home: 198 Mt View Lane Tazewell VA 24651 Office: Riverside Dr North Tazewell VA 24630

DESMOND, MURDINA M. MACFARQUHAR (MRS. JAMES L. DESMOND), physician; b. Isle of Lewis, Scotland, Nov. 14, 1916; d. Alexander and Margaret Muir (Graham) MacFarquhar; B.A., Smith Coll., 1938; M.D., Temple U., 1942; m. James L. Desmond, July 10, 1948; children—Margaret Graham, James Alexander. Intern, Lincoln Hosp., N.Y.C., N.Y. Hosp., N.Y.C., 1942-44; resident D.C. Gen. Hosp., Washington, 1946-47; fellow pediatrics George Washington U., 1947-48; practice medicine, specializing in pediatrics, Houston, 1948-—; mem. staff Methodist Hosp., Tex. Children's Hosp., St. Luke's Hosp.; instr. Baylor U., Houston, 1948-53, asst. prof., 1953-57, asso. prof., 1957-65, prof. pediatrics, head newborn sect., 1965-70, prof. pediatrics and community medicine 1970-—. Diplomate Am. Bd. Pediatrics. Fellow Am. Assn. Mental Deficiency, Acad. Cerebral Palsy; mem. Am. Soc. Pediatric Research, Am. Pediatric Soc. Research into newborn disease and care. Home: 2210 Bellefontaine St Houston TX 77025 Office: Baylor Coll Medicine 1200 MD Anderson Blvd Houston TX 77025

DESNOYERS, THOMAS HOLLISTER, transp. exec.; b. Chgo., Mar. 27, 1928; s. Harry B. and Browning (Hollister) D.; Ph.B., Ill. Wesleyan U., 1951; M.B.A., Northwestern U., 1953; m. Margery N. Foster, Mar. 22, 1952; 1 dau., Aimee Louise. Clk., C. & N.-W. Ry. Co., Chgo., 1950-52, Pa. R.R., Chgo., 1955; asso. editor Ry. Age, Chgo., 1955-58; dir. traffic research C.M., St. P. & P. R.R., Chgo., 1958-66, dir. marketing and research, 1966-67; dir. marketing N. & W. Ry., Roanoke, Va., 1967-69; dir. codes and standards Transp. Data Coordinating Com., Washington, 1969-—. Served with AUS, 1953-55. Mem. Am. Econ. Assn., Transp. Research Forum, Am. Marketing Assn., Phi Kappa Phi, Pi Gamma Mu, Research in field. Home: 8124 Birnam Wood Dr Mc Lean VA 22101 Office: 1101 17th St NW Washington DC 20036

DE SOMBRE, ROBERT MAGNUS, publisher; b. Washington, Oct. 7, 1915; s. John William and Helena (Magnus) de S.; student pub. schs.; m. Patricia Ann Sullivan, Apr. 17, 1948; children—Diane, Patricia Ann, Joanne. With Kiplinger Washington Letters, 1942-50; with Gulf Pub. Co., Houston, 1950-—, v.p., dir., 1956-68, sr. v.p., dir., 1968-—. Mem. Am. Petroleum Inst., Houston C. of C., Direct Mail Advt. Assn. (past gov.). Club: Houston. Home: 4410 Ingersoll St Houston TX 77027 Office: 3301 Allen Pkwy Houston TX 77019

DESOUZA, ANTONIO ALEXANDER, physician; b. Iguatu Ceara, Brasil, May 9, 1913; s. Pedro Alexandre and Maria (Alves) deS.; B.S., Bahia State Agrl. Coll., 1938; M.D., Faculdadede Medicina da Bahia, Brazil, 1945; m. Margaret Elaine Dubendorff, Mar. 29, 1942; children—Maria Lenore (Mrs. James Roan, Jr.), David, Margaret Jeannette. Came to U.S., 1953, naturalized, 1959. Head dept. entomology Bahia State Agr. Coll., 1939-45; intern Prince George Gen. Hosp., Cheverly, Md., 1945-46; resident surgery Orange Meml. Hosp., Orlando, Fla., 1953; resident otolaryngology Ear, Nose and Throat Hosp., New Orleans, 1954-58; practice medicine, Fortaleza, Brasil, 1946-53, specializing in otolaryngology, Plainview, Tex., 1959-—. Diplomate Am. Bd. Otolaryngology Mem. A.M.A., So., Tex. med. assns. Home: 109 Dartmouth Waxahachie TX 75165 Office: 201 Ferris Av Waxahachie TX 75165

DESPAIN, DAYSIE SPENCER (MRS. CHARLES RICHARDSON DESPAIN), pub.; b. Ft. Spring, Ky., Dec. 11, 1894; d. Joseph and Julia (Vaughan) Spencer; student Ky. Western State Tchrs. Coll., 1920; m. Charles Richardson DeSpain, May 15, 1922 (dec. Feb. 1949); 1 son, Charles Richardson. Pub., Anchorage (Ky.) Press. Mem. Nat. League Women's Service, World War I; vol. worker A.R.C., World War II. Mem. Nat. Soc. D.A.R. (registrar 1951-56), Ky. Soc. Mayflower Descs. (corr. sec. 1953-—), U. Ky. Library Assos., English-Speaking Union, Historic Homes Found., Nat. Soc. Magna Charta Dames, Colonial Order of the Crown, Order of Washington, Alden Kindred Am., Wilderness Soc., Anchorage Home Makers No. One, Nat. Trust for Hist. Ky. Hist. Soc., Nat. Soc. Magna Charta Dames, Plantagenet Soc., Sovereign Colonial Soc. Ams. Royal Descent, Knights Most Noble Order Garter. Presbyn. Clubs: Anchorage Civic; Filson. Pub.: Anchorage (Leone Hallenberg), 1959. Home: 11402 Ridge Rd Anchorage KY 40223

DESPALJ, PAVLE, condr.; b. Yugoslavia; grad. Zagreb (Yugoslavia) Music Conservatory, 1956, Zagreb Music Acad., 1960; m. Nadja Radic; 1 dau., Nadja. Dir. Zagreb opera, 1959-66; founder Zadar Chamber Orgn., 1960; dir. Zagreb Chamber Orch. and Zagreb Symphony, 1963-67; mem. Radio City Music Hall Orch., N.Y.C., 1967; violinist Fla. Symphony, Orlando, 1967-68, asso. condr., 1968-69, music dir., condr., 1970-—; composer works for string quartet, piano and strings, orch., chamber orch., sonatas. Address: Florida Symphony Orchestra PO Box 782 Orlando FL 32802*

DESPORTE, JOHN STANLEY, physician; b. New Orleans, Jan. 10, 1911; s. Charles Alexander and Marie Olivia (Meyer) D.; B.S., Tulane U., 1931, M.D., 1935; m. Janet Elizabeth Voorhies, Sept. 14, 1936; children—Elizabeth Ann (Mrs. James Oliphant Lilly), Janet (Mrs. John Edwin Boelte II). Intern, Touro Infirmary, New Orleans, 1935-36; gen. practice medicine and surgery, Bogalusa, La., 1936-66; co. physician Great So. Lumber Co., Gaylord Container Corp., Bogalusa, La., 1936-43; founder Desporte Clinic-Hosp., Bogalusa, La., 1943-66; mem. staff Bogalusa Community Med. Center, 1936-66. Examining physician, med. adviser Selective Service System, Washington Parish, La., 1942-66. Head Civic Music Assn., Washington Parish, La., 1950-60. Bd. dirs. Community Concerts, New Orleans, 1967-68. Mem. Am. Acad. Family Practice, A.M.A., So. Med. Assn., La. State Med. Soc., Alpha Omega Alpha, Nu Sigma Nu, Sigma Chi. Democrat. Episcopalian. Club: Country (New Orleans). Address: 1550 2d St New Orleans LA 70130

DES PORTES, BERNARD BARUCH, corp. exec.; b. Winnsboro, S.C., Mar. 28, 1922; s. Fay Allen and Elise (Lyles) D.; A.B. in Econs., Tulane U., 1951; m. Elise Harleston Ham, Nov. 25, 1953; children—Sally, Faye, Ann. Susan. Personnel mgr. Owen Roofing Co., Columbia, S.C., 1951-52; employee relations mgr. Kendall Co., Charlotte, N.C., 1952-58; labor relations mgr. combustion Engr. Co., Chattanooga, 1958-60; group dir. personnel Deering Milliken, Inc., Spartanburg, S.C., 1960-68; corporate dir. personnel Sonoco Products Co., Hartsville, S.C., 1968-70, v.p. indsl. relations, 1970-71, v.p. adminstrn., 1972-—. Trustee, Byerly Hosp., Hartsville, 1971-—. Served with AUS, 1944-46. Mem. Florence C. of C. (adv. council 1971-—). Episcopalian. Rotarian. Home: Churchill Rd Hartsville SC 29550 Office: 2d St Hartsville SC 29550

DESROSIERS, NORMAN ALFRED, psychiatrist, clergyman; b. East Providence, R.I., Aug. 6, 1924; s. Frederick Israel and Desneiges (Charette) D.; A.B., Duke, 1949, B.D., 1953; M.D., U. N.C., 1959; m. Frances Lorraine Lueders, Sept. 11, 1943; children—Bruce, Paul, David, Mark. Chaplain, John Umstead Hosp., Butner, N.C., 1951-55, staff physician, 1960-62, resident, 1967-69; intern Watts Hosp., Durham, N.C., 1959-60; resident in psychiatry U. N.C., 1961-62; dir. N.C. Alcoholic Rehab. Center, 1962-65; staff psychiatrist, tng. regional dir., 1969-—; med. dir. W.Va. Dept. Mental Health, 1965-66. Served with USNR, 1942-46. Home: 1919 W B St Butner NC 27509 Office: NC Alcoholic Rehabilitation Center E St Butner NC 27509

DETJEN, DON WHEELER, oil co. exec.; b. St. Louis, Oct. 31, 1925; s. C. Wheeler and Irma H. (Grounds) D.; student Ia. State Coll., 1943-44, Ill. State Normal U., 1944; B.S., Mo. Sch. Mines and Metallurgy, 1948; exec. tng. program Ind. U., 1965-66; m. Shirley Anne Pence, Mar. 1, 1947; children—David, Anne, Michael, Joh, Allison. With Ashland Oil Co., Inc. (Ky.), 1948-58; exec. asst. Valvoline Oil Co., Ashland, 1959-68, v.p. operations, 1968-—. Mem. Ashland Zoning Adjustment Bd., 1961-65. Served with USNR, 1943-46. Home: 2931 Lucille St Ashland KY 41101 Office: Ashland Oil Inc Ashland KY 41101

DETJEN, ERVIN WINFRED, sch. prin.; b. Green Bay, Wis., Jan. 24, 1909; s. August Charles and Jennie (Lages) D.; B.S., U. Ill., 1931; M.A., U. Louisville, 1946; m. Mary Elizabeth Ford, June 14, 1938; 1 son, Ervin Winfred. Tchr. indsl. arts Barret Jr. High Sch., Louisville, Ky., 1931-46; prin. Gavin H. Cochran Elementary Sch., Louisville, 1946-58, Hazelwood Elementary Sch., 1958-—. Lectr. elementary edn. and guidance U. Louisville, 1947-60. Bd. dirs. children's Theater, 1953-58, YMCA Central Boys' Club, 1953-58. Mem. Ky. Edn. Assn., N.E.A., Assn. Childhood Edn., Kappa Phi Kappa, Kappa Delta Pi, Tau Kappa Epsilon. Methodist. Mason (Shriner, 32 deg.). Club: Hi-Twelve. Author: Home Room Guidance Programs for the Junior High School Years, 1940; Your Plans for the Future, 1947, 58; Your High School Days, 1947, 58, Canadian Edit., 1950; Elementary School Guidance, 1952, 63, Argentine edit., 1959; So You're in High School, 1958. Contbr. profl. jours. Home: 1956 Deer Park Av Louisville KY 40205 Office: 1325 Bluegrass Av Louisville KY 40215

DETLEFS, DALE RALPH, air filter mfg. co. exec.; b. Stickney, S.D., Jan. 12, 1927; s. William Frederick and Anna (Peterson) D.; student Purdue U., 1945-64; A.B., U. Neb., 1947; J.D., U. Ia., 1950; B.S. in Commerce, U. Louisville, 1961, M.B.A., 1968; m. Claire McIntosh, Aug. 29, 1953; children—Paul Steven, Ann, William Frederick. Admitted to Ia. bar, 1950, Ky. bar, 1957; editor Bur. of Analysis, Davenport, Ia., 1950-51; sales rep. regulatory and legal div. Prentice Hall, Inc., Davenport, 1951-55; indsl. relations asst. Bendix Aviation Corp., Davenport, 1955-56; mgr. central personnel div. Am. Air Filter Co., Louisville, 1956-—. Instr. Grad. Sch. Bus., U. Louisville. Bd. dirs. Louisville Urban League, 1962-70, Louisville chpt. A.R.C. Served with USNR, 1945-46. Mem. Ia., Ky. bar assns., Louisville Personnel Assn. (pres. 1966-67), Am. Mgmt. Assn., Am. Compensation Assn., Am. Soc. Personnel Adminstrn. Presbyn. (deacon). Club: Hurstbourne Country (Louisville). Home: 9001 Peterborough Ct Louisville KY 40222 Office: 215 Central Av Louisville KY 40208

DE TONNANCOUR, PAUL ROGER GODEFROY, library adminstr.; b. Fall River, Mass., May 22, 1926; s. R. Godefroy and Emilie (St. Germain) de T.; A.B. cum laude, Providence Coll., 1952; M.S., Simmons Coll., 1953; m. Mary E. Fenno, Apr. 9, 1955; children—Paul Godefroy, Camille Marie. Asst. librarian Enoch Pratt Library, Balt., 1953-54; chief librarian, tech. analyst Armco Steel Corp., Balt., 1954-56; mgr. Information Services-Gen. Dynamics, Ft. Worth div., 1957-69, manager information programs, 1969-—; cons. Modern Lang. Assn. Am.; cons. on sci. information personnel U.S. Office Edn. John Cotton Dana lectr., 1966. Singer Ft. Worth Opera Assn., Chorus. Active United Fund; mem. exec. com. Big Bros. Tarrant County. Trustee Cosmopolitan Internat., 1961-63. Served with USNR, 1943-46. Named Boss of Year, Am. Bus. Women's Assn., 1965. Mem. Am. Library Assn., Fort Worth Art Assn., Spl. Libraries Assn., (adv. council, chmn. aerospace div.), Am. Soc. Information Sci., Delta Epsilon Sigma. Episcopalian, (vestryman). Mason. Club: Fort Worth Boat. Author: The Exploitation of Technical Information, 1966. Co-author: Science Information Personnel, 1963. Contbr. articles to profl. jours. Home: 6332 Genoa Rd Fort Worth TX 76116 Office: PO Box 748 Fort Worth TX 76101

DETRO, RANDALL AUGUSTUS, librarian; b. Grand Bayou, La., July 6, 1931; s. Clarence Augustus and Clarice Vivian (Lay) D.; B.A., Northwestern La. State Coll., 1952; M.S., La. State U., 1954; Ph.D., 1970; m. Ruby Charlene Lyles, Aug. 23, 1957; children—Barron Randall, Frederick Charles. Library dir. Northeast La. State Coll., Monroe, 1954-55, Mars Hill (N.C.) Coll., 1955-57; serials librarian Northwestern La. State Coll., Natchitoches, 1957-59; library dir. Nicholls State U., Thibodaux, 1959-—. Mem. La. State U. Library Sch. Alumni Assn. (pres. 1962-63), Am., La. library assns., Am. Geog. Soc., Assn. Am. Geographers, Am. Name Soc., Delta Sigma Phi, Alpha Beta Alpha. Home: 1014 Peoples St Thibodaux LA 70301

DEUPREE, CHARLES LAMAR, assn. exec.; b. New Orleans, Feb. 2, 1917; s. Elijah Julius and Della (Morgan) DeuP; B.B.A., U. Tex., 1940; m. Grace Fisher, Mar. 26, 1946; children—Della Grace, Anne Colista, Cecilia Valerie, Elisabeth Frances. Independent oil operator and owner; exec. v.p. Assn. Oilwell Servicing Contractors, Dallas, 1961-—. Mem. exec. com. Nat. Safety Council, 1966-—. Bd. dirs. Tex. Safety Council. Served from pvt. to capt. AUS, 1942-46; ETO. Decorated Purple Heart, Bronze Star medal. Mem. Am. Soc. Assn. Execs. (dir. 1964-—), Tex. Soc. Assn. Execs. (v.p. 1966, pres. 1967-—), U.S. C. of C., Patriotic Soc. Colonial Wars (founder Tex. gentleman council 1966), Am. Petroleum Council (adv. com. 1966-—), Am. Petroleum Inst., Assn. Petroleum Writers, Sigma Nu. Methodist. Mason (32 deg., Shriner), Rotarian. Home: 4414 Alta Vista Lane Dallas TX 75229 Office: Davis Bldg Dallas TX 75202

DEUTSCH, EBERHARD PAUL, lawyer; b. Cin., Oct. 31, 1897; s. Gotthard and Hermine (Bacher) D.; student Tulane U., 1924-25; LL.D. (hon.), U. Messina (Sicily), 1943, Loyola U., New Orleans, 1972; m. Rhea Loeb, Aug. 1, 1929 (dec. Mar. 1961); 1 son, Brunswick G. Admitted to La. bar, 1925, since practiced in New Orleans; spl. asst. to atty. gen. U.S. on Texas City Disaster litigation, 1950-53; prin. legal adviser to Gen. Mark W. Clark in Mil. Adminstrn. of Austria, 1945-46, also chmn. Allied Legal Directorate; dir. Vernon Bank, Leesville, La. Civilian aide for La. to sec. of army; hon. consul gen. of Austria for La. and Miss.; mem. Met. Crime Commn. Chmn. bd. visitors Judge Adv. Gen.'s Sch. of Army; adv. council Sch. Law, Loyola U. Served as lt. with F.A., U.S. Army, 1917-19, col., Gen. Staff Corps, 1942-46. Decorated Silver Star, Bronze Star, Legion of Merit, Purple Heart, Army Commendation; Gold Cross of Merit (Republic Austria); Croix de Guerre with Palm and Fourragere, Order of Lafayette (France). Mem. Internat., Fed., Inter-Am., Am. (chmn. admiralty and maritime law com. 1961-62, com. peace and law through UN 1962-63, 1965-58, mem. council sect. internat. and comparative law 1967-—, mem. com. on marine resources 1968-—), La. (chmn. com. law reform; chmn. commn. on revision of La. corp. law 1962-—, chmn. supreme ct. com. on jury instrns. 1968-—), New Orleans bar assns., Assn. Bar City N.Y., Am. Judicature Soc. (dir. 1935-56), Maritime Law Assn., Am. Soc. Relations Assn. (dir.), Assn. ICC Practitioners, C. of C., Alumni Assn. Tulane U., Scribes, Athene Louisianais, Audubon Soc., Confrerie des Chevaliers du Tastevin, English Speaking Union, Fellowship U.S.-Brit. Comrades, Heroes of '76, Internat. Order of Blue Goose, Order of Lafayette, Le Petit Theatre du Vieux Carre, Met. New Orleans Safety Council, Mil. Govt. Assn., Mil. Order World Wars, Nat. Aero. Assn., Nat. Geog. Soc., Res. Officers Assn., Seldon Soc., 33d Div. War Vets. Assn., Tulane Alumni Fund, Assn. Am. Indian Affairs, Inc., Am. Soc. Legal History, Am. Civil Liberties Union, Internat. Law Assn., Internat. Legal Aid Assn., Assn. of Average Adjusters, Assn. U.S. Army, Information Council of Americas, Nat. Trust Historic Preservation (nat. devel. com.), Am. Arbitration Soc., Research Fellows Southwestern Legal Found., also numerous local assns. and socs. Mason (Shriner); mem. B'nai B'rith. Clubs: Army and Navy, Insurance, International House (dir., mem. exec. com.). Press, University, Knife and Fork, Petroleum, Round Table, Southern Yacht (New Orleans); Lotos, Downtown Athletic (N.Y.C.); Petroleum (Houston); Propeller U.S., Skyriders; Nat. Lawyers, Cosmos (Washington); Nat. Sojourners; City (Baton Rouge); Escoffiers, New Orleans Athletic, New Orleans Yacht, Plimsoll, Rooftop (New Orleans); Tulane Side Lines Mariners. Editor-in-chief Internat. Lawyer, 1968-—. Home: Pontchartrain Hotel New Orleans LA 70140 Office: One Shell Sq New Orleans LA 70139

DEUTSCH, HERMANN BACHER, columnist, restaurant owner; b. Brux, Austria (now Czechoslovakia), Mar. 16, 1889; s. Gotthard and Hermine (Bacher) D.; S.B., U. Chgo., 1910, S.M., 1910, Ph.D., 1915. Newspaperman in Chgo., 1915, New Orleans, 1916-—; asso. editor New Orleans Item (now New Orleans States-Item), 1943-59, editorial page editor, 1947-49, columnist, 1949-—; owner Brennan's Restaurant, New Orleans; dir. Channing Investment Corp., N.Y.C. Bd. dirs. Jr. Achievement New Orleans. Served with Signal Corps, U.S. Army, 1918-19. Author: Incredible Yanqui, 1930; The Wedge, 1933; The Huey Long Murder Case, 1963; also short stories and articles in Cosmopolitan, Sat. Eve. Post, Esquire, others. Home: 16 Tokalon Pl Metairie LA 70001 Office: 615 North St New Orleans LA 70140 Died June 25 1970

DEUTSCH, STANLEY, physician; b. Bklyn., Apr. 4, 1930; s. Elias and Estelle (Press) D.; B.A., N.Y. U., 1950; M.A., Boston U., 1951, Ph.D., 1955, M.D., 1957; m. Margaret Ruth Zuanic, July 11, 1971. Intern U. Pa. Hosp., Phila., 1957-58, resident, 1958-61, asst. prof. anesthesiology, 1963-65; asso. anesthesiology, Harvard Med. Sch., 1965-68, asst. prof., 1968-69; asso. surg. anesthesiolgy Peter Bent

Brigham Hosp., Boston, 1967-69; prof. anesthesiology U. Chgo., 1969-71; chmn. dept. anesthesiology Michael Reese Med. Center, Chgo., 1969-71; prof., chmn. dept., U. Okla. Med. Center, Oklahoma City, 1971—. Cons. VA Hosp., Oklahoma City, 1971—. Served with M.C., AUS, 1961-63. Diplomate Am. Bd. Anesthesiologists. Home: 3004 Rosewood Lane Oklahoma City OK 73112 Office: 800 E 13 St Oklahoma City OK 73190

DEVALL, CHARLES KLINGMAN, newspaper exec.; b. Mount Vernon, Tex., Nov. 7, 1908; s. Charles Robert and Leila (Milam) D.; student John Tarleton State Coll., 1925-26; B.J., U. Tex., 1931; m. Lyde Gwynne Williford, July 15, 1939. Owner-pub. Kilgore (Tex.) Herald, 1935-40, Kilgore Daily News Herald, 1940—; dir. Kilgore Ceramics Corp., Kilgore Nat. Bank, Kilgore Indsl. Found., Inc. Pres., Tex. Good Rds. Assn., 1956-58. Mem. Tex. Democratic party Exec. Com., 1934-38, presdl. elector, 1940. Chancellor's council U. Tex. at Austin. Served to lt. comdr. USNR, 1942-45. Recipient George Washington awards Freedoms Found. Valley Forge, Pa., 1956,63; Appreciation award East Tex. Freedom Forum, 1968. Mem. Tex. Daily Newspaper Assn., So. Newspaper Assn., Tex. (past pres., N.E. Tex. (past pres., award 1964) press assn., Kilgore C. of C. (past pres.), Sigma Delta Chi. Presbyn. (elder). Lion (past pres. Kilgore). Clubs: Laird Country (Kilgore); Cherokee (Longview, Tex.); Headliners (Austin) Home: 820 Crimwood Lane Kilgore TX 75662 Office: 610 E Main St Kilgore TX 75662

DEVANNY, EARL HANNUM, sch. headmaster; b. Buffalo, N.Y., Oct. 30, 1926; s. Earl Hannum and Elsie (Garyin) D.; B.A., Lake Forest Coll., 1950; M.A., The Am. U., 1952; m. Nancy Elaine Ousley, June 4, 1950; children—Earl Hannum III, Christine Laura, Warren Howard, Scott William. Commandant, Howe (Ind.) Mil. Sch., 1953-68; headmaster Presbyn. Day Sch., Memphis,1968—. Mem. Mayor's Council on Drug Abuse, Memphis, 1970—. Bd. govs. Newspaper in the Classroom. Served with AUS, 1943-45. Decorated Army Commendation medal. Mem. Memphis Assn. Ind. Schs. (pres. 1970-72), N.E.A., Elementary Sch. Prins. Assn., Kappa Sigma. Republican. Episcopalian. Home: 520 Colonial St Memphis TN 38117 Office: 4055 Poplar St Memphis TN 38111

DEVAUGHN, JAMES EVERETTE, educator; b. Deatsville, Ala., Apr. 30, 1913; s. Stanly and Medie (Lewis) DeV.; B.S., Auburn U., 1936; M.Ed., Emory U., 1955; Ed.D. (Proctor and Gamble fellow), Columbia, 1964; m. Lillie Hazel Wood, Oct. 26, 1947 (dec. Mar. 1968); children— Kay (Mrs. Joseph Edwards), Emilie Michelle, Wanda Hazel; m. 2d, Jane Gray Rushin, June 14, 1970. Tchr. pub. schs., Atlanta, 1936-52, prin., 1952-61, asst. supt., 1961-68; prof. edn. Ga. State U., Atlanta, 1968—. Cons. various schs. Served with AUS, 1941-45. Mem. P.T.A. (life), Nat. Assn. Sch. Personnel Adminstrs., N.E.A., Am. Assn. Sch. Adminstrs., So. Assn. Colls. and Schs. (exec. sec. Ga. Com., 1969—), Nat. Orgn. Legal Problems in Edn., Phi Kappa Phi. Author; Adminstrative Error in Separation or Reassignment of Professional Personnel in Education, 1964; Teacher Employment, Legal Aspects: Separation and Demotion, 1971; Policies and Procedures for Teacher and Administrator Evaluation, 1971. Home: 60 Burdette Rd NW Atlanta GA 30327

DEVAUGHN, RICHARD LYNN, dentist; b. Henryetta, Okla., May 27, 1942; s. Walter A. and Berta Lee (Stephens) DeV.; B.S., Okla. State U., 1963; D.D.S., U. Mo., 1967; m. Judith A. Ford, Aug. 15, 1964; children— Dustin Lynn, Wendl Lynne. Practice dentistry, Helena, Okla., 1967-69, Enid, Okla., 1969—; dental cons. Okla. Dept. Welfare. Pres., Cedar Canyon Devel. Corp., Enid, 1971—. Elector, Okla. Athletic Hall of Fame, 1970-71. Mem. City Council Enid, 1971—; dir. Enid Mncpl. Authority, 1971—. Mem. Garfield County Dental Soc. (past pres.), Okla. State Alumni Assn. (past v.p.), Am. Bus. Club (dir.), Acacia (life), Delta Sigma Delta (life). Mem. Christian Ch. (bd.). Lion, Elk. Home: 2413 Robin Ridge Enid OK 73701 Office: 330 S 5th St Enid OK 73701

DEVAUGHN, WALTER CALVIN, govt. ofcl.; b. Tampa, Fla., Nov. 3, 1926; s. Ellsworth Calvin and Alice (Pumphrey) DeV.; B.C.S., Benjamin Franklin U., 1948; B.S. in Bus. Adminstrn., Am. U., 1961, J.D., 1963; m. Catherine Virginia Griffith, June 21, 1952; children—David Griffith, Douglas Walter, Lynn Allison. Auditor, Theodore Bollt &Co., C.P.A.'s Silver Spring, Md., 1948-49, Potomac Electric Power Co., Washington, 1949-54; accountant Gen. Accounting Office, Washington, 1954-67; comptroller, gen. counsel U.S. Govt. Printing Office, Washington, 1967-70, acting asst. pub. printer for mgmt. and adminstrn., 1970-71, gen. counsel, 1971—. Prof. accounting Benjamin Franklin U., Washington, 1965—; prof. law Am. Inst. Washington, 1966-67; admitted to D.C. bar, 1964, Supreme Ct. bar, 1967. Pres. Huntington Citizens Assn., Colesville, Md., 1964-66; bd. dirs. Wheaton (Md.) Rescue Squad; treas. Allied Civic Group, Silver Spring, Md., 1966-71. Served with USNR, 1945-46. C.P.A., Md. Mem. D.C., Fed. bar assns., Am. Inst. C.P.A.'s Fed. Govt. Accountants Assn., Washington Club of Printing House Craftsmen, Fed. Exec. Inst. Alumni Assn. Club: Argyle Country, Silver Spring, Md., Nat. Lawyers (Washington). Home: 200 Eldrid Dr Silver Spring MD 20904 Office: US Govt Printing Office N Capitol & H Sts NS Washington DC 20401

DE VAULT, ELMER EMMERT, engr.; b. Bristol, Tenn., Apr. 10, 1916; s. Elmer Emmert and Myrtle (Senter) DeV.; student High Point Coll., 1946-48, U. Tenn., 1948-50; m. Ida Blanche Cunningham, June 4, 1937; one dau., Myrtle Nell (Mrs. Hubert Leroy Brant). Engr. aide U.S. Bur. Pub. Roads, Roanoke, Va., 1938-43, 50-53; supt. constrn. Troitiono Constrn. Co., Asheville, N.C., 1953-56; engr. N.C. State Hwy. Commn., Graham, 1956-66, resident engr., Reidsville, 1966—. Served with AUS, 1943-46; ETO. Registered profl. engr., N.C. Mem. Nat. Soc. Profl. Engrs., N.C. Assn. Professions, D.A.V. Democrat. Home: PO Box 732 Wentworth Rd Reidsville NC 27320 Office: Box 1318 Reidsville NC 27320

DEVAULT, JOHN LEE, geophysicist; b. Kansas City, Mo., Aug. 4, 1937; s. Isaac Henderson and Evelyn (Rowell) DeV.; B. Chem. Engring., Cast Inst. Tech., 1959; B.S. in Math., MacMurray Coll., 1960; m. Audrey McBlaine, Feb. 10, 1966. Geophysicist, Companie Generie de Geophyque, Paris, France, N. Algeria, Libya, Persia, 1960-62; geophysicist United Geophys. Corp., Australia and Alaska, 1962-65, Digital Playback Center, Houston, 1965—. Mem. Soc. Exploration Geophysicists, European Soc. Exploration Geophysicists, Am. Siesmol. Soc., Am. Math. Soc., Soc. Indsl. and Applied Math., Houston, Dallas, S.E. La., S.W. La., Ark.-La.-Tex., Ft. Worth, Alaska geophys. socs., Houston Geol. Soc., Canadian Soc. Exploration Geophysicists. Mason (K.T., 32deg., Shriner), Elk. Home: 1319 M'Ardi St Houston TX 77055

DE VEER, WILLIAM KIPP, banker; b. Hoboken, N.J., Nov. 18, 1914; s. William H. and Henrietta (Kipp) deV.; A.B., N.Y. U., 1937; LL.B., 1940, J.D., 1968; m. Frances Hutchison, June 9, 1945; children—William H., Nancy K. Admitted to N.Y. State bar, 1941; with Bank of Manhattan Co., 1935-37, Empire Trust Co., 1938-42, Chase Nat. Bank, 1946 (all N.Y.C.); pres., dir. Financial Consultants, Inc., Miami, Fla., 1946-65; v.p. First Nat. Bank, Palm Beach, Fla., 1955-57, pres., dir., 1965—; chmn. bd., dir. Palm Beach Mall Bank, 1969—; pres., dir. Arthur V. Davis Co., 1959-65. Mem. Palm Beach Civic Assn., 1955—. Served to lt. comdr. USNR, 1942-46. Mem. Phi Delta Phi. Episcopalian. Clubs: Everglades, Palm Beach Sailfish, Beach (Palm Beach); Miami. Home: 220 Orange Grove Rd Palm Beach FL 33480 Office: 255 S County Rd Palm Beach FL 33480 •

DE VEGA, ARMANDO FERNANDO, pathologist; b. Havana, Cuba, Oct. 23, 1930; s. Armando and Virginia (Leon) De V.; M.D., Havana U., 1955; m. Margaret Nell Newton, June 8, 1958; children—Maria, Suzanne, Elizabeth, Anne, Cynthia. Came to U.S., 1956, naturalized, 1963. Intern, Charleston (W.Va.) Gen. Hosp., 1956-57; resident Birmingham (Ala.) Bapt. Hosps., 1957-61; practice medicine specializing in pathology, Chattanooga, 1961-64, Oak Ridge, 1964—; asst., asso. pathologist Meml. Hosp., Chattanooga, 1961-64; asso. pathologist Oak Ridge Hosp., 1964—. Med. examiner, Anderson County, Tenn., 1967—. Fellow Coll. Am. Pathologists, Am. Soc. Clin. Pathologists; mem. A.M.A., So. Med. Assn., C. of C. Republican. Home: 1056 W Outer Dr Oak Ridge TN 37830 Office: 125 W Tennessee Av Oak Ridge TN 37830

DEVELLE, ROBERT EDOUARD, city ofcl.; b. New Orleans, Nov. 27, 1906; s. Ernest J. and Ambrozine (Jung) D.; student U. Wis. Extension, 1926-29; m. Zoe Jane Carey, Nov. 30, 1935 (dec. Sept. 1956); children— Michael Carey, Robert Edward m. 2d, Gwendola Rosita Laubenthal, Jan. 4, 1958. With Pendleton Shipyards, New Orleans, 1942-46; collector revenue, New Orleans Dept. Finance, 1946-54, dir. finance, 1954—. Treas. City Trusts, Delgado Albania Plantation Commn., commr. Employees Retirement System. Trustee Police and Firemen Pensions' Funds, United Fund. Mem. Municipal Finance Officers Assn. (past pres., chmn. electronic data processing com.), Nat. Inst. Purchasing Agts., Municipal Forum N.Y. C. of C., Lamplighter. Roman Catholic. Club: International House. Home: 6044 Memphis St New Orleans LA 70124 Office: City Hall New Orleans LA 70112

DEVEREAUX, WILLIAM JOSEPH, govt. ofcl.; b. Balt., May 21, 1922; s. Paul and Pauline (Cornwell) D.; B. Mech. Engring., Johns Hopkins U., 1950; M. Engring. Adminstrn., George Washington U., 1960; M.A., U. Pa., 1966; m. Mary Louise Moltz, Sept. 2, 1944; children—William Joseph, Peter Wheaton. Engr., Norden Labs., White Plains, N.Y., 1952-56; sr. engr. Melpar Electronics, Falls Church, Va., 1956-61; chief engr. program mgmt. staff RCA, Moorestown, N.J., 1961-66; instr. econs. Pa. State U., 1966-67; asst. prof. mgmt. Temple U., 1967; mgr. market analysis and planning Atlantic Research Corp., Alexandria, Va., 1967-69; mem. staff Office of Sec., U.S. Dept. Transp., Washington, 1969-70; mem. staff Nat. Aeronautics and Space Council, Exec. Office of Pres., Washington, 1970—; instr. mgmt. Drexel Inst. Tech., 1962-65; asst. profl. lectr. George Washington U., 1968—. Served with USNR, 1942-45. Mem. Am. Econ. Assn., Am. Inst. Aeros. and Astronautics. Home: 8824 Southwick St Fairfax VA 22030 Office: National Aeronautics and Space Council Executive Office of the President Washington DC 20502

DEVERO, KENNETH RAY, city ofcl.; b. Morris, Okla., May 21, 1938; s. Roy W. and Alta (Harrell) D.; B.S., Okla. State U., 1961; M.A., U. Okla., 1969; m. Miriam Locke Jordan, Sept. 1, 1963; children—Kenneth Ray II, Richard Reynolds. City adminstr. City of Newbern (Tenn.), 1965-66; city mgr., exec. dir. housing authority City of Elizabethton (Tenn.), 1966-69, City of Maryville (Tenn.), 1969—. Mem. solid waste adv. com. State of Tenn., 1971. Bd. dirs. United Fund, Sr. Citizens Orgn., local unit Am. Cancer Soc. (all Elizabethton). Served with USMCR, 1961-64; now capt. Res. Mem. Nat. League Cities, Acad. Polit. Sci., Nat., Tenn. (dir.) municipal leagues, Am. Soc. for Pub. Adminstrn., Internat. City Mgmt. Assn., Tenn. City Mgrs. Assn. (pres. 1969-70), Am. Soc. Planning Ofcls. Methodist (adminstrv. bd. 1968-70). Moose, Kiwanian (dir, 1969). Home: 510 Belle Meade Dr Maryville TN 37801 Office: care City Manager Maryville TN 37801

DE VETTE, JUANITA ETHEL, educator; b. Hart, Mich., May 22, 1915; d. J. Minus and Ethel (Larson) de Vette; student Wheaton Coll., 1938, Northwestern U., 1950, U. Ala., 1954, U. Mich., 1955; A.B., Fla. State U., 1948, M.A., 1959; postgrad. U. Fla., 1956-57. Tchr. elementary sch., Fernandina, Fla., 1937-48; librarian Lab. Sch., asso. prof. Sch. Edn., Fla. State U. at Tallahassee, 1949-68, asso. prof. dept. English edn., area of children's lit., 1968—. Vice pres. Fla. Cooperating Council Children and Youth, 1963—. Mem. Assn. Children Edn. Internat., Fla. Hist. Soc., N.E.A., Fla. Assn. Sch. Librarians, Southeastern Library Assn., A.L.A., Nat. Council Tchrs. English, Kappa Delta Pi, Phi Kappa Phi (pres. 1969-70), Delta Kappa Gamma (pres. chpt. 1970-72). Democrat. Baptist. Home: 2314 Jim Lee Rd Tallahassee FL 32301

DEVINE, J. C., physician; b. Bixby, Okla., June 23, 1927; s. James Ed and Velma Lee (Worsham) D.; B.S., Northeastern State Coll., 1949; M.D., U. Okla., 1953; m. Dorothy Jean King, Aug. 25, 1948; children—James Dennis, Cecil Erick. Intern U. Tex. Med. br. John Sealy Hosp., Galveston, Tex., 1953-54; resident internal medicine VA Hosp., Iowa City, 1955-56; resident anesthesiology Univ. Hosps., Iowa City, 1956-58; individual practice medicine, Tulsa, 1954-55; indsl. physician Douglas Aircraft Co., Tulsa, 1954-55; practice medicine, specializing in anesthesiology Milwaukee Hosp., Milw., 1958-62, St. Francis Hosp., Tulsa, 1962-63, St. Joseph, Ouachita Meml. hosps., Hot Springs, Ark., 1964—; asso. prof. anesthesiology U. Mo., 1962. Sec. Hot Springs Municipal Airport Commn., 1969—; sponsor YMCA Coffee House for Youth, Hot Springs, 1970—. Chmn. bd. dirs. Hot Springs Summer Repertoire Theatre Inc. Fellow Am. Coll. Anesthesiology; mem. Garland County Ark. State med. socs., Ark., Am. Socs. anesthesiologists, Milw. Acad. Medicine, Garland County Assn. (dir.). Presbyn. (elder 1971—, lay minister 1968—). Home: 418 Sunset Bay Hot Springs AR 71901 Office: Meyer Bldg Hot Springs AR 71901

DE VITA, VINCENT THEODORE, JR., physician; b. Bronx, Mar. 7, 1935; s. Vincent Theodore and Isabelle (Lo Nano) De V.; B.S. in Chemistry, Coll. William and Mary, 1953-57, M.D., George Washington U., 1961; m. Mary Kay Bush, Aug. 3, 1957; children—Vincent Theodore III, Elizabeth Anne. Intern U. Mich. Med. Center, 1961-62; resident George Washington U. Sch. Medicine, 1962-63, Yale New Haven Med. Center, 1965-66; sr. investigator medicine br. Nat. Cancer Inst., NIH, Bethesda, Md., 1966-68, head solid tumor service, 1968-72, chief medicine br., 1972—; asso. prof. medicine George Washington U., 1971—. Served with USPHS, 1963-65. Decorated Order of the Sun (Peru). Asso. editor Jour. Nat. Cancer Inst., 1968—; sci. editor Cancer Chemotherapy Reports, 1970—. Contbr. articles in field to med. jours. Home: 9925 Juillard Dr Bethesda MD 20034 Office: Nat Cancer Inst Bldg 10 12 N 226 Bethesda MD 20014

DE VOE, DONALD E., coll. coach. Basketball coach Va. Poly. Inst., Blacksburg. Address: Athletic Dept Va Polytechnic Inst Blacksburg VA 24061*

DEVORE, MARGARET BOWEN (MRS. ROBERT N. DEVORE), physician; b. Troy, S.C., Dec. 29, 1930; d. William R. and Ruth (McAlister) Bowen; B.A. magna cum laude, Winthrop Coll., 1951; M.D., Med. Coll. S.C., 1955; m. Robert N. DeVore, Aug. 31, 1952; children—Robert Douglas, Thomas Lee and John Anthony (twins), Margaret Ann and William George (twins). Intern. Med. Coll. S.C., 1955-56; gen. practice Oceana, W.Va., 1957-59, Jackson, S.C., 1959-62; resident anesthesiology, 1962-64; instr. anesthesiology dept. Med. Coll. of Ga., Augusta, 1964-65, asst. prof. anesthesiology, 1966-69, asso. prof., 1969—. Diplomate Am. Bd. Anesthesiology. Mem. A.M.A., Ga., Richmond County med. socs., Am. Soc. Anesthesiologists, Alpha Omega Alpha. Baptist. Home: 405 5th St Jackson SC 29831 Office: Med Coll Ga August GA 30902

DEVOY, CHARLES STEPHEN, port authority exec.; b. N.Y.C., May 12, 1923; s. Harold Edwin and Loretta Veronica (McNamee) D.; B.S., Georgetown U., 1947; postgrad. Northwestern U., 1963; m. Dee Bryan, Nov. 21, 1946; children—Deeanne, Stephen Douglas, Charles Bryan. With Lykes Brothers Steamship Co., Inc., 1947-57, deep sea traffic mgr., Galveston, Tex., 1948-57; dir. Port N.Y. Authority, London, Eng., 1957-62; chief exec. Galveston Wharves, 1963—; dir. Galveston Cotton Exchange, Bd. Trade. Second v.p. Am. Assn. Port Authorities, Inc. Served to capt., USAAF, 1943-46. Mem. Am. Indsl. Devel. Assn., Galveston County Research Assn., Inc. (past dir., mem. exec. com.), Tex. Ports Assn., Inc. (pres. 1965), Gulf Ports Assn., Inc. (pres. 1967-68), Galveston C. of C. (v.p.). Clubs: Propellor, Quarterdeck, Galveston Country. Home: 2 Port aux Princes Galveston TX 77550 Office: PO Box 328 Galveston TX 77550

DEW, JESS EDWARD, chem. engr.; b. Okemah, Okla., July 18, 1920; s. Jess Edward and Colleen (Norman) D.; student Okla. Mil. Acad., 1939-41; B.S. in Chem. Engring., U. Okla., 1943; M.S., Mass. Inst. Tech., 1948; m. Mary Ann Burns, Jan. 3, 1944; children—Anne, Stephen Dodson, David Burns. Asst. chem. engr. Standard Oil N.J., Baytown, Tex., 1943-47; chem. engr. Standard Oil Ind., Tulsa, 1948-52; v.p., John Deere Chem. Co., Pryor, Okla., 1952-63; gen. supt. John Deere Planter Works, Moline, Ill., 1963-65; v.p. Arkla Chem. Corp., Helena, Ark., 1965-69; project mgr. Chem. Constrn. Co., N.Y.C. hdqrs. 1969—, post include Eng., Argentina, Arabia. Pres., dir. Pryor Indsl. Conservation Co., 1961-63. Mem. Pryor Municipal Utility Bd., 1955-60, Pryor City Council; 1962-63; Rivers and Harbor Commn., Helena, 1966-70. Mem. Am. Inst. Chem. Engrs., Sigma Xi, Beta Theta Pi, Tau Beta Pi. Republican. Roman Catholic. Elk. Clubs: Tulsa, Helena Country. Home: 120 S Prairie St Okmulgee OK 74447 Office: c/o Chemico 320 Park Av New York City NY 10022

DEW, MARJORIE, librarian; b. Latta, S.C.; d. Lawrence Edward and Ellen (Allen) Dew; A.B., Furman U., 1928; certificate in L.S. Peabody Library Sch., 1934, B.S. in L.S. George Peabody Coll., 1934, M.A. in L.S., 1941. Librarian, Crescent Jr. Coll., Eureka Springs, Ark., 1930-33, Dickson (Tenn.) Pub. Library 1934-35, Taylors (S.C.) High Sch., 1935-36; librarian Chester (S.C.) High Sch., 1936-42, Slidell (La.) High Sch., 1942-45; asst. prof., periodicals librarian Northwestern State Coll., Natchitoches, La., 1945-46; librarian St. Andrews Parish Schs., Charleston, S.C., 1946-47, Canton (N.C.) High Sch., 1947-48; asst. prof., librarian Wahl-Coats Sch., E. Carolina Coll., Greenville, N.C., 1948-49; librarian Morganton (N.C.) High Sch., 1949-50; bibliographer and spl. aid to students Clemson (S.C.) Coll. Library, 1950-54; librarian Aiken (S.C.) High Sch., 1955-56, Dillon (S.C.) High Sch., 1956-57, John Small Sch., Washington, N.C., 1957-58, Elizabeth City (N.C.) High Sch., 1958-59, Lake Worth (Fla.) Jr. High Sch., 1959-60, Jr. High Sch., St. Augustine, Fla., 1960-61, Kaley Sch., Orlando, Fla., 1961-62, Pineland Coll., Salemburg, N.C., 1962-65, Southwood Coll., Salemburg, N.C., 1965-66; asst. librarian Gardner-Webb Coll., Boiling Springs, N.C., 1966-67; librarian Graham Eckes Sch., Palm Beach, 1967-68; librarian Fairfax Hall, Waynesboro, Va., 1968-71. Active Boy Scouts Am. Mem. D.A.R., U.D.C., A.L.A., N.C., Southeastern library assns. Baptist. Home: 1 King and Zelle Latta SC 29565

DEWAR, JAMES L., state ofcl.; b. Berrien County, Ga., Sept. 18, 1911; student Emory Jr. Coll; B.S., U. Ga., also M.S.; m. Dorothy Herndon; 1 son, James L. Formerly high sch. tchr., basketball coach, prin., county supt. schs.; ins. exec.; pres. Park Av. Bank, Valdosta, Ga.; now mem. Ga. State Bd. Edn., Atlanta. C.L.U. Mem. Valdosta C. of C., Ga. Assn. Supts., Am. Coll. Chartered Life Underwriters. Home: 802 E Park Av Valdosta GA 31601 Office: State Bd Edn Ga Dept Edn State Office Bldg Atlanta GA 30303*

DEWAR, MILDRED (JO) ELLER (MRS. DONALD NORMAN DEWAR), librarian; b. Wilkesboro, N.C., Nov. 9, 1925; d. Charles Franklin and Golda(Velt) Eller; student Brevard Coll., 1942-44; diploma Jr. Coll., 1944; A.B., Berea Coll., 1946; B.S. in L.S., U. N.C., 1948; postgrad. Barry Coll., U. Fla.; m. Donald Norman Dewar, Mar. 6, 1954; 1 dau., Heather. Tchr., librarian Mountain View High Sch., Hays, N.C., 1946-47; chief librarian Tenn. Wesleyan Coll., Athens, 1948-50; dept. head U. Tex. Library, Austin, 1951; librarian U.S. Army Spl. Services, Ft. Jackson, S.C., 1951-52; chief post library system, Ft. Stewart, Ga., 1952-54; librarian Olsen Jr. High Sch., Dania, Fla., 1955-56; librarian Lauderdale Manors Sch., Ft. Lauderdale, Fla., 1956-63; head readers services Miami-Dade Jr. Coll. Library, Miami, Fla., 1963-70; library dir. Miami-Dade Jr. Coll., South, 1970—. Vis. instr. library edn. U. Ga., summer 1967. Co-exec. dir. Nat. Library Week Fla., 1966. Mem. Am. Assn. U. Women (past br. v.p.), Am., Fla. library assns., Nat., Fla. edn. assns., Am., Fla. (past pres.) assns. sch. librarians, Fla. Audio-Visual Assn., Delta Kappa Gamma. Author articles in field. Home: 3520 Crystal View Ct Coconut Grove FL 33133 Office: 11011 SW 104 St Miami FL 33156

DE WELDON, FELIX WELHS, sculptor; b. Vienna, Austria, Apr. 12, 1907; s. Ignaz Weihs and Fredericka (Wenger) de W.; came to U.S., 1937, naturalized, 1945; A.B., Marchetti Coll., Vienna, Austria, 1922-25; M.A., M.S., U. Vienna (Acad. of Creative Arts, Sch. of Architecture), 1927, Ph.D., 1929; postgrad. study in art and architecture, Paris, Rome, Florence, Oxford; m. Margot Kraemer, June 19, 1944. Public monument sculptor, portrait painter; exhibited Vienna, 1925-28, Paris Salon, 1929-30, Cairo, 1932-33, Royal Acad. (London), 1934-37, Montreal, 1938, Archtl. League (N.Y.), 1939. Art Assn. (Newport, R.I.), 1948; executed World War I Monument, Belleau Wood, France; King George VI (coronation bust), 1937; Prime Minister Mackenzie King, Can., 1938; USMC War Memorial (Iwo Jima Flag Raising), Washington, 1954; Nat. Monument for Malayasia, Kuala Lumpur, Malaya; Truman Monument, Athens, Greece; bronze statue of Speaker Rayburn, Bonham, Tex., 1959; equestrian statue Simon Bolivar, 1958; Red Cross Monument, 1959 (both Washington); bronze Pres. Kennedy, 1966, gold medal Pres. Johnson, 1966 (both White House, Washington); equestrian statue of Gen. Garcia, Havana, Cuba, 1958; bronze monument to Adm. Richard E. Byrd for Washington, 1961; bronze of Sgt. Alvin York, Nashville, Tenn.; bronze of Pres. Andrew Jackson, Columbia, S.C. Mem. Commn. of Fine Arts of U.S., 1950-63. Served USN World War II. Mem. Am. Fedn., of Arts, Metropolitan Mus. of Art. English Speaking Union. Home: 2132 Bancroft Pl NW Washington DC 20008 also Beacon Rock Harrison Av Newport RI Office: 219 Randolph Pl NE Washington DC 20002

DEWIRE, KENNETH STEVENS, govt. ofcl.; b. Spooner, Wis., May 18, 1930; s. Donald Stevens and Ethel Bernice Marie (Lemmer) D.; B.A. in Broadcasting, B.E.E. (Syracuse U. Alumni Assn. scholar), Syracuse U., 1953; postgrad. Am. U., 1958-59, Northwestern U., 1958, Georgetown U., 1958-59, Mont. State U., 1962-63. With various comml. TV stas., 1955-57; TV cons. N.Y. State Edn. Dept., 1961-62; instr., ednl. TV cons. Mont. State U., 1962-63; cons. Jansky & Bailey, Washington, 1957-61, 63-64; ednl. TV specialist U.S. Office Edn., Dept. Health Edn. and Welfare, Washington, 1964—, staff Fed. Ednl. Broadcasting Facilities Program, 1964—. Served with USNR, 1953-55. Mem. Alpha Epsilon, Rho, Sigma Pi Sigma, Pi Mu Epsilon, Eta Kappa Nu, Phi Mu Alpha. Home: 2653 Woodley Rd NW Washington DC 20008 Office: Broadcasting Facilities Program US Office Edn Washington DC 20202

DEWITT, ROSCOE PLIMPTON, architect; b. Dallas, Feb. 18, 1894; s. Edgar A. and Imogene (Walker) DeW.; A.B., Dartmouth, 1914, M.A. (hon.), 1937; Harvard, 1917, M.Arch., 1937; m. Elizabeth Boyd Newcomb, 1943; children by previous marriage—Sylvia Louise (Mrs. Tom Ferguson), Elizabeth Frances (Mrs. Julian Acker). Engaged in archtl. practice, Dallas, 1919—. Mem. Tex. Fine Arts Commn., 1967-69. Bd. dirs. Dallas Civic Opera, 1960—. Served from 2d lt. to capt., U.S. Army, World War I; capt. to lt. col. AUS, World War II. Fellow A.I.A., Soc. Am. Registered Architects; mem. Internat. Hosp. Fedn., Soc. Am. Mil. Engrs., Am. Hosp. Assn., Assn. for Hosp. Planning, Royal Soc. Arts, Tex. Soc. Architects (dir. 1956-58), Phi Delta Theta. Clubs: Dallas Athletic, Dallas Country, Brookhollow Golf, City (Dallas); Harvard (N.Y.C.); Cosmos (Washington). Prin. works include: Methodist, Parkland Meml., Presbyn., St. Paul, Tex. Childrens (all Dallas), Hotel Dieu (New Orleans), Sheppard AFB, Carswell AFB hosps., Bay Front Med. Center, St. Petersburg, Fla., St. Vincents Hosp., Jacksonville, Fla.; office bldgs. for Republic Financial Services, N.Y.C., Dallas, Los Angeles, stores and service bldg. for Neiman-Marcus, sch. and coll. bldgs. in Dallas and numerous other Tex. cities, Sam Rayburn Library, Bonham, Tex.; remodeled Cannon House Office Bldg.; (with others) Tex. State Bldg., Dallas Mus. Fine Arts, extension of East Front of Nat. Capitol, James Madison Meml. Bldg. of Library of Congress; housing projects in Dallas and elsewhere. Home: 4657 Mockingbird Lane Dallas TX 75209 Office: 2025 Cedar Springs Rd Dallas TX 75201 also 425 13th St NW Washington DC 20004

DEWITT, TALMAGE, architect, engr.; b. Lubbock, Tex., Dec. 11, 1925; s. Talmage and Allison (Humphreys) D.; student Rice Inst., 1944-45; B. Arch., Tex. Tech. Coll., 1950; m. Vada Lois Graham, June 27, 1944; children—Gail, Nancy. Partner, DeWitt & Maeker, architects and engrs., 1953-60, DeWitt & Spencer, 1960-64, Talmage DeWitt, A.I.A., 1965-70; architect, sr. asso. Page-Southerland-Page, Austin, Tex. 1970—. Served with USNR, 1944-46. Mem. A.I.A. (past state dir., chpt. pres.). Home: 500 E Anderson Lane Austin TX 78752 Office: 602 West Av Austin TX 78701

DEWLETT, HAL J., physician; b., 1918; M.D., Am. U. Beirut (Lebanon), 1944. Practice medicine specializing in preventative medicine; dir. Dallas Health Dept. Mem. Am. Coll. Chest Physicians, Am. Thoracic Soc., Am. Diabetes Assn. Address: 1936 Amelia St Dallas TX

DEWS, MARY JANE, hosp. coordinator; b. Jacksonville, Ill., Jan. 8, 1922; d. William S. and Mary (Reid) Dews; B.S., Fla. State U., 1944; M.Nursing, Yale, 1947, M.S., 1956. Clin. instr. Yale Sch. Nursing, 1947; head nurse, men's medicine New Haven Hosp., 1947-49; instr. nursing arts Yale Sch. Nursing, 1949-51; instr. med. nursing Fla. State U., 1951-54; dir. nursing Gaylord Hosp. and Sanatorium, Wallingford, Conn., 1955-64; mental health cons. Pinellas County Health Dept., Clearwater, Fla., 1964-65, dir. mental health div., St. Petersburg, 1965-66; cons. nursing edn. Fla. State Dept. Edn., 1966-68; asst. prof. advanced med.-surg. nursing Fla. State U., Tallahassee, 1968-72; coordinator ednl. activities Tampa Gen. Hosp., 1972—. Mem. Am., Fla. nurses assns., Nat., Fla. leagues nursing, Fla. Pub. Health Assn., Nat., Fla. rehab. assns., Yale U. Sch. Nursing Alumnae Assn., Alpha Chi Omega. Home: 2109 W Dewey St Apt 202 Tampa FL 33607

DEWTON, JOHANNES LEOPOLD, librarian; b. Vienna, Austria, Sept. 27, 1905; s. Eduard and Elsbeth (Brauchbar) Deutsch; Jur. U. Vienna, 1927; B.S. in Library Scis., U. Ill., 1941, M.S., 1944; m. Hedwig Marianne Strauss, Apr. 7, 1935; children—Elizabeth Ann (Mrs. John B. Cordaro), Doris Jean. Came to U.S., 1939, naturalized, 1944. Court sec., lawyer's asst., Vienna, 1928-34; lawyer, Vienna, 1935-38; cataloger Library U. Ill., Urbana, 1941-45, research asst. English dept., 1944-45; tech. adviser USSTAF, Europe, 1945; with Library Congress, Washington, 1945—, chief shared cataloging div., 1966-67, head Nat. Union Catalog Publ. Project, 1967—. Bd. dirs. Council on Research and Bibliography, N.Y.C., 1962—. Mem. A.L.A., D.C. Library Assn., Beta Phi Mu. Jewish religion. Contbr. to profl. jours. Home: 4201 7th Rd S Arlington VA 22204 Office: Library Congress 10 1st St SE Washington DC 20540

DEXTER, HELEN LOUISE, physician; b. Cin., July 28, 1908; d. William Jordan and Katherine (Weston) Taylor; A.B., Bryn Mawr Coll., 1930; M.D., Columbia, 1937; postgrad. U. Cin. Coll. Medicine, 1948-50; m. Morrie W. Dexter, Jan. 27, 1937; children—Katharine, Helen, Elizabeth Taylor (Mrs. Richard T. Potsubay), William Taylor. Began career as intern Jersey City Med. Center, 1938-39; internist Cin. Babies Milk Fund, Maternal Health Clinic, 1938-45; clinician U. Cin. Med. Sch., 1938-48, instr. dept. dermatology, 1948-53; practice medicine, Clearwater, Fla., 1954—; dermatology cons. VA, 1955—; investigation of carcinogenic effects of shale oil U.S. Bur. Mines, Rifle, Colo., 1950. Mem. Clearwater P.T.A., Clearwater Power Squadron Aux. Recipient Ina Clay trophy Intercollegiate Ski Champion, 1928-30. Mem. A.M.A., Sec. Investigation Dermatology, Am. Acad. Dermatology, S.E. Dermatol. Assn. (v.p. 1963-64), Fla. Dermatol. Soc. (v.p. 1959), Fla. Soc. Dermatology (pres.), Am. Archaeol. Soc., Pan-Am. Dermatol. Soc., Soc. Tropical Dermatology. Presbyn. Club: Clearwater Yacht. Author articles profl. jours. Home: 409 Bayview Dr Belleair FL 33516

DEXTER, WILLIAM A, JR., builder, designer, developer; b. Lansing, Mich., Aug. 17, 1921; s. William A. and Bessie (Spitzer) D.; student Mich. State Coll., 1940-42; m. Mary Catherine Turner, Sept. 22, 1943; children—David, Diane, Timothy, Mark. Self employed painting contractor, 1939-41; bldg. contractor, designer, developer Dexter Built Homes, Dunedin, Fla., 1946—; pres. William Dexter Corp., Dunedin, 1968—; v.p. Tomac of Fla., Dunedin, 1969—; dir. First Nat. Bank, Dunedin. Mem. Planning and Zoning Bd. Dunedin, 1964-67, Dunedin Bd. Adjustment and Appeal, 1968; chmn. Dunedin Housing Authority, 1968—; city commr. Dunedin, 1956, mayor, Dunedin, 1957. Served with AUS, 1942-46. Decorated Bronze Star medal. Recipient various awards including Beautification awards for outstanding design Dunedin City Beautification Com., 1968-69. Mem. C. of C. (treas. 1953-55), Am. Field Service (pres. 1964). Dunedin Pipe and Drum Corp. (pres. 1964). Clubs: Lion. Dale Carnegie, Veteran Motor Car Am. (Bulb Horn mag. corr. 1963). Home: 600 Holly Ct Dunedin FL 33528 Office: 31 Sandpiper Dr Dunedin FL 33528

DEY, JOSEPH CHARLES, JR., sports exec.; b. Norfolk, Va., Nov. 17, 1907; s. Joseph Charles and Martha Lillian (Holt) D.; student U. Pa., 1925-27; m. Rosalie Moran Knapp, Jan. 29, 1937; 1 son, Edward Knapp. Newspaper sports writer, 1923-34; exec. dir. U.S. Golf Assn., 1934-69; commr. tournament players div. Profl. Golfers Assn. Am., 1969—. Sec., World Amateur Golf Council. Served as lt. USNR, World War II. Mem. Sigma Alpha Epsilon. Republican. Episcopalian. Clubs: Creek (Locust Valley); Union League (N.Y.C.); Royal and Ancient Golf (St. Andrews, Scotland); Honourable Company of Edinburgh Golfers (Muirfield, Scotland). Home: Factory Pond Rd Locust Valley NY 11560 Office: 60 E 42d St New York City NY 10017

DEZURKO, EDWARD ROBERT, educator, architect; b. N.Y.C., Mar. 25, 1913; s. Edward and Hattie (Lehman) DeZ.; B.S. in Edn., U. Ill., 1939, B.S. in Architecture with honors, 1940; M.S., Columbia, 1942; Ph.D., N.Y.U., 1954; m. Madith Smith, June 30, 1938 (div. July 1962) children—Robin (Mrs. Ernest E. Sibert, Jr.), Sandra (Mrs. L.C. Krchnak); m. 2d, Grace Crump, Sept. 5, 1964. Asst. prof. Kan. State U., 1942-47; asso. prof. Rice U., 1947-62; prof., chmn. dept. art Austin Coll., 1962-66; prof., mem. grad. faculty U. Ga., Athens, 1966—. Practice architecture, Ill.; Kan.; Conn., 1945-60. Mem. Houston Historic Architecture Preservation Com., 1960-61. Mem. Soc. Archtl. Historians (dir. 1958-61, pres. Houston chpt. 1959-61), Coll. Art Assn., Am. Soc. Aesthetics. Presbyn. Author: Early Kansas Churches, 1948; Origins of Functionalist Theory, 1957. Contbr. articles to profl. jours. Mem. editorial bd. Ga. Rev., 1968—. Home: 284 Valleybrook Dr Athens GA 30601

DIAMOND, HINDI ALTMAN (MRS. WALTER DIAMOND), editor; b. N.Y.C., Sept. 11, 1924; d. Saul and Esther (Kijewski) Altman; student Canal Zone Jr. Coll., Republic of Panama, 1947-49, U. Miami(Fla.), 1966-69; m. Walter Diamond, Nov. 25, 1943; children—Linda, Stephen, Mark. Reporter, photographer The Panama Am. daily English newspaper, 1951-58; Panama corr. McGraw-Hill and Vision mag., 1951-61; pub., editor Panama/This Month, 1958-65; editor Industria Turistica mag. Diamond Pub. Co., South Miami, Fla., 1957—; Miami corr. Nat. Enquirer, 1972—. Bd. dirs. Am. Jewish Com., editor Newsletter, 1969—. Mem. Am. Soc. Mag. Photographers (chmn. Fla. chpt. 1960—), Theta Sigma Phi. Editor Newsletter, Parents Tchrs. Students Assn., Palmetto High Sch., 1970—. Home: 7250 SW 126th St Miami FL 33156 Office: Industria Turistica Box 52 South Miami FL 33143

DIAMOND, JACK LAMAR, govt. ofcl.; b. Houma, La., Dec. 11, 1917; s. Henry Edgar and Lean Marie (Gauthreaux) D.; student Rice Inst., 1936-38; m. Frances C. Eaton, Apr. 25, 1948; children—Frances Marie, Dorothy Louise, Mary Ann. Exec. dir., sec. Housing Authority, Parish of East Baton Rouge, Baton Rouge, 1946—. Served with USAAF, 1942-46. Mem. Nat. Assn. Housing and Redevel. Ofcls., Southwestern Region, La. housing councils, V.F.W., Am. Legion. K.C. Home: 3745 Cathedral Dr Baton Rouge LA 70805 Office: 3002 Mason St Baton Rouge LA 70805

DIAZ, REMEDIOS, glass co. exec.; b. Havana, Cuba, Aug. 22, 1938; s. Casto Rodriguez and Remedios (Gonzalez) R.; B.B.A., Havana U., 1954, Ph.D., 1956; m. Fausto Diaz Oliver, Dec. 13, 1958; children—Rosa Maria, Fausto G. Came to U.S., 1960, naturalized 1969. Vice pres., dir. Havana Bus. Acad. and Havana Bus. Coll., 1956-61; pres., dir. S.P.E.S.A., Havana, 1956-61; v.p. Richford Industries, Inc., Miami, Fla., 1961—; pres. Emmer Importing & Exporting, Inc., Miami, 1964—, Richford Internat., Inc., Miami, 1968—. Pres., Assn. of all Exporters, Freight Forwarders & Mfrs. of Greater Miami, 1968—; cons. New World Sch. Langs., 1967. Recipient E award Pres. Lyndon B. Johnson for excellence in export, 1968. Mem. Nat. Assn. Container Distbrs., Nat. Assn. Wholesalers. Club: Big Five (Miami). Home: 9381 SW 32d St Miami FL 33165 Office: 6250 NW 35th Av Miami FL 33147

DIAZ, RICK, hotel exec.; b. Havana, Cuba, Nov. 6, 1940; s. Juan Enrique and Maria Celida (Castillo) D.; student Sharron-William Comml. Coll., Miami, 1954-56, Walsh Sch. Bus. Sci., Miami, 1956-58, Lindsey-Hopkins Hotel Sch., Miami, 1958-59, Cornell U., summers 1967, 68; m. Georgette Catherine Schufa, Feb. 8, 1964; children—Tashia Marya, Tiara Elleny. Came to U.S., 1960, naturalized, 1965. Page boy, bellman Varadero Internat. Hotel, Cuba, 1951; various positions Robert Clay Hotel, Miami, Fla., 1954-59; various positions to mgr., dir. sales. Taft Hotel, New Haven, Conn., 1961-62; shop mgr., asst. maitreAllison Hotel, Miami Beach, Fla., 1962; asst. reservations mgr., gen. mgr. Antlers Resort Hotel, Lake George, N.Y., summers 1960, 61, 63; resident mgr., exec. asst. mgr. El Convento Hotel, San Juan, P.R., 1962-63; with Causeway Inn Beach Resort, Tampa, Fla., 1964—, gen. mgr., 1964-70, pres., mgr. dir., 1970—. Mem. Fla. Restaurant Assn., Greater Tampa C. of C., Fla. Retail Liquor Dealers Assn. Inc., Fla. Hotel and Motel Assn., Hotel Sales Mgmt. Assn., Pan Am. Commn., Bon Vivants. Address: Causeway Inn Beach Resort Courtney Campbell Causeway Tampa FL 33607

DIAZ-CANALES, FERNANDO LUIS, dentist; b. Vega Alta, P.R., July 14, 1929; s. Luis and Amparo (Canales) D.; student Bluffton Coll., 1947-48, Miami U. at Oxford, O., 1948-49; D.D.S., U. Dominican Republic, 1954, U. Detroit, 1956; m. Maria Esther Martinez, May 26, 1962; children—Gladys Amparo, Fernando Luis, Diana Marta, Tamara Liz. Practice dentistry, Caparra Terrace, P.R., 1956—. Vice pres. Diaz-Canales Enterprise, Vega Alta, 1965—. Mem. Exchange Club Hato Rey, Am. Soc. Clin. Hypnosis (asso.), Am., P.R. dental assns. Club: Nautic Puerto Rico (San Juan). Home: 16 K St Villa Caparra PR 00619 Office: 12 Central Av Caparra Terrace PR 00921

DIAZ-COLLER, CARLOS, physician; b. Villahermosa, Tabasco, Mexico, Sept. 2, 1916; s. Jose Diaz-Coller and Maria Gonzalez; M.D., Army Med. Sch., Mexico, 1945; M.P.H., Harvard, 1948; m. Ana Maria de la Garza, Dec. 17, 1945; children—Carlos, Jose Alberto, Mario, Juan Antonio and Anna Maria Elisa (twins). Del. from Mexico, WHO, 1956, 57, 58; exec. bd. alternate WHO, 1956-57, v.p. exec. bd., 1958-59; del. from Mexico to directing council Pan-Am. San. Orgn., 1956-57, exec. com., 1957-58, pres. exec. com., 1958-59; del. from Mexico, XV Pan Am. San. Conf., 1958; dir. div. exptl. studies in pub. health Ministry Pub. Health and Welfare, Mexico, 1957, 58; now chief dept. profl. edn., chief editorial services Pan Am. Health Orgn. of WHO. Pub. health supr. Mexican Army, 1948-56; dir. Sch. Pub. Health, Mexico, 1953. Mem. Mexican Pub. Health Soc. (pres. 1957-58), Am. Pub. Health Assn., Nat. Geog. Soc. Editor: Jour Mexican Pub. Health Soc., 1955-58. Home: 3505 Dundee Driveway Chevy Chase MD 20015 Office: 525 23rd St NW Washington DC 20037

DIAZ GONZALEZ, CARLOS, editor. Editor newspaper Excelsior, Mexico City, Mexico. Address: Excelsior Reforma 18 Mexico DF Mexico*

DIAZ ORDAZ, GUADALUPE BORJA DE (MRS. GUSTAVO DIAZ ORDAZ), former 1st lady of Mexico, civic worker. Wife former pres. Mexico. Office: Sec for Information Palacio Presidencial Mexico City Mexico*

DIAZ ORDAZ, GUSTAVO, former pres of Mexico; b., 1911; ed. Instituto de Ciencas y Artes Oaxaca, Colegio del Estado de Puebla. Legal, judicial posts, Puebla, Titalangui and Tehuacan, 1937; dep. to Fed. Legislative Assembly, senator, 1946-52, former prof. adminstrn. and labor law Puebla U.; chief officer Secretariat of Govt., 1952-58, sec. Govt., 1958, later minister of interior; candidate Partido Devolucionario Institucional for Presidency of the Republic, 1963; elected pres., July 5, 1964. Address Office of the President State Capital Mexico City MX

DIBRELL, GEORGE EDWARD, city mgr.; b. Dallas, Sept. 22, 1928; s. Waymen Eugene and Maude (Helton) D.; B.B.A., So. Meth. U., Dallas, 1951; LL.B., U. Tex. at Austin, 1957; m. Georgene Valas, May 30, 1953; 1 dau., Deborah Jeanne. Admitted to Tex. bar, 1956; pvt. practice law, Austin, 1956-57; asst. city atty., Port Arthur, Tex., 1958-62, city mgr., 1962—. Mem. State Bar Tex., Jefferson County, Am. Port Arthur bar assns., C. of C., Internat. City Mgmt. Assn., Municipal Finance Officers Assn., Phi Alpha Delta, Sigma Nu. Mason, Rotarian. Home: 3548 Drexel Av Port Arthur TX 77640 Office: City Hall 444 4th St Port Arthur TX 77640

DICE, HENRY KIMMELL, chem. engr.; b. Somerset, Pa., May 31, 1908; s. John E. and Edna (Kimmell) D.; student Antioch Coll., 1926-28, Ohio No. U., 1929-30; B.S., U. Pitts., 1932; m. Janet K. Womer, Sept. 1, 1934; children—Janet (Mrs. Thomas A. Maierhofer, Henry Kimmell. Chem. engr. Celanese Corp., Cumberland, Md., 1934-40, supt. research and devel., 1940-44, prodn. supt., Bishop, Tex., 1944-47, mgr. research and devel., Clarkwood, Tex., 1947-59, v.p. tech. dir., Corpus Christi, Tex., 1959-61, cons., 1963—; sub-dir. gen. Quimica Gen., S.A., Mexico, 1961-63; sr. resident engr. Tex. Hwy. Dept., Houston, 1966—. Mem. Am. Inst. Chem. Engrs., Am. Chem. Soc., Nat. Soc. Profl. Engrs., Alpha Chi Sigma, Sigma Tau. Patentee in field. Home: 10215 Briar Dr Houston TX 77042 Office: 7721 Washington Av Houston TX 77007

DICK, GEORGE WALTER, state ofcl.; b. Berea, Ky., Aug. 24, 1934; s. George Arthur and Alice (Muth) D.; A.B. in Math., Berea Coll., 1956; postgrad. bus. adminstrn., U. Ky., 1962; m. Jane Lee Kavanaugh, Dec. 12, 1958; children—David Arthur, Dana Anne. Trainee, Westinghouse Electric Corp., Pitts., 1956-58; adminstrn. analyst Hwy. Dept., State of Ky., Frankfort, 1960-62, fiscal and personnel officer Dept. Pub. Information, 1962-69, budget dir. Dept. Edn., 1969-71, systems analyst Dept. Finance, 1971—. Developer matching funds program and charge account procedure for state toll facilities for Ky. Served with AUS, 1958-60. Mem. Pub. Personnel Assn. Home: 524 Timothy Dr Frankfort KY 40601 Office: Capitol Annex Frankfort KY 40601

DICK, LOIS A. (MRS. CARL E. DICK), coll. adminstr.; b. Decatur, Ind., June 19, 1907; d. J.F. and Mabel (Schlegel) Hildinger; student Internat. Bus. Coll., Ft. Wayne, Ind., 1926, Mrs. Davis Secretarial Sch., Ft. Wayne, 1929; m. Carl E. Dick, Dec. 31, 1939. Sec., Koerbers Jewelers, Inc., Ft. Wayne, 1932-50; sec. Fruehauf Trailer Co., Ft. Wayne, 1952-53; sec. to registrar Fla. So. Coll., Lakeland, 1956-60; exec. sec. to dean coll. basic studies U. South Fla., Tampa, 1960-62, exec. sec. to dean acad. affairs, 1962-65, adminstrv. asst. to dean, 1965-67, staff asst. to v.p. acad. affairs, 1967-70; part time cons., asso. med. sec. X-Ray dept. Sun Coast Osteo. Hosp., Largo, Fla. Mem. fund raising com. Greater Largo Recreational Complex. Named 1 of 100 outstanding women to attend Conf. Fla., 1964. Mem. Nat. Secs. Assn. (parliamentarian Tampa 1960-61), Lakeland Bus. and Profl. Women's Club (v.p. 1958-59, pres. 1959-60), North Tampa (pres. 1963-64), North Largo bus. and profl. women's clubs, Temple Terrace Bus. and Profl. Women's Club (co-organizer, 2d v.p. 1966), Nat. Assn. Ednl. Secs. Baptist. Mem. Order Eastern Star, White Shrine Jerusalem, Beauceant, Order Amaranth. Clubs: Pilot (parliamentarian Lakeland 1959-60, charter mem. Bay Area); Woman's (U. South Fla.). Home: 79 Rainbow Ct 1159 Clearwater Rd Largo FL 33540

DICKENS, ALBERT EDWARD, economist; b. Mt. Vernon, Ill., May 19, 1904; s. Robert Lee and Laura (Polk) D.; A.B., Ind. U., 1930, M.S., 1939, postgrad. Law Sch., 1932-33; m. Rose Mary Salinardi, Mar. 25, 1954. State statistician Ind., Indpls., 1931-39; dir. research Chgo. Plan Commn., 1941-45; chief surplus property div. Allied Commn., Rome, Italy, 1945-47, chief control br. Joint Export-Import Agy., Frankfurt, Germany, 1947-49; spl. cons. Nat. Acad. Scis., Washington, 1950; owner, prin. Albert E. Dickens & Co., Washington, 1951—. Cons. Internat. Devel. Services, Inc.; expert cons. AID; cons. Washington Bd. Trade. Mem. Am. Econ. Assn., Am. Statis. Assn., Inst. Urban and Regional Affairs, Soc. Internat. Devel., Phi Beta Kappa, Beta Gamma Sigma, Lambda Alpha. Club: Economists (Washington). Author: Growth and Structure of Real Property Uses in Indianapolis, Indiana, 1939. Home: 1500 Massachusetts Av NW Washington DC 20005 Office: 1627 K St NW Washington DC 20006

DICKENS, CHARLES HENDERSON, educator, govt. ofcl.; b. Thomasville, N.C., Nov. 22, 1934; s. Argie Marshall and Edna (Sullivan) D.; B.S., Duke, 1957, M.Ed., 1964, Ed.D., 1966; m. Jane McClung, Aug. 27, 1965; children—Martha Jane, and Anne Elizabeth. Research analyst Dept. Def., Washington, 1957, 1960-62; tchr. Thomasville (N.C.) High Sch., 1962-63; asst. prof. Wake Forest Coll., Winston-Salem, N.C., 1965-67; planning specialist NSF, Washington, 1967-69, asso. program dir. undergrad. instrnl. programs, 1969-70, asso. dir. student-originated studies program, 1970-71; Congl. fellow, 1971-72; legislative asst. to Senator Inouye of Hawaii and Rep. Anderson of Ill., 1972—; staff asst. Senate Appropriations Com., 1972—; asst. dir. NSF Summer Inst., Duke, 1966-67. Cons. math various N.C. Pub. Sch. systems, 1965-67. Campaign worker Winston-Salem United Fund, 1966; class agt. Duke Loyalty Fund, 1960-65, 1967. Served with AUS, 1958-59. Mem. Am. Polit. Sci. Assn., A.A.A.S., Am. Ednl. Research Assn., Nat. Council Tchrs. Math., Phi Beta Kappa. Republican. Baptist. Author: Support of Full-Time Graduate Students in the Sciences, 1967. Home: 1103 Gladstone Pl Wellington VA 22308 Office: NSF Washington DC 20550

DICKENS, H. DERRELL, lawyer; b. Little Rock, Apr. 24, 1918; A.B., Washington and Lee U., 1940, LL.B., 1947; M.B.A., Harvard, 1943. Admitted to Ark. bar, 1947, Tex. bar, 1947, Mo. bar, 1961; atty. legal dept. Lion Oil Co., 1947-55, Lion Oil div. Monsanto Chem. Co., 1955-61, atty. parent co., 1961-65; dir. legal dept., dep. sec. Monsanto Chems. Ltd., London, Eng., 1965; sr. atty., asst. sec. Monsanto Co., 1966-68; now practice law, El Dorado, Ark. Mem. Union County, Ark., Am. bar assns., State Bar Tex., Order Coif, Phi Beta Kappa, Phi Delta Phi. Address: 814 Lion Oil Bldg El Dorado AR 71730*

DICKENSON, RUSSELL ERRETT, govt. ofcl.; b. Melissa, Tex., Apr. 12, 1923; s. John Errett and Lexie Vivian (Davis) D.; student North Tex. State Coll., 1940-41; B.A., No. Ariz. U., 1947; m. Maxine Moran, Dec. 23, 1947; children—Vivian, Russell. With Nat. Park Service, various field locations, 1946—, dir. Nat. Capital Parks, Washington, 1969—. Served with USMCR, 1942-46, 51. Recipient Meritorious Service award Interior Dept., 1971. Mem. Nat. Parks Assn., Nat. Recreation and Park Assn. Home: 3313 Rose Lane Falls Church VA 22042 Office: 1100 Ohio Dr SW Washington DC 20242

DICKERSON, HERMAN EDWARD, city mgr.; b. Greensboro, N.C., Nov. 1, 1915; s. Raymond Rufus and Blanche Eve (Welker) D.; B.S. in Bus. Administrn., Va. Poly. Inst., 1937; m. Nell Taylor, Dec. 25, 1943; children—Herman E., Robert Taylor, William Lawrence, Dennett Haywood, Thomas Welker, James Marshall, Diane. With Security Nat. Bank, Greensboro, N.C., 1937-40, city of Charlotte

(N.C.), 1950-51; adminstrv. asst. to city mgr., city Laurinburg (N.C.), 1951-55; city mgr., Statesville, N.C., 1955—. Served to maj. AUS, 1940-46. Recipient George C. Franklin award N.C. League Municipalities, 1956. Mem. N.C. League Municipalities (dir. 1961-63), Am. Legion, N.C. Soc. Engrs., Internat. City Mgmt. Assn., N.C. City and County Mhrs. Assn. (pres. 1960-61). Presbyn. (deacon 1948—). Rotarian. Home: 335 Holland Dr Statesville NC 28677 Office: City Hall 227 S Center St Statesville NC 28677

DICKERSON, NANCY HANSCHMAN (MRS. CLAUDE W. DICKERSON), news corr.; b. Milw.; d. Frederick R. and Florence (Conners) Hanschman; student Clarke Coll., Dubuque, Ia.; grad. U. Wis., 1948; postgrad. Harvard; H.H.D., Am. Internat.Coll., Springfield, Mass.; m. Claude Wyatt Dickerson, Feb. 24, 1962; children—Elizabeth, Ann, Jane, Michael, John Frederick. Tchr. pub. schs., Milw.; staff asst. Senate Fgn. Relations Com., Washington; producer CBS News, 1956-60, corr., 1960-63; news corr. NBC, 1963-70; pres., producer Dickerson Co., syndicated TV programs, 1971—; reporter Pres. Kennedy's funeral, Republican and Democratic convs., Civil rights March on Washington; rep. pub. broadcasting at conversation with Pres. Nixon, 1971; originator Inside Washington news insert. Recipient Collegian award LeSalle Coll., Phila.; Spirit of Achievement award Albert Einstein Coll., Yeshiva U.; Sigma Delta Chi award Boston U.; Pioneer award New Eng. Women's Press Assn. Asso. fellow Yale, 1972. Mem. Washington Press Club (past v.p.), Radio-Television News Analysts. Home: Merrywood Chain Bridge Rd McLean VA 22101 Office: 1750 Pennsylvania Av NW Washington DC 20006

DICKERSON, THOMAS MILTON, educator; b. nr. Sebree, Ky., Feb. 2, 1898; s. Daniel Webster and Mina (Witherspoon) D.; B.B.A., Bowling Green (Ky.) U., 1924; A.B., Western Ky. State Tchrs. Coll., 1926; M.B.A., Northwestern U., 1929; m. Nell Caldwell Vaughn, Nov. 28, 1922; 1dau., June Nell (Mrs. John Edward Sturgis). Prin. high sch., Simpson County, Ky., 1921-23; asst. prof. accounting Bowling Green Coll. Commerce, 1923-30, head accounting dept., 1928-30; grad. teaching fellow Northwestern U., 1928-29; asst. prof. econs. U. Louisville, 1930-31; asst. sec. Nat. Assn. Accountants, N.Y.C., 1931-34; chief staff accountant Nat. Com. Municipal Accounting, Chgo., 1934-35; asso. prof. Western Res. U., 1935-42, prof., 1942-63; lectr. accounting and chief systems analyst U. South Fla., 1963-68; vis. prof. Stanford, summer 1956; cons. in field. Trustee Cleve. Hearing and Speech Center, 1940-63. Served with U.S. Army, 1918. C.P.A., Ky., Ohio. Mem. Am. Inst. C.P.A.s, Ohio Soc. C.P.A.s, Nat. Assn. Accountants (dir. 1939-46), Am. Accounting Assn. (v.p. 1952), Internat. Congress Accounting, Am. Hearing Soc. (dir. 1960-63), Delta Sigma Pi, Beta Alpha Psi, Beta Gamma Sigma. Democrat. Baptist (trustee). Contbr. articles to profl. jours. Address: Charlotte House 1323 Queens Rd Charlotte NC 28207

DICKEY, FRANK GRAVES, ednl. ofcl.; b. Wagoner, Okla., Dec. 1, 1917; s. Joseph Stone, Jr., and Katherine (Bridges) D.; A.B., Transylvania Coll., 1939; M.A. U. Ky., 1942, Ed.D., 1947; LL.D., Berea Coll. Jacksonville U., Loyola U., New Orleans, U. Ky.; D.Litt., Transylvania Coll.; L.H.D., Findlay Coll.; m. Elizabeth Joan Drymon, Oct. 18, 1940; children—Frank Graves, Joseph Terry, Ann Elizabeth. Tchr. pub. schs., Lexington and Fayette County, Ky., 1939-43; successively instr., asst. prof., asso. prof. edn. U. Ky., 1947-49, prof. edn. dean coll. edn., 1949-56; pres., 1956-63; exec. dir. So. Assn. Colls and Schs., 1963-65; exec. dir. Nat. Commn. Accrediting, 1965—. Mem. exec. com. So. Regional Edn. Bd., 1962-63; Army Adv. Panel on R.O.T.C. Affairs, 1961-63; bd. curators Transylvania Coll., 1959-63, 68-70; bd. dirs. Ky. Heart Assn., 1959-63, Ky. Soc. Crippled Children, 1959-63; v.p. Internat. Conv. Disciples of Christ, 1964-66; chmn. nat. commn. study ministerial edn. Christian Ch., mem. commn. on non-traditional study, commn. for optometric edn. bd. visitors Air U., 1967-70. Served with AUS, 1943-46. Fellow edn. Harvard, 1952-53. Recipient Alma Magna Mater award U. Ky., 1962, Distinguished Alumnus award, 1965. Mem. Am. Council Edn. (dir., exec. com., chmn. commn. accreditation service experiences), N.E.A., Ky. Edn. Assn., S.A.R., S.R., Order Ky. Cols., Newcomen Soc., Delta Pi Epsilon, Phi Delta Kappa, Kappa Delta Pi, Omicron Delta Kappa, Kappa Alpha, Alpha Zeta, Alpha Omega. Mem. Disciples of Christ. Clubs: Kenwood Country, Spindeltop, Cosmos. Author: (with others) Principles of Supervision: Principles of Student Teaching. Office: 1 Dupont Circle NW Washington DC 20036

DICKEY, JAMES, poet, critic; b. Atlanta, Feb. 2, 1923; s. Eugene and Maibelle (Swift) D.; student Clemson Coll., 1942; B.A., Vanderbilt U., 1949, M.A., 1950; m. Maxine Syerson, Nov. 4, 1948; children—Christopher Swift, Kevin Webster. Poet in residence Reed Coll., Portland, Ore., 1963-64, San Fernando (Cal.) Valley State Coll., 1964-65, U. Wis., 1966; cons. in poetry Library of Congress, 1966-68; now writer in residence U. S.C. Served with USAAF and USAF, World War II, Korea. Decorated Air medal. Recipient Union League prize, 1958; Vachel Lindsay award, 1959; Longview award, 1959; Melville Cane award, 1965-66. Sewanee Rev. fellow, 1954-55; Guggenheim fellow, 1962-63; Nat. Inst. grant of, 500, 1966. Author: (poems) Into the Stone, 1960; Drowning With Others, 1962; Helmets, 1964; Two Poems of the Air, 1964; Buckdancer's Choice, 1965 (Nat. Book Award for poetry 1966); Poems, 1957-67; (criticism) The Suspect in Poetry, 1964; Babel to Byzantium, 1968. Address: 4620 Lelia's Ct Lake Katherine Columbia SC 29206

DICKEY, JAY W., lawyer; b. Ft. Worth, Sept. 14, 1906; J.D., U. Ark., 1934. Admitted to Ark. bar, 1934, also U.S. Dist. Ct. bar, U.S. Ct. Appeals bar, 1938, U.S. Supreme Ct. bar; mem. firm Dickey, Dickey & Drake, Pine Bluff, Ark. City atty., Pine Bluff, 1936-48. Trustee U. Ark., 1939-49. Mem. Jefferson County (pres. 1949-50), Ark. (mem. exec. com. 1955), Am. bar assns., Blue Key, Phi Alpha Delta. Address: 208 E 5th Av Pine Bluff AR 71601*

DICKINSON, FRED OTIS, JR., state ofcl.; b. West Palm Beach, Fla., Mar. 28, 1922; s. Fred Otis and Georgia (Bell) D.; student U. Fla., 1941-42; LL.B., John B. Stetson U., 1948; m.Mildred Goddard, Jan. 4, 1952; children—Fred Otis III, Douglas Edward, Catherine Campbell, Dwight D., John Daniel. Mem. Fla. Ho. of Reps., 1954; mem. Fla. Senate, 1957-58; mgr. Fla. Democratic Presdl. Campaign, 1960; spl. counsel Fla. Senate Edn. Com.; comptroller by appointment, 1965; comptroller State of Fla., 1966—. Active YMCA, Fla. Hist. Soc. Bd. dirs. Fla. Children's Home Soc., Jacksonville; trustee Fla. Sheriff's Boys Ranch. Served with USMCR, 1942-45. Recipient Ben C. Williard award Stetson U.; named Fla. Outstanding Young Man, 1957, Outstanding First Term Legislator, Outstanding Fla. Citizen of Year, 1962, Outstanding Young Man of Year, West Palm Beach Jr. C. of C., 1965. Mem. V.F.W., Am. Legion, DeMolay. Mason (Shriner), Kiwanian, Elk. Home: 7500 Buck Lake Rd Tallahassee FL 32301 Office: Monroe St Tallahassee FL 32304

DICKINSON, JOHN DAVID, banker; b. Little Rock, July 18, 1945; s. Louie Leon and Willibell (Aubrey) D.; student Ouachita Bapt. U., 1965-66; m Mary Joyce Kennedy, Dec. 8, 1964. Vice-pres. First Nat. Ins. Agy., Inc., Nashville, Ark., 1966—; v.p. First Nat. Bank, Nashville, Ark., 1970—, dir., 1967—. Rotarian. Methodist (adminstrv. bd.). Home: 801 Sunset Dr Nashville AR 71852 Office: 101 N Main St Nashville AR 71852

DICKINSON, JOSHUA CLIFTON, JR., museum dir.; b. Tampa, Fla., Apr. 28, 1916; s. Joshua Clifton and Mary (Martin) D; B.S., U. Fla., 1940, M.S., 1946, Ph.D., 1950; student U. Va., 1936-39, Cornell U., summer 1938; m. Lucy Freeman Jackson, Apr. 13, 1936; children—Joshua Clifton III, Martin Freeman, Susan Ellissa. Mem. faculty U. Fla., 1946—, asso. prof. zoology, 1955—; curator Fla. State Mus., 1952—, chmn. natural scis., 1953-60, acting dir., 1959-61, dir., 1961—; research fellow Harvard, 1951-52; vis. investigator Woods Hole Oceanographic Inst., 1952; expdns. to Honduras, 1948, Bahamas, 1960-67, Jamaica, 1959, Baffin Island, 1955, Sombrero Island, 1963, Navassa Island, 1965. Chmn. Fla. Commn. Archives and History, 1964-69; adv. council N.E.A., 1970—. Served to comdr. USCGR, 1942-45, Grantee Nat. Park Service, 1952-54, NSF, 1955-57. Mem. Am. Ornithologists Union, Am. Soc. Naturalists, Am. Assn. Museums (council 1964—, sec. 1970), A.A.A.S., Am. Soc. Zoologists, Wilson, Soc., Assn. Systematic Collections (pres. 1972-73), Am. Assn. Sci. Mus. Dirs. (v.p. 1967-69), Sigma Xi, Phi Sigma, Alpha Tau Omega. Democrat. Rotarian (pres. Gainesville 1967-68). Author: Monographs; sci. papers. Home: 1804 SW 35th Pl Gainesville FL 32601 Office: Fla State Museum Museum Rd Gainesville FL 32601

DICKINSON, RONALD IRVIN, horticulturist; b. Lafayette, Ind., May 30, 1941; s. William Jacob and Barbara Eleanor (Rodenbarger) D.; student Purdue U., 1959-61; B.S., Miss. State U., 1966, M.S., 1968. Researcher insect genetics Agr. Research Sta. U.S. Dept. Agr., State College, Miss., 1961-63; owner Raven Landscaping, Starkville, Miss., 1967-68; ornamentalist Fla. Extension Service, Manatee County, Bradenton, Fla., 1969-71; owner, editor The Plant Doctor Reports mag., Bradenton, 1971—; cons. landscaping and maintenance, Bradenton, 1971—. Mem. Manatee County Parks and Recreation Bd., 1970—. Mem. Manatee County African Violet Soc. (founder 1970, lifetime hon. mem.), Sarasota Succulent Soc. (hon.), Fla. Nurserymen Growers Assn., Fla., Am. hort. socs., African Violet Soc. Am., Am. Gloxinia and Gesneriad Soc., Garden Writers Assn. Am., Saint Paulia Internat., Nat. Assn. County Agrl. Agts. Author: African Violet Book, 1972. Office: 3106 Manatee Av W Bradenton FL 33505

DICKINSON, WILLIAM ANDREW, lawyer; b. Roanoke, Va., Sept. 15, 1916; s. George Nelson and Shirley Carter (Hart) D.; B.S., U. Va., 1939, LL.B., 1941; m. Nancy McQuown Ring, Jan. 10, 1942; children—William Andrew, Michael W., Nancy Adele. Admitted to Va. bar, 1940; law clk. Judge Herbert Gregory Va. Supreme Ct. Appeals, 1941-42; asso. firm Hazlegrove, Carr & Shackelford, Roanoke, 1946-49; partner firm Hazlegrove, Carr, Dickinson, Smith & Rea, Roanoke, 1949—. Bd. dirs. Roanoke United Fund, 1956-58, Roanoke Symphony, 1964-67, YMCA, 1961-64. Trustee, v.p. Roanoke Hosp. Assn., 1956—. Served to lt. USNR, 1942-46. Mem. Roanoke C. of C. (dir. 1957-58), Roanoke Bar Assn. (dir., pres. 1958-59). Episcopalian. Clubs: Roanoke Country; Shenandoah. Home: 2616 Stanley Av Roanoke VA 24014 Office: 202 S Jefferson St Roanoke VA 24011

DICKINSON, WILLIAM BOYD, JR., editor; b. Kansas City, Mo., Feb. 21, 1931; s. William Boyd and Aileen (Robinson) D.; A.B., U. Kan., 1953; student George Washington U. Law Sch., 1957-58; m. Betty Ann Landree, Feb. 1, 1953; children—William Boyd IV, David Alan. With U.P.I., 1955-59, mem. staff overnight desk, Washington, 1957-59; staff writer Editorial Research Reports, Washington, 1959-66, editor, 1966-72; editor Congl. Quar., Inc., 1972—; discussion leader Am. Press Inst., 1966—. Winston Churchill Traveling fellow, summer 1968. Served with AUS, 1953-55. Mem. Internat. Press Inst., English-Speaking Union (dir. Washington chpt.), Alpha Tau Omega, Omicron Delta Kappa. Club: National Press (Washington). Supervisory editor Congl. Quarterly's Congress and the Nation, Vol. II. Home: 5430 N 22d Rd Arlington VA 22205 Office: 1735 K St NW Washington DC 20006*

DICKINSON, WILLIAM LOUIS, congressman; b. Opelika, Ala., June 5, 1925; s. Henry K. and Bernice (Lowe) D.; LL.B., U. Ala., 1950; m. Mary Patterson Stanfield, 1948; children—Chris, Mike, Tara, William Louis. Admitted to Ala. bar, 1950; practiced in Opelika, 1950-63; judge Opelika City Ct., 1951-53; judge Ct. Common Pleas, 1953-59; judge Juvenile Ct. Lee County, 1953-59; judge 5th Judicial Ct. Ala., 1959-63; asst. v.p. So. Ry. System, Montgomery, Ala., 1963-64; mem. 89th-92d congresses from 2d Ala. Dist.; mem. com. on govt. operations, com. on house adminstrn. Chmn. Opelika Bd. Edn., 1960-61; mem. Gov.'s Indsl. Com. of 100, 1963-64; dir. Lee County Civil Def., 1961-62. Past pres. Ala. Mental Health Assn. Chmn. Ala. Republican Congl. Delegation. Pres., bd. dirs. Lee County Mental Health Clinic; bd. dirs. Lee County Rehab. Center. Served with USNR, World War II; now capt. USAF Res. Named Man of Year Opelika Jr. C. of C., 1961, One of Four Outstanding Young Men in Ala., 1961. Mem. Ala. Bar Assn., Ala. Alumni Assn., Sigma Alpha Epsilon. Mason, Kiwanian, Elk. Home: 6236 Edgewater Dr Falls Church VA 24041 Office: Cannon House Office Bldg Washington DC 20515

DICKS, JOSEPH LEWIS, JR., dentist; b. Augusta, Ga., Oct. 9, 1935; s. Joseph Lewis and Wesley Townsend (O'Neall) D.; student Acad. Richmond County, 1949-53, Emory-at Oxford Coll., 1953-55; D.D.S., Emory U. Sch. Dentistry, 1959; M.S., Tufts U. Sch. Dentistry, 1969; m. Dorothy Ann Lowery, July 1, 1970. Individual practice dentistry, Columbus, Ga., 1961-63; staff dentist Gracewood (Ga.) Hosp., 1963-64; instr. Arhus (Denmark) Sch. Dentistry, 1964-65; instr. Royal Coll. Dentistry, Copehagen, Denmark, 1965-67; dir. dental program Ga. Retardation Center, Atlanta, 1969—. Cons. Atlanta Cerebral Palsy Assn., 1969-70; instr. Emory U. Sch. Dentistry, U. Ga., 1969—. Served to capt. USAF, 1959-61. Recipient Outstanding Unit award 837th Tactical Hosp., 1961. Mem. Am., Ga. dental assns., Ga. Pub. Health Assn., So. Assn. Institutional Dentists, Xi Psi Phi. Home: 914 Collier P-3 Atlanta GA 30318 Office: 4770 N Peachtree Rd Atlanta GA 30341

DICKSON, ALFRED GRANBERY, newspaper exec.; b. Liberty, S.C., Oct. 28, 1908; s. John G. and Cora (Mauldin) D.; student North Carolina State University, 1925-26, Wofford College, 1926-29; m. Cornelia E. Weaver, Oct. 18, 1932 (dec. Sept. 1958); 1 son, John Hines; m. 2d, Maggie Lee Madry, June 27, 1959; 1 stepson, Robert W. Madry, Jr. Reporter, Wilmington (N.C.) News, 1929, 30-36; sports editor Durham (N.C.) Morning Herald, 1929-30; mng. editor Wilmington (N.C.) Star, 1936-41; mng. editor Wilmington (N.C.) News, 1941-47; editor Wilmington News and Wilmington Star, 1947-55, exec. editor Star-News Newspapers, Wilmington, 1955-70, asst. to pub., 1970—; sec. Jackson & Bell Co. Bd. dirs. Cornelia Nixon Davis Nursing Home, Wilmington chpt. A.R.C., Lower Cape Fear Hist. Soc. Former pres. N.C. Assn. Asso. Dailies; pres. UPI Editors Assn. N.C., 1963-64, Asso. Daily Newspapers N.C., 1966-67. Recipient Forrestal citation, 1947; 6 awards ann. editorial competition N.C. Press Assn., 1954-63; award in new plant competition Am. Press mag., 1969. Mem. Am. Soc. Newspaper Editors, Sigma Delta Chi (Distinguished Service award for journalism in editorial writing 1965), Alpha Phi Gamma, Lambda Chi Alpha. Democrat. Methodist. Clubs: Cape Fear, Rotary. Author: Histories of N.C. Shipbuilding Co. Home: Route 1 Box 603 Wilmington NC 28401 Office: PO Box 840 Wilmington NC 28401

DICKSON, FRANK ALEXANDER, journalist, author; b. Townville, S.C., Oct. 29, 1911; s. Frank Alexander and Laura (Holland) D.; grad. high sch.; m. Renthy Pruitt, Feb. 10, 1938; children—Larry Pruitt (dec.), Milton Alexander, Horace Ansel. Feature writer, columnist Anderson (S.C.) Ind. Anderson Daily Mail, 1929—; columnist Writer's Digest, Cin., 1939—, asso. editor, 1967—; editorial staff Quote Mag., Anderson, 1965—. Democrat. Methodist. Author: 2000 Articles You Can Write and Sell, 1955; Freelancer's Treasury of Article Ideas 1961; Editor: Writers Digest Handbook of Article Writing, 1968. Co-editor: Writer's Digest Handbook of Short Story Writing, 1969. Contbr. articles to newspapers, mags. syndicated publs. Home: 1006 Elizabeth St Anderson SC 29621 Office: 115 E Market St Anderson SC 29621

DICKSON, KENNETH PEARL, hosp. adminstr.; b. New Summerfield, Tex., June 29, 1935; s. Coy and Esther (Richey) D.; B.A., North Tex. State Coll., 1957, M.A., 1962; m. Lucy Ellen Baker, Oct. 26, 1963; children—Kenneth Lowell, Kevin Neal. Lab., X-ray technician, Med. Surg. Clinic, Lewisville, Tex., 1953-63; adminstr. Newton County (Tex.) Hosp., 1963-64, Hardeman County Hosp., Quanah, Tex., 1964-68; adminstr. Simmons Meml. Hosp., Sweetwater, Tex., 1968—. Vice pres. Am. Cancer Soc., Nolan unit, Sweetwater, Tex., 1970-71. Served with AUS, 1958-60. Recipient Pub. Service award Am. Radio Relay League, 1966. Mem. Tex. Hosp. Assn. (pres. midwestern hosp. div. 1967-68; pres. S.W. hosp. div. 1970-71; del. 1968-72), N.W. Tex. Hosp. Assn. (trustee). Presbyn. (deacon). Mason, Lion. Home: 1411 Sunnyvale St Sweetwater TX 79556 Office: 1301 Hailey St Sweetwater TX 79556

DICKSON, LEWIS, dist. Judge, Harris County (Tex.). Office: County Court House Houston TX 77002*

DICKSON, LILLIAN DURHAM, author, editor, artist, art gallery exec.; b. Atlanta; d. Joseph Idelbert and Annie Rosbell (Meeks) Durham; student Sch. Fine Arts, Washington U., St. Louis, 1910-12, Ft. Worth Conservatory Music, 1928, Tex. Christian U., 1930-31; m. Ienry McHaney Dickson, Sept. 16, 1917 (dec. July 1956); 1 son, Henry McHaney; m. 2d, B. Houston Cogdell, Sept. 5, 1966 (div.). Propr. real estate firm, Ft. Worth, 1914-59; mgr., supr. Lloyd Surveying and Engring. Co., Houston, 1958-60; mgr. Tarrant County Surveyor's Office, Ft. Worth, 1961-63; dir., mgr. Westbrook Hotel Art Gallery, Ft. Worth, 1963-64, 69-72; art tchr., propr. Four-Arts Studio, Ft. Worth, 1964—; dir. Westbrook Art Gallery; founder, pub., editor mag. Composers, Authors, Artists Am., 1940—, chief editor, 1940-43, 48-49, contbg. editor, 1943—; contbr. poetry, articles mags., newspapers, 1920—; exhibited paintings in ann. group shows Tex. Fine Arts Soc., Ft. Worth, 1920—, also other regional shows; one-man shows, 1969-71; chmn. Tex. Council Promotion Poetry, Austin, 1949-59, co-chmn., 1960-66; nat. cultural coordinator Avalon Poetry Shrine, San Antonio, 1941-44; Tex. chmn. Nat. Poetry Day Com., Austin, 1960-65; nat. pres. Composers, Authors, Artists Am., 1940-43, historian, 1948-50, 60-67, hon. life pres., 1944—, organizer Ft. Worth br., pres., 1938, v.p., 1951-52; organizer Ft. Worth Water Color Soc., 1952, bd. dirs., 1952-67, recipient art awards, 1952, 53, 54, 63, 68-70; pres. Ft. Worth Poetry Soc., 1960-61. Recipient award of merit, Gold medal Tex. Press Woman's Assn., Houston, 1948, also awards in poetry and music, art exhibits. Mem. Nat. League Am. Pen Women (v.p. Ft. Worth br., 1951-52), Poetry Soc. Tex., A.S.C.A.P., Tex. Fine Arts Assn., Ft. Worth Poetry Soc., Marquis Biog. Library Soc. (adv. mem.). Clubs: Euterpean, Music Study, O'Henryettes (Ft. Worth). Author: The Enchanted Mesa, 1937; Amber In The Sun, 1947. Composer: Sentimental Over Texas, 1946. Home: 200 Burnet St Fort Worth TX 76102

DICKSON, ROY SHELTON, petroleum co. exec.; b. Lewiston, Ida., Aug. 29, 1933; s. Roy S. and Ethel (Means) D.; B.S., U. Tulsa, 1958; children—Laura Ann, Julia Kay. Sci. computer programmer research and devel. Phillips Petroleum Co., Bartlesville, Okla., 1957, systems analyst computing dept., 1958-61, supt. computing systems computing dept., 1961-62, supr. tech. programming systems, 1962-65, dir. computing systems and evaluations, 1965-67, asst. mgr. operations div., 1967-69, mgr. operations div., 1969—. Vice pres. SHARE, Internat., 1964-65, pres., 1965-66. Served with USMCR, 1952. Mem. Assn. Computing Machinery. Home: 201 W 9th Dewey OK 74029 Office: Computing Dept Phillips Petroleum Co Bartlesville OK 74003

DIDEA, ARTHUR ANTHONY, dentist; b. N.Y.C., Jan. 4, 1925; s. Charles and Rebecca (Schmeltzer) DiD.; B.S. with honors, U. City N.Y., 1945; postgrad. Washington U., St. Louis, 1945-47; D.D.S., U. Ill., 1952; m. Viola Mae Rodenmayer, Feb. 8, 1947; children—Barbara (Mrs. David Haines Phillips), Mark Brian, Linda Katherine, Gregory Scott, Karen Lee. Tchr. gen., qualitative and quantitative chemistry Harris Tchrs. Coll., St. Louis, 1947; research bacterial chemist St. Louis Health Dept. Endemic Typhus Fever Study, 1948; practice dentistry, Orlando, Fla., 1955—; asst. prof. oral histology, pathology and operative dentistry U. Ill., 1952-53; dental staff Winter Park (Fla.) Hosp., also Fla. Hosp., Orlando, 1956-62. Chief Hawkeye tribe Indian Guides of YMCA, Orlando, 1963-64, nation chief, 1965; pres. P.T.A., 1970; active Little League, Cub Scouts Am. Bd. dirs. Civic Theater, 1963-66. Served as 1st lt. AUS, 1953-55. Mem. Fla. (ins. chmn. 1965), Orange County (program chmn. 1970) dental socs., Kappa Alpha, Phi Beta Pi, Omicron Kappa Upsilon, Psi Omega. Episcopalian (mem. vestry 1970—). Mason (Shriner); mem. Order Eastern Star. Clubs: Executive (pres. 1966-68); Sertoma (chmn. bd. 1963-65, pres. 1964); University (Winter Park). Contbr. articles to profl. jours. Mailing Address: 2815 Corrine Dr Orlando FL 32803 Home: 1921 N Forest Av Orlando FL 32803

DIDIER, LYDIA MARCHIVE, guidance counselor; b. Baton Rouge, Dec. 23, 1922; d. Marcel M. and Jewel (Furlow) Marchive; B.S., La. State U., 1951, M.Ed., 1953; m. Fabius Odell Didier, Sept. 3, 1940 (dec. 1949); 1 son, Marcel Furlow. Librarian, Gonzales (La.) High Sch., 1951-55, Pride High Sch., Baton Rouge, 1955-59; guidance counselor Westdale Jr. High Sch., Baton Rouge, 1959—. Tutor retarded children, 1958—; vocational counselor Presbyn. Ch., 1960—. Active A.R.C., East Baton Rouge Mental Health Assn., Broadmoor Assn. Greater Baton Rouge, Baton Rouge Little Theater, Broadmoor P.T.A., Westdale Jr. High Sch. P.T.A., La. Assn. Mental Health. Mem. Am. La., personnel and guidance assns., Am. Sch. Counselor Assn., East Baton Rouge Parish Guidance Assn. (pres. 1966, 67), La. Tchrs. Assn., Assn. Classroom Tchrs. East Baton Rouge Parish, Royal Order Daffy, Daffy Daffodil, Phi Lambda Phi (certificate of Merit 1953), Theta Xi (Mothers' Club), Beta Sigma Phi. Democrat. Presbyn. Clubs: Womans', Readers' (Baton Rouge). Home: 2545 Woodland Ridge Blvd Baton Rouge LA 70815 Office: 5650 Claycut Rd Baton Rouge LA 70815

DIEDERICH, JOHN WILLIAM, pub. co. exec.; b. Ladysmith, Wis., Aug. 30, 1929; s. Joseph Charles and Alice Florence (Yost) D.; Ph.B., Marquette U., 1951; M.B.A. with high distinction Baker scholar, Harvard, 1955; m. Mary Theresa Klein, Nov. 25, 1950; children—Mary Theresa, Robert Douglas, Charles Stuart, Michael Mark, Patricia Anne, Donna Maureen (dec.), Denise Brendan, Carol Lynn, Barbara Gail, Brian Donald, Tracy Maureen, Theodora Bernadette, Tamara Alice, Lorraine Angela. Research dir. Landmark Communications, Inc., Norfolk, Va., 1955-61, controller, 1961-64, sec.-treas., 1964-65, v.p., treas., dir., 1965—; instr. Boston U., 1954, Old Dominion U., 1955-59. Bd. dirs. De Paul Hosp., Landmark Charitable Found., Virginian-Pilot and Ledger-Star Joy Fund Found., Norfolk. Served to lt. col. USMC, 1951-53; Res. ret. Mem. Nat. Assn. Accountants, Inst. Newspaper Controllers and Finance Officers, Inst. Broadcasting Financial Mgmt., Am. Numismatic Assn., Nat., Wis. geneal. socs., Geneal. Soc. Pa., Sigma Delta Chi. Roman Catholic. Clubs: Harbor, Mallory Country (Norfolk). Home: 615 Shirley Av Norfolk VA 23517 Office: 150 W Brambleton Av Norfolk VA 23501

DIENHART, CHARLOTTE MARIE, educator; b. Sioux Falls, S.D., Aug. 14, 1923; d. Arthur Peter and Mae (Donahue) Dienhart; B.S., Coll. St. Catherine, 1945; M.S., State U. Ia., 1947; postgrad. U. Minn., 1956-58, Emory U. Sch. Medicine, 1962-64; Ph.D., Mich. State U., 1960. Research asst. U. Minn., 1947-48, grad. teaching asst. physiology, 1957-58; instr. dept. biology Coll. St. Catherine, 1948-57; grad. teaching asst. anatomy Mich. State U., 1958-60; mem. faculty Emory U., Atlanta, 1960—, asst. prof. anatomy, 1966—. Lt. comdr. Med. Specialists Corps, USNR. Mem. A.A.A.S., N.Y. Acad. Scis., So. Soc. Anatomists, Ga. Acad. Sci., Sigma Xi, Sigma Delta Epsilon, Omicron Nu, Beta Beta Beta. Author: Basic Human Anatomy and Physiology, 1967. Home: 1943 N Decatur Rd NE Atlanta GA 30307

DIERCKS, FREDERICK OTTO, govt. ofcl.; b. Rainy River, Ont., Can., Sept. 8, 1912 (parents Am. citizens); s. Otto Herman and Lucy (Plunkett) D.; B.S., U.S. Mil. Acad., 1937; M.S. in Civil Engring., Mass. Inst. Tech., 1939; M.S. in Photogrammetry, Syracuse U., 1950; m. Kathryn Frances Transue, Sept. 1, 1937; children—Frederick William, Lucy Helena. Commd. 2d lt. U.S. Army, 1937, advanced through grades to col., 1952; comdg. officer U.S. Army Map Service, Washington, 1957-61; dir. U.S. Army Coastal Engring. Research Center, Washington, 1964-67; ret., 1967; asso. dir. U.S. Coast and Geodetic Survey, Rockville, Md., 1967—. U.S. mem. commn. cartography Pan. Am. Inst. Geography and History, OAS, 1961-67. Decorated Legion of Merit (U.S.); Grand Cross of Order of King George II (Greece); Most Exalted Order of White Elephant (Thailand). Registered profl. engr., D.C. Fellow Am. Soc. C.E.; mem. Am. Soc. Photogrammetry (pres. 1970-71), Sigma Xi. Republican. Presbyn. Mason. Home: 9313 Christopher St Fairfax VA 22030 Office: 6001 Executive Blvd Rockville MD 20852

DIES, DOUGLAS HILTON, assn. exec.; b. St. Paul, Sept. 9, 1913; s. Edward Jerome and Mareeta (Cole) D.; A.B., Harvard, 1934; post-grad. Oxford U., 1934-35; m. Mary Frances Doreen Harding, Nov. 25, 1939; children—Harding Mogridge, Andrea Frances. Editorial staff Grand Forks (N.D.) Herald, summer 1933, Mpls. Star, summer 1934, London Sunday Chronicle, summer 1935; staff London bur. U.P., 1935-38, Knoxville (Tenn.) Jour., 1938-40; pub. relations dept. Westinghouse Electric Co., 1940-41; staff A.P., Cleve., 1941-42; pub. relations staff U.S. Bd. Econ. Warfare, Washington, 1942-43; pub. relations, Washington, 1946—; asso. world trading corps, 1947—; asst. to pres. Nat. Inst. Oilseed Products, 1947—; Washington rep. Pillsbury Co., 1956-64, East Asiatic Co., 1956—, Woodward & Dickerson, Inc., 1958—; asst. sec., bur. raw materials Am. Vegetable Oils and Fats Industries, 1961-62, sec., 1962—; exec. sec. Am. Council Independent Labs., 1963—; guest lectr. fgn. trade Georgetown U., 1966—. Mem. Republican City Com., Alexandria, 1953-61. Served from ensign to lt. comdr., USNR, 1943-46. Mem. S.R. (gov. D.C. 1956-62), Mil. Order World Wars, Sigma Alpha Epsilon. Episcopalian (vestryman). Clubs: Harvard (N.Y.C., Washington); University, Oxford-Cambridge (Washington). Editor: Chemurgic Digest, 1950-53. Home: 505 Robinson Ct Alexandria VA 22302 Office: 1026 17th St NW Washington DC 20036

DIES, MARTIN, JR., state ofcl.; b. Greenville, Tex., Dec. 21, 1921; s. Martin and Myrtle (McAdams) D.; B.S., Stephen F. Austin State U., 1942; J.D., So. Meth. U., 1948; m. Ruth White, Feb. 6, 1946; children—Martin W., Dianne, David. Admitted to Tex. bar, 1948, since practiced in Lufkin; mem. Tex. Senate, 1959-67, pres. pro tem, 1963; gov. of Tex., 1963; sec. of state State of Tex., 1969—. Served to lt. (j.g.) USNR, 1943-46. Recipient Most Distinguished Alumni award Stephen F. Austin State U., 1967. Fellow Tex. Bar Found.; mem. Tex. Bar Assn., V.F.W., Pi Kappa Alpha. Democrat. Mason. Office: State Capitol Bldg Austin TX 78711*

DIETRICH, EDWIN JERRY, cons. engr., lawyer; b. Shreveport, La., July 14, 1926; s. Merwyn and Vera (Eaves) D.; student Centenary Coll., Shreveport, 1944, Miss. Coll., Clinton, 1944, Tulane, 1945; B.S., U. Tex. at Austin, 1949; LL.B., So. Tex. Coll., 1958; m. Adele Marie Odom, June 5, 1946; children—Shelle (Mrs. Michael Dean Wright), Melanie Gae. Field engr. Farnsworth & Chambers, Houston, 1949; head reports and specifications Lockwood Andrews & Newman, Houston, 1950-56; sr. v.p. Bernard Johnson, Inc. engrs., architects, planners, Houston, 1956—; admitted to Tex. bar, 1958, U.S. Supreme Ct. bar, 1966. Bd. dirs. Greater Houston Council Camp Fire Girls, Inc., 1965-68. Served to capt. USMCR, 1944-47, 51. Fellow Am. Soc. C.E.; mem. Houston Bar Assn., Cons. Engrs. Council, Houston C. of C., Tex. Soc. Profl. Engrs. Clubs: Houston, University. Home: 23 Hickory Ridge Houston TX 77024 Office: 5050 Westheimer St Houston TX 77027

DIETRICH, NEIL KITTRELL, ret. naval officer, museum dir.; b. Hopkinsville, Ky., Sept. 29, 1901; s. Charles Henry and Marian (Lander) D.; B.S., U.S. Naval Acad., 1923; m. Janet Jenkins; 1 dau., Diane (Mrs. Lemuel C. Shepherd III). Commd. ensign U.S. Navy, 1923, advanced through grades to rear adm., 1951; served U.S.S. Colorado, 1923-26, destroyer Greer, 1926-30; instr. English and history U.S. Naval Acad., 1930-32, 35-37; with aircraft carrier Langley, 1932-33, cruiser Marblehead, 1933-35; exec. officer battleship Alabama, 1942-43; logistics officer, dep. chief staff U.S. Naval Forces Europe, 1943-45; aide, flag sec. Comdr. in Chief U.S. Fleet and Chief Naval Operations, 1945, adminstrv. aide, 1946; comdr. cruiser Houston, 1946-47; chief staff to comdr. 6th Task Fleet Mediterranean, 1948-49; comdr. destroyer Flotilla 2, Atlantic Fleet, 1950-52; U.S. Naval attache and attache for air Am. embassy, London, Eng., 1952-53; dep. comdr. mil. sea transp. service, Washington, 1953-56; comdr. mine force Atlantic Fleet, 1956-57; comdr. Hawaiian Sea Frontier, comdr. 14th Naval Dist., 1957-58; ret. 1958; v.p. Hazeltine Corp., N.Y.C., from 1958; now exec. dir. Truxtun-Decatur Naval Mus., Washington. Decorated Legion of Merit; Croix de Guerre (France); comdr. Order Brit. Empire. Address: 1610 H St NW Washington DC 20006

DIETZ, ROBERT SINCLAIR, govt. ofcl.; b. Westfield, N.J., Sept. 14, 1914; B.S., U. Ill., 1937, M.S., 1939, Ph.D. in Geology, 1941; m. 1955; 2 children. Asst. Ill. State Geol. Survey, 1935-37; with Scripps Instn., Cal., 1937-39; oceanographer U.S. Naval Electronics Lab., 1946-52, 54-58; with U.S. Coast and Geod. Survey, Rockville, Md., 1958—; lectr. in field. Served to lt. col. USAAF, 1941-46. Fulbright scholar, Tokyo, Japan, 1952-53. Fellow Brit. Geol. Soc.; mem. Am. Astron. Soc., Am. Geophys. Union, Soc. Limnology and Oceanography, Am. Mineral Soc., Am. Meteoritical Soc., Marine Tech. Soc., Oceanography Soc. Japan. Address: 365 Heather Lane Key Biscayne FL 33149*

DIETZEL, PAUL FRANKLIN, football coach; b. Fremont, O., Sept. 5, 1924; s. Clarence Harlan and Catherine (Bihmer) D.; student Duke, 1942-43; B.S. in Edn., Miami U., Oxford, O., 1948; m. Anne Wilson, Sept. 25, 1944; children—Stephen Paul, Katherine Anne. Asst. football coach U.S. Mil. Acad., West Point, N.Y., 1948, 53-54, named head football coach, 1962; asst. football coach U. Cin., 1949-50, U. Ky., Lexington, 1951-52; head football coach La. State U., Baton Rouge, 1955-61; now athletic dir., head football coach U. S.C., Columbia. Served with USAAF, 1943-46. Decorated Air medal with oak leaf cluster; named Coach of Yr., 1958. Mem. Am. Football Coaches Assn. (trustee, sec. bd. trustees; nat. pres. 1969), Fellowship Christian Athletes (nat. pres. 1963-65), Omicron Delta Kappa, Kappa Delta Pi. Author: Wing T and the Chinese Bandits, 1959. Contbr. numerous articles to profl. jours. Home: 327 Harrow Dr Whitehall Columbia SC 29210

DIEZ, FLORENCIO, coll. dean; b. Salamanca, Spain, Apr. 28, 1933; s. Jose Antonio and Natalia (Pacho) D.; B.A., La Santa Coll., 1952; S.T.B., St. John's Coll., 1958; M.A., U.Salamanca, 1959. Ph.D., 1962; came to U.S., 1963. Tchr. philosophy La Santa Coll., 1959-62; gen. sec. Nat. Inst. Spirituality, Madrid, 1962-63; asso. prof. philosophy Cath. U. Puerto Rico, Ponce, 1963-71, prof., 1971—, dean Coll. Arts and Humanities, 1968—. Mem. Am. Cath. Philos. Assn., Am. Assn. U. Profs. Roman Catholic. Author: Los Complutenses, 1962. Home: San Antonio Devel Ponce PR 00731

DIEZ, PABLO, banker. Vice pres. Banco Nacional de Mexico, Mexico City. Address: Banco Nacional de Mexico Isabel La Catolica 44 Mexico 1 DF Mexico*

DIEZ-RIVAS, FEDERICO MANUEL, physician; b. Caguas, P.R., June 17, 1920; s. Carlos and Elvira (Rivas-Soto) Diez-Ramos; B.S., U. P.R;, 1941; M.D., Med. Coll. Va., 1944; m. Elsie Cardona, July 28, 1963; children— Elsie Marie, Federico, Juan Carlos. Intern Med. Coll. Va. Hosp., Richmond, 1944-45; resident U. Mich. Hosp., Ann Arbor, 1945-49; practice medicine, specializing in internal medicine and cardiology, San Juan and Caguas, P.R., 1950—; mem. staff San Juan City, San Rafael hosps., Rio Piedras Med. Center; chief cardiology clinic Caguas Subregional Hosp., 1972—; asst. prof. medicine U. P.R. Sch. Medicine 1950-58. Served to 2d lt. with AUS, 1942-44. Diplomate Am. Bd. Internal Medicine. Fellow A.C.P.; mem. A.M.A., P.R. (past pres.), Am. heart assns., P.R. (past pres.), Pan-Am. med. assns. Contbr. articles in field to profl. jours. Address: 572 Munoz Rivera Av Hato Rey PR 00918

DI FILIPPI, ARTURO, operatic mgr.; b. Lucera, Italy, Aug. 15, 1894; s. Henry and Frieda di F.; came to U.S., 1913; student Highland Park Coll., 1914-15; student Kan. Wesleyan U., 1915-19, hon. doctorate, 1946; student Juilliard Sch. Music, 1919-22; m. Dec. 5, 1933. Studied and sang in Germany and Italy, 1922-28; debut as operatic tenor Cin. Summer Opera, 1928; mem. Roxy Gang, Radio City Music Hall, N.Y.C., also tenor with numerous symphony and opera orgns. throughout U.S., 1929-39; founder Opera Guild Greater Miami, 1939, artistic dir., gen. mgr., 1939—; chmn. singing dept. U. Miami (Fla.), 1939-63, also prof. Mem. Fla. Arts Council. Recipient awards for outstanding operatic activities Italian Govt., gov. of Salzburg (Austria), French Govt., Presdl. citation Nat. Fedn. Music Clubs, 1965. Mem. Am. Assn. U. Profs., Nat. Assn. Tchrs. Singing (past pres. Miami chpt., regent South Fla.). Mason (32 deg., Shriner). Rotarian. Club: Flamingo Dinner. Home: 625 SW 29th Rd Miami FL 33129 Office: 1200 Coral Way Miama FL 33145

DIGGS, MELVIN M., lawyer; b. Trenton, Tex., Apr. 11, 1914; s. Harvey Washington and Juanita (Moore) D.; A.B., Tex. Christian U., 1936; LL.B., Georgetown U.,1941; m. Virginia Haley, May 3, 1948; children—Susan, Nancy, Ann. Admitted to Tex. bar; lawyer U.S. Govt., Ft. Worth, 1945—; U.S. atty. No. Dist. Tex., Ft. Worth, 1965-68. Served with AUS, 1941-45. Mem. State Bar. Tex., Fed., Tarrant County bar assns., Mil. Intelligence Assn., Texas Christian U. Ex-Lettermen's Assn. Club: Colonial Country (golf com.) (Ft. Worth). Home: 4316 Briar Haven Rd Fort Worth TX 76109 Office: US Court House Fort Worth TX 76101

DIGGS, WALTER WHITLEY, hosp. adminstr.; b. Memphis, June 8, 1932; s. L. W. and Beatrice (Moshier) D.; B.S., Washington and Lee U., 1954; M.H.A., U. Minn., 1956; m. Ann Carol Thobae, Nov. 29, 1958; children—Jennifer, Thomas, Andrew. Adminstrv. resident Stormont-Vail Hosp., Topeka, 1955-56; asst. chief personnel records div. U.S. Naval Hosp., Chelsea, Mass., 1957-58, adminstrv. asst., 1958-59; adminstrv. asst. outpatient services Johns Hopkins Hosp., Balt., 1959-61, asst. adminstr. Wilmer Ophthalmological Inst., 1962-66; adminstr. hosp. and clinics Med. Coll. Ga., Eugene Talmadge Meml. Hosp., Augusta, 1966-70; asst. dir. Memphis Regional Med. Program, 1971—; asst. prof. preventative and community medicine U. Tenn. Coll. Medicine, 1971—; adj. asst. prof. Ga. State Coll. Program Hosp. Adminstrn.; adj. faculty Ga. Tech. Program Hosp. and Med. Systems. Vice pres. Hartford-Alemeda Neighborhood Assn., Balt., 1965-66; treas. Third Dist. Citizens for Good Govt., Balt., 1966. Trustee Columbus Blue Cross. Served to lt. (j.g.) Med. Service Corps, USNR, 1956-59. Mem. Nat. League Nursing, Am. Hosp. Assn., Am. Coll. Hosp. Adminstrs., Am. Pub. Health Assn. Home: 257 S Perkins Memphis TN 38117 Office: 969 Madison Memphis TN 38104

DILL, BILLY CLIFF, elec. engr.; b. Sulligent, Ala., Aug. 28, 1935; s. Ernest Albert and Flora Mae (Burnett) D.; B.S. in E.E., U. Ala. 1963; m. Emma Kathryn Lankford, Dec. 11, 1965; 1 dau., Susan Kathryn. Design engr. Brown Engring. Co., Huntsville, Ala., 1963-64, Chrysler Corp., Huntsville, Cape Canaveral, Fla., 1964-66, Rust Engring. Co., Birmingham, Ala., 1966—; instr. U. Ala. Sch. Engring. at Birmingham, 1966-67. Served with USMCR, 1954-57. Registered profl. engr., Ala., Ga. Mem. I.E.E.E., Instrument Soc. Am. Home: 5401 10th Ct Birmingham AL 35222 Office: Rust Engring Co 1130 S 22d St Birmingham AL 35201

DILL, OVID CLYDE, hosp. adminstr.; b. Sullivan, Mo., Aug. 4, 1927; s. Hugh Edwin and Edith Jane (Jackson) D.; grad. high sch.; m. Betty Lee Martin, Dec. 23, 1946; children—Mary Alice (Mrs. Hal R. Rachman), Melanie Sue. Joined U.S. Army, 1946, advanced through grades to master sgt., 1956; mem. staff Army Hosp., Ft. Sam Houston, Tex., 1946-50, Ft. Hood, Tex., 1955-63, 98th Gen. Hosp., Neubrucke, Germany, 1963-66; ret., 1966; adminstr. Denton (Tex.) Osteopathic Hosp., 1966-68, Hamilton City (Tex.) Gen. Hosp., 1968—. Vice pres. Cancer Soc. Hamilton County, 1970-71. Chmn. bd. Licensed Vocational Nurse Sch., Hamilton, 1969—. Mem. C. of C. (pres., 1969-70), Tex. Hosp. Assn., Central Tex. Hosp. Group. Presbyn. (deacon). Mason, Lion. Club: Perry Country (dir.). Home: Route 1 Hamilton TX 76531 Office: 400 N Brown St Hamilton TX 76531

DILLABER, PHILIP ARTHUR, program analyst; b. Springfield, Mass., Aug. 24, 1922; s. Ralph E. and Grace (Holman) D.; B.A., Am. Internat. Coll., 1949; M.B.A., Ind. U., 1950; postgrad. U. Mich., 1950; m. Jacqueline M. Bertin, July 16, 1946; children—Anne Erline, Katherine Marie, John Phillip, Patricia Elizabeth. Clk. research and devel. div. Springfield Armory, 1946-47; research asst. dept. econs. Ind. U., 1951, lectr. econs., 1955-57; orgn. and methods examiner U.S. Air Force, Gulfport, Miss., 1952-53; mgmt. analyst 5th U.S. Army, Chgo., 1954-61; program progess and resources mgmt. analyst Continental Army Command, Ft. Monroe, Va., 1962-67; adminstrv. officer U.S. Army NIKE-X System Office, Alexandria, Va., 1967; program analyst Office Asst. Chief Staff Force Devel., Dept. Army, Washington, 1967—; guest lectr. econs. Purdue U., 1959-61. Served with AUS, 1943-46. Mem. Am. Econ. Assn., Am. Soc. Pub. Adminstrn., Beta Gamma Sigma. Home: 3003 N Arkendale St Woodbridge VA 22191 Office: Dept Army Office Asst Chief Staff Force Devel Pentagon Washington DC 20301

DILLAHUNTY, WILBUR HARRIS, U.S. atty.; b. Memphis, June 30, 1928; s. Joseph Silas and Octavia (Jones) D.; J.D., U. Ark., 1954; m. Emma Cox, Nov. 25, 1948; 1 dau., Sharon Kaye. Admitted to Ark. bar; practiced, West Memphis, Ark., 1954-58; U.S. dist. atty., Eastern Ark., Little Rock, 1968—. West Memphis city atty., 1958-68. Served with AUS, 1945-48. Names Young Man of Year, Crittenden County, Ark., 1961. Mem. Crittenden County Bar Assn. (past pres.), Omicron Delta Kappa, Delta Theta Phi. Club: Meadowbrook Country (West Memphis). Home: 9710 Catskill Rd Little Rock AR 72207 Office: Courthouse Bldg 5th and Gaines Sts Little Rock AR 72203

DILLAMAN, AUDREY BOROK (MRS. DONALD GENE DILLAMAN), educator; b. N.Y.C., Feb. 16, 1941; d. Arthur and Ruth (Jaffe) Borok; B.Ed., U. Miami, 1963; M.Ed., U. Md., 1968. Classroom tchr. Miami (Fla.) Schs., 1963-65; pre-sch. tchr. Migrant Edn. Project, Miami, 1966; team tchr., team coordinator Colonial Dr. Elementary Sch., Miami, 1966-69; kindergarten tchr. South Miami Heights Elementary Sch., Miami, 1969-70; master tchr. Title I Project Lang. Arts Devel. Program, Shadowlawn Elementary Sch., 1970—; instr. early childhood edn. U. Miami, 1969—. Mem. women's com. Jewish Family and Children's Service; vol. Children's Psychiat. Inst., Jackson Meml. Hosp., 1969—; mem. St. Albans Day Nursery, Big Sisters of Dade County. Mem. Nat., Fla. edn. assns., Nat. Assn. for Edn. Young Children, So. Fla. assns. on children under six, Council for Exceptional Children, Dade County Classroom Tchrs. Assn., Assn. for Childhood Edn., Internat. Reading Assn., Dade County Assn. Retarded Children, U. Miami Alumni Assn., Miami Women's Panhellenic Assn., Mortar Bd., Phi Sigma Sigma (supreme council, nat. chmn.). Jewish religion. Home: 11410 SW 81 Rd Miami FL 33156

DILLARD, JAMES WILLIAM, coll. pres.; b. Lubbock, Tex., June 28, 1910; s. Robert Jefferson and Mary (Gearing) D.; student Clarendon Jr. Coll., 1929-31; B.S. and M.A., W. Tex. State Coll., 1939; m. Edna Gerlach, Aug. 22, 1932; children—Barbara Elaine, Edna Carolyn. Supt. Alanreed (Tex.) pub. Sch., 1931-37; prin. Spring Creek Pub. Sch., Borger, Tex., 1937-46; supt. Hutchinson County Schs., Borger, 1946-48; dean Frank Phillips Coll., Borger, 1948-55, pres., 1955—. Dist. chmn., area exec. com. Adobe Walls council Boy Scouts Am. Served as lt. USNR, 1943-46. Decorated Am. Theatre, Phillippine Asiatic-Pacific, Victory medals. Mem. N.E.A., Am. Assn. Sch. Adminstrs., Tex. Tchrs. Assn., Tex. Jr. Coll. Tchrs. Assn., Panhandle Plains Supts. Assn. (past pres.), Tex. Jr. Coll. Athletic Conf. (past pres.), Alpha Chi. Methodist. Mason, Rotarian (past pres.). Home: 1105 College Av Borger TX 79007

DILLARD, KATHERINE SHANNON RAWLINGS (MRS. TOM CLINTON DILLARD), editor; b. Sulphur, Okla., Oct. 13; d. Frank Hill and Floy (Dickinsheets) Rawlings; student Tex. Christian U., 1938-39; m. Tom Clinton Dillard, Sept. 5, 1942; 1 dau., Shannon Howard (Mrs. Shyam H. Gurbaxani). Feature editor, soc. and amusements editor Ft. Worth Star-Telegram, 1937-42; feature writer, asst. to city editor San Antonio Light, 1942-45; feature writer Dallas Morning News, 1945-47, women's editor, 1947—. Mem. women's bd. Dallas Civic Opera. Recipient Matrix award Theta Sigma Phi, 1969. Mem. Nat. Soc. Interior Designers, Nat. Home Fashions League, Delta Kappa Gamma, Fashion Group Inc., Theta Sigma Phi. Methodist. Clubs: Dallas Athletic, Lakewood Country. Home: 7022 Merrilee Lane Dallas TX 75214 Office: Communications Center Dallas TX 75222

DILLARD, MAX MURRAY, oil drilling co. exec.; b. Lueders, Tex., Nov. 21, 1935; s. Alva Clemens and Effie Carroll (Murray) D.; B.S., U. Tex. at Austin, 1959; student Ranger Jr. Coll., 1953-55; m. Carol Gayle Jenkins, Dec. 27, 1957; children—Denise Gayle, Pamela Deann, Julie Ann. Drilling engr. Offshore Co., Houston, 1959-61, Great Western Drilling Co., Midland, Tex., 1961-63; operations mgr. Arrow Drilling Co., Tulsa, 1963-64; Western states sales mgr. Reed Drilling Tools, Inc., Los Angeles, 1964-67; operations mgr. Peter Bawden Drilling, Inc., Long Beach, Cal., 1967-69; chmn. bd., pres. Bandera, Inc., 1969—; pres. Bandera Drilling Co., Dallas, 1969—, also dir. Mem. Los Angeles Petroleum Club, Am. Petroleum Inst., Nat. Soc. Profl. Engr. Republican. Club: Los Angeles Athletic. Contbr. articles to profl. jours. Home: 7949 LaCosa St Dallas TX 75240 Office: Banders Inc 160 Meadows Bldg Dallas TX 75206

DILLARD, OLIVER W., army officer; M.S. in Internat. Affairs, George Washington U. Commd. officer U.S. Army, advanced through grades to brig. gen., 1971; formerly tng. brigade comdr., Ft. Dix, N.J.; then sr. province adviser U.S. Mil. Assistance Command, Vietnam. Decorated Silver Star, Bronze Star. Address: 9340 Reid Circle Washington DC 20022*

DILLARD, RICHARD HENRY WILDE, educator; b. Roanoke, Va., Oct. 11, 1937; s. Benton Oscar and Mattie Lee (Mullins) D.; B.A., Roanoke Coll., 1958; M.A. (Woodrow Wilson fellow), U. Va., 1959, Ph.D. (DuPont fellow), 1965; m. Annie Doak, June 5, 1965. Instr. English, U. Va., 1961-64; asst. prof. English Hollins Coll., Va., 1964-68, asso. prof. English, 1968—, dir. Grad. Program in English and Creative Writing Sequence, 1971—. Mem. James Branch Cabell Soc., Bibliog. Soc. U. Va., Count Dracula Soc., Authors Guild, Phi Beta Kappa. Democrat. Baptist. Author: The Day I Stopped Dreaming About Barbara Steele and Other Poems, 1966; (editor with Louis D. Rubin, Jr.) The Experience of America, 1969; News of the Nile, 1971; (editor with George Garrett and John Rees Moore) The Sounder Few, 1971; After Borges, 1972. Editorial bd. The Hollins Critic, 1966—. Home: 6910 Ardmore Dr NW Roanoke VA 24019 Office: Box 9671 Hollins College VA 24020

DILLARD, SAMUEL DOUGLAS, religious pub. relations exec.; b. Temple, Tex., July 11, 1929; s. Clarence Young and Aleene (Lynch) D.; B.A., Baylor U., 1951; M.R.E., Southwestern Bapt. Theol. Sem., 1953; m. Marah Snyder Martin, Jan. 15, 1953; children—Deborah Irene, David Lewis, Donna Aleene. Ordained to ministry Bapt. Ch., 1947; minister edn. 1st Bapt. Ch., Nederland, Tex., 1954-57, Riverside Bapt. Ch., San Antonio, Tex., 1957-59, 1st Bapt. Ch. Oak Cliff, Dallas, 1959-65; founder, partner Ministry of Ideas pub. relations and advt., Dallas, 1965—. Free lance cartoonist, 1960—; edit. cartoonist Bapt. Standard, Dallas, 1968—. Recipient Honor Certificate award Freedoms Found., 1971. Mem. Fellowship of Christians in the Arts, Media and Entertainment, Oak Cliff C. of C., Pub. Relations Soc. Am., Religious Pub. Relations Soc. (pres., 1970-71), Author, cartoonist: Meet Bro. Blotz, 1965; Bro. Blotz the Builder, 1967. Illustrator: L.S.D.: Trip or Trap, 1968, Primer for Teachers and Leaders, 1963, Using the Lecture in Teaching and Training, 1968; also color film strips. Home: 833 Goldwood Dr Dallas

TX 75232 Office: Ministry of Ideas 351 W Jefferson Blvd Dallas TX 75208

DILLINGHAM, FAYE ELIZABETH, educator; b. Kemp, Okla., June 26, 1915; d. Earnest Hayden and Moneta (Davis) Dillingham; B.A., Southeastern Okla. State, 1936; M.Ed., U. Okla., 1945; postgrad. Columbia, 1956, W. Tex. State U., 1958, U. Colo., 1959, Tex. Woman's U., 1960; Ed.D., N. Tex. State U., 1966. English tchr. Lawton (Okla.) High Sch., 1936-46; head English dept. Amarillo (Tex.) High Sch., 1946-65; asst. prof. edn. N. Tex. State U., Denton, 1965-66, Central Mo. State Coll., Warrensburg, 1966-69; asso. prof. English; Okla. Christian Coll., Oklahoma City, 1969-71. Dir. Secondary Sch. English Curriculum Guides, multilevel annotated reading lists for Secondary Sch. English, top ten selected for ednl. edition Readers' Digest; judge achievement awards Nat. Council Tchrs. English, 1960-65; supr. student interns in teaching secondary sch. English 1965-69. Mem. N.E.A., Okla. Edn. Assn., Nat. Council Tchrs. English, Modern Lang. Assn., Assn. for Tchr. Educators, Assn. Supervision and Curriculum Devel., Am. Assn. U. Profs., Am. Assn. U. Women, Kappa Delta Pi. Democrat. Mem. Ch. Christ. Home: 3425 Baird Dr Edmond OK 73034

DILLINGHAM, JOHN OLIVER, educator; b. Nashville, Nov. 9, 1912; s. Ollie Martin and Allie Mai (McDowell) D.; LL.B., Nashville YMCA Law Sch., 1935; grad. Lipscomb Jr. Coll., 1940; A.B., Harding Coll., 1942; M.A., George Peabody Coll., 1943; postgrad. Vanderbilt U., 1963-64; m. Marie Chunn, Dec. 22, 1942; children—Susan Diane, John Michael. Admitted to Tenn. bar, 1936; ordained to ministry Ch. of Christ, 1943; minister Ch. of Christ chs., Atlanta, 1943-54, Selma, Ala., 1954-57; tchr. Maury County Pub. schs., 1957-60; asst. prof. history Middle Tenn. State U., Murfreesboro, 1961-66; asso. prof., chmn. div. social sci. Columbia (Tenn.) State Community Coll., 1966—. Mem. Am. Assn. U. Profs., So. Hist. Assn., Phi Gamma Mu. Democrat. Home: Liberty Hall Route 1 Columbia TN 38401

DILLMAN, GEORGE FRANKLIN, operating co. exec.; b. Coronado, Cal., Sept. 5, 1934; s. Wilbur Mitchell and Meadie (Ables) D.; student Abilene Christian Coll., 1952; B.S., B.B. A., U. Tex., 1958; m. Virginia Gayle Yeary, Sept. 1, 1961; children—Leesa Gayle, Mitchell Lynn, Virginia Louise, Laura Lynn. Asso. Bus. Research Corp. Tex., Austin, 1957-61; dir. econ. research Pacific Western Properties, Inc., Los Angeles, 1961; dir. corporate relations, econ. research Diversa, Inc., Dallas, 1961-62, Corporate Sec., 1962-65, v.p., corp. sec., dir., 1965-67; chmn. bd., pres. Bonanza Internat., 1965-67; chmn. Dillman-Berry & Assos., Dallas, 1968—; chmn. exec. com., dir. Trini's Restaurant, Inc., 1968-69; dir. Richardson Savs. & Loan Assn. Mem. univ. bd. Pepperdine Coll., Los Angeles. Mem. bd., pres. Dallas Assembly; vice chmn. Tex. Tourist Devel. Agy., Urban Rehab. Standards Bd. City of Dallas. Served with USNR, 1952-55. Mem. Tex. Pub. Relations Assn. (dir.), Pub. Relations Soc. Am., Alpha Delta Sigma. Democrat. Mem. Ch. of Christ. Clubs: Royal Oaks Country, Dallas Press (Dallas); Headliners (Austin). Contbr. articles in field to profl. and ch. jours. Home: 13361 Peyton Dr Dallas TX 75214 Office: Noel Page Bldg Dallas TX 75206

DILLMAN, H. GRANT, journalist; b. Columbus, O., May 4, 1918; s. Herschel G. and Daisy (Fothergill) D.; student Franklin U., 1939-40; m. Jeanne L. Ford, 1940; 1 dau., Mrs. Daniel F. Kunkle; m. 2d, Audrey Maslow, June 30, 1945; children—Darryl, Craig. With Columbus (O.) Dispatch, 1938-42; with pub. relations dept. Curtiss-Wright Corp., 1942; with UPI (formerly United Press), 1942—, Ohio legislative corr., 1942-43, mgr. Columbus bur., 1944, trans. to Washington staff, 1945—, editor night news, 1950-63, Washington news editor 1963—. Mem. Sigma Delta Chi. Clubs: Gridiron, Nat. Press, Internat. Home: 6604 Rosecroft Pl Falls Church VA 22043 Office: Nat Press Bldg Washington DC 20004

DILLON, GORDON MATT, city ofcl.; b. Athol, Mass., Mar. 16, 1910; s. William and Harriet L. (Phinney) D.; student New Eng. Sch. Accounting, 1930; m. Rosalynd C. Oriani, Dec. 31, 1940; children—William F., Robert D., Gordon A., Paul B. City mgr., Quincy, Mass., 1951-53, Claremont, N.H., 1953-57, North Adams, Mass., 1957-58, Ipswich, Mass., 1959-60, North Miami Beach, Fla., 1960-63, Melbourne, Fla., 1963-66, Oakland Park, Fla., 1968—. Mem. adv. bd. Broward Community Coll., since 1969—. Served with US. Maritime Service, 1942-43. Mem. Internat. City Mgmt. Assn. Home: 1799 NW 39th Pl Oakland Park FL 33309 Office: 3650 NE 12th Av Oakland Park FL 33307

DILLON, IRA GUSTAF, educator; b. Wheatland, Wyo., Oct. 22, 1919; s. Herbert Michael and Hildur Nellie (Rydberg) D.; B.S. in Chem. Engring., Ore. State U., 1942; M.S., Ill. Inst. Tech., 1947, Ph.D., 1965; m. Virginia Stead, Nov. 25, 1953. Chem. engr. Sinclair Research Labs., Harvey, Ill., 1942-49; asso. chem. engr. Argonne Nat. Lab., Lemont, Ill., 1949-65; prof. mech. engring., head dept. Tuskegee (Ala.) Inst., 1965—. Mem. Am. Soc. M.E. (chmn. Chattahochee subsect. 1971-72), Am. Inst. Chem. Engrs., Am. Nuclear Soc., Am. Soc. Elec. Engrs. Mason (Shriner), Lion. Contbr. numerous articles to profl. jours. Home: PO Box 722 Tuskegee AL 36083

DILLON, ROBERT CHESTER, lawyer; b. Birmingham, Ala., May 17, 1931; s. Chester C. and Martha R. (Keith) D.; A.B., U. Ala., 1953, LL.B., 1957; m. Helen C. Frizzle, Sept. 20, 1957; children—Robert C., Susan B., Helen Leigh. Admitted to Ala. bar, 1957; law clk. Supreme Ct. Ala., 1957-58; asst. atty. gen. Ala., 1958-59; individual practice law, Anniston, Ala., 1959—; mem. firm Knox Jones Woolf & Merrill. Chmn. Calhoun County A.R.C., 1970-71. Served to 1st lt. AUS, 1953-55. Mem. Am., Ala., Calhoun County (pres. 1972) bar assns. Rotarian. Club: Anniston Country. Home: 421 Wildwood Rd Anniston AL 36201 Office: PO Box 580 Anniston AL 36201

DILLON, ROBERT MORTON, research exec.; b. Seattle, Oct. 27, 1923; s. James Richard and Lucille (Morton) D.; student U. Ill., 1946-47; B.Arch., U. Wash., 1949; M.Arch., U. Fla., 1954; m. Mary Charlotte Beeson, Jan. 6, 1943; children—Robert Thomas, Colleen Marie, Patrick Morton, Draftsman, Williams and Longstreet, Architects, Greenville, S.C., 1949-50; designer G. Lyles, Bissett, Carlisle &Wolf, Architects, Columbia, S.C., 1950, Robert M. Dillon and Wm. B. Eaton, Architects, Gainesville, Fla., 1952-55; staff architect, proj. dir. Bldg. Research Adv. Bd., Nat. Acad. Scis.-NRC, Washington, 1955-58, exec. dir., 1958—, exec. sec. U.S. nat. com. for Conseil Internat. du Batiment, 1962—. Asst. prof. architecture Clemson Coll., 1949-50; instr., asst. prof. architecture U. Fla., 1950-55; lectr. civil engring. Catholic U. Am., 1957-63; distinguished faculty Acad. Code Adminstrn. and Enforcement, U. Ill., 1972—. Cons. Ednl. Facilities Labs., N.Y.C., 1958-71. Mem. adv. com., low-income housing demonstration program Dept. Housing and Urban Devel., Washington, 1964-67; mem. sub-panel on housing White House Panel on Civilian Tech., Washington, 1961-62. Served with USNR, 1942-45. Mem. A.I.A. (mem. com. on research for architecture 1962-67, chmn. 1969; chmn. com. archtl. barriers 1967-68, mem. housing com. 1970—), Sigma Lambda Chi. Author: (with S.W. Crawley) Steel Buildings: Analysis and Design, 1970. Home: 811 Arrington Dr Silver Spring MD 20901 Office: 2101 Constitution Av Washington DC 20418

DILWORTH, BILLY D., newspaperman; b. Martin, Ga., Oct. 4; 1934; s. B.Q. and Pearl (Davis) D.; student journalism U. Ga. Ga. editor Anderson (S.C.) Ind., 1953-63; state editor Atlanta Times, 1964-65, Athens (Ga.) Daily News, 1967—; host programs radio sta. WLET, Toccoa, Ga., 1960—, sta. WSPA-TV, Spartanburg, S.C., 1968—. Mem. Ga. Scholarship Commn., 1971—. Recipient A.P. award reporting and news photo, 1963. Address: Box 117 Carnesville GA 30521

DILWORTH, JAMES WELDON, lawyer; b. San Antonio, Jan. 1, 1928; s. William H. and Bertie (Lawrence) D.; student U. Houston, 1949-51; LL.B. cum laude, Baylor U., 1953; m. Marie Miller, Mar. 10, 1945; children—Patricia Ann, Pamela Sue, James Weldon. Admitted to Tex. bar, 1953; asso. Andrews, Kurth, Campell & Jones, Houston, 1953-64, partner, 1964—. Spl. counsel for trustee in charge investigation Westec Corp., Houston, Dallas, Chgo., N.Y.C., 1966—. Mem. Houston Heritage Soc., Mus Fine Arts. Served with AUS, 1946-47. Mem. Tex. Bar. Am. (mem. anti-trust, family law sects.), Houston bar assns. Methodist. Clubs: Houston Country, Petroleum (Houston). Home: 1 Hedwig Ct Houston TX 77024 Office: Humble Bldg Houston TX 77002

DIMBATH, MERIE FREDERICK, SR., educator; b. Dayton, O., Mar. 21, 1939; s. Merle S. and Zella (Shadowens) D.; B.S., U. Va., 1961; M.A., U. Fla., 1962, Ph.D., 1964; m. Joyce Rose Dollings, Feb. 3, 1962; children— Merle Frederick, Richard Scotmond, Sesilie Joy. Asst. prof. San Jose State Coll., Sch. Bus., 1964-65; asst. to asso. prof. Coll. Bus. Adminstrn., U. So. Fla., Tampa, 1965-67; chmn. dept. econs. and bus. Fla. So. Coll., Lakeland, 1967-68; Polk County supt. pub. instrn., Bartow, Fla., 1968-69; exec. dir. Fla. Pub. Sch. Bd., Tallahassee, 1969; chmn. dept. bus. and econs. Fla. So. Coll., Lakeland, 1969—. Pres., Dimbath Devel. Co. Mem. Am., So. econs. assns., Am., So. marketing assns., Delta Upsilon, Alha Kappa Psi. Lutheran. Rotarian. Contbr. articles to profl. lit. Home: 4733 Tierra Alta Ct Lakeland FL 33803

DIMLING, JOHN ARTHUR, JR., assn. exec.; b. Pitts., Apr. 9, 1938; s. John A. and Elizabeth (Powell) D.; A.B., Dartmouth, 1960; M.S., Carnegie Inst. Tech., 1962; m. Anne Stewart Hogg. Sept. 10, 1960. Trainee U.S. Steel Corp., Pitts., 1960-62, cost analyst, 1962-63; sr. scientist Spindletop Research, Lexington, Ky., 1965-67, mgr. communications and systems, 1967-69; v.p. Nat. Assn. Broadcasters, Washington, 1969—. Sec.-treas. Broadcast Rating Council, N.Y.C., 1971—; adviser Ky. Ednl. TV Authority, 1968-69. Served to 1st lt. AUS, 1963-65. Mem. Operations Research Soc. Am., Inst. Mgmt. Scis., Am. Econ. Assn., Am. Assn. for Pub. Opinion research. Spindletop Hall, Phi Beta Kappa. Club: Dartmouth (N.Y.C.). Home: 7923 Inverness Ridge Potomac MD 20854 Office: 1771 N St NW Washington DC 20036

DIMMITT, KATHRYNE ELDER COOKSEY (MRS. JAMES E. COREY), artist; b. Washington, May 8, 1910; d. Claude Bonifant and Bessie (Suite) Cooksey; A.B., U. Conn., 1932; m. E. Hewitt Dimmitt, July 11, 1939 (dec. Aug. 1957); m. 2d, James E. Corey, Jan. 19, 1971. Illustrator, mus. preparator artist Nat. Park Service, Dept. Interior, Washington, and Yorktown, Va., 1934-35, illustrator Bur. Reclamation, Washington, 1935-38, 40-45, 60-65; diorama artist Office of Exhibits, N.Y. World's Fair, 1938-40. Exhibited in groups shows at Smithsonian Instn., 1946-52, Corcoran Gallery of Art, 1944-46, Arts Club Washington, 1962-70. Recipient 1st prize Mid-Atlantic Regional Art Exhibit, 1955; 1st prize landscape Nat. League Am. Pen Women, 1948, 55, 63, best oil in show, 1963; Superior Performance award Dept. Interior, 1961. Mem. Nat. League Am. Pen Women (nat. art bd. 1956-66), Miniature Painters, Sculptors and Gravers Soc. Washington (pres. 1970-72), Arts Club Washington (exhibits chmn. 1968-70), Conn. Coll. Alumnae Assn. (chpt. pres. 1943-44), P.E.O. (chpt. pres. 1953-55). Home: 5801 Massachusetts Av Washington DC 20016

DING, GAR DAY, educator; b. Canton, China, Nov. 14, 1929; s. Chew Cheung and Ho (Nagan) C.; came to U.S., 1966; B.Arch., U. New Zealand, 1953; B.E. (Hume Industries scholar, C.S. McCully scholar), U. Canterbury (New Zealand), 1959; M.Tech., U. New South Wales (Australia), 1961; m. Maisie Young, Aug. 28, 1954; children— David, Judy, Derek, Walter. Architect, 1953-54, New Zealand, part-time 1955-58; sr. lectr. U. Sydney (Australia), 1959-66, acting head archtl. sci., 1962, 65; chmn. environmental studies Va. Poly. Inst., Blackburg, 1965—, Cons. architect, engr., 1959-66; cons. environmental studies, 1966—. Found. hon. sec. Bldg. Sci. Forum Australia, 1964-66. Recipient various awards in architecture, 1957, 60, 65. Mem. Archtl. Inst. New Zealand, Archtl. Inst. Australia, Archtl. Inst. Eng., Am. Concrete Inst., Am. Soc. C.E., Australian Instn. Engrs. Author: (with H.J. Gowan and J.S. Gero) Model Methods in Architecture, 1968. Home: Box 44 Newport VA 24128 Office: Va Poly Inst Blacksburg VA 24061

DINKLER, CARLING LOUIS, JR., club exec.; b. Atlanta, Aug. 4, 1919; s. Carling Louis and Alice (Huthnance) D.; student U. Ga., Loyola U., New Orleans; m. Cornelia D. Vandagaer, June 26, 1939; children—Gayonne (Mrs. Harold Pate), Carling Louis III, Derek, Kendel. Owner Palm Bay Club, Miami, Fla., 1965—; owner Le Club Internat., Fort Lauderdale, Fla., 1968—. Co-chmn. Golden Wagon United Fund, Miami, 1969-71. Bd. dirs. Hollywood Coll. Served with USAAF, 1942-45. Named Hotel Man of Year, 1959. Clubs: Indian Creek Country, Surf, Peachtree Golf, Atlanta Country, 200. Home: 720 NE 69th St Miami FL 33138 Office: Palm Bay Club Miami FL 33101

DINSMORE, DWIGHT REGINALD, aerospace co. exec.; b. Fremont, Ia., June 14, 1914; s. Charles Clarence and Mildred (Filmer) D.; B.A., Ia. Wesleyan Coll., 1935; m. Virginia Irene Warren, June 14, 1942; children—Diana Lynn (Mrs. Dale Lee Cowles), Charles Warren. Commd. 1s lt. USAF, 1943, advanced through grades to col., 1960; instr. Craig AFB, Selma, Ala., 1947-49; pilot Berlin Airlift, 1949; dep. dir. information Scott AFB, 1950-51; dir. internat. relations, Iceland, 1951-52; instr. Air Command and Staff Coll. Air U., Maxwell AFB, Ala., 1952-56; dep. dir. information USAF in Europe, 1956-59, chief pub. information div. office sec. Air Force, Washington, 1963-66; pub. relations mgr. LTV Aerospace Corp., Washington, 1966—. Mem. Air Force Assn., Assn. U.S. Army, Navy League, Pub. Relations Soc. Am., Nat. Security Indsl. Assn., Airline Pilots Assn., Aerospace Writers Assn., Am. Ordnance Assn., Armed Forces Mgmt. Assn., Ret. Officers Assn., Nat. Press Club, Nat. Aviation Club, Soc. for Preservation and Encouragement Barbershop Quartet Singing in Am., Inc., Fairfax Jubilaires (pres. 1970). Potomachords, Phi Delta Theta. Methodist. Home: 6011 Claiborne Dr McLean VA 22101 Office: 1155 15th St NW Washington DC 20005

DI PIETRO, ROBERT JOSEPH, sci. linguist; b. Endicott, N.Y., July 18, 1932; s. Americo and Mary Di P.; B.A., Harpur Coll., State U. N.Y. at Binghamton, 1950-54; M.A., Harvard 1955; Ph.D., Cornell U., 1960; m. Vincenzina Angela Giallo, Sept. 5, 1953; children—Angela Maria, Mark Andrew. Instr. English, Boston Sch. Modern Lang., 1955-56; instr., grad. fellow Cornell U., 1957-60; jr. lectr. linguistics U. Rome (Italy), 1960; asst. prof. linguistics Georgetown U., Washington 1961-64, asso. prof., 1964-69, prof., 1969—, head div. Italian, 1966-68, sr. lectr. linguistics U. Madrid (Spain), 1963-64; Spanish lang. proficiency tester Peace Corps Vols., Venezuela, 1965; cons. editor Ginn-Blaisdell Pub. Co., Waltham, Mass., 1964-72. Fulbright grantee, 1960, 63. Mem. Am. Assn. Tchrs. Italian (chpt. pres. 1968-69), Linguistic Soc. Am., A.A.A.S., Am. Anthrop. Assn., Washington Linguistics Club (pres. 1967-68). Author: (with F.B. Agard) Sounds of English and Italian (Vol. I), 1965; Grammatical Structures of English and Italian (vol. II), 1965, 2d edit., 1969; Language Structures in Contrast, 1971. Book rev. editor Modern Lang. Jour., 1972—. Contbr. articles in field to profl. jours. Home: 6723 Haycock Rd Falls Church VA 22043 Office: Georgetown U Washington DC 20007

DIPLACIDO, FRANCIS PAUL, JR., dentist; b. Phila., Dec. 25, 1934; s. Francis Paul and Elizabeth Marie (deMaria) DiP.; B.S. in Biology, St. Josephs Coll., 1956; D.D.S., U. Pa. Sch. Dentistry, 1962; postgrad. U. Pa. Grad. Sch. Medicine, 1965; m. Noreen M. Bamford, June 14, 1969; 1 son, Francis Paul, III. Resident oral surgery U. Pa., 1965-68; pvt. practice oral surgery, Fort Myers, Fla., 1968—. Sec., Mooney Aircraft Southwest Fla., 1970-71; pres. Southwest Amusements, Inc., 1970-71; v.p. Palace Constrn. Co., Inc., 1971—. Served with AUS, 1962-65. Diplomate Am. Bd. Oral Surgery. Mem. Am., Fla. dental assns., Am. Soc. Oral Surgeons, Internat. Assn. Oral Surgeons, Internat. Soc. Maxillofacial Surgeons, Am. Dental Soc. Anesthesiology. Republican. Roman Catholic. Clubs: Cypress Lake Country, Royal Palm Yacht (Fort Myers). Home: 1604 S Hermitage Rd Fort Myers FL 33901 Office: 3900 S Broadway Fort Myers FL 33901

DIRECTOR, HERMAN, furniture co. exec.; b. Bremen, Germany, May 15, 1915; s. Simon and Bertha (Yeserski) D.; m. Lillian Rosenzweig; children—Steven, Dennis, Toby. Came to U.S., 1934, naturalized 1939. Pres. Dir. Enterprises, Inc., Savannah, Ga., 1970—. Pres., Savannah Jewish Council, 1959-61; chmn. Israeli Bond drive, 1960-61; mem. Park and Tree Commn., 1961-66; mem. Bd. Edn., 1963-69, pres., 1969. Bd. dirs. A.R.C., 1960-62. Served with USAAF, 1942-46. Mem. Savannah Retail Furniture Assn. (pres. 1959-61), Greater Downtown Bus. Assn. (pres. 1971). Home: 4710 Fairfax Dr Savannah GA 31405 Office: 401 W Broughton St Savannah GA 31402

DISANTO, FRANK MICHAEL, industrialist; b. N.Y.C., July 12, 1924; s. Rocco and Filomena (DiBiase) DiS.; B.S., Phila. Textile Inst., 1949; m. Grace Johanna DeMarco, Aug. 30, 1946; children—Frank Richard, Bernadette Mary, Roxanne Judith. Plant mgr. Housatonic Dyeing & Printing Co., Derby, Conn., 1951-54; pres. Bay State Dyeing & Finishing Corp., Bondsville, Mass., 1954-61; pres. Morganton Dyeing & Finishing Corp. (N.C.), 1961—; sec. Grace Sales Corp., N.Y.C.; pres. Mimosa Specialty Co., Morganton, Rank Realty Co., Morganton; v.p. Joel Finishing, Inc., Wilmington, Del; sec. Astro Chem. Corp., Morganton; dir. Wachovia Bank & Trust Co., Western Carolina Industries; mem. exec. com. Attacoa, Inc. Bd. dirs. United Fund, Western Piedmont Community Coll. Found. Served with USNR, 1943-46. Mem. Am. Assn. Textile Colorists and Chemists, Community Mgmt. Soc. (pres.), Newcomen Soc. N.Am., C. of C., Phi Psi. Roman Catholic. Clubs: Catawba Valley Executives, Mimosa Golf, Lenoir Country; Asheville City, Grandfather Golf and Country. Home: 218 Riverside Dr Morganton NC 28655 Office: Morganton Dyeing and Finishing Corp Morganton NC 28655

DI SANTO, GRACE JOHANNE DEMARCO (MRS. FRANK MICHAEL DI SANTO), civic worker; b. Derby, Conn., July 12, 1924; d. Richard and Fannie (DeMarco) De Marco; student N.Y. U. Sch. Journalism, 1941-43; m. Frank Michael Di Santo, Aug. 30, 1946; children— Frank Richard, Bernadette Mary, Roxanne Judith. Newswriter, Australian Asso. Press, N.Y.C., 1942-43; staff reporter Ansonia Sentinel, Derby, 1943-45; feature writer, drama critic Bridgeport Herald, New Haven, 1945-46; editor monthly bull. Pa. State Coll. Optometry, Phila., 1947-48; free-lance writer, 1949-54; founder, pres. bd. Investors Ltd., Morganton, N.C., 1966-67. Pres., Catholic Ladies' Guild, Morganton, 1965-66, Morganton Garden Club, 1966-67, Burke County chpt. N.C. Symphony Soc., 1968-70; mem. exec. bd. Community Concerts Assn., 1962-71; mem. Am. Field Service program Burke County, 1969—; active Burke County Heart Fund, Burke County Council Garden Clubs; mem. exec. bd., chmn. room reps. Forest Hill P.T.A., 1968-70; Burke County chmn. nat. humanities series Woodrow Wilson Fellowship Found. Bd. dirs. Burke county chpt. March of Dimes, 1966—; trustee N.C. Symphony Soc., 1965-68, 69-70. Republican. Roman Catholic (pres. St. Charles Borromeo Ladies Guild 1965-66. Clubs: Schubert Music; Morganton Friday Afternoon Bridge, Lenoir Country (N.C.); Grandfather Golf and Country (Linville, N.C.); Mimosa Hills Golf. Address: 218 Riverside Dr Morganton NC 28655

DISHMER, RYLAND, supt. schs.; b. Pattonsville, Va., Oct. 26, 1925; s. John William and Cora Alice (Fickle) D.; B.S., Emory and Henry Coll., 1949; M.Ed., Va. Poly. Inst., 1957; postgrad. U.Va., 1967; m. Helen B. Smith, Dec. 29, 1950; children—Ryland, Charles William, Tammy Shawn. Tchr., coach pub. sch., Castlewood, Va., 1949-54; asst. prin., 1954-56; asst. prin. pub. sch., Dublin, Va., 1956-59; prin. Central High Sch., Woodstock, Va., 1959-63, Fauquier High Sch., Warrenton, Va., 1963-65; asst. supt. schs., Warrenton, 1965-68, supt. schs., 1968—. Dist. chmn. Boy Scouts Am., 1961-62. Bd. dirs. Fauquier County Family Guidance Center, Fauquier CountyAssn., No. Va. Ednl. TV. Served with USNR, 1944-46; PTO. Recipient Outstanding Citizen award K.C., Warrenton, 1971. Mem. Nat., Va., Fauquier edn. assns., Va. Assn. Sch. Adminstrs., No.Va. Sch. Supts. (sec., treas. 1970—, chmn. several secondary sch. evaluation coms. 1965—), Internat. Platform Assn. Methodist. Lion (past dir. Warrenton). Home: Route 1 Warrenton VA 22186

DISHONGH, HOWARD ALLAN, lawyer, state legislator; b. Little Rock, Sept. 22, 1931; s. Howard Allen and Sarah (Crosby) D.; student Tulane U., 1950-51, Little Rock U., 1960-61; LL.B., Ark. Law Sch., 1962; m. Joan Gilbert, July 30, 1965; 1 dau., Sarah Wood. Admitted to Ark. bar, 1962; claims adjustor, 1960-63; partner Longstreth &Dishongh, Little Rock, 1963-65, Sloan, Butler, Ragsdale & Dishongh, Little Rock, 1965—; mem. Ark. Ho. of Reps., 1966—. Partner, Fail-Safe, Ltd., Little Rock. Served with USMC, 1951-54. Mem. Am. Trial Lawyers Assn., Pulaski County Bar Assn., Little Rock C. of C. Democrat. Mem. Christian Ch. Mason (32 deg., Shriner, Jester). Home: 10 River Ridge Rd Little Rock AR 72207 Office: Nat Investors Bldg Little Rock AR 72202

DISMAS, SISTER MARY, educator. Supt. Catholic schs., Diocese Ponce, P.R. Address: Gen Delivery Station 6 Catholic Univ Ponce PR 00731*

DISSTON, GEOFFREY WHITMORE, corp. exec.; b. Greenwich, Conn., Apr. 30, 1933; s. Harry and Valerie (Duval) D.; B.A., Amherst Coll., 1956; m. Joan Stuart Lyman, 1955 (div. 1962); children—Deborah Whitmore, Stuart Lyman and Geoffrey Whitmore (twins); m. 2d, Audrie Brown, Aug. 13, 1964; (div.); 1 son, Jason Manning. With J. P. Morgan N.Y., 1956-59, Morgan Guaranty, N.Y., 1959-61, Chas. F. Quincey, N.Y., 1961-62; v.p. Harris Trust and Savs. Bank, Chgo., 1962-67; chmn. bd., chief exec. officer Multi Channel Response Corp., N.Y.C.; pres. Keswick Corp. (Va.); owner G. W. Disston and Co., Chgo., 1967—. Bd. dirs. Lyric Opera Guild. Served to capt. AUS, 1964. Mem. Beta Theta Pi. Club: Union (N.Y.C.). Home: Keswick VA 22947 Office: 444 Madison Av New York City NY 10022

DISSTON, HARRY, author, polit. adminstr.; b. Red Bank, N.J., Nov. 23, 1899; s. Eugene John Kauffmann and Frances Matilda Disston; A.B., Amherst Coll., 1921; m. Valerie Ivy Duval, Mar. 26, 1930 (dec. 1951); children—Robin John Duval, Geoffrey Whitmore; m. 2d, Catherine Sitler John, Aug. 26, 1960. With N.Y. Telephone Co., 1921-32, with Am. Tel. & Tel. Co., N.Y.C. 1932-60, exec. tng. student, dist. traffic supt., sales engr., dist. mgr., adv. staff engr., adv. staff exec. ind. co. relations, 1951-60; coordinator devel. activities. Grad. Sch. Bus. Adminstrn., U. Va. Aide-de-camp to gov. Va.; chmn. Louisa County Electoral Bd.; mem. Va. Bd. Mil. Affairs; chmn. finance com. Republican party Va.; chmn. Louisa County Rep. Com. Vice pres., dir. Park Av. Assn. Exec. com. Diocese of Va. Trustee Grant Monument Assn. Served from maj. to col., cav. and gen. staff corps, 1941-46; PTO; comdg. officer 107th Regtl. Combat Team, N.Y.N.G., 1947-57; brig. gen. ret. Awarded Legion of Merit, Bronze Star with oak leaf cluster; comdr. Order of Boliver; Philippine Liberation Medal; Medal of Merit with Swords, Free Poland. Mem. Am. Horse Shows Assn. (judge), Vets. 7th Regt., N.Y. Soc. Mil. and Naval Officers World Wars (past pres.), Vet. Corps Arty., Mil. Order Fgn. Wars, Mil. Order World Wars, Am. Legion, St. Georges Soc., St. Andrews Soc., Va. Thoroughbred Assn., U.S. Pony Clubs (gov.), Phi Beta Kappa, Phi Kappa Psi. Clubs: Union; Amherst; Church of New York; Farmington Country, Jack Jonett Bridle Trails (Charlottesville, Va.); The Pilgrims; Keswick Hunt, Keswick of Va. Author: Equestionnaire, 1947; Riding Rhymes, 1951; Know About Horses, 1961; Young Horseman's Handbooks, 1962; Elementary Dressage, 1971; several mag. articles on mil., equine and bus. subjects; contbr. to Ency. Britannica. Home: Hidden Hill Farm Keswick VA 22947

DISTEFANO, SAM ANTHONY, supt. sch.; b. Plaquemine, La., May 15, 1910; s. Sam Nickolas and Antoinette Marian (Ferittita) D.; B.A., Southwestern La. Inst., 1934; M.Ed., La. State U., 1949; m. Lillie Lenora Engolio, Dec. 23, 1934; children—Sam Anthony, Pauline (Mrs. John Mixon Higdon). With Iberville Parish Sch. Bd., Plaquemine, La., 1934—, supr. edn., 1964—. Mayor, North Plaquemine, 1953-57; mem. Plaquemine Recreation Commn., 1956—, pres., 1970—; mem. Plaquemine Zoning Commn., 1964, Rabies Control Bd., 1958—, Iberville Parish Water Bd., 1958—. Mem. S. Central La. Supts. Assn. (pres., 1970—), La. Tchrs. Assn., N.E.A., La. Supts. Com. Elk. Office: PO Box 151 Plaquemine LA 70764

DISTELHORST, CARL FREDERICK, financial cons.; b. Burlington, Ia., May 16, 1906; s. Charles H. and Augusta (Loose) D.; B.S. in Commerce, U. Ia., 1928; M.Litt., U. Pitts., 1936; m. Josephine Harris Smith, July 9, 1932; children—Craig T., Lynn H. Instr. accounting and Finance U. Tenn., 1928-30; instr. accounting U. Pitts., 1930-38, Am. Inst. Banking, 1930-42, Am. Savs. and Loan Inst., 1931-42; asst. to pres. Fed. Home Loan Bank Pitts., 1938-42; staff v.p. U.S. Savs and Loan League, also sec. Am. Savs. and Loan Inst., 1942-43; pres. Council Insured Savs. Assns. N.Y. State, 1943-46; exec. v.p. Am. Savs. and Loan Inst., exec. dir. Grad. Sch. Savs. and Loan, 1946-55; exec. v.p. Fla. Savs. and Loan League, 1955-62; financial cons., Winter Park, Fla., 1962—; dir. Winter Park Fed. Savs. & Loan Assn., Farm & Home Savs. Assn., Nevada, Mo., Comml. Loan Ins. Corp., N.Y. Guaranty Ins. Corp., MGIC Investment Corp.; dir. Mortgage Guaranty Ins. Corp. Wis., 1960—, mem. exec. com., 1965—; dir., mem. exec. com. MGIC Financial Corp., Financial Data Scis., Inc.; dir. Am. Municipal Bond Assurance Corp., Fla. Informanagement Services, Inc., Bus. and Real Estate Trends, Inc., Caltrop Corp., Caltex Corp., Asso. Services, Inc., Internat. Lang. and Devel. Corp., Fiscanex, Ltd. (Can.). Mem. Savs. and Loan Adv. Com. to Sec. Treasury, 1956-71; mem. adv. council on naval affairs 6th Naval Dist., 1957-63. Mem. Highland Park (Ill.) Dist. Sch. Bd., 1950-53. Bd. dirs., sec. Savs. and Loan Found., Washington. Mem. Am. Savs. and Loan Inst. (hon. life trustee dir.); Nat. Planning Assn. (nat. council), Royal Soc. Arts (London, Eng., Benjamin Franklin fellow), Navy League U.S., Am. Finance Assn., Lambda Alpha, Beta Gamma Sigma, Omicron Delta Kappa, Alpha Sigma Phi, Delta Sigma Pi. Republican. Presbyn. Rotarian. Club: Citrus (Orlando, Fla.). Contbr. to books, encys., profl. jours. Address: 141 Alexander Pl Winter Park FL 32789

DIVEN, JAMES LEWIS, research engr.; b. Houston, Aug. 19, 1936; s. Homer Francis and Macy (Stunkel) D.; B.A., Rice U., 1958, B.S. in M. E., 1959; M.S. in M. E., Wichita State U., 1962; m. Doris Ezella Hall, Feb. 20, 1965; children—Aletha Louise, James Lewis. With Boeing Co., Wichita, Kan., 1959-62, asso. research engr., 1961-62; with Brown Engring. Co., Huntsville, Ala. 1962-68, sr. research engr., 1966-68; aerospace engr. U.S. Army Missile Command, Redstone Arsenal, Ala., 1968—. Registered profl. engr., Ala. Mem. Am. Soc. M.E., Am. Inst. Aeros. and Astronautics, Am. Astronautical Soc. Home: 506 Delaney Rd NW Huntsville AL 35806 Office: Army Missle Command AMSMI-RSD Bldg 5400 Redstone Arsenal AL 35809

DIVERS, ALAN GERALD, banker; b. Detroit, Sept. 17, 1935; s. Earle Leland and Dorotha Evelyn (Unger) D.; B.S. in Bus. Adminstrn. U. Fla., 1957; m. Jean Bacon, Apr. 18, 1964; children—Alan Blaec, Brett Devereux. With Exchange Nat. Bank of Tampa, Fla., 1961—, v.p., 1967—; dir. Bank of Osceola, Kissimmee, Fla. Pres., Southwest Fla. Blood Bank, Inc., 1970—; treas., Fla. West Coast Ednl. TV, 1967—. Bd. dirs. Community Coordinating Council, Fla. State Fair and Gasparilla Assn. Served to lt. comdr. USNR, 1957-61. Mem. Robert Morris Assos., Am. Inst. Banking, Phi Delta Theta. Republican. Episcopalian. Rotarian. Clubs: Merrymakers, University, Ye Mystic Krewe of Gasparilla (Tampa). Home: 812 Bayside Dr Tampa FL 33609 Office: PO Box 1809 Tampa FL 33601

DIXON, ALVIN TERRELL, mgmt. cons.; b. Okmulgee, Okla., July 4, 1909; s. Alvin Ernest and Minnie (Ramsey) D.; student U. Mo., 1926-27; B.A., U. Okla., 1962; m. Virginia Lee Francis, Sept. 17, 1938; 1 son, Terrell Francis. Prodn. mgr. Denver Producing & Refining Co., Oklahoma City, 1930-37; chief accountant Seaboard Oil Co. Del., Dallas, 1937-43; dir. controls Nat. Geophys. Co., Dallas, 1943-45; propr. Dixon-Dallas, Bus. Consultants, 1945-48; comptroller Okla. State Tech. Coll., 1949-55; cost accountant Ball Bros. Glass Co., Okmulgee, Okla., 1955-57; mgmt. cons. USAF, Oklahoma City, 1958—. Bd. dirs. Creek Nation council, Boy Scouts Am., Okmulgee, 1955-57, Ark. River Devel. Com., 1956-57. Mem. Am. Inst. C.P.A.'s, Am. Accountants Assn., Tex., Okla. State socs. C.P.A.'s, Fed. Govt. Accountants Assn., Tinker AFB Mgmt. Club, Delta Sigma Pi. Republican. Mem. Christian Ch. Clubs: Rotary, Toastmasters (pres. 1954-55). Home: 1215 Caddell Lane Norman OK 73069 Office: Tinker AFB USAF Logistics Command Oklahoma City OK 73145

DIXON, ANDREW DERART, educator; b. Belfast, No. Ireland, Oct. 27, 1925; s. Andrew and Martha (Stewart) D.; Licentiate in Dental Surgery, Queens U., Belfast, 1948, B. Dental Surgery, 1949, M. Dental Surgery, 1953, B.S. (Nuffield Found. dental fellow), 1954, D.Sc., 1965; Ph.D., U. Manchester (Eng.), 1958; m. Mary Elizabeth Henderson, Oct. 14, 1948; children—Penelope Jane, Melinda Sara, Alison Mary. Came to U.S., 1963, naturalized, 1972. Mem. Faculty U. Manchester (Eng.), 1954-63, lectr. anatomy, 1956-62, sr. lectr., 1962-63; prof. dental sci. U. N.C. at Chapel Hill, 1963-69, prof. oral biology, 1969—, prof. anatomy, 1965—, asst. dean, coordinator research Sch. Dentistry, 1966-69, dir. Dental Research Center, 1967—, asso. dean research, 1969—. Vis. asso. prof. anatomy U. Ia., 1959-61. Mem. dental tng. com. NIH, 1970—, chmn., 1972—. Recipient Outstanding Educator of Am. award, 1972; Fulbright sr. travel award, 1959-61; Commonwealth Fund Travel fellow, 1961. Mem. Anat. Soc. Gt. Britain and Ireland, Am. Assn. Anatomists, Brit. Dental Assn., Internat. Assn. Dental Research, Electron Microscopy Soc. Am., A.A.A.S., Am. Soc. Cell Biology, N.Y. Acad. Sci., Internat. Soc. Craniofacial Biology, Sigma Xi, Omicron Kappa Upsilon, Psi Omega. Author: (with J.H. Scott) Anatomy for Students of Dentistry, 1959, 66, 72. Contbr. numerous articles to profl. jours. Studies on early devel. and growth of the jaws, sex chromatin in oral smears as a diagnostic tool, nerve supply to oral mucous membrane, facial tissues and temporomandibular joint, facial skeletal growth, trigeminal pathway, including trigeminal ganglion, using histological, histochem. and electron microscopy methods. Home: 1514 Cumberland Rd Chapel Hill NC 27514

DIXON, CHARLIE, extension service specialist; b. Skyline, Ky., Nov. 28, 1914; s. Willie and Polly Jane (Griffie) D.; B.S., U. Ky., 1937; M.S., Cornell U., 1939; M.Pub. Adminstrn., Harvard, 1958; m. Goldia Jeanne Boggs, Dec. 23, 1937; children—Larry Donald, Phyllis (Mrs. Lawrence Dale Abernathy), Linda. Vocational-agr. supr., Lincoln County, 1937; asst. county agt. U. Ky. Coop. Extension Service, Fayette, Whitley, Laurel Counties, 1939-41, area specialist farm and home devel., 1954-57, state specialist rural devel., 1958-65, program specialist, 1965—. Sec. Ky. Devel. Com., 1959—; vice-chmn. orgn. Ky. Farm-City Com., 1960-70. Team leader United Way, 1971; profl. adv. mem. White House Conf. on Children and Youth, 1970—; co-chmn. fund drive A.R.C., 1948—. Trustee Clear Creek Bapt. Sch. Recipient Distinguished Service award Nat. County Agrl. Agts. Assn., 1951, Outstanding Service award Epsilon Sigma Phi, 1968. Mem. Nat. Community Devel. Soc. (mem. profl. improvement com. 1970-71), Ky. Assn. Continuing Edn., Extension Specialists Assn., Gamma Sigma Delta. Baptist (deacon 1947—). Home: 153 Zandale Dr Lexington KY 40503 Office: Cooper House U Ky Lexington KY 40506

DIXON, EVA CRAWFORD JOHNSON, librarian; b. Evinston, Fla., Aug. 28, 1909; d. William Alpheus and Willie (Crawford) Johnson; A.B. in Edn. with honors, U. Fla., 1937, M.A., 1948; postgrad. Fla. State U., 1950, Appalachian State Tchrs. Coll., 1955; m. Thomas Gordon Dixon, Dec. 14, 1935 (div. 1944). Tchr., English, librarian Jefferson High Sch., Monticello Fla., 1945-47; audio-visual dir. Jefferson County Schs., 1948-50; tchr. English, librarian Meigs (Ga.) High Sch., 1954-55; librarian Chipola Jr. Coll., Marianna, Fla., 1955-57, dir. library services, 1958—, chmn. student aid and scholarship com., 1961-65. Mem. Jefferson County Edn. Assn. (pres. 1948-50), Fla. Edn. Assn. Honor Socs. (chmn. 1950-51), Bus. and Profl. Women's Club (pres. 1958-59, 62-63), Fla. Fedn. Bus. Profl. and Women's Clubs (dist. dir. 1962-63), Women of 1st Presbyn. Ch. (pres. 1962-65), Kappa Delta Pi. Contbr. articles to profl. jours. Home: 506 Kelson Av Marianna FL 32446 Office: Chipola Jr Coll Marianna FL 32446

DIXON, HAL BERNARD, ch. exec.; b. Wake Forest, N.C., Mar. 6, 1928; s. Dudley Burgwin and Cynthia Lou (Crowder) D.; grad. Wake Forest Coll., 1951; student N.C. State Coll., 1951, U. Chattanooga, 1962-63; m. Starr Faye Stone, Sept. 29, 1951; children—Hal Bernard, Valerie Starr, Candace Starr, Vanessa Starr. Successively credit and sales mgr., sales mgr., gen. sales mgr., dir. marketing Ch. of God Pub. House, Cleveland, Tenn., 1955—; v.p., dir. Dixon Food Service, Inc., Wilson, N.C. Chmn. Bradley County Bd. Edn., 1970—. Pres. North Cleveland Towers. Served with AUS, 1946-47. Mem. Christian Booksellers Assn. (dir. Colorado Springs 1969-70, sec. 1967-69). Rotarian. Club: Cleveland Optimist (pres. 1966-67). Home: 3550 Edgewood Circle NW Cleveland TN 37311 Office: 1080 Montgomery Av Cleveland TN 37311

DIXON, JACK OWENS, fabricated metal co. exec.; b. Portsmouth, O., Dec. 3, 1929; s. Norman T. and Minnie (Clare) D.; C.E., U. Ala., 1952; m. Cora Lee Barnard, Aug. 31, 1952; children—James Lee, Judy Lynn, Jack Owens, Jr. Jr. engr. Brunswick Corp., Marion, Va., 1952-56; with Panelfab, Inc. (name changed to Panelfab Internat. 1969), Miami, Fla., 1956—, v.p. sales, 1969—. Served with USMC, 1950-51. Mem. Ednl. Industries Assn. (dir. 1969-71), Metal Builders Assn., Alpha Sigma Phi. Republican. Moose. Club: Quarter Back (Hollywood, Fla.). Home: 6960 SW 28th St Miramar FL 33121 Office: 1600 NW LeJeune Rd Miami FL 33126

DIXON, JEANE, realtor, author, columnist, psychic. Realtor, Washington; proponent extrasensory perception. Founder, pres. Children to Children Found., Washington. Recipient Woman of World award Internat. Orphans, Los Angeles, 1969; Internat. L'Enfant award Holy Family Found., Los Angeles, 1970; Internat. Loreto award Loreto (Italy) Shrine, 1970. Author: My Life and Prophecies; Reincarnation and Prayers To Live By; the Call to Glory. Subject of book: A Gift of Prophecy. Address: Children to Children Found 1144 18th St NW Washington DC 20036

DIXON, JOHN ALLEN, JR., judge; b. Orange Tex., Apr. 8, 1920; s. John A. and Louella (Stark) D.; B.A., Centenary Coll., 1940; LL.B., Tulane U., 1947; m. Imogene K. Shipley, Oct. 20, 1945; children—Stella, Diana (Mrs. L. C. Morehead, JR.), Jeanette. Tchr., coach Tallulah High Sch., 1940-42; admitted to La. bar, 1947; pvt. practice law, Shreveport, La., 1947-57; asst. dist atty., Shreveport, 1954-57; judge First Dist. Ct., 1957-68, La. Ct. Appeal, Shreveport, 1968-70; asso. justice La. Supreme Ct., 1971—. Bd. dirs. Woolworth Found., 1968—. Served with AUS, 1942-45. Democrat. Methodist. Mason. Home: 3718 Bobbitt St Shreveport LA 71107 Office: 301 Loyola Av New Orleans LA 70112

DIXON, JOHN WAINWRIGHT, corp. exec.; b. Lexington, Ky., Mar. 12, 1920; s. Thomas H. and Mary (Edmonds) D.; postgrad. George Washington U., 1948-49; A.B., U. Houston, 1948; M.A., U. Miami (Fla.), 1951; m. Doris I. Sowell, May 13, 1961; children—Jacqueline P., Frederick D.R., Clinton M. Asst. to v.p. planning Convair Gen. Dynamics, San Diego, 1956-61; asst. comptroller, dir. systems planning Office Asst. Sec. Def., Washington, 1961-62; dir. planning Ling Temco Vought, Inc., Dallas, 1962-67, became v.p. planning, 1967; now chmn., pres., chief exec. officer LTV, Inc. Mem. Dallas Council World Affairs. Served with AUS, 1941-46. Mem. Am. Ordnance Assn., U.S. Army Assn. Club: Dallas Economists (pres. 1968). Home: 6949 Lake Shore Dr, Dallas, TX 75214 Office: PO Box 5003 Dallas TX 75222

DIXON, MELVIN T., state ofcl. Dir. State of Fla. Div. Vets. Affairs, St. Petersburg. Address: Box 1437 St Petersburg FL 33731*

DIXON, PAUL RAND, govt. ofcl.; b. Nashville, Sept. 29, 1913; s. James David and Sarah (Munn) D.; A.B., Vanderbilt U., 1936, LL.B., U. Fla., 1938; m. Doris Busby, Oct. 11, 1939; children—David Leslie, Paul Randall. Admitted to Tenn. bar, also Fla. bar; asst. football coach U. Fla., 1936-38; trial atty. FTC, 1938-57, chmn., 1961-70, commr., 1970—; chief counsel, staff dir. subcom. antitrust and monopoly U.S. Senate, 1957-61. Area rep. Glen Mar Park Council, Bethesda, Md., 1955-56. Mem. alumni bd. dirs. Vanderbilt U. Served with USNR, 1942-45. Mem. Fed. Bar Assn., Tenn. Soc. (pres. Washington, 1958-59, exec. bd. 1960-61), Vanderbilt U. Alumni Assn. (pres. Washington 1954-55), Am. Bar Assn., Nat. Lawyers Club, Phi Delta Phi, Alpha Tau Omega. Democrat. Methodist. Mason. Clubs: Naval Officers, Kenwood Golf and Country (Bethesda); Nashville Quarterback. Home: 5911 Carlton Lane Glen Mar Park Washington DC 20016 Office: Fed Trade Commn Washington DC 20580

DIXON, RICHARD REMY, city ofcl.; b. New Orleans, Oct. 13, 1911; s. Richard Andrew and Marie (Charles) D.; student Loyola U., New Orleans, 1932-36, Tulane U., 1931-32; m. Mimi Eddy, Sept. 12, 1936; children—Richard Lawrence, Marie F. (Mrs. Frank Perez), Jeanne E. Pub. relations dir. City of New Orleans, 1961-65, exec. sec. to mayor, 1955-61, asst. dir. pub. recreation, 1950-54; mng. dir. New Orleans Municipal Auditorium, 1965—; editor, pub. Westside News, 1932-36. Chmn. Algiers unit A.R.C., 1967-70. Mem. Democratic Party Exec. Com., 1952-69. Trustee Our Lady of Holy Cross Coll., Sunshine Club. Mem. New Orleans C. of C., Young Mens Bus. Club, La. Hist. Soc. and Assn., Internat. House. Author: History of Algiers, 1954; This is Algiers, 1718-1970, the Centennial History of Algiers, 1971. Contbr. articles profl. jours., newspapers. Home: 1236 Shirley Dr New Orleans LA 70114 Office: 1201 St Peter St New Orleans LA 70116

DIXON, SAMUEL MCCLURE, constrn. co. exec.; b. Parrall, W.Va., July 19, 1906; s. Fred Fenwick and Anna (McClure) D.; B.S. in Civil Engring., Tri-State Coll., 1926; m. Sara Courtney, Oct. 12, 1930. Pres., dir. S.M. Dixon Constrn. Co., Warren, Ark., 1947—, Michey's Inc., Warren 1946—, Bradco Constrn. Inc., Warren, 1962—; dir., mem. exec. com. Mo. Pacific R.R. Co., First Nat. Bank Little Rock; dir. First Sav. & Loan, Warren. Chmn., Ark. Contractors Licensing Bd., 1945-70. Pres., YMCA, Warren, 1946-49, bd. dirs., 1945—. Chmn. Oaklawn Jockey Club, Hot Springs, Ark., 1970—. Recipient R.L. Newton award YMCA, 1966. Mem. Asso. Gen. Contractors Am. (pres. Ark. chpt. 1950-51). Methodist. Clubs: Warren Country, Little Rock Country. Office: 307Chestnut St Warren AR 71671

DIXON, WILLIAM VICTOR, dentist; b. Ripley, Miss., Aug. 19, 1916; s. Arthur W. and Etta Love (May) D.; student Miss. State Coll., 1934-38; D.D.S., U. Tenn., 1942; m. Doris Erlene Downs, Mar. 20, 1949; children—Deborah Downs, William Victor. Pvt. practice dentistry, Corinth, Miss., 1946—; dental cons. Corinth Hosp. Bd. dirs. Corinth YMCA, 1955-57. Served to capt. Dental Corps, AUS, 1942-45. Decorated 4 Bronze Stars. Mem. Am., Miss. (dir. 1961-62) dental assns., Northeast Miss. Dental Soc. (sec.-treas. 1957-59), Corinth Dental Soc. (pres. 1952-53), Pierre Fauchard Acad. Rotarian (dir. 1957-59, pres. 1960-61). Club: Hillandale Country (pres. 1954-55). Home: 2209 Willow Rd Corinth MS 38834 Office: 601 Jackson St Corinth MS 38834

DI ZEREGA, MARY ALLENE HEADLEY (MRS. RICHARD GREEN DI ZEREGA), educator; b. Callao, Va., July 13, 1906; d. William Edward and Goldia Allene (Weymouth) Headley; B.S. in Edn., Mary Washington Coll., 1927; postgrad. George Washington U., 1953, Am. U., 1964; m. Richard Green di Zerega, Sept. 21, 1929; children—Mary Allene (Mrs. Dennis John Dee), John William. Founder, dir., tchr. Mrs. Dee's Nursery Sch., 1950-70; Mrs. Dee's Preschool and Kindergarten, 1970—; faculty Marjorie Webster Jr. Coll., Washington, 1957-60; faculty Dunbarton Coll., Washington, 1960—, instr., 1968—, dir. career services, 1968—. First aid instr. A.R.C., 1962—. Active Catholic Youth Activities. Mem. Met. Intercollegiate Sports Assn. for Women (sec. 1963-65, pres. 1965-66), D.A.R., Northumberland Hist. Soc., Kappa Delta Epsilon (sponsor Beta Zeta chpt. 1970—). Home: 2916 New Castle Av Silver Spring MD 20910 also Callao VA 22435 Office: Dunbarton College 2935 Upton St NW Washington DC 20008

DOANE, HAROLD EVERETT, record co. exec.; b. N.Y.C., Oct. 17, 1904; s. Thomas J. and Mary S. (Blaisdell) D.; student Edison Sch. Arts, 1919-23, Columbia, 1924; m. Mary G. Gardner, Dec. 20, 1936 (div. 1941); m. 2d, Faith S. Tracy, Oct. 17, 1943 (div. 1966); children— Priscilla Clare, Richard Henry Tracy; m. 3d Vivian Dillon Dunn, May 3, 1966. Asst. cameraman D.W. Griffith Orienta Point Studios, Mamaroneck, N.Y., 1921-22; radio announcer sta. WGBU, Fulford, Fla., 1925-26, WBNY, N.Y.C., 1926-27, WMCA, 1927 WKBQ, 1927-28; owner radio sta. WCOH, Mt. Vernon, N.Y., 1928-29; research engr., N.Y.C., 1929-35; dir. Gramercy Pictures Corp., N.Y.C., 1935-37; producer Spotlight Prodns., Inc., 1940-41; tech. operations dir. War Finance Com., N.Y. State div. U.S. Treasury Dept., N.Y.C., 1941-44; gen. mgr. Art Records, Miami, Fla., 1945-59, pres., 1959—; dir. Mizmor Internat., Inc., Hollywood, Fla. Mem. Nat. Acad. Rec. Arts and Scis., N.Y. Advt. Club. Republican. Home: 5800 Marlin Dr Plantation Isles FL 33314 Office: 991 SW 40th Av Plantation FL 33314

DOBBINS, INNES WILSON, JR., banker; b. Fulton, Ky., Feb. 16, 1908; s. Innes Wilson and Mignonne (Murphey) D.; A.B., U. Louisville, 1930; m. Anne Cooper Parker, Oct. 26, 1935; children—Anne Cooper, Innes Wilson III, Stephen A. With mortgage loan and trust dept. Ky. Trust Co., Louisville, 1931-33; with Liberty Nat. Bank and Trust Co., Louisville, 1933—, exec. v.p., 1965-67, pres., 1967—, also dir.; dir. W. D. Gatchel & Sons, Bus. Devel. Corp. Ky., Gatchels, Inc. Cons., Louisville Urban Renewal Com., 1963—; mem. Mayor of Louisville's Com. on Urban Renewal, 1954—, chmn. Civic Center Study Com., 1965—, chmn. center city com., 1966-69; mem. consumer relations com. Ky. Emergency Resource Planning Com., 1964; mem. athletic com. U. Louisville, 1965. Pres. Louisville Family and Children's Agy., 1952—, bd. dirs., 1956—; chmn. bd. dirs. U. Louisville Assos., 1966—; bd. dirs. Louisville Central Area, 1966—; bd. govs. Kosair Crippled Children Hosp.; mem. pres.'s civic council Bellarmine Coll., 1964—; trustee Sts. Mary and Elizabeth Hosp. Mem. Louisville C. of C. (dir.), Am. (dir., governing council), Ky. bankers assns. (pres. 1970-71), Delta Upsilon, Presbyn. Mason (32 deg.). Clubs: Louisville Country, Pendennis, Wynn-Stay (Louisville). Home: 347 Mockingbird Valley Rd Louisville KY 40207 Office: 416 W Jefferson St Louisville KY 40202

DOBBINS, JACK HOWARD, educator; b. Coweta, Okla., Dec. 6, 1929; s. Deed and Cleo (Lee) D.; B.S., Northeastern Okla. State Coll., 1951; M.S., Okla. State U., 1956; Ed.D., U. Tulsa, 1969; m. Zula Belle Linder, June 5, 1952; children—Michael Kent, Mark Linder, Howard Jack. Head basketball coach Haskell (Okla.) High Sch., 1951-53; basketball coach Shidler (Okla.) High Sch., 1953-54, Tahlequah (Okla.) High Sch., 1954-59; head basketball coach, athletic dir., chmn. health, phys. edn. div. Northeastern Okla. State Coll., Tahlequah, 1959—. Mem. program com. Tahlequah Little League Baseball, 1965—. Named Tchr. of Year, Northeastern Okla. State Coll., 1968, Alumnus of Year, 1969; Citizen of the Year, Tahlequah, Okla., 1968, Mem. N.E.A., Okla. Edn. Assn., Nat. Assn. Intercollegiate Athletics Basketball Coaches Assn., Basketball Coach of Year 1968, Okla Coaches Assn., Kappa Delta Pi. Mem. Christian Ch. (chmn. deacons 1968-70). Lion. Home: 802 W Downing St Tahlequah OK 74464

DOBBS, GLENN, JR., pub. relations mgr.; b. McKinney, Tex., July 12, 1920; s. Glenn and Mary Tennie (McGraw) D.; B.A., U. Tulsa, 1943, postgrad., 1962-63; m. June Marie Manchester, Jan. 16, 1942; children—Glenn III, John Saxon. Owner stock ranch, Tulsa, 1946-53; profl. football player Bklyn. Dodgers, 1946-47, Los Angeles Dons, 1947-49; profl. football player, backfield coach Sask. Roughriders, 1951-53; football coach U. Tulsa, 1961-68, dir. athletics, 1955-70;

pub. relations mgr. Jim Harrell Pontiac, Tampa, Fla., 1971—. Football coach U. Tulsa at Bluebonnet Bowl, 1964, 65; coach teams in Miami N.-S. Shrine Game, 1964, Blue-Gray games, 1965, 66. Mem. Tampa chpt. Nat. Football Found. and Hall of Fame, 1971—; charter mem. bd. dirs. Okla. Sports Hall of Fame; mem. sports adv. com. Hillsboro Jr. Coll., Tampa, 1971—. Served as 1st lt. USAF, 1943-46. Named to Consensus All— Am. football team, 1942, All-Pro team, 1946, Canadian All-Pro team, 1951, Helms Hall of Fame, 1952; elected to Okla. Sports Hall of Fame, 1970; named Rookie of Year, 1946, Most Valuable Player, All-Am. Conf., 1946, Most Valuable Player, Canadian Football League, 1951, Most Valuable Player, Chgo. Tribune All-Star Game, 1944. Mem. Tampa C. of C., Pi Kappa Alpha. Mem. Christian Ch. Rotarian. Home: 3712 Carrollbrook Rd Tampa FL 33618 Office: 3800 W Hillsborough St Tampa FL 33614

DOBBS, HENRI TALMAGE, JR., ins. exec.; b. Atlanta, Oct. 14, 1915; s. Henri Talmage and Maggie Stanton (Austin) D.; student Emory U., 1932-34; B.C.S., Ga. State U., 1939; m. Ruth Reynolds, Mar. 21, 1941; children— Henri Talmage III, Joan, Nancy, Ruth. With Life Ins. Co. of Ga., Atlanta, 1933—, v.p., treas., 1953-63, exec. v.p. finance, 1963-72, dir., 1948-72. Trustee Trinity Presdl. Trust Fund, Ga. State U. Found. Served with USNR, 1944-45. Chartered financial analyst. Mem. Alpha Kappa Psi, Delta Tau Delta. Presbyn. Rotarian. Club: Capital City (Atlanta). Home: 439 Blackland Rd NW Atlanta GA 30342 Office: 600 W Peachtree St Atlanta GA 30308

DOBBS, HUBERT LEE, hosp. adminstr.; b.Cameron, Tex., Feb. 3, 1908; s. S.H. and Velma (Fuller) D.; grad. Bus. Coll., 1928; LL.D. (hon.), Georgetown (Ky.) Coll., 1960; m. Eugenia Cook, Dec. 22, 1934; children—Velma Gene (Mrs. James Wright), Hubert Lee. Adminstr., Ky. Baptist Hosp., Louisville, 1935—; exec. dir. Hosp. Commn. Ky., 1951—, Hosp. Commn. of Ky. Baptist Hosps., 1965—; pres. Ky. Baptist Hosps., Inc., 1969—. A founder Blue Cross-Blue Shield programs, 1935, bd. dirs., 1935—. Fellow Am. Coll. Hosp. Adminstrs.; mem. Ky. Hosp. Assn. (past pres.), Am. Hosp. Assn., Am. Protestant Hosp. Assn. (pres. 1962—). Baptist. Mason, Rotarian. Club: Big Spring Golf (Louisville). Home: 2539 Seneca Dr Louisville KY 40205 Office: 810 Barret Av Louisville KY 40204

DOBBS, ROBERT LEE, football coach; b. Munday, Tex., Oct. 13, 1922; s. Glenn and Mary T. (McGraw) D.; B.S., U.S. Mil. Acad., 1946; m. Joanne Meeks, July 8, 1947; children—John R., Suzanne, Michael L. Commd. 2d lt. U.S. Air Force, 1946, ret., 1955; asst. coach U.S. Mil. Acad., West Point, N.Y., 1952-54; head coach Tulsa U., 1955-60, Calgary (Ont., Can.) U., 1961-64; head football coach U. Tex. at El Paso, 1965—. Home: 5712 Bonneville St El Paso TX 79912 Office: U Tex El Paso TX 79901

DOBBS, SOLON CARTER, dentist; b. Akron, O., Sept. 13, 1919; s. Solon Levelle and May Plen (Carter) D.; student U. Miss., 1937-39; D.D.S., U. Tenn., 1943; m. Kathleen Hathorn, Apr. 25, 1943 (dec. 1963); children—Solon Carter, Jimmy Gage, Frances Maybelle; m. 2d, Marjorie House, Jan. 3, 1964. Individual practice dentistry, Calhoun City, Miss., 1948—; mem. staff Hillcrest Hosp.; missionary dentist, San Blas Islands, Panama, 1967, 69-72. Chmn. various fund drives. Chmn. A.R.C., Calhoun County, 1960—; v.p. scoutmaster Pushmataha Council Boy Scouts Am., 1950-64. Recipient Silver Beaver award Boy Scouts Am., 1964. Alderman, Calhoun City, 1965-69, mayor pro-tem, 1965-69. Served to lt. Dental Corps USNR, 1943-48; PTO. Mem. North Miss. (past pres.), Miss. (v.p. 1959-60) dental assns. Baptist (deacon). Rotarian, Mason. Editor San Blas Newsletter, 1969-71. Home: Monroe at Wells St Calhoun City MS 38916 Office: Calhoun City MS 38916

DOBBS, WALTER EDWARD, pub. accountant; b. Haskell, Ark., Nov. 18, 1922; s. Dewell Gann, and Hester (Caple) D.; B.S., B.A., U. Ark., 1947; m. Marilyn R. Middleton, Dec. 22, 1946; children—Scott, Jeffrey, Douglas. With R.A. Lile & Co., C.P.A.'s, 1949-56; pub. accountant Hennigen, Croft & Cotham, C.P.A.'s, Little Rock, 1958-60; controller A. Tenenbaum Co., Inc., Little Rock, 1960-63; practice of accounting, Little Rock, 1963-68; partner Dobbs, Albright & Co.; C.P.A.'s, Little Rock, 1968—. Served as 1st lt. USMC, 1943-46. Decorated Purple Heart. Mem. Am. Inst. C.P.A.'s, Ark. Soc. C.P.A.'s (sec. 1971—). Lion (sec. 1959-63). Home: 64 White Oak Lane Little Rock AR 72207 Office: Tower Bldg Little Rock AR 72201

DOBBS, WAYNE, basketball coach; b. Smyrna, Ga., June 12, 1939; s. L.F. and Floy (Herren) D.; B.A., Oglethorpe U., 1961; M.A., Peabody Coll., 1964. Head basketball coach S.W. Dekalb High Sch.; Decatur, Ga., 1961-63, head basketball coach, athletic dir. Bronton Parker Jr. Coll., Mt. Vernon, Ga., 1963-64; Belmont Coll., Nashville, 1964-66; head basketball coach George Washington U., Washington, 1966-70; asst. basketball coach Vanderbilt U., Nashville, 1970—. Author: Basketball's Stunting Defenses, 1964. Home: 1199 Murfreesboro Rd Nashville TN 37217

DOBEN, HYMEN JOSEPH, govt. ofcl.; b. St. Louis, Oct. 3, 1913; s. Joseph and Rose (Wallerstein) D.; A.B., Washington U., St. Louis, 1936, M.A., 1942; M.S. in Pub. Adminstrn., George Washington U., 1968; m. Mary Tropp, Mar. 3, 1946; children—Lois Ann (Mrs. David Hunt), Stephen Michael. With Nat. Youth Adminstrn., Jefferson City, Mo., 1936-42, WPB, Washington, 1942, Tb Soc. St. Louis and St. Louis County, Mo., 1948; with VA, Washington, 1946-47, 48—, mem. adminstr.'s adv. council, 1966—. Pres., Westchester Civic Assn., 1966-67, v.p., 1965, treas., 1964. Served with C.E., AUS, 1943-46; ETO, PTO. Recipient VA Meritorious award for work in chemo-therapy of Tb, 1951. Mem. Am. Statis. Assn., D.C. Sociol. Soc., Alpha Kappa Delta. Jewish religion (mem. Sunday sch. faculty 1965-68). Contbr. articles to profl. lit. Home: 1820 Reedie Dr Silver Spring MD 20902 Office: 810 Vermont Av NW Washington DC 20420

DOBKIN, JOHN HOWARD, govt. ofcl.; b. Hartford, Conn., Feb. 19, 1942; s. Louis P. and Ruth G. (Ward) D.; B.A., Yale, 1964, postgrad. Instut d'Etudes Politiques, 1964-65; J.D., N.Y. U., 1968; m. Immaculada Habsburg, Dec. 18, 1969; 1 son, Carlos Eduardo. Confidential asst. to sec. Smithsonian Instn., Washington. Home: 1343 28th St NW Washington DC 20007

DOBRIANSKY, LEV EUGENE, educator, economist; b. N.Y.C., Nov. 9, 1918; s. John and Eugenia (Greshchuk) D.; B.S. (Charles Hayden Meml. scholar), N.Y.U., 1941, Hirshland Polit. sci. fellow, 1943-44, tchg. fellow econ., 1942-43, M.A., 1943, Ph.D., 1951; LL.D., Munich, Germany, 1952; m. Julia Kusy, June 29, 1946; children—Larisa Eugenia, Paula Jon. Faculty mem. N.Y.U., 1942-48; asso. editor Ukrainian Quar., 1946-58, chmn. editorial bd. 1958—; econs. editor Washington Report, Am. Security Council, 1963—; asst. prof. econ. Georgetown U., 1948-52, became asso. prof. econs. 1952, acting chmn. dept. econs., 1953-54; mem. faculty Nat. War Coll., 1957-58; prof. econs. Georgetown U., 1960—; lectr. on Soviet Union; econ. research and cons.; cons. USIA, also State Dept., 1971—; splty. Thorstein Veblen, Ukraine. Mem. Economists' Nat. Com. on Monetary Policy exec. com., Free World Forum; chmn. National Captive Nations Com., 1959—. Asst. sec. Republican Nat. Conv., 1952; Rep. Nat. Com. 1956; Rep. Com. Program and Progress, 1959. Col. Res. 352d Civil Affairs Mem. Acad. Polit. Sci., Nat. Acad. Econs. and Polit. Sci., Am. Assn. U. Profs., Am. Acad. Polit. and Social Sci., Am., Cath. econ. assns., Am. Finance Assn., Nat. Soc. Study Edn., Shevchenko Sci. Soc., Common Cause, Inc. Ukrainian Cong. Com. Am. (chmn.), Fedn. Am. Central and E. European Descent (exec. v.p.), N.Y.U. Alumni Assn., Gold Key Soc. Beta Gamma Sigma, Delta Sigma Pi. Author: A Philosophico-Economic Critique of Thorstein Veblen. 1943; The Social Philosophical System of Thorstein Veblen, 1950; Free Trade Ideal, 1954; Veblenism, A New Critique, 1957; The Great Pretense, 1956; The Crimes of Khrushchev, 1959; Decisions for a Better America, 1960; Nations, Peoples, and Countries in the USSR, 1964; (with others) Peace and Freedom Through Cold War Victory, 1964; The Vulnerable Russians, 1967; U.S.A. and the Soviet Myth, 1971. Contbr. articles field. Radio and TV appearances. Home: 4520 Kling Dr Alexandria VA 22312 Office: Georgetown U Washington DC 20001

DOBSON, CHARLES WILLIAM, dentist; b. Morganton, N.C., Aug. 11, 1925; s. Cecil Burgin and Mary Virginia (Sparks) D.; B.S., Wake Forest Coll., 1951; D.D.S., Emory U., 1953; m. Stella Flora Smith, Mar. 17, 1956; 1 son, Carl Wilhelm. Commd. 2d lt. Dental Corps U.S. Army, 1952, advanced through grades to lt. col., 1966; chief prosthetics, Nurnberg, Germany, 1956-59; chief hosp. dental service, Ft. Gordon, Ga., 1963-65; chief preventive dentistry, Ft. Gordon, 1967-69; ret., 1969; pvt. practice dentistry, Flat Rock, N.C., 1969—. Pres. parents panel Cerebral Palsy Assn., Columbus, Ga., 1961. Served to lt. (j.g.) Air Corps, USNR, 1943-47. Mem. Am., N.C., Buncombe, Henderson County (pres.) dental assns., Am. Legion, V.F.W., Ret. Officers Assn., Assn. U.S. Army. Presbyn. (deacon). Club: Henderson Country. Author, producer, star TV movie preventive dentistry, U.S. Army, 1968. Home: Route 7 Box 120 Hendersonville NC 28739 Office: Box 458 Flat Rock NC 28731

DOBSON, GWEN ARMSTRONG (MRS. ROBERT V. DOBSON), journalist; b. Fairfax County, Va., May 17, 1930; d. J. Sherman and Helen V. (Dove) Armstrong; grad high sch.; m Robert V. Dobson, Feb. 26, 1949; children—Michael C., Robyn Leslie, John Lindsey. Gen. reporter Alexandria (Va.) Gazette, 1947-50, women's editor 1956-61; Sunday women's editor The Washington Star, 1961-64, women's editor, 1964—. Clubs: Women's Nat. Press, Am. Newspaper Women's (pres.). Home: The Meadows Delaplane VA 22025 Office: 2d and Virginia Av SE Washington DC 20003

DOBSON, JOHN HARRISON, librarian; b. Greeneville, Tenn., June 1, 1924; s. Benjamin H. and Leta S. (McAmis) D.; student Tusculum Coll., 1942-43; B.A., U. Tenn., 1948; M.S., Columbia, 1951. Librarian, Greeneville (Tenn.) High Sch., 1951-54, Tusculum Coll., 1952-54; sr. cataloger U. Tenn. Library, Knoxville, 1954-59, spl. collections librarian, 1959—, curator Estes Kefauver Collection, 1966—, archivist, 1971—. Bd. dirs. Greene County Library, 1954-56. Served with AUS, 1943-46. Mem. Am., Southeastern, Tenn. library assns. Editor U. Tenn. Library Lectures, 1955-57, Tenn. Librarian, 1962-67, U. Tenn. Libraries Occasional Publ., 1970—. Home: 1111 Kenesaw Av Knoxville TN 37919

DOBSON, WILLIAM JACKSON, educator; b. Sherman, Tex., Aug. 8, 1915; s. William Jack and Ida (Eccles) D.; B.A., Austin Coll., 1939; Ph.D., U. Tex., 1946; m. Virginia Lee Smith, Nov. 23, 1944; 1 son, George Ray. Instr. zoology U. Tex., 1942-46, vis. prof., 1954; asst. prof. zoology Miss. State U., 1946, U. Cal. at Los Angeles, 1947; asso. prof. biology Tex. A. and M. U., College Station, 1947-54, prof., 1954—, dir. U. Adj., 1967. Fellow Kerchkoff Marine Labs., Cal. Inst. Tech., 1947; vis. prof. biology U. Houston, 1964. Mem. Am. Soc. Zoologists, Am. Inst. Biol. Scis., Am. Assn. U. Profs., Tex. Acad. Sci., Tex. Assn. Coll. Tchrs. A.A.A.S., Sigma Xi. Home: 1101 Ashburn Av College Station TX 77840

DOBYNS, NORMAN LESTER, can co. exec.; b. Lynchburg, Va., Jan. 13, 1933; s. Lloyd Allen and Helen (Stokes) D.; B.A., Washington and Lee U., 1954; postgrad. Wharton Sch. Bus. U. Pa., 1957-58; masters certificate communication Am. U., 1971; m. Yvonne Elizabeth Fox, Nov. 28, 1958; children—Cynthia Lynn, Barbara Diane. Adminstrv. asst. Rep. T. Downing, Newport News, Va., 1960-67; with Am. Can Co., Washington, 1967—, dir. govt. relations, 1969-71, v.p. govt. relations, 1971—. Pres. West Springfield (Va.) Civic Assn., 1964-67; mem. Fairfax (Va.) Council Cultural Com., 1965-66; pres. Springfield Community Council, 1965-66. Served with AUS, 1954-56. Recipient Savs. Bond Sales award Treasury Dept., 1956. Mem. Washington and Lee Alumni Assn., Phi Beta Kappa, Kappa Sigma. Clubs: University, George Town (Washington). Home: 8501 Brook Rd McLean VA 22101 Office: 1660 L St NW Washington DC 20036

DOCKERY, JAMES WILLIS, JR., architect; b. San Antonio, Oct. 13, 1929; s. James Willis and Cynthia Lee (Cotter) D.; student Baylor U., 1947-49; B.Arch., Tex. A. and M. U., 1958; m. Peggy Jeanne Wickinson, June 4, 1949; children—Laurie (Mrs. Carl Edwin Gulley), Jan, Paul. Planner Continental Can Co., Los Angeles, 1949-53; draftsman Tex. Hwy Dept., Hearn, Tex., 1954-57; architect Noonan, Krocker, Dockery, San Antonio, 1958—. Cons. vocational edn. Harlandale Ind. Sch. Dist., 1971-72. Pres. Winston Churchill High Sch. Band Parents, 1970-71, N.E. ind. Sch. Dist. Band Parents, San Antonio, 1971-72. Mem. Tex. Soc. Architects, A.I.A. Baptist (deacon). Mason (Shriner), Lion. Office: 2002 N St Marys St San Antonio TX 78284

DOCKRAY, GEORGE HENRY, editor; b. Phila., May 4, 1920; s. George L. and Mary (Finan) D.; B.S., Phila. Coll. Textiles and Sci., 1948; m. Louise Stedman, Nov. 9, 1942 (dec. May 1970); children—Karen E., George Henry, Andrea. Textile research asso. Research Inst. Temple U., Phila., 1948-49; textile engr. Nat. Cotton Council Am., Washington, 1949-53; asso. editor Textile Industries, Atlanta, 1953-56, exec. editor, 1956-57, editor, 1957-68, editor-in-chief 1968—; v.p., dir. W.R.C. Smith Pub. Co., Atlanta. Served with AUS, 1941-45. Mem. Fiber Soc., Textile Inst. (Eng.), Am. Assn. Textile Chemists and Colorists, Sigma Delta Chi, Delta Kappa Phi. Home: 4053 Shawnee Lane NE Atlanta GA 30319 Office: 1760 Peachtree Rd NW Atlanta GA 30309

DOCTERMAN, GERT N., mfg. co. exec.; b. Stuttgart, Germany, July 9, 1933; s. Alfred N. and Else (Bornstein) D.; came to U.S., 1955, naturalized, 1961; student LaSalle U. Extension, 1961; B.B.A., Ga. State U., 1967; m. Edna Richards, Feb. 7, 1959; children— Michael, Anna, Mark. Accountant Union Camp Corp., Atlanta, 1956-63; exec. v.p., dir. Vintage Enterprises, Atlanta, 1963—. Mem. Nat. Assn. Accountants, Am. Mgmt. Assn., Ga. Mobile Home Assn. (dir., 1971-72). Home: 350 Lighthouse Point Atlanta GA 30328 Office: 3825 NE Expressway Atlanta GA 30340

DODD, DANIEL PHILLIPS, veterinarian; b. St. Louis, July 8, 1919; s. George Deming and Nellie (Phillips) D.; D.V.M., Ia. State U., 1942; m. LaVern Shattuck, June 15, 1946; children—Barbara Ann, Carol Jean. Research asso. Ia. State Coll., 1946-47; pvt. practice vet. medicine, Washington, 1947—. Served from pvt. to maj., AUS, 1942-46 lt. col. U.S. Army Res., ret. Mem. Am., D.C. vet. med. assns., D.C. Acad. Vet. Medicine, Ia. State U. Vet. Assn., Assn. Mil. Surgeons U.S., Ia. State U. Alumni Assn., Sigma Nu. Republican, Methodist. Lion (local pres., zone chmn, dep. dist. gov.). Home: 9806 Ashby Rd Fairfax VA 22030 Office: 317 Massachusetts Av NE Washington DC 20002

DODD, FADRA REBECCA DEAN, govt. ofcl.; b. Corinth, Miss., Dec. 23, 1924; d. Sam. Richard and Ruby Pearl (Meeks) Dean; student Miss. State U., 1942-43; m. James R. Dodd, Feb. 25, 1945 (div. Dec. 1951); children—James Andre, Myra Kathryn. Dept. circuit clk., part-time 1952-57; legal sec. county atty., 1952-57; solicitor, sec. Mut. Ins. Agy., 1957-60; circuit ct. clk., county registrar Alcorn County, 1960— (all Corinth). Chmn., Alcorn County Polio Assn., Corinth, 1960. Mem. Circuit Clks. Assn. Miss. (legislative com. 1960-62, 67-70, pres. 1965, exec. com. 1966, sec.-treas. 1967-69), Internat. Platform Assn., Bus. and Profl. Women's Club Corinth (corr. sec. 1968-69, chmn. legislative com. 1967—), Miss.-Tenn. Peace Officers Assn., C. of C. Baptist. Home: 2010 E 6th St Corinth MS 38834 Office: Alcorn County Courthouse Waldron St Corinth MS 38834

DODD, JAMES BEAUPRE, librarian; b. Eldorado, Ill., Sept. 21, 1926; s. Thomas Leo and Harris Monroe (Ridenhower) D.; student Vanderbilt U., 1943; B.S., So. Ill. U., 1948, M.S. in Ed., 1950, M.S. in Library Sci., 1952; m. Betty Georgene Barcroft, Sept. 1, 1947; 1 son, James Barcroft. Tchr. English, head lang. arts Olney (Ill.) High Sch., 1948-51; asst. librarian Nat. Reactor Testing Sta. Library AEC, Idaho Falls, Ida., 1952-54, librarian, 1954-55; head information services sect., atomic energy div. Babock & Wilcox Co., Lynchburg, Va., 1955-62; sci. librarian No. Ill. U., DeKalb, 1962-67; grad. librarian, head tech. information service Ga. Inst. Tech., Atlanta, 1967—. Mem. tech. information panel AEC, 1957-62; instr. U. Va. extension at Lynchburg, 1960-61; cons. Office Ill. Supt. Pub. Instrn., 1966, Ga. Tech. Services Program, 1968-71; spl. libraries cons., various companies, 1965—. Chmn. interim com. for City-Wide Pub. Library, Lynchburg, 1961-62, Va. Com. for Nat. Library Week, 1960-61; active Boy Scouts Am. Served with AUS, 1945-46. Mem. Ga., Southeastern library assns., Spl. Libraries Assn. (pres. South Atlantic chap., 1970-71), Phi Kappa Sigma. Presbyn. (elder). Asso. editor Illinois Libraries, 1966-67, The Generator, 1959-60, Metals Div. News, Spl. Libraries Assn., 1958-61. Home: 2898 Rockingham Dr NW Atlanta GA 30327

DODD, LAMAR, artist, educator; b. Fairburn, Ga., Sept. 22, 1909; s. Francis Jefferson and Etta Irene (Cleaveland) D.; student Ga. Sch. Tech., 1926-27, Art Students League of N.Y., 1929-33; L.H.D., LaGrange Coll., 1949; A.F.D., U. Chattanooga, 1959; m. Mary Lehmann, Sept. 25, 1930; 1 dau., Mary Irene. Art tchr., Five Points, Ala., 1927-28; asst. mgr. Spivy-Johnson Co., Birmingham, Ala., 1933-37; asso. prof. art U. Ga., Athens, 1937-40, prof. art, 1940—, head dept. art, 1940—, Regents prof., 1948—, chmn. dept. fine arts, 1960—. Chmn. Ga. Art Commn.; mem. com. on arts U.S. Dept. State. Numerous awards and prizes 1936-57; 2d award, Painting of Year, Pepsi-Cola Art Exhbn., 1947; Va. Biennial Purchase award, 1948; 1st purchase prize Southeastern Art Exhbn., 1949; Nat. Inst. Arts and Letters grantee, 1950; Grumbacher Oil award Fla. Internat. Exhibit, 1952; Edwin Palmer Meml. prize N.A.D., 1953; 1st transparent watercolor prize, Southeastern Art Assn. Exhbn., 1953. Exhbn. Am. Art (N.Y. World's Fair), 1940. Exhibited throughout U.S. 1930-57; Whitney Mus. Ann. Exhbn. (1937-57), Neb. Ann. Exhbn. (1940), Carnegie Internat. (Pittsburgh, 1936), N.Y. World's Fair (1939, 1940), San Francisco Fair (1939); work represented in Met. Mus., N.Y.C., by "Sand, Sea and Sky," also in collections of Telfair Acad., Savannah, High Mus., Atlanta, Pa. Acad. Fine Arts, Whitney Mus. Am. Art, many pvt. collections, One man shows: various mus. and galleries, such as Corcoran Museum, Washington, 1942; Grand Central Art Gallery, N.Y., Rochester Meml. Art Gallery, 1949; Witte Meml. Mus., San Antonio, 1951; and many others. Nat. Academician. Mem. Phi Kappa Phi, Sphinx. Author articles on art subjects. Home: 590 Springdale St Athens GA

DODD, PHILIP W., newspaper reporter. Reporter Chgo. Tribune Press, Washington. Address: 1750 Pennsylvania Av Washington DC 20006*

DODD, RICHARD WINNE, physician; b. Syracuse, N.Y., Mar. 18, 1934; s. Donald Cameron and Irene (Winne) D.; B.S., St. Lawrence U., 1956; M.D., State U. N.Y., 1960; m. Jean Susan Petrock, Nov. 12, 1961; children—Richard Paul, Helen Jeanine. Intern U. Va. Hosp., 1960-61; resident J. Hillis Miller Health Center, Gainesville, Fla., 1961-62; practice family medicine, Daytona Beach, Fla., 1962—; mem. active hosp. staff Halifax Dist. Hosp., 1962—, vice-chmn. family practice resident teaching program, 1970—, mem. credential com. and exec. com., 1969-71. Pres. Mental Health Bd. Volusia County, 1971. Bd. dirs. Daytona Beach Symphony Soc., 1967-70, Fla. Internat. Music Festivals, Inc., 1969. Named Doctor of the Day Fla. Legislature, 1970. Diplomate Am. Acad. Family Physicians. Mem. A.M.A., Fla. Med. Assn., Am., Fla. (ed. com. chmn. 1969-71) acads. gen. practice, Volusia County Med. Soc. (pres. 1971-72), C. of C. (med. facilities com. chmn. 1969). Republican. Editor Volusia County Med. Soc. Bull., 1967-68. Home: 513 Riverview Blvd Daytona Beach FL 32018 Office: 157 S Halifax Av Daytona Beach FL 32018

DODD, ROBERT L., athletic dir. Athletic dir. Ga. Inst. Tech. Office: Athletic Dept Ga Inst Tech Atlanta GA 30332*

DODD, WILLIAM JOSEPH, lawyer; b. Liberty, Tex., Nov. 25, 1909; s. Daniel David and Virginia (Sapp) D.; A.B., Northwestern State Coll., Natchitoches, La., 1934; J.D., La. State U., 1947, postgrad. speech, 1937; m. Verone Ford, Aug. 27, 1939; children—William Ford, Leonard Bruce. Admitted to La. bar, 1947, since practiced in Baton Rouge; partner firm Dodd, Hirsch, Barker, Avant & Wall, 1952—; partner Overton & Dodd, farm operations, 1948—; supt. pub. instrn. State La., 1964—. Mem. La. Ho. of Reps., 1940-48; lt. gov. La., 1948-52, auditor State of La., 1956-60; pres. La. Bd. of Edn.; mem. La. Democratic Central Com., 1952-56, 60—. Dir. Civil Def. La., 1950; rep. Gov. La. on La. Tidelands Claim, Washington, 1948-50. Served with AUS, 1942-45. Mem. Am., La. bar assns., Am. Judicature Soc., La. Tchrs. Assn. (pres., council), La. P.T.A. (legislative chmn.), Northwestern State Coll. Alumni Assn. (v.p.). Baptist. Mason (Shriner), Elk. Home: 4472 Whitehaven St Baton Rouge LA 70808 Office: 249 Government St Baton Rouge LA 70802

DODDS, JOSEPH J., surgeon; b. Farrell, Pa., Feb. 9, 1929; s. Joseph Burns and Julia (Scott) D.; B.S., Univ. Pitts., 1951, M.D., 1955; m. Vina Mae Elder, June 19, 1954; children—Lynn Eider, Sandra Allison. Intern, Shadyside Hosp., Pitts., 1955-56; resident Mayo Clinic, Rochester, Minn., 1958-62; practice medicine specializing in surgery, Chattanooga, 1962—; dir. S.E. Tenn. Area Health Edn. Center, Inc., Profl. Systems Inc., Chattanooga. Mem. Tenn. Manpower Commn. Bd. dirs. Ga.-Tech. Regional Health Commn. Served with USAF, 1956-58. Diplomate Am. Bd. Surgery. Fellow A.C.S., Southeastern Surg. Congress, Am. Soc. Abdominal Surgeons, Royal Soc. Health, Pan. Pacific Surg. Assn., Pan. Am. Med. Assn.; mem. A.M.A., So. Med. Assn., Fedn. Am. Hosps. (pres. 1971-72, dir.), Tenn., Chattanooga and Hamilton County med. socs. Republican. Presbyn. Lion. Club: Capital. Home: 1105 E Brow Rd Signal Mountain TN 37377 Office: 525 McCallie Av Chattanooga TN 37402

DODDS, STANLEY, newspaper editor. Bus. financial editor Times-Picayune and States-Item, New Orleans. Address: 3800 Howard Av New Orleans LA 70140*

DODEK, SAMUEL MAYER, physician; b. Chgo., June 14, 1902; s. Mayer B. and Lena (Ettinger) D.; A.B., George Washington U., 1923; M.D., Jefferson Med. Coll., 1927; M.A. in Obstetrics, Western Res. U., 1932; m. Miriam Joyce Selker, Apr. 13, 1936; children—Marianne (Mrs. Benjamin Brauzer), Samayla (Mrs. John M. Deutch). Intern, Albert Einstein Med. Center, Phila., 1927-29; asst. house surgeon N.Y. Lying-in Hosp., N.Y.C., 1929; resident, fellow, teaching fellow dept. obstetrics and gynecology Western Res. U., Cleve., 1929-32; practice medicine specializing in obstetrics and gynecology, Washington, 1932-—; sr. attending staff George Washington Hosp.; chmn. dept. obstetrics and gynecology Washington Hosp. Center, 1959-64, now sr. adv. staff; faculty George Washington U. Sch. Medicine, 1932-—, clin. prof. obstetrics and gynecology, 1960-72, prof. emeritus, 1972-—. Chmn. med. adv. com. Planned Parenthood, Inc., 1962-67. Bd. dirs. Research Found. Washington Hosp. Center. Chmn., Obstet. Bd. D.C., 1965-—; chmn. allied professions group United Jewish Appeal, 1950-53; mem. profl. com. United Givers Fund, 1952. Diplomate Am. Bd. Obstetrics and Gynecology. Fellow A.C.S., Am. Coll. Obstetrics and Gynecology; mem. Am. Fertility Soc., A.M.A., Med. Soc. D.C. (1st v.p. 1954, chmn. profl. conduct and ethics com. 1970-72), Washington Gynecol. Soc. (pres. 1953), So. Med. Assn., Sigma Xi. Clubs: Woodmont Country, Internat. Med., Bass Rocks Beach, Nat. Press, George Washington University. Author: Shakespere's Knowledge of Medicine. Cons. editor Gynecology; Am. Jour. Proctology; editorial staff Obstetric-Gynecology News. Contbr. numerous articles in field to profl. jours. Invented instrument for study human uterine physiology, 1932; co-developer isotope localization of human placentia, 1963. Home: 2930 Woodland Dr Washington DC 20008 Office: 5480 Wisconsin Av Washington DC 20015

DODGE, DONALD W., artist; b. New Albany, Ind., Apr. 21, 1934; B.S., Ind. U., 1956, also postgrad.; M.A., U. Louisville, 1957. One man shows Art Center Assn. U. Louisville, 1958, Moorehead State Coll., 1960, Downtown Gallery, New Orleans, Ohio U., Cin. Art Museum, So. Ind. Studio Gallery, 1961, Bellarmine Coll., 1962, U. Ala., 1963, Ligoa Duncan Gallery, 1964, others; represented in pvt. collections; now head art dept., prof. art Georgetown Coll. Recipient Nat. Soc. Arts and Letters award, 1962; Prix de Paris, 1963, 64. Address: 315 Warrendale Ct Georgetown KY*

DODGE, HARRY ROBERT, educator; b. St. Louis, Sept. 17, 1929; s. Harry Varnum and Jeanne (Groeniger) D.; B.S., Ohio State U., 1951, M.B.A., 1954, Ph.D., 1962; m. Donna Jean Broughman, Aug. 6, 1960; children— Melody Jean, Kevin Robert. Instr., U. Neb., Lincoln, 1954-55, Ohio State U., Columbus, 1955-57; asst. prof. Fla. State U., Tallahassee, 1957-58; research asso. Knox Assos., Toledo, 1958-59; asst. prof. Cal. State U. at Los Angeles, 1959-64; asso. prof. U. Tex., Arlington, 1964-65; prof. marketing Memphis State U., 1965-—. Marketing cons. bus. firms, banks, 1956-—. Fellow in bus. So. Pacific Co., 1960, So. Cal. Edison, 1964. Served to capt AUS, 1951-53. Mem. Am. Marketing Assn. (sec. Memphis chpt. 1969-70), Beta Gamma Sigma. Author: Industrial Marketing, 1970. Home: 5450 Heritage Av Memphis TN 38118

DODGE, JOSEPH JEFFERS, artist, art mus. adminstr.; b. Detroit, Aug. 9, 1917; s. Joseph Morrell and Julia (Jeffers) D.; grad. with honors Choate Sch., 1936; B.S. in Fine Arts with honors, Harvard, 1940; postgrad. Wayne U., 1941; m. Jane Halliday Pike, 1938 (div. 1947); m. 2d, Dorothy MacArthur, Sept. 24, 1949; children—Joseph Morrell II, Dorothy, Julia, Jeffers, Lisa. Curator, Hyde Collection, Glen Falls, N.Y., also tchr. drawing and painting, 1942-62; dir. Cummer Gallery Art, Jacksonville, Fla., 1962-—. Tchr. art history Hamilton Coll., 1947, Adirondack Community Coll., 1961-62; tchr. drawing and painting Ft. Edward Art Center, 1952-62; exhibited one-man shows at Wildenstein Galleries, N.Y.C., Hirschl and Adler Galleries, N.Y.C., Cummer Gallery Art, Jacksonville, Fla., Tampa (Fla.) Art Inst., Group Gallery, Jacksonville, Fla., Columbus (Ga.) Mus. Arts and Crafts, George Thomas Hunter Gallery Art, Chattanooga, Ga. Mus. Art, U. Ga., Athens, Columbia (S.C.) Mus. Art, Jacksonville (Fla.) U., Mint Mus., Charlotte, N.C., U. Fla., Gainesville, Gibbes Gallery, Charleston, S.C. Mem. Fla. Art Mus. Dirs. Assn., Jacksonville C. of C. (fine arts com.), Historic Preservation Council Jacksonville, Jacksonville Council Arts (pres. 1968-69), Am. Inst. Interior Designers. Rotarian. Clubs: Harvard, Torch, University, Fla. Yacht (Jacksonville). Home: 1836 Elizabeth Pl Jacksonville FL 32205 Office: 829 Riverside Av Jacksonville FL 32204

DODSON, BERTRAM FELIX, exterminating co. exec.; b. Lynchburg, Va., June 9, 1927; s. Albert Sydnor and Hallie Turpin (Holland) D.; student pub. schs.; m. Dorothy Lee Hayes, Mar. 8, 1952; children—Bertram Felix, Karen Lee, Bonny Lynn. Founder, chief exec. officer Dodson Bros. Exterminating Co., Inc., Lynchburg, 1944-—, pres., chmn. bd. 41 branches; owner, officer Dodson Florist, Lynchburg, 1961-—, Dodson Real Estate, Lynchburg, 1962-—, Dodson Farms and Aireactor Chem., Lynchburg, 1966-—, Hapiday Motor Lodge, Pearisburg, Va., 1963-—. Pres. Va. Counties Assn., 1960-61, Campbell County Rescue Squad, 1969-70; mem. P.T.A., 1960-71. Pres. Campbell County Bd. Suprs., 1958-61. Bd. dirs. Lynchburg United Fund, 1964-65, A.R.C., 1963-64, Lynchburg Gen. Hosp., 1957-64, U. Va. Extension Coll. at Lynchburg, 1960-63. Mem. C. of C., Pest Control Assn. Va. (pres. 1954-55), Nat. Pest Control Assn., Ruritan. Presbyn. Mason (Shriner), Lion, Elk. Club: Lynchburg Track. Home: 1022 Oakmont Circle Lynchburg VA 24502 Office: 3712 Campbell Av Lynchburg VA 24505

DODSON, DURWOOD RANDOLPH, supt. schs.; b. Picton, Tex., Sept. 3, 1915; s. Joel Marshall and Della Lou (Randolph) D.; B.S., E. Tex. State U., 1937, M.S., 1947; m. Joe Louise Amos, June 2, 1938; children— Keith, Mark. Supt. schs. Rural High Sch., Tahoka, Tex., 1941-43, Merit, Tex., 1946-51, Roxton, Tex., 1951-57, Honey Grove, Tex., 1958-65, Cameron, Tex., 1965-—. Mem. faculty So. Meth. U., 1946. Active Community Chest, 1966-71. Served with AUS, 1943-45. Mem. Am., Tex. assns. sch. adminstrs., Tex. State Tchrs. Assn., Phi Delta Kappa. Mason, Lion, Rotarian. Home: 702 E 7th St Cameron TX 76520 Office: PO Box 712 Cameron TX 76520

DODSON, EUGENE BENEDICT, TV exec.; b. Woodward, Okla., Nov. 25, 1912; s. William Benedict and Minnie (Richard) D.; B.A., U. Okla., 1933; m. Grace Beaulieu, Apr. 4, 1941; children—Jean Ann (Mrs. Jean D. Hibbs), George. Reporter, Okla. News, Oklahoma City, 1933-34, Daily Oklahoman, Oklahoma City, 1934-42; reporter, deskman Asso. Press, Washington, 1945-47; news editor Daily Transcript, Norman, (Okla.), 1947-49; promotion mgr. WKY Television System, Oklahoma City, 1949-51, adminstrv. asst. 1951-54, dir. radio operations, 1954-55, asst. mgr., 1955-56, acting mgr., 1956-57; mgr. WSFA-TV, Montgomery, Ala., 1957-58, WTVT, Tampa, Fla., 1958-—; exec. v.p. WKY Television System, Inc., 1970-—. Past mem. CBS-TV affiliates adv. bd. for Dist. No. 3. Campaign chmn. Tampa United Fund, 1965, pres., 1968-69; pres. Tampa Horse Show Assn., 1966-—, Tampa Citizens Safety Council, 1965, Tampa Philharmonic Assn., 1962-66; fellow U. Tampa. Bd. dirs. U.S. Fla. Found. Served with AUS, 1942-45. Decorated Legion of Merit (U.S.); Order of Vasco Nunez de Balboa (Republic of Panama); named Citizen of Yr., Civitan Club, Tampa, 1967. Mem. Fla. Assn. Broadcasters (dir. 1961-68, past pres.), Broadcast Pioneers, Nat. Press Club, Greater Tampa C. of C. (pres. 1969-70), Sigma Delta Chi. Episcopalian. Rotarian (pres. Tampa club 1966-67). Clubs: University, Tampa Yacht and Country, Palma Ceia Golf and Country. Home: 10703 Carrollwood Dr Tampa FL 33618 Office: PO Box 22013 Tampa FL 33622

DODSON, JAMES MARVIN, ednl. adminstr.; b. Bonnieville, Ky., Mar. 29, 1910; s. Clive and Cola (Riggs) D.; A.B., Western Ky. U., 1936, M.A., 1942; Ph.D., Ind. U., 1960; m. Narvilla Burns, Dec. 28, 1931; 1 dau., Barbara Ann (Mrs. Joseph Macaluso). Classroom tchr., Bonnieville, Ky., 1931-38; prin. Meml. High Sch., Hardyville, Ky., 1938-42; supt. Hart County Schs., 1942-43, Horsecave Schs., 1943-48; dir. pupil transp. Dept. Edn., 1948-50; dir. pub. relations Ky. Edn. Assn., Louisville, 1950-54, exec. sec., 1954-—. Mem. N.E.A., Nat. Council State Edn. Assns., Horace Mann League, Am. Assn. Sch. Adminstrs., Sigma Phi Sigma, Phi Delta Kappa. Methodist. Mason (Shriner). Author: Desirable Practices in Promoting State Legislation, 1960. Home: 925 Packard Av Louisville KY 40217 Office: 101 W Walnut St Louisville KY 40202

DODSON, JOHN WILLIAM, county extension agt.; b. Cin., Apr. 15, 1910; s. William Homer and Lillie (Bond) D.; student La. Poly, Inst., 1929-32; B.S. in Agr., U. Ark., 1937; postgrad., 1941, 50, 63, 66; m. Annie Ruth Askew, Dec. 12, 1939; 1 dau., Ruth Ann (Mrs. Harry Keith Wilson), Asst. in agrl. conservation Clark County (Ark.), 1937-38; asst. county agt. Clark and Quachita counties, 1938-39; county extension agr. Columbia County (Ark.), 1939-47, Johnson County, 1947-53, Drew County, Monticello, 1953-—. Area bd. mem. Boy Scouts Am., Monticello, 1959-60; tech. adviser Drew County Fair and Livestock Show, 1953-—. Recipient Distinguished Service award Nat. Assn. County Agrl. Agts., 1953, Found scholarship Ark. County Agts., 1967. Mem. Ark. County Agts. Assn., Agrl. Extension Workers Credit Assn., County Agrl. Stabilization and Conservation Service, Monticello Pink Tomato Growers Inc. (bd. mem. 1957-—), Farm Bur., Monticello C. of C. (chmn. agrl. com. 1957-68), Squanto, Alpha Lambda Tau, Epsilon Sigma Phi. Presbyn. (deacon, chmn. bd. deacons 1964, elder). Mason. Home: 512 S Main St Monticello AR 71655 Office: Box 508 Courthouse Monticello AR 71655

DODSON, ROBERT W., editor. City editor Ledger-Star, Norfolk, Va. Office: 150 W Brambleton Av Norfolk VA 23501*

DOENGES, RUDOLPH CONRAD, educator; b. Tonkawa, Okla., Dec. 7, 1930; s. Rudolph Soland and Helen (Lower) D.; A.B. magna cum laude, Harvard, 1952, M.B.A., 1954; D.Bus. Adminstrn., U. Colo., 1965; m. Ellen Ione Gummere, Oct. 5, 1963; children—Rudolph Conrad, John Soland. Marketing analyst Ford Motor Co., Dearborn, Mich., 1954; gen. mgr. Doenges-Long Motors Inc., Colorado Springs, Colo., 1958-61; asst. prof. U. Tex. Grad. Sch. Bus., Austin, 1964-67, asso. prof., 1967-—, asso. dean, 1972-—. Dir. Doenges-Glass, Inc., Aurora, Colo. Served to lt. (j.g.) Supply Corps, USNR, 1954-58. Harvard Nat. scholar, 1948-54; Ford Found. Dissertation fellow, 1963-64. Mem. Am. Econ. Assn., Am., Southwestern (pres.) finance assns., Financial Mgmt. Assn., Midwest Bus. History Conf., Phi Beta Kappa, Beta Gamma Sigma, Delta Sigma Pi. Republican. Methodist (adminstrv. bd. 1969-—). Rotarian. Author: (with others) Case Problems in Financial Management, 1968; (with G.A. Jentz) Consumer Credit in Texas, 1969. Editor: (with H.A. Wolf) Readings in Money and Banking, 1968; asso. editor finance Social Sci. Quar., 1966-—. Home: 3500 Hillbrook Circle Austin TX 78731

DOENGES, WILLIAM CONRAD, mem. Democratic Nat. Com.; b. Maple Park, Ill., May 24, 1907; s. Rudolph Conrad and Lulu (Soland) D.; A.B., Oklahoma City U., 1929; m. Elizabeth Shannon, Oct. 23, 1929; children—William Soland, Robert Shannon, James, Rebecca. Pres. Doenges Inc., Tulsa, 1946-—; v.p. Heildis, Inc., Tulsa, 1948-—; ind. oil and gas producer, Okla., Kan. and Tex. Den-Tex Oil Co., Dallas; partner Shibley Oil Co., Bristow, Okla., Langford Oil Co., Dewey, Okla.; dir. Home Savs. & Loan Assn., Bartlesville, Okla., Century Geophys. Co., Inc., Tulsa, Bartlesville Ford Inc., Coffeyville Motor Co., Tonkawa Motor Co. Mem. Dem. Nat. Com. for Okla., 1951-—. Trustee Oklahoma City U. Mem. Nat. (dir.), Okla. (pres.) amateur athletic unions, Olympic Com., Sigma Alpha Epsilon. Home: Box 339 Bartlesville OK 74003 also 5th and Detroit Tulsa OK 74003

DOGGETT, LOWELL, judge; b. Council Grove, Kan., Jan. 6, 1917; s. Walter Martin and May (Jasper) D.; A.B., U. Okla., 1938, LL.B., 1940; m. Shirley Ruth Jackson, June 6, 1947; children—Bruce Jackson, Robert Lowell. Admitted to Okla. State bar, 1940; pvt. practice law, Ponca City, Okla., 1940-48 county atty. Kay County Okla., 1948-52; county judge Kay County, Okla., 1959-69; asso. dist. judge 8th Judicial Dist. Okla., 1969-71, dist. judge, 1971-—. Pres., No. Okla. Coll. Found., 1966; pres. Ponca City YMCA, 1957-58; pres. Kay County Tb. Assn., 1950-51. Served with AUS, World War II. Mem. Okla. Assn. County Judges (pres. 1966-67), Okla. Assn. County Bar Pres. (pres. 1963), Kay County (pres. 1962), Am., Okla. bar assns., Am. Judicature Soc., Nat., Okla. councils juvenile ct. judges, Ponca City C. of C., Kay Council Community Services, Kay County Assn. Child Guidance, Am. Legion (comdr. 1953). Methodist (lay leader). Club: Exchange (dist. gov. 1956). Home: 2509 Robin Rd Ponca City OK 74601 Office: Kay County Courthouse PO Box 424 Newkirk OK 74647

DOGGETT, WESLEY OSBORNE, educator; b. Brown Summit, N.C., Jan. 24, 1931; s. Banks Chandler and Elizabeth (Dobbs) D.; B. Nuclear Engring., N.C. State U., 1952; B.E.E., 1953; M.A. in Physics, U. Cal. at Berkeley, 1954, Ph.D. in Nuclear Physics, 1956; m. Leonor Pinzon, June 13, 1953; children—Kevin W., Marc G., Norman A., Eric L., Valerie G., Nydia L., Steven N., Glen P. Physics research asso. U. Cal. at Berkeley, 1954-56; tech. project coordinator Air Force nuclear engring. test reactor Wright Air Devel. Center, Ohio, 1956-58; faculty N.C. State U., Raleigh, 1958-—, prof. physics, 1962-—, asst. dean Sch. Phys. Scis. and Applied Math., 1964-68. Dir. Troxler Electronic Labs., Inc., Raleigh; cons. Research Triangle Inst., 1962-—, Office Civil Def., 1963-—. Served from 2d lt. to capt. USAF, 1956-58. NSF predoctoral fellow, 1952-54. Recipient N.C. Acad. Sci. Poteat award, 1961-62, Sigma Xi Research award, 1962. Mem. Am. Phys. Soc., Am. Inst. Physics, Am. Assn. Physics Tchrs., Am. Nuclear Soc., A.A.A.S., Am. Soc. Engring. Edn., Sigma Xi, Phi Kappa Phi (chpt. pres. 1963). Research in plasma physics. Home: 2452 Oxford Rd Raleigh NC 27608

DOGGETT, WILLIAM TATE, architect; b. High Point, N.C., Aug. 25, 1939; s. Joseph Granville and Nannie Naomi (Tate) D.; student U. Ill., 1962; B.Arch. N.C. State U., 1966; m. Elizabeth Ann Ford, July 20, 1963; children—Laura Elizabeth, Christy Diane. Individual practice architecture W.T. Doggett, A.I.A., Waynesville, N.C., 1967-70; partner Tolson-Doggett, Asso. Architects, Raleigh, N.C., and Waynesville, 1970-71; partner Tolson-Doggett-Buie, asso. architects and planning cons., 1971-—. Mem. A.I.A., Waynesville C. of C. Home: Box 392-B Route 1 Waynesville NC 28786 Office: 232 North Main St Waynesville NC 28786

DOHERTY, HERBERT JOSEPH, JR., educator, historian; b. Jacksonville, Fla., Feb. 4, 1926; s. Herbert Joseph and Marie (Bishop) D.; B.A., U. Fla., 1948, M.A., 1949; Ph.D., U.N.C., 1953. Mem. faculty U. Fla., 1949-50, 53-—, chmn. social scis., 1963-—, prof. history and social sci., 1964-—; lectr. Far East div. U. Md., 1959-60, European div., 1960-61. Mem. adv. commn. Fla. Bd. Archives and History, 1968-70; adv. bd. Fed. Records Center, Atlanta, 1967-—. Served with USAAF, 1944-46. Mem. Am. Assn. U. Profs., Orgn. Am. Historians, Am., So., Fla. (bd. dirs. 1962-72, pres. 1968-70, editor quar. 1962-64) hist. assns., Phi Beta Kappa, Phi Kappa Phi, Phi Alpha Theta, Delta Tau Delta, Fla. Blue Key. Democrat. Author: Richard Keith Call: Southern Unionist, 1961; The Whigs of Florida, 1845-1954, 1959; also articles. Home: 415 NE 5th Av Gainesville FL 32601

DOHERTY, JAMES EDWARD, govt. ofcl.; b. Oak Park, Ill., Jan. 12, 1929; s. Daniel Joseph and Alice (Proteau) D.; B.S. cum laude, Loyola U., Chgo, 1951; m. Mary Jo Kennedy, Dec. 7, 1964; 1 son, Michael James. Self-employed pub. relations, free lance writer, ind. theatrical prodn. J.D. Prodns., Oak Park, 1956-66; mem. staff TV news dept. WSB, Atlanta, 1966-69; pub. information officer Ga. Water Quality Control Bd., Atlanta, Ga., 1967-—; chmn. copy com. The Georgia Operator ofcl. organ Ga. Water & Pollution Control Assn., 1969-—; pub. relations cons. Tech. Assn. Pulp and Paper Industry, 1971-—; dir. Continental Set Prodns., 1968-—. Vice-chmn. publicity The Broadcast Good Music Com. 1968-—. Mem. Water Pollution Control Fedn., Ga. Water and Pollution Control Assn. Playwright: Whimsy on a Pogo Stock, 1964. Home: 2548 Wood Trail Lane Decatur GA 30033 Office: 47 Trinity Av SW Atlanta GA 30334

DOHERTY, JAMES PAUL, banker; b. Central Falls, R.I., Dec. 20, 1914; s. James and Mary (Brady) D.; Ph.B., Providence Coll., 1935; m. Miriam Louise Barnett, Mar. 3, 1943; children—James Paul, Mary (Mrs. John F. Lally III), Miriam, Patrick, John. Tchr. high sch., Central Falls, 1935-41; v.p., mgr. Cotton Products Co., Inc., 1945-58; v.p., trust officer Am. Bank and Trust Co., Opelousas, La., 1958-—. Vice pres. Evangeline Area council Boy Scouts Am., 1948-—; sec. Krotz Springs Port Commn., 1966-—; pres. Acad. Immaculate Conception Parent Tchr. Club, 1960-61. Bd. dirs. Regional Export Expansion Commn. Served to capt. AUS, 1941-45. Recipient Sertoma Service to Mankind award, 1965; Silver Beaver award Boy Scouts Am., 1969; named Citizen of Year, C. of C., 1966, Man of Year, Acad. Immaculate Conception, 1962. K.C. (3 deg, 4 deg). Roman Catholic (mem. ch. council 1968-—). Home: Route 1 Box 30 Opelousas LA 70570 Office: PO Box 271 Opelousas LA 70570

DOHERTY, RICHARD P., economist, indsl. relations and TV exec.; b. Wilton, N.H., May 5, 1905; s. Edward and Myra J. (Duval) D.; A.B. magna cum laude, Clark U., 1925; A.M., Brown U., 1926, grad. fellow, 1927-28; m. Dorothea M. Sullivan, May 30, 1933; 1 dau., Judith Dale. Prof. econs. Boston U., 1928-46, head dept., 1940-45; v.p., dir. labor relations Nat. Assn. Radio and TV Broadcasters, 1946-54; pres. TV-Radio Mgmt. Corp., 1954-—, TV-Radio Properties Corp., 1964-—. U.S. mgmt. del. ILO, Geneva, Switzerland, 1949-67; mgmt. mem. Internat. Social Security Experts Com., 1962-70; industry mem. WSB, 1951-52; founder, exec. dir. Indsl.Relations Council Met. Boston, 1940-46; industry adviser Pres. Truman's Labor Mgmt. Conf., 1945. Dir. Mass. State Civil Def., 1941-45; chmn. East Coast Civil Def. Council, 1942-45. Awarded Pres. Certificate of Merit for civil def., 1945. Mem. Am. Econs. Assn., Am. Assn. Bus. Economists, Broadcast Pioneers, Broadcasters club Assn., Phi Beta Kappa. Clubs: Circumnavigators, Broadcasters (Washington). Author: Interpretation Business and Financial Conditions, 1934; Structure American Business, 1937; Economic Organization of Society, 1939; Essentials of Collective Bargaining, 1946; Broadcasting and Business Cycles, 1950; Taft Hartley Act and Broadcasting Industry, 1948; Wage Policy and Administration, 1954; Pitfalls in Collective Bargaining, 1955; TV; America's Growth Industry, 1964; Appraisal of the International Labor Organization, 1965. Contbr. articles to profl. jours. Home: Bleak House Downs Dennis MA 02638 Office: 1735 DeSales St NW Washington DC 20036

DOHERTY, ROBERT J., museum dir. Dir. Allen R. Hite Art Inst., U. Ky., Louisville. Address: Allen R Hite Art Inst Belknap Campus 3d St U Ky Louisville KY 40208*

DOHERTY, THOMAS ROSS, dentist; b. Pine Bluff, Ark., Aug. 13, 1938; s. Neumie Ray and Pocahontas (Guthrie) D.; student Ark. A. and M. U., 1956-59; D.D.S., Washington U., 1964; m. Ruth Esther Willoughby, Dec. 31, 1963; children—Christopher Michael, Johnathan Maxwell. Asso. of Drs., Pine Bluff, Dumas, Ark., 1966-67; pvt. practice dentistry, Pine Bluff, 1967-—; mem. dental staff Jefferson, Davis hosps., sec. dental staff, 1968. Chmn., Nat. Children's Dental Health Week, 1968-69; dental dir. Office Econ. Opportunity, 1967-—. Served to capt. Dental Corps, AUS, 1964-66. Diplomate Am. Bd. Oral Implantology. Mem. Am. Dental Assn., Ark., Jefferson County, Armed Forces dental socs., Acad. Gen. Dentistry, Flying Dentists, Quiet Birdmen, Xi Psi Phi. Mason. Clubs: World Traders (Los Angeles); Little Rock Hanger. Home: 904 Wisconsin St Pine Bluff AR 71601 Office: 1700 Doctors Dr Pine Bluff AR 71601

DOKE, MARSHALL J., JR., lawyer; b. Wichita Falls, Tex., June 9, 1934; s. Marshall J. and Mary Jane (Johnson) D.; B.A. magna cum laude, Hardin-Simmons U., 1956; LL.B. magna cum laude, So. Meth. U., 1959; m. Betty Orsini, June 2, 1956; children—Gregory J., Michael J., Laetitia Marie. Admitted to Tex. bar, 1959; practiced in Dallas, 1959, 62-—; partner Rain, Harrell, Emery, Young & Doke, 1965-—. Lectr. govt. contract law So. Meth. U., 1965-—. Mem. bd. visitors So. Meth. U. Law Sch., Dallas, 1966-69; mem. bd. young assos. Hardin-Simmons U., Abilene, Tex., 1964-69; bd. dirs. Hope Cottage-Children's Bur., Dallas, 1964-—, pres., 1969-70. Served with Judge Adv. Gen.'s Corps, AUS, 1959-62. Mem. Am. (chmn. sect. pub. contract law 1969-70, mem. ho. of dels. 1970-—), Fed., Dallas bar assns., State Bar Tex. Methodist (chmn. com. edn. 1967-68). Home: 9473 Spring Branch Dallas TX 75238 Office: Republic Bank Tower Dallas TX 75201

DOLAN, JACQUELYN WARREN (MRS. WILLIAM WILSON DOLAN), editor; b. Gettysburg, Pa., Sept. 28, 1937; d. Elmer Willard and Gladys (Palmer) Warren; B.A., U. Miami, 1958; postgrad. Am. Inst. Pub. Relations, Chgo., 1970; m. William Wilson Dolan, July 8, 1961. Sales rep., asst. prodn. McMurray Printing Co., Miami, Fla., 1958-59; publicity asst. Fla. Power & Light Co., Miami, 1960-62, publicity rep., 1963-70, communications specialist, 1971-—, mng. editor Sunshine Service News, 1966-69, editor, 1970-—. Recipient Best Feature Story award Fla. Mag. Assn., 1966, Best Picture Story award, 1967, Gen. Excellence award for an internal mag., 1966, 67, 70, 71; Gold Quill award Am. Assn. Indsl. Editors, 1970. Mem. Internat. Assn. Bus. Communicators, Am. Women in Radio and TV, Theta Sigma Phi (pres. Miami chpt. 1967-68; co-chmn. nat. conv. 1971), Alpha Sigma Epsilon, Delta Delta Delta. Home: 6840 SW 129th Terrace Miami FL 33156 Office: Fla Power & Light Co PO Box 3100 Miami FL 33101

DOLCE, CARL JOHN, coll. dean; b. New Orleans, June 3, 1928; s. John and Nina (Puglia) D.; B.A., Tulane U., 1947; M.Ed., Loyola U. of South, 1955; Ed.D., Harvard, 1963; m. Nancy Lockwood, July 27,

1955; children—Carla, John. Elementary sch. tchr. 1948-54; secondary sch. tchr., 1954-55; acting supr. textbooks, 1955; prin. jr. high sch., 1955-63; faculty Harvard, 1963-65; supt. pub. schs. City of New Orleans, 1965-69; dean Sch. Edn., N.C. State U., 1969—. Mem. vis. com. Harvard Grad. Sch. Edn., 1967—; mem. adv. com. for new ednl. media U.S. Office Edn, 1966-68; mem. Nat. Citizens Com. for Pub. TV, 1967-68, Inst. for Services to Edn., Inc., Washington, 1967—. Served with AUS, 1951-53. Home: 801 Macon Pl Raleigh NC 27609

DOLCE, JOSEPH DOMENICK, dentist; b. N.Y.C., May 28, 1929; s. Joseph and Lily Ann (Idaspe) D.; B.S., U. Ala., 1953; postgrad. Harvard Sch. Dental Medicine, 1950-52; D.M.D., U. Ala. Sch. Dentistry, 1956; m. Judith Anne Dennis, Aug. 23, 1952; children—Jeffrey Joseph, Stephen Philip. Pvt. practice dentistry, Birmingham, Ala., 1958—; mem. staff Childrens Hosp., Birmingham. Tchr. clin. dentistry Children's Hosp., Birmingham, intermittently 1960-65. Served with USAF, 1956-58. Mem. Am., Ala. dental assns., Birmingham Dist. Dental Soc., Birmingham Soc. Advanced Dentistry (pres. 1971), Acad. Gen. Dentistry, Xi Psi Phi. Presbyn. (deacon 1967-71). Clubs: Sailing, Great Dane (pres. 1970-72) (Birmingham). Home: 2405 Monte Vista Dr Birmingham AL 35216 Office: 1830 14th Av S Birmingham AL 35205

DOLCE, PETER SEBASTIAN, dentist; b. Chgo., Sept. 9, 1923; s. Sebastian Anthony and Rosaria Elizabeth (Dolce) D.; D.D.S., Loyola U., Chgo., 1947; m. Joan Haberkorn, Apr. 16, 1952; children—Kathryn Ann, Peter Joseph. Practice oral reconstrn., Oak Park, Ill., 1947-52, 54-57, Delray Beach, Fla., 1957—. Prof. prosthetics U. Seoul, Korea, 1952-53. Served with AUS, 1943-45; with USNR, 1952-55; Korea. Mem. Am., Dental Assn., East Coast, Palm Beach dental socs., Am. Acad. Dental Practice Adminstrn., Pierre Fauchard Acad. (Fauchard medal 1953), Acad. of 100. Roman Catholic. Kiwanian. Club: Delray Beach; Loyola University (Chgo.). Inventor mouth irrigation device, de-burring mechanism. Mailing Address: 1045 E Atlantic Av Delray Beach FL 33444 Home: 1227 Harbor Dr Delray Beach FL 33444

DOLEZAL, HENRY, judge; b. Perry, Okla., Jan. 11, 1905; s. James H. and Ella (Kasl) D.; A.B., U. Okla., 1926, LL.B., 1933; student U. Chgo., 1930-31. Admitted to Okla. bar, 1933, pvt. practice, Perry, 1933-35, 37-38, 46-68; asso. dist. judge, Noble County, Okla., 1969—; county atty. Noble County, 1935-37, county judge, 1938-41; city atty., Perry, 1937-38. County adviser to registrants under Selective Service Law, 1940-41, 46—; mayor City of Perry, 1947-49, 51-57; mem. Okla. Ho. Reps., 1957-64. Chmn. finance com. Noble County Rep. Central Com., 1948-52, chmn. central com. 1954-58. Served to maj. AUS, 1941-46. Mem. Am., Okla., Noble County (pres. 1953-55) bar assns., Am. Judicature Soc., V.F.W. (comdr. post 1948-49), Am. Legion (chaplain Okla. dept. 1960), 40 and 8, Phi Delta Phi. Presbyn. (elder, clk. session 1966-69). Mason (32 deg., Shriner, K.T.), Rotarian (pres. Perry 1946-47), Odd Fellow, Knight of Pythias. Home: 1102 Delaware St Perry OK 73077 Office: County Courthouse Perry OK 73077

DOLIVE, EARL, mfg. co. exec.; b., 1917; m. With Genuine Parts Co., Atlanta, 1937—, Formerly mgr., Charlotte, N.C., mgr., Mpls., 1959-62, returned to Atlanta, 1962, exec. v.p., 1965—, also dir. Office: 299 Piedmont Av NE Atlanta GA 30312*

DOLL, MAX, paper co. exec.; b. Soldiers Grove, Wis., Feb. 21, 1932; s. Leo E. and Genevieve (Martin) D.; student Loras Coll., 1950-51, Wis. State Coll., 1951-52; m. Karen Mary Bender, Dec. 28, 1955; children—Peter, Mark, Christopher, Mary Kathryn, John. With Cellu Products Co., Patterson, N.C., 1955—, v.p., 1958—, sec., 1968—. Trustee Caldwell Community Coll. and Tech. Inst. Served with AUS, 1953-55. Rotarian (pres. 1969-70). Home: Pine Hill Patterson NC 28661 Office: Cellu Products Co River and Roby Martin Rd Patterson NC 28661

DOLSON, CHARLES HERBERT, air line exec.; b. St. Louis, May 13, 1906; s. Frank Edward, and Hattie Mae (Harbison) D.; B.S. in Civil Engring., Washington U., St. Louis, 1928; m. Bonnie Gooch, May 27, 1935 (dec.); m. 2d, Clara Allison, Aug. 30, 1962. Test pilot Curtiss Wright Airplane Co., St. Louis, 1930-31; pilot Am. Airlines, Inc., 1931-34; pilot Delta Air Lines, Inc., Atlanta, 1934-40, chief pilot, 1940-42, 1945-47, operations mgr., 1947-48, v.p. operations, 1948-59, exec. v.p., 1959-65, pres., 1965-70, chmn. bd., chief exec. officer, 1970-71, chmn. exec. com., 1971—, also dir.; dir. Trust Co. Ga., Fla. Nat. Banks of Fla., Inc., Multiventure, Inc. Served as lt. comdr. USNRF, 1928-30, 42-45. Mem. Nat. Aviation Club, Soc. Automotive Engrs., Transp. Assn. Am. (dir.), Alpha Tau Omega. Elk. Clubs: Cherokee Town and Country, Wings. Home: 660 W Conway Dr NW Atlanta GA 30327 Office: Delta Air Lines Inc Atlanta Airport Atlanta GA 30320

DOMEIER, DOUGLAS DRATH, journalist; b. Berwyn, Ill., June 30, 1939; s. Erwin Jesse and Julia Katharine (Drath) D.; B.J., U. Mo., 1961. Reporter, Dallas Morning News, 1965—, religion editor, 1965-66, editor for aviation, sci. and space, 1966—. Served with AUS, 1962-65. 3times winner Dealey award for outstanding reporting Dallas News; winner Best Spot News Story, Dallas Press Club, 1968; co-recipient S.W. Journalism Forum award, 1969. Mem. Sigma Phi Epsilon, Sigma Delta Chi. Home: 3900 W Northwest Hwy Dallas TX 75220 Office: Young & Houston Sts Dallas TX 75222

DOMENECH, FERNANDO JUAN, accountant; b. Isabela, P.R., Dec. 30, 1912; s. Fernando and Teresa (Esteves) D.; diploma in Higher Accountancy, LaSalle Extension U., 1933; M. Socorro Paonessa, Nov. 19, 1945; children—Fernando J., Rafael Enrique; 1 dau. (by previous marriage)—Awilda Maria. With Sparrow, Waymouth & Co., C.P.A.'s, San Juan, P.R., 1939-55, partner, 1948-55; partner Deloitte, Plender, Haskins & Sells (merger Sparrow Waymouth & Haskins & Sells), 1955-63; partner Haskins & Sells, San Juan, 1963—. Auditor, Casa de Ninos Manuel Fernandez Juncos, 1968-71, v.p., 1971—, also dir. Active fund-raising campaigns Cancer League P.R. Mem. Am. Accounting Assn., Nat. Soc. Accountants for Co-ops. (dir. 1965-66), Nat. Assn. Accountants, P.R. Inst. C.P.A.'s (pres. 1960, chmn. ethics com. 1969—), P.R. C. of C. (treas. 1967—). Club: Casino de Puerto Rico (Santurce). Home: 708 La Paz St Santurce PR 00907 Office: Chase Manhattan Bank Bldg Hato Rey PR 00919 also PO Box 140 San Juan PR 00902

DOMENGEAUX, JEROME ERASTE, judge; b. Lafayette, La., Mar. 3, 1919; s. Joseph Rodolph and Marthe (Mouton) D.; B.A., U. Southwestern La., 1940; postgrad. Georgetown U. Sch. Law, 1941; LL.B., Tulane U., 1948, J.D., 1968; m Julia Marie Harvey, Oct. 5, 1945; children—Jane Ann (Mrs. William J. Bayard), Julia Martha, Joan Marie, Jerome E. Jr., James H. Admitted to La. bar, 1948; gen. practice law, Lafayette, 1948-62; mayor, Lafayette, 1956-60; judge 15th Jud. Dist. Ct. La., Lafayette, 1962-70, 4th La. Ct. of Appeal, New Orleans, 1969-70, 3d Circuit Ct. Appeal, 1970—. Served to capt., AUS, 1942-46. Decorated Bronze Star; recipient Mayor of Distinction award La. Municipal Assn. 1959. Home: 1217 Myrtle Blvd Lafayette LA 70501 Office: War Memorial Bldg Lafayette LA 70501

DOMINEY, FREDERICK DAVID, petroleum economist; b. Huntsville, Tex., Dec. 28, 1921; s. David E. and Fredda (Baldwin) D.; B.S., U. Tex., 1942, B.A., 1947; postgrad. U. Cal. at Berkeley, 1958; m. Lois Heflin, Oct. 8, 1948; children—David, Kim Lex. Statistician, Humble Oil &Refining Co., Houston, 1947-55, petroleum economist, 1958-67; petroleum economist Tidewater Oil Co., San Francisco, 1955-58, Cities Service Oil Co., Tulsa, 1967—. Mem. petroleum subcom. of fgn. supply com. Dept. Interior, 1970—. Served with AUS, 1942-45. Mem. Ind. Petroleum Assn. Am. (supply-demand com. 1968-71), Am. Petroleum Inst. (supply and consumption com. 1971—), Nat. Assn. Bus. Economists, Bus.-Industry Polit. Action Com. Republican. Elk. Home: 5651 S Gary Av Tulsa OK 74105 Office: Box 300 Tulsa OK 74102

DOMINGUEZ, BUFETE VIRGILIO, lawyer; grad. Faculty Law Nat. U. Mexico, 1933. Admitted to Mexican bar, 1933; prof. law, dean Sch. Law Nat. U. Mexico, 1945-48; now practice law, Mexico City. Mem. Barra Mexicana-Colegio de Abogados (pres. 1961-62), Academia Mexicana de Derecho Procesal, Internat. Bar Assn. Author: El Materialismo Historico, 1933. Address: San Juan De Letran 11 Mexico 1 DF Mexico

DOMINGUEZ, JAMES FRANCIS, dentist; b. New Orleans, June 13, 1920; s. James Louis and Frances Beatrice (Buchert) D.; B.S., Tulane, 1943; D.D.S., Loyola U. at New Orleans, 1945; m. Estelle Viola Haase, Jan. 24, 1945; 1 dau., Carlos Ann (Mrs. Gary Jude Danos). Individual practice dentistry, New Orleans, 1945—. Dir. Assn. Upper State St. Inc., 1966—. Served with USNR, 1943-45, 52-54. Mem. C. Victor Vignes Hon. Dental Fraternity, Am., La., New Orleans dental assns., Xi Psi Phi. Roman Catholic. Home: 2323 State St New Orleans LA 70118 Office: 2233 Jefferson Hwy New Orleans LA 70121

DOMINGUEZ, JOSE RAMON, physician; b. Perico, Matanzas, Cuba, Oct. 28, 1924; s. Jose Ramon and Margarita (Daniel) D.; B.S. in Letters and Sci., La Progresiva Presbyn. Coll., 1942; M.D., Havana U., 1952; m. Elise Whetsell, Dec. 3, 1967; 1 dau., Elyse Joley. Intern Christian Hosp., St. Louis, 1953-55; surg. resident St. Francis Hosp., Miami Beach, Fla., 1955-56; gen. practice resident Halifax Dist. Hosp., Daytona Beach, Fla., 1956-58; practice medicine, specializing in geriatrics, West Palm Beach, Fla., 1959-68, Daytona-Ormond Beach, Fla., 1968—; sec.-treas. med. staff Ormond Beach Meml. Hosp., 1970—. Fellow Am. Geriatrics Soc.; mem. A.M.A., Fla. Med. Assn., Volusia County Med. Soc. Mason (32 deg.). Home: 4 Bayberry Dr Ormond Beach FL 32074 Office: 1184 Ocean Shore Blvd Ormond Beach FL 32074

DOMINY, FLOYD E., govt. ofcl.; b. Hastings, Neb., Dec. 24, 1909; s. Charles M. and Emma (Shay) D.; student Hastings Coll.; B.A., U. Wyo., 1932, postgrad., 1932-33, LL.D. (hon.), 1966; postgrad. Columbia, 1944; m. Alice M. Criswell, Dec. 23, 1929; children—Janice Elaine, Charles Elgin, Ruth Ellen. Instr. vocational agr. Hillsdale High Sch., 1933-34; county agrl. agt. Campbell County, Gillette, Wyo., 1934-38; field rep. western div. A.A.A., Washington, 1938-42; asst. dir. food supply div. Office Coordinator Inter-Am. Affairs, Washington, 1942-44; chief allocation and repayment br., asst. dir. div. irrigation Bur. Reclamation, Dept. Interior, 1946-53, chief div. irrigation, 1953-57, asso. commr., 1957-59, commr., 1959—. Served as lt. USNR, 1944-46; assigned mil. govt. Guam. Decorated knight comdr. Order Isabel the Catholic (Spain), 1966, Star Order Thailand, 1966; recipient Distinguished Service award Dept. Interior, 1966; named Pub. Works Man of Yr., Am. Pub. Works Assn., 1966. Mem. Am. Legion, Sigma Xi, Phi Kappa Phi, Alpha Zeta. Mason, Lion (past pres. Gillette, Wyo. club). Home: Box 240 Route 1 Oakton VA 22124 Office: Department of Interior 18th and C Sts NW Washington DC 20242

DONAHUE, THOMAS REILLY, trade union ofcl., govt. ofcl.; b. N.Y.C., Sept. 4, 1928; s. Thomas Reilly and Mary E. (Purcell) D.; B.A., Manhattan Coll., 1949; J.D., Fordham U., 1956; m. Natalie A. Kiernan, Nov. 11, 1950; children—Nancy Angela, Thomas Reilly III. Dir. edn. local 32B, Bldg. Service Employees Internat. Union, AFL-CIO, 1949-52; dir. contract dept., 1952-57; European labor program coordinator Free Europe Com., Inc., Paris, France, 1957-60; asst. to pres. Bldg. Service Employees' Internat. Union, 1960-67; asst. sect. for labor-mgmt. relations Dept. Labor, 1967-69; exec. sec. Service Employees Internat. Union, 1969-71, v.p., 1971—. Served with USNR, 1945-46. Democrat. Home: 7210 Exfair Rd Bethesda MD 20014 Office: 900 17th St NW Washington DC 20006

DONALD, JAMES ROBERT, agrl. economist; b. Omega, Ga., Dec. 31, 1933; s. Clinton Ernest and Lorena (Branan) D.; B.S., U. Ga., 1954; M.S., N.C. State U., 1957; m. Nancy Ripple, Sept. 16, 1961; children— Gordon, Mary. Agrl. economist U.S. Dept. Agr., Washington, 1957—. Served with AUS, 1957. Mem. Am. Agrl. Econ. Assn., Alpha Zeta. Editor: Cotton Situation, 1962—. Author: The Demand for Textile Fibers in the United States, 1963. Home: 1046 Carper St McLean VA 22101 Office: 500 12th St SW Washington DC 20250

DONALDSON, FLETCHER WILLIAM, educator; b. Carlysle, Ky., Oct. 30, 1912; s. Alpheus Fletcher and Elizabeth (Williams) D.; B.A., U. Ky., 1934, M.A., 1936; Ph.D., U. Tex., 1955; m. Myrtle Norma Schneider, Feb. 12, 1943; children—Patricia Annette, Rebecca Joyce. Instr. research mathematician U. Tex., 1945-51; staff mem. U. Cal., Los Alamos, 1951-53; sr. aerophysics engr. Gen. Dynamics Corp., Ft. Worth, 1953-56; applied math. cons. Gen. Electric Corp. MSVD Dept., Phila., 1956-58; mem. sr. staff, head operations and programming Ramo-Wooldridge Corp., also Bunker-Ramo Corp., Ft. Huachuca, Ariz., 1958-65; cons. scientist, project mgr., information processing Lockheed Missiles & Space Co., 1965-69; prof. computer scis. U. Tenn. Space Inst., 1969—. Mem. Tex. Dist. Bd. Parish Edn., Luth. Ch., 1954-56, mem. Tucson Bd., 1960-65. Served to capt. AUS, 1942-44. Fellow Soc. Advanced Med. Systems; mem. Assn. Computing Machinery (chmn. So. Ariz. chpt. 1962; chmn. program com. Bay Area chpt., chmn. Spring symposium 1969), Lutheran Acad. Scholarship, Am. Assn. Univ. Profs., Sigma Xi, Kappa Delta Pi, Pi Mu Epsilon, Phi Delta Kappa. Home: 521 Sharondale Dr Tullahoma TN 37388

DONAN, WILLIAM PAGE, lawyer; b. Morganfield, Ky., May 17, 1914; s. David C. and Adeline (Callaway) D.; LL.B., Cumberland U., 1939; m. Helen Pauline Hinch, Oct. 19, 1940; 1 son, Thomas Arthur. Asst. warehouse mgr. Pitts. Steel Co., Evansville, Ind., 1935-36, St. Louis, 1936-38; clk. land dept. Phillips Petroleum Co., Bartlesville, Okla., 1940; asso. Newton Belcher, attys., Greenville, Ky., 1940-42; partner Belcher & Donan, 1945-51; pvt. practice, 1951-56; partner Donan & Vick, 1956—; atty. Greenville, 1946-48, judge, 1954-70. Pres. Greenville Indsl. Devel. Corp., 1960-67. Mem. Gov.'s Judicial Adv. Council, 1972—. Mem. Muhlenberg County Library Bd., 1969-70. Trustee Greenville Boy Scouts; fund campaign chmn. A.R.C., 1956. Trustee Med. Research Found., Greenville, Muhlenberg County Law Library, Lon Rogers Ednl. Trust, Jessie Rogers Ednl. Trust. Served to 1st lt. AUS, 1942-45. Decorated Bronze Star, Silver Star. Fellow Am. Coll. Probate Counsel; mem. Greenville C. of C. (pres. 1960-62), Muhlenberg County Bar Assn., Sports Philatelists Internat., Am., Ky. (ho. dels.; chmn. ho. dels. 1968-69, v.p. 1970-71, inquiry tribunal 1971—) bar assns., Am. Judicature Soc., Law-Sci. Acad. of Am., Am. Philatelic Soc., Am. Topical Assn., Ky. Hist. Soc., Ky. Bar Found. (dir.), Am. Legion, V.F.W., S.A.R., Blue Key. Presbyn. Democrat. Mason. Clubs: Kiwanis (past pres., lt. gov. div. 2 Ky.-Tenn. dist.), Greenville Country (past pres.). Home: 306 E Main Cross St Greenville KY 42345 Office: 110 E Court Sq Greenville KY 42345

DONAUBAUER, ELTON HENRY, univ. administr; b. Marion, Tex., Nov. 9, 1921; s. Edwin O. and Melanie (Schultze) D.; B.A., Sul Ross State Coll., 1949, M.A., 1950; M.Ed., George Peabody Coll. for Tchrs., 1951; m. Dorothy Mauryne Lindley, Oct. 17, 1947; children—Melanie, Allyn, Craig. Asst. mgr. J. C. Penney Co., New Braunfels, Tex., 1939-42, 1946; prof. edn., polit. sci. S.W. Tex. Jr. Coll., Uvalde, 1949-50; dir. pub. relations Community Chest, Nashville, 1951-54, Allegheny County, Pitts., 1954-55; regional dir., dir. information services Pa. United Fund, 1955-57; instr. Watkins Inst. High Sch., Nashville, 1952-54; mem. pub. relations adv. com. United Community Funds and Councils of Am., Inc., 1955-57, mem. United Fund adv. com., 1957-60; exec. dir. United Fund of Shenango Valley Area, Sharon, Pa., 1957-60; exec. dir. Community Chest, United Fund, Health and Welfare Council, Pulaski County, Little Rock, 1960-64; dir. devel. and planning George Peabody Coll. for Tchrs., also lectr. Sociology and Social scis. Watkins Inst., Nashville, 1964-68; dir. devel. U. Ark., Fayetteville, 1968—; pres. S.W. Regional Conf. United Community Funds and Councils of America, 1963—; part-time instr. social scis. Little Rock U. Chmn. United Fund Campaign, 1970; co-chmn. Ridgehouse campaign, Fayetteville; chmn. Washington County United Way. Vice chmn. Fayetteville Planning Commn. Mem. bd. Westark Boy Scout Council; bd. dirs. pres. United Fund Fayetteville, United Community Services, Fayetteville. Served with USAAF, 1942-46. Mem. Pub. Relations Soc. Am., Ark., Fayetteville chambers commerce, Internat. Platform Assn., Phi Delta Kappa, Kappa Delta Pi. Methodist (bd., pres. Meth. men). Rotarian (dir.). Home: 1101 Woolsey Fayetteville AR 72701

DONAVAN, GEORGE EDGAR, JR., banker; b. Jackson, Miss., Feb. 23, 1916; s. George Edgar and Annie Mivian (Nelson) D.; student Miss. State U., 1933-34; B.S., U. Miss., 1937; postgrad. La. State U., 1964; m. Katie Bell Holmes, Dec. 3, 1938; children—George Edgar III, Carl Howard. With Lamar Life Ins. Co., Jackson, 1937-43; state mgr. Scharff & Jones, Inc., investment bankers, New Orleans, 1946-60; sr. v.p. First Nat. Bank, Jackson, 1960—. Pres. Magnolia Speech Sch.; state fund dir. A.R.C., Am. Cancer Soc. Served with USNR, 1943-46. Mem. Pi Kappa Alpha, Omicron Delta Kappa. Episcopalian. Rotarian. Clubs: Jackson (past pres.), Capital City Petroleum (Jackson). Home: 3949 Eastwood Dr Jackson MS 39211 Office: First Nat Bank Jackson MS 39205

DONEHUE, JOHN DOUGLAS, newspaper exec.; b. Cramerton, N.C., July 5, 1928; s. John Sidney and Annie (Shepherd) D.; student Am. Press Inst., Columbia, 1965; m. Mary Phelps (dec. 1964); children—Teresa Jean, Marilyn Phelps; m. Sylvia Louise McKenzie, Feb. 11, 1966 (dec. 1971); children—Hayden Shepherd, John Douglas. Sports writer Charleston, S.C. News and Courier, 1947, telegraph editor, 1956, state editor, 1959-62, city editor, 1962-68, mng. editor, 1968-71, dir. promotion and pub. service, 1971—, compiler News and Courier Style Book, 1969; sports editor Orangeburg (S.C.) Times and Democrat, 1948-50; polit. reporter Montgomery (Ala.) Advertiser, 1954-55; faculty advisor Bapt. Coll. at Charleston Student Newspaper. Spl. adviser comdt. 7th USCG dist. for establishment dist.-wide pub. information program, 1960-61; journalism lectr. Baptist Coll., Charleston, sec. 1st bd. founders, 1969. Mem. bd. S.C. Commn. for Blind, 1969—, S.C. Tricentennial Parade Com., 1969—. Mem. exec. com. Low Country Council Boy Scouts Am.; mem. adv. bd. Salvation Army. Served with USAF, 1950-54. Recipient Freedoms Found. award, 1971. Mem. John Ancrum Soc. of Soc. Prevention Cruelty to Animals, Carolina Art Assn., YMCA, Toastmasters Internat. (charter mem. Okinawa club), Okinawa Soc. Baptist (deacon, Sunday sch. supt.). Clubs: Country, Rotary (Charleston). Home: 66 Bull St Charleston SC 29401 Office: 134 Columbus St Charleston SC 29401

DONKIN, ROBERT GORDON, mgmt. exec.; b. Cleve., Apr. 16, 1923; s. Robert Forster and Louise (Hess) D.; B.S. in Mech. Engring., Case Inst. Tech., 1944; grad. student U.S. Naval Acad., 1944; m. Marilyn Ann Mitzel Dec. 23, 1944; children—Marilyn Ann (Mrs. Roger E. Walters), Elizabeth Louise (Mrs. Woodroe T. Ayers), Diana Jeanne (Mrs. Alan R. Gregg). Design engr. Towmotor Corp., Cleve., 1946-47; chief engr. Webster Products Co., 1947-48; chief mech. designer Swartwout Co., 1949-50; asst. gen. supt., 1951-54, mgr. steam specialities mfg., 1955-56; gen. supt. Rockwell Mfg. Co., Chgo., 1957-58, works mgr. 1959-62, gen. mgr., Tulsa, 1962-63; mng. asso., gen. mgmt. cons. mgmt. services div. Arthur Young & Company, 1964-66, prin., 1967-68, dir., partner, 1969—, dir. mgmt. information and control planning Southwestern region, 1969—; dir. Convotrol Corp., Chgo. Served to ensign USNR, 1942-46. Mem. Nat. Assn. Accountants, Am. Prodn. and Inventory Control Soc., Petroleum Accountants Soc. Okla., Internat. Platform Assn., C. of C., Phi Delta Theta. Mason. Clubs: Tulsa Country, Harvard, Cup, Summit. Patentee. Home: 5408 E 38th St Tulsa OK 74135 Office: First Nat Bank Bldg PO Box 1529 Tulsa OK 74101

DONLEY, MARSHALL OWEN, JR., edn. editor and writer; b. Christiana, Pa., Mar. 20, 1932; s. Marshall O. and Edna (Detweiler) D.; B.A., Pa. State U., 1954; postgrad. U. So. Cal., 1954-55; M.A., Am. U., 1966, Ph.D., 1971; m. Margaret T. Reagan, Sept. 18, 1971. Newspaper reporter Lancaster (Pa.) Intelligencer Jour., 1950-52; radio-tv writer WGAL and WGAL-TV, Lancaster, 1953; linguist U.S. Army Security Agy., Ft. Meade, Md., 1955-58; edn. writer, exec. editor N.E.A., Washington, 1958—. Instr. spl. sessions U. N.Y. at Buffalo, summers 1964-65. Served with AUS, 1955-58. Mem. Ednl. Press Assn. (chpt. past pres.), N.E.A. (dept. editorial cons. 1960-67; pres. staff orgn. 1967-68), Phi Kappa Phi, Phi Delta Kappa, Phi Sigma Kappa, Sigma Delta Chi. Contbr. articles to profl. jours. Home: 2850 27th St NW Washington DC 20008 Office: 1201 16th St NW Washington DC 20036

DONNAHOE, ALAN STANLEY, newspaper exec.; b. Asheville, N.C., Aug. 27, 1916; s. Paul Albert and Kate (Stanley) D.; student pub. schs.; m. Elsie Pitts., 1938; children—Kate Stanley (Mrs. C. Porter Vaughan, III), Maureen. Dir. research Richmond C. of C., 1936-46 asst. exec. mgr., 1946-50; exec. sec. Richmond (Va.) Inter-Club Council, 1938-41, Va. Soc. Pub. Accountants, Richmond, 1946-50; dir. research Richmond Newspapers, Inc., 1950-55, v.p., 1956-59, exec. v.p., asst. pub., 1959-66, pres., 1966—, also dir.; pres., dir. Tribune Co.; pres., chief exec. officer Media Gen., Inc., 1969—; pres., dir. Southeast Media, Inc., Metro Guide, Inc., Media Gen. Financial Weekly, Inc., Westover Pub. Co., Yellow Tavern Corp. (all Richmond), Cablevision Fredericksburg Inc. (Va.); dir. Evening News Pub. Co., Newark, Piedmont Pub. Co., Winston-Salem, Garden State Paper Co., Garfield, N.J., Morgan Mills, Lititz, Pa., WFLA, Inc., Tampa, Beacon Press, Richmond, Golden Triangle Printing Co., Greensboro, N.C., Security Fed. Savs. & Loan Assn., Richmond, Newspaper Preprint Corp., N.Y.C., United Va. Bank, Richmond, Computer Corp., Richmond. Mem. bus. adv. com. U.S. Bur. Labor Statistic, 1948-49, U.S. Bur. Census, 1948-49; mem. exec. com. Va. Tb

Assn., 1948-50, state fiscal study com. Va. Adv. Legislative Council, 1956-58; evaluation steering com. Va. Adv. Council Ednl. TV, 1971—. Bd. govs. United Fund, 1960-63, 66-69, mem. steering com., 1959, chmn. commerce and industry div., 1962, budget com., 1963, exec. com., 1963; bd. dirs. Collegiate Schs., pres., 1968; bd. dirs. Tuckahoe YMCA, 1958—, River Rd. Civic Assn., 1958—, Richmond chpt. A.R.C., 1957—, Richmond Meml. Hosp., 1958—, Better Richmond, United Givers Fund; bd. dirs. Richmond Eye Hosp., pres., 1970; bd. dirs., pres. RPI Found.; bd. dirs. Richmond Area Community Council. Served from pvt. to 1st lt., C.E., AUS, 1943-46, ETO; 1st lt. AUS, 1950-52. Mem. Am. Newspaper Pubs. Assn. (news research com. 1969—), U.S. (communications com. 1970—), Richmond (dir. 1956-59, v.p., pres. 1968) chambers commerce, Am. Statis. Assn., Atlantic Rural Expn. (dir. 1957-60), Am. Marketing Assn. (pres. Va. 1954-55). Contbr. numerous articles to profl. jours. Home: 8912 Alendale Rd Richmond VA 23229 Office: 333 E Grace St Richmond VA 23219

DONNELLAN, THOMAS A., bishop; b. N.Y.C., Jan 24, 1914; s. Andrew and Margaret (Egan) D.; A.B., St. Joseph's Sem., 1939; J.C.D., Catholic U. Am., 1942. Ordained priest Roman Catholic Ch., 1939; vice chancellor Archdiocese of N.Y., 1947-50, chancellor, 1958-62; synodal judge Marriage Tribunal, 1950-58; rector St. Joseph's Sem., 1962-64; bishop of Ogdenburg, N.Y., 1964-68, archbishop of Atlanta, 1968—. Decorated knight grand cross Knights Holy Sepulchre. Mem. Nat. Conf. Catholic Bishops (adminstrv. bd.), Sacred Congregation Religious and Secular Insts. Address: 136 W Wesley Rd NW Atlanta GA 30305

DONNELLY, ALDEN STUART, geol. engr.; b. Denver, Apr. 29, 1907; s. S. Clifford and Prudence Middleton (Jennings) D.; Geol. Engr., Colo. Sch. Mines, 1928; postgrad. U. Tex., 1942; m. Adelaide Field, Oct. 9, 1929. Mining geologist N.M., 3 mo. 1928; petroleum geologist Honolulu Oil Corp., 1928-31, surface, sub-surface petroleum geologist, oil scout, Midland, Tex., 1931-36, div. devel. engr., mgr. prodn., 1936-44, div. gen. supt. West Tex., N.M., 1944-46, div. mgr. Mid-Continent div., 1946-49, mgr. Mid-Continent div., v.p., dir., Honolulu Oil Corp., 1949-60, exec. v.p., dir., 1960-62, now petroleum cons. Mem. industry adv. com. on petroleum engring. dept. orgn. petroleum prodn. and natural gas Tex. Technol. Sch. Engring. Sch., Lubbock, 1948-50, 54-61; mem. industry adv. com. Petroleum Engring. Sch., U. Tex., 1956-58. Served as 2d lt., 2d combat engrs., U.S. Army Res., 1928-34. Recipient Distinguished Achievement medal Colo. Sch. Mines, 1957; citation for service Am. Petroleum Inst. Registered profl. engr., Tex. Fellow Geol. Soc. Am.; mem. Am. Assn. Petroleum Geologists, Am. Inst. Mining, Metall. and Petroleum Engrs., Am. Petroleum Inst. (1st chmn. S.W. div. oil prodn. 1954-55, chmn. exec. com. S.W. div. 1955-56, gen. com. div. prodn. 1958-61), Soc. Econ. Paleontologists and Mineralogists, Ind. Petroleum Assn. Am. (exec. com., past v.p. Tex. Permian Basin area, nat. treas. 1966-67), Gen. Mid-Continent (dir.), N.M. oil and gas assns., Tex. Mfrs. Assn. (dir.), Midland C. of C. (dir. 1953-56), Tex. Research League (dir. 1956-58), West Tex. Geol. Soc., A.A.A.S., Tau Beta Pi, Sigma Alpha Epsilon, Theta Tau. Episcopalian. Clubs: Petroleum, Country (Midland); Ft. Worth, Contbr. articles to profl. publs. Home: 1505 W Ohio Av Midland TX 79701 Office: Box 5003 Midland TX 79701

DONNELLY, DONALD TRACY, editor; b. Chester, Mass., Mar. 29, 1915; s. Samuel J. and Lucy (Mahan) D.; B.S., U. Mass., 1936; m. Dorothy M. Joyce, May 28, 1938; 1 son, John Samuel. Editor, Mass. Agrl. Extension Service, Springfield, 1936-46; editor Conn. State Farm Bur., New Haven, also Conn. Milk Producers Assn., Hartford, 1946-51; editor Am. Farm Bur. Fedn., Washington, 1951—. Asso. editor Am. Farmer, 1954—; editor Farm Bur. News, 1951—; farm broadcaster, 1936—. Republican. Roman Catholic. Home: 6760 Baron Rd McLean VA 22101 Office: 425 13th St NW Washington DC 20004

DONNELLY, EDWIN GREGORY, publishing exec., cartoonist; b. Crossville, Tenn., Nov. 6, 1904; s. Henry M. and Martha (Shellito) D.; grad. Pleasant Hill (Tenn.) Acad., 1920, Jefferson High Sch., Los Angeles, 1926; m. Gertrude Kennedy, Sept. 13, 1930; children—Edward A., Robert S., John H. Asst. pressman Fibreboard Prodn. Co., Los Angeles, 1926-28; farmer, Tenn., 1928-33; laborer then supt. 3 cos., Work Projects Adminstrn., Tenn., 1933-42; asst. mgr. Trade-A-Plane Co., Crossville, Tenn., 1942-45; mgr., cartoonist Trade-A-Plane and Rock & Dirt publs., 1945-61; pub. Boats and Harbors, 1958; chmn. Crossville Meml. Airport Com. Mem. Upper Cumberland Devel. Assn. Mem. Cumberland C. of C. Democrat. Mem. Christian Ch. Clubs: Exchange, Crossville Aero. Home: Crossville TN 38555 Office: 501-B W 4th St Crossville TN 38555

DONOGHUE, GERALD THOMAS, horse breeder; b. Beaumont, Tex., Sept. 17, 1906; s. Thomas Joseph and Mary Evangelist (Sullivan) D.; grad. Canterbury Sch. (New Milford, Conn.), 1925; B.A., Holy Cross Coll., 1929; m. Louise Huggins, Jan. 27, 1932; children—William T., Clare (Mrs. T. T. Beck, Jr.), Timothy H. Reporter, asst. city editor Houston Chronicle, 1929-43; founder Donoghue Arabian Farm, Goliad, Tex., 1943—. Pres. Arabian Horse Owners Found., 1970-71. Served with AUS, 1944-45, Mem. Am. Horse Shows Assn., Internat. Arabian Assn. (v.p.), Arabian Horse Club Tex. (past pres.). Author: For Peace Comes Dropping Slow, 1946. Contbr. articles to popular mags. including The Atlantic, Esquire. Address: Donoghue Arabian Farm Goliad TX 77963

DONOHOE, STANISLAUS DOLAN, real estate exec.; b. Washington, Aug. 28, 1894; s. John Francis and Emily Frances (Jenkins) D.; A.B., Cath. U., 1916; m. Isabelle Cain, Oct. 30, 1923; children—Grace (Mrs. Murray Toomey), Alice (Mrs. Eugene F. Ford). Automobile dealer Donohoe Motor Co., Washington, 1916-30, Donohoe Chevrolet, 1931-39; pres. John F. Donohoe & Sons, realtors, 1945—; v.p., dir. Nat. Capital Bank; dir. Eastern Savings and Loan Assn. Bd. dirs. Met. Washington Bd. Trade. Recipient award Cath. U., 1963, 66. Mem. Washington Bd. Realtors (pres. 1945-46). Club: Columbia Country. Home: 6204 Garnett Dr Kenwood MD 20014 Office: 3601 Cohn Av Washington DC 20008

DONOHOO, HORRIE VAN WALDO, mining co. exec.; b. Tucumcari, N.M., June 7, 1914; s. Horrie Van Waldo and Pearl (Wilson) D.; student Drake U., 1931-34; student Colo. Sch. Mines, 1936-39, 1945-46, Columbia, 1947; m. Norma Stegmann, Dec. 1, 1933; children—Michael O., Van Brian. Seismic computer Stanolind Oil & Gas Co., 1939-40, Phillips Petroleum Co., Gulf Coast, Tex., La., 1940-41; instr. mechanics Cornell U. Buffalo campus, 1941-43; instr. geophysics Colo. Sch. Mines, 1945-46, Columbia, 1947; asst. prof. geophysics U. Utah, 1947-51; exploration geophysicist Columbia-Geneva div. U.S. Steel Corp., San Francisco, 1953-57; chief geophysicist, asst. mgr. exploration Tex. Gulf Sulphur Co., N.Y.C., 1957-61, Houston, 1961-66, gen. mgr. potash div., Moab, Utah, 1966-67, v.p., gen. mgr. potash div., 1967-70, v.p. agrl. div., Raleigh, N.C., 1970-71, sr. v.p., 1972—. Served to lt. comdr. USNR, 1943-45, 51-53. Recipient medal Colo. Sch. Mines, 1968. Mem. Am. Assn. Petroleum Geophysics, Soc. Exploration Geophysicists, European Assn. Exploration Geophysicists, Soc. Econ. Geologists, Am. Inst. Mining and Metall. Engrs., Mining and Metall. Soc. Am., Newcomen Soc. N. Am., Raleigh C. of C., Canadian Geophys. Soc. Home: 5309 Parkwood Dr Raleigh NC 27609 Office: Tex Gulf Sulphur Co 410 Oberlin Rd Raleigh NC 27605

DONOHUE, FRANCIS JOSEPH, clergyman, editor; b. Phila., July 11, 1924; s. Charles Francis and Mary Loretta (Reynolds) D.; A.B., Mount St. Mary's Coll., Emmitsburg, Md., 1950; postgrad. Mount St. Mary's Sem., 1950-54. Ordained priest Roman Catholic Ch., 1954; asst. rector Cathedral St. John the Baptist, Savannah, Ga., 1954-57; pastor Our Lady of Lourdes Ch., Port Wentworth, Ga., 1957-68; editor The So. Cross, Savannah, 1957—; dir. dept. communications Cath. Diocese of Savannah, 1970—. Served with AUS, 1944-46. Mme. Cath. Press Assn. (several awards), Cath. Broadcasters Assn. K.C. Club: Savannah Press Home: 556 E Gordon St Savannah GA 31401 Office: PO Box 10027 Savannah GA 31402

DONOVAN, EDWARD LAURENCE, educator; b. N.Y.C., Sept. 4, 1941; s. Laurence Joseph and Margaret Mary (McLean) D.; A.B. magna cum laude, Aquinas Inst. Philosophy, 1964, M.A. magna cum laude, 1961, Ph.D., summa cum laude, 1970; student Providence Coll., 1959-60, Loras Coll., 1960-61; m. Kathleen McNerney, Aug. 5, 1967; children—Karen Marie, Michael Riordon. Instr. philosophy Catherine Spalding Coll., Louisville, 1965-68; asst. prof., chmn. philosophy dept. St. Dominic Coll., St. Charles, Ill., 1968-69; acad. dean, asso. prof. philosophy and Am. studies Sacred Heart Coll., Belmont, N.C., 1969—. Mem. exec. bd. Charlotte Area Ednl. Consortium, 1969—, exec. bd. Coll. Transfer Student, N.C. Bd. Higher Edn., 1970—. Mem. Am. Assn. Acad. Deans, N.C. Assn. Acad. Deans, N.C. Edn. Assn., Am. Cath. Philos. Assn., N.C. Assn. Philosophers, Popular Culture Assn., Belmont C. of C. (exec. bd., edn. com. 1970—. Kiwanian (chmn. operation drug alert 1969). Home: 1213 Monroe Dr Gastonia NC 28052 Office: Dept of Philosophy Sacred Heart College Belmont NC 28012

DOOLEY, MARIE LOUISE BOYETT, ednl. adminstr.; b. Bryan, Tex.; d. Oran H. and Mary (Mitchell) Boyett; B.S., Tex. Woman's U., 1954, M.S. in Home Econs. Edn., 1956; M.Ed., East Tex. State U., 1961; Ed.D., 1972; m. James C. Dooley, May 5, 1942 (div. Nov. 1966); children—Bobby Curtis, Marilu. Tchr. home econs. Garland Ind. Sch. Dist., 1954-55; tchr. home econs. Richardson Ind. Sch. Dist., 1955-60, counselor, 1958-66; dir. spl. project drug and crime prevention edn. Tex. Edn. Agy., Austin, 1967—. Mem. Am., Tex. (pub. relations com. 1966) personnel and guidance assns., Am. (membership chmn. 1966, 67), Tex. (pres. 1966-67, exec. bd. 1967) sch. counselors assns., Richardson Edn., Assn. (pres. 1957-58), Tex. Tchrs. Assn., Am. Vocational Assn., North Central Tex. Vocational Guidance Assn. (sec. 1963), Am., Tex. home econs. assns., Phi Sigma Alpha (chpt. charter mem.). Methodist. Club: Altrusa Internat. (chpt. charter mem.). Home: 3 Sugar Shack St Austin TX 78761 Office: Tex Edn Agy 201 E 11th St Austin TX 78701

DOOLEY, VINCENT JOSEPH, football coach; b. Mobile, Ala., Sept. 4, 1932; s. William Vincent and Nellie Agnes (Stauter) D.; grad. Bus. Adminstrn., Auburn U., 1954, M.A. in History, 1963; m. Barbara Anne Meshad, Mar. 19, 1960; children—Deanna, Danny, Denise. Asst. football coach Auburn (Ala.) U., 1956-63; head football coach U. Ga., Athens, 1963—. Served as lt. USMCR, 1954-56. Decorated Nat. Def. medal. Mem. Demosthenian Lit. Soc. (hon.), Omicron Delta Kappa. Roman Catholic. Rotarian. Home: 755 Milledge Circle Athens GA 30601

DOOLEY, WALLACE TROY, physician; b. Conway, Ark., June 15, 1917; s. Thomas Pierce and Dalice (Hawkins) D.; A.B., Kan. U., 1939, M.A., 1941; M.D., Meharry Med. Coll., 1947; m. Orealia Clara Robinson, Dec. 10, 1939; children—Wallace Troy, Orealia Leola. Intern Hubbard Hosp., Nashville, 1947-48, resident, 1948-51; practice medicine specializing in orthopedic surgery Nashville, Tenn., 1955; mem. staff George W. Hubbard Hosp., Riverside Hosp. (both Nashville); resident orthopedic surgeon Mercy Hosp., Iowa City, Ia, 1951-53; orthopedic resident Children's Hosp., State U. Ia., Iowa City, 1953-55; with Meharry Med. Hosp., Nashville, 1955—, head dept. orthopedic surgery, 1955—, asso. prof. surgery, 1955-68, prof. orthopaedic surgery, 1968—. Mem. Frontiers Am., med. adv. bd. Nat. Found., 1959-60; co-chmn. March of Dimes, 1957-58; bd. dirs. N.A.A.C.P., 1958-61; pres. Community Conf. Employment, 1960-64. Bd. dirs. Nat. Found. Fellow Royal Soc. Health; mem. R.F. Boyd Med. Soc. (sec.), Vol. State Med. Assn., Nat. Med. Assn., Am. Congress PM and R., Assn. Med. Rehab. Dirs. and Coordinators, Nashville C. of C., N.Y. Acad. Sci., A.A.A.S., Kappa Pi. Kappa Alpha Psi. Republican. Baptist. Elk. Home: 3404 Geneva Circle Nashville TN 37209 Office: 1005 18th Av N Nashville TN 37208

DOOLEY, WILLIAM GERALD (BILL), football coach; b. Mobile, Ala., May 19, 1934; s. William Vincent and Nellie Agnes (Stauter) D.; student Miss. State U., 1956; m. Mary Christine Paolucci, July 14, 1962; children—Jim Bill. Asst. coach Miss. State U., 1956-57, head freshman coach, 1958-60, offensive line coach, 1963; head line coach George Washington U., 1961-62; head offensive coach U. Ga., 1964-66; head coach U.N.C., 1967—. Rotarian. Home: 110 Fern Lane Chapel Hill NC 27514

DOOLITTLE, JESSE SEYMOUR, educator; b. Bethany, Conn., Sept. 20, 1903; s. Walter Wales and Alice (Russell) D.; B.S., Tufts U., 1925; M.S., Pa. State U., 1937; m. Grace M. Ballou, Sept. 7, 1927. Student engr. Gen. Electric Co., Lynn, Mass., 1925-27; instr. mech. engring. Cast Inst. Tech., Cleve., 1927-31; faculty Pa. State U., State College, 1931-47, asso. prof. mech. engring., 1942-47; prof. mech. engring. N.C. State U., Raleigh, 1947—. Cons.; mem. N.C. Adv. Com. Sci., Engring. and Specialized Personnel, 1956-71, vice chmn., 1961-71. Recipient Tchr. of Year award N.C. State U. Alumni, 1963; Named One of Outstanding Tchrs. N.C. State U. faculty selection panel, 1967. Registered profl. engr., Pa., N.C. Life fellow Am. Soc. M.E.; mem. Am. Soc. Engring. Edn. (Western Electric award 1965, Burks award mech. engring. div. 1970), Am. Assn. U. Profs. (N.C. State U. pres. 1951-52), A.A.A.S., Sigma Xi (pres. N.C. State U. 1965-66), Tau Beta Pi, Pi Tau Sigma, Phi Kappa Phi (N.C. State U. pres. 1970), Pi Kappa Phi. Author: Mechanical Engineering Laboratory, 1957; Thermodynamics for Engineers, 1959, 64; (with Alexander H. Zerban) Engineering Thermodynamics, 1948, 54, 63; Energy Conversion, 1970. Home: 813 Graham St Raleigh NC 27605

DOOLITTLE, JESSE WILLIAM, JR., lawyer; b. Wheaton, Ill., May 19, 1929; s. Jesse William and Selma (Schacht) D.; A.B., DePauw U., 1951; LL.B., Harvard, 1954; m. Annette Danforth Bush, May 5, 1962; children—Danforth Bush, Alice Walters. Admitted to D.C. bar, 1954; law clerk U.S. Supreme Ct. Justice, Felix Frankfurter, Washington, 1957-58; associated with the firm Covington & Burling, Washington, 1958-61; asst. to solicitor gen. of U.S., U.S. Dept. of Justice, Washington, 1961-63, 1st asst., civil div., 1963-66; gen. counsel U.S. Dept. Air Force, 1966-68, asst. Sec. Air Force, 1968-69; partner firm Prather, Levenberg, Seeger, Doolittle, Farmer & Ewing, Washington, 1969—. Mem. council Harvard Law Sch. Assn., 1964-68; mem. Harvard Coll. overseers' com. to visit ROTC programs, 1967-69, com. to visit Law Sch., 1969—, overseer Harvard Law Rev., 1967-72; pres., bd. dirs. Nat. Child Research Center, 1972—. Served to 1st lt., AUS, 1954-57. Recipient Career Service award Nat. Civil Service League, 1968, Air Force Exceptional Civilian Service award, 1969. Mem. Am. Law Inst., Bar Assn. D.C., Delta Chi, Phi Beta Kappa. Clubs: Metropolitan, Internat. (Washington). Episcopalian (vestryman). Home: 4238 50th St NW Washington DC 20016 Office: 1101 16th St NW Washington DC 20036

DOOLITTLE, MARGARET MASTERS (MRS. CHARLES WARREN DOOLITTLE), city ofcl.; b. Jasper, Mo., Dec. 28, 1909; d. Grover Troy and Annie (Winder) Masters; grad. high sch.; m. Charles Warren Doolittle, Dec. 24, 1945. Sec., First Nat. Bank, McAlester, Okla., 1928-46, pvt. sec. to chmn. bd., 1946-48; credit mgr. McAlester Gen. Hosp., 1953-58; sec. Anderson Constrn. Co., 1958-62; office mgr. Active Bus. Credit, 1962-66; city clk., McAlester, 1968—. Bd. dirs. McAlester Boys' Club, Inc. Recipient medallion Boys Club, Inc., 1970. Mem. Okla. Assn. Municipal Clks., Treas. and Finance Officers Assn. Mem. Disciples of Christ Ch. Home: 410 E Wichita St McAlester OK 74501 Office: Box 578 McAlester OK 74501

DORAN, ADRON, univ. pres.; b. Graves County, Ky., Sept. 1, 1909; s. Edward C. and Elizabeth (Clemons) D.; A.A., Freed-Hardeman Jr. Coll., 1930; B.S., Murray State Coll., 1932, M.A., 1948; Ed.D., U. Ky., 1950; LL.D., Ashland Coll., 1967; m. Mignon McClain, Aug. 23, 1931. Tchr. high sch., coach, prin. Boaz (Ky.) High Sch., 1932-35, Sylvan Shade (Ky.) High Sch., 1935-38; prin. Wingo (Ky.) High Sch., 1938-48; mem. Ky. Legislature, 1944-51; speaker of Ky. House Reps., 1950-51; editor Fulton (Ky.) Daily Leader, 1946-48; vis. prof. edn. U. Ga., 1951; dir. div. tchr. edn. and certification Ky. Dept. Edn., 1952-54; pres. Morehead (Ky.) State U., 1954—. Organizer, dir. Legislative Work Conf., So. Regional Edn. Bd., 1952, 53, 54, cons., 1952-54; assisted formation of Western Interstate Commn. on Higher Edn., 1950-52; mem. White House Conf. Edn., Washington, 1954, 65, So. Regional Conf. Edn. Beyond High Sch., 1958; commr. Edn. Commn. of States; mem. Adv. Com. on Edn. to Appalachian Commn. Ordained to ministry Ch. of Christ, 1928. Mem. Eastern Ky. Regional Planning Commn., So. Regional Edn. Bd.; mem. Nat. Adv. Council Edn. Professions Devel., 1967—. Bd. dirs. Central Midwestern Regional Ednl. Lab., Inc., 1967; trustee Ohio Valley Coll., 1967. Recipient award of merit Ky. Assn. Colls., Secondary and Elementary Schs., 1946, award for outstanding service Soil Conservation Dists. Ky., 1958, Lincoln Key award Ky. Edn. Assn., 1959; Man of Year, Morehead (Ky.) C. of C., 1959; Kentuckian of Year, Ky. Press Assn., 1959; Distinguished Kentuckian award, 1966; named Knight Ky. Derby, 1962; Boss of Yr., Morehead Jr. C. of C., 1967; Outstanding Alumnus, U. Ky., 1966; Horatio Alger award, 1971. Mem. N.E.A. (mem. legislative commn. 1963-66, chmn. 1965-66), Ky. Edn. Assn. (past pres.), Ky. Council on Pub. Higher Edn., Phi Delta Kappa, Kappa Delta Pi. Home: 328 University Blvd Morehead KY 40351

DORATI, ANTAL, composer-conductor; b. Budapest, Hungary, Apr. 9, 1906; s. Alexander and Margit (Kunwald) D.; student composition and piano, Acad. of Music, Budapest, diploma, 1924; student U. Vienna, 1923-25; Mus.D., Macalester Coll., 1957; m. Klara Korody, July 14, 1929; 1 dau., Antonia Klara. Came to U.S., 1934, naturalized, 1947. Condr. Budapest Royal Opera House, 1924-28, Dresden State Opera, 1928-29, Munster State Opera, 1929-32, Ballet Russe de Monte Carlo, 1933-37; mus. dir. original Ballet Russe, 1938-40, Ballet Theatre, 1940-44; mus. dir. Dallas Symphony Orch., 1945-49; mus. dir. Mpls. Symphony Orch., 1949-60; chief condr. BBC Symphony Orch., London, 1962-66; chief condr. Stockholm Philharmonic, 1966—; music dir. Washington Nat. Symphony, 1969—; guest condr. all maj. orchs., U.S., Europe, Latin America, Australia. Compositions include string quartet, quintet for oboe and strings, divertimento for small orchestra, three American serenades for string orchestra, cello concerto; 2 Hungarian Peasant Tunes for violin and piano, 1945; arranger La Vie Parisienne by Offenbach, for New Opera Co., 1941; The Way of the Cross (Cantata); The Two Enchantments of Li Tai Pe (lyric scene for baritone and small orchestra); Symphony (for large orchestra); Missa brevis (for mixed choir and percussion instruments); Magdalena (ballet); 7 Pieces for Orchestra; Octet for Strings; Madrigal Suite (chorus and orch.); Largo Concertato for String Orchestra; Chamber Music for Soprano and String Orchestra; ballet arrangements include: Graduation Ball, Bluebeard, Helen of Troy, Pavillon, Fair at Sorochinsk, Harvest Time. Records for Mercury Recording Co. EMI, Philips, RCA-Victor, Decca. Home: Via del Fregagli 74 Rome Italy Office: care Nat Symphony Orch 2480 16th St NW Washington DC 20009

DORENKAMP, HENRY JOSEPH, JR., accountant, lawyer; b. Louisville, May 25, 1925; s. Henry Joseph and Mary J. (O'Hern) D.; B.S., Xavier U. 1949; LL.B., U. Louisville, 1952, J.D., 1952; m. Mary Virginia Rassinier, May 31, 1952; children—Stephen Henry, Jill Ann, Kent Robert, Dayle Ann. Admitted to Ky. bar, 1953; individual practice, Louisville; owner Glendale Office Center; treas. Seignior, Inc. Served USAAF, 1943-46. Decorated Air medal with oak leaf cluster. C.P.A., Ky. Mem. Am. Inst. C.P.A.'s Ky. Soc. C.P.A.'s, Am. Assn. Atty.-C.P.A.'s, Ky., Louisville bar assns., Am. Legion. Home: 2340 Gladstone Av Louisville KY 40205 Office: Glendale Office Center 2305 Taylorsville Rd Louisville KY 40205

DO RIO BRACNO, JOAO PAULO DA SILVA PARANHOS, Brazilian diplomat; b. Pelotas, Brazil, July 9, 1922; s. Paulo Agenor se Silva Paranhos and Francisca (Lebert) do Rio B.; B.A. in Math. and Philosophy, Paris, France; M.A. in Econs., Tulane U., now postgrad.; m. Adrienne McArdle; children—Sandra, Virginia. With Brazilian diplomatic service, 1942—, now consul gen., New Orleans. Home: 3735 Pin Oak Av New Orleans LA 70114 Office: Brazilian Consulate General 1306 Internat Trade Mart New Orleans LA 70130

DORLAND, GILBERT MEDING, steel co. exec.; b. N.Y.C., Nov. 26, 1912; s. Gilbert Grant and Louise(Eckhardt) D.; student Rensselaer Poly. Inst., 1931-32; B.S., U.S. Mil. Acad., 1936; M.S. in Civil Engring., U. Cal. at Berkeley, 1940; m. Lillian Okkerse, Mar. 21, 1937; children—Gilbert N., John H., Peter G., Richard L., Diane L. Commd. 2d lt. U.S. Army, 1936, advanced through grades to col., 1944; with Manhattan Dist., C.E., Armed Forces Spl. Weapons Project, Oak Ridge and Albuquerque, 1946-50; asst. dist. engr. Alaska Dist., C.E., 1950-52, dist. engr. Nashville Dist., 1952-56; ret., 1956; exec. v.p. Nashville Bridge Co., 1956-61, pres., 1962-69; pres. Bessemer Galvanizing Works (Ala.), 1962-68; v.p. Torres Mexicannas, S.A., 1962-68; exec. v.p. Carolina Steel Corp., Greensboro, 1969-70, pres., 1971—; dir. Wachovia Bank & Trust Co., Greensboro. Pres. Middle Tenn. council Boy Scouts Am., 1954-56; now mem. Nat. council; past chmn. Tenn-Tombigbee Waterway Devel. Authority; pres. Cumberland Valley Assn., 1958-69. Decorated Legion of Merit. Bronze Star medal, Order Brit. Empire. Recipient Outstanding Civilian Service award Dept. Army, 1968. Registered profl. engr., Tenn. Fellow Am. Soc. C.E.; mem. Nat. Soc. Profl. Engrs., Soc. Am. Mil. Engrs., Am. Ordnance Assn., Presidents Assn., Am. Inst. Steel Constrn. (pres. 1970—), Nat. Waterways Conf. (pres. 1963-65). Episcopalian. Kiwanian (past pres. Nashville). Clubs: Army and Navy (Washington); Greensboro Country. Home: 1916 Granville Rd Greensboro NC 27408 Office: PO Box 20888 Greensboro NC 27420

DORMAN, DONALD WILBUR, accountant; b. Los Angeles, Dec. 9, 1928; s. Wilbur Alanson and Helen (Baxter) D.; student Texas A. and M. U., 1945-46, Tyler Jr. Coll., 1946; B.B.A., Tex. Technol. U.,

1950; m. Mildred Nelson, May 2, 1952; children—Donna, David, Dean, Daniel. Staff accountant Condray, Pratas & Smith, C.P.A.'s, Lubbock, Tex., 1951-55; propr. Donald W. Dorman, C.P.A., Lubbock, 1955-57; partner Dorman & Newsom, C.P.A.'s, Dorman Newsom & Caraway, Dorman & Caraway, Dorman, Caraway & Howard, 1957-66; mng. partner Lubbock office Main Lafrentz & Co., C.P.A.'s 1966-—; pres., dir. Donall, Inc.; v.p., dir. Dorman & Co. Past pres. S. Plains Trust and Estate Council. Bd. dirs. Lubbock United Fund, chmn. budget div., 1969-—, v.p., 1971; bd. dirs. Tex. Technol. U. Found.; past pres., trustee Ednl. Found. Tex. Soc. C.P.A.'s. Recipient award for meritorious service to pub. accounting profession in Tex., Tex. Soc. C.P.A.'s, 1968. Mem. Am. Inst. C.P.A.'s, Tex. Soc. C.P.A.'s (past v.p.), Lubbock Chpt. C.P.A.'s (past pres.), Beta Alpha Psi (hon.). Home: 3202 57th St Lubbock TX 79413 Office: 1st Nat Pioneer Bldg Lubbock TX 79401

DORMAN, EUGENE ANDERSON, realtor; b. Conway, S.C., Oct. 18, 1923; s. Luther Stanley and Maggie Marie (Anderson) D.; student U. S.C., 1945-46; m Louise Glasgow, July 21, 1946. children—Stephen E., Kathryn Ellen. Life ins. agt., mgr. Durham Life Ins. Co., 1946-56; realtor Dorman Realty & Ins. Co., Inc.,Conway, S.C., 1956-—; pres. Dorman Enterprises, Inc., Coastal Heights, Inc., Beach Motels, Inc., Horry Enterprises, Inc., Premium Finance Corp., exec. v.p. Bucksport Plantation Golf Club, Inc. Chmn., Horry County Airport Commn., 1964-—. Bd. dirs. Devel. Bd. Served with AUS, 1942-45; prisoner of war, 1944-45. Decorated Silver Star, Purple Heart. Mem. C. of C. (award of appreciation for civic work 1961). Methodist (trustee). Rotarian. Home: 108 Park Av Conway SC 29526 Office: 604 Main St Conway SC 29526

DORMAN, JOHN FREDERICK, genealogist; b. Louisville, July 25, 1928; s. John Frederick and Sue Carpenter (Miller) D.; B.S., U. Louisville, 1950; M.A., Emory U., 1955. Asst. archivist Coll. of William and Mary, 1953-55; genealogist, Washington, 1955-—; lectr. Am. U. Inst. Geneal. Research, 1963-—. Fellow Am. Soc. Genealogists (treas. 1959-66); mem. Soc. of Cincinnati, Soc. Colonial Wars (dep. registrar gen. 1969-—), Soc. War of 1812, S.R., S.A.R. (D.C. pres. 1967-68), Newcomen Soc., Nat. Geneal. Soc. (v.p. 1958-59, 68-70, librarian, 1959-60), Children Am. Revolution (sr. nat. registrar 1960-62, sr. nat. treas. 1962-64, 66-68, sr. nat. 2d. v.p. 1968-70), Descs. Colonial Govs. (1st dep. gov. gen. 1970-—), Deses. Lords Md. Manors (registrar 1971-—). Republican. Episcopalian. Editor: The Va. Genealogist, 1957-—. Home: 2022 Columbia Rd NW Washington DC 20009

DORN, WILLIAM JENNINGS BRYAN, congressman; b. Greenwood, S.C., Apr. 14, 1916; s. Thomas Elbert and Pearl (Griffith) D.; ed. pub. schs., Greenwood; LL.D., Lander Coll., 1965, Clemson U., 1970; m. Millie Johnson; children—Briana (Mrs. Wade T. Batson III), Olivia Byrd, Debbie Gail, William Jennings Bryan II, Johnson Griffith. Mem. S.C. Ho. of Reps., 1939-40; mem. S.C. Senate, 1940-42; mem. 80th, 82d-92d congresses from 3d S.C. Dist., vice chmn. vets affairs com., mem. pub. works com., house steering com., sec., organizer informal textile com. Served with AUS, 1942-45; ETO. Mem. Am. Legion, V.F.W., Amvets, Greenwood C. of C., 40 and 8, Air Force Assn., Farm Bur., Woodman of World, Grange. Democrat. Baptist. Mason. Home: Barratt House RFD 1 Greenwood SC 29646 Office: Rayburn Bldg Washington DC 20515

DORNAUS, WALTER PERRY, lawyer; b. Bloomington, Ill., Apr. 27, 1915; s. Walter J. and Minnie E. (Perry) D.; A.B., Ill. Wesleyan U., 1937; LL.B., U. Okla., 1939; m. Aragene Lane, Sept. 15, 1938; children— Elizabeth Ann, Sara Jeanne, Margaret Lane, Vera Carolyn. Admitted to Okla. bar, 1940, Tex. bar, 1945; asso. firm Crouch, Rhodes & Crowe, Tulsa, 1940-42, Milsten & Milsten, Tulsa, 1942; with legal dept. Shell Oil Co., Tulsa, 1942-44, Stanolind Oil & Gas Co., Ft. Worth, also Tulsa, 1944-52; chief counsel, head legal dept. Kewanee Oil Co., Tulsa, 1952-71; practice law, Tulsa, 1971-—; past bd. suprs. Nat. Oil Co. of Libya; dir., sec. Sound Refining, Inc., Tacoma; v.p., dir. Bromandor Corp., Tulsa. Mem. legal com. Interstate Oil Compact Commn., 1963-71; lectr. legal insts. Southwestern Legal Found., Dallas, 1952-53. Mem. Tulsa Mayor's Com. for Charter Revision, 1959-60. Mem. City-County Republican Exec. Com., [illegible]9-60, chmn. state speakers bur., 1950. Mem. State Bar Tex., Okla., Tulsa County, Am. (chmn. oil com. of mineral sect. 1964-65, chmn. spl. ad hoc com. congl. pub. and law rev. commn. 1966) bar assns., Mid-Continent (exec. com.), N.M., Ill. oil and gas assns., Oil Industry Information Council, Independent Petroleum Assn., Petroleum Club Tulsa, S.A.R. (Tulsa pres. 1966-—, state pres. 1969-71), Tau Kappa Epsilon, Pi Kappa Delta, Phi Alpha Delta. Methodist. Mason (Shriner), Author: The Fountain and Other Poems. Contbr. articles to law revs.

DORR, ANNIE MAUDE DEAN (MRS. WILLIAM HENRY DORR), educator; b. Ashland, Ala.; d. William Thomas and Dora (Griffin) Dean; A.B. cum laude, diplomas in piano and speech, Judson Coll., 1928; M.A., George Peabody Coll., 1945; m. William Henry Dorr, June 22, 1954. Tchr. English, Tallapoosa County High Sch., Dadeville, Ala. 1928-32, Clay County High Sch., Ashland, 1932-43; dir YWCA-USO, Carolina Beach, N.C., 1943-44, Durham, N.C., 1944, Montgomery, Ala., 1945-47; asst. prof. edn. and psychology Huntingdon Coll., 1947-48; tchr. English, St. Petersburg (Fla.) High Sch., 1948-—, chmn. dept., 1958-65, 68-—; tchr. English, St. Petersburg Jr. Coll., evening div., 1956-62. Chmn. constitution and by-laws com. Pinellas County Tchrs. English Council, 1965-66. Fla. sponsor Nat. Honor Soc., 1962-63. Mem. Pinellas (2d v.p. 1953-54, pres. 1954-55, 62-63, 1st v.p. 1963-64), Fla. (treas. 1955-57, chmn. textbook evaluation com. 1962-64, chmn. state conv. 1960), Nat. (membership com. 1962, del. 1954, 62), councils tchrs. English, Pinellas County Classroom Tchrs. Assn., St. Petersburg Civic Music Assn., St. Petersburg Little Theater, Alph Delta Kappa (chpt. corr. sec.). Baptist (organist 1938-43). Mem. Order Eastern Star. Home: 1300 6th Av N St Petersburg FL 33705 Office: St Petersburg High Sch 2501 5th Av N St Petersburg FL 33713

DORSEY, JASPER NEWTON, communications co. exec.; b. Marietta, Ga., Jan. 19, 1913; s. John Tucker and Annie (Coryell) D.; A.B., U. Ga., 1936, postgrad. Lumpkin Law Sch., 1935-36; m. Callender Weltner, Oct. 16, 1937; children—Sally (Mrs. David L. Wilsey), John Tucker (dec.). With So. Bell Tel. & Tel. Co., Inc., 1937-61, 68-—, v.p., Atlanta, 1968-—; mgr. govt. relations Am. Tel. & Tel., Washington, 1962-68; dir. Fulton Nat. Corp., Fulton Nat. Bank, Atlanta, Ga. Motor Club, Inc., Atlanta. Mem. adv. bd. Salvation Army, Atlanta, 1970-—. Bd. dirs. Ga. Easter Seal Soc., Ga. Safety Council, Am. Cancer Soc., Atlanta Boys Club, Nat. Conf. Christians and Jews; trustee, mem. exec. com. U. Ga. Found., Atlanta, Kennesaw Jr. Coll. Found., Marietta, Ga., Ga. Student Ednl. Fund, Athens; bd. visitors Emory U., Atlanta; treas., mem. exec. com. Richard B. Russell Found., Atlanta; trustee Gordon Mil. Coll., Barnesville, Ga. Served to lt. col. Inf. AUS, 1941-46. Recipient Blue Key award U. Ga., 1967; Outstanding Contbn. to U. Ga. award, 1969; Alumni Merit award U. Ga., 1970; Georgian of Year award Ga. Assn. Broadcasters, 1971. Mem. Ga. (v.p., dir.), Atlanta (dir.) chambers commerce, U. Ga. Alumni Assn. (nat. pres., 1967-69, chmn. bd., 1969-—), Blue Key, Sphinx, Gridiron, Greek Horsemen, Omicron Delta Kappa, Sigma Delta Chi, Phi Delta Theta. Presbyn. (elder). Kiwanian. Clubs: Capital City, Commerce, Peachtree Golf, Piedmont Driving (Atlanta); Nat. Press, Army-Navy, Kenwood (Washington). Office: So Bell Telephone & Telegraph Co 805 Peachtree St Atlanta GA 30308

DORSEY, ROBERT WYLIE, investment co. exec.; b. West Alexander, Pa., Feb. 12, 1917; s. Frank Wylie and Elisabeth Fuller (Shearer) D.; A.B., Morris Harvey Coll., 1938; M.B.A., U. So. Cal., 1949; m. Julia B. Martin, Mar. 10, 1945; 1 son, Donald Blaine. Accountant Cohen Drug Co., Charleston, W.Va., 1938-40; asst. prof. econs. Morris Harvey Coll., Charleston, 1946-49; economist Atlantic Richfield Corp., Dallas, 1950-54; dir. research Southwestern Securities Co., Dallas, 1954-56; sr. asso. Bruce Payne & Assos. of Mexico, Mexico City, 1957-58; investment analyst Brown Allen &Co., Inc., Dallas, 1958-—. Vice pres., dir. Central Am. Mining &Oil Corp., Tegucigalpa, Honduras, 1966-—; sec., dir. Caribbean Energy Corp., Dallas, 1968-—; pres. Dallas So. Corp., 1959-—. Mem. Dallas County Republican Exec. Com., 1952-54, 56-58; del. Rep. State Conv., 1954, 56, 70; asst. election judge precinct 227 Dallas, 1970-—. Served to capt. AUS, 1941-46. Mem. Dallas C. of C., Mil. Order World Wars (perpetual), Assn. U.S. Army (exec. com.), Dallas Assn. Investment Analysts, Inst. Chartered Financial Analysts. Elk. Club: Lancers. Home: 854 Lake Terrace Dr Dallas TX 75218 Office: Brown Allen & Co Empire Life Bldg Dallas TX 75201

DORTCH, LAWRENCE, lawyer; b. Columbia, Tenn., Jan. 21, 1914; B.A., Duke, 1936; LL.B., U. Va., 1940. Admitted to Tenn. bar, 1939; mem. firm Waller Lansden Dortch & Davis, Nashville. Mem. Nashville, Tenn., Am. bar assns., Phi Delta Phi. Address: Waller Lansden Dortch & Davis 12th Floor Am Trust Bldg Nashville TN 37201*

DORWALD, DICK, advt. agy. exec.; b. Middleport, N.Y., Aug. 16, 1933; s. G. Rollin and Mary Ellen (Greeley) D.; B.A., Bob Jones U., 1956; m Yvonne Colleen McElroy, June 2, 1956; children—Richard S., Julia Ellen, Laura Esther. Continuity dir. WMUU Radio, Greenville, S.C., 1958-62, sales mgr., 1964-65; pres. Dick Dorwald Assos., Greenville, S.C., 1964-72; partner Dorwald-Swiger Assos., 1972-—. Pres., S.C. Gideons Internat., 1968-71. Served with AUS, 1956-58. Home: 224 Azalea Ct Greenville SC 29607 Office: PO Box 10181 618 E Washington St Greenville SC 29603

DOSS, JAMES HOUSTON, bank dir.; b. Weatherford, Tex., Mar. 15, 1915; s. James Houston and Annie Lee (Goodman) D.; grad. Weatherford Jr. Coll., 1934; B.B.A., U. Tex., 1936; postgrad. Sch. Bus. Adminstrn. Harvard, 1937-38; m. Dorothy Jane Smith, Aug. 17, 1940; children—Nancy (Mrs. Billy Francis Knight), James Houston III, John Edgar. With Weatherford Mchts. and Farmers State Bank, 1937-—, pres., 1945-55, dir., 1940-—; dir. Continental State Bank, Boyd, Tex. Tchr. accounting Weatherford Jr. Coll., 1938-39; owner, devel. Shepherd Mall, Oklahoma City, 1964-—; builder S.W. area James Doss Enterprises, 1952-63. Vice pres. Weatherford Pub. Schs., 1958; mem. adv. bd. Southwest Med. Center, Dallas, 1958-61. Trustee Weatherford Jr. Coll., 1938-45; mem. bd. control Weatherford Mcpl. Water and Electric, 1945-48; trustee Trinity U., San Antonio, 1955-—, mem. finance com., 1960-—. Recipient Outstanding Civic Service citation Weatherford, 1958; named Outstanding Layman of Tex., Tex. Council Chs., 1961. Mem. Weatherford C. of C. (bd. dirs. 1942-48). Lion. Presbyn. (pres. Synod Tex. Found., 1954-—, mem. United Presbyn. Found. 1972-—. Home: 616 Baylor St Weatherford TX 76086 Office: James Doss Enterprises 536 Braniff Tower Dallas TX 75235

DOSS, SHANNON LOWELL, govt. ofcl.; b. Wilmar, Ark., Aug. 24, 1923; s. Elvin Payton and Jewell (Ault) D.; B.S., Ark. A. & M. U., 1949; M.S., U. Ark., 1952; student U. Tex., 1968-71; m. Robbye Lee Thompson, July 1, 1948; children—Debra Jo, David Shannon, Dayna Lee. Tchr. pub. schs., Monticello, Ark., 1949-51; prin., Springdale, Ark., 1952-55; asst. prin., counselor Wilson and Matthews jr. high schs., Lubbock, Tex., 1955-61; supt. schs., Claude, Tex., 1961-64; supt. schs., Memphis, Tex., 1964-66; supt. schs., San Marcos, Tex., 1966-70; chief govtl. relations div. Office of Economic Opportunity, Dallas, 1970-—; mem. adv. bd. ednl. TV sta. KLRN, Austin, Tex. Bd. dirs. San Marcos Community Action Agy. Served with USMCR, 1942-45. Decorated Air medal. Mem. Dallas Fed. Bus. Assn. (dir. 1970-—), Tex. Assn. Sch. Adminstrs., Tex. State Tchrs. Assn. (dist. pres. 1968-69); N.E.A., Am. Assn. Sch. Adminstrs., Tex. Congress Parents and Tchrs., San Marcos C. of C. (dir. 1968-70). Methodist (steward 1948-—). Mason. Rotarian, Lion (dir. 1954-66). Home: 3205 Greenbriar Plano TX 75074 Office: Office of Economic Opportunity 1100 Commerce St Dallas TX 75202

DOSSETT, JAMES KEARNEY, lawyer; b. Sanford, Miss., Feb. 10, 1914; s. Jesse Christopher and Mary Elizabeth (Lott) D.; B.S., U. So. Miss., 1939; LL.B., Jackson Sch. Law, 1954; m. Ina Fewell, May 31, 1941; children—James Kearney, Anita Kathryn (Mrs. James Harrold Jones), William Edward. Tchr. Miss. pub. schs., 1939-41; office mgr. Farm Security Adminstrn., Prentiss, Miss., 1941-42; agt. Internal Revenue Service, Jackson, Miss., 1952-54, chief rev. staff, 1954-58; admitted to Miss. bar, 1954; practice law, Jackson, 1958-—. Mem. Estate Planning Council Miss., 1963-64; mem., chmn. delegation S.E. Region Tax Liaison Com., 1967-72; vice chmn. legislative affairs com. Miss. Econ. Council, 1971-72. Trustee Clarke Meml. Coll., Newton, Miss., U. So. Miss. Found. Served with USNR, 1942-45. Mem. Hinds County (chmn. continuing legal edn. com. 1971-72), Miss. (chmn. taxation com. 1965-70), Am. (mem. taxation sect.) bar assns., Miss. Bar Found. (trustee 1962-65), Phi Kappa Phi, Sigma Delta Kappa. Baptist (deacon; adult sch. supt.). Kiwanian. Clubs: Country, Knife and Fork (Jackson). Home: 353 Northside Circle Jackson MS 39206 Office: 1801 Deposit Guaranty Bank Bldg Jackson MS 39201

DOSSETT, WALTER BROWN, JR., furniture co. exec.; b. Waco, Tex., Aug. 20, 1927; s. Walter Brown and Alethea Halbert (Sleeper) D.; B.B.A., U. Tex. at Austin, 1950; m. Mary Martha Dickie, Aug. 4, 1951; children— Walter Dickie, Markham Brown, Susan Sleeper, Martha Beckham, Pauline Reeder. Asst. sec., treas. Exporters & Traders Compress &Warehouse Co., Waco, Tex., 1952-65, sec., treas.; 1965-70; chmn., chief exec. officer Royal Seating Corp., Cameron, Tex., 1970-—; dir. 1st Nat. Bank Waco, Tex. Life Ins. Co., Waco, Rogers Delinted Cotton Seed Co., Waco; pres., Central Tex. Compress Co., Waco, 1965-—. Chmn. Waco Library Commn., 1961-62; pres. United Fund Waco, 1969-70. Mem. Waco City Council, 1970-72. Served with AUS, 1950-52. Mem. Kappa Sigma. Episcopalian (exec. bd. Tex. 1967-69). Rotarian. Club: Ridgewood Yacht. Home: 1609 College Dr Waco TX 76708 Office: PO Drawer 1339 Waco TX 76703

DOSTER, ROBERT MCMANUS, mfg. co. exec.; b. Lancaster, S.C., Sept. 26, 1917; s. Thomas Edwin and Pearle (McManus) D.; student U. Miami, 1936-37; A.B., U. S.C., 1940, LL.B., 1941; m. Jean Stewart, Jan 3, 1948; children—Robert, Anne (Mrs. Grady Britt), Jean, Elizabeth, Louise, Christian. Admitted to S.C. bar, 1941; pres. Chesterfield Shops, Lancaster, 1950-60; pres. DAM Coffee Co., Lancaster, 1951-71; prin. R.N. Doster & Assos., Lancaster, 1960-71; pres. Sculptures Steel, Lancaster, 1960-71; regional marketing mgr. Bernardi Brothers div. Lionel Corp., Lancaster, 1970-—; dir. Lancaster & Chester Ry. Co. Mem. S.C. Finance com. Republican party, 1964-65. Served as fighter pilot USAAF, 1941-45. Decorated 3 Air medals. Mem. Fla. Oil Jobbers Assn. Rotarian. Address: Brook Dr Lancaster SC 29720

DOSWELL, JAMES MARSHALL, JR., textile mills exec.; b. Richmond, Va., Aug. 13, 1921; s. James Marshall and Margaret Lewis (Miller) D.; B.S., Hampden-Sydney Coll., 1942; postgrad. Drake U., 1947-48, U. N.C., 1967-68; m. Gloria Virginia Stacy, Dec. 22, 1947; children—Julia, Margaret, Laura. News editor Chgo. Bur., A.P., 1948-55; editor Covington (Va.) Virginian, 1956; asso. editor, mng. editor Evening Herald, Rock Hill, S.C., 1957-62; dir., v.p. pub. relations Springs Mills, Inc., Ft. Mill, S.C., 1962-—. Bd. dirs. S.C. State Library, Rock Hill Speech and Hearing Center, Rock Hill Sheltered Workshop. Served with AUS, 1942-46. Internat. Press Inst. grantee, 1958; recipient Distinguished Reporting award Atlanta chpt. Sigma Delta Chi, 1960. Mem. Rock Hill C. of C. (pres. 1961), Pub. Relations Soc. Am. (pres. S.C. chpt. 1971), Charlotte Pub. Relations Soc. (pres.), S.C. Textile Mfrs. Assn. (chmn. pub. relations div. 1965), Presbyn. Men of Ch. Bethel Presbytery (pres. 1970), Sigma Delta Chi. Home: Route 1 Box 449 Rock Hill SC 29730 Office: Springs Mills Inc Exec Office Bldg Fort Mill SC 29615

DOTSON, BOBBY JOE, supt. schs.; b. Pound, Va., Sept. 3, 1931; B.A., Emory & Henry Coll., 1954; M.Ed., U. Va., 1963; m. Nancy Collins, Dec. 27, 1957; children—Lisa, Elizabeth. Tchr. high schs., Coeburn, Va., 1954-60, prin. high sch., 1961-67; adminstrv. asst. Rep. William C. Wampler, Washington, 1968; supt. schs. Norton, Va., 1968-—. Sec., Dotson Aviation Corp., Wise, Va., 1960-71. Appointee Council Higher Edn. Gov. Holton, 1971. Vice chmn. Wise County Republican Com., 1969-70, sec., 1970-71. Mem. Va., Nat. assns. sch. adminstrs., Wise County and Lonesome Pine Prins. Assn. (chmn. 1963-64), Va. High Sch. League (Va. chmn. 1964), Emory and Henry Coll. Alumni Assn. (regional v.p. 1970-71), Phi Delta Kappa. Home: Box 112 Wise VA 24293 Office: Wayne Av Norton VA 24273

DOTY, DONALD D., banker; b. Independence, Kan., June 30, 1928; s. Laton L. and Dorothy (Russell) D.; B.S., Okla. State U., 1950; grad. Grad. Sch. Banking, U. Wis., 1963; m. Cheri F. Montgomery, June 14, 1952; children—John Scott, Susan Dorothy, Mark Montgomery. Cattle rancher, nr. Bartlesville, Okla., 1950-53; with First Nat. Bank Bartlesville, 1955-—, asst. cashier, 1956-60, asst. v.p., 1960-62, v.p., 1962-69, exec. v.p., 1969-—, also dir.; v.p., dir. Rocking D Land & Cattle Co., Bartlesville, 1969-—; dir. New Camp Minerals, Inc. Bd. dirs. Bluestem Cattlemens Assn., 1966; pres. Bartlesville Credit Bur., 1971; pres. Bartlesville Area Indsl. Devel. Co., 1971; chmn. bd. trustees Jane Phillips Epsicopal Meml. Med. Center, 1971. Served to capt. USAF, 1953-55. Recipient Distinguished Service award Bartlesville, 1957; named Outstanding Local Jaycee Pres., 1958, Outstanding Young Man in Okla., 1958. Mem. Bartlesville C. of C. (dir. 1966-—), Wis. Sch. Banking Alumni Assn. (pres. Okla. 1966). Republican. Presbyn. (pres. bd. trustees 1970). Mason (32 deg., Shriner, Jester). Club: Hillcrest Country (Bartlesville). Home: 1447 Valley Rd Bartlesville OK 74003 Office: Box 999 Bartlesville OK 74003

DOTY, LOCKWOOD RICHARD, II, pub. relations and advt. exec.; b. Lockport, N.Y., Mar. 24, 1921; s. Lockwood West and Flora (Weaver) D.; student Trinity Coll.; D.Bus. Adminstrn. (hon.), Ind. No. U., 1971; m. Mary Alice Brayer, Oct. 6, 1945; children—Mary Louise Brayer, Jennifer West (dec.), Sara Cady. News editor WCOP, Boston, 1945-47, WCON, Atlanta Constn., 1947-49; commentator NBC, N.Y.C., 1949-52; asso. news dir. WOR-TV, N.Y.C., 1953; program dir. WHAM, Rochester, 1953-57; pres. Blue Skies Broadcasting Corp., 1957-60; exec. v.p., gen. mgr. Fla. Air Power, Inc., 1960-61; v.p. WINZ, Miami, 1961-62; newscaster WTVJ, Miami, 1962-67; pres. Group One, Inc., 1967; sr. v.p. Campbell-Dickey Advt., 1967; pres. Dick Doty & Assos. Inc., pub. relations, advt. and marketing, Ft. Lauderdale, 1968, Prestige Letters, Inc., 1971-72; exec. v.p., sec.-treas. PRAMtee, Inc., 1972-—. Trustee Ft. Lauderdale U. Mem. Pub. Relations Soc. Am., Sales and Marketing Execs. Assn., Greater Ft. Lauderdale Advt. Fedn. (pres. 1970-71), Fla. Pub. Relations Assn. (dir., pres. Gold Coast chpt. 1971-72), Sigma Delta Chi (pres. Fla. E. Coast chpt. 1965-67). Republican. Episcopalian. Rotarian. Home: 2749 NE 19th St Fort Lauderdale FL 33305 Office: Suite 310 2701 E Sunrise Blvd Fort Lauderdale FL 33304

DOUGHARTY, MARCUS HILLMAN, banker; b. nr. Jasper, Tex., May 17, 1923; s. Francis Arthur and Sarah Beulah (McLemore) D.; A.A., Lamar Jr. Coll., 1942; B.B.A., U. Tex., 1947; m. Dorothy Mae Kohler, Sept. 27, 1949; children—Dana Katherine, Steven Wade, Sarah Elizabeth. Tax auditor State of Tex., Houston, 1947-48; agt. Internal Revenue Service, Beaumont, Tex., 1948-53; credit dept. mgr. First Security Nat. Bank, 1953-63, sr. v.p., 1969-—. Treas., Salvation Army Adv. Bd., 1969-—, A.W. Schlesinger Geriatric Center, 1969-—. Served with USAAF, 1943-46. C.P.A., Tex. Mem. Tex. Soc. C.P.A.'s, Am. Inst. C.P.A.'s, Robert Morris Assos. Home: 1130 20th St Beaumont TX 77706 Office: PO Box 3391 Beaumont TX 77704

DOUGHERTY, EDDIE LEE, cons. engr.; b. Kansas City, Kan., Dec. 1, 1925; s. Henry Leslie and Sylvia (Garrett) D.; B.S., U. Mo., 1949; m. Mary Lucille Campbell, June 9, 1948; children—Sylvia Louise, Mary Lorrice, Vicky Lee, Patricia Lorraine, Michael Leslie, Terry Lynn, Denny Leroy. Constrn. engr. Mo. Dept. Hwys., 1949-50; field engr. Howard, Needles, Tammen & Bergendoff, 1950-54, resident engr., Wheeling, W.Va., 1954-55, Emporia, Kan., 1955-56, Sault Ste. Marie, Mich., 1956-58, Rock Island, Ill., 1958-61, project engr., Orlando, Fla., 1961-64, New Castle, Del., 1964-66, engr. in charge, Richmond, Va., 1966-70, project mgr. Greater Buffalo Airport, 1970-71; asso. W.K. Dougherty, Cons. Engrs., Miami, Fla., 1971-—. Com. chmn. Boy Scouts Am., 1967-69. Served with AUS, 1943-45. Decorated Air Medal with 6 oak leaf clusters. Registered profl. engr., Mo., Fla., N.Y., Del., N.J., N.C., Va. Mem. Am. Soc. C.E., Nat. Soc. Profl. Engrs., Fla. Engring. Soc., N.J. Soc. Profl. Planners, Aero Club of Buffalo, Engrs. Club, Theta Tau. Home: 7565 SW 135th St Miami FL 33156 Office: PO Box 1162 Kendall Branch Miami FL 33156

DOUGHERTY, FRANK MARION, judge; b. Diboll, Tex., July 26, 1912; s. Frank E. and Della M. (Fitts) D.; LL.B., Baylor U., 1949; LL.B., Loyola U., New Orleans, 1950; m. Paulyn Gill, Feb. 17, 1946; children—Glenda Ruth, John Michael. Admitted to La. bar, 1950; pvt. practice law, Homer, 1952-57; judge 2d Jud. Dist. Ct., Homor, La., 1958-—. Served with USMC and USNR, 1942-45. Mem. Am., La. bar assns., Am. Judicature Soc., La. Law Inst., N. La. Hist. Soc. Mason (32 deg., Shriner). Baptist. Home: 722 S Main St Homer LA 71040 Office: 1 Public Sq Homer LA 71040

DOUGHERTY, GORDON B., mfg. rep., furniture co. exec.; b. Lewisburg, Tenn., May 6, 1897; s. Joe Clark and Lula Albertine (Wallace) D.; ed. pub. schs.; m. Mary Elizabeth Adkins, Dec. 26, 1928; 1 dau., Nancy (Mrs. Robert Davidson Erwin, Jr.). Salesman Nashville Chair Co., 1922-32; mfrs. rep. representing factories Southwest and So. states, 1933-—; dir., v.p. Bradfords Furniture Co., Nashville, 1950-—. Active civic charity drives. Trustee Martin Coll., Pulaski, Tenn.; bd. dirs. Nashville Big Bros. Served with C.E. U.S. Army, 1918. Mem. Tenn. Furniture Travelers, Southwest Roadruners. Methodist (mem. ofcl. bd. 1935-70, chmn. bd., 1949-51; trustee, 1969-—). Clubs: Merchants and Manufacturers (Chgo.);

Richland Country (Nashville). Home: 2004 Kingsbury Dr Nashville TN 37215 Office: 4100 Hillsboro Rd Nashville TN 37215

DOUGHERTY, J(OHN) CHRYS(OSTOM), lawyer; b. Beeville, Tex., May 3, 1915; s. John Chrysostom and Mary V. (Henderson) D.; B.A., U. Tex., 1937; LL.B., Harvard, 1940; diploma, Inter-Am. Acad. Internat. and Comparative Law, Havana, Cuba, 1948; m. Mary Ireland Graves, Apr. 18, 1942; children—Mary Ireland, John Chrysostom IV. Admitted to Tex. bar, 1940; atty. Hewit & Dougherty, 1940-41; partner Graves & Dougherty, 1946-50, Graves, Dougherty & Greenhill, Austin, Tex., 1950-57, Graves, Dougherty & Gee, 1957-60, Graves, Dougherty, Gee & Hearon, 1961-66, Graves, Dougherty, Gee, Hearon, Moody & Garwood, 1966—; spl. asst. atty. gen., 1949-50. Dir. Austin Nat. Bank. Hon. French consul for Tex., Austin, 1971—. Mem. Tex. Submerged Lands Adv. Com., 1963—, Tex. Bus. and Commerce Code Adv. Com., 1964-66, Gov.'s Com. Marine Resources, 1970, Colo. River Basin Water Quality Mgmt. Study Com., 1972—. Bd. dirs. Advanced Religious Study Found.; trustee Nat. Pollution Control Found., 1966—, St. Stephen's Episcopal Sch., 1966—, U. Tex. Law Sch. Found., 1971—. Served as capt. C.I.C., U.S. Army, 1941-44, Judge Adv. Gen. Corps. 1944-46, maj., 1953—. Fellow Tex. Bar Found., Am. Bar Found.; mem. Am. Arbitration Assn. (mem. nat. panel arbitrators 1958—, S.W. adv. council 1965—) Am., Travis County bar assns., State Bar Tex. (chmn. sect. taxation 1965-66), Internat., Am. fgn. law assns., Am. Law Inst., Am. Soc. Internat. Law (exec. council 1959-62), Inter-Am. Bar Assn., Cum Laude Soc. (hon.), Phi Beta Kappa, Phi Eta Sigma, Beta Theta Pi (dir. Tex. Beta Students Aid Fund). Presbyn. Rotarian. Co-editor: Texas Appellate Practice, 1964. Contbr. Bowe, Estate Planning and Taxation; Texas Lawyers Practice Guide, 1967, 71, How to Live and Die with Texas Probate, 1968; Texas Estate Administration, 1972. Home: 6 Green Lanes Austin TX 78703 Office: PO Box 98 Austin TX 78767

DOUGLAS, BARTON THRASHER, lawyer; b. Gainesville, Fla., Mar. 23, 1908; s. James Byers and Rebecca (Hicklin) D.; J.D., U. Fla., 1932; m. Monica Karlene Darling, May 30, 1958; children—Barton A. J. Zachariah Hicklin II, Alexander Scott II, Monica Karlene. Admitted to Fla. bar, 1932, Tex. bar, 1935; practiced in Gainesville, 1932—. Served to lt. comdr. USNR, 1942-45. Mem. Am., Fla. State, Tex. State, Fed. bar assns., Academia Internationali Lex Et Scientia, Eighth Jud. Bar Assn. (past pres.), Delta Chi. Democrat. Presbyn. (elder). Elk, K.P. Home: 612 NE 4th Av Gainesville FL 32601 Office: 103 N Main St Gainesville FL 32601

DOUGLAS, CHARLES HERBERT, univ. research adminstr.; b. Loughman, Fla., Dec. 2, 1926; s. Herbert and Delia (Sutton) D.; student La. State U., 1943-44, 46-47; Mus.B., Converse Coll., 1949, Mus.M., 1958; Ph.D., Fla. State U., 1965; m. Jane Caroline Long, Aug. 25, 1949; children—Daron Maudel, Carolyn Grove. Tchr. pvt. schs., New Orleans, 1950-57; asst. prof. Converse Coll., Spartanburg, S.C., 1957-60; asst. prof. U. Ga., Athens, 1961-65, asso. prof., 1965-67, asst. dean arts and scis., 1967-68, asst. v.p., 1968-71, dir. gen. research, 1971. Guest lectr. Agnes Scott Coll., 1966; clinician, adjudicator Ga. Music Educators Assn., 1961-66; dir. Spartanburg Civic Band, 1959-61. Served with USNR, 1943-45, 51-53. Spartanburg Found. teaching fellow, 1957-58. Mem. Nat. Council U. Research Adminstrs., Ga. Composers (pres. 1966-67), Phi Mu Alpha, Pi Kappa Lambda. Presbyn. Author: Harmony, 1954; Rhythmic Excerpts, 1954; Piano Class Teaching Method, 1955; Basic Music Theory, 1965; Playing Social Instruments, 1972. Mus. composer: Symphonic Suite for Band, 1958; Rhapsody for String Orchestra, 1962; String Quartet, 1963. Home: 460 Forest Rd Athens GA 30601

DOUGLAS, HENRY CLAY, JR., grove and cattle co. exec.; b. Dora, Ala., Feb. 20, 1921; s. Henry Clay and Annie May (Hodges) D.; B.S. with Honors, U. Fla., 1951; m. Dorothy Christine Krusen, Aug. 7, 1947; children—Susanne, Jennifer Lynn, Andra Christine. Mng. partner West Coast Flying Service, 1946-47; mgr. Krusen Grove and Cattle Co., Inc., Zephyrhills, Fla., 1951-57, v.p. charge of Operations, 1957-67, pres., 1967—; dir. Bank of Zephyrhills. Mem. SHARE com. U. Fla., 1971—. Mem. Zephyrhills City Council, 1960, v.p., 1962-67, pres., 1967—. Served with AUS, 1941-42; with USAAF, 1942-45. Decorated Air medal with 4 oak leaf clusters, D.F.C. Mem. Pasco County Cattleman's Assn. (pres. 1956-59), Eastern Charolais-Charbray Assn. (pres. 1961-63), Am. Internat. Charolais Assn. (pres. 1971), Fla. Cattleman's Assn. (treas. 1970—), Alpha Gamma Rho. Democrat. Baptist. Mason, Rotarian (pres. Zephyrhills 1961-62). Clubs: Zephyrhills Quarterback (pres. 1952-54); University (Tampa, Fla.). Mailing Address: PO Box 577 Zephyrhills FL 33599 Home: 204 21st St Zephyrhills FL 33599

DOUGLAS, JACK, editor. Mng. editor Star-Telegram, Fort Worth. Office: 400 W 7th St Fort Worth TX 76101*

DOUGLAS, NATHANELL LEN, supt. schs.; b. Hamilton, Tex., Sept. 18, 1915; s. Eli E. and Nettie L. (Johnson) D.; B.S., Howard Payne U., 1947; M.E., Tex. Tech. U., 1952-53; m. Juanita McAnelly, Feb. 19, 1935; children—Leon, Gary, Beverly. Prin., pub. schs., Union-Hamilton County, Tex., 1936-39; prin. White Hall Sch., Coryell County, 1939-41; supt. schs. Hale Center, Hale County, 1946-63, Belton Ind. Sch. Dist., 1963—. Mem. Zoning Com., City of Belton, 1968-72; chmn. United Fund Drive, 1971; mem. State Com. for Computer Services, 1970-72. Bd. dirs. West Tex. Sch. Study Council, 1958-63. Served with USNR, 1945-46. Named Man of the Year, Belton C. of C., 1969. Mem. Am., Tex. (state exec. com. 1970-72, chmn. fed. relations com. 1969-71) assns. sch. adminstrs., Nat., Tex., Belton edn. assns., Tex. Tchrs. Assn., Belton C. of C. (dir. 1968-69). Methodist (chmn. adminstrv. bd. 1970-72). Lion. Home: 221 E 21st St Belton TX 76513 Office: Box 269 Belton TX 76513

DOUGLAS, OMER RAY, ednl. adminstr.; b. Hamilton, Tex., May 4, 1919; s. Eli Erwin and Nettie Laura (Johnson) D.; B.S., Howard Payne Coll., 1942; M.A., North Tex. State U., 1949; Ed.D., Tex. Tech U., 1965; m. V. Pauline Fergusson, Aug. 14, 1940; children—Donna Kay (Mrs. Darrell Franks), Randal Ray, Phyllis Jo, Bruce Wayne. Prin., Hess-Averitt Sch., San Angelo, Tex., 1939-42; prin. Winters (Tex.) High Sch., 1942-44, 46-49; prin. Brownfield (Tex.) High Sch., 1949-51; supt. Brownfield pub. schs., 1951-67; exec. dir. Edn. Service Center-Region XVII, Lubbock, Tex., 1967—. Gen. fund chmn. Brownfield Community Chest, 1959. Served with AUS, 1944-46. Mem. Tex. Assn. Sch. Adminstrs. (past pres. Dist. IV and XIII), Tex. Tchrs. Assn. (past pres. Dist. IV). Lion (pres. 1952-53). Home: 6221 Lynnhaven Dr Lubbock TX 79413 Office: 700 Citizens Tower Lubbock TX 79401

DOUGLAS, SAMUEL HORACE, educator; b. Ardmore, Okla., May 10, 1928; s. Harrison and Corine (Gunn) D.; B.S., Bishop Coll., 1948; M.S., Okla. State U., 1959, Ph.D., 1967; children—Carmen, Samuel, Emanuel. Head dept. math Prairie View (Tex.) Coll., 1962-63, asst. prof., 1959-63; prof., head dept. math. Grambling (La.) Coll., 1967—. Dir. Summer Inst. Math., Acad. Yr. Inst. Math., Grambling Coll.-NSF; adviser evaluation grants NSF. Served with AUS, 1943-46. Sci. Faculty fellow, 1963-65. Mem. Math. Assn. Am. (chmn. La.-Miss. sect., vis. lectr.). Home: 120 Dunbar St Gramblin LA 71245

DOUGLAS, THOMAS EDWIN, realtor; b. Burnley, Va., Mar. 5, 1899; s. Thomas Gillum and Ollie (Tisdale) D.; B.S., Ia. State U., 1922; B.S. magna cum laude, Lynchburg Coll., 1923; m. Kathleen Leah Taylor, Aug. 12, 1924; 1 son, Thomas E. County agrl. agt. U.S. Dept. Agr., 1924-30; merc. and investment co. exec., 1930-49; realtor, West Point, Miss., 1949—; dir. Miss. Industries. Chmn., A.R.C., West Point and Clay County, 1952-55. Trustee E. Miss. Jr. Coll. Served with U.S. Army, World War I. Mem. Nat. Real Estate Assn., Miss. Brokers Assn., West Point Bd. Realtors, Am. Legion, 40 and 8, Alpha Zeta, Alpha Kappa Delta. Methodist (steward, trustee, pres. men's club). Mason (Shriner), Odd Fellow, Rotarian. Home: 725 E Main St West Point MS 39773 Office: Douglas Bldg 208 Jordan Av West Point MS 39773

DOUGLAS, WILLIAM ORVILLE, asso. justice U.S. Supreme Ct.; b. Maine, Minn., Oct. 16, 1898; s. William and Julia Bickford (Fiske) D.; B.A., Whitman Coll., 1920, LL.D., 1938; LL.B., Columbia, 1925; hon. M.A., Yale, 1932; LL.D., Wesleyan U., 1940, Washington and Jefferson Coll., 1942, Coll. William and Mary, 1943, Rollins Coll., 1947, Nat. U., 1949, New Sch. Social Research, 1952, U. Toledo, 1956, Bucknell U., 1958; m. Mildred Riddle, Aug. 16, 1923; children—Mildred Riddle (Mrs. Norman T. Read), William Orville; m. 2d, Mercedes Hester, Dec. 14, 1954; m. 3d, Joan Martin, Aug. 5, 1963; m. 4th, Cathleen Heffernan, July 15, 1966. High school tchr., Yakima, Wash., 1920-22; admitted to N.Y. bar 1926; practiced N.Y.C., 1925-27; law faculty Columbia 1925-28, Yale, 1928-34; bankruptcy studies Yale Inst. Human Relations and U.S. Dept. Commerce, 1929-32; sec. Com. Bus. Fed. Courts, Nat. Commn. on Law Observance and Enforcement, 1930-32; dir. protective com. study SEC, Washington, 1934-36, commr. and chmn., 1936-39; nominated asso. justice U.S. Supreme Ct. by Pres. Roosevelt Mar. 20, 1939, confirmed by Senate Apr. 4, 1939, and took seat on bench Apr. 17, 1939. Served as pvt. U.S. Army, 1918. Mem. Royal Geog. Soc. (London), Phi Beta Kappa, Beta Theta Pi, Phi Alpha Delta, Delta Sigma Rho. Democrat. Presbyn. Mason. Clubs: Yale; Himalayan (Delhi, India); University (Washington); Overseas Press. Author various law case books, also following books: Of Men and Mountains, 1950; Strange Lands and Friendly People, 1951; Beyond the High Himalayas, 1952; North from Malaya, 1953; An Almanac of Liberty, 1954; We The Judges, 1955; Russian Journey, 1956; The Right of the People, 1958; Exploring the Himalaya, 1958; West of the Indus, 1958; My Wilderness, The Pacific West, 1960; My Wilderness: East to Katahdin, 1961; A Living Bill of Rights, 1961; Muir of the Mountains, 1961; Democracy's Manifesto, 1962; Mr. Lincoln and the Negros. 1963; The Anatomy of Liberty, 1963; AWilderness Bill of Rights, 1966; Farewell to Texas, 1967; Towards a Global Federalism, 1969; Points of Rebellion, 1970; International Dissent, 1971; Holocaust or Hemispheric Co-op, 1971. Contbr. law jours. Home: Goose Prairie WA 98929 Office: US Supreme Ct Washington DC 20543

DOUGLASS, FRANK EUGENE, florist; b. Houston, June 29, 1925; s. Young Eugene and Ethel (Haag) D.; B.B.A., Tex. Technol. Coll., 1951; m. Virginia Dale Lankford, Mar. 1, 1951; children—Stephen Frank, Cary Dale. Sales rep. Procter & Gamble, Ft. Worth, 1951-54; sales mgr. Blue Bonnet Drug Sales, Arlington, Tex., 1954-57; non-foods purchasing agt. Affiliated Foods, Dallas, 1957-66; mayor pro-tem City of Euless (Tex.) 1968-72. Sec., Euless (Tex.) Planning and Zoning Bd., 1962-63, chmn., 1963-64; councilman, Euless 1964-68; sec., treas., mem. adv. council Northeast Cities, 1964-72. Served with USNR, 1942-45. Lion (pres. 1962-63). Home: 502 Martin Lane Euless TX 76039 Office: 298 N Main St Euless TX 76039

DOUGLASS, H(ILTON) L(EE), lawyer, bus. exec.; b. Van Buren, Ark., Jan. 12, 1905; s. George Lee and Pearl (McEachin) D.; LL.B., U. Kan., 1926; m. Marian Cooke, December 5, 1928; children—Diane Lee (Mrs. John Arthur Philbin), George Lee. Admitted to Okla. bar, 1925; asst. county atty. Pushmataha County, Antler, 1926-28; pvt. practice, Hugo, 1928-30, Oklahoma City, 1930—; mem. firm Cantrell, Douglass, Thompson & Wilson, attys.; v.p. Lyon Devel. Co., 1946—; pres. Marian Land Co., Comml. Bldg. Co., Park View Homes, Inc. Mem. Oklahoma City Park Bd. Served as lt. comdr. Amphibious Forces, USNR, 1943-46. Recipient Philippines Liberation Medal for assault landing on Luzon; Asiatic-Pacific medal for landing on Iwo Jima. Mem. Am., Okla. and Oklahoma County bar assns., Delta Upsilon, Phi Alpha Delta, Sachem. Episcopalian (chancellor). Clubs: Kiwanis (pres. Oklahoma City 1965), Oklahoma City Golf and Country, Beacon, Men's Dinner. Home: 6815 N Country Club Dr Oklahoma City OK 74127 Office: First Nat Bldg Oklahoma City OK

DOUGLASS, JESSE BURTON, food exec.; b. Johnson City, Tenn., Apr. 12, 1914; s. Sidney B. and Mary (Edwards) D.; student Washington and Lee U., 1936; U. Ky., 1937; m. Joan Colgan, July 3, 1941; children—Sidney Barns, Jesse Burton, Daniel O. Mgr. Jellico Grocery Co., Harlan, 1946—; pres. Bryan-Hunt Co., Lexington, Ky., Tri-State Wholesale Co., Middlesboro, Ky., Jellico Grocery Co. (Tenn.). Former dir. Harlan County Planning & Devel. Assn.; commr. Harlan Municipal Water Works; former mem. Blue Grass council Boy Scouts Am., Lexington, voted scouter of the year Harlan dist., 1950. Served to master sgt. USAAF, 1941-45. Mem. Nat. Am. Wholesale Grocers Assn., Ky. Wholesale Grocers (pres. 1964, dir.), Pi Kappa Alpha. Presbyn. (chmn. 1958-59, trustee). Clubs: Kiwanis (dir., pres. 1963, lt. gov. div. 10 Ky-Tenn. dist. 1964, chmn. pub. and bus. affairs com. Ky-Tenn. dist.), Harlan Country (pres.) (Harlan, Ky.). Home: Good Neighborhood Rd Loyal KY 40854 Office: 102 E Rail Rd Harlan KY 40831

DOUGLASS, JOSEPH HENRY, govt. ofcl.; b. Washington, June 26, 1917; s. Haley George and Evelyn (Dulaney) D.; A.B., Fisk U., 1937, M.A. (Nat. Youth Adminstrn. fellow), 1941; Ph.D. (Gen. Edn. Bd. fellow, Rosenwald fellow), Harvard, 1946; m. Katherine E. Washington, Nov. 19, 1938; children—Betty K. (Mrs. William J. Herbert), Jo Ann (Mrs. Aubrey Myers). Spl. rep. of sec. Dept. Health, Edn. and Welfare, Washington, 1954-56, dir. Clearinghouse of Info., Nat. Inst. Mental Health, 1960-62, chief interagy. liaison NIMH, 1963-66, cons. Pres.'s Task Force on Talented, 1967, exec. dir. White House Conf. on Children and Youth, 1968, dir. vol. and profl. orgns. White House Conf. on Children and Youth, 1969—. Cons. Ford Found., 1960, Pres.'s Com. on Handicapped, 1966, Peace Corps, 1966; Fulbright lectr. Sch. Social Work, Cairo, Egypt, 1952-53. Bd. dirs. Nat. Com. for Children and Youth, Nat. Budget and Consultation Com., Assn. for Hearing and Speech Agys., Found. for Human Resources Devel.; trustee Nat. Conf. Christians and Jews. Recipient Ballington and Maud Booth award, 1969, Salvation Army award, 1969. Fellow Royal Soc. Health (London), 1965, Royal Geog. Soc. (London), Am. Sociol. Assn. Author various govtl. publs. Home: 3314 16th St Washington DC 20018 Office: PO Box 19 Washington DC 20044

DOUGLASS, PAUL F., polit. scientist, educator; b. Corinth, N.Y., Nov. 7, 1904; s. Rev. George C. and Mabel (Parker) D.; A.B., Wesleyan U., 1926, LL.D., 1946; A.M., U. Cin., 1929, Ph.D. (Taft fellow), 1931; student U. Chgo., 1928, U. Berlin, 1931-33 unmarried. Reporter, Cin. Post, 1926-27, ednl. editor, 1927-28; corr. Chgo. Bur. Christian Sci. Monitor, 1928-30; dir. study of courts of limited jurisdiction and Cin. Municipal Court for Inst. of Law, John Hopkins, in Hamilton County, O., 1930-31; ordained to ministry C.E. Ch., 1933; pastor Meth. Ch., Poultney, Vt., 1933-41; pres. Am. U., Washington, 1941-52; now prof. polit. sci. Rollins Coll., also dir. Center for Practical Politics (Falk Found.). Adviser to pres. of Republic of Korea, counsel to ministry foreign affairs, 1952-55; chmn. nat. adv. com. on recruitment, tng. and placement recreation personnel Nat. Recreation Found., 1960-65; mem. Pa. Gov.'s Recreation Council, 1956-58; chmn. Settlement Ho. Study Com., United Community Services, Wash., 1951-53; chmn. Christian Friends Korea; v.p. Arthur and Anne Haskell Found. (Detroit), 1942-50; trustee Nat. Recreation and Park Assn., 1965—; chmn. task force on leisure National Council Chs., 1965—. Awarded the Haakon VII Cross (Norway), 1948; Order of Ascending Star with Rosette (China), 1948; Order of Taiguk (Korea), 1950. Admitted to Vt., D.C. Bars. Mem. Vt. Ho. of Reps., 1937-39, 39-41; Vt. Senate, 1941-43. Mem. numerous profl. assns. and orgns., past officer several. Clubs: University, National Press, Cosmos. Metropolitan (Washington, D.C.). Author: several books 1929—, some of later ones being, Six Upon the World, 1954, The Group Workshop Way, 1958; Communication through Reports, 1957; Learned on Learning, 1959; How to be an Active Citizen, 1960; The ABC of Industrial Parks, 1960; The Theory of Leisure Experience, 1966. Editor several books, latest, Recreation in Age of Automation, 1957. Contbr. to Ency. Americana. Home: Langford Hotel Winter Park FL 32789 Office: Knowles Hall Rollins Coll Winter Park FL 32789

DOUGLASS, ROBERT JOSEPH, forest products co. exec.; b. Moline, Ill., Sept. 8, 1913; s. Ralph Allison and Fannie Josephine (Moore) D.; student Augustana Coll., 1933-34; B.S., U. Miss., 1937; m. Hattie Jane Holmes, Feb. 2, 1947; children—Jane (Mrs. John E. Rhodes, Jr.), Robert Joseph. Area mgr. Weyerhaeuser Corp., Tacoma 1954-61; v.p. marketing Gen. Plywood Corp., Louisville, 1961-63; pres., chmn. bd. Gamble Brothers, Inc., Louisville, 1963—; dir. Ernest Homes, Co., Chattanooga, Reliance Universal, Inc., Plastic Parts, Inc., Shelbyville, Ky., Martin Sweets Co., Louisville, Trustee Old Ky. Home council Boy Scouts Am., 1968. Served to lt. comdr. USNR, 1941-46. Mem. Ky. Forestry Council, Nat. Forest Products Assn. (dir. 1966), Internat. Woodworking Machinery and Furniture Supply Fair (dir. 1969—), Ky. Wood Industry Assn. (dir. 1967—), Sigma Chi. Rotarian. Clubs: Flight, Louisville Country, Pendennis, Rock Creek Riding (Louisville). Home: 6213 Glen Hill Rd Louisville KY Office: 4601 Allmond Av Louisville KY 40221

DOUGLASS, ROBERT SATTERFIELD, educator; b. Senath, Mo., Apr. 1, 1919; s. Robert S. and Allie (Hogue) D.; Mus.B., N. Tex. State U., 1948, Mus.M., 1953, Ph.D., 1963; m. Elaine Killen, June 4, 1951; children—Robert Killen, Melanie Elaine. Tchr., McKinney (Tex.) Pub. Schs., 1947-49, Kingsville (Tex.) Pub. Schs., 1949-53; instr. N. Tex. State U., 1953-54; prof. musicology Southwestern Bapt. Theol. Sem., Fort Worth, 1954—, chmn. grad. studies, 1967—. Music critic Fort Worth Star Telegram, 1963—; program annotator Fort Worth Symphony Orch., 1965—. Bd. dirs. Fort Worth Civic Music Assn., Van Cliburn Quadrennial Piano Competition. Served with AUS, 1940-45. Decorated Bronze Star medal; recipient Pi Kappa Lambda commendation, 1953. Mem. Am. Musicological Soc., Pi Kappa Lambda, Phi Mu Alpha. Baptist. Author: Church Music Through the Ages, 1967; The Mechanics of Research, 1970. Writer radio and TV scripts on music, 1963—. Home: 5736 Wedgmont Circle Fort Worth TX 76133

DOUMA, JACOB HENDRICK, civil engr.; b. Hanford, Cal., May 30, 1912; s. Hendrik Jackob and Gertje (Kok) D.; B.S., U. Cal. at Berkeley, 1935; m. Allene Vartia, Apr. 4, 1939; children—Mark Hendrick, Allen Jacob. With C.E. U.S. Army, various locations, 1935—, chief hydraulic engr., Washington, 1961—. TAMS, N.Y.C., 1961-70, CASECO, Vancouver, B.C., Can., 1964-71, Quinones Assos., P.R., 1965-71. Mem. Am. Soc. C.E., Nat. Acad. Engring., Internat. Commn. Irrigation, Drainage and Flood Control, Internat. Commn. Large Dams, Internat. Assn. Hydraulic Research, Permanent Internat. Assn. Navigation Congresses, Tau Beta Pi, Chi Epsilon. Contbr. to profl. jours. Home: 1001 Manning St Great Falls VA 22066 Office: 1000 Independence Av Washington DC 20314

DOUMA, JOHN HENRY, oil co. exec.; b. Oilfields, Cal., July 20, 1914; s. Hendrick J. and Geertje (Kok) D.; B.S. in Petroleum Engring., U. Cal. at Berkeley, 1938; m. Eloise Moore, Aug. 20, 1939; children—Sharon Wilma, Robert Warren. With Barnsdall Oil Co., (merged with Sunray Oil Corp., 1950); 1938-50, supt. mid-continent div., 1948-50; with Sunray Oil Corp., 1950-55, (merged with Mid-Continent Petroleum Corp. to become Sunray Mid-Continent Oil Co., 1955, name changed to Sunray DX Oil Co., 1962), mgr. engring., 1954-55; v.p., mgr. Western div., Denver, 1960-63, v.p. prodn. dept., 1963-66, sr. v.p. extractive, 1966-68, co. merged with Sun Oil Co., 1968, dir., sr. v.p. extractive DX div. Sun Oil Co., 1968-70, dir., v.p. prodn., 1970—. Mem. Internat. Oil and Gas Ednl. Center of Southwest Legal Inst. Bd. dirs. Internat. Petroleum Expn. Mem. Ind. Petroleum Assn. Am. (dir.), Western Oil and Gas Assn. (dir.), Am. Petroleum Inst., Soc. Petroleum Engrs. of Am., Inst. Mining, Metall. and Petroleum Engrs., Rocky Mountain Oil and Gas Assn. (dir.), Mid-Continent Oil and Gas Assn. Clubs: Dallas Petroleum, Brook Hollow Golf. Home: 7210 Stonetrail Dallas TX 75230

DOWD, EDWARD JOSEPH, JR., assn. exec.; b. Holyoke, Mass., May 24, 1921; s. Edward Joseph and Nora M. (Kennedy) D.; A.B., Am. Internat. Coll., 1947; M.Ed., Springfield Coll., 1952; m. Henrietta Laura Moran, Dec. 21, 1943; children—John Edward, Nancy Beth, Christopher John. Restaurant owner, Springfield, Mass., 1947-50, mgmt. trainee Libby-Owens-Ford Glass Co., Toledo, 1952-53; employment supr., tng. dir. Toledo Edison Co., 1953-55; exec. sec. Employers' Assn. Toledo, 1955-58; v.p., pres. Central Piedmont Industries, Charlotte, N.C., 1958—; vocational cons. Dept. Health, Edn. and Welfare, Washington, 1962—. Exec. com. N.C. Manpower Devel. Com.; bd. mem. Belmont Abbey Coll., Belmont, N.C. Served with USNR, 1943-46. Mem. Am., Southeastern, N.C. psychol. assns., Nat. Indsl. Council (exec. com. 1960-63, chmn. indsl. relations group), Am. Soc. Assn. Execs., Charlotte Execs. Club. Clubs: University (N.Y.C.); Rotary, Charlotte City, Carmel Country. Home: 3500 Fielding Av Charlotte NC 28211 Office: 420 Hawthorne Lane Charlotte NC 28204

DOWDEN, CHARLES MERRILL, newspaper editor; b. Louisville, Jan. 26, 1903; s. John W. and Laura (Smith) D.; A.B., U. Ky., 1926; m. Regina Celestine Popham, May 25, 1930; children—Donald Smith, Carroll Vincent. Staff Courier-Jour., Louisville, 1926—, state editor, 1945—. Chess cons., lectr. Mem. C. of C., Sigma Delta Chi. Democrat. Roman Catholic. Clubs: Filson, Louisville Chess, Business and Professional Men's. Author: Childhood Heroes of Famous Americans. Writer chess column The King's Men, 1945. Home: 2312 Village Dr Louisville KY 40205 Office: 6th and Broadway Sts Louisville KY 40202

DOWDY, JOE HOLLAND, dentist; b. High Springs, Fla., Mar. 29, 1930; s. Terrell Joe and Azilene (Holland) D.; B.Mech. Engring.with high honors, U. Fla., 1951; D.D.S. with highest honor, Baylor U., 1960; m. Billye Clarice Arledge, Oct. 26, 1952; children—Kaye Ann, David William. Engr., Westinghouse Electric Corp., Pitts., 1951; pvt. practice dentistry, High Springs, Fla., 1960—. Served to 1st lt. USAF,

1951-55. Mem. Alacha County Dental Soc. (pres. 1971-72), Fla. Dental Assn. (dist. del. 1970-71), High Springs, (dir.), Greater Gainesville (com. of 100) chambers commerce, Phi Kappa Phi, Omicron Kappa Upsilon, Delta Sigma Delta. Democrat. Baptist (deacon, trustee, supt young people dept. 1964—). Home: 230 NE 7th Av High Springs FL 32643 Office: 60 S Main St High Springs FL 32643

DOWDY, JOHN, congressman; b. Waco, Tex., Feb. 11, 1912; s. Carroll Vernard and Lula Mae (Jamison) D.; student E. Tex. Bapt. Coll., 1929-31; m. Mary Ellen Fite, Sept. 14, 1932 (dec. Dec. 1943); children—Carol Sue (Mrs. Forrest Earle Roberts, Jr.), John; m. 2d, Johnnie D. Riley, Aug. 20, 1946. Admitted to Tex. bar, 1940; practiced law, Athens, 1940-52; dist. atty. 3d Jud. Dist. of Tex., 1944-52; mem. 82d Congress (elected spl. election 1952), 82d-92d Congresses, 2d Tex. Dist. Democrat. Methodist. Odd Fellow, Kiwanian. Home: Athens TX 75551 Office: House Office Bldg Washington DC 20036

DOWDY, LEWIS CARNEGIE, coll. ofcl.; b. Eastover, S.C., Sept. 1, 1917; s. William Wallace and Alice (Shivar) D.; A.B., Allen U., Columbia, S.C., 1939, Litt.D., 1962; M.A., Ind. State Coll., 1949; Ed.D., Ind. State U., 1965; m. Elizabeth Smith, June 26, 1943; children— Lewis Carnegie Lemuel, Elizabeth. Prin. schs., Eastover and Aiken, S.C., 1939-51; mem. faculty A. and T. Coll., Greensboro, N.C., 1951—, dean instr., 1960-64, pres., 1964-72, chancellor, 1972—. Pres. Greensboro Human Relations Coll.; active United Fund Greensboro, Greensboro Community Council. Mem. N.C. Colls. and Univs. Assn., Nat. Assn. State Univs. and Land-Grant Colls. (exec. com.), N.E.A., N.C. Tchrs. Assn., Assn. Social Sci. Tchrs., Nat. Soc. Study Edn., Greensboro C. of C., Kappa Delta Pi, Sigma Rho Sigma, Alpha Kappa Mu. Democrat. Baptist. Clubs: Greensboro Rotary, Greensboro Men's. Author articles. Home: 900 Bluford St Greensboro NC 27411

DOWIS, WILLIAM SHAFER, JR., architect; b. Sumter, S.C., Dec. 23, 1923; s. William Shafer and Patricia (Bunn) D.; student Wofford Coll., 1941-43; B.S. in Architecture with honors, Clemson Coll., 1950; m. Joyce Norfleet Deckinson, Apr. 3, 1947; children—William Shafer III, George Dickinson, Mary Norfleet. Architect, specifications writer J.E. Sirrine Co., Greenville, S.C., 1950-54; partner firm Lewis && Dowis, Florence, 1954-71; prin. firm William S. Dowis, Jr., Florence, 1972—. Mem. S.C. Arts Commn., 1967—; chmn. S.C. Art Collection Com., 1970—. Trustee Florence (S.C.) Mus., pres. 1960-70. Served with inf. AUS, 1943-46. Decorated Bronze Star; recipient Distinguished Service award Jr. C. of C., Florence, 1969. Mem. A.I.A. (pres. S.C. 1961), Constrn. Specifications Inst., Guild S.C. Artists (pres. 1970). Methodist. Elk. Lion. One-man shows paintings Florence Mus., Banks Haley Gallery, Albany Ga., Sandlapper Gallery, Columbia, S.C., The Art Center, Spartanburg, S.C. (all 1971). Home: 322 W Pine St Florence SC 29501 Office: PO Box 368 Florence SC 29501

DOWLING, FRED BENNY, environmental cons.; b. Jackson, Miss., Jan. 3, 1937; s. Harry E. and Lozelle (Beasley) D.; B.S., Millsaps Coll., 1959; B.S. in Chemistry, La. State U., 1961; m. Betty Jean Burgdorff, May 23, 1959; children—James Hampton, Charles Edward. With Kem-Tech Labs., Inc., Baton Rouge, 1961—, chemist, 1961-62, air pollution chemist, 1962-65, air pollution chemist, sec.-treas., dir., sec. bd., 1965—, v.p., 1972—. Mem. Am. Chem. Soc., Air Pollution Control Assn., Aircraft Owners and Pilots Assn. Methodist. Club: Fairwood Country. Contbr. articles to profl. jours. Patentee in field. Home: 12270 E Milburn St Baton Rouge LA 70815 Office: 16550 Highland Rd Baton Rouge LA 70808

DOWLING, G.G., lawyer; b. Greenwood, S.C., Sept. 29, 1915; A.B., U. S.C., 1936, LL.B., 1938. Admitted to S.C. bar, 1946; now mem. firm Dowling Dowling Sanders & Dukes, Beaufort, S.C. Hwy. commr. S.C. 14th Hwy. Dist. Mem. S.C. Ho. of Reps., 1949-50. Mem. Phi Delta Phi. Address: Dowling Dowling Sanders & Dukes Drawer 1027 Bay St Beaufort SC 29902*

DOWLING, JOAB MAULDIN, lawyer; b. Greenwood, S.C., Nov. 26, 1917; s. Grafton Geddes and Leonora Connors (Mauldin) D.; B.S., U. S.C., 1939, J.D., 1941; m. Katharine Elizabeth Douglas, Mar. 23, 1943; children— Jane (Mrs. Sherwood N. Fender), Joab Mauldin, John D., Katharine Louisa, May D. Admitted to S.C. bar, 1941, U.S. Supreme Ct. and all state and fed. cts.; partner firm Dowling, Dowling, Sanders & Dukes, P.A. and predecessors, Beaufort, S.C., 1941—. Chmn. bd. Palmetto State Savs. & Loan Assn.; dir., officer Sea Island Investment Co., 1st Beaufort Corp., Coastal Securities Corp.; dir. Blue Channel Corp. Trustee Dowling Found., Bapt. Found. S.C., Beaufort Acad. Served with USNR, 1943-45. Mem. Am., S.C., Beaufort County bar assns., Am. Judicature Soc., Am. Legion, Beaufort County C. of C. (past v.p.). Elk, Rotarian (past pres. Beaufort Club). Home: Fuller Pkwy Beaufort SC 29902 Office: 1105 Bay St Beaufort SC 29902

DOWNEY, FRED MCEWEN, ret. chain drug co. exec.; b. Pleasantville, Tenn., Feb. 12, 1906; s. William Lee and Minnie (Little) D.; grad. Max Morris Coll. Pharmacy, Macon, Ga., 1926; m. Lorraine Church Beasley, June 11, 1932; 1 son, Fred McEwen. Mgr., Coble's Drug Store, Centerville, Tenn., 1926-29; with Peoples Drug Stores Inc., Washington, 1929—, v.p., 1955-66, exec. v.p., 1966-70, vice chmn. bd., 1970-71, also dir. Bd. dirs. Washington Restaurant Assn., 1951-66, treas., 1959; mem. Washington Bd. Trade. Bd. dirs. York County (Pa.) Community Chest, 1946-51, pres., 1949-51; bd. dirs. York and Adams Counties council Boy Scouts Am., 1946-51; adv. com. food service tech. program No. Va. Tech. Coll. Mem. D.C. Pharm. Assn., Friendly Sons St. Patrick, Newcomen Soc. N.A. Mason, Rotarian. Clubs: Kenwood Golf and Country (Bethesda, Md.); University (Washington). Home: 5200 Brittany Dr S St Petersburg FL 33715

DOWNEY, WILLIAM GERALD, JR., lawyer, banker, ret, army officer; b. Bklyn., June 20, 1914; s. William Gerald and Mary Veronica (Ryder) D.; B.S.S., Coll. City N.Y., 1937; M.A., Catholic U., 1938; J.D., Georgetown U., 1951; certificate internat. law, U. Mich., 1937, Latin Am. area tng., 1946; student U. Iceland, 1941-42; grad. Command and Gen. Staff College, 1962; m. Ellen Wagle, Apr. 17, 1942 (dec.); 1 son, William G., III (dec.); m. 2d, Laufey Arnadottir, June 5, 1947; children—Richard, Elizabeth, Mary, Catherine, William Gerald IV, Karen. Commd. 2d lt. inf. res., 1936, advanced through the grades to col. Judge Adv. Gen.'s Corps, 1964, ret., 1969; chief internat. law br., 1946-50, Group Judge Adv., Formosa, 1952-54; sr. partner Downey & Lennhoff, Springfield, Va.; practice law, Va. and Washington; founder, chmn. bd., gen. counsel. No. Va. Bank; pres. Springfield Corp.; pres., dir. Springbank Corp.; fellow internat. law Cath. U., 1936-37, Georgetown U., 1937-40, instr. govt., 1937-40; prof. internat. law Soochow U. Law Sch., 1952-54. Mem. Fairfax County Dem. Com.; del. Va. Dem. Conv., 1960, 64, 68; candidate Va. State Senate, 1963. Mem. Springfield C. of C. (pres. 1961-62, dir.), Washington, Va. bar assns. Clubs: Army-Navy, Army-Navy Country; Morgan Horse, Kiwanis (pres. Springfield 1961-62). Author articles on mil. and internat. law. Contbr. Ency. Britannica. Home: Roscrea 5611 Guinea Rd Fairfax VA 22030 Office: No Va Bank Bldg Springfield VA 22150

DOWNING, AVERY R., supt. schs. City sch. supt., Waco, Tex. Office: Drawer 27 Waco TX 76710*

DOWNING, HUDSON URQUHART, stock broker; b. Columbus, Ga., Feb. 26, 1923; s. Lemuel Tyler and Frances Ruth (Hudson) D.; grad. Truman and Smith Inst., 1942, N.Y. Inst. Finance, 1960; m. Barbara Ann Parker, Oct. 11, 1953. Tchr. pub. schs. Va., Phenix City. Ala., 1946-50; mgr. Ala., Ga. Cigarette Service, Columbus, Ga., 1950-56; asst. mgr. Western Auto Supply Store, Columbus, 1956-59; v.p., partner First Southeastern Co., brokerage firm, Columbus, 1963—; organizer, bd. dirs. Phenix Nat. Bank, Phenix City. Served with USAAF, 1942-46. Presbyn. Club: Stock Investment (Phenix City). Home: Route 1 Box 870 Phenix City AL 36867 Office: 103 12th St Columbus GA 31901

DOWNING, THOMAS NELMS, U.S. congressman; b. Newport News, Va., Feb. 1, 1919; s. Samuel and Lucille (Nelms) D.; B.S., Va. Mil. Inst., 1940; LL.B., U. Va., 1947; m. Virginia Dickerson Martin, Feb. 17, 1947; children—Susan Nelms, Samuel Dickerson Martin. Admitted to Va. bar, 1947; with Downing, Andrews & Durden, Hampton, Va., 1955-58; substitute judge Municipal Ct., City of Warwick (now Newport News), 1953-58; mem. 86th-92d congresses 1st Va. Dist.; mem. mcht. marine and fisheries com., sci. and astronautics com. Bd. visitors Mcht. Marine Acad., Kings Point, N.Y. College. Served from 2d lt. to maj. Cav., AUS, World War II. Decorated Silver Star. Mem. Am. Legion, Am., Va. State, Hampton, Newport News-Warwick (past pres.) bar assns., Assn. U.S. Army, V.F.W. Democrat. Episcopalian (trustee). Jr. Order United Am. Mechanics. Clubs: Propeller, Lions. Home: 27 Indigo Dam Rd Washington DC 20007 Office: Rayburn House Office Bldg Washington DC 20515

DOWNS, ELDON WILSON, air force officer; b. Buffalo, Okla., Feb. 7, 1918; s. Hawley Wilson and Pearl (Clark) D.; A.B., Okla. State U., 1940, M.A., 1941; Ph.D., U. Wis., 1959; m. Elyn Dorothy Howell, Feb. 14, 1947; children—DeAnne, Denise, Danielle, DeLys. Served from pvt. to maj. AUS, 1941-46; instr. polit. sci. Okla. State U., 1946, grad. asst. history U. Wis., 1946-49, instr. history, 1949; instr. history, counselor Stephens Coll., 1949-51; recalled as lt col. U.S. Air Force, 1951; prof. mil. history Air U., 1951-54, chief hist. office, 1951-54; historian Allied Air Forces, Central Europe, NATO, 1954-58; asst. prof. history U.S. Air Force Acad. (Colo.), 1960-61, asso. prof., dir. instrn., 1961-62, asso. prof., dep., 1962-63, asso. prof., spl. asst., 1963-64; plans and programs officer Aerospace Studies Inst., Air U., Maxwell AFB, Ala., 1964—, editor Air Univ. Rev., 1965—. Cons. curriculum Officer Tng. Sch., San Antonio, 1962. Recipient mil. commendation for U. Press Study, 1964. Mem. Am., Western hist. assns., Orgn. Am. Historians, Air Force Hist. Found., Am. Mil. Inst., Am. Aviation Hist. Soc., Phi Kappa Phi, Phi Alpha Theta. Baptist (former mem. bd.). Author: Histories of Headquarters AIRCENT, 1955-58; Army and the Airmail-1934, 1962. Editor: Golden Arrow, 6 vols., 1965; The U.S. Air Force in Space, 1966. Co-author: Readings in Military History. Office: Editor Air U Rev Maxwell AFB AL 36112

DOWTIN, MAUDE CHILES, librarian; b. Troy, S.C., Oct. 27, 1912; s. Robert Lee and Clifford Gallagher (Chiles) D.; student Winthrop Coll., 1930-32; A.B., U. S.C., 1934; A.B. in L.S., Emory U., 1939. Tchr. pub. schs., S.C., 1934-38; library supr. state-wide library project WPA, Columbia, S.C., 1939-43; librarian Post Library No. 4, Fort Jackson, S.C., 1943-45, No. 5, 1945-46, chief librarian, Post Library System, 1946—. Mem. Am., Southeastern, S.C. library assns. Home: 3012 Manchester Rd Columbia SC 29204 Office: Post Library Fort Jackson SC 29207

DOXEY, WALL, JR., lawyer; b. Memphis, Jan. 11, 1926; s. Wall and Myrtle (Johnson) D.; B.B.A., LL.B., U. Miss., 1950; m. Sarah Mozelle Smith, Apr. 19, 1945; children—Ralph Hindman, Helene. Admitted to Miss. bar, 1950; practiced in Holly Springs, Miss., 1950—; county atty. Marshall County, Miss., 1952-56; now atty. Marshall County Bd. Suprs. Served with USAAF, 1943-46. Mem. Am., Miss. bar assns., Phi Delta Theta, Delta Sigma. Home: 510 Randolph St Holly Springs MS 38635 Office: Doxey Bldg Memphis St Holly Springs MS 38635

DOYAL, CLYDE, city ofcl.; b. Lecompte, La., June 19, 1928; s. Flossie Camuel and Alvin (Clark) D.; LL.B., S. Tex. Coll., 1959; m. Mollie B. Poe, June 12, 1953; children—Scot, Mark Bret, Eric. Admitted to Tex. bar, 1959; practice law, Pasadena, Tex., 1960-65; mayor City of Pasadena, 1965—. Mem. Pasadena Sch. Bd., 1961-65. Served with USNR, 1946-48. Democrat. Baptist. Home: 2210 S Memorial Ct Pasadena TX 77502 Office: 1st Pasadena State Bank Bldg Pasadena TX 77501

DOYLE, CHARLES THOMAS, investments, mgmt. cons.; b. Mangum, Okla., Aug. 3, 1934; s. Roy Leo and Mattie (Carter) D.; A.A., Kemper Mil. Acad., 1954; B.B.A., U. Okla., 1956; M.B.A., U. Houston, 1961; m. Mary Ellen Hipp, Aug. 25, 1956; children—Matthew, David, Denise, Patrick, Christopher. With Mangum Brick & Tile Co., 1952-56; indsl. relations Union Carbide Corp., Texas City, Tex., 1956-69; investments and real estate broker, Houston, 1969—; impartial arbitrator labor mgmt. arbitration, 1964—; pres., dir. First Nat. Corp., 1st Nat. Life Ins. Corp. (both Houston); dir. Buffalo Savs. & Loan Assn., Copperstone Constructors Inc., O'Neill, Anderson & Assos. Inc. (all Houston), 1st State Bank, Hitchcock, Tex.; chmn. bd. U.S. Mgmt. Corp., Houston. Adult adviser Catholic Youth Orgn., 1964-68. Mayor pro tem, Texas City, 1964—; pres. Galveston County Mayors and Councilmens Assn., 1968-69. Bd. dirs. Galveston County Community Action Council, 1964-68. Served to capt. Armored Div., AUS, 1956-58. Recipient Texas City Distinguished Service award, 1963; named One of Five Outstanding Young Texans, 1965. Mem. Texas City Jr. (life), Texas City (dir.) chambers commerce, Beta Gamma Sigma, Sigma Iota Epsilon, Omicron Chi Epsilon, Phi Gamma Delta. Contbr. articles profl. jours. Home: 1526 19th Av N Texas City TX 77590 Office: First Nat Life Bldg Main and Rusk Sts Houston TX 77001

DOYLE, JOHN F., dist. ct. judge; b. Kansas City, Mo.; grad. Rockhurst (Mo.) Coll., Georgetown U. Law Sch. Formerly mem. staff U.S. Atty.'s office; mem. staff Ho. of Reps. appropriations com., 1952; then asst. gen. counsel U.S. Cath. Conf., Washington; now judge U.S. Dist. Ct., Washington. Address: Constitution Av and John Marshall Pl Washington DC 20010*

DOYLE, MARK DANIEL, advt. agy. exec.; b. Menominee, Mich., July 28, 1935; s. Thomas Francis and Carolyn Elizabeth (Phelps) D.; student Marquette U., 1953-57; m. Mary Sharon View, Sept. 22, 1962; children—James Edward, Anne Marie, Amy Elizabeth. Office boy Klau-Van Pietersom-Dunlap, Inc., Milw., 1957-58, media asst., 1958, copy-writer, 1960-64; advt. asst. Blackhawk Mfg. Co., Milw., 1958-60; copy supr. Leo Burnett Co., Chgo., 1964-68; v.p., creative dir. Cargill, Wilson & Acree, Inc., Charlotte, N.C., 1968—. Instr. Confrat. Christian Doctrine, Deerfield, Ill., 1966-67. Recipient Certificate of Merit, N.Y. Art Dirs. Club, 1970, 71. Mem. Charlotte Soc. Communicating Arts (dir. 1968-71, pres. 1969). Home: 6932 Thermal Rd Charlotte NC 28211 Office: 700 Kenilworth Av Charlotte NC 28204

DOYLE, ROBERT E., assn. exec. Exec. v.p., sec. Nat. Geog. Soc. Address: Nat Geog Soc 17th and M Sts NW Washington DC 20036*

DOYLE, WALTER ARNETT, dentist; b. Los Angeles, Aug. 9, 1933; s. Walter James and Ruth (Journey) D.; student Glendale Coll., 1951-52, U. Hawaii, 1952-53, Joliet Jr. Coll., 1953-54, U. Ill., 1954-55; D.D.S., Emory U., 1959; M.S. in Pedodontics, Ind. U., 1961; m. Betty Ann Parrott, Dec. 28, 1957; children—Shannon, Elizabeth, Sally, Walter Arnett. Practice dentistry, specializing in pedodontics, Lexington, Ky., 1962—; pres. Bluegrass Orthodontic-Pedodontic Labs., Inc., Lexington, 1971—; instr. pedodontics U. Ky., Lexington, 1964-65, guest lectr., 1965—; mem. staff St. Joseph's Hosp., Central Baptist, Good Samaritan hosps., Lexington. Partner Coca Cola Bottling Co., Campbellsville, Ky., 1971—. Mem. Com. Am. Dental Assn. Task Force Nat. Dental Care Program, Chgo., 1970-71; mem. Blue Grass Trust for Historic Preservation, 1970—. Recipient Travel South photography award, 1968. S.S. White teaching fellow. Fellow Internat. Coll. Dentists; mem. Am. Bd. Pedodontics (examining mem.), Am. (pres. 1964), Ky. socs. dentistry for children, Internat. Assn. Dental Research (pres. 1969) Southeastern Soc. Pedodontics, Ky. Dental Service Corp. (past dir.), Lexington C. of C. Rotarian. Clubs: Polo, Keeneland, Athletic (Lexington). Contbr. to profl. jours. and textbooks. Home: 3800 Nicholasville Rd Lexington KY 40503 Office: 1628 Nicholasville Rd Lexington KY 40503

DOZIER, B(ESSIE) EUPLE, county atty.; b. Fulton, Miss., Nov. 10, 1908; d. Samuel Lee and Maranda (Googe) Dozier; student Ala State Tchrs. Coll., 1932-33, Jackson (Miss.) Sch. Law, 1953. Admitted to Miss. bar, 1953; sec., clk. U.S. Dept. Justice, Oxford, Miss., 1942-55, asst. U.S. atty. No. Dist. Miss., 1955-64; county atty., Itawamba County, Miss., 1964—. Vice chmn. Tenn. Valley Regional Housing Authority. Recipient citation Woman of Achievement, Oxford and Lafayette County, 1955; candidate Freedoms Found. award, 1956. Mem. Miss., Fed. bar assns., Bus. and Profl. Women's Club (past dist. chmn.), Miss. Fedn. Bus. and Profl. Women's Clubs (pres. 1969-70). Mem. Order Eastern Star (past sec., treas. Oxford chpt.). Baptist. Club: Civic. Home: 408 N Cummings St Fulton MS 38843 Office: Courthouse Fulton MS 38843

DOZIER, BEVERLY FISHER, govt. ofcl.; b. Branford, Fla., Nov. 2, 1932; d. Eugene Varnadoe and Grace Woodward (Rowell) Fisher; student Centre Coll., 1950-52, U. Fla., 1952-54; B.A., Fla. State U., 1955, then postgrad.; m. Laurie L. Dozier, Jr., Apr. 9, 1970; children (by previous marriage); Thomas Etheridge Gilman, III, David West Gilman. Tchr. English, Elizabeth Cobb Jr. High Sch., Tallahassee, 1959-60; sec. to Senator Gong, Fla., to Senator de la Parte, Fla.; cultural arts coordinator Fla. Devel. Commn., Tallahassee, 1964-67; recruitment specialist II State Personnel Bd., Tallahassee, 1967-71; dir. Div. Cultural Affairs Dept. State, Tallahassee, 1971—. Mem. Tallahassee Jr. League, 1962—; chmn. Leon County, Fla., Heart Assn., mem. Fla. Heart Fund Bd., 1962-63, treas. county bd., 1962-64, state bd., 1963; mem. Tri-Med. Aux., 1971. Bd. dirs., charter mem. Fla. Arts Council. Mem. Zeta Tau Alpha. Democrat. Methodist. Home: 2830 Pine Ridge Rd Tallahassee FL 32303 Office: Div Cultural Affairs Dept State The Capitol Tallahassee FL 32304

DOZIER, MABRY FRAZIER, lumber sales co. exec.; b. Mobile, Ala., Apr. 4, 1927; s. Mabry F. and Frances (Gray) D.; student Spring Hill Coll., 1946-47; m. Frances Gay, Dec. 24, 1955; children—Mabry Frazier III, Frances. Sales mgr. Alber-Sullivan Lumber Co., Century, Fla., 1963, v.p. sales, dir. Alger-Sullivan Co., Century, 1965—; dir. Clancy Lumber Co., Grayson, Ala. Trustee, Escambia County Hosp. Served with AUS, 1945-46. Mem. So. Pine Assn., Tri-City C. of C. (pres. 1965-66), Hoo-Hoo Internat. Methodist. Lion (pres. Century 1967-68), Toastmaster (pres. Tri-City 1964-65). Home: 100 N Jefferson Av Century FL 32535 Office: Century FL 32535

DOZIER, MAURICE FRANCIS, corp. exec.; b. Richmond, Va., Aug. 20, 1920; s. Curtis M. and Rosa (Conaty) D.; B.S.S., Georgetown U., 1941; m. Ann T. O'Connor, May 7, 1949; children—Curtis M. and Ann O'C. (twins), Thomas C. Sales rep. Hamilton Paper Corp., Richmond, 1949-51; pres. Colonial Paper Co., Inc., Richmond, 1951-54; sales mgr. Richmond Container Corp., 1954-64; pres. Commonwealth Corp., Richmond, 1964—; v.p., treas. Fibre Tube Corp., 1969—. Republican dist. chmn. 3d Congl. Dist. Va., 1952-56. Served with AUS, 1941-46. Decorated Purple Heart (3), Bronze Star. Roman Catholic. Home: 5900 S Crestwood Av Richmond VA 23226 Office: 1003 Commerce Rd Richmond VA 23224

DRAKE, JERRY EDWARD, educator; b. Edna, Tex., Sept. 22, 1907; s. Robert Alonzo and Clara (Bronaugh) D.; B.A., So. Meth. U., 1929, B.B.A., 1946; M.B.A., N. Tex. State U., 1949; Ph.D., U. Tex., 1956; m. Jean Gray, Apr. 20, 1940; children—Jean Elizabeth (Mrs. John M. Watson), Mary Dianne, Alicelyn, Jerry Edward. Salesman advt. Dallas Dispatch, 1929, Dallas Times Herald, 1930-31; grad. mgr. publs. So. Meth. U. Students' Pub. Co., 1931-46; instr. marketing So. Meth. U., Dallas, 1946-50, asst. prof., acting chmn. marketing, 1950-56, asso. prof., chmn. marketing, 1956-58, prof., chmn. marketing. 1958—. Ind. cons. Drake Research & Cons. Service, Dallas, 1956—. Mem. Am. Marketing Assn., Nat. Marketing Theory Seminar, Advt. Fedn. Am., Dallas Advt. League, Dallas Sales and Marketing Execs. Club, Alpha Kappa Psi, Alpha Delta Sigma (nat. v.p. 1957-61). Methodist. Author: (with Frank Millar) Marketing Research, 1969. Home: 3409 Wentwood Dr Dallas TX 75225

DRAKE, ROBERT ELISHA, research corp. exec.; b. Boston, Oct. 14, 1908; s. Robert A. and Verena (Hinds) D.; grad. Williston Acad., 1934; student Am. Internat. Coll., 1934-36; student U. Md. Coll. Engring., 1943-44; m. Doris Anderson, Aug. 25, 1956; 1 dau., Susan H. Engr. Martin Aircraft Co., Balt., 1940-45, Nat. Plastics, Inc., Nashville, 1949-52; chief engr. Winner Mfg. Co., West Trenton, N.J., 1945-49; devel. engr. Lavelle Aircraft Co., Newtown, Pa., 1952-55; adminstr. Young Devel. and Research Lab., Princeton, N.J., 1955-57; mgr. Plastics div. Piper Aircraft Co., Vero Beach, Fla., 1958-70; pres. Radmo, Inc., Vero Beach, 1970—; dir. First Fed. Savs. & Loan Bank, Vero Beach, Fla. Charter dir. United Fund, Vero Beach. Mem. Soc. Plastics Engrs., Am. Water Ski Assn. (charter dir.), Aircraft Owners Pilots Assn., Vero Beach C. of C. (dir. 1963—), Soc. Automotive Engrs., Presbyn. Clubs: Kiwanis (local dir. 1960—, pres. 1967), Vero Beach Country. Designer, builder 1st prodn. plastic boat, 1946, 1st all plastic airplane, 1958-62, 1st molded house, 1970-72. Home: 3265 11th Av Vero Beach FL 32960 Office: Radmo Inc Vero Beach FL 32960

DRAKEFORD, JOHN WILLIAM, educator, psychologist; b. Sydney, Australia, Sept. 26, 1914; s. Walter and Elsie (Curtis) D.; B.A., U. Sydney, 1949; diploma in edn., Sydney Tchrs. Coll., 1950; M.A., Tex. Christian U., 1958, Th.M., 1960; D.Religous Edn., Southwestern Sem., 1956, Ed.D., 1967; m. Robina Balie, Dec. 13, 1941; children—Warwick, Brenton. Came to U.S., 1954, naturalized, 1964. Ordained to ministry Baptist Ch., 1941; pastor in Australia, 1937-42, Haberfield (New S. Wales) Bapt. Ch., 1945-49; youth dir. Bapt. Union New S. Wales, 1949-54; prof. psychology Southwestern Sem., 1954—. Served with Australian Army, 1943-45. Author: Counseling for Church Leaders, 1961; Red Blueprint for the World, 1962; Psychology in Search of a Soul, 1964: The Home: Laboratory of Life, 1965; The Great Sex Swindle, 1967; Integrity Therapy, 1967;

The Awesome Power of the Listening Ear, 1967; Farewell to the Lonely Crowd, 1969; This Insanity Called Love, 1969; Games Husbands and Wives Play, 1971; Forbidden Love, 1971. Co-author: An Introduction of Pastoral Counseling, 1959; Religion and Medicine, 1967. Home: 3228 Spanish Oak Dr Fort Worth TX 76109

DRANGUET, CHARLES EDWIN, JR., banker; b. Natchitoches, La., May 16, 1937; s. Charles Edwin and Cleo (McBride) D.; B.S. in Bus. Adminstrn., Northwestern State U., Natchitoches, 1961; m. Mary E. Bergeron, Dec. 31, 1961; children—Madeline, Charles Edwin III, Molly, Marilyn, Benjamin. With Exchange Bank & Trust Co., Natchitoches, 1961—, asst. cashier, 1963-65, asst. v.p., 1965-69, v.p., 1969—; owner Vienna Acres, Natchitoches, 1967—; pres. Terre Noire Realty Corp., Natchitoches, 1971—. Financial dir. A.R.C., Natchitoches Parish, 1963, Natchitoches Parish, Boy Scouts Am., 1965-66. Bd. dirs. Natchitoches Mental Health Assn., Natchiches Christmas Festival, Pres.'s Council on Aging. Served with USMCR, 1957-59. Named outstanding young man of year Natchitoches Parish, 1971. Mem. La. Bankers Assn. Edn. (dir. 1969—), La. Bankers Assn. (dir. northwestern group 1972—), Natchitoches C. of C. (dir. 1967—), Natchitoches Golfers Assn. Democrat. Roman Catholic. Kiwanian (dir. 1969—), Elk. Clubs: St. Denis Investment (Natchitoches), Natchitoches Country. Home: 202 Sirod St Natchitoches LA 71457 Office: 700 Front St Natchitoches LA 71457

DRAPER, CLARE HILL, III, bldg. material co. exec.; b. Anderson, S.C., June 17, 1928; s. Clare Hill and Helen (Watkins) D.; student bus. adminstn. U. Va., 1946-48; B.S. in Textile Mfg., Clemson Coll., 1952; m. Eulalie Thomas Jenkins, Dec. 8, 1956; children—Clare Hill IV, Eulalie Crommelin, Raleigh Jenkins. Salesman Pacific Mills, Inc., Atlanta, 1954-55; exec. asst. to v.p. Pacific Mills, N.Y.C., 1955-56, asst. mdse. mgr., 1956-57, sales and merchandising mgr., 1957-58; v.p. Jenkins Mfg. Co., Anniston, Ala., 1958—; dir. Nat. Sash & Door Jobbers Assn., Chgo., 1971-73. Bd. dirs. United Fund, Calhoun County, 1970-73. Served to 1st lt. inf. AUS, 1952-54. Mem. Anniston C. of C. (dir. 1972-74), Chi Phi. Episcopalian. Rotarian. Club: Anniston Country. Home: 940 Montvue Rd Anniston AL 36201 Office: 315 W 17th St Anniston AL 36201

DRAPER, DANIEL D., supt. schs.; b. Elk Point, S.D., June 26, 1911; s. Jesse Sylvester and Bertha (Sawtelle) D.; elementary certificate Northeastern State Coll., 1933, B.A., 1937; M.A., Okla. State U., 1949; postgrad. U. Ark., 1957-59; m. Elva Anderson, July 3, 1937; children—Shirley Ann (Mrs. Don Allen Gard), Daniel D., Marjorie Kay (Mrs. William E. Miller). Prin., Stone Chapel Sch., Cherokee County, Okla., 1931-40; supt. Pierce (Okla.) Pub. Schs., 1945-54, Colcord (Okla.) Pub. Schs., 1954—. Mem. Okla. Ho. Reps., 1938-42; chmn. Dem. Central Com., Delaware County; mayor Colcord, Okla. Mem. Anti-Thief Assn. (nat. pres.), Cherokee County (pres. 1940-41), McIntosh County (pres. 1951-52), Delaware County (pres. 1958-59) tchrs. assns., N.E. Dist. Sch. Adminstrs. Assn. (pres.), Colcord C. of C. (pres.). Mason. Address: 102 W Blocker St Colcord OK 74338

DRAPER, EARLE SUMNER, planning, housing cons.; b. Falmouth, Mass., Oct. 19, 1893; s. Frederic Ward and Bertha (Sumner) D.; grad. high sch., Milford, Mass., 1911; B.S., Mass. State Coll., Amherst, 1915; Dr. Landscape Architecture (hon.). U. of Mass., 1950; studied and traveled in Europe, 1922; m. Norma Farwell, May 26, 1917; children—Frederic Farwell, Earle Summer, Norman Claflin (killed in action 1944), Charles Alfred. Norma (dec. 1934); m. 2d, Elizabeth Jordan. Landscape architect, Cambridge, Mass., 1915; settled at Charlotte, N.C., 1917; pioneer in landscape architecture in southern states. Prin. works include: T.V.A. projects; estates and towns throughout the South. Vis. prof. Lowthorpe Sch. of Landscape Architecture, 1931-32, Harvard U. Sch. of Landscape Architecture, 1932. Dir. land planning and housing T.V.A., 1933-37, dir. dept. of regional planning studies, TVA, 1937-40; asst. adminstr. FHA, 1940-41, dep. commr., 1942-45; in own office, housing and planning cons., since 1945. Cons. Nat. Resources Com. and the Md. State Planning Bd. on Balt.-Washington-Annapolis Area Report, 1936-37, Ga., Ala. State Planning Bds., 1937; acting regional counselor, Southeast, Nat. Resources Planning Bd., 1937-40; lectr. in field. Fellow Am. Soc. of Landscape Architects (former v.p., dir.); mem. Am. Inst. of Planners (pres. 1940-42), Am. Soc. of Plan Ofcls. (past bd. dirs.). Phi Kappa Phi, Alpha Sigma Phi. Mason. Clubs: Cosmos, Congressional Country (Washington). Contbr. to publs. Home: 936 E Causeway Blvd Vero Beach FL 32960*

DRAPER, ROBERT BRUCE, architect; b. Gainesboro, Tenn., July 28, 1927; s. Herbert Ridley and Hallie (Reeves) D.; student U. Chgo., 1947-48. Frank Lloyd Wright Found., 1948-50; m. Jane Helen Caplinger, Dec. 11, 1953; children—Cynthia, Christopher Louis, Elizabeth. Draftsman, designer Chgo. firms William F. Deknatel, and Barancik & Conte, 1951-52; draftsman, designer Marr & Holman, Nashville, 1952-53; gen. practice architecture, Nashville, 1953—. Served with USNR, 1945-46. Mem. Soc. Am. Registered Architects. Unitarian. Home: 613 Estes Rd Nashville TN 37215 Office: 2535 Franklin Rd Nashville TN 37204

DRAPER, ROBERT SARGENT, artist; b. Rutland, Vt., Feb. 15, 1920; s. Fred Barton and Abbie (Sargent) D.; B.A., U. Fla., 1941. One man shows Mirell Gallery, Miami Beach Art Center, Atlanta High Mus., Maitland (Fla.) Research Center; group shows Ringling Mus., Sarasota, Fla., 1955, Riverside Mus., N.Y.C., 1958, Columbia Mus., Columbia, S.C., 1959, Columbus Mus., Columbus, Ga., 1961, Springfield Mus., Springfield, Mass., 1962, represented in collections Norton Gallery, Lowe Gallery, Am. Sch. Madrid Mus., Columbus (Ga.) Mus., also Emory U., Atlanta; research dir. Playhouse Gallery, Coconut Grove, Fla., 1959-60; dir., owner Mirell Gallery, Coconut Grove, Fla., 1961—; One Man Show, Ednl.-TV series, 1962-63; exhibited Fla. Artist Group Show, 1963, Blue Dome Ann., 1971. Co-trustee Myrtle Taylor Bradford Art Fellowship Fund, 1959-61. Recipient 1st prize oil Miami Art League, 1950, 51, 55, 2d prize oil Miami Soc. of Four Arts, 1954. Mem. Fla. Artist Group (regional dir. 1959-61), Miami Artists Assn. (pres. 1959-61), Blue Dome Fellowship (pres. 1961-62, 66-68, treas. 1970-71), U. Miami Arts Council, Delta Chi. Democrat. Unitarian. Home: 7719 SW 69th Av Miami FL 33143 Office: 3421 Main Hwy Coconut Grove FL 33143

DRAPER, WILLIAM CLAUDIE, banker; b. Wichita Falls, Tex., May 20, 1928; s William Haskell and May Pearl (Andrus) D.; grad. Am. Inst. Banking, 1971; m. Georgia Ruth Johnson, Nov. 10, 1948; children—Alice Elaine (Mrs. Larry Dan Crabb), Thomas, William Curtis, Merollee. With 1st Wichita Nat. Bank, Wichita Falls, 1945—, installment loan officer, 1955—, v.p. time credit, 1969-72. Bd. dirs. Water Improvement Dist., 1958-62. Mem. City View Sch. Bd., 1957-61. Bd. dirs. Concern, 1970-72. Mem. C. of C. Methodist (trustee). Home: 1013 Landon Lane Wichita Falls TX 76305 Office: PO Box 540 Wichita Falls TX 76307

DRAUGHON, CLYDE OSBORNE, ret. banker; b. Mobile, Ala., June 17, 1903; s. Peter Edwards and Belle Lindsey (Parker) D.; grad. certificate Am. Inst. Banking, 1937; grad. Financial Pub. Relations Sch., Northwestern U., 1950; m. Bertha Godwin, Oct. 6, 1926; children—Eulalie (Mrs. Willis R. Brown), Clyde Osborne. With Mchts. Nat. Bank, Mobile, 1920-71, asst. cashier, 1939-44, asst. v.p., 1944-51, v.p., 1951-71, dir. bus. devel. activities, 1923-44, 1951-71. Instr. pub. relations and pub. speaking Mobile chpt. Am. Inst. Banking, 1950-58. Active United Fund. Mem. Financial Advertisers Assn. (dir. 1938—), Am. Inst. Banking (pres. Mobile chpt. 1938—). Episcopalian (vestryman 1965-68). Lion (past pres.). Author: Practical Bank Letter Writing, 1971. Home: 350 Thornton St Mobile AL 36609

DRAY, CLIFFORD JAMES, drug co. exec.; b. Exline, Ia., Dec. 25, 1909; s. Henry James and Icel (Hutchison) D.; B.S., Purdue U., 1934; m. Marian Kathleen McKeown, Dec. 20, 1941; children—Susan Diane, Linda Jean, Sally Kathleen. With Walgreen Drug Co., Hammond, Ind., 1934-35, Woods Drug Co., Evansville, Ind., 1936-41, Eli Lilly & Co., Hopkinsville, Ky., 1941-44; pres. Major-Dray Drug Co., Inc., Hopkinsville, 1944—. Mem. Am. Ky. pharm. assns., Nat. Assn. Retail Druggists, C. of C., Purdue U. Alumni Assn., Kappa Psi. Elk. Odd Fellow. Club: Hopkinsville Golf and Country. Home: 2121 S Main St Hopkinsville KY 42240 Office: 200 E 9th St Hopkinsville KY 42240

DREIFUSS, FRITZ EMANUEL, educator; b. Dresden, Germany, Jan. 20, 1926; s. Alfred and Erika (Ballin) D.; student Wanganui Collegiate Sch., New Zealand, 1939-42; M.B., U. Otago, New Zealand, 1950, Ch.B., 1950; m. Daphne Guthrie, Feb. 11, 1954; children—Simone, Donald Alfred. Came to U.S., 1958, naturalized, 1964. Intern neurosurgery Anckland Hosp., New Zealand, 1951-52, resident, 1953; resident, resident med. officer Nat. Hosp., Queen Square, London, 1955-57; practice medicine specializing in neurology, Anckland, N.Z., 1958; mem. staff U. Va. Hosp., Charlottesville, 1959—; asst. prof. neurology U. Va. Sch. Medicine, Charlottesville, 1959-64, asso. prof., 1964-68. prof., 1968—. Clin. dir. Commonwealth Va. Child Neurology Program, 1959—. Fellow Am. Acad. Neurology; mem. Royal Coll. Physicians, Royal Australian Coll. Physicians, A.A.A.S., A.M.A., Assn. for Research in Nervous and Mental Diseases, So. Electro Encephalogrphic Soc., N.Y. Acad. Scis. Home: 1614 Yorktown Dr Charlottesville VA 22901

DREIZEN, SAMUEL, physician; b. N.Y.C., Sept. 12, 1918; s. Charles and Rose (Schneider) D.; B.A., Bklyn. Coll., 1941; D.D.S., Western Res. U., 1945; M.D., Northwestern U., 1958; m. Jo Gilley, Aug. 3, 1956; one dau., Pamela L. Intern, Chgo. Wesley Meml. Hosp., 1958-59; practice medicine, Chgo., 1959-66; research asso. Nutrition Clinic Hillman Hosp., Birmingham, Ala., 1945-47, asst. sci. dir., 1947-60; instr. dept. nutrition and metabolism Northwestern U. Med. Sch., 1949-50, asst. prof. 1950-59, asso. prof., 1959-66; prof. dental sci. dental br., mem. Inst. for Dental Sci., U. Tex., 1966—, prof. grad. sch. biomed. scis., 1968—. Served as 2d lt. AUS, 1942-44. Clayton Found. research fellow, 1948-53. Fellow A.A.A.S., Soc. Research Child Devel.; mem. Internat. Assn. Dental Research, Am. Assn. Phys. Anthropology, Am. Dental Assn., World Med. Assn., N.Y. Acad. Scis., Sigma Xi, Omicron Kappa Upsilon, Alpha Omega Alpha. Home: 5218 Dumfries Dr Houston TX 77035

DRELL, ANNIE DEE FLINN (MRS. THEODORE LOUIS DRELL), realtor; b. Fulton, Ky., June 11, 1916; d. Dillingham Dodson and Alma (Bradley) Flinn; student real estate appraising Tulane U., 1966-67; m. Theodore Louis Drell, Aug. 31, 1935; children— Barbara Anne (Mrs. Austin Allen), Robert Louis (dec.), Theodore Louis III, Dee Dodson. Sec.-treas. Ted Drell, advt. art & design, 1939—; real estate agt. Carriere & Harper, New Orleans, 1959-66; broker, 1966-67; v.p. Waguespack, Pratt, Inc., 1967; staff broker Stan Weber & Assos., New Orleans, 1968—. Organizing mem. Lake Terrace Woman's Club, New Orleans, 1957, rec. sec. 1969-70, v.p., 1970-71, 72-73; mem. Methodist Hosp. Woman's Aux., 1968—. Mem. D.A.R. (charter Bayou St. John chpt. regent chpt. 1958-59, 62-63, treas. 1970-72), U.D.C., Jefferson Bd. Realtors, Nat. Assn. Real Estate Bds. (treas. women's council New Orleans chpt. 1972), Real Estate Bd. New Orleans. Baptist. Home: 1336 New York St New Orleans LA 70122 Office: 6244 Argonne Blvd New Orleans LA 70124

DRENNEN, WILLIAM MILLER, U.S. judge; b. Jenkins, Ky., Mar. 1, 1914; s. Everett and Louise Bright (Miller) D.; B.S., Ohio State U., 1936, LL.B., 1938; m. Margaret Morton, Nov. 30, 1940; children—Margaret Penelope, William Miller, David Holmes, Dale Louise. Admitted to W.Va. bar, 1939; asst. to clk. Supreme Ct. of Ohio, 1937-38; law clk. to judge U.S. Dist. Ct., So. Dist. W.Va., 1938-40; with firm Jackson, Kelly, Holt & O'Farrell, and predecessor firms, 1940-58, partner, 1947-58; judge Tax Ct. of U.S., Washington, 1958-67; chief judge 1967—. Active Boy Scouts Am. Served as lt. comdr. USN, 1942-45. Mem. Am., W.Va., Charleston bar assns., W. Va. Tax Inst. (past pres.), Family Service Charleston. Republican. Episcopalian. Clubs: Chevy Chase (Md.); Metropolitan (Washington). Home: 8001 Aberdeen Rd Bethesda MD 20014 Office: US Tax Ct Box 70 Washington DC 20044

DRESSEL, RICHARD LOUIS, dairy exec.; b. Columbis, O., Jan. 4, 1915; s. Charles Louis; B.S., Ohio State U., 1936; m. Elizabeth Davidson, Aug. 1, 1946; children—Richard C., Diann (Mrs. William Martin), Gary, John, Elizabeth Ann, Barbara, Mary, Carol. Salesman, Hamilton Milk Co., Columbus, O., 1936-37; lab. technician M & R Dietetic Labs., 1937-41; owner Dressel Dairy Farm, Miami, Fla., 1941-67; pres., Dressel Dairy, Inc., Avon Park, Fla., 1967—; dir. Barnett Bank, Sebring, Fla., Mem. Fla. Livestock Bd., 1955-65. Mem. Higlands County Hosp. Commn., 1963-67. Mason (Shriner), Elk, Rotarian (pres. 1971). Clubs: Riviera Country (Miami, Fla.); Placid Lakes Golf and Country (Lake Placid, Fla.). Home: PO Box 506 Lake Placid FL 33852 Office: PO Box 398 Avon Park FL 33825

DREVES, ROBERT GEORGE, govt. ofcl.; b. Bklyn., Oct. 24, 1914; s. George A. and Emma (Cordes) D.; student N.Y. U., 1932-36; m. Emily H. Swan, June 5, 1938; children—Janet E. (Mrs. Robert B. Hall), Donald A. With U.S. Naval Tng. Device Center, Orlando, Fla., 1946—, head operational flight trainer br., 1952-55, head air weapons system trainers div., 1955-60, head aerospace trainers dept., 1960-65, dir. field engring., 1965—. Served to lt. USNR, 1943-46. Recipient Superior Civilian Service award USN, 1960. Mem. A.A.A.S., Am. Inst. Aeros. and Astronautics, Soc. Logistics Engrs. Home: 1215 Ensenada Dr Orlando FL 32807 Office: Naval Tng Device Center Orlando FL 32813

DREVO, WILLIAM LUK, SR., architect; b. Pacov, Czechoslovakia, May 27, 1905; s. Joseph and Johanna (Lukova) D.; brought to U.S., 1905, naturalized, 1939; Diploma Architecture, Md. Inst., Balt., 1925; student George Washington U., 1929-31; research studies Richard J. Neutra Inst., 1966-70, George Washington U., 1970—; m. Olga Nenadal, Mar. 25, 1931; children—William L., Richard N. Asso. architect Fed. Constrn. Agys., 1927-43; sr. engr. applied physics lab. Johns Hopkins, Silver Spring, 1943-46; asso. architect firm Frank Grad & Sons, Washington, 1946-51; archtl. planning cons. William L. Drevo, Sr., Washington, 1951—. Cons. Graphics Ednl. Communications Assn., 1949-56. Active campaigns various Congl. ofcls., 1952—. Recipient Civilian award Navy Dept., 1946. Mem. A.I.A., George Washington U. Alumni Assn., Soc. Am. Mil. Engrs. Republican. Presbyn. Nat. Accelerator Lab. site studies, 1964. Performing pianist, 1930—. Home: 6125 29th St NW Washington DC 20015 Office: 6125 29th St NW Washington DC 20015

DREW, E(DWIN) HARRIS, ret. judge; b. Fargo, Ga., Oct. 28, 1903; s. William T. and Idella (Edwards) D.; LL.B., John B. Stetson U., 1923, LL.D. (hon.) 1956; m. Edith Turner, June 10, 1927; 1 dau., Melanie May. Admitted to Fla. bar, 1923, practiced West Palm Beach, 1923-52, as mem. Drew, Burns, Middleton & Rogers; atty. Town of Palm Beach, 1923-52; justice Fla. Supreme Ct., 1952-71, chief justice Fla. Supreme Ct., 1955-57, 63-65. Former mem. bd. commrs. Port Palm Beach. Vice pres. bd. overseers Stetson U. Coll. Law; pres., dir. The Law Center Found. Mem. Associated Municipalities Palm Beach Co. (past pres.) Am., Fla. (past pres.), Palm Beach Co. (past pres.), bar assns., Am. Law Inst., Stetson Alumni Assn. (past pres.), Am. Judicature Soc., Delta Sigma Phi, Phi Alpha Delta. Mason. Club: Tusca Willa. Contbr. articles profl. jours. Address: 2922 N Monroe St Tallahassee FL 32303

DREW, ELIZABETH BRENNER, editor. Washington editor Atlantic mag.; moderator program Thirty Minutes With..... Pub. Broadcasting Service. Address: 3112 Woodley Rd NW Washington DC 20016*

DREWRY, MRS. CARLETON (ELISABETH DREWRY), educator; b. Buchanan, Va., May 15, 1916; d. John Sutton and Bess Irene (Phlegar) McDonald; A.B., Roanoke Coll., 1934-38; M.A., Columbia, 1942; m. Guy Carleton Drewry, Apr. 2, 1942; children—Barbara Louise, Guy Carleton. Head English dept. Pulaski (Va.) High Sch., 1938-40; music supr. city schs., Roanoke, Va., 1940-47; English tchr. Jefferson Sr. High Sch., 1947-61; tchr. English, Patrick Henry High Sch., Roanoke, 1961—, chmn. English dept., 1961-63. Poetry readings for various coll. groups, poetry socs.; condr. weekly book rev. program radio sta. WDBJ Radio-TV, 1955-60. Chmn. local and state creative writing contests Am. Assn. U. Women, 1960-62; organizer Great Books Reading Group, Roanoke, 1958. Bd. dirs. Roanoke City Pub. Library, 1958—, pres. 1962—. Mem. Poetry Soc. Va., N.E.A., Va. Edn. Assn., Am. Assn. U. Women (pres. Roanoke 1966-70), Va. Library Assn. (sec. trustees sect. 1970-72), Va. Assn. Tchrs. English (sec.-treas. 1956-57), Alpha Psi Omega. Episcopalian. Home: 2305 Maiden Lane SW Roanoke VA 24015 Office: 2000 Grandin Rd Roanoke VA

DREWRY, GUY CARLETON, author; b. Stevensburg, Va., May 21, 1901; s. Rev. Samuel Richard and Julia Harriet (Pinckard) D.; student pub. schs. Va.; m. Margaret Elizabeth McDonald, Apr. 2, 1942; children— Barbara Louise, Guy Carleton. Asso. editor The Lyric, 1929-49; vis. lectr. English, Am. poetry Hollins Coll., 1952-53; instr. creative writing U. Va. Extension Div. Counselor Blue Ridge Writers Colony, 1965-66. Contbr. poetry to The Dial, later The Nation, The New Republic, Poetry: A Magazine of Verse also Voices. Work appears in N.Y. Times, N.Y. Herald Tribune, The Ga. Rev., Prairie Schooner, Sat. Rev., Queen's Quar., Va. Quar. Rev. and Yale Rev.; included in following anthologies: American Writing, Lyric Virginia Today, Moult's Best Poems, Virginia Reader, Poetry Awards (1949, 51). Proud Horns, 1933: The Sounding Summer, 1948; A Time of Turning, 1951; The Writhen Wood, 1953. Winner The Voices Award, 1940; Lyric Virginia Today, No. 2, The Best Poems of 1956; Cloud Above Clocktime, 1957. Poetry Awards prize for best book of poetry pub. in 1951; poet laureate Va. Mem. Poetry Soc. Va. (pres. 1952-55, mem. adv. bd.), Poetry Soc. Am. (regional v.p.), Authors Guild of Authors League Am. Club: Virginia Writers (hon.). Editor of Southern Issue of Voices, 1952. Home: 2305 Maiden Lane SW Roanoke VA 24015

DREWRY, LYMAN AUBREY, JR., univ. dean; b. Richmond, Va., Feb. 25, 1934; s. Lyman Aubrey and Evelyn (Hawthorne) D.; B.S., U. Va., 1954; M.A., 1956, Ph.D., 1960; m. Elizabeth Stebbing Allen, Oct. 14, 1967; 1 son, Timothy Allen. Instr. econs. N.C. State Coll., Raleigh, 1957-58; asso. prof. econs. Queens Coll., Charlotte, N.C., 1958-60; Fulbright lectr. econs. U. Ceylon, Peradeniya, 1960-61; prof. banking and finance U. Ga., Athens, 1961-69; asso. dean Sch. Bus. Western Carolina U., Cullowhee, N.C., 1969-70, dean, 1970—. Vis. prof. U. Va., 1959-60, U. Wyo., 1965, World Campus Afloat; Chapman Coll., Cal., 1968; group leader for Expt. in Internat. Living to India, 1966, Ceylon, 1967, Greece, 1968. Mem. Raven Soc., Gridiron Secret Soc., Beta Gamma Sigma, Delta Sigma Pi. Editor: Money, the Market and the State, 1968. Contbr. articles to profl. jours. Home: PO Box 1312 Cullowhee NC 28723

DREWRY, WILLIAM ALTON, educator; b. Dyess, Ark., Oct. 23, 1936; s. C. Clarence and Cathleen (Ford) D.; Asso. Sci., Ark. Tech., 1956; B.S., U. Ark., 1959, M.S., 1961; Ph.D., Stanford, 1968; m. Bette Ann Cooper, Sept. 5, 1959; children—William Boyd, Bette Cathleen, Leslie Ann. Instr., U. Ark., Fayetteville, 1960-62, asst. prof., 1965-68; research asst. Stanford, Palo Alto, Cal., 1962-65; asso. prof. dept. civil engring. U. Tenn., Knoxville, 1968—. Cons. U. Ark., Oak Ridge Nat. Lab. Mem. Tenn. Bd. Certification Water and Wastewater Operators, Knox County Utility Bd. Adv. and Study Commn. Mem. Am. Pub. Health Assn., Am. Assn. Profs. in Environmental Engring., Am. Soc. C.E., Am. Soc. Engring. Edn., Water Pollution Control Fedn., Am. Water Works Assn., Nat. Soc. Profl. Engrs., Knoxville Tech. Soc., Clean Environment Council Knoxville, Sigma Xi, Tau Beta Pi, Chi Epsilon. Contbr. articles to profl. jours. Home: 3729 Cherrylog Rd Knoxville TN 37921

DREXLER, DAVID, savs. and loan exec.; b. Wynne, Ark., Jan. 8, 1903; s. Meyer Mike and Dora (Glass) D.; student Wynne Bus. Coll., 1921-22; m. Christine Elizabeth West, May 12, 1943. With Drexlers' Dry Goods Store, Wynne, 1920-30; owner David's cafe and soda fountain, Wynne, 1930-42; owner Wynne Ins. and Loan Co., 1943-70; dir. Wynne Fed. Savs. and Loan Assn., 1934, pres., 1964—; dir. Cross County Bank. Mem. Wynne Planning Commn., 1952—, chmn., 1956-69. Served with AUS, 1942-43. Mem. Jewish religion. Rotarian; mem. B'nai B'rith. Club: Razorback (Wynne). Home: 909 Hamilton Av Wynne AR 72396 Office: 363 E Union Av Wynne AR 72396

DREYFUS, DANIEL AUGUSTUS, engineer, govt. ofcl.; b. Bklyn., Mar. 5, 1931; s. James and Edna (Hogan) D.; student Northwestern U., 1950-52; B.C.E., George Washington U., 1957, M.E.A., 1965; student Am. U., 1966—; m. Josephine Catherine Sime, Sept. 21, 1957; children— Barbara, Patrick, Teresa, Karin, Lisa. Civil engr. Tex. Co., Lockport, Ill., 1957-59; civil engr. U.S. Corps Engrs., Anchorage, Alaska, 1959-61; planning engr. U.S. Bur. Reclamation, Washington, 1961-68; profl. staff mem. U.S. Senate, Washington, 1968—. Served with AUS, 1952-54. Mem. Am. Soc. C.E., Nat. Soc. Profl. Engrs., Soc. Am. Mil. Engrs., Theta Tau. Roman Catholic. Home: 1536 Forest Lane McLean VA 22101 Office: New Senate Office Bldg Washington DC 22101

DRIGGERS, J(AMES) CLYDE, coll. pres.; b. Ft. Green, Fla., Jan. 10, 1917; s. Uria Alonzo and Mary (Stephens) D.; B.S.A., U. Fla., 1938, Ph.D., 1949; m. Doris Esther McCullough, Aug. 25, 1940; children— David, Billie Kay (Mrs. John Pehler), Stephen, James McCullough. Instr. poultry husbandry U. Fla., 1939-40, asst. prof., 1946-49, asso. prof., 1949-55, prof., 1955-57; chmn. poultry div. U. Ga., 1957-64; pres. Abraham Baldwin Coll., Tifton 1964—. Served with AUS, 1941-46; col. Res. Mem. Poultry Sci. Assn. (past pres.), World's Poultry Sci., Assn. So. Agrl. Workers (past chmn. poultry sect.), Ga. Poultry Fedn., Sabres, Fla. Blue Key, Sigma Xi, Gamma Sigma Delta (past chpt. pres.), Alpha Tau Alpha, Alpha Gamma Rho (past grand pres.), Alpha Zeta (past high censor), Kappa Kappa Psi, Gamma Sigma Epsilon, Sigma Delta Psi. Democrat. Methodist. Clubs: Rotary (past pres., zone chmn. Rotaract) (Tifton, Ga.); F (U. Fla.). Home: Abraham Baldwin Coll Tifton GA 31794

DRIMMER, BERNARD EDWARD, govt. ofcl.; b. N.Y.C., July 31, 1917; s. David and Rebecca (Kupferschmidt) D.; B.S., Coll. City N.Y., 1938; m. Mary E. Bauckman, Sept. 3, 1966. Analytical chemist Washington Navy Yard, 1941-42, U.S. Bur. Mines, College Park, Md., 1942-44; with Carbide & Carbon Chem. Corp., Oak Ridge, 1944-46; research engr. Naval Ordnance Lab., White Oak, Md., 1946-50, br. head explosion dynamics div., 1956-63; project engr. Office Chief Ordnance, Dept. Army, Washington, 1950-52; prodn. engr. prodn. div. U.S. AEC, Washington, 1952-53; Brussels rep. Ordnance Tech. Office, London, Eng., 1953-56; br. head propulsion and energy conversion br., research div. Bur. Naval Weapons, Navy Dept., Washington, 1963-66, dir. energy conversion and materials div. Naval Ordnance Systems Command, 1966—. Mem. Am. Phys. Soc., A.A.A.S., Soc. Motion Picture and Television Engrs. (bd. editors). Patentee in field detonation physics and explosive warheads. Home: 4841 S 9th St Arlington VA 22204 Office: Navy Ordnance Systems Command Nat Center No 2 Washington DC 20360

DRISKELL, DAVID CLYDE, educator, artist; b. Eatonton, Ga., June 7, 1931; s. George W. and Mary L. (Clyde) D.; A.B., Howard U., 1955 M.F.A., Cath. U. Am., 1962; student Skowhegan Sch. Painting and Sculpture, 1953, Rijksbureau voor Kunsthistorisches Documentatie, The Hague, 1964; m. Thelma G. DeLoatch, Jan. 9, 1952; children—Daviryne Mari, Daphne Joyce. Asso. prof. art Talladega Coll., 1955-62; asso. prof., acting chmn. dept. art Howard U., 1963-64; prof. art, chmn. dept. Fisk U., 1966—, dir. div. cultural research, 1968—; vis. prof. Inst. African Studies, U. Ife, Ile-Ife, Nigeria, 1970; exhbns. include Rhodes Nat. Gallery, Salisbury, Rhodesia, 1957, Smithsonian Instn., 1962, The White House, 1966, U. Cal. at Los Angeles Galleries, 1967, Oakland (Cal.) Mus., 1967, N.A.D., 1968, Norfolk (Va.) Mus., 1969, Corcoran Gallery, 1965, Whitney Mus. Am. Art, 1971. Cons. Life mag. on Black History, 1968, Nat. Def. Edn. Act Insts. on Negro Culture and History, 1968. Trustee Am. Fedn. Art, Mus. African Art and Frederick Douglass Inst., Tenn. Arts Commn. Visual Arts Panel. Danforth Found. fellow, 1961; Rockefeller Found. fellow, 1964, 67; Govt. of the Netherlands fellow, 1964. Co-author: Black Dimensions in Contemporary American Art, 1971. Home: 1601 Phillips St N Nashville TN 37208

DRISS, RACHID, Tunisian diplomat; b. Tunis, Tunisia, Jan. 27, 1917; grad. Sadiki Coll., Tunnis; m. 1 child. Mem. Neo-Destour Party, 1934—, dir. party newspaper El Amal, 1955, mem. polit. bur., 1958—; civil servant dept. finance during French rule; exiled, 1946-55; a founder Office Arab Maghreb, Cairo, also engaged in missions to Arab States, Indonesia, India and Pakistan during exile; dep. Constl. Assembly Tunisia, 1956, participated drafting constn. and proclamation of republic, 1957; sec. of state for post office and communications, 1957; elected mem. Nat. Assembly Tunisia, 1958; tour Latin Am. as presdl. rep., 1961; rep. Tunisia Conf. African Ministers Fgn. Affairs, Dakar, 1963; A.E. and P. of Tunisia to U.S., also ambassador to Mexico, 1964— consul gen. of Tunisia. Address: 5131 Broad Branch Rd NW Washington DC 20008

DRIVER, LOTTIE ELIZABETH, librarian; b. Newport News, Va., Dec. 6, 1918; d. James W. and Lottie (Williams) Driver; student Averett Coll., 1936-37; B.S., Mary Washington Coll. of U. Va., 1939; A.B. in L.S., Coll. William and Mary, 1944. Band instr. Hampton (Va.) Sch. System, 1939-41; asst. librarian Newport News Pub. Library, 1941-47, librarian, 1947-69; asst. dir. Newport News Pub. Library System, 1970—. Author book rev. column in Daily Press, 1945—; library news reporter radio sta. WGH, 1959. Active United Fund. Named Outstanding Employee, City of Newport News, 1970. Mem. Am., Southeastern, Va. library assns., Am. Assn. U. Women, P.E.O., D.A.R., Phi Theta Kappa, Alpha Phi Sigma. Baptist. Author articles for library supply house. Home: 14 Westover Rd Warwick Newport News VA 23601 Office: 108 Main St Newport News VA 23601

DRIVER, WILLIAM JOSEPH, chem. exec.; b. Rochester, N.Y., May 9, 1918; s. John J. and Bridget Anna (Farrell) D.; B.B.A. cum laude, Niagara U., 1941; LL.B., George Washington U., 1952, M.A., 1965; m. Marian R. McKay, Aug. 18, 1947; children—William Joseph, Kellie McKay. Dir. compensation and pension service VA, Washington, 1956-59, chief benefits dir., 1959-61, dep. adminstr. vets. affairs, 1961-65, adminstr. vets. affairs, 1965-69; pres. Mfg. Chemists Assn., 1969—. Mem. Pres.'s Council Aging, 1965—, Pres.'s Com. Employment Physically Handicapped, 1965—, Pres.'s Com. Equal Opportunity in Housing, 1965—, Pres.'s Com. on Consumer Interests, 1967—, Pres.'s Com. Health Manpower, 1967—. Served to lt. col. AUS, 1941-45, AUS, 1951-53. Decorated Legion of Merit, Bronze Star medal; Order British Empire; Croix de Guerre (France); recipient Meritorious Service medal VA, 1957, Exceptional Service medal, 1960, Career Service award Nat. Civil Service League, 1964, Achievement award Soc. Advancement Mgmt., 1965; Alumni Achievement award George Washington U., 1967. Mem. Bar Assn. D.C. Home: 215 W Columbia St Falls Church VA 22046

DROBA, HENRY JOHN, ret. dentist; b. Banska Bystrica, Czechoslovakia, June 16, 1899; s. Andrew and Suzan (Chmelko) D.; came to U.S., 1911, naturalized, 1918; student Ill. Inst. Tech., 1920-22, U. Chgo., 1922-23; D.D.S., U. Ill., 1928; m. Helen G. Newey, Oct. 16, 1930; children—Janet (Mrs. Harold K. Rice), Lynn (Mrs. James L. Click), Kathryn. Gen. practice dentistry, Chgo., 1928-65; asso. prof. U. Ill. Coll. Dentistry, Chgo., 1929-48; chmn. bd. dirs. Park Rubber Co., Lake Zurich, Ill., 1947-65. Chmn. Polk County (N.C.) A.R.C., 1968-71. Mem. Glencoe (Ill.) Sch. Bd., 1948-54. Bd. dirs. Southeast Regional Blood Program A.R.C., 1971. Served with U.S. Navy, 1917-19. Mem. Internat. Coll. Dentists, Am., Ill., Chgo. dental assns., Odontographic Soc. Chgo. (sec. 1944; pres. 1945), U. Ill. Dental Alumni Assn. (pres. 1937), Inst. Medicine Chgo., Delta Sigma Delta, Alpha Tau Omega, Omicron Kappa Upsilon. Republican. Club: Tryon (N.C.) Country. Home: Route 2 Green Hills Mill Spring NC 28756

DROZE, WILMON H., state ofcl. Librarian, archivist State of Tenn., Nashville. Address: 1112 Overton Lea Rd Nashville TN 37220*

DRUCE, HERMAN L., milling co. exec.; b. Cordell, Okla., May 12, 1910; s. Arthur Jack and Ursula Ann (Perkins) D.; student Draughans Bus. Coll., West Falls, Tex., 1930; m. Myrtle Claire Hassman, Sept. 10, 1938; children—Linda Ann (Mrs. Gabriel Zablatnik), Teddy Katherine (Mrs. Herman Moore Jr.), Martha Jean (Mrs. Jerry Derby). Traffic clk. Gen. Mills, Inc., Wichita Falls, Tex., 1931, Oklahoma City, 1931, El Reno, Okla., 1932-35, traffic mgr., Oklahoma City, 1935-38, Wichita Falls, 1938-45, asst. div. traffic mgr., Oklahoma City, 1945-53; traffic mgr., grain buyer Morrison Milling Co., Denton, Tex., 1953-60, v.p. purchasing and traffic, 1960—. Mason, Lion. Home: 2619 Robinwood St Denton TX 76201 Office: Morrison Milling Co 319 E Prairie St Denton TX 76201

DRUCKER, MELVIN BRUCE, psychologist; b. Phila., May 27, 1927; s. Maxwell Lionel and Sylvia (Layton) D.; B.S., Western Res. U., 1950; M.A., Ohio U., 1951; Ph.D., George Peabody Coll. for Tchrs., 1956; m. Miriam Elizabeth Koontz, Aug. 22, 1957. Intern clin. psychology S.C. Mental Health Commn., 1955-56; psychologist Fulton County Child Guidance Clinic, Atlanta, 1956-58; chief psychologist community mental health service Ga. Dept. Pub. Health, Atlanta, 1958-65; clin. and research psychologist Georgian Clinic div. Ga. Mental Health Inst., Atlanta, 1965-70; chmn., asso. prof. dept. Mental Health Assts., Sch. Allied Health Scis., also asso. prof. urban life Ga. State U., 1970—. Diplomate in clin. psychology Am. Bd. Examiners in Psychology, Mem. Ga. Psychol. Assn. (sec. 1965-68, pres. 1970). Author: (with Fox, Dominick, Crow) Pilot Project for the Clinical Training of Clergymen in the Field of Alcoholism, 1967. Home: 424 Glenndale Av Decatur GA 30030 Office: Dept Mental Health Assts Ga State U Atlanta GA 30303

DRUMMOND, ALFRED ALEXANDER, cattle rancher, oil producer; b. Pawhuska, Okla., Dec. 2, 1896; s. Fred and Addie (Gentner) D.; B.S., Okla. A. and M. Coll., 1915; postgrad. U. Ill., 1916; m. Madelaine Russell, June 2, 1920; children—Madelaine II (Mrs. Oliver F. Bush); m. 2d, Ferne Boles, Jan. 22, 1943; 1 adopted son, James Alexander. Cattle rancher, Madill, 1920—; First Nat. Bank, Hominy, 1924-30; organizer, mgr. Okla. Live Stock Marketing Assn.; organizer Nat. Livestock Credit Corp., Oklahoma City, 1932; dir. Fed. Land Bank Assn. of Durant, 1956—; adv. com. Okla. to Fed. Land Bank Wichita, 1961-64; nat. adv. com. Washington Fed. Land Bank System representing 9th dist. Okla., Kan., Colo., N.M., 1962-64. Served from 2d lt. to capt., U.S. Army, 1917-19; served from maj. to lt. col., AUS, 1942-46. Mem. Okla. Fedn. of Fed. Land Bank Assns. (pres. 1960, dir. 1958-64), Am. Nat. Cattlemen's Assn., Tex. State and Southwestern Cattle Raisers Assn., Okla. Cattlemen's Assn., Scabbard and Blade, Phi Gamma Delta. Presbyn. Rotarian. Address: 510 W Tishomingo St Madill OK 73446

DRUMMOND, CHARLES EDGERTON, JR., civil engr.; b. Cedar Rapids, Ia., Mar. 5, 1898; s. Charles E. and Lula (Pollans) D.; B.A., Cornell Coll., Ia., 1920; m. Beulah Mae Tull, Aug. 12, 1924; children—Nancy Lee (Mrs. Howard H. McCall III). Draftsman, Caldwell Engring. Co., Jacksonville, Ill., 1920-24; engr. Clinchfield Portland Cement Co., Kingsport, Tenn., 1924-25, Mees & Mees, Charlotte, N.C., 1925-26; head bridge dept. Piedmont & No. Ry., Charlotte, 1926-29; engr. Robert & Co., Atlanta, 1929-30; self-employed as cons. engr., Atlanta, 1930-34; with Wiedeman & Singleton, Atlanta, 1934—, partner, 1959-71, cons., 1972—. Mem. Ga. Environmental Health Task Force, 1969—. Served with S.A.T.C., 1918. Recipient Bedell award Ga. Water and Pollution Control Assn., 1956, Wyckoff award, 1968. Registered profl. engr., Ala., Fla., Ga., N.C., S.C., Tenn., Va. Mem. Am. Inst. Cons. Engrs., Am. Soc. C.E. (Ga. pres. 1954), Nat. Soc. Profl. Engrs., Ga. Engring. Soc. (pres. 1952), Am. Acad. Environmental Engrs. (charter), Water Pollution Control Fedn. (dir. Ga. 1953-56). Episcopalian. Kiwanian. Clubs: Atlanta Athletic, Commerce. Home: 4700 Dudley Lane NW Atlanta GA 30327 Office: 1789 Peachtree Rd NE Atlanta GA 30309

DRUMMOND, KENNETH HERBERT, diversified co. exec.; b. Riverside, Cal., Jan. 19, 1922; s. Finlay Mackay and Eva Mary (Holland) D.; student Bates Coll., 1941-43; B.S., U. Ariz., 1949; postgrad. Tex. A. and M. U., 1950-57; m. Marion Emily Deane, May 14, 1955; children—Laurie, Finlay, Carter. Asso. in oceanography Tex. A. and M. U., College Station, 1950-57; asst. to dir. Smithsonian Astrophysical Obs., Cambridge, Mass., 1957-60; asst. to chancellor U. Cal. at San Diego, 1960-62; Washington rep. Tex. Instruments, 1960-67; exec. sec. panel industry and investment Commn. on Marine Sci., Exec. Office Pres., Washington, 1967-68; dir. program devel. Teledyne, Inc., Washington, 1969-72; asst. to pres. Ensco, Inc., Springfield, Va., 1972—. Mem. adv. council La. State U., 1969—. Served with USNR, 1943-46; PTO. Fellow A.A.A.S., Tex. Acad. Sci., Explorers Club; mem. Nat. Space Club, Marine Tech. Soc., Nat. Oceanographic Soc. (bd. dirs. 1966—). Mason (32 deg.). Club: Washington Hilton Racquet. Author: (with Eloise Engle) Sky Rangers, 1965. Editor: (with C.A. Whitten) Contemporary Geodesy, 1959. Home: 9104 Santayana Dr Fairfax VA 22030 Office: 5804 A Port Royal Rd Springfield VA 22151

DRUMMOND, ROSCOE, columnist; b. Theresa, N.Y.; s. John Henry and Georgia Estella (Peppers) D.; B.S.J., Syracuse U., 1924; Litt.D., Dartmouth, 1947; D.H.L. (hon.), Principia Coll., Elsah, Ill.; LL.D., Syracuse U., 1955, Ricker Coll., 1962; m. Charlotte Bruner, Sept. 11, 1926; 1 son, Geoffrey. Reporter Christian Science Monitor, Boston, 1924, successively asst. city editor, asst. to exec. editor, chief editorial writer, European editorial mgr., gen. news editor, mem. editorial board, exec. editor, 1934-40, chief Washington News Bur., 1940-53, also creator State of the Nation column; on leave as dir. information ECA in Europe, Paris, 1949-51; chief Washington Bur., N.Y. Herald Tribune, 1953-55, also author syndicated column; Washington columnist for Los Angeles Times Syndicate. Chmn. bd. trustees Freedom House, 1962-67. Recipient prize for best editorial pub. in Am. newspaper on significance of Internat. Press Exhbn. at Cologne, 1928; George Arents award for proficiency in Journalism, 1946. Mem. Am. Soc. Newspaper Editors, Alpha Kappa Psi, Sigma Phi Epsilon, Beta Gamma Sigma, Sigma Delta Chi. Clubs: Gridiron, Overseas Writers, National Press, Metropolitan, Cosmos (Washington). Author: (with Gaston Coblentz) Duel at the Brink, 1960. Contbr. to Am. and Brit. mags. Mason. Home: 3029 Cambridge Pl NW Washington DC 20007 Office: 1290 Nat Press Bldg Washington DC 20004

DRUMMOND, THEODORE HAMILTON, govt. ofcl.; b. Salt Lake City, June 17, 1908; s. Elza H. and Grace J. (Surline) D.; B.S. in Civil Engring., U. Utah, 1931; part-time student U. So. Cal., 1943-45; m. Mary V. Lafferty, Sept. 12, 1947 (dec. Feb. 1965); 1 dau., Mary Karen; m. 2d, Harriet Thorstad, July 23, 1967. Surveyor, 1931-37, engr. draftsman, 1937-42; topographic draftsman to chief photogrammetry sect. C.E., Los Angeles, 1942-48; engr.-illustrator Bur. Land Mgmt., Dept. Interior, 1948-57, asst. mgr. records improvement project, 1957-58, adminstr. Dept. Interior Mus., 1958—; paintings, etchings, sculpture exhibited Los Angeles, San Francisco, Salt Lake City, N.Y.C., Lexington, Ky., permanent exhbn. Dept. Interior Mus.; designer gold medal valor award, also deptl. service pins, Dept. Interior. Recipient Outstanding Performance award Bur. Land. Mgmt., 1956. Mem. Nat. Presbyn. Mariners, Am. Mus. Assn., Am. Mus. Natural History (asso.). Presbyn. (past nat. officer Nat. Presbyn. Mariners; past pres. Mariners Washington Presbytery). Compiler, composer, illustrator: A Syllabus of Measurement, 1954; The Public Land Records, 1959. Home: 1212 Tanley Rd Silver Spring MD 20904 Office: Dept Interior Washington DC 20240

DRUMMOND, WINSLOW, lawyer; b. Phila., Jan. 29, 1933; A.B., Wooster Coll., 1954; LL.B., Duke, 1957. Admitted to Ark. bar, 1957; mem. firm Wright, Lindsey & Jennings, Little Rock. Mem. Ark. Supreme Ct. civil com., 1962—, criminal com., 1970—. Mem. Pulaksi County, Ark., Am. (mem. ins., negligence and compensation law sect.) bar assns., Fedn. Ins. Counsel, Order Coif. Asso. editor Duke Law Jour., 1956-57. Address: Wright Lindsey & Jennings 2200 Worthen Bank Bldg Little Rock AR 72201*

DRUMWRIGHT, GEORGE WELLS, dentist; b. Washington, Sept. 2, 1924; s. Leo O. and Emma (Wells) D.; student Western Md. Coll., 1942-43; D.D.S., Georgetown U., 1947; m. Mary Ann Spicer, Nov. 12, 1948; children—Marie (Mrs. William Joseph Pepper Jr.), George Wells, Janet Lee. Individual practice dentistry, Washington, 1947—. Served with USAF, 1953-55. Mem. Am. Dental Assn., D.C. Dental Soc., Dental Progress Study Club, Columbia Dental Study Club, D.C. Acad. Gen. Dentistry (pres. elect 1971-73). Club: Civitan of Washington. Home: 3 Whitingham Terrace Silver Spring MD 20904 Office: 1722 Eye St NW Washington DC 20006

DRURY, THOMAS JOSEPH, bishop; b. County Sligo, Ireland, Jan 4, 1908; s. Michael and Margaret (Lannon) D.; student St. Benedict's Coll., Atchison, Kan., 1926-29; A.B., Kenrick Sem., 1931-35. Ordained priest Roman Catholic Ch., 1935; asst. and pastor Sacred Heart Cathedral, Amarillo, Tex., 1935-45; pastor St. Elizabeth's Ch., Christ the King Ch., Lubbock, Tex., 1956-61; bishop Diocese of San Angelo, 1961-65; consecrated, 1962; bishop Diocese of Corpus Christi, 1965—. Sec. Matrimonial Ct., 1935, promotor of justice, 1938—, defender of the bond, 1939—; diocesan dir. Confraternity of Christian Doctrine, 1936, Soc. Propagation of the Faith, 1936—, Cath. Action, Holy Name Soc.; mem. bd. Diocesan Adminstrn., 1938—. Chmn. Amarillo council Boy Scouts Am.; v.p. Amarillo Cath. Welfare Bur. Served to maj. Chaplains Corps, USAAF, 1945-47, USAF, 1949-55. Editor, bus. mgr. Texas Panhandle Register, 1936-38. Home: 4109 Ocean Dr Corpus Christi TX 78411 Office: 620 Lipan St Corpus Christi TX 78401

DRY, WILLIAM ARTHUR, interior designer; b. Apollo, Pa., Nov. 16, 1928; s. Victor George and Daisy (Hugas) D.; grad. N.Y. Sch. Interior Design, 1955. Interior designer Ruth Miller Interiors, Winston Salem, N.C., 1957-61, Modern Day Furniture, Knoxville, Tenn., 1961-62, Bromberg & Co., Birmingham, Ala., 1962—. Served with AUS, 1951-53. Mem. Am. Inst. Interior Designers (pres. Ala., 1971-72). Home: 2930 Clairmont Av Birmingham AL 35205 Office: 123 N 20th St Birmingham AL 35203

DRYE, RICHARD LEVEN, lawyer; b. Bradfordsville, Ky., Sept. 16, 1912; s. Don Victor and Edna Baker (Thornton) D.; A.B., U. Ky., 1937; LL.B., U. Louisville, 1940; B.Fgn.Trade, Am. inst. Fgn. Trade, Phoenix, 1948; acad. postgrad., diploma in law, London Sch. Econs. and Polit. Sci., U. London, 1953-54; postgrad. Queens' Coll., Cambridge U., 1954. Admitted to Ky. bar, 1940; asst. atty. gen., Commonwealth of Ky., 1946-48; pvt. practice, Louisville, 1948—; asst. Jefferson County atty., 1964-70; treas. Don. V. Drye, Inc., Lebanon, Ky.; mem. Neighborhood Devel. Corp. Rep. candidate for rep. of Ky., 1957. Served as spl. agt., CIC, AUS, 1942-45; 2d lt. Ky. N.G., 1946-48. Mem. Am., Ky., Louisville bar assns., St. James Ct. Assn., V.F.W., Kappa Alpha. Mem. Christian Ch. Club: Lincoln of Kentucky (sec. 1958-59). Home: 1453 St James Ct Louisville KY 40208 Office: 112 S 5th St Louisville KY 40202

DRYER, DOROTHEA MERRILL (MRS. EDWIN JASON DRYER), lawyer; b. Salt Lake City; d. George Edmund and Lillian (Chapman) Merrill; A.B., Stanford, 1936; LL.B., Yale, 1940; m. Edwin Jason Dryer, Feb. 28, 1942; children—Diana Claire, Faith Ellen. Admitted to Utah bar, 1941; clk. for Chief Justice Wolfe of Utah Supreme Ct. 1941; atty. Bur. Immigration, Dept. Justice, Washington, 1941-42; pvt. practice Salt Lake City, 1943-47, Washington, 1948—; dep. county atty., Salt Lake City, 1947-48; admitted to bar U.S. Supreme Ct., U.S. Ct. Mil. Appeals. Fellow Am. Assn. Criminology; mem. Am., Fed., Utah bar assns., Internat. Platform Assn., Oral History Assn., Jr. League Washington, Nat. Assn. Women Lawyers, Nat. Assn. for Gifted Children, Assn. for Gifted, Kappa Kappa Gamma. Unitarian. Clubs: Nat. Lawyers, Potomac Business and Professional Women's Luncheon. Home: 5126 Palisade Lane NW Washington DC 20016 Farm: Running Brook Farm Browntown VA 22610

DRYPOLCHER, WILLIAM ORTHEL, educator; b. Bklyn., Aug. 22, 1905; s. Louis H. and Florence (Orthel) D.; Chem. Engr., Bklyn. Poly. Inst., 1928; postgrad. N.Y. U.; m. Gladys Thuren, Sept. 3, 1931; children—Barbara (Mrs. Bernard Sciacca), William Orthel. Chief engr. Markwell Mfg. Co., N.Y.C., 1930-59, adminstrv. asst. pres., v.p., 1959-61; Instr. Pinellas Vocational Tech. Inst., Clearwater, Fla., 1963—, chmn. sci. dept., 1968—. Registered profl. engr., Fla., N.Y. Mason (32 deg). Patentee in field. Home: 6849 17th Lane N St Petersburg FL 33702 Office: 6100 154th Av N Clearwater FL 33516

DUANE, FRANK, author; b. Chgo., Aug. 8, 1926; s. Frank and Florence (Kednay) Rosengren; B.A., U. Chgo., 1951; fellow Yale, 1955-56; m. Emily Camille Sweeney, Jan. 13, 1951; 1 dau., Emily Duane Ferry. Vice pres. Rosengrens Bookshop, San Antonio, program cons. Sta. KENS-TV, San Antonio, 1963—; staff writer Omnibus, 1956-57; workshop coordinator Elinor Morgenthau New Dramatists Workshop, N.Y.C., 1954-55; producer On The Spot, KENS-TV, 1961—; chief spl. features HemisFair, 1968; editor El Abrazo, 1963—; exec. producer KLRN-TV, San Antonio-Austin, 1968—; exec. dir. Presentation Assos. Bd. dirs. Music Theatre, Inc.; chmn. adv. bd. Coll.-Community Creative Arts Center, Our Lady of Lake Coll. Served with USAAF, 1944-46. Mem. Dramatists Guild, Writers Guild of Am., New Dramatists Com., Acad. Television Arts and Scis., Nat. Assn. Ednl. Broadcasters, San Antonio Theatre Council, U. Chgo. Alumni Assn. Writer various plays, motion picture, TV shows including: Jimmy and the River, 1958; Prophets of Light, 1966; Pilgrims to the West, 1971. Home: 801 Garraty Rd San Antonio TX 78209

DUBACH, HAROLD WILLIAM, oceanographer, sci. cons.; b. St. Joseph, Mo., Nov. 25, 1920; s. Henry William and Susan (Cornelius) D.; A.B., Baker U., 1942; postgrad. U. Chgo., 1942-43, Johns Hopkins U., 1949-51; m. Roberta Pauline Rose, Sept. 26, 1946; children—Linda Joy, Deborah Ann, Nancy Lee, David Wesley. Research meteorologist Thunderstorm Project, U.S. Weather Bur., Chgo., 1946-48; research oceanographer U.S. Naval Hydrographic Office, Washington, 1948-60; oceanographer, dep. dir. Nat. Oceanographic Data Center, Washington, 1960-69; oceanographer, asst. dir. Center for Marine Devel., Coastal Plains Regional Commn., 1969—. Panel examiner in meteorology U.S. Civil Service Commn., 1957-60, in oceanography, 1954-63; mem. Fed. Adv. Com. Water Pollution, 1966-69; chmn. U.S. delegation Working Group on Marine Data Systems, Internat. Council Exploration of Seas, 1968. Pres. Bellemead (Md.) Citizens Assn., 1955-56; lay del. Balt. Conf. Meth. Ch., 1956-71. Bd. dirs. Youth Services Inc., Landover Hills, Md., 1956-57. Served to capt. USAAF, 1942-46. Recipient Central Intelligence Agy.-U.S. Navy Commendation, 1959; Superior Accomplishment award U.S. Navy, 1962, commendation award for invention, 1967, Distinguished Alumni award Baker U., 1970. Mem. Am. Meteorol. Soc., Am. Soc. Limnology and Oceanography, Am. Soc. Testing and Materials (chmn. com. natural environmental testing, chmn. com. G-1 subcom. IX sect. 2 corrosion in natural waters 1967), Instrument Soc. Am. (chmn. data processing com. 1966—), Geophys. Information Soc., Internat. Sci. Information Services (chmn. finance com. 1968), Marine Tech. Soc. (coastal zone mgmt. com. 1969—), Oceanographical Soc. Japan, Marine Tech. Soc., Australian Marine Scis. Assn. Methodist (trustee 1956-57; ofcl. bd. 1956—, mem. social concerns com. 1967; steward). Author tech.

reports, book reviews and papers profl. jours. Mem. editorial bd. Geoscience Documentation (London, Eng.). Patentee in field. Home: 4609 Dean Dr Wilmington NC 28401 Office: Center for Marine Devel Service Box 3643 U NC -Wilmington Wilmington NC 28401

DUBBIN, MURRAY H., state legislator; b. Miami, Fla., Aug. 1, 1929; B.A., U. Fla., 1949, LL.B., 1951; m. Helene Faye Shonbrun; children— Clifford B., Samuel J., David C., Eric S. Admitted to Fla. bar; spl. asst. atty. gen. State of Fla., 1962; mem. Fla. Ho. of Reps., 1963-—, chmn. legislative com. commerce, 1968-69, chmn. house interim and standing com. constn. revision, 1968-69, chmn. com. rules and calendar, 1970. Group chmn. Dist. 7 Democratic com.; mem. Dem. exec. com., 1954-58. Mem. Dade County, Fla. bar assns., Miami-Dade County C. of C., Tau Epsilon Phi (Alumni Heart Service award 1968), Phi Alpha Delta. Jewish religion. Address: 514 DuPont Plaza Center Miami FL 33131*

DUBERG, HELMUTH PRINCE JOHN, banker; b. Des Moines, Feb. 21, 1907; s. Helmuth Frederick Christian and Kathryn Prince (Needham) D.; A.B., Yale, 1930; postgrad. N.Y. U., 1931, U.S. Naval War Coll., 1953; m. Dorys Hall McConnell, June 24, 1964. With Otis & Co., N.Y.C., 1930; with City Trust Co., Bridgeport, Conn., 1931-—, trust officer, 1935-—. Mem. adv. com. YMCA, Palm Beach, Fla., 1967-—; mem. exec. com., finance com., bd. govs. Nature Conservancy, Washington, 1968-—. Bd. dirs., v.p. Pestalozzi Found. of Am., N.Y.C., N.Y., 1955-—. Comdr., Conn. Naval Militia, 1952-—. Served to capt. USNR. Episcopalian. Home: Gomez Rd Jupiter Island Hobe Sound FL 33455 Office: City Trust Co Bridgeport CT 06602

DUBERG, JOHN EDWARD, research scientist; b. N.Y.C., Nov. 30, 1917; s. Charles Augustus and Mary (Blake) D.; B.S., Manhattan Coll., 1938; M.S., Va. Polytech. Inst., 1940; Ph.D., U. Ill., 1948; m. Mary Louise Andrews, June 11, 1943; children—Mary Jane, John Andrews. Field engr. Caulowell Wingate Builders, N.Y.C., 1938-39; research fellow Va. Polytech. Inst., 1939-40; research asst. U. Ill., 1940-43; aero. research scientist Langley Labs., NACA, Langley Field, Va., 1943-46; research engr. Standard Oil Co. (Ind.), Chgo., 1946-48; chief structures research Langley Lab. NACA, 1951-56; mgr. aero. mechanics Aeronutronics, Glendale, Cal., 1956-57; prof. structures U. Ill., 1957-59; asst. to chief theoretical mechanics div. Langley Research Center, NASA. Langley AFB, Va., 1959-61, tech. asst. to asso. dir., 1951-64, asst. dir., 1954-68, asso. dir., 1968-—; instr. U. Va. Extension, 1944-45; adj. prof. George Washington U.; dir. Joint Inst. Acoustics and Flight Scis., 1971. Dir. Newport News Savs. & Loan Assn. Mem. NACA adv. com. on materials, 1950, 60-63, adv. com. on structures, 1951-56; mem. materials adv. bd. Nat. Acad. Scis., 1950; mem. subcom. profl., sci. and tech. manpower Nat. Manpower Adv. Com., Dept. Labor, 1971; participant Fed. Exec. Inst., Charlottesville, Va., 1971. Trustee Peninsula United Fund, 1963-—, campaign chmn. 1965-66; exec. bd. Peninsula council Boy Scouts Am., 1968-—; sci. adv. bd. Va. Asso. Research Center; dir. Peninsula Jr. Nature Mus. Fellow Am. Inst. Aeros. and Astronautics (asso.), Research Soc. Am. (pres. Hampton chpt. 1963), Soc. Indsl. and Applied Math., Engrs. Club Va. Peninsula (pres. 1955), Gamma Alpha, Phi Kappa Phi, Tau Beta Pi, Sigma Xi. Episcopalian (mem. vestry). Clubs: James River Country; Warwick Rotary (pres. 1967-68), Huntington (founding mem., dir., pres. 1972-73) (Newport News, Va.), Contbr. numerous articles to profl. jours. Home: 4 Museum Dr Newport News VA 23601 Office: Langley Station Hampton VA 23365

DUBILIER, LOUIS DAVID, pathologist, educator; b. Jersey City, N.J., Dec. 28, 1934; s. Herbert and Ida (Perkel) D.; A.B. with honors, Johns Hopkins, 1956; M.D., U. Rochester, 1960; m. Vera Joyce Landsberger, Aug. 24, 1958; children—Karen Lee, Gerald Allen, Ellen Jean, Sandra Gail. Intern, U. Rochester Sch. Medicine, 1960-61, resident pathology, 1963-65, instr. pathology, 1963-65; asst. prof. U. Ky. Coll. Medicine, Lexington, 1965-—. Served to capt. U.S. Army Res., 1962-63. Mem. A.M.A., Am. Soc. Clin. Pathologists, Coll. Am. Pathologists, Ky., Fayette County med. socs., Phi Beta Kappa, Omicron Delta Kappa, Delta Phi Alpha. Home: 665 Bayswater Way Lexington KY 40503 Office: Pathology and Cytology Lab Lexington KY 40506

DUBOSE, DOROTHY GAMBLE (MRS. WILLIAM SHELTON DUBOSE), civic worker; b. St. Louis, Dec. 23, 1925; d. Andrew Suter and Dorothy (Collier) Gamble; student Swarthmore Coll., 1942, 43, Tex. Christian U., 1964, 67; m. William Shelton DuBose, Jan. 14, 1944; children—Dorothy, Frances, Julie, William Shelton, Suter Gamble. Vice pres. W. S. DuBose, Inc., Ft. Worth, 1956-—. Bd. mem. Family Service Assn. Tarrant County (Tex.), 1964-66; v.p. Fort Worth (Tex.) Art Center Guild, 1963; mem. Charitable Solicitations Commn., Fort Worth, 1965-—; asso. mem. Mayor's Com. on Status of Women, 1971. Bd. mem. N. Tex. chpt. Arthritis Found., Tarrant County YWCA. Mem. Soc. for Study Democratic Instns., Am. Civil Liberties Union (bd. mem., pres. Greater Ft. Worth chpt. 1971), Nat. Orgn. Women (pres. Ft. Worth chpt. 1970-72, legislative coordinator Tex.). Democrat. Episcopalian. Home: 2928 Owenwood St Fort Worth TX 76109 Office: 3022 Sandage St Fort Worth TX 76109

DUBOSE, JAMES DAULTON, dentist; b. Turbeville, S.C., July 14, 1938; s. Robert Alvin and Olive (Dennis) DuB.; B.S., U. S.C., 1961; D.M.D., U. Louisville, 1965. Practice dentistry, Bishopville, S.C., 1965-70, Aiken, S.C., 1970-—. Chmn. Heart Fund, Lee County, S.C., 1966. Mem. Am. Dental Assn., Am. Soc. Dentistry for Children, Augusta Dental Soc., Delta Sigma Delta. Mason. Clubs: Century (Columbia, S.C.); Sertoma (Aiken, S.C.). Home: 321 Laurens St Apt 4B Aiken SC 29801 Office: 117 Trafalgar Lane Aiken SC 29801

DUBOSE, ROBERT N(EWSOM), clergyman; b. Hartsville, S.C., Sept. 4, 1914; s. John Boyd and Belle (Newsome) DuB.; A.B., Wofford Coll., 1936; B.D., M.Div., Duke, 1942; D.D., Salem Coll., 1946; m. Marie King, Sept. 10, 1937; children—Mary Virginia (Mrs. Jean Derrick), Barbara Anne (Mrs. J.M. Terry). Ordained to ministry Meth. Ch., 1939; pastor, Jamestown, 1937-39, Lake View, 1939-40; asso. pastor Asbury Ch., Durham, N.C., 1940-41; dir. religious activities Duke U., 1945-48; exec. sec. Commn. Christian Higher Edn., Assn. Am. Colls., 1948-51; pastor First Meth. Ch., Whitmire, S.C. 1951-54, Shandon Meth. Ch., Columbia, S.C., 1954-60; dist. supt. Spartanburg Dist., S.C. Conf., 1960-65; pastor Buncombe St. Meth. Ch., Greenville, S.C., 1965-71, 1st United Meth. Ch., Myrtle Beach, S.C., 1971-—. Mem. bd. edn. S.C. Conf., Meth. Ch. Past pres., dir. Columbia chpt. A.R.C., S.C. fund chmn., 1963-65; pres. S.C. Crippled Children's Soc.; chmn. Caroling Program, 1969-70; mem. S.C. Tricentennial Com., 1969-70, Mayor's Adv. Com., 1969-70; adv. bd. Mental Health Clinic; dir. Jr. League Speech and Hearing Clinic. Vice chmn. bd. trustees Wofford Coll; chmn. bd. trustees Spartanburg Jr. Coll., 1967-68, exec. com., 1969-72. Vice Chmn. bd. dirs. U.S.C. Wesley Found.; trustee Meth. Home Aging; chmn. S.C. Meth. Credit Union. Served as chaplain AUS, 1943-45; PTO. Mem. S.C. Conf. Meth. Ch. (chmn. conf. com. Christian vocation, chmn. credit com., chmn. interboard com.), Lambda Chi Alpha. Rotarian, Kiwanian (conf. bd. edn.). Author articles on Christian edn. Editor: College and Church (ofcl. publ. Assn. Am. Colls.), 1948-51. Home: 5408 Hampton Circle Myrtle Beach SC 29577 Office: 1st United Methodist Church Myrtle Beach SC 29577

DUCKER, JOHN LACKNER, state senator; b. Ft. Thomas, Ky., Sept. 3, 1922; s. Stuart Reilly and Margaret (Lackner) D.; student U. Ia., 1943, U. Neb., 1944; B.A., Yale, 1944, LL.B., 1950. Admitted to Fla. bar; mem. Fla. Senate, 1968-—. Mem. Fla. Ho. of Reps., 1960-68; mem. Orange County (Fla.) Republican exec. com. Served with USAAF, 1943-46. Mem. Fla., Orange County bar assns., Am. Legion, Nat. Rifle Assn., Orlando Area C. of C., Fla. Edn. Assn., Orange County Sportsmen's Assn. Episcopalian. Elk, Optimist. Club: University (Winter Park, Fla.). Home: 2810 W Fairbanks Av Winter Park FL 32789 Office: 205 E Jackson St Orlando FL 32801*

DUCKETT, CHARLES HOWARD, physician; b. Asheville, N.C., Nov. 11, 1932; s. Virgil Howard and Maude (Johnson) D.; B.S., Wake Forest Coll., 1954; M.D., Bowman Gray Sch. Medicine, 1957; m. Evelyn Carolyn Garrison, Apr. 1, 1956; children—Deborah Lynn, Ralph Howard, Charles Garrison, Sarah Carolyn. Intern U. Va. Hosp., Charlottesville, 1957-58; practice medicine, specializing in family practice, Canton, N.C., 1958-—; asso. Midway Clinic, 1959-—; mem. staff Haywood County Hosp., chief staff, 1967-—. Pres. Midway Inc., Canton, 1968-—; dir. Canton Savs. and Loan Assn. Alderman, City of Canton, 1967-—; mem. exec. com. Haywood County Council of Govt., 1971-—. Served to capt. USAF, 1961-63. Diplomate Am. Bd. Family Practice. Mem. A.M.A., Am., N.C. acads. family practice, N.C., Haywood County (pres. 1965-—) med. socs., Omicron Delta Kappa. Democrat. Home: 11 Forest Hill Dr Canton NC 28716 Office: Midway Clinic Canton NC 28716

DUCKETT, JAMES WILLIAM, coll. adminstr.; b. Greenwood, S.C., July 8, 1911; s. James William and Eva (Hattaway) D.; B.S., The Citadel, 1932; M.S. in Chemistry, U. Ga., 1934; Ph.D., U. N.C., 1941; m. Gertrude Elizabeth Hass, Dec. 26, 1936; children—Elizabeth Eva (Mrs. Thomas J. Krilowicz), Gertrude Hass (Mrs. John E. Reeves), James William. Mem. faculty The Citadel, 1934-—, prof. organic chemistry, 1946-54, registrar, 1954-62, adminstrv. dean, 1962-63, dean coll., 1963-68, v.p., 1968-70, pres., 1970-—. Mem. commn. colls. So. Assn. Colls. and Schs.; mem. chem. biol. and radiol. adv. council Dept. Def. Served with Chem. Corps, AUS, 1941-46. Decorated Legion of Merit, Commendation ribbon. Mem. Am. Chem. Soc., S.C. Acad. Sci., Greater Charleston C. of C., Assn. Mil. Colls. and Schs. U.S. (exec. com.), Sigma Xi, Pi Mu Epsilon. Lion. Spl. research syntheses N1-isocyclic sulfanilamides, resene in pinus carrebae. Home: Qtrs 1 The Citadel Charleston SC 29409

DUCKWORTH, KENTON M., govt. ofcl.; b. Mt. Olive, Miss., July 2, 1917; s. Cooper E. and Heneritta (Barnes) D.; grad. Soule Bus. Coll., 1936; B.C.S., Benjamin Franklin U., 1940, M.C.S., 1942; m. Ruth L. Parrish (dec. Mar. 1958); children—Kenton M., Thomas C.; m. 2d, Maxine M. Manley, 1960; stepchildren—Leslie (Mrs. Richelsen), Susan Jane Manley. Cost auditor Gen. Accounting Office, 1936-46; adminstrv. analyst USPHS, 1946; auditor, accountant CAA, 1946-51, NPA, 1951-53; with Agy. Internat. Devel., Dept. State, 1953-—, exec. officer, 1954-57, sr. mgmt. analyst, 1958-59, spl. asst. to sec. state for adminstrn., 1958, asst. chief personnel operations div., 1959-61, chief Overseas Employment br. Office Personnel, 1962-64, chief performance evaluation br., 1964-65, spl. asst. for mgmt. and adminstrn. Office Material Resource, 1965-67; dir. mgmt. staff Office War on Hunger, 1967-69, chief spl. operations br. Office of Personnel and Manpower, 1969-—. Served with inf. AUS, 1944-46. Mason. Home: 3132 Holmes Run Rd Falls Church VA 22042 Office: 1601 N Kent St Arlington VA 22209

DUCKWORTH, WALTER DONALD, curator; b. Athens, Tenn., July 19, 1935; s. James Clifford and Vesta Katherine (Walker) D.; student U. Tenn., 1953-55; B.Sc., Middle Tenn. State U., 1957; M.Sc., N.C. State U., 1960, Ph.D., 1962; m. Sandra Lee Smith, June 17, 1955; children— Clifford Monroe, Laura Lee, Brent Cullen. Asso. curator dept. entomology Smithsonian Instn., Washington, 1962-—. Cons. entomol. program PP PMayaguez, 1970-—. NSF, grantee, 1963-65, Am. Philos. Soc. grantee, 1964, Entomol. Soc. Am. grantee, 1964, Smithsonian Research Found. grantee, 1969. Mem. Entomol. Soc. Am., Entomol. Soc. Washington (sec. 1966-68), Assn. Tropical Biology (exec. dir. 1971-—), Soc. Systematic Zoology, Gamma Sigma Delta, Sigma Xi. Presbyn. Mason. Contbr. profl. jours. Home: 3712 Maryland St Alexandria VA 22309 Office: Dept Entomology Smithsonian Instn Washington DC 20560

DUCKWORTH, WILLIAM HENRY, judge; b. Blairsville, Ga., Oct. 21, 1894; s. John Frank and Laura Jane (Noblet) D.; ed. Young Harris (Ga.) Coll., 1915-17; studied law in law office; m. Willibel Pilcher, July 2, 1922; children—Mary (Mrs. L. L. Gellerstedt), Dorothy (Mrs. W. N. Todd), William Henry. Admitted to Ga. bar, 1919, gen. practice law, Cairo, 1919-37; asst. atty. gen. State of Georgia, 1937-38; asso. justice Supreme Court of Ga., 1938-48, chief justice, 1948-—. Served in U.S. Naval Res., 1918. Mem. Am., Ga. bar assns., Am. Legion. Baptist. Mason, Elk. Clubs: Capital City, Atlanta Athletic (Atlanta). Home: 2484 Tanglewood Rd Decatur GA 30033 Office: State Judicial Bldg Atlanta GA

DUCKWORTH, WILLIAM THOMAS, JR., real estate appraiser; b. Asheville, N.C., Mar. 7, 1920; s. William Thomas and Margaret (Ball) D.; A.A., Mars Hill Coll., 1940; B.S., Wake Forest Coll., 1942; postgrad. Duke Div. Sch., summer 1953; m. Mary Watson Corpening, June 16, 1942; 1 dau., Lynne Revell. Partner, W. T. Duckworth Co., Asheville, 1946-60, owner, 1960-—; dir. Asheville Fed. Savs. & Loan Assn. Mem. bd. adjustment Asheville Zoning and Planning Commn., 1950-—; mem. Asheville Housing Authority, 1952-55; mem. chmn. bd. Buncombe County Welfare Bd., 1952-58. Sec., Young Democrats Club, 1951-52. Trustee Revell Meml. Mission, 1960-—. Mars Hill Coll., 1955-58, Realtors Inst., 1958-61; past dir. YMCA; mem. Greater Asheville Council. Served with AUS, 1942-46. Mem. Am. Inst. Real Estate Appraisers, Soc. Real Estate Appraisers (sr.), Central Asheville Assn. (pres. 1965), Asheville Jr. C. of C. (life, pres. 1954), C. of C. (past dir.), Asheville Mchts. Assn. (dir. 1969-71), Kappa Sigma. Baptist. Clubs: Rhododendron Royal Brigade Guards (chief of staff 1972), Asheville Country (gov.), Asheville City, Rotary. Home: 32 Maywood Rd Asheville NC 28804 Office: Northwestern Bank Bldg Asheville NC 28801

DUDEK, RICHARD A., educator. Prof., chmn. dept. indsl. engring. Tex. Tech. U., Lubbock, also founder Center Biotech. and Human Performance. Fellow Am. Inst. Indsl. Engrs. Address: Tex Tech U Lubbock TX 79409

DUDGEON, EDWARD KINGSTON, rubber co. exec.; b. Holyoke, Mass., Feb. 8, 1929; s. Harold Anthony and Ella Valentine (Stevens) D.; B.S., Lowell Tech. Inst., 1955; m. Carol Kay Weidenthal, Mar. 17, 1953; children—Christine, Constance. Jr. buyer B.F. Goodrich Co., Akron, O., 1955-57, buyer, 1957-62, mgr. purchasing, Miami, Okla., 1967-—. Pres., Norse Campus Ministries, Inc., 1971. First v.p. Ozark area council Girl Scouts U.S.A., 1969-—. Served with AUS, 1952-54. Episcopalian (jr. warden 1971, vestryman, licensed lay reader 1965-—). Rotarian. Home: 2217 Johnson Dr Miami OK 74354 Office: PO Drawer 31 Miami OK 74354

DUDGEON, FARNHAM F(RANCIS), editor; b. St. James, Minn., Feb. 16, 1912; s. Hugh G. and Mary Josephine (Nugent) D.; student, St. John's U., 1928-29; B.S., U. N.D., 1934; m. Gould Crook, July 6, 1937; children— Michael, Patrick, Timothy, Colleen. Labor relations, investigative work N.D. state, fed. agys., 1934-39; mem. editorial staff, Western Newspaper Union, 1939-42, editor-in-chief, 1942-52; editor, pub. Feature Publns., Inc., 1952-—. City commr., Mayor pro tem, Frankfort, 1965-68. Mem. Sigma Delta Chi, Theta Chi, Phi Delta Kappa. Roman Catholic. K.C. Contbr. weekly news analysis to 2,500 community newspapers, 1940-43. Home: 105 Dakota Rd Frankfort KY 40601 Office: 100 E Main St Frankfort KY 40601

DUDLEY, GUILFORD, JR., ins. exec.; b. Nashville, June 23, 1907; s. Guilford and Anne (Dallas) D.; student Loomis Inst., Peabody Coll.; A.B., Vanderbilt U., 1929; children—Guilford, Robert Lusk; m. Jane Anderson; 1 dau., Trevania Dallas. Chmn. bd. dirs. Life & Casualty Ins. Co. Tenn., WLAC Radio, WLAC-TV, Casualty Ins. Co. Tenn.; dir. Am. Gen. Life Ins. Investors, 3d Nat. Bank, Nashville; U.S. ambassador to Denmark, 1969-72. Bd. dirs. YMCA, United Givers Fund, Jr. Achievement, So. States Indsl. Council, Ensworth Sch., Tenn. Bot. Gardens and Fine Arts Center, Vanderbilt U., Cumberland Coll. Mem. Nashville C. of C. (dir), Phi Delta Theta. Episcopalian. Clubs: Vanderbilt; Cumberland; River, Turf and Field (N.Y.C.); Hillsboro Hounds Hunt, Belle Meade Country, Seminole Golf, Bath and Tennis, Everglades, Lost Tree (Palm Beach, Fla.); Palm Bay (Miami); Turf (London); Royal Danish Yacht, American (Copenhagen); Washington Republican. Home: Harding Pl at Hillsboro Rd Nashville TN 37215 also 1820 S Ocean Blvd Palm Beach FL 33480 Office: Life and Casualty Tower Nashville TN 37219

DUDLEY, HENRY ANDERSON, lawyer; b. Alta Vista, Va., Apr. 28, 1913; s. Henry Anderson and Mae (Cabell) D.; student Roanoke Coll., 1932-33 A.B., U. Va., 1934, LL.B., 1937; m. Lavinia Ward Payne, Oct. 5, 1942; children—Henry Anderson, Spottswood P. Admitted to Va. bar, 1937, Washington bar, 1948; practiced in Roanoke, Va., 1937-41; clk. Va. Senate, 1941; counsel Fgn. Liguidation Commn., 1945-46, dep. fgn. liquidation for P.I. and China, 1946; sr. partner McNutt, Dudley & Easterwood, attys., Washington, 1947-—, Vice chmn., mem. bd. 1st & Mchts. Nat. Bank Va.; dir. Stone Indsl. Corp. Pres., Def. Orientation Conf. Assn., 1958-59; v.p. Washington Nat. Ballet Found., 1961-64; trustee Marjorie Merriweather Post Found. D.C., Nat. Symphony Orch. Mem. Democratic Nat. Finance Com., 1964-—. Trustee Oblate Coll., Cath. U., Washington, Roanoke (Va.) Coll. Served from ensign to lt. comdr. USNR, 1941-45. So. Soc. N.Y.C., La. Confrerie des chevaliers du Tastevin (sous commanderie de Washington). Clubs: Farmington Country (Charlotteville, Va.) Rolling Rock (Pitts.) International, George Town, Army-Navy, Chevy Chase. Home: 3510 Overlook Lane NW Washington DC 20016 Office: Barr Bldg 910 17th St NW Washington DC 20006

DUDLEY, VIRGINIA (EVELYN), artist; b. Spring City, Tenn.; d. Charles Newton and Laura (Thompson) Dudley; student U. Chattanooga, 1937-40, Art Students League, N.Y.C., 1940-45, New Sch. Social Research, 1942-43, 45, Atelier 17, N.Y.C., 1945-46, N.M. Coll., 1947-48, Coll. William and Mary, 1958-59, U. Md., Seoul, Korea, 1959-60; M.F.A. Claremont (Cal.) Grad. Sch., 1950; m. Joseph Spenser Moran, Apr. 20, 1946. Works exhibited Met. Mus. Art, San Francisco Mus. Art, Library of Congress, also London, Eng., San Francisco, Buffalo, Los Angeles, Phila., Vancouver, Washington, other; one man shows U. Chattanooga, 1943, Hunter Gallery Art, Chattanooga, 1952; Ga. Mus., Athens, 1954, Newport News, Va., 1959, Rome, Ga., 1964, 69, 71, Columbus (Ga.) Mus. Art, 1970, Reinhart Coll., Walleska, Tenn., 1971, So. Missionary Coll., Collegedale, Tenn., 1972; represented permanet collections, including Met. Mus. Art, N.Y.C., Library of Congress, Scripps Coll., Ga. Mus. Art, U. Miami, Art Students League, Everson Mus. Art, Pa. State Mus., Albright Mus. Art, U. Tenn., Columbus (Ga.) Mus. Asso. prof. art Shorter Coll., Rome, 1963-71; pres. Next Door Gallery; dir. Am. Craftsmen, Rising Fawn, Ga., Virginia Dudley Studios lectr. at large on Southeast Asia and the Orient. Regional bd. dirs. Am. Crafts Council, also Ga. rep. Recipient Rosenwald fellowship painting and lithography, 1943, 1st award So. Highland Handicraft Guild, 1953, Sarasota Found. Craft and Sculpture Show, 1953, Internat. Crafts Show, Canadian Pacific Expn., Vancouver, 1945, Nat. Ceramic Exhbns., Everson Mus. Fine Arts, 1956, others. Art dir. Coronado Playmakers, N.M. State Coll., 1947-48 art editor Rio Grande Writer, lit., mag., 1947-48; staff arts and crafts dir. Hdqrs. Eighth Air Force, Westover, Mass., Mem. Internat. Art Guild, Ga. Designer Craftsmen, So. Highland Handicraft Guild, Soc. Am. Graphic Arts, Chattanooga Art Assn., Royal Asiatic Soc., So. Assn. Sculptors, World Crafts Council, Internat. Inst. Arts and Letters. Home and studio: Lookout Mountain Route 2 Rising Fawn GA 30738

DUDMAN, GEORGE THOMAS, SR., food processing co. exec.; b. Westfield, N.J., Nov. 8, 1913; s. George G. and Ethel A. (Dewey) D.; grad. Phillips Exeter Acad., 1931; B.S., Harvard, 1935. With Allen V. Smith, Inc., food processors, 1936-—, pres., Skaneateles, N.Y., 1947-67, Fort Lauderdale, Fla., 1967-—, also dir. Trustee Village of Skaneateles, 1956. Served from ensign to lt. comdr. USNR, 1941-45; comdr. Res., ret. Presbyn. (ch. trustee 1955-56). Club: Coral Ridge Yacht (Fort Lauderdale) (sec. 1971). Home: 2820 NE 7th St Pompano Beach FL 33062 Office: 2425 E Commercial Blvd Fort Lauderdale FL 33308

DUDMAN, RICHARD BEEBE, newspaperman; b. Centerville, Ia., May 3, 1918; s. Virgil Ernest and Wilma (Beebe) D.; A.B., Stanford, 1940; Nieman fellow, Harvard, 1953-54; m. Helen Sloane, Mar. 14, 1948; children—Janet Sloane, Martha Tod. Reporter, photographer Oroville (Cal.) Mercury-Register, summer 1937; reporter Denver Post, 1946-49; reporter St. Louis Post-Dispatch, 1949-—, mem. Washington bur., 1954-—, chief bur., 1969-—. Served with USNR, 1942-45. Clubs: Nat. Press, Gridiron (Washington). Author: Men of the Far Right, 1962; 40 Days with the Enemy, 1971; also articles. Home: 3409 Newark St NW Washington DC 20016 Office: 1701 Pennsylvania Av NW Washington DC 20006

DUDNEY, DORIS ANN, lawyer; b. Sebring, Fla., June 9, 1934; d. Fred Stanton and Opal (Laine) Dudney; B.A., Vanderbilt U., 1954, LL.B., 1956. Admitted to Fla. bar, 1956, since practiced in Tampa; asso. firm Fowler, White, Gillen, Humkey & Trenam, 1956-61; mem. firm Fowler, White, Gillen, Humkey, Kinney & Boggs, P.A., and predecessor firms, 1961-—. Vice chmn., sec. Law Inc. Hillsborough County (Fla.), 1967-70, pres., chmn. bd., 1970-—, also dir. Bd. dirs., vice chmn. YWCA Tampa, 1964-69, 71-—; bd. dirs. Big Sisters, Tampa, 1966-69; bd. dirs. Girls Club, Tampa 1966-—, pres., 1971-72, nat. bd. dirs., 1972-—; bd. dirs. Hillsborough Assn. Retarded Children, Mental Health Assn. Hillsborough County. Named Outstanding Young Woman Am., Vanderbilt U. and Tampa chpt. Am. Assn. U. Women, 1966. Mem. Am., Tampa, Hillsborough County bar assns., Fla. Bar (chmn. standing com. on econs. of law practice 1970-72), Am. Assn. U. Women, Am. Judicature Soc., Nat. Legal Aid and Defenders Assn., Greater Tampa C. of C., Order of Coif, Kappa Delta. Republican. Clubs: Zonta (local pres., dist. lt. gov. 1972-—), Palma Ceia Golf and Country (Tampa); Boston Terrier (Miami); Tampa Bay Kennel; Tampa Woman's (courtesy mem.). Home: 2407 Ardson Pl Tampa FL 33601 Office: Fowler White Gillen Humkey Kinney & Boggs PA 220 Madison St Tampa FL 33601

DUERKSEN, LELAND EMERSON, hotel co. exec.; b. Reedley, Cal., Jan. 10, 1927; s. Daniel Emerson and Lelah (Shelton) D.; student Mont. State U., 1944-48, Jefferson City Jr. Coll., 1947-48; m. Lois Lucile Calavan, Feb. 2, 1952; children—Debrah Lee, Daniel Charles. With Holiday Inns, Inc., Memphis, 1963—, dir. indsl. relations, 1967—, v.p., 1969—. Served with USAF, 1950-56. Elk. Home: 5295 Dargen Av Memphis TN 38118 Office: 3742 Lamar Av Memphis TN 38118

DUFEK, GEORGE J(OHN), museum dir.; b. Rockford, Ill., Feb. 10, 1903; s. Frank and Mary (Wachuta) D.; B.S., U.S. Naval Acad., 1925; grad. Flight Tng. Sch., 1933; student Indsl. Coll. Armed Forces, 1947; LL.D., Carleton Coll.; L.H.D., LeMoyne Coll., D.Sc., Rockford (Ill.) Coll.; m. Murial Thomson Bones, 1947; children—Mary Ellen (Mrs. Bellit), Barbara Bones (Mrs. Phillips), George Cruzen, David Frank. Commd. ensign U.S. Navy, 1925, advanced through grades to rear adm., 1955; assigned U.S.S. Maryland, 1925-27; asst. navigator, asst. communications officer U.S.S. Canopus, 1927-28; aviator U.S.S. Concord, 1933-36; navigator U.S.S. Saratoga, 1936-38; exec. officer U.S.S. Lexington, 1938-39; navigator U.S.S. Bear, flagship Antarctic Devel. Project, 1939; assisted constrn. devel. new naval air sta., Jacksonville, Fla., 1940; spl. U.S. Naval observer for aviation, London, 1942; sr. naval aviator, invasion North Africa, 1942; assisted devel. invasion plans for So. France; comdr. U.S.S. Bogue, 1944; comdg. officer naval air base, Ominato, Japan, also air transport service terminal nr. Tokyo, 1945; staff Naval Regulations Bd., Washington, 1946; chief staff officer on expdn. to establish weather bases northern Polar Regions, 1946; comdr. eastern group Task Force 68, to develop unknown coast line between Palmer Peninsula and Little America; comdr. Task Force 80 to supply existing weather stations and establish new stations nr. North Pole, 1947; mem. logistics planning sect. Joint Chiefs Staff, Washington, 1949-50; comdr. U.S.S. Antietam, 1951; head spl. Antarctic Planning Group, Washington, 1954; comdr. logistic and operational task force Naval Operation Deepfreeze, 1955-59; 1st Am. at geographic South Pole, 1956; retired, 1959; dir. Mariners Museum, Newport News, Va., 1960—. Decorated Legion of Merit with 2 gold stars, Antarctic Expdn. medal; D.S.M. (U.S.); comdr. Order of Crown (Belgium); hon. companion Order of Bath (Eng.); Croix de Guerre, Legion of Honor (France); Andre Medal, Swedish Geog. Soc.; Hubbard medal Nat. Geog. Soc. U.S., 1959. Mem. Am. Soc. Naval Engrs., Nat. Geog. Soc., Am. Geophys. Union. Clubs: James River Country; Army-Navy, Explorers. Author: Operation Deep Freeze; Through the Frozen Frontiers, 1959. Home: 101 Museum Pkwy Newport News VA 23606 Office: Mariners Mus Newport News VA

DUFF, JAMES CLYDE, civil engr.; b. Bonham, Tex., June 30, 1927; s. Clyde and Mae (Smith) D.; student Tex. A. and M. Coll., 1944-45; studied civil engring. Internat. Corr. Schs.; m. Joan Brumback, Feb. 9, 1946; children—Anna Jo (Mrs. Rodney W. Adamek), Julia Carol. Asso. resident engr. Tex. Hwy. Dept., Bonham, 1946-57; dir. pub. works, city engr. City of Greenville (Tex.), 1957-63; cons. engr., Greenville, 1963-64; partner Garland Engring. Co. (now Duff Cons. Engrs., Inc.), Waco, Tex., 1964-65, owner, 1965—. Registered profl. engr., Tex., Okla., Ark., Ida., N.M., La., N.C. Mem. Am. Pub. Works Assn., Tex. Soc. Profl. Engrs. (past pres. N.E. Tex. chpt. 1960-61). Home: 4816 Scottwood Dr Waco TX 76708 Office: 1401 Jefferson St Waco TX 76702

DUFFEL, JOHN ANTHONY, librarian; b. New Orleans, Dec. 23, 1941; s. John Edward and Alice Mae (Lacoste) D.; B.A., La. State U., 1966, M.S., 1968; m. Sarah Elizabeth Covington, Aug. 3, 1968. Librarian, New Orleans Pub. Library, 1968—. Recipient legislative scholarship La. Ho. of Reps., 1961; scholarship New Orleans Pub. Library, 1966. Mem. La. Library Assn., Tau Kappa Epsilon, Alpha Beta Alpha. Home: 1405 Aris Av Metairie LA 70005 Office: 219 Loyola Av New Orleans LA 70140

DUFFIELD, LATHEL F(LAY), archeologist, educator; b. Collinsville, Okla., Dec. 1, 1931; B.A., U. Okla., 1953, M.A., 1957; Ph.D. (NSF fellow), U. Wis., 1970; m. 4 children. Dir. Ark. Mus. Natural History and Antiquities, Little Rock, 1953-55; asst. curator Thomas Gilcrease Inst. Am. History and Art, 1955-57; research scientist Tex. Archeol. Salvage Project, U. Tex., 1958-63; exec. dir. Tex. Archeol. Research Lab., 1963-64; asst. prof. anthropology Eastern Ky. U., 1964-69; asso. prof. U. Ky., Lexington, 1969—, chmn. anthropology dept., 1972—; dir. Ky. Mus. Anthropology, 1969—; Ky. Archeologist, 1969—. Mem. Ky. Heritage Commn., 1970—. Fellow Soc. Am. Archeology, Am. Anthrop. Assn. Contbr. articles in field to profl. jours. Research in Tex. prehistory, paleoecology of man, skeletal studies of prehistoric bison. Office: Dept Anthropology U Ky Lexington KY 40506

DUFFIELD, PAULINE, librarian; b. Sutton, W.Va., June. 30, 1910; d. John Byrn and Mary (Marlow) Duffield; B.S., George Peabody Coll., Nashville, 1936, B.S. in L.S., 1940; student Chgo. Normal Sch. Phys. Edn., Chgo., 1929. Tchr., librarian Richwood (W. Va.) High Sch., 1930-41; librarian Parker Dist. High Sch., Greenville, S.C., 1941-43; asst. librarian Vanderbilt U. Sch. Med., Nashville, 1944-45; librarian Med. and Chirurg. Faculty of Md., Balt., 1945-52, Tex. Med. Assn., 1952—. Mem. Med. Library Assn. (treas. 1954-58, chmn. recruitment com. 1961-63, chmn. nominating com. 1968-69), Tex. Med. Assn. Assts. (hon.), Spl. Library Assn., Tex. Council Health Sci. Libraries (sec.-treas. 1968-72), Austin Library Club (v.p. 1961-62). Club: Zonta. Home: 1219 Castle Hill Austin TX 78703 Office: 1801 N Lamar Blvd Austin TX 78701

DUFFY, BERNARD READ, chem. engr.; b. Oklahoma City, Dec. 7, 1926; s. William and Bessie (Bayless) D.; B.S., Oklahoma City U., 1949; m. Mary Louise Bezner, May 31, 1963; children—William J., Julia Dyan. Chemist, pres., div. engr. N. Tex. div. Oil Well Mud Co., Inc., Gainesville, Tex., 1952—; Served with USNR, 1944-47. Mem. Am. Petroleum Inst., Am. Chem. Soc., Am. Legion, Petroleum Club, Beta Beta Beta, Phi Chi Phi. Democrat. Roman Catholic. Home: 1925 Tulane St Gainesville TX 76240 Office: 1618 N Dixon St Gainesville TX 76240

DUFFY, JAMES JOSEPH, JR., lawyer; b. Mobile, Ala., Aug. 4, 1931; s. James Joseph and Regina (Tobler) D.; grad. Marion Mil. Inst., 1951; A.B., U. Ala., 1953, LL.B., 1957; m. Hunter Williams, Jan. 3, 1953; children—James Joseph III, Lucy Hunter. Admitted to Ala. bar, 1957; practiced in Mobile, 1957—; mem. Inge, Twitty, Duffy & Prince, Mobile, 1957—. Trustee St. Paul's Episcopal Day Sch. Served to 1st lt. AUS, 1953-55. Mem. Am., Ala., Mobile bar assns., Maritime Law Assn. U.S., Am. Judicature Soc., Internat. Assn. of Ins. Counsel, Internat. Assn. Barristers, Delta Kappa Epsilon, Phi Delta Phi. Episcopalian. Clubs: Mobile Touchdown (dir.), Athelstan Mobile Country; Lakewood Country (Point Clear, Ala.); Downtown (Birmingham). Home: 109 Pinebrook Dr Spring Hill Mobile AL 36608 Office: Mchts Nat Bank Bldg Mobile AL 36601

DUFFY, JOHN JOSEPH, ednl. adminstr., educator; b. Charleston, S.C., Apr. 25, 1931; s. John Joseph and Mary (McMahon) D.; student Fordham U., 1948-49; B.S., Coll. Charleston, 1952; M.A., U. S.C., 1955; Ph.D., U. S.C., 1963; m. Marcia Fletcher Tinkham, Aug. 15, 1959; children—Katharine, John Joseph, Eleanor. Dir. U. S.C. at Beaufort, 1959-66, acad. coordinator Coll. Gen. Studies at Columbia, 1966-67, asst. provost for regional campuses, 1967-68, asso. provost for regional campuses, 1968—, asso. prof. history 1964—. Dist. chmn. Midlands council Boy Scouts Am., 1969—. Served with AUS, 1954-56. Named Young Man of Year Beaufort County Jaycees, 1964; recipient Garnet and Black award for distinguished service U. S.C., 1969. Mem. So., U. S.C. hist. assns., Phi Beta Kappa. Democrat. Roman Catholic. Elk. Home: 315 Harden St Columbia SC 29204

DUFOUR, CHARLES, editor. Music editor States-Item, New Orleans. Home: 3800 Howard Av New Orleans LA 70140*

DUGAN, CHARLES CLARK, physician; b. Penn Yan, N.Y., Jan. 24, 1921; s. Charles Emmanuel and Wilhelmina May (Clark) D.; A.A., Wentworth Mil. Jr. Coll., 1940; A.B., Cornell U., 1942; M.D., Jefferson Med. Coll., 1946; m. Ruth Louise Fugh, Dec. 2, 1966; children— Charles Clark II, Douglas Craig, Timothy Gene, C. Dain Walters, C. Jay Walters. Jr. resident in psychiatry Pa. Psychiat. Hosp., Phila., 1946; rotating intern Harrisburg (Pa.) Gen Hosp., 1946-47; resident in dermotology and syphilogy U. Colo. Med. Center, Denver, 1956-57; resident in dermotology and syphilogy Henry Ford Hosp., Detroit, 1957-59; resident in allergy U. Ohio, Columbus, 1961, Montefiore VA Hosp., Pitts., 1962; practice medicine, specializing in dermotology and allergy, West Palm Beach, Fla., 1959—; staff Good Samaritan, Bethesda Meml., Lake Worth, Palm Beach Gardens hosps. Served to lt. col. M.C., USAAF, USAF, 1943-56. Recipient Meritorious Service award Am. Cancer Soc., 1960. Diplomate Am. Bd. Dermotology, Am. Bd. Preventive Medicine. Fellow Am. Coll. Preventive Medicine, Am. Acad. Dermatology, Am. Assn. Dermatology, Am. Coll. Allergy and Immunology; mem, A.M.A., Aerospace (asso.), So., Pan Am., Fla. med. assns., Am. Acad. Allergists, Noah Worcester Dermatol. Assn., Soc. Investigative Dermatologists, Am. Soc. Dermatol. Surgeons, Fla. Dermatol. Soc., S.E., S. Central dermatol. assns., Internat. Corr. Soc. Allergists, Internat. Congress Dermatology, Internat. Congress Allergology, Internat. Soc. Tropical Medicine and Dermotology, N.Y. Acad. Scis. Republican. Mason. Club: Catillian. Research in short-time accelerations and cerebral concussion. Home: 2600 Broadway West Palm Beach FL 33407 Office: MD Center 2600 Broadway West Palm Beach FL

DUGGAN, EDMUND B., dist judge; s.; William Young and Margaret Anna (Grafton) D.; B.A., Rice U., 1928; LL.B., S. Tex. Coll. Law, 1936; m. Grace Olivia Nelson, Aug. 2, 1930; children—Edmund, Paul Nelson. Admitted to Tex. bar, 1936, practiced in Houston, 1949-54; asst. dist. atty., Harris County, Tex., 1939-42, 45-49; judge 14th Dist. Ct., Houston, 1954—. Instr. criminal law S. Tex. Coll. Law, 1949-67. Trustee S. Tex. Jr. Coll., S. Tex. Coll. Law; bd. dirs. Houston Legal Found. Served with USNR, 1942-45. Decorated Bronze Star medal with Combat V. Mem. Phi Alpha Delta. Episcopalian (vestryman, sr. warden). Home: 7521 Creekwood Dr Houston TX 77042 Office: 301 San Jacinto St Houston TX 77002

DUGGAN, MINOR, med. editor, writer; b. Cork, Ireland, Apr. 9, 1924; s. Cornelius and Eugenia (Sposchum) D.; M.B., B.Ch., B.A.O., Univ. Coll., Cork, Nat. U. Ireland 1952; m. Doloria Arlene Zelasko, July 10, 1959. Came to U.S., 1958; naturalized, 1963. Asst. editor Merck Manual, Merck Sharp and Dohme, 1961-64; dir. med. services White Labs., Inc., div. Schering Corp., Kenilworth, N.J., 1967-72; dir. med. illustration and publs. dept. Miami (Fla.) Heart Inst., 1972—. Mem. Assn. Med. Dirs., Am. Med. Writers Assn., Am. Assn. for History Medicine, Drug Information Assn., Brit. Med. Assn. Home: 251 Winston Blvd Apt 1820 Miami Beach FL 33160 Office: Miami Heart Inst 4701 N Meridian Av Miami Beach FL 33140

DUGGER, RONNIE E., writer; b. Chgo., Apr. 16, 1930; s. W.L. and Mary (King) D.; B.A., U. Tex., 1950, student 1954; student Oxford U., 1951-52; m. Jean Williams, June 13, 1951; children—Gary McGregor, Celia Williams. Journalist, Tex. newspapers, 1947-52; asst. to exec. dir. Nat. Security Tng. Commn., Washington, 1952-54; editor, gen. mgr. Tex. Observer, 1954-61, 63-65, editor-at-large, pub., 1965—. Rockefeller fellow, 1969; Research fellow Inst. Indsl. Relations, U. Cal. at Los Angeles, 1969-70. Mem. Authors Guild, Am. Civil Liberties Union (nat. com.), New Democratic Coalition, Tex. Inst. Letters, Tex. Folklore Soc., Philos. Soc. Tex. Club: Town and Gown (Austin). Author: Dark Star, Hiroshima Reconsidered in the Life of Claude Eatherly of Lincoln Park, Texas, 1967; also articles. Editor: Three Men in Texas, Bedichek, Webb and Dobie, 1967. Home: 1017 W 31st St Austin TX 78705 Office: 504 W 24th St Austin TX 78705

DUKE, CHARLES MOSS, JR., astronaut; b. Charlotte, N.C., Oct. 3, 1935; s. Charles Moss and Willie (Waters) D.; B.S., U.S. Naval Acad., 1957; M.S., Mass. Inst. Tech., 1964; grad. USAF Aerospace Research Pilot Sch., 1965; m. Dorothy Meade Claiborne, June 1, 1963; children—Charles Moss III, Thomas Claiborne. With 526th Fighter Interceptor Squadron, Germany, 1958-62; instr. USAF Aerospace Research Pilot Sch., 1965-66; astronaut NASA, Houston, 1966—. Mem. Air Force Assn., S.A.R. Episcopalian. Landed on moon abroad Apollo 16, Apr. 1972. Home: 410 Lakeshore Dr Seabrook TX 77586 Office: Code CB NASA-MSC Houston TX 77058

DUKE, CURTIS CECIL, accountant, educator; b. Goochland County, Va., May 2, 1922; s. Nathaniel C. and Grace M. (Jackson) D.; B.S., Va. State Coll., 1948; M.B.A., N.Y. U., 1950, postgrad., 1950-52; m. Florence Byrd, Sept. 21, 1960. Instr., Ky. State Coll., 1950-51, St. Paul's Coll., 1951-53; asso. prof. accounting Va. State Coll., Petersburg, 1953—, head accounting dept., 1956—. Owner, Curtis C. Duke. C.P.A., Richmond, Va., 1958—; cons. accounting, mgmt. Commr., Capitol Region Park Authority, 1968—; sec.-treas. Chesterfield County (Va.) Indsl. Devel. Authority, 1969—. Served with Q.M.C., AUS, 1943-46. C.P.A., Va. Mem. Am. Inst. C.P.A.'s, Am., Nat. accounting assns., Am. Econ. Assn., Am. Mgmt. Assn., N.E.A. Home: Route 1 20006 Oakland Av Colonial Heights VA 23834 Office: Box 509 Va State Coll Petersburg VA 23803

DUKES, LEE STOLL, JR., city ofcl.; b. Branchville, S.C., May 11, 1920; s. Lee Stoll and Carrie (Ott) D.; B.S., Davidson Coll., 1942; M.P.H., N.C. U., 1951; m. Doris Jean Neal, July 2, 1944; children—Lee Stoll III, Sylvia Jean, Doris Elaine. Self-employed grocer, Charlotte, N.C., 1946-48; chemist Charlotte (N.C.) Water Dept., 1948-50, supr. water and sewage treatment, 1951-65, asst. supt., 1968—; chief engring. sect. N.C. State Bd. Health, Raleigh, 1965-68. Served with USNR, World War II. Mem. N.C. Water Pollution Control Assn. (dir. 1957-60), Am. Water Works Assn. (chmn. N.C. sect. 1970-71), N.C. Waterworks Operators Assn. (chmn. 1968-69), Water Pollution Control Fedn., N.C. Pub. Health Assn. Democrat. Methodist (mem. ofcl. bd. 1970—, counselor sr. high youth 1969—). Home: 2834 Eastburn Rd Charlotte NC 28210 Office: 600 E Trade St Charlotte NC 28202

DUKES, PHILIP DUSKIN, plant pathologist, educator; b.Reevesville, S.C., Jan. 16, 1931; s. Henry L. and Roberta E. (Reeves) D.; B.S., Clemson U., 1953; M.S., N.C. State U., 1960, Ph.D., 1963; student Colo. State U., 1957; m. Marlene Hart, July 28, 1956; children—Marla Hart, Philip Duskin. Plant chief clk. Davison Chem. Corp., Savannah, Ga., 1953-54; asst. county agt. S.C. Extension Service, Saluda, 1956-58; research asst. N.C. State U., Raleigh, 1958-62; asst. prof. U. Ga., Tifton, 1962-67, asso. prof., dept. plant pathology, 1967-70, research plant pathologist U.S. Vegetable Breeding Lab., Agrl. Research Service, U.S. Dept. Agr., Charleston, S.C., 1970—. Mem. Tobacco Variety Adv. Com., 1967-70; chmn. Tobacco Disease Evaluation Com., 1969-70, Sweetpotato Disease Com., 1970-71. Mem. local bd. SSS. Served with Signal Corps, AUS, 1954-56. Mem. Am. Phytopath. Soc., Mycol. Soc. Am., Bot. Soc. Am., Internat. Soc. Tropical Root Crops, So. Agrl. Workers, Nat. Sweetpotato Cooperator Group, Sigma Xi, Phi Kappa Phi, Alpha Zeta. Methodist. Research on physiology of phytopathogenic fungi, physiology of parasitism of root and stem pathogens, breeding disease resistant vegetables. Home: US Vegetable Breeding Lab PO Box 3348 Charleston SC 29407

DULANEY, GENE LANDIS, lawyer; b. Murray, Ky., Nov. 27, 1919; s. James A. and Edith (Bourland) D.; B.A. magna cum laude, Vanderbilt U., 1942; LL.B., St. Mary's U., San Antonio, 1949; m. Mary Arthur Bloomer, Sept. 2, 1948; children—Mary Jean, John Landis. Admitted to Tex. bar, 1949; pvt. practice law, San Antonio, 1949-50, Snyder, 1950—; city judge, Snyder, 1964—. Mem. Snyder Sch. Bd., 1960-63. Mem. Republican State Exec. Com., 1964-66; del. Rep. Nat. Conv., 1964. Bd. dirs. Colorado River Municipal Water Dist., Scurry County Boys Club. Served to 1st lt. USAAF, World War II; ETO. Decorated Air medal, D.F.C., Purple Heart. Mem. Am., Tex. bar assns., Snyder C. of C. (past pres., dir.). Republican. Episcopalian. Rotarian. Home: 3112 Av X Snyder TX 79549 Office: W Tex State Bank Bldg Snyder TX 79549

DULANEY, LUTHER THOMAS, JR., distbg. co. exec.; b. Oklahoma City, Feb. 23, 1939; s. Luther T. and Virginia (Piersol) D.; student U. Okla., 1957-61; m. Barbara Holmes, Feb. 16, 1963; children—Luther Thomas III, Lisa, Geoffrey P. Partner, L. T. Dulaney Co., Oklahoma City; pres. Dulaneys, Inc.; dir. First Nat. Bank & Trust Co. Bd. dirs. Salvation Army Oklahoma City, 1967—, Oklahoma City Symphony, 1967—, A.R.C., 1968—, Okla. Sci. and Arts Found., 1968—, Oklahoma City Better Bus. Bur., 1969—, Oklahoma City Beautiful, 1970—, Southwestern Coll. of Oklahoma City; exec. com. Frontiers of Sci. Found. of Okla., 1971—, Water Devel. Found. Okla., 1966—. Mem. Young Presidents Orgn., Oklahoma City C. of C. (dir. 1967-71), Phi Gamma Delta. Episcopalian (vestryman). Rotarian (v.p. 1971-72, pres. 1972-73). Clubs: Oklahoma City Golf and Country, Young Mens Dinner. Office: PO Box 1292 100 NW 44th St Oklahoma City OK 73101

DULIN, WILLIAM EASTERDAY, electronic engr.; b. Washington, June 28, 1911; s. Charles Thomas and Mary (Easterday) D.; student George Washington U., 1944, 60-62, 65; B.S., Phoenix U., 1959; grad. Capitol Radio Engring. Inst., 1943; postgrad. Am. U., 1951; Ph.D., Taylor U., 1970; m. Mary Barker Wintringham, Mar. 28, 1952; 1 son, Charles Thomas II. With Dulin Radio Service, Dulin Audio Lab., Washington, 1930-36; in charge radio dept. Warfield Motor Co., 1937-38; buyer, estimator Lighthouse Electric Co., 1939; radio technician Md. State Forestry Radio Network, Laurel, 1940; contract radio engr. Naval Research Lab., Washington, 1941; chief engring. aide Office of Chief Signal Officer, War Dept., 1942; electronic engr. FCC, 1945-48, electronic engr. chief tech. br. Marine Div., 1948-51; industry analyst, chief radio communication equipment sect. Electronics div. Nat. Prodn. Authority, 1951-53; indsl. specialist, asst. to dir. for moblzn. planning Electronics div. Bus. and Def. Services Administrn., 1953-55; sci. staff asst., research and devel. Nat. Security Agy., 1955-56, gen. engr., 1956-57; electronic engr., chief radio propagation unit Frequency div. USIA, 1957-60, supervisory electronic engr., dep. chief, 1960—. Grad. instr. Concept Therapy Inst., 1971. Founder, mem. World U., also mem. World U. Roundtable. Served to lt. USNR, 1942-45. Registered profl. engr., D.C., Va. Mem. Va. Soc. Profl. Engrs., I.E.E.E., Internat. Platform Assn., Armed Forces Communications and Electronics Assn., Audio Engring. Soc., Mensa, S.A.R. Methodist. Home: 3522 Washington Ct Alexandria VA 22302 Office: Frequency Div US Information Agy Washington DC 20547

DULMAGE, HOWARD TAYLOR, microbiologist, govt. ofcl.; b. Bridgeport, Conn., July 13, 1923; s. Harlan and Margaret Park (Taylor) D.; grad. Phillips Acad., 1940; B.S., U. Ill., 1947; Ph.D., Rutgers U., 1951; m. Eileen Mary Alders, May 30, 1953; children—Howard Taylor, Mary-Margaret Eileen. Sr. research microbiologist Abbott Labs., North Chicago, Ill., 1950-62; dir. research Nutrilite Products, Inc., Lakeview, Cal., 1962-67; research microbiologist, cotton insects br. Agrl. Research Service, U.S. Dept. Agr., Brownsville, Tex., 1967—. Served with AUS, 1943-46. Recipient Merit certificate for outstanding research U.S. Dept. Agr., 1970. Fellow Am. Inst. Chemists; mem. Soc. Invertebrate Pathologists, Am. Soc. Microbiology, Entomol. Soc. Am., Am. Chem. Soc. Mason, Kiwanian. Prodn. and standardization of microbial insect control agts. Home: 8 Edgewater Pl Brownsville TX 78520 Office: US Agr Dept PO Box 1033 Brownsville TX 78520

DUMAS, WOODROW WILSON, city ofcl.; b. Opelousas, La., Dec. 9, 1916; s. Juble Earl and Margaret A. (Jernigan) Dumas; student Baton Rouge Bus. Coll., 1938, Pope Secretarial Sch., 1939, Diesel Engring. Sch., 1944; m. Carol Epperson, Jan. 18, 1940; children—Diane, Woodrow Huntley. Pipefitter Humble Oil & Refinery Co., Baton Rouge, 1938, personnel, 1941-63; mayor Baton Rouge, 1965—. City-Parish councilman, 1953-64; v.p. Greater Baton Rouge Port Commn., 1956; chmn. constrn. com. Baker (La.) High Sch. Stadium, 1952—, also Greenwood Golf Course, nr. Baker, 1962—; chmn. steering com. for erection Lane Meml. Hosp., Zachary, La., 1959—; pres. Baton Rouge Kids' Baseball Clinic, 1966-67; mem. Nat. Adv. Com. on Hwy. Beautification, Miss. Valley Flood Control Assn., 1965—, La. Air Control Commn., 1965—, Nat. Hwy. Safety Adv. Com. Mem. La. Democratic Central Com., 1964—. Served with USN, 1934-38, 1942-49. Recipient Outstanding Service award La. Recreation and Park Assn., 1964. Mem. La. Police Jury Assn. (pres. 1963, Outstanding Police Juror 1963, dist. pres. 1953-61), Nat. Assn. Counties (pres. 1965—), Am. Legion, V.F.W. Methodist (Steward 1954-58). Lion (pres. Baker 1960), Eagle, Moose. Home: Route 1 Baker LA 70714 Office: Municipal Bldg Baton Rouge LA 70821

DUNAGAN, JOHN CONRAD, bottling co. exec.; b. Midland, Tex., Dec. 31, 1914; s. John C. and Ada L. (Hicks) D.; student U. Tex., 1937; m. Kathlyn Cosper, Aug. 21, 1933; children—Deanna, John C., Carol, Kathleen, William C. Mgr. Midland Bottling Co., 1931-33; mgr. Coca-Cola Bottling Co., Monahans, Tex., 1933-35, 41-46, pres., 1946-71, chmn. bd., 1971—; asst. cashier 1st State Bank, Monahans, 1937-39, dir., v.p., 1942—, chmn. bd., 1968—; asst. bank examiner Fed. Res. Bank, Dallas, 1940-41; chmn. bd. Tex. Savs. & Loan Assn., Monahans, 1965—; dir. Kermit State Bank (Tex.) 1943—; pres. Monahans Enterprises, Inc., 1953—. Midessa TV, Inc., Midland, 1954—. Mem. Tex. Finance Adv. Commn., 1960, U. Tex. Bus. Adminstrn. Adv. Council, 1960-61; mem. standardization com. Bottlers of Coca-Cola (U.S.), 1960—, chmn., 1968-72; mem. Tex. Good Neighbor Commn., 1955-62; pres. Monahans Sandhills Park Assn., 1958-61. Bd. dirs. Tex. Hist. Found., 1971—. Mem. Tex. Bottlers Assn. (pres. 1958), Tex. Hist. Assn., Tex. Folklore Soc.

(councilor 1968—), Tex. Permian Hist. Soc. (pres. 1962-63), Nat. Soft Drink Assn. (exec. bd.), Rotarian (pres. Monahans 1952-53). Home: 1107 S Dwight Av Monahans TX 79756 Office: 500 S Main Av Monahans TX 79756

DUNAHOO, MARK, judge; b. Winder, Ga., May 1, 1908; s. Joe E. and Cora (Chandler) D.; student Athens Bus. Coll., 1929-30; LL.B., Washington Coll. Law, 1939; m. Eva Holliday, Sept. 16, 1937. Mem. Ga. Revenue Com. Taxation, Atlanta, 1930-33; secretarial aide Senator Russell, Ga., Atlanta, 1933-1943, Washington, 1933-43; admitted to Ga. bar, 1945; practiced in Winder, 1945-63; judge Superior Ct. Piedmont Circuit, Winder, 1964—. Mem. Ga. Senate, 1951-53. Served with AUS, 1943-45; ETO. Mem. Am., Ga. bar assns., Am. Judicature Soc., V.F.W., Am. Legion. Democrat. Mem. Christian Ch. Mason (Shriner), Elk; mem. Order Eastern Star. Club: Civitan (past pres.). Home: 1025 E Broad St Winder GA 30680 Office: Court House Winder GA 30680

DUNAVANT, BILLY GLENN, educator; b. Hot Springs, Ark., Oct. 4, 1925; s. Sam and Marie (Staudenmayer) D.; student David Lipscomb Coll., 1947-49; B.S., George Peabody Coll, 1950, M.A., 1953; Ph.D., Purdue U., 1959; m. Ruth Wallis Parker, June 12, 1949. Instr. sci. Freedhardeman Coll., Henderson, Tenn., 1950-54; asst. to dir. isotopes div. U.S. AEC, Oak Ridge, 1954-56, cons. div. nuclear edn. and tng., 1962-66; instr. radiobiology Purdue U., West Lafayette, Ind., 1956-58, radiation control officer, 1956-60, asst. prof. health physics, 1959-60; asso. prof. radiation biology Coll. Medicine, U. Fla., Gainesville, 1960—, prof. nuclear sci., 1967—, dir. nuclear scis., 1967—. Del. 2d Cong. Internat. Radiation Protection Assn., Brighton, Eng., 1970, Mem. program com., 1969-70. Fellow A.A.A.S.; mem. Soc. Nuclear Medicine, Health Physics Soc. (chmn. publicity com. 1962, sci. program com. 1968-69; annual meeting place com., 1970, pres. chpt. 1967—), Am. Assn. Physicists in Medicine, Sigma Xi, Rho Chi, Phi Lambda Upsilon. Rotarian. Home: 5409 SW 13th St Gainesville FL 32601

DUNAWAY, JAMES LEE, JR., sch. adminstr.; b. Molino, Fla., Nov. 4, 1922; s. James Lee and Jahaza (Rooks) D.; B.S., U. Fla., 1948, M.Agr., 1952, Rank I Advanced Post grad. Teaching Certificate, 1955; m. Frances DuBose, Aug. 10, 1950; children—Michael Lee, Frances Ann, Rosemary. Tchr. vocational agr. Columbia High Sch., Lake City, Fla., 1948-56; owner farm supply bus. Mobile Feed Mill, Jasper, Fla., 1955-69; tchr. sci. and vocational edn. Columbia High Sch., 1948-55, Lake City Jr. High Sch., 1961-62; tchr. vocational agr. Jasper High Sch. and Hamilton High Sch., 1962-69; supt. Hamilton County Schs., Jasper, 1969—. Active North Fla. council Boy Scouts Am., 1963—; registered donor North Fla. Eye Bank for Restoring Sight, Inc., Jasper through Gainesville area, 1969—. Councilman, Jasper, 1959-69; mayor pro-tem. Jasper, 1966-68. Served with arty. AUS, 1942-45; ETO. Decorated Purple Heart with oak leaf cluster; recipient complete mobile feed mill as 1st prize Nat. Feed Dealers' Essay Contest, 1956. Am. Assn. Sch. Adminstrs. travel grantee, Europe, 1971. Mem. Jasper P.T.A. (past pres.), Hamilton County Farm Bur., Fla., Nat. vocational tchrs. assns., Hamilton County, Fla. tchrs. assns., Hamilton County, White Springs chambers commerce, V.F.W., Alpha Gamma Rho, Alpha Tau Alpha. Methodist (dir.). Lion. Home: 102 SW 10th St Jasper FL 32052 Office: Box 192 County Court House Jasper FL 32052

DUNBAR, JAMES CURTIS, physician; b. Mountain Home, Ark., Nov. 21, 1921; s. Felton F. and Eilleen (Love) D.; M.D., U. Ark., 1946. Intern Luth. Hosp., Cleve., 1946-47; practiced medicine Mountain Home, 1949—. Served from lt. (j.g.) to lt. comdr. M.C., USNR, 1943-49; PTO. Fellow Am. Coll. Angiology, Am. Geriatrics Soc.; mem. N.Y. Acad. Scis., A.M.A., Ark., Baxter County med. socs., U. Ark. Alumni Assn. Mem. Christian Ch. Home: 806 E 9th St Mountain Home AR 72653 Office: 617 S Baker St Mountain Home AR 72653

DUNBAR, JOHN BURTON, univ. adminstr.; b. Birmingham, Ala., June 24, 1929; s. Collis Burton and Unavay (Gandy) D.; D.M.D., U. Ala., 1953; Dr.P.H., Tulane U., 1963; m. Ruby Frances Berry, June 29, 1953; 1 dau., Inga. Asst to v.p. U. Ala., Birmingham, 1963-65, coordinator of research, 1965-67, dir. Urban Inst., 1969-70, v.p. student and community affairs, 1970—; chief program projects br. Heart Inst. NIH, 1968-69. Pres. Jefferson County Com. for Econ. Opportunity, 1967; mem. bd., exec. com. local Office Econ. Opportunity program, 1969—; mem. Mayor's Opportunity Council, 1970—, Birmingham Festival of Arts, 1971—, Birmingham Area Manpower Commn., 1972—. Bd. dirs. Met. YMCA, 1971—. Served with USAF, 1954-56; ETO. Mem. A.A.A.S., Sigma Xi. Unitarian (v.p. 1966-67). Home: 3220 Dundale Rd Birmingham AL 35216

DUNBAUGH, FRANK MONTGOMERY, author; b. Pueblo, Colo., Sept. 13, 1895; s. Frank M. and Sallie (Bennett) D.; grad. Phillips Andover Acad., 1913, Yale, 1917; postgrad. Toulouse U., 1919; m. Alice Ashby, Aug. 20, 1938; children—Edwin Lane, Frank Montgomery III. Pres., North Shore Newspapers, Inc., N.Y.C., 1926-34; account exec. Albert Frank Guenther Law, N.Y.C., 1934-38; v.p. Colonial Nav. Co., N.Y.C., 1938-43; instr. U. Miami, 1949-52, asso. prof., 1952-62. Pres., Ambassadors of Friendship, Miami, Fla., 1950—; tourist cons. Republic Haiti, 1948-49; cons. Industrias Unidas, Venezuela, 1950; U.S. del. internat. bus. confs., Bogota, Colombia, 1963, Lima, Peru, 1964. U.S. del. Assemblies of UN assns., Geneva, 1954, Warsaw, 1960; del. Rotary Internat. Conv., Nice, 1967; U.S. del. Congress Internat. Fedn. Orgns. for Sch. Corr. and Exchange, Brussels, 1969. Bd. dirs. The Vizcayans, Miami. Served to 2d lt. F.A., U.S. Army, 1917-19, to lt. col. AUS, 1943-46. Decorated Croix de Guerre (France). Mem. Phi Beta Kappa, Alpha Delta Sigma, Beta Theta Pi. Rotarian. Club: Yale (Miami). Author: Going to Florida, 1926; Marketing in Latin America, 1960; Portugal, Bargain Adventure, 1969; Youth Draws Us Toward the World of Tomorrow, 1972. Contbr. articles to profl. jours. Address: 4300 Lennox Dr Miami FL 33133

DUNCAN, A. BAKER, headmaster; b. Waco, Tex., Dec. 29, 1927; s. A. Baker and Frances (Higginbotham) D.; grad. Woodberry Forest (Va.) Sch., 1945; B.A., Yale, 1949; M.A., U. Tex., 1952; m. Sally P. Witt, Jan. 31, 1953; children—Addison Baker III, Richard Witt, Andrew Prescott. Master, Hill Sch., Pottstown, Pa., 1949-51; partner Rotan Mosle & Co., investment bankers, Houston, 1953-61; headmaster Woodberry Forest Sch., 1962—. Trustee Highlands Sch., Warrenton, Va., 1965—; vice chmn. Ind. Ednl. Services, 1968—. Mem. Chi Psi. Democrat. Episcopalian. Address: Woodberry Forest Sch Woodberry Forest VA 22989

DUNCAN, DAVID TURNER, lawyer; b. Bowie, Tex., Feb. 4, 1929; s. John Thomas and Lee (Turner) D.U. Tex., 1956; m. Betty Virginia Watson, Aug. 25, 1956; children—David Turner, Marshall Thomas, Brian Randolph, John William. With F.B.I., Houston, 1951; admitted to Tex. bar, 1956; practiced in Baytown, Houston, 1956-61, Brownsville, Tex., 1961—; mem. firms Cunningham, Yznaga & Duncan, 1961-65, Cox, Wilson, Duncan & Clendenin, 1965-69, Cox, Wilson, Duncan & Black, 1969—. Adv. dir. Pan Am. Bank, Brownsville. Devel. fund chmn. Tex. A. and M. U., 1965. Trustee, Brownsville Pub. Schs., 1964-67; dir., co-chmn. Brownsville Music Festival, 1962-63; dir., trustee Rio Grande Valley council Boy Scouts Am. Served to 1st lt. USAF, 1951-53. Fellow Tex. Bar Found.; mem. State Bar Tex., Am., Cameron County bar assns., Am. Judicature Soc., Tex. Assn. Def. Counsel, Def. Research Inst., Law Sci. Acad. Am., C. of C., Delta Theta Phi. Episcopalian. Clubs: Rotary (pres. 1965-66), Aggie (dir. 1963—). Home: 1404 Mulberry Lane Brownsville TX 78520 Office: 422 E Elizabeth St Brownsville TX 78520

DUNCAN, DAWN DELIGHT NEAL (MRS. WALTER CARLYLE DUNCAN), educator; b. Temple, Tex., Nov. 25, 1923; d. Tom Wright and Elsie (Oates) Neal; B.S., Mary Hardin-Baylor Coll., 1945; M.S., Tex. Womans U., 1964; m. Walter Carlyle Duncan, June 1, 1946. Tchr. pub. schs., Bell County, Tex., 1942-44; home economist Tex. A. and M. U., Agrl. Extension Service, Robertson County, Franklin, 1945-48, Burnet County, Burnet, Tex., 1948-54, Matagorda County, Bay City, 1954-61, Kaufman County, Kaufman, 1962—. Writer corr. courses Tex. Agrl. Extension Service. Bd. dirs., sec., pres. Longhorn Recreation Lab., 1952-60; dir. Kaufman County Women for Better Govt., 1962—. Mem. Am., Tex. home econs. assns., Nat. Assn. Extension Home Economists (So. councilor 1957-59, Distinguished Service citation 1959, nat. 3d v.p. 1968-70), County Home Demonstration Agts. Assn. Tex. (dir. 1951-54, pres. 1955-57), Internat. Platform Assn., Tex. Agrl. Workers Assn., C. of C., Epsilon Sigma Phi (dir.). Club: Pilot (dir., pres. 1972-73) (Terrell, Tex.). Home: 1600 Anthony St Kaufman TX 75142 Office: Courthouse Kaufman TX 75142

DUNCAN, EDWIN, banker, state senator; b. Sparta, N.C., June 25, 1905; s. David C. and Della L. (Woodruff) D.; A.B., U. N.C., 1925; m. Katherine R. Reeves, Aug. 31, 1926 (div. 1934); 1 son, Edwin; m. 2d, Bessie L. Wellborn, June 29, 1935; children—Jane C., David C. (dec.). Cashier Bank of Sparta, 1926-37; exec. v.p. Northwestern Bank, North Wilkesboro, N.C., 1937-58, pres., 1958-70; pres., dir. Northwestern Financial Corp., 1970—; sec.-treas. Northwestern Finance Co., North Wilkesboro, 1940—; chmn. bd. Lowe's Cos., Inc., 1963—; partner Wythe Finance Co., Wytheville, Va., 1949-70; pres. Alleghany Devel. Corp., Sparta, N.C., 1953—; dir. Brad Ragan Enterprises, Floyd Pike Electric Co., Northwestern Financial Investors, Holly Farms Poultry Industries, Wilkesboro; mem. N.C. Senate, 1953-55, 58-60. Mem. N.C. Banking Commn. Chmn. Northwestern Devel. Corp., Industrial Com. N.C. Mem. election com. 9th Dist. N.C. Chmn. finance com. Allegheny County Dist. N.C. Chmn. finance com. Alleghany County Hosp. Mem. Cattle and Dairy Assn. Am. Democrat. Clubs: Roaring Gap (N.C.), Twin City (Winston-Salem, N.C.). Home: 1 Duncan St Sparta NC 28675 Office: Northwestern Bank North Wilkesboro NC 28697

DUNCAN, ELMER HUBERT, educator; b. Fullerton, Ky., May 26, 1933; s. Homer Earl and Elizabeth Augusta (O'Roark) D.; A.B., U. Cin., 1958, M.A., 1960, Ph.D., 1962; m. Rosemary Hack, June 9, 1956. Mem. faculty Baylor U., Waco, Tex., 1962—, asso. prof. philosophy, 1965-70, prof., 1971—. Served with AUS, 1953-56. Taft teaching fellow, 1958-62. Mem. Southwest (sec.-treas., 1964-66), Am. philos. assns., Am. Soc. Aesthetics, Aristotelian Soc. Asst. editor bibliography Jour. Aesthetics and Art Criticism, 1970—. Home: 4813 Lake Englewood St Waco TX 76710 Office: Dept Philosophy Baylor U Waco TX 76703

DUNCAN, GEORGE WALTON, physician; b. Forsyth, Ga., May 29, 1915; s. William and Clyde (Moore) D.; M.D., Emory U., 1938; m. Louise Davis Apr. 6, 1944; children—George, Suzanne, Scott and Bruce (twins). Intern, Vanderbilt U., Hosp., 1938-39, resident surgery and sur. pathology, also neurosurgery, also research asst., 1939-41; William Stewart Halsted fellow Johns Hopkins Hosp. and Sch. Medicine, 1941-43, asso., 1941-48, chief resident surgeon, 1943-44, 47, instr., 1943-44, 46-47; asst. prof. U. Washington, 1948; practice medicine specializing in gen. surgery, Harlingen, Tex., 1949—; mem. staffs Tex. State tb Hosp., Mission, 1951-55, Harlingen, 1951-62, Valley Bapt. Hosp., Harlingen, Knapp Meml. Hosp., Weslaco, Tex., Mercy Hosp., Brownsville, Tex., Dolly Vinsant Hosp., San Benito, Tex.; bd. med. cons. Harlingen State Mental Health Unit. Served with USNR, 1944-46. Decorated Bronze Star; Presdl. Citation. Diplomate Am. Bd. Surgery. Fellow A.C.S. (sect. on trauma 1955-58); Blalock Soc., A.M.A., So., mem. Tex. med. assns., Cameron Willacy Med. Soc., Tex., Pan Pacific surg. socs., Johns Hopkins Med. and Surg. Soc., Caduceus, Sigma Xi, Sigma Nu Phi Chi. Contbr. articles primarily on traumatic shock to profl. jours. Home: 561 Lake Dr Office: 1716 Ed Carey Dr Harlingen TX 78550

DUNCAN, JAMES LOUGHLIN, bishop; b. Greensboro, N.C., Sept. 11, 1913; s. Robert and Mary (Loughlin) D.; B.A., Emory U., 1935, M.A., 1936; B.D., U. of South, 1939, D.D., 1962; m. Evelyn Burgess, July 25, 1943 (dec. Jan. 1967); children—Mary Anna (Mrs. Edward B. Waters), John Robert, James Loughlin; m. 2d, Mrs. Elaine B. Gaither, Oct. 7, 1967. Ordained to ministry Episcopal Ch., 1938; asst. rector in Atlanta, 1939-40; rector in Rome, Ga., 1940-45, Winter Park, Fla., 1945-50, St. Petersburg, Fla., 1950-61; suffragan bishop Episcopal Diocese So. Fla., 1961-69; bishop S.E. Fla., 1969—. Exchangee, U.S.-S. African Program, 1961. Chmn. Dade County Community Relations Bd., 1965. Mem. Kappa Alpha (knight comdr. 1957-58). Home: 3800 Alhambra Ct Coral Gables FL 33134 Office: 525 NE 15th St Miami FL 33132

DUNCAN, JOHN ALEX, govt. appraiser; b. Marianna, Fla., Aug. 22, 1944; s. Finley J. and Vivian Marie (Johns) D.; A.A., Chipola Jr. Coll., 1964; B.S., Troy State Coll., 1966. Trainee Fla. Pub. Welfare Dept., Marianna, 1966-67; cashier Fla. Bank at Chipley, 1967-71; mgr. service center Agrico Chem. Co., Chipley, 1971-72; state R/W appraiser, Dept. Transp., 1972—. Bd. dirs. Chipley Housing Authority, 1970-74, Holmes Valley Authority, 1971-75. Meml. chmn. Am. Cancer Dr. Washington County, 1971. Mem. Bank Adminstrn. Inst. (v.p. 1970-71). Democrat. Baptist. Lion. Club: Quarterback (treas.). Home: 801 S 8th St Chipley FL 32428 Office: Dept Transp Chipley FL 32428

DUNCAN, JOHN JAMES, congressman; b. Scott County, Tenn., Mar. 24, 1919; m. four children. Asst. atty. gen., 1947-56; dir. law, Knoxville, Tenn., 1956-59, mayor, 1959-64; mem. 89th-92d congresses 2d dist. Tenn. Served with AUS, 1942-45. Mem. Am., Tenn., Knoxville bar assns., Am. Legion (comdr. Tenn. 1954), Knoxville C. of C., Knoxville Tourist Bur., V.F.W. Presbyn. Republican. Home: 5403 E Sunset Rd Knoxville TN 37914 also 3803 Cameron Mills Rd Alexandria VA 22305 Office: Cannon House Office Bldg Washington DC 20515

DUNCAN, POPE ALEXANDER, coll. adminstr.; b. Glasgow, Ky., Sept. 8, 1920; s. Pope Alexander and Mabel (Roberts) D.; B.S., U. Ga., 1940, M.S., 1941; Th.M., So. Bapt. Theol. Sem., 1944, Th.D., 1947; postgrad. U. Zurich, 1960-61; m. Margaret Flexer, June 30, 1943; children—Mary Margaret, Annie Laurie, Katherine Maxwell. Instr. physics U. Ga., 1940-41; fellow So. Bapt. Theol. Sem., 1944-45; dir. religious activities Mercer U., 1945-46, Roberts prof. church history, 1948-49; prof. religion Stetson U., 1946-48, 49-53; prof. ch. history Southeastern Bapt. Theol. Sem., 1953-63; dean Brunswick Coll., 1964; pres. S. Ga. Coll., Douglas, 1964-68; v.p. Ga. So. Coll., Statesboro, 1968-71, pres., 1971—. Pres. Wake Forest Civic Club, 1959-60, Ga. Assn. Colls., 1968-69. Mem. Am. Hist. Assn., Am. Soc. Ch. History, Douglas-Coffee County C. of C. (dir. 1966-68), Statesboro-Bulloch County C. of C. (dir. 1971—), Phi Beta Kappa, Omicron Delta Kappa, Phi Kappa Phi, Phi Delta Kappa, Kappa Delta Pi, Pi Mu Epsilon, Phi Eta Sigma, Sigma Phi Sigma. Democrat. Baptist. Rotarian (dir. 1965-66, 1970—, pres. 1967-68). Author: Our Baptist Story, 1958; The Pilgrimage of Christianity, 1965 Hanserd Knollys, 1965. Home: 16 Golf Club Circle Statesboro GA 30458

DUNCAN, WILLIAM ADOLPHUS, JR, electric utility exec.; b. Washington, Aug. 2, 1912; s. William Adolphus and Sue (Ellis) D.; B.S. in Mech. Engring., U. Ky., 1935; m. Dorothy Decker McElrath, Nov. 14, 1939; children—Dorothy, Sara Sue, Mary Patton. Pres., dir. Ky. Utilities Co., Old Dominion Power Co., dir. Electric Energy, Inc., Commonwealth Life Ins. Co., Ohio Valley Electric Corp. Trustee High Temperature Reactor Devel. Assn. Pres. Central Ky. Music Soc., 1965, bd. dirs., 1962—; bd. dirs. Central Baptist Hosp., mem. Ky. Bapt. Hosp. Commn. Men. I.E.E.E., Civil War Roundtable Triangle Frat. Baptist. Clubs: Optimist, Pyramid (Lexington, Ky.). Home: 120 S Limeston St Lexington KY 40507

DUNKIN, MILLARD LEE, dentist; b. Ala., Mar. 20, 1931; s. Robert Lee and Sarah Ruth (Drake) D.; B.S., U. Ala., 1958, D.M.D., 1961; m. Mary Lou Boerschel, Dec. 27, 1953; children—Jeffery, Bethany, Gregory, Malcolm. Practice dentistry, Columbia, S.C., 1961—. Served with USAF, 1951-55. Mem. Central Dist. Dental Soc. (sec.-treas. 1968-70), Am., S.C. (sec., 1970—) dental assns., Greater Columbia Dental Soc., S.C. Acad. Practice Adminstrn., Am. Acad. Dental Electrosurgery, Am. Soc. Dentistry for Children, So. Acad. Clin. Nutrition, Omicron Delta Kappa, Delta Sigma Delta. Optimist (lt. gov., 1967-68). Home: 6909 Longbrook Rd Columbia SC 29206 Office: 2800 Rosewood Dr Columbia SC 29205

DUNKLEBERGER, ALVAND C., newspaper editor; b. Elida, N.M. Apr. 20, 1907; s. Augustus C. and Addie (Foreman) D.; m. Pauline Sechrest, Aug. 22, 1934; children—Paul A., Sandra, Carolyn. Editor, Johnson City (Tenn.) Staff-News, 1933-35; Sunday editor Knoxville (Tenn.) Jour., 1937-38; asso. editor Nashville Banner, 1935, editor, 1942—. Mem. Am. Soc. Newspaper Editors. Mem. Church of Christ. Club: Nashville Executives. Home: 1140 Pierce Av Madison TN 37115 Office: Nashville TN 37201

DUNLAP, ESTELLE CECILIA DIGGS (MRS. LEE A. DUNLAP), educator; b. Washington, Sept. 26, 1913; d. John F. and Mary F. (Chasley) Diggs; B.S., D.C. Tchrs. Coll., 1937; M.S., Howard U., 1940; m. Lee A. Dunlap, May 16, 1941; children—Gladys C. (Mrs. Kimbrough), Dolly A. (Mrs. Sparkman). Tchr. math. Garnet-Patterson Jr. High Sch., Washington, 1941-56, head dept. math., 1950-56; tchr. math., sci. MacFarland Jr. High Sch., Washington, 1956—. Vis. instr. math. D.C. Tchrs. Coll., 1963—. Mem. N.W. Boundary Civic Assn., Washington, 1954—, rec. sec., 1964-66. NSF fellow, 1959. Fellow Intercontinental Biog. Assn.; mem. A.A.A.S., Nat. Edn. Council, Nat. Council Tchrs. Math. Nat. Aviation Edn. Council, Internat. Platform Assn., Washington Performing Arts Soc., Soc. Indsl. and Applied Math., Am. Ordnance Assn., Am. Math. Soc., Math. Assn. Am., Washington Urban League. Republican. Club: Stardusters' V.I.P. (Waldorf, Md.). Home: 719 Shepherd St NW Washington DC 20011 Office: Iowa Av and Webster St Washington DC 20011

DUNLAP, JERRY J., lawyer; b. Chelsea, Okla., Feb. 12, 1925; B.S. in M.E., U. Okla., 1948; J.D., U. Tulsa, 1952. Admitted to Okla. bar, 1952, U.S. Supreme Ct. bar, 1969; practiced in Oklahoma City, 1952—; mem. firm Dunlap, Laney, Hessin & Dougherty. Asst. prof. patent trademark and copyright law Oklahoma City U., 1962-67. Served to lt. (j.g.) USNR, 1943-46, 52-53. Registered profl. engr., Okla. Mem. Nat. Soc. Profl. Engrs., Am., Oklahoma County, Okla. bar assns., Am. Patent Law Assn. Office: 200 Lawyers Bldg 219 Couch Dr Oklahoma City OK 73102*

DUNLAP, JOE EVERETT, dentist; b. Delaware, O., May 11, 1930; s. Arthur Calvin and Mary Irene (Jones) D.; student Ohio Wesleyan U., 1949-50, 54; D.D.S., Ohio State U., 1959; m. Mary Susan King, June 17, 1959; children—Marlene, Todd, David, Sherrie, Dru. With Fla. Instl. Dental Service, Gainesville, Ft. Myers, 1959-60; pvt. practice dentistry, Clearwater, Fla., 1961—; sr. mem. dental group Dunlap, Vance, Strupp & Noyes. Vice pres., bd. dirs. Clearwater Mental Health Assn. Served to 2d lt. Med. Service Corps, AUS, 1950-53. Mem. Am., Fla., West Coast Dist. dental assns. Home: 1816 Lombardy Dr Clearwater FL 33515 Office: 1455 Sunset Point Rd Clearwater FL 33515

DUNLAP, ROY L., civil engr.; b. Canyon, Tex., Aug. 15, 1927; s. Richard and Leona Blanche (Easter) D.; B.S. in Civil Engring., Tex. Technol. Coll., 1949; m. Riley Fae Butler, Jan. 29, 1950; 1 son, Roy Joe. Asst. design engr. City of Lubbock (Tex.), 1950-53; engr. City of Snyder (Tex.), 1953-54, mgr., 1955-62; manager, City of Killeen, Texas, 1962-68; coordinator City of Hamlin (Tex.), 1954-55; asst. to sr. v.p., head project mgmt. div. Turner, Collie & Braden, Inc., cons. engrs., Houston, 1969-71; chief engr. Wilkinson Welding, Killeen, Tex., 1971-72; pres., owner Dunlap & Assos., 1972—. Bd. dirs., sec. Scurry County Indsl. Found., Snyder, Tex. Served with USMCR, 1945-46; now capt. CEC, USNR; recalled to active duty comdg. officer U.S. Naval Constrn. Bn. 22, 7 mos. So. Vietnam, 1968-69. Decorated Legion of Merit; named Outstanding Young Man, Snyder Jr. C. of C., 1957. Registered prof. civil engr., Tex. Mem. Am. Soc. C.E., Internat., Tex. city mgrs. assn., Am. Legion (sch. award Crosbyton, Tex. 1944), V.F.W., Navy League, Killeen C. of C. Methodist. Mason. Rotarian (pres. Snyder 1957-58). Home: 1512 Alta Mira Killeen TX 76541 Office: 5902 E Hwy 190 Killeen TX 76541 also 211 N 2d St Temple TX 76540

DUNLAP, WILLIAM DEWAYNE, JR., postal adminstr.; b. Austin, Minn., Apr. 8, 1938; s. William DeWayne and Evelyn (Hummel) D.; B.A., Carleton Coll. (Scholar), 1960; m. Lois-Mary Apple, Sept. 23, 1961; children—Kristin Mary, Leslie Kathrin, Brenda Jean. With Procter & Gamble Co., Cin., 1960-69, brand marketing mgr., 1964-69; asst. postmaster gen. for product mgmt. U.S. Postal Service, Washington, 1970—. Am. Field Service exchange student, Germany, 1955. Home: 13204 Valley Dr Rockville MD 20850 Office: US Postal Service 12th and Pennsylvania Sts Washington DC 20260

DUNLEAVY, JOSEPH CHARLES, advt. mgr.; b. Phila., Sept. 22, 1923; s. Charles J. and Sophie (Byrne) D.; student U. Ill., 1943-44, Shrivenham U., Eng., 1945; B.A. in Sociology, La Salle Coll., 1955; postgrad. Temple U., 1962; m. Anna Mae Maksimowicz, Feb. 26, 1949; children—Charles, Michael, Brendan, Joseph. Passenger agt. Pa. R.R., Phila., 1942-59; graphic arts coordinator RCA, Camden, 1959-63; advt. dir. Family Finance Mgmt. Corp., Miami, Fla., 1963-66; advt. mgr. Sunbeam Electronics, Ft. Lauderdale, Fla., 1966-68; advt. mgr. Bendix Avionics Div., Ft. Lauderdale, 1968—; substitute tchr. Phila, 1955-56. Jr. Achievement adviser, Miami, 1965-66. Bd. dirs. Broward County United Fund, co-chmn. maj. firms div.; bd. dirs. Broward County March of Dimes. Served with AUS, 1943-46; ETO. Mem. Advt. Club Greater Miami, Ft. Lauderdale Advt. Club, Ft. Lauderdale C. of C., Indsl. Editors Assn. S. Fla. Clubs: Toastmasters (local v.p.), Bendix Management (v.p.), Bendix Employees Activities (dir.). Home: 5713 NE 15th Av Fort

Lauderdale FL 33308 Office: 2100 NW 62d St Fort Lauderdale FL 33310

DUNLOP, DONALD D., scientist; b. Brunswick, Ga., Sept. 6, 1922; B.S., U. Tex., 1947, M.S., 1948; Ph.D., Tex. A. and M. U., 1952. Sr. engr. Esso Research and Engring. Co., Baton Rouge, 1952-61; mgr. research and devel. Oil Recovery Corp., Norman, Okla., 1961-64; pres. Prodn. Research Corp., Norman, Creative Enterprises Internat., Norman, 1964-69; asst., sci. adviser to Sec. of Interior, Washington, 1969-71; mgmt. cons., 1971—; vis. prof. Mgmt. Sch., U. Okla., Norman, 1964-69. Served to 1st lt. USAF, 1943-46. Mem. Am. Inst. Chem. Engrs. (outstanding speaker award 1957), Sigma Xi, Omega Chi Epsilon, Phi Lambda Upsilon. Patentee in field. Home: 3508 Prince William Dr Fairfax VA 22030 Office: 18th and C Sts NW Washington DC 20240

DUNLOP, JAMES NATHANIEL, JR., missile co. exec.; b. Yonkers, N.Y., Apr. 19, 1921; s. James Nathaniel and Katharine W. (Lyon) D.; B.S. in Engring., Princeton, 1942; E.E., 1943; m. Rosemary Royce, Jan. 12, 1948; children—James, William, Rosemary, Paul Dunlop. Engr., Kelex Corp., Silver Spring, Md., 1946-47; with Martin Co., Balt., 1947-55, dir. quality, Orlando, Fla., 1959-61; dir. electronic programs Martin Marietta Corp., Orlando, 1961-69, operations dir. communications and electronics, 1969—. Past bd. dirs. Orange County chpt. A.R.C. Served as lt. USNR, 1942-46. Mem. Armed Forces Communications and Electronics Assn. (regional v.p.), Am. Ordance Assn., I.E.E.E. Assn. U.S. Army, U.S. Naval Inst., Winter Park C. of C. (dir.). Republican. Episcopalian. Home: 1807 Via Amalfi Winter Park FL 32784 Office: Martin Marietta Corp Orlando FL 32805

DUNLOP, JOHN W., pub. TV exec. Gen. mgr. Pub. TV System, V.I. Address: Public Television System*

DUNN, ADOLPHUS WILLIAM, physician; b. Leaksville, N.C., Nov. 23, 1922; s. Adolphus William and Sally (Gray Ivie) D.; B.S., Wake Forest Coll., 1942; M.D., Duke, 1945; m. Doris Margery Nash, Mar. 14, 1945; children—John Bullard Ray, Adolphus William III. Intern New Haven Hosp., 1945-46; commd. lt. (j.g.) 1945, med. officer, 1946-65, ret. as capt. M.C.; head dept. orthopaedic surgery Ochsner Clinic and Ochsner Found. Hosp., New Orleans, 1967—; clin. asso. prof. orthopaedic surgery Tulane U. Sch. Medicine, New Orleans. Diplomate Am. Bd. Orthopaedic Surgery. Fellow A.C.S., Am. Acad. Orthopaedic Surgeons; mem. Am. Orthopaedic Assn., Phi Beta Kappa. Republican. Home: 6909 Wilty St Metairie LA 70003 Office: 1514 Jefferson Hwy New Orleans LA 70121

DUNN, CARROLL HILTON, army officer; b. Lake Village, Ark., Aug. 11, 1916; s. William Lewis and Ruth Sheldon (Dewey) D.; B.S., U. Ill., 1938; M.S., State U. Ia., 1947; m. Letha Estelle Jontz, Nov. 11, 1939; children—Carolyn (Mrs. Douglas Lee Caldwell), Carroll Hilton. Commd. 2d lt. U.S. Army, 1938, advanced through grades to lt. gen., 1971; dir. waterways exptl. sta. C.E., Vicksburg, Miss., 1952-55; exec. officer to chief engrs., Washington, 1955-58; constrn. supr. Greenland and U.S. Ballistic Missile Facilities, 1959-62; div. engr., Dallas, 1962-64; dep. chief staff, 8th U.S. Army, Korea, 1964-66; dir. constrn. U.S. Mil. Assistance Command, Vietnam, 1966; asst. chief staff for logistics, Vietnam, 1966-67; dir. mil. constrn., dep. chief Office Chief Engrs., Washington, 1967-71; dir. Def. Nuclear Agy., Def. Dept., Washington, 1971—. Decorated D.S.M., Silver Star, Legion Merit with oak leaf cluster, Bronze Star with oak leaf cluster, Purple Heart; Croix de Guerre with palm (France). Fellow Am. Soc. C.E.; mem. Soc. Am. Mil. Engrs. Baptist (deacon). Home: Quarters 58 Fort Belvoir VA 22060 Office: Defense Nuclear Agency Def Dept Washington DC 20305

DUNN, CHARLES JEROME, state ofcl.; b. Phila., June 29, 1934; s. Charles Rome and Lelia Mae (Whitley) D.; A.B., U. N.C., Chapel Hill, 1956, postgrad., 1956-60; m. Martha Ellen Sherrill, Dec. 29, 1963; children—Sherrill, Jay. With Chapel Hill Weekly, 1951-52, Durham Morning Herald, 1956-63; legislative asst. to Congressman Horace Kornegay, 1963-64; spl. asst. to Gov. Dan Moore, N.C., 1965-68; dir. State Bur. Investigation, Raleigh, 1969—. Served with AUS, 1957-59. Mem. Am. Polit. Sci. Assn. Democrat. Methodist. Home: 6512 Raceview Terrace Raleigh NC 27609 Office: 421 N Blount St Raleigh NC 27601

DUNN, CHARLES THOMAS, clergyman, psychologist; b. Brookhaven, Miss., Apr. 4, 1920; s. John W. and Josephene (Norman) D.; B.A., Abilene Christian Coll., 1949; M.A., U. Houston, 1952; m. Celeste Mae Cate, Mar. 14, 1946; children—James Nelson, Deanne Lee, Dianna Lynn. Ordained to ministry Church of Christ, 1947; minister in Abilene, Tex., 1948-49, Corpus Christi, 1950, Turkey, 1951, Baytown, 1952, Rodeo Cal., 1954; minister, bishop Hardy and Hopper St. Church of Christ, Houston, 1954—; guidance dir. psychologist Channelview Sch. Dist., 1954-71; prin. Marathon (Tex.) High Sch., 1971-72; supt. schs., Waelder, Tex., 1972—. Served with AUS World War II. Mem. Am., Tex. personnel and guidance assns., Nat. Vocational Guidance Assn., Tex. Edn. Assn., Am. Sch. Counselors Assn. Republican. Contbr. numerous articles to Gospel Tidings. Address: PO Box 564 Waelder TX 78959

DUNN (WILLIAM) EDWIN, journalist; b. Cleveland, Miss., Aug. 21, 1938; s. Sam Edwin and Rachel (Reed) D.; B.A., Memphis State U., 1959. Copywriter, WCLD Radio, Cleveland, Miss., 1959-60; mgr. WDLT Radio, Indianola, Miss., 1960-61; writer Delta-Democrat Times, Greenville, Miss., 1961-63; edn. editor Memphis Press-Scimitar, 1963-69, bus. editor, 1969—. Recipient Superior Writing award Tenn. Edn. Assn., 1965; Sch. Bell award Memphis Edn. Assn., 1966. Mem. Edn. Writers Assn., Maywood Civic Club. Home: Route 1 Box 62A Olive Branch MS 38654 Office: 495 Union St Memphis TN 38101

DUNN, HENRY ARTHUR, entomologist; b. Shirley, Mass., July 15, 1911; s. Arthur Garfield and Josie Elizabeth (Pember) D.; B.S., U. N.H., 1934; Ph.D., Rutgers U., 1952; m. Elise E. Dickerman, July 1, 1939; 1 son, Thomas D. Entomologist Merck & Co., Rahway, N.J., 1947-48; sr. entomologist Diamond Alkali Co., Richmond, Va., 1952-55; dep. asst. adminstr. Cooperative Research Ser., U.S. Dept. Agr., Washington, 1956—. Served with AUS, 1942-46. Mem. Entomol. Soc. Am. Author bull.: Review of Research on the Boll Weevil, 1962. Home: 6801 Galax Ct Springfield VA 22151 Office: Cooperative Research Service Agr Dept Independence Av and Jefferson Dr Washington DC 20250

DUNN, HENRY HAMPTON, editor; b. Floral City, Fla., Dec. 14, 1916; s. William Harvey and Nannie L. (Hemrick) D.; student Mercer U., Macon, Ga., U. Tampa (Fla.); m. Charlotte Rawls, Aug. 16, 1941; children—Janice Kay, Henry Hampton, Dennis Harvey. Staff mem. Tampa (Fla.) Times, 1936-58, city editor, 1946-51, mng. editor, 1951-58; polit. analyst and newscaster WCKT-TV, Miami, 1958-59; pub. relations dir. Peninsula Motor Club, 1959—, also v.p.; editor Fla. Explorer. Advisory council Gordon Keller Sch. Nursing, 1955—, chmn. 1956-59, adv. bd. Salvation Army, 1953—, chmn., 1955-56; dir. United Cerebral Palsy of Tampa, state pres.; dir., treas. Tampa A.R.C.; selections com. Girl Scouts; dir., v.p. Vis. Nurses Assn. Greater Tampa 1956—; mem. Nat. AAA Traffic and Safety Com., Nat. AAA Pub. Relations Com.; charter trustee Historic Pensacola Preservation Bd.; trustee Historic Tallahassee Preservation Bd.; pres. DWI Counterattack Tampa-Hillsborough County; mem. Carrollwood Civic Assn.; dir. Girl's Club of Tampa, Hillsborough County unit Am. Cancer Soc.; adv. com. Hillsborough Community Coll. Major USAF, World War II; MTO. Decorated Bronze Star, 5 Battle Stars. Recipient award for best news story A.P., 1946; Award of Merit, Fla. Hist. Soc.; Torch award Citrus County C. of C., 1969. Mem. Am. Legion, Tampa C. of C. (tourist com., mem. hwy. com.), Fla. Hist. Soc., Hist. Assn. So. Fla., U. Tampa Alumni Assn. (past pres.), Asso. Press Assn. Fla. (pres. 1955-56), Internat. Platform Assn., Tampa Hist. Soc. (v.p.), Old Timers Assn. Hillsborough County (dir.), Sigma Delta Chi (pres. Fla. West Coast chpt. 1954-55). Baptist. Mason, Rotarian (pub. relations chmn., bd. dirs., pres. Tampa, dist. gov.); mem. Order Eastern Star. Author: Re-Discover Florida; WDAE, Florida's Pioneer Radio Station; Yesterday's Tampa; Re-explore Florida. Hist. writer Fla. Trend mag., Tampa Tribune, Tampa Times; writer syndicated hist. column. Home: 10610 Carrollwood Dr Tampa FL 33618 Office: 1515 N Westshore Blvd Tampa FL 33607

DUNN, IRIS CHRISTINE PIPPIN (MRS. MARCE ODIS DUNN), pharmacist; b. Bristol, Va., Mar. 11, 1935; d. Harley Albert and Hazel (Dye) Pippin; gen. cultural degree Va. Intermont Coll., 1955; B.S., Med. Coll. Va., 1959; m. Marce Odis Dunn, Jan. 15, 1962; children—Ramona, Stephanie. Pharmacist, Dunn's Pharmacy, Inc., Bristol, Tenn., also Abingdon, Va., 1959—, v.p., 1962—. Chemistry tchr. Va. Intermont Coll., Bristol, Va., 1964. Mem. Hosp. Aux., Bristol, 1961—. Mem. Am., Va. pharm. assns., Va. Intermont Coll. Alumnae Assn., Med. Coll. Va. Alumni Assn., Wesleyan Service Guild (v.p. 1967-68), Kappa Epsilon. Clubs: Pilot of Bristol (treas. 1965-66); Carolina Caribbean (Banner Elk, N.C.). Home: 100 Ambers Dr Candlewyck Bristol TN 37620 Office: 340 Edgemont Av Bristol TN 37620

DUNN, J. D., educator, labor arbitrator; b. Freeport, Tex., Jan. 18, 1928; s. James Arlee and Martha (Gipson) D.; student Tex. A. and M. U., 1945-46; B.F.A., U. Tex., 1951, M.B.A., 1955; Ph.D., U. Ala., 1961; m. Paula Ann Huston, June 17, 1950; 1 son, Gary Paul. Asst. prof. bus. adminstrn. U. Tex., Arlington, 1955-58; chmn. bus. adminstrn. dept. Ala. Coll., Montevallo, 1960-63; prof. bus. adminstrn. N. Tex. State U., Denton, 1963—, dir. Tech. Information and Mgmt. Services Center, 1963—; labor arbitrator, Denton, 1965—. Cons. Victor Equipment Mfg. Co., Denton, 1966. Served with AUS, 1946-47, 1st lt., 1951-53. Mem. Am. Arbitration Assn., Indsl. Relations Research Assn. (chpt. pres. 1965-66). Author: (with Frank M. Rachel) Wage and Salary Administration), 1971; (with Elvis C. Stephens) Management of Personnel: Manpower Management and Organizational Behavior, 1972. Contbr. articles to profl. jours. Home: 1311 Greenwood St Denton TX 76203

DUNN, JOSEPH WILLCOX, newspaper exec.; b. Richmond, Va., March 9, 1937; s. Joseph Willcox and Lelia (Taylor) D.; grad. Episcopal High Sch., Alexandria, Va., 1955; student U. Va., 1955-57; m. Alice Smiley Hubard, Aug. 17, 1957; children—Joseph Willcox III, Pauline Taylor. Reporter, Princess Anne Free Press, Virginia Beach, Va., 1957-62; with Virginian-Pilot, Norfolk, Va., 1962—, telegraph editor, 1964-65, acting news editor, 1965-66, city editor Virginia Beach Bur., 1966-68, mil. writer, 1968, mng. editor, 1968—. Office: Virginian-Pilot Norfolk VA 23501

DUNN, LEON ALGERNON, JR., diversified pub. corp. exec.; b. Greenville, N.C., Oct. 6, 1938; s. Leon Algernon and Mary Magdalene (Tripp) D.; B.S., U. N.C., 1960; m. Pattie Gene McCay, Apr. 27, 1963; children— Mary Eugenie, Jane McCay. Tchr. pub. schs., Chesapeake, Va., 1960-61; trust adminstr. Wachovia Bank & Trust Co., Winston-Salem, N.C., 1965-66; exec. v.p., dir. Guardian Corp., Rocky Mount, N.C., 1966-72, pres., 1972—, chief adminstrv. officer, 1972—, also dir. 15 subsidiaries; bd. mgrs. Planters Nat. Bank & Trust Co., Rocky Mount. Bd. dirs. Rocky Mount area Wesleyan Coll. Found., 1971—, United Fund, 1971-73. Served to capt. USMCR, 1961-64. Mem. N.C. Health Care Facilities Assn. (pres. East dist. 1967-68, treas. 1968-69, sec. 1969-70, dir. 1967-70), Sigma Phi Epsilon. Republican. Episcopalian. Kiwanian. Club: Benvenue Country (dir.). Home: 3712 Winchester Rd Rocky Mount NC 27801 Office: Sunset Av W Rocky Mount NC 27801

DUNN, NEAL JOSEPH, lawyer; b. Steubenville, O., Oct. 26, 1919; s. Neal Joseph and Anna (Behne) D.; student Ohio State U., 1937-46; LL.B., U. Miami, 1951. Children—Felica Ayn, Ayn, Alan Reid. Admitted to Fla. bar, 1951; gen. practice Miami, 1951—. Served with AUS, 1942-46. Home: 821 NW 39th Ct Miami FL 33132 Office: 23 NW Le Jeune Rd Miami FL 33126

DUNN, PARKER SOUTHERLAND, chem. co. exec.; b. Portsmouth, O., Aug. 25, 1910; s. Joseph Sidney and Florence (Bowen) D.; B. Chem. Engring., Ohio State U., 1930; M.S., Mass. Inst. Tech., 1931; m. Mayde Smith, July 15, 1939; children—Joseph Smith, Dwight James. Tech. asst. Mead Corp., Chillicothe, O., 1930-32; foreman Columbia So. Corp., Barberton, O., 1932-33, asst. plant supt., Corpus Christi, Tex., 1934-38, tech. dir., 1938-41; research dir. Potash Co. Am., Carlsbad, N.M., 1941-46, resident mgr., 1946-51; asst. v.p. Am. Potash & Chem. Corp., Trona, Cal., 1951-52, v.p., Los Angeles, 1952-63, dir., 1958—, pres., 1963-69, chmn., 1969-71; v.p. Kerr McGee Corp., Oklahoma City, 1968—; v.p., dir. Am. Lithium Chems. Co., 1959-64, San Antonio Chem. Co., 1957-71. Recipient Benjamin Garver Lamme medal Ohio State U., 1966. Mem. Am. Inst. Chem. Engrs., Am. Inst. Mining. Metall. and Petroleum Engrs., Am. Nuclear Soc., N.M. Mining Assn. Episcopalian. Clubs: Beacon, Whitehall, Quail Creek Golf and Country (Oklahoma City). Home: 3332 Quail Creek Rd Oklahoma City OK 73120 Office: Kerr McGee Bldg Oklahoma City OK 73102

DUNN, ROY SYLVAN, educator, archivist; b. Nixon, Tex., Mar. 29, 1921; s. Roy and Jailey (Day) D.; B.A., U. Tex., 1948, M.A., 1951; postgrad. Am. U., 1950; m. Elaine Helen McCoy, Aug. 30, 1947; children—Gloria Daye, Roy Edgar, Janet Elaine. Asst., Tex. Archives, Austin, 1947-48, asst. state archivist, 1949-50, coordinator reorgn. Tex. State Library, 1951, state librarian, 1951, records examiner, 1952-53; auditor Office State Comptroller, Austin, 1953-56; archivist Tex. Tech. U., Lubbock, 1956-63, dir. archives, 1963—, asst. prof., 1957-63, asso. prof. sociology, 1963—. Served with USAAF, 1942-46. Recipient H. Bailey Carroll award for best hist. articles in Southwestern Hist. Quar., 1967. Fellow Tex. Hist. Assn. (exec. council); mem. Am., Southwestern, So. sociol. assns., W. Tex. Hist. Assn., Soc. Am. Archivists (com. coll. and univ. archivists), Soc. S.W. Archivists, Orgn. Am. Historians, Western History Assn. Mason. Contbr. articles to profl. jours. Home: 5011 45th St Lubbock TX 79414 Office: Box 4559 Lubbock TX 79409

DUNN, THOMAS T(INSLEY), lawyer; b. Petersburg, Va., Aug. 27, 1901; s. George W. and Emma (Tinsley) D.; B.S., U. Va., 1925, LL.B., 1926; m. Elizabeth Campbell, Dec. 31, 1927; children—Janet E., Thomas C. Asst. trust officer Old First Nat. Bank, St. Petersburg, 1926-30; v.p., trust officer United Savs. Bank, Detroit, 1930-35; asst. v.p. Pub. Nat. Bank & Trust Co., N.Y., 1935-36; dir. trust new business Citizens and Southern Nat. Bank, Atlanta, 1938-41; v.p., trust officer First Nat. Bank, St. Petersburg, Fla., 1941-54; pvt. law practice, 1954—; dir. First Nat. Bank, St. Petersburg. Co-founder Goodwill Industries-Suncoast, Inc. Candidate U.S. Congress, Rep. primary, 1954. Mem. Am. Judicature Soc., Fla., Va. bars, S.A.R., Soc. Mayflower Descs., Huguenot Soc., Newcomen Soc. N.Am., Alpha Chi Rho, Phi Alpha Delta. Clubs: St. Petersburg Yacht, Bath, Kiwanis. Co-author: Trust Accounting Act, 1951. Contbr. articles to profl. jours. Home: 7400 Sun Island Dr S St Petersburg FL 33707 Office: 3023 Central Av St Petersburg FL 33713

DUNN, WILLIAM EDWARD, trade assn. exec.; b. Ohio, Ill., July 30, 1909; s. James Patrick and Anna (Manning) D.; LL.B., DePaul U., 1937; m. Margaret Lyons, Apr. 19, 1937; children—James Albert, Mary Virginia (Mrs. Robert T. Metz), William Frederick, Roger, Mary Suzanne. Admitted to Ill. bar, 1937, U.S. Supreme Ct., 1947; practice in Chgo., 1937-44; regional atty. WLB, Chgo., 1945-46; mem. staff Asso. Gen. Contractors Am., Washington, 1946—, exec. dir., 1961-72, exec. v.p., 1972—. Mem. Pres.'s Missile Sites Labor Commn., 1962—; mem. nat. coms. apprenticeship and tng. Labor Dept., 1961—; bd. dirs. Programs Safety in Constrn., 1960—; mem. Citizen's Adv. Com. on Transp. Quality. Clubs: Nat. Lawyers, Georgetown (Washington); Moles (N.Y.C.). Home: 4828 Fort Sumner Dr Washington DC 20016 Office: 1957 E St NW Washington DC 20006

DUNN, WILLIAM HARP, constrn. co. exec.; b. nr. Salisbury, N.C., Nov. 17, 1935; s. Robert Ernest and Frances Eltra (Harp) D.; B.S. in Civil Engring. with honors, N.C. State U., 1957; m. Molly Ann Elledge, Sept. 9, 1956; children—Leo Elledge, Jennifer Ann, Sally Mae. Draftsman, J.N. Pease Co., architects and engrs., Charlotte, N.C., 1957-58; estimator C.D. Spangler Co., Charlotte, 1958-61; v.p. estimating and engring. Foster-Sturdivant Co., Inc., North Wilkesboro, N.C., 1961—; dir. Foster Sturdivant Co., Inc., 1966—. Mem. bd. commrs. Redevel. Commn., North Wilkesboro, 1967—, sec., 1968-71; active Boy Scouts Am., 1948—, committeeman Old Hickory council Boy Scouts Am., 1969—. Mem. Profl. Constrn. Estimators Assn., Home Builders Assn. (sec. 1968-70; pres. 1971). Republican. Methodist. Mason. Home: 76 Townsend St North Wilkesboro NC 28659 Office: Box 1009 North Wilkesboro NC 28659

DUNN, WILLIAM ROBERT, supt. edn.; b. Shoals Junction, S.C., Mar. 21, 1911; s. Larkin Barmore and Sara E. (Barmore) D.; B.S., U. S.C., 1933, LL.B., 1935; m. Ruth E. Polatty, June 23, 1943; children—Jane Barmore, William Robert. Admitted to S.C. bar, 1935; practicing atty., Greenwood, 1935-41; county supt. edn. Greenwood County, 1943-71; asst. supt. for bus. Greenwood Sch. Dist. 50, 1971—. Chmn. Greenwood County Bd. Edn., 1943-65. Served with AUS, 1941-43. Mem. N.E.A., S.C., Greenwood County edn. assns., Am. Legion (past adj.), S.C. Assn. County Supts. (pres. 1960), Am. Assn. Sch. Adminstrs., S.C. Bar. Baptist. Club: Greenwood Kiwanis (sec.-treas. 1952—). Home: 223 Gracemont Dr Greenwood SC 29646 Office: Adminstrv Bldg Magnolia St Greenwood SC 29646

DUNN, WINFIELD, gov. Tenn.; b. Meridian, Miss., July 1, 1927; s. Aubert C. and Dorothy (Crum) D.; B.B.A., U. Miss.; postgrad. Memphis State U.; D.D.S., U. Tenn.; m. Betty Jane Prichard, Dec. 30, 1950; children—Charles W., Donna Gayle, Julie Claire. Field rep. Aetna Casualty & Surety Co., New Orleans, 1950-51; practice gen. dentistry Memphis, 1956-70; gov. Tenn., 1970—. Chmn. Shelby County (Tenn.) Republican Com., 1964-68, mem. exec. com., 1962-70. Trustee Memphis-Shelby County Hosp., 1968-70. Served with USNR, 1945-47. Mem. Am., Tenn. dental assns., Memphis Dental Soc., Kappa Alpha, Omicron Kappa Upsilon, Omicron Delta Kappa, Delta Sigma Delta, Delta Sigma Pi. Home: Governor's Mansion Curtiswood Lane Nashville TN Office: State Capitol Nashville TN 37219

DUNNAVANT, JOHN MARSHALL, JR., educator; b. Charlotte Court House, Va., Oct. 18, 1927; s. John Marshall and Sallie Mae (Cox) D.; B.S., Va. Poly. Inst., 1950; M.Ed., U. Va., 1959, Ed.D., 1969; m. Nancy Ely, Apr. 25, 1959; children—Julie, Christie. Tchr., asst. prin. Pittsylvania County Schs., 1950-59; prin. pub. schs., Charlottesville, Va., 1959-61, asst. to supt., 1961-63; asst. prof. edn. Mary Washington Coll., Fredericksburg, Va., 1963-64; instr. U. Va., Charlottesville, 1964-68, research asst. to dean edn., 1968-69, asst. prof. edn., dir. Richmond Center, 1969—. Cons. edn. various sch. systems Va. Served with USNR, 1946-48. Mem. Phi Delta Kappa, Kappa Delta Pi. Home: Route 1 Box 381 Manakin-Sabot VA 23103 Office: 4907 Augusta Av Richmond VA 23230

DUNNING, HUBERT RAY, educator; b. Slaydon, Tenn., Oct. 26, 1926; s. Scott and Gussie Lee (Shelton) D.; B.A., Trevecca Nazarene Coll., 1948; B.D., Nazarene Theol. Sem., 1951; M.A., Vanderbilt U., 1953, Ph.D., 1969; m. Bettye J. Dunning, July 10, 1952; children—William Carey, Dennis Ray, Joy Amaris. Ordained to ministry Nazarene Ch., 1947; pastor Ch. of the Nazarene, Tenn., Ark., 1952-64; prof. philosophy and religion Trevecca Nazarene Coll., Nashville, 1964—. Carre fellow Vanderbilt U. Sch. Religion, 1963-64. Mem. Am. Acad. Religion, Wesleyan Theol. Soc. Author: Search the Scriptures, 3 vols., 1958, Our Standard of Conduct, 1959. Home: 419 Southwood Dr Nashville TN 37217

DUNNING, WILHELMINA FRANCES, cancer researcher, pathologist; b. Topsham, Me., Sept. 12, 1904; d. Fred J. and Evelyn (Williams) Dunning; A.B., U. Me., 1926, D.Sc., 1960; M.A., Columbia, 1928, Ph.D., 1932. Asso. cancer research Columbia, 1930-41; instr. pathology Wayne State U., 1941-48, asst. prof. oncology, 1948-50; asso. cancer research Detroit Inst. Cancer Research, 1944-50; prof. zoology U. Miami, 1950-52, research prof. exptl. pathology 1952—, dir. cancer research lab., 1950-71, sr. scientist Papanicolaou Cancer Research Inst., 1971—. Mem. bd. dirs. Coconut Grove Civic Club, Coconut Grove Residents Club. Mem. A.A.A.S., Am. Assn. for Cancer Research (bd. dirs.), Am. Soc. Zoologists, Genetics Soc. Am., Soc. for Exptl. Biology and Medicine, N.Y. Acad. Scis. Club: Pilot (Miami). Home: 2850 Coconut Av Miami FL 33133 Office: Papanicolaou Cancer Research Inst 1155 NW 14th St Miami FL 33136

DUNTON, JAMES GERALD, assn. exec.; b. Circleville, O., Nov. 10, 1899; s. Oscar Howard and Florence (Nightengale) D.; A.B., Harvard, 1923, M.Ed., 1928; m. Dorothy Winfough, Oct. 10, 1944. Free lance author, 1925-34; Fed. Projects dir., Ohio, 1935-37; spl. rep. Fed. N.W. Terr. Sesquicentennial Commn., 1938; editor Ohio Democracy, 1939-40; Ohio field rep. Office Govt. Reports, Exec. Office of Pres., 1940-41; dir. spl. activities Office Sec. Def., 1950-61; assn. exec., Washington, 1962—; adv. council Oliver Wendell Holmes Assn., 1966—; exec. dir. Va. Nursing Home Assn., 1965—; Washington rep. Am. Chess Found., 1962—. Mem. vets. com. Presdl. Inaugurations, 1965, 69; pres. Nat. Capital U.S.O., Washington, 1966-67; mem. Nat. Council of U.S.O., 1966—; Va. State Adv. Com. Adult Services, 1972; distinguished sponsor 100th Anniversary 1st Battle of Bull Run, 1961. Served with Ambulance Corps, A.E.F., U.S. Army, 1918-19, to maj. AUS, World War II. Recipient certificate of appreciation Nat. Press Club, 1955, Commendation award Pres.'s Com. on Employment of Handicapped, 1963; decorated Army Commendation medal. Mem. Nat. Assn. Execs. Club, Am. Legion, Vets. World War I (dir. pub. relations 1969), V.F.W., Res. Officers Assn., Va. Soc. Assn. Execs., Mil. Order World Wars, Ohio Soc.

Washington, Soc. of Va. Presbyn. (elder). Club: Harvard (Washington). Author: Wild Asses, 1925; Murders in Lovers Lane, 1927; Maid and a Million Men, 1928; Counterfeit Wife, 1930; Honey's Money, 1933; Queen's Harem, 1933; (anthology) C'est La Guerre, 1927. Contbr. articles to mags., newspapers. Address: 2820 Bisvey Dr Falls Church VA 22042

DUNWODY, EUGENE COX, architect; b. Macon, Ga., July 19, 1933; s. W. Elliott and Mary Bennet (Cox) D.; B.S., Ga. Inst. Tech., 1955, B.Arch., 1956; m. Susan Howe Foxworth, June 15, 1957; children—Susan Howe, Eugene Cox, George Foxworth, Mary Betty Cox. With archtl. firm W. Elliott Dunwody, Jr. Architect Inc., and successor Dunwody Dunwody & Assos. Architects, Inc., Macon, Ga., 1959-69, 1st v.p., treas., 1966; pres. Dunwody & Co., Architects, 1969—. Chmn., Macon Bibb County Planning and Zoning Commn. Trustee United Givers Fund; pres. Macon Nursery Schs., Inc. Served with C.E.C., USNR, 1956-59. Mem. A.I.A., Constrn. Specifications Inst. (past pres. Macon chpt.), Kappa Alpha. Presbyn. Rotarian (pres. elect). Home: 330 Wesleyan Dr Macon GA 31204 Office: 205 Broadway Macon GA 31021

DUPEPE, F(RANK) CLANCY, lawyer, real estate exec.; b. New Orleans, Mar. 6, 1934; s. Vernon Wilfred and Eunice (Clancy) D.; B.A., Tulane U., 1955; LL.B., Loyola U., 1962. Children—Michele Tanguis, Mignon Wattigny, Andree Nicole. Tchr., Jefferson Parish (La.) Sch. System, 1958-60; pres. Dupepe and Assos., Ltd., New Orleans, 1971—; admitted to La. bar, 1962; practiced in New Orleans, 1962—; chmn. bd. Provincial Motor Hotels, Inc., 1962—; pres. La. Boucherie, Inc., Duman Investments, Inc.; dir. Mchts. Trust &Savs. Bank, French Market Corp. Bd. dirs. Vieux Carre Action Assn.; treas., bd. dirs. Greater New Orleans Tourist and Conv. Commn. Served to 1st lt. USMCR, 1955-58. Mem. S.A.R., La. Bar Assn., Tulane, Loyola alumni assns., C. of C. Clubs: Le Moyne de Bienville, Iris, Bacchus. Home: 1922 3d Kenner LA 70062 Office: 1024 Chartres St New Orleans LA 70116

DUPRE, GRACE ANNETTE, portrait painter; b. Spartanburg, S.C.; d. Daniel Allston and Helen Capers (Stevens) DuPre; student Converse Coll. and Converse Coll. Sch. Music. Grand Central Sch. Art, 1931-32; pvt. studies various tchrs., including Wayman Adams and Frank V. DuMond. Solo violinist, tchr. violin painter, 1932—. Several one man shows; exhibited Fine Arts League of Carolinas, Gibbs Art Gallery, Mint Museum, Charlotte, Blue Ridge, N.C., Allied Artists Am., Nat. Arts Club, Audubon Artists, Am. Artists Profl. League, Ogunquit (Me.) Nat. Exhbn. Paintings; portraits include judges of U.S. Ct. Appeals, 7th Circuit, Chgo., chief justice S.C. Supreme Ct., pres. of Wofford Coll., gov. of S.C., others; portraits in permanent collections Columbia U., N.Y.C., Main P.O., N.Y.C., U. Ind. Law Bldg., White House, U.S. Supreme Ct., U.S. 7th Circuit Ct. of Appeals, Chgo., Charleston (S.C.) City Hall Collection of Portraits, S.C. State House, numerous pub. and ednl. instns., pvt. collections. Recipient various awards including award 31st Ann. Exhbn. Am. Paintings, Ogonquit, Me., 1951, portrait prize Catherine Lorillard Wolfe Art Club ann. show N.Y.C., 1955. Mem. M.B.L.S. Mem. Grand Central Art Galleries, Inc., Pen and Brush, Nat. Arts Club N.Y.C., Am. Artists Profl. League (nat. exec. bd.), Allied Artists Am., Carolina Art Assn., Gramercy Park Assn., Huguenot Soc. S.C., Portraits, Inc. Clubs: Woman's Music (life mem.) (Spartanburg, S.C.); Catherine Lorillard Wolfe Art (N.Y.C.). Studio: 361 Mills Av Spartanburg SC 29302 also 302 S Pine St Spartanburg SC 29302

DUPRE, LOUIS, educator; b. Veerle, Belgium, Apr. 16, 1925; s. Clemens and Francisa (Verlinden) D.; Ph.D., U. Louvain, Belgium, 1952, L.S.T., 1958; m. Constance Pierson, Dec. 17, 1965; 1 son, Christian. Cameto U.S., 1958, naturalized, 1967. Faculty dept. philosophy Georgetown U., 1958—, prof., 1966—. Served with Belgian Army, 1950-51. Recipient Study Grant Danish Govt., 1956. Fellow Am. Council Learned Socs.; mem. Am. Cath. Philos. Assn. (pres. 1970-71), Am. Philos. Assn., Am. Metaphys. Soc. Author: Kierkegaard As Theologian, 1963; Contraception and Catholics, 1964; The Philosophical Foundations of Marxism, 1966; The Other Dimension, 1972. Home: 2328 37th St NW Washington DC 20007

DUPRE, ROBERT EMERY, physician, surgeon; b. Plaisance, La., June 7, 1905; s. Robert and Emily (Soileau) D.; student Southwestern La. Inst., 1928-30; pre-med. (Breaux scholar), Tulane U., 1934; m. Hazel Ardain, Dec. 30, 1928; children—Haidee Marie, Elizabeth Emily. Sec. Evangeline Parish Sch. bd., Ville Platte, La., 1923-25; cotton buyer L. M. Huey, Rayne Farm Produce, Lake Charles, 1925-28; intern Charity hosp., New Orleans, 1934-35; with Dr. R. E. Dupre hosp. & clinic (formerly Ardoins Sanitarium), Ville Platte, 1935—, now full owner; rancher and planter, Villa Platte, 1945—, Dir. Am. Security Bank, Ville Platte, Tideland Life Ins. Co., Bunkie, La. Mem. La. Hosp. Bd. Mem. Evangeline Parish Med. Soc., A.M.A., Alpha Kappa Kappa. Home: 824 W Main St Ville Platte LA 70586 Office: 916 W Main St Ville Platte LA 70586

DUPREE, JAMES HENRY, retail trade exec.; b. N.C., June 28, 1929; s. Paul Earnest and Dixie Pauline (Lamm) D.; grad. high sch.; m. Frances Deloris Mayo, Nov. 12, 1950; children—Kimberly Ann, Connie Frances. Asst. office mgr. Nat. Biscuit Co., Greenville, N.C., 1947-52; bookkeeper M.O. Blount & Sons, Bethel, N.C., 1954-60; gen. mdse. gen. mgr., sec. L.J. Whitehurst & Sons, Inc., Bethel, 1960-64; gen. mdse. sec., mgmt. exec. M.O. Blount & Sons, Inc., Bethel, 1964—, Blount Fertilizer Co., Inc., Greenville, N.C., 1964—, Allied Petroleum Corp., Greenville, N.C., 1965—, Ayden Tractors, Inc., (N.C.), 1965—; v.p. Superior Wholeseale Distbg., Inc., Bethel, 1968—. Dir. Mut. Tobacco Barn Fire Ins. Assn., Robersonville, N.C. Sec., treas. Bethel Little League, 1958-60; commr. Town of Bethel, 1969—, mayor, 1971—. Bd. dirs. Greenville Christian Acad., Bethel Better Bus. Bur. Served with AUS, 1952-54. Baptist (treas. 1958-69). Rotarian, Lion (sec. Bethel 1957-58). Home: McWhorter St Bethel NC 27812 Office: 225 W Railroad St Bethel NC 27812

DUPREE, JIM, ednl. adminstr. Mem. bd. edn. State of Ark. Office: State Bd Edn Edn Bldg Little Rock AR 72203*

DUPREE, JIMMIE GAINES, physician; b. Coushatta, La., Mar. 2, 1924; s. William Daniel and Annie (Gahagan) D.; B.S., Southwestern State U., Lafayette, La., 1944; M.D., Southwestern Med. Found., Dallas, 1947; m. Mary Elise Addison, July 15, 1947; children—Daniel Gaines, Ellyce (Mrs. William Goins). Intern Confederate Meml. Hosp., Shreveport, La., 1947-48, resident in surgery, 1948-49; practice gen. medicine, surgery, Bunkie, La., 1949-64, partner gen. practice and surgery McConnell Dupree Clinic and Hosp.; 1949-64 with La. Dept. Health, Alex, 1964-71, area med. cons., Alex, 1964-68, asst. dir. bur. community health, 1968—. Dir. Tidelands Life Ins. Co., Bunkie, med. dir. 1956; mem. exec. com., dir. Fidelity Credit Co., Bunkie, 1957-71. Med. dir. Avoyelles Parish Civil Def., 1964—; chmn. Avoyelles Parish Bd. of Health, Marksville, La. Bd. dirs. Avoyelles chpt. A.R.C., Cenla Health Planning Council, Alex; bd. dirs. Chronically Ill and Aging Council, Marksville, med. adviser, 1965—. Served with USNR, 1943-45, 53-55; Korea. Mem. Avoyelles Parish Med. Soc. (past pres.), Skull and Key (hon.), Phi Beta Pi. Democrat. Baptist. Rotarian, Mason. Home: 403 S Holly St Bunkie LA 71322 Office: McArthur Dr Alexandria LA 71301

DUPRIEST, BETTE RUTH HORTON (MRS. DENNIS BLACK DUPRIEST, JR.), club woman; b. Dallas, June 8, 1922; d. Frederick Reece and Frances Mellersh (Martyn) Horton; student Tex. State Coll. Women, 1941; B.A. in Spanish, B.S. in Journalism, So. Meth. U., 1944; m. Dennis Black DuPriest, Jr., Nov. 28, 1958. Staff, Internat. News Service, Dallas 1944-45, Dallas Morning News, 1945-49; with Petroleum Engr. Pub. Co., Dallas, 1955-57; translator Spanish and French letters Trinity Portland Cement div. Gen. Portland Cement Co., Dallas, 1950-58. Recipient Sigma Delta Chi scholastic award, 1944. Chpt. pres. Delta Zeta, 1942-44, mem. chpt. alumnae adv. bd., 1950-53, 67-68, Dallas chpt. pres., 1955-56; corr. sec., pub. relations chmn. Maj. James McGregor chpt. Colonial Dames of XVII Century, 1967-69, curator, 1969—. Mem. Magna Charta Dames (registrar 1970-72), Local History and Geneal. Soc., Colonial Order of Crown, Sovereign Colonial Soc., Ams. Royal Descent, Tenn. Geneal. Soc., Maury County Hist. Soc., Script and Score, Mortar Bd., Sigma Delta Pi, Pi Sigma Alpha, Theta Sigma Phi. Presbyn. Home: 5621 McCommas Av Dallas TX 75206

DUPUIS, EASTEN PIERRE, real estate exec.; b. Cecelia, La., Sept. 16, 1917; s. Aurelien J. and Noamie (Willis) D.; ed. Tex. A. and M. U., La. State U.; m. Jeanne Marie Guidry, May 25, 1940; children—Amelie (Mrs. Roland J. Dugas), Gay (Mrs. P. J. St. Romain), Easter Pierre, Richard, Joel, Denise. With So. Pacific R.R., 1941-46; salesman Michawauka Rubber Co., 1946-49; with Sunray Produce Co., Lafayette, La., 1949-55; bldg. contractor ins. and real estate, Lafayette, 1955-61; chief of police, Lafayette, 1961-72; real estate exec., contractor, 1972—. Pres. Easten Dupuis, Contractors, Inc., Lafayette, 1955—. Dir. Breaux Bridge Bank & Trust (La.). Mem. Lafayette Parish Police Jury, 1960. Mem. Lafayette C. of C., Internat. Assn. Chiefs of Police, La. Peace Officers, Internat. Assn. for Identification. Democrat. Roman Catholic. K.C. Home: 705 Landry Dr Lafayette LA 70501 Office: PO Box 3001 Lafayette LA 70501

DUPUY, CLARENCE O., JR., city ofcl. Dist. councilman, New Orleans. Address: 6943 Argonne Blvd New Orleans LA 70124*

DUQUE, HOMER ADOLPH, housing authority ofcl.; b. Belcher, La., Mar. 27, 1918; s. Adolph and Ann (Bullard) D.; student La. Poly., 1939-40; B.A., Centenary Coll., La., 1947; m. Melba Juanita Sisemore, Feb. 15, 1940; 1 dau., Melba Kathryn. Dist. mgr. Shreveport Times, 1946-50; mgr. B.H. Rainwater Ins. Agy., Ruston, La., 1950-55; exec. dir. Ruston Housing Authority, 1956—. Sec., v.p., pres. Housing Council La., 1967—. Served with USNR, 1943-45; PTO. Mem. Nat. Assn. Housing and Redevel. Ofcls., Am. Legion, V.F.W. Democrat. Baptist. Home: 1805 Huey Dr Ruston LA 71270 Office: 615 N Farmerville St Ruston LA 71270

DUR, PHILIP FRANCIS. educator; b. St. Louis, June 30, 1914; s. Alphonse and Sarah (Ralston) D.; A.B., Harvard, 1935, Ph.D., 1941; postgrad. Fgn. Service Inst., 1961; m. Elena Delgado, June 30, 1942; children—Elena (Mrs. Philip A. Morris), Philip, Stansbury, Carmen (Mrs. Norman B. Conley, Jr.), Jacqueline, John. Consul, pub. affairs officer, Lyon, France, 1948-51; chief Office Pub. Affairs, Office U.S. High Commr. for Germany, Bonn, 1951-52; consul. exec. officer, Bremen, Germany, 1952-53; comml. controls officer Mil. Security Bd., Coblenz, Germany, 1953-54; consul Colon, Panama, 1954-55, Yokohama, Japan, 1955-58; pub. affairs adviser Dept. State, 1958-61; consul, Nagoya, Japan, 1961-65; Jefferson Caffery prof. polit. sci. U. Southwestern La., Lafayette, 1965—, faculty senate, 1969—. Adviser, Council for Devel. French in La., 1968—; pres. France-Amerique de la Louisiane Acadienne, 1970—. Served to lt. comdr. USNR, 1942-46. Mem. Am. Fgn. Service Assn., Am. Polit. Sci. Assn., Internat. Studies Assn., Soc. for French Hist. Studies, Phi Beta Kappa. Home: 517 Woodvale Av Lafayette LA 70501

DURAN, OTIS S(AMUEL), ins. and real estate broker; b. nr. Haywood, Okla., Dec. 17, 1911; s. Montgomery Samuel and Fannie (Plunkett) D.; student Hershey Bus. Coll., 1930-32, Walton Sch. Commerce, 1932-34; m. Alberta Mary Sites, June 21, 1932; children—Sim, Annette; m. 2d. Evelyn Sewell, Oct. 7, 1946; children—Robert, Christine; 1 stepdau., Mrs. Mary Minyard, Mgr. Duran & Duran, ins. and real estate brokers, 1930—; owner also mgr. Duran Investment Co., McAlester, Okla.; pres. Duran Mortgage Co., Inc., McAlester; partner McAlester Devel. Co.; sec.-treas. Profl. Bldg. of McAlester, Inc.; dir. First Nat. Bank of McAlester. Councilman, McAlester, 1948-53. Pres. Berry Manor Nursing Home, McAlester; active Boy Scouts Am.; bd. dirs. McAlester United Fund, pres., 1962; v.p. McAlester Ambulance Authority; Bd. dirs. McAlester Boys Club, pres., 1968; bd. dirs. Bapt. Found. Okla., 1971—; trustee McAlester Hosp. Found., McAlester Gen. Hosp. (pres. 1957—); adv. bd. Kiamichi Vo-Tech Schs. Served in USAF, 1943-45. Dir., officer Jr. C. of C., 1933-42. Mem. Okla. Assn. for Crippled Children (life mem.), Okla. Assn. Real Estate Bds. (dir. 1953-62), McAlester Bd. Realtors (pres. 1954-55, 68-69), Eastern Okla. Frontiers Sci. (charter), C. of C. (pres. 1959, dir.), McAlester Ins. Assn. (pres. 1962), Am. Legion, V.F.W. (trustee 1946—), Navy League. Baptist (deacon, trustee, pres. Brotherhood 1967, 68). Mason (32 deg., Shriner). Clubs: Rotary (pres. 1955-56), Knife and Fork (pres. 1958). Home: Red Bud at Hickory Bend McAlester OK 74501 Office: Profl Bldg 10 E Washington McAlester OK 74501

DURAND, L. EUGENE, banker; b. Collinsville, Okla., Aug. 3, 1916; s. Lloyd Eugene and Sue (Smith) D.; student Tex. Technol. Coll., 1935-37, Eastern N.M. Coll., 1938-39; m. Betty Larkin, July 22, 1940; children—Douglas Durand, Deborah (Mrs. Tom Jordan). Engr.-supt. Oberman & Co., Harrison, Ark., 1941-50; pres. Ark. Acceptance Corp., Harrison, 1950-71; pres. The Security Bank, Harrison, 1971—, Acceptance Investment Corp., Harrison, 1952—; dir. Save-A-Stop Midwest, Inc., Harrison. Pres. Harrison Youth Assn., 1952-54, Harrison Planning Commn., 1961—. NoArk council Girl Scouts U.S., 1967-70; mem. Gov.'s Council on Pub. Edn., 1970—. Pres. Harrison Sch. Bd., 1952. Bd. dirs. Community Fund. Mem. Am., Ark. bankers assns., Am. Indsl. Bankers Assn. (dir.). Presbyn. (v.p. nat. bd. pensions, Phila. 1963—). Mason (Shriner, 32 deg.), Elk. Home: 1 Circle Dr Harrison AR 72601 Office: 221 W Stephenson St Harrison AR 72601

DURANT, CLARENCE OLIN, elec. engr.; b. Cottageville, S.C., July 26, 1900; s. William Augustus and Elizabeth (Ackerman) D.; B.S. in E.E., Clemson U., 1921; m. Frances Elizabeth Stoltmann, Sept. 2, 1945; children—Patricia Jo, Joan Alef. Supt., Smoaks (S.C.) High Sch., 1921-22; elec. engr. Westinghouse Electric Corp., Pitts., 1923-27, Commonwealth Power Corp., Jackson, Mich., 1927-29; fed. appraiser Fed. Land Bank, U.S. Forest Service, 1930-41; elec. engr. C.E., U.S. Army, Oak Ridge, Savannah, Ga., 1947-68; chief elec. sect. U.S. Air Force, Charleston (S.C.) AFB, 1968-72; instr. Charleston Tech. Center, 1972—; elec. cons., 1972—. Tchr. engring. night sch. Armstrong Coll., 1965. Served from lt. (j.g.) to comdr. USNR, 1941-46. Registered profl. engr., Ga. Mem. Nat. Soc. Profl. Engrs., I.E.E.E. (sect. chmn. Savannah 1955-56). Home: 1719 Weston Av Charleston SC 29407 Office: Charleston AFB Civil Engring Office Charleston SC 29404

DURANT, FREDERICK CLARK, III, museum exec.; b. Ardmore, Pa., Dec. 31, 1916; s. Frederick Clark, Jr. and Cornelia Allen (Howel) D.; B.S. in Chem. Engring., Lehigh U., 1939; postgrad. Phila. Mus. Sch. Indsl. Arts, 1946-47; m. Carolyn Griscom Jones, Oct. 4, 1947; children—Carolyn M., William C., Stephen H. Engr., E.I. duPont de Nemours & Co., Inc., 1939-41; rocket engr. Bell Aircraft Corp., 1947-48; dir. engring. Naval Air Rocket Test Sta., 1948-51; cons., Washington, 1952-53; mem. sr. staff Arthur D. Little, Inc., 1954-57; dir. Maynard Ordnance Test Sta., 1954-55; exec. asst. to dir. Avco-Everett Research Lab., 1957-59; dir. pub. and govt. relations, research and advanced devel. div. Avco Corp., Wilmington, Mass., 1959-61; sr. rep. Bell Aerosystems Co., Washington, 1961-64; asst. dir. astronautics Nat. Air and Space Mus., Smithsonian Instn., Wash., 1964—, participant ann. congresses Internat. Astronautical Fedn., 1951—, pres., 1953-56; mem. organizing com. Project Orbiter, 1954. Served to comdr. AC, USNR, 1941-46, 48-52. Registered profl. engr., D.C., Mass. Recipient spl. medal L'Assn. Pour l'Encouragement de l'Aeronautique et de l'Astronautique, 1963. Fellow Am. Astronautical Soc. (chmn. awards com. 1961), Am. Inst. Aeros. and Astronautics, Am. Rocket Soc. (pres. 1953); mem. Internat. Acad. Astronautics, Nat. Space Club (gov. 1961); hon. fellow or mem. numerous fgn. rocket and space flight socs. Contbg. editor Missiles and Rockets, 1956-58. Clubs: Cosmos; Sherwood Forest. Contbr. to Ency. Brit., Ency. Americana; contbr. (space terms) Am. Heritage Dictionary. Home: 109 Grafton St Chevy Chase MD 20015 Office: Nat Air and Space Mus Smithsonian Instn Washington DC 20560

DURANT, JOHN, writer; b. Waterbury, Conn., Jan. 10, 1902; s. Harold R. and Mary (Walker) D.; A.B., Yale, 1925; m. Alice Rand, Aug. 6, 1942. Reporter N.Y. Times, 1927-28; mem. N.Y. Stock Exchange, 1929-44; free lance writer, contbr. nat. mags., 1936—. Served as lt. USNR, 1942-44. Mem. Outdoor Writers Assn. Am., Soc. Am. Travel Writers, Salt Water Fly Rodders Am. Republican. Presbyn. Clubs: Racquet and Tennis (N.Y.C.); Yale (N.Y.); Naples (Fla.) Yacht. Author: Come Out Fighting, 1946; The Story of Baseball, 1947; The Dodgers, 1948; The Yankees, 1949; Predictions, 1956; (with Otto Bettman) Pictorial History of American Sports, 1952; (with Alice R. Durant) Pictorial History of American Ships, 1953; Pictorial History of American Presidents, 1955; Pictorial History of the American Circus, 1957; The Heavyweight Champions, 1960; Highlights of the Olympics, 1961; Highlights of the World Series, 1963; The Sports of Our Presidents, 1964; (with Les Etter) Highlights of College Football, 1970. Editor: Yesterday in Sports, 1956. Home: 1851 Gulf Shore Blvd N Naples FL 33940

DURANT, PAUL DILLINGHAM, II, ins. co. exec.; b. Ann Arbor, Mich., Feb. 20, 1931; s. Wentworth Tenney and Katherine (Henning) D.; B.B.A., N. Tex. State U., 1958; m. Carolyn Peterson, June 2, 1967; children— (by former marriage) Marie Nicole, Paul D. III. Staff accountant Peat, Marwick, Mitchell & Co., Dallas, 1958-59; comptroller Steere Tank Lines, Inc., Dallas, 1959-64; accountant Paul D. Durant, C.P.A., Dallas, 1964-65; v.p., controller, asst. treas. Gt. Commonwealth Life Ins. Co., Dallas, 1965-68; pres., dir. Investers Found. Life Ins. Co., Dallas, 1969; cons. Finance and Acquisitions, Dallas, 1968-69; exec. v.p., treas., dir., co-founder Am. Bus. & Comml. Life Ins. Co., Dallas, 1969—. Served with Signal Corps, AUS, 1951-53. Mem. Am. Inst. C.P.A.'s, Am. Accounting Assn., Tex. Soc. C.P.A.'s. Methodist. Club: Lancers. Home: 6905 Kingsbury Dr Dallas TX 75231 Office: Praetorian Bldg Dallas TX 75201

DURANT, WENTWORTH T(ENNEY), lawyer; b. Milw., Sept. 27, 1907; s. Paul Dillingham and Frances Josephine (Linck) D.; A.B., U. Mich., 1930, LL.B., 1932; postgrad. So. Meth. U., 1950-51; m. Katherine Louise Henning, Feb. 8, 1926 (dec. 1971); children—Paul II, Patricia, Wentworth, Frederick. Admitted to Mich., Wis. bars, 1933, D.C. bar, 1944, Tex. bar, 1949; practiced in Milw., 1933-43; with law office Robert Ash, Washington, 1944-48; partner Durant, Mankoff, Davis & Wolens, and predecessor firms, practice restricted to tax law field, Dallas; lectr. fed. taxation N.Y. Inst., 1948, Am. U., 1948, Southwestern Legal Found., First Ann. Inst. Fed. Taxation, 1949, So. Meth. U. Law Sch., 1952, Tex. Technol. Tax Inst., 1962. Mem. Am. (mem. tax ct. procedure sect. taxation 1948-70), Dallas bar assns., State Bar Tex. Mason. Contbr.: Handbook of Tax Techniques, 1951; also legal mags. Home: 10808 Pagewood St Dallas TX 75230 Office: 1st Nat Bank Bldg Dallas TX 75202

DURBIN, GILBERT JOSEPH, sugar league exec.; b. Gilliam, La., Jan. 6, 1914; s. Marshall Charles and Janie D. (Graham) D.; B.S. in Agr., La. State U., 1935, M.S. in Agrl. Econs., 1951; m. Rachel Wallice O'Quin, Dec. 18, 1938; children—Elaine Marie (Mrs. Edward Charles Abell, Jr.), Doris Wallice (Mrs. John Gregory Heard). Various adminstrv. positions U.S. Dept. Agr., La., 1935-40, state adminstrv. officer farm programs in La., 1941, 42, 44, in-charge cotton marketing quotas So. states, Washington, 1943, dist. fieldman farm programs in La., 1949, state exec. officer farm programs in La., 1950, 51; partner, mgr. Smith and Durbin Feed and Seed Stores, Monroe La., 1945-46; asso. agronomist La. State U. Agrl. Extension Service, Baton Rouge, 1947, asso. editor, 1948; v.p., gen. mgr. Am. Sugar Cane League U.S.A., New Orleans, 1952—. Mem. Western La. Producers Assn. (sec., treas. 1952—), S. La. Agrl. Improvement Assn. (sec., treas. 1963—), Am., Internat. socs. sugar cane technologists, So. Farm Forum (chmn. 1962, 63), La. State U. Found., New Orleans C. of C. (chmn. agrl. com. 1961, 62), Phi Kappa Phi, Alpha Zeta. Democrat. Presbyn. Club: Timberlane Country (Gretna, La.). Home: 6303 General Meyer New Orleans LA 70114 Office: Am Sugar Cane League USA Whitney Bldg New Orleans LA 70130

DUREK, THOMAS ANDREW, computer exec.; b. Sharpsville, Pa., July 1, 1929; s. Joseph A. and Helen B. (Ondish) D.; B.A., Pa. State U., 1953; M.A., Baylor U., 1957; M.S., Stanford, 1959. Commd. officer USAF, 1953-65; assigned as mathematician, mgmt. sci. analyst at Hdqrs. USAF, 1959-65; head data processing and analysis space and information systems div., Project Cloud Gap, N.Am. Aviation, 1965-68; sr. staff engr. software and information systems div. TRW, Inc., Washington, 1968—; asst. prof., lectr. statistics George Washington U., 1961-66. Mem. Am. Statis. Assn., Assn. Computing Machinery, Inst. Mgmt. Scis. (treas. D.C. chpt. 1969-70, treas. internat. meeting 1971), Washington Operations Research Council. Home: 2510 Virginia Av NW Washington DC 20037 Office: Westgate Research Park McLean VA 22101

DURFEE, JAMES RANDALL, judge; b. Oshkosh, Wis., Nov. 3, 1897; s. Thomas H. and Mary (Rossiter) D.; student Huron (S.D.) Coll., 1917, 20; LL.B., Marquette U., 1926; m. Mona Burns, July 17, 1933; children— Mary (Mrs. David Clarke), James Randall, John. Admitted to Wis. bar, 1926, practiced in Antigo, 1927-51; dist. atty. Langlade County, Wis., 1928-32; court commr. 10th Jud. Circuit, 1934-50; commr. Pub. Service Commn. Wis., 1951-53, chmn., 1953-56; chmn. CAB, Washington, 1956-60; judge U.S. Court of Claims, 1960—. Served with U.S. Army, 1917-19; maj. Wis. State Guard, 1941-45. Mem. Am., Wis., Dane County bar assns., Am. Legion, Delta Theta Phi. Home: 4 Carvel Circle Westmoreland Hills MD Office: US Ct Claims Bldg 1325 K St NW Washington DC 20005

DURHAM, HENRY CURTIS, JR., educator; b. San Diego, July 18, 1924; s. Henry Curtis and Agnes (Heisler) D.; B.A., San Diego State Coll., 1953; M.A., U. Munich (Germany), 1955, Ph.D. cum laude, 1959; postgrad. U. Md., 1960-61; m. Miriam Louise Hyman, Apr. 1, 1968; 1 son (by previous marriage), Mark Wolfgang. Mem. staff War Dept., 1946-48; lectr. econs. U. Md., 1962-63; asst. prof. econs., U.S.

Naval Acad., 1963-66, 67-68; asst. prof. econs. U.S. Naval Postgrad. Sch., 1966-67; asso. prof., head dept. econs. Ga. So. Coll., Statesboro, 1968-71; asso. prof. econs. Jacksonville (Ala.) State U., 1971—. Cons. majors program in econs. Monterey (Cal.) Inst. Fgn. Studies, 1966-67; Instr., evening coll. Johns Hopkins U., Balt., 1967-68. Served with AUS, 1943-46. Decorated Purple Heart. Mem. Am. Econ. Assn., Indsl. Relations Assn., List Gesellschaft, Omicron Delta Epsilon, Delta Phi Alpha. Author: Die Auswirkungen des Collective Barg auf die Situation des aelteren Arbeitnehmers in den USA, 1958; (with Y.P. Chau) Land Distribution in Densely Populated Developing Countries, 1968. Home: 806 3d Av Jacksonville AL 36265

DURHAM, HUGH NELSON, univ. basketball coach; b. Louisville, Oct. 26, 1937; s. Samuel Hayes and Mary S. (Sparrow) D.; B.S. in Bus. Adminstrn., Fla. State U., 1959, M.S., 1961; m. Malinda Jane Dixon, June 1, 1959; children—David, Douglas, James. Asst. basketball coach Fla. State U., Tallahassee, 1960-66, head basketball coach, 1966—. Home: 914 Ivanhoe St Tallahassee FL 32303

DURHAM, JOSEPH THOMAS, ednl. adminstr.; b. Raleigh, N.C., Nov. 26, 1923; A.B., Morgan State Coll., 1948; Ed.M., Temple U., 1949; Ed.D., Columbia, 1962. Instr. edn., dean Coll. Edn., Va. Sem. and Coll., 1949-51; acting dir. student teaching Morgan State Coll., 1951-56; core tchr. English and social studies New Lincoln Sch., N.Y.C., 1956-58; asso. prof. edn. So. U., 1958-60; prof. Coppin State Coll., 1960-63, prof. edn. and dean, 1965-68; prof. Albany State Coll., 1963-65; prof. edn., asso. dean Coll. Edn., Ill. State U., 1968-71; dean Sch. Edn., Howard U., Washington, 1971—; sr. cons. Research Corp. Am., 1968—. Mem. Am. Assn. Supervision and Curriculum Devel., Alpha Phi Alpha, Phi Delta Kappa. Co-author chpt. in Readings on the Culturally Disadvantaged, 1969; author: Compensatory Education—Who Needs It. 1969. Office: Howard Univ 2401 6th St NW Washington DC 20001

DURHAM, JOSEPH WILLIAM, sportsman, banker; b. Hinton, Okla., July 24, 1922; s. Obie E. and Maude B. (Lee) D.; student U. Tours summers, 1936, 37, 38. Okla. U., 1938-39, Phillips U., Enid, Okla., 1957. With State Guaranty Bank, Okeene, Okla., 1939—, cashier, 1948—, now v.p., dir.; relations, publicity mgr. Rattlesnake Roundup, 1949-55, Rattlesnake Enduro Motorcycle Cross Country Race, 1955-56, also promotor of air shows, wheat festivals; news photographer and reporter Enid Morning News, Okla. Daily Oklahoman, 1952-71; operator farm, Okeene, 1950—; profl. outboard boat racer, 1948—; vice chmn. Barefoot Park Pow Wow; publicity dir. Arapahoe Pow Wow, vice chmn., 1972; Midwest rep. Northwest Flyer; photography staff Antique Airplane News. Official photographer National Air Shows N.W. Okla. Sportsman Club. Housing commr. Cheyenne Arapaho Tribes. Vice pres. Blaine County Anti Thief Assn., 1966-71; mem. Okeene Aviation Council. Lt. 66th Fighter Squadron, RAF; nominated brig. gen. Confederate States Air Force. Recipient Key Man award Okla. Jr. C. of C., 1953; named Nat. Champ, Rattlesnake Roundup, 1959, 2d place award, 1958; internat. service award plaque Exptl. Aircraft Assn., 1963; service award plaque Fairview Flight Club, 1966. Mem. Air Force Assn., Blaine County Hist. Soc. (founder, dir., v.p.), Nat. Flying Farmers, Antique Airplane Assn. (publicity and news dir., ofcl. photographer 1966), Experimental Aircraft Assn., Path Guild, Aircraft Owners and Pilots Assn., Nat. Aero. Assn. Okeene Jr. C. of C. (charter), Aviation Space Writers Assn., Flying Bankers, Assn., Am. Motorcycle Assn., Tau Omega (1st place award U. Okla. chpt. 1959). Democrat. Clubs: Internat. Press (Tokyo); Fairview Flying (Okla.) (treas., dir.); Dragon Motorcycle (award for promotions in club 1956) (Enid); Oklahoma Boat Race (Sportsman of Year award 1958) (Tulsa); Roman Nose Flying (Watonga, Okla.); OX5; Aerobatic of Am.; Prospectors. Author: My Cargo Rattled, 1956, Handfull of Hell, 1956. Photojournalist, contbr. aviation mags. Dual trophy donor Nat. Fly-In Conv., Exptl. Aircraft Assn., 1961-67, Nat. Antique Airplane Assn. Conv., 1960-67. Home: 402 S 5th St Okeene OK 73763 Office: 202 N Main St Okeene OK 73763

DURHAM, NORMAN NEVILL, scientist, educator; b. Ranger, Tex., Feb. 14, 1927; s. Harold H. and Bernice (Griffith) D.; B.S., N. Tex. State U., 1949, M.S., 1951; Ph.D., U. Tex., 1954; m. Jane Harriet Stovall, July 26, 1952; children—Susan Lynne, Janet Anne, Diane Elizabeth, Linda Jane. Student instr., research asst. N. Tex. State U., Denton, 1947-51; research asso., teaching asst. U. Tex., 1951-54; faculty dept. microbiology Okla. State U., Stillwater, 1954-66, prof., 1961-66, dean Grad. Coll., prof. microbiology, 1967—. Cons. biol. scis. communication project NASA, 1963—; vis. lectr. U. Okla. Sch. Medicine, 1963, Kan. State Tchrs. Coll., 1963, 65; program dir. molecular biology and cellular genetics U.S. AEC, 1966-67. Evaluation team Nat. Council Accreditation Tchr. Edn., 1968; mem. evaluation panel sci. faculty fellowships NSF, 1968; mem. adv. council manpower planning U.S. Office Edn. Served with USNR, 1944-45. Recipient Coll. Arts and Scis. award, 1963; Distinguished Alumni citation N. Tex. State U., 1970. Fellow Am. Acad. Microbiology, Okla. Acad. Sci.; mem. Am. Soc. Microbiology (councilor 1961-65), Biochem. Soc., Soc. Gen. Microbiology, A.A.A.S., Am. Assn. U. Profs., Sigma Xi (chpt. pres. 1960-61), Pi Kappa Alpha, Phi Delta Kappa, Beta Beta Beta, Phi Kappa Phi. Presbyn. (elder). Elk, Kiwanian (v.p. 1966-67). Contbr. articles to profl. publs. Home: 3005 N Monroe St Stillwater OK 74074

DURHAM, RICHARD, Democratic nat. committeeman. Chmn. Dem. Nat. Com. from P.R. Address: Banco de Ponce Bldg Ponce de Leon Av Santurce PR 00907*

DURICK, JOSEPH ALOYSIUS, bishop; b. Dayton, Tenn., Oct. 13, 1914; s. Stephen and Bridget (Gallagher) D.; student St. Bernard Coll., Cullman, Ala., 1930-33; B.A., St. Mary's Sem., Balt., 1936; B.Th., Urban Coll. Propagation of Faith, Rome, Italy, 1940. Ordained priest Roman Catholic Ch., 1940, domestic prelate, 1952—, aux. bishop, 1955—; chaplain St. Mary's Summer Camp for Children, Batties Wharf, Ala., 1940; asst. to Rev. Frank Giri, Birmingham, later priest St. John's Ch., Birmingham; dir. North Ala. Missions, 1940-57; pastor St. Margaret's Ch., Birmingham, 1949-57, St. Francis Xavier Ch., Mountain Brook, Birmingham, 1957-64; aux. bishop Mobile-Birmingham, 1955-62, became vicar gen. Mobile-Birmingham, 1962; coadjutor bishop Diocese of Nashville, 1964-65, vicar gen., 1965-66, apostolic adminstr., 1966—, now bishop of Nashville. Founder, dir. Catholic Information Center, Birmingham; dir. Nocturnal Adoration Movement, Birmingham Holy Name Soc.; asst. diocesan dir. Confraternity of Christian Doctrine; diocesan dir. Priests Eucharistic League, 1954—. Mem. Holy Name Union, Toy Bowl Assn. K.C. (4 deg.). Club: Catholic Men's (past chaplain, trustee). Home: 4000 Brookhaven Dr Nashville TN 37204 Office: 421 Charlotte Av Nashville TN 37219

DURIG, JAMES ROBERT, educator; b. Washington County, Pa., Apr. 30, 1935; B.A., Washington and Jefferson Coll., 1958; Ph.D. in Phys. Chemistry (Woodrow Wilson fellow 1958-59, Union Carbide Corp. fellow 1960-61), Mass. Inst. Tech., 1962. Asso. prof. chemistry U. S.C., 1962—. Served with Chem. Corps, AUS, 1963-64. Mem. Am. Phys. Soc., Am. Chem. Soc. Research in infrared and Raman spectra of polyatomic molecules, especially molescules having low frequency vibrations, chemistry of palladium. Office: Dept Chemistry Univ South Carolina Columbia SC 29208*

DURKEE, WILLIAM CARL, beverage co. exec.; b. St. Louis, Mich., Oct. 2, 1921; s. Robert L. and Mary E. (Faunce) D.; m. Katherine J. Barber, Apr. 3, 1943; children—Susan, Stephen, William Carl. In soft drink bus., 1939-63; with Pepsi-Cola Co., 1950-63, v.p., mgr. Central div., Chgo., 1955-58, v.p. marketing, N.Y.C., 1958-61, sr. v.p. marketing 1961-63; pres. Rival Pet Foods, Chgo., 1963-66; exec. v.p., dir. Royal Crown Cola Co., Columbus, Ga., 1966-69, pres. chief exec. officer, 1969—, also dir.; dir. 1st Bank. Served to capt. AUS, 1942-46. Home: 2221 Hilton Av Columbus GA 31906 Office: Royal Crown Cola Co 1000 10th Av PO Box 1440 Columbus GA 31902

DURKIN, MARY LUCILE, librarian; b. Battle Creek, Mich.; d. James Henry and Ella M. (McQuillen) Durkin; B.S., Simmons Coll., 1936; B.A., U. Tenn., 1944; M.A., Columbia, 1955; Advanced Master in L.S., U. Mich., 1972. Librarian, Chattanooga Sch. System, 1938-41; dist. supr. U.S. Govt. Program, Chattanooga, 1941-42; supr. city sch. library and Negro brs., Chattanooga, 1942-44; dir. field clubs A.R.C., Eng., Scotland, Germany, 1944-45; dir. USIS Libraries, Egypt, Morocco, Greece, 1948-58; librarian U.S. Army Aviation Sch., Ft. Rucker, Ala., 1959—. Home: 207 Westview Dr Enterprise AL 36330 Office: Bldg 5907 Fort Rucker AL 36360

DURRENBERGER, JOHN ANTHONY, sci. adminstr.; b. Perham, Minn., Aug. 22, 1920; s. John George and Angela (Wiebeler) D.; student St. John's U., 1938-39; B.Aero. Engring., U. Minn., 1942; postgrad. U. Miami, 1945—; m. Erlene Bailey, June 19, 1946; children—Diane (Mrs. Richard Levy), Thomas Edward, Alan Anthony. Design engr. Douglas Aircraft Co., 1941; sr. liaison engr. Glenn L. Martin Co., 1946-47; aero. engr. Naval Air Sta., Pensacola, Fla., 1947-49; test engr. Air Proving Ground Command, Fla., 1949-58; supervisory operations analyst USAF Air Def. Command, Colo., 1958-61; chief scientist USAF Tactical Air Warfare Center, Elgin AFB, Fla., 1964-67; dep. dir. operations analysis U.S. Air Forces in Europe, 1961-64, dir. operations analysis, 1967-72; chief Scientist USAF Tactical Air Warfare Center, Elgin AFB, Fla., 1972—. Pres. Civilian Welfare Council, Elgin AFB, Fla., 1955-56. Served to Comdr. USNR, 1942-46. Recipient citation Pres. Johnson, 1965; Sec. of Air Force Decoration for exceptional civilian service, 1965. Mem. Am. Ordnance Assn. (Fla. post v.p. 1965-67), Mil. Operations Research Soc. (bd. dirs.), Operations Research Soc. Am. Address: USAF Tactical Air Warfare Center PSC Box 3489 Elgin AFB FL 32542

DURYEA, LYMAN CHANDLER, physician; b. Boston, Jan. 10, 1898; s. Lyman C. and Alice E. (Adelstein) D.; M.D., U. Vt., 1931; M.P.H., Johns Hopkins, 1939; m. Myrtle Holland Ryder, Sept. 6, 1924; children—Arthur Warren (dec.), Lyman Chandler. Intern Da Gresbriand Hosp., Burlington, Vt., 1933-34; resident Bklyn. State Hosp.; practice gen. medicine, Ewa Plantation, Oahu, Hawaii, 1931, Sheldon Springs, Vt., 1935, Lyndonville, Vt., 1939; asso. dir. div. med. care N.Y. State Temporary Emergency Relief Adminstrn., 1935-38; dir. div. physically handicapped Dept. Health, N.Y.C., 1938-41; mem. com. for study care and edn. physically handicapped children pub. schs., N.Y.C., 1938-41; dist. health officer N.M. State Dept. Health, 1958-63; dep. dir. N.M. Dept. Pub. Health, from 1963—; mem. staff Sunland Hosp., Orlando, Fla., 1964-70; ret., 1970. Lectr. part-time Columbia, Fordham U. Bd. dirs. Cerebral Palsy Assn., Inc. Served to col. M.C., AUS, 1941-58. Decorated Army Commendation Ribbon, Legion of Merit. Rockefeller Found. fellow, 1939. Fellow Am. Pub. Health Assn., Am. Sch. Health Assn.; mem. Retired Officers Assn., Assn. U. S. Army, N.Y. State, N.M., West End med. socs., Fed. Hosp. Inst. Alumni Assn., Advt. Execs. Club. Contbr. articles to profl. jours. Home: 2727 Amsden Rd Winter Park FL 32789

DUSCHA, JULIUS CARL, journalist; b. St. Paul, Nov. 4, 1924; s. Julius William and Anna (Perlowski) D.; student U. Minn., 1943-47; A.B., Am. U., 1951; postgrad. (Nieman fellow), Harvard, 1955-56; m. Priscilla Ann McBride, Aug. 17, 1946; children—Fred C., Steve D., Suzanne, Sally Jean. Reporter, St. Paul Pioneer Press, 1943-47; publicist Democratic Nat. Com., 1948, 52; writer Labor's League Polit. Edn., AFL, 1949-52, Internat. Assn. Machinists, 1952-53; editorial writer Lindsay-Schaub Newspapers, Ill., 1954-58; nat. affairs reporter Washington Post, 1958; now news corr. A.P. Recipient award for distinguished Washington corr. Sigma Delta Chi, 1961. Mem. Kappa Sigma. Club: National Press (Washington). Author: Taxpayers' Hayride; The Farm Problem From the New Deal to the Billie Sol Estes Case, 1964. Contbr. articles to mags. including Harpers, Reporter, New Republic. Office: 1404 Crestwood Dr Alexandria VA 22302

DUSON, CURLEY PHARR, investment banker; b. El Campo, Tex., May 24, 1921; s. Curley Pharr and Clarice (Koch) D.; B.B.A., U. Tex., 1942; m. Betty Jo Tomforde, Mar. 18, 1944; children—Betty M., Molly C., Stephen P. With Rotan, Mosle & Co., Houston, 1947-65, partner, 1953-65; pres., dir., mem. exec. com. Rotan, Mosle-Dallas Union, Inc., Houston, 1966—; dir. Western Nat. Bank, Houston, Fairmont Foods Co., Omaha. Bd. dirs. Family Service Bur., Houston, 1957-60, Harris County Mental Health Assn., 1963—. Served to capt. AUS, 1942-46. Mem. Nat. Assn. Securities Dealers (gov. 1964-66), Investment Bankers Assn. (chmn. Tex. 1967), Kappa Sigma. Republican. Presbyn. (ruling elder). Home: 61 Briar Hollow Lane Houston TX 77027 Office: Bank of Southwest Bldg Houston TX 77002

DUTRIZ, RICARDO, El Salvadorian diplomat. Consul gen. of El Salvador, Miami, Fla. Active mem., vice dean Consular Corps. Adv. mem. Bd. Internat. Trade Greater Miami, Inc. Rotarian. Home: 3126 Le Jeune Rd Coral Gables FL 33134 Office: Suite 208 150 SE 3d Av Miami FL 33131

DUTTON, BENSON LEROY, civil engr.; b. Phila., Jan. 7, 1910; s. Bert Leroy and Beatrice (Thomas) D.; B.S., Pa. State U., 1933, C.E., 1949; postgrad. Lehigh U., summer 1955, U. Pa., 1956-57; m. Josephine Olivia Brown, June 24, 1939; children—Marie Elizabeth, Benson Leroy, Michael Eric. Chief-of-party Bur. Engring., 1933-34; constrn. engr. F. Massiah, contractor, Phila., 1935-36; project engr. Nat. Park Service, U.S. Dept. Interior, 1937-40; asst. prof., cons. engr. Hampton Inst., Va., 1940-47; dean engring. Tenn. State U., Nashville, 1947-56; chief design engr. bridges City of Phila., 1956-65; mgmt. engr. U.S. Office Edn., Dept. Health, Edn. and Welfare, Washington, 1965-67, chief constrn. service operations, 1967-70, dir. Office Federally Assisted Constrn., 1970—. Asst. dir. radiol. def. Civil Def., Nashville, 1953-56. Pres., bd. dirs. Mt. Airy/Rittenhouse YMCA; bd. dirs. N.Phila. Area Health and Welfare Council, W.Mt. Airy Neighbors; trustee Germantown YMCA, Phila.; chmn. bd. mgrs. Mt. Airy YMCA, Phila. Recipient prize for welded structures Lincoln Found., 1966; Distinguished Alumnus award Pa. State U., 1971. Registered profl. engr., D.C., Pa., Tenn., Va. Fellow Am. Soc. C.E.; mem. Am. Pub. Works Assn., Assn. Sch. Bus. Ofcls. Planner sch. engring. Tenn. State U., 1949; designer Spring Garden St. bridges over Schuylkill River, Phila.; improvements Art Mus. Complex, 1963-65. Home: Town Sq Towers 700 7th St SW Washington DC 20024 Office: 400 Maryland Av Washington DC 20202

DUVAL, CHARLES NATHAN, electronic engr.; b. Norfolk, Va., Oct. 3, 1926; s. Nathan Henry and Bessie (Holloman) DuV.; student Coll. William and Mary, 1947-48, Old Dominion Coll., 1962-63, U.S. Army and Gen. Staff Coll., 1970. Chief radio officer U.S. Mcht. Marine, 1943-46; TV transmitter supr. WTAR Radio TV Corp., Norfolk, 1949—; pres. Framidouk Co., Inc., Virginia Beach, Va., 1964—; instr. Tech. Inst. Old Dominion Coll., 1963-65. Maj. Signal Corps, AUS Res., 1949—. Mem. I.E.E.E., Va. Beach C. of C. Clubs: Capes Beach and Cabana, Cavalier Beach and Cabanna. Home: 1437 Laurel View Dr Virginia Beach VA 23451 Office: 720 Boush St Norfolk VA 23510

DUVAL, CLAUDE BERWICK, lawyer; b. Houma, La., Oct. 24, 1914; s. Stanwood and Mamie (Richardson) D.; student La. State U., 1931-32; LL.B., Tulane U., 1937; m. Betty Bowman, Apr. 6, 1938; 1 dau., Dorothy. Admitted to La. bar, 1937 practiced in Houma, La., 1937—; mem. law firm Duval, Arceneaux & Lewis. Dir. Pelican Lake Oyster & Packing Co., Ltd., Duval-Whitney-Stevenson, Inc, Citizens Nat. Bank of Houma. Mem. La. Senate, 1967—. Mem. com. A.R.C., 1947-48; chmn. 3d Congl. dist. Area Cancer Drive, 1949-50; mem. devel. council, Tulane U., 1958; mem. bd. trustees Pub. Affairs Research Council; bd. dirs. Council for Better La.; state chmn. Radio Free Europe, 1968. Campaign mgr. deLesseps S. Morrison, Democratic candidate for gov. La., 1959; candidate for lt. gov. La., 1963. Served from 2d lt. to capt. USMCR, 1941-46; PTO. Decorated Bronze Star, Purple Heart. Letter of Commendation, Presdl. Unit Citation; recipient award as Outstanding Young Man of Year, Houma Jr. C. of C., 1947. Mem. Am., La. (mem. house of dels. 1957-60, mem. law reform com.) bar assns., Am. Legion (La. comdr. 1950; mem. nat. exec. com. 1952-54), La. State (pres. 1961-62), Houma (pres. 1959) chambers of commerce, Young Mens' Bus. Clubs of La. (state pres. 1948). Democrat. Episcopalian. Mason (Shriner), Elk. Clubs: Rotary (pres. 1958), Houma Exchange (pres. 1940). Home: 18 Country Club Dr Houma LA 70360 Office: 504 Belanger St Houma LA 70360

DUVAL, MERLIN K., JR., govt. ofcl.; b. Montclair, N.J., Oct. 12, 1922; s. Merlin Kearfott and Margaret (Smith) D.; A.B., Dartmouth, 1943; M.D., Cornell U., 1946; m. Carol Nickerson, June 21, 1944; children— David K., Barbara L., Frederick P. Intern N.Y. Hosp., N.Y.U., 1946-47, Roosevelt Hosp., N.Y.C., 1949-50; resident surgery VA Hosp., Bronx. N.Y., 1951-54; instr., then asst. prof. surgery State U. N.Y. Coll. Medicine, 1954-56; asst prof., then prof. surgery U. Okla. Med. Center, 1956-63; dean Coll. Medicine U. Ariz., 1964-70; apptd. asst. sec. for health and sci. affairs Dept. Health, Edn. and Welfare, 1971; cons. VA, USPHS. Served with USNR, 1943-45, 47-49. Home: 10 CalleEncanto Tucson AZ 85716

DUVAL, MILES P., JR., retired naval officer; b. Portsmouth Va., Apr. 19, 1896; s. Miles P. and Minnie Lee (Chalkley) DuV.; B.S., U.S. Naval Acad., 1918, student U.S. Naval War Coll., 1925-26; U.S. Naval Post Grad. Sch., 1930-31; M.F.S., Fgn. Service Sch., Georgetown U., 1937; unmarried Commd. ensign, 1918, and advanced to capt., 1945; served as comdg. officer, U.S.S. Dupont, 1933-35, participated in naval demonstration off Cuban ports, 1933-34; sec. Shore Sta. Development Bd., Navy Dept., Washington, D.C., 1936-38; comdg. officer U.S.S. Antares, 1939-40; capt. of port, Balboa, C.Z., in charge marine operations of Pacific subdiv. of Panama Canal, 1941-44; planned and coordinated enlargement of Balboa Harbor, 1942-43; developed high level terminal lake plan for improvement of Panama Canal, 1943; comdg. officer U.S.S. Dade, 1944-46, participated in Okinawa campaign, 1945; designated as Navy Dept. liaison officer and coordinator for modernizing studies of Panama Canal by Sec. of Navy, 1946; ret. active service, 1949. Decorated Legion of Merit (Army), 1945, World War I Victory medal with Atlantic and Grand Fleet clasps, 1918, Am. Defense with Fleet and Base clasps, 1939-41, Am. campaign, 1941-44, Asiatic-Pacific campaign with bronze star, 1945. Mem. bd. Gorgas Meml. Inst. Tropical and Preventive Medicine. Fellow A.A.A.S.; mem. Va. Hist. Soc., Naval Hist. Found., Soc. of Va. in Washington (past v.p.), Permanent Internat. Assn. Nav. Congresses (life), U.S. Naval Inst., Soc. Am. Mil. Engrs., Panama Hist. Soc. (corr. mem.), Panama Canal Soc. of Washington (pres.), Phi Alpha Theta, Panama Canal Natural History Soc. (past v.p.). Clubs: Explorers; Propeller of U.S., Cosmos, Army and Navy (Washington); Yacht (N.Y.C.). Author: Series on Panama Canal: Cadiz to Cathay, 1940; And the Mountains Will Move, 1947; Matthew Fontaine Maury: Benefactor of Man Kind, 1964; Sam Houston: The Washington of the Vast Southwest, 1966; George Rogers Clark: Conqueror of the Old Northwest, 1970; also papers on interoceanic canal problems. Home: 5120 King William Rd Richmond VA 23225

DUVALL, CHARLES DOUGLAS, city ofcl.; b. nr. Frankfort, Ky., July 18, 1924; s. Woodson Bryan and Ivy (Armstrong) D.; grad. high sch.; m. Pauline Bryant, July 12, 1952; children—Michael Douglas, Marjorie Kay, Rebecca Lynn, Clayton Stephen. With Frankfort Fire Dept., 1958—, fire chief, 1968—. Instr. radiol. monitoring, State Ky., 1959—. Served with USN, 1945-46, 50-51. Mem. Internat. Assn. Fire Chiefs, Southeastern Fire Chiefs Assn., Internat. Assn. Arson Investigators (state dir. 1970-72), V.F.W., Central Ky. Firemen's Assn. (pres. 1971-72), Ky. State Firemen's Assn. (v.p. 1971-72). Elk. Home: 330 Westland Dr Frankfort KY 40601 Office: Fire Dept Frankfort KY 40601

DUVALL, EDWARD, JR., banker; b. Washington, Aug. 7, 1912; s. Edward Smith and Marie (Palmer) D.; LL.B., Columbus U., 1936; post-grad. Stonier Grad. Sch. Banking, Rutgers U., 1949-51; m. Elizabeth Daniels Oct. 29, 1938; children—Robert E., Daniel Parker. With Riggs Nat. Bank, Washington, 1933—, sr. v.p., 1970—; dir., mem. exec. com. Dist. Realty Title Ins. Co., Washington. Bd. dirs. Washington Soc. for the Blind, 1957-72, pres., 1965. Served to lt. comdr. USNR, 1942-46. Clubs: Metropolitan, Congressional Country (Washington); Farmington Country (Charlottesville, Va.). Home: 2809 N Underwood St Arlington VA 22213 Office: 1503 Pennsylvania Av NW Washington DC 20005

DUVALL, RICHARD ALBERT, indsl. cons., state ofcl.; b. Benton, Ark., Nov. 12, 1905; s. Elisha H. and Ida (Jaco's) DuV.; student Ark. Poly. Coll., 1929; B.S., U. Ark., 1932; m. Miriam Stauffer, May 31, 1938; children—Elizabeth Ann (Mrs. Frank Gomez, Jr.), Mary Catherine (Mrs. Norbert Kordsmeier), Richard Kenneth. Analyst, Fed. Land Bank, St. Louis, 1933-38; div. credit and call mgr. John Deere Plow Co., St. Louis, 1938-42; indsl. specialist WPB, 1942-45, U.S. Dept. Commerce, NPA, Civilian Prodn. Adminstrn., 1945-51; indsl. cons. resources and devel., Little Rock, 1953-55; indsl. cons. Ark. Indsl. Devel. Commn., Little Rock, 1955-63, acting exec. dir., 1963-64, asst. exec. dir., 1964—. State chmn. prodn. task group, Office Emergency Planning Exec. office President U.S. Adv. council S.W. Tech. Inst. Recipient certificate of service WPB, 1945. Mem. Am. Inst. Indsl. Engrs., Am. Soc. Appraisers (past pres. Ark.; past nat. treas.), So. Indsl. Devel. Council, Kappa Alpha. Home: Pamela Dr Little Rock AR 72207 Office: State Capitol Bldg Little Rock AR 72203

DUVALL, RICHARD MAREEN, JR., mfg. co. exec.; b. Richmond, Va., Oct. 1, 1930; s. Richard Mareen and Azele Pogue (Mehl) D.; student Randolph-Macon Coll., 1949-50; B.S., Va. Poly. Inst., 1958; m. Shirley Christine Jones, Sept. 22, 1951; children—Edward Mehl, Julie Lynne, Richard Mareen III. With Albemarle Paper Mfg. Co., Richmond, 1959-67, maintenance supt., 1964-66, asst. paper mill supt., 1966-67; chief engr., asst. to pres. Georgia Bonded Fibers, Inc., Buena Vista, Va., 1967-71, v.p. operations, 1971—; dir. Bontex S.A.,

Stembert, Belgium. Pres. Va. Heights Civic Assn., Henrico County, 1960. Served with USAF, 1951-54. Mem. Paper Industry Mgmt. Assn., Blue Ridge Safety Assn. (bd. dirs., 1970—). Methodist. Kiwanian. Home: 605 Ross Rd Lexington VA 24450 Office: PO Box 751 Buena Vista VA 24416

DUVALL, WILLIAM CLYDE, JR., ednl. adminstr.; b. Farmville, Va., Feb. 4, 1917; s. William Clyde and Harriet King (Bugg) D.; student Hampden-Sydney Coll., 1934-36, Washington Mus. Inst., 1936-38, U. Va., 1951, Coll. William and Mary, 1962-63, Old Dominion U., 1946; m. Ruth Elizabeth Jones, Sept. 30, 1939; children—William Clyde III, George Drummond, Charles Montgomery, Elizabeth Leigh, Thomas King. Tchr. band pub. schs. Charlotte County (Va.), 1939-43, Norfolk County (Va.), 1945-51; dir. music Norfolk County Schs., 1951-55, dir. music and teaching materials, 1955-63; dir. music and teaching materials Chesapeake (Va.) Pub. Schs., 1963—. Band clinician, music festival adjudicator. Pres., Chesapeake Friends of Music, 1967-68. Bd. dirs. Young Audiences, Inc., Norfolk, 1970—. Served with USNR, 1943-45. Mem. Va. Band and Orch. Assn. (pres. 1953-54), Pi Kappa Alpha. Democrat. Episcopalian. Author: High School Band Director's Handbook, 1960. Home: 4714 River Shore Rd Portsmouth VA 23703 Office: 300 Cedar Rd Chesapeake VA 23320

DWIGGINS, CLAUDIUS WILLIAM, JR., chemist; b. Amity, Ark., May 11, 1933; s. Claudius William and Lillian (Scott) D.; B.S., U. Ark., 1954, M.S., 1956, Ph.D. (Am. Oil Co. fellow, Coulter-Jones scholar), 1958. With U.S. Dept. Interior Bur. Mines, Bartlesville (Okla.) Research Center, 1958—, chemist, 1958-60, project leader surface physics project, 1960-65, project leader petroleum composition research project, 1965—. Mem. Am. Chem. Soc., N.Y. Acad. Scis., A.A.A.S., Sigma Xi (sec. 1966-67), Alpha Chi Sigma, Delta Sigma Phi (treas. 1952). Contbr. articles to profl. jours. Home: 1211 S Keeler St Bartlesville OK 74003 Office: US Bur Mines Petroleum Research Center Bartlesville OK 74003

DWIGHT, ROBERT ELMER, ednl. adminstr.; b. Ardmore, Okla., Aug. 2, 1923; s. Clyde O. and Lena Ruth (Gray) D.; B.S., Concord Coll., 1948; M.A., W.Va. U., 1961; m. Nancy Sue Grimm, June 12, 1946; children— Dorothy Sue (Mrs. Gary Harvey), Ruth, Robert Elmer III. Supr. tourist bur. State of Va., 1948-51; editor, Raleigh Register, Beckley, W.Va., 1951-58; prin., Samrorwood (Tex.) Sch., 1958-63, supt., 1964-71; supt. schs., Bartlett, Tex. 1971—. Active Boy Scouts Am. Mem. Collingsworth County exec. com. Democratic party, 1969-71; del. State Dem. Conv., 1970. Served to lt. USAAF, 1943-46. Recipient Silver Beaver award Boy Scouts Am., 1971; Mem. Am., Tex. assns. sch. adminstrs., N.E.A., Tex. State Tchrs. Assn. (pres. Collingsworth County 1960-61). Methodist (lay leader 1962-71). Mason (Shriner), Lion (named Best Sec. 1963). Address: Drawer 170 Bartlett TX 76511

DWYER, CORNELIUS JOHN, economist; b. New Rochelle, N.Y., Oct. 13, 1917; s. George W. and Isabel Agnes (Foley) D.; A.B., Yale, 1939; postgrad. London Sch. Econs., 1946-47; m. Mary Cecilia McDonough, Dec. 7, 1942; children—Cornelius John, Michael Richard, Rosemary Jeanne. With news wire services and radio stas., 1939-42; with State Dept. and Econ. Coop. Adminstrn., 1946-54; with Nat. Bur. Econ. Research, 1954-60; with State Dept., 1960-64; econ. cons. W.R. Grace & Co., Robert R. Nathan Assos. & others, 1964-68, Commerce Dept., 1968-69, AID State Dept., Washington, 1969—. Cons. to First Nat. City Bank, W.R. Grace & Co., M.W. Kellogg Co., McGraw-Hill, Model, Roland & Co., J.H. Whitney & Co., Depts. State, Commerce, Interior and Transp., Govts. El Salvador, Israel, Pakistan, State La. Served to capt. USAAF, 1946. Decorated 2 battle stars. Mem. Am. Econ. Assn., Nat. Press Club, Am. Inst. Mining, Metall. and Petroleum Engrs. (council econs.), Am. Fgn. Service Assn., Nat. Economists Club, Soc. Internat. Devel. Contbr. articles to profl. jours. and revs. Home: 2030 F St NW Washington DC 20006 Office: Dept State Agy Internat Devel Washington DC 20523

DWYER, DANIEL KERRIGAN, banker; b. New Iberia, La., Nov. 8, 1929; s. Rees Lawrence and Mary (Herbert) D.; student Sch. Consumer Banking, U. Va., 1965; postgrad. Am. Inst. Banking, 1967—; m. Wilma Theresa Haydell, May 14, 1955; children—Daniel Kerrigan, Bridget, Robyn, Kathy, Nancy, Keith. With United Credit Plan, Inc., Baton Rouge, 1951-55; mgr., New Orleans 1955-61; mgr. installment credit dept. Am. Bank and Trust Co., Baton Rouge, 1961-62; mgr. installment loan dept. La. Nat. Bank, Baton Rouge, 1962-67, v.p., 1967—; v.p., dir. La. Nat. Leasing Corp., Baton Rouge, 1971—. Instr. installment credit Am. Inst. Banking, 1969—; mem. by-laws com. Baton Rouge Lenders' Exchange. Bd. dirs. Family Debt Counseling Service, Baton Rouge. Served with USNR 1947-48. Mem. Consumer Bankers Assn. (bd. govs. 1969—), La. Bankers Assn. (mem. installment credit com. 1967—, mem. legislative com. 1971—), Baton Rouge C. of C. Kiwanian. Clubs: k Camelot, Sherwood Forest Country (bd. govs. 1970—) (Baton Rouge). Home: 10453 Firelight Dr Baton Rouge LA 70815 Office: 451 Florida St Baton Rouge LA 70801

DYAL, WILLIAM M., research inst. exec. Exec. dir. Inter-Am. Social Devel. Inst., Rosslyn, Va. Office: Inter-Am Social Devel Inst 1515 Wilson Blvd Rosslyn VA 22209*

DYAR, JEFFERSON FREDERICK, dentist; b. Marshall County, Ala., Mar. 28, 1923; s. Joseph Daniel and Lou (Malone) D.; student Snead Jr. Coll., 1941-42, U. Ala., 1942-43; D.D.S., U. Tenn., 1950; m. Linda Lee Shuff, Feb. 2, 1966; children—Jefferson Frederick, William A. Practice gen. dentistry, Boaz, Ala., 1950—. Served with USAAF, 1943-46. Mem. Am., Ala., 5th Dist. (v.p. 1959-60, pres. 1961-62) dental assns., N.E. Ala. Dental Study Club, Boaz C. of C., Boaz Civitan Club, Am. Legion, Delta Sigma Delta (life). Republican. Baptist. Mason. Club: Boaz Country. Home: 812 N Main St Boaz AL 35957 Office: Highland Av Boaz AL 35957

DYE, DEWEY ALBERT, JR., lawyer; b. Bradenton, Fla., June 12, 1926; s. Dewey A. and Lucy (Edmondson) D.; student Duke, 1944; B.A., U. Fla., 1948, LL.B., 1949; m. Charlotte F. Healey, Feb. 1, 1948; children— Deborah Lucy, James Dewey, Stephen Richard. Admitted to Fla. bar, 1949; practiced in Bradenton, 1949—; partner firm Dye, Dye, Cleary & Scott; atty. Manatee County, 1954-56; gen. counsel West Coast Inland Nav. Dist. of Fla. 1954—; dir. Island Bank, Holmes Beach, Fla., Manatee Nat. Bank, Bradenton. Mem. Manatee County Hist. Commn. Bd. dirs. South Fla. Mus., Eaton Found. Served with USNR, 1944-46, 51-53. Fellow Acad. Fla. Trial Lawyers (dir. 1966); mem. Fla. Waterways Assn. (pres. 1965-66), Gulf Intracoastal Canal Assn. (dir.), Am., Fla., Manatee County (past pres.) bar assns., Bradenton C. of C. (v.p.), Hernando DeSoto Hist. Soc. (past pres., dir.), Naval Res. Assn. (past chpt. pres.), Sigma Alpha Epsilon, Phi Delta Phi. Kiwanian. Home: 1303 51st St W Bradenton FL 33505 Office: 920 Manatee Av W Bradenton FL 33505

DYE, DICK (STERLING DICKEY), interior designer; b. Sherman, Tex., Mar. 29, 1922; s. Benjamin Dolpha and Sarah (Dickey) D.; student Priscilla Beach Acad. Dramatic Arts, 1941, Amarillo Coll., 1940, West Tex. State U., 1945-46 Partner, interior designer Western Bus. Supply. Amarillo, Tex., 1946-52; interior designer Gen. Office Supply, Amarillo, 1952-57, Furniture Fashions, Inc., Amarillo, 1957-63. Contract Furniture, Inc., Amarillo, 1963-64; partner, interior designer Design Gallery, Dick Dye Interiors, Amarillo, 1965—. Design cons. Northwest Tex. Hosp. Dist., 1957. Mem. steering com., judge Forensic Speech Tournament, Amarillo, 1962; chmn. decorations com. Amarillo Symphony Ball, 1959-63; active Amarillo Little Theatre, 1955-56. Served with USAAF, 1942-45. Mem. Presidents Hall of Fame, 1948-51. Mem. Am. Inst. Interior Designers (chmn. W. Tex. assn. 1965), W. Tex. Art Guild, Alpha Psi Omega (hon.). Republican. Mem. Ch. of Christ. Home: 2123 Jackson St Amarillo TX 79109 Office: 2123 Jackson St Amarillo TX 79102

DYER, BOYCE LOUIS, state ofcl.; b. Metasville, Ga., Dec. 23, 1913; s. James Thomas and Maggie (Candler) D.; student Young Harris Jr. Coll., 1931-33; B.S. in Agrl. Engring., U. Ga., 1939; m. Frankie Ruth Greene, Apr. 27, 1947; children—Vicki (Mrs. Whitie Gibbs), Beverly, Craig. Tchr. pub. schs., 1933-35; maintenance asst. Hydro Electric plant S.C. Power Co., 1935-37; asst. rural engr. Ga. Power Co., 1939-40; conservationist Soil Conservation Service, 1941-52; dairy farmer, 1952-55; dir. marketing programs Ga. Dept. Agr., Atlanta, 1955—. Served with USNR, 1943-45. Mem. Agr. Honor Soc., Nat. Assn. Marketing Ofcls., Alpha Zeta. Methodist (chmn. finance com. 1969-70). Lion (pres. 1954-55). Home: 2941 Toney Dr Decatur GA 30032 Office: Agr Bldg Capitol Sq Atlanta GA 30334

DYER, DAVID WILLIAM, circuit judge; b. Columbus, O., June 28, 1910; s. Joseph H. and Nelle (Peters) D.; student Ohio State U., 1928-32; LL.B., John B. Stetson, Coll. Law, 1933, LL.D., 1967; m. Helen Hannah, June 28, 1932; children—David William, Hannah. Admitted to Fla. bar, 1933; pvt. practice law, 1933-35; mem. firm Batchelor & Dyer, Miami, Fla., 1935-42, Smathers, Thompson & Dyer, Miami, 1945-61; U.S. Dist. judge, 1961-62; chief judge U.S. Dist. Ct., 1962-66; judge U.S. Ct. of Appeals, 5th Circuit, Miami, 1966—. Pres., Southeastern div. Children's Home Soc. Fla., 1955-57. Served to maj. Judge Adv. Gen.'s Dept., AUS, 1942-45. Recipient Distinguished Citizen award Stetson U. Coll. Law, 1961. Mem. Am. Bar Assn., Internat. Assn. Ins. Counsel (vice chmn. com. on aviation law), Sigma Chi, Phi Delta Phi. Democrat. Presbyn. Kiwanian. Home: 4920 E Sunset St Miami FL 33143 Office: 300 NE 1st Av Miami FL 33101

DYER, ELBA LORRAINE, social worker; b. Wardensville, W.Va., Apr. 19, 1906; s. Thomas A. and Mary Alice (Orndorff) Dyer; B.A., Shepherd Coll., 1933; diploma Columbia, 1939; M.Ed. in Sociology, Temple U., 1941 Med. social worker Lankenau Hosp., Phila., 1939-41; psychiat. social worker, student supr. Norristown (Pa.) State Hosp., 1941-47; med. social work cons. Ariz. Dept. Pub. Welfare, 1947-49; chief psychiat. social worker Child Guidance Clinic, Des Moines, 1949-51, Tulsa, 1951-55; chief psychiat. social worker, acting dir. Cumberland County Guidance Center, Fayetteville, N.C., 1955-61; chief psychiat. social worker, supr. students Psychiat. Clinic, Portsmouth, Va., 1961-66; psychiat. social worker aftercare program Dept. Hosps. and Mental Hygiene, Roanoke (Va.) Guidance Center, 1966—. Fellow Am. Orthopsychiat. Assn.; mem. Nat. Assn. Social Workers (pres. Montgomery County Welfare Conf. 1945-46), Mental Health Assn. Roanoke, Nat. Conf. Social Welfare, Internat. Council Social Welfare, Phi Delta Gamma. Democrat. Lutheran (deaconess 1933-41). Club: Pilot. Home: PO Box 4361 Roanoke VA 24015 Office: 1125 2st St SW Roanoke VA 24016

DYER, EVERETT DIXON, sociologist, educator; b. Bristol, Vt., Mar. 23, 1918; s. Everett Wallace and Winnefred May (Dixon) D.; B.A., U. Houston, 1941; M.A., U. Tex., 1947; Ph.D., U. Wis., 1955; m. Jacqueline Lesh, Jan. 12, 1945; 1 dau., Janette. Instr., asst. prof. sociology U. Houston, 1947-50; teaching asst. in sociology U. Wis., 1952-54; mem. faculty U. Houston, 1954—, prof. sociology, 1961—, chmn. dept. sociology and anthropology, 1961—. Dir. curriculum S.Am. Youth Leaders Program, Houston, 1961—. Dir. city bd. Neighborhood Centers Assn., Houston, 1958—. Served with AUS, 1941-45. U. Houston grantee for travel and research in Europe, 1964, summer research grants, 1966, 67. Fellow Am. Sociol. Assn.; mem. Southwestern Sociol. Assn., (v.p. 1967, pres. 1968), Nat. Council Family Relations, Am. Assn. U. Profs., Houston C. of C., Phi Kappa Phi, Alpha Kappa Delta. Mason (32 deg.). Sociology editor Southwestern Social Sci. Quar., 1962—; asso. editor Forum Mag. (U. Houston), 1965—. Home: 5026 Creekbend St Houston TX 77035

DYER, JOHN RAYMOND, newspaper editor; b. Oklahoma City, Aug. 27, 1931; s. Raymond Joseph and Helen (Campbell) D.; B.A., U. Okla., 1953; m. Patsy Jean McWhorter, Aug. 22, 1953; children—Shanon Helen, Raymond Thomas, Kelly Kathryn, Sean Edward, Patricia Ann, Erin Jane. Reporter Elk City Daily News, 1955-56; editor El Reno (Okla.) Tribune, 1956—. Served from 2d. lt. to 1st lt. AUS, 1953-55. Mem. El Reno C. of C. (pres. 1969), Okla. Assn. Press Mng. Editors (pres. 1967-68), Sigma Delta Chi (pres. 1968). Roman Catholic. Kiwanian, Elk. Club: Oklahoma City Gridiron. Home: 1607 Ridgecres Dr El Reno OK 73036 Office: 201 N Rock Island El Reno OK 73036

DYER, ROSS WATKINS, state justice; b. Halls, Tenn., Mar. 10, 1911; s. Clarence W. and Zona (Smith) D.; student U. Tenn., 1929-30, Cumberland U., 1930-31; LL.B., YMCA Law Sch., Nashville, 1937; m. Agnes Rebecca Moss, Nov. 1, 1936; 1 son, Thomas Ross. Inspector, Tax Dept. Tenn., 1933-39; admitted to Tenn. bar, 1939; adjustor various ins. cos., 1939-41; pvt. practice, Halls, Tenn., 1941-61; asso. justice Supreme Ct. Tenn., 1961—. Mayor of Halls, 1947-49; mem. Tenn. Constl. Conv., 1953; mem. Tenn. Senate, 1957-59. Trustee Lauderdale County Hosp. Served from pvt. to 1st lt. AUS, 1943-46. Methodist. Mason. Home: Halls TN 38040 Office: Supreme Ct Tenn Nashville TN 37203

DYER, SALLIE (MRS. ROBERT FRANCIS DYER), genealogist, club woman; b. Washington, Oct. 16, 1891; d. Nathaniel Talmadge and Emma (Hutchins) Worley; student Cazenovia Jr. Coll., 1908-12, George Washington U., 1912-13, Strayer's Bus. Coll., 1914; m. Robert Francis Dyer, Jan. 2, 1926; children—Robert F., Nancie (Mrs. Edward C. Santelmann), Richard Hutchins, David Marcus. Sec., Brit. Embassy, Washington, 1914-15, Adj. Gen.'s Office, War Dept., 1915-16; owner Dyer's Geneol. Office, Washington, 1914-26. Pres. Washington alumnae club Pi Beta Phi, 1946-47; mem. war work com. D.A.R., 1943-45, vice-regent Dorothy Hancock chpt., 1945—, del. Eastern Shore Va. chpt. to nat. congresses, 1952-72. Mem. spl. com. U.S.O., 1941-45, mem. Belasco Theater, 1942-45; nurse's aid A.R.C., 1943-45; woman's bd. George Washington U. Hosp., 1946-56; mem. George Washington U. Alumni Assn. Recipient service award A.R.C., 1945; Golden Arrow award Pi Beta Phi. Mem. So. Dames Am. (charter mem., state v.p. 1963-66), Tex. Geneal. Soc. Clubs: Washington, Chevy Chase Woman's, Arts. Home: 3813 Garrison St NW Washington DC 20016

DYKE, JAMES (PARVIN), librarian; b. Breckenridge, Tex., Sept. 10, 1920; s. James Elvy and Glenna (Butler) D.; A.B., Hardin-Simmons U., 1942; B.A. in L.S., U. Okla., 1946; M.S., U. Ill., 1950, Ph.D., 1957; m. Thelma Margaret Tiner, Sept. 14, 1941; children—Glenna Margaret, Thelma Lane, James Tiner. Asst. librarian Hardin-Simmons U., 1946-48; mgr. Tiner Drug Store, Munday, Tex., 1948-49; research asst. unit on evaluation U. Ill., 1949-51; librarian Eastern N.M., U., Portales, 1951-66; library dir., prof. Tex. A. & M. U., College Station, 1966—. Vis. prof. U. Okla., summer 1959. Served to capt. USAAF, 1942-45. Decorated D.F.C., Air medal with three oak leaf clusters. Mem. A.L.A. (chmn. membership com. 1959-60), Assn. Coll. and Reference Librarians, Southwestern, N.M. (sec. 1956-57, v.p. 1957-58, pres. 1958-59), Tex. library assns., N.M. Edn. Assn., N.M. Audio-Visual Assn. (dir. 1955-57), Am. Assn. U. Profs. Democrat. Baptist. Mason, Lion (dist. cabinet sec. 1959-60, pres. Portales 1961-62). Home: Box 3926 Bryan TX 77801 Office: Tex A & M U College Station TX 77843

DYKES, ARCHIE REECE, univ. chancellor; b. Rogersville, Tenn., Jan. 20, 1931; B.S., E. Tenn. U., 1952, M.A., 1956; Ed.D. (Ford Found. fellow), U. Tenn., 1959. Tchr., Church Hill Sch., 1952-55, prin., 1955-58; supt. Greenville City Schs., 1959-62; prof., dir. Center Advanced Grad. Studies, U. Tenn.-Memphis State U., 1962-66; Am. Council Edn. fellow U. Ill., 1966-67; chancellor U. Tenn., 1967—; cons. U.S. Office Edn., Louisville and Jefferson County sch. systems. Mem. Tenn. Hist. Commn. Mem. Tenn. Coll. Assn. (pres. 1969-70), Am. Council Edn., Am. Assn. Sch. Adminstrs. (co-chmn. com. sch. bd.-supt. relations), Am. Assn. Higher Edn., Phi Kappa Phi. Author: School Board and Superintendent, 1965; (with others) Philosophic Theory and Practice in Educational administration, 1966; Faculty Participation in Academic Desicion Making, 1968; Presidential Leadership in Academe, 1967; Faculty Participation in Governance, 1968; Campus 1980: The Shape of the Future in American Higher Education, 1969. Office: Office of the Chancellor Univ Tenn Knoxville TN 37916*

DYSON, EARL EUGENE, assn. exec.; b. Columbia, S.C., Nov. 8, 1939; s. Earl Powell and Bessie (Best) D.; student U. S.C., 1957-58, 60-62; student Ga. State U., 1963-65; m. Margaret Fennell Dyson, Mar. 18, 1961; children—Johnny Graham, Suzanne Rhett. Mem. pub. relations dept. S.C. State Devel. Bd., Columbia, S.C., 1961-63; mem. personnel dept. Gen. Motors Corp., Atlanta, 1963-65; exec. v.p. Georgia Bus. & Industry Assn., Atlanta, Ga., 1965—. Pres. Internat. Dietary Information Found.; bd. dirs. Nat. Soc. Prevention of Blindness; chmn. bd. dirs. Ga. Soc. Prevention of Blindness. Served with USNR, 1958-60. Mem. Ga. Soc. Assn. Execs. (pres. 1969-70), Friends of Mexico Soc. (exec. v.p. 1971—). Home: 1874 Chisholm Ct Tucker GA 30084 Office: 181 Washington St SW Atlanta GA 30303

DYSON, SAMUEL ARCHER, librarian; b. Shreveport, La., Sept. 3, 1928; s. Leslie Paul and Bessie (Archer) D.; student Tulane U., 1945-46; B.S., Northwestern State Coll., Natchitoches, La., 1950; postgrad. N. Tex. State U., 1951-52, La. Coll., 1957, La. Tech. U., 1967-69; M.S., La. State U., 1953; m. June Katherine Wallace, May 6, 1950; children—Stuart Alan, Karen Ernestine. Head librarian La. Coll., Pinesville, 1953-60; asso. librarian La. Tech. U., Ruston, 1960-66, dir. libraries, 1966—, asso. prof. library sci. Coll. Edn., 1966—. Sec. treas. adv. bd. Recreation Program for Blind, YWCA, 1960; mem. exec. bd. Quachita Valley council Boy Scouts Am., 1966—; range and information officer Ruston Civil Air Patrol, 1964. Served with USNR, 1948. Mem. La. Library Assn. (1st v.p. 1972-73), La. Coll. Conf. (chmn. library sect. 1957, 63), Conf. La. Acad. Librarians (chmn. 1958), Alpha Tau Omega, Alpha Beta Alpha. Lion. Author: Library Automation, 1971. Editor: Planning and Implementing Academic Library Automation Programs, 1970. Editor abstracts of theses, 1968—. Home: 2 Westwood Hills Ruston LA 71270 Office: Prescott Library La Tech Univ Ruston LA 71270

EAGAN, FRED. L., state senator; grad. Tulane U.; m. Peggy Hopkins; children— Dickey, Polly, Debbie, Ellen. Vice pres. Eagan Ins. Agy.; also with Leitz-Eagan Cos.; mem. La. Senate, 1963—, chmn. legislative com. r.r.s, mem. commerce, ins., finance coms. Active United Fund; chmn. Greater New Orleans March of Dimes, 1971. Served with USNR, World War II. Mem. Greater Magazine St. Bus. Men's Assn. (past pres.), Am. Legion, Holy Name Soc., Delta Sigma Phi. Lion, K.C. Address: 1127 Philip St New Orleans LA 70130*

EAGER, JAMES LESLIE, pub. relations exec.; b. Wendell, Ida., Feb. 22, 1931; s. Leslie H. and Mary G. (Huckaby) E.; B.J., U. Tex., 1953, Journalism, 1955; m. Martha Prescott Cody, Oct. 14, 1962; 1 son, Thomas Prescott. Supr. financial relations Tex. Eastern Transmission Corp., 1959-63, asst. pub. relations dir., 1971—; asst. v.p., pub. relations dir. So. Nat. Bank of Houston, 1963-65; mgr. pub. relations Armco Steel Corp., Houston, 1965-71; asst. pub. relations dir. Tex. Eastern Transmission Corp., Houston, 1971—. Lectr. public relations U. Houston, 1965—. Pres., Friends of Houston Pub. Library, 1969-70, bd. dirs., 1960—. Served to lt. (j.g.) USNR, 1956-59 Mem. Pub. Relations Soc. Am. (chpt. dir.). Office: Tex Eastern Transmission Corp Box 2521 Houston TX 77001

EAGER, WILLIAM GORONWY, JR., security dealer; b. Valdosta, Ga., Dec. 25, 1915; s. William Goronwy and Eugene (Johnston) E.; student Emory Jr. Coll., 1932-34; B.S., Ga. Tech. Inst., 1937; m. Dorothy Gerard Hopkins, Sept. 6, 1941; children—William Goronwy III, Robert C., Josefa N. H. Dir. navy sales Glenn L. Martin Co., 1950-55; v.p. Robinson-Humphrey Co., Valdosta, 1962—. Bd. dirs. United Fund. Mem. Nat. Assn. Security Dealers, N.Y. Stock Exchange, C. of C. (v.p. 1970-71), Sigma Alpha Epsilon. Episcopalian (bd. govs. 1970—, sr. warden 1970-71). Rotarian. Club: Valdosta Country (pres. 1960). Home: Route 1 Country Club Rd Valdosta GA 31601 Office: 100 N Patterson St Valdosta GA 31601

EAGLETON, JAMES RICHARDSON, lawyer; b. Pawnee, Okla., June 17, 1903; s. William L. and Mattie (Saunders) E.; B.A., U. Okla., 1924, LL.B., 1925; m. Ruby M. Moffett, Nov. 30, 1923 (dec. Apr. 1971); children—Suzanne (Mrs. Don R. Nicholson II), Robert M. (dec.); m. 2d, Rosemary E. Callahan, June 24, 1972. Admitted to Okla. bar, 1925; lease buyer and requirements, land dept. Foster Oil Co., Tulsa, 1926-30; gen. practice, Oklahoma City, 1931-40, 1945—; legal asst. Okla. Supreme Ct., Oklahoma City, 1941-44; pres., dir. Royalties, Inc., Oklahoma City, 1970—. Mem. Am., Okla., Oklahoma County bar assns., Phi Alpha Delta, Sigma Chi. Democrat. Presbyn (elder). Home: 1214 NW 21st St Oklahoma City OK 73106 Office: 217 N. Harvey St Investors Capital Bldg Oklahoma City OK 73102

EANES, EDWIN COLEY, real estate exec.; b. Sapulpa, Okla., Dec. 18, 1921; s. Arthur Musgrove and Floy Glenn (Coley) E.; B.S., U. Tulsa, 1949; M.S. in Indsl. Adminstrn., USAF Inst. Tech., 1955; m. Betty Jo Winton, May 27, 1945; children—Donna Jo, Edwin Coley. Commd. 2d lt. U.S. Army, 1945, advanced through grades to lt. col. USAF, 1965; resident rep. of auditor gen., San Antonio, Tex., 1955-59; supervisory mgr. Auditor Gen.'s Office, 1959-61, exec. officer, 1961-67; chief research and plans div. USAF, 1965-67; chief mgmt. review, 1967; ret., 1967; gen. mgr. Ray Conard Constrn. Co., Tulsa, 1967-71; mgr. properties Tri State Devel., Tulsa, 1971—. Decorated D.F.C., Air medal with clusters. Formed and headed 1st research orgn. in internal audit in U.S., 1965. Home: 2217 E 59th St Tulsa OK 74105 Office: 2217 E 59th St Tulsa OK 74105

EANES, GORDON LEA, financial exec.; b. Danville, Va., June 24, 1937; s. Douglas R. and Grace (Dehart) E.; B.S., U. Richmond, 1962; student Va. Poly. Inst., 1958-60; m. Nancy Carolyn Hodnett, Aug. 21,

1960; children—Gordon Lea, Leila Carolyn. With Price Waterhouse & Co., Charlotte, N.C., 1962-65, Atlanta, 1965-70, mgr., 1967-70; v.p. finance Air Treads, Inc., Forest Park, Ga., 1970—. Served with USAF, 1954-58. C.P.A., Ga., N.C. Mem. U.S. Jr. C. of C., Am. Inst. C.P.A.'s, Ga., N.C. Socs. C.P.A.'s, Alpha Kappa Psi. Republican. Home: 2338 Kings Point Dr Atlanta GA 30341 Office: 5075 Pine Tree St Forest Park GA 30050

EARLE, BRASHEAR, physician; b. Winnsboro, La., Nov. 9, 1922; s. William Thompson and Sallie Ann (Bowden) E.; B.S., La. State U., 1948, M.D., 1953; m. Jimmie Louise Fussell, Dec. 12, 1954; children— Sallie Ann, Charles Brashear, Alice Claire. Intern Confederate Meml. Hosp., Shreveport, La., 1953-54; resident E.A. Conway Meml. Hosp., Monroe, La., 1954-55; med. staff Winnsboro (La.) Sanitarium, 1955-59; practice medicine specializing in family practice, Winnsboro, La., 1959—; mem. staff Franklin Parish Hosp., Winnsboro; coroner, Franklin Parish, 1957-64; med. adv. Selective Service Bd., 1960-71. Bd. dirs. Dixie Youth Baseball, 1969-71. Served with AUS, 1943-44. Decorated Purple Heart. Mem. Franklin Parish Med. Soc. (pres. 1971-72). Democrat. Presbyn. Lion. Home: 803 8th St Winnsboro LA 71295 Office: 310 Main St Winnsboro LA 71295

EARLE, JULIUS RICHARD, physician; b. Walhalla, S.C., Apr. 1, 1928; s. Harry Utley and Allie Mae (Woolbright) E.; B.S., Clemson A. and M. Coll., 1949; M.D., Med. Coll. State S.C., 1953; m. Myrtle Vivian Corbitt, June 5, 1953; children—Julius Richard, Suzanne Elizabeth, Dennis Paul, Helen Belinda. Intern White Cross Hosp., Columbus, O., 1953-54; gen. practice medicine Walhalla, S.C., 1954—; staff mem. Oconee Meml. Hosp., Seneca, S.C., chief anesthesia service, 1959-64, chief of staff, 1970-72. Mem. County Bd. Sch. Trustees, Walhalla, 1961—. Served to lt., USNR, 1956-58. Mem. A.M.A., Internat. Platform Assn., Nat. Rifle Assn., So., S.C. med. assns., N.Y. Acad. Sci. Democrat. Methodist. Mason (32 deg., Shriner). Home: RFD 2 Box 239A Earlestead SC 29691 Office: RFD 2 Earlestead Walhalla SC 29691

EARLE, RONALD DALE, judge; b. Fort Worth, Tex., Feb. 23, 1942; s. Charles Cloyd and Lowleta (Muse) E.; B.A., U. Tex., 1964, J.D., 1967; m. Barbara Ann Leach, June 7, 1963; children—Elisabeth Ashlea, Charles Jason. Admitted to Tex. bar, 1967; legal asst. Officer of Gov., Austin, Tex., 1967-69; now presiding judge Municipal Ct., Austin. Cons. race relations Office of the Gov. Recipient Hildy's Cutback award U. Tex. Law Sch. Mem. Am., Tex., Travis County bar assns., Am. Judicature Soc., N. Am. Judges Assn., Phi Alpha Delta. Contbr. articles to profl. jours. Home: 3103 Catalina Dr Austin TX 78741 Office: 700 E 7th St Austin TX 78701

EARLEY, DOUGLAS CHARLES, entomolgist; b. Olean, N.Y., Aug. 2, 1918; s. Samuel Judd and Onnolee Marion (Higbee) E.; B.S., Tex. A. and M. U., 1940; m. Elizabeth Ann Tandy, Dec. 27, 1941; children—Judd Mark, Cleve Martin, Annalyn. Chief entomologist Port Fertilizer & Chem. Co., Los Fresnos, Tex., 1940-60; entomologist, mgr. tech. services Niagara Chem. div. FMC Corp., Los Fresnos, Tex., 1960—; dir. Pan Am. Bank, Brownsville, Tex. Pres. Brownsville Soc. for Crippled Children, 1959-60; mem. adv. bd. Tex. A. and M. U., Research Center, Weslaco, Tex., 1960-71. Bd. dirs. Cleve H. Tandy Found., Brownsville, Tex.; trustee, chmn. bd. Pan Am. Sch., Kingsville, Tex. Served to maj., AUS, 1941-45. Decorated Bronze Star. Mem. Entomol. Soc. Am. (mem. gov. bd. 1968-70). Presbyn. (elder 1950-71). Home: 205 Acacia Lake Dr Brownsville TX 78520 Office: PO Box 337 Los Fresnos TX 78566

EARLEY, HUBERT RANDOLPH, dentist; b. Epworth, Ga., July 20, 1936; s. Homer Cleve and Frankie Iowa (Queen) E.; student U. Fla., 1954-57; D.D.S., Emory U., 1961; m. Lynn Elizabeth Williams, June 8, 1957; children—Jeffrey Thorpe, Clay Randolph. Individual practice dentistry, Orlando, Fla., 1963—. Served to capt. USAF, 1961-63. Mem. Am., Fla., Orange County dental assns., Phi Delta Theta. Republican. Presbyn. Club: Country, University (Orlando). Home: 2112 Santa Antilles Rd Orlando FL 32806 Office: 1319 S Orange Av Orlando FL 32806

EARLY, JACK JONES, assn. exec.; b. Corbin, Ky., Apr. 12, 1925; s. Joseph M. and Lela (Jones) E.; A.B., Union Coll., Barbourville, Ky., 1948; M.A., U. Ky., 1953, Ed.D. (So. scholar 1955-56), 1956; B.D., Coll. of Bible, Lexington, Ky., 1956; D.D., Wesley Coll., Grand Forks, N.D., 1961; LL.D., Parsons Coll., 1962; Litt.D., Dakota Wesleyan U., 1969; LL.D., Ia. Wesleyan Coll., 1972; m. Nancye Bruce Whaley, June 1, 1952;children—Lela Katherine, Judith Ann, Laura Hattie. Ordained to ministry Methodist Ch., 1954; pastor Rockhold Circuit (Ky.), 1943-44, Craig's Chapel and Laurel Circuit, London, Ky., 1944-47, Trinity Ch., Oak Ridge, summer 1945, Hindman Ch. (Ky.), 1947-52; dean of men Hindman Settlement Sch., 1948-51; asso. pastor Park Ch., Lexington, Ky., 1952-54; asst. to pres., dean Athens (Ala.) Coll., 1954-55; v.p., dean of coll. Ia. Wesleyan Coll., Mt. Pleasant, 1956-58; pres. Dakota Wesleyan U., 1958-69, Pfeiffer Coll., Misenheimer, N.C., 1969-71; exec. dir. edn. The Am. Bankers Assn., Washington, 1971—. Active Boy Scouts Am. Mem. Ky. Ho. of Reps., 1952-54; v.p. Young Republican Clubs of Ky., 1949-50. Dir. S.D. Found. Pvt. Colls., S.D. Meth. Found., YMCA. Recipient Spoke award Mitchell Jr. C. of C., 1959, Distinguished Service award, 1960; Distinguished Service award S.D. Jr. C. of C., 1960; named Outstanding Former Kentuckian, 1963. Hon. fellow Wroxton Coll., Oxfordshire, Eng. Mem. Jr. C. of C. (dir. 1959), C. of C., Blue Key, Kappa Delta Pi, Phi Delta Kappa, Kappa Phi Kappa, Alpha Psi Omega, Theta Phi, Pi Tau Chi. Home: 4202 Mt Vernon Memorial Hwy Alexandria VA 22309 Office: American Bankers Assn 1120 Connecticut Av Washington DC 20036

EARLY, JOHN LEVERING, lawyer; b. Staunton, Va., Dec. 19, 1896; s. Charles E. and Ida (Clark) E.; A.B., Washington and Lee U.; LL.B., U. Va., 1923; m. Maebelle C. Brooks, June 2, 1924; 1 son, Charles Edward. Admitted to Va. bar, 1923, W.Va. bar, 1924, Fla. bar 1924; practice law Welch, W.Va., 1923-24, Sarasota, Fla., 1924—; cattleman, breeder thoroughbred Shorthorns. Mem. Sarasota-Bradenton (Fla.) Airport Authority, 1951-53. Mem. Ho. Reps., 1933-39; municipal judge, 1944-46; mayor City Sarasota, 1951-53. Served as pvt., inf., 1918-19. Mem. Sarasota County Bar Assn. (pres.), Am. Legion, D.A.V., Helping Hands (pres.), Rodeheavers Boy's Ranch Assn., Founders Club, Fla. Sheriffs Boys Ranch, Order of Coif. Methodist. Mason, Odd Fellow. Home: 1841 Oak St Sarasota FL 33577 Office: 515 Palmer Bank Bldg Sarasota FL 33577

EARNEST, FRANK, JR., supt. schs.; b. Berry, Ala., Mar. 9, 1928; s. Frank and Dora Ann (Johnston) E.; B.S., Florence State U., 1951; M.A., U. Ala., 1954, postgrad., 1955-63; postgrad. Columbia, 1960—; m. Bertha Dean Best, Dec. 21, 1946; children—Gerry Blake, Clinton Frank, Dayle. Tchr., Tuscaloosa County, Ala., 1946-51, prin., 1951-52; asst. supt. schs., Dallas County, Ala., 1960-63, supt., 1963—. Mem. Am., Ala. (sec.-treas. 1969-72) assns. sch. adminstrs., So. States Work Conf. (state rep. 1970-71), Ala. Edn. Assn. (pres. dist. 1964-65), Central Ala. Fair Assn. (pres. 1965-66), Ala. Sight Conservation Assn. (pres. 1970-71), Kappa Delta Pi, Phi Delta Kappa. Home: 514 Merrimac Pl Selma AL 36701 Office: PO Box 1056 Selma AL 36701

EARNGEY, WILLARD PHELPS, JR., hosp. adminstr.; b. Chgo., July 21, 1915; s. Willard Phelps and Elizabeth (Gardner) E.; A.B., Duke, 1938, certificate hosp. adminstrn., 1939; LL.D. (hon.), Tex. Wesleyan U., 1967; m. Irma Lawson McCaleb, Dec. 19, 1953; children—Willard Phelps III, Lynne, (Mrs. Ferdie R. Fisher III), Martha Ann. Supt., Cherokee County Hosp., Gaffney, S.C., 1939-41, Norfolk (Va.) Gen. Hosp., 1941-44, 46-51; adminstr. Harris Hosp., Ft. Worth, 1951—. Pres. Ft. Worth Soc. Crippled Children and Adults, 1963-64, Va. Hosp. Assn., 1948-49, N.W. Tex. Hosp. Assn., 1961-62, Tex. Hosp. Assn. 1958-59, Tex. Assn. Hosp. Accountants, 1954-55; chmn. bd. Tarrant County (Tex.) Heart Assn., 1967-68. Served to lt. (j.g.) USNR, 1944-46. Recipient Med. Staff award merit Harris Hosp., 1966; Distinguished Mem. award Tex. Assn. Hosp. Accountants, 1968; Boss of Year award Nat. Secretaries Assn., 1966. Fellow Am. Coll. Hosp. Adminstrs., Royal Soc. Health (Eng.). Home: 3101 Tanglewood Trail Fort Worth TX 76109 Office: 1300 W Cannon St Fort Worth TX 76104

EARTHMAN, WILLIAM FLETCHER, banker; b. Nashville, Jan. 21, 1926; s. William Fletcher and Georgia (Bell) E.; student Cornell U., 1944-45; B.S., U.S. Mil. Acad., 1949; m. Alice Warfield Tyne, June 24, 1950 (div. 1966); children—William Fletcher III, Thomas, Elizabeth, John Christopher Burch; m. 2d, Dorothy Ann Bartlett, Sept 7, 1968. Commd. 2d lt. U.S. Army, 1949, advanced through grades to capt., 1954; ret., 1954; capt. Res.; with Commerce Union Bank, Nashville, 1954—, pres., 1961—, also dir., mem. exec. com. Mem. Am. Bankers Assn., Assn. Res. City Bankers, Tenn. Bankers Assn. Home: 105 Belle Meade Blvd Nashville TN 37205 Office: 400 Union St Nashville TN 37219

EASLEY, OWEN RANDOLPH, JR., newspaperman; b. Martinsville, Va., July 30, 1922; s. Owen Randolph and Cassie (DuVal) E.; A.B., Washington and Lee U., 1948; A.M., U. N.C., 1955; m. Louise Craven Langhorne, June 24, 1961; 1 dau., Eleanor Vanderslice. Reporter Southside Va. News, Petersburg, 1948-49, Altavista (Va.) Jour., 1949-50, Smythe County News, Marion, 1955-56, Ledger-Star, Portsmouth, 1956—. Instr., Coll. of William and Mary, Williamsburg, 1959—. Served with AUS, 1942-46. Mem. Am. Polit. Sci. Assn., Sigma Delta Chi. Unitarian-Universalist (trustee). Club: Torch (Portsmouth pres. 1967-68). Home: 2941 Tyre Neck Rd Chesapeake VA 23321 Office: 101 High St Portsmouth VA 23704

EASON, GERALD, govt. ofcl.; b. Evans County, Ga., July 24, 1935; s. Abraham Darlington and Minnie (Fields) E.; student Armstrong State Coll., 1953-54, 57, 59, 64, 69-70; m. Johnnie Fay Taylor, Dec. 12, 1955; children—Debra Kay, Janice Loy, David Gerald. Biol. aid technician Agrl. Research Service, Stored-Products Research and Devel. Lab., Savannah, Ga., 1954-55, agrl. research technician, 1960-71, biol. research technician biochemistry, 1971—. Recipient certificate of Merit, U.S. Dept. Agr., 1971, Certificate of Appreciation, U.S. Dept. Agr., 1966. Mem. Entomol. Soc. Am., Ga. Entomol. Soc., U.S. Dept. Agr. Club (v.p. 1964), Nat. Fedn. Fed. Employees (v.p. local chpt. 1970-71, pres. 1972-73), Am. Bus. Men's Clubs (gov. 1970-71, 71-72, sec. 1972-73, editor Strictly Bus., 1970-71, co-editor 1971-72). Methodist. Co-author sci. publs. in fields of methods, rates and frequency of application, detection, residues and biol. effects of insecticides and fumigants. Co-inventor apparatus for dispensing insecticides. Home: 136 E 60th St Savannah GA 31405 Office: 3401 Edwin Av S Savannah GA 31403

EASON, HELGA RUTH HALVORSEN (MRS. MORRIS JACKSON EASON), librarian; b. Nebraska City, Neb.; d. Lee Roy and Luella (Strong) Halvorsen; student Evansville (Ind.) Coll., 1924-25; A.B., Ohio Wesleyan U., 1927; B.S., Simmons Coll., 1929; m. Morris Jackson Eason, Nov. 23, 1947. Circulation asst. N.Y. Pub. Library, 1930-39; br. librarian Evansville Pub. Library, 1941-45; head reference dept. Miami (Fla.) Pub. Library, (name Miami-Dade Pub. Library System 1971—), 1947-52, head community relations dept., 1952—. Mem. program com. WTHS-TV Community TV Found. South Fla., 1955-70. Bd. dirs. Miami Finance Welfare Employees Fed. Credit Union, 1949-72, sec., 1963-72; bd. dirs. Miami League Women Voters, 1952-53. Recipient certificate of merit Fla. Fedn. Womens Clubs, 1964; John Cotton Dana Publicity awards for library, 1952-54. Mem. Am. (past dir., com. chmn., 2d. vice pres. adult services div. 1968-69; now adult services rep.), Fla. (Nat. Library Week award 66, sect. pres., com. chmn.), Dade County (past pres.) library assns., City Miami Pub. Library Staff Orgn. (past pres.), Nat. League Am. Pen Women (sec., dir., past v.p. Greater Miami br., editor Owls Feather 1970-72, 1st v.p. 1972—), Laramore Rader Poetry Group (pres. 1959-61). Contbr. articles to profl. jours. Home: 152 NE 46th St Miami FL 33137 Office: 1 Biscayne Blvd Miami FL 33132

EAST, CHARLES E., univ. press exec.; b. Shelby, Miss., Dec. 11, 1924; s. Elmo M. and Mabel (Gradolph) E.; B.A., La. State U., 1948, M.A., 1962; m. Sarah Simmons, 1948; 1 son, Charles E. Editorial asst. Collier's mag., N.Y.C., 1948-49; reporter, then Sunday mag. editor Morning Advocate, Baton Rouge, 1949-55; staff writer, then asst. city editor State-Times, Baton Rouge, 1955-62; editors, then asst. dir., then asso. dir. La. State U. Press, Baton Rouge, 1962-70, dir., 1970—. Mem. La. Bicentennial Commn., 1971—. Recipient Henry H. Bellamann award, 1965. Mem. La. Geneal. and Hist. Soc. (editor Geneal. Register; founder, charter mem.), Kappa Alpha, Phi Kappa Phi, Phi Eta Sigma. Author: Where the Music War, 1965; (with Elemore Morgan) The Face of Louisiana, 1969. Contbr. articles to mags. Home: 1455 Knollwood Dr Baton Rouge LA 70808 Office: La State U Press Baton Rouge LA 70803

EASTER, RUFUS, JR., assn. exec. Exec. coordinator Hampton (Va.) Assn. Arts and Humanities. Address: Hampton Assn Arts and Humanities 123 E Queen St Hampton VA 23369*

EASTERLING, GLENDON MARTELL, poultry co. exec.; b. Leona, Tex., Dec. 25, 1924; s. Arthur McIver and Vinnie Ola (Ward) E.; student Allen Mil. Acad. Jr. Coll., 1947-48; B.S., Sam Houston State U., 1950; m. Mayme Hazle Kazmeier, Mar. 13, 1948; children—William Truitt, Mary (Mrs. Ronald Wayne Gooch). Salesman, Kazmeier-Sherrill Hatchery, Bryan, Tex., 1950-53, v.p., Kazmeier Poultry Farm, 1953-63, pres., owner, 1964—; pres., owner Kazmeier Hatchery, 1964—; pres., owner Kazmeier Broiler Hatchery, 1964—; v.p., dir. S & E., Inc., 1965—; dir. Triangle Bowling Alley, First Fed. Savs. & Loan Assn., First Nat. Bank; partner E & E Co., 1965—. County campaign mgr. William Blakely, 1959, Nixon-Lodge, 1960. Served with USAAF, 1943-46. Mem. Tex. Poultry Improvement Fedn., Bryan C. of C. (bd. dirs. 1962-64), Ex-student Assn. Sam Houston State U. (dir. 1965—). Methodist (finance com. 1969-71). Mason (Shriner). Clubs: Briacrest Country, Knife and Fork. Home: 205 S Coulter St Bryan TX 77801 Office: P O Box 791 1806 S College St Bryan TX 77801

EASTERLING, HENRY CLIFTON, dentist; b. Stigler, Okla., June 24, 1920; s. Carl Lloyd and Pearle Belle (Hall) E.; B.S., U. Okla., 1942; D.D.S., Baylor U., 1945; m. Wilma Aldene McGuire, June 25, 1944; children— Susan (Mrs. Jack Calvin Herron, Jr.), Henry Clifton II. Individual practice dentistry, Norman, Okla., 1946-52, 54—. Mem. adv. com. Oscar Rose Jr. Coll., Sch. Dental Hygiene, U. Okla. Sch. Dental Hygiene. Served to H. comdr., USNR, 1945-46, USAF, 1952-54. Mem. Am., Okla. dental assns., Am. Soc. Dentistry for Children, Pierre Fauchard Acad., Delta Chi, Psi Omega, Kappa Psi. Democrat. Methodist. Lion (bd. dirs. 1952). Club: Petroleum (Oklahoma City). Home: 2644 Smoking Oak Rd Norman OK 73069 Office: 230 Alameda St Norman OK 73069

EASTERLY, JOE A., librarian; b. Big Sandy, Tex., May 31, 1907; s. Charles Joseph and Surena Kate (Dow) E.; B.A., E. Tex. State U., 1932; M.A., U. Tex., 1933; M.S., George Peabody Coll., 1940; m. Ruth Pope, June 16, 1940; children—James Arlin, Joanna. Tchr. pub. schs., Tex., 1933-39; documents and periodicals librarian E. Tex. State U., Commerce, 1939-43, asst. librarian, 1945-46; engring. librarian Ordinance Aerophysics Lab., Daingerfield, Tex., 1946-64; asst. librarian Jay-Rollins Library, McMurry Coll., Abilene, Tex., 1964-68, dir., 1968—. Mem. city council, Daingerfield, Tex., 1954-56. Served with USAAF, 1943-46. Mem. Am., Southwestern, Tex. library assns., Phi Beta Kappa. Lion. Home: 1026 Westridge St Abilene TX 79605 Office: Jay-Rollins Library McMurry Coll Abilene TX 79605

EASTERWOOD, HENRY, artist; b. Ga., 1934; student West Ga. Coll., 1953-54; B.F.A., Memphis Acad. Arts, 1958; student Royal Tapestry Mfr., Madrid, Spain, 1965; pupil Franka Rasmussen, Denmark, 1965, Weverij de Uil, Netherlands, 1965. Tapestries exhibited Museum Contemporary Crafts, N.Y.C., Am. House, N.Y.C., Kansas City Art Inst., Ark. Arts Center, Atlanta Art Assns., Tulane U., Winston-Salem Mus., Memphis Acad. Arts, Huntsville (Ala.) Arts Center, Am. Swedish Inst., Mpls., U. Wis., Tweed Gallery U. Minn., others; chmn. textile dept. Memphis Acad. Arts, 1959—; tchr. Haystack Mt. Sch. Crafts, Deer Isle, Me., 1966. Mem. adv. panel crafts Tenn. Arts Commn. Recipient Craft Horizon award Atlanta Arts Festival, 1965; Nat. Merit award Am. Craftsmen's Council, 1966, Mississippi River Crafts award, 1965, 67, 69, A.I.A. Craftmanship award, 1969, others. Mem. Am. Craftsmen's Council (Tenn. rep. council 1964-65), Tenn. Craftsmen's Assn. Address: 643 McConnell St Memphis TN 38112

EASTHOPE, JOE, county judge; b., 1928; ed. U. Fla. Admitted to Fla. bar, 1950; Broward County judge. Address: County Court House Fort Lauderdale FL 33301*

EASTLAKE, MARY GAHAGAN, ret. nurse; b. Mt. Jewett, Pa., Nov. 5, 1902; d. John Spencer and Elizabeth (Ledig) Gahagan; R.N., Johns Hopkins Hosp., 1926; B.S., Columbia, 1942, M.A., 1948; m. Fred L. Eastlake, Feb. 12, 1948 (dec.). Head nurse Johns Hopkins Hosp., Balt., 1927-32; supr. Panama, C.Z., U.S. Govt., 1932-33; nurse dir. Bur. Indian Affairs, 1933-38, nurse cons., 1938-43, 46-55; with USPHS, 1955-65, ret. as chief nursing services, Div. Indian Health. Served from lt. to maj. Nurse Corps U.S. Army, 1943-46; ETO. Decorated Bronze Star medal, Meritorious Service unit plaque; recipient Meritorious Service award USPHS, 1962. Mem. Am. Hosp. Assn., Am. Pub. Health Assn., Am. Nurses Assn., Nat. League Nursing, Johns Hopkins nurses alumnae assns., Tchrs. Coll. P.E.O. Mem. Order Eastern Star. Author articles in field. Home: 3140 Wisconsin Av NW Washington DC 20016

EASTLAND, JAMES O., U.S. senator; b. Doddsville, Miss., Nov. 28, 1904; s. Woods Caperton and Alma (Austin) E.; student U. Miss., 1922-24, Vanderbilt U., 1925-26, U. Ala., 1926-27; m. Elizabeth Coleman, July 6, 1932; children—Nell, Anne, Sue, Woods Eugene. Admitted to Miss. bar, 1927, practiced Forest, Miss.; moved to Sunflower County, 1934; apptd. to U.S. Senate to fill vacancy, June-Sept. 1941; elected U.S. senator, 1943—, chmn. senate com. on judiciary, 1956—. Mem. Miss. House of Reps., 1928-32. Democrat. Home: Doddsville MS 38736 also 5116 Macomb St Washington DC 20016

EASTMAN, JAMES ROBERT, pub. relations agy. exec.; b. Saginaw, Mich., Feb. 19, 1928; s. Lawrence Cleone and Blanche Evelyn (Eastman) Hitchcock; student U. Cal. at Los Angeles, 1945; Los Angeles City Coll., 1947; m. Loretta Irene Grissom, May 1, 1950; children—Lisa Devon, Charles Kent, James Chris, Robert Bruce. News dir. WSIX Radio, Nashville, 1960-64, WMAK Radio, Nashville, 1964-67; pub. relations dir. Communication Arts Inc., Nashville, 1967-68; pres. pub. relations PR Assos., Inc., Nashville, 1968—; exec. v.p., sec.-treas. Advt. Assos., Inc., Nashville, 1969—. Press sec. Hooker for Gov., 1966; dir. advt. and pub. relations Congressman William R. Anderson, 1968, 70, 72; press sec. Crockett for Senate, 1970. Served with USNR, 1946-53. Named Young Man of the Year Warren County Jr. C. of C., 1958; recipient news awards A.P., 1967, Radio-TV Connie award, 1964. Mem. Pub. Relations Soc. Am., Gideons (service sec. 1971—). Sigma Delta Chi. Baptist (deacon 1966—). Mason. Club: Capitol (Nashville). Home: 209 Wallace Rd Nashville TN 37211 Office: 1005 Murfreesboro Rd Nashville TN 37217

EASTMOORE, EUGENE LEGARE, lawyer; b. Jacksonville, Fla., May 22, 1929; s. Theodore Harold and Harriet (Manning) E.; B.A., U. Fla., 1950, J.D., 1952; m. Jeanine Herrington, June 8, 1952; children—Katherine Harriet, Theodore Charles, John Riley. Admitted to Fla. bar, 1952; practiced in Palatka, Fla., 1954—; mem. firm Eastmoore & Nichols, 1954—; atty. City of Palatka, 1956-59, 61—. Bd. dirs. Rodeheavers Boys Ranch, Putnam County Blood Bank (pres. 1967-71). Served with AUS, 1951-54; lt. col. Fla. N.G., 1954—. Mem. Am., Putnam County bar assns., Fla. Bar, Nat. Inst. Municipal Law Officers, Am. Legion, Nat., Fla. skeet shooting assns., C. of C., V.F.W. Episcopalian. Elk, Kiwanian (pres. 1963; lt. gov. 1967). Club: Palatka Skeet (pres. 1966). Home: 2210 Palma Ceia Palatka FL 32077 Office: 329 St Johns Av Palatka FL 31077

EASTON, CAMERON HERNDON, JR., county ofcl.; b. Oxford, N.C., Feb. 25, 1934; s. Cameron Herndon and Frances (Landis) E.; B.S., Salem Coll., 1958; m. Janet Ann Robinson, May 7, 1959; children—Charlotte Virginia, Cameron Herndon III. Claims adjuster Nationwide Mutual Ins. Co., 1960-66; tax supr. Gaston County (N.C.), Gastonia, 1966-71; tax adminstr. Forsyth County (N.C.), 1971—. Bd. dirs. Winston-Salem Kidney Found. Served with AUS, 1958-60. Mem. N.C. Tax Suprs. Assn. (outstanding Tax Supr. award, 1970; chmn. edn. com. 1967-71, chmn. legislative com. 1971-72), N.C. Tax Collectors Assn., Internat. Assn. Assessing Officers (N.C. state rep. 1970-72, Com. of 100 1971-72). Episcopalian (vestryman). Lion (1st v.p. 1969), Elk (esquire 1969). Club: Exchange of Greater Winston-Salem. Home: 431 Burkeridge Ct Winston-Salem NC 27104 Office: 607 Government Center Winston-Salem NC 27104

EASTWOOD, RALPH ALLEN, educator; b. Wheatland, Wyo., Feb. 20, 1919; s. Edward Allen and Marie Ella (Backhaus) E.; B.S., U. Wyo., 1940; M.S., Cornell U., 1947, Ph.D., 1951; postgrad. Sorbonne U., 1945, Northwestern U., 1956; m. Ann Bromley, Aug. 22, 1956; children—Ralph Allen, Edward Bromley. Grad. asst. Cornell U., Ithaca, N.Y., 1940-41, 46-48; exec. sec. Milk for Health, Inc., Grange League Fedn. Exchange, Ithaca, N.Y., 1950-51; chief research sect. agrl. research dept., Swift & Co., Chgo., 1951-52; dir. dept. affiliated unit services Nat. Dairy Council, Chgo., 1954-57; instr. Coll. Commerce and Bus. Adminstrn. undergrad. div. U. Ill., Chgo., 1953, asst. prof., 1953-54; prof. dept. agrl. econs. U. Fla., Gainesville, 1957—. Asst. county agt.-at-large Bur. Agrl. Econs., U.S. Dept. Agr., U. Wyo., Laramie, 1940; economist Coop. Research and Service Div.,

U.S. Dept. Agr., Washington, 1948-49. Pres. Southtown YMCA, Chgo., 1952; sec. Four-State Com. on Coop. Research and Edn., 1970-71. Served from 2d lt. to lt. col., Q.M.C., AUS, 1941-46; now col. Res. ret. Mem. Am. Agrl. Econs. Assn., Fla. Extension Workers Assn., Fla. Farm Bur. Fedn. (mem. dairy adv. com. 1969—), Fla. Grape Growers Assn., N.Y. Acad. Scis., So. Agrl. Econs. Assn., Fla. Peach Growers Assn., Sigma Xi, Gamma Sigma Delta, Omicron Delta Epsilon, Phi Kappa Phi. Clubs: Gainesville Golf and Country. Author: Economics of the Dairy Industry in Costa Rica, 1969. Home: 3210 NW 18th Pl Gainesville FL 32601

EASTWOOD, RICHARD TRUMAN, med. adminstr.; b. Pawnee County, Neb., Nov. 19, 1912; s. Frank Wesley and Elizabeth (Wilkinson) E.; A.B., Tarkio (Mo.) Coll., 1936; M.A., U. Neb., 1939; Ph.D. in Econs. (Richard T. Ely scholar 1939-40), U. Wis., 1954; m. Elizabeth Comer, Apr. 5, 1942; children—Elizabeth Ann, Barbara Jean. Instr., Maysville (Mo.) High Sch., 1936-38; grad. asst. U. Neb., 1938-39; instr. econs. U. Ala., 1939-43, asst. supr. engring., sci. and mgmt. war tng. program, 1941-43, asst. prof. mgmt., then asso. prof., 1946-54, dir. commerce extension service, 1946-51, prof. econs., 1954-62, dir. Birmingham Center, 1951-58, asso. dean extension div., 1956-58, exec. dir. univ. affairs in Birmingham, 1958-62; exec. v.p. Tex. Med. Center, Houston, 1962—. Cons. NIH, 1961—; mem. nat. adv. council Inst. Gen. Med. Scis.; chmn. Com. Aging Jefferson County, Ala., 1954, 56-60; mem. Gov. Ala. Adv. Com. Planning for White House Conf. Aging, also del., 1961; chmn. Ala. Subcom. Housing Needs for Older Persons, 1960-61; sec. Tex. Coordinating Com.-Regional Med. Programs; v.p., sec. Tex. Med. Center Housing, Inc. Bd. dirs. Jefferson County Coordinating Council Social Forces, 1956-62. Served to lt. USNR, 1943-46. Am. Christian Palestine Com. scholar for study tour Middle East, 1955. Mem. Soc. Advancement Mgmt. (pres. Ala. 1953-54), Nat. U. Extension Assn. (sec. eve. div. 1958-59), Am., So. econ. assns., Indsl. Relations Research Assn., Alpha Kappa Psi, Phi Beta Pi. Presbyn. (permanent theol. com. Gen. Assembly). Home: 6135 Doliver Dr Houston TX 77027

EATON, JAMES NATHANIEL, educator; b. Richmond, Va., Sept. 14, 1930; s. John Jasper and Sarah (Cousins) E.; B.A., Fisk U., 1952, M.A., 1959; postgrad. Duke, 1962-63, (Danforth teaching fellow), 1964-66; m. Elsie Delores McLeod, Aug. 6, 1961; children—Jacqueline A., Sabrina Elizabeth, James Nathaniel, Robert Hiliary, Samuel Kenyatta. Instr. history Miles Meml. Coll., 1953-55; lab. technician Sonotone Co., Chgo., 1955-56; patrolman Richmond Police Dept., 1956-57; asst. prin. Hanover (Va.) Sch. for Boys, 1957-58; prof. history, Fla. A. and M. U., Tallahassee, 1958-69, asso. prof. history, chmn. dept. history and geography, 1969—, also dir. Afro Am. studies program. Mem. Fla. Heritage Found., 1967—. Named Most Outstanding Tchr. Fla. A. and M. U. ROTC; 1960, Tchr. of Year, Fla. A. and M. U. Student Govt., 1963. Mem. So. Hist. Assn., Am. Assn. U. Profs. (chpt. pres.), Am. Hist. Assn., Assn. for Study Negro Life and History. Kappa Alpha Psi, Pi Gamma Mu. Democrat. Baptist. Clubs: Fisk University Alumni (Tallahassee pres. 1963—), Fla. A. and M. University Faculty Men's (pres. 1960-61), Fla. A. and M. University Veteran's (adviser 1967—). Home: Lonnbladh Rd Route 3 Box 1068 Tallahassee FL 32301

EATON, JOE O., dist. judge; b. Monticello, Fla., Apr. 2, 1920; s. Robert Lewis and Mamie (Gireadeau) E.; A.B., Presbyn. Coll., 1941; LL.B., U. Fla., 1948; m. Patricia MacVicar, Sept. 25, 1942; children—Joe Douglas, Linda Juliet, Janet Patricia. Admitted to Fla. bar, 1948; practice law, Miami, Fla., 1948-51, 55-59; asst. state atty. Dade County, Fla., 1953; circuit judge, Miami, 1954-55, 1959-67; U.S. dist. judge So. Dist. Fla., 1967—; mem. Fla. Senate, 1956-59; mem. law firm Eaton & Achor, Miami, 1955-58, Sams Anderson, Eaton & Alper, Miami, 1958-59. Instr. law U. Miami Coll. Law, 1954-56. Served with USAAF, 1941-45, with USAF, 1951-52. Decorated D.F.C., Air medal. Methodist. Kiwanian (dir. Miami 1961-63). Home: 4901 SW 59th Av Miami FL 33155 Office: 300 NE 1st Av Miami FL 33132

EATON, RAMONE S(TANLEY), A.R.C. exec.; b. Alexandria, Va., Aug. 29, 1907; s. George H. and Irene M. (Beach) E.; student Southeastern U., Washington, 1925-26, George Washington U., 1928, U. Ga., 1931; m. June L. Clark, Jan. 16, 1933; children—June Elaine, Lyndle Stanley. Dir. pub. recreation, Alexandria, 1926, phys. edn., YMCA, Washington 1927; field rep. 1st aid and life saving, Am. Nat. Red Cross, 1928-39, asst. nat. dir., 1st aid and life saving, 1937-40, dir. roll call, 1940-41, adminstrv. asst. mgr. North Atlantic area, 1942-43; mgr. Eastern area and Pacific area, 1943-48, v.p., 1948-68, sr. v.p., 1968—. Mem. Pub. Relations Soc. Am., Am. Canoe Assn., Phi Pi Phi, Alpha Sigma Phi. Episcopalian. Clubs: Rotary (gov.), National Press (Washington); Fairfax Hunt (Va.); Toc-H; Commonwealth of Cal. (San Francisco); Court House Country (Va.). Contbr. articles on recreation, camping and safety edn., youth and drug edn. to publs. Home: 1400 S Joyce St Arlington VA 22310 Office: American National Red Cross 17th and E Sts Washington DC 20013

EATON, REGINALD CURREN, physician; b. Blomidon, N.S., Can., July 8, 1917 (came to U.S., 1955, naturalized, 1960); s. Victor Bigelow and Leta (Chisholm) E.; B.S., Acadia U., 1938; M.D., Dalhousie U., 1949; m. Isobel F. Carson, Aug. 12, 1944; children—Janice, Nancy, James. Intern, resident Victoria Gen. Hosp., Halifax, N.S., 1949-52; practice medicine, specializing in psychiatry, Darmouth, N.S., 1952-53; Supt. Provincial Hosp., Campbellton, N.B., 1953-55; Supt. South Fla. State Hosp., Hollywood, 1960-65; dept. dir. Fla. div. mental health, also dir. Fla. Community Health, 1965-69; dir. Mental Health Center, Ft. Pierce, Fla., 1969—. Served with Canadian Navy, 1941-45. Diplomate Royal Coll. Physicians and Surgeons. Mem. Am. Psychiat. Assn., Am. Hosp. Assn. Address: 1701 S 8th St Fort Pierce FL 33450

EAVES, GRADY JYLES, lawyer; b. Louisville, Miss., Nov. 6, 1933; s. William Andrew and Pearl (Rogers) E.; B.A., Miss. State U., 1960; J.D., U. Miss., 1962; m. Juan Dean Herrington, Aug. 25, 1962; 1 dau., Juanita Pearl. Admitted to Miss. bar, 1962, since practiced in Jackson, Louisville, 1964—; sr. mem. Eaves & Eaves, 1963—; dist. atty. Fifth Circuit Ct. Dist. Miss., 1967-72. Vice pres. Louisville-Winston Ednl. Found., Inc. Served with Hosp. Corps, USNR, 1956-57. Mem. Winston County Bar Assn. (past pres.), Am. Legion, Phi Alpha Delta. Democrat. Baptist. Mason (Shriner). Home: East Ridge Dr Louisville MS 39339 Office: 114 S. Columbus Av Louisville MS 39339

EAVES, JOEL HARRY, athletic dir.; b. Copperhill Tenn., June 3, 1914; s. Rufus Harry and Mabel (Puckett) E.; B.S. in Edn., Auburn U., 1937; m. Wealthy Elizabeth Lindsay, Jan. 20, 1946; children—Wealthy Joanne, Joel Harry. Basketball coach, asst. in football U. of South, 1937-41, Boys High Sch., Atlanta, 1946-47; basketball coach, head football Murphy High Sch., Atlanta, 1947-49; basketball coach Auburn U., 1949-63, asst. in football, 1949-60; athletic dir. U. Ga., Athens, 1963—. Mem. U.S. Olymic Basketball Com.; mem. basketball tournament com. Nat. Collegiate Athletic Assn. Served to lt. col. F.A., AUS, 1941-45. Named S.E. Conf. Basketball Coach of Year, 1958, 60, 62; named to Ga. Athletic Hall Fame, 1972. Presbyn. Author: Basketball's Shuffle Offense, 1960. Home: 550 Forest Rd Athens GA 30601 550 Forest Rd Athens GA 30601

EBAUGH, ELIZABETH BROWN (MRS. FRANK WRIGHT EBAUGH), civic worker; b. Jacksonville, Tex.; d. John Lemuel and Jewel (Newton) Brown; B.A., U. Colo., 1925; M.A., Tchrs. Coll., Columbia, 1927; m. Frank Wright Ebaugh, Feb. 22, 1930; 1 dau., Betty Jane (Mrs. Gordon B. McFarland, Jr.). Kindergarten tchr., Port Arthur, Tex., 1927-30. Mem. bd. Jacksonville (Tex.) Pub. Library, 1944—, pres., 1944-46, curator, organizer Vanishing Texana Mus., 1965—. Mem. Cherokee County Hist. Survey Com., 1964—. Mem. D.A.R. (charter; registar 1965—), Chi Omega. Presbyn. (historian 1965-66). Home: 428 S Patton St Jacksonville TX 75766

EBAUGH, FRANK WRIGHT, cons. indsl. engr., investments exec.; b. New Orleans, July 31, 1901; s. John Lynn and Mary (Wright) E.; B. in Chem. Engring., Tulane U., 1923; m. Elizabeth Brown, Feb. 22, 1930; 1 dau., Betty Jane (Mrs. Gordon B. McFarland, Jr.). Engr., asso. mgmt. Texas Co., 1923-34; partner retail firm, Jacksonville, Tex., 1934-54; mgr., partner Ebaugh & Brown Investments, Jacksonville, 1955-62; dir. Palestine Savs. & Loan Assn. Pres. Upper Neches River Municipal Water Authority; dir. Tex. Indsl. Devel. Council; vice chmn. Tex. Mapping Adv. Com.; sec. Tex. Coordinating Water Com.; pres. Neches River Devel. Assn.; Mem. panel chmn. Cherokee County (Texas) War Price and Ration Board, 3 years. Mem. regional com. of Girl Scouts Am.; mem. Cherokee County Hist. Survey Com. Bd. dirs. Neches River Conservation Dist. Named Man of Month, East Tex. C. of C., 1953; named Man of Year, Lions Club, 1953; honored as Distinguished Visitor Tex. Senate; Appreciation Plaque erected in Jacksonville Library, 1969. Mem. Nat., Tex. (chmn. Water Com.) socs. profl. engrs., East Texas, Jacksonville (past pres., dir., chmn. water resources com.) C.'s of C., Am. Chem. Soc., A.A.A.S., Tex. Acad. Sci., Tex. Water Conservation Assn., Texas Water Pollution Control Assn. Presbyn. (elder). Clubs: Headliners (Austin); Rotary, Country of Jacksonville (past pres.), Dallas Athletic, Country. Patentee Ebaugh Mixer. Home: 428 S Patton St Jacksonville TX 75766 Office: Box 1031 Jacksonville TX 75766

EBER, VICTOR ISRAEL, accounting firm exec.; b. N.Y.C., May 21, 1924; s. Louis and Clara (Lande) E.; student Coll. City N.Y., 1940-43; B.B.A., U. Miami, 1947; m. Betty Lopez Meruelo, Nov. 11, 1955; children— Steven Lande, Susan Elizabeth. Established, owner firm Victor I. Eber, C.P.A., Miami, Fla., 1950—. Faculty, U. Miami, 1950-61; lectr., coordinator mgmt. courses Havana (Cuba) Bus. U., 1955; feature columnist taxation Miami and Broward Revs.; pres. Med. Computer Services, Inc., Miami, 1965—; treas. Jerry's Inc., Miami, 1969—. Chmn., Gov.'s Profl. Adv. Com., 1968—; mem. Fla. Textbook Inquiry Commn., 1968—. Fla. Indsl. Devel. Commn., 1969—. Trustee Miami-Dade Jr. Coll. Served with USAAF, 1942-46. Mem. Jr. C. of C. (v.p. 1950). Republican. Kiwanian, Mason. Club: Toastmasters Internat. (local pres. 1957). Author: The Pros and Cons in Financial Management, 1971. Contbr. articles to publs. Home: 4975 SW 82d St Miami FL 33143 Office: 1101 Brickell Av Miami FL 33131

EBERHARDT, HOMER CHRISTIAN, state judge; b. Banks County, Ga., Oct. 31, 1904; s. Linton W. and Josephine (Wheeler) E.; B.S. U. Ga., 1925; LL.B., Mercer U., 1927; m. Ruby Jones, Oct. 14, 1931 (dec. July, 1958); children—Gretchen (Mrs. Wilby C. Coleman), Jan (Mrs. L. Howard McCurdy); m. 2d, LaForrest Smith, Aug. 1, 1959. Admitted to Ga. bar, 1927; practiced, Valdosta, 1928-61, sr. partner Eberhardt, Franklin, Barham & Coleman, 1958-61; judge Ga. Ct. Appeals, 1961—. Dir. Valdosta Fed. Savs. & Loan Assn., Citizens & So. Nat. Bank, Valdosta. Member Ga. Bd. Bar Examiners, 1958-61; mem. rules com. Supreme Ct. Ga., 1957-61. Mem. Valdosta Bd. Edn., 1948-61. Trustee Mercer U. Fellow Am. Coll. Probate Counsel; mem. Am. (Appellate Judges Conf.), Ga. (pres. 1960-61), Valdosta bar assns., So., Ga. hist. socs. Methodist. Elk, Mason. Home: RFD 2 Lake Park GA also Peachtree Towers Atlanta GA Office: Judicial Bldg Capitol Sq Atlanta GA 30334

EBERLY, ARTHUR LEE, JR., physician; b. Charleston, W.Va., Jan. 14, 1932; s. Arthur Lee and Salome Topham (Bernheim) E.; B.S., Fla. So. Coll., 1954; M.D., U. Miami, 1960; m. Jane Ellen Demaree, Sept. 30, 1961; children—Arthur Lee III, John Brewer, Sarah Elizabeth. Intern Marion County Gen. Hosp., Indpls., 1960-61; staff physician Polk County Hosp., Bartow, Fla., 1961; practice medicine specializing in family practice, Lighthouse Point, Fla., 1962—; clin. vol. asst. prof. family medicine U. Miami, 1967—; pres. staff No. Broward Hosp., 1968, chief of staff, 1969. Vice-pres. Broward Citizens Bd., U. Miami, 1970-71. Bd. dirs. Broward County unit Am. Cancer Soc., 1964—. Served with AUS, 1952-54. Diplomate Am. Bd. Family Practice. Mem. A.M.A., Am. Acad. Gen. Practice, Broward County Med. Assn. (treas. 1965-66), Sigma Alpha Epsilon. Methodist (pres. ofcl. bd. 1965-67; lay leader 1968—). Home: 3501 NE 27th Av Lighthouse Point FL 33064 Office: 2261 NE 36th St Lighthouse Point FL 33064

EBERT, MYRL LUA-FRANCES, librarian, educator; b. Louisville, Oct. 20, 1913; d. Clifford William and Ella Mae (Pitt) Ebert; B.S. George Peabody Coll., 1943; B.S. in L.S., George Peabody Library Sch., 1945; M.S., Columbia, 1951. Clerical asst. Vanderbilt U. Med. Sch. Library, also joint univ. libraries, Nashville, 1939-45; reference asst. Columbia U. Sch. Med. Library, N.Y.C., 1945-46; reference asst., asst. reference librarian, periodical librarian N.Y. Acad. Medicine, N.Y.C., 1946-51; library asso. N.Y.U. Bellevue Med. Center Library, N.Y.C., 1951-52; dir. Health Affairs Libraries div. U. N.C., Chapel Hill, 1952—, prof. Sch. Library Sci., 1958—. Cons. med., hosp. libraries, instns.; med. library cons. U. Saigon Med. Center, 1966—; cons. medlars program Nat. Library Medicine, 1965— bd. dirs. U.S. Book Exchange. Mem. Med. Library Assn. (chmn. so. regional group 1953-54, sec. 1962-64), Spl. Libraries Assn., N.C. Library Assn. (rec. sec. 1957-59), Am. Assn. History Medicine. Author: Introduction to Literature of the Medical Sciences, 3d edit., 1970. Contbr. articles to profl. jours. Home: Route 6 Box 126 Chapel Hill NC 27514

EBLEN, MERVIN KOHL, lawyer; b. Henderson, Ky., June 30, 1896; s. Mathew Floyd and Kate (Kohl) E.; LL.B., U. Ky., 1921; m. Helen Cole, Nov. 15, 1930; children—Katheryn Cole (Mrs. Robert Jessup), Margaret Louise (Mrs. John Evans Bowling), Helen Elizabeth (Mrs. Gordon Jones), James Milton, Mervin Kohl. Admitted to Ky. bar, 1921; practiced in Hazard, Ky.; city atty., 1923-27; mem. firm Helm & Eblen. Dir. Citizens State Bank, Hazard Coal Corp., Ky. Union Co., Eblen Coal Co., Margo Coal Co., Sun Trucking Co., Home Lumber Co. (all Hazard). Mayor Hazard, 1934, 52. Mem. bd. regents Morehead State U.; trustee Ky. Wesleyan Coll., Union Coll. Mem. Hazard Bar Assn. (past pres.), Hazard Coal Operators Assn. (past pres.), Ky. Coal Assn. (past pres.), Hazard C. of C. (past pres.), Ky. State C. of C. (dir. 1965—), Sigma Alpha Epsilon. Methodist. Lion (past pres.). Home: 301 Kentucky Blvd Hazard KY 41701 Office: 112 Main St Hazard KY 41701

ECHEVERRIA, LUIS, pres. of Mexico; b. Jan. 17, 1922; ed. U. Nacional Autonoma de Mexico. Pvt. sec. to pres. of exec. com. Partido Revolucionario Institucional, 1940-52, also dir. press and propaganda, 1949-52; dir. accounts and adminstrn. to sec. of marine, 1952-54; sr. ofcl. of sec. pub. edn., 1954-57; sr. ofcl. central exec. com. Partido Revulucionario Institucional, 1957; under-sec. of interior, 1958-63, sec. interior, 1963-70; pres. of Mexico, 1970—. Asst. prof. law U. Nacional de Mexico.‡

ECHOLS, WILBURN OLIVER, supt. schs.; b. nr. Greenville, Tex., Mar. 18, 1916; s. William Oliver and Martha Lorraine (Pickle) E.; B.S., So. Meth. U., 1940; M.S., E. Tex. State U., 1947; m. Sara Roddey Riley, July 26, 1941; children—Ann (Mrs. Jack E. Hanna, Jr.), Ruth (Mrs. Phillip L. Adams), Wilburn Oliver. Supt., Olney Pub. Schs., 1952-59; supt. schs. Grapevine (Tex.) Pub. Schs., 1959-61, Gainesville, 1961—. Pres. United Fund, 1969. Served with USNR, 1942-45. Mem. Am., Tex. assns. sch. adminstrs., Tex. Tchr. Assn., Nat. (life mem.), Tex. (life mem.) congresses of parents and tchrs. assns., C. of C. Baptist (deacon 1961—). Mason (32 degree, Shriner), Rotarian. Home: 30 Shadowood Lane Gainesville TX 76240 Office: 1201 Lindsay St Gainesville TX 76240

ECKART, WILLIAM JOSEPH, stage designer, educator; b. New Iberia, La., Oct. 21, 1920; s. William Joseph and Annette Cecile (Brown) E.; B.S. in Architecture, Tulane U., 1942; M.F.A. in Stage Design, Yale, 1949; m. Jean Levy, Aug. 28, 1943; children—Peter, Julie. Designer, CBS, N.Y.C., 1950-51; free lance designer scenery, costumes and lighting for Broadway plays and films, N.Y.C., 1951-71; prof. theatre So. Meth. U., Dallas, 1971—. Served with AUS, 1942-46. Mem. United Scenic Artists. Home: 6822 Westlake Dallas TX 75214

ECKBERG, LLOYD ELLSWORTH, orgn. exec.; b. Shinnston, W.Va., Nov. 11, 1929; s. William Quinn and Emma (Rhodes) E.; student, Fairmont State Coll., 1947-50; m. Glenna Maxine Tacy, Aug. 26, 1950; children—Tim Edward, Sharri Ann. Gen. mgr. Burnham Warehouses, Columbus, Ga., 1952-59; life underwriter N.Y. Life Ins. Co., Columbus, 1959-60; exec. dir. Warner Robins (Ga.) C. of C., 1960-63; exec. v.p. Thomasville-Thomas County C. of C., Thomasville, Ga., 1963—. Bd. dirs. Salvation Army. Served with AUS, 1950-52. Mem. Ga. C. of C. Execs. Assn. (pres. 1967-68), Am. C. of C. Execs. Assn., So Assn. C. of C. Execs. (dir. 1964-69), So. Indsl. Devel. Council. Methodist. Club: Optimist. Home: 527 E Jefferson St Thomasville GA 31792 Office: 401 S Broad St Thomasville GA 31792

ECKBERT, WILLIAM FOX, physician; b. New Cumberland, Pa., May 25, 1914; s. Chester Arthur and Angeline (Mapes) E.; student U. Del., 1932-35; M.D., Duke U., 1939; m. Sarah Ann Wilson, Apr. 9, 1939; children— William Fox, Patricia Ann. Intern Balt. City Hosps., 1939-40; resident contagious diseases Sydenham Hosp., Balt., 1940-41; gen. practice medicine Garrett Meml. Hosp., Crossnore, N.C., 1941-42; pvt. practice medicine, Cramerton, N.C., 1946—; mem. staff Gaston Meml. Hosp., chief of staff, 1959-60. Pres. Gaston County Cancer Soc., 1962-63; mem. Cramerton Sch. Bd., 1951-58. Bd. dirs. Gaston County Heart Assn. Served to capt. AUS, 1942-46. Decorated Bronze Star medal. Mem. Am., So. med. assns., N.C. State Med. Soc., Am. Acad. Gen. Practice, Am. Assn. Physicians and Surgeons, Gaston County Med. Soc. (pres. 1955-56), Sigma Nu, Alpha Kappa Kappa. Republican. Presbyn. (trustee, ruling elder). Kiwanian (pres. 1952), Elks. Club: Gaston Country. Home: Box 501 Belvue Terrace Rt 4 Gastonia NC 28052 Office: Box 317 Cramerton NC 28032

ECKELS, ROBERT Y., ins. co. exec.; b. Temple, Tex., July 24, 1929; s. Robert Y. and Mildred Louise (Daniel) E.; B.S., Sam Houston State Coll., 1949; M.Ed., U. Houston, 1955; m. Carolyn Bickley, Dec. 20, 1949; children—Robert Allen, Carol Ann. Tchr., Houston Ind. Sch. Dist., 1949-57; ins. agt. Bob Eckels & Assos., 1963-70, gen. agt., 1957-60, co. mgr., 1960-63; pres. Sur-Agts., Inc., Houston, 1970—; dir. Mark III, Gulf Coast Nat. Bank; dir., v.p. R.T.G. Mem. Houston Ind. Sch. Dist. Bd. Edn., 1961-69, pres., 1964-65, 68-69. Mem. Life Underwriters Assn., Tex., Houston ind. agts. assns., Tex. Leaders Roundtable, Sam Houston Alumni Assn. (pres. 1970-71), P.T.A. Mason (32 deg., Shriner). Home: 32 E Shady Lane Houston TX 77042 Office: 6733 Stella Link Houston TX 77005

ECKENFELDER, WILLIAM WESLEY, JR., educator; b. N.Y.C., Nov. 15, 1926; s. William Wesley and Martha (Richter) E.; B.Civil Engring., Manhattan Coll., 1946; M.S., Pa. State U., 1948; M.Civil Engring., N.Y.U., 1954; m. Barbara Jean Allen, Dec. 19, 1965; children—Lawrence William, Janice Kathrine. Pres. Eckenfelder Assos., Inc., 1950; asst. prof. Manhattan Coll., 1952-56, asso. prof., 1956-64; v.p. Weston, Eckenfelder & Hood, 1952-56; pres. Hydrosci., Inc., 1962-65; prof. U. Tex., 1965-70; pres. AWARE, 1970-71; Distinguished prof. environmental and water resources engring. Vanderbilt U., Nashville, 1970—. Cons. UN, 1965-70, numerous industries and municipalities; chmn. bd. review Water for Israel Ltd., 1972. Recipient Kenneth Allen award N.Y. Water Pollution Control Assn., 1957, Indsl. Wastes medal Water Pollution Control Fedn., 1957. Mem. Internat. Assn. Water Pollution Research, Am. Chem. Soc., Am. Inst. Chem. Engrs., Am. Soc. C.E., Am. Inst. Chemists, Water Pollution Control Fedn., Inst. Water Pollution Control. Author: (with D.J. OConnor) Biological Waste Treatment, 1961; Industrial Water Pollution Control, 1967; Water Quality Engineering, 1970; contbg. author Advances in Water Quality Improvement, 1967, 70; Advances in Biological Waste Treatment, 1963. Contbr. articles to profl. jours. Home: 4505 Harding Rd Nashville TN 37205 Office: Box 6222 Vanderbilt U Nashville TN 37203

ECKERT, ALLAN W., author; b. Buffalo, Jan. 30, 1931; s. Edward Russell and Ruth Rose (Roth) E.; student U. Dayton, 1951-52, Ohio State U., 1953; m. Joan Dowling, May 14, 1955; children—Joseph Matthew, Julie Anne. Formerly reporter, columnist Dayton Jour. Herald, also asso. editor N.C.R. News, Dayton; free-lance writer, 1960—; created course article writing Writer's Digest; cons. La Salle Extension U., Chgo. Trustee Dayton Mus. Natural History, 1963-65; bd. dirs. W. Charlotte County Civic Assn., Englewood, Fla. Served with USAF, 1948-52. Recipient Ohioana Book award, 1968; Best Book award Friend Am. Writers, 1968; Honor Book award, Newberry medal A.L.A., 1972. Life mem. Dayton Soc. Natural History; mem. Outdoor Writers Assn Am. (bd. dirs.), Soc. Mag. Writers. Author: The Great Auk, 1963; A Time of Terror, 1965; The Silent Sky, 1965; Wild Season, 1967; The Frontiersmen, 1967; Bayou Backwaters, 1967; The Crossbreed, 1968; Blue Jacket, 1968; The King Snake, 1968; The Dreaming Tree, 1968; Wilderness Empire, 1968; In Search of a Whale, 1969; The Conquerors, 1970; Incident at Hawk's Hill, 1970; (with Karl E. Karalus) The Owls of North America, 1972; The Court Martial of Daniel Boone, 1972; (screenplays) A Tale of a Cat, 1971, The Legend of Koo-Tan, 1972; Tecumseh (drama), 1971; 18 TV scripts for Wild Kingdom, NBC, 1971-72; also numerous short stories and articles. Address. 185 Sabal Lane Englewood FL 33533

ECKERT, ANDREW WILBURN, ednl. adminstr.; b. Galveston, Tex., Nov. 27, 1915; s. Fred Andrew and Cora B. (Northington) E.; A.A., U. Houston, 1935; B.B.A., U. Tex., 1941; M.Ed., Tex. Tech. U., 1959; m. Winona Helen Sloan, May 11, 1937; children—Andrea (Mrs. Tom Harold Watters), Andrew Wilburn, Sherry, Maribeth. Bus. mgr. Orange Ind. Sch. Dist. (Tex.), 1947-51; bus. mgr. Lubbock (Tex.) Ind. Sch. Dist., 1951-63; asso. supt. bus. Mpls. Pub. Schs., 1963-70; mgr. ednl. resources Dallas Pub. Schs., 1970—. Vis. instr. U. Wis. Sch. Bus. Workshop, 1968—; cons. Tex. Tech. U., Tex., 1951-63. Pres. Camp Fire Girls, 1952-54. Bd. dirs. A.R.C., United Fund. Recipient commendations A.R.C., 1963. Ednl. Facilities Lab. grantee, 1967. Mem. Am. Assn. Sch. Adminstrs., Assn. Sch. Bus. Ofcls., Tex. Assn. Sch. Bus. Ofcls. (pres. 1955), Metro Sch. Facilities Council,

Tex. State Tchrs. Assn., Dallas Sch. Adminstrs. Assn., Phi Delta Kappa, Sigma Iota Epsilon. Democrat. Methodist. Rotarian, Kiwanian. Home: 5977 Fox Hill Lane Dallas TX 75232 Office: 3700 Ross St Dallas TX 75204

ECKERT, ROBERT MASON, physician; b. Houston, May 1, 1930; s. Louis Frederick and Beatrice (Hunter) E.; B.S., Baylor U., 1951, postgrad., 1951-52; postgrad. U. Houston, 1955-56; M.D., U. Tex., 1960; m. Nancy Lavern Nance, May 18, 1952; children—Robert Mason, Kim, Jay, Dan, Ben. Clk. personnel dept. then asst. to safety dir., Hughes Tool Co., Houston, 1951-56; Intern, Meml. Hosp., Corpus Christi, Tex., 1960-61; gen. practice medicine, Hitchcock, Tex., 1961-64, Houston, 1964—; pres. bd., adminstr. Fourth Ward Kennedy Bros. Health Clinic, Houston, 1969—; mem. staffs St. Joseph Hosp., Houston, Pasadena Gen. Hosp.; clin. instr. dept. community medicine Baylor Med. Coll., Houston, 1970—. City health officer, Hitchcock, Tex., 1962-63. Trustee Inlet, Houston; bd. dirs. Houston Teen Challenge. Recipient Faith in God award Houston Jr. C. of C., 1970-71. Mem. Am. Acad. Gen. Practice, A.M.A., Tex. Acad. Gen. Practice, Tex. Med. Assn., Harris County Med. Soc. Episcopalian (dir. evang. ministries 1964—). Lion. Home: 4341 N MacGregor Way Houston TX 77004 Office: 302 1/2 Pierce St Houston TX 77002

ECKERT, WILLIAM ALTHEN, JR., lawyer; b. New Orleans, Sept. 1, 1919; s. William A. and Eluina (Walt) E.; A.B., La. State U., 1939; LL.B. with honors, U. Ark., 1948; m. Lillian V. Crumpler, Dec. 31, 1942; children—Julie Claire, William Althen III. Admitted to Ark. bar, 1948; partner firm Crumpler & Eckert, Magnolia, Ark., 1948-53; individual practice law, Magnolia, 1953-55; partner firm Keith, Clegg & Eckert, Magnolia, 1956—; municipal judge, Magnolia, 1956—; dir. First Nat. Bank Magnolia, 1958—, So. Extrusions, Inc., 1962—. Served to maj. USAF, 1941-46. Mem. Am., Ark., Columbia County bar assns., Am. Legion, 40 and 8. Methodist. Mason, Lion. Home: 528 Margaret Magnolia AR 71753 Office: McAlester Bldg Magnolia AR 71753

ECKHARDT, ROBERT CHRISTIAN, congressman; b. Austin, Tex., July 16, 1913; s. Joseph Carl Augustus and Norma (Wurzbach) E.; B.A., U. Tex., 1935, LL.B., 1939; m. Orissa Stephenson (dec.), children—Orissa, Rosalind; m. 2d, Nadine Ellen Cannon, Mar. 8, 1962; children—Sidney, Shelby, Willie, Sarah. Tchr., Coleman (Tex.) Flying Sch., 1942-44; S.W. regional dir. Office Coordinator Inter Am. Affairs, Austin, 1944-46; admitted to Tex. bar, 1939, practice law Austin, 1939-42, 46-48, Dallas, 1948-50, Houston, 1950-67; mem. Tex. Ho. of Reps., Austin, 1958-67; mem. 90th to 92d Congresses from 8th Tex. Dist., mem. Interstate and fgn. commerce, com. Served with USAAF, 1942-44. Mem. State Bar Tex. Democrat. Home: 3312 N St NW Washington DC 20007 Office: Longworth House Office Bldg Washington DC 20515

ECKLAND, BRUCE KENT, sociologist, educator; b. Chgo., Mar. 19, 1932; s. Everett Byron and Louise (Kessler) E.; B.S., U. Ill., 1957, M.A., 1961, Ph.D., 1964; m. Bobette Schrotberger, June 7, 1959; children— Lorraine Michel, Eric Kent, Diane Carol. Instr., U. Conn., Storrs, 1962-64; asst. prof. sociology U. N.C., Chapel Hill, 1964-66, asso. prof., 1967-70, prof., 1971—. Research asso. Inst. for Research in Social Sci., 1965—; vis. research sociologist Ednl. Testing Service, Princeton, N.J., 1966-67; co-chmn. task force on human deprivation NIH, 1968; mem. com. on basic research in edn. NRC. Served with AUS, 1952-54. Mem. Am., So. sociol. socs., Am. Eugenics Soc. (bd. dirs.), Soc. Human Genetics, Am. Ednl. Research Assn., Behavior Genetics Assn. Contbr. articles to profl. jours. Asso. editor Social Forces, 1964—, Am. Social Rev., 1968—, Behavioral Genetics, 1969—, Sociology of Education, 1971—, Social Biology, 1971—, Am. Jour. Sociology, 1972—. Home: Lone Pine Rd Chapel Hill NC 27514

ECKLUND, GEORGE NORMAN, govt. ofcl.; b. Odebolt, Ia., June 7, 1920; s. George Milton and Anna Naomi (Peterson) E.; B.A., Drake U., 1945; M.A., U. Minn., 1953, Ph.D., 1962; m. Dolores Lula Newberg, Mar. 16, 1945; children—Carol, Paula, Valerie. Mem. pub. relations staff Pillsbury Mills, Inc., Mpls., 1946-49; economist CIA, Washington, 1953-69; dir. Office Econ. Research, U.S. Tariff Commn., 1969—. Professorial lectr. econs. Am. U., Washington, 1962-69. Served with USAAF, 1942-45. Recipient certificate of Distinction, CIA, 1969. Mem. Am. Econs. Assn. Club: Tacomis (Washington). Author: Financing the Chinese Government budget, 1950-59, 1966. Home: 4211 Woodlark Dr Annandale VA 22003 Office: United State Tariff Commn Washington DC 20436

EDDIN, M. SHEHAB, educator; b. Cairo, Egypt, July 20, 1932; s. Mohammed Hassan Shehab and Asala (Eltabeiy) E.; B.A., U. Cairo, 1958; M.A., Am. U., Washington, 1963, Ph.D., 1966, postdoctoral research, 1967; postdoctoral research U. Stockholm (Sweden), 1967, Grad. Sch. Dept. Agr., Washington, 1967-68; m. Mary Edna Wright, Oct. 1, 1964; 1 dau., Ahlam. Came to U.S., 1960, naturalized, 1970. Mgr. tannery, Cairo, 1946-50; tchr. English and Arabic, Syria, U.A.R., 1950-60; supr. distbn. World Confn. Orgns. of Teaching Professions, Washington, 1962-65; asst. prof. polit. sci. and econs. Western Carolina U., Cullowhee, N.C., 1967-69; prof. Gardner-Webb Coll., Boiling Springs, N.C., 1969—; owner, dir. pvt. evening sch. adult edn., Cairo, 1952-55; adminstrv. asst., asst. dir. Mus. Rokn-Helwan, Cairo, 1955-58; mem. Egyptian Ednl. Mission to Syria, 1958-60, also instr. English civilization and Arabic, Shaabiya Inst., Syria. Mem. Am. Polit. Sci. Assn., Am. Soc. Internat. Law, Am. Acad. Polit. and Social Scis., Internat., So. polit. sci. assns., Middle East Inst., Am. Friends of Middle East, Internat. Platform Assn., Am. Civil Liberties Union, Acad. Polit. Sci., Pi Sigma Alpha. Author: Pan-Arabism and the Islamic Tradition: Ideology and Political Consensus, 1967. Contbr. articles to jours. Rotarian. Home: PO Box 934 Boiling Springs NC 28017 Office: Gardner-Webb Coll Dept Polit Sci Boiling Springs NC 28017

EDDLEMAN, ELVIA ETHERIDGE, JR., physician; b. Birmingham, Ala., Oct. 20, 1922; B.S., Howard Coll., 1944; M.D., Emory U., 1948; m. Jane Eddleman; 1 son, John Steven. Straight med. intern Grady Meml. Hosp., Atlanta, 1948-49; asst. resident internal medicine Parkland Hosp., Dallas, 1949-50; research fellow internal medicine Med. Coll. Ala., Birmingham, 1952-53, research fellow, instr., 1953-54, asst. prof. medicine, 1954-57, asso. prof., 1957-62; asst. chief med. service, chief cardiovascular sect. VA Hosp., Birmingham, 1954-57, acting chief med. service, 1957, chief med. service, 1957-62, asso. chief staff research and edn., 1954—; prof. medicine U. Ala. Sch. Medicine, Birmingham, 1962—, asso. prof. physiology and biophysics, 1966—. Mem. panel study sect. Nat. Heart and Lung Inst., 1971-72. Diplomate Am. Bd. Internal Medicine. Fellow A.C.P.; mem. Am. Coll. Cardiology; mem. Ala. (pres. 1967-68), Am. heart assns., A.M.A., Ballistocardiograph Research Soc., Birmingham Soc. Internists, Jefferson County Med. Soc., Laennec Cardiovascular Sound Group, Med. Assn. Ala., So. Soc. Clin. Investigation, Sigma Xi, Alpha Omega Alpha. Contbg. author: Methods in Medical Research, 1958; Clinical Cardiopulmonary Physiology, 1960; The Heart, 1966; Principles of Internal Medicine, 1966. Contbr. articles to profl. jours. Address: 511 Yorkshire Dr Birmingham AL 35209

EDDLEMAN, HENRY LEO, editorial cons.; b. Morgantown, Miss., Apr. 4, 1911; s. Richard Aaron and Lucille (Power) E.; A.B., Miss. Coll., 1932; Th. M.,So. Bapt. Theol. Sem. Louisville, 1935, Ph.D., 1942; D.D., Georgetown Coll., 1949; m. Sarah Fox, Sept. 7, 1937; children—Sarah Enfield, Evelyn Lucille. Ordained to ministry Bapt. Ch., 1930; ednl. and religious work, Palestine, 1935-41; tchr. O. T., Hebrew, New Orleans Bapt. Sem., 1941-42; pastor Parkland Ch., Louisville, 1942-52; faculty O. T., Hebrew, So. Bapt. Sem., Louisville, 1950-54; pres. Georgetown Coll., 1954-59, New Orleans Bapt. Theol. Sem., 1959-70; editorial cons. Sunday Sch. Bd. So. Baptist Conv., 1970—. Asst. moderator Gen. Assn. Bapts. Ky., also chmn. state bd., chmn. budget com., chmn. com. for nominations, 1954; bd. mgrs. Western Recorder (Bapt. state paper); mem. hosp. bd., pres. state bd. missions Ky. Bapts., also adv. com. Home for Aged; mem. fgn. mission bd., chmn. com. on ministerial edn, for Negroes, So. Bapt. Conv.; pres. So. Assn. Bapt. Colls., 1958. Bd. dirs. Miss. Coll. Alumni Assn., trustee La. Moral and Civic Found. Mem. Internat. Platform Assn., Nat. Assn. Profs. Hebrew of Am. Author: To Make Men Free, 1954; Teachings of Jesus in Matthew 5-7, 1955; Missionary Task of a Church, 1961; Mandelbaum Gate, 1963; (with others) The Second Coming, 1963; Trustees And Higher Education, 1966; Guidlines to Ecumenicalism, 1967; (with others) Last Things: Eschatology, 1968; Federal Aid, Trustees and Higher Education, 1969. Home: 901 Capitol Towers Nashville TN 37219

EDDLEMAN, JAMES CHRISTIAN, supt. schs.; b. Springfield, Ky., Aug. 3, 1903; s. John William and Mary (Lydanne) E.; A.B., Transylvania Coll., 1925; M.A., U. Ky., 1934; m. Ella M. Richardson, Jan. 8, 1926; children—James Christian, Alice Faye (Mrs. Thomas Allen Mitchell). Prin. Lynnvale (Ky.) High Sch., 1925-26, Crittenden (Ky.) High Sch., 1926-37; prin. Pineville (Ky.) High Sch., 1937-44; supt. schs., Pineville, 1944-49, Paintsville, Ky., 1949-58, Stanford, Ky., 1958-65; asst. supt. Lincoln County (Ky.) Schs., 1965—. Mem. Ky. Assn. Sch. Adminstrs. (dir.), Phi Delta Kappa. Mem. Christian Ch. (elder). Kiwanian (pres. Pineville 1948). Author bulletin. Home: 1 Anderson Heights Stanford KY 40484 Office: Somerset St Stanford KY 40484

EDDLEMAN, WILLIAM ROSEMAN, lawyer; b. Shelby, N.C., May 21, 1913; s. William Peter and Nellie Holland (Roseman) E.; student U. N.C., 1930-34, Pace Inst., 1934-35, Washington Coll. Law, 1935-37; LL.B., Gonzaga U., 1939; m. Elizabeth Carp, 1966; 1 son (by previous marriage), William Lammers. Admitted to Wash. bar, 1939, U.S. Supreme Ct., 1945; mem. firm Eddleman & Wheeler, Seattle, 1945-64, Perez, Verdia, Eddleman, 1963-64; law faculty National U. of Mexico, 1964—, Licenciado en Derecho, Mexico, 1968—. Del. Inter-Am. Bar Assn. meeting, Mexico, 1944. Exec. bd. Chief Seattle council Boy Scouts Am., 1959-61. Republican dist. leader, 1949-52, mem. exec. com., 1950-52. Mem. Internat. (charter patron), Am. (nat. chmn. jr. bar conf. 1948-49, ho. dels. 1949-50), Wash. (chmn. world readjustment and traffic court coms. 1944-46), Whitman County (pres. 1943-44) bar assns., Fedn. Ins. Counsel (v.p. 1960-61), Comml. Law League Am. (pres. 1961-62), Selden Soc., Federacion Interamericana de Abogados. Odd Fellow (sovereign grand rep. 1954). Lion (dir. 1963-64). Clubs: Spokane; Arctic (Seattle). Author: Legal Aspects of Economics Integration in Latin America, 1967. Home: Poniente 81 28 Mexico 18 DF Mexico Office: 4014 Republic Bank Tower Dallas TX 75230

EDDS, GEORGE TYSON, educator, pharmacologist; b. Heidenheimer, Tex., Jan. 9, 1913; s. John Cleveland and Eunice (Tyson) E.; student U. Tex., 1930-31; B.S., Tex. A. and M., 1936, D.V.M., 1936, M.S., 1938; Ph.D., U. Minn., 1952; m. Lorene Keith, Aug. 30, 1931; children—Charles Mack, Pamela (Mrs. Richard C. West), Cynthia Ann. Instr., Tex. A. and M., 1936-38, asst. prof. 1938-40, asso. prof. 1940-44, prof. 1944-50; v.p. Fort Dodge (Ia.) Labs., 1950-62; prof. vet. sci. U. Fla., Gainesville, 1962—, chmn. dept., 1962-71. Cons. Health, Edn. and Welfare Vet. Medicine, Health Manpower, 1967—. Chmn. bd. dirs. Sioux Falls Coll. Gen. Edn. Bd. fellow 1948-49. Mem. Toxicology Soc. Am. (exec. com. 1969—), U.S. Animal Health Assn. (chmn. pharm. com. 1965-70), Fla. Vet. Med. Assn. (chmn. edn. com.). Kiwanian, Lion (program chmn.), Rotarian. Home: 7616 SW 36th Av Gainesville FL 32601

EDDY, LEONARD MAX, librarian; b. Stamps, Ark., Apr. 26, 1932; s. Odis Milborn and Thelma Lula (Cheatham) E.; B.S., So. State Coll., Magnolia, Ark., 1954; M.L.S., U. Okla., 1961; m. Marjorie JoAnn Bristow, Oct. 30, 1954; children—Stephen Odis, Paul Wayne. Tchr., librarian Mt. Holly (Ark.) Pub. Schs., 1954-55; tech. librarian ACF Industries, Albuquerque, 1957-59; sci. area librarian U. Okla., Norman, 1961-62, asso. prof., dir. Med. Center Library, Oklahoma City, 1962—, asst. prof. library sci., 1967—. Chmn. Moore (Okla.) Library Bd., 1964-65; vice chmn. Pioneer Multi-County Library Bd., 1967-68. Served with AUS, 1955-57. Mem. Assn. Am. Library Schs., Am. Assn. History Medicine, Med. (chmn. So. regional group 1967-68), Okla. (treas. 1971—) library assns., Beta Phi Mu. Home: 113 Kelley Dr Moore OK 73060 Office: 800 NE 13th St Oklahoma City OK 73104

EDEN, WILLIAM GIBBS, educator; b. Talladaga, Ala., May 3, 1918; s. George G. and Maude (Parnell) E.; B.S., Auburn U., 1940, M.S., 1946; Ph.D., U. Ill., 1950; m. Evelyn Smith, June 1, 1940; children—Brenda (Mrs. W. F. Powell), Jane (Mrs. James M. Buttram). Asst. county agrl. agt. Auburn U., 1940-43, asst. prof., 1948-51, asso. prof., 1951-57, prof., 1957-65; chmn. dept. entomology U. Fla., 1965—. Mem. Auburn (Ala.) City Council, 1960-65. Served with USNR, 1944-46. Mem. Entomol. Soc. Am. (pres. 1972), Gamma Sigma Delta, Phi Kappa Phi, Sigma Xi, Pi Chi Omega. Club: Rotary (Gainesville). Research in econ. entomology. Home: 4411 NW 17th Pl Gainesville FL 32601

EDENFIELD, NEWELL, lawyer, judge; b. Stillmore, Ga., Aug. 10, 1911; s. John and Elizabeth (McCord) E.; LL.B., U. Ga., 1938; m. Theresa Pope, Apr. 8, 1938; children—Nancy, Newell, Bruce, Stephen, James, David. Admitted to Ga. bar; legal editor Edward Thompson Co. div. West Publishing Co., 1938-41; practice of law, Atlanta, 1941—; mem. law firm Edenfield, Heyman & Sizemore; U.S. dist. judge No. Dist. Ga., 1967—; instr. Atlanta Law Sch., 1946-50. Served to lt. (j.g.) USNR, 1942-45. Recipient Nathan Burkan Meml. award U. Ga. Law Sch., 1938. Fellow Am. Coll. Trial Lawyers; mem. Am., Ga. (pres. 1959-60), Atlanta (pres. 1954-55) bar assns. Home: 119 The Prado NE Atlanta GA 30303 Office: Fulton Fed Savs Bldg Atlanta GA 30303

EDENS, JAMES DRAKE, JR., mem. Republican Nat. Com.; b. Blaney S.C., May 13, 1925; s. J. Drake and May (Youmans) E.; B.S. in Bus. Administrn., U. S.C., 1949; m. Ferrell McCracken, May 28, 1946; children— Robert Manning, Jenny, Vice pres. Edens Food Stores, Inc., Columbia, S.C., 1946-55; pres. Edens-Turbeville Gen. Ins. Agy., Columbia, 1956-63. Active Rep. Party, 1960—; chmn. S.C. Rep. Party, 1963-65; mem. Rep. Nat. Com. for S.C., 1965—, vice-chmn., also mem. coordinating com., 1965—. Mem. nat. adv. bd. for sport fisheries and wildlife U.S. Dept. Interior, 1970—. Pres., S.C. chpt. Nat. Arthritis Found. Served with USMCR, 1943-46; PTO. Methodist (lay preacher). Mason. Clubs: Palmetto, Forest Lake Country, Spring Valley Country, Camellia Ball. Home: 905 Arbutus Dr Columbia SC 29205

EDGAR, JAMES WINFRED, commr. edn.; b. Briggs, Tex., Sept. 15, 1904; s. James William and Sarah (Morris) E.; B.A., Howard Payne Coll., 1928; M.A., U. Tex., 1938, Ed.D., 1948; LL.D., Austin Coll., 1958; D. Litt., Southwestern U., 1967; m. Sue Oaklay, Aug. 22, 1927; children—Frances Ruth, Sarah Elizabeth, Susan Elaine. Tchr., Burnet County, Tex., 1923-27; prin., Heidenheimer, Tex., 1928-29; asst. supt. schs., Victoria, Tex., 1936-39; supt. schs., Mirando City, Tex., 1929-36; Orange, Tex., 1939-47, Austin, Tex., 1947-50; state commr. edn., Tex., 1950—. Nat. com. on scouting in schs. Boy Scouts Am. Mem. Am. Assn. Sch. Adminstrs. (mem. 1950 Yearbook commn.), Tex (pres. 1942-44, chmn. edn. policies com. 1947-48) assns. sch. adminstrs., Tex. Tchrs. Assn. (exec. com. 1947, legislative com. 1947-49), N.E.A., Phi Delta Kappa. Presbyn. (mem. adv. council higher edn. U.S.). Editorial bd. Sch. Execs. mag., 1947-52. Home: 1517 Parkway Austin TX 78703 Office: Tex Edn Agy State Capitol Austin TX 78711

EDGE, DONALD RICHARD, architect; b. Detroit, Jan. 25, 1927; s. Ernest Richard and Grace Louise (Beymer) E.; B.Arch., U. Mich., 1951; m. Alice Nan Divine, June 2, 1956; children—Carol, Karl, Nancy. Draftsman, C. L. T. Gabler, Detroit, 1951-52, Byron Simonson, Palm Beach, Fla., 1952-54, William M. King, Palm Beach, Fla., 1954-56; self-employed as architect, Palm Beach, Fla., 1956—. Pres., Joint Coop. Council Fla., Inc., 1965-65. Joint Coop. Council Palm Beach County, 1960, 66. Bd. dirs., exec. com. Crippled Childrens Soc., Palm Beach, Fla. Served with USNR, 1945-46. Recipient award of recognition Fla. Bd. Architecture, 1970. Mem. A.I.A. (pres. Palm Beach chpt. 1960), Urban Land Inst., Constrn. Specifications Inst., Nat. Fire Prevention Assn., Am. Hosp. Assn., Am. Assn. for Hosp. Planning, Fla. Constrn. Industry Council (pres. 1967), Fla. State Bd. Architecture (pres. 1968-69), Fla. Planning and Zoning Assn., Sigma Chi. Prin. archtl. works include Fla. Hosp., Orlando, Palm Beach County Ct. House. Home: 800 Atlantic Dr SE Lantana FL 33460 Office: Phipps Plaza Bldg Palm Beach FL 33480

EDGERTON, JAMES BRYANT, civil engr.; b. Florence, S.C., Dec. 18, 1900; s. John William and Emmeline Haralson (Hall) E.; B.S., Citadel, 1922; m. Grace Regina Kelly, Feb. 23, 1929; children—James Bryant (dec.), Grace Annmarie. Civil engr. A.C.L. R.R., 1922-24, L. & N. R.R., 1924-25, S.C. Hwy. Dept., 1927-31; engr. C.E., 1925-27, Huntington, W.Va., 1932-37, Mobile, Ala., 1937-39, Providence, 1939-46, asst. chief engring. div. Savannah (Ga.) Engring. Dist., 1946-71. Registered profl. engr., Ohio, Ga., S.C. Mem. Am. Soc. C.E. (pres. Savannah chpt. 1959), Internat. Commn. Large Dams, Sons of Revolution in Ga. Episcopalian. Club: Savannah Yacht. Home: 526 E 51st St Savannah GA 31405

EDMAN, JOHN DAVIS, scientist; b. Willmar, Minn., Jan. 20, 1938; s. Joel R. and Agnes E. (Hough) E.; B.S., Gustavus Adolphus Coll., 1959; M.S., U. Neb., 1961; Ph.D., Kan. State U., 1964; m. Lillian A. Hanson, Dec. 20, 1959; children—Scott Joel, Stacy Jill, Sean Jeffrey. Research asst. U. Neb., Lincoln, 1959-62, Kan. State U., Manhattan, 1962-64; research med. entomologist Fla. Div. Health, Entomol. Research Center, Vero Beach, 1964—, asst. dir., 1969—. Cons. NIH, Bethesda, Md., 1967—, WHO, Geneva, Switzerland, 1970—. Recipient Nat. Def. Edn. Act fellowship, 1960, Pub. Health Service pre-doctoral fellowship, 1963. Mem. Entomol. Soc. Am., Am. Mosquito Control Assn., A.A.A.S., Fla. Anti-Mosquito Assn. Elk. Home: 1415 35th Av Vero Beach FL 32960 Office: Entomol Research Center Vero Beach FL 32960

EDMONDS, FRAZER, real estate exec.; b. Cumby, Tex., Feb. 12, 1910; s. William and Daisy (Frazer) E.; student N. Tex. Agrl. Coll., 1928-30, E. Tex. State Tchrs. Coll., 1930-31; m. Opal Louise Dusek, Apr. 2, 1941; 1 dau., K. Louise. Engring. dept. W. Tex. Utilities Co., 1930-39; jobber bldg. materials Frazer Edmonds Co., Abilene, Tex., 1941-53; partner Cumby Storage and Warehouse Co., Tex., 1953—; mgr. real estate, also apts., 1971—; city mgr. City of Wamego, Kan., 1957-58; city mgr., Commerce, Tex., 1959-71. Del. Dem. Nat. Conv., 1956, sch. trustee City of Cumby, 1955-57. Mem. Internat. City Mgrs. Assn., Tex. Municipal League. Presbyn. Mason. Office: 2613 Taylor St Commerce TX 75428

EDMONDS, HELEN GREY, educator, historian; b. Lawrenceville, Va., Dec. 3, 1911; d. John Edward and Ann (Williams) Edmonds; A.B., Morgan State Coll., 1933, LL.D., 1958; M.A., Ohio State U., 1938, Ph.D., 1946; postdoctoral research U. Heidelburg (Germany), 1954-55. Dean women, prof. Greek, Latin and history Va. Sem., Lynchburg, 1933-35; instr. history St. Paul Norman Sch., Lawrenceville, 1935-40; cons. social scis. Va. Dept. Edn., summer 1940; prof. history Grad. Sch., N.C. Coll. at Durham (now N.C. Central U.), 1940—, dean Grad. Sch., 1964—, mem. interim com. charge operation coll., 1966. Leader-specialist State Dept. to Germany, 1955, to Sweden, Denmark, Germany, Austria and France, 1957; rep. President Eisenhower to dedication ceremonies Liberian Capitol Bldg., Monrovia, 1957; del. 8th nat. conf. U.S. commn. UNESCO, Boston, 1961; now del. UN, N.Y.C. Trustee St. Paul's Coll., Va. Gen. Edn. Bd. grantee, 1943-44, Carnegie Found. grantee, 1949, Fund Advancement Edn. grantee, 1954-55; recipient Woman of Year plaque Bachelors-Benedicts Civic Club, 1958; named Woman of Year in So. Area, Nat. Links, 1965. Mem. Council Grad. Deans, Am. Hist. Assn., Assn. Social Sci. Tchrs., Am. Tchrs. Assn., Assn. Study Negro Life and History, Va. Soc. Research, Nat. Links (dir. nat. and internat. trends and services), Phi Alpha Theta, Alpha Kappa Delta, Pi Gamma Mu, Alpha Phi Gamma, Kappa Delta Pi, Delta Sigma Theta. Episcopalian. Author: The Negro and Fusion Politics in North Carolina, 1951; also monographs, articles and hist. pageants. Co-editor: Appropriate Directions for the Modern College in the Challenging New Educational Era, 1962. Home: 118 Nelson St Durham NC 27707

EDMONDS, THOMAS NEWTON, realtor; b. Kemper, Miss., May 21, 1904; s. James Nathanial and Dora (Syanzy) E.; student LaSalle Extension U., 1959-60, U. Houston, 1961-63; m. Vivian McClain Dial. Oct. 5, 1928; children—Betty Frances (Mrs. Davis), Ruth (Mrs. Lincoln), Thomas Newton II. Foreman, Sumpter Lumber Co., Electric Mills, Miss., 1921-24; timekeeper Fla. East Coast R.R., Jupiter, Fla., 1925-26; revenue analysis clk. Houston Lighting and Power Co., Houston, 1927-40; owner, operator Edmonds & Co., realtors and appraisers, Houston, 1940—; dir. Homestead Bank, Houston. Mem. Nat. Assn. Ind. Fee Appraisers (sr. mem.; past pres. Houston chpt.), Am. Soc. Appraisers (sr. mem.; past chpt. dir.), Soc. Real Estate Appraisers (sr.), Right of Way Assn. Mason (Shriner), Lion: Club: North Side Lyons. Home: Route 2 21518 Cosby-Eastgate Rd Crosby TX 77532 Office: 10028 Jensen Dr Houston TX 77016

EDMONDSON, ED, congressman; b. Muskogee, Okla., Apr. 7, 1919; s. Edmond Augustus and Esther (Pullen) E.; grad. Jr. Coll., Muskogee, 1938; A.B., U. Okla., 1940; LL.B., Georgetown U., 1947; m. June Maureen Pilley, Mar. 5, 1944; children—James Edmond, William Andrew, John M., June E., Brian. Newspaperman Muskogee (Okla.) Daily, also United Press, 1936-40; spl. agt. F.B.I., 1941-43; Washington corr. Muskogee Phoenix, Sapulpa Herald, Holdenville News, Daily Ardmoreite, 1946-47; admitted to D.C. bar, 1947, Okla., 1947, since practiced in Muskogee; asso. J. Howard Edmondson, 1948; co. atty. Muskogee Co., 1949-52; mem. 83d-92d Congresses, 2d Dist. Okla. Served as lt. USNR, World War II. Mem. Am. Legion,

V.F.W., Okla. Bar Assn., Phi Beta Kappa, Phi Delta Phi, Delta Sigma Rho, Phi Gamma Delta. Mason, Elk, Kiwanian. Home: PO Box 11 Muskogee OK 74401 Office: Rayburn House Office Bldg Washington DC 20515

EDMONDSON, JERRY HOLLIS, clergyman; b. Newellton, La., Sept. 13, 1933; s. Frank G. and Opal (Colvin) E.; B.S., La. Poly. Inst., 1955; B.D., New Orleans Bapt. Theol. Sem., 1964; Th.D., Luther Rice Sem., 1971; m. Patsy Carole Pippen, Dec. 16, 1962; 1 son, Eric. Constrn. engr., 1959-60; mission pastor La. Bapt. Conv., 1961-66; ordained to ministry Bapt. Ch., 1962; pastor Mooringsport Bapt. Ch. (La.), 1966-70, Fair Park Baptist Ch., West Monroe, La., 1970—. Dist. v.p. La. Bapt. Conv., 1968—, 2d v.p. conv., 1972—. Trustee La. Bapt. Children's Home, Monroe. Served to 1st lt. USAF, 1955-58. Mem. N. Caddo Bapt. Assn. (moderator 1966-69). Mason. Address: 4100 White's Ferry Rd West Monroe LA 71291

EDMONSON, GEORGE HAMPTON, JR., dentist; b. Magee, Miss., Feb. 9, 1937; s. George Hampton and Lanelle (Russell) E.; student Miss. State Coll., 1955-58; B.S., U. Miss., 1961; D.D.S., Emory U., 1969; m. Linda Ray Hartfield, May 8, 1964; children—Mark David, Amy Lynn. Pharmacist, Patterson-Welch Drug Store, Jackson, Miss., 1961-62, Walnut St. Pharmacy, Hattiesburg, Miss., 1962-64, Emory U. Hosp., Ga. Bapt. Hosp., Atlanta, 1965-68; individual practice dentistry, Brookhaven, Miss., 1969—. Organizer, adviser Andrew Jackson Council Boy Scouts Am., 1971-72. Bd. dirs. United Givers Fund Lincoln County. Mem. Am., Miss. dental assns., Gideons, Miss. Pharm. Assn., Xi Psi Phi, Kappa Alpha, Kappa Psi, Phi Eta Sigma. Baptist. Kiwanian. Club: Exchange (Brookhaven, Miss.). Home: 1116 S Church St Brookhaven MS 39601 Office: 232 W Court St Brookhaven MS 39601

EDMUNDS, GEORGE BEAUREGARD, printer, pub.; b. Augusta, Ga., Apr. 11, 1907; s. William Oscar and Irene (Gray) E.; ed. pub. schs.; m. Madeleine Matilda Lang, Dec. 25, 1928; 1 dau., Gloria Ann (Mrs. Walter Gerald Glover). With art and editorial dept. King Feature Syndicate, Inc., N.Y.C., 1927-34; founder, pres. Dixie-Rush Co., Decatur, Ga., 1937-48; pres., treas. Atlanta Dixie-Rush Bottling Co., 1938-48; founder, owner Mountain City (Ga.) Press, 1961—. Mem. Humanitarian Soc., Nat. Ry. Hist. Soc., Gypsy Lore Soc. Methodist. Mason (32 deg.). Home: 357 Electric Av Mountain City GA 30562 Office: PO Drawer E Mountain City GA 30562

EDMUNDS, LAFE REES, ednl. adminstr.; b. Salt Lake City, June 22, 1924; s. David Galloway and Dora (Rees) E.; B.S., U. Utah, 1947, M.S., 1949; Ph.D., Ohio State U., 1952; m. June LaFawn Law, Dec. 19, 1947; children—Jeffrey Garth, Mark Lafe, Alan Law. Sr. asst. scientist USPHS, Mitchell, Neb., 1952-54; asst. prof. Miss. State U., Starkville, 1955-56; prin. entomologist Engr. Research and Devel. Lab., Fort Belvoir, Va., 1956-59; asso. program dir. NSF, Washington, 1959-65, exptl. projects coordinator for edn., 1968—; spl. cons. to Mexican govt. WHO, 1965-68. Cons., Salt Lake City Mosquito Abatement Dist., Armed Forces Pest Control Bd. Expt. Sta., Miss. State U., Surgeon Gen's. Office, 1955-56. Served with AUS, 1943-46. Mem. Am. Inst. Biol. Scis., Entomol. Soc. Am., Entomol. Soc. Washington, Washington Acad. Sci., Sigma Xi. Club: Toastmasters (pres. 1963-64) (Alexandria, Va.). Home: 6003 Leewood Dr Alexandria VA 22310 Office: 1800 G St NW Washington DC 20550

EDMUNDSON, WALTER FLETCHER, dermatologist; b. Pitts., 1917; M.D., Hahnemann Med. Coll., 1941; M.Sc. in Pharmacy, U. Miami (Fla.). Intern Shadyside Hosp., Pitts., 1941-42; asst. resident in dermatology U. Mich. Hosp., Ann Arbor, 1945-46; practice medicine specializing in dermatology, 1946—; staff Venereal Disease Research Lab., also chief dermatology sect. U.S. Marine Hosp., S.I., N.Y., 1946-48; with dermatol. clin. investigations br. Div. Indsl. Hygiene, USPHS, Washington, 1950-51, asso. dir., also chief clin. investigations sect. Venereal Disease Research Lab., Chamblee, Ga., 1952-54, chief Out Patient Dept., USPHS Hosp., San Francisco, 1962-63; med. dir. Inst. Interam. Affairs, Pub. Health Service, Mexico, 1951-52; dir. Okla. Prevention and Control Center, 1954-55; chief tech. services Pesticides Research Lab., Fla. Dept. Agr., Perrine, 1964-66, with Perrine Pvt. Research Lab., 1971—. Teaching fellow dermatology Grad. Sch. Pub. Health, U. Pitts., 1948-49, instr. dermatology, also adj. asst. prof. Dept. Epidemiology, 1955-62; asst. prof. Dept. Medicine, U. Miami (Fla.), 1970—. Asst. dir. Community Studies on Pesticides, Dade County (Fla.)-USPHS, Miami, 1966-70. Served to capt. M.C., AUS, 1942-45. Decorated Air medal. Diplomate Am. Bd. Dermatology. Mem. Am. Acad. Dermatology, Am. Pub. Health Assn., Soc. Investigative Dermatology, A.M.A. Address: 1390 NW 14th Av Miami FL also PO Box 490 Perrine FL 33157

EDRINGTON, ROBERT EUGENE, tax cons.; b. Chgo., July 21, 1930; s. Robert Ernest and Edna Irma (Newman) E.; B.S., U. Fla., 1954; m. Fiona Florence Nichols, July 18, 1969; children—Robert Bruce, Cynthia Leigh. Vice pres. Planning Corp. Am., St. Petersburg, Fla., 1970—; owner R. Edrington & Assos., Tampa, Fla.; v.p. Lamonse-Salmberg Corp.; dir. Univ. Center Constrn. Co., Inc., St. Lucie Industries, Miami Engring Co.; tax cons. to corps. in Fla., Ga. and N.C. Steinberg Found. grantee, 1968. Mem. Am. Accounting Assn., Internat. Assn. Financial Cons. (charter). Mason. Clubs: Commerce; Explorers (Liverpool, Eng.). Author: How to Net More Dollars from Your Business After Taxes, 1966; Why Every Business Needs a Tax Consultant, 1969. Home: 10320 Carrollwood Lane Tampa FL 33618 Office: 6090 Central Av St Petersburg FL 33707

EDSON, MERRITT AUSTIN, JR., designer, editor; b. Pensacola, Fla., July 2, 1922; s. Merritt Austin and Ethel (Robbins) E.; student Georgetown Sch. Fgn. Service, 1941-43, postgrad., 1954-56; B.S. in Fgn. Service, Villanova Coll., 1943-44. Sub-accountant Nat. City Bank N.Y., 1946-48; co-owner Harding Hill Farm, Mt. Sunapee, N.H., 1949-51; marine display and research cons., 1957—; engr. asst. Alan M. Voorhees & Assos., Inc., McLean, Va., 1966-70; designer Planning Research Corp., McLean Va., 1970, Alan M. Voorhees & Assos., Inc., 1970—; editor Nautical Research Jour., 1965-69, editorial adviser, 1969—. Permanent exhibits marine life Smithsonian Instn. Served to 2d lt., USMCR, 1943-46, to capt., 1st Marine Div., 1951-57. Mem. Naut. Research Guild, Soc. Naut. Research, Nat. Rifle Assn., 1st Marine Div. Assn. Republican. Conglist. Club: Army and Navy (Washington). Contbr. articles to nautical research publs. Address: 6413 Dahlonega Rd Washington DC 20016

EDWARDS, ALFRED LEROY, govt. ofcl.; b. Key West, Fla., Aug. 9, 1920; s. Eddie E. and Kathleen L. (Sands) E.; B.A., Livingstone Coll., Salisbury, N.C., 1948; M.A., U. Mich., 1949; Ph.D., State U. Ia., 1958; m. Willie Mae Lewis, June 4, 1949; children—Beryl Laurette, Alfred Leroy. Instr. econs. dept. social sci. So. U., Baton Rouge, 1949-54; instr. econs. State U. Ia., 1956-57; asst. prof. econs. Mich. State U., 1957-60, 62-63; econs. adviser U. Nigeria, Nsukka, W.Africa, 1960-62; dep. asst. sec. for rural devel. and conservation U.S. Dept. Agr., Washington, 1963—; lectr. dept. econs. Howard U. Mem. Nat. Adv. Com. on Vocational Edn., 1964—, D.C. Adv. Com. on Vocational Rehab., 1965—. Bd. mgmt. Met. YMCA. Served with Signal Corps. AUS, 1943-46. Recipient Livingstone Coll. Alumni Achievement award, 1967, Distinguished Service award U.S. Dept. Agr., 1969. Danforth Faculty fellow, summer 1958, Postdoctoral fellow U. Mich., summer 1960, Ford Found. Faculty fellow in econs., 1963-64. Author: A Study of Local Government Debt in Michigan, 1960; The Detroit Income Tax, 1963. Home: 819 6th St SW Washington DC 20024 Office: 12th and Independence Av SW Washington DC 20250

EDWARDS, CHARLES HAYDEN, railroad exec.; b. Louisville, June 24, 1924; s. James P. and Margaret (Wathen) E.; A.B., Harvard, 1948; LL.B., U. Va., 1951; m. Sara Hulette Cummins, June 7, 1958 children—Richard Wathen, Cecilia Barber. Admitted to Ky. bar, 1952; practiced in Louisville, 1955-57; asst. city atty., Louisville, 1952-57; with L. & N. R.R., Louisville, 1958—, sec., gen. atty., 1963-66, sec., treas., dir., 1967—; sec. Carrollton R.R.; sec., treas. Cybernetics & Systems, Inc., Central Transfer Ry. & Storage Co.; dir., sec.-treas. Ky. Central Ry. Co., Houston-McCord Realty Co., L & N Investment Corp.; sec., dir. Louisville, Henderson & St. Louis Ry. Co., Nashville & Decatur R.R. Co., Paducah & Ill. R.R. Co. Bd. overseers Louisville Country Day Sch. Served with inf. AUS, 1943-46. Mem. Am., Louisville bar assns., Ky. State Bar. Democrat, Roman Catholic. Clubs: Louisville Country, Filson, River Valley, Tavern (Louisville); Harmony Landing Country (Goshen, Ky.). Home: 465 Lightfoot Rd Louisville KY 40207 Office: 908 W Broadway Louisville KY 40201

EDWARDS, CHARLES HENRY, county ofcl.; b. Relief, N.C., Feb. 10, 1908; s. Elbert Henry and Emily (Peterson) E.; B.S. in Agrl. Edn., U. Tenn., 1939, M.S. in Agrl. Extension, 1962; postgrad. Cornell U., 1946, U. Ark., 1956; m. Ruby Jewel Grimsley, July 25, 1936; children—Charles Henry, Kenneth Creighton, Linda Ruth (Mrs. Charles Wright Sydnor, Jr.). Asst. county agt., Monroe County, 1939-40; county agrl. agt. Morgan County, Tenn., 1940-46, Greene County, Tenn., 1946-50; sr. agrl. expert Govt. Thailand, 1950-51; co. agrl. agt. Blount County, Maryville, Tenn., 1952—, Del., Nat. Conf. Econ. Issues in Agr., Washington, 1963. Recipient Gov.'s citation for services as war fund chmn. Morgan County 1945; Outstanding County Agt. award Tenn., 1959, 61; Fed. Civilian Career Service award, 1962; Distinguished Service award Nat. Assn. County Agrl. Agts., 1967. Mem. Nat. (chmn. recognition and awards com. 1954-55), Tenn. (sec. 1947-48) county agts. assns., Exchange Club, C. of C., Epsilon Sigma Phi, Alpha Zeta, Phi Epsilon, Biologia, Phi Delta Kappa, Phi Kappa Phi. Methodist (steward). Rotarian. Author: Tobacco Production in Thailand, 1951. Editor Tenn. Farmer Mag., 1938-39. Contbr. over 1,000 articles to newspapers, mags. Home: Route 8 Maryville TN 37801 Office: Courthouse Annex Maryville TN 37801

EDWARDS, CLAUDE REYNOLDS, judge; b. Chester, S.C., Aug. 29, 1922; s. Claude R. and Mary (Walsh) E.; A.B., Wofford Coll., 1943; LL.B., Yale, 1949; m. Sarah Chapman Walker, Sept. 27, 1948; children—Sarah, Claude R., James A. Asst. dir. Inst. of Govt., Chapel Hill, N.C., 1949-50; legal cons. to gen. counsel Econ. Stabilization Agy., Washington, 1950; admitted to Fla. bar, 1950; practiced in Deland, 1950-51, Orlando, 1951-68; circuit judge State Fla., Orlando, 1968—. City councilman, Orlando, Fla., 1955-58; mem. Orlando Traffic Commn., 1955-58. Mem. Orange County Republican Exec. Com., 1955-67; pres. Orange County Young Republican Club, 1958. Bd. dirs. Orlando Civil Service, 1960-67; trustee Orlando Pub. Library, 1958-70, pres., 1969-70. Served with AUS, 1943-46. Mem. Am., Fla., Orange County, Osceola County bar assns., Blue Key, Phi Delta Phi, Sigma Alpha Epsilon, Pi Gamma Mu. Methodist. Rotarian. Office: 447 Orange County Courthouse Orlando FL 32801

EDWARDS, EARLE LARUE, coach; B.S., M.A., Pa. State U. Head football coach N.C. State Coll., Raleigh. Address: Athletic Dept NC State Coll Raleigh NC 27607*

EDWARDS, EDWIN WASHINGTON, gov. La.; b. Marksville, La., Aug. 7, 1927; s. Clarence W. and Agnes (Brouillette) E.; J.D., La. State U., 1949; m. Elaine Schwartzenburg, Apr. 5, 1949; children—Anna Laure, Victoria Elaine, Stephen Randolph, David Edwin. Admitted to La. bar, 1949; gen. practice in Crowley, La 1949-66; sr. founding partner firm Edwards & Edwards, 1954—; mem. Crowley City Council, 1954-62, La. Senate from 35th dist., 1964-65; mem. 89-92d congresses 7th dist. La.; gov. of La., 1972—. Served with USNR, World War II. Mem. Internat. Rice Festival, Crowley C. of C., Crowley Indsl. Found., Am. Legion. Democrat. Catholic. Lion. Home: 1226 N Av J Crowley LA 70526 Office: State Capitol Baton Rouge LA 70804

EDWARDS, ELTON, lawyer, state senator; b. nr. Goldsboro, N.C., Aug. 14, 1923; s. Charles Henry and Lillie (Thornton) E.; A.B., U. N.C., 1943, J.D., 1948; m. Jessie Macon Sapp, Mar. 27, 1954; children—Elton Thornton, Ruth Macon. Admitted to N.C. bar, 1948; practiced in Greensboro, 1949—; partner firm Moseley, Edwards & Greeson, Greensboro, N.C., 1954-71, Edwards, Greeson & Toumaras, 1971—; mem. N.C. Ho. of Reps., 1964-68, N.C. Senate, 1968-70, 72—. Chmn. Handi-Clean Family Found. Served with AUS, World War II, now lt. col. USAF Res. Mem. N.C., Greensboro bar assns., Phi Alpha Delta. Democrat. Presbyn. (elder). Mason (32deg., Shriner). Home: 309 N Tremont Dr Greensboro NC 27403 Office: PO Box 37 Greensboro NC 27402

EDWARDS, EMMETT WELDON, clergyman, lectr.; b. Fort Worth, Dec. 10, 1924; s. Emmitt Houston and Winley (Box) E.; D.D., Trinity Hall Coll. and Sem., 1956, B.D., 1960; LL.B., LaSalle Extension U., 1969 Joined USAF, 1954, served until 1965; pastor Centeral Bible Temple, Chateauroux, France, 1956-59, Universal Harmony Temple, San Antonio, 1960-63; lectr., Haltom City, Tex., 1962—; pastor Open Door Prayer Chapel, Ft. Worth. Mem. Am. Ministerial Assn., Trinity Hall Coll. and Sem. Alumni Soc., Epsilon Delta Chi. Mason. Author: Faith Healing. 1958. Address: 3317 Azle Av Fort Worth TX 76106

EDWARDS, EUNICE HARRIS, Christian Sci. practitioner; b. Gainesville, Fla.; d. Joseph Thomas and Nancy Rhoades (Parker) Harris; student U. Fla., 1946, Jacksonville U., 1963; m. John Edwards, July 21, 1941. With Atlanta Constn., 1925, Jefferson Standard Life Ins. Co., 1932-39, Pa. Dutch Shop, Ardmore, Pa., 1939-41; buyer, mgr. antiques Ovington's Fifth Av. Shop, N.Y.C., 1941-43; mem. Christian Sci. Ch., 1936—; joined Mother Ch., 1936, Christian Sci. practitioner, 1948—; 1st reader Jacksonville Beach, Fla., 1956-59; star People, Places and Things, Sta. WKTX, 1965-66. Chmn. Ribault Flower Show, 1959-60, Beaches Hispanic Garden Fund Com.; com., Jacksonville, Fla.; leader Girl Scouts of U.S.A., Broomall, Pa., 1946-47. Mem. U.D.C. (pres. 1963-64), D.A.R. (sec. 1962, lineage chmn. 1963-64, chpt. vice regent 1968-70), St. Augustine Hist. Soc., Friends of Library. Democrat. Clubs: Women's Ribault Garden; Atlantic Beach Garden (pres. 1968-70); Ponte Vedra Woman's. Traveled in India, 1961; lectr. on India to garden clubs. Home: 89 S Oleander Dr Port Vedra Beach FL 32082 Office: 88 S Oleander Dr Ponte Vedra Beach FL 32082

EDWARDS, HAROLD MILLS, lawyer; b. Anson County, N.C., Nov. 20, 1930; s. William H. and Bertha (Baucom) E.; B.S., Wake Forest U., 1953, LL.B., 1959. Admitted to N.C. bar, 1959; since practiced in Charlotte; judge Charlotte Municipal Ct., 1964-68; pres. Keystone Investment Corp. Mem. N.C. Bd. Alcoholic Control, 1970—. Mem. various bar assns. Home: 1701 Garden Terrace Charlotte NC 28203 Office: Johnston Bldg Charlotte NC 28202

EDWARDS, HARRY LEON, ins. co. exec.; b. LaFayette, Ga., June 12, 1921; s. William Fred and Hattie Mae (Harrison) E.; student Berea Coll., 1939-41, George Washington U., 1942; m. Mary L. Hamm, Jan. 21, 1944; children—Thomas W., Richard M., Linda A. Dist. mgr. Black Hills Power & Light Co., Rapid City, S.D., 1947-59, sales promotion mgr., 1959-64; with Stockman Nat. Life Ins. Co., 1964-69, pres., 1968-69; exec. v.p. Nat. Western Life Ins. Co., Austin, Tex., 1969-70, pres., 1970—, also dir., dir. Comml. Adjusters, 1970—. Served with U.S. Maritime Service, 1942-46. Named Boss of the Year, Austin Jr. C. of C., 1971. Mem. C. of C. (pres. 1953-54). Elk. Home: 8707 Silverhill Lane Austin TX 78759 Office: 1302 Guadalupe St Austin TX 78776

EDWARDS, JACK, congressman; b. Birmingham, Ala., Sept. 20, 1928; s. William Jackson and Sue (Fuhrman) E.; B.S. in Commerce and Bus. Adminstrn., U. Ala., 1952; LL.B., U. Ala., 1954; m. Jolane Vander Sys, Jan. 30, 1954; children—Susan Lane, Richard Arnold. Admitted to Ala. bar, 1954; pvt. practice, Mobile, 1954-58; gen. atty. G., M. & O. R.R., 1958-64; legal adviser Emergency Port Operations Mobile, 1961-64; mem. 89th-92d Congresses, 1st Dist. Ala. Chmn. America's Jr. Miss Pageant, 1960; pres. Ala. Deep Sea Fishing Rodeo, 1956-57; div. chmn. Mobile United Fund, 1960; mem. transp. adv. com. Mobile City Planning Commn., 1960-64; an organizer Freedom over Communism Com., Mobile, 1962. Served with USMC, 1946-48, 50-51. Named one of outstanding young men U.S. Jr. C. of C., 1964. Mem. Am., Ala., Mobile (sec. 1956) bar assns., Mobile Jr. Bar Assn. (pres. 1957), Mobile Jr. C. of C. (pres. 1961-62), Kappa Alpha (pres. 1951-53), Omicron Delta Kappa. Presbyn. (elder, Sunday Sch. tchr.). Home: 1910 Hunter Av Mobile AL 36606 Office: House Office Bldg Washington DC 20515

EDWARDS, JAMES BURROWS, dentist; b. Hawthorne, Fla., June 24, 1927; s. O. Morton and Bertie (Hieronymus) E.; B.S., Coll. Charleston, 1950; D.M.D., U. Louisville, 1955; postgrad. U. Pa., 1957-58; m. Ann Norris Darlington, Sept. 1, 1951; children—James B., Catherine Darlington. Resident Henry Ford Hosp., Detroit, 1958-60; practice dentistry, specializing in oral surgery, Charleston, S.C., 1960—; clin. asso. oral surgery Med. U. S.C., Charleston, 1968—. Cons. USPHS, Charleston, 1964—; lectr. to profl. groups, U.S., Eng. Vice pres. East Cooper Pvt. Sch. Corp., Mt. Pleasant, S.C., 1966—. Bd. dirs. Coastal Carolina council Boy Scouts Am., 1969-72; trustee Charles County Hosp., 1966-70, Greater Charleston YMCA, 1965-70, East Cooper chpt. Sertoma Internat., 1963-66. Nominee 1st. Congl. Dist. S.C. to U.S. Ho. of Reps., Republican party, 1971; chmn. Charleston County Rep. Com., 1964-69, also mem. steering com., 1969-72; chmn. 1st Congl. Dist. S.C. Rep. com., 1969-70; mem. steering com. S.C. Rep. com., 1968-70; del. Nat. Conv., 1968. Served with U.S. Maritime Service, 1944-47, with USNR, 1955-57. Diplomate Am. Bd. Oral Surgery. Fellow Am. Coll. Dentists, Internat. Coll. Dentists; mem. S.C. (past pres., founder, charter mem.), Brit. socs. oral surgeons, Am., S.C. dental assns., Coastal Dist. (past pres.), Charleston dental socs., Chalmers Lyons Acad. Oral Surgery, Internat. Soc. Oral Surgeons, Fedn. Dentaire Internat., Greater Charleston C. of C. Home: 1 Darlington Lane Mount Pleasant SC 29464 Office: 61 Gadsden St Charleston SC 29401

EDWARDS, JAMES EDWIN, lawyer; b. Clarkesville, Ga., July 29, 1914; s. Gus Calloway and Mary Clara (McKinney) E.; student U. Tex., 1931-33; B.A., George Washington U., 1935, J.D., 1946; m. Frances Lillian Stanley, Nov. 22, 1948; children—Robin Anne, James Christopher, Clare (Mrs. Ronald C. Wilkson). Admitted to Fla. bar, 1938, practiced, Cocoa, Fla., 1938-42; divisional asst. Dept. of State, 1945-50; practice law, Ft. Lauderdale, 1951—; mem. firm Bell, Edwards, Coker, Carlon & Amsden, 1956-59; asst. city atty., Ft. Lauderdale, 1961, 63-65; city commr., Coral Springs, Fla., 1970-71, mayor, 1972—; pres., dir. Peninsula Land Co., Ocean Beach Improvement Co. Chmm., Ft. Lauderdale for Eisenhower, 1952; Republican county parliamentarian, 1954-59; pres. Rep. Attys. Club Broward County, 1960-64. Served to lt. USCGR, 1942-45; lt. col. USAF Res. ret. Mem. Am., Fla., Broward County bar assns., Res. Officers Assn. (state judge adv. 1960-61, state v.p. for air, 1961-62), Fla. Sportsmen's Assn. (pres. 1967-68), Delta Sigma Rho, Pi Gamma Mu, Phi Delta Phi, Phi Sigma Kappa. Club: Broken Woods Golf and Country (Coral Springs). Home: 10 Covered Bridge Dr Coral Springs FL 33065 Office: 2822 E Commercial Blvd Fort Lauderdale FL 33308 also 112 Home Center Coral Springs FL 33065

EDWARDS, JUDSON EMERSON, govt. ofcl.; b. Bedford, Ind., Aug. 24, 1927; B.S. in Commerce, U. Louisville; m. 3 children. Pub. information officer Ky. State Police, Frankfort, 1949-61; exec. asst. to commr. Ky. Dept. Pub. Safety, Frankfort, 1961-68; asst. dir. community devel. Montgomery County Dept. Community Devel., Rockville, Md., 1968; exec. dir. No. Va. Transp. Commn., Arlington, 1968—. Adminstrv. asst. to gov. of Ky., part-time 1960-63. Former mem. Ky. Beautification Com., Ky. Gov.'s Safety Adv. Com. Recipient Outstanding Young Men in Capitol City award Ky. Jr. C. of C., 1962. Mem. Am. Assn. Motor Vehicle Adminstrs. (nat. com. on pub. edn. and pub. safety), Am. Soc. Pub. Adminstrn., Internat. City Mgmt. Assn., Southeastern Community Devel. Assn. Home: 6721 Grey Fox Dr Springfield VA 22150 Office: No Va Transportation Commn Radio Bldg 1st Floor 2030 16th St N Arlington VA 22201*

EDWARDS, LENCIL, librarian; b. Bell Buckle, Tenn., May 16, 1909; d. Clarence Douglas and Lucy Pamela (Harrison) Edwards; student Randolph Macon Woman's Coll., 1927-31; grad. library sch., George Peabody Coll., 1941. Tchr., Bell Buckle High Sch., 1932-41; librarian Haywood County High Sch., Brownsville, 1941-50, Isaac Litton, Nashville, 1950-53; librarian, head dept. library service Middle Tenn. State U., Murfreesboro, 1953—. Dir. library insts., 1967, 69. Mem. Nat. (life mem.), Tenn. edn. assns., Tenn., Southeastern library assns., Am. Assn. U. Women, Delta Kappa Gamma. Home: 1135 E Clark St Murfreesboro TN 37130

EDWARDS, LYMAN MAHLON, electronics engr.; b. Springfield, Mo., Jan. 13, 1908; s. Lyman Paul and Lela Louise (Bedell) E.; B.S., U. Okla., 1932; m. Thelma Imogene Weldon, Apr. 16, 1933; children—James Paul, Robert Bruce, Kent Martin. Engr., Mid Continent Research Corp., Enid, Okla., 1933-36, Schlumberger Well Surveying Corp., Houston, 1938-41; mgr. research and labs. Pan Geo Atlas Corp., Houston, 1952, now mgr. engring. Dresser Atlas Corp., Houston. Served to lt. USN, 1936-38, to comdr., 1941-47. Decorated Bronze Star medal. Mem. Houston Geol. Soc., Am. Inst. Mech Engrs., Soc. Profl. Well Log Analysts, Am. Radio Relay League. Patentee in field. Home: 3638 Aberdeen Way Houston TX 77025 Office: PO Box 1407 10201 Westheimer Houston TX 77001

EDWARDS, MAX NIXON, lawyer; b. Wichita, Kan., Dec. 4, 1921; s. Walter Lee and Jane (Nixon) E.; A.B., Dartmouth, 1947; LL.B., U. Ariz., 1950; m. Leona Timko, Dec. 2, 1967. Admitted to N.M. bar, 1950; practiced in Hobbs, 1950, 54-60; mem. firm Edwards & Reese, 1954-60; asst. dist. atty. 5th Jud. Dist. N.M., 1951-53; gen. counsel N.M. Senate, 1959; asst. to sec., legislative counsel Dept. Interior, 1961-67, asst. sec. water quality and research, 1967-69; partner

Collier, Shannon, Rill & Edwards, Washington, 1969—. Chmn. Presdl. Adv. Bd. Water Pollution Control, 1968; lectr. environmental subjects. Adviser Democratic Nat. Com., 1960. Trustee Environic Found. internat.; vice chmn. Nat. Pollution Control Found. Mem. Bar Assn. D.C., N.M., Ariz. bar assns., Bar Assn. U.S. Supreme Ct., V.F.W. Club: Nat. Golf Links of Am. (Southampton, L.I., N.Y.). Contbr. articles on pollution control to various publs. Home: 4201 Cathedral Av NW Washington DC 20016 Office: 1625 Eye St NW Washington DC 20006

EDWARDS, RAY WARREN, furniture co. exec.; b. Stanleytown, Va., June 19, 1938; s. George Oliver and Mildred (Reynolds) E.; B.S., Va. Poly. Inst., 1961; m. Judith Jessup, June 27, 1959; children—Christopher T., Suzanne R. Jr. accountant Ernst & Ernst, Charlotte, N.C., 1961; v.p. Jessop Furniture Co., Collinsville, Va., 1961—; v.p., dir. Jessup Realty Corp.; sec.-treas. Collinsville Land Corp. Chmn. Republican party Henry County, 1964, vice chmn., 1970-72; vice chmn. Fifth Dist. Rep. Com., 1970-72. Mem. Va. Water Control Bd., 1970—. Pres. Collinsville Vol. Fire Dept.; treas., bd. dirs. Collinsville Recreation Center; bd. dirs., chmn. Martinsville-Henry County chpt. A.R.C.; bd. dirs. Martinsville-Henry County United Fund, 1967—, pres., 1971-72. Recipient Distinguished Service awards Bassett, 1967, Collinsville, 1968; named Outstanding Vice Pres. Va. Jaycees, 1967; one of ten outstanding State Vice Pres. in U.S., U.S. Jaycees, 1967; one of five Outstanding Young Men in Va., 1968. Mem. U.S. (past nat. dir.), Martinsville-Henry County C. of C. (pres. 1972—), Va. (sec.-treas., past v.p.), Collinsville Jr. chambers commerce, Alpha Kappa Psi. Baptist. Lion. Home: 109 Plantation Dr Collinsville VA 24078 Office: 205 Virginia Av Collinsville VA 24078

EDWARDS, REM BLANCHARD, educator; b. Washington, Ga., Oct. 2, 1934; s. Rem Blanchard and Ann Opal (Vickers) E.; A.B., Emory U., 1956; B.D. (Danforth fellow), Yale, 1959; Ph.D., Emory U., 1962; m. Alta Louise Blalock, Aug. 5, 1962; children—Rem, Cherron. Asst. prof. philosophy Jacksonville (Fla.) U., 1962-66; asso. prof. philosophy U. Tenn., Knoxville, 1966-70, prof., 1970—. Mem. Am. Assn. U. Profs., So. Soc. Philosophy and Psychology, So. Soc. for Philosophy of Religion, Am., Tenn. philos. assns., Mind Assn., Phi Beta Kappa. Author: Freedom, Responsibility and Obligation, 1969, Reason and Religion: An Introduction to the Philosophy of Religion, 1972. Home: 8709 Longmeade Dr Knoxville TN 37919 Office: Dept Philosophy University of Tenn Knoxville TN 37916

EDWARDS, ROBERT A., county ofcl. Former city adminstr. City of College Park (Md.), 9 years; chief adminstrv. officer Prince George's County (Md.), 1971—. Address: 7308 Rhode Island Av College Park MD 20740*

EDWARDS, ROBERT COOK, univ. pres.; b. Fountain Inn, S.C., Mar. 25, 1914; s. John T. and Effie (Cook) E.; B.S. in Textile Engring., Clemson Agrl. Colyl., 1933; LL.D., The Citadel. 1959, Wofford Coll., 1960; m. Louise Odom, May 30, 1935; children—Robert Cook, Nancy Louise. Supr. quality control lab., Dunean Mill of J.P. Stevens &Co., Inc., Greenville, S.C., 1933-34; designer, then supt. Charles B. Thomas Co., Inc., textile mfg. plant, Red Springs, N.C., 1934-37; supt. weaving Aberfoyle, Inc., Norfolk, Va., 1937-39, plant supt., 1939-42; plant mgr. Abbeville Mills Corp. (S.C.), 1946-48; treas., gen. mgr. Abbeville group Deering-Milliken Mills, 1948-56; v.p. devel. Clemson Coll., 1956-58, acting pres., 1958-59, pres., 1959—. Dir. Charlotte br. Fed. Land Bank of Richmond, Duke Power Co., Dan River Inc. Bd. dirs. So. Regional Edn. Bd. (vice chmn. 1969-70), Piedmont Tb-Respiratory Disease Assn. Served from 2d lt. to maj. AUS, 1942-46. Mem. Assn. U.S. Army (dir. 1965-68), S.C. Council Econ. Edn. (dir.). Home: Parkway Clemson SC 29631

EDWARDS, ROBERT DAVID, indsl. co. exec.; b. N.Y.C., Mar. 22, 1919; s. Albert H. and Blanche (Gans) E.; B.S., N.Y.U., 1938; m. Jean Bauer, Dec. 12, 1946; children—Richard Charles, Marjorie Edith. Pres., Holley-Edwards Sales, Inc., Jacksonville, Fla., 1946—, HESCO, Inc., White Star Sales, Inc. Pres. Temple Brotherhood, 1949-51; sponsor, hon. mem. Jacksonville Overseas Womans Club, 1959—; active Boys Service Council, 1953-58; mem. Com. 100, 1962—. Bd. dirs. Jacksonville YMCA; treas. Jacksonville Symphony Assn., 1970—. Served to 1st lt., AUS, World War II. Recipient Temple Brotherhood Service award, 1951, YMCA Outstanding Service award, 1958, Employees award, Holley-Edwards Sales, Inc., 1961; named Boss of Year Nat. Secs. Assn., Internat., 1956. Mem. Fla. C. of C. (mem. nat. affairs com. 1961—), Beta Gamma Sigma. Clubs: River, Beauclerc Country, St. Johns Dinner; University (charter); Bay Meadows Country. Home: 1112 River Oaks Rd Jacksonville FL 32207 Office: 1738 E Adams St Jacksonville FL 32201

EDWARDS, RODERICK YERKES, coast guard officer; b. Phila., Sept. 20, 1909; s. David William and Elizabeth (Yerkes) E.; student Rutgers U., U. N.Y., Am. U., U. San Francisco; m. Rita Thiele, July 10, 1937; children—Roderick Yerkes, David Thiele. With Am. Export Lines, 1927-40; maritime tchr. N.Y. Bd. Edn., 1940-41; insp. hulls Bur. Marine Inspection and Navigation, 1941-42; commd. lt. USCG, 1942, advanced through grades to rear adm., 1967; chief pub. and internat. affairs, 1966—. U.S. del. Internat. Maritime Consultive Orgn., 1966; alternate chmn. Mcht. Marine Council, 1966; vice chmn. IMCO com. Marine Pollution, 1967; mem. Nat. Cargo Bur., 1966, Am. Boat and Yacht Council, 1963. Bd. dirs. Nat. Air and Space Museum. Decorated Navy Commendation medal, Legion of Merit; named hon. citizen Antwerp, Belgium. Clubs: Army-Navy, Nat. Aviation, Propellor (Washington); Commercial (San Francisco). Home: 1600 S Eads St Arlington VA 22202 Office: 1300 E St NW Washington DC 20004

EDWARDS, ROGER CHADWICK, lawyer; b. Abbeville, La., June 29, 1923; s. William Pierpont and Ruth Edna (Chadwick) E.; B.S., Southwestern La. Inst., 1947; LL.B., Tulane U., 1950; m. Jean Martin, Aug. 5, 1950; children—Katherine Elizabeth (Mrs. John Clyde Prejean), Roger Chadwick. Admitted to La. bar, 1950; practiced in Abbeville, La., 1950—; mem. firm Kibbe, Edwards, Cooper & Sonnier, 1962-69. Dir. First Nat. Bank, Abbeville, La. Pres. Marshall & Edwards Ins. Agy., 1953—. Appeal's agt. Selective Service Local Bd., 1958—; U.S. Savings Bond chmn. Vermilion Parish, 1960—. Sec. Vermilion Parish Democratic Com., 1965—. Served with USNR, 1943-46. Mem. Am. Judicature Soc., Am., La. (mem. com. publs., medico-legal com.), Vermilion Parish bar assns. Episcopalian. Mason. Club: Abbeville High School Quarterback (pres. 1970-71). Home: 111 S Hollingsworth St Abbeville LA 70510 Office: 110 S State St Abbeville LA 70510

EDWARDS, SCOTT SAMUEL, JR., lawyer; b. Atlanta, Apr. 16, 1915; s. Scott Samuel and Maggie (Harris) E., Sr.; LL.B., Woodrow Wilson Coll., 1941; m. Jeanette Victoria Smith, Nov. 14, 1945; 1 son, David Scott. Admitted to Ga. bar, 1941, practiced in Marietta, Ga., 1946—; asst. county atty., Cobb County, 1948-53; atty. City of Marietta, 1948-60, City of Marietta Hosp. Authority, 1948—; now mem. firm. Edwards, Awtrey & Parker. Served with Signal Corps, AUS, 1941-45; PTO. Mem. Am., Ga., Cobb County (pres. 1955-56) bar assns., Am. Legion. Presbyn. Club: Civitan (pres. 1952-53). Home: 330 S Woodland Dr Marietta GA 30060 Office: 199 Roswell St Marietta GA 30060

EDWARDS, WALTER ALDEN, corp. exec.; b. Logansport, Ind., Mar. 15, 1913; s. Edwin Jathan and Edna Mae (DeWitt) E.; student Purdue U., 1931-32; B.S., Ind. U., 1937; m. Elizabeth Knowlson, July 17, 1943; children—DeWitt, Timothy. Asst. to exec. v.p. Pullman-Standard Car Mfg. Co., Chgo., 1937-42, sales exec., 1945-50; mgr. govt.-industry relations dept. Owens-Ill. Glass Co., Toledo, 1950-53, Washington rep., 1954-58; dep. dir. containers and packaging div., spl. asst. to dir. NPA, also asst. adminstr. Bus. and Def. Services Adminstrn., U.S. Dept. Commerce, 1953-54, dep. asst. sec. commerce for domestic affairs, 1958-61, asst. sec. of commerce, 1961; exec. Chrysler Corp., Washington 1961—. Served as lt. comdr. USNR, 1942-45. Clubs: University (Chgo.); Army and Navy, Congressional Country, Burning Tree (Washington). Home: Millboro Springs VA 24460 Office: 1700 K St NW Washington DC 20006

EDWARDS, WILLARD, newspaperman; b. Chgo., Ill., Dec. 7, 1902; s. Evan William and Mary (Kilday) E.; student St. Ignatius Acad., 1918-21; m. Leila Sullivan, Jan. 17, 1931; 1 son, Lee Willard. Reporter City News Bur., Chgo., 1921; with Chgo. Tribune, 1925—, became N.Y. corr., 1934, mem. Washington bur., 1935—. Republican. Columnist, Capital Views, 1967—. Home: 101 4th St SE Washington DC 20003 Office: 1750 Pennsylvania Av NW Washington DC 20005

EDWARDS, WILLIAM RAYMOND, dentist; b. Richmond Hill, N.Y., Apr. 10, 1914; s. Vivian and Mabel Lucy (Keay) E.; student U. Fla., 1932-33, U. Miami, 1933-34; D.D.S., Washington U., St. Louis, 1938; m. Shirley Bonawit, Nov. 14, 1959; children—Bonnie Keay, Barbara Sisson. Individual practice dentistry, Fort Lauderdale, Fla., 1938-41, 45—. Served with AUS, 1941-45. Fellow Fla. State Dental Soc.; mem. Am. Dental Assn., Fla. Acad. Dental Practice Adminstrn., East Coast Dist. (pres. 1955-56), Broward County dental socs., Pi Kappa Alpha, Xi Psi Phi. Home: 3080 NE 47th Ct Fort Lauderdale FL 33308 Office: 3015 Bayview Dr Fort Lauderdale FL 33306

EFRON, MARVIN, optometrist; b. Aiken, S.C., May 30, 1930; s. Harry H. and Mary (Fadem) E.; student U. S.C., 1947-48, Ohio State U., 1958; Dr. Optometry, So. Coll. Optometry, 1951; M.A., U. S.C., 1965, Ph.D., 1969; m. Sara Lyon Timmerman, June 20, 1956; children— Leslie Kay, Susan Frances. Practice of optometry, Edgefield, S.C., 1952-58, West Columbia, S.C., 1958—. Lectr., U.S.C. Coll. Edn., 1970—; mem. adv. com. programs for edn. of handicapped S.C. Dept. Edn. Trustee S.C. Opportunity Sch., cons. various indsl. concerns, Reading Clinic U. S.C. Chmn. Recreational Needs Survey for areas of West Columbia. Cayce and Springsdale, S.C., 1961-63; past chmn. Lexington County Commn. Higher Edn. Trustee United Community Services Lexington and Richland Counties. Recipient Distinguished Service award, 1966; best Scientific paper on vision in South, 1966, 70; Distinguished Service award S.C. Otometric Assn., 1969, Optometrist of Year award, 1970. Mem. S.C. (past chmn.) Central (pres. 1968-69) optometric assns., So. Council Optometry, Am. Psychol. Assn., Am. Optometric Found., West Columbia-Cayce (pres. 1965-66), Greater Columbia (dir.) chambers commerce, Phi Epsilon Pi. Mason, Woodman of World. Home: 1212 Canary Dr West Columbia SC 29169 Office: 1205 D Av West Columbia SC 29169

EGAN, MARTIN DAVID, educator; b. Trenton, N.J., Feb. 13, 1941; s. Martin James and Madolyn (Brown) E.; B.C.E., Lafayette Coll., 1962; M.C.E., Mass. Inst. Tech., 1966; m. Dorothy Jean Strong, Aug. 5, 1967. Mech. engr. Shell Oil Co., New Orleans, La., 1966-68; cons. Bolt, Beranek & Newman, Cambridge, Mass., 1968-69; prof. arch. Tulane U., 1969—; cons. archtl. acoustics and noise control, 1970—; lectr. Auburn U., Clemson U., La. State U., U. Okla., Rice U., U. Tenn., So. U. Served with AUS, 1962-64. Mem. Nat. Council Acoustical Consultants, Acoust. Soc. Am., Phi Gamma Delta. Republican. Methodist. Author: Concepts in Architectural Acoustics, 2d edn., 1971. Home: 6950 Milne Blvd New Orleans LA 70124 Office: School of Architecture Tulane U New Orleans LA 70118

EGAN, MICHAEL JOSEPH, JR., lawyer, legislator; b. Savannah, Ga., Aug. 8, 1926; s. Michael Joseph and Elise (Robider) E.; B.A., Yale, 1950; LL.B., Harvard, 1955; m. Donna Cole, Apr. 14, 1951; children— Moira, Michael, Donna, Cole, Roby, John. Admitted to Ga. bar, 1955; partner Sutherland, Asbill & Brennan, Atlanta and Washington, 1960—; mem. Ga. Ho. of Reps., 1965—, minority leader, 1970—. Home: 97 Brighton Rd Atlanta GA 30303 Office: First Nat Bank Tower Atlanta GA 30303

EGGERS, ALFRED JOHN, JR., govt. ofcl.; b. Omaha, June 24, 1922; s. Alfred John and Golden (Myers) E.; A.B., U. Omaha, 1944; M.S., Stanford, 1949, Ph.D., 1956; m. Elizabeth Ann Hills, Sept. 9, 1950; children— Alfred John III, Philip Norman. With NASA, and predecessor, 1944-71, chief vehicle environment div., Ames Research Center, 1959-63, asst. dir. research and devel. analysis and planning, 1963-64, dep. asso. adminstr. advanced research and tech. NASA Hdqrs., 1964-68, asst. adminstr. policy, 1968-71; asst. dir. research appliations NSF, 1971—; Hunsaker prof. Mass. Inst. Tech., 1969-71; spl. research supersonic and hypersonic aerodynamics, aerodynamics heating, aerospace vehicles aerospace research and devel., mgmt. planning and policy analysis and devel. Mem. sci. adv. bd. USAF, 1958—. Vice chmn. Los Altos (Cal.) Sch. Community Devel. Com., 1963-64. Served to lt. (j.g.) USNR, 1942-46. Recipient Arthur S. Fleming award, 1956; named One of Ten Outstanding Young Men of Year, U.S. C. of C., 1957; recipient Outstanding Alumni award U. Omaha, 1958, H. Julian Allen award NASA, 1969. Fellow Am. Inst. Aeros. and Astronautics (founder, dir.; Sylvanus Albert Reed award 1962, founder chmn. of pres.'s forum com. on interactions aerospace tech. and soc. 1966-70); mem. Am. Acad. Polit. and Social Sci., A.A.A.S., Am. Ordnance Assn., Nat. Acad. Engring., Sigma Xi, Tau Beta Pi. Home: 4425 N 33d Rd Arlington VA 22207 Office: Code RA Nat Science Found Washington DC 20550

EGGERS, PAUL WALTER, lawyer; b. Seymour, Ind., Apr. 20, 1919; s. Ernest H. and Ottile (Carre) E.; B.A., Valparaiso U., 1941; LL.B., U. Tex., 1948; m. Frances Kramer, Dec. 29, 1946; 1 son, Steven Paul. Admitted to Tex. bar, 1948; practiced in Wichita Falls, 1948-69; mem. firm Eggers, Sherrill & Pace, 1952-69; gen. Counsel U.S. Treasury Dept., Washington, 1969-70; practice, Dallas, 1971—. Pres., Wichita Falls Symphony, 1960-62. Chmn., Wichita County Republican Party, 1966-67; chmn. Rep. State Task Force on Revenue and Fiscal Policy, 1967; Rep. candidate for gov. of Tex., 1968, 70. Commr. Pres. Assay Commn., 1972—. Trustee Am. Ch. Bldg. Fund Commn., Dallas Symphony Orch. Served to maj. AUS, 1941-46. Mem. State Bar Tex., Am. Bar Assn., Am. Judicature Soc. Episcopalian. Home: 10511 Ravenscroft Dr Dallas TX 75202 Office: 1407 Main St Dallas TX 75202

EGGLESTON, JOHN WILLIAM, ret. judge; b. Charlotte, Va., June 18, 1886; s. David Quinn and Sue (Daniel) E.; student Hampden-Sydney Coll., Va., 1902-04; B.A., Washington and Lee U., 1906, M.A., 1907, LL.B., 1910, LL.D., 1949; m. Ella Carrington, Oct. 15, 1912; children—Mary (Mrs. W. Perry Moore, Jr.), Suzanne (Mrs. William W. Simpson), Eleanor Carrington (dec.). Tchr., Washington and Lee U., 1906-07, 1908-10, McGuire's Prep. School, Richmond, Va., 1907-08; admitted to Va. bar, 1909; practiced at Norfolk, Va., 1910-35; mem. firms Baker & Eggleston; Hughes, Vandeventer &Eggleston; Vandeventer, Eggleston & Black; mem. Va. State Sen., 1932-35, chmn. legislative com. which drafted Alcoholic Beverage Control Act; justice Supreme Ct. of Appeals of Va., 1935-58, chief justice, 1958-69. Mem. Va. Hist. Soc., Order of Coif, Phi Beta Kappa, Omicron Delta Kappa, Kappa Sigma, Phi Delta Phi. Democrat. Presbyn. Clubs: Princess Anne Country (Virginia Beach); Virginia (Norfolk). Home: 1115 Langley Rd Norfolk VA 23507 Office: City Hall Bldg Norfolk VA 23510

EHLE, JOHN MARSDEN, SR., ins. exec.; b. Morgantown, W.Va., May 5, 1904; s. John F. and Nancy (Marsden) E.; student Bingham Mil Sch., Asheville, N.C., 1923-24; m. Gladys Starnes, Feb. 21, 1925; children— John, Robert Starnes, Mary Ann, David Bolton, Nancy Elizabeth. With Imperial Life Ins. Co., Asheville, N.C., 1927-57, agt., 1927-28, asst. advt. mgr., 1929, advt. mgr., 1930-40, agy. sec., 1940—, mgr. ordinary dept., 1945-48, v.p., 1949-57; 2d v.p. Western & So. Life Ins. Co., 1957-60; regional mgr. Western N.C., Franklin Life Ins. Co., 1960—. Asst. chief aux. police, Asheville civilian def., 1942—; chmn. Christmas Cheer Fund, 1948, 49; chmn. adv. bd. Salvation Army; chmn. Gospel Projects, Inc.; dir. Asheville Jr. Achievement Inc.; publicity chmn, United Appeal. Trustee, mem. exec. com. Asheville Orthopedic Hosp., sec. Orthopedic Hosp. and Rehab. Center; treas. Ben Lippen Sch.; chmn. bd. trustees Eliada Homes, Inc., Faith Cottage. Mem. C. of C., Ins. Agy. Mgmt. Assn., Life Advertisers Assn. (charter mem., past chmn., sec. So. roundtable, mem. nat. exec. com.), Nat., Asheville (past pres., sec.) assns. life underwriters, Carolina Home Office Underwriters (charter mem., past chmn.)., Gideons. Mem. Gospel Tabernacle (trustee). Kiwanian (hon.). Club: Men's (past pres.). Editor The Imperial Indicator (weekly), 1930-55. Contbr. to life ins. publs. Home: 8 Cedarcliff Rd Asheville NC 28803 Office: 217 E Merrimon Av Asheville NC 28801

EHLERS, WALTER HENRY, educator; b. N.Y.C., May 3, 1912; s. Gustave and Frieda S. (Natusch) E.; B.S., N.Y. U., 1936, M.A., 1942; D.S.W., Brandeis U., 1962; m. Sabine Lila Bardack, June 1, 1935; children—Rhea Judith (Mrs. R. John Maxwell), Joyce Reed, Carol Joan (Mrs. Thomas McMahon). With YMCA, 1937-52, exec. sec., Ventura Cal. also Kauai, Hawaii, 1942-52; exec. dir. Palama Settlement, Honolulu, 1952-59; dist. coordinator Action for Boston Community Devel., 1961-62; dir. urban planning dept. United Community Services, Boston, 1962-65; prof. social work Fla. State U., Tallahassee, 1965—. Mem. faculty Northeastern U., 1963-65, Simmons Sch. Social Work, 1964-65, Boston Coll. Sch. Social Work, 1964-65; cons. E. & E. Assos., Tallahassee, 1965—; project dir. improving social work edn. U.S. Dept. Health, Edn. and Welfare, 1969—. Recipient McInerney grant, 1956—. Mem. Nat. Assn. Social Workers, Council Social Work Edn., Am. Assn. U. Profs., Internat. Conf. Social Work, Fla. Conf. Social Welfare, Phi Delta Kappa. Author: Proposal for a Local Planning Organization Within United Community Services, 1964; Mothers of Retarded Children: How They Feel, Where They Seek Help, 1966. Contbr. chpt. to book, articles to publs. Home: 2006 Lee Av Tallahassee FL 32303

EHNI, FREDERICK MARION, architect; b. Moncks Corner, S.C., Aug. 21, 1935; s. Adolph Gustav and Lula Mae (Metts) E.; B.Arch. with honors, Clemson U., 1964; m. Frances Anne Owens, July 28, 1957. Architect, Beachum & Wood, Greenville, S.C., 1959, Lucas & Stubbs Assos., Charleston, S.C., 1964-68; self-employed as architect, Charleston, 1968—. Chmn. Downtown Council Parking Com., 1971. Mem. Charleston County Zoning Bd. Adjustment, 1971—, chmn., 1971-72; exec. committeeman Democratic party, Charleston County, 1971—. Served with USNR, 1957-59. Recipient Minaret award Clemson U., 1961, award S.C. Concrete Masonry Assn., 1961, Rudolph E. Lee award Clemson U., 1963, award of merit for design excellence AIA, 1967. Mem. A.I.A., Architects' Council Charleston (pres. 1970), Charleston Trident C. of C., Historic Ansonborough Neighborhood Assn. (pres. 1969), Tau Sigma Delta. Club: Exchange. Prin. archtl. works include S.C. Dept. Corrections, Coastal Community Pre-Release Center, Village Shaftsbury (a planned-unit devel.). Address: 66 Society St Charleston SC 29401

EHRLICH, JAMES BURTON, airline exec.; b. Chgo., Nov. 20, 1929; s. Max Charles and Amanda (Palmquist) E.; student Carleton Coll., 1947-49; B.A., Ill. Wesleyan U., 1952; m. Audrey Ann Evans, Sept. 21, 1956; 1 stepdau., Karen Schuyler Choate; children—Andrew Carl, Evan Peter. Intelligence officer C.I.A., Washington, 1956-59; asst. to v.p. fed affairs Air Transport Assn. Am., Washington, 1959-68; dir. civic affairs Trans World Airlines, Inc., Washington, 1968—. Served to lt. (j.g.) USNR, 1952-55. Mem. Sigma Chi. Club: University (Washington). Home: 2116 Belle Haven Rd Alexandria VA 22307 Office: 1000 16th St NW Washington DC 20036

EHRLICHMAN, JOHN DANIEL, govt. ofcl.; b. Tacoma, Wash., Mar. 20, 1925; s. Rudolph I. and Lillian (Danielson) E.; B.A., U. Cal. at Los Angeles, 1948; LL.B., Stanford, 1951; m. Jeanne Fisher, Aug. 21, 1949; children—Peter, Jan, Thomas, Jody Ann, Robert. Admitted to Cal. bar, 1951, Wash. bar, 1951; founder firm Hullin & Ehrlichman, Seattle, 1951; partner firm Hullin, Ehrlichman, Roberts & Hodge, Seattle, 1951-68; counsel to Pres. Richard M. Nixon, 1968-69, asst. to Pres. for domestic affairs, 1969—; instr. land use law U. Wash., 1967. Dir. conv. activities Republican Nat. Conv., 1968; tour mgr. Nixon campaign, 1968. Bd. trustees Adventure Unltd., St. Louis. Served to 1st. lt. USAAF, 1943-45. Decorated D.F.C., Air medals. Mem. Cal., Wash., Am. bar assns., Kappa Sigma, Phi Delta Phi. Christian Scientist. Home: 330 Chesapeake Dr Great Falls VA 22066 Office: The White House Washington DC 20500

EHRMAN, LEFEVRE MARIA, Panamanian diplomat; b. Panama; d. Juan and Ana (Lefevre) Ehrman; ed. Panama, Balt., Boston, Paris, France. Attache, Panamanian Embassy, France, 1947-51; consul gen., Le Havre, France, 1952-65, Beirut, Lebanon, 1965-66, Istanbul, Turkey, 1966-69, Houston, 1969—. Home: PO Box 682 Panama Republic Panama Office: 3400 Montrose Blvd Houston TX 77006

EICHENBAUM, E. CHARLES, lawyer; b. Little Rock, May 30, 1907; s. Ephraim Harris and Sadie (Cohn) E.; J.D., Washington U., St. Louis, 1928; m. Helen Lockwood, July 9, 1933; 1 dau., Peggy (Mrs. Leo Richard Jalenak, Jr.). Admitted to Ark. bar, 1928, since practiced in Little Rock; sr. partner Eichenbaum, Scott & Miller, 1932—; lectr. regional and nat. tax insts. and seminars. Pres. Capital Av. Bldg. Co., Profl. Bldg. Co.; dir. Sterling Stores Co., Inc., Dillard Dept. Stores, Inc., Little Rock, Boston Store, Ft. Smith, Ark., United Dollar Stores, Inc., Dumas, Ark., Ike Kempner Bros., Inc., 555, Inc., Pfeifer Plumbing & Heating Co., Little Rock. Mem. Ozark Cultural Commn., 1969-71. Trustee Nat. Conf. Christians and Jews, Leo N. Levi Hosp. Fellow Am. Bar Found.; mem. Am. (past com. chmn.), Ark. (com. chmn.), Pulaski County bar assns., Am. Judicature Soc., Pralma, Thurntene, Zeta Beta Tau. Jewish religion (trustee temple). Mem. B'nai B'rith, Rotarian. Contbr. articles to profl. jours. Home: Summit House Apts 400 N University St Little Rock AR 72205 Office: Tower Bldg Little Rock AR 72201

EICKHOFF, ANDREW ROBERT, coll. dean; b. N.Y.C., Oct. 3, 1924; s. Andrew B. and Ruth L. (Wolfe) E.; B.S., Loyola Coll., Balt., 1944; S.T.B., Boston U., 1949, Ph.D., 1953; certificate in ecumenics U. Geneva, Switzerland, 1956; m. Joan Jordan Dietz, Dec. 22, 1946; children—Andrew Robert, Joan Jordan. Acting head dept. religion Columbia (S.C.) Coll., 1953-55; head dept. religion Bradley U., Peoria,

Ill., 1956-67; dean faculty Union Coll., Barbourville, Ky., 1967—. Mem. council social work edn. Nat. Com. Undergrad. Social Work Programs. Active United Christian Campus Found., Bradley U., Central Vol. Bur., Peoria, Ill., Cumberland River Mental Health-Mental Retardation Assn. Served to lt. (j.g.) USNR, 1943-46. Mem. Am. Conf. Acad. Deans, Am. Assn. U. Profs. (pres. Bradley U. chpt. 1960-61), Am. Acad. Religion (pres. Midwest sect. 1966-67), Acad. Religion and Mental Health (pres. Peoria chpt. 1961-62), UN Assn. U.S.A. (dir. Ill. div. 1964-67), Am. Psychol. Assn., Soc. Psychol. Study Social Issues, World Fedn. Mental Health, Acad. Deans So. States. Methodist. Author: A Christian View of Sex and Marriage, 1966. Home: 916 N Main St Barbourville KY 40906

EIDSON, JOHN OLIN, coll. pres.; b. Johnston, S.C., Dec. 10, 1908; s. Olin Marvin and Margaret (Rushton) E.; A.B., Wofford Coll., 1929, Litt.D. (hon.), 1954; M.A., Vanderbilt U., 1930; Ph.D., Duke, 1941; m. Perrin Cudd, Aug. 7, 1952. Faculty U. Ga., Athens, 1936-68, beginning as instr. English, successively dean Coordinate Coll., dir. U. Center in Ga., dean Coll. Arts and Scis., 1957-68; pres. Ga. So. Coll., Statesboro, 1968-71; vice chancellor U. System of Ga., 1971—; vis. prof. Am. lit. U. Freiberg, Germany, 1956. Mem. senate Nat. Assn. State Univs. and Land-Grant Colls., 1963-66. Served from lt. to maj., inf., AUS, 1942-46; lt. col. Res. Recipient M.G. Michael award for research, 1950. Mem. Am. Studies Assn. (v.p. southeastern 1964-66, pres. 1966-68), Am. Assn. State Colls. and Univs. (mem. grad. com.), Conf. Acad. Deans So. States (pres. 1967-68), Nat. Council Colls. Arts and Scis. (mem. exec. bd. 1965-68), English Assn., Tennyson Soc. Modern Lang. Assn. Am., S. Atlantic Modern Lang. Assn., Newcomen Soc. N. Am., Sphinx, Phi Beta Kappa (chmn. S. Atlantic dist. 1958-61, pres. Coastal Ga.-Carolina 1970-71), Pi Kappa Delta, Phi Kappa Phi, Delta Phi Alpha (nat. sec. 1929-34, mem nat. council 1969—), Tau Kappa Alpha, Kappa Delta Pi, Phi Delta Kappa, Kappa Phi Kappa. Methodist. Rotarian. Author: Tennyson in America, 1943; Charles Stearns Wheeler: Friend of Emerson, 1951; (with W. W. Davidson) Reading for Pleasure, 1948. Editor: Georgia Review, 1950-57, mem. editorial bd., 1957—. Contbr. articles and revs. to scholastic jours. Home: 362 Valley Green Dr NE Atlanta GA 30342 Office: 244 Washington St SW Atlanta GA 30334

EIDSON, PERRIN CUDD (MRS. JOHN OLIN EIDSON), club woman; b. Spartanburg, S.C., May 19, 1914; d. Alfred Perry and Pleasant (Bishop) Cudd; A.B., Converse Coll., 1932; M.A., Columbia, 1949; m. John Olin Eidson, Aug. 7, 1952. Tchr., counselor Spartanburg Sr. High Sch., 1934-52. Del., Intellectual Life Conf., Pugwash, N.S., Can., 1960. Pres., S.C. Dean of Women Assn., 1952; pres. Woman's Club of U. Ga., Athens, 1959-60, adviser to newcomers, 1967-68; historian Ga. So. Coll. Dames Club, 1969-70. Bd. dirs. Community Concert Assn., Athens; exec. com. Gen. Hosp. Aux. 1967-68. Mem. D.A.R., Athens Hist. Soc., Soc. for Preservation Old Athens, Am. Assn. U. Women, U.D.C. (v.p. chpt. 1959—), Tennyson Soc., Delta Kappa Gamma, Alpha Xi Delta (nat. steering com. 1966—). Clubs: Ga. Tech. Women's, South Carolina (Atlanta). Address: 362 Valley Green Dr NE Atlanta GA 30342

EIGENBROD, WALTER FREDERICK, lawyer; b. New Orleans, Dec. 5, 1912; s. Walter H. and Vivian (Madel) E.; B.A., La. State U., 1935; J.D., Tulane U., 1941; m. Marie Elizabeth Vail, Nov. 7, 1942. Admitted to La. bar, 1941, Ala. bar, 1947; practiced in New Orleans, 1945-46, Huntsville, Ala., 1947—; mem. Arbitration Panel, Fed. Mediation and Conciliation Service, Washington, 1953—; mem. Am. Arbitration Assn. Vol. Labor Arbitration Panel, N.Y.C., 1953—. Dir. South Huntsville Land Development Co., Inc., Ideal Baking Co., Ardmore, Inc. Mem. Presdl. Emergency Bd., 1962. Pres., Madison County Tb Assn., 1947-49; chmn. Madison County March of Dimes, 1950; mem. bd. advisers Huntsville Little Theater, 1958—. Adviser on ofcl. U.S. delegation to 5th Session Trade and Devel. Bd. UN Conf., Geneva, 1967. Mem. Ala. State Democratic exec. com. Served to capt. USAAF, 1941-45. Mem. Am. (co-chmn. labor arbitration and law of collective bargaining agreements 1967-68, 68-69), La., Huntsville-Madison County (pres. 1963-64) bar assns., Nat. Acad. Arbitrators, Ala. State Bar (chmn. local bar activities State Ala.), Assn. U.S. Army (chpt. pres.), Huntsville-Madison County C. of C., Huntsville Indsl. Expansion Com., Am. Legion (past post vice-comdr.), 40 and 8. Democrat. Roman Catholic. Kiwanian (pres. Huntsville 1958). Home: 2208 Briarcliff Rd Huntsville AL 35801 Office: Terry-Hutchens Bldg Huntsville AL 35801

EISELE, DONN FULTON, astronaut; b. Columbus, O., June 23, 1930; s. Herman E. and June (Davisson) E.; B.S., U.S. Naval Acad., 1952; M.S. in Astronautics, USAF Inst. Tech., 1960; m. Susan Harter Hearn, Aug. 2, 1969; children—Melinda Sue, Donn Hamilton, Kristin C., Jon J., Andrew D. Commd. 2d lt. USAF, 1953, advanced through grades to col.; assigned Rapid City, S.D., 1953-55, Wheelus AFB, Libya, 1955-58, Wright-Patterson AFB, O., 1960-61, Aerospace Research Pilot Sch., Edwards AFB, Cal., 1962; exptl. flight test officer Kirtland AFB, N.M., 1962-63; astronaut NASA Manned Spacecraft Center, Houston, 1964-70, command module pilot Apollo 7, first manned Apollo space flight, Oct. 1968. Decorated D.F.C. Mem. Nat. Geog. Soc., Soc. Exptl. Test Pilots, A.F.T.R.A., Tau Beta Pi. Home: 149 Indian Springs Rd Williamsburg VA 23185 Office: NASA Langley Research Center Hampton VA 23365

EISEMAN, BYRON M., JR., lawyer; b. Greensville, Tenn., Nov. 24, 1936; s. Byron M. and Mary (Quillen) E.; student Carson-Newman Coll., 1954-56; B.S., U. Tenn., 1956, 1960; LL.M. in Taxation, N.Y.U., 1964; m. Carol Lisbeth Cole, June 16, 1962; children—Mary Melissa, Christopher Cole, Robyn Renee. Admitted to Tenn. bar, 1964, Ark. bar, 1964; asst. prof. law East Carolina U., 1961-63; partner firm Smith, Williams, Friday Eldredge & Clark, Little Rock, 1964—; lectr. U. Ark. Sch. Law. Ark. legal and legislative chmn. United Cerebral Palsy, 1970. Mem. Ark., Am. bar assns., Pi Kappa Alpha, Phi Alpha Delta. Baptist. Author: (with William H. Bowen and Mitchell Moore) Arkansas Estate Planners Workbook, 1967. Home: 16 Huntington Rd Little Rock AR 72207 Office: 1100 Boyle Bldg Little Rock AR 72201

EISENBERG, JOHN F(REDERICK), zoologist, educator; b. Everett, Wash., June 20, 1935; B.S., Wash. State U., 1957; M.A. (NSF fellow), U. Cal. at Berkeley, 1959, Ph.D. in Zoology (Nat. Acad. Sci. fellow), 1962; m. 2 children. Asst. prof. zoology U. B.C., 1962-64; asst. prof. zoology U. Md., College Park, 1964-65, research asso. prof., 1965—. Resident scientist Nat. Zool. Park, Smithsonian Instn., Washington, 1965—. Research on animal behavior, analysis of social structure, factors responsible for limiting population growth, philosophy of sci. Office: University of Md College Park MD 20742 also Nat Zoological Park Rock Creek Valley Rd NW Washington DC 20009*

EISENBERG, KENNETH SAWYER, restoration expert; b. Newark, Dec. 30, 1932; s. William C. and Elsie G. (Greenfield) E.; B.S., N.Y. U., 1954, LL.B., 1961; m. Ruth Miller, Aug. 15, 1965. Engaged in devel. plans for hist. restoration programs Universal Engring. Newark, 1961-69; inventor Permo Bond/Dekosit Process for re-creating stone, 1963; founder Universal Restoration, Inc., Washington and Copenhagen, Denmark, 1967, pres., chmn. bd., 1969—. Adviser, restoration tech. Nat. Park Service. Served to lt. USAF, 1955-57. Mem. Nat. Trust for Historic Preservation, Nat. Capital Hist. Soc., Soc. for Preservation Ancient Bldgs. (London, Eng.). Clubs: International, Touch Down (both Washington). Restored original Corcoran Gallery of Art (now Renwick Mus.), Washington; restored and preserved Castle Clinton Nat. Monument, N.Y.C., Pioneer Ct. House, Portland, Ore., Independence Hall, Wheeling, W.Va.; restored Lafayette Sq. Hist. Row Houses. Home: 2801 New Mexico Av NW Washington DC 20007 Office: 1010 Vermont Av NW Washington DC 20005

EISENSTADT, HEINZ BERNHARD, physician; b. Berlin, Germany, Dec. 15, 1905; s. Ludwig and Elise (Schmulewitz) E.; M.D., U. Berlin, 1929; m. Ruth Haase, Dec. 12, 1934; 1 dau., Rita Marion (Mrs. David Danziger). Intern, Rudolf Virchow Hosp., 1929-30; resident internal medicine and roentgenology in Berlin, 1930-35, King's Daus. Hosp., Temple, Tex., 1937-38; gen. practice internal medicine Port Arthur, Tex., 1938—; dir. S. Jefferson County Tumor Clinic, 1957—. Diplomate Am. Bd. Internal Medicine. Fellow A.C.P. (life), Am. Coll. Gastroenterology (life; trustee, v.p.), Am. Coll. Chest Physicians (life); Am. Coll. Cardiology; mem. Nuclear Soc. (charter), Am., Tex. Socs. internal medicine (charter), Tex. Acad. Medicine. Contbr. to book, articles to profl. jours.Home: 210 4th Av Port Arthur TX 77640 Office: 2900 Commerce St Port Arthur TX 77640

EKERS, ERIC NORTON, internat. orgn. exec.; b. Essex, Eng., Mar. 30, 1922; s. Ernest William and Winifred Amy (Norton) E.; B. Sc. with honors, U. London (Eng.), 1949; M.A. (Fulbright scholar 1949-51), U. Cal. at Berkeley, 1951, M.P.H., 1962; postgrad. Ecole des Sciences Politiques, Paris, France, 1952; m. Dagmar Hedvika Novakova, 1955 (div. 1962); 1 dau., Viveca Joy. Ins. ofcl., London, 1939-42; economist U.S. Mut. Security Agy., Paris, 1952-54; editor Internat. Bank Reconstrn. and Devel., Washington, 1954-55; tng. officer WHO, Washington, 1956-61, cons. pub. health, Central Am., 1962-65; prof. pub. health edn. WHO/U. Jamaica, 1963-64; head Washington center Orgn. Econ. Cooperation and Devel., 1966—. Propr. Norton Properties. Bd. govs. Royal Hosp. and Home for Incurables, London. Served with RAF, 1942-46. Fellow Royal Soc. Tropical Medicine, Am. Pub. Health Assn.; mem. Am. Econ. Assn. Club: Fairfax Racquet. Editor Pan Am. Health Quar., 1956-58. Contbr. articles to profl. jours. Home: 939 26th St NW Washington DC 20037 Office: 1750 Pennsylvania Av NW Washington DC 20006

EKSTROM, WILLIAM FERDINAND, educator; b. Rockford, Ill., June 14, 1912; s. Anton Ivar and Mabel Elizabeth (Mattoon) E.; B.A., U. Ill., 1935, M.A., 1936, Ph.D., 1947; Indsl. Adminstr., Harvard, 1943. Instr. English, U. Ill., 1946-47; asst. prof. English, U. Louisville, 1947-51, asso. prof. English, 1951-56, head dept. 1955-67, prof. English, 1956—, v.p. acad. affairs, 1967-72, acting pres., 1972—. Mem. curriculum study com. Commonwealth of Ky. Pub. Edn. Commn., 1961. Served with USAAF, 1943-45; instr. Chinese Air Force. Bd. dirs. Louisville Presbyn. Sem., Young Men's Christian Assn. Greater Louisville; exec. council Presbytery of Louisville Union. Mem. Am. Assn. U. Profs. (pres. Ky. Conf. 1955-56), Ky. Council Tchrs. English, Modern Lang. Assn., Coll. English Assn., Nat. Council Tchrs. English, Am. Assn. U. Profs., Am. Studies Assn. (pres. Ky.-Tenn. 1961-62). Modern Humanities Research Assn., English-Speaking Union, Newcomen Soc. N.Am., Phi Beta Kappa, Phi Kappa Phi, Lambda Chi Alpha. Presbyn. Club: Jefferson (Louisville). Author: Toward Better English, 1940; Guide to Composition, 1953. Home: 8911 Shelbyville Rd Louisville KY 40222

ELAM, ANDREW GREGORY, II, ins. co. exec.; b. Winchester, Va., Feb. 6, 1932; s. Andrew Gregory and Francis Clayton (Gold) E.; A.B., Presbyn. Coll., 1955; m. Rebecca Rhea Cole, Oct. 26, 1958; children—Andrew Gregory III, Philip Cole, Dawna Francis. Adminstrv. asst. Citizen's and So. Nat. Bank, Columbia, S.C., 1955-56; nat. exec. dir. Pi Kappa Phi, Sumter, S.C., 1956-59; pres. Carolina Potato Co., Inc., West Columbia, S.C., 1959-61; mem. pub. relations staff Kendavis Industries Internat., Inc., Fort Worth, 1961-63; dir. sales promotion Pioneer Am. Ins. Co., Fort Worth, 1963-64, dir. pub. relations and sales promotion, 1964-66, asst. v.p., 1966-68, v.p., mem. exec. com., 1968-71, dir., 1970-71; v.p. pub. relations and sales promotion Gt. Am. Res. Ins. Co., Dallas, 1971—. Mem. pub. relations adv. council Inst. Life Ins., N.Y.C., 1971—; mem. pub. relations com. Tex. Life Conv., 1970-71. Mem. pub. information adv. com. Am. Cancer Soc., Tex. div., 1969-72; vice-chmn. pub. relations com. Tarrant County United Fund, 1967; campaign leader Community Pride Campaign Performing Arts, 1969. Bd. dirs. Fort Worth Community Theatre; bd. dirs., treas., vice-chmn. Tarrant County unit, Am. Cancer Soc. Mem. Life Ins. Advertisers Assn. (dir. communications workshop 1970-71), Pub. Relations Soc. Am., Tex. Pub. Relations Assn. (dir. 1966), Indsl. Editors Fort Worth (pres. 1968), So. Round Table (vice-chmn. 1971), Advt. Club Fort Worth, Dallas-Fort Worth Art Dirs. Club, Fort Worth C. of C. (chmn. publ. com. 1970). Presbyn. (deacon 1966-68; ruling elder 1969-71). Lion. Club: Ridglea Country (Fort Worth). Home: 7730 Chattington St Dallas TX 75240 Office: 2020 Live Oak Dallas TX 75221

ELAM, HARPER JOHNSTON, III, city ofcl., textile lawyer; b. Greensboro, N.C., Sept. 30, 1926; s. Harper Johnston and Elizabeth (Martin) E.; B.S. in Commerce, U. N.C., 1950, LL.B., 1952; m. Mary Carolyn Glendinning, Aug. 30, 1947; children—George Martin, John Claibourne, Erin Patricia. Asst. prof. pub. law and govt. U. N.C., Chapel Hill, 1952-54; admitted to N.C. bar, 1952; asst. to city atty. Greensboro, 1954-57, city atty., 1957-61; corp. counsel, asst. sec. Cone Mills Corp., Greensboro, 1961-68, gen. counsel, 1968—. Lectr. Inst. Govt., U. N.C., 1954—, mem. U. N.C. Law Found. Council, 1961—. Mayor pro tem Greensboro, 1965-69, 71—, mayor, 1969-71. Served with USNR, 1944-46; PTO; now comdr. Res. Recipient Bancroft-Whitney award in constl. law, U. N.C. Law Sch., 1952. Mem. U. N.C. Law Alumni Assn. (past pres.), Am. Mgmt. Assn. (seminar chmn. 1962—), Nat. Inst. Municipal Law Officer (past treas.), Am., N.C. bar assns., Lawyers' Assn. Textile Industry (pres.), N.C. League Municipalities (pres.), Textile Lawyers Assn. (bd. govs.), Phi Delta Theta, Phi Delta Phi. Methodist. Mason, Odd Fellow. Home: 110 S Park Dr Greensboro NC 27401 Office: 1201 Maple St Greensboro NC 27405

ELAM, THEODORE MARINUS, lawyer; b. Enid, Okla., Dec. 18, 1934; s. Roy J. and Sara (Godschalk) E.; student U. Colo., 1952-54; B.B.A., U. Okla., 1957, LL.B., 1959; m. Lyn Pryse, Feb. 2, 1958 children—Pryse Roy, Elain, Elizabeth. Admitted to Okla. bar, 1959; asso. firm Mosteller, Fellers, Andrews, Snider, Baggett, Oklahoma City, 1959-61, partner, 1961-64; mem. firm, pres. Andrews, Mosburg, Davis, Elam, Legg & Kornfeld, Oklahoma City, 1964—. Asst. prof. bus. law U. Okla., 1959, spl. lectr. securities law, 1969, 72, asst. prof. law, 1972. Chmn., Outstanding Citizen of Oklahoma City, 1963. Mem. Am., Okla. (co-chmn. pub. relations com.), Okla. County bar assns., Jr. C. of C., Young Pres.'s Orgn., Order of Coif, Omicron Delta Kappa, Phi Delta Theta, Phi Alpha Delta. Republican. Contbr. articles to profl. jours.Home: 6638 Avondale Oklahome City OK 73116 Office: United Founders Tower Oklahoma City OK 73112

ELARTH, HERSCHEL ANDERSON, architect; b. Omaha, Oct. 15, 1907; s. Gustave Adolph and Amanda Corinne (Anderson) E.; B.S., U. Ill., 1929, M.Arch., 1930; postgrad. L'Ecole des Beaux Arts, Paris, France, 1931-32, Mass. Inst. Tech., 1946; m. Wilhelmina van Ingen, Apr. 2, 1942 (dec. Jan. 7, 1969; m. 2d, Eva Robert Frook, July 2, 1971; stepchildren—Robert C. Frook, Susan (Mrs. John Dunlop). Prof. architecture U. Okla., 1938-46, U. Man., 1947-54, Va. Poly. Inst. and State U., Blacksburg, 1954—; pvt. practice architecture H.A. Elarth & C.S. Worley, Jr., architects, Blacksburg, 1955—; cons. Indsl. Park Plan, Washington, 1968. Nat. chmn. membership Assoc. Collegiate Schs. Architecture, 1959-60. Trustee Unitarian Fellowship, Blacksburg, 1967—. Served to 1st lt. AUS, 1942-46. Recipient W.E. Wine award Va. Poly. Inst. and State U., 1967, Langley scholarship A.I.A., 1941. Mem. A.I.A. (chpt. profl. practice com. 1969), Va. Acad. Scis., Am. Assn. U. Profs., Va. Mus. Fine Arts, Nat. Parks Assn., Audubon Soc., Wilderness Soc., Victorian Soc., Archtl. Faculty Assn., Assn. Preservation Va. Antiquities, UN Assn. U.S., Tau Sigma Delta. Exhibits (with C.S. Worley Jr.), Va. Mus., 1958, Boston Mus. Fine Arts, 1962, Jour. Archl. Edn., 1960, Canada Massey Exhibit, 1952. Home: 706 York Dr NE Blacksburg VA 24060

ELDER, EDWARD LESLIE, ins. agt.; b. Loretto, Ky., May 3, 1924; s. Leslie B. and Hazel (Albright) E.; B.S., U. Ky., 1947; m. Jeanette Reynolds, June 7, 1947; children—Leslie, Betsy, James Edward, David Douglas. Fire protection engr. Ky. Insp. Bur., Louisville, 1947-50; fire protection engr., spl. agt. Firemen's Ins. Co. of N.J., 1950-52; mgr. Louisville office Agrl. Ins. Co., 1952-57; pres., Francis, Francis & Trivette, Inc., Pikeville, Ky., 1957—. Bd. dirs. Pikeville Rescue Squad; mem. bd. trustees Meth. Hosp. Mem. Pike County C. of C. (dir.), Ky. Agts. Assn. (dir.), Nat. Fire Protection Assn., U. Ky. Alumni Assn. (trustee), Pi Tau Sigma, Triangle, Blue Goose. Methodist (steward). Rotarian (past pres., dir. Pikeville). Home: 104 Cherry Lane Pikeville KY 41501 Office: Pikeville Nat Bank Bldg Pikeville KY 41501

ELDER, REX ALFRED, hydraulic engr., govt. ofcl.; b. Laquin, Pa., Oct. 4, 1917; s. George Alfred and Harriet Jane (White) E.; B.S. in Civil Engring., Carnegie Inst. Tech., 1940; M.S. in Hydraulic Engring., Ore. State Coll., 1942; m. Janet Stevens Alger, Aug. 10, 1940; children—John Alfred, Carol Stevens (Mrs. William Jones), Susan Annette, William Perdue. Hydraulic engr. hydraulic lab. TVA, Norris, Tenn., 1942-47, lab. head, 1948-61, dir. engring. lab., 1960—. Vice chmn. Pellissippi dist. Gt. Smoky Mountain council Boy Scouts Am. Chmn., Norris Planning Commn., 1949-54, Norris Water Commn., 1954—. Served with USNR, 1945-46. Mem. Am. Soc. C.E. (chmn. numerous coms., James Laurie prize 1949), Am. Soc. M.E., Internat. Assn. Hydraulic Research (chmn.-elect com. on hydraulic machinery 1972—), Internat. Assn. Nav. Congresses, Sigma Xi, Phi Kappa Phi, Theta Tau, Chi Epsilon. Research in fields of steam and nuclear power plants and asso. environmental problems. Home: 117 W Norris Rd Norris TN 37828 Office: PO Drawer E Norris TN 37828

ELDRIDGE, BRUCE FREDERICK, entomologist; b. San Jose, Mar. 26, 1933; s. Arthur Julius and Ruth Myrtle (Pracht) E.; A.B., San Jose State Coll., 1954; M.S., Wash. State Coll., 1956; Ph.D., Purdue U., 1965; m. Shirley Jean Tate, Apr. 20, 1957; children—Deborah Jean, Stuart Warren, Kenneth Robert. Commd. 2d lt. U.S. Army, 1956, advanced through grades to lt. col., 1968; entomologist Army Med. Service Sch., 1956-58, 37th Preventive Medicine Co., Korea, 1960, Atlantic-Pacific Interoceanic Canal Study Commn., Panama, 1966-68; entomologist, Walter Reed Army Inst. Research, 1958-60, 61-63, chmn. dept. entomology, 1969—; chmn. Armed Forces Pest. Control Bd., 1971—. Decorated Meritorious Service medal, Army Commendation Medal with one oak leaf cluster. Mem. Entomol. Soc. Am., Am. Mosquito Control Assn., Am. Soc. Tropical Medicine and Hygiene, Sigma Xi. Home: 11855 Route 108 Clarksville MD 21029 Office: Dept. Entomology Walter Reed Army Inst Research Washington DC 20012

ELDRIDGE, FRANCIS R., JR., physicist; b. Augusta, Ga., July 21, 1916; s. Francis R. and Kathleen (Sanzo) E.; student N.Y. U., 1933-34, George Washington U., 1934-41, Johns Hopkins, 1949-50; m. Margaret Jeannette Cook, Apr. 18, 1942; 1 son, Francis R. III. Research asst. Carnegie Instn. of Washington, 1938-39; asso. physicist Naval Ordnance Lab., Washington, 1939-43; physicist Jones & Lamson Machine Co., Springfield, Vt., 1943-47; spl. electronics engr. Glenn L. Martin Co., Balt., 1947-48; research scientist Johns Hopkins Inst. for Coop. Research, Balt., 1948-52, dir. Controls Research Lab., 1952-55; phys. sci. and project leader RAND Corp., Santa Monica, Cal., 1955-62; spl. asst. for command, control and communications Dept. Def. OASD, Systems Analysis, Pentagon, Washington, 1962-66; dept. asso. dir. Office Telecommunications Mgmt., Exec. Office Pres., Washington, 1966-67; v.p. Kelly Sci. Corp., Washington, 1967; mem. research council Research Analysis Corp., McLean, Va., 1968-70; mem. div. staff Mitre Corp., McLean, Va., 1971—. Mem. N.Y. Acad. Sci., I.E.E.E., Sigma Xi, Sigma Pi Sigma. Patentee voice response computer devices. Home: 4557 32d Rd N Arlington VA 22207 Office: Mitre Corp Westgate Research Park McLean VA 22101

ELDRIDGE, WILLIAM BUTLER, lawyer, govt. ofcl.; b. Greensboro, N.C., Jan. 26, 1931; s. James Eiffel and Clara Mae (Butler) E.; A.B., Duke, 1953, LL.B., 1956; postgrad. U. Chgo., 1961-62; m. Barbara Galloway, June 15, 1957; children—Mark, Julia. Admitted to Mo. bar, 1956; practiced law in St. Louis, 1956-57; mem. firm Coburn & Croft; asst. exec. dir. Am. Bar Found., Chgo., 1960-68; dir. research Fed. Jud. Center, Washington, 1969—. Served with AUS, 1957-60; Mem. Am. Bar Assn. Author: Narcotics and the Law, 2d edit., rev. 1967. Contbr. articles to legal jours. Home: 11209 Old Post Rd Potomac MD 20854 Office: Federal Judicial Center 1520 H St NW Washington DC 20005

ELEDGE, WILLIAM WALTER, JR., hosp. adminstr.; b. Englewood, Tenn., Sept. 4, 1916; s. William Walter and Stella Belle (Liner) E.; B.S., Carson-Newman Coll., 1939; postgrad. U. Tenn., 1940-41, U. Pa., 1947-48; m. Pauline Bullard, Jan. 23, 1943; children—Margaret (Mrs. Leonard Taylor Lee), William Walter III. Tchr., coach, prin., McMinn County, Tenn., 1936-41; entered U.S. Army as pvt., 1944, advanced through grades to col. USAF, 1961; med. adminstr.; adminstr. Woods Meml. Hosp., Etowah, Tenn., 1967—. Mem. Etowah City Planning Commn., 1969—. Chmn. bd. dirs. McMinn County Mental Health Center. Decorated Legion of Merit. Fellow Am. Coll. Nursing Home Adminstrs.; mem. Am. Coll. Hosp. Adminstrs. Democrat. Baptist. Mason, Lion, Rotarian. Home: Route 2 Box 255L Etowah TN 37331 Office: Woods Memorial Hospital Etowah TN 37331

ELFIN, MEL, mag. editor; b. Bklyn., July 18, 1929; s. Joseph and Bess (Margulies) E.; A.B., Syracuse U., 1951; M.A., Harvard, 1952; student New Sch. Social Research, 1955-58; m. Margery Lesser, June 21, 1953; children—David, Dana. Copywriter, Marvin and Leonard, advt., Boston, 1953-54; successively reporter, travel editor, asst. city editor L.I. Daily Press, Jamaica, N.Y., 1954-58; mem. staff Newsweek mag., 1958—, gen. editor, 1964-65, chief Washington bur., 1965—. Cons. Ednl. Facilities Lab., N.Y.C.; cons. Guidance Assos., Inc., Pleasantville, N.Y. Served as officer, SAC, USAF, 1952-53. Recipient George Polk Meml. award reporting, 1957, N.Y. Newspaper Guild Page One award, 1957; award Edn. Writers Assn., 1966. Mem. White House Corr. Assn., Phi Beta Kappa. Clubs: International, Fed. City (Washington). Author: (with others) Bricks and Mortarboards, 1963; also articles. Home: 2804 29th St NW Washington DC 20008 Office: 1750 Pennsylvania Av NW Washington DC 20006

ELIEL, LEONARD PAUL, physician, educator; b. Los Angeles, Sept. 14, 1914; s. Paul and Harriet (Judd) E.; B.S., Harvard, 1936, M.D. cum laude, 1940; m. Marjorie Blake, Jan. 14, 1943; children—Alan, Suzanne. Intern, Mass. Gen. Hosp., Boston, 1940-42; pediatric fellow Children's Hosp., Boston, 1946-48; Damon Runyon sr. clin. research fellow, asso. Sloan-Kettering Inst., 1949-51; asst. prof. Cornell Med. Coll., 1950-51; head cancer research sect. Okla. Med. Research Found., Oklahoma City, 1951-64, v.p., dir. research, 1965-70; prof. research medicine U. Okla., Oklahoma City, 1956-66, prof. medicine, 1966—, asso. dir., also asso. dean Grad. Coll. Med. Center, 1970, interim exec. v.p., dir. Health Scis. Center 1970-71, exec. v.p., also dir. Health Scis. Center, 1971—; exec. dir. Okla. Med. Research Found., 1959-65. Pres. Oklahoma City Symphony Soc., 1968-69. Served to lt. USNR, 1944-46. Fellow A.C.P.; mem. Am. Assn. Cancer Research, Am. Clin. and Climatol. Assn., Am. Soc. Clin. Investigation, Endocrine Soc. Episcopalian. Rotarian. Contbr. numerous articles to sci. jours. Research in cancer endocrinology and parathyroid physiology. Home: 2541 Wilshire Blvd Oklahoma City OK 73116 Office: 800 NE 13th St Oklahoma City OK 73104

ELIOT, MILTON EARL, steel co. exec.; b. Dallas, Dec. 14, 1914; s. William Mack and Etta (Cundiff) E.; B.S. in Civil Engring., U. Tex., 1935; M.S., U. Ill., 1936; m. Agnes Field, Feb. 14, 1943; children—Emily Ann (Mrs. Charles Oren Hon III), William Eugene, Charles Scott. Draftsman, Mosher Steel Co., Houston, 1936-39, chief engr., Dallas, 1939-56, v.p. and works mgr., 1956-64, exec. v.p., Houston, 1964-66, pres., 1968—, also dir.; dir. Mosher Steel Co. of La., Comml. Iron Works, Trustee Mosher Found., United Fund of Houston and Harris County. Fellow Am. Soc. C.E.; mem. Tau Beta Pi, Chi Epsilon, Delta Kappa Epsilon. Home: 2220 Looscan Lane Houston TX 77019 Office: 3910 Washington Av Houston TX 77007

ELIOT, THEODORE LYMAN, JR., govt. ofcl.; b. N.Y.C., Jan 24, 1928; s. Theodore Lyman and Martha Williams (Bigelow) E.; B.A., Harvard, 1948, M.P.A., 1956; m. Patricia F. Peters, Apr. 14, 1951; children—Sarah Winslow, Theodore Lyman III, Wendy Peters, Peter Bigelow. Vice consul, 3d sec. Am. embassy, Colombo, Ceylon, 1950-52; U.S. information and cultural officer, Germany, 1953-55; 2d sec. Am. embassy, Moscow, USSR, 1956-58; spl. asst. to under sec. state, 1959-61, to sec. treasury, 1961-62; 1st sec. Am. Embassy, Tehran, Iran, 1963-66; country dir. Iran, Dept. State, 1966-69; exec. sec. Dept. State, also spl. asst. to sec. state, 1969—. Adviser U.S. delegation to meeting Inter-Am. Devel. Bank, Rio de Janeiro, 1961, NATO meeting, Paris, 1961, others. Mem. Am. Fgn. Service Assn. (vice chmn. bd. 1967-69, pres. 1970—). Home: 6601 Virginia View Ct Washington DC 20016 Office: Dept State Washington DC 20520

ELIZONDO, EDUARDO A., lawyer; b. Monterrey, Mexico, Dec. 7, 1922; licentiate law U. Neuvo Leon, 1933. Admitted to Mexican bar, 1944; prof. law U. Neuvo Leon, 1946-50, prof. comml. and banking law Inst. Tech., Monterrey, 1946-50; past dir. Comision de Fomento Industrial y Desarrollo Economico del Estado de Neuvo Leon, Servicios de Agua y Drenaje de Monterrey; pres. State U. Neuvo Leon, 1965-67; now mem. firm Bufete Santos de La Garza-Elizondo, Monterrey. Constl. gov., Neuvo Leon, 1967-71. Author: Creditos Documentarios, 1944. Address: Bufete Santos de la Garza-Elizondo Cuauhtemoc 757 Sur 2 Piso Monterrey Mexico*

ELKIN, BENJAMIN JAMES, bank exec.; b. Lexington, Ky., May 7, 1930; s. Z. F. and Rose (Moller) E.; B.S., U. Ky., 1952; postgrad. La. U., 1965-67, Ohio State U., 1968-69, Okla. U., 1969; certificate Am. Inst. Banking, 1963; m. Nita L. Myers, Jan. 17, 1951; children—Kathleen L., Fielding, Julie C. Trainee First Security Nat. Bank, Lexington, Ky., 1956-58, teller, 1958-59, note teller, 1959-60, asst. cashier operations, 1959-60, credit dept. mgr., 1960-61, asst. cashier comml. lending, 1961-62, asst. v.p. comml. lending, 1962-66, v.p. comml. lending, 1966—; dir. G. F. Vaughan Tobacco Co. Instr. Ky. Sch. Banking, 1965-67. Chmn. Easter Seals, 1968; vice-chmn. campaign United Community Fund, 1969, campaign chmn. Lexington-Fayette County, 1970. Served with AUS, 1952-54. Mem. Lexington Mortgage Bankers Assn. (sec. 1971-72), Ky., Greater Lexington area C. of C.'s, Delta Tau Delta, Delta Sigma Phi. Rotarian. Home: 1893 Blairmore Rd Lexington KY 40502 Office: 167 W Main St Lexington KY 40502

ELKINS, BILLY BOB, ednl. adminstr. tech. sch.; b. Henrietta, Tex., Mar. 29, 1940; s. Claude C. and Anne Lee (Morrow) E.; B.S., So. Meth. U., 1963; m. Laura Ann Poindexter, July 29, 1966; 1 dau., Laura Sue. With Elkins Inst., Inc., Dallas, 1958—, pres., 1969—; dir. Elkins Industries, Inc., Elkins Ednl. Research Found. Mem. I.E.E.E., Nat. Rehab. Counciling Assn., Nat. Assn. Radio Engrs., Tex. (dir. 1955-71), Dallas Area rehab. assns., So. Meth. U. Alumni Assn. (dir. 1969-71), Delta Chi. Home: 5320 Pebblebrook Dr Dallas TX 75229 Office: 2727 Inwood Rd Dallas TX 75235

ELKINS, FRANCIS CLARK, coll. adminstr.; b. Scranton, Ark., Feb. 24, 1923; s. Frank V. and Auby (Moore) E.; B.A., State Coll. Ark., 1943; M.A., U. Ark., 1948; postgrad. U. N.C., summers 1948, 49; Ph.D., Syracuse U., 1953; postgrad. U. Minn., summer 1956; m. Norma Trice, Aug. 18, 1946; 1 dau., Annette. Faculty, Henderson (Ark.) State Coll., 1946-61, prof., 1955-61, chmn. social sci., 1957-61; pres. Chadron (Neb.) State Coll., 1961-67; pres. N.E. Mo. State Coll., 1967-69; coordinator U. Coll., Ark. State U., 1969-70, v.p. instrn., 1970—. Examiner, cons. Nat. Council Accreditation of Tchr. Edn., North Central Assn. Colls. and Secondary Schs.; cons. Am. Assn. Colls. for Tchr. Edn., 1967—. Mem. adv. council Mo. 4-H Found., 1968-69; exec. com. Neb. Council on Ednl. TV for Higher Edn., 1965-67; mem. Nat. Commn. on Accrediting, 1967-69. Served with USAAF, 1943-45. Decorated D.F.C., Air medal with 4 oak leaf clusters. Mem. N.E.A. (life), Ark. Edn. Assn., Sigma Tau Gamma, Phi Alpha Theta, Phi Delta Kappa. Elk, Rotarian. Contbr. articles to tech. jours. Home: 1400 Linden Av Jonesboro AR 72401 Office: PO Drawer K State University AR 72467 mailing address: PO Drawer K State University AR 72467

ELKINS, JAMES ANDERSON, JR., banker; b. Galveston, Tex., Mar. 24, 1919; s. James Anderson and Isabel (Mitchell) E.; grad. Hill Sch., 1937; B.A., Princeton, 1941; m. Margaret Wiess, Nov. 24, 1945; children— Elise, James Anderson III, Leslie K. With First City Nat. Bank, Houston, 1941—, v.p., 1946-50, pres., 1950-60, chm. bd., 1960—, also dir.; dir. Eastern Airlines, Almeda State Bank, Houston, Cameron Iron Works. Trustee U. Houston, Baylor Coll. Medicine, St. John's Sch., Princeton. Mem. Houston C. of C. (exec. com., dir.). Episcopalian (trustee Diocese of Tex.). Home: 101 Farish Circle Houston TX 77024 Office: First City Nat Bank Houston TX 77001

ELKINS, RUTH ELLA MCKEOWN, home economist; b. Quincy, Fla., Feb. 10, 1912; d. Oliver Lee and Mattie (Clark) McKeown; B.S., Fla. State U., 1939, postgrad., 1941-56; postgrad. U. Fla., 1952; m. Bryan W. Elkins, Aug. 30, 1927 (dec.); children—Sarah Ruth (Mrs. Chalmers Holmes), Bronna Mae (Mrs. Grant Godwin). Tchr. home econs., gen. sci. Escambia Farms High Sch., Mt. Pleasant, Fla., 1939-40, Mt. Pleasant High Sch., 1940-42; extension home econs. agt., home demonstration agt. Taylor County, Fla., 1942-53, Polk County, Fla., 1953—, vice chmn. agrl. extension service 1964—. Chmn. home econs. div. Polk County Youth Fair, 1953; sec., v.p., pres. Polk County Nutrition Com.; mem. Gov.'s Conf. on Safety, Juvenile Delinquency and Little White House Conf. Fla., 1942—; mem. White House Conf. on Children and Youth, 1960. Trustee Leukemia Soc. Polk County Fla., 1967-68. Recipient Distinguished Service award as most outstanding demonstration agt. in Fla., 1955; U.S. Treasury Dept. citation for patriotic vol. service. Mem. Fla. Extension Home Econs. Assn. (past treas.), Nat. Extension Home Econs. Agts. Assn., Fla. Agrl. Extension Workers Assn. (past pres.), Extension Home Econs. Assn. (chmn. for distinguished service, 1967), Epsilon Sigma Phi (analyst, sec., worthy chief, 1962-63). Clubs: Pilot (exec. bd. 1954—, pres.), Business and Profl. Woman's (charter, dist. chmn.), Perry Garden, (Perry, Fla.), Barstow Federated Women's (pres. 1970-72). Baptist. Contbr. articles to newspapers. Appeared on TV and radio with ednl. programs. Home: 1855 S Margaret Av Bartow FL 33830 Office: PO Box 1049 Bartow FL 33830

ELKOURI, JIM RAY, librarian; b. Chickasha, Okla., Aug. 7, 1938; s. David and Adel (Elkouri) E.; B.A. with distinction, U. Okla., 1960, M.L.S., 1962; postgrad. Oklahoma City U., 1965-66. Documents cataloger Okla. State U., Stillwater, 1962-63; documents librarian Oklahoma City U., 1963-65, catalog librarian, asst. prof. library sci., 1965—. Mem. Am., Okla. library assns., Phi Beta Kappa, Beta Phi Mu, Phi Alpha Theta. Home: 2332 NW 16th St Oklahoma City OK 73107

ELLEDGE, LARRY FRANCIS, editor; b. Poplar Bluff, Mo., May 22, 1941; s. John Elwood and Barbara (Dysinger) E.; B.S., Ark. State U., 1963; m. Ethel Jean Wyatt, June 29, 1963; 1 dau., Selena Grace. Sports editor Springdale (Ark.) News, 1963-64; asst. sports editor Pine Bluff (Ark.) Commercial, 1964; news editor Mt. Vernon (Ind.) Democrat, 1966-67; editor Piggott (Ark.) Banner, 1967-69; city editor Texarkana (Tex.-Ark.) Gazette and Daily News, 1969, mng. editor; 1969-71; exec. editor Hot Springs (Ark.) Sentinal Record & New Era, 1971—. Mem. Hot Springs C. of C., Tex. United Press Editors Assn. (dir. 1970-71), Lambda Chi Alpha. Methodist. Kiwanian. Home: 105 Fernwood Hot Springs AR 71901

ELLEN, JOHN CALHOUN, JR., educator; b. Dillon, S.C., Apr. 4, 1921; s. John Calhoun and Grevelle (Hounshell) E.; B.A., Emory and Henry Coll., 1941; A.B. in Journalism, U. Ga., 1949; M.A., U. S.C., 1954, Ph.D., 1958; m. Dorothy Elizabeth Humphreys, Aug. 20, 1961; children—Elizabeth Delaney, Kathryn Lynn. Grad. teaching asst. U. S.C., 1956-58; asst. prof. history East Carolina Coll., Greenville, N.C., 1959-62, asso. prof., 1962-69, prof, 1969—, dir. Nat. Def. Edn. Act History Inst., summer, 1965. Served with AUS, 1942, USAAF, 1943-45. Mem. So., S.C. hist. assns., N.C. Lit. and Hist. Assn., Orgn. Am. Historians, S.C. Hist. Soc. Author: Political Newspapers of the Piedmont Carolinas during the 1850's 1958. Contbr. articles, book revs to hist. publs. Home: 1504 S Brownlea Dr Greenville NC 27834

ELLENDER, ALLEN JOSEPH, U.S. senator; b. Montegut, Terrebonne Parish, La., Sept. 24, 1890; s. Wallace Richard and Victoria (Javaux) E.; hon. A.M., St. Aloysius Coll., New Orleans; LL.B., Tulane U., 1913; m. Helen Calhoun Donnelly, March 19, 1917 (dec. Sept. 1949); 1son, Allen Joseph. Admitted to La. bar, 1913; city atty., Houma, La., 1913-15; dist. atty. Terrebonne Parish, 1915-16, del. Constl. Conv. of La., 1921; mem. La. State Ho. of Rep., 1924-36, floor leader, 1928-32, speaker, 1932-36; U.S. senator from La., 1937—, pres. pro tem, 1971—, chmn. com. agr. and forestry, 1951-52, 55-71, appropriations com., 1971—. Dem. Nat. committeeman from La., 1939-40; mem. Dem. Policy Com., 1971—. Served with U.S. Army, 1918-19. Mem. Delta Theta Phi, Pi Kappa Alpha. Democrat. Home: 235 E Park Av Houma LA 70360 Address: Senate Office Bldg Washington DC 20510 Died Oct. 1972

ELLER, JAMES EDGAR, lumber co. exec.; b. Bristol, Tenn., Aug. 6, 1931; s. Don James and Wilma (Bentley) E.; student U. of South, 1951, U. Tenn., 1952, 54, N.C. State U., 1954; m. Retha Lois Ragan, Sept. 16, 1950; children—Michael Edgar, Deborah Rai; m. 2d, Connie Charlene Wilcox, Apr. 30, 1971; stepchildren—Thomas Brian Wilcox, John Brett Wilcox. With Cortrim Hardwood Parts Co., Bristol, 1947-58, dry kiln technician, 1951-53, mill room supr., 1953-57, sales mgr., 1959-61, gen. mgr., 1961—; sales engr. Harris Mfg. Co., Johnson City, Tenn., 1958-59. Mem. C. of C. (mem. exec. council 1966-67). Methodist. Mason, Moose, Elk. Home: 213 Sparkling Brook Dr Bristol TN 37620 Office: 1320 Georgia Av Bristol TN 37620

ELLIMAN, GEORGE TROWBRIDGE, govt. ofcl.; b. N.Y.C., Dec. 17, 1905; s. Douglas Ludlow and Theodora Polhemus (Trowbridge) E.; grad. St. Paul's Sch., 1923; A.B. magna cum laude, Princeton, 1928; grad. Nat. War Coll., 1958; m. Natica De Acosta, June 4, 1931; 1 son, Peter Bogert. With Doubleday, Doran & Co., 1928-33; advt. mgr. Sat. Rev. Lit., 1933-36; with Butler & Baldwin, real estate, N.Y.C., 1936-39; with U.S. Govt. agys. engaged in def. and war work, 1939-42; exec. dir. Office Fgn. Liquidation, State Dept., 1945-48; asst. dir. tech. assistance div. ECA, 1948-51; dir. fgn. div. NPA, 1951-52; adviser fgn. activities Dept. Commerce, 1952-59; joined U.S. fgn. service, 1959; comml. attache, Am. embassy, Rome, Italy, 1959-64; dir. internat. activities staff Bus. and Def. Services Adminstrn., U.S. Dept. Commerce, 1964-69, dir. U.S. trade and indsl. devel. mission to Ireland and Portugal, 1966-67, spl. asst. ILO affairs, mem. U.S. delegation to ILO, 1967-69; mem. Fgn. Service selection bd., 1969. Served to lt. comdr. USNR, 1942-45. Home: The Plains VA 22171

ELLING, LAWRENCE JOHN, civil engr.; b. Riviera, Tex., Mar. 30, 1915; s. Fred John and Clara Teresa (Hertzberg) E.; B.S. in Math., Tex. A. and I. U., 1946, B.S. in Engring., 1952, M.S., 1953; m. Mary Elizabeth Rich, Apr. 20, 1948; 1 son, John Frederick. Surveyor Tex. Hwy. Dept., Kingsville, 1946-49; mem. civil engring. dept. Houston Natural Gas Corp., Corpus Christi, Tex., 1953-57, Houston, 1957—. Instr. mech. drawing Del Mar Jr. Coll., Corpus Christi, 1954-57. Mem. Planning and Zoning Com., Spring Valley, Houston, 1964-68. Served with AUS, 1941-45. Recipient Meritorious Service awards Engrs. Council Houston, 1962, 64. Registered profl. engr., Tex.; registered land surveyor. Fellow Am. Soc. C.E.; mem. Tex. Soc. Profl. Engrs., Engrs. Council Houston (pres. 1961), Houston Engring. and Sci. Soc., Houston C. of C. (mem. water supply and conservation com. 1964—). Home: 8718 Winningham Lane Houston TX 77055 Office: PO Box 1188 Houston TX 77001

ELLINGER, CHARLES WILLIAM, dental educator; b. Lancaster, O., June 8, 1934; s. LeRoy Edward and Mable Bernice (Behrens) E.; D.D.S., Ohio State U., 1959, M.Sc., 1965; m. Janet D. Murphy, Mar. 23, 1958; children—Susan, Stacy Ann, Charles William II. Intern, Fla. Instl. Internship Program, Ocala, 1959-60; individual practice dentistry, Lima, O., 1960-62; mem. staff dept. prosthodontics U. Ky., Lexington, 1965—, now asso. prof., dir. complete dentures. Cons. VA Hosp., Lexington, Ky., 1967-72, Nat. Inst. Mental Health, Hosp., Lexington, 1971-72. Served to capt. AUS, 1963-64. Mem. Am. Dental Assn., Blue Grass Dental Soc., Internat. Assn. Dental Research, Am. (nomenclature com. 1971-72), Carl O. Boucher (mem. nominations com. 1968-69), Southeastern (mem. membership com. 1969-70) prosthodontic socs., Psi Omega. Lutheran. Author: (with J. H. Rayson, J. A. Terry, A. O. Rahn) Synopsis of Complete Dentures, 1972. Contbr. articles to profl. jours. Home: 1866 Parkers Mill Lexington KY 40504

ELLINGTON, BUFORD, former gov. Tenn.; b. Holmes County, Miss., June 27, 1907; s. Abner E. and Cora (Grantham) E.; m. Catherine Cheek; children—John Earl. Ann. Mgr., Tenn. Farm Bur. Ins. Service, 1949-51; commr. agr. State of Tenn., 1953-58; gov. of Tenn., 1959-63, 67-71. Chmn. Regional Adv. Com. on Nuclear Energy, 1959-60, So. Regional Edn. Bd., 1960-61, So. Gov.'s Conf., 1960-61, Gov.'s Com. on Roads and Hwy. Safety, 1961—; mem. Nat. Com. on Employment of Youth, 1962—. Chmn. Cordell Hull Found., 1959—. Methodist. Mason (32 deg., Shriner). Home: Curtiswood Lane Nashville TN 37204

ELLIOT, DAVIS HASKINS, elec. engr.; b. Fall River, Mass., Jan. 26, 1907; s. Arthur Frank and Edith Emma (Haskins) E.; B.Sc., U. Mass., 1930; m. Elizabeth Flourney Adams, Dec. 15, 1934; 1 son, William Davis. From clk, distbn. dept. to asst. mgr. Appalachian Electric Power Co., Roanoke, Va., 1930-42; chmn. bd. Davis H. Elliot Co., Inc., elec. constrn., Roanoke and Lexington, Ky., 1946—. Pres. Community Fund, 1950-51; v.p. Roanoke Fine Arts Center; pres. Southwestern Va. chpt. Trout Unlimited. Mem. State Apprenticeship Council, 1953—. Served from lt. (j.g.) to lt. comdr., USNR, 1942-46; comdr. Mine Div. 33, 1945. Recipient Savs. Bond program award U.S. Treasury, 1958. Mem. I.E.E.E., English-speaking Union (br. pres. 1960—, mem. nat. bd.), Roanoke C. of C. (pres. 1957). Episcopalian (warden). Clubs: Roanoke German, Roanoke Country, Shenandoah (pres. 1952), (Roanoke); Commonwealth (Richmond); Army and Navy (Washington); Norfolk (Va.) Yacht and Country, Anglers (N.Y.); Fly Fishers (London, Eng.). Home: 3266 White Oak Rd Roanoke VA 24014 Office: 1920 Progress Dr SE Roanoke VA 24013

ELLIOT, REED A., govt. ofcl. Dir. water control planning div. TVA, Knoxville, Tenn. Address: Water Control Planning Div TVA Knoxville TN 37902*

ELLIOTT, CLARENCE WILLARD, educator, accountant; b. Hampton, Ark., Oct.9, 1936; s. Clarence Willard and Madge (Lyon) E.; B.S., Ark. A. and M. Coll., 1958; M.B.A., U. Ark., 1960, Ph.D., 1964; m. Sherry Carolyn Kennedy, Sept. 3, 1960; children—Clarence Willard III, Erin Gaye. Cost accountant Duracraft Boats, Inc., Monticello, Ark., 1957-58; instr. U. Ark., Fayetteville, 1959-62; asst. prof. accounting St. Josephs Coll., Rensselaer, Ind., 1962-64; asso. prof. accounting La. State U., Baton Rouge, 1964—, also dir. placement Coll. Bus. Adminstrn. Auditor, R.J. Flynn, C.P.A., Rensselaer, 1962-64; cons. internat. div. Ethyl Corp., Baton Rouge, summer 1966; cons. Harbor Banana Distbrs., Inc., Long Beach, Cal., Aluminum Products Co., New Orleans; cons. edn. and tng. Arthur Young & Co., 1968-69; mem. faculty Inst. Ins. Marketing. Recipient service award La. LP-Gas Assn., 1968. C.P.A., La. Mem. Am. Inst. C.P.A.s La. Soc. C.P.A.'s (chpt. pres.), Am. Accounting Assn., Alpha Chi, Beta Alpha Psi, Beta Gamma Sigma. Contbr. numerous articles to profl. jours. Home: 3848 N Bluebonnet Rd Baton Rouge LA 70809

ELLIOTT, DONALD RICHARD, data processing exec.; b. Peoria, Ill., Aug. 23, 1914; s. Jesse P. and Ruth (Bowman) E.; student U. Ia., 1932-33; m. Marjorie Elizabeth Mackley, July 21, 1934; children—Ruth Ann (Mrs. Robert Lee Schwaner), Roxy Mackley. Profl. musician various name dance bands, Chgo., N.Y.C., 1934-42; IBM technician, supr. Caterpillar Tractor Co., Peoria, 1947-54; asst. sec., data processing mgr. Ins. Co. of Tex., Presdl. Ins. Co., Jacksonville, Fla., 1955-56; v.p., dir. servicing and data processing Fed. Title & Ins. Corp. and Republic Mortgage Corp., Miami, Fla., 1956-64; pres. Doriel, Inc., Computer Service Center, Miami, 1965-66; dir. computer operations Lon Worth Crow Co., mortgage bankers, Miami, 1966—; dir., v.p. Bank Directory, Inc., Miami, 1964—. Served with C.E., AUS, 1943-45. Mem. Mortgage Bankers Assn. (loan adminstrn. chmn. 1964), Data Processing Mgmt. Assn., Nat. Machine Accountants Assn. (pres., nat dir. 1958, 63). Mason. Home: 2910 NW 175th St Opa Locka FL 33054 Office: 75 SE 14th St Miami FL 33131

ELLIOTT, FLOYD AVERY, bank exec.; b. Chester, S.C., Feb. 14, 1928; s. John Alexander and Minnie Frances (Cassells) E.; B.A., Duke, 1949; student banking La. State U., 1966; m. Ola Wilkerson Matlock, Apr. 23, 1955; children—Floyd Matlock, John Avery, Robert Wilkerson. Asst. cashier Peoples Nat. Bank, Chester, S.C., 1955-60, asst. v.p., asst. trust officer, 1960-68, v.p., asst. trust officer, dir., 1968—. Mem. Chester County Bd. Devel. and Commerce, 1969-72; sec. Chester Metropolitan Sewer Dist., 1964-73. Bd. dirs. United Fund. Served with AUS, 1950-52. Mem. Nat. Asso. Bank Auditors and Comptrollers (dir. S.C. 1967-68), Young Bankers S.C. (dir. 1966-68). Democrat. Baptist (deacon 1964—). Lion. Home: 107 Hillcrest Dr Chester SC 29706 Office: 120 Church St Chester SC 29706

ELLIOTT, J.H., JR., dir. Atlanta Mus. Office: Atlanta Mus 537-39 Peachtree St Atlanta GA 30308*

ELLIOTT, J(AMES) ROBERT, dist. judge; b. Gainesville, Ga., Jan. 1, 1910; s. Thomas M. and Mamie Lucille (Glenn) E.; Ph.B., Emory U., 1930, LL.B., 1934; m. Brownie C. Buck, Aug. 3, 1949; children—Susan G., James Robert. Admitted to Ga. bar, 1934, engaged in corporate and trial practice; U.S. dist. judge Middle Dist. Ga., 1962—. Mem. Ga. Ho. of Reps., 1937-49; mem. Democratic Nat. Com., 1948-56. Served as lt. (s.g.) USNR, World War II; PTO. Mem. Ga. Jr. C. of C. (pres. 1941-42), Ga. Bar Assn., Lambda Chi Alpha, Phi Delta Phi. Kwianian. Home: 2612 Carson Dr Columbus GA 31906 Office: US District Court Columbus GA 31901

ELLIOTT, JOHN M., govt. ofcl. Chief collections br. Nat. Armed Forces Museum Adv. Bd., Smithsonian Instn., Washington. Address: Smithsonian Instn Washington DC 20560*

ELLIOTT, JOHN MONTGOMERY, labor union ofcl.; b. Phila., Aug. 10, 1913; s. William J. and Catherine (Montgomery) E.; m. Marie Lindtner, Sept. 19, 1934; children—John Montgomery, Catherine Marie. Internat. rep. Amalgamated Assn. of Street, Electric Ry. and Motor Coach Employees of Am. (name now Amalgamated Transit Union), AFL-CIO, 1945-48, v.p., 1948-57, mem. gen. exec. bd., asst. to pres. internat. hdqrs., 1955-57, exec. v.p., 1957-59, internat. pres., 1959—; dir., exec. com. Union Labor Life Ins. Co.; trustee, mem. planning com. Venice (Fla.)-Nacomas Bank. Exec. bd. Internat. Transport Workers Fedn. Home: 2714 Sheridan St Hollywood FL 33020 Office: 5025 Wisconsin Av NW Washington DC 20016

ELLIOTT, JULES LOMBARD, civil engr.; b. Jacksonville, Fla., Sept. 29, 1939; s. Robert Buster and Dorothy Ann (Nagle) E.; B.C.E., U. Fla., 1964; m. Norma Janice Allen, Sept. 2, 1960; children—Julie Lynne, Laura Leigh, David Allen. Designer, Black Crow & Eidsness Engrs., 1960-64; asst. mgr. Va. office Russell & Axon Engrs., 1964-65; founding partner Martin Clifford & Assos. Engrs., Stafford, Va., 1966-69; owner, prodn. mgr. Elliott & Assos., engrs.-planners, Alexandria, Va., 1969—; dir. Bragg Hill Corp. Owner, Kleen Quik Corp. Mem. finance com. United Givers Fund, Fredericksburg, Va., 1969. Registered profl. engr., Va., W.Va., Pa., Md., Fla. Mem. Am. Soc. C.E., Profl. Engrs. in Pvt. Practice, Va. Soc. Profl. Engrs. (state dir. 1968-71), Cons. Engrs. Council Va., F Club, Beta Theta Pi. Club: Fredericksburg Country (golf chmn. 1969). Home: 301 Braehead Dr

Fredericksburg VA 22401 Office: Suite 1000 4660 Kenmore Av Alexandria VA 22304

ELLIOTT, KENNETH CHARLES, transp. co. exec.; b. Burkburnett, Tex., May 31, 1924; s. Wilbur A. and Zebie (Gray) E.; B.B.A., U. Tex., 1945; m. Marcene Simmons, Dec. 2, 1944; children—Linda (Mrs. Gary Osborn), Kenneth Clayton. Asst. plant traffic mgr. Armour & Co., Fort Worth, 1946-57; v.p. traffic and sales Commercial Oil Transport, Fort Worth, 1957-67; exec. v.p. Bray Lines Inc., Cushing, Okla., 1967—. Mem. Nat. Tank Truck Carriers, Inc. (dir. 1970-71), Asso. Motors Carriers Okla. (v.p., dir. 1970-71), Okla. Safety Council (dir. 1970-71), Tulsa Traffic Club, Oklahoma City Traffic Club, Oklahoma City Petroleum Club. Methodist. Republican. Mason (32 degree, Shriner), Rotarian. Club: Cushing Country. Home: 935 E Cherry St Cushing OK 74023 Office: 1401 N Little St Cushing OK 74023

ELLIOTT, LLOYD HARTMAN, univ. pres.; b. Clay County, W.Va., May 21, 1918; s. John and Belva (Stone) E.; A.B., Glenville State Coll., 1937; M.A., W.Va. U., 1939, LL.D., 1967; Ed.D., U. Colo., 1948; LL.D., U. N.H., 1963, Colby Coll, 1965, Concord Coll., 1966, U. Me., 1969, Husson Coll., 1970, Georgetown U., 1971; m. Evelyn Elder, Aug. 25, 1936; children—Lloyd Gene, Patricia Ann. Tchr. pub. schl, Widen, W.Va., 1937-39, elementary, high sch. prin., 1939-42; INSTR. U. Colo., summer 1947; asst. supt. Boulder Pub. Sch., 1947-48; vis. prof. U. Tex., 1948; asst. prof. edn. Cornell U., 1948-50, asso, prof. edn., 1950-54, dir. summer session, 1953-56, prof. ednl. administrn., 1954-58, exec. asst. to pres., 1956-58; pres. U. Me., Orono, 1958-65, George Washington U., Washington, 1965—. Dir. Chesapeake & Potomac Telephone Co., Acacia Mut. Life Ins. Co., Am. Security and Trust Co. Trustee Greater Washington Ednl. TV Assn., Inc.; trustee, mem. exec. com. Washington Center Met. Studies; mem. Commrs. Adv. Council Higher Edn., Am. Council on Edn.; pres. Assn. Urban Univs., 1971; bd. dirs. Consortium Washington Univs.; pres. Nat. Commn. on Accrediting, 1972—. Mem. Am. Assn. Sch. Adminstrs., N.E.A., Nat. Geog. Soc. (bd. trustees), Phi Delta Kappa, Phi Kappa Phi. Clubs: Cosmos. Contbr. articles profl. publs. Home: 2330 Tracy Pl NW Washington DC 20008

ELLIOTT, MORRIS FRANCIS, clergyman; b. Phila., Mar. 26, 1909; s. Matthew and Elizabeth Margaret (Morris) E.; B.A., William and Mary Coll., 1933; B.D., Va. Theol. Sem., 1936; D.D., Daniel Baker Coll., 1953; m. Margaret Ann Miller, May 23, 1938; 1 dau., Barbara Ann. Ordained to ministry P.E. Ch. as deacon, 1936, priest, 1937; asst. rector Galveston, Tex., 1936-38; rector Houston, 1938-41, Lufkin, Tex., 1941-49; rector Emmanuel Ch., San Angelo, Tex., 1949—. Mem. Com. State of Ch., 1950-51; chmn. examining chaplains Diocese of N.W. Tex., 1950-60, mem., 1960—, mem. exec. bd., 1960; del. Provincial Synod, 1951, 54, 57, 66, 69, 72. Mem. adv. bd. Planned Parenthood, San Angelo, 1959—. Mem. bd. Servicemen's Center, 1964—, pres., 1967-70; adv. bd. Parents Without Partners; president San Angelo Council of Churches, 1968-69; mem. San Angelo Council on Alcoholism, 1966—. Trustee, Daniel Baker Coll., Brownwood, Tex., 1950-51; Sem. of S.W.; bd. dirs. San Angelo Symphony Orch.; 1949-60, San Angelo Art Gallery, 1954. Mem. San Angelo Ministerial Alliance (v.p. 1950, pres. 1951). Mason, Elk, Rotarian. Home: 2228 Waco St San Angelo TX 76901 Office: 3 S Randolph St San Angelo TX 76901

ELLIOTT, ROBERT BURL, orthopaedic surgeon; b. Kirksville, Mo., Dec. 30, 1919; s. Burl Dennis and Beatrice (Corbin) E.; A.B., U. Ia., 1941, M.D., 1943; M.S., U. Minn., 1951; m. Georgia Anne Lindley, Aug. 24, 1950; children—Robert Burl, Stephen Corbin, Gregory Taylor. Intern, Md. Gen. Hosp., Balt., 1944; Cole fellowship in orthopaedic surgery U. Minn., Mayo Clinic, 1944-47; practice orthopaedic surgery, Houston, 1948—; instr. orthopaedic surgery Lillie Jolly Sch. Nursing, Meml. Hosp.; chmn. orthopaedic sect., former chief surgery, now dir. acad. orthopaedics Meml. Bapt. Hosp.; instr. clin. faculty Baylor U. Med. Sch.; asso. prof. U. Tex. Med. Sch. Diplomate Am. Bd. Orthopaedic Surgery, Am. Acad. Orthopaedic Surgery. Fellow A.C.S., Internat. Coll. Surgeons (pres. Tex. 1971-72); mem. Am. Fracture Assn. (pres. 1969-71; bd. govs.), Tex. Orthopaedic Soc., So., Pan-Am. med. assns., Houston Surg. Soc., Am. Soc. Testing Materials (com. F-4 surg. implants; sub.-com. performance and implant application; chmn. implant application com. 1968—), Western Orthopaedic Assn., Houston Orthopaedic Club, Doctors Club, Am. Quarter Horse Assn., Sam Houston Trail Assn. (bd. dirs. pres. 1971—), Sociedad Latino-Americana de Ortopedia y Traumatologia, Sigma Alpha Epsilon, Phi Rho Sigma. Mason (K.T., Shriner), Elk. Clubs: Spectators Orthopaedic; International. Home: 10902 Wickwild Dr Houston TX 77024 Office: 1010 Louisiana St Houston TX 77002

ELLIOTT, VANCE JOHNSON, physician; b. Knoxville, Ia., July 10, 1917; s. Jake and Lena (Johnson) E.; M.D., State U. Ia., 1939; m. Albert J. Mater, Oct. 8, 1932; children—Vancene, Cathy; m. 2d Jean C. Stubbs, Dec. 31, 1959 (div. Dec. 1969); one son, Vance II. Intern and resident Charity Hosp., La., 1939-40; pvt. practice, Knoxville, Ia., 1945-47, Odessa, Tex., 1947—; staff Collins Meml. Hosp., Knoxville, 1945-47; staff Med. Center Hosp., Odessa, Tex., 1950—, chief of staff, 1955—; pres. V.J.E., Inc., owner chief obstet. and gynecol. service, 1950-56, pres., Profl. Building Clinic; dir. Corp. Gt. S.W., Inter-Continental Corp., Trinity Valley Ranch Corp., Gt. S.W. Life Ins. Co., Big D Devel. (all Dallas); asso. Harding-Elliott ranches of Texas and Ia. Dir. Community Chest, Odessa. Served as flight surgeon, from lt. to maj., USAAF, 1940-45. Decorated Bronze Star medal. Fellow Am. Coll. Obstetrics and Gynecology, Am. Soc. Study of Sterility, Am. Geriatrics Soc., Am. Soc. Abdominal Surgeons, Am. Coll. Geriatrics, Royal Soc. Health; mem. Pan Am. Cancer Cytology Soc., A.M.A. (chmn. polit. action com. 11 Congl. dist.), So., Tex. (chmn. polit. action com. 11th Congl. district) med. assns., Am. Assn. Physicians and Surgeons, Aero. Med. Soc., Tex., W. Tex. surgeons assns., Tex. Cattlemens Assn., Am. Legion, C. of C. U. Ia. Alumni Assn., Phi Gamma Delta. Methodist. Home: 809 W 15th Odessa TX 79760 Office: 313-B N Alleghaney St Odessa TX 79760

ELLIOTT, WILLIAM FLOYD, ednl. adminstr.; b. Tyler, Tex., Aug. 9, 1928; s. Albert R. and Lillian (Jernigan) E.; B.S., E.Tex. State Coll., 1950, M.Ed., 1951; Ed.D., N.Tex. State U., 1964; postgrad. U. Okla., 1957, 60, Cornell U., 1959; m. Vera Joyce Petty, May 28, 1948; children—David Lynn, Susan Ruth. Tchr., adminstr. Overton (Tex.) Ind. Sch. Dist., 1950-62; inst. Kilgore (Tex.) Coll., 1962-64; prof. edn., dir. tchr. edn. div. U. Corpus Christi (Tex.), 1964-65; asso. prof. edn. Tex. Coll. Arts and Industries, Kingsville, 1965-66; asst. to pres., dir. research and devel. Tex. A. and I. U., Kingsville, 1966-68, v.p. for student affairs, 1968—. Ednl. cons. U.S. Office Edn., Tex. Edn. Agy., Ednl. Projects, Inc., S.W. Edn. Devel. Lab., Pub. Sch. Dists. Mem. Am. Assn. U. Profs., Nat. Council U. Research Adminstrs., Tex. Assn. Coll. Tchrs., Phi Delta Kappa. Developer, Elliott Sociometric Scale, 1964, spl. edn. programs for tchrs. of migrant, educationally deprived children, 1965-67. Home: 102 University Blvd Kingsville TX 78363

ELLIOTT, WILLIAM YOUNG, author; b. Leeds, Ala., Apr. 18, 1902; s. James Barnett and Ida Lee (Vann) E.; B.S., Birmingham-So. Coll., 1926; M.A., U. Ala., 1929; postgrad. George Peabody Coll. for Tchrs., summer 1937; m. Laura Emily Bozeman, Feb. 25, 1928; children—William Young, Dorothy Emily, Robert Collier. tchr. pub. schs., Jefferson County, Ala., 1926-29, Tarrant City, Ala., 1929-37, Birmingham, Ala., 1937-42; with pyrometry dept. Tenn. Coal, Iron & Ry. Co. (now known as Fairfield Works, U.S. Steel), Birmingham, Ala., 1942-67. Author: Skylights (poems), Book I, 1951, Book 2, 1954, Book 3, 1958, Most Lovely Lizzie, 1958; Voices, Book I (poems): Voices, Book II (poems): Wings (poems), 1969; works included in Oberfirst's Anthology of Best Short Stories, Volume 4, 1955, Volume 6, 1958, Volume 7, 1959, Vol. 8, 1960; cover poet Scimitar and Song mag., May 1957; also readings, essays, stories. Leader poetry study group Ala. Writers Conclave, 1959, poetry panel leader, 1967, now treas., dean of poetry, 1971. Recipient 1st prize The Prairie Poet mag., Winter issue, 1957-58; Emil Hess award, poetry contest, Birmingham Festival of Arts, 1958, 2d prize, poetry contest, 1963; 1st prize, ann. poetry contest New Work Writers Guild, 1961; 6 prizes short stories, articles poems Ala. Writers Conclave; 1st prize religious poem Mid-S. Poetry Festival, 1st prize free verse, 1968; 1st prize blank verse, 1969, 2d prize in category, 1971; 1st prize, peace poem contest, Am. Poets Fellowship Soc., 1967; commendable excellence award Cal. Olympiad of Arts, 1968; Distinguished Service citation World Poetry Soc., 1970. Mem. Am. Poetry League (bd. advisers), Am. Poets Fellowship Soc. (1st prize in category 1970), Ala. Poetry Soc. (Poet of Year 1971), Centro Studi E Scambi Internazionali (Rome), Am. Radio Relay League, Internat. Platform Assn. Methodist. Home: 3516 Mariposa Rd SW Huntsville AL 35805

ELLIOTT, WYLEY J., ednl. adminstr.; b. Camden, Ark., Sept. 16, 1926; s. Wyley Madison and Ruby Irene (Womack) E.; B.S., Ouachita Bapt. U., 1948; M.A., George Peabody Coll., 1951; postgrad. Auburn U., 1958-69, Columbia, 1960, U. Ark. 1971; m. Evelyn Gillespie, Dec. 23, 1951; children—Laura, David, Melinda. Biology and sci. tchr. Camden (Ark.) Sr. High Sch., 1948-51; prin. Arkadelphia Sr. High Sch., 1951-56; prin. Camden Sr. High Sch., 1956-66; supt. Camden Pub. Schs., 1966—. Mem. Gov's. Adv. Council on Community Service and Continuing Edn., 1967—; mem.-at-large Commn. on Secondary Schs. of North Central Assn.; mem. U.S. Sch. Study Mission to Germany and Denmark, 1970. Mem. local adv. council Democratic party, 1969—. Served with AUS, 1945-46; PTO. Recipient Distinguished Service award Arkadelphia Jr. C. of C., 1952. Mem. N.E.A. (dir. 1970—), Ark. Edn. Assn. (pres. 1968-69), Ark. Assn. Secondary Sch. Prins. (pres. 1965-66), Camden C. of C. Baptist (deacon 1958). Rotarian. Clubs: Camden Country; Little Rock Capital. Home: 1087 Westwood Rd NW Camden AR 71701 Office: 737 Jefferson Dr NW Camden AR 71701

ELLIOTT, YANCEY CALDONIA, JR., apparel products co. exec.; b. Raleigh, N.C., Nov. 11, 1935; s. Yancey Caldonia and Sarah Lucille (Martin) E.; student N.C. State U., 1954-57; B.S., U. N.C., 1960; M.B.A., East Carolina U., 1969; m. Myrtha LaRue Lockerman, May 15, 1965; 1 son, Yancey Caldonia III. Vice-pres., asst. trust officer Edgecombe Bank & Trust Co., Tarboro, N.C., 1960-68; sec., Runnymede Mills, Inc., Tarboro, N.C., 1968—. Chmn. supervisory devel. com. Edgecombe Tech. Inst., 1969—; chmn. Citizens' Adv. Com., 1970-71; gifts chmn. Friends of the Edgecombe County Meml. Library. Bd. dirs., treas. Edgecombe United Fund; trustee Tarboro Student Aid Assn. Served to 1st lt. USNGR, 1960-67. Mem. Nat. Assn. Accountants, East Carolina Estate Planning Council, Tarboro Mchts. Assn. (pres. 1967-68), Tarboro C. of C., Sigma Chi. Baptist. Home: 1009 Panola St Tarboro NC 27886 Office: 1004 Fountain St Tarboro NC 27886

ELLIS, ANDREW JACKSON, JR., lawyer; b. Ashland, Va., June 23, 1930; s. Andrew Jackson and Sue (Carter) E.; A.B., Washington and Lee U., 1951, LL.B., 1953; m. Dorothy Lichliter, Apr. 24, 1954; children—Elizabeth C., Andrew C., William D. Admitted to Va. bar, 1952; partner Campbell, Ellis & Campbell, Ashland, Va., 1955-70, Mays, Valentine, Davenport & Moore, Richmond, Va., 1970—; substitute Hanover County judge, 1958-63; police justice Ashland, 1958-63; commonwealth atty. Hanover County, 1963-69; county atty. Hanover County, 1970—; dir. Ashland and Montpelier br. First & Mchts. Nat. Bank. Councilman, Ashland, 1956-63; mayor, Ashland, 1958-63. Trustee Hanover Acad., J. Sargeant Reynolds Community Coll. Served to 1st lt., Judge Adv. Gen.'s Corps, AUS, 1953-55. Mem. Am., Va. (mem. council), 15th Jud. (past pres.), Richmond bar assns., Va. Trial Lawyers Assn., Ashland C. of C., S.A.R., Phi Kappa Sigma, Phi Alpha Delta. Kiwanian. Home: Broomfield Route 2 Box 218 Beaverdam VA 23015 Office: PO Box 1122 Ross Bldg Richmond VA 23219

ELLIS, BENJAMIN THOMAS, dentist; b. Shelby, N.C., Feb. 13, 1941; s. Bruce Herbert and Vivian Adams (Adams) E.; B.S., U.N.C., 1964, D.D.S., 1967; m. Elizabeth Pearson Falls, Aug. 23, 1963; children—Sara Hines, Elizabeth Falls, Mary Catherine, Carolyn Whitten. Individual practice dentistry, Grover, N.C., 1967—. Mem. 1st Dist. N.C., Isothermal (sec., treas. 1969-70, pres. 1971-72) dental socs., Am. Soc. Preventive Dentistry, Am. Endodontic Soc., Am. Dental Assn., Acad. Gen. Dentistry, U. N.C. Ednl. Found., Delta Sigma Delta. Episcopalian (mem. vestry 1970-72). Elk, Lion. Club: Cleveland Country (Shelby, N.C.) Home: 904 Montrose Dr Shelby NC 28150 Office: Laurel Av Grover NC 28073

ELLIS, CAREY JAMES, JR., lawyer; b. New Orleans, July 21, 1920; s. Carey Jay and Innes (Morris) E.; B.A., Tulane U., 1942, LL.B., 1943; m. Linda Annette Hudson, June 3, 1943; 1 son, Carey Jay III. Admitted to La. bar, 1943; practiced in Rayville, La., 1946—. Dir. Richland State Bank, Rayville Delta Finance Co., Rayville, Econ. Devel. Co., Inc., Rayville. Franklin Loan Co., Inc., Winnsboro, La. Dist. atty. 5th Jud. Dist., 1958-60. Bd. dirs. Richland Parish Library, 1950-58. Served with USNR, 1943-45; PTO. Mem. Am. Judicature Soc., La. State Bar Assn. (mem. ho. of dels. 1956-57), Am. Legion, V.F.W. Episcopalian (mem. vestry 1970—). Home: 904 Smith St Rayville LA 71269 Office: 105 S Julia St Rayville LA 71269

ELLIS, CHARLES GRANT, museum ofcl. Research asso. Oriental rugs Textile Mus., Washington. Address: Textile Museum 2320 S St NW Washington DC 20008*

ELLIS , DAVID BRADLEY, physician; b. nr. New Albany, Miss., Mar. 29, 1920; s. William Augustus and Della Dee (Teer) Ellis; B.A. in Agr., Miss. State U., 1947, B.S., U. Miss., 1953; M.D., U. Tenn., 1956; m. Nancy Margaret (Mrs. Frederick Robbins Rogers), Mary Corinne (Mrs. Samuel Carroll Pace), Elizabeth Ann, Martha Jane, David Bradley, John McKinstry. Asst. county extension agt., Lafayette County, Miss., 1948-49; asso. county extension agt., Prentiss County, 1949-50; county agt., Clay County, 1950-51; intern, John Gaston Hosp., Memphis, 1955-56; practice medicine specializing in gen. practice, Ripley, Miss., 1956-57, New Albany, 1957—; chief staff Union County Gen. Hosp., New Albany, 1970—; farmer, land owner. Served with USAAF, 1942-46. Mem. Am., Miss. med. assns., Am. Acad. Family Practice, North Miss., Union County med. socs., Alpha Kappa Kappa. Democrat. Presbyn. Home: Hwy 15 N New Albany MS 38652 Office: 701 Hwy 30 W New Albany MS 38652

ELLIS, ELMO ISRAEL, broadcasting exec.; b. Birmingham, Ala., Nov. 11, 1918; s. Samuel B. and Bertha F. (Seletz) Israel; A.B., U. Ala., 1940; M.A., Emory U., 1948; postgrad. Am. Mgmt. Assn., 1959, Emory U., 1965; m. Ruth M. Ballinger, Dec. 26, 1944; children—Janet Faye, William Bryan. Dir. publicity, prodn. mgr. WSB, Atlanta, 1940-42, dir. scripts and prodn., 1947—, prodn. mgr., 1948-52, mgr. programming WSB Radio (AM-FM), 1952-63, v.p., gen. mgr., 1963—; v.p. Cox Broadcasting Corp., 1969—; writer-producer network radio programs NBC, ABC, CBS and Mut. Broadcasting System, 1942-46; writer-producer We The People radio program, Great Jury Trials, FBI in Peace and War. CBS Sch. of the Air, Continental Celebrity Club, 1946; Vice pres. Ga. Safety Council, 1968-69; mem. nat. publicity com. Freedoms Found., 1968-69; radio-TV rep. Nat. Heart Assn., 1969; mem. Gov.'s Com. on Employment Handicapped, 1972, adv. panel Ga. Nutrition Council, 1972; mem. S.E. regional adv. bd. Anti-Defamation League, B'nai B'rith. Asst. to dir. Democratic Nat. Convs., 1952, 56, 60, 64. Vice pres. exec. bd., nat. sponsor Ga. Easter Seal Soc.; bd. dirs. Arthritis Found., Ga. Mental Health Assn., Am. Jewish Com.; mem. president's council Oglethorpe Coll. Served to capt. USAAF, 1942-46. Recipient Silver medal award Atlanta Advt. Club, 1965, Peabody award, 1966, Alfred P. Sloan award, 1966, Distinguished Service award Freedoms Found.; named Citizen of Year, Ga. Assn. Broadcasters, 1965; recipient Abraham Lincoln award So. Baptist Radio-TV Commn., 1972; Silver Beaver award Boy Scouts Am., 1972; Pioneer Broadcaster Ga. award Di Gamma Kappa, 1972. Mem. Ga. Asso. Press Broadcasters (chpt. pres.), Sigma Delta Chi. Mem. B'nai B'rith (bd. dirs.). Clubs: Standard, Commerce. Author: (with others) Radio Station Management; Happiness Is Worth The Effort; Sleepy Hollow Poems. Home: 6345 Aberdeen Dr NE Atlanta GA 30328 Office: 1601 W Peachtree St NE Atlanta GA 30309

ELLIS, ERIC HANS, educator; b. Mannheim, Germany, Aug. 25, 1935; s. Morris and Beatrice (Guthmann) E.; came to U.S., 1938, naturalized, 1944; B.S. in Physics, Syracuse U., 1956, Ph.D. in Physics, 1965; m. Barbara Joan Dresner, June 29, 1958; children—Richard Morris, Susan Ruth, Ralph Loeb, Beatrice Rose. Grad. asst. Syracuse (N.Y.) U., 1956-64; instr. physics U. of South, Sewanee, Tenn., 1964-66, asst. prof. physics, 1966-72, asso. prof., 1972—; dir. Sewanee Summer Inst. Sci. and Math., 1969. Pres. Cumberland Mountain Learning Disabilities Center, Sewanee, Tenn., 1969—. Sec., Sewanee Civic Assn., 1967, v.p., 1969—. Mem. Am. Assn. Physics Tchrs., Am. Assn. U. Profs. (chpt. pres. 1968), Syracuse U. Alumni Rowing Assn., Am. Phys. Soc., Tenn. Acad. Sci., Sigma Xi (chpt. pres. 1968-70), Sigma Pi Sigma. Research in infrared spectral emissivity of terrain, atmospheric optical noise, fluorescence of bone, spectroscopic analysis of bone, trace elements in tendon collagen. Home: SPO Box 1004 Sewanee TN 37375

ELLIS, FRANCES LORENE ARNOLD (MRS. PRINTIS E. ELLIS), civic worker; b. Greenville, Tex., Jan. 8, 1913; d. Horace Robert and Fay (Hall) Arnold; A.A., Wesley Jr. Coll., Greenville, 1932; B.A., E. Tex. State U., 1933; B.S., Tex. Woman's U., 1937; postgrad. Ia. State U., 1951-52; m. Printis E. Ellis, Apr. 19, 1954. Tchr. phys. edn. Wesley Jr. Coll., 1932-33; sec. Hunt County Agrl. Extension Office, Greenville, 1933-35; home demonstration agt. Red River, Cass and Lamar Counties, Tex., 1937-47; home econ. editor agrl. extension service, Tex. A and M U., 1947-53; asst. dir. Nat. Project in Agrl. Communications, Mich. State U., East Lansing, 1953-54; free lance writer home econs. subjects Humble Oil Co. Family mag., Progressive Farmer, Farmer Stockman, Together mag., others, 1947—. Corr. sec., treas., auditor dist. III, Tex. Garden Clubs, 1959-65, gov., 1965-67, state awards chmn., 1967-69, editor Lone Star Gardener, 1971-73; chmn. Lamar County Sr. Citizens Com., 1967; mem. Gov.'s Com. on Aging, 1970; del. White House Conf. on Aging, 1971. Sec. bd. dirs. Paris (Tex.) Pub. Library, 1965—, Liberty Cemetery Assn., Greenville; Adv. Bd. Health for Paris and Lamar County 1971. Recipient Nat. Radio award Nat. Assn. Agrl. Coll. Editors, 1947, Distinguished Alumna award Tex. Women's U., 1971. Mem. Am., Tex., Lamar County econs. assns., Delta Kappa Gamma, Theta Sigma Phi, Epsilon Sigma Phi. Methodist (pres. 1965-67, chmn. commn. on evangelism 1972). Editor ch. sect. 100th anniversary edit. Paris News, 1969. Home: 1003 S Main St Paris TX 75460

ELLIS, JAMES, engr.; b. Memphis, Dec. 22, 1898; s. S. J. and Elise (Crockett) E.; student Memphis pub. schs.; m. Josephine Morris, Oct. 16, 1928. With Comml. Chem. Co., Memphis, 1922-25; draftsman Tenn. Eastman Co., div. Eastman Kodak Co., Kingsport, 1925, since mech. engr., supt. engring. div., gen. supt. in charge engring., constrn. and power; dep. works mgr. Clinton Engr. Works, Oak Ridge, Tenn., 1943-45; asst. v.p. Tenn. Eastman Co., Kingsport, 1958-64, ret. Profl. engr., Tex., Tenn. Named Engr. of Yr., Tenn. Soc. Profl. Engrs., 1963. Fellow Am. Soc. M.E.; mem. Am. Legion, V.F.W., Tau Beta Pi. Episcopalian. Mason (Shriner). Contbr. articles to tech. jours. Home: 1708 Orchard Lane Kingsport TN 37660

ELLIS, JAMES GARFIELD, JR., assn. exec.; b. Beaver, Pa., Sept. 13, 1908; s. James Garfield and Trudie E. (Whitney) E.; A.B., George Washington U., 1941; LL.B., Southeastern U., 1941; m. Marian A. Bissell, Sept. 19, 1929; children—James Garfield III, Marianne B. (Mrs. Duane Alexander), Kaethe (Mrs. Courtney Brown). Dir. information Nat. Bituminous Coal Commn., 1935-36; White House corr. Chilton Publs., 1936-41; pub. relations counsel, Washington, 1958-67; Washington mgr. Automobile Mfrs. Assn., Inc., 1967—; exec. sec. Council Def. and Space Industry Assns., 1966-67, 72-73. Mem. faculty, bd. mgrs. Northeastern Inst. Assn. Mgmt., Yale, 1950-57; lectr. Indsl. Coll. Armed Forces, 1970-71, U. Md., Am. U., George Washington U., 1960-71; mem. bus. adv. council fed. reports Office Mgmt. and Budget, Exec. Office Pres., 1971—. Served to lt. USNR, 1944-47. Mem. Pub. Relations Soc. Am. (pres. Washington chpt. 1960), Am. (dir. 1962-65), Washington (pres. 1961-62) socs. assn. execs., Nat. Assn. Execs. Club (dir. Washington 1958-61), Phi Beta Gamma. Methodist. Clubs: Nat. Press, Army and Navy (Washington). Author: (Kenneth B. Anderson) Association Management, 1958. Contbr. articles to profl. jours. Home: 3309 Stephenson Pl Chevy Chase MD 20015 Office: 1619 Massachusetts Av Washington DC 20036

ELLIS, JAMES LEWIS, lawyer, banker; b. Louisville, Ala., Jan. 15, 1892; s. James L. and Pearla (Hobdy) E.; m. Marybel Hixon, Oct. 21, 1939. Admitted to Ga. bar, 1916, since practiced in Americus; city atty., Americus, 1933. Pres. 1st Fed. Savs. & Loan Assn., 1950-56, dir., chmn. bd., chmn. exec. com., exec. mgr., 1950—. Mem. Adv. Com. Naval Affairs. Mem. U.S. Savs. and Loan League (mem. investments and mortgage lending com. 1958-59, dir. Southeastern Conf. 1961-62, mem. com. on fed. home loan bank system 1969—), Navy League U.S., Americus and Sumter County C. of C. (dir. 1961-62), Nat. Rivers and Harbors Congress, Flint River Valley Devel. Assn. (dir., v.p.), Am. Judicature Soc., Am., Ga., Americus bar assns. Methodist. Mason. Clubs: Commerce (Atlanta); Elks, Kiwanis (past pres.; lt. gov. Ga. dist. 1922). Home: 1301 S Lee St Americus GA 31709 Office: First Federal Savings Bldg Americus GA 31709

ELLIS, MARVIN ELLIOTT, county agr. agt.; b. Cordele, Ga., Feb. 26, 1935; s. George Marvin and Irene (Taylor) E.; B.S., U. Ga., 1956; m. Lucile Forehand Busbee, Dec. 22, 1955; children—Michael Elliott, Bradley Phillip, Keith Marvin. Asst. county agt. Harris County, Ga., 1956-57, Spalding County, Ga., 1957-62; county agt. Hancock County, 1962-69, Morgan County, 1969—. Mem. Epsilon Sigma Phi. Baptist. Clubs: American Business of Griffin (past sec.), Kiwanis,

Lions (pres. 1967). Home: Lakeview Dr Madison GA 30650 Office: PO Box 413 Madison GA 30650

ELLIS, ROBERT RUFUS, III, drug co. exec.; b. Memphis, Apr. 1, 1939; s. Robert Rufus and Martha Jane (Dickinson) E.; B.B.A., U. Miss. Asst. to sales mgr. Ellis-Bagwell Wholesale Drug Co., Memphis, 1961-63, sales mgr., 1963-65, pres., 1965—; pres E-B Data Co., 1968—, Drug Service, Memphis, 1971—. Kiwanian. Club: Memphis Country. Home: 3564 Lily Lane Memphis TN 38111 Office: 455 S Front St Memphis TN 38102

ELLIS, ROBERT WILLIAM, JR., coll. dean; b. Richmond, Va., Oct. 16, 1939; s. Robert William and Odessa (Thompson) E.; B.S., Va. Poly. Inst., 1962, M.S., 1963, Ph.D., 1966; m. Donna Lee Bell, Mar. 22, 1960; children—Robert William III, Richard Berkeley, John Stephen, Donna Elaine. Materials engr., cons. Polysci. div. Litton Industries, Blacksburg, Va., 1962-63; Nat. Def. Edn. Act fellow engring. Va. Poly. Inst., 1962-65; asst. prof. engring. U. South Fla., Tampa, 1965-66, asso. prof., 1967-68, asst. dean engring., 1969-71, asst. v.p. acad. affairs, 1971-72; dean Sch. Tech., Fla. Internat. U., Miami, 1972—; cons. in field. Pack master Tampa council Boy Scouts Am. Registered profl. engr., Fla. NASA fellow, 1969. Mem. Am. Soc. Metals, Am. Soc. Engring. Edn., Soc. Exptl. Stress Analysis, Am. Inst. Mining and Metall. Engrs., Nat. Soc. Profl. Engrs., Sigma Xi, Omicron Delta Kappa, Phi Kappa Phi, Sigma Pi Sigma, Tau Beta Pi, Alpha Sigma Mu. Home: 520 Navarre Coral Gables FL 33134

ELLIS, RYAN BRADFORD, mfg. and mgmt. cons.; b. Ayden, N.C., Apr. 17, 1932; s. L. Ryan and Nancy (Arnold) E.; B. Indsl. Engring., Ga. Inst. Tech., 1954; m. Shirley Fullagar, Jan. 30, 1956. Prodn. engr. Raytheon Co., Waltham, Mass., 1954-56, equipment application engr., 1957, Atlanta, 1957-60; asst. v.p. Marketing Sci. Atlanta, Inc., 1960-61; USAF engring. adviser quality control; dept. mgr. plant 6 Lockheed Aircraft, Marietta, Ga., 1961-62; indsl. engr., contracts adminstr. U.S. Army, Dallas, 1962-65; mfg. and mgmt. cons. Syntron, Inc., Dallas, 1965; various mfg., marketing and mgmt. positions TRACOR, Inc., Austin, Tex., 1965-70; cons. engr. and gen. mgmt.; pres. TIE Inc. investments, 1970—. Served with USAF, 1954-57, 68-69. Registered profl. engr., Tex. Mem. Am. Inst. Indsl. Engrs., Nat., Tex. socs. profl. engrs. Lion (sec. 1964-65, pres. 1972—). Home: 2512 Great Oaks Pkwy Austin TX 78756 Office: 4101 Medical Pkwy Austin TX 78756

ELLIS, WALTER LEE, III, dairy mfg. co. exec.; b. Kosciusko, Miss., June 30, 1925; s. Walter Lee and Catherine (McGee) E.; student La. State U., 1943; B.S., Miss. State U., 1949; m. Lucretia Ann Graham, June 22, 1947; children—Claudia Michele, Michaela Rynn, Walter Lee IV. With LuVel Dairy Products, Inc., Kosciusko, Miss., 1949—, treas., 1953—, gen. sales mgr., 1951—, chmn. bd., 1967—. Chmn. Kosciusko Planning Commn., 1966—, Kosciusko Redevel. Authority, 1969—. Bd. dirs. Andrew Jackson council Boy Scouts Am. Served with Inf., AUS, 1943-45. Decorated Purple Heart with three oak leaf clusters, Bronze Star medal with oak leaf cluster, Silver Star. Mem. Am. Dairy Products (mem. exec. com. 1968—, bd. dirs.), Miss. (mem. exec. com. 1962-72, pres.), Dixie (bd. dirs.) dairy products assns., Am. Legion, V.F.W., Miss. Econ. Council (mem. exec. com. 1966—, dir.), Miss. State U. Alumni Council (dist. pres. 1967-69), Kosciusko-Attala C. of C. (pres. 1963). Methodist (chmn. finance com., long range planning com. 1968-69). Rotarian (bd. dirs.), Moose. Home: 331 E Adams St Kosciusko MS 39090 Office: 101 N Huntington St Kosciusko MS 39090

ELLIS, WILLIAM LEIGH, govt. ofcl.; b. Petoskey, Mich., Jan. 26, 1908; s. William E. and Gertrude May (Webb) E.; A.B., Hillsdale (Mich.) Coll., 1929; LL.B., George Washington U., 1933, LL.M., 1936; m. Norma Foster, Nov. 16, 1935; children—William L., Amy Foster. In govt. service, 1930—, State Dept., TVA, 1930-35; atty. Gen. Accounting Office, 1935-45, asst. to comptroller gen., 1945-49, chief investigations, 1949-55; lectr. law George Washington U., 1942-52; trial atty. Fed. Power Commn., 1955-57, hearing examiner, 1960—; dep. dir. Adminstrv. Office U.S. Courts, 1957-60; admitted to Mich. bar, 1935. Mem. Fed. Bar Assn. (pres. 1952-53). Mason. Club: Cosmos. Home: 1307 New Hampshire Av Washington DC 20036 Office: Fed Power Commn Washington DC 20426

ELLISON, ABE LANE, dentist; b. Oudtshoorn, South Africa, Oct. 23, 1911; s. Morris J. and Hannah B. (Kaplan) E.; came to U.S., 1932; D.D.S., Loyola U., New Orleans, 1937; m. Mary Louise Peacock, Apr. 3, 1948; children—Jack William, Morris Julius. Practice dentistry, New Orleans, 1937-43, Shreveport, La., 1946—; mem. dental staff Drs. Hosp., Shreveport, Confederate Meml. Med. Center, Shreveport. Served to maj. USAAF, 1943-46. Mem. Am., La. dental assns., 4th Dist. Dental Soc., Kells Odentological Soc., Air Force Assn., Air Force Res. Officers Assn. (surgeon gen. La. dept.), Heroes of '76. Democrat. Jewish religion. Mason (Shriner), Lion (dir. Shreveport club), Elk; mem. Order Eastern Star. Home: 2409 Parham Dr Shreveport LA 71109 Office: 1121 Louisiana Av Shreveport LA 71101

ELLISON, ARNOLD DANIEL, assn. exec.; b. Charleston, S.C., Mar. 4, 1917; s. Charles and Frances Lillian (Reisman) E.; A.B., U. N.C., 1937, M.A., 1940; m. Anne Witten, Sept. 11, 1943; children—Paula (Mrs. Richard Woolf), Elaine M. Research fellow La. State U., 1938; dist. membership dir. Dist. Grand Lodge, B'nai B'rith, Atlanta, 1956-63, exec. sec., 1963-67, exec. dir., 1967-69, exec. v.p., 1969—. Mem. tech. adv. com., Fulton and DeKalb Counties, 1965-68. Trustee Leo N. Levi Meml. Hosp., Hot Springs, Ark., Nat. Jewish Hosp., Denver. Served with inf. AUS, 1941-45; ETO. Mem. Pi Sigma Alpha. Mem. B'nai B'rith. Author: History of Civil Service in North Carolina, 1939. Home: 3446 Buford Hwy Apt I-10 Atlanta GA 30329 Office: 805 Peachtree St NE Atlanta GA 30308

ELLISON, JAMES O., lawyer; b. St. Louis, Jan. 11, 1929; B.A., U. Okla., 1949, LL.B., 1951. Admitted to Okla. bar, 1951; now mem. firm Boone, Ellison & Smith, Tulsa. Mem. Tulsa County, Okla. bar assns., Phi Alpha Delta. Address: Boone Ellison & Smith World Bldg 914 Tulsa OK 74103*

ELLISON, O(VID) ERNEST, JR., state ofcl.; b. Panama City, Fla., Sept. 16, 1923; s. Ovid Ernest and Alice (Petty) E.; student U. Fla., 1946-47; B.S., Fla. State U., 1952; m. Evelyn M. Whitney, June 22, 1946; children—Sharon Alice, Ernest Whitney. Auditor, Price Waterhouse & Co., N.Y.C., 1952-53; auditor Office State Auditor Fla., Tallahassee, 1953-59, asst. state auditor, 1959-63, state auditor gen., 1963—. Served with USAAF, 1943-46. Mem. Fla. Inst. C.P.A.'s, Nat. Assn. State Auditors, Comptrollers and Treas., Municipal Finance Officers Assn. Kiwanian. Home: 2030 Chowkeebin Nene Tallahassee FL 32301 Office: Carlton Bldg Tallahassee FL 32304

ELLISON, STELLA CHRISTINE PUREFOY (MRS. HERMAN THEODORE ELLISON), educator, civic worker; b. Furman, Ala., Jan. 7, 1913; d. Judge Thomas and Annie Sophronia (McElroy) Purefoy; B.S., Ala. Coll., 1933; m. Herman Theodore Ellison, July 28, 1935; children—Elva Anne (Mrs. Bogart Scott Reed), Herman Theodore, Walter Frank. Tchr. home econs. Russell County High Sch., 1933-35, substitute tchr., 1935-60. Chmn. Coll. Alumnae Assn. and Scholarship drive chmn. for Russell County, 1955; bd. dirs. Russell County-March of Dimes, 1940-50; vice chmn. bd. dirs. Russell County Pensions and Securities, 1948—, Russell County Anti-Tb Assn., 1953—, A.R.C., 1940-50, 61—, Russell County Farm Bur.; founder, dir. Hurtsboro Youth Club. Named Woman of The Year Bus. and Profl. Women's Clubs, 1961. Mem. U.D.C. (pres. Hurtsboro-Jefferson-Davis chpt. 1960-65, 71-72, registrar 1965-70), Colonial Dames of XVIIth Century (state chmn. spl. activities and awards 1968—), D.A.R. (regent of Reuben Long chpt.; chmn. press book Ala. Soc; chpt. registrar 1970—; state chmn. Ala. Trophy Day), Huguenot Soc., Ala. Soc. Dames of Magna Charta (state chaplain), Am. Assn. Univ. Women, Ala. Hist. Soc., Nat., Soc. Magna Charta Dames, East Ala., Ala. geneal socs., Plantagenet Soc., Daus. Am. Colonies (chpt. historian), Colonial Order of Crown. Democrat. Methodist (sec. Woman's Soc. Christian Service 6 yrs.; tchr. adult class 1968—). Club: Union Springs Country. Home: Church St Hurtsboro AL 36860

ELLISON, THORLEIF, engr.; b. Lyngdal, Norway, May 13, 1902; s. Andreas Emanuel and Gemalie (Svensen) E.; C.E., Christiania Coll. Tech., 1924; postgrad. George Washington U., Va. U.; m. Reidun Ingeborg Skonhoft, Jan. 1, 1932; children—Earl Otto, Thorleif Glenn, Sonja Karen. Came to U.S., 1928, naturalized, 1933. Supervising engr. Gen. Services Adminstrn., Washington, 1948-57; supervising airport and airways service engr. FAA, 1957-61, chief airways engring. AID, Iran, W. Pakistan, Turkey, 1961-67; cons. engr., Washington, Va., 1942—; mission dir.-Israel, Holy Land Christian Mission, Kansas City, 1968-71. Active Christian Bus. Men's Com., Washington, Boy Scouts. Mem. Am. Soc. Profl. Engrs., Am. Norwegian Soc. (treas.). Presbyn. (ruling elder). Home: Svennevik Rosfjord 4580 Lyngdal Norway also 6324 Telegraph Rd Alexandria VA 22310

ELLISTON, LURA DUFF (MRS. FRED ADDISON ELLISTON), club woman; b. Leesville, La., May 28, 1907; d. James Edward and Kate (Williamson) Duff; B.A. summa cum laude, Rice Inst., 1928; m. Fred Addison Elliston, May 21, 1932 (dec. 1970); 1 dau., Lura Duff (Mrs. George Edward Nowotny, Jr.). Pres., Jr. Woman's Club, Ft. Worth, 1933-34, Thursday Study Club, Ft. Worth, 1950-51, Friday Lecture Club, Ft. Worth, 1955-56, 61-62; mem. Round Table, Ft. Worth, Tex. Christian U. Fine Arts Found. Guild, Ft. Worth; founder J.E. Duff Fund, Ft. Worth; v.p. Ft. Worth Opera Assn.; chmn. fine arts com. Ft. Worth C. of C. Bd. dirs. Opera Guild, Ft. Worth, 1950—, Community Theatre, 1963—, Ft. Worth Art Assn., 1967—; bd. dirs. William Edrington Scott Theatre, 1965— (with husband) named patron of arts, 1967, chmn. theater bd., 1968—. Republican. Mem. Christian Ch. Home: 2222 Winton Terrace E Fort Worth TX 76109

ELLSWORTH, LEVOY CARL, trucking co. exec.; b. McCloud, Okla., Sept. 28, 1920; s. Delbert and Donnie (Arrington) E.; student Coll. Bus., Okmulgee, Okla., 1939-40; m. Lucille Elizabeth Niemeier, Jan. 8, 1947; children—Linda Kay, Levoy Carl. Dir. warehousing and storage Texaco, Inc., 1945-46; founder, pres., chmn. bd. Ellsworth Bros. Truck Line, Inc., 1947-70; owner Bennett Van & Storage, Inc., Stroud, Okla., 1971—; v.p. Sorco Products, Inc., Stroud, Okla., 1956—. Mem. adv. bd. Retarded Children's Assn. Okla., 1961-69; v.p. Dad's Day Assn., Okla. U., Norman, 1970-71. Served with AUS, 1942-45; ETO. Mem. Am. Trucking Assn. (v.p. at large 1970-73), Good Roads and Streets Assn. (dir. 1966), Gen. Contractors Okla., Asso. Motor Carriers (chmn. bd. 1961-62), Stroud C. of C. (pres. 1959-60), Am. Legion., Petroleum Club Tulsa. Democrat. Mem. Christian Ch. (mem. bd. elders 1961-71). Lion. Clubs: Propeller (dir. 1969-72), Summit (Tulsa); Stroud (Okla.) Golf and Country. Home: 1101 Circle Dr Stroud OK 74079 Office: 623 E 3d St Stroud OK 74079

ELMER, WARREN PHILO, JR., educator; b. St. Louis, Aug. 14, 1920; s. Warren Philo and Frances (Jennings) E.; A.B., Princeton, 1942; postgrad. Washington U., St. Louis, 1946-49, U. Edinburgh, 1965; M.A., Washington U., St. Louis, 1968; m. Lucy Tabb Love, Nov. 26, 1943; children—Virginia Elmer (Mrs. Blakeney Stafford), Warren P. III, Mary Armstrong. Tchr., bus. mgr. St. Louis Country Day Sch., 1946-49; asst. alumni sec. Princeton, 1949-56, regional dir. devel. office, 1956-62, dir. placement office, 1962-64; headmaster St. Christophers Sch., Richmond, Va., 1964-72; exec. dir. St. Stephen's Sch., Rome, Italy, 1972—. Exec. com. Nat. Assn. Episcopal Schs. Chmn. bd. Princeton Country Day Sch., 1962-64; past dir. Princeton chpt. A.R.C., YMCA, Princeton Chapel Council, Procter Found. Served to capt. AUS, 1942-46. Decorated Purple Heart. Clubs: Nassau, University Cottage (Princeton, N.J.); Commonwealth (Richmond); Princeton (N.Y.C., Washington). Home: 713 St Christophers Rd Richmond VA 23226 Office: St Stephen's School Via Aventina 3 00153 Rome Italy

ELMORE, FRANKLIN HARPER, judge; b. Jacksonville, Fla., Mar. 22, 1903; s. F. H. and Anna Madeleine (Daniel) E.; ed. Sewanee (Tenn.) Mil. Acad.; LL.B., U. Fla., 1926; m. Vivian Gay, April 27, 1927; children—Elisabeth Gay (Mrs. G. W. Gilleland, Junior), Madeleine (Mrs. Henry H. Beckwith) Mary C. (Mrs. D. M. Harrell). Admitted to Fla. bar, 1926, practiced law in Jacksonville, 1926-34; asst. counsel, N.R.A., Washington, 1934-36; spl. asst. atty. gen., 1936-37; partner Latham & Elmore, attys., Jacksonville, 1937-38, 47-52, Elmore & Clark, 1955-60; circuit judge 4th Jud. Circuit of Fla., 1960—; spl. asst. atty. gen. U.S. Dept. of Justice, Washington, 1938-43; partner Wise, Corlett & Canfield, Washington, 1944-46; legal counsel for Arab States, FOA, Am. Embassy, Cairo, Egypt, 1953-55. Pres. Council of Social Agys., Jacksonville, 1948-50. Mem. Am., Fla. (bd. govs. 1950-52), Jacksonville (pres. 1950) bar assns., Jacksonville (past pres.), Fla. Hist. Socs. Kappa Alpha Order, Phi Delta Phi. Democrat. Episcopalian. Club: Florida Yacht. Home: 5039 Timuquana Rd Jacksonville FL 32210 Office: Duval County Court House Jacksonville FL 32202

ELMORE, WILLIAM EARL, univ. adminstr.; b. Etowah, Tenn., Mar. 7, 1922; s. Alfred Menefee and Amee (Bates) E.; B.S., Citadel, 1943; student Inst. Bus. Accounting, Atlanta, 1947-49, Emory U. Law Sch., 1949; m. Mary Patricia Gardner, Jan. 18, 1947; children—William Earl, Patricia Gardner. With Jacksonville, (Fla.) office Internal Revenue Service, 1946-47, Respess & Respess C.P.A.'s, Atlanta, 1947-50; with U. Fla., 1950—, auditor, 1950-53, asst. comptroller, 1953-54, asst. bus. mgr. health center, 1954-55, asst. bus. mgr., 1955-59, asso. bus. mgr., 1959-65, bus. mgr., 1965-67, v.p. bus. affairs, 1967—; dir. Citizens Bank Gainesville (Fla.). Served to capt. CIC, AUS, 1943-46. Mem. So. Assn. Coll. and Univ. Bus. Officers, Ga. Soc. C.P.A.'s, Delta Upsilon. Presbyn. Kiwanian (treas. 1965, 1st v.p. 1966, pres. 1967—. Home: 1777 NW 14th Av Gainesville FL 32601

ELMQUIST, KARL ERIK, educator; b. Evanston, Ill., Jan. 7, 1912; s. Axel Louis and Minna Louise (Harter) E.; B.A., So. Meth. U., 1932; postgrad. U. Chgo., 1932-35; M.A., U. Tex., 1939, postgrad. 1948-50; postgrad. U. Mich. Linguistic Inst., summer 1950; m. Anne Marie Siegel, Feb. 23, 1943; children—Judy Angela, Mark Paul, John Peter, James Martin. Instr., YWCA, Dallas, 1931-32; student asst. So. Meth. U., Dallas, 1931-32; fellow dept. English, U. Chgo., 1934-35; instr. English, Tex. A & M U., College Station, 1935-39, asst. prof., 1941-43, 1945-47, asso. prof. English, 1947—, dir. continuing edn. writing clinics, 1969—; dir. writing clinic New Careers U.S. Dept. Labor, Austin, 1971; instr. North Park Coll., Chgo., 1939-40; research analyst U.S. War Dept., Washington, 1941-43; mem. Grad. Faculty Tex. A & M U.; dir. writing workshops Agrl. Stblzn. and Cons. Service, U.S. Dept. Agr., 1970—. Served to capt. AUS, 1943-45. Recipient Battalion student newspaper awards for debate coaching and supervising student publs., 1948, 57. Mem. Linguistic Soc. Am., Nat. Council Tchrs. English, Tex. Council Tchr. English (publs. editor 1967-68), Conf. Coll. Tchrs. English (Tex.), Am. Assn. U. Profs., Tex. Assn. Coll. Tchrs., Phi Kappa Phi, Sigma Delta Chi, Alpha Theta Phi. Editor: Texas Aggie, part-time 1955-66. Contbr. articles to profl. jours. Home: Drawer H College Station TX 77840

ELMS, BILL GEORGE, accountant; b. Savanna, Okla., June 2, 1935; s. Clarence L. and O. Lorene (Key) E.; A.B., Odessa Coll., 1954; m. Anita Childress, Aug. 6, 1953; children—Tracy K., Terri L., Clark C., Steven W. Partner, Faris, Chapman & Marsh, Odessa, Tex., 1961-65, Chapman, Stroka & Elms, C.P.A.'s, Odessa, 1965-68, Bill Elms & Co., C.P.A.'s, Odessa, 1968-70; mng. partner Elms, Faris & Co., C.P.A.'s, 1970—; pres., dir. Panaquad, Inc., Odessa, 1967—; sec.-treas., dir. Cone & Kerley, Inc., Odessa, 1968—, Gibson Products Co., San Angelo, Tex., 1967—; sec.-treas. Panaquad Oil Co.; pres., dir. Gibson Products Co., Monahans, Tex., 1968—, Gibson Products Co., Newnan, Ga., Gibson Products Co., Kermit, Tex. County commr. Ector County, Tex., 1969—. Treas., Permian Playhouse of Odessa, 1967-69; pres. Odessa Beautiful Assn., 1966-67; v.p. Ector County United Fund, 1971—. Bd. dirs., v.p. Odessa Boys Clubs, 1965-69. Mem. Am. Inst. C.P.A.'s, Tex. Soc. C.P.A.'s, Jr. C. of C. (pres. 1965-66), C. of C. (dir. 1965-66, 72—). Home: 3300 Sherbrook Country Club Estates Odessa TX 79763 Office: 1st National Bldg Odessa TX 79761

ELROD, DAN BERLIN, SR., physician; b. Gainesville, Ga., Oct. 16, 1930; s. Frank Lee and Ethel Cozetta (Leach) E.; student Emory U., 1947-49, U. Ga., 1949-50, 53-54; M.D., Med. Coll. Ga., 1959; m. Ivalene Lazelle Chitwood, Dec. 31, 1952; children—Deborah, Danny, Joanie, Marion, Clifford. Intern Macon Hosp., 1959-60; practice gen. medicine, Hazlehurst, Ga., 1960—; chief staff Clyde Duncam Meml. Hosp., Hazlehurst. Mayor, City of Hazlehurst, 1970—. Served with USAF, 1951-53. Mem. A.M.A., Ga. Med. Assn., Ga. Municipal Assn. Mason. Home: 500 Burketts Ferry Rd Hazlehurst GA 31539 Office: PO Box 8 Hazlehurst GA 31539

ELROD, RUSSELL, lawyer; b. Moseley, Okla., Nov. 30, 1904; A.A., John Brown U., 1928; LL.B., U. Ark. Admitted to Ark. bar, 1933, U.S. Dist. Ct. bar, 1940; practice law, Silaom Springs, Ark., sec. Liberty Savs. & Loan Assn., 1967—. City atty., Siloam Springs, 1934-45, dep. pros. atty., 1937-41. Mem. Ark. Senate, 1945-68. Mem. Benton County (pres. 1953-54), Ark. (chmn. 1955-56) bar assns. Address: 115-117 N Broadway Siloam Springs AR 72761*

ELSASSER, ROBERT W(ILLIAM), mgmt. and econ. analyst; b. N.Y.C., Mar. 10, 1900; s. William Carl and Clara Anna (Koppe) E.; A.B., Dartmouth, 1921, M.C.S., 1922; m. Minnie Helen Pelton, Apr. 10, 1922. Instr. econs. Dartmouth, 1921-22, 24-26; accountant, statistician Eastman Kodak Co., 1922-24; from asso. to prof. bus. statistics and mgmt. Tulane U., 1926-39, prof. econs. and mgmt., 1939-42, spl. asst. to adminstrs. Tulane Ednl. Fund, 1946-47; personnel dir., v.p. for personnel Pendleton Shipyards Co., Inc., 1942, v.p., gen. mgr., 1942-46; profl. practice mgmt., econ. and statis. analysis, 1947—; course coordinator Sch. of Banking of South, La. State U., 1950—; dir. Lake Lawn Park & Mausoleum, Inc., I.L. Lyons & Co., Ltd. Chmn. citizens com. on economy and revenues City New Orleans, 1955-56, 61-62, citizens com. on finances Orleans Parish Sch. Bd., 1958. Mem. New Orleans Indsl. Dispersion Com., New Orleans Census Tract Com. Bd. dirs. New Orleans Hosp. Service Assn., Bur. Govtl. Research of New Orleans; trustee Com. Econ. Devel. C.F.A. Fellow Acad. Mgmt.; mem. C. of C. (pres. 1956; dir.), Am. Econ. Assn., Am. Statis. Assn., Am. Accounting Assn., Am. mgmt. Assn., Soc. Advancement Mgmt. (pres. New Orleans 1950), So. Econ. Assn., New Orleans Assessment Study Com. (vice chmn. 1963-65), Financial Analysts New Orleans (pres. 1965-66), Phi Beta Kappa, Beta Gamma Sigma, Omicron Delta Kappa, Chi Phi. Clubs: Internat. House (dir., exec. com. 1956-61, v.p. 1965), Round Table, Pickwick (New Orleans). Home: 8004 Feret St New Orleans LA 70118 Office: 833 Howard Av New Orleans LA 70113

ELSBERG, PAUL, physician; b. Warendorf, Westfalen, Germany, Apr. 9, 1907; s. David and Ricka (Windmueller) E.; student U. Vienna, 1927-28, U. Freiburg/Breisgau, 1928, U. Breslau, 1929-30; M.D., U. Giessen (Germany), 1932; student N.Y.U., 1942; m. Elizabeth M. Swartz, Jan. 30, 1943; children—Betty Lee (Mrs. William F. Hubbard), David Donald. Came to U.S., 1938, naturalized, 1943. Intern, Gen. Barmbeck Hosp., Hosp., Hamburg, Germany, 1933, Gen. Hosp., Saranac Lake, N.Y., 1938-40; intern Emergency Hosp., Washington, 1940-41, resident anesthesiology, 1941-43; pvt. practice medicine, specializing in anesthesiology, Washington, 1943—; chmn. dept. obstetrical anesthesiology Garfield Hosp., Washington, 1954-57; mem. exec. and teaching staff Doctor's Hosp., Washington, 1958—, mem. post-grad. edn. com., 1969—. Bd. dirs., violinist Alexandria (Va.) Symphony Orch. Mem. Royal Soc. Medicine (Eng.), N.Y. Acad. Scis., Am., So. med. assns., Am. Soc. Anesthesiologists, D.C. Med. Soc., D.C. Soc. Anesthesiology, Washington Heart Assn. Club: Old Dominion Boat Club (Alexandria, Va.). Home: 914 Timber Branch Pkwy Alexandria VA 22302 Office: 1815 Eye St NW Washington DC 10005

ELSILA, DAVID AUGUST, editor; b. Detroit, Feb. 2, 1939; s. Edward J. and Sylvia (Mikkola) E.; B.A., Eastern Mich. U., 1960, postgrad., 1962; m. Kathlyn Deutch, July 17, 1965. Tchr. pub. schs., Livonia, Mich., 1960-64; editor-in-chief Livonia Observer, 1964-65; dir. publs., editor Am. Tchr., also Changing Edn., Am. Fedn. Tchrs., Washington, 1965—. Editor ofcl. publs. Am. Civil Liberties Union, Ill., Mich., 1964-67. Recipient Page 1 award Chgo. Newspaper Guild, 1967, 1st awards in Journalism, Internat. Labor Press Assn., 1968, 69, Ednl. Press Assn. Am., 1968. Mem. Washington-Balt. Newspaper Guild (exec. bd.), Ednl. Press Assn. Am. (pres. Washington chpt., 1971, treas. 1968), Am. Civil Liberties Union, Phi Delta Kappa. Home: 1774 Hobart St NW Washington DC 20009 Office: 1012 14th St NW Washington DC 20005

ELSWICK, D.E., state ofcl. Dir. div. research Ky. Dept. Edn., Frankfort. Address: State Dept Edn State Supt's Office Frankfort KY 40601*

ELVOVE, JOSEPH TEVYA, resort and land devel. exec.; b. Washington, Aug. 19, 1914; s. Elias and Etta (Milatiner) E.; B.S., U. Md., 1934, M.A., 1936; postgrad. Harvard, 1940-41. Dep. dir. sugar div. U.S. Dept. Agr., Washington, 1936-50; dept. head W. R. Grace & Co., N.Y.C., 1950-52; exec. v.p. dir. Pacific Molasses Co., San Francisco, N.Y.C., 1952-63; v.p. Savannah Food Industries, Inc. (Ga.), 1963-71; pres. Resort Cons., Harbor Ventures Ltd. (both Hilton Head, S.C.), 1970—; v.p. Calibogue Properties, Inc.; cons. Sea Pines Co., Hilton Head, 1970—; dir. Stevens Shipping &Terminal Co., Atlantic Towing Co., 1968-71. Trustee Historic Savannah Found., Telfair Acad. Arts and Scis. Served with USNR, 1942-45. Republican. Episcopalian. Clubs: Sugar, India House (N.Y.); Oglethorpe; Chatham

(Savannah, Ga.); Plantation (Hilton Head Island, S.C.). Home: Sea Pines Plantation Hilton Head Island SC 29928 Office: Sea Pines Co Hilton Head Island SC 29928

ELWOOD, WILLIAM KENT, educator; b. Ashtabula, O., Oct. 15, 1928; s. Price Alonzo and Alta May (MacDowell) E.; B.A., Ohio Wesleyan U., 1950; M.S., Ohio State U., 1953, D.D.S., 1957; Ph.D., Wayne State U., 1965; m. Persis Townsend, Dec. 22, 1956; children—Persis, Holly, Bryan. Research asso. Henry Ford Hosp., Detroit, 1957-65; NIH spl. fellow, guest investigator Rockefeller U., N.Y.C., 1965-66; asst. prof. anatomy Med. Center, U. Ky., Lexington, 1966—, asst. prof. restorative dentistry, 1966-70, asst. prof. oral biology, 1970—. Mem. A.A.A.S., Am. Assn. Anatomy, Internat. Assn. Dental Research, Am. Soc. Cell Biology, Electron Microscopy Soc. Am., Ky. Dental Assn., Am. Assn. Dental Schs., Bluegrass Dental Soc., Sigma Xi, Alpha Sigma Phi, Delta Sigma Delta, Omicron Delta Kappa. Contbr. articles to profl. jours. Home: 755 Bravington Way Lexington KY 40503

ELY, THOMAS SOUTHGATE, physician; b. Jonesville, Va., June 8, 1914; s. Thomas Bascom and Jennie (Edds) E.; A.B. magna cum laude, Emory and Henry Coll., 1935; M.D., Med. Coll. Va., 1939; m. Barbara Ellen Dixon, Sept. 7, 1940; children—Thomas Harrison, Maria Jane. Intern hosp. div. Med. Coll. Va., 1939-40; practice gen. medicine, Jonesville, 1945—; med. examiner, coroner Lee County, Va. Pres. Jonesville Drug Co., Inc., 1951—; dir. Powell Valley Nat. Bank, Jonesville, Lee Farmers' Tobacco Warehouse, Pennington Gap, Va. Chmn. Jefferson Forest dist. Boy Scouts Am. Chmn. Jonesville Town Planning and Zoning Com., Lee County Sch. Electoral Bd.; med. adviser Lee County Selective Service Bd., 1964—. Bd. trustees Holston Conf. Colls., 1961—; exec. com. Emory and Henry Coll., 1962—. Served to maj. M.C., AUS, 1941-46; ETO, N. Africa. Decorated N. Africa-ETO medal with 7 battle stars; recipient De Molay Legion of Honor, 1970. Mem. Am. Legion (local post positions to dept. comdr., dept. rehab. chmn., nat. med. adv. bd., vice chmn. nat. legislative Commn.; nat. exec. committeeman from Va.), 40 and 8 (life, cheminot nat. 1958-59), Lee County C. of C. (organizer, pres. pro-tem., dir.), Lee County Med. Soc. (past sec.-treas., (past pres.), Med. Soc. Va., A.M.A., Am. Acad. Gen. Practice, Emory and Henry Alumni Assn. (pres. 1963—), The Cabiri, Blue Key, Tau Kappa Alpha, Pi Gamma Mu, Kappa Phi Kappa, Theta Kappa Psi, Sigma Zeta. Methodist (chmn. bd. stewards, lay leader, chmn. bd. trustees, pres. dist. laymen's orgn. 1959-60, mem. bd. hosps. and instns. Holstein Conf.). Mason (K.T., 32 deg., Shriner, Jester), Odd Fellow, Woodman of World; mem. Order Eastern Star (past patron). Club: Lions (past pres. Jonesville; zone chmn. 1959-60; dist. gov. 1961-62; internat. counsellor 1962—, Lion of Year, Achievement award). Address: PO Box 115 Jonesville VA 24263

EMBREE, MARTHA LOUISE, organic chem. mfg. co. exec.; b. Houston, Nov. 30, 1936; d. Elisha D. and Alma (Bedell) Embree; B.F.A., U. Houston, 1958. Copy trainee, prodn. mgr. Erwin Wasey Advt., Houston, 1959-60; film mgr., prodn. asst. KPRC-TV, Houston, 1960-62; copy chief R.S. Townsend Advt., Kansas City, Mo., 1962-63; advt. asst. Chemagro, Kansas City, 1963-66; free lance copywriter, 1966-68; marketing asst. Glidden-Durkee div. Sem Corp., Jacksonville, Fla., 1968-70, supr. advt., 1970-71, mgr. communications, 1971—. Mem. N.E. Fla. Bus. Communicators (1st v.p. 1970-71, pres. 1971-72), Advt. Fedn. Jacksonville (chmn. bulletin 1971-72). Home: 14660 Stacey Rd Jacksonville FL 32250 Office: PO Box 389 Jacksonville FL 32201

EMBRY, CARLOS BROGDON, newspaper pub.; b. Baizetown, Ky., Jan. 21, 1906; s. Marion Armstrong and Lola (Albin) E.; A.B., Western Ky. U., 1929; student U. Ariz., 1949-50; m. Zora Romans, June 30, 1940; children—Jane Carroll (Mrs. Morris J. Hardwick, Jr.), Carlos Brogdon. Prin. jr. high sch., Bulloch County, Ga., 1926-27, Lynnvale High Sch., White Mills, Ky., 1928-29; owner-pub. Ohio County Messenger, Beaver Dam, Ky., 1930—; pres. Embry Newspapers, Inc., Beaver Dam; builder, owner Embry's Valley Shopping Center. Beaver Dam; pres. Kentucky Weekly Newspaper Assn., 1967-68, chmn. bd. dirs., 1968-69, v.p. legislation, 1969—. Dir Ky. Republican Com., 1944; mem. Ky. Senate, 10th dist., 1945-49. Recipient Ky. Statesman award, 1964; Ky. Col. Mem. Beaver Dam Bd. Trade, Ky. Hist. Soc. Baptist. Clubs: Lions (Beaver Dam); Filson. Author: America's Concentration Camps—The Facts About Our Indian Reservations Today, 1956; Beaver Dam and the Green Valley, 1970. Contbr. articles mags. and newspapers. Home: 211 N Main St Beaver Dam KY 42320 Office: 220 N Main St Beaver Dam KY 42320

EMERSON, HORACE MANN, r.r. exec.; b. Wilmington, N.C., Jan. 22, 1914; s. Horace Mann and Laura Placida (Clark) E.; student pub. and pvt. schs., Sumter, Columbia, S.C.; m. Susan LeRoy Carr, June 1, 1943; children—Susan C. (Mrs. Nicholas H. Bancks), Laura C. Clk., A.C.L. R.R., Wilmington, N.C., 1934-47, gen. agt., Jacksonville, Fla., 1947-51, asst. gen. freight agt., Wilmington, N.C., 1952-57, asst. treas., 1957-58, treas., Wilmington and Jacksonville, 1958-61, asst. v.p. traffic, 1967-68; sr. asst. v.p. traffic, dir. Seaboard Coast Line R.R. Co., Jacksonville, 1967-68, v.p. freight traffic, 1968—; v.p., dir. Louisville & Nashville R.R.; dir. Central R.R. Co. S.C., Columbia, Newberry & Laurens R.R., Seacoast Transp. Co., S.C. Pacific Ry. Co. Served to capt. U.S. Army, 1946-52. Mem. Assn. ICC Practitioners, Nat. Freight Traffic Assn., Fla. Traffic Assn., N.Y. Traffic Club, Jackson Area C. of C. Democrat. Episcopalian (mem. vestry 1970—). Clubs: Timuquana Country, River, University, Meninak, Ponte Vedra (Jacksonville, Fla.). Home: 4805 King Richard Rd Jacksonville FL 32210 Office: 908 W Broadway Louisville KY 40201

EMERSON, KARY CADMUS, biologist, govt. ofcl.; b. Sasakwa, Okla., Mar. 13, 1918; s. Earle Evans and Diva (Wilkins) E.; B.S., Okla. State U., 1939, M.S., 1940, Ph.D., 1949; m. Mary Rebecca Williams, Aug. 13, 1939; children—William K., James B., Robert E. Joined U.S. Army, 1940, advanced through grades to col., 1962, instr. U.S. Army Command and Staff Coll., 1955-58, ret., 1966; asst. for research to the asst. sec. of the Army, 1961—. Adj. prof. Okla. State U., 1971—. Mem. U.N. Mil. Armistice Commn. in Korea, 1958-59. Dir. Biol. Soc. of Washington, Research asso. Smithsonian Inst., 1959—. U.S. mem. NATO Panel for long term Sci. Studies, 1970—. Decorated Bronze Star medal, Purple Heart, Legion of Merit. Fellow Washington Acad. Sci.; mem. Am. Soc. Parasitologists, Am. Soc. Tropical Medicine and Hygiene, Wildlife Disease Assn., Entomol. Soc. Am., Biol. Soc. Wash., Entomol. Soc. Washington, Am. Inst. Biol. Scis., A.A.A.S., Sigma Xi. Contbr articles in field to profl. jours. Home: 2704 N Kensington Arlington VA 22207 Office: Office Sec of the Army Washington DC 20310

EMERSON, MARVIN CHESTER, lawyer, state ofcl.; b. Cromwell, Okla., Dec. 28, 1928; s. Earle Evans and Diva (Wilkins) E.; B.A., U. Okla., 1950, LL.B., 1953; m. George Etta Killingsworth, Feb. 7, 1954; children—Mary Caroline, George Marvin. Admitted to Okla. bar, 1953; practiced in Coalgate, Okla., 1953-55; county atty. Coal County (Okla.), 1955-56; asst. county atty. Pontotoc County (Okla.), 1956-57; asst. dir. State Soil Conservation Bd., Oklahoma City, 1957-61, exec. dir., 1961-71; first asst. atty. gen., Okla., 1971—. Served with USAAF, 1946-47. Named Outstanding Soil Conservationist in Okla., Okla. chpt. Nat. Wildlife Fedn., 1965. Mem. Okla. Bar Assn. Mason (32deg.).Home: 7216 Comanche Av Oklahoma City OK 73132 Office: Atty Gens Office State Capitol Oklahoma City OK 73105

EMERSON, MAXWELL, ret. army officer, educator; b. Newton Center, Mass., Mar. 25, 1903; s. Howard and Ada (Maxwell) E.; student Dartmouth, 1921-23; B.S.C., Roosevelt U., 1957; M.A., Memphis State U., 1960; m. Mary Byram Millet Aug. 18, 1927; 1 son, David M.; m. 2d, Dorothy Jane Kerr, Aug. 1, 1945; 1 dau., June Alice. Plantation overseer United Fruit Co., Guatemala, 1924-26; store mgr. Loft, Inc., Newark, 1927-32; sales dept. Shell Oil Co., N.Y.C., 1933-38; commd. 2d lt. U.S. Army, 1938; advanced through grades to col., 1950; q.m. worldwide assignments, ret., 1958; asst. prof. mgmt. Memphis State U. Coll. Bus. Adminstrn., 1960-72. Decorated Silver Star, Bronze Star medal, Army Commendation medal with oak leaf cluster. Mem. Def. Supply Assn., Mayflower Soc., S.A.R. (pres. Tenn. 1970-71, pres. Memphis chpt. 1968-69), Descs. Colonial Clergy, Tenn. Soc. Colonial Wars (sec.), New Eng. Hist.-Geneal. Soc., Mil. Order World Wars (nat. staff 1940, comdr. Tenn. soc. 1972—), Descs. Colonial Govs., Tenn. Huguenot Soc., Baronial Order Magna Carta, Order Crown of Charlemagne in U.S., Order Colonial Lords Manors in Am., Adam Hawkes Family Assn., Stetson Kindred, Delta Sigma Pi, Phi Sigma Kappa. Methodist. Mason. Home: 223 Lorece Lane Memphis TN 38117

EMERSON, O. D., accountant; b. Hillsboro, Tex., June 25, 1909; s. Ollie D. and Sudie (Johnson) E.; B.B.A., Baylor U., 1932; spl. courses LaSalle U., also the N.Y. Univ.; m. Myrtle Mae Hennigan, Feb. 17, 1933; 1 son Philip Edward. Disbursing officer Tex. Relief Commn., 1933-36; agt. U.S. Bur. Internal Revenue, 1936-45; pub. accounting O. D. Emerson, Jr., C.P.A., Hattiesburg and McComb, Miss., 1945-61, Emerson & Emerson, C.P.A.'s, Hattiesburg, Columbia and McComb, Miss., 1961—; sec., treas. Pearl River Land Co.; dir. S. Miss. Oil Corp. Meridian Vendors, Inc. Auditor City Lumberton; former lectr. accounting U. So. Miss. Mem. Am. Inst. Accts., Tex., Miss. socs. C.P.A.'s. Methodist. Mason. Club: Metropolitan. Home: 610 W Pine St Hattiesburg MS 39401 Office: 606 W Pine St Hattiesburg MS 39401

EMERSON, ROBERT BISCAL, chemist, physicist; b. Nashville, Mar. 17, 1909; s. Winiford Frank and Roberta (Griffith) E.; M.S., La. State U., 1950; grad. Army Command and Gen. Staff Coll., 1948; m. Opal Lynelle Duke, Nov. 3, 1934; children—Robert B., Dorothy Jeanne (Mrs. Tim Davis). Commd. 2d lt. U.S. Army, 1935, advanced through grades to col., 1952; mem. Spearhead Planning Staff, 1944, top secret control officer, 1944-46, G-4 Base sect., ETO, 1944-46, dir. command and gen. staff dept. U.S. Army Res. Sch., 1951-57, instr. or dir. for command and gen. staff subjects, Fort Sill, Okla., 1953-57, Fort Sam Houston, Tex., 1957, comdg. officer 4225 Logistical Command (C), 1957-62; ret., 1962; asst. to forensic chemist State of Fla., Tampa, 1926; control chemist Victor Chem. Works, Nashville, 1927; chief chemist Fla. Match Co., St. Petersburg, 1928-29; owner Emerson Testing Labs., St. Petersburg, Fla., 1930-38; forensic chemist State of Fla., St. Petersburg, 1930-38; asso. chemist Gable Clin. Labs., St. Petersburg, 1930-38, Hurst Labs., St. Petersburg, 1936-38; owner Emerson Testing Labs., Baton Rouge, 1948—; physics instr. La. State U., 1948-53; sr. research chemist, staff research asso Chem. Aluminas, Kaiser Chems., Baton Rouge, 1953—. Decorated Legion of Merit, Bronze Star medal. Mem. Am. Phys. Soc., Am. Chem. Soc., T.A.P.P.I., A.A.A.S., Inst. Fundamental Studies Assn., Internat. Platform Assn, Community Leaders Am., So. Rubber Group, Catalysis Soc., Mil. Order of World Wars, Phi Eta Sigma, Phi Lambda Upsilon, Phi Kappa Phi, Sigma Pi Sigma. Home: 1560 Stephens Av Baton Rouge LA 70808 Office: PO Box 1031 Baton Rouge LA 70821

EMERSON, WALLACE HARLIN, JR., bank exec.; b. Sulphur Springs, Tex., July 25, 1938; s. Wallace Harlin and Verna Ruth (Dillard) E.; B.B.A., Tex. Technol. U., 1961 1 son, Jeffery Farris. Comptroller currency Nat. Bank Examiner, 1961-65; exec. v.p. First Nat. Bank, Ashdown, Ark., 1965-66, First State Bank, Goald, Ark., 1966-69; sr. v.p. Nat. Bank Commerce, Dallas, 1969—. Capt. Heart Fund Drive. Mem. Kappa Sigma. Democrat. Methodist. Mason, Lion. Home: 7923 Shining Willow Lane Dallas TX 75230 Office: PO Box 2249 Dallas TX 75221

EMERY, FRED JOSEPH, govt. ofcl.; b. Buffalo, Oct. 12, 1933; s. Frederick Mead and Frances (Dahlem) E.; A.B., Union Coll., 1954; LL.B., Albany Law Sch., 1957; m. Lola Louise Meyer, Apr. 6, 1958; children— Jean, Alan, Andrew. Admitted to N.Y. bar, 1957; legal cons. Dept. Audit and Control, N.Y. State, Albany, 1958, atty. Bd. Equalization and Assessment, 1959-63; atty. FAA, 1963-67, chief Air Carrier and Ops. br., Gen. Counsel's Office, Washington, 1967-68; dep. asst. Gen. Counsel Regulations Transp. Dept., Gen. Services Adminstrn., 1968-70, dir. sec. adminstrv. com. Fed. Register, 1970—. Served to 2d lt. USAF, 1957-58, 61-62, 67-68. Mem. Fed., Am., N.Y. State bar assns. Home: 3526 Quesada St NW Washington DC 20015 Office: Nat Archives Bldg 18th and F Sts NW Washington DC 20408

EMERY, H. GENE, lawyer; b. Hobart, Okla., Oct. 19, 1923; A.B. with highest honors, U. Ill., 1945; LL.B. cum laude, Harvard, 1948. Admitted to Ind. bar, 1948, Tex. bar, 1955; chmn. Oil and Gas Taxation Inst., Southwestern Legal Found., 1962, mem. faculty fed. taxation studies, 1966-69; now practice law, Dallas. Pres. Dallas Estate Council, 1970-71. Fellow Am. Coll. Probate Counsel; mem. Dallas, Am. bar assns., State Bar Tex. (mem. council sect. taxation 1965-68), Phi Beta Kappa. Address: 4654 Fairfax Av Dallas TX 75209*

EMERY, IRENE, museum ofcl. Curator tech. studies Textile Museum, Washington. Address: Textile Museum 2320 S St NW Washington DC 20008*

EMERY, MARSHALL THOMAS, educator, athletic coach; b. Bridgeport, Conn., June 6, 1932; s. Marshall N. and Adele (Holmes) E.; B.S., Winston-Salem Tchrs. Coll., 1954; M.A., N.Y. U., 1961; m. Patricia E. Holman, Aug. 24, 1958; tchr., coach Cary (N.C.) Sch., 1954-56; tchr. pub. schs. Newark, 1960-61; tchr., coach Winston Paisley High Sch., Winston-Salem, 1961-66; coach basketball Howard U., 1966—. Served with AUS, 1956-58; Alaska. Named Tournament Coach of Year, Central Inter-Collegiate Athletic Assn., 1967. Mem. Omega Phi Psi. Home: 50 Hawaii Av NE Washington DC 20001

EMERY, ROBERT FIRESTONE, economist; b. Kenton, O., Jan. 18, 1927; s. Clayton Sprague and Sarah Webster (Firestone) E.; B.A., Oberlin Coll., 1951; M.A., U. Mich., 1952, Ph.D., 1956; m. Phyllis Eileen Swanson, June 29, 1957; children—Ross David, Ann Elaine, Hope Roberta. Teaching fellow U. Mich., 1954-55; economist Bd. Govs. Fed. Res. System, Washington, 1955—; adj. prof. econs. Southeastern U., Washington, 1960—, chmn. dept. financial adminstrn., 1963-65, dean sr. div., 1965-68. Instl. rep. Troop 255, Boy Scouts Am., Chevy Chase, Md., 1970—. Served with U.S. Mcht. Marine, 1945-47. U. Mich. fellow, 1952-53, Fulbright Grad. Research student U. Rangoon, Burma, 1953-54. Mem. Am. Econ. Assn. Republican. Methodist. Author: Financial Institutions of Southeast Asia, 1971. Home: 3421 Shepherd St Chevy Chase MD 20015 Office: Fed Res Bd Washington DC 20051

EMMANUEL, SISTER MARY, hosp. adminstr. exec. v.p. Mercy Hosp. Office: Mercy Hosp 3663 S Miami Av Miami FL 33133*

EMMANUELLI, JUAN BAUZA, dentist; b. Ponce, P.R., Apr. 2, 1940; s. Juan R. and Elena (Bauza) E.; B.S., Cath. U. P.R., 1959; D.M.D., U. P.R., 1963; M.S., Loyola U., Chgo., 1967; m. Madeleine Benvenuti, Mar. 4, 1967; 1 dau., Madeleine S. Individual practice dentistry specializing in orthodontics, Mayaguez, P.R., 1967—. Comdr. USCG Aux., 1970-71. Served to capt., Dental Corps, AUS, 1965-67. Mem. Am. Dental Assn., Am. Assn. Orthodontists, Middle Atlantic Assn. Orthodontists, P.R. Orthodontic Assn. Colegio de Cirujanos Dentistos de P.R. (pres. western region 1967-68), Xi Psi Phi, Phi Eta Mu. Rotarian. Clubs: Mayaguez Playa (1st v.p. 1970-71), Comodore Deportivo del Oeste (v.p. 1971-73) (Mayaguez, P.R.). Home: Ramonita at Cruz St Urb Bellas Lomas Mayaguez PR 00708 Office: 52 N Post St Mayaguez PR 00708

EMMER, JOHN WILTZ, dentist; b. New Iberia, La., Apr. 27, 1903; s. Albert George and Marie (Wiltz) E.; B.A. magna cum laude, St. Charles Coll., 1920; D.D.S. cum laude, Loyola U., 1925; m. Allene A. Garrett, Apr. 1, 1943; 1 dau., Karen S. Gen. practice dentistry, New Iberia, 1925-42; practice dentistry specializing in periodontics, New Iberia, 1943—; owner, research dir. NDK Co., New Iberia, La., 1949—, pres., 1952—. Diplomate Am. Bd. Periodontology. Mem. La., Third Dist (pres. 1936-38) dental assns. Democrat. Home: 343 Hilltop Circle New Iberia LA 70560 Office: 440 Charles St New Iberia LA 70561

EMMERICH, THEODORE H., accountant; b. Covington, Ky., June 16, 1926; s. Theodore H. and Freida E. (Maier) E.; B.B.A., U. Cin., 1950, M.B.A., 1963. Partner, Ernst & Ernst, Cin., 1950—. Served with AUS, 1944-46, 51-52. Decorated Combat Inf. Badge, Purple Heart; recipient Sell's award Am. Inst. C.P.A.'s, 1954. C.P.A., Ohio. Mem. Ohio Soc. C.P.A.'s (pres. Cin. chpt. 1963, dir. 1970-71), Am. Mgmt. Assn., Am. Accounting Assn., Am. Inst. C.P.A.'s, Beta Gamma Sigma, Beta Alpha Psi. Clubs: Cincinnati, Bankers (Cin.). Home: 714 Winston Hill Dr Covington KY 41015 Office: Dubois Tower Cincinnati OH 45202

EMMONS, MORELLE, sch. supt.; b. Jonesboro, La., Oct. 20, 1907; s. James Redden and Lula (Walker) E.; B.A., La. Poly. Inst., 1936; M.A., La. State U., 1940; m. Trissielee Wyrick, Aug. 3, 1935; children—Barbara Ann (Mrs. James C. Logan), Martha Elizabeth (Mrs. James Davis Green). Tchr. rural schs., Winn Parish, La., 1926-28, Jackson Parish, La., 1929-31, Jonesboro (La.) High Sch., 1931-33; prin. Hodge (La.) Elementary Sch., 1933-37, Simsboro (La.) High Sch., 1937-47; supervising prin. elementary schs., Ruston, La., 1947-48; supt. Lincoln Parish schs., Ruston, 1948—. Pres. La. Bapt. Brotherhood, 1948-50. Mem. bd. dirs. Ruston Parks and Recreation Bd., 1947—; pres. Greater Tech. Found., 1968. Fulbright fellow, 1960. Mem. La. Sch. Supts. Assn. (pres. 1951), La. Tchrs. Assn., Am. Assn. Sch. Adminstrs. (state chmn. centennial 1964), Ruston C. of C. (pres. 1957). Democrat. Kiwanian (pres. 1950). Home: 1102 D'Arbonne St Ruston LA 71270 Office: 300 S Farmerville St Ruston LA 71270

EMMONS, RONALD REECE, accountant; b. Canton, Okla., Feb. 21, 1941; s. William Reece and Gladys (Prigmore) E.; B.S., U. Tulsa, 1963; m. Eleanor Gail Storey, June 1, 1962; children—Kevin Reece, William Bradford, Carrie Kathleen. Tax mgr. Arthur Andersen & Co., Tulsa, 1963-69, tax mgr., 1971—; asst. treas., controller Ednl. Devel. Corp., Tulsa, 1969-71. Mem. Am. Inst. C.P.A.'s, Okla. Soc. C.P.A.'s, Tulsa U. Alumni Assn., Okla. Ofcls. Assn., N.G. Assn. Home: 3527 S Joplin Pl Tulsa OK 74135 Office: Fourth Nat Bank Bldg Tulsa OK 74119

EMMONS, WILLIAM REECE, finance ofcl.; b. Arnett, Okla., Feb. 20, 1915; s. Vernon LeRoy and Dollie (Platt) E.; B.S., Southwestern State Coll., Weatherford, Okla., 1938; postgrad. Tulsa U., 1961-64; m. Gladys Prigmore, June 5, 1937; children—Ronald Reece, Peggy Joyce (Mrs. William F. Combs). Tchr. bus. edn. Canton (Okla.) Pub. Schs., 1938-42; accountant Glenn R. Davis, C.P.A., Muskogee, Okla., 1947-54; agt. Internal Revenue Service, Tulsa, 1942-47, 54-60, field audit group supr., 1960-69, large case audit mgr., 1969—. Capt., Community Chest drive, 1967-68. C.P.A., Okla. Mem. Am. Inst. C.P.A.'s, Okla. Soc. C.P.A.'s, Delta Theta Phi. Methodist. Mason. Home: 5045 E Admiral Blvd Tulsa OK 74115 Office: 15 W 6th St Tulsa OK 74119

EMRICK, EDWARD, JR., petroleum exec.; b. Aledo, Ill., Feb. 17, 1909; s. Edward Everett and Nannie May (Love) E.; B.S., U. Ill., 1931; m. Mary Bentley Woods, Mar. 17, 1934; children—Robert E., Ann Bentley, Katherine W., William P. Asst. treas. Ashland Oil, 1932, chief accounting officer and asst. sec., 1939, purchasing agt., 1942, dir., 1947, exec. asst., 1949; with Ashland Oil & Refining Co. and affiliated cos. (Ky.), 1931-70, exec. asst., 1949-51, dir. purchases, 1952-70, treas., 1959-70; dir. 3d Nat. Bank; treas., dir. Ashland Overseas Corp., 1968-70; dir. 3d Nat. Bank; treas., dir. Ashland Overseas Corp., 1969-70; dir. Rosenblooms, Inc., Gablers, Inc., Ironton, O., Palais Royal, Richmond, Ind. Active Boyd County Community Chest, 1942. Mem. Nat. Assn. Purchasing Agts., Am. Petroleum Inst. Presbyn. (elder). Club: Lion (past dir.). Home: 1725 The Oaks Dr Ashland KY 41101 Office: 1409 Winchester Av Ashland KY 41101

ENCK, RUDOLPH ROBERT, state ofcl.; b. Seguin, Tex., Jan. 7, 1910; s. Dan Henry and Selma (Weniger) E.; student Tex. Lutheran Coll., 1929-30; m. Myrtle Lorayne Teas, Dec. 25, 1931; 1 dau., Sandra Kay (Mrs. James Joseph West). Bookkeeper, Seguin Cotton Oil Co., 1930-41; with R.R. Commn. Tex., 1941—, dir. records services, Austin, 1963—. Hon. mem. Seguin (Tex.) Fire Dept. Named Boss of Year, Am. Bus. Womens Assn., 1963. Mem. Christian Ch. (bd. elders 1966-68). Home: 2402 Bridle Path Austin TX 78703 Office: Ernest O Thompson Bldg Austin TX 78711

ENDSLEY, ELKIN DOUGLAS, state ofcl.; b. Orlando, Fla., Apr. 29, 1935; s. Jack Gordon and Thurma Wenona (Alchin) E.; B.S. in Communications, U. Fla., 1957; m. Joyce Marie Garland, Apr. 1, 1961; children—Cydne Nanette, Jack Douglas. Dir., Community Council of Escambia County, Pensacola, Fla., 1962-63; exec. dir. Community Service Council of Broward County, Ft. Lauderdale, 1964-70; dir. Fla. Div. Family Services, Jacksonville, 1971—. Pres. Fla. Com. for Youth and Children, 1971—. Served with USAF, 1958-61. Mem. Fla. Assn. United Fund and Council Execs. (pres. 1969), Sigma Phi Epsilon. Methodist. Kiwanian (pres. Ft. Lauderdale 1970). Home: 8102 Parkridge Circle S Jacksonville FL 32211 Office: PO Box 2050 Jacksonville FL 32203

ENDSLEY, FRED ROBERT, educator; b. Moline, Ill., Aug. 17, 1930; s. Matt and Bessie (Erickson) E.; B.A., Grinnell Coll., 1952; M.B.A., Ind. U., 1958; Ph.D., La. State U., 1967; m. Peggy Ann Dupre, Sept. 13, 1953; children—Pamela Dawn, Kim Yvette. Mgr., Reliable Implement Store, Marshalltown, Ia., 1954-57; asst. prof. bus. U. Ga., Athens, 1958-60; asst. prof. mgmt. Eastern Ill. U., Charleston, 1963-64; instr. marketing La. State U., Baton Rouge, 1964-65, asso. prof. mgmt., marketing, 1969—, head corr. study dept., 1965-70, asst. dean Coll. Bus., 1970-72, asso. dean, acting chmn. marketing dept.,

1972—. Vice pres. Econ. & Indsl. Research, Inc., 1971—. Cons. mgmt., marketing. Mem. troop com. Boy Scouts Am., Baton Rouge, 1966-68. Served to 2d lt. USAF, 1952-54. Mem. Am. (faculty adviser 1969-70), So. marketing assns., Sales and Marketing Execs. Internat., Southwestern Social Sci. Assn., Nat. U. Extension Assn. (nat. sec.-treas. ind. study div. 1968-70), Red Red Rose, Delta Sigma Pi, Pi Sigma Epsilon, Beta Gamma Sigma. Methodist. Clubs: Civitan, Baton Rouge Advertising (hon.). Home: 3064 Brandywine Dr Baton Rouge LA 70808

ENELOW, MORTON LEONARD, physician; b. Pitts., Dec. 30, 1925; s. Isadore Maurice and Rose (Kasdan) E.; M.D., U. Louisville, 1948; student W.Va. U., 1943-44; m. Sylvia Solomon, June 21, 1953; children—Richard Ian, Robert Stewart, Thomas, James Morton. Intern, Touro Infirmary, New Orleans, 1948-49; resident medicine Louisville Gen. Hosp., 1949-50; practice medicine, New Orleans, 1950-51; fellow psychiatry Tulane U., 1951-54, trainee psychoanalysis, 1951-56; practice medicine, specializing in psychiatry, psychoanalysis, New Orleans, 1955—; mem. sr. staff Touro Infirmary; sr. vis. physician Charity Hosp. La.; asst. prof. clin. psychiatry Tulane U., 1957-64, asso. prof. clin. psychiatry, 1964—, tng. analyst, psychoanalytic tng. program, supervising analyst, 1956—, dir., coordinator psychoanalytic tng., 1966—. Dir. Met. Crime Commn., New Orleans, 1959—. Diplomate Nat. Bd. Med. Examiners, Am. Bd. Psychiatry and Neurology. Fellow Am. Psychiat. Assn., Am. Acad. Psychoanalysis; mem. Am. Psychosomatic Soc., World Fedn. Mental Health, A.A.A.S., A.M.A. Author chpt. in textbook on sexual perversions, chpt. in textbook on dreams in psychoanalysis. Research treatment coll. problems, homosexuality, nature of psychotherapy, dreams in psychotherapy and psychoanalysis. Home: 485 Audubon St New Orleans LA 70118 Office: 4510 St Charles Av New Orleans LA 70115

ENGEL, WALBURGA VON RAFFLER (MRS. A. FERDINAND ENGEL), linguist; b. Munich, Germany, Sept. 25, 1920; d. Friedrich J. and Gertrud (Kiefer) von Raffler; D.Litt., U. Turin (Italy), 1947; M.S., Columbia, 1951; Ph.D., Ind. U., 1953 came to U.S., 1949, naturalized, 1955; m. A. Ferdinand Engel, June 2, 1957; children—Lea Maxine, Eric Robert von Raffler. Faculty, Bennett Coll., Greensboro, N.C., 1953-55, Morris Harvey Coll., Charleston, W.Va., 1955-57, Coll. City N.Y., Adelphi U., 1957-58, N.Y. U., 1957-59, U. Florence (Italy), 1959-60, Istituto Post Universitario Organizzazione Aziendale, Italy, 1960-61, Bologna Center of Johns Hopkins U., 1964-64; faculty Vanderbilt U., Nashville, 1965—, asso. prof. linguistics, 1966—; vis. prof. U. Ottawa, 1971-72. Free lance journalist, 1949-58. Mem. Am. Assn. U. Profs., A.A.A.S., Internat. Linguists Assn., Linguistic Soc. Am., Societas Linguistica Europea, Internat. Phonetics Assn., Internat. Assn. Biophonetics. Author: Il Prelinquaggio Infantile, 1964. Contbr. articles to publs. Home: 3520 West End Av Nashville TN 37205

ENGEL, WILLIAM PERRY, real estate co. exec.; b. Cottondale, Ala., Sept. 23, 1895; s. Michael P. and Sophia (Kronenberg) E.; student Wheeler Bus. Coll., Birmingham, Ala., 1912-13; m. Bess Goldstein, Aug. 23, 1917 (dec. 1971); 1 son, Marvin R. Chmn. bd. Engel Cos., Birmingham, 1917—, Engel Realty Co., Engel Agy.; pres. Morris Av. Corp.; dir. Protective Life Ins. Co., Birmingham Trust Nat. Bank. Chmn. chmn. Jefferson County Community Chest, 1948-49. Pres. Jewish Community Center; v.p., dir. Am. Jewish Com.; sec.-treas., bd. dirs. Warrior-Tombigbee Devel. Assn., Childrens Hosp., Eye Hosp., Salvation Army. Served from 2d lt. to capt. F.A., U.S. Army, World War I. William P. Engel Thyroid Study Unit named in his honor Sch. Medicine, U. Ala. at Birmingham, 1971. Mem. Birmingham C. of C. (named One of Ten Top Men in 100-yr. history of Birmingham, past pres.), Am. Legion. Jewish religion (past pres.) temple). Rotarian. Clubs: Pine Tree Country, The Club, Relay House. Home: 3100 Sterling Rd Birmingham AL 35213 Office: Bank for Savs Bldg Birmingham AL 35203

ENGELHARDT, LLOYD JOHN, city ofcl.; b. New Orleans, Apr. 7, 1924; s. Emile Theodore and Rosalie Mary (Silva) E.; B.S., Okla. State U., 1962; m. Betty Marie Silva, Feb. 7, 1946; children—John, Laine, Melodie. Commd. aviation cadet U.S. Marine Corps, 1942, advanced through grades to lt. col., 1962; served in Far East, 1945-50, Korea, 1950-51, 54; various positions, 1954-65; ret., 1965; pres. So. Helicopters, Greenwood, Miss., 1965-66; asst. to pres. Holmes Jr. Coll., Goodman, Miss., 1967-71; exec. dir. Farmville (N.C.) Econ. Council, 1968—; sec.-treas., exec. dir. Farmville Housing Authority, 1969—. Mem. adv. bd. Mid-East Econ. Devel. Commn., 1968-70. Dir. Civil Def., Farmville, 1968—. Bd. dirs. Pitt County (N.C.) chpt. A.R.C., Salvation Army, Farmville. Decorated D.F.C., Silver Star, Air medals. Rotarian (treas. Farmville, 1968). Home: 508 N Walnut St Farmville NC 27828 Office: Farmville Housing Authority 172 Anderson Av Farmville NC 27828

ENGLAND, ANTHONY WAYNE, astronaut; b. Indpls., May 15, 1942; s. Herman U. and Betty (Steel), E.; S.B., S.M. (NSF grantee), Mass. Inst. Tech., 1965, Ph.D., 1970; m. Kathleen Ann Kreutz, Aug. 31, 1962; children— Heidi, Lynd, Heather Ann. With Texaco Co., summer 1962; student field geology Ind. U., mont., summer 1963; NSF grantee, 1965-67, scientist-astronaut NASA, 1967—; qualified jet pilot, 1968. Mem. Am. Geophys. Union, Am. Geol. Inst., Am. Inst. Aeros. and Astronautics, Soc. Exploration Geophsicists, N.Y. Acad. Scis., Sigma Xi. Office: NASA Houston TX 77058

ENGLAND, IRA ALBERT, educator, clergyman; b. Ottumwa, Ia., Aug. 8, 1915; s. Ira Albert and Margaret (England) Brown; student Parsons Coll., 1933-37; Ph.B., Carroll Coll., 1939; S.B., Central State Tchrs. Coll., 1940; M.A. in Edn., U. Fla., 1954, Edn. Specialist, 1955, Ed.D., 1957. Ordained to ministry P.E. Ch., 1942; rector. Lincoln, Ill., 1944-49; headmaster St. Johns Parish Day Sch., 1951-53, St. Stephens Episcopal Day Sch., 1961-62; asso. sec. unit evaluation Dept. Christian Edn., Nat. Council Episcopal Ch., 1957-61; prof. anthropology and sociology Miami-Dade Jr. Coll., 1962—. Sec. Diocese of Springfield (Ill.), chmn. dept. Christian edn., 1946-48; asst. in adminstrn., research U. Fla Gainesville, 1953-55; cons. gen. research, 1957—, cons. Indian work, 1962—. Mem. Am., Fla. anthrop. assns., Religious Edn. Assn., Phi Delta Kappa, Kappa Delta Pi, Alpha Kappa Delta, Phi Alpha Theta. Mason (K.T.), Rotarian (past exec. sec. Lincoln, Ill.), Lion. Author: The Allapattah Study, 1967; A Community in Crisis, Allapattah and Cosmopolis. Home: 9674 NW 10th Av Miami FL 33150

ENGLAND, KENNETH MURCHISON, educator; b. Wadley, Ga., Nov. 25, 1917; s. Kenneth Murchison and Mattie Emma (McDaniel) E.; B.S., Ga. Tchrs. Coll., 1937; M.A., U. Ga., 1939; Ph.D., Vanderbilt U., 1957. Prin. Matthews Pub. Sch., Wadley, Ga., 1937-38; head English dept. Fitzgerald (Ga.) Pub. Sch., 1939-42; asst. prof. N. Ga. Coll., 1942-45, Ga. Inst. Tech., 1945-46, 47-52; asst. prof. N.C. State Coll., 1946-47; prof. English, Ga. State U., Atlanta, 1952-57, prof. English, dean men, 1957-62, prof. English, dean students, 1962—. Mem. Am. Assn. U. Profs., Nat. Assn. Student Personnel Adminstrs., Ga. Edn. Assn., S. Atlantic Modern Lang. Assn., Alpha Kappa Psi, Phi Eta Sigma, Kappa Phi Kappa, Sigma Nu. Home: 2077 Fairhaven Circle Atlanta GA 30305

ENGLAND, WALTER DONALD, coll. dean; b. Elm Store, Ark., Oct. 10, 1919; s. Marion Nixon and Dora (Hall) E.; B.S. in Edn., Ark. State Coll., 1949; M.S. in Edn., U. Miss., 1953; postgrad. U. Colo., 1956, U. Miss., 1957-63; m. Louise Horner, June 3, 1951; children—Cynthia, Janie, Amber Dawn. Tchr. elementary schs., Couch, Mo., 1941-42, Elm Store, Ark., 1942-45; coach, bus. tchr., Paragould, Ark., 1945-47; prin. schs., Paragould, 1947-50; supt. Cash (Ark.) High Sch., 1950-55, Alton (Mo.) High Sch., 1955-64; dean Ark. State Coll., Beebe, 1964—. Mem. White County Community Action Program. Mem. Orgen County Adminstrs. Assn. (pres. 1960—), Ark. Jr. Coll. Assn. (v.p. 1969-70), Kappa Delta Pi. Baptist (deacon; tchr. Sunday sch. and tng. union, mem. ch. pulpit com., bldg. com. 1970—). Kiwanian (pres. 1967, bd. mem. 1968). Home: Center St Beebe AR 72012

ENGLE, JOE H., astronaut; b. Abilene, Kan., Aug. 26, 1932; s. Abner Ethan and Margaret (Beaver) E.; B.S. in Aero. Engring., U. Kan., 1955; m. Mary Catherine Lawrence, Oct. 6, 1956; children—Laurie Jo, Jon Lawrence. Commd. 2d lt. USAF, 1956, advanced through grades to lt. col.; fighter pilot, George AFB, Cal., 1957-61, fighter test pilot, Edwards AFB, Cal., 1962-63, X-15 rocket research pilot NASA/USAF, Edwards AFB, 1963-66, astronaut Manned Spacecraft Center, NASA, Houston, 1966—. Recipient Lawrence Sperry award Am. Inst. Aeros. and Astronautics, 1966, Air Pioneer award, 1966; named Outstanding Young Officer, USAF, 1964, One of Ten Outstanding Young Men of Am., 1964. Mem. Soc. Exptl. Test Pilots, Aviation Hall of Fame, U.S. Jr. C. of C., Theta Tau. Methodist. Home: 1906 Back Bay Ct Houston TX 77058 Office: Manned Spacecraft Center NASA Houston TX 77058

ENGLER, LESTER, govt. ofcl.; b. N.Y.C., Oct. 29, 1914; s. Max and Dora (Bernfeld) E.; B.A., N.Y. U., 1938, J.D., 1938; m. Patricia S. Eary, Sept. 26, 1956; children—Pamela Jo, Paula Ann (Mrs. Donald Powell). Practiced law, 1939-70; U.S. atty. for Dist. C.Z., Ancon, 1970—. Mem. Legacy Bequest Com. Nat. Jewish Hosp., Phoenix; chmn. Maricopa County (Ariz.) Air Pollution Hearing Bd., 1970. A founder, bd. dirs. Camp Tatiyee, Ariz.; bd. dirs. Jewish Community Center, Phoenix, 1969, Melvin Jones Blind Center, Phoenix, 1970. Served with USNR, 1942-46; ETO, PTO. Mem. Am., Maricopa County, Fed. bar assns., Am. Trial Lawyers Assn. Republican. Mason (Shriner), Lion (recipient certificates of appreciation). Home: 104 Balboa Heights Balboa Canal Zone Office: District Court House Ancon Canal Zone

ENGLER, RICHARD EMIL, JR., social scientist; b. Los Angeles, Dec. 31, 1925; s. Richard E. and Janet (Thompson) E.; B.A., U. Cal. at Los Angeles, 1949; M.A., U. So. Cal., 1953, Ph.D., 1957. Research sociologist Child Welfare League Am., N.Y., 1957-59; human factors scientist Ramo-Wooldridge, Denver, 1959-60; social scientist System Devel. Corp., Falls Church, Va., 1961-65; cons. Greenleigh Assos., Inc., N.Y., 1966-67, Systemetrics, 1968—; sr. research scientist Human Scis. Research, Inc., 1967-68; dir. research Koba Enterprises, Washington, 1969-70; sr. asso. Roy Littlejohn Assos., Inc., Washington, 1970—. Bd. dirs. Washington Ghetto Indsl. Devel. Corp. Served with AUS, 1944-46, 50-52. Fellow Am. Sociol. Assn., Soc. Applied Anthropology; mem. A.A.A.S., Internat. Platform Assn. Author: The Challenge of Diversity, 1964; (with Henry S. Maas) Children in Need of Parents, 1959. Home: 4921 Seminary Rd Alexandria VA 22311

ENGLERT, ROY THEODORE, govt. ofcl., lawyer; b. Nashville, Sept. 11, 1922; s. Roy T. and Ruth Rowe (Tindall) E.; B.A., Vanderbilt U., 1943; LL.B., Columbia, 1951; LL.M., George Washington U., 1953; m. Helen Frances Wiggs, Sept. 25, 1948; children—Lee Ann, Roy Theodore. Asst. supr. Nat. Life & Accident Ins. Co., Nashville; admitted to Tenn. bar, 1951, D.C. bar, 1952, also Supreme Ct. bar; asst. counsel Office Comptroller of Currency, U.S. Treasury Dept., 1951-58, chief counsel, 1958-62, asst. gen. counsel of dept., 1962-66, dep. gen. counsel, 1966—. Mem. Sr. Seminar in Fgn. Policy, Dept. State, 1963—; lectr., writer on banking law. Served from apprentice seaman to lt. USNR, 1943-46. Mem. Fed., Am., Tenn. bar assns. Presbyn. Clubs: Nat. Lawyers (Wash ington); Springfield Golf and Country. Home: 6720 Bellamy Av Springfield VA 22152 Office: Main Treasury Bldg Washington DC 20224

ENGLES, ROBERT EVERET, surgeon; b. Henryetta, Okla., Aug. 21, 1929; s. Earl Franklin and Lily Florence (Lawson) E.; B.S., Southeastern State Coll., 1950; M.D., U. Okla., 1954; m. Phyllis Maria Pyrum, Dec. 22, 1962; children—Ann Elaine, Robert Everet. Intern Wayne County Gen. Hosp., Eloise, Mich., 1954-55; resident in gen. surgery Dallas Meth. Hosp., 1957-59, chief resident, 1960-61; practice medicine, Durant, Okla., 1959-60, specializing in gen. surgery, 1961—. Served with USPHS, 1955-57. Fellow A.C.S.; mem. A.M.A., Okla. State Med. Assn., Atoka-Bryan-Coal County Med. Soc. (pres. 1965-66), U. Okla. Med. Sch. Alumni Assn. (pres.-elect) C. of C., Sigma Tau Gamma. Democrat. Presbyn. Kiwanian. Home: Star Route Durant OK 74701 Office: 323 Waco St Durant OK 74701

ENGLESMITH, GEORGE, architect, indsl. designer; b. Liverpool, Eng., May 31, 1914; s. George and Agnes Beatrice (Dean) E.; B.Arch., Liverpool U., 1937; m. Lydia Julia Johnson-Briet, Sept. 9, 1939; children—Suzelle, Tejas. Came to U.S., 1920, naturalized, 1962. Chief asst. to archtl. adviser to dir. of works Ministry of Works, U.K., 1938-46; prin. G. Englesmith Asso., 1946-52; project designer J.B. Parkin Assos., 1952-54; partner Kohl & Englesmith, 1954-56; project architect Wyatt Hedrick; 1957-59; project designer Frank Dill, 1960-62; project architect Manned Spacecraft Center, NASA, 1962; asso. Floyd & James, 1962-65; design cons. Rustay, Martin, Vale, Architects, Houston, 1965-68; pvt. practice architect, planning and design cons., Houston, 1968—. U.S. del. Internat. Council Socs. Indsl. Design, London, Eng., 1969. Sec.-treas. Brit. Benevolent Fund Com., Tex., 1962—; mem. adv. com. U. Houston, 1956—. Coronation medalist, 1953. Registered architect Nat. Council Archtl. Registration Bds. Fellow Royal Soc. Arts (life); mem. Tex. Soc. Architects, Archtl. Assn. London, Soc. Indsl. Artists and Designers, Assn. Canadian Indsl. Designers, Royal Inst. Brit. Architects, Royal Archtl. Inst. Can., Tex. Hosp. Assn. Office: 7839 Fondren Houston TX 77036

ENGLISH, GEORGE W(ASHINGTON), lawyer; b. Vienna, Ill., Feb. 19, 1898; s. George W. and Lillie May (Farris) E.; B.S., U. Ill., 1921; LL.B., Harvard, 1924; Dr. Humanities, Nova U. Advanced Tech.; m. Alma R. Witt, Sept. 11, 1935; 1 son (by previous marriage), George W. III. Admitted to Fla. bar, 1925; sr. mem. English, McCaughan & O'Bryan; chmn. bd. First Nat. Bank, Ft. Lauderdale, Fla., Guaranty First Nat. Bank, Ft. Lauderdale, Plantation 1st Nat. Bank (Fla.); chmn. Consol. Bankshares Fla., Inc., First Fed. Savs. & Loan Assn. of Broward County (Fla.), Fla. Power & Light Co., Wright & Putnam, Inc., Caulley Steel & Supply Co., Harbor Beach Cos., State dir. Orange Bowl Com., 1958-68; trustee U. Fla. Endowment Fund, 1959-69, Nova U., 1964-69; mem. bd. control Fla. Instns. of Higher Learning, 1952-55, Mem. Ft. Lauderdale Hist. Soc. (trustee), So. Fla. Econ. Soc. (dir.). Rotarian. Clubs: Harvard (Ft. Lauderdale); 100 of Broward County; Lauderdale Yacht; University (N.Y.C.). Home: 1636 SW 15th Av Ft Lauderdale FL 33312 Office: First Fed Bldg Ft Lauderdale FL 33301

ENGLISH, JAMES STEPHEN, city ofcl.; b. Jacksonville, Fla., Aug. 11, 1925; s. Connie C. and Leah C. (Yongue) E.; B.S., The Citadel, 1951; m. Betty Duncan, July 7, 1946; children—Stephen Craig, James Martin. Jr. engr., City of Jacksonville, 1951-53, asst. engr., 1953-60, civil engr., 1960-65, asst. city engr., 1965-68, dir. pub. works, 1968—. Served with USAAF, 1943-45. Mem. Fla. Engring Soc. (chpt. pres. 1964-65), Am. Pub. Works Assn. (dist. rep. 1966-68), Inst. Municipal Engrs. (mem. exec. council 1970-73). Home: 2326 Hirsch Av Jacksonville FL 32216 Office: 220 E Bay St Jacksonville FL 32202

ENGLISH, JOE HAL, cons. engr.; b. Hamilton, Tex., May 7, 1920; s. Jesse Dee and Betty (Roberts) E.; B.S., Tex. A. and M. U., 1941; m. Winifred Byrom, Dec. 7, 1941 children—Virginia (Mrs. William H. Traynham), Betty Lynn. Self-employed mech. contractor engr., Abilene, Tex., 1949-58; self-employed cons. engr. surveyor, Abilene, 1958-65, San Antonio, 1965—; tech. writer, 1958—. Committeeman Chisholm Trail council Boy Scouts Am.; pres. Varsi-teen Club, 1961. Served as ensign USNR, World War II. Registered profl. engr., pub. surveyor, Tex. Mem. Nat. Soc. profl. Engrs., Am. Ordnance Assn., Am. Water Works Assn., Am. Soc. Heating Refrigeration and Air-Conditioning Engrs., Tex. Surveyors Assn., Internat. Platform Assn. Baptist (deacon). Clubs: Nat. Writers; Kiwanis, Contbr. to nat. mags. Home: 1706 Timber Oak San Antonio TX 78232

ENGLISH, ROBERT GOODRICH, supt. schs.; b. Belton, S.C., Dec. 9, 1932; s. John Waymon and Grace (McAllistor) E.; B.S., Eriskine U., 1955; M.Ed., U. S.C., 1964; m. Nancy Juanita Malone, Apr. 29, 1955; children— Patti Darlene, Robert Mark, John Steven. Tchr., Mount Zion High Sch., Winnsboro, S.C., 1958-61, prin., 1961-64; prin. Edito High Sch., Cordova, 1964-69, McCormick (S.C.) High Sch., 1969; supt. Swansea (S.C.) Pub. Schs., 1969—. Served with AUS, 1955-57. Mem. McCormick County Tchrs. Assn. (pres. 1966-67). Lion. Address: Box 128 Swansea SC 29160

ENGLISH, RONALD WILLIAM, clergyman; b. Atlanta, Feb. 20, 1944; s. Jethro and Auretha (Jolly) E.; B.A., Morehouse Coll., 1967; student Andover Newton Theol. Sch., 1968-69, Interdenom. Theol. Center, 1966—; m. Myrtolyn Jones, Jan. 15, 1967; 1 dau., Rondalyn Kristia. Ordained to ministry Baptist Ch.; asst. minister, youth adviser Ebenezer Bapt. Ch., Atlanta, 1966—; dir. pub. relations and alumni affairs Interdenom. Theol. Center, Atlanta, 1969—. Mem. commn. theology Nat. Com. Black Churchmen. Mem. Soc. Bib. Lit., Alpha Phi Alpha. Home: 1881 Bayberry Dr SW Atlanta GA 30311 Office: 671 Beckwith St SW Atlanta GA 30314

ENGLUND, GOSTA, chem. co. exec.; b. Ramvik, Sweden, May 12, 1908 (came to U.S. 1926, naturalized 1932); s. Karl Oscar and Ida Kristina (Nyberg) E.; student Ramviks Folkhogskola (Sweden), Pratt Inst.; m. Joan Marie Epperson, Sept. 20, 1945. Sales mgr. and v.p. Prior Chem. Co., N.Y.C., 1940-58; v.p. F.H. Ross & Co., Charlotte, N.C., 1958-71; v.p. Ashland Chem. Co., Columbus, O., 1971—. Served with U.S. Army, 1942-45. Mem. Chem. Salesmens Assn. N.Y., Chemists Club N.Y., Sky Club N.Y. Republican. Lutheran. Clubs: Siwanoy Country (Bronxville, N.Y.); Boca Raton Country. Home: 701 E Camino Real Boca Raton FL 33432 Office: 410 Park Av New York City NY 10022

ENGLUND, RALPH CALDWELL, constrn. co. exec.; b. Gaffrey, S.C., Mar. 29, 1925; s. Carl G. and Anna (Hall) E.; B.S. in C.E., Ga. Inst. Tech., 1945; m. Sallie Bozier Allen, Nov. 26, 1949; children—John, Susan, Virginia. With Daniel Internat. Corp., Inc., Birmingham, Ala., 1946—, estimator, project mgr., 1946-54, asst. div. mgr., 1954-58, div. mgr., 1958-62, v.p., 1962—; v.p. Daniel Realty Corp., Birmingham, 1970—. Served with USNR, 1943-46. Mem. Am. Mgmt. Assn. Methodist. Kiwanian. Home: 2901 Warrington Rd Birmingham AL 35223 Office: 1900 Daniel Bldg Birmingham AL 35233

ENGMAN, LEWIS AUGUST, lawyer; b. Grand Rapids, Mich., Jan. 6, 1936; s. H. Sigurd and Florence (Lewis) E.; A.B., U. Mich., 1957; postgrad. London Sch. Econs., Univ. Coll., Eng., 1957-58; LL.B., Harvard, 1961; m. Jacqueline Ransford Graham, Sept. 16, 1961; children— Geoffrey Ponton, Jonathan Lewis. Admitted to Mich. bar, 1961, D.C. bar, 1971, also U.S. Ct. Appeals 6th Circuit bar, U.S. Supreme Ct. bar, U.S. Tax Ct. bar; practiced in Grand Rapids, 1961—; asso. Warner, Norcross & Judd, 1961-65, partner, 1965—, on leave of absence, 1970—; lawyer, gen. counsel Office Consumer Affairs, White House, Washington, 1970—. Dir. Interpreter Pub. Co., Grand Rapids, 1968-70, Clarino Sales Corp. Am., Rockford, Mich. 1967-70. Chmn. Kent County Health Planning Unit, 1969-70; mem. Greater Grand Rapids Areaurde Comprehensive Health Planning Unit, 1969-70. Mem. Mich. Young Republican Bd. Control, 1955-57, Kent County Rep. Finance Com., 1965. Pres., bd. dirs. Grand Rapids Symphony Soc., 1968-70; sec. Dyer-Ives Found.; bd. dirs. Opera Assn. Western Mich., 1969; trustee Blodgett Meml. Hosp., 1968—, sec., 1969-70; mem. Grand Valley Coll. Friends of Art Adv. Bd. Mem. Am., Grand Rapids bar assns., State Bar Mich., Soc. Hosp. Attys., Am. Hosp. Assn., 6th Circuit Jud. Conf., Harvard Law Sch. Alumni Council on Placement, Phi Beta Kappa, Delta Sigma Rho, Phi Kappa Phi, Phi Eta Sigma. Presbyn. Rotarian. Clubs: Kent Country, University, Athletic (all Grand Rapids). Home: 2731 Oakwood Dr SE Grand Rapids MI 49506 also 6016 Claiborne Dr McLean VA 22101 Office: Gen Counsel Office Consumer Affairs Washington DC 20506

ENIX, (AGNES) LUCILLE, mag. editor; b. Drummond, Okla., Jan. 17, 1933; d. James Robert and Alma (Hodges) Enix; B.S., Okla. State U., 1955; M.S., Northwestern U., 1966. Dietetic intern VA Hosp., Los Angeles, 1955-56, staff dietician, 1956-57; nutritionist Dairy Council of Greater Kansas City, Mo., 1957-61; asso. dir. materials devel. dept. Nat. Dairy Council, Chgo., 1961-65; reporter, features writer Chgo. Tribune, 1966-67; copywriter Rogers & Smith Advt. Agts., Dallas, 1967-68; editor Dallas mag. Dallas C. of C., 1968—. Mem. com. Wednesday Noon Forum program, Dallas, 1969—. Recipient Southwest Journalism Forum award, 1970, Journalism award Tex. Med. Assn., 1971. Mem. Am. Dietetic Assn. Theta Sigma Phi (Matrix award 1971), Omicron Nu, Phi Upsilon Omicron, Alpha Delta Pi. Club: Dallas Press (dir., sec.). Home: 2622 Highland Rd Dallas TX 75228 Office: 1507 Pacific Av Dallas TX 75201

ENO, CHARLES FRANKLIN, educator; b. Atwater, O., May 21, 1920; s. Clarence and Alice (Rhoads) E.; B.S., Ohio State U., 1942, M.S., 1948; Ph.D., Purdue U., 1951; m. Fern Alea Imler, Sept. 8, 1948; children—Charles Franklin, Mark Imler. Asst. prof. dept. soils U. Fla., 1951, 1952-56, asso. prof. 1956-63, prof., 1963—, chmn. dept. soils, 1965—. Served as capt. AUS, 1942-46, 1951-52. Decorated Bronze Star medal. Fellow Am. Soc. Agronomy; mem. Fla. State Hort. Soc., Soil and Crop Sci. Soc. Fla., Res. Officers Assn., Gamma Sigma Delta, Alpha Gamma Sigma, Phi Sigma, Sigma Xi. Methodist. Club: Gainesville Golf and Country. Home: 600 NW 36th Terrace Gainesville FL 32601

ENSENAT, LOUIS ALBERT, physician; b. Merida, Mexico, Oct. 24, 1916; s. Frank and Guadalupe F. (Ensenat) E.; B.S., Tulane U., 1937, M.D., 1941; M.Sc. in Medicine, U. Pa., 1953; m. Ruth Ogden, July 9, 1943; children—Gloria Louise, Tinita Ruth, Louis Albert, Rita Joan, Barbara Jean, Michael Monroe. Intern, Charity Hosp., New Orleans, 1941-42; resident surgery Charity Hosp., Monroe, La., 1942,

Lakeshore Hosp., New Orleans, VA hosp., New Orleans, Batavia, N.Y.; fellow in surg. pathology Tulane U. Sch. Med.; preceptership in surgery Biloxi (Miss.) VA Hosp.; staff surg. VA Hosp., Montgomery, 1946-52; pvt. practice surgery, Pasadena, Tex., 1952-63, New Orleans, 1963-—; adminstr. Mercy Hosp. Pasadena, 1954-63, chief surgery, 1954-63. Founder, dir. Gulf Coast Home Bulders, Inc. Trustee Big State Factors Corp. Served from lt. (j.g.) to lt. comdr. USN, 1942-46. Decorated Purple Heart. Diplomate Am. Bd. Surgery, Am. Bd. Abdominal Surgery. Fellow French Soc. Phlebology, Am. Coll. Angliology (v.p.); mem. Hawthorne Surg. Soc., Am. Soc. Abdominal Surgeons, N.Y. Acad. Scis., Am. Med. Writers' Assn. Author articles in field. Home: 7630 Jeannette Pl New Orleans LA 70118 Office: 2839 Gen Pershing New Orleans LA 70115

ENSMINGER, JOHN FREDRIC, apparel mfg. co. exec.; b. Chgo., Jan. 8, 1924; s. Fred and Clara Viola (Kliebenstein) E.; student New Eng. Conservatory Music, 1942-43; A.B., Brown U., 1949; m. Katherine Hyde Hedberg, Oct. 16, 1944; children—John Fredric, Jeffrey A., James A. Dist. sales mgr. closure div., Waterbury, Conn. dist. Socvill Mfg. Co., Greensboro, N.C., 1949-66; dir., pres., chief exec. officer, treas. Anderson Bros., Inc., Danville, Va., 1966-—. Mem. devel. council Stratford Coll. Bd. dirs., treas. Apparel Research Found., Washington, Danville chpt. A.R.C. Served with USAAF, World War II. Decorated Air medal with two oak leafs. Mem. Am. Inst. Indsl. Engrs., Am. Apparel Mfrs. Assn., Va. Mfrs. Assn., Central Va. Industries, Va., Danville chambers commerce, Brown Football Assn. Rotarian. Club: Danville Golf. Home: PO Box 2071 Danville VA 24541 Office: 506 Floyd St Box 800 Danville VA 24541

ENSMINGER, LUTHER GLENN, govt. ofcl.; b. Mt. Perry, O., Oct. 17, 1919; s. Charles Henry and Mary E. (Koehler) E.; B.S. in Bus. Adminstrn., Ohio State U., 1942, B.S. in Food Tech. cum laude, 1948; m. Jean Couch, May 12, 1951; children—Luther Glenn, Douglas, Phillip, Deborah. Chemist FDA, Cin., 1948-56, Los Angeles, 1956-59, methods research coordinator, Washington, 1959-—. Sec. Lee-Ballston Citizens Assn., 1965-—. Served with AUS, 1942-45. Fellow Assn. Ofcl. Analytical Chemists (exec. sec. 1967-—); mem. P.T.A., Capitol Dance Soc., Beta Gamma Sigma. Presbyn. (chmn. bd. trustees; elder). Contbr. articles to profl. jours. Home: 1407 N Lincoln St Arlington VA 22201 Office: FDA 200 C St SW Washington DC 20204

ENSTAM, RAYMOND ANDERS, lawyer; b. New Britain, Conn., Apr. 1, 1937; s. Reuben Anders and Rita Margaret (Belleveau) E.; student Trinity Coll., 1956-58; B.A., Marietta Coll., 1960; J.D., Duke U., 1963; LL.M., N.Y. U., 1968; m. Mary Elizabeth York, Aug. 6, 1963; 1 dau., Gwendolyn Elizabeth. Admitted to N.Y. State bar, 1964, Tex. bar, 1969; practiced in Dallas, 1971-—; atty. investment div. Met. Life Ins. Co., N.Y.C., 1963-68; gen. counsel, sec. Data Automation Co., Inc., 1968-71, gen. counsel, 1968-—; dir., v.p., sec., gen. counsel Worldcom, Inc., Dallas. Mem. Am., Tex. bar assns. Home: 4132 Lomita Lane Dallas TX 75220 Office: First Nat Bank Bldg Dallas TX 75202

EPHRAIM, CHARLES, lawyer; b. Chgo., Sept. 18, 1924; s. Max H. and Margaret (O'Neil) E.; Ph.B., U. Chgo., 1948, J.D., 1951; m. Marguerite Marie Lamont, Dec. 23, 1944 children—Linda Patrice, Charles Lamont. Admitted to D.C. bar, 1951; gen. practice, Washington, 1951-—; asso. Posner, Berge, Fox & Arent, 1951-53; mem. firm Layne & Ephraim, 1953-56; gen. practice, 1956-69; mem. firm Ephraim & Clark, 1969-—. Sec.-dir. Herner & Co. Served to 1st lt. USAAF, 1943-47. Mem. Am. Bar Assn., Motor Carrier Lawyers Assn., Order of Coif, Phi Beta Kappa. Contbr. articles profl. jours. Home: 5604 Western Av Chevy Chase MD 20015 Office: 1250 Connecticut Av NW Washington DC 20036

EPPS, AUGUSTUS CHARLES, lawyer; b. Richmond, Va., Feb. 2, 1916; s. John Lindsey and Lily Madeline (Becker) E.; B.S., U. Va., 1936, LL.B., 1938; m. Rosalie Suzanne Garrett, Aug. 17, 1946; children—Augustus Charles, George Garrett, John Daniel. Admitted to Va. bar, 1937; practice in Richmond, 1938-42, 46-—; asso. atty. Christian, Barton & Parker, 1938-42; partner Christian, Barton, Parker, Epps & Brent, 1946-—. Dir., gen. counsel Richmond Life Ins. Co.; dir. Universal Acceptance Corp., Universal Finance Co., Newsome Air Conditioning Co., Va. Suppliers Inc., Community Heating & Air Conditioning Co., Inc. Mem. Richmond Sch. Bd. 1964-—. Past pres. bd. dirs. Friends Richmond Pub. Library; vice chmn., bd. dirs. Richmond YMCA; bd. dirs. Richmond Library, Richmond Citizens Assn.; bd. dirs. exec. com. Legal Aid Soc. Met. Richmond. Served to maj. AUS, 1942-46. Fellow Am. Coll. Trial Lawyers; mem. Am. (past chmn. com. legal edn., admission to bar), Va. State (pres. 1966-67, past chmn. joint com. legislation, law reform, mem. exec. com.), Richmond (past pres.) bar assns., Am. Judicature Soc., Internat. Assn. Ins. Counsel, Assn. Life Ins. Counsel, Fed. Jud. Conf., U. Va. Law Sch. Assn. (mem. council, chmn. com. scholarships), Order Coif, Phi Beta Kappa, Phi Delta Phi, Alpha Tau Omega. Episcopalian. Bd. editors, bd. mng. editors Va. Law Review, 1937-38. Contbr. articles to profl. jours. Home: 6323 Ridgeway Rd Richmond VA 23226 Office: 909 E Main St Richmond VA 23219

EPPS, JAMES HAWS, III, lawyer; b. Johnson City, Tenn., Sept. 15, 1936; s. James H. and Anne (Sessoms) E.; grad. Episcopal High Sch., Alexandria, Va., 1955; B.A. U. N.C., 1959; J.D., Vanderbilt U., 1962; m. Nancy Jane Atkinson, Nov. 30, 1958; children—James Haws IV, Sara Stuart. Admitted to Tenn. bar, 1962, U.S. Supreme Ct., 1967, other fed. cts.; now partner Epps, Powell, Weller, Taylor &Miller, Johnson City, Tenn. City atty. Johnson City, 1967-—. Dir. Farmers & Mchts. Bank, Limestone, Tenn. Mem. Tenn. Law Revision Commn., 1970-71. Mem. budget com. United Fund, Johnson City, 1964-68, now mem. bd. dirs.; mem. Appalachian council Girl Scouts Am., legal adviser, 1969-—; mem. Civil Def. Adv. Bd. Mem. county exec. com. Democratic party. Bd. dirs. Tenn. Mental Health Assn, Washington County Mental Health Assn., Salvation Army. Mem. Am., Tenn. (mem. continuing legal edn. com.), Washington County (past pres.) bar assns., Am. Judicature Soc., Tenn. Municipal Attys. Assn., Assn. Interstate Commerce Commn. Practitioners (mem. com. profl. ethics and grievances), Motor Carrier Lawyers' Assn. (bd. govs. Transp. Law Jour.), Am. Counsel Assn., Nat. Assn. R.R. Trial Counsel, Nat. Inst. Municipal Law Officers, C. of C. (govtl. affairs com.), Tenn. Taxpayers Assn., Internat. Platform Assn., Nat. Legal Aid Defender Assn., Tipton Haynes Hist. Assn. (dir.), Phi Delta Phi, Phi Delta Theta. Episcopalian (vestryman, 1965-68, 70-71, clk. 1968, 70, 71, layreader). Kiwanian, Elk (legal counsel 1963-67). Clubs: North Johnson City Business (dir., pres. 1966-67), Hurstleigh, Johnson City Country; Nat. Lawyers, Unaka Rod and Gun, Highland Stable. Home: 1222 Ridgeway Rd Johnson City TN 37601 Office: 2101 N Roan St Johnson City TN 37601

EPSTEIN, ARTHUR WILLIAM, physician, educator; b. N.Y.C. May 15, 1923; s. Jacob E. and Anne (Bass) E.; A.B. Columbia, 1944, M.D., 1947; m. Leona Cruce, Mar. 2, 1955; children—David Byron, Nona Kathryn, Emily Vera, James Jacob. Intern, Mt. Sinai Hosp., N.Y.C., 1947-48, resident, 1949-50; clin. asst. Norristown (Pa.) State Hosp., 1948-49; faculty Tulane U., New Orleans, 1954-—, asso. prof. psychiatry and neurology, 1959-64, prof., 1964-—; pvt. practice medicine, specializing in neuropsychiatry, New Orleans, 1954-—; vis. physician Charity Hosp., New Orleans, 1951-—; cons. U.S. Army Hosp., New Orleans, 1958-64, VA Hosp., New Orleans, 1969-—. Med. adviser Social Security Adminstrn., 1968-—. Bd. dirs. Ednl. Research and Treatment Center, New Orelans. Served with M.C., USNR, 1956-58. Fellow Am. Psychiat. Assn. (leisure time and its uses com.), Am. Acad. Psychoanalysis, A.A.A.S., Am. Acad. Neurology; mem. Soc. Biol. Psychiatry, Soc. Clin. Neurologists, Soc. for Neurosci., Am. Epilepsy Soc., Alpha Omega Alpha. Author: An Anatomist's Dream of Love, 1966. Contbr. articles profl. jours. Home: 1664 Robert St New Orleans LA 70115 Office: 1430 Tulane Av New Orleans LA 70112

EPSTEIN, BARRY RONALD, assn. exec.; b. N.Y.C., Mar. 22, 1942; s. Irving H. and Libby F. (Ertel) E.; B.S., Kent State U., 1964; m. Judy L. Stender, Jan. 19, 1964; children—Larry Marc, Lori Ann. Promotion mgr. White Plains (N.Y.) C. of C., 1964-66; asst. mgr. Ypsilanti (Mich.) C. of C., 1966-67; exec. v.p. Warren County (Pa.) C. of C., 1967-71, Greater Hollywood (Fla.) C. of C., 1971-—. Mem. Am., Fla. assns. C. of C. execs., Am. Retail Assn. Execs. (dir. 1970-72). Office: 330 N Federal Hwy Hollywood FL 33022

EPSTEIN, ELENI SAKES (MRS. SIDNEY EPSTEIN), editor; b. Washington, May 17,, 1925; d. Constantine and Aspasia (Economon) Sakes; student George Washington U., 1943-45, Columbia, 1947;; m. Sidney Epstein, Mar. 30, 1957. Copygirl, women's staff writer Washington Star, 1945-46, fashion editor, 1946-—. Recipient J.C. Penney Fashion Writing award U. Mo., 1961, citation Nat. Women's Party, 1966. Mem. Washington Fashion Group, Advt. Club Washington, Women's Nat. Press Club (sec. 1949-50), Am. Newspaper Women's Club (v.p. 1952-54). Greek Orthodox. Home: 2807 Cathedral Av NW Washington DC 20008 Office: 225 Virginia Av SE Washington DC 20003

EPSTEIN, FREDERICK, real estate exec.; b. N.Y.C., Jan. 2, 1924; s. Harold H. and Theresa (Friedman) E.; B.S., U. Mich., 1947; m. Joan Hewitt, Sept. 10, 1952; 1 dau., Terrie. Founder, chief exec. officer Devel. Internat. Corp., L.I., N.Y., 1949-55, San Juan, P.R., 1955-71, Coral Gables, Fla., 1971-—; pres., chmn. bd. Devel. Internat. Corp., Coral Gables, 1962-—. Served to 2d lt. USAAF, 1943-46. Mem. Young Presidents Orgn. (past chmn. Carribean chpt.), Nat. Assn. Home Builders. Home: 660 Arvida Pkwy Coral Gables FL 33156 Office: 2801 Ponce de Leon Blvd Coral Gables FL 33134

EPSTEIN, SIDNEY, editor; b. Wilmington, Del., Oct. 11, 1920; s. Abraham and Ida (Kelrick) E.; student George Washington U., 1937-41;; m. Eleni Sakes, Mar. 30 1957; 1 dau., Diane. With Washington Herald, 1937-54; city editor Washington Times-Herald, 1952-54; city editor Washington Star, 1958-68, asst. mng. editor, 1968-—. Served to capt. USMC, 1942-46. Home: 2807 Cathedral Av NW Washington DC 20008 Office: 2d and Virginia Av SE Washington DC 20003

ERBELE, LEO ALBERT, physician; b. Mandan, N.D., Jan 8, 1927; s. Albert Frederick and Anna (Goldmann) E.; student Creighton U., 1944-45; B.A., U. N.D., 1949, B.S., 1950; M.D., Bowman Gray Sch. Medicine, 1952; m. Marian Cooper, June 3, 1950; children—John, Olivia, Peter, Mary. Intern City Hosp., Winston-Salem, N.C., 1952-53; gen. practice medicine, Clover, S.C., 1953-54, Marion, N.C., 1954-55; residency tng. Bowman Gray Sch. Medicine, Winston-Salem, 1955-59; asso. pathologist Macon (Ga.) Hosp., 1959-61, dir. labs., 1961-65; now engaged in pvt. practice. Served as sgt. USAAF, 1945-47. Diplomate in anatomic pathology and clin. pathology Am. Bd. Pathology, Am. Bd. Nuclear Medicine. Fellow Am. Soc. Clin. Pathologists, Coll. Am. Pathologists; mem. A.M.A., So. Med. Assn., Soc. Nuclear Medicine. Home: 3379 Osborne Pl Macon GA 31204 Office: 1021 Daisy Park Macon GA 31208

ERBS, HAROLD JOHN, chem.-mineral co. exec.; b. St. Louis, Mar. 31, 1932; s. Oliver F. and Louise Irene (Rolves) E.; B.S. in Accounting, St. Louis U., 1954; m. Marilyn L. Metcalf, Feb. 6, 1954; children—Susan Marie, James, Mary Lou. Accountant, Price Waterhouse & Co., St. Louis, 1956-57; systems analyst Mississippi River Fuel Corp., 1957-58; with Milchem, Inc., Houston, 1958-—, v.p., treas., adminstrv. v.p., 1966-—, also dir.; dir. Oleum, Inc. (formerly Trice Prodn. Co.), Longview, Tex., Galleria Bank, Houston. Chmn. Houston Diocesan Financial Adv. Bd., 1971-72. Served with AUS, 1954-56. Mem. Financial Execs. Inst., Mensa. Roman Catholic. Lion (pres. 1966). Clubs: St. Louis University; Westbury Civic (pres. 1961), Meyerland (pres. 1972)(Houston). Home: 5130 Braesheather St Houston TX 77035 Office: PO Box 22111 Houston TX 77027

ERDEY, MICHAEL ROLAND ALEXANDER, educator; b. Mezobereny, Hungary, Oct. 2, 1927; s. Andras and Magdolna (Eiler) E.; M.S. in Math., Physics, Sci., U. Szeged, Hungary, 1952; Ph.D. in Elec. Engring., U. Leeds (Eng.), 1959; m. Eva S.L. Varga, Apr. 28, 1956; children— Violet Ildiko, Raymond Michael Atilla, Edward Robert Zoltan. Came to U.S., 1960, naturalized, 1966. Observer, evaluator seismol. measurements Eotvos Lorand Geophys. Inst., Budapest, Hungary, 1951-53; head field group Water Research Inst., Budapest, 1954; research asst. elec. engring. dept. U. Leeds, 1957-60; asst. prof. elec. engring. Mich. State U., East Lansing, 1960-63; prof. elec. engring. Tuskegee (Ala.) Inst., 1963-—, head dept., 1963-69. Bd. dirs. Polish-Hungarian Fedn. Registered profl. engr. Mem. I.E.E.E., (sr.), Am. Soc. Engring. Edn., Ala. Acad. Sci., A.A.A.S., Sigma Xi, Eta Kappa Nu. Home: PO Box 357 Oslin Dr Route 1 Box 19 Tuskegee AL 36083

ERDREICH, BENJAMIN LEADER, state legislator; b. Birmingham, Ala., Dec. 9, 1938; s. Stanley M. and Corinne (Leader) E.; B.A., Yale, 1960; J.D., U. Ala., 1963; m. Ellen Cooper, May 30, 1965; children—Jeremy Cooper, Anna Bethia. Admitted to Ala. bar, 1963; asso. Kaye, Scholer, Fierman, Hays & Handler, N.Y.C., 1965-66; partner Cooper, Mitch & Crawford, Birmingham, Ala., 1967-—; mem. Ala. Ho. of Reps., 1970-—. Served to 1st. lt. AUS, 1963-65. Mem. Am., Ala., Birmingham bar assns. Home: 4326 Kennesaw Dr Birmingham AL 35213 Office: 409 N 21st St Birmingham AL 35203

ERFFT, KENNETH REYNDERS, ednl. adminstr.; b. Chgo., Nov. 14, 1908; s. Victor Athen and Ethel (Reynders) E.; A.B., No. Mich. U.; 1932; M.A., U. Richmond, 1936, D.S.C., 1967; Litt.D., Maclean College, 1947; LL.D., No. Mich. U., 1961; m. Nancy Fontaine Creath, June 8, 1940. Instr. Ironwood (Mich.) High Sch., 1932-34; clk. bd. edn. Petersburg (Va.) pub. schs., 1936-42; bus. mgr. Furman U., Greenville, S.C., 1946-54; comptroller Pa. State U., 1954-57; v.p., treas. Rutgers State U., 1957-62, Thomas Jefferson U., 1962-64; pres. Kenneth R. Erfft Assos., Inc., ednl. cons., Phila. 1964-66; v.p. Duquesne U., Pitts., 1966-72; exec. dir. Nationwide Conf. Edn. Centers, Inc., Atlanta, 1972-—. Chmn. bd. dirs. Afuture Fund, Afortress Fund. Mem. adminstrv. com. for Cal. and Western Conf. Cost and Statis. Study, 1955-57. Served from lt. (j.g.) to comdr. USNR, 1942-46. Mem. Eastern Assn. Coll. and U. Bus. Officers (pres.), Am. Assn. U. Profs., Middle States Assn., Delta Sigma Phi, Phi Epsilon, Tau Kappa Alpha, Omicron Delta Kappa, Theta Omicron Rho. Clubs: International Torch, University (Pitts.). Co-author: Administrators in Higher Education, 1962. Editorial com. College and University Business Administration, rev. edits. Home: 240 Lady Astor Pl Danville VA 24541 817 W Peachtree St NE Atlanta GA 30383

ERICKSON, ERIC FREDERICK, wholesale trade exec.; b. Helsingland, Sweden, July 18, 1919; s. Ole and Bertha M. (Michelsson) E.; student Am. Tech. Soc. Sch., 1940-42; m. Judy Schleicher, Dec. 28, 1939; children— Glen, Donna Sue (Mrs. Jerry Parker). Came to U.S., 1924, naturalized, 1944. Mgr. retail food store, Chgo., 1938-40; merchandiser Salerno-Magowen Biscuit Co., 1940-42; sales supr. Consol. Biscuit Co., 1942-45; asst. sales mgr. Schulze-Burch Biscuit Co., 1945-46; gen. sales mgr. Ill. Chem. Co., 1946-47; v.p. sales Wortz Biscuit Co., Fort Smith, Ark., 1947-67; sales dir. Blue Springs Fish Hatchery, Birmingham, Ala., 1967-—. Instr. salesmanship Fort Smith Jr. Coll., 1961; lectr. Small Bus. Adminstrn. Inst., 1962; coordinator salesmanship course U. Ala., 1969. Mem. Sales and Marketing Execs. Club (pres. 1956, 61). Lutheran (v.p. ch. council 1964-66). Mason (Shriner), Elk. Club: The Club (Birmingham). Home: 163 Glenview Dr Birmingham AL 35213 Office: PO Box 6611 Birmingham AL 35210

ERICKSON, ERIC LEROY, civil engr.; b. Chgo., Oct. 8, 1896; s. John Edwin and Hulda (Magnuson) E.; student Highland Park Coll., 1912-14; student civil engring. State U. Ia., 1914-16; m. Velma Fondren, Jan. 29, 1924; children—Susanne (Mrs. Maurice Chamblee), William M. Bridge designer Ind., N.C. Hwy. Commns., 1919-23; asst. state bridge engr. La. Hwy. Commn., 1923-41; bridge engr. southeastern div. U.S. Bur. Pub. Rds., 1941-46, asst. chief bridge engr., 1946-48, chief bridge engr., 1948-66; cons. Office. Sec. Transp., Washington, 1966-—. Cons. Govt. Victoria, Australia, 1962, Govt. Netherlands, 1967; mem. bd. cons. Panama Canal Bridge at Balboa, 1958-63. Mem. research adv. com. U. Ill., Lehigh U. Served with AUS, 1917-19. Recipient Silver Medal award Dept. Commerce, 1956, Gold Medal award, 1964; Charles S. Whitney award Am. Concrete Inst., 1969; Arthur J. Boaze award Reinforced Concrete Research Council Am. Soc. Engrs., 1972. Mem. Am. Soc. C.E. (life), Am. Rd. Builders Assn. (life), Nat. Acad. Sci. (hwy. research bd.), Prestressed Concrete Inst. (hon.). Mason. Home and Office: 501 Dumbarton Dr Shreveport LA 71106

ERICKSON, FREDERICK KENNETH, san. engr.; b. Missoula, Mont., Apr. 11, 1916; s. David William and Elin (Erickson) E.; student Mont. State Coll. 1934-35, 1937; B.S., U. Wash., 1940; SM., Harvard, 1943; m. Esther Mae McGlone, Jan. 29, 1944; children—Elin Katherine, Frederick Kenneth, Diane Marie. Jr. engr. U.S. Army Engrs., Ketchikan, Alaska, 1940-41; san. engr. Pierce County Health Dept., Tacoma, 1941-42; asst. and sr. asst. san. engr. USPHS, La. Fla., Egypt, Italy, Yugoslavia, Washington, 1943-46; asst. prof. Wash. State Coll., 1946-50, asso. prof. civil engring., head water pollution research, 1950-51; sr. san engr. USPHS, Fed. Civil Def. Adminstrn., 1951-54; prof. san. engring. India Inst. Hygiene, Calcutta, 1954-56; san. engring. dir. Office Engring. Resources, Washington, 1656-61; asso. regional health dir. USPHS Kansas City, Mo., 1961-66; dep. dir. div. of Allied Health Manpower, USPHS, Arlington, Va., 1967-68; asst. commr. tng. and manpower devel. Environmental Control Adminstrn., Rockville, Md., 1968-71; dir. environmental affairs Ryckman, Edgerley, Tomlinson & Assos., 1971-—. Recipient Clements Herschel award, 1943. Registered profl. engr., Pa., Wash. Diplomate Am. Acad. San. Engrs. Fellow Am. Soc. C.E., Am. Pub. Health Assn.; mem Am. Soc. Engring. Edn., Nat. Soc. Profl. Engrs. Home: 8016 Falstaff Rd McLean VA 22101 Office: 7600 Old Springhouse Rd McLean VA 22101

ERICKSON, RALPH H., govt. ofcl. Asst. atty. gen. Office Legal Counsel, Dept. Justice, Washington. Address: Office Legal Counsel Justice Dept Washington DC 20530*

ERICSON, JOE ELLIS, educator; b. Throckmorton County, Tex., June 9, 1925; s. Lester Y. and Lena Agnes (Ellis) E.; student U. Tex., 1943-44, postgrad., 1948-51; B.S. in Edn., Tex. Technol. Coll., 1946, M.A., 1948, Ph.D., 1957; m. Carolyn Reeves, July 16, 1955; children—Linda Dianne, Joseph Reeves, John Ellis. Instr. W. Tex. State U., 1951-53; instr. Arlington State Coll., 1955-57; mem. faculty Stephen F. Austin State Coll., Nacogdoches, Tex., 1957-—, prof. polit. sci., head dept., 1964-—. Precinct committeeman Democratic Party, Nacogdoches, 1968-—. Mem. Am. Polit. Sci. Assn., Am. Studies Assn. (pres. Tex. 1971-72), Alpha Chi (hon.), Pi Sigma Alpha, Pi Kappa Alpha. Mason. Home: 1614 Redbud St Nacogdoches TX 75961

ERICSSON, RALPH LOUIS, chem. co. exec.; b. Ridgway, Pa., Sept. 20, 1908; s. Louis F. and Florence (Siggins) E.; B.S. in Chemistry, Carnegie Inst. Tech., 1933; m. Ruth E. Jacobson, Oct. 18, 1941; 1 dau., Carol A. With Westvaco Chlorine Products Corp. (name later changed to FMC Corp.) N.Y.C., 1933-41, chief chemist, Carteret, N.J., 1934-37, mgr. tech. service, N.Y.C. 1937-41; asst. mgr. tech. service Comml. Solvents Corp., Terre Haute, Ind., 1941-44, asst. to v.p. sales, 1944-45, asst. mgr. pharm. div., 1945-48; sales mgr. Sumner Chem. Co., Inc. div. Miles Lab., N.Y.C., 1948-53, v.p. sales, 1951-54, dir., 1952-56, exec. v.p., gen. mgr., 1954-56; sales mgr. Tex. Butadiene & Chem. Corp., N.Y.C. 1957-59, v.p. marketing, 1958-62; v.p., dir. Tex. Butadiene & Chem. Internat., Ltd., Montreal Que., Can., 1958-62; owner, operator Ericsson Chem. Services, Inc., Houston, 1962-—. Mem. Salesmen's Assn. Am. Chem. Industry (dir. 1948-51, 52-55), Am. Chem. Soc., Mfg. Chemists Assn. Clubs: Chemists (trustee 1955-56, 60-62), (N.Y.C.); Houston, Petroleum. Contbr. articles to tech. publs. Patentee, fields textile treating, tobacco conditioning, pharm. chems. Home: 11108 Meadowick St Houston TX 77024 Office: 2100 Travis St Houston TX 77002

ERIKSON, SHELTON WILLARD, chem. exec.; b. Pecan Island, La., July 23, 1926; s. John Erik and Veronica (Vaughn) E.; student pub. schs.; m. Theresa Bourgeois, Jan. 1, 1954; children—Shelton Leonard, Sylvia Reed (Mrs. Robert W. Feller). Owner Erikson Chem. Corp., New Iberia, La., 1967-—, also Erikson Pollution Control, Inc. Served with AUS, 1944-46. Decorated Purple Heart, 3 Bronze Stars. Mason (Shriner). Home: Route B Box 237 New Iberia LA 70560 Office: PO Box 1424 New Iberia LA 70560

ERLACHER, ARTHUR ROBERT, dentist; b. New London, Conn., Aug. 27, 1918; s. Adolph Joseph and Aimee Alice (Mullan) E.; B.S., Temple U., 1941, D.D.S., 1951; children—Aimee Ellen, Suzanne; m. 2d, Frances Jeannette Bass, June 22, 1963; children—Sandra Annette, Patricia Anne, Lori. Practice dentistry, Orlando, Fla., 1953-—. Dir. Fla. Cinema, Inc., Orlando, 1959-—, sec., 1959-61. Mem. staff Fla. San. and Hospital, Orlando, 1954-—, Winter Park Meml., Orange Meml. hosps. Mem. Com. to Improve Pub. Sch. Edn. Bd. dirs. Northside Boys Club, Orlando, 1961. Served to lt. comdr. USNR, 1941-46; to capt. USAF, 1951-53; PTO. Mem. Am., Fla., Central Fla. dental assns., Central Fla. Soc. Advancement Ethical Hypnosis (dir.), Frederic James Hon. Clin. Pathology Soc., Dr. John A. Kolmer Hon. Med. Soc., Orlando C. of C., Sigma Phi Epsilon, Delta Sigma Delta. Lion (treas. Orlando 1955, pres. 1963-64; pres. Council of Presidents Orange County; developer, exec. dir. Sight Clinic Central Fla.). Club: Rio Pinar Country. Contbr. articles to dental jours. Home: 5112 Duban Av Orlando FL 32809 Office: 710 W Vassar Av Orlando FL 32804

ERMUTLU, ILHAN MEHMET, state ofcl., physician; b. Istanbul, Turkey, June 24, 1927; s. Sami and Ihsan (Emin) E.; M.D., U. Ankara, 1952; came to U.S., 1954, naturalized, 1964; m. Karen Harper, Sept. 9, 1956; children—David Sami, Gary Deniz. Intern, Knickerbocker Hosp., N.Y.C., 1954-55; resident psychiatry Bellevue and Hillside hosps., Glen Oaks, N.Y., 1955-58; resident neurology Goldwater Meml. Hosp., N.Y.C., 1958-59; chief service Eastern State Hosp., Williamsburg, Va., 1959-61; dir. Tidewater Mental Health Clinic, Williamsburg, 1961-63; practice of medicine specializing in psychiatry, Richmond, 1963-64; asst. dir. div. mental health Ga. Dept. Pub. Health, Atlanta, 1964-70; supt. Ga. Regional Hosp., Savannah, 1970—; asso. in psychiatry Emory U. Sch. Medicine, Atlanta, 1964—. Served with Turkish Army, 1953-54. Fellow Am. Psychiat. Assn., Am. Pub. Health Assn.; mem. A.M.A., Ga. Psychiat. Assn., Med. Assn. Ga., Ga. Pub. Health Assn., Ga. Med. Soc. Club: Savannah Exchange. Home: 401 Arlington Rd Savannah GA 31406 Office: PO Box 13607 Savannah GA 31406

ERVIN, RICHARD WILLIAM, justice Fla. Supreme Ct.;; b. Carabelle, Fla., Jan. 26, 1905; s. Richard William and Carrie Marvin (Phillips) E.; LL.B., U. Fla., 1928; m. Frances Blois Baker, Nov. 23, 1933; children—Richard William, Sara Eve. Admitted to Fla. bar, 1929; practiced Clearwater, Fla., 1929, Palatka, Fla., 1930-36; right-of-way atty. Fla. State Rd. Dept., Jacksonville, 1936-37; resident atty. State Rd. Dept., Tallahassee, 1937-43 atty. Overseas Rd., Toll Bridge Dist., Marathon, Fla., 1937-43; asst. atty. gen. Fla., 1943-45; sec. Fla. R.R., Pub. Utilities Commn., 1945; resident atty. Fla. State Rd. Dept., 1945-48; atty. gen. Fla., 1949-64; now chief justice Supreme Ct. Fla. Recipient Good Govt. award, Fla. State Jr. C. of C., 1950. Mem. Nat. Assn. Attys. Gen. (chmn. So. group; pres., 1959-60), Woodmen World Life Ins. Soc. (chmn. bd. trustees), Phi Kappa Tau, Omicron Delta Kappa, Phi Alpha Delta. Democrat. Baptist. Mason. Elk. Club: Exchange. Home: 601 Ingleside Av Tallahassee FL 32304 Office: Supreme Ct Tallahassee FL 32304

ERVIN, ROBERT MARVIN, lawyer; b. nr. Ocala, Fla., Jan. 19, 1917; s. Richard William and Carrie (Phillips) E.; B.S. in Bus. Adminstrn., U. Fla., 1941, LL.B., 1947; m. Frances Anne Cushing, Dec. 25, 1941; children—Anne Cushing (Mrs. Henry Lamar Rowe), Robert Marvin. Admitted to Fla. bar, 1947; practice in Tallahassee, 1947—; partner firm Ervin, Pennington, Varn & Jacobs, 1954—. Referee in bankruptcy No. Dist. Fla., 1952—; mem. Fla. Constn. Revision Commn., 1965—. Dir. Wilson Nat. Life Ins. Co.; sec., dir. Interstate Groves Corp., M & L Devel. Corp.; treas., dir. Leon Abstract Co.; pres. REFG, Inc., Tallahassee, 1961—; gen. counsel Fla. Home Builders Assn., 1955—. Trustee U. Fla. Law Center Assn. Served with USMCR, 1941-45; PTO; col. Res. Recipient Distinguished Service award for legal edn. John B. Stetson U., 1966. Distinguished Service award Armed Forces League, 1966. Fellow Am. Bar Found.; mem. Fla. Bar (pres. 1965-66. Distinguished Service award 1966), Am. Bar Assn. (ho. of dels.). Nat. Conf. Referees in Bankruptcy (pres. 1963-64). Res. Officers Assn., Marine Corps Res. Officers Assn., Fla. Blue Key, Phi Alpha Delta, Alpha Kappa Psi. Democrat. Baptist. Elk. Home: 1434 Crestview Av Tallahassee FL 32303 Office: 305 S Gadsden St PO Box 1567 Tallahassee FL 32302

ERVIN, SAM J., III, judge; b., 1926; B.S., Davidson Coll.; LL.B., Harvard. Judge, Superior Ct., N.C., 1967—. Mem. N.C. Ho. of Reps., 1965-67. Home: 4 Woodside Pl Morganton NC 28655

ERVIN, SAMUEL JAMES, JR., U.S. senator; b. Morganton, N.C., Sept. 27, 1896; s. Samuel James and Laura T. (Powe) E.; A.B., U. N.C., 1917, LL.D., 1951; LL.B., Harvard, 1922; LL.D., Western Carolina Coll. 1955, George Washington U., 1972, Davidson Coll., 1972, St. Andrews Presbyn. Coll., 1972; Dr. Pub. Adminstrn., Suffolk U., 1957, Wake Forest U., 1971; m. Margaret Bruce Bell, June 18, 1924; children—Samuel James, Margaret Leslie (Mrs. Gerald M. Hansler), Laura Powe (Mrs. William Edward Smith). Admitted to N.C. bar, 1919; licensed to practice before ICC, Tax Ct. of U.S., and U.S. Supreme Ct.; engaged in gen. practice of law, Morganton, N.C., 1922—; rep. from Burke County, N.C. gen. assembly 1923, 25, 31; judge, Burke County Criminal Ct., 1935-37, N.C. Superior Ct., 1937-43; rep. in Congress from 10th N.C. Dist., Jan. 1946-Jan. 1947; asso. justice N.C. Supreme Ct., 1948-54, U.S., senator from N.C., 1954—, now mem. judiciary com., also chmn. sub-com. on codification and revision of laws. Chmn. Commn. for Improvement of Adminstrn. of Justice in N.C., 1947-49. Trustee Morganton Graded Schs., 1927-30, U. of N.C., 1932-35, 1945-53, Davidson Coll., 1948-58. Served with Co. I, 28th inf., 1st div., France, 18 months (twice wounded in action, twice cited for gallantry in action), World War I. Awarded French Fourragere, Purple Heart with 1 oakleaf cluster, Silver Star, Distinguished Service Cross. Mem. N.C. State Bd. of Law Examiners, 1944-46; N.C. State Dem. exec. com., 1930-37. Mem. Am., N.C. bar assns., N.C. State Bar, Junior Order United Am. Mechanics, Am. Legion, V.F.W., D.A.V., Soc. 1st Div., Legion of Valor, Morganton C. of C., N.C. Literary and Hist. Assn., So. Hist. Assn., Soc. Mayflower Desc. State N.C. (gov. 1950-52), Gen. Alumni Assn. U. N.C. (pres. 1947-48), Am. Judicature Soc., Am., S.C. hist. assns., N.C. Soc. Preservation Antiquities, Soc. Cin. Sons of Am. Revolution, Sigma Upsilon, Phi Delta Phi. Democrat. Presbyterian (elder). Mason (33 deg., K.T., Kiwanian. Home: Morganton NC 28655 Office: Senate Office Bldg Washington DC 20525

ERWIN, GEORGE MONTAGUE, ins. co. exec.; b. Howell, Mich., Oct. 3, 1917; s. Harold A. and Kittie (Montague) E.; student Bates Coll., 1935-38; m. Ann Ansley, Aug. 20, 1941; children—Diane Elizabeth Baxter, Susan Ansley Carswell, Kittie Montague. With Atlantic-Richfield Co. (formerly Atlanta Refining Co.), 1939-49, asst. dist. mgr., Worcester, Mass., 1941-42; partner Johnson-Erwin Ins. Agy., Atlanta, 1949-59; pres. Ins. Agts., Inc., Atlanta, 1959-64; founder Am. Agy. Life Ins. Co., Atlanta, 1964, pres., 1964—; pres. Am. Agy. Financial Corp., Atlanta, 1969—. Pres., Ga. Assn. for Mental Health, 1958-59, Atlanta chpt. Multiple Sclerosis Soc., 1958-59. Served to maj. C.E., AUS, 1943-46. Named Ins. Agt. of Year, 1963, recipient Edgar Dunlap award Ga. Assn. Ins. Agts., 1960. Mem. Atlanta C. of C., Mil. Order Word Wars, Atlanta Assn. Ins. Agts. (past pres.), Ga. Assn. Ind. Ins. Agts. (past pres.). Episcopalian. Rotarian (past pres.; past dist. gov.). Home: 2575 Peachtree Rd NE Atlanta GA 30319 Office: 1252 W Peachtree St NW Atlanta GA 30309

ERWIN, HOWELL C., JR., lawyer; b. Athens, Ga., Oct. 14, 1917; A.B., LL.B., U. Ga. Admitted to Ga. bar, 1940, since practiced law, Ga., 1940—. Mem. State Bd. Bar Examiners, 1959-65. Fellow Am. Coll. Probate Counsel, Am. Bar Found.; mem. Am., Athens, Western Circuit bar assns., State Bar Ga. (pres. 1969-70), Phi Beta Kappa, Phi Delta Phi, Phi Kappa Phi. Address: PO Box 1587 Athens GA 30601

ERWIN, JOHN PRESTON, JR., physician; b. Hemphill, Tex., Mar. 16, 1939; s. John Preston and Clemence Eloise (Buckley) E.; B.S., Lamar State Coll., 1960; M.D., U. Tex., 1964; m. Martha Jo Phillips, Jan. 31, 1965; children—John Preston III, Bryan, Mark. Intern John Peter Smith Hosp., Ft. Worth, 1964-65, gen. practice resident, 1964-66; partner Family Diagnostic Center, Hillsboro, Tex., 1968—; chief staff Grant-Buie Hosp., Inc., 1970—. Vice-chmn. Hillsboro Housing Authority, 1970—; pres. Hill County Cancel Soc., 1970-72. Chmn. Hill County Republican party, 1971—. Served to capt. USAF, 1966-68. Recipient Tng. Grant NIH, 1960, 61. Diplomate Am. Bd. Family Practice. Mem. A.M.A., Tex. Acad. Gen. Practice (mem. membership and credentials com. 1971—), Mu Delta, Phi Rho Sigma. Episcopalian (mem. vestry 1968-69). Mason, Lion. Home: 112 Mockingbird St Hillsboro TX 76645 Office: 101 Circle Dr Hillsboro TX 76645

ESCARDO, MAURICIO ENRIQUE, educator; b. Montevideo, Uruguay, Sept. 4, 1914; s. Victor and Alicia (Berlan) Escardo y Anaya; B.A., Instituto de Humanidades, Cordoba, Argentina, 1936; Ph.L., Facultad de Filosoffa, San Miguel, Argentina, 1941; M.A., Universidad Nacional del Litoral, Santa Fe, Argentina, 1952; Ph.D., Instituto Libre de Humanidades, Santa Fe, Argentina, 1952; J.D., Loyola U., 1962; diploma Instituto de Derecho Comparado, Universidad Autonoma de Mexico, 1962; m. Margot Gallofre, May 21, 1960. Came to U.S., 1956, naturalized, 1962. Acting dean, prof. law Universidad Iberoamerica, Sch. Law, Mexico City, 1953-56; asso. prof. philosophy Loyola U., New Orleans, 1957-63; asso. prof. theology and philosophy Georgetown U., Washington, 1963-66, lectr. law Sch. Law, 1964-65; prof. dept. humanities, chmn. dept. Coll. V.I., St. Thomas, 1968—. Mem. Am. Philos. Assn., Am. Assn. U. Profs., La. Bar Assn. Author: Graficos de Historia de la Filosofia, 1940. Address: Coll VI St Thomas VI 00801

ESCARRAZ, DONALD RAY, educator; b. Chgo., Nov. 24, 1932; s. Enrique and Edith May (Porter) E.; B.S., U. Tampa, 1960; M.B.A., U. Wis., 1961; Ph.D. (Nat. Def. Teaching Act fellow), Okla. State U., 1964; m. Barbara Fay Swartz, May 24, 1952; children—Pamela, Paul, Peter, Patricia, Phyllis, Philip. Buyer, N. Shure Co., Chgo., 1950-53; bus. mgr. O. J. Swartz Co., Melrose Park, Ill., 1954-57; asst. prof. U. Fla., Gainesville, 1964-66; asso. prof. pub. finance U. Ga. Athens, 1966—. Served with AUS, 1953-54. Mem. Nat. Tax Assn., Pub. Choice Soc., Center for Study Democratic Instns., Am., So. econ. assns., So. Finance Assn., Phi Epsilon Phi. Presbyn. (elder 1969-70). Mason. Home: 121 Stafford Dr Athens GA 30601

ESCHENBACH, ARTHUR EDWIN, psychologist; b. N.Y.C., Jan. 31, 1918; s. Karl G. and Magdelen (Rupert) E.; student Queens Coll., 1940-41; A.B., Cornell U., 1947; M.A., U. Fla., 1949, Ph.D., 1955; m. Patricia Lucille Flowers, Apr. 29, 1944; children—Mary Patricia, Karl Arthur; m. 2d, Marie L. Perez, June 22, 1968; children—Roxanne, Charmion, Deborah. Commd. 2d lt. U.S. Air Force, 1942, advanced through grades to lt. col., 1966; research psychologist Air U., 1951-56, Personnel Lab., Lackland AFB, Tex., 1956-57, Occupational Health Research Lab., Cape Canaveral, Fla., 1957-62, Ballistic Systems div., Norton AFB, Cal., 1962-65, Air Proving Ground, Eglin AFB, Fla. State U., 1965—; asso. prof. Trinity U., 1956-57, U. Pacific, 1966-67, Jacksonville U., 1967—; instr. Rollins Coll., 1958-61. Licensed psychologist, Fla. Mem. Am., Fla. psychol. assns., N.Y. Acad. Scis. Author articles profl. jours. Home: 11440 Starboard Jacksonville FL 32225

ESCOBEDO, MANUEL G(REGORIO), lawyer; b. Zacatecas, Zacatecas, Mexico, May 9, 1896; s. Enrique and Ana Maria Diaz de Leon Escobedo; Ph.B., Licentiate in Law, Instituto Cientificio de Mexico, 1907-14; Nat. U., 1914-15, Law Sch. Mexico City, 1916-20, U. Paris, 1921-22, London U., 1922-25; m. Elsie Fulda, Aug. 22, 1931; children—Elena, Miguel. Prof. comml. law Escuela Libre de Derecho, 1927-37; asso. Basham & Ringe, 1927-34; senior partner Noriega y Escobedo, Mexico City, 1934—; prof. civil law Nat. U., 1947-62, Escuela Libre de Derecho, 1965—; dir. Asbestos de Mexico, S.A., Banco del Atlantico, S.A., Cinzano de Mexico, S.A., Ciba de Mexico, S.A., Devoe de Mexico, S.A., Gen. Motors Acceptance Corp., de Mexico, S.A., Johnson & Johnson de Mexico, S.A., Olivetti Mexicana, S.A., Productos de Maiz, S.A., Reaseguradora Patria, S.A., Sanborn Hermanos, S.A., Sanborn Monterrey, S.A., Cia de Equipo Industrial Acme de Mexico, S.A., Cia Mercantil Internacional, S.A., Steeinbock de Mexico, S.A., Garlock de Mexico, S.A., Cia Mexicana Impresora de Valores, S.A., Pre-Concreto del-Pacifico, S.A., Ascensores Schindler Mexicana, S.A., Sulzer Hermanos, S.A., Becton Dickenson de Mexico, Vitos de Mexico, S.A., Underwood Mexicana, S.A., Norton de Mexico, S.A. de C.V., Preconcreto, S.A., Quimica Niagara de Mexico, S.A., Electroquimica Mexicana, S.A., Mem. Internat. (past-pres.), Am. Inter-Am. bar assns., Assn. Bar City N.Y., Union Iberoamericana de Colegios y Agrupaciones de Abogados (v.p. 1957—), Nat. Coll. Lawyers, Mexico City Bar, Nat. Acad. Law and Jurisprudence. Home: 23 Historiadores Mexico City 20 Mexico Office: 14 Av Juarez Mexico City 1 Mexico

ESKEW, HERMAN, city editor Nashville Tennessean. Office: 1100 Broadway Nashville TN 37203*

ESKEW, RHEA TALIAFERRO, press assn. exec.; b. Lebanon, Tenn., Nov. 16, 1923; s. Robert Edward and Sammie (Taylor) E.; student U. Tenn., 1941-42; B.A., Emory U., 1948; m. Nancy Portlock Hall, June 13, 1953; children—Rhea Taliaferro, Elizabeth Vaughan, Tucker Alexander, Hall Edward. With U.P., 1948-55, bus. rep. N.C., S.C., Va., 1951-55; pub. relations with So. Bell Telephone Co., 1955-56; with U.P.I., and predecessor, 1956—, gen. mgr. communications, N.Y.C., 1964, So. div. mgr., Atlanta, 1964—, also cons. communications. Served with AUS, 1942-45; ETO. Mem. Sigma Delta Chi (dir. region 3). Republican. Methodist. Club: Atlanta Commerce. Home: 339 Camden Rd Atlanta GA 30309 Office: 1211 William St Atlanta GA 30309

ESLICK, JACK W., telephone co. exec.; b. Fayetteville, Tenn., July 7, 1923; s. Aron J. and Mae (Pigg) E.; A.B. in Econs., Duke, 1951; m. Mary Anna Hamilton, June 3, 1950; children—Jackson Lindsay, Cynthia Ann, Melissa Leigh. With So. Bell Telephone & Telegraph Co., 1951—, group mgr., Jacksonville Beach, Fla., 1959—. Bd. dirs. United Fund, Jacksonville Beach. Served with USAAF, 1943-46. Recipient various civic awards. Mem. Jacksonville Beach C. of C. (v.p. 1969, pres. 1969-70, dir.), Phi Delta Theta. Rotarian (pres. 1967-68). Clubs: Jacksonville Beaches Quarterback (pres. 1971); Ponte Vedra. Home: 3722 Coronado Rd Jacksonville FL 32217 Office: 411 Pablo Av Jacksonville Beach FL 32250

ESPINA, ANGEL BEAUNONI (STAGE NAME NONI ESPINA), educator, singer; b. Ayuquitan, Negros Oriental, Phillippines, July 29, 1923; s. Angel Colomiana and Wenceslina (Salatandre) E.; B.S.E., Silliman U., 1947; S.M.M., Sch. Sacred Music, Union Theol. Sem., 1950, S.M.D., 1962; M.A., Ind. U., 1951; postgrad. Juilliard Sch. Music, 1962-63. Came to U.S., 1956. N.Y. recital debut Carnegie Hall, 1958, others, 1964; recitals, solo appearances throughout U.S., 1949-51, 1956—; recitals Central Am., 1949, Philippines, 1951-56, 65-66, 69, Japan, Hong Kong, Thailand, India, 1966, 69; radio, oratorio, opera appearances U.S., Philippines, 1951—; prof. Wagner Coll., 1960-61; asst. prof. Drury Coll., 1963-65; vis. prof. U. Colo., 1966-67; vis. prof., exec. v.p. Coll. Maasin, 1965-66; prof. music Jacksonville (Ala.) State U., 1967—. Lectr. Columbia U., U. Colo., States Mo., Kan., Ala., Philippines, 1964-69. Trustee Coll. Maasin, 1956—. Recipient McFadden Fellowship award, 1948-49, Dodge Fellowship award, 1956-57, Presbyn. award, 1949, Outstanding Alumni award in Music and Art, Coll. Maasin, 1969. Mem. Am. Musicological Soc., Assn. Am. Choral Conductors, Soc. Ethnumusicology, Internat. Folk Music Council, Am. Anthrop. Assn., Presbyn. Published Song Star, 1947, Vocal Solos for Protestant Services, also song cycles, 1968, 69. Contbr. articles to newspapers. Office: Jacksonville State U Jacksonville AL 36265

ESPINOSA YGLESIAS, MANUEL, banker; b. Puebla, Mexico, May 9, 1909; s. Ernesto Espinosa and Guadalupe Yglesias; ed. Colegio Catolico, Colegio del Estado, Academia de Comercio Leon Pararan (all Puebla); Dr. honoris causa Universidad de las Americas; m. Amparo Rugarcia, June 27, 1940; children—Amparo (Mrs. Julio Serrano, Jr.), Angeles (Mrs. Jose Antonio Alonso), Manuel, Guadalupe (Mrs. Jorge Larrea, Jr.). Mgr. Compania Operadora de Teatros, 1944-45, Ingenio de Atencingo Puebla, 1945-50; with Banco de Comercio, Mexico City, Mexico, 1950—, dir., 1955—, chmn. bd. gen. dir., 1958—; mem. bd. all banks Bancos de Comercio System; chmn. bd. Financiera Bancomer S.A., Hipotecaria Bancomer S.A., Seguros de Mexico Bancomer. Pres. Mary Street Jenkins Found. Decorated comdr. Order San Gregorio Magno; cross of honor Asociacion del H. Colegio Militar; great cross Civil Merit (Spain). Mem. Bankers Nat. Assn. (pres. 1965-66, 71-72). Clubs: Banqueros, Golf Mexico, Americano, University, Industriales, Campestre, Libanes, Espana, Jockey (all Mexico). Author papers; lectr. profl. orgns. Address: Venustiano Carranza 44 Mexico City Mexico

ESPY, ISAAC PUGH, civil engr.; b. Clarksville, Tenn., Mar. 23, 1939; s. Goodman Basil and Dacy Clyde (Pugh) E.; B.S. in Civil Engring., U. Ala., 1961, postgrad., 1961-62, J.D. (William Hepburn scholar), 1972; m. Carol Janet Carpenter, May 29, 1960; children—Jami Lucretia, Isaac Pugh, Amanda Susan. Part-time instr. U. Ala., 1961-62; profl. engr., land surveyor, Jackson, Ala., 1965-69; partner G. B. Espy Jr. & Son, Jackson, 1965-69; with Gilbreath, Foster & Brooks, Inc., Tuscaloosa, Ala., 1969—, chief structural engr., 1969-70, v.p., chief engr., 1971—. Del. Ala. State Republican Conv., 1966-68. Served with C.E., USNR, 1962-65. Registered profl. engr., Ala., Fla. Mem. Am. Soc. C.E. (mem. com. 1969-71), Am. Congress on Surveying and Mapping, Ala. Soc. Profl. Land Surveyors. Republican. Baptist (deacon 1966-71, chmn. bd. trustees 1972). Mason. Home: 93 Woodland Hills Tuscaloosa AL 35401 Office: PO Box 1966 Tuscaloosa AL 35401

ESSRICK, ABRAHAM JOSEPH, govt. ofcl.; b. Phila., Feb. 8, 1914;; s. Jacob and Rachel (Pressman) E.; B.A., George Washington U., 1956; J.D. cum laude, Rutgers U., 1940; post-grad. U. Grenoble, France, 1945; m. Riva Krakuzin, Feb. 14, 1943 (dec. Aug. 1959); children— Helene (Mrs. Feldsher), Carol; m. 2d, Pearl Gibel, May 20, 1972; children—Frances H. Gibel, Bonnie (Mrs. Schneider). Admitted to D.C. bar, 1941, U.S. Supreme Ct., 1964; atty. adviser SEC, Washington, 1946-53; atty. advisor ICC, Washington, 1953-59. hearing examiner, 1959—. Mem. Phila. Speakers Council, 1942, Jewish Educators Council, 1958-60; mem. bd. dirs. govt. div. United Jewish Appeal of Greater Washington, Inc., 1958—, mem. exec. com., 1964-65, trustee, 1960-61, 64—, vice chmn. exec. com. govt. div., 1965. Served with Signal Intelligence Div., ETO, 1944-45. Mem. Am., Fed. bar assns., Am. Judicature Soc., Nat. Lawyers Club, Fed. Trial Examiners Conf., Internat. Platform Assn. Jewish religion. Mem. B'nai B'rith. Club: Rutgers (Washington). Home: 905 Kenbrook Dr Silver Spring MD 20902 Office: ICC 12th and Constitution Av NW Washington DC 20423

ESTEB, ADLAI ALBERT, editor; b. La Grande, Ore., Nov. 17, 1901; s. Lemuel Albert and Addretta (Koger) E.; B.Th., Walla Walla Coll., 1931; M.A., Cal. Coll., Peiping, China, 1953; Ph.D., U. So. Cal., 1944; m. Florence Edna Airey, Feb. 5, 1923; children—Adeline, Lucille (Mrs. Cleat Laney). Ordained to ministry Seventh Day Adventist Ch., 1923; missionary to China, 1923-37; pastor Seventh Day Adventist Ch., Long Beach, Cal., 1938-40; sec. Home Missionary Dept., So. Cal. Conf. Seventh Day Adventist Ch., 1940-46, Pacific Union Conf. Seventh Day Adventist Ch., Glendale, Cal., 1946-50; editor Go, Jour. for Adventist Laymen, gen, conf. Seventh Day Adventist Ch., Washington, 1950—; vis. prof., lectr; Christian ethics Andrews U., Berrien Springs, Mich., 1955—. Cited as poet laureate of denomination by pres. World Conf., 1966. Mem. China Soc. of So. Cal. (pres. 1946-50), Oriental Fellowship (pres. 1963), Phi Beta Kappa, Phi Kai Phi, Phi Kappa Phi. Author: Driftwood, 1947; Firewood 1952; Sandalwood, 1955; Morning Manna, 1962; Rosewood, 1964; Scrapwood, 1967; (poetry) Redwood, 1970. Home: 8013 Sligo Creek Pkwy Washington DC 20012 Office: 6840 Eastern Av Washington DC 20012

ESTES, DEWITT OCIE, county agrl. agt.; b. Lafayette, Ala., June 4, 1914; s. Olen J. and Corine (Hamilton) E.; B.S., Ala. Poly. Inst., 1949; m. Sarah Elizabeth Edwards, Oct. 24, 1950. With Extension Service, U.S. Dept. Agr., 1949—, asst. county agt. Monroe County, Ala., 1949-50, Sumter County, Livingston, Ala., 1950-52; asst. county agt. Washington, County, Chatom, Ala., 1952-60, county agt., 1960-66, county extension chmn., 1966—. Adviser, Chatom Indsl. Bd., 1962—. Served with USAAF, 1942-45. Decorated Air medal with bronze oak leaf cluster. Recipient certificate of Achievement for outstanding 4-H work Ala. Assn. County Agts., 1958. Mem. Ala. Assn. County Agrl. Agts., Epsilon Sigma Phi. Baptist (deacon). Mason. Home: 205 E Pinehurst Dr Chatom AL 36518 Office: Frank Turner Hall PO Box 280 Chatom AL 36518

ESTES, JOE EWING, dist. judge; b. Commerce, Tex., Oct. 24, 1903; s, Joe Guinn and Della Marshall (Loy) E.; student E. Tex. State Tchrs. Coll., 1923-24; LL.B., U. Tex., 1927; m. Carroll Virginia Cox, Dec. 1, 1931; children—Carl Lewis II, Carol Lynn. Admitted to Tex. bar, 1927; partner Crosby & Estes at Commerce, 1928-30, Phillips, Trammell, Estes, Edwards & Orn, Ft. Worth, 1930-45, Sanford, King, Estes & Cantwell at Dallas, 1946-52, Estes & Cantwell, 1952-55; dist. judge, No. Dist. Tex., Dallas, 1955—, now chief judge U.S. Dist. Ct., No. Dist. Tex.; also judge Emergency Ct. Appeals of U.S., 1972—. Chmn. exec. com. bd. trustees St. Marks Sch. of Tex., Dallas, 1951-55; chmn. Oil and Gas Inst. of S.W. Legal Found.; trustee, mem. exec. com. S.W. Legal Found. Served as lt. comdr. USNR, 1942-45; mem. Res. Fellow Am. Bar Assn. (chmn. sect, jud. adminstrn., ho. of del., joint com. for effective adminstrn. justice); mem. Jud. Conf. U.S. (exec. com. adv. com. rules evidence, chmn. com. on trial practice and technique), Nat. Conf. Commrs. on Uniform State Laws, Am. Law Inst., Fed., Dallas (v.p.), Ft. Worth (dir.) bar assns,, State Bar Tex., Chancellors, Am. Judicature Soc. (dir.), Nat. Lawyers Club, Am. Legion, Philos. Soc. Tex., Newcomen Soc., Order of Coif, Phi Delta Phi, Kappa Sigma. Methodist. Mason (33 deg., Shriner). Author: (with others) Handbook for Effective Pretrial Procedure; Handbook for Newly Appointed U.S. Judges. Bd. editors Manual for Complex and Multidistrict Litigation. Contbr. profl. jours. Home: 5846 Desco Dr Dallas TX 75225 Office: US Courthouse Dallas TX 75202

ESTES, KENNETH ALLEN, educator; b. Lewisport, Ky., Dec. 11, 1913; s. Carl and Mary Effie (Brown) E.; B.A., Western Ky. U., 1936; M.A., George Peabody Coll., 1948, Ed.D., 1966; m. Dorothy Madison Smith, Oct. 10, 1936; children—Patricia Ann (Mrs. Frank Podlipec), Sava Jill (Mrs. Thomas Dantic). Tchr. rural schs., 1931-37, Lewisport (Ky.) High Sch., 1937-39; elementary prin. Owensboro (Ky.) City Schs., 1939-48, bus. mgr., 1948-54, supt., 1954-68; prof. sch. adminstrn., dir. lab. experience Western Ky. U., Bowling Green, 1968—. Pres. United Fund Campaign, Owensboro, 1967; state dir. Ky. Soc. Crippled Children, 1951-66. Bd. dirs. Owensboro Heart Assn. Recipient Liberty Bell award Daviess County Bay Assn., 1966.

Mem. Ky. Edn. Assn. (pres. 1969-70), N.E.A., Ky. Assn. Sch. Adminstrs., Am. Assn. Sch. Adminstrs., Phi Delta Kappa (v.p. 1971). Kiwanian (pres. 1954). Home: 1326 Woodhurst St Bowling Green KY 42101

ESTES, MOREAU PINCKNEY, IV, business exec.lb. Nashville, Oct. 10, 1917; s.; Moreau Pinckney and Lillian (Cole) E.; student Vanderbilt U., 1937; LL.B., Cumberland U. Law Sch., 1938; m. Bertha Lewis, Jan. 14, 1941; children—Moreau Pinckney V, Robert Lewis, Victoria Susanne. Admitted to Tenn. bar, 1938; practiced in Nashville, 1938-41; bldg. contractor, Nashville, 1940-42; asst. employees service dir. Vultee Aircraft, Nashville, 1942; bldg. contractor, Nashville, 1946-53; dir. Davidson County Farm Bur., Nashville, 1950-56; v.p. Davidson Farmers Co-Op, 1955-56; gen. mgr. Harpeth Valley Utilities Dist. of Davidson and Williamson Counties, Tenn., 1963-67; now pres. Hillsboro-Harpeth Corp.; property adminstr. State of Tenn., 1964-67, atty. property div., 1962-64; dir. So. Title Guaranty Corp. of Tenn. Del. Democratic County Dem. Primary Commn., 1967-69. Served as 1st lt., Signal State Conv., 1951-68; sec. Williamson Corps, AUS, 1942-46. Mem. Nashville Home Bldrs. Assn. (pres. 1951, dir. 1952), Tenn. Horsemens Assn., (dir. 1964), Tenn. Hist. Assn., Nashville Tennis Assn., Tenn., Nashville bar assns., Am. Judicature Soc., Internat. Platform Assn., Davidson Cou;ty Farm Bur., Am. Legion, Delta Kappa Epsilon. Democrat. Methodist (steward 1940-50). Clubs: Inglewood Sch. Men's (past pres.), Percy Priest Sch. Men's (pres., 1963), Wildwood Swimming and Tennis (founder, 1st chmn. bd.). Home: Beech Creek Rd Route 2 Brentwood TN 37027 Office: Am Trust Bldg Nashville TN 37201

ESTES, NOLAN, supt. schs.; b. Rio Hondo, Tex., June 22, 1930; s. Clarence M. and Eva (Boyd) E.; B.S., U. Corpus Christi, 1950; M.Ed., U. Tex., 1954; postgrad. Baylor U., 1956; D.Ed., Harvard, 1958; m. Mildred Johnson, Aug. 9, 1951; children—Dennis, Blake, Kevin, Brian. Tchr. math. and sci., athletic dir. Bruni (Tex.) High Sch., 1950-51; adminstrv. intern Bur. Lab. Schs., U. Tex., Austin, 1953-54; elementary tchr. Waco (Tex.) Ind. Sch. Dist., 1954-55, prin. Lake Waco Sch., 1955-59; ednl. tv instr. Tex. Dept. Edn. and Baylor U., Waco, 1956-57; staff mem. Center for Field Studies, Harvard Grad. Sch. Edn., 1957-58; asst. supt. instrn. Chattanooga Pub. Schs., 1959-62; vis. lectr. edn. U. Chattanooga, 1960-62; vis. lectr. edn. U. Ariz., summer 1962; supt. schs. Sch. Dist. Riverview Gardens, St. Louis County, Mo., 1962-66; Washington intern in edn. as spl. asst. to asso. commr. edn. Bur. Elementary and Secondary Edn., 1965-66, dir. div. Plans and Supplementary Centers, 1966, dep. asso. commr., 1966-67, asso. commr. edn., 1967-68; supt. schs. Dallas Ind. Sch. Dist., 1968—. Mem operations adv. com. Nat. Com. on Assessing Progress of Edn.; mem. adv. and policy com. ERIC Clearing House on Tchr. Ednl; mem. exec. com. Research Council Gt. Cities Program for Sch. Improvement. Vice chmn. Greater Chattanooga United Fund, 1962; pres. St. Louis County Sch. Dist. AV Corp. Bd., 1964. Bd. dirs. Circle Ten council Boy Scouts Am., Chattanooga Symphony Orch.; mem. adv. bd. trustees Carson-Newman Coll., Jefferson City, Tenn.; trustee, mem. exec. com. St. Louis Ednl. Television Commn.; trustee U. Corpus Christi. Served with AUS, 1951-53. Decorated Bronze Star medal. Recipient Outstanding Officer of Year award Chattanooga Jr. C. of C., 1961-62, Sch. of Year award Nation's Sch. Competition as supt. schs., 1965, Distinguished Alumnus awards U. Corpus Christi, 1966, Dallas Bapt. Coll., 1969. S.D. Shankland Meml. scholar, 1968. Mem. N.E.A. (life), Assn. for Supervision and Curriculum Devel. (past dir.), Tex. Assn. Sch. Adminstrs., Tex. Tchrs. Assn., Tex. Elementary Sch. Prins. Assn. (past dist. pres.), Tenn. Assn. for Supervision and Curriculum Devel. (past pres.), Sigma Epsilon, Phi Delta Kappa. Home: 4008 Allencrest St Dallas TX 75234 Office: 3700 Ross Av Dallas TX 75204

ESTRADA, ANDRES, educator; b. Sarita, Tex., Dec. 9, 1924; s. Guadalupe and Guadalupe (Leal) E.; B.S., Tex. A. and I. Coll., 1947, M.S., 1950; m. Maria Christina Vela, Mar. 31, 1948; children—Carl David, Teresa Ann, Andres, Kathryn Marie, Christina Michelle. Asst. prof. St. Mary of Woods Coll., Terre Haute, Ind., 1950-52; analytical chemist S.W. Labs., Harligen, Tex., 1952; instr. Eastern Okla. A. and M. Coll., 1953-59; asst. prof. Pan Am. Coll., Edinburg, Tex., 1959-69, asso. prof., 1970—; with AID, Guatemala, C.Am., summers 1967-68. Pres. Sacred Heart Sch. Bd., 1968—. Republican precinct chmn. several county coms., 1962-64. Bd. dirs. Intercollegiate Knights Found. Mem. Am. Chem. Soc. (vice chmn. local sect.), Am. Assn. U. Profs. (pres. chpt.), Tex. Acad. Sci., Tex. Assn. Coll. Tchrs. (treas. chpt.) A.A.A.S., Phi Kappa Theta (internat. trustee 1971—). Roman Catholic. Intercollegiate Knights (nat. exec. sec., Founder award 1970), Kiwanian (pres. 1972—). Author: Officers Manual, Intercollegiate Knights Fraternity, 1960. Home: 521 N 12th St Edinburg TX 78539

ETCHISON, ANNIE LAURIE, librarian, artist; b. Cana, N.C., Dec. 5, 1908; d. John W. and Nana (Cain) Etchison; A.B., Western Res. U., 1939, B.L.S., 1940. Librarian, Cleve. Pub. Library, 1941-42; chief librarian Langley AFB, Va., 1942-44; supervisory librarian U.S. Army, Hawaii, 1945; chief librarian Armed Forces Western Pacific, Phillipines, Okinawa 1945-46; command librarian 2d Dist. U.S. Army, Europe, 1947-49, U.S. Air Force, Alaska, 1950-52; librarian recruiter U.S. Army, Washington, 1952-54; staff librarian U.S. Army, Korean Communication Zone, 1954-55; librarian Dept. Navy, 1956; dir. libraries, Ft. Bragg, N.C., 1957-63; staff librarian 3d U.S. Army, 1963-70; chief librarian, Ft. McPherson, Ga., 1970-72, staff librarian Hdqrs. 3d Army, Ft. McPherson, 1972—. Cons. automation of libraries, library design and facilities, personnel mgmt. Home: RFD 5 Box 58 Mocksville NC 27028 Office: Hdqrs US Army Bldg 219 Fort McPherson GA 30330

ETGEN, GARRET JAY, educator; b. Hackensack, N.J., Aug. 20, 1937; s. Harold Theodore and Barbara (Neighmond) E.; B.S., Coll. William and Mary, 1959; M.S. (Woodrow Wilson fellow), U. Wis., 1961; Ph.D., U. N.C., 1964; m. Charlotte Lee Tolley, Aug. 20, 1960; children—John Theodore, Garret Jay; Michael Peter. Teaching fellow U. N.C. at Chapel Hill, 1961-62, instr., 1962-64; asst. chief applied math. br., Hdqrs. NASA, Washington, 1964-67; asst. prof. math. U. Houston, 1967-69, asso. prof., 1969—. Instr. Coll. William and Mary, Williamsburg, Va., summers 1961, 62; asst. professional lectr. George Washington U., Washington, 1965-67. Served to capt. AUS, 1964-66. Mem. A.A.A.S., Am. Math. Soc., Math. Assn. Am., Phi Beta Kappa, Sigma Xi, Omicron Delta Kappa, Pi Mu Epsilon. Home: 8815 Concho St Houston TX 77036

ETHEREDGE, ROBERT FOSTER, lawyer, state legislator; b. Birmingham, Ala., July 14, 1920; s. Joel H. and Nell (Cain) E.; A.B., U. Ala., 1946, LL.B., 1949; m. Joanna Carson, Aug. 28, 1948; children—Robert Foster, Carson, Nancy. Admitted to Ala. bar, 1949; since practiced in Birmingham, Ala.; mem. firm Spain, Gillon, Riley, Tate, & Ansley, and predecessor, 1949—. Mem. Ala. Ho. of Reps., 1963—. Mem. adv. com. Family Ct.; pres. Ala. Soc. Crippled Children and Adults, 1971-72; chmn. profl. div. United Appeal. bd. dirs. Jefferson County Socs. for Crippled Children and Adults., N. Central Ala. Rehab. Facility. Served to 1st lt. AUS, 1943-46. Mem. Am. (mem. state legislative com.), Birmingham bar assns., Ala. State Bar, Am. Legion, V.F.W., Relay House, Ala. Law Inst., Farrah Law Soc., Ala. Def. Lawyers Assn., Internat. Assn. Ins. Counsel, Am. Judicature Soc., Omicron Delta Kappa, Pi Kappa Alpha. Democrat. Methodist. Elks, Eagles, Rotarian. Club: Country of Birmingham. Home: 3748 Locksley Dr Birmingham AL 35223 Office: John A Hand Bldg Birmingham AL 35203

ETHERIDGE, JACK PAUL, judge; b. Atlanta, Mar. 16, 1927; s. Anton Lee and Jessie Shephard (Brown) E.; grad. Darlington Sch., Rome, Ga., 1945; B.S., Davidson Coll., 1949; LL.B., Emory U., 1955; m. Ursula Schlatter, Feb. 2, 1952;children—Jack Paul, Margaret, Mary Elizabeth. Admitted to Ga. bar, 1955, practiced in Atlanta, 1955-66, partner firm Huie, Etheridge & Harland, 1958-66; judge Superior Ct., Atlanta Jud. Dist., 1966—; lectr. law Woodrow Wilson Law Sch., 1958-61. Adv. bd. Juvenile Ct. Atlanta, 1961-64. Mem. Ga. Gen. Assembly from Fulton County, 1961-65. Mem. State Crime Commn. Bd. dirs. Atlanta Legal Aid Soc., 1960—; trustee Davidson Coll., Atlanta Hist. Soc., Arts Festival of Atlanta, Inc. Served with USNR, 1945-46; with AUS, 1950-52. Named Young Man of Yr. in Professions, Atlanta Jr. C. of C., 1962. Mem. Atlanta Bar Assn. (pres. 1962-63), Beta Theta Pi. Presbyn. Home: 4715 Harris Trail NW Atlanta GA 30327 Office: Courthouse Atlanta GA 30303

ETHINGTON, GROVER CLEVELAND, JR., state ofcl.; b. Shelby County, Ky., Aug. 24, 1923; s. Grover C. and Samantha G. (Hulker) E.; B.S. in Elec. Engring., U. Ky., 1950; certificate Yale, 1964; m. Virginia M. Watkins, Nov. 22, 1951; children—Jerry Wayne, Candy Marie. Engr., Joe Wakefield, contractor, Shelbyville, Ky., 1950; project engr. Schenley Distillers, Inc., Frankfort, Ky., 1950-54; traffic engr. Ky. Dept. of Hwys., Frankfort, 1954-61, chief traffic engr., 1961-64, asst. dir. traffic, 1964—. Served with AUS, 1942-45, 61-62. Mem. Inst. Traffic Engrs., Triangle, Scabbard and Blade, Eta Kappa Nu. Democrat. Baptist. Home: 245 Hawkeegan Dr Frankfort KY 40601 Office: State Office Bldg Dept Hwys Frankfort KY 40601

ETHRIDGE, SAMUEL BROUGHTON, assn. exec.; b. Brewton, Ala., Dec. 22, 1923; s. Frank and Lillie (Foster) E.; student Stillman Jr. Coll., 1940-42; A.B., Howard U., 1948; M.Ed., U. Cin., 1957; m. Cordia Elizabeth Baylor, Nov. 11, 1946; children—Samuel David, Sherman George, Camille LaVerne, Steven Edsel. Tchr., Central High Sch., Mobile, Ala., 1948-54; prin. Chickasaw Terrace Sch., Mobile County, 1954-56; supr. secondary schs,, Mobile, 1956-58; asst. dir. intergroup relations Nat. Found.-March of Dimes, N.Y.C., 1958-60; free lance fund raising, pub. relations, N.Y.C., 1960-62; dir. So. region United Negro Coll. Fund, Atlanta, 1962-64; asst. sec. Commn. on Profl. Rights and Responsibilities, N.E.A., Washington, 1964-65, asso. sec., 1965-68, asst. exec. sec., dir. Center Human Relations, 1968-69, asst. exec. sec. tchr. rights, 1969—. Camping chmn. Mobile Area, Boy Scouts Am., 1951-58; chmn. alumni fund dr. Stillman Coll., 1966-68. Bd. dirs. Nat. Com. Against Discrimination in Housing. Served with USAAF, 1943-46. Mem. Am. Bridge Assn. (pub. relations dir. 1965-67). Home: 1602 Allison St NW Washington DC 20011 Office: 1201 16th St NW Washington DC 20036

ETTELDORF, JAMES NICHOLAS, physician. Intern, resident John Gaston Hosp.; resident St. Louis Children's Hosp.; mem. attending staff Frank T. Tobey Children's Hosp., Le Bonheur Chidlren's Hosp.; cons. pediatrician St. Joseph Hosp., Methodist Hosp., Baptist Meml. Hosp.; Goodman prof. pediatrics, dir. pediatric research lab. U. Tenn. Diplomate Am. Bd. Pediatrics, also ofcl. examiner. Fellow Am. Acad. Pediatrics; mem. Soc. for Pediatric Research, Am. Pediatric Soc., Alpha Omega Alpha, Sigma Xi. Address: 848 Adams Av Memphis TN 38103

EUBANK, RAYMOND HENRY, petroleum co. exec.; b. Dallas, Aug. 10, 1927; s. Joseph Henry and Fannie Pearl (Riddle) E.; B.S. in Petroleum Engring., Tex. A. & M. U., 1950; m. Ora May Davis, Nov. 28, 1951; children—Richard Henry, Sheri Janece, Dennis Ray. Petroleum engr. Sun Oil Co., 1950-56, Hunt Oil Co., 1956-65; petroleum cons., Dallas, 1965-67; exec. v.p. Triton Oil & Gas Corp., Dallas, 1967—, also dir. Dir. New Zealand Petroleum Co., Ltd., Electrothermic Co. Served to 1st lt. AUS, 1946-48, 1951-53. Registered profl. engr., Tex. Mem. Soc. Petroleum Engrs. of Am. Inst. Mining Engrs., Petroleum Engrs. Club, Dallas Petroleum Engrs. Club. Methodist (mem. bd. 1968-69). Club: Royal Oaks Country (dir. 1970—; v.p. 1971—) (Dallas). Home: 9626 Estate Lane Dallas TX 75238 Office: 2310 Republic Bank Tower Dallas TX 75201

EUBANKS, LUTHER BOYD, dist. judge; b. Caprock, N.M., July 31, 1917; s. J. P. and Evie (Downs) E.; A.B., U. Okla., 1941, LL.B., 1943; m. Lois Marie Stevens, Sept. 5, 1942; children—Nancy Lou (Mrs. Rutledge McClaran), Carolyn Sue, Stephen Don. Admitted to Okla. bar, 1944; atty. Cotton County, Okla., 1946-49; mem. Okla. Ho. of Reps., 1949-53; dist. judge, Lawton, Okla., 1956-65; U.S. dist. judge Western Dist. Okla., Oklahoma City, 1965—. Served with AUS, 1943-45. Recipient Silver Beaver award Boy Scouts Am., 1963; Gulick award Camp Fire Girls, 1963. Mem. Phi Delta Phi. Democrat. Methodist. Rotarian. Home: 2933 Charing Cross Rd Oklahoma City OK 73120 Office: Box 1883 Oklahoma City OK 73101

EUBANKS, RALPH, banker; b. Elko, Ga., Oct. 18, 1908; s. C. E. and Maye (Smith) E.; A.B., B.S.C., Mercer U., 1928; m. Dorothy Slappey, Feb. 21, 1945; children—Donald Charles, David Ralph, John Smith. With Citizens & So. Nat. Bank, Macon, Ga., 1939—, v.p., 1949-57, exec. v.p., 1957—, also mem. adv. bd.; dir. Bank of Warner Robins (Ga.). Pres. Macon United Givers Fund, 1965; mem. Macon Housing Authority, 1961—, Bibb County Bd. Edn., 1959—. Served with AUS, 1942-44. Mem. Nat. Assn. Bank Auditors and Controllers, Am. Bankers Assn., Macon C. of C. (treas. 1966-67), Delta Sigma Pi (past pres. Macon). Baptist. Elk, Lion. Clubs: Idle Hour Country (Macon, Ga.); Houston Lake Country (Perry, Ga.); Milledgeville (Ga.) Country. Home: 1414 Twin Pines Dr Macon GA 31201 Office: PO Box 4007 Macon GA 31208

EULISS, JACK MANNING, automobile dealer, state legislator North Carolina; b. Burlington, N.C., Aug. 27, 1921; s. Cyrus Manning and Myrtle (Cooper) E.; student Wake Forest Coll., 1938-42; m. Ione Cheek, Feb. 25, 1943; children—Jack Manning, Ann Cheek, Williams McAdoo. Gen. sales mgr. Alamance Motors, Inc., 1946-48, gen. mgr., 1948—, treas., 1950—, dir., 1953—; treas., dir. Manning-Cooper Co., Inc., 1955—; automotive cons., treas., dir. United Service Assos., 1958—; treas., dir. Burlington Garment Mfg. Co., 1957—. Mem. N.C. Council on Mental Retardation, 1967. Councilman, City of Burlington, 1959-62, also mayor pro tem; mem. N.C. Ho. of Reps., 1963—. Trustee N.C. Bapt. Children's Home, 1955-59, Campbell Coll. Served with USAAF, 1942-45. Recipient Jaycee Citizenship award, 1953, Alamance County Citizen of Year award, 1958. Democrat. Baptist. Mason (Shriner), Kiwanian (pres. Burlington 1954, lt. gov. dist. 1957); mem. Order DeMolay (Legion of Honor 1957), Loyal Order Moose. Home: Lake Dr E PO Box 913 Burlington NC 27215 Office: 508 S Church St Burlington NC 27216

EURE, THAD, state ofcl.; b. Gates County, N.C., Nov. 15, 1899; s. Tazewell A. and Armecia (Langstun) E.; student U. N.C., 1917-19 Law Sch., 1921-22; LL.D., Elon Coll., 1958; m. Minta Banks, Nov. 15, 1924; children—Mrs. J. Norman Black, Jr., Thad. Lawyer; mayor City of Winton, 1923-28; atty. Hertford County, 1923-31; prin. clk. N.C. Ho of Reps., 1931, 33, 35, 36; sec. state State of N.C., Raleigh, 1936—. Keynote speaker N.C. Democratic Conv., 1950, permanent chmn., 1962. Chmn. bd. trustees Elon Coll. Mem. Nat. Assn. Secs. of State (pres. 1942, dean 1961), Am. Legion, 40 and 8, Theta Chi. Conglist. Elk. Home: 2345 New Bern Av Raleigh NC 27601 Office: State Capitol Bldg Raleigh NC 27601

EUSTON, ANDREW FRANCIS, JR., govt. ofcl.; b. New Haven, Conn., Sept. 8, 1934; s. Andrew Francis and Kathleen (Holwell) E.; grad. Hotchkiss Sch., 1952; B.A., Yale, 1956, B.Arch., 1959. Designer A.F. Euston (Sr.), Architect, New Haven, 1956-59; architect firm McLoed, Ferrara & Ensign, Washington, 1962, firm W.H. Metcalf Assos., Washington, 1963-65; urban designer firm Cooper & Auerbach, Washington, 1965-66; dir. urban programs A.I.A., Washington, 1966-68; dir. urban design br. Office Community Devel., Dept. Housing and Urban Devel., Washington, 1968-70, prin. urban design officer Environmental and Land Use Planning div., 1970—; mem. adv. staff Tech. Adv. Panel on Housing, Commerce Dept., 1968; vis. critic Grad Sch. Design, Harvard, Cambridge, Mass., 1971-72; columnist Capitol Hill News, Washington, 1964-65. Treas. The Seversmith Found., 1966-72; mem. Capitol Hill Community Council, 1962-68, Neighborhood Commons Archtl. Adv. Com., 1964-66, Emergency Recreation Com. for Capitol East, 1966-68; dir. Assn. Study Man-Environment Relations, 1969—, Washington Ethical Soc., 1972—, World Future Soc., 1968—. Bd. dirs. humanist involvement div. Am. Humanist Assn., 1966-68, pres. Washington Chpt. 1962—. Served as 1st lt. M.C., USAF, 1959-62. Loeb fellow in advanced environmental studies, Harvard, 1971-72. Mem. A.I.A. (mem. com. urban design, com. govt. affairs), Am. Soc. Planning Ofcls., Nat. Assn. Housing and Redevel. Ofcls., Nat. Trust for Historic Preservation. Clubs: Yale (Washington); Faculty (Harvard). Author: (with Archibald C. Rogers) Check-list for Cities, 1968; (with others) Socio-Physical Technology: A State-of-the-Art Report, 1971. Home: 122 12th St SE Washington DC 20003 Office: Rm 7126 Dept Housing and Urban Development Washington DC 20410

EVANS, ALLEN B., county extension agt.; b. Laverne, Okla., Nov. 24, 1930; s. Hershal J. and Velma E. (Brillheart) E.; B.S. in Agr. Edn., Okla. State U., 1960; m. Alene Beall, July 2, 1954; children— Allen B. III, Andrea Sue. With Extension Service, Okla. State U., 1960—, 4-H agt., Beaver County, 1960-61, Woodward County, 1961-66, extension dir. Dewey County, Taloga, Okla., 1966—. Served with USNR, 1950-54. Mem. Woodward C. of C. Baptist (deacon 1969; tng. union dir. 1970-71). Kiwanian (agr. chmn. 1966—; vice chmn. 1971-72). Contbr. articles and short stories to mags. Address: Box 188 Taloga OK 73667

EVANS, ARTHUR PICKETT, JR., state ofcl.; b. Louisville, Dec. 1, 1916; s. Arthur P. and Joanna (Morton) E.; B.S., Wilberforce U., 1937; certificate civil engring. Bklyn. Poly. Inst., 1942; M.S., U. Louisville, 1971; LL.D. (hon.), U. Liberia, 1960; m. Theo Wilson Bradshaw, Sept. 1, 1943; children—Joanne M. (Mrs. Cecil R. Sanders), Constance M. (Mrs. Robert E. Smith). Supr. recreation Louisville Dept. Recreation, 1938-40; v.p. Campbell Coll., Jackson, Miss., 1940-41; owner Evans Studio Photography, Louisville, 1945-60; asso. dir. human relations City of Louisville, 1963-65; exec. dir. Youth Commn., City Louisville and Jefferson County, 1965-70; Jefferson County field office adminstr. pub. assistance Ky. Dept. Econ. Security, 1970—. Pres., Chestnut St. YMCA, 1965—. Bd. dirs. Parkhill Community Corp., Vietnam Meml. Non Profit Corp. Served with AUS, 1942-45. Mem. Photographers Assn. Am., Community Devel. Soc., Nat. Assn. Pub. Youth Agys. Alpha Phi Alpha. Methodist (trustee). Clubs: Optimist (pres. 1968-69), Epicurean (pres. 1969-70). Home: 1917 Yale Dr Louisville KY 40205 Office: 400 S. 6th St Louisville KY 40203

EVANS, CHARLES HARMON, city ofcl.; b. nr. Prattville, Ala., Aug. 22, 1932; s. Jessie and Martha J. (Manning) E.; B.S. in Bus. Adminstrn., Auburn U., 1958; m. Cecelia Ann Minor, Oct. 29, 1961; 1 son, Christopher Charles. Salesman Ala. Machinery & Supply Co., Montgomery, 1951-53, 55; accounting lab. asst. Auburn (Ala.) U., 1955-58; coordinator White's Furniture & Appliance Co., Pensacola, Fla., 1958-59; accountant Creel & Dennison, Ft. Walton Beach, Fla., 1959-61; city clk., finance dir., City Fort Walton Beach, 1961—. Div. co-chmn. United Fund, Ft. Walton Beach, 1969-71; mem. govt. subcom. Okaloosa County Com. Goals and Objectives, 1971. Bd. dirs. YMCA, Ft. Walton Beach; mem. adult studies adv. council Okaloosa Walton Jr. Coll., 1967-71. Served with AUS, 1953-55. Named Boss of Year Nat. Secs. Assn., 1969-70. C.P.A., Fla. Mem. Fort Walton Power Squadron, Fla. Municipal Finance Officers Assn. (mem. com. 1971-72), Nat. Assn. Accountants, Am., Fla. Insts. C.P.A.'s, Internat. Inst. Municipal Clks., Fla. Municipal Finance Officers Assn., Nat. Secs. Assn., Delta Sigma Pi. Baptist. Home: 19 Mimosa St NW Fort Walton Beach FL 32548 Office: PO Box 1449 Fort Walton Beach FL 32548

EVANS, CHARLES HARRISON, supt. schs.; b. Bastrop, Tex., Nov. 23, 1925; s. Charles Harrison and Lilly Ann (Hemphill) E.; B.A., Baylor U., 1949; M.S., Tex. Coll. Arts and Industries, 1956; m. June Marie Hensley, Dec. 24, 1949; children—Marcus Eugene, Keith Byron. Tchr., coach, Marble Falls (Tex.) Ind. Sch. Dist., 1949-50, Port Lavaca Ind. Sch. Dist., 1950-53; prin. high sch. coach Sundeen Ind. Sch. Dist., Corpus Christi, 1953-56; prin. high sch. Agua Dulce Ind. Sch. Dist., 1956-57, supt. schs., 1 57-67; supt. schs. Bastrop (Tex.) Ind. Sch. Dist., 1967—. Served with USAAF, 1944-45. Mem. Phi Delta Kappa. Methodist. Mason (Shriner), Elk, Lion (chmn. 1971-72). Home: Route 2 Box 151A Bastrop TX 78602 Office: Box 709 Bastrop TX 78602

EVANS, CHARLES WAYNE, sem. ofcl.; b. Happy, Tex., Jan. 16, 1919; s. Joseph George and Bertie Mae (Mulkey) S.; B.S., Hardin-Simmons U., 1940, LL.D., 1961; studied Tex. Christian U., U. Ky.; m. Zona Elizabeth Horn, June 9, 1940; children—David, Lyn, Jan. Stockman-farmer, Hereford, Tex., 1940-46; dealer Internat. Harvester Co., 1946-53; bus. mgr. Southwestern Bapt. Theol. Sem., Fort Worth, 1954—. Past chmn. budget com. United Fund Fort Worth and Tarrant County; past pres. Ft. Worth Assn. for Retarded Children. Trustee Hardin-Simmons U., 1947-66. Recipient Outstanding Citizen of Year award, Hereford, Tex., 1946, John J. Keeter Jr. Meml. Alumni award Hardin-Simmons U., 1951. Mem. Nat., So. assns. coll. and univ. bus. officers, Bapt. Gen. Conv. Tex. (exec. bd. 1952-64), Am. Assn. Sem. Staff Officers, Adm. Mgmt. Soc., Nat. Assn. Ednl. Buyers, Am. Guild Organists, Hereford-Deaf Smith County C. of C. (past pres.). Baptist (deacon). Mason (32 deg.). Home: Route 3 Box 23A Fort Worth TX 76134 Office: PO Box 22000 Fort Worth TX 76122

EVANS, DAVID A., constrn. co. exec.; b. Texas City, Tex., Feb. 4, 1925; s. Adolph Roemer and Augusta (Henderson) E.; student U. Ark., 1943-44; diploma in Bldg. Contracting, Internat. Corr. Schs., 1949; LL.B., LaSalle U., 1965. Owner, operator Evans Constrn. Co., Texas City, 1949—; pres. Evans Asso. Industries, Inc., Texas City; dir. Texas City Hotel Corp., Provident Security Ins. Co., Houston, 1960-62. Sec. bd. pilot commrs. Ports of Galveston and Texas City, 1962—. Chmn. tax equalization bd. Texas City Schs., 1959; dir. Texas City Civil Def., 1961. Bd. dirs. Tex. Lions Camp Crippled Children, Kerrville. Served with AUS, 1943-45; ETO. Recipient Good Neighbor award Continental Oil Co., 1960. Mem. Nat. Tex. (dir.) home builders assns. Methodist (steward, lay del. ann. conf.

Meth. Chs.). Lion (internat. pres. 1968-69, presidents award 1960, 62-68). Address: 1617 Fannin St 1205 Houston TX 77002

EVANS, EARL, JR., assn. exec.; b. Canton, Miss., June 20, 1906; s. Earl and Minnie (Lewis) E.; student Bowling Green Coll. 1926-29; m. Fay O'Malley, Mar. 30, 1930. Accountant, Evans Co., Canton, 1929-32; farm machinery dealer Earl Evans & Son, Canton, 1932-40; spl. agt. FBI, Washington, 1942-45; pres. Evans Furniture Mfg. Co., Canton, 1945-62; dir. Commn. Budget and Accounting, 1961-66, Alcoholic Beverage Control Commn., 1966-68; exec. v.p. Miss.-Ala. div. Midcontinent Oil and Gas Assn., Jackson, Miss., 1968—; pres. New Evans Gin Co. Mem. State Edn. Finance Com., 1952-56, Pub. Employees Retirement Bd., 1952-56; chmn. Miss. Medicaid Commn., 1969—. Mem. Miss. Senate, 1940-43, 47-62, pres. pro-tem, 1956-60, chmn. finance com., 1950-60. Named Citizen of Year, City of Canton, 1959. Mem. Miss. (past v.p.), Canton (past pres.) chambers commerce. Episcopalian. Lion. Club: Canton Country (past pres., dir.). Home: PO Box 185 Canton MS 39046 Office: 455 N Lamar St Jackson MS 39202

EVANS, EDGAR ERNEST, educator; b. Pittsview, Ala., Jan. 20, 1908; s. Ebenezer Ernest and Mary G. (Day) E.; B.A., Fisk U., 1930; M.A., U. Mich., 1948; m. Zelia V. Stephens, Dec. 25, 1940. Prin., Apopka (Fla.) Jr. High Sch., 1931-34, Winter Garden (Fla.) Jr. High Sch., 1934-38, Starke (Fla.) High Sch., 1938-41, Siluria (Ala.) Jr. High Sch., 1941-42, Rosenwald High Sch., Waidsboro, Va., 1946-48; asso. prof. edn. Ala. State Coll., 1949—. Vice pres. Farm & City Enterprises, Inc., 1952-59, pres., 1961—. Served with USAAF, 1942-45. Fellow Royal Soc. of Health; mem. Am. Pub. Health Assn., Royal Soc. Pub. Health, N.E.A., Am. Sociol. Assn., Internat. Platform Assn., Am. Assn. U. Profs., Phi Delta Kappa, Phi Beta Sigma (state dir. 1953, pres.). Democrat. Member A.M.E. Ch. (1st v.p. Laymens League, 3d state v.p., mem. state edn. com, 2d v.p. lay orgn.). Mason (33 deg.), Elk (asso. state dir. edn.). Home: 1433 Cleveland Av Montgomery AL 36108

EVANS, ELLA ADDIE SMITH (MRS. ROBERT KERR EVANS), clubwoman; b. Raleigh, N.C., Sept. 7, 1902; d. Robert Ira and Maggie Nancy (Bagwell) Smith; tchrs. certificate N.C. State Coll., 1923; certificate Kings Bus. Coll., 1926; m. Robert Kerr Evans, Nov. 9, 1928; children—Nancy Errol (Mrs. David Hazlett Hainlin), Robert Smith. Tchr., Raleigh Pub. Schs., 1923-24; adminstrv. sec. to pres. Meredith Coll., Raleigh, 1936; adminstrv. sec. to dean grad. sch. N.C. State Coll., Raleigh, 1927-31; head of hall, gen. hostess state camps N.C. Future Farmers Am.; administrv. sec. to dean sch. sci. and lit. Auburn (Ala.) U., 1944-64, ofcl. notary public, 1961-64. Mem. Woman's Aux., Lee County Hosp., Opelika, Ala., 1964-65. Mem. U.D.C. (registar, chmn. membership com., mem. edn. com., del. to state conv. Adm. Semmes chpt. 57), D.A.R. (chmn. nominating com., mem. program com. Light Horse Harry Lee chpt., treas.), Colonial Dames XVII Century (charter mem., v.p., mem. screening com., alternate del. to state conv. Capt. Thomas Yale chpt., chpt. v.p. 1968—, nat. and state awards for book), Nat. Soc. Magna Charta Dames, Soc. Descs. Colonial Clergy, Daus. Am. Colonists (charter mem., treas.-sec. 1968—), chpt. chaplain), Sovereign Colonial Soc., Ams. Royal Descent, Soc. Descs. Knights Most Noble Order of the Garter, Plantagenet Soc., Colonial Order of Crown, Nat., E. Ala. geneal. socs., Jamestowne Soc., Nat. Huguenot Soc., Nat. Soc. So. Dames Am., Nat. Ret. Tchrs. Assn. Democrat. Methodist (v.p. Wesleyan Service Guild 1964-65). Clubs: Woman's of Auburn (over-all hostess chmn. 1965-66), Auburn University Campus, Auburn Minerva (pres. 1956-58), Ala. Minerva (state pres. 1956-58). Co-compiler: The Captain Thomas Yale Chapter—Colonial Dames XVII Century—1967. Home: 4015 Camelot Dr Raleigh NC 27609

EVANS, ERNEST PIPKIN, JR., govt. ofcl.; b. St. Petersburg, Fla., Mar. 6, 1944; s. Ernest P. and Carrie (McLeod) E.; student Jacksonville U., 1963-65; B.A., U. Md., 1970. Exec. dir. Jacksonville (Fla.) Youth Council, 1962-64, Nat. Youth Councils, Washington, 1964-66; profl. staff mem. Urban Am., Inc., Washington, 1966-67, U.S. Senate Select Com. Small Bus., Washington, 1967—. Dir. Fourteen-Twenty-one Market Research Inc., Washington; dir., cons. Bartholomew Assos., Inc., Washington. Youth dir. Citizens for Johnson, Humphrey, Jacksonville, 1964. Recipient citation of merit Reader's Digest, 1965; Service to Mankind award Sertoma Internat., 1964. Mem. Am. Soc. Assn. Execs., Nat. Com. Children and Youth, Capitol Hill Restoration Soc. Clubs: Nat. Aviation, U.S. Senate Staff. Home: 318 10th St SE Washington DC 20003 Office: Old Senate Office Bldg Washington DC 20510

EVANS, GEORGE E(DWARD), JR., coal mining exec.; b. Charleston, W.Va., June 7, 1918; s. George E. and Nell (Harrington) E.; B.S.C., Notre Dame, 1940; m. Josephine Collins, Feb. 16, 1942; children—Patricia Ellen (Mrs. Neal J. Crowley), Mary Josephine (Mrs. Phillip R. Johnson), Jane Collins. Pres. Beaver Creek Consol. Coal Co., Evans Industries, Inc., Big Creek Devel. Co. (all subsidiaries Nat. Steel Corp.); dir. 1st Guaranty Bank, Martin, Ky.; dir., mem. exec. com. Bank Lexington (Ky). Mem. coal mining research com. U. Ky.; sec. Inst. Mining Research, Morehead (Ky.) State U. Dist. chmn. Boy Scouts Am., 1954; mem. Ky. Racing Commn. Bd. dirs., mem. exec. com. Spindletop Research, Lexington; trustee Appalachian Regional Hosps., Alice Lloyd Coll., Pippa Passes, Ky.; adv. council Prestonsburg Community Coll., U. Ky. Mem. Am. Inst. Mining and Metall. Engrs., Am. Mining Congress (adv. council), Ky. Coal Assn. (chmn.), Big Sandy Elkhorn Coal Operators Assn. (chmn), Ky. Mining Inst. (pres.). Lion (pres. Wayland 1952). Home: 1711 Fairway Dr Lexington KY 40502 Office: PO Box 8125 Lexington KY 40503 also PO Box 295 Wayland KY 41666

EVANS, GILES L., JR., state ofcl. Mgr. Fla. Canal Authority, Jacksonville. Address: 803 Rosselle St Jacksonville FL 32204*

EVANS, GROSE, govt. ofcl. Curator index Am. design and decorative arts Nat. Gallery Art, Washington. Home: 2307 Glasgow Rd Alexandria VA 22307 Office: Nat Gallery Art Constitution at 6th St Washington DC 20565*

EVANS, HAROLD LEROY, civil engr.; b. Rockwell, Tex., Nov. 13, 1930; s. George W. and Alice I. (Brewer) E.; B.S., So. Meth. U., 1960; m. Sally M. McGlon, Oct. 4, 1952; children—Scott W., Suzanne, H. Craig. Asst. div. engr. M.-K.-T. R.R., Waco, Tex., 1960-65; engr. Magnolia Pipe Line Co., Houston, 1965-66; chief civil engr. Davis & Assos., Dallas, 1966-68; pvt. practice civil engring. Harold L. Evans, cons. engr., Dallas, 1968-70; v.p. Evans-Robertson, Inc., cons. engrs., Dallas, 1970—, chmn. bd., 1972—. Served with USMCR, 1952-54. Mem. Tex. Soc. Profl. Engrs., Am. Soc. C.E. Democrat. Baptist. Mason, Rotarian. Home: Route 1 Box 109 Forney TX 75187 Office: PO Box 28355 Dallas TX 75228

EVANS, HAWTHORNE CLOUGH, JR., coll. pres.; b. Morristown, Tenn., Aug. 18, 1927; s. Hawthorne Clough and Lily (Myers) E.; B.A., Carson-Newman Coll., 1950; M.A., Columbia, 1951; Ed. D., U. Tenn., 1958; postgrad. U. Colo., 1956, Lafayette Coll., 1951; m. Barbara Teagarden, Dec. 18, 1963; 1 son, Mark Richard. Band dir. Morristown (Tenn.) Jr. High Sch., 1951-54; guidance counselor Morristown City Schs., 1954-55; prin. Rose Elementary Sch., Morristown, 1955-56, Roberts Elementary Sch., Morristown, 1958-60; asso. prof. edn., psychology Carson-Newman Coll., Jefferson City, Tenn., 1960-62, placement dir., 1962-63, dir. student teaching, 1963-67, chmn. dept. psychology and edn., dir. tchr. edn., 1966-67; pres. Lees-McRae Coll., Banner Elk, N.C., 1967—. Dir. N.C. Nat. Bank. Dir. Camp at Buck Hill Falls (Pa.), 1962-67; mem. exec. bd. Daniel Boone council, asst. dist. chmn. Boy Scouts Am.; Ky.-Tenn. chmn. Circle K.; dir. charge organizer Boys Club Jefferson City, Inc., former mem.bd. dirs.; adviser Cherokee Tribe; dir. Blue Ridge Health Council; trustee N.C. Found. Ch. Related Colls.; commr., chmn. Presbyn. survey com. Presbyn. Ch. U.S. Gen. Assembly. Served with USAAF, 1946-48; maj. USAF Res. Named Young Man of Year, Morristown Jr. C. of C., 1955; Tenn. Tchr. of Year, Tenn. Fedn. Women's Clubs, 1957; U.S. Airman of Year, USAF Res.; recipient Silver Beaver award Boy Scouts Am., 1958. Mem. Nat. (life mem.), Tenn. (past chmn. guidance sect.), Morristown (past pres.) edn. assns., Nat., Tenn. assns. student teaching, Internat. Platform Assn., Tenn. P.T.A. (life), Phi Kappa Phi, Phi Delta Kappa. Presbyn. (elder. Kiwanian (lt. gov. Carolina dist. 1972-73). Contbr. to mags. and newspapers. Home: Box 35 Banner Elk NC 28604 Office: Lees McRae Coll Banner Elk NC 28604

EVANS, HAZEL ATKINSON, polit. ofcl.; b. Atlanta, Aug. 16, 1931; d. Alex P. and Hazel (Thomas) Robert; student Marjorie Webster Jr. Coll., Washington, 1951; m. W. Reed Talley, Sept. 11, 1951; children— W. Reed Talley, Alex R.; m. 2d, Robert Winfield Evans, Nov. 30, 1968. Mem. State Democratic Com. Manatee, Pinellas County, 1962—; mem. Dem. Nat. Com., 1968—; mem. State Central Com. Dem. Exec. Com., Fla., 1966—; sec. Young Dem. Clubs Fla., 1962-63, v.p., 1963-64; del. Dem. Nat. Conv., 1964, 68, 72. Mem. Gov.'s Adv. Com. Pinellas County; Commr. Pinellas County Housing Authority, 1972—. Bd. dirs. Fla. Heart Assn., Fla. Mental Health Assn., Ringling Mus. Art, United Fund Manatee, Pinellas County. Recipient Meritorious award Am. Heart Assn., 1960, 64, 66, President's award Young Democrats Fla., 1963, 64. Mem. Beta Sigma Phi. Home: 1146 41st Av NE St Petersburg FL 33703

EVANS, ISHAM HARRISON, JR., owner agrl. co.; b. West Point, Miss., Jan. 17, 1898; Died 10/30/71; s. Isham Harrison and Margaret Lillian (Nunn) E.; ed. Marion Inst., 1914-15, U. Miss., 1916-17, U. Wis., 1918-19, Sheffield Sci. Inst., Yale, 1920; m. Gladys Temple, Feb. 25, 1921; children—Isham Harrison III, Franklin Temple, Augustus Temple. Formerly farm mgr. E. F. Nunn & Co., Shuqualak, Miss., then mgr., mgr.owner; distbr. Shell Oil, Internat. Harvester Co.; dir. Mchts. and Farmers Bank, Macon, Miss. Bd. dirs. Noxubee Gen. Hosp., chmn. bd. Served with USN, 1919-20. Mem. Miss. Econ. Council, Noxubee County Agrl. Stablzn. and Conservation Service (past chmn. bd.), Noxubee Soil Conservation Service, Am. Soc. Agronomy (sect. pres.), Miss. Cattle Assn. Am., Am. Mgmt. Inst. Baptist (chmn. bd. deacons). Clubs: Downtown, Meridian (Meridian, Miss.); Capital City Petroleum (Jackson, Miss.). Address: PO Box 7 Shuqualak MS 39361 Died 10/30/71

EVANS, JAMES CONALLY, clergyman; b. Wasioto, Ky., May 18, 1924; s. Leonard Maxwell and Mary Adline (Proffitt) E.; B.A., Carson-Newman Coll., 44; Th.M., Southwestern Bapt. Theol. Sem., 1948; D.D. (hon.), Howard Payne Coll., 1955; m. Naomi Brothers, Feb. 27, 1948; children—Christopher Conally, James Eric. Melanie Kay. Ordained to ministry Bapt. Ch., 1942; pastor Second Ch., Newport, Tenn., 1943-45, First Ch., Cresson, Tex., 1946-48, First Ch., Wink, 1948-50, Belmont Ch., Odessa, 1950-62, First Ch., Ocala, Fla., 1962-71, Woodlawn Baptist Ch., Bristol, Tenn., 1971—; dir. Rainbow Mining Co., Terlinga, Tex.; tchr. police ethics, recruit sch. Central Fla. Jr. Coll., 1966—. Mem. adv. council Crusade of Americas, 1965—; mem. Joint Com. Pub. Affairs 1962-69; chaplain U.S. Ho of Reps., 1959-60, Ocala (Fla.) City Police Dept., 1964—; Bd. dirs. Marion County Community Chest, Marion County Cancer Soc. Fla., Boys Clubs Am., Salvation Army, State Mental Hosp. Tex. Named Young Man of Year Odessa Jr. C. of C., 1957. Mem. Pi Kappa Delta, Alpha Psi Omega. Mason (Shriner, 32 deg.). Rotarian. Contbg. author to books. Home: 488 Plantation Rd Bristol VA 24202 Office: 1400 Southside Av Bristol TN 37620

EVANS, JAMES WILLIAM, JR., educator; b. Red Bluff, Cal., July 13, 1936; s. James William and Suzanne (Laveley) E.; student Shasta Coll., 1956; B.S., Campbellsville Coll., 1963; M.A., Western Ky. U., 1966; m. Mary Ann Moore, Jan. 31, 1960; children—James William III, Barbara Ann. Asst. sta. mgr. Standard Oil of Cal., Dunsmuir, 1953-56; owner Green Jersey Restaurant, Greensburg, Ky., 1960-63; tchr. Greensburg High Sch., 1963-65; programs coordinator Green County Schs., Greensburg, 1965-68; dir. Green County Vocational Sch., 1968—; edn. specialist Western Ky. U., 1970. Chmn. bd. West Lake Cumberland Area Devel. Council, 1967; chmn. Cumberland Community Action Agy., 1967—; chmn. Lake Cumberland Area Devel. Dist., 1969-72. Served with USAF, 1956-60. Mem. Greensburg Hist. Soc. (v.p. 1962-67), C. of C. (v.p. 1965). Republican. Presbyn. (elder). Rotarian (pres. 1966). Home: Route 5 Box 11 Greensburg KY 42743

EVANS, JOHN MARTIN, ednl. adminstr.; b. Whitesville, Ala., Oct. 12, 1916; s. Martin Luther and Naomi Ruth (Duke) E.; student Jones County Jr. Coll., 1940-42; B.A., Miss. Coll., 1947; B.D., Southwestern Bapt. Theol. Sem., 1949; M.A., U. So. Miss., 1953, Ed.D. (teaching fellow 1964-66), 1972; m. Esther McQuagge, June 30, 1944; children—Paul, Ruth (Mrs. Duane Jensen). Tchr. Beat Four High Sch., 1942-43; ordained to ministry Bapt. Ch., 1949; pastor Crystal Springs Bapt. Ch., Tylertown, Miss., 1949-51, McLaurin (Miss.) Bapt. Ch., 1951-56, Sunflower (Miss.) Bapt. Ch., 1956-64; instr. Jones County Jr. Coll., Ellisville, Miss., 1966-68, registrar, 1968—. Mem. Miss. Bapt. Conv. Bd., 1961-63. Served with USAAF, 1943-46. Mem. Am. Personnel and Guidance Assn., Southwestern Bapt. Theol. Sem. Alumni Assn. (chpt. pres. 1958-59), U. So. Miss. Alumni Assn., Phi Delta Kappa, Phi Alpha Theta. Rotarian (pres. 1962). Home: 412 Harrison St Ellisville MS 39437

EVANS, JOHN MCCALLUM, physician, educator; b. Hamburg, N.Y., July 18, 1913; s. George Frank and Daisy (Wells) E.; B.A., Denison U., 1935; M.D., U. Buffalo, 1939; m. Marion Jane Cornwell, Nov. 22, 1941; 1 son, Gregory. Intern, Buffalo Gen. Hosp., 1939-40, resident, 1940-41; resident Peter Bent Brigham Hosp., Boston, 1946-48; practice medicine, specializing in cardiology, Washington, 1948—; instr. medicine U. Buffalo, 1940-41; asst. in medicine Harvard, 1946-48; asst. prof., asso. prof. George Washington U., 1948-60, prof. medicine, 1960—, lectr. Cath. U., 1957—; cons. cardiology N. D. Baker Hosp., Mt. Alto Hosp., Washington Hosp. Center; dir. cardiology George Washington U. Hosp. Served with AUS, 1941-46. Fellow A.C.P., Am. Coll. Cardiology; mem. N.Y. Acad. Scis., Acad. Medicine Washington, Assn. U. Cardiologists, Washington Heart Assn. (dir. 1952—, v.p. 1962-63), Am. Heart Assn. (fellow council clin. cardiology), So. Soc. Clin. Investigation. Contbr. numerous articles profl. jours. Home: 7104 Lenhart Dr Chevy Chase MD 20015 Office: 1250 Connecticut Av NW Washington DC 20036

EVANS, KEITH WILLIAM, aluminum co. exec.; b. Detroit, Nov. 30, 1920; s. Walter and Ethel (Constable) E.; pre-med. student Mich. State Coll., 1939-41; Chem.E., Mich. Coll. Mining and Tech., 1946; m. Aubrey Bowling, July 13, 1959; children—Gerald, Dawn, Linda. Adminstrv. officer Ordnance Tank Auto Command, Detroit, 1950-56; gen. mgr. Fla. Enterprises, Miami, 1956-59; v.p., gen. mgr. Cinco Screens Inc., Miami, 1959-60; pres., gen. mgr. Fla. Aluminum Enterprises, Miami, 1960-71; v.p. Warren Industries, 1971-72; exec. v.p. Advance Metals, 1971—, also dir.; pres., gen. mgr. Fla. Screen Enterprises, Inc., 1972—. Served with USNR, 1942-45. Mem. Community Ch. (elder). Home: 19540 NW 8th Av North Miami FL 33161 Office: 1707 W 32d Pl Hialeah FL 33012

EVANS, LEONARD O., state ofcl.; b. Williamsburg, Ky., Nov. 17, 1908; student pub. schs.; m. Nell Cobble; children—Leonard O., Mintha Marie. Successively trustee, v.p., pres. Local 309, United Steelworkers Am., later internat. rep.; state pres. CIO, later 1st v.p. AFL-CIO of Tenn.; now commr. of labor Tenn. Dept. Labor. Baptist. Office: care Tenn Dept Labor Cordell Hull Bldg Nashville TN 37219*

EVANS, MALCOLM GLENMORE, bldg. trade assn. exec.; b. Texarkana, Tex., Mar. 24, 1919; s. Roy Glenmore and Maude (Kizer) E.; B.S., U. Richmond, 1940; postgrad. Old Dominion U., 1964-66; m. Martha Louise Woodson, Feb. 11, 1942; children—Martha (Mrs. Larry Hunter), Charles G., Thomas R. Commd. ensign U.S. Navy, 1940, advanced through grades to comdr., 1952; commanding officer Destroyer and Destroyer Escort, 1948-51, U.S. Naval Amphibious Sch., Little Creek, Va., 1961-62; ret., 1968; exec. dir. Tidewater Assn. Home Builders, Inc., Norfolk, Va., 1968—. Guest lectr. Ednl. TV, 1963-64. Scoutmaster Boy Scouts Am., 1960-68, council scout commr., 1966-68, chmn. Scout dist., 1971; pres. Pony League, 1962. Bd. dirs. Tidewater Assn. Home Builders Scholarship Found., Inc., Tidewater Council exec. com. Boy Scouts Am. Recipient Silver Beaver award Boy Scouts Am., 1962. Mem. Va. Beach (mem. com. 1969-71), Norfolk (mem. com. 1970-72) chambers commerce, Ret. Officers Assn., Kappa Alpha. Baptist. Home: 909 Red Coat Ct Virginia Beach VA 23455 Office: 5665 Virginia Beach Blvd Norfolk VA 23502

EVANS, MARY LANGSTON (MRS. DENNIS E. EVANS), state ofcl.; b. Goldsboro, N.C., May 30, 1911; d. John Dallas and Mary (Williamson) Langston; A.B., Duke, 1932; grad. study Vanderbilt, summer 1938, U. N.C., 1939, U. Chgo., 1940; m. Dennis Ethelbert Evans, July 14, 1942. Tchr. social studies, English, pub. schs., Greenville, N.C., 1932-34, Goldsboro, N.C., 1934-40; field sec. N.C. Classroom Tchrs. and N.C. Edn. Assn., 1940-42; tchr., prin. Dare Co. (N.C.) Schs., 1942-49, co. supr. instrn., 1949-51, supt. schs., 1951-66; regional curriculum project coordinator N.C. Dept. Pub. Instrn., 1966-68, dir. comprehensive sch. improvement project, 1968-71, State Experimentation in Ednl. Devel., 1971—. Mem. Dist. Health Bd.; chmn. Dare County Health Bd., 1961-65. Mem. N.C. Edn. Assn. (dir. 1943, pres. co. unit 1942, 46; pres. N.E. dist. div. supts. 1963), Delta Kappa Gamma, Zeta Tau Alpha. Democrat. Methodist. Club: Manteo Women's (dist. pres. 1947-49). Home: Raleigh Apts Raleigh NC 27605 Office: NC Dept Pub Instrn State Edn Bldg Raleigh NC 27602

EVANS, MELVIN HERBERT, gov. V.I.; b. Christiansted, St. Croix, V.I., Aug. 7, 1917; s. Charles Herbert and Maude (Rogiers) E.; B.S., Howard U., 1940, M.D., 1944; M.P.H., U. Cal. at Berkeley, 1967; m. Mary Phyllis Anderson, Aug. 26, 1945; children—Melvin Herbert, Robert Rogiers, William Charles, Cornelius Duncan. Intern, Harlem Hosp., N.Y.C., 1944-45; physician-in-charge Frederiksted, Govt. V.I., 1945-58, 50-51; sr. asst. surgeon USPHS, Washington, 1948-50; chief municipal physician, St. Croix, 1951-56, 57-59; fellow cardiology Johns Hopkins Hosp., 1956-57; commr. health for V.I., 1959-67; pvt. practice medicine, specializing in internal medicine, St. Croix, 1967-69; gov. V.I., 1969—. Trustee New St. Croix Savs. Bank. Chmn. Bd. Med. Examiners, 1959-67. Mem. Gov.'s Commn. on Civil Def. 1961-66; chmn. Gov.'s Commn. on Human Services, 1962-66; mem. U.S. Selective Service Bd. Appeals, 1967-69. Chmn. bd. trustees Coll. V.I.; bd. dirs. Good Hope Sch., St. Croix; bd. advice St. Dunstan Sch., St. Croix, Island Center St. Croix. Fellow A.C.P.; mem. A.M.A., Nat., Pan Am. med. assns., V.I. Med. Soc. (past pres.), Am. Assn. Pub. Health, Physicians, Am. Pub. Health Assn., St. Croix C. of C., Phi Beta Sigma, Kappa Pi. Methodist. Mason, Rotarian. Club: St. Croix Yacht. Home: La Grande Princesse Christiansted St Croix VI 00820 Office: Govt House Charlotte Amalie St Thomas VI 00801

EVANS, MORTIMER DANIEL, hotel exec.; b. N.Y.C., Feb. 27, 1930; s. Earle and Essie (Applegreen) E.; B.S. in Aeros., St. Louis U., 1951; postgrad. Jacksonville U., 1969-70 children by previous marriage—Stanley Paul, Ilene Claire, Roy Alan; m. 2d, Bobbie Gene Barnett, Aug. 25, 1971. Sales, field engr. Gen. Electric Co., Syracuse. N.Y., 1953-56, Fort Wayne, Ind., 1956-58; chief financial officer Price Co., Inc., Jacksonville, Fla., 1958-66, Atlantic Consol., Inc. (merged with Price Co., Inc. 1966), Jacksonville, 1966-70; pres. 1061 Corp., Mobile Ala., 1971—, Motor Inn Mgmt. Corp. Am., New Orleans, 1971—. Cons. ind. motel owners, 1968—. Vice pres., bd. dirs. Jacksonville Jewish Center, 1967-70, bd. chmn. bldg. fund, 1968-70; trustee Jacksonville Art Mus., 1969-71; bd. dirs. River Garden Hebrew Home, 1970. Kiwanian, Mason (32 degree, Shriner). Office: PO Box 1007 2231 Vets Hwy Kenner LA 70062

EVANS, NATHAN LYLE, elec. supply co. exec.; b. Baton Rouge, Jan. 14, 1926; s. Oscar and Bernia (Fuselier) E.; student Gulf Coast Mil. Acad., 1943, Northwestern U., 1948, N.Y. U., 1949; B.A. in Journalism, La. State U., 1950; m. Gloria Jane Weir, July 26, 1952; children—Peggy Jane, David Lyle. With Evans Elec. Supply, Inc., Baton Rouge, 1951—, v.p., 1956—. Bd. dirs. Fish Vols., Baton Rouge Symphony Orch. Served with AUS, 1945-46, 1950-51. Mem. Baton Rouge C. of C., Ls. State U. Alumni Fedn., Gideons, Internat. Episcopalian (past vestryman). Club: Bocage Racquet (Baton Rouge). Home: 5885 Eastwood Dr Baton Rouge LA 70806 Office: 1060 Nicholson Dr Baton Rouge LA 70821

EVANS, OVERTON CHENAULT, II, mfg. co. exec.; b. Aucon, C.Z., Feb. 22, 1912; s. Joe Ashby and Minnie (Williams) E.; student Ky. Wesleyan U., 1930; A.B., Morehead State U., 1934; m. Madge Durham, July 6, 1940; children—Peter Chenault, David Overton. Pres., O. C. Evans Equipment Corp., mfg. co., Mount Sterling, Ky., 1934—; partner Oldshaw and Evans, land developers and home builders, 1964-72; dir. Montgomery Nat. Bank, Mount Sterling. Mem. Mount Sterling Water Commn. 1971-72; mem. Mount Sterling Sch. Bd., 1962-64. Bd. dirs. Mount Sterling Indsl. Found. Served with AUS, 1942-43. Mem. Mount Sterling C. of C. (dir. 1966—), Am. Legion. Baptist (trustee 1960—). Mason, Lion. Club: Mount Sterling Golf and Country (dir. 1960—). Home: 307 Sycamore St Mount Sterling KY 40353 Office: 9 Wilson St Mount Sterling KY 40353

EVANS, PAUL LEWIS, journalist; b. Alpena, S.D., Oct. 31, 1914; s. John David and Margaret Vida (Smith) E.; B.S., Dakota Wesleyan U., 1937; Nieman fellow Harvard, 1946-47; m. Lelah Everly Hayes, Jan. 8, 1938; children—Lance Darrel, Thomas John, Mary Paula, Marcia Lee. Reporter, sports editor Mitchell (S.D.) Daily Republic, 1937-40, exec. editor, 1943-50; information specialist A.A.A., Dept. Agr., 1941-42; editor Redfield (S.D.) Jour.-Observer, 1943; prof. journalism Ohio Wesleyan U., 1950-51; asst. dir. information TVA, 1951-52, dir. information, 1952—. Mem. S.D. Asso. Press Mng. Editors' Assn. (pres. 1949), So. Assn. Nieman Fellows (v.p. 1958-59, 60-61), Nieman Alumni Council, Norris Religious Fellowship. Home:

29 E Norris Rd Norris TN 37828 Office: New Sprankle Bldg Knoxville TN 37902

EVANS, PETER KENNETH, advt. exec.; b. Brighton, Eng., Apr. 18, 1935; s. Percy Edward and Doris (McCoy) E.; ed. in Eng.; m. Juana Santana Ramirez, Mar. 31, 1956; children—Luis Miguel, Linda Rosa Del Rocio, Pilar De Los Angeles. Dental technician E.J. Steele, Shoreham, Eng., 1950-51, John Williams, Brighton, Eng., 1951-53, W.G. Hetherington, Salisbury, Eng., 1955-58; art dir. Grant Advt., Toronto, Ont., Can., 1958-61; art dir., writer Goodis, Goldberg & Soren, Toronto, 1961-63; creative dir., v.p. Baker Advt., Toronto, 1963-65; creative dir. Kenyon & Eckhardt, Toronto, 1965-66, Mexico, 1967-68; creative dir., exec. v.p. Vladimir & Evans, Inc., Miami, Fla., 1968-71; pres. Peter Evans Advt., Inc., 1971—. Served with RAF, 1953-55. Recipient numerous medals from advt. orgns. Home: 285 W Mashta Dr Key Biscayne FL 33149 Office: 800 Douglas Entrance Coral Gables FL 33134

EVANS, RONALD ELLWIN, astronaut; b. St. Francis, Kan., Nov. 10, 1933; s. Clarence E. and Marie A. (Priebe) E.; B.S. in Elec. Engring., U. Kan., 1956; M.S. in Aeros., U.S. Naval Postgrad. Sch., 1964; m. Janet M. Pollom, Dec. 22, 1957; children—Jaime Dayle, Jon Pollom. Commd. ensign USN, 1956, advanced through grades to comdr., 1965; fighter pilot, 1957-62, pilot, Vietnam, 1964-66, astronaut NASA, Manned Spacecraft Center, Houston, 1966—, support crew Apollo 7 and 11, back up command module pilot Apollo 14, crew command module pilot Apollo 17. Decorated 8 Air medals, Navy Commendation medal. Mem. Sigma Xi, Tau Beta Pi, Eta Kappa Nu, Sigma Nu. Home: 1310 Woodland Dr Seabrook TX 77586 Office: Code (CB) NASA-Manned Spacecraft Center Houston TX 77058

EVANS, ROSEMARY KING (MRS. HOWELL DEXTER EVANS), librarian; b. Forsyth, Ga., Nov. 16, 1924; d. Wiley Gwin and Mary (Goggans) King; B.S., Tift Coll., 1957; librarian's certificate Woman's Coll. of Ga., 1963; M. Library Edn., U. Ga., 1972; m. Howell Dexter Evans, June 29, 1945; children—Joseph Williams, Curtis McKenney. Tchr. elementary sch., Forsyth, Ga., 1946-48, 54-62; librarian Mary Persons High Sch., Forsyth, 1962—, now head librarian. Spiritual edn. chmn. P.T.A., 1960-61. Named Star Tchr., 1966. Mem. Nat., Ga., Monroe County (sec. 1959-60, v.p. 1961-62, pres. 1962-63) edn. assns., Internat. Platform Assn., Ga. Library Assn. (dist. pres. 1965), A.L.A. Methodist (chmn. local edn. bd. 1964-65, chmn. commn. on Christian Vocation 1965—, tchr. adult Bible class). Clubs: Jaycettes, Woman's (1st v.p. 1955-56, chmn. edn. dept. 1959-60, chmn. pub. affairs dept. 1961-62) (Forsyth). Home: Smarr GA 31086 Office: Mary Persons High Sch Brooklyn Av Forsyth GA 31029

EVANS, ROWLAND, JR., newspaper columnist; b. White Marsh, Pa., Apr. 28, 1921; s. Rowland and Elizabeth Wharton (Downs) E.; grad. Kent Sch., 1939; student Yale, 1940-41; A.A., George Washington U., 1950; m. Katherine Winton, June 18, 1949; children—Rowland Winton, Sarah Warren. With A.P., 1945-55; mem. staff N.Y. Herald Tribune, 1955-63, syndicated columnist, 1963—; contbr. Sat. Eve. Post, Harpers, Reporter, New Republic; TV panelist and commentator. Served with USMCR, 1941-44. Author: (with Robert Novak) Lyndon B. Johnson: The Exercise of Power, 1966; Nixon in the White House: The Frustration of Power, 1971. Home: 3125 O St NW Washington DC 20007 Office: 1750 Pennsylvania Av Washington DC 20006

EVANS, ROY RALPH, labor union exec.; b. Oklahoma City, Feb. 13, 1925; s. Clyde Richards and Majel Vesta (Goad) E.; ed. U. Tex., So. Meth. U.; m. Hazel Robertson, Dec. 19, 1948; children—Dickie, Andy, Jimmy, Johnny. Active labor union movement, 1948—, organizer United Auto Workers union Chance Vought Aircraft Plant, North Tex., 1948, successively unit leader to pres. local union; pres. Dallas CIO Council, from 1951; pres. United Auto Workers Citizenship Council, 1951-61; United Auto Workers adminstrv. v.p. Tex. CIO Council, to 1961; sec.-treas. Tex. AFL-CIO, 1961-71, pres., 1971—. Mem. S.W. Regional Manpower Adv. Com., Tex. and nat. coms. labor problems. Served with USNR. Mem. Internat. Assn. Machinists, Internat. Union Elec., Radio and Machine Workers, Am. Newspaper Guild, Am. Acad. Polit. and Social Sci., Internat. Platform Assn., Indsl. Relations Research Assn., Austin Fgn. Policy Assn. Contbr. articles to union publs.; author, producer radio and TV shows in field. Home: 1422 Larkwood St Austin TX 78723 Office: Texas AFL-CIO 308 W 11th St Austin TX 78701

EVANS, MRS. SILLIMAN, SR., pub. co. exec. Pres. Nashville Tennessean. Address: Nashville Tennessean 1100 Broadway Nashville TN 37201*

EVANS, THOMAS ALFRED, architect; b. Buffalo, Apr. 22, 1930; s. John Hugh and Helen Elizabeth (Ryan) E.; B.S., B.Arch. (V.B. Higgins scholar 1956; Lyles Bisset Carlyle and Wolf scholar 1957), Clemson U., 1957; M.Arch., U. Pa., 1959. Project architect Barrows Parks Marin Hall & Brennan, architects, Rochester, N.Y., 1959-62; chief designer Mills Petticord & Mills, architects, engrs., Washington, 1962-64; head design dept. McLeod Ferrara & Ensign, architects, Washington, 1964-68; asso. Thomas E. Stanley & Assos., architects, engrs., Dallas, 1968-72, Warden & Evans, architects, planners, 1972—. Teaching fellow Ga. Inst. Tech., 1958; critic U. Ohio, 1968. Served with USNR, USMCR, 1948-52. Recipient 1st prize So. Brick and Tile competition, 2d prize Armstrong Tile competition, A.A.S.A. Honor award, 1965-69. Mem. A.I.A. (medal 1957; Honor award 1962, 63), Nat. Council Archtl. Registration Bd., Phi Eta Sigma. Home: Box 19112 Dallas TX 75219 Office: Box 2189 Dallas TX 75221

EVANS, THOMAS PEABODY, govt. ofcl.; b. Wade, N.C., Oct. 9, 1912; s. William and Lillian (May) E.; B.S., U. S.C., 1937; grad-student Duke, 1938; m. Valree Lide, Aug. 8, 1955. Tchr. pub. schs., Columbia, S.C., 1937-41; statistician S.C. Employment Security Commn., Columbia, 1941-46, chief research and statistics, 1946-65; dir. staff service, S.C. Employment Security Commn., 1965-66; dir. statistical research, S.C. Budget and Control Bd., 1966—; mem. com. research and reporting Interstate Conf. Employment Security Agys., 1956-58, 64; cons. U.S. Employment Service, Bur. Employment Security, Washington. Trustee, vice chmn. Fed. Statistics Users' Conf. Served with USNR, 1942-46; now lt. comdr. ret. Mem. Am. Statis. Assn. (pres. S.C. 1970), S.C. State Employees Assn. Presbyn. Club: Optimist. Author: (with S. M. Derrick) The Cost of Unemployment Insurance in South Carolina, 1954; (with William B. Richey) Benefit Financing in South Carolina, 1959. Home: 1505 Greenhill Rd Columbia SC 29206 Office: R L Bryan Bldg PO Box 11038 Columbia SC 29211

EVANS, TRUMAN, airline exec.; b. San Antonio, Oct. 10, 1917; s. Truman and Lucinda (Latimer) E.; B.S. in C. E., Okla. State U., 1941; m. Henrietta Louise Mackay, Aug. 29, 1952; 1 dau., Marcia Joan (Mrs. Robert William Specht). Control engr. C.E., U.S. Army, Tulsa, Kansas City, Mo., 1941-44; plant indsl. engr. Pitts. Plate Glass Co., Clarksburg, W.Va., Creighton, Pa., 1945-47, divisional controller for window glass, Pitts., 1947-52, mgr. prodn. planning for glass div., 1952-61; dir. inventory control Am. Airlines, Tulsa, 1962-64, dir. mgmt. systems planning, 1964—. Instr. physics Okla. State U., 1944-45. Mem. Mayor's Com. for Joint Systems Devel. for City, County, Sch. Bd., 1968—; mem. Tulsa Govtl. Mgmt. Study Com., 1968-69; mem. Data Processing Adv. Commn. State Okla., 1972—; mem. mgmt. adv. bd. Concentrated Employment Program for Tulsa, 1972—; chmn. Welfare Services Study Com. for Tulsa County, 1969—; mem. Com. on Study of Rehab. Services in Tulsa, 1969—; mem. adv. bd. for curriculum devel. Tulsa Jr. Coll., 1972—. Bd. dirs. Community Service Council Greater Tulsa, 1969—; bd. dirs., exec. com., chmn. health care com. St. John's Hosp., 1972—. Recipient Citation of Recognition Ind. U. and OEEC, 1961. Registered profl. engr., Okla. Mem. Nat., Okla., Tulsa socs. profl. engrs., Am. Inst. Indsl. Engrs., Inst. Mgmt. Scis., Engrs. Council for Profl. Devel. (mem. ethics com. 1968—), Nat. Mgmt. Assn., Am. Prodn. and Inventory Control Soc. (founder, charter mem.), Tulsa C. of C. (vice-chmn. edn. com. 1967-68, mem. com. for Tulsa Jr. Coll. devel. fund 1972—, com. for health care edn. 1972—). Presbyn. (elder 1956—). Mason (32 deg., Shriner). Home: 3614 E 55th St Tulsa OK 74135 Office: 3800 N Mingo Rd Tulsa OK 74151

EVANS, WILLIAM NEY, commnr. U.S. Ct. Claims; b. West Plains, Mo., June 18, 1898; s. William Nelson and Sarah Annis (Smith) E.; A.B., Duke, 1920; LL.B., Harvard, 1923; m. May Alcott Thompson, July 26, 1930. Admitted to Mo. bar, 1923, and practiced in West Plains and Houston, Mo., until 1925; prof. law U. Ark., 1925-27, U. N.C., 1927-28; admitted to N.C. bar, 1928; practice in Greensboro and High Point, 1923-34; asst. gen. counsel Textile Labor Relations Bd., 1935; atty. Dept. Labor, 1936; atty. U.S. Maritime Commn., 1936-40, legislative counsel, 1940-42; asst. gen. counsel War Shipping Adminstrn., 1943-45; commnr. U.S. Ct. Claims, 1942, 45—, chmn. com. rules, 1960—. Served with U.S. Army, 1918, to lt. comdr. USNR, 1942-45. Mem. Am., Fed., N.C. bar assns., Order of Coif, Sigma Chi. Democrat. Methodist. Mason. Clubs: Tavern, University, Cosmos, Nat. Lawyers (Washington). Author articles. Home: 4651 Kenmore Dr NW Washington DC 20007 Office: US Court Claims Washington DC

EVEREST, HARVEY PETTIT, banker; b. Hutchinson, Kan., Apr. 10, 1895; s. Claude Harrison and Martie (Pettit) E.; student U. Okla., 1914-17; m. Ruth Whetstone, 1915; children—Jean I., Howard H. With Mid-Continent News Co., Pubs. News Co., Oklahoma City, mag. distbrs., 1912—, now chmn.; v.p., treas. Darby-Everest Cadillac, Inc., 1955—; dir. Liberty Nat. Bank & Trust Co., Oklahoma City, 1946—, exec. com., 1947—, pres., 1955-70, hon. chmn. bd., 1970—. Past pres. Community Chest, Oklahoma City. Chmn. trustees Phillips U.; bd. dirs. United Community Funds and Councils Am., YMCA, A.R.C., Goodwill Industries, Family and Children's Service, Okla. Med. Research Found. Served as lt. USNR, World War II. Mem. Am. Bankers Assn., Oklahoma City C. of C. Mem. Christian Ch. (mem. bd., exec. com.). Home: 7414 North Country Club Dr Oklahoma City OK 73116 Office: PO Box 25848 Oklahoma City OK 73125

EVERHART, OSCAR CHARLES, librarian; b. Danville, Ill., July 2, 1909; s. Charles E. and Maud Amy (Chatfield) E.; student U. Md., 1926-28; B.A., Pomona Coll., 1948; M.A. in L.S., Ind. U., 1950. Head librarian Jeffersonville (Ind.) Pub. Library, 1948-51; field cons. extension div. Ind. State Library, Indpls., 1951-53, aquisitions librarian, asst. to dir., 1953-58; asso. librarian Miami Beach (Fla.) Pub. Library, 1958, chief librarian, 1958—. Library rep. A. C. McClurg & Co., Chgo., 1929-46. Served with AUS, 1942-45. Mem. Am., Fla., Southeastern, Dade County library assns. Home: 4490 Royal Palm Av Miami Beach FL 33140 Office: 2100 Collins Av Miami Beach FL 33139

EVERS, JAMES CHARLES, mem. Democratic nat. com.; b. Decatur, Miss., Sept. 11, 1922; s. Jim and Jessie (Wright) E.; B.A., Alcorn A. and M. Coll., Lorman, Miss., 1951; m. Nanie Magee, June 2, 1947; children— Patricia, Carolyn, Sheila, Yvonne. Dem. candidate for Congress, 1968; mem. Dem. Nat. Com. for Miss., 1968—; mayor Fayette, Miss., 1969—. Address: PO Box 605 Fayette MS 39069

EVERSOLE, ALEX GORDON, supt. schs.; b. Krypton, Ky., Aug. 9, 1932; s. App and Cassie (Pennington) E.; B.S. in Edn., Eastern Ky. U., 1959, M.A. in Edn., 1960; m. Golda Witt, Dec. 26, 1952; children— Dwight, Steven, Alexis Ann. Tchr. M.C. Napier High Sch., Hazard, Ky., 1959-62; prin. D. Wooton Elementary Sch., Hazard, 1962-63; asst. supt. Perry County Schs., Hazard, 1963-67, supt., 1967—. Served with USAF, 1952-56. Mem. Perry County Edn. Assn. (pres. 1961-62), Ky. Edn. Assn. (mem. bd. 1969—), N.E.A. Lion (bd. dirs. 1969-71). Home: Krypton KY 41754 Office: Perry County Schs Hazard KY 41701

EVERT, CHARLES MICHAEL, lawyer, former county ofcl.; b. Chgo., June 7, 1920; s. Charles J. and Christine (Grotz) E.; B.S., North Central Coll., Naperville, Ill., 1947; J.D., Northwestern U., 1950; m. Ruth Haywood, May 26, 1945; children—Constance, Katherine, Barbara, Janice, Michael. Admitted to Ga. bar, 1950; individual practice law, Columbus, 1950—; asst. atty. Muscogee County (Ga.), 1953-56, county atty., 1956-70. Mem. Ga. Bar Assn. (chmn. local govt. sect. 1969). Home: 2807 Carson Dr Columbus GA 31906 Office: 912 2d Av Columbus GA 31907

EVETTS, EDGAR RAY, retail exec.; b. Moaffet, Tex., Dec. 1, 1915; s. Edgar Roy and Nannie Elizabeth (Evans) E.; grad. Hillsboro (Tex.) Jr. Coll., 1935; m. Mary Juanita Huff, Feb. 13, 1938; children—Robert Craig, Betty Joan (Mrs. John Robert Kuehl). Asst. mgr. S. H. Kress, Inc., Waxahachie, Tex., 1930-36, asst. mgr. all-chain variety stores, 1936-51; with Perry Bros., Mineola, Tex., Mineral Wells, Tex. and Lufkin, Tex., 1940-51; with Winns Stores, Inc., San Antonio, 1951—, exec. v.p., 1969—. Dir., v.p. Winn Western Real Estate, San Antonio, 1957—; pres., dir. S& W Wholesale Corp., San Antonio, 1954-72; rancher, Stockdale, Tex., 1969—. Served with AUS, 1944-45. Home: 215 Hillview Dr San Antonio TX 78209 Office: 1235 Gembler Rd San Antonio TX 78219

EVINS, JOSEPH LANDON, congressman; b. DeKalb County, Tenn., Oct. 24, 1910; s. James Edgar and Myrtie (Goodson) E.; A.B., Vanderbilt U., 1933; LL.B., Cumberland U., 1934, LL.D., 1958; postgrad. George Washington U., 1938-40; m. Ann Smartt, June 7, 1935; children— Joanna, Jane, Mary. Admitted to Tenn. bar, 1934; engaged in gen. law practice, Smithville, 1934-41; atty. FTC, Washington 1935-38, asst. sec., 1938-40; v.p. 1st Nat. Bank, Smithville, Tenn., 1944-54, pres., 1954-63, chmn. bd., 1963—; men. 80th-92d Congresses, 4th Congl. Dist.; mem. com. appropriations, chmn. subcom. pub. works AFC appropriations, mem., former chmn. subcom. housing-space-sci.-vets. appropriations, chmn. select com. small bus. Chmn. Tenn. Democratic Campaign Com., 1964. Served to maj. AUS, 1942-46; ETO. Received Dem. nomination as state senator, 12th Tenn. senatorial dist. (declined to serve during war), 1944. Mem. Am. Legion, V.F.W., Army Res. Corps, 40 and 8, Amvets, Phi Kappa Sigma, Phi Delta Phi. Mason (33 deg., Shriner), Elk. Clubs: Lions, Commodore, Army-Navy. Author: Understanding Congress, 1962. Home: 300 E Main St Smithville TN 37166 also 5044 Klingle St NW Washington DC 20016 Office: Rayburn House Office Bldg Washington DC 20515

EVITT, JAMES EDWARD, JR., telephone co. exec.; b. Ringgold, Ga., Sept. 1, 1912; s. James E. and Annie (Ward) E.; grad. McCallie Sch.; student U. Ga., 1929-33, U. Chattanooga, 1931; m. Malley Thornton, Sept. 6,1961; 1 dau., Alice Lee. Druggist, Ringgold Drug Co., 1934-53; owner, mgr. Ringgold Telephone Co., 1948-58, pres., 1958—; treas. Catoosa Industries, Inc.; dir. Bank Ringgold. Dir. Chattanooga Area Met. Council; dir. of YMCA OF Ga.; chmn. Ga.-Tenn. Regional Health Commn., 1970—; mem. Catoosa County Bd. Health; dir. Coosa Valley Planning Com., Chattanooga Full Employment Com., Inc., 1969—. Dep. clerk of Superior Court of Catoosa County, 1933-44; mem. Ga. Ho. of Reps., 1945-51; pres. Ga. Young Democratic Club, 1945-46. Treas. Hutchison Meml. Tri-County Hosp., Ft. Oglethorpe, Ga., 1947-67, vice chmn., 1967—; pres. Ga. Hosp. Governing Bd. Assn., 1957; mem. Ga. Hosp. Indigent Care Council, 1957-59. Mem. Ga. Telephone Assn. (pres. 1961-62; dir.), Nat. R.E.A. Telephone Assn. (dir.), Greater Chattanooga C. of C. (dir. 1969-71), Ind. Pioneer Telephone Assn. Clubs: Rotary, Quarterback. Address: Ringgold GA 30736

EWAN, JOSEPH ANDORFER, botanist, educator; b. Phila., Oct. 24, 1909; s. Horace Gilbert and Emma (Magill) E.; student U. Cal., Los Angeles, 1929-33; A.B., U. Cal., Berkeley, 1934; m. Ada Nesta Dunn, Aug. 20, 1935; children—Kathleen Kilburn (Mrs. Richard Harris), Dorothy Saranne (Mrs. Stephen Nemecek), Marjorie Magill. Asst. phanerogamic botany U. Cal., Berkeley, 1933-37; instr. biology U. Colo., 1937-44; botanist Fgn. Econ. Adminstrn., Colombia, 1944-45; asst. curator div. plants Smithsonian Instn., 1945-46; asso. botanist Bur. Plant Industry, Dept. Agr., Beltsville, Md., 1946-47; asst. prof. Tulane U., New Orleans, 1947-52, asso. prof., 1952-57, prof. botany, 1957—; lectr. botany U. Hawaii, summer 1967. Bd. adminstrs. Longue Vue Gardens, New Orleans. Recipient grants Am. Philos. Soc., 1949-52, 54, 58, 64, 69, NSF, 1959-61. Guggenheim fellow, 1954. Mem. A.A.A.S., Am. Fern Soc. (pres. 1958-59), Am. Soc. Plant Taxonomists, History of Sci. Soc., Soc. Bibliography of Natural History, Torrey Bot. Club, Cooper Ornithol. Soc., Bot. Soc. Am., Sigma Xi. Author: North American Delphiniums, 1945; Rocky Mountain Naturalists, 1950; William Bartram: botanical and zoological drawings, 1968. Editor: Classica Botanica Americana, 1967—; Short History of Botany in the U.S., 1969; John Banister and his Natural History of Virginia, 1678-1692, 1970. Home: 4320 Pitt St New Orleans LA 70115

EWBANK, ROBERT CHAPMAN, JR., dentist; b. Chgo., July 19, 1941; s. Robert Chapman and Grace Ethel (White) E.; student Milligan Coll., 1959-61; D.D.S., Northwestern U., 1965; additional study East Carolina U., 1966; postgrad. W. Va. U., U. Tenn.; m. Mary Daisy Read, June 16, 1962; children—Michael Andrew, Robert Charles. Practice gen. dentistry, Johnson City, Tenn., 1967—; mem. staff Meml. Hosp., Johnson City. Asst. prof. biology Milligan Coll., Johnson City, 1967-71, asst. basketball coach, 1971-72; pres. Holmes Enterprises, Inc., Johnson City, 1970—. Dir. Co-op. Vocation Edn. Program, Boones Creek High Sch., Jonesboro, Tenn. Served to capt. USAF, 1965-67. Mem. United Comml. Travelers, Tenn. Dental Soc., Am. Dental Assn., Delta Sigma Delta. Mem. Christian Ch. (bd. sec. 1970-71). Clubs: Civitan (dir. 1968—; pres. 1971-72, lt. gov. Appalachian dist. 1972-73), Monday Study (Johnson City). Home: 1609 Woodridge Dr Johnson City TN 37601 Office: 408 N Roan St Johnson City TN 37601

EWEN, DAVID, musician, educator, author; b. Lemberg, Austria, Nov. 26, 1907; s. Isaac and Helen (Kramer) E.; student Coll. City of N.Y. 3 yrs.; received musical edn. with private tutors and in spl. courses at Columbia U.; m. Hannah Weinstein, Sept. 11, 1936; 1 son, Robert. Music editor Cue, 1937-38; serious music record critic Stage, 1938-39; editor Musical Facts, 1940-41. Dir. Allen, Towne & Heath, Inc., 1946-49; adj. prof. music U. Miami, 1965—. Bd. dirs. Greater Miami Philharmonic Orch. Served with U.S. Army, 1944-45; authorized to write history of American paratroopers. Mem. Friends Chamber Music Miami (dir.), Miami Beach Music and Arts League (hon. life). Contbr. many articles on music. Author many books on musicians, 1933-46; Haydn: A Good Life, 1946; Songs of America, 1947. American Composers Today, 1949; The Story of Irving Berlin, 1950; The Story of Arturo Toscanini, 1951; The Complete Book of Twentieth Century Composers, 1952; The Story of Jerome Kern, 1953; European Composers Today, 1953; (with Milton Cross) The Milton Cross Encyclopedia of Great Composers, 1953, rev. edit., 1969; The Home Book of Musical Knowledge, 1954; Encyclopedia of the Opera, 1955, rev. edit., 1971; A Journey to Greatness: The Life and Music of George Gershwin, 1956, rev. edit., 1970; Panorama of American Popular Music, 1957; Richard Rodgers, 1957; The Complete Book of the American Musical Theatre, 1958, rev. edit., 1970; Ency. of Concert Music, 1959; The World of Jerome Kern, 1960; Leonard Bernstein: A Biography for Young People, 1960; The Story of the American Musical Theater, 1961; David Ewen Introduces Modern Music, 1962; The Book of European Light Opera, 1962; With A Song in His Heart (a young people's biography of Richard Rodgers), 1963; The Life and Death of Tin Pan Alley, 1964; The Complete Book of Classical Music, 1965; The Cole Porter Story, 1965; Great Composers: 1300-1900, 1966; American Popular Songs: From The Revolutionary War to the Present, 1966; Famous Modern Conductors, 1967; The World of Twentieth Century Music, 1968; Composers Since 1900, 1969. Composers for the American Musical Theatre, 1968; Composers of Tomorrow's Music, 1971; Opera, 1972. Address: 2301 Collins Av Miami Beach FL 33139

EWERS, JOHN CANFIELD, museum adminstr.; b. Cleve., July 21, 1909; s. John Ray and Mary Alice (Canfield) E.; A.B. Dartmouth, 1931, D.Sc., 1968; M.A., Yale, 1934; LL.D., U. Mont., 1966; m. Margaret Elizabeth Dumville, Sept. 6, 1934; children—Jane (Mrs. Robinson), Diane (Mrs. Peterson). Field curator Nat. Park Service, Wash., Morristown, N.J., Berkeley, Cal., Macon, Ga., 1935-40; curator Mus. Plains Indian, Browning, Mont., 1941-44; asso. curator ethnology U.S. Nat. Mus., Smithsonian Instn., Washington, 1946-56, planning officer, 1956-59, asst. dir. Mus. History and Tech., 1959-64, dir., 1964-65, sr. scientist Office Anthropology, 1965—, now sr. ethnologist Office Anthropology. Museum planning cons. Bur. Indian Affairs, 1948-49, Mont. Hist. Soc., 1950-54; cons. Am. Heritage, 1959. Served with USNR, 1944-46. Recipient 1st Exception Service award Smithsonian Instn., 1965. Fellow Am. Anthrop. Assn.; mem. Am. Indian Ethno logist Conf. (pres. 1960-61), Am. Assn. Museums, Anthrop. Soc. Washington. Author: Plains Indian Painting, 1940; The Horse in Blackfoot Indian Culture, 1955; The Blackfeet: Raiders on the Northwestern Plains, 1958; Artists of the Old West, 1965; Indian Life on Upper Missouri, 1968. Editor: Adventures of Zenas Leonard, Fur Trader, 1959; Crow Indian Medicine Bundles, 1960; Five Indian Tribes of the Upper Missouri, 1961; O-Kee-Pa, AReligious Ceremony and Other Customs of the Mandans (George Catlin), 1967. Editor Jour. Washington Acad. Scis., 1955-56. Editorial bd. The American West, 1965—. Contbr. articles to profl. publs. Home: 4432 26th Rd N Arlington VA Office: Smithsonian Instn Washington DC 20560

EWING, BETTY, society editor Houston Chronicle. Address: 512-20 Travis St Houston TX 77002*

EWING, GEORGE H., business exec.; b. San Antonio, June 11, 1925; s. H. L. and Miriam (Galloway) E.; B.S. in C. E., Tex. A. and M. U., 1948; m. Doris Ann Cannan, May 31, 1947; children—Susan,

Beverly, Mary, Bryan. With Tex. Eastern Transmission Corp., Houston, 1948-—, supr. plans and research div., 1956-58, supervising engr., 1958-64, v.p., chief engr., 1965-71, v.p. engring. and supplemental fuels and devel., 1971-—. Served with USNR, 1943-46. with USNR, 1943-46. Registered profl. engr., La. Mem. Am. Soc. M.E., Am. Gas Assn., Ind. Natural Gas Assn. Houston. Presbyn. Club: Petroleum (Houston). Home: 502 W Forest St Houston TX 77024 Office: PO Box 2521 Houston TX 77001

EWING, TILLMAN REAL, gas co. exec.; b. Belden, Miss., Feb. 12, 1914; s. Claude T. and Maude (Rial) E.; student pub. schs.; m. Dessie Grant, Aug. 10, 1928; children—Mary (Mrs. Wayne Harlow), James T., Peggy (Mrs. Lester Grump). Foreman, Carnation Co., 1936-39; salesman Life Ins. Co. of Ga., 1939-41, J.J. Rogers & Sons, Inc., 1941-44; partner, mgr. Butane Gas of Miss. and Ala., Inc., 1946-51; owner, gen. mgr. Ewing Gas Co., Inc., 1951-—; sec.-treas. Ewing Mobile Homes, 1962-— (all Tupelo, Miss.), C. & E. LP Gas Co.; pres. Tombigbee Finance Co.; dir. East Heights Devel. Corp., Modern Dixie Life Ins. Co., Jackson, Miss., Tombigbee Water Valley Mgmt. Dist., Tupelo, Action Industries Furniture Mfg. Co., Tupelo. Col. on Gov.'s Staff. Served with AUS, 1944-46. Mem. Miss. LP Gas Dealers Assn. Baptist. Club: Civitan (pres. 1962-63). Home: Route 4 Tupelo MS 38801 Office: 778 E Main St Tupelo MS 38802

EYDE, RICHARD HUSTED, botanist; b. Lancaster, Pa., Dec. 23, 1928; s. Richard H. and Thelma (Somers) E.; B.S., Franklin and Marshall Coll., 1956; M.Sc., Ohio State U., 1957; Ph.D., Harvard, 1962; m. Lorraine Sylvia Dittrich, June 8, 1957; children—Douglas Alan, Dana Everest. Fulbright scholar Birbal Sahni Inst. Palaeobotany, Lucknow, India, 1960-61; research asst. dept. botany Smithsonian Instn., Washington, 1961-62, asso. curator, 1962-69, curator, 1969-—. Home: 2400 S Arlington Ridge Rd Arlington VA 22202 Office: Dept Botany Smithsonian Instn Washington DC 20560

EYEINGTON, CHARLES DAVID, city ofcl.; b. Buffalo, Aug. 19, 1919; s. David F. and Mira (Pettit) E.; B.A., Baylor U., 1953; m. Tillie Hejl, Nov. 28, 1946; children—Charlotte (Mrs. John MacClelland), Charles David II, Emily, Thomas, James, Mary Beth, Robert. Plant supt. SWS Mfg. Co., 1951-54; mgr. C. of C., Hughes Springs, Tex., 1954-55, Daingerfield, 1955-58; city mgr. City of Daingerfield, 1958-65, City of Georgetown, 1965-68, City of Mission, 1968-—. Served bith AUS, 1941-46. Mem. Internat., Tex. city mgrs. assns., Municipal Finance Officers Assn., N.G. Assn. U.S. and Tex. Lion. Home: 1223 Doherty Av Mission TX 78572 Office: 900 Doherty Av Mission TX 78572

EYRES, DEREK EDMUND CRESSWELL, interior decorator; b. Bombay, India, July 1, 1913; s. Charles Lionel and Ethel Vera (French) E.; matriculated Dolwich Coll., London, Eng., 1928-31, Magdalen Coll., Oxford U. (Eng.), 1931-33; m. Kathryne Mary Woodson, July 1, 1958; 1 dau., Kathryne Avon (Mrs. Joseph Alan Towler). Came to U.S., 1950, naturalized, 1962. Owner Derek Eyres, Ltd., London, 1945-50; partner Edwards & Eyres, Ltd., N.Y.C., 1950-53; interior designer W & J Sloane, N.Y.C., 1953-56, Beverly Hills, Cal., 1962-65; owner London Studio Interior Design, Richmond, Va., 1967-—. Served with Royal Navy, 1939-45. Decorated Distinguished Service Cross (Eng.). Mem. Am. Inst. Interior Designers. Clubs: Junior Naval and Military Overseas, Royal Automobile (London). Home: Darbytown House 7515 Darbytown Rd Richmond VA 23231 Office: 7515 Darbytown Rd Richmond VA 23231

EZELL, FRANCIS HAYS, librarian; b. Chapel Hill, Tenn., Jan. 5, 1933; d. Edward Swanson and Sara (Bailey) Ezell; B.S. in Elementary Edn., Middle Tenn. State U., 1954; M. in Library Sci., George Peabody Coll., 1960. Tchr. Muscogee County Sch. System, Columbus, Ga., 1955; library asst. Main Post Library, Ft. Benning, Ga., 1955-59; librarian Free Library Phila., 1960-61; asst. regional librarian Upper Cumberland Regional Library Center, Cookeville, Tenn., 1961-68; sr. librarian Tenn. State Library and Archives, Nashville, 1968-70; dir. Tenn. Library for Blind and Physically Handicapped, Nashville, 1970-—. Mem. Tenn., Southeastern library assns., Am. Assn. Workers for the Blind, Bus. and Profl. Women, Am. Assn. U. Women (v.p. 1961-64). Home: 2601 Hillsboro Rd Nashville TN 37212 Office: 5200 Centennial Blvd Nashville TN 37209

EZELLE, SAM, III, labor union exec.; b. Evansville, Ind., July 16, 1920; s. Samuel Wahl and Augusta (Culley) E.; LL.B., Jefferson Law Sch., Louisville, 1948, U. Louisville, 1951; m. Ruby Gordon Layman, Sept. 16, 1939; 1 son, Sam IV; m. 2d, Dorothy W., Dec. 16, 1967; children—Kent, Dale. Began career as a structural ironworker, 1941-46; dir. dept. research and edn. Ky. Fedn. Labor, 1946-52, exec. sec., 1952-58; exec. sec. Ky. AFL-CIO, 1958-—; sec.-treas. Ky. Labor News, Inc., 1952-—. Labor edn. specialist Mut. Security Agy., 1952; mem. Ky. Atomic Energy Commn., 1961-—, U.S. Labor-Mgmt. Manpower Com., 1956-—. Bd. regents Western State Coll., Bowling Green, Ky., 1957-59; bd. trustees U. Ky., 1960-68. Served with USAAF, 1942-43. Democrat. Home: 2422 Dundee Rd Louisville KY 40205 Office: 706 E Broadway Louisville KY 40202

EZZARD, GEORGE PIERCE, physician; b. Lawrenceville, Ga., June 7, 1935; s. Webster Pierce and Doris Virginia (Cooper) E.; grad. Emory-at-Oxford Jr. Coll., 1953; B.S., U. Ga., 1955, B.A., 1956; M.D., Emory Med. Sch., 1961; m. Polly Anne Efird, Aug. 15, 1959; children— Mary Anne, Margaret Lynn, Carolyn Marie. Intern Crawford W. Long Hosp., Atlanta, 1961-62; practice gen. medicine, Lawrenceville, 1962-—; mem. staff Button Gwinnett Hosp., Lawrenceville. Dir. Gwinnett Comml. Bank, Lawrenceville. Mem. Chattahoochee Med. Soc., Phi Chi. Methodist. Home: Route 3 Lawrenceville GA 30245 Office: Ezzard Bldg Lawrenceville GA 30245

FABER, CHARLES FRANKLIN, educator; b. Moravia, Ia., Dec. 6, 1926; s. Richard Andrew and Inez (McAlister) F.; B.A., Coe Coll., 1948; M.A., Columbia, 1952; Ph.D., U. Chgo., 1961; m. Patricia Jane Utt, June 8, 1947; children—Deborah, Daniel, Melinda. Pub. sch. tchr., adminstr., Ill., 1949-59; asst. prof. edn. Ia. State U., 1961-64; prof. edn., chmn. dept. ednl. adminstrn. Peabody Coll., Nashville, 1964-71; prof. edn., chmn. dept. ednl. adminstrn. U. Ky., Lexington, 1971-—; cons. sch. systems and other ednl. agys., Ill., Ia., Mo., Ky., Tenn., Ala., Fla. Served with USNR, 1944-46. Mem. Am. Ednl. Research Assn., Am. Assn. Sch. Adminstrs., Nat. Conf. Profs. Ednl. Adminstrn., Phi Delta Kappa. Author: (with Gilbert Shearron) Elementary School Adminstration: Theory and Practice, 1970. Sect. editor: Educational Administration Abstracts, 1968-71. Contbr. articles to profl. jours. Home: 3569 Cornwall Dr Lexington KY 40503

FABRY, PAUL ANDREW, internat. assn. exec.; b. Budapest, Hungary, June 19, 1919; s. Andrew and Ilona (Gombos) F.; B.A., Godollo Jr. Coll., 1937; Ph.D., U. Budapest, 1942, J.D., 1943; m. Louise Hitchcock Fair, May 15, 1958 (div. 1968); children—Lydia Louise, Alexa Fair; m. 2d, Angela Andrews Rutledge, May 8, 1971. Came to U.S., 1949, naturalized. War corr. Central European Press Service, Warsaw, Poland, Berlin Germany, Vienna, Austria, Zurich, Switzerland, Budapest, 1943-44; sec. Fgn. Office, Budapest, 1945; head Prime Minister's Cabinet, Budapest, 1945-46; charge d'affaires of Hungary, Ankara, Turkey 1946-47; fgn. corr. Istanbul, Turkey, 1948-49; sect. chief Radio Free Europe, N.Y.C., 1950-53; free lance writer, lectr., N.Y.C., 1954; pub. relations adviser E.I. du Pont de Nemours & Co., Wilmington, Del., 1955-62; mng. dir. Internat. House, New Orleans 1962-—. Rep. Internat. Red Cross, Vienna-Budapest, 1945-46; adv. bd. Istanbul U., 1948-49, Internat. Econ. Cooperation Com., N.Y.C.; v.p. Cultural Services, Inc., N.Y.C., 1953-54; moderator Fact and Opinion, WYES-TV, 1965-—. Active United Fund, Wilmington, 1955-60. Trustee, mem. exec. com. New Orleans Ednl. TV Found., 1970-—. Served as capt. Royal Hungarian Artillery, 1943. Mem. Pub. Relations Soc. Am., Miss. Valley World Trade Council (dir., mem. exec. com. 1963-—); World Trade Centers Assn. (v.p., treas. 1969-—). Fgn. Press Assn., New Orleans Bd. Trade, C. of C. Home: 1127 Bourbon St New Orleans LA 70116 Office: 607 Gravier St New Orleans LA 70130

FACKELMAN, ROBERT HENRY, newspaper exec.; b. Ponca, Neb., Oct. 19, 1907; s. Herman Carl and Jeanette (Pomeroy) F.; student Midland Coll., 1923-25; B.J., U. Mo., 1927; postgrad. Harvard, 1941-42; m. Anna Laura Torbert, June 6, 1928; 1 dau., Ann Karen (Mrs. Frank Nixon). Editor, pub. Baxter Springs (Kan.) Citizen, 1927-28, Raymondville (Tex.) Chronicle, 1929-40, Morristown (Tenn.) Sun, 1950-52; editor, gen. mgr. Winter Haven (Fla.) News-Chief, 1943-50; pub. Cleveland (Tenn.) Banner, 1952-54; v.p. So. Newspapers, Inc., 1954-58; pres. Newspaper Service Co., Inc., 1953-—; pres. Gulf Coast Newspapers, Inc., 1958-—; pres. Ruston (La.) Pubs., Inc., Minden (La.) Newspapers, Inc., Tarpon Springs (Fla.) Leader, Inc. v.p. Slidell Newspapers, Inc.; sec. Panhandle Press Pubs. Served in USAAF, 1941-42. Mem. So. Newspaper Pubs. Assn. (dir. 1970-—). Address: 408 S Bonita Av Panama City FL 32401

FADDIS, EDWARD LEROY, architect; b. Mobile, Ala., Nov. 5, 1925; s. LeRoy and Edna Lucille (Hilburn) F.; student Va. Mil. Inst., 1943, U. Ala., 1946-47; B.Arch., Auburn U., 1951; m. Anne Shannon, Aug. 20, 1949; children—Sara Shannon, John Paige. Draftsman, Pearson & Tittle, architects, Montgomery, 1947; draftsman Pearson, Tittle &Narrows, architects, Montgomery, 1951-53, chief draftsman, 1953-56, job capt., 1951-58; job capt. Platt Roberts & Co., architects, Mobile, 1958-59; individual practice architecture, Mobile, 1959; partner Harry Inge Johnstone & Edward L. Faddis, architects, Mobile, 1962-70; prin. Architects Group, Inc., Mobile, 1971-—. Mem. archtl. rev. bd. City of Mobile, 1965-70, chmn., 1970. Served with USAAF, 1943-45. Mem. A.I.A. (chpt. treas. 1971), Scarab. Presbyn. (deacon 1969-—). Club: Exchange (dir. Mobile 1966-67). Prin. archtl. works include Library Bldg., U. South Ala., 1967, Bus. and Mgmt. Studies Bldg., U. South Ala., 1969, First Fed. Tower, Mobile, 1970. Home: 118 E Ridgelawn Dr Mobile AL 36608 Office: 1860 Government St Mobile AL 36606

FADNER, FRANK LESLIE, univ. regent; b. Neenah, Wis., Jan. 11, 1910; s. Frank L. and Elizabeth Theresa (Regenfusz) F.; A.B., M.A., Georgetown Coll., 1940; Licenciate in Philosophy, Woodstock Coll., 1939, Th.L., 1943; Ph.D., U. London, 1949. Ordained priest Soc. of Jesus, Roman Cath. Ch., 1943; exec. asst. regent Sch. Fgn. Service, Georgetown U., 1949-55, regent, 1955-61, asso. prof. Russian history, 1949-62, prof. of Russian history, 1962-—; regent Inst. Langs. and Linguistics, 1961-—. Decorated Fundacion Internacional Eloy Alfaro; knight comdr. Orden de Isabel la Catolica; Gran Oficial Al Merito, Peru, 1961. Mem. Am. Cath. Hist. Assn., Am. Hist. Assn., Nat. Fedn. Modern Lang. Tchrs. Assn., U.S. Naval Inst., Jesuit Ednl. Assn. Delta Phi Epsilon, Pi Gamma Mu, Gamma Rho Sigma, Delta Sigma Pi. Author: Seventy Years of Pan-Slavist Thought in Russia, 1800-1870, Karazin to Danilevskii, 1962. Home: Georgetown U 37 and O Sts NW Washington DC 20007

FAGAN, MAURICE JAMES, dentist; b. Coventry, R.I., Dec. 4, 1921; s. Maurice James and Ellen Louisa (Albro) F.; B.S., Providence Coll., 1943; student Balt. Coll. Dental Surgery 1944-47; D.D.S., U. Md., 1947; m. Ruth Pearl Mcdonald, June 28, 1947; children—Maurice James III, Malford, Mark, Mitchell, Laurie Anne, Margo Jean. Practice dentistry, Wakefield, R.I., 1947, Atlanta, 1956-—; asso. in geriatrics, cons. Malford Thewlis Geriatric Clinic, 1947-56, Dental Masters, Inc.; founder dental health program South Kingston (R.I.) Sch. Dept. 1948, dir., 1948-50; instr. USAF Med. Service, Atlanta, 1959-64; pres. Dental Practice Plan Inc. Founder, 1960, since pres., chmn. bd. dirs., trustee Maurice J. Fagan Meml. Dental Hosp., Dentistry for Aged, Handicapped, Atlanta. Served from pvt. to lt. col., USAF, 1942-72. Fellow Am. Acad. Gen. Dentistry, Internat. Coll. Oral Implantologists (a founder 1972); mem. Inst. Advanced Dental Research, So. Acad. Oral Implantology (founder; pres. 1969-70), Am. Acad. Implant Dentistry, Am., Ga. dental assns., No. Dist. Dental Soc., Am. Soc. Dentistry for Children, Acad. Dentistry for Handicapped, Am. Geriatric Soc., Am. Soc. Geriatric Dentistry, Res. Officers Assn., Am. Soc. Clin. Hypnosis, Acad. Gen. Dentistry, Soc. Study and Research of Oral Implants. Author: Dental Practice Planning; How to Succeed in Dentistry; New Concepts in Implant Dentistry. Home: 5360 Peachtree-Dunwoody Rd NE Atlanta GA 30342 Office: 960 Johnson Ferry Rd NE Atlanta GA 30342

FAGAN, WAYNE STANTON, accountant; b. Nekoosa, Wis., Nov. 3, 1918; s. Ralph R. and Opal (Brower) F.; B.B.A., U. Wis., 1946-48; m. Elizabeth Ann Guill, June 18, 1954; children—Michael Wayne, Patricia Ann. Supervising sr. accountant Touche, Ross, Bailey & Smart, Chgo. and Houston, 1948-53; treas., plant mgr. Bernhard Altmann Tex. Corp., San Antonio, 1953-56; supervisory auditor U.S. Army, San Antonio, 1956-61; sr. price analyst, contract negotiator USAF, San Antonio, 1961-64; asst. regional audit mgr. NASA, Houston, 1964-—. Served with USAAF, 1942-45. Decorated Air medal. C.P.A., Ill., Tex. Mem. Am. Inst. C.P.A.'s, Fed. Govt. Accountants Assn., Am. Legion, Phi Beta Kappa, Beta Gamma Sigma. Home: 2214 Lillian St Pasadena TX 77502 Office: NASA Manned Spacecraft Center Houston TX 77058

FAHIEN, RAYMOND WILLIAM, educator; b. St. Louis, Dec. 26, 1923; s. John H. and Alice K. (Schubkegel) F.; B.S., Washington U., St. Louis, 1947; M.S., Mo. Sch. Mines, 1950; Ph.D., Purdue U., 1954. Instr., Mo. Sch. Mines, 1947-50; process design engr. Ethyl Corp., Baton Rouge, 1953-54; asst. prof. Ia. State U., 1954-57, asso. prof., 1957-59, acting dept. head, summer 1959; engr. U.S. AEC, Ames Lab., 1954-64; vis. prof. U. Wis., 1959-60; Fulbright lectr. div. chem. engring. U. Brazil, Rio de Janeiro, 1964; prof., chmn. chem. engring. dept. U. Fla., Gainesville, 1964-—. Mem. Am. Inst. Chem. Engrs. (tech. program chmn., research comm. 1962-—), Am. Chem. Soc., Am. Assn. U. Profs. (chpt. pres.), Am. Soc. Engring. Edn., A.A.A.S., Sigma Xi, Phi Kappa Phi, Alpha Chi Sigma. Editor: Jour. Chem. Engring. Edn., 1967. Contbr. articles to profl. jours. Home: 2306 SW 13th St Gainesville FL 32601

FAIL, THOMAS ALLEN, contractor; b. Jackson, Tenn., Nov. 13, 1922; s. Thomas Allen and Nela (Myracle) F.; student Lambuth Coll., 1946-47, Union U., 1947; student Vanderbilt U., 1948-49; m. Beverly Townsend, June 3, 1949; children—Beverly Jessica, Sherri Lisa, Allycin Clair. Engr., G., M. & O. R.R. Co., Jackson, Tenn., 1940-44; resident mgr. Townsend Electric Co., Memphis, 1949-56, v.p., Jackson, 1956-—; v.p. Townsend Supply Co., Jackson, 1956-—, also dir. Served with C.E., AUS, 1944-46: PTO. Mem. I.E.E.E., V.F.W., Elec. Apparatus Service Assn. (co. rep. 1956-—), Jackson and Madison County Area C. of C. Methodist (supt. youth dept. 1963-—). Mason. Club: Golf and Country (Jackson, Tenn.). Home: 54 Fair Oaks Dr Jackson TN 38301 Office: 128 Johnson St Jackson TN 38301

FAIN, DOUGLAS WILSON, carpet co. exec.; b. Weatherford, Tex., Sept. 30, 1919; s. Douglas Wythe and Mary (Barber) F.; A.A., Weatherford Jr. Coll., 1938; B.B.A., Tex. U., 1942; m. Bette Jane Harder, Jan. 16, 1960; children—Gregorl, Mary Tanya. Cashier, Mchts. & Farmers State Bank, Weatherford, Tex., 1946-50; partner Berhard-Fain Carpets, Dallas, 1950-—; dir., mem. exec. com. Inwood Nat. Bank. Mem. city council, Dallas, dep. mayor pro tem, 1971-—. Served with Mil. Intelligence Corps, AUS, 1942-45; ETO. Decorated Bronze Star. Mem. N. Dallas C. of C. (pres. 1963-64). Mason (32 deg., Shriner), Lion (past pres. Park Cities club.). Home: 4444 Lovers Lane Dallas TX 75229

FAIN, ROBIN PAULINE, librarian; b. nr. Nicholasville, Ky., Apr. 14, 1912; d. Larkin Davis and Minnie (House) Fain; A.B., U. Ky., 1941, M.A., 1952, postgrad., 1953, 58, 69; postgrad. U. Denver, 1962. Elementary tchr. Jessamine County (Ky.) Schs., 1930-45; tchr. English, Wilmore High Sch., 1946-58; librarian Jessamin County High Sch., Nicholasville, 1958-—; instr. summer sch. U. Ky., 1961, 63-66. Named Outstanding Ky. Sch. Librarian, Ky. Library Trustees Assn., 1967. Mem. N.E.A. (life), Ky. Edn. Assn., Jessamine County Tchrs. Assn. (past pres.), Southeastern, Ky. library assns., Ky. Assn. Sch. Librarians (past pres.), Delta Kappa Gamma. Republican. Methodist. Home: Route 2 Nicholasville KY 40356 Office: Route 4 Jessamine County High Sch Nicholasville KY 40356

FAIRBANKS, CHARLES LEO, football coach; b. Detroit, June 10, 1933; s. Ronald J. and Grace (Qubish) F.; B.S. in Phys. Edn., Mich. State U.; m. Virgeleen Thomson, June 9, 1951; children—Charles Leo, Gwenn, Melissa, Tyler John, Tobin J. Student asst. Mich. State U., 1955; high sch. football coach, Ishpeming, Mich., 1955-57; defensive backfield coach Ariz. State U., 1958-61; backfield coach U. Houston, 1962-64, asst. head coach in charge of offense, 1965; defensive backfield coach U. Okla., Norman, 1966-67, head coach, 1967-—. Presbyn. Home: 1620 Holliday Dr Norman OK 73069 Office: 180 W Brooks St Norman OK 73069

FAIRCHILD, CLARE E., investment, bldg. exec.; b. Marietta, S.D., Dec. 15, 1911; s. Fred Lamont and Eleanor (Stobbs) F.; student U. Wash., 1933-34; m. Eleanore Marie Donoghue, Jan. 27, 1947; children— Linda Jean, Brenda, Mark. Photographer Atlas Photos, N.Y.C., 1935-39; ad man Clovis (Cal.) Tribune, 1939-41; steelworker C.P.N.A.B., Honolulu, Hawaii, 1942-44; insp. Bahrein Petroleum Co., Persian Gulf, 1944-45, treas. Fairchild Bros., Inc., Rutland, Mass., 1945-48; pres., treas. Brentwood Realty Corp., Worcester, 1948-—; designer, builder Fairbrook Hotel. Pres., treas. Capital Investors, Inc., Holden, 1954-—; pres. C. A. Turner Co. of Florida, 1964-—; v.p. U.S. Water Conservation Corp.; developed Brentwood Estates; pres., treas. Fairchild Products Corp., West Palm Beach, Fla., Ofcl. Equipment Co. Bd. dirs. Barker Players, Inc., Worcester Art Mus., Worcester Found. Exptl. Biology; nat. dir. Child Safety Edn. Assn. Inc. Mem. Nat. Assn. Home Builders, Fla. Sheriff's Assn., Palm Beach County Sheriff's Aux., Nat. Assn. Real Estate Bds., Master Home Builders Assn. Worcester County (v.p.), Worcester C. of C. Mason. Clubs: Fairbrook Country (treas.); Quinsigamond Yacht; Nat. Exchange, Holden Country (treas.); Palm Beach Yacht, Palm Beach Athletic. Home: 142 Peruvian Av Palm Beach FL 33480 Office: 512 24th St West Palm Beach FL

FAIRCHILD, RAYMOND EUGENE, geologist; b. Bowling Green, O., June 25, 1923; s. Ira Ethalbert and Bessie Louise (Gearhart) F.; B.S., Ohio U., 1948; M.A., U. Mo., 1950; m. Linda Fee, Oct. 11, 1952; children— Charles Patterson, William Gearhart, Katherine Louise. Geol. scout Pan Am. Prodn. Co., Shreveport, La., 1950-51, geologist, Abilene, Tex., 1951-54, Houston, 1954-56; dist. geologist Trunkline Gas Co., Houston, 1956-60, dist. mgr. exploration, 1960-63, mgr. exploration and chief geologist, 1963-67; Gulf coast div. exploration mgr. Anadarko Prodn. Co., Houston, 1967-—. Commr., Spring Branch Fire Dept., Houston, 1962; alderman, City of Hunter's Creek Village, Tex., 1962-67, mayor, 1967-72. Served with AUS, 1943-46. Mem. Am. Assn. Petroleum Geologists, Houston Geol. Soc. (v.p. 1962-63), Gulf Coast Assn. Geol. Socs. (pres. 1965), Independent Petroleum Assn. Am. Republican. Presbyn. (elder). Clubs: Sagewood Country (pres. 1961), Houston. Home: Hedwig House 9029 Gaylord Houston TX 77024 Office: C & I Bldg Houston TX 77002

FAIRCHILD, WILEY, constrn. co. exec.; b. Covington County, Miss., Sept. 19, 1912; s. William Robert and Susie (Ingram) F.; student pub. schs.; m. Marie Ishee, May 21, 1956; children—Redditt Andrew, Wiley Jean (Mrs. Paul W. Commiskey). With W.R. Fairchild Constrn. Co., Hattiesburg, Miss., 1924-—, gen. partner, 1945-—, gen. mgr., 1948-—; an organizer So. Nat. Bank of Hattiesburg, 1965, v.p., dir., now chmn. bd., 1972-—; chmn. bd. Fairchild-Fla. Constrn. Co., Monticello, Fla., 1950-—; v.p. Fairco Contractors, Inc., Hattiesburg, 1965-—; pres. F-S Prestress, Inc., Hattiesburg, 1954-—; dir. Miss. Valley Cement Industries, Inc., Magna Corp., Pine Belt Savs. & Loan Assn., Pik-A-Pak Delicatessen & Service Co., Inc. Mem. Nat. UN Day Com., 1971. Trustee William Carey Coll., Hattiesburg, chmn. trustees, 1972-—. Clubs: Hattiesburg Country, Lamplighters. Home: 114 S 24th Av Hattiesburg MS 39401 Office: PO Box 1609 Hattiesburg MS 39401

FAIRCLOTH, EARL, atty. gen. Fla.; b. Chiefland, Fla., Sept. 24, 1920; s. Joseph William and Emma (Hogan) F.; B.A., LL.B., U. Fla.; m. Wilma Smith, June 5, 1945; children—Amy Lynn, David Earl. Admitted to Fla. bar; practiced in St. Petersburg and Tallahassee until 1953; mem. firm Hector, Faircloth & Davis, and predecessor firms, Miami; atty. gen. Fla., 1965-—. Organizer Fla. Com. for Fair Apportionment, 1959; candidate Fla. Senate, 1960; mem. Fla. Ho. of Reps., 1963-64. Served with C.E., AUS, 1944-45. Named Outstanding Young Man, Jr. C. of C., 1964. Mem. Am., Dade County bar assns., Fla. Bar, Am. Judicature Soc., Am. Legion, V.F.W., Miami-Dade C. of C., Blue Key, Delta Theta Phi, Tau Kappa Alpha. Baptist. Woodmen of World. Home: 1103 Kenilworth Rd Tallahassee FL 32303 Office: Office Atty Gen Capitol Bldg Tallahassee FL 32304

FAIRLEY, FRANCIS HILLIARD, lawyer; b. Monroe, N.C., Oct. 3, 1915; s. Frank Hilliard and Janie (Phifer) F.; B.A. with honors, U. N.C., 1935, student and teaching fellow, Grad. Sch., 1935-36, LL.B., 1939; student Columbia U. Sch. Law, 1936-38; m. Ella Doris McGuinn, Aug. 24, 1951; children—Mary Jane, Ella Frances. Admitted to N.c. bar, 1939, also U.S. Dist. Ct., Circuit Ct. Appeals, U.S. Supreme Ct., Ct. Claims, ICC, FCC, Tax Ct., Treasury Dept., U.S. Customs Ct.; law clk. to chief judge U.S. Ct. Appeals, 4th Circuit, 1939-40; sr. partner firm Fairley, Hamrick, Monteith & Cobb, Charlotte, N.C., 1939-—; pros. atty. City of Charlotte, 1941; sr. asst. U.S. atty. Western Dist. N.C., 1948-53. Dir. So. Nat. Bank, Catawba Loan & Finance Co., Daniels Constrn. Co., Lenoir Finance Co., J.V. Griffith Co.; instr. negotiable instruments and comml. law Am. Inst. Banking, 1946-49, 51-52. Mem. Charlotte Estate Planning Council. Mem. N.C. Democratic Exec. Com., 1960-—. Bd. dirs. N.C. Law Found. Served to lt. comdr. USNR, 1941-45. Fellow Am. Bar Found.,

Am. Coll. Probate Counsel, Comml. Law Found; mem. Am. Acad. Polit. and Social Scis., Acad. Polit. Sci., Am. Law Inst., Am. Judicature Soc., Assn. Bar City N.Y., Internat., Inter-Am., Fed., Am. (life; ho. dels. 1962—), 26th Jud. Dist. (exec. com. 1950-54, past chmn. programs com. 1949-55) bar assns., N.C. State Bar (pres. 1962-63, past v.p., chmn. exec. com., mem. council), Am. Legion (post comdr.), 40 and 8, Comml. Law League Am. (bd. govs. 1963-69, v.p. 1966-67, pres. 1967-68), S.A.R., S.C.V., Fedn. Ins. Counsel, Nat. Assn. Probate and Bank Attys., U. N.C. Law Alumni Assn. (dir. 1953-64, pres. 1959-60), V.F.W., U.N.C. Gen. Alumni Assn. (life; dir. 1948-51), Charlotte Opera Assn., Charlotte C. of C., Scribes, Phi Beta Kappa Assos., Phi Beta Kappa, Phi Delta Phi (province pres., 1947-64, nat. pres. 1967-69, chief justice 1969—). Episcopalian (sr. warden, lay leader). Clubs: Executives, Cotillion; Charlotte Country, Carmel Country (pres. 1957) (Charlotte). Contbr. articles to profl. jours. Home: 424 Eastover Rd Charlotte NC 28207 Office: Law Bldg East Trade St Charlotte NC 28202

FAIRLEY, WALTER EUGENE, dentist; b. Service, Ala., Aug. 7, 1927; s. Robert Dewey and Laura May (Tew) F.; student Jones County Jr. Coll., 1944-45, 46-47; B.A., Baylor U., 1949, D.D.S., 1952; m. Cora Virginia Matheny, June 16, 1949; children—Karen (Mrs. Willis Mark Turner), Dawn, Laura Nan, Erin Margaret. Practice dentistry, Indianola, Miss., 1952-53, Okolona, Miss., 1953-55, West Point, Miss., 1955—. Chmn. Okolona chpt. A.R.C., 1953; pres. West Side Sch. P.T.A., West Point, 1959-60; pres. West Point Jr. High Sch. P.T.A., 1961-63; sec. Bi-Racial Com., 1971—. Served with USCGR, 1945-46. Mem. Am., Miss., N.E. Miss. dental assns. Democrat. Methodist. Rotarian. Home: 216 Travis St West Point MS 39773 Office: 209 Commerce St West Point MS 39773

FAIRLY, JACK, city editor Jackson (Miss.) Daily News. Address: 311 E Pearl St Jackson MS 39201*

FAIRSTEIN, EDWARD, elec. co. exec.; b. Bklyn., Dec. 14, 1922; s. Sidney Samuel and Katherine (Bader) F.; B.S. in E.E., City Coll. N.Y., 1944; grad. U. Tenn., 1951; m. Helen Chastain, July 9, 1949 (div. Oct. 1971); children—John Elliot, Joel Alan. Trainee, Tenn. Eastman Corp., Oak Ridge, 1945-46; sr. engr. Oak Ridge (Tenn.) Nat. Lab., 1946-59; sec.-treas., chief engr. FairPort Instruments, Inc., 1959-60; pres., chief engr. Tennelec, Inc., Oak Ridge, 1960—; dir. Tennecomp Systems, Inc., Hamilton First Nat. Bank, Oak Ridge, Assn. Nuclear Instrument Mfrs., Chgo.; sec. Rockwood Modular Industries, Inc. (Tenn); v.p. Grove Devel. Corp., Oak Ridge. Vice-pres. Indsl. Devel. Bd., Oak Ridge, 1969—. Fellow I.E.E.E. (chpt. dir. 1970), mem. Sci. Research Soc. Am., Am. Phys. Soc., A.A.A.S. Editorial bd. Review Sci. Instruments, 1958-61. Contbr. articles to profl. jours. Patentee in field. Home: 228 Outer Dr Oak Ridge TN 37830 Office: Box D Oak Ridge TN 37830

FAISON, FRANK ALLEN, city mgr.; b. Richmond, Va., Nov. 14, 1929; s. Patrick L. and May (Trusheim) F.; B.S., Va. Poly. Inst., 1951, M.S., 1952; postgrad. U. Chgo., 1959-60; m. Marilyn Roth, Sept. 14, 1958; children—E. Lawrence, David L., Elizabeth L., Patricia L. Adminstrv. asst. City LaGrange Park (Ill.), 1956-59, city mgr., 1961-67; dir. pub. works City of St. Charles (Ill.), 1959-61; city mgr., Danville, Va., 1967-71, Pensacola, Fla., 1971—. Lectr. Va. Commonwealth U., Pensacola Jr. Coll. Bd. dirs. Pensacola United Fund. Served with C.E., U.S. Army, 1952-56, now lt. col. Res. Decorated Bronze Star medal. Mem. Internat. City Mgmt. Assn., Omicron Delta Kappa, Chi Epsilon. Lion, Kiwanian, Rotarian. Home: 4745 Howe Av Pensacola FL 32504 Office: City Hall Pensacola FL 32502

FAKLIS, NICK VASILE, dentist; b. Tarpon Springs, Fla., Nov. 28, 1931; s. Vasile George and Dikea (Valsamis) F.; B.S., U. Tampa, 1954; D.M.D., U. Louisville, 1964; m. Anna Marie Athanason, Sept. 11, 1966; 1 children—Theda Marie, Debra Ann. Trainer dental nurses, operator Hillsborough County Dental Research Clinic, 1964-65; individual practice dentistry, Clearwater Beach, Fla., 1965—. Served with AUS, 1954-56. Mem. Am., Fla., Ky., Pinellas County dental assns., Royal Soc. Health, Am. Soc. Geriatric Dentistry, Fedn. Dentaire Internationale, Acad. Gen. Dentistry, Delta Sigma Delta. Democrat. Greek Orthodox. Rotarian. Contbr. to We Like These Ideas, 1970; also articles profl. jours. Home: 331 Leeward Island Clearwater Beach FL 33515 Office: 491 Mandalay Av Clearwater Beach FL 33515

FALCON, CARROLL JAMES, educator; b. Rayne, La., Mar. 15, 1941; s. Wilfred and Edith (Trahan) F.; B.S., U. Southwestern La., 1963; M.S., U. Ky., 1965, Ph.D., 1967; m. Deanna Jean Hickman, Apr. 6, 1968. Research asst. U. Ky., 1963-67; asst. prof. animal sci. Nicholls State U., Thibodaux, La., 1967-71, asso. prof. animal sci., head agr. dept., 1971—. Mem. Am. Soc. Animal Scis., A.A.A.S., Am. Inst. Biol. Scis., Soc. for Study Reprodn., Am. Farm Bur. Fedn., La. Animal Sci. Assn., Sigma Xi, Gamma Sigma Delta, Phi Mu Epsilon, Phi Kappa Theta. Roman Catholic. K.C. Contbr. articles to publs. Home: RFD 2 Box 571-E Thibodaux LA 70301

FALIK, HAROLD M., business exec.; b. N.Y.C., 1922. Exec. v.p. retailing, chmn. exec. com. J. Weingarten, Inc. Dir., Topco Assos. Home: 415 Little John Houston TX 77071 Office: 600 Lockwood Dr Houston TX 77001*

FALK, CHARLES EUGENE, ofcl. NSF; b. Hamm, Germany, Oct. 20, 1923; s. Eric J. and Lucy (Kaiser) F.; came to U.S., 1938, naturalized, 1944; B.A., N.Y. U., 1944, M.S., 1946; D.Sc., Carnegie-Mellon U., 1950;; m. Lillian Mandell, Dec. 26, 1948; children—Michael K., Gary M., Jeffrey D. With Brookhaven Nat. Lab., Upton, N.Y., 1950-56, 58-66, asst. dir., 1960, asso. dir., 1961-66; with AEC, Washington, 1956-58; planning dir. div. sci. resources and policy studies NSF, Washington, 1966—. Served with AUS, 1944-46. Mem. Am. Phys. Soc., A.A.A.S., Sigma Xi. Home: 8116 Lilly Stone Dr Bethesda MD 20034 Office: 1800 G St NW Washington DC

FALK, ELMER M, fgn. service officer; b. New Bedford, Mass., May 6, 1911; s. Elmer H. and Selma P. (Larsen) F.; B.S. in Econs., Wharton Sch. U. Pa., 1931, M.S. in Edn., 1933; m. Margaret Fulton, Nov. 9, 1940; children—Christine M., Martin E. With Pa. Dept. Pub. Assistance, 1934-43, 46; dir. assembly center UNRRA, Salzburg, Austria, 1945-46; with Vocational Rehab. and Edn. Office, VA, Phila., 1946-48; dep. dept. chief, then dept. chief Internat. Refugee Orgn., Germany, 1948-51; dep. European coordinator, then coordinator U.S. Displaced Persons Commn., Frankfurt, Germany, 1951-52; chief U.S. escapee program for Germany, Dept. State, FOA/ICA, 1952-54; dep. chief intergovtl. refugee program div. ICA, Washington, 1954-56; with Office Internat. Adminstrn., Dept. State, Washington, 1956-62; dir. office refugee and migration affairs, 1962-68. Recipient Superior Honor award Dept. State, 1966. Home: 7828 Lee Av Wellington Alexandria VA 22308 Office: Dept State Washington DC

FALK, JACK ARNOLD, circuit judge; b. Bridgeport, Conn., Nov. 8, 1927; s. Louis E. and Bessie (Adelman) F.; B.A. cum laude, U. Miami, 1949, J.D. magna cum laude, 1950; m. Corinne Clifton, Oct. 17, 1957; children—Andrew, Jack Arnold, Elizabeth. Admitted to Fla. bar, 1950; practiced law, Miami, 1950-60; dep.commr. Fla. Indsl. Commn., 1958-60; judge Criminal Ct. of Record, Dade County, 1960-66, Circuit Ct. 11th Jud. Circuit, Miami, 1966—. Pres. Dade County (Fla.) U.S.O. Council, 1966-70. Served with U.S. Army, 1946-48; maj. Res., 1959-69. Mem. Am., Dade County bar assns., Fla. Bar (chmn. Dade County grievance com. 1960). Res. Officers Assn. (chpt. sec. 1963-64), U. Miami Law Alumni (v.p. 1964), Phi Kappa Phi. Mason (32 deg, Shriner). Clubs: Optimist (pres. 1958-59). Home: 1835 SW 82d Ct Miami FL 33155 Office: Dade County Courthouse Miami FL 33130

FALK, LESLIE ALAN, physician, educator; b. St. Louis, Apr. 19, 1915;. s Albert F. and Eleanor (Allina) F.; A.B., U. Ill., 1935; D.Phil. (Rhodes scholar), Oxford U., 1940; M.D., Johns Hopkins, 1942; m. Joy Hume, Dec. 29, 1943; children—Gail, Theodore, Donald, Beth. Intern, John Hopkins Hosp., Balt., 1942-43; fellow Med. Adminstrn. Service and Com. on Research in Med. Econs., 1943; med. officer UNRRA, Eastern Europe, 1946; med. dir. Migratory Labor Health Assn. USPHS, Atlanta, 1947; mem. staff Med. Group Practice Study div. Pub. Health Methods, Washington, 1948; area med. adminstr. UMWA Welfare and Retirement Fund, Pitts., 1948-67; project co-dir. Meharry Neighborhood Health Center, Nashville, 1967-69; lectr. Am. U. Sch. Pub. Affairs, 1948; lectr. U. Pitts. Sch. Social Work, 1949-67; lectr. med. care adminstrn. U. Mich. Sch. Pub. Health, 1965—; adj. asso. prof. med. and hosp. adminstrn. U. Pitts. Grad. Sch. Pub. Health, 1950—; prof., chmn. dept. family and community health Meharry Med. Coll., 1967—; health cons. food industry health and welfare plan Pub. Sch. Edn., St. Louis. Served with M.C., AUS, 1943-46. Diplomate Am. Bd. Preventive Medicine and Pub. Health. Home: 1476 Clairmont Pl Nashville TN 37215 Office: Meharry Med Coll Nashville TN 37208

FALKENSTEN, RICHARD GEORGE, dentist; b. L.I., N.Y., June 25, 1940; s. Richard Nelson and Lorraine D. (Duerr) F.; student U. Okla., 1958-59, U. Tulsa, 1959-62; D.D.S., U. Mo., Kansas City, 1966; m. Sandra Marie Knebel, Aug. 17, 1965; children—Richard Christopher, Michele Marie. Staff doctor Tulsa City-County Health Dept., 1968; individual practice dentistry, Tulsa, 1968—; tchr., cons. Tulsa Dental Asst.'s Sch. Vocational Tng.; cons. Tulsa Jr. Coll.; mem. staff Hillcrest Hosp.; founder, mem. staff Charity Dental Clinic at Tulsa Boys Home. City dir., chmn. com. for Explorers, 1970—; mem. Okla. Com. Continuing Edn. in Dentistry. Bd. dirs. Tulsa Boys Home; mem. exec. bd. Indian Nations council Boy Scouts Am. Served with AUS, 1966-68. Recipient Vol. of Year award Tulsa Boys Home, 1970. Mem. Am., Okla. (mem. peer rev. com., bd. govs. 1972—) dental assns., Tulsa County Dental Soc. (com. chmn. dental health and community service, 1970-71; mem. constn. and by-laws com. 1971-72; dir. edn. 1972-73), Tulsa Endodontic Study Club, Am. Soc. Analgesia, Acad. Gen. Dentistry, Am. Soc. Preventive Dentistry, Psi Omega. Club: Tulsa Optimist. Office: 4515 S Yale Av Tulsa OK 74135

FALLIS, GORDON, city editor Tulsa Tribune. Address: 315 S Boulder Av Tulsa OK 74102*

FALLS, ANONA JENKINS (MRS. GEORGE E. FALLS), librarian; b. Clarksdale, Miss.; d. James Talmadge and Effie (Turney) Jenkins; student Goucher Coll., Balt., 1922-25; summer study U. Ill., 1938; certificate library sci. Carnegie Library Sch., Carnegie Inst. Tech., 1940. With Carnegie Pub. Library, Clarksdale, Miss., 1936—, successively library asst. children's librarian, asst. librarian, 1936-48, head librarian, 1948—. Mem. sec., bd. commrs. Miss. Library Commn., 1955-58. Mem. A.L.A. (Miss. rep. council 1954-58, mem. recruiting network 1961—, notable books council adult services div. 1970—), Miss. (exec. bd. 1950-59, pres. 1952-53, chmn. adult edn. com. 1960-61), Children's (membership regional chmn. 1944-46, state membership chmn. 1942). Southeastern library assns., Bus. and Profl. Women's Club, D.A.R., Delta Kappa Gamma, Gamma Phi Beta. Home: 229 Maple St Clarksdale MS 38614 Office: Carnegie Pub Library Clarksdale MS 38614

FALLS, LEE WAYNE, statistician; b. Cleve., Mar. 17, 1929; s. George B. and Winifred (Jaycox) F.; student Fenn Coll., 1953; B.S., Kent State U., 1959; M.S., U. Ga., 1965; postgrad. U. Ala., 1966; m. Phyllis Brazo, Aug. 28, 1955 (div. Aug. 1968); children—Tad Lee, David Wayne, Randall Allan. Aerospace engr. George C. Marshall Space Flight Center, NASA, Huntsville, Ala., 1965—. Mem. Am. Statis. Assn. Home: 604 Stella Dr Madison AL 35758 Office: NASA Marshall Space Center R-Aero-YT Huntsville AL 35812

FALTERMAN, JAMES BONIN, physician; b. St. Martinville, La., Mar. 3, 1935; s. Charles Henry and Marie (Carlos) F.; student U. Southwestern La., 1957; M.D., La. State U., 1962; m. Lorayne Walker, Jan. 11, 1957; children—James Bonin, Mary, Corinne, Charles, David, Stephen, John. Intern, Touro Infirmary, New Orleans, 1962-63; gen. practice medicine, Jeanerette, La., 1962—; mem. staff Iberia Parish Hosp., 1955—, chief staff, 1966; mem. staff Dauterive Hosp., New Iberia, La. Adv. bd. dirs. Peoples Nat. Bank, Jeanerette. Asst. coroner Iberia Parish, 1965—; alderman City of Jeanerette, 1967—, police commr., 1967—. Pres. St. Joseph Sch. Bd., 1970. Named Intern of Year Touro Infirmary, 1963. Mem. Am., La. acads. gen. practice, So. Med. Assn., La., Iberia Parish (pres. 1971) med. socs. K.C. Home: 537 Druilhet St Jeanerette LA 70544 Office: 1411 Church St Jeanerette LA 70544

FANGUY, JUNIUS JOHN, hosp. adminstr.; b. Houma, La., Apr. 7, 1927; s. Clifford John and Evelyn (Tivet) F.; certificate Columbia, 1958-59; student Loyola U., 1953-54; A.A., Marion Mil. Inst., 1951-53; B.B.A., Phoenix U., 1954-56; M.B.A., 1956; Ph.D., U. Minerva, 1959; m. Annabelle C. Provost, Dec. 28, 1951;children—Junius John, Brian Keith, Timothy Synge, Michael James. Asst. comandant Cadets, Marion Mil. Inst., 1951-53; asst. adminstr. Sara Mayo Hosp., New Orleans, 1953-54; adminstr. Webster County Meml. Hosp., Webster Springs, W.Va., 1956-59, Abrom Kaplan Meml. Hosp., Kaplan, La., 1959-69; exec. dir. Vermilion Nursing Home, Kaplan, 1962-70; adminstr. St. Bernard Hosp. and Med. Center, Chalmette, La., 1969-70; adminstr. Many (La.) Clinic and Hosp. div. Extendicare, 1970-71, Brentwood Hosp. div. Extendicare, Shreveport, La., 1971—. Cons. Hosp. Service Dist. 1, Vermilion Parish, La., sec., treas., 1963-69; cons. Savoy Meml. Hosp., Mamou, La., Mamou Nursing Home, Vermilion Nursing Home and Mgmt. Corp., Kaplan, A. Kaplan Meml. Hosp.; pres. Acadiana Internat. Trading Co., 1964—, Fanguy Seafood Co., Houma, La., 1964-71, Seaport Leasing Corp., Houma, 1965—; chmn. adv. bd. Sch. Practical Nursing, Gulf Area Vocational Tech. Sch., Abbeville, La., 1965-67. Chpt. chmn. A.R.C., Kaplan, 1961-65; vice chmn., bd. dirs. S.W. La. Rehab. Center, 1963-68. Served with USNR, 1944-46, USCG, 1947-51; Korea. Fellow Royal Soc. Health, Am. Coll. Nursing Home Adminstrs., Am. Acad. Med. Adminstrs.; mem. Am. Legion, V.F.W., Am. Coll. Hosp. Adminstrs.; Federation Internationale Des Hopitaux, Am. Hosp. Assn. Nat. Assn. for Mental Health, Shreveport C. of C. K.C. (4 deg.) Home: 3824 Creswell St Shreveport LA 71106 Office: PO Box 4426 Shreveport LA 71104

FANKHAUSER, GLENN HENRY, citrus mgmt. co. exec.; b. Burlington, Okla., Aug. 16, 1910; s. Henry Isaac and Lucy Louise (Schwab) F.; student Tex. A. and M. U., 1928-31; m. Dorothy Woods, Apr. 16, 1936. Hort. foreman Am. Land Co., Harlingen, Tex., 1931-34; agt. Franklin Life Ins. Co., Houston and Mission, Tex., 1935; mgr. Valley Growers Chems., Mission, 1936; constrn. foreman Dodds & Wedegartner, San Benito, Tex., 1936-40; supt. Am. Investment Corp., Mission, Tex., 1940-64; tchr. Farm Hand Gen. fed. program instrn. to farm labor, Edinburg, Tex., 1965; pres., owner Citrus Mgmt. Corp., Mission, 1970—. Active land and citrus appraiser and broker. Chmn. Democratic Precinct, Hidalgo County, Tex., 1962-72. Bd. dirs. Hidalgo County Water Control and Improvement Dist. 6, 1972—. Mem. Edinburg Citrus Assn. (dir. 1966-72), Tex. Citrus Mut. (dir. 1971-72). Mason. Address: Box 965 Mission TX 78572

FANNIN, CASEY CARY, city ofcl.; b. Madisonville, Tex., Feb. 6, 1916; s. Roy F. and Mary F. (DeFee) F.; B.S. in Petroleum Engring., A. and M. Coll. Tex., 1934-38, student econs. and accounting, 1945-46, postgrad. municipal adminstrn., 1947, B.A. in Econs., 1958; m. Oleta Estelle Crouch, Oct. 2, 1941; children—Pamela, Casey, Michael. Petroleum engr. Pan Am. Prodn. Co., 1938-40, Tide-Water Seabord Oil Co., 1940; service sta. attendant, 1940-41; tax assessor, collector Madison County, Tex., 1941-47; city mgr., Tex., 1947, Pittsburg, 1948-49, Odessa, 1949-52, Bryan 1953-58, Columbia, Mo., 1958-61, Tyler, Tex., 1961—; local tax specialist; cons. Japanese Nat. Govt., Tokyo, 1949; v.p. Tellyer Pipe Co. Tex. 1952-53; treas. W. Tex. Concrete Products, Inc., 1953. Bd. dirs. Bryan Indsl. Found.; adv. com. Tex. Police Tng. Sch. A. and M. Coll. Tex.; dist. committeeman Boy Scouts Am. Mem. E. Tex., Bryan (dir.) C.'s of C., Internat., Tex. (regional dir.) city mgrs. assns., Tax Assessors Collectors Assn. Tex. (life), Am. Pub. Works Assn., A.I.M., Tex. Water Sewage Works Assn., Former Students' Assn. A. and M. Coll. Tex., Civic Music Assn. Methodist (ofcl. bd., chmn. finance com.). Mason (32 deg., K.T., Shriner), Rotarian. Home: 2720 Sunnybrook Dr Tyler TX 75701 Office: 1411 Winrock St Houston TX 77027

FANNIN, TROY EDWARD, optometrist, educator; b. Sandy Hook, Ky., Jan. 19, 1925; s. Floyd Mitchell and Elizabeth (Hayes) F.; B.S., U.S. Mcht. Marine Acad., 1945; B.S., Dr. Optometry, Ohio State U., 1952; m. Cecile Mae Owen, Nov. 24 1949; 1 dau., Heather Fay. Marine engr. Isthmian S.S. Co., 1945-46, Coastwise S.S. Co., 1946-47; instr. U. Houston Coll. Optometry, 1954-56, asst. prof., 1965-68, asso. prof., 1968—; vis. asso. prof. U. Cal. at Berkeley, summer 1969; pvt. practice optometry, Houston, 1956-65. Lt. USNR. Diplomate Nat. Bd. Optometry. Mem. Am. Acad. Optometry (chmn. sect. meetings), Am., Tex., Harris County optometric assns., Am. Assn. U. Profs., Tex. Assn. Coll. Tchrs., Editorial Council Am. Acad. Optometry, Assn. Optometric Educators, Beta Sigma Kappa. Unitarian. Home: 13334 Bretagne Dr Houston TX 77015

FANNING, CHARLES BUCKNER, clergyman; b. Houston, Mar. 13, 1926; s. Charles A. and Beryl (Buckner) F.; B.A., Baylor U., 1949; B.D., So. Bapt. Theol. Sem., 1954; D.D., Howard Payne U., 1962; m. Martha Howell, June 5, 1949; children—Michael Buckner, Stephen Scott, Martha Lisa. Ordained to ministry Baptist Ch., 1948; pres. Buckner Fanning Evangelistic Found., Dallas, 1955-59; pastor Trinity Bapt. Ch., San Antonio, 1959—. Vice pres. Bapt. Gen. Conv. Tex., 1963; speaker before various groups in U.S., overseas 1947—; mem. fgn. mission bd. So. Bapt. Conv. Mem. exec. council Boy Scouts Am., 1961—; mem. Citizens Com. to Provide Treatment Center for Narcotic Addicts, San Antonio, 1965—; bd. dirs. Planned Parenthood; spl. pub. relations cons. Hemisfair '68; chmn. Billy Graham Hemisfair Crusade, 1968; mem. Gov.'s Council Lifetime Sports, Urban Coalition of San Antonio. Trustee Bapt. Meml. Hosp., San Antonio. Served with USMCR, 1943-46. Mem. C. of C. (human resources council). Contbr. articles to religious jours. Home: 2327 Blanton Dr San Antonio TX 78212 Office: 319 E Mulberry St San Antonio TX 78209

FANSEEN, JAMES FOSTER, govt. ofcl.; b. Balt., Feb. 3, 1928; s. Foster Hooker and Lillian (Seguine) F.; A.B., U. N.C., 1950; LL.B., U. Md., 1954; grad. Inst. Police Community Relations, Mich. State U., 1958. Admitted to Md. bar, 1954, D.C. bar, 1968; magistrate Balt. City Police Ct., 1955-59; partner Fanseen & Chlan, Balt., 1959—; commr. Fed. Maritime Commn., 1967—, acting chmn., 1969, vice chmn, 1969-71; prof. polit. sci. Community Coll. Balt., 1963-70. Mem. Nat. Conf. Christians and Jews, 1965—; mem. Criminal Justice Commn., 1965—, pres., 1966-68. Served to maj. USAF Res., 1950-69. Mem. Am., Md., Balt. bar assns., Trial Judges Assn., Md. Law Enforcement Officers, Edgar Allan Poe Soc., Gamma Eta Gamma (past pres.), Phi Delta Theta. Republican. Methodist. Mason (Shriner). Clubs: Metropolitan, University (Washington); Baltimore Country; Yacht, Power Squadron (Annapolis, Md.). Home: 29 Blythewood Rd Baltimore MD 21210 Office: 1405 I St NW Washington DC 20573

FANSHIER, CHESTER, metal products mfg. exec.; b. Wilson County, Kansas, March 2, 1897; s. Thomas J. and Nora Belle (Maxwell) F.; m. Ina Muriel Goens April 12, 1918; 1 dau., Norma Elaine (Mrs. Robert B. Rice). Gen. mgr. Bart Products Co., 1932-39; pres. gen. mgr. Metal Goods Mfr. Co., 1939—. Commr. Tulsa Presbytery to 156th Gen. Assembly, Presbyn. Ch. U.S.A., 1944; pres. Sunday Eve. Fedn. (chs.), 1937-38. Recipient Wisdom award Honor, 1970. Registered profl. engr. Okla. Mem. Am. Soc. M.E., Am. Soc. Testing Materials, Bartlesville C. of C., Am. Ordnance Assn. (life), Nat. Rifle Assn. Am. (life), Nat., Okla. (charter) socs. profl. engrs., Okla. Rifle Assn., Profl. Photographers Am. Presbyn. (elder). Clubs: Rotary (pres. 1956-57), Engineers of Bartlesville (charter mem.; past dir.). Home: 1328 Cherokee Av Bartlesville OK 74003 Office: 309 W Hensley Blvd Bartlesville OK 74003

FANT, ELENA BEDFORD (MRS. GEORGE FANT), bus. exec.; b. nr. Bridgeport, Tex., Aug. 15, 1908; d. John Wesley and Beatrice (Acord) Newsom; student Tex. Bus. Coll., 1925-26; m. George Fant, Apr. 26, 1941 (dec. Sept. 1962). Sec., First Nat. Bank, Weatherford, Tex., 1926-40, asst. cashier, 1941-45, v.p., dir. 1946-49; sec. and clk. Mut. Bldg. & Loan Assn., 1926-40, asst. sec., 1941-49, v.p., 1950-58, pres., 1959—, also dir. Hon. mem. 4-H Club, Parker County. Founder, George Fant Found., George Fant-Stephens Catholic Ch. Found. Trustee E. D. Farmer Relief Fund. Mem. Soc. Savs. and Loan Controllers, Soc. Real Estate Appraisers (asso.), A.I.M. (pres.'s council 1967-69). Baptist. Clubs: Jim Wright Congressional, Weatherford Kangaroo Booster, Live Oak Country. Home: 508 W Baylor St Weatherford TX 76086 Office: 133 College Av Weatherford TX 76086

FANT, JULIAN EARLE, JR., banker; b. Jacksonville, Fla., Mar. 11, 1939; s. Julian Earle and Nathalie Lorraine (Beville) F.; B.S., U. Fla., 1961; M.B.A., U. Pa., 1962; m. Dorothy Stephenson, Sept. 2, 1966; children—Julian Earle III and Jennifer Lynne (twins). Pres., First Guaranty Bank & Trust Co., Jacksonville, 1962—; vice chmn. Five Points Guaranty Bank; faculty U. Fla., Fla. Sch. Banking. Mem. city council, Jacksonville, 1971—. Bd. dirs. N.E. Fla. Heart Assn., Jacksonville Childrens Hosp. Mem. Fla. Bankers Assn. (dir.), Kappa Alpha. Democrat. Episcopalian.Home: 4415 Pirates Cove Rd Jacksonville FL 32210 Office: 1234 King St Jacksonville FL 32205

FANTL, S. JOSEPH, pub. relations exec.; b. Newark, Mar. 16, 1920; s. Richard and Sarah (De Jonge) F.; B.S., U. Chgo., 1940; M.F.A., New Sch. for Social Research, N.Y.C., 1948; postgrad. Cornell U., 1950; m. Shirley Ruth Chesler, June 8, 1947; children—Brian I., Stephanie Jan, Robin, Richard David. Trainee to supr. textile industry, 1948-58; advt., pub. relations Am. Homes, Inc. and Louis P.

Batson Co., textiles, Greenville, S.C., 1958-67; pub. relations coordinator Greenville Tech. Edn. Center, 1967-71, also tchr. creative thinking; chmn. bd. Ideas, Inc.; tchr. creative writing Furman U.; dir. coll. relations Prince George's Community Coll., Largo, Md., 1971—. Pres., Southside P.T.A., 1971-72. Served with AUS, 1941-45. Decorated Purple Heart. Mem. Pub. Relations Soc. Am., Am. Assn. Textile Colorists and Chemists, Am. Assn. Jr. Colls., So. Assn. Colls. and Schs. (cons., chmn. pub. relations com.), Greenville C. of C. Mason. Club: International (pres.) (Greenville). Author: Brown House of Black Anna (play) (finalist Sergel Internat. Drama Competition 1968); Public Relations in the Junior Community College, 1972. Patentee mechanic, lit. and novelty ideas. Home: 12101 Foxhill Lane Bowie MD 20715 Office: Prince George's Community Coll 301 Largo Rd Largo MD 20870

FARABEE, DALE HENRY, state mental health ofcl.; b. New Albany, Ind., Oct. 15, 1926; s. George and Lula Dale (Pollard) F.; A.B. in Psychology, Ind. U., 1951; M.D., U. Louisville, 1958; m. Laura Hutchens, Feb. 12, 1960. Intern, Louisville Gen. Hosp., 1958-59, resident, 1960; resident Central State Hosp., Louisville, 1959, 60-61, Norton's Meml. Infirmary, Louisville, 1961-62; dir. Eastern Ky. region Div. Community Services, Ky. Dept. Mental Health, Lexington, 1962-64, commr. dept., Frankfort, 1965—; chief psychiat. sect. U. Ky. Student Health Service, Lexington, 1964-65. Asst. prof. psychiatry U. Ky., 1962-71, U. Louisville, 1962—; cons. Nat. Inst. Mental Health, 1967—; mem. Nat. Adv. Council on Alcohol Abuse and Alcoholism, 1971—. Served with AUS, 1947-48, 51-53; Korea. Mem. Am., Ky. psychiat. assns., Fayette County (Ky.) Med. Soc. Design and devel. Ky. Comprehensive Mental Health Center program, 1963-65. Home: 2538 Westmoreland Rd Lexington KY 40504 Office: Ky Dept Mental Health PO Box 678 Frankfort KY 40601

FARABOW, FORD FRANKLIN, JR., lawyer; b. Charlotte, N.C., Jan. 6, 1938; s. Ford F. and Louise (Botts) F.; B.S. in Chem. Engring., Clemson U., 1959; J.D., George Washington U., 1963; m. Lynne LaFuze, Aug. 12, 1962; children—Ford Franklin III, Amy Kathryn, Andrew Leighton. With law dept. Swift & Co., Washington, 1959-62; admitted to S.C. bar, 1963, D.C. bar, 1965; asso. Cooper, Gary, Nexsen & Pruet, Columbia, S.C., 1962-64; with patent dept. Hercules, Inc., Wilmington, Del., 1964-65; partner Finnegan, Henderson & Farabow, Washington, 1965—. Mem. Am. Judicature Soc., Am., S.C. bar assns., Bar Assn. D.C., Am. Patent Law Assn., U.S. Trademark Assn., Nat. Lawyers Club, Am. Chem. Soc., Clemson Alumni Assn., Order of Coif, Tiger Brotherhood, Phi Eta Sigma, Delta Theta Phi. Clubs: Bethesda Country, Touchdown (Washington); Clemson IPTAY. Home: 11523 LeHavre Dr Potomac MD 20854 Office: 1775 K St NW Washington DC 20006

FARFEL, BERNARD, physician; b. N.Y.C., May 21, 1911; s. Hyman and Fannie (Azinski) F.; B.S., N.Y.U., 1932, M.D., 1935; m. Bettie Harriet Braunstein, Nov. 7, 1937; children—Carol (Mrs. Barry Goodfriend), Linda Gene (Mrs. Herbert A. Lesser), Helen (Mrs. Larry A. Rose). Intern Fordham Hosp., N.Y.C., 1935-36, house physician 1936-37; vol. asso. intern M. D. Anderson Hosp., Houston, 1956-65; practice medicine, specializing in internal medicine, Mt. Vernon, N.Y., 1937-39, Houston, 1939—; mem. staff Methodist, St. Lukes Episcopal, Hermann, Jefferson Davis, M. D. Anderson hosps. (all Houston); instr. Baylor U., 1945-50, asst. prof. 1950-61, asso. prof. internal medicine 1961—. Dir. 1630 Financial Corp., Spring Branch Bank, Houston. Pres. Jewish Family Service, 1966-69, now mem. bd.; chmn. bd. Jewish Inst. Med. Research; trustee Inst. Religion (both Tex. Med. Center); bd. dirs. Jewish Community Council. Served as 1st lt. M.C., USAF, 1942-43. Recipient Max H. Nathan award for S.W., 1968; award Nat. Conf. Christians and Jews, 1970. Fellow Gerontol. Soc., Royal Soc. Health (U.K.); mem. N.Y. Acad. Scis., A.M.A., Tex., Harris County med. socs., A.C.P., So. Med. Assn., Am., Houston (pres. 1967) socs. internal medicine, Internat. Platform Assn., Am. Coll. Gastroenterology, Am. Heart Assn., Houston Soc. Gastroenterology, Tex. Soc. Gastroenterologists and Proctologists, Phi Delta Epsilon. Author articles in profl. jours. Abstract editor Am. Jour Gastroenterology, 1956-66. Home: 2503 Bellefontaine St Houston TX 77025 Office: Med Towers 6600 Main St Houston TX 77025

FARIES, BELMONT, newspaper editor; b. Wilmington, Del., June 3, 1913; s. Clarence D. and Elva (Eddingfield) F.; B.A., U. Pa., 1935; m. Bette Jane Bonine, Sept. 5, 1945; children—Jain, Nancy, Jennifer. Reporter, Jour.-Every Evening, Wilmington, Del., 1935-38; copy editor Evening Star, Washington, 1938-55, news editor, 1955—, stamp editor, 1956—. Editor Soc. Philatelic Ams. Jour., 1962—. Minkus Stamp Jour., 1966—. Mem. Postmaster Gen.'s Stamp Adv. Com., 1967-69, 71—. Served to 2d lt. AUS, 1942-46; capt. Res. ret. Mem. Am. Philatelic Congress (mem. council 1966—), Phi Beta Kappa. Home: 11713 Chapel Rd Clifton VA 22024 Office: 225 Virginia Av SE Washington DC 20003

FARIOLETTI, MARIUS, economist; b. Turin, Italy, Apr. 22, 1908; s. Joseph and Josephine (Pasquino) F.; brought to U.S., 1913, naturalized, 1926; B.B.A. cum laude, Chattanooga U., 1932; M.A. in Econs. (fellow), Oberlin Coll., 1933; postgrad. (univ. teaching fellow), Duke, 1933-35; m. Elizabeth Byrd Venable Mar. 28, 1935; children—Mary Jo (Mrs. David Portch), Elizabeth. Economist, A.A.A., 1935-39; economist, asst. dir. tax research U.S. Treas. Dept., 1939-48; tax advisor, asst. dir. plans and policy div. U.S. Internal Revenue Service, Washington, 1948-65, dir. planning and analysis div., 1966-70, econ. cons. tax and tax adminstrn. systems, 1970—. Lectr., Cath. U., 1937-39; chmn. Equalization Bd., 1951-53, Fiscal Affairs Com., 1958-59 (both Arlington County, Va.). Recipient Superior Work Performance award Internal Revenue Service, 1960, Commr.'s award, 1966; Treasury's Albert Gallatin award, 1970; Treasury's Meritorious Service award, 1970. Mem. Nat. Tax Assn., Nat. Press Club. Home: 4822 3d St N Arlington VA 22203 Office: Nat Press Bldg Washington DC 20004

FARIS, ROBERT K., athletic dir. George Washington U. Office: George Washington U Washington DC 20006*

FARIS, WILLIAM LAWRENCE, educator; b. Beaumont, Tex., Dec. 2, 1925; s. William C. and Emma (Fulwilder) F.; B.S., U. Houston, 1956; m. Geneva Clara Flynn, Apr. 20, 1947; children—Eugene William, Laurrie Kay, Kathleen Lynn, Mary Gayle. Instr. vocations Lamar State Coll. Tech., 1951-54, instr. engring., 1954-66; instr., heat air conditioning tech. San Jacinto Coll., Pasadena, Tex., 1966—. Tech. adviser Dacca, East Pakistan (now Bengladesh), 1969-71. Cons. Indsl. Engring. Co., Beaumont, Tex., 1951—. Served with USAAF, 1943-45. Decorated Air medal with two oak leaf clusters. Mem. Am. Soc. Heating, Refrigerating and Air Conditioning Engrs., Tex. Jr. Coll. Tchrs. Assn. Kiwanian (treas. 1968). Home: 10435 Winding Trial LaPorte TX 77571 Office: 8060 Spencer Hwy Pasadena TX 77505

FARISH, STEPHEN THOMAS, JR., singer, educator; b. Columbia, VA., May 5, 1936; s. Stephen Thomas and Jessie (Jones) F.; B.S., E. Carolina Coll., 1958; MusM., U. Ill., 1959, D.Mus. Arts, 1962; pvt. study Bruce Foote, Paul Ulanovsky, George Reeves, Caro Carapetyn; m. Anna Withers Montgomery, May 31, 1958; children—Stephen David, Virginia Kaye. Singer, 1956—; appearances include tv, radio, recitals, concerts; appeared with Chgo. NBC Symphony, Tex. Boys Choir, W. Coast Symphony, Fort Worth Opera Assn.; faculty N. Tex. State U., Denton, 1962—, asso. prof. music, 1967-72, prof. music, 1972—; vis. asso. prof. Okla. U., summer 1963; contest adjudicator, clinician, Okla., Tex., Mo., La., Ill.; minister music First Meth. Ch., Urbana, Ill., 1961-62, St. Andrew Presbyn. Ch., Denton, 1964-72, Univ. Christian Ch., Ft. Worth, 1972—; mus. dir. Denton Community Chorus. Mem. Phi Mu Alpha Sinfonia, Phi Kappa Phi, Pi Kappa Lambda, Kappa Delta Pi. Presbyn. Kiwanian. Home: 1900 Emerson Dr Denton TX 76201

FARLEY, JACK EMORY, lawyer; b. Pikeville, Ky., Jan. 4, 1939; s. Lewis Clyde and Mary (Emory) F.; B.A., U. Ky., 1962; J.D., Am. U., 1967; m. Margaret Rose Saad, Jan. 26, 1963; children—Aletha Claire, Jennifer Lucille, Dana Rose. Admitted to D.C. bar, 1968, Ky. bar, 1969; communications security specialist Def. Dept., Washington, 1962-67; trial atty. Justice Dept., Washington, 1967-68; exec. dir. Pike County C. of C. Pikeville, Ky., 1968-72; practice law, Pikeville, 1972—. Counsel Pikeville-Pike County Airport Bd., 1969—, Pikeville Urban Renewal Agy., 1970—; chmn. Pike County Headstart Policy Com., 1970-71; v.p. Eastern Highlands Tourism Region, 1970-72. Bd. dirs., v.p. Big Sandy Area Devel. Council. Served with AUSR, 1956-64. Named Ky. Col., 1962. Mem. Am., So., Ky. assns. C. of C. execs., Am., Fed., Ky. bar assns., Democrat. Methodist. Home: PO Box 90 Smith Hill Pikeville KY 41501 Office: PO Box 897 Pikeville KY 41501

FARLEY, WILLIAM EDWARD, educator; b. Louisville, June 12, 1929; s. Raymond Lee and Dora (Walker) F.; B.A., Centre Coll., 1950; B.D., Louisville Presbyn. Theol. Sem., 1953; Ph.D. (Kent fellow), Columbia, 1958; m. Doris June Kimbel, Aug. 11, 1951; children—Mark Kimbel, Wendy Lee, Amy Catherine. Ordained to ministry Presbyterian Ch., 1953; asst. prof. DePauw U., Greencastle, Ind., 1957-62; asso. prof. theology Pitts. Theol. Sem., 1962-69; prof. theology Div. Sch., Vanderbilt U., Nashville, 1969—. Mem. Presbytery of Nashville, 1970-72. Recipient fellowship in religion Lilly Found., 1961-62; faculty fellowship Am. Assn. Theol. Schs., 1970-71. Mem. Soc. Religion in Higher Edn., Am. Philos. Assn., Am. Assn. Religion, New Haven Theol. Discussion Group. Democrat. Author: The Transcendence of God, 1958; Requiem for a Lost Piety, 1966. Home: 415 Grayson Dr Nashville TN 37205

FARLOW, ELBERT ALLISON, motel exec., lawyer; b. Wilmington, N.C., June 12, 1929; s. Elbert Allison and Lillian Irene (Leath) F.; B.S., The Citadel, 1951; J.D., U. S.C., 1956; m. Patricia Leatherwood, June 12, 1961; children—Elizabeth Allison, Leath Anne, William Allison. Admitted to S.C. bar, 1956, since practiced in Myrtle Beach; owner Waterside Motel, Myrtle Beach, 1959—; pres. The Breakers, Myrtle Beach, 1970—. Chmn. S.C. Travel Council, 1968; mem. Myrtle Beach City Council, 1968, 69, 72—; vice chmn. Myrtle Beach Planning and Zoning Commn., 1970-71; vice chmn. Horry County Devel. Bd., 1967—. Mem. adv. bd. Horry County Salvation Army. Served as lt. arty. AUS, 1951-53. Named Citizen of Yr., Myrtle Beach C. of C. Mem. Am. (chmn. S.C. Jr. Bar Conf. 1959), S.C. (circuit v.p. 1960), Horry County bar assns., S.C. (dir. 1965-66), Greater Myrtle Beach (pres. 1966) chambers commerce, S.C., Horry County (pres. 1970) hist. socs., Long Bay Power Squadron (comdr. 1964), S.A.R. (pres. S.C. 1960), Phi Delta Phi. Democrat. Presbyn. (Sunday sch. supt. 1966-68, chmn. bd. deacons 1969, elder 1970—). Mason, Rotarian (pres. 1971). Club: Dunes Golf and Beach (dir. 1967—, sec. 1967—) (Myrtle Beach, S.C.). Home: 4801 N Ocean Blvd Myrtle Beach SC 29577 Office: 1908 N Ocean Blvd Myrtle Beach SC 29577

FARMAN, IRVIN SAMUEL, pub relations exec.; b. L.I., N.Y., Aug. 23, 1921; s. Samuel and Goldie (Elkins) F.; B.J., U. Mo., 1943; m. Rosalyn Graves, June 7, 1947; 1 son, Richard Kent. Sports writer Dallas Morning News, 1946, A.P., 1946; reporter, columnist Fort Worth StarTelegram, 1946-53; with Witherspoon & Assos., Inc., Ft. Worth, 1953—, exec. v.p., dir., 1960—. Mem. faculty pub. relations course Tex. Christian U. Evening Coll., 1965—. Exec. sec. Greater Ft. Worth Planning Com., 1956-61; commr. Fort Worth Housing Authority, 1965—, vice chmn. 1967—; bd. dirs. Tarrant County Assn. Mental Health, Friends of Ft. Worth Library. Served to capt. AC, AUS, 1943-46. Mem. Pub. Relations Soc. Am. (chpt. v.p. 1964—), Ridotto, Newcomen Soc. N.Am., Sigma Delta Chi (chpt. pres. 1955—), Kappa Tau Alpha, Phi Eta Sigma. Republican. Methodist. Clubs: Kiwanis (pres. 1970-71), River Crest Country. Home: 409 Ridgewood Rd Fort Worth TX 76107 Office: 321 S Henderson St Fort Worth TX 76104

FARMER, BERKWOOD MALCOLM, univ. adminstr.; b. Danville, Va., Aug. 3, 1938; s. Isham Malcolm and Aubria (Mylum) F.; B.S., N.C. State U., 1960, M.S. (Nat. Def. Edn. Act fellow), 1963, Ph.D., 1970; m. Mariah Anderson, July 14, 1958; children—Donna Louise, Katherine Lynn, Berkwood Malcolm. Instr. dept. econs. N.C. State U., 1963-64; commd. 2d lt. U.S. Army, 1964, advanced through grades to maj., 1968; asst. prof. dept. social scis. U.S. Mil. Acad., 1968-71; asst. prof. econs. U. Richmond, Va., 1971-72, asso. dean U. Coll., 1972—. Decorated Bronze Star medal; recipient Wall St Jour. Student Achievement award N.C. State U., 1960. Mem. Am. Econs. Assn., Am. Agrl. Econs. Assn., Lambda Chi Alpha. Baptist. Club: Richmond Country. Contbr. articles to profl. jours. Home: 9402 Midvale Rd Richmond VA 23229 Office: 7 W Franklin St Richmond VA 23220

FARMER, FRANCES, librarian; b. Keysville, Va., Dec. 5, 1909; d. Horatio Weldon and Florence (Womack) Farmer; A.B., U. Richmond, 1931, LL.B., 1933. Sec. to dean, law sch. U. Richmond, 1931-38, law librarian, 1938-42; law librarian U. Va. 1942—. Mem. Am. Assn. Law Libraries (pres. 1959-60), Va. State Bar Assn., Va. State Bar, alumnae assn., Westhampton Coll., U. Richmond (former pres.), Order of the Coif, Phi Beta Kappa. Author: (with M. Ray Doubles) Manual of Legal Bibliography, 1947. Editor The Woodrow Wilson Reader, 1956. Home: 2031 Hessian Rd Charlottesville VA 22903 Office: U Va Law Library Clark Hall Charlottsville VA 22204

FARMER, JAMES, govt. ofcl.; b. Marshall, Tex., Jan. 12, 1920; s. James Leonard and Pearl Marion (Houston) F.; B.S., Wiley Coll., Marshall, 1938; B.D., Howard U., 1941; HH.D., Morgan State Coll., Balt., 1964; m. Lula A. Peterson, May 21, 1949; children—Tami, Abbey. Founder, Congress of Racial Equality (CORE), 1942, nat. chmn., 1942-44, 50, nat. dir., 1961-66; race relations sec. Fellowship of Reconciliation, 1941-45; organizer Upholsterer's Internat. Union N. Am., 1945-47; lectr. race and labor problems, 1948-50; student field sec. League Indsl. Democracy, 1950-54; internat. rep. State, County and Municipal Employees Union, 1954-59; program dir. N.A.A.C.P., 1959-61; leader CORE Freedom Ride, 1961; dir. Center for Community-Action Edn., 1966-69; asst. sec. adminstrn. Dept. Health, Edn. and Welfare, Washington, 1969-70; pres. Center for Study of Goals and Strategies, Minority Peoples Think Tank, 1970—. Mem. nat. exec. bd. Am. Com. on Africa, 1959-64; chmn. Council United Civil Rights Leadership, 1963—; sponsor Am. Negro Leadership Conf. on Africa, 1962—; prof. social welfare Lincoln U., Oxford, Pa. Vice chmn. Liberal Party N.Y. County, 1954-61. Bd. dirs. League Indsl. Democracy, Am. Civil Liberties Union, Americans for Democratic Action. Recipient Am. Friendship Club award, 1961, Am. Vets. Com. award, 1962, John Dewey award League Indsl. Democracy, 1962, Distinguished Postgrad. Achievement Alumni award Howard U., 1964, Omega Psi Phi award, 1961, 63. Author: Freedom-When, 1965; also essay and numerous articles. Home: 5129 Chevy Chase Pkwy NW Washington DC 20008

FARMER, JOHN MILBURN, physician; b. Linn Creek, Mo., May 3, 1937; s. Lee Wendall and Abigail (Roach) F.; A.B., U. Mo., 1959, M.D., 1963; m. Carol Sue Dunn, Dec. 22, 1957; children—Rebecca Sue, Teressa Jon, John Milburn III. Intern, St. Louis County Hosp., 1963-64; gen. practice medicine, Magnolia, Ark., 1966—; mem. staff Magnolia City Hosp. Served to capt. USAF, 1964-66. Mem. Am. Acad. Family Physicians, A.M.A., Ark., Columbia County med. socs. Home: 910 Peach St Magnolia AR 71753 Office: 104 E Columbia St Magnolia AR 71753

FARMER, LEON, JR., lawyer, wholesale exec.; b. Athens, Ga., May 23, 1937; s. H. L. and Eloise (Harmon) F.; B.B.A., U. Ga., 1964, J.D., 1967; m. Marilyn Therese Wade, Apr. 26, 1958; children—Terri Leigh, Lisa Rene, Joni Denise, Leon III. Admitted to Ga. bar, 1966, since practiced in Athens, 1966—; exec. v.p., gen. mgr. Premium Distbg. Co., Inc., Athens; mem. Ga. Ho. of Reps., 1967-71. Mem. Ga. Manpower Planning Council, 1971—. Ofcl. del., temp. floor chmn., reg. Ga. delegation Democratic Nat. Conv., 1968; mem. exec. com. Dem. party Clarke County, 1969-71. Served with USMCR, 1957-59; comdt. Ga. Marine Corps, 1967-71. Mem. State Bar Ga., Am., Athens bar assns., Chi Phi, Phi Alpha Delta. Home: 1000 Old Creek Rd Athens GA 30601 Office: Farmer Bldg 1700 Commerce Rd Athens GA 30601

FARMER, LESTER FRANKLIN, banker; b. Tuckerman, Ark., Feb. 17, 1907; s. Joseph F. and Ann (Butler) F.; Okla. Bapt. U., 1926-27, U. Ark., 1928-29; m. Katchie Jones, Aug. 16, 1929; 1 son, Joseph F. With U.S. Dept. Agr., Newport, Ark., 1933-35; editor Newport Daily Ind., 1935-37; cashier 1st Nat. Bank, Tuckerman, Ark., 1937-45, pres., 1945—; dir. 1st Nat. Bank, Newport, Zenith Seed Co., Tuckerman, Ark., Citizens Power & Light Co., Tuckerman. Chmn., Jackson County Bd. Edn., 1940-50, Jackson County Welfare Bd., 1936-50; sec. Tuckerman Sch. Bd., 1946-56. Sec., Democratic Central Com., 1935-55. Baptist. Mason (32 deg.). Address: Tuckerman AR 72473

FARMER, RALPH NUCKOLLS, ins. exec.; b. Woodlawn, Va., Aug. 17, 1919; s. James F. and Irena (Worrell) F.; student W.Va. Bus. Coll., 1939, Indsl. Coll. Armed Forces, 1960; m. Ethel Scism, Jan. 17, 1942; children—James Ralph, Harriet Elaine. Pub. accountant, Charlotte, N.C., 1945-48; accountant Thermoid Co., 1949-50; asst. treas. Hardware Mut. Ins. Co. of Carolinas, 1951-55, treas., 1956-59, v.p., 1960-62, exec. v.p., 1963-64, pres., dir., 1965—; pres., dir. Acme Ins. Agy., HMC Corp., Pathway Ins. Agy. Mem. adv. com. Citizens Safety Assn.; mem. estate planning com. Campbell Coll. Bd. dirs. N.C. chpt. Multiple Sclerosis Soc., 1965-68. Served with USAAF, 1941-45. Mem. Charlotte C. of C. Baptist. Clubs: Charlotte Executives; Carmel Country. Home: 710 Jefferson Dr Charlotte NC 28211 Office: 1356 E Morehead St Charlotte NC 28201

FARMER, THOMAS ALBERT, JR., educator; b. Smithfield, N.C., Jan. 28, 1932; s. Thomas Albert and Oma Martha (Adams) Farmer; student Davidson Coll., 1950-51; B.S., U. N.C., 1953, M.D., 1957; m. Nancy Josephine Nussear, Aug. 25, 1956; children—Thomas Albert III, David Crown, Steven Adams, Kelly Elizabeth. Asst. prof. medicine, asst. dean curriculum matters U. Ala. Med. Center, Birmingham, 1965-67, asso. dean, dir. student affairs and curriculum, 1967-68, asso. prof. medicine, 1967-69, exec. asso. dean, dir. undergrad. med. edn., 1968—, prof. medicine, 1969-72; dean Sch. Medicine, U. Tenn., Memphis, 1972—. Served to capt. AUS, 1961-63. Diplomate Am. Bd. Internal Medicine. Fellow. A.C.P.; mem. Am. Fedn. Clin. Research, Endocrine Soc. Contbr. articles to profl. pubs. Home: 6503 Kirby Woods Dr Memphis TN 38103

FARNHAM, JERRY JOE, city ofcl.; b. Oklahoma City, June 28, 1933; s. John B. and Eva A. (Barns) F.; student East Central State Coll., 1968, U. Okla., 1971—; m. Mamie F. Arney, Oct. 31, 1952; children—Mark Allen, Peggy Jo. Traffic mgr. Evergreen Mills, Inc., Ada, Okla., 1952-63; shipping supr. Ideal Cement Co., Ada., 1963-67; dir. finance City of Ada, 1967—. Mem. State Bd. for Certification of Municipal Clks., Treasurers and Finance Officers. HUD fellow for grad. work in pub. adminstrn., 1971-75. Mem. Municipal Clks., Treasurers and Finance Officers (state pres.). Kiwanian. Home: 2204 Foster Dr Ada OK 74820 Office: 13th and Townsend Sts Ada OK 74820

FARNSWORTH, JERRY, artist; b. Dalton, Ga., Dec. 31, 1895; s. Samuel and Lavinia (Pou) F.; studied at the Corcoran Sch., Washington, D.C., and with Charles W. Hawthorne, Provincetown, Mass.; m. Helen Alton Sawyer, Aug. 26, 1924. Exhibited in N.Y.C., Chgo., Washington, Phila., Toledo, St. Louis, Cleveland, and others. Carnegie vis. prof. art, artist in residence. U. Ill., 1942-43; dir., instr. Farnsworth Sch. of Art, North Truro, Mass. and Sarasota, Fla. Represented in Met. Museum N.Y.C. by "Annabella," bought 1940; Whitney Museum Am. Art by "My Neighbor Miss Williams," bought 1942; represented in permanent collection Syracuse U. Awards include honorable mention Chgo. Art Inst., 1940; Portrait prize, Nat. Arts Club, N.Y.C., 1941; purchase prize, Los Angeles Museum, 1945; First purchase prize, High Mus., Atlanta, for Loraine of Truro, 1946; Maynard Portrait Prize, Nat. Acad., 1952; purchase prizes Chrysler Mus. Art, Provincetown, Mass. Asso. Nat. Academician, 1933. Nat. Academician, 1935. Mem. Washington Soc. Artists, Provincetown Art Assn. Clubs: Salmagundi, Nat. Arts (N.Y.C.) Author: Painting with Jerry Farnsworth, Learning to Paint in Oil; Portrait and Figure Painting. Home: 3482 Flamingo Sarasota FL 33581

FARNUM, LEON VERNON, JR., dentist; b. Birmingham, Ala., Dec. 14, 1916; s. Leon Vernon and Rose Lambert (Tyus) F.; B.S., Birmingham So. Coll., 1938; D.D.S., Northwestern U., 1944; m. Martha Reeves McGahee, Dec. 27, 1943; children—Nancy (Mrs. David Alan Calkins), Leon Vernon III. With Tenn. Coal, Iron & R.R. Co., 1939-41; pvt. practice dentistry, Birmingham, 1946—; asst. prof. U. Ala. Dental Sch., 1948-58. Dir. Pacific Am. Corp., Life Ins. Co. Am., Investors Corp. Am., Internat. Resorts, Inc. Asst. commr. Southside Little League Baseball, 1968-69; mem. Colonel's Club, Woodlawn High Sch., 1968—. Bd. dirs. Crestwood Youth Athletic Assn., 1963-69, Community Service Council. Served to lt. Dental Corps, USNR, 1944-46. Mem. Acad. Gen. Dentistry, Am., Ala. dental assns., Birmingham Dist. Dental Soc. (v.p.), Birmingham Dental Study Group (pres. 1967-68), Xi Psi Phi. Methodist. Club: The Club (Birmingham). Home: 5721 10th Av S Birmingham AL 35222 Office: 2114 10th Av S Birmingham AL 35205

FARQUHAR, ROBERT JOHN, III, newspaper editor; b. Oklahoma City, July 5, 1939; s. Robert John and Lucille (McCrary) F.; B.A., Central State Coll., Edmond, Okla., 1964; postgrad. Am. Press Inst., Columbia, 1966, Medill Sch. Journalism, Northwestern U., 1967; m. Odessa June Wilson, June 7, 1964; children—Sherrie Lou, Lance Richard. Reporter, Oklahoman and Times, Oklahoma City, 1959; feature editor Fort Bliss (Tex.) News, 1959; feature, sports and news editor The Vista, Central State Coll., 1960-64; asst. state editor Oklahoman, 1963, asst. city editor, 1965; asst. city editor Oklahoma City Times, 1966-68, city editor, 1969—. Instr. journalism Oklahoma City U., 1969. Mem. exec. com. Gridiron Found., 1965, 66, 67, 69, 70. Served with AUS, 1959-60. Named Journalism Student of the Year, Central State Coll., 1961. Mem. Okla. Collegiate Press Assn. (treas. 1961). Club: Gridiron (author, dir. 1965, 66, 67, 69, sec. 1969-70) (Oklahoma City). Home: 1308 N Bradley St Oklahoma City OK 73103 Office: 500 N Broadway Oklahoma City OK 73125

FARRELL, JAMES D., editor. Exec. editor Brookings Instn., Washington. Address: Brookings Instn 1775 Massachusetts Av NW Washington DC 20036*

FARRELL, JOSEPH MICHAEL, shipping co. exec.; b. Yonkers, N.Y., June 7, 1922; s. Joseph Michael and Mary Elizabeth (Powers) F.; B.S. in Econs., U.S. Mcht. Marine Acad., 1943; postgrad. Columbia, 1948-50, Fordham U., 1947-48; m. Cloatta Grace Pennington, Dec. 6, 1945; children—Cloatta M., Anthony J., Christopher J., Janice E. Commd. ensign U.S. Navy, 1944, advanced through grades to capt., 1960; ret. 1960; mgr. Great Lakes Service, States Marine Lines, 1960-62; European mgr., Bremerhaven, Germany, 1962-65; v.p. Waterman S.S. Corp., Washington, 1965—; v.p. Hammond Leasing Corp., Mobile, Ala., 1967—, Waterman S.S. Co. of Del. Mem. Propeller Club U.S. (v.p., bd. govs. 1967-68), Nat. Def. Transp. Assn., Navy League. Clubs: Congressional Country, University, George Town, Army-Navy (Washington). Home: 5607 Wilson Lane Bethesda MD 20014 Office: 910 17th St NW Washington DC 20006

FARRELL, KENNETH ROYDEN, govt. ofcl.; b. Ottawa, Ont., Can., Jan. 17, 1927; (came to U.S. 1950, naturalized 1958); s. William R. and Velma V. (Wood) F.; B.S., U. Toronto, 1950; M.S., Ia. State U., 1955, Ph.D., 1958; m. Mary Christine Souter, Sept. 7, 1951; children—Janet, Betty, Deborah, Robert, Patricia, Lisa. Economist, U. Cal. at Berkeley, 1957-69, asso. dir. Gianniai Found., 1969-71; dep. adminstr. Econ. Research Service, U.S. Dept. Agr., Washington, 1971—. Econ. cons. U.S. firms. Mem. Am. Agrl. Econs. Assn., Am. Econs. Assn., A.A.A.S., Gamma Sigma Delta, Phi Kappa Phi. Home: 11312 Handlebar Rd Reston VA 22070 Office: 500 12th St SW Washington DC 20250

FARRELL, RAYMOND FRANCIS, govt. ofcl.; b. Pawtucket, R.I., Feb. 6, 1907; s. James E. and Jennie (Moran) F.; J.D., Georgetown U., 1931; m. Charlotte M. Griedel, Nov. 11, 1961. Spl. asst. to gen. counsel joint com. U.S. Senate and House Investigating TVA, 1938-39; with FBI, 1931-33, Dept. Interior, also PWA, 1934-41; asst. commr. U.S. Immigration and Naturalization Service, 1952-58, asso. commr. 1958-62, commr., 1962—. Chmn. fed. govt. div. United Givers Fund, Washington, 1960; del. White-House Conf. Children and Youth, 1950; adv. council Nat. Council Nationality and Citizenship, 1949—; mem. Select Commn. on Western Hemisphere Immigration, 1966—, Nat. Council on Organized Crime, 1970-71; del. U.S.-Mexico Cabinet Consultations on Control Narcotics, Marihuana and Other Dangerous Drugs, 1969-71. Served to lt. col. AUS, 1942-46. Decorated Bronze Star medal; grand ufficiale Order of Merit (Italy); recipient Alumni Achievement award Georgetown U., 1961; named R.I. Man of Year, 1967; Roger Williams award, 1967; R.I. Heritage award, 1970, Founders award Assn. Nationality Lawyers, 1972. Mem. Soc. Former Agts. FBI, Am. Legion. Club: Nat. Press (Washington). Home: 2500 Q St NW Washington DC 20007 Office: 119 D St NE Washington DC 20007

FARRELL, SALLIE JOHNSON, librarian; b. Brookhaven, Miss., Dec. 29, 1909; d. William Henry and Ora Lee (Johnson) Farrell; B.A., Miss. State Coll. Women, 1931; B.S. in L.S. cum laude, U. Ill., 1932. Tchr.-librarian Picayune (Miss.) High Sch., 1932-33; asst. Queens Borough Pub. Library, Jamaica, N.Y., 1934-36, Tulane U. Library, 1936; reference librarian La. State Library, Baton Rouge, 1936-38; parish librarian Shreve Meml. Library, Shreveport, 1939, Winn, Rapides and Calcasieu parishes, La., 1940-46; field rep. La. State Library, 1946-54, dir. field services, 1954-62, state librarian, 1962—. Trustee Pub. Affairs Research Council. Mem. U.S.-USSR Libraries Exchange Mission, 1961. Mem. Am. (v.p. 1954-55, council 1963-67), La. (pres. 1943-44), Southwestern library assns., Nat. Fedn. Bus. and Profl. Women's Clubs, Alpha Delta Kappa, Delta Kappa Gamma. Methodist. Contbr. to profl. jours. Home: 1922 Ramsey Dr Baton Rouge LA 70808 Office: La State Library Baton Rouge LA 70803

FARRINGER, JOHN LEE, JR., surgeon; b. Bowling Green, Ky., Sept. 4, 1920; s. John Lee and Zora (Lawson) F.; B.A., Vanderbilt U., 1942; M.D., U. Tenn., 1945, M.S., 1950; m. Mary Margaret Smith, Mar. 8, 1947; children—John Lee, III, Janice Ann, Mary Jill. Intern, Harris Meml. Meth. Hosp., Ft. Worth, 1946; resident John Gaston and U. Tenn. Hosp., Memphis, 1949-54; practice surgery, Nashville, 1954—; asst. clin. prof. surgery Vanderbilt U. Sch. Medicine, 1956—; chief surgery Baptist Hosp., Nashville, 1966-69. Coordinator, Battle Nashville Centennial Commemoration, 1964—; chmn. Met. Hist. Commn., Nashville, 1966—; exec. bd. Middle Tenn. council Boy Scouts Am., 1961—. Bd. dirs. Davidson County unit Am. Cancer Soc., Davidson County Council Retarded Children, Police Assistance League, Profl. Systems Nashville; trustee Parkview Hosp. Served with AUS, 1943-45. Diplomate Am. Bd. Surgery. Fellow A.C.S., Southeastern Surg. Congress, So. Surg. Assn., Am. Geriatric Soc.; mem. Nashville Acad. Medicine (dir. 1970—), Davidson County Med. Soc. (dir. 1970—), So. Med. Assn., Nashville Surg. Soc. (pres. 1973), Co. Mil. Historians, Nashville Area C. of C., Alpha Kappa Kappa. Clubs: Richland Country, Nashville City, University (Nashville). Contbr. articles to surg. jours. Home: 2325 Golf Club Lane Nashville TN 37215 Office: 1907 Hayes St Nashville TN 37203

FARRIS, ANTHONY J.P., U.S. dist. atty. for so. Tex. Address: 2006 Du Barry St Houston TX 77018*

FARRIS, BILLY RALPH, dentist; b. Kansas, Ala., Oct. 30, 1936; s. James Clespy and Amanda Lucille (Mayo) F.; B.S., U. Ala., 1959, D.M.D., 1963; m. Ann Jeanine Meadows, May 27, 1961; children—Wendy Meadows, Sarah Lucille, Billy Ralph, James Glynn. Individual practice gen. dentistry, Decatur, Ala., 1965—. Charter mem. John C. Calhoun Jr. Coll. Warhawk Booster Club. Served with Dental Corps, USNR, 1963-65. Mem. Am., Ala. dental assns., Ramage Dental Study Club, Delta Sigma Delta. Baptist. Lion (pres. 1972-73). Club: Burningtree Country (Decatur). Home: 2312 Meadowbrook Dr SE Decatur AL 35601 Office: 2002 Flint Rd SE Decatur AL 35601

FARRIS, DONN MICHAEL, librarian; b. Welch, W.Va., Nov. 4, 1921; s. Robert Coleman and Aileen (Hutson) F.; A.B., Berea Coll., 1943; B.D., Garrett Theol. Sem., 1947; postgrad. Northwestern U., Yale; M.S., Columbia 1950; m. Joyce Gwendolyn Lockhart, Nov. 20, 1956; children—Evan Michael, Amy Virginia. Gen. asst. Yale Div. Sch. Library, 1948-49; cataloging asst. Gen. Theol. Sem. Library, N.Y.C., 1949-50; librarian Duke Div. Sch., 1950—, asst. prof. theol. bibliography, 1959-64, asso. prof., 1964-71, prof., 1971—. Mem. Am. Soc. Ch. History, Am. Theol. (v.p. 1961-62, pres. 1962-63, editor Newsletter 1953—), N.C., Southeastern library assns. Democrat. Presbyn. Contbr. articles to profl. jours. Home: 921 Buchanan Blvd Durham NC 27701

FARRIS, FRANK MITCHELL, JR., lawyer; b. Nashville, Sept. 29, 1915; s. Frank Mitchell and Mary Frances (Lellyett) F.; B.A., Vanderbilt U., 1937; student N.Y. Law Sch., 1939; m. Genevieve Baird, June 7, 1941; 1 dau., Genevieve Baird. Admitted to Tenn. bar, U.S. Supreme Ct. bar; mem. firm Clayton & Farris, 1939-40, 40-41; conciliation commr., def. counsel 12th Naval Dist., Treasure Island, Cal., 1944; partner firm Farris, Evans & Evans, Nashville, 1946-71, Farris, Warfield & Samuels, 1972—. Dir., gen. counsel Cherokee Ins. Co., Nashville, 1947—; exec. com., dir., counsel 3d Nat. Bank, Nashville; dir. Cherokee Equity Corp. Chmn. commrs. Watkins Inst., Nashville. Trustee, gen. counsel, exec. com. George Peabody Coll.; chmn. bd. dirs. Oak Hill Sch.; asso. Grad. Sch. Vanderbilt U. Served to lt. USNR, World War II. Mem. Bar Assn. Tenn., Beta Theta Pi, Phi Delta Phi. Presbyn. Clubs: Cumberland, Belle Meade Country, City (Nashville). Home: 940 Overton Lea Rd Nashville TN 37220 Office: 3d Nat Bank Bldg Nashville TN 37219

FARRIS, MILTON GLENN, lawyer; b. Rockwood, Tenn., Oct. 13, 1906; s. Oscar Alexander and Myrtle Amy (Derrick) F.; LL.B., Atlanta Law Sch., 1935; m. Elizabeth Herzberg, Nov. 15, 1934; children—Sandra Glenn, Janet Gail, Milton Carl, William, Stuart. Admitted to Ga. bar, 1935, and practiced in Atlanta 1935—; asso. Gulf Oil Corp., Atlanta div., 1927—, mgr. bus. analysis, market research, 1954-59, mgr. marketing services, 1960-62, mgr. Atlanta div., 1962-65, v.p., 1965-72, ret. Councilman, Atlanta, 1952-71; Fulton County Commr., 1971—. Bd. dirs. W.End Businessmen's Assn., Met. Atlanta Boys Club, Atlanta Conv. Bur., Central Atlanta Progress, Big Bros. Assn., Ga. Bus. and Industry Assn.; adv. bd. Emory U., Salvation Army. Pres. bd. trustees Atlanta Pub. Library, 1949—, awarded Trustee Citation at ALA Chgo. Conf. 1951. Mem. Am.; Ga. bar assns., West End Bus. Men's Assn. (dir.). Methodist. Mason (past master), Lion (past pres.), Kiwanian. Clubs: Commerce, Capital City, (Atlanta). Home: 580 River Valley Rd NW Atlanta GA 30328 Office: 165 Central Av SW Atlanta GA 30303

FARRISH, GIBB, fire chief; b. Cruger, Miss., Jan. 11, 1919; s. Gibb and Clara Bell (Day) F.; grad. high sch.; m. Lina Bario Mitchel, Mar. 4, 1942; children—Linda Ann (Mrs. Phil Farone), George Malcolm, Gibb. With Greenwood (Miss.) Fire Dept., 1946-54; fire chief Yazoo City (Miss.) Fire Dept., 1954—. Instr. first aid. Greenwood Sch. Nursing, 1947-54. Bd. dirs. A.R.C., 1947—, instr., 1947-66; bd. dirs. Miss. State Fire Sch., Sch. Nursing Lepre County, Miss. Served with AUS, 1941-45. Mem. Miss. Firemens Assn., Miss. Fire Chiefs Assn., Southeastern Assn. Internal Fire Chiefs. Presbyn. (deacon 1964-70). Elk, Rotarian. Home: 1608 Swayze St Yazoo City MS 39194 Office: 200 Washington St Yazoo City MS 39094

FARSON, WILLIAM J., ret. labor union ofcl.; b. Phila., Dec. 9, 1904; student Swarthmore Coll. Advt. salesman Phila. Pub. Ledger, Phila. Inquirer; organized Phila.-Camden Advt. Guild, AFL, 1936; mem. internat. exec. bd. Am. Newspaper Guild, 1937-40, 43-47, dir. orgn. of Guild, 1947-51, sec.-treas., 1951-55, exec. v.p., 1955-69; v.p. for N. Am. of Internat. Fedn. Journalists, Brussels, Belgium, until 1970. Mem. U.S. Nat. Commn. for UNESCO, until 1969. Home: 4100 W St NW Washington DC 20007

FARST, DON DAVID, veterinarian; b. Wadsworth, O., Feb. 25, 1941; s. Walter K. and Ada K. (Stetler) F.; D.V.M., Ohio State U., 1965; m. Mollye Ann Beale, Dec. 16, 1961; children—Julie, Jenny. Gen. practice vet. medicine, Franklin, Pa., 1965-69; resident veterinarian Columbus (O.) Zoo, 1969-70; faculty Ohio State Coll. Vet. Medicine, 1969-70; asso. dir. Gladys Porter Zoo, Brownsville, Tex., 1970—. Mem. Am. Vet. Med. Assn., Am. Assn. Zoo Veterinarians, Am. Assn. Zoos, Parks and Aquariums. Elk. Home: 24 Cowan Terrace Brownsville TX 78520 Office: 500 Ringgold St Brownsville TX 78520

FARTHING, KENNETH JOEL, educator; b. Prairie Hill, Mo., Feb. 4, 1928; s. Nova Joel and Bertha Ellen (McCart) F.; B.S., N.E. Mo. State Tchrs. Coll., 1952, M.A., 1957; Ph.D. (research fellow), U. Ia., 1969; m. Nelda Rose Lewis, July 4, 1952; children—Larry Joel, Janet Sue, Shawna Kay. High sch. tchr. Cairo (Mo.) Pub. Schs., 1954-57; supt. Cainsville (Mo.) Pub. Schs., 1957-59; supt. Moulton-Udell Pub. Schs., Moulton, Ia., 1959-61; supt. Danville (Ia.) Community Schs., 1961-67; research asso. Ia. Center for Research in Sch. Adminstrn., 1967-69; asso. prof. dept. ednl. adminstrn. Coll. Edn., U. Ark., Fayetteville, 1969—. Served with USMCR, 1946-48. Mem. Ark. Edn. Assn., Am. Assn. Sch. Adminstrs., Nat. Orgn. on Legal Problems Edn., Phi Delta Kappa. Rotarian. Asso. editor: Epsilon Bull., 1969. Home: 133 Miller St Fayetteville AR 72701

FARTHING, WILLIAM HOWELL, dentist; b. Wytheville, Va., May 10, 1937; s. Fred Grey and Effie (Winebarger) F.; student Carson-Newman Coll., 1954-57; D.D.S., Med. Coll. Va., 1961; m. Nancy Wheeler, June 23, 1964; children—William Howell, Samuel Lee. Practice dentistry, Roanoke, Va., 1964—. Served with USNR, 1961-63. Mem. Roanoke Jr. C. of C. Presbyn. Mason (Shriner); Lion. Club: Sertoma (Roanoke). Home: 1848 Dorset Dr SW Roanoke VA 24015 Office: 2022 Brambleton Av SW Roanoke VA 24015

FARVER, ALVIN D, dentist; b. Topeka, Ind., Oct. 25, 1893; s. Moses A. and Mary Elizabeth (Hostetler) F.; D.D.S., Ind. U., 1914; m. Marie Ellen Troyer, June 20, 1918; children—Frances Charlene (Mrs. Jack E. Farley), Gloria Jean (Mrs. Richard L. Payton), Patricia Ann (Mrs. Jerry R. Lusk). Practice gen. dentistry, Middlebury, Ind., 1914-27, restorative dentistry, Miami Beach, Fla., 1940—; presented clinics to numerous dental groups, 1945—; instr. gold inlays, crown and bridge group Dade County Dental Research Clinic, 1948—; cons. in restorative dentistry Miami VA, 1954-58. Served to 1st lt. Dental Corps, U.S. Army, 1917-19; AEF. Fellow Am., Internat. colls. dentists; mem. Am. Dental Assn. (1st v.p. 1962-63), Ind., Fla. (pres. 1959-60), East Coast Dist. (pres. 1942-43), Miami (pres. 1940—), Miami Beach, Chgo. dental socs., Dade County Dental Research Clinic (pres. 1952-53), Am. Acad. Restorative Dentistry, Am. Legion, 40 and 8, Xi Psi Phi. Conglist. Mason (Shriner, K.T.). Home: 4291 Nautilus Dr Miami Beach FL 33140 Office: 333 Arthur Godfrey Rd Miami Beach FL 33140

FARVER, FRANCIS FRANKLIN, dentist; b. Middleburg, Ind., Jan. 29, 1899; s. Moses A. and Mary Elizabeth (Hostetler) F.; D.D.S., Ind. U., 1922; m. Mary Celia Wheeler, June 25, 1922. Practice dentistry, S. Bend, Ind., 1922-25; practice specializing in restorative dentistry, Miami Beach, Fla., 1925—; asso. mem. Dade County Research Dental Clinic, 1948—. Pres. St. Joseph Dental Soc., 1922-25; mem. Fla. Bd. Exam. to Practice Dentistry and Dental Hygiene, 1956—, chmn., 1960-64, 68-71. Served with U.S. Army, World War I; to comdr. USNR, 1942-45. Fellow Internat. Coll. Dentistry, Am. Coll. Dentistry, S.E. Acad. Prosthodontics; life mem. Am. Dental Assn.; mem. Fedn. Dentaire Internat., E. Coast, Miami, Miami Beach, Chgo. dental socs., Pierre Fauchard Acad., So. Conf. Dental Deans, Am. Legion, Xi Psi Phi. Mason (Shriner). Clubs: La Gorce, Surf (Miami). Home: 5431 Alton Rd Miami Beach FL 33140 Office: 605 Lincoln Rd Miami Beach FL 33139

FASCELL, DANTE B(RUNO), congressman; b. Bridgehampton, L.I., N.Y., Mar. 9, 1917; s. Charles A. and Mary (Gullotti) F.; J.D., U. Miami, 1938; m. Jeanne-Marie Pelot, Sept. 19, 1941; children—Sandra J., Toni F., Dante J. Admitted to Fla. bar, 1938, practiced in Miami, 1938-41, 46—; mem. Turner, Hendrick, Fascell, Guilford, Goldstein & McDonald, and predecessor firms, 1950-71. Legal attache and state legislative delegation Dade County, 1947-50; mem. Fla. Ho. of Reps., 1950-54; mem. 84th-92d congresses from 12th dist. Fla. Served as officer U.S. Army, 1942-46. Named one of ten outstanding legislators Fla. Legislature, 1951, 53; one of five outstanding men in Fla., Fla. Jr. C. of C., 1951. Mem. Miami Jr. C. of C. (pres. 1947-48), Am., Dade County, Coral Gables bar assns., Fla. Bar, Am. Legion, Mil. Order World Wars, Kappa Sigma. Democrat. Clubs: Lions, Italian-American (pres. 1947-48), Dade County Young Democratic (pres. 1947-48) (Miami, Fla.). Home: 6300 SW 99th Terrace Miami FL 33156 Office: House Office Bldg Washington DC 20515

FASKEN, DAVID R(OBERT), oil producer; b. Toronto, Ont., Can., Apr. 22, 1915; s. Robert Winstanley and Mae (Ferland) F.; student San Rafael Mil. Acad. Jr. Coll., 1932-34, U. San Francisco, 1935. Livestock breeder, Tex., Cal., 1939—; pres. Midland Farms Co., Tex., 1943-44, Palafox Exploration Co., Midland and Laredo, Tex.; ind. oil producer, 1953—; chmn. Sedgemoor Prodns. Ltd., London, Eng. Republican. Episcopalan. Club: Olympic (San Francisco). Home: Circle Dr Ross CA 94957 Office: First Nat Bank Bldg Midland Tx

FASTI, ALBERT JAMES, dentist; b. Wilmington, Del., Jan. 31, 1943; s. Albert James and Evelyn Virginia (Buchanan) Fasti; student U. Del., 1961-63; D.M.D., U. Pa., 1967; m. Irene Doris Greenway, Aug. 8, 1964; children—Christopher Alan, Michelle Lynn. Pvt. practice dentistry, Houston, 1969—. Clin. instr. preventive dental medicine U. Tex. Dental Br., 1969-72; bd. dirs. Dental Asst. Tng. Program, 1971-72. Served with Dental Corps, USAF, 1967-69. Mem. Am. Soc. Preventive Dentistry (v.p. 1969-71), Am. Soc. Dentistry for Children, Rocky Mountain Analgesia Soc., Am. Dental Assn., Houston Dist. Dental Assn. Republican. Roman Catholic. Home: 12442 Briar Forest Dr Houston TX 77042 Office: 14465 Memorial Dr Houston TX 77024

FATZINGER, CARL WARREN, entomologist; b. Albany, N.Y., June 9, 1938; s. Carl Peters and Mildred Elizabeth (Warren) F.; Asso. Arts and Scis., Paul Smith's Coll., 1958; B.S., U. Mich., 1960, M.F., 1961; Ph.D., N.C. State U., 1968; m. Dianne Jean Miley, Nov. 25, 1967. Research entomologist Southeastern Forest Experiment Sta., Olustee, Fla., 1962—, prin. research entomologist, 1970—. Mem. Entomol. Soc. Am., Entomol. Soc. Can., Fla. Entomol. Soc., U.S. Power Squadron, Sigma Xi, Xi Sigma Pi. Contbr. articles to profl. jours. Home: Route 2 Box 187-C Lake City FL 32055 Office: PO Box 3 Olustee FL 32072

FAUBION, JERRY TOLBERT, fiber and chem. co. exec.; b. Pidcoke, Tex., June 9, 1917; s. Roy Arthur and Lilly (Pendleton) F.; B.S. in Engring. Adminstrn., Tex. A. and M. U., 1940; m. Rena Louise Derouen, July 20, 1940; 1 son, Roy Michael. Mech. and chem. engr. Dow Chem. Co., Freeport, Tex., 1942-43, supt. prodn. control, 1943-55, mgr. prodn. coordination, 1955-57, mgr. planning and distbn., 1957-63, mgr. organic chems., Midland, Mich., 1963-64, mgr. packaging dept., 1964-65; pres. Dow Badische Co., Williamsburg, Va., 1966—, also dir.; dir. United Va. Bank of Williamsburg, Lurex N.V., Lurex Co., Ltd., Castlecreek Fabrics, Inc., Bentex Mills, Inc., Universal Textured Yarns, Inc.; mem. internat. council United Va. Bankshares. Mem. city council City of Freeport (Tex.), 1950-51; mem. Brazosport (Tex.) Ind. Sch. Bd., 1952-57, pres., 1955-57. Trustee Community Hosp., Freeport, Tex., 1960-61; bd. dirs. Williamsburg (Va.) Community Hosp., Carpet and Rug Inst. Registered profl. engr., Tex. Presbyn. (elder). Home: Box BT Williamsburg VA 23185 Office: Dow Badische Co Williamsburg VA 23185

FAUBION, R(OSCOE) MORRIS, automobile dealer, sci. cons.; b. Austin, Tex., Feb. 13, 1937; s. Roscoe H. and Myrtle (Jennings) F.; B.S., Southwestern U., 1959; m. Janice Lea Whiteley, Feb 6, 1959; children—Robert Morris, Julia Lea. Research scientist Mil. Physics Research Lab., Austin, 1959-61; asst. chief research and devel. Electro-Mechanics Co., Austin, 1961-64; engr., sci. TRACOR, Inc., Austin, 1964-70; owner, operator cattle ranch, Travis County, Tex., 1961-70; owner Faubion Chevrolet, Mason, Tex., 1970—, J. & R. Co., Mason, 1970—. Faubion Ins. Agy., Mason, 1970—; sci. cons., Mason, 1970—. Treas. Round Mountain Community Club, 1962-67; pres. Lake Travis Assn., 1966-69. Mem. Assn. of Old Crows, Am. Phys. Soc., Nat., Tex. automobile dealers assns., Tex. and Southwestern Cattle Raisers Assn., Mason C. of C. (dir. 1972—), Mason County Hist. Soc. (dir. 1970—), Blue Key, Kappa Alpha. Mem. Ch. of Christ. Mason. Contbr. articles to profl. pubs. Home: 208 Rainey Mason TX 76856 Office: 403 San Antonio Rd Mason TX 76856

FAULCONER, HUBERT LLOYD, banker; b. Lynchburg, Va., Aug. 7, 1926; s. Henry Edward and Edna (Bailey) F.; student Sch. Consumer Banking, U. Va., 1954-57; m. Elva Moore, Dec. 20, 1947; children—Sharon Scott, Hubert Lloyd. Shipping clk. Dunlop Tire & Rubber Co., Richmond, Va., 1956; with Fidelity Nat. Bank, Lynchburg, Va., 1956—, asst. cashier, asst. v.p., installment loan officer, 1953-65, v.p. sales finance, 1965-70, v.p. loan adminstrn., 1970-71, v.p. charge liquidations and recovery dept., 1971—. Instr. Am. Inst. Banking; thesis advisor Sch. Consumer Banking, U. Va. Served with USNR, 1943-52. Clubs: Sandusky (treas. 1952-70) (Lynchburg); Colonial Hills (Forest, Va.). Home: 720 Chinook Pl Lynchburg VA 24502 Office: 901 Main St Lynchburg VA 24505

FAULK, E. WARD, banker. With Mchts. Nat. Bank, Mobile, 1925—, sr. v.p., 1952-63, pres., 1963—, also dir. Campaign chmn. United Fund Mobile County, 1955, now pres. Mem. U.S. C. of C. (dir., past chmn. fgn. commerce com.). Home: Riviere du Chien Rd Route 4 Box 50 Mobile AL Office: 110 St Francis St Mobile AL 36602*

FAULK, JOHN HENRY, author, lectr.; b. Austin, Tex., Aug. 21, 1913; s. John Henry and Martha Cynthia (Miner) F.; B.A. in English, U. Tex., 1936, M.A. in English, 1940; m. Elizabeth Peake, May 29, 1965; 1John Henry III; children by previous marriage—Tannehill, son, Johanna, Evelyn, Frank Dobie. Mem. faculty English dept. U. of Tex., 1942; fellow Julius Rosenwald Found., 1941-42; field dir. A.R.C., Cairo, Egypt, 1942-44; star radio programs CBS, N.Y.C., 1946-48; star John Henry Faulk Show, sta. WCBS, 1951-57, It's News to Me, Leave It to the Girls, Walk a Mile for a Camel, CBS-TV, 1953-55; lectr. on humor and Am. heritage, 1949-65; author-performer Pear Orchard, USA, 1970-71; columnist Take It Easy, 1971-72; appeared in movies All the Way Home, 1963, The Best Man, 1964. Precinct chmn. Austin Democratic Com.; mem. Travis County Dem. Exec. Com. Served with AUS, 1944-46. Mem. A.F.T.R.A. (past v.p.), Screen Actors Guild, Internat. Platform Assn. (bd. govs. 1967—). Author: Fear on Trial, 1964. Home: 1420 Red Bud Trail Austin TX 78746

FAULK, LILLIAN MILDRED TIBBELS (MRS. RAYMOND B. FAULK), ednl. adminstr.; b. Smithville, Ark., Aug. 3, 1912; d. Charles D. and Aurelia J. (Shaver) Tibbels; B.S. Edn., Ark. State Tchrs. Coll., 1940; M.A., George Peabody Coll. Tchrs., 1947; Specialist in Edn., U. Tenn., 1970; m. Raymond B. Faulk, Mar. 19, 1954 (dec. Aug. 1955). Tchr., Black Rock (Ark.) Elementary Sch., 1936-40; tchr. Hulbert (Ark.)-West Memphis Schs., 1940-49, elementary sch. prin., 1949-69; elementary sch. supr. West Memphis Pub. Schs., 1969—; instr. edn. Ark. State Coll., Jonesboro, summer 1956. Chmn. elementary sch. council Ark. Dept. Edn., 1965-68. Named Favorite Tchr. in Ark. and Mo., Memphis Comml. Appeal, 1959; Woman of Year, West Memphis Jr. C. of C., 1966. Mem. N.E.A. (Ark. rep. dept. elementary sch. prins. 1963-69), Ark. Edn. Assn. (mem. com. profl. rights and responsibilities 1965-68), Ark. Assn. Supervision and Curriculum Devel. (pres. 1961-62), Ark. Elementary Sch. Prins. (sec. 1952-53), Pi Gamma Mu, Kappa Delta Pi, Delta Kappa Gamma (state treas. 1965-67), Alpha Tau (pres. 1960-62). Baptist. Mem. Order Eastern Star. Clubs: West Memphis Quota, Beethoven Music. Home: 508 Gibson St West Memphis AR 72301 Office: Adminstrv Annex PO Box 261 West Memphis AR 72301

FAULK, LLOYD BUFORD, banker; b. Hawkins, Tex., Aug. 28, 1915; s. John William and Libbie (Crow) F.; grad. Sch. Bank Audit, Control and Operations, U. Wis., 1956; m. Marion Elouise Jones, Dec. 27, 1939; 1 dau. Barbara Louise. With First Nat. Bank, Ft. Worth, 1935—, auditor, 1954—. Served with USAAF, 1942-45; to capt. USAF, 1950-52. Decorated D.F.C., Air medal with two oak leaf clusters. Mem. Tex. Bankers Assn. (past sect. chmn.), Nat. Assn. Bank Auditors and Controllers (past chpt. pres., dir., past state, dist. dir.), Inst. Internal Auditors. Mason (Shriner). Home: Route 2 Box 308 Azle TX 76020 Office: 1 Burnett Plaza Fort Worth TX 76102

FAULKNER, JAMES HERMAN, editor; b. Lamar County, Ala., Mar. 1, 1916; s. Henry L. and Ebbie (Johnson) F.; B.J., U. Mo., 1936; m. Evelyn Irwin, Apr. 16, 1937; children—James Herman, Henry Wade. Co-owner, co-pub. The Baldwin Times, Bay Minette, Ala., 1936—, also The Onlooker, Foley, Ala., Fairhope (Ala.) Courier; pres. Faulkner Radio, Inc., Bay Minette Mills, Inc.; owner radio stations WLBB, Carrollton, Ga., WBCA, Bay Minette, WGAA, Cedartown, Ga., WAOA, Opelika, Ala.; sr. v.p. David Volkert & Assos., architects and engrs., Mobile, Ala., Washington, Baton Rouge, Miami, Fla. Mayor, Bay Minette, 1940; mem. Ala. Dem. Com.; del. Dem. Conv. in Phila., 1948; Ala. state senator, 1951-55; candidate gov. Ala. Chmn. Baldwin County Hosp. Bd., Bay Minette Housing Authority; chmn. adv. bd. James H. Faulkner State Coll. Dir. Ala. Crippled Children's Soc.; dir. Ala. div. Am. Cancer Soc., chmn., 1960-61; state chmn. Cancer Fund Drive, chmn. bd. trustees Ala. Christian Coll., Montgomery. Served with USAAF, World War II. Named Man of Year, Bay Minette, 1965; named Journalist of Year (weekly newspaper), U.S. Steel Corp., 1966. Mem. Ala. Press Assn. (pres. 1939), Ala. (dir.), Bay Minette (pres.) chambers commerce, Am. Legion, 40 and 8, Sigma Delta Chi. Rotarian. Home: 705 E 5th St Bay Minette AL 36507 Office: Baldwin Times Bay Minette AL 36507

FAULKNER, JAMES HERMAN, JR., publisher; b. Bay Minette, Ala., May 31, 1938; s. James Herman and Elyyn (Irwin) F.; A.A., Marion Mil. Inst., 1958; B.A., U. Ala., 1960; m. Roxie Anne Allen, Aug. 25, 1960; children—James Herman III, Jenny, Mary Jane, Rebecca, Rachel. Co-pub. Baldwin Times, Bay Minette, 1969—; sec.-treas. Faulkner Radio, Inc., 1961—; partner Baldwin Times, The Onlooker, Foley, Ala., Fairhope (Ala.) Courier. Pres. Ft. Pierce Wildlife Assn. Served with inf., U.S. Army, 1961. Mem. Ala. Press Assn. (past dir.). Mem. Ch. of Christ. Rotarian (past pres.). Pub.: A History of Baldwin County, 1970. Home: Lee Av Extension Bay Minette AL 36507 Office: Court Sq Bay Minette AL 36507

FAULSTICH, ALBERT JOSEPH, govt. ofcl.; b. New Orleans, May 28, 1910; s. Albert and Mary (Balser) F.; B.S. in Accounting and Econs., Columbus U., Washington, 1938, M.S. in Accounting and Finance, 1948; m. Anna Emily Collignon, June 30, 1940; children—Albert Joseph, Richard Charles. With Treasury Dept., 1939—, dir. salary and wage adminstrn., 1946-53, asst. to dir. personnel, 1954-60, acting dir. personnel, 1960, asst. to under sec. treasury, 1961, dir. Office of Security, 1962, asst. to comptroller of currency, 1962-65, dep. comptroller of currency for FDIC affairs, 1965—, dir. FDIC, 1965—, mem. bd. rev., 1966—, mem. com. on liquidations, loans and purchases of assets, 1966—. Chmn. comptroller currency orgn. for nation-wide campaign for Kennedy Library Fund, 1964. Served to lt. USNR, 1943-46. Decorated Commendation medal; recipient commendation Treasury Dept., 1962, Meritorious award, 1972. Democrat. Roman Catholic. Home 505 Elderwood Rd Silver Spring MD 20904 Office: 550 17th St NW Washington DC 20429

FAUNT, JOAN SCHREINER REYNOLDS, librarian; b. Columbia, S.C., Nov. 24, 1918; d. John Schreiner and Emily Simms (Bellinger) Reynolds; student Randolph-Macon Woman's Coll., 1935-37; certificate L'Institute de Touraine, Tours, France; 1938; A.B., U. S.C., 1939; M.A. in English, U. N.C., 1940; m. Douglas Faunt, Feb. 3, 1945; children—Douglas, Emily Simms Bellinger (Mrs. James William Clarkson). Tchr., S.C., 1940-42; reporter State Newspaper, Columbia, S.C., 1942-45; editor U.S.C. Alumni News, 1954-56; asst. dir. U. S.C. News Service, 1956-58; sec. S.C. Confederate War Centennial Commn., 1959-62; state librarian S.C., 1965—; free lance writer, pub. relations cons., 1945—. Mem. Am., S.C. library assns., Am. Assn. Law Libraries (chmn. publicity com. 1967—) Am. Legion Aux., D.A.R. (regent Ann Pamela Cuningham chpt. 1952-54, officer S.C. 1953-59), S.C. Hist. Soc., Nat. Trust Historic Preservation, S. Carolinian Soc., Alpha Delta Pi. Episcopalian. Club: New Century (Columbia). Author: History of The Class of 1910, University of South Carolina, 1961; (with John A. May) South Carolina Secedes, 1960; (with Emily Bellinger Reynolds) The Senate of South Carolina, 1776-1962, 1962; History of the Class of 1907, The Citadel, 1963; (with Emily Bellinger Reynolds) Biographical Directory of the Senate of South Carolina, 1776-1964, 1964. Home: 310 Holly St Columbia SC 29205 Office: State House Columbia SC 29201

FAUNTROY, WALTER E., congressman; b. Washington, Feb. 6, 1933; s. William T. and Ethel V. F.; A.B. cum laude, Va. Union U., 1955, D.D., 1968; B.D., Yale, 1958, D.D., 1969; LL.D., Muskingum Coll., 1971; m. Dorothy Simms; 1 son, Marvin Keith. Ordained to ministry Baptist Ch.; pastor New Bethel Bapt. Ch., Washington, 1969—; mem. 92d congress from D.C. Coordinator March on Washington for Jobs and Freedom, 1963; coordinator Selma (Ala.) to Montgomery March, 1965; chmn. D.C. Coalition Conscience, 1965-66; nat. coordinator Poor People's Campaign, 1969; former dir. So. Christian Leadership Conf., Washington. Vice chmn. Washington City Council, 1967-68; chmn. D.C. Met. Transit Authority, 1967; del. Democratic nat. conv., 1972. Bd. dirs. Martin Luther King Jr. Meml. Center, Atlanta; chmn. bd. dirs. Model Inner City Community Orgn. Mem. Inter-religious Com. Race Relations, Leadership Conf. Civil Rights, other civil rights orgns. Address: 1330 Longworth House Office Bldg Washington DC 20515*

FAUSH, E.R., program dir. WENN, Birmingham, Ala. Address: 1428 5th Av N Birmingham AL 35201*

FAUST, JOHN MOGAN, dentist; b. McComb, Miss., Jan. 12, 1922; s. Thomas Dixon and Gertrude Helen (Lyall) F.; student U. Miss., 1939-41; D.D.S., U. Tenn., 1944, certificate in orthodontics, 1951; m. Della Rose Harris, Oct. 5, 1947; children—John Mogan, Susan. Individual practice dentistry, Corinth, Miss., 1947-50, Hattiesburg, 1951—. Trustee Hattiesburg Teen Center. Served with Dental Corps, AUS, 1943-47. Fellow Am. Coll. Dentists, Internat. Coll. Dentists, Acad. Internat. Dentistry; mem. Am. (trustee 1971-73), Miss. (pres. 1966) dental assns., So. Soc. Orthodontics (pres. elect 1971), Forrest County Dental Soc. (pres. 1959), Dist. Dental Soc. (pres. 1961). Kiwanian (lt. gov. 1962). Presbyn. (deacon 1949—). Home: 125 S 28th Av Hattiesburg MS 39401 Office: 116 10th Av Hattiesburg MS 39401

FAVI, MORRIS JOHNNY, SR., rubber co. exec.; b. Shelby, Miss., Apr. 26, 1936; s. Fattie and Estrnia (Capocaccia) F.; B.S., Miss. State Coll., 1958; m. Mary Ann Davis, Feb. 8, 1964; children—Morris Johnny, Tiffany Ann, Chris. Cost supr. Emhart Corp., Clarksdale, Miss., 1958-66, personnel mgr., 1966, prodn. supr., 1966-68; plant comptroller Cooper Tire & Rubber Co., Clarksdale, 1968—. Served with AUS, 1957-63. Mem. Clarksdale C. of C. Lion. Home: 1516 Camellia St Clarksdale MS 38614 Office: 2205 4th St Clarksdale MS 38614

FAVRET, ANDREW GILLIGAN, educator; b. Cin., May 9, 1925; s. James Raymond and Helen Marie (Gilligan) F.; B.S., U.S. Mil. Acad., 1945; M.S. in Elec. Engring., U. Pa., 1950; postgrad. Mass. Inst. Tech., 1954-55; B.Eng., Cath. U. Am., 1964; m. Loretta Moore, Sept. 10, 1949; children—Andrew A., Peter J., Michael J., Patrick J., Thomas R., Mary A., James V., Loretta M., Martin A., John D., Anne M. Staff mem. Mass. Inst. Tech. Lincoln Lab., Lexington, 1954-55; dept. mgr. advanced research dept. Am. Machine and Foundry Co., Alexandria, Va., 1955-59; sr. sci. adviser Army Intelligence, Dept. Army, Washington, 1959-63; prof. elec. engring. Cath. U., Washington, 1963—, dir. computer center, 1968—; dir. Computer &Logistics Tech., Inc., Arlington, Va. Cons. Hdqrs. NASA, Washington, Chesapeake Instrument Corp., Shadyside, Md., Am. Kennel Club, N.Y.C. Trustee Cath. U., 1970—. Served from 2d lt. to capt. AUS, 1945-54. Mem. I.E.E.E., Assn. for Computing Machinery, Sigma Xi. Roman Catholic. Author: Digital Computer Applications, 1965; Digital Computer Principles and Applications, 1972. Home: 2105 Gatewood Pl Silver Spring MD 20903

FAW, DENNIS BOYDE, cons. chemist; b. nr. Winston-Salem, N.C., Jan. 2, 1921; s. Noah Henry and Mary (Foltz) F.; student Guilford Coll., 1939, Duke, 1948; B.S., High Point Coll., 1949, B.A., 1956. Tchr. high sch., Forsth County, N.C., 1949-50; chemist Carolina Paint &Varnish Co., Greensboro, N.C., 1956-57; chemist Research Lab., Cone Mille Corp., Greensboro, 1957-70; cons. chemist Lockette Corp., Greensboro, 1970-71; cons. chemist, 1971—. Mem. A.A.A.S., Am. Chem. Soc., Am. Assn. Textile Colorists and Chemists. Home: Route 4 Winston Salem NC 27107

FAWLEY, JOHN JONES, banker; b. Phila., Oct. 1, 1921; s. James L. and Edna (Jones) F.; B.S. in Econs., Wharton Sch., U. Pa., 1948; grad. Rutgers U. Grad. Sch. Banking, 1957; m. Ann Kemp, Jan. 8, 1944; children—Jo Ann (Mrs. Richard High), Christine, James K. With First Pa. Bank, Phila., 1948-69, sr. v.p., 1968-69; pres. United Va. Bank/First & Citizens Nat. Bank, Alexandria, Va., 1969—; lectr. Comml. Lending Sch., U. Okla., 1969. Served with AUS, 1942-45. Mem. Robert Morris Assos. (past pres. Phila., past nat. dir., nat. pres. 1972-73). Presbyn. (past trustee). Mason. Home: 4318 Adrienne Dr Alexandria VA 22309 Office: 515 King St Alexandria VA 22314

FAWSETT, EDWARD HARVEY, newspaper exec.; b. Washington, Aug. 1, 1916; s. Clifford Cleveland and Lillie (Peters) F.; B.S., U. Fla., 1939; m. Talulah Frances Doggett, Sept. 5, 1942; children—Judith Chandler (Mrs. James S. Wilder), Robert Hastings, Clifford Carleton, Jane Leslie. Teller, Morris Plan Bank, Washington, 1939-41; fed. govt. bank examiner Fed. Home Loan Bank Bd., Winston-Salem, N.C., 1941-43; auditor, credit mgr. Washington Star, 1943-58, controller, 1958-67, asst. bus. mgr., 1967-69, asst. to pres., 1969—; v.p., treas. Tal-Star Computer Systems, Inc., 1969—; treas. Washington Star Syndicate, 1969—. Recipient Carley award for writing Inst. Newspaper Controller and Finance Officers. Mem. Financial Execs. Inst., Inst. Newspaper Controllers and Finance Officers, Phi Delta Theta. Episcopalian. Contbr. articles to profl. jours. Home: 3509 34th St NW Washington DC 20008 Office: 225 Virginia Av SE Washington DC 20003

FAXON, LOUIS HENSLIE, JR., architect; b. Wadena, Minn., July 13, 1930; s. Louis Henslie and Edna Dell (McFall) F.; B.S., La. State U., 1958; m. Martha Anne Hill, Oct. 31, 1970; 1 son (by previous marriage), Louis Henslie III. Designer, A. Hays Town, architect, Baton Rouge, 1958-59; architect B.G. Buquoi, architect, Baton Rouge, 1960-61, Perry L. Brown, Inc., Baton Rouge, 1961-66, v.p., 1964-66; pres. Louis H. Faxon, Inc., Architects, Baton Rouge, 1966—. Asst. prof. architecture La. State U., Baton Rouge, 1966—. Pres. bd. Baton Rouge Symphony Assn., 1966-67; asst. scoutmaster Istrouma Area council Boy Scouts Am., 1963-64; mem. sch. plants and facilities com. East Baton Rouge Parish Sch. Bd., 1969-71. Bd. dirs. Baton Rouge Community Concert Assn., Baton Rouge Gallery. Served with USAF, 1950-53. Decorated Air medal with oak leaf cluster. Mem. A.I.A., La. Architects Assn., Council Ednl. Facilities Planners, Internat. Flying Dutchman Assn., Tau Beta Pi. Methodist. Clubs: Baton Rouge Rifle and Pistol; Pelican Yacht, City, Camelot (Baton Rouge). Home: 10436-F Jefferson Hwy Baton Rouge LA 70809 Office: 3104 Convention St Baton Rouge LA 70806

FAY, FREDERIC ALBERT, housing exec.; b. Oneonta, N.Y., July 4, 1911; s. Earl D. and Madoline (Lewis) F.; B.S. in Landscape Architecture, Syracuse U., 1933; m. Wray Hass, Feb. 9, 1936 (dec.); 1 dau., Anne Madoline; m. 2d, Virginia Easton Ford, Feb. 11, 1961. Asst. landscape architect Central N.Y. State Parks Commn., Syracuse, 1933-34; asst. landscape architect Nat. Park Service, Gatlinburg, Tenn. and Richmond, Va., 1934-41; tech. dir., asst. exec. dir. Portsmouth (Va.) Redevel. and Housing Authority, 1941-49; architect, engr. George T. McLean Co., Inc., Portsmouth, 1949-50; exec. dir. Richmond Redevel. and Housing Authority (Va.), 1950—; chmn. Va. Housing Devel. Authority, 1972—. Mem. slum clearance adv. com. HHFA, 1951-52; mem. Va. Adv. Legislative Council, 1957. Bd. dirs. Richmond Symphony, A.R.C., Jr. Achievement Richmond; trustee Old Dominion Symphony Council. Named Ky. col. Fellow Am. Soc. Landscape Architects; mem. Am. Soc. Planning Ofcls., Am. Inst. Planners, Nat. Assn. Housing and Redevel. Ofcls. (pres. Southeastern regional council 1957-58, gov. 1957—, pres. 1965-67), Nat. Housing Conf., Va. Assn. Redevel. and Housing Authorities (pres. 1946, 54-57), A.I.A. (hon.). Democrat. Episcopalian. Rotarian. Club: Commonwealth (Richmond). Home: 801 St Christopher Rd Richmond VA 23226 Office: PO Box 26887 Richmond VA 23261

FAY, PETER THORP, judge; b. Rochester, N.Y., Jan. 18, 1929; s. Lester Thorp and Jane (Baumler) F.; B.A., Rollins Coll., 1951; J.D., University of Florida, 1956; m. Claudia Pat Zimmerman, Oct. 1, 1958; children—Michael Thorp, William, Darcy. Admitted Fla. bar, 1956, U.S. Supreme Ct. bar, 1961; partner, Nichols, Gaither Green, Frates & Beckham, Miami, 1956-61; partner Frates, Fay, Floyd & Pearson and predecessors, Miami, 1961-70; U.S. dist. judge, Miami, 1970—. Prof., Fla. Jr. Bar Practical Legal Inst., 1959-65; lectr. Fla. Bar Legal Insts. Dist. collector United Fund, 1957-70. Served with USAF, 1951-53. Mem. Law Sci. Acad., Nat., Fla. assns. compensation and claimants attys., Fla., Fla. Jr. (gov.), Dade County Jr., John Marshall (pres.) bar assns., U. Fla. Alumni Assn. (dir.), Miami C. of C., Order of Coil, Phi Delta Phi (pres.), Medico Legal Inst., Omicron Delta Kappa (pres.), Pi Gamma Mu (pres.), Phi Kappa Phi, Phi Delta Theta (sec.). Republican. Catholic. Clubs: Miami, University, Riviera Country, Snapper Creek Lakes, Jockey, Ocean Reef (Miami, Fla.). Home: 11000 Snapper Creek Rd Miami FL 33156 Office: US Post Office and Court House Miami FL 33101

FAY, WILLIAM MICHAEL, fed. judge; b. Pittston, Pa., May 14, 1915; s. William Morris and Carolyn (Runner) F.; student Georgetown U., 1939; LL.B., Cath. U. Am., 1942; m. Jean Burke, Sept. 8, 1945; 1 son, W. Michael. Admitted to D.C. bar, 1942; asst. counsel atomic energy com. U.S. Senate, 1946; exec. sec. to U.S. Senator McMahon, 1946-48; with Chief Counsel's Office, Internal Revenue Service, 1948-61, asst. regional counsel, 1957-61; judge Tax Ct. U.S., 1961—. Served with USNR, 1942-45. Mem. Am., D.C., Fed. bar assns., U.S. Senate Assn. Adminstrv. Assts. and Secs. Home: 5809 Highland Dr., Kenwood Chevy Chase MD 20015 Office: Tax Ct of US Washington DC 20044

FEAGIN, ROBERT R., newspaper publisher. Pres., pub. Jacksonville (Fla.) Times-Union. Office: One Riverside Av Jacksonville FL 32201

FEAGINS, CARROLL SPURGEON, educator; b. Jesup, Ga., July 28, 1917; s. Walter Brown and Clyde Ruby (Tobelar) F.; A.B., Duke, 1938; M.A., U. Mich., 1939; Ph.D., Northwestern U., 1954; m. Mary Ellen Brown, Sept. 10, 1941; children—Carroll Spurgeon, David Willcutts. Instr., Sullins Coll., Bristol, Va., 1941-44; asst. prof. philosophy Guilford Coll., Greensboro, N.C., 1946-56, asso. prof., 1956-66, prof., 1966—. Asso. dir. S.E. Asia Confs. and Seminars Program, New Delhi, India, 1965-66. Assignee to Civilian Pub. Service Camp No. 108, Gatlinburg, Tenn., 1944-46. Mem. Am. Assn. U. Profs., Am. Philos. Assn. Democrat. Mem. Soc. Friends. Home: 1505 Nathan Hunt Rd Greensboro NC 27410 Office: Archdale Hall 206 Guilford Coll W Friendly Av Greensboro NC 27410

FEAREY, PORTER, distbg. and sales co. exec.; b. Albany, N.Y., June 17, 1918; s. Porter and Elizabeth B. W. (Martin) F.; student Williams Coll., 1938-39, S.W. Tex. State Coll., 1946-48; m. Mary King Estill, May 14, 1944; 1 dau., Mary King Estill (Mrs. James McEwan Dewar). Began career as salesman Westchester Pubs., Inc., Noel Macy Chain, Yonkers, N.Y., 1940-41; marketing supr. Gulf Oil Corp., N.Y.C., 1941-45, Tex. Co. (Texaco, Inc.), Houston, 1945-46; owner, pres. Water Service Co., San Antonio, 1948—; pres., dir. Apartimientos S.A., Monterrey, Mexico, 1958-68; owner, pres. Ice Service, Inc., San Antonio. Mem. central exec. com. Episcopal Diocese West Tex., 1960—, mem. finance dept., 1963—, mem. exec. bd., 1963-66, 69-72, mem. central exec. com. Episcopal Advance Fund; del. Tex. Council Chs., 1968; del. Tex. Conf. Chs., 1969-72. Del. Tex. State Republican Conv., 1960; del. Comal County (Tex.) Rep. Conv., 1956. Served with USAAF, World War II; ret. Mem. S.W. Found. Research and Edn., Comal County (dir.), New Braunfels (dir.), San Antonio chambers commerce, Good Govt. League (dir.), Episcopal Churchmens Assn., Williams Coll. Alumni Assn., Am. Legion, Mil. Order Loyal Legion U.S. (comdr. Tex. commandery 1965—), Mil. Order World Wars, Res. Officers Assn., Ret. Officers Assn., Armed Forces Communications and Electronics Assn., Am. Ordnance Assn., San Antonio Zool. Soc., Comal County Hist. Soc. (dir.), New Braunfels Conservation Soc. (dir.), Mil. Order Fgn. Wars U.S., St. Nicholas Soc. N.Y.C., N.Y. So. Soc., St. Georges Soc. N.Y., S.R. (bd. mgrs. Tex. soc.), Soc. Colonial Wars, Vets. Assn. 7th Regiment N.Y. N.G., Assos. Engr. Corps 7th Regiment N.Y. N.G., Mil. Order World Wars, Am. Geog. Soc., Kappa Alpha. Republican. Episcopalian (vestryman, sr. warden); diocesan exec. bd.; del. Rotarian, Elk. Clubs: Explorers (N.Y.C.); San Antonio Press, St. Anthony, Press (San Antonio); Williams (N.Y.C.). Home: 100 Paseo Encinal San Antonio TX 78212 Office: care Water Service Co Maverick Bldg San Antonio TX 78205

FEARN, ROBERT MORCOM, educator; b. Paterson, N.J., Oct. 10, 1928; s. William and Violet Emily (Bray) F.; A.A., Boston U., 1950; B.S., Ohio U., 1952; M.A., Washington State Coll., 1954; Ph.D., U. Chgo., 1968; m. Priscilla Anne Southard, Sept. 15, 1951; children—Diane, Deborah, Priscilla, Robert. Grad. asst. Washington State Coll., Pullman, 1952-54; intelligence officer CIA, Washington, 1954-63; asst. prof. econs. N.C. State U., Raleigh, 1965-68, asso. prof., 1968—. Vice pres. West Raleigh Civic Assn., 1970, pres., 1971. Served with AUS, 1946-48. Recipient grant N.C. State U., 1966-71. Mem. Am., So. econ. assns., Indsl. Relations Research Assn., Beta Gamma Sigma. Unitarian. Contbr. articles to profl. pubs. Home: 1202 Kent Rd Raleigh NC 27606 Office: 220 Patterson Hall North Carolina State University Raleigh NC 27607

FEARS, ALFRED DANIEL, lawyer; b. Flovilla, Ga., Apr. 23, 1919; s. Robert Lee and Alberta (Pope) F.; J.D., U. Ga., 1948; B.C.S., 1950; m. Mildred E. Andrews, Feb. 19, 1949; children—Marcia Denise, Deborah Jean, Alfred D., William Andrews. Admitted to Ga. bar, 1948; practiced in Jackson, Ga., 1948—. Mem. Ga. Ho. of Reps., 1951-52; chmn. Butts County Bd. Commrs., 1969—. Served with USNR, 1941-45. Mason (32 deg., Shriner). Home: 339 Watkins St Jackson GA 30233 Office: 38 Mulberry St Jackson GA 30233

FEARS, ERNEST D., JR., state ofcl. Dir. SSS Va., Richmond. Address: Selective Service Hdqrs 400 N 8th St Richmond VA 23224*

FEASTER, JOHN PIPKIN, educator; b. St. Petersburg, Fla., Oct. 1, 1920; s. Orion O. and Juanita (Pipkin) F.; B.A., Coll. William and Mary, 1943; M.S., Emory U., 1948; Ph.D., U. N.C., 1951; m. Marian Elizabeth Leach, June 2, 1944; children—John William, Pamela Audry, Deborah Ann. Biochemist, Dept. Animal Sci., U. Fla., Gainesville, Fla., 1951—, prof. biochemistry, 1968—. Served to 2d lt. AUS, 1943-46; lt. col. Res. AEC grantee, 1955, NIH grantee, 1963. U.S. Dept. Agr. grantee, 1967. Mem. Am. Inst. Nutrition, Am. Chem. Soc., Am. Soc. Animal Sci., Sigma Xi. Contbr. articles to profl. pubs. Home: 3021 SW 70th Lane Gainesville FL 32601

FEATHERSTON, C. MOXLEY, U.S. judge; b. Jayton, Tex., June 6, 1914; s. William Matthew and Fannie Eva (Roberts) F.; A.B., Hardin-Simmons U., 1935; J.D., George Washington U., 1939; m. Rose Danlington Ross, Dec. 29, 1938; children—Ross Moxley, Neal Roberts, Rose Anne. Admitted to D.C. bar, 1939, Tex. bar, 1940; pvt. practice, Hereford, Tex., 1940-41; atty. Dept. Agr., 1941-42, War Relocation Authority, 1942-45; asst. gen. counsel Inst. Inter-Am. Affairs, 1949-51; atty. Dept. Justice, 1945-49, 51-67; judge U.S. Tax Ct., 1967—. Mem. Order of Coif, Alpha Chi. Baptist. Home: 2010 Lorraine Av McLean VA 22101 Office: US Tax Ct 12th and Constitution Av Washington DC 20044

FEATHERSTON, ERRETT GLENN, ret. ednl. adminstr.; b. Callao, Mo., Oct. 15, 1900; s. E. C. and Mattie (Cunningham) F.; student Central Coll., 1920-22; B.S., U. Mo., 1929, M.A., 1931, Ed.D., 1940; m. Sophia Nelle Eubank, Aug. 19, 1931; 1 dau., Jean Ellen. Tchr., prin. high sch., supt. schs., Madison, Mo., 1922-28; prin. high sch., Prairie Hill, Mo., 1928-29; prin. high sch., supt. schs., Huntsville, Mo., 1929-38; dir. research Mo. Dept. Edn., Jefferson City, 1938-41, asst. state supt. schs., 1941-43; with U.S. Office of Edn., 1943—, successively specialist for pupil transp., asst. dir., dir. adminstrn. br., acting asst. commr. edn., 1943-58, asst. commr. edn., dir. div. state and local sch. systems, 1958-62, dep. asso. commr. research and devel., 1962-65, dep. dir. div. state agy. cooperation, 1965-68, dep. asso. commr. for fed.-state relations, 1968-70. Mem. N.E.A., Am. Assn. Sch. Adminstrs., Am. Ednl. Research Assn., Mo. Tchrs. Assn., Mo. Soc. (pres. Washington 1960-61). Co-author: Pupil Transportation; also author numerous articles and bulls. on pupil transp. Home: 6427 Quincy Pl Falls Church VA 22042

FEATHERSTON, RICHARD HENRY, aluminum co. exec.; b. Hurtsboro, Ala., Jan. 28, 1918; s. William Edward and Ruth (Herin) F.; B.S., U. Ala., 1940; m. Virginia Frances Azbell, June 17, 1943; children—William Edward, Robert Henry, Francis Bruce. Chem. analyst Gulf States Paper Corp., Tuscaloosa, Ala., 1938-40; chem. engr. Reynolds Metals Co., Sheffield, Ala., 1941-46, chief process engr., 1946-47, plant supt., 1947-54, asst. plant mgr., Bauxite, Ark., 1954-56, plant mgr., 1956-67, plant mgr. Sherwin plant, Corpus Christi, Tex., 1967—. Bd. dirs. Asso. Industries Ark., Inc., 1962-65, dir. Bd. Trade Port of Corpus Christi, 1967—, v.p., 1971. Bd. dirs. Ouachita River Valley Assn., 1960-65, v.p., 1965; bd. govs. United Community Service, Corpus Christi. Mem. Corpus Christi C. of C. (dir. 1971—), Tex. Chem. Council (pres. 1972—), Tex. Mfrs. Assn. (dir. 1970—). Methodist. Rotarian (local pres. 1962). Home: 5414 Chevy Chase Corpus Christi TX 78412 Office: PO Box 9177 Corpus Christi TX 78408

FEBLES-VIZCARRONDO, FRANCISCO, physician; b. San Juan, P.R., Mar. 12, 1929; s. Francisco and Rosalia (Viscarrondo-Llompart) Febles-Martinez; B.S., George Washington U., 1950, M.D., 1955; m. Maria Esther Morales-Yordan, July 26, 1953; children—Mayra Jean, Francisco III, Maria Eugenia, Adrian Febles. Intern, Providence Hosp., Washington, 1955-56; resident in pathology and internal medicine U. P.R., San Juan, 1961-65, asst. prof. internal medicine dept., 1969—; practice medicine, specializing in internal medicine and gastroenterology, Hato Rey, P.R., 1971—. Treas., El Centro Profl. Group, Inc., 1971—. Pres. com. human resources P.R. Dept. Health, 1967-68. Served to lt. comdr. USPHS, 1958-61. Mem. A.M.A. (Med. Achievement award 1971), A.C.P., Am. Soc. Tropical Medicine, Am. Fedn. Clin. Research, Am. Soc. Mil. Surgeons, P.R. Med. Assn., P.R. Soc. Gastroenterology (sec.-gen.), George Washington U. Med. Alumni Assn. (pres. P.R. chpt. 1966-68), Phi Eta Mu, Phi Chi. Roman Catholic. Club: Casino de P.R. Contbr. articles to med. jours. Research on tropical sprue, schistosomiasis, peptic ulcer. Home: 5 Castana Urb San Patricio Guaynabo PR 00657 Office: 500 Munoz-Rivera Av Condominium El Centro I Hato Rey PR 00919

FECHTMANN, FRED, banker; b. Woodhaven, N.Y., Mar. 15, 1916; s. Reinhart and Emily Margaret (Koch) F.; bus. certificate Bob Jones Coll., 1937; m. Dora Elizabeth Cline, Apr. 18, 1944; children—Virginia (Mrs. Thomas R. Coughenour), Freddie Ann, Elizabeth E. Supr., L.I. Feather Marketing Corp., 1937-41; cashier Harrisonburg Loan & Thrift Corp. (Va.), 1946-56; asst. cashier, mgr. consumer loan dept. First Nat. Bank, Harrisonburg, 1957-62, v.p., comml. loan officer, 1962-68, sr. v.p., chief lending officer, 1968-70; sr. v.p. Va. Nat. Bank, Harrisonburg, 1970—, mgr., 1972—. Served to 1st lt. AUS, 1941-46. Mem. Robert Morris Assos. Lutheran (v.p., trustee). Club: Exchange (past dist. gov., past pres. Harrisonburg). Home: Box 372 Harrisonburg VA 22801 Office: P O Box 1212 Harrisonburg VA 22801

FEFFERMAN, ARTHUR STANLEY, govt. ofcl.; b. Bklyn., Apr. 18, 1918; s. Louis and Esther (Morris) F.; B.A., Bklyn. Coll., 1939; M.A., Columbia U., 1941; Ph.D., New Sch. Social Research, 1950; m. Liselott Ruth Stern, Dec. 21, 1946; children—Charles, Robert. Fiscal economist U.S. Treasury Dept., Washington, chief personal taxation staff, 1945-63; dir. econ. analysis Am. Life Convention, Washington, 1963-69; chief economist, Joint Com. Internal Revenue Taxation, Congress of U.S., Washington, 1969—. Mem. Am. Econ. Assn., Am. Finance Assn., Nat. Assn. Bus. Economists., Nat. Economists Club. Home: 9006 Linton St Silver Spring MD 20901 Office: Room 1010 Longworth Building Washington DC 20515

FEGGANS, EDWARD LELAND, univ. ofcl.; b. Atlantic City, Mar. 5, 1919; s. Edward Leland and Ethel M. (McIntyre) F.; student Suffolk U., 1946-48, Howard U., 1949-51; m. Ozra Young, Feb. 25, 1950; children— James Enoch, Helen Anna. Clk., 1st Nat. Bank of Boston, 1948; teller, asst. auditor Indsl. Bank of Washington, 1949-50; adminstrv. clk. U.S. Navy Yard, Washington, 1951-52; ry. mail clk. U.S. Post Office, 1952-53; regional salesman Sch. Jewelry, Herf Jones Co., 1953-54; asst. sales mgr. Kaplan & Crawford Dodge and Plymouth Agy., Washington, 1954-57; sales mgr. Fuller Products Co., Washington, 1957-64; bus. counselor United Planning Orgn., Washington, 1964-66; trade assn. officer Small Bus. Guidance and Devel. Center, Howard U., Washington, 1966—. Tchr. bus. mgmt. D.C. Pub. Schs., 1964. Sec. Nat. Bus. League, 1969; bd. mgmt. YMCA, Washington, 1963-64; mem. com. for rights Washington Bus. Community, 1963-66; financial sec. Uptown Progress Com., 1964-67; dir. Health and Welfare Council Nat. Captal Area, 1964-66; vice comdr. USCG Flotilla 75, 5th Dist. Mem. D.C. Republican Com., 1964—, vice chmn., 1971, Mem. D.C. C. of C. (v.p. 1969, dir. 1971). Episcopalian (lay reader). Mason (K.T., Shriner). Clubs: Neptune Yacht (commodore Balt. 1964-67); Seafarers Yacht (vice commodore). Bus. columnist Washington Informer, 1964-66, Washington Afro Am., 1966-69. Home: 2504 S Dakota Av NE Washington DC 20018

FEHR, CARL AUGUST, educator, musician; b. Austin, Tex., Nov. 29, 1907; s. Herman Reno and Selma (Kilian) F.; B.A., U. Tex., 1928, M.A., 1930; Mus.M., U. Mich., 1942; Ed.D. in Music and Music Edn., Columbia, 1950; m. Alice Theresa Knippa, June 3, 1933. Tchr., organist St. Paul's Ch., 1931-33; music instr. Austin pub. schs., 1933-45; mem. faculty Coll. William and Mary, 1945—, prof. music, 1961—; organist, choir dir. in chs., Austin and Williamsburg, 1923-69; music dir. Common Glory, 1947-67, The Founders, 1957, 58, 64; adjudicator choral festivals, dir. choral workshops in Va., 1947—. Recipient George Washington honor medal Freedoms Found. at Valley Forge, 1969. Mem. Am. Choral Dirs. Assn. (charter), Music Educators Nat. Conf., Va. Music Educators Assn., Pi Kappa Lambda, Phi Mu Alpha, Kappa Delta Pi. Home: 108 Spring Rd Williamsburg VA 23185

FEHRENBACH, T(HEODORE) R(EED), author; b. San Benito, Tex., Jan. 12, 1925; s. Theodore R. and Mardel (Wentz) F.; A.B., magna cum laude, Princeton, 1947; m. Lillian Breetz, Aug. 22, 1951. Pvt. practice as ins. broker San Antonio, 1956-70, ins. cons., 1970—; mgr. Fehrenbach Trusts; pres. Royal Poinciana Corp., San Antonio. Chmn. adv. com. Inst. Pub. and Internat. Affairs, St. Mary's U. Pres. Republican Citizen's Com. of Bexar County, 1965-66. Served from pvt. to 1st sgt. AUS, 1943-46; served as 1st lt., AUS, 1951-53; ret. lt. col., Res. Mem. Am. Numis. Soc., Tex. Inst. Letters, Authors Guild, Sons Republic Tex., Mil. Order World Wars. Episcopalian. Author: Battle of Anzio, 1962; U.S. Marines in Action, 1962; Crisis in Cuba, 1963; This Kind of War, 1963; This Kind of Peace, 1966; The Swiss Banks, 1966; Crossroads in Korea, 1966; FDR's Undeclared War, 1967; Elkdom USA, 1968; UN in War and Peace, 1968; Lone Star, 1968; Fight for Korea, 1969; also stories and articles in U.S. and European mags., including Sat. Eve. Post, Argosy, Esquire, Atlantic. Home: 131 Mary D Av San Antonio TX 78209 Office: 7078 San Pedro AV San Antonio TX 78216

FEIGHNER, JAMES WILBUR, food co. exec.; b. Marion, Ind., Sept. 17, 1916; s. Harry Wilbur and Lucille (Ferguson) F.; B.S. in Mech. Engring., Purdue U., 1939; grad. Advanced Mgmt. Program, Harvard, 1955; m. Margaret Gordon Richards, Aug. 23, 1941; children—Barrett Gordon, Katherine, James Wilbur. Sales engr. Westinghouse Electric Corp., 1939-41; applications engr. Servel, Inc., 1941-42; with Tom Huston Peanut Co., Columbus, Ga., 1945—, v.p., 1951-58, pres., 1958—, also dir.; now exec. v.p., dir. of Gen. Mills, Inc., Mpls.; pres., dir. Muscogee Sales Corp., Columbus; dir. First Nat. Bank, Columbus, Bickerstaff Clay Products, Columbus. Trustee Walter Alan Richards Found.; past pres. Muscogee County chpt. A.R.C. Served with USAAF, 1942-45. Mem. Nat. Confectioners Assn. (dir.), Columbus C. of C. (past pres.), N.A.M. (dir.). Home: 1420 Wynnton Rd Columbus GA 31906 Office: 900 8th Av Columbus GA 30901

FEIGLE, WALTER LEONARD, JR., police chief; b. Galveston, Tex., Dec. 9, 1932; s. Walter Leonard and Angelina (Amato) F.; grad. high sch.; student various police tng. schs., narcotics sch., 1957-64, Coll. of Mainland, 1971; m. Bonnie Mae Hall, June 28, 1951; children— Walter Leonard III, Alys Ann, Ricky Wayne, Vincent Heath. Patrolman police dept., Galveston, Tex., 1955-56; patrolman police dept., LaMarque, Tex., 1956-58, asst. chief, 1958-67, chief police, 1967—. First asst. dir. civil def., LaMarque, 1970-71; mem. adv. bd., steering com. Galveston County Crime Squad. Bd. dirs. Child Day Care Center, 1969-70; v.p. bd. dirs. City Employees Credit Union, 1965; hon. trustee Policemans Hall of Fame; mem. adv. bd. Coll. of Mainland; founder LaMarque chpt. Boys Club Am. Recipient letters of commendation Treasury Dept., Bur. Customs, Houston office; named Outstanding Law Enforcement Officer, 1964. Mem. Tex. Police Assn., E. Tex. Peace Officers Assn. Mem. Ch. of Christ. Elk. Home: 1820 Bayou St LaMarque TX 77568 Office: 320 Laurel St LaMarque TX 77568

FEIJO, OLAVO GUIMARAES, educator; b. Livramento, Rio Grande de Sul, Brazil, Feb. 27, 1930; s. Octavio Garcia and Maria (Guimaraes) F.; B.A., Sao Paulo State Coll., 1947; B.D., S. Brazil Bapt. Theol. Sem., 1951; postgrad. U. Rio de Janeiro, 1957-60; M.R.E., Southwestern Bapt. Theol. Sem., 1962, Ed.D., 1969; m. Denise Francoise Keller, July 19, 1952. Ordained to the ministry Baptist Ch., 1951; pastor Central Bapt. Ch., Rio De Janeiro, Brazil, 1951-61; prof. Hebrew, religious edn., sociology, Old Testament, S. Brazil Bapt. Theol. Sem., Rio de Janeiro, 1952-61; prof. psychology, edn., Portuguese, religious edn., counselor Bapt. Inst. Religious Edn., Rio de Janeiro, 1952-61; editor, announcer Radio and TV Commn., Brazilian Bapt. Conv., 1956-61, dir. student dept., adolescents tng. dept. Sunday Sch. Bd., 1950-61; lang. missionary Howe Mission Bd., So. Bapt. Conv., Tex., 1962-70; tchr. philosophy, Bible, Tex. Wesleyan Coll., Fort Worth, 1964-66; tchr. philosophy, psychology, humanities, counselor Weatherford (Tex.) Coll., 1966—. Lectr., free lance writer. Chmn. polit. action Rio de Janeiro City Council, 1958-59; chmn. Bank Campaign, Rio de Janeiro, 1958. Annuity Bd., Brazilian Bapt. Convention, 1952-61. Named Hon. Citizen, Rio de Janeiro City Council, 1960, City of Fort Worth, 1964. Mem. Internat. Platform Assn., Am. Assn. U. Profs., Southwestern Philos. Soc., N. Tex. Philos. Assn., Tex. Tchrs. Assn., Southwestern Bapt. Religious Edn. Assn., Am. Automobile Assn. Author: Seroes Dominicais, 1952. Editor: Revista da Uniao Intermediaria, Brazil, 1950-61. Contbr. articles to profl. pubs. Author pub. lyrics of religious and secular songs. Home: 6871 Chickering 243 Fort Worth TX 76116

FEILD, JAMES RODNEY, physician; b. Memphis, Mar. 12, 1934; s. Roscoe Adam and Georgia (Bledsoe) F.; student Southwestern U. at Memphis, 1952-54; M.D., U. Tenn., 1957, postgrad. biol. sics., 1966—, Mayo Grad. Sch., 1964; m. Nancy Tanner, June 14, 1958; children—Mary Janet, Frederick Duane, Jamie Lee, John Alan, Nancy Glynn. Intern John Gaston Hosp., Memphis, 1958; resident neurosurgery U. Tenn., 1960-63; pvt. practice medicine specializing in neurosurgery, Memphis, 1965—; asst. prof. anatomy U. Tenn., 1965-70. Mem. health ins. benefits adv. council Medicare, Dept. Health, Edn. and Welfare, 1971—. Diplomate Am. Bd. Neurosurgery. Mem. A.M.A., Tenn., Memphis and Shelby County med. assns., Congress Neurosurgeons, Internat. Coll. Surgeons, Alpha Omega Alpha. Contbr. articles profl. jours. Home: 2254 N Parkway Memphis TN 38112 Office: 910 Madison St Memphis TN 38103

FEINDLER, CHARLES RICHARD, city ofcl.; b. Sacket Harbor, N.Y., Oct. 10, 1935; s. Edmund and Mary Elizabeth (Johnson) F.; B.B.A., N. Tex. State U., 1961; postgrad. U. Md., 1967-70; M.S., So. Ill. U., 1972; m. Joyce Janell Wood, Sept. 17, 1960; children—John Eric, Carl Edwin. Office mgr. Fireman's Fund Am. Ins. Cos., Washington, 1961-66; office operations supr. Allstate Ins. Co., Hyattsville, Md., 1966-67; asst. city adminstr., city treas., College Park, Md., 1967-71; town mgr., Herndon, Va., 1971—. Mem. No. Va. Cigarette Tax Bd., 1971—, No. Va. Regional Purchasing Officers Council, 1971—, Gov's Alcohol Safety Action Project Com., 1971—; mem. recreation and open space tech. adv. com. Washington Met. Council Govts., 1967-71, mem. chief adminstrs. com., 1971—, mem. purchasing officers tech. com., 1970-71. Served with USAF, 1954-57. Mem. Internat. City Mgmt. Assn., Municipal Finance Officers Assn., Am. Soc. Pub. Adminstrn., Md. Pub. Relations Assn. (pres. Prince George's County 1971), Md. Winter Sports Assn. (dir. 1971), Soc. Preservation and Encouragement Barber Shop Quartet Singing in Am. Episcopalian. Lion. Home: 613 Missouri Av Herndon VA 22070 Office: 57 Elden St Herndon VA 22070

FEINGOLD, S. NORMAN, psychologist; b. Worcester, Mass., Feb. 2, 1914; s. William and Aida (Salit) F.; A.B., Ind. U., 1937; M.A., Clark U., 1940; Ed.D., Boston U., 1948; m. Marie Goodman, Mar. 24, 1947; children—Elizabeth Anne, Margaret Ellen, Deborah Carol, Marilyn Nancy. Dir. vocational service and ednl. and vocational dir. Hecht Neighborhood House, Boston, 1940-43; exec. dir. Boston Jewish Vocational Service and Work Adjustment Center, 1946-58; nat. dir. B'nai B'rith Career and Counseling Services, Washington, 1958—; exec. adviser Rehab. Services. Boston, 1953-58; dir. ednl. and vocational workshop United Cerebral Palsy of Greater Boston, Inc., 1957-58; cons. to Scholarships, Fellowships and Loans News Service to state and fed. govts.; instr., spl. lectr. Boston U., 1951-58; cons. Social Security Adminstrn., 1962—; professorial lectr. Am. U. Rehab. Counseling Adv. Panel, 1963-65; mem. Am. Bd. Counseling Services, 1962-65, 70—; chmn. Washington Bus.-Industry Group, 1963-64. Chmn., Gov.'s Council on Aging, 1956-58; mem. President's Com. on Employment Handicapped, 1950—; mem. adv. com. Nat. Health Council; mem. Nat. Home Study Accrediting Commn. Served from pvt. to 1st lt. AUS., 1943-46; ETO and PTO. Recipient Community Service award B'nai B'rith, 1957, Brotherhood and Americanization award, 1958. Fellow Am. Psychol. Assn.; mem. Greater Boston (pres. 1952-53), Am. personnel and guidance assns., Mass., Eastern psychol. assns., Nat. Vocational Guidance Assn. (past pres.), Am. Assn. Adult Edn., A.A.A.S., Am. Coll. Personnel Assn., Am. Gerontol. Assn., Indsl. Relations Assn., Mass. Conf. Social Work, Nat. Council on Measurements Used Edn., Nat. Soc. Study Edn., Nat. Rehab. Assn., Phi Delta Kappa. Clubs: Torch, New Century (dir. 1957-58). Author: Jobs in Unusual Occupations; Scholarships, Fellowships and Loans (5 vols.); How to Choose that Career, Words for Work: How to get College Scholarships: Finding Part-time Jobs; The Job Finder; It Pays to Advertise; Occupations and Careers, 1969; The Vocational Expert in the Social Security Disability Program, 1969. Editor: Counselors Information Service. Home: 9707 Singleton Dr Bethesda MD 20034 Office: 1640 Rhode Island Av Washington DC 20036

FEINSTONE, W(OLFFE) HARRY, scientist; b. Pultusk, Poland, Oct. 1, 1913 (naturalized U.S. citizen); B.S., U. Ark., 1936; Sc.D. in Bacteriology (scholar), Johns Hopkins, 1939; m. 1938; 3 children. Asst. chemotherapy Johns Hopkins, 1937-39; research bacteriologist Am. Cyanamid Co., 1939-43; dir. biol. research Pyridium Corp., 1943-46; dir. research Central Pharmacological Co., 1947-48; sci. dir. C.B. Kendall Co., 1949-58; v.p. sci. adminstrn. Plough, Inc., Memphis, 1958—; cons. in field, 1949-58. Mem. A.A.A.S., Am. Chem. Soc., Soc. Exptl. Biology, Soc. Microbiology, Inst. Chemists. Home: 3745 S Galloway Dr Memphis TN 38122 Office: Plough Inc 3022 Jackson Av Memphis TN 38112

FEISS, CARL, educator, city planner; b. Cleve., June 18, 1907; s. Paul Louise and Edith (Lehman) F.; B.F.A., U. Pa., 1931; student Cranbrook Acad. Arts, 1931-33; M.City Planning, Mass. Inst. Tech. 1938; m. Alleen Kelly, Oct. 10, 1941; children—Caroline Lehman, Alison Kelly Hays. Dir. planning and housing div. Columbia, 1936-42; dir. Denver Planning Commn., 1942-45; dir. sch. architecture and planning, dept. bldg. industry and real estate U. Denver, 1945-47; chief planning and engring. br., div. slum clearance and urban redevel. HHFA, Washington, 1950-54; planning and urban design cons., 1954—; prof. architecture and urban studies U. Fla., 1971—. Planning and devel. cons., Bratenahl, O., Columbia, S.C. State of Ohio, East Central Fla. Regional Planning Council, Tampa Bay Regional Planning Council, P.R., V.I., others; historic preservation cons., Beaufort, S.C., Charleston, S.C., Columbus, Ga., New Orleans, Washington, others; urban renewal planning and other consultation, Buffalo, Rochester, Syracuse, N.Y., Caracas, Venezuela, others,; cons. Balt. Art Mus., 1970-71, Urban Studies Bur. U. Fla., 1971. Mem. Denver Planning Commn., 1948-50; v.p. planning Found. Am. Mem. White House Conf. Children and Youth, 1963, White House Conf. on Natural Beauty, 1963. Trustee Denver Art Mus. Recipient grant Nat. Found. on Arts and Humanities, 1966. Fellow A.I.A. (Spl. Services award; mem. Nat. Assn. Housing and Redevel. ofcls., Nat. Housing Conf., Am. Inst. Planners (past dir.), Internat. Housing and Town Planning Assn., Am. Soc. Planning Ofcls. (past dir.), Internat. Commn. on Monuments and Sites (Am. com.), Internat. Union of Architects, Soc. Archtl. Historians, Nat. Trust Historic Preservation (trustee). Club: Cosmos. Author: (with N.S. Keith) Report on the Renewal Possibilities of the Historic Triangle of the City of San Juan, The Future of Buffalo, 1958; A Community Renewal Program for the City of Rochester, N.Y.; co-author With Heritage So Rich, The New City; also contbr. articles to profl. jours. Home: 3227 33d Pl NW Washington DC 20008

FEKETEKUTY, GEZA, govt. ofcl.; b. Budapest, Hungary, June 15, 1940; s. Laszlo and Margit (Von Kern) F.; A.B., Columbia, 1962; M.A., Princeton, 1964. Came to U.S., 1954. Statis. analyst Book of the Month Club, N.Y.C., 1959-62, cons., 1962-65; spl. asst. 1st Nat. City Bank of N.Y., 1965; instr. econs. Princeton, 1965-67; vis. prof. Cornell U., 1967-68; economist, budget examiner Office of Mgmt. and Budget, Exec. Office of Pres., Washington, 1968—. Internat. Finance fellow, 1962-64. Mem. Am. Econ. Assn., Phi Beta Kappa. Editor in chief The Am. Economist, 1962-65. Home: 1533 Crescent Dr Reston VA 22070 Office: Office of Management and Budget Executive Office of the President Washington DC 20500

FELD, WERNER JOACHIM, educator; b. Dusseldorf, Germany, Apr. 10, 1910; s. Bruno and Irma (Loebl) F.; law degree Friedrich Wilhalm U., Berlin, Germany, 1933; Ph.D., Tulane U., 1962; m. Elizabeth Lloyd Tandy, Oct. 1, 1957. Came to U.S., 1938, naturalized, 1944. Sales exec. E. Edelmann & Co., Chgo., 1938-43; pres. Dixie Splty. Co., Inc., wholesale distbr., Mobile, Ala., 1946-61; prof. polit. sci. N. Ga. Coll., 1961-62, Moorhead (Minn.) State Coll., 1962-65; prof., polit. sci., dept. head. La. State U., New Orleans, 1965—. Adviser, asst. sec. state for European affairs, 1966-69; cons. Dept. State, 1965-70. Civil Def. dir., Mobile, Ala., 1955-57. Served with AUS, 1943-46, 50-52. Fulbright scholar, 1968-69; Ford Found. grantee, 1965. Mem. Am. Polit. Sci. Assn., So. Polit. Sci. Assn. (sec. 1967-68), Internat. Studies Assn. (pres. South 1969-70). Author: Reunification and West German-Soviet Relations, 1963, The Court of the European Communities, New Dimension in International Adjudication, 1964; The European Common Market and the World, 1967; The Enduring Questions of Politics, 1969; Transnational Business Collaboration Among Common Market Countries: Implications for Political Integration, 1970. Contbr. numerous articles to profl. pubs. Home: 2362 Killdeer St New Orleans LA 70122

FELDMAN, ABROM LEWIS, chem. co. exec.; b. Hartwell, Ga., Mar. 17, 1896; s. Morris Bernard and Minna (Shobelstock) F.; student Ga. Inst. Tech., 1913-15; D.H.L., John Marshall U.; m. Jennie Eutice Saul, Jan. 28, 1920; children—Carlyn (Mrs. Ted Victor Fisher), Brena (Mrs. W.H. Frey). Chmn. bd. Puritan Chem. Co., Atlanta, 1920—; chmn. bd. Churchill Co.; pres. River Land Co., Feta Corp. Bd. dirs. Community Chest, 1953-54, co-chmn. fund campaign, 1953; chmn. Fulton County Heart Fund, 1958, Jewish Welfare Fund, 1953-54; chmn. Ga. Tchr. Scholarship Plan, 1958; co-chmn. So. Conf. on Quality Edn., 1958; chmn. Gov.'s Conf. on Edn., 1958; mem. Ga. Nuclear Adv. Commn., 1964-71. Bd. dirs., mem. adv. council Ga. State U. Found.; bd. dirs. Atlanta Area council Boy Scouts Am., Health Careers Council Ga.; trustee Miles Coll., Birmingham, Ala.; past trustee St. Josephs Hosp.; mem. adv. com. Atlanta-Fulton County Vocational Edn. Schs. Recipient Ga. State Golden Staff award, 1971; named Alumnus of Year, 1969; named Man of Year B'nai B'rith, 1954. Mem. Fedn. Jewish Social Service (past pres.), Nat. Alumni Assn. Ga. State U., Ga. C. of C. (past chmn. edn. com.), Kappa Phi Kappa, Alpha Kappa Psi, Alpha Epsilon Pi, Omicron Delta Kappa. Mem. B'nai B'rith, Rotarian. Home: 3596 Castlegate Dr NW Atlanta GA 30327 Office: 916 Ashby St NW Atlanta GA 30318

FELDMAN, ARNOLD HAROLD, dentist; b. Chgo., July 10, 1903; s. Emil and Esther (Gruenwald) F.; student Lewis Inst., 1926-27; D.D.S., Northwestern U., 1931; m. Clara Lolita Michael, May 11, 1934; children—Eleanor (Mrs. John Michael Murphy), David, Daniel. Practice Dentistry, Chgo., 1931-41, DeKalb, Ill., 1946-50; commd. 1st lt. U.S. Army, 1941, advanced through grades to Col., 1963; presented dental clinics U.S., India, Okinawa, Germany, 1939-63; cons. Ruyukus Govt., 1952-53; organized, presented Dental Sci. Health Fair, Germany, 1963; ret. 1963; pub. health dentist Ga. counties, 1964-66; dental cons. LSI Service Corp., 1966; evaluator

Headstart Programs LSI Service Corp., 1966. Chmn. Service Corps Ret. Execs., Columbus, Ga., 1966-67. Decorated Army Commendation medal. Mem. Am. Dental Assn., Ill., Fox River Valley dental socs. Methodist. Mason (32 deg.), Elk. Club: Officer (Orlando). Home: 1126 E Gore St Orlando FL 32806

FELDMAN, NANCY (MRS. RAYMOND G. FELDMAN), educator; b. Oct. 4, 1922; student Vassar Coll., Northweatern U.; B.A., U. Chgo., 1944, J.D., 1946; m. Raymond G. Feldman. Mem. faculty U. Tulsa, now asst. prof. sociology. Mem. Council Social Work Edn. Mem. Pres. Johnson's Talent Bank Women, 1967; adminstr. Heartland White House Conf. Youth, 1969; chmn. Okla. adv. com. to U.S. Commn. Civil Rights; mem. Okla. Gov.'s Com. Children and Youth. Recipient U. Chgo. Pub. Service award, 1968. Mem. Am. Sociol. Assn., Southwest Social Sci. Assn., Okla., Ill. bar assns., Okla., Tulsa County assns. health and welfare. Home: 2120 E 46th St Tulsa OK 74105

FELDMAN, NORMAN JOSEPH, typographer; b. Cherniachov, Russia, Aug. 15, 1907; s. Joseph and Braina (Weinerman) F.; came to U.S. 1935, naturalized 1940; student N.Y.U., 1930-31; m. Claire Ruchlin, July 13, 1935; children—Barbara Joy, Alvin Jay. Compositor, Nat. Printing Co., Toronto, Ont., Can., 1922-28; compositor, proofreader, Sumner Printing & Pub. Co., Windsor, Ont., 1933-35; proofreader Morning Telegraph, N.Y.C., 1935-36; owner Quality Printing Co. Bklyn., 1936-41; composing room foreman Bowling Green Printing Co., N.Y.C., 1941-44; asst. foreman Morris and Walsh Typesetting Co., N.Y.C., 1944-52; foreman Homestead (Fla.) News, 1952-53; dir. Monotype Composition Corp., Miami, Fla., 1953-56; owner Norman Typographic Service, Miami, 1956—; pres. Norman Typographic Service, Inc., Miami, 1962-69, chmn. bd., 1969—; dir. Alphabet Innovations Fla., Inc. Mem. Advt. Typographers Assn. Am. Mason, K.P. Home: 10060 SW 213th Terrace Miami FL 33157 Office: 247 SW 17th Av Miami FL 33135

FELICIANO, HECTOR ANIBAL, physician; b. Maricao, P.R., Dec. 26, 1925; s. Lino V. and Eva R. (Rodriguez) F.; B.S., U. P.R., 1945; M.D., Hahnemann Med. Coll. of Pa., 1953; m. Nereida Mal Donado, June 6, 1946; children—Nereida, Hector, Jose. Intern San Juan (P.R.) City Hosp., 1953-54; gen. practice medicine, Rio Piedras, 1954—; clin. preceptor in family medicine U. P.R. Sch. Medicine. Lay dir. Movement for Better World, Cath. Ch. Served with M.C., AUS, 1944-45. Diplomate Am. Bd. Family Practice, Nat. Bd. Med. Examiners. Mem. Alpha Omega Alpha. Rotarian. Home: 213 Rossi St Hato Rey PR 00918 Office: 1124 Vallejo St Rio Piedras PR 00925

FELIX, OTIS LEANDER, govt. ofcl.; b. Christiansted, St. Croix, V.I., Nov. 7, 1915; s. James and Sarah (Barnwell) F.; N.Y. Police Acad., 1951; Cin. Police Acad., 1955; Boston Sch. Criminology, 1962; FBI Nat. Acad., 1964; Ph.D. in Pub. Adminstrn., 1968; m. Edna Steele, Aug. 9, 1940; children—Priscilla (Mrs. Adrian Plunkett), Rita, Ramon, Otis. Mem. V.I. police dept., 1941—, chief detectives, 1949-55, chief police, 1955-62, commr. pub. safety, 1962-69, spl. asst. to commr. pub. safety Govt. V.I., 1972—. Vice-pres. Internat. Assn. Identification, V.I. Assn. Criminology. Dir. P.A.L. Served in World War II, 1945-47. Mem. A.C.S., FBI Nat. Acad. Assos. Odd Fellow. Democrat. Home: No 12 Constant St Thomas VI 00801

FELIX, SYLVANUS GEORGE, lawyer; b. Los Angeles, Feb. 25, 1910; s. Sylvanus George and Nettie (Poindexter) F.; A.B., Oklahoma City U., 1935; B.B.A., U. Okla., 1936, J.D., 1939; m. Mary Gay Lyon, June 3, 1945 (dec. 1970); children—Barbara E. (Mrs. Ralph E. Combes), Charles Sylvanus, Sylvanus George III. Admitted to Okla. bar, 1939, Tax Ct. U.S., 1940, U.S. Supreme Ct., 1946; asso. Yancey & Douglass, Oklahoma City, 1939-41; partner Felix, Bowman, McIntyre & McDivitt, and predecessor firms, Oklahoma City, 1941—, specializing in formation corps., fed. income and estate tax matters; pres. Standard Devel. Co., Inc., Park Estates Investment Co., Inc., Tower Bldg. Co., Casady Heights Developers, Inc., Felix Devel. Co., Inc., Inc.; v.p. Park Estates Devel. Co., Okla. Nat. Mortgage Co., Allied Devel. Co. Mem. Nat. Assn. Home Builders (dir.), Oklahoma City Home Builders Assn., C. of C. (dir.), Order of Coif, Phi Delta Phi, Kappa Alpha. Mason (Shriner, 32 deg.). Clubs: Oklahoma City Young Men's, Lawyers, Beacon, Oklahoma, Petroleum, Oklahoma City Golf and Country; Lawyers (N.Y.C.). Home: 1708 Kingsbury Lane Oklahoma City OK 73116 Office: City National Bank Tower Oklahoma City OK 73102

FELKER, REX ANDERSON, assn. exec.; b. Gainesville, Tex., Feb. 10, 1911; s. John Anderson and Mary Jessie (Viars) F.; student Hardin Simmons U., 1936-39; m. Kathleen Mitchell, Mar. 15, 1946; 1 son, Rex Stephen. Mgr. Quanah (Tex.) C. of C., 1957-59, Colorado City (Tex.) C. of C., 1959-61, Haskell (Tex.) C. of C., 1951-57, 68—. Mgr. Haskell County Celebration, 1958, Hardeman County Centennial Celebration, 1959; organized Haskell County Fair Assn., 1968, exec. sec., treas., 1968—. Served with inf. AUS, 1941-45. Rotarian, Lion. Home: 1001 North J St Haskell TX 79521 Office: 112 1/2 N Av E Haskell TX 79521

FELLER, RICHARD TABLER, cathedral adminstr.; b. Fairmont, W.Va., Mar. 14, 1919; s. Richard Roeder and Ethel (Tabler) F.; B.S. in Civil Engring., W.Va. U., 1942; m. Wilma Gertrude Stenger, June !, 1943; children—Richard Stenger, Nancy Carol (Mrs. James M. Bogart). Supervising engr. Def. Plant Corp., Indpls., 1942-45; v.p. Huber, Hunt & Nichols, Inc., Indpls., 1945-47; gen. mgr. Richard R. Feller Co., Martinsburg, W.Va., 1947-51; engr. Ceco Steel Products Co., Washington, 1952-53; mgr. purchasing and accounting, Washington Cathedral, 1953-57, clk. of works, 1957—; Trustee Stone Cutters and Carvers Welfare Fund, 1965—; dir., treas. Frat. Housing Corp., Washington, 1952-69, exec. v.p., 1969—. Mem. Guild for Religious Architecture, Christian Art Guild, Soc. Archtl. Historians, Kappa Alpha (exec. council 1961-71, nat. pres. 1971—). Episcopalian (sr. warden). Mason. Club: Arts (bd. govs. 1969-71, v.p. 1970-71) (Washington). Author: (with Marshall W. Fishwick) For Thy Great Glory, 1965. Contbr. articles to religious periodicles. Home: 8014 Maple Ridge Rd Bethesda MD 20014 Office: Washington Cathedral Mt St Alban Washington DC 20016.

FELLERS, BONNER FRANK, ret. army officer; b. Ridgefarm, Ill., Feb. 7, 1896; s. Frank and Florence (Newlin) F.; student Earlham Coll., 1914-16; B.S., U.S. Mil. Acad., 1918; grad. Command and Staff Sch., Ft. Leavenworth, Kan., 1933-35, War Coll., 1938-39; m. Dorothy Ross Dysart, Nov. 25, 1925; 1 dau., Nancy Fellers Lear. Commd. 2d lt. U.S. Army, 1918, advanced through grades to brig. gen., 1942; liaison officer between Gen. MacArthur and Pres. Queson, P.I., 1935-38; U.S. combat observer with Brit. in Libyan desert, 1940-42; mem. staff Gen. MacArthur, 1943-46; chief joint planning, dir. psychol. warfare, mil. sec. to Gen. MacArthur; sec.-gen. Allied Council for Japan; ret., 1946. Chmn. Citizens Fgn. Aid Com., 1958-68. Trustee Ams. for Constl. Action, 1958-69. Asst. to chmn. Republican Nat. Com., 1947-52. Decorated D.S.M. with oak leaf cluster (U.S.); Distinguished Service Star (Philippines); 2d Order Sacred Treasure (Emperor Japan). Mem. V.F.W. (dir. pub. relations 1946-47). Clubs: Army-Navy, Army-Navy Country, Capitol Hill. Author: Wings for Peace-A Primer for a New Defense, 1953. Home: 3535 Springland Lane NW Washington DC 20008

FELLOWS, KENNETH, utility exec.; b. Lansing, Ia., 1908; grad. U. Ia., 1931 Vice pres., sec. Houston Natural Gas Corp.; sec., dir. Houston Pipe Line Co.; v.p., sec., dir. Houston Natural Gas Prodn. Co., Valley Gas Transmission Inc., HNG Petrochems., Inc., Valley Pipe Lines, Inc., Liquid Carbonic Corp. Home: 11713 Chapel Rd Clifton VA 22024 Office: Houston Natural Gas Bldg Houston TX 77002*

FELOS, PETE GUS, physician; b. Jacksonville, Fla., Aug. 16, 1916; s. Gus C. and Georgia E. (Manousopoulos) F.; M.D., U. Athens, Greece, 1941; m. Anna Ramos, Dec. 23, 1954; 1 son, Chris. Intern Wyckoff Heights Hosp., Bklyn., 1946-48; resident Sea View Hosp., N.Y.C., 1948-49; asst. med. dir. Fla. Tb Hosp., Tampa, 1949-51; practice medicine, Starke, Fla., 1951—; chief of staff Bradford County Hosp., Starke, 1957-58, 68-69. Vice pres. Community State Bank, Starke. Mem. World Med. Assn., A.M.A., Am. Coll. Chest Physicians (asso.), Alachua County Med. Soc. (Gainesville, Fla.). Greek Orthodox (trustee). Elk. Address: P O Box 843 Starke FL 32091

FELT, ARTHUR FAIRFIELD, JR., newspaper editor; b. Kansas City, Mo., June 28, 1914; s. Arthur Fairfield and Elizabeth (Osborn) F.; student La. State U., 1932-35; m. Charlotte Mae Yocum, May 5, 1941; children— Melinda Lou, Robert Yocum, Rebecca Goodwin. Sports writer New Orleans Item, 1931-36; mem. staff Times-Picayune, New Orleans, 1936-41, night city editor, 1941-45, city editor, 1945-64, mng. editor, 1964-69, asso. editor, 1969—. Mem. La.-Miss. A.P. Assn. (pres. 1969-70), A.P. Mng. Editors Assn., New Orleans C. of C., Sigma Delta Chi, Delta Kappa Epsilon, S.A.R. Club: New Orleans Country. Home: 244 Bellaire Dr New Orleans LA 70124 Office: 3800 Howard Av New Orleans LA 70140

FELT, W. MARK, govt. ofcl.; b. Twin Falls, Ida., Aug 17, 1913; s. Mark Earl and Rose (Dvgert) F.; B.A., U. Ida., 1935; LL.B., George Washington U., 1940, J.D., 1968; m. Audrey Isabelle Robinson, June 15, 1938; children—Audrey Joan, W. Mark. Admitted to D.C. bar, 1941. U.S. Supreme Ct. bar, 1955; adminstrv. asst. to Senator D. Worth Clark 1938-41; atty. FTC. Washington, 1941; spl. agt. FBI. 1942—, supr. counterintelligence operations, Washington, 1942-45, agt. charge, Salt Lake City, 1956-58, Kansas City, Mo., 1958-62, asst. dir. insp. div., Washington, 1962-71, dep. asso. dir., 1971—. Home: 3216 Wynford Dr Fairfax VA 22030 Office: FBI Dept Justice 9th and Pennsylvania NW Washington DC 20535

FELT, WILLIAM NORCROSS, educator; b. Northboro, Mass., Sept. 24, 1904; s. George Herbert and Ella Winchester (Norcross) F.; B.A., Clark U., 1926; M.A., Middlebury Coll., 1931, D.M.L., 1951; postgrad. U. Bordeaux (France), U. Grenoble (France), U. Paris (France), U. Madrid (Spain), Harvard, Ohio State; m. Elizabeth Fay Pease, Aug. 29, 1931; 1 dau., Marcia (Mrs. John C. Abernethy). Tchr. French and history Acton (Mass.) High Sch., 1926-27; from instr. to asst. prof. Denison U., Granville, O., 1927-47; from asst. prof. to asso. prof. U. N.C., Greensboro, 1947—; asso. dir. French NDEA Inst., U. Alaska, 1965. Franco-American Exchange scholar, Bordeaux, 1929-30; named Chevalier dans l'Ordre des Palmes académiques. Mem. Modern Lang. Assn., Am. Assn. U. Profs. (mem. nat. council, 1945-48), Am. Assn. Tchrs. French (mem. nat. council 1960-65, v.p., 1967-69, mng. trustee 1969—), South Atlantic Modern Lang. Assn., Am. Assn. Tchrs. Spanish and Portuguese. Contbr. articles to profl. jours. Home: 1003 Westridge Rd Greensboro NC 27410

FELTER, JAMES WARREN, artist; b. Bainbridge, N.Y., Aug. 25, 1943; s. Warren G. and Margaret J. (Carney) F.; B.A., U. So. Fla., Tampa, 1964. One man shows at Town Hall, Walton, N.Y., 1961, Korman Galleries, Tampa, Fla., 1964; exhibited mems. shows Tampa Art Inst., 1962, 63; 138th Ann. Exhbn. N.A.D., 52d Ann. Exhbn. Art Assn. Newport (R.I.); represented in collections Univ. Center Art Collection, U. So. Fla., also pvt. collections in Europe, S.Am. and U.S. Art critic campus edit. Tampa Times. Dir. Galeria de OCEPA, Quito, Ecuador, 1965-66. Peace Corps vol. with Latin Am. Regional Arts and Crafts, 1964-66. Recipient Citizenship award D.A.R., 1958. WCS Tchrs. Assn. scholar, 1961. Mem. Tampa Art Inst. Contbr. poetry to collections; pub. poems in Spanish. Home: 108 W Curtis St Tampa FL 33603 Office: Design Dept OCEPA Artesanas del Ecuador Box 2948 Quito Ecuador

FELTNER, DONALD RAY, ednl. adminstr.; b. Hazard, Ky., Aug. 31, 1933; s. Clarence E. and Dora (Feltner) F.; B.S., Eastern Ky. U., 1956, M.A., 1960; postgrad. U. Ky., intermittently 1963—; m. Marthalyn Holliday, Aug. 25, 1956; 1 son, Derek Ray. Sports corr. Louisville Courier-Jour., 1950-52; staff Eastern Ky. U., Richmond, 1956-57, dir. publicity and publs., 1959-63, coordinator pub. affairs, 1963-66, dean pub. affairs, 1966-70, v.p. pub. affairs, 1970—; adviser weekly student newspaper, univ. yearbook, 1960—. Active various community drives. Served to lt. AUS, 1957-59; capt. Ky. N.G. Named Ky. col. Mem. N.E.A., Ky. Edn. Assn., Assn. for Higher Edn., Columbia Advisers Assn., Ky. Intercollegiate Press Assn. (exec. dir.), Nat. Council Coll. Publs. Advisers (state dir. 1965-67, dist. V chmn., 1967; v.p. 1969—), Am. Coll. Pub. Relations Assn., Phi Delta Kappa. Democrat. Presbn. Club: Madison Country. Editor: Eastern Alumnus, 1961—. Contbr. articles to publs. Home: 406 Barnes Mill Rd Richmond KY 40475

FELTNER, JOHN CONRAD, agrl. extension agt.; b. London, Ky., Apr. 23, 1912; s. James Michael and Cora Allie (Black) F.; student Sue Bennett Jr. Coll., 1931-32; B.S., U. Ky., 1935; M.S., U. Wis., 1957; m. Sarah Elizabeth Trumbo, July 10, 1938; children—Conrad Wade, Helen Maret (Mrs. Richard Stephen Garard). Asst. county agt. U. Ky., Southern Madison and Rockcastle Counties, 1935, county agt., McCreary County, 1936-37, Breathitt County, 1938-46, Owen County, 1946-54, field agt. 4-H, 1954-65, 4-H program spl., 1965-70, asst. extension dir. for 4-H, Lexington, Ky., 1970—. Chief cons. Ky. Rural Youth div. Whitehouse Conf. on Children and Youth, 1969; mem. Woodford County Recreation Bd., 1970—; mem. Owen County Fair Bd., 1946-54. Recipient Golden Key award U. S. Dept. Agr., 1968; Distinguished Service award Nat. County Agts. Assn., 1968; Distinguished Service award Nat. 4-H Agt. Assn., 1970; Distinguished Service award Epsilon Sigma Phi, 1964. Mem. Ky. Extension Specialists Assn. (pres. 1964-65), Epsilon Sigma Phi, Gamma Delta. Democrat. Presbyn. (deacon 1970—). Mason, Rotarian (pres. 1952-53, 71-72), Kiwanian (pres. 1943-44). Home: Route 4 Versailles KY 40383 Office: University of Ky Lexington KY 40506

FELTS, CORNELIUS BUFORD, JR., elevator co. exec.; b. Kansas City, Mo., Mar. 31, 1928; s. Cornelius Buford and Hazel (Vandivier) F.; B.A., U. Mo., 1950; m. Jeannine Troupe, June 7, 1947; children—William Thomas, Mary Michelle, Richard Neal. Pub. accountant Arthur Young & Co., Kansas City, 1950-57; treas., dir. Simpson, Laybourne, Miller & Stark-Colo. Grain Co., Salina, Kan., 1957-59; treas. Grain Mchts., Inc., Topeka, 1959-63; pres. Garvey Elevators, Inc., Ft. Worth, 1963—; dir. Jim Garvey Ranches, JaGee Corp., Rafter-J Ranch, Inc.; corp. officer Jim Garvey Ranches, Inc., Garvey Ranch Mgmt., Inc., J.C.R. Ranches, Inc. Mem. Chgo., Kansas City bds. trade, Ft. Worth Grain Exchange. Sec.-treas. Garvey Tex. Found. Served with USN, 1945-47. Mem. Am. Inst. C.P.A.'s, Financial Execs. Inst., Ft. Worth C. of C. Episcopalian. Mason. Clubs: Ridglea Country (Fort Worth), Colonial Country. Home: 4104 Harlanwood St Fort Worth TX 76109 Office: PO Box 1688 Fort Worth TX 76101

FELTS, JACK LEON, author, pub.; b. Blanchard, Okla., Jan. 7, 1921; s. W.B. and Cordelia B. Cross F.; m. Beth Kramer, Feb. 27, 1953 (dec. Sept. 1970). Author short stories, lit. miscellany, 1953—. Internat. dir. Individualist Soc., 1959—, pub. Tablet. Author: Money Magnetism, 1966; Money Mail, 1966. Office: PO Box 156 Tahlequah OK 74464

FELTS, JAMES RONE, JR., trust adminstr.; b. Charlotte, N.C., Aug. 5, 1912; s. James Rone and Alma (Query) F.; student U. N.C., 1930-32; m. Frances Isabelle Miller, Sept. 29, 1945; children—Julian (Mrs. John A. Miller, Jr.), James Rone III. With Duke Power Co., Charlotte, N.C., 1933-37; adminstrv. asst. Charlotte Meml. Hosp., 1940-41; bus. mgr. Cabarrus Meml. Hosp., Concord, 1941-42; with Duke Endowment, Charlotte, 1937-40, 45—, exec. dir. hosp. and child care sect., 1966—, asst. sec., 1961—, trustee, 1971—. Clin. instr. hosp. adminstrn. Duke U. Med. Center, Durham, 1950—, mem. bd. visitors, 1971—. Vice pres. United Community Services, Charlotte, 1966-68, 70—, chmn. budget bd., 1966-68; mem. Social Planning Council, Charlotte, 1968—, chmn., 1970—; treas. bd. pensions Western N.C. conf. United Methodist Ch., 1964—; mem. N.C. Med. Care Commn., 1969—. Chmn., trustee Eugene M. Cole Found. Served to maj. AUS, 1942-45. Mem. Am., Southeastern, N.C., S.C. hosp. assns., Council Assn. Devel., N.C. Hosp. Assn. Methodist (chmn. adminstrv. bd.). Rotarian. Club: Carmel Country. Home: 1534 Andover Rd Charlotte NC 28211 Office: NC Nat Bank Bldg Charlotte NC 28202

FENDER, DARWIN EUGENE, forester; b. Lawton, Okla., Sept. 4, 1921; s. Isaac Nelson and Edna (Langston) F.; B.S., U. Ga., 1942; m. Alice Cain Neal, Apr. 11, 1943; children—Rebecca (Mrs. William Aiken Peck), Jeffrey Neal. Forester, Internat. Paper Co., Nacogdoches, Tex., 1946-51, 53-57, tech. supr., Mobile, Ala., 1957-65, dir. forest research, Bainbridge, Ga., 1965-70, chief forester, Mobile, 1970—. Served to capt. AUS, 1942-46, 51-53. Decorated Bronze Star. Mem. So. Forest Disease and Insect Research Council (chmn. 1971), Soc. Am. Foresters. Republican. Methodist. Contbr. articles to profl. jours. Home: 958 Highpoint Dr E Mobile AL 36609 Office: PO Box 2328 Mobile AL 36601

FENDLER, OSCAR, lawyer; b. Blytheville, Ark., Mar. 22, 1909; s. Alfred and Rae (Sattler) F.; B.A., U. Ark., 1930, LL.B., Harvard, 1933; m. Patricia Shane, Oct. 26, 1946; children—Tilden P. Wright III (stepson), Frances Shane. Admitted to Ark. bar, 1933; practice in Blytheville, 1933-41, 46—; spl. justice Ark Supreme Ct., 1965. Mem. Ark. Jud. Council, 1959-60; pres. Conf. Local Bar Assn., 1958-60; pres. bd. dirs. Ark. Law Rev., 1961-67. Mem. Miss. County Democratic Central Com., 1948—. Served with USNR, 1941-45. Fellow Am. Coll. Probate Counsel, Am. Bar Found.; mem. Am. (chmn. gen. practice sect. 1966-67, mem. council sect. gen. practice 1964—, mem. ho. of dels. 1968—), Ark. (chmn. exec. com. 1956-57, pres. 1962-63) bar assns., Am. Judicature Soc. (dir. 1964-68), Nat. Conf. Bar Pres.'s (exec. council 1963-65), Blytheville C. of C. (past v.p., dir.), Navy League, Am. Legion. Rotarian (past pres.). Club: Blytheville Country. Home: 1062 W Hearn St Blytheville AR 72315 Office: 104 N 6th St Blytheville AR 72315

FENDLER, R. E., lawyer; b. Manila, Ark., Feb. 22, 1917; s. Alfred and Rae (Sattler) F.; student U. Ark., 1934-36, Ariz. State U., 1940-42, Emory U., 1946-48; m. Dorothy Louise Erwin, July 16, 1949; children—Alan Irwin, Jeffery Scott, Viviane Linn. Admitted to Ga. bar, 1948, since practiced in Atlanta. Chmn. bd., chief exec. officer Matador Mills, Inc.; pres. Am. Industries, I.E.I., Inc. Finance chmn. Democratic Party Ga., 1960-64. Mem. exec. bd. Atlanta Area council Boy Scouts Am. Served with USNR, 1941-46. Decorated Navy Cross, D.F.C., Air medal; recipient Silver Beaver award Boy Scouts Am., 1957. Presbyn. Clubs: Cherokee Town and Country, Commerce, Stadium (Atlanta); Dalton (Ga.) Country. Home: 4675 Northside Dr Atlanta GA 30327 Office: P O Box 28955 Atlanta GA 30328

FENDLEY, CHARLES WILLIAM, chemist; b. Tamburo, Miss., Feb. 17, 1941; s. William Coy and Lucille (Brewer) F.; student Miss. State U., 1959-65; B.S., Delta State Coll., 1968; m. Patricia Louise Campbell, July 16, 1965; children—Charles William II, James Coy. With Ark. Best Freight System, Greenville, Miss. and Columbus, O., 1965-68; researcher Geigy Chem. Corp., Greenville, 1968-69; chemist Corry Foam Co., div. Firestone Co., Milan, Tenn., 1969—. Vice-pres. Babe Ruth League, Milan, 1971—. Mem. Milan Jr. C. of C. Club: Milan Country. Home: Route 4 Denwood Apartments 17 Milan TN 38358 Office: Kefauver Rd Milan TN 38358

FENIMORE, JACK CURTIS, supt. schs.; b. Littlefield, Tex., May 31, 1933; s. Tony Barty and Ima Dean (Clark) F.; B.S., Central State Coll., Edmond, Okla., 1955; M.S., Southeastern State Coll., Durant, Okla., 1963; Dr. Ednl. Adminstrn., Okla. State U., 1972; m. Winnie Mae DeShazo, July 7, 1952; children—Vivian Sue, Jack Curtis, Vareeda Gale. Jet mechanics instr. Amarillo (Tex.) AFB, 1955-56; tchr. math., coach Collinsville (Okla.) pub. schs., 1956-64; supt. Loyal (Okla.) pub. schs., 1964-66; supt. Drummond (Okla.) pub. schs., 1966—. Chmn. bd. control Garfield County (Okla.) Schs., 1967-70, Okla. Schs., Inc.; mem. nominating com. Okla. Athletic Hall of Fame; mem. seminar team which visited Soviet Union Schs., 1971. Mem. Okla. Edn. Assn., Am., Okla. assns. sch. adminstrs. Baptist (trustee). Home: Box 193 Drummond OK 73735

FENN, HARRY TALBOT, accountant; b. Battle Creek, Mich., Sept. 22, 1911; s. Frank Edward and Harriet Bernice (Barker) F.; B.C.S., Ga. State Coll., 1949; J.D., Woodrow Wilson Coll. Law, 1955; m. Rachael Elizabeth Grier, June 8, 1946; children—Frank S., Donald, Harriet. C.P.A., Napier & Hamrick, Atlanta, 1954-55, Harry T. Fenn, Chamblee, Ga., 1955-64, Fenn & Gordon, Chamblee, 1964—; dir. C & S Bank Chamblee, 1961—. Served with A.C., AUS, 1942-46. C.P.A., Ga. Mem. DeKalb C. of C. (com. chmn. 1966—, v.p. 1971-72), Am. Inst. C.P.A.'s, Ga. Soc. C.P.A.'s (chpt. v.p. 1965-66), Am. Ga. socs. attys.-C.P.A.'s, Nat. Assn. Accounting, Am., Ga., Atlanta bar assn. Lion (pres. 1964-65). Home: 2612 Clairmont Rd Atlanta GA 30329 Office: 2508 Carroll Av Chamblee GA 30341

FENNELL, EARLE JAMES, civil engr., assn. exec.; b. Velva, N.D., Dec. 8, 1905; s. James and Oleanna (Finstad) F.; B.S. in Civil Engring., U. N.D., 1933; m. Helen Ann Holm, Feb. 11, 1931; 1 dau., Susan Earle (Mrs. Richard K. Bambach). With U.S. Geol. Survey, 1925-67, asso. chief topographic engr., Washington, 1960-67; exec. dir. Am. Congress on Surveying and Mapping, Washington, 1968—. Recipient Distinguished Service award U.S. Dept. Interior, 1965. Mem. Am. Soc. C.E. (chmn. exec. com. surveying and mapping div. 1960-61), Am. Congress on Surveying and Mapping (pres. 1966-67, chmn. delegation to permanent com. meeting Yugoslavia 1966), Assn. Am. Geographers, Am. Soc. Photogrammetry, Explorers Club. A.A.A.S., Am. Polar Soc., Canadian Inst. Surveying, Lambda Chi Alpha. Conglist (deacon, vice-moderator). Mason. Contbr. articles to profl. publs. Home: 4613 Merivale Rd Chevy Chase MD 20015 Office: Woodward Bldg 733 15th St NW Washington DC 20005

FENNER, HARRY WOLCOTT, circus exec.; b. Norfolk, Va., Mar. 24, 1911; s. Harry Mosely and Ruby Shelton (Davis) F.; B.S., U. Va., 1933; postgrad. George Washington U., 1937; m. Mildred Lee Sandison, Feb. 1, 1940. Auditor, project mgr. U.S. Govt., 1933-37; certified property mgr. Mark Winkler Mgmt., Washington, 1937-52; with Feld Bros. Orgn., Washington, 1952-—, asst. controller, v.p. Super Shows, Inc., 1957-67, v.p. Ringling Bros. and Barnum and Bailey Circus, 1967-71, sr. v.p., 1971-—. Tchr. bus. subjects, adult edn.; profl. singer road show N.Y. Co. St. of Bleecker St., 1954-—. Mem. Nat. Citizens for Johnson Com., 1964, Nat. Citizens for Humphrey Com., 1968. Democrat. Episcopalian (pres. brotherhood chpt. 1949-52). Club: Chicago Press. Compiler, editor (with Mildred S. Fenner) The Circus: Lure and Legend, 1970. Home: 530 N St SW Washington DC 20024 Office: 1015 18th St NW Washington DC 20036

FENNER, MILDRED SANDISON (MRS. H. WOLCOTT FENNER), editor; b. Huntsville, Mo., July 9, 1910; d. John Forte and Minnielee (Holliday) Sandison; B.S., Northwest Mo. State U., 1931; M.A., George Washington U., 1938, Ed.D., 1942; Litt. D., Glassboro (N.J.) State Coll., 1962; m. H. Wolcott Fenner, Feb. 1, 1940. With N.E.A. Jour. (now Today's Edn.), 1931-—, beginning as mem. staff, successively asst. editor, mng. editor, 1931-54, editor, 1954-—. Recipient 1st annual Distinguished Alumni award N.W. Mo. State U., 1970, George Washington U., 1972. Mem. Am. Assn. U. Women, Edn. Press Assn. Am. (nat. sec.-treas. 1951-60; rep. Internat. Ednl. Editors' Workshop, Manila, summer 1956. Amsterdam 1961), Nat. Council Adminstrv. Women in Edn., Am. Newspaper Women's Club. Horace Mann League (1st woman mem., nat. pres. 1972-73), Pi Lambda Theta, Sigma Sigma Sigma. Methodist. Author: (with Eleanor Fishburn) Pioneer American Educators, 1944; NEA History, 1945; (with H.W. Fenner) The Circus Lure and Legend, 1970; Schools Are People, 1971; also articles in field. Home: 530 N St SW Washington DC 20024 Office: 1201 16th St Washington DC 20036

FENNO, RICHARD MONTGOMERY, physician; b. Milw., Feb. 7, 1918; s. Montgomery Rae and Lillian (Weiss) F.; B.S., U. Wis., 1941, M.D., 1949; M.P.H., Johns Hopkins, 1955; m. Gratia Bettina Witter, Feb. 21, 1942; children—Laura Jean (Mrs. Roland V. Flail), Lillian Lynn (Mrs. James M. Hunt), Lani Louise (Mrs. Dennis Reid). Intern, Queen's Hosp., Honolulu, 1949-50; commd. 1st lt. U.S. Air Force, 1949, advanced through grades to lt. col., 1965, resident aerospace medicine, 1953-57; dir. air medicine Kanto (Japan), 1962-65; dir. communicable disease div. Houston Health Dept., 1965-68, Kelsey Seybold Clinic, Houston, 1968-—; also dep. project mgr. occupational and aerospace medicine NASA, Houston, 1968-—; mem. courtesy staff Alvin's Gulf Coast Hosp., Alvin, Tex., Clear Lake (Tex.) City Hosp., Space Center Meml. Hosp., Nassau Bay, Tex. Served with AUS, 1942-46. Decorated Purple Heart, Bronze Star medal with oak leaf cluster. Diplomate Am. Bd. Preventive Medicine. Fellow A.C.P., Am. Coll. Preventive Medicine; mem. A.M.A., Tex., Harris County med. assns. Mason. Home: Route 2 Box 74B Alvin TX 77511 Office: NASA Manned Spacecraft Center Houston TX 77058

FENTON, ALBERT B., restaurant chain exec.; b. Centerville, Ia., Mar. 11, 1934; s. A. B. and Edwyna (Payton) F.; B.A., U. Ia., 1952-56; J.D., U. Tex., 1961; m. Janey R. Birdwell, Sept. 19, 1964; 1 dau., Susan Elizabeth. Admitted to Tex. bar, 1961; asst. city atty., Dallas, 1961-65; asst. gen. counsel Diversa, Inc., holding Co., 1965-67; v.p., gen. counsel, sec., dir. Bonanza Internat., Inc., Dallas, 1967-—. Served to lt. AUS, 1956-58. Mem. Am., Tex., Dallas bar assns., Naval Res. Assn. Presbyn. Elk. Home: 3410 White Hall Dr Dallas TX 75229 Office: 300 First Bank and Trust Co 811 S Central Expressway Richardson TX 75080

FENTRISS, GRAYSON GOLDZIER, ins. co. exec., lawyer; b. Danville, Va., Oct. 1, 1929; s. Robert Bernard and Janie (Thompson) F.; student George Washington U., 1947-48, 51; B.A., U. Va., 1951; J.D., William and Mary Coll., 1969; m. Joan Dorothy Copeland, Oct. 21, 1950; children—Stephen, Laurence, Cynthia. Agt., underwriter Acacia Mut. Ins. Co., Washington, 1951-53; underwriting clk. Prudential Ins. Co., Jacksonville, Fla., 1953-54, underwriting approver, 1954-55, asst. underwriter, 1955-57, life, sickness and accident underwriter, 1957-58; chief underwriter Fidelity Bankers Life Ins. Co., Richmond, Va., 1958-60; state sales mgr. Peoples-Home Life Ins. Co. Ind., 1960-64; organizer Williamsburg Life Ins. Co. (Va.), 1964, pres., 1964-67; pres. Flexibility Unitd., Inc., 1967-—, Flexibility Investment Corp. Internat., 1970-—. Life Underwriter's Tng. Council chmn., City of Williamsburg, 1965-67. C.L.U. Mem. Internat., Richmond (past pres.) assns. health underwriters, Am. Richmond (past ednl. chmn.) socs. C.L.U., Va., Richmond (dir.) assns. life underwriters, A.I.M. (pres.'s council), Nat. Assn. Life Ins. Cos. (v.p. 1965-68), Richmond Jr. C. of C. (sec. 1959), Am. Fedn. Police (v.p. 1971). Home: 7802 Hillview Av Richmond VA 23229 Office: 700 Bldg Richmond VA 23219 also Penniman Rd and Wickre St Williamsburg VA 23185

FERDIE, RONALD D., aerospace engr.; b. Chgo., Nov. 8, 1934; s. Jack and Evelyn (Lustgarten) F.; B.S., U. Miami (Fla.), 1956; m. Diane Rease Skor, Mar. 15, 1964; children—Moreen Ann, Pamela Irene, Michael Herman. Asso. test engr. Martin Co., Middle River, Md., 1956-57; jr. san. engr. Gen. Devel. Corp., Miami, Fla., 1957-58; project engr. Chrysler Corp. Space Div., Huntsville, Ala., 1958-64; sr. project engr. Brown Engring. Co., Huntsville, 1964-67; staff engr. IBM, Huntsville, Ala., 1967-—. Pres., acting chmn. bd. Rocket City Astron. Assn., Swanson Obs., Monte Sano Planetarium; lectr. space exploration. Served with AUS, 1959. Registered profl. engr., Ala. Mem. Am. Inst. Astronautics and Aeros., Am. Soc. C.E., Rocket City Astron. Assn., Astron. League, Tau Epsilon Phi. Jewish religion. Home: 7901 Regent Circle SW Huntsville AL 35802 Office: 150 Sparkman Dr, NW Huntsville AL 35805

FEREBEE, CLAUDE WILLIAM, JR., lawyer, trucking co. exec.; b. Vernon, Tex., July 10, 1925; s. Claude William and Anne Belle (Bennett) F.; B.B.A., So. Methodist U., 1948; J.D., Loyola U. of South, 1971; m. Dorothy Jean Smith, June 3, 1948; children—William Curtis, David Warren, Dayna. Self employed in grocery bus., 1948-58; pres., dir. Tom Hicks Transfer Co., Inc., Harvey, La., 1958-—; admitted to La. bar, 1971; dir. Plaquimine Loan & Investment Co. Past mem. bd. dirs. Jefferson Plaquemine Drainage Dist. Served with USNR, 1943-46; PTO. Mem. La. Oilfield Haulers Assn. (past pres., dir.), Am. Trucking Assn. (chmn. oilfield haulers div.), La. Motor Transp. Assn. (dir.). Mem. Christian Ch. (past chmn. bd.). Home: 14 Noble Dr Belle Chasse LA 70037 Office: Box 283 Harvey LA 70058

FERGUSON, CHARLES AUSTIN, JR., newspaper editor; b. New Orleans, Mar. 16, 1937; s. Charles Austin and Josephine (Gessner) F.; B.A., Tulane U., 1958, LL.B., 1961; postgrad. (Nieman fellow) Harvard, 1965-66; m. Jane Pugh, Dec. 21, 1961; children—Elizabeth Hayes, Caroline Pugh. Admitted to La. bar, 1961; gen. assignment reporter New Orleans States-Item, 1961-63, state capital corr., 1963-65, asso. editor, 1966-—; host news program, WYES-TV. Participant, Met. Leadership Forum New Orleans, Met. Area Com. and Tulane U., 1967-68; exec. com. Greater New Orleans Tourist and Conv. Commn.; mem. Bur. Govtl. Research New Orleans; vice chmn. task force state and local govt. Goals for La., 1969-70; mem. men's adv. com. League Women Voters New Orleans; mem. Mayor's Adv. Com. on Cultural Resources. Bd. dirs. Interracial Council for Bus. Opportunity, Urban League New Orleans, 1970-71; pres. bd. trustees Inst. Politics, Loyola U., New Orleans. Served with USAF, 1958. Mem. La. State Bar Assn., Am. Soc. Newspaper Editors, New Orleans C. of C. (bd. dirs., exec. com.), L.Q.C. Lamar Soc. (dir.), Alpha Tau Omega. Unitarian-Universalist. Clubs: International House, New Orleans Lawn Tennis. Home: 831 Calhoun St New Orleans LA 70118 Office: 3800 Howard Av LA 70140

FERGUSON, CHARLES RAY, labor union exec.; b. Dellslow, W.Va., Aug. 25, 1906; s. Charles Edwin and Frances Burnette (Grimm) F.; student pub. schs.; m. Elsie Stolting, Dec. 7, 1928; children—Donald Ray, Charles Edwin. Coal miner, safety dir., asst. mine foreman, 1920-39; sec.-treas. Supervisory Union of Mineworkers, 1939-42; internat. rep. United Mine Workers Am., 1942-48, safety dir., 1948-—; dep. adminstr. Def. Solid Fuels Adminstrn., 1950-52. Mem. Fed. Coal Mine Safety Bd. of Rev., 1951-—; mem. joint industry safety com. President's Conf. on Occupational Safety, President's Com. on Nat. Employment the Physically Handicapped Week. Served with Naval Air Arm, USN, 1943-45. Mem. Mine Inspector's Inst. Am., Coal Mining Inst. Am., Nat. Mine Rescue Assn., Ill., Ky. mining insts. Moose, Elk, Eagle. Home: 455 Fourth Av New Kensington PA 15068 Office: 1435 K St Washington DC 20005

FERGUSON, CHESTER HOWELL, lawyer; b. Americus, Ga., July 1, 1908; s. Sidney Hugh and Barbara (White) F.; student Mercer U., U. Ala.; LL.B., U. Fla., 1930; m. Louise Lykes, Dec. 2, 1939; children—Stella Louise, Howell Lykes. Admitted to Fla. bar, 1930; with Macfarlane, Ferguson, Allison & Kelly, predecessors, Tampa, 1930-—, mem. firm, 1935-—. Chmn., dir. Lykes Bros., Inc., 1945-—; chmn. First Financial Corp., 1st Nat. Bank in Palm Beach; vice chmn. Lykes Youngstown Corp.; dir. First Nat. Bank of Tampa, Lykes Bros. S.S. Co., Inc., Pasco Packing Co., Knight & Wall Co., Bank of Clearwater, Kennesaw Life & Accident Insurance Company, First Nat. Bank, Miami, Fla. Dir. civil def. Hillsborough County, also Gulf Coast dist. Fla., 1947-63. Trustee U. Tampa, 1950-—; mem., former chmn. bd. regents Fla. State U. System. Served from 1st lt. to col., USAAF, 1942-46; asst. chief staff CBI. Decorated Air medal, Legion of Merit, Bronze Star medal, also Chinese decoration. Mem. Fla., Greater Tampa chambers commerce, Am. Legion, Air Force Assn., Mil. Order World Wars, Newcomen Soc., Am., Fla., Tampa bar assns., Am. Coll. Trial Lawyers, Internat. Ins. Counsel Assn., Maritime Law Assn., Am. Coll. Probate Counsel, Blue Key. Phi Delta Theta, Omicron Delta Kappa. Phi Delta Phi. Episcopalian (sr. warden). Rotarian. Clubs: University, Tampa Yacht and Country, Palma Ceia Golf and Country, Merrymakers, Ye Mystic Krewe of Gasparilla (Tampa). Home: 5400 Interbay Blvd Tampa FL 33611 Office: 512 Florida Av Tampa FL 33601

FERGUSON, DON K., city ofcl. Formerly city editor Knoxville (Tenn.) News-Sentinel; mem. Knoxville City Council, 1971-—. Address: 2901 Avondale Av NE Knoxville TN 37917*

FERGUSON, FRANK DANIEL, educator; b. Pleasant City, O., Oct. 4, 1910; s. Henry D. and Missouri (Crewell) F.; B.S., Kent State U., 1948, M.A., 1950; postgrad. Ohio State U., 1950, 52, 53; Ph.D., La. State U., 1958; m. Gertrude Smith, July 19, 1939; children—Janie Elizabeth (Mrs. Robert Neale McBee), Katherine Louise (Mrs. John Hannie). Personnel mgr., instr. Kent State U., 1948-49; head dept. bus. Urbana Coll., 1950-52; faculty La. State U., Baton Rouge, 1952-—, prof. secretarial adminstrn., bus. edn., head dept., 1965-—. Vis. prof. N.M. State U., summer 1952; cons. pvt. bus. schs., Esso Corp.; chmn. evaluation team for accreditation Bus. Colls. Am., 1957-—; mem. Accrediting Commn. for Bus. Schs., Washington, 1969-72. Served with AUS, 1944-45. Mem. Nat. Office Mgmt. Assn. (Diamond Merit award 1963, pres. 1959-60), Am. Vocational Assn., N.E.A., Nat. Bus. Tchrs. Assn. (pres. 1968), Am. Assn. U. Profs., La. Tchrs. Assn. (council mem. 1960-67), Delta Pi Epsilon, Beta Gamma Sigma, Alpha Sigma Lambda, Phi Delta Kappa, Contbr. articles to profl. publs. Home: 395 College Hill Dr Baton Rouge LA 70803

FERGUSON, GARLAND PERRY, educator; b. Lytton Springs, Tex., July 14, 1921; s. Homer Anderson and Ella Rachel (Perry) F.; B.S., S.W. Tex. State Coll., 1942, M.Ed., 1949; m. Bonnie Muriel Mason, Oct. 2, 1943; children—Bonnie Kay, Bobby Dwight. Tchr., San Marcos (Tex.) Bapt. Acad., 1945-46, Union Grove High Sch., Gladewater, Tex., 1946-49; prin. Union Grove Elementary Sch., Gladewater, 1949-54; supt. schs. Union Grove, Gladewater, 1954-—. Chmn. legislative council Univ. Interscholastic League, 1962; mem. Tex. Surplus Property Agy. Bd. Served to lt. USCG, 1942-45. Mem. Am., Tex. (dist. dir. 1966) assns. sch. administrs., Tex. State Tchrs. Assn. (pres. 1965-66, state membership chmn. 1968-72, chmn. organizational affairs com.), N.E.A. Mason, Rotarian (pres. 1969-70). Contbr. articles in field to profl. jours. Address: PO Box 1447 Gladewater TX 75647

FERGUSON, GEORGE ROBERT, lawyer; b. Learned, Miss., Aug. 13, 1933; s. George R. and Eugenia (Williams) F.; B.S., Miss. State U., 1955; LL.B., Jackson Sch. Law, 1964; m. Martha Gillespie, July 5, 1959; children—Martha Elizabeth, George Robert, Cade Drew. Admitted to Miss. bar, 1965; sales rep. Procter & Gamble Co., 1958-60; dir. advt., pub. relations Standard Life Ins. Co., 1960-64; v.p. advt., pub. relations L. E. Davis & Assos., 1964-65; pvt. practice law, Raymond, Miss., 1965-—; mem. Miss. Ho. of Reps., 1967-—; owner, pub. Miss. Valley Stockman-Farmer mag., 1965-—; v.p., dir. Statewide Savings and Loan Assn., 1971-—. Mem. Miss. Classification Commn., 1970-—; chmn. Hinds County Christmas Seal campaign, 1971. Bd. dirs. Hinds County TB Assn., Jackson, Miss., 1969-—. Served with AUS, 1956-58. Named among Outstanding Young Men of Am., Nat. Jr. C. of C., 1969. Mem. Miss., Hinds County bar assns. Presbyn. (elder 1963-—). Lion (pres. 1969-70, zone chmn. 1970-71), Mason (Shriner), Moose. Home: PO Drawer 89 Oak Street Raymond MS 39154 Office: Main St Raymond MS 39154

FERGUSON, L. BENTON, advt. exec.; b. Watonga, Okla., Nov. 2, 1909; s. Walter Scott and Lucia (Loomis) F.; student Washington and Lee U., 1926-27; A.B., U. Okla., 1931; m. Grace Wilkinson, Apr. 1, 1965; 1 dau., Carole S. (Mrs. Jack Shakely). With Scripps Howard Newspapers, 1932-38; v.p. Tex. State Network, Fort Worth, 1938-40, Campbell Mithun Advt. Agy., Mpls., 1940-48; founder, pres. Ferguson Advt. Agy., Tulsa, 1950, owner, 1950-—. Prof. advt. Tex. Christian U., 1949-50. Bd. dirs. Tulsa Philharmonic Soc., Planned Parenthood Assn. Tulsa; mem. adv. bd. Salvation Army Tulsa, 1960-—. Mem. Pub. Relations Soc. Am. (state pres. 1962-—), Blue Key, Kappa Alpha, Alpha Delta Sigma. Republican. Unitarian-Universalist. Mason (Shriner, 32 deg.). Contbr. book reviews, articles to publs. Home: 2112 E 59th St Tulsa OK 74105 Office: Atlas Life Bldg Tulsa OK 74103

FERGUSON, MALCOLM DOUGLAS, banker; b. Marble Falls, Tex., Sept. 24, 1925; s. William Malcolm and Virginia Maude (Rowney) F.; student U. Tex., 1942-46; grad. Stonier Grad. Sch. Banking of Rutgers U., 1964; m. Marilyn Joyce Houston, Apr. 19, 1947. With Alamo Nat. Bank, San Antonio, 1946-49; v.p. Tex. State Bank, Austin, 1949-69; sr. v.p. Univ. State Bank, Austin, 1969-—. Dir. Arts Council of Austin; treas., dir. All Faiths Chapel Corp. Mem. Robert Morris Assos., Delta Sigma Pi. Methodist. Mason (Shriner). Clubs: University Area Kiwanis, Westwood Country (Austin). Home: 7602 Mesa Dr Austin TX 78731 Office: 1904 Guadalupe St Austin TX 78705

FERGUSON, ROWENA, editor, writer; b. Little Rock, Dec. 24, 1904; d. William Benson and Mary (Proudfoot) Ferguson; A.B., Randolph-Macon Woman's Coll., 1925; postgrad. Vanderbilt U. Div. Sch., Columbia Sch. Journalism; D.D. (hon.), Ia. Wesleyan Coll., 1967. Editor, Methodist Pub. House, Nashville, 1930-—, dir. dept. youth publs., 1958-71; cons. curriculum Bd. Edn., Meth. Ch. 1958-71; ofcl. recorder World Conf. Christian Youth, Oslo, Norway, 1947, Travancore, India, 1952. Ofcl. del. World Council Christian Edn., Birmingham, Eng., 1957, Toronto, Can., 1950, White House Conf. Children and Youth, 1960. Mem. Tenn. Council on Human Relations, Phi Beta Kappa. Author: Hunger and Hope, 1955; Teen-agers, Their Days and Ways, 1950; Everywhere, The Story of the World-wide Church, 1961; Youth and the Christian Community, 1954; Editing the Small Magazine, 1958; The Church's Ministry with Senior Highs, 1963, rev. edit., 1968. My Life: What Will I Make of It 1966. Home: 3525 West End Av Nashville TN 37205

FERGUSON, THOMAS CAMPBELL, lawyer; b. Roswell, N.M., Sept. 3, 1906; s. William Marion and Martha Ann (Harvey) F.; grad. high sch.; m. Vera Elizabeth Foster, Apr. 20, 1930. Owner-editor Liberty Hill Index, 1921-23, Blanco Courier, 1923-24; pub. Burnet (Tex.) Bull., 1924-26; floor foreman, advt. mgr. Superior (Ariz.) Sun, 1926-27; dep. dist. clk. Burnet County, 1927-28; admitted to Tex. bar, 1929, U.S. Supreme Ct., 5th Circuit Ct. of Appeals, U.S. Dist. Ct.; practiced in Burnet, 1929-—; city atty., Burnet, 1932-36, Marble Falls, Tex., 1930-42, 63-66; spl. counsel County of Burnet, 1932-38; atty. Home Owners Loan Corp.; atty. City of Johnson City, 1963-68. County judge Burnet County, 1945-47; dist. judge 33d Jud. Dist. Tex., 1947-60, ret.; chmn. State Bd. Ins., 1961-62; sec.-treas. Burnet Nat. Farm Loan Assn.; dir. First State Bank of Burnet, Moore State Bank of Llano (Tex.), Moursund Abstract Co., Johnson City. Mem. Burnet County Sch. Bd., 1934-41; chmn. Def. Bond sales Burnet County, 1941-42; county officer U.S.O., 1940-42; county chmn. A.R.C., 1946-47; adult scouter Boy Scout program, 1940-72. Chmn. Burnet County Democratic Com., 1928-30; mem. Tex. Ho. of Reps., 1931-32; mem. State Dem. Exec. Com. from 10th Dist., 1933-34; mayor, Burnet, 1939-43. Bd. dirs. Lower Colorado River Authority, 1935-37, 45, 65-71; chmn. adv. bd. to registrants SSS for Burnet County, 1939-47. Served with AUS, 1942-45. Mem. Am., Tex., Hill Country bar assns., Am. Judicature Soc., Tex. Heritage Found. (life), Nat., Tex. hist. assns., Washington-on-the-Brazos Park Assn., Am. Legion, 40 and 8. Mem. Christian Ch. Mason. Home: 208 E Post Oak St Burnet TX 78611 Office: P O Box 38 Burnet TX 78611

FERMAN, IRVING, lawyer, educator; b. N.Y.C., July 4, 1919; s. Joseph and Sadie (Stein) F.; B.S., N.Y.U., 1941; LL.B., Harvard, 1948; m. Bertha Paglin, June 12, 1946; children—James Paglin, Susan Paglin. Admitted to La. bar, 1948; partner Provensal, Faris & Ferman, attys., New Orleans, 1948-52; v.p. Internat. Latex Corp., 1960-66; pres. Piedmont Theatres Corp., 1966-69; adj. asso. prof. mgmt. N.Y.U., 1964-67; prof. law Howard U. Law Sch., Washington, 1968-—; adj. prof. law Am. U., 1971-—; dir. Washington office Am. Civil Liberties Union, 1952-59, vice chmn. Nat. Civil Liberties Clearing House, 1952-54. Mem. citizens adv. com. U.S. Commn. on Govt. Security, 1957; vice chmn. Pres.'s Com. Govt. Contracts, 1959-60; mem. Am. Com. Cultural Freedom, 1954-—, D.C. Health and Welfare Council; bd. dirs. New Orleans Acad. Art, 1948-51; mem. Com. of Arts and Scis. for Eisenhower, 1956; chmn. Washington Police Complaint Rev. Bd., 1965-—; mem. Dept. Health, Edn. and Welfare Reviewing Authority, 1969-—. Served from cadet to 1st lt. USAF, 1942-46. Mem. Am., La., New Orleans bar assns. Jewish religion. Clubs: Capitol Hill, International (Washington); Harvard, Caterpillar (N.Y.C.). Home: 3818 Huntington St Washington DC 20015 Office: Howard U Law Sch 6th St and Howard Pl NW Washington DC 20001

FERNALD, CHARLES EDWARD, transp. co. exec.; b. Downingtown, Pa., Sept. 28, 1902; s. Joshiah Pennell and Sophia (Weltner) F.; student mech. engring. Drexel Inst. Tech., 1921-24; student Wharton Sch., U. Pa., 1926-30; m. Gertrude Marie Connell, Oct. 17, 1936; 1 son, Charles Edward. With credit dept. Notaseme Hosiery Co., 1919-22; purchasing agt. Haslett Chute & Conveyor Co., Oaks, Pa., 1922-24; sr. partner Fernald & Co., Phila., 1924-63; sec., dir., chmn. finance com. Chem. Leaman Tank Lines, Inc., Downingtown. Active Republican Com. Past pres., trustee Credit Research Found., Inc. Served as lt. (j.g.) spl. assignments USN, USCG Res., World War II. C.P.A., Pa., N.J., N.Y., Ill. Mem. Am. Inst. C.P.A.'s, Pa., N.J., N.Y., Ill. Socs. C.P.A.'s, Credit Mgmt. Assn. Delaware Valley, Mgmt. (past nat. pres.). Clubs: Poor Richard, Seaview Country, Union League (Phila.); Union League (Chgo.); Internat. House (New Orleans); PGA Nat. Golf (Palm Beach Gardens, Fla.). Home: 2600 N Flagler Dr West Palm Beach FL 33407 Office: 1813 Ranstead St Philadelphia PA 19103

FERNANDEZ, JORGE MARQUEZ, physician; b. Santurce, P.R., Aug. 5, 1925; s. Francisco D. and Georgina Marquez (Fernandez) M.; B.S., U. P.R., 1946; M.D., Nat. U. Mex., 1953; m. Manola Pato Soto, Mar. 28, 1951; children—Francisco, Georgina. Intern Presbyn. Hosp., Santurce, 1953-54; resident obstetrics and gynecology Instituto de Salubridad, Mexico City, Mexico, 1954-55, surgery, Auxilio Mutuo Hosp., Hato Rey, P.R., 1955-56, psychiat. resident, 1956; practice medicine specializing in gen. practice, Santurce, 1956-—. Pres., Farmacia Plaza, Inc., Santurce, 1959-71; aviation med. examiner U.S. Fed. Govt., 1967-71; med. examiner life ins. companies, 1957-71. Fellow Am. Acad. Family Practice, Acad. Psycho-Somatic Medicine; mem. P.R. Med. Assn., Am. Geriatric Soc., Aerospace Med. Assn., Gerontol. Soc., Am. Assn. Planned Parenthood Physicians, Am. Acad. Air Traffic Control Medicine, Pan Am. Med. Assn., World Med. Assn., Civil Aviation Med. Assn., Aerospace Med. Assn., Am. Assn. History Medicine, Royal Soc. Health (London). Home: 661 McKinley St Santurce PR 00907 Office: 2067 Borinquen Av Santurce PR 00915

FERNANDEZ-BARILLO, JUAN B., fed. judge. Judge Fed. Dist. Ct., Dist. P.R., San Juan. Address: US Dist Ct San Juan PR 00936*

FERNANDEZ-MARINA, RAMON, physician; b. San Juan, P.R., Sept. 16, 1909; s. Ramon and Sofia (Marina) Fernandez-Abarca; B.S., U. Madrid (Spain), 1930, M.S., 1931, M.D., 1933;; m. Luz Petrovich, Aug. 31, 1941; 1 son, Ramon. Intern, San Juan City Hosp., 1933-34; St. Elizabeth's Hosp., Washington, 1945, Chestnut Lodge, Rockville, Md., 1945-47; practice medicine specializing in internal medicine, Bayamon, P.R., 1933-45, specializing in psychiatry and psychoanalysis, Santurce, P.R., 1947-—; dir. State Psychiat. Hosp., Rio Piedras, P.R., 1952, P.R. Inst. Psychiatry, Bayamon, 1952-—; asst. prof. psychiatry U. P.R. Sch. Medicine, 1952-57, lectr. Sch. Law, 1963-65. Television lectr. sta. WIPR, Santurce, 1961-63; instr. residents in psychiatry P.R. Inst. Psychiatry, 1956-—; pres. Mountain Camp Resort, Inc., Rosario, P.R., 1956-—. Trustee Camp Rosario Rehab. Center. Recipient several medals, diplomas for poetry, short stories. Diplomate Am. Bd. Psychiatry and Mental Hosp. Adminstrn. Washington Sch. Psychiatry, Washington Psychoanalytic Inst. Fellow

Am. Acad. Psychoanalysis, Am. Psychiat. Assn., A.A.A.S., N.Y. Acad. Sci.; mem. Am. Psychoanalytic Assn., P.R. Med. Assn., P.R. Pub. Health Assn. (past pres.), P.R. Psychiat. Sect. (past pres.), Argentine Child and Adolescents Psychiat. Assn. (hon.). Clubs: Caparra Country, Yacht (San Juan). Author (with Ursula von Eckardt) The Horizons of the Mind, 1965; The Sober Generation, 1968; also articles. Patentee diving mask. Home: Box 789 Hato Rey PR 00919 Office: Profl Bldg Santurce PR 00909

FERNANDEZ-MARTINEZ, JOSE, physician; b. San Juan, P.R., Apr. 17, 1930; s. Telesforo and Luisa (Martinez) F.; B.S., Villanova (Pa.) U., 1951; M.D., U. Pa., 1955; m. Carmen Dolores Noya, Dec. 26, 1954. Intern, Hosp. U. Pa., 1955-56, resident internal medicine, 1956-59, fellow in hypertension and cardiovascular diseases, 1956-57; pvt. practice medicine, specializing in internal medicine and cardiovascular diseases, Santurce, P.R., 1961—; asso. attending in internal medicine San Juan City Hosp., 1961—. Served to capt. U.S. Army, 1959-61. Diplomate Am. Bd. Internal Medicine, also splty. cardiovascular diseases. Fellow A.C.P.; asso. fellow Am. Coll. Cardiology; mem. P.R. Med. Assn. (pres. sci. council 1968). Home: 54 King's Ct Santurce PR 00911 Office: Ashford Med Center Ashford and Washington Sts Santurce PR 00907

FERRARA, ANTHONY BENVENUTO, architect; b. Bovino, Italy, Aug. 8, 1903 (came to U.S., 1913); s. Vincent Paul and Elvira (Icolari) F.; student Columbia U., 1928, Beaux Arts Inst. Design, 1930, George Washington U., 1946; m. Lucille Campana, Jan. 7, 1934; children—James Joseph, Robert Anthony, Marcia Lucille. Draftsman, Guilbert & Betelle, A.I.A., Newark, 1932; sr. draftsman C. Godfrey Poggi, A.I.A., Elizabeth, N.J., 1936; founding partner McLeod & Ferrara, A.I.A., Elizabeth, N.J., 1936; sr. architect U.S. Engrs. on Design of the Pentagon, 1941; sr. architect War Prodn. Bd., 1943; founding partner McLeod, Ferrara and Ensign, A.I.A., Washington, 1964. Instr. adult edn. Montclair (N.J.) High Sch., 1936. Bd. govs. Washington Bldg. Congress, 1960-64. Mem. A.I.A. (div. pres. 1962), Guild for Religious Architecture (pres. 1964), Washington Urban League, Nat. Trust for Historic Preservation, Bldg. Research Inst. Acad. Scis. Presbyn. (elder 1966-72). Prin. archtl. works include Library Bldg., Haile Selassie U., Addis Ababa, Ethiopia, 1966-69, Staging Bldg. Am. Embassy, Brasilia, Brazil, 1960. Home: 10809 Admirals Way Potomac MD 20854 Office: 1705 DeSales St Washington DC 20036

FERRARO, HILDA FULLER (MRS. LOUIS R. FERRARO), ret. librarian; b. Bernice, La., Mar. 8, 1906; d. Young Smith and Wihlema (Pittard) Fuller; student Tulane U., 1923-25, Columbia, 1930; B.S., Northwestern U., 1927; B.S. in L.S., La. State U., 1941; m. Louis Ferraro, Sept. 16, 1949. Coll. tchr., Ala., 1927-30; pub. sch. tchr. La., 1930-35; supr. secondary schs., La, 1935-41; became reference librarian La. State U., 1941, now ret. Cons. secondary edn. pub. sch. music Bd. dirs. YWCA, 1955-57. Mem. Am., La. library assns., Delta Kappa Gamma. Episcopalian. Clubs: Faculty, Baton Rouge Library (pres.). Home: 630 DuBois Dr Baton Rouge LA 70808

FERRE, ANTONIO LUIS, publisher. Publisher El Nuevo Dia, San Juan, P.E. Address: 164 Ponce de Leon C P 1964 San Juan PR 00901*

FERRE,, GEORGE FRANS, physician; b. Malmberget, Sweden, Apr. 26, 1904; came to U.S., 1919, naturalized, 1925; s. Frans A. and Maria (Wickman) F.; Th.B., Bethel Theol. Sem., 1923; M.D., Boston U., 1931; postgraduate work in surgery, Vienna, Austria and Stockholm, Sweden, 1937; m. Elna Dagmar Peterson, Aug. 3, 1929; children— Barbara (Mrs. Marion Phillips), George Allen, Paul Gordon. Dir. edn. N.E. Conf. Bapt. Ch., 1923-25; ordained to ministry, Bapt. Ch., 1925; pastor First Ch., Canton, Miss., 1925-27; pastor, Swedish Temple, Boston, 1927-31; intern, resident in surgery Queens Hosp., Honolulu, 1931-33; plantation physician Hamakau Coast, Hawaii, 1934-36; practice gen. surgery, Manchester, N.H., 1938-41, Miami, Fla., 1945-70; surg. cons. Munroe Meml. Gen. Hosp., Ocala, Fla., 1970—. Owner cattle ranch, registered cattle, Ocala, Fla. Trustee Miami Bapt. Hosp., Inc. Served as lt. M.C., AUS, 1939-41; as lt. comdr. M.C., USNR, 1942-45. Mem. Internat. Coll. Surgeons (past regent, mem. bd. govs. 1955—), Am., Fla., Miami med. assns., Mil. Order World Wars, Ry. Physicians Assn. and others. Bapt. Mason (K.T., 32 deg., Shriner), Kiwanian (past pres. Miami Shores). Home: Silver Acres Ranch Route 1 Box 46 Fort McCoy FL 32637

FERRE, JOSE A(NTONIO), corp. ofcl.; b. Ponce, P.R., Sept. 13, 1902; s. Antonio and Mary Aquayo (Casals) F.; B.B.A., Boston U., 1924; M.B.A., U. Miami, 1955; m. Patricia Christensen; children—Maurice, Mary Ann, Jo, Noel, Jose, Emile Christina. Salesman P.R. Iron Works, Inc., 1924-34, v.p., 1934—; exec. v.p. Ponce Cement Corp., 1941—; co-chmn. Puerto Rican Cement Co., Inc.; pres. P.R. Marine Corp., Pan Am. Investment, Inc., P.R. Cement Corp., Cementos Nacionales, S.A., P.R. Drydock & Marine Terminal, Ponce Products, Inc., 1947—; v.p. P.R. Glass Corp., P.R. Clay Corp., P.R. Paper & Pulp Corp., Ferre Export Corp., N.Y.C., 1947—; chmn. Maule Industries, Inc., Miami, Fla., 1956—. Adviser P.R. delegation Caribbean Commn., 1952; hon. consul for Brazil, San Juan, P.R. Pres. Ponce Harbor Bd., 1937-38. Chmn. A.R.C., Ponce, 1943; pres. finance com. Cath. U. P.R.; pres. bd. trustees Dr. Phila.'s Hosp., Ponce, 1955-57; pres. Cancer Hosp. Bldg., Com., San Juan. Trustee Boston U., Pan Am. Hosp., Miami, U. Miami, Catholic U. P.R. Mem. Navy League. Elk. Clubs: Rotary, Athletic, Advertising (N.Y.C.); Yacht (Havana, San Juan, Miami); Bankers; Surf; La. Gorce. Home: Ponce PR 00731

FERRE, LUIS ALBERTO, gov. of P.R., mem. Republican Nat. Com.; b. Ponce, P.R., Feb. 17, 1904; s. Antonio and Mary (Aguaqyo) F.; B.S., Mass. Inst. Tech., 1924, M.S., 1925; LL.D., Springfield Coll., 1959; D.C.L., U. P.R., 1965, Pace Coll., 1966; D. Hum., Interam. U. P.R., 1966; LL.D., Harvard, 1970, Amherst Coll., 1970; L.H.D., N.Y. U., 1970; m. Lorencita Damirez de Arellano, May 30, 1931; children—Antonio Luis, Rosario (Mrs. Benigno Trigo). With P.R. Iron Works, 1925—; an organizer P.R. Cement Corp., 1941, served as co-chmn. bd., dir.; pres., chmn. several indsl. concerns Ferre Industries, 1950—; chmn. bd., pres. Ponce Hotel Corp., 1959—; treas. Central Igualdad Inc., 1950—; gov. P.R., 1969—; dir. Banco de Ponce. Gen. chmn. devel. P.R. YMCA, 1950, pres. Fedn. YMCA'S P.R., 1964; mem. Citizens Adv. Com. Govt. Security, 1957. Rep. candidate for gov. P.R., 1956, 60, 64; mem. P.R. Ho. of Reps. at large, 1952-56; mem. Republican Nat. Com., 1964—. Organizer Luis A. Ferre Found., 1956; founder, pres. Ponce Mus. of Art. Named P.R. of Year, Knights of St. John of Chgo., 1958; decorated Order Vasa (Sweden), 1958; knight Order Holy Sepulchre (Pope John XXIII); recipient Freedom award Order of Lafayette, 1969. Mem. C. of C. P.R., A.I.A. (hon.). Home: 2 Reina Mora Ponce PR 00731 Office: PO Box 82 San Juan PR 00902

FERRELL, CAREY ELWYN, JR., educator; b. Palatka, Fla., Oct. 8, 1930; s. Carey Elwun and Lois (Smith) F.; B.S., Stetson U., 1956; M.Ed., U. Fla., 1966; m. Elizabeth Ann Hiers, Dec. 28, 1956; children—John Michael, Robert Alan. Mgr., Wattles Office Supply, Palatka, 1956-61; asst. finance officer Putnam County Bd. Pub. Instrn., Palatka, 1961-63, dir. bus. affairs, 1963-66, supt. pub. instrn., 1966-71; Fla. Dept. of Education, Tallahassee, Consultant in Sch. Adminstrn., 1971—. Chmn., Putnam County Cancer Crusade, 1966; treas. County Mental Health Assn., 1966-67; mem. exec. bd. Putnam County United Fund, Inc., 1966-67. Bd. dirs. Putnam County Tchrs. Credit Union, 1965-66. Served with USAF, 1951-55. Mem. Fla. Sch. Plant Mmgt. Assn. (state dir. 1966), Am. Assn. Sch. Adminstrs., Assn. Sch. Bus. Ofcls. U.S., Fla. Assn. County Sch. Supts., C. of C., Am. Legion, Putnam County Hist. Soc., Sigma Nu. Kiwanian (treas. 1965-66). Home: 2806 Sweetbriar Dr Tallahassee FL 32303 Office: 129 West Jefferson St Tallahassee FL 32303

FERRELL, GEORGE FRANKLIN, city clk.; b. Portsmouth, Va., Nov. 27, 1943; s. Hagen Sherman and Anne (Roberts) F.; student Roanoke Coll., 1960-61; Asso. in Accounting, Nat. Bus. Coll., 1963; student Va. Western Community Coll., 1970-71; m. Rosetta Epperly, Oct. 25, 1963; children—James Franklin, Paul Flemming. Asst. mgr. Roanoke Truck & Trailer Service Co. (Va.), 1962-63; city clk., chief accountant City of Salem, Va., 1963—. Mem. Am., Va. (membership chmn.) municipal finance officers assns., Internat. Municipal Clks. Assn., Salem Jr. C. of C. Home: 736 Elizabeth Av Salem VA 24153 Office: 19 N College Av Salem VA 24153

FERRELL, ORVILLE LEE, hosp. adminstr.; b. Glenalum, W.Va., Mar. 31, 1921; s. Willie and Ava (Carter) F.; student N.C. State U., 1946, Hardbarger Bus. Coll., 1946-47; A.B., Marshall U., 1950; m. Rachel May, Mar. 29, 1945; children—Richard Daniel, William James, Robert Gordon. With Williams & Wall, C.P.A.'s, 1947-49, N.C. Med. Care Commn., 1950-51; asst. adminstr. St. Agnes Hosp., 1951-53, Rowan Meml. Hosp., 1953-58; adminstr. Cherokee County Meml. Hosp., Gaffney, S.C., 1958-61, Meml. Hosp., Waycross, Ga., 1961-69, Riverside Nursing Home, Waycross, 1965-69, Ormond Beach (Fla.) Meml. Hosp., 1969-72, Baldwin County Hosp., Milledgeville, Ga., 1972—; Instr. Waycross (Ga.) Ware Vocational Tech. Sch., 1968—, Daytona Beach (Fla.) Community Coll., 1970; cons. adminstrn. Southeast council Ga. Hosp. Assn., 1967—. Chmn. Waycross chpt. Am. Cancer Soc., 1968—; bd. dirs. Mental Health Assn., Waycross, United Fund, Waycross. Served to lt. USNR, 1942-46. Fellow Am. Coll. Hosp. Adminstrs.; mem. Fla. Hosp. Assn. Methodist. Rotarian. Home: PO Box 690 Milledgeville GA 31061

FERRER, JOSE LUIS, physician; b. Santurce, P.R., June 3, 1927; s. Luis and Juanita (Cutierrez) F.; B.A., Poly. Inst. P.R., 1948; M.D., Madrid Sch. Medicine, 1954; m. Conchita Garcia, Mar. 27, 1954; children—Jose Luis, Nora C. Intern Aquadilla (P.R.) Dist. Hosp., 1954-55; med. dir. Sabana Grande (P.R.) Municipal Hosp., 1955-57; attending physician Mayaquez Municipal Hosp., 1956-57; practice gen. medicine, Trujillo Aito, P.R., 1957—; mem. staffs Profl. Hosp., Santurce, P.R., San Martin Hosp., Rio Piedras, P.R.; faculty mem. Centro Clinico Metro Politano, 1958-70. Mem. P.R. Med. Assn. Club: Exchange (dist. pres. 1971-72). Home: 380 Holy Cross Rpto Univ Rio Piedras PR 00926 Office: 22 Munoz Rivera St Trujillo Aito PR 00760

FERRETTI, LEWIS CLEMENT JOSEPH, communications services agy. exec.; b. New Bedford, Mass., Jan. 30, 1932; s. Clement Armando and Stella (Sorenti) F.; B.S. in Bus. Adminstrn., Providence Coll., 1953; M.B.A., Boston Coll., 1970; m. Helen Mae Eaton, Aug. 11, 1955; children—Lewis Clement Joseph, Kevin J., Peter J., Joseph M. Staff accountant Boyden, Yardley, McManus & Guay, Boston, 1955-57; successively mgmt. devel. trainee, cost gen. accounting supr., staff asst. to div. controller Raytheon Co., Waltham and Norwood, Mass., 1957-61; successively asst. div. controller, div. controller, asst. to gen. mgr. for planning and devel. Singer Co., Pickens, S.C. and Hight Point, N.C., 1961-66; corporate controller, now v.p. finance and adminstrn., treas. Alderman Studios, Inc., High Point, 1966—, also dir.; dir. Lynn Photo Co., Inc., Lenoir, N.C., Alderman Photo Co., Inc., High Point, Stuart Studios, Greensboro, N.C., HF/TV, Inc., High Point, Piedmont Asso. Industries, Inc., Greensboro; partner Marketplace Devel. Co., High Point. Mem. dist. advancement com. Uwharrie council Boy Scouts Am., 1971, chmn. dist. long-range planning and devel. com., 1972; committeeman Troop 26, Boy Scouts Am., High Point, 1967—. Bd. dirs., mem. exec. com. Business-Oriented Polit. Action Com., Greensboro, 1972—. Served to 1st lt. USMC, 1953-55; now lt. col. Res. Mem. High Point C. of C. (mem. congl. action com. 1965—), Marine Corps Res. Officers Assn. (nat. dir. 1970-72, nat. exec. council 1972—), Res. Officers Assn., Am. Mgmt. Assn., Soc. for Advancement of Mgmt., Marine Corps Assn., Providence Coll. Alumni Assn., Boston Coll. Alumni Assn. Republican. Roman Catholic (mem. parish adv. council 1965-67, 72—). K.C., Elk. Clubs: Willow Creek Golf, Southern Furniture (High Point). Home: 1710 Windsor Dr High Point NC 27260 Office: 2055 Francis St High Point NC 27261

FERRIN, ROBERT WAYNE, constrn. co. exec.; b. Oklahoma City, Apr. 20, 1931; s. Horace Harlan and Lorene Lovinia (Richardson) F.; student U. Okla., 1949-53, Okla. A. and M. U., 1950, Oklahoma City U. Law Sch., 1954, West Tex. State U., 1957; m. Koletyo Belvin, Oct. 8, 1954; children—Robert Sterling, Stephen Craig. With Southwestern Pub. Service Co., Amarillo, Tex., 1956-59; owner Bob Ferrin Constrn. Co., Amarillo, 1959—; pres. Ferrin Enterprises, Inc., Ferrin-Standefer Co.; dir. North State Bank, Armarillo. Pres. Tex. Panhandle Home Builders Assn., 1964. Served with U.S. Army, 1954-56. Recipient Honor Man award USN, 1952. Methodist. Home: Route No 1 Box 332 Amarillo TX 79106 Office: 3213 Western St Amarillo TX 79109

FERRIS, FREDERICK JOSEPH, social work adminstr.; b. Troy, N.Y., June 2, 1920; s. John and Amelia (Deeb) F.; B.A. cum laude, State U. N.Y. at Albany, 1942; M.S., Columbia, 1949, D.S.W., 1968; m. Ellen J. Walsh, June 12, 1965. Head social studies dept. Heatly High Sch., Green Island, N.Y., 1946-47; sec. Information Service, Greater N.Y. Fund, N.Y.C., 1949-51; exec. sec. N. Met. div. United Community Services, Boston, 1951-53, mem. Research div. com., 1953-57; dir. community orgn., asst. prof. Boston Coll. Sch. Social Work, 1953-57; dean, prof. Nat. Catholic Sch. Social Service, Catholic U. Am. 1960-69; asso. dir. planning and research Am. Assn. Ret. Persons and Nat. Ret. Tchrs. Assn. 1972—, A.A.R.P.-N.R.T.A. coordinator White House Conf. on Aging, 1970—. Adj. asso. prof. Fordham U. Sch. Social Service, 1957-60; lectr. Adelphi and Rutgers univs., 1959-60; social planning cons. Am. Found. for Blind, 1958-59; cons. Inst. Community Studies, United Way Am., 1970-71, Psychiat. Inst. Found., 1970. Vice chmn. Joint Legislative Com., Boston, 1954-57. Bd. dirs. Social Service Exchange, Boston, 1955-57, Child Welfare League Am., 1966-70, Cath. Internat. Union Social Service, 1967—, Christ Child Soc. Washington, 1967—; treas., mem. bd. Nat. Conf. Catholic Charities, 1971—. Chmn. Washington com. 13th Internat. Conf. Schs. Social Work, 1965-66. Served from pvt. to capt. AUS, 1942-46. Recipient Lasker Doctoral fellowship Columbia, 1957-58. Mem. Nat. (chpt. treas. 1956-57), Am. (chmn. div. pub. policy and social work, exec. com. 1953-55) assns. social workers, Mass. Conf. Social Work (bd. dirs., chmn. nominating com. 1956-57), Alumni Assn. Columbia U. Sch. Social Work (chpt. chmn. 1954-55, dir. 1956-59), United Community Funds and Councils Am. (nat. adv. com. health and welfare services 1955-57, council planning execs. 1957-59), Nat. Assn. Hearing and Speech Agys. (nat. tng. adv. com. 1963-70), Acad. Certified Social Workers, Council Social Work Edn. (deans adv. com. fed. welfare agys. 1962-64, 66-68), Nat. Conf. Social Welfare, Social Welfare History Group, Nat. Council on Aging, Gerontological Soc. Home: 5101 River Rd Washington DC 20016

FERRY, ALAN LONGSTAFF, interior designer; b. Phila., Feb. 29, 1916; s. Asa J. and Anna (Mundell) F.; student U. Wichita, 1934-35, Art Inst. Chgo., 1935-57; M.A., Yale, 1940; m. Sarah Click, Apr. 8, 1942; children—Joseph L., Alan Eugene. Scenic designer, N.Y.C., 1939-41; staff designer Rich's Dept. Store, Atlanta, 1946-48; pres. Alan L. Ferry, Designers, Inc., Atlanta, 1948—. Bd. dirs. Atlanta Arts Festival. Served to capt. C.E., AUS, 1941-46. Mem. Am. Inst. Interior Designers (dir. 1965-68), Nat. Soc. Indsl. Designers, Illuminating Engring. Soc., Am. Inst. Store Planners. Presbyn. (deacon, elder). Kiwanian (dir. 1950-54). Home: 387 Manor Ridge Dr Atlanta GA 30305 Office: 34 11th St Atlanta GA 30309

FESHBACH, MURRAY, economist; b. N.Y.C., Aug. 8, 1929; s. Benjamin and Lilly (Harfenist) F.; A.B., Syracuse U., 1950; M.A., Columbia, 1951; postgrad. Am. U., 1957—; m. Muriel Joan Schreiner, Dec. 30, 1956; children—Michael L., David S. Research asst. Nat. Bur. Econ. Research, N.Y.C., 1955-56; analyst fgn. demographic analysis div. Bur. Census, 1957-67, chief USSR br., 1967-68, chief USSR/East Europe br., 1969-72; supervisory economist Bur. Econ. Analysis, Washington, 1972—. Research asso., bibliog. cons. NSF projects, 1963-71; lectr. Indsl. Coll. Armed Forces, 1962-71, Am. U., 1968, Syracuse U., 1970, Pa. U., 1971; mem. Fgn. Area Research Coordination Group, USSR and Eastern Europe subcom., U.S. Dept. State, 1969—. Served with AUS, 1951-55. Mem. Am. Econ. Assn., Assn. for Study Soviet-Type Econs. (mem. exec. com. 1970-71) Am. Assn. Advancement Slavic Studies (mem. nat. bibliog. and documentation com. 1971—).Omicron Delta Epsilon. Author: Manpower in the USSR, U.S. Congress Joint Econ. Com., New Directions in the Soviet Economy, 1966. Contbr. articles to profl. jours. Home: 11403 Fairoak Dr Silver Spring MD 20902 Office: Dept Commerce Washington DC 20230

FESMIRE, FRANCIS MILLER, physician; b. Baxter, Tenn., July 21, 1933; s. William J. and Eulu (Hoy) F.; student U. of South, 1951-53; M.D., U. Tenn., 1957; postgrad. Oak Ridge Inst. Nuclear Studies, 1959; m. Carolyn Block, Nov. 9, 1957; children—Carolyn Lee, Francis Miller, Mary Ann. Intern, U. Ala. Hosp., 1957; resident 3d U.S. Army Med. Lab., 1958-61; trainee in clin. pathology Kennedy VA Hosp., Memphis, 1962-64; asst. pathologist Meth. Hosp., Memphis, 1964; pathologist Rutherford Hosp., Murfreesboro, Tenn., 1964-71; asso. pathologist Baroness Erlanger Hosp., Chattanooga, 1971—. Mem. adv. com. Tenn. Mid-S. Regional Med. Program, 1968—. Bd. dirs. Nat. Regional Red Cross Center, Nashville. Served to capt. M.C., AUS, 1958-61. Diplomate in anatomical and clin. pathology Am. Bd. Pathology. Fellow Coll. Am. Pathology, Am. Assn. Clin. Pathology; mem. Am. Assn. Blood Banks, Am. Nuclear Soc., A.M.A., Alpha Tau Omega. Methodist (mem. ofcl. bd.). Rotarian. Contbr. articles to med. jours.Home: 13 Fairhills Dr Chattanooga TN 37403 Office: Erlanger Hospital Chattanooga TN 37403

FESMIRE, HAROLD LUNN, banker; b. Lexington, Tenn., Mar. 1, 1929; s. Thompsie Wesley and Pauline (Lunn (F.; student Okaloosa Walton Jr. Coll., 1961; m. Eva Ruth Jones, May 19, 1950; 1 dau., Sharon Lynn. Dep. sheriff, counselor Juvenile Ct., Okaloosa County, Fla., 1956-59; owner A & W Root Beer franchise, 1957-71; dir. 1st Nat. Bank, Ft. Walton Beach, Fla., 1964—; adv. council A & WCorp., 1966-69. Co-sponsor Jamaica Mission Program, Isle of Jamaica, 1971. Bd. dirs. Mental Health Assn. Okaloosa County, 1961, Ala. Christian Coll., Wiregrass Youth Camp, Enterprise, Ala.; bd. dirs., officer Okaloosa div. West Fla. Heart Assn. Served with USNR, 1950-52. Mem. Ft. Walton Beach C. of C. Mem. Ch. of Christ (deacon, treas.). Home: Route 1 Box 26D Fort Walton Beach FL 32548 Office: 55 Eglin Pkwy Fort Walton Beach FL 32548

FESPERMAN, TOM, mng. editor Charlotte (N.C.) Observer. Address: 600 S Tryon St Charlotte NC 28201*

FESTA, SALVATORE ANTONIO, ednl. adminstr.; b. Vineland, N.J., Nov. 23, 1921; s. Anthony Joseph and Mary Anna (Tomasello) F.; A.B., Elon Coll., 1943; M.Ed., U. N.C., Greensboro, 1953; postgrad. Duke, 1960, U. N.C., Chapel Hill, 1965; m. Helen Deanne Yarborough, Oct. 18, 1947; children—Anita Marie, Donna Cecilia, Carmella Anne. Purchase service clk., expeditor Western Electric Co., Burlington, N.C., 1946-50, tech. asst. engr., summers 1956-57; sci. instr. Bessemer High Sch., Guilford County, N.C., 1950-53; prin. Brightwood Elementary Sch., 1953-55; dir. pub. relations audio-visual and sci. Burlington (N.C.) city schs., 1955-62; prin. Broad St. Jr. High Sch., 1962-66, dir. instructional materials services, 1966—. Night prin. Tech. Inst. of Alamance, 1958-60, speed reading instr., 1960-61; speed reading instr. Forsyth Tech. Inst., 1961; vis. instr. U. N.C., Greensboro, 1967, 69; tchr. grad. courses in extension U. N.C., 1966-70, U. Va., 1968-71; mem. Almanance County Human Relations Council, 1972—; instr. Media Inst. for N.C. Dept. Pub. Instrn. at Burlington, summer 1970; cons. Durham County Schs., Audio-Visual Workshop, 1967, Montgomery County Schs., Audio-Visual Workshop, Troy, N.C., 1969, State Adv. Council on Tchr. Edn.; mem. adv. coms. N.C. Dept. Pub. Instrn. NDEA-Audio-Visual and Sci. Civil def. coordinator, 1955-60; mem.-at-large Alamance County Community Council, 1955—; capt. United Fund, 1971—; instnl. rep. Boy Scouts Am., 1966—, leadership tng. chmn. dist. com., 1968—; pub. relations chmn., treas. Parents League, 1965; mem. alumni exec. com. Elon Coll., 1968-70. Precinct del. State Conv. Democratic party, 1964. Served with Med. Dept., AUS, 1943-46. Mem. N.E.A. (life), N.C. Assn. Edn. (pres. ednl. media assn. 1972—), Am. Assn. Sch. Adminstrs., Assn. for Ednl. Communications and Tech. (dir. 1959-60, state legislative chmn. 1971—), N.C. Acad. Sci. (pres. Guilford County 1959, 60), N.C. Dept. Audio-Visual Edn. (pres. 1959-60). Roman Catholic. K.C., Moose. Home: 2914 Amherst Av Burlington NC 27215 Office: 217 Union Av Burlington NC 27215

FETTER, WILLIAM HUTCHINSON, oil refining co. exec.; b. Jenkintown, Pa., Dec. 1, 1916; s. A. Leroy and Elizabeth H. (Smith) F.; B.S., Pa. State U., 1938; m. Jean C. Agster, Aug. 6, 1940; children—Lee (mrs. Lee Anderson), Sally (Mrs. John Winslow), Lynn (mrs. Dudley Smith). With Atlantic Oil Co., Phila., 1938-39; mgr. petroleum Pa. Farm Bur., Harrisburg, 1939-51; pres. Texas City Refining, Inc. (Tex.), 1951—; dir. Bank of the Mainland, LaMarque, Tex. Bd. dirs. United Fund, Region IV Ednl. Service, Galveston County Research Council; past pres. bd. trustees LaMarque Ind. Sch. Dist. Served with AUS, 1942-44. Recipient certificate of merit LaMarque Pub. Schs., 1966, Distinguished Service award LaMarque Jr. C. of C., 1970; named Sr. Citizen of LaMarque, 1970. Registered profl. engr., Tex., Pa. Mem. Nat. Petroleum Refiners Assn., Am. Petroleum Inst., Texas City/LaMarque C. of C. (v.p.), Sigma Alpha Epsilon, Presbyn. (trustee, pres.). Home: 2215 Carriage Lane LaMarque TX 77568 Office: Box 1271 Texas City TX 77590

FETTERMAN, JOHN, journalist; b. Danville, Ky., Feb. 25, 1920; s. John Lawrence and Zora (Goad) F.; B.S., Murray State U., 1948; postgrad. U. Ky., 1949-51; m. Evelyn Alline Maner, Nov. 2, 1944; children—Phyllis Lee (Mrs. John Terry), Mindy Nelle. Editor, Ledger & Times, Murray, Ky., 1945-46; writer Nashville Tennessean, 1950-56; writer-photographer Louisville Courier-Jour., 1957—. Served with USNR, 1942-45; PTO. Co-recipient Pulitzer prize, 1967; recipient Pulitzer prize, 1969, Nat. Headliner award, 1969; named Distinguished Alumnus, Murray State U., 1971. Methodist. Author:

Stinking Creek, 1967. Home: 4425 Greenbriar Rd Louisville KY 40207

FETZER, CARL STEPHAN, JR., agr. exec.; b. Lakewood, O., Jan. 13, 1927; s. Carl Stephan and Bessie (Haffemeister) F.; student Western Res. U., 1946-48; m. Martha Jeanne Smith, June 21, 1949; children—Carl Stephan III, Mark, Gayle. Distbr. for Scott & Fetzer Co., Cleve., 1949-59; pres. Sefco, Inc., Vero Beach, Fla., 1959—. Vice chmn. Indian River Grapefruit Com., 1971-72. Bd. dirs. Indian River Citrus League. Served with USAAF, 1944-46. Republican. Christian Scientist (dir.). Home: 917 Lady Bug Lane Vero Beach FL 32960 Office: P O Box 2226 Vero Beach FL 32960

FICHANDLER, ZELDA DIAMOND (MRS. THOMAS C. FICHANDLER), theater producer, dir.; b. Sept. 18, 1924; d. Harry and Ida (Epstein) Diamond; B.A., Cornell U., 1945; M.A., George Washington U., 1950; L.H.D. (hon.), Hood Coll., 1962; m. Thomas C. Fichandler, Feb. 17, 1946; 2 sons. Founder, producer, dir. Arena Stage; mem. exec. com. Theatre Communication Group. Recipient ann. award Nat. Theater Conf., 1971, Margo Jones award, 1971. Mem. Phi Beta Kappa. Home: 3120 Newark St NW Washington DC 20008 Office: Arena Stage 6th and M Sts SW Washington DC 20024*

FICHTER, GEORGE SIEBERT, author; b. Hamilton, O., Sept. 17, 1922; s. Matthew and Hazel Evelen (Siebert) F.; A.B., Miami U., 1947; M.S., N.C. State U., 1948; postgrad. U. N.C., 1948-49; m. Nadine Kay Warner, Feb. 10, 1945; children—Susan Kay, Thomas Matt, Jane Ann. Instr. zoology and conservation Miami U., Oxford, O., 1948-50; zoology editor Jour. Sch. Sci. and Math., Chgo., 1949-50; v.p., editor-in-chief Fisherman Press, Inc., Oxford and N.Y.C., 1950-55; asst. exec. v.p. Sport Fishing Inst., Washington, 1955-57; dir. Golden Guides, Western Pub. Co., N.Y.C., 1967-68; free lance writer and editor of pubs. in area of natural history. Mem. A.A.A.S., Am. Entomological Soc., Am. Littoral Soc., Sigma Xi, Phi Kappa Phi. Author of numerous nature books including Insect Pests, 1966, Animal Kingdom, 1968, Snakes and Other Reptiles, 1968, Airborne Animals, 1969, Your World--Your Survival, 1970, Birds of Florida, 1971, Bicycling, 1972. Contbr. articles, and papers to profl. pubs. Editor: Golden Encyclopedia of Natural History, 1962, Golden Bookshelf of Natural History, 1963, and numerous other nature books. Address: P O Box 1368 Homestead FL 33030

FICKLEN, JACK HOWELLS, editorial cartoonist; b. Waco, Tex., Apr. 18, 1911; s. Fielding and Bessie (Howells) F.; student art So. Methodist U., 1930-32, Dallas Creative Center, 1964—; m. Mary Alice Brown, Oct. 21, 1950; children—Molly-Bess, Jack Howells, Robert F. Copyboy, Dallas News, 1928-35, layout artist, photog. retoucher, 1935-37, sports cartoonist, 1937-40, editorial cartoonist, 1937-40, 46—; syndicated cartoonist Register & Tribune Syndicate, Des. Moines, 1940-45, Bell-McClure Syndicate, 1959-62, Ledger Syndicate, N.Y.C., 1967—. Book illustrator, free-lance cartoonist, 1930—; owner, mgr. Avalon Features Syndicate, editorial cartoon service, Dallas, 1960—; work exhibited Archives Am. Art, Detroit, U. Mo. Sch. Journalism, Wayne State U., dept. journalism U. Ariz.; permanent exhbn. Assn. Am. Editorial Cartoonists Assn., Dallas Hall of State. Dir. communications Dallas County Civil Def., 1958-60. Bd. dirs. Tex. Council for Wildlife Protection. Served with AUS, 1940-46; ETO; officer Res., ret. Decorated Bronze Star, Croix de Guerre avec palme (Belgium). Mem. Am. Editorial Cartoonists Assn., Res. Officers Assn., Artists and Craftsmen Asso., Dallas. Democrat. Presbyn. Fundamental Principles of Driving, 1945; Self Government by Texans, 1950. Home: 6657 Avalon Av Dallas TX 75214 Office: Dallas Morning News Dallas TX 75222

FICKLING, AUSTIN LECOUNT, judge; b. Washington, May 11, 1914; s. F. Douglas K. and M. Viola (Henderson) F.; LL.B., Terrell Law Sch., 1942; m. Julia Young, Apr. 2, 1935 (dec.); children—Ralph L., Phyllis (step-dau.). Admitted to D.C. bar, 1943; prof. of law Terrell Law Sch., 1945-50; pvt. practice law, Washington, 1943-54; asst. U.S. Atty., 1954-56; judge D.C. Ct. Gen. Sessions, 1956-68, D.C. Ct. Appeals, 1968—. Mem. Am. Bar Assn., Am. Judicature Soc. Home: 1716 Allison St NW Washington DC 20011 Office: 400 F St NW Washington DC 20001

FIEDOTIN, ARNOLDO, physician; b. Parana, Argentina, May 25, 1936; s. Aaron Adolfo and Paulina (Spector) F.; B.A. cum laude, Coll. Nac Nicolas Avellaneda, Buenos Aires, Argentina, 1954; M.D., U. Buenos Aires, 1961; m. Rosa L. Ludner, June 9, 1961; children—Diana Sylvia, Richard Alan, Norma Alexandra. Came to U.S., 1961, naturalized, 1967. Intern, Pontiac (Mich.) Gen. Hosp., 1961-62; resident St. Joseph's Hosp., Pontiac, 1962-65; NIH fellow N.J. Coll. Medicine, 1965-66; fellow in cardiology Cleve. Clinic, 1966-67; practice of medicine, specializing in cardiology, Atlanta, 1967—; dir. cardiac services St. Joseph's Infirmary, Atlanta, 1967—; asst. clin. prof. medicine Emory U., 1968—. Cons. cardiology Office Vocational Rehab., Ga. Dept. Edn., 1968—. Mem. Am. Coll. Cardiology (asso. fellow), A.C.P. (asso. fellow), A.M.A., Am. Heart Assn., Am. Soc. Internal Medicine, Ga. Med. Assn., Med. Assn. Atlanta, Atlanta Forum Cardiology. Home: 1818 W Wesley Rd NW Atlanta GA 30327 Office: 265 Ivy St NE Atlanta GA 30303

FIEKOWSKY, SEYMOUR, govt. ofcl.; b. Detroit, Dec. 19, 1921; s. Hyman Beryl and Elizabeth (Berman) F.; B.A., Wayne State U., 1942; M.A., Harvard, 1948, Ph.D., 1959; m. Hortense Vivian Firestone, Mar. 28, 1943; children—Lisa, Nicholas, Peter. Asst. prof. econs. Reed Coll., Portland, Ore., 1949-54; asso. prof. econs. and statistics Cal. State Coll., Los Angeles, 1956-59; dir. resource analysis div. Center for Naval Analyses, Arlington, Va., 1960-67; chief bus. taxation staff Office Tax Analysis, U.S. Treasury, Washington, 1967—, acting dir. Office Indsl. Econs., Internal Revenue Service, 1971—. Served with AUS, 1942-45. Mem. Am. Econ. Assn., Econometric Soc., Am. Statis. Assn., Nat. Tax Assn. Home: 5425 39th St NW Washington DC 20015 Office: 15th and Pennsylvania Ave NW Washington DC 20220

FIELD, RICHARD LANE, editor; b. Balt., Sept. 12, 1897; s. Charles Carter and Mary Virginia (Lane) F; A.B., Johns Hopkins, 1920; m. Camilla L. Chewning, June 25, 1932; children—Richard Lane, William Carter. Reporter, Baltimore Sun, 1920-23, night city editor, 1923-24; swing editor Baltimore Am., 1925; asst. make-up editor New York Herald-Tribune, 1926, asst. editor Sunday Mag., 1926-35; article editor This Week Mag., 1935-45; asso. editor Holiday mag., 1945-47, mng. editor, 1947-57, prodn. dir. Holiday mag., 1957-64; city editor High Springs (Fla.) Herald, 1966; cons., part-time editor The Floridian, Sunday mag. of St. Petersburg (Fla.) Times, 1966—. Participated in founding Herald Tribune Sunday mag., 1926, This Week mag., 1935, Holiday mag., 1945, The Floridian, 1966. Dir. mag. information O.P.A., Washington, 1945. Served as pvt. U.S. Army, 1918. Mem. Kappa Alpha. Clubs: Dutch Treat, Johns Hopkins, P.E.N. (New York). Contbr. articles to nat. mags. Home: Ivanhoe House 5955 30th Av S Gulfport FL 33707

FIELD, ROBERT JOSEPH, petroleum Co. exec.; b. Langdon, N.D., May 24, 1924; s. William Hansford and Florence Esther (Quick) F.; B.S., Colo. Coll., 1948, M.A., 1951; m. Freddie Jean Morgan, Jan. 26, 1952; children—James, Murray, Laurie. Engr., Eastman Oil Well, Long Beach, Cal., 1949-50; geologist Deep Rock Oil Co., Denver, 1951-54; div. geologist Sohio Petroleum Co., Houston, 1954-61; exploration mgr. Morgan Drilling Co., Oklahoma City, 1961-63, An-Son Corp., 1963-65; pres. Morgan Petroleum Co., 1965—. Served with USMCR, 1943-45. Mem. Am. Assn. Petroleum Geologists., Okla City Geol. Soc., Kappa Sigma. Club: Petroleum (Oklahoma City). Office: 2000 Liberty Tower Oklahoma City OK 73102

FIELD, STANLEY, govt. ofcl.; b. Ukraine, May 20, 1911; s. Henry and Nina (Cibulsky) F.; brought to U.S., 1914, naturalized, 1924; B.A., Bklyn. Coll., 1934; m. Joyce Stillman, Dec. 7, 1935; children—Jeffrey Michael, Constance Elyse. Program dir. Radio sta. WLTH, N.Y.C., 1935-37, writer NBC, 1937-38; copywriter Emil Mogul Advt. Agy., 1939-40; free lance writer, Washington, 1941—; information specialist Dept. Army, Washington, 1941—. Instr. Bklyn Coll., 1938-40, Grad. Sch. Dept. Agr., 1969—, Adult Edn. div. Arlington County, Va., 1967—; adj. prof. Am. U., 1953-67. Recipient Emmy award Acad. TV Arts and Scis., spl. award YMCA Internat, 1947. Mem. The Author's Guild, Assn. Profl. Broadcasting Edn., Nat. Assn. Ednl. Broadcasters. Author: Television and Radio Writing, 1958; Guide to Opportunities in the Sciences, 1968; Bible Stories for Adults, 1969; Writing for the Broadcast Media, 1972; also numerous TV and radio documentary and dramatic scripts. Home: 3520 Duff Dr Falls Church VA 22041 Office: Broadcast Pictorial Branch U.S. Army Command Information Unit Washington DC 20315

FIELDER, ROBERT ECHOLS BARNES, investor; b. Arlington, Tex., Nov. 23, 1906; s. James Park and Mattie (Barnes) F.; student Tex. U.; m. Dorothy Umphress Taylor, Mar. 15, 1928; children—Julia Caroline (Mrs. Robert J. Jeffress), James Park III. Owner Fielderdale Farms, Venus, Tex., 1927—; mgr. Taylor Grain Co., Inc., Van Alstyne, Tex., 1929-58; owner Fielder Lumber and Supply, Van Alstyne, 1945—, Plano, Tex., 1954—; owner Discount Warehouse, Van Alstyne, 1962-64. Chmn. Grayson County Bldg. Program; pres. Grayson County Devel. Council; chmn. Grayson County Child's Welfare Bd.; exec. bd. Texoma Valley council Boy Scouts Am., 1944-58, 68—, pres., 1969—; gen. chmn. Arlington High Sch. Tri-Ann. Roarin' 20's Roundup, 1964, 67, 70, 73; mem. exec. County chpt. A.R.C., 1948—, pres. bd., 1969—; exec. bd. bd. Grayson Texoma Regional Planning Commn., 1969—; charter mem. bd. Grayson United Fund, 1970, county campaign chmn., 1971; pres. Van Alstyne Sch. Bd., 1941-43; donor Fielder Outstanding Student award Arlington High Sch., 1932—. Trustee Grayson Jr. Coll., 1964—, pres., 1969—; bd. dirs. Old Settlers Village, Grayson County, C.C. Young-Blanton Gardens Methodist Home for Aged, Dallas. Served as liberation leader, World War II, 1942-44. Recipient Am. Legion Citizen medal. Van Alstyne, 1945; Bronze Plaque World War II Service Men award, Van Alstyne, 1945; named Outstanding Citizen, Van Alstyne C. of C., 1960. Mem. Van Alstyne C. of C. (past pres., sec.), Tex. Landrace Assn. (charter pres.), Santa Gertrudis Breeders Premier Assn. (dir.), North Tex. Hatchery Assn. (past pres., sec.), North Tex. Lumber Dealers (dir. 1967), Sigma Alpha Epsilon. Methodist (charge lay leader, chmn. ofcl. bd., dist. trustee, bd. missions, mem. ministers salary com. North Tex. Conf.). Lion (pres.). Home: 701 S Waco St Van Alstyne TX 75095 Office: Main at Stephens Sts Van Alstyne TX 75095

FIELDING, ELIZABETH M., govt. ofcl.; b. New London, Conn., May 16, 1917; d. Frederick James and Elizabeth (Martin) Fielding; B.A., Conn. Coll. Women, 1938; M.A., Am. U., 1944. Research writer Republican Nat. Com., 1940, acting dir. research, 1944, asst. dir. research, 1948-53; govt. statistician, personnel clk., economist, 1941-42; staff writer, spl. cons. several U.S. Congressmen, 1944-52; exec. sec., legislative asst. U.S. Senator Alexander Wiley, 1953-54; asso. dir. research Rep. Nat. Com., 1954-57, research, speech writer, 1960-61; legislative analyst, newsletter editor Nat. Assn. Electric Cos., 1957-60; pub. relations dir. Nat. Fedn. Rep. Women, 1961-68; editor Republican Clubwoman, 1961-68; dir. spl. activities women's div. United Citizens for Nixon-Agnew, 1968; finance coordinator Inaugural com., 1969; spl. asst. to asst. Postmaster Gen., 1969-71; pub. affairs dir. Pres. Council on Youth Opportunity, Washington, 1970-71; asst. adminstr. pub. affairs Nat. Credit Union Adminstrn., 1971—, editor bull., 1971—. Mem. Am. Polit. Sci. Assn., Am. Acad. Polit. and Social Sci., A.A.A.S., D.C. League Rep. Women, Am. Mgmt. Assn., Am. Soc. Pub. Adminstrn., Fed. Editors Assn., Govt. Information Orgn., Am. Soc. Tng. and Devel., Nat. Soc. Historic Preservation, Phi Beta Kappa. Methodist. Clubs: Antique Automobile Am.; Nat. Press, Washington Press, Am. Newspaper Women's Capitol Hill (Washington). Author: A History of the Republican Party, 1854-1948; also party pubs. Home: 3701 Thornton Pkwy Oxon Hill MD 20022 Office: 2025 M St NW Room 3320 Washington DC 20456

FIELDS, ARCHIE REID, librarian; b. Whitesburg, Ky., Sept. 2, 1917; s. Felix Gilbert and Minnie (Adams) F.; B.S., U.S. Naval Acad., 1941; M.A., Stanford, 1962; M.L.S., U. Wash., 1964; m. Dorothy Elizabeth Province, June 17, 1942; children—Patti, Alan, James, Jennifer. Commd. ensign U.S. Navy, 1941, advanced through grades to comdr., 1952; served in European and Pacific areas, World War II, Korean action; ret., 1961; tchr. sci. Kalapooya Jr. High Sch., Albany, Ore., 1963; cataloger U. N.C. Library, Chapel Hill, 1964-66, chief of circulation, 1966—. Decorated Purple Heart. Home: Route 6 Arboretum Dr Chapel Hill NC 27514 Office: L R Wilson Library U N C Chapel Hill NC 27514

FIELDS, HUBERT, dentist; b. London, Ky., May 20, 1923; s. Hubert and Mary Eileen (Warner) F.; certificate Sue Bennett Jr. Coll., London, 1943; student U. Wis., 1943-44; D.M.D., U. Louisville, 1947; m. Jean Elizabeth Sheets, June 15, 1950; 1 son, Douglas Scott. Asst. dental surgeon USPHS, 1947-49, sr. asst. dental surgeon, 1949-53; asst. prof. prosthodontics U. Louisville, 1953-57, asso. prof., 1957-60, prof., 1960—, chmn. dept. prosthodontics, 1972—; cons. Ky. Bd. Dental Examiners, 1968-70. Mem. Fed. Dental Service Com., 1963-65, chmn., 1965. Leader troop Boy Scouts Am., 1964-65. Served with AUS, 1943-44. Fellow Am. Coll. Dentists (sec. Ky. sect.); mem. Am., Ky. (ho. of dels. 1966—), Louisville (dental trade and dental lab. relations com. 1969-71) dental assns., Am. Prosthodontic Soc., Southeastern Acad. Prosthodontics, Am. Assn. Dental Schs., Omicron Kappa Upsilon, Delta Sigma Delta, Phi Delta. Mason. Contbr. articles to profl. jours. Home: 4325 Foeburn Lane Louisville KY 40207

FIELDS, JOHN CAM, banker; b. Sparta, N.C., Sept. 29, 1897; s. Wiliam Callahan and Josephine Virginia (Jones) F.; student William Jewell Coll., 1913-14, U. Richmond, 1914-17; m. Anna Graham Halsey, Sept. 18, 1937; children—William Jackson, Nancy Rosamond. Pres. 1st Nat. Bank of Troutdale, 1921-32; dir. Grayson Nat. Bank, 1932—, pres., 1945-69, chmn. bd., 1969—; sec.-treas. Fields Mfg. Co., Mouth of Wilson, Va. Mem. Dem. State Central Com., Grayson County Dem. Exec. Com., 1940—; mem. Grayson County Sch. Bd., 1933—, chmn., 1938—. Trustee Oak Hill Acad.; mem. coll. bd. Wytheville Community Coll. Mem. Business Men's Club, Sigma Phi Epsilon. Baptist (deacon, past mem. Va. gen. bd.). Home and office Mouth of Wilson VA 24363

FIELDS, REUBEN ELBERT, physicist; b. Society Hill, S.C., Sept. 30, 1916; s. Ephraim Duncan and Susan Margaret (Hay) F.; B.S.E.E., Ga. Inst. Tech., 1940; M.S. in Physics, U. Wis. 1951, Ph.D., 1954; m. Lucile Courtenay Stark, Oct. 20, 1945; children—Lucy Margaret (Mrs. James L. Walden), Sara Eugenia, Julia Elizabeth. Asso. engr. U.S. Dept. Agr. Rural Electrification Adminstrn., Washington, St. Louis, 1940-42; asso. physicist Argonne Nat. Lab., Chgo., 1944-46, 48, 50; sta: sci. Gen. Dynamics Corp., Ft. Worth div., 1954—; adj. prof. physics Tex. Christian U., 1960—. Cons. Nuclear Safety USAF Directorate of Nuclear Safety. Served with AUS, 1942-46. Mem. Am. Nuclear Soc., Am. Phys. Soc., Sigma Xi. Contbr. articles to profl. jours. Home: 4132 Clayton Rd West Ft Worth TX 76116 Office: P O Box 748 Ft Worth TX 76101

FIELDS, WILBERT OSBORNE, JR., state ofcl.; b. nr. Selma, N.C., Sept. 12, 1928; s. Wilbert Osborne and Mary Eliza (Worrell) F.; B.S., U. N.C., 1950, M.Ed., 1957, Ph.D., 1962; m. Jean Mozelle Kirby, Dec. 22, 1951; children—Sara, Frank. Elementary and secondary sch. tchr., Johnston County, N.C., 1953-56; elementary and secondary sch. prin., Bertie County, N.C., 1956-61; exec. sec. N.C. State Sch. Buss. Assn., Chapel Hill, 1961-63; asst. supt. Rocky Mount, N.C., 1963-66, supt. schs., 1966-70; asst. supt. State Dept. Pub. Instruction, Raleigh, 1970—. Mem. N.C. State Adv. Com. Vocational Edn., 19——; mem. Gov.'s Commn. to Study Pub. Schs., 1968. Bd. dirs. Rocky Mount United Fund, Nash Edgecombe Manpower Devel. Commn., Nash County Cancer Soc. Served with AUS, 1950-52. Mem. Am. Assn. Sch. Adminstrs., N.E.A., N.C. Assn. Educators (pres. unit 1959-60, 65-66), So. Assn. Colls. and Schs. (mem. state com. 1967-71), Methodist. N.C. Conf. Bd. Laity, N.C. Conf. Bd. Edn., N.C. Conf. Bd. Coll. Visitors, N.C. Conf. Bd. Commn. on Higher Edn.). Home: 3917 Quail Hollow Dr Raleigh NC 27609 Office: N C Dept Public Instruction Raleigh NC 27602

FIELDS, WILLIAM HENRY, newspaper editor; b. Edison, Ga., Mar. 6, 1915; s. Edward Blount and Lura (Rish) F.; student U. Ala., 1931-35; m. Hazel Cobb, June 19, 1943; children—William Cobb, Nancy Virginia. Sports editor, gen. assignment reporter Dothan (Ala.) Eagle, 1935; various editorial positions Nashville Tennesseean, Savannah (Ga.) Morning News, 1935-47; editorial asst. Atlanta Constitution, 1947, asso. editor, 1947-51, mng. editor, 1951-64; mng. editor Atlanta Jour., 1964-67; exec. editor Atlanta Jour. and Atlanta Constitution, 1968—, v.p., 1970. Served with USMCR, 1941-45. Mem. Marine Corps Res. Officers Assn., Sigma Delta Chi. Clubs: River Bend Gun, Northside Kiwanis, Commerce. Home: 5330 Timber Trail NE Atlanta GA 30342 Office: 72 Marietta St Atlanta GA 30303

FIERST, HERBERT A., lawyer; b. N.Y.C., 1914; A.B. summa cum laude, Harvard, 1935; LL.B., Yale, 1939. Admitted to N.Y. bar, 1939, D.C. bar, 1951, Md. bar, 1961; asso. counsel N.Y. State Commn. Quasi-Jud. Action Adminstrv. Agys., 1940-41; atty. Bd. Econ. Warfare, 1942; legal officer SHAEF, 1944-45; spl. asst. to asst. sec. state occupied areas, 1946-49, to asst. sec. state UN affairs, 1950-55; now practice law, Washington. Mem. Bar Assn. D.C., Am., Fed. bar assns., Yale Law Sch. Assn. Washington (pres. 1965-66), Order Coif, Phi Beta Kappa. Address: Ring Bldg 1200 18th St NW Washington DC 20036*

FIGG, ROBERT MCCORMICK, JR., lawyer; b. Radford, Va., Oct. 22, 1901; s. Robert McCormick and Helen Josephine (Cecil) F.; grad. Porter Mil. Acad., Charleston, S.C., A.B., Coll. of Charleston, 1920, Litt.D., 1970; student law Columbia, 1920-22; LL.D., U. S.C., 1959; m. Sallie Alexander Tobias, May 10, 1927; children—Robert McCormick III, Emily (Mrs. Richard A. Dalla Mura), Jefferson Tobias. Admitted S.C. bar, 1922, since practiced in Charleston; circuit solicitor 9th Jud. Circuit of S.C., 1935-47, spl. circuit judge, 1957; dean Law Sch., U.S.C., 1959-70. Dir. Palmetto State Life Ins. Co., Home Fed. Savs. & Loan Assn. Mem. S.C. Ho. of Reps., 1933-35; mem. S.C. Reorgn. Commn., 1948—, chmn., 1951-55, 71—. Pres., Coll. Charleston Found., 1970—. Fellow Am. Coll. Trial Lawyers; mem. Am., Inter-Am., Charleston County (pres. 1953) bar assns., Am. Law Inst., Am. Judicature Soc., Am. Soc. Internat. Law, S.C. State Bar (pres. 1970-71), Blue Key, Phi Beta Kappa, Phi Delta Phi. Mason (grand master S.C. 1972—). Home: 1522 Deans Lane Columbia SC 29205

FIGUEROA, MIGUEL, JR., physician; b. San Lorenzo, P.R., Nov. 19, 1922; s. Miguel and Maria Luisa (Mangual) F.; B.S., Fordham U., 1943; M.D., N.Y. Med. Coll., 1948; m. Lillian Grossberg, July 26, 1949. Intern, Fordham Hosp., Bronx, N.Y.C., 1948-49; gen. practice medicine, San Juan, P.R., 1949-51; resident anesthesia San Juan City Hosp., 1951-53; practice medicine, specializing in anesthesiology, 1954, Miami, Fla., 1957—; trustee Abbey Hosp. Med. Center and Found., Coral Gables, Fla.; mem. bd. dirs. Palmetto Gen. Hosp., Hialeah, Fla.; clin. prof. anesthesiology U. Miami, 1970—; chief div. anesthesiology Parkway Gen. Hosp., North Miami Beach, Fla., Palmetto Gen. Hosp., Hialeah, Fla. Served to capt. USAF, 1954-56. Mem. Am., So., Fla. med. assns., Am., Fla. (pres. 1969-70, bd. dirs. 1966-71), P.R. (pres. 1953-54) socs. anesthesiologists, Am. Heart Assn. Home: 11111 Biscayne Blvd Miami FL 33161 Office: 2121 Biscayne Blvd Miami FL 33137

FIKE, JOHN WILLIAM, govt. ofcl.; b. Autaugauille, Ala., Jan. 4, 1922; s. Walter and Willie (Fuller) F.; B.S., U. Ala., 1949; postgrad. U. Tenn., U. Ala., U. Mich., Mass. Inst. Tech.; M.S. in Mgmt., Fla. State U., 1972; m. Sara Katherine McKee, Dec. 24, 1943; children—Susan Katherine, Mary Ellen, John W. Communication engr. TVA, Chattanooga, 1949-56; prof. engring. State of Tenn., 1953-56; research engr. Army Rocket and Guided Missiles Agy., Red Stone Arsenal, Ala., 1956-62; prof. engring. State of Ala., 1960-63; engring. mgr. G. C. Marshall Space Flight Center, 1962-63; contract mgr. J. F. Kennedy Space Center, Fla., 1963-68, chief office, 1968—. Served with USNR, 1941-45. Registered profl. engr. Mem. Am. Soc. Engring. Edn., Nat. Soc. Profl. Engrs., V.F.W., Am. Legion. Mason (K.T., Shriner). Contbr. articles to profl. jours. Home: 114 High View Dr Cocoa FL 32922 Office: Kennedy Space Center FL 32899

FIKE, STANLEY REDFIELD, govt. ofcl.; b. Warrensburg, Mo., June 7, 1913; s. Lyman Walter and Bethana (Redfield) F.; student Kansas City Jr. Coll., 1930-31; m. Mildred Curry, July 10, 1935; children— Margaret (Mrs. Anthony Gray), Bethana (Mrs. John Cartland, Jr.), Joann Dorace. Gen. mgr., editor Inter-City Press, Inc., Fairmount-Independence, Mo., 1930-53; v.p. Jackson County Times, Inc., Grandview, Mo., 1952-53; pres. Lee's Summit (Mo.) Jour., 1949-65; administrv. asst. to senator Stuart Symington, 1953—. Founder, 1st pres. Jackson County Community Chest, Independence, Mo.; organizer Jackson County YMCA, Del., Democratic Nat. Conv., 1952; exec. dir. Symington for Pres., 1960. Bd. dirs. Kansas City Area council Boy Scouts Am. Mem. Mo. (pres. 1949), N.W. Mo. (pres. 1944) press assns., U. Mo. Sch. Journalism Alumni Assn. (hon.), Mo. Acad. Squires, Sigma Delta Chi. Mem. Reorganized Ch. of Jesus Christ of Latter-Day Saints. Kiwanian (past lt. gov. Mo.-Kan.-Ark. dist). Club: Kansas City Press. Home: 511 Boston Av Takoma Park MD 20012 Office: Senate Office Bldg Washington DC 20510

FIMMEL, GUSTAV ADOLF, III, civil engr.; b. Milltown, N.J., Oct. 3, 1922; s. Gustav A. and Olga (Harmel) F.; B.S. in Civil Engring., Newark Coll. Engring., 1943; B.S., Pelman Inst., 1940; m. Bonny I.C.

Bitthien, Apr. 18, 1942; 1 son, Jon Ernest. Various engring. positions Bethlehem Steel Co., Elizabethport, N.J., Yara Engring. Co., Elizabeth, N.J., A.P. & R.K. Michaels, Orlando, Fla., George M. Brewster & Son, Inc., Bogota, N.J., Berger Assos., Harrisburg, Pa., 1943-54; self-employed in engring. and surveying, Orlando, Fla., 1954-57; sr. engr. Reynolds, Smith & Hills, Jacksonville, 1957-58; engr.-programmer Martin Co., Orlando, 1958; field engr. R.F. Ball Constrn. Co., Pinecastle, Fla., 1959; city engr. City of Melbourne (Fla.), 1960-61, City of Cocoa (Fla), 1961-63; pres. The Cape Seminole Co., Inc., Forest City (Orlando) Fla., 1963—. Mem. Fla. Engring. Soc. (sr. life), Fla. Sheriffs Assn. (hon.), Nat. Soc. Profl. Engrs. (life), Forest City Community Assn. (life), Tau Beta Pi (life). Home: Route 2 Box 712 Maitland FL 32751

FINCH, CHARLES CLIFTON, lawyer; b. nr. Pope, Miss., Apr. 4, 1927; s. Carl B. and Christine (McMinn) F.; pub. adminstrn. degree U. Miss., 1956, LL.B., 1958; m. Zelma Lois Smith, Nov. 20, 1952; children— Janet, Anne, Charles Clifton II, Stephen Nicholas. Admitted to Miss. bar, 1958, since practiced in Batesville; mem. Miss. Ho. Reps., 1959-64; dist. atty. 17th Circuit Ct. dist., 1964-72. Served with AUS, 1945-47. Mem. Batesville, C. of C., Vets. Fgn. Wars, Am. Legion, Farm Bur. Baptist. Mason (Shriner). Clubs: Lions (pres.), Civitan. Home: westmoreland Heights Batesville MS 38606 Office: Finch Bldg Batesville MS 38606

FINCH, EDWIN PERKINS, tobacco co. exec.; b. Henderson, N.C., May 9, 1910; s. Edwin G. and Ida (Fox) F.; A.B. in Bus. Adminstrn., Duke, 1932; m. Lucy Marshall Goode, Feb. 3, 1940; 1 dau. Anne Marshall. With Brown & Williamson Tobacco Corp., Louisville, 1932—, dir., 1953—, v.p., 1956-62, exec. v.p., 1962-64, pres., 1964—; dir. Export Leaf Tobacco Co., Richmond, Va.; dir. First Nat. Bank Louisville; mem. Ky-Tenn. adv. bd. Liberty Mut. Ins. Co., 1964—. Mem. Louisville Fund, 1963—; mem. Pres.'s Civic Council Bellarmine Coll., Louisville, 1964—. Bd. overseers U. Louisville. Mem. Louisville C. of C. Tobacco Inst. (dir.), Council for Tobacco Research (Dir.). Episcopalian. Clubs: Louisville Country, Pendennis (Louisville). Home: 4010 Napanee Rd Louisville KY 40207 Office: 1600 W Hill St Louisville KY 40201

FINCH, HUGH EDSEL, state legislator, ins. exec.; b. Spartanburg, S.C., June 21, 1928; s. Robert Lewis and Rosalee (Watt) F.; A.B., Wofford Coll., 1952 div.; children—Deborah Elaine, Susan Denise. Newspaper reporter Spartanburg (S.C.) Herald Jour., 1952-54; tchr. Pacolet (S.C.) Hgh Sch., 1955-56; operator, owner Hugh E. Finch Agy., ins. and real estate, Spartanburg, 1958. Mem. S.C. Ho. of Reps., 1956-66, 69—. County chmn. March of Dimes, 1968. Mem. Nat., S.C., Spartanburg County ins. assns. Methodist. Mason (Shriner), Lion. Club: Ruritan (past pres.). Home: 1265 Asheville Hwy Spartanburg SC 29303 Office: Asheville Hwy Spartanburg SC 29303

FINCH, JAMES MITCHELL, JR., banker; b. Maysville, Ky., Sept. 14, 1909; s. James Mitchell and Carrie (Smith) F.; grad. mil. sch.; m. Mary Jane Kehoe, Feb. 15, 1939; children—Barbara, James Anderson. Vice pres. Standard Tobacco Co., Inc., Maysville, Ky., 1932—, Key Broadcasting Co., Marathon, Fla., 1958—, Ky., O. Cable Vision Co., Maysville, Ky., 1964—; pres. Bank Maysville, 1958—; chmn. bd. Home Tobacco Warehouse Co., Maysville, 1959—; pres. Finch Oil Co.; v.p. Cable Vision Ohio; dir. Mason County Bldg. and Loan, Maysville. Bd. dirs. Boys' Club Am., Maysville. Bd. dirs. Hayswood Hosp., Maysville. Served to maj. AUS, 1942-45. Mem. Maysville (pres. 1967-70), Ky. (dir.) chambers commerce, Army Ordnance Assn. Clubs: Maysville Country; Hidden Valley (Gaylord, Mich.). Home: The Point Maysville KY 41056 Office: 20 W 2d St Maysville KY 41056

FINCH, JERALD ALLEN, newspaper editor; b. Huntington, W.Va., June 17, 1927; s. Plynn Jerald and Annabelle Virginia (Allen) F.; A.B. with high distinction, U. Ky., 1950; m. Nancy Tynes St. Clair, Nov. 30, 1963; children—Jerald Kelly, Laura Plynn, Allen St. Clair, Thomas Tynes. Reporter, sports writer, makeup editor Lexington (Ky.) Leader, 1948-55; with Richmond (Va.) News Leader, 1955—, successively copy editor, asst. city editor, asso. city editor, now city editor. Served with USAAF, 1944-46. Home: 923 Cowan Rd Bon Air VA 23235 Office: 333 E Grace St Richmond VA 23219

FINCH, JOHN IGNATIUS, oil co. exec.; b. New Orleans, Jan. 1, 1928; s. John C. and Nancy B. (Bertucci) F.; B.S., Rice U., 1950; postgrad. U. Houston, 1954-56; m. Patsy Sengel, Feb. 27, 1954; children— Kevin, Jayne Ann, Allan, Julie. Sect. head controllers dept. Humble Pipe Line Co., 1952-64; asso. earnings coordinator Humble Oil & Refining Co., 1964-66; controller, treas. Carter Oil Co., Houston, 1966—. Mem. BIPAC, 1968-71. C.P.A., Tex. Mem. Am., Tex., Houston socs. C.P.A.'s. Club: Civic (Houston). Home: 606 Bendwood Dr Houston TX 77024 Office: PO Box 2180 Houston TX 77002

FINCH, ROBERT HUTCHISON, govt. ofcl.; b. Tempe, Ariz., Oct. 9, 1925; s. Robert L. and Gladys (Hutchison) F.; B.A. in Polit. Sci., Occidental Coll., 1947; J.D., U. So. Cal., 1951; m. Carol Crothers, Feb. 14, 1946; children—Maureen, Kevin, Priscilla, Cathleen. Admitted to Cal. bar, 1951, since practiced in Los Angeles; partner firm Finch, Bell, Duitsman & Margulis, and predecessor, 1951-68; lt. gov. State Cal., 1967-69; sec. U.S. Dept. Health Edn. and Welfare, 1969-70; counsellor to Pres. U.S., mem. Pres.'s cabinet, 1970—; mem. domestic council, cabinet com. on edn. Organizer, 1st pres. Palos Verdes Savs. & Loan Assn., 1956-58; chmn. bd. Marina Fed. Savs. & Loan Assn., 1958-59; organizer, counsel Guaranty Bank, Torrance, Cal., 1961. Chmn. Pres.'s Council Aging, 1969-70, Fed. Radiation Council, 1969-70, Pres.'s Com. Retardation, 1969-70; mem. Air Quality Adv. Bd., 1969-70, Econ. Opportunity Council, 1969-70, Com. Status Women, 1969-70; mem. adv. com. on intergovtl. relations Richard Nixon Found. Exec. sec. U.S. Congressman Poulson, 1947-48; vice chmn. Los Angeles County Central Republican Com., 1954-56; del. Rep. Nat. Conv., 1948, 56; Rep. nominee for U.S. Congress, 1952-54; chmn. Los Angeles County Rep. Central Com., 1956-58; trustee Rep. Assos., 1958-66; adminstrv. asst. to Vice Pres. Nixon, 1958-60; campaign dir. for Nixon Presdl. Campaign, 1960; adviser for Nixon Presdl. campaign, 1968; chmn. Senatorial Campaign of George Murphy, 1964; chmn. exec. com. Rep. Assos., 1964-65. Trustee Occidental Coll., 1965-68, Cal. State Coll., 1967-68; regent U. Cal., 1967-68; trustee John F. Kennedy Center Performing Arts, 1969-70; adv. com. Coro Found., 1961-68; adv. bd. Marymount Coll., 1960-63; bd. dirs. Centinela Valley YMCA, 1954-58; trustee, counsel Palos Verdes Coll., 1953-56; mem. Los Angeles County Com. Long Term Bldg. Needs, 1953-54. Mem. Legion Lex, Kappa Sigma, Phi Alpha Delta. Clubs: California, Los Angeles Athletic, Town Hall (Los Angeles); Commonwealth of Cal. Office: The White House Washington DC 20500

FINCH, ROBERT MACON, physician; b. Little Rock, Dec. 19, 1933; s. Joe E. and Beulah Ann (Jernigan) F.; student E. Tex. State Tchrs. Coll., 1951-52, Ouachita Bapt. Coll., 1952-54, Hendrix Coll., 1958-60; B.S., U. Ark., M.D., 1964; m. Myra Sue Beasley, Aug. 27, 1961; 1dau., Laura Lee. Intern, Ark. Bapt. Hosp., Little Rock, 1964-65; gen. practice medicine, Forrest City, Ark., 1965-66, Caraway, Ark., 1966-67, Paragould, Ark., 1967—; mem. staff Community Meth. Hosp. Bd. dirs. Crowleys Ridge council Girl Scouts Am. Served with USAF, 1954-58. Mem. Ark., Greene-Clay County med. socs. Home: Finch Rd Paragould AR 72450 Office: 1001 Kingshighway Paragould AR 72450

FINCH, THOMAS AUSTIN, JR., furniture mfg. co. exec.; b. Thomasville, N.C., Aug. 12, 1922; s. Thomas Austin and Ernestine (Lambeth) F.; grad. Woodberry Forest Sch., 1940; B.S. in Engring., Princeton, 1943; m. Meredith Clark Slane, June 4, 1949; children—Thomas Austin III, John Lambeth, David Slane, Sumner Slane, Meredith Kempton. With Thomasville Furniture Industries, Inc., 1946—, pres., 1961—; sr. v.p. parent co. Armstrong Cork Co., 1968—; dir. Wachovia Bank and Trust Co., Carolina and Northwestern R.R., Integon Corp. Trustee Duke, 1963—, Woodberry Forest Sch., 1967—, Community Gen. Hosp., Thomasville, 1964-71. Served to lt. (j.g.) USNR, World War II. Named Furniture Man of Year, Am. Furniture Mart Corp., 1963. Mem. Phi Beta Kappa. Methodist (past chmn. ofcl. bd.). Rotarian (pres. Thomasville 1958). Home: Pine Needle Lane Thomasville NC 27360 Office: 401 E Main St Thomasville NC 27360

FINCHER, CHARLIE ERNEST, JR., govt. ofcl.; b. Arlington, Ga., Nov. 16, 1917; s. Charlie Ernest and Clyde (Jordan) F.; B.C.S., Columbus U., 1944; m. Liliana Palma, Apr. 4, 1966; children—Romina Liliana, Deborah Charlene, Anastasia Josephine. Cost accountant U.S. Mint, 1945-51; systems accountant U.S. Gen. Accounting Office, Washington, 1951-56; dep. comptroller U.S. Govt. Printing Office, Washington, 1956-58; chief finance div. U.S. Bur. Pub. Rds., Washington, 1958-63; finance officer UN FAO, Rome, Italy, 1963-67; self employed C.P.A., Savannah, 1967-69; chief, prodn. planning div. Bur. Mint, Washington, 1969—. Served with USMCR, 1942-45. Named lt. col., aide-de-camp gov. Ga. C.P.A., Ga. Mem. Am. Inst. C.P.A.'s, Ga. Soc. C.P.A.'s, Fed. Govt. Accountants Assn. Mason (Shriner). Home: 8315 Garfield Ct Springfield VA 22152 Office: US Treasury Dept Bur Mint Washington DC 20220

FINCHER, DICK, automobile dealer, state senator; b. Rochester, N.Y., Sept. 27, 1927; s. Harry West and Lucille C. (Schmitz) F.; B.A., Cornell U., 1949; m. Gloria De Haven, Jan. 19, 1957; children—Harry West, Faith Frances. Pres., Fincher Motors, Inc., 1952—; mem. Fla. Ho. of Reps., 1963-65, Fla. Senate, 1967—. Mem. Orange Bowl Com.; mem. brain trust com. Hire the Handicapped; mem. citizens bd. U. Miami; chmn. Heart Assn. Greater Miami. Del., Democratic Nat. Conv., 1968. Served to 2d lt. AUS, 1953-54. Mem. Miami Automobile Dealers Assn. (past pres.), Phi Delta Theta. Democrat. Roman Catholic. Clubs: Indian Creek Country, La Gorce Country. Home: 1800 W 24th St Sunset Island 3 Miami Beach FL 33140 Office: 1740 NE 2D Av Miami FL 33132*

FINCHER, DORSEY RAY, cons. engr.; b. Rosston, Ark., July 1, 1927; s. Earl and Helen Gould (Murry) F.; B.S., Tex. A. and M. U., 1948; m. Bette Corinne Pyland, Nov. 29, 1946; children—Stephen Ruell, David Bruce. Engr. Getty Oil Co., 1948-70; cons. engr., mfr. splty. instruments and devices Fincher Engring. Co., Houston, 1970—. Registered profl. engr., Tex. Mem. Nat. Assn. Corrosion Engrs. (dir.), Am. Petroleum Inst., Nat. Gas Processors Assn., Am. Inst. Mining, Metall. and Petroleum Engrs., Am. Inst. Chem. Engrs. Mason. Contbr. articles to tech. jours. Patentee in field. Home: 13306 Havershire Houston TX 77024 Office: 6839 Mayard St Houston TX 77040

FINCHER, GEORGE TRUMAN, zoologist; b. Arlington, Ga., Sept. 28, 1939; s. George Thomas and Vera Ethel (Tindol) F.; student Abraham Baldwin Agrl. Coll., 1957-59; B.S., U. Ga., 1961, M.S., 1966, Ph.D., 1968; m. Brooksy Ann McCain, Mar. 2, 1963; children—George David, Stephen Clay. Research zoologist vet. scis. research div. Agrl. Research Service, U.S. Dept. Agr., Animal Parasite Research Lab., Tifton, Ga., 1968—. Active Cub Scouts Am. Bd. dirs. Tift County Tng. Center for Mentally Retarded. Mem. Am. Soc. Parasitologists, Am. Entomol. Soc., Helminthological Soc. Washington, Southeastern Soc. Parasitologists, Wildlife Disease Assn., Ga. Acad. Sci., Ga. Entomol. Soc., Coleopterists Soc., Am. Mus. Natural History, Sigma Xi, Alpha Zeta, Phi Sigma. Contbr. articles to profl. pubs. Home: 511 E 18th St Tifton GA 31794 Office: Coastal Plain Experiment Station Tifton GA 31794

FINCHER, HANDLEY HERMAN, furniture mfg. co. exec.; b. Roanoke, Ala., Feb. 17, 1935; s. Dewey Olin and Lauzie Lucille (Johnson) F.; student Huntingdon Coll., 1954-59; B.S., Auburn U., 1961; m. Betty Glenda Nelson, Dec. 24, 1954; children—Ginger Maria, Leslie Lucille. With Drexel Enterprises (N.C.), 1961—, dir. research and devel., 1968—. Mem. adv. bd. Western Piedmont Coll., 1971-72. Served with USAF, 1954-58. Mem. Soc. Plastic Engrs., So. Furniture Mfrs. Assn., Xi Sigma Pi, Alpha Zeta. Lion. Home: 104 Hawthorne Lane Morganton NC 28655 Office: Drexel Enterprises Drexel NC 28619

FINCHER, JOHN ALBERT, coll. pres.; b. Union, S.C., Sept. 8, 1911; s. Robert C. and Addie (Murphy) F.; B.S., U. S.C., 1933, M.S., 1935; Ph.D., U. N.C., 1939; postgrad. U. Minn., 1952; m. Ruby C. Broom, Aug. 19, 1939; children—Judith Ellen (Mrs. William E. Neill), Janice Manette, John Albert. Prin., Pineview Sch., 1933-34; instr. U. S.C. 1934-35; Grad. asst. U. N.C., 1935-39; instr. biology Cumberland Coll., 1939-40; asst., asso. prof. Millsaps Coll., 1940-46; prof., head dept. Samford U., Birmingham, Ala., 1946-57, asst. to pres., 1955-57, dean, 1957-68; pres. Carson-Newman Coll., Jefferson City, Tenn., 1968—. Chmn. edn. commn. So. Bapt. Conv., 1962-66. Trustee Gorgas Scholarship Found., 1958-68; pres. Mid. Appalachia Coll. Council, Inc., 1969—; chmn. Tenn. Council Pvt. Colls., 1971—; bd. East End Meml. Hosp., 1957-68, v.p. bd., 1966-68; bd. dirs. Douglas Cherokee Econ. Authority, 1970—. Fellow A.A.A.S.; mem. Assn. Ala. Coll. Administrs. (pres. 1959-60), Am. Assn. Higher Edn., Ala. Acad. Sci. (pres. 1952-53), Am. Soc. Zoology, Assn. Southeastern Biologists, Tenn. Edn. Assn., Am. Assn. Sch. Administrs., Jefferson City C. of C. (pres. 1972), Phi Beta Kappa, Sigma Xi, Alpha Epsilon Delta (nat. councilor 1954-60, nat. v.p. 1960-62), Omicron Delta Kappa (province dep. 1968), Pi Kappa Alpha, Beta Beta Beta, Phi Sigma Tau, Blue Key. Democrat. Bapt. Rotarian. Contbr. sci. articles jours. Home: Route 1 Laurel Hills Jefferson City TN 37760 Office: Carson Newman Coll Jefferson City TN 37760

FINCO, DELMAR ROY, educator; b. Roundup, Mont., Nov. 5, 1936; s. Albin and Mary Cecelia (Kuzara) F.; B.S., U. Minn., 1957, D.V.M., 1959, Ph.D., 1966; m. Clarissa Irene Fowler, June 10, 1959; children— Deborah, Paul, Timothy, Brian. Pvt. practice vet. medicine, Chgo., 1959-61; research fellow U. Minn., St. Paul, 1961-66, asst. prof., 1966-70; prof. U. Ga., Athens, 1970—. Recipient NIH research grant, 1969—. Mem. Am. Vet. Med. Assn., Am. Animal Hosp. Assn., Am. Assn. Vet. Clinicians, Conf. Research Workers in Animal Diseases, Phi Zeta, Gamma Sigma Delta. Home: 285 Kings Rd Athens GA 30601

FINDLAY, ALEXANDER CARSTAIRS, statistician; b. Chgo., Sept. 27, 1900; s. Alexander and Mary (Carstairs) F.; B.S., U. Chgo., 1921, student, 1941; m. Jeannette Manning Child, May 18, 1929; children—Emily (Mrs. Emily Brown), Andrew M., Mary L. With constrn. cos., Chgo. 1929-34; asst. dir Flint (Mich.) Community Fund, 1935-41; economist U.S. Bur. Labor Statistics, Washington, 1941-53, Pub. Housing Adminstrn., Washington, 1953-57; chief facilities and equipment br., housing div. U.S. Bur. Census, Washington, 1957—. Mem. Am. Econ. Assn., Am. Statis. Assn. Unitarian. Patentee in field of locks. Home: 3010 26th St NE Washington DC 20018 Office: Census Washington DC 20233

FINDLAY, ROBERT CLYDE, real estate exec.; b. Springfield, Mo., Aug. 17, 1920; s. Clyde P. and Lettie Mae (St. Clair) F.; B.S. magna cum laude, Abilene Christian Coll., 1943; M.B.A., Harvard Bus. Sch., 1947; m. Opal Callie Carlton, Feb. 12, 1943; children—Steven, Bruce, Elaine. Pres., Brazosport Savs. & Loan Assn., Freeport, Tex., 1953-65; owner Findlay Enterprises, Arlington, Tex., 1965—. Bd. dirs. A.R.C. Served to 1st lt. AUS, World War II. Named Brazosport Outstanding Citizen of Year, Brazosport C. of C., 1958; Arlington Realtor of Year, 1971. Mem. Arlington C. of C. (treas.), Urban Land Inst., Nat. Assn. Homebuilders (land use task force), Builders Assn. Ft. Worth (past pres.). Home: 1600 Royal Mile Dr Arlington TX 76015 Office: 1405 W Mayfield Rd Arlington TX 76015

FINE, J(AMES) ALLEN, ins. co. exec.; b. Albemarie, N.C., May 2, 1934; s. Samuel Lee and Ocie (Loflin) F.; student Pfeiffer Coll., 1957-58; B.S., U. N.C., 1961, M.B.A., 1965; m. Marie Nan Morris, Sept. 1, 1957; children—James A(llen), William Morris. Sr. accountant Haskins & Sells, C.P.A.'s Charlotte, N.C., 1961-62, Watson, Penry, & Morgan, Asheboro, N.C., 1962-64; instr. U. N.C., Chapel Hill, 1964-65; asst. prof. Pfeiffer Coll., Misenheimer, N.C., 1965-66; treas., v.p. adminstrn. Nat. Lab. for Higher Edn. (formerly Regional Edn. Lab. Carolinas and Va.), Durham, N.C., 1966-72; organizer, pres., treas., dir. Investors Title Ins. Co., Inc., Chapel Hill, 1972—. Lectr. accounting U. N.C., Chapel Hill, 1967-70. Area officer ann. alumni giving U. N.C., Chapel Hill, 1968-69, 71, 72. Served with USN, 1953-57. Recipient Haskins & Sells Found. award for excellence in accounting, 1961; N.C. Assn. CPAs award for most outstanding accounting student U. N.C., 1961. Mem. Am. Inst. C.P.A.'s, N.C. Assn. C.P.A.'s, Am. Accounting Assn., CEDAR Bus. Mgrs. (chmn. nat. exec. com. 1971), Phi Beta Kappa, Beta Gamma Sigma (treas. 1961). Home: Route 1 Chapel Hill NC 27514 Office: University Sq Chapel Hill NC 27514

FINGAR, WALTER WIGGS, educator; b. Nashville, Jan. 14, 1934; s. Julian Russell and Murphy (Vaden) F.; student Middle Tenn. State U., 1952-54; D.D.S., U. Tenn., 1957; M.S., U. Ia., 1965; m. Mildred Annette Heinz, July 15, 1955; children—Mildred Elizabeth, Linda Elaine, Walter Brian, William Russell, Amy Jo, Rachel Lynn. Practice dentistry, Nashville, 1959-63; USPHS fellow, instr., asst. prof. U. Ia., Iowa City, 1963-67; asst. prof. U. Tenn., Memphis, 1967-68; asso. prof. operative dentistry Med. S.C., Charleston, 1968—, chmn. dept. operative dentistry-endodontics, 1971—; mem. staff Med. U. S.C. Hosp. Served to capt. Dental Corps, AUS, 1957-59. Mem. Am., Tenn., Memphis dental assns., Am. Assn. U. Profs. Am. Assn. Dental Schs., Am. Coll. Prosthodontists (asso.), Am. Acad. Operative Dentistry, Am. Acad. Gen. Dentistry. Home: 766 Norfolk Dr Charleston SC 29401

FINGER, HOMER ELLIS, JR., bishop; b. Ripley, Miss., Oct. 8, 1916; s. Homer Ellis and Bertha (Rogers) F.; A.B., Millsaps Coll., Jackson, Miss., 1937; student Emory U., Atlanta, 1938-39; B.D., Yale, 1941; student Union Theol. Sem., N.Y.C., 1946; D.D. (hon.), Centenary Coll. La., 1954; m. Mamie Lee Ratliff, Oct. 6, 1942; children—Homer Ellis, William Ratliff, Elizabeth Ellen. Math. tchr. Aberdeen (Miss.) high sch., 1937-38; ordained to ministry Methodist Ch., 1941; pastor, Coldwater, Miss., 1941-43, Oxford, Miss., 1946-52; pres. Millsaps Coll., 1952-64; resident bishop Meth. Ch., Nashville, 1964—. Mem. commn. on colls., exec. council So. Assn. Colls. and Secondary Schs.; mem. univ. senate Meth. Ch.; mem. Southeastern Jurisdictional Council, 1956—; chmn. United Meth. Commn. on Chaplains and Related Ministries, 1968-72; mem. exec. com. World Meth. Council, mem. bd. Christian social concerns. Served as chaplain USNR, Air Sta., Pensacola, Fla., 1944-45, with 75th constrn. bn., P.I., 1945-46. Mem. Jackson C. of C. (dir.), Pi Kappa Alpha, Omicron Delta Kappa, Eta Sigma Phi (past nat. pres.). Rotarian (dir. Jackson). Home: 301 Hillwood Dr Nashville TN 37205 Office: 95 White Bridge Rd Nashville TN 37205

FINK, DONALD ALFRED, economist; b. Hammond, Ind., Jan. 16, 1930; s. Lee Edward and Jane (Dye) F.; B.A., Yale, 1952, M.A., 1955; postgrad. Am. U., 1963-65; m. Beatrice C. Freeman, June 11, 1955; children— Alan Lee, Marc Louis. Research asso. Carnegie Inst. Tech., 1959-62; cons. Govt. of Columbia, 1962-63; sr. economist Pan Am. Union, Washington, 1963—, chief Andean countries, 1965-67, chief Caribbean countries, 1967-68; economist Nat. Assn. Wool Mfrs., 1968-71; sec., treas. McLean Products Internat., Inc., 1971—, also dir.; dep. mng. dir. Skoko Ltd., 1971—, also dir.; dir. UNCO, Inc. Econ. cons. Latin Am. Iron and Steel Inst., Latin Am. Free Trade Assn. Bd. dirs. Springfield Boys Club. Served with USN, 1955-59; now comdr. Supply Corps Res. Mem. Am. Econ. Assn., Royal Econ. Soc. Eng., Am. Finance Assn. Home: 6111 Madawaska Rd Bethesda MD 20016 Office: Suite 838 815 15th St NW Washington DC 20005

FINK, ELI HARRY, lawyer; b. Jacksonville, Fla., June 18, 1909; s. Harry and Sophie (Starr) Finkelstein; A.B., Washington and Lee U., 1932, LL.B., J.D., 1935; m. Emily Morgenstern, Feb. 14, 1946; children—Elizabeth Sue, Eli Harry, Edward Lawrence. Admitted to Fla. bar, 1935; practiced in Jacksonville, 1935—; asst. city atty., 1937-42; city solicitor, 1946; counsel Sears, Dunlap & Sears, 1969—. Dir. So. Indsl. Bank, Jacksonville. Past pres., bd. dirs., mem. exec. com. St. Lukes Hosp.; past pres., bd. dirs. Jacksonville Civic Music Assn.; bd. regents Fla. Bd. Control, 1949-53. Served to lt. comdr. USNR, World War II. Mem. Am., Fla., Jacksonville bar assns., Omicron Delta Kappa, Zeta Beta Tau. Jewish religion. Clubs: River, University (Jacksonville). Home: 1205 Jean Ct Jacksonville FL 32207 Office: Am Heritage Life Bldg Jacksonville FL 32202

FINK, JOHN BERNARD, newspaper advt. exec.; b. N.Y.C., Apr. 6, 1935; s. Edward Bernard and Kathryn (Long) F.; student pub. schs.; m. Cheryl Dorothy Hurst, Mar. 28, 1969; 1 son, Glen Patrick. Police officer, Hallandale, Fla., 1961-66; classified salesman Miami Herald, 1966-69, classified office mgr., 1969-70; classified advt. mgr. Tallahassee (Fla.) Democrat, 1970—. Disaster chmn. Leon County A.R.C., 1970-71. Served with USMC, 1953-57. Mem. Tallahassee Advt. Fedn. (pres. 1971), Tallahassee Auto dealers Assn., Tallahassee Builders Assn., Tallahassee Realtors Assn., Tallahassee C. of C. (mem. pres.'s council 1970-71). Mem. Fraternal Order Police. Home: 2030 Wahalaw Nene Tallahassee FL 32302 Office: 277 N Magnolia Dr Tallahassee FL 32302

FINKELSTEIN, MORRIS B., judge; b. New Haven, Mar. 7, 1897; s. Henry and Lena (Fogelson) F.; LL.B., Chattanooga Coll. Law, 1920; m. Rose Baras, June 6, 1922; children—Marvin, Farol Faye (Mrs. Martin B. Seretean). Admitted to Tenn. bar, 1920; practiced in Chattanooga, 1920-55; judge Tenn. Chancery Ct., Chattanooga, 1955—. Nat. dir. Joint Distbn. Com., 1954—. Bd. dirs. Little Theatre, Chattanooga, B'nai Zion Trust Fund. Served with USN, 1918-19. Recipient awards, citations for patriotic service; named Man of Year Am. Legion, 1954, S.A.R., 1958. Mem. Bar Assn. Tenn., Tenn. Jud. Conf. (sec.-treas. 1957-58, 1965-66), Am., Chattanooga (sec.-treas. 1952-53) bar assns., Judicature Soc., Chattanooga Jewish Welfare Fedn. (dir.), Am. Jewish Com. Jewish religion. Elk. Home: 1238 Duane Rd Chattanooga TN 37405 Office: Courthouse Chattanooga TN 37402

FINKNER, ALVA LEROY, research co. exec.; b. Akron, Colo., May 8, 1917; s. A. Ed G. and Iona A. (Roszell) F.; B.S., Colo. State U., 1938; M.S., Kan. State U., 1940; Ph.D., N.C. State U., 1950; m. Betty Jane Rabeler, Feb. 17, 1946; children—Patricia (Mrs. Rodney Boyette), Stephen Glen, Judith Lynn. With statis. reporting service U.S. Dept. Agr., Raleigh, N.C., 1940-50, agrl. statistician, head Raleigh research office, 1946; asso. prof. N.C. State U., Raleigh, 1950-55, prof., 1955-60, adj. prof., 1960—; with Research Triangle Inst., Research Triangle Park, N.C., 1960—, sr. statistician, dir. statistics research div., 1964-71, v.p. for social scis. and human resources, 1971—. Served to maj. AUS, 1942-46. Decorated Bronze Star. Fellow Am. Statis. Assn.; mem. Inter-Am. Statis. Inst. (asso.), Am. Farm Econs. Assn., (mem. joint com. agrl. statistics with Am. Statis. Assn.), Sigma Xi, Phi Kappa Phi, Gamma Sigma Delta, Alpha Zeta. Author: (with Robert Monroe) Principles of Test Design, 1955; (with John Monroe) Handbook of Area Sampling, 1959. Home: 3909 Arrow Dr Raleigh NC 27612 Office: PO Box 12194 Research Triangle Park NC 27709

FINLEY, ROBERT VAN EATON, missionary exec.; b. Charlottesville, Va., May 2, 1922; s. William Walter and Melissa (Hoover) F.; B.A., U. Va., 1944; postgrad. U. Chgo. Div. Sch., 1946-47; Litt.D. (hon.), Houghton Coll., 1952; m. Ethel Drummond, Dec. 23, 1949; children— Deborah Ann, Ruth Ellen. Evangelist, Youth for Christ Internat., Chgo. and Inter-Varsity Christian Fellowship, Chgo., 1945-46, overseas, 1948-51; pastor Temple Bapt. Ch., Washington, 1965-66; founder, pres. Internat. Students, Inc., Washington, 1952-67, chmn., 1968-70; founder, gen. dir. Christian Aid Mission, Washington, 1953-70, pres., 1970—; founder, gen. dir. Overseas Students Mission, Toronto, Ont., Can., 1954-68, pres., 1969—; ordained to ministry Bapt. Ch., 1957. Bd. dirs. Sino-American Cultural Soc., Washington. Mem. Omicron Delta Kappa. Republican. Home: 4518 Western Av Washington DC 20016 Office: 5028 Wisconsin Av Washington DC 20037

FINLEY, WILLIAM WALTER, JR., civil engr.; b. nr. Charlottesville, Va., Jan. 24, 1928; s. William Walter and Milissa (Hoover) F.; B.S., Va. Poly. Inst., 1953, M.S., 1968; m. Mae Elliott, Aug. 7, 1953; children—John Weldon, Walter Gordon, Martha Sharon, James Edward. Civil engr. TVA, Knoxville, Tenn., 1953-55; structural engr. Burns & Roe, Inc., N.Y.C., 1955-59; sr. civil engr., chief div. of waste treatment City of Richmond, Va., 1959-63; partner Blue & Finley, cons. engrs., Charlottesville, 1965-66; san. engr., chief planning and reports Chesapeake Bay-Susquehanna River Basins project Fed. Water Pollution Control Adminstrn., 1966-70; project mgr. WHO Master Plans Waste Disposal and Drainage, UNDP Spl. Fund Project Ibadan, Nigeria, 1970—; instr. civil engring. Va. Poly. Inst., 1964-65; lectr. civil engring. U. Va., 1965-66. Served to 1st lt. AUS, 1946-47. Registered profl. engr. Diplomate Am. Acad. Environmental Engrs. Mem. Water Pollution Control Fedn., Va. Soc. Profl. Engrs. Baptist (deacon). Address: Free Union VA also PMB 5036 Ibadan Nigeria

FINN, BERNARD S., chmn. sci. and tech. Nat. Mus. History and Tech., Washington. Home: 6819 Connecticut Av Chevy Chase MD 20015 Office: Nat Museum History and Technology Constitution Av at 12th St Washington DC 20560*

FINNEGAN, FREDERICK JOHN, dentist; b. N.Y.C., June 5, 1921; s. Frederick Leo and Julie Isabelle (Cahill) F.; student Columbia, 1944-45, Cornell U., 1943-44; D.D.S., N.Y.U., 1950; m. Doris Jeanette Wells, May 26, 1956, 1 son, Jeffrey. Commd. lt. (j.g.) USN, 1950, advanced through grades to capt., 1958; head prosthodontics dept. Naval Dental Clinic, Norfolk, Va., 1970—. Decorated Silver Star. Diplomate Am. Bd. Prosthodontics. Mem. Am. Dental Assn., Am. Prosthodontics Soc., Southeastern Acad. Prosthodontics, Am. Coll. Prosthodontists. Roman Catholic. Home: 3212 Sunnybrook Lane Virginia Beach VA 23452 Office: Naval Dental Clinic Norfolk VA 23511

FINNEGAN, MARCUS BARTLETT, patent lawyer; b. Morristown, N.J., Sept. 15, 1927; s. George Bernard and Elisabeth (Morgan) F.; B.S., U.S. Mil. Acad., 1949; LL.B., U. Va., 1955; LL.M., George Washington U., 1957; m. Betsy Neil Hammer, June 3, 1950; children—Nancy Lee, Susan Bartlett, Katharine Elisabeth. Admitted to Va., D.C. bars, 1955, U.S. Supreme Ct., N.Y. bars, 1960; U.S. patent adviser to Japan, Tokyo, 1957-59; atty. firm Morgan, Finnegan, Durham & Pine, N.Y.C., 1959-63, Irons, Birch, Swindler, & McKie, Washington, 1963-65; sr. partner Finnegan, Henderson Farabow & Garrett, Washington, 1965—. Professorial lectr. law George Washington U., 1971—; lectr. various profl. groups; invited expert tech. licensing, group meeting experts UNIDO, Vienna, Austria, 1972. Served to capt. U.S. Army, 1949-59. Mem. Raven Soc., Bar Assn. D.C., Am., Fed., Va., Interam. bar assns., Am., N.Y., N.J. patent law assns., U.S. C. of C. (antitrust and trade regulation com.), N.Y. County Lawyers Assn., Assn. Bar City of N.Y., Am. Soc. Metals, U. Va. Law Sch. Found., Inst. Mil. Law, Internat. Legal Soc. Japan, Va. State Bar, Am. Judicature Soc., Assn. Grads. U.S. Mil. Acad., West Point Soc. D.C., Army Athletic Assn., Licensing Execs. Soc. (v.p. Eastern region 1971-72, pres.-elect 1972—), Am. Mgmt. Assn., Internat. Patent and Trademark Assn., World Peace Through Law Center, Patent and Trademark Inst. Can., Phi Delta Phi, Omicron Delta Kappa, Order of Coif. Episcopalian. Clubs: Touchdown (Washington); Army and Navy, Nat. Lawyers, International, George Washington University (Washington); Tokyo (Japan) Am.; Army Navy Country, Washington Golf and Country (Arlington, Va.); Congressional Country, Kenwood Country (Bethesda, Md.). Author: (with Richard W. Pogue) Federal Employee Invention Rights—Time to Legislate, 1957. Contbg. editor Les Nouvelles Jour. Home: 5001 Wyandot Ct Fort Sumner Bethesda MD 20016 Office: 1775 K St NW Washington DC 20006

FINNELL, WILLIAM CONRAD, lawyer; b. Cleve., Nov. 20, 1938; s. William Theodore and Beatrice Ellen (Presswood) F.; B.S., U. Tenn., 1959, LL.B., 1962; m. Warnie Elizabeth Dooly, June 4, 1960; 1 dau., Jennifer Ellen. Salesman, Southwestern Co., Nashville, 1955-62; admitted to Tenn. bar, 1962; practice law, Cleveland, Tenn., 1962—; sr. partner law firm. Finnell, Thompson, Scott & Logan, 1962—; prin. Travena Grammar Sch., Cleveland, Tenn., 1958; partner Finnell, Thompson & Cannon Apartments, Cleveland, Tenn., 1968—; dir Founders Security Life Ins. Co., Memphis. Pres. Cleveland Bradley County Citizens for Better Schs., 1964-65; boxing coach YMCA, 1962-63. Bd. dirs. Cleveland Bradley County March of Dimes Campaign, 1965. Recipient Man of the Year award Cleveland (Tenn.) Jr. C. of C. Mem. Am., Tenn. bar assns., Am., Tenn. trial lawyers assns., Am. Judicature Soc., Cleveland Jr. C. of C., V.F.W., Lambda Chi Alphi. Republican. Mem. Ch. of Christ. Lion. Home: 2620 Springplace Rd Cleveland TN 37311 Office: 213 Broad St Cleveland TN 37311

FINNERTY, HUGH JAMES, investment co. exec.; b. St. Louis, Sept. 29, 1918; s. Hugh Joseph and Lena (Schultz) F.; student St. Louis U., 1936-37, U. Minn., 1942; m. Kathryn Joy Mutz, Nov. 28, 1946; children—Mark Hugh, Danny James. Sports dir. KOTV, tv. sta., Tulsa, 1953-56, regional sales mgr., 1956-59; sales mgr. KTUL-TV, 1959-61; gen. mgr. Tulsa Baseball Club, 1961-65; pres. Tex. Baseball League, 1965-69; v.p. Ada Securities Corp., Houston, 1969—; pres. bd. Tulsa Speedway, Inc., 1971—. Vice-pres. bd. Tulsa YMCA, 1967. Served with AUS, 1941-45. Mem. Sales and Marketing Execs. of Tulsa (pres. 1961), Sales and Marketing Execs. Inst. (council pres. 1970-71). Clubs: Coat of Arms (pres. 1968—), Petroleum (Tulsa). Home: 4625 S Lewis St Tulsa OK 74105 Office: Box 4196 Tulsa OK 74104

FINNEY, THOMAS DUNN, JR., lawyer; b. Idabel, Okla., Jan. 20, 1925; s. Thomas D. and Bettie (Higgs) F.; A.B., U. Okla., 1945, LL.B., 1948; m. Sally Van Horn, June 25, 1945; children—Susan Deuell (Mrs. Richard Ford), Kathleen, Deirdre, Thomas. Admitted to Okla. bar, 1948, D.C. bar, 1963; with Finney & Finney, Idabel, Okla., 1948-51; polit. officer U.S. Fgn. Service embassy Copenhagen (Denmark), 1952-55; with Foliart, Hunt & Shepherd, Oklahoma City, 1955-57; adminstrv. asst. to U.S. Senator A.S. Mike Monroney, 1957-63; with Clifford, Warnke, Glass, McIlwain, & Finney (formerly Clifford & Miller) Washington, 1963—. Dep. spl. asst. to pres. for fgn. trade policy, 1962; spl. counsel to credentials com. Democratic Nat. Conv., 1964. Served to lt. (j.g.) USNR, 1943-46. Mem. Phi Gamma Delta, Phi Delta Phi, Delta Sigma Rho. Home: 9000 McDonald Dr Bethesda MD 20034 Office: 815 Connecticut Av Washington DC 20006

FIRESTONE, GEORGE, indsl. security co. exec., state legislator; b. N.Y.C., May 13, 1931; s. Benjamin and Sally (Gollon) F.; student pub. schs., Miami, Fla.; m. Helene A. Eiserman, Aug. 28, 1952. Ins. broker Berkshire Life Ins. Co., 1952-56, Guardian Life Ins. Co., 1956-61; with Gray Security Service, Miami, Fla., 1961-72; sec., treas. Investco, Inc., Miami, 1972—; mem. Fla. Ho. of Reps., 1966—. Pres., N.W. Miami Property Owners Assn., 1957; v.p. Dade County Council Civic Orgns., 1957; chmn. Miami Econ. Adv. Bd., 1962, Dade County Personnel Adv. Bd., 1965. Bd. dirs. Here's Help. Served with AUS, 1948-52. Mem. Nat. Soc. State Legislators (pres.-elect), Greater Miami Jr. C. of C. (pres. 1960). Home: 861 San Pedro St Coral Gables FL 33156 Office: 777 NW 72d Av Miami FL 33144

FISCHER, ERNEST FREDERICK, JR., researcher, investment exec.; b. Houston, Feb. 11, 1940; s. Ernest Fredrick and Margaret Louise (Fitzgerald) F.; B.A., Gustavus Adolphus Coll., 1962; M.A., U. Tex., 1964; m. Jeanne Serur, Apr. 4, 1964; children—Charlotte Jean, Jason Frederick. Asst. prof. U.S. Army-Baylor U. program health care adminstrn., San Antonio, 1966-69, also asst. prof. San Antonio Coll., 1966-70, and lectr. St. Mary's Grad. Sch. Bus., San Antonio, 1969-70; research asso. A.M.A., Chgo., 1969-70, also project dir. Hosp. Research and Ednl. Trust, Chgo., 1969—; pres., dir. Urban Am. Corp., Austin, Tex., 1968—; dir. Urban Am. Investments, Inc. Adminstrv. asst. Rep. Nat. Comitteeman of Tex., 1965. Served to Capt. M.S.C., AUS, 1966-69. Mem. Chgo. Assn. Bus. Economists, Am. Econs. Assn. Republican. Lutheran. Author: HoustonSite for Industrial Location, 1967; Annotated Bibliography on the Sharing, Centralization and Consolidation of Clinical Laboratory and Related Diagnostic Facilities, 1971. Office: P O Box 731 Austin TX 78767

FISCHER, GEORGE WALLACE, pub. health vet.; b. San Antonio, Jan. 10, 1921; s. Earnest Augustus and Marie (Holzlohner) F.; D.V.M., Tex. A. and M. Coll., 1944; M.P.H., U. Mich., 1963; m. Nina Mae Sisley, May 16, 1962. Practice vet. medicine, San Antonio, 1944; meat insp. City Health Dept., San Antonio, 1944-46; vet. livestock insp., fgn. and exotic disease specialist USDA Bur. Animal Industries 1946-55; dir. milk inspection services Health Dept., San Antonio, 1955-62; dir. vet. services Corpus Christi (Tex.)-Nueces County Health Dept., 1963—. Bd. dirs., treas. Beautify Corpus Christi Assn. Fellow Tex. Pub. Health Assn.; mem. Am. Pub. Health Assn., Tex., S. Tex. sanitarians assns., Tex. Vet. Med. Assn., Coastal Bend Vet. Med. Assn. (pres. 1967). Home: 2944 Japonica St Corpus Christi TX 78410 Office: 1111 Navigation Blvd Corpus Christi TX 78407

FISCHER, MABEL JULIA THOMAS (MRS. THEODORE C. FISCHER), librarian; b. Reading Pa.; d. Costa and Katharine Irene (Kalbach) Thomas; A.B., Albright Coll.; M.A., Temple U.; M.L.S., Tex. Woman's U.; m. Theodore C. Fischer. Br. librarian Reading Pub. Library, 1944-48; children's asst. Tulsa Pub. Library, 1949-50; dept. head Ft. Worth Pub. Library, 1950-62, asst. dir., 1964-70, dir., 1970—; br. head Dallas Pub. Library, 1963-64. Mem. summer faculty Tex. Woman's U., 1962-70. Bd. dirs. YWCA, Ft. Worth. Mem. A.L.A., Tex. (pres., sec.-treas. pub. library div., chmn. dist. planning com), S.W. library assns., Am. Assn. U. Women, Ft. Worth Bus. and Profl. Women's Club. Club: Altrusa. Home: Route 1 Box 132 Roanoke TX 76262 Office: Ft Worth Public Library 9th and Throckmorton Sts Fort Worth TX 76102

FISCHER, STEWART CLARENCE, city ofcl.; b. Fischer Store, Tex., Jan. 25, 1924; s. Adolph H. and Anna (Lueders) F.; B.S. in Civil Engring., U. Tex., 1948; student East Tex. State Tchrs. Coll., 1945; Certificate in Hwy. Traffic Yale, 1951; m. Myra Lea Katt, Sept. 10, 1946; children—Nancy D., Kenneth L. Engr. trainee Tex. Hwy. Dept., Houston, 1948-52; traffic engr. City San Antonio, 1952-62, dir. traffic, transp., 1962—. Instr. U. Houston, 1950. Served with AUS, 1943-46; ETO. Decorated Purple Heart. Mem. Inst. Traffic Engrs. Methodist. Lion. Home: 9615 Lantana Dr San Antonio TX 78217 Office: PO Box 9066 San Antonio TX 78204

FISCHER, WILLIAM AUGUST, geologist; b. Litchfield, Ill., Jan. 6, 1919; s. August Ernst and Juliette Maria (Niemeyer) F.; B.S., McKendree Coll., Lebanon, Ill., 1940; student U. Ill., 1940-41; m. L. Blanche Youngblood, Sept. 8, 1941; children—Judith Lynn (Mrs. Court Soloff), William Jeffrey. Tchr. chemistry, physics Christopher (Ill.) High Sch., 1941; with U.S. Geol. Survey, 1941-44, 46-66, chief photogeology sect., 1950-60, charge lunar probe photometric analyses, 1960-62, research geologist charge remote sensing project, 1962-66; mgr. Earth Resources Observation Systems Program, Dept. Interior, 1966—, prin. lectr. pilot course aerial surveys for geology UN, Tokyo, Japan, 1961. Rep. Dept. Interior orgn. meeting Orgn. Europeenen d'Etudes Photogrammetriques Experimentales, Brussels, Belgium, 1952; chmn. U.S. delegation UN seminar aerial survey methods, Bangkok, Thailand, 1960; chief U.S. rep. orgn. meeting UNESCO conf. integrated surveys, Paris, France, 1963; chief U.S. delegation Internat. Congress Photogrammetry, 1964. Served as officer USNR, 1944-46. Mem. Am. Soc. Photogrammetry (pres. 1964-65, dir., mem. exec. com.), Dept. Interior Recreation Assn. (pres. 1961). Club: Cosmos (Washington). Author numerous papers and maps. Home: 228 Noland St Falls Church VA 22046 Office: US Geol Survey Washington DC 20242

FISH, MARJORIE, occupational therapist; b. St. Louis, Oct. 20, 1905; d. Edwards Russell and Ida (McBride) Fish; B.A., Swarthmore Coll., 1927; M.A., Columbia, 1952; postgrad. Boston Sch. Occupational Therapy, 1932. Organizer occupational therapy depts. Columbia, 1941-51, hosps. and tng. centers, Australia, 1948-50; exec. dir. Am. Occupational Therapy Assn., N.Y.C., 1951-64; cons. occupational therapy, div. tng. Vocational Rehab. Adminstrn., 1964—. Mem. panel Pres.'s Commn. Health Needs of the Nation, 1951-52; U.S. del. World Fedn. Occupational Therapists, 1954-62; cons. rehab. Phys. Medicine and Rehab. Service, VA, 1955-60; adv. panel on rehab. WHO, 1957—; tech. adv. com. Office Vocational Rehab., 1956-57; com. Internat. Exchange of Persons for Fulbright lecturing and research awards, 1957-62. Mem. Internat. Soc. Welfare Cripples (U.S. com. 1950-59), Am. (chmn. council edn. 1945-46, v.p. 1946-49), N.Y. (pres.) occupational therapy assns. Author: (with Holland Hudson) Occupational Therapy in the Treatment of the Tuberculosis Patient, 1943; also articles in field. Home: 503 6th St SE Washington DC 20003 Office: Vocational Rehab Dept Health Edn and Welfare Washington DC 20201

FISHBACK, ELLA SCOTT, wholesale trade co. exec.; b. Lexington, Ky., July 30, 1918; d. Robert Edward and Bessie Mae (Scott) Fishback; student U. Ky., 1935-37. Clk. dairy and poultry plant Swift & Co., Inc., Lexington, Ky., 1939-41, chief clk., 1941-55; office mgr. Ky. Ignition Co., Inc., Lexington, 1955-67, sec., 1963—, controller, dir., Louisville, 1967—; sec., dir. S.E. Gasket & Parts Warehouse, Atlanta. Mem. Am. Soc. Women Accountants (dir., past treas.). Club: Altrusa (dir.) (Louisville). Home: 4834A Westport Rd Louisville KY 40222 Office: 737 S 3d St Louisville KY 40202

FISHBEIN, MORRIS, microbiologist; b. N.Y.C., Oct. 31, 1916; s. Samuel and Mollie (Snitowski) F.; B.S., Coll. City N.Y., 1938; M.S., U. Ky., 1941; Ph.D., U. Md., 1952; m. Eleanor Levin, July 20, 1945; children—David P., Susan Leslie, Sanford Shawn. Lab. asst. U. Ky., 1938-40; lab. chief Pensacola Lab., Fla. Bd. Health, 1940-42; chief biologist Schwarz Labs., N.Y.C., 1945-46; research fellow U.S. Fish and Wildlife Service, Dept. Interior, Washington, 1946-48; research microbiologist U.S. FDA, Washington, 1948—. Served with USAAF, 1942-45; ETO. Decorated Air medal with oak leaf cluster. Mem. A.A.A.S., Am. Soc. Microbiology, Assn. Ofcl. Analytical Chemists, N.Y. Acad. Scis., Sigma Xi. Home: 11512 Soward Dr Silver Spring MD 20902 Office: FDA 200 C St SW Washington DC 20204

FISHBURNE, FRANK BEATTY, hydraulic press mfg. co. exec.; b. Columbia, S.C., July 13, 1915; s. Frank Beatty and Anita L. (Bellinger) F.; grad. high sch.; m. Mary Alice Whitton, Mar. 18, 1938; children—Frank Beatty III, Willard B., Carolyn A., Mary Janette. Plant engr. Pacific Iron & Steel Co., Los Angeles, 1942-45; pres. Standard Designers, Inc., Ashville, N.C., 1946-54; engr. Engring. Assos., Inc., Asheville, N.C., 1955-59; pres. Fishburne Equipment Co., Ashville, 1960—; pres. Asheville (N.C.) Ceramic Equipment Co., Fishburne Internat., Inc. Bd. dirs. N.C. World Trade Assn. Patentee in field. Home: 24 Summit Dr Arden NC 28704 Office: Airport Rd Arden NC 28704

FISHEL, CLARK RAMSEY, journalist; b. East Orange, N.J., Feb. 28, 1921; s. Newell Herbert and Muriel Elizabeth (Bush) F.; B.S., U. Ill., 1942; m. Iva Wilma Simmer, Dec. 20, 1947; children—Clark, Mark, Dawn, Dallas, Parke. Sales promotion and advt. copywriter Gen. Electric Co., Milw., 1946-49; indsl. advt. coordinator Allis-Chalmers, Milw., 1949-53; corp. information mgr. Tex. Instruments, Dallas, 1953-66, personnel activities mgr., 1966—. Heavy industry unit chmn., Tex. Instruments campaign coordinator Dallas United Fund, 1966-70; savs. bond chmn. Tex. Instruments, 1966-69; active Community Concert Greater Dallas. Served with USAAF, 1942-46. Mem. Assn. Indsl. Advertisers (chpt. pres. 1955-57, nat. dir. 1956-58), China-Burma-India Vets. Assn. (adj. 1970, historian 1972), S.W. Electronics Conf. (chmn. 1966), Dallas Press Club, Nat. Rifle Assn., Chili Appreciation Soc., Tex. Parks and Recreation Assn., Dallas Art Assn., Armadillo Breeders Assn., Am. Quarter Horse Breeders Assn., Nat. Indsl. Recreation Assn. (nat. dir. 1972—), Pi Kappa Phi, Sigma Delta Chi (v.p. 1966), Methodist. Clubs: Sportsmen's of Tex., Dallas Woods and Waters. Home: PO Box 149 Allen TX 75002 Office: PO Box 5474 Dallas TX 75222

FISHEL, RACHAEL ROBINSON (MRS. EDWARD KEITTH FISHEL), educator; b. Wilmington, N.C., Oct. 13, 1921; d. Jem and Anna (Johnson) Robinson; A.B., U. N.C., 1942; M.Ed. East Carolina U., 1967; m. Edward Keith Fishel, June 20, 1946 (dec. June 1968); children—Edwarth Keith II, Anna Elizabeth. Tchr., Littleton, N.C., 1942-47; GUIDANCE DIR. Warren County (N.C.) Schs., Warrenton, from 1964, now gen. supr. schs. Dir. Warren County Headstart Program, summer, 1966. Chmn. Warren County Com. Mental Retardation, 1967—; mem. Franklin-Vance-Warren County Mental Health Council, 1965—; mem. dist. com. Reynold's Scholarship, U. N.C., Greensboro, 1963; troop leader Girl Scouts Am., 1959-62; den mother Boy Scouts Am., 1957-59. Sec. Littleton Sch. Bd., 1960-62, chmn., 1962-64. Mem. Am., N.C. personnel and guidance assns., Am. Sch. Counselors Assn., N.E.A., N.C., Warren County (v.p. 1969—) edn. assns., Dirs. Guidance Services in Eastern N.C. (sec. 1969—), Delta Kappa Gamma, Kappa Delta Pi. Democrat. Methodist (v.p. womens soc. Christian services 1969—). Home: 205 College Av Littleton NC 27850 Office: PO Box 110 Warrenton NC 27589

FISHER, ALLAN CARROLL, JR., editor; b. Cumberland, Md., Feb. 17, 1919; s. Allan C. and Ella (Rees) F.; A.B., U. Md., 1941; m. Mary Alice Michael, Jan. 20, 1944; children—Suzanne de Cessna (Mrs. Roger A. Eichholz), Martha Rees. Staff writer Washington Post, 1941, Balt. Sun, 1941-43; editorial staff N.Y. bur. A.P., 1943-47; N.Y. pub. relations rep. Kaiser-Frazer Corp., 1947-48; v.p. Booke & Fisher, Inc., pub. relations, Houston, 1948-49; asso. Hammond Assos., pub. relations, Balt., 1949-50; mem. staff Nat. Geog. Mag., 1950—, asst. editor charge articles, 1963-65, sr. asst. editor, 1965-70, sr. asst. editor, staff adminstrn., 1971—. Recipient James J. Strebig Meml. award Aviation Writers Assn., 1956, 60. Mem. Aviation/Space Writers Assn., Nat. Assn. Sci. Writers, Nat. Aero. Assn., A.A.A.S. Democrat. Episcopalian. Clubs: Nat. Space (bd. govs. 1961-62), Nat. Press. Nat. Aviation, Aero, Clipper (Washington); Annapolis Yacht. Contbr. numerous articles Nat. Geog. Mag. Home: Beaumaris Bywater Rd Annapolis MD 21401 Office: Nat Geog Soc 17th and M Sts N W Washington DC 20036

FISHER, BEN COLEMAN, assn. exec., educator; b. Webster, N.C., May 27, 1915; s. Ben Franklin and Amy (Long) F.; A.B., Wake Forest U., 1938, D.D., 1971; B.D., Andover-Newton Theol. Sch., 1942; LL.D., Campbell Coll., 1968; m. Sara Gehman, Dec. 27, 1940; children—David Lincoln, Hugh Robert. Ordained to ministry Bapt. Ch., 1938; pastor Bapt. chs., Nashville, 1942-45, Newton, N.C., 1945-47; chmn. English dept. Gardner-Webb Jr. Coll., 1947-48, exec. asst. to pres., dir. pub. relations, 1948-52; asso. sec. Edn. Commn. So. Bapt. Conv., exec. sec. dept. Christian edn. Gen. Assn. Bapts. in Ky., 1952-54; chmn. pub. relations adv. com., 1959-60, chmn. edn. commn., 1968-70; asso. editor Educator, 1952-54; adminstrv. asst. to pres., dir. pub. relations Southeastern Bapt. Theol. Sem., 1954-62; exec. sec. Council on Christian Higher Edn., Bapt. State Conv. N.C., Raleigh, 1962-70; exec. sec.-treas. edn. commn. So. Bapt. Conv., Nashville, 1970—. Mem. New Eng. Town and Country Ch. Commn., 1941-42; mem. ednl. survey team Bapt. Colls. in Miss. and Ga., 1952; mem. N.C. Bd. Higher Edn. adv. com. on inter-instl. cooperation, 1967, mem. adv. com. on role pvt. higher edn., 1968, cons., 1968-70; coordinator N.C. Assn. Ind. Colls., 1969-70; mem. N.C. Commn. on Study of Statutes Relating to Vis. Speakers at State-supported Instns.,

1965; chmn. bd. Bibl. Recorder; trustee Campbell Coll. Recipient citation merit Trustees Gardner-Webb Jr. Coll., 1953; Tar Heel of Week award News and Observer, 1963, Distinguished Alumni award Wake Forest U., 1966, gov.'s citation for contbns. to devel. of N.C., 1967. Mem. Am. Coll. Pub. Relations Assn., Am. Alumni Council, So. Bapt. Pub. Relations Assn. (past pres.), Grange. Democrat. Lion, Rotarian. Author: Public Relations Manual for Church Related Colleges, 1954; Communications Manual, 1961; A Manual for College Trustees, 1965; Duties and Responsibilities of College Trustees, 1969; An Orientation Manual for College Trustees, 1971. Editor: Outlook, Southeastern Bapt. Theol. Sem., 1954-62, Educator, 1970—. Home: 3415 West End Av Nashville TN 37203 3415 West End Av Nashville TN 37203 Office: 460 James Robertson Pkwy Nashville TN 37219

FISHER, CHARLES RAY, physician; b. McHenry, Ky., Jan. 25, 1922; s. William Lee and Lodema (Fulkerson) F.; student Gary (Ind.) Coll., 1946-48; B.S., U. Louisville, 1951, M.D., 1953; m. Violet Shields, Jan. 31, 1946; children—Charles S., Timothy Ray. Intern Louisville Gen. Hosp., 1953-54; individual practice medicine, Flemingsburg, Ky., 1954; staff physician Trover Clinic, Madisonville, Ky., 1954—; chief of staff Hopkins County Hosp. Dir. Madisonville Realty Corp. Served with USNR, 1942-45. Mem. Ky. Acad. Family Practice (dist. dir.), Ky. Med. Assn. (county del.). Democrat. Home: 1035 McPherson Dr Madisonville KY 42431

FISHER, FRANCENIA ELEANORE, plant pathologist; b. Green Cove Springs, Fla., Sept. 23, 1924; d. Roy Dexter and Daisy (Sparkman) Fisher; B.S., Fla. State U., 1945; postgrad. U. Chgo., 1945; M.S., Mich. State U., 1946. Plant Pathologist Citrus Expt. Sta., U. Fla., Lake Alfred, 1946—; researcher, cons., 1946—, adviser county agts., grad. students, 1946—. Mem. A.A.A.S., Soc. Econ. Botany, Am. Phytopath Soc., Internat. Soc. Plant Pathology, Internat. Platform Assn., Fla. Hort. Soc., Mediterranean Phytopath. Union, Internat. Soc. Plant Pathology, Smithsonian Assos., Internat. Congress Plant Protection, Internat. Orgn. Citrus Virologists, Seminarium Botanicum (hon.), Ancient Order Ranales (hon.), Sigma Xi. Democrat. Episcopalian. Club: Lake Region Yacht and Country (charter mem.). Contbr. articles on citrus diseases caused by fungi, chem. control, biol. control fungus diseases of insects and mites attacking citrus to profl. jours. and trade mags. Home: 1507 W Lake Cannon Dr PO Box 242 Winter Haven FL 33880 Office: U Fla Agricultural Research and Education Center Lake Alfred FL 33850

FISHER, GERALD HOMER, supt. schs.; b. Mulberry, Ark., Sept. 1, 1927; s. Gilford Homer and Ethel (Trotter) F.; B.A., Coll. of Ozarks, 1949; M.A., U. Ark., 1950, Ed.D., 1961; m. Melba Ruth Cole, Sept. 29, 1950; children—Cindy, Christopher Cole, Sarah, Gregory Thomas. Secondary tchr. pub. schs., Cedarville, Ark., 1950-51, Fort Smith, 1951-52; dean Sr. High Sch., Fort Smith, 1952-55; counselor Ark. Rehab. Service, 1955-60; adminstr. Hot Springs (Ark.) Rehab. Center, 1960-66, dir., 1966-69; dir. Ark. Rehab. Research and Tng. Center, Hot Springs, 1966-69; supt. city schs., Hot Springs, 1969—. Mem. Commn. Accreditation of Rehab. Facilities, 1967—. Pres. United Fund, Hot Springs, 1964—, campaign chmn., 1963—, bd. mem., 1963—; bd. mem. YMCA, A.R.C., Community Players. Served with AUS, 1946-50. Recipient Distinguished Service award Hot Springs Jr. C. of C., 1964, Coll. of Ozarks Alumni Achievement Award, 1964. Mem. Nat. Rehab. Assn. (mem. policy com. 1966—), Assn. Rehab. Centers, C. of C. (bd. mem.). Methodist (bd. mem.). Mason, Rotarian (pres. 1968-69, dist. gov. 1971-72). Address; 140 Border St Hot Springs AR 71901

FISHER, JOEL HILTON, lawyer; b. Bklyn., Mar. 28, 1918; A.B. magna cum laude, Syracuse U., 1939, J.D., 1941. Admitted to N.Y. State bar, 1941, U.S. Supreme Ct. bar, 1949, U.S. Ct. Appeals for D.C., 1949, U.S. Dist. Cts. So and Eastern Dists. N.Y., 1953, Md. bar, 1954, U.S. Dist. Ct. Balt., 1955; asst. to solicitor Dept. Commerce, 1945-46; now partner firm Fisher & Gelband, Washington. Mem. Am., Internat. (patron), Inter-Am., Fed. (com. on taxation, aviation law com. 1958-65) bar assns., Bar Assn. D.C. (com. on adminstrv. law, aviation law com. 1958—), UN League Lawyers, Decalogue Soc. Lawyers, Am. Soc. Internat. Law. Office: 1522 K St NW Suite 1000 Washington DC 20005*

FISHER, JOSEPH FRANKLIN, physician; b. Clinton, N.C., Aug. 3, 1926; s. Walter Harrison and Lossie Salena (Herring) F.; student Wake Forest Coll., 1943-45; M.D., Bowman Gray Sch. Medicine, 1949; m. E. Jean Wilson, June 9, 1951; children—Joseph Franklin, Andra Harrison, Walter Clark. Intern, Nashville Gen. Hosp., 1949-50; gen. practice medicine, Sparta, Tenn., 1950-52, Arlington, Tex., 1952-55, McMinnville, Tenn., 1957—. Chmn. bd. dirs. Plateau Mental Health Clinic, Cookeville, Tenn. Served to capt. USAF, 1955-57. Mem. A.M.A., Tenn., Warren County med. assns. Methodist. Club: McMinnville Flying. Home: Oak Hill Dr McMinnville TN 37110 Office: Plaza Shopping Center McMinnville TN 37110

FISHER, JOSEPH JEFFERSON, dist. judge; b. San Augustine County, Tex.; s. Guy B. and Lula (Bland) F.; student Stephen F. Austin Coll., 1929; LL.B., U. Tex., 1936; m. Kathleen Clark, Sept. 22, 1938; children—Leila Beth (Mrs. Walter G. Thomas), Joseph Jefferson, John Clark, Guy Cade, Kathleen Anne (Mrs. F. Thomas Winslow). Admitted to Tex. bar, 1936; county atty. San Augustine County, 1936-39; dist. atty. 1st Jud. Dist. Tex., 1939-46, dist. judge, 1956-59; partner firm Fisher, Tonahill & Reavley, Jasper, Tex., 1941-56; U.S. dist. judge Eastern Dist. Tex., 1959—. Adv. bd. Salvation Army. Recipient Silver Beaver award Boy Scouts Am., 1952. Mem. Am. (chmn. jud. sect. 1957), 1st Jud. (pres. 1956), Tex. bar assns., State Bar Tex. (legislative and exec. coms. 1957-59), Jasper (pres. 1943-45), E. Tex. (past dir.) chambers commerce, Am. Judicature Soc., Tex. Hist. Assn., Ex-Student Assn. U. Tex. (life), Sons Republic Tex., Delta Kappa Epsilon. Methodist. Lion (dist. gov., internat. dir., mem. exec. com. 1952-59), Mason (Shriner). Home: 130C Caldwood Beaumont TX 77704 Office: PO Bldg Beaumont TX 77704

FISHER, JOSEPH LYMAN, economist; b. Pawtucket, R.I., Jan. 11, 1914; s. Howard Colburn an ' Caroline (Nash) F.; B.S., Bowdoin Coll., 1935; postgrad. London Sc Econs., 1935-36; M.A., Harvard, 1938, Ph.D. (teaching fellow 1946-47), 1947; M.A. in Edn., George Washington U., 1951; D.Sc., Bowdoin Coll., 1965; LL.D., Allegheny Coll., 1966; L.H.D., Starr King Sch. for Ministry; m. Margaret Saunders Winslow, June 21, 1942; children—H. Benjamin, Caroline, Robert W., William B., Elizabeth, James H., Barbara W. Instr. econs. Allegheny Coll., 1938-40; planning tch. Nat. Resources Planning Board 1939-43; economist Dept. State 1943; economist, exec. officer Council Econ. Advisers, Washington, 1947-53; asso. dir. Resources for Future, Washington, 1953-59, pres., 1959—; vis. prof. U. Colo., 1957, U. Cal., 1970; staff dir. Cabinet Com. Energy Supplies and Policies, 1955; cons. to govt. agys. Mem. Arlington County Bd., 1964—, chmn., 1965, 71. Trustee Unitarian Universalist Assn., 1961-65, moderator, chmn. bd. trustees, 1965—; trustee Tchrs. Ins. and Annuity Assn., 1966—, United Planning Orgn., 1966-71; bd. dirs. Washington Met. Area Transit Authority, Washington Met. Council Govts. (pres. 1969, chmn. 1970); bd. overseers Bowdoin Coll. Served with inf. AUS, 1943-46. Mem. Am. Forestry Assn. (dir. 1967—), Am. Soc. Pub. Administrn., A.A.A.S., Regional Sci. Assn., Arctic Inst. N.A., Phi Beta Kappa, Phi Delta Kappa. Club: Cosmos (Washington). Author: (with others) Resources in America's Future; World Prospects for Natural Resources; also chpts. in books, articles profl. jours. Home: 2608 N 24th St Arlington VA 22207 Office: 1755 Massachusetts Av NW Washington DC 20036

FISHER, KING, marine contracting co. exec.; b. Port Lavaca, Tex., Jan. 14, 1916; s. Charles Everett and Kittie (Moss) F.; student pub. schs., Port Lavaca; m. Jewel Tanner, Aug. 13, 1937; children—Ann (Mrs. Waymon Boyd), Linda. Pres. King Fisher Marine Service, Inc., Port Lavaca, 1941—; treas. Fisher Channel & Dock Co., Port Lavaca, 1954—. Mem. Tex. Mid-Coast Water Devel. Assn., Port Lavaca C. of C. Home: Hillcrest Chocolate Bay Port Lavaca TX 77979 Office: PO Box 108 Port Lavaca TX 77979

FISHER, MARION LEROY, JR., educator, clergyman; b. Detroit, Nov. 20, 1925; s. Marion LeRoy and Clela Mae (Smith) F.; B.A., Defiance Coll., 1947; M.Div., Duke U, 1950; M.Ed., Bowling Green State U., 1959. Ordained to ministry Meth. Ch., 1951; minister Harmony (N.C.) Meth. Ch., 1950-52; instr. chemistry, physics Holgate (O.) High Sch., 1952-58, prin., 1958-60; supervising prin. Poynor Jr. High Sch., Florence, S.C., 1964-67, Moore Jr. High School, 1964-66; instr. U. S.C., 1966-67; dir. fed. programs and adult edn. Florence Sch. Dist. 1, from 1967; now supt. schs. Weldon (N.C.) City Schs. Dir. S.C. State Sci. Fair, 1962-64, regional sci. fair, 1961-65. Mem. Council of Del., Florence County, 1963-66, del. Ohio Edn. Assn., 1959. Scoutmaster, Boy Scouts Am. Named Sci. Tchr. of the Year, O. Acad. Sci., 1960. Mem. Nat., S.C., Edn. Assn., A.A.A.S., N.C. Assn. Educators, N.C. Assn. Sch. Adminstrs., Travelers Protective Assn. Am. Mason, Rotarian. Contbr. articles to jours. Home: PO Box 246 Weldon NC 27890 Office: PO Box 31 Weldon NC 27890

FISHER, MILTON NATHAN, mfg. co. exec.; b. Newark, N.J., Nov. 25, 1921; s. Davis and Maria (Rapaport) F.; B.S. in Bus. Adminstrn., U. Fla., 1946; m. Berna Braunstein, June 9, 1946; 1 son, Jerome Peter. Pres., dir. Panelfab Internat. Corp., Miami, Fla., 1951—; pres., dir. Decor Internacional de Cuba, 1958-59; pres., dir. Dicoa Corp., 1958—; pres., dir. Panelfab Pacific, Inc., 1965—, Panelfab P.R., Inc., 1967—; dir. Nihon Panelfab, Ltd., Japan, 1967—, Panelfab Europe, Ltd. Mem. regional export expansion council U.S. Dept. Commerce. Bd. dirs. International Trade, now pres.; pres., dir. Internat. Center, Greater Miami, Fla. Served to maj. USAAF, 1942-45. Decorated D.F.C., Air medal with 3 oak leaf clusters. Mem. Tau Epsilon Phi, Beta Alpha Psi, Beta Gamma Sigma. Mason. Club: Kings Bay Yacht (Coral Gables, Fla.). Home: 535 Reinante Av Coral Gables FL 33156 Office: 1600 N W Le Jeune Rd Miami FL 33126

FISHER, O. CLARK, congressman; b. nr. Junction, Tex., Nov. 22, 1903; s. Jobe B. and Rhoda (Clark) Fisher; student U. Tex.; LL.B., Baylor U., 1929; m. Marian DeWalsh, Sept. 12, 1927; 1 dau., Rhoda. Admitted to Tex. bar, 1929; county atty., Tom Green County, 1931-35; state rep., 1935-37; dist. atty., 51st Jud. Dist., 1937-43; mem. 78th-92d U.S. Congresses from 21st Tex. Dist. Democrat. Mem. Acacia. Mason; mem. Order Eastern Star; K.P., Rotarian. Author: It Occurred in Kimble, 1937; The Texas Heritage of the Fishers and the Clarks, 1963; King Fisher, his Life and Times; co-author: Great Western Indian Fights, 1960. Home: San Angelo TX 78206 Office: Rayburn Office Bldg Washington DC 20515

FISHER, PAUL, economist; b. Vienna, Austria, July 9, 1908; s. Ernst and Irma (Loebl) Fischer; student U. Paris (Sorbonne), 1926-27; J.D., U. Vienna, 1930; m. Susan Schwarz, June 5, 1948. Came to U.S., 1938, naturalized, 1944. Instr. dept. econs. William and Mary Coll., Williamsburg, Va. 1938-40, U. Me. at Orono, 1941-43; asst. prof. dept. econs. Clark U., Worcester, Mass., 1943-46, Dartmouth Coll., Hanover, N.H., 1946-51; chief labor econ. br., dep. dir. div. planning assistance Agy. for Econ. Devel., Washington, 1952-63; chief internat. staff Social Security Adminstrn., Dept. Health, Edn. and Welfare, Washington, 1963—; sr. research economist ILO, Geneva, Switzerland, 1968-69; adj. prof. econs. Am. U., Washington, 1952—. Mem. Am. Econ. Assn., Indsl. Relations Research Assn. Contbr. numerous articles in field to profl. jours. Home: 7024 Bybrook Lane Chevy Chase MD 20015 Office: 1875 Connecticut Av NW Washington DC 20009

FISHER, RANDALL HACKNEY, contractor; b. Cleveland, Tenn., Dec. 23, 1937; s. Homer Burton and Arda DeEtte (McClure) F.; student Carson-Newman Coll., 1956-60; m. Judith Lee Melton, Mar. 26, 1960; children— Melodie Lee, Melissa DeEtte. Pres., Randall Fisher Constrn. Co., Inc., Cleveland, 1960—; pres. Fisher Real Estate Co., 1962—, D.E.F. Developers, 1968—, E & F Devel. Co., 1969—; v.p. Rain-Flow of Cleveland Inc., 1970—, Ervin Fisher & Headrick Devel. Co., 1970—. Mem. Cleveland Home Builders Assn. (pres.). Republican. Baptist (deacon). Home: 605 Forest Lane Cleveland TN 37311 Office: 755 Wildwood Av Cleveland TN 37311

FISHER, RICHARD LEE, dentist; b. Nathalie, Va., Sept. 3, 1929; s. Joe T. and Effie (Fariss) F.; B.S. in Chemistry, U. Richmond, 1953; D.D.S., Med. Coll. Va., 1955; m. Kate Hughes, June 25, 1955; children—Debra Rene, Richard Lee. Pvt. practice dentistry, Brookneal, Va., 1958—. Vice-mayor, Brookneal, Va., 1960-64; town councilman, 1960—; mem. Campbell County Planning Commn., 1964—. Served from 1st lt. to capt. AUS, 1955-57. Mem. Am., Va., Piedmont dental assns., Jr. C. of C. (pres. 1960-61, life mem. Va.), Phi Beta Kappa, Omicron Kappa Upsilon, Gamma Sigma Epsilon, Sigma Zeta, Phi Kappa Sigma, Psi Omega. Democrat. Baptist deacon, Sunday sch. supt.). Lion (pres. 1962-63). Home: Clark St Brookneal VA 24528 Office: Main St Brookneal VA 24528

FISHER, ROBERT B., librarian Mt. Vernon (Va.) Ladies Assn. Address: Mt Vernon Ladies Assn Mount Vernon VA 22121*

FISHER, ROBERT DALE, economist; b. Memphis, July 30, 1924; s. Hollis Welton and Anna Sue (Parrish) F.; student Tex. Christian U., 1940-44; B.A., Am. U., 1959; m. Joy Lee Chandler, Mar. 30, 1946. Commn. ensign USN, 1944, advanced through grades to comdr., 1963; served with various ships and stas.; tng. officer Polaris Missile program, 1956-59; comdr. U.S.S. McCaffery, 1960-63; ret., 1963; now with R.R. duPont Glore Forgan, Inc., mem. N.Y. Stock Exchange, Washington. Mem. Internat. Platform Assn., Am. Econ. Assn., Naval Inst. Methodist. Kiwanian (pres. Falls Church). Club: Navy League (Washington). Contbr. articles to profl. jours. Home: 6033 Chesterbrook Rd McLean VA 22101 Office: 1211 Connecticut Av NW Washington DC 20036

FISHER, ROBERT HENRY, yacht broker; b. Boston, May 20, 1925; s. Milton and Mae (Gurson) F.; student Mass. Inst. Tech., 1948, Boston U., 1948; m. Peggy von Lindenmayer, Aug. 3, 1954. Vice pres., gen. mgr. Gloucester Marine Railways Corp., Rocky Neck Shipyards, Inc., Gloucester, Mass., 1950-59; v.p. Breen-Fisher & Assos., yacht brokers, Ft. Lauderdale, Fla., 1960-64; pres., chief exec. officer Northrop & Johnson, Inc., yacht brokers, Ft. Lauderdale, 1964—. Pvt. marine cons. Bd. dirs., mem. marine adv. com. Fla. Atlantic U.; bd. dirs. Fla. Ocean Scis. Inst. Served with USN, 1941-46. Mem. North Am. Yacht Racing Union, So. Yacht Brokers Assn. (pres. 1964-65). Clubs: Storm Trysail (fleet capt. So. sta.), Coral Reef Yacht (Miami, Fla.), Royal Norwegian Yacht (Oslo), Propellor, Gulfstream Sailing (Ft. Lauderdale); Boston Yacht (Marblehead, Mass.). Home: 2629 Clematis Pl Fort Lauderdale FL 33301 Office: 2190 SE 17th St Fort Lauderdale FL 33316

FISHER, STANLEY MILTON, ins. co. exec.; b. Mansfield, O., Dec. 23, 1921; s. Joseph Clarence and Mildred Lucille (Van Antwerp) F.; J.D., Wayne State U., 1949; m. Joan Pauline Frederiksen, Mar. 27, 1943; children—Richard Brage, Peter Jay. With Abstract & Title Guaranty Co., Detroit, 1940-51, office mgr., to 1951; admitted to Mich. bar, 1949; individual practice law, Lincoln Park, Mich., 1951-55; pres. Am. Title Co. of Mich., Detroit, 1955-59; sr. v.p. Am. Title Ins. Co., Detroit, 1959-69, exec. v.p., Miami, 1969—; pres. Am. Title Trust Co., Phoenix, 1970—; dir. Attys. Title Guaranty Fund, Inc., Denver. Served to 1st lt. USAAF, 1942-45. Decorated Air medal with 12 oak leaf clusters. Mem. State Bar Assn. Mich., Detroit, Macomb, Am., Down River bar assns., Mich. Real Estate Assn., Detroit Real Estate Bd., Nat. Assn. Real Estate Bds., Mortgage Bankers Assn. Mich. Club: Detroit Yacht. Home: 68 Greenbriar Lane Grosse Pointe Shores MI 48236 Office: 150 S E 3d Av Miami FL 33131

FISHER, WILLIAM HOOVER, educator; b. Lima, O., Nov. 15, 1927; S. Vernon Arthur and Palleene (Hoover) F.; B.A., U. Miami, Coral Gables, Fla., 1955, M.Ed. in Guidance, 1959; postgrad. in History, U. Me., summers 1962-63; postgrad. U. Pitts., 1965; m. Hilma Hannah Hagelin, Aug. 12, 1953; 1 stepdau., Barbara Elaine (Mrs. George L. Hobson); children—Mark Edward, Valerie Sue, Richard Joseph, Robin Connie. Tchr. history Coral Gables (Fla.) Sr. High Sch., 1955—, guidance counselor, 1961—, tennis coach, 1955-60; tchr. history evening div. Miami (Fla.) Sr. High Sch., 1957—, counselor-supr., 1966, program adviser Miami-Dade Jr. Coll., 1967; guidance specialist, human relations cons. S. Central sch. dist. Dade County Schs.; coordinator counselor edn. program; vis. instr., group process leader U. Miami. Served with USNR, 1945-48, 51-52. Mem. Nat. Assn. Pub. Sch. Adult Educators, Dade County Guidance and Personnel Assn., Fla., Fla. Adult edn. assns., Dade County Classroom Tchrs. Assn. Club: Optimist (dir.). Home: PO Box 2335 Oceanview Br Miami Beach FL 33140 Office: 2201 SW 4th St Miami FL 33143

FISHMAN, JACOB ROBERT, psychiatrist, educator; b. N.Y.C., Aug. 6, 1930; s. Samuel and Fannie (Goldin) F.; A.B., Columbia, 1952; M.D., Boston U., 1956; m. Tamar Hendel, June 1, 1958; children—Marc Judah, Risa Esther, Zalman, Rebecca Anne. Intern, medicine Einstein Coll. Medicine, Bronx, N.Y., 1956-57, resident psychiatry, 1957-59; research psychiatrist Nat. Inst. Mental Health, Washington, 1959-62; prof. psychiatry Howard U. Coll. Medicine, Washington, 1962-71; dir. Howard-D.C. Comprehensive Mental Health Center, 1966-68; chmn. bd., pres. Univ. Research Corp., Washington, 1968—, Am. Health Services, Inc.; pres. Center for Human Services, 1968—. Cons. various govtl. agys. including U.S. Dept. Labor, numerous pvt. corps. Bd. dirs. Webster Coll., Washington, Center for Human Services, 1967—, Nat. Capital Day Care Assn., 1966-68; mem. D.C. Pub. Health Adv. Council, 1966-68; attending psychiatrist Freedman's Hosp., Washington Vets. Hosp., D.C. Gen. Hosp. Served with USPHS, 1959-61. Fellow Am. Pub. Health Assn.; mem. Am. Psychiat. Assn., D.C. Psychiat. Soc., A.A.A.S., D.C. Pub. Health Assn. Author numerous profl. articles and books. Bd. editors Nat. Jour. Research on Crime and Delinquency, 1965-71. Home: 1717 Poplar Lane NW Washington DC 20012 Office: 4301 Connecticut Av NW Washington DC 20008

FISHMAN, ROBERT JACK, pub., editor; b. Memphis, Nov. 1, 1934; s. Saul Jack and Katherine (Little) F.; B.S., Memphis State U., 1955; postgrad. U. N.C. Inst. for Orgn. Mgmt., 1956-61, U. Okla. Indsl. Devel. Inst., 1963-65; m. Nancy Allen, Nov. 25, 1955; children— Jeffrey Daniel, Robert M. Mgr. Jesup-Wayne County C. of C., Jesup, Ga., 1956-59, Morristown (Tenn.) C. of C., 1959-65; exec. dir. Middle Tenn. Indsl. Devel. Assn., Nashville, 1965-66; editor, pub. Citizen Tribune, Morristown, Tenn., 1966—. Tchr. bus. mgmt. clinic Carson-Newman Coll., 1962, Environmental Health Clinic, Cin., 1962-63, Southeastern Inst. for Orgn. Mgmt., U. Ga., 1963-65. Sec. bd. trustees Morristown Hamlen Hosp. Chmn. 2d dist. Citizens Commn. on Compensation; chmn. Tenn. Indsl. and Agrl. Devel. Commn., Tenn. Indsl. Finance Com., Morristown Indsl. Devel. Bd.; vice chmn. Gov.'s Econ. Study Com.; mem. Gt. Smoky Mountain council, finance chmn. Cherokee dist. Boy Scouts Am. Named Tenn. Young Man of Year, 1964. Mem. Tenn. (past pres.), Am., So. assns. chambers commerce execs., So., Am., E. Tenn. (pres. 1962), indsl. devel. councils, Holston River Devel. Assn. (v.p. 1963-65), Gov. Tenn. Travel and Tourist Promotion Council, Pi Delta Epsilon, Kappa Sigma, Theta Kappa Omega (nat. pres. 1955-56). Episcopalian (sr. warden). Elk, Kiwanian (dir.). Home: 2114 Collins Av Morristown TN 37814 Office: 1609 W 1st at North St Morristown TN 37814

FISHWICK, JOHN PALMER, r.r. exec.; b. Roanoke, Va., Sept. 29, 1916; s. William and Nellie (Cross) F.; A.B., Roanoke Coll., 1937; LL.B., Harvard, 1940; m. Blair Wiley, Jan. 4, 1941; children—Ellen Blair, Anne Palmer, John Palmer. Admitted to Va. bar, 1939; asso. Cravath, Swaine & Moore, N.Y.C., 1940-42; asst. to gen. solicitor N. & W. Ry., Roanoke, Va., 1945-47, asst. gen. solicitor, 1947-51, asst. gen. counsel, 1951-54, gen. solicitor, 1954-56, gen. counsel, 1956-58, v.p., gen. counsel, 1958-59, v.p. law, 1959-63, sr. v.p., dir., then pres., chief exec. officer, dir., 1963—; former chmn., chief exec. officer Erie Lackawanna Ry. Co.; former pres., chief exec. officer Del. and Hudson Ry. Co., Dereco, Inc., now dir.; dir. Trailer Train Co., Akron, Canton & Youngstown R.R., Va. Commonwealth Corp., Pocahontas Land Corp., Va. Holding Corp. Pres., United Fund of Roanoke Valley, 1960, dir., 1959-62, campaign chmn. 1959. Trustee Roanoke Coll., Salem, Va.; bd. dirs. Roanoke Fine Arts Center. Served as lt. comdr. USNR, 1942-45. Mem. Am., Va. (exec. com. 1959-62), Roanoke bar assns., Am. Law Inst., Newcomen Soc. N.Am., Va. (dir. 1959-62, 65—), Roanoke (pres. 1958) chambers commerce, Kappa Alpha, Tau Kappa Alpha. Episcopalian. Clubs: City Tavern Assn. (Georgetown); Commonwealth, Shenandoah (Roanoke); Duquesne (Pitts); Metropolitan (Washington). Home: 535 Market St Salem VA 24153 Office: 106 N Jefferson St Roanoke VA 24011

FISTER, JAMES ROBERT, county ofcl.; b. Danville, Ky., May 15, 1933; s. Fred Marion and Willia (Slattery) F.; B.S., Clemson U., 1958; M.S., Ga. Inst. Tech., 1964; m. May Alicia Horne, June 8, 1957; children—Anne Marie, Jane Frances, James Robert, Sandra Lynn. Asst. planning engr. Ga. State Hwy. Dept., 1960-65; traffic engr. City of Savannah, Ga., 1965-67, dir. pub. works, 1967-69; dir. pub. works DeKalb County, Decatur, Ga., 1969—. Served with inf., U.S. Army, 1953-55. Registered profl. engr., Ga., La. Mem. Am. Soc. C.E., Inst. Traffic Engrs., Am. Pub. Works Assn. Author: (with R.J. Paquette) Economical Stabilzation of Soils in Georgia, 1964. Home: 4225 Waterloo Circle Tucker GA 30084 Office: 556 N McDonough St Decatur GA 30030

FITCH, WALTER R., postmaster; b. Bedford, Tex., Dec. 13, 1912; s. William Reece and Nora (Bobo) F.; student Tex. Christian U., 1931-32, Navy Petroleum Sch., Bayonne, N.J., 1945; m. Mina Evelyn

Wilkerson, Apr. 15, 1933; children—Walter Bobo, William Randy. Owner-mgr. Fitch's Gen. Merc., 1933-61; postmaster, Bedford, 1950—; town clk., Bedford, 1953-63. Dir. Haltom City State Bank. Bd. dirs. Mid-Cities Hosp., 1968-69. Served with USNR, 1942-45; PTO. Mem. Nat. Assn. Postmasters (past pres. Tex. chpt., mem. nat. exec. com.), Bedford C. of C. (past pres.). Mem. Ch. of Christ. Mason (Shriner), Kiwanian, Lion. Home: 1801 Bedford Rd Bedford TX 76021 Office: 1901 Bedford Rd Bedford TX 76021

FITE, ROBERT CARL, educator; b. Brinkman, Okla., July 26, 1915; s. Ernest Elias and Myrtie (Frost) Fite; A.B., Central State Coll., Okla., 1937; M.S., Okla. State U., 1947; Ph.D., Northwestern U., 1951; m. Lucy Lou Smith, Apr. 6, 1940; children—Cynthia Ann, Priscilla Jane. Tchr. high sch. math., Okla., 1927-42; prof. geography and meteorology Okla. State U., Stillwater, 1947-56, prof., 1956—, dir. arts and scis. extension, 1956-68, dir. programs for professorials, 1968—. Fulbright lectr., Uruguay, 1966; asso. program dir. NSF, 1967-68. Served to lt. comdr. USNR, 1943-46. Decorated Air medal. Mem. Nat. Sci. Tchrs. Assn., A.A.A.S., Am. Meteorol. Soc. Author: Weather Elements, 1957, latest rev. edit., 1965. Home: 1019 W Knapp St Stillwater OK 74074

FITE, ROBERT HUNTER, utilities exec.; b. Nashville, July 26, 1902; s. Robert Hunter and Alma (McCarthy) F.; B.E., Vanderbilt U., 1923; m. Mary Josephine Cotton, May 14, 1932; children—Peter Hunter, Robert Cotton. With Gen. Electric Co., 1923-25; head rate dept. to gen. sales mgr. Fla. Power & Light Co., Miami, 1926-36; with Ebasco Services, Inc., N.Y.C., 1936-45, as sales sponsor, head sales dept., mgr. Washington office; with Fla. Power & Light Co., 1945—, successively v.p. and dir., v.p. and gen. mgr., pres. and gen. mgr., 1954-68, pres., chief exec. officer, 1968—, vice chmn. bd., 1969-72. Mem. Beta Theta Pi. Conglist. Clubs: Miami, Kiwanis (Miami); Riviera Country (Coral Gables, Fla.). Home: PO Box 3100 Miami FL 33101 Office: Fla Power & Light Co Miami FL 33101

FITZGERALD, DON WALLACE, banker; b. Pauls Valley, Okla., June 16, 1936; s. Roy Erwin and Allie Mae (Stapp) F.; B.B.A., U. Okla., 1958; postgrad. Stonier Grad. Sch. Banking, Rutgers U., 1966-69; m. Sonja So Relle Land, June 28, 1958; children—Kelly Denise, Jay Land, Erin Leigh. Dist. rep. Philips Petroleum Co., Jefferson City, Mo., 1958-65; v.p. City Nat. Bank, Tulsa, 1965-68; v.p. Guranty Nat. Bank, 1968-69; chmn. bd. First Wagoner Bank & Trust Co., Wagoner, 1969—; vice-chmn. bd. First Okla. Bank & Trust Co., Sulphur, Okla., 1968—; chmn. bd., pres. Plaza Mgmt. Co., Inc., Oklahoma City, 1969—; vice chmn. Plaza Nat. Bank, Bartlesville, Okla. Bd. dirs., Okla. Good Roads and Streets Assn., v.p. 1971-72; bd. dirs. U. Okla. Bd. Visitors, Okla. Alumni Devel. Fund. Mem. Okla. Bankers Assn., Fellowship of Christian Athletes, Okla. U. Alumni of Oklahoma City (v.p. 1970-71). Democrat. Methodist. Mason (Shriner, Jester), Kiwanian (pres. 1966-67). Clubs: Okla. Touchdown, Quail Creek Golf and Country (Oklahoma City); Tulsa. Address: 5834 S 78th E Av Oklahoma City OK 73120

FITZGERALD, JOEL LUTHER, physician; b. New Orleans, July 22, 1939; s. James Arthur and Grace Mae (Keen) F.; B.S., Southeastern La. U., 1961; M.D., La. State U., 1965; m. Ethel Harriet Tycer, Apr. 21, 1961; children—Joel Luther, Brett Kelly, Shannon Kay. Intern, Charity Hosp., New Orleans, 1965-66; resident Lafayette (La.) Charity Hosp., 1966-67; practice medicine, Westwego, La., 1967—; v.p. Av C Clinic, med. corp., 1971—; mem. staff W. Jefferson Gen. Hosp., 1967—, chief family practice sect., 1972. Mem. La., Jefferson Parish med. socs., Alpha Omega Alpha. Lion. Home: 2525 Crestwood Rd Marrero LA 70072 Office: 880 Av C Westwego LA 70094

FITZGERALD, ROBERT DEMARS, ins. co. exec.; b. Hartford, Conn., May 11, 1923; s. John Joseph and Viola Helen (DeMars) F.; B.A., U. Conn., 1948; diploma in mgmt. Am. Coll. Life Underwriters, 1965; m. Glenna Gibbs Cady, July 14, 1951. Second v.p. Fed. Life & Casualty Co., Battle Creek, Mich., 1965-67; v.p. Bankers Security Life Ins. Soc. (N.Y.), Washington, 1967-68; exec. v.p. Bankers Financial Life Co. (Okla.), Washington, 1968-71; exec. v.p., sec. Consumers United Ins. Co. (Del.), Washington, 1971—; dir. Consumer Credit Ins. Assn. Pres. Young Republican Club, U. Conn., 1948. Served with USAAF, 1943-45. C.L.U. Mem. Nat. Assn. Life Underwriters, Gen. Agts. and Mgrs. Conf., Am. Soc. C.L.U.'s, Hartford Alumni Assn. (pres. 1957-59), Sigma Alpha Epsilon. Home: 620 Bennington Dr Silver Spring MD 20910 Office: 2100 M St Washington DC 20037

FITZGERALD, THOMAS ROLLINS, univ. adminstr.; b. Washington, Feb. 23, 1922; s. Thomas Rollins and Bessie (Sheehy) F.; B.A., Woodstock (Md.) Coll., 1945, M.A., 1948; S.T.L., Facultes St. Albert de Louvain (Belgium), 1953; Ph.D., U. Chgo., 1957. Joined Soc. of Jesus, 1939, ordained priest Roman Catholic Ch., 1952; instr. classics Novitiate St. Isaac Jogues, Wernersville, Pa., 1957-58, dean studies, asst. prof. classics, 1958-64; dean Coll. Arts and Scis., Georgetown U., 1964-66, acad. v.p., 1966—. Mem. adminstrv. com. Consortium of Univs., Washington, 1968—. Trustee Gonzaga High Sch., Washington, 1969—; chmn. bd. trustees St. Peter's Coll., Jersey City, 1969—. Mem. Am. Philol. Assn. Democrat. Address: Georgetown Univ 37th and O Sts NW Washington DC 20007

FITZMORRIS, JAMES E., JR., lt. gov. of La.; b. New Orleans, Nov. 15, 1921; student Loyola U., New Orleans; m. Gloria Lopez; 1 dau., Lisa Marie. With K.C.S. Ry., New Orleans, 1940-72, v.p., until 1972; lt. gov. State of La., Baton Rouge, 1972—. Active numerous civic activities, including mem. La. Bd. Pub. Welfare, 1952-54, Regional Planning Commn., 1965-66; mem. citizen adv. com. New Orleans Recreation Dept.; regional v.p. Nat. Municipal League, 1966-71; pres. Mississippi Valley World Trade Council, 1968; nat. nat. adv. bd. Small Bus. Adminstrn., 1966-72; pres. Cultural Attractions Fund Greater New Orelans, 1971; mem. Nat. Def. Exec. Res., Office Emergency Transp.; mem. President's Hwy. Safety Com., 1957-63; La. chmn. March of Dimes, 1968-69. Mem. New Orleans City Council, 1954-66. Bd. dirs. New Orleans Bd. Trade, 1967-69, Internat. House, New Orleans Philharmonic Symphonic Soc., Youth Concerts Assn., New Orleans chpt. Nat. Conf. Christians and Jews, 1967-71, Camp Fire Girls, 1967-71; trustee Delgado Art Mus., 1958-62, United Fund for Greater New Orleans Area, 1965-70, Leukemia Soc., Nat. Cystic Fibrosis Research Found., 1967-68. Served from pvt. to maj., AUS, 1942-46. Recipient deLesseps S. Morrison Meml. award, 1965, Distinguished Citizens award Nat. Municipal League, 1968, various others. Mem. New Orleans Area C. of C. (hon. life, v.p. 1966-68), Young Men's Bus. Club Greater New Orleans (hon. life, past pres.), World Trade Club Greater New Orleans (hon. life), Nat. Def. Transp. Assn. (nat. v.p. 1968-69). KC (4 deg.). Home: 700 Emerald St New Orleans LA 70124 Office: State Capitol Bldg Baton Rouge LA 70804*

FITZPATRICK, HUGH, physician; b. Richmond, Va., Dec. 6, 1921; s. Hugh and Ruby Amoretta (Gilliam) F.; B.S., Hampden Sydney Coll., 1943; M.D., Med. Coll. Va., 1950; m. Rachel Anne Lewis, Dec. 21, 1948; children—Hugh E., Stuart L., Julia L., Anne L. Intern, U.S. Naval Hosp., Phila., 1950-51; practice medicine, Asheboro, N.C., 1951-70; emergency room physician High Point (N.C.) Meml. Hosp., 1970—; health dir. Randolph County, N.C., part-time, 1970—; mem. staff High Point Meml. Hosp.; mem. courtesy staff Randolph Hosp., Asheboro; county coroner, 1954-58. Pres. bd. Randolph County Tb. and Health Assn., 1956-58; mem. Asheboro City Sch. Bd., 1962-68. Bd. dirs. Randolph Center for Exceptional Children, United Fund. Served to lt. (j.g.) USNR, 1943-46, 50-51. Mem. N.C., Randolph County (pres. 1957) med. socs., Am. Acad. Gen. Practice, Am. Coll. Emergency Physicians, Theta Chi, Alpha Kappa Kappa. Presbyn. (ruling elder 1957). Democrat. Kiwanian (bd. dirs. 1956-58). Home: 117 S Main St Asheboro NC 27203

FITZPATRICK, JOE WARREN, educator; b. Waco, Tex., Mar. 18, 1925; s. Frank M. and Winnie (Warren) F.; B.S., Baylor U., 1948; M.A., U. Tex., 1950; m. Donna P. Davis, Nov. 3, 1951; children—Wynn Davis, Scott Warren. Research physicist Monsanto Chem. Co., Texas City, Tex., 1950-54; faculty Trinity U., San Antonio, 1956-66, prof. math., 1960-66; prof. math U. Tex., El Paso, 1966—. Active Yucca council Boy Scouts Am. Mem. Math. Assn. Am., Soc. Indsl. and Applied Math., Nat. Council Tchrs. Math., A.A.A.S., Tex. Acad. Sci., Internat. Platform Assn., Sigma Pi Sigma. Home: 5813 Viewmont St El Paso TX 79912

FITZPATRICK, JOHN J., clergyman; b. Trenton, Ont., Can., Oct. 12, 1918; ed. Propaganda Fide Coll. (Italy), Our Lady of Angels Sem. (U.S.) Ordained priest Roman Catholic ch., 1942; named titular bishop of Cenae and aux. of Miami (Fla.), 1968, consecrated, 1968; named bishop of Brownsville, 1971, installed, 1971. Address: PO Box 2279 Brownsville TX 78520

FITZPATRICK, THOMAS, JR., assn. exec.; b. Birmingham, Ala., Mar. 22, 1932; s. Thomas H. and Faustine (Crawford) F.; B.Indsl. Mgmt., Auburn U., 1954; postgrad. Inst. for Organisational Mgmt., U. N.C., 1961, U. Ga., 1965, Mich. State U., 1970; m. Peggy Dierks, Dec. 27, 1955; 4 children. Mgr. govtl. affairs Tampa (Fla.) C. of C., 1958-62; gen. mgr. Sarasota County (Fla.) C. of C., 1962-67; exec. v.p. Greater Columbia (S.C.) C. of C., 1967—. Instr., Inst. for Organisational Mgmt., 1964—. Served to 1st lt. AUS, 1954-57. Named Sarasota Outstanding Young Man of Year, 1963. Mem. Am. (chmn. com.), S.C. (dir., v.p. 1971) assns. C. of C. execs., Phi Delta Theta. Rotarian. Author: Guide to Hillsborough County Government. Office: PO Box 1333 Columbia SC 29202

FITZPATRICK, WILLIAM HENRY WALTER, editor; b. New Orleans, May 23, 1908; s. Harry William and Clara Mary (Bertel) F.; student Tulane U.; m. Francis Westfeldt, Aug. 31, 1940; children—William Whitfield, Peter Bryan, Victor Vaughan Owen, Francis James Gasquet. Reporter, New Orleans Item, 1933-35, Times-Picaynue, 1935-40; city editor New Orleans States, 1940-41, mng. editor, 1941-45, editor, 1945-52; v.p., dir. The Times-Picaynue Pub. Co., 1948-52; dir. Internat. House, New Orleans, 1949-50; editor Wall Street Jour., 1952-60; editor Norfolk-Portsmouth (Va.) Ledger-Star, 1960—. Bd. visitors Tulane U., 1953-64; mem. La. selection com. for Root-Tilden scholarships at N.Y. U. Sch. of Law, 1950-52. Served from lt. to lt. comdr. USNR, 1942-45; PTO. Recipient Pulitzer prize for distinguished editorial writing, 1950; Freedoms Found. medal, 1952. Mem. S.A.R., Am. Soc. Newspaper Editors, La. Soc. Colonial Wars, N.Y. Soc. Colonial Wars (council 1956-58), Beta Theta Pi, Sigma Delta Chi. Roman Catholic. Clubs: Louisiana, Boston, Wrong Day Duck (New Orleans); National Press (Washington); Racquet and Tennis (N.Y.C.); Baltimore (N.C.) Forest Country; Cedar Point (dir.); Princess Anne Country. Home: 109 Oak Grove Rd Norfolk VA 23505 Office: 150 W Brambleton Av Norfolk VA 23501

FITZSIMMONS, FRANK E., labor union ofcl. Gen. v.p., then pres. Internat. Brotherhood Teamsters. Office: 25 Louisiana Av NW Washington DC 20001*

FIX, ROBERT EUGENE, san. engr.; b. Dallas, Tex., Dec. 18, 1916; s. George Joseph and Florence Anna (Dorst) F.; B.S., Tex. A. and M. U., 1938, M.S., 1940; m. Ida Faye McGuire, Apr. 26, 1941; children—Ronald Edward, Thomas Allen, Alice (Mrs. Roy Lee Fry), Frances (Mrs. Frances Lowry). Engr. stream pollution Tex. Dept. Health, Austin, 1940-43; process engr. Filtrol Corp., Jackson, Miss., 1943-47; cons. engr. Wisenbaker, Fix, & Assos., Tyler, Tex., 1947—; partner Municipal Service Co., 1950—; dir., sec.-treas. E. Texas Water Co., White Oak Water Co., Springhill Water Co., So. Utilities Co., Natural Gas Service Co. Bd. dirs. Tyler Youth Found. Mem. Tex., Nat. socs. profl. engrs., Am. Soc. C.E., Am. Inst. Chem. Engrs., Am. Water Works Assn., Water Pollution Control Fedn., Am. Radio Relay League, Aircraft Owners and Pilots Assn., Confederate Air Force. Mason, Rotarian. Home: 2700 Sunnybrook Dr Tyler TX 75701 Office: 1400 Peoples Bank Bldg Tyler TX 75701

FLACK, JOE FENLEY, ins. co. exec.; b. Menard, Tex., Feb. 23, 1921; s. Frank H. and Evelyn (Fenley) F.; B.B.A., U. Tex., 1943; m. Ann Tarry, Jan. 21, 1945; children—Kate Scott, Joan Rudolph, Joe Fenley. Jr. accountant Ernst & Ernst, C.P.A.'s, 1946-47; v.p., treas., dir. Am. Gen. Ins. Co., 1947-69, sr. v.p., treas., dir., 1969—; v.p., dir. Md. Casualty Co., Robert Hampson & Son, Ltd., Whyburn & Co., Am. Gen. Mgmt. Co., Marcasco Co., Inc.; partner John L. Wortham and Son, Houston, 1947-65; auditor Hawaiian Life Ins. Co., Ltd.; v.p. Assurance Co. Am., Me. Bonding & Casualty Co., No. Ins. Co. N.Y.; v.p., treas., dir. Md. Am. Gen. Ins. Co., Nat. Standard Ins. Co., Am. Gen. Leasing &Financing Corp., Am. Gen. Investment Corp., Am. Gen. Realty Co., Atlas Realty Co., Channing Financial Corp., Knickerbocker Corp.; asst. v.p. Emmett A. Larkin Co., Inc.; dir. Chanstat Services, Inc. Mayor pro-tem City of Bunker Hill Village, Tex., 1959-61, mayor, 1961-65. Chmn. finance com. Boy Scouts Am.; bd. dirs., gen. campaign chmn. Salvation Army, Greater Services Campaign; v.p. Spring Br. Sch. Dist. Trustee Kappa Sigma Found., U. Tex. Served as lt. (s.g.) USNR, 1943-45. C.P.A., Tex. Methodist (bd. govs.). Home: 301 Mayerling Dr Houston TX 77024 Office: PO Box 3247 Houston TX 77001

FLAGG, ROGER HOLMES, dentist; b. Buffalo, Aug. 7, 1930; s. Lloyd Eugene and Luella (Breed) F.; D.D.S., U. Buffalo, 1954; m. Nancy Jane Mabee, Dec. 10, 1954; children—David Kenneth, Peter Wesley, Mark Holmes, Susan Carroll. Commd. 2d lt. U.S. Navy, 1954, advanced through grades to Capt., 1971; intern, U.S. Naval Hosp., Camp Pendleton, Cal., 1954-55; staff dental officer Comdr. Constrn. Battalions, U.S. Atlantic Fleet, 1963-64; sr. dental officer U.S.S. Grand Canyon, 1964-66; Clin. supr., prosthodontist Naval Dental Clinic, Washington, 1966-70; dental officer U.S.S. Intrepid, 1970-72. Guest lectr. U. Philippines, and U. Far East, Manilla, 1960-61, Kent County (R.I.) Dental Soc., 1971. Awards chmn., treas. troop Cub Scouts Am., Vienna, Va., 1967-69. Recipient certificate of appreciation Philippines Dental Assn., 1961, certificate of recognition R.I. Dental Soc., 1962. Mem. Am. Dental Assn., Am. Acad. Oral Medicine. Methodist (v.p. men's club 1968-69). Home: 8401 Stonewall Dr Vienna VA 22180 Office: USS Intrepid (CVS-11) C/O FPO New York City NY 09501

FLAHERTY, DAVID THOMAS, state senator, advt. exec.; b. Boston, Dec. 9, 1928; s. Thomas Patrick and Mabel (Seely) F.; B.S. in Bus. Adminstrn., Boston U., 1955; m. Nancy Ann Hamill, Dec. 6, 1952; children— David Thomas, Stephen F., Deborah A., Jon E. Sales rep. Broyhill Furniture Factories, Lenoir, N.C., 1955-56, jr. exec., 1956-58, asst. sales mgr., 1958-60, gen. mgr. Broyhill Plastics, Inc. (div. Broyhill Industries), 1960—. Mem. N.C. Senate, 1969—, mem. appropriations com., hwy. safety com., mental health com., ins. com., mfg., labor and commerce com., edn. com. Del. NATO Youth Conf., Bonn, Germany, 1963; dist. chmn., council tng. chmn. Boy Scouts Am.; founder, pres. Bunny Maynard Midget Football League. Mem. N.C. Republican Exec. Com., 1949-52; nat chmn. Young Rep. Com., 1965; nat. committeeman Nat. Fedn. Young Reps., 1964, 65, state chmn., 1963, vice chmn. pub. relations, 1962, nat. co-chmn. campaign com., 1966. Recipient Scouters key Boy Scouts Am., 1961, Council Pres.'s trophy, 1968, Silver Beaver award Boy Scouts Am., 1968; named Outstanding Young Republican N.C., 1964. Mem. Scarlet Key, Lock, D.A.V. (comdr. Lenoir chpt.), Alpha Kappa Psi. Clubs: Lenoir Golf, Cedar Rock Country. Optimist (bd. govs., chmn. oratorical contest, 1957, 60). Home: 803 Hospital Av Lenoir NC 28645 Office: Broyhill Park Lenoir NC 28645

FLAHERTY, J. LOUIS, clergyman; b. Norfolk, Va., May 13, 1910; ed. Holy Cross Coll., N.Am. Coll. and Gregorian U. (Italy) Ordained priest Roman Catholic ch., 1936; army chaplain, World War II; formerly supt. schs., Richmond Diocese; pastor Blessed Sacrament Ch., Norfolk, Va.; consecrated titular bishop of Tabuda and aux. of Richmond, 1966. Address: 170 Painter St Norfolk VA 23505

FLAMMIA, DOMINICK ANTONIO, ry. co. exec.; b. Long Island City, N.Y., Dec. 21, 1921; s. Domencio Antonio and Maria (Del Visco) F.; student Duke U., 1942; B.A., Wake Forest Coll., 1948; m. Lidie Lee Walters, Sept. 12, 1970; children by previous marriage—Shelly (Mrs. Phil Greer), Dayle Andrew, Grady Walters, Lyn. Sch. tchr. Millbrook High Sch., Raleigh, N.C., 1952-55; salesman Peden Steel Co., Raleigh, 1959-64; v.p. marketing Norfolk So. Rwy., Raleigh, 1964-70, sr. v.p., 1970—. Served with USMCR, 1942-46. Methodist. Clubs: N.Y. Traffic; Eastern N.C. Traffic; Ponte Vedra (Fla.); Raleigh Civitan (pres. 1964), North Ridge Country (Raleigh). Home: 1108 Hardimont Rd Raleigh NC 27609 Office: 2424 North Blvd Raleigh NC 27609

FLANAGAN, CLIFFORD PETER, apparel co. exec.; b. New Bedford, Mass., Nov. 1, 1918; s. John J. and Lucy (Sullivan) F.; student New Bedford Textile Sch., 1939, Washington and Lee U., 1943; m. Pearl D. Rodgers, May 21, 1948; children—Patricia Ann, Teresa Rose, Michael Patrick. Dyer, Acme Dye Works, Pulaski, Va., 1939-42; founder, partner Charlotte Finishing Co. (N.C.), 1946-68, pres., 1954-68 (merged into Huntley of York, Ltd., York, S.C.), pres., 1968—, dir., 1968—. Chmn. bd. dirs. Divine Saviour Hosp., York, 1971; bd. dirs. United Fund, York, 1970-71. Served to maj. AUS, 1942-45. Decorated Bronze Star. Mem. Am. Assn. Textile Chemists and Colorists, Nat. Knitted Outerwear, Am. Apparel Mfg. Assn. Roman Catholic. Club: Golf (York). Home: Route 1 Box 31D York SC 29745 Office: PO Box 419 York SC 29745

FLANAGAN, MIKE D., polit. editor Tulsa World. Nieman fellow. Address: 315 S Boulder St Tulsa OK 74102*

FLANARY, CARL FRANKLIN, dentist; b. Jonesville, Va., Mar. 1, 1920; s. James Monroe and Orra Elizabeth (Graham) F.; A.B., Lincoln Meml. U., 1940; postgrad. U. Tenn., 1946-47; D.D.S., Med. Coll. Va., 1952; m. Gladys Imogene Dean, Dec. 24, 1948; children—Carl Franklin II, James Monroe. Tchr. pub. schs., Va., 1940-41; aluminum tester Aluminum Co. Am., Alcoa, Tenn., 1942; pvt. practice dentistry, Waynesboro, Va., 1952—; sec.-treas. Karalot, Inc., Waynesboro, 1970—; mem. med. adv. com. Blue Ridge Community Coll., 1971—. Served with USNR, 1942-46. Decorated Bronze Star. Mem. Am., Va., Shenandoah Valley (pres. 1969-70) dental assns. Presbyn. (deacon 1963-65). Elk. Home: 2024 Cheroke Rd Waynesboro VA 22980 Office: 361 S Linden Av Waynesboro VA 22980

FLANDERS, DONALD HARGIS, mfg. co. exec.; b. Memphis, Apr. 26, 1924; s. Henry Jackson and Mae (Hargis) F.; student Tex. Christian U., 1943; B.B.A., Baylor U., 1947; m. Phala Katherine Davis, Dec. 15, 1946; children—Donald Hargis, Dudley Kennedy, Phala Katherine. Purchasing agt., cost accountant McCoy-Couch Furniture Mfg. Co., Benton, Ark., 1947-50; dir. cost accounting and purchasing Garrison Furniture Mfg. Co., Ft. Smith, Ark., 1950-54; pres., gen. mgr. Flanders Mfg. Co., Ft. Smith, 1954-70; pres. Flanders Metal Products, Inc., 1970—; dir., chmn. exec. com. City Nat. Bank Ft. Smith, 1960-71. Chmn. exec. com. Ft. Smith Freight Bur., 1960-61; chmn. furniture bd. govs. Dallas Market Center, 1968; mem. exec. com. Ark. Council on Econ. Edn., 1964-67; mem. Small Bus. Adv. Council, Ark., 1966-68. Chmn. Ft. Smith United Fund, 1962; dist. chmn. Boy Scouts Am., Ft. Smith, 1960-62, pres. Westark area council, 1963-65, mem.-at-large nat. council, 1963—, regional exec. com., 1964—, vice chmn. Region 5, 1967-69, chmn. Region 5, 1969-71, rep. nat. council, 1968—, mem. nat. exec. bd., 1969—, Silver Antelope, Silver Beaver, Distinguished Eagle Scout awards; mem. Com. of 100, 1965—. Trustee Sparks Regional Med. Center, Hendrix Coll. Served from apprentice seaman to lt. (s.g.) USNR, 1943-46. Named Industrialist of Year, Ft. Smith Realtors Bd., 1965; recipient Free Enterprise award, 1964. Mem. Southwestern Furniture Marketing Assn. (pres. 1963), Ft. Smith C. of C. (dir. 1961-63). Ark. Retail Furniture Assn. (dir. 1960), Ark. Wood Products Assn. (dir. 1965-68), Delta Sigma Pi. Methodist (trustee conf.). Mason (K.T., 33 deg., Shriner). Home: 20 Berry Hill Rd Fort Smith AR 72901 Office: 1801 Wheeler Av Fort Smith AR 72901

FLANDERS, FRANCES VIVIAN, librarian; b. Howe, Okla., Sept. 18, 1908; d. Frank and Vivian Moore (Fair) Flanders; grad. Mansfield Female Coll., 1927; A.B., Northwestern State Coll., 1929, B.S. in Library Sci., La. State U. 1936. Tchr. pub. sch., Pelican, La., 1929-35; librarian Neville High Sch., Monroe, La., 1936-46; dir. Ouachita Parish Pub. Library, Monroe, La., 1946—; instr. library sci. Southwestern La. Inst., summers 1938-39, Northwestern State Coll., summers 1944-45; bldg. cons. to La. State Library, 1947—. Mem. Am., La. (pres. 1951) library assns., D.A.R. (regent Ft. Miro chpt., 1952-52, state librarian, 1954-57, vice-chmn, S.W. region conservation com., 1956-59), Am. Assn. U. Women (pres. Monroe br., 1941), Daus. Founders and Patriots (state officer, 1954-57), Colonial Dames 17th Century (chpt. v.p. 1971-72), Phi Kappa Phi, Delta Kappa Gamma, (pres. chpt., 1944-45), Phi Mu (chpt. pres. alumnae 1963-64). Presbyn. (bd. deacons).Home: 1703 N 3d St Monroe LA 71201 Office: 1800 Stubbs Av Monroe LA 71201

FLANDERS, HENRY JACKSON, JR., educator; b. Malvern, Ark., Oct. 2, 1921; s. Henry Jackson and Mae (Hargis) F.; B.A., Baylor U., 1943; B.D., So. Bapt. Theol. Sem., 1948, Th.D., 1950; postgrad. U. Tenn., 1943, Union Theol. Sem., 1963, Hebrew Union Coll., 1948; m. Tommie Lou Pardew, Apr. 19, 1944; children—Janet, Jack III. Ordained to ministry Bapt. Ch., 1940; prof., chmn. dept. religion, chaplain Furman U., 1950-62; pastor First Bapt. Ch., Waco, Tex., 1962-69; prof. religion Baylor U., Waco, 1969—. Trustee Baylor U., Hillcrest Bapt. Hosp.; chmn. bd. Golden Gate Bapt. Theol. Sem.; mem. exec. bd. Bapt. Gen. Conv. Tex.; pres. bd. dirs. Econ. Opportunity Advancement Corp.; bd. dirs. Heart of Tex. Red Cross. Served with USAAF, 1943-45. Decorated Air medal with clusters. Mem. Baylor Ex-students Assn. (pres.), Waco Bapt. Ministerial Assn. (pres.), Assn. Bapt. Profs. Religion (pres.), Soc. Bibl. Lit., Am. Assn. U. Profs. (chpt. pres. 1971—), Am. Acad. Religion. Mason, Rotarian.

Club: Western S.C. Torch (Greenville, S.C.). Author: People of the Covenant, 1963. Home: 3820 Chateau St Waco TX 76710

FLANIGAN, PETER M(AGNUS), govt. ofcl.; b. N.Y.C., June 21, 1923; s. Horace C. and Aimee (Magnus) F.; grad. cum laude Portsmouth Priory, R.I.; B.A. summa cum laude, Princeton, 1945; m. Brigid Snow, Nov. 27, 1954; children—Brigid Snow, Sheila Magnus, Timothy, Megan, Robert. With Dillon, Read & Company, Inc., 1947-69, v.p., 1954-69; asst. to Pres. U.S., Washington, 1969—; dir. Adolphus Busch Estate. Financial analyst ECA Mission to U.K., 1949-50. Asst. treas., trustee N.Y. U.-Bellevue Med. Center; trustee Am. Mus. Natural History; adv. bd. N.Y. Foundling Hosp. Clubs: Recess (gov., v.p.), The Links (N.Y.C.); Round Hill (Greenwich, Conn.); Clove Valley (North Clove, N.Y.). Office: The White House 1600 Pennsylvania Av Washington DC 20500

FLANIGEN, JOHN M., elec. engr., city ofcl.; b. Athens, Ga., Nov. 25, 1895; s. Cameron Douglas and Mary (Nevitt) F.; B.S. in Elec. Engring., Ga. Sch. Tech., 1917; m. Hannah Scofield, Oct. 15, 1924; children—John M., Anna (Mrs. Edwin Scott), Charlotte (Mrs. Bruce E. Paine), William Scofield. Engr. in tng. Cities Service Co., 1919-20, engr., supt. various utility properties, Conn., Md., O., 1920-27; asst. supt. distbn. Ga. Power Co., 1927-39, plant engr., 1939-60. Alderman City of Atlanta, 1962—. Served to 1st lt. U.S. Army, 1917-19; AEF in France. Registered profl. engr., Ga. Fellow I.E.E.E. (dir. 1945-48); mem. Beta Theta Pi. Episcopalian. Mason. Address: 245 3d Av SE Atlanta GA 30317

FLANNAGAN, BENJAMIN COLLINS, IV, lawyer; b. Richmond, Va., Sept. 7, 1927; s. Benjamin Collins and Virginia Carolyn (Gay) F.; B.A., U. Va., 1947, M.A., 1948, LL.B., 1951; LL.M., Georgetown U., 1956. Admitted to Va. bar, 1951; trial atty. Internal Security div. Justice Dept., 1955—. Served as 1st lt. Judge Adv. Gen.'s Corps, 1952-55; maj. Res. Mem. Va. Bar Assn., Beta Gamma Sigma. Clubs: Country of Virginia, Deep Run Hunt, Virginia Boat (Richmond). Episcopalian. Book rev. editor Va. Law Rev., 1950-51. Home: 3000 39th St NW Washington DC 20016 Office: US Dept Justice Washington DC 20530

FLANNERY, THOMAS A., U.S. dist. atty., Washington. Office: 5607 Jordan Rd Springfield VA*

FLASHING, DONALD JOSEPH, dentist; b. Chgo., Feb. 19, 1937; s. Michael Joseph and Evelyn (Tansley) F.; student Tex. A. and M. U., 1956, Arlington State Coll., 1960-63; D.D.S., Baylor U., 1967; m. Patricia Ann Campbell, Nov. 26, 1964. Pvt. practice dentistry, Garland, Tex., 1967—; v.p. F. and G. Roofing Co., Inc., Garland, 1971—; mem. staff Meml. Hosp., Speegle Clinic, Garland Clinic, Garland. Bd. dirs. Garland Welfare Bd., 1968-69. Served with USAF, 1956-60. Mem. Am., Tex. dental assns., Dallas County Dental Soc., Phi Kappa Theta, Zi Psi Phi (pres. 1966-67), Garland Jr. C. of C. (bd. dirs. 1968). Kiwanian (bd. dirs. 1969-71). Patentee crown and splint remover, 1971. Home: 1821 Meadowcrest St Garland TX 75042 Office: Forest Tower Bldg Garland TX 75042

FLATT, WILLIAM PERRY, univ. adminstr.; b. Newbern, Tenn., June 17, 1931; s. Carl Hadley and Evelyn Inez (Kelso) F.; student Bethel Coll., 1948-49; B.S., U. Tenn., 1952; Ph.D., Cornell U., 1955; postgrad. Rowett Research Inst. (Scotland), 1967-68; m. June Nesbitt, Apr. 9, 1949; children—Melynda Claire, Katherine Ann. Dairy cattle nutritionist, head energy metabolism lab. Agrl. Research Services, U.S. Dept. Agr., Beltsville, Md., 1956-68, asst. dir. animal husbandry research div., 1968-69; prof. animal sci., head animal sci. div. U. Ga., Athens, 1969-70, dir. agrl. expt. stas. Coll. Agr., 1970—. Recipient NSF fellowship, Cornell U., 1953-55, Presidential Citation, U.S. Dept. Agr., 1965. Superior Service award, 1968, award Am. Feed Mfrs. Assn., 1965, Hoblitzelle Nat. award Tex. Research Found., 1968. Mem. A.A.A.S., Am. Soc. Animal Sci., Am. Dairy Sci. Assn., Am. Inst. Nutrition. Rotarian. Contbr. articles to profl. jours. Home: 110 Broomsedge Trail Athens GA 20601

FLAX-JAFFE, HERMAN JACOB, physician; b. Richmond, Va., Mar. 31, 1917; s. Bernard Nathan and Jennie (Jaffe) F.; B.S., U. Richmond, 1936; M.D., Med. Coll. Va., 1940; M.Med. Sci. in Phys. Medicine, U. Pa., 1952; m. Josefina Guarch, Sept. 13, 1940; children—Hjalmar, Judith, Jennifer. Intern, Stuart Circle Hosp., Richmond, 1940-41; resident surgery Charity Dist. Hosps., Bayamon, Arecibo, P.R., 1941; fellow phys. medicine and rehab. Workmens Compensation Bd., Rehab. Center, Toronto, Ont., Can., 1947, Malton, Ont., 1948-51, Inst. Phys. Medicine and Rehab., N.Y.C., 1951; practice medicine specializing in phys. medicine and rehab., San Juan, P.R., 1951—; dir. pub. charities, Manati, P.R., 1941-44; med. insp., chief phys. medicine and rehab. State Inc. Fund, San Juan, 1945-51; chief phys. medicine and rehab. San Juan VA Center, Clinica Dr. E. Fernandez Garcia, Profl. Hosp., 1951— (all San Juan); attending U. Hosp., Municipal Hosp., Auxillo Med. Mutuo, Clinica Mimiya, Drs. Hosp.; cons. Presbyn. Hosp., Dept. Vocational Rehab., 1952— (all San Juan); from asst. prof. to prof. phys. medicine and rehab. U. P.R. Sch. Medicine, 1952—. Med. cons., organizer P.R. chpt. Crippled Children and Adults Assn., 1950—; mem. Pres.'s Com. on Hiring Physically Handicapped, 1956-60; mem. med. research study section Social Security Agy., Dept. Health, Edn. and Welfare, 1969—. Diplomate Am. Bd. Phys. Medicine and Rehab. Fellow A.C.P.; mem. Internat. Soc. Rehab. Disabled (dir., med. cons. U.S. com.), P.R., Ind. med. assns., A.M.A., Am. Congress Rehab. Medicine (pres. 1970-71), Am. Acad. Phys. Medicine and Rehab., Assn. Phys. and Mental Rehab., Assn. Med. Rehab. Dirs. and Coordinators, Assn. Mil. Surgeons U.S., Am. Assn. Electromyography and Electrodiagnosis, Am. Acad. Cerebral Palsy, Nat. Rehab. Assn., Am. Soc. Med. Hydrology, Phi Sigma Delta, Phi Delta Epsilon, Sigma Pi Sigma. Contbr. numerous articles to sci. jours. Home: Luhn 2 Urb Victor Braegger Villa Caparra Bayamon PR 00619 Office: 310 de Diego Santurce PR 00909

FLEET, IRVING JOSEPH, dentist; b. Live Oak, Fla., Jan. 23, 1924; s. William Abraham and Anna Mildred (Blate) F.; A.A. with honors, U. Fla., 1943; D.D.S., Northwestern U., 1946, M.S. in Dentistry, 1951; m. Anita Kant, Aug. 26, 1956; children—Martin L., Charles S., Philip B., Ann Caroline. Practice dentistry specializing in orthodontics, Tallahassee, Fla., 1951—. Cons. Fla. State U. Sch. Home Econs. and Cleft Palate Clinic. Pres. LeMoyne Art Found., 1967; soloist Tallahassee Symphony Orch., 1963). Served to capt. AUS, 1947-49. Mem. Leon County Dental Soc. (pres. 1957), Northwest Dist. Dental Soc. Fla., (pres. 1960-61). Home: 1575 Hickory St Tallahassee FL 32303 Office: 437 E College St Tallahassee FL 32301

FLEETWOOD, BARROW TILSON, social worker; b. Hertford, N.C., Mar. 22, 1911; s. Barrow A. and Blanche (Tilson) F.; A.A., Mars Hill Coll., 1930; B.S., Western Carolina U., 1934; postgrad. Duke U., 1939; M.S.W., U. N.C., 1942; m. Dorothy Madeleine Young, Dec. 20, 1938; children—Stephen T., Barrow S. Tchr., Mars Hill, N.C., 1934-39; dir. Henderson County Dept. Pub. Welfare, Hendersonville, N.C., 1945-47, Lenoir County Dept. Pub. Welfare, Kinston, N.C., 1957-61; dir. social service Bapt. Childrens Homes, Thomasville, N.C., 1948-51, dir. social work G. Pierce Wood Meml. Hosp., Arcadia, Fla., 1961—; social worker VA, Oteen, N.C., 1952-57. Served from pvt. to capt. AUS, 1942-45, 51-52; Korea; lt. col. ret. Decorated Bronze Star medal. Mem. Nat. Assn. Social Workers. Home: 5211 Commonwealth Rd Palmetto FL 33561 Office: Box 189 Arcadia FL 33821

FLEETWOOD, JOSEPH ANDERTON, physician; b. Jackson, N.C., Jan. 27, 1894; s. Robert Wilson and Harriet Rebecca (Burnette) F.; B.S., Wake Forest Coll., 1919; M.D., Tulane U., 1921; m. Caroline Lane, Dec. 27, 1924; 1 son, Joseph Anderton. Intern, St. Vincent Hosp., Norfolk, Va., 1921-22, City Hosp., Macon, Ga., 1922, Walker Meml. Hosp., Wilmington, N.C., 1922-23; physician Atlantic Coast Line Hosp., Atlantic Coast Line R.R., Rocky Mount, N.C., 1923; practice medicine, Conway, N.C., 1923—; mem. staff Roanoke Rapids Hosp. Examiner, Selective Service, 1942-46. Mem. Conway Sch. Bd., 1934-42, town council, 1942-50. Mem. Am. Acad. Gen. Practice, A.M.A., N.C., Northampton-Halifax County med. socs., Seaboard Coastline R.R. Surgeons, N.C. Hist. Soc. Baptist. Mason (32 deg.). Address: Main St Conway NC 27820

FLEISCHMAN, WILLIAM EDWARD, economist; b. Fanwood, N.J., Jan. 25, 1939; s. Edward Joseph and Frances (Weller) F.; A.B., Rutgers U., 1960; M.A., U. Mich., 1966, Ph.D., 1971; m. Martha Gardner Wellman, Aug. 21, 1967. Adminstrn. asst. Port of N.Y. Authority, N.Y.C., 1960-61; asst. prof. econs. New Coll., Sarasota, Fla., 1968-71; staff economist Nat. Commn. State Workmen's Compensation Laws, Washington, 1971—. Cons., Nat. Endowment for the Humanities, Washington, 1971. Ford Found. research fellow, 1966-67. Mem. Am. Econ. Assn., Assn. Evolutionary Econs., Labor Historians. Home: 2013 O St NW Washington DC 20036 Office: National Workemen's Compensation Commn 1825 K St NW Washington DC 20006

FLEMING, BILL GORDON, retail food co. exec.; b. Morganton, N.C., July 4, 1931; s. William Thomas and Camelia Blanche (Garrison) F.; student Western Carolina Tchrs. Coll., 1949-50, Clemson U., 1948-49; m. Lois June Waldrop, Aug. 20, 1954; children—Starr, Heidy, Bill Gordon. Spl. agt., pub. relations exec. Richmond Fredricksburg & Potomac R.R., Richmond, Va., 1955-61; pub. relations exec. Armour & Co., Jacksonville, Fla., 1961-68; pres. Fleming & Hobbs, Inc., food brokers, Dunnellon, Fla., 1967—; pres. Fleming, Inc. doing bus. as Shop Rite Super Markets, Dunnellon, 1969—. Chmn. Kirk for Gov., 1968. Served with USMCR, 1950-55. Decorated Bronze Star medal, Purple Heart. Mem. Greater Dunnellon C. of C. (pres. 1969-72), Mchts. Assn. (pres. 1969), V.F.W. Baptist (youth sch. tchr. 1964-66). Elk, Lion. Home: Route 1 Box 611 Dunnellon FL 32630 Office: Box 656 Donnellon FL 32630

FLEMING, DERYL EDWARD, pub. relations exec.; b. Graettinger, Ia., Jan. 5, 1931; s. Curtiss F. and Idella (Murphy) F.; B.A. cum laude (Murray fellow), U. Ia., 1958; m. Verena Marie Werner, Nov. 1954; children—Geoffrey, Linda, Pandra; m. 2d, Carolyn Gorman, Aug. 1971. Pub. relations mgr. Nat. Assn. Retail Clothiers and Furnishers, Washington, 1958-59; asst. to dir. com. pub. affairs Am. Petroleum Inst., N.Y.C., 1960-61; mem. account staff Carl Byoir & Assos., N.Y.C., 1961-62; dir. pub. relations Kellogg Co., Battle Creek, Mich., 1962-69, Washington rep., 1969—. Bd. dirs. Calhoun (Mich.) County Red Cross, Nottawa Trails council Boy Scouts Am., Greater Battle Creek United Fund, Battle Creek Civic Theater. Served with USAF, 1951-55. Recipient Brewer Press Key, Journalism Sch. U. Ia., 1958. Mem. Pub. Relations Soc. Am., Sigma Delta Chi. Club: Nat. Press (Washington). Home: 9433 Forest Haven Dr Alexandria VA 22309 Office: Suite 4400 485 L'Enfant Plaza SW Washington DC 20024

FLEMING, EDWARD STITT, physician; b. Washington, Apr. 11, 1930; s. Robert Walton and Emma Scott (Stitt) F.; B.A. in Psychology, U. N.C., 1951; M.A. in Psychology, U. Tex., 1952; M.D. cum laude, George Washington U., 1957. children—Edward Stitt, Edith Page, Richard B. Intern, U. N.C. Sch. Medicine, 1957-58; resident in psychiatry Yale Sch. Medicine, 1958-61, instr. psychiatry, 1961-63, also physician-in-charge psychiat. outpatient clinic Yale-New Haven Hosp., 1961-63; career tchr. Nat. Inst. Mental Health, 1963-65; dir. inpatient psychiat. services George Washington U. Hosp., Washington, 1963-67; asst. clin. prof. psychiatry George Washington U. Sch. Medicine, 1963-65, asso. clin. prof., 1965—; postgrad. med. tng. Washington Psychoanalytic Inst., 1963-67; founder, pres. Psychiat. Inst. Washington, 1966—, Psychiat. Insts. Am., 1967—; v.p., bd. dirs. Psychiat. Inst. Found., 1968—; bd. dirs. Tidewater Psychiat. Inst., Norfolk, Va., 1970—; chmn. governing bd. Elmcrest Psychiat. Inst., Portland, Conn., 1971—. Psychiat. Cons. to VISTA, U.S. Civil Service Commn. Served to capt. USAF, 1951-53. Fellow Am. Psychiat. Assn.; mem. A.M.A., D.C. Med. Soc., World, Washington psychiat. socs., N.Y. Acad. Scis., Soc. Lee's of Va., Smith-Reed-Russell Honor Frat., Kane-King Honor Soc., William Beaumont Honor Med. Soc., Alpha Omega Alpha. Episcopalian. Clubs: International (Washington); Gibson Island; Princess Anne. Office: Psychiatric Insts America 1825 K St NW Washington DC 20006

FLEMING, GWENNETH DWAINE, banker; b. Cleburne, Tex., Mar. 20, 1934; s. Cecil Sylvester and Vera Corrine (Wilson) F.; grad. Am. Inst. Banking, 1962; student San Jacinto Jr. Coll., Pasadena, Tex., 1963-64, U. Wis., 1969; m. Dorothy Calissa Brasher, Sept. 6, 1952; children—Cecil Dwaine, Ricky Lynn, Demiria Ann, Kirby Loren. With Houston br. Fed. Res. Bank, 1952-66, asst. mgr. transit dept., 1963-66; v.p., cashier, auditor First Pasadena State Bank (Tex.), 1966—; instr. Houston chpt. Am. Inst. Banking. Pres. Pasadena Livestock Show and Rodeo Assn.; sec.-treas. Pasadena Nat. Little League. Mem. Am. Inst. Banking (past treas., dir. Houston chpt.), Bank Adminstrn. Inst. (Gulf Coast chpt.), Tex. Bankers Assn., Pasadena C. of C. Optimist (dir.). Home: 238 Crescent St Pasadena TX 77502 Office: 1001 E Southmore St Pasadena TX 77502

FLEMING, HUGH JOSEPH, educator; b. Detroit, Apr. 16, 1922; s. Hugh Joseph and Clara Belle Cecilia (Scott) F.; B.S., U. Detroit, 1944; B.S. Fgn. Service, Sch. Fgn. Service, Georgetown U., 1946; M.B.A., U. Detroit, 1956; m. Hilda Rodriguez-Hernandez, Sept. 27, 1947; children—Sheila, Hugh Joseph, III, Ann, Nieves, Maria. Asso. prof. econs. Sch. Fgn. Service, Georgetown U., Washington, 1946-52; def. accountant Packard Motor Car Co., Detroit, 1952-54; chmn. dept. bus. and econs. Marian Coll., Indpls., 1954-57; life underwriter Aetna Life Ins. Co., Indpls., 1956-57; financial analyst Ford Motor Co., 1957-63; asso. prof., chmn. personnel mgmt. St. Mary's U., San Antonio, 1963-72, grad. dir. Sch. Bus. Adminstrn., 1972—. Ford Found. grantee, U. Tex., 1964. Mem. Am., Cath. econ. assns., Soc. for Advancement Mgmt. San Antonio Personnel and Mgmt. Assn. (v.p. research and devel. 1969), Pi Gamma Mu, Delta Phi Epsilon. Roman Catholic. K.C. Home: 5402 Inwood Circle San Antonio TX 78228 Office: 2700 Cincinnati St San Antonio TX 78228

FLEMING, JAMES FURMAN, assn. exec.; b. Conway, S.C., Mar. 31, 1937; s. Irvin McLaurn and Martha (Denton) F.; A.A., N. Greenville Jr. Coll., 1960; student St. Bernard Coll., 1969; m. Martha Ann Capps, July 12, 1958; children—James Furman, William Keith. Partner, Fleming Bros. Photo Service, Conway, S.C., 1955-56; news editor Georgetown Times (S.C.), 1956-58, 60-61; staff mem. Greenville News (S.C.), 1958-60; field rep. S.C. Farm Bur., Columbia, 1962-64, dir. dept. promotions, 1964-66; exec. v.p. Ala. Poultry Industry Assn., also sec.-treas. Ala. Poultry and Egg Council, 1966-70; dir. pub. and govtl. relations United Egg Producers, Atlanta, 1970—. Recipient Outstanding Leadership award in poultry industry Poultry and Egg Nat. Bd., 1963. Mem. Am. Soc. Assn. Execs. (Mgmt. award 1970), State Poultry Exec. Secs. Assn. (dir. 1966-67, sec.-treas. 1967-70). Baptist (deacon). Home: 4184 Idlevale Dr Tucker GA 30084 Office: 1001 International Blvd Atlanta GA 30354

FLEMING, JULIAN DENVER, JR., lawyer; b. Rome, Ga., Jan. 12, 1934; s. Julian Denver and Margaret (Mangham) F.; student U. Pa., 1951-53; B.Chem. Engring. with highest honors, Ga. Inst. Tech., 1955, Ph.D., 1959; J.D. with distinction, Emory U., 1967; m. Sidney Mack Howell, June 28, 1960; 1 dau., Julie Adrianne. Research asst., instr. Ga. Inst. Tech., Atlanta, 1955-59, research asso., asst. prof., 1959-61, research engr., asso. prof., 1961-66, research engr., prof. chem. engring., 1966-67; admitted to D.C. and Ga. bars; now practicing in Atlanta. Research project dir. for programs of U.S. Army, USN, AEC; engring. cons. Oak Ridge Nat. Lab., Rayonier, Inc., Glasrock Products, Inc., Buckman Labs., Bd. dirs. Ga. Mental Health Assn., Met. Atlanta Mental Health Assn. Registered profl. engr., Ga., Cal. Fellow Am. Inst. Chemists; mem. Am., Ga. bar assns., Sigma Xi, Tau Beta Pi, Omicron Delta Kappa, Phi Lambda Epsilon, Phi Kappa Phi, Phi Delta Theta. Republican. Author profl. papers, govt. and pvt. research reports. Editor-in-chief Jour. Pub. Law, 1966-67. Patentee in field. Home: 2238 Hill Park Ct Decatur GA 30033 Office: 1st Nat Bank Bldg Atlanta GA 30303

FLEMING, LAWRENCE DURWOOD, univ. pres.; b. Sulphur Springs, Tex., Aug. 9, 1914; s. John Payne and Alice Lucile (Rash) F.; B.A., So. Meth. U., 1937, Th.M. 1940; D.D., McMurry Coll., 1957; m. Lurlyn January, Mar. 19, 1940; children—Jon Hugh, Pamela (Mrs. J. Kenneth Shamblin, Jr.), Martha Ann (Mrs. Stephen Curtis). Ordained to ministry Meth. Ch., 1940; pastor, Caddo-Mills-Salem, Tex., 1940-42, Dallas, 1942-44, Eastland, Tex., 1944-45; founding pastor St. Luke's Ch., Houston, 1945-61, pres. Southwestern U., 1961—. Past pres. Tex. Council Ch.-Related Colls.; mem. World Meth. Council, also del. confs., 1961, 66, gen. and jurisdictional confs., 1960, 64, 66; mem. exec. com. Ind. Colls. and Univs. of Tex. Bd. dirs. Tex. United Community Services; mem. Gov.'s Adv. Council Language Handicapped Children, Tex. Planning Commn. Recipient Distinguished Alumnus award So. Meth. U., 1965. Mem. Tex. Meth. Coll. Assn. (past pres.), Am. Assn. Ind. Coll. and Univ. Presidents, Philos. Soc. Tex. Mason, Rotarian. Home: 111 Taylor Rd Georgetown TX 78626

FLEMING, LLOYD LESLIE, JR., fire chief; b. Pensacola, Fla., May 23, 1924; s. Lloyd Leslie and Ethel Hazel (Anderson) F.; student Pensacola Trade Sch., 1942, Fla. State Fire Coll., 1948, Pensacola Jr. Coll., 1961-63; m. Selma Elaine Goelz, July 26, 1942; children—Jan Faye, Marianne Leda. With Pensacola News Jour., 1937-41; fireman Pensacola Fire Dept., 1945-53, driver, 1953-60, capt., 1960-61, asst. fire chief, 1961-62, fire chief, 1962—, asst. drill master, 1959-60. West Area dir. Urban Fire Def., 1963—. Bd. dirs., mem. exec. bd., past chmn. govt. div. Pensacola United Fund; bd. dirs. Escambia Lighthouse for Blind. Named News Boy of Year, 1939, Lion of Year, 1969. Mem. Indsl. Mgmt. Assn. (past mem. exec. bd.). Mem. Ch. of Christ (deacon). Lion. Home: 619 South D St Pensacola FL 32501 Office: 239 N Spring St Pensacola FL 32501

FLEMING, LOUISE ELIZABETH, coll. ofcl.; b. Greenville, N.C., Apr. 8, 1900; d. James Lawson and Loula (White) Fleming; A.B., Meredith Coll., 1921; M.A., Columbia, 1922, postgrad., 1928, profl. diploma, 1958; postgrad. Union Theol. Sem., 1933, U. Wash., 1937. Gen. sec. Winthrop Coll. YWCA, Rock Hills, S.C., 1923-26, U. Wash. YWCA, Seattle, 1926-37, Northwestern U. YWCA, Evanston, Ill., 1937-42; mem. staff nat. bd. YWCA, asso. in adminstrn. and personnel, tng. for coll. and univ. div., N.Y.C., 1942-50; dean students Meredith Coll., Raleigh, N.C., 1950-69, spl. asst. to pres., 1969-70, dean emeritus, 1970—. Mem. Nat., N.C. assns. women deans and counselors, Am. Personnel and Guidance Assn., Am. Coll. Personnel Assn., Nat. Assn. Social Workers, Am. Assn. U. Women, N.C. Lit. and Hist. Soc., N.C. Art Soc., Nat. Soc. Colonial Dames Am., Mortar Bd., Kappa Delta Pi, Pi Lambda Theta, Sigma Alpha Iota. Baptist. Club: Woman's (Raleigh, N.C.). Address: 3939 Glenwood Av Raleigh NC 27609

FLEMING, SAMUEL M., banker; b. Franklin, Tenn., Apr. 29, 1908; s. Samuel M. and Cynthia Graham (Cannon) F.; student Battle Ground Acad., 1919-24; A.B., Vanderbilt U., 1928; m. Josephine Cliffe, Dec. 30, 1930; children—Joanne Cliffe, Daniel Milton. Asst. credit mgr., N.Y.C. Trust Co., 1928-31; with Third Nat. Bank, Nashville, 1931—, dir., 1947—, pres., 1950—; dir. Williamson Co. Bank, Jack Daniel Distillery, Geneso, Inc., Tennessee Tufting Co., Murray-Ohio Mfg. Co., Seaboard Coast Line Industries, Nat. Life & Accident Ins. Co.; pres. NLT Corp. Trustee Battle Ground Acad., Vanderbilt U., Meharry Med. Coll. Lt. USNR, 1942-45. Mem. Res. City Bankers Assn., Robert Morris Assos., Am. Bankers Assn. (pres. 1961), Tenn. Hist. Soc. (treas.) S.A.R., Newcomen Soc. Eng., New York So. Soc., Sigma Alpha Epsilon (hon. eminent supreme archon). Presbyn. Clubs: National Golf (Augusta, Ga.); Cumberland, Belle Meade Country Richland Golf (Nashville); Links, University (N.Y.C.). Home: 810 Jackson Blvd Nashville TN 37205 Office: Third Nat Bank Nashville TN 37219

FLEMING, STANLEY LOUIS, dentist; b. Johnson City, Tenn., Oct. 21, 1933; s. Smith George and Vivian Cecile (Richardson) F.; student U. Denver, 1951-52, Wayne State U., 1955-58; D.D.S., Howard U., 1962; M.S. in Physiology, Georgetown U., 1972 children—Stanley Louis, Ron D., Lovie T., Tanya R. Instr., Coll. Dentistry, Howard U., 1963-66, asst. prof., 1966-69; dentist Dental Health Clinic, Washington, 1963-67; individual practice dentistry, Washington, 1963—; NIH postdoctoral research fellow Georgetown U., 1969-71. Vol. dentist Resurrection City, Washington, 1968; dentist Head Start Program and Med. Assistance Program. Served with USAF, 1951-55. Mem. Am., Nat. dental assns., D.C., Robert T. Freeman dental socs., Washington, Nat. Negro golf assns., Chi Delta Mu, Omega Psi Phi. Methodist. Home: 4000 Tunlaw Rd NW Washington DC 20007 Office: 231 Atlantic St SE Washington DC 20032

FLEMING, THOMAS PRINCE, govt. ofcl.; b. Russellville, Ark., May 24, 1920; s. Thomas Prince and Margery (Hill) F.; student Little Rock Jr. Coll., 1938-41; B.S. in Chem. Engring., U. Ark., 1947; M.S., U. Tenn., 1956; m. Marilyn L. Long, June 19, 1948 (dec. Mar. 1965); children—Michael Richard, Terry Lynn; m. 2d, Rebecca Elizabeth Plumley, June 4, 1968. With Weather Bur., 1938-41; engr. Union Carbide Nuclear Co., Oak Ridge, 1952-65, Armour Agrl. Chem. Co., Cherokee, Ala., 1965-66; project engr., head isotopes sect. programs br. Naval Facilities Engring. Command, Fort Belvoir and Falls Church, Va., 1966-70, head isotopes programs, programs br., Arlington, Va., 1970—. Justice of Peace Gray Twp. (Ark.), 1951. Served to 1st lt. USAAF, 1943-46, USAF, 1948. Mem. Nat. Soc. Profl. Engrs., Am. Chem. Soc., Am. Mgmt. Assn., Soc. Am. Mil. Engrs., Pi Kappa Alpha. Presbyn. Home: 6309 Charnwood St Springfield VA 22152 Office: Yards and Docks Bldg Washington DC 20390

FLESHOOD, ARNOLD PENDLETON, coll. dean; b. LaCrosse, Va., Sept. 11, 1923; s. Otis Arnold and Josephine (Roberts) F.; B.A., U. Richmond, 1950; M.S., Va. Poly. Inst., 1954; Ed.D., Columbia, 1961; m. Carrie Louise Allen, Dec. 27, 1950; children—William Arnold, Martha Louise. Tchr. English, Martinsville (Va.) High Sch., 1950-53; prin. Joseph Martins Sch., Martinsville, 1953-56; gen. supr. Martinsville Sch., 1956-58, dir. instrn., 1958-60; dir. instrn., asst. supt. Lynchburg (Va.) City Sch. System, 1961-65; prof., head dept. elementary edn. Richmond (Va.) Profl. Inst. (now Va. Commonwealth U.), Richmond, 1965-68, dean Sch. Edn., 1968-71, asst. v.p. academic affairs, 1971—. Vis. prof. Randolph Macon Womans Coll., Lynchburg Coll., 1960-61. Dalhousie U., Halifax, N.S., Can., summers 1963-64; chief cons. Richmond City Schs.; mem. Va. Textbook Evaluation Com., adv. com. on higher edn.; cons. Chesterfield County (Va.) Schs. Mem. bd. edn. Va. Meth. Conf., 1968-70. Bd. visitors Buford Acad. Served with USNR, 1943-46. Recipient Outstanding Community Service award Martinsville Exchange Club, 1961. Mem. Phi Delta Kappa, Theta Chi. Club: Richmond Exchange (pres.) Home: 204 Roslyn Hills Dr Richmond VA 23229

FLETCHER, ALBERT LEWIS, clergyman; b. Little Rock, Oct. 28, 1896; s. Thomas M. and Helen (Wehr) F.; A.M., Little Rock Coll., 1917; student St. John's Home Mission Sem., 1917-20. Ordained priest Roman Catholic Ch., 1920; asst. prof. Little Rock Coll., 1920-23, pres. 1923-25; faculty St. John's Sem., 1925-39; chancellor Little Rock Diocese, 1926-33; apptd. vicar gen. Little Rock Diocese, 1933; made papal chamberlain, 1929, domestic prelate of papal household, 1934; elected to titular see of Samos, 1939, and apptd. aux. bishop of Little Rock; consecrated aux. bishop, 1940; apptd. bishop of Little Rock by Pope Pius XII, 1946. Apptd. pres. of Diocesan Publ. Soc., 1937. Home: 4605 Crestwood Dr Little Rock AR 72207 Office: 305 West 2d St Little Rock AR 72114

FLETCHER, CHARLES PORTER, dentist; b. Norfolk, Va., Apr. 9, 1926; s. Bluker Ehringhaus and Catharine (Price) F.; student U. Biarritz, So. France, 1946; A.A., Coll. William and Mary, 1949; B.S., Va. Poly. Inst., 1951; D.D.S., Med. Coll. Va., 1956; m. Juanita Joyce Underdown, Apr. 1, 1950; children—Terry Lynn, Catharine Anne. Practice dentistry, Virginia Beach, Va., 1956—; dir. First and Mchts. Nat. Bank, WVAB radio, Virginia Beach, Princess Anne Investment Corp., Virginia Beach. Part time instr. Sch. Dental Hygiene, Old Dominion U., 1968-71. Mem. sch. bd. Virginia Beach Pub. Schs., 1966—. Mem. Am., Va., Virginia Beach, Tidewater dental assns., Seaboard Dental Study Club, Sigma Zeta, Psi Omega. Democrat. Presbyn. (ruling elder 1958—). Home: 1200 Kent Lane Virginia Beach VA 23454 Office: 424 Woodway Lane Virginia Beach VA 23462

FLETCHER, JOHN LYNN, psychologist, educator; b. Springdale, Ark., Apr. 18, 1925; s. Lynn Harrington and Elsie (Jones) F.; B.A., U. Ark., 1950, M.A., 1951; postgrad. U. Md., 1951-53; Ph.D., U. Ky., 1955; m. Mary Lou Campbell, Aug. 29, 1949; children—Lynn Gray, Jana Lee. Commd. 2d lt. U.S. Army, 1952, advanced through grades to lt. col., 1966; research psychologist Med. Research Lab., Fort Knox, Ky., 1952-70; prof. psychology, speech and hearing Memphis State U., 1970—. Vice pres., dir. Hearing Conservation, Inc., Virginia, Minn., 1964-70; lectr. U. Ky., Fort Knox, 1960—; cons. to various cos.; mem. hearing and bioacoustics com. NRC-Nat. Acad. Scis., 1956—, mem. exec. council, 1970—. Mem. Fort Knox (Ky.) Sch. Bd., 1962—; bd. dirs. Jr. Sci. and Humanities Symposium, Fort Knox, 1962—. Served with AUS, 1943-46. Decorated Bronze Star medal. Fellow Acoustical Soc. Am.; mem. Psychonomic Soc., Sigma Xi. Baptist. Patentee hearing protection devices. Home: 5305 N Clover Dr Memphis TN 38117

FLETCHER, JOSEPH O., oceanographer, govt. ofcl.; b. Rygate, Mont., May 16, 1920; B.S. in Geophysics, U. Okla., 1940; certificate in meteorology Mass. Inst. Tech., 1941; M.S. in Physics, U. Cal. at Los Angeles; m. Caroline Fletcher; children—Margaret, Christina, Joseph, Richard, Jonathon. Chief Project Icicle, 1952; program mgr. Project Corrode, U.S. Air Force, 1953; mem. concepts evaluation staff Air War Coll., 1954-57; chief air sect. Mil. Assistance Adv. Group, Oslo, Norway, 1958-61; chief long-range plans group Directorate of Plans, Hdqrs. U.S. Air Force, 1962-63; sr. research scientist RAND Corp., Santa Monica, Cal., 1964-71; research prof. oceanography and atmospheric scis. U. Wash., Seattle, 1970-71; head Office Polar Programs, nat. and internat. programs NSF, Washington, 1971—. Chmn. sci. adv. com. U.S. Coast Guard; mem. adv. com. U. Alaska Geophys. Inst.; mem. U.S. nat. com. for internat. hydrological decade, panel on glaciology Nat. Acad. Scis. Fellow Norwegian Polar Inst., Norwegian Geog. Soc.; mem. Am. Meteorol. Soc., Arctic Inst. N.Am. (gov.), Sigma Xi, Tau Beta Pi, Sigma Tau. Contbr. articles on climatic and Arctic research to profl. publs. Home: Sherry Towers 2117 E St NW Washington DC 20037 Office: Nat Sci Found 1800 G St NW Washington DC 20550*

FLETCHER, LLOYD, commnr. U.S. Court Claims; b. Amarillo, Tex., Jan. 5, 1915; s. Lloyd and Florence (McKenzie) F.; B.B.A., U. Tex., 1936; J.D., George Washington U., 1939; m. Lola Slaight, Apr. 25, 1940; children—Diane, Bruce. Admitted to D.C. bar, 1940; practiced law, Washington, 1940-59; professorial lectr. law Am. U., 1946—; commnr. U.S. Ct. Claims, 1960—. Served to lt. (j.g.) USCGR, World War II. Mem. Am., D.C., Fed. bar assns., The Barristers (Washington), Order of Coif, Phi Kappa Psi. Mason (Shriner). Contbr. articles to legal jours. Home: 4851 Maury Lane Alexandria VA 22304 Office: US Court Claims Washington DC 20506

FLETCHER, ORLIN KENYON, JR., state ofcl.; b. Augusta, Ga., Nov. 25, 1908; s. Orlin Kenyon and Mary (Heckle) F.; B.S., U. Ga., 1942; M.P.H., U. N.C., 1948; m. Dorothy Roberta Harris, Apr. 1, 1934. Biologic aide U.S. Bur. Fisheries div. sci. inquiry, 1935-37; biologic technician U. Ga., 1937-42; biologist Ga. Dept. Health, Albany, 1942-68, asst. epidemiologist, 1968—. Cons. local health units, USAF, USN, other govtl. agys. Mem. Ga. Entomol. Soc. (pres. 1960-61), Am. Assn. Econ. Entomologists, Pub. Health Engr., Sigma Xi, Phi Beta Kappa. Episcopalian (founder St. Mark's ch., Albany 1950, warden 1953-63). Contbr. articles to publs. Inventor apparatus for collection, measurement specimens. Home: 117 Redbud Rd Albany GA 31705 Office: 1109 N Jackson St Albany GA 31705

FLETCHER, RILEY EUGENE, lawyer; b. Eddy, Tex., Nov. 29, 1912; s. Riley Jordan and Lelih (Gill) F.; B.A., Baylor U., 1950, J.D., 1950; m. Hattie Inez Blackwell, June 11, 1954. Admitted to Tex. bar, 1950; asst. county atty. Navarro County, Tex., 1951-52, county atty., 1952-54; pvt. practice law, Corsicana, Tex., 1955-56; asst. atty. gen. Tex., 1956-62, chief law enforcement div., atty. gen.'s dept., 1958-61; chief taxation div., atty. gen.'s dept., 1961-62; asst. gen. counsel Tex. Municipal League, Austin, 1962-63, gen. counsel, 1963—. Lt. col. arty. U.S. Army Res. ret. Mem. Am., Travis County bar assns., State Bar Tex., Am. Judicature Soc., Res. Officers Assn., Assn. U.S. Army (chpt. pres. 1965-66), Am. Legion, Judge Advs. Assn. Baptist. Mason. K.P. Home: 8100 Balcones Dr Austin TX 78759 Office: Vaughn Bldg Austin TX 78701

FLETCHER, THOMAS WILLIAM, city ofcl.; b. Portland, Ore., Mar. 1, 1924; s. Irving A. and Florence (Cooper) F.; B.S. in Bus. Adminstrn., U. Cal. at Berkeley, 1951; m. Margerie Frances Muller, Dec. 27, 1945; children—Thomas William, Heidi, Dean. Asst. to city mgr., San Leandro, Cal., 1951-52; city adminstr., Davis, Cal., 1952-55; asst. to city mgr., San Diego, 1955-61, city mgr., 1961-66; pres. Franchise Corp., 1966-67; dep. asst. sec. Dept. Housing and Urban Devel., 1967; dep. mayor of Washington, 1967—. Vice pres. San Diego County council Boy Scouts Am., 1959—. Bd. dirs. San Diego YMCA, 1961-64. Served with AUS, 1943-46. Named Outstanding Young Man of Year in San Diego, San Diego Jr. C. of C., 1960. Mem. League Cal. Cities (pres. city mgrs. dept. 1965-66, chmn. electronic data processing com. 1965-67), Western Govt. Research Assn. (pres. 1963-64), Am. Soc. Pub. Adminstrn. (pres. San Diego 1960-61), Internat. City Mgrs. Assn., Nat. League Cities (chmn. nat. joint com. uniform traffic control devices 1965-66), Nat. Municipal League (mem. council). Kiwanian. Author articles in field. Home: 3001 Veazey Terrace NW Washington DC 20008 Office: Dist Bldg 14th and E Sts NW Washington DC 20004

FLICKINGER, W(ALTER) GARRETT, lawyer, educator; b. Erie, Pa., July 9, 1928; s. Carlton Phillip and Kathleen (Garrett) F.; A.B. with high honors, Yale, 1950; J.D., U. Mich., 1953; postgrad. Columbia, 1967-68 Admitted to N.Y. bar, 1953, Ky. bar, 1969; asso. White & Case, N.Y.C., 1953, 55-60; asst. prof. law Boston U., 1960-63; vis. asso. prof. law U. Ky., 1963-64, asso. prof., 1964-67, prof., 1967—. Bd. govs. Citizens Assn. for Planning, Lexington, 1964-70; trustee LSATC Council, 1969-71. Served with AUS, 1953-55. Mem. Am. Bar Assn. (mem. com. on successions 1966—), Assn. Bar City N.Y., Phi Beta Kappa, Delta Theta Phi, Order of Coif, Omicron Delta Kappa. Democrat. Episcopalian. Home: 1416 Cochran Rd Lexington KY 40508

FLINT, CHARLES W., JR., chmn. bd. Flint Steel Co. Trustee, Tulsa U. Address: 3730 S Birmingham St Tulsa OK 74105*

FLINT, CORT RAY, clergyman; b. Leedey, Okla., Mar. 17, 1915; s. Corties Ray and Kathryn (Logan) F.; B.A., Southwestern State Coll., 1935; postgrad. U. Okla., summers 1937, 39; Th.M., So. Bapt. Theol. Sem., 1943, Th.D., 1952; m. Wilma Ilene Moore, Nov. 24, 1920; children—Sue Ann, Cort Ray. Tchr. pub. schs., Okla., 1935-40; ordained to ministry, Bapt. Ch., 1940; pastor, New Haven, Ky., 1941-43, Pleasant Grove Ch., Hodgenville, Ky., 1941-42, 46-47; asst. pastor Southside Bapt. Ch., Birmingham, Ala., 1947-48; pastor First Ch., Olney, Tex., 1948-50, Lynn Acres Ch., Louisville, 1951-53; adminstrv. asst. So. Bapt. Theol. Sem., Louisville, 1952-55; pastor First Ch., Anderson, S.C., 1955—; interim pres. Anderson Coll., 1957—; pastor Meadows of Dan Bapt. Ch., Va.; dir., pres. Anderson Sch. Theology for Laymen; vice chmn. bd. PACA. Various offices Bapt. convs., Tex., Ky., 1948-53; chmn. stewardship com. S.C. Bapt. Conv., 1957-58, gen. bd., 1957—; finance com. Saluda Bapt. Assn. S.C., 1955-58. Active YMCA, Anderson County Tb Assn.; exec. bd. Blue Ridge council Boy Scouts Am. Vice chmn. bd. trustees So. Bapt. Theol. Sec., Louisville; trustee Furman U. Served as lt., chaplain, USNR, 1943-46; PTO. Mem. Anderson Ministerial Assn. (pres. 1956-57), Internat. Platform Speakers Orgn. Mason, Odd Fellow. Clubs: Rotary, Kiwanis. Author: Grief's Slow Wisdom; To Thine Own Self Be True; Better Men or Bitter Men; Grief Is Love; The Best Is Yet To Be. Editor: The Quotable Dr. Crane; The Quotable Billy Graham. Home: The Recluse Route 2 Box 174 Hillsville VA 24343

FLINT, EINAR P(HILIP), chemist; b. Wardner, Ida., Aug. 10, 1908; s. Oscar Frederick and Mathilda Charlotte (Peterson) F.; B.S., U. Wash., 1930; A.M., George Washington U., 1932; Ph.D., U. Md., 1936; m. Adele Cavanagh, Nov. 6, 1937; children—Robert Bryan, James Frederick. Research chemist clay and silicate products div. Nat. Bur. Standards, Washington, 1930-44; supr. inorganic chem. sect. Armour Research Found., Chgo., 1944-46, became chmn. ceramics and minerals dept., 1946; dir. inorganic research Mallinckrodt Chem. Works, St. Louis, 1954-56; head inorganic research Arthur D. Little, Inc., Cambridge, Mass., 1956-62; asst. to pres. Ipsen Industries, Inc., Rockford, Ill., 1962-65; mgr. materials Am. Machine & Foundry Co., 1965-66; mem. hdqrs. staff U.S. Bur. Mines, 1966—. Fellow Am. Ceremic Soc., Washington Acad. Scis., mem. Inst. Ceramic Engrs., Am. Inst. Mining and Metall. Engrs., Am. Chem. Soc. Club: Cosmos (Washington). Contbr. articles to tech. jours. Home: 6229 Radcliff Rd Alexandria VA 22307 Office: Interior Bldg Washington DC 20240

FLIPPEN, LLEWELLYN TUCKER, dentist; b. Richmond, Va., July 8, 1933; s. James Howard and Evelyn (Tucker) F.; B.A., U. Richmond, 1954; D.D.S., Va. Commonwealth U., 1958. Rotating dental intern Wilford Hall Hosp., San Antonio, 1958-59; pvt. practice dentistry, Richmond, 1961—; asst. clin. prof. restorative dept., also chmn. part time faculty com. Sch. Dentistry, Va. Commonwealth U., 1961—. Mem. alumni interfraternity council U. Richmond, 1966—. Served to capt. USAF, 1958-61. Mem. Met. Acad. Dentistry (treas. 1969), Richmond Dental Soc. (bd. dirs., sec.), Va. Assn. professions, Am. Profl. Practice Assn., S.A.R. (chpt. pres. 1966, bd. mgrs. 1964-69), Omicron Kappa Upsilon, Kappa Alpha, Delta Sigma Delta, Alpha Sigma Chi, Sigma Zeta. Presbyn. (chmn. bd. deacons 1971-72, elder 1972—). Club: Bull and Bear. Home: 4310 Old Brook Rd Richmond VA 23227 Office: 4100 Brook Rd Richmond VA 23227

FLIPSE, DAVID ERLE, govt. economist; b. Monrovia, Cal., Nov. 12, 1922; s. Cornelius Ivan and Jane Louise (Ellis) F.; B.S., Cal. Poly. Coll., 1948; m. Floy Esme Strayer, July 21, 1945; children—Jane Ann (Mrs. Stephen C. Getman), Patricia Kay, Mark Reed. Agriculturist, agrl. economist, gen. economist Bur. Reclamation, Dept. Interior, Visalia, Fresno and Sacramento, Cal., 1948-56, bus. and gen. economist, supervisory gen. economist, chief econs. br. Div. Planning, Washington, 1956—. Served to 2d lt. USAF, 1942-45. Decorated Purple Heart. Recipient certificate of superior performance Dept. Interior, 1959. Mem. Am. Econs. Assn., Am., Western agrl. econs. assns., Nat. Econs. Club, Soc. Govt. Economists, A.A.A.S. Home: 10400 Trumpeter Ct Vienna VA 22180 Office: Department of the Interior Bureau of Reclamation 18th and C Sts NW Washington DC 20240

FLOCKS, KARL W., lawyer; b. N.Y.C., Apr. 27, 1910; B.E. in Mech. Engring., Johns Hopkins U., 1930; J.D., George Washington U., 1934. Admitted to D.C. bar, 1933, U.S. Ct. Customs and Patent Appeals bar, 1934, U.S. Supreme Ct. bar, 1955; patent examiner U.S. Patent Office, 1930-37; now with Karl W. Flocks and Assos., Washington. Mem. Am. Bar Assn., Bar Assn. D.C. (council sect. patent, trademark and copyright law 1960), Am. Trial Lawyers Assn., Am. Patent Law Assn., Tau Beta Pi. Home: 4848 Loughboro Rd NW Washington DC 20016 Office: Munsey Bldg Washington DC 20004*

FLORA, BEN VIVIAN, supt. schs.; b. Owingsville, Ky., May 23, 1909; s. Perry Edward and Rada (Triplett) F.; A.B., Ky. Wesleyan Coll., 1932; postgrad. U. Ky., 1933; M.A., Xavier U., 1955; m. Irene Rogers, Dec. 24, 1934. Tchr. pub. schs. Montgomery County (Ky.), 1932-33; asst. coach pub. schs., Mount Sterling, 1933-38, supt. schs., 1957-59; tchr., coach pub. schs., Raceland, Ky., 1938-43; tchr., coach secondary schs., Bellevue, Ky., 1943-55, prin. high sch., 1955-57, supt. schs., 1962—; Supt. schs., Irvine, Ky., 1959-62. Kiwanian, Rotarian. Home: 910 Clayton St Bellevue KY 41073 Office: 200 Center St Bellevue KY 41073

FLOREN, MARVIN JOHN, dentist; b. Chulumami, Bolivia, S.A., Sept. 3, 1941 (parents Am. citizens); s. Roger Chevalier and Pearl Marvie (Hubbard) F.; student Andrews U., 1960-61; D.D.S., Loma Linda U., 1967; m. Carol Conard Morgan, July 31, 1966; children—John Wesley, Jeffery Dean. Research asst. restorative dept. Loma Linda U., 1965, 66; clin. instr. crown and bridge dept. Emory U., Atlanta, 1969—; clinician Ben Massell Dental Clinic, 1969-70. Recipient awards Loma Linda U. Dental Clinic, 1966, Ben Massell Dental Clinic, 1970. Mem. Am., Ga. dental assns., S.A.R. Mem. Ch. of Seventh Day Adventist. Home: 1861 N Decatur Rd NE Atlanta GA 30306 Office: 3312 Piedmont Rd NE Atlanta GA 30305

FLORES, ADOLPH ANTHONY, JR., physician; b. Mansfield, La., Oct. 16, 1921; s. Adolph Anthony and Kathleen Garland (Rambin) F.; B.S., La. State U., 1942, M.D., 1944. Intern, Charity Hosp., Shreveport, La., 1944-45; gen. practice medicine, Pleasant Hill, La., 1946-50; resident in medicine Charity Hosp. La., New Orleans, 1950-53, asst. dir., 1955-59; practice medicine specializing in internal medicine, New Orleans, 1959—; asst. cardiologist So. Bapt. Hosp., New Orleans; clin. prof. medicine La. State U. Sch. Medicine, New Orleans, 1971—. Head med. div. New Orleans Civil Defense, 1965-66. Bd. dirs. La. Med. Polit. Action Com., 1964-68, Greater New Orleans Area Wide Health Planning Council; charter mem. Vis. Nurses Assn. Greater New Orleans. Served with USNR, World War II, Korea. Diplomate Am. Bd. Internal Medicine. Mem. A.M.A., A.C.P., Assn. Am. Physicians and Surgeons, Am. Soc. Internal Medicine, So. Med. Assn., La. State Med. Soc., New Orleans Acad. Internal Medicine (pres. 1967-68), Orleans Parish Med. Soc. (dir. 1970-72), Phi Chi. Roman Catholic. K.C. Home: 1737 Milan St New Orleans LA 70115 Office: 4500 Magnolia St New Orleans LA 70115

FLORES, ARTURO FRANCISCO, importer-exporter; b. Eagle Pass, Tex., Sept. 20, 1928; s. Arturo and Margaret (Streigler) F.; student Tex. A and M Coll., 1945-48; B.B.A., Sul Ross State Coll., 1950; m. Martha Henderson, Jan. 31, 1950; children—Deborah Kay, Arturo Francisco. Purchasing agt. La Consolidada, S.A., 1954-59, forwarding agt., 1959—; dir. Hallmark Aviation, San Antonio, First Nat. Bank, Eagle Pass, Tex. Mem. exec. bd. Concho Valley council Boy Scouts Am., 1964-72; mem. Criminal Justice Council Tex., 1969-72; mem. Regional Export Expansion Council, 1967—; pres. region Tex. Municipal League, 1967-68. Mayor, City of Eagle Pass, 1966-72; del. Nat. Democrat Conv., 1968. Served with USMCR, 1952-54. Mem. Eagle Pass C. of C. Rotarian. Home: Box 707 Eagle Pass TX 78852 Office: 840 Main St Eagle Pass TX 78852

FLORES, JOHN DEE, JR., wholesale trade co. exec.; b. Bethany, La., July 24, 1924; s. John Dee and Virginia Gaynell (Fortson) F.; grad. high sch.; m. Melba Jean Jackson, Sept. 10, 1946; children—Michael Wayne, Gene Rene. With Morris & Dickson Co., Shreveport, La., 1941—, v.p., 1970—. Served with USNR, 1941-46; PTO. Democrat. Baptist. Home: 6127 Canal Blvd Shreveport LA 71108 Office: 220 Travis St Shreveport LA 71101

FLORES, PATRICK FERNANDEZ, aux. bishop Diocese of San Antonio. Office: PO Box 13190 San Antonio TX*

FLORES, RUBEN, educator, city ofcl.; b. Del Rio, Tex., Nov. 17, 1939; s. Jesus Ramon and Maria (Paredes) F.; A.A., San Antonio Coll., 1963; B.A. in Internat. Relations, St. Mary's U., 1965; m. Acenete Hernandez, Nov. 24, 1967. Chmn. social studies San Felipe Ind. Sch. Dist., Del Rio, Tex., 1965—. Area coordinator Texans for Ednl. Advancement of Mexican-American, San Antonio. Mem. city council, Del Rio, 1968—; mem. sch. bd. San Felipe Del Rio Consol. Sch. Dist., 1972—. Served with USMCR, 1957-60. Mem. Tex. State Tchrs. Assn. (pres. 1968-69, chmn. adv. com.), Am. G.I. Forum, Theta Sigma Chi. Democrat. Roman Catholic. Club: Optimist. Home: 314 E Adobe St Del Rio TX 78840

FLORY, ALDEN EARL, ins. co. exec.; b. Whiting, Kan., Mar. 13, 1916; s. Edwin E. and Kathleen (Whitson) F.; Ph.B., Washburn Coll., Topeka, 1938, LL.B., 1947; m. Lolita Tebbets, Dec. 31, 1938; 1 dau., Linda Joyce (Mrs. Michael L. Rigsby). Admitted to Kan. bar, 1947, Mo. bar, 1948, Va. bar, 1950; claims atty. Mo. Farm Bur. Ins. Co., Jefferson City, 1947-50; organizer, chief exec. officer Va. Farm Bur. Ins. Co., Richmond, 1950-70; organizer, pres., chief exec. officer Early Settlers Ins. Co., Richmond, 1961-70; dir., co-organizer Second Nat. Bank, Richmond, 1966—. Dir. Va. Hosp. and Med. Service assns. (Blue Cross-Blue Shield), Va. Fire Ins. Rating Bur. Pres. Canterbury Assn., 1961-62. Served to 1st lt. AUS, 1940-45. Mem. Am., Va., Richmond bar assns., Am. Mgmt. Assn., Def. Research Inst., Internat. Assn. Ins. Counsel. Democrat. Clubs: Executives, Downtown, Richmond Country (dir.). Home: 1209 Giltspur Rd Richmond VA 23229 Office: 2015 Staples Mill Rd Richmond VA 23261

FLORY, DAVID PAUL, communications engr.; b. Phillipsburg, O., Aug. 3, 1919; s. David Chleo and Della (Fox) F.; B.A., Denison U., 1941; m. Virginia Ruth Knox, Mar. 20, 1943; children—Katharine Knox (Mrs. Winston Michael Fox), Carol Wallace (Mrs. Harold H. Wingerd, Jr.), David Paul. Engr., Western Electric Co., Chgo., 1946-49; partner D.C. Flory & Sons, Gen. Contractors, Dayton, O., 1949-52; engr. So. Bell Tel. & Tel. Co., Charlotte, N.C., 1952-63, supervising engr., 1963—. Served to lt. USAF, 1941-46; now lt. col. Res. Registered profl. engr., N.C. Mem. Nat. Soc. Profl. Engrs., Phi Gamma Delta. Democrat. Episcopalian. Home: 3301 Eastburn Rd Charlotte NC 28210 Office: PO Box 240 Charlotte NC 28201

FLORY, ROBERT ALLAN, chemist; b. Sullivan, Ind., Nov. 12, 1924; s. James Ivan and Winnie (McCain) F.; B.S., Ball State U., 1951; m. Aletha M. Ammerman, Dec. 4, 1945; children—Michele Lynn (Mrs. James E. Hardie), Craig Alan. Chemist, Ball Bros. Co., Muncie, Ind., 1951-53; chemist Hawkeye Rubber Co., Cedar Rapids, Ia., 1953-60; plant mgr. H. B. Egan Mfg. Co., Muskogee, Okla., 1960—. Active YMCA, Muskogee, Okla., 1963—. Republican precinct chmn., 1964. Served with AUS, 1942-45. Decorated Purple Heart, Bronze Star medal (U.S.); Belgian Fourragere. Mem. Am. Chem. Soc. Presbyn. Mason. Address: Route 2 Webbers Falls OK 74470

FLORY, ROBERT MIKESELL, govt. ofcl.; b. Bridgewater, Va., Feb. 21, 1912; s. John Samuel and Vinnie (Mikesell) F.; B.A., Bridgewater Coll., 1932; M.A., U. Va., 1938, postgrad., 1938-40; postgrad. U. Chgo., 1946-47; m. Thelma Louise Thomas, Sept. 14, 1942; 1 dau., Pamela. Tchr., coach Rockingham County (Va.) Schs., 1932-37; psychol. test technician U.S. Employment Service, Boston, 1940-42; job and systems analyst United Air Lines, Inc., Chgo., 1945-48; asst. to v.p. Fairbanks, Morse & Co., Chgo., 1949-60; lectr. U. Chgo., 1960-61; employment service adviser U.S. Dept. Labor, Chgo., 1961-62; information systems designer USDA, Washington, 1963—. Instr. bus. adminstrn. Roosevelt U., Chgo., 1955-60. Served to lt. comdr. USNR, 1942-45. Mem. Inst. Mgmt. Sci., Assn. Systems Mgmt., Washington Operations Research Council, Am. Statis. Assn., Tau Kappa Alpha. Toastmaster (pres. 1968—). Home: 5535 Columbia Pike Arlington VA 22204 Office: US Dept Agr Washington DC 20250

FLORY, WALTER S., JR., geneticist, botanist; b. Bridgewater, Va., Oct. 5, 1907; s. Walter Samuel and Ella May (Rehard) F.; A.B., Bridgewater Coll., 1928, Sc.D. (hon.), 1953; A.M. (Blandy fellow, 1928-31), U. Va., 1929, Ph.D., 1931; Nat. Research fellow biol. Scis., research asso. Harvard 1935-36; m. (Nellie) Maude Thomas, Apr. 24, 1930 (dec. Jan. 1971); children—Kathryn Sue (Mrs. Walter Maier), Walter Samuel, Thomas Reherd. In charge tech. work Shaver Bros., Inc., Jacksonville and Tampa, Fla., 1931-32; instr. sci. Greenbrier Coll., Lewisburg, W.Va., 1932-34; prof. biology Bridgewater Coll., 1934-35; horticulturist Tex. Agrl. Expt. Sta., 1936-44, Va. Agrl. Expt. Sta., 1944-47; prof. exptl. horticulture U. Va., 1947-63; vice dir., mgr. Blandy Exptl. Farm, 1947-63, vis. prof., summer 1964; curator O. E. White Research Arboretum, 1955-63; bd. dirs. Winston-Salem Nature Sci. Center, 1964-70, treas., 1965-66; Babcock prof. botany Wake Forest U., Winston-Salem, N.C., 1963—; dir. Reynolda Gardens, 1964-71; instl. lectr. Piedmont U. Center, 1965-70; collaborator U.S. Dept. Agr., 1945-48. Del. Internat. Botany Congress, Paris, 1954, Montreal, 1959, Edinburgh, 1964; mem. Internat. Genetics Congress, Montreal, 1958, Tokyo, 1968, Internat. Hort. Congress, 1966. Invited lectr. Internat. Chromosone Seminar, Calcutta, 1968. Trustee, mem. exec. com. Highlands Biol. Sta., pres., 1969-72; trustee Bridgewater Coll. Recipient J. Shelton Horsley Research award Va. Acad. Sci., 1949; Pres. and Visitors Research prize U. Va., 1951; Bridgewater Coll. Alumni award, 1956. Fellow A.A.A.S.; mem. Am. Soc. Hort. Sci., Genetics Soc. Am., Am. Genetics Assn., Soc. Study Evolution, Bot. Soc. Am. (chmn. southeastern sect. 1951-52), Assn. Southeastern Biologists (pres. 1962-63), Am. Boxwood Soc. (co-founder, treas., editor 1961-63), Am. Assn. Bot. Gardens and Arboretums (editorial bd. 1962-64), Am. Begonia Soc. (hon.), Fairchild Tropical Garden (life), So. Appalachian Bot. Club (v.p. 1962), Am. Plant Life Soc., Va. Acad. Sci. (pres, 1956; chmn. publs. com. 1964—, chmn. biology sect. 1962-63, I.F. Lewis award 1969), La. Soc. Hort. Research (hon.), Am. Magnolia Soc. (v.p. 1968-72), Phi Beta Kappa, Sigma Xi (pres. Wake Forest chpt. 1970), Tau Kappa Alpha, Phi Sigma. Democrat. Mem. Ch. of Brethren. Club: Torch. Contbr. articles on genetics, cytology and hort. subjects in profl. jours. and mags. Home: 2025 Colonial Pl Winston-Salem NC 27104

FLOURNOY, EDWIN ELLIOTT, JR., physician; b. Jackson, Miss., Nov. 30, 1935; s. Edwin Elliott and Josephine (Cotten) F.; B.S., Millsaps Coll., 1956; M.D., U. Miss., 1960; m. Mary Beth Brandon, June 29, 1957; children—Elizabeth Lynn, Katherine Elliott. Intern, Womack Army Hosp., Ft. Bragg, N.C., 1960-61; resident gen. practice Lafayette (La.) Charity Hosp., 1964-65; practice medicine specializing in family practice, 1965—; mem. staff Phoebe Putney Meml. Hosp., Albany, Ga.; med. v.p. Dougherty County branch Am. Cancer Soc., 1970—; mem. med staff, trustee Palmyra Park Hosp. Served with USAF, 1960-64. Mem. Ga. Acad. Family Physicians, Am., So. med. assns., Med. Assn. Ga., Dougherty County Med. Soc. Baptist. Elk, Kiwanian. Home: 508 Greenwood St Albany GA 31705 Office: 1009 N Monroe St Albany GA 31701

FLOWERS, CHARLES ELY, JR., physician; b. Zebulon, N.C., July 20, 1920; s. Charles Ely and Carmen, (Poole) F.; B.S., The Citadel, 1941; M.D., Johns Hopkins, 1944; m. Juanita Bays, Nov. 23, 1944 (dec.); children—Charles Ely III, Carmen Eva. Intern, Johns Hopkins Hosp., Balt., 1944, resident, 1945-50; instr. State U. N.Y., 1950-51, asst. prof., 1951-53; asso. prof. U. N.C., 1953-61, prof., 1961-66; prof., chmn. dept. obstetrics and gynecology Baylor U., Houston, 1966-69; prof., chmn. dept. obstetrics and gynecology U. Ala. Sch. Medicine, Birmingham, 1969—; obstetrician and gynecologist-in-chief U. Ala. Med. Center. Cons. NIH; asso examiner Am. Bd. Obstetrics and Gynecology; gen. chmn. 6th World Congress Obstetrics and Gynecology; adv. com. oral contraceptives Internat. Planned Parenthood; mem. nat. clin. adv. com. Nat. Found. Served to capt. M.C., AUS, 1946-48. Recipient Teaching award Baylor Coll. Medicine, 1968; Distinguished Service award U. N.C. Mem. A.M.A., Continental Gynecol. Soc., Am. Gynecol. Soc., Am., Central assns. obstetricians and gynecologists, A.C.S. (obstetrics and gynecology council), Am. Coll. Obstetricians and Gynecologists (chmn. com. obstetric anesthesia and analgesia), Internat. Coll. Anesthetists. Mem. editorial bd. Obstetrics and Gynecology, 1970. Research in obstet. anesthesia, analgesia, population control and toxemia of pregnancy, physiology of endometrium. Home: 3757 Rockhill Rd Birmingham AL 35223 Office: U Ala Sch Medicine Univ Sta Birmingham AL 35294

FLOWERS, ELLIOTT GALETIN, lawyer; b. Houston, Mar. 10, 1913; s. Louis Irwin and Hazel (Lawshae) F.; B.A., Rice U., 1934; LL.B., Tex. U., 1937; m. Elizabeth Sinclair, Jan. 22, 1957; children—Leigh (Mrs. L.F. Bonner, Jr.), Elliott Galetin, Lynn Zarr, Lucy (Mrs. A.J. Foyt, Jr.). Admitted to Tex. bar, 1937; practiced Houston, 1939-41, 47—; gen. counsel McCarthy Oil & Gas Corp., Houston, 1947-52; asso. gen. counsel Allied Chem. Corp., Houston, 1952-71, asst. gen. counsel, 1971—; exec. asst. to pres. Union Tex. Petroleum, Houston, 1952—. Served to lt. comdr. USNR, 1942-47. Mem. Am., Tex. bar assns., Fed. Power Bar Assn., Ind. Petroleum Assn. (v.p. 1963-66, dir. 1966—, Mid-Continent Oil and Gas Assn. (mem. exec. mgmt., legis., legal coms. 1964— finance com. 1964-68, dir. 1970—), So. Gas Assn. (adv. council 1962-63), Houston Bar Assn. (finance and budget com. 1963-64). Author: Municipal Officials in Texas, 1939. Contbr. articles on municipal law to profl. jours. Home: 3330 Del Monte Houston TX 77019 Office: 3000 Richmond Av Houston TX 77006

FLOWERS, JEFFERSON MCDOWELL, JR., physician; b. Dallas, Jan. 30, 1929; s. Jefferson McDowell and Mary Lois (York) F.; B.A., Erskine Coll., 1948; M.D., Med. Coll. S.C., 1957; m. Marilyn Mansfield, July 9, 1968; children by previous marriageVirginia, Jerry, Jefferson McDowell III, John, Sam, Kay, Kimberly, Kellye, James, Paul. Chemist, E.I. Dupont Co., Chattanooga, 1948-50; intern Spartanburg Gen. Hosp., 1957-58; practice medicine, Charleston, S.C., 1958-65, Sanderson, Tex., 1965-68, Victoria, Tex., 1968—; chief surgery Citizens Meml. Hosp., Victoria, 1971; med. dir. Devereaux Schs. Tex., 1968—; exec. dir. Community Orgn. Drug Abuse Control, 1971—. Served with AUS, 1950-52. Mem. Phi Chi. Rotarian. Home: 304 Cannon Rd Victoria TX 77901 Office: 1501 E Red River Victoria TX 77901

FLOWERS, PAUL ABBOTT, newspaper columnist, educator; b. Trenton, Tenn., Mar. 30, 1905; s. F. C. and Louise (Dance) F.; student La. Coll., Pineville, 1925-26; B.A., Ohio State U., 1940, M.A., 1942; D.Litt., Erskine Coll., 1960; m. Louise Templeton, Dec. 26, 1936; 1 son, Frank Templeton. Reporter, Lake Charles (La.) Am.-Press, 1922-25, Alexandria (La.) Town Talk, 1926-27, Shreveport (La.) Times, 1927-28; copyreader Birmingham (Ala.) News, 1928; telegraph editor Age-Herald, Birmingham, 1929, also news editor Lake Charles Am.-Press; feature writer, photographer The Enterprise, Beaumont, Tex., 1929-30; reporter Comml. Appeal, Memphis, 1931, The Times, El Paso, Tex., 1931; copyreader News and Age-Herald, Birmingham, 1933-37; telegraph editor Ohio State Jour., Columbus, 1937-41; asst. prof. journalism W.Va. U., 1941-43; columnist, book editor The Comml. Appeal, Memphis, 1943-71; instr. creative writing Southwestern U., 1945; asso. prof. polit. sci. Memphis State Coll., 1946-47; asst. prof. polit. sci. Sch. Nursing U. Tenn. Extension, 1948—; asst. prof. journalism Miss. State Coll. for Women, Columbus, 1964-66. Mem. exec. com., dir. Memphis Heart Assn. Mem. Sigma Delta Chi, Kappa Tau Alpha. Presbyn. Home: 30 N Highland St Memphis TN 38111 Office: Joint Univ Center 127 Madison Av Memphis TN 38103

FLOWERS, WALTER, congressman; b. Greenville, Ala., Apr. 12, 1933; s. Walter W. and Ruth (Swaim) F.; A.B., U. Ala., 1955, LL.B., 1957; Rotary Found. fellow, U. London, 1957-58; m. Margaret V. Pringle, Aug. 21, 1958; children—Vivian Victoria, Walter Winkler III, Victor Woodley. Admitted to Ala. bar, 1957, Miss. bar, 1960; sr. partner firm Flowers and Shelby, Tuscaloosa, Ala., 1961-68; mem. 91st-92d Congresses, 5th Dist. Ala. Past mem. Black Warrior council Boy Scouts Am., Tuscaloosa YMCA; former mem., chmn. Tuscaloosa Civil Service Bd.; past pres. Tuscaloosa County Mental Health Assn.; past bd. dirs. Tuscaloosa County chpt. A.R.C., Tuscaloosa Tb Assn. Served to 1st lt. U.S. Army Res., 1958-59. Mem. Am., Miss., Ala., Tuscaloosa County bar assns., U. Ala. Alumni Assn. (past pres. Tuscaloosa County), Phi Beta Kappa, Omicron Delta Kappa, Jasons Soc., Phi Delta Phi, Sigma Alpha Epsilon. Democrat. Episcopalian. Rotarian.Home: 2111 14th St Tuscaloosa AL 35401 Office: House of Representatives Washington DC 20515

FLOWERS, WILLIAM HOWARD, JR., food processing exec.; b. Thomasville Ga., Nov. 14, 1913; s. William Howard and Flewellyn (Strong) F.; B.A. in Bus. Adminstrn., Washington and Lee U., 1933; m. Fontaine Maury Tice, June 22, 1936; children—Fontaine Maury (Mrs. Thomas Garcin Parker), Maury deGraffenried, Daphne Howard (Mrs. Charles Martin Wood III), Thornton Taliaferro. With Flowers Baking Co., Inc. (name changed to Flowers Industries, Inc.), Thomasville, Ga., 1933—, chmn. bd., chief exec. officer, 1965—; former dir. Quality Bakers Am. Coop., Inc., N.Y.C.; dir. Am. Heritage Life Ins. Corp., Rollins Internat., Inc. Mem. Ga. Citizens Com. on Crime and Delinquency, 1961—, Dept. State Spl. Adv. Com. Pub. Opinion, 1970—. Mem. Ga. Senate, 1964-68. Trustee William Howard Flowers Found. Named Man of Year Thomasville-Thomas County C. of C., 1964. Mem. Nat. Assn. Mfrs., Ducks Unlimited, Chief Execs. Forum, Kappa Alpha. Episcopalian (vestryman, sr. warden). Elk, Rotarian. Clubs: Ga.-Fla. Field Trial (sec. 1952-68), Glen Arven Country, Farmington Country, Sapphire Valley Country; Lyford Cay (Nassau); Wildcat Cliffs Country (Highlands, N.C.). Home: Merrily Plantation Thomasville GA 31792 Office: PO Box 1219 Thomasville GA 31792

FLOYD, ALPHA CARLIE, ret. acountant b. Tureville, S.C., Aug. 17, 1912; s.; Willie Edward and Effie (Coker) F.; student U. S.C., 1946, U. Ala., 1951-52; m. Mary Beck Dennis, Mar. 1, 1936; children—Shirin Alpha (Mrs. Thomas H. Turnbull), Robert Carlisle. With USDA, 1938-48; self employed C.P.A., 1948-57; staff accountant comptroller's office Hdqrs. Air U., Maxwell AFB, Ala., 1957-72. Treas., dir. Maxwell-Gunter Fed. Credit Union, 1965-69. Served with USMC, 1929-35, 44-46. C.P.A., Ala. Recipient Certificate recognition Nat. Assn. Accountants, 1968. Mem. Am. Inst. C.P.A.'s, Ala. Soc. C.P.A.'s, Nat. Assn. Accountants (chpt. dir. 1966-71, v.p. 1971), Am. Soc. Mil. Comptrollers (chpt. v.p. 1969). Democrat. Methodist (mem. ofcl. bd. 1966-69). Toastmaster (local pres. 1969—). Home: 2632 Girard St Montgomery AL 36106

FLOYD, CARLISLE, composer, educator; b. Latta, S.C., June 11, 1926; s. Carlisle Sessions and Ida (Fenegan) F.; Mus.B., Syracuse U., 1946, Mus. M., 1949; m. Kay Reeder, Nov. 28, 1957. Mem. faculty Sch. Music, Fla. State U., Tallahassee, 1947—, now prof. music; composer Slow Dusk (mus. play), 1949, Susannah (mus. drama), 1954, Pilgrimage, 1955, Sonata For Piano, 1957, Wuthering Heights (mus. drama), 1958, The Mystery, 1960, The Passion of Jonathan Wade (mus. drama), 1962, The Sojourner and Mollie Sinclair (comedy-drama), 1963; Markheim (mus. drama), 1965, Of Mice and Men (mus. drama), 1970; Flower and Hawk (monodrama), 1972. Recipient Citation of Merit, Nat. Assn. Am. Composers and Conductors, 1957, N.Y. Music Critics Circle award, 1957; named one of ten Outstanding Young Men, U.S. Jr. C. of C., 1959; Guggenheim fellow, 1956. Mem. A.S.C.A.P., Am. Guild Mus. Artists, Pi Kappa Lambda, Phi Mu Alpha, Delta Omicron. Democrat. Episcopalian. Home: 806 Middlebrook Circle Tallahassee FL 32303

FLOYD, D.S., athletic dir.; b. Charleston, Ark., May 27, 1929; s. Lawton A. and Verna (Sharp) F.; B.S., Ark. Poly., 1953; M.S., Ark. State U., 1964; m. Betty Jo Pickens, May 30, 1954; children—Donna Marie, Martha Jo. Head coach football Charleston, Ark., 1953-57, Stuttgart, Ark., 1957-63; asst. coach football Ark. State U., Jonesboro, 1963-67, dir. athletics, 1967—. Served with AUS, 1950-52. Clubs: Lions, Exchange (Jonesboro, Ark.). Home: 1201 Tory Dr Jonesboro AR 72401

FLOYD, HENRY BASCOM, III, indsl. engr.; b. Floyd Dale, S.C., Sept. 6, 1927; s. Henry Bascom and Isabelle (Sanders) F.; B.S. in C.E., The Citadel, 1949; M.S. in Indsl. Mgmt., Ga. Tech., 1966; m. Rubie Mae Fore, Mar. 27, 1948; children—Rebecca Anne (Mrs. Alan H. Arrington), Henry Bascom IV, Jennette Isabelle, Tina Fore. Constrn. engr. DuPont, Camden, S.C., Martinsville, Va., Pensacola, Fla., 1950-54; cons. engr. Townsend Builder's Supply, Whiteville, N.C., 1954-55; plant engr. Serv-Air Aviation Corp., Kinston, N.C., 1955-57; dep. base engr. USAF, Seymour Johnson AFB, Goldsboro, N.C., 1957-62; tech. mgr. NASA, Marshall Space Flight Center, Huntsville, Ala., 1963-66, mgr. facilities and logistics Saturn program, 1966—, dep. project mgr. Skylab Expt. project, 1971—, also project mgr. Skylab student project. Founding dir. Boy's Home Inc., Lake Waccamaw, N.C. Served with USNR, 1945-46; PTO. Registered profl. engr., Ala., N.C. Methodist. Mason. Clubs: Civitan, Greenwyche Community Club and Pool, Valley Inc. Home: 4017 Dobbs Dr Huntsville AL 35802 Office: Marshall Space Flight Center Huntsville AL 35812

FLOYD, HUGH JOHNSON, supt. schs.; b. Heath Springs, S.C., Jan. 12, 1919; s. Thomas Johnson and Mae (Sims) F.; B.A., Oglethorpe U., 1943; M.Ed., U. S.C., 1953; m. Eloise Outen, Aug. 30, 1940; children—Joseph Randolph, Frankie (Mrs. Harrell Clark Royer), Martha (Mrs. McAdoo Pershing White), Edward Sims. Tchr., Ga. Mil. Acad., 1943-44; supt. Flat Creek Schs., Lancaster County, 1947-51; prin. McColl High Sch., 1951-54, Heath Springs Elementary Sch., 1954-57, Summerville High Sch., 1957-62; supt. Harleyville Ridgeville Schs., 1962-67; supt. Denmark-Olar Schs., Denmark, S.C., 1967—. Scoutmaster, Kershaw (S.C.) council Boy Scouts Am., 1954-57; coach Little League, Summerville, 1958; chmn. March of Dimes, Dorchester County, 1966, 67. Served with Submarine Service, USNR, 1944-46. Mem. S.C. Tchrs. Assn. (council of dels.), Dorchester County Edn. Assn. (past pres.), Blue Key, Alpha Lambda Tau. Baptist (deacon). Mason (Shriner), Elk, Lion. Club: Crestwood Golf (Denmark). Home: Legare St Denmark SC 29042 Office: Beech Av Denmark SC 29042

FLOYD, LOUIS CARL, physician; b. Malakoff, Tex., Nov. 22, 1914; s. Marion Avery and Minnie Ada (Payne) F.; student Tex. Christian U., 1931; B.A., Rice Inst., 1938; M.D., U. Tex., 1942; m. Aera Margaret Allsup, Sept. 20, 1938 (dec. 1952); children—Marilyn Jo, Louis Carl; m. 2d, Margery Francis Johnson, June 8, 1957; stepchildren—Martha Jo, Barbara Lynn. Commd. asst. surgeon, 1st lt., USPHS, 1943; advanced through grades to col., 1961, ret., 1964; intern USPHS Hosp., Balt., 1942-43; resident USPHS Hosp., Boston, 1945-47; chief med. officer Fed. Reformatory, Pettersburg, Va., 1952-58, El Reno, Okla., Fed. Correctional Instrn., San Pedro, Cal., 1958-63, dep. chief surgery USPHS Hosp., Chgo., 1963-64, ret.; pvt. practice medicine specializing in geriatrics and surgery, Yukon, Okla., 1964—. Pres. Floyd Enterprises Okla., Inc., 1965—. Mem. A.M.A., Okla. Med. Assn., Am. Acad. Family Practice, Nu Sigma Nu, Alpha Omega Alpha. Democrat. Baptist. Mason, Moose. Home: 703 S Holly Yukon OK 73099 Office: 800 W Main PO Box D Yukon OK 73099

FLOYD, PICOT DE BOISFEUILLET, research orgn. exec.; b. Savannah, Ga., Aug. 18, 1931; s. Marmaduke Hamilton and Marie Dolores (Boisfeuillet) F.; A.A., St. Bernard Coll., 1951; A.B., St. Mary's Coll., Balt., 1953; M.A. in Govt., George Washington U., 1965; postgrad. in pub. adminstrn. U. Ga., 1965-66; m. Mary Mullarky Keating, Dec. 26, 1959; children—Geoffrey Keating, John Adam Fendin, Picot de Boisfeuillet. Staff writer Savannah Morning News, 1959-60; asst. city mgr. City of Savannah, 1960-62, city mgr., 1967-71; city mgr. City of Alexandria (Va.), 1962-65; area coordinator Ala.-Miss. community action programs U.S. Office Econ. Opportunity, 1965-66; dir. field services program Inst. of Govt., U. Ga., Athens, 1966-67; sr. v.p., corporate sec. Pub. Tech., Inc., state and local govt. research and devel. orgn., Washington, 1971—. Former mem. Chatham County-Savannah Met. Planning Commn. Served to lt. (j.g.) USCGR, 1955-59. Mem. Internat. City Mgmt. Assn., Am. Soc. for Pub. Adminstrn., Am., So. polit. sci. assns., Assn. for Systems Mgmt., Urban and Regional Information Systems Assn., Ga. Hist. Soc. (curator). Roman Catholic. Contbr. articles to profl. jours. Home: 507 Monticello Blvd Alexandria VA 22305 Office: 1140 Connecticut Av NW Suite 305 Washington DC 20036

FLOYD, W.C., county judge; b. Conway, S.C., Oct. 4, 1904; s. William Thomas and Charlotte (Johnson) F.; student pub. schs., S.C.; m. Ruth Smith, Sept. 16, 1923; children—Eugene C. Mozelle, Billie Roy Nichols, Sidney T. Farmer, Horry County, 1923-34; owner Floyd Supply Co., Conway, S.C., 1934-58; probate judge Horry County, Conway, S.C., 1959—. Mason, Lion. Home: 411 Beaty St Conway SC 29526 Office: Court House Conway SC 29526

FLUGRATH, JAMES MARION, audiologist; b. St. Joseph, Mich., Sept. 23, 1934; s. Ralph and Helen (Bischoff) F.; A.B., U. Mich., 1961; M.A., Wayne State U., 1963, Ph.D., 1965; m. Nancy Louise Sharp, May 30, 1962. Adult aphasic counselor U. Mich., 1961; speech pathologist St. Clair Shores (Mich.) pub. schs., 1961-62; audiologist Wayne State U., 1962-65, Eastern Ill. U., 1965-68; dir. clin. audiology Memphis State U. Speech and Hearing Center, 1968-71; chief audiology and speech pathology Mountain Home (Tenn.) VA Center, 1971—. Cons. audiologist, Memphis, 1968-71. Served with AUS, 1953-56. Mem. Am. Speech and Hearing Assn. (recipient certificates in basic hearing, 1961, basic speech, 1961, clin. competence in audiology, 1968, in speech pathology, 1969), Acoustical Soc. Am., Volta Bur., Am., Tenn. speech and hearing assns. Soc. Preservation Barbershop Quartet Singing Am. (publicity chmn.). Contbr. articles to profl. jours. Home: 1812 McClellan Dr Johnson City TN 37601 Office: VA Center Mountain Home TN 37684

FLUNO, JOHN ARTHUR, cons. entomologist; b. Appleton, Wis., July 21, 1914; s. Arthur Swetland and Elsie (Younger) F.; B.S., Rollins Coll., 1937; M.S., Ohio State U., 1939; m. Ruth Margaret Johnson, Aug. 15, 1942; children—Ruth Adaire, Jo Anne. Field aide U.S. Dept. Agr., Orlando, Fla., 1937-38, entomologist, Orlando, Fla., Beltsville, Md., 1946-72; asst. Ohio Biol. Survey, Columbus, 1938-40; instr. Rollins Coll., Winter Park, Fla., 1941; jr. entomologist USPHS, 1941-46; now cons. Served with AUS, 1943-46. Mem. Am. Mosquito Control Assn., Entomol. Soc. Am., Entomol. Soc. Washington, Rollins Coll. Alumni Assn. (past pres.). Home and office 1234 Lakeview Dr Winter Park FL 32789

FLY, JOHN WESLEY, city ofcl.; b. Zellwood, Fla., Aug. 17, 1915; s. E. W. and Leila (King) F.; B.S., U. Fla., 1937; M.S., U. Ill., 1941; m. Bessie Faye Mires, Sept. 3, 1938; children—John Wesley, Walter Mires, James Lawrence. Asst. prof. accounting U. Fla., 1938-41; partner Pribble, Wells & Fly, C.P.A.'s, Orlando, Fla., 1946-48; exec. in gas and equipment cos., Orlando, 1948-64; dir. finance City of Orlando, 1965—; dir. Plaza First Nat. Bank. Sec. Fla. State Racing Commn., 1954. Trustee Fla. Meth. Childrens Home. Served to maj. USAAF, 1942-45. C.P.A., Fla. Mem. Blue Key, Theta Chi, Beta Alpha Psi, Phi Kappa Phi. Methodist (trustee). Kiwanian. Clubs: University, Country (both Orlando). Home: 2050 Fawsett Rd Winter Park FL 32789 Office: 400 S Orange Av Orlando FL 32801

FLY, STERLING HARPER, JR., physician; b. Sabinal, Tex., Feb. 11, 1925; s. Sterling Harper and Mary Eloise (Sutherland) F.; student Tex. A. and M. Coll., 1942-43; M.D., U. Tex.,1950; m. Bobbie Lou Kirkpatrick, Feb. 23, 1952; children—Ruth Marguerite, Sterling Harper III, Suzanne, Bruce. Intern, Phila. Gen. Hosp., 1950-51; resident Robert B. Green Hosp., San Antonio, 1951-52; gen. practice medicine, Uvalde, Tex., 1952-53, 54—. Dir. Uvalde County Hosp. Authority, 1962—, pres. bd., 1971. Dir. 1st State Bank of Uvalde; pres. Uvalde Land Co., Amber Sky Corp. Mem. exec. com. Concho Valley council Boy Scouts Am. Served with USNR, 1943-45, AUS, 1953-54. Named Outstanding Citizen, Uvalde C. of C., 1968. Mem. A.M.A., Tex. Med. Assn., Am. Acad. Family Practice, Tex. Acad. Gen. Practice, Alpha Omega Alpha. Methodist. Rotarian. Home: N 4th St Uvalde TX 78801 Office: 1042 Garner Field Rd Uvalde TX 78801

FLYNN, LIGON BROADUS, architect; b. Sandy Plains, N.C., Feb. 24, 1931; s. Broadus Bryan and Myrtle Eula (Shields) F.; B.Arch., N.C. State U., 1959; m. Susan Lane Hardin, Nov. 16, 1962; children—Ligon Haywood, Susan Brooks. Archtl. apprentice various firms including Charles H. Wheatley & Assos., Charlotte, N.C., 1959-63; instr. Sch. Design, N.C. State U., 1963-67; pvt. practice architecture, Raleigh, 1967—. Served to 1st lt. C.E., AUS, 1954-56. Recipient merit award N.C. chpt. A.I.A., 1969, 70, 71. Mem. A.I.A. Prin. archtl. works include Visitors Reception Center, Brookgreen Gardens, S.C., 1969. Office: Figure Eight Island PO Box 738 Wilmington NC 28401

FLYNN, RICHARD JAMES, lawyer; b. Omaha, Dec. 6, 1928; s. Richard T. and Eileen (Murphy) F.; student Cornell U., 1944-46; B.S., Northwestern U., 1950, J.D., 1953; m. Joanne Elizabeth Resseguie, Aug. 31, 1951; children—Richard McDonnell, William Thomas, Kathryn Eileen, James Daniel. Admitted to D.C. bar, 1953, Ill. bar, 1954; law clk. to Chief Justices Vinson and Warren, 1953-54; asso. Sidley, Austin, Burgess & Smith, Chgo., 1954-63, partner, Washington, 1963-66, Sidley & Austin, 1967—. Mem. Met. Washington Planning and Ad Com., 1971—. Served with USN, 1946-48. Mem. Am. (chmn. subcom. transp. antitrust sect. 1971—), Chgo., (antitrust com. 1961-63), Fed. bar assns., Bar Assn. D.C. (vice-chmn. com. lobbying), Nat. Lawyers Club, ICC Practioners, Washington Lawyers Commn. Civil Rights Under Law, Order of Coif, Phi Beta Kappa, Phi Delta Phi, Sigma Chi. Republican. Presbyn. (deacon). Clubs: Metropolitan (Washington), Economic of Chicago, Legal, Kenwood Golf and Country. Contbr. articles to profl. jours. Home: 5000 38th St NW Washington DC 20016 Office: 1625 I St NW Washington DC 20006

FLYNN, THOMAS E., labor union ofcl.; b. Chgo., July 1, 1906; s. Patrick P. and Katherine (Nolan) F.; m. Mildred Wanetta Brandeberry, June 16, 1923; children—Robert Thomas, Jerome Patrick, Colleen (Mrs. Robert S. Schwenger) and Maureen (Mrs. John P. Treanor) (twins). Mem. Internat. Brotherhood of Teamsters, 1923—, internat. dir. Eastern conf., 1953—, internat. 4th v.p., 1957—, gen. sec.-treas., 1969—. Democrat. Roman Catholic. Home: 4815 Broadbrook Dr Bethesda MD 20014 Office: 100 Indiana Av NW Washington DC 20001

FLYNT, JOHN JAMES, JR., congressman; b. Griffin, Ga., Nov. 8, 1914; s. John James and Susan Winn (Banks) F.; student Ga. Mil. Acad.; A.B., U. Ga., 1936; postgrad. Emory U., 1937-38; J.D., George Washington U., 1940; grad. Command and Gen. Staff Sch., Air Corps Advanced Flying Sch., Brooks Field, Tex.; m. Patricia Irby Bradley; children—Susan Banks, John James III, Crisp Bradley. Admitted to Ga. bar, 1938; asst. U.S. atty. No. Dist. Ga., 1939-41, 45-46; mem. Ga. Ho. of Reps., 1947-48; solicitor gen. Griffin Jud. Circuit, 1949-54; mem. 83d-88th congresses, 4th Ga. Dist.; mem. 89th-93d congresses, 6th Ga. Dist. Chmn. bd. visitors U.S. Air Force Acad., Colo.; trustee LaGrange (Ga.) Coll., Woodward Acad. Served in U.S. Army, 1936-37, 41-45, col. Res. Decorated Bronze Star medal. Mem. Ga. (pres.), Am. (com. jud. selection, tenure, compensation) bar assns., Am. Legion, V.F.W., Phi Delta Phi, Sigma Alpha Epsilon. Democrat. Methodist (chmn. bd. stewards). Mason (Shriner). Home: Griffin GA 30223 Office: House Office Bldg Washington DC 20515

FLYTHE, SIMON SUTTON, banker; b. Jackson, N.C., Mar. 15, 1907; s. Jesse Thomas and Acree (Lassiter) F.; student Trinity Coll., Duke; m. Virginia White, Sept. 6, 1926; children—Walter W., Simon Sutton, Margaret F. (Mrs. Francis B. Teague, Jr.), James Thomas. Vice pres., cashier Bank of Fieldale, Va., 1928-47; exec. v.p. First Nat. Bank of Martinsville and Henry County, Martinsville, Va., 1947-54, pres., 1954—, also dir.; dir. Fieldale Ins. Agy., Inc., Bassett-Walker Knitting Co., Inc., Bassett, Va., Martinsville Novelty Corp., INTEGON Corp., Winston-Salem, N.C., Martinsville Cablevision, Inc. Mem. State Hwy. Commn., 1954-65, sec., 1963-65; mem. Nat. council Boy Scouts Am. Mem. Henry County Sch. Bd. Bd. dirs. Martinsville Med. Center, Va. Dept. Welfare and Instns., 1968-71; trustee Martinsville-Henry County Meml. Hosp.; mem. adv. bd. Patrick Henry Coll.; bd. visitors Med. Coll. Va., 1966-67. Mem. Am. (mem. exec. com. Va.), Va. bankers assns. Kiwanian. Club: Chatmoss Country. Home: 1101 Sam Lions Trail Martinsville VA 24112 Office: PO Box 4911 Martinsville VA 24112

FOARD, SUSAN LEE, editor; b. Asheville, N.C., Aug. 1, 1938; d. Carson Cowan and Anne (Brown) Foard; A.B., Salem Coll., 1960; M.A., William and Mary Coll., 1966. Asst. editor Inst. Early Am. Hist. and Culture, Williamsburg, Va., 1961-66, asso. editor, 1966; editor U. Press of Va., Charlottesville, 1966—. Active League of Women Voters. Office: Box 3608 University Station Charlottesville VA 22903

FODELL, HARVEY WALLACE, dentist; b. Houston, Dec. 1, 1930; s. George Neiman and Matilda (Curry) F.; D.D.S., Baylor U., 1958; m. Kathleen Coe, July 28, 1954; children—Cynthia, Nanette. Individual practice dentistry, Houston, 1958—; dir. Gulf Coast Nat. Bank. Mem. Am., Tex. dental assns., Harris County Dental Soc. Republican. Mason (32 deg., Shriner). Clubs: C, Cougar Cager (Houston). Home: 803 Monte Cello St Houston TX 77024 Office: 2519 Sage Rd Houston TX 77027

FOGARTY, WILLIAM JOSEPH, educator; b. Toronto, Ont., Can., Nov. 18, 1932 (brought to U.S., 1934); s. Eugene Martin and Josephine Alice (Serosky) F.; B.S.C.E., U. Miami, 1958; M.S. in Civil Engring., Purdue U., 1961; Ph.D., Ga. Inst. Tech., 1968; m. Zoraide Perez, Aug. 2, 1958; children—William Joseph, John Martin, Alyce Diane. Constrn. designer Fla. State Road Dept., Bartow, 1958-59; instr. Purdue U., Lafayette, Ind., 1959-61; asst. prof. U. Miami Sch. Engrs., Coral Gables, Fla., 1961-67, asso. prof., 1968—. Cons. environmental engring., traffic safety, Coral Gables, 1968—. Served to 2d lt. AUS, 1952-54. Recipient Brownell award, outstanding engring. grad., U. Miami, 1958; Outstanding Tchr. award, U. Miami, 1969; Fla. Govs. Conservation award, 1970. Mem. Am. Soc. C. E. (v.p. 1970-71). Home: 5800 SW 63rd St Miami FL 33143 Office: Sch Engring U Miami Coral Gables FL 33124

FOGLEMAN, JOHN ALBERT, justice Ark. Supreme Ct; b. Memphis, Nov. 5, 1911; s. John Franklin and Julia (McAdams) F.; student U. Ark., 1927-31; LL.B., U. Memphis (now Memphis State U.), 1934; m. Annis Adell Appleby, Oct. 24, 1933; children—John Albert. Annis Adell (Mrs. Henry M. Rector), Mary Barton (Mrs. Charles L. Williams, Jr.). Admitted to Ark. bar, 1934; dep. circuit ct. clk. Critenden County, 1933-34; pvt. practice law, 1934-44; partner Hale & Fogleman, West Memphis, Ark., 1944-66; dep. pros. atty., Crittenden County, 1946-57; asso. justice Ark. Supreme Ct., 1967—. Mem. State Bar Examiners, 1960-63; chmn. Ark. Jud. Commn., 1963-65; mem. Ark. Constl. Revision Study Com., 1967, Ark. Criminal Code Revision Com., 1972—. Active Ark. and Crittenden County Democratic central com. Served to 1st lt. AUS, 1944-45, Fellow Am. Coll. Trial Lawyers; mem. Ark. (past pres.), N.E. Ark. (past pres.), Crittenden County (past pres.) bar assns. Mason, Rotarian. Home: 67 Cherry St Marion AR 72364 Office: Justice Bldg State Capitol Grounds Little Rock AR 72201

FOISIE, PHILIP MANNING, journalist; b. Seattle, Mar. 14, 1922; s. Francis Patrick and Wynifred (Shaw) F.; B.A., Harvard, 1947; m. Margaruitte van Tschurin, Apr. 3, 1948; children—Gregory, Geoffrey, Christina, Timothy. City editor China Press, Shanghai, 1948-49; reporter, telegraph editor Santa Rosa (Cal.) Press-Democrat, 1949-53; copy editor Louisville Courier-Jour., 1953-56; cable editor Washington Post, 1956-60, fgn. editor, 1960-68, asst. mng. editor, 1968—. Served with AUS, 1942-46. Home: 812 Timber Branch Pkwy Alexandria VA 22302 Office: Washington Post 1515 L St NW Washington DC 20005

FOLEN, VINCENT J., physicist; b. Scranton, Pa., Jan. 17, 1924; s. Joseph William and Josephine (Maldonate) F.; B.A., LaSalle Coll., 1949; M.A., U. Pa., 1954; Ph.D., Am. U., 1972; m. Doris Ruth Braun, Feb. 14, 1954. Physicist, U.S. Naval Research Lab., Washington, 1954-59, head ferromagnetism sect., 1959—. Served with USAAF, 1943-46. Recipient award for outstanding performance U.S. Naval Research Lab., 1962; Research Publs. award U.S. Naval Research Lab., 1968, 70; Pure Sci. award Sci. Research Soc. Am., 1971. Fellow Am. Phys. Soc.; mem. Research Soc. Am., Philos. Soc. Washington, Alpha Epsilon. Contb. articles profl. jours. Co-founder magnetoelectric effect, 1961. Home: 203 Tecumseh Dr Washington DC 20021 Office: US Naval Research Lab Washington DC 20390

FOLEY, JAMES B., v.p. adminstrn. A.R.C. Address: 1218 Falster Rd Alexandria VA 22308*

FOLEY, LESTER WILLIAM, lumber exec.; b. Mpls., Aug. 13, 1903; s. J. S. and Marie (Scanlon) F.; student Ga. Inst. Tech., 1920; A.B., U. Notre Dame, 1924; m. Edith Klug, Apr. 20, 1926; children—Jerry S. III, Patricia F. Stedeford. Pres. Foley Lumber Industries, Jacksonville, Fla., Beiswenger-Hoch & Assos. Mem. adv. bd. U. Notre Dame. Mem. Soc. Am. Mil. Engrs., Navy League U.S. (dir.), Friars. Roman Catholic. Clubs: Florida Yacht, Seminole, Deerwood, Ponce de Leon, Quarterback, Timuguana Country, Ponte Vedra, River. Home: 3626 Richmond St Jacksonville FL 32207 Office: Gulf Life Towers Jacksonville FL 32207

FOLGER, JOHN DALTON MURPHY, govt. ofcl.; b. Thunderbolt, Ga., Oct. 15, 1915; s. William Clayton and Lilly May (Doane) M.; A.B., Emory U., 1951, M.L.S., 1954; m. Florence Mary Schloss, Feb. 15, 1947. Librarian Ga. State Library, Atlanta, 1951-56; asst. state librarian, Atlanta, 1956-59, state librarian, 1959—. Served as med. lab. technician AUS, 1942-46; ret. master sgt. Res. Mem. A.L.A., Am. Assn. Law Librarians. Home: 1861 Boulderview Dr SE Atlanta GA 30316 Office: Jud Bldg Capitol Hill Sta Atlanta GA 30334

FOLGER, JOHN KENNETH, state ofcl.; b. Atlanta, Mar. 13, 1924; s. Dagnall Frank and Vivian (Rowland) F.; student W. Ga. Coll., Carrollton, 1940-42; A.B., Emory U., 1943; M.A., U. N.C., 1950, Ph.D., 1951; m. Marjorie Bullock, July 27, 1947; children—Karen, John Kenneth, Carol Anne; m. 2d, Mary J. Harrison, May 10, 1958; children—Susan, Dagnall, James. Chief tech. services Human Resources Research Inst., U.S. Air Force, Montgomery, Ala., 1951-53; research asso. So. Regional Edn. Bd., Atlanta, 1953-57, asso. dir., 1957-61; dean Grad. Sch., Fla. State U., Tallahassee, 1961-65, 67-68; dir. Tenn. Commn. Higher Edn., 1968—; dir. Commn. Human Resources, Nat. Acad. Scis., 1965-67. Mem. tech. adv. com. 1960 and 1970 Census. Served lt. (j.g.) USNR, 1944-46. Fellow Am. Sociol. Assn.; mem. Am. Statis. Assn., Population Assn. Am. Author: Education of the American Population, 1967; Human Resources and Higher Education, 1969. Home: 5437 Camelot Rd Brentwood TN 37027

FOLGER, LEE MERRITT, investment co. exec.; b. Washington, May 5, 1934; s. John Clifford and Mary Kathrine (Dulin) F.; A.B., Harvard, 1956; m. Nancy Sue McElroy, Feb. 11, 1961; children—Neil, Peter, Nicholas. With Folger Nolan Fleming Douglas, investments, Washington, 1959—, v.p. sales and sales mgmt., 1962—; pres. Cumberland Trust Co., Knoxville, Tenn., 1962—; v.p. Piedmont Mortgage Co., Washington, 1960—. Chmn. D.C. chpt. A.R.C., 1971—. Bd. govs. St. Albans Sch., Washington; chmn. bd. govs. Corcoran Gallery of Art.; v.p. The Folger Fund, Washington, 1958—. Served to lt. (j.g.), USNR, 1956-58. Mem. Nat. Assn. Securities Dealers (dist. com. 1971—), The Downtown Assn. Episcopalian (vestryman 1969—). Clubs: The Book (NYC); Chevy Chase, Metropolitan (Washington). Home: 2918 33d Place Washington DC 20008 Office: 725 15th St N.W Washington DC 20005

FOLK, OLIVER HAROLD, cons.; b. Moselle, S.C., Dec. 26, 1915; s. Oliver Perry and Ursula (O'Quinn) F.; B.S., Clemson U., 1937; M.A., U. Va., 1938; m. May Day Wyatt, Nov. 14, 1940; children—May Day, Ruth, Frances. Fellow, Econ. Devel. Inst., 1957; agrl. economist U.S. Dept. Agr., Washington, 1938-40; asst. exec. Selective Service System, Washington, 1940-47; loan officer Internat. Bank for Reconstrn. and Devel., 1947-61; chief devel. adviser Govt. Saudi Arabia, Riyadh, 1961-63; cons., Washington, 1963-64; dep. asst. adminstr. AID, 1964-69; cons., Washington, 1970—; pres. Harold Folk Enterprises; dir. Resource Devel. Corp., Asia Devel. Corp. Comdg. officer Selective Service Army Res. Unit, Washington. Pres., Washington Council Presbyn. Men, 1951-52; v.p. Internat. Christian Leadership, 1947-52; chmn. dept. finance Washington Fedn. Chs., 1951-53. Bd. dirs. Fellowship Found., 1948-54, Sr. Research Inst. Arts and Scis.; bd. dirs. Presbyn. Lay Com. Washington. Served from lt. to col. AUS, 1940-46. Mem. Soc. Internat. Devel., Am., Inter-Am. statis. assns., A.A.A.S., Am. Fgn. Service Assn., Mil. Order World Wars, U. Va. Alumni Assn., Iran-Am. Soc., UN Assn., Order Lafayette, Am. Econ. Assn., Am. Finance Assn., Am. Acad. Polit. and Social Sci., Acad. Polit. Sci., Population Assn. Am., Clemson U. Alumni Assn. (pres. Washington chpt. 1948-49), Am. Legion, Res. officers Assn. (pres. Lewis B. Hershey chpt. 1964-65), Nat. Planning Assn., World Future Soc. Presbyn. (elder). Mason (32 deg., Shriner). Clubs: National Economists; International; Foreign Service Officers; Sprinx. Author: White House Task Force Proposal on Urban Devel. Bank, 1968. Home: 3351 Stephenson Pl NW Washington DC 20015 Office: 5480 Wisconsin Av Washington DC 20015

FOLSOM, JAMES CANNON, govt. ofcl.; b. Sweetwater, Ala., Oct. 11, 1921; s. Douglas L. and Lillian McMillan (Hart) F.; student Livingston State Coll., 1939-41, U. Ariz., 1941, U. Ala., 1942, U. Ala. Med. Coll., 1942-44; M.D., Wash. U. Sch. Medicine, 1946; m. Ruth Becton, Aug. 1947 (div. 1950); m. 2d, Geneva Scheihing, Dec. 29, 1958; children—Ivy (Mrs. John E. Gary Simpson), Lisa Kay. Intern, Jefferson-Hillman Hosp., Birmingham, Ala., 1946-47; spl. course neurology and psychiatry U. Vienna, summer 1948; resident in psychiatry Timberlawn San., Dallas, 1950-52; resident physician, fellow Menninger Sch. Psychiatry VA Hosp., Topeka, 1952-53; psychiatrist Hill Crest San., Birmingham, 1949; staff psychiatrist Timberlawn San., Dallas, 1952; admission physician VA Hosp., Topeka, 1953-55, chief phys. medicine and rehab., 1955-60; clin. dir. Mental Health Inst., Mt. Pleasant, Ia., 1960-62; chief staff VA Hosp. Tuscaloosa, Ala., 1962-66, dir. hosp., 1966-71; dep. commr. hosps. Ala. Dept. Mental Health, 1971—; mem. faculty Menninger Sch. Psychiatry, 1953-60; asso. clin. prof. psychiatry Med. Coll. U. Ala., 1963—. Mem. Interagy. Bd. U.S. Civil Service Examiners N. Ala., 1966-71; mem. central bd. mgmt. Tuscaloosa County YMCA, 1966; mem. adv. com. Planning a Program for Overcoming Deprivation in Aesthetic Experiences, Tuscaloosa County, 1967; mem. steering com. Tuscaloosa County Comprehensive Community Mental Center, 1967; mem. Assn. Regional Planning Dirs. and Adminstrs. Ala. Regional Med. Program, 1968; mem. adv. bd. Tuscaloosa County Salvation Army, 1967; mem. Ala. Gov.'s Com. on Employment of Handicapped, 1967; mem. adv. bd. Ala. Jaycees Mental Health-Mental Retardation Com., 1967; chmn. Ala. State White House Conf. on Aging, 1971. Bd. dirs. Ala. Assn. for Mental Health, Tuscaloosa County Assn. for Mental Health, Boys' Club Tuscaloosa County, United Fund Tuscaloosa County; trustee The Menninger Found. Served to 1st lt. M.C., AUS, 1947-49. Recipient William C. Porter award in psychiatry Assn. Mil. Surgeons U.S., 1971. Fellow Am. Coll. Psychiatrists, Am. Psychiat. Assn. (1st editor Kan. Dist. br., Ala. Dist. br. Newsletter), Am. Geriatric Soc.; mem. A.M.A., Assn. Med. Supts. Mental Hosps. (pres. elect 1971, council), Ala. Acad. Neurology and Psychiatry (pres. 1968-69), Tuscaloosa County Med. Soc., Menninger Sch. Psychiatry Alumni Assn. (pres. 1958-59, editor Alumni Bull. 1954-57, mem. nat. alumni adv. com. 1969), Am. Hosp. Assn. (governing council psychiat. hosp. sect. 1969—, mem. spl. adv. panel assn. type I mental health instns. and services 1968-69), Tuscaloosa C. of C. (state-fed. hosps. action com. 1966). Kiwanian (pres. 1965). Editorial bd. Staff Mag. Contbr. articles to med. jours. Home: Bryce Hosp Tuscaloosa AL 35401

FOLSOM, JOHN ROY, savs. and loan assn. exec.; b. Hartsville, S.C., Dec. 30, 1918; s. William Arthur and Flora (Newsom) F.; B.A., Furman U., 1940; m. Anita Anderson, Oct. 18, 1941; children—Anita Marie (Mrs. Harold A. Boney, Jr.), Dale (Mrs. Reginald Davies Heinitsh, Jr.), John William, George Anderson. With Aiken Loan and Security Co., Florence, S.C., 1940-41, Surety Life and Liberty Life Ins. Co., Greenville and Columbia, S.C., 1941-43, 46-60, with Home Fed. Savs. Loan Assn., Columbia, 1960—, pres., 1963-(—, also mem. exec. com. loan com., dir.; dir. Investors Nat. Life Ins. Co. Financial adv. com., Erskine Coll., Mental Health Assn. S.C. Trustee United Fund Columbia, 1968-70, bd. dirs., 1958-60; past treas., past vice chmn., chmn. S.C. Heart Fund, 1969-70. Mem. Citizens Com., Bd. Adminstrs., Richland County, 1968—; mem. S.C. Gov.'s Council on Housing. Recipient Good Egg award S.C. Heart Assn. Mem. S.C. Savs. and Loan League (pres. 1968-69), Columbia C. of C. (dir., v.p. indsl. devel.), Furman U. Alumni Assn. (pres. 1953-54, mem. athletic council 1955), Columbia Real Estate Bd., Columbia Real Estate Appraisers, Columbia Home Builders Assn. Methodist (chmn. Finance com., bd. dirs.). Rotarian, Lion. Clubs: Palmetto, Forest Lake, Spring Valley Country (Columbia). Home: 1515 Adger Rd Columbia SC 29205 Office: 1500 Hampton St Columbia SC 29201

FOLSOM, MARION BAYARD, JR., educator; b. Rochester, N.Y., June 8, 1926; s. Marion Bayard and Mary (Davenport) F.; A.B., Princeton, 1950; certificate Sorbonne, 1953; M.A. (teaching fellow), U. Rochester, 1956; postgrad. Harvard, 1950, 51, U. N.C. (teaching fellow), 1958-59; m. Christine Maria Groth, May 27, 1954; children—Catherine Marie, Frederic Groth. Tchr. English, Allendale Sch., Rochester, N.Y., 1950-53, head dept., 1951-53; fgn. service staff officer USIA, Tehran, Iran, 1956-58; teaching asst. U. N.C., 1959-61; asst. prof. English, Rollins Coll., Winter Park, Fla., 1961-66, asso. prof. English, chmn. dept., 1967—, chmn. Rollins Coll. Writers' Conf., 1969—, research grantee, 1970. Served with USNR, 1944-45, AUS, 1953-55. Danforth Tchr. grantee, 1966-67; Danforth Asso., 1963—. Mem. Fla. Coll. English Assn. (pres. 1969-70, bd. dirs. 1970-71), Coll. English Assn. (chmn. regional program com. 1970-71), Modern Lang. Assn., S. Atlantic Modern Lang. Assn., Nat. Council Tchrs. English, Conf. on Coll. Composition and Communication, Conf. Christianity and Lit., Am. Assn. U. Profs., Alliance Francaise, English Speaking Union. Clubs: Princeton (N.J.) Quadrangle; Princeton (N.Y.C.); Country (Rochester); Greater Orlando Torch. Home: 691 Williams Dr Winter Park FL 32789

FOLTS, HOWARD ALLEN, univ. dean; b. Springville, N.Y., Feb. 5, 1918; s. Allen William and Pearl (Taft) F.; A.B., U. Ala., 1946, M.B.A., 1952; m. Kathryn Fletcher Harris, Feb. 1, 1942; children—H. Allen, William Edward. Copywriter, news editor, announcer WJRD, Tuscaloosa, Ala., 1938-47; asst. prof. econs. and bus. communications U. Ala., University, 1947-57, asst. dean Sch. Bus. Administrn., 1959—; state dir. Survival Planning Commn., Montgomery, 1957-59. Cons.-adviser on civil def. to gov. of Ala., 1958-59; spl. adviser to Ala. dir. SSS, 1958-59; mem. Ala. Sci. Adv. Com., 1958—. Served with AUS, 1941-46. Mem. So. Coll. Placement Officers Assn., Ala. Acad. Sci., Beta Gamma Sigma, Alpha Kappa Psi, Delta Tau Delta, Pi Epsilon Delta. Home: 252 Woodland Hills Tuscaloosa AL 35401 252 Woodland Hills Tuscaloosa AL 35401 Office: Sch Commerce PO Box J University AL 35486

FOLTZ, JOHN CHARLES, govt. ofcl.; b. West Lafayette, O., Feb. 23, 1933; s. Ralph Monroe and Mary Ruth (Karr) F.; B.S. in Agr., Ohio State U., 1955, postgrad. 1957, 65-67, M.S. in Agr., 1971; postgrad. Am. U. Washington, 1966-68; m. Anne Clark, June 24, 1956; children—John Clark, Mary Elizabeth. Instr. vocational agr., adviser Future Farmer Am., Washington Local Sch., Dublin, O., 1957-58, regional advt. mgr. Nat. Future Farmer, Alexandria, Va., 1958-62, advt. mgr., 1962-65; information specialist Future Farmers Am., Washington, 1965-67, coordinator Future Farmers Am. Found., Inc., Washington, 1967-68; pub. relations mgr. Future Farmers Am., Washington, 1968-69; confidential asst. to adminstr. Agrl. Stblzn. and Conservation Service, U.S. Dept. Agr., Washington, 1969; legislative officer U.S. Dept. Agr., 1969-71; dir. congl. relations Cost of Living Council, Exec. Office of Pres., 1971—. Pres., Washington-Balt. Founder Fellowship of Am. Youth Found., Washington, 1964-65, Mount Vernon Terrace (Va.) Community Assn., 1962-64; v.p. Washington Mill Sch. P.T.A., Alexandria, 1964-65, pres., 1965-66; bd. govs. Mount Vernon Guard, 1966-69; pres. Walt Whitman Sch. P.T.A., Alexandria, 1971-72. Trustee Mount Vernon Terrace Community Assn. Served to lt. (j.g.) USNR, 1955-57. Recipient degree Am. Farmer, Future Farmers Am., 1953; certificate Merit, U.S. Dept. Agr., 1970. Mem. Nat. Grange, Agrl. Relations Council, Towers, Alpha Zeta (trustee Found., high council, high scribe), Gamma Sigma Delta. Republic. Methodist (bd. stewards 1960—, asso. lay leader 1963-65, vice chmn. ofcl. bd. 1967-68, chmn. pastorial relations 1967-69, chmn. adminstrv. bd. 1968-69, council ministries 1969—, co-chmn. worship 1970—). Mason. Club: Mansion House (Mt. Vernon, Va.); Capitol Hill (life mem.) (Washington). Home: 5301 Remington Dr Alexandria VA 22309 Office: Office of Sec US Dept Agr Washington DC 20250

FONDREN, WILLIAM MERLE, army officer; b. Cleveland, Miss., Aug. 31, 1914; s. Lester Banks and Lilly (Ruff) F.; B.S., Miss. State U., 1938; grad. Command and Staff Coll., 1948, Army War Coll., 1955-56; m. Evelyn Blaird, Dec. 28, 1938; children—William Merle, Evelyn. Commd. 2d lt. U.S. Army, 1938, advanced through grades to maj. gen., 1968; with 7th Army, North Africa and Sicily, 1943, Allied Forces, Italy, 1944; with Army Ground Forces, Washington and Ft. Monroe, Va., 1945-47; mem. staff Dept. Army Gen. Staff Plans and Operations div., 1948-51; asst. chief staff, 1952-53; Comdg. officer 140th Tank Bn., Korea, 1953; comdg. officer 3d Armored Div., Ft. Knox, Ky.; mem. staff Dep. Chief Staff for Logistics, Army Dept., 1956-58; mem. staff Office Joint Chief Staff, dep. dir. Joint Mil. Assistance Affairs Directorate, 1968-61; dir. mil. assistance U.S. So. Command, 1961-64; dir. Western Hemisphere region Office Asst. Sec. Def., 1964-65; asst. div. comdr. 24th Inf. div., 1965-67; then dep. dir. logistics, Europe; chief staff First U.S. Army, Ft. George G. Meade, Md., 1968-70; commr. Ala. Bd. Corrections, 1970-71. Decorated D.S.M., Silver Star, Legion of Merit with oak leaf cluster, Croix de Guerre (France); Ulchi (Korea). Mem. Kappa Sigma, Omicron Delta Kappa, Beta Beta Beta. Home: 150 Grove Park Rd Memphis TN 38117 Office: City Hall 125 N Main St Memphis TN 38103

FONFRIAS, ERNESTO JUAN, lawyer, author; b. Toa Baja, P.R., Nov. 7, 1909; s. Juan B. and Aracelis (Rivera) F.; student N.Y.C. Coll., 1929-30; B.A., U. P.R., 1932, LL.B., 1935; m. Rafaela Otero, Mar. 24, 1938; 1 son, Ernesto Juan. Mem. P.R. Senate, 1944—. Mem. constl. assembly, 1952. Bd. dirs. Hispanic-Am. Inst. Lexicography. Mem. Am., Fed., P.R. bar assns., Puerto Rican Inst. Lit. Nat. Pres Club, Royal Acad. Spanish (corr.), Puerto Rican Writers Assn. (pres.), Puerto Rican Acad. Polit. Sci., Puerto Rican Acad. Arts and Scis., League Writers and Editors of Uraguay, Interam. Soc. Writers, Am. Assn. Writers and Artists, Pen Club Puerto Rico (founder, sec.), Nat. Press Club, Puerto Rican Inst. N.Y. (award 1963), P.R. Writers Assn. (pres. 1950), Spanish Acad. Langs. Decorated Order Isabel la Catolica (Spain). Roman Catholic. Author: Hebras de Sol., 1934; Al Calor de la Lumbre, 1935; Bajo la Cruz del Sur journeys, 1944; Cosecha, 1955; Conversao en el Batey, 1957; Guasima, 1958; Una Voz en la Montana, 1959; Sementera, 1962; Espigas de Oro, 1962; Raiz y Espiga, 1962. Home: El Batey Candelaria Rd Toa Baja PR 00759 Office: PO Box 2229 San Juan PR 00903

FONTAINE, CHARLES ENGLISH, dentist; b. Pontotoc, Miss., Nov. 8, 1918; s. John Brooks and Katherine English (Crawford) F.; B.A., U. Miss., 1940; M.A., Columbia, 1942; D.D.S., U. Tenn., 1949, M.S., 1951; m. Grace May Fleming, Nov. 25, 1944; children—Katherine, May, Charles English, Margaret. Practice dentistry, specializing in orthodontics, Mobile, Ala., 1951—. Served with USCGR, World War II. Decorated Navy Cross, Silver Star medal. Mem. Am. Dental Assn., Am. Assn. Orthodontics. Clubs: Mobile Country, Bienville. Home: 1910 Oak Knoll Dr Mobile AL 36607 Office: 257 Azalea Rd Mobile AL 36609

FONTAINE, DOUGLASS LATIMER, motel exec.; b. Boston, June 12, 1932; s. John Eaton and Sidney Hosford (Latimer) F.; student Vanderbilt U., 1951; B.A., U. Miss., 1955; m. Bertha Mae VanLandingham, May 28, 1961; children—Douglass Latimer II, Rebecca Van, Patrick Lamar. Mgr., Allison's Wells Resort, Way, Miss., 1948-55; resident mgr. King Edward Hotel, Beaumont, Tex., 1958; mgr. Holiday Inn, Pascagoula, Miss., 1958-62; pres. LaFont Inn, Pascagoula, 1963—. Mem. Com. of 60, Inst. Higher Learning Miss., 1968—; Jackson County chmn. Hwys. Our Pressing Emergency, 1971—; pres. Lake Elementary P.T.A., 1968-69, Fair Elementary P.T.A., 1971-72. Served with AUS, 1955-57. Recipient Distinguished Service award Jr. C. of C., 1961; Distinguished Service citation Baylor Sch. for Boys, 1962. Mem. Am. Hotel and Motel Assn., Miss. Coast (pres.), Miss. (pres.) innkeepers assns., Pascagoula C. of C. (past pres.), Am. Legion, V.F.W., S.A.R. Episcopalian. Rotarian. Home: 2703 Denny Av Pascagoula MS 39567 Office: P O Box 1028 Pascagoula MS 39567

FONTELLIO-NANTON, H. I., ednl. exec.; b. Panama, C.Z., May 15, 1908; s. P. F. and Palmyrah (Ferdinand) F.-N.; B.A., Wesleyan U., 1928; M.A., U. Ia., 1945, Ph.D., 1947; m. Lillian Nunn, Aug. 2, 1962; children—James, Walter. Asso. editor Commerce and Industry, N.Y.C., 1928; mng. editor Carolina Times, Durham, N.C., 1932; owner-pub. Carolina Tribune, Raleigh, N.C., 1933-44; grad. asst. U. Ia., 1946; editor San Francisco Reporter, 1947-48; adminstrv. asst. to pres. Tex. So. U., Houston, 1948-51, head dept. journalism, 1951-58; prof. journalism, chmn. planning and devel. St. Augustine's Coll., Raleigh, 1959-62; dean Allen U., Columbia, S.C., 1962-65; acad. dean Voorhees Coll., Denmark, S.C., 1967-69; dir. social sci. div. Hampton (Va.) Inst., 1969-71, dir. devel., 1971—. Supr. N.C. Housing Survey, Raleigh, 1938; dep. adminstrv. asst. Nat. Youth Adminstrn., Raleigh, 1941; information specialist Venereal Ednl. Inst., USPHS, 1943. Mem. gov.'s adv. com. Manpower Devel. and Tng. Act, Raleigh. Named Man of Month, Pitts. Courier. Mem. Am. Assn. U. Profs., Am. Sociol. Soc., Nat. Dean and Registrar's Assn., Palmetto Edn. Assn., Am. Acad. Polit. and Social Sci., Sigma Delta Chi (Pencil Club award U. Ia. chpt. 1946), Alpha Phi Alpha. Author: Facts for Teen Age Folks, 1944; (with Doaks) What Every Woman Should Know, 1944. Address: Hampton Inst Hampton VA 23368

FONTENOT, TERRY JOHN, physician; b. Eunice, La., Dec. 25, 1933; s. Edwin C. and Ethel (Vellion) F.; M.D., La. State U., 1961; m. Barbara J. Caldwell, Feb. 24, 1970; children—Terry John, Rickey Lynn, Carla Annette, Thomas. Intern, Charity Hosp., New Orleans, 1961-62, resident, 1962-63; gen. practice medicine and surgery, Bridge City, Tex., 1963—. Mem. Tex. Med. Polit. Action Com., 19—. Recipient certificate of merit Internat. Who's Who in Poetry, 1971. Poet laureate Tex., 1971. Mem. A.M.A., Tex., So. med. assns., Orange County Med. Soc., Am. Geriatrics Soc., World Poetry Soc., Am. Acad. Am. Poets, Poetry Soc. Tex., Internat. Platform Assn., Internat. Traders Assn., Smithsonian Assn., Am. Quarterhorse Assn., Flying Physicians Assn., Orange, Bridge City chambers commerce, Tex. 4-H. Optimist. Home: 227 Baker St Bridge City TX 77611 Office: 2515 Texas Av Bridge City TX 77611

FONT SALDANA, JORGE, sec. of treasury P.R.; b. Havana, Cuba, Jan. 14, 1907; s. Jorge Font Ruiz and Maria Duisa Saldana; m. Carmen Maria Gonzalez Olivieri; children—Alma, Marta, Maria Eugenia, Jorge. Mem. bd. editors El Imparcial, La Democracia, El Mundo, also P.R. Illustrado, 1932-47; editor mag. Bohemia Puertorriquena, 1963; formerly adminstrv. asst. to treas. P.R., exec. asst. to gov. P.R., chmn. bd. dirs. P.R. Cement Corp., mem. Indsl. Com. P.R., supt. ins. P.E., sec. senate P.R., pres. P.R. Finance Commn., vice speaker P.R. Ho. of Reps.; now sec., treas. P.R. and chmn. bd. dirs. Govt. Devel. Bank. P.R. Rep. of P.R. to Jose Marti Centennial, Havana, 1953, Pro-Democracy and Liberty Congress, Maracay, Venezuela, 1960; formerly sec. commn. on preamble and sec. commn. style P.R. Constl. Conv. Mem. central com. and presdl. commn. Popular Democratic Party. Recipient Journalism award Inst. P.R. Lit., 1939, 53. Mem. P.R. Soc. Pub. Adminstrn. (pres. 1964-65), P.R. Atheneum (bd. dirs.), Royal Spanish Acad., P.R. Acad. Arts and Scis., P.R. Soc. Journalists. Lion (past pres. San Juan). Home: 706 Paz St Miramar Santurce PR 00908 Office: Dept of Treasury San Juan PR 00901

FONT ZELINSKI, JUAN EDUARDO, dentist; b. Balt., Dec. 22, 1927; s. Juan and Mary Zelinski (de Font) Font Suarez; D.D.S., Ind. U., 1956. Individual practice dentistry, Santurce, P.R., 1957—; pub. health dentist Health Dept. Commonwealth of P.R., 1957—. Mem. Met. Opera Guild, 1967—. Mem. Colegio de Cirujanos Dentistas de P.R. Roman Catholic. Home: Box 10056 Santurce PR 00908 Office: Doctors Med Center Av Hipodromo 800 Santurce PR 00908

FORBES, HENRY WILLIAM, govt. ofcl.; b. Vienna, Austria, Nov. 9, 1918; s. Isidor and Ida (Loewy) F.; came to U.S., 1941, naturalized, 1942; A.A., U. Cal. at Los Angeles, 1948, B.A., 1949; Ph.D. in Internat. Relations, Georgetown U., 1959; grad. Army War Coll., 1970; m. Alice Berger, Oct. 23, 1959; children—Evelyn, Monica, Jessica. Chief logistics div. Ordnance Tech. Intelligence Agy., Dept. Army, Washington, 1951-63, chief econ. br. Def. Intelligence Agy., 1963—. Lectr. George Washington U., 1959-66, U. Va., Richmond extension, 1967—. Served to capt. arty., AUS, 1942-45. Mem. Am. Econ. Assn., Am. Ordnance Assn., Am. Goethe Soc. Lutheran. Author: The Strategy of Disarmament, 1962. Home: 3208 Annandale Rd Falls Church VA 22042 Office: Def Intelligence Agy Washington DC 20301

FORBES, SARAH ELIZABETH, physician; b. Currituck, N.C.; d. Dexter Thomas and Mary (Brock) Forbes; B.A. U. Rochester, 1949; M.D., Med. Coll. Va., 1954. Intern, Norfolk (Va.) Gen. Hosp, 1954-55, resident, 1956-58; resident Johnston-Willis Hosp., Richmond, Va., 1955-56; practice medicine specializing in obstetrics and gynecology, Newport News, Va., 1958—; mem. staff, teaching staff Riverside Hosp. Pres., Soc. for Prevention Cruelty to Animals, 1967—; dir. Cancer Soc., 1960-69; chmn. Research for Cancer Soc., 1961-69, now v.p.; mem. bd. Family Planning Council, 1969—. Fellow Am. Coll. Obstetrics and Gynecology; mem. Tidewater Obstet. and Gynecol. Soc., Va. Peninsula Acad. Medicine (sec.-treas.), Newport News Med. Soc., Va. Med. Soc., A.M.A. Home: 5 Merry Point Terrace Newport News VA 23606 Office: 12420 Warwick Blvd Newport News VA 23606

FORD, ARCHIE W., state ofcl.; b. Wooster, Ark., Jan. 25, 1906; s. Thomas N. and Minnie (Clements) F.; B.E., Ark. State Tchrs. Coll., 1928; M.S., U. Ark., 1948; LL.D., Ouachita Bapt. Coll., Arkadelphia, Ark., 1962; m. Ruby Lee Watson, Dec. 24, 1927; children—Justin Turner (dec.), Harold Watson (dec.), Joe Thomas. Formerly tchr. and ednl. adviser Civilian Conservation Corps; staff Ark. State Dept. Edn., 1941—, commr. edn., 1953—. Mem. N.E.A., Ark. Edn. Assn., Council Chief State Sch. Officers (pres. 1962-63), Phi Delta Kappa, Kappa Delta Pi. Democrat. Baptist. Mason. Contbr. articles to profl. jours. Home: 1221 Mitchell St Conway AR72032 Office: Edn Bldg Little Rock AR 72203

FORD, BILL KENTON, supt. schs.; b. Denison, Tex., Feb. 8, 1927; s. Roscoe Virgil and Bertha Lorene (Landreth) F.; B.E., Tex. Wesleyan Coll., 1950; M.Ed., Tex. Christian U., 1951; Ed.D., Baylor U., 1967; m. Florence Maxine Waters, May 15, 1948; 1 dau., Sharla Kay. Tchr., coach, prin. pub. schs., Glen Rose, Tex., 1950-53; supt. schs., Eula, Tex., 1953-54, Baird, Tex., 1954-60, Belton, Tex., 1960-63, Texarkana, Tex., 1963-70, Denison, 1970—. Served with USNR, 1944-46. Mem. N.E.A., Am., Tex. assns. sch. adminstrs., Tex. Tchrs. Assn., P.T.A. Baptist (deacon 1953—). Lion. Home: 607 Royal Ridge St Denison TX 75020 Office: 800 S Mirick St Denison TX 75000

FORD, BLANCHARD FRED, JR., physician; b. Florence, S.C., Sept. 19, 1913; s. Blanchard Fred and Vera (Ratcliffe) F.; B.S., U. S.C., 1933; M.D., Med. Coll. S.C., 1938; m. Marjorie Nell Wells, July 6, 1940; children—Diane (Mrs. Roy E. Young), Blanchard Fred III. Intern Roper Hosp., Charleston, S.C., 1940-41; resident McLeod Infirmary, Florence, S.C., 1941-42; practice medicine, Maxton, N.C., 1946-68, Shallotte, N.C., 1968—; chief staff Scotland County Meml. Hosp., 1955-56; health dir. Horry and Georgetown counties, S.C., 1957-64. Served to lt. comdr. M.C., USNR, World War II. Mem. Am., So. med. assns., New Hanover, Scotland County (pres. 1956-57) med. socs., Am. Legion. Mason, Lion. Home: Copa Shores Shallotte NC 28459 Office: N Main St Shallotte NC 28459

FORD, EDSEL WILLIAM, psychiat. social worker; b. Muskogee, Okla., Nov. 4, 1930; s. Robert Lee and Florence (Detherage) F.; B.S. in Edn., Northeastern State Coll., 1955; M.S.W., U. Okla., 1961; m. Ruth Stark, Dec. 17, 1953; children—Edsel William, Kelly Carl. With Okla. Dept. Pub. Welfare, 1955-62, field rep., 1960-62; with Family Service Center, Oklahoma City, 1962-64; with Okla. Dept. Mental Health, Oklahoma City, 1964—, regional supr. of after care, 1966—. Mem. profl. adv. bd. Okla. State Council on Crime and Delinquency, 1966—. Bd. dirs. Okla. Health and Welfare. Served with USN, 1948-52; capt. Civil Air Patrol, USAF Aux., 1970—. Mem. Nat. Assn. Social Workers (chpt. chmn. 1965-67, mem. exec. bd. 1967—), Okla. Health and Welfare Assn. (bd. mem., pres. 1970-71). Baptist (dept. supt. 1964-68). Mason. Home: 11221 Jeffords St Nicoma Park OK 73066 Office: 1615 N Lincoln Blvd Oklahoma City OK 73104

FORD, EDWIN D., JR., lawyer; b. La Crosse, Wis., Nov. 7, 1899; B.S., Whitman Coll., 1921; B.A. in Jurisprudence, B.C.L. (Rhodes scholar), Oxford (Eng.), 1924, M.A., 1949. Admitted to Ida. bar, 1924, Minn. bar, 1925, N.Y. State bar, 1937; partner firm Reid & Priest, N.Y.C., 1937-70; now with firm Ortiz, Ramos & Inman, Mexico D.F., Mexico. Mem. Am., Inter-Am. (council), Internat. bar assns., Assn. Bar City N.Y., Am. Soc. Internat. Law. Address: Morelos 98 303-304 Mexico 1 DF Mexico*

FORD, HOMOR TAYLOR, JR., govt. ofcl.; b. Springfield, Mo., Nov. 6, 1911; s. Homor Taylor and Eugenia (Morice) F.; student S.W. Mo. State Coll., 1929-30; B.S. in E.E., Mo. Sch. Mines, 1934; m. Rosemary McKenna, Nov. 21, 1935; children—Judith Anne (Mrs. Ronald J. Groeger), Homor Taylor III, Rosemary Vicki. Vice pres. Ford Electric Co., Springfield, 1934-38; engr., contractor Springfield, 1938-40; with VA Hosps., 1946—, engr. officer, Springfield, 1946-51, asst. mgr. trainee, Hines, Ill., 1951-52, asst. dir., 1962-63, asst. mgr., Memphis, 1952-55, asst. dir., St. Louis, 1955-62, dir. engring. service VA Dept. Medicine and Surgery, Washington, 1964-71, dir. VA Hosp., Fayetteville, N.C., 1971—. Served with AUS, 1941-46. Registered profl. engr., Mo. Fellow Am. Coll. Hosp. Adminstrs.; mem. Mo., Nat. socs. profl. engrs., Soc. Am. Mil. Engrs., Am. Legion, Lambda Chi Alpha. Roman Catholic. Rotarian. Home: 2340 Ramsey St Fayetteville NC 28301 Office: VA Hosp 2300 Ramsey St Fayetteville NC 28301

FORD, J. CLARK, physician; b. Ruston, La., Oct. 29, 1930; s. Amos W. and Elizabeth (Clark) F.; B.S. magna cum laude, La. Poly. Inst., 1953; M.D., La. State U., 1955; m. Mildred Mae Weatherly, Dec. 19, 1956; m. Elizabeth Ann, Richard Clark, Joe Edward. Intern Charity Hosp., New Orleans, 1955-56, resident, 1956-59; practice medicine, specializing in internal medicine, Davidson's Clinic, Lake Worth, Fla., 1961—; chief medicine John F. Kennedy Hosp., Atlantis, Fla., 1968-70; mem. staff John F. Kennedy Hosp., Bethesda Meml. Hosp., Boynton Beach, Fla. Served with USNR, 1959-61. Diplomate Am. Bd. Internal Medicine. Fellow Am. Coll. Cardiology; mem. Fla. Heart Assn., Am. Soc. Internal Medicine, A.C.P., Fla., Palm Beach County med. assns., A.M.A. Baptist. Home: 457 N Country Dr Atlantis FL 33460 Office: 601 S Fed Hwy Lake Worth FL 33460

FORD, JOHN WILLIAM, govt. ofcl.; b. Louisville, May 19, 1920; s. John M. and Leila (Waters) F.; student U. Louisville, 1939-40, Jefferson Law Sch., Louisville, 1940-42, 46-47, FBI Acad., Quantico, Va., 1943; grad. Nat. War Coll., 1961; m. Mercedes Barreda, Jan. 13, 1945; children—John Henry, Douglas William, Walter Paul, Richard, Glen, Robert. With FBI Dept. of Justice, 1939-44, 46-47; attache U.S. Embassy, Caracas, Venezuela, 1947-49, Mexico City, 1949-50. Paris, France, 1950-51; asst. chief and chief div. of security Dept. of State, 1952, dir. Office of Security, 1953; attache Am. Embassy, Manila, 1953-55, 1st sec. and consul, 1955-56; 1st sec. and consul Mexico City, 1956-60, assigned to Dept. State, Washington, 1960—, exec. sec. policy planning council, 1962-64, dir. Inter-Am. polit. affairs, 1967—; consul gen., Barcelona, Spain, 1964-67. Served with C.I.C., U.S. Army, 1944-46, 2d lt. Mil. Intelligence Res. Recipient Commendable Service award Dept. of State, 1958, 61, 64; 20 year Govt. Service Recognition, 1959. Home: 104 Myrtle Av Alexandria VA 22301

FORD, JON CHARLES, journalist; b. Cushing, Tex., Nov. 27, 1920; s. John Charles and Monterie (Swearingen) F.; B.J., U. Tex., 1942; m. Marian Benson Colley, June 17, 1942; children—Jon Michael, Mary Jane, Charles Colley, Ann Shelley. Reporter Honolulu Advertiser, Hawaii, 1945; mng. editor Odessa Am., Tex., 1946-48; reporter San Antonio Express and News, 1948-49, successively mng. editor, 1949-51, asso. editor, 1952-54, state capital bur. chief, 1955-60, 63—; chief state capital bur. Harte-Hanks Newspapers, 1970—; adminstrv. asst. Gov. Price Daniel of Tex., 1960-62. Tex. writer C.S. Monitor; Tex. delegation reporter Republican and Democratic nat. convs. NBC News, 1968. Bd. dirs. Gonzales (Tex.) Warm Springs Found. Served with AUS, 1942-45; PTO. Recipient citation for distinguished writing Headliners Club, Austin, Tex., 1957. Mem. Sigma Delta Chi. Home: 13 Peak Rd Austin TX 78746 Office: Box 12126 State Capitol Station Austin TX 78711

FORD, L(ESTER) HARLAN, ednl. adminstr.; b. Troy, Tex., Mar. 27, 1929; s. Ben F. and Pearl A. (Dockray) F.; B.S., S.W. Tex. State Coll., 1950, M.Ed., 1955; Ed.D., Colo. State Coll., 1960; m. Jo Ann Cravens, Dec. 26, 1950; children—Robert Harlan, William Harlan. Tchr., Junction (Tex.) Pub. Schs, 1947-50; dean San Marcos (Tex.) Mil. Acad., 1951-59; ednl. cons., Greeley, Colo., 1959-60; prof. secondary edn. Howard Payne Coll., Brownwood, Tex., 1960-61; dir. tchr. edn. Sul Ross State Coll., Alpine, Tex., 1961-63, dean of coll., 1963-67, interim pres., 1964-65; exec. dir. region XIX Edn. Service Center, El Paso, Tex., 1967-68; asst. commr. tchr. edn. and instrn. Tex. Edn. Agy., Austin, 1968—. Dir. W. Tex. Innovative Edn. Center, 1965-66; vis. prof. U. Alta., Edmonton, Can., 1964. Chmn., Big Bend Community Action Com., 1965—, Boy Scouts Am., 1965—, Salvation Army, 1964— (all Alpine); mem. City Planning Com., Alpine, 1965—, State Planning Council for Tex. Ednl. Devel., 1967—. Trustee, Mary Hardin Baylor Coll., Belton, Tex., 1972—. Served with AUS, 1951-53. Recipient Distinguished Service award Alpine Jr. C. of C., 1966; Educator of Month award Tex. Sch. Bus. Publs., 1971; Meritorious award Tex. Indsl. Arts Assn., 1972; Meritorious award Tex. Assn. Health, Phys. Edn. and Recreation, 1970. Mem. Tex. State Tchrs. Assn. (dist. pres. 1966—), Nat. Assn. Drs. U.S., N.E.A., Phi Delta Kappa, Kappa Delta Pi, Phi Alpha Theta. Democrat. Baptist. Lion (dir.). Author: History of San Marcos Academy, 1960; Guide for Administrative Interns, 1964: Ideas. Resources. Results, 1965. Home: 801 Country Club Rd Georgetown TX 78626 Office: Tex Edn Agy 11th and Brazos Austin TX 78711

FORD, MARION GEORGE, JR., peridontist; b. Houston, Aug. 22, 1937; s. Marion G. and LaVerne (Hanks) F.; student Wiley Coll., 1954-55, U. Ill., 1955-57; B.S., U. Tex., 1958, D.D.S., 1962; Ms.D. (Fulbright fellow), U. Bonn, 1963; m. Jacqueline Elaine Tillman, Mar. 30, 1957; children—Inge Brechelle, Erika Jane. Common laborer Internat. Longshoremen's Assn., 1953-55; hydro-engr. City of Houston, 1958-62; sci. German translator U. Tex. Dental Br., 1958-62; research fellow U. Tex., 1959-61; pvt. practice as peridontist, Houston, 1964—; asst. chief oral surgery Lockwood Hosp. Sec., Lockwood Profl. Grouping; dir. Lockwood Profl. Pharmacy. Dir. Franklin Bank. Cons. Head Start, 1968-69; edn. dir. Model Cities Program, Houston, 1969—; mem. Mayor's Citizens Comm. for Police Dept., 1968-69; mem. N.E. Houston Sch. Bd., 1967; sec. Harris County Grand Jury, 1969—. Bd. dirs. Houston Met. Ministries, Julia C. Hester House. Mem. Am. Dental Assn., Charles A. George Dental Soc., U. Tex. Ex-Students Assn., Jewish Community Center, Phi Beta Tau, Alpha Alpha Alpha. Methodist. Author: Blood Calcium Effects of Parotin, 1960; Color Schematics in Denture Acrylic Resins, 1961. Home: 10338 Cheeves St Houston TX 77016 Office: 4315 Lockwood St Houston TX 77026

FORD, NORMAN DENNIS, author; b. High Wycombe, Eng., Jan. 8, 1921; s. Frederick William and Jessie (Shortland) F.; ed. in Wales; m. Angela McNair, Sept. 10, 1964; children—Eric, Kirk. Came to U.S., 1947, naturalized, 1949. Freelance travel writer, 1951—; travel editor Harvest Years Mag., 1961—. Served with Royal Navy, 1939-45. Yogi. Clubs: Sierra (San Francisco); Cyclists Touring (Godalming, Eng.). Author: Where to Retire on a Small Income, 1971; Fabulous Mexico-retiring and investing in Mexico, 1971; All Mexico at Low Cost-tourist guide, 1971; America by Car, 1971; What to see in All America, 1971; Todays Best Buys in Travel, 1971; Harian's Favorite Travel Discoveries, 1970; Today's Best Buys in Freighter Travel, 1971; Bargain Paradises of the World, 1971; How to Travel Without Being Rich, 1970; Utopia is an Island, 1971; Norman Ford's Florida, 1971; Off The Beaten Path, 1971; How to Travel and Get Paid for It, 1970; Freighter Days, 1971.‡

FORD, RUBYE LOUISE, banker; b. Buhl, Ala.; d. Samuel Emmett and Maude (Gramling) Food; student Florence State Normal, 1923; standard certificate Am. Inst. Banking, 1957; m. William Wilson Peebles, July 5, 1931 (div. May 1935). With Bank for Savs. & Trust, Birmingham, Ala., 1924-63, asst. treas., 1941-43, treas., 1943-63; cashier Birmingham Trust Nat. Bank, 1963—. Mem. Nat. Assn. Bank Women, Am. Inst. Banking (past pres., v.p., treas., dir.), Women's Jr. Co. of C. (past pres., v.p., treas., finance chmn., dir.). Baptist. Clubs: Women's Com. of 100 for Birmingham (treas. 1964-70), Downtown, Relay House. Home: 508 Town House 2008 8th Av S Birmingham AL 35233 Office: PO Box 2554 Birmingham AL 35202

FORD, RUTLEDGE FREDERICK, agronomist; b. Crossett, Ark., Nov. 17, 1926; s. Frederick Rice and Pauline Ester (Dunn) F.; student Ark. A. and M. Coll., 1949-50; B.S., U. Ark., 1953, M.S., 1961; m. Alma Lucille Orr, Sept. 1, 1957; 1 dau., Rebecca Suzanne. Asst., asso. county agrl. agt. Ark. Agrl. Extension Service, Pine Bluff, 1958-64, county agrl. agt., DeWitt, 1964-66, area agronomist for cotton, Jonesboro, 1966-68; area agronomist cotton and cotton agronomist, agronomy dept. U. Ark., Jonesboro, 1968—. Cons. Wheeler Crop Conditioning, Inc., Leachville, Ark., Brycot Seed Co., Jonesboro. Served with AUS, 1945-46. Recipient research grant Nationwide Chem. Co., 1969. Mem. County Agrl. Agts. Assn. (retirement ins. chmn. 1964-66), Ark. Pesticide Assn., Farm Bur. (dir. at large 1964-66), Epsilon Sigma Phi. Methodist (adminstrv. bd. 1965—). Mason (Shriner), Rotarian (chmn. interact com. 1968-69); mem. Order Eastern Star. Home: 1832 Rosemond St Jonesboro AR 72401 Office: P O Box 1405 Federal Bldg Jonesboro AR 72401

FORD, THOMAS JEFFERS, indsl. and econ. devel. specialist; b. Charleston, S.C., Sept. 9, 1930; s. Rufus and Mildred (Jeffers) F.; A.B., Wofford Coll., 1952; postgrad. U. N.C., 1956-58, 59-61, U. Okla., 1965-67; m. Barbara Jean Jackson, Dec. 28, 1954; children—Thomas Jeffers, Edward Rufus. Asst. mgr. Albany (Ga.) C. of C., 1956; mgr. Rock Hill (S.C.) C. of C., 1957-58; dir. trade devel. Greenville (S.C.) C. of C., 1959-60, dir. bus. and indsl relations, 1961; exec. dir. Marlboro County Devel. Bd., Bennettsville, S.C., 1962-65, Lakeland (Fla.) Indsl. Bd., 1965-67; dir. Chesterfield-Marlboro Tech. Edn. Center, Cheraw, S.C.,1968—. Served with USN, 1952-53. Mem. S.C. Indsl. Developers Assn. (founder, 1st pres. 1965), Am., So. (past dir.) indls. devel. councils, S.C. Assn. C. of C. Execs. (past officer, dir.), Blue Key, Sigma Alpha Epsilon. Methodist. Rotarian (past pres.). Club: Cheraw Country. Home: 15 Hamden Circle Cheraw SC 29520 Office: PO Box 928 Cheraw SC 29520

FORD, THOMAS WELLBORN, educator; b. Houston, Dec. 23, 1924; s. Harry H. and Natalia (Wellborn) F.; B.A., Rice U., 1950; M.A., U. Tex., 1951; Ph.D., 1959; m. Cora M. Lewis, Aug. 29, 1953; children—Thomas W., Emily Lewis. Instr. English, Kinkaid Prep. Sch., Houston, 1953-55; instr. English, U. Tex., 1958-59; asst. prof. Am. lit. U. S.C., 1959-66; asso. prof. Am. lit. U. Houston, 1966-71, prof., 1971—. Served with USAAF, 1943-46. Decorated Bronze Star; recipient fellowships U. Tex., 1956-57, 57-58, grant U. Houston, 1969. Mem. Modern Lang. Assn., Coll. Conf. Tchrs. English, Coll. English Assn., S. Central Modern Lang. Assn. Episcopalian. Author: Heaven Beguiles the Tired: Death in the Poetry of Emily Dickinson, 1966, A.B. Guthrie, Jr., 1968. Contbr. articles and poems to profl. pubs. Home: 6126 Sugar Hill Houston TX 77027

FORD, WENDELL HAMPTON, gov. Ky.; b. Owensboro, Ky., Sept. 8, 1924; s. Ernest M. and Irene (Schenk) F.; student U. Ky., 1942-43; grad. Md. Sch. Ins., 1947; m. Jean Neel, Sept. 18, 1943; children—Shirley Jean, Steven. Partner Gen. Ins. Agy., Owensboro, 1959-67; chief asst. to gov. (Ky.), 1959-61; mem. Ky. Senate, 1965-67; lt. gov. Ky., 1967-71, gov., 1971—. Chmn. Legislative Research Commn., Ky., mem. Ky. Property and Bldgs. Commn., Ky. Turnpike Authority. Served with AUS, 1944-46; Ky. Nat. Guard, 1949-62. Mem. U.S., Ky. (pres. 1954-55) jr. chambers commerce (nat. pres. commerce (pres. 1956-57), Jr. C. of C. Internat. (v.p. N. Am.

1958-59), U.S. C. of C. (bd. dirs.). Democrat. Baptist. Elk. Home: 333 Maple St Owensboro KY 42301 Office: State Capitol Frankfort KY 40601

FORD, WILLIAM LAMONTE, dentist; b. Ardmore, Okla., Feb. 4, 1941; s. Lester Bill and Peggy Mary (Ford) F.; B.S., Baylor U., 1963, D.D.S., 1967; m. Jaqueline Ann Jordan, June 6, 1964; 1 dau., Kerri Elaine. Practice dentistry, Hamilton, Tex., 1967—; dir. 1st Nat. Bank, Classic Candles, Inc., Hamilton, 1969-70. Chmn., City Planning Commn., Hamilton, 1970-71. Mem. Tex. Soc. Dentistry for Children, Am. Dental Assn., Central Tex. Dist. Dental Soc., Psi Omega, Hamilton C. of C. (pres. bd. 1970-71), Hamilton Jr. C. of C. Baptist (chmn. stewardship com. 1967-71, ch. bldg. com. 1970-71). Lion. Home: Navajo Trail Hamilton TX 76531 Office: 310 E Main St Hamilton TX 76531

FORD, WILLIAM OZZIE, social service adminstr.; b. Forest City, N.C., Apr. 6, 1922; s. James Louis and Mamie (Camp) F.; B.A., N.C. Coll., 1951; M.S.W., Howard U., 1955; m. Mary Frances Fulton, Jan. 10, 1952; children—Mazetta Francena, Rita Denise. Dir. ch. center group work project Christ Child Settlement House, Washington, 1955; youth work sec. 12th St. YMCA, Washington, 1956-57; caseworker Child Welfare Div., D.C. Dept. Pub. Welfare, Washington, 1957-61, supr. social work child welfare div., 1961-67, chief instl. care sect. 1967-68; dep. chief social service D.C. Welfare Children Center, Laurel, Md., 1968-69, acting chief, 1969-70; chief ater care Bur. Youth Services, Social Services Adminstrn., D.C. Dept. Human Resources, Washington, 1970-71; professorial lectr. Am. U., Washington, 1971—. Life mem. D.C. Congress P.T.A. Bd. dirs. N.W. Settlement House, 1958-68. Served with USNR, 1942-46. Mem. Nat. Assn. Social Workers, Acad. Certified Social Workers, N.C. Coll. Alumni Assn. (chpt. pres. 1962-64), Howard U. Social Work Alumni Assn. (treas. 1958-67), Washington Urban League, Omega Psi Phi. Democrat. Methodist. Home: 5929 2d Pl NW Washington DC 20011 Office: 122 C St NW Washington DC 20001

FORDERHASE, EARL DUANE, educator; b. Keytesville, Mo., Feb. 18, 1934; s. Earl August and Goldie Faye (Barnes) F.; B.A., William Jewell Coll., 1955; B.D., Southwestern Bapt. Theol. Sem., 1959; M.A., U. Okla., 1962, postgrad., 1965—; m. Carol Ann Cave, Feb. 14, 1959; children—Gregory Duane, Andrea Alision. Asst. prof. philosophy Parsons Coll., 1965-67; grad. teaching asst. U. Okla., 1967-69; asst. prof. philosophy Austin Peay State U., Clarksville, Tenn., 1969—. Instr. philosophy Altus Air Force Base, Okla., 1967-68, Fort Campbell, Ky., 1969. Chmn. dr. A.R.C., Lindsey, Okla., 1964, Am. Heart Fund Drive, Lindsay, 1965—. Mem. Governing Bd., Bapt. Student Union. Mem. Am. Assn. Univ. Profs., Southwestern, Tenn. Ia. philos. assns., Southeastern Assn. Tchrs. Religion, So. Assn. Library Internal Study (chmn. library com. 1971-72), Alpha Tau Omega, Sigma Tau Delta. Mason, Rotarian. Home: 230 Trahern Lane Clarksville TN 37040

FORDICE, DANIEL KIRKWOOD, constrn. co. exec.; b. Russellville, Ind., Dec. 27, 1901; s. Morton William and Ella (Guilliams) F.; student Purdue U., 1921, 23, U. Tenn., 1938, 39; m. Clara Aileen Augustine, Dec. 31, 1929; children—Grace Aileen (Mrs. William M. Holt), Daniel K. Engr., U.S. Army Corps of Engrs., Memphis, 1922-42; partner Fordice Constrn. Co., Memphis, 1946—; pres. Abraham & Fordice, Inc., 1956-69. Served with AUS, 1942-46. Mem. Asso. Gen. Contractors of Am. (dir.), Cons. Constructors Council Am., Soc. Am. Mil. Engrs., Asso. Gen. Contractors Miss. Valley Flood Control (br. pres. 1957). Republican. Address: 3350 Highland Park Pl Memphis TN 38111

FORDICE, DANIEL KIRKWOOD, JR., constrn. co. exec.; b. Memphis, Feb. 10, 1934; s. Daniel Kirkwood and Clara Aileen (Augustine) F.; B.S., Purdue U., 1956, M.S., 1957; m. Patricia Louise Owens, Aug. 13, 1955; children—Angela Leigh, Daniel Kirkwood III, Hunter Lloyd, James Owens. Engr., Humble Oil & Refining Co., Baton Rouge, La., 1956-62; partner Fordice Constrn. Co., Delta, 1962—; pres. Fordice Constrn. Co., Inc., Vicksburg, Miss., 1970—, dir., 1970—; dir. Vicksburg Sand & Gravel, Inc.; pres., Vicksburg Quality Edn., Inc., 1971—. Served to 1st lt. C.E., AUS, 1957-59. Recipient Distinguished Service award Vicksburg Jr. C. of C., 1969. Mem. Am. Soc. C.E., Aircraft Owners and Pilots Assn., Pilots Internat. Assn., Asso. Gen. Contractors Am. (nat. bd. dirs. 1970—, pres. Miss. Valley flood control br. 1970), Sigma Chi, Tau Beta Pi, Chi Epsilon. Clubs: Army Navy, Engineers (Vicksburg, Miss.). Home: 1457 Parkside Dr Vicksburg MS 39180 Office: PO Box 37 Delta LA 71233

FORDYCE, PHILLIP RANDALL, educator; b. Lyons, Ind., May 28, 1928; s. Russell and Agnes (Fulk) F.; B.S., Butler U., 1951, M.S., 1954; m. Lois Marilyn Lamb, Dec. 27, 1947; children—Deborah, Natalie, Marilyn, Kerry, Timothy. Asst. prof. sci. edn. Fla. State U., Tallahassee, 1963-67, asso. prof., 1967-70, prof., 1970—, asst. dean Coll. Edn., 1965-67, asso. dean, 1967-69, dean, 1969—. Cons. U.S.-AID Sci. Edn. in India Program, summer 1964; dir. 38 NSF-USOE Grant projects. Fellow A.A.A.S.: mem. Am. Inst. Biol. Scis., Nat. Assn. for Research in Sci. Teaching, Assn. for Edn. Tchrs. in Sci., Nat. Assn. Biology Tchrs. (editor newsletter 1965-68, pres. 1963), Phi Delta Kappa, Kappa Delta Pi. Contbr. articles to profl. jours. Home: 2805 St Leonard Dr Tallahassee FL 32303

FOREHAND, ART, state ofcl. Chief Bur. Community Med. Facilities Fla. Dept. Health, Tallahassee. Address: 908 S Borough St Tallahassee FL 32304*

FOREHAND, WILLIAM WHITEHURST, ins. agt.; b. Shiloh, N.C. Oct. 14, 1912; s. Wm. Gregory and Elizabeth (Whitehurst) F.; grad. high sch.; m. Geneva Hughes, Aug. 4, 1935; children—Billie Faye, Winfred Brian. Mem. Civilian Conservation Corps, 1933-34; mcht. Shiloh, N.C., 1936-40; gen. ins. agt., Shiloh, 1941—. Mem. N.C. Ins. Adv. Bd., 1965-69; chmn. Camden County Planning Bd., 1965-69, Camden County Bd. Elections, 1958-69. Chmn., Democratic Exec. Com., 1948-50; polit. leader Camden County, 1952—. Trustee, Museum of Albemarle. Mason (master 1952, sec. 1958-69). Baptist (ch. historian, deacon 1947-51, 68—, treas. 1941-56). Club: South Camden Ruritan (sec. 1948-50, pres. 1968, gov. Albemarle zone 1970, dist. gov. 1971). Writer articles on history Camden County. Home: Shiloh NC 27974

FOREMAN, BARNEY SIMPSON, retail trade exec.; b. Lake Charles, La., June 26, 1917; s. Homer and Aldea (Bushnell) F.; B.A., U. Southwestern La., 1939; m. Fleurette Emile Kahn, Apr. 1, 1942; children—Julian Brian, Glenn Barney. Tchr., coach, Crowley (La.) High Sch., 1939-42, Lake Charles (La.) High Sch., 1942-44; with Mefvine Kahn Co., retail trade, Rayne, La., 1944—, sec.-treas., mgr. hardware and appliance dept., 1944—. Chmn. Rayne Youth Program, 1962-69; active Little League Football, Boy Scouts Am. Mem. Rayne Council, 1946-50, mayor prot-tem, 1946-50. Baptist. Mason (shriner). Home: 309 E Jeff Davis St Rayne LA 70578 Office: PO Box 29 Rayne LA 70578

FOREMAN, PERCY, lawyer, lectr.; b. Polk County, Tex., June 21, 1902; s. Ransom Parson and William Pinckney (Rogers) F.; LL.B., U. Tex., 1927; m. Marguerite Obert, Apr. 21, 1957; children— William Pinckney Rogers 111, Marguerite. With Nat. Lyceum, then Chautauqua lectr.; admitted to Tex. bar, 1927, since practiced in Houston. Mem. Am., Tex., Houston bar assns., Nat. Assn. Def. Lawyers Criminal Cases (pres. 1963-64). Home: 200 Carnarvon St Houston TX 77002 Office: 1116 Capitol Av Houston TX 77002

FOREMAN, RICHARD JESSE, truck leasing co. exec.; b. Augusta, Ga., Jan. 16, 1918; s. Simkins and Gertrude (Baker) F.; grad. high sch.; m. Claudine M. Bentley, Aug. 13, 1939; children—Gertie (Mrs. William W. McElmurray), Richard Jesse Foreman. Owner, pres. R.J. Foreman Trucking Co., Jackson, S.C., 1935—; v.p., dir. First State Nat. Bank. Mem. Aiken County Planning and Devel. Bd., 1960-68, Aiken County Sch. Bd., 1958-64. Baptist. (Mason (32 deg., Shriner), Lion. Club: Silverton Agriculture (pres. 1962-63) (Jackson). Address: Route 1 Jackson SC 29831

FOREMAN, WILLIAM EDWIN, educator; b. Columbus, O., Sept. 6, 1929; s. Ira Luce and Helen Marie (McCarthy) F.; B. Engr. Mines, Ohio State U., 1953; M.S., Va. Poly. Inst., 1961; Ph.D., Pa. State U., 1965; m. Dorothy Elaine Reed, Feb. 2, 1957; children—Douglas, John, Michael. Research and devel. engr. Basic, Inc., Cleve., 1953-57; asso. prof. mining engring. Va. Poly. Inst. and State U. at Blacksburg, 1957—; corporate dir. Mining Cons., Blacksburg. Carborundum fellow, 1961-63. Mem. Va. Acad. Sci., Am. Inst. Mining Engrs., Sigma Xi, Sigma Gamma Epsilon. Home: 907 Mason Dr Blacksburg VA 24060

FOREMAN, WILMER LOUIS, agrl. orgn. exec.; b. Eden, Miss., June 8, 1912; s. Daniel Henry and Bessie Belle (Faulk) F.; student Delta State Coll., Cleve., Miss., 1932, U. Ala., 1937-40; m. Virginia Sims, Apr. 4, 1941; 1 dau., Laura Virginia. Editor, Atmore (Ala.) Advance, 1941-42; asso. editor Huntsville (Ala.) Times, 1946-47; editor Comml. Dispatch, Columbus, Miss., 1947-48; pub. relations staff Nat. Cotton Council, Memphis, 1948-53, pub. relations mgr., 1953-70, dir. pub. relations and promotion, 1970—. Served to comdr. USNR, 1942-46. Mem. Pub. Relations Soc. Am. (mem. nat. exec. com. 1958), Agrl. Relations Council (pres. 1961), Nat. Assn. Farm Broadcasters (asso.), Am. Assn. Agrl. Coll. Editors, Lambda Chi Alpha. Republican. Methodist. Author: Cotton From Field to Fabric, 1966. Contbr. articles to profl. publs. Home: 297 Mary Ann Dr Memphis TN 38117 Office: 1918 North Pkwy Memphis TN 38112

FORESMAN, BOB, newspaperman; b. Tulsa, July 20, 1912; s. Frank and Mabyl (Weldon) F.; A.B., U. Tulsa, 1934; m. Betty Louise McDaniel, Dec. 15, 1940; 1 dau., Elizabeth Ann. With Tulsa Tribune, 1935—, bus. editor, 1958—, author weekly column. Founder, Tulsa Tribune Send-a-Kid-to-Camp Fund, 1936. Fund chmn. Tulsa Expressway Beautification Com., 1963-64. Bd. dirs. Okla. Hist. Soc. Served to lt. comdr. USNR, 1943-46; PTO, ETO. Recipient Spl. Merit award Okla. Pub. Expenditure Council, 1955. Mem. Tulsa Press Club (past pres.), Navy League, Sigma Delta Chi, Lambda Chi Alpha. Methodist. Clubs: University Tulsa Lettermens', Petroleum, University (Tulsa), Indian Springs Country. Home: 2347 S Delaware Pl Tulsa OK 74114 Office: 315 S Boulder Av Tulsa OK 74102

FORESMAN, HENRY JOYCE, lawyer; b. East Liberty, Pa., Nov. 9, 1919; s. Robert All and Helen (Joyce) F.; B.A., Va. Mil. Inst., 1941; student Tulane U. La. Coll. Law, U. Colo. Sch. Law, 1947; J.D., Washington and Lee U., 1948; m. Helen Tilden Williamson, Apr. 19, 1952; children—Henry Joyce, Lee Gephart, Robert Holmes, George Williamson. Admitted to Va. bar, 1949, practice law, Buena Vista, Va, 1949-59, Lexington, Va., 1959—; town atty. Glasgow, Va., 1951—; city atty. Buena Vista, 1952-55, atty. for commonwealth, 1952-56; sec. Lexington Electoral Bd., 1966-69; spl. asst. to supt. Va. M.I. Inst., 1971—. Mem. Buena Vista City Democratic Com., 1952-59; del. State Dem. Convs., 1952, 56, 60, 64. Trustee Kappa Alpha Scholarship Fund, 1965-71. Served to capt. AUS, 1941-45; PTO. Decorated Bronze Star medal, Air medal, Purple Heart. Recipient George Washington Honor Medal award Freedoms Found., 1967. Mem. Am., Va., Lexington-Buena Vista-Rockbridge (pres. 1952-53) bar assns., Virginia State Bar (council 1953-56), Nat. Inst. Municipal Law Officers, Am. Judicature Soc., Kappa Alpha Order (nat. pres. 1965-67). Phi Delta Phi. Episcopalian. Home: 408 Highland Rd Lexington VA 24450 Office: 20 W Washington St Lexington VA 24450

FORGOSH, ELLIOTT HAROLD, govt. ofcl.; b. Bklyn., Aug. 12, 1919; s. Louis and Anna (Stang) F.; B.B.A., Coll. City N.Y., 1940; M.B.A. in Mgmt., N.Y. U., 1956; m. Bernice M. Sumergrade, Mar. 6, 1955; children—Errol Martin, Leslie Bryan. Accountant, Joseph Getz & Co., N.Y.C., 1940-48; asst. controller Century RibbonMills, N.Y.C., 1948-53; cost officer N.Y. region U.S. Postal Service, 1955-63, financial mgr., Washington, 1963-70, mgr. accounting systems, 1971—. Asst. profl. lectr. George Washington U., 1964-68; instr. Montgomery Coll., Rockville, Md. Served with AUS, 1942-46. C.P.A., N.Y. Mem. Am. Inst. C.P.A.'s, N.Y. Soc. C.P.A.'s Nat. Assn. Accountants, Fed. Govt. Accountants Assn. Home: 8213 Cindy Lane Bethesda MD 20034 Office: 1200 Pennsylvania Av Washington DC 20260

FORLAND, MARVIN, physician, educator; b. Newark, N.J., Mar. 29, 1933; s. Aaron and Fay Betty (Garfinkel) F.; B.A., Colgate U., 1954; M.D., Columbia U., 1958; m. Ellinor Salinger Klein, Dec. 19, 1965; 1 son, Aaron Hans. Intern, U. Chgo. Hosps., 1958-59, resident, 1959-62; asst. prof. dept. medicine U. Chgo. Sch. Medicine, 1964-68; asso. prof., chief sect. renal disease, dept. physiology and medicine U. Tex. Med. Sch., San Antonio, 1968—; attending physician Bexar County Hosp., 1968—; mem. task force on heart Tex. Regional Med. Program, 1970—. Served to capt. USMCR, 1962-64. Mem. Central Soc. Clin. Research., Am. Soc. Nephrology, Internat. Soc. Nephrology, A.C.P. Contbr. articles to profl. pubs. Home: 519 Country Lane San Antonio TX 78209 Office: 7703 Floyd Curl Dr San Antonio TX 78229

FORMAN, FRANK (SHANE, III), govt. ofcl.; b. Kansas City, Mo., Oct. 28, 1944; s. Frank Shane, Jr., and Dorothy Jean (Roberts) F.; B.A., U. Va., 1966, M.A. (Ford Found. U. Scholar and fellow 1964-67; NSF grad. fellow, 1966-68), 1968; m. Sarah Stirling Banks, Feb. 2, 1968. Industry economist CAB, Washington, 1969—. Contbr. articles to profl. jours., bulls. Home: 1742 Corcoran St NW Washington DC 20009 Office: B-15 Civil Aeronautics Board Washington DC 20428

FORMAN, HAMILTON COLLINS, banking and nursery co. exec.; b. Ft. Lauderdale, Fla., Apr. 3, 1919; s. Hamilton Mc Lure and Blanche (Collins) F.; student U. Tenn., 1939-43; m. Doris Marie Davis, Jan. 7, 1945; children—Miles Austin, Hamilton Collins. Owner, mgr. Forman's San. Dairy, 1945-55; dir., v.p. Fern Crest Quarries, 1955-62; owner, mgr. Forman's Palm Nursery, Fern Crest Village, Fla., 1955—; dir., v.p. United Fed. Savs. & Loan Assn., Ft. Lauderdale, 1965—. Pres., Hamilton M. and Blanche C. Forman Christian Found., 1955—; commr., treas., chmn. bd. North Broward Hosp. Dist., 1961—; mem. nat. adv. bd. Berea in Korea Found. and Sch., 1960—; mem. nat. adv. council Lynchburg (Va.) Coll., 1967—; commr., treas., town clk. Fern Crest Village, 1955—; pres., dir. Fern Crest Improvement Dist., 1957—; mem. Gov.'s Com. Interstate Land Sales of Fla., 1963, Ft. Lauderdale Opera Guild; commr. Tindall Hammock Irrigation and Soil Conservation Dist.; mem. Fla.-Columbia Alliance, Taxpayers League Broward County, Broward County Narcotics Guidance Council, Gov.'s Com Tax Reform. Trustee Bethany (W. Va.) Coll., Nova U. Advanced Tech.; bd. dirs. Nova Gold Key Assn. Served with USAAF, World War 11. Mem. Fla. Hosp. Commrs. and Trustees Assn. (vice chmn., dir.), S.A.R., Phi Eta Sigma, Kappa Sigma. Democrat. Mem. Christian Ch. (Elder, chmn. bd.). Kiwanian (award Ft. Lauderdale 1966), Gideon. Clubs: Fort Lauderdale Yacht, Rolling Hills Golf and Country (dir., treas. 1960—), Gold Coast Rotunda, Tiger Bay (Ft. Lauderdale). Home: 1524 Coral Ridge Dr Fort Lauderdale FL 33304 Office: 3600 N Federal Hwy Fort Lauderdale FL 33308

FORMAN, WILLIAM HARPER, JR., lawyer; b. Houston, Aug. 13, 1936; s. William Harper and Ermaleen (Lukas) F.; B.A., Tulane U., 1958, J.D., 1961; postgrad. Coll. William and Mary; M.A., La. State U., 1970; m. Olive Goodwill Roberts, June 17, 1967. Commd. 1st lt. USAF, 1961, advanced through grades to capt., 1963, regular officer, 1966-67; asst. staff judge adv. Clark Air Base, Phillipines, 1961-63; staff judge adv. Bossier Base, Shreveport, La., 1963-67; atty. Gulf South Research Inst., 1968-69; atty. FTC, New Orleans, 1969—, pub. information officer, 1971—. Sec., Consumer Adv. Bd., New Orleans, 1970—, Consumer Protection Com., New Orleans, 1970—. Bd. dirs. La. Consumers' League. Capt., USAF Res. Recipient 1st place award for hist. articles Deep South Writers and Artists Conf., 1971, for book-length biography, 1971. Mem. Am. (mem. local govt. law sect.), Fed., La. State (mem. pub. relations com. 1970—) bar assns., St. Thomas More Cath. Lawyers Assn., Soc. Colonial Wars, S.A.R., Soc. War of 1812, Soc. Cincinnati, La. Hist. Assn., Air Force Assn. Order of Stars and Bars, Judge Advs. Assn., La. Hist. Soc., La. Landmarks Soc., Friends of Cabildo, Am. Humane Assn., Vietnam Vets. Against War, Phi Delta Theta, Phi Delta Phi, Pi Sigma Alpha. Club: Pendennis (New Orleans). Contbr. articles to profl. jours. Home: 3102 Coliseum St New Orleans LA 70115 Office: 333 St Charles St New Orleans LA 70130

FORNEY, DAISY (ELENORE) CUNDIFF (MRS. SILAS DURAN FORNEY), educator; b. Lafayette, Ind., Mar. 24, 1913; d. Edward E. and Mattie (Moore) Cundiff; student Purdue U., 1931-32; primary certificate Butler U., 1934; B.S., Sul Ross State Coll., 1956; m. Silas Duran Forney, Dec. 20, 1941. Primary tchr. Ford Sch., Lafayette, 1937-41, Oakland City, Ind., 1943-44; elementary tchr. Pease Sch., Odessa, Tex., 1954—. Com. mem. art textbooks Ector County Ind. Sch. Dist., 1960, handwriting textbooks, 1967. Mem. Tex., Classroom tchrs. assns., Panhellenic, Odessa Art Assn., Sigma Sigma Sigma (past pres.), Kappa Kappa Iota (chpt. v.p.). Mem. Order Eastern Star. Home: 1207 W 26th St Odessa TX 79760

FORREST, HERBERT EMERSON, lawyer; b. N.Y.C., Sept. 20, 1923; s. Jacob K. and Rose (Fried) F.; B.A., George Washington U., 1948, J.D., 1952; student Coll. City N.Y., 1941, Ohio U., 1943-44; m. Marilyn Lefsky, Jan. 12, 1952; children—Glenn Clifford, Andrew Matthew. Admitted to Va., D.C. bars, 1952, Md. bar, 1959; law clk. Bolitha J. Laws, Chief Judge U.S. Dist. Ct., Washington, 1952-55; practiced in Washington, 1952—; mem. firm Welch & Morgan, 1955-65, Steptoe & Johnson, 1965—. Chmn. D.C. Criminal Justice Act Adv. Bd., 1972—. Served with AUS, 1943-46. Mem. Am. Judicature Soc., Am. (chmn. com. agy. rule making), Va. State, Fed., Fed. Commn. (chmn. publs. com.) bar assns., Bar Assn. D.C. (sec., dir., mem. exec. com.), N.A.M. (telecommunications com.), Order of Coif, Phi Beta Kappa, Pi Gamma Mu, Artus, Phi Eta Sigma, Phi Delta Phi. Democrat. Jewish religion. Book editor Fed. Commn. Bar Jour. Contbr. articles to profl. jours. Home: 7001 Whittier Blvd Bethesda MD 20034 Office: 1250 Connecticut Av Washington DC 20036

FORREST, PHILIP RYDER, JR., banker; b. N.Y.C., July 25, 1919; s. Philip Ryder and Marie (Shannon) F.; A.B., Spring Hill Coll., 1942; m. Anne Martina Dermeranville, Feb. 14, 1942; children—Philip Ryder III, Marie S. (Mrs. Douglas Perryman), Helena P., Anne H. Reporter, feature writer Mobile (Ala.) Press Register, 1940-42; mem. staff indsl. personnel and pub. relations Ala. Drydock & Shipbldg. Co., 1942-44; with A.P., N.Y.C., 1944-46; owner Shoppers Delivery Service, Mobile, 1946-48; with Morris Timbes Advt. Agy.-Howard Barney Advt. Agy., 1948-50; promotion mgr., program dir. WABB Radio, 1950-57; promotion dir., news dir. WALA-TV, 1957-59; owner Phil Forrest Advt. Agy., 1959-63; pub. relations dir. Am. Jr. Miss Pageant, Inc., 1963-69; dir. advt. and pub. relations Mchts. Nat. Bank of Mobile, 1969—. Pres. St. Catherine Sch. P.T.A., 1966-68. Campaign dir. Young Republicans for Eisenhower, 1952-56. Recipient Exceptional Achievement award Pub. Relations Council Ala., 1970. Mem. Overseas Press Club Am., Am., Ala. pub. relations socs., Pub. Relations Council Ala. (dir. 1972), Pub. Relations Council Mobile (pres. 1972), Am. Bankers Assn., Bank Marketing Assn., Spring Hill Coll. Alumni Assn. K.C. (4 deg.). Clubs: International Trade, Athelstan. Home: 304 Siena Vista St Mobile AL 36607 Office: PO Box 2527 106 St Francis St Mobile AL 36622

FORREST, WILLIAM A., JR., bussiness exec., b. 1929; U. Va., 1951, LL.B., 1956; m. Admitted to Va. bar, 1956; atty. McGuire, Woods, King, Davis & Patterson Assos. (name now McGuire, Woods & Battle), 1956-61, partner, 1961-66; asst. gen. counsel, asst. sec. A.H. Robins Co., Inc., Richmond, Va., 1966-67, sec., asst. gen. counsel, 1967-69, sec., gen. counsel, 1969—; dir. Capital Savs. and Loan Assn., Va. Trust Co. Trustee Crippled Chidren's Hosp.; bd. dirs. Team of Progress, 1970—, Senior Center, 1966-69. Served to 1st lt. AUS, 1951-53. Mem. Richmond Tennis Patrons Assn. (pres. 1969-71), U. Va. Alumni Assn. (pres. Richmond chpt. 1968-70). Address: 1407 Cummings Dr Richmond VA 23220

FORRESTER, BRUCE M(ILLAR), U.S. judge; b. Kansas City, Mo., Dec. 26, 1908; s. James M. and Bertha (Wilkinson) F.; J.D., U. Mo., 1935; m. Anne Lee Broaddus, Nov. 9, 1937; children—Anne Norris, Jean Bruce, Bruce Millar. Admitted to Mo. bar, 1935, practiced in Kansas City, 1935-57; mem. firm Watson, Ess, Groner, Barnett & Wittaker (now Watson, Ess, Marshall & Enggas); judge U.S. Tax Ct., Washington 1957—. Charter trustee Holton-Arms Sch., Washington. Served with AUS, 1944-45; instr. ROTC. Mem. Fed. Am., Mo., Kansas City bar assns., Mo. Bar, Am. Law Inst., Lawyers Assn. Kansas City, Sigma Alpha Epsilon (past pres., trustee). Episcopalian. Home: 7017 Beechwood Dr Chevy Chase MD 20015 Office: 12th S and Constitution Av Washington DC 20044

FORRESTER, EUGENE NORWOOD, physician; b. Jacksonville, Fla., July 1, 1924; s. Vinson T. and Mary Alice (Moore) F.; A.B., Duke U., 1949, M.D., 1954; m. Mary Frances Hickman, Jan. 28, 1947; children—Cynthia Patrice, Eugene Norwood, John Vinson, David Kevin. Intern U.S. Naval Hosp., St. Albans, L.I., N.Y., 1954; pvt. practice medicine, Clayton, N.C., 1956-58, Winter Park, Fla., 1958—. Dir. Semovan Atlantic Bank, Casselberry, Fla., 1972—. Served with USNR, 1943-45, 1953-55. Mem. Fla., So., Am. med. assns., Orange County Med. Soc. Home: 406 Park North Ct Winter Park FL 32789 Office: 2035 Glenwood Dr Winter Park FL 32789

FORRESTER, LELAND S., reporter. Chgo. Tribune Press. Office: 1750 Pennsylvania Av Washington DC 20006*

FORT, ARTHUR TOMLINSON, III, physician, educator; b. Lumpkin, Ga., Sept. 24, 1931; s. Thomas Morton and Gladys (Davis) F.; student N. Ga. Coll., 1948-50; B.B.A., U. Ga., 1952; student Memphis State U., 1957-58; M.D., U. Tenn., 1962; m. Jane Wilmer McClelland, June 15, 1957;children—Abby Lucinda, Arthur Tomlinson Jr., Juliana Melody, Ernest Arlington II. Intern, Bapt. Meml. Hosp., Memphis, 1962-63; resident obstetrics and gynecology U. Tenn., 1963-66, asst. prof., 1966-70; prof., head dept. gynecology and obstetrics La. State U. Med. Sch., Shreveport, 1971—; pvt. practice obstetrics and gynecology, Memphis, 1966-70. Mem. med. com., bd. dirs. La. Family Planning Program, Caddo Parish, 1971—; mem. nat. adv. council Nat. Center Family Planning Program Devel. Served with USAF, 1952-57. Recipient Student Golden Apple award A.M.A., 1969. Diplomate Am. Bd. Obstetrics and Gynecology. Fellow Am. Coll. Obstetrics and Gynecology; mem. Am. Fertility Soc., Am., So. med. assns., S.-Central Obstet. and Gynecol. Soc., Soc. for Study Reprodn., Nat. Assn. Family Planning Program Dirs., Nat. Planning Forum. Democrat. Presbyn. Home 503 Forest Av Shreveport LA 71104 Office: 1541 Kings Hwy Shreveport LA 71103

FORT, GEORGE EDWARD, petroleum engring. cons.; b. Rolla, Mo., July 28, 1916; s. Rowe and Maude (Eddleman) F.; B.S., Mo. Sch. Mines, 1940; hon. profl. petroleum engring. degree U. Mo. at Rolla, 1967; m. Mary Anne Reeves, July 5, 1947 (dec. 1970); children—Georgiann, William R., George Edward 11. With Pan Am. Petroluem Corp., 1940-58, successively engr. trainee S. Tex., S. La., engr. Houston, petroleum engr. S. La., field engr. Western Kan., dist. engr. Shreveport, La., 1947-50, sr. engr., Oklahoma City, 1951-58; petroleum cons. Oklahoma City 1959; partner Fort and Miller, petroleum cons. firm, 1960—. Served from pvt. to 1st lt. USAAF, 1942-45. Decorated Air medal with cluster, Purple Heart. Registered profl. engr., Okla. Mem. Engring. Club Oklahoma City, Oklahoma City Geol. Soc., Am. Petroleum Inst., Am. Inst. Mining, Metall. and Petroleum Engrs., Okla. Ind. Petroleum Assn. (dir.), Soc. Ind. Profl. Earth Scientists, Lambda Chi Alpha. Republican. Methodist. Club: Petroleum (dir.). Home: 3939 NW 34th St Oklahoma City OK 73112 Office: First Nat Bank Bldg Oklahoma City OK 73102

FORT, HOMER T(HOMAS), JR., museum exec.; b. Hillsboro, Tex., Sept. 2, 1920; s. Homer Thomas and Gesna Vern (Higgins) F.; B.J., U. Tex., 1941, B.A., 1942; m. Ruth Elsie Hotchkiss, July 21, 1945; children—Barbara Ann (Mrs. Dorriss Beasley), Thomas Allen. Indsl. journalism Magnolia Petroleum Co., Beaumont, Tex., 1945-54, asst. mgr. pub. relations, Dallas, 1954-57, mgr. pub. relations, 1957-59; mgr. N.Am. pub. relations Mobil Oil Corp., N.Y.C., 1959-61, mgr. corp. pub. relations dept., 1961-69; exec. v.p. Permian Basin Petroleum Mus., Midland, Tex., 1969—. Served with USAAF, World War II. Mem. Pub. Relations Soc. Am., Tex. Museums Assn. Methodist. Rotarian. Club: Ranchland Hills Country (Midland). Author: (with Drucilla Stovall Jones) A Family Called Fort, 1970. Contbr. articles profl. jours. Home: 9 Fairfax Ct Midland TX 79701 Office: PO Box 1310 Midland TX 79701

FORT, RUFUS E., JR., ins. exec.; b. Nashville, Aug. 29, 1910; s. Rufus E. and Louise (Clark) F.; B.S. in Elec. Engring., Va. Mil. Inst., 1931; m. Agnes M. Stokes, June 17, 1933; children—Agnes S., Julia G., Eugenia W., Louise C. Instr. elec. engring. Va. Mil. Inst., 1931-32; with Nat. Life & Accident Ins. Co. of Nashville, 1932-66, successively life ins. agt., Detroit, supt., mgr., Nashville, asst. mgr. ordinary life dept., agy. sec., mgr. manpower devel. div., supt. agys., 1932-53, v.p. charge field research planning and devel., 1953-62, sr. v.p. selling and servicing, 1962-64, sr. v.p. spl. assignments, 1964-66, dir., 1940—, mem. exec. com., 1959—. Trustee, vice chmn. bd. Tenn. Retirement System, 1949—; bd. trustees Checkwood-Tenn. Bot. Garden and Fine Arts Center. Served as 2d lt. AUS, 1942-46, adj. gen. Tenn., 1946. Recipient meritorious commendation 4th Service Command; named mem. Exec. and Profl. Hall of Fame. Mem. Life Ins. Agy. Mgmt. Assn. (dir. 1957-60), Life Underwriters Tng. Council (trustee 1962). Episcopalian. Elk. Clubs: Belle Meade Country, Cedar Creek, Cumberland, Exchange (Nashville); Capital City (Atlanta); Internat. (Chgo.); University (N.Y.C.). Home: 116 Jackson Blvd Nashville TN 37205 Office: PO Box 2641 Nashville TN 37219

FORTAS, ABE, lawyer; b. Memphis, June 19, 1910; s. William and Ray (Berson) F.; A.B., Southwestern Coll. at Memphis, 1930; LL.B., Yale, 1933; m. Carolyn Eugenia Agger, July 9, 1935. Mem. faculty law Yale, 1933-37, 46; asst. chief Legal Div. A.A.A., 1933-34; asst. dir., corporate reorgn. study SEC, 1934-37, cons., 1937-38, asst. dir. Pub. Utilities Div., 1938-39; gen. counsel, Pub. Works Adminstrn., 1939-40, Bituminous Coal Div., 1939-41; dir. Div. of Power, Dept. Interior, 1931-42; under-sec. interior, 1942-46; mem. law firm Arnold, Fortas & Porter, Washington, D.C., 1947-65; asso. justice Supreme Ct. U.S., 1965-69; practice law, Washington, 1969; mem. law firm Fortas & Koven, Washington, 1970—. Acting gen. counsel Nat. Power Policy Com., 1941; mem. bd. legal examiners Civil Service Commn., 1941-43; mem. Pres.'s Com. to Study Changes in Organic Law of P.R., 1943; adviser to U.S. delegation to UN, San Francisco, 1945, London, 1946. Trustee Carnegie Hall Corp., Kennedy Center Performing Arts; bd. govs. Nat. Guild Community Music schs.; bd. dirs. Nat. Symphony Orch.; chmn. bd. A.K. Rice Inst. Washington sch. Psychiatry; overseer Coll. V.I. Mem. Order of Coif, Phi Beta Kappa, Omicron Delta Kappa. Home: 3210 R St NW Washington DC 20007 Office: 1054 31st St NW Washington DC 20007

FORTENBERRY, JOHN LAMAR, supt. schs.; b. Sumrall, Miss., Sept. 11, 1922; s. William Edward and Pearlie (Wilks) F.; B.S., Southeastern La. Coll., 1948; M.A., U. So. Miss., 1950; Ed.D., U. Miss., 1956; m. Mary Margaret Mosal, Sept. 10, 1964; children—Lisa Mosal, John Lamar. Asst. prof. edn. U. Miss., 1950-52; prin. high sch., Bay St. Louis, Miss., 1952-55; state supr. edn. State Dept. Edn., Jackson, Miss., 1956-65; supt. schs., Canton, Miss., 1965—; instr. extension classes U. Miss., Miss. State U., U. So. Miss. Served with USNR, 1942-47. Mem. Am. Assn. Sch. Adminstrs., Miss. Ednl. Assn., Am. Legion, Phi Delta Kappa, Kappa Delta Pi. Mason (32 deg.). Rotarian. Author: Fortenberry's Mississippi School Guide, 1958. Home: 226 Rebecca Dr Canton MS 39046 Office: 403 E Lincoln St Canton MS 39046

FORTH, STUART, librarian; b. Manistee, Mich., Aug. 13, 1923; s. Wade S. and Nan (Rumans) F.; B.A., U. Mich., 1949, M.A. in L.S., 1950; Ph.D. in History, U. Wash., 1961; m. Pearl Brown, Dec. 24, 1951. Catalog librarian Ore. State U., 1950-52, adminstrv. asst. to dir. libraries, 1952-54; reference librarian Seattle Pub. Library, 1954-59; undergrad. librarian U. Kan., 1959-61, asso. dir. libraries, 1961-64, acting dir. libraries, 1964-65; dir. libraries U. Ky., 1965—, v.p. for student affairs, 1968-70; teaching fellow history U. Wash., 1954-55, 57-58; tchr. dept. Western civilization U. Kan., 1960-65. Mem. Kan. Library Com., 1964-65. Served with USAAF, 1942-45; PTO. Mem. Am. Assn. U. Profs. (pres. U. Kan. chpt. 1965), Am. Hist. Assn., Orgn. Am. Historians, Bibliog. Soc. Am., Pacific Northwest (sec. 1953-54), Kan. (chmn. coll. and univ. library sect. 1963-64), Ky., Am. Library assns., Am. Civil Liberties Union. Democrat. Episcopalian. Clubs: Caxton (Chgo.); Filson (Louisville). Contbr. to profl. jours. Home: 1277 Colonial Dr Lexington KY 40504

FORTSON, BENJAMIN WYNN, JR., Ga. sec. state; b. Tignall, Ga., Dec. 19, 1904; s. Benjamin Wynn and Lillie (Welborn) F.; student Emory U., 1919-20, Starkes U., 1920-23, Ga. Inst. Tech., 1923-24; LL.D., John Marshall Law Sch., 1949; m. Mary Cade, May 15, 1926 (dec.); 1 dau., Ann McNeill (Mrs. George Mandus). With Citizens Nat. Bank, Washington, Ga., 1924-25, Atlanta and Lowry Nat. Bank, 1925-26; asst. cashier Washington Loan and Banking Co., 1927-29; sec. state State of Ga., Atlanta, 1946—. Sec., treas. Wilkes County chpt. A.R.C.; pres. Ga. Soc. for Crippled Children, 1954-56. Mem. Ga. Senate, 1939-40, 41-42; mem. Ga. Ho. of Reps., 1943-46. Trustee, Mary Willis Library. Mem. Nat. Assn. Secs. of State (pres. 1954), Alpha Kappa Psi (hon.), Pi Sigma Alpha (hon.), Demonsthenian Lit. Soc. U. Ga. (hon. life). Democrat. Methodist. Mason, Moose. Home: Box 428 Washington GA 30673 Office: State Capitol Atlanta GA 30334

FORTUNATO, LEONARD HENRY, educator; b. Pitts., Mar. 17, 1909; s. John B. and Rosalie (D'Anna) F.; B.S. in Edn., Duquesne U., 1932; postgrad. Western Theol. Sem., Pitts., 1933-35; M.Litt., U. Pitts., 1936, postgrad., 1937-42; postgrad. Columbia, summer 1942, U. So. Cal., 1954, Coll. of Charleston, 1970-71, Boston U., summer 1971; m. Maxine Wipperman, Mar. 4, 1933; children—Margot (Mrs. Robert L. Kriel), D'Anna Elizabeth. Instr. history, Italian and history of art Pitts. Adult Evening Sch., 1932-42; lt. col., asso. prof. history Citadel, Charleston, S.C., 1946—, faculty adviser Citadel Demolay Club. Tchr. history U. S.C. Extension, 1958-64; lectr. evening sch. Bapt. Coll. Charleston, 1965-66; lectr. Coll. Gen. Studies, U.S.C. at Charleston Naval Base, 1968-71; past performer, bd. dirs. Charleston Symphony Orch., 1948—. Frick Found. fellow, 1941; Danforth Found. fellow, 1954. Mem. So., S.C. (exec. com., pres. 1964-68) hist. assns., S.C. Hist. Soc., Nat. Trust for Historic Preservation Charleston Masonic Research Soc., Charleston Preservation Soc., Nat. Sojourners (chmn. Americanism-Youth com.), Am. Assn. U. Profs., Phi Alpha Theta (charter mem.). Democrat. Presbyn. Mason. Hist. cons. Freedom's Four Square Miles (J. Percival Petit), 1964. Home: 6 Formosa Dr Charleston SC 29407

FORTUNE, EDMOND M., state legislator; b. Milton, Fla., Nov. 23, 1932; s. Perry Fortune and Nora (Lowery) F.; student Pensacola Jr. Coll.; B.S., Howard Coll., 1958; m. Erma Ruth Stewart, Jan. 28, 1956; children—Felicia Ann, Edmond Dwayne, Terry Leon. Mem. Fla. Ho of Reps., 1966—, mem. appropriations com., 1959-71, vice chmn., 1971, chmn. subcom. pub. funding, 1969-71. Trustee West Fla. Tb Assn., 1966—, Fla. Welfare Bd. Dist. 1, 1967—. Served with AUS; ETO. Recipient Man of Year award Pace Civitan Club, 1967. Mem. Fla., Am., Santa Rosa pharm. assns. Baptist. Home: 807 Lake Av Milton FL 32570 Office: PO Box 1086 Pace FL 32570*

FOSBERG, IRVING ARTHUR, psychologist; b. N.Y.C., Jan. 22, 1916; s. Albert and Julia (Greenfield) F.; B.S., N.Y. U., 1937 Ph.D., 1940; M.A., Columbia, 1938; m. Betty Pearlman, Feb. 11, 1945; children— Ben, Orin, Barry. Cons. psychologist, N.Y.C., 1940-41; asst. prof. psychology Farragut Coll., Farragut, Ida., 1946-47; dir. Bur. Psychol. Service, Tulane U., New Orleans, asst. prof. psychology, 1947-48; chief psychologist VA Hosp., New Orleans, 1952-57; pres. Psychol. Service Center New Orleans, Inc., 1955—; asso. prof. Loyola U. Sch. Bus. Administrn., New Orleans, 1960-67, prof., 1967—, also mgmt. cons. to pres. univ. Cons. psychologist Cerebral Palsy Clinic, Civil Service Commn. New Orleans; vocational cons. U.S. Dept. Health, Edn. and Welfare. Served with USNR, 1941-68; now comdr. ret. Fellow Am. Psychol. Assn., A.A.A.S., Rorschach Inst.; mem. So. Soc. Philos. Psychology, Am. Assn. U. Profs., La. Psychol. Assn. (past pres.). Contbr. articles to profl. jours. Home: 350 Lowerline St New Orleans LA 70118 Office: 8116 Hampson St New Orleans LA 70118

FOSBERG, MORTON FREDRIC, govt. ofcl.; b. N.Y.C., May 3, 1919; s. Albert and Julia (Greenfield) F.; B.S., Coll. City N.Y., 1939; M.A., Columbia U., 1940, postgrad., 1940-41; postgrad. U.S. Army War Coll., 1963-64; m. Barbara Ann Bonner, Sept. 4, 1946; children—Deborah Jayne, Stephen Lawrence. Examining asst. N.Y.C. Civil Service Commn., 1940-41; research asst. Office Radio Research, N.Y.C., 1941-42; chief research br. Office Mil. Govt., Hesse, Germany, 1946-48; chief statis. research sect. Voice Am., N.Y.C., 1949-54; chief research staff USIS, Bonn, Germany, 1954-59, information officer, Havana, Cuba, 1959-60, regional research officer, Lima, Peru, 1960-63; chmn. Latin Am. area course, coordinator and asso. dean Center for Area and Country Studies, Fgn. Service Inst., U.S. Dept. State, Washington, 1964-67; br. pub. affairs officer USIS, Guayaquil, Ecuador, 1967-69; with office of asst. dir. Latin Am., USIA, 1969—. Vice pres. Cresskill (N.J.) Civic Assn., 1952, pres., 1953; vice-chmn. community council Am. embassy, Bonn, Germany, 1958; asst. troop scoutmaster Montgomery County council Boy Scouts Am., 1965-66. Served with AUS, 1942-46. Mem. Am. Statis. Assn., Am. Sociol. Assn., World Assn. Pub. Opinion Researchers. Home: 5805 Overlea Rd Washington DC 20016 Office: Office of Asst Dir Latin Am USIA Washington DC 20547

FOSHEE, LILLIAN SERENA MITCHELL (MRS. CHARLES CECIL FOSHEE), educator; b. Verbena, Ala., Mar. 15, 1914; d. Columbus White and Lillian (Cooper) Mitchell; normal tchr's. degree, TroyState U. (Ala.), 1936; student Ala. Coll., summer 1961-68; m. Charles Cecil Foshee, Oct. 5, 1940; children—John Clinton II, Charles Mitchell. Tchr. elementary schs., Clanton, Ala., 1936-43, Shelby County Sch., Vincent, Ala., 1943-44; tchr. spl. class Clanton Elementary Sch., 1962—. Civil Defense tchr., Chilton County, Ala., 1966. Mem. U.D.C. (chpt. pres. 1958-66, chpt. sec. 1966-68), Internat. Platform Assn. Methodist. Home: Route 1 Box 24 Verbena AL 36091 Office: Clanton Elementary Sch Clanton AL 35045

FOSHEE, WAYNE OTIS, constrn. co. exec.; b. Hot Springs, Ark., Jan. 17, 1937; s. Otis B. and Greta Edna (Smith) F.; student U. Va., 1955-56, U. So. Cal., 1957, Santa Monica City Coll., 1958-59; B.A. in Philosophy, U. Cal. at Los Angeles, 1961; m. Dorothy Lee Westerman, May 31, 1957; children—Michael Wayne, Kevin Otis. Tchr. social studies secondary schs., 1961-63; co-founder Brown &Foshee Constrn. Co., Hot Springs, 1963, partner, 1963—; profl. draftsman, 1957—; dir. Trail's Inn, Inc., Shelter, Inc., Gt. Western Land Corp.; founding partner, dir. Am. Letter, Inc.; co-founder, partner Paul Wayne Devel. Co., Nat. Realty Developers & Investment Co. Pres. Garland County Property Owners Assn., 1964. Recipient Am. Legion Citizenship award, 1955, D.A.R. Citizenship award, 1952. Mem. Nat. Assn. Homebuilders, Ark. (pres., dir.), Hot Springs (past pres., dir.) homebuilders assns. Republican. Methodist. Home: 1003 Prospect St Hot Springs AR 71901 Office: PO Box 1217 Hot Springs AR 71901

FOSS, ARTHUR HAZEN, educator; b. Haverhill, Mass., Jan. 23, 1930; s. Hazen Arthur and Lillian (Thompson) F.; A.B., Boston U., 1951, M.A., 1959; postgrad. U. Fla., 1964-65. Tchr., Wamogo Regional High Sch., Litchfield, Conn., 1955-57; Edgewater High Sch., Orlando, Fla., 1957-60; instr. Jr. Coll. Broward County, Ft. Lauderdale, Fla., 1960—, head dept. math., 1963-69, pre-profl. math. program coordinator, 1967-68. Mem. Fla. Task Force in Math. Articulation, 1965—. Served with USNR, 1951-54. Mem. Math. Assn. Am., Am. Assn. U. Profs., Phi Beta Kappa, Phi Delta Kappa, Alpha Phi Omega. Democrat. Baptist. Kiwanian. Home: 5007 SW 88th Terrace Ft Lauderdale FL 33314

FOSS, ROBERT EDWIN, oil exec.; b. Glendale Cal., July 7, 1910; s. Raymond P. and Mary Ann (Peters) F.; B.S., Cal. Inst. Tech., 1932; m. Olive Lorene Easley, July 13, 1935; children—David Easley, Dixon Keith. Jr. engr. Barnsdall Oil Co., 1935-40, chief engr., 1940-42, gen. supt., 1942-45, v.p. in charge Cal. prodn., 1945-49; joined Sunray Oil Corp. (Sunray-Barnsdall merger), 1950, v.p., 1950, v.p. in charge exploitation and prodn., Tulsa, 1952-55, (co. merged with Mid-Continent Oil Corp. 1955), v.p., mgr. prodn. dept. Sunray DX Oil Co., 1955-59, dir., 1958—, sr. v.p. prodn., 1959-64, exec. v.p. mfg. and marketing, 1963, pres., 1964-68, (co. merged with Sun Oil Co., 1968), exec. v.p., dir. Sun Oil Co., Dallas, 1968—; pres. Sun Oil Co. (Del.), 1971—; dir. First Nat. Bank Tulsa. Bd. dirs., nat. chmn. central com. tng., nat. chmn. exec. com. standardization of oilfield equipment and materials Am. Petroleum Inst. Mem. Twenty-Five Year Club Petroleum Industry. Home: 3310 Fairmount Dallas TX 75201 Office: PO Box 2880 Dallas TX 75221

FOSTER, AUBREY ALFRED, ret. govt. ofcl.; b. Los Angeles, Oct. 20, 1912; s. Ernest W. and Elsie (Dryhurst) F.; B.S., Cornell U., 1939, Ph.D., 1945; m. Grace Mathilda Kuchler, Sept. 13, 1941; children—David, George, Ruth Kathleen (Mrs. Donald J. Cole), Betty Jo (Mrs. Ward Haskell Duke). Plant breeder Francis C. Stokes Co., Vincentown, N.J., 1936-41; plant pathologist Central Fla. Expt. Sta., Sanford, 1946-48; asso. prof. plant pathology Cornell U., Farmingdale, N.Y., 1948-50; forest pathologist U.S. Forest Service, Macon, Ga., 1953-61; supr. tree improvement TVA, Norris, Tenn., 1961-72. Recipient Meritorious Service award U.S. Dept. Agr., 1956. Fellow A.A.A.S.; mem Am. Inst. Biol. Sci., Am. Phytopath. Soc. Home: 110 Dale Rd Norris TN 37828

FOSTER, CHARLES BRADFORD, JR., civil engr.; b. Hope, Ark., Aug. 27, 1915; s. Charles B. and Nancy (Lightle) F.; B.S. in Civil Engring., Tex. A. and M. U., 1938; postgrad. Tex. U. Water Utility Mgmt. Inst., 1962; m. Cecile L. Gatlin, Sept. 23, 1944; children—Charles Bradford III, Nancy Lightle II. Civil engr. Tex. Hwy. Dept., Childress, 1938-39; with Dept. Water Utilities, Shreveport, La., 1939-71, gen. supt. dept., 1962-71; dir. sch. plant Caddo Parish (La.) Schs., 1971—. Comdg. office U.S. Army Reserve Sch., 1966-71. Decorated Legion of Merit. Registered profl. engr., La., Tex., Ark. Fellow Am. Soc. C.E.; mem. Nat. Soc. Profl. Engrs., Engrs. Joint Council, La. Engring. Soc., Am. Water Works Assn. Episcopalian (ch. sch. tchr. 1953—). Lion, Elk. Club: Shreveport Tex. A. and M. Home: 247 Preston St Shreveport LA 71105 Office: Caddo Parish Schs Shreveport LA 71101

FOSTER, DANIEL W., physician, educator; b. Marlin, Tex., Mar. 4, 1930; B.A., Tex. Western Coll. of U. Tex., 1951; M.D., U. Tex. Southwestern Med. Sch. at Dallas, 1955; m. 3 sons. Intern in internal medicine Parkland Meml. Hosp., Dallas, 1955-56, asst. resident, 1956-58, chief resident, 1958-59; USPHS Postdoctoral fellow U. Tex. Southwestern Med. Sch., Dallas, 1959-60; sr. asst. surgeon USPHS, 1960-62; investigator Intermediary Metabolism sect. Nat. Inst. Arthritis and Metabolic Diseases, NIH, Bethesda, Md., 1960-62; instr. medicine U. Tex. Med. Sch., Dallas, 1962-63, asst. prof., 1963-68, asso. prof. internal medicine, 1968-70, prof. internal medicine, 1970—; attending physician Parkland Meml. Hosp.; cons. internal medicine and research VA Hosp., Dallas. Mem. metabolism study sect. NIH, 1968-70, chmn., 1970—. Mem. Dallas Bd. Edn. Recipient Career Devel. award Nat. Inst. Arthritis and Metabolic Diseases, NIH, 1963. Mem. Am. Fedn. for Clin. Research, Dallas County Med. Soc., Am., Tex. med. assns., Am., So. socs. for clin. investigation, Am. Soc. for Biol. Chemists, Sigma Xi, Alpha Omega Alpha. Presbyn. (ruling elder; moderator N.E. Tex. presbytery 1968). Mem. editorial bd. Metabolism, Clin. and ExpH. Office: 5323 Harry Hines Blvd Dallas TX 75235

FOSTER, DEE ROBERT, physician; b. Grapevine, Tex., Oct. 10, 1902; s. William Jordan and Nancy Angeline (Valentine) F.; B.S., U. Tex., 1923, M.D., 1927; m. Albertine Kent, July 1921 (dec. Nov. 1934); m. 2d, Anna D. Williams, Mar. 19, 1936; children—Maradee (Mrs. Charles E. Wendt), Thala (Mrs. William D. Stalls), Albertine (Mrs. Neil Schacht), Carol Ann (Mrs. W. Kent Kerbel). Intern, Hermann Hosp., Houston, 1927-28; practice medicine, Malone, Tex., 1928-37, Itasca, Tex., 1938-46, Lockney, 1946-51, Hales Center, Tex., 1951—; mem. staff Lockney Gen., Hales Center hosps. Served with S.A.T.C., 1917-18. Mem. N.M. Bd. Med. Examiners, 1962—. Mem. Am., Tex. med. assns., Hale Floyd Briscoe County Med. Soc. (sec.-treas. 1949), Am. Acad. Gen. Practice (charter). Home: 431 Stevenson St Hale Center TX 79041 Office: Hi Plains Hospital Hale Center TX 79041

FOSTER, EDITH LENORE, librarian, educator; b. Carrollton, Ga., Mar. 6, 1906; d. Robert Ellis and Margaret (Byrom) Foster; A.B., La Grange Coll., 1926; A.B. in L.S., Emory U., 1944, postgrad.; postgrad. West Ga. Coll., U. Ga., Milw. U., Fla. State U. Tchr. Buena Vista (Ga.) High Sch., 1926-27; drama coach Wayne P. Sewell Producing Co., 1927-28; head English Dept. Choctaw County High Sch., Butler, Ala., 1928-33, Trion (Ga.) High Sch., 1933-40, Tallapoosa (Ga.) High Sch., 1940-41, Gordon meml. High Sch., Chickamauga, Ga., 1941-43; dir. West Ga. Regional Library, Carrollton, 1944—; instr. English West Ga. Coll., Carrollton, summers 1944-45, asst. prof. library edn., 1958—. Cons. Fla. State U. Adult Edn. Inst., summer 1955; library cons. for Carroll, Douglas, Haralson, Heard, Paulding counties, Ga., 1944—. Mem. Carrollton City Hall Bldg. Com., 1955-57. Bd. dirs. Carroll Service Council. Recipient Betty Crocker award of honor, 1950, Nat. Library Week awards 1960, 61; Distinguished Service award Carrollton C. of C., 1969; named Carroll County's Outstanding Citizen, 1952; Carroll County's Outstanding Woman in Edn., 1964. Mem. Am. (pres. adult edn. sect. 1955, mem. Ga. assembly adult edn. 1956, chmn. operation nat. library project 1958-59, council 1960-63), Ga. (pres. 1961-63, chmn. library devel. com. 1964, chmn. intellectual freedom com. 1965-67; handbook com., govt. relations com., chmn. Nix-Jones distinguished service award, manual com. 1969-71), Southeastern (chmn. recruitment com. 1952-56) library assns., Ga. Sch. and Coll. Library Assn. (mem. adv. bldg. com. 1969-71), Carroll Hist. Soc. Democrat. Methodist. Author: Beside the Wishing Well, 1937; To Wind a Chain, 1951; A Libraria's Memorial Tribute to Lucile Nix. Contbr. articles to profl. jours. Home: 219 E Sims St Carrollton GA 30117 Office: Rome St at Spring St Carrollton GA 30117

FOSTER, FORREST KENDALL, graphic arts exec.; b. Butler, Pa., Nov. 27, 1916; s. Frank Forrest and Grace Myrtle (Coleman) F.; A.B., Allegheny Coll., 1939; m. Helen P. Vorwerk, Nov. 6, 1943; children—Caroline (Mrs. B.D. Carter), Susan (Mrs. Gerald Fritsche), Barbara. Salesman Pitts. Outdoor Advt. Co., 1939-41, Thomas Publishing Co., N.Y.C., 1941-48; pres. Foster Co., Austin, Tex., 1948-52; sales mgr. Steck Warlick Co., printing, Austin, Tex., 1952—. Served with USAAF, 1943-46. Mem. Austing Sales and Marketing Execs. (pres. 1956-57), Austin Advt. Club (pres. 1954-56), Austin C. of C., Phi Beta Kappa. Lutheran (council v.p. 1958-60). Home: 5804 Overlook Dr Austin TX 78731 Office: PO Box 968 Austin TX 78767

FOSTER, HOWARD JERRY, educator; b. Gadsden, Ala., Sept. 22, 1926; s. Lewis H. and Lois (DuPree) F.; B.A. magna cum laude, Fisk U., 1954, M.A., 1957; Ph.D. (citation for outstanding acad. performance), Cath. U. Am., 1964; postgrad. Atlanta U. 1941, U. Chgo., 1959; m. Margaret Earline Drake, Mar. 15, 1953 (div. Mar. 1968); children—Jeanne Renee, Gary Lewis, Kathy Denise, Tracy Anne. Instr., research asst. Fisk U., Nashville, 1952-57, also with AMP, Inc., Harrisburg, Pa.; project leader, solid-state physicist inst. materials research U.S. Bur. Standards, Washington, 1957-65; prof., head dept. physics and math. Ala. A. and M. Coll., Normal, 1965—; physicist U.S. Army Missile Command, Redstone Arsenal, Ala., 1967; vis. prof. physics Oakwood Coll., Huntsville, Ala., 1966-67, U. Ala., Huntsville, 1969—, Mass. Inst. Tech., 1970-71; cons. math. Madison County Bd. Edn., Huntsville, 1966—, IBM Corp., Huntsville, 1968, U.S. AEC, Washington, 1969—, Litton Industries, Inc., Monterey, Cal., 1971—, NASA, 1967—, N.Am. Aviation Corp., Los Angeles, 1968—, Howard U., Washington, 1966—. Mem. orgn., extension com. Creek Dist. Boy Scouts Am., 1966-67. Trustee Roxbury Med.-Tech. Inst., Boston. Served with AUS, 1945-46. Recipient E. Harris Harbison award for gifted teaching Danforth Found., 1970. Mem. Am. Phys. Soc., Ala. Acad. Sci., Am. Assn. Physics Tchrs. (council physics in edn.), Am. Math. Soc., Nat. Inst. Sci., Soc. Religion in Higher Edn., Ala. Consortium Devel. Higher Edn. Sigma Xi, Beta Kappa Chi, Omega Psi Phi. Contbr. articles to profl. jours. Home: 4414 Grizzard Rd NW Huntsville AL 35810

FOSTER, J(OHN) EDWIN, ednl. administr.; b. Stoughton, Sask., Can., Jan. 6, 1917; s. Gloyd and Lydena (Scott) F.; B.A., U. Sask., 1939, B.Ed., 1942; M.S., Ind. U., 1948, Ed.D., 1950; m. Marjorie Kathleen Currie, Aug. 22, 1942; 1 son, Scott Percy. Prin., Radisson (Sask.) High Sch., 1939-41; supr. Aux. War Services Overseas, Canadian Army, 1942-46; field rep. Nat. Film Bd. Can., 1946-47, supr., 1950-52; dir. Med. Film Inst., Chgo., 1952-57; audio visual dir. Am. Heart Assn., N.Y., 1957-61; exec. dir. Ednl. Media Council, N.Y., 1961-65; dir. learning systems Howard U., Washington, 1965—. Cons. U.S. Office Edn., 1965. Mem. Nat. Assn. Ednl. Broadcasters, Phi Delta Kappa. Patentee in field. Home: 6012 Namakagan Rd Washington DC 20016 Office: 2400 6th St NW Washington DC 20001

FOSTER, LAWRENCE, music dir.; b. Los Angeles, 1941; pupil Fritz Zweig; student Bayreuth Festival Masterclasses. Debut as orch. condr. Young Musicians' Found. Debut Orch., 1960, condr., mus. dir., 1960-64; asso. condr. San Francisco Ballet, 1964-65; asst. condr. Los Angeles Philharmonic Orch., 1965-68; chief guest condr. Royal Philharomic Orch., Eng., 1969—; guest condr. Houston Symphony, 1970-71, condr.-in-chief, 1971-72, now music dir.; guest condr. orchs. U.S., Europe. Recipient Koussevitsky Meml. Conducting prize, 1966, Eleanor R. Crane Meml. prize Berkshire Festival, Tanglewood, Mass., 1966. Home: 2316 Auburndale St Houston TX 77023 Office: 615 Louisiana Av Houston TX 77002*

FOSTER, LUTHER HILTON, coll. pres.; b. Lawrenceville, Va., Mar. 21, 1913; s. Luther Hilton and Daisy (Poole) F.; B.S., Va. State Coll., 1932, Hampton Inst., 1934; M.B.A., Harvard, 1936; M. A., U. Chgo., 1941, Ph.D., 1951; Dr. Pub. Service, Adams State Coll., 1957; LL.D., U. Liberia, 1958. Va. State Coll., 1959, U. Mich., 1967, Colby Coll., 1971; L.H.D., Loyola U., 1970; m. Vera Chandler, Aug. 27, 1941; children—Adrienne Maria, Luther Hilton 111. Budget officer Howard U., 1936-40; bus. mgr. Tuskegee Inst., 1941-53, pres., 1953—. Mem. adv. council Sch. Edn. U. Chgo. Mem. Am. Revolution Bicentennial Commn. Bd. dirs. Race Relations Information Center, chmn., 1970); bd. dirs. Overseas Devel. Council, Council on Financial Aid to Edn., United Negro Coll. Fund, So. Regional Council, Inst. Ednl. Mgmt.; trustee Coll. Retirement Equities Fund, Resources for Future, George Washington Carver Found., Nat. Found. Recipient Alumni award, Hampton Inst., 1954. Mem. Phi Delta Kappa, Alpha Phi Alpha, Sigma Phi Boule. Home: 520 Montgomery Rd Tuskegee AL 36088

FOSTER, MINARD I., govt. ofcl.; b. Miami, Fla., Dec. 8, 1915; s. Irwin Bell and Mary Jessie (Johnstone) F.; B.B.A., U. Miami, 1950, M.A., 1951; Ph.D., U. Fla., 1953; m. Margaret Elizabeth Freeman, Mar. 30, 1946; children—Mary (Mrs. Josiah A. Harrison), Michael, Robert. Economist div. power marketing TVA, Chattanooga, 1954-59, supr. borrowings and investments sect., financial planning staff, 1959-61, chief nav. resources br., Div. Nav. Devel., Knoxville, Tenn., 1962-67, dir. Div. Nav. Devel. and Regional Studies, Knoxville, 1968—; lectr. econs. and marketing U. Chattanooga, 1954-62. Mem. permanent internat. and U.S. commns. Permanent Internat. Assn. Nav. Congresses. Mem. adv. bd. U. Tenn. Tech. Assistance Center. Mem. Am., So. econ. assns., Order Artus, Phi Beta Kappa, Alpha Kappa Psi. Author: The Nature of the Demand for Electric Power, 1953. Home: 5205 Shady Dell Trail Knoxville TN 37914 Office: TVA 511 Arnstein Bldg Knoxville TN 37902

FOSTER, THOMAS LEE, educator; b. Roseland, Va., June 9, 1922; s. Howard L. and Annie (Plunkett) F.; B.S., Okla. State U., 1949, M.S., 1951; Ed.D., U. Neb., 1957; m. Mary Dale Fetzer, Feb. 24, 1946; children—David Lee, Richard Dale, Debra Beth (dec.), Michael Dean (dec.). Asst. prof. bus. edn. San Jose (Cal.) State Coll., 1961-65, asst. prof. edn., 1966-67; prof., chmn. div. bus. and econs. Houston Bapt. Coll., 1965-66; instr. bus. De Anza Coll., Cupertino, Cal., 1967-68, San Jose City Coll., 1967—; asso. prof. bus. edn. Southwestern State Coll., Weatherford, Okla., 1968—. Cons. associational student work com. San Jose So. Bapt. Assn., 1967, dir. Bapt. Student Union San Jose Assn., 1966-67. Served with AUS, 1942-46. Mem. Nat., Mountain-Plains, Okla. (S.W. dist. rep. exec. bd.) bus. edn. assns., N.E.A., Nat. Educator's Fellowship, Okla. Edn. Assn., Phi Delta Kappa, Delta Pi Epsilon, Pi Omega Pi. Baptist (deacon). Rotarian. Home: 1204 N Illinois St Weatherford OK 73096

FOSTER, TOLBERT EDWARD, TV exec.; b. Center, Tex., May 30, 1929; s. Tom E. and Ruth L. (Smith) F.; student U. Tex., 1947-48; m. Betty Harper, Nov. 17, 1949; children—Bonnie Ruth, Tolbert Lamar, James Robert. With Center Broadcasting Co., KDET, Center, 1948—, gen. mgr., partner, owner, 1951—; chief exec. officer v.p., dir. Tucson TV Co., Inc., 1956-61; pres., dir. KPRO, Inc., Riverside, Cal., 1961-66, KREO, Inc., Indio, Cal., 1961-66, KROP, Inc., Brawley, 1961-66, KYOR, Inc., Blythe, 1961-66; v.p., dir. Grants Broadcasting Co., Inc., Grants, N.M., 1960-66; owner JBF Co., broadcast cons., Center, 1966—; v.p., dir. McAlister TV Enterprises, Inc., Lubbock, Tex., 1969—; pres., dir., chief exec. Channel Twenty-Four Corp., Austin, Tex., 1969—; partner Foster & Foster, Double F. Ranch, Pushmataha County, Okla., 1957—, Foster-Stamper, Breedlove, Lone Rock, Pushmataha County, 1966—; partner, chief exec. Blake-Dyche-Foster-Foster & Younger, real estate, Riverside, 1961—; pres., dir. chief exec. Van Buren Heights, Inc., Indio, 1966—; partner Foster Assos., real estate, Sabine County, Tex., 1968—; sec., dir. Toledo Yacht Club and Marina, real estate, Sabine County, Tex., 1969—; pres., dir. Pendleton Harbor Corp., real estate, Sabine County, Tex., 1969—; pres., dir., chief exec. Center Cable TV, Inc. (Tex.), 1969—; pres., dir., chief exec. San Augustine Cable TV, Inc., San Augustine, Tex., 1969—; dir. Terry Ford Sales, Inc., car dealership, Kilgore, Tex., 1968—, Peoples State Bank, Marshall, Tex., 1964—. Trustee, Thomas M. Foster Trust. Served with USNR, 1948-53. Mem. Tex. Assn. Broadcasters, Nat. Assn. Broadcasters, Tex., Nat. cable TV assns. Methodist. Elk. Clubs: Center Country, Center Hunting. Home: 6500 Sumac Dr Austin TX 78731 Office: 3201 Steek Av Austin TX 78758

FOSTER, WILLIAM BELL, JR., clothing co. exec.; b. Washington, June 27, 1923; s. William Bell and Jennie May (Hardwick) F.; B.A., Cornell U., Ithaca, N.Y., 1947, M.B.A., 1948; m. Martha Elizabeth Walker, Jan. 29, 1953; children—Dorothy, Nancy. Dir., Hardwick Clothes, Inc., Cleveland, Tenn., 1948—, sec., 1951—, v.p. marketing, 1966—. Trustee, Cleveland (Tenn.) Day Sch. Served to capt. AUS, 1942-46; now col. Res. Mem. Soc. Mayflower Descs., Res. Officers Assn., Assn. of U.S. Army, Mil. Order of World Wars, Am. Legion, V.F.W., Kappa Sigma. Methodist. Elk. Clubs: Cleveland Country (pres. 1953); Cornell (N.Y.C.). Home: 2701 Highland Dr Cleveland TN 37311 Office: 445 Church St Cleveland TN 37311

FOSTER, WILLIS ROY, sci. adminstr.; b. New Orleans, Dec. 8, 1928; s. Horace Frank and Opal (Norman) F.; B.A., La. State U., 1950, M.S., 1957, M.D., 1957; postgrad., U. N.C., 1950-52, George Washington U., 1957-58, Johns Hopkins, 1958-59. Profl. asso. Bioscis. Information Exchange, Smithsonian Instn., Washington, 1959-61, chief of life scis. div. Sci. Information Exchange, 1962-71, asso. dir., 1962-71, dir. sci. div., v.p., 1972—. Mem. Am. Chem. Soc., A.A.A.S., Kappa Sigma, Nu Sigma Nu. Democrat. Unitarian. Contbr. articles to profl. jours. Home: 6117 Greentree Rd Bethesda MD 20034 Office: 1730 M St NW Washington DC 20036

FOTIS, CHARLES WILLIAM, govt. ofcl.; b. Lynn, Mass., Nov. 1, 1914; s. William P. and Eva (Mougoss) F.; A.B., Tufts, U., 1937, Ed.M., 1939; postgrad. Harvard, 1940; Ph.D., Am. U., 1959; m. Dorothea S. Girdis, July 24, 1949; children—Charles William, Linda Diane, Stephen Charles. Instr. math. and scis. Dean Jr. Coll., 1939-42; tng. analyst Central Office VA, 1946-48; chief pre-assignment tng. Naval Ordnance Lab., White Oaks, Md., 1948-50; chief profl. and career devel. div. Air Force Systems Command, Washington, 1950-64; dir. Employee tng. career devel. Dept. Def., Washington, 1964—; vis. prof. U. Okla. at Norman; adj. prof. Am. U.; cons. to industry and govt. Past pres., charter partner Westgrove Investment Fund. Mem. U.S. Civil Service Commn. Edn. Pub. Mgmt. Adv. Group; cons. Commn. Govt. Procurement; co-chmn. Govt. Task Force on Continuing Engring. Studies; mem. Joint Com. on Continuing Engring. Studies. Past pres., dir. Westgrove Citizens Assn., 1956-58. Mem. adv. com. on computer assistance instrn. Am. U. Served with USNR, 1942-46. Recipient Meritorious Civilian Service award; Leadership award Am. Soc. for Tng. and Devel. Mem. Soc. Pub. Adminstrn., Am. Assn. U. Profs., Soc. Personnel Adminstrn., Am. Soc. Tng. and Devel. (Leadership award 1965, chmn. workshop and insts. com.), Am. U. Alumni Assn. (bd. govs., exec. com., co-chmn. fund campaign 1971, chmn. fund campaign 1972), Am. Acad. Polit. and Social Studies, Pi Sigma Alpha. Mason (32 deg., Shriner). Author: Organization and Policy Control of Scientific Research and Development in the Federal Government, 1959. Contbr. Ency. of Edn., also profl. jours. Home: 6901 Andover Dr Alexandria VA 22307 Office: Office Sec Def Pentagon Washington DC 20301

FOUCH, GEORGE EDGAR, govt. ofcl.; b. Mt. Vernon, O., Apr. 11, 1909; s. Rollin James and Nellie Elizabeth (Michaux) F.; B.Sc., Ohio State U., 1931, M.B.A., 1937; m. Beulah Clarinda Snyder, June 29, 1940; children—Gregory George, Roger Brent, Barbara Nell. Asst. prof. bus. adminstrn. Wittenberg U., 1935-36; dir. comml. research Goodyear Tire & Rubber Co., 1937-42; asst. to gen. mgr. Goodyear Aircraft Corp., 1942; v.p., gen. mgr. Sterrett Motors, 1947-48; planning and logistics support Berlin Airlift, Mil. Air Transport Service, 1948; chief spl. projects div. Exec. Office Sec. Navy, 1949-52; mgr. subcontracting J-47 program Gen. Electric Co., 1952, gen. mgr. jet engine dept., 1953-54, gen. mgr. Evendale operations, aircraft gas turbine div., 1955-57, gen. marketing cons. pres.'s office, 1957-62; dep. asst. sec. equipment maintenance and readiness, installations and logistics Dept. Def., 1962-68, dep. asst. sec. logistics mgmt. systems and programs, installations and logistics, 1968—. Served to comdr. USNR, 1943-46. Recipient Distinguished Pub. Service award Dept. Navy, 1956; Distinguished Service award Soc. Am. Value Engrs., 1965; Engring. News Record mag. citation, 1966. Mem. Am. Ordnance Assn., Soc. Am. Value Engrs. (hon. v.p. 1968), Am. Soc. Zero Defects (chmn. adv. bd.), Am. Inst. Aeros. and Astronautics, Soc. Automotive Engrs. Author: Graphic Management Control, 1943. Home: 6859 Tulip Hill Terrace NW Washington DC 20016 Office: The Pentagon Washington DC 20301

FOUKE, HARRY, athletic dir. U. Houston. Office: U Houston Houston TX 77004*

FOUNTAIN, BENJAMIN EAGLES, JR., ednl. adminstr.; b. nr. Rocky Mount, N.C., July 20, 1929; s. Benjamin Eagles and Emmie (Green) F.; A.B., U. N.C., 1950, M.Ed., 1952, Ph.D. (Kellogg fellow 1957-58), 1961; m. Norma Fagan, Apr. 9, 1955; children—Stephanie, Claire, Benjamin Eagles III, Susan. Tchr., prin. Rocky Mount (N.C.) Schs., 1950-55; sec. N.C. Sch. Bds. Assn., Chapel Hill, 1955-57; prof. U. N.C., 1958-61; supt. schs., Elizabeth City, 1961-65; pres. Lenoir Community Coll., Kinston, 1965-71; state pres. N.C. Dept. Community Colls., Raleigh, 1971—. Dir. Raleigh Bd. Br. Banking & Trust Co. Bd. dirs. Nat. Lab. for Higher Edn. Named Citizen of Year, Kinston C. of C., 1970. Mem. Am. Assn. Sch. Adminstrs., N.E.A., N.C. Assn. Educators, N.C. Assn. Community Coll. Presidents (chmn. 1967-68), So. Assn. Colls. and Schs. (mem. commn. colls.). Democrat. Presbyn. Club: MacGregor Downs Country (Cary, N.C.). Home: 422 S West St Cary NC 27511 Office: Dept Community Colls State Bd Edn Raleigh NC 27602

FOUNTAIN, LAWRENCE H., congressman; b. Leggett, N.C., Apr. 23, 1913; s. Lawrence H. and Sallie (Barnes) F.; A.B., U. N.C. (Wiley P. Mangrim Oratorial medal), 1934, LL.B. (Mary D. Wright Debate medal 1935), 1936; m. Christine Dail, May 14, 1942; 1 dau., Nancy Dial. Admitted to N.C. bar, 1936; reading clk. N.C. Senate, 1936-41; sec., treas. Coastal Plains Broadcasting Co., radio sta. WCPS, Tarboro, now exec. v.p.; mem. 83d-92d Congresses, 2d Dist. N.C., mem. com. fgn. affairs, chmn. Near East sub. com. of govt. operations com.; chmn. inter-govtl. relations sub-com; del. to UN, 1967. Mem. exec. com. E. Carolina council Boy Scouts Am. Trustee St. Andrews Coll. Mem. N.C. State Senate from 4th Senatorial Dist., 1947-52; pres. Edgecombe Young Dem. Club, 1940; eastern organizer, past chmn. 2d dist. exec. com. Young Dem. Clubs N.C. Enlisted AUS as pvt., 1942, disch. as maj. J.A.G.O., O.R.C., 1946. Elected Tarboro's Man of Year, 1948. Mem. Am., N.C., Edgecombe County bar assns., N.C. Farm Bur., N.C. Grange, Am. Legion. Democrat. Presbyn. (elder). Elk, Kiwanian (past pres., lt. gov. 6th N.C. div.). Home: 1102 Panolo St Tarboro NC 27886 also 4000 Cathedral Av Washington DC 20006 Office: House Office Bldg Washington DC 20515 also US Post Office Tarboro NC 27886

FOUTAIN, (PETE) PETER DEWEY, JR., clarinet player; b. New Orleans, July 3, 1930. Played clarinet in sch. band, 1942; with Jr. Dixieland Jazz Band, 1948-49, Phil Zito, 1949-50, Basin Street Six, 1950-54; appeared New Orleans, also Jazz Ltd. and Blue Note, Chgo., 1949-53; formed group Pete Fountain and His Three Coins, 1954-57; leader Dixieland combo Lawrence Welk Orch., ABC-TV series, 1957-59. Address: Lake Vista LA 70124

FOUNTAIN, SILAS DAVID, osteo. physician; b. Wild Cherry, Ark., Oct. 29, 1915; s. Alfred Wesley and Mary (Locke) F.; D.O., Kansas City Coll. Osteopathy and Surgery, 1937; m. Lillian Grey McLamb, Nov. 25, 1936; children—Henry Mac, Mary, David, Nellie, John. Intern Conley Clin. Hosp., Kansas City, Mo., 1938; practice osteopathic medicine specializing in surgery, Noel, Mo., 1938—; mem. staff McDonald County Osteo. Hosp., Cardwell Meml. Hosp. Pres. bd. dirs. Cardwell Meml. Hosp., Inc. Mem. Am. Osteo. Assn., Mo. Assn. Osteo. Physicians and Surgeons, S.W. Mo. Assn. Osteo. Physicians and Surgeons (v.p.), Am. Acad. Osteo. Surgeons (bd. govs.), Am. Med. Soc. Vienna (life). Methodist (sec. bd. dirs.). Home: Sulphur Springs AR 72768 Office: Noel MO 64854

FOURIER, ARTHUR ERNEST, educator; b. Chgo., Nov. 2, 1917; s. Arthur Ernest and Rose (Buske) F.; B.S., U. Ill., 1940; postgrad. Chgo. Tchrs. Coll., 1940-41; M.A., George Peabody Coll., 1949, Ph.D., 1954; m. Mary Ruth Gasser, Sept. 30, 1944; children—Arthur Ernest, Barbara Renee. Asst. football coach Foreman High Sch., Chgo., 1940-41; tchr. University High Sch., Columbia, S.C., 1945; instr., asst. prof. U. S.C., Columbia, 1945-61; prof., head dept. health, phys. edn. and recreation Auburn (Ala.) U., 1961—. Served to ensign USNR, 1941-44. Mem. A.A.H.P.E.R., N.E.A., Nat. Recreation and Parks Assn., Am. Assn. U. Profs., Nat. Coll. Phys. Edn. Assn. for Men, Phi Delta Kappa. Home: 477 Cary Dr Auburn AL 36830

FOURNET, BERNIE LEE, city ofcl.; b. Donaldsonville, La., Aug. 21, 1926; s. Walter Joseph and Lillian (Richard) F.; student Millsaps Coll., 1944, U. Southwestern La., 1946, 47, 69, La. State U., U. Tex.; m. Doris May Chataignier, Dec. 15, 1947; children—Ernie, Lee Marie (Mrs. Jim Hyde), Kerry, Valery. With Bur. Identification and Investigation, La. State Police, 1948-51; fingerprint expert St. Martin Parish Sheriff's Dept., 1951-60, chief criminal dep., 1960-64; chief police, City of New Iberia, La., 1964—. Served with USNR, 1943-46. Mem. Internat. Chiefs of Police Assn., La. Chief's Assn., Nat. Sheriffs Assn., La Peace Officers Assn., Municipal Peace Officers Assn., Internat. Assn. Identification Officers. Democrat. Roman Catholic. Home: 603 N Lewis St New Iberia LA 70560 Office: PO Box 387 New Iberia LA 70560

FOURNET, JOHN BAPTISTE, judge; b. St. Martinville, La., July 27, 1895; s. Louis Michel and Marcelite (Gauthier) F.; grad. La. State Normal, 1915; LL.B., La. State U., 1920, LL.D., 1956; m. Rose M. Dupuis, Feb. 1, 1921 (div.); children—Lela Mae Ann (Mrs. Roger Vincent), John Dupuis; m. 2d Sylvia Ann Fournet. Admitted to La. bar, 1920; practice law, St. Martinville, 1920, Baton Rouge, 1921-22, Jennings, 1922; mem., speaker La. Ho. of Reps., 1928-32; lt. gov. of La., 1932-35; asso. justice Supreme Ct. La., 1935-49, chief justice, 1949-70. Served as pvt. U.S. Army, 1918. Mem. Am., La. bar assns., Am. Judicature Soc., Conf. Chief Justices, Order of Coif, Blue Key, Gamma Eta Gamma, Phi Alpha Delta, Pi Lambda Beta, Pi Gamma Mu. Democrat. Mason (32 deg., Shriner). Clubs: Lamplighters; New Orleans Country. Home: 200 Kings Rd Lafayette LA 70501 also Apt 405 211 St Charles Av New Orleans LA 70130

FOURNET, LEON FRANCIS, dentist; b. New Orleans, June 9, 1940; s. Earl Joseph and Lucia Marie (Cuccia) F.; D.D.S., Loyola U., New Orleans, 1964; m. Sandra Fonseca, June 5, 1961; children—Leslie, Kevin and Keith (twins), Monique. Intern oral surgery Charity Hosp., New Orleans, 1964-65; resident Ochsner Found. Hosp., New Orleans, 1967-70; pvt. practice dentistry specializing in oral surgery Suburban Med. Plaza, Metairie, La., 1970—; part time asst. clin. prof. oral surgery Charity Hosp., La. State U. Med. Center, New Orleans, 1971—. Served to capt. AUS, 1965-67. Recipient Dean Echoles award Ochsner Found. Hosp., 1969. Diplomate Am. Bd. Oral Surgeons. Mem. Am., New Orleans dental assns., Am., Southeastern socs. oral surgeons, Psi Omega. Democrat. Roman Catholic. Home: 5013 Avron Blvd Metairie LA 70002 Office: 4324 Veterans Blvd Metairie LA 70002

FOURRIER, BROTHER FELICIAN, supt. schs.; b. Baton Rouge, Sept. 17, 1914; s. J.D. Lawrence and Felicie Marie (Landry) F.; B.S. in Chemistry, Loyola U., New Orleans, 1945; M.S. in Edn., Fordham U., 1951. Headmaster, prin., U.S., Can., Kenya, Uganda; asst. supt. schs. Archdiocese of New Orleans, 1967-69; supt. schs. Diocese of Baton Rouge, 1969—. Dir. studies Bros. of Sacred Heart. Home: 2021 Terrace Ave Baton Rouge LA 70806 Office: PO Box 2028 Baton Rouge LA 70821*

FOUST, GEORGE PERSIA, dentist; b. Huntington, Tenn., Jan. 29, 1927; s. O. Quay and Georgia (Fry) F.; B.S., Memphis State U., 1958; D.D.S., Loma Linda U., Cal. Dental Coll., 1960; m. Georgia Ruth Davis, Sept. 19, 1948; children—Pamela Ruth, Blake Evan. Tchr. microbiology Loma Linda U., 1959-60; gen. practice dentistry, Memphis, 1964—. Officer, Memphis Jr. Acad. Sch. Bd., 1953—, Loma Linda U. Dental Sch. Bd., 1966-69. Internat. Inst. Health grantee, 1961-64. Mem. Am. Dental Assn., Memphis Dental Soc., Nat. Assn. Seventh-day Adventist Dentists, Dental Legion Dental Soc. Club: Optimist. Contbr. articles profl. jours. Home: 5558 Knight Arnold Rd Memphis TN 38118 Office: 5420 Knight Arnold Rd Memphis TN 38118

FOUST, ROSCOE THORNTON, JR., geologist; b. Elizabeth, N.J., Aug. 2, 1928; s. Roscoe Thornton and Mary Edith (Sparks) F.; student Kenyon Coll., 1947-48; B.S., Tex. A. and M. U., 1956; m. Doris Jane Jones, Feb. 4, 1950; children—Patricia Jane, Roscoe Thornton III, Melvin Jones, Leah Catherine. Geologist, Stanolind Oil & Gas Co., San Antonio and Corpus Christi, Tex., 1956-60; dist. geologist Brazos Oil & Gas Co., Houston and Lafayette, La., 1960-68; chief geologist So. Union Prodn. Co., Dallas, 1968—. Served to 1st lt. USAF, 1948-53. Mem. Dallas Geol. Soc., Am. Assn. Petroleum Geologists. Episcopalian. Home: 3401 Sherry St Plano TX 75074 Office: 1429 Fidelity Union Tower Dallas TX 75201

FOUTCH, HENRY C., lawyer; b. Nashville, Sept. 21, 1910; student U. Tenn.; LL.B., Cumberland U., 1932. Admitted to Tenn. bar, 1933, U.S. Dist. Ct. bar, 1935, U.S. Ct. Appeals, 1958, also U.S. Supreme Ct. bar; asst. atty. gen. State Tenn., 1937-67; now mem. firm Foutch and Neil, Nashville. Served to 1st lt. AUS, 1942-46. Mem. Nashville, Tenn. bar assns. Address: Foutch and Neil Life & Casualty Tower Nashville TN 37219*

FOUTZ, SHIRLEY VEIRS, real estate exec.; b. Oklahoma City, Oct. 19, 1924; d. Robert Calvin and Elnora (Hauser) Veirs; B.S., Oklahoma City U., 1945; M.S. in Physics, U. Okla., 1962; m. Bill D. Foutz, May 11, 1946; children—Sherri Ann, Donna Kay. Former x-ray technician, dept. head Balyeat Asthma-Hay Fever Clinic, Oklahoma City, office mgr. Container Corp. Am., pvt. sec. to sec.-treas. Kerr-McGee Corp., accountant Central Exploration Co., owner-mgr. Canyon Park Corp., mgr. Newport-Granada Apts, Capital Arms Apts., asso. Contract Furnishings, Inc.; real estate broker Shirley Foutz Co., pres. Interiors by Shirlee, Oklahoma City, 1967—. Instr., Evelyn Woods Reading Dynamics Inst., Oklahoma City, 1966—. Mem. Okla. Soc. Profl. Engrs. Aux. (pres. 1959-60), Am. Assn. U. Women, Nat. Assn. Real Estate Brokers, Oklahoma City

Met. Bd. Real Estate Brokers, Okla. Real Estate Exchangors, Phi Beta Kappa, Alpha Chi Omega. Methodist. Kiwanian (pres. wives' group 1955-56). Home: 3409 Windsor Terrace Oklahoma City OK 73122 Office: 3900 N Tulsa St Oklahoma City OK 73112

FOWINKLE, EUGENE W., physician, state ofcl.; b. Memphis, 1934; M.D., U. Tenn., 1958. Intern City of Memphis Hosps., 1959; resident in pub. health State of Tenn., 1962-64, now commr. pub. health, Nashville. Asst. prof. Dept. Preventive Medicine, U. Tenn. Diplomate Am. Bd. Preventive Medicine. Mem. Am. Pub. Health Assn. Office: Cordell Hull Bldg 436 6th Av Nashville TN 37219

FOWLER, EARLE BROADUS, lawyer, accountant; b. Georgetown, Ky., June 9, 1914; s. Earle B. and Susan A. (Covington) F.; A.B., U. Louisville, 1941, J.D., 1948; m. Grace W. Towles, Sept. 7, 1940; children— Martha C. (Mrs. David Dean), Mary Carol (Mrs. John E. Crabtree), E. Douglas. Admitted to Ky. bar, 1948; practiced in Louisville, 1948—; mem. firm Sales, Lynch, Fowler, 1969—; exec. sec. Ky. State Bd. Accountancy, Louisville, 1947-52; partner Youngblood, Reich & Fowler, C.P.A.'s, Louisville, 1952—. Instr. accounting, income taxes, real estate Ind. U., Jeffersonville, Ind., 1957—; pres. Ky. Newsclip, Inc., Middletown, Ky., 1970—. Mem. Am., Ky., Louisville bar assns., Am. Inst. C.P.A.'s, Ky. Soc. C.P.A.'s, Urban and Regional Information Systems Assn. (pres. Ohio Valley sect. 1970—), C. of C. Home: Dow Knob Rd Route 1 Box 215-B Borden IN 47106 Office: Marion E Taylor Bldg Louisville KY 40202

FOWLER, GEORGE EDWARD, III, naval officer; b. Dallas, Dec. 1, 1938; s. George Edward and Mabel (Frantz) F.; B.A., Rice U., 1962, B.S., 1962; M.S., U.S. Naval Postgrad. Sch., Monterey, Cal., 1970; m. Susanne Elaine Alford, May 4, 1968. Commd. ensign U.S. Navy, 1962, advanced through grades to lt. comdr., 1969; aide, spl. asst. to chief C.E.C., Washington, 1967-68; asst. officer charge constrn. Subic Bay Naval Base, Philippines, 1968; asst. officer program mgmt. OICC, S.W. Pacific, 1968-69; level of effort officer, officer in charge constrn. Rep. of Vietnam, Saigon, 1971; now comdg. officer Constrn. Equipment div. Naval Constrn. Bn. Center, Port Hueneme, Cal. Decorated Bronze Star medal, Meritorious Service Medal; William Ward Watkins traveling fellow, 1962; named one of outstanding young men of Am., 1968. Mem. Soc. Am. Mil. Engrs., (Morrell medal 1968; sec. Manila post 1969), Rice Archtl. Alumni Assn. Presbyn. Elk. Home: 2817 Westminster St Dallas TX 75205 Office: Comdg Officer Constrn Equipment Div Naval Constrn Bn Center Port Hueneme CA 93041

FOWLER, HAMMOND, lawyer, state ofcl.; b. Rockwood, Tenn., Apr. 6, 1901; s. Hammond and Zoe (Leland) F.; student U. Tenn., 1918-19, 21-22, Maryville Coll., 1919; LL.B., Cumberland U., 1929; m. Netha McCorkle, Apr. 26, 1952. Pres., Times Printing Co., also pub. Rockwood Times, 1922-42; admitted to Tenn. bar, 1929; practice law, Rockwood, 1931—; atty. City of Rockwood, 1933-53; dir. Rockwood Fed. Savs. & Loan Assn., 1934—, v.p., 1946—; gen. counsel Tenn. Dept. Employment Security, 1939-47. Mem. Tenn. Pub. Service Commn., 1948-72; dir. indsl. devel. bd. City of Rockwood, 1964—. Mem. Tenn. Senate, 1934-36; mem. Roane County Democratic Exec. Com., 1922—. Served from lt. to lt. comdr. USNR, 1942-45. Mem. Tenn., Am., Roane County bar assns., Nat. Assn. Regulatory Utilities Commrs., Am. Legion, V.F.W., S.A.R. (pres. Tenn. Soc. 1971-72), Soc. Colonial Wars, Mil. Order World Wars, Lambda Chi Alpha. Rotarian (hon.). K.P. Clubs: Civitan, Rockwood Golf and Country. Home: 421 S Douglas Av Rockwood TN 37854 Office: Cordell Hull Bldg Nashville TN 37219

FOWLER, HAROLD HENDERSON, banker; b. Montgomery, Pa., Sept. 20, 1914; s. Harold Sherman and Mary Helen (Henderson) F.; B.S., Temple U., 1936; m. Marian Annette Shuman, Jan. 8, 1943; 1 dau., Marian Elizabeth (Mrs. Harry Landon Pearce). Supr. audit div. Westinghouse Electric Corp., East Pittsburgh, Pa., 1944-45; comptroller, office mgr. Campbell Chain Co., York, Pa., 1946-50; auditor Western Nat. Bank, York, 1951-58; auditor Broward Nat. Bank, Ft. Lauderdale, Fla., 1958-67, v.p., cashier, 1967—. Served with AUS, 1942-44. Mem. Nat. Office Mgmt. Assn. (past pres.), Nat. Assn. Cost Accountants (past dir.). Mason (Shriner). Home: 3496 NE 19th Av Fort Lauderdale FL 33306 Office: 25 S Andrews Av Fort Lauderdale FL 33302

FOWLER, JOHN THOMAS, lawyer; b. Louisville, Mar. 8, 1917; s. John T. and Catherine (Glenn) F.; A.B., U. Louisville, 1939, LL.B., 1941; m. Lucille Kinnarney, Jan. 15, 1944; children—John T. III, Marilyn. Admitted to Ky. bar, 1941; gen. practice, Louisville, 1941—; cons. trial practice and criminal law practice. Served with AUS, 1942-46. Decorated Bronze Star. Mem. Am., Ky., Louisville (past pres.) bar assns., V.F.W., Ky. Assn. Trial Lawyers (pres. 1962), Am. Trial Lawyers (bd. govs. 1965). K.C. Home: 4604 S 3rd St Louisville KY 40214 Office: Republic Bldg Louisville KY 40202,

FOWLER, SISTER MARY CHARLOTTE, coll. pres.; b. Mechanicsville, Md., Aug. 26, 1899; d. Thomas Henry and Charlotte (Burch) Fowler; student St. Mary's Acad., Leonardtown, Md., 1916-17, 18-19, U. Ky., summers 1921-25, Sisters' Coll., Washington, 1926-27; Ph.D., Cath. U. Am., 1938. Joined Congregation Sisters of Charity of Nazareth, 1920; tchr. high sch. to 1933, coll. math., 1937—; faculty Nazareth Coll. (name changed to Catherine Spalding Coll.), 1937-61, head dept. math., 1950-61, pres., 1961—. Mem. Math. Assn. Am., Am. Math. Soc. Address: Catherine Spalding Coll Louisville KY 40203

FOWLER, ROBERT DOBBS, newspaper pub.; b. Marietta Ga., Sept. 1, 1930; s. Ralph W. and Irma (Dobbs) F.; B.A., U. South, Sewanee, Tenn., 1952; m. Judith Knox Lidstone, Sept. 8, 1956; children—Nancy Adair, Elizabeth Louise. Editor, Cobb County Times, Marietta, 1956-58, Marietta Daily Jour., 1958-64; pub. Gwinnett Daily News, Lawrenceville, Ga., 1964—; v.p. N. Ga. Radio, Inc., Dalton, 1961—, also dir.; pres. Gwinnett Pub. Co., Lawrenceville, 1964—, also dir. Dir. Ga. Newspaper Service. Trustee Ga. Press Ednl. Found., Atlanta, Atlanta Crime Commn. Served to 1st lt. USAF, 1952-56. Mem. Ga. Press Assn. (pres. 1966-67), Gwinnett (Ga.) C. of C., Kappa Alpha, Sigma Delta Chi. Episcopalian. Kiwanian. Home: 174 Maplewood Dr Lawrenceville GA 30245 Office: 394 Clayton St NE Lawrenceville GA 30245

FOWLER, VANCE, real estate co. exec.; b. Norfolk, Va., Mar. 1, 1918; s. Daniel Lee and Marion Gertrude (Forrest) F.; A.B., Coll. William and Mary, 1940; M.B.A. with distinction, Harvard, 1952; m. Marjory Johnston, Dec. 13, 1943; children—Joan (Mrs. Henry Joseph Endt), Thomas Vance, Carole. Vice-pres. adminstrn. and plantation services, Hilton Head, S.C., 1967—; pres. Airport Co., Hilton Head, 1968—; pres. Six Oaks Cemetery Corp., Hilton Head, 1968—. Bd. dirs. U.S. Navy Supply Corps Found. Served to capt. U.S. Navy, 1941-67. Mem. Theta Delta Chi. Republican. Presbyn. Rotarian (pres. 1965-66). Clubs: Army Navy Country (Washington, D.C.); Plantation (Hilton Head, S.C.). Home: 6 Sylvan Lane Sea Pines Plantation Hilton Head SC 29928 Office: Sea Pines Co. Hilton Head SC 29928

FOWLER, WILMA SIM, ins. co. exec.; b. Gustine, Tex., Jan. 10, 1920; s. William Sim and Nettie Vera (Estis) F.; student John Tarleton Coll., 1939-40; B.S., U. Tenn., 1948; postgrad. in ins. marketing La. State U.; m. Sarah Frances Livingston, Dec. 20, 1947; children—Sarah Frances, William Hilary. Athletic dir., head coach pub. high schs., Lexington, Tenn., 1948, Corinth, Miss., 1949-50; pres., gen. mgr. Dr. Pepper Seven-Up Bottling Co., Kosciusko, Miss., 1951-67; sr. v.p. Dixie Nat. Life Ins. Co., Jackson, Miss., 1966—, also dir., mem. exec. com.; sec.-treas., dir. Natchez-Trace Savs. & Loan, Kosciusko, 1965—; mgr. Kosciusko-Attala Airport, Kosciusko, 1956-60; dir. Jackson Savs. & Loan, Attala Nat. Bank, Kosciusko, Fisher Oil Guard, Dixie Nat. Corp. Chmn., Heart Fund, Attala County, 1957. Bd. dirs., pres. Miss. YMCA. Served to comdr. AC, USNR, 1941-46. Decorated Silver Star medal, D.F.C. with Gold Star, Order of Red Star, others. Mem. Nat. Football Hall of Fame Found. (charter), Am. Legion (comdr. 1955), V.F.W., V-5 Assn., Tarleton Ex-Students Assn. (life), T Club U. Tenn. C. of C., Pi Kappa Alpha. Republican. Presbyn. Mason (Shriner), Moose. Clubs: Nat. Exchange (dist. gov. 1953-54), Kosciusko Exchange (past pres.), Kosciusko Golf. Home: Liberty Hall PO Box 309 Columbus MS 39701 Office: 1 Dixie Plaza Jackson MS 39205

FOWLIE, WALLACE, author, literary critic; b. Brookline, Mass., Nov. 8, 1908; s. Wallace Bruce and Helen (Adams) F.; A.B., Harvard, 1930, A.M., 1933, Ph.D., 1936. Fellow Ezra Stiles Coll., Yale; faculty French lit. Yale, 1940-45, U. Chgo., 1945-49, Bennington (Vt.) Coll., 1950-62; James B. Duke prof. French, Duke, 1964—. Guggenheim fellow, 1948-49. Author: Sleep of the Pigeon, 1948; Pantomime, 1951; Age of Surrealism, 1953; Mallarme, 1953; Paul Claudel: Studies in Modern European Literature and Thought, 1957; A Guide to Contemporary French Literature: from Valery to Sartre, 1957; Dionysus in Paris, 1960; A Reading of Proust, 1964; Andre Gide: His Life and Art, 1965; Rimbaud: A Critical Study, 1965; Jean Cocteau: The History of a Poet's Age, 1955; Climate of Violence: The French Literary Tradition from Baudelaire to the Present, 1967; The French Critic: 1549-1967, 1968. Translator: The Journals of Jean Cocteau, 1955; Seamarks (Saint-John Perse), 1958; Two Dramas of Claudel, 1960; Complete Works of Rimbaud, 1966; many other French works. Fgn. editor Poetry mag., 1950-70. Home: 17 D Valley Terrace Durham NC 27707

FOX, BILLY JOE, fire chief; b. Texarkana, Tex., June 6, 1925; s. Joseph Thomas and Katy May (Rafters) F.; student Tex. A. and M. U. Firemen's Tng. Sch., 1960-62, 65-66, Nat. Fire Dept. Mgmt. Sch., So. Meth. U., 1971; m. Peggy Jane Lucas, Jan. 9, 1949; children—William Terry, Karen Jane. Fire fighter Texarkana (Ark.) Fire Dept., 1947-51; fire fighter, driver, engr., capt., asst. chief, fire marshall Texarkana (Tex.) Fire Dept., 1951-68, fire chief, 1968—; instr. Tex. A. and M. Firemans Tng. Sch.; asso. tchr. fire tech., chmn. adv. com. Texarkana Coll. Chmn. health and safety com. Boy Scouts Am., 1968-71; first aid instr. A.R.C., 1959-71; pres. Texarkana Area chpt. Muscular Dystrophy Assn., 1970-71. Bd. dirs. Tri-State chpt. A.R.C. Served with USMCR, 1943-46. Recipient Lloyd Bennett award A.R.C., 1964. Mem. S.W., Tex. fire chiefs assns., Internat. Assn. Fire Chiefs. Mem. Christian Ch. (deacon). Home: 220 Melrose Dr Texarkana TX 75501 Office: PO Box 1967 Texarkana TX 75501

FOX, BUCK VAN, paraffin co. exec.; b. Okla., Sept. 18, 1920; s. Boyd Floyd and Oma Belle (Paslay) F.; grad. high sch.; m. Yvonne Brashears, Sept. 26, 1940; children—Craig, Loreda (Mrs. Phillip White), Vicki. Owner, Fox Paraffin' Service, Denver City, Tex., 1953—, incorporated, 1969, pres., 1969—; dir. B & F Leasing Co., Denver City, B. & F. Ranch, Sallisaw, Okla. Served with USCG, 1942-45. Mem. Acid Engrs. Tex. (bd. dirs. 1965—), Acid Engrs. La. (bd. dirs. 1966—), United Dollar Stores of Ark., Okla. (bd. dirs. 1968—). Address: Drawer 1380 Denver City TX 79323

FOX, CROCKETT CARTER, grocery exec.; b. Crowell, Tex., Dec. 29, 1915; s. Crockett Carter and Addie (Rader) F.; student McMurray Coll., 1937; m. Peggy Thompson, June 20, 1936; children—Laurie Jo, Mary Jane. Br. mgr. Anheuser-Busch Co., Houston, 1938-42; dist. mgr. McCormick & Co., Dallas, 1948-50; gen. mgr. Thornton's Grocery Stores, Abilene, Tex., 1952-60; gen. mgr. Foodway Stores, Ardmore, Okla., 1960—. Served with USAAF, 1942-46. Mem. Retail Grocers Assn. Okla. and Tex. Methodist (ofcl. bd.). Mason (Shriner, 32 deg.). Home: 226 Meadow Rd Ardmore OK 73401 Office: 202 S Mills St Ardmore OK 73401

FOX, DONALD RAY, banker; b. Elizabethtown, Ky., Mar. 30, 1944; s. Norton Boyd and Mary Kathleen (Edlin) F.; diploma Draughon's Bus. Coll., 1964; student U. Ky., 1967-68, Louisville chpt. Am. Inst. Banking, 1965-70; m. Phyllis Darlene Cornett, June 5, 1965; children—Donald Ray, Phyllis Elaine. Asst. v.p., cashier, dir. Citizens Bank of Elizabethtown (Ky.), 1964—. Treas. Hardin County unit Am. Cancer Soc., Hardin County unit Arthritis Found.; bd. dirs. Hardin Meml. Hosp. Served with Ky. N.G., 1964. Mem. U.S., Elizabethtown (past treas.) jr. chambers commerce, Travelers Protective Assn. (dir.). Baptist (trustee). Optimist. Home: Route 1 Box 303-A Elizabethtown KY 42701 Office: 425 W Dixie Av Elizabethtown KY 42701

FOX, EDWARD MARK, paper co. exec.; b. Montreal, Que., Can., Apr. 8 (came to U.S. 1954, naturalized 1960), 1924; s. George James and Sarah Lucida (Blakely) F.; B.Commerce, McGill U., Montreal, 1950; m. Marilyn Adrienne Huguenin, July 17, 1954; children—Jeffrey Numa, Jorja-An Dubois. Sales mgr. Celanese Plastics Co., Newark, 1956-63; marketing mgr. Weyerhaeuser Co., N.Y.C., 1963-66; v.p. marketing Perfect Fit Industries N.Y.C., 1966-67; dir. marketing services Standard Packaging Corp., N.Y.C., 1967-68; v.p. marketing and sales Eastern Fine Paper Inc. div. Eddy Paper Co. Ltd., Brewer, Me., 1968—, also dir.; dir., v.p. parent co., 1970—. Served with Royal Canadian Navy, 1943-45. Mem. McGill U. Alumni Assn., Delta Sigma Phi. Home: 613 Citrus Ct Melbourne Beach FL 32951 Office: Eastern Fine Paper Inc PO Box 129 Brewer ME 04412

FOX, FREDERICK ALVIN, stock broker; b. Plainfield, N.J., Aug. 27, 1940; s. Frederick Francois and Judith Esterbrook (Eason) F.; certificate Municipal Bond Sch., 1963; m. Sandra Mary Babcock, Feb. 4, 1967; 1 dau., Alexandra Noelle. Charter fishing boat owner and capt., Brielle, N.J., 1961-63; municipal bond salesman Banco Credito, N.Y.C., 1963-64; account exec. Moore & Schley, N.Y.C., 1965-66; with various brokerage firms, 1966-69; v.p., mgr. Paul R. Dean & Co., Inc., Atlanta, 1969-72; sr. v.p. Seaney Jones & Co. Inc., Atlanta, 1972—; dir. Three Barrells Ltd. and Four Barrells Ltd., Atlanta, v.p., 1970—; dir. Brat Haus Internat. Ltd., Atlanta, sr. v.p., 1971—; partner F & M Leasing, Atlanta, 1970—. Served with USNR, 1958-61. Mem. Nat. Assn. Security Traders, Ga. Security Dealers Assn. Club: Flint River Sportsmen (Thomaston, Ga.). Home: 210 Azalea Dr Roswell GA 30075 Office: 3379 Peachtree Rd Atlanta GA 30326

FOX, G(EORGE) ROBERT, educator; b. Cleve., Mar. 31, 1918; s. Clarence G. and Eleanor M. (Barber) F.; A.B., U. Mich., 1941; M.A. in Sch. Adminstrn., Western Res. U., 1948, Ph.D., 1962; m. Marilou Farnsworth, June 17, 1944; children—Cynthia Lynn, Bruce Kevin. Supt. schs., North Fairfield, O., 1948-50, Plain City, O., 1950-53, West Ceauga Schs., Chesterland, O., 1953-57; prof. edn., chmn., dir. dept. Hiram Coll., 1957-69; chmn. grad. div. Stetson U., 1969—. Mem. Adv. Council Grad. Edn., Dept. Health, Edn. and Welfare, 1971-72. Served to lt. col. USAF, 1941-45. Nat. Def. Fgn. Lang. fellow Ind. U., 1967; Fulbright-Haya lectr. Am. Edn., Yugoslavia, 1968-69. Mem. Am. Assn. Sch. Adminstrs., Nat. Orgn. Legal Problems Edn., Assn. Tchr. Educators, Nat. Assn. Fgn. Student Affairs, Fla. Adult Edn. Assn., Kappa Delta Pi. Republican. Methodist. Mason, Rotarian; mem. Order Eastern Star. Author: Problems of Adjustment of Beginning Teachers, 1962. Contbr. articles to profl. jours. Home: 540 N McDonald Av DeLand FL 32720

FOX, GERALD GEORGE, city mgr.; b. Chgo., Nov. 11, 1932; s. John E. and Dolores (Chess) F.; B.A., Beloit Coll., 1954; M.P.A., U. Kan., 1963; m. Dolores Condon, Sept. 27, 1958; children—Stephen Edward, Gerald George, Carol Elizabeth. Administrv. asst. to city mgr., San Antonio, 1957-59; city manager, Ennis, Tex., 1959-62, Camden, Ark., 1963-66. Fayetteville, Ark., 1966-69, Wichita Falls, Tex., 1969—. Mem. state and local govt. adv. commn. Office Econ. Opportunity; mem. information and statistics task force to Nat. Adv. Commn. on Criminal Justice Standards and Goals, Dept. Justice. Served with AUS, 1954-56. Mem. Internat., Tex. (bd. dirs., chmn. scholarship com.) city mgmt. assns., Am. Soc. Pub. Adminstrn., Municipal Finance Officers Assn., Tex. Municipal League (mem. human resources com., com. on future), Urban and Regional Information Systems Assn. (pres. elect, dir.), Phi Kappa Psi, Omicron Delta Kappa. Roman Catholic. Rotarian. Contbr. articles to profl. jours. Office: City Manager City Hall Wichita Falls TX 76307

FOX, HARRISON WILLIAM, savs. and loan exec.; b. Galway, N.Y., Aug. 6, 1919; s. Harrison Edgar and Frances Belle (Brown) F.; B.C.E., N.C. State Coll., 1941; B.S., Cal. Inst. Tech., 1945; postgrad. Ind. U., 1964; m. Ruth Pirtle, Nov. 8, 1941; children—Harrison William, Mary (Mrs. Charles Franckle), Charlotte. Partner, Fox & Fox Bldg. Contractor, St. Petersburg, Fla., 1946-56; asst. project engr. Hamilton Standard, St. Petersburg, 1956-58; project engr. Fla. Builders, St. Petersburg, 1958; v.p. Home Fed. Savs. & Loan Assn., St. Petersburg, 1959-63; sr. v.p. First Fed. Savings & Loan Assn., St. Petersburg, 1963—, pres. First St. Petersburg Service Corp. subsidiary, 1970—. Mem. Fed. Home Loan Bank Bd. Task Force, 1970-71. Chpt. chmn. constrn. div. United Fund Pinellas County, 1966; mem. gen. contractors exam. bd. City of St. Petersburg, Fla., 1951-56; mem. blue ribbon zoning com. City of St. Petersburg, Fla., 1965-67; mem. Fla. selection com. R.O.T.C., 1971; chmn. Carpenters Joint Apprenticeship Com., St. Petersburg, 1950-53. Bd. dirs., treas., mem. adv. bd. St. Petersburg Salvation Army. Served to comdr. USNR, 1941-46. Mem. St. Petersburg Home Bldg. Assn. (charter sec., dir. 1946), Contractors and Builders Assn. Pinellas County (pres. 1949), St. Petersburg C. of C. (gov. 1968-71), Mortgage Loan Officers Soc. West Coast Fla. (pres. 1965, dir. 1961-66), Am. Orchid Soc., Assn. Gen. Contractors (mem. nat. com. apprenticeship 1952), Suncoasters, Engr. Council, Blue Key, Pine Burr, Scabbard and Blade, Tau Beta Pi, Theta Tau, Navy League (v.p. St. Petersburg 1969-72). Presbyn. (elder, deacon 1951). Mason. Clubs: Yacht, Commerce (St. Petersburg). Home: 3230 Walnut St NE St Petersburg FL 33704 Office: PO Box 1509 St Petersburg FL 33731

FOX, IRWIN CLIFFORD, govt. ofcl.; b. Wichita, Kan., Apr. 30, 1935; s. Ernest Lyle and Ila T. (Gaumer) F.; B.S. in Civil Engring., U. Okla., 1960; m. Jerre Lou Boully, June 26, 1953; children—Jerre Gayle, Clifford Dale. Hwy. engr. U.S. Forest Service, Albuquerque, 1960-61; hwy. engr. U.S. Bur. Pub. Rds., Ft. Worth, 1961-63, area engr., Baton Rouge, 1963-65, pavement design engr., Washington, 1965-67, regional pavement design engr. and maintenance engr., Ft. Worth, 1967-69, dist. engr., Austin, Tex., 1969—. Registered profl. engr., Okla., Tex. Home: 2401 Remuda Trail Austin TX 78745 Office: 826 Fed Office Bldg Austin TX 78701

FOX, LEO, govt. ofcl.; b. Boston, June 3, 1917; s. David I. and Rhoda (Fox) F.; B.S., Boston Coll., 1938; M.A., Boston U., 1948, Ph.D., 1966; m. Helen R. Leavitt, Mar. 18, 1943; children— Elizabeth (Mrs. Anthony S. McMahon), James H., Robert M., William I. Chief spl. weapons protection br. Army Research Lab., Natick, Mass., 1955-62; research dir. Inst. Indsl. Launderers, Washington, 1962-64; chief human research NASA, Washington, 1964-67, dep. dir. div. human research and biotech., 1967-71, dir. aero. life scis. div., 1971—. Asso. dir. Nat. Inst. Neurol. Diseases and Stroke. Served with AUS, 1942-46. Mem. A.A.A.S., Biophys. Soc., Aerospace Med. Assn., Sigma Xi. Home: 6100 Greentree Rd Bethesda MD 20034 Office: 600 Independence Av SW Washington DC 20546

FOX, LESTER IRVING, physician; b. Lawrence, Miss., Aug. 19, 1912; s. James L. and Ethel (Hacker) F.; student Bates Coll., 1930-31; A.B., Johns Hopkins, 1934; M.D., U. Md., 1938; m. June White, Apr. 29, 1946; children—Susan Scott, William Peyton, Elizabeth Forrest. Commd. 1st lt. M.C., U.S. Army, 1938, advanced through grades to maj., 1945; intern Quincy City Hosp., 1939-40; active duty, 1940-42; Japanese prisoner of war, 1942-45; resident physician VA Hosp., Richmond, Va., 1947-48; resident allergist, instr. medicine Med. Coll. Va., 1948-49; chief medicine, 1949-63, chief profl. services U.S. Army Health Clinic, Fort Monroe, Va., 1949—. Decorated Silver Star Medal, Purple Heart. Diplomate Am. Bd. Internal Medicine. Fellow A.C.P., Am. Geriatric Assn.; asso. fellow Am. Coll. Cardiology; mem. Am. Acad. Allergy, Am., Peninsula (2d v.p.) heart assns., Peninsula Acad. Medicine, Briarcliffe Acres Assn. Clubs: Army-Navy (Washington); Langley Air Force Base Golf; Beachwood Golf (N. Myrtle Beach, S.C.). Home: 67 Ingals Rd Fort Monroe VA 24574 Office: US Army Health Clinic Fort Monroe VA 24574

FOX, MARK, accountant; b. N.Y.C., Apr. 28, 1923; s. Abraham and Rose (Rosenbaum) F.; B.B.A., Coll. City N.Y., 1943; m. Del Franklin, Jan. 15, 1951; children—Andrew Eric, Steven Allen. Sr. accountant Samuel Fishman & Co., C.P.A.'s, 1948-51; mgr., supr. Rieders, Fink & Co., C.P.A.'s, 1951-59; gen. practice pub. accounting, tax cons., mgmt. cons., Sarasota, Fla., 1959—. Served with AUS, 1943-46. Mem. Am., Fla. insts. C.P.A.'s, N.Y. State Soc. C.P.A.'s. Mason (32 deg. Shriner), Elk. Club: University. Home: 4634 Higel Av Sarasota FL 33581 Office: 1272 N Palm Av Sarasota FL 33577

FOX, PORTLAND PORTER, cons., geologist; b. New Hope, N.C., Aug. 10, 1908; s. William Ross and Dora (Mayes) F.; B.S. in Geology, U. N.C., 1937; m. Sarah Pearl Monk, June 8, 1935. Geologist U.S. Geol. Survey, Chapel Hill, N.C., 1934, TVA, Knoxville, Tenn., 1943, Metals Res. Corp., Washington, Brazil, 1943, TVA, Fontana Dam, 1943-45, U.S. Bur. Reclamation, Billings, Mont., 1945-47, Brazilian Light and Power Co., Sao Paulo, 1947-53; cons. many hudro-elec. projects, Cleveland, Tenn., 1953—. Bd. cons. Northfield (Mont.) Pumped Storage Project, 1967—, Blenheim-Gilboa Pumped Storage (N.Y.), 1968-72, Bear Swamp Pumped Storage (Mass.), 1970—. Fellow Am. Soc. C.E., Geol. Soc. Am.; mem. Tenn. Acad. Sci. (v.p. 1945), Assn. Engring. Geologists, Am. Inst. Profl. Geologists, Sigma Xi, Sigma Gamma Epsilon. Mem. Christian Ch. (chmn. bd. 1963-64). Mason. Address: 500 Hiwassee St NE Cleveland TN 37311

FOX, ROBERT LLOYD, state ofcl.; b. Alexandria, Ind., Sept. 17, 1908; s. Lloyd Alvin and Lillian Blanche (Porter) F.; student U. Ala., 1933; J.D., Samford U., 1935; student Command and Gen. Staff Coll., 1949; m. Louise Elizabeth Walters, Sept. 2, 1936; children— Louise, Robert Lloyd. With power sales dept. Tenn. Electric Power Co., Nashville, 1936-37; with sales and service dept. Am. Mut. Liability

Ins. Co., Nashville, 1937-39; partner Walters & Fox Gen. Ins. Agy., Nashville, 1939-60; dir. civil def. and emergency preparedness State of Tenn., Nashville, 1950—. Mem. U.S. Surgeon Gen.'s Adv. Com. on Emergency Health Preparedness, 1963-69. Served to col. USAF. Mem. Nat. Assn. Civil Def. Dirs. (pres. 1970-71), Mil. Order World Wars (comdr. 1968-69), Air Force Assn., Am. Legion, Sigma Alpha Epsilon. Home: 207 Woodmont Circle Nashville TN 37205 Office: Emergency Operations Center Sidco Dr Nashville TN 37204

FOX, SAMUEL MICKLE, III, physician, assn. exec.; b. Andalusia, Pa., 1923; M.D., U. Pa., 1947. Intern Pa. Hosp., Phila., 1947-48, resident in medicine 1950; resident fellow gastro-enterology U. Pa. Hosp., 1948-49, resident in pathology, 1949; acting chief gastro-enterology Nat. Naval Med. Center, Bethesda, Md., 1950-51, chief cardiological services, 1954; head Dept. Clin. Investigation, U.S. Naval Med. Research Unit 3, Cairo, Egypt, 1954-56; chief cardiological services, U.S. Naval Hosp., Portsmouth, Va., 1956-57; sr. staff Nat. Heart Inst., NIH, 1957-59, co-chief cardiodynamics, 1959-61, asst. dir., 1961-62; asso. dir. Cardiopulmonary Research Tng. Program, VA Hosp., Washington, 1960-63; cons., NASA, 1959-63, mem. research adv. com. for bio-tech. and human research, 1963-68; dep. chief Heart Disease Control Program, USPHS, 1963-64, chief, 1965-70. Asst. instr. medicine U. Pa., 1948-49, instr. pathology, 1949, instr. medicine, 1950; vis. prof. medicine Ein Shams U.; resident asso. Kasr-el-Aini Faculty Medicine, Cairo, 1955-56; clin. asst. prof. medicine Georgetown U., 1959-70; prof. medicine George Washington U., 1970—. Served to comdr. M.C., USNR, 1950-57. Diplomate Am. Bd. Internal Medicine. Fellow Am. Coll. Cardiology (pres. 1972—), A.C.P.; mem. A.M.A., Am. Heart Assn. Address: George Washington U 2029 G St NW Washington DC 20006 also 2150 Pennsylvania Av NW Washington DC 20037

FOX, THEODORE BERT, educator; b. Jacksonville, Ala., Oct. 25, 1912; s. Cass and Jennie Magnolia (Taylor) F.; student Selma U., 1929-30, Gen. Motors Inst., 1935-36; certificate Ala. State U., 1954, Allen Electric Co. Sch., 1950, Ala. A. and M. U., 1956; m. Agnes Marshall Watley, Apr. 7, 1933; children—Sydney (Mrs. Eugene Reid, Jr.), June (Mrs. J. Mason Davis), Barbara (Mrs. Franklin Todd), Sandra (Mrs. Thomas Sudduth). Supr., Anniston (Ala.) Army Ordnance Depot, 1940-46; vocational instr. Anniston City Bd. Edn., 1946—, tchr. Anniston Area Vocational Tech. Sch. Mem. City Council, Jacksonville, Ala., 1968—; bd. dirs. Ala. Democratic Com., 1970—. Pres. Jacksonville Civic League; bd. dirs. Jacksonville Child Care Center; mem. exec. bd. Choccolocco council Boy Scouts Am. Recipient Silver Beaver award Boy Scouts Am., 1962. Mem. N.E.A., Anniston Edn. Assn. (pres.), N.A.A.C.P. Baptist. Home: 157 Spring St Jacksonville AL 36265 Office: Anniston High Sch Anniston AL 36201

FOX, VERNON BRITTAIN, educator, criminologist; b. Boyne Falls, Mich., Apr. 25, 1916; s. John Lorenzo and Ethel (Hamilton) F.; A.B., Mich. State U., 1940, certificate in social work, 1941, M.A., 1943, Ph.D., 1949; m. Laura Grace Ellerby, Mar. 22, 1941; children—Karen, Vernon, Loraine. Dir. case work, coach Starr Commonwealth, Albion, Mich., 1941-42; psychologist State Prison So. Mich., 1942-46, dep. warden, 1949-52; psychologist Cassiday Lake Tech. Sch., Mich. Dept. Corrections, 1946-49; prof., sch. social welfare Fla. State U., 1952—, also dir. delinquency control inst. Mem. Fla. Adv. council on Adult Corrections and Prison Industries; mem. Gov.'s Adv. Council Law Enforcement Edn. Bd. visitors U.S. Army Mil. Police Sch., Fort Gordon, Ga. Served with AUS, 1945-46. Mem. Am. Correctional Assn., Am. Sociol. Soc., Fla. Psychol. Assn., C. of C. Clubs: Capital City Country, Tallahassee Exchange. Author: Violence Behind Bars 1956; Guidelines for Education in Corrections in Community and Junior Colleges, 1969. Mem. internat. bd. editors Exerpta Criminologica; bd. editors Internat. Behavioral Scientist. Home: 644 Voncile Av Tallahassee FL 32303

FOXWORTH, ELEANOR WINN, educator; b. Kingstree, S.C., Oct. 15, 1920; d. John Gary and Elizabeth (Winn) Foxworth; B.S., Winthrop Coll., 1941; postgrad. Yale Div. Sch., 1943-44. Sec. to treas. Liberty Life Ins. Co., Greenville, S.C., 1941-42; sec. to pres. YMCA Grad. Sch., Blue Ridge, N.C., and Nashville, 1942-43; dir. student work Presbyn. Ch. of U.S.A. (So. br.) at La. State U., Baton Rouge, 1945-47; field sec. exec. com. Christian edn. coll. and sem. level and ministerial relief Presbyn. Ch. U.S. (So.), Louisville, 1947-50, asso. dir. dept. campus Christian life (offices moved from Louisville), Richmond, Va., 1950-53; tchr. Kingstree High Sch., 1953-55; alumnae exec. sec. and treas. Winthrop Coll. Alumnae Assn., Rock Hill, S.C. 1955-65, speaker at coll. gatherings, fund raiser for alumnae giving to coll., 1955-65, organizer alumnae chpts., 1955-65, organizer tours to Europe and around world, 1963-64; asst. to dir. guidance and placement Winthrop Coll., Rock Hill, 1965-68, asst. dir. instl. research, 1968-69, statistician instl. research, 1969-71; dir. pub. relations Williamsburg Regional Manpower Tng. Center, Kingstree, S.C., 1971—. Represented Presbyn. Ch. at various ch. and religious meetings in U.S., Can., Europe. Mem. Pilot Club, Delta Kappa Gamma. Democrat. Presbyn. (Bible tchr., mem. christian edn. com.). Editor: Avalanche of Summer Opportunities, 1952; co-editor (devotional booklet) Thy Will—My Will, 1951-53. Contbr. to Day by Day, devotional quar. Sandlapper, other mags., newspapers. Home: 1301 Woodland Dr Kingstree SC 29556

FOY, THOMAS JOSEPH, JR., banker; b. Charleston, S.C., Oct. 6, 1925; s. Thomas Joseph and Ethel Vivian (Purse) F.; student Coll. Charleston, 1942-43, The Citadel, 1946-48, U. Wis. Sch. Banking, 1956-58; m. Nona Willette Snipes, June 4, 1949; children—Barry Joseph, Thomas Patrick, Lee Ann, Janice Maureen, Thomas Joseph. With Citizens and So. Nat. Bank of S.C., Columbia, 1948—, v.p., 1965—, adv. bd., 1965—. Instr., Columbia chpt. Am. Inst. Banking, 1966-67. Treas. Spartanburg County Heart Fund, 1958-59. Bd. dirs. Salvation Army, Spartanburg, 1957-58, United Cerebral Palsy, Spartanburg, 1957-58. Friendship Center Columbia, Central Tb Assn. Served with USNR, 1944-46. Mem. Am. Inst. Banking (pres. chpt. 1959-60, bd. govs. chpt. 1960-61), Nat. Assn. Bank Auditors and Comptrollers (pres. conf. 1957-58, nat. program commn. 1966), Internat. Adminstrv. Mgmt. Soc. (v.p. 1971-72), Bank Adminstrn. Inst. (chmn. nominating com. 1970), Columbia C. of C. Lion (bd. dirs. 1970-71). Clubs: Citadel (treas. 1956-57) (Spartanburg); Columbia (S.C.) Country (bd. dirs. 1970—, treas. 1970—). Home: 3835 Rockbridge Rd Columbia SC 29206 Office: PO Box 727 Columbia SC 29202

FOYE, LAURANCE V., JR., physician, govt. ofcl.; b. Seattle, 1925; M.D., U. Cal., 1952. Intern San Francisco Gen. Hosp., 1953-53; resident in internal medicine VA Hosp., San Francisco, 1953-55, 56-57, attending physician in medicine, 1957-58, asst. chief med. services, 1958-66, chief Cancer Chemotherapy Sect., 1960-66; resident in internal medicine Stanford Hosp., 1955-56; chief Cancer Therapy Evaluation Br., Nat. Cancer Inst., 1966-68, chief Clin. Investigation Br., 1968-70; dir. ednl. services VA Central Office, Washington, 1970—. Research asso. Cancer Research Inst., also asst. clin. prof. medicine U. Cal., 1962-66. Diplomate Am. Bd. Internal Medicine. Fellow A.C.P.; mem. Am. Soc. Clin. Oncology. Office: 810 Vermont Av Washington DC 20420 also VA Central Office Vermont at H St NW Washington DC 20420

FRAILEY, ROBERT H., athletic dir. Am. U. Office: American U Washington DC 20016*

FRALISH, MARVIN LEWIS, JR., ednl. adminstr.; b. High Wycombe, Eng., Nov. 6, 1943; came to U.S., 1947, naturalized, 1953; s. Marvin Lewis and Brenda G. (Smith) F.; student U. Ga., 1962-63; A.B., Ga. State Coll., 1966; M.Ednl. Adminstrn., Ga. State U., 1970; m. Mildred Christine Sorrow, Sept. 27, 1963; children—Marcus Paul, Stephan David. With Atlanta (Ga.) Jour., 1961-62; shipping clk. Grinnell Co., Atlanta, 1962-64; English asst. Ga. State Coll., 1964-66; secondary tchr. Cobb County Bd. Edn. (Ga.), 1966-67; secondary tchr. DeKalb County Bd. Edn., 1967-69, elementary tchr., 1969-70; prin. Oakcliff Sch., Doraville, Ga., 1970—. Recipient Achievement in Edn. award Jr. C. of C., Atlanta, 1970. Mem. Ga. (rep. 1971), DeKalb County (rep. 1968-71) edn. assns., DeKalb Classroom Tchrs. Assn. (sec. 1970), DeKalb Elementary Prins. Assn. (rep. 1971-72), Northeast Improvement Assn. (publicity chmn. 1971-72), P.T.A., Assn. Supervision and Curriculum Devel., Ga. Dept. Elementary Prins., Ga. State U. Alumni Assn., Pi Kappa Alpha Alumni Assn., Sigma Tau Delta. Club: Civitan (chmn. jr. civitan com. 1971-72). Home: 4348 Tucker North Court Tucker GA 30084 Office: 3150 Willow Oak Way Doraville GA 30340

FRANCE, ROGER JAMES, electronic co. exec.; b. Bismarck, N.D., Feb. 8, 1930; s. Oscar J. and Rebecca (Neuman) F.; B.S., Jamestown Coll., 1952; student George Washington U., 1960. Exec. v.p. Control Sci. Corp., Alexandria, Va., 1962-64, pres., 1964—, dir., 1962; pres., dir. Aquarius Enterprises, Inc., Alexandria, 1969—; treas., dir. Spectra Research Corp., Alexandria, 1969—; dir. Amron, Inc., Alexandria, Va. Served with AUS, 1953-55. Mason. Home: 3726 N Oakland St Arlington VA 22207 Office: 4810 Beauregard St Alexandria VA 22312

FRANCIS, AMADEO I. D., assn. exec.; b. St. Croix, V.I., Oct. 22, 1931; s. Amadeo I. and Ethanie (Smith) F.; B.A., InterAm. U., San German, P.R., 1951; M.S., U. London, 1954; M.P.A., U. P.R., 1959; m. Pami Hernandez, Mar. 31, 1958 (div. 1971); children—Lloyd, Lorraine. Economist, Office Econ. Research, Econ. Devel. Adminstrn., Santurce, P.R., 1955-59, asst. dir., 1959-61; chief Progress Reporting div. Bur. Pub. Works Programming, P.R. Planning Bd., 1960; dir. econ. research Econ. Devel. Adminstrn., 1961-63, exec. asst. to adminstr. econ. affairs, 1963-67; exec. dir. P.R. Mfrs. Assn., 1967—. Treas., P.R. chpt. A.R.C., 1966-67; pres. Commonwealth Job Devel. Center, P.R. Jobs Inc.; mem. pres.'s council InterAm. U. P.R.; mem. P.R. Olympic Com. Mem. Am. Econ. Assn., Am. Statis. Assn., Soc. Internat. Devel., P.R. Assn. Econs. and Statistics (past sec., v.p.), P.R. Amateur Athletics Fedn. (pres. 1966—), InterAm. U. P.R. Alumni Assn., P.R. Council Assn. Execs. (pres.), Am. Soc. Assn. Execs. Home: Apt 16A Los Robles Rio Piedras PR 00926 Office: 420 Ponce de Leon Av Hato Rey PR 00918

FRANCIS, HORACE, supt. schs.; b. Stockman, Tex., Dec. 18, 1920; s. Eugene A. and Medie (Murray) F.; B.S., Stephen F. Austin State Coll., 1941, M.A., 1950; m. Johnnie Williams, Feb. 21, 1942; children—Horace Francis, David Anthony. Prin. pub. schs., Stockman, Tex., 1941-43, Garrison, Tex., 1948-51; supt. pub. schs., Garrison, 1951—. Postmaster, Stockman, Tex., 1942-52. Mem. Nat., Tex. edn. assns., Tex. Assn. Sch. Adminstrs., Tex. Small Schs. Assn. (past pres.). Methodist. Mason. Lion. Home: PO Box 308 Garrison TX 75946

FRANCIS, JAMES HARRIS, physician; b. Memphis, Tex., Feb. 14, 1928; s. Roy N. and Zephyr Lee (Wills) F.; B.A., Tex. U., 1956, then M.S., M.D., 1959; m. Bera Meade Miller, May 5, 1951; children—Alan Kirk, Marsha Ann. Intern Orange County (Cal.) Gen. Hosp., 1959-60; individual practice medicine, Fullerton, Cal., 1959; practice medicine specializing in family practice, Garland, Tex., 1961—; chief staff Garland Clinic & Hosp., 1966-67, now mem. staff, mem. staff Meml. Hosp. of Garland. Pres. HFC Corp., Garland, 1963-72. Bd. dirs. Garland (Tex.) YMCA, 1967-68; bd. dirs. Garland Clinic & Hosp., 1967-71, chmn. bd., 1972—. Diplomate Am. Bd. Family Practice. Mem. C. of C., Dallas County Med. Soc., Am. Acad. Family Practice (v.p. since 1971—), Tex. Med. Assn., A.M.A. (Physicians Recognition award 1970). Mem. Ch. of Christ. Home: 3106 Ridgedale St Garland TX 75041 Office: 325 N Shiloh Rd Garland TX 75042

FRANCIS, JAMES WALLACE, real estate and ins. broker; b. Ballinger, Tex., Aug. 21, 1895; s. James Wallace and Kate (Fentress) F.; student Tex. A. and M. U., 1918; m. Roberta Beryl May, Feb. 28, 1924; 1 dau., Beryl Kathryn (Mrs. Arvel R. Ponton). Equipment engr. Tex. Hwy. Dept., 1919-25; owner James W. Francis Co., 1925-33, James W. Francis Truck Co., 1927-33, Motor Equipment Corp., 1930-57, Delphian Devel. Corp., 1927-33; bonds, ins. rec. agt. and real estate broker, San Antonio, 1958—; dir. Valley-Hi Nat. Bank. Served as 1st lt. Signal Corps, Aviation Sect., U.S. Army, 1917-18, from capt. to lt. col. ordnance, AUS, 1942-45. Mem. San Antonio Safety Council (pres. 1957-58), U.S. Hwy. 87 Improvement Assn. (pres. 1960, 71), San Antonio C. of C. (1st v.p. 1957, dir. 1955-57), Tex. Good Roads Assn. (dir.). Presbyn. (chmn. bd. deacons, mem. bench elders). Mason (32 deg., Shriner). Clubs: Quarterback (pres. 1951), Conopus (dir. 1936), San Antonio (1st v.p. 1953), San Antonio Country. Home: 214 Terrell Rd San Antonio TX 78209

FRANCIS, JANET BOTTS (MRS. HANSFORD P. FRANCIS), educator; b. Roanoke, Va., Oct. 18, 1906; d. James Berrey and Janet (Hilleary) Botts; B.A., Converse Coll., 1928; M.Ed., U. Va. 1959; postgrad. U. N.C., 1963—; m. Hansford Payne Francis, Dec. 26, 1933; children—Janet Hilleary (Mrs. Robert Hinton Crittenden), Ann Tilghman, Hansford. Tchr., Roanoke (Va.) Pub. Schs., 1928-33; propr. Knitting & Gift Shop, Roanoke, 1929-35; reporter, soc. editor Roanoke Times, 1942-44; tchr., counselor Lee Jr. High Sch., Roanoke, 1952-61; coordinator of guidance Jefferson Sr. High Sch., Roanoke, 1961-62; guidance dir., counselor Eastern High Sch., Mebane, N.C., 1962-66; counselor Durham (N.C.) High Sch., 1966-72. Pres., Jr. League of Roanoke, 1942-43; dir. Family Service Assn., Roanoke, 1942, Children's Home Soc., 1942-43. Recipient Freedoms Found. Tchrs. Medals; Gen. Electric fellow in guidance, 1966. Mem. N.E.A., N.C., Durham City assns. educators, Am., N.C. (rep. Triangle chpt.) personnel and guidance assns., Mental Health Assn., Nat., N.C. (pres.) vocational guidance assns., Am. Sch. Counselor Assn., Assn. Coll. Admissions Counselors, Am., N.C. assns. women deans and counselors, Kappa Delta Pi (life), Delta Kappa Gamma. Democrat. Episcopalian. Research to establish counselor scale for the Strong Vocational Interest blank 1968 women's. Home: 505 Dogwood Dr Chapel Hill NC 27514

FRANCIS, JOHN DARRELL, banker; b. Campbell, Tex., Feb. 3, 1904; s. William Foster and Rachel Tennessee (Yancey) F.; student pub. schs.; m. Martha Elizabeth Jordan, Mar. 17, 1932; children—Darrell Shannon, John Foster, Robert Connor and Raymond Edwin (twins), Martha Elizabeth. With Mercantile Bank, Dallas, 1925, v.p., 1939-51, sr. v.p., 1951-57, exec. v.p., 1957-61, pres., 1961-66, chmn. exec. com., 1966-69, chmn. exec. com., chief exec. officer, 1969—, also dir.; dir. Dallas Power & Light Co., Gen. Telephone Co. S.W., San Angelo, Tex., Republic Nat. Life Ins. Co., Lomas & Nettleton Financial Corp., Strickland Transp. Co., Summers Electric Co., Capital S.W. Corp., Allied Finance, Republic Financial Services, Rangaire Corp., Cleburne, Tex.; trustee Lomas & Nettleton Mortgage Investors. Mem. Dallas Citizens Council. Bd. dirs. Tex. Research League, 1969—; trustee Southwestern Med. Found. Mem. Assn. Res. City Bankers, Dallas C. of C. (mem. com. Trinity River devel.). Mem. Community Ch. Mason (33 deg., Shriner). Clubs: Dallas Country, Dallas Athletic, Dallas, Petroleum, Chapaaral, Cipango (Dallas). Home: 3604 Lexington St Dallas TX 75205 Office: PO Box 5415 Dallas TX 75222

FRANCIS, JOHN HUBERT, JR., petroleum co. exec.; b. Meridian, Miss., Apr. 27, 1928; s. John H. and Mary (Stevenson) F.; student Miss. State Coll., 1945-46; B.A., U. Ala., 1952; M.A. La. State U., 1966; m. Carolynne B. Vann, Jan. 23, 1949; 1 dau., Kathryn Alayne. Staff asst. U. (Ala.) Press Bur., 1952; employee information supr. So. Bell Tel. & Tel. Co., Atlanta, 1953-54; sr. dist. rep. Am. Petroleum Inst., 1955-59; asso. dir. La Petroleum Council, 1959-67; southwest pub. relations mgr. Humble Oil & Refining Co., 1967—. Pres., La. Travel Council, 1967; mem. adv. com. La. Tourist Devel. Commn. Served from pvt. to staff sgt. AUS, 1946-48, capt., 1950-52. Recipient Inter Frat. Congress publ. award 7 times, 1950-56, 59, Citation for Service, La. Oil and Gas Industry, Distinguished Service to Journalism award; named Man of the Year, 1959, 1960; named Friend of Tex. Press, 1971. Mem. Inter Frat. Congress (pres. 1958-59), C. of C., Res. Officers Assn., Pub. Relations Soc. Am., Tex. Bur. Econ. Understanding, Assn. Petroleum Writers, Tex. Press Assn., N.M. Press Assn., Tex. Assn. Broadcasters, Assn. Edn. Journalism, Sigma Delta Chi (pres. 1960-61; Distinguished Service award), Omicron Delta Kappa, Theta Kappa Omega (nat. pres. 1950-56), Kappa Alpha. Kiwanian. Clubs: Marlin, Rococo; Krewe of Iduna. Home: 850 Myrtlea Lane Houston TX 77024 Office: PO Box 2180 Houston TX 77001

FRANCIS, LEON WALTER, dentist; b. Prescott, Ark., Mar. 17, 1926; s. John Ricks and Mary Ada (Still) F.; student Ark. A. and M. Coll., 1944-46; B.S., U. Ark., 1947; D.D.S., U. Tenn., 1962; m. Esther Lougene Thornton, May 22, 1948; children—Jacquelyn Ruth, Lee Thornton. High sch. tchr. math. and sci., Altheimer, Ark., 1947-50; cotton farmer, Altheimer, 1950-59; practice dentistry, Pine Bluff, Ark., 1963—; farm operator, 1967—. Pres. Pine Bluff Bd. Edn., 1969-71. Bd. dirs. Teen Town. Served with USNR, 1944-46. Mem. Am., Ark. dental assns., S.E. Ark., Jefferson County dental socs., Am. Farm Bur. Fedn., Omicron Kappa Upsilon. Mason (32 deg., Shriner), Kiwanian. Club: Pine Bluff Country. Home: 25 Longmeadow Pine Bluff AR 71601 Office: 1616 Cherry St Pine Bluff AR 71601

FRANCIS, LEWIS, physician; b. Troy, O., Dec. 16, 1921; s. Jesse Bernard and Joy Louise (Miller) F.; B.A., Ohio State U., 1943, M.D., 1945; m. Jean Davis, June 14, 1941; children—Carol (Mrs. Carol Parkhurst), Patricia, Joy. Intern Harris Hosp., Ft. Worth, 1945-46; resident Mass. Gen. Hosp., Boston, 1948-50; instrn., asst. anesthesia Harvard U. Med. Sch., Boston, 1950; practice medicine, Oakland, Cal., 1950-51; instr. anesthesia Stanford Med. Sch., San Francisco, 1952; dir. anesthesia Central Bapt. Hosp., Lexington, Ky., 1954—; asst. prof. clin. anesthesia U. Ky. Med. Sch., Lexington, 1962—; cons. anesthesia USPHS, Lexington. Mem. Fayette County Republican Adv. Com., 1967-71, Ky. Ednl. Med. Polit. Action Com., 1965-72. Bd. dirs. Central Ky. Youth Music Symphony, 1964-65, Lexington YMCA, 1963—; chmn. bd. trustees Sayre Sch., 1963. Served with AUS, 1942-46, USPHS, 1946-48. Recipient Community Service to Youth award YMCA, Lexington, 1965. Diplomate Am. Bd. Anesthesiology. Fellow Am. Coll. Anesthesiologists; mem. Am., Ky. (pres. 1959) socs. anesthesiologists, Internat. Anesthesia Research Soc., A.M.A., Ky., Fayette County med. socs., Assn. Am. Physicians and Surgeons, Phi Chi. Presbyn. (deacon 1961-64, trustee 1964-66). Lion (dir. 1965-66). Club: Lansdowne (Lexington,). Home: 3022 Breckenwood Dr Lexington KY 40502 Office: First Nat Bank Bldg Lexington KY 40507

FRANCIS, MURIEL BULTMAN, publicity and personal rep.; b. New Orleans; d. A. Fred and Pauline (Geschwind) Bultman, Jr.; B.A., U. Ala., 1928; student Sorbonne, Paris, France, 1928-29; m. Harold Owen Francis, Aug. 9, 1932 (dec. 1943). Promotion rep. Grace Denton, Chgo., 1934; publicity rep. New Orleans Philharmonic Symphony Orch., 1936-37; personal rep. for Hollywood Workshop of Max Rheinhardt, 1930-40; pres. Pioneer Assurance Co., New Orleans, 1940-43; account exec. for radio and TV programs Earl Ferris Assos. N.Y.C., 1943-45; publicity and personal rep. Muriel Francis Assos., N.Y.C., 1946-61; head artists div. Nat. Concerts and Artists Corp., 1962-64; pres. Bultman Mortuary Service, Inc., New Orleans, 1964—; cons. Edgar Vincent Assos., 1961-65. Mem. Pres. Eisenhower's Person to Person Music Com., 1956-62. Pres., Isaac Delgado Mus. Art, New Orleans, 1968-69; bd. dirs. St. Charles Gen. Hosp., New Orleans Philharmonic Symphony Orch., New Orleans Opera House Assn., New Orleans Spring Fiesta Assn., New Orleans Speech and Hearing Center, English Speaking Union New Orleans, New Orleans Mus. Art, Russell Holman Vocational Center. Mem. Phi Beta Kappa, Delta Zeta. Roman Catholic. Home: 116 E 65th St New York City NY 10021 Office: 3338 St Charles Av New Orleans LA 70115 also: 1525 Louisiana Av New Orleans LA 70115

FRANCIS, RICARDO HUGH, lawyer; b. San Juan, P.R., July 4, 1935; s. Hugh Richard and Mercedes (Lajara) F.; B.A., Harvard, 1955, LL.M., 1962; LL.B., U. P.R., 1958; m. Vanessa Vassallo, June 27, 1958; children— Valerie, Hildren. Admitted to P.R. bar; partner firm Trias, Saldana & Francis, Hato Rey, P.R.; prof. taxation, corp. law and bus. planning U. P.R. Law Sch., 1962—. Dir. Boricua Broadcasting Corp., Mercantile Investment Co., Enterprising Realty Corp., P.R. Auto Corp., Hato Rey Supply, Inc. Mem. adv. council to Gov. P.R. Mem. Am., P.R. bar assns., Am. Assn. Trial Lawyers, Nat. Assn. Mfrs., Nu Sigma Beta. Clubs: San Juan Yacht; Metropolitan Shooting. Home: 603 Condominio San Luis San Juan PR 00609 Office: 1900 Popular Center Bldg Hato Rey PR 00609

FRANCIS, SIR FRANK (CHALTON), librarian, mus. dir.; b. Liverpool, Eng., Oct. 5, 1901; s. Frank W. and Elizabeth (Chalton) F.; B.A., U. Liverpool, 1923, Litt.D., 1963; M.A., U. Cambridge, 1925, Litt.D., 1968, Litt. D. (hon.), U. B.C., 1960, Trinity Coll., Dublin, 1962, U. of Exeter, 1966, U. Leeds, 1967, U. N.B., 1967, U. Oxford, 1968, U. Wales, 1968; m. Katrina F. McClennon, Apr. 20, 1927; children—Jane, Jeremy J. F., Guy. Asst. master Holyhead County Sch., 1925-26; asst. keeper British Mus., 1926-46, sec., 1946-47, keeper dept. printed books, 1948-59, dir., prin. librarian, 1959-67; lectr. bibliography Univ. Coll., London, 1945-59; David Murray lectr. U. Glasgow (Scotland), 1957. Chmn. Internat. Com. Library Experts, UN, 1948, Council Brit. Nat. Bibliography, 1949-59; v.p. internat. adv. com. bibliography UNESCO, 1954-60. Hon. fellow Emmanuel Coll. Cambridge U. Pierpont Morgan Library. Decorated Knight Comdr. of the Bath (Eng.). Fellow Soc. Antiquaries, Museums Assn. (pres. 1965-66), Library Assn. (pres. 1965); mem. Internat. Fedn. Library Assns. (pres. 1964-70), Anglo-Swedish Soc. (chmn. 1964-68), Mass. Hist. Soc. (corr.), Bibliog. Soc. (hon. sec. 1938-64, pres. 1964-66), King Gustav Adolfs Akademien Sweden (hon.), Inst. de France (corr.), Oxford, Cambridge, Edinburgh, Am. bibliog. socs., Assn. Spl. Libraries and Information Bur. (pres. 1957-59); hon. fgn. mem. Am. Acad. Arts and Scis. Club: Grolier (hon.). Author: Robert Copland, Sixteenth Century Printer and Translator, 1961; also articles in field. Editor: The Library, 1936-53, The Bibliographical Society 1892-1942, Studies in Retrospect, 1945; Facsimile of The Compleat Catalogue, 1680, 1956. Co-editor: Jour. of Documentation, 1947—. Home: The Vine Nether Winchendon Aylesbury Bucks England Office: Council on Library Resources Inc One Dupont Circle Washington DC 20036

FRANCK, ISAAC, social worker; b. Russia, Mar. 15, 1909 came to U.S., 1923; naturalized, 1936; s. George and Minnie (Babin) F.; B.S., N.Y. U.-Washington Sq. Coll., 1934; postgrad. Columbia U., 1934-37, 47-49, Harvard, 1937-40, U. Mich., 1940-43; Ph.D., U. Md., 1966; m. Pearl C. Crystal, Oct. 21, 1934; children—Walter B., Phyllis S. Dir. clubs Jewish Center, Port Chester, N.Y., 1934-37; exec. dir. Jewish Community Center, Manchester, N.H., 1937-39; edn. dir. Jewish Center, Detroit, 1939-41; exec. dir. Jewish Community Council, Detroit, 1941-46; exec. dir. Bklyn. Jewish Council, 1946-47; exec. sec. Am. Fund for Israel Instns., N.Y.C., 1947-49; exec. v.p. Jewish Community Council Greater Washington, 1949—. Spl. lectr. polit. sci. dept. Wayne U., Detroit, 1943-46; adj. prof. philosophy and sociology Am. U., Washington, 1956—. Sec. Interreligious Com. on Race Relations, 1963—; sec. Met. Washington Urban Coalition, 1968—. Recipient Stephen S. Wise Medallion award Am. Jewish Congress, 1962. Mem. Am. Philos. Assn., Am. Sociol. Assn., Nat. Assn. Intergroup Relations Ofcls., Nat. Conf. Jewish Communal Service, Assn. Jewish Community Relations Workers, Nat. Assn. Social Workers, Acad. Certified Social Workers. Co-author: American Jewry: The Tercentenary and After, 1958; Trends in Jewish Communal Service 1898-1958; English transl. The Tale of the Scribe (by S.Y. Agnon). Contbr. articles in field to profl. jours. Home: 1415 Crestridge Dr Silver Spring MD 20910 Office: 1330 Massachusetts Av NW Washington DC 20005

FRANCK, JAMES RICHARD, county extension exec.; b. Richlands, N.C., Aug. 20, 1923; s. James Roscoe and Grace Aline (Whitaker) F.; B.S., N.C. State U., 1949, M.S., 1970; m. Dorothy Grey Senter, Aug. 16, 1947; children—James Richard, Edward Senter, Rebecca Leigh. Asst. agrl. agt. N.C. Agrl. Extension, Washington, 1949-52; county extension chmn., Trenton, N.C., 1952—. Scoutmaster, East Carolina council Boy Scouts Am., 1953-69. Served with AUS, 1943-46. Decorated Combat Inf. badge; recipient Silver Beaver award, 1968. Mem. Am. Legion (past comdr.). Democrat. Methodist. Rotarian. Address: Box 218 Trenton NC 28585

FRANCO, JOHAN (HENRI GUSTAVE), composer; b. Zaandam, Netherlands, July 12, 1908; s. S. Franco and Margaretha J. E. C. (Gosschalk) F.; grad. First Coll., The Hague; studied composition with Willem Pijper, Amsterdam, 4 yrs.; m. Eloise Lavrischeff, Mar. 28, 1948. Came to U.S., 1934, naturalized, 1942. Entire program of his compositions was presented at Town Hall, N.Y., 1938; collaborated with Oscar Thompson on Sect. on Contemporary Dutch composers in the Cyclopedia of Music and Musicians, 1938. Served with AUS, 1942-43. Mem. Am. Composers Alliance, Southeastern Composers League. Prin. works: 5 symphonies; Divertimento for Flute and Strings, 1946; many songs, 2 cello sonatas, 1 viola sonata 6 partitas piano, 9 partitas and other compositions for carillon, classical guitar, flute, saxophone; As the Prophets Foretold (cantata); Fantasy for cello and orch.; The Stars Look Down (oratorio); The Prodigal string quartet; Songs of the Spirit for soprano and woodwind quintet; The Song of Life (for mixed chorus a cappella); Concerto Lirico No. 1 for violin and orch.; Concerto Lirico No. 2 for cello and orch.; Concerto Lirico No. 3 for piano and orch.; Concerto Lirico No. 4 for percussion and orch.; Concerto Lirico No. 5 for guitar and orch.; incidental music for the Book of Job, Romans by St. Paul; the Pilgrim's Progress, Electra and the Tempest for the Everyman Players produced and directed by Orlin Corey; Supplication-Revelation-Triumph for orch.; also recs. Home: 403 Lake Dr Virginia Beach VA 23451

FRANCOIS, EVAN A., Republican nat. committeeman. Office: PO Box 276 St Thomas VI 00802*

FRANK, GEORGE WILLARD, oil co. exec.; b. Beloit, Kan., Mar. 2, 1923; s. George N. and Catherine (Wideman) F.; B.S. in Petroleum Engring., U. Kan., 1946; m. Elaine Wells, June 22, 1947; children—Janis, Barbara. Engr., Phillips Petroleum Co., 1947-50; asst. supt. Progress Petroleum Co., Houston, 1950-56; gen. supt. Austral Oil Co., Inc., Houston, 1956-59, v.p., 1959-65, sr. v.p., 1965—; mng. dir., sr. v.p. Austral Nuclear Engring. Co., 1970—; dir. Austral Petroleum Gas Co., Austral Minerals, Austral Oil Co. (U.K.) Ltd. Mem. panel on peaceful uses Internat. AEC, Vienna, Austria, 1971; lectr. World Petroleum Congress, Moscow, USSR, 1971. Active Am. Cancer Soc., United Fund, Heart Fund. Served to lt. USNR, 1946. Mem. Am. Petroleum Inst., Houston Geol. Soc., Am. Inst. Mining, Metall. and Petroleum Engrs., Ind. Petroleum Assn. Am., Atomic Indsl. Forum (chmn. plowshare com. 1969-72; dir. 1971—). Club: Lakeside Country (v.p. 1968; dir. 1965-68). Contbr. articles to profl. jours. Home: 6223 Holly Springs St Houston TX 77027 Office: 2700 Humble Bldg Houston TX 77002

FRANK, MORRIS, columnist Houston Chronicle. Address: 512 Travis St Houston TX 77002*

FRANKEL, MAX, journalist; b. Gera, Germany, Apr. 3, 1930; s. Jacob A. and Mary (Katz) F.; came to U.S., 1940, naturalized, 1948; A.B., Columbia, 1952, M.A. in Polit. Sci., 1953; m. Tobia Brown, June 19, 1956; children—David M., Margot S., Jonathan M. Mem. staff N.Y. Times, 1952—, chief Washington corr., 1968—; lectr., also TV news analyst. Served with AUS, 1953-55. Mem. Council Fgn. Relations, Phi Beta Kappa. Home: 5607 Montgomery St Chevy Chase MD 20015 Office: 1920 L St NW Washington DC 20036

FRANKFORD, JOSEPH, social worker; b. Phila., Feb. 11, 1918; s. Samuel and Regina (Halberthal) F.; A.B. in Psychology, U. Pa., 1949, postgrad., 1956; M.A. in Social Work, Ohio State U., 1950; m. Ethel Braverman, (div.); children—Susan, Peter, Shellie, Leanard, Steven; m. 2d, Gladys Dellinger, Sept. 6, 1968. Program dir. Jewish Community Center, Canton, O., 1950-52; program asst. Jewish Community Center, Balt., 1952-54; sch. social worker Balt. Schs., Balt., 1958-63; dir. social work Charlotte-Mecklenburg Schs., N.C., 1963-71; adminstrv. dir. Coastal Plain Mental Health Center, Greenville, N.C., 1971—. Lectr. U. N.C. Sch. Social Work, Charlotte, 1966—; asso. prof. Sch. Allied Health Professions, East Caroline U. Pres. Community Execs. Congress, Charlotte, 1966-68. Served with AUS, 1941-45. Mem. Nat. Assn. Social Workers (pres. South Piedmont chpt. 1966-68), N.E.A. Home: Route 8 Box 462 Greenville NC27834 Office: 1827 W 6th St Greenville NC 27834

FRANKLAND, WALTER LESLIE, JR., assn. exec.; b. Jackson, Tenn., June 4, 1924; s. Walter Leslie and Sarah (Moore) F.; B.S., U.S. Mil. Acad., 1946; M.A., U. Fla., 1955; m. Carol Elizabeth Armstrong, June 20, 1946; children—Walter, Mary Elizabeth. Commd. 2d lt. Inf., U.S. Army, 1946, advanced through grades to lt. col., 1963; served in Japan, 1947-49; with 10th Tng. Div., Ft. Riley, Kan., 1950-51; assigned to Armored Sch., 1951-52; 2d Inf. Div., Korea, 1952-53, U.S. Mil. Acad., 1955-58, French Army Staff Coll., 1958-59, Am. embassy, Paris, 1959-63, Armed Forces Staff Coll., Norfolk, 1963; officer Office Chief Information, Dept. Army, Washington, 1964-66; ret., 1966; exec. sec. Silver Users Assn., Washington, 1966, exec. dir., 1967-71, exec. v.p., 1971—; partner Scott & Frankland, mgmt. cons. Pres., Arlington-Forest (Va.) Citizens Assn., 1970, Washington-Lee High Sch. Boosters Club, 1971—. Decorated Combat Inf. badge, Bronze Star medal, Commendation medal; French Croix de Guerre Otre Mere (Korea). Mem. Pub. Relations Soc. Am. (dir. Nat. Capital chpt.), Radio TV News Dirs. Assn., Am. Soc. Assn. Execs., West Point Soc. D.C. (treas., dir.), Nat. Press Club, Tenn. State Soc. (v.p.), Sigma Delta Chi. Clubs: Nat. Press, Army-Navy (Washington); Army-Navy Country (Arlington, Va.). Home: 2674 Marcey Rd Arlington VA 22207 Office: 1625 Eye St NW Washington DC 20006

FRANKLIN, BEN A., journalist. Mem. Washington bur. N.Y. Times. Recipient Weatherford award Appalachian journalism, 1971. Home: 1140 Rockby St Garrett Park MD 20766 Office: NY Times 1920 L St NW Washington DC 20005*

FRANKLIN, CHARLES BOB, diversified industry exec.; b. Dallas, May 4, 1928; s. Arlie H. and Mary Ann (Edwards) F.; Asso. Aero. Engring., Spartan Coll. Engring., Tulsa, Okla., 1951; m. Jeannine Hart, Mar. 19, 1949; children—Judith Elaine, Donna Carol, Kenneth Bob. Chief project engr. LTV Aerospace Corp., Dallas, 1961-62, dir. vehicle programs, 1963-67; v.p., gen. mgr. engring. systems div. Service Tech. Corp., subsidiary LTV Aerospace Corp., 1968-69, pres., 1970—. Served with AUS, 1946-49. Home: 7130 Mossvine St Dallas TX 75240 Office: 2345 W Mockingbird St Dallas TX 75235

FRANKLIN, HENRY BLAND, JR., agriculturist; b. Raleigh, N.C., May 14, 1934; s. Henry Bland and Mary (Keith) F.; B.S. in Agr., N.C. State Coll., 1956; M.S. in Sociology, N.C. State U., 1966; m. Mary Frances Fulp, Dec. 7, 1957; children—Henry Bland, Benjamin Paul, Shelley Francine. Extension agt. N.C. Coop. Extension Service, Rockingham County, Reidsville, 1960-64; community devel. specialist N.C. State U., Raleigh, 1965; with extension service Va. Tech. U., Richmond, 1966—, program leader, 1966-68, extension specialist, 1968-72, asso. prof., 1972—. Recipient Valley Forge Freedom's Found. award, 1969. Served with USNR, 1956-59. Mem. Va. Citizens Planning Assn., Va. Extension Service Assn., Naval Res. Assn. Baptist (dir. Sunday Sch.). Home: 9125 Redington Dr Richmond VA 23235

FRANKLIN, J. STUART, JR., civil engr.; b. Richmond, Va., May 2, 1920; s. James Stuart and Gaynelle (Phillips) F.; B.S., Va. Poly. Inst.; m. Margaret Elizabeth May, June 12, 1948. Field engr. Mason & Hanger, Dublin, Va. and Baraboo, Wis., 1941-42; insp. Fred Bur. Rds., Blue Ridge, Parkway, Va., 1946-47; civil engr., structural design for numerous schs., chs., hosps., indsl. bldgs., Eubank & Caldwell, Inc., Roanoke, Va., 1948-55; structural designer Am. Bridge div. U.S. Steel Corp., 1955-58; v.p., gen. mgr. Cates Bldg. Spltys., Inc., 1958-60; partner Eubank, Caldwell & Assos., architects and engrs., 1961-66, Eubank, Caldwell, Dobbins, Sherertz & Franklin, 1966-70, Sheretz & Franklin, 1970—. Served as staff sgt. C.E., AUS, Africa, Hawaii, 1942-46. Registered profl. engr., Va. Fellow Am. Soc. C.E. (pres. Roanoke br. 1955-56, pres. Va. sect. 1968, mem. nat. com. on student chpts.); mem. Va. Soc. Profl. Engrs. (sec.-treas. Roanoke chpt. 1955, v.p. 1956), Roanoke C. of C., Tau Beta Pi, Chi Epsilon. Baptist (deacon). Mason, Kiwanian (pres. 1967, lt. gov. 1970-71), Elk. Home: 3256 Woodland Dr SW Roanoke VA 24015 Office: First Fed Bldg Roanoke VA 24011

FRANKLIN, JAMES DADE, petroleum co. exec.; b. Cushing, Okla., Feb. 21, 1918; s. James Taylor and Elfreda (Shotwell) F.; grad. Cushing High Sch., 1938; spl. tech. courses Am. Tech. Soc., also John Deer Plow Co.; m. Flora Deane York, Mar. 15, 1947; children—Dean Markel, Leota Jean, James Charles; m. 3d, Eva Lee Harding, Jan. 22, 1961; children—Daphne Lee, Eric Boyd, Tony Allen. Carrier, reporter Tulsa Daily World, 1934-38; partnership owner John Deere Plow Co., implement sales and service, Cushing, 1938-42; dist. salesman Willis Sales, Inc., Chgo., 1947-50; sales mgr. Lester M. List, automobile dealers, Bartlesville, Okla., 1950-55; oil producer, Bartlesville, 1950-56; engring. standards asst. Phillips Petroleum Co., Bartlesville, 1955—. Mem. Lincoln-Mercury Sales Council, 1950-55; panel mem. Tom McKay Hill Nat. Automobile Survey, 1950-55. Served with USAAF, 1942-46. Decorated Meritorious Service award. Mem. Am. Legion, S.A.R., Frank Phillips Mens Club. Democrat. Baptist. Inventor mail zip code, 1942. Home: 1507 Saddle Lane Bartlesville OK 74003 Office: Phillips Bldg Bartlesville OK 74004

FRANKLIN, MARY ANNE GUY, tv ednl. exec.; b. Columbia, S.C.; adopted dau. Lynn Trimble and Roberta (Mitchell) Guy; B.A., U. Richmond, 1935; M.A., U. Va., 1943; m. Samuel Howell Franklin Jr., Oct. 16, 1946 (div. Nov. 1952). Tchr. pub. schs., Richmond Va., 1936-58, ednl. TV cons., 1956-64; v.p., program dir. ednl. WCVE/WCVW-TV, Richmond, 1964-71; dir. ednl. TV, Va. Dept. Edn., 1971—; tchr. English evening sch. Richmond Profl. Inst., 1960-64, summer insts. U. Mich., Ann Arbor, 1955; Madison Coll., Harrisonburg, Va., 1962, U. Richmond, 1963. Cons. ednl. TV workshops Del. 1965, W. Va., 1968; field cons. Nat. Project for Improvement TV Instrn., Nat. Assn. Ednl. Broadcasters, 1966—. Mem. State Bd. Community Colls., 1966—, Regional Council for Continuing Edn., Richmond, 1967—, steering com. for ednl. TV, State Council Higher Edn., 1967—. Bd. dirs. Va. Ednl. TV, Inc. Winifred Cullis lecture fellow. Eng., Scotland, 1953; Fulbright fellow, Thailand, 1958-59; exchange tchr., London, Eng. 1948-49. Mem. Am. Assn. U. Women (past pres.), English Speaking Union (past v.p.), Phi Beta Kappa (past pres. Richmond). Democrat. Baptist. Club: Willow Oaks Country. Home: 1829 Hanover Av Richmond VA 23220 Office: 9th St Office Bldg Richmond VA 23216

FRANKLIN, PHILIP EARLE, economist; b. Detroit, Jan. 11, 1928; s. Edward Earle and Minnie (Evans) F.; B.A., George Washington U., 1949, M.A., 1955; Ph.D., Am. U., 1968; m. Jacqueline Jo Rogers, Dec. 28, 1949; children—Debora, Janice, Stephanie, Diana, Jennifer. Bus. economist Office Bus. Econs., Dept. Commerce, 1950-51; indsl. analyst Govt. Patents Bd., Exec. Office Pres., 1952-55; gen. economist Bur. Fgn. Commerce, Dept. of Commerce, 1955-56; transp. specialist Commodity Stblzn. Service, Dept. Agr., 1956-57; transp. economist Maritime Adminstrn., Dept. Commerce, 1957-60, gen. economist Office of Area Devel., 1960-61, transp. economist Office of Under Sec. of Commerce for Transp., 1961-62, internat. economist Bur. Internat. Commerce, 1962-64, gen. economist Office Undersec. Transp., 1964-67; coordinator for water resources Office of Sec., Dept. Transp., 1967-70, chief econs. and spl. project div., 1971—; transp. cons. UN, 1965. Pres. Eastpines Citizens Assn., Riverdale, Md., 1955-57. Served with USAAF, 1945-47. Served as 1st lt. AUS, 1951-52. Mem. Am. Econ. Assn., Council on Fgn. Relations, Am. Water Resources Assn., Soc. Govt. Economists, Regional Sci. Assn., Econ. History Assn., A.A.A.S., Am. Soc. Pub. Adminstrn., Am. Acad. Polit. Social Sci., Delta Phi Epsilon (pres. Washington alumni assn. 1965-66). Home: 3734 Northampton St NW Washington DC 20015 Office: Office of Sec Dept Transp Washington DC 20590

FRANKLIN, PHYLLIS PINE (MRS. IRWIN FRANKLIN), educator; b. N.Y.C., Apr. 21, 1932; d. Matthew and Helen (Lutsky) Pine; A.B., Vassar Coll., 1954; M.A., U. Miami (Fla.), 1965, Ph.D. (Danforth Found. fellow), 1969; m. Irwin Franklin, Apr. 22, 1957 (div.); children—James, Jody. Asst. prof. English, U. Miami, Coral Gables, Fla., 1969—. Mem. Modern Lang. Assn., South Atlantic Modern Lang. Assn., Nat. Orgn. for Women, Nat. Council Tchrs. English. Author: Show Thyself A Man; AComparison of Benjamin Franklin and Cotton Mather, 1969. Contbr. articles to profl. jours. Home: 1429 Garcia Av Coral Gables FL 33146

FRANKLIN, WILLIAM MCHENRY, historian; b. Cin., Sept. 6, 1913; s. Ward and Hazel (McHenry) F.; B.A., U. Cin., 1934, M.A., 1935; exchange student U. Konigsberg, 1935-36; Ph.D., Fletcher Sch. Law and Diplomacy, 1941; m. Alicelia Hoskins, May 25, 1939; children—Hayward H., Charles E. Research sec. Council Fgn. Relations, 1939-40; div. asst. State Dept., 1941-45, sr. div. asst., 1945-51, asst. chief hist. div., 1951-62, dir. Hist. Office, 1962—; professorial lectr. diplomatic history Georgetown U., 1964—. Served to lt. USNR, 1943-45. Recipient Meritorious Service award State Dept., 1963. Mem. Am. Hist. Assn., Am. Polit. Sci. Assn., Am. Soc. Internat. Law, Phi Beta Kappa. Author: Protection of Foreign Interests, 1947; also articles. Home: 6617 Barnaby St SW Washington DC 20015 Office: Hist Office State Dept Washington DC 20520

FRANKS, CHARLES LESLIE, banker; b. Columbus, Miss., Jan. 21, 1934; s. Leslie J. and Almeda (Morris) F.; B.S. in Accounting Summa cum laude, Miss. State U., 1956; m. Cecil Alice Cronovich, Feb. 7, 1959; children—Carolyn Anne, Charles Christopher. Accountant, Arthur Andersen & Co., Houston, 1959-61; chief internal auditor Bank S.W., N.A., Houston, 1966-71; gen. auditor S.W. Bancshares, Inc., Houston, 1972—. Lectr. Bank Adminstrn. Inst. Sch. U. Wis. Served to capt. USAAF, 1956-59. C.P.A., Tex. Mem. Bank Adminstrn. Inst., Am. Inst. Banking, Tex. Soc. C.P.A.'s, Inst. Internal Auditors, Arnold Air Soc., Alpha Kappa Psi, Phi Kappa Phi, Phi Eta Sigma. Roman Catholic. Home: 6106 Cheena St Houston TX 77035 Office: 910 Travis St Houston TX 77002

FRANKS, THOMAS KENNETH, educator; b. Stockman, Tex., Nov. 9, 1912; s. Thomas and Florence (Echols) F.; B.S., Stephen F. Austin, 1946, M.Ed., 1951; m. Iva Powell, July 15, 1949; children—Kenneth, Karen, Kyle, Keith, Kim. High sch. prin. Pineland (Tex.) Ind. Sch. Dist., 1946-55; supt. Joaquin (Tex.) Ind. Sch. Dist., Joaquin, Tex., 1955-61; supt. West Sabine Ind. Sch. Dist., Pineland, Tex., 1961—. Served with inf. AUS, 1943-46; ETO. Decorated Bronze Star with oak leaf clusters, Purple Heart. Mem. Am. Legion (post comdr.), N.E.A., Nat., Tex. assns. sch. adminstrs. Methodist. Home: Pines Av Pineland TX 75968 Office: Flagpole Rd Pineland TX 75968

FRANTZ, RAY WILLIAM, JR., librarian; b. Princeton, Ky., Aug. 17, 1923; s. Ray William and Marjorie (Kevil) F.; student Grinnell (Ia.) Coll., 1941-42; A.B., U. Neb., 1948; M.L.S., U. Ill., 1949, M.A. in English, 1951, Ph.D., 1955; m. Doris H. Methvin, Aug. 26, 1951; children—Kathie Kevil, Paul William. Librarian, U. Richmond (Va.), 1955-60; asst. dir. Ohio State U. Library, 1960-62; dir. libraries U. Wyo., 1962-67; librarian U. Va. Library, Charlottesville, 1967—; library cons. for proposed coll. at Sun City, Ariz., 1964; vice chmn. library adv. com. Va. Council Higher Edn., 1971. Served with inf. AUS, 1943-46. Mem. Am., Southeastern library assns., Bibliog. Soc. Am., Bibliog. Soc. U. Va. Club: Torch (Charlottesville). Home: 1859 Fendall Av Charlottesville VA 22903

FRANZMATHES, JOSEPH EDWARD, lawyer; b. Beloit, Kan., Dec. 8, 1907; s. Joseph W. and Grace (Shafer) F.; student Kan. Wesleyan Coll., 1927-29; LL.B., U. Mo., 1937; m. Elizabeth M. Lutz, July 1, 1950. Admitted to Mo. bar, 1937; accountant Am. Service Co., 1931-39; atty., auditor Consumers Pub. Service Co., 1939-42; atty. passport office State Dept., Washington, 1945—. Served with CIC, AUS, 1942-45. Mem. Am., Fed., Mo. bar assns., Am. Legion (vice comdr. 1959-60). Home: 5415 Connecticut Av NW Washington DC 20015 Office: McPherson Bldg 1425 K St Washington DC 20524

FRANZUS, BORIS, educator; b. Chgo., July 23, 1924; s. Louis and Ida (Berkowitz) F.; A.A. summa cum laude, Chgo. City Coll., 1948; M.S., U. Chgo., 1950; Ph.D., U. Colo., 1955; m. Bettylene Welsch, Sept. 6, 1948; children—Benjamin, David, Martin. Research chemist Phillips Petroleum Co., Bartlesville, Okla., 1954-60; sr. research chemist Esso Research & Engring. Co., Linden, N.J., 1960-67; prof. chemistry East Tenn. State U. at Johnson City, 1967—. Served with USAAF, 1943-46. Mem. Am. Chem. Soc., London (Eng.) Chem. Soc., Phi Lambda Upsilon. Democrat. Jewish religion (bd. congregation). Contbr. articles profl. jours. Research in organic reaction mechanisms and nuclear magnetic resonance spectroscopy. Patentee in field. Home: RFD 2 Hillmont Dr Hillmont Heights Johnson City TN 37603

FRASE, ROBERT WILLIAM, economist, assn. exec.; b. Chgo., Jan. 1, 1912; s. Otto Paul and Lillian (Jones) F.; A.B., U. Wis., 1934; A.M., Harvard, 1944; m. Eleanor J. Stockwell, June 10, 1939; children—Mary (Mrs. Raymond Williams), Richard Stockwell, Katharine Gordon. Staff mem. Social Sci. Research Council, Washington, 1934-36; adminstr., economist Dept. Labor, Washington, 1938-40, Dept. Agr., 1940-42, War Relocation Authority, 1942-43, WPB, 1943; spl. asst. to Sec. Commerce, Washington, 1945-50; asso mng. dir., economist Am. Book Pubs. Council, Washington, 1950-60; dir. Joint Washington office Am. Book Pubs. Council and Am. Ednl. Pubs. Inst., 1960-70; v.p., economist Assn. Am. Pubs., Washington, 1970—. Served to 1st lt. AUS, 1943-45. Guggenheim fellow, 1948-49. Mem. Phi Beta Kappa. Clubs: Cosmos, International, Nat. Economists, Harvard (Washington). Author: The Administration of Unemployment Insurance in Germany, 1938; (with H. Guinzburg, T. Waller) Books and the Mass Market, 1953; (with C. McKinley) Launching Social Security, 1970; (with R. Bernstein, M. Carroll, E. McCabe, W. B. Wiley) Book Publishing in the U.S.S.R., 1971. Contbr. articles to profl. jours. Home: 6704 Haycock Rd Falls Church VA 22043 Office: 1826 Jefferson Pl NW Washington DC 20036

FRASER, DONALD HINES, U.S. atty.; b. Hinesville, Ga., Feb. 27, 1906; s. Donald and Beulah Lee (Hines) F.; student Mercer U., 1923-25; LL.B., U. Fla., 1927; m. Evelyn Hughey Green, July 13, 1933; 1 dau., Jane Evelyn (wife of Lt. William E. Bowen). Admitted to Ga. and Fla. bars, 1928; judge city ct., Darien, Ga., 1943-45, Hinesville, Ga. 1933-49; solicitor gen. Atlantic Jud. Circuit, 1950-51; pvt. practice law, Hinesville, 1951—; asst. U.S. atty. So. Dist. Ga., 1951-61, U.S. atty., 1961—. Mem. Ga. Gen. Assembly from Liberty County, 1930-31, 71—; mem. Hinesville City Council, 1931-33. Mem. Ga. Bar Assn. (db. govs. 1950), St. Andrews Soc. Savannah, S.A.R. Democrat. Methodist. Club: Exchange. Home: 503 Oglethorpe Hwy Hinesville GA 31313 Office: PO Box 472 Hinesville GA 31313

FRASER, JAMES ROY NAIRN, civil engr.; b. Belize, Brit. Honduras, Mar. 27, 1924; came to U.S. 1937, naturalized 1942; s. Cuthbert Nairn and Alice (Cran) F.; B.Civil Engring., Ga. Inst. Tech., 1950; m. Eileen Dolores Kavulish, Apr. 16, 1946; children—Eileen (Mrs. Bill Taffs), James Nairn. Asst. div. engr. Seaboard Airline R.R., Jacksonville, Fla., Raleigh, N.C., 1950-55; design and sales engr. Albany (Ga.) Concrete Products Co., 1955-57; div. engr. materials, handling Link-Belt Co., Atlanta, 1957-61; sr. structural engr. Eastern Engring. Co., Atlanta, 1962-64; prin. cons. engring. firm J. Roy Fraser & Assos., Atlanta, 1964—. Served with AUS, 1942-45; ETO.

Registered profl. engr., Ga., Fla., N.C., S.C. Recipient Lincoln Fedn. award for paper, 1972. Mem. Am. Soc. C.E. (Ga. treas., bd. dirs., 1958-62), Nat. Soc. Profl. Engrs., Prestressed Concrete Inst. Presbyn. (supt. Sunday Sch. 1957-62). Contbr. articles to profl. jours. Designer, engr. for 2 longest permanent overland belt conveyors in world, Ada, Okla., 1958-59, Reynolds, Jamaica, West Indies, 1967-68. Home: 3426 Finesse Dr Decatur GA 30032 Office: Hensley-Schmidt Inc 290 Interstate Northern Pkwy Atlanta GA 30339

FRASER, THOMAS AUGUSTUS, JR., bishop; b. Atlanta, Apr. 17, 1915; s. Thomas Augustus and Lena Lee (Connell) F.; B.A., Hobart Coll., 1938, S.T.D., 1965; B.D., Va. Theol. Sem., 1941, D.D., 1960; special student U. Jena (Germany), 1937; D.D., U. of South 1960, Wake Forest Coll., 1961; m. Marjorie Louise Rimbach, May 29, 1943; children—Thomas Augustus III, Constance Louise Fraser. Ordained to ministry Episcopal Ch. as deacon, 1941, priest, 1942, bishop, 1960; missionary Diocese L.I., N.Y., 1941-42; sec., chaplain Bishop of L.I., 1942; sr. asst., N.Y.C., 1942-44; rector in Alexandria, Va., 1944-51, Winston-Salem, N.C., 1951-60; bishop coadjutor Diocese of N.C., Raleigh, 1960-65, diocesan bishop, 1965—. Mem. edn. com. Anglican Cong., Toronto, Can., 1963; chmn. joint commn. on edn. Holy Orders Am. Episcopal Ch.; sec. commn. on priesthood Lambeth Conf., 1968. Mem. Community Nursing, Alexandria, Va., 1944-50, Winston-Salem, N.C., 1951-60, Alcoholic Rehab., Winston-Salem, 1954-59; United Fund, Winston-Salem, 1957-60, Family and Child Welfare, Winston-Salem, 1955-57, Children's Psychol. Clinic, Winston-Salem, 1955-57. Trustee, U. of South, Sewanee, Tenn., St. Mary's Jr. College, Raleigh, N.C.; chmn. bd. trustees St. Augustine's Coll., Raleigh. Mem. exec. com. Gov.'s Commn. on Piedmont Crescent, 1964—. Mem. Tau Kappa Alpha, Sigma Chi. Home: 1200 Glen Eden Dr Raleigh NC 27609 Office: Diocesan House 201 St Albans Dr Raleigh NC 27609

FRASER, WHITMAN, physician; b. Wichita Falls, Tex., Oct. 24, 1926; s. Wallace Winn and Jen (Whitman) F.; student Okla. A. and M. U., 1944, Va. Poly. Inst., 1945, Midwestern U., Wichita Falls, 1947, Rice Inst., 1947-50; B.A., U. Tex., 1952, M.D., 1956; m. Mary Lou Snead, Mar. 23, 1951; children—Sherry Lynn, Mary Gwynn, Clint. Sr. asst. surgeon USPHS Hosps., New Orleans, 1956-57, Savannah, Ga., 1957-58; individual practice gen. medicine, Hinesville, Ga., 1958—; chief of staff Liberty Meml. Hosp., 1961—. Chmn. Liberty County Bd. Health, 1963—; organizer, speaker Liberty County Com. on Drug Abuse, 1970—. City councilman, Hinesville, 1963-67; del. Republican State Conv., 1964; county chmn. Rep. Party, 1968—. Trustee Rabun Gap-Nacoochie Sch. Served with AUS, 1944-47; PTO. Mem. Am. Assn. Physicians and Surgeons, Savannah Presbytery Men of the Ch. (pres. 1968). Presbyn. (elder). Address: PO Box 406 Hinesville GA 31313

FRASHER, JAMES HOWARD, petroleum exploration co. exec.; b. Gardner, Colo., Mar. 28, 1919; s. Jonah J. and Susan C. (Simms) F.; student Colo. State U., 1936-41; m. Venna Singleton, Nov. 19, 1946; children—James Howard, Linda S., Barbara A. With Nat. Geophys. and Teledyne Exploration, geophysicists, Houston, 1946—, pres., 1970—. Served with USAAF, 1942-45. Decorated Bronze Star. Mem. Soc. Exploration Geophysicists, Am. Assn. Petroleum Geologists, European Soc. Exploration Geophysicists, Internat. Assn. Geophys. Contractors (treas. 1971-72), Houston C. of C. Club: Lakeside Country. Home: 14751 Quail Grove St Houston TX 77024 Office: 5825 Chimney Rock Rd Houston TX 77036

FRASIER, RALPH KENNEDY, lawyer, bank exec.; b. Winston-Salem, N.C., Sept. 16, 1938; s. LeRoy Benjamin and Katheryn O. (Kennedy) F.; B.S. in Bus. Adminstrn., N.C. Central U., 1962, J.D., 1965; m. Annie Mae Spaulding, Sept. 16, 1961; children—Karen Denise, Gail Spaulding, Ralph Kennedy, Jr., Keith Lowery. Admitted to N.C. bar, 1965; legal asst. Wachovia Bank & Trust Co., Winston-Salem, 1965-66, asst. sec., 1966-68, asst. v.p., 1968-69, v.p., mgr. legal dept., 1969-70; v.p., asso. gen. counsel Wachovia Corp. (parent co. Wachovia Bank & Trust Co.). 1970. Bd. dirs. Family Services, Inc., 1966—, asst. sec., 1967-68, chmn. pub. relations com., 1968-69; vice chmn. Winston-Salem Transit Authority, 1968—; bd. dirs. Research for Advancement Personalities, Inc., N.C. United Community Services, Inc.; bd. dirs., sec. Winston-Salem Citizens for Fair Housing, 1969—. Served with AUS, 1958-60. Mem. N.C., Forsyth County bar assns., Southeastern Lawyers Assn., Am. Bar Assn., Greater Winston-Salem C. of C., N.A.A.C.P. (mem. exec. bd. 1966-67), Alpha Pi Lambda, Alpha Phi Alpha. Home: 3222 Pennington Lane Winston-Salem NC 27106 Office: PO Box 3099 301 N Main St Winston-Salem NC 27102

FRASURE, CHARLES REED, ins. co. agt.; b. Neon, Ky., Aug. 16, 1940; s. Wilburn Reed and Matilda Sue (Johnson) F.; grad. life underwriter course Ashland Jr. Coll., (Ky.), 1965-66; m. Alva Jean Church, Jan. 12, 1963; children—Teresa Jean, Timothy Reed. Retail sales mgr. Patton Lumber Co., Ashland, Ky., 1962-64; agt. Lincoln Inc. Life Ins. Co., 1964, staff mgr., 1964-69, 69-70, indsl. agt., Ashland, Ky., 1970—. Juvenile probation officer Boyd County, Ky., 1971—; mem. Mayors Citizens Adv. Com., 1966-71, Ashland Bd. Zoning and Adjustment, 1969—, vice chmn., 1971—; co-chmn. Uni Govt. Community Heart Fund and Community Chest, 1965-66. Trustee, New Horizons, center for mental retarded, Ashland. Served with USNR, 1958-62. Decorated Am. Sprit Honor Medal; named Key Man, Ashland Jr. C. of C., 1968, Jaycee of Quarter, 1968; recipient Hagan award Ky. Jr. C. of C., 1970, Martin Wardman Meml. award, 1970, award of honor, 1970. Jaycee of the Year Spark Plug award, 1970, Ashland C. of C. (dir. 1969), Ashland Assn. Life Underwriters (pres. 1968), Am. Legion. Home: PO Box 412 Ashland KY 41101 Office: PO Box 327 Ashland KY 41101

FRAY, LLOYD LEE, hosp. adminstr.; b. Decatur, Ill., July 7, 1932; s. Charles Lee and Bessie Vernon (Howe) F.; B.A. in Mgmt., U. Ill., 1955, B.A., 1955; m. Charlotte Brown, Dec. 28, 1955; children—Charlie, Lee, Carol. Bus. mgr. Outlar and Blair Clinic, Wharton, Tex., 1958—; adminstr. Carney Valley Meml. Hosp., Wharton, 1959—. Pres. Coastal Bend Tb Assn., 1970-71, Wharton Tb Assn., 1970, Wharton Little League, 1970; treas. East Wharton County Heart Assn., 1970. Sec. Wharton Indsl. Found., 1970; bd. dirs. Wharton Babe Ruth League, 1971. Served with USAF, 1955-58. Mem. Med. Group Mgmt. Assn., Hosp. Financial Mgmt. Assn., Tex. Assn. Hosp. Accountants, Nat. Rehab. Assn., Tex. Hosp. Assn. (chmn. Gulf Circle area com. 100 1970). Methodist (mem. ofcl. bd. 1959-61). Lion (sec. 1970). Home: 1305 Kelving Way Wharton TX 77488 Office: 3007 N Richmond Rd Wharton TX 77488

FRAZER, JOHN STANLEY, state ofcl.; b. Furman, Ala., Aug. 1, 1911; s. George Stanley and Mary Elizabeth (Williams) F.; student Southwestern Coll., 1928-30; B.A., U. Fla., 1932; M.A., U. N.C., 1933; m. Eleanor Beatrice Carlton, May 19, 1944; 1 dau., Beatrice Carolyn. Sr. personnel technician Ala. Personnel Dept., Montgomery, 1939-41, dep. dir., 1945-53, dir., 1954—; sr. examiner La. Dept. State Civil Service, Baton Rouge, 1941-42; mem. field staff Pub. Adminstrn. Service, Sao Paulo. Brazil, 1953-54. Served from ensign to lt. USN, 1942-45; now lt. comdr. Res. ret. Mem. Pub. Personnel Assn. (chmn. So. Regional Conf. 1959-60, mem. exec. council 1960-64). Democrat. Methodist. Home: Route 1 Box 399 Millbrook AL 36054 Office: State Adminstrv Bldg Montgomery AL 36104

FRAZIER, CHALMER HAYNES, hosp. adminstr.; b. Martin, Ky., Sept. 28, 1911; s. Noah Melvin and Laura (Maggard) F.; B.A., Berea Coll., 1934; M.A., U. Ky., 1939; m. Kathryn Stumbo, Apr. 11, 1935; children—Kay Anne (Mrs. Stephen Wilborn), Elizabeth Lynn (Mrs. John W. Sutherland), William C. Tchr. high sch., 1934-40, prin., 1940-48; supt. schs., Prestonsburg, Ky., 1948-58; adminstr. Prestonsburg (Ky.) Gen. Hosp., 1958—. Recipient Silver Beaver award Boy Scouts Am., 1965. Mem. Am. Coll. Hosp. Adminstrs., Ky. (pres. 1970-71), Bluegrass (pres. 1968-69) hosp. assns. Kiwanian (local pres. 1965-66, lt. gov. div. 1967-68). Home: 102 E Court St Prestonsburg KY 41653 Office: 28 1st Av Prestonsburg Ky 41653

FRAZIER, DWIGHT EAROLL, lab. exec.; b. West Palm Beach, Fla., Apr. 13, 1923; s. Frank James and Josie (Roebuck) F.; B.S., U. Fla., 1948, M.S., 1950; m. Frances Eleanor Berglund, Feb. 13, 1948; children—Frans Earoll, Claire. Bacteriologist, Fla. Bd. Health, Jacksonville, 1948-52, dir. Miami regional lab., 1953-55, 63-66, v.p., gen. mgr. La Huis Clin. Lab., 1955-63, dir. Pesticide Research Lab., 1964-66; pres., dir. Biochemistry Assos. Internat., Miami, Fla., 1966—. Co-investigator Armed Forces Epidemic Bd., 1963-64; clin. asst. prof. preventive medicine U. Miami Sch. Medicine, 1965—; adviser Miami Dade Jr. Coll. Div., 1966-67; cons. pesticide research project Dade County, Fla., 1966-67. Served to 1st lt. F.A., AUS, 1943-47. Mem. Am., Fla. (chmn. lab. sect. 1965) pub. health assns., Am. Soc. Microbiologists (v.p. S. Fla. br. 1966-67), Fla. Soc. Med. Technologists (pres. 1955-56, award 1955). Clubs: Meninak (sec. Miami); Exchange (Jacksonville). Contbr. articles profl. jours. Home: 8615 SW 20th Terrace Miami FL 33155 Office: One NE 19th St Miami FL 33132

FRAZIER, JAMES, JR., govt. ofcl. Dir. civil rights Dept. Transp., Washington. Address: Dept Transportation 400 7th St SW Washington DC 20024*

FRAZIER, JAMES COY, cons. engr.; b. Dodson, Tex., Sept. 29, 1936; s. James Coy and Macie Fern (Ford) F.; B.S., U. Ark., 1958; m. Elaine Marie Camel, July 28, 1959; children—Scott Paul, James Martin. Test engr. McDonnell Aircraft Co., St. Louis, 1958-59; asst. resident engr. Ark. Hwy. Dept., Little Rock, 1959-62, resident engr., Forrest City, Ark., 1962-64; cons. engr., Helena, Ark., 1964—. City engr., Helena, 1967—; engr. Helena Improvement Dist., 1968—. Pres., Helena Mayor's Adv. Com., 1968-69. Mem. Nat., Ark. socs. profl. engrs., Jaycees (pres. 1968-69), Tau Beta Pi, Pi Mu Epsilon. Democrat. Methodist. Home: 832 Arkansas St Helena AR 72342 Office: 706 Cherry St Helena AR 72342

FRAZIER, JO WOOD (MRS. JOHN MARTIN FRAZIER), club woman; b. Batesville, Ark.; d. Jo Shelby and Allie (Johnson) Wood; B.A., Ark. Coll.; M.A. George Peabody Coll. Tchrs., 1931; m. John Martin Frazier, Sept. 4, 1930; 1 dau., Josephine (Mrs. John Kenneth Davidson). Tchr. pub. schs., Batesville, Ark., 1925-30; asst. prof. history U. So. Miss., 1930-32; tchr. Ravenswood Pub. Schs., Palo Alto, Cal., 1950-51, Sacred Heart Parochial Sch., Hattiesburg, Miss., 1954-59. Chpt. vice regent D.A.R. 1967-69, chpt. regent, 1969-71, Miss Am. heritage chmn., 1965-68, state librarian, 1968-71, state chaplain, 1971—; state 1st v.p. Nat. Assn. Parliamentarians, 1965-67; pres. Miss. State Assn. Parliamentarians, 1967-69. Mem. Daus. Am. Colonists, Nat. Geneal. Soc., Children Am. Revolution (state v.p. 1951-54), John Dodd Soc. (sr. pres. 1952-55), Nat. Soc. Colonial Dames XVII Century, Nat. Soc. Magna Charta Dames. Am. Assn. U. Women, Sorosis Lit. Soc. (pres. 1946-47), Delta Kappa Gamma (chpt. parliamentarian 1964-66). Episcopalian. Club: Faculty Wives (pres. 1964-65, parliamentarian 1968, historian 1971-72). Home: 305 Transylvania Av Hattiesburg MS 39401

FRAZIER, JOHN MARTIN, educator; b. Cleveland, Tenn., June 20, 1900; s. Thomas Martin and Louvenia (Westmoreland) F.; student Tenn. Technol. U., 1920-22; B.S., George Peabody Coll. Tchrs., 1927, M.A., 1929; postgrad. U. Chgo., 1933, Stanford, 1950-51. Prin. Flint Springs High Sch., Cleveland, 1922-24, Clarkrange (Tenn.) High Sch., 1923-24, Tassol (Tenn.) High Sch., 1925-26; tchr. sci. high sch., Elizabeth City, N.C., 1927; tchr. biology Tenn. Technol. U., 1928; faculty U. So. Miss., Hattiesburg, 1928-68, ret., dir. field health service for schs., 1946-49, dir. project in applied econs., asso. prof. practical arts, 1949-52, asso. prof. conservation and natural resources, 1952-64, curator Mus. Natural History, dir. Arboretum, 1964-68, asso. prof. dept. sci. edn., 1964-69, asso. prof. emeritus, 1969—, dept. chmn., 1949-64. Served to lt. col. AUS, 1942-46. Mem. A.A.A.S., Am. Edn. Assn., Ecol. Soc. Am., Miss. Ornithol. Soc. (past pres.), S.A.R., Order White Boar, Soil Conservation Soc. Am. Mason. Contbr. column natural history to newspapers. Research on ecol. factors inducing flatheaded apple-tree borers to attack peach trees. Home: 305 Transylvania Av Hattiesburg MS 39401

FRAZIER, SAMUEL DAVID, coll. pres.; b. Blaine, Tenn., July 18, 1931; s. William Dewey and Nancy (Jarvis) F.; A.B., Carson-Newman Coll., 1953; M.S., U. Tenn., 1956; Ph.D., Fla. State U., 1962; m. Bobbye Jeane Frazier, June 3, 1956; children—Nelson David, DeAnne Lynn. Tchr. high sch., 1953; sch. counselor, Jacksonville, Fla., 1956-58; prin. Minta (Tenn.) Sch., 1958-59; admissions counselor U. Ga., 1959-61; dean of students and admissions Young Harris (Ga.) Coll., 1962-65; pres. Peace Coll., Raleigh, N.C., 1965—. Bd. dirs. United Fund; dir. Raleigh Concert Music Assn., 1960. Served with AUS, 1953-55. Mem. N.C. Jr. Coll. Assn. (pres. 1968-70), N.C. Assn. Ind. Colls. (treas., mem. exec. com.), N.C. Assn. Colls. and Univs. (pres. elect 1971-72). Presbyn. (elder). Kiwanian. (dir.). Home: 2017 St Marys St Raleigh NC 27608

FREAS, ANNIE BELLE HAMILTON (MRS. MAURICE HENRY FREAS), constrn. co. exec.; b. Delrose, Tenn.; d. James N. and Emma (McLaughlin) Hamilton; grad. Martin Jr. Coll., Pulaski, Tenn., 1923; m. Maurice Henry Freas, June 6, 1931. Sec. law firm Bass, Berry & Sims, 1923-24; coml. tchr., bookkeeper Martin Coll., 1924-25; bookkeeping machine operator, head accounting dept., asst. comptroller T. L. Herbert & Sons, W. G. Bush & Co., Sangravl Co., Nashville, 1925-58; bookkeeper, co-owner M. H. Freas, gen contractor, Nashville, 1958-63; sec., gen. bookkeeper Freas & Houghland Gen. Contractors, Inc., Nashville, 1963-67; sec.-treas. Freas Constrn. Co., Inc., 1967—; office mgr. Pres. Women of Ch. Downtown Presbyn. Ch., 1961-63, recipient life membership pin, 1964. Mem. Ladies Hermitage Assn., Cheekwood YWCA, Assn. for Preservation Tenn. Antiquities, Tenn. Bot. Gardens and Fine Arts Center. Recipient medal Underwood Typewriter Co., 1923. Mem. Women in Constrn. (pres. Nashville 1964-66, regional dir. 1966-68, mem. nat. bd. dirs. 1966—, named WIC of Year 1965, nat. orgn. and extension chmn.), Internat. Platform Assn. Club: Zonta (treas., dist. chmn. pub. affairs S. and S.W.; chpt. pres, 1970). Address: 3003 Natchez Trace Nashville TN 37215

FREDE, RALPH EDWARD, coll. adminstr.; b. Floydada, Tex., Sept. 28, 1921; s. Elmer Fred and Marjorie (King) F.; B.J., U. Tex., 1943, M.A., 1947; m. Martha Camilla Chambers, Dec. 25, 1946; children—Phyllis, Bethann, Ellen, Sarah Jane. Mgr. pub. relations, edn. Austin (Tex.) C. of C., 1947-48; dir. Student Employment Bur., U. Tex., Austin, 1948-50; state rep. Nat. Found. for Infantile Paralysis, Austin and Jefferson City, Mo., 1950-56; dir. devel., exec. dir. U. Houston Found., 1956-70; dir. devel. and pub. relations Baylor Coll. Medicine, Houston, 1970—; lectr. U. Houston. Pres., bd. dirs. Protestant Charities Houston, 1966-67; bd. dirs. United Fund Houston, 1968; adv. dir. Alley Theater. Served to lt. USNR, 1943-46. Recipient Silver Beaver award Boy Scouts Am., 1950; Exceptional Achievement award Am. Coll. Pub. Relations, 1964, 65; Silver Anvil award Pub. Relations Soc. Am., 1965. Mem. Pub. Relations Soc. Am. (dir.), Am. Coll. Pub. Relations Assn. (dist. chmn. 1969), Press Club Houston, Friars U. Tex., Sigma Delta Chi. Episcopalian. Rotarian. Home: 849 Hickorywood Lane Houston TX 77024

FREDERICK, CAROLYN HALL ESSIG (MRS. HOLMES W FREDERICK), state legislator; b. Atlanta; d. Philip Martin and Lillian (Hall) Essig; A.B., Agnes Scott Coll., 1928; m. Holmes Walter Frederick, Oct. 1, 1933; children—Lynn (Mrs. John Grant Williamson), Rosa Margaret (Mrs. Glen Clayton Smith). Asso., Rich's, Atlanta, 1928-29; advt., promotion dir. Burdine's, Miami, Fla., 1931-33, Jordan Marsh, Boston, 1934; asso. dir. Greenville (S.C.) County Community Chest and Council, 1950-53; pub. relations cons., Greenville, 1954—; mem. S.C. Ho. of Reps., 1967—, sec. Greenville delegation, 1967, 68. Mgr. Greenville (S.C.) Symphony Assn., 1954-70; S.C. state rep. to U.S. com. for UNICEF, 1963-65; mem. masters art teaching program com. Converse Coll., 1961-66; initiator, exec. dir. Arts Festival Greenville, 1963-65; pub. relations dir. Greenville YWCA 1958-64, bd. dirs.; mem. State-Wide Master Planning Com. Nursing Edn., 1971—; adv. com. arts John F. Kennedy Center for Performing Arts, 1970—. Named Outstanding Woman in Community Service, Greenville Piedmont, 1963; Career Woman of Yr., Greenville Zonta, 1967; S.C. Woman of Yr., S.C. Conf. Status Women, 1970. Mem. Nat. League Am. Penwomen, Am. Assn. U. Women (br. pres. 1944-45, 57-58, mem. nat. mass media com. 1958-63, S.C. state pres. 1959-61, mem. nat. nominating com. 1963, bd. dirs. S.C. div.), Aux. S.C. Soc. Profl. Engrs. (charter pres. 1956). Presbyn. Clubs: Women's Republican (dir.), Women's of Greenville (dir.). Home: 326 Chick Springs Rd Greenville SC 29609

FREDERICK, LAFAYETTE, educator; b. Friarspoint, Miss., Mar. 19, 1923; s. James Davis and Ellen (Johnson) F.; B.S., Tuskegee Inst., 1943; M.S., U. Rhode, 1950; Ph.D., Wash. State U., 1952; m. Antoinette Arlene Reed, Dec. 24, 1950; children—Lewis Reed, Karla Mae, David Warren. Asso. prof., prof. biology So. U., Baton Rouge, 1952-62; prof. biology Atlanta U., 1962—, chmn. dept. biology, 1963—. Commr., Commn. on Undergrad. Edn. Biol. Scis., 1970-71; mem. biology achievement test com. Ednl. Testing Service, 1971—. Mem. Southeastern Forestry Research adv. com.; mem. gen. support adv. com. NIH. Trustee Ga. Conservancy. Served with USNR, 1944-46. Recipient 2d Ann. Trustees award for excellence in teaching, 1964. Mem. A.A.A.S., Bot Soc. Am., Mycol. Soc. Am., Am. Phytopathol. Soc., Assn. Southeastern Biologists, So. Appalachian Bot. Club (v.p.), Ga. Acad. Sci. (councilor-at-large 1970—), Sigma Xi, Phi Sigma, Beta Beta Beta, Phi Kappa Phi. Presbyn. Home: 672 Beckwith St SW Atlanta GA 30314 Office: 223 Chestnut St SW Atlanta GA 30314

FREDERICK, PHILIP, JR., physician; b. Atlanta, Ga., Aug. 11, 1929; s. Philip and Mary Ella (Arnold) F.; B.S., U. Richmond, 1950; M.D., Med. Coll. Va., 1954; m. Margaret Ann Peery, June 21, 1958; children—Mary Helen, Clair Peery, Philip III. Intern, U. Minn., 1954-55; resident internal medicine Med. Coll. Va., 1957-59; fellow gastroenteology Ochsner Clinic, New Orleans, 1959-60; practice medicine, specializing in internal medicine and gastroenterology, Richmond, Va., 1960—; mem. staff Med. Coll. Va., Johnston-Willis Hosp., Richmond. Served to lt. USNR, 1955-57. Diplomate Am. Bd Internal Medicine. Fellow A.C.P.; mem. Phi Beta Kappa, Omicron Delta Kappa, Alpha Omega Alpha. Home: 4108 Cambridge Rd Richmond VA 23221 Office: 2208 Monument Av Richmond VA 23220

FREDERICKS, MARY PATE (MRS. GEORGE W. FREDERICKS), librarian; b. Elizabethton, Tenn., Oct. 11, 1912; d. George W. and R. Charlotte (Boothe) Pate; B.S., E. Tenn. State U., 1936; m. George W. Fredericks, July 15, 1932; 1 son, George W. III. Head librarian Mayne Williams Pub. Library, Johnson City, Tenn., 1940—. Mem. Boone Tree Library Club (past sec.), Am., Southeastern, Tenn. library assns. Club: Johnson City Altrusa. Home: Route 1 Sciota Rd Unicoi TN 37692 Office: 205 S Roan St Johnson City TN 73601

FREDERICKSON, EVAN LLOYD, physician, educator; b. Spring Green, Wis., Mar. 1, 1922; s. Edward and Rebecca Lloyd (Jones) F.; B.S., U. Wis., 1947, M.D., 1950; M.S., U. Ia., 1953; m. Ruth Evans Murphey, Sept. 17, 1946; children—Mary Evans (Mrs. Clinton H. Joiner), Helen Lloyd, Edward Dent. Intern, Walter Reed Army Hosp., Washington, 1950-51; resident State U. Ia. Hosps., 1951-53; practice medicine, specializing in anesthesiology, Atlanta, 1965—; instr., asst. prof. U. Kan. Med. Sch., 1953-56, prof., 1959-65; asst. prof., asso. prof. U. Wash. Sch. Medicine, 1956-59; prof., dir. anesthesia research Emory U. Sch. Medicine, Atlanta, 1965—; vis. prof. U. Rochester Sch. Medicine, U. Mo. Sch. Medicine, U. Miami Sch. Medicine, U. Tex. Sch. Medicine, San Antonio. Dir. Computer Dynamics; mem. NIH Tng. Com. Bd. dirs. Immunologic Cancer Research Fund. Served with AUS, 1943-46, 50-51. Diplomate Am. Bd. Anesthesiology. Fellow Am. Coll. Anesthesiologists; mem. Am. Soc. Anesthesiologists, A.M.A., A.A.A.S., Pan Am. Med. Assn. Asso. editor Surveys of Anesthesiology, 1964—, Clin. Anesthesia, 1967—. Contbr. articles profl. jours. Home: 961 Castle Falls Dr NE Atlanta GA 30329

FREDRICKS, SIMON, plastic surgeon; b. N.Y.C., Feb. 14, 1926; s. Samuel and Esther (Baumann) F.; B.A., N.Y.U., 1947, M.B., Chgo. Med. Sch., 1951, M.D., 1952; m. Rhoda Brand, Oct. 30, 1960; children— Marta Allison, Brent David. Intern, Kings County Hosp., Bklyn., 1951-52; resident Nassau Hosp., Mineola, N.Y., 1952-53; resident Baylor U., 1956-58, instr. plastic surgery, 1959-66, clin. asst. prof. plastic surgery, 1966-69, clin. asso. prof. plastic surgery, 1969—; fellow Johns Hopkins Hosp., 1958-59; pvt. practice plastic surgery, Houston, 1959—; mem. staff Meth., Hermann, Meml. Bapt., St. Lukes, St. Joseph's, Pasadena Bayshore, Southmore hosps.; asso. chief plastic surgery Hermann Hosp.; asst. staff plastic surgery sect. St. Luke's Episcopal Hosp.; cons. Ben Taub, VA Hosps., Tex. Inst. Rehab. and Research; mem. courtesy staff 17 hosps. Pres., Collector's Collection, Inc. Served as capt. M.C., USAF, 1953-55. Diplomate Am. Bd. Plastic Surgery. Fellow A.C.S., Internat. Coll. Plastic Surgeons; mem. Am. Soc. Plastic and Reconstructive Surgeons, A.M.A., So., Tex., Harris County med. socs., Am. Assn. Cleft Palate Rehab., Internat. Coll. Surgeons (regional splty. chmn. 1970—), Am. Assn. Physicians and Surgeons, Nat. Rehab. Assn., Brit., Tex. assns. plastic surgeons, Am. Soc. Aesthetic Plastic Surgery (founding mem., nat. sec. 1968-72), Internat. Soc. Aesthetic Plastic Surgery (charter, sec. gen. 1971—, asst. sec. N.Am. Continent), Chgo. Soc. Plastic Surgery (hon.). Contbr. articles to profl. jours. Office: Med Towers Houston TX 77002

FREDRICKSON, ARTHUR ALLAN, newspaper exec.; b. Grand Island, Neb., May 30, 1923; s. Edmond Russell and Jeannette (Burlingame) F.; student Doane Coll., 1940-42; m. Joyce Meredith Walls, June 3, 1949; children—Jeannette Walls, Arthur Allan. Mng. editor Blytheville (Ark.) Courier News, 1950-54, city editor, 1947-49, sports editor, 1946-47, asso. editor, 1949-50; copy editor, state news desk Times Union, Jacksonville, Fla., 1954-60, women's news editor, 1960-67, asst. exec. editor Fla. Pub. Co., Jacksonville, 1967—. Served with USNR, 1942-46. Mem. Fla. Soc. Newspaper Editors. Democrat. Episcopalian. Home: 2918 Princeton Av Jacksonville FL 32210 Office: 1 Riverside Av Jacksonville FL 32202

FREDRICKSON, LUTHER ERICK, veterinarian; b. Ironwood, Mich., Oct. 18, 1912; s. Erick and Maren (Arneson) F.; A.A., Gogebic Jr. Coll., 1934; D.V.M., Mich. State U., 1937; M.P.H., U. Minn., 1954; certificate attendance-Oak Ridge (Tenn.) Inst. Nuclear Studies. 1958, Nat. Communicable Disease Control Center, 1968; m. Mildred Howard, 1962. Dairy sanitarian St. Louis Health div., 1937-40, dairy sanitarian supr., 1940-50, rabies control officer, 1951-53, pub. health veterinarian, 1953-55; milk sanitarian Atlanta Health Dept., 1940-41; field veterinarian Wis. State Dept. Agriculture. Madison, 1941; pub. health veterinarian Tenn. Dept. Pub. Health, Nashville, 1956—; dir. pub. health vet. sect., 1969—; lectr. Ga. Inst. Tech., 1941, St. Louis U., 1955, E. Tenn. State Coll., 1958—, Vanderbilt U., 1962—, Tenn. Tech. U.; cons. Ga. Dept. Health. Named Veterinarian of Yr., Tenn. Vet. Med. Assn., 1969. Mem. Am. Soc. Mammalogists, Am. (mem. sci. program com. 1971—), Tenn. veterinary med. assns., U.S. Livestock Sanitary Assn., Internat. Assn. Milk, Food Sanitarians, Am., Tenn., So. pub. health assns., Conf. Pub. Health Veterinarians (program chmn. 1970), Assn. State Pub. Health Veterinarians (pres. 1962-64). Lutheran. Elk. Club: Collector's Gallery (Blowing Rock, N.C.). Spl. research in brucellosis control, also rabies epizootiology. Home: Apt R323 2131 Elm Hill Pike Nashville TN 37210 Office: 101 Capitol Towers Nashville TN 37219

FREDRICKSON, MILDRED LOUISE HOWARD (MRS. LUTHER E. FREDRICKSON) nursing educator; b. Union City, Tenn.; d. James Albert and Esther (Carter) Howard; Grad. Nurse, U. Tenn., 1944; B.S. in Pub. Health Nursing, U. Mich., 1951; M.A., Memphis State U., 1955; m. Luther E. Fredrickson, Dec. 1, 1962. Pub. health nurse Bedford County Health Dept., 1945, Rutherford County Health Dept., 1947-48, Obion County (Tenn.) Health Dept., 1948-49; dir. div. pub. health nursing Oak Ridge Pub. Health Dept., 1949-53; asso. prof. U. Tenn. Coll. Nursing, Memphis, 1953-67, chmn. dept. pub. health nursing, 1953-63, dir. continuing edn., 1963-66. Vice chmn. Tenn. Bd. Nursing, 1962-64, chmn., 1964-66, sec., cons., 1966-67, exec. dir., 1967—; mem. nursing com. Tenn. Heart Assn., 1963-64; nurse A.R.C., 1944—; vice chmn. Council State Bds. Nursing. Recipient faculty medal U. Tenn., 1944. Fellow Am. Pub. Health Assn. (chmn. field teaching conf. So. br. 1960-62, chmn. nursing sect. 1964-65); mem. Am. (chmn. council state bds. 1972-73), Tenn. (treas. 1952-56, v.p. 1956-60, pres. dist. 1, 1958-62) nurses assns., Nat. League Nursing (accreditation visitor), Tenn. Assn. Student Nurses (adviser). Democrat. Home: Apt R323 2131 Elm Hill Pike Nashville TN 37210 Office: 354 Capitol Hill Bldg 301 7th Av Nashville TN 37219

FREE, ANN COTTRELL, writer; b. Richmond, Va.; d. Emmett Drewry and Emily (Blake) Cottrell; grad. Collegiate Sch. for Girls, Richmond, 1934; student Richmond div. Coll. William and Mary, 1934-36; A.B., Barnard Coll., Columbia, 1938; m. James Stillman Free, Feb. 24, 1950; 1 dau., Elissa. Reporter Richmond Times Dispatch, 1938-40; Washington corr., Newsweek, 1940-41. Chgo. Sun, 1941-43, N.Y. Herald Tribune, 1943-46; pub. information dir. UNRRA China Mission, Shanghai, 1946-47; corr. Middle and Nr. East and Europe, 1947-48; writer-photographer Marshall Plan, Washington and Western Europe, 1949-50; contbr. N. Am. Newspaper Alliance Syndicate, Washington Eve. Star, Washingtonian Mag. Founding mem. Friends Nat. Zoo, Eleanor Roosevelt Meml. Commn.; pres. Nat. Humane Services Fund; mem. adv. com. Council Livestock Protection; mem. editorial bd. Potomac Valley Conservation and Recreation Council; assembly mem. Inst. Ecology. Bd. govs. Montgomery County Human Soc. Recipient Dodd Mead-Boys' Life Writing award, 1963, Albert Schweitzer medal, Animal Welfare Inst., 1963, Jr. Book award certificate Boys Clubs of Am., 1964; Humanitarian of Yr. awards Washington Animal Rescue League, 1971, Montgomery County Humane Soc., 1971. Episcopalian. Clubs: Am. Newspaper Women, Washington Press. Author: Forever the Wild Mare, 1963. Home: 4700 Jamestown Rd Washington DC 20016

FREE, JAMES, newspaper corr.; b. Gordo, Ala., Nov. 5, 1908; s. James S. and Nettie (Bell) F.; A.B., U. Ala., 1929; B.Litt., Columbia, 1930; m. Ann Cottrell, Feb. 24, 1950; 1 dau., Elissa. With Tuscaloosa (Ala.) News, Birmingham (Ala.) News, Richmond (Va.) Times-Dispatch, Washington Star, Chgo. Sun (Washington bur.), 1930-47; Washington corr. Birmingham News, 1947—, Newhouse Nat. Service, 1962—. Served as lt. USNR, World War II, Carribean Sea Frontier and Amphibious Forces, Pacific Ocean Area; capt. Res., now ret. Chmn. Standing Com. of Correspondents, U.S. Capitol, 1959. Mem. Omicron Delta Kappa, Phi Kappa Sigma, Sigma Delta Chi. Democrat. Clubs: Nat. Press, Gridiron, Internat. (Washington. Contbr. to nat. mags., newspaper syndicates. Home: 4700 Jamestown Rd Washington DC 20016 Office: 1750 Pennsylvania Av NW Washington DC 20006

FREEAR, LANDON A., banker; b. Weatherford, Tex., Aug. 25, 1906; s. Robert Everett and Mary Alice (Pierce) F.; grad. high sch.; m. Loraine Bird, June 10, 1936. With First Nat. Bank, Ft. Worth, 1924-32, William N. Edwards & Co., investment bankers, Ft. Worth, 1932-62, Barron McCulloch & Co., investment bankers, Ft. Worth, 1962-65; v.p. Continental Nat. Bank, Ft. Worth, 1965—; dir. R. L. Smith Mfg. Co. Served to maj. USAAF, 1942-46. Mem. Soc. Colonial Wars (sec. Tex.). Home: 4021 El Campo St Fort Worth TX 76107 Office: PO Box 910 Fort Worth TX 76101

FREED, SAMUEL WELLS, investment co. exec.; b. Washington, Jan. 7, 1926; s. Samuel and Della (Wells) F.; B.A., U. N.C., 1949, M.S., 1951; m. Shirley Ann Weber, Sept. 7, 1955; children—Deborah Ann, David Alan. Research, Fort Detrick, Md., 1951-59; entered brokerage bus., 1959; v.p., dir. Pressman, Frohlich & Frost, Inc., Washington, 1966—; dir. Sentinel Resources Corp. Allied mem. N.Y. and Am. stock exchanges, 1966; mem. Phila., Balt. stock exchanges, 1971. Served with USNR, 1943-46. Mem. Bond Club Washington, Mut. Fund Council Million Dollar Producers, Zeta Beta Tau. Mason (Shriner). Club: Touchdown (Washington). Home: 9019 LeVelle Dr Chevy Chase MD 20015 Office: 1100 17th St NW Washington DC 20036

FREEDLAND, JACOB BERKE, dentist; b. Wilmington, N.C., Mar. 19, 1913; s. Morris and Molly (Burke) F.; student U. N.C., 1930-32; D.D.S., Emory U., 1936; m. Charlotte Soble, Sept. 7, 1939; children—Martin Berke, Leslie Ann (Mrs. Malcolm Frederick Locke, Jr.). Individual practice gen. dentistry, Charlotte, N.C., 1938-41, 46-63, specializing in endodontics, Charlotte, 1963—; cons., lectr. USN Dental Corps, U.S. Army Dental Corps, Naval Dental Sch., Nat. Naval Med. Center, Bethesda, Md., U.S. Naval Hosp., Portsmouth, Ft. Knox, Ky., Ft. Benning, Ga., Ft. Bragg, N.C., U.S. Army Inst. Dental Research; cons. Am. Dental Assn. Council on Dental Edn.; prof. dept. endodontics U. N.C. Sch. Dentistry. Bd. dirs. Charlotte Symphony, Jr. Achievement Am., Mecklenburg County chpt. A.R.C., Blood Bank, Am. Assn. Endodontists Endowment and Meml. Found., Dental Found. N.C., John Motley Morehead Found. Selection Com. Served to maj., Dental Corps, AUS, 1941-46; ETO. Recipient Thomas P. Hinman medallion for meritorious service, 1964, Charlotte Dental Soc. award, 1965, Am. Assn. Endodontists Appreciation award, 1967, Thomas P. Hinman Appreciation award, 1969. Deplomate Am. Bd. Endodontics. Fellow Am. Coll. Dentists; mem. Internat. Coll. Dentists, Am. Assn. Endodontists (past pres.), Am. Dental Assn., N.C. 2d Dist. Dental Soc. (past pres.), Am. Acad. Dental Medicine (past v.p.), Am. Acad. Dental Practice (past dir., editor), Am. Inst. Oral Scis. (past chmn.), Am. Acad. Oral Pathology, Internat. Assn. Dental Research, Omicron Kappa Upsilon. Mem. editorial bd. Jour. of Oral Surgery, Oral Medicine and Oral Pathology, 1964—. Contbr. articles profl. jours. Home: 811 Hempstead Pl Charlotte NC 28207 Office: Doctors Bldg 1012 Kings Dr Charlotte NC 28207

FREEDMAN, BEN, physician, state ofcl.; b. Wilmington, Del., Apr. 11, 1905; s. David and Henrietta (Kiel) F.; student Loyola U., New Orleans, 1926-28; M.D., Tulane U., 1935; M.P.H., Johns Hopkins, 1940; m. Miriam Katz, Aug. 17, 1931. Intern, resident Hotel Dieu, New Orleans, 1935-36; with La. Dept. Health, New Orleans, 1936—, dir. Bur. Health Conservation, 1967—; prof. pub. health adminstrn. dept. tropical medicine and pub. health Tulane U. Med. Sch., New Orleans, 1949—. Cons. USPHS, 1951-64. Served with AUS, 1942-44. Recipient Medal of Freedom (Norway). Fellow Am. Pub. Health Assn. (exec. com., governing council So. br., past pres. So. br., chmn. com. pub. health history); mem. A.A.A.S., A.M.A., Am. Acad. Polit. and Social Scis., Nat. Assn. Sanitarians (citation 1960, Mangold award 1969), La. state Med Soc., Am. Assn. for History Medicine, Assn., State Maternal and Child Health and Crippled Children Dirs. (exec. com., pres. elect), Assn. Research Health Depts. (pres.), Am. Assn. Pub. Health Physicians (past pres., editor Bull. 1958—, Distinguished Service award 1966), La. Pub. Health Assn. (past pres., Dr. C. B. White Meml. award 1954, Dr. Edward Hall Barton Meml. award 1958), La. Assn. for Retarded Children, La. Heart Assn., Delta Omega (chmn. publs. com. 1959—). Author: Sanitary Inspector's Manual, 1942; Sanitarians's Handbook: Theory and Administrative Practice, 1957. Contbr. numerous articles to pub. health and med. jours. Home: 1321 Frankfort St New Orleans LA 70122 Office: State Office Bldg 325 Loyola Av New Orleans LA 70112

FREEDMAN, JOSEPH, internat. agy. ofcl.; b. Brighton, Mass., Oct. 16, 1923; s. Edwin Arkiva and Fanny (Wine) F.; B.S. in Pub. Health Engrng., Ga. Sch. Tech., 1943; M.S. in San. Engrng. (fellow), U. N.C., 1945; S.M. in San. Engrng., Harvard, 1955; groundwater devel. certificate U. Minn., 1959; m. Emily Ann Feltman, Nov. 4, 1959. Jr. san. engr. Homes & Narver Co., Okinawa, 1946-48; chief san. engr. Mariannas Bonins Command Dept. Army, Guam, 1948-49; exec., partner Continental Devel. Co., Mexico, 1949-50, 51-52; designer Charles T. Main., Inc., Boston, 1950-51, 52-53; san. engr. adviser to Govt. Honduras, WHO, Tegucigalpa, 1955-61; san. engr., adviser Govt. of Bolivia AID, 1961-63, Govt. of Paraguay, 1963; sr. specialist project analysis div. Interam. Devel. Bank, 1964—. Registered profl. engr., Mass. Mem. Am. Soc. C.E., Inter-Am. Soc. San. Engrs., Royal Soc. Health, Am. Water Works Assn., Am. Pub. Works Assn., Sigma Xi, Phi Kappa Phi, Phi Eta Sigma. Home: 6504 Elgin Lane Bethesda MD 20034 Office: 808 17th St NW Washington DC 20577

FREEDMAN, MAX, columnist Daily News Washington, 1962—. Recipient Internat. Freedom award, Internat. Freedom Festival, Windsor, Ont.

FREEDMAN, WALTER, lawyer; b. St. Louis, 1914; A.B., Washington U., 1937, LL.B., 1937; LL.M., Harvard, 1938. Admitted to Mo. bar, 1947, U.S. Supreme Ct. bar, 1940, D.C. bar, 1946; atty. SEC, 1938-41; chief legal research sect. Bituminous Coal div., 1941-42; chief counsel Office Export Control, 1942-43; dep. dir., then dir. export control Fgn. Econ. Adminstrn., 1943-45; now mem. firm Freedman, Levy, Kroll & Simonds, Washington. Mem. Bar Assn. D.C., Fed., Am. bar assns., Am. Law Inst., Order Coif, Phi Beta Kappa, Omicron Delta Kappa. Editor-in-chief Washington U. Law Quar., 1936-37. Address: Freedman Levy Krolls & Simonds 1730 K St NW Washington DC 20006*

FREEMAN, BERNICE, educator; b. LaGrange, Ga., Aug. 8, 1909; d. Thomas Norman and Everette (Jenkins) Freeman; A.B., Tift Coll., 1930; M.A. in English, U. N.C., 1932; Ed.D. in English, Columbia, 1952. Tchr. math. pub. schs., Dublin, Ga., 1930-31; tchr. social studies pub. schs., La Grange, Ga., 1932-42; tchr. social studies, English Peabody Demonstration Sch., Ga. State Coll. Women, 1942-48, prin., tchr. 1948-51; dir. curriculum Troup County Schs., La Grange, 1951-67; asso. prof. edn. West Ga. Coll., Carrollton, Ga.; 1967-69, prof. edn., 1969—, also coordinator secondary edn. Del. Washington Conf. Academically Talented, 1958, White House Conf. Children and Youth, 1960; chmn. English curriculum guide com., Ga. Pub. Schs., 1960-64, mem. steering com., English curriculum guide com., 1965-68; pres. Ga. Dept. Instructional Supervision, 1961-62, co-dir. English Study in Ga., 1951-62. Bd. dirs. Troup-Harris-Cowetta Regional Library. Mem. League Women Voters (pres. Carrollton br. 1970-72), Am. Assn. U. Women (pres. Ga. div. 1957-59), Ga. Council Tchrs. English (pres. 1947-48), Ga. Writers Assn., Ga. Acad. Social Scis., Nat. Council Tchrs. English, Pi Lambda Theta, Kappa Delta Pi, Pi Gamma Mu, Delta Kappa Gamma. Preparation ednl. materials (with Lydia A. Thomas) The Reader's Digest, N.E.A. (exec. com. dept. rural education 1965-69), Reading Skill Builder, Grade 5, Part 3, 1960. Home: 305 Park Av LaGrange GA 30240 Office: West Ga Coll Carrollton GA 30117

FREEMAN, CHARLES MADDRY, govt. ofcl.; b. Raleigh, N.C., Nov. 1, 1921; s. Lemuel Elmer MacMillan and Katherine (Parker) F.; B.A., Wake Forest Coll., 1942; M.A., U. N.C., 1944; Ph.D., N.C. State Coll., 1956; m. Flora Elizabeth Navitt, May 11, 1950; children—Renuka, Sunil Kumar, Anita. Asso. prof. rural sociology Pa. State U. extension at University Park, 1958-61; program leader Nat. 4-H Club Found., Washington, 1961-69; asso. community educator Cooperative Extension Service, Fed. City Coll., Washington, 1969—. Fulbright prof., India, 1956-58; Am. Inst. Indian studies research fellow, 1965. Mem. Adult Edn. Assn., Rural Indian sociol. socs., Mem. Soc. of Friends. Author: Adventures in Citizenship: A Leader's Handbook, 1968. Home: 1603 Sherwood Rd Silver Spring MD 20902 Office: 1424 K St NW Washington DC 20005

FREEMAN, DAVID, lawyer, orgn. exec.; b. Los Angeles, Oct. 15, 1927; s. David and Viola Eretta (Grubbs) F.; student U. Cal. at Berkeley, 1951-52; B.B.A., U. Mich., 1952; J.D., Stanford, 1955; m. Anna Johanne Horton, Aug. 6, 1949. Admitted to Cal. bar, 1955; practiced in Los Angeles, 1955-60; mem. firm Trippet, Yoakum, Stearns & Ballantine; asst. dean sch. Law, asso. dir. univ. devel. Stanford, 1960-64; tng. officer, coordinator, S. Am. tng. Peace Corps, Washington, 1964, dep. asso. dir. Asia, Near East, N. Africa div. U. Relations and Tng., 1964-66; owner, dir. Edn. Process Innovation Center, Washington, 1966-68, also cons.; owner, sr. exec. Mgmt. Talent Bank, cons. firm, 1970-71; chief hearing examiner, spl. counsel Action Agy., Washington 1971—. Mem. Town Hall, Los Angeles, 1955-61; exec. dir Washington Met. Area Jobs Council, Inc., 1967-68; mem. panel of arbitrators Fed. Mediation and Conciliation Service. Asso. in urban affairs Nat. Inst. Pub. Affairs, 1967; admitted to U.S. Supreme Ct. bar; exec. dir. Merit Employment and Tng. Council Met. Washington Bd. Trade, 1968-70; commr. Econ. Opportunity Commn., Alexandria, Va., 1969-71; mem. Washington Urban Coalition Task Force on Expanding Econ. Opportunity, 1969-70. Served with USNR, 1945-46. Recipient Indigent Criminal Defense citation Los Angeles Bar Assn., 1957-58. Mem. Am. (standing com. on econs. law practice 1963-64), Cal., (com. on group legal services 1963-64), Palo Alto (past chmn. constl. rights adv. com.), Los Angeles (past chmn. com. def. indigent criminal defendants) bar assns., Delta Theta Tau, Phi Alpha Delta. Author, editor: Stanford Law Sch. Fund President's Report, 1960-64; A Unified System for Employment Resources, 1969. Editor: Stanford Lawyers Directory, 1963. Home: 726 S Lee St Alexandria VA 22314 Office: 806 Connecticut Av NW Washington DC 20525

FREEMAN, DONALD WILFORD, financial exec.; b. Brooksville, Fla., Sept. 25, 1929; s. Fred Maxwell and Dovie (Keef) F.; B.S., U. Ala., 1953, LL.B., 1953; LL.M., N.Y. U., 1957; m. Ruby Jane Lewis, Aug. 6, 1931; children—Clifton Lewis, Susan Anne. Accountant Ernst & Ernst, Atlanta, 1953-55; admitted to Ala. bar, 1953; tax atty. Office Chief Counsel, U.S. Treasury Dept., N.Y.C., 1955-57, West Point Mfg. Co. (Ga.), 1957-58; asst. treas. Ryder System, Inc., Miami, Fla., 1958-61; v.p., dir., Henderson's Portion Pak, Inc., 1961-63; pres. Biscayne Capital Corp., 1963-66; asso. Lazard Freres & Co., N.Y.C., 1967-69; financial adviser James A. Ryder & Assos., Miami, 1969—. Served with AUS, 1946-48; PTO. C.P.A., Ga. Mem. Fla. Inst. C.P.A.'s, Phi Kappa Sigma, Beta Gamma Sigma. Episcopalian. Home: 13026 Nevada St Coral Gables FL 33156 Office: 2701 S Bayshore Dr Miami FL 33133

FREEMAN, EDWARD, newspaper editor; b. Vanndale, Ark., Mar. 11, 1914; s. C. K. and Mary (Craig) F.; A.B., Murray State Coll., 1937; m. Lois Aline Farley, July 13, 1939; children—Edward Michael, Mary Elizabeth. Editor, Ledger & Times, Murray, Ky., 1937-40, Inland Empire News, Richland, Wash., 1940; reporter Nashville Tennessean, 1940-43, city editor, 1943-64, mng. editor, 1964—. Served from ensign to lt (j.g.), USNR, 1944-46. Mem. Sigma Delta Chi. Home: 4960 Stillwood Dr Nashville TN 37211 Office: 1100 Broadway Nashville TN 37201

FREEMAN, EDWIN RUTHVEN, govt. ofcl.; b. San Diego, Aug. 6, 1917; s. Edwin Ruthven and Elizabeth (Woods) F.; A.B., U. Cal. at Berkeley, 1941; M.A., Georgetown U., 1948; m. Mary Douglas Blackwood, Mar. 2, 1951; children—Veronica Woods, William Patrick, Margaret Michelle. Instr. polit. sci. Pottsville, Pa. State U., 1947-48; intelligence research analyst, specialist State Dept., Washington, 1948-60; research specialist U.S. I.A., Washington, 1960—. Served to lt.(j.g.) USNR, 1942-46. Home: 605 Manor Dr NE Vienna VA 22180 Office: 1750 Pennsylvania Av NW Washington DC 22180

FREEMAN, GEORGE CLEMON, JR., lawyer; b. Birmingham, Ala., Jan. 3, 1929; s. George Clemon and Annie Laura (Gill) F.; B.A. magna cum laude, Vanderbilt U., 1950; LL.B., Yale, 1956; m. Anne Colston Hobson, Dec. 6, 1958; children—Anne Colston, George Clemon III, Joseph Reid Anderson. Admitted to Ala. bar, 1956, Va. bar, 1958; law clk. to Justice Black, U.S. Supreme Ct., 1956; asso. firm Hunton, Williams, Gay, Powell & Gibson, Richmond, Va., 1957-62, partner, 1962—. Cons. Va. Outdoor Recreation Study Commn. Va. Gen. Assembly, 1964-65, gov's. spl. com. on water resources, 1966. Mem. Richmond Democratic Com., 1964—, chmn., 1969-72. Bd. dirs. Richmond Symphony, 1958-64, sec., 1960-64; trustee Am. the Beautiful Fund. Served to lt. (j.g.) USNR, 1951-54. Mem. Am. (chmn. standing com. on facilities Law Library of Congress 1967—, mem. continuing legal edn. com. sect. corporate banking and bus. law 1966—, chmn. trade assn. com. 1969—), Va., Richmond bar assns., Am. Law Inst., Nature Conservany (chmn. Va. chpt. 1962-64), Phi Beta Kappa, Phi Delta Phi, Omicron Delta Kappa. Episcopalian. Clubs: Country, Deep Run Hunt (Richmond); Knickerbocker (N.Y.C.). Contbr. articles to profl. jours. Home: 10 Paxton Rd Richmond VA 23226 Office: 700 E Main St Richmond VA 23226

FREEMAN, HARRY LYNWOOD, accountant; b. Los Angeles, May 5, 1920; s. Edward Church and Mildred Eaton (Noyes) F.; B.S., U. Cal. at Los Angeles, 1942; m. Ruth Turner, Feb. 14, 1941; children—Tracy Ruth (Mrs. Richard W. Flatow), Martin Harry. With Price Waterhouse & Co., C.P.A.'s, 1942—, partner, Mexico City, 1956—. Chmn. auditing com. Am. British Cowdray Hosp., 1962-68. Bd. dirs., mem. finance exec. com. Inst. Mexicano-Norteamericano de Relaciones Culturales, 1960—; bd. dirs., treas. YMCA Mexico. Served with AUS, 1944-46. C.P.A., 7 states. Mem. Am. Inst. C.P.A.'s, Cal. Soc. C.P.A.'s Am. C. of C. Mexico (past pres.), U.S. C. of C. (Mexico-U.S. com. internat. com.), Assn. Am. Chambers Commerce in Latin Am. (past pres., treas.). Clubs: Bankers, University (Mexico City); Chapultepec Golf (Lomas, Mexico). Home: Sierra Paracaima 855 Mexico City 10 Mexico Office: Paseo de la Reforma 243 Mexico City 5 Mexico

FREEMAN, JAMES POLK, JR., dentist; b. Knoxville, Tenn., Mar. 31, 1929; s. James Polk and Dovie Mae (Jones) F.; student E. Tenn. State Coll., 1950; D.D.S., U. Tenn., 1954; m. Joyce Joan Leinart, June 26, 1955; children—James Polk III, Daniel, Joyce. Asso., Glen A. Bibee, Fountain City, Tenn., 1954-55; practice dentistry, LaFollette, Tenn., 1958—; mem. dental staff E. Tenn. Bapt. Hosp., 1954-55, 57—, chief surg. dental dept., 1960; mem. dental staff LaFollette Community Hosp., 1959—. Committeeman, troop 23 Boy Scouts Am., LaFollette, 1960—; chmn. Campbell County Indsl. Com., 1966-67. Vice mayor, chmn. finances City of LaFollette, 1967-71, mayor, 1971—. Bd. dirs. Clinch Powell River Valley Assn.; bd. dirs. LaFollette Housing Authority, 1964—. Served with USAF, 1955-57. Mem. Campbell County Health Dept. Mem. Am., Tenn., 2d Dist. (v.p. 1962, mem. exec. council 1963, 65-68) dental assns., Bapt. Brotherhood (sec. 1965-66), Powells Valley Conservation League, Pierre Fauchard Acad. Dentistry, LaFollette C. of C. (pres. 1966-67, dir. 1969—), Delta Tau Delta, Xi Psi Phi. Baptist (trustee 1961—, chmn. bd. trustees 1962-64). Mason (32 deg, Shriner). Clubs: Optimist (charter mem., past dir., pres. 1962-63, chmn. membership and attendance com. dist. 11 1963-64, lt. gov. Tenn. dist. 1965-66). Home: 312 W Central Av LaFollette TN 37766 Office: Davis Clinic Bldg LaFollette TN 37766

FREEMAN, JOHN W., scientist. Mem. faculty dept. space sci. Rice U., Houston, also scientist NASA. Home: 9206 Mullins St Houston TX 77035 Office: Rice U 6100 Main St Houston TX 77001*

FREEMAN, JOHN WRIGHT, JR., educator; b. Chgo., July 12, 1935; s. John Wright and Evelyn (Laier) F.; B.S., Beloit Coll., 1957; M.S., U. Ia., 1961, Ph.D. in Physics, 1963; postgrad. U. Minn., 1957-58; m. Phyllis Ann Palmer, June 10, 1957; children—Laura, David. Staff scientist NASA, Washington, 1963-64; research asso. Rice U., Houston, 1964-65, asst. prof., 1965-68, asso. prof. space sci., 1968-72, prof., 1972—; NSF vis. scientist, 1965—; vis. scientist Royal Inst. Tech., Stockholm, Sweden, U. Bern (Switzerland), 1972; cons. numerous spacecraft missions NASA. U.S. Steel Found. fellow, 1958-61. Recipient Apollo Achievement award NASA, 1969. Mem. Am. Geophys. Union, A.A.A.S., Internat. Union Geophysics and Geodesy, Sigma Alpha Epsilon. Prin. investigator numerous space experiments including a lunar surface experiment deployed by Apollo 12, 14, and 15 astronauts. Home: 9206 Mullins St Houston TX 77035

FREEMAN, JOSEPH H., economist-statistician; b. N.Y.C., Aug. 21, 1914; s. Harry and Jeanet (Guterman) Feingold; student U. Ariz., 1932-33, U. Mich., 1933-35; B.A., Clark U., 1936, M.A., 1937; postgrad. Am. U., 1946-56; m. Cecile E. Freeman, Sept. 14, 1941; children— Diane Jean, Lois Alison. Asst. regional dir., regional dir. Bldg. Permits Survey, Bur. of Labor Statistics, U.S. Dept. of Labor, Washington, 1938-41; economist WPB, 1941-46, Housing & Home Finance Agy., 1946-48; customer relations dir. Hecht Co., Washington, 1948-57; chief consumer price indexes br. Bur. Labor Statistics, U.S. Dept. of Labor, Washington, 1957-60; chief export statistics br. Fgn. Trade div. Bur. of Census, U.S. Dept. Commerce, 1960-63, asst. div. chief, 1963—; cons. Am. U., 1950-53, lectr., 1957-61. Served with USAAF, 1943-46. Mem. Am. Econ. Assn., Am. Statis. Assn. Contbr. articles to profl. jours. Home: 6805 Millwood Rd Bethesda MD 20034 Office: Fgn Trade Div Bur of Census US Dept of Commerce Washington DC 20233

FREEMAN, LESTER, assn. exec. Exec. v.p. Greater Miami (Fla.) C. of C. Address: 1200 Biscayne Blvd Miami FL 33132*

FREEMAN, MILTON V., lawyer; b. N.Y.C., Nov. 16, 1911; s. Samuel and Celia (Gelfand) F.; A.B., Coll. City of N.Y., 1931; LL.B., Columbia, 1934; m. Phyllis Young, Dec. 19, 1937; children—Nancy Lois (Mrs. Gans), Daniel Martin, Andrew Samuel, Amy Martha. Admitted to N.Y. bar, 1934; D.C. bar, 1946, U.S. Supreme Ct. bar, 1943; with gen. counsel's office, S.E.C., 1934-42, asst. solicitor, 1942-46; with securities div., F.T.C., 1934; practice with firm Arnold & Fortas, Arnold, Fortas & Porter, Arnold & Porter, Washington, 1946—. Lectr. law schs. Trustee, Inst. for Internat. and Fgn. Trade Law, Georgetown U. Mem. Am., D.C., Fed. bar. assns. Home: 3405 Woolsey Dr Chevy Chase MD 20015 Office: 1229 19th St NW Washington DC 20036

FREEMAN, NELSON WRIGHT, corp. exec.; b. Charleston, Ill., Aug. 6, 1908; s. Ernest and Mabel (Wright) F.; student U. Ill.; m. Norma Greenlese, Sept. 11, 1928; children—Nancy (Mrs. Henry Hughes), Jody Greenwood. Br. mgr. Univeral Credit Corp., Detroit, 1929-34; pres., gen. mgr. Freeman & Riesen Motor Co., Milw., 1934-38; mgr. Assos. Investment Co., Houston, 1938-42; personnel and safety dir. Lummus Co., 1942-43; mgr. personnel dept. Tenn. Gas Transmission Co. (co. name now Tenneco. Inc.), 1943-47, asst. to pres., 1947-50, v.p., 1950-54, sr. v.p., 1954-59, pres., dir., 1966—, also chief exec. officer, 1968—; pres. Midwestern Gas Transmission Co., 1954-61; natural gas cons., 1962-64; pres., dir. Houston Nat. Bank, 1964-66, dir., chmn. exec. com., 1966—; chmn. bd., dir. J. I. Case Co., Newport News Shipbldg. & Dry Dock Co. Tenneco Corp., Midwestern Gas Transmission Co., East Tenn. Natural Gas Co., Channel Industries Gas Co.; dir. Tenneco Oil Co., Tenn. Gas Transmission Co., Packaging Corp. of Am., Tenneco Internat., Inc., Heggblade-Marguleas-Tenneco, Inc., Tenneco West, Inc.; Tenneco Properties, Inc., Tenneco Realty, Inc., Tenneco Walker Mfg. Co.; pres., dir. Houston Nat. Co.; dir. Petro-Tex Chem. Corp., Phila. Life Ins. Co., Tenn. Life Ins. Co., Farmers Nat. Bank, Brenham, Tex.; adv. dir. Bayshore Nat. Bank, LaPorte, Tex. Bd. dirs. U. St. Thomas, Houston; trustee United Fund of Houston and Harris County; chmn. 1970 and 1971 Payroll Savs. Bond Drive, Houston-Harris County. Mem. Houston C. of C. (dir.). Clubs: River Oaks, Ramada (Houston); Links, Board Room (N.Y.); Chicago; Burning Tree (Washington). Home: 1233 Post Oak Park Dr Houston TX Office: Tenneco Bldg Houston TX 77002

FREEMAN, RICHARD W(EST), beverage mfr.; b. New Orleans, Jan. 4, 1913; s. Alfred Bird and Ella Moore (West) F.; B.B.A., U. Tulane U., 1934; m. Montine McDaniel, Oct. 15, 1936; children—Richard W., Louis, Tina. Salesman, Milw. Coca-Cola Bottling Co., 1934-35; asst. to pres. Gt. Lakes Coca Cola Bottling Co., 1936-38; pres. Wis. Coca Cola Bottling Co., also plants in Mich., Ohio, 1938-42; dir. Coca Cola Co., Chgo., 1938-42, 58-61; asst. to pres. La. Coca Cola Bottling Co., Ltd., 1946-47, pres., 1947-70, chmn. bd., 1971—; dir. Coca Cola Bottling Co., Lake Charles, La., 1950—; chmn. finance com. Delta Air Lines, Atlanta; dir. Hibernia Nat. Bank, Coca Cola Co., Middle States Utilities, New Orleans Pub. Service, Inc. Pres., dir. Bur. Govtl. Research; mem. Miss. River Bridge Commn., 1954-65; pres. New Orleans Community Chest, 1952; mem. Bd. Liquidation City Debt, New Orleans. Trustee Alton Ochsner Med. Found.; bd. adminstrs. Tulane U.; bd. dirs. YMCA, New Orleans. Mem. S.A.R., Sons Colonial Wars, C. of C., Phi Delta Theta. Democrat. Presbyn. Clubs: International House, Louisiana, Boston, Picwick, Stratford, New Orleans Country, Southern Yacht (New Orleans). Home: 295 Walnut St New Orleans LA 70118 Office: PO Box 50400 New Orleans LA 70150

FREEMAN, SIMON DAVID, ofcl. Pres. Office Sci. and Tech.; b. Chattanooga, Jan. 14, 1926; s. Morris and Lena (Matzkel) F.; B.S. in Civil Engring., Ga. Inst. Tech., 1948; LL.B., U. Tenn., 1956; m. Marianne Beatrice Cohn, Jan. 22, 1950; children—Anita, Stanley, Roger. Admitted to Tenn. bar, 1957, Supreme Ct. bar, 1964, D.C. bar, 1965; engr., atty. TVA, Knoxville, Tenn., 1948-61; asst. to chmn. FPC, 1961-65; partner Swidler & Freeman, Washington, 1966-67; dir. energy policy staff Office Sci. and Tech., Exec. Office of Pres., Washington, 1967-70, asst. dir. for energy, natural resources and environment, 1970—. Served with US Mcht. Marine, 1944-45. Mem. Am., Fed. bar assns., Order Coif, Phi Delta Phi. Club: National Press (Washington). Home: 7211 Pyle Rd Bethesda MD 20034 Office: Office Sci and Tech Exec Office Pres Washington DC 20506

FREEMAN, THOMAS JASPER, librarian; b. nr. Roanoke, Ala., Mar. 29, 1930; s. Carl Jasper and Ellie Mae (Walker) F.; B.S., Jacksonville State U., 1956; M.Ed., Auburn U., 1958; M.A., George Peabody Coll., 1961; m. Marian Laney, Dec. 21, 1956; children—Kevin, Carl. Librarian, Calhoun County Ala. Schs., 1956-61; acquisitions librarian Jacksonville (Ala.) State U., 1961—. Served with AUS, 1951-53. Mem. Ala., Southeastern library assns., Ala. Edn. Assn., Kappa Delta Pi, Kappa Phi Kappa, Sigma Tau Delta. Episcopalian. Home: 719 Bain Av Weaver AL 36277 Office: Romona Wood Library Jacksonville State U Jacksonville AL 36265

FREEMAN, WAYNE WOODROW, editor; b. Pickens County, S.C., Nov. 9, 1916; s. Norman Benjamin and Elizabeth (Jones) F.; student Furman U., 1936-38; Litt.D., Clemson Univ., 1959; m. Tinie Hill, Oct. 10, 1941; children—Martha, Michael Wayne, John David, Benjamin James. Clk., Duke Power Co., Greenville, S.C., 1935-39; reporter Greenville (S.C.) Piedmont, 1939-42, asst. city editor, 1946; state capital corr. Greenville News, 1946-48; editor Piedmont, 1948-55; editor Greenville News, from 1955. Lectr., Furman U., Clemson Coll.; vis. lectr. Limestone Coll. Mem. Gov.'s Commn. on Mental Health Planning; sec. S.C. Special Sch. Com., 1951—; pres. Childrens Center, 1951-54; pres. Community Council, 1949; mem. Govt. Study Com., Greenville County, 1959-60; 1st chmn. bd. trustees United Fund; projects com. County Found. Served with AUS, 1942-46. Member S.C. C. of C. (dir.), Am. Soc. Newspaper Editors, Sigma Delta Chi. Episcopalian (lay leader). Home: 109 Sunset Dr Greenville SC 29605 Office: News Bldg 301 S Main St Greenville SC 29601

FREEMAN, WILLIAM M., educator, govt. ofcl.; b. Selma, Ala.; B.S., U. Denver, also M.A., Ph.D.; M.R. Ed., Dever Sch. Religion; postgrad. (So. Fund fellow) U. So. Cal. Mem. faculty So. U., Baton Rouge, 1957—. Goodwill ambassador U.S. Dept. State, 1959; now rep. State Dept. Confs. Internat. Relations Far East and Middle East. Mem. Omega Psi Phi (scholarship dir.). Baptist. Mason (32). Home: 1755 79th Av Baton Rouge LA 70807*

FREI, EMIL, physician. Research scientist leukemia therapy Nat. Cancer Inst., Bethesda, Md. Address: Nat Cancer Inst 9000 Rockville Park Bethesda MD 20014*

FREIDBERG, EDITH LIPSIG (MRS. HEBALD FREIDBERG), civic worker; b. N.Y.C., Jan. 18, 1920; d. Irving A. and Bertha (Evans) Lipsig; student Radcliffe Coll., 1937-39; LL.B., St. Lawrence U., 1943; m. Selian Hebald, June 28, 1940 (dec. Feb. 1959); children—Anne, Selian; m. 2d, Sidney Freidberg, June 11, 1962. Pres., Forest Knolls Corp., N.Y.C., 1960—, Norman Homes Corp., N.Y.C., 1968—. Nat. sec. Women's Am. Orgn. for Rehab. through Tng., 1950; pres. Radcliffe Club of Washington, 1969, Radcliffe Club, N.Y., 1959, 63; chmn. clubs Radcliffe Alumnae Assn., 1966; mem. founders com. Am. Symphony Orch. N.Y., 1962. Trustee Allergy Found. Am. Fellow Pierpont Morgan Library, N.Y. Home: 1525 34th St NW Washington DC 20007

FREMOUW, GERRIT DANGREMOND, govt. ofcl.; b. Newark, N.Y., Jan. 21, 1909; s. John A. and Ida Jane (Dangremond) F.; B.S. in Civil Engring. cum laude, Clarkson Coll. Tech., 1931, C.E., 1934; m. Ruth Schurink, Nov. 3, 1962; children—William John, Jane Ellen (Mrs. William Swanson). Commd. 1st lt. C.E. U.S. Army, 1942, advanced through grades to col. USAF, 1969; chief missiles and spl. installations br. SHAPE, Paris, France, 1958-59; engr. Hdqrs. 14 Air Force, China, 1944-45; dep. dir. civil engring. Hdqrs. SAC, 1951-58, dep. chief staff civil engring. hdqrs., 1961-69; ret., 1969; cons. engr. Leo Daly Co., Washington, 1969-70; dir. Facilities Engring. and Constrn. Agy., Dept. Health, Edn. and Welfare, Washington, 1970—. Decorated Legion of Merit, Bronze Star, Distinguished Service medal; recipient Outstanding Achievement award as most Outstanding Civil Engr. Officer USAF, 1965. Registered profl. engr., N.Y. Fellow Am. Soc. C.E.; mem. Omaha Post Soc. Am. Mil. Engrs. (pres. 1968—), Tau Beta Pi. Mason. Home: Penthouse 3000 Spout Run Pkwy Arlington VA 22201 Office: 330 Independence Av SW Washington DC 20201

FRENCH, CLARICE PAXTON (MRS. WALTON W. FRENCH), librarian; b. Jester, Okla.; d. Guyde B. and Emily Pearl (Moore) Paxton; B.S., Southwestern State Coll., 1932; M.L.S., U. Okla., 1964; m. Walton W. French, May 22, 1926 (dec. Mar. 1958); 1 son, Eddie Carroll. Head English dept. Westview Sch., Hollis, Okla., 1930-40, Canute (Okla.) Pub. Sch. 1946-56, Dill City (Okla.) Pub. Sch., 1956-60; head librarian Burns Flat (Okla.) and Clinton Sherman AFB, 1960-64; head librarian Okla. Christian Coll., Oklahoma City, 1964—, also asso. prof. Vice chmn. Southwestern English Conv., 1959, Southwestern Dist. Library Conv., 1964. Mem. Am. (del. 1972), Okla. (sec. coll. div. 1968-69), S.W. Regional library assns., Okla. Ednl. Assn., Am. Assn. U. Women, Delta Kappa Gamma. Mem. Ch. of Christ. Home: 3121 Meadow Lane Edmond OK 73034 Office: Memorial Rd and Eastern St Oklahoma City OK 73111

FRENCH, LESTER EUGENE, city ofcl.; b. Nevada, Ia., May 12, 1905; s. Guy Davis and Edith (Hyden) F.; grad. high sch.; m. Daisy Campbell, Mar. 16, 1948. Owner, French Chevrolet Co., Newkirk, Okla., 1947-66; exec. dir. Newkirk Housing Authority, 1966—; exec. dir. Newkirk C. of C.; pres. Newkirk Indsl. Devel. Corp. Recipient Achievement award Newkirk C. of C., 1966. Mason (Shriner). Rotarian. Home: French Acres Newkirk OK 74647 Office: 311 N Main St Newkirk OK 74647

FRENCH, TRISTRUM CLYDE, hosp. adminstr.; b. Muskogee, Okla., Apr. 7, 1911; s. Daniel Harvey and Florence (Adams) F.; student Southwestern State Coll., 1962-63; m. Helen Darlene Rich, Sept. 21, 1945; children—Clark, Daniel, David, Sara Jane. Owner, French Drilling Co., Wagoner, Okla., 1935—; with Wagoner (Okla.) Hosp., Okla., 1953—, hosp. adminstr., 1966—. Served with USAAF, World War II. Mem. Christian Ch. Lion. Home: 800 SE 4th St Wagoner OK 74467 Office: 410 E Cherokee St Wagoner OK 74467

FRENCH, WARREN B., JR., chmn. state Republican com.; b. Woodstock, Va., Apr. 14, 1923; s. Warren B. and Lena (Sheetz) F.; B.S. in Elec. Engring., U. Va., 1947; m. Patricia Teale, Sept. 17, 1949; children—Anne E., Cynthia E., Warren B. III, Christopher E. With long lines dept. Am. Tel. & Tel., 1947-54; gen. mgr. Shenandoah Telephone Co., Edinburg, Va., 1954—, v.p., 1963—; dir. Farmers Bank Edinburg. Pres. Shenandoah Indsl. Devel. Corp., 1963; mem. exec. bd. Shenandoah area council Boy Scouts Am. Formerly 1st sec. dist. Republican com.; then precinct chmn. Rep. com., Arlington, Va.; pres. Electoral Coll. Va., 1952; mgr. state senatorial campaign, 1965; del. Rep. nat. conv., 1968; chmn. 7th Va. dist. Rep. com., 1966-70; chmn. Va. Rep. com., 1970—. Bd. dirs., v.p. Shanandoah County Meml. Hosp., 1968—. Served with USNR, 1943-46; lt. Res. Mem. Va. Ind. Telephone Assn. (past pres.). Methodist (trustee). Rotarian. Address: Route 2 Box 209-A Edinburg VA 22842*

FRENKEL, EUGENE PHILLIP, physician; b. Detroit, Aug. 27, 1929; s. David Eugene and Eva (Antin) F.; B.S., Wayne State U., 1949; M.D., U. Mich., 1953; m. Dr. Rhoda Smilay, Dec. 18, 1958; children—Lisa Michelle, Peter Alan. Intern, Wayne County Gen. Hosp., Eloise, Mich., 1953-54; resident Boston City Hosp., 1954-55, U. Mich. Med. Center, 1957-59, research asso., 1959-62; asst. prof. internal medicine Southwestern Med. Sch. of U. Tex., 1962-64, asso. prof., 1964-69, prof., 1969—; cons. VA Hosp., Dallas, Brooke Army Hosp., San Antonio, Baylor, Presbyn., Meth. hosps., Dallas. Served with USAF, 1955-57. Diplomate Am. Bd. Internal Medicine. Fellow A.C.P.; mem. Am., Internat. socs. hematology, Am. Fedn. Clin. Research, So. Soc. Clin. Research, Am. Assn. Cancer Research, Am. Soc. Clin. Oncology, Am. Cancer Soc. (pres. Dallas County unit 1970-71). Contbr. articles profl. jours. Home: 4028 Shady Hill Dr Dallas TX 75229 Office: 5323 Harry Hines Blvd Dallas TX 75235

FRENZEL, CHARLES HERMAN, hosp. adminstr.; b. Jersey City, Sept. 6, 1919; s. Charles H. and Carolyn (Reichert) F.; A.B., Duke, 1941, certificate hosp. adminstrn., 1951; m. Virginia LeGlise, Jan. 6, 1945; 1 son, James Charles. Dir. N.C. Hosp. Study Commn., 1951-52; S.C. Hosp. Care Study, 1952-53; adminstr. Bedford County Meml. Hosp., Bedford, Va., 1953-56; asst. dir. Duke Med. Center, 1956-58, dir., 1958—; prof. hosp. adminstrn. Duke, 1962—, dir. grad. program in hosp. adminstrn., 1967—. Dir. Central Carolina Bank & Trust Co., Durham. Mem. Gov.'s Adv. Com. Med. Assistance; mem. exec. com. Assn. U. Programs in Hosp. Adminstrn. Served to 1st lt. AUS, 1941-46. Fellow Am. Hosp. Coll. Adminstr.; mem. Am. (mem. ho. of dels. 1967—), N.C. (chmn. council hosp. financing 1965) hosp. assns., Assn. Am. Med. Colls., Am. Coll. Hosp. Adminstrs., Nat. Rehab. Assn., Durham C. of C. (chmn. health services com.). Rotarian. Author: Hospital Care of the Indigent in South Carolina, 1953. Home: 3950 Bristol Rd Durham NC 27707 Office: Duke U Med Center Durham NC 27706

FRETZ, EUGENE CAMP, advt. agy. exec.; b. Knoxville, Tenn., Jan. 23, 1922; s. Eugene Camp and Elizabeth (Sprankle) F.; B.A., U. Tenn., 1943; LL.B., U. Va., 1948; m. Llewellyn Bane Sprigg, Feb. 11, 1950; children—Elizabeth Llewellyn, Thomas Robertson. Reporter, copy editor Knoxville Jour., 1941-45; copy editor Portland (Ore.) Oregonian, 1945-46; copy editor Tulsa World, 1948; copy editor, Sunday mag. editor, book reviews Ark. Gazette, Little Rock, 1949-59; with Gene Fretz & Assos., Inc., advt., pub. relations, 1959-63; account exec. Brooks-Pollard, advt., pub. relations, 1963-66; with R.K. Butcher & Assos., Inc., Little Rock, 1966—, dir. pub. relations, 1968—. Organizer, Stop This Outrageous Purge, 1959. Mem. Pub. Relations Soc. Am., Ark. Press Club, Phi Gamma Delta. Democrat. Episcopalian. Clubs: Country of Little Rock, Little Rock; Cherokee Country (Knoxville). Home: 305 Crystal Ct Little Rock AR 72205 Office: Union Life Bldg Little Rock AR 72201

FREUDBERG, LEOPOLD V., ins. exec., lawyer; b. Libau, Latvia; s. S. F. and Lea (Effenbach) F.; LL.B., Washington Coll. (now Am. U.), 1918; student George Washington U.; m. Rose Ruth Bersh, Nov. 24, 1921; children—Grace Mignon Berlow, Richard Lee. Admitted to D.C. bar, 1918, U.S. Supreme Ct., 1925, Tax Ct., 1946; prof. ins. law Am. U., 30 yrs.; law instr. Life Ins. Inst., D.C.; dir. Nat. Bank Washington. Past v.p. Jewish Community Center; past pres. United Jewish Appeal Corp. Greater Washington, gen. campaign chmn., 1955, 56; chmn. State of Israel Bonds, Greater Washington, 1951; trustee Jewish Commn. Council; bd. dirs. Big Bros. Am., Kaufmann Camp for Washington Boys and Girls, past pres. D.C. Life Ins. Trust Council. Served with USMC, World War I. Recipient Gold Medal Humanitarian award B'nai B'rith, Community Service award Jewish Theol. Sem. U.S., Good Name award Adas Israel Congregation, Wilner Meml. award D.C. Underwriters Assn., Wisdom award of honor Wisdom Soc.; honored with planting of forest in Kennedy Peace Forest in Israel by Jewish Nat. Fund. Fellow Hebrew U. Jerusalem. Mem. D.C. Golf Assn. (past pres.), Md. Golf Assn. (past v.p.). Am., D.C. bar assns., Million Dollar Round Table of Nat. Life Underwriters Assn. (life), Zionist Orgn. Am. (past pres. Washington dist.). Jewish religion (trustee, past v.p. congregation). Mason; mem. B'nai B'rith (trustee youth services). Clubs: Nat. Press, Variety, Amity, Woodmont Country (past pres.; hon. life mem., mem. bd. govs.). Home: 3538 Albermarle St NW Washington DC 20008 Office: Freudberg Bldg 4201 Connecticut Av Washington DC 20008

FREY, GERARD LOUIS, bishop; b. New Orleans, May 10, 1914; s. Andrew and Maria Therese (DeRose) F.; D.D., St. Joseph's Sem. at St. Benedict's La., 1933; D.D., Notre Dame Sem., New Orleans, 1933. Ordained priest Roman Cath. Ch., 1938; asst. pastor, Taft, La., 1938-46; asst. dir. Confraternity Christian Doctrine, Archdiocese New Orleans, also asst. St. James Ch., New Orleans, dir. Confraternity Christian Doctrine, Archdiocese New Orleans, also asst. pastor St. Leo the Great Paris, 1946-67; founding pastor St. Francis Cabrini Ch., New Orleans, 1942-63; pastor St. Frances de Sales Parish, Houma, La., 1962-67; clergy rep. 2d Vatican Council, 1964; dir. Diocesan Friendship Corps, New Orleans, 1966; bishop of Savannah, Ga., 1967—; Episcopal moderator Theresians Am., 1968—. Recipient Bishop Tracy Vocation award St. Joseph's Sem. Alumni Assn., 1959. Address: PO Box 8789 225 Abercorn St Savannah GA 31402

FREY, LOUIS, JR., congressman; b. Rutherford, N.J., Jan. 11, 1934; s. Louis and Mildred (Engel) F.; B.A. cum laude, Colgate U., 1955; J.D. with honors, Mich. Law Sch., 1961; m. Marcia Turner, Nov. 1956; children—Julia, Lynne, Louis, Lauren, Christine. Admitted to Fla. bar, 1961; practice in Orlando; asst. county solicitor, 1963; asso., partner firm Gurney, Skolfield & Frey, Winter Park, 1963-67; partner firm Mateer, Frey, Young & Harbert, Orlando, 1967; mem. 91st-92d Congresses from 5th Dist. Fla. Acting gen. counsel Fla. Turnpike Authority, 1966-67. Mem. Fla. Republican State Exec. Com.; treas., chmn. Fla. Fedn. Young Reps.; legal counsel Nat. Fedn. Young Reps., 1965-66. Bd. dirs. Winter Park Youth Center, Am. Cancer Soc. Orange County; mem. asso. bd. Fla. Symphony. Served to lt (j.g.) USNR, 1955-58; comdr. Res. Mem. Order of Coif, Phi Gamma Delta, Phi Delta Phi. Lutheran. Home: 139 Genius Dr Winter Park FL 32789 Office: 214 Cannon House Office Bldg Washington DC 20515

FRICK, HERMAN L., educator; b. Chapin, S.C., Nov. 11, 1907; s. John (Adam) and Martha (Cannon) F.; A.B., Newberry Coll., 1929; M.A., U. S.C., 1936; Ph.D., Ohio State U., 1941; m. Harriet Permelia Douglass, June 14, 1934; children—Ann Marcesta (Mrs. Dooley Culbertson II), Herman Douglass. Tchr. high sch., Walterboro, S.C., 1929-35; tchr., prin. city schs., Columbia, S.C., 1935-37, 39-40, Gen. Edn. Bd., 1941; fellow Ohio State U., 1937-38, grad. asst., 1940-41; supt. tng. sch., dir. tchr. edn. Winthrop Coll., Rock Hill, S.C., 1941-49; prof. ednl. adminstrn. Fla. State U., Tallahasse, 1949—, acting head dept. ednl. adminstrn., 1968-70. Developed plan for edn. and certification tchrs. S.C., 1944; dir. sch. surveys; ednl. cons. S.C., N.C., Ga., Ala., Ark., Miss., La., Tex., Fla. Active Boy Scouts Am., 1947-48. Chmn. Fla. com. Commn. on Secondary Schs., 1961-64, 67—; mem. adminstrv. council So. Assn. Colls. and Schs., 1968—. Served as lt. USNR, 1944-46. Mem. Am. Assn. Supervision and Curriculum Devel., Fla. Assn. Supervision and Curriculum Devel., Am. Ednl. Research Assn., Nat. Assn. Secondary Sch. Prins., Nat. Soc. Study Edn., S.C. Sch. Adminstrs. Assn. (pres. 1942-43), N.E.A., John Dewey Soc., Phi Delta Kappa (faculty sponsor Fla. State U. chpt. 1960-61). Contbr. articles to edn. jours. and yearbooks. Home: 2003 Lee Av Tallahassee FL 32303

FRIDAY, WILLIAM CLYDE, univ. pres.; b. Raphine, Va., July 13, 1920; s. David L. and Mary E. (Rowan) F.; student Wake Forest Coll., 1937; B.S., N.C. State Coll., 1941; LL.B., U. N.C., 1948; LL.D., Belmont Abbey Coll., Wake Forest Coll., 1957, Duke, Princeton, 1958, Elon Coll., 1959, Davidson Coll., 1961, U. Ky., 1970; m. Ida Howell, May 13, 1942; children—Frances H., Mary H., Ida Elizabeth. Admitted to N.C. bar, 1948; asst. dean student U. N.C., 1948-51, asst. to pres., 1951-55, sec. of univ., 1955-56, acting. pres., 1956, pres., 1956—. Past pres. N.C. div. Am. Cancer Soc.; past chmn. Am. Council on Edn.; past mem. central adv. council Marshall Scholarship Scheme; chmn. Pres.'s Task Force on Edn., 1966-67; vice chmn. So. Regional Edn. Bd., 1967-69, mem. exec. com., 1969—; mem. nat. council Boy Scouts Am. Trustee Carnegie Found. for Advancement Teaching; bd. visitors Davidson Coll.; mem. Carnegie Commn. on Higher Edn. Served as lt. USNR, World War II. Mem. Assn. Am. Univs. (pres. 1971). Democrat. Baptist. Home: 402 E Franklin St Chapel Hill NC 27514

FRIDDELL, WILLIAM THURMAN, theatre owner; b. Pickens, S.C., Nov. 11, 1908; s. E. N. and Mary Hattie (Hawkins) F.; grad. elec. engring. course Internat. Corr. Schs., 1928; m. Lois Elizabeth Thornely, Dec. 25, 1938 (div.); children—Lois, Loretta, William Thurman; m. 2d, Mary James Easterlin, Aug. 4, 1962; 1 son, David; 1 step-son, Edward Earl Easterlin. Employee Piedmont Mfg. Co., 1925-26; grocery clk. Hampton Mercantile Co., 1926-28; with Huntington & Guerry, elec. contractors, 1928-29; contract installer sound equipment motion picture theatres in Tenn., Ga., Fla., 1929-30; advt. mgr. Sears Roebuck & Co., Charleston, S.C., 1930-32; civil engr. on govt. work relief program in Berkeley County, S.C., 1932-33; chief engr. power utility co., Moncks Corner, S.C., 1933-35; elect. engr. shipbldg. U.S. Navy Yard, Charleston, 1935-40; opened Berkeley

Theatre in Moncks Corner, 1938; owner, operator theatre in St. Stephen, S.C., 1941-44; operator Gen. Electric appliance store, Moncks Corner, 1945-48; opened Berkeley Drive In Theatre, Moncks Corner, 1951; dir., 1st v.p. Bank of Berkeley; organized in Friddell Engring. Co., 1957; owner WWMC-FM radio sta., Moncks Corner, 1969—. Comdr. Moncks Corner Squadron, Civil Air Patrol. Home: 102 Jolly Lane Moncks Corner SC 29461 Office: Hwy 52 and 17A Moncks Corner SC 29461

FRIDGE, DAVID STEADMAN, dentist; b. Ellisville, Miss., Sept. 25, 1906; s. Benjamen Franklin and Alice Pond (Steadman) F.; student Tulane U., 1926; D.D.S., Loyola U., New Orleans, 1930; m. Carlita Amilie Williams, Aug. 9, 1928; children—David Steadman, Carlita F. (Mrs. Arnold Thames), Dixie F. (Mrs. Ernie J. Tauck). Pvt. practice dentistry, Mobile, Ala., 1930—; county dentist, Mobile County, 1938—; dental surgeon Mobile City Hosp. Dental Clinic, 1932-34, Mobile County Hosp. Clinic, 1934-36, Bur. Cath. Charities Health Clinic, 1936-40. Pvt. tchr. sousaphone. Served with USNR, 1942-44. Mem. Am., Ala. dental assns., First Dist. Dental Soc. (past pres.), Nat. Rifle Assn., Psi Omega. Episcopalian. Mason (Shriner). Inventor, patentee dental instruments. Home: 1709 Springhill Av Mobile AL 36604 Office: Van Antwerp Bldg Mobile AL 36602

FRIEDERSDORF, MAX LEE, govt. ofcl.; b. Grammer, Ind., July 7, 1929; s. John L. and Lola Francis (Fox) F.; A.B. in Journalism, Franklin Coll., 1952; M.A. in Communications, Am. U., 1969; m. Priscilla Jones, Oct. 17, 1953; children—Kristine, Fritz. With Indpls. News, Chgo. Daily News, Louisville Times; former adminstrv. asst. Congressman Richard L. Roudebush; then asso. dir. for Congl. relations Office Econ. Opportunity, Washington; now spl. asst. to Pres., Washington. Recipient Congl. fellowship Am. Polit. Sci. Assn., 1966. Home: 7617 Leith Pl Alexandria VA 22307 Office: 1200 19th St NW Washington DC 20506

FRIEDHEIM, JERRY WARDEN, govt. ofcl.; b. Joplin, Mo., Oct. 7, 1934; s. Volmer Havens and Billie Alice (Warden) F.; B.J., U. Mo., 1956, A.M., 1962; m. Shirley Margarette Beavers, Oct. 17, 1956; children— Daniel Volmer, Cynthia Dianne, Thomas Eric. Reporter, editor, editorial writer Neosho (Mo.) Daily News, Joplin (Mo.) Globe, Columbia Missourian, 1956-61; instr. U. Mo. at Columbia, 1961-62; mem. staff Ho. of Reps., Washington, 1962; legislative asst., press sec., exec. asst. U.S. Senator John Tower, Washington, 1963-69; dep. asst. Sec. Def. for Pub. Affairs, Washington, 1969—. Served to capt. AUS, 1956-58. Congressional fellow Am. Polit. Sci. Assn.; mem. Sigma Delta Chi. Author: Where Are the Voters, 1968. Home: 3412 Old Dominion Blvd Alexandria VA 22305 Office: The Pentagon Washington DC 20301

FRIEDLANDER, BLAINE PEYSER, lawyer; b. Washington, June 26, 1928; s. Mark P. and Helen (Finkel) F.; B.A., U. Va., 1948; M.A., George Washington U., 1953; LL.B., Georgetown U., 1959; m. Phyllis Gabel, June 19, 1961; children—Blaine Peyser, Diane Elizabeth. Tchr., Fairfax (Va.) High Sch., 1948-55; supervising clk. civil div. Municipal Ct. of D.C., 1957-59; admitted to D.C. bar, 1959; partner Friedlander & Friedlander, Washington, 1959—. Vice pres. Falls Hill Civic Assn., Falls Church, Va., 1965-68, pres., 1968—; pres. Shrevewood P.T.A., 1969-70; del. Fairfax County (Va.) Fedn. Civic Assns., 1965—; mem. Fairfax County Zoning Rev. Study Com., 1966-67. Served with AUS, 1950-52. Mem. Bar Assn. D.C., Va. Bar Assn., V.F.W. (post adv. 1955—, post comdr. 1968—). Jewish religion. Home: 2341 Dale Dr Falls Church VA 22043 Office: 3932 Old Lee Hwy Fairfax VA 22030

FRIEDLANDER, JACKSON H., hosp. adminstr.; b. N.Y.C., 1909; M.D., L.I. U., 1934. Intern L.I. Coll. Hosp., 1934-35; intern Kings County Hosp., Bklyn., 1935-36, resident in medicine, 1936-39, asso. vis. physician, later asso. Cardiology Dept.; later chief med. services Northport Hosp., L.I., N.Y.; later chief, resident and internship div. VA, Washington, also dir. edn., also area med. dir.; now dir. VA Center, Bay Pines, Fla. Served to maj. AUS, 1942-46. Diplomate Am. Bd. Internal Medicine. Fellow Am. Coll. Cardiology, A.C.P.; mem. A.M.A., Am. Heart Assn. Office: VA Center Bay Pines FL 33504

FRIEDMAN, BAYARD HARRY, banker; b. Ft. Worth, Tex., Oct. 7, 1926; s. Harry Bayard and Mayme (Potishman) F.; LL.B., U. Tex., 1950; m. Cornelia Cheney, June 10, 1950; children—Harry Bayard II, Walker Cheney, Alan Douglas, Cornelia. Admitted to Tex. bar, 1950; partner firm Stone, Parker, Snakard, Friedman and Brown, Ft. Worth, 1950-65; sr. v.p. Ft. Worth Nat. Bank, 1965—. Vice pres. Nat. Municipal League, 1966—; mem. Joint Dallas-Ft. Worth Airport Bd., 1965—. Mem. Ft. Worth City Council, 1962-65; mayor of Ft. Worth, 1963-65. Vice Chmn. bd. of trustees Tex. Christian U. Research Found. Served with AUS, 1945-46. Named Ft. Worth Salesman of Year, Sales and Marketing Execs. Ft. Worth, 1965; Ft. Worth Outstanding Citizen, B'nai B'rith, 1965; recipient Golden Deeds award Ft. Worth Exchange Club, 1966; Royal Purple award Tex. Christian U., 1967; Distinguished Citizen's award Nat. Municipal League, 1968. Mem. Am., Ft. Worth-Tarrant County bar assns. State Bar Tex. Home: 5100 Crestline Rd Fort Worth TX 76107 Office: PO Box 2050 Fort Worth 76101

FRIEDMAN, SAMUEL JOHN, research co. exec.; b. Cleve., Jan. 25, 1918; s. Adolph Jacob and Margaret Helen (Smith) F.; B.S., Case Western Res. U., 1939, M.S., 1941; m. Saralee Long, Oct. 21, 1950; children—Alden James, Brion David. Chem. engr. E.I. duPont de Nemours & Co., Wilmington, Del., 1941-47, indsl. engr., Parlin, N.J., 1947-48, chem. engr., Wilmington, 1948-50, sr. engr., Camden, S.C., 1950-52, group leader, 1952-53, research supr., Waynesboro, Va., 1953-57, sr. tech. supr., 1957-62, research mgr., Wilmington, 1962-63, tech. supt., 1963-69, lab. dir., Old Hickory, Tenn., 1969—. Mem. A.A.A.S., Am. Inst. Chem. Engrs., Am. Chem. Soc., Am. Soc. M.E., Nashville C. of C., Phi Kappa Tau, Gamma Phi, Tau Beta Pi, Sigma Xi. Club: Hillwood Country (Nashville). Patentee in field. Contbr. articles to profl. pubs. Home: 708 Summerly Dr Nashville TN 37209 Office: Textile Fibers Dept Old Hickory TN 37138

FRIEDMAN, SUZANNE LOIS NEUMAN (MRS. THEODORE FRIEDMAN), social worker; b. Cleve., Dec. 14, 1931; d. Bertram Morton and Gertrude (Miller) Neuman; A.B., U. Ky., 1953; M.S., Case Western Res. U., 1958; m. Theodore Friedman, Apr. 12, 1959; children—Greta Ruth, Aron David. Field dir., camp dir. Dayton (O.) Girl Scout Council, 1953-56; with Eastern State Hosp., Lexington, Ky., 1958—, program dir. community placement program, 1969—. Pres., Jewish Community Assn., 1970-71. Bd. dirs. Sarah Fox Ades Nursery Sch., Lexington. Mem. Nat. Assn. Social Workers, Phi Sigma Sigma. Jewish religion (synagogue trustee, chmn. edn. com. 1968-70). Home: 307 Lakeshore Dr Lexington KY 40502 Office: 627 W 4th St Lexington KY 40508

FRIEMEL, JEROME LOUIS, feed co. exec.; b. Canyon, Tex., Dec. 9, 1932; s. Herbert Joseph and Josephine Teresa (Wieck) F.; student West Tex. State U., Canyon, 1970; m. Romilda Mary Gerber, Apr. 24, 1957; children—Rebecca Marie, John Barry, Anna Beth, Karen Teresa, Randall Louis. Ind. agr. businessman, Deaf Smith, Oldham, Dallam and Carson Counties, Tex. and Otero County, N.M., 1957—; sec., dir. Latigo Co., Inc., Hereford Grazing Co.; sec.-treas., dir. Tularosa Farms, Inc.; mgr., sec.-treas., dir. Friemel Bros., Inc.; dir. S.W. Feed Yards, Inc. Chmn. judges panel N.M. Maid of Cotton Pageant, 1971; mem. Vets. Land Bd., 1968-72. Dir. Deaf Smith County Farm Bur. Served with U.S. Army, 1953-55. Mem. Nat. Farmers Orgn., Deaf Smith County Water Assn., Grain Sorghum Producers Assn., Tex. Wheat Growers Assn., Tex.-N.M. Sugar Beet Growers Assn. K.C. Patentee in field. Home: Route 4 Hereford TX 79045 Office: Box 1351 Hereford TX 79045

FRIEND, EDWARD MALCOLM, lawyer; s. Edward M. and May (Gusfield) F.; A.B., U. Ala., 1933, LL.B., 1935; m. Hermione Frances Curjel, Sept. 22, 1938 children—Ellen (Mrs. Frederick John Elsas), Edward M. Admitted to Ala. bar, 1935; individual practice law, Birmingham, 1935—. Mem. bd. Nat. Legal Aid and Defender Assn., 1959-62; gen. co-chmn. Jefferson County (Ala.) United Fund, 1959; pres. Legal Aid Soc., Birmingham, 1954-55; pres. Family Counseling Assn., Jefferson County, 1958-59; pres. Ala. Law Sch. Found., 1969-71. Trustee Ala. Law Sch. Found., Children's Hosp., Meth. Hosp., Birmingham Symphony Orch.; bd. dirs. Jefferson County A.R.C.; mem. nat. bd. Nat. Conf. Christians and Jews, 1969-71. Served with AUS, 1941-45; brig. gen. Res. ret. Decorated Legion of Merit, Bronze Star medal with cluster (U.S.); Croix de Guerre with palm (France); recipient Daniel J. Meador Outstanding Alumnus award U. Ala. Law Sch., 1971; Outstanding Service award U.S. Army. Mem. Ala. State Bar Assn., Birmingham Bar Assn. (v.p. 1970, pres. 1971), Birmingham C. of C. (bd. dirs.), Phi Beta Kappa, Omicron Delta Kappa, Zeta Beta Tau. Rotarian. Home: 22 Woodhill Rd Birmingham AL 35223 Office: First Fed Bldg 2030 1st Av N Birmingham AL 35203

FRIEND, RALPH EDWARD, accountant; b. Satanta, Kan., Sept. 17, 1934; s. Raymond E. and Julia (Stidd) F.; B.S., U. Southwestern La., 1956; m. Beverly Castille, Apr. 6, 1958; 1 son, Brian E. Staff accountant Peat, Marwick, Mitchell & Co., C.P.A.'s, New Orleans, 1960-64, Paul Crochet, C.P.A., New Iberia, La., 1964-65; partner Crochet, Dressel & Friend, C.P.A.'s, New Iberia, 1965-70, Crochet, Friend & Co., C.P.A.'s, New Iberia, 1970—. Mem. Am. Inst. C.P.A.'s, La. Soc. C.P.A.'s (treas. Lafayette chpt. 1968-69, sec. 1969-70, v.p. 1970-71, pres. 1971-72) Methodist. Rotarian. Home: 618 Myra St New Iberia LA 70560 Office: 302 Hacker St New Iberia LA 70560

FRIERSON, EDWARD CLARENCE, educator; b. Akron, O., Dec. 22, 1933; s. Eugene C. and Bernice (Stuver) F.; B.A., Wheaton (Ill.) Coll., 1955; M.Ed., U. Miami (Fla.), 1959; Ph.D., Kent State U., 1964; m. Bettye Davies, Aug. 20, 1955; children—Suzan Kay, Dianne Elaine, Deborah Ellyn, Julie Davies and Edward Davies (twins), Robert Eugene. Tchr., Coventry Twp. Sch., Akron, 1955-57; counselor, dir. guidance pub. schs., Coventry, Hudson, O., 1959-61; instr. Kent State U., 1961-64; dir. Ga. Gov's. Honors Program, Atlanta, 1964; asso. prof. spl. edn. George Peabody Coll., Nashville, 1964—; exec. dir. Nashville Learning Center, 1970—; vis. prof. U. Vt., U. Houston, U. Cal. at San Francisco Med. Center, U. Wyo.; lectr. U. Tenn., 1969—. Pres., Middle Tenn. Council for Exceptional Children, 1967-68; chmn. legislative com. Assn. for Gifted, 1966-68; pres. Edn. Corp. Am. Served with AUS, 1957-58. Recipient Pres.' Distinguished Service award Assn. Children Learning Disabilities, 1969. Mem. Am. Psychol. Assn., Am. Personnel and Guidance Assn., N.E.A. (div. pres. 1968-69), Am. Acad. Polit. and Social Sci., Phi Delta Kappa, Kappa Delta Pi. Author: Educating Children with Learning Disabilities, 1967; Biennial Review of Research on Giftedness; 1968. Contbr. articles in field to profl. jours. Home: 925 Davidson Dr Nashville TN 37205

FRIES, STUART GILBERT, ret. army officer, research engr.; b. Washington, Dec. 8, 1913; s. Amos Alfred and Elizabeth (Wait) F.; B.S., U.S. Mil. Acad., 1935; M.S. in M.E., U. So. Cal., 1949; m. Helen S. Haynes, May 5, 1938. Commd. 2d lt. U.S. Army, 1935, advanced through grades to col., 1965; comdr. 747th Tank Battalion Normandy Invasion, 1944; dep. comdr. 2d Army Corps, 1963-65; ret., 1965; joined Boeing Co., Huntsville, Ala., 1966, research engr., 1966-70, lead engr. on systems engring., on Saturn-Apollo spacecraft, 1966-70. Pres., West Point Soc. Tennessee Valley, 1968-69; sec., treas. West Point Soc. Ala., 1971. Decorated Silver Star, Legion Merit, Bronze Star with oak leaf cluster, Purple Heart (U.S.); Croix de Guerre with palm (France); Order Oassim Alouite (Morrocco). Mem. Am. Soc. M.E., S.A.R. Republican. Episcopalian. Mason (Shriner). Clubs: Boeing Toastmasters (pres. 1968-69); Army-Navy, Army-Navy Country. Home: 409 Zandale Dr Huntsville AL 35801

FRIESE, HARRISON LEONARD, city ofcl.; b. L.I., N.Y., July 17, 1907; s. Herman A. and Marie Louise (Elcholtz) F.; grad. St. Paul's Sch., 1923; A.B. in Econs. and Banking, Colgate U., 1927; m. Grace M. Fellows, May 6, 1933 (dec. Oct. 1966); children—Harrison Leonard, John F.; m. 2d, Bette H. Hinsdale, June 29, 1968. With Fellows Engring. & Constrn., Hollis, N.Y., 1934-37; v.p. Fellows and Friese Constrn., 1938-42; planning Grumman Aircraft, Bethpage, L.I., 1942-47; owner, operator Sunrise Nursery, landscape constrn. and design, Fort Lauderdale, Fla., 1948-68; vice mayor, Fort Lauderdale, 1967-69; city commr. Fort Lauderdale, 1963-71. Vice chmn. Fort Lauderdale Planning and Zoning Bd., 1961-63; mem. Fort Lauderdale-Hollywood Internat. Airport Zoning Bd,, 1965-67; mem. area planning bd. Community Shelter Com. Broward County, 1969-71; mem. Broward County Erosion Prevention Bd., 1967-71; mem. Ft. Lauderdale Little Yankee Stadium Com. Republican precinct committeeman, Ft. Lauderdale, 1961-63. Bd. dirs. Fort Lauderdale Mus. Arts, Fort Lauderdale Symphony Orch. trustee Ft. Lauderdale Parker Play House, 1967-69; bd. dirs., hon. alumnus Nova. U. Recipient V.I.P. award Little League Baseball League, 1970. Mem. Fla. League Municipalities (legislative com. 1967-69), Taxpayers League Broward County (v.p. 1960), Fla. Nurserymen and Growers Assn. (charter), Gilchrist County C. of C., Fla. Planning-Zoning Assn., Broward County Traffic Assn., U.S. Power Squadron, Phi Kappa Psi. Episcopalian. Mason (Shriner), Elk, Rotarian. Clubs: Colgate Gold Coast Alumni (pres. 1962), Harbor Beach Surf (pres. 1963-65); Gainesville (Fla.) Golf and County. Home: Rt 2 Box 97 Trenton FL 32693 also 4900 Bay View Dr Fort Lauderdale FL 33308

FRIETSCH, HERMAN MICHAEL, JR., mfg. co. exec.; b. Chgo., Feb. 26, 1940; s. Herman Michael and Alice Dorothy (Deschermeier) F.; B.S. magna cum laude, Rockhurst Coll., 1960; M.B.A., U. Chgo., 1962; m. Karen S. Cornelius, Nov. 28, 1959; children—Katherine Carol, Steven Cornelius, Michael Thomas. With Standard Oil Co., N.J., 1962-65, sr. finance analyst, N.Y.C., 1965; with Internat. Systems & Controls Corp., diversified engring., mfg. and finance operations, Houston, 1965—, asst. to chmn., 1968, v.p., 1968-70, sr. v.p., 1970—. Mem. N.Y. Commodity Exchange, 1970—. Bd. dirs., chmn. Nat. Children's Activities Centers, Inc., Montessori Nursery Schs., Houston. Club: Houston. Home: 14334 Cindywood St Houston TX 77024 Office: 2727 Allen Pkwy Houston TX 77019

FRIMET, ARTHUR A., architect; b. Bronx, N.Y., Sept. 1, 1925; s. Louis A. and Goldie E. (Weiss) F.; certificate art and architecture Cooper Union, 1947; B.Arch., U. Okla., 1950; m. Lois R. Sokolow, Dec. 4, 1966; children—Jeffrey A., Lisa A., Adam T., Wendy R. Owner, Arthur A. Frimet, architect, Hollywood, Fla., 1954-70; partner, Frimet-Novick Assos., architects, planners, designers, Hollywood, Fla., 1970—. Mem. Hollywood (Fla.) Planning and Zoning Bd., 1966-69; mem. Broward County Area Planning Bd., 1970—; chmn. South Broward Communities United Fund, 1971. Bd. dirs. Seven Lively Arts Found. Served with AUS, 1943-45; ETO. Mem. Nat. Council Archtl. Registration Bds., A.I.A. (pres. Broward chpt. 1972), Am. Soc. Planning Ofcls., Urban Land Inst., Fla. Planning and Zoning Assn., Hollywood C. of C. (dir. 1969—, v.p. 1970—). Mason. Prin. archtl. works include Driftwood Elementary Sch., Forum Bldg., Moy's Restaurant, West Broward Hosp., Dania Nursing Home. Home: 4212 Roosevelt St Hollywood FL 33021 Office: 208 S 28th Av Hollywood FL 33020

FRISBIE, WILLIAM MORRIS, lawyer, city ofcl.; b. Sturgeon, Mo., Apr. 4, 1929; s. Haden Reed and Linnie Francis (Morris) F.; J.D., U. Mo., 1956; postgrad. Internat. Accountants Soc., 1960-62; m. Janet Lynell Pruitt, June 10, 1961; 1 dau., Joellyn Elizabeth. With Continental Casualty Co., Chgo., 1957-61; with Space div. Chrysler Corp., New Orleans, 1961-62; admitted to Miss. bar, 1964; practiced law, Bay St. Louis, 1964—; with Gen. Electric Co., Bay St. Louis, Miss., 1969—; instr. U. So. Miss. Extension Service; commr. pub. utilities, Bay St. Louis, 1969—. Trustee Christ Episcopal Day Sch., Inc., CEDS Coast Episcopal High Sch. Served with AUS, 1951-53. Mem. Am., Miss., Ill., Mo. bar assns., Am. Legion, V.F.W., Bay St. Louis C. of C., Sigma Chi, Phi Delta Phi. Episcopalian. Mason (32 deg., Shriner), Rotarian. Home: 958 S Beach Blvd Bay St Louis MS 39520 Office: PO Box 406 Bay St Louis MS 39520

FRITSCH, SISTER MARY ROBERTA ANN, educator; b. Louisville; d. William Henry and Mary (Uebelhor) Fritsch; B.Ed., Nazareth Coll., 1951; M.Ed. in adminstrn., Xavier U., 1959. Joined Sisters of Mercy of the Union, 1938; tchr. St. Aloysius Sch., Louisville, 1940-48, St. Aloysius Sch., Pewee Valley, Ky., 1949-54, St. John's Sch., Paducah, Ky., 1954-56, St. Mary Magdalen Sch., Louisville, 1956-60, St. Aloysius Sch., Louisville, 1960-61; prin. St. Athanasius Sch., 1961-68; tchr. grade 6 Holy Family Sch., 1967-68; tchr. grade 8 St. Polycarp Sch., Pleasure Ridge Park, Ky., 1968-71, head social studies dept., 1969-71; tchr. grade 6 St. Basil Sch., Louisville, 1971—. Address: St Paul Convent 6901 Dixie Hwy Pleasure Ridge Park KY 40258

FRITZ, GEORGE SPAULDING, accountant; b. Louisville, Dec. 31, 1912; s. George and Lena (Hennemann) F.; student LaSalle Extension U., 1939-43; m. Mary Rose Feldman, Apr. 3, 1937; 1 son, George P. Comptroller, Ordnance Plant Am. Well and Prospecting Co., Corsicana, Tex., 1941-42; asst. comptroller The Mengel Co., Louisville, 1942-43; chief accountant parts div. Reynold Metals Co., 1943-46; pvt. practice pub. accounting, Louisville, 1946-56; partner Fritz & Banet, C.P.A.'S. 1957-67; staff mem. Lybrand, Ross Bros. & Montgomery, 1967-69; bus. mgr. Hartstern, Shnell & Assos.; architects, Louisville, 1969-71; accountant Brown-Formann Distillers, Inc., Louisville, 1971—. Tchr. accounting Tex. A. and M. Coll., 1942, Am. Inst. Banking, 1947-48. Chmn. spl. gifts Muscular Dystrophy Assn. campaign, 1962, treas., 1962-63; treas. Louisville chpt. Muscular Dystrophy Assn., 1965; police judge, Lynnview, Ky., 1963. Personnel officer, lt. col. Civil Air Patrol, Great Lake Region, 1960—, mem. nat. finance com., 1965. Mem. Am. Inst. C.P.A.'s, Ky. Soc. C.P.A.'s. Republican. Roman Catholic. K.C. (4 deg.), Lion. Club: Jefferson. Home: Wayside Lane Goshen KY 40059 Office: Brown-Formann Bldg Louisville KY 40210

FRITZE, JULIUS ARNOLD, marriage counselor; b. Albuquerque, Dec. 30, 1918; s. Martin Herman and Mary (Staerkel) F.; student St. Paul's Jr. Coll., 1937-39; diploma Concordia Sem., 1944; B.A., in Edn., U. N.M., 1943; M.S., Central Mo. State Coll., 1969; m. Marion Caroline Becker, June 4, 1944 children—Christine, Timothy. Ordained to ministry Lutheran Ch., 1944; pastor in Corpus Christi, Tex., 1944-48, Higginsville, Mo., 1948-57; exec. dir. Marriage and Parenthood Center, Dallas, 1957-59; pvt. practice marriage counseling, Dallas, 1959—. Cons. Mo. Snyod, Luth. Ch., St. Louis, 1961; lectr. to profl. and laymen's insts., 1956—; lectr. Dallas County Jr. Coll. Mem. Am. Assn. Marriage Counselors, Am. Personnel and Guidance Assn., Nat. Vocational Guidance Assn., Nat. Council Family Relations, Am., Southwestern, Tex. psychol. assns. Author: The Essence of Marriage, 1969. Contbr. series of articles to nat. mags. Home: 10025 Ridgehaven St Dallas TX 75238 Office: Suite 112 2919 Welborn Dallas TX 75219

FRIZZELL, WILLIAM, city ofcl.; b. Union City, Tenn., Feb. 25, 1910; s. Henry T. and Mary Ann (Redford) F.; student U. Tenn., 1956-57; student spl. courses U. Chgo., Internat. Corr. Schs.; m. Ada Wheatley, Feb. 14, 1931; children—Peggy Jane (Mrs. Earl W. Pride), Beverly Kay (Mrs. Milton Magee), Diane (Mrs. Thomas Barger). Partner automobile dealership 1936-50; commr. Pub. Works, Union City, Tenn., 1950-54; field engr. Portland Cement Assn., Memphis, 1954-61; city mgr., Union City, Tenn., 1961—. Mem. Tenn. Law Enforcement Planning Comm. Dist. commr. Boy Scouts Am., Union City, 1950-54. Mem. Nat., Tenn. socs. profl. engrs., Internat., Tenn. (pres. 1964, chmn. state intergovtl. com. 1966-69) city mgrs. assns., Tenn. Municipal League (pres. 1968-69, dir.). Methodist. Kiwanian. Clubs: Union City (bd. dirs., lt. gov. 1954), Memphis Engineers. Home: 820 Pierce St Union City TN 38261 Office: 408 Depot St Union City TN 38261

FRIZZELL, WILLIAM RAYMOND, architect; b. Punta Gorda, Fla., Sept. 29, 1929; s. Roy Stanley and Sarah Lee (Thompson) F.; B.S., Ga. Inst. Tech., 1952, B.Arch., 1953; m. Margaret Morrow, Jan. 3, 1953; children—Leigh, Roy Tyler. With Lockheed Aircraft Corp., Marietta, Ga., 1951, Toombs & Co. Architects, Atlanta, 1952, Finch & Barnes Architects, Atlanta, 1953, Mark Hampton Architect, Tampa, Fla., 1954, McBryde & Frizzell Architects, Fort Myers, Fla., 1955-65; pres. W. R. Frizzell Architects, Inc., Fort Myers, 1965—; pres. Frizzell/Vickrey Architects/Planners, Inc.; sec. Sanibel Devel. Corp.; dir. 1st Fed. Savs. & Loan Assn. Bd. dirs. S.W. Fla. council Boy Scouts Am. Mem. A.I.A., Council Ednl. Facility Planners, Fort Myers C. of C. (dir.), Phi Delta Theta. Democrat. Presbyn. Rotarian, Elk. Clubs: Cypress Lake Country, Royal Palm Yacht (commodore). Important works include S. Fla. Jr. Coll., Edison Jr. Coll., Fort Myers City Hall, Riverdale High Sch. Home: 1601 Llewellyn Dr Fort Myers FL 33901 Office: Lee County Motor Bank Fort Myers FL 33901

FROEHLKE, ROBERT FREDERICK, govt. ofcl.; b. Neenah, Wis., Oct. 15, 1922; s. Herbert O. and Lillian (Porath) F.; LL.B., U. Wis., 1949; m. Nancy Jean Barnes, Nov. 9, 1946; children—Bruce, Jane, Ann, Scott. Admitted to Wis. bar, 1949; with firm McDonald & MacDonald, Madison, 1949-50; mem. faculty U. Wis. Law Sch., 1950-51; with Sentry Ins. Co., 1951-69, resident v.p., Boston, 1968-69; asst. sec. def. for adminstrn., 1969-72; sec. of the Army, 1972—. Treas., mem. bd. Laird Youth Leadership Found., 1968. Bd. dirs. St. Michael's Hosp., Stevens Point, Wis., Wis. Regional Med. Program. Served to capt. AUS, 1943-46. Mem. Am., Wis. bar assns., Order of Coif. Psi Upsilon. Republican. Presbyn. Home: 5440 Jordan Rd Washington DC 20016 Office: The Pentagon Washington DC 20310

FROHBERT, JOHN HENRY, city ofcl.; b. Gillisonville, S.C., Sept. 26, 1907; s. Henry Nicholas and Emma Florence (Moore) F.; student U. Ga., 1926-27; m. Julia Cheshire, Feb. 1, 1934; 1 dau., Julianne

(Mrs. Clarence Saxby Chambliss). Freight clk. Atlantic Coast Line Railroad, Thomasville, Ga., 1927-35; office mgr. Kirby Evans Material Co., Thomasville, 1935-40, sec.-treas., 1940-62; treas. City of Thomasville, Ga., 1962—. Bd. dirs. YMCA, Thomasville, 1956-59. Mem. Ga. Finance Officers Assn. (bd. dirs. 1968-69), C. of C. (bd. dirs. 1956-58). Methodist (chmn. bd. stewards 1958). Rotarian (pres. 1959). Club: Glen Arven Country (Thomasville). Home: 909 E Washington St Thomasville GA 31792 Office: 144 E Jackson St Thomasville GA 31792

FROHMAN, ALICE PATRICIA, lawyer; b. Washington, Mar. 16, 1930; d. Philip Hubert and Olivia (Avery) Frohman; student George Washington U., 1948-49; J.D., 1955; A.B., Wellesley Coll., 1952. Admitted to D.C. bar, 1955; atty. Lawyers Title Ins. Corp., Washington, 1955-57; law clk. Judge Burnita S. Matthews, U.S. Dist. Ct., Washington, 1957-63; asst. U.S. atty., Washington, 1963—. Chmn. dist. fund-raising Wellesley Coll., 1965-67. Treas., Washington Forum, 1969-70; trustee Legal Aid Soc., Washington, 1968-72. Recipient Young Lawyer of the Year award D.C. Bar Assn., 1966. Mem. Women's Bar Assn. D.C. (pres. 1963-64, dir. 1966-69), D.C. Bar Assn. (dir. 1967-69, sec. 1968-69), Chevy Chase Bus. and Profl. Womens Club (pres. 1964-65), State Fedn. Bus. and Profl. Womens Clubs D.C. (corr. sec. 1968-69, treas. 1969-70), Order of Coif, Kappa Beta Pi, Delta Gamma. Republican. Roman Catholic. Home: 5245 43d St NW Washington DC 20015 Office: US Attys Office US Court House Washington DC 20001

FROHOCK, FRED CLIFTON, civil engr.; b. Lake Jackson, Fla., May 15, 1909; s. Luther Russell and Weltha (Cowart) F.; B.S. in C.E., U. Fla., 1934; m. Marie Domenech, Dec. 22, 1935; children—Fred Manuel, Patrick Anthony. Engr., C.E., Jacksonville, Fla., 1938-41; dir. engring. div. U.S. Navy Dept., Key West, Fla., 1941-52, dir. tech. div., Port Lyautey, Frech Morocco, 1952-53; chief engr. Paul Smith Constrn. Co., Miami, Fla., 1953-55; engr. Maurice H. Connell & Assos., Miami, 1955-66; dir. U.S. Navy Aqueduct, Key West, 1966—. Chmn. S. Fla. Tech. Socs. Council, 1961. Registered profl. engr., Fla., S.C. Mem. Nat. Soc. Profl. Engrs., Soc. Am. Mil. Engrs., Am. Soc. C.E., Fla. Engring. Soc. (chpt. pres. 1959, state dir. 1965), Am. Water Work Assn., Sigma Tau. Home: PO Box 82 Summerland Key FL 33042 Office: US Naval Sta Key West FL 33040

FROMHERZ, FRANK C(HARLES), civil san. engr.; b. New Orleans, Sept. 5, 1921; s. Alvin M. and Alice (Spetz) F.; B.E., Tulane U., 1943; S.M., Harvard, 1947; m. Jocelyn Nyland, Sept. 12, 1946; children—Frank Charles II, Martha Joanne. Stress analyst Goodyear Aircraft Corp., 1943-45; with USPHS, 1945-46; pub. health engr. La. Dept. Health, 1947-48; partner Fromherz Engrs., cons. civil, mech. elec. and municipal engrs., 1948—. Mem. Water Pollution Control Fedn., Am. Soc. C.E. (past pres. La. sect.), Am. Water Works Assn., La. Engring. Soc., Nat. Soc. Profl. Engrs., Am. Inst. Cons. Engrs., Am. Assn. Port Authorities, Cons. Engrs. Council, Sigma Chi. Contbr. articles profl. jour. Home: 1327 Pine St New Orleans LA 70130 Office: 1539 Jackson Av New Orlaens LA 70130

FROMM, ERICH, psychoanalyst; b. Frankfurt, Germany, Mar. 23, 1900; s. Napthali and Rosa (Krause), F,; Ph.D., U., of Heidelberg, 1922; student U. Munich, 1923-24; student Psychoanalytic Inst., Berlin; m. Frieda Reichmann, June 16, 1926 (div.); m. 2d, Henny Gurland, July 24, 1944 (dec. 1952); m. 3d, Annis Freeman, Dec. 18, 1953. Lectr. Psychoanalytic Inst., Frankfurt, Inst. for Social Research, U. Frankfurt, 1929-32, Internat. Inst. Social Research, N.Y.C., 1934-39; guest lectr. Columbia U., 1940-41; lectr. Am. Inst. Psychoanalysis, 1941-42; Terry lectr. Yale, 1949; faculty Bennington (Vt.) Coll., 1941-50; fellow faculty William Alanson White Inst. Psychiatry, N.Y.C.; prof. Nat. U. of Mexico, 1951-67, Mich. State U., 1957-61; adj. prof. N.Y. U., 1962—. Diplomate in clin. psychology Am. Psychol. Assn. Fellow N.Y. Acad. Sci.; mem. Washington Psychoanalytic Soc., Mexican Nat. Acad. Medicine (hon.). Author books including: Psychoanalysis and Religion, 1950; The Forgotten Language, 1951; The Sane Society, 1955; Sigmund Freud's Mission, 1958; the Art of Loving, 1962; The Dogma of Christ and Other Essays on Religion, Psychology and Culture, 1962; The Heart of Man, 1964; The Crisis of Psychoanalysis, 1970. Address: 180 Riverside Dr New York City NY 10024 also Patricio Sanz 748-5 Mexico City 12 Mexico

FROSCH, CURTIS EUGENE, banker; b. Lexington, Tex., Nov. 1, 1936; s. Herbert Otto and Lena Anna (Winkler) F.; pre-standard certificate Am. Inst. Banking, 1959; m. Mary Ann Urban, May 6, 1956; 1 dau., Deborah Gail. Bookkeeper, teller Austin Nat. Bank (Tex.), 1956-60; with First Nat. Bank of Giddings, Tex., 1960—, cashier, 1961-63, v.p., 1963—. Chmn. Salvation Army drive, 1967, Boy Scouts Am. drive, 1969; co-chmn. Giddings Centennial Com., 1971. Mem. C. of C. (dir. 1962-65), Lion (dep. dist gov. 1969-70, treas. 1968—). Home: 413 S Williams Av Giddings TX 78942 Office: Box 269 Giddings TX 78942

FROSH, STANLEY B., lawyer, banker; b. Denver, Jan. 9, 1919; s. Joseph and Anna (Wabeck) F.; B.S., Northwestern U., 1939, J.D., 1942; m. Judith Lee Wirkman, May 7, 1943; children—Brian Esten, Robin Dale, Wendy Joan. Admitted to D.C. bar, U.S. Supreme Ct. bar, also state and fed. cts.; practiced in Washington, 1945—, Montgomery County, Md., 1949—; partner firm Frosh, Lane & Edson, Washington; chief rent atty. Chgo. regional office OPA, 1942-43; sr. litigation atty. OPA, Washington, 1945-47; lectr. internat. law Am. U., Washington, 1947-49; lectr. as Am. specialist in polit. sci. and internat. law USIA and Dept. State in Africa, 1964, Asia, 1966. Chmn. bd. gen. counsel, State Nat. Bank Bethesda (Md.). Bd. dirs. Washington Housing and Planning Assn., 1962-68, Montgomery County Arts Found.; mem. nat. panel arbitrators Am. Arbitration Assn.; mem. Montgomery County Council, 1958-62, pres. pro-tem, 1961-62. Bd. dirs. Washington met. area Community Chest and Council, 1948-57, Montgomery County, 1949-57. Vice pres. The Bridge (internat. univ.), 1965—. Served with AUS, 1942-45; ETO. Decorated Bronze Star. Mem. Montgomery County Bar Assn., Bar Assn. D.C. Mem. B'nai B'rith (pres. met. Washington council, 1950-52, chmn. Montgomery County Am. Civil Liberties Union). Club: Internat. (dir. and gen. counsel 1962—) (Washington). Home: 6100 Bradley Blvd Bethesda MD 20034 Office: 1430 K St NW Washington DC 20005 also Nat Bank Bldg Bethesda MD 20014

FROST, LAURENCE LEONARD, psychologist; b. North Platte, Neb., Feb. 18, 1925; s. Leonard Laurence and Agnes (Greenwood) F.; B.A., U. Denver, 1949, Ph.D., 1952; m. Alice Louise Cecil, Apr. 14, 1956; children—Laurence Leonard III, Amy Louise. Clin. psychologist div. psychosomatic medicine U. Colo. Med. Center, 1952-53; chief sect. clin. psychology Nat. Inst. Neurol. Diseases and Blindness, NIH, Bethesda, Md., 1953-57; dir. Child Guidance Clinic, D.C. Juvenile Ct., 1957-64; supervising psychologist St. Elizabeths Hosp., Washington, 1964—. Mem. Am., D.C., Md. psychol. assns., A.A.A.S., Am. Acad. Neurology, Am. Orthopsychiatric Assn. Home: 11214 Ashley Dr Rockville MD 20853 Office: St Elizabeths Hosp Washington DC 20032

FRUECHTENICHT, RICHARD WILLIAM, textile co. exec.; b. Fort Wayne, Ind., Apr. 4, 1920; s. George P. and Charlotte (Buesching) F.; B.S., Butler U., 1942; m. Marion C. Carlson, Oct. 27, 1945; children—Richard William, Lynn. With Gen. Electric Co., Schenectady, N.Y., 1942-46, Montgomery Ward & Co., Chgo., 1946-65, Allied Radio Corp., Chgo., 1965-68; exec. v.p. textile div. Nat. Distillers and Chem. Corp., Swannanoa, N.C., 1968—; pres., dir. Textiles Largaespada, Managua, Nicaragua, 1969—, dir. Swannanoa Warehouse Corp. Patron, Montreats Anderson Coll., 1969—; trustee Asheville Orthopedic Hosps.; bd. dirs. Community Fund, Asheville. Served to capt. USAAF, 1943-46. Decorated D.F.C. Mem. Asheville C. of C. (bd. dirs. 1970-74), Better Bus. Bur., Am. Mgmt. Assn., Financial Execs. Inst. Club: Biltmore Forest Country, Asheville City, Mountain City (Asheville, N.C.). Home: 16 Amherst St Asheville NC 28801 Office: National Distillers and Chemical Corp Swannanoa NC 28778

FRUGE, J. CLEVELAND, judge; b. nr. Basile, La., Oct. 17, 1900; s. Augustine and Alice (Reed) F.; student St. Charles Coll., Grand Coteau, La., 1914-16, St. Paul's Coll., Covington, La., 1916-18; LL.B., Loyola, New Orleans, 1922; m. Georgiana Tate, June 30, 1919 (dec. July 1963); children—Jack C., James F.; m. 2d, Heloise Boudreaux, Aug. 17, 1964. Admitted to La. bar, 1922, practiced in Ville Platte, 1922-35; asst. dist. atty., 13th Jud. Dist. La., 1930-35, dist. judge, 1935-60, presiding judge La. Ct. Appeal, 3d Circuit, 1960—; justice Supreme Ct. La., 1949. Mem. La. Legislature, 1928-30. Past pres. Evangeline area council Boy Scouts Am. Mem. La. Bar Assn. K.C. (4 deg., state retreat chmn. La. State). Rotarian (past pres.). Home: 204 Hi-School Dr Ville Platte LA 70586 Office: PO Box 3000 Lake Charles LA 70601

FRY, DAVID DONALD, civil engr.; b. Canton, O., Oct. 4, 1924; s. Don David and Mary J. (Petch) F.; student Kan. State Coll., 1943-44; B.C.E., Case Inst. Tech., 1949; m. Ann Selden Nicholson, Apr. 25, 1958; 1 dau., Constance Louise. Engr. Ohio Dept. Hwys., Ravenna, 1949-53; engr. Peter Kiewit Sons Co., Portsmouth, O., 1953-54; area engr. Arabian Am. Oil Co., Dhahran, S.A., 1954-56; design engr. M. H. Connell & Assoc., Inc., Miami, 1956-60; asst. dir. pub. works City Coral Gables, Fla., 1960-67; v.p. charge Fla. Office Brighton Engring. Co., 1967-69; project engr. Clarkeson, Kononoff & Smith, Inc., Coral Gables, 1970-71; chief engr. Pavlo Engring. Co., Inc., Coral Gables, 1971—. Registered profl. engr., Ohio Fla. Mem. Theta Chi. Presbyn. Home: 6001 SW 81st St South Miami FL 33143 Office: 2012 Ponce de Leon Blvd Coral Gables FL 33134

FRY, J. HAYDEN, athletic dir.; m. Hue Leita Zachry, Dec. 29, 1951; children— Hayden Randolph, Zachry Hodge, John Kelly, Adrian Warren, Robin Elaine. Dir. athletics, head coach football So. Meth. U.; lectr. football clinics. Bd. dirs. Pop Warner Little League. Named S.W. Conf. Coach of Yr., 1962, 66, 68; Tex. Sports Writers Assns.'s Sr. Coll. Coach of Yr., 1962; Coach and Athlete's Coach of Yr. in S.W., 1962; Nat. Coach of Week, 1963, 65, 66, 67. Mem. Am. Football Coaches Assn., Fellowship of Christian Athletes. Home: 4409 Goodfellow Dallas TX 75229 Office: Box 779 So Meth U Dallas TX 75222

FRYBURGER, L(AWRENCE) BRUCE, lawyer; b. Cin., Apr. 7, 1933; s. Lawrence W. and Norma C. (Hunsicker) F.; B.A., (Sutphin law scholar), U. Cin., 1956, LL.B., U. Tex., 1958; m. Ann Elizabeth Plankey, June 24, 1961; children—Craig William, Lawrence Kent. Admitted to Tex. bar, 1959; asso. firm. Clemens, Knight, Weiss & Spencer, San Antonio, 1959-65; individual practice labor relations law offices L. Bruce Fryburger, San Antonio, 1965—. Originator Ann. Tex. Young Lawyers Inst., 1964. Chmn. lawyers div. United Fund, San Antonio and Bexar County, 1967-68; mem. Bd. Adjustment, City of San Antonio, 1969-72. Bd. dirs. March of Dimes, San Antonio. Served with USAF, 1958-59. Recipient Outstanding Young Lawyer of San Antonio award, 1967. Mem. State Bar of Tex., Am., Tex. Jr. (bd. dirs. 1964-66), San Antonio, San Antonio Jr. (pres. 1963-64) bar assns., Tex. Cradle Soc. (dir., v.p. 1969-70), Am. Judicature Soc., Phi Delta Phi (v.p. San Antonio alumni assn. 1966-68), Sigma Chi. Presbyn. (bd. deacons). Club: San Antonio German. Contbr. articles to profl. jours. Mem. editorial bd. Tex. Lawyers Practice Guide, 1964. Office: Frost Nat Bank Bldg San Antonio TX 78205

FRYE, CLARENCE EDWARD, accountant; b. Bristol, Tenn., July 24, 1930; s. William Edward and Ella (Cross) F.; student King Coll., Bristol, 1949-50, 52-53; B.S., U. Tenn., 1955; m. Lena Elizabeth Latham, June 4, 1954; children—Mark, Scott, Stuart, Tara. With U.S. Army Audit Agy., 1955—, mgr. internal audits, Washington, 1968-71, asso. dist. mgr. So. dist., Atlanta, 1971—. Served with AUS, 1950-52. C.P.A., Tenn. Home: 1315 Martina Dr Dunwoody GA 30338 Office: US Army Audit Agy So Dist 100 Edgewood Av NE Atlanta GA 30303

FRYE, DOLAN BRUCE, textile co. exec.; b. Albemarle, N.C., Oct. 26, 1918; s. David Alexander and Nellie S. (Staton) F.; B.S., N.C. State U., 1950; m. Eva Louise Webb, July 26, 1947; children—Richard Dolan, Mark Reid. Overseer, supt. Wiscassett Mills Co., Albemarle, N.C., 1950-60; gen. mgr., 1960-65; mgr. Kendall Co., Albertville, Ala., 1965-69, mgr. Pelzer (S.C.) upper plant, 1969, mgr. Pelzer plants, 1970—. Pres., United Givers Fund, Albertville, 1969; chmn. Marshall County dist. Boy Scouts Am., Albertville, 1969; v. p. Wiscassett YMCA, Albemarle, 1962-65; Bd. dirs. Stanly County Hosp., Albemarle, 1965; trustee Wiscassett YMCA, 1962-65. Served with USNR, 1942-45. Mem. C. of C. (bd. dirs. 1968-69). Methodist (trustee 1963-65). Lion (pres. 1962), Rotarian (dir. 1967-69). Home: 18 Lebby St Pelzer SC 29669 Office: PO Box 396 Pelzer SC 29669

FRYE, JAMES MARION, JR., food co. exec.; b. nr. Mount Airy, N.C., Oct. 3, 1930; s. James M. and Thelma R. (Williamson) F.; B.S. in Bus. Adminstrn., U. Richmond, 1953, M.B.A., 1959; postgrad. Brookings Inst. Advanced Study, 1965; m. Virginia Nash, Nov. 24, 1962. With Philip Morris, Inc., Richmond, Va., 1953—, mgr. community relations, Richmond, 1964-68, dir. corporate relations, N.Y.C., 1968-69, dir. community relations, Richmond, 1969—. Pres. U. Richmond Alumni Council, 1968; v.p. United Givers Fund, 1970—, bd. dirs., 1970—; bd. dirs. Va. Council Health and Med. Care, 1964-67, Richmond Boys Club, 1969-70, Press Club Va., 1965—, Big Brothers, Nat. Tobacco Festival, Va. Thanksgiving Festival, Va. Coll. Fund. Served with AUS, 1953-55. Mem. Pub. Relations Soc. Am. (dir. 1970—), Richmond Pub. Relations Assn. (v.p. 1970-71), Richmond Indsl. Personnel Club (pres. 1959), Richmond C. of C., Va. C. of C. Rotarian. Clubs: Capitol Hill (Washington); Westwood Racquet, Downtown (Richmond, Va.). Home: 109 S Wilton Rd Richmond VA 23226 Office: 4001 Commerce Rd Richmond VA 23234

FRYE, JOHN H., JR., metall. engr.; b. Birmingham, Ala., Oct. 1, 1908; s. John H. and Helen (Mushat) F.; B.A. (with honors), Howard Coll., 1930; M.S., Lehigh U., 1934; D.Phil., Oxford (Eng.) U., 1942; m. Helen Lewis Johnston, Sept. 21, 1935; children—John H., III, Helen (Mrs. Grant Van Siclen Parr), Kathleen (Mrs. Walter T. Woods, Jr.). Asst. prof. metallurgy Lehigh U., 1937-40, asso. prof. metallurgy, 1940-44; civilian employee Office Sci. Research and Devel., 1944; research engr. Bethlehem Steel Co., 1944-48; dir. metals and ceramics div. Oak Ridge Nat. Lab., (Tenn.), 1948—; lectr. U. Tenn. Grad. Sch., 1950—; hon. adj. prof. U. Ala. Coll. Engring., 1964-67. Dir. Bank Oak Ridge, 1956—. Tech. adviser on U.S. delegation to 2d Internat. Conf. on Peaceful Uses Atomic Energy, Geneva, Switzerland, 1958. Fellow A.A.A.S., Am. Soc. for Metals (mem. handbook com. 1969-72); mem. Am. Inst. Mining, Metall. and Petroleum Engrs. (exec. com. inst. metals div. 1959-60), Am. Nuclear Soc., Sigma Xi. Episcopalian. Club: Oak Ridge Country. Editorial adv. bd. Jour. Less-Common Metals, 1962—, Nuclear Tech., 1965—. Contbr. articles to profl. jours. Home: 210 Outer Dr Oak Ridge TN 37830 Office: PO Box X Oak Ridge TN 37830

FRYE, OZRO EARLE, JR., state ofcl.; b. Petersburg, Tenn., Oct. 8, 1917; s. Ozro Earle and Mabel (Wooten) F.; B.S., U. Fla., 1939, M.S., 1941, Ph.D., 1954; postgrad. Tex. A. and M. Coll., 1941-42; m. Barbara Ann Landstreet, Oct. 8, 1949; children—Scott Walton, Leslie Ann. Research asst. Ala. Coop. Wildlife Research Unit, Auburn, 1940; Tex. A. and M. Coll., College Station, 1941-42; research biologist Fla. Game and Fresh Water Fish Commn., Tallahassee, 1944-48, chief wildlife biologist, 1948-51, asst. dir., 1951-65, dir., 1965—. Chmn., Atlantic Waterfowl Council, 1970—, Land Acquisition Commn., 1957-64, Nat. Waterfowl Council, 1960-61. Pres., Tallahassee Little Theater, 1954-55. Served to lt. USNR, 1942-46. Decorated Air medal with two gold stars; recipient Conservation award Am. Motors Corp., 1966, Fla. Conservation award Ft. Myers Rod and Gun Club, 1966. Mem. Wildlife Soc. (award 1957), Southeastern Assn. Game and Fish Commrs. (pres. 1968-69), Audubon Soc., Ecol. Soc. Am., Wilderness Soc., Wilson Ornithol. Club, Fla. Acad. Scis. (past pres.), Internat. Assn. Game, Fish and Conservation Commrs. (chmn. exec. com. 1971). Home: 758 DuParc Circle Tallahassee FL 32303 Office: Fla Game and Fresh Water Fish Commn 620 S Meridian St Tallahassee FL 32304

FRYE, VERNON LESTER, publisher; b. Niagara Falls, N.Y., Sept. 5, 1915; s. Reinhart B. and Cora B. (Carl) F.; student U. Cal. at Los Angeles, 1947-50; m. Judith Eleen Minor, Apr. 1, 1954. Accountant, McLaren, Goode & West, C.P.A.'s, Los Angeles, 1950-51; br. chief accountant Philco Corp., Los Angeles, 1951-54; chief accounting officer Centinela Valley Union High Sch. Dist., Hawthorne, Cal., 1955-60; partner Imperial Printing Co., Los Angeles, 1955-68; pub. New Era Mag., Los Angeles, 1962—. Served with AUS, 1941-45; ETO. Mem. Laundry and Cleaners Allied Trades Assn., Nat. Automatic Laundry and Cleaning Council, Laundry and Drycleaning Suppliers, Nat. Automatic Coin Laundry Equipment Operators. Office: 7915 S Western Av Los Angeles CA 90047

FRYER, JOHN RUSSELL, pharm. co. exec.; b. Wellsburg, W.Va., Aug. 22, 1921; s. Harry and Jane (Eddy) F.; B.S. in Pharmacy, U. Okla., 1949; m. Lillian R. Ferguson, Sept. 21, 1944; children—Kenneth R., Jane A. Asst. mgr. Stephenson Drug, El Reno, Okla., 1949-50; asst. mgr. Allison Drug, Wichita Falls, Tex., 1951-52; drug buyer, asst. mgr. Blvd. Pharmacy, Lawton, Okla., 1952-56; sales rep. Ciba Pharm. Co., Waco, Tex., 1956—. Served with USAAF, 1942-45. Decorated Air Medal with 8 oak leaf clusters. Mem. Kappa Psi. Republican. Mason (Shriner). Home: 2013 Mountainview Dr Waco TX 76710

FRYER, THOMAS W., JR., jr. coll. pres. Pres. Downtown Campus Miami-Dade County Jr. Coll., Miami, Fla. Mem. Fla. Assn. Pub. Colls. (pres.). Address: 16116 S W 102d Ct Miami FL 33144*

FRYER, THOMAS WAITT, SR., clergyman; b. Chadbourn, N.C., Jan. 14, 1908; s. Matthew Alexander and Frances Etta (Parker) F.; student Roanoke Coll., 1927-30, D.D., 1954; student So. Bapt. Theol. Sem., 1931-32; m. Pauline Harp, July 8, 1931; children—Thomas Waitt, Laura Frances, Mary Ann. Ordained to ministry Baptist Ch., 1932; pastor chs. in Clintwood, Va., 1932-34, Scottsburg, Va., 1934-36, Starling Av. Ch., Martinsville, Va., 1936-40, First Bapt. Ch., Dunn, N.C., 1940-42, First Bapt. Ch., New Bern, N.C., 1942-49, West End Ch., Suffolk, Va., 1949-51, Moffett Meml. Chm., Danville, Va., 1951-54, Stanton Meml. Ch., Miami, Fla., 1954-59, Immanuel Bapt. Ch., Florence. S.C., 1959-63, College Park Bapt. Ch., Florence, 1963—. Moderator Blue Ridge (Va.) Bapt. Assn., 1938, Atlantic Bapt. Assn., N.C., 1948. Trustee, treas. Harnett County Hosp., Dunn, N.C.; trustee N.C. Bapt. Hosp. Mem. 0 x 5 Club of Am. Mason (32 deg.). Rotarian (past pres. New Bern N.C.), Lion. Home: 2128 S Converse Dr Florence SC 29501 Office: 1450 Mars Hill Circle Florence SC 29501

FRYER, WILLIAM NEAL, psychologist; b. Cin., Mar. 10, 1920; s. Roy Charles and Alice (Carson) F.; B.A., Harding Coll., 1948; M.A., Columbia, 1953, Ed.D., 1965; m. Dorothy Elizabeth McClain, May 11, 1942; children—Bonnie Jean, Debra Lynn. Aircraft painter Aero. Corp. Am., Cin., 1937-39; salesman Sears, Roebuck & Co., Covington, Ky., 1940-41; minister Bklyn. Ch. of Christ, 1948-56; asst. prof. psychology Abilene (Tex.) Christian Coll., 1956-65, asso. prof., 1965-68, part-time tchr. psychology, 1968-70; chief psychologist Abilene State Sch., 1968—. Mem. Mayor's Com. on Mental Retardation, Abilene, 1964-65; mem. exec. com., profl. adviser Abilene Suicide Prevention Service. Bd. dirs., mem. profl. adv. com. Abilene Assn. for Mental Health, pres., 1958-59; past bd. dirs. Tex. Assn, for Mental Health. Served to capt. USAAF, 1941-46. Mem. Am., Southwestern, Tex., Abilene (past pres.) psychol. assns., A.A.A.S., N.Y. Acad. Sci., Am. Assn. Mental Deficiency, Phi Delta Kappa, Kappa Delta Pi. Mem. Ch. of Christ. Kiwanian. Author: (with Orval Filbeck, Max Leach) College, Classroom, Campus, and You, 1959. Home: 833 EN 10th St Abilene TX 79601 Office: Box 451 Abilene TX 79604

FRYER, WOODRING MANN, real estate broker; b. Henderson, Ky., Jan. 1, 1923; s. Charles Alvin and Rebekah (Mann) F.; grad. high sch.; m. Vonda Lee Moore, Dec. 6, 1941; children—Rebekah Virginia, Charles Herman, William Mann, Vonda Suzanne, Juli Anne, Patricia Kae. Pres., mgr. Fryer Realty Co., Henderson, Ky., 1945—; mgr. Property Sales Corp., 1964—; pres. Appraisers Asso., Inc.; sec. Lively Homes, Evansville, Ind. Pres., dir. Grantwood Hills, Inc., Melwood Developments, Inc., Eastgate Center, Inc. (all Henderson). Served with USN, 1943-45. Named Ky. col. Mem. Henderson Bd. Realtors (past pres.), Nat. Assn. Ind. Fee Appraisers (nat. dir. 1972, mem. nat. edn. com., chmn. nat. membership com., past pres. Greater Evansville chpt.), Nat. Assn. Real Estate Bds., Nat. Inst. Real Estate Brokers, Soc. Real Estate Appraisers, Henderson C. of C., Nat. Inst. Real Estate Bds., Nat. Assn. Real Estate Bds., Evansville Bd. Realtors. Mason (32 deg., Shriner). Club: Internat. Traders. Home: 235 Water St Henderson KY 42420 Office: 139 N Main St Henderson KY 42420 also Old Nat Bank Bldg Evansville IN 47708

FU, SHANG-LING, educator; b. Swatow, China, Mar. 7, 1902; s. Shao Chung and Ching-Hui (Cheng) F.; came to U.S., 1958; B.A., U. Shanghai, 1921; Docteur-es-Lettres, Societe Internationale de Philologie, Scis. et Beaux-Arts, 1931; postgrad. U. London, 1925-28, Case Inst., 1960; m. Chen-Te Chang, Aug. 10, 1933; children—Pearl Elizabeth Te-Ling (Mrs. Dennis Pindar Magovern), Victoria Ruth Chia-Ling, David Tsao. Dean, prof., head sociology and history dept. Fukien Christian U., 1929-30; prof. Nat. Tsing Hau U., Yenching U., and Nat. Normal U., Peiping, 1930-32; pres. Tientsin Anglo-Chinese Coll., 1932-33; head sociology dept., dir. Inst. Social Research, Nat. Sun Yatsen U., 1932-39; prof. Nat. Central U., Chungking U., Fu Tan U., Chungking and Nanking, 1939-49; vis. prof. Chung Chi Coll., also lectr. U. Hong Kong, 1952-58; prof. sociology, also dir. Non-Western studies Bennett Coll., Greensboro, N.C., 1959-70, prof. sociology,

1970—; lectr. Instnl. Lectrs. program Piedmont U. Center, N.C., 1966-70. Pres. Christian Mission to Chinese Seamen, 1952-58; chmn. United Com. of Hong Kong World U. Service, 1957-58; adv. mem. Acad. Human Rights, 1958—. Fellow China Acad., Am. Sociol. Assn.; mem. Internat. Sociol. Assn., Council Chinese Sociol. Assn. (hon.), Am. Assn. U. Profs., Nat. Soc. Sci. Honor Soc., Pi Gamma Mu. Author: Anglo-Chinese Dictionary of Sociology, 1936; Contemporary Chinese Sociology, 1962; Founding Father of the Republic of China and Modern Sociology, 1965. Home: 805 Plummer Dr Greensboro NC 27410

FUELSCH, DON JAMES, editor, pub.; b. St. Louis, Jan. 16, 1921; s. Arthur George and Verna (Kamier) F.; m. Lerah Mae Moreland, May 27, 1945; m. 2d, Janet Williams Griffin, Dec. 30, 1968. Editor Outdoor Field, Hot Springs, Ark., 1950—, pub., 1960—. Cons. advt. sales, design of outdoor products. Served as liaison pilot USAAF, 1942-43. Mem. Outdoor Writers Assn. Am. Author: Southern Angler's and Hunter's Guide, 1961, rev. edit., 1962, 63, 64, 65, 67. Office: PO Box 2188 Hot Springs AR 71901

FUENTES, CARLOS, author, b. 1928; ed. U. Mexico, also Institut des Hautes Etudes Internationales, Geneva. Mem. Mexican delegation ILO, Geneva, 1950-52; asst. head press sect. Ministry Fgn. Affairs, Mexico, 1954; asst. dir. cultural dissemination U. Mexico, 1955-56; head dept. cultural relations Ministry Fgn. Affairs. Editor: Revista Mexicana de Literatura, 1954-58, Siempre and Politica, 1960—; co-editor: El Espectador, 1959-61. Author: Los dias enmascarados, 1954; La region mas transparente, 1958; Las buenas conciencias, 1959; Aura, 1962; The Death of Artemio Cruz, 1962; Whither Latin America, 1963; Cantar de Ciegos, 1964; Zona sagrada, 1967; Cambio de piel (Biblioteca Breve prize Barcelona), 1967; Paris La Revolucion de Mayo, 1968; La Nueva Novela Hispanoamericana, 1969; Cumpleanos, 1969; Casa con dos puertas, 1970; Todos los Gatos son pardos, 1970; El Tuerto es Rey, 1971; Tiempo Mexicano, 1971. Address: 2a Cerrada de Galeana 16 San Angel Mexico City 20 Mexico also care Brandt & Brandt 101 Park Av New York City NY 10017 also care Gallimard 5 rue Sebastien Bottin Paris 6e France

FUGATE, DOUGLAS BROWN, hwy. adminstr.; b. Reed Island, Va., Aug. 14, 1906; s. Jesse Honaker and Elizabeth (Brown) F.; B.S., Va. Mil. Inst., 1927; m. Mary Addison Latham, June 15, 1940; 1 son, Douglas Brown. Civil engr. Va. Dept. Hwys., Richmond, 1927-42, asst. chief engr., chief engr., dep. commr., 1956-64, commr., 1964—; dir. toll facilities State of Va., Norfolk, 1946-56. Chmn., Elizabeth River Tunnel Commn., 1964—; mem. Va. Outdoor Recreation Commn., 1965—; mem. exec. com. Hwy. Research Bd. Served to lt. col. C.E., AUS, 1942-46. Recipient Exceptional Service award Am. Road Builders Assn., 1970; Thomas H. McDonald award for exceptional service in hwy. engring. Am. Assn. State Hwy. Ofcls., 1971. Fellow Am. Soc. C.E. (past pres. Va. sect); mem. Nat. Soc. Profl. Engrs., Am. (past pres.), Southeastern (past pres.) assns. state hwy. ofcls., Am. Rd. Builders Assn. (regional v.p.). Episcopalian. Home: 18 Lexington Rd Richmond VA 23226 Office: 1221 E Broad St Richmond VA 23219

FUGUA, DON, congressman; b. Jacksonville, Fla., Aug. 20, 1933; s. J. D. and Lucille (Langford) F.; B.S. in Agrl. Econs., U. Fla., 1957; m. Doris Akidakis, Dec. 20, 1955; children—Laura, John Eric. Mem. Fla. Ho of Reps. from Calhoun County, 1958-62; mem. 88th-92d Congresses, 2d Dist. Fla. Served with M.C., AUS, Korean War. Named one of five outstanding young men in Fla., Fla. Jr. C. of C., 1963. Mem. Future Farmers Am. (state pres. 1950-51), Am. Legion, Fla. Blue Key, Fla. Gold Key, Alpha Gamma Rho, Gamma Sigma Delta. Presbyn. (elder). Mason (32 deg., Shriner, Jester), Elk, Woodman of World, Rotarian. Home: Altha FL 32421 Office: House Office Bldg Washington DC 20515

FULBRIGHT, GARLAND W., state ofcl.; b. nr. Hillsboro, Tex., Nov. 30, 1909; s. Edward H. and Maude B. (Barnes) F.; student Southwestern Jr. Coll., 1926-27; m. Marjorie Ruth Trimble, Apr. 27, 1935; children—Donald G., Larry Ray, Linda Jean. With San Antonio Fire Dept., 1929-42, 47-71, fire marshal, 1952-63, 1st asst. fire chief and exec. officer, 1963-71; exec. dir. Tex. Commn. on Fire Protection Personnel Standards and Edn., Austin, 1971—; 1st asst. chief in charge crash fire fighting Kelly AFB, San Antonio, 1942-47; dir. 8th Service Command Crash Fire-fighting Sch., 1942; instr. Tex. A. and M. College Fire Sch., 1939—; mem. fire ins. rate study com. Tex. Municipal League, San Antonio; pres. bd. dirs. Tex. Arson Conf., Inc., Austin, 1958-68; fire cons. for Hemisfair, 1967-68. Dir., treas. San Antonio Fed. Credit Union, 1948-70, pres., 1971; pres. Highland Park Little League Stadium, Inc., San Antonio, 1950-64; safety chmn, Bob Hill dist. Boy Scouts Am., 1951-53, advancement chmn., 1953-57; chmn. formation and control Fiesta Flambeau, San Antonio; pres. Northwood Elementary Sch. P.T.A., 1960-62; coordinator San Antonio Civil Def., 1958-60, chief staff, 1960-71. Bd. dirs. Nat. Found., San Antonio (exec. com. county chpt., chmn. ednl. com.), Firemen's Benevolent Fund, San Antonio; Bexar County campaign dir. March of Dimes. Recipient various awards San Antonio Civil Def., 1958, Tex. Civil Def., 1958, Tex. A. and M. Coll., 1958, Treasury Dept., 1944; Guy Cude award for fireman making most outstanding contbn. to community and civic projects. Exchange Club, 1961; named Outstanding Fireman of Year, 1962. Mem. Internat. Assn. Firefighters, Nat. Fire Protection Assn. (chmn. subcom. useful statistics 1963—, mem. fire reporting com., mem. steering com.), Fire Marshals' Assn. N.A., Tex. Firemen's and Fire Marshall's Assn. (pres. 1970-71), San Antonio C. of C. (mem. fire prevention com. 1947—, certificate of merit 1951), Hermann Sons Tex., San Antonio Power Squadron. Methodist (mem. ofcl. bd. 1949-61). Mason (Shriner). Developer fire demonstration equipment. Home: Apt 206 2211 W North Loop Austin TX 78756 Office: Suite B 2209 Hancock Dr Austin TX 78756

FULBRIGHT, JAMES WILLIAM, U.S. Senator; b. Sumner, Mo., Apr. 9, 1905; s. Jay and Roberta (Waugh) F.; A.B., U. Ark., 1925; B.A., Oxford U., Eng., 1928, M.A., 1931; LL.B., George Washington U., 1934; m. Elizabeth Williams, June 15, 1932; children—Elizabeth Williams (Mrs. John Lowrie Winnacker), Roberta Waugh (Mrs. Edward Thaddeus Foote II). Admitted to D.C. bar, 1934; spl. atty. Anti-Trust Div., U.S. Dept. of Justice, 1934-35; instr. in law, George Washington U., 1935-36; lectr. in law, U. Ark., 1936-39, pres., 1939-41; Mem. 78th Congress, 3d Dist. Ark., 1943-45; U.S. Senator from Ark., 1945—; mem. finance com., chmn. com. fgn. relations. Mem. Sigma Chi, Order of Coif. Democrat. Mem. Disciples of Christ Ch. Rotarian. Home: Fayetteville AR 72701 also 2527 Belmont Rd NW Washington DC Office: New Senate Office Bldg Washington DC 20510

FULCHER, GEORGE CORDON, publisher; b. Naples, Tex., Aug. 24, 1909; s. Henry Clarence and Emma Kate (Baker) F.; student Wichita Falls Jr. Coll., 1927-28, U. Tex., 1928-31; m. Ruth M. Moore, Apr. 4, 1931; children—Ruth (Mrs. Julian L. Biggers, Jr.), Todd Moore (dec.). Reporter, Wichita Falls Record News, 1927-28; news editor Austin (Tex.) Am., 1928-36, mng. editor, 1936-41; editor Austin Am.-Statesman, 1941-45; pub. The Tex. Star, Austin, 1945—; contractor Gordon Fulcher Constrn. Co., Austin, 1945-63. Mem. Tex. Water Quality Bd., 1968-69, chmn., 1969—. Mem. Tex., N. and E. Tex. press assns., Advt. Club Dallas, Phi Kappa Psi. Democrat. Methodist. Clubs: Indian Hill Country (Atlanta); Citadel, Headliners (Austin); Press (Dallas). Address: PO Box 2234 B Austin TX 78767

FULCHER, HELEN MCCRACKEN(MRS. TYLER FULCHER), psychiat. social worker; b. Canton, China, Jan. 29, 1908; d. Josiah Calvin and Helen (Newpher) McCracken; A.B., Lake Erie Coll., 1929; grad. N.Y. Sch. Social Work, 1929-31; M.A., N.Y. U., 1933; m. Tyler Fulcher, June 19, 1936; children—Helen, Irene, Mary. Bus., indsl. girls sec. YWCA, Lynchburg, Va., 1931-42; chief psychiat. social worker Lynchburg Tng. Sch. and Hosp. for mentally retarded, 1954—. Mem. exec. com. Central Va. Health Services Devel. Council. Bd. dirs. Lynchburg Sheltered Workshop. Registered social worker, Va. Mem. Nat. Assn. Social Workers, Acad. Certified Social Workers, Am. Assn. Mental Deficiency. Home: RFD 1 Madison Heights VA 24572 Office: Lynchburg Tng Sch and Hosp Lynchburg VA

FULENWIDER, JOHN OSBORNE, JR., physician; b. Monroe, N.C., Sept. 30, 1910; s. John Osborne and Mirian (Cline) F.; B.S., Wake Forest Coll., 1934; M.D., U. Va., 1936; m. Catherine L. McNally, Aug. 28, 1939; children— John Osborne III, Catherine Lindsay. Intern, USMC Hosp. and Grant Hosp., Chgo., 1936-37; gen. practice medicine, Pageland, S.C., 1938—; mem. staff Chesterfield County Meml. Hosp. Served with AUS, 1942-45. Mem. A.M.A., S.C. Med. Soc., Kappa Alpha, Nu Sigma Nu. Club: Charlotte (N.C.) City. Home: Route 4 Pageland SC 29728 Office: 405 W McGregor St Pageland SC 29728

FULFORD, WILLIAM EDMOND, state legislator; b. Orlando, Fla., July 9, 1923; s. Jesse Curtis and Effie (Hansel) F.; ed. U. Fla., 1941; m. Mary Ramsey, June 22, 1943; children—Danny, Mickey, Patt, Jeff. Pres. Fulford Van & Storage Co., Inc., Orlando, 1948—; mem. Fla. Ho. of Reps., 1966—, vice chmn. natural resources com. Served with USAAF, 1942-45; CBI. Decorated Air medal, D.F.C. Mem. Orange County (past pres.; hon. life), Dist. 50 sportsmen's assns., Fla. Wildlife Fedn. (past dir.), C. of C., Farm Bur. Home: 3221 Alamo Dr Orlando FL 32805 Office: PO Box 1226 Orlando FL 32801*

FULGENZI, JOHN ALFRED, civil engr.; b. Madrid, Spain, Jan. 19, 1930; s. Ben and Cecilia Pearl (Ridgeway) F. (parents Am. citizens); B.S. in Civil Engring., Okla. State U., 1952; postgrad. U. N.M., 1961-63; m. Kay Charlotte Lofley, July 29, 1966; stepchildren—Stephen Faulkner, John Faulkner. Div. engr. marketing Continental Oil Co., Albuquerque, 1954-58; dist. engr. Continental Pipeline, Wichita Falls, Tex., 1958-59; constrn. supt. Blumenthal Bros. Constrn. Co., Albuquerque, 1960-61; pres. Fulgenzi Engring., Albuquerque and Amarillo, Tex., 1962—; v.p. Panhandle Engrs. and Contractors, Inc., 1971—. Coach Kids, Inc., Amarillo, 1968-71, bd. govs., 1971—; active YMCA. Commr., Randall County, Tex., 1971—. Served to 1st lt. USAF, 1952-53; maj., liaison officer U.S. Air Force Acad., 1953—. Registered profl. engr., N.M., Tex., Colo., Ariz. Mem. Nat. Soc. Profl. Engrs., Am. Soc. C.E. Methodist. Editor West Tex. sect. Am. Soc. C.E. paper, 1971. Home: 6704 Dreyfuss St Amarillo TX 79106 Office: 216 S Lipscomb St Amarillo TX 79105

FULK, FRANK FLOYD, geologist; b. Atlanta, Neb., Feb. 24, 1904; s. Osee Allen and Zona (Baker) F.; B.A., Tex. U., 1927; m. Dorothy Louise Montgomery, Oct. 19, 1930. With So. Crude Oil Purchasing Co., 1927-31; farmer, racher, 1931-33; torsion balance operator Ohio Oil Co., 1933-34; with Stanolind Oil and Gas Co., 1934-45; ind. petroleum geologist, Fort Stockton, Tex., 1945—. Supr., Tex. Soil and Water Conservation, 1948—; chmn. Tex. Agrl. Water Com., 1968—. Mem. Fort Stockton City Council, 1959-64. Mem. Am. Assn. Petroleum Geologists, Soc. Ind. Profl. Earth Scientists, W. Tex. Geol. Soc., Fort Stocton Hist. Soc. (pres.), Sigma Gamma Epsilon. Republican. Mem. Christian Ch. Home: 600 Colpitts St Fort Stockton TX 79735 Office: 220 S Main St Fort Stockton TX 79735

FULKER, EDMUND NORMAN, ednl. adminstr.; b. Pittsfield, Mass., June 14, 1927; s. Herbert E.C. and Albina (Archambault) F.; student Dartmouth, 1945-46, U. Cal. at Los Angeles, 1946, U. Mass., 1946-47; B.S., Purdue U., 1951, M.S. in Psychology, 1952; Ed.D., Am. U., 1970; m. Jeanette R. Fletcher, July 31, 1948; children—Pamela J., Glen H. Instr., Purdue U., 1952-54; head reading improvement Hdqrs. USAF, Pentagon, 1954-57; dir. U.S. Dept. Agr. Reading Improvement Lab., Washington, 1957-59, exec. sec. tng. in mgmt. Office of Sec., 1957-59, also asst. dir. Grad. Sch.; mem. faculty psychology dept. Am. U., 1955-59; cons. Ford Found., Delhi, India and Nepal, 1970-71. Served with USNR, 1945-46. Recipient Individual Trainer award Am. Soc. Tng. and Devel., 1963; named Outstanding Chpt. Pres., Am. Soc. Tng. and Devel., 1964-65. Mem. Am. Psychol. Assn., Am. Soc. for Tng. and Devel. (past chpt. pres.), Am. Soc. Pub. Adminstrn. (past chpt. v.p.), Sigma Xi, Phi Delta Kappa. Home: 6109 Rivanna Dr Springfield VA 22150 Office: US Dept Agr Grad Sch Washington DC 20250

FULKERSON, BETTY FULK, editor; b. Little Rock, Aug. 12, 1916; d. Augustus Marion and Elizabeth (Keane) Fulk; grad. Little Rock Jr. Coll., 1935; A.B., Vassar Coll., 1938; m. Baucum Fulkerson, Sept. 21, 1940 (dec.); children—Catherine Embry, Josephine Bond (dec.). Mgr., Club Travel Agy., Little Rock, 1950-52; woman's editor Ark. Gazette, Little Rock, 1952—. Mem. Consumer's Affairs com. Gov. Ark.'s Commn. Status of Women, 1966-70. Bd. dirs. All Saints Episcopal. Sch., Vicksburg, Miss., 1961-63, Family Life Board, Pulaski County Health and Welfare Council; adv. bd. Women's auxiliary U. Ark. Med. Center, 1958. Mem. Phi Theta Kappa. Contbg. editor The Delta Rev. Home: 1 Beverly Pl Little Rock AR 72207 Office: Ark Gazette 3d and Louisiana Sts Little Rock AR 72201

FULLEN, EUGENE FRANCIS, oil well service co. exec.; b. Duluth, Minn., Feb. 2, 1914; s. Ferman F. and Alice (Crane) F.; student pub. schs., Robinson, Ill.; m. Mildred Chapman, Feb. 28, 1934; children—Phyllis Anne (Mrs. L.W. Lewis), Alice Ruth (Mrs. Tom Hull). Began career as truck driver for Fred S. Endsley, Robinson, 1932-36; roughneck D.D. Feldman, Jennings, La., 1936-37; roustabout, foreman Pan Am. Prodn. Co., Houston area, 1937-46; supt. Pan Am. Prod. Co. Houston area, 1946-52; mgr. expln. and devel. Columbia Carbon Co., Monroe, La., 1952-53; owner, pres. Mallard Well Service, Lafayette, La., 1952—, Drake Rentals Inc., 1968—; dir. La. Gulf Coast Oil Expn., Lafayette. Mem. Am. Assn. Oilwell Drilling Contractors, Am. Petroleum Inst. Mining, Metall. and Petroleum Engrs., Greater Lafayette C. of C. (past chmn. oil industry com.). Methodist. Mason (Shriner). Club: Oakbourne Country (pres. 1968). Home: 100 Hampton Rd Lafayette LA 70501 Office: 106 Heymann Blvd Lafayette LA 70501

FULLENWIDER, HARLAN DRUE, dentist; b. Mechanicsburg, Ill., Sept. 4, 1893; s. Henry Thomas and Sarah Connet (Lindsly) F.; D.D.S., Northwestern U., 1916; m. Maryland Virginia Darnall, Aug. 30, 1916; 1 dau., Virginia (Mrs. Henry M. Poppenga); m. 2d, Alberta Sudbrink, Mar. 12, 1967. Practice dentistry, Crystal Falls, Mich., 1916-18, Springfield, Ill., 1919-52; ret., 1952. Served to 1st lt., Dental Corps, U.S. Army, 1918-19. Mem. Am., Ill., Springfield dental assns., Omega Kappa Upsilon. Republican. Methodist. Mason (K.T.), Optimist. Clubs: Exchange (past pres.) (Springfield). Home: 700 John Ringling Blvd Sarasota FL 33577

FULLER, BANDY EARL, textile co. exec.; b. Lafayette, Ga., July 23, 1910; s. Earl Roscoe and Buelah (Bandy) F.; student Emory U., 1929-30; m. Mary Virginia Barclay, Mar. 10, 1944; children—Earl Bandy, James Allison, Mary Louise, Gina. Dept. mgr. B.J. Bandy Co., tufted bedspreads co., Dalton, Ga., 1930-37; gen. mgr. J. & C. Bedspread Co., Ellijay, Ga., 1938-57; pres. Hampton Mills, Inc., tufted rugs, Ellijay, 1958—. Mayor, Sugar Valley, Ga., 1930-32; mayor pro-tem, Ellijay, 1940-42. Baptist (deacon 1950—). Lion (pres. 1943). Home: Blue Ridge Rd Ellijay GA 30540 Office: Industrial Blvd Ellijay GA 30540

FULLER, DONALD RAY, social worker; b. DeRidder, La., Sept. 19, 1934; s. Clarence Gerald and Annie (Johnson) F.; Mus. B., Northwestern State Coll., 1956; M.S.W., La. State U., 1962; m. Mary Yvonne Welch, June 2, 1956; children—William David, Nancy Lynne. With La. Dept. Pub. Welfare, Baton Rouge, 1956—, welfare case worker, 1956-58, children's case worker, 1958-62, children's case supr., 1962-63, welfare tng. cons., 1963-68, asst. dir. div. pub. assistance, 1968-72, dir., 1972—. Mem. Nat. Assn. Social Workers, Acad. Certified Social Workers, Am. Pub. Welfare Assn., La. Conf. Social Welfare. Democrat. Methodist. Home: 1255 Sharnwood Dr Baton Rouge LA 70808

FULLER, EARL HOUSTON, textile co. exec.; b. Columbia, S.C., Mar. 23, 1916; s. Linzey Thurmond and Sue Ethel (Stover) F.; B.S., Clemson U., 1938; m. Claudia Marian Wallace, Mar. 30, 1937; children— Judith (Mrs. Drew C. Smith), Claudia (Mrs. Marshall F. Thompson, Jr.), Earl Houston. Various positions to supt. Simmons Co., 1939-55; supt., plant mgr. J.P. Stevens & Co., Inc., 1956-66, group gen. mgr., 1966-70, group v.p., Roanoke Rapids, N.C., 1970—; bd. mgrs. Planters Nat. Bank. Chmn. Halifax County Draft Bd., 1949-54, Roanoke Rapids Recreation Commn., 1953-55; mem. Roanoke Rapids Bd. Edn., 1961-67. Bd. Advisers Chowan Coll. Served to maj. AUS, 1942-46; ETO. Decorated Bronze Star with oak leaf cluster, Purple Heart; named Young Man of Year, Roanoke Rapids Jr. C. of C., 1951. Mem. Roanoke Rapids C. of C. (pres. 1966). Presbyn. (elder). Clubs: Roanoke Rapids Lions (past pres.), Chockoyotte Country of Roanoke Rapids (dir.). Home: 100 Glenn Wayne Rd Roanoke Rapids NC 27870 Office: J P Stevens & Co Inc Roanoke Rapids NC 27870

FULLER, FRANK GARDNER, educator; b. Providence, Oct. 26, 1916; s. N. Byron and Marie (Gardner) F.; B.S., Aurora Coll., 1939; M.A., George Washington U., 1947, Ed.D., 1957; m. Bernadette A. Klich, June 5, 1943; children—Ellen Marie, Stephen Byron, Marilyn Joan. Tchr. sci. Hardwick High Sch., Gilbertville, Mass., 1940-42; vocational counselor George Washington U., 1946-47, admissions examiner, counselor 1948-49; counselor Gwynn Park High Sch., Brandywine, Md., 1947-48; faculty, counselor educator East Carolina U., Greenville, N.C., 1949—, asso. prof. edn., 1949-58, prof. edn., 1958—, cons. sch. guidance programs, 1949—, chmn. dept. counselor edn.; mem. instn. vis. team So. Assn. Colls. and Secondary Schs., N.C. Dept. Pub. Instrn., 1955-63; bd. advisers Sacred Heart Jr. Coll., 1963-69; chmn. mental health task force N.C. Study in Vocational Rehab. Pres. Pitt County Mental Health Assn., 1961-63. Mem. Greenville (N.C.) City Council, 1967—. Dir. N.C. Assn. Mental Health. Served with AUS, 1942-45. Mem. Nat. Vocational Guidance Assn., N.C. Personnel and Guidance Assn. (pres. 1962-63), N.C. Edn. Assn. (pres. 1963-64), Am. Personnel and Guidance Assn. (senator 1970-72), N.E.A. (mem. resolutions com. 1967-72), N.C. Congress Parents and Tchrs. (bd. mgrs., mental health chmn. 1966-70, 2d v.p. 1971—), Phi Delta Kappa (chpt. pres. 1961-62). Moose (local gov. 1962-63). Contbr. articles profl. jours. Home: 912 E 14th St Greenville NC 27834

FULLER, G.M., lawyer; b. Anadarko, Okla., Aug. 6, 1920; A.B., U. Okla., 1941, LL.B., 1946. Admitted to Okla. bar, 1942, U.S. Tax Ct. bar, 1957, U.S. Supreme Ct. bar, 1961; now mem. firm Fuller, Tubb & Pomeroy, Oklahoma City. Mem. Nat. Conf. Commrs. Uniform State Laws, 1958-67. Mem. Okla. Ho. of Reps., 1952-60. Served to maj. USAAF, 1942-45. Mem. Oklahoma County, Okla., Am. bar assns., Order Coif, Phi Delta Phi. Address: Fuller Tubb & Pomeroy 2500 First Nat Bank Bldg Oklahoma City OK 73102*

FULLER, GEORGE GREGG, fgn. service officer (ret.), educator; b. Rochester, N.Y., Oct. 29, 1886; s. George R. and Helen (Gregg) F.; A.B., Yale, 1910; A.M., Queen's U., 1934; grad. study U. Berlin; m. Therese Alson Williams, Feb. 27, 1926; children—George Havemeyer, Gregory Alston, Therese Brevoort. Officer various telephone cos., 1910-13; successively v.p. Standard Automatic Machine Co., Lindsay-Fuller, Inc., and dir. Bjornsen & Co., Oslo and Berlin; vice consul. Oslo and Trondhjem, Norway, 1920. Malmo, Sweden, 1921. Reval, Esthonia, 1922; vice consul, judge Consular Ct., Jerusalem, Palestine, 1923, Bushire and Teheran, Persia (Iran), 1924-25; successively consul Berlin, Niagara Falls, Kingston, Winnipeg, St. John (N.B.), Can.; consul gen., Antwerp, Tunisia, Malta and Tripolitania; assigned Dept. of State, 1922-23, asst. chief div. polit. and econ. information, sec. interdept. econ. liaison com. western Europe, 1927, trade cons. sec. state, 1934-37; prof. internat. econs. Fgn. Service Sch., Georgetown U., Am. U., U. Va.; pres. Sch. Advanced Study Internat. Understanding. Mem. President's Com. for Reciprocity Information, White House Conf. on Aging; organizer, chmn. Theatre Alliance. Served in Mexican Border campaign, N.Y. Cav.; maj. gen. staff, Washington, World War I; maj. M.I. Res. Mem. Ret. Army Officers Assn. (founder, exec. dir.), Diplomatic and Consular Officers Ret. S.A.R., Soc. Mayflower Desc., Brit. Embassy Players, Mt. Vernon Players, Tunis-Am. C. of C. (hon. pres.), Psi Upsilon, Delta Phi Epsilon, Clubs: St. John Figure Skating (founder); Metropolitan. Washington Figure Skating. Chevy Chase, Dacor (Washington); Yale (N.Y.C.). Author articles on internat. economics. Home: 3816 Huntington St NW Washington 15

FULLER, HELEN, editor; b. Cullman, Ala.; d. Arthur Wright and Lela E. (Thompson) Fuller; A.B., U. Ala., 1933, M.A., 1934, student law sch., 1935. Spl. atty. U.S. Dept. of Justice, 1935-39; asst. to adminstr. Nat. Youth Adminstrn., 1939-41; joined New Republic, 1941, asst. editor, 1944-46, Washington editor, 1946-48, polit. editor, 1948-51, mng. editor, 1951—. Bd. dirs. MEDICO, Inc., bd. dirs. Pub. Welfare Found. Mem. Am. Polit. Sci. Assn., Phi Beta Kappa. Author: Year of Trial, 1962. Home: 3242 Woodland Dr NW Washington DC 20037 Office: 1244 19th St NW Washington DC 20036

FULLER, JAMES WOODROW, clergyman; b. nr. Ashland, Miss., Dec. 15, 1914; s. Geoffrey C. and Jane (Hunsucker) F.; B.A., Union U., 1935; postgrad. So. Bapt. Theol. Sem., 1937, 39, 46; B.D., Southwestern Bapt. Theol. Sem., 1949; D.D., Howard Payne Coll., 1955; postgrad. So. Meth. U., 1968; m. June Wynne, Oct. 31, 1942; children—Ann (Mrs. Bill Coffman), James W., Ginny (Mrs. Ed Johnson), Robert Jack. Ordained to ministry Bapt. Ch., 1931; pastor Bapt. chs., Tenn., Ky., Ga., Tex., 1935-49; supt. missions Tarrant Bapt. Assn., Ft. Worth, 1950-52; asso. exec. sec. Bapt. Gen. Conv. Tex., 1953-64; asso. pastor First Bapt. Ch., Dallas, 1964-67, cons. long range plan com.; 1964-65; asso. supt. missions Dallas Bapt. Assn., 1967-69; dir. missions div. Fla. Bapt. Conv., Jacksonville, 1969—. Cons. goals Cliff Temple Bapt. Ch., Dallas, 1968-69. Mem. adv. com. Dallas Community Chest Found., 1968-69. Served to maj. USAF, 1941-45. Mem. Alpha Tau Omega. Rotarian (dir. program chmn.

1967-69). Author: Texans Around the World, 1958. Home: Apt 125 D 5201 Atlantic Blvd Jacksonville FL 32207 Office: 1230 Hendricks Av Jacksonville FL 32207

FULLER, MAYNARD GERALD, civil engr.; b. Ft. Cobb, Okla., Apr. 21, 1907; s. Martin Luther and Christina Barbara (Patten) F.; B.S. in Civil Engring., Okla. U., 1930; m. Ethel Mae Munson, June 6, 1931; children—Maynard Gerald, Alen Munson, Ingrid Ellen(Mrs. Michael Hogue). Surveyor, Gypsy Oil Co., Tulsa, 1928; resident engr. Okla. Hwy. Dept., 1930-38,40-41; constrn. engr. Holway & Neuffer, cons. engr. Grand River Dam Authority, 1938-40; sr. engr. C.E., Tulsa Dist., 1941-44, Hdqrs. 8th Service Command, Dallas, 1944-46; sr. engr., chief rds., r.r.'s runways-engr. sect. hdgrs. 4th Army, San Antonio, 1946-54; sr. engr., civilian asst. post engr. U.S. Army, Ft. Sill, Okla., 1954-58; contractor hwy. and heavy Freeman, Inc., Lawton, Okla., 1958-61; co-founder, partner Dambold & Fuller, Cons. Engrs., 1961-64; cons. civil engr., founder, owner M.G. Fuller and Assos., Inc., Cons. Engrs., Lawton, Okla., 1964—. Co-promoter registration law for profl. engrs. in Okla., 1934-35. Co-founder Christian Serviceman's Center, San Antonio, dir., 1951-54; co-founder Christian Serviceman's Center, Lawton, Okla., dir., 1959—, pres. bd., 1959. Recipient certificate appreciation for civilian war service with war dept. Sec. War, 1946; certificate achievement U.S. Army Arty. and Missile Center, 1958. Registered profl. engr., Okla., Tex., Ark., Kan., Pa., Va. Mem. Okla. Soc. Profl. Engrs. (co-founder, charter mem., dir., sec.-treas. 1942, v.p. 1943, pres. 1944), Am. Soc. Planning ofcls., Am. Congress Surveying and Mapping, Am. Water Works Assn., Frontiers Sci., Profl. Soc. Nuclear Def. (charter), U.S. Com. Dams, Sigma Tau. Democrat. Baptist (deacon 1944—, tchr. bible 1945—). Author: Focal Paths of Revelation, 1969. Contbr articles to profl. jours. Home: 4908 Gore Lawton OK 73501 Office: 1313A Av Lawton OK 73501

FULLER, PARRISH, lumber mfr.; b. Madison, Wis., May 21, 1892; s. William Wilson and Minnie Lou (Parrish) F.; student Wabash Coll., 1910-11, M.A., 1949, LL.D., 1954; m. Hester Porter, Oct. 18, 1919; children—Mary Margaret (Mrs. James D. Voorhees), William Porter. Gen. mgr. J. O. Parish Lumber Co., Shelbyville, Ind., 1914-18; asst. to pres. Hillyer Deautsch Edwards, Inc., Oakdale, La., 1919-20, v.p., gen. mgr., 1920—; v.p. Hillyer Edwards Fuller, Inc., Glenmora, La., 1923-40; gen. partner King Edwards-Fuller Co., St. Francisville, La., 1940-47, Avoyelles Timber Co., Bordelonville, La.; v.p. King Lumber Industries, Canton, Miss., 1946-50, Canton (Miss.) & Carthage R.R. Co., 1946-53, Heflands, Inc., 1939—, Porter Steel Specialties, Inc., Shelbyville, Ind., 1946-51; dir., chmn. forest lands and products Celotex Corp., Chgo.; pres. J. O. Parrish Lumber Co., Shelbyville, Ind.; gen. partner Fuller Farms, Shelbyville, Edwards & Fuller, Oakdale, La.; dir. Nat. Bank of Commerce, New Orleans, South Shore Oil and Devel. Co., New Orleans, Lower Coast R.R. Chmn., Citizens Adv. Com. on La. Edn., 1964. State Salvage chmn. 1942-45, United War Fund, 1943-45; pres. Pub. Affairs Research Council La., Inc., 1958; mem. Coordinating council La. State Colleges and La. State U., 1948-52; mem. La. State Bd. Edn., 1929-52, pres., 1952; vice chmn. La. Commn. Higher Edn., 1955-56. Bd. visitors Tulane U., 1953; bd. govs. Ochsner Med. Found., New Orleans; trustee Wabash Coll. Served as 2d lt. aviation sect. O.R.C., 1919. Received Citizenship Citation, La. div. V.F.W. (14th Good Citizenship medal for pub. service in a vital war effort); pub. service citations So. U., 1952, La. Council Coll. Pres., 1953; award merit Wabash Coll., 1960; named Humanitarian of Yr., Abbeville, La., 1960. Mem. Sigma Chi. Presbyn. Clubs: The Chicago; Boston, International House, Plimsell (New Orleans). Address: Box 60 Oakdale LA 71463

FULLER, W(ILLIAM) SIDNEY, lawyer; b. Auburn, Ala., Aug. 9, 1931; s. William Melton and Ernestine (Tolbert) F.; B.A., Auburn U., 1953; LL.B., U. Ala., 1956; m. Joyce Jeffrey, Nov. 5, 1953; children—Jeffrey Melton, Barbara Rush. Student asst. to dean of law sch. U. Ala., 1952-53; admitted to Ala. bar, 1956; law clk. U.S. Dist. Judge, Montgomery, Ala., 1956-57; practiced in Andalusia, Ala., 1957—; mem. firm Tipler, Fuller & Barnes Mem. Am., Ala. (mem. grievance com.), Covington County bar assns., Am., Ala. (pres. 1968, mem. adv. com.) trial lawyers assns., Ala. Plaintiff Lawyers Assn., Phi Delta Phi, Kappa Alpha, Alpha Phi Omega. Presbyn. (deacon, trustee). Club: Andalusia Country (pres.). Home: 100 S Ridge Rd Country Club Park Andalusia AL 36420 Office: Tipler Bldg Andalusia AL 36420

FULLERTON, CHARLES GORDON, astronaut; b. Rochester, N.Y., Oct. 11, 1936; s. Charles Renwick and Grace (Sherman) F.; B.S., Cal. Inst. Tech., 1957, M.S. in M. E., 1958; m. Marie Jeanette Buettner, July 6, 1968. Commd. 2d lt. U.S. Air Force, 1958, advanced through grades to maj., 1969; completed pilot tng., 1959; bomber pilot SAC, Davis-Monthan AFB, Tucson, 1960-64; completed aerospace research pilot sch. Edwards AFB, 1965; bomber flight test pilot, 1966; astronaut USAF Manned Orbiting Lab., 1966-69, NASA Manned Spacecraft Center, Houston, 1969—. Decorated USAF Commendation medal, Outstanding Unit award, Nat. Def. Service medal. Mem. Soc. Exptl. Test Pilots (asso.), Tau Beta Pi. Home: 16006 Torry Pines Rd Houston TX 77058 Office: Astronaut Office NASA Manned Spacecraft Center Houston TX 77058

FULLERTON, SAMUEL BAKER, constrn. co. exec.; b. St. Louis, July 10, 1931; s. Samuel Baker and Mary (Styron) F.; grad. Lawrenceville Sch., 1950; student Duke U., 1950-51; B.S., B.A., U. Ark., 1955; m. Tomme Fairfax Triplett, July 31, 1953; children—Samuel Baker III, Fairfax Triplett, Arthur King. Accounting trainee Bradley Lumber Co., Warren, Ark., 1954-55, asst. to pres., 1956-58; incorporator Moro Gravel Co., Warren, Ark., 1959-63; pres., treas. Moro, Inc., constrn., 1961—; dir. First Nat. Bank. Served to capt. USAF, 1955-56; now capt. Res. ret. Mem. Asso. Gen. Contractors Am., Asso. Gen. Contractors Ark. (bd. dirs. 1967-68), Kappa Sigma. Presbyn. (deacon 1961—). Rotarian. Clubs: Warren Country, Pine Bluff (Ark.) Country, Little Rock Country, Capitol, Little Rock. Home: 416 S Myrtle St Warren AR 71671 Office: Box 232 Warren AR 71671

FULTON, JAMES WAYTE, JR., clergyman; b. Stuart, Va., Feb. 23, 1911; s. James Wayte and Mary Ward (King) F.; B.A., Davidson Coll., 1933; B.A., Union Theol. Sem., 1936; D.D., Belhaven Coll., 1956; m. Jerry Liddell, Mar. 9, 1946; children—Alyce, Christine, Frances Anne, Jerry Virginia, Kathleen Bell. Ordained to ministry Presbyn. Ch., 1937; pastor First Ch., Gloucester, Va., 1937-39, Bishopville, S.C., 1939-41, Royal Oak Ch., Marion, Va., 1946-49; dir. Christian Edn., Synod La., New Orleans, 1949-52; pastor Shenandoah Ch., Miami, Fla., 1952-69, Meml. Presbyn. Ch., West Palm Beach, Fla., 1969—. Trustee Davidson Coll.; bd. dirs. Christianity Today; served with Chaplains' corps, USNR, 1941-46; now capt. Res. Mem. U.S. Naval Inst., S.A.R. Kiwanian. Home: 200 Ellamar Rd West Palm Beach FL 33405 Office: 1300 S Olive Av West Palm Beach FL 33401

FULTON, JOSEPH FRANK, economist; b. Newark, Apr. 5, 1920; s. Frank and Rose (Ruggear) F.; B.A., N.Y. U., 1946, M.A., 1948; m. Frances E. Simpson, Dec. 4, 1954; children—Alice, Amy. Instr. econs. N.Y. U., 1947-48, Mich. State U., 1949-50; economist U.S. Dept. Labor, Washington, 1950-64, U.S. Internal Revenue Service, 1964-69, Library Congress, Washington, 1969—; securities analyst Salomon Bros. & Hutzler, N.Y.C., 1948. Served with USNR, 1941-45. Mem. Am. Econ. Assn., Indsl. Relations Research Assn., Nat. Economists Club. Contbr. articles profl. jours. Home: 6544 Placid St Falls Church VA 22043 Office: Library Congress Washington DC 20540

FULTON, RICHARD ALSINA, lawyer; b. N.Y.C., Feb. 27, 1926; s. Robert B. and Consuelo (Alsina) F.; A.B., U. Fla., 1949; J.D., Tulane U., 1957; m. Susan Breakfield. Admitted to La. bar, 1957; practiced in Baton Rouge, 1957-60; asst. gen. counsel La. Dept. Hwys., 1957-58, La Dept. Revenue, 1959-60; asst. to U.S. Senator Allen J. Ellender, 1961; exec. dir., gen. counsel United Bus. Schs. Assn., 1962—; gen. counsel Accrediting Commn. for Bus. Schs. Project dir. Manpower Devel. and Tng. Act, Research and Demonstration Project for Health, Edn. and Welfare-U.S. Office Edn., cons. fed. relations Nat. Fedn. Licensed Practical Nurses. Trustee, Nat. Licensed Practical Nurse Edn. Found. Served with U.S. Mcht. Marine, World War II, Korea. Mem. Am., Fed., La. bar assns., D.C. Tulane Alumni Assn. (past pres., treas.). Sigma Chi, Phi Delta Phi. Democrat. Episcopalian. Mason. Clubs: University, Nat. Lawyers, Potomac Boat (Washington). Author: Your Career as a Secretary, 1963; Accounting for Your Future, 1966. Editor in chief The Compass, 1962—. Contbg. editor Ency. Ednl. Research, 1969, Nat. Bus. Edn. Yearbook, 1969. Contbr. articles profl. jours. Home: 1533 Foxhall Rd NW Washington DC 20007 Office: 1730 M St NW Washington DC 20036

FULTON, RICHARD HARMON, congressman; b. Nashville, Jan. 27, 1927; s. Lyle Houston and Labina (Plummer) F.; student U. Tenn., 1946-47; m. Jewel Simpson, Dec. 23, 1945; children—Richard, Michael, Barry, Donna, Linda. Real estate broker Fulton & Riddle Realty Co.; mem. Tenn. Senate 1959-60; mem. 88th-92d Congresses, 5th Tenn. Dist. Served as seaman USNR, 1945-46. Democrat. Methodist. Mason (Shriner). Home: 911 Preston Dr Nashville TN 37206 also 104 Schott's Ct NE Washington DC Office: House Office Bldg Washington DC 20515

FUNDERBURK, EARL COLUMBUS, educator; b. Ansonville, N.C., Mar. 24, 1914; s. Curtis Milton and Anne Elizabeth (Gibson) F.; A.B., U. N.C., 1934, MA., 1946; m. Marjorie Alethia Pritchard, Aug. 31, 1939; 1 son, Ronald Baxter. Tchr., athletic coach Pine Level Sch., Johnson County, N.C., 1935-37, Selma (N.C.) High Sch., 1937-39; prin. Pine Level High and Elementary Sch., 1939-42; high sch. prin. Elizabeth City (N.C.) Schs., 1946-49, supt., 1949-55; supt. Asheville (N.C.) City Schs., 1955-60, New Hanover County Schs., Wilmington, N.C., 1960-61, Fairfax County Schs., Fairfax, Va., 1961-69; dir. supervisory-adminstv. services N.E.A., Washington, 1969—. Pres. Pasquotank County Tb Assn., 1948-50; N.E.A. rep. 1960 White House Conf. on Youth. Mem. Fairfax City Council 1971. Mem. No. Va. Coll. Bd., 1969—. Served to lt. USNR, 1942-46. Named Man of Yr., Fairfax County, 1969; Outstanding Educator of Yr., Phi Delta Kappa, 1969; Citizen of Yr., City of Fairfax, 1971; recipient Am. Educators Medal award Freedoms Found., 1971. Mem. N.E.A., Va., Fairfax County edn. assns., Am., Va. assns. sch. adminstrs., Am. Acad. Polit. and Social Sci., Horace Mann League (dir. 1964-67), C. of C. (dir. 1965-70), Phi Delta Kappa. Methodist (mem. ofcl. bd). Kiwanian. Home: 3800 Haynesworth Pl Fairfax VA 22030 Office: 1201 16th St NW Washington DC 20036

FUNDERBURK, JAMES ERNEST, ret. dentist; b. Pageland, S.C., Nov. 24, 1887; s. James Thomas and Mary (Welch) F.; D.D.S., U. Md., 1908, postgrad. degree in Oral Surgery and Anesthesia, 1910; m. Mary Eliza Sellers, Dec. 29, 1909 (dec. Apr. 1934); children—James Ernest, Julius Sellers, Benjamin Jackson, Thomas Alexander, George Wilson (dec.), Louise (Mrs. Harry Willis), Mary Sinclair (dec.), Eugenia (Mrs. Harold Smoak), Nancy (Mrs. Edwin Waterman Robeson); m. 2d, Effie Ingram Wall, Aug. 29, 1936; 1 son, Ervin. Practice dentistry, Cheraw, S.C., 1908-66. Chmn., Chesterfield County Dept. Welfare, 1945-54. Precinct pres. Cheraw Democratic Com., 1954-70. Recipient citations for doing free dental work for mil. conscripts from Pres. of U.S., 1941, 45. Fellow S.C. Dental Assn. (hon., exec. bd. 1908-66, past chmn. numerous coms.); mem. Am. Dental Assn. (life), Pee Dee Dental Soc. (charter), Psi Omega (citation for distinguished service to fraternity and dentistry 1966). Presbyn. (ruling elder 1964-68). Mason (Shriner, K.T.), Kiwanian. Address: 506 Kershaw St Cheraw SC 29520

FUNDERBURK, SAPP, cons.; b. Columbia, S.C., Sept. 12, 1916; s. Virgil F. and Virginia (Sapp) F.; student Furman U., 1939; m. Frances Norwood, Mar. 2, 1940; children—George Norwood, Sapp. Asst. v.p., asst. treas. Auto Finance Co., Greenville, S.C., 1939-61, asst. treas., 1958-61, asst. v.p., 1955-61, also asst. v.p. Am. Discount Co., Greenville, 1955-61; v.p. installment loan dept. Citizens and So. Nat. Bank S.C., Greenville, 1961-67, adv. bd., 1958-67; mem. 5th Fed. Res. Dist. Adv. Bd.-Installment Credit, 1961—. Adv. Com. S.C. Tech. Tng. Com. Chmn. United Fund campaign, 1959; mem. Greenville County Planning and Devel. Bd., 1961—. Bd. dirs. Carolinas United Community Services, 1961—; chmn. bd. dirs. Broner Home; bd. dirs. Greenville YMCA; chmn., trustee Greenville County Found.; mem. adv. council Furman U., St. Francis Hospital; campaign chmn. Furman U. Devel. Fund; bd. dirs. Greenville County chpt. A.R.C., 1959-62; Served to maj. USAAF, World War II. Decorated Bronze Star. Recipient Distinguished Alumni award Furman U., 1963. Mem. Greenville C. of C. (past pres., dir., chmn. indsl. com., chmn. Better Bus. div.), Furman U. Alumni Assn. (pres.), Furman U. Athletic Council (past chmn.), Kappa Alpha (ct. of honor). Methodist. Mason, Elk, Rotarian (past pres., dir.). Clubs: Touchdown (past pres.), Greenville Cotillion, Poinsett (all Greenville). Address: 417 Belmont Av Greenville SC 29601

FUNKE, FRANCIS JOSEPH, educator; b. Indpls., June 11, 1915; s. Anthony and Caroline A. (Reimer) F.; A.B. magna cum laude (Liberal Arts scholar 1936-37), Butler U., 1937; M.A. (Legislative scholar 1937-38), U. Wis., 1938; postgrad. U. Pa., 1940, George Washington U., 1953-54; Ph.D., Fla. State U., 1964; m. Bertha Julia Sainz, Aug. 20, 1941; 1 son, John Anthony (dec.). Tchr. modern lang. Riverside Mil. Acad., Gainesville, Ga., 1938-41; Spanish tchr. Reitz High Sch., Evansville, Ind., 1941-43; tchr., Culver (Ind.) Mil. Acad., 1943-45; pharm. translator Eli Lilly Internat. Corp., Indpls., 1945-50; translator, interpreter U.S. Govt., Washington, 1950-55; adult edn. tchr. Good Neighbor Sch., Washington, 1951-53; tchr., North Miami High Sch., 1955-60; prof. Spanish-French Miami-Dade Jr. Coll., 1960—. Mem. Am. Assn. Tchrs. Spanish and Portuguese, Am. Assn. Tchrs. French, Modern Lang. Assn., Am. Dialect Soc., So. Atlantic Modern Lang. Assn., Dade County Spanish Tchrs. Assn. (pres. 1960-61), Fla. State Alumni Assn. (sec. bd. Dade County 1967—), Kappa Delta Pi, Phi Kappa Phi, Sigma Delta Pi, Pi Delta Phi, Alpha Mu Gamma. Home: 6700 Brookline D Country Club Miami Hialeah FL 33015

FUQUA, ANN A., museum ofcl. Curator museum Robert E. Lee Mansion, Arlington (Va.) Nat. Cemetery. Address: Robert E Lee Mansion Arlington Nat Cemetery Arlington VA 22211*

FUQUA, FRANK GORDON, cable television exec.; b. Bluefield, W.Va., Oct. 14, 1927; s. I. N. and Pansy M. (Meek) F.; B.S., W.Va. U., 1949; m. Shirley A. Cole, Aug. 26, 1960; children—Scott, Mark, Lynn, Kelly. With Citizens Underwriters Co., 1949-52; mgr. Bluefield TV Cable Co., 1952-61; tech. supr. Nat. Gen. Corp., Los Angeles, 1961-64; exec. v.p. TeleVision Communications, Inc., N.Y.C., 1964-70; pres. Electra Communications, Charlotte, N.C., 1970—. Served with USAAF, 1944-47. Mem. Nat. Cable TV Assn. (sec., dir., mem. exec. com.), Mid-Atlantic (pres.), W.Va. (pres.) CATV assns. Clubs: Clover; Bluefield Country (Bluefield), Carmel Country, River Hills Plantation (Charlotte). Home: 91 Brittany Ct Charlotte NC 28211 Office: 1515 Mockingbird Lane Charlotte NC 28209

FUQUA, JOHN BROOKS, business exec.; b. Prince Edward County, Va., June 26, 1918; s. J. B. and Ruth (Fuqua) Elam; student pub. schs. Va.; m. Dorothy Chapman, Feb. 10, 1945; 1 son, John Rex. Chmn. bd., chief exec. officer Fuqua Industries, Inc., Atlanta, 1965—; chmn. bd. Fuqua TV, Inc., owners WJBF-TV, Augusta, Ga.; owner Fuqua Investment Co., Inc.; dir. Central Ga. R.R. Co., Winston Devel. Corp.; chmn. exec. com., dir. Gable Industries, Inc. Mem. Ga. State Univ. Adv. Council; past mem. Ga. Sci. and Sci. and Tech. Commn.; mem. Augusta Aviation Commn., 1945-67; past mem., past finance chmn. Augusta Hosp. Authority; mem. Chief Exec. Forum, Inc., World Bus. Council, Inc. Mem. Ga. Ho. of Reps., 1957-62; mem. Ga. Senate, 1963-64; chmn. House Banking Com., 1959-62, Senate Banking and Finance Com., 1963-64; chmn. Democratic Exec. Com. Ga. and Dem. Party Ga., 1962-66. Bd. visitors Emory U.; trustee Ga. State U. Found. Named Boss of Year, Augusta Jr. C. of C., 1960, Ga. Broadcaster Citizen of Year, 1963. Mem. Young Presidents Orgn. (past v.p.), Augusta (pres. 1962), Atlanta (past dir.) chambers commerce. Club: Augusta Exchange (past pres.). Home: 3574 Tuxedo Rd NW Atlanta GA 30305 Office: 3800 First Nat Bank Tower Atlanta GA 30303

FUQUA, RAYMOND FABIOUS, city ofcl.; b. nr. Luling, Tex., Dec. 31, 1922; s. Leslie Fabious and Mary Alice (Hand) F.; B.B.A., tchrs. certificate, Southwest Tex. State Coll., 1949; m. Noveleene Bone, Aug. 10, 1950; children—Suzette, Michele. Clk., Kewanee Oil Co., Odessa, Tex., 1950-52; tax assessor, city sec., dir. finance, City of Odessa, Tex., 1952—. Cons. tax assessing and appraising. Bd. dirs. Odessa Community Chest, United Fund, 1950. Served with USCGR, 1952-56. Mem. Date Processing Mgmt. Assn., Municipal Finance Officers Assn. U.S. and Can., Tex. chpt. Municipal Finance Officers, Tex. Assn. Assessing Officers, Am. Pub. Works Assn., C. of C. Lion. Home: 4222 Locust St Odessa TX 79760 Office: PO Box 4398 Odessa TX 79760

FUQUAY, JOHN WADE, educator; b. Burlington, N.C., July 31, 1933; s. Wade Flem and Margaret Hazel (Zachary) F.; B.S., N.C. State U., 1955, M.S., 1966; Ph.D., Pa. State U., 1969; m. Charlotte Ann Kesler, Aug. 22, 1970; 1 son, Michael Wade. Herd mgr. Fuquay's Jersey Farm, Snow Camp, N.C., 1959-64; grad. asst. N.C. State U., 1964-66, Pa. State U., 1966-69; asst. prof. dairy sci. Miss. State U., 1969—. Pres. Eli Whitney Community Devel. Assn., 1962-64. Bd. dirs. N.C. Dairy Found., 1963-65. Served with USAF, 1956-59. Mem. Am. Dairy Sci. Assn., Am. Soc. Animal Sci., Assn. So. Agrl. Workers, Sigma Xi, Phi Kappa Phi, Gamma Sigma Delta. Methodist. Club: Starkville (Miss.) Civitan. Home: Box 3311 State College MS 39762

FURBEE, CHARLES E., state ofcl. Exec. dir. West Coast inland naval dist. State Fla., Bradenton. Address: Box 786 Bradenton FL 33505*

FURBUSH, R. A., ins. exec.; b. Salem, Mass.; student Middlebury Coll.; B.S., Dartmouth, 1927; m. Consuelo Furbush; children—Michael R., William Van Reed. Past chmn., chief exec. officer Am. Nat. Ins. Co. Galveston; v.p., dir. Commonwealth Life & Accident Ins. Co., St. Louis; dir. Am. Printing Co., Galveston. Mem. joint com. field relations Am. Life Conv.-Life Ins. Assn. Am. Trustee Nat. Cystic Fibrosis Research Found.; life trustee Rosenberg Library, Galveston. Mem. Health Ins. Assn. Am. (dir.), Ins. Econs. Soc. Am. (exec. com.), Tex. Life Conv. (dir.), Galveston C. of C. (bd. dirs.). Home: Galvez Hotel Galveston TX 77550 Office: Am Nat Ins Co Moody Av at 21st St Galveston TX 77550

FURCHTGOTT, ERNEST, psychologist, educator; b. Zlate Morauce, Czechoslovakia, Nov. 2, 1922; s. Adalbert and Sara (Schor) F.; A.B., U. Cal., Los Angeles, 1946, M.A., 1948, Ph.D., 1950; m. Mary Wilkes, July 23, 1953; children—Margaret A., David G., Harold W. Came to U.S., 1938, naturalized, 1944. Asst. prof. to prof. psychology U. Tenn., 1949-69; head dept. psychology U. S.C., Columbia, 1969—; cons. USPHS, U.S. AEC, VA; mem. NIH Study sect., 1964-67, 68-72. Mem. U.S. Delegation to UN Com. on Effects of Atomic Radiation, 1967-69; mace bearer U. Tenn., 1969. Fellow Am. Psychol. Assn., A.A.A.S.; mem. Southeastern (mem. council 1966-69), S.C. psychol. assns. Home: 4600 Perry Ct Columbia SC 29206

FUREY, FRANCIS JAMES, bishop; b. Summit Hill, Pa., Feb. 22, 1905; s. John and Anna (O'Donnell) F.; student St. Charles Sem., Overbrook, Pa., 1920-24; Ph.D., Pontificio Seminario Romano, Rome, 1926, S.T.D., 1930; LL.D., La Salle Coll., Phila., 1944, St. John's U., Bklyn., 1946, Villanova U., 1947, St. Joseph's Coll., Phila., 1949. Ordained priest Roman Catholic Ch., 1930; pvt. sec. to Cardinal Dougherty, 1930-36; pres. Immaculata (Pa.) Coll., 1936-46; rector St. Charles Sem., 1946-58, St. Helena's Parish, Phila., 1958-63; consecrated bishop, 1960; auxiliary bishop Phila., titular bishop Temnus, 1960-63; bishop San Diego, Cal., 1963, now bishop, San Antonio. Dir. Cath. Charities Appeal, Phila., 1958. Bd. dirs. Misericordia Hosp., Phila., St. Joseph Hosp., Phila., Ravenhill Acad., Germantown, Pa.; trustee Roman Cath. High Sch., Phila. Named Domestic Prelate by Pope Pius XII, 1947; knight comdr. Legion Cedars Lebanon. Mem. Nat., Pa. Cath. ednl. assns., Assn. Coll. Presidents Pa., John Henry Newman Soc. Address: PO Box 13190 San Antonio TX 78284

FURINO, ANTONIO, economist; b. Rome, Italy, May 7, 1931; J.D., U. Rome, 1955; M.A., U. Houston, 1965, Ph.D., 1972. Free lance writer, Rome, 1950-58; research asst. Center for Research in Bus. and Econs., U. Houston, 1960-63; chmn. depts. hunanities Sacred Heart Dominican Coll., Houston, 1963-65, teaching fellow dept. econs., 1965-66; asst. prof. to asso. prof. econs. St. Edwards U., Austin, Tex., 1967-70; dir. regional analysis Alamo Area Council Govts., San Antonio, 1970—; econ. cons. Tex. Nat. Bank of Commerce, 1966-68. Mem. Am., So. econ. assns., Regional Sci. Soc., Urban Regional Information Systems Assn., Southwestern Social Sci. Assn., Modern Lang. Assn., Dante Cultural Soc. (pres. Houston 1963-65), Latin Am. Studies Assn. (asso.), Omicron Delta Epsilon (pres. chpt. 1964). Home: 3800 Parkdale Dr San Antonio TX 78229

FURLONG, EDWARD COLSON, JR., educator; b. Morgantown, W.Va., May 31, 1913; s. Edward C. and Mary Jane (Edgar) F. Sr.; student W. Va. U., 1931-33, Potomac State Coll., Keyser, W.Va., 1934-36; B.S., John B. Stetson U., DeLand, Fla., 1938, A.M., 1940; m. Charlotte D. Werwage, July 27, 1942; children—Edward C., James Joseph, Jane Vesta, William Robert, and Elsbeth Charlotte. Mem. faculty, John B. Stetson U. 1938— (mil. leave, 1942-46), asso. prof. econs., 1946-47, dean, Sch. Bus., 1947—, prof. of bus. adminstrn., 1947—, bus. mgr., 1957-63. City commr. DeLand, Fla. 1949-53, mayor, 1953-56; mem., incorporator Valusia County Indsl. Bd.; chmn. DeLand Housing Authority. Regent Fla. Episcopal Coll.; trustee Diocese South Fla., Episcopal Ch., 1963-68 bd. dirs. DeLand Meml.

Hosp. Served to capt., inf., AUS, 1942-46. Carnegie Found. for Advancement of Teaching, grantee, 1949. Mem. Am. Acad. Polit. and Social Sci. Am., So. econ. assns., Am. Bus. Law Assn., So. Intercollegiate Athletic Assn. (v.p.), N.E.A., DeLand C. of C. (pres. 1963), United Bus. Edn. Assn., Sigma Phi Epsilon, Episcopalian. Editor, Stetson Survey (a method of measuring the effectiveness of radio advertising), 1948. Home: 201 W Pennsylvania Av DeLand FL 32720

FURLONG, RICHARD WILSON, educator; b. Norwalk, O., Mar. 30, 1929; s. Norman Burr and Dorothy May (Wilson) F.; B.S. in Civil Engring., So. Meth. U., 1952; M.S. in Civil Engring., Washington U., St. Louis, 1957; Ph.D., U. Tex., 1963; m. Helen Corinne Prince, Sept. 7, 1951; children—John Norman, Sara Catherine. Stress engr. McDonnell Aircraft Corp., St. Louis, 1952-53; detailer, checker Petroleum Equipment Co., St. Louis, 1953-55; design engr. F. Ray Martin, Inc., cons. engrs., St. Louis, 1955-58; asst. prof. U. Tex., Austin, 1958-65, asso. prof., 1965-71, prof. civil engring., 1971—. Pres. P.T.A., 1962; active Austin Cerebral Palsy Center, Austin Assn. Retarded Children. Ford Found. fellow, 1961; NSF fellow, 1962. Registered profl. engr., Tex. Mem. Am. Soc. C.E. (chmn. structural div. Tex. sect. 1970-71, chmn. Austin br. 1971-72), Am. Concrete Inst. (chmn. com. 428 limit design), Nat. Soc. Profl. Engrs. Presbyn. (deacon 1963-66, elder 1969—). Club: Balcones Country (Austin). Home: 8815 Balcones Club Dr Austin TX 78759

FURLOUGH, ROBERT REGINAL, social worker; b. Creswell, N.C., Feb. 15, 1936; s. Henry Samuel and Myra Mae (Gibbs) F.; A.B., Fla. So. Coll., 1958; M.S.W., Fla. State U., 1961, now postgrad. in child devel.; certificate Advanced Continuing Edn., U. N.C., 1969; m. Louise Elizabeth Jerrell, June 10, 1956; children—Robert Reginal, Darinda Kay, Stanley Jerrell, Dayna Michele. Social worker Fla. Dept. Pub. Welfare, Sarasota, 1958-59; asst. dir. social services dept. Fla. State Hosp., Chattahoochee, 1961-63; exec. dir. Northcentral div. Childrens Home Soc., 1963-68; adminstr. spl. programs and interstate services State of Fla. Div. Mental Health, Tallahassee, 1969—, mem. adv. council Bur. Aging, Project Instep. Instr. undergrad. program dept. social welfare Fla. State U., Sch. Social Welfare, 1967-68; v.p. Posterity, Inc. Mem. Adv. Council on Planning of Workshops for Handicapped, State Div. Vocational Rehab. Bd. dirs. Fla. Health and Welfare Council. Mem. Nat. Assn. Social Workers, Acad. Certified Social Workers, Gideons Internat., Leon County Assn. Community Services (past pres.), Nat., Southeastern councils on family relations, Pi Gamma Mu (life). Club: Civitan International (lt. gov. Fla. dist., past pres. Tallahassee). Home: 2514 Hartsfield Rd Tallahassee FL 32301 Office: Larson Bldg 200 E Gaines St Tallahassee FL 32304

FURMAN, DAVID CHARLES, educator; b. Waco, Tex., Oct. 6, 1910; s. Herbert I. and Gertrude (Connor) F.; B.S., Rice U., 1935; M.A., Columbia, 1937, Ed.D., 1950; m. Mary Elizabeth Bendall, Dec. 25, 1936; children—David Charles, Mary Ann. Recreation leader Horace Mann Elementary Sch., N.Y.C., 1935-37; tchr. Lincoln Sch., N.Y.C., 1937-42; instr., asst. to dean Columbia Coll., N.Y.C., 1942-50; prof. phys. edn. U. P.R., Rio Piedras, 1950—. Mem. exec. bd. P.R. council Boy Scouts Am., dist. chmn., 1954—, recipient Silver Beaver award. Mem. A.A.H.P.E.R., Nat. Coll. Phys. Edn. Assn., P.R. Assn. for Health, Phys. Edn. and Recreation. Home: PO Box 22682 Univ Sta Rio Piedras PR 00931

FURNESS, BETTY, state ofcl., actress, TV personality; b. N.Y.C., Jan. 3, 1916; d. George Choate and Florence (Sturtevant) Furness; student Brearly Sch., N.Y.C., Bennett Sch., Millbrook, N.Y.; m. John Waldo Green, Nov. 27, 1937 (div. Aug. 1943); 1 dau. Barbara Sturtevant; m. 2d, Hugh B. Ernst, Jr., Jan. 3, 1945 (dec. Apr. 1950); m. 3d, Leslie Midgeley, Aug. 15, 1967. Movie actress, 1932-37; appeared stage plays Golden Boy, My Sister Eileen, Doughgirls; commls. for Westinghouse Corp., 1949-60; own shows include Penthouse Party, 1951, Success Story, 1951, Meet Betty Furness, 1953, At Your Beck and Call, 1961, Dimension of a Woman's World (radio), Answering Service (TV), Ask Betty Furness (radio); spl. asst. to Pres. U.S. for consumer affairs, 1967-69; chmn. Pres.'s Com. Consumer Interests, 1967-69; exec. sec. Consumer Adv. Council, 1967—; columnist McCall Mag., 1969-70; chmn., exec. dir. N.Y. State Consumer Protection Bd., 1970—. Address: Exec Office Bldg Pennsylvania Av and 17th St Washington DC 20006

FURNISH, VICTOR PAUL, educator; b. Chgo., Nov. 17, 1931; s. Reuben McKinley and Mildred Lorraine (Feller) F.; A.B., Cornell Coll. (Ia.), 1952; B.D., Garrett Theol. Sem., 1955; M.A., Yale, 1958, Ph.D., 1960; m. Vida Joann Carmichael, May 25, 1963; children—Brianna Ruth, Rebecca Joann. Instr. New Testament, Perkins Sch. Theology, So. Meth. U., Dallas, 1959-60, asst. prof., 1960-65, asso. prof., 1965-71, prof., 1971—. Bd. dirs. Greater Dallas Housing Opportunity Center. Recipient Philosophy prize Cornell Coll., 1951. Howes fellow Garrett Theol. Sem., 1955, Am. Assn. Theol. Schs. fellow, 1964, Research fellow Alexander von Humboldt Found., 1965-66. Mem. Studiorum Novi Testamenti Societas, Soc. Bibl. Lit., Am. Acad. Religion, New Testament Colloquium, Archeol. Inst. Am., Phi Beta Kappa, Tau Kappa Alpha. United Methodist. Author: Theology and Ethics in Paul, 1968; The Love Command in the New Testament, 1972. Contbr. to The Interpreter's One Volume Commentary on the Bible, 1971. Contbr. articles profl. jours. Home: 6806 Robin Rd Dallas TX 75209

FURNISS, JAMES P(INE), financial exec.; b. Pelham, N.Y., Feb. 1, 1920; s. Henry Dawson and Ruth (Pine) F.; grad. Phillips Exeter Acad., 1937; B.A., Yale, 1941; m. Laleah Adams Sullivan, June 15, 1948; children—Laleah A., James P. Reporter The Atlanta Constn., 1941, 45-48; asst. v.p., advt. mgr. Citizens & So. Nat. Bank, Atlanta, 1952-54, v.p. marketing, 1954-69; gen. mgr., dir. Jamaica Citizens Bank, Kingston, 1967-69; mng. trustee Great Am. Mortgage Investors, 1969-72, chmn., 1972—. Served to capt. AUS, 1941-45; ETO, NATO, N. Africa. Mem. Soc. Colonial Wars, Episcopalian. Clubs: Links, Yale (N.Y.C.); Piedmont Driving, Peachtree Golf (Atlanta). Home: 36 Wakefield Dr NE Atlanta GA 30309 Office: 3930 First Nat Bank Towers Atlanta GA

FURR, CARL AUGUSTUS, educator; b. Georgeville, N.C., Nov. 19, 1895; s. Walter Columbus and Rena (Little) F.; A.B., Loyola U., New Orleans, 1920; M.A., U. N.C., 1931; m. Blanche B. Current, June 7, 1930; children—Flora and Carl Augustus (twins). Prin. Winecoff Sch., Cabarrus County, N.C., 1921-24, Woodleaf Sch., Rowan County, 1924-39; teaching fellow U. N.C., 1926; became supt. Cabarrus County Sch., 1939, now supt. emeritus Cabarrus County Bd. Edn.; instr. Catawba Coll., Salisbury, N.C., summer 1927-30, Appalachian State Tchrs. Coll., Boone, summers 1939-40. Chmn. Cabarrus County Bd. Health, 1960—; chmn. Concord City Library, 1949—. Mem. adv. council N.C. Bd. Edn., 1960-63. Served as seaman 1st class USNRF, 1917-18. Mem. N.E.A. (exec. com. dept. of supts., dept. of rural edn. 1964-67), C. of C., Am. Assn. Sch. Adminstrs., Nat. (life), N.C. (pres. div. supts. 1960) edn. assns., South Piedmont Dist. Sch. Master's Club (pres. 1938), Internat. Platform Assn., Am. Legion, 40 and 8. Democrat. Presbyn. Rotarian. Clubs: Cabarrus Country. Home: 93 Eastover Av Concord NC 28025 Office: County Bldg Concord NC 28025

FURR, ROBERT EARL, dentist, air force officer; b. Greenville, N.C., Mar. 27, 1929; s. James Elisha, Sr., and Viola (Carpenter) F.; student Wake Forest Coll., 1947-50; D.D.S., U. N.C., 1954; certificate postgrad tng. prosthetics U. Ala., 1960-62; m. Danny Marie Hayes, Sept. 12, 1953. Individual practice dentistry, Wilmington, N.C., 1956-57; commd. 2d lt. U.S. Air Force, 1954, advanced through grades to lt. col., 1966; chief prosthetics Maxwell AFB, Ala., 1971—. Dir. J.E. Furr, Inc. Decorated Bronze Star. Mem. Am. Dental Assn., Delta Sigma Delta. Baptist. Home: Quarters 614-A 7th St Maxwell Air Force Base AL 36113 Office: Maxwell Regional Hospital Maxwell Air Force Base AL 36113

FURTADO, JOSEPH EDWARD, dentist; b. West Warwick, R.I., Oct. 23, 1931; s. Joseph and Theresa Marie (Farias) F.; A.B., Providence Coll., 1954; D.D.S., U. Md., 1961; m. Marilyn Dietrich, Mar. 21, 1959; children—Martha Ann, Joseph Edward, Nathan Farrand, James Dietrich. Individual practice gen. dentistry, Carnegie, Okla., 1963—; mem. staff Tri-County Hosp. Chmn. Big-One, 1969, pres., 1971. Cubmaster Boy Scouts Am. Served with AUS, 1954-56, 61-63. Mem. Am. Dental Assn., Okla., Southwestern Dist. dental socs. Rotarian. Home: 103 Carol St Carnegie OK 73015 Office: 6 N Broadway Carnegie OK 73015

FUSON, NELSON, educator; b. Canton, China, Sept. 4, 1913 (parents Am. citizens); s. Chester Garfield and Phebe (Meeker) F.; A.B., Coll. of Emporia, 1934; M.A., U. Kan., 1935; Ph.D. (Rackham fellow), U. Mich., 1939; postgrad. Columbia, 1942-43; m. Marian Haines Darnell, June 23, 1945; children—Allan Darnell, Dan Meeker. Instr., Rutgers U., 1938-41; drafted conscientious objector, 1941-45; research asso. U. Mich., 1945; research asso. Johns Hopkins, 1945-48; asst. prof. physics Howard U., 1948-49; asso. prof. physics Fisk U., Nashville, 1949-52, prof., 1952—, dir. infrared Spectroscopy Research Lab., 1949-67, dir. Infrared Spectroscopy Inst., 1950—; vis. prof. U. Bordeaux, France, 1956-59; vis. prof. Vanderbilt U., summer 1960; cons. AMP, Inc. Exec. Soc. Nashville U. Center Council, 1969—; participant numerous NSF and Com. on Coll. Physics Rev. confs. on coll. physics curricula. Mem. Am. Chem. Soc., Am. Phys. Soc., A.A.A.S., Am. Assn. Physics Tchrs., Am. Assn. U. Profs., Coblentz Soc. (pres. 1966-68), Soc. Social Responsibility in Sci. (chmn. membership com. 1959-63), Optical Soc. Am., Sigma Xi. Co-author Infrared Determination of Organic Structures, 1949. Contbr. articles profl. jours. Home: 911 18th Av N Nashville TN 37208

FUSSELLE, WARNER EARLE, coll. pres.; b. High Springs, Fla., June 22, 1915; s. James Isaac and Allie Loyce (Dampier) F.; A.B., U. Fla., 1939; Th.M., So. Bapt. Theol. Sem., 1943, Th.D., 1950; m. Ruth Trotter Boone, Aug. 21, 1943; children—Warner Earle, Alicia Ruth. Ordained to ministry Bapt. Ch., 1941; pastor 1st. Bapt. Chs., Ft. Thomas, Ky., 1944-45, Taylorsville, Ky., 1946-49, Rivermont Av. Bapt. Ch., Lynchburg, Va., 1949-54, 1st Bapt. Ch., Gainesville, Ga., 1955-64; pres. Truett McConnell Coll., Cleveland, Ga., 1964—, trustee, 1956-61, 62—. Chmn. edn. com. Ga. Bapts.; pres. Ga. Assn. Jr. Colls.; mem. Gov.'s Staff; program writer Bapt. Tng. Union Adult Quar. Vice pres. Lynchburg Guidance Center, 1953-54; pres. Piedmont Heart Assn., Lynchburg, 1952-54; regional chmn. N. Ga. Cancer Soc., 1966—. Bd. dirs. Assn. Retarded Children, Gainesville, Hall County Cancer Soc. Named Citizen of Year Gainesville, 1963-64. Mem. Beta Theta Pi. Rotarian, Kiwanian. Contbr. articles profl. jours. Home: 1101 S Olive Av West Palm Beach FL 33401

FUTRAL, JOHN GORDON, agrl. engr.; b. Griffin, Ga., Jan. 3, 1914; s. John Brown and Ethel Ophelia (Gray) F.; B.S., Ga. Inst. Tech., 1934; postgrad. U. Ga., 1939-40; m. Mamie Fullilove, July 5, 1941; children—Carol Ann (Mrs. Thomas B. Hawkins), Donald Gordon. Asso. agronomist Ga. Expt. Sta., 1934-52; head dept. agrl. engring. Ga. Expt. Sta., Experiment, 1952—. Mem. Griffin (Ga.) Sch. Bd., 1965-69. Mem. Am. Soc. Agrl. Engrs., Phi Kappa Phi, Gamma Sigma Delta. Baptist (deacon 1945-71). Contbr. articles to profl. jours. Home: 1133 Skyline Dr Griffin GA 30223 Office: Ga Expt Sta Experiment GA 30212

FUTRIS, STEVE CHARLES, dentist; b. Memphis, Aug. 1, 1928; s. Charles Petro and Magdeline (Kalimanis) F.; student Christian Bros. Coll., 1947-48, Southwestern Memphis U., 1948-50; B.S., Memphis State Coll., 1952; D.D.S., U. Tenn., 1955; m. Zoe Theodore, Dec. 27, 1953; 1 dau., Valerie. Practice dentistry, Memphis, 1957—. Prof. crown and bridge dept. U. Tenn. Dental Coll., 1969—; mem. courtesy staff Meth. Hosp., Memphis. Served to capt. Dental Corps, AUS, 1955-57. Mem. Am. Dental Assn., Fedn. Dentaire Internat., Memphis Dental Soc., Gnathological Study Clubs Am., Dental Legion, Memphis C. of C., Dean's Hon. Odontological Soc., Kappa Alpha, Delta Sigma Delta. Greek Orthodox. Clubs: Sertoma, Chickasaw Country, Summit (Memphis). Home: 182 E Chickasaw Pkwy Memphis TN 38111 Office: 100 N Main Bldg Memphis TN 38103

GABBARD, TOM LEMUEL, supt. schs.; b. Newport, Ky., Jan. 15, 1925; s. Houston B. and Lou Etta (Creech) G.; B.S. U. Cin., 1949; M.A., Xavier U., 1952; Ph.D., Burton Coll. and Sem., 1961; m. Dorothy Rechtin, June 5, 1948; children—Cathy Lou, Susan Lee, Nanci Lynn, Tom Lemuel. Tchr. ind. schs., Silver Grove, Ky., 1949-50, supt. schs., 1950-69; supt. schs., Newport, Ky., 1969—. Asst. prof. air sci. U. Cin., 1951-63; liaison officer U.S. Air Force Acad., 1957—. Mem. adv. council Ky. Dept. Surplus Property, 1951-59; mem. Ky. Regional Crime Commn., 1971—; mem. Community Action Exec. Bd., Edn. and Community Devel. Bd., 1971. Named Man of the Year, Jr. C. of C. Campbell County, Ky., 1950; nat. award Edn. of the Handicapped Program, 1971. Distinguished Service award Midway Jr. Coll., 1969. Mem. Am., Ky., Newport assns. sch. adminstrs., No. Ky. C. of C. (edn. com. 1971—)., Christian Englistment Bd., Early Childhood Edn. Bd., Mem. United Ch. of Christ (ch. council 1960-63, deacon 1964-68). Mason. Home: 46 Sterling Av Fort Thomas KY 41075 Office: 8th and Washington Av Newport KY 41071

GABBAY, MEIR S., govt. ofcl.; b. Basra, Iraq, Sept. 5, 1925; s. Abraham S. and Sara (Habbob) G.; student Am. U. (Beirut, Lebanon), 1947; B.A., Elon Coll., 1949; M.B.A., Ind. U., 1950; postgrad U. N.C., 1949-50; m. Florence E. Ritchie, May 6, 1950; children— Sarah, Lisa, Helene, Yvonne, Michael. Came to U.S., 1947, naturalized, 1955. Jr. accountant Strand. Skees & Jones, C.P.A.'s, Greensboro, N.C., 1951; semi-sr. accountant A. M. Pullen & Co., C.P.A.'s, Danville, Va., 1951-54; sr. accountant Price Waterhouse & Co., Washington, 1954-57; supervisory accountant U.S. Gen. Accounting Office, Washington, 1957-59, 59-61; controller Roscoe Ajax Constrn. Co., Washington, 1959; dep. dir. internal audit div. U.S. Dept. Agr., Washington, 1961-62, asst. dir. inventory mgmt. div., 1962-66; chief financial systems staff, chief accountant U.S. Dept. of Commerce, Washington, 1966—. Pub. accountant, Alexandria, Va., 1955—. Recipient Dept. Commerce Gold Medal, 1971. Mem. Am. Inst. C.P.A.'s, Fed. Govt. Accountants Assn. Fed. Exec. Alumni Assn. Home: 805 Timberbranch Pkwy Alexandria VA 22302 Office: 14th St and Constitution Av NW Washington DC 20230

GABERINO, ELIZABETH MCCAFFERTY(MRS. JOHN ANTHONY GABERINO), club woman; b. Scammon, Kan., Oct. 3, 1913; d. William and Bridget (Gardiner) McCafferty; student Okla. Catholic Coll. for Women; m. John Anthony Gaberino, June 12, 1939; children— Margaret Mary, John Anthony. Pres., St. Stephens Altar Soc., McAlester Deanery Cath. Women; state home and sch. chmn. Okla. Council Cath. Women; chmn. Deanery Nat. Council Cath. Women; civic improvement v.p. Holdenville (Okla.) C. of C.; mem. Holdenville Meml. Hosp. Fund; local pres. Schubert Music Club; pres. local P.T.A.; pres. Garden Club; ednl. chmn. Cancer Dr., Heart Dr.; chmn. Polio Dr.; pres. Roosevelt for Pres. Club; pres. Antlers (Okla.) chpt. Bus. and Profl. Women's Club; v.p. Literary Club, McAlester; chmn. nominating com. Betterment Pub. Schs. Edn. in Okla.; den mother Boy Scouts Am.; leader Brownie Scouts; mem. dist. com. Girl Scouts; bd. Community Chest; ch. youth leader; mem. coll. com. Elk Club; dist. conservation chmn. Garden Club, dist. chmn. home and sch. program; mem. Mayor's City Improvement Com.; active Community Chest; mem. Meml. City Rose Garden; patroness Beta Beta chpt. Epsilon Sigma Phi. Chmn. ch. unity Mcalester Dist. Cath. Women; mem. Holdenville Gen. Hosp. Heart Bd., Holdenville Gen. Hosp. Aux.; hon. bd. mem. Harry S. Truman Library; clothing chmn. Holdenville Red Cross, 1968-69. Mem. bd. Holdenville Community Chest, Holdenville Concert Assn., Decorated Lady of Equestrian Order Holy Sepulchre (Pope Pius XII). Mem. Internat. Platform Assn. Roman Catholic. Club: Our Lady of Cincinnati College Mother's. Home: 424 E 10th St Holdenville OK 74848

GABIANELLI, VINCENT JAMES, educator; b. Bridgeport, Conn., July 8, 1932; s. Joseph Charles and Emily (Gabianelli) G.; A.B. in Zoology, U. Vt., 1954; M.Ed., U. Miami, 1959; m. Allene Jane Caise, Aug. 14, 1954; children—Mary Emily, Kathy Ann, Vincent James, Laura Ann. Sci. tchr., Norwalk, Conn., 1955-57; curator edn. Museum Sci., Miami, 1957-60, dir., 1960-66; dir. Museum Sci. and Space Transit Planetarium, Miami, 1966-68; chmn. dept. interpretation Fla. State Mus., Gainesville, 1968-69; dir. Ocean Space Center, Internat. Oceanographic Found., Miami, Fla., 1969-71. Bd. govs. Center, Fla. Zool. Soc., Tropical Audubon Soc. Mem. Southeastern Museums' Conf. Recipient Miami Jaycees Man of the Year award, 1966. Fellow A.A.A.S.; mem. Am. Assn. Museums, Fla. Defenders of Environment. K.C., Rotarian. Conducted spl. tng. program in STP instrument for Spitz Labs. Home: 8811 SW 52d St Miami FL 33165 Office: Fla State Museum U Fla Gainesville FL 32601

GABLE, JAMES JACKSON, JR., physician; b. Oklahoma City, Apr. 3, 1918; s. James Jackson and Naomi (Jones) G.; B.S., U. Okla., 1940, M.D., 1942; m. Joan Rice, June 8, 1941; children—Diane, Robert Phillips, Susan, Howard Yelding, Rebecca, Ann, James Jackson III. Intern Good Samaritan Hosp., Portland, Ore., 1942-43; resident internal medicine San Diego County Hosp., 1945-46, VA Hosp., U. Okla. Med. Center, 1946-48; practice medicine specializing in internal medicine and cardiology, Oklahoma City, 1948—; partner, trustee Oklahoma City Clinic, 1948—; mem. active staff, trustee Wesley, Presbyn. hosps., 1948—; attending physician VA Hosp., 1950—; asso. prof. medicine U. Okla. Sch. Medicine and U. Hosps., 1961—; trustee Oklahoma City Clinic Bus. Trust; dir. Oklahoma City Clinic Bldg. Corp.; chief med. service Presbyn. Hosp., 1964, 68. Trustee Presbyn. and Wesley Hosp. Found. Served with AUS, 1943-45, 50-52. Decorated Bronze Star medal with cluster. Diplomate Am. Bd. Internal Medicine. Fellow A.C.P.; mem. A.M.A., Am. Heart Assn., Osler Soc., Diabetes Assn., N.Y. Acad. Scis. Club: Golf and Country, Mayfair (Oklahoma City). Contbr. articles to profl. jours. Home: 829 NW 41st St Oklahoma City OK 73118 Office: 301 NW 12th St Oklahoma City OK 73103

GABLE, ROBERT ELLEDY, coal and lumber co. exec.; b. N.Y.C., Feb. 20, 1934; s. Gilbert E. and Paulina (Stearns) G.; grad. Deerfield (Mass.) Acad.; B.S., Stanford, 1956; m. Emily Brinton Thompson, July 5, 1958; children—James, Elizabeth, John. With Stearns Coal & Lumber Co. Inc. (Ky.), 1958—, asst. to pres., 1958-60, sec., 1960-70, treas., 1961-62, v.p., 1962-70, chmn. bd., 1970—, also dir.; v.p., dir., sec. Ky. & Tenn. Ry., Stearns; chmn. bd. B.R. Campbell, Inc., Stearns; v.p., dir. King Lumber Co., Inc., Stearns; dir. McCreary County Bank. Commr. Ky. Dept. Parks, 1967-70; mem. pub. lands com. Interstate Oil Compact Commn., 1968-70; mem. adv. com. Ky. Ednl. TV, 1971—. Past pres., past dir. McCreary County Indsl. Devel. Corp.; trustee Stearns Recreational Assn., Inc., sec., 1962-68; bd. dirs. Ky. Mountain Laurel Festival Assn.; mem. McCreary County Air Bd., 1967-70. mem. adv. bd. U. Ky. for Somerset Community Coll. Trustee George Peabody Coll. for Tchrs. Served to lt. (j.g.) USNR, 1956-58. Named Ky. Col., Mr. Coal of Ky., 1970. Mem. Ky. Hotel-Motel Assn. (dir. 1968-70), Ky. Travel Council (dir. 1969-70), Nat. Assn. State Park Dirs., Nat. Recreation and Park Assn., Assn. Southeastern State Park Dirs. (v.p. 1969-70), Res. Officers Assn. U.S., Ky. Coal Assn., Ky. Hist. Soc., Ky. C. of C. (regional v.p., dir. 1971—), McCreary County Devel. Assn. (dir. 1970), McCreary County Jaycees (past pres.), Tau Beta Pi, Alpha Kappa Lambda (past chpt. pres.). Episcopalian. Clubs: Lions (Whitley City, Ky.); Steanrs (Ky.) Golf; Frankfort (Ky.) Country; City (Knoxville, Tenn.); Franklin County Lincoln (dir.). Home: 1 Stearns Lane Stearns KY 42647 also 290 Leawood Dr Frankfort KY 40601 Office: Stearns Coal & Lumber Co Stearns Ky 42647 also McClure Bldg Frankfort KY 40601

GABRIEL, PAT (MRS. GENE F. GABRIEL), club woman; b. Rock Island, Ill., May 2, 1922; d. Max Voyle and Faye (Crist) Wolfe; grad. Canterbury Sch. Fine Arts, 1939; m. Gene Floyd Gabriel, Mar. 8, 1941; 1 dau., Patricia Gene. Society columnist Coral Gables Times-Guide. Drama chmn. Morgan Park Jr. Woman's Club, Chgo., 1952-54, 3d Dist Jrs., 1952-54; children's theatre dir. Beverly Hills Jr. Woman's Club, Chgo., 1954; dist. coordinator Mothers March of Dimes, Chgo., 1952-55, Coral Gables, Fla., 1956-61; publicity chmn. woman's com., pres. woman's com. Variety Children's Hosp., pres. women's com., 1968-70; pres. Theatre Arts League, Inc., 1971-73; chmn. Com. of Allied and Performing Arts of City of Coral Gables; 2d v.p. Dade County Women's Com. Project Hope. Women's campaign mgr. Senator Doyle Carlton, Jr. for Gov., Coral Gables, 1960. Mem. D.A.R. (rec. sec. 1962-64), Fla. Fedn. Women's Clubs (drama co-chmn. 1960-62). Methodist. Club: Coral Gables Senior Women's (1st v.p, 1962-64). Home: 3915 Monserrate St Coral Gables FL 33134

GABRILES, GEORGE ANTONIO, mech. engring. co. exec.; b. Barcelona, Spain, June 24, 1926; s. Demitrius and Mary (Cohen) G.; brought to U.S., 1937, naturalized, 1949; B.M.E., U. Houston, 1954; m. Delphia Reeder, Nov. 10, 1947; children—Glenda, Gary, Jerel, Lorie. Gen. supervising engr. Monsanto Co., Texas City, Tex., 1954-67, maintenance supt., Trenton, Mich., 1968-69; v.p. Mallay Freeport Corp., Freeport, Tex., 1969—, dir., 1969—; v.p. Mono Valve Corp.; pres. Brazoria Aviation Enterprises Corp. Instr. Dale Carnegie Leadership Course, Dale Carnegie Supervisory and Mgmt. Course; maintenance engring. cons. Tng. dir. Explorers, Boy Scouts Am. Bd. dirs. Lake Jackson (Tex.) United Fund, Bay Area chpt. Am. Heart Assn. Served with USNR, 1944-46. Mem. Am. Inst. Plant Engrs. (regional v.p. 1964-65), U. Houston Alumni Assn. Texas City C. of C. v.p.). Lion, Rotarian. Home: 53 Willow Ct Lake Jackson TX 77566 Office: PO Box 2890 Freeport TX 77541

GADDY, JAMES LEE, JR., transformer mfg. co. exec.; b. Florence, Ark., Aug. 20, 1921; s. James Lee and Ella (Crews) G.; student Ark. A. and M. Coll., 1939-40, Washington U., St. Louis 1945-46; m. Dolores Morrel, Sept. 11, 1948; children—Donna Lee (Mrs. Donald Atkinson), Pamela, Robert Kim. Test and design engr. Molone Elec. Co., St. Louis, 1946-55; mgr. quality control Central Transformer Corp. (Colt Industries), Pine Bluff, Ark., 1955-65, v.p. quality control, 1965—. Mem. adv. com. Ark. Vocational Sch., Pine Bluff, 1962—. Served with AUS, 1941-45; ETO. Decorated Bronze Star medal. Sr. mem. I.E.E.E. Methodist (ofcl. bd., pres. Sunday Sch. class 1963-65), Patentee in field. Home: Route 2 Box 243 Pine Bluff AR 71601 Office: 2400 W 6th Av Pine Bluff AR 71601

GADE, FREDERICK HERMAN, stock broker; b. Rochester, N.Y., Aug. 28, 1908; s. John A. and Ruth (Sibley) G.; student Groton Sch., 1921-27; B.A., Harvard, 1931; m. Allison Rutter, June 25, 1932; children—Ruth (Mrs. Harry M. Ferguson), Patricia (Mrs. Wendell J. Curtis III), Sibley, John. Statistician, Investment Securities, Rutter &Co., N.Y.C., 1933-35; asst. advt. mgr. Procter and Gamble, Phila., and Cin., 1935-37; financial cons., self-employed, Greensboro, N.C. and Jacksonville, Fla., 1935-44; pres. Security Assos., Inc., Winter Park, Fla., 1949-61; partner A.C. Allyn & Co., 1961-63; mgr. Francis I. du Pont & Co., 1963-67; v.p., mgr. Laird, Bissell & Meeds, Inc., 1967—. Occasional lectr. Crummer Bus. Sch., Rollins Coll., Winter Park, Fla., 1968—; dir. Financial Data Sci., Inc., Orlando, Fla., Telesis Investment Corp., Orlando. Bd. trustees Winter Park Library Assn., 1949—, pres., 1969—; bd. dirs. Centra. Fla. Devel. Com. Rollins Coll.; founder, bd. dirs., v.p. Winter Park Meml. Hosp., 1951-58. Mem. Investment Bankers Assn. Republican. Episcopalian (vestry 1949-52). Rotarian (v.p., treas. 1955-57). Clubs: Harvard (N.Y.C.); Harvard (pres. 1945-47) (Central Fla.); University (Winter Park, Fla.); Country (Orlando, Fla.). Home: 1461 Grove Terrace Winter Park FL 32789 Office: 111 S Knowles Av Winter Park FL 32789

GAFFORD, FRANK HALL, univ. dean; b. Afton, Okla., Jan. 11, 1903; s. Benjamin Ford and Elizabeth Newman (Payne) G.; B.A., U. Tex., 1925, M.A., 1927, Ph.D., 1940; m. Anita Marguerite Engerrand, Dec. 28, 1926; children—Eleanor Marguerite (Mrs. Ernest Owen Bransford, Jr.), Frank Hall, Jeanne Engerrand. Instr. history U. Miss., 1927-29, asst. prof., 1929-31; asst. prof. history Coll. of Charleston, S.C., 1931-32, asso. prof., 1932-41, prof., 1941-49; asso. prof. history North Tex. State U., 1949-51, prof., 1951—, chmn. dept., 1951-52, dir., 1952-65, dean Coll. Arts and Scis., 1953—; summer instr. U. of South, 1944, Tulane U., 1949. Mem. Am. Hist. Assn., Am. Assn. U. Profs., Phi Alpha Theta, Pi Sigma Alpha, Pi Kappa Alpha. Home: 2520 Royal Lane Denton TX 76201

GAGE, GEORGE RAYMOND, JR., physician; b. Bklyn., Feb. 13, 1919; s. George R. and Mary A. (Green) G.; B.A., Columbia, 1938, M.D., 1942; m. Mildred Jeanne Cahill, Nov. 15, 1947 (div.); children—Mary, Joanne, Janice, Kathleen, Margaret, George III, Richard. Practice obstetrics and gynecology, Coral Gables, Fla., 1950-72; asst. prof. obstetrics and gynecology U. Miami. Served lt. M.C. USNR, 1943-47. Diplomate Am. Bd. Obstetrics and Gynecology. Fellow A.C.S., Am. Coll. Obstetricians and Gynecologists, South Atlantic Assn. Obstetrics and Gynecology, Internat. Coll. Surgeons; mem. Fraternal Order of Police Assos. K.C. Home: 365 Alcazar Av Coral Gables FL 33134 Office: 365 Alcazar Av Coral Gables FL 33134

GAGE, LESLIE LEON, owner retail furniture co.; b. Austin, Tex., Oct. 2, 1935; s. Louie and Velma (King) G.; student U. Tex., 1953-56; m. Winnie Jane MacIver, Feb. 4, 1955; children—Kyle, Georganne, Cameron, John Ragen. Owner, Gage Furniture, Austin, 1957—; owner Gage Western Investments, 1960—; dir. Union Nat. Bank, Austin, Franklin Fed. Savs. and Loan, Austin. Lectr. Bus. Sch. U. Tex., 1956—. Mem. Model Cities Commn., 1963-64, Travis County Grand Jury, 1967; active United Fund, div. chmn. 1968-71; active Capitol Kidney Found. Councilman, Austin, 1969-71. Mem. Austin Retail Mchts. Assn., Ecumena House, Austin Ballet Soc., Better Bus. Bur., Peace Officers, Campus Crusade for Christ. Presbyn. (elder 1967). Home: 8503 Emerald Hill Dr Austin TX 78759 Office: 5319 N Interregional St Austin TX 78723

GAGE, TOMMY WILTON, dental educator; b. Stamford, Tex., Oct. 6, 1935; s. Carl and Mildred (Hughes) G.; B.S., U. Tex., 1957; D.D.S., Baylor U., 1961, Ph.D., 1969; m. Loyce Marie Voss, June 2, 1956; children—Sharon, Stephen, Susan, Stacey. Individual dental practice, Munday, Tex., 1963-66; asso. prof., chmn. dept. pharmacology Baylor Coll. Dentistry, 1969—. Served with AUS, 1961-63. NIH postdoctoral spl. fellow, 1966-69. Mem. Internat. Assn. Dental Research, Am., Tex. dental assns., Am. Assn. Dental Schs., Sigma Xi, Kappa Psi, Xi Psi Phi. Methodist. Home: PO Box 252 403 Coachlight Rockwall TX 75087 Office: 800 Hall St Dallas TX 75226

GAGLIARDI, FRANK JOSEPH, bus. exec.; b. N.Y.C., June 26, 1933; s. Biagio and Mary (Iraldi) G.; grad. Gettyburg (Pa.) Coll., 1956; m. Suzanne Lee Wickman, Dec. 27, 1958; children—Mary Lee, Laura, Ellen, Gail, Caroline. Tchr., Neptune (N.J.) High Sch., 1958-59; rep. Field Enterprises Edn. Corp., Chgo., 1959, dist. mgr., 1960, regional mgr., 1961, sales mgr. home office, 1962-63, Australian mgr., 1964-65, v.p., gen. sales mgr., 1966-70; pres. Field Creations, Subsidiary Field Enterprises, 1970—. Served with AUS, 1956-58; Korea. Named 1 of 10 Outstanding Young Men Chgo., 1966. Mem. Phi Kappa Psi. Club: Atlanta County. Home: 320 Pine Valley Rd Marietta GA 30060 Office: 2759 Delk Rd Marietta GA 30060

GAGNARD, FRANK, newspaper columnist. Amusements and music columnist New Orleans Times-Picayune. Office: 3800 Howard Av New Orleans LA 70140*

GAGNE, RAYMOND JOSEPH, entomologist; b. Meriden, Conn., Aug. 27, 1935; s. Albert Joseph and Irene (LaQuerre) G.; B.A., U. Conn., 1961; M.S., Ia. State U., 1963; Ph.D., U. Minn., 1967; m. Sarah Ellen Pullar, July 20, 1963; children—Pierre Alexander, Cybele Jacqueline. Research entomologist systematic entomology lab., insect identification and parasite introduction br. Agrl. Research Service, Dept. Agr., Washington, 1965—. Served with U.S. Army, 1955-58. Contbr. articles to profl. jours. Home: 1110 Carson St Silver Spring MD 20901 Office: c/o US Nat Mus Washington DC 20560

GAIENNIE, CHARLES SEYMOUR, JR., banker; b. New Orleans, Nov. 24, 1912; s. Charles Seymour and Emma Cecelia (Waggaman) G.; B.A., U. Southwest La., 1935; certificate U. Va., Sch. Consumer Banking, 1962; m. Elizabeth Jackson Landry, Jan. 2, 1943 (dec. Dec. 1965); children—Gail Elizabeth, Nancy Ann (Mrs. George Michael Rockett). Tchr., Acadia Parish Sch. Bd., Crowley, La., 1935-39; mgr. Universal CIT Credit Corp., Baton Rouge, 1939-42; dist. supr., 1946-53; asst. v.p. La. Nat. Bank, 1953-67; v.p. Am. Bank and Trust Co., 1967—. Instr. Am. Inst. Banking, 1955-69. Active United Givers Fund, 1940—; treas. Baton Rouge Little Theater, 1946-49. Bd. dirs. Istrouma Area council Boy Scouts Am., Jr. Achievement, Audubon council Girl Scouts Am., 1964-68, 66-70. Served with Counter Intelligence Corps AUS, 1942-46. Mem. Am., Consumers, La., Charge Account bankers assns., Kappa Delta Pi. Democrat. Roman Catholic. K.C. Home: 2109 Perkins Rd Baton Rouge LA 70808 Office: PO Box 3317 Baton Rouge LA 70821

GAILLARD, JOHN PALMER, JR., city ofcl.; b. Charleston, S.C., Apr. 4, 1920; s. John Palmer and Eleanor Ball (Lucas) G.; m. Lucy Huguenin Foster, July 15, 1944; children—John Palmer III, William Foster, Thomas Huguenin. Alderman, 1951-59, mayor Charleston, S.C., 1959—. Pres. Municipal Assn. S.C., 1964-65. Served to lt., USNR, 1941-45. Mem. C. of C., St. Andrews Soc., U.S. Conf. Mayors (adv. bd 1969—). Episcopalian. Elk. Clubs: Carolina Yacht, Hbernian, Charleston. Office: City Hall Charleston SC 29401

GAILLARD, SAMUEL SEPTIMUS, steamshipping and shipside warehousing exec.; b. Perdue Hill, Ala., Apr. 9, 1900; s. John Frye and Mamie (Savage) G.; student pub. schs.; m. Elise Davis, Oct. 22, 1924; children—Barbara (Mrs. Alvin Lee Magnon), Mary Frye (Mrs. Roger B. Ray). With Agwilines, Inc., Mobile, Ala., Jacksonville, Fla., Houston, N.Y.C., Tampa, Fla., 1920-43; v.p. Blocks Terminal, Tampa, 1943-66, pres., 1966—; mgr. Lykes Bros. S.S. Co., Tampa, 1946-65. Pres., Tampa Maritime Assn., 1955-69. Bd. dirs. Fla. Ports and Fgn. Trade Council, 1958-69; bd. dirs. Seamens Inst., 1943-69, pres., 1950-52. Mem. Pres. Regional Export Expansion Council, 1967-69. Served with U.S. Navy, 1918-19. Mason (32 deg., Shriner). Club: Propeller. Home: 3016 Lawn Av Tampa FL 33611 Office: 512 N Florida Av Tampa FL 33601

GAINER, RUBY JACKSON (MRS. HERBERT P. GAINER), educator, civic leader; b. Buena-Vista, Ga.; d. William B. and Lovie (Jones) Jackson; student Miles Meml. Coll.; B.S., Ala. State Tchrs. Coll.; M.A. in English and Social Studies, Atlanta U.; postgrad. Fla. A. and M. Coll., Western Wash. State Coll., U. Conn., Okla. State U.; Dr. Humanities (hon.) Selma U., Daniel Payne Coll., 1971; LL.D., Birmingham Bapt. Coll.; m. Herbert P. Gainer; children—Ruby Paulette, James H., Cecil F. Tchr. J.B. Turner High Sch., Milton, Fla., pub. schs., Birmingham, Ala., Washington Jr. High Sch., Pensacola, Fla., prior to 1968; guidance counselor Wedgewood Jr.-Sr. High Sch., Pensacola; English tchr. Woodham High Sch., Pensacola. Brought 2 successful legal cases against Jefferson (Ala.) County Sch. Bd. for equalization of Negro tchr. salaries, 1946-47, re-instatement Negro tchrs. under Tchr. Tenure Act in 1960's; organized 1st tchrs. union, Birmingham; also organized local high sch. chpt. Future Tchrs. Am., local tchr. aide and teen service groups, local and county assns. edn.; local capt. Heart Fund, Mothers March of Dimes, Cancer Fund; active local P.T.A., chmn. Fla. P.T.A. Workshop; participant Gov. Fla. Conf. Edn., Tallahassee, Nat. conf. Profl. Rights and Responsibilities, Arlington, Tex.; participant chmn. numerous profl. ednl. confs. So. U.S.; mem. Escambia County Guidance Council; mem., past officer Fla. Guidance Council; mem., bd. dirs. Partners for Progress. Bd. dirs. Escambia County Tb Assn. Recipient Tchr. of Year Award Dist. 1 Fla. State Tchrs. Assn., also award meritorious service, Distinguished Service award, 1966, DuShane Outstanding Service award; recipient DuShane Outstanding Dir. award Escambia County Tchrs. Assn., 1967, Distinguished Service award civil, human, profl. rights, 1965; recipient Outstanding Tchr. and Leader award Fla. Edn. Assn., honor award N.E.A. and Fla. State Tchrs. Assn., 1966, also numerous awards distinguished service youth, community orgns.; cited newspapers, NAACP. Mem. Jefferson County (past sec., past pres.), Escambia County (past sec., past pres.), Fla. State (past bd. dirs. dist. 1, past pres. dist. 1, mem. tchr. edn. and profl. standards commn. and evaluation com., bd. advisers dept. classroom tchrs.), Ala. (past chmn. secondary sch. tchrs.), Am. tchrs. assns., Am. Assn. U. Women, Jefferson County Tchrs. Union (past pres.), N.E.A., Assn. Classroom Tchrs. (v.p. 1969), Nat. Council English Tchrs., Nat. Council Social Studies Tchrs., Escambia County League Justice, Future Tchrs. Am. Advisers Council, City-Wide Fedn. Women's Clubs (past officer), League Women Voters, Alpha Kappa Alpha. Baptist (mem., pres. Bd. Ushers). Democrat. Mem. Order Eastern Star. Clubs: Mary M. Bethune (officer); New Idea Art and Study (officer). Composer: God Planted You Here, Talking to the Moon, It Is Better Not to Know, In the Quiet of the Day. Contbr. articles, poems, publs. Address: 1516 W Gadsden St Pensacola FL 32501

GAINES, J.H., educator; b. Luling, Tex., Mar. 30, 1931; s. James Henry and Mary Madeline (Renfro) G.; B.S., U. Tex., 1957, M.S., 1959, Ph.D., 1966; m. Mary Jean Van Zandt, Dec. 23, 1952; children— Brenda Ellen, Leslie Ann, Kip Eliot. Research engr. Def. Research Lab., Austin, Tex., 1957-58; lectr. engring. mechanics U. Tex., Austin, 1958-59; engr. Gen. Dynamics, Fort Worth, 1959-62; instr. engring. mechanics U. Tex., Austin, 1962-66; asst. prof. engring. mechanics, U. Tex., Arlington, 1966-68, asso. prof. aerospace engring., 1968-72, prof., 1972—. Engring. cons. specializing in structures and dynamics. Served with USMCR, 1950-53. Mem. Am. Soc. C.E., Am. Inst. Aeronautics and Astronautics, Am. Soc. Engring. Edn., Sigma Xi, Tau Beta Pi. Author: (with Enrico Volterra) Advanced Strength of Materials, 1971. Home: 1721 Ridgeview Court Arlington TX 76012

GAINES, JAMES EDWIN, JR., librarian; b. Dalton, Ga., Feb. 21, 1938; s. James Edwin and Olivia (McCarty) G.; A.B., Emory U., 1961, M. Librarianship, 1964; m. Sally Nichols Martin, Nov. 27, 1965; 1 son, Thomas Martin. English tchr. Marist Coll. High Sch., Atlanta, 1961-62; library asst. Emory U., 1962-64; service librarian U. Cin., 1964-65; asst. librarian tech. services Antioch Coll., 1965-66, dir. reclassification project, 1966-68; dir. library Birmingham-So. Coll., 1968—. Mem. Birmingham Com. Fgn. Relations. Mem. A.L.A., Southeastern (exec. bd. coll. and univ. sect. 1970-72), Ala. library assns., Kappa Phi Kappa. Democrat. Methodist. Home: 922 9th Ct W Birmingham AL 35204

GAINES, JAMES PRESTON, trade assn. exec.; b. Bogalusa, La., Aug. 3, 1924; s. James C. and Clydie (Mitchell) G.; B.S., La. State U., 1947, M.S., 1948; m. Lillian Mary Lemucchi, July 30, 1960; children—Walton Jay, John Edward, Joey William. Asst. prof. agrl. econs. Miss. State U., Starkville, 1948-51; asst. to pres. Rice Millers Assn., Washington, 1951-62, exec. v.p., 1962—. Served to 1st lt. AUS, 1943-45; ETO. Methodist. Home: 8605 Virginia Av Annandale VA 22003 Office: 425 13th St NW Washington DC 20004

GAINES, SYDNEY APPEL, air conditioning co. exec.; b. N.Y.C., Mar. 30, 1895; s. Roy Grundy and Henrietta (Appel) G.; student Dallas pub. schs.; m. Betty Trobett, Aug. 17, 1921 (dec. Oct. 1950); children— Jodelle (Mrs, Maurice W. McCall), Craig T.; m. 2d,, Ethel Pack, Sept. 24, 1951. Circulation mgr. Dallas Times Herald, 1914-17; sec.-treas. Gaines Motor Sales, Wichita Falls, Tex., 1919-28; v.p. Wichita Falls Wholesale Drug Co., 1928-32; co-owner United Elec. Co., Wichita Falls, 1932-64, pres. 1964—. Chmn., Wichita County Crippled Children's Com., 1932-58; v.p. Tex. Soc. Crippled Children, 1937-46; mem. adv. com. Tex. Crippled Children's div., 1941; mem. planning com. A.R.C., 1949, adv. bd. Salvation Army, 1947-51; v.p. YMCA, 1950; chmn. Wichita Falls Park Planning Com., 1949-51; adv. council Citizens Com., 1950-53; adv. bd. vocational tng. Wichita Falls Sr. High Sch., 1949-54; chmn. Wichita County Employ the Handicapped, 1953-54; v.p. N. Tex. Cerebral Palsy Treatment Center, 1951-61; chmn. area devel. com. N.W. Tex., S.W. Okla. Devel. Assn., 1955; arrangements chmn. nat. security seminar United States Armed Forces, 1967. Precinct chmn. Democratic party, 1952; del. state conv., 1952. Served with U.S. Army, 1917-18. Named Citizen of Yr., Lions Club, 1969. Mem. C. of C. (pres. 1961), Wichita Falls Indsl. Found. (pres. 1953-54), Tex. Mfrs. Assn., Am. Soc. Refrigeration Engrs., Air Force Assn. Episcopalian. Mason (Shriner, K.T., 33 deg.). Clubs: Kiwanis (charter mem.), Rotary (dist. gov. 1956-57), Wichita, Wichita Falls Country. Home: 2615 Chase Dr Wichita Falls TX 76308 Office: 501-17 Kell Blvd Wichita Falls TX 76307

GAINEY, JOHN VINCENT, architect; b. Houston, July 18, 1913; s. John Cullen and Ethel May (Stancliff) G.; B.A., Rice U., 1935, B.S. in Architecture, 1936; certificate in Naval Architecture, U. Tex., 1941; m. Margaret Anne Boyett, Feb. 3, 1939; children—Michele Boynton (Mrs. Neil Brent Karlskind), Karen Patrick (Mrs. James Carroll Marrow). Architect, Gulf Oil Co., Venezuela, 1936-39; architect O.L. Hazelwood, Palestine, 1939-41; chief ship surveyor Consol. Steel Co., Orange, Tex., 1941-46; asso. Irving Klein, Architect, 1946-51; architect Walter Kidde Engrs., Houston, 1951-54; sr. asso. Eugene Werlin & Assos., Architect, Houston, 1954—; lectr. U. Houston; critic dept. architecture Rice U. Mem. A.I.A. (past sec. Houston chpt.), Constrn. Specifications Inst. (past dir. Houston chpt.), Houston C. of C. Episcopalian. Home: 1018 River Glyn Dr Houston TX 77042 Office: 3501 Allen Pkwy Houston TX 77019

GAIO, RAYMOND LEE, architect; b. Springfield, Ill., May 3, 1938; s. Americo and Edith E. (Bloom) G.; student Millikin U., summer 1960; profl. architecture degree U. Notre Dame, 1961. Designer, draftsman Spangler, Beall, Salogga & Bradley, Decatur, Ill., 1961-62; designer, planner, draftsman, client relations Leo A. Daly Co., Omaha, 1962-63; schematic design draftsman Perkins & Will, Washington, 1963-64; dir. Dept. of State, chpt. and student affairs A.I.A., Washington, 1964-69; mgr. client relations Vincent G. Kling & Assos., Phila., 1969-70; pres., chief exec. officer, treas. Gaio Assos., Ltd., Washington, also Los Angeles, 1970—; dir. corporate devel. Gruen Assos., Los Angeles, N.Y.C., Washington, Vienna, Teheran, 1970. Lectr. various univs.; archtl. orgn. mgmt. cons. Resource Mgmt. Corp., Bethesda, Md., also Santa Monica, Cal. Adviser, Jr. Achievement, Omaha, 1962-63; mem. Royal Ct. of Ak-Sar-Ben, 1962-63; adviser, lectr. Heights Study House, Washington, 1965; mem. joint engring. council Notre Dame U., 1958-59, 60-61. Licensed architect, V.I. Mem. A.I.A. (corporate, nat. student pres. 1960-61; co-chmn. nat. task force on student action programs), Coral Gables Jr. C. of C. Notre Dame Alumni Assn. Republican. Roman Catholic. Author: A.I.A. Organizational Guidelines Manual; A.I.A. Student Chapter Handbook; The State Organization; Chapter Organization. Contbr. articles to profl. jours. Office: Gaio Assos Ltd 1914 Sunderland Pl NW Washington DC 20036 Office: 895 S Lucerne Blvd Los Angeles CA 90005

GAIR, ROBERT MARION, govt. ofcl.; b. Pittsfield, Mass., May 6, 1929; s. Abraham M. and Dora (Schein) G.; A.B., Bklyn. Coll., 1951; M.P.A., Syracuse U., 1952; postgrad. George Washington U., 1955-56; m. Sondra Joye Sacks Battist, June 22, 1969. Budget analyst Bur. Ships, Dept. Navy-Def., Washington, 1952-53; budget examiner Office Sec., Dept. Health, Edn. and Welfare, Washington, 1955-57; budget officer Office Navy Comptroller, Washington, 1957-61; budget analyst Dept. Housing and Urban Devel., Washington, 1961-72, budget dir. Office Housing Mgmt., 1972—; program dir. Dept. Parks and Recreation, City of Pittsfield, Mass., 1950-51. Served with AUS, 1953-55. Recipient Sustained Superior Accomplishment award Dept. Navy, 1961. Mem. Am. Polit. Sci. Assn., Am. Soc. Pub. Adminstrn. Home: 5134 Wissioming Rd Washington DC 20016 Office: Dept Housing and Urban Devel Washington DC 20410

GAITHER, ROBERT BARKER, educator; b. North Bay, Ont., Can., Aug. 12, 1929; s. Edwin H. and Loyola E. (Barker) G.; B.M.E., Auburn U., 1951; M.S., U. Ill., 1957, Ph.D., 1962; m. Renate-Konstanze Zielke, Dec. 11, 1954; children—Patricia, Vivienne, Francesca. Instr., U. Ill., 1957-62; asso. prof., acad. supr. Palm Beach Grad. Center, U. Fla., 1962-64, chmn. dept. mech. engr., 1964—, prof. mech. engring., 1965—. Cons., State of Ill., E.I. duPont, Gen. Electric Co., Babcock and Wilcox. Treas., Fla. Found. for Future Scientists, 1967—. Served with USNR, 1951-54. Mem. Am. Soc. M.E., (nat. chmn. mech. engring. dept. 1971-72), Am. Soc. E.E., Sigma Xi, Tau Beta Pi, Pi Tau Sigma, Pi Mu Epsilon. Roman Catholic. Home: 2100 NW 63d Terrace Gainesville FL 32601

GAITHER, ROSCOE B., lawyer; b. El Paso, Tex., Aug. 25, 1894; B.S., U. Va., 1917; LL.B., 1923, J.D., 1971; postgrad. Sorbonne U. Paris, 1919. Admitted to N.Y. bar, 1924, also Mexican bar; now practice law, Mexico City. Mem. Assn. Bar City N.Y., Academia Mexicana de Legislacion y Jurisprudencia, Correspondiente a la de Espana. Author: Expropriation in Mexico, 1940. Address: Reforma 51-706 Mexico 1 DF Mexico*

GALANE, IRMA ADELE BERESTON, electronic engr.; b. Balt., Aug. 23, 1921; d. Arthur and Sarah (Hillman) Bereston; B.A., Goucher Coll., 1940; postgrad. Johns Hopkins, 1940-42, Mass. Inst. Tech., 1943, George Washington U., 1945, U. Md., 1958, Army Mgmt. Sch., 1964; 1 dau., Suzanne Felice. Physicist, Naval Ordnance Lab., 1942-43; electronic engr. Navy Bur. Ships, 1943-49, Army Office Chief Signal Officer, 1949-51, Navy Bur. Aeros., 1951-56, Air Research and Devel. Command, USAF, 1956-57, FCC, 1957-60, NASA, 1960-62; supervisory electronic engr. USCG Hdqrs., 1962-64; sci. specialist, engring. Scis. Library of Congress, Washington, 1964-65; project engr., advanced aerial fire support system Army Materiel Command, 1965-66; gen. engr. Navy Dept., 1966-71; project control Spectrum Mgmt. Task Force, FCC, 1971—. Registered profl. engr., D.C. Mem. A.A.A.S., I.E.E.E. (sr.), Am. Inst. Aeros. and Astronautics, Nat. Soc. Profl. Engrs. (chmn. publs. com. 1959-60), Soc. Women Engrs. (sr. mem.; nat. membership chmn. 1952, nat. dir. 1953, mem. nat. scholarship awards com. 1958), Armed Forces Communications and Electronics Assn., Fedn. Profl. Assn., Am. Ordnance Assn., U.S. Naval Inst., Marine Tech. Soc., Smithsonian Instn. (asso.), Johns Hopkins Alumni Assn. Editor: The Met. Washington Profl. Engr., 1958-60. Home: 4201 Cathedral Av NW Washington DC 20016

GALANTY, IRVING MAX, synagogue exec.; b. Bklyn., Apr. 30, 1906; s. Ellis Hyman and Dina Dora (Reiskind) G.; student pub. schs.; m. Fannye Heiman, Aug. 3, 1933; children—Ellen H., Renee L. Organizer, editor Atlanta Jewish News, 1921-22; owner, operator variety stores, Atlanta, 1937-53; exec. dir., campaign dir. Ahavath Achim Congregation, Atlanta, 1955—. Mem. Nat. Assn. Synagogue Adminstrs. (mem. governing bd. 1962—). Mason (32 deg., Shriner). Home: 1766 Johnson Rd NE Atlanta GA 30306 Office: 600 Peachtree Battle Av NW Atlanta GA 30327,

GALASPIE, LEE EDWARD, aluminum co. exec.; b. Hinton, W.Va., Apr. 3, 1908; s. Frank Edward and Margaret (McDaniel) G.; student Morris Harvey Coll., 1926-27, W.Va. Sch. Tech., 1929-30; grad. of laws Smithdeal Massey Coll., 1950; m. Kathleen Ann Garrison, May 30, 1953; children—Barbara (Mrs. Thomas H. Lowe), Charles Edward, Robert. With C.&O. R.R., 1928-39; with Reynolds Metals Co., Richmond, Va., 1939—, gen. traffic mgr., 1948-52, dir. traffic, 1952-64, dir. transp., 1964—. Recipient certificate of award for ednl. activities Asso. Traffic Clubs, 1952; named Transp. Man of Year, Delta Nu Alpha, 1959, Mem. Assn. ICC Practitioners (past pres. Richmond Chpt.), Transp. Assn. Am. (chmn. policy devel. com.), Nat.

Freight Traffic Assn. Home: 1507 Pump Rd Richmond VA 23233 Office: Reynolds Metals Bldg Richmond VA 23218

GALATZAN, MORRIS A., lawyer; b. El Paso, Tex., Jan. 21, 1911; s. Benjamin and Elka (Snider) G.; B.A., U. Tex., 1934; m. Irene Asbach, June 19, 1947; children—Judith, Sandra, David. Admitted to Tex. bar, 1934; judge 65th Jud. Dist. Tex., 1950-57; partner firm Hardie, Grambling, Sims & Galatzan, El Paso, 1957—. Pres. El Paso Jr. C. of C., 1939, Tex. Jr. C. of C., 1941. Served to capt. AUS, 1942-46. Decorated Bronze Star. Mem. El Paso Bar Assn. (pres. 1955), El Paso C. of C. (bd. dirs. 1969). Democrat. Jewish religion. Lion (bd. dirs. 1961); mem. B'nai B'rith (past pres. lodge). Home: 1220 Baltimore St El Paso TX 79902 Office: El Paso Natural Gas Co Bldg El Paso TX 79901

GALBRAITH, JAMES GARBER, physician, educator; b. Anniston, Ala., May 28, 1914; s. Samuel L. and Sarah (Garber) G.; student U. Notre Dame, 1930-32; B.S., St. Louis U., 1936, M.D., 1938; m. Marguerite Stabler, June 6, 1942; children—Ann, Jane, Mary Kay, Laura. Intern, Loyd Noland Hosp., Fairfield, Ala., 1938-39, resident gen. surgery, 1939-40; resident neurol. surgery Neurol. Inst. Columbia Presbyn. Med. Center, N.Y.C., 1940-43, instr. neurology, 1942-43; practice medicine, specializing in neurol. surgery, Birmingham, Ala., 1946—; asso. prof. surgery Med. Coll. Ala., 1946-54, prof. surgery, 1954—, prof., chmn. div. neuro-surgery, 1965. Mem. lay bd. advisers St. Bernard Coll. Served to lt., M.C., USNR, 1943-46. Diplomate Am. Bd. Neurol. Surgery (mem. bd.). Fellow A.C.S.; mem. A.M.A., So. (pres., past chmn. council), Ala. (mem. bd. censors) med. assns., Jefferson County Med. Soc. (past pres.), So. Neuro-surg. Soc. (past pres.), Am. Assn. Neurol. Surgeons, Soc. Neurol. Surgeons, Assn. Research Mental and Nervous Disorders, Birmingham C. of C. (past dir.), Am. Acad. Neurol. Surgery (pres. 1968), Alpha Omega Alpha.Office: 1919 7th Av S Birmingham AL 35233

GALBREATH, WILLIAM DUNCAN, mortgage banker, realtor; b. Memphis, Aug. 15, 1908; s. Percy and Kate (Chadwell) G.; B.A., Vanderbilt U., 1930; m. Mary Powel Abbay, Feb. 20, 1936; children—Mary Abbay (Mrs. Michael E. Jabaley), Ann Litton (Mrs. W. McDonald Thrasher), William Percy. Pres., Percy Galbreath & Son, Inc., Memphis, 1934—, Galbreath Ins. Agy., Inc., Memphis, 1934—; partner Wilson-Galbreath Co., Memphis, 1947—; dir. Union Planters Nat. Bank. Bd. dirs. Memphis Pub. Library. Served to lt. USNR, 1943-46. Named Realtor of Year, Tenn. Assn. Real Estate Bds., 1961, Educator of Year Greater Memphis State, 1963; recipient Bodley award for Americanism, Am. Legion, 1963. Mem. Nat. Assn. Real Estate Bds. (co-chmn. Build Am. Better com. 1957), Mortgage Bankers Assn. Am. (chmn. urban renewal com. 1957), Tenn. (pres. 1967-68), Memphis (pres. 1959-61) mortgage bankers assns., Memphis Real Estate Bd. (pres. 1958), Inst. Real Estate Mgmt. (pres. 1964), Memphis C. of C. (pres. 1969), Sigma Alpha Epsilon. Presbyn. (deacon 1960-64, elder 1964-68). Clubs: Memphis Country; Tennessee. Home: 282 Goodwyn St Memphis TN 38111 Office: N Main Bldg Memphis TN 38103

GALE, HAZEN FREDERICK, agrl. economist; b. Ossipee, N.H., Feb. 10, 1934; s. Parkman D. and Lucille M. (Gray) G.; B.S., U. N.H., 1956; M.S., U. Conn., 1961; postgrad. U. Minn., 1964-65; m. Betty J. Earle, Sept. 1, 1956; children—Hazen Frederick, Janet, Susan. Agrl. economist U.S. Dept. Agr., Washington, 1956-68, 70—; economist U.S. Dept. Labor, 1968-70. Mem. Am. Econ. Assn., Am. Statis. Assn., Am. Agrl. Econs. Assn. Editor: Nat. Food Situation, 1970—. Home: 2460 Stevens St Alexandria VA 22311 Office: 500 12th St SW Washington DC 20250

GALEGAR, WILLIAM CLARK, govt. ofcl.; b. Avant, Okla., Apr. 27, 1924; s. Barton and Ora (Wood) G.; B.S. in Chem. Engring., Okla. State U., 1949; M.S. in Chem. Engring., Okla. U., 1953; m. Viola Jean Snodgrass, Aug. 20, 1947; children—Jeannine Elizabeth, Janice Elaine. Jr. to prin. engr. Okla. State Dept. Health, Oklahoma City, 1949-60; dep. project dir. Ark.-Red River Water Quality Conservation Project, div. water supply and pollution control, Dept. Health, Edn. and Welfare, USPHS, Dallas, 1960-64, dep. regional program dir. Fed. Water Pollution Control Adminstrn., 1964-66; with U.S. Dept. Interior, Fed. Water Pollution Control Adminstrn., 1966—, lab. dir. Robert S. Kerr Water Research Center, Ada, Okla., 1966-67, regional dir. south central region, Dallas, 1967-70; dir. Robert S. Kerr Research Center, Environmental Protection Agy.; guest lectr. occupational medicine Okla. U. Sch. Medicine, 1957-60. Served with AUS, 1943-45. Decorated Purple Heart, Bronze Star medal. Diplomate Am. Acad. San. Engring. Mem. Okla. Soc. Profl. Engrs. Home: 2627 Woodland Dr Ada OK 74820 Office: Robert S Kerr Water Research Center Ada OK 74820

GALFO, ARMAND JAMES, educator; b. Buffalo, Nov. 16, 1924; s. Joseph and Josephine (Sabella) G.; A.B., U. Buffalo, 1949, Ed.M., 1953, Ed.D., 1956; postdoctoral study Ore. State System Higher Edn., 1967; m. Mary I. Faust, Aug. 19, 1950; children—Christopher H., Gregory J. Tchr. West Seneca (N.Y.) Central Schs., 1949-57, Dade County Pub. Schs., Miami, 1957-58; mem. faculty Coll. William and Mary, Williamsburg, Va., 1958—, asso. prof. edn., 1961-68, prof., 1968—, asso. dean, 1966-67. Cons., U.S. Navy, 1960, USAF, 1958—. Served with USAAF, 1942-45; ETO. Decorated Air Medal with 2 oak leaf clusters. Western N.Y. Sch. Study Council research fellow, 1955-56. Contbr. profl. jours. Author: (with Earl Miller) Interpreting Educational Research, 1965. Home: 108 Overlook Dr Kingspoint Williamsburg VA 23185

GALIANO, AUGUST, newspaper exec.; b. Beaumont, Tex., Jan. 14, 1927; s. Augustine and Ida (Hillman) G.; B.B.A., U. Houston, 1955; m. Elizabeth Willis, June 9, 1952; children—Margaret, Elizabeth, Allison August. With Houston Chronicle, 1955—, research and promotion dir., 1971—. Lectr. marketing research U. Houston, 1965—. Served with AUS, 1946-49, 50-51. Mem. Internat. Newspaper Promotion Assn. (pres. So. region 1971—), Am. Marketing Assn. (chpt. dir.). Home: 1011 Cheshire St Houston TX 77018 Office: 512 Travis St Houston TX 77001

GALIFIANAKIS, NICK, congressman, lawyer; b. Durham, N.C., July 22, 1928; s. Mike and Sophia (Kastrinakis) G.; A.B., Duke, 1951, LL.B., 1953; m. Louise Cheatham; children—Stephenie, Katherine, Jon. Began practice law, 1956, formerly partner firm Upchurch & Galifianakis, Durham; instr. bus. law, Duke, 1956-59, asst. prof. bus. law, Sch. Econs., 1959-66; mem. N.C. Ho. of Reps., 1960-66; mem. 90th congress from 5th N.C. Dist., 91st and 92d congresses from 4th N.C. Dist. Active Durham County Dem. party orgn. Bd. dirs. N.C. Bd. Sci. and Tech., March of Dimes, Durham Mental Health Assn. Served with USMCR, 1953-56, now maj. Res. Recipient Distinguished Service award Durham Jr. C. of C., 1963; named Outstanding Young Man of Year, N.C. Jr. C. of C., 1963. Mem. N.C., Durham County, 14th Jud. Dist. bar assns., Am. Assn. U. Profs. (mem. bd.), Am. Hellenic Ednl Progressive Assn., Am. Legion, Omicron Delta Kappa, Pi Kappa Phi, Delta Theta Phi. Greek Orthodox (trustee). Home: 2648 University Dr Durham NC 27707 Office: House of Reps Washington DC 20515

GALINDO, DESIDERIO LEO, physician; b. Allende, Mex., Feb. 6, 1919; s. Arnulfo F. and Maria (Lozano) G.; came to U.S., 1919, naturalized, 1940; B.S., U. Tex., 1940; M.D., Baylor U., 1947; m. Emma Flores, June 11, 1947; children—Denis Leo, Jonathan. Intern, Santa Rosa Hosp., San Antonio, 1947-48, resident, 1948-49; resident Baylor U., Houston, 1949-51; dir. labs. King's Daughters Clinic and Hosp., 1953-54; asst. pathologist St. John's Hosp., Tulsa, 1954-56; dir. labs. R. B. Green Hosp., San Antonio, 1956-66; cons. M. D. Anderson Hosp., 1957—; dir. lab. Luth. Gen. Hosp., 1967—, pres. med. staff, 1969; pres. Pathology Assos., Galindo & Thuss, 1970; pres. med. staff Park North Gen. Hosp., San Antonio, 1972—; clin. prof. pathology U. Tex., S. Tex. Med. Sch. Mem. San Antonio Urban Renewal Adv. Com., 1961—; vice chmn. San Antonio Pub. Library Bd., 1958-64, pres. 1964-66; trustee San Antonio City Water Bd., 1968—, vice chmn., 1972—, Bd. dirs. U.S.O., San Antonio. Served with AUS, 1942-46, 51-53, Diplomate Am. Bd. Pathology. Fellow Am. Coll. Pathologists; mem. Am., Tex. med. assns., Bexar County Med. Soc. (sec.), Am. Soc. Clin. Pathologists, San Antonio Soc. Pathologists (sec.-treas. 1960—), Am. Cancer Soc., Cerebral Palsy, Sembradores de Amistad (charter), Mexican C. of C. Methodist. Home: 338 Club Hill Dr San Antonio TX 78228 Office: Med Arts Bldg San Antonio TX 78205

GALL, LAWRENCE HOWARD, lawyer, corp. exec.; b. Leesville, S.C., Dec. 17, 1917; s. John J. and Bertha (Smyer) G.; A.B., U. S.C., 1939, LL.B., 1941; m. Winifred Belle Nelson, Dec. 18, 1948; children—Sally Patricia, Linda, Constance. Admitted to S.C. bar, 1941, D.C. bar, 1948, Tex. bar, 1966, also U.S. Supreme Ct.; mem. legal dept. E.I. duPont de Nemours & Co., Inc., also asst. to gen. counsel Remington Arms Co., Bridgeport, Conn., 1941-43; asso., then partner firm Disney & Gall, Washington., 1946-52; research dir., gen. counsel Ind. Natural Gas Assn. Am., Washington, 1952-61, exec. dir., 1961-65; v.p., gen. counsel Transcontinental Gas Pipe Line Corp., 1965—. Served to lt. (s.g.) USNR, 1943-46. Mem. Am., Fed. Power bar assns., State Bar Tex., Houston Bar Assn. Clubs: Petroleum (Houston); Congresional Country (Washington). Home: 643 Shartle Circle Houston TX 77024 Office: 3100 Travis St Houston TX 77006

GALLAGHER, BERNARD THOMAS, govt. ofcl.; b. N.Y.C., Jan. 28, 1922; ed. U. Ala.; diploma Command Staff Coll. Air U., 1962; diploma Nucelar Weapons Def. Atomic Support Agy., 1963, U.S. Army Dugway Proving Ground, 1964, Indsl. Coll. Armed Forces. Commd. officer USAAF, 1942, advanced through grades to col. U.S. Air Force, 1965; comdr. test squadron Olmstead AFB, Pa., 1958-62; chief spl. flight br. USAF hdqrs., Washington, 1963-64; chief USAF Diasaster Preparedness Program, Washington, 1964-65; ret. 1965; chief plans and programs br. Office Emergency Preparedness, Exec. office Pres., 1965-66, dep. chief div., 1966-68, chief div. nuclear biology and chem. warfare Office Emergency Preparedness, 1968—; cons. in field. Address: Box 88B Route 2 Leesburg VA 22075

GALLAGHER, JACK EDWARD, diversified industry exec.; b. Cumberland, Ky., July 23, 1937; s. George Washington and Edith (Mullins) G.; B.A., U. Ky., 1959; m. Mary Patricia Dobos, Aug. 9, 1957; children— Christopher George, Mark Edward, Shannon Gale. Pres., Gallagher-Roberts Builders, Inc., Lexington, Ky., 1961—; pres. Blue Grass Foods, Inc., 1968—; v.p. Dickens Linoleum & Carpet Co., Inc., 1968—. Active United Fund Drive, A.R.C. fund drive; active Pee Wee Football and Basketball Leagues; mem. Save the Children Fedn. State co-chmn. Builders for Embretson-Host, 1971-72; finance chmn. for Robert Wooley for Rep., 1968. Recipient builder of year award Lexington Home Builder Assn., 1969, named outstanding new Jaycee, Lexington Jr. C. of C., 1963. Mem. Home Builder Assn. Ky. (pres. 1971), Home Builder Assn. Lexington (bd. dirs. 1966-70), Nat. Assn. Home Builders (bd. dirs. 1964-70). Republican. Methodist. Club: K (Lexington, Ky.). Home: 712 Cumberland Rd Lexington KY 40503 Office: 181 Southland Dr Lexington KY 40503

GALLAGHER, JOHN GEORGE, engr.; b. Pitts., May 15, 1935; s. Edward Francis and Margaret (Clifford) G.; B.S., Cath. U., 1959; m. Anne Mary Baroody, Sept. 12, 1959; children—Catherine Anne, Anne Miriam, Mary Theresa, Rebecca Anne, John Joseph, Judith Elizabeth. Engr. radar lab. staff Melpar, Inc., Falls Church, Va., 1959-64, sr. elec. engr., 1964-67, sr. elec. engr. night vision lab. support br., 1967-69, ground systems lab., 1969—. Mem. Acoustical Soc. Am., Am. Inst. Physics, I.E.E.E., A.A.A.S. Home: 14042 Mathews Dr Woodbridge VA 22191 Office: 7700 Arlington Blvd Falls Church VA 22046

GALLAHER, ART, JR., coll. dean; b. Duncan, Okla., Mar. 22, 1925; s. Art and Mildred (Dunaway) G.; B.A., U. Okla., 1950, M.A., 1951; Ph.D., U. Ariz., 1956; m. Dixie Ann Clower, June 6, 1950; children—Brynn, Kell. From instr. to asso. prof. anthropology and sociology U. Houston, 1956-62; vis. lectr. Rice U., 1961-62; asso. prof. anthropology U. Neb., 1962-63; prof. dept. anthropology, dept. behavioral sci., dep. dir. Center for Developmental Change, U. Ky., Lexington, 1963-70, chmn. dept. anthropology, 1970-72, dean Coll. Arts and Scis., 1972—. Served with USCGR, 1943-46. Fellow Am. Anthrop. Assn., Soc. for Applied Anthropology (sec.-treas.); mem. Am. Ethnol. Soc., Am. Assn. U. Profs., Alpha Kappa Delta, Phi Delta Kappa. Author: Plainville Fifteen Years Later, 1961; Perspectives in Developmental Change, 1968. Home: 3167 Roxburg Dr W Lexington KY 40503

GALLALEE, JACK CAULKINS, lawyer; b. Lookout Mountain, Tenn., Aug. 13, 1918; s. John Morin and Lua (Caulkins) G.; A.B., U. Ala., 1939, LL.B., 1941; m. Jeppie Blacksher Adams, Mar. 17, 1951; children—Margaret Vaughn, John Adams. Admitted to Ala. bar, 1941; since practiced in Mobile; mem. firm Gallalee, Denniston & Edington, and predecessor firms, 1947—. Pres., Acreage Devel., Inc., Gen. Securities, Inc., St. Emanuel Street Corp. Mem. Estate Planning Council, Mobile, Ala. Exec. Com., 1966-67, 70-71; mem. Mobile County Bd. Sch. Commrs., 1961-65, pres., 1964-66; pres. Mobile Tb. Assn., 1956. Mem. Ala. Ho. of Reps., 1950-54. Bd. dirs. Ala. Tb. Assn., Mobile Pub. Library. Served with AUS, 1941-46, maj., 1950-51. Mem. Historic Mobile Preservation Soc., Mobile County Wildlife and Conservation Assn., Am., Ala. State, (chmn. real property probate and trust law sect 1970-72), Mobile County (pres. 1966) bar assns., Newcomen Soc., Ala. Hist. Assn., U. Ala. Alumni Assn., C. of C., (chmn. primary-secondary edn. com. 1970—). Phi Beta Kappa, Omicron Delta Kappa, Delta Kappa Epsilon. Clubs: Mobile Country, Athlestan. Home: 143 Myrtlewood Lane Mobile AL 36608 Office: 50 St Emanuel St Mobile AL 36602

GALLAND, RICHARD I., lawyer; b. Denver, Oct. 13, 1916; s. Raymond F. and Mabel (Wilson) G.; A.B., Yale, 1937, LL.B., 1940; m. Alice Halstead, July 21, 1941; children—Richard I., Holley, John H. Admitted to N.Y. bar, 1940, asso. Cravath, deGersdorff, Swaine & Wood, N.Y.C., 1940-43, Cravath, Swaine & Moore, 1946-50; chief counsel Mathieson Chem. Corp., 1950-55; v.p., gen. counsel Colo. Oil and Gas Corp., 1955-58; pres. Am. Petrofina Co. of Tex., 1958—; pres Am. Petrofina, Inc., 1969—. Served as lt. (j.g.) USNR, 1943-46. Home: 4647 Miron Rd Dallas TX 75220 Office: PO Box 2159 Dallas TX 75221

GALLANDER, CATHLEEN LYRA SPARKS (MRS. THOMAS R. GALLANDER), mus. exec.; b. San Antonio, Feb. 4, 1931; d. Walter C. and Lyra (Haisley) Sparks; A.A., Stephens Coll., 1950; B.A., U. Tex., 1952; m. Thomas R. Gallander, June 15, 1956; 1 dau., Melissa Hope Gallander. Secretarial work various oil cos. 1952-60; exec. sec. Corpus Christi (Tex.) Arts Council, 1961, mem., 1961—; dir. Art Mus. S. Tex., Corpus Christi, 1961—. Mem. Am. Assn. Museums, Am. Fedn. Arts, Coll. Art Assn., Jr. League Corpus Christi, Assn. Art Mus. Dirs., Internat. Inst. Edn., Kappa Alpha Theta Alumni. Home: 321 Claremore St Corpus Christi TX 78412 Office: 1902 N Shoreline St PO Box 1010 Corpus Christi TX 78402

GALLANT, THOMAS GRADY, editor, author; b. Gadsden Ala., June 14, 1920; s. Thomas Grady and Louise (Ralls) G.; student Emory U., 1939-41, 46-47; m. Micheal Ann Snider, Mar. 18, 1946; children—Lacy, Thomas Grady III, Scott. Editor, Cleveland (Tenn.) Daily Banner, 1947-48; reporter Chattanooga News Free Press, 1948-63; columnist Chattanooga Times, 1963-67; columnist, city editor Chattanooga Post, 1966-70; city editor News and Observer, Raleigh, N.C., 1970-71; staff writer, columnist Nashville Banner, 1971—. publicity dir. Cherokee (N.C.) Hist. Assn., 1959-61. Served with USMC, 1941-45. Episcopalian. Author: On Valor's Side, 1963; The Friendly Dead, 1964. Contbr. Marine Corps Gazette. Home: 3314 West End Av Nashville TN 37203 Office: 1100 Broadway Nashville TN 37202

GALLANT, WADE MILLER, JR., lawyer; b. Raleigh, N.C., Jan. 12, 1930; s. Wade M. and Sallie (Jones) G.; B.A. summa cum laude, Wake Forest Coll., 1952, LL.B. cum laude, 1955; m. Nona Hanes Porter, June 15, 1963 (div. Oct. 1969); m. 2d, Margaret Legette, Nov. 27, 1970. Admitted to N.C. bar, 1955; asso. Womble, Carlyle, Sandridge & Rise, Attys. and Counselors at Law, Winston-Salem, N.C., 1955-63, partner, 1963—. Chmn., dir. Cayman Reef Devel. Co. Ltd.; dir. Wacayman Bank & Trust Co., Wacayman Corp. Ltd. (both Grand Cayman), Life Assurance Co. Carolina, Brenner Industries, Inc., Phillips-Foscue Corp., Piece Goods Shops, Inc. Pres., Forsyth County Legal Aid Soc., 1963-67, Asso. Family and Child Service Agy., Winston-Salem, 1962-65, Winston-Salem Symphony Assn., 1965-66. Lectr. continuing legal edn. program N.C. Bar Found., 1966—. Mem. Am., N.C., Forsyth County bar assns., Internat. Fiscal Assn., Am. Judicature Soc., Am. Counsel Assn. (hon.), Phi Beta Kappa, Omicron Delta Kappa, Phi Delta Phi. Clubs: Old Town, Twin City (Winston-Salem); Dunes (Atlantic Beach, N.C.). Home: 224 Roslyn Rd Winston-Salem NC 27104 Office: 2400 Wachovia Bldg Winston-Salem NC 27101

GALLASPY, JOHN NORMAN, lawyer; b. Pelican, La., Nov. 8, 1932; s. Francis Norman and Hazel (Weeks) G.; B.A., La. State U., 1952, LL.B., 1958; m. Dixie Nell Yates, June 14, 1958; children—John Whithurst, Gardner Weeks, Leland Redding. Admitted to La. bar, 1958; practiced in Lake Charles, La., 1958-61, Bogalusa, La., 1961—; asst. dist. atty. 22d Jud. Dist., 1969—. Chmn. City of Bogalusa Bd. of Adjustments, 1963-69, Bogalusa Community Affairs Com., 1965. Dir. Milltown Players, 1964-66. Served to 1st lt. AUS, 1952-54. Recipient Distinguished Service award Bogalusa Jr. C. of C., 1966. Mem. Am. Judicature Soc., Am., La. State bar assns., C. of C. (dir. 1964-66), Sigma Chi, Gamma Eta Gamma. Methodist (chmn. adminstrv. bd. 1968-70). Rotarian (dir. 1962-65). Home: 1737 Gaylord Dr Bogalusa LA 70427 Office: 327 Memphis St Bogalusa LA 70427

GALLEN, THOMAS M., state legislator; b. Tampa, Fla., Dec. 28, 1932; s. Thomas M. and Mary Ellen (Satterfield) G.; student U. Tampa, 1950-52, Fla. State U., 1955-57; LL.B., U. Fla., 1960; m. Linda C. Pruitt; 1 son, Thomas M. Admitted to Fla. bar, now practice, Bradenton; mem. Fla. Ho. of Reps. Served with AUS, 1952-55; ETO. Mem. Manatee County (treas. 1964), Am. bar assns., Fla. Bar, Fla. Acad. Trial Lawyers, U. Fla., Fla. State U. alumni assns., Am. Legion, V.F.W. Roman Catholic. K.C. Home: 5506 9th Av Dr W Bradenton FL 33505 Office: 701 11th St SW Bradenton FL 33505*

GALLETTE, RUSSELL F., banker; b. Toledo, Nov. 4, 1918; s. Russell C. and Ora Ada (Harmon) G.; B.S., U. Toledo, 1942; m. Lucille Elinora Rupley, May 10, 1956; 1 son, Russell F. Vice-pres. First Nat. Bank, Lake Worth, Fla., 1959-63; v.p., Litchfield State Savs. Bank, (Mich.), 1963-68; exec. v.p., sec. Citizens Trust Co., Portsmouth, Va., 1968—; pres., chmn. bd. Portsmouth Local Devel. Co., Inc., 1970—; sec., dir. Citizens Trust Co., 1968—. Chmn. Hillsdale County (Mich.) chpt. Office Econ. Opportunity, 1964-65. Council mem., finance dir., fire commr. Village of Palm Springs, Fla., 1959-61. Bd. dirs. United Fund, Portsmouth, treas. 1970-71, exec. com. 1970-71. Served with USAAF, 1943-46. Mem. Am. Inst. Banking, Bank Adminstrn. Inst., Aircraft Owners and Pilots Assn., Club: Elizabeth Manor Golf and Country (Portsmouth). Home: 3201 Camellia Dr Portsmouth VA 23703 Office: 355 Crawford St Portsmouth VA 23704

GALLEY, JOHN EDMOND, geologist; b. Cleveland Heights, O., Apr. 2, 1905; s. Ernest J. G. and Augusta (Richmond) G.; student Mich. State Normal Coll., 1922-23; A.B., U. Mich., 1926, M.S., 1929; postgrad. La. State U., 1931-33; m. Margret B. Kramer, Aug. 29, 1931 (dec. Feb. 1968). Geologist, Shell Oil Co., Kan., and Okla., 1929-31, 33-34, dist. geologist, Amarillo, Tex., 1934-38, div. geologist, Wichita, Kan., 1940-45, area geologist, Tulsa, 1938-40, 45-48, research geologist, Midland, Tex., 1948-60, chief geologist, Midland, 1960-63; geol. cons., Midland, 1963-68, Kerrville, Tex., 1968—. Adviser radioactive waste mgmt. U.S. AEC, 1958-67; regional coordinator com. on petroleum resources U.S., Nat. Petroleum Council adv. to U.S. Dept. Interior. Mem. Am. Assn. Petroleum Geologists, Am. Ornithologists Union, Cooper, Wilson, Okla., Tex. (pres. 1955-57) ornithol. socs. Contbr. articles to profl. jours. Home: 1600 Sheppard-Rees Rd Kerrville TX 78028 Office: PO Box 1346 Kerrville TX 78028

GALLIANO, ALBERTO M., physician; b. Sancti-Spiritus, Las Villas, Cuba, Sept. 8, 1927 (came to U.S. 1958, naturalized 1963); s. Domingo and Enriqueta Maria (Galliano) G.; B.S., Instituto de Segunda Ensenanza de Sancti-Spiritus, Las Villas, Cuba, 1945; M.D., Havana (Cuba) Med. Sch., 1953; m. Maria Rosa Mendiboure, July 9, 1951; children—Rosa Maria, Alberto Enrique, Carlos Enrique. Rotating intern Ga. Bapt. Hosp., Atlanta, 1959-60, resident gen. surgery, 1960-62; resident gen. practice Halifax Dist. Hosp., Daytona, Beach, Fla., 1962-64, now mem. staff; practice medicine specializing in family practice, Daytona Beach and Ormond Beach, Fla., 1964—; mem. staff Ormond Beach Meml. Hosp., mem. exec. com. 1968-70. Diplomate Am. Bd. Family Practice. Mem. Am., Fla., Volusia County med. assns., Am., Fla. acads. gen. practice, Fla. Diabetes Assn., Ormond Beach C. of C. Roman Catholic. Home: 165 Royal Dunes Circle Ormond Beach FL 32074 Office: 722 S Atlantic Av Ormond Beach FL 32074

GALLIANO, VERNON FREDERICK, univ. pres.; b. Cut Off, La., Apr. 26, 1923; s. Emile D. and Josephine (Vega) G.; B.S. (Univ. acad. scholar), U. Southwestern La., 1947; M.S., La. State U., 1954, Ph.D. (Univ. fellow), 1960; m. Josephine Bennett, Apr. 13, 1945; children—Vernon Frederick, Timothy, Gregory, Jonathan. Tchr. Vocational agr. Larose-Cut Off High Sch., Lafourche Parish, La., 1947-54; supervising tchr. Southwestern La. Inst. (now U. Southwestern La.), Lafayette, 1948-54, prof. agrl. edn., dir. tchr. tng., 1954-60; dean edn. Nicholls State Coll., Thibodaux, La., 1960-63, pres. Nicholls State U., Thibodaux, 1963—. Dir. Citizens Bank & Trust Co., Thibodaux; trustee Gulf S. Research Inst. Mem. adv. com. La. State Supt. Edn., 1965-66; chmn. adv. council for vocational and tech. edn. La. Bd. Edn., 1969—; mem. adv. council for federally assisted programs La. Dept. Edn., 1967—; mem. La. Gov.'s Legislative Com. Study Coordination Higher Edn., 1968—, La. Indsl. Adv. Com., 1968—, Council for Devel. French-Speaking La., 1968—. Dist. finance campaign chmn. Boy Scouts Am., 1965; v.p. La. Sci. Found., 1967-68, pres., 1969—; mem. com. community action and crime La. Commn. Law Enforcement and Adminstrn. Criminal Justice, 1968—, citizens adv. com. Greater Lafourche Port Commn., 1969—, adv. com. Lafourche Parish Airport Dist., 1964-65. Chmn. St. Charles-St. John the Baptist Bridge and Ferry Authority, 1968-70. Bd. dirs. St. Joseph Hosp., Thibodaux, 1965-69; bd. advisers St. Joseph Sem., St. Benedict, La.; bd. commrs. Hosp. Service Dist. 3 Lafourche Parish. Served to lt. USNR, 1943-45, 61-62; lt. comdr. Air Res. ret. Recipient Hon. State Farmer degree La. Assn. Future Farmers Am., 1955, commendation Houma-Terrebonne C. of C., 1966. Mem. So. Educators Corp. (bd. govs. 1968—), Gulf S. (Athletic) Conf. (pres. 1971—), Am. Assn. State Colls. and Univs. (environment com. 1970—), La. State Colls. and Univs. Presidents' Council (chmn. 1964-66), La. Tchrs. Assn. and Dept. Higher Edn., Thibodaux C. of C., Am. Legion, V.F.W., John Henry Cardinal Newman Hon. Soc., Blue Key, Phi Kappa Phi, Phi Kappa Delta, Delta Tau Alpha. Democrat. Roman Catholic. K.C., Rotarian (pres. Thibodaux club 1966-67). Propeller of the U.S. (Port of Orleans). Contbr. articles to ednl. jours. Home: President's Home Nicholls State University Thibodaux LA 70301 Office: Box 2001 Nicholls University Station Thibodaux LA 70301

GALLIEN, JOHN HURST, dentist; b. Waynesboro, Tenn., Dec. 10, 1937; s. Glenn S. and Mary Belle (Hurst) G.; D.D.S., U. Tenn., 1960; m. Shelby Webb, July 13, 1957; children—Mary Susan, Jean Anne, Jane Ellen. With Tenn. Dept. Pub. Health, 1960; pvt. practice dentistry, Savannah, Tenn., 1961—. Mem. Savannah Zoning and Planning Commn. Bd. dirs. Hardin United Givers Orgn. Mem. Am., Tenn. dental assns., Seventh Dist. Dental Soc. (chmn. dental health com.), Pierre Fauchard Acad., Savannah C. of C. (pres.). Xi Psi Phi. Methodist. Mason (32 deg.), Lion (pres. Savannah club). Home: 1016 Church St Savannah TN 38372 Office: 903 College St Savannah TN 38372

GALLINGHOUSE, GERALD J., U.S. dist atty. for eastern La. Address: 2552 Valentine Ct New Orleans LA 70114*

GALLION, MACDONALD, lawyer, state ofcl.; b. Montgomery, Ala., Apr. 5, 1913; s. Thomas Travis and Varina Ann (George) G.; LL.B., U. Ala., 1937; m. Velma Lee Biddy, July 10, 1942; children—Thomas Travis III, Frances Mallory (Mrs. Francis Mallory Gallion Bear). Admitted to Ala. bar, 1937; practiced in Birmingham, 1937-42, Montgomery, 1950-54; asst. atty. gen., Ala., 1945-50, chief asst. atty. gen., 1955-58, atty. gen., 1959-63, 67—; mem. firm Gallion & Hare, 1963-66. Spl. counsel for Ala., Phenix City crime cleanup, 1954. Exec. bd. Central Ala. council Boy Scouts Am. Served as 1st lt. USMCR, 1942-45. Mem. Am. Legion (nat. law and order com. 1969-70), V.F.W., Sons Confederate Vets., Nat. Assn. County and Pros. Attys., Am., Montgomery bar assns., Ala. State Bar, Nat. Assn. Attys. Gen. (So. regional chmn., mem. exec. com.), Ala. Sheriffs and Peace Officers Assn., Montgomery C. of C., Alpha Tau Omega. Democrat. Presbyn. Elk, Moose, Mason; mem. Woodmen of World (head consul Ala. 1959-61, nat. dir. 1964—, trustee 1967—). Clubs: Montgomery Country, Men of Trinity (Montgomery). Past asso. editor The Ala. Lawyer, ofcl. pub. Ala. Bar assn. Home: 1013 Lynwood Dr Montgomery AL 36111 Office: Washington Bldg Montgomery AL 36104

GALLMAN, DAVID CLINTON, ins. co., real estate agy. exec.; b. Resaca, Ga., Feb. 27, 1922; s. Dennis J. and Mamie (Hall) G.; student N.C. State Coll., 1943; m. Lida Elizabeth Bolton, Mar. 21, 1943 (div.); children—Sharon Nelle (Mrs. Robert L. Bramblett, Jr.), Gary C., David Christopher. Owner, operator photog. studio, Calhoun, Ga., 1946-51; asst. factory rep. Advance Aluminum Castings Corp., Ga., 1951-55; dist. supr. state circulation Atlanta Newspapers, Inc., 1955-60; supr. agts. David C. Gallman Ins. Agy., Monroe, Ga., 1960—. Cons. home loans, auto financing. Pres. Monroe PTA, 1963-64. Served to sgt. USAAF, 1943-45. Decorated Air medal with oak leaf cluster, 3 battle stars; recipient Distinguished Leadership award Boy Scouts Am., 1961; Certificate of Leadership award Rotary Club, 1963. Mem. Life Underwriters Assn. (sec.), Internat. Platform Assn., Monroe Assn. Life Underwriters (pres. 1967-68), Monroe C. of C., Internat. Biog. Assn. Baptist (deacon). Mason. Clubs: Lions, Rotary (local pres. 1962-63, zone chmn. dist. gov.'s staff 1964), Toastmasters (pres. 1969-70). Home: 144 Maddox St Lawrenceville GA 30245 Office: 414 E Spring St Monroe GA 30655

GALLOWAY, ALEXANDER H(ENDERSON), mfg. co. exec.; b. Winston-Salem, N.C., Dec. 27, 1907; s. Alexander H. and Mamie (Gray) G.; student Woodberry Forest Sch., Orange, Va., 1921-25; A.B., U. N.C., 1929; m. Martha Erckman, May 10, 1930; children—Alexander Henderson, Robert Galloway, James G. With R. J. Reynolds Tobacco Co., 1929—, asst. treas., 1937-51, treas., 1951-55, v.p., treas., 1955-59, exec. v.p., 1959-60, pres., 1960-70, chmn. bd., 1969-70, also chief exec. officer, 1967-70, chmn. exec. com., 1962-70; chmn. bd., chief exec. officer R.J. Reynolds Industries, Inc., 1970—. Dir. Wachovia Corp., Am. Ind. Oil Co., In., McLean Industries, Inc., Piedmont Aviation, Inc., Allendale Mut. Ins. Co. Mem. Grocery Mfrs. Am. (dir.), Soc. of Cincinnati, Phi Beta Kappa, Beta Theta Pi. Democrat. Episcopalian. Clubs: Rotary, Twin City, Old Town, Bermuda Run, Ltd., Country of N.C., Augusta Nat. Home: 1048 Arbor Rd Winston-Salem NC 27104 Office: RJ Reynolds Industries Inc Winston-Salem NC 27102

GALLOWAY, EDGAR, physician, hosp. adminstr.; b. nr. Atlanta, Tex.; s. James and Mary E. (Perkins) G.; B.A., La. State U., 1915; M.D., Tulane U., 1921; m. Clara Elizabeth Tompkins, June 3, 1919; children—Mrs. James Urban Morrison, Mrs. George T. Brown, Margaret Ann (Mrs. Burch), Martha Elaine. Intern Shreveport (La.) Charity Hosp., 1921-22, adminstr., 1940-48, 54-56, 61—; adminstr. Confederate Meml. Med. Center; practice medicine, Shreveport, 1921-40; adminstr. Duval Med. Center, Jacksonville, Fla., 1949-54; field rep. Joint Commn. on Accreditation Hosps., 1957-61. Served to 1st lt., inf., U.S. Army, World War I. Mem. Am. Coll. Hosp. Adminstrs., La. Hosp. Assn. (past pres.). Democrat. Baptist. Mason (Shriner). Home: 7857 Broadacres Rd Shreveport LA 71109 Office: 1541 Kings Hwy Shreveport LA 71103

GALLOWAY, FRANK AMEND, indsl. engr.; b. Tulsa, Nov. 12, 1938; s. Frank H. and Odessa M. (Amend) G.; B.S. in Indsl. Engring., Okla. State U., 1961, M.B.A., 1962; m. Verna C. Mason, June 4, 1960; children— Mary Catherine, Linda Kay. Systems engr. IBM, Oklahoma City, 1962-69, staff engr., Washington, 1969—. Mem. Am. Inst. Indsl. Engrs. (chpt. pres. 1968-69). Kappa Sigma. Democrat. Presbyn. (deacon 1967-69). Elk. Home: 4918 Gadsen Dr Fairfax VA 22030 Office: 1825 St NW Washington DC 20006

GALLOWAY, GRADY RANSOM, state ofcl.; b. Whittier, N.C., Apr. 13, 1919; s. Elbert Daniel and Sarah (Ward) G.; B.S., Western Carolina U., 1941, M.A., 1961; m. Irene Graham, Oct. 20, 1950; children—Karen, Neal, Mark. Rehab. counselor, Asheville, N.C., 1946-55; dist. rehab. supr., Asheville, 1955-65; asst. dir. div. vocational rehab., Raleigh, N.C., 1965; exec. dir. N.C. Commn. for Blind, Raleigh, 1965-70; asst. dir. Vocational Rehab. Agy., N.C. Dept. Human Resources, 1970—. Mem. Gov.'s Council on Comprehensive Health Planning, 1968-70. Bd. dirs. Raleigh Lions Clinic; past trustee Am. Printing House for Blind; mem. adv. com. on rehab. U. N.C., E. Carolina U. Served with USCGR, 1942-46. Decorated Silver Star medal. Mem. Am. Assn. Workers for Blind (past (chpt. pres.), Am. Legion, Naval League (sec.-treas.), N.C. Rehab. Assn. (past. pres.), Rehab. Counseling Assn. (past regional pres.), N.C. Assn. for Blind (past dir.), Soc. for Prevention Blindness (chpt. dir.). Baptist. Lion. Home: 104 Shirley Dr Cary NC 27511 Office: 303 1/2 W Martin St Raleigh NC 27602

GALLOWAY, JAMES HARRISON, oil co. exec.; b. Sour Lake, Tex., May 11, 1908; s. James Harrison and Katherine (Williams) G.; B.S., Tex. A. and M. Coll., 1930; grad. Advanced Mgmt. Program, Harvard, 1954; m. Marie Muenster, Jan. 20, 1934. With Humble Oil & Refining Co., Houston, 1930—, asst. mgr. prodn. dept., 1954, dir., 1958, v.p. Central region, 1962—, dir. Houston, 1963, v.p., dir., 1967—. Served to capt. C.E., AUS, 1942-45. Decorated Bronze Star with Oak leaf cluster. Registered engr., Tex. Mem. Am. Petroleum Inst., Am. Inst. Mining, Metall. and Petroleum Engrs., Mid-Continent Oil and Gas Assn., Tex. Soc. Profl. Engrs., Houston Engring. and Sci. Soc. Episcopalian. Clubs: Houston Country, Petroleum, Houston (Houston). Home: 327 Westminster Dr Houston TX 77024 Office: PO Box 2180 Houston TX 77001 ALSO 800 Bell Av Houston TX 77002

GALLOWAY, PAUL VERNON, bishop; b. Mountain Home, Ark., Apr. 5, 1904; s. James Jesse and Ella (Burkhead) G.; student Hendrix Coll., 1921-22, D.D., 1951; A.B., Henderson-Brown Coll., 1926; student So. Meth. U., 1926-27, LL.D. (hon.), 1964; B.D., Yale, 1929; student U. Chgo., 1933; LL.D., Ark. A. and M. Coll., 1947; L.H.D., Oklahoma City U., 1960; Litt.D., McMurray Coll.; m. Elizabeth Boney, June 14, 1932; 1 son, Paul Vernon. Ordained to ministry Meth. Ch., 1929, consecrated bishop, 1960; pastor in Ark., 1925-50, Okla., 1950-60; bishop of San Antonio-North West Texas area, 1960-64; bishop Ark. area, 1964—; pres. Gen. Bd. Health and Welfare Ministries, 1968-72, now ret.; visitor to mission fields abroad, 1947, 54, 58, 59, 61, 62. Chmn. conf. hosps. and homes Meth. Ch., 1939-48, chmn. commn. world service and finance, 1952-60, program chmn., also chmn. commn. entertainment, 1952-60, chmn. commn. camp activities, 1964—, chmn. campus commn., mem. Com. on Christian Vocations; mem., v.p. nat. div. of Bd. Missions. Mem. Gov. Ark. Com. to Study Vocational Tng., 1939; rep. Ark. A. and M. Coll. on Ednl. Com. Colls. and Higher Edn., 1936-50. Trustee Meth. Hosp., Memphis, Meth. Childrens Home, Little Rock; bd. dirs. So. Meth. U., Lydia Patterson Inst., El Paso, McMurry Coll., Southwestern U., Ark. A. and M. Coll.; bd. mgrs. Ark. Indsl. Schs. Mem. Delta Chi, Pi Kappa Delta (pres. 1925-26; Diamond key 1926). Mason (32 deg., grand chaplain Ark.). Home: 200 Center Plaza Tulsa OK 74119 Office: 723 Center Little Rock AR 72201

GALPHIN, BRUCE MAXWELL, writer; b. Tallahassee, Aug. 11, 1932; s. Lawrence Tatum and Helen (Hoskins) G.; A.B., Fla. State U., 1954. With Atlanta Constn., 1954-69, polit. corr., 1956-60, race relations specialist, 1960-62 editorial asso., 1963-69; Atlanta bur. chief The Washington Post, 1969-70; mng. editor Atlanta mag., 1971—. Nieman fellow, Harvard, 1962-63; named Outstanding Young Man in Professions, Atlanta Jr. C. of C., 1967. Mem. Atlanta Press Club (pres. 1968). Author: The Riddle of Lester Maddox, 1968. Contbr. articles to various mags. including Saturday Rev., N.Y. Times mag., Gentleman's Quar., New Republic, Nation. Contbg. editor Atlanta mag., 1963-71. Home: 217 Westminstr Dr NE Atlanta GA 30309 Office: Commerce Bldg Atlanta GA 30303

GALUSHA, BRYANT LEROY, physician; b. Morgantown, W.Va., Nov. 28, 1927; s. Harold Leroy and Edna (Sines) G.; A.B., W.Va. U., 1948; M.D., Western Reserve U., 1952; m. Shirley McCann, July 8, 1950; children— Janice, Sherlyn, Katherine. Intern Univ. Hosp., Cleve., 1952-53, resident, 1953-55; practice medicine, specializing in pediatrics, Charlotte, N.C., 1957-62; dir. med. edn. Charlotte Meml. Hosp., 1962—; asst. clin. prof. pediatrics U. N.C., 1965—. Mem. N.C. Bd. Med. Examiners, 1968—. Served with M.C., AUS, 1955-56. Fellow Am. Acad. Pediatrics; mem. Phi Beta Kappa, Alpha Omega Alpha. Home: 3308 Ferncliff Rd Charlotte NC 28211 Office: Charlotte Meml Hosp Charlotte NC 28203

GAMBATESE, JOSEPH MICHAEL, profl. assn. exec.; b. Cleve., Mar. 13, 1912; s. Joseph and Concetta (Vaccariello) G.; student Miami U., Oxford, O., 1929-30; A.B., Western Res. U., 1933; m. Betty Antonelli, Sept. 8, 1934; children—Roger, Richard. Reporter, Cleve. Plain Dealer, 1934-42; information dir. press sect. Nat. War Labor Bd., Washington, 1943-45; information dir. Nat. Wage Stablzn. Bd., Washington, 1945; reporter Washington bur. McGraw-Hill, 1946-53; communications cons. Gen. Electric Co., N.Y.C., 1953-54; asso. editor Nation's Business, Washington, 1953-65; mgr. news dept. C. of C. of U.S., Washington, 1965-71, communications gen mgr., 1971—. Mem. Indsl. Relations Research Assn., Pub. Relations Soc. Am., Nat. Press Club (treas. 1965). Editor: Golf Guide, 1963—. Home: 7119 Exfair Rd Bethesda MD 20014 Office: 1615 H St NW Washington DC 20006

GAMBEE, BUDD LESLIE, educator; b. Auburn, N.Y., Nov. 16, 1917; s. Budd Leslie and Maude (Henry) G.; B.A., U. Rochester, 1940; A.B. in L.S., U. Mich., 1941, M.A. in L.S., 1949, Ph.D., 1963; m. Ruth Blanche Richter, May 30, 1944. Reference librarian Aurora (Ill.) Pub. Library, 1941-43; sr. asst. librarian Detroit Pub. Library, 1943-48; chief audio-visual aids dept. W.Va. U., 1948-51; film librarian, asst. prof. library sci. Ball State U., Muncie, Ind., 1951-58; asso. prof. dept. librarianship State U. N.Y. at Albany, 1958-61; asso. prof. Sch. Library Sci., U. N.C., Chapel Hill, 1963-71, prof., 1971—; Fulbright lectr. library sci. Am. Coll. for Girls and Ibrahim U., Cairo, Egypt, 1952-53; vis. lectr. Sch. Library Sci. U. Mich., 1963; vis. prof. North Tex. State U., Denton, summer 1970; lectr. Nat. Def. Edn. Act Insts., summers 1965, 67, 68; audio-visual workshops Raleigh Pub. Schs., 1969, Kanawha County Schs., Charleston, W.Va., 1970; audiovisual cons. J. Murrey Atkins Library, U. N.C. at Charlotte, 1971. Bd. dirs. Muncie Art Assn., 1954-58. Recipient Hull prize and Charles Ellis Caldwell prize U. Rochester, 1940. Mem. Am. (sec.-treas. tchrs. sect. library edn. div. 1966-69), N.C. (sec. commn. on edn. for librarianship) library assns., Am. Assn. U. Profs., Am. Assn. Library Schs., N.C. Art Soc., Chapel Hill Hist. Soc. Contbr. articles to profl. jours. Home: 121 Markham Dr Chapel Hill NC 27514 Office: Sch Library Sci Manning Hall UNC Chapel Hill NC 27514

GAMBLE, ROBERT ALAN, librarian; b. Duncan, Okla., June 1, 1940; s. Maurice Dean and Cleta Mae (Sharp) G.; B.A., Okla. State U., 1963; postgrad. U. Kan., 1963; M.L.S., U. Okla., 1965. Govt. documents librarian Oakland U., Rochester, Mich., 1965-67; govt. documents librarian U. Tex. at Arlington, 1967-69, dir. Tex. labor archives, 1969—. Mem. Soc. Am. Archivists, Western History Assn. Home: 930 Peach St Arlington TX 76011 Office: Texas Labor Archives University of Texas Arlington TX 76010

GAMBLE, ROY JACKSON, forester; b. nr. Hanceville, Ala., June 5, 1924; s. Ota K. and Ivela (Parsons) G.; B.S., Auburn U., 1951; m. Mary Jane Duren, Apr. 18, 1953; children—David Jackson, Steven Roy, Julia Dale, John Neil, Barbara Jane. Asst. forester Gulf States Paper Corp., 1951-52, asst. dist. forester, 1952-54, dist. forester, 1954-61, dist. supt., 1961—; intermittent cons.-dist. chmn. Ala. Tree Farm Com., 1962—; now pulpwood dealer, Cullman, Ala. Active Boy Scouts Am. Vice chmn. Bibb County Republican Com., 1964—. Served with USMCR, 1944-46. Mem. Soc. Am. Foresters, Forest Farmers Assn., Ala. Registered Foresters. So. Methodist. Mason. Contbr. articles to co. jours. Home: 741 Scenic Dr NE Cullman AL 35055 Office: PO Box 253 Hanceville AL 35077

GAMBLE, WILLIAM BELSER, JR., physician; b. Andrews, S.C., Apr. 17, 1925; s. William Belser and Anna (Moyd) G.; B.S., U. S.C., 1945; M.D., Med. Coll. S.C., 1948; M.P.H., U. N.C., 1972; M. Margaret Florence DuBose, June 7, 1947; children—William Belser III, Richard Ervin, Heather Moyd. Intern, Roper Hosp., Charleston, S.C., 1948-49; resident pediatrics, teaching fellow Med, Coll. S.C., Charleston, 1953-56, asst. prof. pediatrics; practice medicine specializing in pediatrics, Charleston, 1956-71; state epidemilogist State Bd. Health, Columbia., S.C., 1972—; mem. staffs Med. Coll., Roper, St. Francis hosps., Charleston. Pres., Coastal Carolina Tb. and Health Assn. Dist. dir. S.C. Bd. of Health, 1972. Bd. dirs. Charleston County Mental Health Assn., Charleston County Tb Assn., Charleston. Served with M.C., AUS, 1951-53. Diplomate Am. Bd. Pediatrics, Am. Bd. Clin. Allergy and Immunology. Mem. A.M.A., Am. Acad. Pediatrics, Am. Acad. Allergy, Phi Beta Kappa, Alpha Kappa Kappa, Kappa Sigma, Alpha Omega Alpha. Methodist (mem. ofcl. bd.). Rotarian (past pres.). Contbr. articles to profl. jours. Address: Bd Health J Marion Sims Bldg Columbia SC

GAMBRELL, BARMORE P., lawyer; b. Belton, S.C., Jan. 27, 1894; s. Enoch Pepper and Macie (Latimer) G.; B.A., Furman U.; Washington and Lee U.; LL.B., Georgetown U. Clk. office of sec. of U.S. Senate, 1 1/2 years; in practice of law, Atlanta, 1920—; mem. law firm Arnold, Arnold & Gambrell, 1930-33, Arnold, Gambrell & Arnold, 1933-52, Arnold & Gambrell, 1952-57; pvt. practice, 1957—. Served with U.S. Navy, World War I. Recipient Distinguished Alumnus award Furman U., 1968. Fellow Am. Coll. Trial Lawyers, Am. Bar Found.; mem. Am., Atlanta bar assns., State Bar Ga., Am. Judicature Soc., Lawyers Club, Am. Legion (comdr. Atlanta post 1922-23). Democrat. Baptist. Clubs: Capital City, Piedmont Driving (Atlanta). Home: 2025 Peachtree St NE Atlanta GA 30309 Office: 1512 William-Oliver Bldg Atlanta GA 30303

GAMBRELL, DAVID HENRY, lawyer; b. Atlanta, Dec. 20, 1929; s. E. Smythe and Kathleen (Hagood) G.; B.S., Davidson Coll., 1949; LL.B. cum laude, Harvard, 1952; m. Luck Coleman Flanders, Oct. 16, 1953; children—Luck Coleman, David Henry, Alice Kathleen Hagood, Mary Latimer. Admitted to Ga. bar, 1951; pvt. practice, Atlanta, 1952-54; teaching fellow Harvard Law Sch., 1954-55; practice in Atlanta, 1956—; partner firm Gambrell & Mobley, 1963—; U.S. senator, 1970—. Bd. dirs. Ga. YMCA, 1965—, V.P., 1965-66; trustee Met. Atlanta Commn. Crime and Juvenile Delinquency, 1966-68; bd. dirs. Nat. Legal Aid and Defender Assn., 1965—. Mem. Am., Atlanta (pres. 1965-66) bar assns., State Bar Ga. (bd. govs. 1964-66. pres. 1967-68), Lawyers Club Atlanta, N.C. Soc. Cincinnati, Sigma Alpha Epsilon, Omicron Delta Kappa. Democrat. Presbyn. Kiwanian. Clubs: Piedmont Driving, Atlanta Country, Capital City (Atlanta). Home: 3820 Castlegate Dr NW Atlanta GA 30327 Office: Senate Office Bldg Washington DC 20510

GAMBRELL, E(NOCH) SMYTHE, lawyer; b. Belton, S.C., Jan. 29, 1896; s. Enoch Pepper and Macie Amanda (Latimer) G.; A.B., U. S.C., 1915, LL.D., 1953; LL.B., Harvard, 1922; LL.D., So. Meth. U., 1956, U. Montreal, 1956, Emory U., 1964; m. Kathleen Hagood, Feb. 24, 1927 (dec. 1932); children—Robert H. (dec.), David H. Prin. pub. sch., Bannockburn, S.C., 1915-16; supt. schs., Pelzer, S.C., 1916-18; admitted to Ga. bar, 1922, since practiced in Atlanta; sr. partner law firm Gambrell, Russell, Killorin, Wade & Forbes; gen. counsel, adv. dir. Eastern Air Lines, Inc.; dir. Southwire Co.; counsel numerous indsl., ins., transp., other cos.; prof. law Emory U., 1922-40. Served with Machine Gun Co., 324th Inf., 81st Div., AEF, 1918-19; was instr. AEF Univ., Beaune, France, Pres. Atlanta Legal Aid Soc., 1924-41 (organizer); mem. Ga. state council YMCA, 1931—; trustee U. S.C. Edn. Found. Fellow Am. Coll. Trial Lawyers; mem. Ga. C. of C. (pres. 1952-54), Am. Bar Assn. (pres. 1955-56, gov. 1955-57), Ga. (v.p. 1934), Atlanta bar assns., Assn. Bar City of N.Y., Air Law Inst., Internat. Assn. Ins. Counsel, Am. Law Inst., Am. Judicature Soc. (v.p. 1956-58), Acad. Polit. Sci., Lawyers Club of Atlanta (pres. 1948-49), Harvard Law School Assn. (mem. overseers vis. com.), Am. Bar Found. (pres. 1955-56, chmn. fellows, 1956-57), Order of Coif, Phi Beta Kappa, Phi Delta Phi, Sigma Alpha Epsilon. Baptist. Clubs: Capital City, Harvard, Chair Endowment of Univ. S.C. (chmn.) Piedmont Driving. Contbr. articles to legal pubs. Home: 1327 Peachtree St Atlanta GA 30309 Office: 1st Nat Bank Tower Atlanta GA 30303

GAMBRELL, HERBERT, historian; b. Tyler, Tex., July 15, 1898; s. Joel Halbert Gambrell; B.A., M.A., So. Meth. U.; postgrad. U. Nacional de Mexico; Ph.D., U. Texas; m. Virginia Leddy, Aug. 4, 1940. Mem. faculty So. Meth. U., chmn. history dept., 1948-64; hist. dir. Tex. Centennial, 1936; dir. museum Tex. Hall of State, Dallas Hist. Soc., Dallas, 1938-48, hist. dir., 1948—. Decorated officer Acad. France; recipient Collins award Tex. Inst. Letters, 1948; Faculty Achievement award So. Methodist U. Alumni Faculty, 1958. Fellow Royal Soc. Arts; mem. Tex. Inst. Letters (sec., editor, pres. 1950-52), Newcomen Soc. New Eng., Philos. Soc. Tex. (sec., editor, pres. 1968-69), French Council History and Heraldy (corr.), Soc. Am. Historians, Tex. State Hist. Assn. (pres. 1950-52), Phi Beta Kappa. Author: Texas Yesterday and Today; Mirabeau Buonaparte Lamar, Troubadour and Crusader; Anson Jones, the Last President of Texas; (with Virginia Gambrell) A Pictorial History of Texas, 1960 (Summerfield G. Roberts award for best Tex. book of year Sons of Rep. of Tex., 1960). Address: Tex Hall of State Fair Pk Dallas TX 75226

GAMBRELL, VIRGINIA LEDDY (MRS. HERBERT GAMBRELL), museum dir.; b. Greenville, Tex., Aug. 7, 1910; d. Charles A. Leddy; B.A., U. Tex., 1933; postgrad. So. Meth. U., 1934; m. Herbert Gambrell, Aug. 4, 1940. Archivist, Dallas Hist. Soc., 1934-48, dir. museum Tex. Hall of State, 1948—. Mem. Tex. Library and Hist. Commn., 1944-51, chmn., 1949-51. Fellow Royal Soc. Arts; mem. Am. Assn. State and Local History (v.p. 1948-68), Soc. Am. Archivists (mem. council 1945-48), Phi Beta Kappa. Author: (with Herbert Gambrell) A Pictorial History of Texas, 1960 (Summerfield G. Roberts award for best Tex. book of year Sons of Rep. of Texas, 1960). Address: Tex Hall of State Fair Pk Dallas TX 75226

GAMER, SAUL RICHARD, lawyer; b. New Haven, Mar. 27, 1906; s. Samuel and Bertha (Resnik) G.; Ph.B., Yale, 1927, LL.B., 1929; m. Ethel Huchberger, June 28, 1934; children—Janet G. (Mrs. T.S.L. Perlman), Susan J. (Mrs. W.B. Blacklow). Admitted to Conn. bar,

1929, N.Y. bar, 1931, D.C. bar, 1939, U.S. Supreme Ct., 1935; faculty research asst. Yale Law Sch., 1929-30; charge investigations for Report Nat. Commn. on Law Observance and Enforcement (Wickersham Commn.), on Lawlessness in Law Enforcement, 1930-31; asso. Engelhard, Pollak, Pitcher & Stern, N.Y.C., 1931-34; atty. NRA, Dept. Agr., Rural Electrification Adminstrn., 1934-37; practice law, New Haven, 1938; supervisory loan atty. Rural Electrification Adminstrn., chief court claims sect., civil div. Dept. Justice, 1939-58; commr. U.S. Ct. of Claims. Washington, 1958-72, chief commr., 1972—. Recipient merit citation Nat. Civil Service League, 1958. Mem. Am., Fed. bar assns., Phi Beta Kappa. Bd. editors Yale Law Jour., 1928-29. Contbr. legal periodicals. Home: 2818 Kanawha St NW Washington DC 20015 Office: Court of Claims Washington DC 20005

GAMMIE, JOHN GLENN, educator, clergyman; b. N.Y.C., Jan. 20, 1929; s. John and Helen Virginia (Sims) G.; A.B., Dartmouth, 1950; B.D., Union Theol. Sem., 1953; student U. Tubingen, 1956, U. Basel, 1958; Ph.D., U. Edinburgh, 1962; m. Catherine Elizabeth Widdowson, Dec. 7, 1957; children—Helen, John, Stephen, Alison. Ordained to ministry Presbyn. Ch., 1953; minister, North Shore Presbyn. Ch., Great Neck, N.Y., 1958-63; asst. prof. religion, U. Tulsa (Okla.), 1963-68, asso. prof., 1968—, faculty research fellow, 1965, 67, 70. Mem. exec. com. Barnard P.T.A., 1970—. Bd. dirs., Tulsa Urban League, 1964-66, Concerttime, Inc., Friends of Tulsa Pub. Library. Served with AUS, 1953-55. Mem. Soc. Bibl. Lit., Cath. Bibl. Assn., Am. Acad. Religion (sec. S.W. region 1968-71), Am. Schs. Oriental Research, Am. Assn. U. Profs., Phi Beta Kappa. Contbr. articles on O.T. to religious jours. Home: 1628 S Atlanta Av Tulsa OK 74104

GAMMON, GERALD, pub. relations exec.; b. DuQuoin, Ill., Nov. 16, 1925; s. James Harley and Lora (Jones) G.; student Nat. U. Mexico, 1943, U. Mo., 1942-44, 46-48; m. Flora Dean Southworth, July 15, 1950; children—Gay Lee, Gregg. Writer, The Courier-Jour., Louisville, 1948-52; asst. to dir. pub. relations Reynolds Metals Co., Louisville, 1952-58, dir. information, Richmond, 1960-63; dir. pub. relations Robertshaw Controls Co., Richmond, Va., 1958-60, 63—. Served with USNR, 1944-46. Mem. Pub. Relations Soc. Am., Sigma Delta Chi. Club: Downtown. Home: 4319 Stuart Av Richmond VA 23221 Office: 1701 Byrd Av Richmond VA 23226

GAMMON, WILLIAM HOWARD, educator, computer specialist; b. Danville, Va., Mar. 9, 1910; s. William Edward and Nannie Ellen (Fallin) G.; B.A., George Washington U., 1941, D.B.A., 1971; M.A., Am. U., 1956; m. Martha Winters, Sept. 3, 1937; children—Robert Winston, Richard Harriss, Lawrence Edward, Philip Lee. With Fed. civil service, 1930-70, orgn. and methods examiner U.S. Bur. Budget, Washington, 1945-55; automatic data processing systems analyst Office Sec. Def., Washington, 1955-63; asst. to dir. Nat. Bur. Standards, Washington, 1963-66, asst. to dir. Center for Computer Scis, and Tech., 1966-70; asst. prof. Center for Tech. and Adminstrn., Am. U., Washington, 1970—. Served to lt. (j.g.) USNR, 1944-46. Recipient Evening Star trophy Arlington Civic Fedn., 1956. Mem. Assn. for Computing Machinery, Am. Soc. Pub. Adminstrn., I.E.E.E., Harvard Bus. Sch. Club Washington, Acad. Mgmt., Soc. for Mgmt. Information Systems, A.A.A.S., Am. Assn. U. Profs. Home: 5740 N 18th St Arlington VA 22205 Office: Center for Tech and Adminstrn Am U Washington DC 20016

GAMMON, WILLIAM HUGH, oil co. exec.; b. St. Louis, Mar. 8, 1926; s. James Blakely and Floy Mabel (Randolph) G.; B.S., U. Mo., 1949, Chem.E., 1968; m. Dorothy L. Scheips, Nov. 25, 1948; children—Nancy (Mrs. Peter Dienna), Janice Lynn, William Hugh. Pilot plant engr. Sinclair Research Labs., Harvey, Ill., 1949-55; devel. supr. Ashland Oil, Inc. (Ky.), 1955-60, asst. dir. research and devel., 1960-63, mgr. research and devel. united carbon div., Houston, 1963, dir. research and devel., 1964; pres. united carbon div., 1964-68, v.p., 1966; sr. v.p. Ashland Chem. Co., Columbus, O., adminstrv. v.p., Ashland, Ky., 1970—, also dir. Chmn. bd. Spindle Top Research, Lexington, Ky. Pres. P.T.A., 1961-62. Served with USMCR, 1944-46. Decorated Purple Heart. Kiwanian. Clubs: Bellefonte Country (Ashland); Lakeside Country (Houston). Home: 1718 Oaks Dr Ashland KY 41101 Office: PO Box 391 Ashland KY 41101

GAMST, FREDERICK CHARLES, educator; b. N.Y.C., May 24, 1936; s. Rangvald Julius and Aida (Durante) G.; A.A., Pasadena City Coll., 1959; A.B., U. Cal. at Los Angeles, 1961; Ph.D., U. Cal. at Berkeley, 1967; m. Marilou Swanson, Jan. 28, 1961; 1 dau., Nicole Christina. Anthrop. fieldwork North Central Ethiopia, 1964-65; instr. anthropology Rice U., Houston, 1966—, asst. prof., 1967—; faculty asso. Lovett Coll., 1968—. Acting dir. Houston Inter-U. African Studies Program, 1969—, Woodrow Wilson Nat. fellow, 1961-62; Ford Found. fgn. area fellow, 1962-63; Social Sci. Research Council and Am. Council of Learned Socs. Fgn. area fellow, 1963-64, 64-65, 66. Fellow Am. Anthrop. Assn., Soc. for Applied Anthropology, African Studies Assn.; mem. Internat. African Inst., Sigma Xi. Author: The Qemant, A Pagan-Hebraic Peasantry of Ethiopia, 1969. Home: 7910 Burning Hills Dr Houston TX 77071

GANDY, EDYTHE EVELYN, state ofcl.; b. Hattiesburg, Miss., Sept. 4, 1922; d. Kearney C. and Abbie (Whigham) Gandy; student U. So. Miss., 1939-40; LL.B., U. Miss., 1944 Admitted to Miss. bar, 1944; practiced in Hattiesburg, 1948-56; atty. Miss. Dept. Pub. Welfare, 1954-58; asst. atty. gen. Miss., 1959; treas. Miss., 1960-64, 68-72; commr. of ins. State of Miss., 1972—. commr. pub. welfare, 1964-67. Mem. Miss. Econ. Council, 1968—, Miss. Mental Health Commn., 1964-67, Miss. Cabinet Women in Pub. Affairs, 1948—; mem. Gov.'s Commn. on Status Women, 1964—; mem. Miss. Bd. Savs. and Loan Assns. Mem. Miss. Ho. of Reps., 1948-52. Bd. dirs. Miss. Hosp. and Med. Service. Mem. Am., Miss., Hinds County, Forrest County bar assns., Am. Judicature Soc., Am. Assn. U. Women., Am. Assn. Women Accountants, Am. Pub. Welfare Assn., Miss. Conf. on Social Welfare, Miss. Fedn. Bus. and Profl. Womens Clubs (past pres.), Miss. Congress P.T.A., Miss. Ofcl. Womens Club. Democrat. Baptist. Club: Altrusa (Jackson, Miss.). Home: 727 Arlington St Jackson MS 39202 Office: Walter Sillers Bldg Jackson MS 39205

GANDY, THOMAS WHITNEY, coll. dean; b. Foley, Ala., Oct. 18, 1919; s. John William and Amye (Daniel) G.; B.S., Berry Coll., 1942; B.S., Auburn U., 1947, M.S., 1950; Ed.D., U. Ill., 1953; m. Theodora H. Nettles, Oct. 25, 1944; 1 dau., Suzanne Nettles. Tchr. vocational agr., Opelika, Ala., 1945-46, 47-50; instr. agrl. edn. Auburn (Ala.) U., 1950-51, asso. prof., 1953-61; research asst. U. Ill., Urbana, 1951-53; adminstrv. asst. to pres. Womans Coll. Ga., Milledgeville, 1961-63; v.p. Berry Coll. and Berry Acad., Mt. Berry, Ga., 1963-69, acad. dean Berry Coll., 1969-71; dean Sch. Edn., dir. pub. services Valdosta (Ga.) State Coll., 1971—. Pres. Lee County (Ala.) Mental Health Assn., 1958-59; drive dir. Auburn Community Chest, 1959-61. Trustee, Berry Coll., 1954-56; devel. dir. Found. Womans Coll. Ga., 1961-63. Served with USNR, 1942-45. Mem. Berry Alumni Assn. (nat. pres. 1954-56), Ala. Vocational Assn. (sec.-treas. 1959-61), Phi Kappa Phi, Gamma Sigma Delta, Phi Delta Kappa, Kappa Delta Pi. Rotarian. Editor: The Agrl. Edn. Mag., 1961-62. Address: 2102 Sherwood Dr Valdosta GA 31601

GANGAROSA, LOUIS PAUL, educator; b. Rochester, N.Y., June 8, 1929; s. Biagio and Carmella (Bellassai) G.; B.A. with high distinction, U. Rochester, 1952; D.D.S., U. Buffalo, 1955; M.A., U. Rochester, 1961, Ph.D., 1965; m. Clara Amalfi, Sept. 4, 1950; children— Michael, Louis Paul, Maria, Alyssa. Pvt. dental practice, Rochester, 1958-61; asst. prof. dental research, instr. pharmacology, U. Rochester, 1965-67, asst. prof. dental research and pharmacology, 1967-68; asso. prof. oral biology and pharmacology Med. Coll. Ga., 1968-71, prof. oral biology, coordinator pharmacology, 1971—; clin. research asso. Eastman Dental Center, Rochester, 1966-68. Cons. Dental Pharms.; cons. tng. Nat. Inst. Dental Research, 1970; dental dir. migrant health program U. Rochester, 1966-68. Served to capt. USAF, 1954-55, 55-58. Fellow Am. Coll. Dentists; mem. Am. Soc. Pharm. and Exptl. Therapeutics, Internat. Assn. Dental Research, Sigma Xi. Club: St. Mary's of Augusta, Men's. Home: 3055 Eton Ct Augusta GA 30904 Office: 1459 Gwinnett St Augusta GA 30902

GANGSTAD, EDWARD OTIS, botanist; b. Chippewa Falls, Wis., Dec. 18, 1917; s. John Otis and Della (Brunberg) G.; B.S., U. Wis., 1942, M.S., 1947; Ph.D., Rutgers U., 1950; m. Ruth Margaret Fletcher, Aug. 22, 1946; children—James Otis, John Erik, Karl Edward, Lillis Marie. Research asst. U. Wis., 1946-47; teaching asst. Rutgers U., 1947-50; research agronomist U.S. Dept. Agr., Agrl. Research Service, Belle Glade, Fla., 1950-54; agronomist Tex. Research Found., Renner, 1954-58, sr. agronomist, 1959-61, prin. agronomist, 1962-65; mgmt. agronomist Dept. of Army, Washington, 1966-69, botanist, 1969—. Served as capt. AUS, 1943-45. Fellow A.A.A.S., Am. Inst. Chemists; mem. Am. Soc. Agronomy, Weed Soc. Am., Biometric Soc., Sigma Xi, Phi Eta Sigma, Alpha Zeta. Republican. Unitarian. Club: Toastmaster. Contbr. articles to profl. jours. Home: 7909 Greeley Blvd Springfield VA 22152 Office: Dept Army DAENCWP-V-APC Washington DC 20315

GANNON, J(OHN) DEANE, govt. ofcl.; b. Madison, Wis,, Mar. 2, 1907; s. Thomas C. and Anna (Welsh) G.; A.B., U. Wis., 1930; m. Doretha V. Schoman, Aug. 29, 1936; children—James T., John D. Spl. agt. Aetna Life Ins. Co., 1931-33; bank examiner Wis. Banking Dept., Madison, 1933-38, securities examiner, 1938-39, supr. credit union div., 1939-53; dir. bur. fed. credit unions U.S. Dept. Health, Edn. and Welfare, 1953-70; dep. adminstr. Nat. Credit Union Adminstrn., 1970—. Staff mem. President's Com. on Financial Institutions, 1963. Recipient Presdl. Citation, 1964. Home: 4806 Dover Rd Washington DC 20016 Office: 2025 M St NW Washington DC 20456

GANO, ELVIS RICE, JR., bottling co. exec.; b. Mascott, Fla., Aug. 21, 1922; s. Elvis Rice and Ada (Drawdy) G.; ed. Tampa (Fla.) Bus. Coll.; m. Angelina St. Paul, Oct. 17, 1948; children—Patricia June, Richard Allen, Marcia Ann. Gen. mgr. Pepsi-Cola Bottling Co., Tampa, 1967—; sec.-treas. Seven-Up Bottling Co. Tampa, 1968—; pres. Service Leasing Co., Tampa, 1971—. Served with USCGR, 1942-46. Mem. C. of C. (com. of 100), Fla. West Coast Bottlers Assn., Fla. Bottlers Assn., Hillsborough Wildlife Assn. Baptist. Club: Temple Terrace Golf and Country. Home: 7517 Veve Lane Tampa FL 33610 Office: PO Box 17175 Tampa FL 33612

GANS, JOHN DAVID, diversified mfg. co. exec.; b. Milw., Apr. 10, 1928; s. Thomas S. and Ruth Renee (Rubens) G.; B.A., Amherst Coll., 1949; M.S., Columbia, 1951; m. Marcia Cummings, Oct. 17, 1953; children—Thomas Cummings, Timothy Hunt, Patrick Winslow. With Rubbermaid, Inc., Wooster, O., 1956—, v.p. marketing, 1965—, mem. corporate council, 1963—, pres. Rubbermaid Comml. Products, Inc., Winchester, Va., 1970—; dir. RCP, Inc., Winchester. Bd. dirs. Meml. Hosp. of Winchester, Winchester-Frederick Devel. Corp., Boys Clubs Am. Mem. Va. (dir.); Winchester chambers commerce, Beta Theta Pi. Served as 1st lt. USAF, 1943-46. Decorated Flying medal. Presbyn. Rotarian. Clubs: Winchester Golf, Menauhaut Yacht (East Falmouth, Mass.). Home: Shockey Dr Route 6 Winchester VA 22601 Office:

GANSLER, JACQUES SINGLETON, govt. ofcl.; b. Newark, Nov. 21, 1934; s. Fred H. and Doris (Eisner) G.; B.Engring., Yale, 1956; M.S., Northeastern U., 1959; M.A., New Sch. Social Research, 1971; m. Alison Friend, June 29, 1955; children—Gillian, Douglas. Tech. dir. spl. programs, missile and space div. Raytheon Co., Bedford, Mass., 1956-62; program dir. Kearfott div. Singer Co., Wayne, N.J., 1962-70; v.p., dir. bus. devel. ITT Avionics, Nutley, N.J., 1970-72; asst. dir. electronics Def. Directorate of Research & Engring., Office Sec. Def., Washington, 1972—; instr. grad. courses serve mechanisms Tufts U. Extension, 1959-61. Mem. Internat. Inst. Strategic Studies. Author numerous papers. Home: 7210 Maple Av Chevy Chase MD 20015 Office: OSD/ODDR & E Pentagon Washington DC

GANT, DUPLAIN RHODES, govt. ofcl.; b. Washington, June 24, 1924; s. Wallace Porter and Carrie (Rhodes) G.; A.B., Dillard U., 1948; M.S., Howard U., 1951; D.S.W., Catholic U., 1958; m. Lois Alva Williams, July 24, 1949; children—Adrienne Cecelia, Duplain Rhodes. Supervisory social worker Pub. Assistance Div., D.C. Dept. Pub. Welfare, Washington, 1958-62, chief research sect. planning and research div., 1964-67, chief Bur. Spl. Services, 1967—. Spl. cons. Pres.'s Commn. on Crime in D.C. Chmn. Foundry-Met. Community Council, Inc., 1968-69. Trustee United Planning Orgn., 1969. Served with AUS, 1943-46. Mem. Nat. Assn. Social Workers, Am. Pub. Welfare Assn., D.C. Pub. Health Assn., Am. Pub. Health Assn. Home: 6308 16th St NW Washington DC 20011 Office: 1875 Connecticut Av NW Washington DC 20009

GANT, JAMES QUINCY, JR., physician; b. Detroit, May 26, 1906; s. James Q. and Alice (Black) G.; A.B., Ohio State U., 1930, M.S., 1931; M.D., Med. Coll. Va., 1935; m. Irene S. Ellis, May 21, 1938 (dec. Feb. 1962); m. 2d, Helen Relic Fentress, June 30, 1962; stepchildren—William George, Carole Ann, Janet Marie Fentress. Interne, Stuart Circle Hosp., Bellevue Hosp.; with USPHS, 1939-46; pvt. practice, 1946—, practice ltd. to dermatology; chmn. skin and allergy service U.S. Vets. Hosp., Washington, 1946-66; emeritus prof. clin. dermatology and syphilology George Washington U. Sch. Medicine. Pres., Assn. Res. Officers USPHS, 1962-65, bd. govs., 1966—. Med. dir. USPHS ret. reserves, 1946-71; active duty D.C. Civil Def., 1959—. Diplomate Am. Bd. Dermatology, Am. Bd. Immunology and Clin. Allergy. Fellow Am. Acad. Dermatology and Syphilology, Am. Acad. Allergy; mem. A.M.A., Med. Soc. D.C., British Astron. Soc., Royal Astron. Soc. Can., Internat. Lunar Soc. (pres. 1958-62, sec. gen. 1963—), Washington Acad. Scis., Assn. Lunar and Planetary Observors (lunar recorder Eastern U.S.), Med. Arts Soc. Greater Washington (pres. 1960-61), Va. Med. Soc., Va. Acad. Sci., Richmond Acad. Medicine, So. Med. Assn., Am. Venereal Disease Assn., Assn. Mil. Surgeons, Washington Acad. Sci., Am. Geophys. Union, Internat. Assn. Planetology. Club: Cosmos (Washington). Author articles. Episcopalian. Home: 4349 Klingle St NW Washington DC 20016 Office: 1835 I St NW Washington DC 20006

GANTT, AUBREY DOYLE, physician; b. Pelion, S.C., Feb. 9, 1924; s. Grover and Blanche (Holley) G.; student Clemson Coll., 1940-43; M.D., Med. Coll. S.C., 1946; m. Jane Henricks Jones, Dec. 22, 1948; children—Rebecca (Mrs. John W. White Jr.), Aubrey Doyle, George Grover. Intern Roper Hosp., Charleston, S.C., 1946-47; gen. practice medicine, Williston, S.C., 1950—; mem. staff Barnwell County Hosp. Mem. adv. bd. Am. Bank & Trust Co. Mem. dist. com. health Boy Scouts Am., 1963-72. Mayor pro-tem, Williston, 1947-59; Councilman, Williston, 1953-55. Trustee Williston Schs., 1958-67; bd. visitors Clemson U., 1968. Served with USNR, 1943-50. Fellow Am. Acad Family Practice; mem. A.M.A., S.C., So., Barnwell County med. assns., Assn. So. Ry. Surgeons. Baptist. Mason, Elk, Woodman. Home: 701 Springfield St Williston SC 29853 Office: 101 W Main St Williston SC 29853

GANTT, FRED, JR., educator; b. Foreman, Ark., Nov. 12, 1922; s. Fred and Margaret Elizabeth (Taaffe) G.; A.A., So. State Coll., 1941; B.A., So. Meth. U., 1943, M.A., 1948; Ph.D., U. Tex., 1962. Instr. So. Meth. U., Dallas, 1947-51; teaching fellow U. Tex., 1951-52; adminstrv. asst. to personnel dir. Lone Star Ordnance Plant, Texarkana, Tex., 1952-55; instr., dir. evening sch. Texarkana (Tex.) Coll., 1955-58; teaching fellow U. Tex., 1958-60; instr. Tex. A. and M. U., College Station, 1961-62; faculty North Tex. State U., Denton, 1962—, prof. polit. sci., 1966—, chmn. dept., 1969—. Vis. prof. U. Tex., Austin, 1968, research asso. Inst. Pub. Affairs, 1969; cons. Tex. Constl. Rev. Commn., 1967, Com. on Reorgn. Exec. Br., Nat. Govs. Conf., 1968. Del. Tex. State Democratic Conv., 1964. Served with AUS, 1944-46. Mem. Am. Assn. U. Profs., Am. Soc. Pub. Adminstrn., Am., Southwestern (pres. 1970-71), Midwest, So. polit. sci. assns., Tex. Assn. Coll. Tchrs., Pi Sigma Alpha, Phi Theta Kappa, Psi Chi. Democrat. Methodist. Author: The Chief Executive in Texas, 1964; (with I. O. Dawson and L. G. Hagard) Governing Texas, 1966, rev. edit., 1970. Home: 1900 Westminister Dr Denton TX 76201

GANTZ, HALLIE GEORGE, univ. pres.; b. Durham, Okla., May 13, 1910; s. John Gottfred and Letetia Paine (Thomas) G.; A.A., Randolph Jr. Coll., Cisco, Tex., 1929; B.A., Phillips U., Enid, Okla., 1931, M.A., 1932, B.D., 1933, L.H.D., 1956; B.D., Yale, 1937; D.D. (hon.), Tex. Christian U., 1946; m. Sylvia Lee Baker, Nov. 7, 1933; children—Charles Baker, Gwendolyn (Martin), Kaye (Gates). Ordained to ministry Christian Ch., 1933; minister in Ft. Worth, 1933-36 Ft. Trumbull, Conn., 1936-37, Lubbock, Tex., 1938-48, Tulsa, 1948-61; pres. Phillips U., 1961—. Pres. Tex. Conv. Christian Chs., 1945-46, Tulsa Council Chs., 1950; chmn. com. ministry Disciples of Christ Ch., 1950; chmn. program and arrangements com. St. Louis Assembly Internat. Conv. Christian Chs., 1958. Pres. trustees Okla. Christian Missionary Soc., 1954-55; bd. dirs. Nat. Benevolent Assn. Disciples of Christ, 1952-56; trustee United Christian Missionary Soc., 1957-60, Hillcrest Med. Center, Tulsa, 1956-61; mem. commn. restructure of Christian Ch., mem. commn. Christian Unity Christian Ch., Disciples of Christ, chmn. board higher education, 1968—; trustee Christian Bd. Publ., 1967—. Recipient Pawnee Dist. Conservationist award, 1954, Okla. Lay Conservationist award, 1955. Mason (Shriner), Rotarian. Home: 2602 E Maine St Enid OK 73701

GANUS, CLIFTON LOYD, JR., clergyman, coll. pres.; b. Hillsboro, Tex., Apr. 7, 1922; s. Clifton Loyd and Martha Jewel (Bearden) G.; B.A., Harding Coll., 1943; M.A., Tulane U., 1946, Ph.D., 1953; profl. diploma Tchrs. Coll., Columbia, 1956; m. Louise Nicholas, May 27, 1943; children—Clifton Loyd III, Deborah Lynn, Charles Austin. Ordained to ministry Ch. of Christ, 1943; minister, Charleston, Miss., 1943-45; asso. prof. history Harding Coll., Searcy, Ark., 1946—, dean Sch. Am. Studies, 1952-65, v.p., 1956-65, pres., 1965—. Dir. Finest Foods, Inc., New Orleans, First Security Bank, Searcy. Treas., bd. dirs. Johnnie Donaghey Wallace Found.; pres. Ark. Found. Asso. Colls.; bd. dirs. Quapaw Area council Boy Scouts Am. Recipient medals Freedoms Found., 1955, 56, 57, 58, 59, 67. Mem. Am. Studies Assn., So. Hist. Assn., Ark. Acad. Scis., Phi Alpha Theta, Psi Delta Sigma, Sigma Chi. Lion. Author: History of the Freedmans Bureau in Mississippi, 1953. Home: 208 S Cross St Searcy AR 72143

GARBER, AUBREY, investment broker; b. Jonesville, Va., Feb. 26, 1917; s. Samuel V. and Myrtle B. (Smith) G.; C.E., U. Tenn., 1943; m. Virginia Dare Ratliff, Jan. 26, 1957; children—Jan, Phillip. With lab. Tenn. Eastman Corp., 1937-40, Crosley Corp., 1940-41; supr. planning Alcoa, 1941-43; smoke jumper U.S. Forest Service, 1943-45; engr. Tenn. State Planning Commn., 1946-48; wholesale broker, 1948-52; radio broadcasting news and sales, 1953-64; investment broker, Grundy, Va., 1964—; sec. Va.-Ky. Broadcasting Corp.; dir. Grundy Nat. Bank, Levisa Ins. Agy.; pres. Modern Homes, Inc.; owner Continental Constrn. Co. Comdr. Civil Air Patrol; chmn. Airport Commn. Ky. col. Mem. Grundy C. of C. (pres. 1968), Bus. and Profl. Assn., Three State Coin Club (pres. 1959-63), Tri-State Antique Car Club (pres. 1960-64), Appalachian Confedn. Coin Clubs (pres. 1961), Internat. Platform Assn., Am. Numismatic Assn. Moose, Lion (pres. 1967). Home and office: Box 818 Grundy VA 24614

GARBER, PAUL EDWARD, museum curator; b. Atlantic City, N.J., Aug. 31, 1899; s. Paul Greenwood and Margaret (Sithens) G.; student McKinley Tech. Sch., Washington, 1917, U. Md., 1918; student aero. engring. Research U., Washington, 1920-21; Nat. Aviation Sch., Washington, 1927-28, U.S. Grad. Sch., 1939-40, 47-48, 52; m. Irene Tusch Reece, May 10, 1952; children—(by previous marriage) Paul James, Edward Willimas, Barbara Jane. Joined Postal Aviation Service, 1918; with Smithsonian Instn., 1920—, asso. curator div. engring., curator Nat. Air Museum, Washington, 1946, head curator, 1952-65, asst. dir. aeros., 1965-69, historian emeritus and Ramsey fellow, 1969—. Served as sgt. U.S. Army, World War I; comdr. spl. devices div. Bur. Aero., USNR, World War II. Recipient Washington Air Derby Assn. trophy, 1954; Air Line Traffic Assn. citation, 1955; Frank G. Brewer Trophy, for air-youth edn., 1959, Elder Statesman of Aviation award, 1964, Crocciero Atlantica medal (Italy), 1964; Santos Dumont medal of Merit, Brazil, 1967; Order of Rio Branco, 1969; Citation for Exceptional Service Smithsonian Instn., 1969. Mem. Nat. Aero Assn., Air Mail Pioneers, Early Birds Aviation (archivist, historian, pres. 1969). Episcopalian. Clubs: National Rocket (gov.), OX-5. Author: Building and Flying Model Aircraft, 1928; Kites, 1931; The Nat. Aeronautical Collections, 1956; also handbooks, pamphlets, ency. and mag. articles on aeros. Home: 310 N Jackson St Arlington VA 22201 Office: National Air and Space Museum 10th and Independence Av Washington DC 20560

GARCIA, CLOTILDE PEREZ, physician; b. Victoria, Mexico, Jan. 11, 1917; d. Jose Garcia and Faustina (Perz) Garcia; A.A., Edinburg Jr. Coll., 1936; B.A., U. Tex., 1938, M.Ed. 1950, M.D., 1954; m. Hipolito Canales, May 25, 1943; 1 son, Jose Antonio. Tchr. pub. schs. Mercedes, Tex., 1944-50; intern Meml. Hosp., Corpus Christi, Tex., 1954-55, now mem. staff; practice medicine, specializing in family practice, Corpus Christi, 1954—. Founding mem. Parents and Friends Club, Carmelite Day Nursery, Corpus Christi, 1968; mem. nat. program rev. com. Nurse Tng. Act, Dept. Health, Edn. and Welfare, 1967—; mem. adv. com. on aging to U.S. Senate, 1971—, to Gov. Tex., 1971—; mem. Tex. Rehab. Assn., 1971—; Tex. dir. for health, mem. com. aging Am. GI Forum Ladies Aux., 1971-72. Nat. bd. dirs. Service, Employment and Devel. Com. Office Econ. Opportunity and Manpower Dept. Labor; bd. dirs. Nueces County Anti-Poverty Community Com., Nueces County Cerebral Palsey Assn.; mem. bd. regents Del Mar Coll., Corpus Christi. Mem. A.M.A., Nueces County (mem. disaster com.), Tex. med. socs. Nueces County Hist. Socs. and Geneology, Tex. Hist. Assn. Home: 3017 Ocean Dr Corpus Christi TX 78405 Office: 2601 Morgan St Corpus Christi TX 78405

GARCIA, JULIO SHERER, newspaper exec. Dir. gen. newspaper Excelsior, Mexico City, Mexico, 1968—. Recipient Maria Moors Cabot award Inter-Am. Journalism, 1971. Address: Excelsior Reforma 18 Mexico DF Mexico*

GARCIA, LEOPOLDO, psychiatrist; b. Ponce, P.R., 1913; M.S., Tulane U., 1913. Intern Hotel Dieu Hosp., New Orleans, 1939-40; resident VA Hosp., Bedford, Mass., 1949-50, Cushing VA Hosp., Framingham, Mass., 1950-51, VA Hosp., West Roxbury, Mass., 1951, VA Mental Hygiene Clinic, Boston, 1952; now practice medicine specializing in psychiatry; mem. courtesy staff Presbyn. Hosp., San Juan, P.R. Served to lt. col. M.C., AUS, 1940-46. Diplomate in psychiatry Am. Bd. Psychiatry and Neurology. Mem. A.M.A. Address: San Martin Bldg Ponce de Leon Av and Parque St Santurce San Juan PR 00902*

GARCIA, NICOLAS LOPEZ, agrl. agt.; b. Yabucoa, P.R., Feb. 3, 1925; s. Claudino Lopez and Angelina (Sanchez) D.; B.S. in Agr., Coll. of Agr. and Mech. Arts (Mayaguez, P.R.), 1950, M.S. in Agr., 1967; m. Damiana Perez, May 29, 1949. Tchr. vocational agr. Dept. Edn. P.R., 1950-53; sales rep. Procter & Gamble Comml. Co., P.R., 1953-55; agrl. extension agt. U. P.R., Humacao, 1955-61, asst. regional dir., 1961—. Dir. Oriental Fed. Savs. & Loan Assn., Humacao. Dir. funds campaign Mentally Unfit Children, Humacao, 1970. Served with USAAF, 1943-46. Mem. Coll. Agronomists P.R., Assn. Agrl. Agts. (bd. dirs. 1967), Epsilon Sigma Phi, Gamma Sigma Delta. Club: Exchange (Humacao). Home: Road 924 K2 Humacao PR 00661 Office: Dufresne Humacao PR 00661

GARCIA-CUELLAR, SAMUEL, lawyer; b. Mexico City, Mexico, Feb. 28, 1909; M.L.L., Escuela Libre de Derecho. Admitted to Mexican bar, 1934; mem. staff Internat. Cooperation Office, Mexican Secretariat Pub. Edn., 1955-56; now mem. firm Garica-Cuellar, Zepeda Vega, Mexico City. Mem. Mexican Bar Assn.-Coll. Advs., Illustre y Nacional Colegio de Abogados de Mexico (v.p. 1969), Am. Bar Assn. (hon.). Author: Corporate Law and Practice in Mexico, 1964. Address: Garcia-Cuellar Zepeda Vega Avenida Yuarex 88 Mexico 1 DF Mexico*

GARCIA-GONZALEZ, EFRAIN, physician; b. Lares, P.R., Mar. 21, 1932; s. Pablo and Emilia (Gonzalez) Garcia; B.S., U. P.R., 1951, M.D., 1955; m. Rosemary Kendrigan, Aug. 20, 1958; children—Margarita, Rosanne, Alicia, Sara, Carmen. Intern Med. Coll. Va. Hosp., 1955-56, resident internal medicine, 1957-59; resident cardiovascular diseases Brooke Gen. Hosp., 1960, asst. chief cardiology, 1962-65; dir. cardiac catheterization lab. VA Hosp., Houston, 1966; cardiologist Kelsey Seybold Co., 1965-71; asst. med. dir. Tex. Heart Inst., Houston, 1971—; asst. prof. medicine Baylor U.; cons. Tex. Children's Hosp., Kelsey Seybold Clinic, Center Pavillion Hosp. Served with AUS, 1955-65. Fellow A.C.P., Am. Coll. Cardiology; mem. Am. Heart Assn. (fellow council clin. cardiology). Home: 7603 Meadowvale St Houston TX 77042 Office: 6720 Bertner St Houston TX 77025

GARCIA GUERRERO, GUSTAVO, lawyer; b. Mexico City, Mexico, 1923; ed. Nat. U. Mexico. Admitted to Mexican bar, 1945; asst. sec. Minister Nat. Properties, Mexico, 1949-51; pres. Ct. Appeals, Colima State, Mexico, 1951-54; asst. dir. Immigration Bur. Mexican Dept. Interior, 1954-55; now mem. firm Escobar, Garcia, Adler & Antolinos, Mexico City. Address: Escobar Garcia Adler & Antolinos Paseo de la Reforma No 122 7 Piso Section C Mexico 6 DF Mexico*

GARCIA-MENDEZ, MIGUEL A., polit. party ofcl.; b. Aguadilla, P.R., Nov. 17, 1902; s. Juan Bautista Garcia-Figueroa and Carmen Mendez-Elias; LL.B., U. P.R., 1922; diploma in constl. law, Princeton, 1922; m. Fredeswinda Ramirez de Arellano-Bartoli, June 25, 1926; children—Ileana (Mrs. Leonard B. Carr), Fredeswinda (Mrs. Antonio Frontera). Pres., Mayaguez Ins. Service, Inc., 1942-52, Super-A Fertilizer Works, Inc., 1942-52, Western Distilling & Devel. Co., Inc., 1942-52; chmn. bd. Central Eureka, Inc., Central Igualdad, Inc., Atlantic Quality Constrn. Corp., Mayaguez Motors Corp., Western Realty, Inc., Mayaguez Realty Corp., Western Fed. Savs. and Loan Assn., Integrated Industries, Inc., Publicaciones Editorial, Inc. (El Impareial; judge Municipal Ct. of San German, P.R., 1923-24; mem. P.R. Ho. of Reps., 1932-33, floor leader, 1933; mem. Republican Party of P.R. Minority Constl. Conv., 1951-52; senator-at-large, P.R. Legislative Assembly, 1953-69, also floor leader; mem. Commn. on Status of P.R.; pres. directory com., state chmn. Statehood Republican Party, P.R., 1952—; dep. Republican Nat. Conv., 1968. Mem. Am. Bar Assn., Lawyers' Coll. P.R., Assn. of U.S. Army, Ateneo Puertorriqueno, Sociedad de Periodistas, Assn. Sugar Producers of P.R. Roman Catholic. Lion. Clubs: Bankers (P.R.); Congressional (Washington). Address: PO Box 599 Cerro Las Mesas Mayaguez PR 00709

GARCIA-MOLINER, LUCIO RAMON, physician; b. Leon, Spain, May 4, 1931 (came to U.S., 1956, naturalized, 1960); s. Lucio and Luisa (Gonzalez-Requeral) G.; M.D., U. Madrid, Spain, 1956; m. Graciela Basora, June 20, 1956; children—Graciela, Clara Eugenia, Maria Luisa. Intern, Ponce (P.R.) Dist. Hosp., 1957, resident in pathology, 1958, resident in internal medicine, 1959-60; practice medicine specializing in internal medicine, Ponce, P.R., 1961-62; attending physician, chief sects. Ponce (P.R.) Dist. Hosp., 1963-71; cons. in internal medicine Lafayette Hosp., Arroyo, P.R., 1964—; chief dept. medicine Oncologic Clinic, Ponce, 1968—; mem. asso. staff Clinica Dr. Pila, St. Lukes Hosp., Ponce; mem. courtesy staff Damas Hosp., Ponce. Mem. exec. com. Plan Ponce, Blue Cross, 1970-71. Home: Calle G 552 Extension La Rambla Ponce PR 00731 Office: Condominio San Vicente Concordia 43 Ponce PR 00731

GARCIA-PALMIERI, MARIO RUBEN, physician, educator; b. Adjuntas, P.R., Aug. 2, 1927; s. Rafael Garcia-Borregon and Mercedes (Palmieri-Ferri) G.-P.; B.S. magna cum laude, U. P.R., 1947; M.D., U. Md., 1951. Intern, Fajardo (P.R.) Dist. Hosp., 1951-52, head dept. med., 1955-56; resident in medicine Bayamon (P.R.) Dist. Hosp., 1952-53, cons., 1953—; resident in medicine San Juan VA Hosp., asst. in medicine U. P.R. Sch. Medicine, San Juan, 1953-54, Nat. Heart Inst. fellow in cardiology, 1954-55, instr. medicine, 1955-56, asso. in medicine, 1956-58, asst. prof., 1958-60, asso. prof., 1960, prof., head dept. medicine, chief sect. cardiology, 1961-66, 68—, prof., chief sect. cardiology, 1967-68, lectr. cardiovascular epidemiology, 1968—; head dept. medicine and sect. cardiology U. Hosp., San Juan, 1961-66, 67—; sec. health of P.R., 1966-67; pres. bd. dirs. P.R. Med. Center, 1966-67; cons. Presbyn., San Jorge, San Juan City, Auxilio Mutuo, Drs., Tchrs. hosps. Vis. prof. Seton Hall Coll. Medicine, 1963, U. Fla. Sch. Medicine, 1963, N.Y. Med. Coll., 1971, Downstate Med. Center Sch. Medicine, Bklyn., 1971; vis. lectr. Ind. U. Sch. Medicine, 1963, Bklyn. Jewish Hosp., 1964, Central U. Venezuela, 1964; guest lectr. U. Md., 1965; lectr. Postgrad. Course on Adminstrn. Med. Care Services, Dominican Republic, 1966, 68. Recipient certificate of merit Fajardo Dist. Hosp., 1965, certificate of distinction Associacion de Hospitales de P.R., 1970. Diplomate Am. Bd. Internal Medicine. Fellow A.C.P., Am. Coll. Cardiology (gov. P.R. chpt. 1966-69); mem. Am. Heart Assn. (fellow council clin. cardiology, council on epidemiology, editorial bd. Jour. 1965-70), Internat. (dir. 1964-68, v.p. 1968-72, founder, mem. sci. council on epidemiology and prevention 1968—), P.R. (pres. 1968-69), Dominican (hon.) socs. cardiology, Pan. Am. (Latin Am. v.p. sect. cardiovascular diseases 67—), P.R. (editor Bull. 1960-66, pres. sect. cardiology 1968-69, certificate of merit 1965) med. assns., A.A.A.S., Am. Fedn. for Clin. Research, Am. Soc. Tropical Medicine and Hygiene, Assn. Am. Med. Colls., Am. Soc. Internal Medicine, Am., P.R. pub. health assns., Royal Soc. Health, Soc. for Epidemiologic Research, Assn. Univ. Cardiologists, Assn. Am. Physicians, Soc. Soc. Clin. Investigation, P.R. Soc. Gastroenterology, P.R. Acad. Arts and Scis., Alpha Omega Alpha. Author: (with R.C. Rodriguez and C. Girod) The Electrocardiogram and Vectorcardiogram in Congenital Heart Disease, 1965. Mem. bd. advisers Buhiti. Contbr. numerous articles to med. jours. Home: Box DG Caparra Heights Sta San Juan PR 00922 Office: Dept of Medicine University of PR Medical Sciences Campus San Juan PR 00905

GARDEA, RAYMOND ANGEL, physician; b. El Paso, Tex., Jan. 23, 1922; s. Juan and Luz (Soto) Gardea; B.A., U. Tex., 1951, M.D., 1955; m. Eleanor Covell, Dec. 27, 1954; children—Ann Marie, Elena, Louise, Raymond Angel, Margaret. Intern, R. E. Thomason Gen. Hosp., El Paso, 1955-56; gen. practice medicine, El Paso, 1956—; mem. staff Hotel Dieu, Sun Towers, Providence, Thomason Gen. hosps., El Paso; v.p. Paisano Med. Clinic, El Paso, 1969—. Mem. Nat. Adv. Council to Surgeon Gen. on Med., Dental, Optometric and Podiatric Edn., 1966-67; mem. Regional Health Adv. Commn., 1968-72; v.p. S.W. Ednl. Devel. Lab., 1971-72; adviser Project Head Start, El Paso Sch. System, 1968-72. Bd. dirs. Urban Coalition, mem. exec. com., 1971. Served with USAAF, 1942-46. Named Outstanding Ex-Student, U. Tex. at El Paso, 1971. Mem. Am. Acad. Gen. Practice, A.M.A., Am. Cancer Soc. (pres. El Paso chpt. 1966-67, dir. Tex. div. 1966-67), El Paso County Med. Soc., Theta Kappa Psi. Elk. Club: El Paso Tennis. Home: 625 E Kerbey St El Paso TX 79902 Office: 5301 Alameda Av El Paso TX 77515

GARDNER, CLARENCE ELLSWORTH, JR., surgeon; b. Bucyrus, O., Feb. 27, 1903; s. Clarence Ellsworth and Anna (Startzman) G.; A.B., Wittenberg, U., 1924, D.Sc., 1950; M.D., Johns Hopkins, 1928; m. Beatrice Ina Lockwood, June 8, 1928; 1 dau., Jane Lockwood. Intern, asst. resident surgery Johns Hopkins Hosp., also instr. surgery Johns Hopkins Sch. Medicine, 1928-30; resident surgery Duke Hosp., asso. surgery Duke Sch. Medicine, Durham, N.C., 1928-30, ast. prof. surgery, 1930-34, asso. prof., 1934-37, prof., 1937—, chmn. dept. surgery, 1960-64, emeritus prof. surgery, 1968—. Served to col. M.C., AUS, 1942-45. Diplomate Am. Bd. Surgery. Fellow A.C.S.; mem. A.M.A., So., Orange, Durham med. assns., So., Am. surg. assns., Soc. U. Surgeons, Internat. Surg. Soc., Phi Beta Kappa, Alpha Omega Alpha. Contbr. articles to surg. lit. Home: Route 1 Box 72 Astor FL 32002

GARDNER, ELIZABETH ANN HUNT (MRS. VERNON EVERETT GARDNER), artist; b. Chgo., Aug. 8, 1916; d. William Luther and Elizabeth (Miller) Hunt; student Wilson Tchrs. Coll., Washington, 1934-35; m. Vernon Everett Gardner, Mar. 25, 1950. Art instr. Studio 6624, Falls Church, Va., 1968—; vol. arts tchr. Anderson Orthopedic Hosp., Arlington, Va., 1958-66; certified flower judge, Nat. Capital Garden Club League; exhibited in all important area art shows and flower shows. Mem. Arts Club Washington, Arlington Arts Craft Club, Palette Club, Emerald Shillelagh. Unitarian. Club: Washington Figure Skating. Address: 6624 Kirby Ct Falls Church VA 22043

GARDNER, ELLIS, physician, state ofcl. Mem. Ark. Bd. Edn., Little Rock. Address: Ark Bd Edn Edn Bldg Little Rock AR 72203*

GARDNER, GEORGE PERCY, JR., motel exec.; b. Jackson, Tenn., Nov. 26, 1914; s. George Percy and Helen Ruth (Kesselus) G.; student Memphis State Coll., 1934-35, Bowling Green Bus. U., 1935-36; m. Ardis Margaret Worthington, June 18, 1936; children—George Percy III, John Worthington. With George Anna Motel, Jackson, 1927—, mgr., 1936-41, partner, 1941, pres., gen. mgr., 1963—; dir. Jackson State Bank. Active United Fund drives. Bd. dirs. Jackson area Council Alcoholism and Drug Abuse, treas., 1969-72. Mem. Am. Motor Hotel Assn. (dir. 1950-68, gov. bd. 1959-60), Tenn. Motel Assn. (founder, pres. 1950), Jackson C. of C. (dir. 1954-56, v.p. 1955-56). Mason (Shriner), Elk, K.P., Moose. Baptist (supt. jr. dept. 1954-57, supt. young peoples dept. 1957-59). Club: Exchange (dir. 1959-60). Home: 423 Airways Blvd Jackson TN 38301

GARDNER, HAZEL IONE CARTER (MRS. THURMAN C. GARDNER, JR.), librarian; b. Booneville, Miss.; d. John Archie and Caddie (Henson) Carter; B.A., Blue Mountain Coll., 1939; B.L.S., N. Tex. State Coll., 1952; m. Thurman C. Gardner, Jr., May 4, 1942; 1 dau., Amanda (Mrs. John David Price). Train hostess G., M. & O. R.R., St. Louis, 1939-42; instr. N.E. Miss. Jr. Coll., Booneville, Mississippi, 1948-52, librarian, then head librarian, 1952—. Chmn. spl. capaign Nat. Multiple Sclerosis Soc., Prentiss County, Miss., 1959. Trustee Miss. chpt. Nat. Multiple Sclerosis Soc. Mem. Am., Miss., Southeastern library assns., Miss. Edn. Assn., Assn. Coll. and Research Libraries, Bus. and Profl. Women Booneville, D.A.R. (librarian, past chpt. vice regent, regent chpt. 1971—), Dames Magna Charta. Club: Thursday Study (pres. 1972). Home: Foster Park Booneville MS 38829 Office: Cunningham Blvd Booneville MS 38829

GARDNER, HENRY DELOSS, JR., ednl. adminstr.; b. Clinton, N.Y., Feb. 10, 1925; s. Henry DeLoss and Evaline (Gile) G.; B.S., Syracuse U., 1953, M.S., 1953; student U. Md., 1959-64, Am. U., 1968-72; m. Patricia Flannigan, May 31, 1947; children—Marjorie Elizabeth (Mrs. Roger E. Blaine), Henry DeLoss III. Employee Waterville Cleaners, (N.Y.), 1946-49; clk. Hotel Hilton, Syracuse, N.Y., 1949-51, asst. mgr., 1951-53; teacher mentally retarded Rochester (N.Y.) Bd. Edn., 1953-56; head teacher secondary edn. mentally retarded Wakefield High Sch., Arlington, Va., 1956-59; coordinator for Exceptional Children Arlington Pub. Schs., 1950-64, dir. gen. programs, 1964-71, asst. supt. for personnel, 1971—; cons. integration, human relations. Served with USNR, 1943-46. Mem. No. Va. chpt. Council for Exceptional Children (pres. 1962-63; pres. state fedn. 1963-65), Interprofl. Research Commn. on Pupil Personnel Services (mem. adv. com. 1966-69), Am. Assn. on Mental Deficiency, Am. Assn. Sch. Adminstrs., Am. Assn. Sch. Personnel Adminstrs., Phi Delta Kappa, Kappa Phi Kappa. Home: 6401 Lee Hwy Arlington VA 22205 Office: 1426 N Quincy St Arlington VA 22207

GARDNER, JAMES CARSON, hotel exec.; b. Rocky Mount, N.C., Apr. 8, 1933; s. James Cuthrell and Sue (Trenholm) G.; student N.C. State U., 1952-53, 56; m. Marie Tyler, Oct. 5, 1957; children—Sue Elizabeth, Marie Theresa, Christopher Tyler. Vice pres. Gardner Dairy Products, Rocky Mount, 1957-62; exec. v.p. Hardee's Food Systems, Inc., Rocky Mount, 1962-66; pres. So. Sports Corp., Rocky Mount, 1969-70; pres. Carolando Corp., Rocky Mount, 1969-71; pres. Family Inns of Am., Inc., Rocky Mount, 1971—; mem. adv. bd. Peoples Bank & Trust Co., Rocky Mount. Mem. U.S. Ho. of Reps., 1967-69; chmn. N.C. State Republican Party, 1965; candidate Gov. N.C., 1968. Mem. adv. bd. Nat. Inst. for Law, Order and Justice, 1969—. Served with AUS, 1953-55. Club: Optimist. Author: A Time to Speak, 1968. Home: 3820 Woodlawn Dr Rocky Mount NC 27801 Office: 419 Sunset Av Rocky Mount NC 27801

GARDNER, JAMES MADISON, lawyer; b. Wynne, Ark., Apr. 4, 1925; s. Menta G. and Mable R. (Eubanks) G.; J.D., U. Ark., 1949; m. Martha Ann Lintzenich, Oct. 19, 1950; children—Charles Jefferson, Marsha Gail. Admitted to Ark. bar, 1949; practice law, Blytheville, Ark., 1949—; mem. firm Gardner & Steinsiek, 1960—. Spl. chancellor 12th Chancery Dist., 1954, 59. Mem. Ark. Bd. Pardon and Paroles. Trustee Ark. Bapt. Hosp., 1953-59. Served with AUS, 1943-46. Mem. Am., Ark., Blytheville (pres. 1955-56) bar assns., Bar Assn. Ark., Blytheville C. of C. (pres. 1961-62), Blue Key, Delta Theta Phi, Pi Kappa Alpha. Baptist (chmn. bd. deacons 1967-69, trustee 1961—). Home: 1700 Eastgate Lane Blytheville AR 72315 Office: 118 W Walnut St Blytheville AR 72315

GARDNER, JOHN EDWARD, educator; b. Sharon, Tenn., Feb. 2, 1917; s. Jesse Olion and Lester (Allen) G.; B.A., Bethel Coll., 1939; B.D., Cumberland Presbyn. Theol. Sem., 1943; Th.M., McCormick Theol. Sem., 1945; Th.D., Union Sem., 1955; m. Mary Anna Bailey, Mar. 28, 1939; children—John Edward, Mary Ann, James Bailey. Ordained to ministry Presbyn. Ch., 1937; pastor Mt. Vernon Congregation, Ramer, Tenn., 1938-41, Kenton Cumberland Presbyn. Ch., 1941-43, 49-61, Campbell Park Presbyn. Ch., Chgo, 1943-45; prof. homiletics and Christian edn. Memphis Theol. Sem., 1945—. Mem. bd. publ. Gen. Assembly, 1946-54, 62-71, chmn. com. on ministry, 1962-68; mem. exec. com. Tenn. Council Chs., 1969—. Author: Handbook for Committees on Ministry, 1964; Personal Religious Disciplines, 1966. Home: 3628 Oakley Av Memphis TN 38111 Office: 168 E Parkway S Memphis TN 38104

GARDNER, PAUL VICKERS, museum curator; b. Savona, N.Y.; s. George Augustus and Anja (Vickers) G.; B.S. in Ceramic Art, Alfred U., 1930; student Geneseo (N.Y.) State Tchrs. Coll., summer 1928, U. Miami, 1947. Designer Steuben Glass, Corning, N.Y., 1929-32; asst. to art dir. Corning Glass Works, 1933-42; curator Nat. Collection of Fine Arts, Smithsonian Instn., Washington, 1948-57, curator charge div. ceramics and glass Mus. Hist. and Tech., 1957—. Cons. on ceramics and glass White House, 1956. Dept. State, 1960-64, other govt. agys.; lectr. Corning Mus. Glass, Sandwich Mus. Glass, Chgo. Art Inst., Washington Antique Show, Sulgrave Club, Washington. Trustee Alfred U.; bd. govs. Wedgwood Internat. Seminar. Served with USNR, 1942-46. Mem. Am. Ceramic Soc., Am. Guild Organists, Washington Kiln Club (hon.), Lambda Chi Alpha. Methodist. Mason. Contbr. articles to Ency. Britannica, also profl. publs. Home: 3612 Massachusetts Av NW Washington DC 20007 Office: Smithsonian Instn Washington DC 20560

GARDNER, RALPH WEBB, lawyer; b. Shelby, N.C., Jan. 9, 1912; s. O. Max and Fay (Webb) G.; A.B., U. N.C., 1935; LL.B., Yale, 1938; m. Carrie Horn Derby, Sept. 14, 1950. Admitted to N.C. bar, 1938, D.C. bar, 1941; asso. Gardner, Morrison, Sheriff & Beddow, Washington, 1938-64; practice law, Shelby, 1964—. Pres., dir. Gardner Land Co., Shelby, 1942—; dir. Piedmont Aviation, Inc., Winston-Salem, N.C. Mem. Shelby Revitalization Com., 1964-70. Pres. Young Democrats Club N.C., 1938; mem. N.C. Senate, 1939-41. Trustee O. Max Gardner Found., 1947—, pres., 1969—; trustee Gardner-Webb Coll., Boiling Springs, N.C. Served to maj. AUS, 1942-46. Mem. Am., N.C. bar assns., Bar Assn. D.C., Soc. of Cincinnati, S.A.R., Phi Beta Kappa, Phi Delta Phi, Delta Kappa Epsilon. Club: Charlotte (N.C.) City. Breeder purebred Aberdeen-Angus cattle. Home: 1340 E Marion St Shelby NC 28150 Office: 403 S Washington St Shelby NC 28150

GARDNER, RICHARD JACOB, lawyer; b. Quincy, Fla., Apr. 10, 1912; s. Ignatz N. and Olga (Fischl) G.; B.A., U. Fla., 1933, J.D., 1935; m. Lila M. Strouse, June 30, 1945 (dec. June 1968); children—Richard Jacob, Charles Robert, Jane, David Alan. Admitted to Fla. bar, 1935; practiced in Quincy, 1937—; mem. firm Gardner & Lines, 1937-68, individual practice, 1968—. Dir. Quincy State Bank, 1st Fed. Savs. & Loan Assn. Mem. Fla. Jud. Council, 1953-59; legislative counsel Gov. Leroy Collins, 1955-57; pres. Suwannee River Area council Boy Scouts Am., 1953-54, Fla. State U. Found., Inc., 1967—; vice chmn. Fla. Bd. Bar Examiners, 1967-68, chmn., 1968-69. Trustee Fla. State U. Found., 1964—, chmn., 1968-69. Served to capt. USAAF, 1942-46. Fellow Am. Coll. Probate Counsel; mem. Am. Legion, Blue Key, Phi Kappa Phi, Phi Alpha Delta. Mason, Rotarian. Home: 905 Myrtle Av Quincy FL 32351 Office: 4 E Washington St Quincy FL 32351

GARDNER, RUSSELL MENESE, lawyer; b. High Point, N.C., July 14, 1920; s. Joseph Hayes and Clara (Flynn) G.; A.B., Duke, 1942, LL.B., 1948; m. Joyce Thresher, Mar. 7, 1946; children—Winthrop Gillet, Page Stansbury, June Thresher. Admitted to Fla. bar, 1948; asso. McCune, Hiaasen, Crum, Ferris & Gardner, and predecessor firms, 1949-50, partner, 1950—. Dir. Thellian Co., Inc. Charter revision com. City of Fort Lauderdale, 1957; mem., chmn. information and edn. subcom. Ft. Lauderdale Citizens Adv. Committee. Pres., chmn. bd. Jack and Jill Nursery, Inc. Bd. dirs. United Fund Broward County; trustee Ft. Lauderdale Museum Arts, pres. bd., 1964-67; bd. dirs. Boys Clubs of Broward County Cultural Council Greater Ft. Lauderdale, Inc. Served from ensign to lt. Supply Corps, USNR, 1942-46. Mem. Fla. Bar (mem. grievance com.), Am., Broward County (chmn. cts. com.) bar assns., Am. Judicature Soc., Ft. Lauderdale Hist. Soc. (trustee), U.S. Navy League (dir. Ft. Lauderdale council), Phi Delta Phi, Omicron Delta Kappa. Democrat. Presbyn. (trustee, deacon, elder). Kiwanian. Clubs: Hundred of Broward County; Drummer; Coral Ridge Country; Lauderdale Yacht; le Club International. Home: 2412 NE 14th St Fort Lauderdale FL 33304 Office: Broward Nat Bank Bldg Fort Lauderdale FL 33301

GARDNER, SAM JAMES, traffic safety inspector; b. Honey Grove, Tex., July 1, 1908; s. Sam H. and Ella Mae (Mosse) G.; student U. Tex., 1926-28, Northwestern U. Traffic Inst., 1952; m. Margaret L. Byrnes, Aug. 31, 1962; children—Mary Elizabeth (Mrs. Wm. L. Little), Jo Anna (Mrs. James L. Watt). Patrolman, Tex. Hwy. Patrol, 1937-46, sgt., 1946-49, capt. commanding Waco Dist., 1949-69; inspector Hwy. Patrol Service, Tex. Dept. Pub. Safety, Austin, 1969—; instr. Dept. Pub. Safety Police Acad., Tex. A. and M. Extension Service, U. Tex. Extension Service. Chmn. Waco chpt. A.R.C., 1967—. Bd. dirs. Waco YMCA. Rotarian. Home: 500 E Anderson Lane Austin TX 78752 Office: 5805 N Lamar St Austin TX 78751

GARDNER, SAMUEL NEWTON, beverage co. exec.; b. Reynolds, Ga., July 1, 1907; s. Emmett Emerson and Celeste (Thompson) G.; A.B., U. Ga., 1929, M.A. in Exptl. Psychology, 1932; m. Edwina Arnold, Oct. 14, 1932; 1 dau., Lynn Arnold (Mrs. Phillip Swingle). Tchr. pub. schs. Ga., 1929-37; prin. Griffin (Ga.) High Sch., 1937-38, supt. schs., 1938-42; with Coca-Cola Co., 1946—, mgr. bottler sales promotion, 1956-65, v.p., 1962—, staff v.p. plans, 1965-67, spl. asst. to pres., 1967—. Served to lt. comdr. USNR, 1942-45. Mem. Am. Legion, Phi Beta Kappa, Phi Kappa Phi. Methodist. Clubs: Commerce; Univ. Yacht, Confrerie de la Chaine des Rotisseurs. Home: 455 Riverside Pkwy NW Atlanta GA 30328 Office: 310 North Av NW Atlanta GA 30301

GARDNER, THOMAS VINCENT, JR., dentist, army officer; b. Kansas City, Mo., Aug. 5, 1931; s. Thomas Vincent and Francois Tiffany (White) G.; B.S., U. Pitts., 1955, D.D.S., 1955; M.S.,

Georgetown U., 1965; m. Constance Eileen Campbell, Apr. 14, 1954; children—Thomas Lee, Tiffany Eileen. Commd. 1st lt. Dental Corps, U.S. Army, 1955, advanced through grades to col., 1972; practice dentistry Schofield Barracks, Hawaii, 1955-58; chief hosp. dental service Ft. Dix, N.J., 1958-61; practice gen. dentistry Walter Reed Gen. Hosp., 1962-63; mem. faculty asst. chief dept. dental material U.S. Army Inst. Dental Research, 1965-68; comdg. officer 40th Med. Detachment, Vietnam, 1968-69; chief dental clinic 2, dir. intern tng. Ft. Sill, Okla., 1969—. Sponsor South Central Dist. Dental Assts. Soc. Recipient Fairbanks medal Med. Field Service Sch., 1962; decorated Bronze Star with oak leaf cluster, Air medal. Mem. Am. Dental Assn., Dental Materials Group, Internat. Assn. Dental Research, Assn. U.S. Army, Rathskeller Dental Study Club, Delta Sigma Delta. Republican. Presbyn. Mason. Club: Artillery Hunt (Ft. Sill). Home: 531 Lindsay St Ft Sill OK 73503 Office: Dental Detachment Ft Sill OK 73503

GARDNER, WILLIAM BADHAM, town ofcl; b. Edenton, N.C., Dec. 9, 1934; s. William H. and Emma (Badham) G.; A.B., U. N.C., 1957; m. Mary Rhea Spivey, Dec. 28, 1957; children—Virginia Hudgins, Elizabeth Badham, William Badham. Adminstr., Hosp. Care Assn., 1957-61; adminstr. Town of Edenton, 1961—. Dir. Peoples Bank & Trust Co., Edenton. Chmn. Indsl. Devel. Com., Edenton, 1967-69; mem. Chowan County Planning Bd., 1963—; chmn. Historic Edenton Inc., 1967-69; pres. Chowan County Cancer Soc., 1967; sec. Edenton Airport Commn., 1965—; chmn. bd. Albemarle Regional Planning and Redevel. Commn., 1971—; active various community drives. Sec.-treas. Chowan County Democratic Exec. Com., 1967—. Bd. dirs. Chowan Acad., Inc., N.C. League of Municipalities. Served with N.G. Recipient Distinguished Service award Edenton Jr. C. of C., 1969. Mem. Edenton C. of C. (pres. 1967). Clubs: Rotary (pres. 1969). Edenton Cotillion (pres. 1957-60), Chowan Golf and Country (bd. mem. 1965-66). Home: 116 W Church St Edenton NC 27932 Office: S Broad St Edenton NC 27932

GARDNER, WILLIAM HENRY, ret. newspaper editor; b. Austin, Tex., Oct. 30, 1907; s. William Henry and Elizabeth (Jaqua) G.; student U. Tex., 1924-28; m. Mildred Louise McMinn, June 22, 1938; children—Elizabeth (Mrs. William P. Jones), Terry Gardner, Stephen. Reporter, Galveston (Tex.) Tribune, 1928-29, Houston Press, 1929-30; reporter Galveston News, 1930-32, city editor, 1932-34; with Internat. News Service, 1935; telegraph editor Tyler (Tex.) Courier-Times, 1935; reporter, city editor, mag. editor, Austin bur. chief Houston Post, 1935-63, mng. editor, 1963-65, polit. affairs editor, 1965-69, editorial page editor, 1969-71, ret., 1971; adminstrv. asst. to Gov. Allan Shivers, Austin, 1952. Editor news and information service U. Tex., 1946. Mem. Tex. Library and Hist. Commn., Tex. State Ethics commn. Served to capt. USAAF, 1942-45. Mem. Am. Assn. Newspaper Editors, Internat. Press Inst., Sigma Delta Chi (past pres. Austin profl. chpt.). Episcopalian. Clubs: Headliners; Forty Acres (Austin, Tex.). Author: The Texan Citizen, 1955. Home: Route 7 Box 652 Austin TX 78703

GARDNER, WILLIAM LEONARD, mil. sch. supt.; b. nr. Jefferson, S.C., Nov. 22, 1902; s. Benjamin F. and Rosa (Ogburn) G.; A.B., The Citadel, 1928; postgrad. Cornell, 1931, Yale, 1943; M.Ed., U. Va., 1953; m. Mabel Marguerite Stott, Sept. 10, 1930; children—Margaret Lee (Mrs. Manley Patton Caldwell, Jr.), Nancy Alice (Mrs. Coleman DeLynne Carter). Tchr., Staunton (Va.) Mil. Acad., 1928-30, Howe (Ind.) Mil. Acad., 1930-32, Fork Union (Va.) Mil. Acad., 1939-41; comdg. officer Civilian Conservation Corps Camps, N.C., S.C., 1933-39; prof. mil. sci. and tactics The Citadel, 1945; tchr., supt. Augusta Mil. Acad., Ft. Defiance, Va., 1945—. Corporator Kings Daus. Hosp., Staunton, Va. Dir. Ind. Sch. Fund, 1965-66. Active A.R.C., United Fund. Served with AUS, 1941-46; ETO. Mem. Va. Edn. Assn., S.C. Tchrs. Assn. (life), Ret. Officers Assn., Kappa Delta Pi. Baptist (deacon). Mason, Kiwanian. Author: Progress in Reading, 1959. Home: 20 Orchard Rd Staunton VA 24401 Office: Augusta Mil Acad Fort Defiance VA 24437

GARDNER, WILLIAM ROBERT, physician; b. Oklahoma City, June 16, 1931; s. Stearns H. and Mary L. (Venable) G.; B.A., Oklahoma City U., 1955; M.D., Baylor U., 1959; children—Mary Catherine, Russell Morgan, Maurie Ann, Amy Lynn, John Randolph. Intern, then resident John Peter Smith Hosp., Ft. Worth, 1959-61; pvt. practice medicine, Mansfield, Tex., 1961—; adminstr. Cedars Hosp., Mansfield, 1965—; health officer, Mansfield, 1966—. Trustee Mansfield Ind. Sch. System, 1964—. Served with AUS, 1952-54. Diplomate Am. Bd. Family Practice. Mem. Am., Tex. med. assns., Mansfield C. of C. (pres. 1963). Presbyn. (elder, trustee). Lion. (pres. Mansfield 1963). Club: Ft. Worth. Home: Route 2 Mansfield TX 76063 Office: 106 Cedars St Mansfield TX 76063

GARIBI Y RIVERA, JOSE, clergyman; b. Guadalajara, Mexico, Jan. 30, 1889; s. Miguel and Joaquina (Rivera) G.; grad. Guadalajara Sem.; D.D., Gregorian U., Rome, Italy, 1916. Ordained priest, Roman Catholic Ch., 1912, consecrated bishop, 1930; apptd. titular bishop of Rhosus, aux. bishop of Guadalajara, 1929; apptd. titular archbishop of Bizya and coadjutor of Guadalajara, 1934, archbishop of Guadalajara 1936—. Address: Secretaria del Arzobispado Liceo 17 Guadalajara Mexico

GARIKES, ARTHUR GEORGE, ednl. adminstr.; b. Chgo., Sept. 13, 1928; s. George Thomas and Assimo (Tsakiris) G.; student Wilson Jr. Coll., 1947-49; B.S. in Architecture, U. Ill. at Urbana, 1956; m. Betty Jean Tansor, Sept. 27, 1953; children—Sandra Lee, George Charles, Ronald Wayne. Designer, Milw. R.R., Chgo., 1956; asso. Perkins & Will, architects, Chgo., 1956-65; dir. clin. facilities planning, asst. to v.p. health affairs U. Ala., Birmingham, 1965—, faculty mem. Sch. Community and Allied Health Resources, 1967—. Trustee Jefferson Health Found.; bd. dirs. Univ. Credit Union. Served with AUS, 1951-53. Mem. Nat. Council Archtl. Registration Bds., A.I.A. (treas. 1969), Nat. Assn. Power Engrs., Inc., Am. Hosp. Assn., Am. Legion, U. Ill. Alumni Assn., Gresham Athletic Assn. (v.p. 1970-71), Cahaba Heights Athletic Assn. (pres. 1968). Mem. Greek Orthodox Ch. (chmn. bldg. com. 1969—). Clubs: Civitan, Altedena Valley Golf and Country (Birmingham). Home: 2917 Christopher Ct Birmingham AL 35243 Office: 19 S 19th St Birmingham AL 35233

GARLAND, WALTER BROOKS, judge; b. Strawn, Ill., Oct. 18, 1917; s. Pierce N. and Eva (Brooks) G.; B.S., E. Tenn. State U., 1939; LL.B., U. Tenn., 1945; m. Edith Elsie Bradley, June 7, 1939; children—Walda Carole (Mrs. Louis Whitney), Wayne Bradley, Kent Winston. Tchr. Tenn. High Sch., Bristol, 1939-41; admitted to Tenn. bar, 1945; asst. prof. law U. Tenn., Knoxville, 1945-49; practiced law, Erwin, Tenn., 1949-66; mem. firm Garland & Garland, 1949-66; judge Ct. Gen. Sessions, Unicoi County, 1960-66; circuit ct. judge First Jud. Dist., State of Tenn., Erwin, 1966—. Bd. dirs. Erwin Utilities (Tenn.). Chmn. United Fund Campaign, Erwin, 1950, bd. dirs., 1950—; pres. Unicoi County Indsl. Com., 1960-62, bd. dirs., 1957—. Chmn. Unicoi County Republican Party, 1956-62. Mem. Bar. Assn. Tenn., Am., Unicoi County bar assns., Tenn. Jud. Conf., Order of Coif, Phi Delta Phi. Methodist. Mason. Club: Civitan (Erwin pres. 1953-54, dist. lt. gov. 1954-55, bd. dirs.). Home: 453 Ash St Erwin TN 37650 Office: Municipal Bldg Erwin TN 37650

GARMAT, JOHN, economist, educator; b. Vienna, Austria, Feb. 17, 1933; s. Robert and Hilda (Monetti) G.; B.S. summa cum laude, U. Hartford, 1956; M.B.A., U. Conn., 1961; postgrad. George Washington U.; m. Portia Lateiner, Apr. 7, 1951; children— Marcy G., Diana Rosemarie, Richard B. Agt., U.S. Internal Revenue Service, Hartford, Conn., 1956-59, staff asst. to chief audit, 1959-61, tax research analyst, sr. operations research analyst Nat. Office Audit Div., Washington, 1961-67; economist, asst. dir. Office Planning and Program Evaluation, U.S. Treasury Dept., Washington, 1967—; adj. prof. econs. and data processing Southeastern U., Washington, 1961—. Recipient Raymond E. Ellison Outstanding Faculty Mem. award Southeastern U., 1968, U.S. Treasury Dept. Spl. Act award, 1968, Meritorious award Jump Meml. Found., 1969, High Quality Pay award U.S. Treasury Dept., 1970. Mem. Am. Econ. Assn., Am. Statis. Assn., Soc. for Advancement Mgmt. (v.p., dir. research), Washington Operations Research Council. Home: 11100 Oak Leaf Dr Silver Spring MD 20901 Office: Main Treasury 15th and Pennsylvania Av NW Washington DC 20220

GARMENT, LEONARD, govt. ofcl. Spl. cons. to Pres. Nixon. Address: White House Washington DC20500*

GARNER, ANDREW JACKSON, III, govt. ofcl.; b. Birmingham, Ala., Nov. 25, 1913; s. Andrew Jackson and Sallie (Oliver) G., Jr.; student Wake Forest Coll., 1932-33; m. Polly Elizabeth Gosorn, Apr. 16, 1939; children— Andrew Jackson IV, Philip Gosorn. Fountain mgr., drug store, Asheville, N.C., 1933-36; with Post Office, Asheville, 1936—, beginning as clk., successively clk. in charge, foreman, 1936-50, chief accountant (controller), 1955-66, asst. postmaster, 1966, postmaster, 1966—, sect. center mgr., 1971—. Pres., T.C. Roberson PTSA, 1970. Chmn. Buncombe County chpt. Nat. Found. for Infantile Paralysis; chmn. budget. com. panel Buncombe County United Fund; chmn. Fed. Agys. United Fund, 1970; mem. permanent com. Buncombe County Planning Council; mem. Citizens Com. for Better Schs.; dist. chmn. Boy Scouts.; vice chmn. bd. dirs. Eliada orphanage. Served with USNR, 1942-45. Mem. Nat. Fedn. Post Office Clks. (pres. N.C. chpt. 1949), Nat. Assn. Postal Suprs. (pres. 1959 Carolinas br., editor Caronaps Digest 1953, 54), Asheville Fed. Execs. Assn. (pres. 1970-71). Democrat. Baptist (chmn. bd. deacons). Kiwanian (past dir. Asheville, pres. 1964, lt. gov. Carolinas dist.). Home: 29 Willow Springs Rd Asheville NC 28803 Office: Post Office Asheville NC 28801

GARNER, EARL RAY, county ofcl.; b. Varnado, La., May 3, 1920; s. Mike Robert and Rozella (Seal) G.; B.S, in Mech. Engring., U. Ark., 1942; postgrad. U. Pitts., 1954-55; grad. student Bell System Mgmt. Tng. Program, 1949-50; m. Josephine Massaro, July 26, 1945; children—Robert Earl, William Louis, Deborah Ann (Mrs. Robert Lee Burton, Jr.) Cythia Seal (Mrs. David W. House), John Dupont. Supervising engr. Bell System, 1946-56, 60-64; constrn. engr. Mellon Bank, Pitts., 1956-60; cons. Middle West Service Co., Chgo., 1964-65; asst. dir. phys. plant U. Fla., Gainesville, 1965-66; dir. Dept. Inspections and Licenses Fulton County, Atlanta, 1967—. Served to capt. AUS, 1942-46. Recipient W.S. Beaver award W.S.B. Radio Sta., Atlanta, 1967. Registered profl. engr., Pa., Ga., Fla. Mem. Ga. Archtl. and Engring. Soc., Bldg. Ofcl. Conf. Am. Home: 4007 Gladney Dr Atlanta GA 30340 Office: 165 Central Av Atlanta GA 30303

GARNER, JOHN MICHAEL, lawyer, banker; b. Miami, Fla., July 17, 1935; s. James Geston and Alberta (Willis) G.; B.A., Washington and Lee U., 1957, LL.B., 1960; m. Beatrice Marie Keep, Apr. 5, 1958; children—John Michael, Mary Elizabeth. Admitted to Fla. bar, 1960, since practiced in Miami. Pres., dir. Garner Mortgage Co., Miami, 1960—, First State Bank of Miami, 1972—; pres. Garner, Ward & Assos., Inc., Miami, 1968—; dir. Airport First State Bank, Hialeah-Miami Springs First State Bank, North Hialeah First State Bank, Miami Lakes First State Bank, State Mut. Ins. Co. Pres. Dade County Crippled Children's Soc., 1965-67, bd. dirs., 1961—; mem. Fla. Crippled Children's Commn., 1968-71. Trustee Fla. Presbyn. Coll., St. Petersburg. Mem. Am. Bar Assn., Fla. Bar, Sigma Chi, Phi Alpha Delta. Democrat. Presbyn. (deacon 1967—). Clubs: University, Bath, LaGorce Country, Rod and Reel, Ocean Reef. Home: 4580 Bay Point Rd Miami FL 33137 Office: 8017 NE 2d Av Miami FL 33138

GARNER, ROBERT FRANK, investment co. exec.; b. Toccoa, Ga., Oct. 19, 1918; s. Robert Frank and Ella Margaret (Cooper) G.; student North Ga. Coll., 1936-38; B.S., U. Ga., 1938-40; postgrad. Duke U. and U. N.C., 1948-49, George Washington U., 1951, U. Omaha (Carnegie fellow), 1961-62, Armed Forces Staff Coll., 1956-57; m. Virginia Nell Bogue, May 30, 1942; children—Robert Frank III, James R., Margaret J. Vice-pres. bus. affairs Fla. Presbyn. Eckerd Coll., St. Petersburg, 1960-67; pres. Cee Bee Income Properties, 1967—; sec.-treas., dir. R.J. Financial Corp., 1967—; sr. v.p. Raymond, James & Assos., St. Petersburg, 1967—; pres. Planning Corp. Am., 1967—. Ednl. bus. cons. Sec., Fla. Boxing Commn., 1940-42. Active Boy Scouts Am.; mem. Mayor's Goals Com. Mem. devel. bd. Fla. Presbyn. Coll., Clearwater Christian Coll., 1968-71. Served to lt. col. USAF, 1940-60. Decorated Bronze Star. Mem. Am. Ordnance Assn. (charter pres. Fla. chpt.), Symphony Soc. (pres. elect, dir. 1964-68), Lambda Chi Alpha. Republican. Presbyn. (deacon 1947-62, elder 1963-71). Mason, Kiwanian (pres. 1968). Clubs: Toastmasters (Norfolk, Va. and St. Petersburg); Civic Association (St. Petersburg). Home: 5030 39th St S St Petersburg FL 33711 Office: 6090 Central Av St Petersburg FL 33707

GARNICK, DANIEL HARRIS, economist; b. Phila., Jan. 13, 1929; s. Samuel Louis and Minnie Brenda (Sternman) G.; B.S., Temple U., 1951; M.A., U. Pa., 1960; Ph.D., Dorpsie Coll., 1958; m. Toby Schwartzman, Mar. 22, 1951; children—Micah, Sara. Research asso. Dropsie Coll., 1957-59; asst. prof. econs. State U. N.Y. at Buffalo, 1959-63; Fulbright prof. econs. Seoul Nat. U., Korea, 1963-64; adviser, Econ. Planning Bd., Korea, 1964-65; asso., Robert R. Nathan Assos., 1964-67; br. chief, analysis br., regional econs. div., Office Bus. Econs., U.S. Dept. Commerce, Washington, 1967—. Ford Found. fellow, 1962. Mem. Am. Econ. Assn., Am. Statis. Assn., Regional Sci. Assn. Home: 816 Hyde Ct Silver Spring MD 20502 Office: 2400 M St NW Washington DC 20230

GARNSEY, CLARKE HENDERSON, artist, historian; b. Joliet, Ill., Sept. 22, 1913; s. Charles Bushniell and Sibyl Mary (VanPelt) G.; grad. Cleve. Inst. Art, 1947; B.S., Western Res. U., 1947, M.A., 1948, Ph.D., 1962; postgrad. U. Colo., W. Tex. State; m. Jean Sharpless Shoemaker, Oct. 21, 1943. Ednl. staff Cleve. Mus. Art, 1947-49, 57-59; instr. Cleve. Inst. Art, 1957-59; dept. chmn. art. Amarillo Coll., Tex., 1949-63; prof., chmn. dept. art Wichita State U., 1963-66; chmn. dept. art U. Tex., El Paso, 1966—; cons. El Paso Div. Upward Bound. Bd. dirs. Wichita Art Mus. Served with USAAF, 1941-46. Mem. Coll. Art Assn. Am., Soc. Archtl. Historians. Home: 221 Carnival Dr El Paso TX 79912

GARRARD, JEANNE (MRS. GARRARD EBERSOLE), editor, educator, writer; b. Birmingham, Ala., Apr. 9, 1923; d. Oscar and Jeanne (Holoman) Garrard; Stetson U., 1940-42; postgrad. Lindsey Hopkins Hotel Sch., 1959; m. Huber S. Ebersole, Oct. 1, 1957 (div. Nov. 1960). Radio dir., writer, commentator radio sta. WDBO, WLOF, Orlando, Fla., 1942-43; columnist Sentinel-Star, Orlando, 1943; radio commentator, writer for Burdine's, Palm Beach, Fla., 1943, Miami, Fla., 1943-44, radio Sta. WKAT, Miami Beach, 1944-45; commentator Sta. WIOD, Miami, 1944, commentator, writer Sta. WGBS, 1945; program dir. Melody, Inc., Miami Beach, 1945-48; writer Grant Advt., Inc., 1946; columnist Miami Beach Sun Star, 1946; writer for sta. WVCG, Coral Gables, Fla., 1949-50; columnist Miami Beach, 1950, Riviera-Times, Coral Gables, 1950, Miami Daily News, 1950-51; writer for Sta. WIOD, Miami, 1951; feature editor Miami Visitor Publ. Co., Miami Beach, 1952-55, mng. editor, 1955-56, editor, 1956-58; free-lance writer, photographer with work appearing in various publ. including Am. Home mag., Stag mag., numerous newspapers; scout asst. to Better Homes & Gardens, Des Moines, 1959—; asst. mgr., housekeeper Anson Hotel, Surfside, Fla., 1959; asst. to editor, photographer Meredith Pub. Co., Des Moines, 1961; instr. writing adult edn. North Miami (Fla.) High Sch., 1956—; editorial asst. Ortho Garden Guide, Cal. Chem. Co., San Francisco, 1964; became exec. editor Beach and Town, Visitor Pub. Co., Miami Beach, 1964, now cons. editor, bus. mgr. Visitor Pub. Co., until 1971; freelance writer, Miamian, Miami Pictorial, Palm Beach Life, 1971—; also sometime lectr. Bd. dirs. Miami Beach Garden Center and Conservatory. Mem. S. Fla. Orchid Soc., Met. Miami Flower Show Assn., Theta Sigma Phi (chpt. pres. 1966-67), Pi Beta Pi. Club: Miami Beach Garden (pres. 1966-68). Author: Growing Orchids for Pleasure (Nat. Lit. Horticulture award Nat. Council Garden Clubs, 1967); Potted: Flowers of Bermuda, 1970; Tropical Flowers of Florida, 1970; Flowers of Caribbean, 1970; Flowers of Bahamas, 1970; Fairchild Tropical Gardens, 1972. Home: 5768 Pine Tree Dr Miami Beach FL 33140

GARREN, HERBERT EUGENE, design engr.; b. Atlanta, Aug. 2, 1912; s. Ernest T. and Amy (Rowe) G.; student Ga. Inst. Tech., 1939., RCA Insts., 1967; m. Elsie Marsh, Dec. 2, 1937; children—Robert Eugene, Dianne Elaine (Mrs. Bobby Garner). Dept. engr. Am. Moistening Co. div. Grinnell Corp., Atlanta, 1937-49; design engr, Donald Lindstrom &Assos., Atlanta, 1949-70; design engr. McLendon & Holbrook, Inc., Atlanta, 1970—. Registered profl. engr., Ga., S.C. Mem. Am. Radio Relay League, Lake Berkeley Civic Assn. Mason. Home: 60 Lake Shore Dr Duluth GA 30136 Office: 1455 Tully Rd NE Atlanta GA 30329

GARREN, ROBERT DAVIES, dentist; b. Hendersonville, N.C., Sept. 19, 1934; s. Earl Vincent and Dorothy (Davies) G.; B.S. in Sci., Wake-Forest U., 1957; D.M.D., U. Louisville, 1964; m. Barbara Mashburn, Nov. 16, 1957; children—Ashley Dianne, Kristi Lynn. Gen. practice dentistry, Asheville, N.C., 1964—. Mem. exec, com. Citizens Com. for Better Schs., 1968—. Bd. dirs. Fellowship Christian Athletes. Served to 1st lt., arty. AUS, 1957-59. Mem. Am. Dental Assn., N.C., Buncombe County dental socs., Psi Omega. Club: Asheville Optimist (dir. 1965—, pres. 1969). Home: Route 4 Box 335E Candler NC 28715 Office: 5-D Doctors Park Asheville NC 28801

GARRETT, ALEX REID, city ofcl.; b. Letohatchie, Ala., Sept. 2, 1907; s. Alex Reid and Corrie (Mitchell) G.; B.S., Auburn U., 1927; m. Mamie Iceal Burson, Nov. 8, 1942; children—Alex Reid III, Richard Bartlett. With Ala. Power Co., Montgomery and Gadsden, 1928-30; owner Woodside Milling Co., 1930-39; commd. 2d lt. Chem. Corps, U.S. Army, 1941, advanced through grades to lt. col., 1955; ret., 1955; with City of Montgomery, 1957—, city clk., 1965—. Recipient plaques from Boy Scouts Am., United Appeal, Traffic Safety Com. Mem. Internat. Inst. Municipal Clks., Ala. City Clks. Assn. (v.p.), Lambda Chi Alpha. Mem. Ch. of Christ (deacon). Lion. Club: Dalraida Recreation (past pres.) (Montgomery). Author: Chronological History of Montgomery 1817-1967, 1971. Home: 3586 Pelzer Av Montgomery AL 36109 Office: PO Box 1111 Montgomery AL 36102

GARRETT, CHESTER WILLIAM, newspaper exec.; b. Hill, Okla., Oct. 25, 1915; s. William Oscar and Irene (Boozman) G.; student Draughmon's Bus. Coll., 1934; m. Lulu Clairette Hopson, Mar. 9, 1946; children—William Randal, Cynthia Dawn. Dist. mgr. circulation S.W. Times Record, Fort Smith, Ark., 1935-42; dist. advt. mgr. Ark. Democrat Co., Little Rock, 1946-55, circulation promotion mgr., 1955-66, circulation mgr., 1966-68, bus. mgr., 1968—. Served with AUS, 1942-46. Democrat. Baptist. Mason. Home: 9114 S Heights St Little Rock AR 72206 Office: 5th and Scott Sts Little Rock AR 72203

GARRETT, DONALD MITCHELL, ednl. adminstr.; b. Monroe, Ga., Sept. 11, 1933; s. Willie Reese and Ola Jo (Mitchell) G.; student U. Md., 1956, S. Ga. Coll., 1957; B.S., U. Ga., 1959, M.Ed., 1968, Ed. Specialist, 1971; m. Roxie Mae Clegg, Nov. 24, 1960; children—Jennifer Lynn, Margaret Jo, Donald Mitchell. Tchr., Social Circle (Ga.) High Sch., 1959-60, 61-62; teller Nat. Bank Monroe, 1960-61; counselor Ga. Dept. Edn., Milledgeville and Athens, 1962-67; casework supr., Atlanta, 1967-68; prin. Social Circle Elementary Sch., 1968-70; prin., supt. Social Circle City Schs., 1970—. Served with AUS, 1954-56. Named Young Educator of the Year Social Circle Jaycees, 1970. Baptist (deacon, sec. bd. 1968-71). Lion. Home: Route 1 Social Circle GA 30279 Office: PO Box 428 Social Circle GA 30279

GARRETT, FRANKLIN MILLER, historian; b. Milw., Sept. 25, 1906; s. Clarence Robt. and Ada (Kirkwood) G.; LL.B., Woodrow Wilson Coll. Law, 1941; L.H.D., Oglethorpe Coll., 1970; div.; children—Patricia Abbott, Franklin Miller. Br. mgr. Western Union Telegraph Co., Atlanta, 1934-38; salesman Ward Wight & Co., Atlanta, 1939-40; mem. exec. staff pub. relations, historian, Coca-Cola Co., Atlanta, 1940-68. Chmn., Fulton County (Ga.) Civil Service Bd., 1955—. Bd. dirs. Children's Center Met. Atlanta, 1958-70. Served with AUS, 1942-45. Mem. Nat. Ry., Va., Ga., Atlanta (chmn. bd. trustees 1967-68, dir. 1968—), DeKalb County hist. socs., Newcomen Soc. N.Am., Atlanta Art Assn., Atlanta Civil War Round Table, Grand Jurors Assn. Fulton County, Ga. Geneal. Soc. Presbyn. Clubs: Rotary, Commerce, Piedmont Driving, Atlanta City. Author: Atlanta and Environs I-III, 1954, rev. edit., 1969. Home: 3433 Roxboro Rd NE Atlanta GA 30326 Office: 3099 Andrews Dr NW Atlanta GA 30305

GARRETT, JAMES LAMAR, city engr.; b. Topton, Miss., Jan. 24, 1933; s. James Robert and Louise (Hooks) G.; student Meridian Jr. Coll., 1951; B.S., Miss. State U., 1954; m. Barbara P. Merrill, Nov. 12, 1955; children—Jimmy, Robby, Keith. Project engr. Metal Landing Mats. Project, U.S. Army Engrs., Waterways Experiment Station, Vicksburg, Miss., 1954-60; asst. city engr., planning dir. City of Meridian, Miss., 1960-62, city engr., dir. pub. works, 1962—. Registered profl. engr., Miss. Mem. Meridian Municipal Employees Assn. (v.p. 1971-72), Miss. Soc. Profl. Engrs. (chmn. engrs. in govt. sect. 1971-72), Pvt. Sch. Ofcl. Assn., Phi Kappa Phi, Tau Beta Pi, Phi Delta Kappa (pres. 1966-69). Democrat. Baptist. Moose. Club: Briawood Country (Meridian). Home: 4519 30th St Meridian MS 39301 Office: PO Box 1430 Meridian MS 39301

GARRETT, JAMES LEO, JR., educator; b. Waco, Tex., Nov. 25, 1925; s. James Leo and Grace (Jenkins) G.; A.B., Baylor U., 1945; B.D., Southwestern Bapt. Theol. Sem., Ft. Worth, 1948, postgrad., 1949-53, Th.D., 1954; Th.M., Princeton Theol. Sem., 1949; postgrad.

Tex. Christian U., 1954, 56, Catholic U. Am., 1963, U. Oxford (Eng.), 1968-69; Ph.D., Harvard, 1966; m. Myrta Ann Latimer, Aug. 31, 1948; children—James Leo, Robert Thomas, Paul Latimer. Ordained minister Bapt. Ch.; pastor Bapt. chs., rural Tex., 1945-48; mem. faculty Southwestern Bapt. Theol. Sem., 1949-59, asst. prof theology, 1951-54, asso. prof., 1954-57, prof., 1957-59; prof. Christian theology So. Bapt. Theol. Sem., Louisville, 1959—. Mem. adv. council Tuohy Chair Ecumenical Studies, John Carroll U., Cleve., 1965-68; chmn. study commn. on cooperative Christianity, Bapt. World Alliance, 1968—; lectr. Bapt. theol. sems., Colombia, 1955, Mexico, 1958, Brazil, 1963, Eng., 1969; guest Secretariat Promoting Christian Unity, Vatican Council II, 1965. Grad. fellow, Harvard, 1956-57; Am. Assn. Theol. Schs. faculty fellow, 1962-63. Mem. Am. Soc. Ch. History, Am. Acad. Religion, So. Bapt. Hist. Soc. Author: Baptist Church Discipline, 1962; Evangelism for Discipleship, 1964; Baptists and Roman Catholicism, 1965. Editor: (with E.J. Vardaman) The Teacher's Yoke: Studies in Memory of Henry Trantham, 1964; The Concept of the Believers' Church, 1970. Home: 205 Gibson Rd Louisville KY 40207 Office: 2825 Lexington Rd Louisville KY 40206

GARRETT, JAMES LOWELL, constrn. co. exec.; b. Stillwater, Okla., Dec. 29, 1946; s. Calvin Lee and Jetta Lee (Hubble) G.; B.S., Okla. State U., 1970 1 dau., Kristina Dawn. With The Atlas Orgn., Inc., gen. constrn., and devel., Oklahoma City, 1970—, v.p., 1971—; partner Garrett-Andersen, real estate devel. and investments, Dallas; land acquisition agt. Nat. Community Builders, Inc.; partner apt. devel. co. Adviser capital devel. div. Transfinancial of Okla., Inc., 1971—. Mem. loyalty fund Okla. State U., 1970-71. Mem. Oklahoma City C. of C., Okla. State U. Alumni Assn., Lambda Chi Alpha. Club: Athletic. Home: 612 Melbourne Ct Hurst TX 76053 Office: 824 N Peniel St Oklahoma City OK 73127 also Suite 100 1720 Regal Row Dallas TX

GARRETT, JOHN MAXWELL, JR., retail trade exec.; b. Greensboro, N.C., Sept. 14, 1924; s. John Maxwell and Nellie Victoria (Leonard) G.; B.A., Elon Coll., 1948; m. Jean Marie Abell, Dec. 25, 1949; children— Victoria Marie, John Keith. Asst. mgr. Western Auto Supply Co., Knoxville, 1948-49, mgr., 1949-50, Raleigh, N.C., 1950-51, Winston-Salem, N.C., 1951-52, retail sales mgr., Atlanta, Ga., 1952-57; mgr. Lowes Cos., North Wilkesboro, N.C., 1957—. Mem. Profit Sharing Investment Com., 1970—. Bd. dirs. Alcoholic Beverage Control, 1971—. Served with AUS, 1943-45. Decorated Bronze Star. Mem. Alpha Phi Delta. Democrat. Presbyn. (deacon 1970—). Kiwanian (bd. dirs. 1958—). Home: 1114 Brookwood Dr Wilkesboro NC 28697 Office: Lowes Hardware Box 1111 North Wilkesboro NC 28659

GARRETT, JOHN S., state legislator; b. nr. Haynesville, La., Oct. 29, 1921; B.S. in Social and Polit. Sci., La. Poly. Inst. Mem. La. Ho. of Reps., 1948—, speaker, 1958—. Land developer, bus. exec., cattleman; mem. Democratic State Central Com., 1958—; mem. ex-officio State Bond and Bldg. Commn., State Bd. Liquidation, State Bd. Registration. Served with AUS, World War II; ETO. Decorated Bronze Star. Home: 103 Frances Circle Haynesville LA 71038 Office: PO Box 44062 Baton Rouge LA 70804

GARRETT, JULIUS BENJAMIN, JR., micropaleontologist; b. Calhoun, La., June 18, 1913; s. Julius Benjamin and Elizabeth (Gandy) G.; B.S. in Geology, La. State U. 1932, M.S., 1933; m. Irma Dorothy Fonville, June 15, 1940; children—Joan, Richard, Alfred. Micropaleontologist, United Gas System, Houston, 1934-35, Stanolind Oil and Gas. Co., Houston, 1935-42; chief paleontologist Pan Am. Petroleum Corp. (name now Amoco Prodn. Co.), Houston, 1946—. Served to maj. AUS, 1942-46; ETO. Decorated Bronze Star medal. Fellow A.A.A.S., Geol. Soc. of Am.; mem. Am. Assn. Petroleum Geologists, Soc. Econ. Paleontologists and Mineralogists (v.p. 1948-49). Contbr. articles to profl. jours. Home: 24 W Oks St Houston TX 77027 Office: 1646 Old Spanish Trail Houston TX 77025

GARRETT, LARRY, newspaper exec. Pres. Memphis Citizen. Address: 1404 Airways Memphis TN 38114*

GARRETT, MARY KEITH, assn. exec.; b. San Antonio, Dec. 4, 1940; d. Stephen Girard and Mildred (Burrows) Garrett; student U. Tex., E. Tex. State U.; B.S., S.W. Tex. U., 1966; postgrad. Old Dominion U. Dir., Austin (Tex.) Natural Sci. Center, 1963-65; tchr. Austin Pub. Schs., 1966-67; dir. natural history Norfolk (Va.) Mus. Arts and Scis., 1967-70; dir. Soc. Scis. of Tidewater, 1970—. Mem. adv. bd. Tidewater Shell and Fossil Club. Fellow Am. Parks and Recreation Assn.; mem. Natural Sci. for Youth Found. Home: 324 W Freemason St Norfolk VA 23510 Office: Box 3127 Norfolk VA 23510

GARRETT, NORMAN HESSON, JR., physician; b. Mount Kisco, N.Y., Jan. 10, 1927; s. Norman Hesson and Mary (Mellow) G.; M.D., Duke, 1950; m. Anne Rebecca Honeycutt, Mar. 19, 1950; children—Elizabeth Ann, Linda Carol, Mary Katherine, Norman Hesson III. Intern medicine Duke, 1950, Cin. Gen. Hosp., 1951; resident pathology Cin. Gen. Hosp., 1952; resident medicine Duke Hosp., 1953, instr. medicine, 1954; practice medicine specializing in internal medicine, Greensboro, N.C., 1954—; chief staff Moses Cone Hosp., Greensboro, 1968-69; clin. asso. prof. medicine, U. N.C. Medicine, 1967—. Served with AUS, 1945-46. Mem. Am. Soc. Internal Medicine (chmn. membership com. 1968—), N.C. Diabetes Assn. (pres. 1969-70), N.C. Soc. Internal Medicine (pres. 1970-71), Greensboro Acad. Medicine (pres. 1967-68), Alpha Omega Alpha. Presbyn. (elder 1963-66, 68-71). Home: 3932 Madison Av Greensboro NC 27410 Office: 1038 Profl Village Greensboro NC 27401

GARRETT, PAUL HAMILTON, clergyman; b. Erick, Okla., Jan. 26, 1908; s. Ewing Sylvester and Alma Lillard (Hamilton) G.; B.A., Bethany Nazarene Coll., 1931, D.D., 1954; M.A., U. Houston, 1946; m. Sylvia Morris Smith, Jan. 14, 1933; children—Gaylia Suzanne (Mrs. Lorrin L. Dreier), Myrta Paulyn. Tchr. pub. schs., Hajo (Okla.) Consol. Sch.; 1932, Choctaw Sch., Erick, 1933-34; supt. Alfalfa Union Graded Sch., 1935-37; ordained to ministry, Ch. of Nazarene, 1934, pastor Central Park Ch., Houston, 1937-46, First Ch. Texarkana, Tex., 1946-49; supt. Dallas dist. Ch. of Nazarene, 1949—. Chmn. Thunderbird Enterprises; chmn. bd., pres. West Central Found. Mem. commn. on edn. Ch. of Nazarene, 1948-52, pres. Dallas dist. adv. bd., 1949—, del. gen. assembly, 1940, 44, 48, 52, 56, 60, 64, 68, chmn. bldg. and devel., chmn. finance com. bd. trustees Bethany Nazarene Coll.; pres Scottsville Holiness Campmeeting Assn. Dir. Tex. Alcohol-Narcotic Edn., Inc. Bd. dirs., pres. Rest Cottage. Mem. Nat. Rifle Assn. (life), Profl. Photog. Assn., Nat. Geog. Soc., Mag. Home: 2718 Maple Springs Blvd Dallas TX 75235 Office: PO Box 19805 Dallas TX 75235

GARRETT, PEARSON BEVERLY, banker; b. Brenham, Tex., Aug. 22, 1895; s. William Beverly and Elizabeth Overton (Pearson) G.; LL.B., U. Tex., 1915; m. Ruth Evens, 1919; children—Pearson Beverly, Richard Gordon. Admitted to Tex. bar, 1915; partner Garrett & Garrett, 1915-17. Partner, Breg, Garrett & Co., investment bankers, 1919-24; owner Garrett & Co., investment bankers, 1924-45; pres. Texas Bank & Trust Co. of Dallas, 1945-58, vice chmn. bd., 1958—; dir. Shovel Supply Co. Pres. Assn. State Chartered Banks Texas, 1962-63. Served from 1st lt. to capt., Air Service, U.S. Army, 1917-19; AEF. Mem. Am. Bankers Assn. (chmn. econ. edn. com.), Tex. Council on Econ. Edn. (pres.). Home: 3131 Maple Av Dallas TX 75205 Office: 1 Main Pl Dallas TX 75202

GARRETT, ROBERT EDWIN, mfg. co. exec.; b. Saginaw, Ala., Dec. 13, 1908; s. John Allen and Lena Jane (Naish) G.; student U. Ala., 1926-27; m. Annie Cole Smith, Aug. 8, 1931; children—Robert Michael, Joan Elizabeth. Office boy Sloss-Sheffield Steel & Iron Co., 1929; exec. asst., 1945-52, asst. to pres., 1952; v.p. U.S. Pipe & Foundry Co., Birmingham, Ala., 1952-59, exec. v.p., 1959-60, pres., 1960-64, chmn. bd., pres., 1964-70, chmn. bd., 1970—, also dir.; dir. Jefferson Fed. Savs. & Loan Assn., Birmingham, Jim Walter Corp., Tampa, Fla. Methodist. Clubs: Vestavia Country, Downtown, Country (Birmingham). Home: 204 Vestavia Circle Birmingham AL 35216 Office: 3300 1st Av N Birmingham AL 35202

GARRETT, ROLAND LEMUEL, bank dir., civic leader; b. Elizabeth City, N.C., July 14, 1894; s. William Wallace and Sarah (Berry) G.; student Creecy Bus. Coll., Elizabeth City, 1913; m. Nina E. Widgeon, June 5, 1917 (dec. May 1956). With Stevens Jobbing Co., Elizabeth City, 1915; owner Garrett Grocery, 1920-25; co-owner Garrett Hardware Co., 1926-64; postmaster City of Elizabeth City, 1943-64. Pres., Albemarle Savs. and Loan Assn., 1965—, dir., 1947—; dir. Indsl. Comml. Bank. Chmn., trustee Pub. Library, 1967—; bd. dirs. Elizabeth City Boys Club, N.C. State Tb. Assn., A.R.C., United Fund, Econ. Improvement Council, Mayor's Human Relations Council; trustee adv. bd. Salvation Army; trustee Chowan Coll., Murfreesboro, N.C.; treas. Albemarle Orthopedic Clinic. Served with AUS, 1917-19. Named Citizen of Year V.F.W., 1966, Man of the Year, Cosmopolitan Club, 1968. Mem. Mchts. Bur., C. of C. (bd. dirs. 1970—). Kiwanian, Odd Fellow, Red Men. Baptist (bd. deacons 1928-72). Club: Cosmopolitan. Home: 1021 W Church St Elizabeth City NC 27909 Office: 306 W Colonial Av Elizabeth City NC 27909

GARRETT, WILBUR EUGENE, editor; b. Kansas City, Mo., Sept. 4, 1930; s. Clay Dean and Cecil Zora (Melton) G.; B.J., U. Mo., 1954; m. Lucille Hall, Dec. 26, 1950; children—Michael Dean, Kenneth Lewis. Photographer, Hallmark Greeting Card Co., 1948-50; picture editor, then asst. illustrating editor, asso. illustrating editor, now sr. asst. editor Nat. Geog. Soc., 1954—; mem. faculty photojournalism mag. color workshop U. Mo., 1963, 64, 69, 70, 71; designer photog. exhbn. People-to-People lounge U.S. Pavilion, N.Y. World's Fair, 1965; designer-producer Nat. Geog. Soc, exhbns. 23d, 24th, 25th Picture of Year Competition; lectr. in field, 1954—. Served with USNR, 1950-52; Recipient Newhouse citation U. Syracuse, 1963; 14 awards Pictures of Year competition, including Mag. Photographer of Year, 1969. Mem. Nat. Press Photographers Assn., White House News Photographers Assn. Clubs: Overseas Writers University, Cosmos (Washington). Home: 209 Seneca Rd Herndon VA 22070 Office: Nat Geographic Soc 17th and M Sts Washington DC 20036

GARRETT, WILLIAM TARRANT, plastic co. exec.; b. Dallas, May 11, 1925; s. Wilburn T. and Ella Mae (Miles) G.; student U. Pickton, 1950; m. Betty B. Kretchmer, Jan. 25, 1945; children—William T. III, Glenn Herbert, Raymond Wayne. Coordinator, Stanford Univ. Press, 1946-49; sales mgr. A & A Plastic Supply Co., Dallas, 1950-58; pres., gen. mgr. A-1 Plastic Supply Co., Dallas, 1959—. Mem. Circle 10 council Cub Scouts, Boy Scouts of Am., 1954-57; coach Little League Baseball, 1954-56, Midget League Basketball, 1955-57. Served with AUS, 1944-46. Mem. Soc. Plastic Engrs. (sr.), Dallas C. of C. Home: 2534 Crest Ridge Dallas TX 75228 Office: 13700 Gamma Rd Dallas TX 75240

GARRETT, WILLIAM WALTON, JR., elec. engr.; b. Nashville, Sept. 6, 1886; s. William Walton and Mattie (Mitchell) G.; B.S., Auburn U., 1910; certificate corrosion engring. U. Tex., 1961; m. Willie Mae Appling, Sept. 3, 1912; children—Loudel Appling (Mrs. Sanford P. Enslen Jr.), Dorothy Mae (Mrs. James O. Patton, Jr.). Test engr. U.S. Steel Co., Birmingham, Ala., 1910-22, dir. elec. lab., 1922-51; mut. funds Frank Chappelle, Birmingham, Ala., 1960-67; tchr. extension div. U. Ala., 1941-45; cons. corrosion engr. indsl. water, 1950-67. Mem. div. industries Bur. Mines, Com. of Birmingham, 1942. Registered profl. engr., Ala. Mem. Iron and Steel Engrs. (pres. 1927-28), Engring. Council Birmingham (mem. exec. com.), Nat. Assn. Corrosion Engrs. (past chmn. Birmingham chpt.), Lambda Chi Alpha. Methodist (bd. stewards 50 yrs.). Mason (Shriner). Club: National Exchange (Vestavia Hills). Contbr. articles to profl. jours., History of Iron and Steel Engrs., 1920-39. Home: 1105 Wickford Rd Vestavia AL 35216

GARRICK, ISADORE EDWARD, aero research scientist; b. Chgo., Mar. 3, 1910; s. Rubin and Ida (Leavitt) G.; B.S., U. Chgo., 1930; m. Cicely Berlin, Feb. 14, 1937; children—Michael, Linda, Danielle. Physicist aero. research Langley Aero. Lab. NACA (now NASA), 1930—, chief dynamic loads div., 1949—, chief math. scientist, Langley Research Center, Hampton, Va., 1970—; adj. prof. George Washington U.; Jerome Clarke Hunsaker prof. Mass. Inst. Tech., 1956-57. Mem. applied math. adv. council Nat. Bur. Standards, 1947-50; NASA rep. to div. math. scis. Nat. Acad. Scis.-NRC, 1968—. Recipient Exceptional Service award NASA, 1964. Fellow Am. Inst. Aeros. and Astronautics; mem. Am. Phys. Soc., Soc. for Indsl. and Applied Math. Author numerous sci. papers; contbr. tech. articles profl. publs. Home: 2208 Crescent Dr Hampton VA 23361 Office: Langley Research Center Hampton VA 23365

GARRIGA-RODRIGUEZ, FRANCISCO, educator; b. Santiago, Spain, Apr. 3, 1912; s. Francisco and Julia (Rodriguez) Garriga; B.S., U. P.R., 1932; A.B., U. Chgo., 1944, M.A., 1949; Dr. en Filosofia, U. Madrid, 1965; student U. N.C., U. Tex., Princeton, 1957-60; m. Ana Trillo, Nov. 19, 1941; children—Ana Julia, Julia Margarita, Francisco Javier, Margarita Maria, Maria Caridad. Tchr., Utuado (P.R.) High Sch., 1932-41, prin., 1941-42; instr. math. U. P.R., 1942-48, asst. prof., 1948-55, asso. prof., 1955-65, prof. math., 1965—, asso. dean sci., 1959, acting dean, 1969, asso. dean studies, 1961-62, chmn. math. dept., 1962-67. Author: El razonamiento matematico, 1956; The Teaching of Mathematics in Puerto Rico, 1965. Home: N-11 Everglades Rio Piedras PR 00929

GARRIOTT, OWEN K., astronaut; b. Enid, Okla., Nov. 22, 1930; grad. U. Okla., 1953; M.S., Stanford, 1957, Ph.D., 1960; m. Helen Mary Walker; children—Randall, Robert, Richard; Linda. NSF fellow Cambridge (Eng.) U., Radio Research Sta., Slough, Eng., 1960-61; instr. electronics, electro-magnetic theory, ionospheric physics Stanford, 1961-65; now astronaut Manned Spacecraft Center, Houston. Mem. Am. Geophys. Union, I.E.E.E., Am. Astron. Soc., Tau Beta Pi. Former regional editor Planetary and Space Scis. Address: Manned Spacecraft Center Houston TX 77058

GARRIS, HOWARD FRANKLIN, supt. schs.; b. Round, O., Sept. 6, 1906; s. William B. and Minnie (Dodd) G.; B.S. in C.E., The Citadel, 1929; C.E., U. S.C., 1930, M.A., 1938; m. Julia Crider, Aug. 17, 1932; 1 dau., Julia Helen. Testing engr. S.C. Hwy. Dept., 1930-32; tchr., prin. St. George (S.C.) High Sch., 1932-41; supt. Bethune (S.C.) Schs., 1941-43, Blackville (S.C.) Schs., 1943-47; supt. St. Matthews (S.C.) Schs., 1947-72. Mem. Fed., S.C. edn. assns., Am., S.C. assns. sch. adminstrs. Baptist. Mason. Lion. Address: PO Box 215 St Matthews SC 29135

GARRISON, CHARLES CLAYTON, ednl. adminstr.; b. Slocum, Tex., July 6, 1927; s. Emmett Riall and Cora Dell (Skidmore) G.; B.B.A., N. Tex. State U., 1949; M.Ed., Stephen F. Austin State U., 1956; m. Bonnie Faye Roberts, Feb. 3, 1950; children—John Thomas, Frank Anthony. Tchr., Kirbyville Sch. Dist., 1949-62, prin., 1952-53, tax-assessor-collector, bus. mgr., 1954-58; tchr. Deer Park (Tex.) Ind. Sch. Dist., 1962-63, asst. bus. mgr., 1963-68, asst. supt. for bus., 1968—; dir. Nat. Bank Deer Park. Served with USNR, 1945-46. Mem. Assn. Sch. Bus. Ofcls. U.S. and Can., Gulf Coast Sch. Bus. Ofcls. (pres. 1969-70), Tex. State Tchrs. Assn., Deer Park C. of C. (dir. 1970-71), Phi Delta Kappa. Kiwanian. Home: 814 Mark St Deer Park TX 77536 Office: 203 Ivy St Deer Park TX 77536

GARRISON, HARRELL EDMOND, coll. pres. emeritus; b. Hugo, Okla., Nov. 4, 1908; s. James Henry and Cynthia (Adams) G.; A.B., Bethany-Peniel Coll., 1932; M.S., Northwestern U., 1936; Ph.D., George Peabody Coll., 1949; m. Virginia Clarice Taylor, Mar. 5, 1933; children—Linda Clarice, Sandra Sue. Tchr. pub. sch., Swink, Ft. Towson, Durant, Okla., 1932-45; diagnostician child study George Peabody Coll., 1945-48; dir Demonstration Sch. North Tex. Tchrs. Coll., 1949, U. Okla., 1950-51; pres. Northeastern State Coll., 1951-70. Mem. P.T.A. (exec. com. Okla. Congress), Nat., Okla. edn. assns., Am. Assn. U. Profs., Phi Delta Kappa, Kappa Delta Pi. Kiwanian (dist. lt. gov.). Co-author: Phonetic Keys to Reading. Home: Riverview Farm Route 3 Tahlequah OK 74464

GARRISON, J. DON, state ofcl. Sec. Okla. Bd. Edn. Address: Okla Dept Pub Instrn State Capitol Oklahoma City OK 73105*

GARRISON, JAMES EUNICE, dairy exec.; b. Pontotoc, Miss., July 5, 1924; s. Basil E. and Mamie (Cruse) G.; B.S., Miss. State U., 1949; m. Edith Archer, May 12, 1950; children—Beth, David, Nancy. Sales rep. Johnson & Johnson, Chgo., 1949-53; asst. to mgr. Pontotoc Dairy, 1953-56; gen. mgr. Ryan Milk Co., Murray, Ky., 1956-60, pres., 1960—; dir. Nat. All Jersey, Ky. Dairy Products Assn., Bank of Murray. Chmn., Murray Airport Bd., 1967. Bd. dirs. Murray Hosp. Bd., Murray Indsl. Found. Served with USAAF, 1943-46. Decorated Air medal. Mem. Murray C. of C. (dir.). Methodist. Home: 303 Oakdale Dr Murray KY Office: East Chestnut Murray KY 42071

GARRISON, JOAN CARTER HINSON (MRS. FLOYD E. GARRISON), med. record librarian; b. Pinehurst, N.C., Mar. 29, 1935; d. Thomas Evandor and Bessie (Carter) Hinson; A.A., Lees-McRae Coll., 1955; intern Charlotte Meml. Hosp., 1955-56; m. Floyd Elwood Garrison, Sept. 1, 1962; 1 dau., Catherine Ellen Garrison. Head med. records dept. Waddell Hosp., Galax, Va., 1956-58; asst. librarian Annie Penn Meml. Hosp., Reidsville, N.C., 1958-60, chief med. record librarian, 1960—. Mem. N.C. (sec. 1965-66, pres. 1967-68; chmn. nominating com. 1971-72), Am. assns. med. records librarians, Rockingham County Assn. Med. Assts. Home: Route 4 Reidsville NC 27320 Office: 619 S Main St Reidsville NC 27320

GARRISON, RICHARD NEIL, sculptor; b. Ft. Bidwell, Cal., Nov. 26, 1912; s. John Henry and Vera (Bell) G.; student Visalia Jr. Coll., 1930-31; m. Jeanne C. Trimble, Oct. 12, 1969. One man shows at Long Boat Key Art Center, Friends Gallery, Sarasota, Fla.; two-man shows Art League Manatee County, Artisan Shop, Cortez Gallery, Boca Grande; exhibited in group shows at Art League Manatee County, Sarasota Art Assn., Contemporary Gallery, St. Petersburg, Fla., Venice Art Assn,, Cortez Art Sch. and Galleries, Compass Galleries, Nantucket, Mass., Artisan Shop, Cortez Gallery, Latin Quarter Gallery, Tampa; represented in permanent collections at Edison Jr. Coll., Ft. Myers, Fla., also pvt. collections; instr. sculpture, dir. Art League of Manatee County, 1967-68. Pres. Fla. Craftsmen. Mem. Art League Manatee County (life), Sarasota Art Assn., Am. Craftsmans Council, Fla. Craftsmen, Long Boat Key Art Assn. (instr. 1971-72). Home and studio: 5911 Shore Acres Dr NW Bradenton FL 33505

GARRISON, THOMAS ALEXANDER, banker; b. Jackson, Tenn., Aug. 29, 1918; s. Thomas Alexander and Frances Lucile (Hicks) G.; student pub. schs., Memphis; m. Gean Koberlein, Oct. 16, 1945; 1 dau., Linda (Mrs. John W. Ellwood). With Union Planters Nat. Bank, Memphis, 1937—, now sr. v.p., mgr. retail banking div.; dir. Bus. Music Corp. Mem. Memphis Traffic Adv. Commn. Pres., bd. dirs. Memphis Boys Town, Inc.; bd. dirs. St. Joseph Hosp. Served with AUS, World War II; ETO. Decorated Silver Star medal, Bronze Star medal. Rotarian. Home: 8187 Cherryfield Lane Germantown TN 38138 Office: 67 Madison St Memphis TN 38103

GARRISON, WILLIAM CARL, state ofcl.; b. Alfalfa County, Okla., Jan. 8, 1910; s. William and Mary (Lasswell) G.; B.A., U. Okla., 1932; grad. Arty. Sch., 1941, Army War Coll., 1953, Command and Gen. Staff Coll., 1947, Armed Forces Staff Coll., 1947; m. Jessie L. Dunham, June 4, 1933; children—Sharon (Mrs. Thomas L. Lias), Mary Nell (Mrs. Francis Stewart), Linda Carol (Mrs. William D. Clifford). Commd. 2d lt. Okla. N.G., 1935, capt. U.S. Army, 1946, advanced through grades to maj. gen., 1963; instr. Arty. Sch., 1942-43; comdr. arty. bn., then arty. group, also asst. corps arty. officer 3d Army, Europe, 1944-45; mem. faculty Engrs. Sch., 1946-48; personnel officer, U.S. Army, Caribbean, 1948-52; assigned gen. staff Dept. Army, also mil. asst. to undersec. army, 1953-57; adviser V Korean Corps, 1958; comdr. 2d Missile Command, 1959-60; dep. G-3, Continental Army Command, 1960-61; comdg. gen. 24th Div. Arty., also VII Corps Arty., Europe, 1961-63, X U.S. Corps, 1964-65; dep. insp. gen. Dept. Army, 1965-66; insp. gen., 1966-68; fed.-state coordinator Oklahoma Gov.'s Office, Oklahoma City, 1968-70. Mem. Am. Battle Monuments Commn., 1969—. Decorated D.S.M., Legion of Merit, Bronze Star medal with V device and cluster, Army Commendation medal with cluster, D.S.M.; Croix de Guerre with palm (France); War for Fatherland medal (Russia). Home: 3117 NW 61st Terrace Oklahoma City OK 73112

GARRISS, PHYLLIS WEYER (MRS W. P. GARRISS), educator; b. Hastings, Neb., Dec. 25, 1923; d. Frank Elmer and Mabelle (Carey) G.; A.B., Hastings Coll., 1945, Mus.B., 1945; Mus.M., Eastman Sch. Music, U. Rochester, 1948; m. William Philip Garriss, Aug. 28, 1954; children—Daniel Weyer, Meredith Carey, Margaret Elizabeth. Instr. mus. theory, violin DePauw U., Greencastle, Ind., 1948-51; vis. prof. violin Ball State Coll., Muncie, Ind., summers, 1951, 53; asst. prof. violin, advanced theory Meredith Coll., Raleigh, N.C., 1951—. Mem. Tri-City Chamber Symphony, 1951—, Roanoke Symphony, 1954—, Duke U. Symphony, 1954—; tchr. Cannon Music Camp, Appalachian State U., Boone, N.C., summers 1971, 72. Mem. Raleigh Civic Council, 1958-60. Mem. Raleigh Chamber Music Guild (dir.), N.C. Art Soc., N.C. Fedn. Music Clubs, Nat. Assn. Amateur Chamber Music Players, Am. Assn. U. Women, Am. Assn. U. Profs. (sec. chpt. 1961), Am. String Tchrs. Assn. (corr. sec. 1950-54), Music Educators Nat. Conf., Music Tchrs. Nat. Assn., Raleigh Concert Music Assn. (dir.), P.E.O., Mu Phi Epsilon, Pi Kappa Lambda. Presbyn. Home: 3400 Merriman Av Raleigh NC 27607

GARROU, LOUIS WILLIAM, textile co. exec.; b. Morganton, N.C., Apr. 6, 1920; s. Albert F. and Louise (Holloway) G.; grad. Darlington Sch., Rome, Ga., 1937; student Davidson Coll., 1937-39, Lenoir Rhyne Coll., Hickory, N.C., 1939-40, U. N.C., 1959-60; m.

Dora Elizabeth Bowles, Sept. 16, 1939; children—John L.W., Elizabeth Louise, Albert Leith. With Waldensian Hosiery Mills, Inc., Valdese, N.C., 1947-62, exec. v.p., 1957-62; exec. v.p. Alba Hosiery Mills, Inc., Valdese, 1959-62; pres. Alba-Waldensian, Valdese, N.C., 1962—, bd. Redesco, S.A., Paris, France, 1966—. Bd. dirs. Valdese Gen. Hosp., 1958—; trustee Lees-McRae Coll., Banner Elk, N.C. Served with AUS, 1943-45. Mem. Nat. Assn. Hosiery Mfrs. (bd. dirs.). Presbyn. Rotarian (pres. Valdese 1951-52). Home: 405 Louise Rd Valdese NC 28690 Office: 408 Armaud St Valdese NC 28690

GARST, ARTHUR WILHELM, research chemist; b. McPherson, Kan., Mar. 7, 1911; s. Roy Arthur and Bertha (Schelb) G.; B.S., U. Tulsa, 1933; m. Helon Roy, June 6, 1936 (dec. Sept. 1966); children—Marcia (Mrs. James Franklin Caldwell), Paul Henry; m. 2d, Betty Elizabeth Ellis, Apr. 1, 1967. Chemist Dowell Inc., 1936-39; sr. research scientist Pan Am. Petroleum Corp., Tulsa, 1939—; cons. in field. Sponsor Wesley Found. U. Tulsa, 1954-60. Fellow Am. Inst. Chemists. Methodist (bd. mem. 1957-60). Contbr. articles to profl. journs. Home: 2303 S Delaware Pl Tulsa OK 74114 Office: Pan Am Petroleum Corp P O Box 591 Tulsa OK 74102

GARTH, WINSTON FEARN, warehouse co. exec.; b. Huntsville, Ala., Mar. 14, 1913; s. William Willis and Mary Louise (Dodsworth) G.; B.S., Dartmouth Coll., 1935; postgrad. Harvard Bus. Sch., 1936-37; m. Emily Hails Thornton, Apr. 27, 1940; children—Winston Fearn, Robert D., J. Thornton, Thomas F., Emily, John F., Frederick D. With Mills Asso., Deering Milliken, Inc., textile mfg., Ala., S.C., Ga., 1942-61; owner, mgr. Southeastern Freezer Corp., cold storage warehouse, Gainesville, Ga., 1963—; dir. Gainesville Midland R.R., Home Fed. Savs. and Loan Assn. Bd. dirs. Community Chest, 1952-60, A.R.C., 1952-56. Bd. dirs. Brenau Coll. Mem. Nat. Frozen Foods Assn., Phi Kappa Psi. Episcopalian (sr. warden 1958-59). Elk. Clubs: Chattahoochie Country. Home: 1090 Dixon Circle Gainesville GA 30501 Office: P O Box 1212 Gainesville GA 30501

GARVAN, JOSEPH BOND, textile co. exec.; b. Hartford, Conn., Oct. 28, 1925; s. John S. and Louise (Bond) G.; grad. The Gunnery, Washington, Conn., 1943; B.A., Yale, 1951; m. Catherine Wheeler, Aug. 26, 1950; children—Stephen B. Gregory L., Melissa W. Pres., P. Garvan, Inc., Spartanburg, S.C., 1957—; dir. Am. Cotton Waste Exchange, First Citizens Bank & Trust Co. Bd. dirs. Broad River Tb-Respiratory Disease Assn., Spartanburg YMCA, Spartanburg Salvation Army, Spartanburg Animal Shelter, S.C. Arthritis Found.; trustee John S. Garvan Found., Wofford Coll., Spartanburg Day Sch. Served with USAAF, 1943-46. Republican. Episcopalian. Clubs: Wofford Eleven (dir.), Piedmont-Yale (alumni bd. rep.). Home: 35 Montgomery Dr Spartanburg SC 29302 Office: PO Box 1492 Spartanburg SC 29301

GARVIN, OTIS ANDERSON, dentist; b. Lakeland, Fla., Aug. 3, 1936; s. Anderson and Agnes (Hester) G.; student Fla. A. and M. U., 1954-56; B.S., Howard U., 1959, D.D.S., 1963. Analytical chemist Mobil Oil Co., Nichols, Fla., 1965-66; pvt. practice dentistry, St. Augustine, Fla., 1966—. Served to capt. USAF, 1963-65. Recipient award Oral Cancer Soc., 1963, Royal Soc. Health, 1966. Mem. Royal Soc. Health, Am., N.E. Dist. dental assns., Fla. Dental Soc., Nat. Med. Dental Pharm. Assn., Am. Legion, Alpha Phi Alpha, Alpha Phi Omega. Methodist. Mason. Home: 83 Bridge St St Augustine FL 32084 Office: 79 Bridge St St Augustine FL 32084

GARY, JAMES WARREN, lawyer; b. Cameron, Tex., Sept. 22, 1929; s. William Warren and Christine (Esslinger) G.; B.A., Rice U., 1951; LL.B., U. Tex., 1956; m. Dayle Hartkopf, Dec. 11, 1954; children—Jill, Clair Leigh and James Mathew (twins). Admitted to Tex. bar, 1956, since practiced in Corpus Christi; asso. Branscomb & Foy, 1956-60; partner Branscomb, Gary, Thomasson & Hall and predecessor firm, 1960—. Finance chmn., treas. Paisano council Girl Scouts Am., 1968-72. Served with USMCR, 1951-53. Decorated Bronze Star medal with combat V. Mem. Am., Tex., Nueces County bar assns., Am., Corpus Christi assns. petroleum landmen, Delta Tau Delta. Methodist. Rotarian. Home: 4933 Cherry Hills Dr Corpus Christi TX 78413 Office: Hawn Bldg Corpus Christi TX 78401

GARY, NATHAN BENNETT, JR., lawyer; b. Sherman, Tex., May 25, 1934; s. Nathan Bennett and Nadyne Coy (Shumate) G.; student Rice Inst., 1951-52, Tex. Christian U., 1952-54; B.A., U. Tex., 1956; J.D., So. Meth. U., 1966; m. Rebecca Fay Orton, Aug. 12, 1961; children—James Bennett, Sydney Catherine, Marcus Orton. Exec. v.p. Waples-Painter Co., Gainesville, Tex., 1960-63, v.p., 1966—; v.p., Gary-Nees Lumber Co., Bowie, Tex., 1966—; admitted to Tex. bar, 1966; practiced in Bowie, 1966—; dir. First Nat. Bank, Bowie. City atty., Bowie, 1967—. Trustee Bowie Hosp. Authority. Served to lt. comdr. USNR, 1956-59. Mem. Naval Res. Assn., State Bar Tex., Lumbermen's Assn. Tex. (dir. 1971—), Phi Delta Phi. Methodist. Home: 1003 Pebble St Bowie TX 76230 Office: PO Box 1282 Bowie TX 76230

GARZA, REYNALDO G., dist. judge; b. Brownsville, Tex., July 7, 1915; s. Ygnacio and Zoila (Guerra) G.; B.A., LL.B., U. Tex.; LL.D., U. St. Edwards, Austin, Tex., 1955; m. Bertha Champion, June 9, 1943; children—Reynaldo G., David C., Ygnacio Daniel, Bertha Victoria, Monica Bernadette. Admitted to Tex. bar, 1939; pvt. practice, 1939-42, 46-50; partner firm Sharpe, Cunningham & Garza, 1950-60, Cunningham, Garza & Yznaga, 1960-61; U.S. dist. judge So. Dist. Tex., 1961—. Treas. Cameron County Child Welfare Bd., 1950-52; mem. Tex. Good Neighbor Commn., 1957-61. Commr., City Brownsville, 1947-49. Trustee Brownsville Ind. Sch. Dist., 1941-42. Served with USAAF, 1942-45. Recipient Pro Ecclesia et Pontifice medal Pope Pius XII, 1952; decorated knight Order St. Gregory the Great, Pope Pius XII, 1954. Mem. Am., Cameron County bar assns., State Bar Tex. Home: 234 Calle Retama Brownsville TX 78520 Office: PO Bldg Brownsville TX 78520

GARZA, TRINIDAD, lead instrumentation engr.; b. Stockdale, Tex., Sept. 22, 1931; B.S. in Elec. Engring., Tex. A. and M. U.; m. Benilde Garza; children—Jerome, Norma Ruth, Bernice Ann and Denise Ann (twins). Lead instrumentation engr. LTV Vought Aeronautics, Dallas. Chmn. ednl. com. League United Latin Am. Citizens; chmn. planning Community, Council of Greater Dallas; mem. higher edn. task health panel United Fund Budget com.; mem. higher edn. task force Goals for Dallas; mem. adv. com. So. Meth. U. Inst. Urban Studies; 1st v.p. Dallas Community Relations Commn.; past pres. Stevens Park Elementary Sch. P.T.A; mem. Dallas Bd. Edn.; commr. Westview dist. Boy Scouts Am. Bd. dirs. Panel Am. Women, Tejas council Girl Scouts U.S. Bd. dirs. Internat. Council for Bus. Opportunity. Methodist (chmn. Rio Grande Conf. scholarship com., Informational Services Com. Conf. Communication Council, Conf. Program Council, mem. gen. bd. laity, Dallas Met. Planning Commn.). Home: 2235 W Colorado Blvd Dallas TX 75211

GASCH, OLIVER, judge; b. Washington, May 4, 1906; s. Herman E. and Marie (Manning) G.; A.B., Princeton, 1928; LL.B., George Washington U., 1932; m. Sylvia Meyer, Oct. 17, 1942; 1 son, Michael Barrett. Admitted to D.C. bar, 1931; asst. corp. counsel for D.C., 1937-53; prin. asst. U.S. atty. for D.C., 1953-56; U.S. atty. for D.C., Washington, 1956-61; partner Craighill Aiello, Gasch & Craighill, 1961-65; judge U.S. Dist. Ct. for D.C., 1965—; gen. counsel Interstate Commn. on Potomac River Basin, 1940-60; chmn. Council on D.C. Law Enforcement, 1958-62; mem. Jud. Conf. D.C. Circuit; co-chmn. Commrs. Crime Council, 1962-63. Mem. dean's council Georgetown U. Law Center, 1960-65. Served as lt. col. Judge Adv. Gen. Dept. AUS, 1942-46; PTO; U.S. Army Res. ret. Fellow Am. Coll. Trial Lawyers, Am. Bar Found.; mem. Fed. (chmn. com. of gen. counsel of fed. govt. 1960-61), Am. bar assns., Bar Assn. D.C. (dir. 1961-63; pres. 1964-65), Am. Law Inst., Barristers of Washington (pres. 1962-63), Res. Officers Assn. (past pres. D.C. dept.), Inst. Mil. Law, Judge Adv.'s Assn., Mil. Order Fgn. Wars (comdr. D.C. 1956), Law Alumni George Washington U. (pres.), Selden Soc. (London, Eng.), Phi Delta Phi. Republican. Episcopalian (vestryman, chancellor, v.p. exec. council diocese of Washington 1961-64, dep. to gen. conv. 1961, 64). Clubs: University, Lawyers, Princeton (Washington); Counsellors; Princeton (N. Y.C.); Chevy Chase. Home: 3673 Upton St Washington DC 20008 Office: US Courthouse Washington DC 20001

GASKINS, LOSSIE LEONARD, ednl. adminstr.; b. nr. Sparks, Ga., May 25, 1925; s. Joseph Leonard and Sallie Mae (Thornton) G.; diploma Middle Ga. Coll., 1946; B.S., Ga. Tchrs. Coll., 1954; M.A., Ga. Peabody Coll. for Teachers, 1962; m. Eleanor Hambrick, June 11, 1967. Tchr.- coach Nashville (Ga.) High Sch., 1946-51; prin. New River Jr. High Sch., Nashville, 1951-54; tchr. English dept. head Berrien County High Sch., 1954-59; asst. prof. Abraham Baldwin Coll., Tifton, 1959-64; county sch. supt. Berrien County, Nashville, 1964—. Active Boy Scouts Am. Served with USNR, 1944. Mem. N.E.A., Ga., Berrien County assns. educators, Ga. Assn. Sch. Supts. Baptist (deacon; Sunday Sch. supt.). Clubs: Civitan (past sec.), Rotary (past pres.). Home: 615 E Smith Av Nashville GA 31639 Office: PO Box 625 Nashville GA 31639

GASPERONI, ELLEN JEAN LIAS (MRS EMIL GASPERONI), auto wash exec.; b. Rural Valley, Pa.; d. Dale S. and Ruth (Harris) Lias; student Youngstown U., 1952-54, John Carrol U., 1953-54, Westminster Coll., 1951-52; grad. Am. Inst. Banking; m. Emil Gasperoni, May 28, 1955; children—Sam, Emil, Jean Ellen. Bd. dirs. Fill-Up-Up Auto Wash Co., Inc., Ft. Lauderdale, Fla., 1968—, sec., 1968—. Mem. Jr. Business Womens Club (dir. 1962-64). Presbyn. Clubs: Le Club Internat., Coral Ridge Country (Ft. Lauderdale). Home: 4201 NE 25th St Fort Lauderdale FL 33308

GASS, W(ALTER) CONARD, educator; b. Jefferson City, Tenn., July 25, 1918; s. Ernest L. and Callie (Snow) G.; A.B., Carson-Newman Coll., 1941; B.Th., So. Bapt. Theol. Sem., 1944; A.M., U. Louisville, 1949; Ed.D., Duke, 1963; m. Austre Berta Cavazos, Oct. 21, 1944. Chmn. dept. social scis. Campbellsville (Ky.) Coll., 1948-53; from instr. to asso. prof. social scis. Campbell Coll., Buie's Creek, N.C., 1954-63, prof., chmn. dept. social scis., 1963—. Cons. Jr. Coll. A.L.A., 1967. Mem. Am., So. hist. assns., Orgn. Am. Historians, History of Edn. Soc., Kappa Delta Pi, Pi Kappa Delta. Democrat. Baptist. Home: P O Box 368 Buie's Creek NC 27506

GASSAWAY, JIM FOOSHE, lawyer; b. Coalgate, Okla., Aug. 27, 1927; s. Percy Lee and Lillian (Fooshe) G.; B.A. in Edn., East Central (Okla.) State Coll., 1949; J.D., U. Okla., 1955; m. Eva Lou Toler, July 5, 1947; children—Caroline, Kevin T. Admitted to Okla. bar, 1955, since practiced in Ada. Mem. Okla. Bd. Bar Examiners, 1959-66. Bd. dirs. McCall's Chapel Sch. for Exceptional Children. Served with USMCR, 1945-46, 50-52. Mem. Okla. Bar Assn. (v.p. 1966; pres. 1971). Episcopalian. Home: 1316 S Johnston St Ada OK 74820 Office: 207 Townsend Bldg Ada OK 74820

GASSIE, EDWARD WILLIAM, educator; b. Addis, La., Nov. 29, 1925; s. Marion Mark and Cecile M. (Hebert) G.; B.S., La. State U., 1951, M.S., 1958, Ph.D., 1964; m. Helen Madelon Lucas, Feb. 19, 1949; children— Janice, Edward William, Jeffery. County extension agt. La. State U., Baton Rouge, 1951-55, dist. extension supr., 1955-64, tng. specialist, prof. extension edn., 1964—. Served with USNR, 1944-46. Mem. Nat. Extension Curriculum Devel. Com., Assn. So. Agrl. Workers, Am. Legion, Phi Kappa Phi, Gamma Sigma Delta, Alpha Zeta, Epsilon Sigma Phi. K.C. Home: 1043 Rodney St Baton Rouge LA 70808

GASSMAN, RICHARD OLIVER, architect; b. Freeport, Ill., Oct. 22, 1916; s. Oliver August and Leona (Pahl) G.; student Bradley U., 1945-47; B.S., U. Okla., 1950; m. Daisy Cameron Mitchell, Feb. 9, 1945; children—Lanona Ann, Pamela Cheryl. Draftsman, Mills Petticord & Mills, Washington, 1954-55; job capt. Arthur Anderson, architect, Washington, 1955-56; architect Chatelain Gauger & Nolan, architects, Washington, 1956-64, Cafritz Constrn. Co., Washington, 1964-66, Ward Assos., architects, Arlington, Va., 1966-71, VA Constrn. Washington, 1971—. Mem. Prince William County Bldg. Code and Appeals Bd., 1969—. Served with USMCR, 1942-45. Mem. A.I.A., Disabled Am. Vets., Greater Manassas C. of C. Moose. Home: 8819 Wellington Rd Manassas VA 22110 Office: 811 Vermont Av NW Washington DC 20420

GASSMANN, ALBERT HENRY, golf equipment mfg. co. exec.; b. Elmhurst, N.Y., July 8, 1922; s. Albert Charles and Anna Marie (Kurz) G.; B.S. in M.E., U. Wis., 1946; B.S. in Bus. Adminstrn. summa cum laude, Rutgers U., 1952; m. Emily Theresa Prufer, Mar. 23, 1946; children—Janet Lynn, Lorraine Joan, Ellen Annmarie. Mfg. engr. heating and air conditioning equipment Gen. Electric Co., 1950-53; mgr. new products div. Mergenthaler Linotype Co., 1953-60; dir. operations Amfare div., AMF Inc., 1960-67; v.p. mfg. Ben Hogan Co., Fort Worth, 1967—. Served with USNR, 1942-46. Mem. Am. Soc. Tooling and Mfg. Engrs., Soc. Am. Value Engrs., Am. Mgmt. Assn. Mason. Club: Wisconsin Alumni and Nat. "W". Patentee in field. Home: 3904 Stonehenge Rd Fort Worth TX 76109 Office: 2912 W Pafford St Fort Worth TX 76110

GASTON, HUGH WILLIAM, architect; b. Gastonburg, Ala., Oct. 27, 1924; s. Emmet Lamar and Harriet Juan (George) G.; B.Arch., Auburn U., 1950; m. Marion Mikel Matheny, June 5, 1950; 1 son, Hugh William. Prin., Hugh Gaston Assos., Albany, Ga., 1958—. Instl. rep., mem. exec. bd. Chehaw council Boy Scouts Am., 1967; mem. Citizens Adv. Com. for Albany and Dougherty County, 1969—; chmn. Dougherty County Com. on Aging, 1959-60; Ga. del. White House Conf. on Aging, 1961; chmn. Albany-Dougherty County Council on Aging, 1965-66, bd. dirs., 1965—; chmn. Ga. Commn. on Aging, 1965—; mem. nominating panel Ga. Art Commn., 1970—; chmn. Ga. Gov.'s Mansion Com., 1970—. Bd. dirs. Nat. Council on Aging, Albany Little Theatre; pres., bd. dirs. S.W. Ga. Art Assn.; mem. adv. bd. Salvation Army; mem. exec. com. for social devel. Goals for Ga. Program. Served with USAAF, 1943-46. Mem. A.I.A. (past com. chmn. Ga. chpt.), Dougherty County Council Architects and Engrs. (past sec.-treas.), Albany C. of C., Ga. Gerontology Soc. (dir., past trustee, com. chmn., mem. exec. com., John Tyler Mauldin award 1970), Nat. Assn. State Units on Aging (dir., chmn. housing com.), Scarab, Kappa Sigma. Presbyn. (elder). Rotarian, Elk. Important works include numerous schs., colls., hosps., nursing homes, chs., housing projects, office bldgs., indsl. and comml. bldgs. Home: 3210 Old Dawson Rd Albany GA 31705 Office: 1107 4th Av Albany GA 31705

GASTON, JOHN NEWTON, JR., physician; b. Edgemoor, S.C., Oct. 2, 1908; s. John Newton and Mary (Patton) G.; A.B., Presbyn. Coll., 1929; M.D., S.C. Med. U., 1936; m. Martha Moore Wilbur, Sept. 5, 1935; children—John Newton III, William Cuttine. Intern Roper Hosp., Charleston, S.C., 1936-37; gen. practice medicine, Chester, S.C., 1937—; mem. staff Pryor Hosp., Chester, S.C., 1937, Chester County Hosp., 1950—; dir. Peoples Nat. Bank. Pres. Chester County Bd. Commerce and Devel., 1957. Trustee Presbyn. Coll., 1967-70. Mem. S.C. Heart Assn. (dir. 1956-59), S.C. Acad. Gen. Practioners, S.C., Chester County med. assns., Alumni Assn. Presbyn. Coll. (pres. 1966), Pi Kappa Phi. Home: 143 Park Dr Chester SC 29706 Office: 107 Oakland Av Chester SC 29706

GASTON, WILLIAM ROBERT, III, physician; b. San Angelo, Tex., Jan. 23, 1936; s. William Robert and Thelma (Vance) G.; B.A., U. Tex., 1958; postgrad. Washington Sch. Medicine, 1958-60; M.D., Baylor U., 1962; m. Richea Brown, June 21, 1958; children—William Robert IV, Richea K., Angela. Intern, Jefferson Davis Hosp., Houston, 1962-63; resident medicine Baylor U. Affiliated Hosps. Program, Houston, 1963-65; chief resident medicine Ben Taub Gen. Hosp., Houston, 1963-65; chief resident medicine Ben Taub Gen. Hosp., Houston, 1965-66; research fellow cardiovascular disease Baylor Coll. Medicine, 1966-67, asst. prof. medicine, 1969-70, prof. medicine, 1970—; practice medicine specializing in cardiology, Houston; mem. staff Ben Taub Gen. Hosp.; mem. active staff Meth. Hosp., St. Joseph Hosp.; mem. courtesy staff Hermann, Meml. Bapt., St. Lukes hosps.; chief cardiology cons. Rosewood Gen. Hosp., Houston, Montgomery County Hosp., Conroe, Tex. Served to maj., M.C., AUS, 1967-69. Diplomate Am. Bd. Internal Medicine, also cardiovascular splty. Mem. A.C.P., Am. Coll. Cardiology, A.M.A., Tex. Med. Assn., Tex., Houston heart assns., Harris County Med. Soc., Houston Soc. Internal Medicine (treas. 1972), Phi Beta Kappa. Home: 11519 Habersham Houston TX 77024 Office: Med Towers 1709 Dryden St Houston TX 77025

GATCHELL, WILLIAM HENRY, banker; b. Memphis, Mar. 20, 1910; s. Harry Lavender and Hannah May (Ellis) G.; student Memphis Univ. Sch., 1926-28, Am. Inst. Banking, 1929-35; m. Janice A. Northrup, Sept. 19, 1931; 1dau., Barbara Ellen (Mrs. A. Douglas Salmon). With Union Planters Nat. Bank, Memphis, 1929—, sr. v.p. charge nat. accounts div., 1967—. Past treas. local U.S.O., Boy's Town, Muscular Dystrophy Assn. Bd. dirs. Duration Sch., 1966—, treas., 1967-68; chmn. adv. bd. Memphis Salvation Army, 1948, bd. dirs., 1968—. Mem. Memphis Execs. Club (pres. 1957), Memphis C. of C. (life, past chmn. welcome com.), Memphis Secret Soc. (treas.), Memphis Cotton Carnival Assn. (past asst. treas.). Mem. Christian Ch. (vice chmn. bd. elders 1968—). Lion (past v.p., dir.). Club: Chickasaw Country (past v.p., treas.) (Memphis). Home: 36 Wynchewood Dr Memphis TN 38117 Office: 67 Madison Av PO Box 387 Memphis TN 38101

GATES, DONALD D., hotel exec.; b. Mullens, W.Va., June 14, 1930; s. Lewis Otto and Mildred Morrison (Buchanan) G.; student Nat. Bus. Coll., 1950, Am. Motel Sch., 1968; m. Margaret Hester Henderson, July 29, 1956; children—Donald Dean II, Leisa Diane, Lori Anne. With Krish Bros., 1951-57; salesman Am. Motor Inns, Roanoke, Va., 1957—; systems analyst Holiday Inn, Alexandria, Va., 1957-63, gen. mgr., 1963—. Served with USNR, 1950-51. Recipient Community Leader award New Pub. Co., 1969; named Businessman of the Year Jr. C. of C., 1967, 71. Mem. So. Innkeepers Assn. (v.p. 1970-71), Va. Hotel and Motel Assn. (v.p. 1972—), Mt. Varnon/Lee (chmn. bd. 1968), Fairfax County (dir. 1968-69) chambers commerce. Baptist. Mason (32 deg., Shriner). Home: 6429 Carrage Dr Alexandria VA 22310 Office: 2460 Eisenhour Dr Alexandria VA 22314

GATES, ERNEST PLEASANTS, circuit ct. judge; b. Chesterfield, Va., June 16, 1924; s. Ordway Benjamin and Ida (Heath) G.; B.S., Hampden-Sydney Coll., 1947; LL.B., Washington and Lee U., 1950; m. Virginia Yonce, Aug. 18, 1951; children—William Mayo, Ernest Pleasants, David Heath, Elizabeth Williams, Virginia Morehead, Thomas Bass. Admitted to Va. bar, 1950; commonwealth atty., Va., 1954-66; additional judge 37th Jud. Circuit, Va., 1966-68, sr. judge, 1968—. Served to lt. (j.g.) USNR, 1946. Decorated Purple Heart. Mason. Home: 4701 Bruce Rd Chester VA 23831 Office: Courthouse Chesterfield VA 23832

GATES, HOWARD MARION, coll. adminstr.; b. Huntington, Tex., May 3, 1920; s. Davis Beauregard and Cora Stella (Richardson) G.; B.B.A., Stephen F. Austin State U., 1943; M.S., Tex. A. and M. U., 1944; m. Maggie Hazel McKeown, Dec. 26, 1955. Claim investigator Mo. Pacific R.R., Palestine, Tex., 1945-56; accountant, Tex. A. and M. U. System, College Station, 1956-65; bus. mgr. Tex. State Tech. Inst., Waco, 1965-68; bus. mgr. Angelina Coll., Lufkin, Tex., 1968—. Mem. phys. plant operation and maintenance formula study com. Tex. Jr. Colls., 1969. Served with AUS, 1945. Mem. Tex. Assn. Pub. Jr. Coll. Bus. Officers (treas. 1970-72), Tex. State Tchrs. Assn. Methodist (mem. adminstrv. bd.). Home: 1404 Sleepy Hollow Lufkin TX 75901 Office: PO Box 1768 Lufkin TX 75901

GATES, LEON WAINWRIGHT (MRS. HAROLD GATES), ret. educator; b. Phoebus, Va., Sept. 7, 1903; d. John Henry and Mary (Chaney) Wainwright; B.S., Hampton Inst., 1931, M.A., 1940; postgrad. U. Me., 1961, 64, 67; m. Harold Gates, July 18, 1931; children—Meredith D., Gloria C., Dolores W. Tchr. Nottoway Tng. Sch., Blackstone, Va., 1923-24, Gastonia, N.C., 1924-47; prin. Mary N. Smith High Sch., Accomac, Va., 1931-39, 56-70; instr. English, Hampton Inst., 1950-55; adult edn. instr. U.S. Office of Edn., 1947-49. Active Community Center Bd., Tb Bd., W. E. Atkins Auxiliary to Vis. Nurses. Mem. Internat. Speakers Assn., Am., Va. tchr. assns., Nat., Va. prins. assns., Dau of Isis, Pan Hellenic, Sigma Gamma Rho, Omega Sigma. Baptist. Mem. Order Eastern Star, Golden Circle Auxiliary to 32 deg. Masonry. Home: 416 Eaton St Hampton VA 23369

GATES, MAC STUART, clergyman, sch. adminstr.; b. Romeo, Mich., June 24, 1914; s. Ernest E. and Mary (Stuart) G.; student Moody Bible Inst., 1942-44; B.A. cum laude, Ouachita Bapt. U., 1948; student U. Ark., 1950, 53; M.S. in Edn., Henderson State Tchrs. Coll., 1956; m. Mary E. Brown, Jan. 21, 1949; step-children—Mary P. (Mrs. William L. Parker), Rual T. Lee. Ordained to ministry Bapt. Ch., 1945; pastor-evangelist, 1940-48; pastor Glenwood (Ill.) United Ch., 1944-45, 1st Bapt. Ch., Bingen, Ark., 1945-49, Walnut Valley Ch., 1950-56, Riverside Ch., Donaldson, Ark., 1956-59; adminstr. Malvern (Ark.) pub. schs., 1948—; mission pastor 1st Bapt. Ch., Malvern, 1959-65; prin. Malvern Jr. High Sch.; pastor 2d Bapt. Ch., Bryant, Ark., Salem Bapt. Ch., Benton, Ark., 1970—; lectr. series, Edn., Now, 1965—. Mem. Hot Spring County Library Bd., 1955-57; sec., publicity dir. Malvern City Planning Commn., 1952-65; mem. State Com. Guidance and Selection Audio-Visual Materials; chmn. Malvern Housing Authority, 1966-72. Mem. Photographers Internat. Assn., Nat., Ark., Hot Spring County (pres. 1956-57) edn. assns., Ark. Hist. Assn., Ouachita Valley Schoolmasters Assn. (past pres.), Phi Delta Kappa (historian Henderson State Coll. chpt. 1970). Home: 2017 Wilson Malvern AR 72104 Office: 1910 Roosevelt St Malvern AR 72104

GATES, WILLIAM FRED, JR., bishop; b. Lexington, Va., Mar. 29, 1912; s. William Fred and Edna (Brundige) G.; student Hobart Coll., 1931-32; A.B., U. Chattanooga, 1934; B.D., Va. Theol. Sem., 1937, D.D., 1967; D.D., U. of South, 1967; m. Jane Gregory Dillard, Apr. 25, 1938; children—Anne Gregory, Susan Wenrick. Ordained priest Episcopal Ch., 1938; asst. minister Calvary Episcopal Ch., Memphis, 1937-38; priest-in-charge St. John's Ch., Old Hickory, Tenn., 1938-42; rector St. Peter's Ch., Columbia, Tenn., 1943-66; suffragan bishop Episcopal Diocese Tenn., Memphis, 1966—, also mem. bishop and council, standing com., bd. examining chaplains. Chmn. Maury County chpt. A.R.C., 1947-49; pres. Maury County United Givers Fund, 1965-66. Mem. Kappa Alpha. Club: Memphis Country. Home: 5302 Southwood Dr Memphis TN 38117 Office: 692 Poplar Av Memphis TN 38105

GATEWOOD, MAUD F., artist, educator; b. Yanceyville, N.C., Jan. 8, 1934; d. J. Yancey and Mary Lea (Florance) Gatewood; A.B., U. N.C. Woman's Coll., 1954; M.A., Ohio State U., 1955; postgrad. Harvard, summer 1957, U. Vienna, Acad. of Applied Arts Vienna, 1962-63. Instr. art Huntingdon Coll., 1956-58, Tex. Christian U., 1959-62; faculty U. N.C. at Charlotte, 1964—, now asso. prof.; one man shows at Austin Galleries, U. N.C. at Greensboro, Mint Mus. Art, Winston-Salem Gallery Fine Arts, U. N.C. at Charlotte; exhibited in group shows at N.C. Mus. Art, Chapel Hill Art Gallery, Library of Congress, Dallas Mus. Fine Arts, Denver Mus., many others; represented in permanent collections Mint Mus., pvt. collections. Fulbright grantee, 1962-63. Mem. Asso. Artists N.C. Home: 2309 Pender Pl Charlotte NC 28209

GATHRIGHT, JOSEPH RADFORD, banker; b. Louisville, Mar. 23, 1911; s. Jesse N. and Lucy (Farmer) C.; A.B., Dartmouth, 1931; LL.B., U. Louisville, 1934; m. Jane Dobbins, Dec. 7, 1935; 1 son, Joseph Radford. Admitted to Ky. bar, 1934; practice in Louisville, 1934-38; asst. city atty., Louisville, 1935-38; with Ky. Trust Co., Louisville, 1938—, trust officer, 1945—, sr. v.p., 1961-67, exec. v.p., 1967—, also dir.; dir. First Kentucky Co., W.E. Caldwell Co., Commonwealth Land Title Ins. Co. Phila.; co-pub. Will Manual Service, 1955—. Pres. Estate Planning Council, Louisville, 1948; Pres. Legal Aid Soc. Louisville, 1959. Mem. Am., Ky., Louisville bar assns. Presbyn. (deacon). Home: 180 West Wind Rd Louisville KY 40207 Office: 216 S 5th St Louisville KY 40201

GATHRIGHT, PEARL GILMER (MRS. ROBERT HAROLD GATHRIGHT), educator; b. Toccopola, Miss., Sept. 19, 1910; d. Ernest Lavert and Ida (Moor) Gilmer; B.S. in Commerce, U. Miss., 1955, M.Bus. Edn., 1957; m. Robert Harold Gathright, June 30, 1927 (dec. Sept. 1963); children—Eugene Lavert, Sandra Ann (Mrs. Gerald Leroy Tucker). High sch. tchr., Thaxton, Miss., 1951-53, Toccopola, 1953-57; faculty U. Miss., University, 1957—, asst. prof. office adminstrn., 1964—. Univ. supr. Student Tchrs. in Field Bus. Edn., 1963—. Mem. Nat., So., Miss. (pres. 1968) bus. edn. assns., Nat. Assn. Bus. Tchr. Edn., Am. Vocational Assn., Am. Assn. U. Women (pres. Oxford br. 1967-69), Oxford Bus. and Profl. Women's Club (sec. 1965-66), Delta Pi Epsilon (chpt. treas. 1963—), Phi Gamma Nu (chpt. adviser 1959—), Epsilon Gamma Epsilon, Delta Kappa Gamma. Presbyn. (pres. bus. women's circle 1967). Home: 609 Park Dr Oxford MS 38655 Office: Conner Hall University MS 38677

GATLIFF, BEN FANKLIN, physician; b. Macon, Ga., Jan. 19, 1922; s. Benjamin and Mellie (Corley) G.; B.S., U. Ga., 1948; M.D., Med. Coll. Ga., 1952; m. Marion Hays, Aug. 19, 1950; children—Gary Edwin, Eda Marie, Laural Francis. Intern, Orange Meml. Hosp., Orlando, Fla., 1952-53; pvt. practice medicine specializing in gen. practice, Plant City, Fla., 1953—; staff mem. South Fl. Bapt. Hosp., Plant City, chief of staff, 1959-60. Served from pvt. to T/5, AUS, 1943-45; 1st lt. Res. Mem. A.M.A., Fla. Med. Assn., Theta Kappa Psi. Episcopalian. Named Ky. col. Home: 1202 W Baker St Plant City FL 33566 Office: 402 Dort St Plant City FL 33566

GATLIN, DOUGLAS STUART, educator; b. Jacksonville, Fla., May 2, 1928; s. William Arthur and Claire Antoinette (Denby) G.; B.A., U. Fla., 1956, M.A., 1957; Ph.D., U. N.C., 1964. Instr. polit. sci. dept. Wake Forest Coll., 1960-64; asst. prof. polit. sci. Fla. Atlantic U., Boca Raton, 1964-67, asso. prof., 1967-70, prof., 1970—; research cons. Am. pub. opinion and voting behavior. Bd. dirs. Palm Beach chpt. Am. Civil Liberties Union. Served with AUS, 1951-53. Recipient Eagleton Found. grant for study Fla. Legislative Party System, 1968, NSF grantee, 1972; named Distinguished Tchr., Fla. Atlantic U., 1969-70. Mem. Am., So. polit. sci. assns., Southwestern Social Sci. Assn., Am. Assn. Pub. Opinion Research, Am. Assn. U. Profs. (past pres. Fla. Atlantic U. chpt.), Sigma Alpha Epsilon. Editor: (with William J. Crotty and Donald M. Freeman) Political Parties and Political Behavior, 1966. Contbr. to Approaches to the Study of Party Organization, 1968. Home: 495 NW 16th St Boca Raton FL 33432

GATTI, JOHN, mayor. Vice pres., resident mgr. Rauscher Pierce Securities Corp.; mayor, San Antonio, 1971—. Past mem. San Antonio City Council, past mayor pro tem. Address: Mayor's Office Military Plaza City Hall San Antonio TX 78205*

GATTIS, SARAH BREWER, educator; b. Siler City, N.C., Aug. 19, 1925; d. G. Ernest and Bertha (Russell) Brewer; A.B., U. N.C., 1962, M.A., 1962, Ph.D., 1971; m. David Frady, Dec. 1945 (div. Apr. 1950); children—Russell A., Susan Gayle (Mrs. Larry Martin); m. 2d, Clyde Gattis, Apr. 1952 (div. May 1963). Instr., Atlantic Christian Coll., Wilson, N.C., 1962-65, asst. prof., 1965-68; asso. prof., social studies dept., 1968—. Mem. Am. Assn. U. Profs., N.C. Edn. Assn., Am., So. hist. assns., Pi Gamma Mu. Home: 405 Mt Vernon Dr Wilson NC 27893

GATTON, T(HOMAS) HARRY, banking assn. exec.; b. Harmony, N.C., Mar. 10, 1918; s. Thomas Lee and Freddie Cornelia (Moore) G.; A.B., U. N.C., 1940; m. Mary Louise Gordon, Sept. 12, 1942. Newspaper reporter Statesville (N.C.) Daily Record, 1941-42; engaged in broadcasting sta. mgmt., 1946-50; charge radio savs. bond. div. Treasury Dept., 1951-53; administrv. asst. to U.S. Senator Lennon, 1953-54; exec. sec. to U.S. Senator Ervin, 1954-60; exec. dir. N.C. Bankers Assn., 1960-67, exec. v.p., 1967—, also editor, mgr. Tarheel Banker mag. Mem. Am. Battle Monuments Commn., 1961-69, Statesville Civil Service Commn., 1947-48. Trustee Sch. Banking of South, La. State U.; registrar-treas. Carolinas Sch. Banking, U. N.C.; mem. exec. bd. N.C. Dept. Archives and History, vice chmn., 1965—; mem. George Washington Statue Commn., 1968-71; mem. presdl. adv. bd. Campbell Coll., N.C., 1968—; mem. bus. adv. council Peace Coll., chmn., 1971—; bd. dirs. Southeastern Trust Sch., Campbell Coll. Alternate del. Democratic Nat. Conv., 1956; dir. orgn. Young Dem. Clubs N.C., 1950; pres. N.C. Dem. Club, 1958-59. Served with USNR, 1942-45; lt. comdr. Res. Mem. N.C. Lit. and Hist. Soc., Civil War Round Table D.C., Am. Bankers Assn. (bd. dirs. 1971-72, chmn. state assn. div. 1971-72), Conf. So. Banking Assn. Execs. (pres. 1964-65), N.C. Soc. for Preservation of Antiquities (v.p. 1965-66, pres. 1967-70), Wake County Hist. Soc. (pres. 1967-68), Order Golden Fleece, U.S. Senate Adminstrv. Assts. and Secs. Club. Methodist. Mason, Rotarian (pres. 1971-72). Home: 3012 Eton Rd Raleigh NC 27608 Office: Durham Life Bldg Raleigh NC 27602

GATTOZZI, MICHAEL DOMENIC, educator; b. Cleve., July 7, 1929; s. Joseph and Ralphine (Yok) G.; student Ohio State U., 1947-50; Mus.B., Mus.M., Am. Conservatory Music, 1950-53; postgrad. Ind. U., 1963; m. Charlotte Corrine Kruger, June 3, 1950; children—Michael Scott, Constance Ann, Joseph Walter. Instr. music Bethany (W.Va.) Coll., 1953-55; asst. concertmaster Atlanta Symphony, 1955-61; asst. prof. music Middle Tenn. State U., Murfreesboro, 1961-63; asst. prof. music U. Ala., University, 1963-69, asso. prof., 1969—, condr. U. Ala. Symphony Orch., 1969—; 2d violinist Cadek String Quartet U. Ala., 1963—; faculty, conducting staff Brevard (N.C.) Music Center, summers. Mem. Ala. Music Edn. Assn. (chmn. string div.), Am. String Tchrs. Assn., Music Tchrs. Nat. Assn., Music Educators Nat. Conf. Home: 52 The Highlands Tuscaloosa AL 35401

GATZKE, DELMAR ERWIN, housewares mfg. co exec.; b. Auburn, Wis., Nov. 29, 1929; s. Norbert H. and Laura (Backhaus) G.; B. in M.E., Marquette U., 1965; m. Anita C. Brinkmann, Oct. 17, 1953; children—Jean, Paul, David, Diane. Prodn. worker The West Bend Co. (Wis.), 1949-54, indsl, engr., 1954-59, indsl. engring. coordinator, 1959-62, indsl. engring. supr., 1962-65, resident mgr. Sheridan (Ark.) div., 1965—. Dir. Grant County Bank. Vice pres. dist. Quapaw council Boy Scouts Am., 1967-68; mem. Grant County Health Adv. Council, 1970—, pres., 1972; mem. Sheridan City Planning Commn., 1967—; chmn. Bd. Zoning Adjustment, 1968—. Served with AUS, 1951-53. Mem. Soc. Advancement Mgmt., Am. Soc. M.E., Grant County C. of C. (1st v.p. 1968-69, pres. 1970), Grant County Wildlife Fedn. (pres., dir.). Lutheran. Rotarian. Home: Route 1 Box 4G Sheridan AR 72150 Office: Route 1 Box 291B Sheridan AR 72150

GAUB, MARGARET LUISE, physician; b. Guatemala City, Guatemala (parents Am. citizens); d. William H. and Margaret (Lattelle) Gaub; B.S. cum laude, U. Wash., 1954, M.D. (Ethel Young Phillips scholar, Group Health Coop. scholar, Nat. Found. Infantile Paralysis fellow, Nat. Inst. Mental Health grantee), 1960. Research asst. zoology dept. U. Wash., 1951, asst. poliomyelitis lab., 1953, research asst. microbiology dept., 1953-54, research asst. for U.S. Army, pharmacology dept., 1959; bacteriologist Seattle-King County Dept. Health, 1954-56; intern surgery Jackson Meml. Hosp., Miami, Fla., 1960-61, resident surgery, 1961-63; research fellow anesthesiology U. Miami Sch. Medicine, 1963-65, resident anesthesiology, 1965-66, instr. anesthesiology, 1966-70, asst. prof. anesthesiology, 1970—; practice medicine specializing in pediatric anesthesiology, 1966—. Mem. Dade County Opera Guild, Greater Miami Philharmonic Soc., 1965—. Recipient Anna C. Dunlap prize Soroptomist Club, 1958-59. Diplomate Am. Bd. Anesthesiology. Fellow Am. Coll. Anesthesiologists; mem. Phi Beta Kappa, Sigma Xi, (asso.) Phi Sigma, Alpha Epsilon Delta, Iota Sigma Pi, Sigma Epsilon Sigma, Alpha Xi Delta. Contbr. articles to profl. jours. Home: 2451 Brickell Av Apt 17-L Miami FL 33129

GAUDIN, HOMER CHARLES, judge; b. New Orleans, July 14, 1930; s. Regis B. and Inez C. (Grenier) G.; B.A., U. Southwestern La., 1952; LL.B., Loyola U., New Orleans, 1958; postgrad. La. State U., 1950, U. Pa., 1967, U. Nev., 1970; m. Myra Elizabeth Altman, June 8, 1956; children—Melanee Anne, Monique Grenier, Charles Altman. Head football and basketball coach St. Paul's Coll., Covington, La., 1954-55; sports columnist New Orleans States-Item newspaper, 1956-66; admitted to La. bar, 1958; practiced in New Orleans and Gretna, La., 1958-66; dist. judge 24th Jud. Dist. Ct., Gretna, 1966—. State pres. Nat. Cystic Fibrosis Research Found. Served with USAF, 1952-54. Mem. Am., La., Jefferson Parish bar assns., La. Dist. Judges Assn., Am. Judicature Soc., N. Am. Judges Assn., V.F.W., Amvets, Delta Theta Phi. Roman Catholic. Clubs: Lions, Timberlane Country (dir. 1964—). Home: 28 Farnham Pl Metairie LA 70005 Office: New Parish CourthouseGretna LA 70053

GAUER, CHARLOTTE EDWINA, assn. exec.; b. Balt., Jan. 16, 1912; d. Charles E. and Lucinda D. (Smith) Gauer; B.S., U. Ill., 1932, LL.B., 1935. Admitted to Ill. bar, 1935; legal editor Commerce Clearing House, Chgo., 1935-42; legal staff Montgomery Ward & Co., 1942-50, Pub. Housing Adminstrn., 1951-54; exec. dir. Am. Patent Law Assn., Arlington, Va., 1954—. Nat. bd. Med. Coll. Pa., 1953—. Served with Am. Women's Vol. Services, 1942-45. Mem. Women's Bar Assn. Ill. (pres. 1942-43), Nat. Assn. Women Lawyers (pres. 1947-49), Am. Bar Assn., World Peace Through Law, Mortar Bd., Delta Delta Delta, Alpha Alpha Alpha, Kappa Beta Pi. Republican. Conglist. Home: 2111 Jefferson Davis Hwy Arlington VA 22202 Office: 2001 Jefferson Davis Hwy Arlington VA 22202

GAUGH, FAY MERTON, army officer; b. Springfield, O., Aug. 4, 1910; s. Lee and Mellie (Campbell) G.; M.A., George Peabody Coll., 1955; D.D., Am. Bible Coll., 1943; m. Jessie Studebaker, Oct. 25, 1934; children—Joanna (Mrs. Robert Swyers), Brenda (Mrs. Harold Stout, Jr.), Jon Lee. Regional supr. USO, 1941; asst. prin. Sch. for Officers' Tng., 1963; city comdr. Salvation Army, Birmingham, 1964-71, Tulsa, 1971—. Brig. gen. on staff Tenn. Gov. Mem. Nat. Assn. Social Workers, Acad. Certified Social Workers. Author: Social Work Practice, 1962. Address: 2329 Westfield Rd Charlotte NC 28207

GAULTER, LOREN WILLIAM, II, furniture co. exec.; b. Chanute, Kan., Oct. 17, 1932; s. Loren William and Bessie May (Rush) G.; B.B.A., Armstrong Coll., 1957; m. Shirley Ann Galope, Jan. 27, 1967; children— Judith Ann, Loren William III, Constance Elizabeth, Janice Marie; stepchildren—Erin Dolores, Elyse Marie, Eric Severin. Controller, Eldorado Electronics, Concord, Cla., 1963-67, Kearney-Nat., Inc., N.Y.C., 1967-69; v.p. finance and adminstrn. So. Cross Industries, Inc., Atlanta, 1969—; dir. Fabtron Co., Inc. Com. chmn. Mt. Diablo area Boy Scouts Am., 1965-66. Served with USAF, 1951-53. Mem. Nat. Assn. Accountants. Republican. Lutheran (deacon 1969-72). Optimist. Home: 2771 Wileshire Ct Tucker GA 30084 Office: 290 Hunter St SE Atlanta GA 30312

GAUTIER, JEFF D., state legislator. Mem. Fla. Ho. of Reps., mem. com. criminal code and ct. rev. Address: 800 Concord Bldg 66 W Flagler St Miami FL 33030*

GAUTIER, NEWTON PERRY, supt. schs.; b. Gautier, Miss., Mar. 16, 1926; s. Newton Houston and May Omega (Golden) G.; student Perkinston Jr. Coll., 1948, Miss. State U., 1948-49; B.S., U. So. Miss., 1951, M.Ed., 1961; m. Dixie Ann Wieder, Jan. 2, 1953; children—Choyce Mayo, Elizabeth Ann. Tchr., Vancleave Consol. Sch., 1949-52, Pascagoula High Sch., 1952-53; tchr. Ocean Springs High Sch., 1953-54, prin., 1954-59, 65-66; supt. edn. Jackson County, 1960-64; supt. schs. Pascagoula (Miss.) Municipal Separate Sch. Dist., 1966—. Chmn. Jackson County chpt. A.R.C., 1964; pres. Jackson County Heart Fund, 1969. Served with USNR, 1944-46. Mem. Am. Assn. Sch. Adminstrs. (state membership chmn. 1970-71), Council Pub. Schs. (pres. 1971-72, v.p. 1970-71, sec.-treas. 1967-70), Miss. Assn. Sch. Adminstrs., Miss. Supts. Assn., Miss. (chmn. county supts. div. 1964), Pascagoula (pres. 1968-69) edn. assns., Phi Delta Kappa. Methodist (mem. adminstrv. bd. 1953). Home: Star Route Box 156 Gautier MS 39567 Office: PO Box 250 Pascagoula MS 39567

GAVAZZI, ALADINO A., hosp adminstr. Adminstr. VA Hosp., Washington. Address: VA Hosp 50 Irving St NW Washington DC 20422*

GAVENDA, JOHN DAVID, physicist, educator; b. Temple, Tex., Mar. 25, 1933; s. Edward and Rose (Machalek) G.; student U. Chgo.1950-51; B.S., U. Tex., 1954, M.A., 1956; Ph.D. (Edgar Lewis Marston fellow 1957-59), Brown U., 1959; m. Janie Louise Yeoman, Dec. 22, 1952; children—Victor Joseph, Philip Martin. Asst. prof. physics and research scientist U. Tex. Austin, 1959-62, asso. prof. physics, 1962-65, asso. prof. physics and edn., 1965-67, prof. physics and edn.1967—; sr. research fellow Inst. for Study of Metals. U. Chgo., 1963; NATO sr. fellow in sci. U. Oslo, spring 1969. Fellow Tex. Acad. Scis.; mem. Am. Phys. Soc., Am. Assn. Physics Tchrs., A.A.A.S., Phi Beta Kappa, Sigma Xi, Sigma Pi Sigma. Baptist (deacon 1961—). Home: 5709 Bullard Dr Austin TX 78731

GAVETT, THOMAS WILLIAM, govt. ofcl.; b. Milw., Jan. 10, 1932; s. Harold S. and Verona (Reinhold) G.; B.B.A., U. Wis., 1953, M.S., 1954, Ph.D., 1957; m. Patricia Ann Dummer, Aug. 21, 1954; children— Geoffrey, Stephen, Christopher. Lectr., Marquette U., Milw., 1956-57; asst. prof., asso. prof., dir. Inst. of Indsl. Relations, W.Va. U., Morgantown, 1957-66; dep. commr., economist Bur. Labor Statistics, U.S. Dept. of Labor, Washington, 1966—. Chmn., W.Va. State Human Rights Commn., 1961-66. Mem. Am. Econs. Assn., Am. Statis. Assn., Indsl. Relations Research Assn. Home: 513 Springlock Rd Silver Spring MD 20904 Office: Bur of Labor Statistics Washington DC 20102

GAW, JAMES RICHARD, auditorium mgr.; b. Owensboro, Ky., July 12, 1926; s. James William and Josephine (Thompson) G.; student Owensboro Bus. Coll., Brescia Coll.; m. Alma Irene Knott, Aug. 16, 1952; children—Stephen Thomas, Barbara, Monica, James Gerard, Angela, Thersa. Prodn. mgr. Murphy-Miller, Inc., Owensboro, 1947-48; asst. mgr. Owensboro Sportscenter, 1949-52, mgr., 1958—; partner Elite Cigar Co., Owensboro, 1952-57, Magistrate, Daviess County, Owensboro, 1958-61. Pres. Young Democrats Daviess County, 1955; sec. exec. com. Daviess County Dem. Com., 1960-64. Bd. dirs. Spastic Home and Sch., Owensboro, 1956—, chmn., 1959-60. Named Ky. col., 1955. Mem. Internat. Assn. Auditorium Mgrs., Ky. Parks Soc., Ky. Magistrates Assn. (pres. 1960-61), Owensboro Jr. C. of C. (pres. 1954), Ice Skating Inst. Am. (dir.). Democrat. Roman Catholic. K.C., Elk, Moose. Home: 1810 Cecelia Ct Owensboro KY 42301 Office: Owensboro Sportscenter 12th St and Hickman Av Owensboro KY 42301

GAXIOLA, FRANCISCO JAVIER, lawyer; b. Toluca, Mex., Sept. 6, 1898; s. Francisco Javier and Blanca (Zendejas) G.; legal degree Escuela libre de Derecho, 1922; m. Clothilde Ochoa, June 28, 1924, 1 son, Francisco Javier. Admitted to Mex. bar, 1922, practices in Mexico City; pres., bd. dirs. several banks, ins. cos., financing instns. and indsl. cos. Fiscal rep. Mexico, 1919-20; sec. of Govt. in Baja, Cal. 1930; pres. Mexican Labor Ct., 1932; sec. to Pres. Republic Mexico. 1932-34, sec. nat. economy, 1940-44; pres. several gubernamental coms., World War II; mem. Bd. Properties and Concerns of Enemy. World War II; personal rep. of Pres. Mexico to Pres. Roosevelt, 1942. Decorated Orden de honor forense. Mem. Illustrious and Nat. Coll. Lawyers Mexico (pres. 1957—), Colegio de Abogados, Internat. Bar Assn. (co-pres. 1963), Sociedad Mexicana de Geografia y Estadistica y Academia Mexicana de Jurisprudencia. Author: El Juicio Constitucional por Invasion de Jurisdicciones, 1922; El Presidente Rodriquez, 1938; Algunos—proglemas de la Economia Mexicana, 1940; Cuestiones pentientes entre Mexico y Estados Unidos, 1943; Sobre la Creacion de una Secretaria de Justicia, 1960; y Ciudadania y Regimen—Democratico, 1961. Address: Paseo de la Reforma 284 Mexico City 6 Mexico

GAY, LAVERNE WILLIAM, naval officer; b. Chgo., Jan. 10, 1928; s. Loren Thomas and Lucy Helen (White) G.; B.S., Cornell U., 1958; m. Jeanne Elizabeth Davis, Jan. 2, 1947 (div. Sept. 1970); children—Christopher Lee, Elizabeth Ann, William Jon, Michael Kim, Timothy Jos. Enlisted USN, 1945, commd. ensign, 1950, advanced through grades to comdr., 1965; adminstr. naval hosp., ships; service, Vietnam, 1965-66; adminstrv. officer Naval Hosp., Charleston, S.C., 1966-70; med. adminstrv. officer 14th Naval Dist. Decorated Navy Commendation with Gold Star, campaign and unit citations. Mem. Hawaii Hosp. Assn., Phi Kappa Phi. Home: Naval Base BOQ c/O F O San Francisco CA 96610 Office: 14th Naval Dist Med Officer Box 110 c/o F O San Francisco CA 96610

GAYHARTT, HOMER, aerospace exec.; b. Hardburley, Ky., Mar. 30, 1920; s. Curtis and Martha (Williams) G.; diploma, Coyne Elec. Sch., 1938; student Brevard Jr. Coll., 1965, 68-69; m. Dorothy McAdam, Mar. 1, 1947; children—Mary Anne, James Curtis. Joined USN as elec. supr., 1939, advanced to chief warrant officer, 1952; tech. adviser Turkish Navy, 1948-49; spl. weapons assembly officer atomic, Albuquerque, 1952-54; ret., 1959; field insp. Titan Missile, Martin Co., Cocoa Beach, Fla., 1960; supr. Minuteman Launch Complexes, aerospace div. Pan Am. World Airways. Kennedy Air Force Sta., 1960-71; supr. Unmanned Launch Vehicle Complexes, Aerospace div. Pan Am. World Airways, Kennedy Air Force Sta., 1972—. Mem. Ret. Officers Assn. Club: Indian River Yacht (commodore) (Cocoa, Fla.). Home: 42 Scott Lane Rockledge FL 32955 Office: Pan Am World Airways Aerospace Div Patrick AFB FL 32931

GAYLES, ANNE RICHARDSON, educator; b. Marshallville, Ga., June 4, 1923; d. Franklin J. and Marian (Richardson) Gayles; B.S., Ft. Valley State Coll., 1943; M.A., Columbia, 1949, profl. diploma, 1955; Ed.D., Ind. U., 1961; postgrad. Fisk U., 1944-45; postdoctoral Ore. State U., summer 1962. Tchr. high sch. social studies, Sparta, Ga., 1943-44, Grittin, Ga., 1945-46, Marshville, Ga., 1946-48; elementary sch. tchr. Mt. Zion Luth. Sch., N.Y.C., 1948-49; instr. sociology Ft. Valley (Ga.) State Coll., 1949-50, 51-52; head dept. sociology Ark. Bapt. Coll., Little Rock, 1950-51; dir. internship tng. Sillman Coll., Tuscaloosa, Ala., 1952-54, asst. prof. social scis., coll. supr. Albany (Ga.) State Coll., 1954-57; faculty Fla. A. and M. U., Tallahassee, 1957—, prof. edn. dir. internship teaching, 1961-62, prof. secondary edn. head dept. 1962—, coordinator of curriculum and instrn., 1969—, also chmn. dept. secondary edn. and founds. Mem. tchr. edn. program evaluation panel Nat. Council for Accreditation Tchr. Edn., 1966, 68, field reader Bur. Research U.S. Office Edn., 1966—; spl. cons. Fla. Commn. for Quality Edn., 1967; cons. Ann. Coll. and U. Teaching Workshop, Ore. State U., summer 1962, Choice: Books for Coll. Libraries, 1965—, Social Studies Council Fla., Evaluation Com. Elementary Schs. Fla., participant ann. selection outstanding ednl. books NEA Jour., 1966, 67, Internat. Seminar Comparative Edn. Soc., 1967; mem. vis. summer faculty Harvard, 1969. Mem. Assn. Social Sci. Tchrs. (1st v.p. 1966), Fla. Tchrs. Assn. (cons.), Nat. Assn. Coll. Tchrs. Edn., Fla. Assn. Supervision and Curriculum, Fla. Assn. Student Teaching, Nat. Soc. Coll. Tchrs. Edn. (chmn.), Fla. Edn. Assn., Assn. Higher Edn., Assn. Student Teaching Internat. Platform Assn., Nat. Soc. Profs. Edn. (mem. exec. com.), Pi Gamma Mu, Kappa Delta Pi, Pi Lambda Theta, Delta Sigma Theta, Alpha Kappa Mu. Republican. Methodist. Editorial staff Quar. Rev. Higher Education Among Negroes, 1965—. Contbr. articles to profl. jours. Home: 609 Howard Av Tallahassee FL 32304

GAYLIN, GEORGE R(OBERT), newspaperman; b. Cleve., Jan. 21, 1910; s. Philip and Ida (Koppelman) G.; student pub. schs. Cleve.; m. Ida Polay, Mar. 25, 1934; children—Barbara Lou, Harvey Stuart. Joined NEA-Acme (now U.P.I, Newspictures), 1927, Washington photo bur. mgr., 1938—, covered Korean war, also in Japan, 1950-51. Mem. Nat. Press Photographers Assn., White House News Photographers Assn. (pres. 1953). Club: Nat. Press (Washington). Home: 1436 Primrose Rd Washington DC 20018 Office: 1013 13th St Washington DC 20005

GAYLORD, EDWARD KING, editor; b. Muscotah, Kan., Mar. 5, 1873; s. George Lewis and Eunice M. (Edwards) G.; student Colo. Coll., 1894-97, LL.D., 1936; studied law at Cororado Springs, 1900-02; m. Inex Kinney, Dec. 29, 1914; children—Edith Kinney, Edward Lewis, Virginia Elizabeth. Clerk of Dist. Court. Colorado Springs and Cripple Creek, 1897-1900; telegraph editor, editorial writer Colorado Springs Telegraph, 1901; bus. mgr. St. Joseph Gazette 1902; gen. mgr. Daily Oklahoman, Oklahoma City Times, Okla. Farmer-Stockman, 1903—; pres. Oklahoma Pub. Co., 1918—, pub. editor The Daily Oklahoman, Oklahoma Times; pres. Mistletoe Express Co., chmn. bd. WKY Television Systems, Inc.; dir. Southland Paper Mills, Inc., Lufkin, Tex. Mem. commn. in charge constrn. Okla. State Capitol, 1916. Pres. Oklahoma City C. of C., 1915. Mem. A.P., Am., So. Newspaper editors assns. Democrat. Conglist. Mason. Home: 6907 Avondale Av Oklahoma City OK 73116 Office: 500 N Broadway Oklahoma City OK 73102

GAYLORD, EDWARD LEWIS, pub. co. exec.; b. Denver, May 28, 1919; s. Edward King and Inez (Kinney) G.; student Asheville (N.C.) Sch. for Boys, 1936-37; B.A., Stanford 1941; grad. student Harvard Bus. Sch., 1942; LL.D., Oklahoma City U., 1966, Okla. Christian Coll., 1968; m. Thelma Feragen, Aug. 30, 1950; children—Christine Elizabeth, Mary Inez, Edward King II, Thelma Louise. Pres., treas., dir. WKY TV System, Inc., Oklahoma City; sec., treas Mistletoe Express Service, Oklahoma City, 1948—; exec. v.p., asst. gen. mgr., treas., dir. Okla. Pub. Co., Oklahoma City, 1955—. Chmn., trustee Okla. Indusries Authority; pres. Okla. State Fair, 1961-71. Chmn. president's council, adv. bd. Okla. Christian Coll. Served with AUS, 1942-46. Mem. Oklahoma City C. of C. (dir., treas., 1963-69, pres. 1960), So. Newspaper Pubs. Assn. (pres. 1965-66, chmn. bd.). Conglist. Home: 1506 Dorchester Dr Oklahoma City OK 73120 Office: PO Box 25125 Oklahoma City OK 73125

GAYMON, NICHOLAS EDWARD, librarian; b. Pinewood, S.C., Apr. 8, 1928; s. Rufus Dray and Viola James (Boyd) G.; A.B., Morehouse Coll., 1956; M.S., Atlanta U., 1959; postgrad. Fla. State U., 1971; m. Marjorie Sinkfield, Sept. 3, 1955; children—Renwick, Dara, Warren. Structural mechanic Lockheed Aircraft Corp., Marietta, Ga., 1953-59; acquisitions librarian, circulation librarian Atlanta U., 1959-65; head librarian Dillard U., New Orleans, 1965-69; dir. librarier Fla. A. and M. U., Tallahassee, 1969—. Mem. vis. team So. Assn. Colls. and Schs., 1969-71. Served with AUS, 1951-53. Ford Found. travel grantee, 1968. Mem. Am., Southeastern, Fla. library assns., Council on Sci. and Tech. Information (subcom. on Negro Research Libraries 1970-72). Mason. Home: 426 Mercury Dr Tallahassee FL 32304 Office: Fla A and M U Tallahassee FL 32307

GAYNOR, ALAN SIMS, lawyer, state legislator; b. Savannah, Ga., Oct. 11, 1928; s. Sims and Dora (Gittelsohn) G.; B.A., U. Va., 1950, LL.B., 1952. Admitted to Ga. bar, 1951; since practiced in Savannah; partner Bouhan, Williams & Levy, Savannah, 1960—; mem. Ga. Ho. of Reps., 1966—; sec., dir. Topp-Cola Internat., Inc., Savannah; dir. S.A. Allen, Inc., Savannah. Mem. exec. bd. Coastal Empire council Boy Scouts Am., 1957—, v.p., 1971—; vice chmn. Ga. Bicentennial Commn., 1970—. Bd. dirs. Savannah United Community Services, 1964-66; sec., bd. dirs. Goodwill Industries, Savannah, 1965—. Served to capt. Judge Adv. Gen. Dept. USAF, 1952-54, Named Outstanding Young Man of Savannah, Savannah Jr. C. of C., 1964; recipient Silver Beaver, Boy Scouts Am., 1961. Mem. Ga., Am., Savannah bar assns., Mil Order World Wars (chpt. comdr. 1970), Ga. Hist. Soc. (treas., mem. bd. curators 1956-69). Jewish religion. Mason, Rotarian. Home: 440 Lincoln St Savannah GA 31401 Office: Armstrong House Savannah GA 31401

GAYNOR, JAY IRVIN, dentist; b. Chgo., May 13, 1924; s. Sam and Frieda (Dorman) G.; student Theodore Herzl Jr. Coll., 1941-42; B.S., U. Ill. at Urbana, 1943; D.D.S., U. Ill. at Chgo., 1947; m. Elaine Ruth Shure, Oct. 12, 1947 (dec. Dec. 1965); 1 son, Richard, Mitchell; m. 2d, Barbara Legrande Beene, May 15, 1968; stepchildren—Gordon Beene, Debra (Mrs. Ricky White Hamby). Pvt. practice dentistry, Chgo., 1947-56, Hale Center, Tex., 1956-64, Plainview, Tex., 1964—; mem. staff Hi-Plains Hosp., Hale Center, Tex., 1956—, Central Plains Gen. Hosp., Plainview, 1964—. Mem. Hale Center (Tex.) City Council, 1959-63. Trustee, Tex. Tech. U. Dads Assn. Served with AUS, 1942-45. Mem. Acad. Gen. Dentistry, Am., Tex. dental assns., Internat. Assn. Orthodontia, Soc. Dentistry for Children. Lion. Home: 1106 Holiday Dr Plainview TX 79072 Office: 701 Houston St Plainview TX 79072

GAYNOR, ROBERT MITCHELL, orgn. exec.; b. Scranton Pa., Aug. 10, 1911; s. James Lawrence and Katherine (Mitchell) G.; student U. Pa. Extension, 1932-35; B.S., U. Scranton, 1938; m. Margaret Mary Jennings, Jan. 18, 1941; children—Margaret Katherine, Mary Josephine, Barbara Anne, Robert Mitchell. Joined Pa. N.G., 1927, ret., 1947; commd. 2d lt. U.S. Army, 1941, advanced through grades to lt. col., 1946, ret. as col., 1967; comdg. officer 28th Cav. Reconnaissance Troop, 1943; intelligence officer 110th Inf., 1944; asst. intelligence officer 1st U.S. Army, 1945, 2d U.S. Army, 1945; War Dept. Gen. Staff, 1946-47; Central Intelligence Agy., 1947-71; companion Army and Navy Legion of Valor U.S.A., Arlington, Va., 1947-61, nat. adj. and q.m., 1961—. Decorated D.S.C., Intelligence medal of merit, Bronze Star with oak leaf cluster, Purple Heart with oak leaf cluster, Combat Infantryman's badge (U.S.); Croix de Guerre (France). Mem. Nat. Rifle Assn. (life), Mil. History Soc. Ireland, Army and Navy Club, Am. Legion, Disabled Officers Assn., Am. Numis. Soc., Am. Numis. Assn., Mil. Hist. Soc. Gt. Britain, Soc. 28th Div., Pa. N.G. Vets. Assn. Roman Catholic. Address: 621 S Taylor St Arlington VA 22204

GAZZOLO, DOROTHY HAVEN, magazine editor; b. Ft. Wayne, Ind., Apr. 28, 1911; d. Frank R. and Sue (Bolster) Haven; student Ind. U., U. Chgo.; m. Louis J. Gazzolo, Dec. 30, 1940 (dec. Sept. 1958). With Nat. Assn. Housing and Redevel. Ofcls., Chgo., 1939—, dep. exec. dir. nat. orgn., adminstr. Chgo. office, 1950-61, editor Jour. of Housing, 1944—. Mem. Nat. Housing Conf., Internat. Fedn. Housing and Planning, Washington Housing and Planning Assn. (2d v.p., mem. exec. com.), Nat. Conf. on Social Welfare (chmn. com. combined asso. groups), Pub. Housing Assn. Chgo. (dir.). Club: Kenwood Golf and Country. Contbr. housing articles to Municipal Yearbook, Book of the States. Home: 4000 Massachusetts Av NW Washington DC 20016 Office: 2600 Virginia Av NW Washington DC 20037

GEAUGUE, EDWIN PRESTON, publishing co. exec.; b. Phila., Jan. 28, 1901; ed. U. Cal. at Berkeley, Stanford. Formerly reporter San Francisco Chronicle, corr., Europe and Far East; with govt. intelligence staff, World War II; founder Wake-Brook House, Ft. Lauderdale, Fla., 1946, now exec. dir. Founder, exec. dir. Fine Arts Found. Office: Wake-Brook House 3038A North Federal Hwy Times Sq Fort Lauderdale FL 33306 Home: Ft Lauderdale Fl summer Hyannis MA

GEDDIE, EDGAR MCPHAIL, power and light co. exec.; b. Fayetteville, N.C., Jan. 3, 1912; s. Edgar Chestnut and Lottie (Bullard) G.; student Campbell Coll., 1929-30; B.S., N.C. State Coll., 1934; m. Katie Lee Ward, Apr. 2, 1938; children—Edgar McPhail, Kathryn Ward, Donald Thomas. Electrician, Erwin Mills (N.C.), 1934-35; jr. engr. Carolina Power & Light Co., Raleign, N.C., 1935-39, div. dist. engr., 1939-48, div. supt., 1948-62, supt. lines and motor vehicles, 1962-68, asst. v.p. transmission and distbn. dept., 1968-69, v.p. transmission and distbn. dept., 1969—, v.p. div. operations, 1972—. Bd. dirs. Wake County Tb Assn., 1965-70. Mem. Raleigh Engrs. Club, Raleigh C. of C. Methodist (mem. ofcl. bd. 1964-68). Kiwanian. Home: 316 Forsyth St Raleigh NC 27609 Office: 336 Fayetteville St Raleigh NC 27602

GEE, EDWARD FOWLKES, banker; b. Victoria, Va., May 28, 1910; s. Edward Lewis and Ruth Naomi (Gary) G.; student U. Richmond, 1928-29; honor grad. Am. Inst. Banking, 1933; grad. accounting and bus. adminstrn., Va. Mechanics Inst., 1939; grad. Rutgers U. Grad. Sch. Banking, 1940; m. Margaret Osborne Williams; 1 dau., Ruth Ann (Mrs. R. Franklin Skinner IV). With State-Planters Bank of Commerce and Trusts (now United Va. Bank), Richmond, Va., 1929—, v.p., sec., 1952-61, exec. v.p., comml., mem. adv. bd., 1961-63, pres., dir., 1963-71, chmn. bd., 1971—; vice-chmn. United Va. Bankshares, Inc., past chmn. bd. Va. Indsl. Devel. Corp.; dir. Lawyers Title Ins. Corp., Victoria Hardware & Furniture Co., Inc., Mut. Assurance Soc. Va., Overnite Transp. Co. Past instr. U. Richmond Evening Sch. Bus. Adminstrn., Va. Mechanics Inst., also numerous bankers confs. Bd. dirs. Randolph-Macon Coll. Sr. mission officer to North Africa for Lend-Lease Adminstrn., World War II. C.P.A., Va. Mem. Robert Morris Assos. (past pres.), Am. Inst. Banking (past pres. Richmond), Richmond Assn. Credit Men (past pres.), Am. Inst. C.P.A.'s, Newcomen Soc., Va., Richmond (past pres.) chambers commerce. Clubs: Commonwealth, Forum, Country of Virginia (Richmond). Author: The Evaluation of Receivables and Inventories, 1943. Co-author: Analyzing Financial Statements, 1948. Contbr. articles in field. Home: 305 Greenway Lane Richmond VA 23226 Office: 900 E Main St Richmond VA 23219

GEE, ROBERT SANFORD, lawyer, state senate adminstr.; b. Oklahoma City, Feb. 24, 1932; s. Robert Lee and Vernice (Doughty) G.; A.A., Muskogee Jr. Coll., 1951; A.B., U. Okla., 1953, LL.B., 1955; m. Nancy Neil, Aug. 23, 1953; children—Robert Neil, Catherine Ann, Elizabeth Ruth, James Kenneth. Admitted to Okla. bar, 1955; asst. county atty. Ottawa County, Okla., 1955-59, county atty., 1960-64; partner law firm Wallace & Owens, Miami, Okla., 1965—; mem. Okla. State Senate, 1965-69, chmn. jud. com. 1st and 2d session, 1967-68, senate adminstr., 1969—. Vice chmn. Grand Lakes dist. Boy Scouts Am., 1963-65, chmn. orgn., extension com., 1965-67; chmn. Constrnl. Revision Commn. of Okla. Mem. Okla. (mem. adminstrn. justice com. 1967-70, chmn. adminstrn. justice com. 1970-71), Am., Ottawa County bar assns., Miami Jr. C. of C. (pres. 1959-60), Miami C. of C. Presbyn. (elder 1960-64). Home: 421 G NW Miami OK 74354 Office: Savs & Loan Bldg Miami OK 74354

GEENTIENS, GASTON PETRUS, JR., constrn. engring. exec.; b. Garfield, N.J., Apr. 6, 1935; s. Gaston Petrus and Margaret (Piros) G.; B.S. in Civil Engring., The Citadel, 1956; m. Barbara Ann Chamberlain, Oct. 14, 1960; children—Mercedes Frith, Faith Piros. Plant engr. Western Elec. Co., Inc., Kearny, N.J., 1956-58, owner's rep., N.Y.C., 1960-64; v.p. Gentyne Motors, Inc., Passaic, N.J., 1958-60; project engr. Ethyl Corp., Baton Rouge, 1964-65; mgr. Timothy McCarthy Constrn. Co., Atlanta, 1965; asst. to v.p. A.R. Abrams, Inc. and Columbia Engring., Inc., Atlanta, 1965-66; supr. engring. and constrn. Litton Industries, N.Y.C., 1966-71; pres. G.P. Geetiens, Jr., Inc., Charleston, S.C., 1971—. Mem. Ramapo (N.Y.) Republican Com., 1961-64. Served to 1st lt. C.E., AUS, 1956-58. Registered profl. engr., 11 states. Mem. Am. Soc. C.E., Soc. Profl. Engrs., Am. Mgmt. Assn. Home: 7 Fort Royal Dr Charleston SC 29407 Office: 10 Gillon St Charleston SC 29401

GEER, CHARLES HERMAN, trucking co. exec.; b. Brownwood, Tex., Jan. 24, 1929; s. Frank Tobin and Thelma Lucille (Walker) G.; grad. high. sch.; m. Bettye Sue Hicks, May 21, 1948; children—Charles Randall, Jana Sue, Stephen Mark. Partner, Geer Tank Trucks, Inc., Jacksboro, Tex., 1951-65, pres., 1965—; partner Geer Prodn. Co. Mem. Sch. Bd., Jacksboro, 1965-67. Mem. City Council, Jacksboro, 1959-65, mayor, Jacksboro, 1967-69. Bd. dirs. Jack County Hosp. Named Outstanding Citizen, City of Jacksboro, 1967. Lion. Home: 242 Live Oak St Jacksboro TX 76056 Office: PO Box 172 Jacksboro TX 76056

GEER, DANIEL EARL, textile co. exec.; b. Orme, Tenn., Mar. 13, 1918; s. Henry Clay and Mary Lee (Sparkman) G.; student U. Chattanooga, 1935-37, Internat. Accountants Soc., Massey Coll., Chattanooga State Tech. Inst.; m. Mary Elizabeth Moore, Aug. 28, 1949; children—Daniel Earl, Michael Sparkman. Ship clk. Davenport Hosiery Mills, Inc., Chattanooga, 1938-39; accounting clk. U.S. TVA, Chattanooga, 1939-41; accountant A.W. Taber, 1941-46; city auditor City of Chattanooga, 1947-51; controller E-Z Mills, Inc., Cartersville, Ga., 1951-64, Magic Chef, Inc., Cleveland, Tenn., 1964-68; asst. controller Coats & Clark, Inc., 1968-70, dir., 1970—, asst. treas., 1970, mgr. finance dept., 1971—. Tchr. McKenzie Sch. Bus., Chattanooga; adv. bd. Chattanooga State Tech. Inst. Served with AUS, 1946-47. C.P.A. Tenn. Mem. Am. Inst. C.P.A.'s, Ga. Soc. C.P.A.'s, Nat. Assn. Accountants, Data Processing Mgmt. Assn., Assn. for Systems Mgmt. Mem. Ch. of Christ. Home: 2700 Claridge Ct Doraville GA 30340 Office: PO Box 11929 Atlanta GA 30305

GEER, SAMUEL LEE, banker; b. Sparta, Tenn., May 24, 1921; s. Thomas Beecher and Martha Elizabeth G.; student U. Ala., 1943-44; grad. La. State U. Sch. Banking, 1967; m. Mary Esther Bryant, Dec. 30, 1944; children—Martha Gwendolyn (Mrs. David Edward Krebs), Beth (Mrs. Jerold Jennings). Asst. cashier Bank of Cowan, Tenn., 1946-47; teller, asst. cashier, asst. v.p. and cashier, v.p. and cashier, v.p., sr. v.p. Pompano Beach (Fla.) Bank & Trust Co., 1947—. Mem. personnel com. Fla. Bankers Assn., 1966-69. Treas., bd. dirs. 4-H Found. Broward County. Served with USAF, 1943-45. Mem. Am. Inst. Banking (past v.p. Broward County), Greater Pompano Beach C. of C. (past treas., dir.). Mem. Ch. of Christ. Kiwanian. Home: 1003 S W 4th Terrace Pompano Beach FL 33060 Office: 1101 Atlantic Blvd Pompano Beach FL 33060

GEESLIN, DORINE HAWK (MRS. ROBERT JONES GEESLIN), educator; b. Priceville, Ky., June 22, 1918; d. Benjamin Franklin and Rosa (Avery) Hawk; B.A., Western Ky. U., 1938; M.Ed., U. Louisville, 1959; D.Ed., Fla. State U., 1967; m. Robert Jones Geeslin, May 19, 1938; children—Robert Hawk, Franklin Andrew, Melanie Rose. Tchr., Versailles (Ky.) City Schs., 1950-52, Jefferson County Schs., Louisville, 1952-56; supr. of instrn. Elizabethtown (Ky.) City Schs., 1956-64; research asst. Fla. State U., Tallahassee, 1964-65; dir. reading inst. N. Fla. Jr. Coll., Madison, summer 1965; asst. prof. edn. and human devel. Valdosta (Ga.) State Coll., 1965-67; reading cons. DeKalb County Schs. Reading Center, Clarkston, Ga., 1967-70; instr. dept. psychology, asst. prof. edn. Western Ky. U., Bowling Green, 1970—. Mem. N.E.A., Internat. Reading Assn., Am. Assn. U. Women, Am. Assn. U. Profs., Delta Kappa Gamma (pres. 1972—). Presbyn. Democrat. Home: Upton KY 42784 Office: Dept Edn Western Ky U Bowling Green KY 42101

GEESLIN, MARK ALLISON, county agt.; b. Stephenville, Tex., June 25, 1925; s. Mark and Mittie (McKenzie) G.; B.S., Tex. A. and M.U., 1949; postgrad., 1966; postgrad. U. Ark., 1957, Colo. State U., 1961; m. Laudazelle Brown, Aug. 2, 1948; children—Elvis Paul, David Lamar, Deborah Minette. Asst. county agt. Tex. Agrl. Extension Service, Young County, 1950-51, county agt., Kent County, Jayton, 1952—. Bd. dirs. Hosps. and Homes, Meth. Ch. Conf., 1964-68. Served with AUS, 1944-45, ETO. Recipient Silver Beaver award Boy Scouts Am., 1960. Mem. Tex. County Agrl. Agts. Assn. (sec.-treas. 1972). Mason (Shriner), Lion. Home: Box 65 Jayton TX 79528 Office: Kent County Courthouse Jayton TX 79528

GEHRING, DONALD MCGLASHAN, pub. relations exec.; b. Lakewood, O., Apr. 19, 1913; s. Carl Walter and Mabel Mary (McGlashan) G.; A.B., Cornell U., 1935; m. Catherine Margaret Sutter, May 18, 1946. Radio broadcaster, Ohio, Mich., 1935-39, 46-51; advt., pub. relations dir. Wire Reinforcement Inst., Washington, 1953-67; propr. Don Gehring Pub. Relations, Alexandria, Va., 1967—. Served to capt., inf., AUS, World War II, 1951-52. Alexandria Bd. Trade, Constrn. Writers Assn. (past pres.), Washington Bldg. Congress, Am. Rd. Builders Assn., Hwy. Research Bd. (past chmn. spl. com. information), Sigma Nu. Club: Nat. Press. Home: 409 S Pitt St Alexandria VA 22314 Office: 300 N Lee St Alexandria VA 22314

GEIBAVICIUS, EDMUND ERASMUS, ret. educator; b. Lithuania, Jan. 18, 1903; s. Erazm Johan and Franciska-Theodora (Abramavicius) G.; LL.M., U. Vilna (Lithuania), 1938; postgrad. Columbia, 1959-60, U. Heidelberg (Germany), 1968. Came to U.S., 1957, naturalized, 1967. Tchr., Lithuania, 1940-44; translator French High Commr. Office, Innsburck, Austria, 1950-55; asst. prof. fgn. lang. Xavier U., New Orleans, 1961-71. Named hon. citizen New Orleans, 1968. Mem. Am. Assn. Tchrs. Slavic and East European Langs. (La. treas. 1967), Am. Assn. U. Profs., German Assn. Lit. Contbr. anti-Communist articles newspapers. Home: 530 W 163d St New York City NY 10032

GEIER, WOODROW A., journalist, educator; b. Anniston, Ala., Oct. 3, 1914; s. Louis Charles and Minnie (Parsons) G.; B.A., U. Ala., 1938; B.D., Vanderbilt U., 1943, Ph.D., 1959; m. Rosemary Parkman, Dec. 9, 1939; children—Janet Lynn, Gail Ellen, Carl David. Reporter, Anniston (Ala.) Star, 1937; editor Anniston (Ala.) Times, 1938-40; asst. editor Methodist Publishing House, 1940-41, asso. editor of adult publs., 1947-53; asso. dir. pub. relations and finance Bd. of Edn., The Meth. Ch., 1953-57, dir. information and publs., 1957—. Vis. prof. drama Scarritt Coll., 1960—; tchr. journalism extension div. U. Tenn., 1963; vis. prof. Vanderbilt U. Div. Sch., 1965. Trustee Paine Coll. Mem. Am. Alumni Council, Am. Coll. Pub. Relations Assn., Commn. on Higher Edn., Nat. Council of Chs. Author: The Campus Ministry of the Methodist Church; A Wayfarer's Book of Devotion; also numerous articles in religious journals. Editor: Studies in Christian Higher Education. Home: 4036 Overbrook Ct Nashville TN 37204 Office: PO Box 871 Nashville TN 37204

GEIGER, SYDNEY, JR., steel co. exec.; b. Jacksonville, Fla., Dec. 21, 1923; s. Sydney and Bertha (Jacobs) G.; B.S. in Civil Engring., The Citadel, 1948; m. Joan M. Nirenberg, Dec. 21, 1947; children—Beverly, Susan, Steven, Mindy. Engr., Va. bridge plant U.S. Steel Co., Birmingham, Ala., 1948-51; steel engr. Howell Steel Co., Jackson, Miss., 1951-55; pres. Delta Steel Co., Inc., Jackson, 1955—. Mem. social action com. Union Am. Hebrew Congregations, 1964-74, mem. exec. bd., 1970-74; mem. Council Human Relations, Urban League, 1960-72. Bd. dirs. Goodwill Industries. Served with AUS, 1945-48; ETO. Mem. Am. Inst. Steel Constrn., Am. Soc. C.E., Am. Soc. Profl. Engrs. Jewish religion (pres. congregation, trustee, nat. bd. mem.). Mem. B'nai B'rith. Club: North Jackson Civitan (past dir.). Home: 2246 Greenbriar St Jackson MS 39211 Office: P O Box 9266 Jackson MS 39206

GEIGERMAN, CLARICE FURCHGOTT, pub. relations, ins. and real estate agt.; b. Charleston, S.C., Sept. 24, 1916; d. Melvin and Doreta (Brown) Furchgott; student Draughon Sch. Commerce, 1934-35, U. Ga., 1935-36, Am. Inst. Banking, 1936-41; m. Henry David Geigerman, July 4, 1941 (dec. Nov. 1967); children—Henry David, Robert M. Sec. to v.p. investment dept. Citizens & So. Nat. Bank, Atlanta, 1935-41; personnel dir., payroll chief Atlanta Ordnance Dept., 1941-43; pub. relations counselor, 1944—; agt. Nat. Life Ins. Co. Vt., Atlanta, 1968—; agt. First Atlanta Equity Corp., 1972—. Bd. dirs. So. Regional Opera, 1969—, chmn. women's com., 1969—, v.p. exec. com., 1972—; pres. Atlanta Civic Ballet Assos., 1962-64; adv. bd. Muscular Dystrophy Assn., 1968—; bd. sponsors Atlanta Symphony Guild, 1969—, v.p. women's bd., 1966-68, mem. policy bd., 1966—; dir. Active Voters, 1965—; mem. High Mus. Art; mem. women's com. Brandeis U., Alliance Theatre. Mem. Am. Women in Radio and TV, Pub. Relations Soc. Am. Women's C. of C., English-Speaking Union, Italian Cultural Soc., Victorian Soc. Am. Nat. Council Jewish Women, Atlanta Music Club (dir., co-editor newsletter). Jewish religion. Clubs: Atlanta Press, Georgia Writers, Standard, Oaks (Atlanta). Contbg. editor Arts mag., So. Israelite, TV Guide, Seydell Quar., Nat. Messenger. Home: 620 Peachtree St NE Atlanta GA 30308 Office: 151 Ellis St Atlanta GA 30308 also 100 Peachtree St NW Atlanta GA

GEIS, CLARENCE HUGH, ednl. adminstr.; b. Huntington, Ark., July 2, 1907; s. Peter and Nola (Hart) G.; B.S. in Edn., U. Ark., 1930, M.S., 1952; m. Hazel Dawson Baucum, Dec. 26, 1930; children—William Peter, Susan Elaine (Mrs. John Ellerbe Sanford), John Perry. Coach high schs., Jonesboro, Ark., 1930, 39-41, 46-48, Minden, La., 1931-36, Texarkana, Ark., 1936-39, Central High Sch., Little Rock, 1941-44; adminstr. Jonesboro Pub. Schs., 1949—. Served with USNR, 1944-45. Mem. N.E.A., Ark. Edn. Assn. Secondary Sch. Prins. (past pres.), Am., Ark. assns. sch. adminstrs., Ark. Congress Parents and Tchrs. (life), Ark. Sch. Study Council (pres. 1967-68), Ark. Activities Assn. (exec. com.), Phi Delta Kappa. Methodist. Rotarian. Home: 524 W Oak St Jonesboro AR 72401 Office: 1300 S Church St Jonesboro AR 72401

GEIS, DUANE VIRGIL, investment banker; b. Okeene, Okla., Apr. 16, 1923; s. Harry H. and Margareth (Tieman) G.; B.A., Okla. State U., 1947; m. Lois Blakey, Mar. 11, 1944; children—D. Gregory, Paul Geoffrey. Accounting machine sales IBM, Houston, 1947-54; with Rotan Mosle Dallas Union, Inc., Houston, 1954-70, exec. v.p., 1966-69, 1st sr. v.p., mem. exec. com., also dir., 1969-70; partner Paine, Webber, Jackson & Curtis, 1970—. Bd. dirs. Star of Hope Mission; trustee Annuity Bd. So. Bapt. Conv. Mem. Houston C. of C. (life), Kappa Sigma, Phi Eta Sigma, Beta Alpha Psi, Phi Kappa Phi, Blue Key. Baptist. Clubs: Houston Country, Coronado (Houston). Home: 522 Shady Wood St Houston TX 77027 Office: Tenneco Bldg Houston TX 77002

GEIS, HAROLD LORENZ, geologist; b. Okeene, Okla., Jan. 22, 1906; s. Karl and Lydia (Lorenz) G.; A.B., U. Ill., 1930, M.S., 1933; student U. Wis., 1928-29; postgrad. U, Chgo., 1933-35; m. Dorothy Cansler, June 28, 1936; children—Robert Koenig, Sarah Louise; m. 2d, Peggy Ayer, Dec. 27, 1949 (div. 1957); 1 step-dau., Annes Yvonne; m. 3d, Jessie Brewer McGaw, Aug. 28, 1964; stepchildren—Miriam, Vernon. Paleontologist Shell Oil Co., 1935-38; paleontologist stratigrapher Atlantic Refining Co., 1938-43; div. geologist Barnsdall Oil Co., 1943-50, cons. geologist, engr., 1950—; pres. Pano Tech. Exploration Corp., 1959—, also dir.; pres. Geis Petroleum Research Inc., 1960-65; dir., sec.-treas. RWH Oil Corp., 1968— (all Houston). Dir. Ongoing Northwestern Gulf Mollusk Population Survey, 1965—. Exec. dir. Houston Zool. Soc., 1967-68; bd. dirs. CEDAM Internat., 1967—. Mem. Tex., N.Y. acads. sci., Marine Tech. Soc., Am. Soc. Oceanography (founder, pres.), Internat. Oceanographic Found., Houston Aquarium Soc. (hon. life), Houston Conchology Soc., Houston Philos. Soc., Am. Assn. Petroleum Geologists, Sigma Xi, Gamma Alpha, Kappa Epsilon. Editor: Am. Oceanography, 1965-67. Contbr. articles profl. jours. Home: 2405 Dickey Pl Houston TX 77019 Office: C & I Bldg Houston TX 77002

GEISBERG, HARRY, textile co. exec.; b. Anderson, S.C., Oct. 27, 1918; s. Harry and Sadie (Cohen) G.; B.S. in Textile Engring., Clemson U., 1938; m. Carol Rosenbaum, Nov. 30, 1940; 1 son, Harry Irvin. With Louisville Textiles, Inc., 1938—, pres., 1967—; sec. Cane Run Lanes, Inc., 1954—. Served to capt. AUS, 1943-46. Decorated Army Commendation medal. Jewish religion (v.p. temple). Mason, Kiwanian. Home: 415 Country Lane Louisville KY 40207 Office: 1318 McHenry St Louisville KY 40217

GEISER, MARVIN DOYLE, JR., utility exec.; b. San Antonio, Dec. 29, 1931; s. M.D. and Anna (Wise) G.; B.S., Tex. Agrl. and Indsl. U., 1959; m. Rosa Lee Dennis, Aug. 29, 1958; children—Karen Lee, Cheryl Lynn, James Doyle. Utilization engr. Lone Star Gas Co., Ft. Worth, 1959-65, air conditioning sales supr., 1965-67, mdse. sales mgr., 1967-68, promotion projects mgr., 1968-69, dist. mgr., Cleburne, Tex., 1969, gen. supt., Ft. Worth, 1969-71, regional mgr. San Angelo, Tex., 1971—. Loaned exec. Tarrant County United Fund, 1960-69; adviser Jr. Achievement, 1961-63. Served with Signal Corps, AUS, 1954-56. Registered profl. engr., Tex. Mem. Tex. Soc. Profl. Engrs. (chpt. treas. 1964), Tarrant County Home Builders Assn. (dir. 1969), Tarrant County Apt. Assn. (dir. 1969). Republican. Baptist. Mason (K.T.), Rotarian. Clubs: Optimist (v.p. and dir. 1969) (Ft. Worth, Tex.). Home: 2738 Chimney Rock Lane San Angelo TX 76901 Office: 111 W Twohig St San Angelo TX 76901

GEISLER, JERRY HUBERT, lawyer; b. Big Stone Gap, Va., July 6, 1934; s. Ernest Keith and Marie (Killen) G.; student Milligan Coll., 1951-52; B.A., Emory and Henry Coll., 1955; LL.B., U. Richmond, 1959; m. Betty Lou Coyle, June 30, 1961; children—Jennifer Hope, Byrum Lynn, Brett Lorne. Admitted to Va. bar, 1959; practiced in Hillsville, 1959—. Chmn. Va.-N.C. New River Compact Study Commn., 1970-71; mem. Va. Consumer Credit Study Commn., 1970-71. Chmn. Carroll County Republican Com., 1963-67; mem. State Rep. Central Com., 1965—; mem. Va. Ho. of Dels., 1966-71. Mem. Va. State Bar Assn., Va. Trial Lawyers Assn., Carroll County Jr. C. of C. (v.p. 1961, pres. 1962), Izaak Walton League (pres. 1963-65), Delta Theta Phi. Home: Hillsville VA 24343

GEISS, JACQUELINE SUZANNE, lawyer, certified pub. accountant; b. Evanston, Ill., May 18, 1936; d. Frederick William and Suzanne (La Velle) Geiss; student U. Colo., 1952-55, Baylor U., 1961-63; LL.B., U. Tex., 1961. Admitted to Tex. bar, 1961; practiced law Waco, Tex., 1961-62; accountant Scott-Timmons & Co., C.P.A.'s Waco, 1962-64; sr. law clk. to U.S. Dist. Judge, San Antonio, 1964-66; tax specialist Peat, Marwick, Mitchell & Co., C.P.A.'s, 1967-69; asst. gen. counsel, also asst. corporate sec. Data Automation Co., Inc., Dallas, 1969-70; gen. counsel, corporate sec. Alcorn Combustion Co., N.Y.C., 1970—. Mem. Tex. Bd. Pub. Accountancy. C.P.A.'s, Tex. Mem. Am., San Antonio bar assns., State Bar Tex., Am. Inst. C.P.A.'s, Am. Women's Soc. C.P.A.'s, Am. Soc. Women Accountants, Sigma Alpha Iota (sec. 1952-53), Kappa Beta Pi (pres. 1959-61), Beta Alpha Psi (sec. 1962-63), Beta Gamma Sigma. Presbyn. Asso. editor Dicta (U. Tex. Law Sch. newspaper), 1960-61. Address: PO Box 2266 Dallas TX 75221

GELBAND, STEPHEN L., lawyer; b. N.Y.C., Feb. 13, 1931; A.B., Yale, 1952; J.D., Harvard, 1955. Admitted to N.Y. bar, 1955, D.C. bar, 1961, U.S. Ct. Appeals bar, 1963; atty. Office U.S. Atty. So. Dist. N.Y., 1955; legal assistance adviser, Ft. Myer, Va., 1956-57; trial atty. Bur. Econ. Regulation, CAB, 1957-60; now mem. firm Fisher & Gelband, Washington. Mem. Bar Assn. D.C. (mem. internat. law com), Fed. Bar Assn. Address: Fisher & Gelband 1522 K St NW Washington DC 20006*

GELLERSTEDT, MARY NEAL MCCOY (MRS. WRIGHT W. GELLERSTEDT), religious youth ofcl.; b. Commerce, Ga., June 20, 1926; d. Hoyt and Burruss (Gailey) McCoy; student pub. schs., U.Ga.; m. Wright W. Gellerstedt, Oct. 21, 1961. Edn. sec. 1st Bapt. Ch.; Atlanta, 1945-55, bus. mgr., 1955-61, recreation dir., 1961-64, youth dir., 1964—. Sponsor Youth Congress, Atlanta, 1968—. Bd. dirs. Bapt. Home Mission Bd., 1968—. Mem. Atlanta Womens C. of C. Home: 1723 Council Bluff Dr Atlanta GA 30329 Office: 754 Peachtree St Atlanta GA 30308

GELPI, DONALD LOUIS, clergyman, educator; b. New Orleans, May 30, 1934; s. Albert Joseph and Alice Marie (Delaup) G.; A.B. magna cum laude, St. Louis U., 1957, M.A. magna cum laude, St. Louis U., 1957, M.A. magna cum laude, 1958, Ph.L., 1958, Th.L., magna cum laude, 1966; postgrad. Coll. St. Albert, Louvain, Belgium, 1961-63, St. Marys Coll. (Kan.), 1963-65; Ph.D., Fordham U., 1970. Joined Soc. of Jesus; instr., Jesuit High Sch., New Orleans, 1958-61; ordained priest Roman Catholic Ch., 1964; pastoral work, Auriesville, N.Y.,1965-66; asst. prof. philosophy Loyola U., New Orleans, 1968—. Mem. Phi Beta Kappa. Author: Life and Light; A Guide to the Theology of Karl Rahner, 1969; Functional Ascetisicm: A Guideline for American Religious, 1969; Discerning the Spirit: Foundations and Futures of Religious Life, 1970; Pentecostalism: A Theological Viewpoint, 1971; Pentecostal Piety, 1972. Contbr. articles to profl. jours. Address: 6363 St Charles Av New Orleans LA 70118

GEMMILL, HENRY, news corr.; b. Toledo, June 11, 1917; s. Robert Bringhurst and Mary (Mehaffie) G.; A.B., Yale, 1939; m. Ann-Mari Andersson, Feb. 11, 1940; children—Elisabeth (Mrs. Steven Izenour), John, Ann-Mari. Reporter, Washington Evening Star, 1939-42; reporter Washington Bur. Wall St. Jour., 1942-46, news editor, 1946-50, 1954-59, mng. editor, 1950-54, chief of corrs., London, 1959-60, chief Washington News Bur., 1960-67, asso. editor, 1968-71; editor Nat. Observer, 1971—. Clubs: Federal City, Press (Washington): Gridiron. Home: 638 G St SE Washington DC 20003 Office: 11501 Columbia Pike Silver Spring MD 20910

GENDEL, BENJAMIN ROBERT, physician; b. N.Y.C., Apr. 29, 1911; s. Aaron and Fannie (Litt) G.; B.S., Tulane U., 1931, M.D., 1935; m. Rena Spector, Aug. 1, 1937. Intern Greenpoint Hosp., Bklyn., 1935-37; practice medicine specializing in internal medicine, New Haven, 1937-42, Atlanta, 1955-71, Memphis, 1971— vis. prof. pediatric research unit Guy's Hosp. Med. Sch., London, Eng., 1968-69; chief med. service VA Hosp., Memphis, 1971—; cons. internal medicine and hematology Grady Meml. Hosp. and VA Hosp., Atlanta, 1956-71; prof. medicine Emory U. Sch. Medicine, 1955-71; prof., asso. chmn. dept. medicine U. Tenn. Coll. Medicine, 1971—. Served with AUS, 1942-46. Diplomate Am. Bd. Internal Medicine. Fellow A.C.P., Internal Soc. Hematology; mem. Am. Fedn. Clin. Research, Am. Soc. Human Genetics, Am. Soc. Hematology, A.M.A., Phi Beta Kappa, Alpha Omega Alpha. Home: 435 N Highland St Memphis TN 38122 Office: 1030 Jefferson Av Memphis TN 38104

GENERES, LOUIS F., supt. schs.; b. New Orleans, Nov. 20, 1927; s. Louis F., Jr. and Pauline A. (Toujan) G.; B.S. in Elec. Engring., La. State U., 1948, B.S. in Secondary Edn., 1949, M.Ed., 1952; student Cath. U. Am., 1950-52, Notre Dame Sem., New Orleans, 1952-56. Ordained priest Roman Cath. Ch., 1956; asst. pastor various ch. parishes, 1956-63; asst. supt. sch. Archdiocese New Orleans, 1961-63; chaplain Ursuline Acad., 1963-64; prin. St. John Vianney Prep. Sch., New Orleans, 1964-68; supt. schs. Archdiocese New Orleans, 1968—. Mem. Total Community, Inc., Young Audiences Inc., Tb Assn. Greater New Orleans, WYES-TV Greater New Orleans Ednl. TV Found., C. of C. New Orleans Area, La. Arts and Sci. Center Adv. Com., La. Adv. Com. Tchr. Edn. and Certification, Jr. Achievement Greater New Orleans; mem. adv. council vocational edn. La. Bd. Edn. Home: 2705 State St New Orleans LA 70118 Office: 7887 Walmsley Av New Orleans LA 70125

GENGLER, NORMAN JOHN, physician; b. Oak Park, Ill., May 22, 1924; s. Michael Joseph and Adeline E. (Oldenberg) G.; M.D., Northwestern U., 1948; m. Faith Rita Larkin, Aug. 30, 1947; children—Pamela (Mrs. John E. Fuss), Michael J. Intern St. Anne's Hosp., Chgo., 1948-49, staff anesthesiologist St. Francis Hosp., Evanston, Ill., 1953-65; individual practice medicine specializing in anesthesiology, Sarasota, Fla., 1965—; staff Sarasota Meml. Hosp., chief of staff, 1972-73. Served with USNR, 1943-46, 51-53. Diplomate Am. Bd. Anesthesiology. Mem. Am. Soc. Anesthesiologists, Internat. Soc. Anesthesia and Analgesia, Fla. Soc. Anesthesiologists (pres. 1971-72), A.M.A., Fla. Med. Assn., Sarasota C. of C., Phi Chi. K.C. (4 deg.). Home: 4258 Featherbed Lane Sarasota FL 33581 Office: Medical Arts Bldg Sarasota FL 33579

GENNETT, NATHANIEL CHAPMAN WEEMS, JR., lumber mfr., lawyer; b. Franklin, N.C., Aug. 10, 1915; s. N. C. W. and Nina Burdick (Porter) G.; B.S., Yale, 1936; LL.B., U. Va., 1940; m. Matilann Thoms; children—Virginia (Mrs. Leverett S. Miller), Nathaniel Chapman Weems, III, Matilann Selene. Legal tng. Cravath, de Gersdorff, Swaine & Wood, also Fulton, Walter & Halley, N.Y.C., 1942-46; admitted to N.C. bar, 1941, N.Y. bar, 1943; asso. counsel Com. on Mcht. Marine and Fisheries, Ho. of Reps., 79th Congress; partner, gen. counsel Gennett Lumber Co., N.C., S.C., Tenn., Ky, N. Ga., 1947—; dir. Gennett Oak Flooring Co., W & G Corp., Winnett, Inc. Clubs: Biltmore Forest Country, Asheville Country; Everglades (Palm Beach,) Beaver Lake Golf; University (N.Y.C.). Home: 77 Elk Mountain Scenic Hwy Asheville NC 28801 Office: 52 Page Asheville NC 28801

GENSLER, PHILIP, JR., stock broker; b. New Orleans, Mar. 7, 1936; s. Philip and Louise (Tusson) G.; B.A., Tulane U., 1957, postgrad. 1957-58; m. Elizabeth Turner Pratt, Nov. 27, 1957; children—Philip III, David Scott, Nina Pratt. Sales mgr. J.R. Quaid, Inc., New Orleans, 1960-61; account exec. Merrill Lynch, Pierce, Fenner & Smith, Inc., New Orleans, 1961—. Active United Fund, Am. Cancer Soc. Bd. dirs. Met. Crime Commn., 1967—, sec., 1970. Mem. C. of C., Sigma Chi (pres. alumni 1968-69). Roman Catholic. Clubs: Young Mens Business, Boston, Stratford. Home: 1824 Octavia St New Orleans LA 70115 Office: 915 Common St New Orleans LA 70130

GENTLE, EDGAR CUTHBERT, JR., telephone co. exec.; b. New Orleans, Oct. 7, 1918; s. Edgar Cuthbert and Edvige Louise (Fernandez) G.; B.S. in Elec. Engring., Auburn U., 1942; postgrad. Williams Coll., 1956; m. Marie Jeanne Thibodeau, June 29, 1946; children—Judith (Mrs. Chester B. Adams), Patricia (Mrs. W. Michael Rees), Edgar Cuthbert III, Diane Frances, Paul F., Thomas W. Engr., So. Bell Tel. & Tel. Co., Birmingham, Ala., 1940-56, chief engr., Atlanta, 1956-59, gen. plant mgr., Atlanta, 1959-62; adminstr. data communications planning Am. Tel. & Tel. Co., N.Y.C., 1962-68; v.p. South Central Bell Telephone Co., Birmington, 1968—. Bd. dirs. Arthritis Found. Ala.; mem. engring. alumni council Auburn U. Served with AUS, 1942-46; PTO. Decorated Bronze Star. Registered profl. engr., Ala., Ga. Mem. Am. Inst. E.E. (ednl. activities bd. N.Y.C. 1970—), Briaerean Soc., Birmingham C. of C., Scabbard and Blade, Phi Kappa Phi, Tau Beta Pi, Eta Kappa Nu. Roman Catholic. Clubs: Birmingham, The Club, Downtown Kiwanis, Vastavia Country (Birmingham). Author: Data Communications in Business, an Introduction, 1965. Home: 3533 Spring Valley Ct Mountain Brook AL 35223 Office: South Central Bell Tel Co PO Box 771 Birmingham AL 35201

GENTRY, JACK WEAR, city ofcl.; b. Denton, Tex., Dec. 6, 1923; s. J. D. Alex and Irene (Powell) G.; student Tex. A. and M. U., 1958-61, So. Meth. U., 1967; m. Anna Ruth O'Dell, Apr. 3, 1947; children—Julianna, Belinda. With Denton Fire Dept., 1942—, vol. fireman, 1946, fireman, 1947-58, fire chief, 1958—. Instr. Tex. Firemen's Tng. Sch., 1962-71. Active Boy Scouts Am., various community drives. Served with USNR, 1943-45; PTO. Recipient Silver Beaver award Boy Scouts Am., 1967, Reaford Scholarship, Internat. Assn. Fire Chief's, 1966. Mem. Internat. Assn. Fire Chiefs, Tex. Fire Chief's Assn., Tex. Firemen's and Fire Marshals Assn., North Tex. Firemen's Assn. (pres. 1970), Denton County Fire Fighters Assn. (pres. 1969). Presbyn. (elder 1969-71). Club: Optimist (pres. Breakfast Club) (Denton). Home: 1423 Michial St Denton TX 76201 Office: 215 E McKinney St Denton TX 76201

GENTRY, MARIE ELIZABETH FADDIS (MRS. GEORGE V. GENTRY), physician; b. Chgo., July 5, 1905; d. Wallace Ray and Elsa (Rockener) Faddis; A.B., Syracuse U., 1926; Ph.D., U. Tex., 1933; M.D., U. Chgo., 1936; m. George V. Gentry, Feb. 21, 1930. Intern, Women's and Children's Hosp., Chgo., 1936; practice medicine, Austin, Tex., 1937-42; med. cons. Tex. Health Dept., 1942-45, dir. mental health div., 1947-51; resident pediatrics Raymond Blank Meml. Hosp., Des Moines, 1944-45; asst. dir. Austin Travis County Health Dept., 1951-70, dep. dir., 1970—. Fellow Am. Acad. Pediatrics; mem. A.M.A., Tex., Travis County med. socs., Am., Tex. pub. health assns., Am., Tex. assns. pub. health physicians. Club: Zonta (pres. 1952-53) (Austin). Home: 317 Ridgewood Rd Austin TX 78746 Office: 1313 Sabine St Austin TX 78701

GENTRY, WILLIAM C., JR., educator; b. Hope, Ark., July 15, 1935; s. William C. and Agnes (McDowell) G.; B.A., Hendrix Coll., 1957; Th.M. (Am. Assn. Theol. Schs. Sr. Honors scholar Lilly Found., So. Meth. U., 1960, Ph.D., 1968; m. Elizabeth Brooks, Sept. 5, 1959; children—William Brooks, Robert McDowell. Ordained to ministry Methodist Ch., 1960; Meth. minister, Mena, Ark., 1960-61; Meth. campus minister Little Rock U., U. Ark. Med. Sch., 1961-65; asso. prof. philosophy Henderson State Coll., Arkadelphia, Ark., 1968—. Bd. dirs. West End Day Care Center, Arkadelphia, Ark. Named Outstanding Young Man Am., 1971. Mem. Am. Acad. Religion, Am. Soc. Christian Ethics. Home: 1631 Walnut St Route 1 Arkadelphia AR 71923

GENTRY, WILLIAM HUNTER, JR., realty and ins. co. exec.; b. Crozet, Va., July 2, 1926; s. William Hunter and Ora (Short) G.; attended Sch. Banking, U. Wis., 1951-54, La. State U., 1962; m. Frances Louise Hutchinson, Mar. 5, 1949; children—Mark H., Eric L. Asst. cashier various banks, Va., 1948-62; sr. v.p. So. Nat. Bank, Southern Pines, N.C., 1962-64; exec. v.p. Barnum Realty & Ins. Co., Southern Pines, 1964-67, pres., owner, 1967—. Vice pres., dir. Mile-away Farms, Inc., Southern Pines, 1966-70; pres. Five Mile Farms Inc., Southern Pines, 1968—. Bd. dirs., treas. Moore County Tb Assn., 1966-68; bd. dirs. Mid-State Tb and Respiratory Disease Assn.; bd. dirs., treas. Moore County (N.C.) Charitable Found., 1968—. Served with USAAF, 1944-46. Mem. Nat. Assn. Real Estate Bds., Southern Pines Bd. Realtors (sec. 1967—), Sandhills Area C. of C. (pres. 1968, v.p. 1970—, dir.). Episcopalian (vestryman). Kiwanian. Home: 915 E Indiana Av Southern Pines NC 28387 Office: 124 NW Broad St Southern Pines NC 28387

GEORGE, CHARLES KAY, lawyer; b. Detroit, Mar. 14, 1929; s. G.K. and Florence (Joudi) G.; student U. Miami, 1948-51, J.D., 1956; m. Mary Carol Pittman, June 9, 1950; children—Cary Ann, Charles M.P., Curtis Allen. Admitted to Fla. bar, 1954; mem. firm. Admas, George & Wood, Miami, Fla., 1956—. Dir. Allmand Boat Co., Miami. Chmn., Orange Bowl Stadium Adv. Com., 1963-69; sec. Everglades Found., 1962-64; mem. Rev. Bd. and Civil Def. Bd., Coral Gables, Fla. Bd. dirs. Citizen's League, Miami, U. Miami Hall of Fame, Dade County (Fla.) Citizens Safety Council. Served with USAF, 1954-56. Mem. Internat. Assn. Ins. Counsel, Am. Judicature Soc., Am., Fla., Dade County bar assns., Delta Alpha Delta, Phi Alpha Delta, Sigma Alpha Epsilon. Democrat. Roman Catholic. Clubs: University, Fla. Athletic, Jockey, (Miami); Riviera Country (Coral Gables). Home: 11210 Mendavia Av Coral Gables FL 33143 Office: Concord Bldg Miami FL 33131

GEORGE, DESMOND ALVIS, chemist, physicist; b. Jacksonville, Tex., June 7, 1917; s. John H. and Willie (Durrett) G.; student Jacksonville Jr. Coll., 1934-36; B.S., Stephen F. Austin, 1941; postgrad. George Washington U., 1947-59; m. Sadie Dee Davis, Dec. 26, 1935; 1 dau., Desma Kay (Mrs. George F. Middleton). Tchr., Anderson County, Tex., 1937-42; with Nat. Bur. Standards, 1942-60; with Sci. Liaison and Adv. Group, sr. chemist U.S. Army, 1960—. Served to comdr., USNR, 1944-46, 61-62. Mem. Am. Soc. Testing Materials (subcom. chmn. 1954-59), Am. Phys. Soc., Alpha Chi Sigma. Address: 509 N Manchester St Arlington VA 22203

GEORGE, DIMITRA STEVE, state ofcl.; b. N.Y.C., Jan. 26, 1925; d. Steve and Amelia (Petalas) George; A.B. in Sociology, U. N.C., Greensboro, 1946; M.A., U. Chgo., 1954. Caseworker, Welfare Dept., Wilmington, N.C., 1946-50; supr. Welfare Dept., Concord, N.C., 1950-52; chief psychiat. social worker Richland Mental Health Clinic, Columbia, S.C., 1954-64; mental health cons. S.C. Dept. Mental Health, Columbia, 1964—. Instr. sociology and psychology U. S.C., Columbia, 1958—; cons. Mem. adult edn. adv. com. Columbia (S.C.) Sch. Dist. 1, 1960—. Mem. Nat. Assn. Social Workers (mem. leadership training program 1969-71), So. Community Execs. Inst. Blue Ridge (mem. exec. com. 1964-69), S.C. Council Family Relations (pres. 1969-71), Chief Social Workers in State Mental Health Programs (mem. exec. com. 1968-69), League Women Voters, Daus. of Penelope. Club: Soroptimist. Home: 1509 Brennen Rd Columbia SC 29206 Office: 2414 Bull St Columbia SC 29202

GEORGE, EDWARD YOUSSEF, educator; b. WadiHalfa, Sudan, July 23, 1925; s. Youssef and Fortune (Dwani) G.; B.Sc. in Chem. Engring., Cairo U., 1947, M.A. in Polit. Sci., 1953; B.A. in Social Sci. with honors, Am. U., Cairo, 1957; Ph.D. in Econs., New Sch. Social Research, 1962; m. Mary E. Morgan, Jan. 28, 1961; children—Mary Lynn, Edward Nabeel, Ann Elaine. Came to U.S., 1957, naturalized, 1965. Asst. fgn. editor Al Ahram Newspaper, 1953-57; press sec. UAR delgation at UN, N.Y.C., 1958-62; asst. to asso. prof. Bentley Coll., Boston, 1962-66, prof. econs., dir. of research, 1967-69; asso. prof. mgmt. sci. Northeastern U., 1966-67; prof. bus. and quantitative methods U. Tex. at El Paso, 1969—; project dir. Input/Output Study for State of Tex., 1969—. Mgmt. cons. computers and operations research. Mem. Council of Social Data Systems, Inc.; mem. New Eng. Council for Econ. Devel., 1965-69. Mem. Am. Statis. Assn., Asso. Univ. Burs. Bus. and Econ. Research, Am. Econ. Assn., Regional Sci. Assn., Inst. Mgmt. Sci., Operations Research Soc, Am., Data Processing Mgmt. Assn. Author: Economic Impact of Tourism and Travel in Eastern Massachusetts; Diagnostic Tools for Data Management-IBM Monograph; numerous articles for profl. jours. Home: 780 DeLeon Dr El Paso TX 79912

GEORGE, JAMES COLLIN, II, surgeon; b. Tampa, Fla., June 20, 1917; s. Sawnie McKinney and Lula (McDougal) G.; student Tex. Southmost Coll., 1933-35, U. Tex., 1935-38; M.D., Baylor U., 1942; m. Jane Jarvis, June 1, 1942; children—Jane Elizabeth, James Collin III, Robert Jarvis. Intern, Robert B. Green Meml. Hosp., San Antonio, 1942-43, resident in surgery AAF Regional Hosp., Salt Lake City, 1943-44, Baylor U. Hosp., Dallas, 1946-47, Ball Meml. Hosp., Muncie, Ind., 1947-48; practice medicine specializing in surgery, Brownsville, Tex., 1948—; mem. staff Mercy Hosp., 1948—, chief surgery, chief staff; county health officer Cameron County, Tex 1963—. Dir., v.p. Nat. Bank of Commerce, Brownsville. Founder, organizer City County Health Clinic, 1951, chmn., 1951-52; founder, organizer Brownsville Soc. Crippled Children, 1950, med. dir., 1950-58. Chmn. Brownsville Bd. City Devel., 1955-56; mem. Brownsville Indsl. Commn., 1960-61; organizer Cameron County Community Project, Nat. Econ. Opportunity Act, 1966, chmn., 1966-67; mayor City of Brownsville, 1959-61; mem. Brownsville Pub. Utility Bd., 1960-61. Served with USAAF, World War II. Fellow A.C.S.; mem. Am., Tex. med. assns., Southwestern, Pan Pacific med. socs., Am. Bd. Abdominal Surgeons, Internat. Acad. Medicine, Internat. Coll. Proctology, Skull and Key, Sigma Alpha Epsilon, Phi Chi. Episcopalian. Home: 285 Calle Cenizo Brownsville TX 78520 Office: 705 W Jefferson St Brownsville TX 78520

GEORGE, JAMES FREDERICK, state ofcl.; b. Oklahoma City, Feb. 2, 1910; s. William Samuel and Bertha (Leckner) G.; B.S., Okla. A and M., 1931; m. Marie Louise Lloyd, Nov. 23, 1939; children—Frances Louise, William Lloyd, Caroline Ann. Survey party chief Okla. Hwy. Dept., 1931-41, resident engr. constrn., 1941-53, div. constrn. engr., 1953—. Bd. dirs. Okla. Hwy Dept. Credit Union, 1966—. Mem. Sigma Phi Epsilon. Episcopalian (vestry 1960—, sr. warden 1966). Home: 1710 W Locust St Durant OK 74701 Office: 503 SW D St Antlers OK 74523

GEORGE, JOSEPH JOHNSON, meteorologist; b. West Plains, Mo., June 20, 1909; s. William and Bess (Johnson) G.; student U. Cal. at Los Angeles, 1926-29, Cal. Inst. Tech., 1933-34; m. Mary Beale Sasscer, Oct. 16, 1937; children—Mary B., Margaret Lynn, Penelope, Joseph Sasscer. Weather and dispatch dept. Western Air Express, Los Angeles, 1929-34; supt. meteorology Eastern Airlines, Atlanta,

1934-41, 46-64, dir meteorology, Miami, Fla., 1964—. Chmn. adv. com. on weather services Dept. Commerce, 1953—; mem. Pres.'s Adv. Com. on Weather Control, 1953; mem. NACA sub com. Meteorol. Problems, 1946-56; mem. tech. adv. bd. to adminstr. FAA; mem. nat. adv. com. Oceans and Atmosphere, 1971-74. Served from capt. to col., weather service, USAF, 1942-46. Recipient Meisinger award for aero. research Am. Meterol. Soc., 1941; Losey Award Inst. Aero. Scis., 1944. Fellow Am. Meteorol. Soc. (v.p. 1950-52; award, applied meteorology 1955); mem. Nat. Acad. Scis. (mem. panel on rivers and weather services, 1968-69). Author: Weather Forecasting for Aeronautics; also numerous papers on weather forecasting. Home: 2521 N Greenway Dr Coral Gables FL 33134 Office: Eastern Airlines Miami Internat Airport Miami FL 33148

GEORGE, KALANKAMARY PILY, educator; b. Kadayirupe, India, June 13, 1933; s. Kalankamary Varkey and Sarah (Varkey) Pily; B.E., Nat. Inst. Engring., Mysore, 1956; Ph.D., Ia. State U., 1963; m. Mani, Aug. 19, 1958; children—Sarah, Paul. Came to U.S., 1959, naturalized, 1966. Asst. prof. U. Miss., University, 1963-65, asso. prof., 1965-68, prof. civil engring., 1968—. Mem. Am. Soc. C.E. Contbr. articles profl. jours. Home: Box 525 Oxford MS 38677 Office: Civil Engring Dept U Miss University MS 38677

GEORGE, LEWIS DUDLEY, chem. co. exec.; b. Richmond, Va., Feb. 15, 1905; s. Henry H. and Lillian B. (Wright) G.; B.S., U. Richmond, 1923; C.E., Cornell U., 1926; m. Sally Gibson Barret, June 1, 1935. Constrn. engr. Stone & Webster Engring. Corp., 1926-31; engr. City of Richmond, 1933-34; constrn., engr. DuPont, 1934-35; with Richmond Guano Co., 1935—, sec., 1937-56, v.p., 1956-59, pres., 1959—, also dir.; dir. Bank of Commerce & Trusts, 1952-56, Suburban Bank, 1959-62. Chmn. Port of Richmond Adv. Commn., 1970—. Trustee U. Richmond. Served from capt. to lt. col., C.E., AUS, 1942-46. Decorated Army Commendation medal. Mem. Nat. Plant Food Inst. (chmn. bd. 1958-59), Ind. Chem. Industries (v.p.), Antiquarian Soc. Richmond, Lambda Chi Alpha. Mem. Christian Ch. (chmn. bd. trustees). Rotarian. Club: Commonwealth (Richmond). Home: 210 Ampthill Rd Richmond VA 23226 Office: P O Box 544 Richmond VA 23204

GEORGE, MILDRED A. MILLER (MRS. SAMUEL F. GEORGE), assn. exec.; b. Tiffin, O., Sept. 17, 1916; d. Grover A. and Clara (Dellinger) Miller; grad. Tiffin U., 1937; ed. Am. Savings & Loan Inst., 1951; m. Samuel F. George, Feb. 11, 1956. Sec., teller Citizens Savs. & Loan Assn., Tiffin, O., 1937-44, bookkeeper, 1944-50; bookkeeper Anacostia Fed. Savs. & Loan Assn., Washington, 1950-56, asst. treas., 1951-56; asst. controller Perpetual Bldg. Assn., Washington, 1956-68; asst. v.p., mgr. s.w. br., Perpetual Bldg. Assn. in L'Enfant Plaza, Washington, 1968—. Mem. Ft. Washington Estates Citizens Assn., 1958—, sec., 1959-60, v.p., 1971-72. Mem. Nat. Soc. Controllers and Financial Officers of Savs. Instns., Kappa Delta Phi. Methodist. Soroptomist. Home: 9341 Reid Circle Oxon Hill MD 20022 Office: 965 L'Enfant Plaza N Washington DC 20024

GEORGE, RONALD BAYLIS, physician; b. Zwolle, La., Nov. 17, 1932; s. Ronald Lee and Theodora Virginia (Baylis) G.; B.A., U. Ala., 1954; M.D., Tulane U., 1958. Intern Charity Hosp., New Orleans, 1958-59, resident internal medicine, 1959-60, 62-64; fellow pulmonary diseases Tulane U., New Orleans, 1964-66, chief inhalation therapy and emphysema sect. VA Hosp., New Orleans, 1966-71; asso. prof. medicine, head pulmonary diseases sect. La. State U. Med. Center, Sch. Medicine, 1972—; chief physician inhalation therapy Confederate Meml. Med. Center, Shreveport, 1972—. Served to capt. USAF, 1960-62. Diplomate Am. Bd. Internal Medicine. Fellow Am. Coll. Chest Physicians, A.C.P.; mem. Am. Thoracic Soc., Alpha Omega Alpha. Home: 208 Villa Contessa Shreveport LA 71106 Office: 3720 Blair St Shreveport LA 71103

GEORGE, THEODORE ALEXANDER, aero. engr.; b. Detroit, Nov. 1, 1926; s. Alexander T. and Nada (Braun) G.; B.A., George Washington U., 1950; B.Mech. Engring., Cath. U., 1959, M.Aero. Engring., 1960; m. Lillian C. Clark, Nov. 14, 1953. Aero. engr. Dept. Army, Washington, 1950-58; mgr. project discoverer Office Sec. Def., Washington, 1960-61; dept. dir. nuclear test detection, 1961-64; prin. engr. Office Manned Space Flight, NASA, Washington, 1964-67, mgr. Earth Resources Tech. Satellite, 1967-70; asst. to water quality commr. Environmental Protection Agy., 1970-71; mgr. earth observing advanced programs NASA, 1971-72; asst. for arms control ODDR&E Office Sec. Def., 1972—. Guest lectr. applied math. U. Va., Fairfax. Served with AUS, 1946-47. Registered profl. engr., Md., D.C. Mem. Soc. for Indsl. and Applied Math., Am. Inst. Aeros. and Astronautics, N.Y. Acad. Sci., Nat. Soc. Profl. Engrs., Tau Beta Pi. Author: Principles of Atmospheric Reentry, 1961. Home: 4132 N River St Arlington VA 22207 Office: Pentagon Bldg Washington DC 20301

GEORGESCU-ROEGEN, NICHOLAS, educator; b. Constantza, Romania, Feb. 4, 1906 (came to U.S., 1948); s. Stavru and Maria (Niculescu) Georgescu; license U. Bucharest, 1926; D.Stat., Sorbonne, 1930; m. Otilia Busuioc, Sept. 2, 1934. Prof. U. Bucharest, 1932-46, also asst. dir. Central Statis. Inst., Bucharest, 1932-38, econ. adviser Treasury Dept., Bucharest, 1938-39, and dir. Bucharest Bd. Trade, 1939-44; lectr., research asso. Harvard, 1948-49; prof. econs. Vanderbilt U., 1949-69, distinguished prof., 1969—; Rockefeller Found. prof., Japan, 1962-63; Ford Found. lectr., Brazil, 1964, 66, 70. Romanian del. to Com. on Peaceful Change of League of Nations, 1938; sec. gen. Romanian Armistice Commn., 1944-45. Guggenheim fellow, 1958-59. Fellow Am. Econ. Assn. (distinguished fellow), Econometric Soc., Internat. Inst. Sociology, Internat. Inst. Statistics; mem. A.A.A.S., So. Econ. Assn., Societe de Statistique de Paris, Omicron Delta Epsilon. Club: Foreign Relations (Nashville). Author: Metoda Statistica, 1933; Analytical Economics: Issues and Problems, 1966; La science economique: Ses problemes et ses difficultes, 1970; The Entropy Law and the Economic Problem, 1971; The Entropy Law and the Economic Process, 1971. Editor: (with T. C. Koopmans et.al.) Activity Analysis of Production and Allocation, 1951. Contbr. articles to profl. jours. Home: 2614 Hemingway Dr Nashville TN 37215

GEORGIADE, NICHOLAS GEORGE, physician; b. Lowell, Mass., Dec. 25, 1918; s. George Nicholas and Stephanie C. (Englisch) G.; student Fordham U., 1937-40; D.D.S., Columbia, 1944; M.D., Duke, 1949, B.S., 1950; m. Ruth Catherine Sauer, Sept. 21, 1942; children—Greg, Robert, Nancy. Intern oral surgery Kings County Hosp. Med. Dept., 1944; intern Duke Med. Sch. Dept. Surgery, 1949-50, asst. resident, 1950-52, resident plastic and maxillofacial surgery, 1952-54; cons. plastic, maxillofacial and oral surgery Durham's VA Hosp., U.S. Army, Air Force, NIH, 1956; practice medicine, specializing in plastic and maxillofacial surgery, Durham, N.C.; mem. staff Duke U. Med. Center; prof. plastic, maxillofacial and oral surgery Duke U. Med. Center, Durham, 1954—. Dir. Liberty Bank and Trust Co. Served with AUS, 1944-46. Diplomate Am. Bd. Plastic Surgery (mem. exec. com.). Fellow A.C.S. (chmn. adv. com. plastic and maxillofacial surgery); mem. Am. Soc. Maxillofacial Surgeons (pres. 1965-66), Am. Assn. Plastic Surgeons (trustee 1971-73, sec.), Am. Soc. Plastic and Reconstructive Surgery (mem. exec. com. 1967-68), Am. Cleft Palate Assn. (trustee 1967-71), A.M.A. (chmn. sect. plastic surqery 1968), Am. Burn Assn., So. Surg. Assn. Contbr. to books on plastic and reconstructive surgery, burns, and aesthetic surgery, numerous articles to profl. jours. Office: Duke Univ Med Center Durham NC 27710

GERACCI, JAMES PAUL, dentist; b. Niagara Falls, N.Y., Sept. 17, 1930; s. Rocco and Rose Mary (Fruscione) G.; B.S., Niagara U., 1952; D.D.S., U. Buffalo, 1957; postgrad. Tufts U., 1964-66; m. Louise Martha D'Anna, June 7, 1955; children—Gary James, James Jay. Commd. 1st lt. USAF, 1957, advanced through grades to lt. col., 1969; dental officer McGuire AFB, N.J., 1957-61, Panama Canal Zone, 1961-64; periodontist, dental health officer, mil. cons. in periodontics Maxwell AFB, Ala., 1966—. Clin. asst. dept. periodontology Tufts U. Sch. Dental Medicine, 1965-66; mil. cons. periodontics Surgeon Gen., USAF, 1970—. Shelter comdr. Civil Defense, 1967-71. Pres. Maxwell AFB Sch. Bd., 1970-71. Mem. Am. Dental Assn., Am. Acad. Periodontology, Am. Soc. Periodontists, Omicron Kappa Upsilon, Xi Psi Phi. Club: Spanish-Am. (Montgomery); Maxwell AFB Officers (Ala.). Home: 529-A Catalpa Dr Maxwell AFB AL 36113 Office: Box 10335 USAF Regional Hosp Maxwell AFB AL 36112

GERALD, REX ERVIN, anthropologist, mus. dir.; b. Lenorah, Tex., Mar. 18, 1928; s. Cecil Leroy and Mary E. (Donaldson) G.; B.A., U. Ariz., 1951; M.A., U. Pa., 1957; postgrad. (NIH fellow, NSF fellow) U. Chgo., 1963-66; m. Elgie Zaiz, Feb. 14, 1961; children— Rosemary Elaine, Eric Campbell (by previous marriage); Elgie Lisette, Rex Ervin II, Lorenzo Xocotzin, Camille Nenetzin. Archaeologist, Ft. Vancouver Nat. Monument, Wash., 1950; field archeologist Amerind Found., Inc., Dragoon, Ariz., 1957; dir. El Paso Centennial Mus., 1958—; asst. prof. anthropology, U. Tex., El Paso, 1959—; Cons. archaeology Nat. Park Service, 1959—; anthropology cons. to Tigua Indians of of Ysleta del Sur, Indian Claims Case, 1970. Chmn., Hueco Tanks Co. Park Adv. Com., 1965-67. Served with Judge Adv. Gen. Corps, Q.M.C., 1946-48, 51-54. Tex. Western Coll. Faculty fellow, 1963-64. Mem. Sigma Xi (asso.). Contbr. to profl. textbooks. Home: 3901 Emory Rd El Paso TX 79922

GERBER, ISRAEL J., clergyman, author; b. N.Y.C., July 30, 1918; s. Max and Sadie (Shuster) G.; B.A., Yeshiva U., 1939; M.S., City Coll. N.Y., 1940; Ph.D., Boston U., 1950; m. Sydelle Reba Katzman, Jan. 9, 1943; children—Barbara J., Sharon M., Wayne S. Tchr. N.Y.C. schs., 1941-42; prof. of Old Testament Livingstone Coll., Hood Sem., Salisbury, N.C., 1960—; prof. psychology Johnson C. Smith U., Charlotte, N.C., 1969—; rabbi Beth Jacob Synogogue, Plymouth, Mass., 1943-44, Congregation Agudath Achim, Fitchburg, Mass., 1944-53, Temple Emanu-El, Dothan, Ala., 1953-59, Temple Beth El, Charlotte, 1959-72; lectr. U. N.C., Charlotte, 1968—. Chaplain Boston Psychopathic Hosp., 1948-50; cons. psychologist Southeast Ala. Gen. Hosp., 1956-59. Chmn. Mecklenburg (N.C.) County Soc. for Crippled Children; mem. Charlotte-Meckenburg Council on Human Relations, Multiple Sclerosis Soc., Citizens Safety Assn.; v.p. Mental Health Assn. Charlotte and Mecklenburg County; pres. Mecklenburg County Soc. for Crippled Children and Adults, chmn. Hearthstone Half-Way House; chmn. Charlotte chpt. Nat. Conf. Christians and Jews; trustee Florence Crittendon Home. Bd. govs. Inst. Pastoral Care. Served as chaplain, AUS, 1951-52. Recipient Award in Religion, Charlotte Jr. Womens Club, 1962. Mem. New Eng. Zionist Region, Southeast Assn. Reform Rabbis (sec.-treas. 1956-59), B'nai B'rith (lodge pres. 1956-58), Am., Southeastern, N.C., Ala., Mecklenburg County psychol. assns., Am. Assn. U. Profs., Am. Acad. Religion, Soc. Sci. Study Religion, Nat. Assn. Biblican Instrs., Jewish Chaplains Assn., Acad. Religioun and Mental Health; hon. mem. Internat. Mark Twain Soc. Mason, Rotarian, Kiwanian. Author: The Psychology of the Suffering Mind, 1951; Man on a Pendulum, 1956; Immortal Rebels, 1963; Rabbinical Counseling, 1966. Contbr. articles to religious mags. Home: 5727 Riviere Dr Charlotte NC 28211 Office: 5727 Riviere Dr Charlotte NC 28211

GEREAU, MARY M. CONDON, ednl. assn. exec.; b. Winterset, Ia., Oct. 10, 1916; d. David Joseph and Sarah Rose (Stack) Condon; student Mt. Mercy Jr. Coll., 1935-37; B.A. in English, State U. Ia., 1939, M.A., in U.S. History, 1941, postgrad., 1948—; m. Gerald R. Gereau, Jan. 14, 1961. Tchr. English, history high sch., Colo., Ia., 1941-42, Creston, Ia., 1942, 43; program dir. A.R.C., India, 1943-45, field cons. Mont., N.D., S.D., 1945-46; dean students Eastern Mont. Coll. Edn., 1946-48; supt. pub. instrn. Mont., Helena, 1949-57; specialist U.S. Senate Com. Interior Affairs, Washington, 1957; adviser Pa. Council Edn., Harrisburg, 1957; asst. dir. rural services N.E.A., 1957-61, legislative cons., 1961—, pres. staff orgn., 1961. Sec. Mont. Bd. Edn., 1949-57; vice-chmn. Mont. Land Bd., 1949-57; chmn. Mont. Tchrs. Retirement System, 1949-57, council chief state sch. officers, dir., 1953-55, pres., 1956; chmn. nat. com. sch. savs. U.S. Treasury Dept., 1950-56; chmn. Mont. Conf. Children and Youth, 1950; del. White House Conf. Edn., 1955; mem. profl. staff White House Conf. Edn., 1965. Del. Democratic Nat. Conv., 1956; mem. platform com. Mont. Dem. Party; exec. dir. Educators for Johnson-Humphrey, 1964, Educators for Humphrey-Muskie 1968; chmn. Women's Joint Congl. Com., 1969—. Recipient spl. citation V.F.W., 1954; named Conservationist of Year, Mont., 1950; recipient Distinguished Service award Council of Chief State Sch. Officers, 1956; made hon. princess Blackfeet Indian Tribe. Mem. N.E.A. (life), Mont. Edn. Assn. (life), Am. Assn. Sch. Adminstrs. Democrat. Roman Catholic. Home: 1234 Massachusetts Av NW Washington DC 20005 Office: 1201 16th St NW Washington DC 20036

GERECHT, ASHER, editor; b. Kansas City, Mo., Nov. 23, 1922; s. Ben and Golda Reva (Englander) G.; B.A., Washington U., St. Louis, 1949; M.A., U. Chgo., 1950; m. Gloria Lantz, Nov. 21, 1951; children—Ellen, Mike, Danny. Writer short fiction Harpers and Esquire mags., 1945-51; reporter Hobbs (N.M.) News-Sun, 1947, Savannah (Ga.) Morning News, 1948, Fairchild Publs., Chgo., and Washington, 1950-61; founder Housing Affairs Letter, Washington, 1961, editor, 1961—; founder Housing and Renewal Index, 1965. Served with AUS, 1943-45. Mem. Ind. Newsletter Assn. (founder 1962, pres. 1962-64). Club: Nat. Press (Washington). Home: 1109 Ruppert Rd Silver Spring MD 20903 Office: 1319 F St NW Washington DC 20004

GERLACH, FREDERICK HERMAN, govt. ofcl.; b. Milw., Aug. 8, 1938; s. Arthur John and Margaret (Williamson) G.; B.A., U. Wis., 1961; M. Internat. Affairs, Columbia, 1963, Ph.D., 1968; m. Brigitte Steinberg, Oct. 21, 1967. Asso. operations officer, editor Operations Center, Dept. of State, Washington, 1966-68, staff aide, counsellor Dept. of State, 1968; internat. transp. specialist Office Of Internat. Coop., Dept. of Transp., Washington, 1968-70; consul, polit. officer Am. Embassy, Rabat, Morocco, 1970—. Sec. Cherrydale Citizens Assn., Arlington, 1969-70, Arlington (Va.) Civic Fedn., 1969-70. Mem. Am. Fgn. Service Assn., Am. Polit. Sci. Assn., German Lang. Soc., Phi Beta Kappa, Phi Kappa Phi, Phi Eta Sigma, Alpha Delta Phi. Mem. United Ch. of Christ. Home: 1711 N Quincy St Arlington VA 22207 Office: Box 99 FPO New York City NY 09544

GERMAN, JOHN PAUL, educator; b. Livingston, Tex., June 10, 1917; s. Sam Houston and Martha (Peters) G.; B.S., U. Tex., 1940, M.S., 1949, Ph.D., 1955; m. Mary Frances Keith, Aug. 2, 1941; 1 dau., Margaret Keith (Mrs. John W. Halsell). Asso. prof. elec. engring. Purdue U., Lafayette, Ind., 1955-58; prof. elec. engring. Tex. A. and M. U., College Station, 1958—. Served to capt., Signal Corps, AUS, 1942-46. Mem. I.E.E.E., Am. Soc. E.E., Sigma Xi, Tau Beta Pi, Eta Kappa Nu, Sigma Pi Sigma, Phi Kappa Phi. Research in properties of ionosphere, in electromagnetic radiation. Home: 807 S Rosemary Dr Bryan TX 77801 Office: Elec Engring Dept Tex A and M U College Station TX 77843

GERMANY, EUGENE WILSON, petroleum mining exec., mayor; b. Grand Saline, Tex., Mar. 11, 1916; s. Eugene Benjamin and Maggie Lee (Wilson) G.; B.S., So. Meth. U., 1937; m. Jennie Margaret Blackman, Jan. 17, 1940; children—Wesley H., Joan Lee. Partner, E. B. Germany & Sons, Dallas, 1937—; partner Germany Investment Co., 1948—; pres. Calto Oil Co., 1956—; dir., vice chmn. bd. Preston State Bank; dir. Southwestern Gen. Life Ins. Co.; mayor, University Park, Tex., 1970—. Mem. City Commn., University Park, 1959-70. Pres. Dallas YMCA; bd. dirs. Meth. Hosp. Dallas; trustee So. Meth. U. Mem. Am. Assn. Petroleum Geologists, Am. Assn. Petroleum Landmen, Petroleum Assn. Am., Dallas Petroleum Club, Phi Delta Theta, Alpha Kappa Psi. Methodist (trustee). Mason. Clubs: Dallas Country, Preston Trail Golf, Northwood (Dallas). Home: 3508 Wentwood St Dallas TX 75225 Office: 8111 Preston Rd Dallas TX 75225

GERMANY, JAMES CLYDE, biologist; b. Atoka, Okla., Dec. 25, 1934; s. Clyde and Ernestine (Houchin) G.; B.S., N.M. State U., 1964, M.S., 1969; m. Elizabeth M. Steinke, Nov. 29, 1963; children—William Clyde, Jenny Lynne, James Clyde, Justin Wesley. Wildlife research technician N.M. State U., 1964-69; biologist Fla. Div. Health and Rehab. Services, 1969—; owner Hitchen Post Fountain and Sundries, Capitan, N.M., 1965-69; mayor, Capitan, 1966-68; owner Fashion Gallery. Mem. Capitan Fire Dept., 1964-69. Bd. dirs. Lincoln County Devel. Assn. Served with AUS, 1957-59. Mem. Wildlife Soc. (past pres. N.M.-Ariz. sect.), Nat. Wildlife Fedn., Fla. Wildlife Soc. Methodist. Lion. Contbr. articles to profl. jours. Research on transferable diseases to man from wildlife. Home: 7211 Crane Av Apt 31 Jacksonville FL 32216

GERON, JAMES MICHAEL, investment co. exec.; b. Dallas, Oct. 25, 1937; s. Bedford Tanner and Frances Agnes (Crook) G.; B.S., U. Tex., 1960; m. Suzanne Pitts, Aug. 1, 1959; children—Mary Frances, James Michael. Exec. training program, credit analyst First Nat. Bank, Dallas, 1960-62; stockbroker, Walker Austin & Waggener & Co., Inc., Dallas, 1962-66, Paine Webber Jackson & Curtis, Dallas, 1966-69; v.p., resident mgr. Underwood Neuhaus & Co., Inc., Dallas, 1969—. Div. leader United Fund, 1970-71; active Cancer Crusade, Heart Fund. Mem. Dallas Security Dealers Assn., Phi Kappa Psi. Republican. Methodist. Clubs: Woods and Waters (v.p., dir. 1964-70), Country. Home: 3548 Marquette St Dallas TX 75250 Office: 3130 1 Main Pl Dallas TX 75250

GERRISH, ROBERT GRANT, investment banking co. exec.; b. Boston, Feb. 9, 1921; s. John Jordan and Alice (Grant) G.; student Tufts Coll., 1938-39; Boston U., 1939-42; m. Bernadine A. Taylor, Feb. 27, 1945; children—Grant T., Gail V., Conrad J., Thomas R. Salesman, Whiting Weeks & Stubbs, Boston, 1945-50; mgr. syndicate and municipal bond depts. G.H. Walker & Co., Providence, 1950-59; partner Oscar E. Dooly & Co., Miami, Fla., 1959-64; pres. Dooly, Gerrish & Co., Inc., 1964-70; account exec. Reynolds Securities Inc., Miami, 1970—; Past pres. United Way of Fla., Inc. Mem. R.I. Pub. Expenditures Council, Providence, 1956-59, Com. State Budget, 1957-59, Taxation Com., 1957-59, Met. Govt. Com., 1957-59. Trustee, R.I. United Fund, 1955-59; bd. dirs. Big Brothers of Greater Miami, Hearing and Speech Center of Dade County, United Fund of Dade County, Crime Commn. Greater Miami. Served with USNR, 1942-45. Mem. Investment Bankers Assn. Am. (edn. com.), N.Y. Stock Exchange (investors information com.). R.I. Assn. Investment Firms (founder 1959), Nat. Security Traders Assn. (edn. com.), Fla. Security Dealers Assn. (pres.), Security Dealers Assn. Greater Miami (past pres.). Clubs: Boston Investment (founder 1946, pres. 1946-48); Country (Coral Gables, Fla.); Miami. Home: 820 Castile Av Coral Gables FL 33134 Office: 202 SE 1st St Miami FL 33131

GERSCHEFSKI, EDWIN, educator, composer; b. Meriden, Conn., June 10, 1909; s. Otto J. and Josephine (Sturmer) G.; Ph.B., Mus. B., Yale, 1931 (1st recipient Charles Ditson fellowship for year's study abroad); diploma (Jeffrey Reynolds scholar), Matthay Pianoforte Sch. (London), 1932; postgrad. study piano with Artur Schnabel, Como, Italy; m. Ina Magnuson, June 18, 1931; children—Jo Ellen, Peter, Martha, Michael, John. Mem. piano faculty Yorkville Music Sch., N.Y.C., 1933-37, Turtle Bay Music Sch., N.Y.C., 1937-40; dir. music dept. Home Thrift Assn., N.Y.C., 1938-40; tchr. piano, theory and composition Converse Coll., Spartanburg, S.C., 1940-59, dir. Summer Sch. Music, 1942-45, dean Sch. Music, 1945-59, tchr. piano and composition Cummington Sch., summer 1943; guest faculty Appalachian State Tchrs. Coll., Boone, N.C., summer 1956; composer, radio performer, recordings and motion picture scores; chmn. dept. music U. N.M., 1959-60, U. Ga., 1960—. Mem. bd. New Music Recordings, 1938-43; judge Young Artists Contest, Nat. Fedn. Music Clubs, 1954, 1961; mem. founders bd. Southeastern Composers League, 1952—; mem. scholarship com. The Presser Found.; participant Danforth Found. Workshop, Sarah Lawrence Coll., summer 1957. Recipient invitation to spend 2 summers Yaddo Found., Saratoga Springs, N.Y., 1936-37; award radio commn. League Composers, 1937; winner band music competition N.Y. World's Fair, 1939; recipient Carnegie grant, 1947, Fund for Advancement Edn. grant, 1952; gold medal Arnold Bax Soc. for Musical Composition in Harriet Cohen Internat. awards, 1963. Mem. Nat. Assn. Schs. Music (regional v.p. 1953-55, examiner 1955—, chmn. library com. 1962-65), Music Tchrs. Nat. Assn., Ga. Composers (pres. 1961-63), Ga. Music Council (pres. 1962-64), Phi Beta Kappa, Phi Kappa Phi, Pi Kappa Lambda, Phi Mu Alpha. Contbr. articles to publs. Composer: Classic Symphony, 1944; Half Moon Mountain (women's chorus, baritone), 1948; Song of the Mountains (for piano), 1957; Saugatuck Suite (orch.), 1958; Salutation of the Dawn (mixed chorus), 1964; 100th Psalm (mixed chorus), 1965; also numerous manuscripts. Regional editor Jour. Music Theory, 1957-62. Home: 765 Riverhill Dr Athens GA 30601

GERSCHEVISKI, MARTHA, violoncellist, educator; b. Spartanburg, S.C.; student Juilliard Sch. Music; pupil Andre Narvarra, Paris, France; student (scholar) Accademia Musicale Chigiana, Siena, Italy. Formerly asso. prin. cellist Am. Symphony Orch.; concertized U.S., 1968, under U.S. Cultural Presentation Abroad, Europe, 1969; now instr. music Ga. State U., Atlanta. Recipient Brevard Music Center Distinguished Alumni award, 1971-72. Address: Ga State U 33 Gilmer St SE Atlanta GA 30303

GERSTEIN, RICHARD E., state atty. Dade County (Fla.). Address: Met Justice Bldg 1351 NW 12th St Miami FL 33125

GERSTENBERGER, ROLAND WALTER, machinery co. exec.; b. Frankfurt, Germany, Apr. 21, 1938 (came to U.S. 1957, naturalized 1963; s. Walter and Lina Frieda (Birn) G.; B.S., U. Miami, 1964; m. Johanna Herrmann, Mar. 5, 1962; children—Elke, Steven. Mech. engr. Sjostrom Automations, Boca Raton, Fla., 1964-65; chief prodn. engr. Lundy Tech. Center, Pompano Beach, Fla., 1965-66; exec. v.p., dir. Jensen Machinery, Inc., Ft. Lauderdale, Fla., 1966—. Mem. Am. Soc. M.E., Sales and Marketing Execs. Kiwanian. Home: 4021 NE

22d Av Ft Lauderdale FL 33308 Office: 1101 NW 69th St Ft Lauderdale FL 33309

GERSTNER, HENRY GEORGE, sugar co. exec.; b. New Orleans, Apr. 14, 1905; s. Henry and Annie Evelyn (Krennerich) G.; B.E., Tulane U., 1926; m. Verlin C. Boutte, June 8, 1932; children—Janet (Mrs. R. A. Monica), Merrill Henry, Catherine (Mrs. D. L. Teijelo), Gretchen. Asst. chemist Colonial Sugars Co., Gramercy, La., 1926-29, chief chemist, 1939-34, asst. supt., 1934-44, gen. supt., 1944-48, asst. mgr., 1948-56, gen. mgr., 1956—, v.p., 1963—; dir. St. James Bank & Trust Co., N.Am. Sugar Industries. Mem. U.S. Nat. Com. on Sugar Analysis, 1958—; pres., dir. Sugar Industry Technologists, Inc., Cane Sugar Refining Research Project, 1969-70. Chmn. Selective Service Bd., 1958-65; mem. Parish Hosp. Bd., 1965-71; pres. Gramercy Recreation Commn., 1965-67; pres. St. James Parish Symphony Assn., 1966-69. Recipient Honor award Sugar Industry Technologists, 1970. Mem. Am. Chem. Soc., Am. Inst. Chem. Engrs., Am. Soc. Food Technologists, Am. Soc. Sugar Technologists, Sugar Research Found. (mem. industry adv. bd. 1957-68), Alpha Chi Sigma. Democrat. Lutheran. Lion. Home: 5 Park Av Gramercy LA 70052 Office: Colonial Sugars Co 1 5th Av Gramercy LA 70052

GERTZ, JOSEPH BARRY, investments exec.; b. Detroit, May 7, 1942; s. Harold Morris and Geneva Rice (Skirvin) G.; A.B., Stanford, 1964; M.B.A., U. Cal. at Los Angeles, 1966, C.Phil., 1970. Investment analyst Bank of Am., Los Angeles, 1961-63; officer tng. program Shearson Hammill & Co., Los Angeles, 1965; research asso. finance U. Cal. at Los Angeles, 1966-68; asst. prof. finance U. Tex., 1968-71; pres. J.B. Gertz & Co., Austin, Tex., 1969-72; owner Faubion Ranch, Leander, Tex., Town Lake Apts., Austin; cons. Competitive Capital Corp.; editorial cons. on investments to pubs.; lectr. investment banking and portfolio mgmt.; dir. Innovation Research Assos. of Prescott (Ariz.) Coll. Trustee Endowment for Commonwealth, Gertz Found. Mem. Econometric Soc., Am. Econ. Assn., Am. Finance Assn., Am. Mgmt. Assn., Inst. Mgmt. Sci., Beta Gamma Sigma, Delta Sigma Pi. Club: Los Angeles Athletic. Home: 5204 Ridge Oak Dr Austin TX 78731 Office: PO Box 5370 Austin TX 78763

GESELL, GERHARD ALDEN, judge; b. Los Angeles, June 16, 1910; s. Arnold Lucius and Beatrice (Chandler) G.; grad. Phillips Andover Acad., 1928; A.B., Yale, 1932, LL.B., 1935; m. Marion Holliday Pike, Sept. 19, 1936; children—Peter Gerhard, Patricia Pike. Admitted to Conn. bar, 1935, D.C. bar, 1941; with SEC, Washington, 1935-40, tech. advisor to chmn., 1940, acted for Commn. as spl. counsel Temporary Nat. Econ. Com., study legal res. life ins. cos.; mem. Covington & Burling, Washington, 1941-67; judge U.S. Dist. Ct. of D.C., 1968—; chief asst. counsel Joint Congl. Com. on Investigation Pearl Harbor Attack, 1945-46; chmn. Pres.'s Com. Equal Opportunity in Armed Forces, 1962-64; chmn. com. on adminstrn. of justice jud. Council. Mem. Am. Bar Assn., Bar Assn. D.C., Am. Law Inst., Am. Coll. Trial Lawyers, Yale Law Sch. Assn., Phi Delta Phi, Zeta Psi. Clubs: Metropolitan (Washington); Casino (N. Haven, Me.). Co-author: Study of Legal Reserve Life Insurance Cos., 1940; Families and Their Life Insurance, 1940. Home: 3304 N St Washington DC 20007 Office: US Courthouse Washington DC 20001

GESS, WILLIAM BUSH, lawyer; b. Lexington, Ky., Oct. 16, 1906; s. William and Naomi (Bush) G.; A.B., U. Ky., 1928, LL.B., 1930; m. Jane Elizabeth Hamilton, Sept. 2, 1931; children—William Bush, Mary Hamilton (Mrs. William J. Germond), Alexander. Admitted to Ky. bar, 1930; asso., J. Pelham Johnston, 1930-35, Job D. Turner, Scott Reed, Jack F. Mattinghly, 1953-54; partner, Gess, Mattingly, Saunier & Atchison, Lexington, Ky., 1954—; dir., gen. counsel 2d Nat. Bank & Trust Co., Lexington, Ky.; v.p., dir. WLEX-TV, Inc. Asst. corp. counsel, City of Lexington, Ky., 1931-35. Bd. dirs. Greater Lexington YMCA, Community Chest. Mem. Am. Judicature Soc., Am. Law Inst., Am., Ky. State (pres. 1944), Fayette County bar assns. Rotarian (pres. 1941). Clubs: Lexington (pres. 1960), Idle Hour Country (Lexington). Home: 2721 Tates Creek Rd Lexington KY 40502 Office: Citizens Union Nat Bank Bldg Lexington KY 40507

GESSMAN, ALBERT MILOSLAV, educator; b. Vienna, Austria, Dec. 12, 1916 (came to U.S. 1954, naturalized 1959); s. Albert Julius and Natalia (Buric) G.; M.A., Charles U. (Prague), 1939; Ph.D., Rudolf U. (Vienna), 1950; m. Anna Blazek, Dec. 29, 1940; children—Milada, Nadina, Milan. Prof. modern langs. Acad. Commerce, Mlada Boleslav, Czechoslovakia, 1939-48, editor Narodni Republika, 1945-48, headmaster Inst. Modern Languages, 1947-48; intelligence officer U.S. Army in Europe, 1950-54; head dept. modern langs., prof. Talladega Coll., 1954-61; chmn., prof. dept. classics and ancient studies U. South Fla., 1961—, editor-in-chief The U. South Fla. Language Quarterly, 1962—; lectr. adult edn. Congregation Shaarai Zedek, Tampa, Fla.; cons. The Choice, Middletown, Conn., 1969—. Served with AUS, 1950-54. Mem. Czechoslovak Soc. Arts and Scis. in America, Coll. Language Assn. (mem. exec. com. 1959-61), Birmingham Anthropol. Soc. (pres. 1959-60), Torch Internat. (pres. Tampa chpt. 1967-68), Linguistic Soc. Am., Am. Class. League, Ala. Archeol. Soc., Nat. Geographic Soc. Author: The Codes of Language, 1964; The Tongue of the Romans, 1970; The Tongues of the Bible, 1971. Home: 10905 N 19th St Tampa FL 33612 Office: U South Fla 4202 Fowler Av Tampa FL 33620

GESUND, HANS, educator; b. Vienna, Austria, Sept. 18, 1928 (came to U.S. 1940, derivative citizen); s. Carl and Else (Sternberg) G.; B.E. with honors, Yale, 1950, M. Engring., 1953, D. Engring., 1958; m. Irmgard Orth, Jan. 28, 1951; children—Peter J., Ann M. Instr. civil engring. Yale, 1954-58; asst. prof. structural engring. U. Ky., Lexington, 1958-60, asso. prof., 1960-64, prof., 1964—. Served from lt. to capt. AUS, 1950-52, 61-62, now maj. Res. ret. Registered profl. engr., Conn., Ky. Fellow Am. Soc. C.E.; mem. Am. Concrete Inst., Am. Soc. Engring. Edn., Am. Soc. Testing and Materials, Internat. Assn. Bridge and Structural Engring., Internat. Assn. Shell Structures, Sigma Xi, Tau Beta Pi, Chi Epsilon. Jewish religion (trustee 1965—, pres. congregation 1971-73). Mem. B'nai B'rith (dir. lodge). Home: 844 Celia Lane Lexington KY 40504

GETLEIN, FRANK, journalist; b. Ansonia, Conn., Mar. 6, 1921; s. Frank J. and Katherine (Sheehan) G.; B.S., Holy Cross Coll., 1942; M.A., Catholic U. Am., 1947; m. Dorothy Woollen, May 26, 1943 (dec. Aug. 1965); children—Christine, Stephen, Mary, William, Karl; m. 2d, Jean Franklin, Apr. 16, 1966. Art editor Milw. Jour., 1956-59; art critic New Republic, 1956-67, Washington Star, 1961—; syndicated polit. columnist Washington Close-Up, 1965—. Mem. Fulbright com. on art and architecture, 1961-64; mem. acquisitions com. Pan Am. Union, 1965—. Served with inf. AUS, 1942-45; MTO. Decorated Purple Heart; recipient award of merit Lotus Club, 1963. Mem. Internat. Assn. Art Critics. Clubs: Cosmos, Washington Press (Washington). Author: Christianity in Art, 1958; Christianity in Modern Art, 1959; A Modern Demonology, 1962; The Bite of the Print, 1963; Abraham Rattner, 1961; Jack Levine, 1965; Herman Maril, 1967; Walt Kuhn, 1967; Peter Blume, 1968; 100 Art Treasures, 1968; The Politics of Paranoia, 1969; Milton Hebald, 1971; Playing Soldier, 1971; (opera libretto) The Decorator, 1959. Home: 915 Prince St Alexandria VA 22314 Office: 225 Virginia Av SE Washington DC 20003

GETTIG, CARL WILLIAM, optometrist; b. Cleve., June 15 1928; s. Edmund Elmer and Arlie (Williams) G.; O.D., No. Ill. Coll. Optometry, 1949; student U. Ala., 1952-53, Spring Hill Coll., 1957; A.B., Oberlin Coll., 1962, B.M., 1962; attended Mozarteum, Salzburg, Austria, 1959-60. Individual practice optometry, Norwalk, O., 1949-50, Mobile, Ala., 1952-58, Foley, Ala., 1963—; part-time music tchr., Foley and Robertsdale, Ala., 1955—. Co-founder Performing Arts Assn., Foley, 1967, pres,, 1968-69, 72-73. Served with AUS, 1950-52. Mem. Am. Optometric Assn., Am. Optometric Found., Am. Pub. Health Assn., Am. Guild Organists, Nat. Fellowship Meth. Musicians, A.L.A., Am. Forestry Assn. Composer piano sonata, 1961. Home: 1515 N McKenzie St Foley AL 36535 Office: 1517 N McKenzie St Foley AL 36535

GETTINGS, BRIAN P., U.S. dist atty. for eastern Va. Address: 8331 Queen Elizabeth Blvd Annandale VA 22003*

GETTY, JAMES RAHN, railroad exec.; b. Oaks, Pa., Sept. 26, 1914; s. Claude W. and Lorene (Stadon) G.; B.R., U. Pa., 1936; m. Jean Hutchison, Apr. 14, 1956; 1 son, James Hutchison; 1 stepson, Winfield A. Worth III. Tour agt. Am. Express Co., Chgo., San Diego, summers 1934, 35; ticket agt. Pa. R.R., Wilmington, Del., 1936; passenger agt., Seaboard R.R., Phila., 1937-40, dist. passenger agt., 1940-43, gen. passenger agt., Miami, Fla., 1943-48, passenger traffic mgr., Norfolk, Va., 1948-52, head gen. passenger traffic mgr., Richmond, Va., 1952; v.p. passenger traffic Seaboard Coast Line, R.R., Richmond, 1967—; v.p. passenger traffic Louisville & Nashville R.R., 1972—; dir. Nat. Ry. Publ. Co., N.Y.C., Richmond Terminal Ry. Co. Mem. travel adv. com. U.S. Dept. Commerce, Richmond bd. Bank of Va. Decorated order of So. Cross (Brazil); Distinguished Transp. Service award Costa Rica. Mem. Am. Assn. Passenger Traffic Officers (pres. 1962-63), Nat. Assn. Travel Orgns. (former dir.), Nat. Def. Transp. Assn. (life). Episcopalian. Kiwanian (dir. Richmond). Home: 15 Summit Dr Glenbrooke Hills Richmond VA 23229 Office: PO Box 27581 3600 W Broad St Richmond VA 23261

GETTYS, THOMAS SMITHWICK, congressman; b. Rock Hill, S.C., June 19, 1912; s. John E. and Maud (Martin) G.; student Clemson U., 1929-30; A.B., Erskine Coll., 1933; postgrad. Duke, Winthrop Coll.; m. Mary Phillips White, Dec. 9, 1947; children—Julia Martin, Sara Elizabeth. Tchr., coach Rock Hill High Sch., 1933-35; prin. Central Sch., Rock Hill, 1935-41; sec. to Congressman Richards, 1941-51, postmaster, Rock Hill, 1951-54: admitted to S.C. bar, 1953; practice in Rock Hill, 1954-64; mem. 88th to 93d congresses from 5th S.C. Dist., mem. banking and currency com., house adminstrn. com. Pres. Rock Hill YMCA, 1960; chmn. Rock Hill United Fund campaign, 1955; chmn. trustees Rock Hill Sch. Dist. 3. Served with USNR, World War II; PTO. Mem. Am., S.C., York County bar assns., Am. Legion, V.F.W., Rock Hill C. of C. (past pres.). Democrat. Presbyn. (elder). Elk, Rotarian (past pres. Rock Hill). Home: Rock Hill SC 29730 Office: House Office Bldg Washington DC 20515

GETZ, MILTON GERALD, orthodontist; b. Houston, Nov. 7, 1929; s. Jacob Charles and Rose (Markowitz) G.; B.A., U. Tex., 1950, D.D.S., 1955; M.S., U. Houston, 1951; postgrad. U. Ala., 1958, Washington U., 1961, U. Tenn., 1970; m. Shirley Sherman, Mar. 6, 1953; children— Michael David, Karen Lee, Ricky Bryan. Instr. chemistry U. Houston, 1950; individual practice orthodontics, Port Arthur, Tex., 1956—. Dir. First State Bank of Groves. Cons. Hughen Sch. Crippled Children, 1958—, Sunnyside Speech and Hearing Clinic, 1958—. Trustee Port Arthur (Tex.) Ind. Sch. Dist., 1969—, pres., 1970. Bd. dirs. Community Home. Served to capt. USAF, 1955-57. Fellow Acad. Internat. Medicine and Dentistry; mem. Am. Assn. Orthodontists, Am., Tex. dental assns., Southwestern Soc. Orthodontists, Sabine Dist. Dental Soc. (dir. 1969-72). Jewish religion (trustee 1958-69). Mason (32 deg., Shriner), Rotarian. Club: Towne (Port Arthur, Tex.). Home: 3849 Purdue St Port Arthur TX 77640 Office: 3701 Doctors Dr Port Arthur TX 77640

GEVANTMAN, LEWIS HERMAN, chemist, govt. ofcl.; b. N.Y.C., Sept. 12, 1921; s. Benjamin and Ida (Goldberg) G.; B.Engring., Johns Hopkins, 1942; Ph.D. in Phys. Chemistry, U. Notre Dame, 1951; m. Leatrice Black, Aug. 22, 1948; children—Sandra Cay, Janis Mara. Chem. operator Johns Hopkins, also Bethlehem Steel Co., 1942-43; research chemist Clinton Labs., Manhattan Project, 1943-46; supervisory research chemist U.S. Naval Radiol. Def. Lab., San Francisco, 1951-56, acting head applied research br., 1956-59, head radiation chemistry br., 1959-61, sci. research adminstr., head chem. tech. div., 1961-64; sr. sci. adviser U.S. mission Internat. Atomic Energy Agy., 1964-67; program mgr. Office of Standard Reference Data, Nat. Bur. Standards, 1967—, U.S. dept. Commerce coordinator NBS-AEC programs, 1967—, Nuclear Sci. and Engring. Corp., 1956-59; mem. Bd. Civil Service Examiners, 1958-61. Mem. Am. Chem. Soc. (chmn. civil def. com. No. Cal. sect. 1961-64, civil def. and disaster com. 1969—), Am. Soc. Testing Materials (ad hoc com. dosimetry), A.A.A.S., Radiation Research Soc., N.Y. Acad. Scis., Sigma Xi. Contbr. articles to profl. jours. Patentee in field. Address: Nat Bur Standards Washington DC 20234

GEWIN, WALTER PETTUS, judge; b. Nanafalia, Ala., Dec. 9, 1908; s. John Walker and Julia (Crenshaw) G.; A.B. cum laude, Birmingham So. Coll., 1930; B.A. in Library Sci., Emory U., 1932; LL.B., U. Ala., 1935; m. Anna Fidelia Sledge, Dec. 5, 1936; children—Walter Pettus, James William, Margaret Juliette. Admitted to Ala. bar, 1935, practiced in Birmingham, 1935, Greensboro, 1936-51, Tuscaloosa, 1951—; state pros., Hales County, Ala., 1942-51; judge Fifth Circuit, U.S. Ct. Appeals, 1961—. Mem. Code Com. of Ala., 1940. Mem. Ala. Ho. of Reps., 1939-43; mem. Ala. Democratic Exec. Com., 1943-47. Served as sgt., judge adv. gen. dept., AUS, 1944-45. Mem. Am., Ala. (pres), Tuscaloosa bar assns., Am. Coll. Trial Lawyers. Presbyn. (elder). Mason (Shriner), Kiwanian. Home: 35 The Downs Tuscaloosa AL 35401 Office: Federal Bldg Tuscaloosa AL

GEYELIN, PHILIP LAUSSAT, journalist; b. Devon, Pa., Feb. 27, 1923; s. Emile Camille and Cecily (Barnes) G.; grad. Episcopal Acad., Overbrook, Pa., 1940; B.A., Yale, 1944; m. Cecilia Sherman Parker, Jan. 28, 1950; children—Mary Sherman, Emile Camille, Philip Laussat, Cecily, Parker. With Washington bur. A.P., 1946-47; mem. staff Wall St. Jour., 1947-66, diplomatic corr., 1960-67; mem. editorial staff Washington Post, 1967—, editor editorial page, 1968—. Bd. dirs. Alliance Francaise, Washington, 1964—, Served to 1st lt. USMCR, 1943-46. Fellow Inst. Politics, Harvard Sch. Govt., 1967; recipient Pulitzer prize for editorial writing, 1969. Clubs: Gridiron, Metropolitan, Overseas Writers, Federal City (Washington). Author: Lyndon B. Johnson and the World, 1966. Home: 4511 Cathedral Av NW Washington DC 20016 Office: 1515 L St Washington DC 20005

GHEESLING, JOHN LINDSEY, motel exec.; b. Ashford, Ala., Dec. 6, 1927; s. John Lindsey and Jesse (Collier) G.; student Berry Schs., Rome, Ga.; m. Rose Tillich, May 15, 1949; children—John Lindsey III, Debra Eve, Karen Jo, Richard Peter, Ann Collier. Various positions to sr. insp. Retail Credit Co., 1950-69; owner Bikini Motel, Panama City Beach, Fla., 1957—. Mem. Planning Bd., Panama City Beach, 1970—, Panama City News Bur., 1968—. Served with USNR, 1946-50. Named Good Neighbor by local news media, 1971, Outstanding Businessman by news media, 1971. Mem. Bay County C. of C. Lion. Address: 11000 W Hwy 98 Panama City Beach FL 32401

GHIARDI, JOHN FELIX LINUS, govt. ofcl.; b. Negaunee, Mich., Mar. 6, 1918; s. Martin Catherine (Chiabotto) G.; B.A., Sacred Heart Sem., 1939; M.A., Catholic U., 1947; m. Lucille Torreano, Apr. 7, 1947; children—Christopher, Giancarlo. With U.S. Treasury Office of Internat. Finance, Washington, 1949-66, treas. rep. middle east, 1950-53, Rome, Italy, 1954-66; dept. asst. Sec. Internat. Monetary Affairs, State Dept., Washington, 1966-68; adv., internat. div., bd. govs. Fed. Reserve System, Washington, 1968-72; dir. office econ. research State Dept., Washington, 1972—. Served with AUS, 1942-46. Decorated Bronze Star, Purple Heart. Mem. Am. Econ. Assn. Roman Catholic. K.C. Home: 12 Park Overlook Ct Bethesda MA 20034 Office: 21st and C Sts Washington DC 20520

GHOLSON, HUNTER MAURICE, lawyer; b. Columbus, Miss., Feb. 19, 1933; s. Leon Carter and Marie (McDoniell) G.; B.A., U. Miss., 1954, LL.B., 1955, J.D. 1968; m. Hortense Jones, June 3, 1961; children—Emily Jones, William Webster. Admitted to Miss. bar, 1955; since practiced in Columbus; mem. firm William G. Burgin, 1955-56, Burgin, Gholson, Hicks & Nichols, and predecessor firm, 1959—. Sec., dir. Realty Rentals Corp., 1961—, Meml. Leasing Co., 1962—, Quality Products, Inc., 1963—; dir. Columbus Bottlers, Inc., Egger's dept. store. Chmn., Lowndes County Republican Party, 1960-64. Sec., dir. Columbus Ednl. Found., 1965-70; founder, dir. Stephen D. Lee Found. Served to lt. USNR. 1956-59. Mem. Am., Miss. (exec. com. jr. bar conf. 1963-64), Lowndes County (sec. 1960-62) bar assn., Lowndes County Hist. Soc. (pres. 1964-65), Columbus C. of C. (dir. 1969—), Ole Miss Alumni Assn. (chpt. pres. 1964-65), Claiborne Soc., Phi Delta Theta, Phi Delta Phi. Episcopalian. Kiwanian (v.p. 1964, dir. 1960-64). Home: 1100 N Sixth St Columbus MS 39701 Office: 516 N 2d Av Columbus MS 39701

GHOLSTON, LAFAYETTE EDWONE, agronomist; b. Baldwyn, Miss., July 27, 1919; s. Marcus D. and S. Alice (Camp) G.; B.S., Miss State U., 1942, M.S., 1947; m. Vadie Lorene LeCroy, Nov. 7, 1942; children—Robert Ed, Patricia Alice. Instr. agronomy Miss. State U., State College, 1947-48; asst. agronomist Miss. Agr. Extension Service, State College, 1948-54, asso. agronomist, 1954-62, leader soil testing dept., 1962—. Served to 1st lt. AUS, 1942-45. Mem. Am. Soc. Agronomy (pres. Miss. sect. 1962), Miss. State U. Alumni Assn. (chpt. pres. 1960, 61, state membership chmn. 1960, 64), Alpha Zeta. Mem. Christian Ch. Mason. Contbr. articles to Coop. Extension Service publs. Home: Route 1 Box 5-A Starkville MS 39759 Office: Box 5405 State College MS 39762

GIAM, CHOO SENG, educator; b. Singapore, Apr. 2, 1931; s. Chong-Hing and Eng-Keow (Tan) G.; M.S., U. Sask., Can., 1961, Ph.D., 1963; m. Mun-Yung Ng, Feb. 25, 1956; children—Benny Y.B., Patrick Y.Y., Michael Y.K. Research chemist Imperial Oil Research Dept., Sarnia, Can., 1963-64; postdoctoral fellow Pa. State U., 1964-65; research asso. U. Cal., Irvine, 1965-66; asst. prof. Tex. A. and M. U., College Station, 1966-70, asso. prof., 1970—. Mem. Am., Canadian chem. socs., Royal Inst. Chemistry, N.Y. Acad. Scis., Sigma Xi, Phi Lambda Upsilon. Contbr. articles profl. jours. Patentee in field. Home: 1108 Dona Dr Bryan TX 77801 Office: Chemistry Dept Tex A and M U College Station TX 77803

GIAMMITTORIO, GEORGE MARVIN, judge; b. Alexandria, Va., May 6, 1921; s. David and Rosina (Recchiuti) G.; LL.B., George Washington U., 1941, LL.M., 1942; m. Mary Lucy Parrish, Nov. 16, 1946; children—Eugene Robert, David Carrington, Rosemary Parrish, Ruthanne Miller, Gregory Mark. Admitted to Va. bar, 1942; practiced in Alexandria, 1946-64; judge Corp. Ct., Alexandria, 1964—. Pres., chmn. bd., dir. Peoples Bank & Trust Co. of Fairfax. Chmn. Alexandria council Boy Scouts Am., 1955-56; life mem. Friendship Fire Co. Co-founder, pres., regent Ascension Acad. Served with USNR, 1942-46. Recipient Outstanding Citizenship award Order of Eagles, 1965. Mem. Am., Fed., Va. bar assns., Am. Legion (past post comdr.), Sigma Delta Kappa. Roman Catholic. K.C. Home: 2416 Ridge Road Dr Alexandria VA 22302 Office: City Hall Alexandria VA 22314

GIARDINI, ARMANDO ALFONZO, educator; b. Salamanca, N.Y., June 5, 1925; s. Giardino B. and Rose (Ferrara) G.; B.S., U. Mich., 1951, M.S., 1953, Ph.D., 1956; m. Anne Morton Johnston, Aug. 20, 1950; children— Michele, Richard, Melissa, Peter. Phys. scientist electrotech. lab. U.S. Bur. Mines, Norris, Tenn., 1952; sr. research engr. research and devel. div. Carborundum Co., Niagara Falls, N.Y., 1953-55; physicist, project leader high pressure research U.S. Army Electronics Lab., Ft. Monmouth, N.J., 1957-65; prof. geology U. Ga., 1965—; prof. U. Cal. Lawrence Radiation Lab. at Livermore, summers 1966-67, 69. Served with USNR, 1943-46. Mem. Am. Mineral. Soc., Am. Geophys. Union, A.A.A.S., Am. Soc. M.E. (chmn. com. pressure tech. 1965—), Sigma Xi. Editor: High Pressure Measurement, 1962. Contbr. articles profl. jours. Patentee in field. Home: 180 Lanier Ct Athens GA 30601

GIARRUSSO, ALFRED PETER, educator; b. New Orleans, Mar. 11, 1913; s. James I. and Anna (Blumstein) G.; student Loyola U., New Orleans, 1933-35; B.E., Tulane U., 1948, M.Ed., 1958; postgrad. La. State U., 1959-60; Ed.D., U. Ark., 1969; m. Zona Turnoy, Sept. 29, 1945; children—Judy Mary, Jerel Monte (Mrs. Robert DeLoney Downing), Joel Iver, Peter James. With R.P. Bellande Co., Biloxi, Miss., 1935-39, Higgins Industries, New Orleans, 1939-41, New Orleans Recreation Dept., 1947-50; supr. Delgado Trades and Tech. Inst., New Orleans, 1950-69; prof. edn., dir. counseling Delgado Coll., 1969—. Tchr. indsl. relations to supr. in industry and for City of New Orleans, 1957—; maj. aux. div. New Orleans Police Dept., 1957—; lectr. human relations New Orleans Police Acad. Served with USNR, 1942-45. Col. on staff Gov. Long, 1958-60, Gov. Davis, 1961-64. Mem. Am. Personnel and Guidance Assn., Am., La. vocational assns., Central Labor Council, La. Fedn. Tchrs. (exec. bd.), La. Guidance Assn., Phi Delta Kappa. Democrat. Roman Catholic. Home: 7943 Edgelake Ct New Orleans LA 70126 Office: 615 City Park Av New Orleans LA 70119

GIBBIN, DON ERIC, dentist; b. Rochester, N.Y., Feb. 2, 1923; s. Clifford Lynn and Helen Olivia (Ericson) G.; student Oberlin Coll., 1940-43; D.D.S., U. Pa., 1946; m. Joyclyn Watrous, July 1, 1948 (div. 1964); children—Candice Lynn, Holly Ann, Don Eric; m. 2d, Eleanore Iris MacCutcheon, Apr. 2, 1964 (div. Dec. 1965); m. 3d, Shiela Stover Smith, May 28, 1966; 1 son, Christopher Holliday; stepchildren—Sherrill, Douglas, Lee Hamilton, David Ashley, Jeffrey Lore. Pvt. practice dentistry, Rochester, N.Y., 1948-50, Alexandria, Va., 1955—; dir. Alexandria (Va.) Dental X-ray Lab, Inc., 1971—. Mem. Alexandria Welfare Council, 1963-67. Served to lt. (j.g.) Dental Corps, USNR, 1946-48, maj. Dental Corps, AUS, 1950-55. Decorated Bronze Star medal, Army Commendation Ribbon. Mem. Royal Soc. Health, Am., Va. dental assns., Alexandria, No. Va. dental socs., Inst. Advanced Dental Research, Am. Soc. Preventive Dentistry, Acad. Gen. Dentistry, Acad. Oral Implantology. Presbyn. Club: Optimist (Alexandria). Home: 6919 Harrison Lane Alexandria VA 22306 Office: 3700 King St Alexandria VA 22302

GIBBONS, ALAN CLARK, educator; b. N.Y.C., Mar. 25, 1938; s. Maurice Clark and Josefina (Abad) G.; B.A., Carleton Coll., 1959; B.D., U. Chgo., 1963; Ph.D. (Fulbright scholar to Germany, 1963-64, 64-65, fellow Deutscher Akademischer Austauschdienst, 1965-69, 71), Albert-Ludwigs-Universitat, Freiburg, Germany, 1969; m. Ingrid Poertner, May 27, 1967; children—David Alan, Steven Frederick, Adrienne-Silke. Instr., Lenoir Rhyne Coll., Hickory, N.C., 1969-70; asst. prof. dept. philosophy East Carolina U., Greenville, N.C., 1970—. Mem. Internat. Husserl and Phenomenological Research Soc., Internat. Phenomenological Soc., Am. Assn. U. Profs., Soc. Phenomenology and Existential Philosophy, So. Soc. Philosophy and Psychology (lectr. 1972). Author: Religion und Sprache, 1970. Office: Dept Philosophy East Carolina U Greenville NC 27834

GIBBONS, CARLOS, assn. exec. Sec.-treas. S.C. Edn. Assn., Columbia. Address: 421 Zimal Crest Dr Columbia SC 29210*

GIBBONS, JOHN WILLIAM, pub. relations exec.; b. Salt Lake City, Mar. 16, 1907; s. John Wood and Margaret (Stuart) G.; student Mount Angel Jr. Coll., 1924-26; A.B., U. Notre Dame, 1930; m. Marcella Marie Butsch, July 28, 1929; children—John, Mary (Mrs. George John), Joan (Mrs. Phil Devore), Sally (Mrs. James Wilding), Susan. With South Bend (Ind.) Tribune, 1930-36; dir. South Bend Safety Council, 1936-39; mgr. pub. relations dept. Automobile Mfrs. Assn., 1939-42; dir. pub. relations Automotive Safety Found., Washington, 1942—. Bd. dirs. Nat. Safety Council. Recipient Distinguished Service award Nat. Safety Council, 1969. Mem. Pub. Relations Soc. Am. (charter mem., chpt. pres. 1953, dist. chmn. 1961, sec. pres. 1966), Inst. Traffic Engrs. (hon.), Internat. Assn. Chiefs Police (hon.). Roman Catholic. Club: Nat. Press (Washington). Home: 9504 Crosby Rd Silver Spring MD 20910 Office: Ring Bldg Washington DC 20036

GIBBONS, JOSEPH HARRISON, educator; b. Turbeville, S.C., Sept. 4, 1934; s. James Harry and Roxie (Morris) G.; B.S. in Chem. Engring., U. S.C., 1956; M.S. in Chem. Engring., U. Pitts., 1958, Ph.D., 1961; m. Geneva Emmalean Floyd, June 10, 1956; children—Karen June, Lisa Ann. With Westinghouse Electric Corp., 1956-63, sr. engr., 1962-63; asso. prof. chem. engring. U. S.C., Columbia, 1963—. Mem. Am. Inst. Chem. Engrs., Am. Chem. Soc., Am. Soc. Engring. Edn., Jr. Engrs. Tech. Soc. (state coordinator 1966—), Phi Beta Kappa, Tau Beta Pi, Omicron Delta Kappa. Baptist (deacon). Home: 6300 Macon Rd Columbia SC 29209

GIBBONS, SAM MELVILLE, congressman; b. Tampa, Fla., Jan. 20, 1920; s. Gunby and Jessie Kirk (Cralle) G.; LL.B., U. Fla., 1947; LL.D., U. So. Fla., 1969; m. Martha Hanley, Sept. 14, 1946; children—Clifford, Mark, Timothy. Admitted to Fla. bar, 1947; mem. Fla. Ho. of Reps. from Hillsborough County, 1952-58, Fla. Senate, 1958-62; mem. 88th-89th U.S. congresses, 10th Dist. Fla., 90th-92d congress, 6th dist. Fla. Bd. dirs. Hillsborough County Heart Assn., Hillsborough County Guidance Center, Fla. Mental Health Assn.; founder, 1st pres. U.S. Fla. Found., 1958. Served to maj. AUS, 1941-45; ETO. Decorated Bronze Star medal; named Outstanding Young Man, Tampa Jr. C. of C., 1954; recipient President's award Tampa C. of C., 1955. Mem. Tampa (dir.), Hillsborough (dir.) bar assns., Greater Tampa C. of C. (dir.), Democrat. Presbyn. (deacon). Home: 940 S Sterling Av Tampa FL 33609 Office: House Office Bldg Washington DC 20515

GIBBS, FREDERICK H., educator; b. Knoxville, Tenn., Mar. 31, 1920; s. William Aaron and Lena Margaret (Durham) G.; student U. Tenn., 1920-21; B.S., U. Md., 1958; M.H.A., U. Minn., 1959; m. Ivy Lois Brooks, May 1, 1931; children—Frederick William, Thomas Cecil, Helen Lois (Mrs. John J. Justy), Mary Barbara (Mrs. Thomas Keith Treichel). Salesman, asst. supt. Cosmopolitan Life Ins. Co., Nashville, 1920-25; joined U.S. Army, 1925, advanced through grades to col.; with Transport Service, 1930-32, hosp. insp. 4th Service Command, 1943-45, exec. office surgeon Far East Command, 1945-48, exec. officer plans and operations Div. Surgeon Gen., 1948-52, organizer Surgeon Gen.'s Hosp. Mgmt. Research Program, 1948-52, dir. dept. adminstrn. Army Med. Service Sch., San Antonio, 1952-56; ret., 1957; dir. grad. program in hosp. adminstrn. Baylor U., 1952-56; for Found. Hosp. Adminstrs., Washington, 1956-70; prof. hosp. adminstrn., coordinator-dir., chmn. dept. health care adminstrn. George Washington U., Washington, 1959-67, Gordon A. Friesen prof. health care adminstrn., 1969-72, emeritus, 1972—; ednl. cons., 1957—; cons., Cath. Hosp. Assn., 1956-57, Office Def. Moblzn., 1960-61, Columbia U's Health Care Continuation Studies, 1956-67; vis. prof. U San Paulo, 1964. Pres. Assn. Univ. Programs in Hosp. Adminstrn., 1964-65, mem. long term care task force, 1965-72; cons. chief med. dir. VA, 1961—. Recipient awards for outstanding ednl. contbns. Surgeon Gen., Fed. Med. Service, 1965, 1970. Fellow Am. Coll. Hosp. Adminstrs. (book awards com., policy com. 1960-68, adv. editorial bd. 1970-72), Am. Coll. Nursing Home Adminstrs. (hon., com. on ethics 1970—); mem. Inter-Agy. Insts. Alumni Assn. (pres. 1953, distinguished service award 1968), Am. Hosp. Assn. (council on adminstrv. practice 1951-55, chmn. com. on methods improvement 1954-55), Am. Nursing Home Assn. (hon.; trustee ednl. trust, Better Life award for lasting contributions to institutions for health care of aged, 1970), Am. Assn. U. Profs., Am. Pub. Health Assn. Contbr. to mags. Home: Box 29 Deale MD 20751 Office: George Washington U Washington DC 20006

GIBBS, JAMES ALANSON, geologist; b. Wichita Falls, Tex., June 18, 1935; s. James Ford and Clovis (Robinson) G.; B.S., U. Okla., 1957, M.S., 1962; m. Judith Walker, June 18, 1966; children—Ford W., John A. Geologist, Cal. Co., New Orleans, 1961-63, Lafayette, La., 1963-64; cons. geologist, oil producer, Dallas, 1964—. Served with USNR, 1957-59. Certified profl. geologist. Mem. Dallas Geol. Soc., Am. Assn. Petroleum Geologists, Am. Inst. Profl. Geologists, Geol. Information Library of Dallas (v.p.), Soc. Ind. Profl. Earth Scientists, Sigma Xi, Sigma Gamma Epsilon, Phi Delta Theta, Petroleum Engrs. Club: Dallas. Republican. Methodist. Home: 6223 Park Lane Dallas TX 75225 Office: Exchange Bank Bldg Dallas TX 75235

GIBBS, RICHARD HENRY, social worker exec.; b. Richmond, Va., Mar. 2, 1925; s. Herbert P. and Lillian (Crew) G.; B.S., Va. Commonwealth U., 1946, M.S.W., 1948; children—Richard H., Robert, Betsy. Dir. teen age activities YWCA, Richmond, 1948-50; child welfare worker State Dept. Welfare, Richmond, 1950-51; casework supr. VA Hosp., Richmond, 1951-56; chief med. assistance div. Dept. Pub. Welfare, Norfolk, Va., 1956-57; med. social cons. State Dept. Health, Richmond, 1957-64, dir. social work, 1964—. Pres. Va. Council Social Welfare, 1971—; bd. dirs. Blue Ridge Inst. So. Community Service Execs., 1966-69; adv. com. Sch. Social Work Va. Commonwealth U., 1970—. Served with USNR, 1942-45. Mem. Nat. Assn. Social Workers, Phi Delta Theta. Home: 7602 Foxhall Lane Richmond VA 23228 Office: 109 Governor St Richmond VA 23219

GIBBS, ROBERT HENRY, JR., zoologist; b. New London, Conn., July 30, 1929; s. Robert Henry and Elizabeth (Kilgore) G.; A.B., Cornell U., 1951, Ph.D., 1955; m. Frigga Katharina Elizabeth Bahr, Mar. 2, 1963; children—Elizabeth, Hans-Martin, Hans-Thomas, Adrienne. Asst. prof. State U. N.Y. at Plattsburgh, 1955-56; research asso. in marine biology Woods Hole Oceanographic Inst., Woods Hole, Mass., 1956-58; asst. prof. Boston U., 1958-62, asso. prof., 1962-63; asso. curator, div. fieshes U.S. Nat. Mus., Washington, 1963-67, curator, 1967—, chmn. dept. vertebrate zoology, 1972—. Mem. editorial bd. Fishes of Western N. Atlantic, 1966—. Mem. Am. Soc. Ichthyologists and Herpetologists (bd. govs. editorial bd. treas. 1967-71), Am. Ornithol. Union, Am. Soc. Mammalogists, Am. Soc. Limnology and Oceanography, Soc. Systematic Zoology, Soc. Study of Evolution, Marine Biol. Assn. U.K. Home: 4017 Simms Dr Kensington MD 20795 Office: Div Fishes US National Museum Washington DC 20560

GIBSON, ALLYN DOUGLAS, social worker; b. Lakeland, Fla., Jan. 26, 1932; s. Horace Wood and Elizabeth (Sneed) G.; A.A., Gardner-Webb Coll., 1952; B.A., Wake Forest U., 1956; M.S.W., Fla State U., 1961; spl. certificate U. Chgo., 1968. Social worker Fla. Dept. Pub. Welfare, Lakeland, 1957-59; sr. caseworker, supr. Family Service Agy., Ft. Lauderdale, Fla., 1961-67; instr., field instr. Barry Coll. Sch. Social Work, Miami, Fla., 1967-69, asst. prof., 1969—; field work instr. Fla. State U., 1963-67; adj. asst. prof. Fla. Atlantic U., Boca Raton, 1971—. Social work cons. Plantation Nursing Home, Fla., 1969-70. Served with AUS, 1953-55, Mem. Nat. Assn. Social Workers (chpt. pres. 1966-68, chpt. del. 1966—), Am. Assn. U. Profs., Acad. Certified Social Workers, Council on Social Work Edn. Home: 3550 Galt Ocean Dr Fort Lauderdale FL 33308 Office: 11300 NE 2d Av Miami Shores FL 33161

GIBSON, AVERY, TV co. exec.; b. Washington, Nov. 23, 1926; s. Percy D. and Ruth (Baker) G.; B.A., U. N.C., 1949; m. Murray Davis, Aug. 31, 1957. Dir. promotion WTOB, Winston-Salem, N.C., 1949-54; v.p. charge research H-R Television, Inc., N.Y.C., 1954-63, v.p. charge H-R Facts div., 1963-66; cons. to pres. Am. Research Bureau subsidiary Control Data, 1966-71, exec. dir. TV council, 1969-71; pres. Camelot Consultants, Hayes, Va., 1971—. Spl. cons. computer standardization Sta. Reps. Assn.; chmn. TV Bur. Advt. Research Adv. Com., 1962-66; pres. Radio-TV Research Council, 1964-65. Mem. Internat. Radio TV Soc., Nat. Acad. TV Arts and Scis. Contbr. articles to trade mags. Address: Camelot on the Severn Route 1 Hayes VA 23072

GIBSON, BEN TERRELL, JR., ins. and real estate co. exec.; b. Union S.C., July 26, 1929; s. Ben Terrell and Marie (Garner) G.; B.S. in Bus. Adminstrn., Davidson Coll., 1951; m. Amelia Ann Douglass, Oct. 16, 1954; children—Ben Terrell III, Preston D. Partner, Gibson Agy., Union, 1951-53, owner, mgr., 1955—; treas., mgr., dir. Cherokee Estates, Inc., Union, 1954—; sec., dir. Cedarbrook, Inc., Union, 1965—; pres., dir. Aimco., Inc., Union. Served with USNR, 1948-49. Mem. Nat., S.C. assns. ins. agts. and realtors, Union Bd. Realtors (pres.), Union Bd. Ins. Agts. (pres.), S.C. (dir.), Union County (dir., pres.) chambers commerce, Nat. Skeet Shooting Assn., Pi Kappa Alpha. Methodist (trustee, mem. choir). Elk, Rotarian (pres., dir.). Home: 1 Cherokee Pl Union SC 29379 Office: 105 S Gadberry St Union SC 29379

GIBSON, DANIEL MORGAN, JR., mech. engr.; b. Seguin, Tex., Aug. 1, 1932; s. Daniel Morgan and Marian (Engel) G.; B.S., Tex. A. and M. U., 1953, M.S., 1958; M.A., Princeton, 1960, Ph.D., 1961; m. Betty Ann Powers, Dec. 20, 1952; children—Daniel Morgan III, Michael, David, Diane. Staff scientist Convair Aerospace div. Gen. Dynamics Corp., Ft. Worth, 1961—; adj. prof. nuclear engring. Tex. A. and M. U., 1964—. Served to 1st lt. AUS, 1953-55. Mem. Am. Soc. M.E., Am. Inst. Aeros. and Astronautics, Sigma Xi, Phi Kappa Phi, Tau Beta Pi. Home: 6220 Greenway Rd Fort Worth TX 76116

GIBSON, EDWARD GEORGE, astronaut; b. Buffalo, Nov. 8, 1936; s. Calder Alexander and Geraldine (Shannon) G.; B.S., U. Rochester, 1959; M.S., Cal. Inst. Tech., 1960, Ph.D. in Engring. and Physics, 1964; m. Julie Anne Volk, Aug. 22, 1959; children—Jannet Lynn, John Edward, Julie Ann, Joseph Michael. With Aronutronic research lab. Philco Corp., Newport Beach, Cal., 1964-65; astronaut Manned Spacecraft Center, Houston, 1965—. Solar physics Subcom. NASA. Mem. Am. Astron. Soc., Inst. Physics, Am. Inst. Aeros. and Astronauts, Sigma Xi, Tau Beta Pi, Theta Chi. Home: 18611 Martinique Dr Nassau Bay Houston TX 77058 Office: Code (CB) Manned Spacecraft Center Houston TX 77058

GIBSON, GEORGE DANDRIDGE, lawyer; b. Richmond, Va., May 8, 1904; s. George Armistead and Alice (McClung) G.; B.A., U. Va., 1924; A.M., Harvard, 1925, LL.B., 1928; m. Edith Ludlow Sedgwick, Feb. 23, 1935 (div. 1966); children—Pamela Sedgwick (Mrs. John T. Farrar), Alice Armistead (Mrs. Malcolm W. Stothers); m. 2d, Roberta Pearson Grymes, Aug. 26, 1966. Admitted to Va. bar, 1928, since practiced in Richmond; asso. Hunton, Williams, Gay, & Gibson and predecessor firms, 1931—, partner, 1934—; gen. counsel Va. Electric & Power Co., Richmond, 1958—. Dir. Richmond Hotels, Inc. Spl. counsel Va. Code Commn. on Corp. Law, 1955-56; mem. Va. Commn. Arts and Humanities; past chmn. Richmond Tax Study Commn. Trustee Va. Mus. Fine Arts, 1952-63. Fellow Am. Bar Found. (chmn. com. model bus. corp. acts 1965-70, mem. adv. com. corporate debt financing); mem. Richmond, Va., Am. (chmn. pub. utility law sect. 1940-41, chmn. sect. corp., banking and bus. law 1959-60, chmn. com. on corporate laws 1962-65, chmn. com. sect. projects 1965-70) bar assns., Am. Law Inst. (mem. joint com. continuing legal edn. 1969-72), Am. Judicature Soc., Assn. Bar City N.Y., Bar Assn. D.C., Edison Electric Inst. (chmn. legal com. 1965-67), Va. Hist. Soc. (exec. com. 1965—), Soc. Colonial Wars, S.R., Richmond, Va. chambers commerce, English Speaking Union (nat. bd. 1964-71), Phi Beta Kappa Assos. (bd. dirs. 1971—), Phi Beta Kappa, Phi Kappa Sigma. Clubs: Forum, German, Commonwealth, Country, Downtown (Richmond); Metropolitan (Washington); Knickerbocker, Century, Brook, Coffee House (N.Y.C.); Buck's (London). Contbr. articles legal jours. Editor: The Bus. Lawyer, 1957-58. Home: 9 River Rd Richmond VA 23226 Office: 700 E Main St Richmond VA 23212

GIBSON, GORDON DAVIS, anthropologist; b. Vancouver, B.C., Can., June 22, 1915; s. Ross Clark and Rebecca (Davis) G.; student Cal. Inst. Tech., 1933-35, U. Cal. at Berkeley, 1935-36; B.A., U. Chgo., 1937, M.A., 1950, Ph.D., 1952; m. Bethune Millen, Jan. 3, 1938; children—Linda Caroline (Mrs. Mohamed Benabdi), Roger Eliot. Instr. math. Kalamazoo Coll., 1943-44; anthropometrist U.S. Dept. of Agr., Beltsville, Md., 1944-45; statistician U.S. Naval Ordnance Test Sta., Inyokern, Cal., 1945-46; self employed, Berkeley, Cal., 1946-49; field research, Bechuanaland, 1953-61, South-West Africa, 1960-61, Angola, 1971, 72, 73; instr. anthropology U. Chgo., 1954-55; asst. prof. anthropology U. Utah, Salt Lake City, 1955-58; curator anthropology Smithsonian Instn., Washington, 1958—. Fellow Am. Anthrop. Assn., African Studies Assn.; mem. Internat. African Inst. Contbr. articles to profl. jours. Home: 9708 W Bexhill Dr Kensington MD 20795 Office: Smithsonian Instn Washington DC 20560

GIBSON, HENRY WRIGHT, physician; b. Batesburg, S.C., June 18, 1924; s. William Thornwell and Kate Bates (Wright) G.; B.S., Wofford Coll., 1946; M.D., Med. U. S.C., 1950; m. Janet Yvonne Gilliland, June 6, 1953; children—Yvonne Kinsley, Amy Susan, Rosalyn Bates, Katherine Wright. Intern Columbia Hosp. Richland County, 1950-51; gen. practice medicine, Barnwell, S.C., 1951—; chief staff Barnwell County Hosp.; surgeon So. Railway System, Seaboard-Coastline R.R.; med. dir. Shuron-Continental; mem. adv. bd. Am. Bank and Trust Co.; pres. Red Oak Farms, Inc., Barnwell; dir. Palmetto Breeder Farms, Barnwell; med. dir. Barnwell Woolen Mills. Trustee Barnwell County Hosp. Served with USAAF, 1943-45. Decorated Air medal with four oak leaf clusters. Mem. A.M.A., Am. Acad. Gen. Practice, S.C., So. Barnwell County (pres. 1972—) med. assns., Am. Legion, Kappa Sigma, Alpha Kappa Kappa. Methodist (bd. stewards 1952—). Home: 2015 Simms Av Barnwell SC 29812 Office: 1802 Wren St Barnwell SC 29812

GIBSON, IVA B., coll. dean.; b. Spartanburg, S.C.; d. Cauthen McKinstree and Iva (Brannon) Gibson; B.A., Winthrop Coll., 1934; M.A., Columbia, 1944. Tchr. pub. schs., Columbia, S.C., 1934-41; dean students, asst. prof. English, Wesleyan Coll., Macon, Ga., 1945-53; dean students Montevallo (Ala.) U., 1953-61; residence counselor, instr. English, Winthrop Coll., Rock Hill, S.C., 1941-45, dean of students, 1961—. Mem. S.C. Assn. Women Deans and Counselors (pres. 1965-66), Nat. Assn. Women Deans and Counselors, Am. Assn. U. Women, Kappa Delta Pi, Alpha Lambda Delta, Pi Lambda Theta, Alpha Psi Omega, Phi Kappa Phi. Home: 638 Oakland Av Rock Hill SC 29730

GIBSON, JOE WALLACE, banker; b. Durant, Okla., Dec. 16, 1916; s. Hade and Anne George (Mason) G.; B.S., Southeastern U., 1938; m. Vivian Dee Crutcher, Sept. 10, 1940; 1 dau., George Ann. With 1st State Bank, Caddo, Okla., 1939-41; with 1st Nat. Bank in Durant, 1941-42, 45-58, 62—, exec. v.p., 1962-72, pres., 1972—, dir., 1962—; exec. v.p. 1st State Bank of Caddo, 1958-59; bank examiner State of Okla., 1959-62. Active Heart Assn., Tb Assn., Boy Scouts Am., Campfire Girls. Mem. Durant City Council; pres. Durant Sch. Bd. Served as lt., USNR, World War II. Mem. D.A.V., Am. Legion, V.F.W. Wars. Methodist. Mason (Shriner), Elk, Rotarian (pres. Durant 1972). Club: Durant Country. Home: Route 2 Durant OK 74701 Office: First National Bank Durant OK 74701

GIBSON, JOHN BOYD, educator; b. Murphy, N.C., July 21, 1931; s. Newton F. and Edythe (Anderson) G.; A.A., Young Harris Jr. Coll., 1951; B.S., Appalachian State U., 1956, M.A., 1959; postgrad. Western Carolina U., 1960, U. Tenn., 1963-69, George Peabody Coll., 1964; m. Eva Nell Wells, May 24, 1953; children—Lamar, Charles, Robert, Walter, George. Tchr., Cherokee County Bd. Edn., Murphy, N.C., 1956-58; minister edn. First Bapt. Ch., Boone, N.C., 1959-62; guidance supr. Watauga County Bd. Edn., Bonne, 1962-63; asst. prof. edn. Carson-Newman Coll., Jefferson City, Tenn., 1963—, dir. reading, 1963—. Cons. Ednl. Devel. Labs., 1966—; group supr. Field Enterprises Edn. Corp., Jefferson City, 1965—. Mem. City Council, Jefferson City, 1969—, City Planning Commn., Jefferson City, 1969—; mgr., bd. dirs. Municipal Baseball League, Jefferson City, 1966—; mem. Coll.-Community Council, 1970—. Served with AUS, 1953-55. Recipient Lane Bryant award, 1970. Mem. N.E.A., Tenn. (chpt. pres. 1968—), E. Tenn. edn. assns., Internat., Coll. reading assns., Nat. Reading Conf., Jefferson City C. of C. (chmn. edn. com. 1971). Baptist (deacon). Home: 609 E Ellis St Jefferson City TN 37760

GIBSON, PAUL EUGENE, life ins. co. exec.; b. Md., May 7, 1924; s. Monroe Henry and Isabel (Walters) G.; B.S., U. Balt., 1950; postgrad. Am. Coll. Life Underwriters, 1963-64; m. Mary Anne Eskridge, June 5, 1948; children—Paula Lee, Scott Eugene, Jill Eskridge. With Sun Life Assurance Co. Can., Washington, 1951—, br. mgr., 1955—. Served with USMCR, 1943-46. Recipient Bernard L. Wilner award D.C. Life Underwriters Assn., 1969. Mem. Nat. Assn. Life Underwriters (treas., mem. exec. com. 1967-72), D.C. Life Underwriters Assn. (pres. 1963-64), Gen. Agts. and Mgrs. Assn. Met. Washington (pres. 1961-62). Home: 8941 Colesbury Pl Fairfax VA 22030 Office: 1250 Connecticut Av NW Washington DC 20036

GIBSON, ROBERT CARL, coll. dean; b. Mason, Ill., May 31, 1917; s. Robert Walter and Ruby (Reed) G.; B.Ed., E. Ill. State Coll., 1938; M.A., U. Ill., 1942; postgrad. U. Neb., 1942-44, George Washington U., 1948; D.Ed., U. Va., 1960; m. Helen Werner Minor, Sept. 2, 1941; children—Carl Reed, Karen Minor. Pub. sch. tchr., Va., 1938-41; instr., supr. adminstr., Army Airplane Mechanics Schs., Ill., Neb., Tex., 1941-44; prin. Sussex County Schs., Waverly, Va., 1946-48, Campbell County schs., Altavista, Va., 1948-53, Radford (Va.) High Sch., 1953-56; dir. instrn. Albemarle County Schs., Charlottesville, Va., 1956-60; dir. student teaching Radford (Va.) Coll., 1960-67, bd. dirs. Wesley Found., 1961-67; chmn. edn. dept. George Mason Coll., Fairfax, Va., 1967-70; dean Radford (Va.) Coll., 1970—. Mem. extension and pub. service adv. com. Va. Council Higher Edn., 1967-69, mem. edn. TV adv. com., 1967-69; cons. legislative commn. on merit pay for tchrs., 1961-62; cons. Va. Sch. Bds. Assn., 1961-62. Served to lt. comdr. USNR, World War II. Mem. Va. Student Coop. Assn. (adv. bd. 1954-67), Nat., Va. edn. assns., Nat. Assn. Student Tching., Va. Dept. Higher Edn. (pres. 1966-69). Methodist (lay speaker 1950—). Rotarian. Contbr. articles to profl. jours. Home: Radford VA 24141

GIBSON, ROBERT FISHER, bishop; b. Williamsport, Pa., Nov. 22, 1906; s. Robert F. and Harriet (McKenney) G.; A.B., Trinity Coll., Hartford, Conn., 1928; A.M., U. Va., 1932; B.D., Va. Theol. Sem., 1940, D.D., 1948; m. Alison Morice, June 1, 1935; children—Robert Fisher III, John V. M., Margaret Alison, Peter McKenney. Ordained priest Protestant Episcopal Ch., 1940; held business and teaching positions, P.I., Dutch East Indies, Balt., also N.Y.C., 1928-38; asso. prof. church history Va. Theol. Sem., 1940-46; liaison officer P.E. Ch. in Mexico, 1946-49; dean Sch. Theology, U. of South, 1947-49; suffragan bishop P.E. Ch., Diocese of Va., 1949-54, bishop coadjutor, 1954-61, diocesan bishop, 1961—. Chmn. Joint Commn. on Ecumenical Relations. Episcopal Ch. Home: 8737 River Rd Richmond VA 23229 Office: 110 W Franklin St Richmond VA 23220

GIBSON, RUSSELL FLEMING, city ofcl.; b. nr. Waycross, Ga., Nov. 11, 1922; s. N. Madison and Ruth (Dean) G.; student U. Ga., 1946-47; m. Helen Faye Barefoot, Aug. 20, 1944; children—Janice Faye (Mrs. James L. Pickett), Lon M., Morris F. Credit mgr. B.F. Goodrich Tire Co., Waycross, 1947-66; exec. dir. Housing Authority, Waycross, 1966—. Bd. trustees Gibson Children's Trust Fund, Waycross. Mem. S.A.R., Nat. Assn. Housing and Redevel. Ofcls. Elk, Lion. Home: 810 E Waring St Waycross GA 31501 Office: PO Box 372 Garlington Heights Waycross GA 31501

GIBSON, VIVIAN LEA, coll. dean; b. Pennington Gap, Va.; d. Olen Clay and Mossie (Quillen) Gibson; A.B., U. N.C., 1934; M.A., U. Ala., 1952; postgrad. Syracuse U., 1957-59. Tchr., Wise County (Va.) schs., 1934, 46, Big Stone Gap Elementary Sch., 1934-35, Wise High Sch., 1935-38, 44-46, East Stone Gap High Sch., 1938-41; prin. Dorchester Elementary Sch., 1941-44; tchr. J. B. Pennington High Sch., Blountsville, Ala., 1946-47; instr. Berry Coll., Mt. Berry. Ga., 1947-48; prin. Harmony Jr. High Sch., Rome, Ga., 1948-51; counselor to women Office of Dean of Women, U. Ala., 1951-57; student dean Syracuse U., 1957-59; dean of women Fairmount (W.Va.) State Coll., 1959-61; dean of women Frederick campus Tidewater Community Coll., 1961-70, also dir. guidance; counselor Coastal Carolina Community Coll., Jacksonville, 1970—. Pres. bd. dirs. Family and

Child Service of Portsmouth, Health Welfare and Recreation Planning Council Portsmouth (Va.) Area. Mem. Va., Ga., Wise County (past pres.), Floyd County (past pres.) edn. assns., Floyd County Prins. Assn., N.C. Assn. Educators, N.C. Student Services Personnel Assn., Nat. Assn. Women Deans and Counselors, Coll. and U. Personnel Assn., Am. Assn. U. Women, W.Va. Personnel Assn., Regional Assn. Women Deans and Counselors, Hampton Roads Guidance and Personnel Assn., Kappa Delta Pi, Pi Lambda Theta, Delta Kappa Gamma, Alpha Phi. Democrat. Presbyn. Clubs: Pilot (1st v.p.) (Portsmouth); Jacksonville Business and Professional Women's (1st v.p. 1972); Surf City (N.C.) Women's (pres. 1971).

GIBSON, WILLIAM EDWIN, mining engr.; b. Weeksbury, Ky., Sept. 16, 1930; s. Edwin Joseph and Irene (Depew) G.; B.S. in Mining Engring., Va. Poly. Inst., 1955; m. Gwenda Jean Wicker, Dec. 15, 1954; children— James Edwin, Barbara Ann. Indsl. engr. U.S. Steel Co., Lynch, Ky., 1956-62; mining engr. Evans Elkhorn Coal Corp., Wayland, 1964-66; indsl. engr. Eastern Coal Corp., Stone Ky., 1962-64, mining engr., 1966-70; mining engr. Ky. Carbon Corp., Phelps, 1970—. Registered profl. engr. Mem. Nat., Ky. socs. profl. engrs., Am. Inst. Mining Metall. and Petroleum Engrs. Mason. Home: Star Route W Box 31-1A Phelps KY 41553 Office: Ky Carbon Corp Phelps KY 41553

GIDDEN, NORMAN L., ins. co. exec., 1916; A.B., Coll. City N.Y., 1937; m. Prodn. mgr. Gaston de Paris, 1937-39; self-employed ins. broker, 1939-40; with Govt. Employees Ins. Co., Washington, 1946—, v.p. adminstrn., 1959-62, 1st v.p., 1963-64, exec. v.p., 1964-66, pres., 1966—, also dir. Dir. Western Pacific Industries, Inc., Western Pacific R.R. Bd. govs. Ins. Inst. Am.; trustee Am. Inst. Property and Liability Underwriters. Served to maj. USMCR, 1940-46. Address: 1705 L St NW Washington DC 20036

GIDEON, RUSSELL ARTHUR, editor; b. Catoosa, Okla., Apr. 20, 1908; s. Arthur Burton and Laura (Bradshaw) G.; student U. Kan., 1927-28, U. Tulsa, summer 1930; B.A., U. Okla., 1931; m. Helen Belt, June 22, 1935 (dec. Oct. 1945); children—Lee Burton, Robert Wesley; m. 2d, Louisa Brown Lovell, Jan. 1, 1949 (div. Aug. 1951); m. 3d, Dorothy Naylor Bowen, Feb. 22, 1957. With Tulsa World, 1932—, asst. sports editor, news reporter, asst. city editor, 1932-45, Sunday editor, 1945—. Mem. Am. Assn. Sunday and Feature Editors (pres. 1964), Okla., Tulsa County (past v.p., dir.) hist. socs., Tulsa Press Club (pres. 1944-45), Kappa Sigma. Home: 2013 S Canton Av Tulsa OK 74112 Office: Tulsa World Box 1770 Tulsa OK 74102

GIDUZ, ROLAND, journalist; b. Fall River, Mass., July 24, 1925; s. Hugo and Edith May (Baker) G.; A.B. in Journalism, U. N.C., 1948; M.S. in Journalism, Columbia, 1949; m. Helen Frances Jeter, Dec. 25, 1949; children—William Roland, Robert Baker, Thomas Tracy. Migrant field rep. Home Missions Council N.Am., 1949-50; staff writer Chapel Hill (N.C.) Weekly, Durham (N.C.) Herald & Sun, 1950-54; state editor N.C. Jr. C. of C., 1951-54; editor Chapel Hill News Leader, 1954-58, News of Orange County (N.C.), 1960-66; editor, pub. Triangle Pointer, Chapel Hill, 1960—. Editor Alumni Rev., U. N.C. at Chapel Hill, 1966—, Univ. Report, 1969—, asso. sec. Gen. Alumni Assn., 1970—; founder Visitor Information Publs., Chapel Hill, 1970, pres., 1970—. Mem. Chapel Hill Bd. Aldermen, 1957-69; mayor pro-tem, Chapel Hill, 1964-69; mem. Orange County Democratic Party Exec. Com., 1964-69. Served as pvt. 399th Inf. Regiment, 100 Div., AUS, 1943-45; ETO. Decorated Purple Heart. Mass Media fellow Fund Adult Edn. Harvard, 1958-59. Mem. Chapel Hill-Carrboro C. of C. (dir. 1969-71). Presbyn. Mason (K.T., Shriner), Toastmaster, Rotarian (pres. Chapel Hill 1972—). Home: Box 44 Chapel Hill NC 27514 Office: Gen Alumni Assn U N C Chapel Hill Box 660 Chapel Hill NC 27514

GIEGER, WILFRED LAWRENCE, constrn. co. exec.; b. Skene, Miss., Dec. 16, 1930; s. William Lloyd and Vonciel (Barron) G.; student U. Ala., 1949-50, Livingston State U., 1952-53; B.S., Auburn U., 1956; m. Henrietta Whittle, July 2, 1950; children—William Lawrence, Elizabeth Kay, Laura Kay. Constrn. engr. Phillips Petroleum Co., Fla. and Ga., 1956-58; pres. Gieger-Jones Constrn. Co., Inc., Orlando, Fla., 1958—. Dist. chmn., mem. exec. bd. Central Fla. council Boy Scouts Am., 1968-71. Democratic nominee Fla. Ho. of Reps., 1964. Served with USAF, 1951-52; with C.E., AUS, 1956. Mem. Asso. Gen. Contractors of Am. (chpt. pres. 1964, nat. dir. 1972—), Orlando Area C. of C. (dir.), Am. Soc. C.E. Mason (32 deg., Shriner). Club: Civitan (pres. Orlando 1963). Home: 541 Virginia Dr Winter Park FL 32789 Office: 663 Harold Av Winter Park FL 32789

GIESELMAN, RICHARD WILLIAM, clergyman, educator; b. St. Louis, Feb. 28, 1913; s. Walter Mary and Gertrude Louise (Simmons) G.; B.A., St. Mary's Sem., Perryville, Mo., 1940; Mus.M., Montreal U., 1948; M.A., Catholic U., 1949; postgrad. St. Louis U., 1949-50. Tchr., St. Vincent Coll., Mo., 1933-34; ordained priest Roman Catholic Ch., 1940; prof. St. Mary's Sem., 1940-45; prof. St. Johns Coll., Camarillo, Cal., 1945-48; prof. Kenrick Coll., 1949-50; prof. St. Thomas Coll., Denver, 1950-58; prof. Assumption Coll., San Antonio, 1958-63; prof. St. Marys Sem., Houston, 1963-64; prof. U. St. Thomas, Houston, 1964—; ecumenical works in Mo., Colo., 1941-62. Mem. Am. Cath. Philos. Assn. K.C. Club: Sierra (Houston). Home: 9845 Memorial Dr Houston TX 77024 Office: 3812 Montrose Blvd Houston TX 77006

GIESEN, FRANK HARTMAN, civil engr.; b. Superior, Wis., Oct. 5, 1932; s. Irving W. and Tracy (O'Donnel) G.; B.S., Marquette U., 1955; m. Mary Margaret Girouard, Aug. 13, 1955; children—David, Stephen, Robert, Tracy, Mary Patrice, Francis Gregory. Mgr., project engr. Consoer, Towsend & Assos., Cons. Engrs., Nashville, 1955-71, partner, 1966—. Dir. Plumbing Examiners and Appeals, City of Nashville, 1965—. Mem. Am. Soc. C.E., Tenn. Soc. Engrs. (treas. 1970, dir. 1966-68), Water Pollution Control Fedn. Club: Civitan (pres. Hendersonville, Tenn. 1963). Home: 513 Freda Villa Madison TN 37115 Office: 404 James Robertson Pkwy Nashville TN 37219

GIESSE, RICHARD JOSEPH, educator, psychologist; b. Cleve., Aug. 10, 1919; s. Carl K. and Anne (Prosek) G.; B.A., Howard Payne Coll., 1950; M.A., Hardin Simmons U., 1958; Ed.D., Northeast La. U., 1972; m. Bernice Evelyn Gossett, Dec. 23, 1944; children—Judith Ann (Mrs. Robert E. Plummer), Richard Joseph, Carl Kern II, Mary Elizabeth, Michelle. Chief psychologist Abilene (Tex.) State Sch., 1953-54; sch. psychologist Abilene Pub. Schs., 1959-62; research project dir. Tex. Christian U., Fort Worth, 1962-63; asst. prof., spl. ednl. psychologist La. Tech. U., Ruston, 1963—. Cons. psychologist Ruston State Sch., 1963—; vis. lectr. Hardin Simmons U., Abilene, 1959-62, McMurray Coll., Abilene, 1960-62. Served with USMCR, 1943-45. Mem. Am., La. psychol. assns. Home: Route 3 Box 395 Ruston LA 71270

GIETZEN, ARTHUR WILLIAM, JR., civil engr.; b. Beaumont, Tex., Jan. 13, 1927; s. Arthur William and Pauline (Andrus) G.; B.S., Lamar State Coll. Tech., 1961; m. Patsy Page Gietzen, Mar. 3, 1956; children—Karen Denise, John Eric. Engring. asst. Tex. Hwy. Dept., Silsbee, 1961-65, resident engr., 1965-67; project engr. Eastex, Inc., Silsbee, 1967—, Served with AUS, 1946-49. Mem. Am. Soc. C.E. (chpt. pres. 1964), Tex. Soc. Profl. Engrs. (pres. 1969). Roman Catholic. Home: 105 Read St Silsbee TX 77656 Office: PO Box 816 Silsbee TX 77656

GIFFORD, MARIE BATTEY (MRS. JOSEPH GIFFORD), radio sta. exec.; b. Cordell, Okla., Jan. 12, 1917; d. John William and Mary (Yoder) Battey; B.F.A., U. Okla., 1937; m. Joseph Gifford, Sept. 2, 1948 (dec. Dec. 1960). Account exec. Sta. KOME, Tulsa, Okla., 1941-44; instr. Baylor U. Sch. Radio, 1944-45; asst. program dir. Sta KWKH, Shreveport, La., 1945-57; account exec. Sta. KTBS, 1947-55, sales mgr., 1955-57; sales mgr. Sta. KEEL, Inc., 1957-62, gen. mgr., 1962—, v.p., 1964-69, pres., 1969—; v.p. Lin Broadcasting, 1966—. Exec. asst. Shreveport Summer Theatre, 1954-60. Bd. dirs. Community Action Program, Caddo-Bossior Parishes, 1969-71. Recipient Broadcaster of Yr. award La. Assn. Broadcasters, 1970. Mem. Shreveport Advt. Club (pres, 1964-65), Advt. Fedn. Am. (dir. 10th dist. 1964-66), La. Assn. Broadcasters (former officer), Shreveport C. of C. dir. 1968-71), Chi Omega. Club: Ambassadors (Shreveport). Home: 3818 Akard St Shreveport LA 71105 Office: 710 Spring St Shreveport LA 71102

GIFFORD, WILLIAM LEO, govt. ofcl.; b. Weston, Conn., Aug. 30, 1930; s. Rolland Wyckoff and Margaret (Clifford) G.; B.A., Fordham U., 1952; student U. Conn., 1952-55; m. Marion Frances Miletti, Oct. 27, 1956; children—Margaret Rose, William Leo, David Wyckoff. Polit. reporter Jamestown (N.Y.) Post-Jour., 1957-59; adminstr. asst. Rep. Charles E. Goodell of N.Y., Washington, 1959-68, Rep. James F. Hastings of N.Y., 1969; spl. asst. Sec. of Labor for Legislative Affairs, Washington, 1969-70; spl. asst. to Pres., 1970—. Mem. Nat. Press Club, Am. Polit. Sci. Assn. Republican. Home: 3908 Terry Pl Alexandria VA 22304 Office: The White House Washington DC 20500

GIGNILLIAT, PEGGY THOMSON (MRS. CHARLES N. GIGNILLIAT, JR.), music educator; b. Spartanburg, S.C., Dec. 29, 1911; d. Webb and Marguerite (Darden) Thomson; pvt. study violin with Francis Macmillen, N.Y.C. and Paris, France, 1930-32; B.A., Converse Coll., 1934, Mus. B., 1944; postgrad. Colo. Coll., 1956; m. Charles N. Gignilliat, Jr., Dec. 4, 1934; children—Marguerite (Mrs. William Old, III), Sally (Mrs. Roland A. Stebbins). Tchr. stringed instrument Spartanburg (S.C.) city schs., 1939-44, coordinator string program, 1952—; violin tchr. S.C. Sch. for Blind, Cedar Spring, 1940-42; prof. violin Converse Coll., 1951-58. Concertmaster, Spartanburg Symphony, 1946—, Little Theatre Orch., 1951—. Pres. Jr. League Spartanburg, 1949-51; chmn. women's div. United Fund, 1948; chmn. women's div. War Bond Sale, 1944; pres. Spartanburg Music Found., 1947-49; mem. S.C. Archives Commn., 1968—. Bd. dirs. Spartanburg County Library, Salvation Army, A.R.C., Mental Health Clinic, Speech and Hearing Clinic. Recipient Mary Mildred Sullivan award Converse Coll., 1964. Mem. Am. String Tchrs. Assn., Music Educators Nat. Conf., Music Tchrs. Nat. Assn., Nat. Trust for Historic Preservation, S.C., Hist. Soc., S.C. Classroom Tchrs. Assn., Confederation S.C. Local Hist. Socs. (pres. 1968-69), S.C. String Tchrs. Assn. (pres. 1961-63), Spartanburg County Hist. Assn. (pres. 1961-67), Pi Kappa Lambda. Presbyn. Home: 1026 Woodburn Rd Spartanburg SC 29302 Office: Box 2565 Spartanburg SC 29302

GILBERT, CARL J., govt. ofcl. Spl. rep. for trade negogiations U.S. Office Spl. Rep. Trade Negogiations, Washington. Address: 1800 G St NW Washington DC 20506*

GILBERT, CHARLES WILLIAM, state ofcl.; b. Gainesville, Fla., Apr. 28, 1937; s. Carroll Willis and Mary Frances (Revell) G.; A.A., Tallahassee Community Coll.; B.S. Fla. State U; m. Betty Joyce Houseman, Nov. 2, 1956; children—Charles William, Randall Jeffery, Mary Ellen, Alan Keith. Fingerprint clk. FBI, Washington, 1956-58; fingerprint technician Fla. Sheriffs' Bur., Tallahassee, 1958-59, supr. identification unit, 1959—. Mem. Internat. (mem. membership com. 1962—), Fla. (sec.-treas. 1959—) assns. identification. Methodist. Home: PO Box 147 Bronson FL 32621 Office: PO Box 1489 Tallahassee FL 32302

GILBERT, CLARENCE MITCHELL, physician; b. Chester, Pa., Dec. 30, 1931; s. Clarence M. and Leila G. (Wilson) G.; B.A., U. Pa., 1953, M.D., 1957; m. Barbara Patterson, Mar. 28, 1953; children—Clarence Mitchell III, Ronald S. Rotating intern Hosp. U. Pa., Phila., 1957-58, asst. resident medicine, 1958-59, resident medicine, 1961-62; asst. instr. medicine, dept. medicine U. Pa., 1958-59, 61-63, instr., 1963-64, fellow in cardiology Robinette Dept., 1962-64; practice medicine specializing in cardiovascular diseases, Orlando, Fla., 1964—; mem. active staff Orange Meml. Hosp., Fla. Sanitarium and Hosp., Mercy Med. Center; mem. cardiology staff Holiday Hosp.; mem. consultation staff Leesburg, Osceola Gen. hosps.; clin. prof. allied health scis., Fla. Tech. U., 1970. Served to capt. USAF, 1959-61. Diplomate Am. Bd. Internal Medicine and cardiovascular sub-splty., Nat. Bd. Med. Examiners. Fellow Am. Coll. Chest Physicians, Am. Heart Assn., Am. Coll. Cardiology, Am. Coll. Angiology; mem. A.C.P., A.M.A., Am. Fedn. Clin. Research, So., Pa., Fla. med. assns., Fla., Central Fla. (pres. 1970) heart assns., Orange County Med. Soc. (v.p. 1971), Med. Study Club Orlando. Rotarian. Home: 1020 Terrace Blvd Orlando FL 32803 Office: 15 W Columbia St Orlando FL 32806

GILBERT, DWAYNE CHAMPION, educator; b. Ladonia, Tex., Sept. 24, 1923; s. Felix M. and Ethel (Champion) G.; M.S., East Tex. State U., 1948; postgrad. Tex. A. and M. U., 1964-65; m. Virginia Ann Graves, Dec. 26, 1946; children—Linda Sue, Sarah Lou. Instr. indsl. arts Port Neches (Tex.) High Sch., 1947-50; elementary sch. prin., Port Neches, 1950-53; asst. prof. indsl. edn. Northwestern State Coll., Natchitoches, La., 1953-60, asso. prof. indsl. edn. and tech., 1960—. Served with U.S. Naval Air Force, 1942-44. Mem. Am., La. vocational assns., Am. Indsl. Arts Assn., Iota Lambda Sigma. Lion (pres. 1952-53). Home: Route 2 Box 770 Natchitoches LA 71457

GILBERT, ELIZABETH ANN DINWIDDIE, librarian; b. nr. Berea, Ky., Apr. 15, 1907; d. Joseph C. and Laminia Walker (Armstrong) Gilbert; B.A., Berea Coll., 1930; B.S., Western Res. U., 1938; postgrad. Columbia, Case Western Res. U. Library supr. circulation Berea Coll., 1930-44, librarian, chmn. dept. library sci., 1944—, prof. library sci., 1965—. Mem. Ky. Librarian's Certification Bd., 1957—. Mem. A.L.A. (Ky. rep. coll. and reference libraries div.), Southeastern (Ky. rep. 1966-68), Ky. (pres. 1945-46) library assns., Am. Assn. U. Profs., Am. Assn. U. Women, Kappa Delta Pi, Phi Kappa Phi. Club: Progress. Contbr. to Libraries in the Southeast, 1949. Home: RFD 1 Berea KY 40403

GILBERT, GORDON JOEL, neurologist, electroencephalographer; b. N.Y.C., Mar. 24, 1933; s. Benjamin L. H. and Lunny (Zelen) G.; A.B. summa cum laude, Harvard, 1953; M.D., N.Y.U., 1957; m. Adele Schwartz, July 10, 1960; children—Benette Lizabeth, Stefanie Celeste, Benjamin Leon. Intern in medicine Johns Hopkins Hosp., Balt., 1957-58; clin. fellow in neurology Yale Sch. Medicine, 1958-59, sr. fellow, 1960-61, instr., 1963-65, asst. prof., 1965; teaching fellow in neurology Harvard, Boston City Hosp., 1959-60; asst. chief neurology West Haven (Conn.) Vets. Hosp., 1963-65; clin. investigator, 1963-65; asso. dept. medicine Grace-New Haven Community Hosp., 1964-65; cons. neurology Bay Pines VA Hosp., 1965-67; neurologist Mound Park Hosp., St. Petersburg, Fla., 1965—; neurologist St. Anthony's Hosp., St. Petersburg, 1965—, med. dir. electroencephalograph lab., 1968—; neurologist Palms of Pasadena Hosp., St. Petersburg, 1965—, med. dir. electroencephalograph lab., 1969—, neurologist All Children's Hosp., St. Petersburg, 1967—, med. dir. muscular dystrophy clinic, also electroencephalograph lab., 1968—; neurologist St. Petersburg Gen. Hosp., 1969—; clin. asso. prof. physiology U. South Fla., 1971—. Served to capt. USAF, 1961-63. Recipient Citation of Merit, Muscular Dystrophy Assn. Am., Inc., 1966, 67, 68. Diplomate in neurology Am. Bd. Psychiatry and Neurology, 1964, Am. Electroencephalographic Soc. Mem. Phi Beta Kappa, Alpha Omega Alpha. Home: 2220 Pelham Rd N St Petersburg FL 33710 Office: 441 33d St N St Patersburg FL 33713

GILBERT, HAROLD STANLEY, warehousing co. exec.; b. Fort Worth, Jan. 22, 1924; s. Sydney Ralph and Reba Samuels (Lever) G.; B.A., U. Tex., 1947, M.Ed., 1949; grad. Air Command and Staff Coll., 1961, Air War Coll., 1970, Indsl. Coll. Armed Forces, 1970; m. Jeanne Schwarz, Apr. 6, 1950; children—Marsha, Mark S., John L. Sci. tchr., coach Houston Ind. Schs., 1949-51; asst. prin., head sci. dept., athletic dir., coach USAF Dependents Sch. System, Germany, 1953-55; v.p. Coastal Bag and Bagging Corp., Houston, 1968-71; v.p. gen. mgr. Coastal Storehouse, Houston, 1968—. Served with AUS, 1943-45, USAF, 1951-53. Decorated Bronze Star, Purple Heart with oak leaf cluster. Mem. Air Force Assn., Res. Officers Assn., Nat. Fedn. Temple Brotherhoods (dir. 1964—), Jewish Chautauqua Soc. (chmn. S.W. region 1964—), T Assn. U. Tex., Houston C. of C. (mil. affairs com. 1969—), Houston, S.W. warehouse and transfer assns., Phi Delta Kappa, Sigma Alpha Mu. Elk, Rotarian (pres. Houston and Harris County 1969-70). Home: 476 N Post Oak Lane Houston TX 77024 Office: PO Box 3207 Houston TX 77001

GILBERT, HAROLD WENDELL, record co. exec.; b. Murray, Ky., Jan. 24, 1939; s. Vernon and Martha (Walls) G.; student Miss. Vocational Coll., 1956-58; B.S., Tenn. A. and I. U., 1958-62; m. Jean Farley, Sept. 7, 1958; children—Kenneth, Keith, King, Kim, Kleetha. Tchr. Hampton High Sch., Dickson, Tenn., 1960-65; pres. Hitsburgh Music Co. & Rec. Co., Gallatin, 1964—; chmn. bd. Hal and Jean Enterprises, Inc.; pres. So. City Records. Served with USAF, 1958-60. Named Mid-Tenn. High Sch. Band Dir. of Yr., 1969. Mem. Nat., Tenn., Clarksville Montgomery edn. assns. Club: Mystery Men Society (treas.). Home: 157 Ford Av Gallatin TN 37066 Office: Hitsburgh Music Bldg Ford Av Gallatin TN 37066

GILBERT, IRWIN HELLINGS, entomologist; b. Frostburg, Md., July 6, 1909; s. Irwin Engel and Margaret (Cook) G.; B.S., U. Md., 1932; M.Sc., Ohio State U., 1941, postgrad., 1941-42, 46; m. Marie Wainwright, July 2, 1938; 1 son, Robert Lee. Mgr. exterminating dept. Sanitation Grocery Co., Washington, 1932-35; asst. entomologist Chipman Chem. Co., N.J., 1936; hort. insp. N.Y. State Dept. Agr., 1936-38; asst. extension entomologist Ohio State U., 1940-42, 46; entomologist U.S. Dept. Agr., 1946-53, Agrl. Research Service, 1953—; prof. entomology U. Fla., 1963—. Specialist, U.S. Army, 1951-53, 65, 67; cons. W.H.O., 1958, 62, 63, 67, 69. Served with AUS, 1942-46; ETO. Recipient Superior Service award U.S. Dept. Agr., 1958, certificate of merit, 1963. Mem. Entomol. Soc. Am., Canadian, Fla. entomol. socs., Sigma Xi, Gamma Sigma Delta. Contbr. articles profl. jours. Home: 218 NW 30th St Gainesville FL 32601

GILBERT, J. CHARLES, theatre mgr.; b. Mpls., Aug. 30, 1900; B.S., Northwestern U., 1923; m. Vivian Kier, June 3, 1922; 1 son, Paul. Instr. romance lang. dept. Northwestern U., 1923-26; appeared as singing-actor in Broadway and touring prodns. of: Blossom Time (as Franz Schubert), The New Moon, The Count of Luxembourg, Firefly, The Student Prince, Maytime, The Chocolate Soldier, 1926-38; mng. dir. Civic Opera House and Civic Theatre, Chgo., 1938-44; mgr. Mansfield Theatre, N.Y.C., and gen. mgr. Broadway prodns.: Lute Song, Twelfth Night, The Barrier, Getting Married, Peter Pan, 1945-51; mng. dir. Civic Opera House, Chgo., 1951-70; gen. mgr. theaters John F. Kennedy Center for Performing Arts, Washington, 1971-72, gen. mgr. Kennedy Center Prodns., Inc., 1972—. Office: John F Kennedy Center for Performing Arts Washington DC 20566

GILBERT, JAMES GILHAMS, law pub.; b. LaGrange, Ind., Feb. 18, 1918; s. Karl D. and Mildred G. (Gilhams) G.; M.E., Purdue U., 1941; m. Marjorie Putnam, Oct. 17, 1946; children—Belinda (Mrs. A. Newton Ticer), Deborah G., James Gilhams. Salesman The Michie Co., Charlottesville, Va., 1946-62, sales mgr., 1963—. Served with AUS, 1941-46. Decorated 4 Purple Hearts, Silver Star. Mem. V.F.W., Am. Legion, D.A.V. Elk, Lions (pres. 1952-53). Clubs: Exchange (pres. 1968-69), Pinehurst (N.C.) Country; Farmington Country (Charlottesville). Home: 509 Berwick Ct Charlottesville VA 22901 Office: 610 E Market St Charlottesville VA 22901

GILBERT, JOSEPH GATLIFF, clin. psychologist; b. Pineville, Ky., Nov. 21, 1920; s. Thomas Joseph and Eva (Gatliff) G.; B.A. cum laude, U. S.C., 1951, M.A., 1952; Ph.D. in Clin. Psychology, U. Tenn., 1954; m. Katherine Armida Jennings, Aug. 30, 1948; children—Armida Jennings, Arthur Herbert, Robert Joseph, Katherine Elizabeth. Clin. psychologist Regional Office VA, St. Petersburg, Fla., 1954-55; chief clin. psychologist VA Mental Health Clinic, Pensacola, Fla., 1955-59, VA Gen. Med. and Surg. Hosp., Fayetteville, N.C., 1959-60; clin. and research psychologist State Hosp., Yankton, S.D., 1960-61; chief clin. psychologist Richland County Mental Health Clinic, Columbia, S.C., 1961-63, Child Devel. Center, S.C. Med. Coll. Hosp., Charleston, 1963-64; chief clin. psychologist Mental Health Center, Anderson, 1964-66; clin. psychologist VA Hosp., Charleston, 1966-69, S.C. State Hosp., Columbia, 1969—. Served with U.S. Mcht. Marine, 1942-46. Mem. Phi Beta Kappa. Author: Clinical Psychological Tests in Psychiatric and Medical Practice, 1969. Research and publs. in field. Home: 14 S Washington St Sumter SC 29150 Office: SC State Hosp Columbia SC 29201

GILBERT, NORMAN SUTCLIFFE, physician, med. sch. adminstr.; b. Butte, Mont., July 8, 1919; s. Norman Sutcliffe and Naomi (Robinson) G.; B.S., La. State U., 1939; M.D., 1943; m. Andrea Armbruster, Apr. 23, 1949; children—Andrea Naomi, Carolyn Sutcilffe. Intern, Charity Hosp., New Orleans, 1943-44, asst. vis. physician in internal medicine, 1946-47, vis. physician, 1950, sr. vis. physician, 1958—; resident internal medicine Shreveport (La.) Charity Hosp., 1958; staff physician Murray Hosp., Butte, 1948-50; instr. La. State U., New Orleans, 1950-51, asst. prof., 1951-57, asso. prof. rehab. medicine, 1958-65, prof., 1965—, asso. dean Sch. Medicine, 1964—, med. dir. Vocational Rehab. Inst., 1966—. Served from 1st lt. to capt. M.C., AUS, 1944-46. Diplomate Am. Bd. Internal Medicine. Mem. Orleans Parish, La. State med. socs., New Orleans Acad. Internal Medicine. Home: 3120 Coliseum St New Orleans LA 70115

GILBERT, TED CURTIS, ednl. administr.; b. Arjay, Ky., Feb. 11, 1917; s. Roland and Cora (Hayslett) G.; A.B., Eastern Ky. U., 1939, M.A., 1947; postgrad. U. Ky., 1948; LL.D., Georgetown Coll., 1962; m. Eva Marie Neal, Feb. 6, 1944; 1 dau., Jane (Mrs. G. McNeely). Tchr., Bell County (Ky.) Elementary Schs., 1937, Breathitt County (Ky.) High Sch., 1939-40; prin. Pineville Elementary Schs., 1940-42, New Albany (Ind.) Jr. High Sch., 1946-49; supt. schs., London,

1949-50, Maysville, 1950-56; with Ky. Dept. Edn., 1956-60, asst. supt. pub. instrn., 1958-60; exec. sec. Ky. Council Pub. Higher Edn., Frankfort, 1960-62, exec. dir., 1964—; asst. supt schs., Louisville, 1962-64. Chmn., Christian edn. com. Ky. Bapt. Conv., 1958-65; mem. exec. com. So. Bapt. Conv., 1966—. Bd. dirs. Ky. Child Welfare Research Found., Frankfort. Served to capt. AUS, 1942-46. Recipient Outstanding Alumnus award Eastern Ky. U., 1963. Mem. Nat. Assn. State Higher Edn. Exec. Officers (pres. 1971), Am. Assn. Higher Edn., Am. Assn. Sch. Adminstrs., Ky. Edn. Assn. (1st v.p. 1952-53), Nat. Assn. Chief State Sch. Officers (mem. study commn. 1958-60). Baptist (deacon). Rotarian (pres. 1955). Home: 305 Ute Trail Frankfort KY 40601 Office: Capital Plaza Office Tower Frankfort KY 40601

GILBERTO, MAYMI, dentist; b. Guaynabo, P.R., June 15, 1939; s. Julio and Jedulfa (Pagan) Maymi; B.A., U. P.R., 1960, D.M.D., 1969; m. Norma L. Perez, May 17, 1963; children—Gilberto, Javier Adolfo. Pvt. practice dentistry, Bayamon, P.R., 1969—. Served to capt. F.A., AUS, 1960-65. Decorated Army Commendation medal. Mem. Am. Dental Assn., Colegio de Cirujana Dentistas de P.R., Delta Sigma Delta. Lion. Home: DB-26 Damasco Sta Juanita Bayamon PR 00619 Office: No 4 Mangirial Forest Hills Bayamon PR 00619

GILBOA, MOSHE A., Israeli diplomat; b. Warsaw, Poland, 1922; ed. Hebrew U.; m. Menuha Ben Shlomo; children—Meir, Erel. Head fgn. currency budget Insrael Ministry Finance, 1955; then econ. adviser, dir. cooperation Hevrat Ovdim; dep. dir. gen. Ministry Commerce and Industry; now consul gen. Israel, Atlanta. Mem. Assn. Social Sci. and Humanities Israel (chmn.). Author: On Democracy; Changes in Labour Economy and Cooperation; The Added Value; Six Years—Six Days, 1968. Contbr. articles to profl. jours. Address: 805 Peachtree St Atlanta GA 30308*

GILBRETH, FRANK BUNKER, JR., writer, newspaperman; b. Plainfield, N.J., Mar. 17, 1911; s. Frank Bunker and Lillian Evelyn (Moller) G.; student St. John's Coll., Annapolis, Md., 1928-29; B.A., U. Mich., 1933; m. Elizabeth Cauthen, Sept. 29, 1934 (dec. 1954); 1 dau., Betsy; m. 2d, Mary Manigault, June 4, 1955; children—Edward, Rebecca Motte. Reporter, N.Y. Herald Tribune, 1933-34; corr. Asso. Press, Raleigh, N.C., 1938-42, cable editor, 1945-47; editorial writer News and Courier, Charleston, S.C., 1947-50, asso. editor, 1951-57, asst. pub., v.p. News and Courier and Charleston Evening Post, 1957—; v.p. Packet Motor Lines, Charleston, 1958—, Beaufort (S.C.) Gazette, 1962—, Aiken (S.C.) Communications, Inc., Aiken Cablevision, Inc., Buenos Aires Herald, Cambridge, Md. Banner. Served from lt. (j.g.) to lt. comdr. USNR, 1942-45. Decorated Air medal, Bronze Star medal. Mem. Alpha Delta Phi. Author: (with Ernestine Gilbreth Carey) Cheaper by the Dozen, 1949, Belles on Their Toes, 1950; (with John Held, Jr.) Held's Angels, 1952; I'm a Lucky Guy, 1951; Innside Nantucket, 1955; Of Whales and Women, 1957; How to Be a Father, 1958; Loblolly, 1959; He's My Boy, 1962; Time Out for Happiness, 1972. Home: 430 Maybank Hwy Charleston SC 29407 also The Shoe Hulbert Av Nantucket MA Office: The News and Courier and The Charleston Evening Post Charleston SC 29402

GILBRETH, HAROLD BRITE, coll. adminstr.; b. Bowling Green, Ky., Dec. 20, 1908; s. Wiley Smith and Eulah (Brite) G.; A.B., Western Ky. U., 1930, Bowling Green Coll. Commerce, 1931; M.A., U. Ky., 1935; Ed.D., N.Y., U., 1940; m. Georgia Mary Lecroy, Dec. 24, 1938. Tchr. pub. high sch. Rome, Ga., 1931-35, Winthrop Coll., Rocky Hill, S.C., 1935-37; teaching fellow N.Y. U., N.Y.C., 1937-38, Western Ill. U., Macomb, 1938-40; chmn. dept. bus. Winthrop Coll., 1940-67, dean Grad. Sch., 1967—. Vis. prof. U. N.C. at Greensboro, summer 1946. Recipient distinguished prof. award, Winthrop Coll., 1960; Found. for Econ. Edn. fellow, 1951. Mem. So. (past pres.), S.C. (past pres.), Ga. (past pres.) bus. edn. assns., S.C. Acad. Sci., Phi Kappa Phi, Delta Pi Epsilon, Pi Gamma Mu. Service editor Bus. Edn. Forum, 1947-52; asst. editor Modern Bus. Edn. Contbr. articles to profl. jours. Home: 616 Guilford Rd Rock Hill SC 29730

GILCHRIST, RALPH EDWARD, petroleum engr.; b. Milw., Dec. 17, 1926; s. Ralph Towns and Anna (Eggert) G.; student Lawrence Coll., 1944-46, Cornell Coll., summer 1945, Colo. Sch. Mines, summer 1946; B.A., Denver U., 1947; B.S., U. Tex., 1950, M.S., 1951; Ph.D., Penn. State U., 1957; m. Mary Ann Gill, Jan. 8, 1955; children—Gayle Lee, Jeffery Towns, Andrew McCord. Research engr., Texaco, Bellaire, Tex., 1951-52; research asst. Pa. State U., University Park, 1954-57; project engr. Sinclair Oil Co., Tulsa, 1957-59; sr. research engr. Phillips Petroleum Co., Bartlesville, Okla., 1959-66; dir. prodn. research Tenneco Oil Co., Houston, 1966-72; mgr. exploration and prodn. research, dept. applied physics Southwest Research Inst., Houston, 1972—; lectr. U. Tulsa, 1958-59. Served to 1st lt. AUS, 1952-54. Mem. Am. Inst. Mining Engrs., Soc. Petroleum Engrs. (founding mem., 1st chmn. Bartlesville Sect. 1962-63), Am. Soc. for Oceanography, S.A.R., Sigma Xi, Sigma Gamma Epsilon, Pi Epsilon Tau, Beta Theta Pi. Republican. Lutheran. Patentee in field. Home: 12218 Taylorcest Houston TX 77024 Office: Southwest Research Inst 3600 Yoakum Blvd Houston TX 77006

GILDEN, ROBERT OREN, govt. ofcl.; b. Anacortes, Wash., Dec. 4, 1922; s. Elmer John and Janie Maria (Lovelace) G.; B.S. in Agrl. Engring., Wash. State Coll., 1947, M.S., 1951 divorced; children—Jack, Ronald, Leanne. Instr. Wash. State Coll., 1947-51; prof. U. Wyo., 1951-56; extension agrl. engr., extension service Dept. Agr., 1956-71, exec. sec. Com. on Safety in Agr., 1971—; coordinator Agrl. Engrs. Internat. 1967—. Served with USAAF, 1942-45. Decorated Purple Heart, Air medal with 2 oak leaf clusters. Mem. Am. Soc. Agrl. Engrs. (chmn. structures and environmental div. 1970-71, chmn. Washington-Md. sect. 1971), Am. Geophys. Union, A.A.A.S., Sigma Tau, Epsilon Sigma Phi. Mason. Home: 1111 Army Navy Dr Arlington VA 22202 Office: ES-USDA Washington DC 20250

GILES, HANNELORE HENDYGAIN (MRS. WILLIAM GARY), physician; b. New Orleans, Nov. 26, 1935; d. Andrew and Gertrud (Runte) Hendygain; B. Med. Tech., Tulane U., 1956; M.D., La. State U., 1963; m. William Gary, May 29, 1956; children—Deborah Lynne, Loren David, Elizabeth Anne. Intern So. Bapt. Hosp., New Orleans, 1963-64; resident internal medicine VA Hosp., New Orleans, 1964-66; fellow cardiology U. Tenn., 1966-68, instr. medicine, 1967-69; cons. heart disease Miss. Health Dept., 1966—; individual practice cardiology, Hattiesburg, Miss., 1969—. Mem. Am. Coll. Cardiology, Am. Heart Assn., So. Miss. Med. Soc., Forrest County Med. Aux. Republican. Lutheran. Contbr. articles to profl. jours. Home: 2503 Arcadia St Hattiesburg MS 39401 Office: 990 Hardy St Hattiesburg MS 39401

GILES, LAWRENCE ELMER, educator; b. Sunset, Wash., Aug. 23, 1914; s. Luther and Kittie (Wear) G.; B.A., Wash. State U., 1936, B.Ed., 1939; M.A., U. Minn., 1948, Ph.D., 1950; m. Margaret Sinclair Smith, Apr. 7, 1942; children—Mary (Mrs. John Clinton McClain, Jr.), Catherine Lynn, Carol Ann, Margaret Sinclair. Instr., U. Minn., 1948-50; asst. prof. U. Ill., 1950-52; prof. social sci. Territorial Coll. of Guam, 1952-54; mem. faculty U. S.C., Columbia, 1954—, prof. edn., 1960—, chmn. psychol. services, 1956-62, chmn. secondary edn., 1962-70, dir. Univ. M.A. in Teaching, 1970—. Served to comdr. USNR, 1942-45. Mem. Am. Psychol. Assn., Assn. Supervision and Curriculum Devel. (past pres. S.C.), Nat. Council Social Studies, Phi Delta Theta, Sigma Delta Chi. Rotarian. Democrat. Presbyn. (elder). Home: 4218 St Clair Dr Columbia SC 29206

GILES, WILLIAM LINCOLN, univ. pres.; b. Oklahoma City, July 5, 1911; s. William L. and Katherine M. (Hill) G.; B.S.A., U. Ark., 1934, M.S., 1935, LL.D., 1967; Ph.D., U. Mo., 1949; m. Jean Presson, July 11, 1946; children—Ginger K., Richard W., John P. Agronomist, U.S. Dept. Agr., Manhattan, Kan., 1937-39, Beltsville, Md., 1939-42, Miss. State U., 1949-52; supt. Delta br. Expt. Sta. 1952-61; v.p. Miss. State U., 1961-66, pres., 1966—. Dir. Memphis br. Fed. Res. Bank St. Louis. Co-chmn. agrl. research policy adv. com. U.S. Dept. Agr. and Nat. Assn. State Univs. and Land-Grant Colls., 1969—; Bd. dirs. So. Regional Edn. Bd., 1966—, mem. council grad. edn. agrl. scis., 1965—, chmn., 1967. Named Man of Year in Agr., Progressive Farmer, 1960, Conservationist of Year, Am. Soc. Soil Conservation, 1963; recipient Distinguished Service award Miss. Farm Bur. Fedn., 1966; Hall of Distinction award Ark. Tech. Alumni Assn., 1968. Fellow A.A.A.S.; mem. Assn. So. Agrl. Workers (pres. 1964), Am. Soc. Agronomy (pres. Miss. sect. 1952), Soil Conservation Soc. Am., Miss. Entomol. Assn., Sigma Xi, Farm House Frat, Alpha Zeta, Alpha Kappa Psi, Phi Kappa Phi, Gamma Sigma Delta, Omicron Delta Kappa (hon.), Phi Chi Theta (hon.), Blue Key (hon.). Methodist. Rotarian. Home: Drawer J State College MS 39762

GILFORD, MURRENE, ins. exec.; b. Trinity, Tex., Dec. 7, 1924; s. Edward and Alma (Smith) G.; B.S., Wiley Coll., 1950; m. Mary Frances Bland, Feb. 18, 1961; children—Dexter Earl, Muriel Yvonne. Spl. rep. Atlanta Life Ins. Co., Tex., 1951-52, staff mgr., Lubbock, Tex., 1951-54, Austin, Tex., 1954-62, dist. mgr., San Antonio, 1962—. Mem. Ecumenical Council on Religion and Health, 1969—, San Antonio Community Relations Commn., 1967—. Chmn. bd. dirs. Alamo br. YMCA, 1967-68; bd. dirs. San Antonio Transit System; trustee San Antonio Jr. Coll., 1960—. Served with USNR, 1943-46. Mem. Nat., Tex., San Antonio assns. life underwriters, Alamo City C. of C. (pres. 1964-69), Alpha Phi Alpha, Beta Kappa Xi. Baptist. Home: 1618 Lone Oak St San Antonio TX 78220 Office: 2756 E Commerce St San Antonio TX 78220

GILGASH, CURTIS ARNOLD, educator; b. nr. Ellicott City, Md., Jan. 15, 1929; s. August P. and Ethel (Wilcox) G.; A.B. magna cum laude, Washington Coll., Md., 1949; M.A., Am. U., 1953, Ph.D., 1956; m. Ruthetta Lippy, June 15, 1957. Tchr. pub. schs. Catonsville, Md., 1949-50; research staff psychologist Spring Grove State Hosp., Balt., 1950-53; clin. sch. psychologist Baltimore County Bd. Edn., 1953-57; clin. sch. psychologist U. Hawaii, Honolulu, 1957-58, asst. prof., gen. counselor, coordinator, 1957-58; dir. spl. edn. Dillard U., New Orleans, 1958-59; chmn. dept. psychology MacMurray Coll., Jacksonville, Ill., 1959-62; prof., chmn. dept. psychology U. Tampa (Fla.), 1962—. Vis. prof. Johns Hopkins, summers 1963, 64. Mem. Md. N.G. 1947-49. Served with AUS, 1945-47. Recipient G. Truman Hunter award as outstanding prof. U. Tampa, 1969. Fellow Internat Council Psychologists, Md. Psychol. Assn.; mem. Am., Southeastern, Fla. psychol. assns., Am. Assn. U. Profs. Contbr. articles to profl. jours. Home: 4503 North A St Tampa FL 33609

GILKERSON, YANCEY SHERARD, editor; b. Laurens, S.C., Mar. 5, 1919; s. Yancey S. and Harriet (Bentz) G.; student Furman U., 1936-38; m. Vashti Keys, July 29, 1941; 1 son, Richard B. City editor The Greenville (S.C.) Piedmont, 1946-48, San Diego Jour., 1949; asst. city editor New Orleans Item, 1950-54; bur. chief Fairchild Publs., Greenville, S.C., 1954-58; editor Women's Wear Daily, N.Y.C., 1958-61; exec. v.p. Textile Hall Corp., 1961-66, pres., treas., 1966—. Home: 112 Lanneau Dr Greenville SC 29605 Office: Exposition Av PO Box 5823 Greenville SC 29606

GILKESON, JAMES WILLIAM, JR., constrn. co. exec.; b. Fisherville, Va., Oct. 9, 1925; s. James William and Zanie Julia (Winchester) G.; B.S. in Civil Engring., Va. Poly. Inst., 1950; m. Emily Thomas Scott, June 27, 1953; children—J. Scott, Julia R., David T., Emily Page. Foreman, Va. Asphalt Paving Co., Inc., 1950-55, mgr. no. dist., 1955-56; v.p. engring., safety dir. Nielsen Constrn. Co., Inc., Harrisonburg, Va., also dir.; dir. Shen Valley Corp., 1968-71. Mem. gen. adv. com. Massanutten Vocation Tech. Center, 1970—; mem. exec. com. bldg. div., constrn. sect. Indsl. Dept., Nat. Safety Council, 1970—; chmn. activities com., dir. Stonewall Jackson Area council Boy Scouts Am., 1970—; mem. local Price Stabilization Bd., 1970—. Mem. Planning Commn., City of Harrisonburg, Va., 1969—, vice-chmn., 1971. Bd. dirs. Va. Safety Assn., Inc., 1970—. Served with USNR, 1943-46. Recipient award Stonewall Jackson area council Boy Scouts Am., 1971. Mem. Am. Soc. C.E. (mem. exec. council, program chmn. Blue Ridge chpt. Va. sect. 1971), Asso. Gen. Contractors Am. (co-chmn. safety com. Va. br. 1967), Harrisonburg Rockingham C. of C. (chmn. safety com. 1968—), Va. Poly. Inst. Alumni Assn. (v.p. Massanutten chpt. 1967-68). Presbyn. (elder 1961—). Mem. Order of the Arrow Brotherhood. Home: 986 S Dogwood Dr Harrisonburg VA 22801 Office: 56 W Johnson St PO Box 591 Harrisonburg VA 22801

GILL, ATTICUS JAMES, physician, educator; b. Okmulgee, Okla., June 8, 1914; s. X.R. and Martha (Trotter) G.; M.D., Duke, 1938; m. Lucille Hodge, Nov. 8, 1941; children—Frank Harrison, Mary, James Hodge. Intern, residency tng. pathology Duke Hosp. and St. Pauls Hosp., Dallas, 1938-41; instr. pathology U. Tenn., 1941-42, asst. prof., 1942-43; asst. prof. pathology Southwestern Med. Sch., 1943-46, asso., prof., 1947-49, prof., 1950—, asso. dean, 1950-51, asst. dean, 1952-55, dean, 1955-67; staff Parkland Meml. Hosp.; cons. staff Baylor Hosp., Presbyn. Hosp., St. Paul's Hosp., Dallas. Diplomate Am. Bd. Pathology. Fellow Am. Soc. Clin. Pathologists, Coll. Am. Pathologists, A.C.P.; mem. A.M.A., So., Tex. med. assns., Tex. Soc. Pathologists, Dallas So. Clin. Soc., Dallas County Med. Soc. (dir. 1956-58), Alpha Omega Alpha, Sigma Phi Epsilon, Phi Chi. Home: 7103 Lakewood Blvd Dallas TX 75214

GILL, CHARLES RICHARD, physician; b. Washington, Aug. 14, 1931; s. Teiser Bass and Ruth Lindon (Kagey) G.; A.B. summa cum laude, Lafayette Coll., 1951; M.D. with distinction, George Washington U., 1955; m. Lois Isabel Snyder, June 26, 1956; children—Richard Marshall, Virginia Louise. Intern, Duke Hosp. Durham, N.C., 1955-56; fellow internal medicine Mayo Clinic, Rochester, Minn., 1956-57, 59-61; practice medicine, specializing in internal medicine, Lexington, Ky., 1961—; staff physician, cons. internal medicine Lexington Clinic, 1961—; asso. clin. prof. medicine U. Ky. Med. Center, Lexington, 1963—. Served with AUS, 1957-59. Mem. A.C.P. (asso.), Am. Rheumatism Assn., Phi Beta Kappa, Alpha Omega Alpha, Sigma Chi, Phi Chi. Republican. Methodist. Home: 631 Tateswood Dr Lexington KY 40502 Office: 1221 S Broadway Lexington KY 40504

GILL, EDWIN MAURICE, state ofcl.; b. Laurinburg, N.C., July 20, 1899; s. Thomas Jeffries and Mamie (North) G.; student Trinity Coll., 1922-24; LL.D., Duke, 1959. Admitted to N.C. bar,1924; mem. firm Gibson and Gill, Laurinburg, N.C., 1924-31, Gardner, Morrison & Rogers, Washington, 1949-50; pvt. sec. to gov. of N.C., 1931-33; commr. paroles State of N.C., 1933-42, commr. revenue, 1942-49; collector, dir. internal revenue, Greensboro, N.C., 1950-53; treas. State of N.C., Raleigh, 1953—. Bd. commrs. Law Enforcement Officers' Benefit and Retirement Fund; mem., investment officer Local Govt. Employees' Retirement System; mem. N.C. Bd. Edn.; former mem. N.C. Probation Commn., N.C. Art Commn. Mem. N.C. Ho. of Reps., 1929, 31. Trustee, N.C. Art Museum. Mem. Am. Legion, Nat. Tax Assn., Nat. Assn. Tax Adminstrs., Sigma Nu Phi, Omicron Delta Kappa, Beta Gamma Sigma. Democrat. Methodist. Address: State Capitol Bldg Raleigh NC 27601

GILL, EUGENE LAVERNE, accountant; b. Kansas City, Kan., Jan. 2, 1929; s. Carl and Anna (Sambol) G.; student La. State U., 1953-59, U. Ala., 1960; m. Mary Alita Williams, Sept. 9, 1967; children—Alita Ann, Carla Gene. Partner firm Carl Gill & Son, Mercantile, New Roads, La., 1950-63; pub. accountant Eugene L. Gill, C.P.A., New Roads, 1962-66; partner Gill & Kendrick, New Roads, 1966—; pres. Ben Morgan Furniture Co.; pres. Poor Boy's Friend, Inc., Gill Land Co., Ltd. Chmn. bd. dirs. Pointe Coupee Gen. Hosp., 1969-70. C.P.A., La., Miss., Ark. Mem. Am. Accounting Assn., Nat. Assn. Accountants, Am. Inst. C.P.A.'s. Soc. La. C.P.A.'s (mem. com. to secure C.P.A. problems 1962-69, chmn. 1963-66, vice chmn. consultation com. 1966-67, mem. profl. devel. council 1967-71), Am. Bus. Law Assn., Am. Judicature Soc., Pub. Affairs Research Council La. (trustee 1968—), Nat. Sourjourners, Farm Bur. Fedn., Am. Radio Relay League. Democrat. Episcopalian (warden, vestryman, lay leader). Mason (32deg., Shriner), Lion (past pres., past treas. New Roads); mem. Order Eastern Star. Clubs: Executive (Baton Rouge); False River Country. Contbr. articles to profl. jours. Home: 311 Gretchen St New Roads LA 70760 Office: 104 W End Dr New Roads LA 70760

GILL, GEORGE NORMAN, newspaperman; b. Indpls., Aug. 11, 1934; s. George E. and Urith (Dailey) G.; A.B., Ind. U., 1957; m. Kay Baldwin, Dec. 27, 1957; children—Norman Alan, George Baldwin. Reporter, Richmond (Va.) News Leader, 1957-60; from copy editor to mng. editor Courier-Jour., Louisville, 1960—. Served with USNR, 1954-56. Recipient Reporting award Va. Press Assn., 1959; named Newspaper Picture Editor of Year, Nat. Press Photographers Assn., 1966. Mem. Am. Soc. Newspaper Editors, A.P. Mng. Editors, Louisville Com. Fgn. Relations, Sigma Delta Chi, Alpha Tau Omega. Mason. Home: 308 Rebel Dr Pewee Valley KY 40056 Office: 525 W Broadway Louisville KY 40202

GILL, GRAYSON WOODWARD, architect; b. Port Clinton, O., Nov. 7, 1893; s. Elmer Ellsworth and Sarah (Woodward) G.; student Ohio State U., 1911-14; B.S., U. Mich., 1921; m. Cornelia Wade Douglas, June 16, 1927; 1 son, Grayson Douglas. Draftsman, Mills Rhines, Bellman & Nordhoff, 1914-16, Am. Bridge Co., 1924-25; asso. prof. A. and M. Coll. Tex., 1922-24; engr. Herbert M. Greene Co., 1925-34; self-employed as architect-engr., Dallas, 1934-58; pres. Grayson Gill, Inc., Dallas, 1959—. Chmn. Dallas Bldg. Code Com., 1946-47; mem. City Plan Commn., 1939-48, Greater Dallas Planning Council, 1948—, Dallas Fire Council, 1964—, Tex. State Commn. Code Com., 1968. Served to 1st lt. U.S. Army, 1916-19. Fellow A.I.A., Am. Soc. C.E.; mem. Bldg. Research Inst., Am. Concrete Inst., Constrn. Specifications Inst., Tex. Soc. Architects. Home: 4000 Rock Creek Dr Dallas TX 75204 Office: 1913 San Jacinto St Dallas TX 75201

GILL, HARRY WILLIAM CYRIL, educator; b. Gillingham, Eng., May 31, 1902; s. Harry and Katherine (Wallace) G.; B.A., U. London, 1923, M.A., 1925; m. Kathleen R. Williams, Apr. 28, 1927; children—Sheila Margaret (Mrs. Donald A. Maser), Barbara Elaine (Mrs. Malcolm Templeton), Humphrey G. Came to U.S., 1943. Asst. prof. Georgetown U., 1946-50; headmaster Fla. Mil. Acad., Ft. Lauderdale, 1953-57; asst. prof., asso. prof. St. Leo (Fla.) Coll., 1957-66, prof. polit. sci. and history, 1966-69, distinguished prof. polit. sci., 1969—; vis. prof. U. Scranton, 1967. Mem. Am. Assn. U. Profs., Am. Polit. Sci. Assn., So. Polit. Sci. Assn., Polynesian Soc. K.C. (4 deg.). Home: PO Box 2301 Saint Leo FL 33574

GILL, JOHN PAUL, educator; b. Warrior-Run, Pa., Jan. 7, 1910; s. John and Hedwig (Ryto) G.; student Pa. State Coll., 1929-31; A.B., U. Ala., 1932, M.A., 1934; Ph.D., U. Tex., 1950; m. Bernice Victoria Alman, May 24, 1932; 1 son, John Paul. Asst. instr. Sch. Bus. Adminstrn., U. Ala., 1932-34, comml. math., 1934-42, instr. bus. statistics, statistician Bur. Bus. Research, 1942-43, asst. prof., 1945-46; head math dept. John E. Brown Coll., summers 1934-35; research statistician, dept. research Fed. Res. Bank, Dallas, 1943-45; chief research and progress analysis div. Houston regional office, War Assets Adminstrn., 1946-47; instr. U. Tex., 1947-49; asst. prof. Fla. State U., 1949-51; prof. econ. statistics, dir. div. research, also editor Atlanta Econ. Rev., Sch. Bus. Adminstrn., Atlanta div. U. Ga., 1951-54, prof. econs., dir. Bur. Bus. Research, coordinator grad. studies, also editor Ga. Bus., Coll. Bus. Adminstrn., U. Ga., 1954-60; prof. Sch. Commerce and Bus. Administrn., U. Ala., 1960—, head dept. bus. statistics, 1960-71. Mem. Am. Assn. U. Profs., Am. Statis. Assn. (pres. Ala. chpt. 1965-66), Southern Econs. Assn., Pi Mu Epsilon, Alpha Kappa Psi, Beta Gamma Sigma (nat. exec. com. 1958-61). Author booklet on indexes of retail sales, also chpt. 1953-54 Credit Mgmt. Year-Book; numerous articles in field. Editor Southeastern Resources Handbook, Vols. I, II, III. Home: 10 C Northwood Northport AL 35476

GILL, JOHN RAYMOND, educator, dentist; b. St. Paul, Mar. 23, 1895; s. John and Hanna (Anderson) G.; D.D.S., U. Minn., 1921; m. Margaret Sutor Hole, Aug. 7, 1941. Instr., U. Minn., 1921-23; prof. U. Cal. at San Francisco, 1923-58; prin., De Montmorency Dental Sch., Lahore, Pakistan, 1949-50; prof. U. Los Andes, Merida, Venezuela, 1959-64; prof. Sch. Dentistry, U. P.R., San Juan, 1964—, dir. dept. restorative dentistry and grad. div., 1966—. Recipient French Acad. Palm; hon. prof. U. Los Andes. Fellow Am. Coll. Dentists, Internat. Coll. Dentists; mem. Am. Dental Assn. (life), Acad. Restorative Dentistry (life), Acad. Crown and Bridge Prosthesis, Acad. Gold Foil Operators, Pacific Coast Prosthetic Soc. (life), Cal., Pakistan dental assns., Ore. Dental Soc., Omicron Kappa Upsilon. Home: Hotel Borinquen Santurce PR 00707 Office: Sch Dentistry U PR San Juan PR 00905

GILL, MICHAEL DOUD, mfg. co. exec.; b. San Antonio, Dec. 14, 1935; s. Richard and Frances (Doud) G.; student U. Va., 1954-57, Am. U., 1958-60; m. Cornelia Elizabeth Stewart, Feb. 19, 1953; children—Julia Frances, Gordon Carlson, Michael Doud. Asst. dir. sanitation, automatic merchandising Govt. Services, Inc., Washington, 1954-55; v.p. Robert G. Lynch Co., Washington, 1955-56; with G.B.L. Service, Inc., Air Freight Clearings, Inc., Washington, 1956-58; pres. Pictagraph, Washington, 1958—, Gill Products, Inc., Washington, 1958—, Michael Doud Gill; Assos., Inc., Washington, Michael Doud Gill Africa Ltd., Zambia, Mgmt. Systems' Sales, Inc., Washington, 1972—; former asst. to chmn. bd., Decker Corp., Bala Cynwyd, Pa., bd. chmn. Oxy Catalyst Co., Berwin, Pa., Nat. Aero. Assn.; asst. to pres. Air Transit Services, Inc.; dir. Wells Industries Corp., North Hollywood, Cal., 1958—; gen. agt. Am. Heritage Life Insurance Co., Washington, Va., Md.; v.p. Internat. Expositions Corp. Asst. to U.S. housing adm.instr. HHFA, 1960-61; del. 2D Atlantic Conf. NATO, 1960, Eric Johnston Conf. Mut. Security, Pres.'s Conf. Reciprocal Trade; Nat. Committeeman Boy Scouts Am., 1964—; Washington coordinator Support Our Boys in Viet Nam Day, 1967-68; pres. Nat. Civic Affairs Bur., 1965; nat. vice-chmn. Nat. Citizen's for Columbus Day, Friends of Korea Com.;

mem. steering com. D.C. Com. Eisenhower Presdl. Library; mem. exec. com. Theodore Roosevelt Centennial Com; mem. diplomatic Council People-to-People Sports Com., 1969—; chmn. teenage program March of Dimes; chmn. of benefits various charitable orgns. Md. and D.C. area, 1956—. Mem. finance com. Rep. State Central Com., D.C., 1955-64; asst. campaign dir. Rep. Nat. Com., 1960; Sgt.-at-arms nat. com. 1960, Rep. Nat. Conv., 1960, chief page, conv., 1964; chmn. Youth Salutes the Pres., 1956, I Miss Ike night, 1962; dir. Speakers and Personal Appearance Bur., 1964; chief staff Nat. Nixon for Pres. Com., 1967, dir. spl. events and activities at nat. conv., 1968; asst. to nat. chmn. United Citizens for Nixon/Agnew, 1968; chmn. United Citizen com. Inaugural Com., 1969. Bd. dirs. Heart Found., Nat. Found.; pres. Free World Forum, Inc. Served with USMCR. Named Outstanding Young Man in Politics Nat. Rep. Women's Club, 1957; recipient citation 2d Atlantic Conf. NATO, 1960. Mem. Internat. Platform Assn., Am. Acad. Polit. and Social Sci., Am. Legion, Washington Bd. Trade, Bahamas Oceanographic Soc. (gen. mgr. 1965—), St. Hubert Soc. Am. Sigma Alpha Epsilon. Toastmaster. Clubs: Capitol Hill (Washington); Jockey (Miami, Fla.). Home: 8712 Ewing Dr Bethesda MD 20034 Office: 2139 R St NW Washington DC 20008

GILL, WILFRED VERNON, govt. ofcl.; b. Boston, June 8, 1915; s. Otis Weld and Wilma Clarene (Richardson) G.; A.B., Harvard, 1936; m. Mary Jane Miller, July 17, 1948; 1 son, Craig Richardson. Claims adjuster Liberty Mut. Ins. Co., N.Y.C., 1936-39; claims examiner U.S. Railroad Retirement Bd., 1939-41; investigator CSC, N.Y.C., 1941, examiner, 1941-47, field ops. supr., Washington, 1947-55, regional dir., Dallas, 1955-61, asst. to chmn., Washington, 1961-69; exec. dir. Fed. Labor Relations Council, 1970—. Served from pvt. to capt., USAAF, 1942-46. Decorated Air Medal. Recipient Distinguished Service award Civil Service Commn., 1968. Mem. Indsl. Relations Research Assn. Home: 8320 Fenway Rd Bethesda MD 20034 Office: 1900 E St NW Washington DC 20415

GILL, WILLIAM GILLETTE, petroleum exec.; b. Bay City, Tex., Mar. 10, 1922; s. Hugh and Eloise (Gillette) G.; B.S., Tex. A. and M. U., 1947; m. Ruth Bayne Bishop, July 5, 1943; children—William Gillette, Marie (Mrs. L. Hollingshead), James S., Richard B. Oil prodn. P.R. Rutherford Co., Houston, 1947-51, F. William Carr, Corpus Christi, Tex., 1951-56; ind. oil producer, 1956-64; pres. TEC. Corpus Christi, 1964—. Served to capt. inf. AUS, 1942-45. Decorated Bronze Star. Mem. Am. Inst. Mining Engrs., Petroleum Club. Patentee inventions for secondary oil recovery. Home: 1 Hewit Dr Corpus Christi TX 78404 Office: Wilson Bldg Corpus Christi TX 78401

GILL, WILLIAM ROBERT, educator; b. McDonald, Pa., July 21, 1920; s. William M. and Della M. (Leiden) G.; B.S., Pa. State U., 1942; M.S., U. Hawaii, 1949; Ph.D., Cornell U., 1955; m. Irene Victoria Majorkiewicz, July 19, 1947; children—William Robert, John P., David C., Michael J., Elaine N. Soil scientist Pineapple Research Inst., Honolulu, 1949-50; soil scientist Nat. Tillage Machinery Lab., Auburn, Ala., 1955-70, dir., 1971—; research lectr. agrl. engring. Auburn U.; exchange scientist USSR, 1970. Served with AUS, 1943-47, 51-53. Christian Scientist (reader). Author: (with G. E. Vander Berg) Soil Dynamics in Tillage and Traction, 1968. Contbr. articles to profl. jours. Home: 283 Hillcrest Dr Auburn AL 36830 Office: PO Box 792 Auburn AL 36830

GILLEMAND, SYDNEY WILLIAM, constrn. co. exec.; b. Chgo., Aug. 9, 1910; s. Sydney Charles and Dagmar Matilda (Assumaa) G.; ed. Harvard (Ill.) pub. schs.; m. Vivian Lucille Wilbur, Mar. 11, 1932; children— Lucille (Mrs. Harold Redlund), Leslie Charles. Mgr., A. & P. Tea Co., 1932-34; salesman Sears, Roebuck & Co., 1934-40; with Bally Mfg. Co., 1940-55; carpenter, Hot Springs, Ark., 1955-60; owner firm Sid Cillemand Custom Builder, Hot Springs, 1963—; pres. Home Builders Rehab. Corp., 1971—. Mem. Hot Springs mayor's Sewer Com., 1971—; chmn. Bd. Adjustments and Appeals So. Bldg. Code, Hot Springs, 1971—. Mem. Ark. (dir. 1971—), Hot Springs (pres.) home builders assns. Address: Rt 6 Box 796 Hot Springs AR 71901

GILLEN, MARY-MARGARET D., lawyer; b. Poughkeepsie, N.Y., May 17, 1941; B.A. magna cum laude, Trinity Coll., 1962; J.D., Georgetown U., 1961, LL.B., 1966. Admitted to D.C. bar, 1966, U.S. Ct. Appeals bar, 1966; now mem. firm Bergson, Borkland, Margolis & Adler, Washington. Mem. Bar. Assn. D.C., Am. Bar Assn. Editor Georgetown Law Rev., 1964-65. Address: Bergson Borkland Margolis & Adler 21 DuPont Circle NW Washington DC 20036*

GILLENWATER, JAY KING, chem. co. exec.; b. Esserville, Va., Mar. 3, 1907; s. J. A. and Nannie (Slemp) G.; student Lincoln Meml. U., 1921-25, U. Va., 1925-28; m. Anne Young, Dec. 21, 1931; children—Jay Young, Joyce (Mrs. J. W. Mottern), John K. Salesman, Tenn. Eastman Co. div. Eastman Kodak Co., 1931-34, asst. sales mgr., 1934-49, purchasing agt., 1949-53, dir. purchases, 1953-61, dir. purchases and traffic, 1961-68, dir. supply and distbn., 1968-69, v.p. supply and distbn., 1969—. Mem. Am. Chem. Soc., Nat. Assn. Purchasing Mgmt., Inc., Tenneva Assn. Purchasing Agts., C. of C., Alpha Chi Sigma. Club: Ridgefields Country (Kingsport, Tenn.). Home: 2221 Charsley St Kingsport TN 37660 Office: PO Box 511 Kingsport TN 37662

GILLER, NORMAN MYER, architect; b. Jacksonville, Fla., Feb. 14, 1918; s. Morris and Esther (Seltzer) G.; student Ga. Inst. Tech. B. Arch., U. Fla., 1945; m. Frances Schwartz, June 30, 1946; children—Ira Dean, Anita Sue, Brian Jay. Architect-owner Norman M. Giller & Assos., Miami Beach, Fla., 1944—; pres., chmn. bd. Jefferson Nat. Bank, Sunny Isles, Fla., 1965—, mem. bd., Miami Beach, 1968—; lectr., cons. in field. Pres. South Fla. chpt. Boy Scouts Am., 1961-62, mem. nat. council and regional exec. com., 1961—; mem. community planning adv. bd. Met. Dade County, Fla., 1964-66; chmn. Miami Beach Housing Authority, 1972—. Campaign mgr. Mayor of Miami Beach, 1971. Bd. dirs. Home for Aged, Miami; mem. archtl. adv. com. U. Miami, 1971. Served with USNR, World War II. Recipient Honor award Am. Assn. Sch. Adminstrs., 1969. Registered architect, Fla., P.R. Mem. A.I.A. (commr. pub. affairs So. Fla. chpt. 1971, treas. So. Fla. chpt. 1972), Nat. Council Archtl. Registration Bds., Miami Beach Taxpayers Assn., Greater Miami Beach C. of C. (pres. 1966-68), Fla. Bankers Assn. (mem. econ. edn. com. 1971). Jewish religion. Mason (Shriner). Home: 4500 Prairie Av Miami Beach FL 33140 Office: 975 Arthur Godfrey Rd Miami Beach FL 33140

GILLESPIE, A(NDREW) C(ECIL), accountant; b. Maryville, Tenn., Feb. 13, 1917; s. James Otha and Velma (Holt) G.; student Maryville Coll., 1934-35, LaSalle Extension U.; m. Marjorie Bennette Turner, Aug. 15, 1942; children—Marjorie Annette, Karol Elizabeth. Cost accountant Aluminum Co. Am., 1940-45; staff accountant Dent K. Burk Assos., C.P.A.'s, 1945-46; self-employed as C.P.A., Maryville and Knoxville, Tenn., 1946—; partner Gillespie & Sherrod, C.P.A.'s, 1969—; dir. Rockford Mfg. Co., Inc., Trotter Pontiac Co., Chattanooga, Supreme Foods Co., Knoxville, C.P.A., Tenn. Mem. Am. Inst. C.P.A.'s, Tenn. Soc. C.P.A.'s. Baptist. Mason (Shriner), Rotarian. Club: Green Meadow Country. Home: RFD 3 Louisville TN 37777 Office: Blount Nat Bank Bldg Maryville TN 37801

GILLESPIE, D. RAY, assn. exec.; b. Dunkirk, O., Dec. 26, 1933; s. Dale Leroy and Margaret Rae (Fletcher) G.; B.S., Bowling Green State U., 1958; postgrad. Mich. State U., 1961, 64, 68; m. Cherie Elizabeth Rahal, Dec. 26, 1952; children—David Robert, Anne Elizabeth, James Ray Fletcher. Asst. exec. Massillon (O.) C. of C., 1958-59; mgr. Ashland (O.) C. of C., 1959-62; exec. v.p. Bloomington (Ill.) Assn. Commerce, 1962-64; exec. v.p. Lexington (Ky.) Area C. of C., 1964—. Mem. Community Health Adv. Bd., 1969-71). Bd. dirs. United Cerebral Palsy, 1967-69, United Community Fund, 1966-70, Fayette County Med. Soc. Found., Community Action Council. Served with USAF, 1951-55. Mem. Am. (pub. relations com. 1962-71), Ky. (1st pres. 1968-69), So. (dir. 1969-71) chambers commerce execs. Republican. Mem. Christian Ch. (deacon, mem. adminstrv. bd. 1967-69). Rotarian. Home: 3192 Roxburg Dr Lexington KY 40503 Office: 239 N Broadway Lexington KY 40508

GILLESPIE, HAROLD EDWIN, state ofcl.; b. Minto, N.D., Aug. 12, 1907; s. Alexander G. and Rosa (Engebretson) G.; student U. Mont., 1924-27; B.A., B.S., B.M., U. Minn., 1932, M.D., 1933; m. Mary Miller Kress, June 29, 1940; children—Angus Kress, Mary Sabra, Cameron Alexander. Commd. lt. (j.g.) U.S. Navy, 1932, advanced through grades to capt., 1945; intern USN Hosp., Mare Island, Cal., 1932-33, St. Francis Hosp., San Francisco, 1933; hosp. comdr. Naval Air Stations, various locations, 1947-59; with Mil. Air Transport Services, 1959-63; ret., 1963; health dir., Williamsburg, Va., 1964-66; dep. commr. health Va. Dept. Health, Richmond, 1966—. Diplomate Am. Bd. Preventive Medicine. Fellow Am. Coll. Preventive Medicine; mem. Iron Wedge, Incus. Home: 1827 Grove Av Richmond VA 23220 Office: 109 Governor St Richmond VA 23219

GILLESPIE, JESSE SAMUEL, JR., research inst. exec.; b. Lynchburg, Va., Dec. 20, 1921; s. Jesse Samuel and Norna Brenda (Wright) G.; B.S., Va. Mil. Inst., 1943; Ph.D. (Tenn. Eastman fellow), U. Va., 1949; m. Nancy Vaughn Blackburn, Sept. 1, 1950; children—Samuel Harrison, Leonard Blackburn, William Wright, Nan Walker. Asst. prof. chemistry U. Richmond (Va.), 1949-51; sr. chemist, group leader, research dept. Va.-Carolina Chem. Corp., Richmond, 1951-54, asst. div. mgr. fiber div., 1954-56, sales mgr., 1956-58; partner Cox and Gillespie, Richmond, 1958-62; sr. research chemist Va. Inst. Sci. Research, Richmond, 1962-68, dir., 1968—. Vis. prof. chemistry Randolph-Macon Coll., 1960-61; adj. prof. chemistry U. Richmond, 1969—; advanced sci. tchr. St. Christopher's Sch., 1964-68; mem. library adv. com. State Council Higher Edn., 1968-71. Mem. Richmond Air Pollution Control Appeals Bd., 1971—; mem. Selective Service State Adv. Com. on Sci., Engring. and Specialized Personnel, 1969-71; regional v.p. Nat. Kidney Found., 1960-63. Served to 1st lt. AUS, World War II. Decorated Purple Heart; recipient Jackson-Hope medal Va. Mil. Inst., 1943. Mem. Am. Chem. Soc. (exec. com. local sect. 1965—), Va. Acad. Sci., Soc. Va. Creepers, Raven Soc., Sigma Xi, Alpha Chi Sigma, Omicron Delta Kappa, Kappa Alpha. Republican. Episcopalian. Rotarian. Club: Country of Va. (Richmond). Contbr. articles to profl. jours. Home: 22 Maxwell Rd Richmond VA 23226 Office: 6300 River Rd Richmond VA 23229

GILLESPIE, RALPH, textile exec.; b. Walhalla, S.C., Oct. 20, 1928; s. Major T. and Inez (Rowland) G.; student U. S.C., 1948-51, Internat. Corr. Schs., 1951-53; m. Rosalina Brandt, Apr. 8, 1951; children—Ralph Michael, Portia Anne, Demillia Sue, Maxwell Brandt. With Deering Milliken, Inc., 1950—, v.p. indsl. spltys. div., 1964-65, v.p. co., 1965—, pres. indsl. div., Spartanburg, S.C., 1965—; pres. Milliken Indsls. Corp., Clemson Automotive Fabrics, Inc.; v.p. Magnolia Industries, Inc.; v.p., dir. Deering Milliken Service Corp.; pres., treas., dir. Lockhart Power Co.; dir. Deering Milliken Ltd., Deering Milliken Research Corp., Milliken Europe N.V., Geonics, Ltd., Alfortex S.A., Milliken Fabrics S.A. Mem. bus. com. Spartanburg County Arts Council. Served with AUS, 1947-49. Mem. S.C. State C. of C., Spartanburg C. of C., S.C. Textile Mfrs. Assn., Am. Textile Mfrs. Inst. Republican. Lutheran. Clubs: Union League (N.Y.C.); Spartanburg Esquire, Piedmont (Spartanburg). Home: 268 Mills Av Spartanburg SC 29302 Office: PO Box 1926 Spartanburg SC 29301

GILLESPIE, ROBERT GILL, chief justice Miss. Supreme Ct.; b. Madison, Ala., Sept. 17, 1903; s. Philander M. and Flora (Gill) G.; student Huntsville Jr. Coll., 1923-24; law student U. Ala., 1924-26; m. Margaret Griffith, June 30, 1930; children—Robert Gill, Virgil Griffith. Admitted to Miss. bar, 1927, practiced in Meridian, 1927-33; spl. agt. FBI, 1934-35; partner Bailey & Gillespie, 1939-43, Gillespie & Minniece, 1945-48, Gillespie, Huff & Williams, 1948-54; chancellor 2d Chancery Ct. Dist. of Miss., 1939; justice Miss. Supreme Ct., 1954-66, presiding justice, 1966-71, chief justice, 1971—. Mem. Miss. Council State Govts., 1944-48. Bd. dirs. Southwestern Coll., 1952-60. Mem. Am. Bar Assn., Miss. State Bar, Am. Judicature Soc., Delta Tau Delta. Presbyn. Home: 432 Dunbar St Jackson MS 39216 Office: Miss State Supreme Ct New Capitol Jackson MS 39201

GILLESPIE, WILLIAM MILLER, state legislator; b. Daytona Beach, Fla., Apr. 19, 1928; s. James U. and Hazel (Moore) G.; A.A., U. Fla., 1951; B.S., Fla. State U., 1952; J.D., Stetson U., 1956; m. Sally M. Igo, Sept. 5, 1958. Admitted to Fla. bar; asst. city atty., New Smyrna Beach, Fla., 1958-59; municipal judge, New Smyrna Beach, 1964-67; city atty., Oak Hill, Fla., from 1964; mem. Fla. Ho. of Reps., 1966—. Served with AUS, 1946-48. Recipient Good Govt. award New Smyrna Beach Jr. C. of C., 1967, Ray Starr award, 1967. Mem. Am., Volusia County (pres. 1968-69) bar assns., Am. Trial Lawyers Assn., Stetson Lawyers Assn. (state dir.), Am. Legion, V.F.W. Episcopalian. Moose, Elk, Mason, Kiwanian. Home: 610 N Peninsular Av New Smyrna Beach FL 32069 Office: PO Box 580 New Smyrna Beach FL 32069*

GILLETT, JOHN SHACKLEFORD, supt. schs.; b. George West, Tex., Sept. 4, 1908; s. Henry Pleasants and Mabel Cordia (Crawford) G.; B.A., Tex. A. and I. U., 1934, M.A., 1938; m. Lela Jo Merideth, July 30, 1945. Tchr. Kingsville (Tex.) pub. schs., 1934-37, prin., 1937-42, 47-52, asst. supt., 1952-56, supt. schs., 1956—. Pres. Community Concerts Assn., Kingsville, 1960-67. Bd. dirs. Kingsville Pub. Library. Served to lt. comdr. USNR, 1942-46. Mem. Tex. State Tchrs. Assn., N.E.A., Tex., Am. assns. sch. adminstrs., Phi Delta Kappa. Home: Box 988 Kingsville TX 78363 Office: Box 871 Kingsville TX 78363

GILLEY, LLOYD JAMES, assn. exec.; b. Ada, Okla., Sept. 30, 1941; s. Louis Lee and Viola May (Olds) G.; student E. Central State Coll., Ada., 1959-60; m. Bobbie Joan Wheeler Johnson, Aug. 13, 1961. Mgr. Spearman (Tex.) C. of C., 1967-68, Kermit (Tex.) C. of C., 1969-72, Weatherford (Tex.) C. of C., 1972—. Bd. dirs. Winkler County Fair Assn., 1971. Mem. C. of C. Execs. Assn. W. Tex. (bd. dirs. 1969-72), Permian Basin C. of C. Execs. Assn. (pres. 1971). Lion (bd. dirs. Kermit 1967-72), Rotarian. Clubs: Winkler County Country, Desert (Kermit); Hansford County Golf (Spearman). Home: 501 Harcourt St Weatherford TX 76086 Office: 119 N Main St Weatherford TX 76068

GILLHAM, JAMES ODELL, banker; b. Greenville, Tex., Oct. 7, 1899; s. James Verner and Etta V. (Chapman) G.; student E. Tex. State Coll., 1914-15, W. Tex. State Coll., 1916-17, Denver U., 1919, m. Ruth Z. Upton, Dec. 25, 1922; children—Eleanor (Mrs. Robert N. Tipps), Helen (Mrs. J. C. Powell) DeLores (Mrs. Robert Lee Craig). Cashier, First State Bank, Happy, Tex., 1921-27; asst. cashier First Nat. Bank, Pampa, 1927-36; with Brownfield (Tex.) State Bank & Trust Co., (Tex.), 1936-71, pres., 1944-68, chmn. bd., 1968-71, also dir.; pres. Yoakum County State Bank, Denver City, 1950-71, also dir.; pres., dir. Brownfield Savs. & Loan Assn. (Tex.), 1951-71; chmn. bd., dir. Levelland State Bank (Tex.), 1944-62. Mem. Tex. Ho. of Reps., 1953-57. Bd. dirs. Tex. Tech. Found. Mem. Ind. (state dir.), Tex. (pres. 1943-44) bankers assns., C. of C. (pres. 1945). Democrat. Methodist. Rotarian (pres. Brownfield 1944-45), Elk. Home: 1620 E Buckley St Brownfield TX 79316 Died June 6, 1971

GILLIAM, DARRELL KAY, physician; b. Wise, Va., Nov. 11, 1928; s. Franklin William and Mary Virginia (Bevins) G.; student Marshall U., 1946-48; B.A., U. Richmond, 1950; M.D., Med. Coll. Va., 1959; m. Nancy Evelyn Giannotti, Mar. 25, 1951; children—Darrell Kent, Shelley Lynn, William Anthony. Rotating intern Stuart Circle Hosp., Richmond, Va., 1959-60, now mem. staff; gen. practice medicine, Richmond, Va., 1960—, mem. staff St. Luke's Hosp., Richmond, Retreat for the Sick, Richmond, Johnston-Willis Hosp., Richmond, Grace Hosp., Richmond, Chippenham Hosp., Richmond; clin. instr. dept. family practice, health sci. div. Va. Commonwealth U., 1970-71. Pres., owner Broad Rock Bldg. Corp. Committeeman Robert E. Lee council Boy Scouts Am., 1970-72. Served with AUS, 1951-53; ETO. Diplomate Am. Bd. Family Practice. Mem. A.M.A., So. Med. Assn., Med. Soc. Va., Va. (dir. 1971), Richmond (pres. 1969-70) acads. gen. practice, Richmond Acad. Medicine (sec. 1968-70), Manchester Med. Soc., Alumnus U. Richmond, Theta Kappa, Sigma Phi Epsilon. Methodist (chmn. bd. trustees 1966-71). Club: Meadowbrook Country (Richmond). Home: 5110 Monza Ct Richmond VA 23234 Office: 3315 Broad Rock Rd Richmond VA 23224

GILLIAM, FRANCIS ERVIN, dentist; b. nr. Burlington, N.C., Dec. 13, 1900; s. John Wesley and Mary Jane (Leath) G.; D.D.S., Emory U., 1924; m. Myrtle Mildred Burch, Dec. 14, 1929; children—Frank Ervin, Jeanette (Mrs. Lawrence Oliver). Practice gen. dentistry, Burlington, 1924—; speaker on dental procedures to profl. groups. Mem. N.C. (sec.-treas. 3d dist. 1945-46), 3d Dist. (pres. 1948), Alamance Caswell dental socs., Pierre Fauchard Acad., Acad. Internat. Dentistry, Am. Dental Assn., Am. Soc. Dentistry for Children. Baptist (deacon). Kiwanian. Club: Alamance Country of Burlington. Home: 1209 Aycock Av Burlington NC 27215 Office: PO Box 448 Burlington NC 27215

GILLIAM, JOHN JACKSON, librarian; b. South Pittsburg, Tenn., Sept. 25, 1927; s. Charles Lester and Lucy (Jackson) G.; B.S. in Edn., Kent State U., 1952, M.S. in L.S., 1954; m. Phyllis Jean Fike, July 16, 1949; children—Charles Kevin, Curtis Kyle. Head bus. and tech. dept. Canton (O.) Pub. Library Assn., 1957-62; head librarian Firestone Tire & Rubber Co. Research Center, Akron, O., 1962; head librarian Babcock & Wilcox Co. Research Center, Alliance, O., 1962-63; head adminstrv. services Thiokol Corp., Brunswick, Ga., 1963-65; dir. libraries Brevard Community Coll., Cocoa, Fla., 1965-69, dean learning resources, 1969—. Served with USNR, 1945-46. Mem. Fla. Library Assn. (mem. intellectual freedom com. 1970-72), Fla. Assn. Pub. Jr. Colls., Phi Delta Kappa. Kiwanian. Home: 828 Mallard Rd Cocoa FL 32922 Office: 1519 Clearlake Rd Cocoa FL 32922

GILLIAM, JOSEPHINE CALDWELL, oil co. exec.; b. Bowie, Tex., June 8, 1912; d. John Walter and Josephine (Ribble) Caldwell; student Trinity U., 1929-30; m. Raymond Arnold Gilliam, June 3, 1932. Typist, Elliot & Waldron Abstract Cos. Inc., Athens, Tex., 1932-35, titleman, 1935-40; mgr. Elliott & Waldron, Quitman, Tex., 1940-42; staff fiduciary trust suit Shell Oil Co., Houston, 1942-43, sr. title clk. land dept., 1943-50; mgr. land dept., corporate asst. sec. J. Ray McDermott & Co., Houston, 1951-68; mgr. land dept., corporate asst. sec. TransOcean Oil Inc., Houston, 1968—. Trans Ocean Oil Can. Ltd., 1971—, Trans Ocean Oil (U.K.) Ltd., 1971—, Trans Ocean (U.K.) Inc., 1971—, corporate asst. sec. brs. J. Ray McDermott Can., Ltd., 1967—. Mem. Am. Bus. Women's Assn. (pres. 1967-68, Woman of Year 1965-66, editor Shamrock chpt. monthly mag. Blarney Stone 1970—). Home: 10626 Chevy Chase Houston TX 77042 Office: 1700 First City East Bldg Houston TX 77002

GILLIAM, THOMAS ETHERIDGE, editor; b. Bassfield, Miss., Aug. 30, 1912; s. Thomas Newton and Birdie Ada (Etheridge) G.; student Northwestern U., 1934, U. Mich., 1938, Auburn U., 1942, U. Ga., 1956; m. Eleanor Darnell, Feb. 26, 1939; children—Judy Darnell (Mrs. F. Daniel Thomas). Writer, actor radio and movies, Detroit, 1933-39; mech. engr. Ala. Power Co., Birmingham, 1940-43, Continental Gin Co., Birmingham, 1945-61; art dir., mag. editor Elton B. Stephens Co. Industries, Birmingham, 1961-65; with Civitan Internat. Birmingham, 1965—, editor Civitan Mag., 1968—. Recipient award Freedoms Found., 1968. Mem. So. Assn. Bus. Communicators (v.p. 1970—). Methodist (mem. ofcl. adminstrv. bd. 1961—). Club: Civitan (pres. Birmingham 1961-62). Home: 543 Durham Dr Birmingham AL 35209 Office: 115 N 21st St Birmingham AL 35203

GILLIARD, JOSEPH WADUS, educator; b. Taylors, S.C., Nov. 23, 1914; s. Josecphus and Anna (Durant) G.; B.S., Hampton Inst., 1941, M.A., 1952; m. Bertha Holder, Mar. 19, 1943; children—Bernard O., Brenda L. Faculty, Hampton (Va.) Inst., 1941—, asst. prof. art, 1949-71, asso. prof. art, 1971—. Ceramic art exhibited at Ceramic Nat., Syracuse Mus. Fine Arts, Richmond Mus. Fine Arts. Instnl. rep., dist. commr. Peninsula council Boy Scouts Am. Served with USNR, 1942-44. Recipient Merit award 2d biennial showing of Chesapeake Craftsmen, Norfolk Museum, 1954; Meritorious award Peninsula Jaycees, 1958; Walter R. Brown award Gamma Ita chpt. Alpha Phi Alpha; Outstanding Achievement award Gamma Epsilon chpt. Omega Psi Phi, 1964; Silver Beaver award Boy Scouts Am., 1966; Outstanding Achievement award Alpha Delta Mu Honor Soc., Hampton Inst., 1965-66. Mem. Am. Ceramic Soc., Am. Indsl. Arts Assn., Am. Assn. U. Profs. Baptist (trustee). Home: 108 W County St Hampton VA 23363

GILLILAN, LOIS ADELL, educator; b. Springville, Utah, June 15, 1911; d. Lew Wallace and Ellen (Benson) Gillian; B.A., Mt. Holyoke Coll., 1935; A.M., Vassar Coll., 1937; Ph.D., U. Mich., 1940; M.D., U. Pitts., 1947. Med. adviser women U. Ill., 1948-49; asst. prof. anatomy Grad. Sch. Medicine, U. Pa., 1949-51, asso. prof., 1951-60; asso. prof. anatomy U. Ky., 1960-63, prof., 1963—; research asso. neuroanatomy, dept. neurology Phila. Gen. Hosp., 1958-60. Fellow Council on Cerebrovascular Disease, Royal Soc. Health (hon.); mem. Am. Assn. Anatomists, Phila. Neurol. Soc. (v.p. 1959), Am. Acad. Neurology, Am. Neurol. Assn., Am. Assn. Neuropathologists, Phi Sigma, Sigma Xi. Home: 954 Wolf Run Rd Lexington KY 40504

GILLILAND, FRANK MARSHALL, JR., lawyer; b. Memphis, Nov. 27, 1927; s. Frank Marshall and Elizabeth (Jordan) G.; B.A., Vanderbilt U., 1949, LL.B., 1951; m. Tandy A. Jones, Dec. 27, 1958; children—Tandy Elizabeth, Mary Josephine, Carol Jordan, Frank Marshall III. Admitted to Tenn. bar, 1951, since practiced in

Memphis; law clk. U.S. Dist. Judge, Memphis, 1955-56; mem. firm Frank M. Gilliland, 1956-69, Pittman, Clay, Cole & Gilliland, 1959—. Pres. Gilliland Co.; sec-treas. Gilliland Farms; sec-treas. DeSoto Properties, Inc. Gen counsel Memphis Cotton Carnival Assn., 1959—. Trustee Webb Sch., Bell Buckle, Tenn., 1961—. Served to lt. (j.g.) USNR, 1951-54. Mem. Vanderbilt Law Rev., Navy League U.S., Order of Coif, Phi Beta Kappa, Omicron Delta Kappa, Phi Delta Theta, Phi Delta Phi. Clubs: Memphis Country, Memhis Univ. Home: 4008 N Galloway Dr Memphis TN 38111 Office: Sterick Bldg Memphis TN 38103

GILLILAND, JOHN ALVIN, real estate co. exec.; b. Hartselle, Ala., Nov. 11, 1911; s. John Alvin and Lena Marguerite (Boyce) G.; B.S.C., U. Miss., 1933; m. Marion Russell McCrory, Oct. 21, 1940; children—John Alvin, Louisa Christina, Marion Russell. Exec. v.p., dir. Knight Orr and Co., Inc., Jacksonville, Fla., 1945-62; pres., dir. Stockton, Whatley, Davin & Co., Jacksonville, 1962—; dir. State Bank Jacksonville, Title and Trust Co. Fla., Jacksonville, Security Fed. Savs. and Loan Assn., Jacksonville, Investors Central Mgmt. Corp.; trustee Barnett Mortgage Trust, Jacksonville. Bd. dirs. Children's Home Soc. Fla., Jacksonville Children's Hosp. Served to lt. comdr. USNR, 1942-45. Mem. Mortgage Bankers Assn. Am. (pres. 1967), U. Miss. Alumni Assn. Episcopalian (sr. warden). Clubs: Florida Yacht, Deerwood (Jacksonville); Ponte Vedra. Home: 3089 Doctors Lake Dr Orange Park FL 32073 Office: 100 W Bay St Jacksonville FL 32202

GILLILAND, JOHN WESLEY, ednl. adminstr.; b. Springfield, Mo. June 12, 1905; s. William Greene and Laura Etta (Wade) G.; A.B., S.W. Mo. State U., 1927; M.A., U. Mo., 1931; Ed.D., N.Y.U., 1949; postgrad. Columbia, 1935—, Northwestern U., 1940-41, Washington U., St. Louis, 1945; m. Ruth L. Stice, Dec. 24, 1928; children—Marlene (Mrs. Robert Z. Fowler), Gene, Richard. Supt. city schs., Mo., 1927-40; secondary prin., Aurora, Mo., 1931-32; instr. edn. S.W. Mo. State U., 1933; elementary sch. prin., Clayton, Mo., 1940-46; prof. edn., dir. sch. planning lab. U. Tenn., 1951-70; dir. ednl. facility planning U. Fla., Gainesville, 1970—. Mem. Am. Assn. Sch. Adminstrs., Council Ednl. Facility Planners, Phi Delta Kappa. Methodist (trustee 1941—). Author: Selection and Care of Carpet for Schools, 1971. Home: 10819 NW 11th Av Gainesville FL 32601

GILLILAND, LENO ELWIN, assn. exec.; b. Beebe, Ark., Feb. 2, 1914; s. John B. and Mary Elizabeth (Ray) G.; B.S.A., U. Ark., 1937; m. Margaret Helen Graham, Aug. 22, 1936; children—Rebecca (Mrs. James L. Chance), Betty Ray, James Elwin, Robert Graham. Tchr. vocational agr., Clarksville, Ark., 1937-39, Rogers, Ark., 1939-45; sales mgr. McNeil Chevrolet Co., Rogers, 1945-47; with Texarkana (Tex.) C. of C., 1947—, exec. v.p., 1950—. Chmn. Ark. Waterways Commn., 1972. Councilman, Rogers, 1944-45. Mem. Ark. C. of C. Execs. (pres. 1960), Tex. C. of C. Mgrs. (pres. 1968). Mason. Club: Texarkana Country. Home: 1509 Hickory St Texarkana AR 75501 Office: PO Box 1468 Texarkana AR 75501

GILLILLAND, THOMAS (MOULTON), govt. ofcl.; b. Bladen, Neb., Feb. 14, 1932; s. Whitney and Virginia (Wegmann) G.; grad. Wentworth Mil. Acad. Jr. Coll., 1952; student State U. Ia.; B.A., Am. U., 1963, M.A., 1967; m. Cora Lee Critchfield, Aug. 23, 1956; children—Shaun, Ruth, Virginia. Land officer, dist. adminstrv. officer Govt. of Pacific Islands Trust Terr., 1957-59, 61-66; adminstrv. asst. U.S. Rep. John Kyl, 1960-61; financial analyst AID, Washington, 1967-68, congl. liaison officer, 1969-70, dep. dir. Office Legislative Affairs, 1970—; cons. environmental impact Office Sec. Transp., 1968-69; instr. history Charles County (Md.) Community Coll., 1966-67. Bd. dirs. Ia. State Soc. Washington. Mem. Soc. for Preservation and Edn. of Barber Shop Quartet Singing Am., Am. Polit. Sci. Assn., Micronesian Acad. Sci. Republican. Conglist. Clubs: Northern Va. Aquatic (Arlington, Va.); Capitol Hill (Washington). Home: 3713 N Glebe Rd Arlington VA 22207 Office: AID Dept. State Washington DC 20523

GILLIS, EVERETT ALDEN, educator, author; b. Cameron, Mo., Mar. 4, 1914; s. Earle Adrien and Pearle (Owens) G.; B.A., Tex. Christian U., 1936, M.A., 1939; Ph.D., U. Tex., 1948; m. Lizzie Mae Allen, Aug. 14, 1943. Asst. prof. English, Tex. Coll. Arts and Industries, Kingsville, 1947-49; prof. English, Tex. Tech U., Lubbock, 1949—, chmn. dept., 1964-69. Served with AUS, 1942-46. Fellow Ford Found., 1955-56. Mem. Modern Lang. Assn., Am. Folklore Soc., Nat. Council Tchrs. English, Tex. Inst. Letters, Poetry Soc. Tex. (v.p. 1951), Tex. Folklore Soc. (pres. 1961). Nat. Writers Club, Southwestern Am. Lit. Assn. (pres. 1970). Author: Sing Your America, 1954; A College Forum, 1963; Oliver La Farge, 1967; (verse) Hello the House, 1944; Who Can Retreat, 1944; Sunrise in Texas, 1949; Angles of the Wind, 1954; (music lyrics) Ballads for Texas Heroes, 1964; also articles. Home: 3209 26th St Lubbock TX 79410

GILLIS, JAMES HILL, newspaperman; b. Poydras Plantation, La., July 2, 1908; s. Gary Eldridge and Stella May (Taylor) G.; B.A., Tulane U., 1931; m. Isadora Bright Myers Wilson, Jan. 25, 1940; 1 dau., Stella Elizabeth (Mrs. Franklin Ronald Waller-Diemont); stepchildren-David C. Wilson, Oren C. Wilson, Jack M. Wilson. Reporter, New Orleans Times-Picayune, 1931-40, ships news reporter and marine editor, 1932-39, city hall reporter, polit. columnist, 1945—, state legislature corr., 1960—. Served to lt. comdr. USNR, 1940-45; PTO. Mem. S.A.R., Press Club of New Orleans, Alpha Tau Omega. Republican. Episcopalian. Home: 5111 Dryades St New Orleans LA 70115 Office: 3800 Howard Av New Orleans LA 70140

GILLIS, JOHN ROBERT, JR., business exec.; b. San Antonio, May 19, 1928; s. John R. and Alma M. (Hirt) G.; student San Antonio Coll., 1949-51, St. Mary's U., 1951-52, Pan Am. Coll., 1957-58, U. Houston, 1959-61; grad. Southwestern Grad. Sch. Banking, So. Meth. U., 1968; m. Lois Jeanenne Holland, June 29, 1949; children—Robert David, Mark Steven, Matthew Jeffrey, Gina Gay. With Southwestern Bell Telephone Co., 1945-65, mgr., 1953-65; comml. loan officer Pan Am. Bank, Brownsville, Tex., 1965-69, sr. v.p., 1969-71; engaged in mortgage, investment, real estate and ins. bus., Brownsville, 1971—; v.p., dir. First State Bank of Alamo (Tex.), 1967—. Program chmn. Brownsville Community Players, 1965-66, v.p., 1966-67; campaign chmn. United Fund, 1963-64, pres. bd., 1964-65; pres. Mr. Amigo Assn., 1966; bd. dirs. Boys Club. Mem. Rio Grande Valley Bankers Assn., C. of C. (v.p. 1965-66). Rotarian. Home: 77 McLelland Blvd Brownsville TX 78520 Office: Suite 211 2100 Boca Chica Blvd Brownsville TX 78520

GILLIS, RICHARD SAMUEL, JR., assn. exec.; b. Lawrenceville, Va., Sept. 10, 1915; s. Richard Samuel and Janie (Wilkins) G.; student U.S. Mil. Acad., 1935; B.A., Randolph-Macon Coll., 1940; m. Margaret Crawford Shelton, July 10, 1948; 1 dau., Margaret Kimbrough. News editor Herald Progress, Ashland, Va., 1940-41; adminstrv. asst. Randolph-Macon Coll., 1945-51; exec. dir. Va. C. of C., Richmond, 1951—; mil. staffs Govs. Mills Godwin and Lynwood Holton, Richmond Export Expansion Council, 1966—. Mem. Va. regional adv. council Small Bus. Adminstrn., mem. State Hosp. Bd. Trustee Jamestown Found., Common Glory Found. Served to capt. AUS, 1941-45. Recipient Distinguished Service awards Randolph-Macon Coll., 1960, Am. Cancer Soc., 1960. Mem. Richmond Pub. Relations Soc. (past pres.), Va. Assn. C. of C. Execs. (past pres.), Am. Legion (past comdr.), Export-Import Club (past pres.). Baptist. Kiwanian. Home: 116 Snead St Ashland VA 23005 Office: 611 E Franklin St Richmond VA 23219

GILLMORE, DONALD WOOD, govt. ofcl.; b. Lorain, O., June 24, 1919; A.B., Williams Coll., 1941; Ph.D., Pa. State U., 1954; m. Johanna E. Mayer, June 10, 1944; children—Susan Elizabeth, Janet Lynne, Judith Ann. With Nat. Lead Co., Sayreville, N.J., 1941-43; chemist Inst. Gas Tech., Chgo., 1943-44, Koppers Co., Kobuta, Pa., 1944-45; with Houdry Process Corp., Marcus Hook, Pa., 1945-48; research fellow Pa. State U., 1948-53; supr. active carbon research Pitts. Coke & Chem. Co., Neville Island, Pa., 1953-60; tech. mgr. Carborundum Co., Niagara Falls, N.Y., 1960-67, plant mgr., 1967-70; research supr. U.S. Bur. Mines, Morgantown, W.Va., 1970—. Mem. Am. Chem. Soc., C. of C. Republican. Home: 661 S View St Morgantown WV 26505 Office: Box 880 Morgantown WV 26505

GILLOCK, RICHARD, hosp. adminstr. Adminstr. Med. Coll. Ga. Hosp. and Clinics, Augusta. Address: Med Coll Ga Hosp and Clinics 1120 15th St Augusta GA 30902*

GILLUM, VIRGIL MARION, coll. adminstr.; b. Burke, Ky., July 29, 1902; s. John William and Maude (Davis) G.; Certificate, Ky. Christian Coll., 1928; B.S., Milligan Coll., 1930; m. Anne Sue Pittman, June 4, 1930; 1 son, John Alvin. With Gen. Mills, Inc., 1930-53; accountant Du Pont Co., Charlestown, Ind., 1954; office mgr., accountant Kelley Paint Co., Louisville, 1955-60; comptroller Ky. Christian Coll., Grayson, 1964—. Ordained elder Ch. of Christ, 1937. Trustee Ky. Christian Coll., 1937-65. Home: 402 N Hord St Grayson KY 41143 Office: Ky Christian Coll Grayson KY 41143

GILMAN, LAUREN CUNDIFF, educator; b. Bozeman, Mont., Nov. 24, 1914; s. Ralph Webster and Pearl (Cundiff) G.; A.B., Baker U., 1936; Ph.D., Johns Hopkins U., 1940. Asst. prof. zoology U. S.D., Vermillion, S.D., 1946-47; asso. prof. zoology U. Miami, Coral Gables, 1947—. Mem. corp. Marine Biol. Lab., Woods Hole, Mass., 1949—. Served from pvt. to capt. AUS, 1941-46. Mem. Am. Inst. Biol. Scis., A.A.A.S. (mem. council 1967), Am. Genetic Assn., Am. Assn. U. Profs., Assn. Southeastern Biologists, Soc. Protozoologists (mem. exec. com. 1957-62), Phi Beta Kappa (pres. Greater Miami assn. 1964), Sigma Xi (treas. Miami chpt. 1959-65), Alpha Delta Sigma, Beta Beta Beta, Gamma Alpha. Democrat. Research in mating types and syngens in Paramecium caudatum; morphol. and physiol. differences among syngens. Home: 423 Majorca St Coral Gables FL 33134

GILMAN, LEE ATTERBURY, pub. relations counselor; b. Chgo., Jan. 7, 1926; s. Victor Boughton and Beulah (Fisk) G.; B.A. in English, U. Tex., 1951; postgrad. U. Cal. at Berkeley, 1951; m. Virginia R. Dana, Oct. 1, 1966. City editor Hillsboro (Tex.) Daily Mirror, 1951; asst. publicity dir. Tex. Ind. Producers and Royalty Owners Assn., Austin, 1952-54; pvt. practice as pub. relations cons., 1954-56; pub. relations asst. Southwestern Life Ins. Co., Dallas, 1956-60; gen. mgr. Gilman & Co., 1960-61, pres., 1961-65; sec., dir. Statewide Plat-Service, Inc. of Tex., 1966—; dir. pub. relations Interstate Life & Accident Ins. Co., 1968—. Served with USNR, 1944-46. Mem. Pub. Relations Soc. Am., Life Ins. Advertisers Assn., Chattanooga Ad Club, Alpha Phi Omega. Republican. Episcopalian. Home: 724 Bacon Trail Chattanooga TN 37412 Office: Interstate Life Bldg Chattanooga TN 37402

GILMAN, STANLEY FRANCIS, mech. engr.; b. Portland, Me., Mar. 31, 1921; s. Frank W. and Elotia (Noyes) G.; B.S. in M.E., U. Me., 1943; M.S., U. Ill., 1948, Ph.D., 1953; m. Jean Elizabeth Murphy, Feb. 4, 1943; children—Susan F. (Mrs. William B. Gentry), Michael J., Kathleen A., Steven C., Christine J. Co-owner, chief engr. Gilman Furnace Co., Portland, 1946-47; instr. U. Ill., Urbana, 1947-48, research asso., 1949-50, research asst. prof. mech. engring., 1950-53; sr. research engr. Carrier Air Conditioning Co., Syracuse, N.Y., 1953-57, asso. dir. research, 1957-59, mgr. compressor devel., 1959-60, mgr. advanced devel., 1960-61, mgr. engring., 1961-70; v.p. engring. Climatrol Industries, Inc., Milw., 1970-71; mgr. environmental control planning Am. Air Filter Co., Inc., Louisville, 1971—. Served to lt. USNR, 1943-46. Registered profl. engr., N.Y. Mem. Am. Soc. Heating, Refrigerating and Air-Conditioning Engrs. (dir. 1964—, pres. 1971-72), Nat. Soc. Profl. Engrs., Sigma Xi, Tau Beta Pi, Pi Tau Sigma, Sigma Alpha Epsilon. Republican. Roman Catholic. Contbr. articles to profl. jours. Patentee in field. Home: 11101 Huntley Pl Middletown KY 40243 Office: PO Box 1100 Louisville KY 40201

GILMORE, ELEANOR LAVERNE, govt. ofcl.; b. Newark, July 25, 1921; s. Leslie Dennis and Nellie (Peterson) Gilmore; student Bethany Coll., 1939-41; B.S., Mich. State U., 1943, M.S., 1944; postgrad. U. Wis., 1949-50. Serologist, Ortho Research Found., Raritan, N.J., 1944-45, research bacteriologist, 1945-59; chief bacteriologist Centaur div. Sterling Drug Corp., Rahway, N.J., 1945; grad. research asst. dept. med. bacteriology U. Wis., Madison, 1949-50, research asst. dept. vet. medicine, 1950-52; chief bacteriologist City of Madison Health Dept., 1952; med. microbiologist U.S. Army Inst. Dental Research, Walter Reed Army Med. Center, Washington, 1952—, head biophysics sect., dept. oral biology, 1966—. Lectr. Georgetown U., Washington, 1963—. Mem. Am. Soc. Microbiologists, N.Y. Acad. Sci., Washington Soc. Electron Microscopy, Sigma Xi. Contbr. numerous articles to sci. jours. Office: US Army Inst Dental Research Walter Reed Army Med Center Washington DC 20012

GILMORE, HUGH REDLAND, govt. ofcl.; b. Bristol, Vt., Aug. 13, 1916; s. John R. and Rubie (Rathbun) G.; Ph.B. magna cum laude, U. Vt., 1937; J.D., Columbia, 1941; m. Marjorie V. Havens, May 8, 1942; children— Douglas H., Anne C., Joan L. Admitted to Vt. bar, 1946, N.Y. State bar, 1948; asso. firm Sylvester & Ready, St. Albans, Vt., 1946-47; atty.-adviser Office Gen. Counsel Air Force, Office Sec. Air Force, Washington, 1949-54, asst. gen. counsel Air Force for personnel and adminstrn., 1954—. Served to maj. AUS, 1942-46, 47-49; col. Air Force Res. Decorated Asiatic-Pacific ribbon with 3 bronze stars, Phillippine Liberation ribbon with 1 bronze star; recipient Exceptional Civilian Service award U.S. Air Force 1965; certificate of spl. recognition Sec. Air Force, 1969. Mem. Fed. Bar Assn., Phi Beta Kappa, Pi Gamma Mu. Mason. Clubs: Overlee Community Assn., Arlington Forest (past dir.). Home: 3020 N Nottingham St Arlington VA 22207

GILMORE, MARJORIE HAVENS (MRS. HUGH REDLAND GILMORE), lawyer, club woman; b. N.Y.C., Aug. 16, 1918; d. William Westerfield and Elsie (Medl) Havens; A.B., Hunter Coll., 1938; J.D., Columbia, 1941; m. Hugh Redland Gilmore, May 8, 1942; children—Douglas Hugh, Anne Charlotte, Joan Louise. Admitted to N.Y. bar, 1941, Va. bar, 1968; research asst. N.Y. Law Revision Comm., 1941-42; asso. firm Spence, Windels, Walser, Hotchkiss & Angell, N.Y.C., 1942, Chadbourne, Wallace, Parke & Whiteside, N.Y.C., 1942-43; atty. U.S. Army, Washington, 1948-53. Sec., Thomas Jefferson Jr. High Sch. P.T.A., 1956-58; parliamentarian Wakefield High Sch. P.T.A., 1959-60, chmn. citizenship com., 1960-61; publicity chmn. Patrick Henry Sch. P.T.A., 1963-64, sec., 1964-65; parliamentarian Nottingham P.T.A., 1966-69; troop leader Girl Scouts U.S.A., 1963-70; mem. extra-curricular activities com. Arlington County Sch. Bd.; area chmn. fund drive Cancer Soc., 1955-56. Recipient Constl. Law award Hunter Coll., 1938. Mem. Columbia Law Sch. Alumni Assn., Alpha Sigma Rho. Presbyn. Club: Williamsburg Women's (publicity chmn. 1969-70, corr. sec. 1970-72, 1st v.p. 1972-73). Home: 3020 N Nottingham St Arlington VA 22207

GILMORE, ROBERT JAMES, communications engr.; b. Tulsa, Aug. 18, 1925; s. James Harvey and Velma (Goforth) G.; student So. Meth. U., 1943, Ga. Tech. U., 1944-45; B.S., U. Tulsa, 1949; postgrad. Washington U., 1965; m. Mary Lee Jenkins, Aug. 30, 1947; children—Gayle, Robert James. Computer, Petty Geophys. Engring. Co., Tulsa and Minot, N.D., 1947-49; with Southwestern Bell Tel. Co., 1950—, sr. engr., Oklahoma City, 1958-66, spl. services engr., 1966-71, equipment maintenance engr., 1971—; cons. income tax, 1952-64. Cub scoutmaster, 1966-67; coach jr. baseball YMCA, 1962-67. Served with USNR, 1943-46. Mem. Nat., Okla. socs. profl. engrs., Armed Forces Communications and Electronics Assn., Lambda Chi Alpha. Mem. Disciples of Christ. Optimist. Home: 3220 NW 54th St Oklahoma City OK 73112 Office: 707 N Robinson St Oklahoma City OK 73102

GILMORE, THOMAS ODELL, nurseryman; b.Julian, N.C., Nov. 15, 1936; s. Glen Gordon and Mary Elizabeth (Haris) G.; B.S., N.C. State U., 1959; m. Betty Lou Shoffner, Aug. 16, 1958; children—Thomas Odell, Dwayne Gordon, Dana Ellen. Sales mgr., v.p., dir. Gilmore Plant &Bulb Co., Inc., 1959—; dir. Dr. Clyde M. Gilmore Meml. Park. Mem. Am., N.C. (v.p.), Piedmont assns. nurserymen, N.C. State U. Alumni Assn. (award 1972), N.C. Mental Health Assn. Presbyn. (elder). Rotarian. Address: Julian NC 27283

GILMORE, WALTER MARSHALL, dentist; b. Meridian, Miss., Dec. 14, 1925; s. George Walter and Jewell Jones (Jones) G.; student Meridian Jr. Coll., 1946-48, Birmingham So. U., 1948-49; D.D.S., Loyola U., 1953; m. Gail Potter Griffin, June 8, 1950; children—David Marshall, Leslie Ann. Individual practice dentistry, Meridian, 1953—; mem. staff Rush, Riley, Anderson hosps. Active Tb Assn., Heart Assn. Served with USNR, 1944-46; PTO. Fellow Internat. Coll. Dentists; mem. Miss. (trustee 1965-66), East Miss. Dist. (pres. 1965-66), Meridian (pres. 1960-61) dental assns., Phi Kappa. Mem. Christian Ch. (chmn. bd. 1971). Clubs: Northwood Country (dir. 1965-68), Exchange (pres. 1960-61) (Meridian). Home: 3441 18th Av Meridian MS 39301 Office: 1428 22d Av Extension Meridian MS 39301

GILMORE, WILLIAM CAMPBELL, JR., banker; b. Rome, Ga., Mar. 11, 1919; s. William Campbell and Susan Glen (Watts) G.; grad. Darlington Sch., 1936; B.S., Davidson Coll., 1940; M.S., Vanderbilt U., 1941; m. Elizabeth Anne McMichael, Dec. 20, 1945; children—Susan Dorsey (Mrs. George R. McSwain), William Campbell, Elizabeth Anne. City traffic mgr. Delta Air Lines Inc., Atlanta, 1946-47; mgr. heating and air conditioning I.W. Phillips & Co., Tampa, Fla., 1947-62; mgr. indsl. Dept. Greater Tampa C. of C., 1962-66; v.p. First Nat. Bank, Tampa, 1966-69, sr. v.p. 1969—. Served to lt. col. USAAF, 1941-46. Mem. Greater Tampa C. of C., Com. of 100, Am. Meteorol. Soc., So. Indsl. Devel. Council, Am. Inst. Banking, Fla. Bankers Assn. Phi Delta Theta, Sigma Phi Sigma. Democrat. Presbyn. (ruling elder 1962—). Clubs: Tampa University, Tampa Yacht and Country. Home: 715 South Blvd Tampa FL 33606 Office: PO Box 1810 Tampa FL 33601

GILROY, WILLIAM ALLEN, JR., architect; b. Elizabeth, N.J., Jan. 9, 1919; s. William Allen and Louise (Hermiston) G.; grad. Pingry Sch., Elizabeth, N.J., 1936; A.B., Princeton, 1940, M.F.A. (fellow), 1947; m. Ridgeley C. Vermilye, Aug. 9, 1941; children—Carolyn L. (Mrs. James W. Standard), Ridgeley Patricia, Joanne Vermilye. Partner, Gamble, Pownall & Gilroy, architects, Ft. Lauderdale, Fla., 1947-66, Gamble & Gilroy, architects, Ft. Lauderdale, 1960-70; v.p. Gamble & Gilroy, Architects, Inc., Ft. Lauderdale, 1970—. Mem. Ft. Lauderdale Bd. Rules and Appeals, 1960-70. Bd. dirs. Fla. mental Health Assn, 1960; bd. dirs. Mental Health Assn. Broward County, 1956-61, pres. 1960. Served with USNR, 1942-46. Mem. A.I.A. Republican. Episcopalian. Club: Lauderdale Yacht (commodore 1968). Prin. archtl. works include S. Fla. State Hosp., Pine Crest Sch. Home: 2524 Barcelona Dr Fort Lauderdale FL 33301 Office: 1628 N Federal Hwy Fort Lauderdale FL 33305

GILSTRAP, JOSEPH CORTEZ, freight transp. cons.; b. Dothan, Ala., Sept. 14, 1925; s. Charles Joseph and Lennie (Nowell) G.; student Northwestern U., 1944, Pensacola Jr. Coll., 1969; m. Wynona Frances James, Apr. 23, 1953; children—James Rodney, Joseph Randall. Various positions Atlanta and St. Andrews Bay Ry., Panama City, Fla., 1945-55, Frisco Ry., Pensacola, Fla., 1955-57; asst. traffic mgr. Newport div. Heyden Newport Chem. Co., Pensacola, Fla., 1957-58; traffic mgr., Newport div. Tenneco Chems., Inc., Pensacola, Fla., 1958-69; freight transp. cons., Pensacola, 1969—. Served with USNR, 1943-45. Mem. So. Traffic League, Pensacola Traffic and Transp. Club (dir. 1950), Pensacola C. of C. Baptist. Club: Am. Propeller. Home: 207 Pine Tree Dr Gulf Breeze FL 32561 Office: Suite 609 Brent Annex Pensacola FL 32501

GILSTRAP, LEWEY OLIVER, JR., control equipment mfg. co. exec.; b. Tecumseh, Okla., Jan. 28, 1927; s. Lewey Oliver and Lessie Marie (Reeves) G.; student U. Tenn., 1944-45; B.S., U. Okla., 1950; postgrad. Cin. U., 1953-56, George Washington U., 1959; m. Virginia Mary Buckman, Sept. 4, 1954. Engr., Gen. Electric Co., 1950-56; sr. engr., Melpar, Inc., 1956-58; research scientist Psychol. Research Assos., Inc., 1958-59; project engr. Melpar, Inc., 1959-61; exec. v.p. Adaptronics, Inc., McLean, Va., 1961—, bd. chmn., 1961—. Pres. bd., trustee Sch. Guidance Center. Served with AUS, 1945-46. Mem. Am. Soc. Cybernetics (v.p. 1971). Patentee in field. Home: 2700 Virginia Av NW Washington DC 20037 Office: 7700 Old Springhouse Rd McLean VA 22101

GINGLES, TOMMY, state ofcl.; b. Little Rock, Nov. 22, 1914; s. T.J. and Ruth (Cobb) G.; B.S. in Civil Engring., Tex. A. and M. U., 1955; M.S. in San. Engring., U. Mo., 1959; m. Cletis Lorraine O'Quinn, Dec. 24, 1935; 1 son, Benjamin Wayne. Project engr. Forrest & Cotton, Engrs., Dallas, 1955-56; instr. civil engring. dept. Tex. A. & M. U., 1956-57; prof. civil engring. U. Miss., 1957-64; prin. B.M. Dornblatt, Cons. Engrs., New Orleans, 1964-66, spl. cons. san. engring., 1966-70; prof. civil engring. Miss. State U., Gulfport, 1966-70, mem. grad. faculty, 1960-64; chief engr. adminstrv. staff Miss. Air and Water Pollution Control Comnn.; cons. engr., 1938-51. Mem. University-Oxford-Lafayette County Planning Commn., 1962-64. Served with AUS, 1943-45; ETO. Registered profl. engr., Tex., Miss., La. Mem. Nat., Miss. (dir. 1961-63, pres. chpt. 1961-62) socs. profl. engrs., Am. Soc. C.E., Water Pollution Control Fedn., (pres. Miss. 1963), Am. Concrete Inst., Miss. Acad. Sci., Am. Pub. Health Assn. Mason. Home: PO Box 306 Long Beach MS 39560 Office: Miss Air and Water Pollution Control Commn PO Box 827 Jackson MS 39205

GINGRICH, DOROTHEA LOHOFF, journalist; b. Lane County, Kan., May 7, 1911; d. Paul and Emma (Thon) Lohoff; student Washington U., 1927-29; B.J., U.Mo. (outstanding woman journalism student), 1931, M.A., 1941; m. R. G. Schlegel, Aug. 29, 1933 (div.); 1 dau., Sandra Kay (Mrs. Tucker Hollamon); m. 2d, Jack Edward Gingrich, July 27, 1941; 1 son, Paul Schuyler. Editor West Plains (Mo.) Jour., 1931-33; dir. journalism and publicity Mary Hardin-Baylor Coll., Belton, Tex., 1936-41, dir. Centennial pub. relations, 1944-45; mem. journalism faculty Tex. Christian U., 1947-49; asso. editor Seguin (Tex.) Enterprise, 1951-53, woman's page, 1953-55, featured columnist, 1954-—; corr. San Antonio Light, 1951-68; head journalism dept. Tex. Luth. Coll. Girl Scout commr., Robstown, Tex., mem. council Ft. Worth, Seguin, Tex.; pres. Seguin Friends of Library, 1961, hon. life mem.; trustee County Library, 1961-—, chmn. bd. 1965-—. Region V mem. Women's Civil Def. Council. Recipient Headliner award Theta Sigma Phi, San Antonio, 1956; 1st place award for column South Tex. Press Assn., 1957; distinction in journalism Tex. Centennial Rangerette Commn., 1936; 1st place award in state for newspaper column Tex. Women's Press Assn., 1960, 61, 63, 65, 66, 67, 69; 1st place Tex. Press Assn., 1960; 3d place Nat. Fedn. Press Women's contest, 1960; Outstanding Community Service award Seguin and Guadalupe County C. of C., 1970; Devoted Service plaque Library Bd., 1970; named Library Trustee of Year, Tex. Library Assn., 1965, chmn. Trustee, Round Table, 1970. Mem. Women's Soc. Christian Service (pres. 1957), Tex. Press Women, Inc. (pres. 1968-69), Nat. Fedn. Press Women (2d v.p. 1969-70), Am. Assn. U. Women (state bd. mem., past pres.), Am. Coll. Pub. Assn. (pres. Tex.-Okla. dist. 1941), Tex. Fedn. Women's Clubs (dist. chmn. edn. dept. 1961-64, pres. Alamo dist. 1968-70, state div. chmn.), Conservation Soc., Tex. Assn. Coll. Jour. Tchrs. (pres. 1959), Theta Sigma Phi (past nat., sec., v.p., regional dir.; distinguished service award 1962), Delta Delta Delta (nat. pub. relations chmn.), Beta Sigma Phi (hon.; order Rose degree 1970), Kappa Tau Alpha, Delta Kappa Gamma. Methodist (steward). Clubs: Seguin Shakespeare (pres. 1965-—), Delphian (pres.). Home: 21 Hampton Dr E Seguin TX 78155 Office: Seguin Enterprise N Austin St Seguin TX 78155

GINIGER, HENRY, newspaperman; b. Bklyn., Jan. 15, 1922; s. Abraham and Bertha (Wolf) G.; B.A. in Social Sci., Coll. City N.Y., 1942; M.S. in Journalism, Columbia, 1943; m. Janine Goldfeil, May 14, 1948; 1 dau., Marianne. Corr., Paris (France) bur., N.Y. Times, 1946-65, cort. for Mexico, Central Am. and Caribbean, 1965-—. Served with USMCR, 1943-46; PTO. Pulitzer traveling fellow, 1946-47. Mem. Fgn. Corr. Assn. Mexico. Club: Overseas Press (N.Y.C.). Home: Lamartine 144-201 Mexico City 5 Mexico

GINN, VALORAN NILE, fertilizer co. exec.; b. Tollesboro, Ky., Oct. 23, 1930; s. Forrest R. and Helen L. (McDaniel) G.; student U. Ky., 1951, Chgo. Inst. Mgmt., 1953-55; m. Dottie Faul, July 29, 1950; children—Deborah (Mrs. Samuel Hampton), Larraine, Troy, Samantha. Chief exec. officer Ohio Valley Fertilizer, Inc., Maysville, Ky., 1955-—, Ky. Plating and Polishing Co., 1970-—; sec.-treas. Ohio Valley Fertilizer Corp., 1964-—. Exec. dir. United Appeal, 1959-62. Served with USNR, 1951-53. Mem. Chem. Engring. Soc., Ky. Plant Food Council. Democrat. Presbyn. Odd Fellow, Lion. Home: Route 4 Box 405 Maysville KY 41056 Office: PO Box 36 Maysville KY 41056

GINSBURG, GILBERT JEROME, lawyer, educator; b. Chgo., Aug. 26, 1936; s. Maurice Israel and Sarah (Ginsberg) G.; A.B., U. Chgo., 1954, A.B. in Law, 1955, J.D., 1957; m. Faith Davida Rosenson, June 28, 1959; children—Yale Maurice, David Bennet, Benjamin Lavin, Raphael Natan. Admitted to Ill. bar, 1957, Supreme Ct. U.S. bar, 1961, D.C. bar, 1968; asst. house counsel Aldens, Inc., Chgo., 1956-57; sec.-treas. Cam Products, Inc., Chgo., 1957-58; atty., labor relations adviser U.S. Army C.E., N. Central div., Chgo., 1958-59; atty. Office Gen. Counsel, NASA, Washington, 1962-66, mem. Bd. Contract Appeals, 1963-64; asst. dir. govt. contracts program George Washington U., Washington, 1966-—, asso. prof. law, 1966-70, prof. law, 1970-—. Lectr. contracting techniques in govt. procurement, Williamsburg, Va., San Francisco, Los Angeles, 1964-—. Pres., Yeshiva High Sch. Greater Washington; del. Jewish Community Council Washington, 1966-—. Trustee United Jewish Appeal. Served to capt. AUS, 1959-62. Mem. Am., Fed. bar assns. Democrat. Jewish religion (pres. synagogue 1965-—). Author: Cases and Materials on Federal Labor Standards and Equal Employment. Contbr. articles to law jours. Home: 810 Whittington Terrace Silver Spring MD 20901

GINSBURG, MARCUS, lawyer; b. Marietta, O., Feb. 16, 1915; s. Louis and Dora (Brachman) G.; student Marietta Coll., 1932-33; A.B., U. Mich., 1936; LL.B., Harvard, 1939; m. Martine Heilbron, Feb. 23, 1949; children—Harold Heilbron, Robert L. Admitted to Tex. bar, 1939, since practiced in Ft. Worth; partner firm McDonald, Sanders, Ginsburg, Phillips, Maddox, & Newkirk, 1951-—. Dir. vice chmn. bd. S.W. Nat. Bank, Ft. Worth; dir., exec. com. Pioneer Am. Ins. Co. Pres. United Fund and Community Services Ft. Worth, 1962, Tarrant Council Community Council, 1966-67, Traveller's Aid Soc., Ft. Worth, 1953-54; vice chmn. city solicitations commn., Ft. Worth, 1963-67; past nat. v.p. Am. Jewish Congress; past v.p. Nat. Community Relations Adv. Council; mem. U.S. nat. commn. UNESCO, 1959-64, exec. com., 1963-64, steering com., 1964, chmn. pub. information com., 1962-64; past v.p., treas. Children's Museum Ft. Worth; mem. Nat. Budget and Consultation Com., 1966-—. Bd. dirs. Ft. Worth Art Assn. Served to 2d lt. USAAF, 1942-45. Decorated Army Commendation medal; recipient award excellency United Fund Ft. Worth; award Ft. Worth Traveller's Aid Soc., Ft. Worth Community Council. Mem. Harvard Law Sch. Assn. (pres. Tex. 1955-56, nat. v,p. 1956-57), Pi Lambda Phi. Jewish religion (v.p. temple). Clubs: Fort Worth, Shady Oaks Country, Ridglea Country (Ft. Worth); Cipango (Dallas). Home: 3860 Bellaire Circle Fort Worth TX 76109 Office: Continental Nat Bank Bldg Fort Worth TX 76102

GIORDANO, HENRY LUKE, govt. ofcl.; b. San Francisco, June 10, 1914; s. Peter L. and Elisabeth M. (Dernbach) G.; Ph.G., U. Cal., 1934; m. Elaine Watson, June 11, 1939; children—Marjorie E., Anne Marie. Registered pharmacist, 1934-41; narcotic agt. Fed. Bur. Narcotics, 1941-43, Seattle, 1946-50, dist. supr., Mpls., 1950-54, Kansas City, Mo., 1954-55, field supr., 1956, asst. dep. commr., 1956-57, asst. to commr., 1957-58, dep. commr. narcotics, 1958-62, became commr. narcotics, 1962; now asso. dir. for enforcement Bur. Narcotics and Dangerous Drugs. Chief investigator subcom. on narcotics House Ways and Means Com., 1955-56; adviser U.S. rep. 14th session UN Commn. on Narcotic Drugs Geneva, Switzerland, also 18th session. Served with USCGR, 1943-46. Home: 9609 New Hampshire Av Silver Spring MD 20903 Office: 1300 E St NW Washington DC 20004

GIPSON, BERNICE B. (MRS. DEWEY E. GIPSON), realtor; b. Comanche, Okla.; d. Abraham Lincoln and Rebecca Ann (Hale) Brown; grad. high sch.; m. Dewey Edward Gipson, Nov. 22, 1933; children—Dewey Colleen (Mrs. Paul Jones), David Michael (dec.), Douglas Edward. Real estate saleslady Lucille Renoudet, Real Estate Broker, 1950-51; owner, operator Bernice B. Gipson Realty Co., New Iberia, La., 1952-—. Charter mem. New Iberia Bd. Realtors, pres., 1960. Active Iberia Parish Cancer Soc. Mem. Order Eastern Star (star point office 1951-54), IOF (bldg. com. 1954-—, adv. bd. to bldg. com. 1970). Home: 1706 Weeks St New Iberia LA 70560 Office: 911 B Charles St New Iberia LA 70560

GIPSON, HANNIBAL MCNEILL, state ofcl.; b. Prattville, Ala., Aug. 1, 1909; s. Henry Edward and Lillie Roberta (McNeill) G.; student Auburn U., 1925-26, U. Ala., 1926-28; m. Emerson Ashmore, Nov. 10, 1934; children—Hannibal McNeill, Philip A., Richard E. With Ala. Hwy. Dept., Montgomery, 1928-46, 56-—, asst. div. engr., 1966-—; owner (name Gipson Auto Service, 1946-56; land surveyor, Prattville, Ala., 1960-—. Mem. Prattville City Council, 1948-52; chmn. Selective Service Bd. 1, Prattville, 1950-—. Mem. Am. Right of Way Assn. (v.p. Ala. chpt. 1968-—). Mason, Lion. Club: Prattville Country (dir. 1967-—). Home: 536 Wetumpka Rd Prattville AL 36067 Office: Ala Hwy Dept 3706 Fairground Rd Montgomery AL 36110

GIPSON, WILEY KAYE, finance exec.; b. Knoxville, Tenn., Aug. 11, 1918; s. Claude Elvie and Elizabeth Forrest (Kauerz) G.; B.S., U. Tampa, 1939; m. Frances Russo, June 29, 1944. Chief authorizer Maas Bros., Tampa, 1939-40; mgr. Time Finance Co., Louisville, also Time Loan Co., Cin., 1940-46; organizer Term Finance Co., Cynthiana, Ky., 1947, gen. mgr., sec., treas., 1947-53, pres., gen. mgr., 1953-—; sec. treas. Term Thrift Plan, Inc., 1959-—; founder, pres., dir. F & W Investors Financial Corp., 1971-—; Adv. com. Ky. commr. banking, 1956-57; mem. com. to draft consumer finance law Ky., 1960-61; mem. Ky. Consumer Affairs Commn., 1968-—, Ky. Consumer Affairs Legislative Subcom., 1968-—. Bd. dirs. Harrison County chpt. Nat. Found. Served with USAAF, 1942-45. Mem. Ky. Consumer Finance Assn. (past pres., dir.), Cynthiana-Harrison C. of C. (past pres.). Rotarian (past pres. dir. Newport, Ky.). Home: 218 Beechwood Rd S Fort Mitchell KY 41017 Office: PO Box 223 Fort Thomas KY 41075

GIRLING, ROBERT GEORGE WILLIAM, social work adminstr.; b. El Dorado, Ark., July 28, 1929; s. Robert G.W. and Mildred (Massey) G.; student Hinds Jr. Coll., 1946-47; B.A., Miss. Coll., 1950, postgrad., 1956-57; B.D., New Orleans Bapt. Theol. Sem., 1954; postgrad. Baylor U., 1959; M.S. in Social Work, U. Tex., 1961; m. Bettie Joyce Moore, Sept. 2, 1960; children—Robert G.W. IV, Maria Julia Anastasia, Samuel Marcus Shaw, Katherine Susan Jane. Ordained to ministry Baptist Ch., 1949; pastor various chs., 1949-55; asst. pastor Calvary Bapt. Ch., Jackson, Miss., 1955-58; counselor Meth. Home, Waco, Tex., 1959; dir. social service Lena Pope Home, Fort Worth, 1961-63; exec. dir., 1963-66; dir. social service Austin (Tex.) State Sch., 1966-71. Pres., dir. Girling & Assos. Home Health Services Inc., Austin, 1969-—; mem. Community Coordinated Child Care Steering Com. for Austin, 1969-70. Bd. dirs. Austin State Sch. Credit Union. Mem. Acad. Certified Social Workers, Nat. Assn. Social Workers, Tex. Pub. Employees Assn. (dir. Austin State Sch. chpt. 1969-70). Rotarian. Home: 2608 Pembrook Trail Austin TX 78731 Office: 1104 W 38th St Austin TX 78767

GIROD, CLARENCE ELBERT, JR., dentist; b. Baton Rouge, Dec. 20, 1919; s. Clarence Elbert and Irene (Heroman) G.; student La. State U., 1936-38; D.D.S., Loyola U., New Orleans, 1942; m. Grace Rieth, June 1, 1942; children—Joel-J. Loupe, Jerold, Rieth, John, Donna. Individual practice dentistry, Baton Rouge, 1945-—; dental surgeon Greenwell Springs (La.) Hosp.; dental surgeon, athletic dept. La. State U., Baton Rouge. Served with USAAF, 1942-45. Mem. Pierre Fauchard Acad., Am., La., 6th Dist. dental assns., Am. Acad. Dental Radiology, Acad. Gen. Practice, A.A.A.S., Nat. Geog. Soc., Sigma Chi, Delta Sigma Delta. Club: Camelot. Research football dental injuries. Home: 2077 Ramsey St Baton Rouge LA 70808 Office: 1940 Perkins Rd Baton Rouge LA 70808

GIROUX, RICHARD ROBERT, math. statistician; b. Springfield, Mass., Oct. 16, 1939; s. George Herman and Gladys Helmerich (Winkler) Gero; student Coll. of Guam, 1957-58; B.S., U. Mass., 1961, M.S., 1965; postgrad. Adelphi U., 1961-62, Fla. State U., 1965; m. Jane Devine Sellgren, July 18, 1959; children—Richard Dana, Yvonne Yvette. Engr. Sperry Gyroscope Co., Great Neck, N.Y., 1959-62; research specialist Nat. Cash Register Co., Dayton, O., 1962-63; program analyst ITT Data Services, Virginia Beach, Va., 1963-66; math. statistician Naval Ship Engring. Center, U.S. Naval Sta., Norfolk, Va., 1966-67; pres., cons. Data Research Service, Virginia Beach, 1967-—; expert cons. Nat. Bur. Standards, Dept. Commerce, Gaithersburg, Md., 1971-—. Instr. math., programming Old Dominion Coll., Norfolk, 1966; asst. prof. computer sci. U. Va. at Norfolk, 1966-69; pres. Giroux Computer Task Group, Inc., Galion, O., 1969-—; sr. cons. engr. Union Switch & Signal div. Westinghouse Air Brake Co., Pitts., 1967-68. Mem. Thoroughgood Civic League, Virginia Beach, 1966-—. Served with USAF, 1955-58. Mem. Am. Statis. Assn., Biometric Soc., Gesellschaft fur Angewandte Math. und Mechanik. Contbr. articles to tech. lit. Home: 4301 Country Club Circle Virginia Beach VA 23455 also Giroux Farm Postal Route 1 Bellville OH 44813 Office: Box 321 Gaithersburg MD 20760

GISH, PAUL TUDOR, state ofcl.; b. Athens, Ala., July 8, 1923; s. Paul Tudor and Margaret (Sanders) G.; student Athens (Ala.) Coll., 1941-42; A.B., U. Ala., 1945, LL.B., 1947; m. Sarah Campbell, May 24, 1952; 1 son, Anthony Paul. Admitted to Ala. bar, 1947, gen. practice law, Athens 1947-53; asst. atty. gen. State of Ala., 1953-—. Mem. Am., Ala. bar assns., Ala. Quadrangle. Phi Delta Phi, Omicron Delta Kappa. Episcopalian. Home: 3869 Pelzer Av Montgomery AL 36109 Office: Adminstrv Bldg State Capitol Montgomery AL 36104

GIST, LEWIS ALEXANDER, chemist; b. Richmond, Va., Nov. 17, 1921; s. Lewis Alexander and Leonia (Hill) G.; B.S., Va. Union U., 1947; M.S., Howard U., 1949; Ph.D., Ia. State U., 1956; m. Grace Naomi Perry, Dec. 25, 1948; children—Marilyn Elaine, Lewis Alexander III. Research asst. Carver Found. Tuskegee Inst., Ala., 1949-52, research asso., 1956, asst. prof., 1956; asso. prof., head chem. dept. Va. Union U., 1956-58; prof., chmn. dept. chemistry Va. State Coll., 1958-64; asso. program dir. summer study program NSF, Washington, 1964-69, asso. program dir. and coordinator for fgn. activities, div. pre-coll. edn. in sci., 1969-—; cons., judge Sci. Fairs in Va., 1956-64. Legislative chmn. Coolidge High Sch., Washington, 1965-67; sci. edn. cons. to India, 1967, 69, to Republic of South Africa, 1972. Served with AUS, 1943-46. Fellow Gen. Edn. Bd., Nat. Med. Fellowships. Mem. Am. Chem. Soc., Am. Inst. Chemists, A.A.A.S., Nat. Inst. Sci. (pres. 1962-63, 71-72) Sigma Xi, Alpha Phi Alpha (v.p. 1962-63), Beta Kappa Chi (v.p. 1956, exec. sec. 1962-64). Home: 1336 Locust Rd NW Washington DC 20012 Office: NSF Washington DC 20550

GITTESS, RONALD MARVIN, dentist; b. Nyack, N.Y., Nov. 10, 1937; s. David and Mildred (Levin) G.; B.S., Columbia, 1959, D.D.S., 1963; postgrad. U. Pa., 1964-66; m. Carol May Block, Apr. 6, 1963; children— Robert Andrew, Leslie Ellen. Intern, Mt. Sinai Hosp., Miami, Fla., 1963-64, now attending dental surgeon; pvt. practice dentistry, specializing in endodontics, Miami, 1966-—; mem. staff Variety Children's Hosp., VA Hosp., Miami, Mt. Sinai Hosp.; cons. Dade County Dental Research Clinic. Asst. coordinator dental div. United Fund Campaign, 1968. Recipient certificate of recognition Jarvie Honor Soc., 1961. USPHS fellow, 1962-63. Diplomate Am. Bd. Endodontics. Mem. Am. Dental Assn., Am. Assn. Endodontics, A.A.A.S., Fedn. Dentaire Internationale, Fla., Miami, Miami Beach, South Dade, East Coast dental socs., So. Endodontic Study Group. Alpha Omega. Home: 14520 SW 84th Av Miami FL 33158 Office: 7400 N Kendall Dr Miami FL 33156

GIVENS, JOHNNIE ESTHER, librarian; b. Pleasant View, Tenn., Sept. 7, 1925; d. Claude Preston and Willie Lena (Brashear) Givens; B.S. in Edn. Austin Peay State Coll., 1946; B.S. in L.S., George Peabody Coll., 1949; A.M., U. Chgo., 1960. Asst. librarian Austin Peay State Coll., 1946-58, head librarian, 1958-—; order librarian George Peabody Coll. library, summer 1947; library cons. coll. and spl. libraries, 1964-—. Bd. dirs. Clarksville Community Concert Assn., Clarksville Community Ambassador Assn. Mem. Am., Tenn. library assns., Nat., Tenn. edn. assns., Am. Assn. U. Profs., Assn. Coll. and Research Libraries, Kappa Delta Pi, Delta Kappa Gamma, Beta Phi Mu. Democrat. Methodist. Contbr. profl. jours. Home: 413 Locust St Springfield TN 37172 Office: Austin Peay State Univ Clarksville TN 37040

GIVHAN, THOMAS BARTRAM, lawyer; b. Lexington, Ky., Sept. 24, 1926; s. Thomas Holman and Eva Mae (Beck) G.; student Ia. State Coll., 1947; LL.B., U. Ky., 1951; m. Sharon Rose Richard, June 11, 1949; children— Elise Charles, Ellen Foster, Aaron Todd. Admitted to Ky. bar, 1951; practice law, Shepherdsville, Ky.; mem. firm Givhan & Porter; city atty., Shepherdsville, 1953-58; county atty. Bullitt County, 1959-62, 66-—. Dir. Echo Telephone Co., Shepherdsville. Chmn. Bullitt County Democratic Com. Served with USMC, 1945-46. Mem. Ky. Bar Assn., Am. Bar Assn., Am. Trial Lawyers Assn., Ky. Trial Lawyers Assn., Sigma Chi. Baptist. Mason. Clubs: Louisville Boat, Jefferson Club (Louisville). Home: 312 Lee St Sheperdsville KY 40165 Office: Professional Bldg Sheperdsville KY 40165

GJERNES, OSCAR, psychologist; b. Oklee, Minn., Aug. 24, 1914; s. Ellef K. and Borghild (Gjeldaker) G.; B.A., Concordia Coll., 1941; M.S., N.D. State U., 1954; postgrad. U. Minn., 1958, U. N.D., 1965; m. Myrdith L. Kronschandbel, Apr. 13, 1941; children—Marylou Diane. Counseling psychologist VA, N.D., 1946-49; with N.D. Employment Service, 1941-65; supr. tech. services, Bismarck, 1957-65; employment service adviser Manpower Adminstrn., Dept. Labor, Washington, 1965-—. Served with AUS, 1942-45, 1951-52. Mem. Nat. Vocational Guidance Assn., Nat. Employment Counselor Assn. (pres. 1969-70), N.D. Assn. Personnel in Employment, N.D. Personnel and Guidance Assn. (past pres.), N.D. Vocational Guidance Assn. (past pres.). Lutheran (deacon). Research in psychol. field. Home: 9039 Sligo Creek Pkwy Silver Spring MD 20901

GLAD, DONALD DAVISON, psychologist, educator; b. Salt Lake City, Apr. 23, 1915; s. Andrew Anderson and Ada (Davison) G.; B.A., U. Utah, 1943, M.A., 1943; Ph.D., Stanford, 1946; m. Virginia Markey Brown, Jan. 13, 1952; children—Lynn B. (Mrs. Al L. Wosk), Dawn G. (Mrs. Erick U. Lundquist), Toni G. (Mrs. Marvin L. Saunders), Sue Ellyn (Mrs. Len Flake Winmill), Roger B. Asst. prof. San Jose State Coll., 1946-47; chief psychologist U. Colo. Med. Sch., 1947-53, dir. accident proneness research, 1953-57; asso. prof. U. Denver, 1957-59; dir. div. psychology Greater Kansas City (Mo.) Mental Health Found., 1959-67; prof. U. Mo. Med. Sch., Kansas City, 1964-67; prof. psychology and psychiatry La. State U., 1967-—; clin. prof. U. Kan. Med. Sch., 1960-61, dir. Midwestern Lab. for Exec. Devel., 1965-67. Cons. Dept. Justice, 1957-59, Dept. Def., 1947-57, Nat. Inst. Mental Health, 1972-—; asso. Nat. Tng. Lab. Inst., 1966-70; dir. La. Community Lab. Learing Inst., 1971-—. Trustee Midwest Group for Human Resources, 1966-69; bd. dirs. Southwest Inst. for Personal and Organizational Devel., 1968-71. Fellow Am. Psychol. Assn.; mem. A.A.A.S., Am. Group Psychotherapy Assn., Sigma Xi, Address: 2304 Fairway Dr Baton Rouge LA 70809

GLADDEN, JAMES WALTER, educator; b. Dunbar, Pa., Nov. 3, 1912; s. T. Milton and Hattie (Rowley) G.; A.B., Waynesburg Coll., 1933; S.T.B., Wesley Theol. Sch., 1936; M.Ed., U. Pitts., 1943, Ph.D., 1946; m. Cynthia E. Hales, June 22, 1935 (dec. June 23, 1971); children—Peg (Mrs. C. F. Hermann), James Walter. Ordained to ministry Meth. Ch., 1938; pastor Meth. chs., Pa., 1935-46; head dept. sociology Mt. Union Coll., Alliance, O., 1946-49; prof. sociology U. Ky., Lexington, 1949-—. Mem. Am., So., Ohio Valley sociol. socs., Nat., Regional, councils on family relations. Democrat. Kiwanian. Contbr. numerous articles in field to profl. jours. Home: 3401 Bellefonte Dr Lexington KY 40502

GLADDING, EVERETT BUSHNELL, electronics exec.; b. New Haven, June 27, 1917; s. Daniel Henry and Grace A. (Brown) G.; B.A., Wesleyan U., 1938; M.A., Johns Hopkins, 1946; m. Harriet Allen Clark, June 7, 1941; children—Nicholas Clark, Brenda Bushnell. Commd. ensign USN, 1941, advanced through grades to capt., 1960; staff SACLANT, 1956-59; chief Nat. Security Agy., Pacific, 1960-63; comdg. officer Naval Communications Sta., Adak, Alaska, 1963-64; chief staff officer Naval Security Group, 1964-66, dir. Naval Security Group, Pacific, 1966-68; ret., 1968; planning specialist LTV Electrosystems, Inc., Greenville, Tex., 1968-—. Judge dog obedience trials, 1957-—. Mem. I.E.E.E. (sr.), Armed Forces Communications-Electronics Assn., U.S. Naval Inst., Modern Lang. Assn., Am. Radio Relay League, Aircraft Owners and Pilots Assn., various dog clubs. Clubs: Quinnipiack (New Haven); Army and Navy (Washington). Home: 5303 Windy Hill Rd Greenville TX 75401 Office: Box 911 Greenville TX 75401

GLADNEY, WILLIAM JESS, entomologist; b. Magnolia, Ark., Sept. 8, 1940; s. Henry Howerth and Rubye Dean (Bussey) G.; B.S., So. State Coll., 1962; M.S., U. Ark., 1964; Ph.D., Va. Poly. Inst., 1967; m. Bonita Elaine Norman, Mar. 27, 1963; 1 dau., Tracy Lynne. Research entomologist U.S. Dept. Agr., Kerrville, Tex., 1967-—, project leader, 1970-—. Mem. Entomol. Soc. Am., Bluebonnet Philatelic Soc., Sigma Xi, Phi Sigma, Kerrville Jr. C. of C. (dir. 1971-—). Methodist (mem. ofcl. bd. 1968-—). Home: 105 Royal Oaks Rd Kerrville TX 78028 Office: PO Box 232 Kerrville TX 78028

GLADSON, IRA RICHARD, ednl. adminstr.; b. Knoxville, Tenn., June 10, 1930; s. Thomas Benjamine and Cordie (Powell) G.; B.S. (Mary Fabian scholar), U. Tenn., 1953, M.S., 1957, postgrad., 1960-65. Tchr., counselor Pi Beta Phi Sch., Gatlinburg, Tenn., 1953-54; counselor South High Sch., Knoxville, 1957-66; supr. guidance Knoxville Sch. System, 1967-—; asst. Student Counseling Center, U. Tenn., 1965. Nat. Def. Edn. Act grantee in guidance and counseling U. Tenn., Knoxville, 1962. Knox County adv. com. Tenn. State Welfare Dept., 1969-70; mem. Youth Com. YMCA, Knoxville, 1968-70; bd. dirs. Florence Crittenton Agy., Knoxville. Served with AUS, 1954-56. Mem. Tenn. (pres. guidance sect. 1963), Nat. edn. assns., Am., Tenn. (pres. 1971-72), East Tenn. (pres. 1961-62) personnel and guidance assns., Nat. Vocational Assn., U. Tenn. Alumni Assn. (gov. 1967-68), Coll. Edn. Alumni Assn. U.Tenn. (pres. 1968), Phi Delta Kappa. Baptist. Kiwanian (vocational guidance chmn. 1968). Clubs: East Tennessee Miss-Mr. (pres. 1965; adviser 1965-66), Senator's Country. Home: 3001 Cherrywood Rd Knoxville TN 37921 Office: Bd Edn Bldg 101 E 5th Av Knoxville TN 37919

GLADWELL, JOHN STUART, water resources engr.; b. Panama, Aug. 21, 1932 (parents Am. citizens); s. John Stuart and Norah (Ford) G.; B.S. in Bus. Adminstrn., Trinity U., 1953; B.S., Tex. A. and M. U., 1959, M.S. in Civil Engring., 1961; postgrad. Wash. State U., 1967-69;

Ph.D. in Agril. Engring., U. Ida., 1967; m. Gail Aldyen Ree, May 7, 1960; children—Jennifer Aldyen, Carolyn Louise. Civil engr. U.S. Forest Service, Alaska, 1959-60; asst. hydraulic engr. Coll. Engring. Wash. State U., 1961-64; asst. prof. civil engring. U. Me., 1964-65; asso. hydraulic engr., asso. prof., asst. dir. Wash. Water Research Center Wash. State U., 1965-70; staff water resources, research and planning engr. Nat. Water Commn., Washington, 1970-71; water research scientist Office Water Resources Research Dept. Interior, Washington, 1971—. Served with AUS, 1954-56. Registered prof. engr., Wash., Me. Mem. Am. Soc. C.E., Nat. Soc. Profl. Engrs., Am. Water Resources Assn., Sigma Xi, Tau Beta Pi, Phi Kappa Phi. Contbr. articles to profl. jours. Home: 8230 The Midway Annandale VA 22003 Office: Dept Interior Office Water Resources Research Washington DC 20240

GLAHN, HARRY ROBERT, meteorologist; b. nr. Shelbyville, Mo., July 28, 1928; s. Harry Richison and Beulah (Melson) G.; B.S., N.E. Mo. State Tchrs. Coll., 1953; postgrad. Okla. A. and M., 1953-54, U. Mo., 1957; M.S., Mass. Inst. Tech., 1958; Ph.D., Pa. State U., 1963; m. Anna Margaret Morgan, May 28, 1949; children—Robert Gale, Gary Lee. Sch. tchr., Shelby County, Mo., 1947-51; meteorologist U.S. Weather Bur., Washington, 1958—. Served with USAF, 1953-57. Mem. Am. Meteorol. Soc. Home: 3233 Holly Hill Dr Falls Church VA 22042 Office: 8060 13th St Silver Spring MD 20910

GLASCOCK, G. GRAHAM, lawyer; b. Mexico City, Mexico, 1925; A.B., U. Cal. at Berkeley, 1949, J.D., 1951; postgrad. Facultad de Derecho y Ciencias Sociales Nat. U. Mexico. Admitted to Mexican bar, 1955; now mem. firm Basham, Ringe & Correa, Mexico City. Address: Basham Ringe & Correa Calle de Liverpool 123 Mexico DF Mexico*

GLASER, HAROLD, govt. ofcl.; b. Kurseni, Lithuania, Aug. 28, 1924; s. Joseph and Emma (Greenspan) G.; B.S., Roosevelt U., 1948; M.S., Northwestern U., 1949, Ph.D., 1953; m. Margaret V. Stoney, Dec. 29, 1945; children—Roberta L., Miriam L., Ruth H. Physicist, sr. staff Applied Physics Lab., Johns Hopkins, 1952-54; head theoretical analysis sect. Naval Research Lab., Washington, 1954-57; physicist electronics br. Office of Naval Research, Washington, 1957-59, physics br., 1959-62; spl. asst. div. for math., physi. and engring. scis. NSF, Washington, 1962; physicist physics br. Office Naval Research, Washington, 1962-64, head nuclear physics br., 1964-66; dep. chief solar physics NASA, Washington, 1966, acting chief solar physics, 1966-67, chief solar physics, 1967-70, long range planning Nat. Bur. Standards, 1970-71, acting dir., dep. dir. Experimental Incentives program, 1972—; mem. staff Office of Sci. and Tech. Office of Pres., 1971-72; cons. Advanced Research Projects Agy., 1966—. Instr., Roosevelt U., 1950-51; lectr. U. Md., 1956; research asso. U. So. Cal., 1959. Served with AUS, 1943-46. Mem. Am. Phys. Soc., Am. Geophys. Union, Am. Astron. Soc., Sci. Research Soc. Am., Internat. Astron. Union, Philos. Soc. Washington (corr. sec. 1968-69, v.p. 1970—), Sigma Xi. Home: 312 Chartwell Dr Silver Spring MD 20904 Office: NBS Washington DC 20234

GLASGOW, BILLY DEAN, mayor, tax accountant; b. Pontotoc, Miss., Mar. 13, 1931; s. Earl Clinton and Grace Jewel (Conlee) G.; B.S., Miss. State U., 1963; m. Jenell Tubb, Aug. 12, 1947; children—Carla Bert (Mrs. Paul Burt), Steven. Mayor City of Amory, Miss., 1969—; tax accountant; partner Simmons Mfg. Co.; owner, mgr. rental property; sec.-treas. Glendale, Inc. Mem. Monroe County Selective Service Bd. Served with USAF, 1951-55. Mem. Am. Legion (past comdr.), V.F.W. Baptist. Mason (Shriner). Home: 104 S 6th St Amory MS 38821 Office: City Hall Amory MS 38821

GLASGOW, CLARENCE OGDEN, mfg. co. exec.; b. Fairview, Okla., Sept. 26, 1908; s. Arthur W. and Floy (McCowan) G.; B.S. in Mech. Engring., Okla. State U., 1934; m. Elizabeth McClung, Feb. 15, 1938; children—Edsel, Melvin. With Nat. Tank Co., Tulsa, 1934-61, v.p., dir., 1949-61; pres. Custom Engring. & Mfg. Corp., Tulsa, 1961—; dir. Tulsa Rubber Co.; owner Spring Valley Ranch, Locust Grove, Okla., 1948—. Bd. regents Oral Roberts U., Tulsa. Mem. Am. Soc. M.E., Okla. Inventors Congress (bd. mem.), Tulsa C. of C. Methodist. Club: Petroleum. Patentee in field. Home: 2620 S Yorktown St Tulsa OK 74114 Office: 1073 N Owasso St Tulsa OK 74150

GLASGOW, JOSEPH LELAND, physician; b. DeQueen, Ark., Nov. 7, 1931; s. John Leland and Minnie Venus (Martindale) G.; B.S., Ouachita Coll., 1953; M.D., U. Ark., 1959; m. Jeanne Rae Bonar, May 30, 1960; children—Leslie Ann, David Leland, John Bonar. Chief nuclear medicine VA Hosp., Jackson, Miss., 1965—, chief med. service, 1970—; asst. prof. medicine U. Miss., 1967-69, asso. prof., 1969—. Served with USMC, 1953-55. Fellow A.C.P., Am. Coll. Chest Physicians; mem. Soc. Nuclear Medicine, A.M.A., Am. Diabetes Assn., A.A.A.S., Sigma Xi. Home: 4730 N Hampton Dr Jackson MS 39211 Office: Veterans Administration Hospital Jackson MS 39216

GLASGOW, ROBERT SAMUEL, JR., lawyer; b. Adamsville, Ala., July 3, 1907; s. Robert Samuel and Louise (Maxwell) G.; A.B., Birmingham-So. Coll., 1928; J.D., U. Ala., 1933; m. Thelma Thompson, Nov. 7, 1935; 1 dau., Gloria Elaine (Mrs. G. Preston Bryant). Admitted to Ala. bar, 1933; pvt. law practice, 1933—; owner Home Supply Co., 1936-41; v.p. Davidson-Pratt Mining Co., Inc., 1943-44; partner Blossburg Mining Co., 1944; chief area atty. Office of Housing Expediter, 1945-51; mayor, Adamsville, Ala., 1953-55, city atty., 1955-56; title agt. Ala. Power Co., Birmingham, 1955-62; partner Glasgow & Sides Devel. Co.; atty for Town of Brookside (Ala.), 1954-56. Gen. and trial atty. Office Price Stblzn., 1951-52; hearing examiner Bur. Hearings and Appeals, Social Security Adminstrn., Birmingham, 1962—. Mem. Am. Ala., Birmingham bar assns., Fed. Trial Examiners Conf., Tenn., Ala., Newberry (S.C.) hist. assns., Sons of Confederate Vets., Theta Chi, Sigma Upsilon, Phi Alpha Delta. Methodist (chmn. adminstrv. bd., trustee). Mason, Lion (past pres., past sec., past zone chmn.) Club: The Club (Birmingham, Ala.). Home: Adamsville AL 35005 Office: 908 S 20th St Birmingham AL 35205

GLASGOW, WILLIAM RODNEY, JR., dentist; b. Fairview, Okla., Jan. 18, 1928; s. William Rodney and Dolores Rillette (Mellor) G.; student No. Okla. Jr. Coll., 1949-51, Kan. U., 1951-52; D.D.S., U. Kansas City, 1956; m. Lola Marie Dobson, Sept. 17, 1951; children—Rodney Dale, Sondra Gayle, Steven Daniel, Michael David, Theresa Marie, Phillip Vincent, Patricia Lynnette. Individual practice gen. dentistry, Hominy, Okla., 1956—. Bd. dirs. Osage County Mental Health Assn., Osage County Mental Health Services, Inc., Pawhuska. Served with USAF, 1946-49. Mem. Am., Okla. dental assns., C. of C. (v.p. 1957), Delta Sigma Delta. Democrat. Roman Catholic. Rotarian (pres. 1958-59). Club: Knife and Fork (Tulsa). Home: Route 1 Box 101 Hominy OK 74035 Office: 115 S Price St Hominy OK 74035

GLASS, ALBERT JULIUS, psychiatrist, state ofcl.; b. Balt., June 16, 1908; s. Simon Barry and Jennie (Miller) G.; Ph.G., U. Md., 1928, B.S., 1928, M.D., 1932; m. Loretta Marie Lesnau, Aug. 6, 1936; children— Susan (Mrs. David Pithkethly), David, Richard, Judith. Intern Gouverneur Hosp., N.Y.C., 1933-34; resident specializing in neurology Central Neurol. Hosp., N.Y.C., 1934-35, Riverside Hosp., N.Y.C., 1936; practice of medicine, Balt., 1936-41; commd. maj. U.S. Army, 1946, advanced through grades to col., 1950; chief psychiatry Far East command, 1950-56, Walter Reed Gen. Hosp., Washington, 1951-56; cons. psychiatry U.S. Surgeon Gen., 1956-61; ret., 1963; dir. Okla. Dept. Mental Health, Oklahoma City, 1963—. Mem. exec. bd. Oklahoma City Council on Alcoholism, 1967—. Served with AUS, 1941-45. Decorated Bronze Star medal, Legion of Merit with oak leaf cluster. Recipient Gorgas medal Assn. Mil. Surgeons, 1959. Fellow Am. Psychiat. Assn.; mem. Group for Advancement Psychiatry. Rotarian. Contbr. chpts. to books, also articles to profl. publs. Home: 2305 NW 57th St Oklahoma City OK 73112 Office: State Capitol Oklahoma City OK 73105

GLASS, BENTLEY, author. Author: Science and Liberal Education, 1959; Science and Ethical Values, 1965, 68; Timely and the Timeless; Problems of Education in the Coming Decades, 1970, others. Address: care U N C Press Box 2288 Chapel Hill NC 27514*

GLASS, HENRY EDWARD, govt. ofcl.; b. East Orange, N.J., Apr. 14, 1914; s. Joseph and Sophie (Begum) G.; B.S. in Econs., N.Y.U., 1939, post-grad. 1939-41, postgrad. Am. U., 1942; m. Lillian L. Silver, Aug. 31, 1941; children—Marcia Lynn, Laura Faye, David Vaughn. Asst. cons. Social Security Bd., 1941; asso. economist, div. research OPA, 1942-43; with Army Air Forces Material Command, 1943-44, chief labor utilization field survey teams, 1943-45; asst. chief indsl. planning sect. Army Air Forces Tech. Service Command, 1946-47; prof. econs., later bus. orgn. USAF Inst. Tech., 1947-51; program analyst for asst. for programming Hdqrs. USAF, 1951-53; comptroller Office Asst. Sec. Def., 1953-65; asst. to sec. and dep. sec. def. Dept. Def., Washington, 1965—. Served to 1st lt. USAAF, 1944-46. Home: 2104 N Quintana St Arlington VA 22205 Office: The Pentagon Washington DC 20301

GLASS, HOLLIS, govt. ofcl.; b. Blossburg, Ala., Apr. 2, 1920; s. William Anderson and Dora Lue (Moore) G.; student Internat. Corr. Schs., 1946-50; m. Maria Elizabeth Nations, June 15, 1946; children—James Luther, Bobbie Jeanne. Sr. insp. Ala. State Hwy. Dept., Rodman, 1941-42, transitman, 1946-47, project engr., 1947-51; county engr. Clay, Houston and Henry Counties, Ala., 1951-60; fgn. project div. U.S. Bur. Pub. Rds., San Francisco, 1960—, hwy. constrn. and maintenance engr., 1963-65, project mgr., 1965-69, dep. div. engr., 1969—. Served with AUS, 1942-45. Decorated Bronze Star. Recipient Silver Medal award Dept. Commerce, 1965, Meritorious Service award Dept. State, 1966. Registered profl. engr., Ala. Mem. Nat. Soc. Profl. Engrs., Am. Road-Builder's Assn., Nat. Assn. Govt. Engrs., Ala. County Engrs. Assn. Mason (32 deg., Shriner). Home: 332 Cullen St Montgomery AL 36105 Office: Am Embassy US AID Bur Pub Roads San Francisco CA 96352

GLASS, JAMES GERBER, pipeline co. exec.; b. N.Y.C., Oct. 12, 1928; s. Joseph and Bessie (Gerber) G.; B.S., U. Tex., 1950; m. Geraldine Eisenberg, Sept. 3, 1950; children—Randall, Joseph, Amy Lyn, Robert, Brett, Bart, Kimberly. Petroleum engr., chief reservoir engr. Midstates Oil Corp., Tulsa, 1953-58, N.Y.C., 1955-56, dir. Middle States Petroleum Corp., La.; N.W.R.R., 1956-58; cons. petroleum engr. Glass & Moove Co., Tulsa, 1958-64; gen. mgr. Bigheart Pipe Line Corp., Tulsa, 1964-72, v.p., 1967-71, sr. v.p., 1971—; gen. mgr. Bigheart Crude Oil Corp., Tulsa, 1969-72, v.p., 1969-71, sr. v.p., 1971—; gen. mgr. Bigheart Transport Co., Tulsa, 1968-72, v.p., 1968-71, sr. v.p., 1971—. Trustee Tulsa Edn. Found., 1963-64. Served with USCGR, 1951-53. Registered profl. engr., Okla. Mem. Am. Inst., Mining, Metall. and Petroleum Engrs., Am. Assn. Petroleum Geologists, Internat. Oil Scouts Assn., Tulsa Engrs. Club, Petroleum Club Tulsa. Office: Amoco E Bldg Tulsa OK 74101

GLASS, JAMES WILLIAM, elec. engr. aerospace technologist; b. Fairburn, Ga., Aug. 1, 1913; s. Lemuel Page and Emmie (Luck) G.; student Jr. Coll. of Augusta (Ga.), 1930-31; B.S. in Elec. Engring., Ga. Inst. Tech., 1935; m. Elsie Wolfe, June 23, 1941; children—Emily Maude (Mrs. Charles Michael Woodward), Alliene Nell. Electrical engr. U. S. Army, C.E., Savannah, Ga. 1946-56; elec. engr., aerospace technologist, dep. br. chief astrionics lab. Army Ballistic Missile Agy. and Marshall Space Flight Center, Huntsville, Ala., 1956—. Served as staff sgt. USAAF, 1942-45. Registered profl. engr., Ala. Sr. mem. I.E.E.E. Baptist. Designer, supr. design ground support equipment Jupiter Weapons Systems, Juno II Space Vehicle, Saturn Space Vehicle. Home: 4205 Tombrook Pl NW Huntsville AL 35805 Office: Marshall Space Flight Center NASA Huntsville AL 35812

GLASS, POWELL, JR., publisher; b. Lynchburg, Va., Feb. 21, 1917; s. Powell and Ann (Cleghorn) G.; B.A., Washington and Lee U., 1938; student London Sch. Econs., 1938-39; postgrad. N.Y. U., 1939-40, U. Pa., 1956; LL.B., U. Va., 1947; m. Marianna Rhett duPont, June 18, 1940 (div. Jan. 1956); children—Anne Cleghorne, Marianna Rhett, Alicia Middleton; m. 2d, Joan Marilyn de Sardon, Nov. 24, 1958. Admitted to Va. bar. 1947; law clk. Isaac W. Diggs, N.Y.C. 1939-40, firm Davies, Auderbach & Hardy, N.Y.C., 1940; co-pub. Lynchburg News, Lynchburg Daily Advance, 1946-50, 51-56, v.p. Lynchburg News, Inc., 1959; v.p. Daily Advance, 1959—; editorial dir. Lynchburg News, also Lynchburg Daily Advance, 1969—; dir. Carter Glass & Sons, Inc., 1959—; instr. law U. Va., 1947-48; asso. prof. law Mercer U., 1956-58; editor-pub. Sea Coast Echo, Bay St. Louis, Miss., 1958-68, pres. MTO Publicity Corp., 1964- . Served with USMC, 1940-46, 50-51. Fellow Internat. Conf. Newspaper Editors; mem. Order Coif, Raven Soc., Hancock County C. of C. (past pres.), Nat. Conf. of Editorial Writers, Kappa Sigma. Rotarian. Contbr. articles to legal jours. Home: 1509 Clayton Av Lynchburg VA 24503 Office: 857 Church St Lynchburg VA 24505

GLASS, THOMAS EDGAR, JR., ednl. adminstr.; b. Tarboro, N.C., July 15, 1928; s. Thomas Edgar and Lilly Mae (Smith) G.; student Campbell Coll., 1947-48; A.B., U. N.C., 1954, M.Ed., 1957; m. Jean Ball DeWitt, Dec. 26, 1953; children—Thomas Edgar III, Janet. Tchr., athletic dir. Charlotte (N.C.) City Schs., 1953-60; self-employed as salesman, 1960-64; evening dir. Durham (N.C.) Tech. Inst., 1964-66, bus. mgr., 1966—. Served with AUS, 1951-53. Mem. N.E.A., Am. Assn. Sch. Adminstrs., Assn. Sch. Bus. Ofcls. U.S. and Can. (state chmn. 1968-70), N.C. Edn. Assn., N.C. Classroom Tchrs. Assn., N.C. Assn. Community Coll. Bus. Ofcls. Club: Willowhaven Country (Durham). Home: 1030 Evergreen Dr Durham NC 27705 Office: 1637 Lawson St Durham NC 27703

GLASS, WILLIAM A., petroleum co. exec.; B.S. in Petroleum Engring., U. Okla., 1959. With Big Chief Drilling Co., Oklahoma City, 1959—, drilling engr., Oklahoma City, 1962, then project engr. AEC project, named chief drilling engr., 1964, mgr. drilling operations, 1966, v.p., mgr. drilling, 1967, now exec. v.p. Mem. com. Scripps Inst. Oceanography. Mem. Am. Petroleum Inst., Am. Inst. Mining Engrs., Mid Continent Oil and Gas Assn., Oklahoma City Petroleum Club. Address: Big Chief Drilling Co 601 N E 63d St Oklahoma City OK 73144

GLASSCOCK, CHARLES GUS, JR., rancher; b. San Antonio, Feb. 19, 1918; s. Charles Gus and Lucille (Freeman) G.; student Baylor U., 1935-38; m. Bonnie Dell Smith, Jan. 25, 1947; children—Charles Gus III, John Donley, James Thomas. Foreman 4 G Ranch, 1938-39, 2 G Ranch, 1939-40, toolpusher Glasscock Drilling Co., Corpus Christi, Tex., 1940-42, partner, 1942-52, v.p., 1952-59; v.p. Glasscock Tidelands Oil Co., 1952-59; pres. Gt. Basins Petroleum Co., 1955-58; owner 2 G Cattie Ranches, Columbus, Tex., Glenderey, Colo., 1960—; chmn. bd. Bell Western Corp.; pres. Coral Pines, Ltd., Freeport, Bahamas. Trustee Houston Bapt. Coll.; devel. council Baylor U. Mem. Tex., Southwestern, Am. cattlemens assns., Aircraft Owners and Pilots Assn., Baylor U. Alumni Assn. (past v.p.), Tex. Mid-Continent Oil and Gas Assn. Clubs: Cherry Hills Country (Denver); Sierra, Baylor Bear (Waco, Tex.). Home: Route 2 Box 84 Columbus TX 78934 Office: 2016 Main St Houston TX 77002

GLAVIN, W(ILLIAM) RICHARD, cons.; b. Mahanoy City, Pa., Nov. 30, 1903; s. David Emmett and Sophia (Molichan) G.; B.C.S., Southeastern U., 1928; m. Edith Ann Williams, June 26, 1926; children—Ann (Mrs. Lewis A. Bristow), Richard. Asst. div. accountant Internat. Tel. & Tel., 1927-31; civil and criminal accounting investigations, 1929-31; spl. agt. FBI, N.Y.C., Phila., Washington, 1931-34, insp., asst. dir. in charge budget and personnel mgmt., 1934-54; lectr. FBI Nat. Acad., 1935-54; asst. sec. East Volusia Mosquito Control Dist., Daytona Beach, Fla., 1957-62; exec. sec. Fla. State Bd. Architecture, Ormond Beach, 1962-70. Alternate mem. adv. staff U.S. Senate Civil Service Com. on Personnel Matters, 1954; chmn. FBI U.S. Civil Service Appeals Com., 1950-54; tax. cons. Daytona Beach (Fla.) C. of C., 1955-56; mem. finance com. Continuing Council for Edn., Volusia County, 1955-57; personnel and budget cons. Halifax Dist. Hosp., 1956-57; mem. Gov's. Tax Study Com. for Volusia County, 1956; cons. personnel budget and finance N.Y. State Police, 1960-62; pres. Halifax area Boys' Clubs Am., 1969—. Served with USMC, 1922-27. Mem. Soc. Former Spl. Agts. FBI (chmn. Southeastern chpt. 1965), Fla. Anti-Mosquito Assn. Kiwanian (dir. Ormond Beach 1965—). Clubs: Riviera Country, Oceanside Country. Home: 461 Pinewood St Ormond Beach FL 32074 Office: 282 N Shore Dr Ormond Beach FL 32074

GLAZER, FREDERIC JAY, librarian; b. Portsmouth, Va., Feb. 20, 1937; s. Moses Herman and Charlotte Esther (Blachman) G.; B.A., Columbia, 1958, M.S., 1964; m. Sylvia Katherine Lerner, Aug. 18, 1963; children—Hoyt Eric, Hilary Alison. Media buyer Dancer-Fitzgerald & Sample, N.Y.C., 1958-60; mil. and civilian library assn. U.S. Army Spl. Services Library, Ft. Lee, Va., 1962-63; librarian, bus., tech. and social scis. dept. Kirn Meml. Library, Norfolk, Va., 1964-67; dir. Chesapeake (Va.) Pub. Library System, 1967—. Chmn. Va. Nat. Library Week, Southeastern Library Assn. Com., 1971. Vice pres. Tidewater Lit. Council, 1970-71, Social Econ. Area Research Clearing House, 1969. Served with AUS, 1960, 61-62. Recipient Presdl. certificate of appreciation for vol. service to project Headstart, 1968, certificate of recognition Nat. Book Com. and Nat. Library Week Com., 1970. Mem. A.L.A. (Nat. Library Week com. 1971-72, nat. publicity chmn. Jr. Mems. Round Table 1971-72), Va. Library Assn. (intellectual freedom com. 1970-71, pub. library devel. com. 1971-72). Creator Library Six-Pack, also Book Bucks, 1969. Home: 525 Redwood Dr Chesapeake VA 23320 Office: Civic Center Chesapeake VA 23320

GLEASON, WILLIAM HENRY, lawyer, judge; b. Eau Gallie, Fla., Jan. 9, 1928; s. William Lansing and Carol (Hurlbut) G.; student Ga. Inst. Tech., 1944-47; J.D., Vanderbilt U., 1950; m. Angela Gleason; 1 dau., Jane Carey. Admitted to Fla. bar, 1951; practiced in Brevard County, Fla., 1953—; mem. firm Gleason, Walker, Pearson & Shreve, Indialantic, Fla., 1964—; city judge, Indian Harbour Beach, 1955—, West Melbourne, Fla., 1968—, Indialantic, 1971—. Organizer, v.p., dir. 1st Nat. Bank, Satellite Beach, Fla., 1963-69; organizer, dir. Harbor City Nat. Bank, Eau Gallie, 1963—; organizer, dir. 1st Fed. Savs. and Loan Assn., Eau Gallie, 1959—, pres., 1966-68. Commr. Indian Harbour Beach, 1961-64, mayor, 1964-66. Bd. dirs. Brevard Heart Fund, 1954—, pres., 1965-66. Served with AUS, 1951-53; Korea. Decorated Bronze Star. Mem. Am., D.C., Brevard County bar assns., Fla. Bar, V.F.W., Phi Delta Phi. Rotarian, Mason (Shriner, 32 deg.). Clubs: Eau Gallie Yacht. Home: 200 Poinciana Dr Indian Harbour Beach FL 32937 Office: 121 5th Av Indialantic FL 32901

GLENDINNING, RICHARD (EDWIN), writer; b. Elizabeth, N.J., Oct. 10, 1917; s. Richard Edwin and Alice May (Summers) G.; A.B., Dartmouth, 1940; m. Sara Helena Wilson, Dec. 27, 1941; 1 dau., Elizabeth Ann (Mrs. Alan Burrell). Writer, Vogue Mag., 1940-41; pub. relations Balt. Mus. Art, 1941; author short stories and articles in nat. publs., radio dramas, novels, hist. non-fiction, 1945—. Mem. Sarasota (Fla.) Library Bd., Sarasota County Library Adv. Bd.; chmn. Sarasota County Hist. Commn.; mem. adv. council Myakka River State Park. Served as lt. comdr. USNR, World War II. Mem. Soc. Am. Historians, Mystery Writers Am. Methodist. Club: Forest Lakes Country (Sarasota). Home: 1638 South Dr Sarasota FL 33579

GLENN, FRANCIS BERKELEY, supt. schs.; b. Staunton, Va., Nov. 17, 1905; s. John Abram and Frances Ellen (Ramsey) G.; B.A., Coll. William and Mary, 1929; M.S., U. Tenn., 1941; m. Jean Brownlee, Dec. 24, 1929; children—Peggy (Mrs. Charles Honeycutt), Francis Berkeley. Prin. elementary sch., McDowell County, W. Va., 1929-30; prin. elementary sch., Waynesboro, Va., 1930-45, prin. high sch., 1946-48, supt. schs., 1948—. Mem. staff ednl. workshops, Va., La., 1946. Bd. dirs. Waynesboro chpt. A.R.C., Waynesboro Community Hosp., Waynesboro YMCA. Mem. Phi Delta Kappa, Kappa Delta Pi. Presbyn. (deacon, supt. Sunday schs.). Contbr. articles to profl. jours. Home: 830 S Ellison Lane Waynesboro VA 22980 Office: 301 Pine Av Waynesboro VA 22980

GLENN, HELEN IRENE, univ. adminstr.; b. Atlanta, Aug. 17, 1918; d. Harry James and Edna (Montanye) Glenn; A.B., Mercer U., 1938; M.A., Ind. U., 1942. Tchr. pub. schs. Porterdale, Ga., 1938-40; dir. pub. relations, asso. prof. journalism Brenau Coll., Gainesville, Ga., 1946-48; grand sec., treas. Alpha Delta Pi, Berkeley, Cal., Kansas City, Mo., Atlanta, 1948-57; dir. pub. relations asso. prof. journalism Wesleyan Coll., Macon, Ga., 1957-61; dean of women, asst. prof. journalism Mercer U., Macon, 1961-70; adviser to married students Auburn (Ala.) U., 1970-71; dir. financial aids Jacksonville (Fla.) U., 1971—. Nat. Panhellenic Conf. del. Alpha Delta Pi, 1959-62; pres. Macon Council Women's Civic Clubs, 1962-64; mem. membership com. YWCA, 1969-70. Served to maj. WAC, AUS, 1942-46. Mem. Am. Assn. U. Women, Assn. Edn. in Journalism, So. Coll. Personnel Assn. (state membership chmn., chmn. job opportunities service; pres. 1969), Nat. Assn. Student Financial Aid Adminstrs., So., Fla., Nat., Ga. (pres. 1967-69) assns. women deans and counselors, Am. Legion, Theta Sigma Phi, Kappa Delta Epsilon, Alpha Delta Pi, Delta Kappa Gamma. Club: Quota (past dist. gov.; past pres. Macon). Home: 3830 University Blvd S Apt 49 Jacksonville FL 32216

GLENN, JACK FITTEN, banker; b. Atlanta, Nov. 16, 1910; s. William Harper and Anne (Fitten) G.; B.S., Ga. Inst. Tech., 1932; m. Anne Amanda Alston, Dec. 18, 1935; children—Jack Fitten, Philip Alston, Robert James, James Lewis. Various positions Coca-Cola Co., Atlanta, 1932-35; salesman unlisted securities, head trading dept. and underwriting dept. Courts & Co., Atlanta, 1936-42, gen. partner, 1942-50, charge br. office operations, 1945-50; became asst. pres. Citizens & So. Nat. Bank Ga., Atlanta 1951-67, chmn. bd., 1967—; dir. Granitesville Co., Citizens & So. Bank Am., Citizens & So. Holding Co. Active United Appeal Community Chest; commr.

Atlanta Housing Authority. Trustee, Darlington Sch., Rome, Ga., Ga. Tech. Found. Served as lt. USNR, 1942-45. Mem. Assn. Res. City Bankers, Ga. C. of C. (dir., treas.), Phi Delta Phi. Clubs: Piedmont Driving (past v.p., pres., dir.), Capital City (past dir.), Peachtree Golf (past dir.), Nine O'Clocks (past pres., dir.), Commerce (past dir., treas.), Homosassa Fishing (past v.p., bd.) (Atlanta). Home: 8 Cherokee Rd NW Atlanta GA 30305 Office: Marietta and Broad Sts Atlanta GA 30303

GLENN, JAMES FRANCIS, surgeon; b. Lexington, Ky., May 10, 1928; s. Cambridge Francis and Martha (Morrow) G.; student U. Ky., 1947-48; B.A., U. Rochester, 1949; M.D., Duke, 1952; m. Gale Brooke Morrison, Dec. 29, 1948; children—Cambridge Francis II, Sara Brooke, Nancy Carrick, James Morrison Woodworth. House officer gen. surgery Peter Bent Brigham Hosp., Boston, 1952-54; resident urology Duke Med. Center, Durham, N.C., 1956-59; asst. prof. urology Yale, 1959-61; asso. prof. Bowman Gray Med. Sch., Winston-Salem, N.C., 1961-63; prof., chmn. urology dept. Duke, 1963—; practice medicine specializing in urologic surgery, New Haven, 1959-61, Winston-Salem, 1961-63, Durham, 1963—; mem. staff Duke, Watts, Lincoln, VA hosps. (all Durham). Cons. U.S. Army, VA, Nat. Acad. Scis., NRC; mem. sci. adv. bd. Nat. Kidney Found., 1964-69. Served to capt. M.C., USAF, 1954-56. Mem. Soc. Univ. Urologists (sec., pres.), A.C.S., Am. Assn. Genito-Urinary Surgeons, Am. Urologic Assn., Am. Fertility Soc., Internat. Urologic Soc. Sigma Xi, Delta Kappa Epsilon, Phi Chi, Alpha Omega Alpha. Author: Diagnostic Urology, 1964; Ureteral Reflux in Children, 1967; Urologic Surgery, 1969. Mem. editorial bd. Urology Digest, 1965—, Human Sexuality, 1967—, Urological Survey, 1968—. Home: 27 Oak Dr Durham NC 27707

GLENN, JOHN H(ERSCHEL), JR., bottling co. exec., former astronaut; b. Cambridge, O., July 18, 1921; s. John Herschel and Clara (Sproat) G.; student Muskingum Coll., 1939, D.Sc., 1961; naval aviation cadet U. Ia., 1942; grad. flight school Naval Air Tng. Center, Corpus Christi, Tex., 1943, Navy Test Pilot Tng. School, Patuxent River, Md., 1954; m. Anna Margaret Castor, Apr. 1943; children—Carolyn Ann, John David. Commd. 2d lt. USMC, 1943, advanced through grades to lt. col.; assigned 4th Marine Aircraft Wing, Marshall Islands campaign, 1944, 9th Marine Aircraft Wing, 1945-46; with 1st Marine Aircraft Wing, North China Patrol, also Guam, 1947-48; flight instr. advanced flight tng., Corpus Christi, 1949-51; asst. G-2/G-3 Amphibious Warfare Sch., Quantico, Va., 1951; with Marine Fighter Squadron 311, exchange pilot 25th Fighter Squadron USAF, Korea, 1953; project officer fighter design br. Navy Bur. Eero., Washington, 1956-59; non-stop supersonic transcontinental Flight, July 16, 1957; astronaut Project Mercury, Manned Spacecraft Center NASA, 1959-64, pilot Mercury-Atias 6, orbital space flight launched from Cape Canaveral, Fla., Feb., 1962. Vice pres. corporate devel., dir. Royal Crown Cola Co. Decorated D.F.C. (five), Air medal (18), Astronaut medal USMC, Navy unit commendation; Korean Presidential unit citation; Distinguished Merit award Muskingum Coll.; Medal of Honor, N.Y.C. Mem. Soc. Exptl. Test Pilots, Internat. Acad. Astronautics (hon.). Presbyn. Co-author: We Seven, 1962. Author: P.S., I Listened to Your Heart Beat. Home: 203 Sleepy Hollow Ct Timbercove Seabrook TX

GLENN, NORVAL DWIGHT, educator; b. Roswell, N.M., Aug. 13, 1933; s. William N. and Mary E. (Cochrain) G.; B.A., N.M. State U., 1954; Ph.D., U. Tex., 1962. Instr., Miami U., Oxford, O., 1960-61; instr. U. Ill., 1961-63, asst. prof., 1963-64; asst. prof. U. Tex., Austin, 1964-65, asso. prof. sociology, 1965-70, prof. sociology, 1970—. Served from 2d lt. to 1st lt., AUS, 1954-56. Mem. Am. Sociol. Assn. Author: (with Leonard Broom) Transformation of the Negro American, 1965. Editor: (with Charles Bonjean) Blacks in the United States, 1969. Compiler: (with Jon Alston and David Weiner) Social Stratification: A Research Bibliography, 1969. Contbr. research articles to profl. jours. Home: 2204 Trail of the Madrones Austin TX 78746

GLENN, WADLEY R., physician, hosp. adminstr. Dir. Crawford Long Meml. Hosp., Emory U., Atlanta. Address: Crawford Long Meml Hosp 35 Linden Av NE Atlanta GA 30308*

GLENN, WAYNE EDWARD, oil col. exec.; b. Fort Worth, Nov. 3, 1915; s. Arthur E. and Lura M. (Hammon) G.; B.S. in Petroleum Engring., U. Okla., 1940; student Am. Mgmt. Sch., 1954; grad. Advanced Mgmt. Program, Harvard, 1957; Ph.D. in Engring., Mont. Sch. Mines, 1960; m. Barbara E. Gamble, July 13, 1941; children—Ellen Gail, Carvel Wayne, Lawrence Edward. With Continental Oil Co., 1936-62, asst. regional mgr. prodn. Rocky Mountain region, Denver, 1952-58, gen. mgr. prodn. dept., Houston, 1958-61, v.p., 1961-62; pres., dir., gen. mgr. Hudson's Bay Oil & Gas Co. Ltd., Calgary, Alta., Can., 1962—; pres., dir. Mic Mac Oils, Ltd.; 1963—; v.p., coordinator world-wide exploration and prodn. activities Continental Oil Co., 1965-67, exec. v.p., 1967-69, pres. Western Hemisphere Petroleum div., 1969—; also dir.; exec. v.p. N. Am. Petroleum Operations, 1968—; 1st v.p., dir. Peace River Oil Pipe Line Co. Ltd.; dir. Security Freehold Petroleum Ltd.; voting trustee Trans-Can. Pipe Lines Ltd. Mem. Canadian Council Christians and Jews. Adv. com. engring. U. Alta. Bd. dirs. Jr. Achievement, United Engrs. Trustees Found. Served to capt. AUS, World War II. Mem. Am. Inst. Mining Metall. and Petroleum Engrs. (v.p.; pres. soc. petroleum engrs. 1960-61). Calgary (past chmn. petroleum and natural gas com.), Canadian, Houston (dir.) chambers commerce, Canadian Petroleum Assn. (vice chmn., bd. govs. 1964-65; dir. Alta. div. 1962-65), Internat. Oil and Gas Center, Canadian Businessmen's Aircraft Assn. (past dir.), Ind. Petroleum Mid-Continent Oil and Gas Assn. (dir.), Nat. Alliance Businessmen (met. chmn.), Am. Petroleum Inst. (past chmn. adv. com., dir.), Tex. Research League (dir.). Republican. Presbyn. (elder). Mason (32 Shriner). Club: Houston Petroleum, River Oaks Country. Home: 5025 Riverway Houston TX 77027 Office: PO Box 2197 Houston TX 77001

GLENN, WILLIAM LAURENCE, JR., elec. engr.; b. Decatur, Ga., July 5, 1931; s. William Laurence and Marie (Pearce) G.; B.E.E., Ala. Polytech. Inst., 1957; m. Patricia Joan Franklin, May 22, 1954; children— William Laurence III, Patricia Kathleen, Karen Ann, James Patrick. Powerplant installation engr., base operations mgr. Pan Am. World Airways, Grand Turk, B.W.I., 1958-59, asst. supt. range operations, program specialist, 1959-61; Saturn operations engr. Douglas Aircraft Co., Cocoa Beach, Fla., 1961-70; pres. Glenn-Terrill Devel. Corp., 1970—. Served with USCGR, 1951-54. Mem. I.E.E.E., Phi Delta Theta. Republican. Roman Catholic. Lion. Home: Route 3 Box 574-A Tequesta Harbor Merritt Island FL 32952 Office: PO Box 2636 Vero Beach FL 32960

GLICK, EDWARD MAURICE, found. exec., author; b. Cleve., May 23, 1920; s. Philip and Lillian (Levin) G.; B.A., Cum laude, Ohio State U., 1943; M.A., Western Reserve U., 1947; Ph.D., Ohio State U., 1960; m. Florence Goldman, Sept. 22, 1946; children—Linda Ruth (Mrs. Samuel Drewen), Ellen Adrienne. Dir. pub. relations Ohio Bur. Unemployment Compensation, 1947-50; chief publs. and reports State and Health, Edn. and Welfare Depts., Washington, 1951-57; pres. Glisand Corp., Washington, 1957-60; editor, pub. Med.-Hosp. Research Digest, Washington, 1957-60; spl. correspondent Times of London, 1960-62; cons. Senate Judiciary Com., U.S. Congress, Washington, 1963-64; mng. dir. Am. Inst. for Polit. Communication, Washington, 1965—. Prof. polit. sci. George Washington U., 1964-65, Md. U., 1965-66; prof. journalism Am. U., 1962-63. Pres., dir. Am. Inst. for Polit. Communication, 1965. Served with AUS, 1943-45. Decorated Purple Heart. Mem. Am., So. polit. sci. assns., Am. Acad. Polit. and Social Sci., Phi Beta Kappa, Sigma Delta Chi. Club: Nat. Press (Washington). Author: The New Methodology: A Study of Political Strategy and Tactics, 1967; The Federal Government-Daily Press Relationship, 1968; Media and Non-Media Effects on Formation of Public Opinion, 1969; co-author Television Station Ownership, 1971. Contbr. to profl. jours. Home: 18604 Walker's Choice Rd Gaithersburg MD 20760 Office: Prudential Bldg Washington DC 20005

GLICK, PAUL C(HARLES), govt. ofcl.; b. Hartsville, Ind., Sept. 22, 1910; s. David E. and Mattie (Morrison) G.; B.A., DePauw U., 1933; M.A., U. Wis., 1935, Ph.D., 1938; m. Joy V. Usher, June 20, 1938; children—Paul Charles, David M. Instr. sociology Whitman Coll., 1938-39, DePauw U., 1937-38; with population div. U.S. Bur. Census, Washington, 1939—, mem., chief family statistics sect., 1939-49, chief social statistics br., 1949-61, asst. chief population div. (for demographic and social statistics programs), 1961—; mem. standing com. pub. health conf. on records and statistics, 1964-68. Served with AUS, 1944-45; ETO. Recipient Silver medal for meritorious service U.S. Dept. Commerce, 1953, Gold medal for exceptional services, 1970, Fellow Am. Pub. Health Assn., Am. Statis. Assn., Am Sociol. Assn.; mem. Population Assn. Am. (pres. 1966-67), D.C. Sociol. Soc. (pres. 1960-61), Am. Sociol. Assn. (chmn. family sect. 1966-67, mem. council 1963-67). Author: American Families, 1957; also chpts. in books; co-author Marriage and Divorce; A Social and Economic Study, 1970. Home: 4706 Pard Rd SE Washington DC 20027 Office: US Bureau Census Washington DC 20233

GLICKMAN, NATHANIEL, physiologist; b. Chgo., Sept. 23, 1911; s. David and Sarah (Herman) G.; B.S., U. Chgo., 1934; M.S., U. Ill. Coll. Medicine, 1936; m. Elisabeth Lewis, Oct. 1, 1944; children—Diane Joy (Mrs. Jeffrey Ram), Marjorie Beth. Asst. in physiology U. Ill. Coll. Medicine, 1935-36, research physiologist atmospheric environment and aero med. research unit, dept. medicine, 1936-47, asst. prof. med., research physiologist, 1947-51; cons. physiologist, Miami Beach, Fla., 1952—; clin. asst. prof. physiology U. Miami (Fla.) Sch. Medicine, 1964-69; cons., dir. research St. Mary of Nazareth Hosp., Chgo., 1971—. Chmn. Commn. on Jewish Edn. for S.E. region United Synagogue Am., 1970—. Mem. Am. Physiol. Soc., A.A.A.S., Sigma Xi. Jewish religion (chmn. sch. bd. 1957—). Mem. B'nai B'rith (pres. lodge 1956-58). Contbr. articles to profl. jours. Research on physiol. responses of humans to ambient environment, tolerance to cold as modified by diet, physiology of convalescence from surgery. Home: 970 South Shore Dr Miami Beach FL 33141

GLICKSTEIN, JOSEPH M(ORRIS), lawyer; b. Jacksonville, Fla. 26, 1899; s. Harry and Fannie B. (Shorr) G.; LL.B., Washington and Lee U., 1920; m.Myra M. Grunthal, Jan. 8, 1924; children—Joseph Morris, Hugh S. Admitted to Fla. bar, 1920, U.S. Supreme Ct. bar, 1933; practiced in Jacksonville; 1920—; now sr. partner Glickstein, Crenshaw, Glickstein, Fay & Allen; atty. City of Neptune Beach (Fla.); gen. counsel R. C. Motor Lines, Inc., So. Indsl. Corp., Fulton Distbg. Co. of Fla., Universal Marion Corp; spl. counsel Merrit-Chapman & Scott Corp.; counsel Bapt. Meml. Hosp., B.B. McCormick & Sons, Ace Electric Supply Co., Harbor View Farm, Daylight Industries, Inc., John Deihl Chevrolet Co.; sr. adviser Barnett Bank of Jacksonville, N.A. Mem. staff govs. Fla., 1937-39, 49—; mem. Duval County Civil Service Commn., 1937-38; mem. registrants adv. bd., No. 3, Jacksonville, World War II. Mayor Town of Neptune Beach, 1945-47, councilman, 1937-45. Trustee Jacksonville Baptist Hosp., 1950—; mem. adv. bd. Fla. Jr. Coll. Mem. Am. Judicature Soc., Am. Legion, Nat. Geographic Soc., Am., Fla. and Jacksonville bar assns., C. of C., Union Am. Hebrew Congregations (past trustee), Robert E. Lee Assos. (charter), Zeta Beta Tau, Omicron Delta Kappa. Democrat. Jewish. Clubs: University (charter), River (charter), Ponte Vedra. Author article. Home: 1008 Ocean Front Neptune Beach FL 32233 Office: Universal Marion Bldg Jacksonville FL 32202 also PO Box 1086 Jacksonville FL 32201

GLISPIN, VERNON LEE, accountant; b. Houston, Nov. 19, 1923; s. Frank Amell and Pearl (Williams) G.; B.B.A., U. Houston, 1950; m. Agnes Pauline McKenzie, Apr. 8, 1951; children—Joanna Lyn, Melissa Lee, Sharla Suzanne. Pub. accountant, Pasadena, Tex., 1952-59, 66—; partner Spain, Glispin & Co., Pasadena, 1959-66; v.p., dir., charter sec. Southmore Savs. Assn., Pasadena, 1959—; dir., sec.-treas. Smith's Appliances, Inc., Pasadena, 1955—, Petro-Chem. Suppliers, Inc., Houston, 1968—; dir., v.p. A-B Distbg. Co., Inc., Harlingen, Tex., 1959—; dir., treas. H & H Apts., Inc., Pasadena, 1967—. Chmn. dist. orgn. and extension com. Sam Houston Area council Boy Scouts Am., 1970-71. Served with USNR, 1943-46, ensign, 1950-55. Mem. Tex. Soc. C.P.A.'s, Am. Inst. C.P.A.'s, Pasadena C. of C., Pasadena Livestock and Rodeo Assn., Nat. Rifle Assn. (life) Optimist (treas. Pasadena 1970-72). Club: Exchange (charter sec. Pasadena 1953-66, charter mem. S.E. Houston). Home: 1311 Jefferson St Pasadena TX 77502 Office: 825 E Southmore St Pasadena TX 77502

GLISSON, DOROTHY W., state ofcl. Dir. div. elections State of Fla., Tallahassee. Address: Div Elections Dept State The Capitol Tallahassee FL 32304*

GLOCKER, THEODORE WESLEY, JR., lawyer; b. Knoxville, Tenn., Aug. 10, 1925; s. Theodore W. and Julia (McClarty) G.; student U. of South, 1943-44, U. Tex., 1944-45; B.S., U. Tenn., 1947; J.D., Harvard, 1950; m. Eleanor Julia Glocker, Nov. 30, 1950; children—Theodore William, Margaret McClarty, Eleanor Julia, David Hansen. Admitted to N.M. bar, 1951, D.C. bar, 1953, Fla. bar, 1956; practiced in Albuquerque, 1950-51, Jacksonville, Fla., 1956—; mem. firm Buck & Drew, 1956-57, Buck, Drew & Glocker, 1958—; trial atty., lands div. Dept. of Justice, Washington, 1952-53; atty. Tax Ct. of U.S., 1953-56. Mem. Spl. Liaison Tax Com. Southeastern Region, Jacksonville, 1956-57, 59-60, 65-67. Chmn. bd. Duval County Beaches Hosp., 1959-63; v.p., bd. dirs. Riverside Presbyn. House, Inc., 1970—. Served with USNR, 1943-46. Mem. Am., N.M., Jacksonville bar assns., Bar Assn. of D.C., Fla. Bar (chmn. tax sect. 1963-64). Sigma Chi, Tau Beta Pi, Beta Gamma Sigma, Phi Kappa Phi. Presbyn. Home: 949 Elder Lane Jacksonville FL 32204 Office: Fla Title Bldg Jacksonville FL 32202

GLOSSER, MORT MARK, supt. schs.; b. Rochelle, Ill., Oct. 5, 1913; s. Mort Wagner and Georgia (Wright) G.; B.S., Cornell Coll., 1934; Mus.M., U. Wis., 1943; Ed.D., Mich. State U., 1954; m. Catherine Cornelia Rogers, Dec. 24, 1938; children—Catherine Anna (Mrs. Robert M. Gleaves), Aurelia Sewall. Dir. band Woodbine (Ia.) High Sch., 1934-36, Gadsden (Ala.) High Sch., 1936-59; asst. supt. city schs., Gadsden, 1959-65, supt. schs., 1965—. Served with USAAF, 1944-46. Mem. Ala. Bandmasters Assn. (past pres.), Ala. Music Educators Assn. (past pres.), N.E.A., Ala. Edn. Assn., Am., Ala. assns. sch. adminstrs., C. of C. (dir. 1965—). Episcopalian. Rotarian (past pres.). Home: 867 Crown Point St Cadsden AL 35901

GLOSTER, HUGH MORRIS, coll. pres.; b. Brownsville, Tenn., May 11, 1911; s. John and Dora (Morris) G.; student LeMoyne Coll., 1927-29; B.A., Morehouse Coll., 1931; M.A. (Univ. fellow), Atlanta U., 1933; Ph.D. (Gen. Edn. Bd. fellow), N.Y.U., 1943; Hon. Doctorate, U. Haiti, 1968, N.Y.U., 1971; m. Louise Elizabeth Torrence, June 1, 1935 (div.); children—Alice Louise, Evelyn Elaine; m. 2d, Beulah Victoria Harold, Sept. 9, 1957; 1 son, Hugh Morris Jr. Insr., asso. prof. English, LeMoyne Coll., 1933-41; prof. English, Morehouse Coll., 1941-43; program dir. USO, Ft. Huachuca, Ariz., 1943-44, asso. regional exec., Atlanta, 1944-46; prof. English, chmn. dept. lang. and lit. Hampton Inst., 1946-67, dir. summer session, 1952-62, dean of faculty, 1963-67; pres. Morehouse Coll., Atlanta, 1967—; prof. English, Atlanta U., summers 1942, 43; guest prof. English, N.Y.U., summers 1949, 62; Fulbright prof. English, Hiroshima U., Japan, 1953-55; lectr. Orientation Center Fgn. Grad. Students, Coll. William and Mary, summer 1955; vis. prof. Am. lit. U. Warsaw, Poland, 1961-62; lectr. tours, 1933-55, 56, 59; summer faculty various univs. and colls. Bd. dirs. Nat. Assn. for Equal Opportunity in Higher Edn., United Bd. for Coll. Devel., Council Protestant Colls. and Univs.; bd. dirs., trustee United Negro Coll. Fund; trustee Atlanta U., Morehouse Coll., Interdenominational Theol. Center, Inst. Ednl. Devel., Martin Luther King Jr. Meml. Center, Ednl. Testing Service, So. Christian Leadership Conf. Recipient research grant Alpha Phi Alpha, summer 1940; research grant Carnegie Found., 1950-51; distinguished contbns. award Coll, Lang. Assn., 1958; Alumnus of Year, LeMoyne Coll., 1967. Mem. Assn. Pvt. Colls. and Univs. Ga. (v.p.), Am. Assn. U. Adminstrs. (dir.), Coll. Lang. Assn. (founder, pres. 1937-38, 48-50, trustee) Assn. Am. Colls. (commn. coll. adminstrn.), Nat. Collegiate Athletic Assn. (long-range planning com., Theodore Roosevelt award Jury), Inst. European Studies (pres.'s council), Am. Assn. Higher Edn. (exec. com. 1967-69), Nat. Reading Council (dir.), Com. on Econ. Devel. (dir.), Phi Beta Kappa, Sigma Pi Phi, Alpha Phi Alpha. Rotarian. Author: Negro Voices in American Fiction, 1948. Co-Editor: The Brown Thrush: An Anthology of Verse by Negro College Students, 1935; My Life—My Country—My World: College Readings for Modern Living, 1952. Contbg. editor Phylon: The Atlanta U. Review of Race and Culture, 1948-53; adv. editor Coll. Lang. Assn. Jour., 1957—. Home: 900 Flamingo Dr SW Atlanta GA 30311

GLOVER, HARRY DOLPHIN, dentist; b. Chautauqua, Kan., Aug. 16, 1906; s. Edward Bruce and Dora (Anderson) G.; D.D.S., U. Kansas City, 1928; m. Edyth Berniece Parker, Aug. 10, 1925; children—Cyntha (Mrs. Richard F. Ward), Shirley (Mrs. James T. Hoke, Jr.), Rhoda (Mrs. Billy G. McGuire), Michael. Practice dentistry, Stillwater, Okla., 1928—. Mem. Am., Okla., Stillwater dental assns., Am. Inst. Oral Biology, So. Med. Assn., Psi Omega. Democrat. Presbyn. Rotarian (past pres.). Home: 3614 S Husband St Stillwater OK 74074 Office: 1604 W 8th St Stillwater OK 74074

GLOVER, ROBERT JULIAN, lawyer; b. Malvern, Ark., Apr. 12, 1909; s. David Delano and Robert T. (Quinn) G.; B.A., Ouachita Bapt. U., 1933; postgrad. Ark. Law Sch., Little Rock, 1933-36; m. Loretta Cornelia Hill, Apr. 8, 1934. Admitted to Ark. bar, 1936; practice law, Hot Springs, Ark., 1936—; firm Glover and Sanders, 1969—; city atty., Hot Springs, 1947-48; pros. atty. 18th Jud. Dist. of Ark., 1949-52. Chmn., De Gray Dam and Reservoir Land Condemnation Commn., 1966-68; pres. Ouachita Area council Boy Scouts Am., 1952-53, recipient Silver Beaver, 1954; chmn. Garland County Election Commn., 1954-68. Served to lt. Col. AUS, 1969. Mem. Am., Ark., Garland County bar assns., Am. Trial Lawyers Assn., Am. Judicature Soc., Am. Legion, 40 and 8. Mason (32 deg., Shriner, Jester). Baptist. Home: 112 Crestwood Rd Hot Springs AR 71901 Office: First Federal Bldg Hot Springs AR 71901

GLOVER, WENDELL JOE, supt. schs.; b. Okmulgee, Okla., Mar. 6, 1931; s. Blain E. and Joyce Mabel (Reed) G.; B.S., E. Central State Coll., Ada, Okla., 1952; M.S., Okla. State U., 1956, Ed.D., 1968; m. Wilma Jean King, July 16, 1954; children—Deborah, David, Daniel, Derald. Tchr., coach Eram Schs., Boynton, Okla., 1952-57; prin. Twin Hills Sch., Okmulgee, 1957-59, Beggs (Okla.) Jr. High Sch., 1959-62; supt. Beggs Pub. Schs., 1962-65; grad. asst. univ. placement services Okla. State U., Stillwater, 1965-66; supt. schs. Stillwater Schs., 1966-69, Woodward (Okla.) Pub. Schs., 1969—; tchr. pub. sch. finance Okla. State U., Stillwater, summer 1968, tchr. extension class in sch. finance, 1969. Mem. manpower planning council Dist. II, Okla. Econ. Devel. Assn., 1971-72. Bd. dirs. Woodward Kids, Inc., Plains Indian Mus. Found. Mem. Am., Okla. (v.p. 1970-71) assns. sch. adminstrs., N.E.A., Okla., Woodward County edn. assns., N.W. Okla. Adminstrs. Orgn. (pres. 1970), Okla. Assn. Sch. Bus. Ofcls., Woodward C. of C. (dir. 1969-72), Phi Delta Kappa. Home: Route 3 Box 94 M Woodward OK 73801 Office: PO Box 668 10th and Main Woodward OK 73801

GLOYNA, EARNEST FREDERICK, educator, cons. san. engr.; b. Vernon, Tex., June 30, 1921; s. Herman E. and Johanna M. (Riethmayer) G.; B.S., Tex. Technol. Coll., 1946; M.S., U. Tex., 1949; D.Eng., Johns Hopkins, 1952; m. Mary Agnes Lehman, Feb. 17, 1946; children— David F., Lisa M. Engr. Tex. Hwy. Dept., 1945; office engr. Magnolia Petroleum Co., 1946; with U. Tex., Austin, 1947—, prof., dir. environmental health engring. labs. research, 1953-70, dir. Center for Research in Water Resources, 1963—, dean Coll. Engring., 1970—; dir. Bur. Engring. Research, 1970—; clin. lectr. indsl. medicine, post grad. sch. medicine U. Tex., 1955-59; research asso. Johns Hopkins, 1950; research participant Oak Ridge Nat. Lab., summer 1949; guest engr. Brookhaven Nat. Lab., summer 1952; sr. nuclear engr. Convair Corp., summer 1956, 58, 59; cons. U.S. Select Com. on Water Resources, U.S. Senate, 1959-60, Nuclear Aircraft Program, 1959-60, UN WHO, 1964-68; spl. cons. USPHS 1954-60, U.S. Army Nuclear Def. Lab., Los Alamos Sci. Lab., U. Cal., USAF, 1962-64, to major industries and state and local on water and wastewater treatment; chmn. tech. adv. com. Tex. Water Pollution Control Bd.; 1962-65; chmn. adv. com. on design, constrn., operation sewage systems Tex. Health Dept.; 1960-62; mem. environmental health review com. of health professions U.S. Dept. Health, Edn. and welfare, 1969-70, also mem. ad hoc water supply com. Bur. Water Hygiene, 1969-71; adv. bd. Water Inc., 1969—; com. natural resources Tex Urban Devel. Commn., 1969-71. Sec.-treas., trustee Environmental Engring. Intersoc. Bd., 1971—. Served from lt. to maj., AUS, 1942-45. Recipient Harrison Prescott Eddy medal Water Pollution Control Fedn. Jour., 1959; Water Resources Div. award Am. Water Works Assn., 1959; meritorious paper award Tex. sect. Am. Soc. C.E., 1968, Distinguished Grad. award Tex. Technol. U., 1971. Diplomate Am. Acad. San. Engrs. Mem. Nat. Acad. Engring., Am. Inst. Chem. Engrs., Am. Environmental Engr. Intersoc. Bd. (com. on certification by invitation), Water Pollution Control Fedn., Am. Water Works Assn., Am. Soc. Engring. Edn., Nat. Soc. Profl. Engrs. (past dir. univs. council on water resources), S.W. Soc. Nuclear Medicine (hon.), Acad. Environmental Engrs., Internat. Assn. Water Pollution Research (nat. com.), Am. Soc. C.E., Am. Assn. Profs. San. Engring. (pres. 1966-68), Radiol. Health Conf., U.S.-Mexico Border Health Assn., Sigma Xi, Chi Epsilon, Tau Beta Pi, Phi Kappa Phi. Lutheran. Author in field; co-author Principles of Radiological Health, 1969; Waste Stabilization Ponds, 1971. Editor (with Eckenfelder) Advances in Water Quality Improvement— Water Resources Symposium No. 1, 1968, Water Quality Improvement by Physical and Chemical Processes, No. 3, 1970, (with Butcher)

Conflicts in Water Resources Planning, No. 5, 1972. Home: 3317 River Rd Austin TX 78703

GLYNN, EMMETT MARTIN, realtor; b. Arbroth, La., Aug. 9, 1912; s. Alexander A. and Felicia (Supple) G.; B.S., La. State U., 1936, postgrad., 1938-40; m. Natalie Jones, Apr. 27, 1946; children—Christine Supple, Martin Alex. Cattle farmer, 1945-53; salesman J. T. Doiron Realtor, Baton Rouge, 1945-49; gen. sales mgr. Anhydrous Ammonia div. Gen. Gas Corp., Baton Rouge, 1954-56; v.p. Glenrich, Inc., 1960-69; pres. Schriever Devel. Co., Inc., 1958-69, Broadmoor Heights, Inc., 1965-69, E.M. Glynn, Inc., Houma, La., 1957—. Mem. La. State U. Alumni Council, 1936-42, chmn. exec. com., 1939-40. Served with A.C., AUS, 1942-45. Roman Catholic. K.C., Elk. Clubs: Bayou Country, R.O.T.C. Parents (Thibodaux, La.). Home: 605 St Philip St Thibodaux LA 70301 Office: 705 Lafayette St Houma LA 70360

GOAD, FRANK ROARK, circuit judge; b. Allen County, Ky., Apr. 14, 1915; s. Frank R. and Anna Laura (Kemp) G.; B.A., U. Mo., 1938; LL.B., U. Louisville, 1941; m. Anne Fuqua, Mar. 27, 1937; children—Margaret (Mrs. William C. Hawkins), Hutch, Frank Roark III. Admitted to Ky. bar, 1942; practice in Louisville, 1942-44, Scottsville, Ky., 1948—; county atty. Allen County, 1950-53; commonwealth atty. 8th Jud. Dist., 1953-55; judge 49th Jud. Dist. Ky., 1970—. Dir. Farmers Nat. Bank, Scottsville; v.p. Mid-South Life Ins. Co., Nashville. Chmn. Ky. Workmen's Compensation Bd. Served with AUS, 1944-48. Mem. Am., Ky. bar assns., Am. Trial Lawyers Assn., Am. Judicature Soc. Elk, Rotarian. Home: Route 1 Woodland Heights Scottsville KY 42164 Office: PO Box 66 Scottsville KY 42164

GOBAR, ASH, educator; b. Georgia, USSR, Apr. 7, 1930; s. Imir G. and Salia (Mirian) G.; A.B., Coll. Wooster, 1952; M.A., U. Chgo., 1954; Ph.D., U. Wis., 1959; postgrad. U. Geneva, Switzerland, 1959-60; m. Anne Boeke, June 15, 1957; children—Penelope, Peter. Research fellow in psychology Nat. Inst. Mental Health, 1959-61; asso. prof. philosophy and psychology Concord Coll., 1961-67; prof. philosophy Transylvania U., Lexington, Ky., 1968—. Named Outstanding Educator Am., 1970. Am. Philos. Soc. grantee, 1968. Mem. Am. Philos. Assn., History of Sci. Soc., Nat. Geog. Soc., Nat. Wildlife Fedn. Republican. Mem. Christian Ch. Author: Philosophic Foundations of Genetic Psychology and Gestalt Psychology, 1968; Philosophy and Modern Life, 1972. Home: 989 Holly Springs Dr Lexington KY 40504

GOCKEL, ASHFORD RAVENSCROFT, petroleum co. exec.; b. Tulsa, Okla., Dec. 10, 1925; s. Edward and Eugenia Jane (Graves) G.; B.E. with high honors, Yale, 1945, LL.B., 1948; m. Gladys Darnell, July 29, 1950; children—Ashford Ravenscroft, Dencie E. Asst. instr. dept. civil engring. Yale, 1945-48; dir. sales adminstrn. Deep Rock Oil Corp., Tulsa, Okla., 1948-53, bulk sales mgr., 1953-55; dir. sales adminstrn. and marketing research Kerr-McGee Corp., Oklahoma City, 1955-63, gen. mgr. petroleum supply and transp., 1963-67, gen. mgr. corp. purchasing and transp., 1967-68, v.p., 1968—; pres. Kerr-McGee Pipeline Corp.; pres., dir. White Shoal Pipeline Corp. Mem. Am. Petroleum Inst. (mem. gen. com. div. refining 1968—), Ind. Petroleum Assn. Am., Nat. Petroleum Refiners Assn., Soc. Advancement Mgmt., Okla. Bar Assn., Oklahoma City Petroleum Club, Sigma Xi, Tau Beta Pi. Republican. Presbyn. (ruling elder 1960). Home: 1208 Glenwood Av Oklahoma City OK 73116 Office: Kerr McGee Bldg Oklahoma City OK 73102

GODARD, LOUIE D., dist. judge; b. Mobile, Ala., Aug. 16, 1908; s. Louie J. and Beulah Emma (Sossman) G.; LL.B., J.D., U. Tex., 1936; m. Glennis Jeannette Birket, Oct. 10, 1946; children—Jeanette, (Mrs. William R. Livesay, Jr.), Tom. Admitted to Tex. bar, 1936; atty. Office Tex. Atty. Gen., 1936-37; with firm Beasley & Beasley, Beeville, Tex., 1937-38, Thornton, Markwell & Godard, Texas City, 1938-40, Godard & Dazey, Texas City, 1940-59; judge 122d Jud. Dist. of Tex., Galveston, 1959—. Dir. Mainland Bank, Texas City. Mem. Tex. Ho. of Reps., 1947-51. Served with AUS, 1942-46. Mem. Am., Tex. bar assns., Am. Judicature Soc. Rotarian (v.p., dir. Texas City 1957), K.C. Home: 1721 Oleander Rd Dickinson TX 77539 Office: Court House Galveston TX 77550

GODBOLD, BRYGHTE DAVIS, educator; b. Coy, Ala., July 8, 1914; s. Edwin Condie and Elsie Lillian (Williamson) G.; B.S., Auburn U., 1936; M.A., Leland Stanford U., 1947; Ph.D., N.Y.U., 1960; m. Lenore Elnora Alkire, Nov. 1, 1945 (dec. Apr. 1965); m. 2d, Patricia Mildred Murphy, Dec. 30, 1969. Commd. 2d lt. U.S. Marine Corps, 1936, advanced through grades to brig. gen., 1958; dir. personnel research Marine hdqrs., Washington, 1947-50; asst. chief staff 1st Marine Div., Korea, 1950-51; dep. dir. Manpower Requirements Def. Dept., Washington, 1951-54; asst. chief staff Fleet Marine Force, Pacific, 1955-56; comdg. officer 4th Marine, Kancohe, Hawaii, 1956-57; asst. to chancellor N.Y.U., 1958-59; exec. v.p. Midwest Program on Airborne TV Instrn., 1960-63; v.p. S.W. Center for Advanced Studies, Dallas, 1963-65; exec. dir. Goals for Dallas Program, 1965—. Cons. Com. on Econ. Devel., 1966-67, Am. Revolution Bicentennial Commn., 1970—, W.Va. Bd. Regents, 1971. Dir. N. Ala. Broadcasters, Huntsville, Eagle Broadcasting Co., Columbus, Ga. Mem. adv. bd. Dallas Health and Sci. Mus., 1969—, Marine Mil. Acad., Harlingen, Tex., 1968—. Trustee Dallas Pub. Library, U. YMCA, Dallas, Area Ednl. TV Found. North Tex., Excellence in Edn. Found., Dallas, Lamplighter Sch., Dallas. Decorated Legion of Merit (2), Bronze Star medal. Mem. Archaeol. Inst. Am., Theta Chi, Tau Beta Pi, Eta Kappa Nu, Omicron Delta Kappa, Kappa Delta Pi. Baptist. Editor: Goals for Dallas: Submitted for Consideration by Dallas Citizens, 1966; Goals for Dallas: Mutual Aims of Its Citizens, 1967; Goals for Dallas: Proposals for Achieving the Goals, 1969; Goals for Dallas: Achieving the Goals, 1970. Home: 6810 Bradbury Lane Dallas TX 75230 Office: 825 1 Main Pl Dallas TX 75250

GODBOLD, CLYDE EVERETT, dentist; b. Rains, S.C., Sept. 16, 1923; s. Fred Monroe and Frances Leona (Grice) G.; student U. S.C., 1946-49; D.D.S., Med. Coll. Va., 1953; postgrad. Dewey Sch. Orthodontics, N.Y. U., 1964, 69, U. Pitts., 1965, 69; m. Elizabeth Arlene Branham, Apr. 10, 1955; children—Sarah, Cheryl, Debbie, Rhett, Walter. Practice gen. dentistry, Myrtle Beach, S.C., 1953—, gen. dentistry and orthodontics, 1963—. Served with USNR, 1944-46; PTO. Mem. S.C., Am. dental assns., Internat. Assn. Orthodontics, Acad. Gen. Dentistry, Civitan Club (dir. 1970-72). Methodist. Mason (Shriner), Elk. Home: 3916 Pine Lakes Dr Myrtle Beach SC 29577 Office: 3409 N Kings Hwy Myrtle Beach SC 29577

GODBOLD, JOHN COOPER, U.S. judge; b. Coy, Ala., Mar. 24, 1920; s. Edwin Condie and Elsie (Williamson) G.; B.S., Auburn U., 1940; J.D., Harvard, 1948; m. Elizabeth Showalter, July 18, 1942; children—Susan, Richard, John C., Cornelia, Sally. Admitted to Ala. bar, 1948; with firm of Richard T. Rives, Montgomery, (Ala.,) 1948-49; partner firm Godbold, Hobbs & Copeland, and predecessors, 1949-66; U.S. circuit judge Ct. of Appeals, 5th Circuit, Montgomery, 1966—. Served with F.A., AUS, 1941-46. Mem. Montgomery County Bar Assn., Ala. State Bar, Alpha Tau Omega, Omicron Delta Kappa, Phi Kappa Phi. Club: Montgomery Country. Home: 3590 Thomas Av Montgomery AL 36111 Office: Federal Bldg Montgomery AL 36102

GODBOLD, PERCY ELLIS, JR., banker; b. Pine Hill, Ala., Feb. 5, 1913; s. Percy Ellis and Kathleen (Davie) G.; B.S., U. Ala., 1933; m. Grace Fuller, Sept. 16, 1937; 1 son, Leonard William. Agt. Internal Revenue Service, Birmingham, Ala., 1945; partner Kirkland, Godbold & Smith, C.P.A.'s, Birmingham, 1951-63; self-employed mgmt. cons., Anniston, Ala., 1964—; chmn. bd. Comml. Bank, Douglasville, Ga., 1961—, Bank of Pine Hill (Ala.), 1972—. Trustee Stringfellow Meml. Hosp., Anniston. Served with AUS, 1943-45. C.P.A., Ala. Mem. Am. Bankers Assn. Baptist. Kiwanian. Club: Country (Anniston) Home: 1038 Michael Lane Anniston AL 36201 Office: PO Box 1176 Douglasville GA 30134 also PO Box 1366 Anniston AL 36201

GODCHAUX, CHARLES RAGLAND, food co. exec.; b. Abbeville, La., Dec. 27, 1930; s. Frank Area and Mary Lawrence (Ragland) G.; B.A., Vanderbilt U., 1952; m. Wilma Polk Monypeny, Mar. 21, 1953; children—Theresa Polk, Rebecca Ragland. With La. State Rice Milling Co., Inc. (name now changed to Lastarmco Inc.), Abbeville, La., 1954—, v.p., 1956—, mem. exec. com., 1964—, also dir.; v.p., dir. Raviana Foods, Inc. Pres. Vermilion Parish Library Bd. Control, 1967—. Served to lt. (j.g.) USNR, 1952-54. Mem. Phi Delta Theta. Episcopalian. Home: Homeplace Abbeville LA 70510 Office: PO Box 269 Abbeville LA 70510

GODCHAUX, FRANK AREA, III, food co. exec.; b. Nashville, Feb. 5, 1927; s. Frank Area and Mary Lawrence (Ragland) G.; B.A. in Bus. Adminstrn., Vanderbilt U., 1949; m. Agnes Kirkpatrick, May 23, 1953; children—Katherine Area, Mary Lawrence, Leslie Kirkpatrick, Frank Kirkpatrick. Pres. Lastarmco Inc. (formerly La. State Rice Milling Co., Inc.), Abbeville, La., 1964—, also dir., mem. exec. com.; chmn. bd. Riviana Foods, Inc., Houston, 1965—, gen. mgr. internat. div., 1967—; chmn. bd. Food Engring. Internat., Inc., Houston, 1965—; dir. Fed. Res. Bank, New Orleans 1958-63, Self Service Restaurants, Inc., New Orleans. Mem. nat. rice adv. com. Dept. Agr., 1964-66, 71-73. Active Boy Scouts Am. Trustee Vanderbilt U.; mem. U. Southwestern La. Found., Council for a Better La. Served with USNR, 1945-46. Mem. Phi Delta Theta. Episcopalian. Home: 502 5th St Abbeville LA 70510 Office: PO Box 278 Abbeville LA 70510

GODDARD, FREDERICK PERCY, bishop; b. Seymour, Conn., Dec. 8, 1903; s. Frederick and Louisa (Marshall) G.; Ph.B., Yale, 1924; B.D., Berkeley Div. Sch., 1927, S.T.D., 1950; D.D., U. South, 1954; m. May Selena Bennett, Sept. 8, 1928 (dec. Apr. 1965); children—Marie Louise (Mrs. John Bullard), Gladys Emily (Mrs. Roger Rishel);; m. 2d Hazel Bennett Falconer, Nov. 17, 1968. Ordained to ministry Episcopal Ch. as deacon, 1927, as priest, 1928; rector St. John's Episcopal Ch., Marlin, Tex., 1927-55; suffragan bishop Diocese of Tex., Tyler, 1955—. Sec., Diocese of Tex., 1939-46; del. gen. conv. Episcopal Ch., 1934, 37, 43, 46, 49, 53; pres. standing com. Diocese of Tex., 1950-55. Chmn. ARC, Falls County, Tex., 1934-42, Community Welfare, Falls County, 1932-48. Trustee U. of South, Sem. of Southwest. Recipient Silver Beaver award Boy Scouts Am. Mem. Tex. Archeol. Soc. Club: Yale Houston. Editor: Texas Churchman, 1930-39. Home: 615 Perry St Marlin TX 76661

GODDARD, JAMES LEE, physician; b. Alliance, O. Apr. 24, 1923; s. Frederick Oscar and Harriet Beryl (Calhoun) G.; student Mt. Union Coll., 1942-43, D.Sc., 1967, Washington and Lee U., 1943-44, Temple U., 1944; M.D., George Washington U., 1949; M.P.H. magna cum laude, Harvard, 1955; D.Sc., U. Mich., 1967; m. Mildred Mae Miller, May 20, 1945; children—Margaret L., Bruce E., Patricia Ann. Asst. surgeon gen. USPHS, Dept. Health, Edn. and Welfare, Washington, 1951-59, chief Communicable Disease Center, Atlanta, 1962-66; commr. FDA, Washington, 1966-69; civil air surgeon FAA, Washington, 1959-62. Nat. adv. council Law-Medicine Research Inst.; sci. adv. council Consumers Union. Recipient John Jeffries award, 1962; award of merit George Washington U., 1966; Distinguished Service award Am. Med. Authors, 1967; Liberty Bell award Fed. Bar Assn., 1967. Fellow Am. Assn. Surgery of Trauma; mem. A.M.A., Am. Pub. Health Assn., Assn. Mil. Surgeons, Aerospace Med. Assn., A.A.A.S., Assn. Food and Drug Ofcls. U.S., Smith-Reed-Russell Honor Soc. George Washington U., Delta Omega. Contbr. articles to profl. jours. Home: 5405 Beech Av Bethesda MD 20014

GODDARD, RUTH, publishing co. exec.; b. Ballinger, Tex., Dec. 5, 1911; d. John Eugene and Dora Ruth (Elder) Gressett; grad. high sch.; m. John H. Hunnicut, Nov. 18, 1927 (dec. Oct. 1948); children—Joann (Mrs. John P. Taylor), Dolores (Mrs. A.L. Delaney, Jr.), Carolyn (Mrs. Charles Scarborough); m. 2d, Walter C. Goddard, Oct. 12, 1952 (dec. Sept. 1971). Script writer U. Tex., 1946-52; copy writer KNOW, Austin, Tex., 1954-60, KTBC, Austin, 1963-67; now asso. editor, pub. relations Jenkins Pub. Co., Austin; writer radio series Tex. Sch. Air. Recipient of 5 nat. awards for radio plays; Theta Sigma award, 1971. Mem. Christian Ch. Author: Live and Help Live, 1953; Ralph Ogden and The Seven Mustangs, 1970. Home: 1108 West 9 Austin TX 78703 Office: 6929 S Interregional P O Box 2085 Austin TX 78767

GODFREY, B. FRANK, govt. ofcl.; b. Clinton, S.C., Apr. 13, 1906; s. B. Frank and Bessie (Cunningham) G.; student Presbyn. Coll., 1923-25; m. Mary Elise Hawkins, Aug. 4, 1936; 1 son, James Frank. Fiscal clk. S.C. Employment Security Commn., Columbia, 1937-40, bus. mgr., 1940-46, dir. Unemployment Compensation div., 1946-65, exec. dir., 1965—. Chmn. state coordinating com. S.C. Cooperative Manpower Planning System; chmn. edn. and manpower adv. council Coastal Plains Regional Commn., vice. chmn. Gov.'s Com. on Employment of Handicapped; mem. Gov.'s Adv. Council on Vocational and Tech. Edn., Gov.'s Council for Aging. Former dir. A.R.C.; pres. Apollo Chorus; active Boy Scouts Am. Presbyn. (elder). Clubs: Executive, Columbia Sailing, Civitan (dir.). Home: 1323 Haynesworth Rd Columbia SC 29205 Office: 1225 Laurel St Columbia SC 29202

GODFREY, GARLAND ALONZO, coll. pres.; b. Booneville, Ark., Nov. 5, 1909; s. William Wylie and Lelar Clay (Courtney) G.; B.S., Okla. A. and M. Coll., 1933, M.A., 1936; Ed.D., Okla. State U., 1957; m. Merriam Jocille Morris, Nov. 4, 1933; children—Merriam Rose, Anna Lee, Joseph William, Jon Thomas. Tchr. Ark. rural schs., summers 1927-28, 28-29, tchr., prin. high sch., Kan., Okla., 1933-35, Pryor, Okla., 1935-39; supt. Pryor pub. schs., 1939-52; supt. schs., Durant, Okla., 1952-60; pres. Central State U., Edmond, 1960—. State chmn. sch. edn. Okla. Congress Parents and Tchrs., 1955-60. Mem. AACTE vis. team to Pakistan, 1964. Recipient citation Okla. Edn. Assn., Distinguished Alumnus award Ark. Tech. U., 1968. Mem. N.E.A. (dir. Okla.), Okla. Edn. Assn. (pres. 1950-51), Okla. Assn. Sch. Adminstrs. (pres. 1949-50), Phi Alpha Theta, Pi Kappa Delta. Baptist. Rotarian (pres. 1957-58). Home: 400 E Hurd St Edmond OK 73034

GODFREY, JAMES LOGAN, educator; b. Roanoke, Va., Aug. 31, 1907; s. James Thomas and Jean Rollins (Logan) G.; A.B., Roanoke Coll., 1931; A.M., U. N.C., 1933; Ph.D.,U. Chgo., 1942; m. Eleanor Elsabeth Smith, June 17, 1937; children—Jean Lee, Eleanor Ann. Instr. dept. history U.N.C. at Chapel Hill, 1936-41, asst. prof., 1941-44, asso. prof., 1944-47, prof. English history, 1947-64, Distinguished Univ. prof. English history, 1964—, chmn. faculty, 1956-57, dean of faculty, 1957-65, chmn. dept. history, 1965—, mem. bd. U. N.C. Press, 1966—. Chmn. Ford Found. Coop. Program in Humanities Duke U.-U. of N.C. President's fellow Brown U., 1951-52; trustee Roanoke Coll.; pres. So. Conf. on Brit. Studies, 1970—. Fellow Royal Hist. Soc.; mem. Am. Assn. U. Profs., Am., So. hist. socs., Sigma Chi. Democrat. Episcopalian. Author: (with C.H. Pegg and others) American Society and the Changing World, 1947; Europe since 1815 (with M.B. Garrett), 1947; Revolutionary Justice, 1951. Editor: The Graduate Sch.; Dissertations and Theses, 1947. Asso. editor: Jour. Brit. Studies, 1961-68. Contbr. articles to jours. Home: Hillcrest Rd Chapel Hill NC 27514

GODFREY, JOHN MUNRO, economist; b. San Antonio, Mar. 20, 1941; s. George Phillips and Frieda (Allen) G.; A.A., Armstrong State Coll., 1964; B.B.A., U. Ga., 1964, postgrad., 1964-67; m. Nancy Falconer Porter, June 4, 1966; 1 son, John Munro. Instr. econs. U. Ga., Athens, 1967-69; economist Fed. Res. Bank Atlanta, 1969—. Nat. Def. Edn. Act fellow, 1964-67. Mem. Am., So. econ. assns., Omicron Delta Epsilon, Chi Phi. Republican. Episcopalian. Home: 548 Echota Dr NW Atlanta GA 30318 Office: 104 Marietta St NW Atlanta GA 30303

GODFREY, RAYMOND VINCENT, aerospace exec.; b. Buffalo, Nov. 6, 1913; s. James J. and Ellen (O'Brien) G.; B.S., State U. N.Y. at Buffalo, 1935; M.A., Columbia, 1938; m. Agnes Watt Mulvey, May 30, 1941; children— James Terrance, Lynn E. (Mrs. Asaad Kelada), Raymond Michael, Susan Marie. Physicist Naval Ordnance Lab., Washington, 1942-46; sci. asst. Naval Ordnance Test Sta., China Lake, Cal., 1946-50; physicist Long Range Proving Ground, Cape Kennedy, Fla., 1950-53; mgr. instrumentation planning RCA, Eastern Test Range, Cape Kennedy, 1953-60; mgr. systems engring., range devel., systems mgmt. Pan Am. World Airways, Cape Kennedy, 1960—. Asso. fellow Am. Inst. Aeros. and Astronautics; mem. Am. Inst. Physics, Am. Ordnance Assn., Am. Rocket Soc. (pres. Cape Canaveral chpt. 1959). Club: Eau Gallie Yacht (Indian Harbor Beach, Fla.). Home: 736 W Espanola Way Melbourne FL 32901 Office: Patrick Air Force Base FL 32925

GODFREY, RICHARD HENRY, lawyer; b. Fairview, Okla., May 20, 1914; s. J. Nile and Mary (Every) G.; student Oklahoma City U., 1933-34, LL.B., 1938; m. Marcella Hill, Jan. 1, 1941; 1 son, Richard Henry. Admitted to Okla. bar, 1937; practiced in Oklahoma City, 1937-40; with investment firm, Levelland, Tex., 1940-42; pvt. practice, Okalhoma City, 1946-60; pres., dir. Am.-First Title & Trust Co., Oklahoma City, 1960—, Capitol Corp., 1962—; dir. Village Bank, Oklahoma City. Mem. Oklahoma World's Fair Adv. Council; vice chmn. Mercy Hosp. Heart Sta., 1958-60; dir. Frontiers of Sci. Found., treas., 1965-72; adv. dir. Salvation Army, 1969-72, mem. finance com., 1971-72. Served from pvt. to capt. USAAF, 1942-45. Mem. Am., Okla. bar assns., Okla. Land Title Assn. (pres. 1966-67), Am. Land Title Assn. (gov. 1968-70), Oklahoma City Bd. Realtors, Oklahoma City Home Builders Assn., Mortgage Bankers Am., Better Bus. Bur. (pres. 1967-68, dir. 1967-72), Oklahoma City C. of C. (dir. 1965-70). Presbyn. (pres. trustees 1968, sec.-treas. 1971-72). Clubs: Revelers (pres. 1964-65), Economic of Oklahoma, Lawyers, Beacon (pres. 1958-60), Quail Creek Golf and Country, Men's Dinner. Home: 6401 N Hillcrest Av Oklahoma City OK 73116 Office: 219 Park Av Oklahoma City OK 73102

GODFREY, WILLIAM AUBREY, JR., physician; b. Dallas, Dec. 9, 1931; s. William Aubrey and Mary Sue (Sherman) G.; student Baylor U., 1951; M.D., U. Tex., 1955; m. Mary Elizabeth Heffington, Sept. 21, 1963; children— Martha Sue, Mary Catherine. Intern, VA Hosp., Dallas, 1955-56, resident, 1956-57, 59-62; practice medicine specializing in internal medicine and diagnosis, Dallas, 1962—; partner, Physicians and Surgeons Clinic, Dallas, 1962—; mem. jr. attending staff Parkland Meml. Hosp.; mem. staff Meth. Hosp. Dallas; mem. cons. staff Colonial Acres-Beverly Hills: asso. clin. prof. internal medicine U. Tex. S.W. Med. Sch., 1970-71. Served with USAF, 1957-59. Diplomate Am. Bd. Internal Medicine. Fellow A.C.P.; mem. Am., Tex. socs. internal medicine, Tex. Acad. Internal Medicine, Dallas Diabetes Assn. (pres. clin. soc. 1971—), Phi Chi. Home: 1547 Cedar Hill Av Dallas TX 75208 Office: 1511 N Beckley St Dallas TX 75203

GODFREY, WILLIAM MELVIN, state ofcl.; b. Lakeland, Fla., July 7, 1927; s. William Edwin and Nettie (Terry) G.; B.C.E., U. Fla., 1950; m. Charlotte Arthur Laird, July 2, 1949; children—Douglas Alan (dec.), James Kenneth. Draftsman, Fla. Rd. Dept., Tallahassee, 1950-51, designer, 1951-56, sr. designer, 1956-62, asst. engr. bridge design, 1962-66, dep. engr. traffic and planning, 1966-69, chief bur. planning, 1969-70, dep. dir. div. planning and programming, 1970—. Mem. com. Suwannee River Area council Boy Scouts Am., 1965—. Served with USNR, 1952-55. Registered profl. engr., Fla. Home: 2010 Wahalaw Nene Tallahassee FL 32301 Office: Haydon Burns Bldg 605 Suwannee Tallahassee FL 32304

GODLEY, G(EORGE) MCMURTRIE, fgn. service officer; b. N.Y.C., Aug. 23, 1917; s. Frederick Augustus and Anne Conyne Wood (Franchot) G.; grad. Hotchkiss Sch., 1935; A.B., Yale, 1939; grad. study U. Chgo., 1940; m. Livia Paravicini, Jan. 4, 1946 (div.); m. 2d, Elizabeth McCray, 1966. Joined U.S. Fgn. Service, 1941—; vice consul assigned Marseilles, France, 1941, 3d sec., Bern, Switzerland, 1941-45; 2d sec., Brussels, Belgium, 1946-48; Dept. of State, 1948-52; 1st sec., Paris, France, 1952-55; counselor of Embassy, Phnom Penh, Cambodia, 1955-57; assigned Dept. of State, 1957; counselor embassy, Leopoldville, Congo, 1961-62; dir. Office Central African Affairs, Dept. State, 1962-64; U.S. ambassador to Democratic Republic of the Congo, Leopoldville, 1964-66, career minister, 1966; fgn. service insp., 1967; dep. asst. sec. state for E. Asian and Pacific Affairs, 1968-69; U.S. ambassador to Laos, 1969—. Served as ensign USNR, 1939-40); served as pvt. USMC Res., 1945; liason officer San Francisco Conf., 1945. Clubs: Metropolitan (Washington); The Brook (N.Y.C.); Chevy Chase. Home: Morris NY Office: care US Dept of State Washington DC

GODSEY, WILLIAM COLE, physician; b. Memphis, Dec. 11, 1933; s. Monroe Dowe and Margaret (Cole) G.; B.S., Southwestern at Memphis, 1955; M.D., U. Tenn., 1958; m. Norma Jean Wilkinson, June 18, 1958; children—William Cole, John Edward, Robert Dowe. Intern, John Gaston Hosp., Memphis, 1958-59; resident U. Tenn., 1960-63; practice medicine, specializing in psychiatry, Memphis, 1964—; mem. staff Tenn. Psychiat. Hosp. & Inst., clin. dir., 1965—; instr. dept. psychiatry U. Tenn., 1963-66, asst. prof., 1966—. Diplomate Am. Bd. Psychiatry and Neurology. Mem. Am. Psychiat. Assn. (past pres. West Tenn. chpt.), Nat. Rehab. Assn., Mid-South Med. Center Council, Tenn. Med. Assn., Memphis and Shelby County Med. Soc., Nat. Rifle Assn., Memphis Music, Inc., Pi Kappa Alpha, Phi Rho Sigma. Methodist. Home: 1446 Estate Dr Memphis TN 38117 Office: 865 Poplar St Memphis TN 38105

GODSHALL, ARTHUR RAY, lawyer; b. Union, S.C., July 19, 1906; s. Leslie Byron and Lillie Belle (Jones) G.; B.A., U.S.C., 1928, J.D., 1932; m. Rachel Elizabeth Pridmore, June 14, 1934; children—Alyce Kathleen (Mrs. Robert Henry Hileman), Evelyn Belle (Mrs. Charles DePass Cathcart). Admitted to S.C. bar, 1932; practiced in Gaffney, S.C., 1932—; chmn. S.C. Pardon Bd., 1935-39; sec. U.S. Senator Olin

D. Johnston, 1945; city atty., Gaffney, S.C., 1971; atty., Cherokee County Sch. Dist., 1971, United Cities Gas Co., 1971; pres., gen. counsel Radio Sta. WFGN, Gaffney, S.C., 1948—; dir., gen. counsel Bank of Gaffney; dir. Gaffney Devel. Co. Mem. adv. bd. Salvation Army, 1969-72. Mem. Cherokee County (pres. 1959-60), S.C., Seventh Circuit (pres. 1953-54) bar assns., S.C. Trial Lawyers Assn., Blue Key, Phi Delta Phi, Sigma Phi Epsilon. Lion. Home: 609 S Limestone St Gaffney SC 29340 Office: 415 1/2 N Limestone St Gaffney SC 29340

GODWIN, ADOLPHUS PILSTON, JR., judge; b. Gatesville, N.C., Oct. 6, 1912; s. Adolphus Pilston and Mabel C. (Hayes) G.; LL.B., Wake Forest Coll., 1937;; m. Mildred Vann, Aug. 10, 1940; children—Adolphus Pilston, Gretchen Vann. Admitted N.C. bar, 1937; mem. firm Godwin & Godwin, Gatesville, 1937-65; spl. agt. FBI, 1942-45; v.p. Tarheel Bank & Trust Co., 1954-65, pres., 1965-66, also dir. Judge N.C. Superior Ct., 1967—. Mem. N.C. Senate, 1953-57, gen. statutes com., 1953-55, 61-62; commr. N.C. Dept. Motor Vehicles, 1965-67. Mem. State Dem. Exec. Com., 1948-66. Mem. 1st Jud. Dist. Bar (pres. 1953-54). N.C. State Bar Inc., N.C. Bar Assn. (gov. 1957-61, 63-64, pres. 1965-66). Baptist. Mason (past master). Address: 2706 Fairview Rd Raleigh NC 27608

GODWIN, WINSTON YUVAWN, physician; b. Summerton, S.C., Nov. 5, 1928; s. Chalmers Luke and Anna Snow (Huggins) G.; B.S., Clemson U., 1949; postgrad. The Citadel, 1955-56; M.D., Med. U. S.C., 1959; m. Mary Hodge, June 3, 1950; children—Winston Yuvawn, Paul L., Michael L., Mary L., David A., Roger T. Self-employed in farm machinery and supplies, ins. agy., automobile sales and repair, 1949-53; intern Med. U.S.C. teaching hosps., 1959-60; practice medicine specializing in family practice, Cheraw, S.C., 1969—; chief staff Chesterfield County Meml. Hosp.; pres., med. dir. Cheraw Nursing Home, Inc., 1965—. Mem. exec. com. S.C. State Bd. Health, 1970—. Mem. Chesterfield County Sch. Bd., 1962—. Served to 1st lt. USAF, 1953-55. Diplomate Am. Bd. Family Practice. Mem. Internat. Flying Farmers, Am. Legion, A.M.A., S.C. Acad. Family Practice (chmn. membership com. 1970—), S.C., Cheraw med. assns., Alpha Omega Alpha. Baptist (trustee 1969-72). Mason. Club: Civitan (dir. 1970—) (Cheraw). Home: Hwy 9 Cheraw SC 29520 Office: 207 Marion St Cheraw SC 29520

GOEHRING, ELEANOR ELIZABETH, librarian; b. Norfolk, Va., Dec. 5, 1904; A.B., Randolph Macon Woman's Coll., 1925; M.S. in L.S., Columbia, 1927; postgrad. U. Tenn. Library asst. Randolph-Macon Woman's Coll., 1925-26; head circulation dept. U. Tenn. Library, 1927-46, reference librarian, 1946—. Librarian Tenn. Civil Def. Survival Plan Study, Knoxville. Mem. A.L.A., Tenn. Library Assn., Phi Beta Kappa. Address: U Tenn Library Cumberland Av SW Knoxville TN 37196*

GOEN, CLARENCE CURTIS, educator; b. San Marcos, Tex., July 4, 1924; s. Clarence Curtis and Velma Irene (Stone) G.; B.S., U. Tex., 1944; postgrad. Ind. U., 1945; B.A., Hardin-Simmons U., 1957; B.D., Southwestern Bapt. Theol. Sem., 1953, Th.D., 1956; M.A., Yale, 1958, Ph.D., 1960; m. Betty Ruth Presnell, Aug. 19, 1944; children—Charles Kyle, John Scott, Robert Curtis. Electronics engr. RCA Victor, Bloomington, Ind., 1944-47; ordained to ministry Baptist Ch., 1948; asso. pastor Hyde Park Bapt. Ch., Austin, Tex., 1947-48; pastor, Bapt. Chs., Rowena, Tex., 1948-51, Allen, Tex., 1951-55, Ada, Okla., 1955-57; research asst. Yale, 1959-60; prof. ch. history Wesley Theol. Sem., Washington, 1960—. Vis. prof. ch. history Sch. Theology at Claremont (Cal.), 1971; adj. prof. U.S. history Am. U., Washington, 1971-73. Recipient George Washington Egleston Hist. prize, Yale, 1960, Frank S. and Elizabeth D. Brewer prize, Am. Soc. Ch. History, 1961, Faculty fellowship Am. Assn. Theol. Schs., 1969-70. Mem. Am. Bapt. Hist. Soc. (bd. mgrs. 1962-71, v.p. 1969-71), Am. Soc. Ch. Hist., Am. Hist. Assn., Orgn. Am. Historians. Democrat. Baptist. Author: Revivalism and Separatism in New England, 1740-1800, 1962, revised edit., 1969. Editor: The Works of Jonathan Edwards, Vol. 4 The Great Awakening, 1972. Contbr. articles to profl. jours. Home: 4507 Verplanck Pl NW Washington DC 20016 Office: 4400 Massachusetts Av NW Washington DC 20016

GOERDT, BROTHER EDWIN, ednl. adminstr. Supt. Catholic schs., San Antonio. Address: Box 13190 9123 Lorene Lane San Antonio TX 78213*

GOERITZ, MATHIAS, artist. Address: Toluca 142 San Angel Tizapan Mexico 20 DF Mexico*

GOETHALS, HENRY WEBB, newspaper corr.; b. Boston, Mar. 16, 1922; s. Thomas Rodman and Mary (Webb) G.; grad. Roxbury Latin Sch., 1940; B.A., Harvard, 1947. Reporter, editor El Paso (Tex.) Herald Post, 1948-50; night editor Mexico City (Mexico) News, 1951-55; corr. McGraw-Hill, Havanna, Cuba, 1956-60; corr. Mexico, Central Am., Copley News Service, Mexico City, 1960-64, mem. news service bur., Washington, 1964—. Served with USAAF, 1943-46. Home: 1801 Clydesdale Pl NW Washington DC 20009

GOETHALS, PAUL LAWRENCE, physician; b. Rock Island, Ill., Oct. 21, 1933; s. Otto A. and Barbara L. (Blasig) G.; B.S., Loyola U., Chgo., 1956, M.D., 1958; M.S. in Otolaryngology, U. Minn., 1963; m. Judith Arlene Albrecht, Apr. 11, 1964; children—Cynthia Marie, Patricia Lynn, Andrea Lee, Paul Lawrence, James. Intern Mound Park Hosp., St. Petersburg, Fla., 1958-59; resident Mayo Clinic, Rochester, Minn., 1959-63; practice medicine specializing in otolaryngology, Winter Park, Fla., 1965—. Served to lt. comdr., M.C., USNR, 1963-65. Diplomate Am. Bd. Otolaryngology. Fellow Am. Acad. Opthalmology and Otolaryngology, A.C.S.; mem. Am., So., Fla. med. assns., Orange County Med Soc., Mayo Alumni Assn., Am. Council Otolaryngology. Republican. Roman Catholic. Rotarian. Club: University (Winter Park). Home: 652 Darcey Dr Winter Park FL 32789 Office: 255 N Lakemont Av Winter Park FL 32789

GOETTEE, JAMES HENRY, ednl. adminstr.; b. Carmona, Tex., July 18, 1907; s. Francis Marion and L. Catherine (Welch) G.; B.S., Sam Houston U., 1933; M.Ed., U. Tex., 1937; D.Ed., U. Houston, 1959; m. Edna Mae Survant, Aug. 23, 1933; 1 son, James Lee. Teaching prin. county schs., Trinity County, Tex., 1927-30; teaching prin. Field's Store Sch., Waller, Tex., 1930-33; supt. Spring (Tex.) Ind. Sch. Dist., 1933-38; tchr. Oates Jr. High Sch., Houston, 1938-42, acting prin., 1942-44; asst. prin. Stephen F. Austin Sr. High Sch., Houston, 1944-49, prin., 1949-66; dir. secondary edn. Houston Ind. Sch. Dist., 1966-68, asst. supt., 1968—. Mem. Tex. Tchrs. Assn. (past v.p.), Houston Council Edn. (past pres.), Houston Assn. Sch. Adminstrs. (past pres.), So Assn. Colls. and Schs. (Tex. com.), Nat. (life), Tex. (life) congresses parents and tchrs., Nat. Assn. Drs. in U.S., S.A.R., San Houston State Coll. Ex-Students Assn. (past pres.), Nat. Assn. Secondary Sch. Prins., Phi Delta Kappa, Delta Kappa Pi. Democrat. Baptist. Mason (33deg., Shriner); mem. Order Eastern Star (past grand patron Tex.), Clubs: Knife and Fork (Houston), Southeastern Houston Kiwanis (past pres. Contbr. to profl. publs. Home: 8106 Beverly Hill Lane Houston TX 77042 Office: 1300 Capitol St Houston TX 77002

GOFF, DEAN CARLSON, optometrist; b. Mankato, Minn., Aug. 22, 1919; s. Hiram Slade and Clara (Carlson) G.; student Los Angeles City Coll., 1938-40; B.S. in Optometry, Los Angeles Coll., 1947, O.D., 1948; m. Mercedes Patakas, Jan. 18, 1948; children—Janise Marie, Evans, Kathleen Elaine. Head clinic staff Los Angeles Coll. Optometry, 1948-55; pvt. practice Pasadena, 1949-55, El Paso, 1955-66; former owner, pres. Carlson Corp.; dir. optometric services, chief optometrist Farah Mfg. Co., El Paso, San Antonio, Victoria, Tex., Las Cruces, N.M., Albuquerque, 1966-72. Bd. dirs. Lighthouse for Blind. Served from aviation cadet to 1st lt., USAF, 1942-45. Mem. El Paso Optometric Soc. (v.p.), Am., Tex. (chmn. occupational vision com., dir.) optometric assns., Omega Delta. Presbyn. (deacon, elder). Rotarian (charter sec., past pres. N.E., El Paso). Home: 1536 Rocky Bluff Rd El Paso TX 79902 Office: 1207 State National Plaza El Paso TX 79901

GOFF, FREDERICK RICHMOND, div. chief Library of Congress; b. Newport, R.I., Apr. 23, 1916; s. Francis Shubael and Amelia Richmond (Seabury) G.; A.B., Brown U., 1937, A.M., 1939, Litt.D., 1965 Asst. to editor Incunabula in Am. libraries, 1937-40, editor 3d census, 1964; asst. to curator, 1940-41, acting chief, 1941-45, chief rare book div. Library of Congress, 1945—. Feldman lectr. U. Tex., 1968; vis. com. Hunt Bot. Library, Pitts.; com. mgmt. Annmary Brown Meml., Providence; mem. adv. com. rare book library Washington Cathedral. Mem. Biblіog. Soc. Va., Am. Antiquarian Soc., A.L.A. (chmn. rare book sect. 1960), Bibliog. Soc. Am. (council, pres. 1968-70), Bibl. Soc. (London), Internat. Bibliophile Assn., Lit. Soc. Washington, Manuscript Soc., Phi Beta Kappa, Theta Delta Chi. Unitarian. Clubs: Grolier (N.Y.); 1925 F Street (Washington). Author: (monograph) The Dates in Certain German Incunabula; Catalog of recent additions to the Lessing J. Rosenwald Collection in the Library of Congress, 1947; Early Belgian Books in the Rosenwald Collection, 1948; Early Music Books in the Rare Book Div. of Library of Congress, 1948; Fifteenth Century Books in the Library of Congress, 1950; The Rare Books Division-A Guide to the Collections and Services, 1950, rev. 1965. Editor: Essays Honoring Lawrence C. Wroth, 1951; The Rosenwald Collection, a Catalogue of Manuscripts, Illustrated Books, Books from Celebrated Presses, and Maps, 1150-1950, 1953; The Hersholt Collection of Anderseniana, 1954; Early Printed Books from the Low Countries, 1958; The Primordia of Bishop White Kennett, 1959; 3rd Census of Incunabula in American Libraries, 1964; The Permanence of Johann Gutenberg, 1970. Contbr. to Library of Congress Quar. Jour.; articles and reviews to various periodicals. Home: 5034 Sherrier Pl NW Washington DC 20016 Office: Library of Congress Washington DC 20540

GOFF, KENNETH HAROLD, lawyer; b. Spring Lick, Ky., Nov. 1, 1926; s. Tom and Beulah (Carter) G.; A.B. in History, Western Ky. State U., 1949; LL.B., U. Ky., 1951; m. Florene Shain, Aug. 1, 1956; children— Kenneth Harold, Thomas H., Laura Jane, John H., Tracy Lynn. Admitted to Ky. bar, 1951, since practiced in Leitchfield; mem. firm Goff & Meredith; judge pro tem Grayson County, Ky., 1951-54, county atty., 1954-66; mem. Ky. Workmen's Compensation Bd., 1968-69; commonwealth's atty. 46th Jud. Dist. Ky., 1968—. Chmn. Caney Creek Watershed Conservancy Dist., 1956-63; sec.-treas. Grayson County Fair, 1956-68; vice chmn. Lincoln Trail Econ. Devel. Dist.; past chmn. Lincoln Trail Comprehensive Health Planning Commn. Del. Republican Nat. Conv., 1960, 64. Bd. dirs. Grayson Housing; past sec.-treas. Grayson County Hosp. Found. Mem. Leitchfield-Grayson County C. of C. (pres. 1968-72). Mason. Home: Route 3 Leitchfield KY 42754 Office: 62 Court Sq Leitchfield KY 42754

GOFF, WAYNE HULEN, govt. ofcl.; b. Imboden, Ark., May 1, 1922; s. Washington Esro and Ruth Etta (Abee) G.; B.S. in Physics and Math., U. S.W. La., 1955; M.A. in Pub. Adminstrn., U. Okla., 1967; Ph.D. in Mgmt., N. Tex. State U., 1972; m. Julia Elizabeth Sanford, Sept. 2, 1943; children—Sandra Janice, Larry Wayne, Ronald Keith, Susan Lynn, Elizabeth Ann, Rebecca Kay. Electronics specialist CAA, Lafayette, La., 1947-58; dep. dist. supr. FAA, 1958-59, dist. supr., 1959-63, chief tech. staff, Ft. Worth, 1963-65, chief engring. br., 1965-67, chief plans and programs br., 1967-68, chief facilities and equipment br., 1968-70, chief electronics engring. br., 1970-72; prof. mgmt. Ark. State U., 1972—. Instr. physics U. S.W. La., also Centenary Coll., 1958-59. Served with USNR, 1940-46. Mem. I.E.E.E. Home: 1620 Dupwe Jonesboro AR 72401 Office: Ark State U Coll Bus State University AR 72467

GOFFMAN, IRVING JAY, educator; b. Montreal, Que., Can., Apr. 21, 1933 (came to U.S., 1959), naturalized; s. William and Ethel (Dumansky) G.; B.A., McGill U., 1954; M.A., Duke, 1957, Ph.D., 1959; m. Judith Barbara Kasler, June 5, 1956; children—Susan, Sandra. Research economist Govt. Can., Ottawa, 1958-59; prof., chmn. dept. econs. U. Fla., Gainesville, 1959—. Cons. Pres. Commn. on Sch. Finance, 1971. Chmn. United Jewish Appeal, Gainesville, Fla., 1971-72. Danforth Asso., 1967—. Mem. Tau Epsilon Phi, Beta Gamma Sigma, Omicron Delta Epislon. Jewish religion. Mem. B'nai B'rith. Editor: Pub. Finance Quarterly. 1971-75. Home: 1424 NW 31st St Gainesville FL 32601

GOFORTH, JOHN LAWRENCE, physician; b., 1897; M.D., Johns Hopkins, 1923. Practice medicine specializing in pathology, Dallas. Cons. pathology Dallas City Health Lab., Med. Arts Hosp., St. Paul Hosp. Mem. Am. Assn. Pathologists and Bacteriologists, A.M.A., A.C.P., Coll. Am. Pathologists, Am. Soc. Clin. Pathologists. Office: Med Arts Bldg 1717 Pacific Av Dallas TX 75201

GOGGINS, HORACE, dentist; b. Hodges, S.C., May 14, 1929; s. Ulysses and Mattie Lou (Butler) G.; B.S., S.C. State Coll., 1950; D.D.S., Howard U., 1954; m. Juanita Willmon, May 13, 1961; 1 son, Horace Willmon. Individual practice dentistry, Rock Hill, S.C., 1956—. Mem. Mayors' Citizens Adv. Com., So. Regional Council, 1965-71. Bd. dirs. Carolina Community Actions, 1965-67. Served to capt., Dental Corps, AUS, 1954-56. Mem. N.A.A.C.P. (sec. Rock Hill br. 1960-67), Am. Soc. Analgesia, Nat., Palmetto dental assns., Beta Kappa Chi, Alpha Phi Alpha. Democrat. Baptist. Home: Route 1 Box 465 Rock Hill SC 29730 Office: 425 S Trade St Rock Hill SC 29730

GOINS, TRUMAN, gen. engr.; b. Peason, La., Nov. 14, 1920; s. John Henry and Elizabeth (Pantalion) G.; B.S., La. State U., 1950; M.S., Ohio State U., 1954, postgrad., 1955-58; m. Mary Beatrice, Aug. 18, 1943; 1 son, Neal Rodney. Asst. prof. Ohio Agrl. Expt. Sta., Columbus, 1950-58; engr. adviser ICA, Tegucigalpa, Honduras, 1958-61; engr. adviser, regional dir. AID, Guayaquil, Ecuador, 1961-63, water resources engr., Vientiane, Laos, 1966-67, Washington, 1967-68; research engr. Agrl. Research Service, Norfolk, Va., 1963-66; civil engr. U.S. Dept. Housing and Urban Devel., Washington, 1968—. Rep. tech. and coordinating coms. Water Resources Council. Asst. scoutmaster Tidewater council Boy Scouts Am., 1964. Served with USCGR, 1939-46; ETO. Decorated Bronze Star (3). Mem. Am. Soc. Agrl. Engrs. (past pres., sec.-treas. Ohio sect.), Nat. Soc. Profl. Engrs., Soil Sci. Soc. Am., Am. Soc. C.E., Phi Eta Sigma, Alpha Zeta, Tau Beta Pi, Phi Kappa Phi, Gamma Sigma Delta. Home: 11610 Hickory Dr Oxon Hill MD 20022 Office: Dept Housing and Urban Devel Washington DC 20410

GOLAND, MARTIN, research inst. pres.; b. N.Y.C., July 12, 1919; s. Herman and Josephine (Bloch) G.; M.E., Cornell U., 1940; LL.D., St. Mary's U., San Antonio; m. Charlotte Nelson, Oct. 16, 1948; children—Claudia, Lawrence Jon, Nelson Stuart. Instr. mech. engring. Cornell U., 1940-42; sect. head structures dept. Research Lab., Curtiss-Wright Corp., research lab. Airplane div., Buffalo, 1942-46; chmn. div. engring. Midwest Research Inst., Kansas City, Mo., 1946-50, dir. for engring. scis., 1950-55; v.p. S.W. Research Inst., San Antonio, 1955-57, dir., 1957-59, pres., 1959—; prof. research (honoris causa) St. Mary's U., San Antonio. Mem. sci. adv. com. Harry Diamond Labs., 1955—; mem. adv. panel com. on sci. and astronautics Ho. of Reps., 1960—; mem. Nat. Commn. on Libraries and Information Sci., 1971—; mem. missile adv. group Army Missile Command; mem. sci. adv. panel Dept. Army; chmn. U.S. Army Weapons Command Adv. Group; mem. materials adv. bd. NRC; mem. research and tech. adv. com. on aeronautics NASA, 1967-71; chmn. lab. adv. bd. on undersea warfare Dept. Navy, 1970—. Pres. San Antonio Symphony Soc., 1968-70, chmn. bd., 1971—. Bd. govs. St. Mary's U., San Antonio. Recipient Spirit of St. Louis Jr. award Am. Soc. M.E., 1945, Jr. award, 1946; Alfred E. Noble prize Am. Soc. M.E., 1947. Fellow A.A.A.S., Am. Inst. Aeros. and Astronautics (pres. 1971, dir. 1972—); mem. Nat. Acad. Engring. (council 1969—), Am. Soc. M.E. (hon.), Am. Ordnance Assn., Sigma Xi, Tau Beta Phi. Editor: Applied Mechanics Rev., 1952-59, editorial advisor, 1959—. Home: 211 Five Oaks St San Antonio TX 78209 Office: 8500 Culebra Rd San Antonio TX 78228

GOLD, ALLEN JAY, apparel co. exec.; b. Newark, Aug. 23, 1927; s. Bernard Leon and Shirley (Brodofsky) G.; student So. Meth. U., 1945-47. Partner, Nardis of Dallas, 1948-65; pres. Nardis of Dallas, Inc., 1965—, also dir. Bd. dirs. Dallas Civic Opera. Served with USCGR, 1945-46. Mason (32 deg., Shriner). Home: 5205 Royal Lane Dallas TX 75215 Office: 1300 Corinth St Dallas TX 75215

GOLD, BILL (WILLIAM EMIL), newspaper reporter; b. Bklyn., Aug. 9, 1912; s. Mayer and Miriam (Feldman) G.; B.S. in Journalism, Ohio State U., 1933; m. Bernice Radine Ellman, 1933; 1 son, Walter Leslie. Reporter, condr. Dist. Line column Washington Post, 1947—. Mem. White House Corrs. Assn., Sigma Delta Chi. Club: Nat. Press. Home: 7036 Wilson Lane Bethesda MD 20034 Office: The Washington Post Washington DC 20005

GOLD, BURTON MALCOLM, carpet co. exec.; b. N.Y.C., Apr. 7, 1929; s. William and Mildred (Heidenreich) G.; B.C.E., Cornell U., 1951; m. Lenore Joan Elis, Aug. 30, 1953; children—Joanne Meredith, Lauren Elizabeth, Janice Hilary, Pamela Alison. Pres., William Gold, Inc., N.Y.C., 1953-67, Stratton Industries, Inc., Atlanta, 1963—, Celestial Carpet Mills, Inc., Atlanta, 1966—; dir. William Gold, Inc., N.Y.C. Mem. auction com. Arts Festival Atlanta, 1970-72. Served to 1st. lt. Ordnance Corps, AUS, 1951-53. Mem. Cornell Soc. Engrs., The Temple, High Mus. Art, Mus. Modern Art, Cartersville C. of C., Carpet and Rug Inst., Chi Epsilon, Phi Sigma Delta, Zeta Beta Tau. Clubs: Cornell (N.Y.C.); Standard (Atlanta); Dalton (Ga.) Golf and Country; Cartersville (Ga.) Country. Home: 3550 Rembrandt Rd NW Atlanta GA 30327 Office: Cartersville GA 30120

GOLD, HERBERT MARVIN, broadcasting exec.; b. Paterson, N.J., Aug. 5, 1930; s. Harry and Rebecca (Levy) G.; student Fairleigh Dickinson Coll., 1948-49; m. Elaine Singer, May 17, 1953; children—David, Cathy, Susan. Photographer, Paterson Evening News, 1946-51, 55-57; photographer WFGA-TV, Jacksonville, Fla., 1957-58, film dir., 1958-62, dir. spl. events, 1962-66, prodn. mgr., 1966—. Asst. to producer Jim Kitchell, space unit, NBC News, 1962-71; pres. TV Program Conf., 1971-72. Mem. planning com. Jr. Achievement, Jacksonville, 1971. Bd. dirs. Jacksonville Symphony. Served with USNR, 1951-55; ETO. Recipient award Nat. Acad. TV Arts and Scis., 1969-70. Mem. Nat. Assn. Press Photographers. Mason. Home: 1829 Pelton Lane Jacksonville FL 32211 Office: 1070 E Adams St Jacksonville FL 32202

GOLD, JOHN, city editor Tulsa World. Address: 315 S Boulder Av Tulsa OK 74102*

GOLD, JOHN M., city ofcl. City mgr. Winston-Salem, N.C. Office: City Hall Winston-Salem NC 27101*

GOLDBERG, ARTHUR SAMUEL, lawyer; b. St. Joseph, Mo., Nov. 20, 1916; s. Benjamin and Dora (Wilk) G.; A.A., St. Joseph Jr. Coll., 1935; A.B., Washburn Coll., 1939; J.D., So. Methodist U., 1939; m. Ruth Miriam Friedman, Oct. 19, 1947; children—Donna Raye, David Victor. Admitted to Tex. bar, 1939, Okla. bar, 1942; U.S. Supreme Ct. bar; practiced in Dallas, 1946—; partner firm Goldberg, Alexander, Sullivan & Strange. Sec. Liberty Steel Co., Friedman Investment Co., M & W Realty Co. Lectr., S.W. Legal Found. Pres. I. Zesmer dist. Zionist Orgn. Am., 1950-51, mem. nat. exec. com., mem. bd. S.W. Region, 1968—; bd. dirs. Jewish Family Service, Jewish Welfare Fedn. Dallas, Schepps Community Center. Served to 1st lt. AUS, 1942-46. Mem. Am., Tex., Dallas bar assns., Am. Judicature Soc., Comml. Law League Am. Jewish religion (dir., past co-treas. congregation). Mason (Shriner); mem. B'nai B'rith. Home: 7701 Yamini St Dallas TX 75230 Office: 1511 Bryan St Dallas TX 75201

GOLDBERG, BARTON SHELDON, banker; b. N.Y.C., Oct. 20, 1933; s. Samuel C. and Shirley (Klepper) G.; B.B.A., U. Miami, 1956, J.D., 1957; diploma Stonier Grad. Sch. Banking, Rutgers U., 1967; m. Rochelle Singer, June 16, 1956; children—Shari, Jeffrey, Michael. Admitted to Fla. bar, 1958; atty. firm Schlissel and Scher, Miami Beach, 1958-63; atty. firm Courshon & Courshon, Miami Beach, 1963-64; with Jefferson Nat. Bank of Miami Beach (Fla.), 1964—, pres., 1970—, also dir.; sec.-treas. Jefferson Bancorp., Inc. Pres. Miami Beach Home Owners Assn., 1972—, Arthur Godfrey Rd. Assn., 1972—; chmn. small bus. div. United Fund, 1972—; chmn. Miami Beach Landlord-Tenant Arbitration Bd., 1972—. Mem. Miami Beach C. of C. (gov. 1972—). K.P. Jewish religion (dir. coms. temple). Home: 4420 N Bay Rd Miami Beach FL 33140 Office: 310 41st St Miami Beach FL 33140

GOLDBERG, FAYE JOAN GIRSH (MRS LEON I. GOLDBERG), educator; b. Phila., May 5, 1933; d. Jack Gould and Rose (Rosenberg) Girsh; A.B., Temple U., 1954; M.A., Boston U., 1955; Ed.D., Harvard, 1962; m. Leon I. Goldberg, Feb. 20, 1958; children—Mark, Claudia. Clin. psychologist Mass. Mental Health Center, Boston, 1958-59; social sci. analyst Nat. Isnt. Mental Health Bethesda, Md., 1959-61; instr. psychiatry Emory U., Atlanta, 1960-61; mem. faculty Morehouse Coll., Atlanta, 1965—, asso. prof. psychology, acting chmn. dept., 1969—. Mem. DeKalb County Bond Study Commn., 1969-70, Criminal Justice Commn., 1969-70. Mem. DeKalb County Democratic Exec. Com., 1966-71 mem. Ga. Dem. Exec. Com., 1966-70. Mem. Am., Ga., Southeastern psychol. assns., Soc. for Research in Child Devel., Soc. for Psychol. Study Social Issues, Am. Assn. U. Profs. (chpt. sec. 1968-69), Am. Civil Liberties Union (dir. Ga. bd. 1966—). Contbr. articles to profl. jours. Home: 317 Hertford Circle Decatur GA 30030 Office: Morehouse Coll Atlanta GA 30314

GOLDBERG, IRVING LOEB, judge; b. Port Arthur, Tex., June 29, 1906; s. Abraham and Elsa (Loeb) G.; B.A., U. Tex., 1926; LL.B., Harvard, 1929; m. Marian Jessel Melasky, Dec. 30, 1928; children—Nancy Paula (Mrs. Jay L. Todes), Julie Elsa (Mrs. Michael Lowenberg). Admitted to Tex. bar, 1929; mem. firms Smith, Crawford & Combs, Beaumont, Tex., 1929-31, Harris Melasky, Taylor, Tex., 1931-32; gen. counsel Murray Co., Dallas, 1932-34; partner firm Winfrey & Goldberg, 1934-43, Thompson, Meek & Goldberg, 1946-50, Goldberg, Akin, Gump, Strauss & Hauer, 1950-66 (all Dallas); judge U.S. Ct. Appeals 5th Jud. Circuit, Dallas, 1966—. Pres. Jewish Welfare Fedn., Dallas, 1950-51; nat. v.p. Am. Jewish Com., 1962-65; vice chmn. Tex. adv. com. U.S. Commn. Civil Rights, 1964-66; bd. dirs. Dallas UN Assn., 1963-65, Dallas Council Social Agys., 1964-66, Hebrew Immigrant Sheltering Soc., 1952-54, Council Jewish Fedns. & Walfare Funds, 1955-57, Nat. Conf. Christians & Jews, 1948-60; pres. Dallas Home & Hosp. for Jewish Aged, 1960-62. Served to lt. USNR, 1942-46. Mem. Am., Dallas bar assns. Clubs: Dallas, Columbian (Dallas). Home: 3701 Turtle Creek Dr Dallas TX 75219 Office: 13-C-6 1100 Commerce St Dallas TX 75202

GOLDBERG, IVAN BAER, bus. exec.; b. Newport News, Va., Apr. 20, 1939; s. David and Sara (Levy) G.; student U. Va., 1957-58, Coll. William and Mary, 1958-60; m. Linda Caffee, Oct. 27, 1969; 1 son, Stephen Morris. Exec. v.p., dir. Bedding Supply Co., Inc., Newport News, 1961—, Goldkress Corp., 1968—, Goldkress Investment Co., 1970—. Served with USCGR, 1962. Mem. Hampton Roads Jr. C. of C., Def. Supply Assn., Va. Mfrs. Assn. Jewish religion. Elk. Home: 120 Tipton Rd Newport News VA 23606 Office: 524-2628 25th St Newport News VA 23607

GOLDBERG, JOSEPH PHILIP, govt. ofcl.; b. N.Y.C., May 1, 1918; s. Max and Fanny (Steltzer) G.; B.S., Coll. City N.Y., 1937; M.A., Columbia, 1938, Ph.D., 1950; m. Selma Takiff, Aug. 22, 1943; children— Seth M., Lise A. Instr., Coll. City N.Y. 1937-38; tchr. high schs., N.Y.C., 1938-42; economist Bur. Labor Statistics, U.S. Dept. Labor, 1942, spl. asst. to commr., 1954—; econ. adviser appeals com. War Labor Bd., 1943-45; labor specialist Office Housing Expediter, 1946-47, Pub. Affairs Inst., 1948-49; labor economist Joint Labor Com., 1949; economist Dept. Labor, 1949-51; div. chief Wage Stablzn. Bd., 1951-53 (all Washington); instr. Am. U., 1948-49; research asso. Littauer Sch., Harvard, 1957-58, U. Mich. Wayne State Indsl. Relations Research Inst., 1964-68. U.S. rep. ILO Seamen's Welfare Com., 1959-61, 66; chmn. U.S. delegation ILO Fishermem's Conf., 1965; mem. U.S. delegation ILO and OAS meetings, 1956, 57, 58, 63; chmn. U.S. delegation ILO Prep. Tech. Maritime Conf., Genoa, 1969; vice chmn. U.S. delegation to ILO Maritime Conf., 1970; govt. adviser to U.S. delegation to Internat. Labor Conf., 1970, 71. Pres. P.T.A., 1953-54, legislative rep., 1964-68, sch. trustee, 1955-61, treas., 1967-68; pres. John F. Kennedy High Sch. P.T.A., 1968-69. Recipient Dept. Labor Meritorious Service award, 1962; Yale Fund Grantee, 1947-48. Mem. Am. Econ. Assn., Indsl. Relations Research Assn. (chpt. pres. 1963-64). Phi Beta Kappa. Author: The Maritime Story, 1957; (with others) Modernization in the Maritime Industry in Collective Bargaining and Technological Change in American Transportation, 1971. Contbr. numerous articles and book revs. on collective bargaining, maritime industry, pub. employees, labor history and ILO to profl. publs. Home: 707 Stonington Rd Silver Spring MD 20902 Office: Labor Dept Gen Accounting Office Bldg Washington DC 20212

GOLDBERG, MICHAEL, engr.; b. N.Y.C., Nov. 13, 1902; s. Harry and Sarah (Pastor) G.; B.S. in Elec. Engring., U. Pa., 1925; M.A., George Washington U., 1929; m. Goldie Back, Aug. 15, 1930; children— Jeremy R., Susan D. (Mrs. Richard G. Wax). Elec. engr. Phila Electric Co., 1925-26; ordnance engr. Bur. of Ordnance, Navy, 1926-45, br. engr. Bur. Naval Weapons, 1945-63; cons., 1963—. Mem. Philos. Soc. Washington (past pres.), Washington Acad. Scis., A.A.A.S., Am. Math. Soc., Math. Assn. Am., Sigma Xi. Contbr. articles to profl. jours. Patentee in field. Home: 5823 Potomac Av NW Washington DC 20016

GOLDBERG, STANLEY IRWIN, bedding supply mfg. co. exec.; b. Newport News, Va., May 13, 1934; s. David and Sara (Levy) G.; student Coll. William and Mary, 1952-54, U. Va., 1954-55; m. Marilyn Levin, Nov. 22, 1963; 1 son, Andrew Garfield. With Bedding Supply Co., Inc., Newport News, 1956—, v.p., 1956-59, exec. v.p., 1960-61, pres. 1962—; dir. Goldkress Corp. Served with USAF, 1957-58. Mem. Va. Mfrs. Assn., Def. Supply Assn. Jewish religion (trustee temple). Elk. Home: 6923 Huntington Av Newport News VA 23607 Office: 524 25th St Newport News VA 23607

GOLDBLATT, KEN, broadcasting exec. Mgr. sta. WAOK, Atlanta. Address: 110 Edgewood Av NE Atlanta GA 30303*

GOLDEN, HARRY, editor, publisher, author; b. N.Y.C., May 6, 1903; s. Leib and Anna (Klein) Goldhirsch; student Coll. City N.Y., 1919-22; m. Genevieve Gallagher, Apr. 20, 1926; children—Richard, Harry, William, Peter. Editor, pub. Carolina Israelite, 1942—. Named Man of Year, Carver Coll., 1957, Johnson C. Smith Coll., 1958, Temple Emanu-El, N.Y.C., 1958. Mem Am. Jewish Congress (mem. bd.), N.A.A.C.P. (life), Shakespeare Soc. Am., Catholic Inter-racial Council. B'nai B'rith. Author: Only in America, 1958; For 2 cents Plain, 1959; Enjoy, Enjoy. 1951; Life of Carl Sandburg, 1961; Five Boyhoods, 1962; You're Entitle, 1962; Forgotten Pioneer, 1963; Mr. Kennedy and the Negroes, 1964; So What Else is New, 1965; A Little Girl is Dead, 1966; Ess Ess Mein Kindt, 1967; The Best of Harry Golden, 1968; Autobiography of Harry Golden, 1969; The Israelis, 1970; So Long as You're Healthy, 1970; Golden Book of Jewish Humor, 1972; The Greatest Jewish City in the World, 1972. Home: 1316 Elizabeth Av Charlotte 1 NC 28204

GOLDEN, JEWEL, educator; b. Birmingham, Ala.; d. Dowdell D. and Alice (Stone) Golden; B.S. with honors, Auburn U., 1933; M.A., Tchrs. Coll., Columbia, 1941; Ph.D., Fla. State U., 1958. Tchr. home econs. Billingsley (Ala.) High Sch., 1933-34, Red Leval (Ala.) High Sch., 1934-35, Selma (Ala.) Jr. High Sch., 1935-41; instr. Winthrop Coll., 1941-42; asst. prof. clothing and textiles Tex. Tech. Coll., 1942-43, Auburn U., 1943-54; asso. prof. clothing and textiles U. Md., 1958-59; asso. prof. clothing and textiles U. So. Miss., Hattiesburg, 1960-62, prof., 1962—, chmn. dept. environmental design, 1971—. Mem. Am. Assn. U. Women (br. v.p. 1963-65), Am., Miss. (chmn. coll. clubs sect. 1960-61, clothing and textiles sect. 1964-66) home econs. assns., Am. Assn. Textile Chemists and Colorists, Nat., Central Region (adv. com. 1971-72) assns. coll. tchrs. textiles and clothing, Mortar Bd., Phi Kappa Phi, Omicron Nu, Kappa Delta Pi, Alpha Phi Epsilon, Chi Delta Phi, Delta Kappa Gamma (pres. 1970-72), Pi Tau Chi. Presbyn. Home: So Sta Box 286 Hattiesburg MS 39401

GOLDEN, JOHN, scientist; b. San Francisco, Mar. 18, 1925; s. S. Sydney and Laura Marie (Melloh) G.; B.A., Lawrence Coll., 1948; M.A., U. Chgo., 1951; m. Jean Knoblock, June 19, 1948; children—Curt Clifton, Mark Jonathan, Karen Vanessa. Field dir. Ben Gaffin Assos., Market Facts Inc., Chgo., 1949-50; Soviet and E. European specialist Dept. State, 1951, asso. dir. Center for Internat. Systems Research, 1965-67; chief social sci. sect. Library of Congress, Washington, 1952-57; sr. scientist weapons systems evaluation group Dept. Def. Washington, 1957-64, dir. command and mgmt. systems devel., 1958-67; dir. Stanford Research Inst., Washington, 1967-71; dir. planning, research and evaluation Corp. for Pub. Broadcasting, Washington, 1971—; mgr. mgmt. systems IBM, 1964-65. Cons. various govt. agys., 1952—; staff dir. sec. def. task force on mgmt. research Def. Dept. 1962-63; adviser on mgmt. systems White House, 1964—; mem. def. sci. bd. Task Force on Research Mgmt., 1966—; mem. Presdl. Commn. on Mass Urban Transp., 1967—. Bd. dirs., vice chmn. bd. Presdl. Classroom for Young Americans; bd. dirs. Girl Scouts U.S.A., 1971—. Served with USNR, 1942-46. Mem A.L.A., Operations Research Soc. Am., Am. Mgmt. Assn., Am. Anthropological Association. Congregationalist (moderator). Author: System, Process and Decision Taking, 1968. Contbr. articles to publs. Home: 2791 N Quebec St Arlington VA 22207 Office: 888 16th St Washington DC 20006

GOLDFARB, RONALD LAWRENCE, lawyer; b. Jersey City, Oct. 16, 1933; s. Robert S. and Aida J. (Weintraub) G.; A.B., Syracuse U., 1954, LL.B., 1956; LL.M., Yale, 1960, J.S.D., 1962; m. Joanne Jacob, June 9, 1957; children—Jody Anne, Nicholas, Maximilian. Admitted to D.C. bar, 1965, U.S. Supreme Ct. bar; practiced in Washington, 1966—; spl. asst. to U.S. atty. gen. organized crime sect., 1961-64; partner firm Goldfarb & Singer, and predecessor, 1966—. Dir., Brookings Instn. Program on Cts. and Adminstrn. Justice. Staff counsel com. on law and social action Am. Jewish Congress, 1960-61. Served to capt. Judge Adv. Gen. Corps, USAF, 1957-60. Recipient Fed. Bar Assn. award for book Ransom, 1966; Arthur Garfield Hays fellow N.Y.U., 1960-61. Mem. Am., Fed., D.C., N.Y., Cal. bar assns., Am. Civil Liberties Union, Am. Acad. Polit. and Social Sci., Am. Judicature Soc., Sigma Alpha Mu, Phi Delta Phi. Club: Cosmos (Washington). Author: The Comtempt Power, 1963; Ransom: A Critique on the American Bail System, 1965; (with Alfred Friendly) Crime and Publicity, The Impact of News on the Adminstr. of Justice, 1967; (with Linda R. Singer) After Conviction: A Review of the American Correction System, 1972. Contbr. articles to profl. jours., popular mags. Home: 7312 Rippon Rd Alexandria VA 22307 Office: 1616 H St NW Washington DC 20006

GOLDMAN, DAVID TOBIAS, physicist; b. Bklyn., Jan. 25, 1933; s. Joseph L. and Frances (Snyder) G.; A.B., Bklyn. Coll., 1952; M.S., Vanderbilt U., 1954; Ph.D., U. Md., 1958; m. Elizabeth Ann Ward, Sept. 15, 1957; children—Daniel, Jonathan, Michael, Benjamin. Physicist Evans Signal Lab., 1952-53; asst. in physics U. Md. 1954-58, adj. prof., 1965—; research asso. U. Pa. 1958-59; theoretical physicist Knolls Atomic Power Lab., Gen. Electric Co., 1959-63; supervisory physicist, 1963-65; chief theoretical physics, reactor radiations div. Nat. Bur. Standards, Washington, 1965-69, program leader standard nuclear reference data, 1965-69; program analyst, 1970-72; acting dept. dir. Inst. Basic Standards, 1972—; program analyst Bur. Budget, 1969-70; Commerce Dept. sci. and tech. fellow, 1969-70. Physicist Naval Research Lab., 1956, Oak Ridge Nat. Lab., 1957-58; adj. asso. prof. Renssalaer Poly. Inst., 1960-65; mem. European Am. Sub-Com. on Nuclear Data Evaluation, 1965-69; chmn. Neutron Cross Sects. and Tech. Conf., 1968. Mem. Schenectady County (N.Y.) Democratic Party Com., 1963-65. Recipient Mgmt. award Gen. Electric Co., 1962. Fellow Am. Phys. Soc.; mem. Am. Nuclear Soc. (div. chmn. 1964-67), Internat. Orgn. for Standards (chmn. nuclear glossary com.), Sigma Xi. Contbr. articles to sci. publs. Home: 8519 Victory Lane Potomac MD 20854 Office: Nat Bur Standards Washington DC 20234

GOLDMAN, JACQUELIN ROBERTA, educator; b. Ocala, Fla.; d. Leon and Mildred B. Goldman; B.A., U. Fla., 1956; M.A., U. Ill., 1959, Ph.D., 1962. Asso. prof. psychology U. Fla., Gainesville, 1961—. Sec., Alacaua Conservation Council, 1969—. Mem. Am., Fla., Southeastern psychol. assns., Soc. Research in Child Devel., Sigma Xi. Office: Dept Clin Psychology U Fla Gainesville FL 32601

GOLDMAN, MARVIN ISRAEL, drug co. exec.; b. Cleve., Sept. 11, 1924; s. Samuel Harry and Dena Zachariah (Sands) G.; student U. Miami, 1940-44; m. Carol Milberg, June 25, 1950; children—Howard, Marjorie, Andrea. Pres. Gulf Drug Co., Hialeah, Fla., 1949—. Chmn. drug div. Combined Jewish Appeal Miami, 1965-71; chmn. gen. med. div. United Fund Dade County, 1971—. Bd. dirs. Greater Miami Jewish Fedn. Served with AUS, 1942-46. Home: 4207 University Dr Coral Gables FL 33146 Office: 425 E 10th Ct Hialeah FL 33011

GOLDMUNTZ, LAWRENCE A., govt. ofcl. Exec. sec. Fed. Council Sci. and Tech., Washington. Address: Office Sci and Tech Executive Office Bldg Washington DC 20506*

GOLDSMITH, ARTHUR A., JR., librarian; b. Portland, Ore., Aug. 24, 1924; B.S., Cornell U., 1951, M.B.A., 1952; M. Librarianship, U. Wash, 1959; m. Martha Dyles. Owner-mgr. retail store, Corvallis, Ore., 1953-57; librarian Queens Borough Pub. Library, Queens, N.Y., 1959-64; audiovisual con. Mid-Hudson Libraries, Poughkeepsie, N.Y., 1964-65; spl. collections cataloger Ariz. State U. at Tempe, 1965-67, spl. collections librarian, 1967-69, circulation librarian, 1969—; librarian Typographic Reference Library, N.Y.C., 1962-65; cons. in field. Mem. A.L.A. (life), Pvt. Libraries Assn., Bibliog. Soc. Va., Ariz. Library Assn. (exhbn. chmn. 1969), Bibliog Soc. London, Book Club Cal., Typophiles, Western Hist. Assn., Phoenix Corral Westerners. Kiwanian. Club: Caxton. Author: How to Catalogue the Private Library, 1961. Address: 42 Hudson Lane Tempe AZ 85281

GOLDSTEIN, HAROLD, govt. ofcl.; b. N.Y.C., Sept. 30, 1914; s. Charles and Susan (Garman) G.; B.A., U. Ill., 1934; M.A., U. Chgo., 1936; m. Sara Saltzman, Mar. 18, 1938; children—Martha (Mrs. Duffield White), Carola. Financial writer N.Y. Evening Jour., 1936-37; clk. Bur. Census, 1937-38; economist wage and hour div. U.S. Dept. Labor, Washington, 1938-42, economist Bur. Labor Statistics, 1942—, asst. commr., 1959—. Lectr., Am. U., 1950-55; cons. on manpower Govt. Israel, 1961, Orgn. Econ. Cooperation and Devel., 1958. Fellow A.A.A.S., Am. Statis. Assn. (mem. nat. council 1968-70); mem. Am. Econ. Assn., Am. Personnel and Guidance Assn., Washington Statis. Soc. (pres. 1965-66), Am. Indsl. Relations Assn. Home: 7012 Wilson Lane Bethesda MD 20034 Office: Bureau Labor Statistics Dept Labor Washington DC 20210

GOLDSTEIN, JOSEPH ISRAEL, leisure and recreation co. exec.; b. Balt., Mar. 8, 1923; s. Goodman and Belle (Butcher) G.; student U. Md., 1942-43; m. Shirley Herman, Nov. 14, 1948; children—Deborah, Jonathan. Mem. Joseph Goldstein Enterprises; chmn. bd., pres. Wilson Line, Washington, 1958—, also subsidiary cos.; founder, pres., Star Enterprises, Ltd., Washington, 1969—, also chmn. bd.; pres., chmn. bd. Fort Washington Marina, Washington, 1969—; pres. dir. Cruise Ships Ltd., Annapolis, Md., 1968—, Cedar Beach Aviation, Prince Frederick, Md., 1965—; chmn. bd. Marshall Hall Park (Md.); mem. Metropolitan Washington Bd. Trade, 1958—. Bd. dirs. Washington Conv. & Visitors Bur., Washington met. Transp. & Planning div. Civil Def.; trustee TTT Inst., Niagara (N.Y.) U. Served with 8th Air Force, USAAF, 1943-45. Mem. Nat. Aviation Club, Washington Soc. Assn. Execs., C. of C. Charles County, Soc. Nav. Architects & Engrs., (asso.). Democrat. Clubs: Washington International; Solomons Island Yacht (Md.); Chesapeake Country (Lusby, Md.); Center (Balt.); Wicomico Hunt (Charles County, Md.). Home: Cedar Beach Farm Prince Frederick MD 20678 Office: Pier 4 Maine Av & 6th St SW Washington DC 20024

GOLDSTEIN, JOSEPH LEON, psychiatrist; b. Louisville, Sept. 4, 1910; s. Samuel and Rebecca (Moseson) G.; student U. Pa., 1926-28; A.B., U. Louisville, 1929, M.D., 1933; m. Sylvia A. Levinson, Nov. 3, 1940. Rotating intern Louisville City Gen. Hosp., 1933-34; resident Worcester (Mass.) State Hosp., 1935-36; practice gen. medicine, Louisville, 1937-40; postgrad. tng. psychiatry Langley Porter Clinic, U. Cal. at San Francisco, 1946, Duke U. Hosp., 1946, Highland Hosp., Asheville, N.C., 1946-47; practice medicine, specializing in psychiatry, Louisville, 1947—; mem. faculty U. Louisville, 1946—, asso. prof. psychiatry, 1956—. Served with AUS, 1940-45. Diplomate Am. Bd. Psychiatry. Fellow Am. Psychiat Assn. (life); mem. A.M.A., Ky. Psychiat. Assn. (pres. 1959), Assn. Advancement Psychotherapy, Alpha Omega Alpha, Phi Delta Epsilon. Jewish religion. Home: 2437 Broadmeade Rd Louisville KY 40205 Office: Med Arts Bldg Louisville KY 40217

GOLIGHTLY, CASEY, microfilm co. exec.; b. Preston, Ida., Oct. 24, 1923; s. Osburn and Myrtle (Dalley) G.; ed. Internat. Bus. Coll., El Paso, Tex.; m. Catherine Marian Alden, Feb. 2, 1944; children—Marjorie (Mrs. Calvin E. Jenson), George Alden, Kenneth Alden, Pauline, Sandra. Pres. Golightly, Payne and Coon Microfilm Co., San Antonio; v.p. Groos Nat. Bank, Straus Frank Co. Co-chmn., bd. dirs. United Fund. Served with Armed Forces, World War II. Mem. Nat. Assn. Credit Mgmt. (exec. sec. chpt.), Nat. Microfilm Assn. (dir.), Nat. Credit Interchange (dir.), Sub-Contractors Assn.(dir.). Mem. Ch. of Jesus Christ of Latter-day Saints (pres. stake). Mason. Home: 107 McNell St San Antonio TX 78228 Office: PO Box 600 San Antonio TX 78296

GOLINO, FRANK RALPH, govt. ofcl.; b. Erie, Pa., Oct. 26, 1936; s. Dominic F. and Mary (Dober) G.; A.B. cum laude Gannon Coll., 1957; M.A., Fordham U., 1960; postgrad. (Italian Fgn. Ministry fellow) Bologna (Italy) Center Sch. Advanced Internat. Studies, 1958-59; m. Lois Mary Jean Tavani, June 21, 1958; children—Fabrizio Raffaele, Louis Raffaele, Frank Ralph. Instr. history and polit. sci. Marymount Coll., 1959-60; Middle East editor Colliers Ency., N.Y.C., 1960-61; 3d sec. Am. embassy, Mogadiscio, 1962-63; vice consul, Tangier, Morocco, 1964-65; 2d sec. Am. embassy, Tripoli, Libya, 1966-68; chmn. Near East and North African area studies Fgn. Service Inst., Dept. State, Washington, 1968-70, planning officer Bur. African Affairs, 1970—. Mem. Am., Internat. polit. sci. assns., Middle East Inst., Am. Fgn. Service Assn. Contbr. articles to profl. jours. Home: 8230 Bradley Blvd Bethesda MD 20034 Office: Bureau of African Affairs Dept State Washington DC 20500

GOLLAHER, LUSTER PAUL, county ofcl.; b. Greenland, Ark., Aug. 1, 1909; s. Noah Frank and Beulah (Talley) G.; A.B., U. Redlands, 1933; postgrad. U. So. Cal., 1935; m. Lois Blanche Hill, Aug. 22, 1933; 1 son, Larry Luster. Social case worker, Cal. Relief Adminstrn., San Bernardino, 1934-37, dist. supr. San Bernardino dist. office, 1937-39; parole officer Fed. Prison Service, Alcatraz, Cal., 1939, Sandstone, Minn., 1940, Texarkana, Tex., 1941-44, parole supr., Lewisburg, Pa., 1946-48, asso. warden, McNeil Island, Wash., 1948-55, warden, Seagoville, Texas, 1955-64; dir. ct. services Dallas County Juvenile Probation Dept., Dallas, 1964—. Mem. citizens adv. com. Tex. Senate Youth Affairs Com.; adv. com. on corrections Tex. Penal Code Revision Project. Chmn. United Fund, Seagoville, 1961; mem. youth com. YMCA. Bd. dirs. Dallas Council Alcoholism, Dallas Youth Commn. Served to lt. USNR, 1944-46. Named Seagoville Man of Year, 1959. Mem. Nat. Council Crime and Delinquency (profl. council), South States Correction Assn. (sec.), Am. Congress Correction, Tex. Police Assn., Dallas Personnel Assn., Tex. Correctional North Tex. Juvenile Officers Assn., Am. Legion. Methodist (chmn. ofcl. bd., dir. stewardship, program chmn.). Elk, Lion (pres. Seagoville 1958, chmn. carnival). Home: 8320 Baumgarten Dr Dallas TX 75228 Office: 4711 Harry Hines Blvd Dallas TX 75235

GOLUMBIC, CALVIN, govt. ofcl.; b. Lock Haven, Pa., Nov. 8, 1912; s. Isaac and Tillie (Miller) G.; B.S. (State of Pa. scholar), Pa. State U., 1934; M.S. (grad. fellow), Rutgers U., 1935, Ph.D., 1937; m. Norma Richman, May 10, 1946; 1 dau., Isabel (Mrs. John Frederick Davison). Research asso. U. Ia., 1937-42; spl. investigator Rockefeller U., 1942-45; asst. prof. chemistry U. Pitts., 1946-47; with U.S. Dept. Interior, 1947-53; with U.S. Dept. Agr., Washington, 1953—, asst. dept. adminstr., 1968—. Recipient Merit certificate U.S. Dept. Agr., 1964, 69. Mem. Am. Assn. U. Profs., Am. Chem. Soc., Inst. Food Technologists, Am. Inst. Chemists, N.Y., Washington acads. sci. Research in vitamin E, nitrogen mustards, synthetic fuels, terpenes, agrl. products. Home: 6000 Highboro Dr Bethesda MD 20034 Office: US Dept Agr Independence Av Washington DC 20250

GOMEZ, ALBERTO FLAVIO, architect; b. Santa Clara, June 22, 1933 (came to U.S., 1960, naturalized, 1968); s. Rafael Eligio and Olimpia (Padron) G.; B.S., Inst. Santa Clara (Cuba), 1950; architect, Sch. Architecture, U. Havana (Cuba), 1956; m. Vilma Ortega, May 29, 1960; children—Albertico, Malvy. Architect Planning Bd., Havana, 1956-58; asso. Abner C. Hopkins, Jacksonville, Fla., 1960-62, Hardwicke & Lee A.I.A., Jacksonville, 1962-63, Robert E. Hansen A.I.A., Ft. Lauderdale, Fla., 1963-65; partner firm Dye & Gomez, Ft. Lauderdale, 1965—; sec. Modulus, Inc., Ft. Lauderdale, 1970—. Recipient Jose Marti's award Inst. Santa Clara, 1950. Mem. A.I.A. (bd. dirs.), Colegio de Arquitectos de Cuba. Lion. Club: Le Club International (Ft. Lauderdale). Home: 1091 Alabama Av Fort Lauderdale FL 33312 Office: 808 E Las Olas Blvd Fort Lauderdale FL 33301

GOMEZ, FORTINO, clergyman; b. Celaya, Gto., Mexico, Aug. 11, 1890; s. Felipe and Dolores (Leon) G.; student Coll. Pio Marieno of Queretaro, Sem. of Monterrey, Coll. Pio Latino Americano, Rome, Italy; Dr. Phil., 1910, Dr. Theology, 1914, Dr. Law, 1916. Ordained priest Roman Catholic Ch., 1913; rector, Sem. of Monterrey, 1934; gen. vicar of archdiocese of Monterrey, 1935, dean, 1937; named archbishop of Antequera or Oaxaca, 1942, consecrated, Feb. 24, 1943; asst. pontifical throne, 1955; pastoral charge of Antequera, 1967; named titular archbishop of Ceramo. Home: Colon 206 Mexico Office: Apdo 368 Celaya Gto Mexico

GONCE, ROBERT EUGENE, orthodontist; b. Haileyville, Okla., Nov. 20, 1927; s. Thompson A. and Abbie R. (Reed) G.; student Okla. U., 1944-46; B.S., Central State U., 1950; D.D.S., U. Mo., 1954, M.S., 1964; m. Geraldine Ethel Lund, Aug. 7, 1954; children— Debra, Robert, Mark, Mike. Pvt. practice dentistry, Oklahoma City, 1954-64, pvt. practice orthodontics, Oklahoma City, 1964—. Asst. prof. surgery Okla. Sch. Medicine, 1965—. Served with AUS, 1946-48. Mem. Am. Orthodontic Soc., Am. Dental Assn., Okla. State, Okla. County dental socs., Southwestern, Okla. State socs. orthodontists, Okla. County Orthodontic Soc. (pres. 1968-70), Oklahoma City C. of C. Democrat. Baptist. Club; Quail Creek Golf and Country (Oklahoma City). Home: 2949 Quail Creek Rd Oklahoma City OK 72120 Office: 3333 NW 63d St Oklahoma City OK 73116

GONG, EDMUND JOSEPH, state senator; b. Miami, Fla., Oct. 7, 1930; s. Joe Fred and Fayline G.; A.B. cum laude, Harvard, 1952, student Sch. Law, 1954-55; LL.B., U. Miami, 1960; m. Sophie Vlachos, July 25, 1957; children—Frances Fayline, Peter, Madeleine, Joseph Fred, Edmond Joseph. Spl. writer Hong Kong Tiger Standard,

1955-56; staff writer Miami Herald, 1958-59; admitted to Fla. bar; asso. firm Helliwell, Melrose & De Wolf, 1960-61; practice law, Miami, 1962—; mem. Fla. Senate, 1966—. Asst. U.S. Atty. So. Dist. Fla., 1961-62; mem. Fla. Ho. of Reps., 1963-66. Fellow Inst. Politics John Fitzgerald Kennedy Sch. Govt., Harvard, 1969-70. Mem. Am., Dade County, Fed. bar assns., Assn. Harvard Alumni (dir.-at-large). Methodist. Home: 7751 S W 78th Ct Miami FL 33143 Office: 1117 First Nat Bank Bldg Miami FL 33131*

GONZALES, BROTHER ALEXIS (JOSEPH M. GONZALES), educator, drama dir.; b. Santa Fe, Oct. 1, 1931; B.A., Coll. Santa Fe, 1957; M.Ed., U. S.W. La., 1960. Mem. teaching order Christian Bros., 1949—; acad. dean Catholic Coll., Negros Occidental, Philippines, 1960-66; tchr. English and religion, drama coach, film producer Antonian High Sch., San Antonio, 1967-70, also organizer amateur theater group; Univ. prof. theatre and communications Loyola U., New Orleans, 1970—. Organizer internat. film festival HemisFair, San Antonio, 1967; dir. summer Creative Arts Festival, San Antonio; organizer Center Social Communications, seminars on media, San Antonio, 1968; mem. planning council Coll.-Community Creative Arts Center, Model Cities, San Antonio, 1969—; bd. consultors Mexican-Am. Social Communications Inst., San Antonio, 1971-72; dir. premier The Serpent, Mexico City; vis. prof. theatre dept. U. Mexico, 1971-72; vis. lectr. Latin Am. Center, Institute Latinoamericano de Investigaciones Pedagogicas y Antropologicas, Mexico, City, 1971-72. Rockefeller Found. grantee cultural center P.I. Mem. ANTA, Am. Ednl. Theatre Assn., Nat. Cultural Theatre Conf., N.E.A., Tex. Audio Visual Assn., Internat. Fine Arts Council S.W., Jesuit Inst. for Arts. Produced, exhibited films An Investigation of All the Lonely People; The Black and White Checkerboard Society, others. Address: Loyola U New Orleans TX 70118

GONZALES, CARLOTTA (MRS. RICHARD LAHEY), painter, sculptress, educator; b. Wilmington, N.C., Apr. 3, 1910; d. Anthony Manuel and Nettie Rivers (van Tharp) Golzales; student Pa. Acad. Fine Arts, 1927-28, N.A.D., N.Y.C., 1928-30, Art Students League, N.Y., 1930-33, Corcoran Sch. Art, Washington, 1934-36; m. Richard Lahey, Dec. 19, 1931. Tchr. children's classes Corcoran Sch. Art, Washington, 1935-37; tchr. sculpture classes Goucher Coll., Towson, Md., 1935-37; staff artist Nat. Geog. Soc., Washington, 1941-47; exhibited in group shows at Nat. Acad. Design, N.Y.C., 1930, Corcoran Biennials, Washington 1936, Goucher Coll., Towson, Md., 1943, Montclair (N.J.) Art Mus., 1945, Balt. Mus., 1946, Richmond (Va.) Mus. Art, 1947, Ogunquit (Me.) Art Assn., 1956-66. Mem. Art Students League N.Y., Ogunquit Art Assn. Illustrator for Nat. Geog. Mag., The Heavens Above, U.S.A., and State Seals, Flags of the Americas, 1941-47; commd. (with Richard Lahey) by Am. Battle Monuments Commn. to design mural for War Meml., Honolulu, 1960, dedicated, 1966; commd. (with Richard Lahey) by Stravon Ednl. Press to write Rembrandt the Artist and His Works, Picasso the Artist and His Works, 1969. Home and studio: 9530 Clark Crossing Rd Vienna VA 22180

GONZALEZ, HAYDEE, broadcasting exec. Mgr. sta. WKVM, San Juan, P.R. Address: PO Box 4189 San Juan PR 00903*

GONZALEZ, HENRY B., congressman; b. San Antonio, May 3, 1916; s. Leonides and Genevieve (Barbosa) G.; student San Antonio Jr. Coll.; B.A., U. Tex.; grad. St. Mary's Law Sch., St. Mary's U., San Antonio; m. Bertha Cuellar, 1940; children—Henry Thomas, Rosemary, Charles A., Bertha, Stephen, Genevieve, Francis, Anna Maria. Tchr. citizenship adult vocational class Ladies Garment Workers Union; slum clearance projects San Antonio Housing Authority; translator; pub. relations counselor for ins. co., San Antonio; chief probation officer Bexar County, Tex., 1946; exec. sec. Jr. Deputies of Am. (predecessor Pan Am. Progressive Assn.); councilman, San Antonio 1953-56, mayor pro-tem, 1955-56; mem. Tex. Senate, 1956-61; mem. 87th to 92d Congresses from 20th Tex. Dist. Past civilian cable and radio censor Mil. and Naval Intelligence, World War II. Home: 238 W King's Hwy San Antonio TX 78212 Office: Rayburn House Office Bldg Washington DC 20515

GONZALEZ, JOSE LOZANO, pub. health engr.; b. Laredo, Tex., June 16, 1924; s. Jose G. and Concepcion (Lozano) G.; B.S. in Civil Engring., Notre Dame U., 1950; M.P.H., Johns Hopkins, 1964; m. Maria Margarita Verduzco, Nov. 18, 1961; children—Alejandra, Gabriela. Asso. resident engr. Tex. Hwy. Dept., Laredo and San Benito, 1950-56; pub. health engr. adminstr. Laredo-Webb County Health Dept., 1956—. Civil def. dir. City of Laredo, 1961—; cons. engr. WHO, 1961—; mem. Gov's Adv. Manpower Council, also Tex. Adv. Council for Constrn. Mental Health Centers; mem. Tex. Health Adv. Com. Campaign chmn. A.R.C., 1959, chmn. Laredo Internat. Bridge Ceremony, 1960—; past. vice chmn., sec. health com. Internat. Good Neighbor Council. Bd. dirs., campaign chmn. Laredo United Fund, Washington's Birthday Assn. Served with USAAF, 1942-46; lt. (j.g.) USN Res. Registered profl. engr., Tex. Mem. Tex. Soc. Profl. Engrs., U.S.-Mexico Border (v.p.) Am., Tex. pub. health assns. Roman Catholic. Rotarian. Contbr. articles to nat. mags. Home: 2310 Frost St Laredo TX 78040 Office: 2600 Cedar Av Laredo TX 78040

GONZALEZ, MARIO FLORES, architect; b. San Antonio, Mar. 4, 1925; s. Braulio Garcia and Arcenia Ancira (Flores) G.; student Bradley U., 1946-48; B.Arch., U. Ore., 1952; m. Consuelo Carvajal, June 15, 1959; children—Mario Flores, Teresa, Sonia. Architect, Hesson & May & Assos., architects, San Antonio, 1952-56; self-employed as architect, San Antonio, 1956—. Mem. Bd. Housing Appeals, San Antonio, 1962-65; chmn. San Antonio Fine Arts Commn., 1966-69. Served with USAAF, 1943-45. Mem. A.I.A., Tex. Soc. Architects, Mexican, San Antonio chambers commerce. Roman Catholic. Club: Optimist (v.p. 1966) (San Antonio). Prin archtl. works include Eastside Pub. Health Center, City of San Antonio, Tex., Anthony Margil Elementary Sch., San Antonio Ind. Sch. Dist., Gus. Garcia Jr. High Sch., Edgewood Ind. Sch. Dist. Home: 334 W Mistletoe St San Antonio TX 78212 Office: 803 River Rd SanAntonio TX 78212

GONZALEZ, MARIO OCTAVIO, educator; b. Matanzas, Cuba, Sept. 14, 1913 (came to U.S. 1961; naturalized, 1969); s. Mario Octavio and Margarita Edelmira (Rodriguez) G.; B.S., Matanzas Inst., 1930; Dr. Physico-math. Scis., U. Havana, 1938; postgrad. Mass. Inst. Tech., 1939; Guggenheim fellow, Princeton, 1940-41; m. Maria Dolores Gutierrez, Oct. 17, 1937; children—Victoria (Mrs. Harold Raley), Alfredo, Laura (Mrs. Wyatt Cooper). Asso. prof. math. U. Havana, 1940-44, prof., 1944-60; vis. prof. U. Ala., University, 1947-48, 53-55, 58-59, prof. math., 1961—. Lectr. U. P.R., 1946, 58, 62, U. Caracas, 1960; statistician Cuban Inst. Tech. Research, 1960. Mem. Am. Math. Soc., Math. Assn. Am., Union Mathematica Argentina, Unione Matematica Italiana, Sociedad Matematica Espanola, Acad. Scis. Lima. Author: Introduction to Mathematical Analysis, 1940; Report on Higher Mathematical Studies, 1942; A Summary of Theory Continuous Groups of Transformations, 1946; Fundamentals of the Theory of Functions of a Complex Variable, 1952; Complements of Arithmetic and Algebra, 1960; Complements of Geometry and Elements of Differential and Integral Calculus, 1960; (with J. D. Mancill) Modern College Algebra, 1960; Modern Elementary Algebra, 1962; Basic College Algebra, 1962, rev., 1968; Contemporary Mathematics, 1966; Elements of Modern Mathematics, 2vols., 1969. Contbr. articles to prof. jours. Home: 47 Arcadia St Tuscaloosa AL 35401 Office: Box 1056 University AL 35486

GONZALEZ VARGAS, AURELIANO, lawyer; b. Chihuahua, Mexico, Sept. 3, 1907; Ph.B., Nat. Prep. Sch., Mexico City; LL.M., Nat. U. Mexico. Admitted to Mexican bar, 1937; now mem. firm Gonzales-Vargas and Gonzalez-Baz, Cuidad Juarez, Chihuahua, Mexico. Pres. Juarez Symphony Assn., 1962-64, City Planning Commn., 1963-64. Head legal dept. City of Juarez, 1962-63., mayor pro tem, 1962-65; spl. counsel to gov., 1962-63. Mem. Juarez (pres. 1952-55), Inter-Am., Nat. bar assns. Rotarian (pres. 1959). Contbg. author: 1001 Questions on Mexican Law. Address: Gonzalez-Vargas and Gonzalez-Baz Abraham Gonzalez 257 Cuidad Juarez Chichauhau Mexico*

GOOCH, ALBERT BARR, computer co. exec.; b. New Orleans, Nov. 4, 1938; s. John Barr and Clarisse (Galatoire) G.; B.S., Tulane U., 1960, M.S., 1962. With Standard Oil (Cal.) New Orleans 1962-67; asst. research scientist Tulane U., New Orleans, 1967-69; pres. Computer Engring., Inc., New Orleans, 1969—. Served with USCGR, 1956. Mem. Am. Soc. C. E., Assn. Computing Machinery, Sigma Xi, Tau Beta Pi. Clubs: Southern, New Orleans Yacht. Home and Office 521 Dauphine St New Orleans LA 70112

GOOCH, JAMES THOMAS, lawyer; b. Vanndale, Ark., Dec. 10, 1913; s. Samuel Amos and Augustus (Halk) G.; student Ark. State U., 1937, Ark. Law Sch., 1940; m. Edris Wyanna Lookadoo, Mar. 9, 1940; children—Edris Johanna (Mrs. Wade Quinn, Jr.), Marilyn Kay (Mrs. Donald Peterson, Jr.). Admitted to Ark. bar, 1940; practiced in Wynne, 1940-46, Arkadelphia, 1954—; mem. firm Gooch & Gooch, 1940-46; U.S. atty. Eastern Dist. Ark, 1946-54; partner Lookadoo, Gooch & Lookadoo, 1954—; pres. U.S. Atty's. Conf., 1948-50. Vice pres., dir. Elk Horn Bank & Trust Co. Mem. War Meml. Stadium, Little Rock, 1946-67. Mem. Ark. Senate, 1940-44; chmn. Clark County Democratic Com., 1960—. Served to lt. USNR, 1942-45; ETO, PTO. Mem. Am. Judicature Soc., Am., Ark., S.W. Ark., Clark County bar assns., Ark. Trial Lawyers Assn. (pres.). Home: 1215 Richardson St Arkadelphia AR 71923 Office: Lookadoo Bldg PO Box 357 Arkadelphia AR 71923

GOOCH, ROBERT DELMAS, JR., stock broker; b. Memphis, Oct. 7, 1937; s. Robert Delmas and Rebie (Perry) G.; grad. Baylor Sch., 1955; B.A., U. of the South, 1959; m. Katharine Butler Harwood, June 6, 1964; children—Robert Delmas III, Perry Butler. Stockbroker, Kohlmyer &Co., 1963-69; v.p., sec., dir. Morgan, Keegan & Co., Inc., Memphis, 1969—. Mem. Housing Rehab. Bd., Shelby County, Memphis, 1969-71; pres. Arthritis Found., 1970-71. Pres. Happy Acres Children's Hosp., 1972. Served to lt. (j.g.) USNR, 1959-62. Mem. Am. Stock Exchange, Memphis Security Dealers Assn., Phi Delta Theta. Clubs: Country, Wolf River Society (Memphis); Ponte Vedra (Fla.). Office: Sterick Bldg Memphis TN 38103

GOOD, ANNE LEEPER (MRS. JOHN CARTER GOOD), civic worker; b. Jackson, Tenn., Nov. 10, 1923; d. Robert Allen and Ola (Crittenden) Leeper; A.B., B.S. cum laude, Lambuth Coll., 1944; m. John Carter Good, Oct. 28, 1945; children—John Robert, Carter Crittenden, William Allen. Co-chmn. Introduction to Washington com. THIS, the Hospitality and Information Service, 1968-71, treas., 1971—; membership chmn. Spanish Portuguese Study Group, 1968-69, v.p., 1969-70, pres., 1970-71; mem. women's bd. House of Mercy, 1970—, treas., 1972—. Bd. dirs D.C. br. Nat. capitol Area YWCA, mem. planning and priorities com., 1971—, also mem. Hannah Harrison Sch. Com.; bd. dirs. Met. Washington chpt. Achievement Rewards for Coll. Scientists, 1971-72. Mem. Nat. Council of Women, Alliance Francaise, Club d'Amitie Franco-Internationale. Clubs: St. Albans School Mothers (pres. Washington 1964-65), Air Force Officers Wives (mem. bd. Washington 1959-61). Home: 3712 Fordham Rd NW Washington DC 20016

GOOD, BERNARD SCOTT, gen. ins. claims adjuster; b. Chgo., July 9, 1916; s. Dr. Bernard Adam and Sophia Ann (Brown) G.; B.A., Notre Dame U., 1939; LL.B., De Paul U., Chgo., 1943; m. Anne Caroline Russell, Dec. 2, 1939; children—Bernard Scott, Caroline Anne. Ins. adjuster Gen. Adjustment Bur., Miami, Fla., 1946-52; developer property holdings on St. Johns River, DeBary, Fla., 1952-57; salesman Peninsular Life Ins. Co., 1957-60; life ins. adjuster, representing various cos. in Miami area, 1960—. Mem. Estate Planning Bd. Volusia County; mem. Life Underwriters Tng. Council. Active in United Fund, A.R.C. Served as com. mem. for election Sec. State Tom Adams, Fla.; com. mem. for Senator George Smathers. Served to 1st lt. 96th Div., AUS, 1941-46. Recipient gold medal award from Gen. C. Marshall and Civilian Mil. Edn. Found. of Washington. Mem. Nat. Assn. Ind. Ins. Adjusters, Ret. Officers Assn. Democrat. Roman Catholic. Optimist (charter). Clubs: Notre Dame (charter) (Miami); Halifax Yacht, Gun, Bath and Tennis (Daytona Beach, Fla.); Ponte Vedra Country (Jacksonville, Fla.). Home: 11072 Monfero St Hammack Oaks Harbor Coral Gables FL 33134 Office: Public Service Mutual Insurance Co 902 SW 2d Av Miami FL 33130

GOOD, EDGAR CLIFTON, JR., pub. relations exec.; b. Washington, May 11, 1939; s. Edgar and Alma Mae (Dunn) G.; A.B., George Washington U., 1961; postgrad. Boston U., 1962; m. Patricia Jeanette Sullivan, Dec. 26, 1961; children—John Clifton, Wendy Marie. Editorial asst. Dow Jones Pub. Co., Washington, 1957-59; dir. news bur. George Washington U., Washington, 1965-67; editor Red Cross Youth Publs., Am. Nat. Red Cross, Washington, 1967-71, dep. dir. Office Pub. Relations, 1971—. Served to capt. USAF, 1961-65. Recipient awards Am. Coll. Pub. Relations Assn., Ednl. Press Assn. Am. Mem. Pub. Relations Soc. Am., Edn. Writers Assn. Republican. Episcopalian. Club: Evergreen Hunt (Mt. Falls, Va.). Home: 900-A Mt Vernon Av Alexandria VA 22301 Office: 18th and D Sts NW Washington DC 20006

GOOD, MARY LOWE (MRS. BILLY JEWEL GOOD), educator; b. Grapevine, Tex., June 20, 1931; d. John W. and Winnie (Mercer) Lowe; B.S., Ark. State Tchrs. Coll., 1950; M.S., U. Ark., 1953, Ph.D., 1955; m. Billy Jewel Good, May 17, 1952; children—Billy, James. Instr., Ark. State Tchrs. Coll., Conway, summer 1949, La. State U., Baton Rouge, 1954-56, asst. prof., 1956-58, asso. prof., New Orleans, 1958-63, prof., 1963—. Bd. dirs. Oak Ridge Asso. Univs., 1971—. Recipient Agnes Faye Morgan research award, 1969; AEC tng. grant, 1967; NSF internat. travel grant, 1968; NSF research grant, 1969-70, NSF grant, 1970-73. Fellow Am. Inst. Chemistry, Chem. Soc. London; mem. Am. Chem. Soc. (dir. 1971—), Am. Nuclear Soc., Sigma Xi, Iota Sigma Pi (regional dir. 1967—), Alpha Chi. Club: Zonta. Contbr. articles in field to profl. jours. Home: 6321 Cartier St New Orleans LA 70122 Office: La State U Dept Chemistry New Orleans LA 70122

GOODALL, DONALD BANNARD, educator; b. Los Angeles, Oct. 8, 1912; s. George Oliver and Margaret (Bannard); G.; A.B., U. Ore., 1935; grad. painting Sch. Art Inst. Chgo., 1936; A.M., U. Chgo., 1938; Ph.D. (fellow) Harvard, 1969; m. Gladys Hobbs, May 5, 1940; children—Brooks, Anne, Hollis. Dir. Utah Art Center, Salt Lake City, 1938-42; with U. Tex., 1942-46, 1959—, chmn. art dept., 1945-46, prof., chmn. dept. art, dir., Univ. art mus., 1959—, acting dean Coll. of Fine Arts, 1965. Acting dean of sch. Todedo Art Mus., 1947-48; chmn. dept. fine arts U. So. Cal., 1948-59; Exec. sec. Utah Inst. Fine Arts, 1940-42; sec. Utah Symphony Assn., 1941-42; exec. bd. Los Angeles Mus. Assn., 1950-56; trustee Pasadena Art Mus., 1956-60; bd. dirs., Tex. Fedn. Fine Arts, 1959—; bd. dirs., trustee Nat. Assn. Schs. of Art. Mem. Coll. Art Assn. (dir.), Am. Studies Assn., Sigma Nu. Club: Headliner's. Home: 836 E 37th St Austin TX 78705

GOODALL, LEON STEELE, ins. co. exec.; b. Lebanon, Tenn., Aug. 24, 1925; s. William Thomas and Effie (Steele) G.; student U. Tenn., 1943; B.S., U. S.C., 1947, LL.B., 1950; m. Billie Rice, Sept. 9, 1949; children—David Christian, Katherine Stuart. Spl. agt. FBI, 1950-52; sr. auditor S.C. Tax Commn., Columbia, 1952-53; sales devel. mgr. Allstate Ins. Co., Charlotte, N.C., 1953-59; agy. v.p. Colonial Life & Accident Ins. Co., Columbia, S.C., 1959-70, pres., 1970—; dir., 1964—; mem. Columbia adv. bd. Am. Bank & Trust Co. Trustee, Columbia Coll. Served with USNR, 1943-47. Mem. S.C. State Bar Assn., Sales Marketing Execs. Club, Soc. Former FBI Agts. Methodist. Club: Sertoma. Home: 6328 Eastshore Rd Columbia SC 29206 Office: 1612 Marion St Columbia SC 29201

GOODALL, VAN DOREN, physician; b. Valley Mills, Tex., July 21, 1909; s. William George and Ethel (Barnett) G.; student Baylor U., 1927-29; M.D., U. Tex., 1933; m. Valorie Birdie Shaw, June 10, 1933; children—Valorie Shaw (Mrs. William Piatt Mooney), Van Doren. Intern, Providence Hosp., Waco, Tex., 1933-34; practice medicine, specializing in internal medicine, Clifton, Tex., 1934—; co-founder, sr. staff mem. Goodall-Witcher Hosp. Found., 1939—, Clifton Med. and Surg. Clinic, 1939—; dir., v.p. Farmers State Bank, Clifton, Tex. Mem. Tex. Hosp. Licensing Bd., 1959—, chmn., 1970. Bd. dirs. Tex. Good Rds. Assn. Mem. A.M.A., Tex. Acad. Gen. Practice (pres. 1958), Tex. Pvt. Clinics and Hosp. Assn. (pres. 1961), Tex. Med. Assn., Bosque-Hamilton County Med. Soc., Clifton C. of C. (v.p. 1970), Baylor U. (pres. 1960), U. Tex. Med. Br. (pres. 1971) ex-students assns. Presbyn. (elder 1945—). Lion. Clubs: Ridgewood (Waco); Bosque Valley Country Meridian, Tex.); Central Tex. Golf Academy (dir. 1971—) (Gatesville, Tex.). Home: 1415 W Hackberry St Clifton TX 76634 Office: 110 N Av F Clifton TX 76634

GOODCHILD, JAMES FISHER, orthodontist; b. N.Y.C., Oct. 11, 1939; s. Chauncey George and Hazel Gertrude (Fisher) G.; B.A., Emory U., 1961, D.D.S., 1965; postgrad. U. Pitts., 1967-69; m. Catherine Erwin Lamons, June 15, 1963; children—James Bradley, Karen Hope. Individual practice orthodontics, Atlanta, 1969—. Served to capt. Dental Corps, AUS, 1965-67. Decorated Army Commendation medal. Mem. Am. Assn. Orthodontists, Am., Ga. dental assns., So. Soc. Orthodontists, No., Fifth Dist. dental socs. Home: 2664 Fleur de Lis Pl Atlanta GA 30340 Office: 4700 Chamblee Dunwoody Rd Atlanta GA 30341

GOODE, MARK IRA, govt. ofcl.; b. Steubenville, O., Mar. 25, 1932; s. Solomon Benjamin and Ceil (Perry) G.; B.S., Northwestern U., 1954; m. Sandra Zogut, July 19, 1959; children—Jill, Leslie, Claudia. Staff dir., then asso. dir. ABC-TV, 1957-67; free lance TV dir., 1967-71; spl. asst. to Pres., Washington, 1971—. Served with AUS, 1954-56. Mem. Dirs. Guild Am. Home: 6235 Kellogg Dr McLean VA 22101 Office: 1600 Pennsylvania Av Washington DC

GOODE, MORTON JACOB, dentist; b. Washington, Feb. 3, 1924; s. Julius and Sadie (Fleisher) G.; B.S., Georgetown U., 1942; D.D.S., Temple U., 1946; m. Amy Lou Harris, Dec. 23, 1945; children—Scott, Robert, Jill. Intern Glendale (Md.) Sanitarium, 1946; asso. Dr. Jack Goldblatt, Washington, 1947-49; individual practice gen. dentistry, Washington, 1949-51, 52-59, gen. dentistry, crown bridge and rehab., 1959—. Pres. Budget Rent-a-Car, (Miami Beach, Fla.); dir. Beverage Control, Inc.; v.p. Derma-Hair; lectr.; staff adviser dental dept. Children's Hosp., Hebrew Home for Aged. Dir. Boy Scouts Am., 1961-62. Served as p.f.c., AUS, 1943-44, as capt. Dental Corps, USAF, 1950-51. Mem. Am. Dental Assn., D.C. Dental Soc. (dir. dental program for treatment of mentally retarded children), Acad. Gen. Dentistry, D.C. Dental Sci. Club (past pres.). Jewish religion (dir. congregation). Kiwanian. Contbr. articles to profl. jours. Home: 5504 Uppingham St Chevy Chase MD 22015 Office: 7723 Alaska Av NW Washington DC 20012

GOODEN, REGINALD HEBER, bishop; b. Long Beach, Cal., Mar. 22, 1910; s. Robert Burton and Alice Leonard (Moore) G.; A.B., Stanford, 1931; S.T.M., Berkeley Div. Sch., New Haven, 1934, S.T.D., 1946; student U. Madrid, 1934-35, Centro de Estudios Historicos, Madrid (Spain), 1934-35; m. Victoria Elena Fernandez de Mendia y Miranda; children—Reginald Heber, Hiram Richard. Ordained to ministry Protestant Episcopal Ch., 1934; hon. asst. chaplain Brit. Embassy Ch., Madrid, 1934-35; priest in charge St. Paul's Ch. and Sch., Camaguey, Cuba, 1935-39; dean Holy Trinity Cathedral, Havana, Cuba, 1939-45; bishop of missionary dist. P.E. Ch. in Panama C.Z., 1945-72, also bishop in charge, Ecuador, 1956-64; asst. bishop Epis. Ch. Diocese La., Shreveport, 1972—. Pres. bd. Colegio Episcopal, Academia de Cristo, Instituto Episcopal. Chmn. bd. dirs., pres. bd. adminstrs. Bella Vista Children's Home, Panama City, C.Z.; mem. com. mgmt. Balboa-Armador Rd. YMCA. Recipient Master Key, Panama Canal Co.; decorated grand cross Order Vasco Nunez de Balboa (Panama); recipient Community Service award and citation Pres. U.S. and Gov. C.Z., 1972. John Henry Watson fellow Berkeley Div. Sch. Mason. Club: The Breakers (Stanford U.). Home: Fairfield Oaks Apts Shreveport LA 71104 Office: 835 Beck Bldg Shreveport LA 71101

GOODFELLOW, THOMAS MACKEY, railroad exec.; b. Altoona, Pa., Oct. 1, 1907; s. Frank Addison and Edith (Mackey) G.; C.E., Cornell U., 1929; LL.D., LI. U.; m. Dorothy Haak, May 26, 1934. With Pa. R.R. Co., 1924-54, successively apprentice, asst. on engring. corps., asst. supr. track, supr. track, asst. div. engr., Phila. Terminal div., 1944-45, div. engr., Colombus, O., 1945-47, Pitts., 1947-48, asst. supt. freight transp., Pitts., 1948, supt., Delmarva div., 1948-51, Fort Wayne div., 1951-53; Pitts. div., 1953-54; v.p., gen. mgr. L.I.R. R., 1954-56, pres., gen. mgr., 1956-67; pres. Assn. Am. Railroads, 1967-70; chmn., 1970—; dir. Riggs Nat. Bank. Chmn. U.S. Nat. commn. Pan Am. Ry. Congress. Chmn. Golden Spike Centennial Celebration Commn., 1967; chmn. Nat. R.R. Com. on Scouting. Bd. dirs. World Safety Inst., Nat. Capital Area council Boy Scouts Am., YMCA Met. Washington. Mem. Phi Delta Theta. Republican. Presbyn. Mason (Shriner) Home: 4917 Rockwood Plwy Washington DC 20016 Office: 1920 L St NW Washington DC 20036

GOODHUE, LYLE DAVID, chemist; b. Newton, Ia., Sept. 30, 1903; s. Thomas Warwick and Kathrine Jane (Engle) G.; B.S., Ia. State U., 1928, M.S., 1929, Ph.D., 1934; m. Helen Elizabeth Hamaker, June 19, 1929; children—Lois Ann (Mrs. Wayne C. Coltrain), Charles, Jackson, Lura Irene (Mrs. John B. Pierce). Instr. chemistry Ia. State U., 1930-34; sr. chemist U.S. Dept. Agr., Beltsville, Md., 1934-46; dir. research Airosol, Inc., Neodesha, Kan., 1946-47; mgr. agrl. chem. research Phillips Petroleum Co., Bartlesville, Okla., 1947-68; cons. in field, 1968—. Recipient Gold Medal, Eastern Br. Entomol. Soc., 1937; John Scott award City of Phila., 1945, Alumni award Ia. State

U., 1948, Rotheim award Fedn. European Aerosol Assns., 1970. Mem. Am. Chem. Soc. (Kenneth Spencer award 1971), Am. Soc. Entomologists, Sigma Xi, Phi Kappa Phi, Phi Lambda Upsilon, Gamma Sigma Delta, Alpha Chi Sigma. Club: Camera (Bartlesville). Contbr. articles to profl. jours. Inventor aerosol, Avitrol repellent method of pest control, others. Home: 1940 S Keeler St Bartlesville OK 74003

GOODING, JESSIE JEWELL SIMS (MRS. ARTHUR RAY GOODING), clubwoman; b. Hartshorne, Okla., May 9, 1902; d. William Poley and Leola (Sullivan) Sims; student Okla. Coll. Women, 1921-22; m. Arthur Ray Gooding, Aug. 16, 1925; children—Jack Bascom, Arthur Gene. Shipping clk. William Volker Wholesale Co., Oklahoma City, 1942-43; bookkeeper, sales clk. Seela Windowshade Co., 1944-51; sales clk. John A. Brown Co., 1957. Recipient Torch award Am. War Mothers, 1966. Mem. Bus. and Profl. Women's Club, Am. War Mothers (charter, chpt. pres. 1955-56, chpt. treas. 1956-62, state treas. 1958-60, chpt. corr. sec. 1963-68, chpt. historian 1969-71, state pres. 1968-70; state alternate rep. in Vets. Voluntary Service 1969-71), Am. War Dads. Aux. (pres. 1965-66, nat. council woman, Okla. historian; life mem.). Baptist. Mem. Order Eastern Star. Clubs: Flower (v.p. 1965—), Home Demonstration, Merry Modern Mothers (past v.p.). Home: 508 SW 35th St Oklahoma City OK 73109

GOODLET, JAMES HARRIS, city ofcl.; b. Columbus, Ga., Sept. 10, 1922; s. Hiram O. and Nona (Harris) G.; B.S., Samford U., 1946; m. Thelma I. Moon, Sept. 17, 1944; children—Janice Gail, Gloria Jean. Asst. to bus. mgr. Howard Coll., Birmingham, Ala. 1946-48; agt. Life Ins. Co. of Ga., Miami, Fla., 1948-49; city clk., treas., personnel dir. City of Hialeah (Fla.), 1949—. Trustee, treas. City of Hialeah Employees Retirement System. Served to lt. USAAF, 1943-45. Decorated Silver Star, Air medals with two oak leaf clusters, Purple Heart. Mem. Fla., Dade County (past pres.) finance officers assns., Fla. Assn. Personnel Agencies (past pres.), Internat. Inst. Municipal Clks. Baptist. Home: 951 E 37th St Hialeah FL 33013 Office: 501 Palm Av Hialeah FL 33010

GOODLOE, JOSEPH WAVERLY, ins. co. exec.; b. Durham, N.C., Oct. 8, 1906; s. Allen and Ross (Bumpass) G.; grad. in bus. adminstrn. Hampton Inst., 1926; LL.D., Shaw U., 1963; m. Betty Alice Wilson, Dec. 23, 1936; 1 dau., Betty Jo. (Mrs. William E. Merritt III). With N.C. Mut. Life Ins. Co., Durham, N.C., 1926—, dir., 1953—, sr. v.p., 1961-64, sec., 1952-67, exec. v.p., 1964-68, pres., chief exec. officer, 1968—; dir. Mechanics and Farmers Bank, Durham, Mut. Savs. & Loan Assn., Durham. Mem. gov.'s study comm. Pub. Sch. System N.C.; mem. nat. adv. com. Housing Underhoused Project; mem. adv. council Minority Bus. Enterprise. Mem. exec. com. Durham Downtown Devel. Assn.; mem. div. finance com. Occoneechee council Boy Scouts Am. Bd. dirs. Shaw U., John Avery Boys' Club, Durham United Fund, Durham County United Fund, Nat. Indsl. Conf. Bd.; pres. Central Orphanage N.C., Goodwill Industries. Mem. Life Ins. Assn. Am. (dir.), Nat. Ins. Assn. (past pres.), Omega Psi Phi. Mason. Baptist (chmn. bd. trustees). Home: 119 Masondale Av Durham NC 27707 Office: Mutual Plaza Durham NC 27701

GOODMAN, BERNARD, museum ofcl. Supervisory interpretive specialist Cumberland Gap Nat. Park, Middlesboro, Ky. Address: Cumberland Gap Nat Park Box 840 Middlesboro KY 40965*

GOODMAN, HILLIARD HERMAN, economist; b. Balt., Apr. 28, 1913; s. Joseph and Rose (Buckner) G.; student Carnegie Inst. Tech., 1931-34; B.S., Am. U., 1948, M.A., 1952; m. Maria del Carmen Pena, Jan. 16, 1945. Economist, Office Econ. Research, U.S. Tariff Commn., Washington, 1950—. Mem. Citizens Transit Improvement Assn., Washington, 1956—, v.p., 1958, exec. v.p., 1959—. Served with AUS, 1943-46. Mem. Am. Econ. Assn., Regional Sci. Assn., A.A.A.S., Internat. Platform Assn., Soc. Govt. Economists, Am. Fedn. Govt. Employees (local v.p. 1969-70). Jewish religion. Mason. Home: 3700 Massachusetts Av NW Washington DC 20016 Office: US Tariff Commn Washington DC 20436

GOODMAN, JAMES JACOB, psychiatrist; b. Boston, Mar. 31, 1922; s. Morris and Rosa (Wolfsen) G.; B.A., Boston U., 1943; M.D., Middlesex U., 1945; m. Janice Annabel Stenson, July 11, 1951; 1 dau., Ann Rosalind. Intern St. Mark's Hosp., Salt Lake City, 1946-47; resident St. Vincent's Sanitarium, St. Louis, 1947-48, Western State Hosp., Ft. Steilacoom, Wash., 1948-50; staff psychiatrist VA Hosp., American Lake, Wash., 1950-51; asst. attending physician dept. psychiatry and neurology Jackson Hosp., Miami, Fla., 1954—, also clin. dir. Miami Med. Center; practice medicine specializing in psychiatry, Miami, 1954-65; staff psychiatrist VA Hosp., Indpls., 1966-69, VA Hosp., Miami, Fla., 1969—. Instr. psychiatry U. Miami, 1955-57, clin. asst. prof. neurology, 1957-59, clin. instr. psychiatry, 1969-72, clin. asst. prof. Sch. Medicine, 1972—. instr. psychiatry Ind. U. Sch. Medicine, 1967-69. Bd. dirs. P.L. Dodge Found. and Meml. Hosp., Miami. Served to capt. M.C., AUS, 1951-54. Mem. Am. Psychiat. Assn. A.M.A. So., Fla., Dade County med. assns. Assn. Am. Med. Colls., Assn. for Psychiat. Treatment of Offenders, Nat. Assn. for Mental Health, Mental Health Soc. S.E. Fla., Assn. Mil. Surgeons, Am. Soc. for Group Psychotherapy and Psychodrama, Acad. Religion and Mental Health, Fla. Council on Aging, Fla. Soc. Neurology and Psychiatry, World Med. Assn. (U.S. com.), Nat. Com. on Alcoholism, N.Y. Acad. Scis., Am. Geriatrics Soc., Am. Acad. Forensic Scis. Home: 6818 Corsica St Coral Gables FL 33146 Office: 1201 NW 16th St Miami FL 33125

GOODMAN, JOSEPH LIPTON, physician; b. Alta., Can., Feb. 10, 1919; s. Joshua Harry and Anna (Briebart) G.; B.S., The Citadel, 1952; M.D., Med. U. S.C., 1951; m. Helen Breetwor, Aug. 26, 1952; children—Debbie, Pamela. Intern, U. Colo. Hosp., Denver, 1952; practice gen. medicine, Charleston, S.C., 1952—; med. dir. research Raybestos Manhattan, Inc., Charleston, 1958—; med. dir. Charleston Rubber Co.; plant physician Am. Brands, Inc., 1955—, Army Depot, Charlotte, 1952, Avco Lycoming, Inc., 1958—; clin. prof. occupational medicine Med. U. S.C., 1968—. Commr., adviser S.C. Dept. Labor. Bd. dirs. Salvation Army. Served with AUS, 1942-46. Fellow Indsl. Med. Assn. Rotarian. Home: 1259 Keble Rd Charleston SC 29406 Office: 623 O'Hear St Charleston SC 29406

GOODMAN, ROBERT CAREY, JR., ednl. adminstr.; b. Phila., Apr. 18, 1930; s. Robert Carey and Gwyn (Mercer).; B.A., Conn. Wesleyan U., 1952; M.A., Memphis State U., 1965; m. Virginia Shea Saunders, June 7, 1955; children—Martha Swann, Robert Carey III, Alice. Instr., Richmond (Va.) Profl. Inst., 1963; headmaster Presbyn. Day Sch., Memphis, 1963-65, Augusta (Ga.) Prep. Sch., 1965-68; instr. Augusta Coll., 1967; pres. Arlington Schs., Atlanta, 1968—. Served with AUS, 1952-54. Rotarian, Kiwanian. Club: Lakeside Country (Atlanta). Home: 1630 Loch Lomond Trail SW Atlanta GA 30331 Office: 2605 Fairburn Rd SW Atlanta Ga 30331

GOODMAN, RONALD H., museum ofcl. Curator South Asian textiles Textile Museum, Washington. Address: Textile Museum 2320 S St NW Washington DC 20008*

GOODMAN, S. OLIVER, newspaper editor; b. Cleve., May 5, 1910; s. Louis and Kate (Korngood) G.; grad. high sch.; m. Sylvia Posner, June 12, 1932; children—Donald E., Abby J., Linda G. Reporter, Cleve. Press, 1926-29; reporter, copy editor, financial editor Buffalo Times, 1929-36; bus. editor Washington Post, 1937—, Bd. dirs. Washington Post Employees Fed. Credit Union. Recipient Ann. Merit award Greater Washington Indsl. Council, 1956. Mem. Soc. Am. Bus. Writers, Am. Newspaper Guild, Washington Advt. Club, Bond Club Washington. Home: 6404 Wilson Lane Bethesda MD 20034 Office: 1515 L St NW Washington DC 20005

GOODMAN, WILLIAM EDWARD, dentist; b. Fairland, Okla., Nov. 11, 1932; s. Eugene G. and Vella (Stelle) G.; A.A., Northeastern A. and M. Coll., 1952; A.B., Okla. Bapt. U., 1957; D.D.S., Marquette U., 1962; m. Glenda Jo Blair, Dec. 21, 1957; children—Mark W., Michael S., Timothy W., B. Daniel. Individual practice dentistry, Miami, Okla., 1962—; organizer Investors Life Ins. Co., Oklahoma City, Estate Security Life Ins. Co., Miami. Pres. Miami Safety Council, 1965-69, Norseman Athletic Scholarship Assn., 1969—; commr. Miami Housing Authority, 1966-69; chmn. dir. Ottawa County (Okla.) March of Dimes, 1964-69; capt. United Fund, Miami, 1965-69; v.p. P.T.A., Miami, 1969. Trustee Ottawa County Cancer Soc., 1965-69. Served with AUS, 1954-56. Mem. No. Dist. (pres. 1969), Am., Okla. dental assns. Baptist (trustee). Mason (Shriner), Kiwanian. Home: 1515 E St SW Miami OK 74354 Office: 1st Nat Bank Miami OK 74354

GOODMAN, WILLIAM WOLF, lawyer; b. Memphis, June 26, 1900; s. Abe and Bobye (Wolf) G.; ed. Memphis U. Sch., Culver Mil. Acad.; B.A., U. Pa., 1920; J.D., Harvard U., 1923; grad. student St. Johns Coll., Cambridge (Eng.) U., 1923-24; Barrister, Lincoln's Inn (London), 1926; m. 1942; 5 children. Sec. Tenn. Planning Commn., 1932-40; chmn. bd. treas. Am. Finishing Co.; chmn. Memphis Cold Storage Warehouse Co., Mid-South Refrigerated Warehouse Co., McCall & Dermon Bldgs. Co.; chmn. Commerce Title Guaranty Co.; pres. Madison Oil & Devel. Co. Pres. commr. Goodwyn Inst.; pres. Lausanne Sch., Memphis. Served with U.S. Army, 1918, World War I; col. USAAF, 1942-45. Decorated Legion of Merit. Army Commendation Ribbon, Royal Yugoslav Aviator's Wings, Honoris Causa; Spl. Breast Award Order of Yun Hui (Cloud and Banner) (China); knight comdr. Order Orange-Nassau (Netherlands); knight comdr. Royal Order St. Olaf (Norway); chevalier Legion of Honor (French); officer Order of Brit. Empire (Eng.). Mem. Am., Tenn. bar assns., Assn. Bar City N.Y., Brit. Barrister, Memphis and Shelby County bar assns., Memphis Freight Bur. (pres. 1951-60). Clubs: Harvard (N.Y.C.); Army and Navy (Washington); University, Ridgeway Country (Memphis). Home: 159 E Parkway N Memphis TN 38114 Office: Commerce Title Bldg Memphis TN 38103

GOODNER, ARMEL HOYT, hosp. adminstr.; b. Boles, Ark., June 24, 1934; s. Orval Kern and Effie Hanna (Taylor) G.; student Ark. Tech. Coll., 1951-53, State Coll. Ark. Corr. Sch., 1953, Okla. State U., 1966; m. Linda Jean Davis, July 30, 1960; children—Karan Lynn, Gregory Todd. Asst. mgr. Waldron Furniture Factory, Ark., 1954-56; asst. parts mgr. Dewitt Oldsmobile Co., Ft. Smith, Ark., 1959; comml. repair S.W. Bell Tel. Co., Stillwater, Okla., 1959-70; adminstr. Scott County Hosp., Waldron, 1970—. Served with AUS, 1956-58. Mem. Waldron C. of C. Lion. Home: Box 81 Waldron AR 72958 Office: Box Q Waldron AR 72958

GOODNIGHT, (ANNIE) CATHERINE SMITH, newspaper editor; b. Dothan, Ala., Sept. 30, 1922; d. Julian L. and Opal (Pierce) Smith; student Enterprise Jr. Coll., 1969; m. Bernard S. Goodnight, Aug. 16, 1941 (div. Jan. 1957); children—Kenneth, Ronnie, Gloria. Editor, advt. mgr., office mgr., circulation mgr. News Herald, Hartford, Ala., 1960—. Mem. Ala.-Fla. council Boy Scouts Am., 1969, Parents Tchrs. Orgn.; active various community drives. Recipient awards for best service to edn. and best feature article Ala. Press Assn., 1967, best service to edn. awards, 1969; Appreication award Hartford Jaycees, 1970; named 1st woman hon. mem. Hartford chpt. Future Farmers Am., 1971; hon. Lt. col. a-d-c Ala. State Militia, 1971. Mem. Bus. and Profl. Orgn. (rec. sec. 1969). Baptist. Mem. order Eastern Star. Home: 403 4th Av S Hartford AL 36344 Office: 102 Commerce St Hartford AL 36344

GOODPASTURE, BENTON CORDELL, publisher, editor; b. Livingston, Tenn., Apr. 9, 1895; s. John Jefferson and Elora (Thompson) G.; B.A., David Lipscomb Coll., 1918; LL.D., Pepperdine Coll., 1955, Magic Valley Coll., 1955; Litt.D., Harding Coll., 1955; m. Cleveland Cliett, Sept. 3, 1918 (dec. Nov. 1964); children—Benton Cordell, Eleanor Pauline (Mrs. Myron L. King), John Cliett; m. 2d, Freddie Joan Goetz, Nov. 11, 1965. Ordained to ministry Ch. of Christ, 1912; minister Main St. Ch. of Christ, Shelbyville, Tenn., 1918-19, West End Ch. of Christ, Atlanta, 1920-27, Poplar St. Ch. of Christ, Florence, Ala., 1927-28, Druid Hills Ch. of Christ, Atlanta, 1927-39, Hillsboro Ch. of Christ, Nashville, 1939-51; editor Gospel Advocate Co., Inc., Nashville, 1939—, pres., 1950—. Bd. dirs. Potter Orphan Home, Atlanta Christian Schs., B.C. Goodpasture Christian Sch. Author: Sermons and Lectures, 1964; (with W.T. Moore) Biographies and Sermons of Pioneer Preachers, 1954, Great Preachers of Today, 1967. Home: 932 Caldwell Lane Nashville TN 37204 Office: 1006 Elm Hill Pike Nashville TN 37210

GOODRICH, BAXTER DEE, utility exec.; b. Oklahoma City, July 9, 1913; s. Robert E. and Moye Aileen (Wilson) G.; student Ala. Poly. Inst., 1931-33; B.S. in Civil Engring., Rice U., 1935; m. Glennis McCrary Aug. 9, 1937. With W. M. Kellogg Co., 1935-36, United Gas Pipe Line Co., 1936-46; chief engr. Arctic Contractors, 1946-47; with Tex. Eastern Transmission Corp., 1947—, pres., 1965-71, chmn. bd., chief exec. officer, 1971—. Mem. gas industry group on tour USSR, 1961. Trustee Inst. Gas Tech. Served to lt. comdr. USNR, 1943-46. Mem. Ind. Natural Gas Assn. (dir.), Am. Gas Assn. (dir., chmn. industry tech. adv. com.; award pipe line research com. 1964), Soc. Am. Mil. Engrs., Sigma Alpha Epsilon. Home: 615 Hunters Grove Houston TX 77024 Office: PO Box 2521 Houston TX 77001

GOODRICH, GEORGE HERBERT, judge; b. Charleston, W.Va., June 19, 1925; s. Edgar Jennings and Beulah Etta (Lenfest) G.; B.A., Williams Coll., 1949; LL.B., U. Va., 1952; m. Nancy Ann Needham, Sept. 3, 1949; children—George Herbert, Craig N., Thomas A. Admitted to D.C. bar, 1953, Md. bar, 1958; practiced in Washington, 1953-69; mem. firm Guggenheimer, Untermeyer & Goodrich, 1953-62, Burton, Heffelfinger, McCarthy & Kendrick, 1962-67, Heffelfinger, Schweitzer & Goodrich, 1967-69; asso. judge Superior Court D.C., 1969—. Law instr. Bus. Sch., Am. U., 1969—. Pres. Homemaker Service Nat. Capitol Area, 1966; v.p. Hillcrest Children's Center, 1969; mem. community adv. com. Jr. League D.C., 1969. Bd. dirs. A.R.C. Served with USNR, 1943-46. Mem. Am., D.C. bar assns. Club: Chevy Chase (Md.); Metropolitan (Washington). Home: 6003 Corbin Rd Washington DC 20016 Office: 4th and E Sts NW Washington DC 20001

GOODRICH, JAMES LYNN, feasibility cons.; b. Tempe, Ariz., Jan. 29, 1905; s. James Bert and Sallie E. (Cummings) G.; student Westinghouse Tech. Schs., 1923-24; m. Gisela Carolina Teran Meltz, Sept. 20, 1946; children—Berthold James, Gisela Martha (Mrs. Michael Webb), James D. (dec.), John R., Lynn (Mrs. Warren Lyon). Chief elec. engr. Allen & Hoshall, cons. engrs., Memphis, 1935-41; power cons. Ashley G. Classen & Assos., El Paso, Tex., 1947-48; exec. dir. Elec. Distbrs., Inc., San Juan, P.R., 1948-50; v.p. cons. Telemusic Corp., San Juan, P.R.; feasibility cons. Pullara, Bowen & Watson, Architects-Engrs., Tampa, Fla., 1957-59, James L. Goodrich & Assos., Tampa, Fla., 1959—; feasibility cons. White Sands Missile Range, N.M., 1961-70; technol. forecaster, long-range planner, gen. engr. Plans Office; spl. cons. U.S. Army Tropic Test Center, C.Z., 1967. Dir., sec.-treas., liaison engr., counselor, now vice chmn. Engring. Guidance Council of El Paso Area, Inc. Exec. dir., gen. mgr. Progress Village, Inc., Tampa, 1958-59; adminstr. Condomino Ponce de Leon, Santurce, P.R., 1960; exec. dir. Mercados de P.R., Inc., and Centro de Expocisiones del Caribe, Inc., adminstr. Tecemomova Realty and Financing Co., 1960. Served with AUS, 1942-45; now lt. col. Res. ret. Registered profl. engr., Tenn., Miss. Mem. I.E.E.E. (chmn. El Paso 1970 rep. Region V, dir. S.W. 1971-74), Illuminating Engr. Soc., Soc. Am. Mil. Engrs. (local dir.), Nat., N.M., Tex. socs. profl. engrs., Southwestern Internat. Fedn. Tech. Socs. (chmn., exec. sec. 1970—), Am. Soc. C.E., Am. Inst. Aeros. and Astronautics (chmn. inland missile range sect. 1969-70, rep. Region IV), East Tampa Bay C. of C. (dir. 1959-70). Home and office: 10304 Rushing Rd El Paso TX 79924

GOODRICH, MAX, univ. dean; b. Calboun, Mo., Dec. 11, 1905; s. Henry Charles and Elma Antionette (Shafer) G.; B.A. cum laude, Westminster Coll., Fulton, Mo., 1927; Ph.D., U. Minn., 1936; m. Marian Jeannette Guyer, Aug. 24, 1919; children—Mary Lee Ann (Mrs. Roy T. Matthews) Marna Jean (Mrs. Clement J. Clarke III). Instr. math. Salt Lake City Collegiate Inst. 1927-29; asst. instr. physics U. Minn., 1929-36; faculty La. State U., Baton Rouge, 1936—, prof. physics, 1950—, dean Grad. Sch., 1961—, on leave as chief grad. acad. programs br. U.S. Office Edn., Washington, 1968-69. Mem. staff War Research Lab., U. Tex. 1945; sr. physicist Oak Ridge Nat. Lab., 1949, summers 1950, 52, 54. Mem. computer com. So. Regional Bd. 1968—. Fellow Am. Phys. Soc., A.A.A.S.; mem. Am. Assn. Physics Tchrs., Am. Assn. U. Profs., La. Acad. Sci., Sigma Xi (past pres. La. State U. chpt.), Sigma Pi Sigma, Omicron Delta Kappa, Phi Kappa Phi. Contbr. articles to profl. jours. Home: 5688 Forsythia Av Baton Rouge LA 70808

GOODRICH, WARREN M., lawyer; b. Lawton, Okla., Jan. 5, 1922; A.B. with honors, U. Fla., 1943, LL.B. with high honors, 1948. Admitted to Fla. bar, 1948; mem. firm Goodrich, Hampton, Thompson and Boylston, P.A., Bradenton, Fla.; pros. atty., 1953-57; Mem. Fla. Constn. Revision Commn., Commn. on Aging. Chmn. Fla. Democratic Exec. Com., 1962—, chmn., 1962-66. Fellow Acad. Fla. Trial Lawyers (pres. 1962-63); mem. Am., Manatee County (pres. 1956-57) bar assns., Fla. Bar (past chmn. com. on econs. of bar, council of bar presidents), Law Sci. Acad., Am. Trial Lawyers Assn. (editor Jour. 1961—, Fla. committeeman 1962-63), Blue Key, Phi Beta Kappa, Phi Delta Phi, Phi Kappa Phi, Tau Kappa Alpha. Editor-in-chief U. Fla. Law Rev., 1949-50. Address: 406 13th St W Bradenton FL 33505

GOODRUM, BERNIE, naturalist. Recreational dir. Wichita (Kan.) Park Commn. Bd., 1937-40, also founder Wichita Zoo; naturalist, authority Indian lore, bird study; artisian Ozark arts and crafts. Address: Eureka Springs AR 72632*

GOODRUM, DANIEL SHEPARD, banker; b. Leslie, Ga., July 11, 1926; s. John W. and Inez M. (Culp) G.; B.S., U. Fla., 1949; m. Margaret Swanson, June 8, 1949; children—John, William. Vice-pres., Fla. Nat. Bank, Jacksonville, 1957-62; sr. v.p. First Nat. Bank of Fort Lauderdale (Fla.), 1962-66; pres. First Nat. Bank, Lake Worth, Fla., The Community Bank, Boca Raton, Fla., Congress Nat. Bank, Palm Springs, Fla., 1966—; v.p. Gen. Financial Systems, Inc., bank holding co., Riviera Beach, Fla., 1966—; dir. Peoples Bank, Gainesville, Marine Nat. Bank, Jacksonville. Served with USAAF, 1943-45, 50-51. Mem. Fla. Bankers Assn. (1st v.p. 1971-72). Democrat. Episcopalian. Club: Sailfish (Palm Beach). Home: 232 Angler Av Palm Beach FL 33480 Office: 114 N J St Lake Worth FL 33460

GOODSON, EDWARD LEE, hosp. adminstr.; b. Leeds, Ala., Feb. 9, 1927; s. Roy E. and Bernice (Lee) G.; B.A., Ala. Polytech. Inst., 1950; m. Mary Lou Mitchell, May 6, 1948; children—Stephen E., William Lee, David Lynn. Rep., Ala. Dept. Pub. Welfare, Montgomery, 1950-60; adminstr. Leeds Hosp., 1960—, sec. bd. dirs., 1960—. Mem. Leeds Planning and Zoning Commn., 1962—, Jefferson County Planning and Zoning Commn., 1961-64; mem. Jefferson County Assn. Mental Health, 1969—; chmn. Leeds Indsl. Devel. Bd., 1969—. Bd. dirs. Leeds Housing Authority, 1968—. Served with USAAF, 1946-47. Mem. C. of C. (dir. 1962-69). Presbyn. (elder). Clubs: Terry Walker Country, Civitan (pres. 1962-63), Quarterback (pres. 1958). Home: 107 Greenbrier Acres Leeds AL 35094 Office: 100 Parkway Dr Leeds AL 35094

GOODSON, JAMES BUTLER, life ins. co. exec.; b. Waco, Tex., Aug. 15, 1923; s. William Lloyd and Susie (Butler) G.; B.B.A., U. Tex., 1948; m. Molly Barnes, Mar. 20, 1949; children—Laurie, Liza, James Butler, Thomas Barnes. Analyst, Rauscher, Pierce & Co., Dallas, 1948-52; with Southland Life Ins. Co., Dallas, 1952—, pres., 1969—, also dir., mem. exec. com.; chmn. finance com., dir., mem. exec. com. Nathan Hale Life Ins. Co. Treas., dir. Boys' Clubs Am., 1962-66; pres., dir. Children's Devel. Center, Dallas, 1967; mem. exec. com. Dallas Council Chs., 1967, bd. dirs., 1968; mem. Dallas Assembly, 1962—, Cotton Bowl Council 1962—; active United Fund, YMCA. Bd. dirs. Goodwill Industries Dallas, Hope Cottage, Dallas, Jr. Achievement Dallas. Served with AUS, World War II. Mem. Salesmanship Club Dallas (dir. 1965-66), Sigma Alpha Epsilon. Presbyn. (chmn. deacons 1961, elder 1962-65, deacon 1961—). Home: 3817 Gillon St Dallas TX 75205 Office: 1800 Southland Center Dallas TX 75201

GOODSON, LOUIE AUBREY, JR., textile co. exec.; b. Caswell County, N.C., Dec. 20, 1922; s. Louie Aubrey and Lenna Sue (Neal) G.; B.S., N.C. State U., 1943; LL.B., Georgetown U., 1951, J.D., 1967; m. Bernice Carroll, July 23, 1945; children—Louie Aubrey III, Gayle, Mark Edward, Mary Ellen. Chemist, patent liaison Dan River, Inc., Danville, Va., 1946-48, house patent lawyer, asst. dir. research, 1951-52, v.p., dir. research, 1959—; patent searcher Fisher & Christen, Washington, 1948-51; partner Fisher, Christen & Goodson, Washington, 1953-62; dir. Danville Industries, First Fed. Savings & Loan Assn., Danville. Chmn., Danville Planning Commn., 1968—. Trustee, mem. exec. com. Averett Coll.; chmn. bd. trustees Textile Research Inst. Served with AUS, 1943-46. Decorated Silver Star, Bronze Star, Purple Heart. Mem. Am. Textile Mfrs. Inst. (mem. research and tech. service com. 1967—). Am. Assn. Textile Chemists and Colorists, Am. Chem. Soc., Am. Assn. Textile Tech., Am. Patent Law Assn., Va. Mfrs. Assn. (mem. water and air control com. 1965—), Am. Bar Assn. Baptist. Republican. Home: 174 Fairmont Circle Danville VA 24541 Office: 2291 Memorial Dr Danville Va 24541

GOODSON, RAYMOND LYLE, JR., civil engr.; b. Burkburnett, Tex., Dec. 11, 1918; s. Raymond Lyle and Gretchen (Brooks) G.; B.S. in Civil Engring., So. Meth. U., 1941; M.C.E., N.Y.U., 1949; m. Ann Clark Meriwether, Aug. 22, 1947; children—James Lyle, David Meriwether, Sarah Ann. Design engr. Myers & Noyes & Assos., cons. engrs., 1941, 46-48; asst. prof. So. Meth. U. Engring. Sch., 1949-51; project engr. Myers & Noyes, 1951-53; owner, Raymond L. Goodson,

Jr., Inc., cons. engrs., Dallas, 1953—. Mem. Greater Dallas Planning Council, 1967-71; bd. devel. Engr. Sch., So. Meth. U., 1970-71. Served to lt. comdr. USNR, 1941-46. Named Civil Engr. Year, Dallas chpt., Nat. Soc. Profl. Engrs., 1971. Registered profl. engr., Tex. Mem. Cons. Engrs. Council U.S.A. (dir. 1965-67), Am. Soc. C.E. (pres. Dallas br. 1967), Nat. Soc. Profl. Engrs., Cons. Engrs. Council Tex. (pres. 1963), Engrs. Club Dallas. Episcopalian. Club: Lakewood Country (bd. govs. 1970-72) (Dallas). Home: 3708 Alderson St Dallas TX 75204 Office: 2909 Lemmon Av Dallas TX 75214

GOODSON, WALTER KENNETH, bishop; b. Salisbury, N.C., Sept. 25, 1912; s. Daniel Washington and Sarah (Peeler) G.; A.B., Catawba Coll., 1934; postgrad. Duke Div. Sch., 1934-37, D.D., 1960; D.D., High Point Coll., 1951; L.H.D., St. Bernard Coll., 1968; LL.D., U. Ala., 1968; m. Martha Ann Ogburn, July 12, 1937; children—Sarah Ann (Mrs. Larry M. Faust), Walter Kenneth, Nancy Craven (Mrs. Thomas S. Johnson). Ordained to ministry Methodist Ch., 1939; pastor in Western N.C. Conf., 1935-64; bishop Birmingham (Ala.) area, 1964-72, Richmond, Va. area, 1972—. Del. World Conf. Meth. Ch., Oxford, Eng., 1951, Lake Junaluska, N.C., 1956; mem. Mission Team to Gt. Britain, 1962, study team to France and Berlin, 1962. Pres. J.B. Cornelius Found., 1946-64. Trustee Brevard Coll., Miles Coll., Birmingham-So. Coll., Duke U., Athens Coll., Huntingdon Coll. Rotarian, Mason (32 deg.). Home: 211 Massie Rd Richmond VA 23221 Office: 4016 Broad St Richmond VA 23230

GOODWIN, CHARLES JAMES, dentist; b. Opelousas, La., Sept. 24, 1939; s. Charles Moulton and Marguerite (Walker) G.; student La. State U., 1957-59; B.S., U. Southwestern La., 1962; D.D.S., U. Tenn., 1966; m. Lou Ellen James, Dec. 28, 1965; 1 dau., Wendy Bryn. Individual practice dentistry, Hickory, N.C., 1968—. Chmn. dental profession United Fund, 1968, 70, 72. Served with USNR, 1966-68. Mem. Western Piedmont Dental Soc. (v.p. 1971-72, pres. 1972-73), Lambda Chi Alpha, Xi Psi Phi. Republican. Methodist. Club: Lake Hickory Country (dir.). Home: Route 5 Box 928 Hickory NC 28601 Office: 935 4th St Dr NE Hickory NC 28601

GOODWIN, GEORGE EVANS, pub. relations exec.; b. Atlanta, June 20, 1917; s. George and Carrie (Clark) G.; A.B. with cert. in journalism, Washington and Lee U., 1939; m. Lois Milstead, Nov. 2, 1940; children—Clark, Allen. Reporter, Atlanta Georgian, 1939, Charleston (S.C.) News and Courier, 1940; Washington Times-Herald, 1940-41, Miami Daily News, 1941-42; staff writer Atlanta Jour., 1945-52; exec. dir. Central Atlanta Improvement Assn., 1952-54; v.p. First Nat. Bank of Atlanta, 1954-64; exec. v.p. Bell & Stanton, Inc., 1965—; exec. sec. Ga. Senatorial Transit Study Com., 1954; dir Roy D. Warren Co., Bell & Stanton, Inc. Trustee Oglethorp U.; vice chmn. bd. trustees Atlanta Arts Alliance. Served to lt. USNR, 1942-45; PTO. Decorated Purple Heart; recipient Pulitzer Prize for local reporting, 1948; Sigma Delta Chi award for gen. reporting, 1948; A.P. of Ga. award for reporting, 1948 (all for story on Telfair Co. (Ga.) vote frauds), Pall Mall Big Story award, 1949. Mem. Pub. Relations Soc. Am., Delta Tau Delta, Sigma Delta Chi, Omicron Delta Kappa. Democrat. Presbyn. (elder). Home: 3302 Ivanhoe Dr NW Atlanta GA 30327 Office: Suite 2016, Peachtree Center Bldg Atlanta GA 30303

GOODWIN, JACK HOWARD, librarian; b. Columbus, O., Mar. 9, 1921; s. Ernest S. and Lucy Rebecca (Hart) G.; B.A., Olivet Nazarene Coll., 1948; M.L.S., U. Ill., 1949; postgrad. U. Edinburgh (Scotland), 1951-52; m. Mary Ellen Wilson, July 25, 1943; children—James Wilson, Jeremy Philip. Librarian, Va. Theol. Sem., Alexandria, 1954—. Served with AUS, 1942-46. Mem. Am. Theol Library Assn. Home: Box 12111 Alexandria VA 22304

GOODWIN, JAMES MONROE, ins. co. exec.; b. Forest, Miss., Sept. 29, 1937; s. Wilbur R. and Thelma (Spillman) G.; B.S. in Edn., Miss. Coll., 1959; m. Katherine Elizabeth Attridge, Apr. 16, 1959; children— Angela Lynne, Katherine Elizabeth. Coach, tchr., Biloxi (Miss.) Schs., 1959-60; agr. Morris Ins. Agy., Forest, 1960-61; pres. Forest Ins. Agy., Inc., 1961—; adv. dir. Farmers & Merchants Bank, Forest. Housing officer, Forest, 1963—. Vice chmn., bd. dirs. S.E. Lackey Meml. Hosp., Forest. Mem. Miss. Mut. Ins. Agts. Assn. (bd. dirs., pres. elect 1972), Forest C. of C. (v.p. 1965, 71, dir. 1964-66, 71-72). Baptist. Mason (Shriner), Lion (sec.-treas. Forest 1965-68). Club: Forest Country (pres. 1970-71). Address: 104 Sunset Dr Forest MS 39074

GOODWIN, JAMES RANDALL, ins. exec.; b. Trinity, Tex., Apr. 4, 1933;; s. Dan Frank and Ollie (Atkinson) G.; student U. Louisville, 1955; B.S., La. State U., 1956; m. Margaret Ann Lee, June 6, 1959; children—James Randall, Lee Ann, Margaret Lynn, Garland Katherine. Pres., gen. mgr. Goodwin-Gauthier Ins. Agy., Baton Rouge, 1955—; dir. Baton Rouge Bank & Trust Co. Mem. City-Parish Planning and Zoning Commn., Baton Rouge, 1963-64, Recreation and Planning Commn., 1963-64; mem. East Baton Rouge Parish Sch. Bd., 1962-71, v.p., 1968-70, pres., 1971—. Bd. dirs. Baton Rouge Symphony, 1966-67; Baton Rouge Sci. Found. Mem. Nat. Assn. Casualty and Surety Agts. (fed. liaison com. 1966—), Sales and Marketing Execs. Baton Rouge (bd. mem., 2d v.p. 1962), Baton Rouge Ins. Exchange (pres. 1964), Fellowship Christian Athletes (chpt. charter mem.), Baton Rouge C. of C., Better Bus. Bur., Kappa Alpha, Eta Sigma Pi. Presbyn. (elder). Clubs: Audubon Kiwanis (dir., chmn. vocational guidance com. 1968—), L, Baton Rouge Country. Home: 1134 W Lakeview Dr Baton Rouge LA 70810 Office: 3968 North Blvd Baton Rouge LA 70806

GOODWIN, MERRILL HARRY, assn. exec., ret. naval med. officer; b. Selma, Ind., May 19, 1911; s. William and India Moore(Dunkin) G.; student Ball State Coll., 1930-32; B.S., Ind. U., 1934; M.D., 1936; m. Josephine Deanne Voynic, Apr. 1, 1943; children—Michael Anne, Kimberley Dane. Intern U.S. Marine Hosp., Balt., 1936-37; commd. lt. (j.g.), M.C., U.S. Navy, 1937, advanced through grades to capt., 1953; grad. USAAF, Sch. Aviation Medicine, 1938, USN Sch. Aviation Medicine, 1939; designated naval flight surgeon, 1939, naval aviator, 1944; exec. med. officer Naval Air Sta.,Pensacola, Fla., 1948-51; head liaison sect. Bur. Medicine and Surgery, 1951-54; sr. med. officer Naval Air Sta., Barbers Point, Hawaii, 1954-56, Quonset Point, R.I., 1956-59; asst. chief for aviation medicine Bur. Medicine and Surgery, 1959-63; comdg. officer U.S. Naval Hosp., Pensacola, Fla., also dep. comdr. U.S. Naval Aviation Med. Center, 1963-67; ret., 1967; exec. v.p., sec.-treas. Aerospace Med. Assn., Washington, 1967—, also mng. editor Aerospace Medicine. Diplomate Am. Bd. Preventive Medicine (trustee; vice chmn. for aerospace medicine 1968-70). Fellow Aerospace Med. Assn. (exec. council 1962-65), Am. Coll. Preventive Medicine: mem. A.M.A., Am. Pub. Health Assn., Am. Inst. Aeros. and Astronautics, Am. Soc. Assn. Execs., Internat. Acad. Aviation and Space Medicine, Am. Assn. Med. Soc. Execs., Profl. Conv. Mgmt. Assn., Quiet Birdmen, Alpha Omega Alpha, Phi Beta Pi. Home: 1321 Macbeth St McLean VA 22101 Office: Aerospace Med Assn Washington Nat Airport Washington DC 20001

GOODWIN, ROBERT LEWIS, oil and gas corp. exec.; b. Dublin, Tex., Aug. 30, 1924; s. Ernest Lloyd and Iva (Whisenant) G.; B.S. in Econs., Centenary Coll. La., 1950; m. Jessica Harris, Dec. 21, 1948. Dist. Landman Mid-Continent Petroleum Corp., Shreveport, La., 1948-50, Seaboard Oil Co., New Orleans, 1950-58; with Exchange Oil & Gas Corp., New Orleans, 1962—, exec. v.p., dir., 1969—. Mem. Mid-Continent Oil and Gas Assn., Ind. Petroleum Assn. Am., Council for Better La., C. of C., Am. Assn. Petroleum Landmen. Clubs: Petroleum, Plimsoll (New Orleans). Home: 1594 Jefferson Av New Orleans LA 70115 Office: 1010 Common St New Orleans LA 70112

GOODWIN, WILLIAM CARROLL, JR., pedodontist; b. Durham, N.C., Dec. 29, 1941; s. William Carroll and Gretchen Louise (Willard) G.; B.S., East Carolina U., 1963; D.D.S., U. N.C. Sch. Dentistry, 1967, M.S., 1971. Individual practice pedodontics, Fayetteville, N.C., 1971—; asso. staff Cape Fear Valley Hosp., Fayetteville. Asst. clin. prof. pedodontics U. N.C. Sch. Dentistry, Chapel Hill, 1971-72. Served to lt. USNR, 1967-69. Mem. Am. Dental Assn., N.C. Dental Soc., Am. Soc. Clin. Hypnosis, Kappa Alpha. Episcopalian. Contbr. articles to profl. jours. Home: 14-J Briar Circle Fayetteville NC 28306 Office: 3415-B Melrose Rd Fayetteville NC 28304

GOODWYN, JOHN LANCASTER, justice Ala. Supreme Ct.; b. Montgomery, Ala., Oct. 13, 1903; s. Robert Tyler and Jessie (Lancaster) G.; A.B., U. Ala., 1925, LL.B., 1926; m. Elizabeth Hudson Hill, Apr. 16, 1931; children—Warren Hudson, Elizabeth Lancaster. Admitted to Ala. bar, 1926; gen. practice, 1926-40, city atty. Montgomery, 1931-40; mayor Montgomery, 1946-51; legal adviser to Gov. Ala., 1951; asso. justice Supreme Court of Ala., 1951—. Served from capt. to col., U.S. Army, 1940-46. Decorated Legion of Merit, Bronze Star with oak leaf cluster Bronze Arrow Head. Mem. Phi Delta Phi, Omicron Delta Kappa. Presbyn. Mason (Shriner). Home: 1567 Gilmer Av Montgomery AL 36104 Office: State Judicial Bldg Dexter Av Montgomery AL 36104

GOODWYN, OTIS JAMES, lawyer, state legislator; b. Warrior, Ala., Dec. 12, 1920; B.S., LL.B., U. Ala.; m. Mary Chalmers Hair; children—Otis James, Susan Anne. Admitted to bar, 1949; mem. firm Goodwyn & Smith, Montgomery, Goodwyn & Smith, Montgomery, Ala; mem Ala. Ho. of Reps., 1954, 58, 62-66, Ala. Senate, 1967—, pres. protem, pres., 1968-69. Am., Ala. bar assns., Phi Alpha Delta, So. Regional Educ. Bd., Nat. Council State Govts. (bd.), C. of C., Jaycees, Exchange Club, K.P., Am. Legion. Presbyn. Address: 325 Bell Bldg Montgomery AL 36104 also Capital Bldg Montgomery AL

GOODYKOONTZ, CHARLES ALFRED, mng. editor Richmond (Va.) Times-Dispatch. Address: 333 E Grace St Richmond VA 23219*

GOOLSBY, THOMAS MORRIS, JR., educator, psychologist; b. Wetumpka, Ala., Apr. 3, 1932; s. Thomas Morris and Lottie Mae (Collier) G.; B.S., U. Ala., 1954; M.Ed., Auburn U., 1960; Ph.D., U. Ia., 1963. Tchr. sci. Robert E. Lee High Sch., Montgomery, Ala., 1958-59, Ramey Base Schs., P.R., 1959-60; research asst. psychol. measurement U. Ia., 1960-63; prof. ednl. psychology, measurement and statistics U. So. Cal., 1963-64; prof. Fla. State U., Tallahassee, 1964-68, dir. univ. test service, 1965-68; prof. U. Ga., Athens, 1968—, asso. dir., research and devel. center in ednl. stimulation, 1969. Measurement and research cons. pub. schs., govtl. agys. and pvt. enterprise. Served to 1st lt. AUS, 1955-57. Mem. Am. Psychol. Assn., Am. Ednl. Research Assn., Am. Acad. Polit. and Social Sci., A.A.A.S., Nat. Soc. Study Edn., Nat. Council Measurement Edn., U.K. Reading Assn., Theta Chi. Episcopalian. Club: Civitan. Contbr. articles to publs. Home: 20 Glenn Forest Athens GA 30603

GOORLEY, JOHN THEODORE, educator; b. Galion, O., Mar. 12, 1907; s. William H. and Emma (Ness) G.; B.S., Ohio State U., 1930; M.S., Purdue U., 1932, Ph.D., 1934; m. Ethel L. Coleman, Nov. 27, 1935; children—John, Alice (Mrs. Harold A. Breard, Jr.), Robert, Richard. Chief control chemist Burroughs Wellcome & Co., Tuckahoe, N.Y., 1933-38; research dir. Labs. Lex, Havana, Cuba, 1939-42, Ben Venue Labs., Bedford, O., 1946-48, Johnson & Johnson de Argentina, Buenos Aires, 1948-50; owner, dir. Labs. Goorley, Buenos Aires, 1950-55; prof. pharm. chemistry Ohio No. U., Ada, 1956-57; v.p., gen. mgr. Inland Alkaloid Co., Tipton, Ind., 1957-58; prof. pharm. chemistry N.E. La. U., Monroe, 1958-68, prof. pharmacognosy, 1968—. Fulbright prof. U. Honduras, 1966-67, cons., 1967—; vis. prof. U. El Salvador, 1968; cons. pharm. industries. Active Little Theater, Monroe. Served to capt. AUS, 1942-46. Col. staff govs. Ky., La. Mem. Am. Pharm. Assn., Am. Chem. Soc., A.A.A.S., Sigma Xi, Rho Chi, Phi Delta Chi, Tau Kappa Epsilon. Research in pharm. chemistry and biochemistry. Contbr. articles to profl. jours. Patentee in field. Home: Route 1 Box 298C West Monroe LA 71291 Office: Route 1 Box 298 C West Monroe LA 71291

GOOSETREE, ROBERT E., lawyer, educator; b. Montgomery County, Tenn., Sept. 23, 1923; B.A., Southwestern U. at Memphis, 1943; M.A., Ia. State U., 1948; Ph.D., 1950; J.D. summa cum laude, Am. U., 1962. Admitted to D.C. bar, 1962; asst. dean Sch. Govt. and Pub. Adminstrn., Am. U., Washington, 1958-62, acting dean, 1959-60, 62-63, prof., 1963—; lectr. law Washington Coll. Law, 1962-63, prof., 1963—, dir. admissions, 1967-68, acting dean, 1970—. Cons. John F. Kennedy Center for Performing Arts, Washington, 1967—. Mem. Task Force on Zoning Procedures, Mountgomery County, Md., 1966-67. Mem. Fed., Am. bar assns., Order of Artus, Pi Sigma Alpha, Omicron Delta Kappa. Contbr. articles to profl. pubs. Office: 1819 H St NW Washington DC 20006*

GORDON, CHESTER MURRAY, govt. ofcl.; b. N.Y.C., Mar. 31, 1918; s. Michael and Bess (Wassell) G.; B.S., City Coll. N.Y., 1938, M.S., 1943; postgrad. Am. U., 1941-42, George Washington U., 1947-48; m. Ruth B. Herson, June 28, 1942; children—Jeffrey B., Shelley B. Free-lance reporter various newspapers, 1934-40; asst. operations chief Bur. Census, Washington, 1940-42; statis. analyst WPB, Washington, 1942-48; mgmt. analyst Dept. Navy, Washington, 1948; indsl. specialist ODM, Washington, 1951-53; with AEC, Washington, 1948-51, 1953—, def. coordinator 1964-71, relocation officer, chief personal property mgmt., 1971—. Real estate investor, Washington, 1956-59. Bd. dirs. Found. Retarded Children, Washington, 1959—, Home for Aged, Rockville, Md., 1963—. Served with Signal Corps, AUS, 1943-46. Mem. Am. Statis. Assn. Mason. Home: 9209 Watson Rd Silver Spring MD 20910 Office: AEC Washington DC 20545

GORDON, DOUGLAS LITTLETON, physician; b. Baton Rouge, Mar. 15, 1924; s. Amos Kilgore and Irma Ruth (John) G.; student La. State U., 1941-43; M.D., Tulane U., 1946; m. Betty Pauline Bishop, Nov. 29, 1947 (dec. Sept. 1960); children—Douglas Littleton, Pamela Gayle; m. 2d, Florence Cecilia Vine, Dec. 30, 1961; children—Stephen Vine, Stewart Thomas. Intern Charity Hosp., New Orleans, 1946-47; fellow in internal medicine Ochsner Clinic, 1947-49; clin. asso. Endocrine Research Lab., Alton Ochsner Med. Found., 1949-51, 53-57; practice medicine specializing in internal medicine and endocrinology, Baton Rouge, 1954—; instr. medicine Tulane U. Sch. Medicine, 1949-51, 53-57; mem. staff sect. endocrinology Ochsner clinic, 1949-51, 53-57; asst. vis. physician Charity Hosp., Tulane unit, 1951; vis. physician, 1953-57, vis. physician La. State U. unit, 1957-61, sr. vis. physician, 1961—; vis. staff Baton Rouge Gen. Hosp., 1954—, chief staff, 1967; vis. staff Our lady of Lake Hosp., Baton Rouge, 1954—; cons. internal medicine East La. State Hosp., Jackson, 1961-63; dep. coroner East Baton Rouge Parish, 1955-70; mem. staff sect. medicine Baton Rouge Clinic, 1959—; clin. asst. prof. medicine La. State U. Sch. Medicine, 1957-62, clin. asso. prof. medicine, 1962-67, clin. prof. medicine, 1967—. Served to capt., M.C., USAF, 1951-53. Diplomate Am. Bd. Internal Medicine. Fellow A.C.P.; mem. A.M.A., Am. Fedn. Clin. Research, Endocrine Soc., A.A.A.S., Am. Diabetes Assn., So. Med. Assn., So. Soc. Clin. Research, N.Y. Acad. Scis., La. State, East Baton Rouge Parish med. socs., New Orleans Acad. Internal Medicine, Baton Rouge Acad. Inernal Medicine (pres. 1962), Sigma Xi, Alpha Omega Alpha. Episcopalian. Contbr. articles to profl. jours. Home: 4534 Woodside Dr Baton Rouge LA 70808 Office: 134 N 19th St Baton Rouge LA 70808

GORDON, EUGENE ANDREW, dist. judge; b. Guilford County, N.C., July 10, 1917; s. Charles Robert and Carrie (Scott) G.; A.B., Elon Coll., 1938; LL.B., Duke, 1941; m. Virginia Stoner, Jan. 1, 1943; children—Eugene Andrew, Rosemary Anne. Admitted to N.C. bar, 1941; practice of law, 1946-64; mem. firm Young, Young & Gordon, Burlington, 1947-64; solicitor Alamance Gen. County Ct., 1947-54; county atty., Alamance County, 1954-64; U.S. judge Middle Dist. N.C., 1964—. Past chmn. adv. bd. Salvation Army. Past nat. committeeman N.C. Young Democrats; past pres. Alamance County Young Dems.; chmn. Alamance County Dem. Exec. Com., 1954-64. Served to capt. AUS, 1942-46; comdg. officer N.G., Burlington, 1946-47. Mem. Alamance County Bar Assn. (past pres.), Burlington-Alamance County C. of C. (past pres.), Phi Delta Phi. Rotarian (past pres.). Club: American Business (Burlington). Home: PO Box 3285 Greensboro NC 27402 Office: Greensboro NC 27402

GORDON, HAMILTON ADAIR, JR., assn. exec.; b. East Orange, N.J., Feb. 24, 1912; s. Hamilton Adair and Caroline (Cochrane) G.; student Newark Sch. Fine Arts, 1931-33, N.Y.U., 1934, C. of C. Insts., 1948-63; m. Margaret C. Morris, Mar. 3, 1938; children—Nancy Cora, Thomas Kipp, Jane Adair. With Catlin-Farish Co., Inc., N.Y.C., 1932-33; bus. mgr. Crow Rock Ranch, Miles City, Mont., 1934-47; exec. v.p. Miles City C. of C., 1948-56; owner, operator motel, Ocala, Fla., 1957-60; exec. v.p. Putnam County C. of C., Palatka, Fla., 1961—. Mem. Mont. Gov.'s State Land Com., 1944-45. Bd. dirs. Rocky Mountain Isnt., 1955-56. Mem. Am., Fla. (dir.) C. of C. execs., Fla. Crown Council of Chambers Commerce (past pres.). Elk. Home: 123 Crestwood Av Palatka FL 32077 Office: Box 550 Palatka FL 32077

GORDON, HUGH WESCOTT, JR., constrn. co. exec.; b. Houston, Sept. 25, 1926; s. Hugh Wescott and Hattie Florence (Tate) G.; student Rice U., 1943-44; B.B.A., U. Tex., 1948; m. Ann Holmes Gordon, Oct. 7, 1956; children—Michael Wescott, William Edward, Raleigh Ann. With Brown & Root, Inc., Houston, 1951—, exec. v.p., 1971—, also dir.; v.p., dir. Brown & Root subsidiary cos.; v.p., dir. Jackson Marine Co., Taylor Diving & Salvage Co., Locher Constrn. Co. Served with USNR, 1944-46. Mem. Kappa Alpha. Clubs: Petroleum, Racquet, (Houston). Home: 930 Briar Ridge Rd Houston TX 77027 Office: PO Box 3 Houston TX 77001

GORDON, JAMES FLEMING, dist. judge; b. Madisonville, Ky., May 18, 1918; s. John F. and Ruby (James) G.; LL.B., U. Ky., 1941; m. Iola Young, Sept. 1, 1942; children—Maurice K. II, James Fleming, Marianna. Admitted to Ky. bar, 1941; practiced in Madisonville, 1941-65; chief judge U.S. Dist. Ct., Western Dist. Ky., Louisville, 1965—. Chmn., Ky. Pub. Service Commn., 1955-59. Speakers chmn. Ky. Democratic Com., 1955, campaign chmn., 1962. Bd. dirs. Clinic Found., Madisonville. Served to 1st lt., Judge Adv. Gen. Dept., AUS, 1941-46; PTO. Mem. Am. Coll. Trial Lawyers, Am. Legion, V.F.W., Phi Delta Phi. Home: 402 Mockingbird Hill Rd Louisville KY 40207 Office: Fed Bldg Louisville KY 40202

GORDON, LINCOLN, polit. economist.; b. N.Y.C., Sept. 10, 1913; s. Bernard and Dorothy (Lerned) G.; A.B., Harvard, 1933; D.Phil. (Rhodes scholar), Oxford U. (Eng.), 1936; LL.D., Fairleigh Dickinson U., 1965, Columbia, 1967, Rutgers U., 1967, U. Md., 1968, Wash. Coll., 1968, U. Del., 1969; L.H.D., Loyola Coll., Balt., 1968; m. Allison Wright, June 25, 1937; children—Anne, Robert W., Hugh, Amy. Instr., faculty instr. govt. Harvard, 1936-41, William Ziegler prof. internat. econ. relations, 1955-61; research technician water, energy resources, U.S. Nat. Resources Planning Bd., Washington, 1939-1940; sr. econ. analyst adv. commn. Council Nat. Def., Washington, 1940; mem. staff requirements com. W.P.B., 1942, asst. and dep.-dir. program bur., 1943-44, dir. program bur., 1944, dep. vice chmn. program, 1944-45, program vice chmn., 1945; dir. bur. reconversion priorities Civilian Prodn. Adminstrn., 1945-46; asso. prof. bus. Harvard, 1946-47, prof. govt. and adminstrn., 1947-50; cons. U.S. Rep. UN AEC, 1946, Army and Navy Munitions Bd., Dept. of State, 1947, ECA, 1948; North Atlantic Council Com. of Three on non-mil. aspects of NATO, 1956; dir. program div. Office ECA spl. rep. in Europe, 1949-50; econ. adviser to spl. asst. to Pres., 1950-51; asst. dir. for Mut. Security Agy., 1951-52, chief mission to U.K., 1952-55, minister econ. affairs in Am. embassy, London, 1952-55; U.S. ambassador to Brazil, 1961-66; asst. sec. state for inter-Am. affairs, 1966-67; pres. Johns Hopkins U., Balt., 1967-71; prof. polit. economy Johns Hopkins Sch. Advanced Internat. Studies, Washington, 1971—. Dir. Equitable Life Assurance Soc. U.S. Bd. dirs. Center Inter-Am. Relations; trustee Com. for Econ. Devel. Decorated Grand Cross Order Quetzal (Guatemala); Grand Cross Order Cruzeiro do Sul (Brazil). Fellow Am. Acad. Arts and Scis.; mem. Am. Polit. Sci. Assn., A.A.A.S., Am. Econ. Assn. Council on Foreign Relations, Royal Econ. Soc., Am. Council Edn. (overseas devel. council), Phi Beta Kappa, etc. Club: Cosmos (Washington). Author: The Public Corporation in Great Britain, 1938; Government and the American Economy (with M. Fainsod), 1941, rev. edit. 1948; Fuel and Power in Industrial Location and National Policy, Nat. Resources Planning Bd., 1942; Representation of the U.S. Abroad (in part), 1956, rev. edit. 1964; (with Engelbert L. Grommers) United States Manufacturing Investment in Brazil, 1961; A New Deal for Latin America, 1963. Editor: Internat. Stability and Progress; U.S. Interests and Instruments, 1957; Fgn. Trade Policy, House Ways and Means Com., 1957. Contbr. articles and book revs. to periodicals. Home: 3069 University Terrace NW Washington DC 20016 Office: Johns Hopkins Sch Advanced Internat Studies 1740 Massachusetts Av NW Washington DC 20036

GORDON, M. MICHAEL, judge; b. San Francisco, Dec. 21, 1911; s. Rudolph and Sarah (Mesinger) G.; B.A., St. Ignatius Coll., 1931; LL.B., U. San Francisco, 1935. Admitted to Tex. bar, 1935, since practiced in Houston; now mem. firm M. Michael Gordon; judge Houston Municipal Ct., 1962—; dir., gen. counsel Sterling Electronics, Inc., Houston. Founder, Teenage Jury System, 1964, judge, 1964—. Pres. Juvenile Delinquency and Crime Commn., Houston 1958-59. Mem. bd. Houston Bd. Pub. Welfare, 1948-56; Bd. dirs. Am. Acad. Jud. Edn., 1970—, Nat. Center for State Cts., 1971—. Served to capt., USAAF, 1942-46. Recipient Disneyland trophy for achievement in reducing juvenile delinquency in U.S. and Can., Nat. Assn. Municipal Judges, 1965. Mem. N.Am. Judges Assn. (gov. 1965—, treas. 1965-66, pres. 1969-70), Am., Houston bar assns., State Bar Tex. Am. Judicature Soc. (dir. 1969-70). Mason (Shriner). Home: 2014 Southgate Houston TX 77025 Office: 5017 Fanin St Houston TX 77004

GORDON, MAURICE MELBOURNE, physician; b. Jamaica, West Indies, Nov. 12, 1905; s. Claudius Alexander and Henrietta (Morrison) G.; came to U.S., 1923, naturalized, 1941; B.S., Howard U., 1929, M.D., 1932; postgrad. eye, ear, nose and throat N.Y. Polyclinic Med. Sch., 1947-48; m. Irene Constance Dabney, June 25, 1938; 1 son, Claudius Alexander II. Intern, Freedmen's Hosp., Washington 1932-33; resident eye, ear, nose and throat Harlem Hosp., 1948-49; gen. practice medicine, Martinsville, Va., 1936-47, practice medicine specializing in eye, ear, nose and throat, Richmond, Va., 1950-—. Vice pres. Union Mut. Savs. & Loan Assn. Chmn. bd. dirs. Peoples Polit. and Civic League, 1959-—; Richmond Democratic committeeman, 1967-—. Mem. Nat., Old Dominion (com. chmn.) med. socs., Phi Beta Sigma. Baptist (trustee). Home: 2706 Griffin Av Richmond VA 23222 Office: 418 N 1st St Richmond VA 23219

GORDON, RICHARD F., JR., profl. football club exec., former astronaut; b. Seattle, Oct. 5, 1929; s. Richard F. and Angela Gordon; B.S. in Chemistry, U. Wash., 1951; postgrad. U.S. Naval Post Grad Sch., Monterey; m. Barbara Jean Field; children—Carleen Elizabeth, Richard F. III, Lawrence Joseph, Thomas Alan, James Edward, Diane Marie. Entered U.S. Navy, 1951, advanced through grades to capt., grad. All-Weather Flight Sch., Test Pilot Sch.; astronaut NASA Manned Spacecraft Center, Houston; pilot Gemini XI, 1966; command module pilot Apollo XII, 1969; ret., 1972; exec. v.p. New Orleans Saints Profl. Football Club, 1972-—. Winner Bendix Trophy Race from Los Angeles to N.Y., 1961. Mem. Soc. Exptl. Test Pilots. Office: 944 St Charles Av New Orleans LA 70130

GORDON, ROBERT LATIMER, JR., banker; b. Richmond, Va., Dec. 3, 1908; s. R. Latimer and Anne Moore (Talbott) G.; student McGuire's U. Sch., Richmond, Va., 1915-25, Episcopal High Sch., Alexandria, Va., 1925-27, U. Va., 1927-29; m. Charlotte Faulconer Epps, June 25, 1936 (dec. 1968); 1 dau., Charlotte Latimer; m. 2d, Lucylle Corey Farmer, Sept. 22, 1969. With First & Merchants Nat. Bank of Richmond, 1929-—, v.p., trust officer, 1951-62, exec. v.p., 1962-66, pres., 1966-68, chmn., 1968-—; also dir. Pres. Estate Planning Council of Richmond, 1962. Vice pres. Richmond area Community Chest, 1954, 58, campaign gen., 1956; chmn. Richmond-Henrico chpt. Nat. Found. Infantile Paralysis, 1954. Chmn. St. Catherine's Sch., Richmond, 1960-63; mem. bd. Sheltering Arms Hosp., v.p., treas. Richmond Eye Hosp., 1952-—; bd. govs., exec. com. United Givers Fund, 1963-68; bd. dirs. J. Sergeant Reynolds Community Coll. Served to lt. comdr. USNR, 1942-45. Mem. Assn. Res. City Bankers, Phi Kappa Psi. Episcopalian (vestry 1949-52, 59-62, treas. 1959-62). Clubs: Commonwealth, Country of Va. (mem. bd., sec.-treas. 1957-59); Downtown (bd. 1962-63) (Richmond). Home: 706 Tiber Lane Richmond VA Office: 9th and Main Sts Richmond VA

GORDON, ROBERT WILLARD, banker; b. Rochester, N.Y., Oct. 1, 1916; s. Nicholas and Evelyn (Lazarus) Gordon; A.B., Harvard, 1938; m. June Elaine Mailman, June 17, 1945; children—Spencer Bruce, Jonathan Richard, Jill Mia. Free lance radio and mag. writer, 1938-42; pres. Robert Gordon Co., Ltd., Montreal, Can., 1946-52; pres. Miramar Corp., real estate devel., Hollywood, Fla., 1952-60; sr. v.p. Hollywood Bank, 1960-—, also dir.; dir. Am. Savs. & Loan Assn. Fla., Miami Beach. Mem. Hollywood Planning Bd., 1962-64; pres. Mental Health Assn. Broward County, 1963-68; Jewish Welfare Fedn., 1969-70; mem. planning bd. S. Broward Hosp. Dist., 1971-—. Mayor, City of Miramar, Fla., 1955-59. Bd. dirs United Fund Broward County, 1965-67. Served with AUS, 1942-46. Mem. Jewish Religion. Clubs: Harvard (Broward County, Fla.), Ocean Reef Yacht (Key Largo, Fla.), Hollywood Yacht. Writer and dir. scripts on network radio, 1939-41. Contbr. articles and short stories Saturday Evening Post, 1936-45. Home: 20001 S Surf Rd Hollywood FL 33020 Office: 1900 Tyler St Hollywood FL 33022

GORDON, ROY IRVING, govt. ofcl.; b. Peekskill, N.Y., Jan. 7, 1921; s. Samuel and Leah (Blaine) G.; B.A., L.I. U., 1941; M.A., N.Y. U., 1942; m. Ethel J. Shohet, Aug. 26, 1951; children—Frederick E., Elizabeth J. Reporter, suburban news editor, columnist Ossining (N.Y.) Citizen Register, 1947-50; religious news, edn. news editor Mt. Vernon (N.Y.), Daily Argus, 1950-53; editor Fall River (Mass.) Transcript, 1953-54; news bur. chief Yankee Mut. Radio Sta. WALE, Fall River, Mass., 1954-55; copy editor N.Y. World Telegram and Sun, 1955-57; with Pub. Affairs office C.E., U.S. Army, Washington, 1958-—, asst. for news media, 1961-—. Prof. journalism U. Md., part-time, 1966-—; adj. prof. journalism Georgetown U., Washington, 1970-—. Vice pres. Alexandria Council P.T.A., 1966-69; sec. Govt. Information Orgn., 1970-71. Served to lt. col. AUS, 1942-45, 60-62. Decorated Bronze Star, Silver Star, Purple Heart. Mem. Pub. Relations Soc. Am., Assn. Edn. Journalism. Club: National Press. Contbr. articles, stories to mags. Home: 601 Prospect Pl Alexandria VA 22304 Office: Forrestal Bldg Army Corps Engrs Washington DC 20314

GORDON, RUTH EVANS (MRS. RALPH GORDON), civic worker; b. Bloomington, Ill.; d. Newton Wallace and Bessie (Holcomb) Evans; student Bethany (W.Va.) Coll.; m. John Paul O'Boyle, Nov. 26, 1936 (div. 1942); children—Ruth (Mrs. James J. Cooke Jr.), Paul Theodore; m. 2d Ralph Gordon, Feb. 12, 1945. Sec.-treas. Pass Christian (Miss.) C. of C.,1962-71, exec. sec., adminstr., 1971-—; sec. Pass Christian Civil Def., 1964-68; sec. to mayor City of Pass Christian, 1968-—; past pres. Harrison County Humane Soc. Recipient Nat. Dog World award, 1965. Mem. Miss. Coast Kennel Club (past dir.), United Spanish War Vets. Aux. (past dept. pres.), Bull Terrier Club Am., Bull Terrier Club Eng., Minature Bull Terrier Club Am. (organizer), Miniature Bull Terrior Club (Eng.), V.F.W. (past pres.). Mem. Christian Ch. Mem. Order Eastern Star. Home: 152 Boisdore Av Pass Christian MS 39571 Office: City Hall Pass Christian MS 39571

GORDON, THOMAS CHRISTIAN, JR., lawyer; b. Richmond, Va., July 14, 1915; s. Thomas Christian and Ruth (Robins) G.; grad. Episcopal High Sch., Alexandria, Va., 1932; B.S., U. Va., 1936, LL.B., 1938. Admitted to Va. bar, 1937; asso. firm Parrish, Butcher & Parrish, Richmond, 1938-40; asso. firm McGuire, Woods & Battk and predecessor, Richmond, 1940-48, partner, 1949-65, 72-—, asso. justice Supreme Ct. Va., Richmond, 1965-72. Lectr., U. Va. Law Sch. Trustee, mem. exec. com. Crippled Children's Hosp., 1948-—, pres., 1954-59. Served from pvt. to maj., AUS, 1941-45. Decorated Bronze Star with oak leaf cluster. Mem. Am., Va. State (pres. 1963-64), Richmond bar assns., Am. Law Inst., Va. State Bar. Episcopalian (vestryman). Contbr. articles to law revs. Home: 300 W Franklin St Richmond VA 23220 Office: 1400 Loss Bldg Richmond VA 23219

GORDON, THOMAS EDWIN, JR., dentist; b. Orlando, Fla., Sept. 12, 1925; s. Thomas Edwin and Lillian (Stover) G.; D.D.S., Emory U., 1948; m. Jeanne Love, Nov. 19, 1949; children—Tina Lynne, Thomas Gary, Karen Anne. Pvt. practice dentistry Decatur, Ga., 1948-50, Orlando, Fla., 1951-53, 1955-—; cons. dentistry in space; attending staff Orange Meml. Hosp., chief laser lab. Bd. dirs. Orange County unit Am. Cancer Soc; trustee Central Fla. Mus. and Planetarium, sec. bd. trustees, 1960-61, chmn. finance com., 1963-—; trustee Constantine Found. Served from 1st lt. to capt. USAF, 1953-55. Fellow Royal Soc. Health; mem. Internat. Soc. Dental Research, Am. Dental Assn., Am. Acad. Implant Dentistry, Soc. Occlusion and Oral Physiology, Am. Acad. Maxillo Facial Prosthesis, Sigma Xi (hon.), Sigma Chi. Author articles publ. profl. jours. Research laser in dentistry and med. research; developer 1st laser welding system and technique for dentistry. Home: 1410 N Westmoreland Dr Orlando FL 32804 Office: 550 N Bumby Av Orlando FL 32803

GORDON, WALTER ARTHUR, dist. judge; b. Atlanta, Oct. 10, 1894; s. Henry B. and Georgia (Bryant) G.; A.B., U. Cal. at Berkeley, 1918, J.D., 1922, LL.D., 1958; m. Elizabeth Fisher, July 22, 1920; children—Walter, Edwin, Betty. Policeman, City of Berkeley, Cal., 1919-30; asst. football coach U. Cal. at Berkeley, 1919-43; admitted to Cal. bar, 1923, practiced law, 1923-44; atty. Golden State Ins. Co., Cal., 1935-44, adminstrv. adviser, 1944-—; gov. V.I., 1955-58; judge Dist. Ct. of V.I., 1958-—. Chmn. Adult Authority, State of Cal., 1945-55. Bd. dirs. YMCA. Mem. Am. Prison Assn., Nat., Cal. parole and probation assns., Alpha Phi Alpha. Elk. Club: Commonwealth (San Francisco). Office: District Court Charlotte Amalie St Thomas VI 00801

GORDON, WILLIAM TALBOTT, banker; b. Richmond, Va., Sept. 4, 1914; s. Robert Latimer and Anne (Talbott) G.; student U. Va., 1934-36; m. Eleanor Stuart Holladay, Aug. 23, 1943; children—Ellen S. (Mrs. Jesse Frank Williams), William Talbot, Anne M., James H. With Bank of Va., Richmond, 1936-—, now pres., dir.; dir. Royal Sch. Labs., Inc., Ashland, Va., 1958-66, Apex Machine Mfg. Co., Inc., Richmond, 1959-64. Chmn. Va. Found. for Ind. Jr. Colls., 1969-71. Treas., bd. dirs. Va. Thanksgiving Festival, Inc.; bd. dirs. League Planned Parenthood. Served to lt. USNR, 1942-45. Mem.Am. Inst. Banking, Va., Richmond chambers commerce, Va. Soc. Creepers. Clubs: Commonwealth, Downtown (dir.) (Richmond). Home: 9912 Drouin Dr Richmond VA 23229 Office: 800 E Main St Richmond VA 23214

GORE, ALBERT ARNOLD, U.S. senator; b. Granville, Tenn., Dec. 26, 1907; s. Allen and Margie (Denny) G.; B.S., State Tchrs. Coll., Murfreesboro, Tenn., 1932; LL.B., YMCA Night Law Sch., Nashville, Tenn., 1936; m. Pauline La Fon, Apr. 17, 1937; children—Nancy, Albert. Admitted to Tenn. bar, 1936, practiced in Carthage, Tenn.; commr. of labor State of Tenn., 1936-37; mem. 76th to 82d congresses from 4th Tenn. Dist.; U.S. senator from Tenn., 1953-—. Mem. Tenn. Edn. Assn. Democrat. Baptist. Home: Carthage TN 37030

GORE, BLANCHE ALLBRITTON (MRS. WILLIAM FRANK GORE), educator, nutritionist; b. Houston, Mar. 3, 1921; d. Luther Lafayette and Lois Jesse (Saunders) Allbritton; student Tex. Women's U., 1938-40; B.S., U. Tex., 1945, M.S., 1947; m. Richard Royster Royall, May 3, 1941 (dec. Dec. 1945); 1 son, Richard Royster III; m. 2d, William Frank Gore, Aug. 23, 1947. Home econs. food cons., nutritionist, Allbritton's Cafeterias, Houston, 1947-—; asso. prof. home econs., U. Houston, 1947-—, chmn. dept., 1964-67. Active Home Econs. Scholarship Group, Houston, 1950-—. Mem. Tex. Nutrition Council. Mem. Am., Tex., S.W. Tex. dietetic assns., Am., Tex., Houston (past pres.) home econs. assns., Home Economists in Bus., Elec. Women's Round Table Tex. (former treas.), Tex. Restaurant Assn. Women's Aux., Zeta Tau Alpha. Rotary Ann. Research work for Latin Am. countries, 1963-—; research work in cereals, 1964-—. Adv. editor Favorite Recipes of Texas, 1964; Favorite Recipes of Texas Meats, 1965. Home: 827 Kuhlman Rd Houston TX 77024

GORE, BLINZY LEE, lawyer, coll. dean; b. Hinton, W.Va., June 13, 1921; s. Isaiah E. and Cora (Pack) G.; B.S. in Edn., W.Va. State Coll., 1945; J.D., State U. Ia., 1950; M.A., N.Y.U., 1958, Ph.D., 1967; m. Gloria Alease Bultman, Oct. 3, 1951; children— Brian Douglass, William Bultman. Admitted to S.C. bar, 1950, since practiced in Orangeburg; asso. prof. law S.C. State Coll., 1950-57, prof., 1958-66, asso. prof. social sci., 1966; dean instrn. Claflin Coll., Orangeburg, 1967-—. Democratic precinct committeeman, 1969. Bd. dirs. Edisto Fed. Credit Union, Orangeburg br. N.A.A.C.P. Served with AUS, 1943-46; PTO. Recipient Distinguished Student award N.Y.U., 1967. Mem. Am., S.C., Ia. State bar assns., N.E.A., S.C. Edn. Assn., Am. Assn. U. Profs., Am. Trial Lawyers Assn., Am. Conf. Acad. Deans, Kappa Alpha Psi. Home: State College Box 1837 Orangeburg SC 29115

GORE, CHARLES MINOR, lawyer; b. Johnson City, Tenn., Oct. 26, 1910; s. Benjamin Stone and Helen (Hayward) G.; A.B., Vanderbilt U., 1933; postgrad. Harvard Law Sch., 1933-34; LL.B., U. Tenn., 1936; m. Mildred Anne Smith, June 20, 1937; children—Charles Smith, Anne Hayward. Admitted to Tenn. bar, 1936; mem. firm Gore & Gore, 1937-54, Gore, Gore & McIntyre, Bristol, Tenn., 1954-63, Gore & Gore, 1963-65, Gore, Gore and Ladd, 1965-68, Gore, Ladd and Gillenwater, 1968-—. Asst. sec., dir. Appalachian Broadcasting Corp., WCYB-TV, 1946-—; sec. Strong-Robinette Bag Co., Inc., 1953-—; dir. Gen. Shale Products Corp., Johnson City. Bd. dirs. United Fund., 1957-59. Served from lt. (j.g.) to lt., USNR, 1943-46. Mem. Am., Tenn., Bristol bar assns. Presbyn. Democrat. Home: Lick Branch Rd Bristol TN 37620 Office: Central Bldg Bristol TN 37620

GORE, HENRY GRADY, real estate broker; b. Belwood, Tenn., Feb. 10, 1895; s. Benton Lemuel and Mary Pondexter (Sampson) G.; LL.B., Cumberland U., 1915, J.D., 1969; m. Jamie Shorter, Apr. 24, 1915; children—Henry Grady, Mary Benton (Mrs. Gordon E. Dean), James Grafton, Louise. Admitted to Tenn. bar, 1915; pvt. practice, Gainesboro, 1915-22; mem. firm Hamilton & Gore, Lebanon and Gainesboro, Tenn., 1922-24; financial corr. Todd Bond & Mortgage Co., Roanoke, Va., 1924-29; real estate broker, Washington, 1929-—; dir. Nat. Mortgage Co., Washington, Atlantic Research Corp., Alexandria, Va., Nuclear Sci. & Engring. Corp., Pitts. Apptd. Col. Tenn. Gov.'s staff, 1939, apptd. col., a.d.c., 1945; mem. Md. Econ. Devel. Commn., 1967-70. Republican candidate for U.S. Senate, 1952. Pres. Montgomery County (Md.) Hist. Soc., 1953-55; mem. Internat. Employees Loyalty Bd., 1952-62. Club: Congressional Country (Bethesda, Md.). Home: 11300 River Rd Rockville MD 20854 Office: 2100 Massachusetts Av NW Washington DC 20008

GORE, JACK WARTER, newspaper editor, pub.; b. Evansville, Ind., Aug. 8, 1916; s. Robert H. and Lorena (Haury) G.; B.S., John B. Stetson U., 1939; m. Betty Lou Stickrod, Nov. 17, 1941; children—John Christopher, Richard Stewart, David Stephen, Laurence Douglas. Bus. mgr. Daytona Beach (Fla.) Sun, 1939-40; auditor Sea Ranch Hotel, Ft. Lauderdale, Fla., 1940-41; Sports editor, editor Ft. Lauderdale News, 1945-68, editor, pub., 1968-—; dir N. Am. Co., Ft. Lauderdale. Pres., Country Club Championship of Am., 1969-—. Mem. C. of C., Sigma Nu. Club: Coral Ridge Country. Home: 2800 NE 40th St Fort Lauderdale FL 33308 Office: 320 SE 1st Av PO Box 131 Fort Lauderdale FL 33302

GORE, ROBERT HAYES, newspaper editor, publisher; b. Knottsville, Ky., May 24, 1886; s. Joseph Henry and Mary (Carrico) G.; B.A., St. Mary's Coll., 1904; LL.D., U. Notre Dame, 1958; m. Lorena Haury, Oct. 3, 1907; children—Robert Hayes, Edward F., Dorothy (Mrs. Jack Firlit), Mary (Mrs. Charles Palmer), John W., Frederick P., Joseph A., George H., Theodore T. Mng. editor Evansville (Ind.) Press, 1909-16; editor, pub. Terre Haute (Ind.) Post, 1916-21; owner, operator R. H. Gore Co., Ins., Chgo., 1921-68, Ft. Lauderdale (Fla.) News, 1929-63; hon. chmn. Gore Newspaper Co., 1963-—; builder Gov.'s Club Hotel, Ft. Lauderdale, 1935, Sea Ranch Resort Hotel, Ft. Lauderdale, 1939, Park Hill Hotel, Hendersonville, N.C., 1948-55, Franklin Hotel, Brevard, N.C., 1949-55, Green Park Hotel, Blowing Rock, N.C., 1947-55, Algren Hotel, Asheville, N.C., 1954-59; gov. P.R., 1933-34; pres., chmn., dir. R. H. Gore Co., Bardstown, Ky., 1949-68, Home Owners Life Ins. Co., Ft. Lauderdale, 1954-61, Instnl. Ins. Co. Am., Chgo., 1955-70, Gore Pub. Co., Ft. Lauderdale, 1929-63, N.A. Co., Ft. Lauderdale, 1931-—, Gore-Milkon Mortgage Co., Ft. Lauderdale, 1958-62, Gore-Calder Investments, Inc., Ft. Lauderdale, 1929-—, Fla. Industries and Warehousing, Inc., Ft. Lauderdale, 1955-—. Writer scenarios Edison, Essanay, Biograph, 1909-10. Mem. Fla. Bd. Control, 1938-42, 56-59. Mem. Nat. Democratic Exec. Com. Campaign, 1932-33. Author: Wampus Cat, 1918; Newsboys' Mystery Novels, 1918. Inventor exercising bed, Ready-Lady chair. Address: Governors Club Hotel Fort Lauderdale FL 33304

GORE, RUTH M, educator, govt. ofcl.; m. Alfonso E. Gore; children—Bargara, Bannie. Asst. prof. edn. and guidance Agrl. and Tech. U., Greensboro, N.C., from 1971, now dir. counseling and testing; apptd. mem. Nat. Postal Service Adv. Council, 1971. Mem. Zeta Phi Beta (nat. v.p.). Home: 1208 Eastside Dr Greensboro NC 27406 Office: 312 N Dudly St Greensboro NC 27411

GORE, T.T., newspaper exec. Pres., Fort Lauderdale (Fla.) News. Address: 320 SE 1st Av Fort Lauderdale FL 33302*

GOREN, CHARLES H., writer; b. Phila., Pa., Mar. 4, 1901; s. Jacob and Rebecca Goren; LL.B., McGill Univ., Montreal, Can., 1922. LL.M., 1923; unmarried. Admitted to Pa. Bar, Sept. 1923; practiced law in Phila., since 1923. Author various books including: Contract Bridge in a Nutshell, 1946; Point Count Bidding, 1950; Contract Bridge Complete, 1951; the Italian Bridge System, 1958; New Contract Bridge in a Nutshell, pub. 1959; An Evening of Bridge with Charles Goren, 1959; Goren's Hoyle, 1961; Goren's Bridge Complete, 1963; Bridge is My Game, 1965, Goren on Bridge, daily column syndicated by Chgo. Tribune syndicate (210 papers in U.S. and Brit.). Weekly Column Sports Illustrated mag., 1944-—. Home: Miami Beach FL*

GORGES, HEINZ AUGUST, research engr.; b. Stettin, Germany, July, 22, 1913; s. Gustav and Marga (Benda) G.; M.E., Tech. U. Dresden (Germany), 1938; Ph.D., Tech. U. Hannover, Germany, 1946; m. Sapienza Teresa Coco, Sept. 2, 1957. Came to U.S., 1959. Group leader LFA Aero Research Establishment, Braunschweig, Germany, 1940-45; with Royal Aircraft Establishment, Farnborough, Eng. 1946-49; prin. sci. officer Weapons Research Establishment, Adelaide, South Australia, 1949-59; sci. asst. George C. Marshall Space Flight Center, NASA, Huntsville, Ala., 1959-61; dir. advanced projects Cook Technol Center, Morton Grove, Ill., 1961-62; scientific adviser Ill. Inst. Tech. Research Inst., Chgo., 1962-66; prin. scientist, dir. research Tracor, Inc., Austin, Tex., 1966-—, asst. v.p. Environmental and Phys. Scis. div., 1970-72, v.p. Tracor-Jitco, Rockville, Md., 1972-—. Prof. Redstone extension U. Ala., 1960. Fellow Am. Inst. Aeros. and Astronautics (asso.); mem. Am. Geophys. Union, Am. Soc. M.E., Acoustical Soc. Am. Research on super and hypersonics, ramjet performance, space scis., system engring. and analysis. Home: 3705 Sleepy Hollow Rd Falls Church VA 22041 Office: 1601 Research Blvd Rockville MD 20850

GORMAN, JAMES EDWARDS, trade assn. exec.; b. Block, Tenn., Aug. 8, 1915; s. James Jerome and Eurfron (Edwards) G.; student Milligan Coll., 1934-35; m. Charlotte May Richey, Mar. 1, 1941; 1 dau., Carol Woolverton. Bookkeeper, accounting mgr. Comml. Credit Co., Knoxville, Tenn. and Montgomery, Ala., 1937-40; auditor, property, supply officer TVA, Knoxville, 1940-43; promotion dir. Ga. C. of C., Columbus, 1946-48; mng. dir. Fla. Chain Store Council, Jacksonville, 1948-57; gen. mgr. Fla. Retail Fedn., Jacksonville, 1957-—, exec. v.p. Mem. Fla. Adv. Council Distbr. Edn.; chmn. Fla. Council on Comml. Frauds, Inc. Past mem. courses of study com. Fla. Dept. Edn.; mem. state adv. com. Distributive Edn.; founder, past v.p. Greater Jacksonville Fair; bd. dirs. Fla. Presbyn. Homes, Bradenton Manor; lifetime dir. Fla. Livestock Show and Sale. Mem. Fla. Council for Econ. Edn., Am. Retail Fedn. (exec. com.), Nat. Council State Retail Assns. (past chmn.), Am. Retail Assn. Execs. (dir.). Presbyn. (elder). Rotarian (past pres.). Home: 1570 Park Terrace W Atlantic Beach FL 32233 Office: Am Heritage Life Bldg Jacksonville FL 32202

GORMAN, (MIKE) THOMAS FRANCIS, reporter, writer; b. N.Y.C., Dec. 7, 1913; s. Frank and Mary (Naughton) G.; A.B., N.Y.U., 1934, postgrad. 1934-36; m. Ernestine Brown, June 3, 1946 (dec. June 1958); children— Michael, Patricia. Advt., free-lance writer, 1936-41; reporter, cover gen. med. run Daily Oklahoman, 1945; writer numerous news stories and editorials in mental hosp. campaign; pioneered in establishment mental hygiene clin. in Okla., also mental hygiene orgn.; chief writer, dir. pub. hearings President's Commn. on Health Needs of Nation, 1950-53; exec. dir. Nat. Com. Against Mental Illness, Washington, 1953-—. Mem. Menninger Found. Nat. Com. Mental Hygiene; exec. bd. Okla. Com. Mental Hygiene. Served with USAAF, 1942-45. Recipient spl. Lasker award 10 outstanding young men U.S. Jr. C. of C., 1949; Edward A. Strecker Meml. medal, 1962, William C. Menninger Meml. medal, 1971. Fellow Am. Pub. Health Assn., Am. Psychiat. Assn. (hon.), Royal Soc. Health (Eng.), N.Y. Acad. Scis.; mem. Nature Conservancy, Phi Beta Kappa. Clubs: Federal City, City Tavern, Nat. Press (Washington). Author: Oklahoma Attacks its Snake Pits, 1948; Every Other Bed, 1956; co-author Impressions of Soviet Psychiatry, 1969. Contbr. articles on psychiat. subjects to mags. Home: 1230 30th St NW Washington DC 20007 Office: 1101 17th St NW Washington DC 20036

GORMAN, THOMAS KIELY, bishop; b. Pasadena, Cal., Aug. 30, 1892; s. John Joseph and Mary Elizabeth (Kiely) G.; student St. Patrick's Sem., Menlo Park, Cal., 1910-14; St. Mary's Sem., Balt., 1914-17; S.T.B., St. Mary's U., Balt.; J.C.L., Cath. U. Am. 1918; Docteur en Sciences Historiques, U. Louvain, 1925. Ordained priest R.C. Ch., 1917; asst. pastor Oxnard, Cal., 1918-19, St. Vibiana's Cathedral, Los Angeles, 1919-22; mng. editor The Tidings (offl. organ Diocese of Los Angeles and San Diego), 1926-31; prof. medieval and modern history, Mt. St. Mary's Coll., Los Angeles, also Immaculate Heart Coll., Hollywood, 1926-31; bishop of Reno, 1931-52; Titular Bishop of Rhasus, coadjutor to bishop of Dallas, 1952-54. became bishop of Dallas-Ft. Worth, 1954, now Titual bishop of Pinhel; chancellor U. Dallas, 1956-—; asst. at Pontifical Throne, 1942. Episcopal chmn. press dept. Nat. Catholic Welfare Conf., 1952-57, asst. Episcopal chmn. Bur. Information, 1961-66. Grand Prior So. lieutenancy, Knight Grand Cross Equestrian Order Knights of the Holy Sepulchre. Democrat. Author: America and Belgium, 1925; Seventy-five Years of Catholic Life in Nevada, 1936. Pub.: The Nevada Register, 1932-52; The Texas Catholic, 1952-—. Home: 6435 Forest Lane Dallas TX Office: 3915 Lemmon Av PO Box 19507 Dallas TX

GORRELL, FRANK C., lawyer, state senator; b. Russellville, Ky., June 20, 1927; s. Lilburn and Mrs. G.; A.B., Vanderbilt U., 1949, LL.B., 1952; m. Bette Jamison; children—Frank C. III, Jamison

Richter. Admitted to Tenn. bar 1952, since practiced in Nashville; former mem. Tenn. senate, former speaker; lt. gov. State of Tenn., 1967-71. Mem. Tenn. council Boy Scouts Am.; chmn. Tenn. Cancer Crusade, 1967-69. Trustee Aquinas Jr. Coll.; bd. dirs. YMCA, Muscular Dystrophy Assn. Mem. Am., Tenn., Nashville (dir.) bar assns., Am. Judicature Soc., Nat. Conf. Lt. Govs. (exec. com.), Nat. Soc. State Legislators (dir.), Vanderbilt Alumni Assn. (dir.). Elk. Clubs: Nashville Vanderbilt; Woodmont School Men's (dir.). Office: State Capitol Bldg Nashville TN 37219

GORTNER, WILLARD AUSTIN, stock broker; b. Morris, Ill., Jan. 25, 1926; s. Peter Franklin and Emma Rachel (Ream) G.; B.S. in Bus. Adminstrn., Northwestern U., 1950; m. Satie Elizabeth Broyhill, Oct. 12, 1968; children—Terri Leigh, Harvey Franklin; stepchildren—Jan E., Kenneth M., Michael H., Robert B. Investigator, Retail Credit Co., St. Petersburg, Fla., 1950-51; spl. agt. FBI, 1951-53; owner, mgr. Gortner Ford & Mercury Sales, Inc., Keyser, W.Va., 1954-60; broker A.G. Edwards & Sons, St. Petersburg, Fla., 1961-62; v.p., mgr. Harris, Upham & Co., Inc., St. Petersburg, 1963—. Chmn. Mineral County (W.Va.) United Fund, 1958. Bd. dirs., treas. St. Petersburg Symphony, 1961-68; bd. dirs. Potomac Valley council Boy Scouts Am., 1954-58; trustee, chmn. investment com. Eckerd Coll. Served with AUS, 1944-46. Presbyn. (chmn. trustees 1966-70). Mason (Shriner). Clubs: Yacht, Lakewood Country (St. Petersburg); East Bay Country (Largo, Fla.); Cedar Rock Country (Lenoir, N.C.). Home: 500 Bluff View Dr Belleair Bluffs FL 33540 Office: 3303 3d Av N St Petersburg FL 33713

GOSE, RICHARD VERNE, lawyer; b. Hot Springs, S.D., Aug. 3, 1927; s. Vernie O. and Mame K. (Thompson) G.; B.S., U. Wyo., 1950; M.S., Northwestern U., 1954; LL.B., J.D., George Washington U., 1967; m. Agnes Jean Allen, Apr. 13, 1952 (div.); children—Beverly Marie, Donald Paul, Celeste Marlene. Exec. asst. to U.S. Senator Hickey, Washington, 1960-62; mgr. Washington office E.G. & G. Corp., 1965-67; admitted to N.M. bar, 1967; Supreme Ct. N.M., U.S. Dist. Ct. of N.M., U.S. Ct. of Appeals, 10th Circuit; practiced in Santa Fe, 1967—. State co-chmn. Citizens for Johnson for Pres., Wyo., co-chmn. Citizens for Jackson for Pres., N.M., 1971—. Served with U.S. Army, 1950-52. Recipient Outstanding Service award N.M. Soc. Profl. Engrs., 1971. Mem. 1st Jud. Dist. Bar Assn. (v.p., past sec. and treas., chmn. judiciary com.), U.S. Senate Assn. Adminstrv. Assts. and Secs., Phi Delta Theta, Pi Tau Sigma, Sigma Tau. Methodist. Mason. Home: 815 Don Gaspar St Santa Fe NM 87501 Office: 301 Johnson St Santa Fe NM 87501

GOSNELL, HAROLD CORNELIUS, clergyman; b. Syracuse, N.Y., July 17, 1908; s. Cornelius Parsons and Carrie (Fawcett) G.; B.A., Syracuse U., 1930; B.D., Episcopal Theol. Sch., Cambridge, Mass., 1930-33; D.D., U. of South, 1956; m. Marjorie O. Adams, Aug. 29, 1932; children— Judith (Mrs. James M. Cavender III), Harold Cornelius. Ordained to ministry Episcopal Ch., 1933; rector St. John's Ch., Marcellus, N.Y., 1933-36, All Saints Ch., Fulton, N.Y., 1936-38, Holy Trinity Ch., Lincoln, Neb., 1938-48, St. Mark's Ch., San Antonio, 1948-68; consecrated bishop coadjutor Diocese W. Tex., 1968; bishop of West Tex., 1968—. Mem. exec. bd., trustee Diocese of West Tex.; mem. Nat. Commn. Ch. in Human Affairs; mem. Armed Forces Commn. Episcopal Ch.; mem. bd. Gen. Commn. on Chaplains and Armed Forces Personnel; dep. Episcopal Gen. convs., 1940, 43, 46, 49, 52, 55, 58, 61, 64, 67; mem. exec. council Episcopal Ch., 1970—. Pres. Allied Children's Services, 1958-64, San Antonio Council of Chs., 1963-64. Bd. dirs. United Fund (pres. 1962-63), Community Chest, also Good Govt. League, 1952— (all San Antonio); trustee St. Mary's Hall, San Antonio; regent U. South, Sewanee, Tenn. Served with USNR, 1943-46; ret. capt. Reserve. Mem. Psi Upsilon. Mason (33 deg., Shriner), Rotarian (past pres. San Antonio). Club: Oak Hills Country (San Antonio). Home: 342 E Terra Alta San Antonio TX 78209 Office: 111 Torcido Dr San Antonio TX 78209

GOSS, JAMES WALTER, oil co. exec.; b. Farmerville, La., Mar. 18, 1924; s. Walter Frank and Louie (Hollis) G.; B.S., La. State U., 1949; m. Mertle Henry, Jan. 1, 1953; children—James Walter, Kimberly. With Gen. Am. Oil Co. Tex., Dallas, 1949— v.p. in charge land dept., 1960-70, exec. v.p., dir., mem. exec. comm., 1970—. Served with USNR, 1943-46. Mem. Ind. Petroleum Assn. Am. (dir.), Am., Dallas (past pres., dir.) assos. petroleum landmen, Midcontinent Oil and Gas Assn., Tex. Ind. Producers and Royalty Owners Assn., Am. Petroleum Inst., Lambda Chi Alpha. Clubs: Dallas Athletic, Petroleum, Texas (Dallas). Home: 3509 Centenary Dr Dallas TX 75225 Office: Meadows Bldg Dallas TX 75206

GOSSETT, EARL FOWLER, JR., educator; b. Birmingham, Ala., Jan. 28, 1933; s. Earl Fowler and Clara May (York) G.; A.B., Birmingham-So. Coll., 1954; B.D., Vanderbilt U., 1957, Ph.D. (Rockefeller fellow), 1961; m. Rhoda Lois Scoates, July 17, 1956; 1 dau., Amelia Gretchen. Instr. theology Scarritt Coll., Nashville, 1959-60; asst. prof. religion U. Miami, Coral Gables, Fla., 1961-65; asso. prof. religion and philosophy Birmingham-So. Coll., 1965-69, prof., 1969—, chmn. dept. religion, 1965—. Mem. program com. Ala. Council on Human Relations, 1971—. Bd. dirs. Birmingham chpt. Nat. Conf. Christians and Jews. Recipient Founders medal Vanderbilt U., 1957. Mem. Am. Acad. Religion (pres. Southeastern sect. 1970-71), Ala. Philos. Assn., So. Soc. Philosophy and Psychology, Omicron Delta Kappa. Home: 1811 Cedar Crest Rd Birmingham AL 35214

GOSSETT, ED, judge; b. Sabine Parrish, La., Jan. 27, 1902; s. Edward L. and Sarah Anne (McKinley) G.; A.B., U. Tex., 1924, L.B., 1927; m. Mary Helen Moseley, May 20, 1939; children—Glenn, Judy, Jane, Melissa, Stephen, Murray. Admitted to Tex. bar, 1927; practiced in Vernon and Wichita Falls, Tex., 1927-32; dist. atty. 46th Jud. Dist. Tex., 1933-37; mem. 76th-81st congresses from 13th Dist. Tex.; gen. atty. for Tex. S.W. Bell Telephone Co., 1951-67; judge Criminal Dist. Ct. No. 5, Dallas County. Dir. Fed. Home Loan Bank of Little Rock. Chmn. U.S. Savs. Bonds Program for Tex., 15 yrs. Regent Tex. Woman's U., 1 term, Tex. sr. colls., 1 term. Mem. Am., Dallas (pres. 1960) bar assns., East Tex. C. of C. Democrat. Presbyn. Mason. Club: Dallas City (v.p.). Home: 3916 Gillon Av Dallas TX 75205 Office: County Courthouse Dallas TX 75202

GOSSETT, OUIDA GRITH (MRS. JAMES W. GOSSETT), club woman; b. Nocona, Tex., Aug. 15; d. Marvin Grey and Louise (Stewart) Griffith; student Tex. Woman's U. 1935-37, Baylor U., 1938-41, U. Tex., 1949; m. James William Gossett, Apr. 3, 1944; children—James Richard, William Griffith. Head nurse Baylor U. Hosp., 1941-42. Dir. Lakeside Activity Center, Parks and Recreation Dept., 1967-71, asst. supr. dept., 1968-71, supr. sr. activities, 1971-72; cons. Gov.'s Committee on Aging Program, 1972—; bd. dirs. Nueces Activity Center, 1965-66, sec.-treas. of trustees, 1964-65. Served with USNR, 1942-44. Mem. Woman's Aux. Tex. Dental Assn. (state pres. 1959-60, adminstrv. com. 1962-65), Tex. Parks and Recreation Soc., Friends of Austin Pub. Library, Women of Univ. Presbyn. Ch., Austin Dist. Dental Aux. (pres. 1950-51), North Austin Rotary-Anns. Presbyn. Club: Westwood Country. Home: 3401 River Rd Austin TX 78703

GOTAUTAS, VITO ADOLPH, cons. geologist; b. Chgo., Dec. 6, 1928; s. John Dominic and Anele (Markevich) G.; A.B., Miami U., 1950; M.S., 1951; postgrad. Yale U., 1955-56; m. Mary Jane Dean, Oct. 4, 1952; children—Jane, Patricia, Anita. Exploration geologist Atlantic Refining Co., Lake Charles, La., 1956-61; v.p., exploration mgr., Century Mineral Corp., 1961-63; independent cons. geologist, 1963—. Served with USNR, 1951-55. ETO. Certified profl. geologist. Mem. Am. Assn. Petroleum Geologists, Am. Inst. Mining Engrs., Soc. Exploration Geophysicists, Am. Inst. Profl. Geologists (nat. membership chmn. 1969-71, pres. La. sect. 1965), Soc. Econ. Mineralogists and Paleontologists Am. Assn. Prof. Well Log Analysts, Lafayette Geol. Soc. (past sec.), Houston Geol. Soc., Lafayette Geophysical Soc., Sigma Xi, Sigma Gamma Epsilon. Clubs: Toastmasters (pres. 1971), Civitan of Lafaytte. Contbr. articles in field to profl. jours. Home: 133 Maurice Lafayette LA 70501 Office: PO Box 51788 OCS Lafayette LA 70501

GOTHARD, NICHOLAS, air pollution control exec.; b. Pecs, Hungary, Dec. 12, 1933 (came to U.S. 1960, naturalized 1966);; s. Jozsef and Margit (Schweiczer) G.; Elec. Engr., Budapest Tech. U., 1956; M.S., Mass. Inst. Tech., 1962; Ph.D. (NASA fellow), Cornell U., 1965; m. Julianna Erdesz, Dec. 21, 1957; children—Anita, Monica. With RCA Victor Co. Ltd., Montreal, Que., Can., 1958-60; research asst. Mass. Inst. Tech., Cambridge, 1960-62; research cons., 1962-63; asst. prof. Pa. State U., University Park, 1965-66; asst. prof. Tex. A. and M. U., College Station, 1967; co-founder Filtronics Corp., (name now Filteron Internat. Inc.) 1967, v.p., 1967—, also dir. Contbr. numerous articles to profl. jours. Home: Preston Tower 6211 W NW Hwy Dallas TX 75225 Office: 2322 Irving Blvd Dallas TX 75207

GOTHIE, DANIEL LLOYD, educator, librarian; b. Lewisburg, Pa., Oct. 3, 1936; s. Daniel Shinton and Mary Elizabeth (Beck) G.; B.A., Princeton, 1958; M.B.A., U. Va., 1964; M.S., Columbia, 1969; m. Katya Francesca Shoemaker, May 6, 1961; children—Mary Francesca, Katya Danielle. Account exec. Compton Advt., Inc., N.Y.C., 1964-66; v.p. Peterson's Guides, Inc., Princeton, N.J., 1966-68; librarian, instr. bus. adminstrn. U. Va. Grad. Sch. Bus. Adminstrn. Library, Charlettesville, Va., 1969—. Ind. cons. to govt. and pvt. bus. on information systems and marketing, 1968-71. Served to lt. USNR, 1958-62. Recipient U. Va. Govs. fellow, 1971-72. Mem. Am., Va. (com. 1970-72) library assns., Spl. Library Assn. (com. 1971-72), Va. Spl. Library Assn. (chmn. com. 1970-71), Nat. Microfilm Assn., Am. Mgmt. Assn., Omicron Delta Kappa. Home: 1707 Old Forge Rd Charlottesville VA 22901 Office: Grad Sch Bus Adminstrn U Va Charlottesville VA 22903

GOTT, CLYDE MORRIS, supt. schs.; b. Anahuac, Tex., Sept. 21, 1912; s. James William and Stella (Palmer) G.; B.S., S.W. Tex. State U., 1934; M.Ed., U. Tex., 1940, Ed.D., 1966; m. Louise Marie Kneuper, Jan. 23, 1937; 1 son, Carroll Deene. Athletic coach, tchr. Hull-Daisetta (Tex.) High Sch., 1934-38, Smithville (Tex.) High Sch., 1938-40; athletic coach, tchr. Burbank High Sch., San Antonio, 1940-41, asst. prin., 1942-52; supt. Smithville (Tex.) Ind. Sch. Dist., 1941-42; asst. prin. Thomas Jefferson High Sch., San Antonio, 1952-56, prin., 1956-60; prin. Thomas Jefferson High Sch., Port Arthur, Tex., 1960-66; supt. Port Arthur Ind. Sch. Dist., 1966—. Mem. Tex. Commn. on Sch. and Coll. Relations, 1965, Tex. Commn. on Sch. Accreditation, 1965. Pres. CavOilcade, Port Arthur, 1968-69; pres. YMCA, 1967. Mem. N.E.A., Am. Assn. Sch. Adminstrs., Tex. Assn. Sch. Adminstrs., Tex. Tchrs. Assn. (dist. chmn. 1957, 71-72), Tex. Congress Parents and Tchrs., Phi Delta Kappa (chpt. pres. 1966-67). Methodist (chmn. bd. stewards 1966-67, lay leader 1967-68). Mason (Shriner), Lion (pres. Part Arthur 1967). Home: 3049 Bryan Av Groves TX 77619 Office: 733 5th St Port Arthur TX 77640

GOTT, PORTER HASTINGS, oral surgeon; b. Akron, O., July 9, 1921; s. Philip Porter and Ethel (Hastings) G.; student Oberlin Coll., 1939-42; D.D.S., Georgetown U. Sch. Dentistry, 1945; postgrad. U. Pa. Grad. Sch. Medicine, 1946-47; m. Ernestine Hudson, July 21, 1945; children—Philip Hudson, Leslie Lorinda. Individual practice oral surgery, Washington, 1948-49, Ft. Lauderdale, Fla., 1949—. Served with USNR, 1944-46, 1951-52. Diplomate Am. Bd. Oral Surgery. Fellow Internat. Coll. Dentists; mem. Fla. Acad. Dental Practice Mgmt., Broward County Dental Assn. (pres. 1955-56), East Coast Dist. Dental Soc. (pres. 1967-68), Am. (del. 1970-71), Fla. (sec. 1960—) socs. oral surgeons, Fla. Dental Assn. Rotarian, Mason. Club: Tennis (Fort Lauderdale, Fla.). Home: 1717 Middle River Dr Ft Lauderdale FL 33305 Office: 906 NE 26th Av Ft Lauderdale FL 33304

GOTTLIEB, BERTRAM, research adminstr.; b. N.Y.C., Feb. 9, 1921; s. Samuel and Bessie (Halpern) G.; B.S., Ill. Inst. Tech., 1949, M.S., 1950; postgrad. U. Wis., 1950-54; m. Phyllis Virginia Jacobson, Mar. 24, 1940; children—Richard Allan, Deborah Ann, Lisa Susan. Instr. econs. Ill. Inst. Tech., 1948-50; instr. labor relations U. Wis., 1950-54, 56-57; research prof. assigned to U. Phillipines, U. Conn., 1954-56; indsl. engr. AFL-CIO, 1957-66, asst. dir. research, 1967-68; prof. bus. adminstrn., U. Ia., 1966-67; dir. research Transp. Inst., Washington, 1968—. Indsl. engring. cons., 1950-54, 56-57, 68—; labor arbitrator Fed. Mediation and Conciliation Service and Am. Arbitration Assn.; mem. tech. adv. bd. U.S. Dept. Commerce, 1967—; mem. prodn., tech. and growth com., wages and indsl. relations com. Dept. Labor, 1957—; mem. central com. to standardize indsl. engring. terminology Am. Nat. Standards Inst., 1964—; speaker, lectr. various univs., profl. socs., radio, tv. Served with USAAF, 1943-46. Mem. Am. Inst. Indsl. Engrs. (sr., editorial bd. 1960, nat. dir. div. indsl. and labor relations 1968—, chpt. dir. 1968—), Nat. Acad. Sci., Indsl. Relations Research Assn. (gov. 1966-68), Sigma Iota Epsilon. Contbr. articles to profl. jours., textbooks. Home: 703 Hillsboro Dr Silver Spring MD 20902 Office: 2000 L St NW Washington DC 20036

GOTTLIEB, LEON, constrn. co. exec.; b. Poland, Sept. 2, 1902; s. Alexander and Bertha (Smolian) G.; brought to U.S., 1907, naturalized, 1930; B.S. in C.E. with highest honors, Auburn U., 1922; postgrad. Oxford U., 1944-45; m. Jessie E. Radford, Oct. 26, 1968. With Ala. Hwy. Dept., 1922-42, prin. hwy. engr., 1934-42; with Wright Contracting Co., Columbus, Ga., 1946—, exec. v.p., dir., 1963—. Served from capt. to lt. col. C.E., AUS, 1942-46. Decorated Croix de Guerre with silver leaf (France); named Distinguished Auburn Engr., Alumni Engring Council, 1970. Registered profl. engr., Ala., Ga. Fellow Am. Soc. C.E. (life); mem. Assn. Asphalt Technologists (life), Am. Soc. Testing Materials, Nat. Asphalt Paving Assn., Asso. Gen. Contractors, Am. Roadbuilders Assn., Am. Assn. State Hwy. Ofcls., Auburn Alumni Assn. (life). Home: 2847 Auburn Av Columbus GA 31906 Office: PO Box 1580 Columbus GA 31902

GOTTSCHALD, ROBERT, govt. ofcl. formerly asst. commr. patents, now commr. patents, Washington. Office: Crystal Plaza Dr S Arlington VA 22202*

GOTTSEGEN, MARSHALL IVAN, dentist; b. New Orleans, Jan. 9, 1940; s. Alexander and Fannye (Feinblum) G.; student Washington and Lee U., 1957-60; D.D.S., Loyola U. of New Orleans, 1964; M.S., U. Pa., 1967; m. Carole Simon Gold, Feb. 23, 1963; children—Andrea Lee, George Bradley, Thomas Eliot. Individual practice specializing orthodontics, New Orleans, 1968—; clin. asst. prof. orthodontics La. State U.; clin. asst. prof., cons. orthodontics Loyola U.; cons. Cleft Palate Clinic of Charity Hosp.; mem. staff Touro Infirmary. Divisional campaign chmn. Jewish Welfare Fund, 1971; dir. Jewish Family and Children's Service. Served to capt., USAF, 1964-66. Recipient award Lemann-Stern Leadership Found., 1969-71. Mem. Am., La., New Orleans dental assns., Am. Assn. Orthodontists, Psi Omega. Home: 1421 Cadiz St New Orleans LA 70115 Office: 3424 Coliseum St New Orleans LA 70115

GOTTWALD, FLOYD DEWEY, JR., chem. co. exec.; b. Richmond, Va., July 29, 1922; s. Floyd Dewey and Ann (Cobb) G.; B.S., Va. Mil. Inst., Lexington, 1943; M.S., U. Richmond, 1951; m. Elisabeth Morris Shelton, Mar. 22, 1947; children—William M., James T., John D. With Albemarle Paper Co., Richmond, 1943-68, sec., 1956-57, v.p., sec., 1957-62, pres., 1962-68, also dir.; exec. v.p. Ethyl Corp., 1962-64, vice chmn. bd., 1964-68, chmn. bd., 1968—, chief exec. officer, 1970—; dir. Va. Commonwealth Bankshares, Inc., Seabord Coast Line R.R. Co. Mem. Port Adv. Commn., Richmond, 1963—. Trustee Va. Mil. Inst. Found., U. Richmond. Served to 1st lt. U.S. Army Res., 1943-46. Decorated Bronze Star medal, Purple Heart. Mem. Va. Inst. Sci. Research (trustee), Am. Petroleum Inst. (dir.). Home: 300 Herndon Rd Richmond VA 23229 Office: 330 S 4th St Richmond VA 23217

GOTWALT, NANCY ANN, educator; b. Harrisburg, Pa., May 23, 1927; d. Lloyd William and Margaret (Wilbert) Gotwalt; B.S, New Haven State Tchrs. Coll., 1949; M.A., Columbia, 1952, profl. diploma, 1960. Elementary sch. tchr., Fairfield, Conn., 1949-60; asst. prof. edn. Upsala Coll., E. Orange, N.J., 1960-69, supr. elementary sch. student tchrs., 1960-69; elementary sch. prin. Lutheran Parish Sch., St. Thomas, U.S. V.I., 1969—. Dir. Camp Mahetu, Bear Mountain, N.Y., 1956-58; co.-dir. Camp Yolijwa, Yucaipa, Cal., 1961; summer ch. sch. dir. for migrant children, Manalapan, N.J., 1960; dir. Camp Hagan, Shawnee-on-Delaware, Pa., 1966-67. Mem. Friends of Denmark Soc. Phi Omega Chi (hon.). Lutheran. Home: 14-16 5th St St Thomas US VI 00801 Office: No. 1 Lille Taarne Gade St Thomas US VI 00801

GOUAUX, FRANK THEOPHILE, JR., dentist; b. Lockport, La., Jan. 15, 1912; s. Frank Theophile and Mathilde Louise (Robichaux) G.; B.A., Springhill Coll., 1932; D.D.S., Loyola U. of South, 1936; m. Lorraine Gladys Weeks, Mar. 2, 1947; children—Jerrylyn (Mrs. Raymond E. McNeely), Frank Thomas. Individual practice dentistry, Lockport, La., 1936—. Mem. LaFourche Parish Sch. Bd., 1950-68; mem. La. State Bd. Dentistry, 1960-68. Mem. bd. alderman Town Lockport, La., 1937-52. Served with Dental Corps USNR, 1944-47. Mem. Am., La. dental assns., Am. Legion, V.F.W., 3d Dist. Dental Soc. Home: RFD Box 184A Raceland LA 70374 Office: 112 Barataria St Lockport LA 70374

GOUGH, CLARENCE RAY, educator; b. Krum, Tex., Dec. 7, 1919; s. Herman Lang and Gertrude (Page) G.; B.S., N. Tex. State U., 1940, M.S., 1941; B.Arch., Ill. Inst. Tech., 1950. Art tchr. Edinburg (Tex.) Ind. Sch. Kist., 1941; interior designer Contemporary House, Dallas, 1950; freelance interior and archtl. designer, Denton, Tex., 1951—; prof. art, chmn. interior design N. Tex. State U., Denton, 1950—. Served with USNR, 1942-46. Mem. Am. Assn. U. Profs., Interior Design Educators Council (chmn. S.W. region, mem. bd. govs. 1969-71), Soc. Archtl. Historians, Am. Inst. Interior Designers, Nat. Soc. Interior Designers, Nat. Trust Historic Preservation, Tex. Assn. Coll. Tchrs., Denton C. of C. Illustrator: Modern Dance for the Youth of America, 1944. Home: 1813 Willowwood Dr Denton TX 76201 Office: Box 6782 N Tex State U Denton TX 76203

GOUGH, ORAN DEAN, broadcasting exec.; b. Detroit, Apr. 3, 1937; s. Henry Dean Gough and Gertrude (Schultz) Gough Kidd; m. Sharon Ann Beals, Dec. 12, 1955 (dec. Feb. 1972); children—Laura Ellen, Oran Dean, Frank Dixon II, Juliann Michelle. Program dir. WIRK-TV, Palm Beach, Fla., 1953-56; pres., gen. mgr. Eloral Assos., Inc., Pub., 1957-59; prodn. mgr., TV dir. Fiorino Advt., 1960-62; mgr. Palm Coast Shopping Center, 1963; program dir. WEAT-TV, West Palm Beach, Fla., 1963-66, prodn. mgr., 1966-70, dir. operations, mem. mgmt. com. WEAT-AM-FM-TV, 1970—; pres. Color Communications Corp., 1967-70. Pub. relations counsel Palm Beach County Republican Exec. Com. Bd., 1968-70. Recipient Outstanding Individual Achievement award 4th dist. Am. Advt. Fedn., 1969. Mem. Palm Beaches Advt. Club (v.p., sec., dir. 1961-64, 69-71 pres. 1972). Home: 2365 Av Barcelona Oste West Palm Beach FL 33406 Office: PO Box 70 West Palm Beach FL 33402

GOUKE, CECIL GRANVILLE, educator; b. Bklyn., Dec. 5, 1928; s. Joseph and Etheline (Grant) G.; B.A., Coll. City N.Y., 1956; M.A., N.Y. U., 1958, Ph.D., 1967; m. Mary Noel, July 19, 1964; 1 son, Cecil Granville. Instr., Fisk U., 1958-60; research asst. Phelps-Stokes Fund, 1960-61; research asst. N.Y. U., 1961-62, instr., 1962; asst. prof. Grambling Coll., 1962-64, asso. prof., 1964-67; chmn. econs. dept. Hampton (Va.) Inst., 1967—. Vis. asso. prof. U. Cal. at Los Angeles, summer 1969; vis. lectr. U. Wis., summer 1970. Served with AUS, 1947-49, 50-51. Mem. Am., So., Western econ. assns., Am. Statis. Assn., Indsl. Relations Research Assn., N.A.A.C.P. (br. exec. bd.). Episcopalian (vestryman). Author: Amalgamated Clothing Workers of America, 1972. Office: PO Box 6607 Hampton Institute Hampton VA 23368

GOULD, BELLE, ret. educator; b. Willis, Tex., Sept. 6, 1899; d. Robert Amos and Fannie (Laylon) Gould; B.M., Tex. Presbyn. Coll., 1918, B.A., 1920; M.A., U. Tex., 1924; summer study Columbia U., U. Tex., Oxford U., U. Toronto. Tchr., head English dept. Davis (Okla.) High Sch., 1920-22; instr. Bolton High Sch., Alexandria, La., 1922-28, head, 1926-28; English dept. head South Park High Sch., Beaumont, Tex., 1928-29; instr. English Lamar Coll., Beaumont, 1929-36; English tchr. Henderson (Tex.) High Sch., 1938-65, Latin dept. head, 1939-65, established sponsored editors Nat. Jr. Classical League paper Torch: U.S., 1952—. Organizer, East Tex. Latin Assn. Pubi. chmn. Nat. Jr. Classical League, 1951-58, pub. relations sponsor, 1950-58, chmn. scholarship com., 1958—. Hon. dept. sheriff Rusk County, Tex., 1958—. Named Ky. col. Mem. Tex. Fgn. Lang. Assn. (hon. life), D.A.R., Delta Kappa Gamma. Presbyn. Ala Krew of the Silver Key, 1969. Home: 315 Wilson St Henderson TX 75652

GOULD, FREDERICK T., dir. Ednl. Advances in Chemistry, Am. Chem. Soc. Address: 1155 16th St NW Washington DC 20036*

GOULD, JAMES ADAMS, educator; b. Flint, Mich., July 11, 1922; s. Edgar Harola and Matilda Louise (Wareham) G.; B.S. in Math., U. Mich., 1947, M.A. in Philosophy, 1948, Ph.D. in Philosophy, 1953; m. Jeanette Cesarini, Mar. 23, 1956; children—Leslie, Francesca, Stephanie. Instr. U. Miami (Fla.), 1953-57; asst. prof. Emory U., Atlanta, 1957-62; asso. prof. Fla. State U., Tallahassee, 1962-64; prof., chmn. dept. philosophy U. South Fla., Tampa, 1964—. Pres. Tampa Am. Civil Liberties Union, 1968-72. Committeeman Democratic Party, 1970—. Served to 1st lt. USAF, 1943-46. Recipient Research Grants, Emory U., 1961, 62, U. Center Ga., 1962. Author: Readings on Logic, 1964; Contemporary Readings in Logical Theory, 1967; Philosophy for a New Generation, 1970; Freedom: The Philosophical Problems, 1970; The Western Humanities, 1971; Classic

Philosophical Questions, 1971; Love, Sex, and Identity, 1972; Violence, 1972. Home: 14701 Carnation Dr Tampa FL 33612

GOULD, KENNETH LAWRENCE, newspaper editor; b. Miami Fla., Jan. 31, 1925; s. Kenneth Leroy and Mary Amanda (Wilson) G.; B.A. in History Coll. William and Mary, 1947; m. Marilynn Brand, Aug. 12, 1950; children—Alison, Brand, Meredith. Mng. editor Richmond (Va.) News Leader, 1969-—; gen. mgr., exec. editor Financial Weekly, Richmond, 1970-—. Served to lt. comdr. USNR, World War II, Korean War. Mem. Sigma Delta Chi. Episcopalian. Club: Salisbury Country. Home: 104 Medina Rd Richmond VA 23235 Office: 119 N 3d St Richmond VA 23219

GOULD, PHILLIP, mech. engr.; b. N.Y.C., Feb. 19, 1940; s. Isaac and Blanche (Handler) G.; B.M.E., City Coll. N.Y., 1961; M.S., Mass. Inst. Tech., 1963, D.Sc., 1965; m. Joanna Grugeon, Apr. 17, 1964; children—David Elliot, Jessica Ann. Asst. prof. mech. engring. Mass. Inst. Tech., Cambridge, 1965-67; mem. Inst. for Def. Analyses, Arlington, Va., 1967-—. Mem. Am. Soc. M.E., N.Y. Acad. Scis., Operations Research Soc. Am., A.A.A.S., Am. Inst. Aeros. and Astronautics, Sigma Xi. Home: 415 S Lee St Alexandria VA 22314 Office: 400 Army-Navy Dr Arlington VA 22202

GOULD, ROBERT ALBERT, city ofcl.; b. Cresent City, Fla., Sept. 29, 1926; s. Albert W. and Anna (Richards) G.; student Orlando Jr. Coll., 1950-53, Stetson U., 1953-54; m. Evelyn Joyce Walker, Dec. 30, 1953; children—Mary Elizabeth, Leila Catherine. With City of Orlando (Fla.), 1947-—, asst. supt., 1957-62, supt., 1962-—, mgr. city auditorium, 1957-—. Commr. Amateur Softball Assn., Orlando, 1971-—. Served with USNR, 1945-46. Baptist (deacon). Home: 903 Silver Dr Orlando FL 32804 Office: 1103 S Westmoreland Dr Orlando FL 32805

GOULD, SYD S., publisher; b. Boston, Dec. 16, 1912; s. Charles M. and Cecelia (Duke) G.; student Coll. William and Mary, 1934; m. Grace Leich, May 22, 1938; 1 dau., Nancy Hamilton (Mrs. Lucien M. Gex, Jr.). Radio bus., Buenos Aires, Argentina, 1934, 36; advt. dept. Call-Chronicle Newspapers, Allentown, Pa., 1936-42; v.p., adv. dir. Baytown (Tex.) Sun, 1943-55; pub.-owner Cleveland (Tenn.) Daily Banner, 1955-—; pres. Cleveland Newspapers, Inc., 1956-67; exec. v.p. Southern Newspapers, Inc., 1963-69; pres. Syd S. Gould Assos., 1966-—, Bolivar Newspapers, Inc., 1967-—, Ironton Tribune Corp. (O.), Franklin Newspapers, Inc. (La.), Comet-Press Newspapers, Thibodaux, La., Milton Newspapers, Inc. (Fla.). Mem. Regional Small Bus. Adv. Council. Sec., Bradley County (Tenn.) Indsl. Devel. Bd., 1961-—; pres. Bradley County Heart Assn., 1960-61. Served with USNR, World War II. Mem. Newspaper Advt. Execs. Assn., Tenn. Press. Assn., Bur. Advt., Am. Newspaper Pubs. Assn., USCG Aux., Sigma Delta Chi. Episcopalian. Clubs: Bayou Country, Mobile Big Game Fishing, Montgomery Country; Isle Dauphine Country. Home: 1816 Pine Needle Rd Montgomery AL 36106 also Route 1 Box 196 Theodore AL Office: 180 2d St Cleveland TN also 2118 Mt Meigs Rd Montgomery AL 36107

GOURAS, PETER, physician, govt. scientist; b. N.Y.C., Apr. 15, 1930; s. James and Julia (Crowley) G.; A.B., Johns Hopkins, 1951, M.D., 1955; m. Ute Keppler, Aug. 29, 1959; children—Eckhart, Gunnar, Roswitha. Surg. intern Johns Hopkins Hosp., 1955-56; research scientist Physiol. lab. Cambridge, (Eng.) U., 1958-59; instr. physiology dept. U. Pa. Med. Sch., 1959-60; research asso. neurosurgery NIH, Bethesda, Md., 1956-57, research asso. ophthalmology, 1957-58, sr. investigator ophthalmology physiology, 1960-68, chief sect. ophthalmology, physiology, 1968-—. Nat. Found. March of Dimes fellow, 1958. Recipient citation Nat. Council To Combat Blindness, 1961. Mem. Am. Physiol. Soc., Soc. Gen. Physiologists, Optical Soc. Am., N.Y. Acad. Sci., A.A.A.S., Phi Beta Kappa. Hon. editorial adv. bd. Vision Research (jour.). Contbr. papers to sci. lit. Home: 6309 Crathie Lane Washington DC 20016 Office: NIH Bethesda MD 20014

GOURLEY, JAMES LELAND, editor, publisher, banker, broadcaster; b. Mounds, Okla., Jan. 29, 1919; s. Samuel O. and Lodema (Scott) G.; B. Liberal Studies, U. Okla., 1963; m. Billie Jo Simpson, Apr. 11, 1943; children—James Leland II, Janna Lynn. Editor, pub., pres. Henryetta (Okla.) Daily Free-Lance, 1946-—; pres. radio sta. KHEN and KHEN-FM, Henryetta, 1955-71; pres. Hugo (Okla.) Daily News, 1953-63; asst. gov. Okla., 1959-63; commr. Okla. Ins. Fund, 1961-62; pres. State Capitol Bank, 1962-67, chmn. bd., chmn. exec. com., 1962-68; chmn., pres. State Capitol Bldg. Corp.; treas. radio sta. KJEM, Oklahoma City, 1963-67. Chmn. Oklahoma City Bond Issue Campaign, 1962; mem. Pres. Nat. Pub. Adv. Com. to Sec. of Commerce, 1963-66; mem. Nat. Council State Govts., 1960-63; dir. So. Regional Edn. Bd., 1959-67; exec. dir. Gov.'s Commn. on Higher Edn., 1960-61; chmn. Okla. Lake Redevel. Authority, 1960-63; mem. Gov.'s Commn. on Tourism, 1967-—. Dist. chmn. Boy Scouts Am., 1962-64. Chmn. adult edn. subcom. U. Okla., 1967-68. Dir. Nat. Cowboy Hall of Fame Okla. Soc., 1965-—; vice chmn. Nat. Finals Rodeo, 1966-68. Democratic candidate for gov. Okla., 1966. Served to maj. AUS, 1941-46. Decorated Bronze Star; recipient 13 Best Small Town Daily Newspaper Okla. awards, Marshall Gregory award for distinguished journalism in edn., 1971. Mem. Am. Newspaper Pubs. Assn., Am. Bankers Assn., Okla. Press Assn., (Newspaper Community Service award 1971), Nat. Assn. Broadcasters, Mil. Order World Wars, Oklahoma City C. of C. (dir.), Sigma Delta Chi, Pi Kappa Alpha. Democrat. Mem. Disciples of Christ Ch. (pres. Okla. laymen 1964-65). Rotarian. Home: 2508 NW Country Club Dr Oklahoma City OK 73116 Office: PO Box 53404 Oklahoma City OK 73105

GOW, ROBERT HAIGH, corporate farming exec.; b. Paris, France, Apr. 26, 1933 (parents Am. citizens); s. Ralph Frederick and Eleanore (Haigh) G.; B.S., Sch. Engring., Yale, 1955; m. Patricia Alice Lawson, July 20, 1957 (div.); children—Laura Lawson, David Frederick, Heather Haigh. Indsl. engr. Electro-Chem. div. Norton Co., Chippawa, Ont., Can., 1955-56, supr. indsl. engring., sec. co. growth com., Worcester, Mass., 1958-61; pres. Champlain-Zapata Plastics Machinery, Inc., Caldwell, N.J., 1961-63; v.p., treas. Zapata Off-Shore Co., Houston, 1963-67; exec. v.p. Zapata Norness, Inc., 1967-69, pres., 1969-70; chmn. bd., chief exec. officer Stratford of Tex., Inc., 1970-—; dir. Southdown, Inc., Australian Land & Cattle Co., Ltd., Digicon, Inc., Terrain King Corp. Served as radar officer, 1st lt. USAF, 1956-58. Mem. Houston Soc. Financial Analysts, Young Pres.'s Orgn., Tau Beta Pi. Club: Yale (past pres.) (Houston). Home: 1110 Potomac St Houston TX 77027 Office: Tenneco Bldg Houston TX 77002

GOZONSKY, MOSES JAMES, govt. ofcl.; b. Laconia, N.H., Sept. 10, 1923; s. Archie and Ida (Halperin) G.; B.S., U. N.H., 1947, M.A., 1950; M.S., Columbia, 1950; m. Eileen Ruth Charney, Oct. 14, 1951; Instr. dept. econs. and bus. adminstrn. U. N.H., 1948-49; bus. economist Bur. Labor Statistics, Dept. Labor, Washington, 1950-51, labor economist wage and hour div., 1951-53; cons. United Steelworkers Am. Com. on Retired and Older Workers, 1957-61, with Murray W. Latimer, indsl. relations cons., Washington, 1954-61; dep. asst. for problems of elderly and handicapped Dept. Housing and Urban Devel., Washington, 1961-—; cons. U.S. Senate Com. on Aging, 1961. Research dir. Sr. Citizens for Kennedy and Johnson, Washington, 1960. Mem. exec. bd. govt. div. United Jewish Appeal, Washington. Served with USAAF, 1943-45. Mem. Alumni Assn. Sch. Bus. Columbia, N.H. State Soc. Washington (dir., past v.p.), Am. Pub. Welfare Assn., Phi Sigma Delta. Club: U. N.H. Alumni (past pres. Washington). Home: 700 7th St SW Washington DC 20024 Office: Dept Housing and Urban Devel 7th and D Sts SW Washington DC 20410

GRACE, CHARLES C(LYDE), physician; b. Belleville, Ark., May 23, 1905; s. William H. and Edna (Harkness) G.; student Hendrix Coll., 1922-24; B.S., U. Ark., 1928, M.D., 1928; m. May H. Clarke, Dec. 26, 1931; children—Charles Clyde, Marilyn. Intern, resident Greenville City Hosp., 1928-30; resident Pitts. Eye and Ear Hosp., 1930-31; ophthalmologist, otolaryngologist, chief staff Flagler Hosp. Dir., Exchange Bank of St. Augustine. North Fla. cons. Council for Blind, 1944-66. Mem. com. otolaryngology Fla. Mid Winter Seminar; dir. Fla. Midwinter Seminar Ophthalmology and Otolaryngology. Diplomate Am. Bd. Otolaryngology. Fellow A.C.S., Internat. Coll. Surgeons; mem. Fla. Med. Assn. (pres.), Fla. Soc. Ophthalmology and Otolaryngology, Am. Laryngol. Rhinol. and Otolog. Soc. (v.p.), Am. Acad. Ophthalmology and Otolaryngology, A.M.A. Democrat. Presbyn. Mason (K.T., Shriner), Kiwanian. Contbr. articles to med. jours. Home: 22 E Park AV St Augustine FL 32084 Office: Doctors Bldg St Augustine FL 32084

GRACIA, VALENTIN, surgeon; b. Panuco, Veracruz, Mexico, May 5, 1929; s. Valentin and Maria (Sanchez) G.; B.S., U. Mexico, 1946, M.D., 1952; m. Joan Oltmann, Mar. 13, 1954; children—Linda Joan, Valentin, Walter Dietrich, Maria, Rita Lynn, Phillip, Irene, Carlos. Came to U.S., 1952, naturalized, 1960. Rotating intern Monmouth Meml. Hosp., Long Branch, N.J., 1952-53; surg. resident St. Luke's Hosp., Bethlehem, 1953-54, Scott & White Clinic, Temple, 1954-57; resident plastic surgery Baylor Med. Center, Dallas, 1957-59; gen. practice medicine specializing in plastic surgery, Ft. Worth, 1959-—; mem. staffs All Saints Episcopal, Harris, St. Joseph's, John Peter Smith, Arlington Meml., Fort Worth Children's Glenview, Cook's Blvd. hosps.; cons. plastic surgeon USPHS Hosp., Ft. Worth. Diplomate Am. Bd. Plastic Surgery. Fellow A.C.S., Internat. Coll. Surgeons; mem. Am. Soc. Plastic Surgery, A.A.A.S., N.Y. Acad. Scis., Am., Tex. Soc. Plastic Surgeons, Ft. Worth Surg. Soc., Internat. Good Neighbor Council, So., Tex., Tarrant County med. assns., Am. Burn Assn., Internat. Soc. Burn Injuries, Internat. Soc. Plastic Surgeons. Mason (K.T., Shriner), Rotarian. Contbr. articles to profl. jours. Home: 2013 Jenson Rd Fort Worth TX 76112 Office: 1001 W Rosedale PO Box 2476 Fort Worth TX 76101

GRADY, JOHN EDWARD, JR., real estate co. exec.; b. Boston, June 15, 1935; s. John Edward and Catherine Agnes (Connolly) G.; A.B., Harvard, 1956, M.B.A., 1965; m. Angela Loretta McDonnell, July 10, 1965; children—John Edward III, Robert Emmet McDonnell, Douglas Anderson. Account exec. Merrill Lynch, Pierce, Fenner & Smith, N.Y.C., 1960-63; sr. asso. Cresap, McCormick and Paget, N.Y.C., 1965-69; v.p., Investment Mgmt. and Research, Inc., St. Petersburg, Fla., 1969-70; v.p. finance, treas. Suncoast Highland Corp., Largo, Fla., 1970-—, also dir. Regional chmn. Harvard Bus. Sch. Fund, 1971-—; mem. pres. roundtable Fla. Presbyn. Coll., 1971-—. Served to lt. (j.g.) USNR, 1956-60. Clubs: Lakewood Country, Harvard West Coast (St. Petersburg, Fla.); Harvard Business School (sec. 1969) (N.Y.C.) Home: 1640 N Dakota Av NE St Petersburg FL 33703 Office: 1180 Jasper St Largo FL 33540

GRADY, LEE TIMOTHY, pharm. researcher; b. Chgo., Mar. 21, 1937; s. Thomas A. and Lentella (Eibel) G.; B.S., U. Ill., 1959, Ph.D., 1963; m. Ann Marie Gill, Aug. 8, 1964; children—Patricia A., Meghan E. Analyst CIA, Washington, 1963-66; research pharmacologist Merck Inst. for Therapeutic Research, West Point, Pa., 1966-68; sr. supr. Drug Standards Lab., Washington, 1968-71, dir., 1971-—. NSF Coop. Grad. fellow, 1959-61. Mem. Acad. Pharm. Scis. (sect. sec. 1971-73), Am. Chem. Soc., Am. Pharm. Assn., Phi Delta Chi, Phi Kappa Phi, Rho Chi. Contbr. to profl. jours. Home: 1205 Carol Raye St McLean VA 22101 Office: 2215 Constitution Av NW Washington DC 20037

GRAFF, HOMER LEVESQUE, physician; b. Texla, Tex., Nov. 2, 1925; s. Homer Levesque and Bessie Lee (Bridges) C.; student Tex. Christian U., 1943-44; M.D., Baylor U., 1951, B.S., 1958; m. Dora Villafane, Dec. 18, 1949; children—Mark, Philip, Laura, Paul, Hans. Intern, Gorgas Hosp., C.Z., 1951-52; resident Ind. U. Med. Center, Indpls. and Baylor U. Hosp. Group, 1953-56; gen. practice medicine, C.Z., 1952-53; specializing in otolaryngology, Houston, 1956-—; mem. staff Hermann, Meml. Bapt., St. Lukes, Tex. Childrens hosps.; clin. instr. Baylor U. Coll. Medicine, 1956-—. Served to lt. (j.g.) USNR, 1943-46. Mem. A.M.A., Tex. Harris County med. socs., Tex. Otolaryngol. Soc., Royal Soc. Medicine (Eng.). Home: 11335 Bothwell Way Houston TX 77024 Office: 6510 Hillcroft St Houston TX 77036

GRAGAN, PHILIP A., dept. store exec.; b., 1931; B.A., George Washington U., 1953, J.D., 1959. Atty., Covington & Burling, law firm, 1959-65; asst. to v.p., sec., treas., Woodward & Lothrop, Inc., Washington, 1965, asst. sec., asst. treas., 1965-68, sec., asst. treas., counsel, 1968-—. Served with AUS, 1953-55. Address: 11th F and G Sts NW Washington DC 20013*

GRAGG, LOGAN, hosp. adminstr.; b. Lexington, Ky., Aug. 30, 1916; s. Logan and Louise (Creighton) G.; A.B., Transylvania Coll., Lexington, 1937; M.D., U. Louisville, 1941; m. Mary Park Avery, June 12, 1940; children—Ann (Mrs. Russell Lay), Wyatt Logan, Susan Park. Intern Good Samaritan Hosp., Lexington, 1941-42; resident Louisville Gen. Hosp., 1945-47; practice medicine, specializing in psychiatry, Lexington, 1947-49; mem. psychiat. staff, chief phys. medicine rehab. VA Hosp., Lexington, 1949-53; clin. dir. Eastern State Hosp., Lexington, 1953-56, supt., 1956-—; dir. Franklin County Child Guidance Clinic, Frankfort, Ky., 1956-64; cons. dept. psychology U. Ky., 1956-60. Bd. dirs. Central Ky. Mental Health Assn., Central Ky. Mental Health Center. Served to capt., M.C., AUS, 1942-45; PTO, ETO. Fellow Am. Psychiat. Assn.; mem. A.M.A., Ky. Med. Assn., Ky. Psychiat. Assn. (past pres.), Alpha Kappa Kappa, Kappa Alpha. Democrat. Mem. Christian Ch. Kiwanian. Home: No 7 Tanglewood Lexington KY 40505 Office: 427 W 4th St Lexington KY 40508

GRAHAM, ALEXANDER H., JR., lawyer; b. Greensboro, N.C., June 11, 1918; A.B., U. N.C., 1939, LL.B., 1941. Admitted to N.C. bar, 1941; spl. agt. FBI, 1941-46; now mem. firm Newsom, Graham, Strayhorn, Hedrick & Murray, Durham, N.C. Mem. Durham County, N.C., Am. bar assns., N.C. State Bar, Order of Coif, Phi Beta Kappa, Phi Delta Phi. Office: Central Carolina Bank Bldg 111 Corcoran St Durham NC 27702*

GRAHAM, AUBREY GUY, postmaster; b. Norfolk, Va., Jan. 14, 1905; s. George A. and Daisy (Bell) G.; student U. Va., 1925; m. Martha Elizabeth Hornaday, Apr. 8, 1939; children—Aubrey Guy, Martha Elizabeth. Dep. clk. Corp. Ct., 1927-38; exec. sec. to city mgr., Norfolk, 1938-44; postmaster, Norfolk, 1944-—. Active in Community Fund, 1929-—; pres. Tidewater council Boy Scouts Am., 1951, 52, 53, mem. exec. bd., 1950-63; chmn. Hampton Roads area Fed. Safety Council, 1959. Bd. dirs. A.R.C., 1939-46. Methodist (steward). Mason (33 deg. Shriner, bd. dirs. Shriners Hosps. for Crippled and Burned Children 1962-—. Home: 515 Carlisle Way Norfolk VA 23505 Office: PO Box 719 Norfolk VA 23501

GRAHAM, CHARLES MOORE, actuary; b. Newark, Apr. 14, 1900; s. Charles L. and Sarah (Moore) G.; student U. Newark, 1919; m. Mildred Ray, Dec. 20, 1945. Enging. estimator Hyatt Bearings div. Gen. Motors Corp., Harrison N.J., 1918-20; asst. statistician Globe Indemnity Co., Newark, 1921-22; actuarial research technician Nat. Council Compensation Ins., N.Y.C., 1922-25; asso. actuary N.Y. State Ins. Fund, 1925-45; chief self-ins. examiner, actuary, Workmen's Compensation Bd., 1945-57; actuarial cons., Largo, Fla., 1957-59, 72-—; fire and casualty actuary Fla. Ins. Dept., 1959-65; actuary S.C. Ins. Dept. 1965-72. Fellow Casualty Actuarial Soc.; mem. Am. Acad. Actuaries (charter). Contbr. articles to Casualty Actuarial Soc. Proc. Home: 13760-104th Terrace N Largo FL 33540

GRAHAM, CLARENCE R., librarian; b. Louisville, Feb. 28, 1907; s. Samuel J. and Lillian Ellen (Paris) G.; student U. N.C., 1924-27; A.B., U. Louisville, 1934; B.S. in L.S., Western Res. U., 1935; postgrad. Northwestern U., 1937-38; m. Esther Charlotte Lothman, Feb. 28, 1930; 1 dau., Carolyn. Student asst. U. N.C. Library, 1925-27; field rep. N.C. Dept. Health, Raleigh, 1924-25; with dept. statistics Brown & Williamson Tobacco Co., Louisville, 1929-30; librarian Parkland Jr. High Sch., 1930-34; asst. to librarian Louisville Free Pub. Library, 1935-36, librarian 1942-—. Vis. asso. prof. dept. library sci. U. Ky.; dir. Nat. Coll. Edn. Library Evanston, Ill., 1936-42; instr. in library scis. U. Louisville, 1946-51. Mem. Louisville Labor-Mgmt. Com. Bd. dirs. Jr. Art Gallery, Louisville Theatrical Assn., Childrens Theatre. Mem. A.L.A. (pres. 1950-51, audio-visual bd.), Ky., (1st v.p. 1946, pres. 1947), Southeastern (pres. 1948-50) library assns., Art Center Assn. (dir.). Adult Edn. Assn. U.S.A. (del. assembly), Arts Club (dir.), Newcomen Soc. N.A., Louisville Urban League. Rotarian. Clubs: Louisville Library (pres. 1948-49), Filson. Co-founder, 1947, and cons. to free neighborhood colls. in br. libraries sponsored by U. Louisville, Free Pub. Library. Author: First Book of Public Libraries, 1959. Contbr. articles to profl. jours. Home: 1028 Cherokee Rd Louisville KY 40204 Office: 301-333 Library Pl Louisville KY 40203

GRAHAM, DANIEL ROBERT, cattle producing co. exec., state senator; b. Coral Gables, Fla., Nov. 9, 1936; s. Ernest R. and Hilda Elizabeth (Simmons) G.; B.A., U. Fla., 1959; LL.B., Harvard, 1962; m. Adele Khoury, Feb. 2, 1959; children—Gwendolynn Patricia, Glynn Adele, Arva Suzanne, Kendall Elizabeth. Vice pres. Graham Co. various locations in Fla., Albany, Ga., 1962-—; v.p., sec. Sengra Devel. Corp., Miami Lakes, Fla., 1962-—; mem. Fla. Senate, 1970-—; admitted to Fla. bar, 1962. Mem. Fla. Ho. of Reps., 1966-70. Chmn. Nat. Found. for Improvement Edn.; mem. exec. com. Edn. Commn. of States. Named Outstanding Young Man, Fla. Jr. C. of C., 1970-71. Mem. Blue Key, Phi Beta Kappa. Mem. United Ch. (chmn. bd.). Kiwanian. Home: 16141 Aberdeen Way Miami Lakes FL 33014 Office: 14420 NW 60th Av Miami Lakes FL 33014

GRAHAM, DUNCAN SMITH, lawyer; b. McRae, Ga., Apr. 17, 1907; s. Eschol Wayne and Eva Mae (Smith) G.; A.B., Emory U., 1929; J.D., U. Ga., 1932; m. Elizabeth Meadows, Feb. 20, 1945; children—Sara Eleanor (Mrs. Peter Hobart Hand), Mary Josephine. Admitted to Ga. bar, 1932; practiced in Vidalia, Ga., 1935-—; city atty., Vidalia, 1956-62; county atty., Toombs County, Ga., 1965-—. Dir. Vidalia Fed. Savs. & Loan Assn., Brice Banking Co., Inc., (all Vicalia). Served to lt. USNR, 1941-45. Mem. Am. Bar. Assn., State Bar Ga., C. of C. Methodist. Club: Vidalia Country. Home: 1019 Center Dr Vidalia GA 30474 Office: 403 Church St Vidalia GA 30474

GRAHAM, FREDERICK BOLLES, banker; b. Wallace, N.C., Mar 2, 1906; s. Benjamin R. and Edith (Bolles) G.; B.S., U. N.C., 1928; postgrad. Wilmington Law Sch., 1931-33; grad. Stonier's Grad. Sch. Banking, Rutgers U., 1947; m. Katherine Carr, Oct. 20, 1934; children—Katherine (Mrs John Daughtridge), Benjamin Robinson III, Frederick Bolles. Bookkeeper, Wilmington Savs. & Trust Co. (N.C.), 1928-32, asst. trust officer, 1932-37, asst. cashier, 1937-50, v.p., 1950-58, dir., 1953-58, pres., 1958; sr. v.p. Wachovia Bank & Trust Co. (merger Wilmington Savs. & Trust Co. and Wachovia Bank & Trust Co. 1958), Wilmington, 1958-—, also mem. bd. mgrs. Past v.p., dir. Cape Fear Holding Co., Wilmington. Chmn., Wilmington-New Hanover County Charter Commn., 1970-71. Pres., dir. Southeastern N.C. Devel. Assn., 1955-64. Mem. bd. aldermen, Wrightsville Beach, N.C., 1945-47, mayor pro tem, 1946-47. Chmn., Wilmington chpt. A.R.C., 1968-69; chmn. exec. com., trustee Wilmington Coll., 1964-68, chmn. bd., 1968-69; a founder, trustee Univ. Found., U. N.C. at Wilmington, 1962-68. Mem. N.C. Bankers Assn. (pres. trust div. 1939), Lower Cape Fear Hist. Soc., Sigma Alpha Epsilon, Episcopalian. Clubs: L'Ariosa German, Cape Fear, Cape Fear Country (Wilmington); Surf, Caroline Yacht (Wrightsville Beach). Home: 1411 Live Oak Pkwy Wilmington NC 28401 Office: PO Box 1422 Wilmington NC 28401

GRAHAM, JACKSON, transp. exec., govt. ofcl.; b. Mosier, Ore., June 27, 1915; s. A.E. and Nada (Clark) G.; B.S. in Civil Engring., Ore. State U., 1936; postgrad. Mass. Inst. Tech., 1939-40; Nat. War Coll., 1958-59; m. Mabel Lee Dowlin, July 4, 1943; children—Ona Lee, Jackson Reade. Commd. 2d lt. C.E., U.S. Army, 1936, advanced through grades to maj. gen., 1963; comdr. combat engr. regt., ETO. World War II; comdr. all aviation engrs., Korea, 1954; dir. civil works Army Engrs., 1963-66, ret., 1967; gen. mgr. Washington Met. Area Transit Authority, 1967-—. Decorated D.S.M., Legion of Merit, Commendation medal; Medal of Merit (Brazil). Mem. Sigma Phi Epsilon. Mason. Home: 2836 Fort Scott Dr Arlington VA 22202 Office: 950 S L'Enfant Plaza SW Washington DC 20204

GRAHAM, KATHARINE (MRS. PHILIP L. GRAHAM), newspaper exec.; b. N.Y.C., June 16, 1917; d. Eugene and Agnes (Ernst) Meyer; student Vassar Coll., 1935-36; A.B., U. Chgo., 1938; m. Philip L. Graham, June 5, 1940 (dec. Aug. 1963); children—Elizabeth Morris (Mrs. Elizabeth Weymouth), Donald Edward, Willaim Welsh, Stephen Meyer. Reporter, San Francisco News, 1938-39; with Sunday, circulation and editorial depts. Washington Post, 1939-45; pres. Washington Post. Co., owners Washington Post, Newsweek mag., various radio and TV stas., 1963-—; dir. Bowaters Mersey Paper Co., Ltd., Liverpool, N.S., Can. Mem. adv. com. John F. Kennedy Sch. Govt. for Inst. of Politics, Harvard U. Trustee Com. Econ. Devel., George Washington U., U. Chgo., Urban Inst., Nat. Center for Resource Recovery, Inc. Mem. Bur. Advt. (dir.), Inter-Am. Press Assn. (dir., exec. com.), Conf. Bd., Sigma Delta Chi, Theta Sigma Phi. Clubs: Nat. Press, Washington Press, 1925 F Street (Washington); Cosmopolitan (N.Y.C.). Home: 2920 R St NW Washington DC 20007 Office: 1150 15th St NW Washington DC 20005

GRAHAM, NATHAN G., U.S. dist. atty. for no. Okla. Address: Dist Atty's Office Civic Center Tulsa OK 74103*

GRAHAM, PAUL PANNELL, educator; b. Montgomery County, Va., May 31, 1936; s. Eugene Paul and Hazel Ethylene (Pannell) G.; B.S. in Animal Husbandry, Va. Poly. Inst., 1956, M.S., 1959; Ph.D. in Food Sci., N.C. State U., 1970; m. Leola Ruth Westmoreland, Aug.

10, 1956; children—Tammy Carol, Cathy Ann. Research asst., then asst. county agt. Va. Agrl. Expt. Sta., 1957-58; mem. faculty Va. Poly. Inst., 1958-—, asst. prof. food sci., 1970-—; food sci. cons. Bd. dirs. New River Valley Mental Health Assn. Environmental Sci. fellow NIH, 1965-67. Mem. Am. Meat Sci. Assn., Am. Soc. Animal Sci., Carolina-Va. Inst. Food Tech., A.A.A.S., Sigma Xi, Phi Tau Sigma. Baptist (deacon). Home: 207 Ardmore St Blacksburg VA 24060

GRAHAM, ROBERT DUKE, savs. and loan assn. exec.; b. Greensboro, N.C., Sept. 8, 1900; s. John Buie and Emma (Fowler) G.; grad. high sch.; m. Edith Brown, Aug. 20, 1937. Pres. C.W. Lampkin Hotels, Bowling Green, Ky., 1926-60; v.p. Fidelity Fed. Savs. & Loan Assn., Bowling Green, 1965-—; mayor Bowling Green, Ky., 1959-64, 1968-72. Chmn. Democratic County Com., 1940-52; chmn. City Bd. Pub. Works, 1953-59. Bd. dirs. Bowling Green Indsl. Found., 1940-71. Presbyn. Lion. Home: 1716 Normal Dr Bowling Green KY 42101 Office: City Hall 10th and College Sts Bowling Green KY 42101

GRAHAM, RONALD AUSTIN, physician; b. Tulia, Tex., Mar. 5, 1919; s. William Smith and Cora Belle (Russell) G.; B.A., Baylor U., 1940; M.D., Baylor U. Coll. Medicine, 1945; postgrad. Aviation Sch. Medicine, 1946, U. Vienna, Austria, 1947; m. Lourene Schell, Sept. 6, 1941 (div.); children—David Austin, James Lee, Barbara Ann (Mrs. Marvin Couey). Intern Jefferson Davis Hosp., Houston, 1945-46; resident Baptist Meml. Hosp., San Antonio, 1947-48; gen. practice medicine, Pharr-McAllen, Tex., 1948-60, Junction, Tex., 1960-61, 68-—, Fayetteville, Ark., 1961-68; v.p. Fayetteville City Hosp. Staff, 1968; mem., chief staff Kimble Hosp., Junction, 1970-71. Health officer Kimble County, Tex., 1969-—. Served as flight surgeon USAF, 1946-48. Mem. Am. Internat. Chorolais Assn., Am., Tex., Ark. med. assns. Republican. Baptist (deacon 1941-60, brotherhood pres. 1960). Mason, Lion. Home: Cedar Creek Rd Junction TX 76849 Office: 701 College St Junction TX 76849

GRAHAM, WESLEY HOPE, county ofcl.; b. Shellmound, Tenn., Nov. 28, 1915; s. John Hope and Minerva (Burnett) G.; student U. Tenn., 1936-39; m. Mary Rachel Thomas, Aug. 1, 1942; children—Judith (Mrs. Troy Blevins), Thomas Wesley, John Paul. Farmer, grain dealer, South Pittsburg, Tenn., 1939-62; Marion County road commr., Jasper, Tenn., 1962-—. Chmn., Marion County Agr. Stblzn. Conservation Com., 1952-56, South Pittsburg Housing Authority, 1957-71. Chmn. Marion County Democratic Party, 1956-61; hon. sgt.-at-arms Tenn. Senate, 1969. Bd. dirs. Sequatchie Valley Devel. Corp. Mem. Tenn. County Hwy. Ofcls. Assn. (pres.), Tenn. County Services Assn. (dir.), Am. Rd. Builders Assn. (dir. county div.), South Pittsburg C. of C., Kappa Alpha. Methodist. Club: Sequatchie Valley Golf and Country (South Pittsburg). Home: Raulstontown Rd South Pittsburg TN 37380 Office: Marion County Hwy Dept Jasper TN 37347

GRAHAM, WILLIAM E., judge; b., 1929; grad. U. N.C. Admitted to N.C. bar, 1956; now asso. judge Ct. Appeals, Raleigh, N.C. Home: 617 Glen Eden St Raleigh NC 27601*

GRAHAM, WILLIAM KARR, editorial cartoonist; b. Coshocton, O., Dec. 14, 1920; s. Lorenzo Karr and Zola (McGinnis) G.; B.S. in Social Sci., Centenary Coll., 1942; m. Wilma Lea Been, Oct. 19, 1945; children—Walter, Joseph. Reporter, cartoonist Coshocton Tribune, 1946-48; editorial cartoonist Ark. Gazette, Little Rock, 1948-—. Traveling exhbns. Nat. Cartoonists Soc., Assn. Am. Editorial Cartoonists; represented in collections U. Kan., Wayne State U., Va. Mil. Inst., U. Mo., Syracuse, U. Cin. Served with AUS, 1942-46. Mem. Nat. Cartoonists Soc., Assn. Am. Editorial Cartoonists, Kappa Sigma. Mem. Ch. of Christ. Mason. Home: 5208 W 24th St Little Rock AR 72204 Office: Ark Gazette Little Rock AR 72203

GRAHAM, WILLIAM RUSSELL, editor; b. Scranton, Pa., Mar. 8, 1927; s. Franklin Stewart and Elsie (Carpenter) G.; student Wentworth Inst., 1945-46, Traffic Mgrs. Inst. of N.Y., Boston, 1947; m. Gloria Stickler, Dec. 25, 1955 (div. June 1968); children—Geoffrey Tye, Robin Dolores; m. 2d, Barbara Jane Cooke, June 25, 1968; 1 stepdau., Deborah Ann Good. With John A. Conkey & Co., Boston, 1947, Air Express Internat., Houston, 1948, Lykes Bros. S.S. Co., 1949, Digest Publs., 1949-50, Hughes Tool Co. mfrs. oil tool products, Houston, 1951-—, editor Hughesnews, 1951-—. Served with USNR, World War II. Mem. S.Tex. Indsl. Editors, Houston Fine Arts Assn. Editor: Diary of William Fairfax Gray, From Virginia to Texas, 1835-1836, 1966; Diary of Millie Gray (Mildred Richards Stone Gray) and the Small Journal, 1967. Home: 9711 Riddlewood St Houston TX 77025 Office: Hughes Tool Co Box 2539 Houston TX 77001

GRAHAM, WILMER ALLEN, accountant; b. Ft. Stockton, Tex., Jan. 15, 1914; s. Joel Allen and Mattie (Pullen) G.; student West Tex. State U., 1946-48;; m. Mary A. Fields, Mar. 19, 1938; children—Betty J. (Mrs. David Hinton), Donald A. With U.S. Dept. Agr., 1938-45; partner Russell, Graham & Brown, Amarillo, Tex., 1948-57, Glover, Graham & Brown, C.P.A.'s, Tulia, Tex., 1957-—. Vis. prof. Sch. Bus., West Tex. State U., Canyon, 1950-67. Bd. dirs. Tulia (Tex.) Indsl. Found. Served with USNR, 1945-46. C.P.A., Tex. Mem. Ch. of Christ. Rotarian (pres. 1963-64, 69-70). Home: 45 Fannin Dr Tulia TX 79088 Office: 125 N Maxwell St Tulia TX 79088

GRAINE, GEORGE NATHAN, govt. ofcl.; b. Bklyn., Mar. 4, 1934; s. Allen Robert and Rosalind Schancupp (Goldberg) G.; B.A., Alfred U., 1955, M.A., 1956; m. Gwendolyn Whiting, Nov. 13, 1958; children—Steven, Robin. Counselor Wiltwyck Sch. Boys, Esopus, N.Y., 1957; research psychologist Human Resources Research Office, Ft. Benning, Ga., 1957-59; research psychologist, 1959-67; head anti-submarine warfare Weapons br. Personnel Research Lab., Washington, 1967-68, asst. for human factors coordination Naval Ship Systems Command, Washington, 1968-—. Bus. mgr. Holmes Run Acres Civic Assn., Falls Church, Va., 1967; publs. mgr. Holmes Run Acres Recreation Assn., 1968-69, 72. Served with AUS, 1957-59. Mem. Human Factors Soc., Am., Eastern, D.C. psychol. assns. Contbr. articles to profl. jours. Home: 7604 Westminster Ct Falls Church VA 22042 Office: Naval Ship Systems Command SHIPS 03H Washington DC 20360

GRAINGER, DAVID ALAN, dentist; b. Sydney, Australia, Sept. 25, 1934; s. William Alan and Sybil Wahl (Baxter) G.; B.D.S. with honors, Sydney U., 1956; D.D.S., Northwestern U., 1957; m. 1960; 5 children. Came to U.S., 1956, naturalized, 1968. Asst. in dental medicine Harvard-Forsyth, Boston, 1957-59; pvt. practice dentistry, London, Eng., 1959-60, Sydney, 1961-64; instr. Tufts Dental Sch., Boston, 1964-65, asst. prof., 1965-68, asso. prof., 1968-69; prof., chmn. operative dentistry U. Fla., Gainesville, 1969-—. Cons. Vets. Adminstrn. Hosp., Gainesville, 1969-—. Served with Australian Nat. Service, 1952-55. Fellow Internat. Coll. Dentists, Australian Coll. Dental Surgeons. Author: (with Bruce Bell) Basic Operative Dentistry Procedures, 2d. edit., 1971. Office: Coll Dentistry U Fla J Hillis Miller Health Center Gainesville FL 32601

GRALLA, STANLEY WILLIAM, architect; b. Great Barrington, Mass., Aug. 29, 1939; s. Stanley John and Victoria M. (Wezevitz) G.; B.Arch., Okla. U., 1964; m. Mary Ann Conley, June 16, 1962; children—Shawn Michael, Todd Conley. Designer Shaw & Shaw, architects, Oklahoma City, 1964-66; project and design architect, asso. dir. Benham-Blair & Affiliates, Inc., Oklahoma City, 1966-—. Mem. A.I.A., Nat. Council Architl. Registration Bds., Oklahoma City C. of C. Club: Ski (Oklahoma City). Home: Route 2 Box 18A Oklahoma City OK 73114 Office: 6323 N Grand Blvd Oklahoma City OK 73118

GRAMLEY, DALE H(ARTZLER), found. exec.; b. Loganville, Pa., Sept. 23, 1905; s. Andrew D. and Ada Laura (Meals) G.; A.B., Albright Coll., 1926, Litt.D., 1949; S.M., Columbia, 1929; LL.D., Moravian Coll. and Theol. Sem., 1950; Litt.D. (hon.), Wake Forest Coll., 1955; LL.D. (hon.), Davidson Coll., 1960; m. Caroline Lois Illick, Dec. 27, 1929; children—Hugh Andrew, William Eugene, Dale Illick, Stephan Edward. Reporter, asst. editor U. York (Pa.) Dispatch, 1926-28; copy-reader N.Y. Jour. of Commerce, 1929; instr. journalism Lehigh U., 1929-33, asst. prof., 1933-35, asso. prof., 1935-42, dir. of courses in journalism, 1931-42, editor of Univ. News, 1936-42; asst. to pres. Moravian Coll. and Theol. Sem., 1942-44; editor Bethlehem (Pa.) Globe-Times, 1944-49; v.p. and dir., Bethlehem Globe-Times, WGPA Charities, Inc., 1947-49; v.p. Old Salem Inc., 1950-—; pres. Salem Acad. and Coll. Winston-Salem, 1949-71; exec. dir., sec.-treas. Z. Smith Reynolds Found., 1971-—; dir. Triangle Broadcasting Co. Alumnus trustee Albright Coll., 1931-40; trustee Moravian Coll. and Theol. Sem., 1947-50; v.p. Moravian Music Found., 1956-71; bd. dirs. Reynolda House, Inc., 1967-71; pres. Piedmont U. Center of N.C., 1964-69. Mem. Winston-Salem C. of C. (pres. 1968, chmn. bd. 1969), Pi Delta Epsilon. Democrat. Moravian, Rotarian. Clubs: Forsyth Country; Winston-Salem Automobile (dir.). Home: 231 Main St Winston-Salem NC

GRAMLICH, EDWARD MARTIN, govt. ofcl.; b. Rochester, N.Y., June 18, 1939; s. Jacob Edward and Harriet (Williams) G.; B.A., Williams Coll., 1961; M.A., Yale, 1962, Ph.D., 1965; m. Ruth Ann Brown, Aug. 29, 1964; children—Sarah Becker, Robert Edward. Mem. staff Fed. Res. Bd., 1965-70; with Monash U., Australia, 1970; dir. policy research div. Office Econ. Opportunity, Washington, 1970-—. Recipient Abramson award Nat. Assn. Bus. Economists, 1970. Editorial bd. Nat. Tax Jour., 1971-—. Home: 11521 Links Dr Reston VA 22070 Office: Office Econ Opportunity Exec Office Pres Washington DC 20506

GRAMLING, ELIZABETH B., clubwoman; b. Carp, Tenn., Mar. 2, 1910; d. James Rhea and Cynthia (Smith) Bogart; R.N., James M. Jackson Hosp. Sch. Nursing, Miami, Fla., 1931; m. William Sanders Gramling, Sept. 11, 1935; 1 son, Frank Robert. Nurse, 1931-35. First vol. instr. home nursing A.R.C., Dade County, 1941, organizer nurses aide corps, 1941, chmn., 1941-42, 44, vice chmn. vol. spl. services Dade County chpt., 1944, bd. dirs., 1949-50; sec. Miami Beach Garden Center and Conservatory Com., 1958-68, treas., 1969-72. Mem., sec. bd. trustees Jackson Meml. Hosp., 1938-42; trustee Opera Guild Greater Miami. Recipient certificates of appreciation for civic work. Mem. U.D.C. (chpt. pres. 1957-60, chmn. state by-laws com. 1959-60, chmn. nat. by-laws com. 1960-—), So. Dames of Am. (founding mem.). Episcopalian. Clubs: Bath, Miami Beach Garden, Coast Guard Officers Wives, Jockey. Home: 251 E San Marino Dr Miami Beach FL 33139

GRANBERRY, GEORGIA LOU, ednl. adminstr.; b. Wesson, Miss., Dec. 25, 1939; d. George Richmond and Lou (Meadows) Granberry; student Millsaps Coll., 1958-59; B.S., U. So. Miss., 1962, M.S., 1966. Organizer, tchr. spl. edn. program Kuhn Meml. State Hosp., Vicksburg, Miss., 1963-64, recreation dir. for the blind Div. State Rehab. Dept., 1963; head resident U. So. Miss., 1964-66; resident counselor Fla. State U., 1966-67; residence hall counselor, Panhellenic adviser La. Tech. U., Ruston, 1967-72. Mem. Nat. Assn. Women Deans and Counselors, Am. Assn. U. Women (1st v.p. Ruston br. 1971), U. So. Miss. Alumni Assn., Phi Delta Gamma, Cwens. Methodist. Club: F, Fla. State University (Tallahassee). Home: 850 N Jefferson St Apt C24 Jackson MS 39202

GRANER, STANLEY, corp. exec.; b. Dallas, Dec. 4, 1925; s. Walter and Marie (Weaks) G.; student So. Methodist U., 1943-44; B.S., U. Tex., 1947, M.B.A., 1948; m. Ann Elizabeth Carnathan, Aug. 13, 1949 children—Ann, Lane, Stanley, Jane. With U.S. Cold Storage Corp., 1948-—, salesman, Dallas, 1948-51, adminstrv. asst., Kansas City, Mo., 1951, adminstrv. asst., asst. treas., Chgo., 1951-53 asst to pres., Kansas City, Mo 1953-54, sales mgr., Ft. Worth, 1954-58, v.p., mgr., 1958-71, exec. v.p., 1971-—. Councilman, mayor pro tem North Richland Hills, Tex., 1958-61. Served to lt. (j.g.) USNR, 1943-46. Mem. Nat. Assn. Refrigerated Warehouses (chpt. past pres., dir. 1970-—), Refrigeration Research Found. (past gov.). Republican. Methodist. Clubs: Rotary, Diamond Oaks Country. Home: 5929 Diamond Oaks Dr Fort Worth TX 76117 Office: 5150 Pulaski St Dallas TX 75247

GRANGER, GILBERT LOFTON, accountant; b. Charleston, S.C., June 25, 1935; s. Warren B. and Dorothy Lofton (Gilbert) G.; A.B., Coll. William and Mary, 1957; m. Ann Cornelia Hill, Sept. 25, 1959; children—Gilinda Dawn, Gray Ann, Gregory Hill. Partner Granger & Lent, C.P.A.'s, Williamsburg, Va., 1961-—; pres. G-Square, Inc., Williamsburg, 1965-—; partner Va. Broadcasters, Williamsburg 1965-—; columnist Va. Gazette, 1969-—. Bd. dirs. Williamsburg Area Recreation Assn., 1964-72, pres., 1969; bd. dirs. Williamsburg Area Day Care Center, 1968-—. Recipient Service award Nat. Found., 1965, Jaycee of Year award, 1963, Distinguished Service award, 1966, Outstanding State Chmn. award Va. Jr. C. of C., 1971. Mem. Am. Inst. C.P.A.'s, socs. C.P.A.'s, Williamsburg Jr. (pres. 1967-68), James City County (dir. 1963-68, pres. 1966-67) chambers commerce, St Andrew's Soc., Mensa, William and Mary Alumni Soc., Lambda Chi Alpha. Presbyn. (deacon 1970-71, chmn. 1971). Elk (pres. 1965-66), Kiwanian (dir. 1967, 71-72). Home: 209 Tyler Brooks Dr Williamsburg VA 23185 Office: 1005 Richmond Rd Williamsburg VA 23185

GRANIK, HANNAH BELLE, TV and radio producer; b. N.Y.C., Nov. 19, 1909; d. Samuel and Regina (Fallick) Hayne; grad. Brown's Bus. Coll., Bklyn., 1927; m. Theodore Granik, June 7, 1931; children—William Robert, Marian Ruby (Mrs. Stephen Good). Supr., coordinator Youth Wants to Know, 1951-—, Am. Forum of the Air, 1928-—, All Am. Wants to Know, 1960-—, Women Want to Know, 1955-—; primitive painter, 1963-—. Vice pres. CATV Enterprises, Inc., Riverdale Sect., Bronx, N.Y. Mem. Nat. Council Jewish Women, Friends Brandeis U. Mem. U.S. Reps. Radio and TV Gallery. Mem. B'nai Brith. Home: 4000 Cathedral Av Washington DC 20016 Office: 1627 K St Washington DC 20016

GRANT, BEN JOSEPH, publisher; b. Dothan, Ala., July 20, 1909; s. Ben Joseph and Ethel (Dowman) G.; B.S., U. Fla., 1931; m. Elizabeth Brubaker, Aug. 9, 1938; children—William Dowman, Richard Martin, Martha Watts (Mrs. Mark A. Bedner). Staff writer AP, Jacksonville, Fla., also Tallahassee, 1935-36, Washington, 1936-42; asso. editor U.S. News and World Report, 1946-52, asso. exec. editor, 1952-68, mng. editor, 1968-70, exec. vice pres. 1970-—. Dir., Madana Realty Corp., U.S. News & World Report, Inc. Served to maj. USAAF, 1942-46. Recipient certificate of merit U. Fla., 1953. Clubs: Nat. Press (pres. 1957), International (Washington); Kenwood Country (Bethesda, Md.); Plantation (Hilton Head Island, S.C.). Home: 7000 Orkney Pkwy Bethesda MD 20034 also North Sea Pines Dr Hilton Head SC 29928 Office: 2300 N St NW Washington DC 20037

GRANT, DAVID ALAN, physician; b. Mart, Tex., Nov. 28, 1926; s. Walter Lee and Emma (Reichert) G.; student Tex. Christian U., 1944-45; B.A., U. Tex., 1947, M.D., 1951; m. Alice Louise Inskeep, Dec. 23, 1949; children—Cynthia Lynn, Karen Ann. Intern, Emory U., 1951-52; resident U. Tex. Med. Br., 1954-60; practice medicine, specializing in plastic surgery, Ft. Worth, 1960-—; mem. staffs St. Joseph's, All Saints Episcopal. Ft. Worth Children's, W. I. Cook Childrens', Glenview hosps.; chief div. surgery Harris Hosp., 1971-73; chief div. plastic surgery John Peter Smith Hosp., 1969-71; spl. lectr. Harris Coll. Nursing, Tex. Christian U., 1963; hon. cons. Carswell Air Force Hosp. Pres. bd. dirs. Tarrant County Easter Seal Soc. for Crippled Children and Adults, 1971-72. Served to lt. (j.g.) M.C., USNR, 1952-54. Diplomate Am. Bd. Surgery, Am. Bd. Plastic Surgery. Fellow A.C.S.; mem. A.M.A., Tex., So. med. assns., Tarrant County Med. Soc., Southwestern Surg. Congress, Ft. Worth Acad. Medicine, Tex., Ft. Worth, Singleton (1st v.p. 1965) surg. socs., Am. Burn Assn., Tex. Soc. Plastic Surgery (v.p. 1969-70, pres. 1971), Am. Soc. Plastic and Reconstructive Surgery, Am. Assn. for Hand Surgery, Am. Assn. Physicians and Surgeons, Sigma Xi, Phi Beta Pi, Alpha Epsilon Delta, Alpha Phi Omega. Rotarian (dir. 1964-66). Home: 2736 Colonial Pkwy Fort Worth TX 76109 Office: 800 8th Av Fort Worth TX 76104

GRANT, ELIZABETH BRUBAKER (MRS. BEN J. GRANT), artist; b. St. Paul, Apr. 3, 1917; d. Delmer Dawson and Maude (Spear) Brubaker; student Sarah Lawrence Coll., 1934-37; m. Ben J. Grant, Aug. 9, 1938; children—William Dowman, Richard Martin, Martha Watts (Mrs. Mark A. Bedner). Exhibited in one-man shows Down East Gallery, Washington, Port Royal Inn, Hilton Head, S.C., 1970; exhibited in group shows at Nat. Press Club Ann. Art Shows, Washington Soc. Artists Show, 1962. Recipient First Popular prize Washington Religious Art Exhibit, 1962, 65, Congl. Club Art Show, 1964, St. Andrews Religious Art Exhibit, 1964, 65, Best of Show Nat. Capital Garden Club Show, 1956, 62. Mem. Nat. Capital Area Fedn. Garden Clubs, Artists Equity Assn. Conglist. Clubs: Kenwood Golf and Country (Bethesda, Md.); Plantation (Hilton Head, S.C.). Home: 7000 Orkney Pkwy Bethesda MD 20034 also North Sea Pines Dr Hilton Head Island SC 29928

GRANT, EMORY BRYAN, coll. adminstr.; b. Griffin, Ga., July 14, 1917; s. Joseph Franklin and Martha Ethel (Weldon) G.; B.S., Ga. Inst. Tech., 1949; m. Lina Beatrice Poteet, July 23, 1937; children—Lyna (Mrs. John L. Taylor) Jim Bryan. Asst. regional dir. U.S. Bur. Census, Atlanta, 1949-52; comptroller Middle Ga. Coll., Cochran, Ga., 1953-66, Dalton (Ga.) Jr. Coll., 1967-—. Mem. evaluation coms. So. Assn. Colls. and Schs. Trustee, treas. Dalton Jr. Coll. Found. Served with AUS, 1942-46. Methodist (chmn. trustees 1965-66, mem. ofcl. bd. 1967-—, mem. Ga. commn. higher edn.). Rotarian (pres. Cochran 1959-60). Home: 1021 E Lakeshore Dr Dalton GA 30720 Office: Dalton Junior Coll Dalton GA 30720

GRANT, GEORGE THOMAS, optometrist; b. Chgo., Oct. 17, 1937; s. George Merton and Juanita (Battistoni) G.; student Ill. State U., 1956-58, Thornton Jr. Coll., 1958-59; D.Optometry, Ill. Coll. Optometry, 1962; m. Kathryn Lucille Racanelli, May 9, 1959; children— Jeffrey Thomas, Matthew Thomas, Brynn Elizabeth. Practice optometry, Perry, Ga., 1962-63, Hinesville, Ga., 1964-71, Cartersville, Ga., 1972-—. Mem. Liberty County Bd. Health Hinesville, 1964-71; Liberty County rep. Comprehensive Health Planning, 1968-71; mem. Liberty County Title I Adv. Com., 1968-71, Liberty County Recreation Commn., 1970-71; pres. Coastal Areawide Comprehensive Health Planning Council, 1970-71; chpt. chmn. Liberty County chpt. A.R.C., 1964-66. Liberty County campaign chmn. Jimmy Carter for Gov., 1970. Recipient award of appreciation A.R.C., 1966; named adm. in Ga. Navy, 1971. Fellow Am. Acad. Optometry (sec.-treas. Ga. chpt. 1970-72, chpt. pres. 1972-—); mem. Am. Ga. (sec.-treas.) optometric assns., Ga. Vision Services (dir. 1971-—), So. Council Optometrists, 1st Dist. (pres. 1965-66), 7th Dist. optometric socs., C. of C. (past pres. Liberty County), Internat. Platform Assn., Tomb and Key, Beta Sigma Kappa. Key. Home: 216 Pioneer Trail Cartersville GA 30120 Office: 310 N Tennessee St Cartersville GA 30120

GRANT, H. DANE, banker; b. Lubbock, Tex., June 23, 1935; s. Homer D. and Dorothy (Allen) G.; B.B.A., Tex. Tech U., 1957; m. Linda Bunger, Jan. 24, 1960; children—Rachel, Jacob Nicholas. Asst. v.p. Lubbock Nat. Bank, 1951-64; sr. v.p. Nat. Bank Commerce, Dallas, 1964-70; chief exec. officer Wynnewood State Bank, Dallas, 1970; pres. First Bank of Houston, 1970-—. Bd. dirs. Found. Children, Houston, Mem. Tex. Tech Ex-Students Assn. (dir.), Phi Delta Theta. Mason (Shriner, (32 deg.). Home: 848 Friar Tuck Houston TX 77024 Office: PO Box 36708 Houston TX 77036

GRANT, JAMES MARSE, editor; b. High Point, N.C., Sept. 13, 1920; s. Lon L. and Elsie (Warren) G.; A.B. with honors, High Point Coll., 1941, L.H.D., 1972; m. Marian Gibbs, June 16, 1942; children—Susan (Mrs. Robert Rawls), Marcia (Mrs. Kenneth Hungate), Carol. With personnel dept. Firestone Textiles, 1943-47; editor Ecusta Paper Corp. (now Olin Mathieson), Pisgah Forest, N.C., 1947; editor Lincoln County News, Lonconton, N.C., 1948, News-Herald, Morganton, N.C., 1949; editor Charity and Children for Bapt. Children's Homes, Bapt. State Conv. N.G., Thomasville, N.C., 1950-60, editor Bibl. Recorder, Raleigh, 1960-—. Mem. N.C. Good Neighbor Council, 1963-71, exec. com., 1963-71; N.C. chmn. March of Dimes, 1964-67. Mem. N.C. Gov.'s Com. Jobs for Ex-Offenders, 1970-—, Raleigh Mayor's Com. Employment of Handicapped, 1970-—, N.C. Adv. Com. Pub. Edn., 1970-72. Mem. So. Bapt. Radio and TV Commn., So. Bapt. Press Assn. (pres. 1970). Author: Whiskey at the Wheel, 1970. Home: 1428 Ridge Rd Raleigh NC 27607 Office: Biblical Recorder PO Box 26568 Raleigh NC 27611

GRANT, JAMES PINEO, found. exec.; b. Peiping, China, May 12, 1922; s. John Black and Charlotte (Hill) G.; A.B., U. Cal., 1943; LL.B., Harvard, 1951; m. Ethel Henck, Dec. 30, 1943; children—John Putnam, James Dickinson, William Joseph. Rep. UNRRA in N. China, 1946-47; cons., spl. asst. to dir. U.S. Econ. Aid Mission to China, 1948-49, 50; asso. Covington & Burling, Washington, 1951-54; regional legal counsel U.S. Econ. Aid missions, South Asia, 1954-56; dir. U.S. Econ. Aid Mission to Ceylon, 1956-58; spl. asst. to dir. ICA, 1958, dep. dir. I.C.A., Washington, 1958-61; dep. asst. sec. of state for Near Eastern and S. Asian affairs, 1962-64; dir. AID Mission to Turkey, 1964-67; asst. adminstr. AID, Washington, 1967-69; pres. Overseas Devel. Council, 1969-70; commr. Commn. on Chs. Participation in Devel., World Council of Chs., 1970-—. Served as capt. AUS, 1943-45; intelligence officer Burma and China. Decorated Bronze Star with cluster; Breast Order of Yun Hui (China); recipient Distinguished Pub. Service award AID, 1961. Mem. Council Fgn. Relations, Bar Assn. D.C. Club: Metropolitan (Washington). Home: 2871 Tilden St NW Washington DC 20008 Office: 1717 Massachusetts Av NW Washington DC 20036

GRANT, LILLIAN, educator; b. Spartanburg, S.C., Mar. 3, 1906; d. Woodson S. and Alice (Wilkens) Grant; A.B., Winthrop Coll., 1927; M.A., Columbia, 1947. Tchr. English and French High Sch., Holly Springs, S.C., 1927-30, Henrietta-Caroleen-Avondale High Sch., 1930-42, Forest City (N.C.) High Sch., 1942-44; tchr. English and civics Cleveland Jr. High Sch., Spartanburg, S.C., 1944-45; English tchr. Spartanburg High Sch., 1945-47; dean women Meredith Coll., Raleigh, N.C., 1947-50; guidance counselor, tchr. English, Spartanburg High Sch., S.C., 1950—. Mem. regional panel of secondary cons. in guidance Coll. Entrance Exam. Bd., 1963-66. Mem. S.C. Com. on Revising Standards for Accrediting Instns. for Tchr. Edn., S.C. Textbook Evaluating and Rating Com. Recipient Teacher of the Year award Spartanburg County, 1958. Mem. Nat. Congress Parents and Tchrs. (hon. life), Spartanburg City Classroom Tchrs. (pres. 1953-54), Spartanburg County Edn. Assn. (pres. 1955-56), S.C. Classroom Tchrs. (pres. 1956-57), Nat. Assn. Women Deans and Counselors (pres. 1957-58), Nat., S.C. (pres. 1958-59, chmn. finance com. 1959-60). mem. high sch-coll. com. 1968-70) edn. assns., Am. Assn. U. Women, Nat. Council Tchrs. English, Am. Personnel and Guidance Assn., Delta Kappa Gamma (state program chmn. 1957-59, state legislative chmn. 1959-61, state 1st pres. 1969-71, state pres. 1971-73). Baptist. Mem. Order Eastern Star. Home: Route 1 Lake Lanier Landrum SC 29356

GRANT, MILTON, broadcasting exec. Pres., WDCA-TV, Washington. Address: 5202 River Rd Washington DC 20016*

GRANT, VERNE, educator; b. San Francisco, Oct. 17, 1917; s. Edwin E. and Bessie (Swallow) G.; B.A., U. Cal. at Berkeley, 1936-40, Ph.D., 1949; m. Karen Alt, Nov. 28, 1960; children (by previous marriage)—Joyce, Brian, Brenda. Translator, U.S. War Dept., Panama, 1942-45; teaching asst. botany U. Cal. at Berkeley, 1946-49; vis. investigator Carnegie Instn. Washington, Stanford, Cal., 1949-50; geneticist, exptl. taxonomist Rancho Santa Ana Botanic Garden, Claremont, Cal., 1952-67; mem. faculty Claremont (Cal.) Grad. Sch., 1952-67; prof. biology Inst. Life Scis., Tex. A. and M. U., College Station, 1967-68; dir. Boyce Thompson Southwestern Arboretum, prof. biol. scis. U. Ariz., Superior, 1968-70, prof. botany U. Tex., Austin, 1970—. Recipient fellowship NRC, 1949-50, award in sci. Phi Beta Kappa, 1964, Certificate of Merit, Bot. Soc. Am., 1971. Mem. Soc. for Study Evolution (pres. 1968), Am. Soc. Naturalists, Genetics Soc. Am., Bot. Soc. Am., Internat. Soc..plant Taxonomists, Am. Soc. Plant Taxonomists, Nat. Acad. Scis., Southwestern Assn. Naturalists. Author: Natural History of the Phlox Family, 1959; The Origin of Adaptations, 1963, The Architecture of the Germplasm, 1964; Flower Pollination in the Phlox Family, 1965; Hummingbirds and Their Flowers, 1968, Plant Speciation, 1971. Editorial bd. Ency. Americana, 1955-64, Brittonia, 1957-62, Evolution, 1960-62, Am. Naturalist, 1964-67. Contbr. articles to profl. jours. Home: 2811 Fresco Dr Austin TX 78731

GRANT, WILLIAM ALEXANDER, JR., coal co. exec.; b. Richmond, Va., Nov 7, 1918; s. William Alexander and Louise (Hooper) G.; B.A., U. Richmond, 1941; m. Marion Louise Bankhead, Aug. 27, 1945; children—William Alexander III, Blossom Grant, Walter Bankhead. Sec.-treas. Bankhead Mining Co. Inc., 1953—; sec. Tri W Broadcasting, Inc., Jasper, 1965—, Bankhead Broadcasting Co., Inc., Jasper, 1964—, Franklin Broadcasting Inc., Russellville, Ala., 1965—, Bankhead Devel. Inc., Jasper, 1960—, Live Line Inc., Jasper, 1968—; chmn. bd. Gatorland Broadcasting Inc., St. Augustine, Fla., 1969—; mng. partner Cobb Coal Co., Jasper; dir. Viking Oil Co., Jasper. Chmn. March of Dimes, 1955. Served as lt. (s.g.) USNR, 1942-46. Decorated Navy Cross, D.F.C., Air Medal with gold star. Mem. Nat. Assn. Accountants, Theta Chi, C. of C. (dir. 1956). Clubs: Downtown (Birmingham); Musgrove Country, Rotary. Home: 912 9th Av Jasper AL 35501 Office: Box 16 29 Jasper AL 35501

GRANT, WILLIAM FRANKLIN, JR., banker; b. Marion, N.C., May 4, 1921; s. William Franklin and Mary Ellen (Allison) G.; student Brevard Jr. Coll., 1938-40, E. Carolina Tchrs. Coll., 1940-42, U. N.C., 1950-54, La. State U., 1962-65; m. Mildred Lenore Ragan, Nov. 16, 1946; children—William Franklin III, Michael Ragan, David Allison. Vice pres., First Nat. Bank, Hickory, N.C., 1950-66; v.p., cashier Alexandria Nat. Bank (Va.), 1966-68, Peoples Nat. Bank, Chester, S.C., 1968—. Tchr. Am. Inst. Banking, 1954-55. Sec.-treas. Hickory Community Found., Inc., 1960-66. Bd. dirs., chmn. United Fund; bd. dirs., treas. Chester County Mental Health Assn.; bd. dirs., vice chmn. S.C. Mental Health Assn.; chmn. bd. dirs. York, Chester, Lancaster Mental Health Center, Rock Hill, S.C., 1972—. Served with USNR, 1942-46. Recipient Distinguished Service award Nat. Polio Found., 1957, Nat. Heart Assn., 1960, United Fund, 1970; named Civitan of the Year, 1970. Mem. Am. Inst. Banking (chpt. pres. 1955-56), N.C., Va., S.C. bankers assns., Am. Legion, Democrat. Baptist. Moose. Club: Civitan (lt. gov. S.C. dist.) (Chester, S.C.). Home: Hill Top Acres Chester SC 29706 Office: Church St Chester SC 29706

GRANT, W(ILLIAM) VANCE, JR., govt. ofcl.; b. Gainesville, Ga., Sept. 3, 1924; s. W. Vance and Myrtle (Haynes) G.; A.B., Piedmont Coll., 1943; B.B.A., U. Ga., 1947; M.A., Columbia, 1948; M.S., Fla. State U., 1951; Ph.D., U. Md., 1968; postgrad. U. London, 1957; m. Earlynn Vance, Aug. 23, 1952; children—James, Jean. Psychometrist, Fla. State U., 1951-52; statistician, test technician State of Fla., Tallahassee, 1952-54; research psychologist U.S. Dept. Army, Washington, 1954-55; specialist ednl. statistics U.S. Office Edn., Washington, 1955—. Served with USNR, 1944-45. Mem. Am. Polit. Sci. Assn. Baptist. Author: (with others) Biennial Survey of Education in the United States, 1957, 59, 62; (with Kenneth A. Simon) Digest of Educational Statistics, 1962-71; (with others) Progress of Public Education in the United States of America, 1967-1968, 1968. Contbr. to Historical Statistics of the United States, Colonial Times to 1957, 1960. Contbr. articles to profl. jours. Home: 211 W Columbia St Falls Church VA 22046 Office: 400 Maryland Av SW Washington DC 20202

GRANTHAM, JOHN RICHARD, oil co. exec.; b. McGregor, Tex., Aug. 8, 1917; s. John Richard and Myrtle (Kirkpatrick) G.; B.S., Tex. A. and M. U., 1939; m. Mary Lois McWhirter, June 23, 1944; children—Mary Gail (Mrs. Charles Stephen LaGrone), Becky Lynn (Mrs. Lyle Wayne Schwedland), Susan Kay, James William. Tng. asst. Humble Oil & Refining Co., Baytown, Tex., 1946-47, indsl. relations research asst., Houston, 1947-48; owner, operator Grantham Bros. (cotton firm), McGregor, 1948-53; mgr. employee relations Phillips Petroleum Co., McGregor, 1953-58; v.p. indsl. relations Apco Oil Corp., Oklahoma City, 1958—. Gen. chmn. Greater Oklahoma City United Appeal, 1967, now pres., mem. bd. dirs.; dir. Oklahoma City and Oklahoma County Community Council. Served to maj. AUS, 1942-46. Mem. Am. Mgmt. Assn., Oklahoma City C. of C. (chmn. petroleum council), Asso. Industries Okla. (v.p., (dir.). Club: Oklahoma City Petroleum (pres. 1969). Home: 2943 Huntleigh Dr Oklahoma City OK 73120 Office: Liberty Bank Bldg Oklahoma City OK 73102

GRASER, MERLE LAWRENCE, banker; b. Toledo, July 18, 1929; s. Ottomar and Irene Olga (Frommer) G.; student U. Miami, 1955-56; B.S. in Bus. Adminstrn., U. Fla., 1959; m. Lila Patricia Woodburn, Nov. 6, 1948; children—Shaun Douglass, Cathleen Patricia. Asst. v.p. City Nat. Bank Coral Gables, Fla., 1960-63; with First Nat. Bank Venice, Fla., 1963—, exec. v.p., 1970-72, pres., 1970-72, chmn. bd., 1972—, Instr. Am. Inst. Banking, 1960-71; dir. Charlotte County Nat. Bank, Port Charlotte, Fla. Bd. dirs. Golden Beach Assn., Venice, Fla., 1964—, Loveland Sch. for Retarded Children, 1964—. Served with USCG, 1951-54. Mem. Delta Sigma Pi. Lion (pres. 1969-70), Rotarian, Elk. Club: Yacht (Venice, Fla.). Home: 612 Hibiscus Dr Venice FL 33595 Office: 200 Nokomis Av S Venice FL 33595

GRASSBAUGH, FRANCIS JOSEPH, mgmt. cons.; b. Akron, O., Nov. 7, 1916; s. Lewis B. and Pearl Florence (O'Neal) G.; student U. Akron, 1937-40; B.B.A., U. Cin., 1948; m. Ruth M. Klug, Apr. 15, 1942; children— Christine (Mrs. James Knioum), David. Accountant various firms, 1948-58; with Rice Well Service, Kingsville, Tex., 1958—, mgmg. cons., 1959—; owner Bus. Mgmt. Service, Corpus Christi, Tex.; sec., treas. Rice Well Service, Coastal Bend Oil Co., Borco Trawlers, Acllimate Constructors; dir. Ace Sales Co., Port Constrn. Co. Active Boy Scouts Am. Treas., Republican Party, Nueces County, Tex., 1952-56, county chmn., 1957. Served with USNR, 1940-45. Decrated Air medal, D.F.C. Mem. Corpus Christi Life Udnerwriters Assn. (exec. sec. 1969—), Al Hambra, Theta Chi. Roman Catholic. K.C. Club: Civitan (sec. 1950) (Corpus Christi, Tex.). Home: 457 Glenmore St Corpus Christi TX 78412 Office: 720 Buffalo St Corpus Christi TX 78403

GRATER, HARRY ALLEN, educator. Dir., sr. counseling psychologist Univ. Counseling Center, U. Fla., Gainesville, also asso. prof. psychology. Office: U Fla Gainesville FL 32601*

GRATTAN, CLINTON HARTLEY, author; b. Wakefield, Mass., Oct. 19, 1902; s. Leonard and Laura (Campbell) G.; A.B., Clark Coll., Worcester, Mass., 1923; D. Litt., Clark U., 1953; m. Beatrice Kay, Oct. 22, 1926 (div. 1934); m. 2d, Marjorie Sinclair Campbell, June 3, 1939; children—Rosalind Campbell (Mrs. Arthur von Au), Jennifer Hartley (Mrs. Alan Corner), Jacqueline Allison (Mrs. Conrad Smeeth), John Hartley. Head dept. English, Urbana (O.) Jr. Coll., 1923-25; writer, 1925-; vis. fellow Australian Nat. U., 1960; curator Grattan Collection of Southwest Pacificana, univ. prof. history U. Tex., 1964—. Author books including: Way We Fought, 1929, 66; Bitter Bierce: A Mystery of American Letters, 1929, 66; The Three Jameses: A Family of Minds, 1932, 62; (with Paxton Hibben) The Peerless Leader: William Jennings Bryan, 1929, 67; Introducing Australia, 1942, rev. edit., 1947; Australia (U. N. Series), 1947; (with Sylvan Hoffman) News of the World, 1953; In Quest of Knowledge, 1955; The United States and The Southwest Pacific, 1961; The Southwest Pacific: A Modern History, 2 vols., 1963. Editor publs. including: Such is Life, by Tom Collins, 1948; American Ideas about Adult Education 1710-1951, 1959, Collaborator News of the Nation, 1944, and others. Contbr. articles on Australia 1945 edit. Ency. Americana. Contbr. to Harpers, Am. Mercury, Scribners and other nat. mags., 1924-; writer on Australian affairs, 1927—. Awarded grant by Carnegie Corp., N.Y.C., to study social devel. of Australia, 1937-38. Home: 702 Spofford St Austin TX 78704

GRAVEL, CAMILLE F(RANCIS), JR., lawyer; b. Alexandria, La., Aug. 10, 1915; s. Camille F. and Aline (Delvaille) G.; student Notre Dame U., 1931-35, La. State U., 1935-37, Catholic U. Am., 1937-39; m. Katherine Yvonne David, Nov. 26, 1939; children—Katherine Ann, Mary Eileen (Mrs. Richard B. Cappell), Martha Louise (Mrs. Thomas A. Antoon), Camille F. III, Grady David, Eunice Holloman (Mrs. Joseph A. Mitchell), Virginia Maureen (Mrs. Charles L. Carbo, Jr.), Margaret Lynn, Mark Alan, Charles Gregory. Mem. U.S. Capitol Police Force, 1937-39; admitted to La. bar, 1940, U.S. Supreme Ct. bar, U.S. 5th Circuit Ct. Appeal bar, U.S. Dist. Cts. of La.; practiced in 1940—; sr. partner firm Gravel, Roy & Burnes; asst. dist. atty. Rapides Parish, La., 1942, atty. for inheritance tax collector, 1943-45; asst. atty. city of Alexandria, 1946-48. Officer, dir. Payne-Gravel Corp., So. Ventures Corp., MYCI Corp. Atty., La. Workmen's Compensation Laws and Tax Laws, 1964-65; spl. counsel on medicare to gov. of La., 1966-67, on health, 1967; mem. La. Interdepartmental Health Policy Commn., 1967-68; gen. counsel La. Labor-Mgmt. Commn. on Inquiry, 1967. Mem. Nat. Citizen's Com. for Community Relations, 1964-68, La. Adv. Com. on Civil Rights, 1965-67, Nat. Adv. Bd. on Community Relations, 1965-67; founding mem. Com. on So. Progress; mem. adv. bd. Catholic Youth Orgn., Diocese of Alexandria. Mem. La. Democratic Central Com., 1948-64; Dem. nat. committeeman for La., 1954-60; rep. on exec. com. Dem. Nat. Com., 1955-60; chmn. La. delegation Dem. Nat. Conv., 1956, chmn. site selection com., co-chmn. credentials com., mem. arrangements com., 1960, del., 1964; mem. Nat. Adv. Council of Dem. Party, 1956-60; co-chmn. La. Lawyers for Johnson-Humphrey Presdl. Campaign, 1964; founding mem. So. Com. on Polit Ethics, So. Polit. Edn. Action Com. Bd. dirs. La. Council on Human Relations, 1965-68, Catholic Charities, Diocese of Alexandria. Decorated Knight of St. Gregory; recipient citation for outstanding achievement in field of politics Catholic U. Am., 1962. Fellow Internat. Acad. Trial Lawyers (dir. 1960-69); mem. Am., La. (gov. 1969-71, chmn. criminal law sect. 1971—), Alexandria (pres. 1949-50) bar assns., Notre Dame Law Assn. (dir. 1960-66, pres. 1962-63), Law Sci. Acad., Internat. Soc. Barristers, Am. Trial Lawyers Assn., Nat. Assn. Compensation Claimant's Attys. (asso. editor Law jour. 1954-68, state v.p. 1958-59), Alexandria-Pineville C. of C., Pub. Affairs Research Council, La. Civil Service League, Am. Legion, Internat. Platform Assn., L.Q.C. Lamar Soc., Catholic U. Am. Alumni Assn. (nat. gov. 1963-67, 71—, past pres. Alexandria chpt.), Phi Delta Phi, Kappa Sigma. K.C. (4 deg.), Elk (past exalted ruler Alexandria). Club: City (Baton Rouge). Home: 3214 Carol Ct Alexandria LA 71301

GRAVELY, CLINTON EUGENE, architect; b. Reidsville, N.C., Sept. 7, 1935; s. William H., Jr. and Mildred (Slade) G.; B.Arch., Howard U., 1959; m. Etta Christine Leath, July 3, 1960; children—Angela Renee, Clinton Eugene, Tyrsa Monnique. Officer in charge plans and projects sect. Post Engrs., Ft. Jackson, S.C., 1960-61; designer, draftsman, fallout shelter analyst, project architect, job supr. Loewenstein, Atkinson & Wilson, Greensboro, N.C., 1961-67; pvt. practice architecture, Greensboro, 1967—; instr. archtl. engring. dept. A. and T. State U., 1968-71. Mem. Greensboro Housing Commmn., 1968—. Mem. finance com. Tarhill Triad council Girl Scouts Am., 1965-67; mem. camping com. YMCA, 1970—; exec. bd. Gen. Greene council Boy Scouts Am. Served with AUS, 1960-61. Recipient 2d Place Design award for Community Bldg. City of Rockville, Md., 1957. Mem. A.I.A., Greensboro Registered Architects, Omega Psi Phi. Home: 607 Callan St Greensboro NC 27405 Office: 500 Banner Av Greensboro NC 27401

GRAVELY, SAMUEL LEE, JR., naval officer; b. Richmond, Va., June 4, 1922; s. Samuel Lee and Marg George (Simon); student Va. Union U., 1938-40, 46-48, B.A. in History, 1948; student U. Cal. at Los Angeles, 1943-44, Columbia, 1944; postgrad. U.S. Naval War Coll., 1963-64, George Washington U., 1964; m. Alma Bernice Clark, Feb. 12, 1946; children—Robert Michael, David Edward, Tracey Ernestine. Commd. ensign U.S. Navy, 1944, advanced through grades to rear adm., 1955; asst. bn. comdr. Naval Tng. Center, Great Lakes, Ill., 1944-45; communications officer, electronics officer, exec. officer, personnel officer USS PC-1264, 1945-46; communications watch officer Fleet Tng. Group, Norfolk, Va., 1946; asst. to officer in charge for recruiting Naval Recruiting Sta. and Officer Procurement, Washington, 1949-51; radio officer U.S.S. Iowa, 1952-53; communications officer U.S.S. Toledo, 1953-55, also asst. operations officer, 1953-55; asst. dist. security officer Hdqrs. 3d Naval Dist., N.Y., 1955-57; operations officer U.S.S. Seminole, 1957-59; mem. staffs Comdr. Destroyer Squadrons Seven and Five, 1959-60; exec. officer U.S.S. Theodore E. Chandler, 1960-61, comdg. officer, 1961, exec. officer, 1961-62; comdr. U.S.S. Falgout, Pearl Harbor, Hawaii, 1962-63; nat. emergency airborne command post programmer. Def. Communications Agy., Arlington, Va., 1964-66; comdg. officer U.S.S. Taussig, 1966-68; coordinator Navy Satellite Communications Program Office Asst. Chief Naval Operations, 1968-70; comdr. U.S.S. Jouett, San Diego, 1970-71; comdr. Naval Communications Command, dir. Naval Communications Div. Chief Naval Operations, Washington, 1971—; ry. postal clerk Richmond (Va.) office. Decorated Bronze Star, Meritorious Service Medal, Joint Services Commendation Medal, Navy Commendation Medal with bronze star and combat V, Nat. Def. medal with 1 bronze star, China Service medal, Korean Service medal with 2 bronze stars, UN Service medal, Armed Forces Expeditionary medal, Vietnam Service medal with 3 bronze stars, Vietnamese Campaign medal, others. Mem. Armed Forces Electronics Assn. (v.p. 1971—), I.E.E.E., Alpha Phi Alpha. Kiwanian (hon.). Home: 7211 Idylwood Ct Falls Church VA 22043 Office: Dept Navy Office Chief Naval Operations OP-941 Washington DC 20350

GRAVES, CRANOR FRANKLIN, vocational rehab. counselor; b. Kinston, N.C., Oct. 26, 1926; s. Charles Franklin and Sarah (Barker) G.; student U. N.C., 1943-44; S.T.B., St. Mary's Sem., Balt., 1950; m. Rita Catherine Gassman, Aug. 6, 1971. Ordained priest Roman Catholic Ch., 1950; editor N.C., Cath., 1954-57; nat. dir. Movement for a Better World, 1965-67; chmn. priests senate, Diocese of Raleigh, N.C., 1968-69; vocational rehab. counselor, 1971—. Mem. Raleigh Community Relations Com., 1969—. Home: 1109 E Morgan St Raleigh NC 27610 Office: 11 S Boylan Av Raleigh NC 27603

GRAVES, DOUGLAS FOCH, banker; b. Appleton, Minn., Nov. 11, 1918; s. James and Pearl (Perrin) G.; B.S., Ia. State U., 1946, M.S., 1948; m. Barbara Giese, Feb. 1, 1942; children—Heidi (Mrs. Downing), Douglas, Thomas, Deborah (Mrs. Reitinger), James, Jeffrey. Extension specialist Ia. State U., 1945-49; asst. sec. No. Trust Co., 1950-58; asst. v.p. Harris Trust & Savs. Bank, 1958-61; v.p., dir. First Nat. Bank, Freeport, Ill., 1962-67; pres., dir. Nat. Mfrs. Bank, Neenah, Wis., 1967-69; exec. v.p., dir. Union Nat. Bank, Little Rock, 1969—; pres., dir., chief exec. officer Nat. Bank Commerce, Jackson, Tenn., 1971—. Trustee Nat. Brain Research Found. Served to capt. AUS, 1942-45. Mem. Am., Ill. socs. farm mgrs., Tenneseans for Better Transp., Phi Delta Theta. Episcopalian. Club: Jackson Golf and Country. Contbr. syndicated agr. and consumer credit column to profl. jours., popular mags. Home: 231 Elmwood Dr E Jackson TN 38301 Office: Nat Bank of Commerce Bldg Jackson TN 38301

GRAVES, EMORY LEA, developing co. exec.; b. New Orleans, Sept. 2, 1923; s. Emory and Esther (Lea) G.; B.A., Tulane U., 1942; postgrad. La. Polytech. Inst., 1942; La. Normal Coll., 1943; U. Ga., 1943; Southeastern La. Coll., 1950-51, La. State U., 1951, Loyola U., 1951-52 m. 2d, Sylvia Acosta; children—Emory Lea, Christy, Ann Elizabeth, Julie. Sales mgr. William B. Reily & Co., Inc., New Orleans, 1946-48; pres. Christy Ann Lea Inc., 1948; Crestmont Devel. Corp., 1964—; owner Emory L. Graves Realty Co., 1950—; Emory L. Graves Enterprises, 1950— (all Slidell, La.). Served with USNR, 1943-46. Mem. Nat. Inst. Farm and Land Brokers, St. Tammany Bd. Realtors (past pres., dir. 1965-68; realtor of year 1964); Am. Legion V.F.W., Res. Officers Am.. Episcopalian (vestryman, lay reader). Mason (Shriner). Home: Treasure Cove on Bayou Liberty Slidell LA 70458 Office: 520 Rigolets Rd Slidell LA 70458

GRAVES, HAROLD HUE, former sch. adminstr.; b. Fort Worth, Sept. 19, 1905; s. Edward and Emma Susan (Wilmore) G.; B.A., Southwestern U., 1928; M.A., Tex. Christian U., 1938; m. Juanita S. Wilkerson, June 4, 1935; 1 dau., Carole Sue (Mrs. George Edward Brandt). Tchr. Southwestern U., Georgetown, Tex., 1927-28, Anatolia Coll., Saloniki, Greece, 1928-31; with Fort Worth Pub. Schs., 1931-71, tchr., 1931-34, adminstr., 1935-57, asst. supt., 1958-66, dir. curriculum, 1967-71, ret., 1971. Bd. dirs. Fort Worth Mus. Sci. and History, 1962-64. Mem. Am. Assn. Sch. Administrs., Nat. Assn. Elementary Sch. Prins., N.E.A., Tex. State Tchrs. Assn., Tex. Elementary Sch. Prins. Assn., Assn. Supervision and Curriculum Devel. Methodist. Lion (pres. 1953-54). Author (with others) Spelling Textbook Series, Steps to Good Spelling, 1950. Home: 5758 Rockhill Rd Fort Worth TX 76112

GRAVES, HENRY THEODORE NORTHCOTT, corp. exec.; b. Luray, Va., Nov. 10, 1922; s. Henry Walton and Katherine (Northcott) G.; grad. Lawrenceville Sch.; student U. Miami; B.S., U. Va.; m. Rebecca Beall Jackson, Nov. 29, 1944; children—Rebecca (Mrs. John R. Hudson, Jr.), Henry Theodore Northcott II, Katherine Murchison, Elizabeth Duval, Cornelia Walton, John Howard Hershey, James Roderick Oughton. Pres. Luray Caverns Corp. (Va.), 1952—, Car & Carriage Daravan, Inc., Luray, 1957—, Luray Service Co., Inc., 1962—, Carillon Properties, Inc., Luray, 1965—, Luray Mfg. & Distbg. Co., Inc., 1963—; Historic Stoners Store, Fredericksburg; dir. Page Valley Nat. Bank, Va. Sky-Line Co., Inc. Richmond. Mem. Gov.'s Travel Adv. Com., Page County Sch. Bd., Page County Selective Service Bd.; mem. Upper Valley Regional Park Authority, Harrisonburg, Va. Mem. adv. com. New Market Battlefield Meml., Woodrow Wilson Found. Served with USAAF, 1942-45. Mem. Va. Travel Council (past pres.), So. Highland Attractions (past pres.), Nat. Caves Assn. (past pres.), Am. Soc. Travel Agts., Sovereign Colonial Soc. Ams. Royal Descent, Kappa Sigma. Conservative Democrat. Episcopalian. Mem. Order Magna Carta Barons; Mason, Rotarian. Clubs: National Press (Washington); Commonwealth (Richmond). Home: PO Box 389 Luray VA 22835

GRAVES, JOHN BRICE, utilities exec.; b. Cullman, Ala., Feb. 11, 1911; s. Charles Burvel and Lucinda Jane (Miller) G.; student Howard Coll., 1931-32; B.S. in Forestry with honors, N.C. State Coll., 1935; m. Eva Lena Castleberry, Oct. 14, 1939; children—John Brice, Edwin Castleberry, Lena Bingham (Mrs. William Alton Murrah, Jr.). Project forester U.S. Forest Service, 1935-46; chief forester land dept., dir. forest mgmt. Ala. Power Co., Birmingham, 1946—; mgr. family farm lands, Ala., 1944—. Sec. Ala. Forestry Council, 1961, chmn., 1962. Chmn. Keep Jefferson County (Ala.) Green Com., 1954. Mem. Ala. Forest Products Assn. (dir. 1967-70), Soc. Am. Foresters (chmn. Ala. chpt. 1953, historian 1958-62; chmn. Southeastern sect. 1969). Baptist (deacon). Mason. Home: 504 South St E Talladega AL 35160 Office: Ala Power Co 600 18th St N Birmingham AL 35202

GRAVES, ROBERT STRICKLER, JR., farmer; b. Cleve., Sept. 19, 1922; s. Robert Strickler and Annabel (Dye) G.; B.A., Va. Poly. Inst., 1944; m. Ellen Russell McMullan, Apr. 1, 1950; 1 dau., Anne McMullan. Vice pres. R.S. Graves Bros., Inc., Syria, Va., 1965—; dir. Shen-Valley Meat Packers; mem. adv. bd. Nat. Bank & Trust Co. (Madison, Va.); mem. adv. bd. ARA Sky-Line, Inc. (Richmond). Chmn. Madison County Sch. Bd., Piedmont Vocational Sch. Bd.; finance chmn. Va. Sch. Bds. Assn., 1970-71; mem. Va. State Apple Commn. Served with USAAF, 1943-46. Mem. Va. Hort. Soc. (pres.),

Fellowship Christian Athletes, Alpha Kappa Psi. Independent. Lutheran. Mason, Lion. Home: Syria VA 22743

GRAVES, WILLIAM LESTER, JR., educator; b. Terry, Miss., Aug. 26, 1915; s. William Lester and Ada Lee (Graves) G.; student Graceland Coll., 1933-36; B.S., N.W. Mo. State Coll., 1945; M.Ed., Drake U., 1948; Ed.D., U. Colo., 1963; m. Kathlyn Earlita Cato, Feb. 20, 1938; children—William Lester III, Pamella Kay (Mrs. Joe Rayford Daniel). Instr. music pub. schs., Mo., 1936-45, Ia., 1945-46, Miss., 1953-61; mem. faculty Graceland Coll., Lamoni, Ia., 1946-53; state supr. music Tenn. Dept. Edn., 1961-64; prof. music Miss State Coll. for Women at Columbus, 1964—. Mem. arts edn. adv. panel Miss. Arts Commn., 1970—; cons. Miss. Textbook Com., 1966; music cons. community, civic music orgns., 1961—. Bd. reps. Columbus Civic Arts Council. Mem. Miss. Music Educators Assn. (bd. reps. 1953-61, 64—, pres. 1960-61; editor Miss. Notes 1966—), Miss. Edn. Assn., Am. String Tchrs. Assn., Nat. Sch. Orch. Assn., Coll. Music Soc., Music Educators Nat. Conf., Phi Delta Kappa, Lambda Delta Sigma. Mem. Reorganized Ch. of Jesus Christ of Latter-day Saints (elder). Author: A Comparison of Three Methods for Improving Intonation in the Performance of Instrumental Music, 1963. Mus. compositions include Passacaglia and Fugue for Strings, 1962, Hear Us, O Lord, from Heav'n Thy Dwelling Place, 1965, Unto Thee Do We Cry, 1969. Contbr. articles profl. jours. Home: Box 2363 Columbus MS 39701

GRAVITT, T(HUR) O(DELL), telephone co. exec.; b. Apperson, Okla., July 10, 1923; s. Miles C. and Winnie C. (Harris) G.; student U. Kan., 1943-44, U. Tulsa, 1947-49; m. Oleta Maye, July 23, 1943; children— Michael T., Patrick D. With Southwestern Bell Telephone Co., 1947—, gen. comml. mgr., Topeka, Kan., 1964-69, v.p. staff, 1969-70, v.p., gen. mgr. San Antonio area, 1970—; dir. Frost Nat. Bank, San Antonio. Bd. dirs. Alamo Area council Boy Scouts Am., YMCA, United Fund, Fiesta Commn.; trustee S.W. Methodist Hosp. Rotarian. Clubs: Oak Hills Country, University, St. Anthony (San Antonio). Home: 503 Squires Row San Antonio TX 78213 Office: PO Drawer 390 San Antonio TX 78292

GRAY, CHARLES DOWD, SR., brokerage exec.; b. Gastonia, N.C., Aug. 21, 1890; s. George A. and Jennie (Withers) G.; student Trinity Coll., 1907-09, Washington and Lee U., 1909-10; m. Clarice Poff, July 9, 1912; children—Charles D., David G., Betty Claire (Mrs. L. S. Summey). Catherine Demaris (Mrs. H. Chapin Jackson). Pres. Gray Cotton Co., 1914-31, Priscilla Spinning Co., 1921-27; salesman Textiles, Inc., 1931-36, dir., 1933—; pres. Gray & Daniel, Inc. 1936—; incorporator Rex Spinning Co., Priscilla Spinning Co., Parkdale Mills, Inc., Ranlo Mfg. Co., Arkray Mills, Inc., Myrtle Mills, Inc. Chmn. adv. council Belmont Abbey Coll. Mem. N.C. State Ports Authority. Mem. Kappa Sigma. Mason (Shriner). Clubs: Kiwanis, Gastonia Country, Biltmore Country. Home: 1805 Country Club Rd Gastonia NC 28052 Office: Box 1238 Gastonia NC 28052

GRAY, CHARLES WEBSTER, mgmt. cons., cons. engr.; b. nr. Clinton, Mo., Sept. 9, 1914; s. Harvey Gant and Mary (Lay) G.; student Central Coll., 1931-33, U. Mo., 1933-36; Pittsburg (Kan.) State Coll., 1949-50; m. Frances Louise Thomas, Sept. 6, 1936; children—Mary Elizabeth, Charles Webster. Jr. engr., supr., asst. state planning engr. WPA, Jefferson City, Mo., 1936-40; design engr., field engr., asst. maintenance supt. Hercules Powder Co., Radford, Va., Wilmington, Del., 1940-46; maintenance and engring cons., Carthage, Mo., 1946; engr., sr. engr., projects supt. Spencer Chem. Co., Quaker Valley Constructors, Inc. subsidiary, Pittsburg, 1947-53; sr. maintenance engr., maintenance supt. Am. Cyanamid Co., New Orleans, 1953-59; maintenance cons., pres. Gray Equipment, Inc., Metarie, La., 1959-61, chmn. bd., 1959—; resident engr. Barnard and Burk, Baton Rouge, Seneca, S.C., 1961-62; chief planner, project supt., project mgr., cons. Catalytic Inc., Orange, Tex., Toledo, Phila., 1962—; mgmt. and engring. cons. on maintenance, constrn. chem. and petroleum industries and critical path method planning for chem. processing cos., oil refining cos., govt. agys., others, 1961—. Recipient numerous commendations, certificates for engring. and mgmt. achievements, distinguished service. Registered profl. engr., Mo., La., Kan. Mem. Internat. Platform Assn., Am. Mgmt. Assn., Nat., Mo. socs. profl. engrs., La. Engring. Soc., Am. Welding Soc. (dir. 1954-55). Democrat. Methodist (ofcl. bd.). Elk. Home: 121 N Livingston Pl Metairie LA 70005 Office: 121 N Livingston Pl Metairie LA 70005 also 1908 Dana Dr Adelphi MD 20783 also care Haskins-Sharp-Ordelheide 1009 Baltimore Kansas City MO 64105 also 613 S Patterson St Gibsonburg OH 43431 also 1528 Walnut St Philadelphia PA 19102

GRAY, CLARENCE JONES, educator, dean; b. Red Bank, N.J., June 21, 1908; s. Clarence J. Sr. and Elsie (Megill) G.; A.B., U. Richmond, 1933; M.A., Columbia U., 1934; postgrad. Centro de Estudios Historicos, Madrid, Spain, summer 1935; Ed.D., U.Va., 1962; m. Jane Love Little, Aug. 25, 1934; children—Frances Elizabeth (Mrs. Harry B. Mark Jr.), Kenneth Stewart. Underwriter Aetna Life Ins. Co., 1925-30; instr. Spanish, Columbia U., 1934-38; gen. sec., mem. exec. council Instituto de las Espanas en los Estados Unidos, 1934-39; instr., sec. dept. Romance langs. Queens Coll., N.Y.C., 1938-46 (on mil. leave 1943-46); dean students U. Richmond (Va.), 1946-68, asso. prof. modern langs., 1946-62, prof., 1962—, dean administrv. services, 1968—, editor bull., 1968—, moderator U. Richmond- WRNL Radio Scholarship Quiz Program. Cons., Commn. on Colls., So. Assn. Colls. and Schs., 1963—. Trustee' Inst. Mediterranean Studies. Served from lt. to lt. comdr., USNR, 1943-46. Mem. Modern Lang. Assn., N.E.A., Am. Assn. Tchrs. Spanish, Am. Coll. Personnel Assn., Am. Personnel and Guidance Assn., Phi Beta Kappa, Phi Delta Kappa, Kappa Delta Pi, Omicron Delta Kappa (nat. sec. gen. council 1966-72, Distinguished Service key 1968), Alpha Psi Omega, Phi Gamma Delta, Alpha Phi Omega. Baptist. Mason. Mem. Legion of Honor, Order of De Molay. Clubs: Country of Va., Colonnade. Contbr. articles to profl. jours. Home: 1 Bostwick Lane U Richmond Richmond VA 23173

GRAY, CLINTON W., veterinarian; b. Wilmington, Del.; D.V.M., Mich. State U., 1943. Veterinarian, Md. Livestock San. Service, 1943-46; gen. practice vet. medicine, 1946-48; supr. Vaccine Prodn. Unit, Dept. Agr., Mexico City, 1948-50; staff biol. dept. Norden Labs., Lincoln, Neb., 1950-55; with dept. Agr., S.Am., 1955-58; with Dept. Pub. Health S.Am., 1958-63; head animal health dept. Nat. Zool. Park, Washington, 1963—. Mem. Am., Md. vet. med. assns., Am. Animal Hosp. Assn., D.C. Acad. Vet. Medicine, Am. Assn. Zoo Veterinarians (sec.-treas. 1970-71). Office: Nat Zool Park Rock Creek Valley Washington DC 20009*

GRAY, FRANK, JR., judge; b. Franklin, Tenn., Feb. 25, 1908; s. Frank and Mary Hall (Philips) G.; LL.B., Cumberland U., 1928; m. Faye Anders, Feb. 14, 1941. Admitted to Tenn. bar, 1928; practiced in Franklin, 1928-61; chief judge U.S. Dist. Ct., Middle Dist. Tenn., 1961—. Mayor of Franklin, 1947-61. Mem. Am., Tenn. (gov. 1956-58) bar assns., Am. Judicature Soc. Democrat. Presbyn. Home: 1003 Adams St Franklin TN 37064 Office: US Courthouse Nashville TN 37203

GRAY, GORDON, broadcasting co. exec.; b. Balt., May 30, 1909; s. Bowman and Nathalie Fontaine (Lyons) G.; A.B., U. N.C., 1930; LL.B., Yale, 1933; m. Jane Boyden Craige, June 11, 1938 (dec. July 1953); children—Gordon, Burton Craige, Boyden, Bernard; m. 2d, Nancy Maguire Beebe; step-children—Cameron, Alexandra, Schuyler Beebe. Admitted to N.Y. bar, 1934, N.C. bar, 1936; asso. Carter, Ledyard & Milburn, 1933-35, Manly, Hendren & Womble, 1935-37; pub. Piedmont Pub. Co., Winston-Salem Jour., Twin City Sentinel, 1935-47, chmn. bd., 1961-69; chmn. bd. Triangle Broadcasting Corp., 1961—; asst. sec. Army Dept. Def., 1947-49; sec. of army, 1949-50; spl. asst. to Pres. U.S., 1950; became pres. U. N.C., 1950; asst. sec. def. for internat. security affairs 1955-57; dir. ODM, 1957-58; spl. asst. to pres. for nat. security affairs, 1958-61; dir. R. J. Reynolds Industries, Inc., Am. Security & Trust Co., Media General. Trustee Fed. City Council, 1962—; mem. Pres.' Fgn. Intelligence Adv. Bd., 1961—. Chmn. Nat. Trust for Historic preservation; trustee Brookings Instn.; bd. dirs. Psychol. Strategy Bd., 1951. Mem. N.C. Senate, 1938-42, 46-47. Served from pvt. to capt. Inf., AUS, 1942-45. Mem. Phi Beta Kappa, Delta Kappa Epsilon, Phi Delta Phi. Episcopalian. Clubs: Alibi, Chevy Chase, Burning Tree, Metropolitan (Washington). Home: 1224 30th St NW Washington DC 20007 Office: 800 17th St NW Washington DC 20006

GRAY, GUY LINCOLN, mfg. co. exec.; b. Cadiz, Ky., Feb. 13, 1909; s. Joe Nathan and Docia H. (Cook) G.; student pub. schs., Paducah, Ky.; m. Gladys Marie Lee, Apr. 9, 1932 (dec. Nov. 1967); children—Judith Lee, Joseph William; m. 2d, Eula Anderson Spradling, Nov. 22, 1968. With Henry A. Petter Supply Co., Paducah, 1925-47; pres. Ohio Valley Supply Co., Inc., Paducah, 1947-66, Guy Gray Mfg. Co., Inc., Paducah, 1958—, A-G Products, Inc., Paducah, 1961—, Lone Oak (Ky.) Recreation Corp., 1964—; formed Guy Gray Supply Co., 1966. Nat. bd. dirs. Boy Scouts Am. Mem. Travelers Protective Assn. (dir. post A). Methodist. Lion (past pres.). Home: Route 1 S Friendship Rd Paducah KY 42001 Office: PO Box 392 Paducah KY 42001

GRAY, HARLEY EUGENE, coop. ofcl.; b. Franklin, N.C., Sept. 2, 1933; s. Jim Slagle and Bessie (Cabe) G.; B.S., N.C. State U., 1955; m. Shirley Brookshire, May 10, 1958; children—James W., Jeffrey E. Asst. agr. agt. N.C. Agr. Extension Service, Jefferson, 1955-60, asso. agr. agt., Sparta, 1962-65, county extension chmn., Sparta, 1965-68; dist. mgr. Blue Ridge Electric Membership Corp., 1968—. Fieldman Kraft Foods, West Jefferson, N.C., 1960-62. Mem. Alpha Zeta, Kappa Phi Kappa, Epsilon Sigma Phi. Presbyn. Lions (past pres.). Home: Box 181 Sparta NC 28675 Office: Box 177 Sparta NC 28675

GRAY, HAROLD, lawyer; b. Ottawa, Ill., May 14, 1926; s. John E. and Mildred (Grady) G.; Ph.B., Ill. Westleyan U., 1949; summer student U. Cal. at Los Angeles, 1947; law student U. Ill., summer 1950; J.D., Valparaiso (Ind.) U., 1951; m. Judith Maddox; children—Nora Alison, Jeffrey John. Admitted to Fla. bar, 1955; established claims dept. State Farm Mut. Automobile Ins. Co., West Palm Beach, Fla., 1951-54; practiced in Miami, Fla., 1955—; of counsel Bolles, Goodwin and Ryskamp; dir., chmn. exec. com. Scotten, Dillon Co., Detroit; partner C.B. Richard, Ellis & Co., N.Y.C.; trial counsel for So. Indemnity Ins. Co., Miami, 1959. Trustee Unitarian Fellowship of Palm Beach County, Fla., 1957-58. Served with USAAF, 1944-46. Mem. Palm Beach County Claim Men's Assn. (pres. 1952), West Palm Beach Jr. C. of C., Fla. Bar Assn., Sigma Chi, Phi Alpha Delta (past justice Halleck chpt., Vaiparaiso U.). Unitarian. Club: Surf (Miami Beach). Home: 828 Valencia Av Coral Gables FL 33134 Office: PO Box 347 Coconut Grove Sta Miami FL 33133

GRAY, HARRY GORDON, civil engr.; b. Brookline, Mass., May 13, 1908; s. David Smith and Mary (Bell) G.; B.C.E., Northeastern U., 1928; m. Beatrice G. Churchil, Sept. 24, 1932; 1 son, Robert Norman. Project and resident engr. Mass. Dept. Pub. Works, Boston, 1932-42, chief engr., exec. asst., 1953-61; project mgr. Metcalf & Eddy, engrs., Boston, 1961-63; dir. Pinellas County Pub. Works & Engring., Clearwater, Fla., 1963—. Mem. Planning Bd., Beverly, Mass., 1960-63. Served with Civil Engr. Corps, USNR, 1942-46, USNR, 1947-48, to capt. Civil Engr. Corps, 1951-53. Registered profl., engr. Mass., N.Y., Fla., Me., N.H., Vt. Fellow Am. Soc. C.E. (br. pres. 1970-71); mem. Fla. Engring. Soc. Home: 1438 Monte Carlo Dr Clearwater FL 33516 4Office: 315 Haven St Clearwater FL 33516

GRAY, HERBERT HAROLD, JR., elec. co. exec.; b. Graysville, Ala., Sept. 20, 1919; s. Herbert H. and Dorothy R. (Jones) G.; B.S., U. Ala., 1943; postgrad. Ga. Inst. Tech., 1961, Stanford Bus. Sch., 1966; m. Mary Ellen Parsons, June 17, 1944; children—Herbert Harold III, Thomas Parsons. Asst. sales engr. Westinghouse Elec. Co., Nashville, 1947-50, sales engr. Chattanooga, 1950-54, area sales mgr., Atlanta, 1954-57, asst. to indsl. mgr. Pitts., 1957-58, mgr., marine, aviation and transp. sales, 1958-60, dist. mgr., Birmingham, Ala., 1960-62, S.E. Zone mgr., elec. utility sales, Atlanta, 1962-67, nat. field sales mgr. power systems, Pitts., 1967-72, southeastern regional v.p., Atlanta, 1972—. Dir. Southeastern Electric Exchange. Mem. Fla. Council 100. Bd. dirs. Ga. div. Am. Cancer Soc. Served to capt. AUS, 1943-46, ETO, PTO. Registered profl. engr. Tenn. Mem. I.E.E.E. Conf. Bd., Ga., Atlanta chambers commerce, Ga. Electrification Council, Theta Tau. Presbyn. (deacon). Clubs: Chartiers Country, University (Pitts); The Club & Birmingham, Ala.) Author: (with E.G. Fischer) Shockproofing For Hardened Bases, 1959. Office: 1299 Northside Dr PO Box 4808 Atlanta GA 30302

GRAY, JAMES ALEXANDER, corp. exec.; b. Winston-Salem, N.C., Dec. 12, 1920; s. James Alexander and Pauline Lizette (Bahnson) G.; A.B., U. N.C., 1941; M.B.A., Harvard, 1943; m. Yvonne Winifred Jackson, Aug. 12, 1944; children—Susan Winifred, James Alexander, David Bahnson. Mfrs. rep., 1946-49; with Jour. and Sentinel newspapers, Winston-Salem, 1949-61, gen. mgr., 1957-59, pub. 1959-61; dir. Piedmont Pub. Co.; dir. Triangle Broadcasting Corp.; exec. dir. Winston-Salem Found., 1961-62 Mem. N.C. Hwy. Commn., 1953-57; chmn. Winston-Salem United Fund campaign, 1958. Bd. visitors Bowman Gray Sch. Medicine, 1959—; trustee Salem Acad. and Coll., 1959—; dir. N.C. Fund, 1963-66; pres. Old Salem, Inc., 1950-53, 63—. Served to lt. (j.g.) USNR, 1943-46. Named Young Man of Year, Winston-Salem Jr. C. of C., 1949. Mem. Home Moravian Ch. (trustee). Rotarian. Club: Torch. Home: 1020 W Kent Rd Winston-Salem NC 27104 Office: 600 S Main St Winston-Salem NC 27108

GRAY, JOHN EDMUND, environmental cons.; b. Woonsocket, R. I., Apr. 13, 1922; s. John Joseph and Alice (Naylor) G.; B.S. in Chem. Engring., U. R.I., 1943; m. Mary Lightbody, Dec. 3, 1944; children—Jane Elizabeth (Mrs. Peter W. Redmond), John Carlton, Jeffrey Naylor. Research engr. Westinghouse Electric Corp., 1943-46; sr. design engr. Engring. div. Gen. Electric Co., Hanford, Wash., 1946-47, head materials sect. atomic power dept. Gen. Engring. and Coss. Lab., Schenectady, 1948-49; materials adminstr. naval reactors br. AEC, U.S. Navy, 1949-50; dir. tech. and prodn. div. AEC, Savannah River Operations Office, 1950-54; project mgr. for Shippingport atomic power sta. Duquesne Light Co., Pitts., 1954-60; pres., chief exec. officer NUS Corp., Rockville, Md., 1960-69, chmn. bd., chief exec. offcer, 1969-72; chmn. bd. Neutron Products, Inc., Rockville, 1962-72. Consultec, Inc., Rockville, 1967-72; dir. Gourdine Systems, Inc., 1968—; dir. Inst. Pub. Transp., N.Y.C., 1972—, Aviation Values Corp., Washington, 1972—. Active Boy Scouts Am. Served with AUS, 1945-46. Registered profl. engr. Mem. Am. Inst. chem. Engrins., Am. Nuclear Soc. Atomic Indsl. Forum (orgn. mem., mem. reactor safety com., task force access to enrichment tech. com.; mem. internat. affairs com.). Clubs: University (Washington); Belle Haven Country (Alexandria, Va). Contbr. articles to profl. publs., Mark's Standard Handbook for Mech. Engrs. Home and office: 2007 Windsor Rd Alexandria VA 22307

GRAY, JOHN LEWIS, forester, educator; b. Falls Church, Va., July 4, 1920; s. Lewis Cecil and Pearl (Patterson) G.; B.S. in Forestry, Pa. State U., 1941; M.F., Yale, 1942; D.F., Duke, 1969; m. Mildred Lorraine Toney, Oct. 18, 1942; children—John T., Barbara J. Asst. extension forester Agrl. Extension Service, N.C. State Coll., Raleigh, 1945-49, in charge of extension forestry, 1950-63; dir. Sch. Forest Resources and Conservation, U. Fla., Gainesville, 1963—. Mem. forestry research adv. com. U.S. Dept. Agr., 1964-69. Served to 2d lt. USAAF, 1942-44. Mem. Soc. Am. Foresters (Outstanding Forester Fla. chpt. 1965), Am., Fla. (dir. ex-officio, recipient award for significant contbns. to industry, 1970) forestry assns., Wildlife Soc., Internat. Union Forestry Research Orgns. (permanent com. 1967), Sigma Xi, Gamma Sigma Delta, Alpha Zeta, Xi Sigma Pi. Democrat. Methodist. Home: 805 NW 36th Dr Gainesville FL 32601

GRAY, JULES, architect, oil co. exec.; b. Haralson, Ga., June 5, 1907; s. Lattimer and Willie (Hodnett) G.; B.S. in Architecture, Ga. Inst. Tech., 1927; m. Ellen Southwell, Sept. 5, 1939; children—James Southwell, Elizabeth (Mrs. David Jamison), Judith Ellen. Draftsman, Hentz, Adler & Shutze, Atlanta, 1930-31; designer Chrysler Bldg. Corp., N.Y.C., 1931-36; asst. to mdse. mgr. Sinclair Co., Atlanta, 1936, field merchandiser, Fayetteville, N.C., 1937, field constrn. engr., 1937-45; Southeastern constrn. engr. Pure Oil Co., Atlanta, 1945-65; div. constrn. mgr. Union Oil Co., Atlanta, 1965-68, regional constrn. mgr., 1968-72. Recipient Gold Certificate, Hall of Fame award Petroleum Council Ga., 1965, Leadership award A.I.A., 1969. Mem. A.I.A., Am. Petroleum Inst. (mem. com. on pub. affairs so. region 1967-72), Atlanta Petroleum Engrs. (chmn. 1961), Alpha Tau Omega. Presbyn. Prin. archtl. works include Sinclairs Nat. Biltmore Type Service Sta., Atlanta, Varsity Drive-In, Atlanta, Daytona Speedway-Nascar Office Bldg., J.H. Williams Oil Co., Butterfly Roof Service Sta., Tampa, Fla., Miller Bookstore Interiors, Atlanta, Jobber Non-Interstate Truck Stop, Columbus, Miss. Home: 515 W Paces Ferry Rd NW Atlanta GA 30305 Office: 13 Corporate Square Box 4147 Atlanta GA 30302

GRAY, KENNETH EUGENE, educator; b. Herrin, Ill., Jan. 11, 1930; s. Ira Lee and Faye (Boles) G.; student So. Ill. U., 1952-53; B.S. (Cal. Co. scholar), U. Tulsa, 1956, M.S. (Stanolind Oil & Gas Co. fellow), 1957; Ph.D. (Shell Oil fellow), U. Tex., 1963; m. Beatrix Irene Wolfe, Aug. 29, 1955; children—David Kenneth, Diana Lynn, Debra Lee. Engr., Cal. Co., Venice, La., 1957-59, Sohio Petroleum Co., Oklahoma City, 1959-60; asst. prof. U. Tex., Austin, 1962-65, asso. prof. petroleum engring, 1965-68, prof., 1968—, Halliburton prof. petroleum engring., 1968—, chmn. dept., 1966—, dir. Center for Earth Scis. and Engring., 1968—. Cons. Continental Oil Co., Ponca City, Okla., 1963-65, Martin Co., Balt., 1966-67. Vice chmn. U.S. Nat. Com. for Rock Mechanics. Served with AUS, 1947-48, 50-51. Mem. Soc. Petroleum Engrs., Am. Soc. Engring. Edn., N.Y. Acad. Scis., Sigma Xi, Tau Beta Pi, Pi Epsilon Tau (nat. pres. 1964-67), Phi Gamma Kappa, Sigma Gamma Epsilon, Phi Eta Sigma, Alpha Phi Omega, Xi Omicron. Republican. Methodist. Editorial bd. Internat. Jour. Rock Mechanics. Contbr. articles to profl. jours. Home: 3930 Sierra Dr Austin TX 78731

GRAY, MAY HARRIS (MRS. THOMAS VIRGIL GRAY), writer; b. Canton, Ky.; d. James Robert and Mary Priscilla (Bridges) Harris; student Northeastern La. Bus. Coll., Fort Smith, Ark., 1917-18; m. Thomas Virgil Gray, June 19, 1920; children—Jean (Mrs. Louis H. Peer), Dorothy (Mrs. Joseph Beech Edwards), Thomas Virgil. Co-owner COIN-Stores, Fort Smith, Ark. and Oklahoma, Tex., 1946—. Mem. womans bd. Sparks Meml. Hosp., Fort Smith, 1936—. Recipient John Gould Fletcher Poetry award, 1964, 68; Jesse Stuart award, 1967; Dylan Thomas award, 1968; Poet Laureate's citation, 1966; Southwest Times Record award Poets Roundtable Ark. Mem. Ft. Smith Poets Roudtable Group (co-founder), Acad. Am. Poets, Nat. Fedn. State Poetry Socs., Nat. League Am. Pen Women (treas. 1968-69), Poetry Soc. Am., Poets Roundtable Ark., University City Poetry Club, P.E.O. (chpt. pres. 1960-61), D.A.R. Baptist. Club: Explorers. Author: In the Garden, 1935; The Voice of the Sea, 1963; Moment Before Summer, 1970; poems pub. in various mags., anthologies, newspapers. Home: 1315-55 Terrace Fort Smith AR 72901 Office: 2300 Rogers Av Fort Smith ARK 72901

GRAY, MURRAY DANIEL, JR., banker; b. Columbus, Ga., Dec. 1, 1933; s. Murray Daniel and Martha (Martin) G.; student Auburn U., 1952-54, W.Ga. Coll., 1954-55; B.S., Auburn, 1957; m. Janet Pulliam, June 11, 1955; children—Roxann Malsby, Murray Daniel III. Jr. accountant Leonard, West, Favors, Columbus, 1955-57; v.p., trust officer Columbus Bank & Trust Co., 1958—, head trust dept., 1970—; dir. United Oil Corp., Columbus, Ga. Treas. Little League Football Columbus, 1970. Bd. dirs. Columbus Opportunity, Inc., 1970—, Columbus Mus., 1970—. Boys Club, 1969—, Orphans Home, 1971—, Muscogee Council Boy Scouts Am., 1971—. Served with AUS, 1957. Mem. Ga. Bankers Assn. (pres. elect, 1972-73), Estate Planning Council Columbus, Columbus Life Underwriters Assn. Baptist. Lion. Club: Country Columbus. Home: 2835 Roswell Lane Columbus GA 31906 Office: PO Box 120 Columbus GA 31902

GRAY, ROBERT ALTON, sch. supt.; b. Stokes, N.C., Nov. 23, 1926; s. Henry Abram and Lucy Elizabeth (Carrington) G.; B.S., East Carolina U., 1949, M.A., 1950; Advanced Adminstrs. Certificate, U. N.C., 1965; m. Marie Whitford, Sept. 1, 1950; children—Robert Alton, Diane Marie. Tchr. sci. Bethel (N.C.) High Sch., 1949-51; prin. Magnolia (N.C.) High Sch., 1951-52, Faison (N.C.) High Sch., 1952-55, Mingo High Sch., Dunn, N.C., 1955-56, Boone Trail Sch., Mamers, N.C., 1956-63; asst. supt. Harnett County Schs., Lillington, N.C., 1963-66, supt., 1966—. Chmn. Lee-Harnett Mental Health, 1963-65, bd. dirs., Harnett County Health Dept.; chmn. bd. Harnett County Library, 1970-71. Served with USNR, 1944-46. NSF, grantee, 1960-61. Mem. N.E.A. (life), N. C. Assn. Educators (life, div. state dir. 1970-71, dist. pres. 1961-62), Am. Assn. Sch. Adminstrs., Nat. Rural Supts. Presbyn. (deacon, elder). Mason, Rotarian. Club: Ruritan (Mamers). Home: PO Box 26 Lillington NC 27546 Office: PO Box 1027 Lillington NC 27546

GRAY, ROBERT LEROY, pub. relations exec.; b. Scranton, Pa., Feb. 2, 1920; s. Francis Bli and Caroline Rosetta (Weed) G.; student Marion Inst. Jr. Coll., 1939-40; B.S. in Communications, Am. U., 1949; m. Patricia Perry, May 1965 (div. Mar. 1972); children—Susanna, Roger. Dir. pub. affairs Nat. Housing Center, Washington, 1959-65; pres. Robert Gray Pub. Relations, Washington, 1965-68; dir. pub. relations Mortgage Bankers Assn. of Am., Washington, 1968—. Served with USNR, 1941-46, PTO, ETO. Mem. Pub. Relations Soc. Am., Am. Pub. Relations Assn. (pres. chpt. 1955). Clubs: Nat. Press, Nat. Aviation (Washington). Author: Communications Manual for Mortgage Banking, 1969. Home: 1205 15th St NW Washington DC 20005 Office: 1125 15th St NW Washington DC 20005

GRAY, ROBERT WINSTON, security analyst; b. Austin, Tex., July 20, 1938; s. Hob and Mary (Tanner) G.; B.S. in Petroleum Engring., U. Tex., 1960; M.B.A., Harvard, 1963; m. Patricia Wadlington, Aug. 5, 1961; children—Susan Patricia, Lauren Ashley. Petroleum engr. Continental Oil Co., Sweetwater, Tex., 1960-61; accountant Arthur Young & Co., Houston, 1963-65; security analyst Underwood Neuhaus & Co., Houston, 1965-70, Rauscher Pierce Securities Corp., Dallas, 1970—. C.P.A., Tex. Mem. Am. Inst. C.P.A.s, Tex. Soc. C.P.A.s, Financial Analysts Fedn., Inst. Chartered Financial Analysts, Dallas Assn. Investment Analysts, Harvard Bus. Sch. Club (dir. 1969-70), Phi Gamma Delta, Tau Beta Pi. Home: 825 Teakwood Pl Richardson TX 75080 Office: 1200 Mercantile Dallas Bldg Dallas TX 75201

GRAY, ROY COOPER, JR., cattle co. exec.; b. Flemingsburg, Ky., June 4, 1928; s. Roy Cooper and Alice Kerr (Hood) G.; B.S., U. Ky., 1956, M.S., 1957; Ph.D., Auburn U., 1964; m. Norma Jean Wright, June 12, 1954; children—Susan, Roy Cooper, Steven. Farmer, Flemingsburg, Ky., 1947-50; staff mem. Auburn U., 1957-64; U. Ky., 1964-70; pres. Purebred Herds of Am., Inc., 1970-71, also dir.; pres., owner Modern Cattle Mgmt. Inc., Lexington, Ky., 1971—; dir. Profl. Services, Inc., Cattle Herds, Inc., Westbrook Cattle, Inc. Served with AUS, 1950-53, 61-62. Decorated Bronze Star medal. Mem. Am. Soc. Animal Prodn., Res. Officers Assn., Am. Legion, Sigma Xi, Gamma Sigma Delta. Kiwanian. Home: Route 5 Nicholasville KY 40356 Office: Box 866 Lexington KY 40501

GRAY, THOMAS TURNER, distillery exec.; b. Topeka, Apr. 24, 1927; s. Ben Foster and Catherine (Turner) G.; B.A., U. Louisville, 1950; postgrad. Ky. Indsl. Devel. Inst., 1966; m. Cynthia Ann Sloane, May 27, 1961; 1 dau., Catherine Lynn. Staff corr. U.P.I., Louisville, 1952-63; pub. relations specialist Dept. Pub. Information, Commonwealth of Ky., Frankfort, 1963-66; mgr. external communications Brown-Forman Distillers Corp., Louisville, 1966—. Served with AUS, 1945-47. Mem. Pub. Relations Soc. Am. (accredited, chpt. treas. 1971, dir. 1972), Louisville C. of C. (tourist council 1971-72). Club: Plantation Country (Louisville). Home: 230 S Peterson St Louisville KY 40206 Office: 850 Dixie Hwy Louisville KY 40210

GRAY, VIRGIL CLAYTON, city ofcl.; b. Brady, Tex., Feb. 10, 1934; s. Elmer L. and Lois E. (Turner) G.; grad. Brownwood Bus. Coll., 1959; m. Emily Grace Lancaster, Mar. 23, 1957; children—Lisa Gaye, Clayton Louis. City sec. City Brownwood, Tex., 1957-62, asst. city mgr., city sec., 1967—; office mgr. Tex. Brick Co., Brownwood, 1962-67. Trustee Tex. Municipal Retirement System, 1968—. Served with USAF, 1953-57. Mem. Municipal Finance Officers U.S. and Tex., Internat. City Clks. and Secs., Tex. City Mgrs. Assn. Kiwanian (pres. 1967). Home: 2502 Belmeade St Brownwood TX 76801 Office: 110 S Greenleaf St Brownwood TX 76801

GRAY, WALTER, JR., dir. Community Workshop; mem. exec. com. Adult Edn. Assn. of U.S.; vice chmn. Am. Inst. Discussion. Author: Manual for Discussion Moderators. Address: Oklahoma County Pub Library 131 NW 3d St Oklahoma City OK 73102

GRAY, WARREN PHILIPS, banker; b. Franklin, Tenn., Oct. 6, 1911; s. William Francis and Mary (Philips) G.; grad. Rutgers U. Grad. Sch. Banking, 1948; m. Nancy Lee Thompson, Dec. 26, 1936; children—Mary Ann (Mrs. William M. Tate, Jr.), Frances Phyllis. Clk., First Bank & Trust Co., Franklin, 1929-31, Harpeth Nat. Bank, Franklin, 1931-34; with Third Nat. Bank, Nashville, 1934—, cashier, 1963—, sr. v.p., 1965—; treas. Presbyn. Apts. Active local A.R.C., United Givers Fund; treas. Tenn. Children's Home Soc. Mem. Bank Adminstrn. Inst. (nat. treas. 1967-69), Financial Execs. Inst. (pres. Nashville 1964-65), Am. Inst. Banking (pres. Nashville 1940-41). Presbyn. (elder). Clubs: Richland Country, City (Nashville). Home: 4103 Estes Rd Nashville TN 37215 Office: Third Nat Bank Bldg Nashville TN 37202

GRAY, WARREN SMITH, architect; b. Glen Ridge, N.J., Jan. 10, 1920; s. Warren and Elizabeth (Smith) G.; B.Arch., U. Pa., 1943, M.Arch., 1948; m. Nora Louise Stokes, Apr. 9,1949; children—Moline Elizabeth, Jon Bel, Gladys Lillian, Nora Louise. Staff architect, designer Vertner Tandy, N.Y.C., 1946, Vahan Hagopian, N.Y.C., 1947, Carroll, Grisdale & Van Alen, Phila., 1952-56; exec. development bd., Lagos, Nigeria, 1958; architect W. Africa, 1956-58, Phila. Mem. archtl. faculty Howard U. Mem. citizens council on city planning; committeeman Boy Scouts Am. Served with AUS, 1945-46. Mem. Am. Inst. Planners, Nat. Tech. Assn., Phila. Housing Assn., Big Bro. Assn., A.I.A. (asso.), Am. Friends Nigeria, Am. Soc. African Culture, Am. Acad. Polit. and Social Sci., World Ship Soc., Urban Am., Nat. Assn. Housing and Redevel. Ofcls. Mem. Soc. of Friends. Club: T Square (Phila.). Address: 410 E Slocum St Philadelphia PA 19119 Office: 212 Rhode Island Av NW Washington DC 20001

GRAY, WELLINGTON BURBANK, educator; b. Albany, N.Y., Apr. 25, 1919; s. Wellington and Lilla Maude (Burbank) G.; B.S., Kutztown (Pa.) State Coll., 1947; M.A., N.Y.U., 1948, Ed.D., 1954; student Pa. State U., U. Philippines; m. Norma Laree Wallace, Dec. 26, 1942; children— Bruce Wellington, Brian Erwin. Art supr. pub. schs., Connellsville, Pa., 1947-49; art dir. Highland Park (Ill.) High Sch., 1949-54; dean Art Sch., Edinboro (Pa.) State Coll., 1954-56; dean Sch. Art, E. Carolina U., Greenville, N.C., 1956—; lectr. fine arts Alliance Coll., 1955-56; instr. N.Y.U., summers 1950, 51. Partner Gray Assos., design cons., Greenville, 1960—; paintings in permanent collections Atlanta, Akron, O., Albany, N.Y., Highland Park, Mobile, Greenville; exhibited Carnegie Inst. Tech., Art Inst. Chgo., Albany Inst. History and Art; one man shows Highland Park, Greenville, Erie, Pa. Sec., Pitt County Republican Com. Served to lt. col. AUS, World War II; PTO. Mem. Am. Assn. U. Profs., Nat. Art Edn. Assn., Am. Inst. Interior Designers, also mem. Southeastern Arts Assn. (co-chmn. coll. tchrs. art com.), Nat. Soc. Interior Designers, Phi Delta Kappa. Kappa Delta Pi, Delta Phi Delta. Episcopalian. Author: Student Teaching in Art, 1960; also articles. Home: 2001 Brook Rd Greenville NC 27834

GRAY, WILLARD FRANKLIN, univ. adminstr.; b. Flint, Tex., Dec. 25, 1913; s. John Franklin and Leona (Booth) G.; B.S. in Elec. Engring., Tex. Tech. Coll., 1934; M.S. in Elec. Engring., Tex. A. and M. U., 1940; m. Clotyde Roberts, Jan. 2, 1937; children—Jay Willard, Paula Kay (Mrs. Clyde Samuel Precise). Jr. engr. Tex. Power and Light Co., Dallas, 1934-37; mem. faculty Tex. Tech. Coll., 1937-46, asso. prof. elec. engring., 1943-46; asst. prof. elec. engring. Mass. Inst. Tech., 1946-47; mem. faculty U. Ala., 1947—, prof. elec. engring., head dept., 1959-66, asst. v.p. acad. affairs, 1966-68, asst. v.p. adminstrn., 1968-71, asso. acad. v.p., dean adminstrn., 1971—; cons. to bus. and industry, 1950—. Mem. panels evaluation applications for undergrad. instructional equipment NSF, 1965-66; mem. Charles LeGeyt Fortescue fellowship panel I.E.E.E. 1966—. Mem. Am. Soc. Engring. Edn. (chmn. elec. engring. div. 1964-65, chmn. prizes and award div. elec. engring. 1967—), I.E.E.E., Nat. Soc. Profl. Engrs., Am. Assn. U. Profs., Tau Beta Pi, Eta Kappa Nu, Theta Tau, Pi Tau Chi, Omicron Delta Kappa. Methodist. Registered profl. engr., Ala. Home: 21 Windsor Dr Tuscaloosa AL 35401 Office: PO Box 3625 University AL 35486

GRAY, WILLIAM PAUL, physician; b. Batesville, Ark., Aug. 14, 1912; s. Frank Alexander and Mary Melissa (Laman) G.; B.A., Ark. Coll., 1934; M.D., U. Ark. Sch. Medicine, 1938; m. Dorothy Hope Landis, Dec. 30, 1950; 1 dau., Mary Ann. Intern Church Home and Infirmary, Balt., Balt. City Hosp.; pvt. practice gen. medicine, Batesville, Ark., 1940—; adminstr. Dr. Gray's Hosp., Batesville, Ark., 1940—. Mem. Ark. (counselor 1960-73), Independence County med. socs., A.M.A., Am. Coll. Chest Physicians, Am. Acad. Gen. Practice. Home: 589 College St Batesville AR 72501 Office: 477 E Main St Batesville AR 72501

GRAYBEAL, WILLIAM SAMUEL, educator; b. Emory, Va., Nov. 7, 1924; s. Henry Clay and June (McConnell) G.; B.S., Emory and Henry Coll., 1947; M.S., Va. Poly. Inst., 1953; Ed.D., George Peabody Coll., 1962. Tchr. Wills (Va.) High Sch., 1947-49; asst. prin. Pearisburg (Va.) High Sch., 1949-50; prin Speedwell (Va.) High Sch., 1950-51; asst. to supt., vis. tchr. Wythe County Schs., Wytheville, Va., 1951-52; high sch. supr., 1952-54; dir. secondary edn. Fairfax County Schs., Fairfax, Va., 1956-60; asst. prof. edn., asso. dir. div. surveys and field services George Peabody Coll., 1962-63; supr. ednl. research State Dept. Edn., Richmond, Va., 1963-65; asst. dir. research div. N.E.A., Washington, 1965—. Served with USNR, 1944-46. Mem. N.E.A., Nat. Soc. Study Edn., Am. Edn. Research Assn., Assn. Supr. and Curriculum Devel., Nat. Council Measurement Edn., Am. Assn. Sch. Adminstrs., Blue Key, Phi Delta Kappa, Kappa Delta Pi. Methodist. Home: 1700 Fox Run Ct Vienna VA 22180 Office: NEA 1201 16th St NW Washington DC 20036

GRAYSON, ERNEST CARSON, sch. supt.; b. Evansville, Ind., Mar. 2, 1926; s. Ernest Clay and Ruby (Tapp) G.; B.S., U. Louisville, 1950, M.B.A., 1956; m. Patsy Sipes, Oct. 1, 1949; children—Deborah, Carson, Amy. Marketing asst. Standard Oil Co., Louisville, 1949-55; asso. supt., treas. Jefferson County Schs., Louisville, 1955—. Treas. WKPC-TV, Louisville, 1969—. Bd. dirs. Am. Jr. Red Cross, U.S.O., Jefferson County Assn. for Children with Learning Disabilities, Boy Scouts Am. Served to capt. USNR, 1944-46, 1950-52; Korea. Decorated Presidential Unit Citation. Mem. Internat. (pres. 1969), Ky. (pres. 1964) assns. sch. bus. ofcls. Methodist (mem. Edn. Commn. 1965—). Mason. Home: 9204 Tiverton Way Louisville KY 40222 Office: 3332 Newburg Rd Louisville KY 40218

GRAZIER, JAMES ALFRED, author, found. exec.; b. Johnstown, Pa., Dec. 18, 1916; s. John H. and Kathryn Estelle (Friedline) G.; A.B., U. Ala., 1939; postgrad. Am. U., 1950-51; m. Iole Lastella, Dec. 1951; children—Kathy, Stella. Editor, Hawthorne (Cal.) Tribune, 1946-48; commd. 2d lt. U.S. Army, 1940, advanced through grades to lt. col., 1958; faculty Army War Coll., 1951-53; chief pub. affairs NATO for Italy, Greece and Turkey, 1953-56; ret., 1956; nat. program dir. AMVETS, 1956-59; AID liaison officer to Brazil, 1961-69; pres. Keimer Found. for Social Devel. and Hist. Research, Washington, 1971, chmn. bd., 1971—; cons. Office Internat. Tng. AID, Dept. State, Washington, 1969; cons. Ludwig Keimer Found., Rome, Italy and Basel, Switzerland. Decorated Purple Heart, Commendation medal, Bronze Star medal; recipient Superior Service award U.S. Army War Coll., 1953. Author: Hydra, 1969; Runts of 61 Cygni C, 1970. Home: Casella Postale 746 Rome Italy 00100 Office: Keimer Found 1150 Connecticut Av NW Washington DC 20036

GREAVES, FRANCIS LANDON, JR., librarian; b. Ferriday, La., Jan. 19, 1938; s. Francis Landon and Frances (Cooper) G.; B.S., La. Tech. U., 1961; M.S., La. State U., 1966; postgrad. Fla. State U., 1971; m. Mary Jo Ellington, Mar. 11, 1961; children—Mark Landon, Melinda Cobb. Head circulation social sci. div. Dupre Library, U. Southwestern La., Lafayette, 1966-69; head librarian Sim's Library, Southeastern La. U., Hammond, 1969—. Bd. dirs. Wesley Found., Southeastern La. U., 1971-73. Served with AUS, 1961. Mem. Am., La. library assns. Home: 1406 Pecan St Hammond LA 70401 Office: Box 302 Univ Sta Hammond LA 70401

GRECO, CHARLES P., clergyman; b. Rodney, Miss., Oct. 29, 1894; s. Frank P. and Carmela (Testa) G.; student Jesuit Coll., New Orleans, 1904-07; Jefferson Coll., Convent, La., 1908; St. Joseph Sem., St. Benedict, La., 1907-13; Am. Coll., Louvain, Belgium, 1910-14; U. of Fribourg, Switzerland, 1914-18. Ordained priest Roman Cath. Church, 1918; asst. pastor, Houma, La., 1918-23, vice chancellor and chancellor of New Orleans, 1923-26, adminstr. and pastor of St. Maurice Ch., 1926-45, bishop of Alexandria, 1946—. Sec., Defender of Marriage Bond, presiding judge of Matrimonial Court, 1923-46; vicar gen. of New Orleans, 1944-46. Editor-in-chief Cath. Action of South, 1944-46. Address: PO Drawer 191 Alexandria LA 71301

GRECO, DICK A., JR., mayor; b. Tampa, Fla., Sept. 14, 1933; s. Dick A. and Evelyn (Cotarella) G.; student U. Fla.; B.S., U. Tampa, 1956; m. Dana Hepinstall, Apr. 3, 1953; children—Richard L., Dana L., Darcy L. Councilman, City of Tampa, 1963-67, mayor, 1967—. Vice pres. King-Greco Hardware Co., Inc. Pres. Travelers Aid Soc.; v.p. Davis Islands Civic Center. Bd. dirs. MacDonald's Tng. Center, Fla. League Municipalities. Named Outstanding Young Man of Year, Jr. C. of C., 1965; mem. Nat. Skeet Champion-All Am. Skeet Team, 1950-51. Mem. C. of C. (dir.). Home: 112 Lodoga St Tampa FL 33606 Office: City Hall Florida Av and JF Kennedy Blvd Tampa FL 33602

GRECO, EDWARD CARL, research scientist; b. Marsala, Italy, Nov. 2, 1911; s. Camelo L. and Domenica (LoGacano) G.; came to U.S., 1914, naturalized, 1941; B.A., Northwestern State Coll., 1934; D.Sc., Centenary Coll., 1963; m. Marcia Scott Dudley, Apr. 20, 1938; children—Edward Carl, Marcia Scott. With Lone Star Ordnance Plant, U.S. Army Ordnance, Texarkana, Tex., 1942-43, E.I. du Pont, Millington, Tenn., 1943-45; with United Gas Corp., Shreveport, La., 1945-67, sr. research asso.; dir. research Supplementary Edn. Center, Northwestern State Coll., Nachitoches, Oa., 1967-70, coordinator sci. and tech., Northwestern State U., Nachitoches, 1970—, dir. Inst. Sci. Research, 1969—, lectr. chemistry. Pres., 2d Internat. Congress on Metallic Corrosion, 1963-66, v.p. 4th internat. congress; speaker various colls. and univs. Fellow Am. Inst. Chemists, A.A.A.S.; mem. Nat. Assn. Corrosion Engrs. (pres. 1962-63), La. Acad. Scis. (pres. 1955-56), Shreveport C. of C. (v.p. 1967), Am. Chem. Soc. Editor: Materials Protection, 1966—; adv. editor Protection of Metals, 1965—. Contbr. prefaces, chpts. to tech. books articles to publs. Home: 918 Harvey St Natchitoches LA 71457

GREEN, ALLEN LELDON, aircraft co. ofcl.; b. Hanceville, Ala., Feb. 15, 1938; s. Onis Leldon and Stella Magnolia (Day) G.; B.S. in Mech. Engring., U. Miss., 1961; children—Cooper Alan, Elizabeth Nicole and Kimberly Kelly (twins). Engr. aide TVA Power Prodn., New Johnson, Tenn., 1960; punter, field goal kicker, line backer Dallas Cowboys, 1961-62, design engr. Chgo. Bridge & Iron Co., Birmingham, Ala., 1962-63, field engr., 1963; punter, field goal kicker Green Bay Packers, 1964; structures engr. B, Chrysler Corp./Space Div., Huntsville, Ala., 1963-64, test, devel. engr. B, 1964-65, test, devel. engr. A, 1965-67, test engr. sr., 1967, test engr. sr. mgmt., 1967-68; organized Tide Corp., Birmingham, 1969, v.p., 1969—; sr. program planner Martin-Marietta Corp., Huntsville, 1969—; owner Allen Green Golf Driving Range, Huntsville, 1969—. Mem. exec. com. Tenn. Valley Boy Scouts Am., 1967. Named Hon. Col., Miss. Gov., 1961. Mem. Nat. Football League Players Assn., Am. Soc. M.E., Am. Soc. Weights Engrs., Chrysler Basketball League, Chrysler Golf League and Tournaments (award 1968). Club: Alabama Hawks Professional Football (award 1967) (Huntsville). Home: 201 Utica Pl Huntsville AL 35806 Office: Martin Marietta Corp PO Box 1107 Huntsville AL 35807

GREEN, ARTHUR GEORGE, accountant; b. Midland, Tex., June 2, 1937; s. Lymond Darrel and Viona (Grant) G.; Asso. Applied Sci., Odessa Coll., 1960; B.B.A., U. Tex., 1962; m. Margaret Hash, June 1, 1959; children—Shane Ann, Sabrina Kay, Amy Suzanne, William Wade. Estimator, Boing Co., New Orleans, 1962-63; staff accountant Main, Lafrentz & Co., Odessa, Tex., 1963-65, Will Faris & Co., Odessa, 1965-67; partner Elms, Faris, Green, Smith & Sims, Odessa, 1968—. Bd. govs., treas. Globe of Gt. S.W., 1969—. Served with USAF, 1954-58. Mem. Am. Inst. C.P.A.'s, Tex. Soc. C.P.A.'s (chpt. v.p. 1969—), Data Processing Mgrs. Assn. (chpt. treas. 1970), Odessa Jr. C. of C. Mem. Christian Ch. (dir.) Mason (K.T., Shriner). Home: 1606 E 13th St Odessa TX 79760 Office: 1st Nat Bank Bldg Odessa TX 79760

GREEN, BEN LAMAR, JR., supt. schs.; b. Monroe, La., Feb. 28, 1921; s. Ben Lamar and Lorraine (Lowe) G.; B.A., La. State U., 1954, M.Ed., 1956; Ed.S., George Peabody Coll. Tchrs., 1964; m. Maxine Boyd, Jan. 6, 1946; children—Ben Lamar III, Terry Boyd, Penny Maxine. Tchr., coach Vidalia (La.) High Sch., 1954-55; tch. bus. edn., coach Ferriday (La.) High Sch., 1956-57; supr. instrn. Concordia Parish Schs., Vidalia, 1958-60; prin. Ferriday Elementary Sch., 1961-69; supt. Concordia Parish Schs., Vidalia, 1969—. Mem. Selective Service Bd., Concordia Parish, 1967—. Served with USMCR, 1942-45. Decorated Purple Heart, Bronze Star. Mem. Phi Delta kappa. Mason (Shriner), Rotarian (pres. 1970-71). Address: Box 548 Vidalia LA 71373

GREEN, BERNARD CLAY, lawyer; b. Shelby County, Ky., Oct. 11, 1904; s. Clarence Evans and Fanny (Baker) G.; student Centre Coll., 1922-25; student Jefferson Sch. Law, 1927-29; LL.B., U. Louisville, 1930; m. Clara Ellen McCammon, Aug. 6, 1936; children—Wanda Mae, Suzette Clay, Earl Mac. Admitted to Ky. bar, 1929; dept. supt. United Merc. Agys., Louisville 1930-36; practiced in Louisville, 1936-40, Owensboro, Ky., 1940—; asst. county atty. Daviess County, Ky., 1953; city prosecutor, Owensboro, 1954-58. Mem. Am., Ky. State, Daviess County (pres. 1970) bar assns., Am. Trial Lawyers Assn., Comml. Law League Am., Am. Judicature Soc., Internat. Acad. Law and Sci., Ky. Hist. Soc. Mem. Christian Ch. (elder, mem. ofcl. bd., past chmn.). Kiwanian (pres. Owensboro 1970-71). Home: 1030 College Dr Owensboro KY 42301 Office: 700 Frederica St Owensboro KY 42301

GREEN, BERNARD REED, athletic dir.; b. Leakesville, Miss., Dec. 10, 1911; s. Samuel James and Cora (Byrd) G.; B.S., U. So. Miss., 1934; m. Rebecca Suzanne Gallaspy, Feb. 9, 1935; children—Rebecca Suzanne (Mrs. A.C. McLeod), James Reed. Freshman football coach U. So. Miss., Hattiesburg, 1934-35, asst. football coach, 1935-37, head football coach, 1937-48, athletic dir., 1948—. Mem. exec. com., dir. Southeastern Life Ins. Co. Mem. Hattiesburg Planning and Zoning Bd. Bd. dirs. U. So. Miss. Found. Served to lt. comdr. USNR, 1942-46. Named to U. So. Miss Sports Hall of Fame, State of Miss. Hall of Fame. Mem. Am. Football Coaches Assn., Nat. Athletic Dirs. Assn., U.S. C. of C. Methodist. Elk. Home: 420 S 21st Av Hattiesburg MS 39401

GREEN, (WILLIAM) COOPER, county ofcl.; b. Birmingham, Ala., Nov. 18, 1900; s. Charles Martin and Mary Elizabeth (Cooper) G.; B.S., Birmingham-So. Coll., 1921, postgrad. in law, 1922-23; grad. Columbia Exec. Program, 1953; m. Hattie Lee Taylor, June 20, 1920; children— William Cooper, Charles T., Margaret (Mrs. Loel Passe), Jane (Mrs. Llewellyn Johns, Jr.), Dorothy (Mrs. Dewey E. Calhoun) (dec.). Tchr., football coach Marbury (Ala.) High Sch., 1922; real estate, ins. broker, Tarrant City, Ala., 1922-23, Birmingham, 1923-33; mem. Ala. legislature, 1931-33; postmaster Birmingham, 1933-40; mayor, Birmingham, 1940-53; v.p., then exec. v.p. Ala. Power Co., Birmingham, 1953-65; pres. Jefferson County (Ala.) Commn., Birmingham, 1965—. Mem. Ala. State Fair Authority, Birmingham, 1958—, pres. bd., 1968-69; mem. Downtown Improvement Assn., Birmingham, 1963—; chmn. Jefferson County campaign A.R.C., 1954; chmn. Ala. Indsl. Adv. Com., 1963-65, Jefferson County U.S. Savs. Bond Campaign, 1965-72; v.p. U.S. Conf. Mayors, 1947-48, pres., 1949-50; represented U.S. in Helsinki, Finland, 1950. Mem. Ala. League Municipalities (pres. 1950-53), Birmingham-So. Coll. Alumni Assn. (past pres.). Clubs: Green Valley Country; Civitan (treas. 1934-35, pres. Birmingham chpt.). Home: 3415 Cherokee Rd Birmingham AL 35223 Office: Court House Birmingham AL 35203

GREEN, DOUGLAS ALVIN, librarian; b. Gilmer, Tex., Feb. 17, 1925; s. Arthur Elmer and Eva Lena (Loyless) G.; student Kilgore Jr. Coll., 1946-48, Harmony Sch. Piano Tech., 1948, Eastern N.M. U., 1949-50; B.A., North Tex. State U., 1951; M.A., East Tex. State U., 1951; diploma Nat. Tech. Schs., 1961; M.S. in L.S., La. State U., 1968; m. Clovis Wayne Elwell, Dec. 15, 1945; 1 son, Danis Ray. Librarian Crystal City (Tex.) High Sch., 1951-52, Woodsboro (Tex.) High Sch., 1956-63; chief bibliographer Gen. Library U. Ark., Fayetteville, 1963-67; librarian Bee County Coll., Beeville, Tex., 1968—. Served with USNR, 1943-46. Mem. Piano Technicians' Guild (craftsman 1953-66), Tex., Ark. (hon.) library assns. Home: 1402 Oriole Lane Beeville TX 78102 Office: Bee County Coll Beeville TX 78102

GREEN, ELEANOR BROOME (MRS. LEON GREEN, JR.), mus. curator; b. Covina, Cal.; d. Charles Samuels and Eleanor Broome; A.B., Vassar Coll., 1949; M.A., George Washington U., 1971; m. Leon Green, Jr. Curator Washington Gallery Modern Art, 1964-67; curator contemporary art Corcoran Gallery Art, Washington, 1967-71; dir. U. Md. Art Gallery, 1972—. Art critic. Mem. Am. Assn. Museums, Jr. League of Washington. Episcopalian. Club: Porto Cervo Yacht. Contbr. articles to profl. publs. Home: 5140 Westpath Way Washington DC 20016 also Villa Green Porto Cervo Sardegna Italy Office:Art Dept U. Md College Park MD 20742

GREEN, FLOYD AARON, constrn. co. exec.; b. Joplin, Mo., Oct. 25, 1922; s. Virgil Ollie and Pearl Verona (Davis) G.; m. Lillan Leona Bates, Jan. 20, 1946; children—Floyd Richard, Don Gerald, Linda Darlene. Riveter, Consolidated Aircraft Corp., San Diego, 1941-43; prodn. mgr. Universal Mfg. Corp., Kansas City, Mo., 1946-49, Nashua Mfg. Corp., Nashua, 1949-64; v.p., dir. Conner Homes Corp., Newport, N.C., 1964-72; v.p. Advance Industries, 1972, pres., 1972—. Served with AUS, 1943-45. Decorated Purple Heart. Baptist. Elk. Club: Morehead Country. Home: Route 1 Box 268 Morehead NC 28557

GREEN, FRANKLIN A., JR., bus. exec.; b. Selma, Ala., Apr. 13, 1931; s. Franklin A. and Louis (Webb) G.; B.S. in Agr., Auburn U., 1954; m. Frances Fuller Green, Apr. 7, 1957; children—Elizabeth, Franklin, Frances Ann, Cary. With Ring Around Products, Inc., and predecessor, Pratville, Ala., 1956—, v.p., 1968—, also dir. Served with AUS, 1954-56. Mem. Soc., Ala. seedsmens assns. Baptist. Kiwanian. Home: 2186 Beverly Dr Montgomery AL 36111 Office: PO Box 589 Montgomery AL 36111

GREEN, GEORGE, dentist; b. Nathalie, Va., Dec. 31, 1925; s. John Collins and Frances (Oliver) G.; student Mars Hill Coll., 1942-44; D.D.S., Med. Coll. Va., 1948; certificate in periodontology, Columbia, 1961. Gen. practice dentistry, Brookneal, Va., 1948—; clin. cons. Columbia U. Dental Sch. Instr. Campbell County chpt. Va. Cancer Soc., 1956-59. Served with USN, 1944-45, 51-53. Mem. Am., Va. dental assns., Piedmont Dental Soc., Am. Legion, 40 and 8, Brookneal C. of C., Delta Sigma Delta. Democrat. Baptist. Mason (Shriner), Elk, Moose, Lion. Clubs: Piedmont, German, Cotillion, Country. Home: Forest St Brookneal VA 24528 Office: Rush St Brookneal VA 24528

GREEN, GEORGE FRANKLIN, physician; b. Bostwick, Ga., Sept. 27, 1924; s. Rice Burkitt and Rubye (Riden) G.; B.S., N. Ga. Coll., 1948; M.D., Med. Coll. Ga., 1951; m. Helen Montine Maxwell, June 4, 1944; children—George F., Helen Claudia, Wallace Maxwell. Intern Brooke Army Med. Center, 1951; pvt. practice, gen. practitioner, Sparta, Ga., 1953—; chief staff Hancock Meml. Hosp.; asso. prof. clin. medicine Duke; asso. prof. clin. and ambulatory medicine U. Ala. Pres. Oconee Valley Investment Corp.; dir. Bank of Hancock County; pres. Hancock Redevel. Corp., Sparta Med. Clinic. Mayor, Sparta, Ga., 1966-70; commr. Hancock County Bd. Rds. and Revenue; past chmn. Oconee Area Planning and Devel. Commn. Bd. dirs. local council Boy Scouts Am. Served as capt. inf. AUS, 1943-46; capt. M.C. AUS, 1951-53. Fellow Am. Geriatrics Soc.; mem. Am., So., Ga. med. assns., Oconee Valley Med. Soc., Am., Ga. (past dir. 6th dist.) acads. practice, V.F.W., Gridiron Soc., Am. Legion, Delta Sigma Pi (hon.) Baptist (deacon). Mason (Shriner, K.T.), Lion (pres. 1961-62). Club: Civitan (past pres. Sparta br., past lt. gov. Ga. dist.). Home: 333 Parkway Dr Sparta GA 31087 Office: 325 E Broad St Sparta GA 31087

GREEN, GEORGE MARVIN, lawyer; b. Tampa, Fla., Sept. 22, 1904; s. William Truman and Maude (Powell) G.; LL.B., U. Fla., 1930; m. Mary Bentley, May 22, 1958; 1 dau., Linda. Admitted to Fla. bar, 1930; partner firm Carlton, Fields, Ward, Emmanuel, Smith & Cutler, Tampa. Mem. Hillsborough County Bd. Pub. Instrn., 1947-67, chmn., 1959-62, vice chmn., 1965. Served to lt. col. USAAF, 1941-46. Mem. Am., Tampa, Hillsborough County bar assns., Fla. Bar, Am. Judicature Soc., Am. Legion, 40 and 8 (chef de gar passe), Sigma Nu, Phi Delta Phi. Mason (Shriner). Home: 3707 Obispo St Tampa FL 33609 Office: Exchange Nat Bank Bldg Tampa FL 33602

GREEN, HAROLD, broadcasting exec. Program mgr. WMAL, Washington. Address: 4461 Connecticut Av NW Washington DC 20008

GREEN, HAROLD DAVID, physician, educator; b. Zanesville, O., Aug. 11, 1905; s. Louis Harold and Laura (Gobel) G.; B.S., Wooster Coll., 1927, D.Sc., 1957; M.D., Western Res. U., 1931; m. Bonnie Louise McClung, June 30, 1934; children—Barbara Holden (Mrs. Jerry A. Trivette), David Louis Darragh. Intern J.D. Archbold Meml. Hosp., Thomasville, Ga., 1931-32; med. house officer Lakeside Hosp.; med. house officer Univ. Hosps., Cleve., 1932-33, asst. resident, 1933; instr. physiology Western Res. U. Med. Sch., 1933-35, sr. instr., 1936-37, asst. prof., 1937-39, asso. prof., 1940-45, Commonwealth Fund fellow, guest prof. Mass. Inst. Tech., 1939-40; instr. physiology Yale U. Med. Sch., 1935-36; chmn. dept. physiology Bowman Gray Sch. Medicine, Winston-Salem, N.C., 1945-72, Gordon Gray prof., asso. in internal medicine, 1945—, asso. in pharmacology, 1963—; practice medicine dept. of clinics, 1945—; mem. staff N.C. Bapt. Hosp., 1945—. Mem. physiology study sect. NIH, USPHS, 1959-62, mem. program com. cardiovascular undergrad. tng. programs, 1960-63; mem. program project com. Nat. Heart Inst., 1966-68; physiology sect. Nat. Bd. Med. Examiners, 1960-63. Fellow A.C.P.; mem. Am. Soc. Pharmacology and Exptl. Therapeutics, A.A.A.S., Biophysical Soc., Am. (basic sci. council 1955—, council on circulation; research allocations com. 1957-59), N.C. (dir.), Forsyth County heart assns., Central Soc. Clin. Investigation, So. Soc. Clin Research, Micro Circulatory Soc. (mem. council 1971), Am. Physiol. Soc. (membership com. 1963-66), Am. Fedn. Clin. Research, A.M.A., N.C., Forsyth County med. socs., Am. Coll. Clin. Pharmacology and Chemotherapy, Phi Beta Kappa, Sigma Xi, Alpha Omega Alpha, Theta Chi Delta. Mem. editorial bd. Circulation, 1945-47, Circulation Research, 1960-67, An. Rev. Physiology, 1956-60; Am. Jour. Physiology and Jour. Applied Physiology, 1957-62. Address: 3619 Dewsbury Rd Winston-Salem NC 27104

GREEN, HOLLIS LYNN, religious assn. exec.; b. Rhea County, Tenn., Jan. 6, 1933; s. Herbert Barton and Grace Irene (Curton) G.; student Beckley Coll., 1952-54, U. Cin., 1957-58, Miami Christian U., 1961-62; B.D., Luther Rice Sem., 1965, Th.D., 1968; m. Peggy Jean Lane, Dec. 8, 1951; children—Barton Lynn, Brian Lane. Ordained to the ministry Ch. of God, 1959; pastor various churches Ohio, S.C., Ind., Fla., 1958-64; state dir. Christian Edn., Ch. of God., 1952-58; mem. gen. youth and Christian Edn. Bd., Cleveland, Tenn., 1958-62; dir. pub. relations Ch. of God Exec. Offices, Cleveland, Tenn., 1962—; pres. Aid, Ltd., Miami, Fla., 1970—; dir. Ch. Funding, Inc., Hialeah, Fla., 1971—; dir. Provident Investment Corp., Atlanta, Ga. Cons. Time Life Books, Protestant Armed Forces Field Rep. Mem. U.S. Postal Forum II, III, 1968-69, Inter-Racial Study Commn. of the South, 1962-64, Dr. King's List of 200, 1966-68. Trustee, Luther Rice Sem.; trustee Internat. Christian Found., pres., 1972—. Served as chaplain (maj.) USAF, 1964-72. Recipient pub. service award U.S. Postal Service, 1968. Fellow Program and Platform Techniques div. Internat. Platform Assn.; mem. Pub. Relations Soc. Am., Religious Pub. Relations Council, Evangelical Press Assn., Soc. Pentecostal Scholars, Nat. Sunday Sch. Assn. (bd. dirs. 1958-62), Internat. Pub. Relations Assn. Republican. Kiwanian. Author: Hitching Your Star to a Wagon, 1958; Dynamics of Christian Discipleship, 1962, Christian Education Cyclopedia, 1965; Marchings As to War, 1969; Understanding Pentecostalism, 1970; Where in the World are you Going, 1971; Why Churches Die, 1972. Home: 917 Hackberry Dr NW Cleveland TN 37311 Office: Keith and 25th Sts NW Cleveland TN 37311

GREEN, HOWARD LEMUEL, county judge; b. Swenson, Tex., Jan. 24, 1921; s. Thomas Lemuel and Della (Hall) G.; B.S., McMurry Coll., 1943; m. Betty Bratton, Jan. 6, 1950; children—Leslie Carole, Howard Lemuel. Sports writer Abilene Reporter-News, 1939-47; pres. Longhorn Baseball League, 1947-48, Gulf Coast Baseball League, 1950-52, Big State Baseball League, 1951-55; mem. Tex. Ho. of Reps., 1957-67; judge Tarrant County, Tex., 1967—. Served with USAAF, 1943-45. Decorated Air medal. Democrat. Methodist. Home: 7316 Oakland Lane Fort Worth TX 76118 Office: Tarrant County Courthouse Fort Worth TX 76102

GREEN, JAMES DOUGLAS, physician; b. Tulsa, Okla., Oct. 18, 1933; s. Marian Floyd and Cornelia (Allen) G.; M.D., U. Okla., 1957; m. Betty Jo Albright, Sept. 7, 1957; children—James Douglas, David Stanley, Karen Elizabeth. Intern St. John's Hosp., Tulsa, 1956-57, resident, 1957-61; practice medicine, specializing in internal medicine, Tulsa, 1961—; mem. staff St. John's Hosp.; vis. staff St. Francis, Hillcrest hosps.; instr. dept. medicine Sch. Medicine, U. Okla., Tulsa, 1971—. Bd. dirs. Tulsa County chpt. Heart Assn. Served with AUS, 1966-68. Recipient Physicians Recognition award A.M.A., 1969. Mem. Tulsa County Internist Soc., A.M.A., C. of C., A.C.P. Presbyn. (elder). Home: 5830 S Delaware Pl Tulsa OK 74105 Office: 3102 S Harvard St Tulsa OK 74135

GREEN, JOHN PLATH, lawyer; b. Dallas, Dec. 11, 1910; s. George Athel and Nora (Rape) G.; LL.B., U. Tex., 1938; m. Marguerite Francine Tatom, Sept. 6, 1941; children—John Randall, Nancy Robin. Admitted to Tex. bar, 1938; asso., partner firm Storey, Sanders, Sherrill & Armstrong, Dallas, 1938-48; partner firm Sanders, Lefkowitz & Green, Dallas, 1950-65, Green, Gilmore, Crutcher, Rothpletz and Burke, Dallas, 1967—. Chmn., Dallas County Hist. Survey Com., 1962—. Trustee Dallas Ind. Sch. Dist., Dallas Pub. Library; pres. Dallas Bd. Edn., 1971—. Bd. dirs. Little Bethel Cemetery Found. Served with AUS, 1942-46. Decorated Legion of Merit, Bronze Star medal. Mem. Am., Dallas bar assns., State Bar Tex., Dallas Local History Soc. (founder, pres.). Presbyn. (elder 1953—). Author: Henry Cabaniss and His Descendants, 1955; Abstracts of Deeds, Rutherford County, North Carolina, 1970; Stephen Tatom and His Descendants, 1971. Home: 7517 Mason Dell Dr Dallas TX 75230 Office: First Nat Bank Bldg Dallas TX 75202

GREEN, JOSHUA, lawyer; b. Jackson, Miss., Nov. 12, 1922; s. Garner Wynn and Winifred (Calhoon) G.; B.A. magna cum laude, Vanderbilt U., 1946, J.D., 1949; m. Myra Louise Allison Hamilton, Apr. 10, 1947; 1 dau., Lynn Hamilton. Admitted to Miss. bar, 1949, U.S. Supreme Ct. bar, 1963; partner firm Green, Cheney, Jones and Hughes (formerly Green, Green and Cheney), Jackson, Miss., 1949—. Dir., Old Trace Marina, Inc., 1970. Trustee St. Andrews Day Sch., Jackson, 1961-65; pres. Allison Art Colony, Way, Miss., 1953; treas. Jackson Civic Art Council, Inc., 1958, v.p., 1961, pres., 1963, dir. 1956-70. Served from pvt. to sgt. AUS, 1943-46. Mem. Miss. State Bar, Am., Hinds County bar assns., Comml. Law League Am., Miss. Art Assn. (pres. 1958), Phi Beta Kappa, Phi Alpha Delta, Phi Delta Theta. Episcopalian. Club: Jackson Yacht (sec.-treas. 1964, commodore 1966). Editor: Mainsheet, 1970. Home: 154 Glen Way Jackson MS 39216 Office: 800 Electric Bldg Jackson MS 39205

GREEN, JOYCE HENS (MRS. SAMUEL GREEN), judge; b. N.Y.C., Nov. 13, 1928; d. James Stanley and Hedy (Bucher) Hens; B.A., U. Md., 1949; LL.B., George Washington U., 1951; m. Samuel Green, Sept. 25, 1965; children—James Harry, Michael Timothy, June Heather. Admitted to D,C. bar, 1951, Va. bar, 1956; practiced in Washington, 1951-68, Arlington, Va., 1956-68; partner (with husband) Green & Green, Washington, until 1968; asso. judge D.C. Ct. Gen. Sessions, 1968-71, Superior Ct. of D.C., 1971—. Trustee D.C. div. Am. Cancer Soc., 1963—. Recipient certificate of merit for outstanding profl. achievement D.C. Profl. Panhellenic Assn. Fellow Am. Acad. Matrimonial Lawyers; mem. Am., Va., Arlington County, D.C. Women's (pres. 1960-62) bar assns., Bar Assn. D.C., Unified Bar of D.C., Va. State Bar, Nat. Lawyers Club, Va. Assn. Trial Attys., U. Md. Alumni Assn., Kappa Beta Pi Home: 1714 N Glebe Rd Arlington VA 22207 Office: Superior Court of DC 4th and E Sts NW Washington DC 20001

GREEN, JUNE LAZENBY (MRS. JOHN CAWLEY GREEN), fed. judge; b. Arnold, Md., Jan. 23, 1914; d. Eugene H. and Jessie T. (Briggs) Lazenby; J.D., Am. U., 1941; m. John Cawley Green, Sept. 5, 1936. Admitted to Md. bar, 1943, D.C. bar, 1945; pvt. practice law in Washington, 1947-68, Annapolis, Md., 1950-68; claims adjuster Lumbermans Mut. Casualty Co., Washington, 1942-43, claims atty., 1943-47; judge U.S. Dist. Ct. for D.C., 1968—. Bar examiner, Washington, 1963-68. Named Woman Lawyer of Year, 1965. Fellow Am. Acad. Matrimonial Lawyers; mem. Inter-Am., Am., Md. bar assns., Bar Assn. D.C, (dir. 1966-68), Women's Bar Assn. D.C. (pres. 1955-57), Kappa Beta Pi. Clubs: Nat. Lawyers, Zonta. Home: 261 Joyce Lane Arnold MD 21012 Office: US Courthouse Washington DC 20001

GREEN, MARGARET KELLY MOORE (MRS. JOHN FONDON GREEN), educator; b. Talladega Springs, Ala., July 11, 1919; d. Sam Curry and Gertrude (Kelley) Moore; B.S., Ala. Coll., 1941; M.S., U. Ala., 1947, postgrad., 1947; postgrad. U. Tenn., 1949; m. John Fondon Green, Mar. 6, 1953. Tchr. vocational home econs. Falkville (Ala.) High Sch., 1941-42; served with WAVES, 1942-46; student asst. Infancy Lab., U. Ala., Tuscaloosa, 1947; asst. prof. clothing and textiles Berry Schs., Mt. Berry, Ga., 1947-50; asst. home econs. Jacksonville (Ala.) State U., 1950-63, asst. prof. clothing and textiles, 1963—, dir. Nursery Sch., 1951-63, Home Mgmt. House, 1962-63. Mem. Am., Ala. home econs. assns., Leone Cole Home Econs. Club, U.D.C., Wesleyan Service Guild. Methodist. Club: Flower Growers Garden (pres. 1960). Home: Box 346 Jacksonville AL 36265

GREEN, RALPH TILLMAN, banker; b. Paxton, Tex., Apr. 10, 1922; s. Ralph Eugene and Nettie Ann (Cammack) G.; B.A., Tex. A. and M. U., 1942, M.S., 1947; Ph.D., Duke, 1954; m. Mary Lou Malone, June 20, 1945; children—Meslissa Ann, Susan Kimberly, Nancy Alison. Financial economist Fed. Res. Bank of Dallas, 1949-55, v.p., 1962—; prof., chmn. dept. econs. Baylor U., 1955-56; exec. dir. Tex. Commn. Higher Edn., 1956-62. Mem. So. Regional Edn. Bd., 1956-62; cons. Va. Council Higher Edn., 1961, So. Regional Edn. Bd., 1958-60, Tex. Coordinating Bd. Higher Edn., 1971; mem. research adv. com. Fed. Res. System; lectr. univs. Mem. tech. adv. com. Goals for Dallas, 1967-70. Bd. dirs. Tex. United Fund, 1968-72. Served to lt., USNR, 1942-46; PTO. Fellow Found. Econ. Edn., Irvington-on-Hudson, N.Y., 1948. Mem. Am., So. econ. assns., Am. Finance Assn., S.W. Social Sci. Assn., Dallas C. of C., Dallas Economists Club (pres. 1967). Home: 4017 Northview Lane Dallas TX 75229 Office: 400 S Akard St Dallas TX 75222

GREEN, ROBERT HAMILTON, engring. co. exec.; b. Bridgeport, Conn., July 3, 1935; s. Albert Arthur and Mary Elizabeth (Hansen) G.; B.S. in Aero. Engring., U. Fla., 1958, B.Indsl. Engring., 1959; postgrad. Ga. Inst. Tech., 1963; m. Paula Hathaway Anderson, Sept. 6, 1958; children—Lydia Anne, Edith Hathaway, Elizabeth Anderson, Cecilia Hamilton. Flight test engr. Mercury Program, Gen. Dynamics Co., Cape Canaveral, Fla., 1958-61; project engr. airlift containerized freight L.I.P., Atlanta, 1961-68; scientist asso. graphite fiber composite materials Lockheed Ga. Co., Marietta, 1968-70. Mem. Sandy Springs Planning Commn., Atlanta, 1967—. Registered profl. engr., Ga., Fla. Mem. Nat., Ga. socs. profl. engrs., Am. Inst. Indsl. Engrs., Ga. Cons. Engrs. Council, Tau Beta Pi, Lambda Chi Alpha. Episcopalian. Clubs: Atlanta Yacht (past fleet capt.); U. Fla. Alumni (Gainesville). Contbr. articles to profl. jours. Patentee in field. Home: 550 High Point Lane NE Atlanta GA 30342 Office: RH Green Engineering Co Inc Atlanta GA 30342

GREEN, THOMAS ROBERT, aviation co. exec.; b. Columbus, O., Aug. 15, 1922; s. Charles William and Reba (Maxwell) G.; student Kenyon Coll., 1940-42; m. Nilda Lopez, Oct. 12, 1945; children—Stephanie, Timothy, Thomas R., Melissa, Juan. Jr. sta. mgr. Pan Am. Airways, 1944-46; area operations mgr., chief dispatcher Transportes Aeroes Central Americanos, 1946-47; pres. Dispatch Services, Inc., 1947—; Air Acgy., Inc., 1949—; Fla. Aviation Fueling Co., Inc., 1952—; Pan African Airlines (Nigeria) Ltd., 1961—; Freeport Flight Services, Ltd., 1965—; Safari Air Services, Ltd., Nairobi, 1968—; dir. Fla. Nat. Bank & Trust Co., Miami, Dania Jai Alai. Served with AUS, 1943-44. Mem. C. of C. of Miami, Aviation Exec. Club (dir., exec. com.), Quiet Birdman. Lion. Clubs: Lucaya Beach Country, Bahama Reef Country (Freeport, Bahamas); Calusa Country; Coral Reef Yacht. Home: 3500 Granada Blvd Coral Gables FL 33134 Office: PO Box 2034 Miami FL 33159

GREEN, WILLIAM CLINTON, lawyer; b. Tyler, Fla., Jan. 14, 1907; s. William Henry and Nettie Loraine (Brooks) G.; student U. Fla., 1926-27, U. Miami (Fla.), 1927; m. Phoebe Diehl, Jan. 28, 1955; children—Clinton Marvin Tyler, Janice (Mrs. Fred Grothe), Marjorie Jeanette, Melinda Jane, Melissa Anne, Melanie Roberta, Marcia Loreen. Admitted to Fla. bar, 1930, since practiced in Miami; mem. firm Green & Hastings, 1961-; dir. U. Miami Law Center, 1960—. Dir. for Fla. compensation dept. Fed. Civil Works Adminstrn., 1934. Served to 1st lt., judge adv. gen. dept. AUS. World War II; 1st lt. Res. Fellow Am. Coll. Trial Lawyers; mem. Am., Fla., Dade County (dir. 1960) bar assns., Law Sci. Acad. Am., Judge Adv. Gen. Assn., Am. Judicature Assn., Soc. Am. Mil. Engrs. Nat. Assn. Claimants Counsel Am., Acad. Fla. Trial Lawyers, Mil. Order World Wars, Res. Officer Assn., Sigma Phi Epsilon. Club: Miami Beach Rod and Reel. Home: 2616 Country Club Prado Coral Gables FL 33134 Office: Biscayne Bldg 19 W Flagler St Miami FL 33132

GREEN, WILLIAM WELLS, civil engr.; b. Sioux City, Ia., Nov. 26, 1911; s. Thomas William and Jessie Eadie (Wells) G.; B.S., U. Notre Dame, 1934; m. Patricia Cecille Gregory, Jan. 10, 1944; children—William Joseph, Mary Teresa. Asst. engr. Ia. Hwy. Commn., Cherokee, 1935-40; asst. engr. City Corpus Christi, Tex., 1940-44; asst. office county surveyor, Nueces County Tex., 1944-54, county surveyor, 1955—. Mem. Tex. Bd. Registration Pub. Surveyors. Bd. dirs. Carmelite Day Nursery. Fellow Am. Soc. C.E.; mem. Am. Congress Surveying Mapping, Tex. Surveyors Assn. (past dir.). Democrat. Roman Catholic. K.C. Home: 3149 Topeka St Corpus Christi TX 78404 Office: 206 Courthouse Annex 409 Mann St Corpus Christi TX 78401

GREENAWAY, DONALD, assn. exec.; b. Frankfort, Mich., Apr. 14, 1911; s. George Henry and Mary Elizabeth (Orr) G.; B.A., Mich. State U., 1934; m. Louise Constance Wadsworth, June 27, 1936; 1 dau., Jeanne Elizabeth (Mrs. Robert Mattice); m. 2d, Lorraine Muellenbach, July 6, 1958; 1 dau., Karen. Engaged in hotel adminstrn. and mgmt., 1934-41; food service exec. Trans World Airlines, 1946-47; prof. hotel adminstrn. Coll. Bus., Wash. State U., 1947-51; prof., adminstr.-dir. Sch. Hotel, Restaurant and Instl. Mgmt., Coll. Bus., Mich. State U., 1951-58; exec. v.p. Nat. Restaurant Assn., Chgo., 1958—. Mem. Gov. Wash. Com. Devel. State Wash., 1950-51; pres., founder Nat. Council Hotel and Restaurant Edn., 1946; bd. dirs. Govs. Confs. Tourism Pacific N.W., 1947-49, Pacific-N.W. Trade Assn., 1947-48; adviser USPHS, USAF World-Wide Food Service; mgmt. cons. Soc. Advancement Food Service Research; mem. U.S. Travel Service, also trade assn. adv. com. U.S. C. of C.; trade missions to Europe auspices Dept. Commerce. Dir. Wilkensburg Hotel Co. (Pa.), Hotel Elkhart (Ind.). Served to capt. USAAF, 1942-46. Mem. Am. Assn. U. Profs., Am. Soc. Assn. Execs., Execs. Forum, Mich. Resort Assn., Mich., Pa. hotel assns., Food Execs. Assn., Fifth Internat. World Food Congress, Internat. Ho-Re-Ca. Confrerie de la Chaine des Rotisseurs, Theta Chi, Alpha Kappa Psi. Rotarian. Author: Manual for Resort Operations, 1950; also monographs, papers, articles. Home: 5580 Longmont St Houston TX 77027 Office: 925 Caroline St Houston TX 77002

GREENBAUM, SAMUEL MEYER, lawyer; b. Washington, July 15, 1916; s. Samuel M. and Estelle (Ball) G.; J.D., Georgetown U., 1939, LL.M., 1942; m. Helen L. Marx, Feb. 15, 1942; children—Steven M., Marcia E. Admitted to D.C. bar, 1939; practiced in Washington, 1939—. Alternate chmn. Commn. on Mental Health, U.S. Dist. Ct. for D.C., 1962-72; instr. Catholic U. Columbus Sch. Law, 1965—; adj. prof. creditor's rights in bankruptcy Georgetown U. Law Center, 1971; professorial lectr. creditor's rights in bankruptcy Am. U., 1971, 72. Sec., dir. Lady Hamilton, Inc., Arlington, Va. Mem. Am., Fed. (chmn. com. on bankruptcy law 1971-72), D.C. (chmn. subcom. on bankruptcy) bar assns., Comml. Law League. Author: Plenary, Summary and Concurrent Jurisdiction under the Bankruptcy Act, 1942. Home: 2840 Brandywine St NW Washington DC 20008 Office: Tower Bldg 14th and K Sts NW Washington DC 20005

GREENBAUM, STUART IRWIN, educator; b. N.Y.C., Oct. 7, 1936; s. Sam and Bertha (Freimark) G.; B.S., N.Y.U., 1958, postgrad. (fellow), 1959-60; postgrad. fellow New Sch. for Social Research, 1960; Ph.D. (fellow), Johns Hopkins, 1964; m. Margaret Elaine Wache, July 29, 1964; 1 dau., Regina Gail. Financial economist Fed. Reserve Bank, Kansas City, Mo., 1962-66; sr. economist, asso. editor Nat. Banking Review, Office Comptroller of Currency, Washington, 1966-67; asso. prof. econs. U. Ky., Lexington, 1967—. Cons. Fed. Reserve Bank Cleve., 1968-70. Mem. Am. Econs. Assn., Econometric Soc., Am. Finance Assn. Contbr. articles to profl. jours. Office: Econ Dept U Ky Lexington KY 40506

GREENBERG, BENJAMIN EDWIN, radiologist; b. N.Y.C., Aug. 25, 1907; s. Samuel and Edith (Goodman) G.; B.A., Columbia, 1929; M.D., N.Y. State U., 1932; m. Mollie Weinstein, June 5, 1932; 1 dau., Barbara J. Intern Beth-Eli Hosp., Bklyn., 1932; practice medicine specializing in radiology, 1933-42; with VA, 1946—, chief radiology service VA Hosp., Memphis, 1950—; prof. radiology U. Tenn., 1965—. Served from 1st lt. to maj., M.C., AUS, 1942-46. Diplomate Am. Bd. Radiology. Fellow Am. Coll. Radiology; mem. Memphis Roentgen Soc. (pres. 1956-57). Home: 294 Aurora Circle Memphis TN 38111 Office: VA Hosp Memphis TN 38104

GREENBERG, PAUL, newspaperman; b. Shreveport, La., Jan. 21, 1937; s. Ben and Sarah (Ackerman) G.; B.Journalism, U. Mo., 1958, M.A. in History, 1959; student Columbia Grad. Sch., 1960-62; m. Carolyn Levy, Dec. 6, 1964; children—Daniel, Ruth Elizabeth. Lectr. Am. history Hunter Coll., 1962; editorial page editor Pine Bluff (Ark.) Comml., 1962-66, 67—; editorial writer Chgo. Daily News, 1966-67; nationally syndicated columnist. Served to capt. AUS, 1969. Recipient Grenville Clark award, 1964; Pulitzer prize for editorial writing, 1969; Best Editorial award Nat. Newspaper Assn., 1968. Republican. Jewish religion. Home: 2406 W 39th St Pine Bluff AR 71601 Office: 300 Beech St Pine Bluff AR 71601

GREENBERG, SANFORD DAVID, research co. exec.; b. Buffalo, Dec. 13, 1940; s. Carl and Sarah (fox) G.; A.B., Columbia, 1962, M.B.A., 1966; M.A., Ph.D. (Woodrow Wilson fellow) Harvard, 1965, postgrad. Law Sch., 1965-66; postgrad. (Marshall scholar) Oxford U. (Eng.), 1964-65; m.Susan Beth Roseno, Aug 12, 1962; children—Paul Eric, James Albert. Asst. prof. govt. Columbia; N.Y.C., 1965; faculty Center for Internat. Affairs, Harvard, 1966; White House fellow, asst. to Pres.'s sci. adviser White House, Washington, 1966-67; dir. corporate devel. Systems Devel. Corp., Washington, 1967-68; chmn. bd. EDP Tech., Inc., Washington, 1968-71; vice chmn. bd. KMS Industries, Inc., Washington, 1971—; Univ. Research prof. U. Md., 1971—. Trustee Nat. Braille Press, Boston, Charles River Acad., Cambridge, Mass., Opera Soc. Washington, Ford's Theatre Soc.; bd. dirs. Nat. Com. on U.S.-China Relations. Named One of 10 Outstanding Young Mem. of Am., U.S. Jr. C. of C., 1966, One of 4 Outstanding Young Men of Mass., Mass. Jr. C. of C., 1966, One of 10 Outstanding Young Men, Boston Jr. C. of C., 1966. Mem. Young

Pres.'s Orgn., Am. Polit. Sci. Assn., Am. Hist. Assn., Oxford Union Soc., Assn. for Computing Machinery, Newcomen Soc. N. Am., Phi Beta Kappa, Zeta Beta Tau. Clubs: Harvard (N.Y.C.); Federal City; Harmonie; International; Bay. Patentee device for compression and expansion of speech. Home: 700 New Hampshire Av NW Apt 106 Washington DC 20037 Office: 600 New Hampshire Av NW Washington DC 20037

GREENBURG, LEONARD, judge; b. Schenectady, N.Y., Sept. 3, 1911; s. Michael and Annie (Shapiro) G.; B.A., Tulane U., 1931, LL.B., 1933; m. Alice Douglas Daspit, June 30, 1942; children—Justin Michael, Douglas Henry. Statis. clerk, asst. legal adv. Emergency Relief Adminstrn., New Orleans, 1934-35; research asst., spl. lectr. La. State U., 1935-40; admitted to La. bar, 1934; practiced in Houma, La., 1938-40, 45-66; spl. agt. F.B.I., 1940-45; asst. dist. atty., Houma, 1948-51, acting dist. atty., 1951-54, dist. atty., 1954-60; dist. judge Houma and Thibodaux, La., 1966—. Instr. French, Tulane U., 1935. Chmn. A.R.C., 1951-52; Active Boy Scouts of Am. Mem. Am., La. bar assns. Democrat. Jewish religion. Home: 900 Liberty St Houma LA 70360 Office: 413 Goode St Houma LA 70360

GREENE, A(LVIN) C(ARL), editor, author; b. Abilene, Tex., Nov. 4, 1923; s. Alvin Carl and Marie (Cole) G.; B.A., Abilene Christian Coll., 1948; student Phillips U., 1942, Kansas State Coll., Pittsburg, 1943, Hardin-Simmons U., 1951; m. Betty Dozier, May 1, 1950; children—Geoffrey, Mark, Eliot, Meredith Elizabeth. Mem. staff Abilene Reporter-News, 1948-52, amusements editor, 1957-60; book store owner, Abilene, 1952-57; spl. instr. Hardin-Simmons U., 1957; book editor, editorial columnist Dallas Times Herald, 1960-68, editor editorial page, 1963-65; staff U. Tex., 1968-69; exec. editor Southwestern Hist. Quar., 1968-69; free-lance writer, 1950—. Served with USNR, 1943-46; PTO, China. Recipient award Nat. Conf. Christians and Jews, 1964; Dobie-Paisano fellow, 1968. Mem. Tex. Inst. Letters (pres. 1969-71; award 1964), Tex. Electric Railroaders Assn. Presbyn. Club: Dallas Press. Author: A Personal Country, 1969; The Last Captive, 1972; The Santa Claus Bank Robbery, 1972. Editor: Living Texas, 1972. Home: 10640 Lennox Lane Dallas TX 75229

GREENE, BARNET, accountant; b. N.Y.C., May 8, 1916; s. Harry and Ceilia (Myerson) G.; B.S., Am. U., 1952; m. Rosalie Maletz, May 29, 1949; children—Ellyn Bailey (Mrs. Steven Allen Stark), Barbara Lynn. Mgmt. analyst Rural Electrification Adminstrn., Washington, 1948-53; with Forrest E. Ferguson, C.P.A., 1953, Burke, Lansburg & Gerber, C.P.A.'s, 1954, Marinus Koster, C.P.A., 1955-58 (all Washington); accountant Bernet Greene, C.P.A., Washington and Silver Spring, Md., 1958—. Instr., Am. U., Washington, 1958-62. Treas., Connecticut Estates Civic Assn., Silver Spring, Md., 1955-56, Parkland Pool Assn., 1965-66. Served with AUS, 1942-46. Mem. Am., D.C. insts. C.P.A.'s Md. Assn. C.P.A.'s (chpt. treas. 1969-70, sec. 1970-71, v.p., pres.-elect 1971-72, pres. 1972-73), Accounting Research Assn. Home: 11300 Gilsan St Silver Spring MD 20902 Office: 3408 Wisconsin Av NW Washington DC 20016

GREENE, CONDON LORNTZ, dentist; b. Lake City, Tenn., Apr. 12, 1895; s. Thomas Wiley and Mary Frances (Pebley) G.; student Carson-Newman Coll., 1916; U. Tenn., 1918-19; D.D.S., U. Tenn. Coll. Dentistry, 1924; m. Gladys Irene Hill, June 29, 1926; 1 dau., Frances Hill (Mrs. Benjamin A. Morton, Jr. Pvt. practice dentistry, Clinton and Lake City, Tenn., 1924—. Chmn. Anderson County Red Cross, 1942; chmn. Crippled Children's program for Shriners, 1930; active Great Smokey Mountain council Boy Scouts Am.; chmn. Anderson County Youth for White House Program, 1958. Recipient Silver Beaver award Boy Scouts Am. Mem. Anderson County Fair Assn. (pres. 1926), Am., Tenn. dental assns., Clinton Literary Soc. (pres. 1941). Methodist. Mason, Lion. Clubs: Civitan, Knoxville Executive, City. Home: Box 126 Clinton TN 37716 Office: Gen Delivery Lake City TN 37769

GREENE, DALLAS WHORTON, JR., city ofcl.; b. Shreveport, La., June 29, 1923; s. Dallas Whorton and Eunice (Lester) G.; student Centenary Coll., 1941; m. Alice Whittington, Oct. 4, 1947; 1 dau., Valerie (Mrs. David Randall Rockett). With La. Fire Dept., Shreveport, 1942—, fire chief, 1965—. Mem. Shreveport Assn. for Blind, 1966—. Mem. governing com. Arthritis Found., 1968—. Served with C.E., AUS, 1943-45. Mem. Internat. Assn. Fire Chiefs (pres. 1971-72), La. State Firemen's Assn., Fraternal Order Fire Fighters (hon.), Nat. Fire Protection Assn., Am. Legion, V.F.W., Am. Ordnance Assn. Lion. Home: 8826 Stonelake Pl Shreveport LA 71108 Office: PO Box 1143 Shreveport LA 71163

GREENE, HAROLD HERMAN, judge; b. Frankfurt, Germany, Feb. 6, 1923 (came to U.S. 1942, naturalized 1944); s. Irving and Edith (Spandau) G.; student George Washington U., 1948-52, J.D. with distinction, 1952; student Biarritz Am. U., 1946; m. Evelyn Schroer, Sept. 19, 1948; children—Michael D., Stephanie A. Admitted to D.C. bar, 1952; asst. U.S. atty., Washington, D.C., 1953-57; atty. Office Legal Counsel, U.S. Dept. Justice, Washington, 1957-58, chief appeals sect. Civil Rights div., 1958-65; judge D.C. Ct. Gen. Sessions, 1965-66, chief judge, 1966-71; chief judge Superior Ct. D.C., 1971—. Served with AUS, 1944-47. Recipient Isiah award for pursuit of justice, 1971; Distinguished Alumnus award George Washington U. Law Sch., 1969. Mem. Am., Fed. bar assns., Bar Assn. D.C. (Distinguished Service award 1970), Am. Judicature Soc., World Peace Through Law Assn., Order of Coif, Phi Delta Phi. Jewish religion. Asso. editor George Washington U. Law Rev., 1951. Contbr. articles to profl. jours. Home: 6417 Tone Dr Bethesda MD 20034 Office: Superior Court Dist Columbia 4th and F Sts NW Washington DC 20001

GREENE, JOHN WILLIAM, JR., physician; b. E. Orange, N.J., July 25, 1926; s. John William and Illinois (Dowler) G.; B.S., U. Pitts., 1948; M.D., U. Pa., 1952; m. Eugenie W. Wuichet, Sept. 4, 1954; children— Eugenie, Susan, Isobel. Intern U. Pa. Hosp., 1952-53, resident obstetrics and gynecology, 1953-56; research fellow, then research asso. obstetrics and gynecology U. Pa. Sch. Medicine, 1956-59, asst. prof., 1959-63; prof. obstetrics and gynecology, chmn. dept. U. Ky. Coll. Medicine, 1963—. Trustee Frontier Nursing Service, 1966—. Served with AUS, 1944-46. Diplomate Am. Bd. Obstetrics and Gynecology (asso. examiner). Fellow A.C.S., Am. Coll. Obstetricians and Gynecologists, mem. A.M.A., Am. Assn. Obstetricians and Gynecologists, Central Assn. Obstetricians and Gynecologists, Soc. Gynecologic Investigation. Author: (with others) Induction of Labor, 1965; also numerous papers. Home: 420 Bristol Rd Lexington KY 40502

GREENE, JOSEPH NATHANIEL, utilities exec.; b. Ft. Logan, Colo., Feb. 1, 1893; s. Lewis Douglass and Lillian Taft (Adams) G.; B.S., U. Ill., 1915; m. Nanine W. Pond, 1917 (div. 1931); children—Joseph Nathaniel, Nicholas Misplee; m. 2d, Margaret Mordock Wright, 1938; children—William Mordock, Elizabeth Kimberly. With Astoria Importing & Mfg. Co., Long Island City, N.Y., 1922-29; officer, dir. Fed. Water Service Corp. or subsidiary firms, 1929-52; pres., dir. Ala. Gas Corp., 1940-52, chmn. bd., 1953-67. Trustee Pelham Manor, N.Y., 1925-27, mayor, 1928-29; coordinator Jefferson County Civilian Def., 1941-46; chmn. local chpt. ARC, 1949-52, chmn. com. on resolutions, 1957, conv. Am. Nat. Red Cross, mem. bd. govs. 1960-66; chmn. Alabama Hall of Fame Bd., 1952—; co-chmn. Birmingham Com. of 100, 1954, chmn., 1955-57. Served as capt. U.S. Army, 1916-19. Mem. Birmingham Symphony Assn. (pres. 1958-62, chmn. bd. 1962-65, trustee), Sigma Nu. Mason. Club: Birmingham Country. Home: 50 Fairway Dr Birmingham AL

GREENE, ROBERT THOMAS, clergyman, writer; b. Vance County, N.C., Aug. 28, 1919; s. Edward Jones and Iola (Gooch) G.; B.A., Wake Forest Coll., 1944; B.D., So. Baptist Theol. Sem., Louisville, 1948; spl. grad. studies Syracuse U., summer 1963; m. Grace Carolyn Bailey, Dec. 24, 1939; children—Ruth Adams, Robert Thomas. Ordained to ministry Bapt. Ch., 1942; pastor Bapt. Center Bapt. Ch., Clayton, N.C., 1942-44, Olive Branch Bapt. Ch., Dillsboro, Ind., 1945-48, Beech Grove Bapt. Ch., Owenton, Ky., 1948-49, Riverside Bapt. Ch., Merry Hill, N.C., 1949-52; missionary for West Chowan Bapt. Assn., Ahoskie, N.C., 1952-53, Cabarrus Bapt. Assn., Concord, N.C., 1953-60; dir. retirement Bapt. State Conv. N.C., 1960-61, sec. dept., stewardship devel., 1963-70, dir. coop program promotion, 1971—; sec. Christian Education Advance, 1962-63. Pub. relations dir. for denominational work in Bapt. assns. in N.C., 1957-58; writer Bible. column for newspapers called Biblical Series, 1952-57; regular writer for Bibl. Recorder, other Bapt. mags. Active in A.R.C. Recipient citation from Editorial Conf. of N.C., 1953. Democrat. Co-author: How To Write and Use a Few Words for an Effective Harvest, 1967. Contrbr. over 1000 articles to Bapt. publs., over 300 to jours. and newspapers. Home: 2700 St Marys St Raleigh NC 27609 Office: PO Box 26508 Raleigh NC 27611

GREENE, WILDA WITT (MRS. WALLACE S. GREENE, JR.), author; b. Falkville, Ala.; d. Frank Thomas and Ida Dixie (Lovelady) Witt; student pub. schs.; m. Wallace S. Greene, Jr., Mar 2, 1936; 1 dau., Donna (Mrs. William T. Miller). Author: Visitation Evangelism, 1955; The Disturbing Christ: A Devotional Study of Hebrews, 1968; numerous articles in field for religious publs. Mem. Nat. League of Am. Pen Women, Authors Guild, Internat. Platform Assn. Clubs: Tenn. Woman's Press and Authors; Nashville Womans' Press and Authors'. Address: 5020 Dovecote Dr Nashville TN 37220

GREENFIELD, CHARLES THOMAS, mfg. co. exec.; b. Toronto, Ont., Can., Jan. 9, 1920; s. Albert Edgar and Emily (Smith) G.; came to U.S., 1920, naturalized, 1946; student U. Cin., 1951-52; m. Martha Jeannetta Connor, June 29, 1941; children—Janet Kay (Mrs. Ronald Hanock), Richard Duane, Susan Carol (Mrs. Michael Julius), Judith Ann (Mrs. Thomas Ward). Tool maker Union Carbide & Carbon Co., 1941-48, Fostoria Machine & Tool Co., 1948-51; tooling supr. Gen. Tire & Rubber Co., 1951-52; chief tool engr. Aerojet-Gen. Corp., Cin., 1952-54; gen. foreman Ex-Cell-O Corp., Lima, O., 1954-57, plant supt., New Breman, O., 1957-60, asst. plant mgr., Elwood, Ind., 1960-63, div. project mgr., Lima, 1963-64, gen. mgr., Black Mountain, N.C., 1964-66; dir. mfg. Duff-Norton Co., Charlotte, N.C., 1966-70; plant mgr. Kay Mfg. Corp., High Point, N.C., 1970—. Served with USAAF, 1942-45. Decorated Air medal. Mem. Am. Ordnance Assn., Am. Rocket Soc., Am. Soc. Tool Engrs., Am. Inst. Aeros. and Astronautics. Republican. Address: 1422 Grantham Dr High Point NC 27260

GREENFIELD, LEO, lawyer; b. Middletown, N.Y., Dec. 25, 1923; s. Alex and Helen (Klein) G.; B.B.A., U. Miami, 1950, J.D., 1948; m. Barbara Merritt, May 2, 1959; children—Jacqueline Beth, Helen Heidi. Admitted to Fla. bar, 1948; partner firm Street & Greenfield, North Miami, Fla., 1948—; pres. Comutrix Corp., Miami, Fla., 1968-70; instr. law U. Miami, 1952-54; dir. Capital Nat. Bank of Miami, Mercantile Nat. Bank; gen. counsel Am. Agronomics Corp. Served with USAAF, 1943-45. Decorated Purple Heart medal, Air medal with four oak leaf clusters, Fourragere (Belgium). Mason (32 degree, Shriner). Club: U. Miami Century. Home: 2040 NE 194th Dr North Miami Beach FL 33161 Office: 12700 Biscayne Blvd North Miami FL 33161

GREENFIELD, MEG, journalist; b. Seattle, Dec. 27, 1930; d. Lewis James and Lorraine (Nathan) Greenfield; B.A. summa cum laude, Smith Coll., 1952; postgrad. (Fulbright scholar) Newnham Coll., Cambridge (Eng.) U., 1952-53. With Reporter mag., 1957-68, Washington editor, 1965-68; editorial writer Washington Post, 1968-70, dep. editor editorial page, 1970—. Mem. Phi Beta Kappa. Home: 1324 35th St NW Washington DC 20007 Office: 1515 L St NW Washington DC 20005

GREENGLASS, BERT, indsl. engr.; b. N.Y.C., Mar. 16, 1932; s. Morris and Hannah (Stark) G.; B.Indsl Engring., N.Y.U., 1955; m. Anne Goldstein, Jan. 30, 1955; children—Gwen Esther, Felice Joy, Leslie Beth. Time and motion study analyst for various cos., N.Y.C., 1950-55; valuation engr. Pub. Service Commn. N.Y. State, 1955-56; prodn. engr. Ideal Toy Corp., N.Y.C., 1956; indsl. engr., program coordinator Army Ballistic Missile Agy., Huntsville, Ala., 1957-60; chief resources office, launch operations center NASA, Cape Kennedy Fla., 1961-65; chief Apollo Program Control, Kennedy Space Center, Fla., 1965-68; dep. dir. mgmt. systems div. NASA, 1968-69; dir. mgmt. information and program control systems Office Research and Tech., Dept. Housing and Urban Devel., Washington, 1969-71, dir. Office of Adminstrn., 1972—. Cons. resource control techniques; v.p. for operations Am. Med. Bldg. Guild, Madison, Wis., 1971-72. Served with AUS, 1956-57. Registered profl. engr., Ala. Mem. Nat., Ala. socs. profl. engrs., Am. Inst. Indsl. Engrs. (local chpt. pres.; past dir. North Ala. chpt.). Home: 2517 Farrier Lane Reston VA 22070 Office: Dept Housing and Urban Devel 451 7th St SW Washington DC 20410

GREENHAW, HAROLD WAYNE, journalist; b. Sheffield, Ala., Feb. 17, 1940; s. Harold Reed and Myrtle (Able) G.; student Instituto Allende (San Miguel de Allende, Mexico), 1959-60; B.S. in English, U. Ala., 1966. Tech. writer, tchr. fed. edn. project Draper Correctional Center, Elmore, Ala., 1965; newspaper reporter, editor Ala. Jour., Montgomery, 1966-71; reporter-editor Ala. Jour.-Montgomery Advertiser, 1966—. Writer for Hidden Faces series NBC-TV, 1969. Recipient Reporting award A.P. Mng. Editors Assn., 1968. Nieman fellow Harvard, 1972-73. Mem. Sigma Delta Chi. Author: The Golfer, 1967; Hard Traveling, 1971; The Making of a Hero (biography Lt. William Calley), 1971; also several short stories. Contbr. profl. jours. Home: 424 Perry St Montgomery AL 36102 Office: Washington St Montgomery AL 36102

GREENHILL, JOE, state justice; b. Houston, July 14, 1914; s. Joe Robert Jr. and Violet (Stanuell) G.; B.A., U. Tex., 1936, B.B.A., 1936, LL.B., 1939; m. Martha Shuford, June 15, 1940; children—Joe Robert IV, William Duke. Admitted to Tex. bar, 1938; partner firm Bryan, Suhr, Bering and Bell, Houston, 1939-41, Graves, Dougherty & Greenhill, Austin, 1950-57; briefing atty. Supreme Ct. of Tex., Austin, 1941-42, 46, asso. justice, 1957—; asst. atty. gen. of Tex., 1947-48, 1st asst. gen. of Tex., 1948-50. Served from ensign to lt., USNR, 1942-46. Mem. Am. Bar Assn., State Bar Tex. (chmn. mineral sect. 1957-58, mem. coms. adminstrn. of justice, rules and statutes, water law, chmn. jud. sect. 1970-71), Am. Judicature Soc. (dir.), Philos. Soc. Texas, Order of Coif, Phi Beta Kappa, Phi Delta Theta. Episcopalian. Mason (33 deg.). Lion (past pres. Austin). Home: 3204 Bridge Path Austin TX 78703 Office: Supreme Court of Texas Austin TX 78711

GREENLEE, WILLIAM PURDY, educator; b. Charleston, W.Va., Sept. 19, 1928; s. William Clarkson and Alma (Purdy) G.; B.A., Vanderbilt U., 1949; M.A., Tex. Christian U., 1965; B.D., Southwestern Bapt. Theol. Sem., 1957, Th.D., 1960; m. Sarah Lynn Estes, July 9, 1955; children—Lisa Beth, Lori Brook, Leighton Brian. Teaching fellow Southwestern Bapt. Theol. Sem., Ft. Worth, 1957-59; reference research librarian, 1959-65, asst. prof. 1960-65; asst. prof. philosophy McNeese State U., Lake Charles, La., 1965-69, asso. prof., 1969—. Served to capt. USAF, 1950-54. Mem. A.A.A.S., Am. Acad. Religion, Alpha Chi Sigma. Democrat. Baptist. Club: Civitan. Author: How to Keep Current, 1962; The Christian Way, 1962, rev. edit., 1969. Home: 408 E Dolby St Lake Charles LA 70601

GREENMAN, JACK NORMAN, co. exec.; b. Kansas City, Mo., July 30, 1912; s. Jack Norman and Josephine (Hershfield) G.; grad. pub. schs.; m. Elise Schoenberg, Dec. 28, 1935; children—Jack Norman, Richard A., Robert L. Clk. Uhlmann Grain Co., Kansas City, Mo., 1929-35, mgr., Amarillo, Tex., 1935-37; pres. Uhlmann Elevators Co., Ft. Worth, 1937-65; pres. Richland Warehouse Co., Ft. Worth, 1954—, Flour Mills of Am., Inc., Ft. Worth, 1965—; pres. dir. Chickasha Cotton Oil Co., Ft. Worth, 1970—; dir. Bank of Commerce, Ft. Worth & Denver Ry. mem. Chgo. Bd. Trade. Pres., Ft. Worth Jr. Achievement, 1959-61. Bd. dirs. Trinity Improvement Assn., 1959, A.R.C., 1960—. Crippled Children's Soc., 1959—; trustee Mt. Olivet Cemetery Assn., Ft. Worth Children's Hosp. Mem. Nat. Grain Dealers Assn. (dir.), Newcomen Soc. N.Am., Nat. Grain Trade Council (dir.). Home: 3905 Monticello Dr Fort Worth TX 76107 Office: 2109 S Main St Fort Worth TX 76101

GREENSPON, HERBERT MITCHELL, cons. investments; b. Bridgeport, Conn., June 26, 1917; s. Abraham and Rebecca (Rivets) G.; student Yale, 1939-43; m. Bernice Taylor, June 28, 1965; children—John Laurence, Arthur Robert, Jeffrey Thomas. Exec. v.p. Columbia Records div. CBS, Inc., N.Y.C., 1935-60; v.p. operations Revlon, Inc., N.Y.C., 1960-62; pres. Nautec Corp., N.Y.C., 1962-64; exec. v.p. Telex Corp., Chgo., 1964-70; pres. Waters Conley Co., Inc., Chgo., 1965-70, Elco Electronics, Inc., Michigan City, Ind., 1966-70; cons. investments, Sarasota, Fla., 1970—. Mem. Bd. Finance, Trumbull, Conn., 1956. Served with USNR, 1945-46. Mem. Electronic Industry Assn. (exec. com. 1957-70). Office: 2295 Gulf of Mexico Dr Sarasota FL 33577

GREENWAY, ZELMAR CARVEY, fire chief; b. Swainsboro, Ga., Nov. 16, 1919; s. Arlie Thomas and Mattie (Davis) G.; student Tampa Bus. Coll., 1938, St. Petersburg Jr. Coll., 1961, 68-69; m. Donnie Mae Thomas, Mar. 12, 1943; 1 dau., Donnie Jean (Mrs. Alan C. Brown). With St. Petersburg (Fla.) Fire Dept., 1946—, fire capt., 1957, tng. officer, 1958-61, fire chief, 1962—. Dir. rescue Pinellas County, 1961; exec. dir. St. Petersburg Civil Def., 1969. Pres. Greater Sun Coast chpt. Muscular Dystrophy Assn. Am.; mem. adv. council Medic Alert. Served with USNR, 1942-45. Recipient Pub. Service citation of merit Muscular Dystrophy Assn., 1963-68; Service Appreciation award A.R.C., 1961. Mem. Internat., Southeastern, Fla. assns. fire chiefs. Democrat. Methodist. Rotarian. Home: 4574 8th Av N St Petersburg FL 33713 Office: 150 14th St N St Petersburg FL 33705

GREENWOOD, EL CAROL VOIGHTMAN, lawyer; b. Seward, Neb., Oct. 2, 1920; s. James Charles and Ella (Voightman) G.; A.B., Hastings Coll., 1941; postgrad. in econs. U. Neb. 1941-42; J.D., U. Mich., 1949; m. Wilma Ernestine Hopson, Nov. 19, 1945; 1 son, Richard Hopson. Admitted to Tex. bar, 1950, since practiced in Houston; mem. firm Fulbright, Crooker & Jaworski, 1949-63, partner, 1963—. Served with USNR, 1942-46. Mem. Maritime Law Assn. (exec. com. 1970—), Am. Judicature Soc., Am., Houston bar assns., State Bar Tex., Propeller Club U.S., Phi Delta Theta. Methodist (steward, trustee). Clubs: Champions Golf, Plaza (Houston). Home: 6223 Rolling Water Dr Houston TX 77069 Office: Bank of Southwest Bldg Houston TX 77002

GREENWOOD, K.R., broadcasting exec.; grad. U. Neb. Pres., Swanco Broadcasting, Inc., Tulsa, 1965—. Past chmn. Gov.'s Adv. Com. Tourism. Office: 1502 S Boulder Av Tulsa OK 74119

GREENWOOD, SAMUEL ROSS, banker; b. Speegleville, Tex., Sept. 1, 1921; s. Samuel Tillian and Rosa (Oliver) G.; student Okla. A. and M. U., Stillwater, City Coll., Los Angeles; postgrad. So. Meth. U.; m. Clara Hejl, Feb. 6, 1943; children—Gayle (Mrs. Richard Edwin Pitts), Samuel T., Fletcher Hejl. Pres., dir. Temple Nat. Bank (Tex.), 1967—, also dir.; dir. Am. Income Life Ins. Co.; pres. Investors Diversified Devel. Corp., Inc., 1965—. Mem. Nat. Mortgage Sch. Faculty, Ohio State U., 1961-69; Mem. exec. com., chmn. finance com. Wesleyan Homes, Inc., 1959—; chmn. Gov.'s State Com. on Aging, 1965—; mem. nat. adv. com. White House Conf. on Aging, 1971; pres. Temple Lions Crippled Children's Found., 1962; mem. Temple Law Enforcement Commn., 1970—; mem. regional adv. group, exec. com., task force allied health sci. Regional Med. Program Tex., 1969—; mem. Tex. United Community Services, 1970-72. Bd. dirs. Tex. Soc. on Aging; bd. dirs., treas. Bell County Mental Health and Mental Retardation Center; trustee, pres. bd. Central Tex. Regional Med. Edn. Found.; mem. lay adv. council So. Meth. U., 1972. Recipient Outstanding Citizen award Temple Jr. C. of C., 1969, Distinguished Service award Tex. Soc. Aging, 1969. Mem. V.F.W., Am. Legion, D.P.T. & D. Hunting Soc., Am. (panel moderator, seminar leader mortgage finance com. 1959-68, mem. nat. mortgage finance com. 1961-66, chmn. com. on housing and urban devel. 1965-66), Tex. (chmn. mortgage finance com. 1968-70) bankers assns., Temple C. of C. (pres. 1966, chmn. transp. and hwy. div. 1971-72). Methodist (chmn. bd. stewards 1957-58). Mason (Shriner), Elk, Lion (pres. Temple 1961). Clubs: Country (Temple); Stagecoach Country (Salado, Tex.); City (Waco, Tex.); Admirals, Lancers (Dallas). Home: 3005 Las Cruces St Temple TX 76501 Office: PO Box 809 Temple TX 76501

GREENWOOD, WILLIAM FRANK, banker; b. Nashville, Aug. 9, 1924; s. Vayne K. and Eleanor (Steele) G.; grad. Rutgers U. Grad. Sch. Banking, 1961; m. Reba Capps, June 14, 1946; children—William Frank, Lisa Claire. Asst. prodn. mgr. Baird Ward Printing Co., Nashville, 1946-47; prodn. supr. Genesco, Inc., 1947-49; account exec. Gen. Outdoor Advt. Co., 1949-51; with First Am. Nat. Bank, Nashville, 1951—, exec. v.p., 1965-69, vice chmn. bd., 1969—, also dir. Pres. Nashville Mental Health Assn., 1966-69, Vis. Nurse Service Nashville, 1962-64; vice chmn. bd. United Givers Fund Nashville, 1960-61; mem. bus. adv. bd. Middle Tenn. State U.; chmn. pres.'s adv. bd. Trevecca Coll. Bd. dirs. Council of Community Services; bd. dirs. Tenn. Mental Health Assn., 1967—, local council Boy Scouts Am., 1964-67, Nashville Salvation Army, 1967—; trustee, treas. Disciples of Christ Hist. Soc., 1961—, Disciples of Christ. Hist. Found., Nashville, 1961—. Served with USNR, 1943-46. Mem. Nashville C. of C., Am. Inst. Banking, Assn. Res. City Bankers. Mason. Club: Belle Meade Country (Nashville). Home: 2318 Woodmont Blvd Nashville TN 37215 Office: 326 Union St Nashville TN 37202

GREEP, HARRY PETERSON, savs. and loan assn. exec.; b. Chgo., Mar. 7, 1914; s. Carl F. and Hulda (Peterson) G.; student U. Ill. at Urbana, 1932, Northwestern U., 1934; grad. Am. Savs. & Loan Inst., Chgo., 1936; m. Catherine E. Portscheller, Apr. 23, 1939; children—Patrice Lea, Stephen Michael, Shari-Lea. Credit man Bell Savs. &

Loan Assn., Chgo., 1935-37; teller, credit man First Fed. Savs. & Loan Assn., Miami, Fla., 1938-44, mortgage officer, 1946; organizer, pres. Greep & Merrill, Inc., Ft. Lauderdale, Fla., 1946-52; founder, 1952, since pres., dir. Atlantic Fed. Savs. & Loan Assn.; organizer Investment Corp. Fla., 1955, chmn. bd., 1955-62, cons., 1963-66; organizer, dir. Home Owners Life Ins. Co., 1960. Cons. AID, 1961—; mem. board adjustment, Ft. Lauderdale, 1953-66; mem. adv. com. naval affairs 6th Naval Dist., 1958—. Nat. asso. Boys Clubs Am., 1961-67; pres. Broward County club, 1966-69, founding dir., 1965; pres. Broward County chpt. Am. Cancer Soc., 1957-60, bd. dirs., 1955—, Fla. Crusade chmn., 1964; v.p., dir. Opera Guild Ft. Lauderdale, 1953—; mem. seminar and inst. adv. com. Nova U. Advanced Tech., Ft. Lauderdale, 1964—; mem. bd. S. Fla. Edn. Center, Ft. Lauderdale, 1964—; hon. dir. Ft. Lauderdale Symphony Soc., 1960—; hon. trustee Pine Crest Sch., Ft. Lauderdale, 1966-68; mem. adv. board Holy Cross Hosp., 1968—. Served with USNR, 1944-46. Recipient Francisco de Miranda Decoration (Venezuela). Mem. Ft. Lauderdale C. of C. (dir. 1964-68), Navy League (founder 1958, past pres. Ft. Lauderdale council), Nat. League Insured Savs. Assns. (pres. 1965-66), Econ. Soc. South Fla. Elk. Clubs: Le Club International (Ft. Lauderdale), Lauderdale Yacht (Fort Lauderdale); Hundred (Broward County). Home: 2222 N Atlantic Blvd Fort Lauderdale FL 33305 Office: 1750 E Sunrise Blvd Fort Lauderdale FL 33304

GREER, ALFRED EDGAR, supt. schs.; b. Snyder, Tex., June 3, 1929; s. Fred T. and Mable (Houston) G.; A.A., Decatur Bapt. Coll., 1949; B.S., N. Tex. State U., 1951; M.S., 1954; postgrad. Tex. Tech. U., 1962-66; m. Jessie Elaine Calloway, Dec. 20, 1952; children—Gerry D., Cheryl L. Elementary prin. pub. schs., Era, Tex., 1951-53, high sch. prin., 1953-54; prin. high sch. Rockwall (Tex.) Ind. Sch. Dist., 1954-55; prin. sch., Ponder, 1955-58, Memphis, Tex., 1966-67; supt. schs. Bridgeport (Tex.) Ind. Sch. Dist., 1967—. Mem. Bridgeport Park Bd., 1967-71. Mem. Tex. Tchrs. Assn., N.E.A., Tex. Assn. Sch. Adminstrs., Hockley County Tchrs. Assn. (v.p. 1966), Bridgeport C. of C. (dir. 1968-71, 3d v.p. 1969-70), Phi Delta Kappa. Mason (Shriner), Lion (dir. 1971). Home: 123 Nottingham Circle Bridgeport TX 76026 Office: 1407 Carpenter St Bridgeport TX 76026

GREER, ELDON GERALD, JR., county extension dir.; b. Enid, Okla., May 10, 1937; s. Eldon Gerald and Matilda Evangeline (Taborsky) G.; Asso. Sci., Connor's Jr. Coll., 1957; B.S., Okla. State U., 1960, M.S., 1971; m. Judith Sue White, Apr. 3, 1965; children—Diana Sue, Brenda Dawn, Marek Tavis. Farmer, Enid, Okla., 1955-61; wage employee Soil Conservation Service, 1961-62; supt. Agr. Research Agronomy Sta., Okla. State U., Cherokee, 1962-69; extension agt. Coop. Extension Service, Watonga, 1969-72, county extension dir., Hollis, 1972—. Neighborhood chmn. Salt Plains council Boy Scouts Am., 1964-66; chmn. Sight Conservation, 1970-72. Served with AUS, 1961. Mem. Am. Soc. Agronomy, Am. Soc. Crop Sci., Am. Soc. Soil Sci., Reserve Officers Assn., Okla. County Extension Agts. Assn. (mem. 4-H and youth com. 1962—), Defense Supply Assn., Okla. Farm Bur., Higher Edn. Alumni Assn. Okla., Okla. State U. Alumni. Methodist. Lion. Home: Agriculture Bldg Hollis OK 73550

GREER, JOHN ONLY, univ. adminstr.; b. Henderson, Tex., Oct. 21, 1933; s. Dolphus Only and Sarah Flonelle (Brison) G.; B.Arch., A. and M. Coll. Tex., 1957; M.Arch., Tex. A. and M. U., 1964; m. Wanda Faye Knight, June 5, 1954; children—Gregg Only, Valorie Ann. Project architect Matthews & Assos., architects and engrs., Bryan, Tex., 1964-66; partner Maynard & Greer, architects, Nacogdoches, Tex., 1966-71; mgmt. services dir. Archtl. Research Center, Tex. A. and M. U., College Station, 1971—, archtl. graphics instr., 1963-65. Pres. Nacogdoches County United Fund, 1969-70. Served to 1st lt. AUS, 1957-59, 61-62. Recipient 2d prize Tex. Soc. Architects, 1956. Mem. A.I.A. (sec. Brazos chpt. 1971), Nacogdoches Jr. C. of C. (pres. 1968-69). Prin. archtl. works include Commercial Nat. Bank, Drive-In Facility, Christ Episcopal Ch. Daysch. Bldg., First Methodist Ch., Sanctuary, Nettie Marshall Elementary Sch. Addition (all Nacogdoches). Home: 506 Brookside St Bryan TX 77801 Office: Archtl Research Center Coll Arch and Environmental Design Tex A and M U College Station TX 77843

GREER, MACK VARNEDOE, physician; b. Valdosta, Ga., July 29, 1927; s. Lloyd Barton and Julie Winn (Varnedoe) G.; A.B., Emory U., 1951; postgrad. Valdosta State Coll., 1955-56; M.D., Med. Coll. Ga., 1960; m. Betty Dame English, Dec. 27, 1951; children—Betty June, Mack Varnedoe. Adjuster, Crawford & Co., ins. adjusters, Atlanta, 1951-52; high sch. math. and sci. tchr., football coach Clinch County (Ga.) and Waycross (Ga.) High Sch., 1952-55; rotating intern Bapt. Meml. Hosp., Jacksonville, Fla., 1960-61; gen. practice medicine and surgery, Homerville, Ga., 1961—; mem. staff Clinch Meml. Hosp.; high sch. athletic physician; coll. physician, also asso. prof. biology Valdosta State Coll., 1972—. Served with USMCR, World War II, Korean Conflict. Mem. A.M.A., So., Ga. med. assns., S.Ga. Med. Soc., Clinch County Bd. Health, Clinch County Athletic Assn., Pi Kappa Alpha, Alpha Kappa Kappa. Methodist. Club: Valdosta (Ga.) Touchdown, Exchange. Home: 213 W Dame Av Homerville GA 31634 Office: 106 W Dame Av Homerville GA 31634

GREER, S. MARCUS, bus. exec.; b. Pittsburgh, Tex., 1899; grad. U. Tex., 1921; m. Margaret Griffith; children—John Marcus, Robert Griffith, Margaret McLean. Dir. Terrell (Tex.) State Bank, Jefferson Standard Life Ins. Co., Greensboro, N.C.; vice chmn. bd. First City Nat. Bank of Houston, pres., 1963-69, now dir.; dir. Moody Nat. Bank, Galveston, Tex., Am. Nat. Ins. Co., Galveston, Heights State Bank, Houston. Trustee Moody Found., Galveston, Baylor Sch. Medicine, Houston, Meth. Hosp., Houston, M.D. Anderson Hosp.; Houston. Home: 5607 Bordley Houston TX 77027 Office: First City National Bank Houston TX 77002

GREER, THOMAS KEISTER, lawyer, newspaper publisher; b. Premier, W.Va., Sept. 28, 1921; s. Moses Theodrick and Goldie (Shaw) G.; B.A. with honors, U. Va., 1947, B.Laws, 1948; m. Dorothy Lucille Leech, Jan. 9, 1943; children—Nancy Taliaferro (Mrs William N. Alexander), Giles Carter, Celeste Claiborne. Admitted to Va. bar, 1948; practiced in Rocky Mount, Va.; asst. U. S. atty. So. Dist. Cal., 1951-54; pub. Franklin County Times, Rocky Mount, 1968—; asst. judge, Franklin County, Va.; 1958—; gen. counsel Salyer Land Co., Corcoran, Cal., 1959—; dir. Peoples Nat. Bank of Rocky Mount. Served to capt. USMC, World War II. Mem. Va., Cal. bars, Va. Hist. Soc., Raven Soc., Order of Coif, Phi Delta Phi. Democrat. Christian Scientist. Clubs: Roanoke (Va.) Country; Willow Creek Country (Rocky Mount); San Diego Yacht. Home: The Grove Rocky Mount VA 24151 Office: 110 Maple St Rocky Mount VA 24151

GREER, VIRGINIA BRADFORD (MRS. JOHN GREER), writer; b. Atlanta, Mar. 30, 1919; d. John and Floy (Jarrett) Bradford; diploma corr. course in journalism Newspaper Inst. Am., 1952; m. John Greer, Dec. 23, 1936; children—Kitty, John, Lynn. Reporter, Mobile (Ala.) Press Register, 1955; free-lance writer, 1951—. Bd. dirs. Mobile Mental Health Center, A.R.C. Recipient nat. 1st pl. award for outstanding journalism in field home laundry, 1962, other service awards. Mem. Nat. League Am. Pen Women (v.p.). Baptist. Club: Octavia LeVert Toastmistress. Author: Give Them Their Dignity, 1968. Address: Route 5 Box 267TG Mobile AL 36608

GREESON, GEORGIANA WHITE, librarian; b. Capps, Ark., Mar. 26, 1921; d. James L. and Agnes (Calvert) White; student Hendrix Coll., 1939-40; B.A., Ark. State Tchrs. Coll., 1943; B.S. in L.S., La. State U., 1951; m. William H. Greeson, Jan. 16, 1946 (div. 1953); 1 dau., Patricia Evlin. Tchr., English jr. high sch., Harrison, Ark., 1943-44; library asst., librarian North Ark. Regional Library, Harrison, 1944-53; children's librarian Los Angeles Pub. Library, 1954; librarian Phillips County Library, Helena, Ark., 1955-57, St. Charles Parish Library, Hahnville, La., 1958—. Mem. Am., La. library assns. Home: Route 2 Box 34C Luling LA 70070 Office: St Charles Parish Library Hahnville LA 70057

GREFE, DONALD CEDERSTROM, air lines exec.; b. Des Moines, Dec. 26, 1912; s. Fred and Hilder Josephine (Cederstrom) G.; B.S., Ia. State U., 1936; m. Mary Elizabeth Balliet, July 6, 1959. Sub-accountant First Nat. Bank N.Y., Panama, 1936-41; sec.-treas. Panama Coca-Cola Bottling Co., Panama, 1945-48; mgr. for Argentina, Chile, Paraguay, Uruguay, Braniff Internat. Airways, Buenos Aires, Argentina, 1948-57; with Eastern Air Lines, Inc., Atlanta, 1957—, regional dir. pub. affairs, 1964—. Group chmn. family services United Appeal, 1967; 1st v.p. Met. Atlanta Traveler's Aid, 1969—, bd. dirs., 1965—; mem. exec. com. Nat. Found. March Dimes, 1970—. Bd. dirs. Ga. Safety Council, 1968—, Ga. Motor Club, 1967—, Am. Cancer Soc., 1965—. Served with USNR, 1941-45. Mem. Atlanta C. of C. (mem. com. 1964—), Pub. Relations Soc. Am., Phi Delta. Mason (Shriner). Clubs: Atlanta Press, Piedmont Driving, Capital City, Commerce (Atlanta). Home: 17 Glenald Way Atlanta GA 30327 Office: 1240 Life Georgia Tower 600 W Peachtree St NW Atlanta GA 30308

GREGG, CECIL MANREN, educator; b. Eustace, Tex., Jan. 20, 1908; s. Guy M. and Minnie (Graham) G.; B.S., Eastern Tex. State U., 1933; M.Ed., Tex. A. and M. U., 1944; Ph.D., Mich. State U., 1950; m. Louie Price, Dec. 22, 1932; children—Cecil Manran, Llelwyn Price. Tchr. pub. schs. Tex., 1930-32, 33-46; prof. agr. S.W. Tex. State Coll., San Marcos, 1946-48, 50-68, 70—; prof. plant sci., researcher Alemoya Coll. Agr., Haile Sellassie I Univ., 1968-70 (on leave); Participant NSF Underground Water Study, N.M. State U., Las Cruces, summer 1964; project leader Tex. Partners of Alliance with Peru, summer 1967, Pueblo Nuevo, Peru; research grantee for forage fertilizer study, 1971-72. Active United Fund. Mem. Tex. Tchrs. Assn., Tex. Assn. Coll. Tchrs., Am. Soc. Agronomy, Internat. Soil Soc., Am. Forestry Assn., Sigma Xi, Delta Tau Alpha (nat. treas. past). Baptist (deacon). Mason, Kiwanian. Home: Box 1126 San Marcos TX 78666

GREGG, FLORENCE CLARA, govt. ofcl.; b. Nevada, Mo.; d. Harry J. and Florence (Edmondson) Gregg; student S.W. State Coll., Springfield, Mo., 1930-32; B.S., Tex. Christian U., 1950. Adminstrn. clerical asst. TVA, Knoxville, Chattanooga, Tenn., 1935-44; adminstrv. asst. UNRRA, Washington, Rome, Italy, 1944-46; adminstrv. officer Chgo.-Cook County Health Survey, 1946; exec. asst. San Antonio Health Dept., 1946-47; sr. analyst, adminstrv. asst. Ft. Worth Health Dept., 1947—. Mem. Am., Tex. pub. health assns., Am. Acad. Health Adminstrs., Alpha Chi. Methodist. Home: 3916 W 4th St Fort Worth TX 76107 Office: 1800 University Dr Fort Worth TX 76107

GREGG, JACK RAYMOND, family planning exec.; b. Clarksdale, Miss., Aug. 4, 1936; s. James Frank and Hallie (Jenkins) G.; B.E.E., Vanderbilt U., 1959; postgrad. Ala. A. and M. U., 1970-71; m. Betty Marie Cobb, June 29, 1962; 1 child, Carrah Leigh. Project engr. NASA-Marshall Space Flight Center, Huntsville, Ala., 1959-65; chief engr. Saturn/Apollo program office N.Am. Rockwell Corp., Huntsville, 1965-71; dir. program planning, control family planning clinics Family Health, Inc., New Orleans, 1971—; sec., treas. Tech. Utilization Corp., Huntsville, 1970—; mem. faculty Tulane U. Sch. Pub. Health. Hon. col.-aide-de-camp governor's staff Gov. Albert Brewer, Ala., 1969-71. Registered profl. engr., Ala. Home: 6424 Worchester Dr New Orleans LA 70126 Office: Family Health Inc 120 S Derbigny St New Orleans LA 70131

GREGG, PERCIVAL PORCHER, civil engr.; b. Florence, S.C., Sept. 28, 1916; s. Percival Porcher and Constance (Ashby) G.; B.C.E. with honors, N.C. State U., 1940; m. Constance Ruth Weiser, Dec. 31, 1960; children—Janet Porcher, Percival Porcher III. Beginning engr. Pitts.-Des Moines Steel Co., 1941; design engr. Seaboard Airline R.R. Co., Norfolk, Va., 1946-51; constrn. positions, 1951-55; asso. John M. Baldwin & Assos., 1955-60; partner, Baldwin & Gregg, Norfolk, Va., 1960-69, pres., 1969—. Bd. dirs. Cape Henry Sch., Virginia Beach, Va. Served with AUS, 1941-46, now lt. col. Res. ret. Registered profl. engr., Va., D.C., N.C., S.C., Fla., La., Ohio. Fellow Am. Soc. C.E.; mem. Soc. Am. Mil. Engrs., Nat., Va. (chmn. profl. engrs. pvt. practice functional sect. 1965-67) socs. profl. engrs., Va. Assn. Surveyors (pres. 1965), Am. Legion. Episcopalian. Clubs: Virginia (dir. 1970—) (Norfolk). Harbor; Princess Anne Country (dir. 1967-70) (Virginia Beach, Va.). Home: 1421 N Bay Shore Dr Virginia Beach VA 23451 Office: PO Box 5783 Norfolk VA 23516

GREGORY, DARRELL WELDON, JR., physiologist; b. Baimbridge, Ga., Aug. 13, 1942; s. Darrell Weldon and Agnes Christene (Matthews) G.; student Emerson Inst., 1960-61; B.S., U. Ga., 1969, M.S., 1971; m. Mary Robette Jay, Aug. 28, 1966; 1 son, Darrell Weldon III. Foreman, Wright Contracting Co., Columbus, Ga., 1961-64; mgr. R.L. Jay Daries, Madison, Ga., 1964-66; research physiologist U.S. Dept. Agr., Agrl. Research Service, Russell Research Center, Athens, Ga., 1971—. Mem. Am. Soc. Animal Sci., Am. Dairy Sci. Assn., Poultry Sci. Assn., Ga. Poultry Fedn., Delta Tau Delta. Home: 135B Georgetown Dr Athens GA 30601 Office: Russell Research Center Coll Sta Rd Athens GA 30604

GREGORY, EDWARD MEEKS, clergyman; b. Richmond, Va., Sept. 30, 1922; s. George Craghead and Constance (Heath) G.; grad. St. Christopher's Sch., Richmond, 1941; A.B., U. Va., 1947, S.T.B., Episcopal Theol. Sch., Cambridge, Mass., 1954; postgrad. George Washington U., 1950. Ordained to ministry Episcopal Ch., 1954; instr. Staunton (Va.) Mil. Acad., 1947-48; master Episcopal High Sch., Alexandria, Va., 1948-51; curate St. Mark's Episcopal Ch., Richmond, Va., 1954-69; vicar St. Peter's Episcopal Ch., Richmond, 1969—; diocesan youth dir., 1956-60; diocesan del. Va. Council Chs., 1967—. Diocesan Dept. on Social Relations, 1970—; pres. Religious Edn. Council, Richmond, 1961-62, Richmond Episcopal Clericus, 1972-73. Bd. dirs. Vol. Service Bur., Richmond, 1960-63, Ednl. Therapy Center, 1964—, Multiple Sclerosis, 1961-66, Va. Am. Civil Liberties Union, 1970-71, Internat. Council, Va. Council on Human Relations, 1965-70, Planned Parenthood, 1969—; pres. Richmond Council Human Relations, 1960-62; pres. Friends' Assn. for Children, 1967-70; mem. Richmond Area Community Council; mem. adv. bd. Richmond Model Neighborhood, 1971—. Served with M.C., AUS, 1942-46. Mem. Richmond Clergy Assn., Jamestown Soc. (gov. 1951-54), Mayflower Soc. (elder Va. co. 1963—), Va. Hist. Soc., Episcopal Soc. Cultural and Racial Unity (chmn. Richmond 1964-66), Assn. for Preservation Va. Antiquities, Va. Mus. Fine Arts, Chi Phi. Clubs: Torch Internat. Home: St Peter's Vicarage 1907 N 23d St Richmond VA 23223 Office: St Peter's Episcopal Ch 1719 N 22d St Richmond VA 23223

GREGORY, EDWARD WADSWORTH, JR., educator; b. Chase City, Va., Sept. 29, 1903; s. Edward Wadsworth and Kate Winn (Cleveland) G.; A.B., U. Va., 1925, M.A., 1926, Ph.D., 1931; m. Margaret Louise Jeffreys, August 28, 1934; 1 son, Allen Wadsworth. Instr. sociology U. Va., 1925-28; asst. prof. sociology U. Ala., 1928-29, asso. prof., 1929-35, prof., 1935-45; prof. sociology U. Md., 1946; prof. sociology U. Richmond (Va.), 1946—. Chmn. Tuscaloosa Co. (Ala.) Bd. Pub. Welfare, 1940-43; pres. Ala. Conf. Social Work, 1941-42; pres. Va. Council Social Welfare, 1950-51; mem. Va. Commn. on Aging, 1962-68, Bd. Welfare and Instns. Va., 1963—. Chmn. adv. bd. Pub. Welfare, Richmond, 1953-55; pres. Richmond Area Community Council, 1951-53. Mem. War Price and Rationing Bd. of Tuscaloosa County, 1942-43; mem. commn. on Reorgn. State Govt., Va., 1947. Commd. lt. USNR, Jan. 1943, lt. comdr., Oct. 1945 (on active duty, Feb. 1943-Jan 1946). Mem. Am. Sociol. Soc., So. Sociol. Soc. (pres. 1939), Nat. Council Family Relations (nat. adv. council 1939-42). Am. Assn. U. Profs., Va. Social Science Assn. (pres. 1951-52), Family and Children's Service Richmond (bd. dirs.), Delta Sigma Phi, Delta Sigma Rho, Phi Beta Kappa, Phi Delta Kappa, Alpha Kappa Delta. Raven. Methodist. Club: Country of Va.; Torch. Author: Introductory Sociology (with Lee Bidgood), 1939. Co-author: Social Control, 1947, rev. ed., 1956. Contbr. articles to jours. Address: University of Richmond Richmond VA

GREGORY, FERDINAND ROCHET, govt. ofcl.; b. Las Marias, P.R., Dec. 20, 1915; s. Candelario Rochet and Emelina (Gregory) Lacourt; B.S., Coll. Agr. and Mech. Arts, 1938; m. Teofila Rodriguez, Apr. 24, 1941; children—Ana Emelina Rochet, Fernando Rochet, Carlos Enrique Rochet. Tchr. vocational agr., Cidra, P.R., 1938-45; reserach agronomist Agrl. Expt. Sta., Rio Piedras, P.R., 1945-47; county agt., Cidra, 1947-60; agrl. extension supr., Caguas, P.R., 1960—. Organizer consumers, farmers and credit coops., Cidra, 1950-55, Farmers Assn. in Swine Prodn. in Caguas, 1968, Community Assn. in Caguas, 1968, House Project for Sr. Citizens. Pres. bd. dirs. CREA House, Caguas. Named Agronomist of Year in P.R., 1969. Mem. Sociedad Agricola de Agronomos (pres.), Coll. of Agronomists (dir. 1967-68, pres. Caguas chpt. 1968-69), Farmers Coop. Cidra (pres. 1963-65). Mason, Lion. Home: 13 Amatista Caguas PR 00625 Office: Gautier Benitez Esq Georgetti St Caguas PR 00625

GREGORY, G. WARREN, indsl. co. exec.; b. Nashville, Aug. 14, 1920; s. Graham O. and Iola (Mackey) G.; student Vanderbilt U., 1937-38, Hampden-Sydney Coll., 1943; B.S. in Engring., Ga. Inst. Tech., 1945; m. Christian May Nevitt, Nov. 19, 1945; children—Catherine, Glenn, George. Inventory control Genesco Inc., Nashville, 1939-42, inventory co-ordinator 1946-47, adminstrv. asst. to dir. purchasing, 1948, purchasing agt., 1948-60, pres. Chem. Div., 1960-68, pres. Mansco div., 1965-68, pres. Mantex div., 1968-71, gov., 1968—, pres. Tower div., 1971—. Served with USNR, 1942-46. Mem. Eta Kappa Nu, Tau Alpha Tau. Baptist. Club: Bluegrass Country. Home: 307 Harbor Island Old Hickory TN 37138 Office: Genesco Inc Tower Div Genesco Park Nashville TN 37202

GREGORY, HERBERT WAYNE, ednl. adminstr.; b. Pittsboro, Miss., Apr. 18, 1921; s. Leonard C. and Leona (Wagner) G.; B.A.E., U. Miss., 1942, M.Ed., 1952, Ed.D., 1954; m. Jeannette Spainhour, June 11, 1955; children—Wayne Porter, Anne Hazel. Tchr., Miss. Pubs. Schs., 1947-50; faculty, chmn. dept. edn. Tift Coll., Forsyth, Ga., 1954-57; faculty, head dept. edn. La. Coll., Pineville, 1957-60; dir. tchr. edn. Southeastern La. Coll., Hammond, 1960-67, asst. to pres. Office of Dean, 1967-68, head dept. student teaching, 1968—. Mem. La. Adv. Com. Tchr. Edn. and Certification, 1958-64. Mem. So. Council Tchrs. Edn., La. Tchrs. Assn. (nat. commn. internships in teaching 1964—), Assn. Student Teaching, La. Assn. Student Teaching (pres. 1964-65), N.E.A., Am. Assn. U. Profs., Kappa Delta Pi, Kappa Phi Kappa, Phi Delta Kappa (La. coordinator 1961—). Rotarian. Home: 126 College Dr Hammond LA 70401

GREGORY, JOHN MASON MOODY, JR., tobacco co. exec.; b. Durham, N.C., Feb. 5, 1907; s. John Mason Moody and Mary (Barksdale) G.; A.B., Duke, 1929; m. Katherine Jamieson, Apr. 18, 1936; children—John Mason Moody III, Andrew Jamieson. With Am. Leaf Orgn., Imperial Tobacco Co. Great Britain and Ireland, Ltd., and predecessor, 1929—, pres., 1963—; pres. British Leaf Tobacco Co. Can., Ltd., 1964—. Mem. Durham City Council, 1945-57. Served with USNR, World War II. Mem. Alpha Tau Omega. Democrat. Episcopalian. Clubs: Hope Valley Country, TOBAC (Durham); Country N.C. (Pinehurst); Dunes Golf and Beach (Myrtle Beach, S.C.); Commonwealth (Richmond, Va.); Wilson Country. Home: 400 Wilshire Circle Wilson NC 27893 Office: PO Box 1848 Wilson NC 27893

GREGORY, LOWELL DEAN, aerospace co. exec.; b. Chickasha, Okla., Feb. 19, 1918; s. Simeon Roscoe and Pearl (Robinson) G.; B.A. in English, U. Okla., 1940, M.A. in Math., 1950; Ph.D. in Math. Statistics (Ling-Temco-Vought fellow), So. Meth. U., 1968; m. Marian Gavin, May 27, 1939; children—Gavin George, Lynn. Instr. math. U. Okla., Norman, 1947-51; sr. analyst Chance Vought Aircraft, Dallas, 1951-55, devel. project engr., 1955-57, supr. advanced weapon systems analysis, 1957-59, chief reliability astro. div., 1959-62; mgr. reliability engring. astro. div. Ling-Temco-Vought Dallas, 1962-64, supr. operations analysis, 1964—. Served to 1st lt. F.A., AUS, 1940-42, to capt. USAAF, 1942-45. Mem. Aerospace industries Assn. (mem. reliability com. 1964—), Am. Astronautical Soc. Assn. (reliability com. 1964—), Am. Astronaut. Soc. North Tex. Operations Research Soc. (dir.), Sigma Xi, Phi Mu Epsilon. Home: 1300 W 2d St Arlington TX 76013 Office: PO Box 6267 Dallas TX 75222

GREGORY, THORNE, banker, state legislator; b. Halifax, N.C., Dec. 25, 1928; s. Fletcher Harrison and Boyd (Thorne) G.; grad. Fisburne Mil. Sch., 1946; A.B. in History, U. N.C., 1952; grad. U. N.C. Sch. Banking, 1960; m. Hester Lockett, Feb. 23, 1957; children— Hester Elizabeth, Boyd Wynn, Ann Harrison, Thorne Gregory. Vice pres., dir. Bank of Halifax (N.C.), 1960-68; sr. v.p., dir. Branch Banking & Trust Co., 1968-73, pres., 1973—; mem. N.C. Ho. of Reps., 1959—, chmn. com. on fed. and interstate cooperation, 1961—, also chmn. com. banks and banking, chmn. com. on finance. Mem. Nat. Hwy. Policy, N.C. Com. on Aviation, N.C. Adv. Budget Com., N.C. Bd. Higher Edn., Rex Hosp. Found. Bd. dirs. Roanoke River Valley Basin Assn.; mem. Atlantic States Marine Fisheries Commn., Nat. Highway Policy Com. Served as 1st lt. USAF, 1952-56. Mem. N.C. Bankers Assn. (mem. adv. bd. Group II), Raleigh C. of C. (dir.), Order of Gimghoul, Zeta Psi. Democrat. Episcopalian. Clubs: Benvenue (Rocky Mt., N.C.); Carolina Country (Raleigh); Kiwanis. Home: 1200 Brookside Dr Wilson NC 27893 Office: Branch Banking & Trust Co Wilson NC 27893

GREINER, PHYLLIS KEITH GOODWIN (MRS. KEITH G. GREINER), educator; b. nr. Eggleston, Va.; d. John Earl and Glenna (Williams) Goodwin; student Radford Coll., 1928-30, U. Va. Extension, 1935-45; B.S., Roanoke Coll., 1953; M.Ed., Va. Poly. Inst., 1959; m. Charles B. Greiner, Mar. 24, 1932 (dec. Jan. 1954); 1 dau., Carolyn Ruth. Tchr., Roanoke County Pub. Schs., Salem, Va., 1930-45, 50-53; tchr. kindergarten North Cross Pvt. Sch., Salem, 1945-50; tchr. Roanoke City Pub. Schs., 1953-61; prin. Wash. Heights and Westside Schs., Roanoke, 1961-64, Acad. State Sch., Salem,

1964-68, Burlington Sch., 1968—. Box office mgr. Roanoke Valley Drama Assn., Salem, summers 1957, 58; mem. edn. Govs. Commn. on Status of Women, 1965; mem. Citizens Com. on status of Women in Va. Mem. Am. Assn. U. Women, N.E.A., Va. State, Va. Dist., Roanoke County edn. assns., Nat. Va., Roanoke County prins. assns., Nat. (exec. bd. 1966-68), Va. (state pres. 1966-68), Roanoke Valley (pres. 1964-66) councils adminstrv. women in edn., UN Assn. of U.S.A., Centro Studi E Scambi Internazionali, Internat. Reading Assn., Internat. Platform Assn., Va. Mental Health Assn., Colonial Dames 17th Century, Alpha Delta Kappa. Methodist. Home: 124 Lewis Av Salem VA 24153 Office: 6533 Peters Creek Rd NW Roanoke VA 24019

GREMILLION, EFFIE GILLIS, clin. social worker; b. Excelsior, La., Nov. 9, 1906; d. Joseph Benjiman and Ada Helen (Phillips) Gillis; student La. Coll., 1949-50; B.A., Tex. U., 1950-53; M.S.W., Wordens Sch. Social Service, 1958; m. Wiley J. Gremillion, Feb. 4, 1928 (div. Mar. 1947); children—Barbara Margaret (Mrs. Linton Bowman, III), Dona Madrice (Mrs. William Weaver Harris), Effie Jeanne (Mrs. Michael Dennis O'Callaghan). Social worker Austin State Hosp., 1954-57; clin. social worker VA Hosp., Shreveport, La., 1958-65, mem. intensive psychiat. staff, 1965—, dir. psychodrama, 1968—. Treas., Austin-Travis County Assn. Mental Health, 1956-57. Bd. dirs. Cadd-Bossier chapt. La. Assn. Mental Health, 1958—. Mem. Nat. Assn. Social Workers, Acad. Certified Social Workers. Methodist. Home: 2829 Doles Pl Shreveport LA 71104 Office: VA Hosp 510 E Stoner St Shreveport LA 71101

GREMILLION, JACK PAUL FAUSTIN, atty. gen. La.; b. Donaldsonville, La., June 15, 1914; s. William Kossuth and Genoa (Henderson) G.; student La. State U., 1931-37; m. Doris McDonald, Jan. 12, 1942; children—Jack Paul Faustin, William McDonald, Wayne Francis, Doris H. Admitted to La. bar, also Fed. Cts., U.S. Supreme Ct., 1941; practice of law, 1937—; atty. Dept. Revenue, 1940-42; 2d asst. Dist. Atty. Parish of East Baton Rouge, 1952-53, 1st asst., 1953-56, atty. gen. State of La., 1956—. Served as 1st lt. 106th and 3d inf. divs., AUS, 1942-45. Mem. Am., La., East Baton Rouge bar assns., Nat. Assn. Attys. Gen., Am. Legion (past post pres.), Mil. Order World Wars, Baton Rouge C. of C., Nat. Assn. County and Pros. Attys. K.C., Elk. Clubs: Lions, Young Men's Business (pres. 1940) (Baton Rouge). Address: 5475 Capital Heights Av Baton Rouge LA

GREMILLION, (CURTIS) LIONEL, JR., hosp. adminstr.; b. Slaughter, La., Feb. 26, 1924; s. Curtis Lionel and Beatrice (Watson) G.; B.A. in Psychology and Music, U. Southwestern La., 1948; postgrad. psychology, La. State U., 1948-49, 53; m. Rosemary Duhon, Dec. 8, 1951; children—Suzanne Lynelle (Mrs. Walden), Curtis Lionel III, Monique Angele. Profl. musician, 1940-43, 46-51; psychologist, asst. dir. psychological and social services, staff E. La. State Hosp., Jackson, 1949-52, dir. psychology and social services depts., 1952-57, asst. supt., 1957-62, adminstr., 1961-64, acting supt., 1964-66, asso. adminstr., 1966—. Chmn. E. Feliciana Parish United Givers Fund, 1960; regional chmn. Am. Heart Assn., 1968—. Bd. dirs. United Givers E. La. State Hosp., 1957-62, A.R.C., 1954-55, Boy Scouts Am., 1964-69, Am. Heart Assn., 1963, Am. Cancer Soc., 1963-64; bd. mem. La. Credit Union Dept. Hosps., 1962-67; bd. dir. So. Behavorial Research Found., 1970—; dir. Regional Council on Alcoholism, 1972—. Served with USNR, 1943-46. Recipient Outstanding Leadership and Service award La. Dept. Hosps., 1966. Charter mem. La. Psychol. Assn.; mem. So. Sociol. Assn., La. Music Therapy Assn. (mem. bd. 1966—), Internat. Platform Assn., Am. Legion, Psi Chi, Sinfonia, Pi Gamma Mu, Kappa Delta Pi. Democrat. Baptist. Lion. Club: New Orleans Jazz. Address: Residence 121 East Louisiana State Hosp Jackson LA 70748

GRENIER, WILLIAM JOHN, educator; b. Havana, Cuba, July 25, 1920; s. Wifrid Alphonse and Concepcion (Cruz-Reyes) G.; B.A., U. Havana, 1943; Ph.D., U. Nacional, 1958; M.A., U. Ga., 1966; m. Nelida Mendez, Mar. 5, 1949; children—William Joseph, Jacqueline Marie. With Cuban Treas. Dept., 1943-46; instr. Spanish, U. Chattanooga, 1946-47; in charge tchrs. record, payroll Bd. Edn., Havana, 1947-59; adviser, supr. internat. procedures Aerolineas Nalair, Havana, 1949-60; prof. French and Spanish, Brenau Coll., Gainesville, Ga., 1961—. Roman Catholic. Home: 808 Perry St NE Gainesville GA 30501

GRENINGER, EDWIN THOMAS, educator; b. Montoursville, Pa., Apr. 12, 1918; s. Fred R. and Martha (Cutler) G.; student Susquehanna U., 1936-38; A.B., Gettysburg Coll., 1941; M.A., Temple U., 1947; Ph.D., U. Pa., 1958; m. Jane Torbert, June 26, 1948 (dec. Mar. 1963);; m. 2d, Gem Kate Taylor, Oct. 26, 1968. Instr. history Valparaiso U., 1948-49, Pa. State U., Ogontz, 1950, 52-53, Wilkes Coll., 1951-52; asst. prof. history E. Tenn. State U., Johnson City, 1958-61, asso. prof. 1961-64, prof. history, 1964—. Mem. com. on higher edn. Synod Va., United Luth. Ch. Am., 1959-63, Southeastern Synod, 1963—. Served with AUS, 1942-46. Mem. So. Hist. Assn. (European sect.), Lexington Group, Am. Assn. U. Profs. (chpt. v.p. 1969-70, pres. 1970-72), Pi Kappa Alpha, Pi Gamma Mu (treas. local chpt. 1961—). Author: Fifteen Days in Russia, 1966. Book rev. editor: Social Science, 1961-62. Home: 2210 Wyndale Rd Johnson City TN 37601

GRESE, EVERETT G., clergyman, supt. schs. supt. Mid-South Dist. Lutheran Schs., Tenn., Ark., Ky. Address: Suite 714 1131 Union Av Memphis TN 38104*

GRESHAM, BATEY MOORE, JR., architect; b. Lebanon, Tenn., Apr. 5, 1934; s. Batey Moore and Elisabeth (Doak) G.; B.Arch., Auburn U., 1957; m. Edna Ann Weaver, Nov. 6, 1957. With U.S. Army Corps Engrs., 1957-59, 61-62; designer, draftsman Clemmons & Gingles, Nashville, 1959-65, Sam H. McLean, architect, Nashville, 1965-66; partner McLean & Gresham, Nashville, 1966; self-employed as architect, Nashville, 1967; partner Gresham & Smith, Nashville, 1967—. Mem. A.I.A., Guild Religious Architecture, Am. Assn. Hosp. Planners, Constrn. Specificiations Inst. (pres. 1971-72), Blue Key, Scarab, Kappa Sigma. Home: 330 Lynwood Blvd Nashville TN 37205 Office: 2220 State St Nashville TN 37203

GRESHAM, CHARLES RUSSELL, educator; b. Erie, Ill., Mar. 20, 1928; s. Fred Earl and Sarah Jane (Duncan) G.; A.B., Manhattan Christian Coll., 1949; postgrad. Phillips U., 1949-50, Perkins Sch. Theology, 1953; M.R.E., Southwestern Theol. Sem., 1956, D.R.E., 1958, Ed.D., 1971; postgrad. Kan. State U., 1961-64, Central State Coll., 1957-58; m. Virginia Ruth Smith, Aug. 3, 1947; children—Michael Ross, Barbara (Mrs. Michael L. Bundy), Timothy Ward, Janelda Rae. Prof. N.T., Dallas Christian Coll., 1951-56; prof. theology and Christian edn. Midwest Christian Coll., 1951-56; prof. theology and Christian edn. Midwest Christian Coll., Oklahoma City, 1956-60; prof. Bible and Christian edn. Manhattan (Kan.) Christian Coll., 1960-66; prof. Christian edn. and pastoral care Emmanuel Sch. Religion, Milligan College, Tenn. Cons. Standard Pub. Co., Cin., 1966—; exec. sec., chaplaincy endorsement commn. Christian Chs. and Chs. of Christ, 1967—. Mem. Disciples of Christ Hist. Soc., Nat. Assn. Evangelicals (sec. chaplains commn. 1971—), Evang. Theol. Soc., Phi Alpha Theta, Sigma Delta Psi. Author: The Adult Department, 1964. Editor: Christian Quar., 1952-56. Christian Educators Jour., 1968—. Home: Route 8 Johnson City TN 37601 Office: Box R Milligan College TN 37682

GRESHAM, SPARKMAN BOOTHE, banker; b. Ashland, Miss., May 10, 1932; s. Marvin and Elizabeth (Johnson) G.; grad. Sch. Banking of South, La. State U., 1964; m. Frances McGill, May 11, 1954; children—Greg, Steve, Anita. With Bank of Holly Springs (Miss.), 1955—, cashier, 1964—, v.p., 1966—, also dir. Served with USAF, 1951-55. Recipient Marshall County Distinguished Service award, 1961. Mem. Holly Springs Jaycees. Baptist. Rotarian (pres. Holly Springs). Home: 710 College St Holly Springs MS 39635 Office: PO Box 250 Holly Springs MS 38635

GRESHAM, VERNON CLIFFE, educator; b. nr. Kirksey, Ky., Dec. 6, 1904; s. John Allen and Senora Essie (Waggoner) G.; B.S., Murray U., 1938; M.A., Peabody Coll., 1940; postgrad. George Washington U., 1947-48, Tex. A. and M. U., 1967; m. Mabel Mathis, Dec. 29, 1928; children—Norman, Neal. Tchr. pub. schs. Graves County, Ky., 1928-34; dir. vocational tng. State Sch., Nashville, 1940-41; supt. war prodn. tng., tchr. indsl. arts Tenn. Tech. U., Cookeville, 1941-43, tchr. indsl. arts, 1946-47, asso. prof. indsl. tech. dept., 1964—; tng. specialist U.S. Navy, 1947-54, Arabian-Am. Oil Co., 1954-59. Served to lt. comdr. with USNR, 1943-45. Recipient award for tng. film Venice Internat. Film Festival, 1953. Mem. N.E.A., Tenn. Edn. Assn., Am. Foundry Soc., Tenn. Acad. Sci., Am. Legion, V.F.W., Baptist. Woodman of World, Lion. Home: 301 Dry Valley Rd Algood TN 38501 Office: Box 148A Tenn Tech U Cookeville TN 38501

GRESSETTE, LAWRENCE MARION, lawyer, state senator; b. nr. St. Matthews, S.C., Feb. 11, 1902; s. J. T. and Rosa (Wannamaker) G.; J.D., U. S.C., 1924; m. Florence Howell, Aug. 18, 1927; 1 son, Lawrence Marion. Practiced in St. Mathews; partner firm Gressette & Gressette; mem. S.C. Senate, 1937—, chmn. jud. com., 1953—, chmn. rules com., 1959—. Chmn., S.C. Sch. Com., 1951-64. Mem. S.C. Democratic Exec. Com., 1948—, chmn., 1953-54; mem. S.C. Ho. of Reps., 1925-28, 31-32. Fellow Am. Coll. Trial Lawyers; mem. Blue Key, Phi Kappa Phi. Baptist. Mason. Home: PO Box 346 St Matthews SC 29135 Office: State House Columbia SC 29201

GRIBBIN, JOHN HAWKINS, librarian; b. Charleston, S.C., Sept. 22, 1920; s. Robert Emmet and Emma (Jenkins) G.; A.B., U. N.C., 1942; B.L.S., U. Cal., Berkeley, 1947, M.L.S., 1950; Ph.D., U. Chgo., 1958; m. Lenore Evelyn Sipes, Mar. 3, 1951. Documents librarian U. Mo., 1947-49; geology librarian, instr. Library Sch., U. Tex., Austin, 1950-51; asso. librarian Rice U., 1953-54; librarian Nat. Acad. Scis., Washington, 1955-61; asso. librarian U. N.C., 1961-66; library dir. Tulane U., New Orleans, 1966—; chmn. sectional com. U.S. Standards Inst. Served as officer AUS, 1942-46. Mem. Am., Southeastern, La. library assns., Kappa Alpha. Episcopalian. Editor: Industrial Research Laboratories of the U.S., 1960; Scientific and Technical Societies of the U.S. and Canada, 1961; The Southeastern Librarian, 1965-66. Home: 19 Central Park Dr Metairie LA 70005

GRICE, BENNING MOORE, justice Supreme Ct., Ga.; b. Hawkinsville, Ga., Sept. 16, 1909; s. Justice Warren and Clara (Rumph) G.; A.B., Mercer U., 1931, LL.B., 1932; m. Mary Calhoun, Oct. 18, 1941; children—Benning Moore, Ann Victoria, Warren C. Admitted to Ga. bar, 1932, pvt. practice, Macon, 1933-60; asso. justice Supreme Ct. of Ga., 1961—. Mem. Ga. Bd. Bar Examiners, 1957-60. Trustee YMCA, 1948-67, Ga. Indsl. Home., 1937-42, 47-49; pres. Central Ga. council Boy Scouts Am., 1955-58. Mem. Ga. Ho. of Reps., 1939-42. Served from lt. (j.g.) to lt. comdr., USNR, 1942-45. Named Macon's Outstanding Young Man by civic clubs, 1940. Mem. Am., Ga., Macon Circuit (pres. 1953-54), Atlanta, Macon bar assns., Mercer U. Alumni Assn. (pres. law chpt. 1950-51). Baptist (deacon). Mason, Kiwanian (pres. 1951). Clubs: Idle Hour Golf and Country (Macon); Atlanta Athletic, Capital City. Home: 3065 High Point Dr Macon GA 31204 Office: State Judicial Bldg State Capitol Atlanta GA 30334

GRIDER, KELLY VERNON, aerospace engr.; b. Scottsboro, Ala., May 28, 1933; s. Kelly Thomas and Mildred Anna (Morris) G.; B.S. in Elec. Engring., U. Ala., 1958, M.S. in Engring., 1965; m. Lula Frances Smith, Mar. 17, 1952; children—Donna Denee, Lisa Susanne, Kelly Vernon. Aerophysics engr. Gen. Dynamics Convair, Ft. Worth, 1958-59; systems engr. Martin Marietta Corp., Orlando, Fla., 1959-61, sr. engr., 1961-62; aerospace engr. Engring. and Missile Systems Lab., Army Missile Command, Directorate of Research, Redstone Arsenal, Ala., 1962-65, research aerospace engr., 1965-69, supervisory aerospace engr., 1969—, chief guidance and control systems analysis, 1967—; instr. elec. engring. U. Ala. at Huntsville, 1968—. Served to staff sgt. USAF, 1951-54. Mem. I.E.E.E., Control Systems Soc., Assn. U.S. Army. Profl. Group Automatic Control (chmn. Huntsville chpt. 1968-69), Tau Beta Pi, Pi Mu Epsilon, Eta Kappa Nu, Phi Eta Sigma, Theta Tau. Baptist. Mason. Contbr. numerous articles tech. jours. Home: 2100 Gladstone Dr Huntsville AL 35811 Office: Army Missile Command Redstone Arsenal AL 35809

GRIER, EDNA CATHERINE GOSSETT, social worker; b. nr. Spartanburg, S.C., Jan. 9, 1897; d. James Hadden and Lillie (Thompson) Gossett; student Draughons Bus. Coll., 1918; student U. S.C., 1942-44, Converse Coll., summers 1966-68; m. James Edward Grier Sr., Oct. 16, 1919 (dec. Dec. 1959); children—James Edward, Galen Marion (Mrs. Wilmot Heinitsh Mitchell, Jr.). Tchr. pub. schs. Georgetown County, S.C., 1916-18; office mgr. Hwy. Dept., Aiken, S.C., 1927-29; dist. supr. WPA projects Union, Cherokee and Spartanburg Counties, S.C., 1938-40; chief counselor Spartanburg Family Ct., 1942-69, vol., 1969—. Chmn. exchange com. Council for Spartanburg County, 1955-57; sec.-treas. Mental Health Clinic Bd., Spartanburg, 1946—; sec. Spartanburg Safety Council, 1964-68, State Bd. Juvenile Corrections, 1946-66; mem. Area Manpower Planning Bd., 1972; mem. fact finding com. S.C. Status of Women Conf., 1968—; mem. adv. com. Pub. Health Nursing, Spartanburg, 1968—. Bd. dirs. S.C. Children's Bureau. Named Career Woman of Year, 1967; recipient certificate appreciation City of Spartanburg, 1969; named Radio Woman of Month, June, 1972. Mem. Spartanburg Social Service Assn. (pres. 1959-60), Spartanburg C. of C. (dir. 1948-50), S.C. Bus. and Profl. Women's Clubs (pres. 1957-59), S.C. Welfare Forum, Nat. Assn. Juvenile Agys., Spartanburg Women's Club (sec. 1960, 65). Methodist. Club: Zonta Internat. Address: 103 Windsor Av Spartanburg SC 29301

GRIER, HAROLD EDWIN, educator; b. McDonough, Ga., Jan. 3, 1921; s. Jefferson and Josephine (Weems) G.; B.S., Savannah State Coll., 1941; M.S., U. Minn., 1948; M.Ed., U. Ill., 1959; Ph.D., Miss. State U., 1971; m. Linelle Nolan, Jan. 30, 1964; children—Alma L., Harold Edward, Lorna M. Tchr., Selma U., 1949-50, Tenn. State U., Nashville, 1948, Ala. A. and M. Coll., Huntsville, 1950-53, Fort Valley (Ga.) State Coll., 1953-56; research cons. U.S. Dept. Agr., U. Ill., Urbana, 1956-63; asso. prof. Alcorn A. and M. Coll., Lorman, Miss., 1963—, project leader agrl. and forestry expt. sta., 1971—, developer coop. program agrl. research with Miss. State U. and Br. Agr. and Forestry Expt. Sta., 1968-69. Served with AUS, 1942-45. Mem. Am. Vocational Assn., Phi Beta Sigma, Gamma Sigma Delta. Address: Alcorn A and M Coll Lorman MS 39096

GRIER, PAUL LIVINGSTON, librarian; b. Clover, S.C., May 26, 1914; s. William Pressly and Nellie Brownlee (Bigham) G.; A.B., Erskine Coll., 1936; A.B. in L.S., U. N.C., 1938; A.M., U. Mich., 1947; m. Eleanor Jane Meacham, Aug. 16, 1947. Library asst., Washington Pub. Library, 1936-40; librarian Hampden-Sydney (Va.) Coll., 1940-42, 46—. Mem. evaluating coms. So. Assn. Schs. and Colls. Served from ensign to lt., USNR, 1942-46. Mem. A.L.A., Southeastern, Va. library assns., Assn. for Preservation Va. Antiquities, Assn. Am. Museums, English-Speaking Union, Sigma Upsilon, Omicron Delta Kappa. Presbyn. (elder). Home: Hampden-Sydney VA 23943

GRIER, WILLIAM HARRIS, textile mfr.; b. Ft. Mill, S.C., Nov. 21, 1901; s. Robert F. and Bessie (Caldwell) G.; B.S., Clemson Coll., 1923; LL.D., 1963; m. Lila Atkinson, Sept. 20, 1930; children—William Harris, John Buford. With Pacific Mills, Lawrence, Mass., 1924-25, Lyman, S.C., 1925-27, Thomaston (Ga.) Mills, 1927-29, Commander Mills, Sand Springs, Okla., 1929-33; with Rock Hill Printing & Finishing Co., 1933—, exec. v.p., 1947-58, pres., 1958—; pres. Lyman Printing & Finishing Co., 1958—; dir. Bus. Devel. Corp. S.C.; bd. dirs. M. Lowenstein & Sons, Inc., N.Y.C., 1950—; dir. Fed. Res. Bank of Richmond, Piedmont & No. Ry., Charlotte. Bd. dirs. Carolinas United Community Services, Charlotte. Trustee of Winthrop College, Rock Hill, N.C. Mem. Rock Hill C. of C., S.C. Mfrs. Assn. (dir.), Soc. Advancement Mgmt. Presbyn. (elder). Club: Executives. Home: 604 Charlotte Av Rock Hill SC 29730 Office: Rock Hill Printing & Finishing Co Rock Hill SC 29730

GRIES, GEORGE ALEXANDER, univ. dean; b. Cambridge, Mass., May 2, 1917; s. John Mathew and Ethel (Goff) G.; A.B., Miami U., Oxford, O.; M.S., Kan. State U., 1940; Ph.D., U. Wis., 1942; m. Mary Lou Carpenter, May 26, 1939; children—James C., Judy L. Asst. plant pathologist Conn. Agr. Expt. Sta., 1942-45; asso. prof., then prof. plant physiology Purdue U., 1945-60; research demonstrator U. Wales, Swansea, 1957-58; prof. plant pathology, head dept. U. Ariz., 1960-66, prof. head biol. scis., 1966-68; dean Coll. Arts and Scis., Okla. State U., Stillwater, 1968—. Mem. Commn. Edn. in Agr. and Natural Resources, 1961-68; cons. Commn. Undergrad. Edn. in Biol. Scis., 1966-69, mem., 1969-72; mem. governing bd. Am. Inst. Biol. Scis., 1970—; cons. examiner North Central Assn. Colls. and Secondary Schs., 1968—. Recipient Silver Beaver award Boy Scouts Am. Mem. Am. Phytopathol. Soc. (councillor-at-large 1966-68), Bot. Soc. Am., Nat. Assn. Biology Tchrs., Nat. Assn. Coll. Tchrs. Agr., Phi Beta Kappa, Sigma Xi, Phi Kappa Phi, Phi Sigma, Omicron Delta Kappa. Contbr. articles to jours. Home: 23 Brentwood Dr Stillwater OK 74074

GRIESSMAN, BENJAMIN EUGENE, sociologist, educator; b. Spartanburg, S.C., Aug. 12, 1934; s. Benjamin F. and Irene (Hill) G.; B.A., Tenn. Temple Coll., 1956; M.A., Baylor U., 1958; B.D., New Orleans Bapt. Theol. Sem., 1962; Ph.D., La. State U., 1966, Sem., 1962,; m. Mary N. Lutz, Sept. 3, 1956; children—Katrina Margene, Sharon, Gloria Gay. Research asso. La. State U., Baton Rouge, 1963-66; spl. lectr. Coll. William and Mary, summer 1965; asso. prof. sociology and anthropology, asso. Sch. Forest Recources, N.C. State U., Raleigh, 1966-70, project dir. Center for Occupational Edn., 1967-70, dir. nat. evaluation Concerted Services in Tng. and Edn., 1967-70; Alumni prof. sociology Auburn (Ala.) U., 1970—, head dept., 1970—. Cons., Ontario East Regional Center, N.Y., 1968, 69. Mem. Am., So., Rural sociol. assns., Am., So. anthropol. assns., Am. Assns. U. Profs., Alpha Kappa Delta. Contbr. articles to profl. jours. Home: 906 Cherokee Rd Auburn AL 36830

GRIFFEY, EARLE BARTLETT, physician, mayor; b. Houston, Oct. 1, 1927; s. Edward W. and May (Bartlett) G.; student Rice U., 1944-45; Ph.B., U. Chgo., 1951, B.S., 1951; M.D., U. Tex., 1956; postgrad. U. Mich., 1956-58; m. Rogene Larsen, Dec. 31, 1962; children—William Earle, Lynn, Anne, Edward Sykes. Intern U. Mich. Hosps., 1956-57, resident 1957-58; gen. practice medicine, Brownsville, Tex., 1958—; mem. staff, exec. com. Mercy Hosp.; city health officer, Brownsville, 1959—; mayor city of Brownsville, 1971—. Dir. Pan Am. Bank. Pres. Am. Cancer Soc., Brownsville, 1965-67, dist. dir., 1967-69. City commr., Brownsville, 1967-69. Bd. dirs. Crippled Childrens Clinic. Served with M.C., USNR, 1945-46. Mem. Cameron County Med. Soc. (v.p. 1968-69), Delta Upsilon, Zeta Phi Chi, Mu Delta. Home: 1144 Belthair St Brownsville TX 78520 Office: 825 Lakeside St Brownsville TX 78520

GRIFFIES, ELMER GERALD, space craft engr.; b. Huffman, Ala., Feb. 24, 1935; s. Elmer Murphy and Mary Winifred (Bailey) G.; B.S. in Mech. Engring., Auburn U., 1957, M.S. in Mech. Engring., 1959; postgrad. U. Tex., 1959-61; m. Anna Louise Carver, June 18, 1955; children— Jerry Murphy, Barbara Ann. Jr. engr. pressure vessel design Chgo. Bridge & Iron Co., Birmingham, Ala., 1956; instr. mech. engring. Auburn (Ala.) U., 1957-59; engr. Sturm and O'Brien, Inc., cons., Auburn, 1957-59; research engr., instr. mech. engring. U. Tex. at Austin, 1959-61; sr. project engr. space craft design, analysis and testing Brown Engring. Co., 1961-67, sr. research engr. anti ballistic missile studies Stanford Research Inst., 1967-71, engr.-scientist tactical weapons systems Northrop Corp., 1971— (all Huntsville, Ala.); asst. prof. engring. mechanics U. Ala. at Huntsville, 1962—. Mem. indian guide program Southeast Huntsville YMCA, 1966-67, chief, 1967, coach football program, 1968, 69, 70; coach Little League Baseball, 1967, 68, 69; scoutmaster Boy Scouts Am., 1969—; mem. Jones Valley Elementary Sch. P.T.A., 1967—, chmn. legislative com., 1969-70. Registered profl. engr., Ala. Mem. Am. Soc. M.E. (faculty adviser Auburn U. 1958-59; PVRC terminal strength subcom. 1966—), Phi Kappa Phi, Pi Mu Epsilon, Pi Tau Sigma, Tau Beta Pi. Baptist (tchr. Sunday sch. adult men's class). Home: 2809 Barcody Rd SE Huntsville AL 35801 Office: Northrop Corp 6025 Technology Dr Huntsville AL 35805

GRIFFIN, CHARLES HENRY, educator, accountant; b. Blooming Grove, Tex., July 3, 1922; s. Lindsay Ira and Fay Dorothy (Pruitt) G.; B.B.A., U. Tex., 1942, M.B.A., 1948, Ph.D., 1953. Staff accountant Peat, Marwick, Mitchell & Co., C.P.A.'s, Dallas office, 1949-50; instr.-lectr. U. Tex., 1950-53; asst. prof. accounting U. Cin., 1953-54, asso. prof., 1954-57; asso. prof. accounting U. Ill., 1957-60, prof., 1960-62, vis. Arthur Young Distinguished prof., 1972-73; prof. accounting U. Tex., Austin, 1962—; vis. prof. U. Birmingham (Eng.), spring 1972. Served as lt. (j.g.) USNR, 1942-46. C.P.A., Tex., Ill. Mem. Am. Accounting Assn., Am. Inst. C.P.A.'s, Nat. Assn. Accountants, Tex., Ill. socs. C.P.A.'s, Beta Alpha Psi, Beta Gamma Sigma, Phi Kappa Phi, Delta Sigma Pi, Phi Kappa Psi. Author: (with T.H. Williams) The Mathematical Dimension of Accounting, 1964; (with Williams, K.D. Larson) Advanced Accounting, rev. edit., 1971; (with Williams) Management Information: A Quantitative Accent, 1967. Editor: Accounting Rev., 1967-70, book rev. editor, 1966-67. Home: 1801 Lavaca Austin TX 78701

GRIFFIN, CHARLES HUDSON, U.S. congressman; b. Utica, Miss., May 9, 1926; s. Charles Farris and Nora (Shelton) G.; student Hinds Jr. Coll., 1943-44, 46-47; B.S., Miss. State U., 1949; m. Angelina Mary Pedrotti, Nov. 8, 1953. Adminstrv. asst. to John Bell Williams, U.S. Rep., Miss., 1949—; mem. 90-92d congresses from 3d Miss. dist. Served with USNR, 1944-46; PTO. Mem. Am. Legion,

V.F.W., (Scottish Rite, Shriner), Moose. Home: Utica MS 39175 Office: 1330 House Office Bldg Washington DC 20515

GRIFFIN, FLOYD SILAS, JR., electronics engr.; b. Bainbridge, Ga., May 28, 1930; s. Floyd Silas and Ethel (Drinkwater) G.; B.S. in Elec. Engring., Ga. Inst. Tech., 1956; m. Laharon Ezell, Sept. 13, 1953; children—Brian Keith, Barbara Wren. Project Engr. Radiation Inc., Melbourne, Fla., 1956-61; lab. dir. Aero Geo Astro, Ft. Walton Beach, Fla., 1961-66; pres. Ordnance Research, Inc., Ft. Walton Beach, 1966-71, sec.-treas., 1971—; owner United Rent-Alls, Ft. Walton Beach, 1964-69. Served with USN, 1948-52. Mem. Am. Ordnance Assn., I.E.E.E. Baptist (deacon, pres. Mens Brotherhood). Lion. Home: Apt 6A 726 N Eglin Pkwy Ft Walton Beach FL 32548 Office: PO Box 1426 Ft Walton Beach FL 32548

GRIFFIN, GEORGE ELLISON, diversified co. exec.; b. St. Louis, Feb. 15, 1921; s. Thomas Joseph and Ursula (Tockstein) G.; B.S. magna cum laude St. Louis U. Sch. Commerce and Finance, 1948, J.D., 1956; m. Beverly Joy Benson, Sept. 9, 1944; children—Dennis Michael, Terence James, Rory Ellison, Maureen Joy, Douglas Paul, Laurie Ann. Admitted to Mo. bar, 1957; staff asst. to controller Stix, Baer & Fuller, St. Louis, 1948-51; sr. tax accountant Touche, Ross Bailey & Smart, Detroit, 1951-54; adminstrv. asst. McDonnell Aircraft Corp., St. Louis, 1954; asst. treas., sec. Orbit Corp., St. Louis, 1955-57; exec. asst. McDonnell Aircraft Corp., St. Louis, 1957-59, mgr. corp. budgets, 1959-61; mgr. profit analysis LTV Corp., Dallas, 1961, mgr. tax, financial planning, 1962, asst. treas., 1963-65, dir. corporate financial planning, 1966, v.p. corp. financial plans, 1967-70, sr. v.p., chief financial officer, 1970—, dir., 1970—; dir. Jones & Laughlin Steel Corp., Wilson & Co., Inc., LTV Aerospace Corp., Altec Corp. Lectr. corp. finance, budgeting St. Louis U. Sch. Commerce and Finance, 1960-61. Served with USNR, 1942-43, USAAF, 1943-45. Decorated Air medal with oak leaf cluster, Purple Heart. C.P.A., Mich. Mem. Financial Execs. Inst. Roman Catholic. Home: 4252 Shady Hill Dr Dallas TX 75229 Office: PO Box 5003 Dallas TX 75222

GRIFFIN, GEORGE RICHARD, banker; b. Tampa, Fla., Sept. 4, 1903; s. James A. and Nannie M. (Johnson) G.; B.S. in Econs., Wharton Sch., U. Pa., 1925; m. Mildred D. Macdonald, July 14, 1952; children—Donald W., Gordon G. With Exchange Nat. Bank of Tampa, Fla., 1925—, dir., 1936—, v.p., 1939-52, pres., 1952-67, chmn. bd., 1967—; vice chmn., dir. Exchange Nat. Bank of Winter Haven, Fla., 1951—; pres., dir. Exchange Bank of Temple Terrace, Fla.; pres. Tampa Investment Securities Co., Tampa; Gen. Telephone Co. Fla., Gen. Portland Cement Co., Dallas, Fla. Steel Corp., Founders Life Assurance Corp., Tampa, Indsl. Devel. Corp. Fla. Trustee U. Tampa. Served from lt. (s.g.) to lt. comdr. USNR, 1942-46. Mem. Fla. Bankers Assn. (pres. 1956). Episcopalian. Home: 3106 Sunset Dr Tampa FL Office: 601 Franklin St Tampa FL

GRIFFIN, HARRIET ELIZABETH, educator; b. Parker County, Tex.; d. Minter Crozier and Lillian (Sumner) Griffin; B.A., Tex. Christian U., 1932, M.A., 1935; postgrad. Colo. State U., U. Cal. at Los Angeles, U. So. Cal. English tchr. Milsap Sch., 1933-35; tchr. Ft. Worth Pub. Schs., 1935-47, dean Tech. High Sch, also supr. Adult Evening Sch., 1947-63, coordinator guidance, testing and vis. tchrs., 1963, dir. profl. relations, 1963—; vis. instr. curriculum and child psychology Tex. Christian U. Del. World Confedn. Orgns. Teaching Profession, 1966, 68, 72. Treas. Community Action Agy.; sec. Mayor's Youth Opportunity Council. Bd. dirs. Fort Worth Human Relations Commn., Traffic Safety Commn., Family Service and Travelers Aid, Nat. Conf. Christians and Jews, Big Bros., Gov.'s Com. Status of Women, Mayor's Com. Status Women. Mem. N.E.A., Am. Assn. Sch. Adminstrs., Tex. Congress Parents and Tchrs. (program chmn.), Tex. P.T.A. (bd. mgrs.), League Women Voters, Bus. and Profl. Women's Club, Tex. Tchrs. Assn. (pres.), Council Adminstrv. Women, C. of C. (edn. com. women's div.), Kappa Delta Pi, Delta Kappa Gamma. Clubs: Altrusa (past pres.), Woman's, Shakespeare, Knife and Fork (v.p.), Bon Soir. Contbr. ednl. column. Ft. Worth Press; producer radio program Education Today. Author articles in field. Home: 2555 Greene Av Fort Worth TX 76109 Office: 3210 W Lancaster Fort Worth TX 76107

GRIFFIN, JAMES CHRISTOPHER, JR., civil, mech. engr.; b. Forney, Tex., Nov. 3, 1917; s. James Christopher and Kate (Linn) G.; B.S. in Mech. Engring., Tex. A. and M. Coll., 1938; m. Claudine Neal, Mar. 15, 1942; children—James Christopher III, Nancy Claudine (Mrs. Larry Victor Pyle). With U.S. Army C.E., 1939—, chief specifications sect., design br. engring. div., Ft. Worth dist., 1958—. Registered profl. engr., Tex. Mem. Nat., Tex. socs. profl. engrs. Democrat. Methodist. Mason. Home: 6208 Woodbine Dr Fort Worth TX 76112 Office: 819 Taylor St Fort Worth TX 76102

GRIFFIN, JOHN ANSLEY, found. exec.; b. Monroe, Ga., July 3, 1912; s. William Hull and Belle (Barr) G.; A.B., Emory U., 1935, M.A., 1938; Ph.D., U. Wis., 1956; m. Wallace Lillard Lyons, June 5, 1943 (dec. Sept. 1960); children—Sarah Lockhart, John Ansley, Mary Earle, William Hull II; m. 2d, Anne Ryland Ricks, June 14, 1968. Faculty, Ga. Inst. Tech., 1935-44; asso. prof. sociology, asst. to pres., dir. community ednl. service Emory U., Atlanta, 1944-59; prof. sociology, dir. univ. relations Fla. State U., 1959-64; asso. dir. for conciliation Community Relations Service, U.S. Dept. Commerce, 1964-65; exec. dir. So. Edn. Found., Atlanta, 1965—. Chmn., S.E. Enforcement Commn., WSB, 1951-52; asso. research dir. Ashmore Project Biracial Edn., 1953-54; cons. White House Conf. to Fulfill These Rights, 1965-66; chmn. So. Regional Conf. Adult and Basic Edn., 1966. Exec. com. So. Regional Council, 1945-64; chmn. program rev. com. Penn Community Center, Frogmore, S.C., 1968-72; nat. profl. adv. bd. Mary Holmes Jr. Coll. and Child Devel. Group, Miss. Bd. dirs. Better Schs. Atlanta; trustee Atlanta U. Recipient Delbert Clark award W. Ga. Coll., 1957. Julius Rosenwald fellow, 1948-49. Mem. Am. Arbitration Assn. (arbitrator fed. mediation and conciliation service 1942—), Phi Delta Kappa, Sigma Delta Chi, Alpha Kappa Delta, Omicron Delta Kappa, Phi Delta Theta. Methodist. Contbr. articles to profl. jours. Home: 1198 Oakdale Rd NE Atlanta GA 30307 Office: 811 Cypress St NE Atlanta GA 30308

GRIFFIN, MARY RUFFIN ROBERTSON (MRS. ORMOND BISHOP GRIFFIN), educator; b. Stoneville, N.C., Aug. 24, 1915; d. Samuel Ruffin and Daisy (Joyce) Robertson; R.N., Roanoke Rapids (N.C.) Hosp. Sch. Nursing, 1938; B.S. in Pub. Health Nursing, Peabody Coll. for Tchrs., 1947; M.P.H., U. N.C., 1965; postgrad. East Carolina U., 1962-63; m. Ormond Bishop Griffin, Dec. 28, 1947. Sch. nurse Roanoke Rapids (N.C.) high sch., 1938-41; field health supr. U.S. Govt. Nat. Youth Adminstrn., Kinston, N.C., 1941; mem. infirmary nursing staff East Carolina U., Greenville, 1941-42; pub. health nurse Chatham County Health Dept., Pittsboro, N.C., 1942-46, Greensboro Health Dept., 1947, Halifax County (N.C.) Health Dept., 1953-62; nurse Dr. K. Mathiesen, Pittsboro, 1948; pvt. duty Mathiesen Clinic, Pittsboro, 1949-52; instr. pub. health nursing East Carolina U., 1962-65; asst. prof. East Tenn. State U., Johnson City, 1965-69, prof., 1969—. Tchr. home nursing A.R.C., 1942-44; chmn. nursing adv. com., bd. dirs. Tenn. Tb and Respiratory Disease Assn. Precinct chmn. Haw River Twp. Democratic Com., Moncure, N.C. Mem. Blountville Bus. and Profl. Women's Club, Am., Tenn. pub. health assns., Am., N.C. (dist. pres. 1964) nurses assns. Nat., Am. leagues for nursing, Tenn., East Tenn. edn. assns., Am. Assn. U. Profs. Baptist. Home: Rural Delivery 4 Blountville TN 37617 Office: East Tenn State U Johnson City TN

GRIFFIN, ROBERT LEWIS, ednl. adminstr.; b. Washington, Ga., Feb. 1, 1926; s. Edward Moore and Linnie Ruth (Johnson) G.; A.B., Olivet Nazarene Coll., 1950, Th.B., 1951; M.A., Butler U., 1959; Ed.D., Okla. State U., 1965; m. Dorothy Maxine Hollingsworth, Oct. 29, 1944; children—Katherine Mary, Timothy Alan, Robert Paul. Ordained to ministry Ch. of Nazarene, 1952; pastor, Logansport, Highland and Crawfordsville, Ind., 1950-59, Cushing and Bartlesville, Okla., 1959-67; prof. philosophy and religion Wesleyan Coll., part-time, 1962-67; asst. prof. philosophy Kan. State Coll., 1963-65; prof., acad. dean, dir. grad. studies Bethany (Okla.) Nazarene Coll., 1967—. Dist. youth pres. Ch. of Nazarene, 1952-66. Served with USAAF, 1944-46. Mem. S.W. Philosophy Edn. Assn., Stillwater Acad. Deans Assn. Conf., Phi Delta Lambda. Kiwanian (chmn. internat. com. 1970-71). Home: 2801 Meridian Court Oklahoma City OK 73127 Office: Bethany Nazarene Coll Bethany OK 73008

GRIFFIN, SAMUEL MARVIN, JR., editor, ednl. adminstr.; b. Bainbridge, Ga., Feb. 12, 1936; s. Samuel Marvin Griffin; B.S. in Indsl. Mgmt., Ga. Inst. Tech., 1958; m. Mary Ann Hill; children—Samuel Marvin III, Virginia Ann. Editor, Bainbridge Post-Searchlight, 1963—. Mem. Ga. Bd. Edn., 1970—. Served with USNR, 1958-63. Mem. Bainbridge C. of C. (past dir.), Bainbridge Jaycees (past dir.), Ga. Press Assn. (treas., past bd. mgrs.), Sigma Alpha Epsilon. Presbyn. (deacon). Rotarian (past dir.). Office: State Bd Edn State Office Bldg Atlanta GA 30303*

GRIFFIN, SUMNER ALBERT, ednl. adminstr.; b. Ashland, N.Y., May 11, 1922; s. Frank A. and Nina (Lee) G.; student N.Y. State Agr. and Tech. Inst., 1939-41; B.S., Cornell U., 1949; M.S., U. Ky., 1950; Ph.D., Mich. State U., 1955; m. Barbara Jean Hammill, Dec. 15, 1951; children—Margaret, Nina, Patricia. Instr., Mich. State U., 1951-55; mgr. animal health and nutrition Mallinckrodt Chem. Works, St. Louis, 1955-57; asso. prof. U. Tenn., Knoxville, 1957-70, dean Sch. Agr., Cookeville, 1970—. Cons., Oak Ridge Nat. Lab., 1967—. Bd. dirs. Bachman Meml. Home. Served with USAAF, 1942-45. Mem. Am. Soc. Animal Sci., Animal Nutrition Research Council, Nat. Assn. Colls. and Tchrs. Agr., Tenn. Edn. Assn., Sigma Xi, Alpha Zeta, Gamma Sigma Delta, Phi Kappa Phi. Presbyn. (deacon 1966-69). Mason, Rotarian. Home: 987 Georgetown St Cookeville TN 38501

GRIFFIN, THOMAS, columnist New Orleans States-Item. Address: 3800 Howard Av New Orleans LA 70140*

GRIFFIN, WILBURN SCOTT, state ofcl.; b. Mantee, Miss., Oct. 15, 1913; s. Virgil Homer and Martha Elizabeth (Davis) G.; B.A., U. Miss., 1941, M.A., 1947; m. Sarah Myrtle Oswalt, Mar. 14, 1941; children— Susan, Georgia. Prin., athletic coach Woodland (Miss.) High Sch., 1936-38, Wathall (Miss.) Elementary Sch., 1938-42; asst. registrar U. Miss., 1945-49; dir. adminstrn. and finance State Dept. Edn., Jackson, Miss., 1950—. Served with USNR, 1942-45. Mem. Am., Miss. assns. sch. adminstrs., Am. Sch. Food Service Assn. (dir. 1954-55), Miss. Edn. Assn. (dir. 1951-52), Phi Delta Kappa., Am. Legion. Mason. Home: 5051 Canton Heights Jackson MS 39211 Office: PO Box 771 Jackson MS 39205

GRIFFIS, CLARENCE ALTON, assn. exec.; b. Waycross, Ga., Oct. 10, 1927; s. Clarence A. and Trudy (King) G.; B.A., Stetson U., 1951; LL.B., Woodrow Wilson Law Coll., 1958; postgrad. Yale, 1959; m. Rose Whitten, Aug. 15, 1953; children—Miriam (Mrs. Lawrence W. Simon), Ronald W., Mark Alton and Michael Allen (twins). With research dept. Pillsbury Mills Inc., 1953-55; with U.S. Brewers Assn., Inc., Atlanta, 1955—, state dir., 1963-69, So. regional dir., 1969—. Mem. Peach and Bowl Com. Trustee Found. Visually Handicapped Children, Atlanta. Served to 1st lt. AUS, 1945-47, 51-53. Recipient Excellence award Ga. Press, 1967, Newspaper citation, 1966. Mem. Ga. Press Assn., Ga. Municipal Assn., Ga. Radio-TV Broadcasters Assn., County Commrs. Assn., Ga. Soc. Assn. Execs., Atlanta C. of C. Clubs: Atlanta Press, Leafmore. Home: 2544 Tanglewood Rd Decatur GA30033 Office: 1655 Tully Circle NE Atlanta GA 30329

GRIFFIS, JAMES TRUMAN, educator; b. Bonham, Tex., Aug. 1, 1909; s. James Arthur and Minnie (Magouirk) G.; B.A., Austin Coll., 1941; B.S., U. Corpus Christi, 1952; M.A., Tex. Coll. Arts and Industry, 1950; Ed.D., U. Houston, 1955; m. Billye Florine Snow, June 5, 1931; 1 son, Bill J. Tchr., prin. rural schs., Fannin County, Tex., 1937-41; field exec. Boy Scouts Am., Corpus Christi, Tex., 1941-48; elementary prin. Flour Bluff Schs., Corpus Christi, 1948-52; instr., research asst. U. Houston, 1953-55; asst. supt. N.E. Houston schs., 1955-59; prof., head dept. edn., dean men Coll. Ozarks, Clarksville, Ark., 1961-64; prof., head dept. elementary edn. Panhandle State Coll., Goodwell, Okla., 1964—. Summer sch. faculty Troy (Ala.) State Coll., 1963-65, Okla. State U., Stillwater, 1966; research cons. Hugoton (Kan.) Schs., 1966—, Okla. Commn. on Tchr. Edn. and Certification, 1965—. Participant 1st World Congress on Reading, Paris, 1966, 2d congress, Copenhagen, 1968. Recipient Hornaday award for distinguished service to wild life, 1940. Mem. Phi Delta Kappa, Kappa Delta Pi. Presbyn. (elder). Mason (Shriner, 32 deg.), Kiwanian (past pres.), Author monograph: Education at Three Cost Levels, 1955. Home: 426 1st St Goodwell OK 73939

GRIFFITH, BRODIE SHEPPARD, newspaper editor; b. Saluda, S.C., Mar. 14, 1899; s. John Franklin and Elizabeth (Keziah) S.; student Erskine Coll., 1916-17; LL.D., Davidson Coll., 1966, Erskine Coll., 1967; m. Thelma Cobb Wilkinson, Dec. 18, 1920; children—Gail Elizabeth (Mrs. W.C. Dowd, II), Myra Elise (Mrs. Norman L. Moore). Reporter, Greensboro (N,C.) Record, 1919-21, Greensboro Daily News, 1921-23; state editor Charlotte (N.C.) News, 1923-25; mng. editor, 1929-48, exec. editor, 1948-55, gen. mgr., 1955-59, editor, gen. mgr., 1959-65, asso. pub., 1965-66; became v.p., sec., gen. mgr. Charlotte News Pub. Co., Inc., 1955; v.p., treas., dir. Knight Pub. Co., v.p., asso. pub. 1968—, gen. mgr. Charlotte Observer and Charlotte News, 1966-72, now ret.; treas., dir. Observer Transp. Co.; editor N.C. Legion News, 1937—; dir. Knight Newspapers, Inc., Bank of Charlotte. Chmn. N.C. Urban Affairs Com. Mem. Charlotte Zoning Bd. Adjustment, 1949-50, mem. and chmn. Planning Bd., 1950-51. Served as sgt. 118th Inf., 30th Div., 1917-19. A.E.F., 1918-19. Mem. Am., So. newspaper pubs. assns., N.C. Press Assn. (v.p.), Am. Legion 40 and 8, Newcomen Soc., Sigma Delta Chi. Baptist. Mason (32 deg. K.T., Shriner). Club: Charlotte City. Home: 330 Ridgewood Av Charlotte NC 28209

GRIFFITH, DAVID NICHOLAS, SR., dentist; b. Bonne Terre, Mo., May 27, 1917; s. Laurence Clinton and Anna Sophia Carolina (Mabuce) G.; B.S., Miss. State Coll., 1949; postgrad. U. Wis., 1950; D.D.S., U. Tenn., 1956; m. Bonnie Jane Bourland, May 29, 1949; children—David Nicholas, Mary Jane. Pvt. practice dentistry, Tallassee, Ala., 1956-63, Dadeville, 1964—. Served with USNR, 1941-45. Mem. Am., Ala., Dist. dental assns., Gideons (v.p. 1971-72), C. of C. Presbyn. Mason, Kiwanian. Club: Horseshoe Bend Garden (Dadeville, Ala.). Home: Lake Martin Dadeville AL 36853 Office: East Tallapoosa Medical Center Dadeville AL 36853

GRIFFITH, ERNEST STACEY, editor, writer; b. Utica, N.Y., Nov. 28, 1896; s. George and Elizabeth (Stacey) G.; A.B., Hamilton Coll., 1917, L.H.D., 1959; D.Phil. (Rhodes scholar), Oxford U., 1925; Litt.D., W. Va. Wesleyan, 1957; m. Margaret Dyckman Davenport, June 8, 1929; children—Margaret Dyckman, Elizabeth Alison, Lawrence S. Cameron, Julia Bourne, Stephen Loyal. Preceptor in econs. Princeton, 1920-21; warden Univ. Settlement, Liverpool, Eng., 1923-28; lectr. dept. govt. Harvard, 1929-30; dean lower div., prof. comparative govt., Syracuse U., 1930-35; dean. Grad. Sch., prof. polit. sci. Am. U., 1935-40; dir. legislative reference service, Library Congress, 1940-58; dean Sch. Internat. Service, Am. U., 1958-65; cons. editor Praeger series U.S. Govt. Depts. and Agys., 1966—; lectr. Swarthmore Coll., 1941; Stokes lectr. N.Y.U., 1951; Fulbright lectr. Oxford, 1951-52, Internat. Christian U., Tokyo, 1966-67; lectr. Birmingham U., Manchester U., U. Oslo, U. Swansea. Pres. Washington Council Social Agys., 1943-47; Washington chmn. Nat. Conf. Christians and Jews, 1940-41. Mem.-at-large. Bd. Missions and Ch. Extension, Methodist Ch., 1947-51; del. World Council of Chs., New Delhi, 1961; mem. Am. Nat. Commn. for UNESCO, 1963-66; cons. in fgn. policy, platform com., 1968; Nat. Republican Com., mem. D.C. Planning Commn., 1946-47. Served with Naval Air Force, 1918. Mem. Am. Polit. Sci. Assn. (exec. council, 1939-42, chmn. research com. 1942-47, program com. 1949, v.p. 1958-59), Nat. Municipal League, Am. Soc. Pub. Adminstrn., Wilderness Soc. (council 1937-55, treas. 1940-50, 58—), Nat. Acad. Econs. and Polit.-Sci. (pres. 1958-63), Nat. Acad. Pub. Adminstrn. (hon.), Phi Beta Kappa, Phi Kappa Phi, Delta Upsilon. Republican. Methodist. Clubs: Potomac Appalachian Trail, Cosmos. Author: The Modern Government in Action, 1942; Congress: Its Contemporary Role, rev. edit. 1967; The American System of Government, 1953, 4th rev. edit., 1966, Italian, German and Korean edits., 1957-58, edits. numerous fgn. langs. Editor and co-author Research in Political Science, 1948. Editor, Congressional Anthology, rev. edit. 1958. Holder misc. speed and endurance records in mountain climbing. Home: 1941 Parkside Drive NW Washington DC 20012

GRIFFITH, HENRY WINTER, physician; b. Atlanta, May 4, 1926; s. James Marvin and Lillian (Winter) G.; B.S., U. S.C., 1947; M.D., Emory U., 1953; m. Julia Ann Dobson, Apr. 3, 1948; children—Edith, Henry, Tracy. Intern, U.S. Naval Hosp., Bethesda Md., 1953-54; resident Dade County Hosp., Miami, Fla., 1954-55; pvt. practice medicine, South Miami, Fla., 1956-66; physician Student Health Service, Fla. State U., Tallahassee, 1966-69, prof. medicine, 1969—; dir. med. edn. Tallahassee Meml. Hosp. Served with USNR, 1943-47, 53-57. Author: Instructions for Patients, 1969. Home: 1202 Domingo Dr Tallahassee FL 32306 Office: care Program in Med Sci Fla State U Tallahassee FL 32306

GRIFFITH, JAMES, govt. ofcl. Dir. Region VI Office Econ. Opportunity, Dallas. Address: 100 Commerce St Dallas TX 75202*

GRIFFITH, JERRY LYNN, librarian; b. George West, Tex., Aug. 29, 1938; s. Ray Septimus and Flossie (Stevens) G.; A.A., Wharton County Jr. Coll., 1958; B.A., N. Tex. State U., 1960; M.S. in Library Sci., E. Tex. State U., 1966. Librarian Ganado (Tex.) High Sch., 1960-66; br. librarian Fort Polk, La., 1966-68; librarian 2d Inf. Div., Korea, 1967-68; adminstrv. librarian Army Spl. Services Library Service Center, Fort Polk, La., 1968—. Mem. Jaycees (treas.), Am., Southwestern, La. library assns. Democrat. Methodist. Home: Route 4 Box 509 DeRidder LA 70634 Office: Spl Services Sect Fort Polk LA 71459

GRIFFITH, JOE WESLEY, banker; b. Ackerman, Miss., Apr. 25, 1929; s. Thomas Jefferson and Ara Ethel (Stephenson) G.; student U. Miss., 1947-49; B.S. in Accounting, Miss. State U., 1955; m. Lulu Jean Love, Dec. 24, 1955; children—Elizabeth, Joe Wesley. Examiner Fed. Deposit Ins. Corp., 1955-64; v.p. Bank of Philadelphia, Miss., 1964-66; cashier Citizens Bank, Philadelphia, 1966-70, cashier, trust officer, 1970—. Treas. Neshoba County Heart Fund, 1967—; treas., meml. chmn. Neshoba County unit Am. Cancer Soc., 1968—. Served with USNR, 1950-54. Mem. Philadelphia-Neshoba C. of C. (treas. 1970). Baptist (leader adult dept. 1965-68, treas., sec. 1965-68, 71—, deacon). Lion (chmn. program Philadelphia 1971—, dir. 1967—). Home: Route 6 Box A15 Philadelphia MS 39350 Office: Box 209 Philadelphia MS 39350

GRIFFITH, LUTHER BAILEY, accountant; b. Mansfield, La., June 25, 1901; s. William Jasper and Elizabeth (Bailey) G.; student Soule Coll., 1922; B.C.S., YMCA Coll., 1931; m. Louie Barnard, Apr. 25, 1931; children—Emelia Gay, Louie. Vice pres. Griffith Lumber Co., Mansfield, 1922-27; clk. La. Oil Co., Shreveport, 1927-34; bookkeeper Haynes Oil Corp., Shreveport, 1934-41; sr. accountant Colbert & Pasquier, C.P.A.'s, 1935-41; partner Griffith and Hettler, C.P.A.'s, Shreveport, 1941—. Mem. La. Soc. C.P.A.'s, Am. Inst. C.P.A.'s, Internat. Lightning Class Yachting Assn. (life; v.p. 1960-61, co chmn. selection 1st site yacht races 1960-61, commodore So. dist. 1963-64), De Soto Parish Hist. Soc., S.A.R., Ga. Geneological Soc. Episcopalian (vestryman). Mason. Clubs: Shreveport Country, Shreveport Yacht; Northwood Country. Home: 3255 Old Mooringsport Rd Shreveport LA 71107 Office: Ray P Oden Bldg Shreveport LA 71101

GRIFFITH, MARY IRENE, physician; b. Ruffin, N.C., July 1, 1909; d. Harry and Nannie (Dameron) Griffith; student Woman's Coll., U. N.C., 1926-29, U. N.C., 1932-33; M.D., U. Tenn., 1942. Intern, N.C. Bapt. Hosp., Winston-Salem, N.C., 1942, obstetrics gynecology staff, 1942, now mem. staff; intern Johns Hopkins Hosp., 1942-43, asst. resident 1943-44, resident obstetrics, 1944-45; asst. resident pathology Boston Lying-In Hosp., 1945, Free Hosp. for Women, 1945-46; practice medicine, specializing in obstetrics, gynecology, Winston-Salem, N.C., 1946—; mem. staff Forsythe Meml. Hosp.; instr. obstetrics, gynecology Bowman Gray Sch. Medicine, 1946, now asst. prof.; med. cons. Nigeria, Ire Welfare Center, W. Africa, 1954, 62, Bapt. Hosp., Paraguay, 1956. Bd. dirs. Friendship House. Diplomate Am. Bd. Obstetrics and Gynecology. Fellow Am. Coll. Obstetricians and Gynecologists; mem. A.M.A., Am. Med. Women's Assn., World, Pan Am. med. assns. Alpha Epsilon, Iota, Alpha Omega Alpha, C. of C. Baptist. Club: Altrusa. Author articles in field. Home: 419 S Hawthorne Rd Winston-Salem NC 27103 Office: 207 S Hawthorne Rd Winston-Salem NC 27103

GRIFFITH, MELVIN EUGENE, govt. ofcl.; b. Lawrence, Kan., Mar. 24, 1912; s. George Thomas and Estella (Shaw) G.; A.B., U. Kan., 1934, A.M., 1935, Ph.D. (fellow in entomology), 1938; postgrad. U. Mich., summers, 1937-40; m. Pauline Sophia Bogart, June 23, 1941. Instr. zoology N.D. Agrl. Coll., Fargo, 1938-39, asst. prof., 1939-41, asso. prof., 1941-42; malaria control entomologist US PHS, La., 1942-43, Okla. 1943-46; Okla. communicable disease center entomologist US PHS-Okla. Dept. Health, 1946-50; communicable disease center rep. Ark.-White-Red River Basins investigations USPHS, Ark., Colo., Kan., La., Mo., N.M., Okla., Tex., 1950-51; chief malariologist ICA, USPHS, Thailand, 1951-60; asso. dir. Malaria Eradication Tng. Center, Jamaica, 1960; regional malaria adviser S.E. Asia, Agy. Internat. Devel., USPHS, New Delhi, India, 1960-62, regional malaria adviser Near East and So. Asia, 1962-64, dep. chief malaria eradication br., Washington, 1964-67, chief., 1967-71; ret., 1971; cons. Office of Health, AID, Washington,

1971—. Asso. prof. zool. scis. U. Okla., Norman, 1946-52, prof., 1952-56. Recipient citation for distinguished service, U. Kan., 1962. Mem. A.A.A.S., Am. Pub. Health Assn., Am., Royal socs. tropical medicine and hygiene, Am. Mosquito Control Assn., Am. Soc. Limnology and Oceanography, Entomol. Soc. Am., USPHS Commd. Officers Assn., Siam Soc., Phi Beta Kappa, Sigma Xi. Club: Bangkok Sports (Bangkok, Thailand). Contbr. articles and monographs on entomology, malaria control, pub. health, Alconeura of U.S. Address: 400 N St SW Washington DC 20024

GRIFFITH, REUBEN WILLIAM, state ofcl.; b. Monroe County, Miss., Dec. 9, 1900; B.A., U. Miss., 1925, M.A., 1939; LL.B., Jackson Sch. Law, 1959; m. 1926; 2 children. Tchr. history and English Miss. Heights Acad., Blue Mountain, Miss., 1920-33; supt., tchr. history Tippah-Union Consol. High Sch., Cotton Plant, Miss., 1933-38, Ripley (Miss.) High Sch., 1938-44; asst. supt. edn. Miss. Dept. Edn., from 1944, now sec. Bd. Edn. Mem. N.E.A. Home: 567 Hickory Ridge Dr Jackson MS 39206 Office: State Bd Edn Woolfolk State Office Bldg Jackson MS 39205*

GRIFFITH, SAMUEL CLARENCE, JR., hosp. adminstr.; b. Asheville, N.C., June 22, 1930; s. Samuel Clarence and Marcia (Sherrer) G.; B.B.A., U. Ga., 1951; certificate in hosp. adminstrn., Ga. State Coll., 1961, M.H.A., 1969; m. Ethel Christine McClure, Dec. 20, 1950; children—Samuel Clarence III, Robert C., Joseph H. Controller, Athens (Ga.) Gen. Hosp., 1956-59; bus. mgr. Henrietta Egleston Hosp. for Children, Atlanta, 1959-63; adminstr. Ponce de Leon Infirmary, Atlanta, 1963—. Founder, pres. Ga. Soc. for Autistic Children, Inc., 1967—; pres. Met. Atlanta Hosp. Council, 1967. Served with AUS, 1951-53. Mem. Am. Coll. Hosp. Adminstrs., Am. Assn. Hosp. Accountants (chpt. pres. 1962), Ga. Hosp. Assn. (trustee 1968-71), Nat. Soc. for Autistic Children (pres. 1970-72), Ga. Hosp. Computer Group (dir. 1968-69). Baptist. Home: 2314 Street de Ville NE Atlanta GA 30345 Office: 144 Ponce de Leon Av NE Atlanta GA 30308

GRIFFITH, WILLIAM HOWARD, electric co. exec.; b. Huntingdon, Pa., Aug. 8, 1925; s. Howard Sidney and Gladys Flora (Prindle) G.; B.S., Pa. State U., 1951; postgrad. Northeastern U., 1952-55; m. Patricia Ruth Carney, May 22, 1948; 1 son, Michael John. Engring. supr. Gen. Electric Co., Knolls Atomic Power Lab., Schnectady, 1955-60; v.p. operations Alloy Freitag Mfg. Co., subsidiary Salem-Brosius, Inc., 1960-61; gen. mgr. Salem-Brosius, Inc., alloy mfg. div., Pitts., 1961-62; project mgr. Westinghouse Atomic Equipment and Atomic Fuel divs., Cheswick, Pa., 1962-64; mfg. projects mgr. atomic equipment div., 1966, naval nuclear project mgr., 1966-67; gen. mgr. Westinghouse Electric Corp., Pensacola (Fla.) div., 1967—; dir., chmn. bd. Commercial Nat. Bank Pensacola (Fla.). Mem. adv. bd. Bapt. Hosp., 1968—, Sacred Heart Hosp., 1968-72. Bd. dirs. United Fund Greater Pensacola, Fla., Charter Bankshares, Inc. Served with USAF, 1951-55. Mem. Navy League U.S., Atomic Indsl. Forum, Asso. Industries Fla., Fla. State (dist. dir. 1970—), Pensacola chmabers commerce. Mason, Rotarian. Home: 257 Sabine Dr Pensacola Beach FL 32561 Office: PO Box 791 Pensacola FL 32502

GRIFFITHS, THOMAS WILLIAM, III, adhesive co. exec.; b. Dallas, Jan. 12, 1913; s. Thomas William and Eva (Lavino) G.; grad. Lawrenceville Sch., 1933; standard certificate Am. Inst. Banking, 1936; student Aetna Casualty Sch., 1937, Dale Carnegie Course, 1941, Dun & Bradstreet Bus. Course, 1966; m. Muriel Carr, Feb. 7, 1942; children—Thomas Carr, Gail (Mrs. Yerger Hill, III). Clk., Nat. Bank Commerce, Dallas, 1933-36; ins. agt. Steele-Fonda Co., Dallas, 1936-42, Great Nat. Life Ins. Co., Dallas, 1941-42; gen. mgr. Indsl. Adhesive Co., Dallas, 1943-46, pres., dir., 1946—; sr. partner, mgr. Lavino-Griffiths Oil Co., 1956-61; asso. Headington Bros., Oklahoma City, 1956—; v.p. Evergreen Investment Co., Dallas, 1963-71; affiliate Onival Corp., Phila., 1967—; asso. M.A. McBee & William D. McBee, Jr., Dallas, 1969—; dir. C & C Mfg. Co., 1963-67, S & F Mfg. & Leasing Co., 1964-67, Trininty Nat. Bank, 1964-65 (all Dallas). Mem. exec. council Highland Park Community League, 1970—. Bd. dirs. Big Bros. Dallas, 1943-45. Mem. Southwestern Soc. Packaging and Handling Engrs. (treas. 1961-62), Tex. Mfrs. Assn., Dallas C. of C., U.S. C. of C., Dallas Sales and Marketing Execs. Republican. Episcopalian. Clubs: City, Northwood Country, Idelwild, Terpsichorean, Hesitation (all Dallas); Garden of the Gods (Colorado Springs, Colo.). Home: 4205 Lakeside Dr Highland Park Dallas TX 75219 Office: 2500-10 Caroline St Dallas TX 75201

GRIGGS, JAMES CHOICE, ednl. adminstr.; b. Milledgeville, Ga., Aug. 24, 1907; s. Mark and Carrie M. (Edwards) G.; A.B., Paine Coll., 1934; M.A., Columbia, 1951, postgrad., 1952; m. Azelma Mobley, Apr. 29, 1956; 1 son, Alton Lavoris (dec.). Tchr. social studies and music Boggs Acad., Keysville, Ga., 1934-39; Sunday Sch. missionary Presbyn. Ch., 1939-41; prin. Cousins Jr. High Sch., Sardis, Ga., 1948-59, Waynesboro (Ga.) High and Indsl. Elementary Sch., 1959-62, Blakeney Elementary Sch., Waynesboro, 1962—. Served with AUS, 1942-45. Mem. N.E.A., Ga. Assn. Educators, Burke County Tchrs and Edn. Assn. (pres. 1950-53). Baptist (organist, choir master). Mason. Home: PO Box 633 Waynesboro GA 30830 Office: Blakeney Elementary Sch Waynesboro GA 30830

GRIGGS, JOSEPH, III, architect; b. Virginia Beach, Va., Nov. 24, 1932; s. Joseph, Jr., and Irene (Masters) G.; B.Arch., Va. Poly. Inst., 1967; m. Joanne Carolyn Jones, Aug. 25, 1957; 1 dau., Adrian. With Mills, Petticord & Mills, 1956-57, Heery & Heery, Atlanta, 1957-61, Mills, Petticord & Mills, Norfolk, Va., 1961-62, Oliver & Smith, Norfolk, 1962-63; pvt. practice architecture, Christiansburg, Va., 1962-63; partner Clay & Griggs, Roanoke, Va., 1966—; pres. Sugarloaf-Highlands Corp., Sugarloaf Devel. Corp., House of Carpets of Roanoke, Inc., Contract Carpets, Inc.; works include Grant Plaza Shopping Center, Sugarloaf Highlands Apts. Mem. Roanoke Sci. Mus. Assn. Served with USAF, 1952-56. Mem. A.I.A., YMCA. Home: 3466 Meadowlark Rd Roanoke VA 24018 Office: 3112 Franklin Rd SW Roanoke VA 24014

GRIGGS, WALTER STALEY, JR., electronics engr.; b. Suffolk, Va., Dec. 13, 1926; s. Walter Staley and Beulah (Odom) G.; student Coll. William and Mary, 1944-45; B.S., Va. Poly. Inst., 1948; postgrad. U. Va., 1951-52; m. Mildred Audrey Melvin, Jan. 26, 1952; children—Walter Staley III, James Melvin. Electronics Project engr. Norfolk Naval Shipyard, Portsmouth, Va., 1948-56, head engr. ship radio div., 1956-57; head engr. shore electronics Fifth Naval Dist., Portsmouth, 1957-58, chief electronics engr. for indsl. mgr. USN, 5th Naval Dist., 1958-66; tech. dir. Naval Electronics Systems Command, Atlantic div., Portsmouth, 1966—. Served with USNR, 1945-46. Recipient Superior Work Performance award, 1960, 71. Mem. Armed Forces Mgmt. Assn., I.E.E.E. (sr.), Aircraft Owners and Pilots Assn., Soc. Profl. Naval Engrs. Baptist. Home: 4739 Rivershore Rd Portsmouth VA 23703 Office: Box 55 Portsmouth VA 23705

GRIGSBY, JAMES KELTNER, geophys. exploration co. exec.; b. Houston, Aug. 11, 1933; s. James Tolivar and Etta (Keltner) G.; B.S. in Geology, U. Houston, 1956; m. Juanita Hartwell, Sept. 22, 1956; children— Clark Hartwell, Matthew Keltner. Geophysicist Teldyne Exploration, Houston, 1956-63, Union Oil Co. California, Houston, 1963-66; mgr. geophys. services Control Data Corp., Houston, 1966-69; mgr. operations and sales Dresser Olympic, Houston, 1969—. Mem. Soc. Exploration Geophysicists, European Assn. Exploration Geophysicists, Geophys. Soc. Houston (sec. 1971-72), Kappa Alpha (pres. 1955). Republican. Methodist. Mason. Home: 8910 Bintliff St Houston TX 77036 Office: PO Box 1407 Houston TX 77001

GRIGSBY, ROBERT LEE, JR., tech. coll. pres.; b. Saluda, S.C., Jan. 25, 1924; s. Robert Lee and Juell (Gregory) G.; B.S., Clemson Coll., 1947; M.S., N.C. State Coll., 1952; m. Hilda Mae Page, May 27, 1946; 1 son, Robert Lee III. Part-time grocery clk., farmer, Saluda, 1937-41; tchr. Gilbert (S.C.) Schs., 1947-51; tchr., asst. prin. Irmo (S.C.) Pub. Sch., 1952-56; mfg. supr. Gen. Electric Co., Irmo, 1956-61; exec. dir. Midlands Tech. Edn. Center, Columbia, 1962—. Mem. Lexington County Bd. Edn., 1963—, sec., 1963—. Chmn., dir. Irmo Youth Center, 1952—. Served with AUS, 1942-45. Decorated Purple Heart. Mem. Am. Vocation Assn., Am. Soc. Engring. Edn. (sec, 1967-69, vice chmn, 1969-71), Am. Vocation Assn., C. of C., Phi Kappa Phi, Kappa Phi Kappa, Am. Assn. Jr. Colls., Am. Tech. Edn. Assn., Internat. Platform Assn., Am. Legion. Methodist. Home: Route 2 Box 420 Columbia SC 29210 Office: 316 Beltline Blvd Columbia SC 29205

GRIGSBY, SHAW EARL, sociologist, educator; b. Winnfield, La., Sept. 4, 1912; s. Reid Earl and Berta Lee (Shaw) G.; B.S., La. State U., 1935, M.S., 1937; Ph.D., Cornell U., 1942; postgrad. Harvard, summer 1943; m. Sigrid Charlotte Werner, May 30, 1952; children—Susan Elizabeth, Shaw Earl. Asst. supr. rural research WPA, La., 1937-39; social sci. analyst Bur. Agrl. Econs., U.S. Dept. Agr., Washington, 1942-43, 46-49; cons. Social Sci. Offices, Mil. Govt., Dept. Army. Frankfurt, Germany, 1949-50; social economist fgn. service Dept. State, also dir. Inst. Social Sci. Research, Darmstadt, Germany, 1951-52; prof. sociology U. Fla., Gainesville, 1953—. Cons., Fla. Probation and Parole Assns., So. Conf. Corrections, Fla. Council Crime and Delinquency, Fla. Conf. Social Welfare, Fla. Alcoholic Rehab. Program, U. Fla. Peace Corps Tng. Program, U. Fla./AID, Costa Rica, Colombia; pres. Research Assos., Gainesville, 1947-59. Bd. dirs. Fla. Tb and Health Assn. Served with USNR, 1943-46. Recipient Outstanding Faculty Adviser award Delta Sigma Phi, 1962, Merit Exhibit award Nat. Tb. Assn., 1963. Mem. Frat. Faculty Advisers Assn. (pres. 1961), Am., So. sociol. assns., Am. Soc. Criminology, Am. Assn. U. Profs., Applied Anthropology, Am. Personnel and Guidance Assn., Fla. Blue Key, Alpha Delta Kappa, Kappa Sigma, Omicron Delta Kappa, Alpha Phi Omega, Gamma Sigma Delta. Home: 4890 NW 20th Pl Gainesville FL 32601

GRIMBALL, BERKELEY, headmaster; b. Charleston, S.C., Nov. 25, 1922; s. Berkeley and Anne (Strohecker) G.; B.A., U. of South, 1943, D.C.L., 1969; M.A., Duke U., 1951; m. Emily-Lawton Kirkland, June 25, 1949; children—Berkeley Lawton, Meta Morris. Owner, headmaster Gaud Sch. for Boys, 1948-63, headmaster, Porter-Gaud Sch., 1963—. Mem. Charleston Playground Commn., 1962-69; trustee Charleston Library Soc., U. of South. Served with AUS, 1943-45. Mem. Nat. Assn. Episcopal Schs. (governing bd. 1971—), St. Cecilia Soc. Episcopalian. Clubs: Rotary, Carolina Yacht. Home: 205 Albermarle Rd Charleston SC 29407

GRIMBALL, WILLIAM H., lawyer; b. Charleston, S.C., Feb. 6, 1917; A.B., Coll. Charleston, 1938; LL.B., U. Va., 1941. Admitted to S.C. bar, 1941; now mem. firm Grimball & Cabaniss, Charleston. Mem. S.C. Ho. of Reps., 1953-58, chmn. Charleston County dels., 1956-58; alderman, Charleston, 1960—, mayor pro tem, 1969. Served to lt. comdr. USNR, 1942-45. Fellow Am. Coll. Trial Lawyers; mem. Charleston County (pres. 1968-69), S.C., Am. bar assns., Coll. Charleston Alumni Assn. (pres. 1953), Order Coif, Phi Alpha Delta. Address: Grimball & Cabaniss 39 Broad St Charleston SC 29402*

GRIMES, CECIL CLAYMON, JR., lawyer, state senator; b. Greenville, Miss., July 23, 1922; s. Cecil C. and Sadie (Ehlers) G.; A.B., U. S.C., 1946, LL.B., 1947; m. Harriet Horry Pyatt, Oct. 4, 1947; children— Harriet Pyatt, Cecil C. III, John Pyatt. Admitted to S.C. bar, 1947; practiced in Georgetown, S.C., 1947—; sr. mem. firm Grimes & Hinds, 1965—; mem. S.C. Ho. of Reps., 1959-62, S.C. Senate, 1962—. Dir. First Fed. Savs. & Loan Assn. of Georgetown. Mem. adv. bd. Brookgreen Gardens. Served with USAAF, 1943-46; PTO. Decorated Air medal with three oak leaf clusters, D.F.C. Mem. Am., S.C. bar assns., Hist. Soc., Pi Kappa Phi. Rotarian, Mason. Clubs: Palmetto, Cotillion, Georgetown Country. Home: 421 Prince St Georgetown SC 29440 Office: 604 Front St Georgetown SC 29440

GRIMES, JUNIUS DANIEL, editor; b. Durham, N.C., May 14, 1940; s. Junius Daniel and Lily Stanfield (Grist) G.; A.B., E. Carolina U., 1963; M.A., (Woodrow Wilson fellow), U. N.C., 1969, postgrad. 1968—; m. Johanna McKevlin, Nov. 21, 1965; 1 dau., Elizabeth. Entertainment editor, asst. Sunday feature editor News and Observer Pub. Co., Raleigh, N.C., 1963-65; dir. publs. Franklin and Marshall Coll., Lancaster, Pa., 1966-68; editor Carolina Quar. Colonial Press, Chapel Hill, 1970—. Pub. relations cons. N.C. Cancer Soc., 1964-65; graphics and pub. relations cons. U. N.C., 1968—. Editor, N.C. Gov.'s Commn. Emotionally Disturbed Children, 1969. Recipient spl. award for outstanding contbn. to pub. understanding of ednl. problems Edn. Writers Assn., 1967. Mem. Am. Coll. Pub. Relations Assn., Am. Alumni Council, Edn. Writers Assn., Modern Lang. Assn. Home: 500 Long Leaf Dr Chapel Hill NC 27514 Office: Box 1117 Chapel Hill NC 27514

GRIMLAND, JOHN MARTIN, JR., accountant, orgn. ofcl.; b. Clifton, Tex., May 11, 1917; s. John Martin and Mayme (Gollihar) G.; B.S. in Commerce, Tex. Christian U., 1939; m. Phyllis Montgomery, Nov. 1, 1947; children—Diane, Donna Jean, Norma Gayle. With Universal C.I.T. Corp., 1940-42, Internal Revenue Service, 1946-47; pub. accountant, Midland, Tex., 1947-51, C.P.A., 1951—; partner Main Lafrentz & Co., 1968—. Mem. Optimist Internat., 1949—, gov. Dist. 7, 1957-58, v.p., 1958-59, chmn. pub. relations com., 1959-62, internat. pres., 1962-63, chmn. internat. community service com., 1966-69; treas. High Sky Girls Ranch, 1961-62; treas. Midland Symphony Assn., 1960-62, pres. 1963-65; pres. Midland United Fund, 1969, Indsl. Found. of Midland, 1971—. Served to lt. USNR, World War II. C.P.A., Tex. Mem. Am. Inst. C.P.A.'s, Tex. Christian U. Alumni Assn. (pres. 1965-66), Midland C. of C. (pres. 1970). Methodist (chmn. bd. 1961-62). Home: 1605 Country Club Dr Midland TX 79701 Office: Gihls Tower East Midland TX 79701

GRINER, ELSIE HIGGS, JR., journalist, entertainer; b. Nashville, Ga., July 15, 1932; d. George and Elsie (Higgs) Griner; student pub. schs., Nashville; m. Hugh D. Alderman, July 20, 1952 (div.); 1 dau., Pandora Dee. Gospel concert singer, song writer Hill & Range, Inc., N.Y.C., 1955-61; recorded with RCA Victor, 1955-61; editor-pub. Nashville (Ga.) Herald, 1962-66; polit. satirist, recording with Lowery Music, Atlanta, 1966—. Mem. Fulton County Democratic Exec. Com., 1970—. Recipient Salvation Army awards, 1964, 66; named Georgia's First Weekly Editorial Columnist, Ga. Press Assn., 1964, 66. Mem. Mensa.Home: 1315 Fairview Rd NE Atlanta GA 30306 Office: 310 Ponce de Leon Av NE Atlanta GA 30383

GRINER, JOHN F., labor union ofcl.; b. Camilla, Ga., Aug. 7, 1907; s. Will and Dollier (Shiver) G.; LL.B., Columbus U., Washington; m. Claranell Nicholson, Nov. 27, 1936; children—John F., Remer Will. With various railroads, 1925-36; adjudicator, liaison officer, labor relations officer U.S. Railroad Retirement Bd., 1936-62; nat. pres. Am. Fedn. Govt. Employees, 1962—. Mem. Order R.R. Telegraphers, Am. Train Dispatchers Assn.; hon. mem. Brotherhood R.R. Trainmen, R.R. Yardmasters Am., Brotherhood R.R. Signalmen. Democrat. Baptist. Mason (Shriner). Home: 10225 Kensington Pkwy Kensington MD Office: 400 1st St NW Washington DC

GRISCOM, RICHARD WILLIAM, scientist; b. Chattanooga, Apr. 15, 1926; s. Frank Norris and Mary Amanda (Kelly) G.; B.S., U. Chattanooga, 1945; M.S., U. Tenn., 1948; m. Mary Elizabeth Line, Dec. 27, 1953; children—Richard William, Daniel Clarence, Grace Elizabeth. Chemist, Monsanto Chem. Co., Anniston, Ala., 1948-49; research chemist Tenn. Products and Chems., Chattanooga, 1949-64; sr. scientist Chemetron Corp., Newport, Tenn., 1964—. Mem. Am. Chem. Soc., Soc. Animal Sci., Morristown Art Assn. (pres. 1969-70), Alpha Chi Sigma. Presbyn. (deacon 1965—). Patentee in field. Home: 1883 Hugh Dr Morristown TN 37814 Office: Rock Hill Lab Route 4 Newport TN 37821

GRISET, HENRY EDWIN, civil engr.; b. Bklyn., Feb. 24, 1912; s. Gustavus B. and Veronica (Mock) G.; B.S. in Civil Engring., N.Y.U., 1934; M.C.E., Bklyn. Poly. Inst., 1945; m. Iona Jacobi, Mar. 13, 1931; children—Arlene (Mrs. Clinton Waynick), Bruce Henry, Kurt Barron; m. 2d, Ursula Williams, Dec. 29, 1967. Asst. engr. Henry I. Mock, Contractor, Bklyn., 1932-35, N.Y.C. Park Dept., 1935-36; surveyman U.S. Army Engrs., 1936-37; structural engr., appraiser Mortgage Corp. of N.Y., N.Y.C., 1937-40; stress analyst Republic Aviation Corp., Farmingdale, N.Y., 1940-41; structural engr. J. G. White Engring. Corp., N.Y.C., 1941-42; instr. Bklyn. Poly. Inst., 1941-43. Coll. City N.Y., 1943-44; asst. prof. Sch. Civil Engring. Cornell U., 1944-47; part time appraiser Equitable Life Assurance Soc. of U.S., 1944-47; asso. prof. N.C. State Coll., Raleigh, 1947-52, prof. in charge constrn. curriculum, 1950-52; owner Allied Engring. Services, Raleigh, N.C., 1952—. Registered profl. engr. N.Y., N.C., Fla. Mem. Am. Soc. C.E., Am. Concrete Inst., Internat. Assn. Bridge and Structural Engrs., Am. Soc. for Engring. Edn., Nat. Soc. Profl. Engrs., Cornell Soc. Engrs., N.Y. Acad. Scis., N.C. Assn. Professions, N.Y. Acad. Scis., Beta Theta Pi, Tau Beta Pi, Chi Epsilon. Home: 1623 Dixie Trail Raleigh NC 27607 Office: PO Box 10532 Raleigh NC 27605

GRISHAM, FRANK PHILLIPS, educator; b. Birmingham, Ala., Aug. 28, 1928; s. James Ernest and Evie Elizabeth (Phillips) G.; A.B., Birmingham So. Coll., 1949; B.D., Vanderbilt U., 1952; M.L.S., George Peabody Coll., 1958; m. Louise Fly, Sept. 23, 1950; children—Elizabeth, Phillip, David, Brian. Dir. religious life Birmingham So. Coll., 1954-56; divinity librarian, asso. prof. Vanderbilt U., Nashville, 1956-64, asst. dir. libraries, asso. prof., 1965-67, asso. dir., asso. prof., 1967-68, dir. libraries, asso. prof., 1968—. Ordained minister North Ala. Conf. The Meth. Ch., 1949—. Vice chmn. Met. Nashville Davidson County Bd. Edn., 1964—. Mem. Am., Tenn., Southeastern library assns., Am. Sch. Bds. Assn., Tenn. Sch. Bds. Assn. Rotarian. Home: 5332 Anchorage Dr Nashville TN 37220 Office: Joint University Libraries Nashville TN 37203

GRISMER, RAYMOND LEONARD, educator, author; b. Schenectady, N.Y., Mar. 30, 1895; s. Charles Valentine and Luna M. (Leonard) G.; A.B., U. Vt., 1916; Rhodes Scholar, Oxford U., Eng., 1916-17; M.A., Ohio State U., 1922; Ph.D., U. Cal., 1930; m. Mildred Best, Aug. 20, 1919; children—Jean, Raymond, William. Tchr., Mercersburg Acad., Pa., 1917-18, The Hill Sch., Pottstown, Pa., 1919-20; instr. romance langs. Ohio State U., 1920-24; head modern lang. dept. Oklahoma City U., 1924-27; asso. Spanish, U. Cal., 1927-31; asst. prof. U. Minn., 1931-34, asso. prof. 1934-49, prof. romance langs., 1949-66, prof. emeritus Romance langs., 1966—. Served with O.T.S., Brit. Army, Oxford, Eng., 1917; lt. inf. O.T.C., U.S. Army, Camp Gordon, Ga., 1917-18; capt. arty. Okla. N.G., Ft. Sill, 1925-27. Mem. Am. Assn. Tchrs. Spanish, Modern Lang. Assn. Am., Phi Beta Kappa, Tau Kappa Epsilon. Author: Pageant of Spain (with D.K. Arjona), 1939; Reference Index to Twelve Thousand Spanish-American Authors, 1939; Sailing the Spanish Main, 1940; New Bibliography of the Literatures of Spain and Spanish America (with M.B. Grismer, J. Magraw; 7 vols.), 1941-46; A Brief Spanish Grammar for Beginners, 1942; Spanish Short Stores (with R.H. Olmsted), 1943; Buenos Vecinos, Buenos Amigos (with C.I. Arroyo), 1943; Short Spanish Review Grammar (with D.K. Ariona), 1943; Tales of Spanish America (with N.R. Adams), 1944; Influence of Plautus in Spain Before Lope de Vega, 1944; Easy Spanish-American Reader (with M.W. Molinos, E.D. Corbett), 1945; Elementary Spanish Conversation (with L. C. Keating), 1946; Cervantes: A Bibliography, Vol I, 1946, Vol. II, 1963; Liberatadores y Defensores (with Roy and Margarita Mills), 1953; Bibliography of Lope de Vega, Vols. I and II, 1964-65; Bibliography of the Drama of Spain and Spanish America, Vols. I and II, 1967; and others. Contbr. articles jours. Home: Town Apts South 101 1847 Shore Dr South Pasadena FL 33707

GRISSETT, WALLACE EDWARD, JR., lawyer; b. Clearwater, Fla., Apr. 24, 1926; s. Wallace Edward and Grace (Clark) G.; student Jacksonville U., 1946-47; B.A., Stetson U., 1950, LL.B., 1953; m. Bonnie Tapley, Apr. 14, 1962; children—David Arthur, Stephen Edward Parks, Elizabeth Helen. Admitted to Fla. bar, 1953; practiced in Green Cove Springs, Fla., 1953-55, Jacksonville, 1957—; mem. firm Scott & Cox, 1957-60, Cox, Grissett & Webb, 1960-66, W. E. Grissett, Jr., 1966-69, Grissett, Humphries & Danese, 1969-70, Grissett and Humphries, 1970—; adjuster State Farm Mut. Auto Ins. Co., Tallahassee, 1955-56. Vice chmn. Local Govt. Study Commn. of Duval County, 1965-67; Mem. City Council Consol. City Jacksonville, 1968-71, pres., 1968-69; mem. Fla. Law Revision Commn., 1968—. Bd. dirs. Gateway Girl Scout Council, 1966-72, Jacksonville Symphony Assn., 1968—, Gator Bowl Assn., 1968-70. Served with USNR, 1944-46. Mem. Am., Jacksonville (pres. 1970) bar assns., Fedn. Ins. Counsel, Internat. Assn. Ins. Counsel, Am. Judicature Soc., Maritime Law Assn. U.S., Nat. Assn. R.R. Trial Counsel, Inter-Am. Bar Assn., Fla. Bar (bd. gov. 1964-68), Jacksonville U. Alumni Assn. (pres. 1959), Omicron Delta Kappa, Phi Alpha Delta, Sigma Nu. Home: 5720 Cherry Laurel Dr Jacksonville FL 32210 Office: 231 E Forsyth St Jacksonville FL 32202

GRISSO, JOHN K., U.S. atty. Dist. atty. for S.C., Columbia. Address: Office Dist Atty Columbia SC 29202*

GRISSOM, EUGENE EDWARD, educator; b. Melvern, Kan., May 15, 1922; s. Edwin Hobart and Elizabeth Alma (Sattler) G.; B.S. in Music and Art, Emporia (Kan.) State Tchrs. Coll., 1958; M.F.A., State U. Ia., 1951; children—(by previous marriage)—Jon F., Joni F.; m. 2d, Dec. 9, 1961. Faculty dept. art U. Ky., Lexington, 1951-53; faculty dept. art U. Fla., Gainesville, 1953—, now prof., chmn. dept. Served with AUS, 1943-46. Mem. Phi Mu Alpha Sinfonia (life), Phi Delta Chi. Home: 4607 Clear Lake Dr Gainesville FL 32601

GRISSOM, TERRY HAMILTON, wholesale food chain exec.; b. Glasgow, Ky., June 7, 1918; s. Robert Hamilton and Verla Jewell (Oliver) G.; grad. high sch.; m. Willa Belle Penn, Dec. 20, 1936; 1 son, Robert Hamilton. Store mgr. Glass Food Stores, chain store, Lexington, Ky., 1934-41; with Nat. Life and Accident Ins. Co.,

Lexington, 1941-42; dist. mgr. Libby, McNeill & Libby, food mfrs., Lexington, 1946-50, Indpls., 1949-50; with Cupples Co., brokers, Lexington, 1950-52; with W.T. Sistrunk & Co., wholesale retail food voluntary chain, Lexington, 1952—, v.p. marketing, 1960—. Cons. food industry activities. Sales contest judge, cons. Jr. Achievement, 1966-71; sales and marketing judge Distributive Edn. Clubs Am., 1970. Served with USCGR, 1942-45. Recipient Most Valuable Member award Lexington Salesmen's Club, 1957. Mem. Nat. Am. Wholesale Grocers Assn. (bd. govs. 1966-68), Nat. Sales Mgmt. Task Force, Nat. Advt. Adv. Council. Mason (Shriner). Clubs: Lexington Salesmen's (pres. 1954, 65), Bluegrass Sales and Marketing Executives, Optimist (sec. Lexington 1971-73). Home: 707 Pasadena Dr Lexington KY 40503 Office: 2155 Young Dr PO Box 1020 Lexington KY 40501

GRISWOLD, MRS. L., society editor New Orleans States-Item. Address: 3800 Howard Av New Orleans LA 70140*

GRITZ, JACK LINTON, clergyman, editor; b. Okmulgee, Olka., Dec. 31, 1916; s. Harry Vernon and Katie (Houston) G.; student Phillips U., 1935-37; A.B., Okla. Bapt. U., 1939; Th.M., Southwestern Bapt. Theol. Sem., 1942; Th.D., So. Sem., Louisville, 1947; m. Veva Chloe Hammack, June 29, 1947; 1 son, Paul Linton. Asso. sec. dept. religious edn. Bapt. Gen. Conv. Okla., 1944-47; pastor First Bapt. Ch., Tahlequah, Okla., 1947-49; editor Bapt. Messenger, Oklahoma City, 1949—. Mem. So. Bapt. Press Assn. (pres. 1968-69). Home: 1419 N Drexel St Oklahoma City OK 73107 Office: 1141 N Robinson Oklahoma City OK 73103

GRIVET, PAUL EDWARD, electronics engr.; b. St. Louis, Oct. 13, 1906; s. Edward Francis and Etta Pearl (Davis) G.; B.S. in Elec. Engring., Washington U., St. Louis, 1931. Various positions teaching elec., electronic maintenance, 1931-42; elec. engr. CAA, 1947-53, Patchen & Zimmerman, 1953-54; electronics engr. Army Missile Command, Redstone Arsenal, Ala., 1954—. Served with Signal Corps, USAAF, 1942-47; maj. Res. ret. Registered prof. engr., Ala. Mem. I.E.E.E., Nat. Soc. Profl. Engrs. Home: 407 Green Acres Dr Huntsville AL 35805 Office: Army Missile Command Bldg 5400 Redstone Arsenal AL 35809

GROAH, WILLIAM JENNINGS, JR., assn. exec.; b. Harrisonburg, Va., May 28, 1931; s. William Jennings and Jean Stuart (Nicholas) G.; B.S., Va. Poly. Inst., 1955; M.S. in Wood Technology, N.C. State U., 1956; m. Helen Virginia Gibbs, Dec. 17, 1960; children—William Michael, Suzanne Lynn. Lab. mgr. Hardwood Plywood Mfrs. Assn., Arlington, Va., tech. dir., 1970—. Served with USNR, 1956-57. Mem. Am. Soc. for Testing and Materials Forest Products Research Soc., Soc. of Wood Sci. and Tech. Xi Sigma Pi, Phi Sigma. Home: 11233 S Shore Rd Reston VA 22070 Office: 2310 S Walter Reed Dr Arlington VA 22206

GROGAN, HIRAM JOHN, lawyer, probation officer; b. Ball Ground, Ga., Aug. 21, 1925; s. Paul and Lila (Stamper) G.; student Oglethorpe U., 1942-43, Ga. So. Coll., 1946; A.B. cum laude, Piedmont Coll., 1948; M.Ed., U. Ga., 1949, Ed. S., 1972; J.D., Woodrow Wilson Coll., 1958; m. Ruth Carney, Oct. 2, 1948. Tchr., prin. Etowah Sch., Cherokee County, Ga., 1950-51; tchr., coach Blackwell Sch., Cobb County, Ga., 1951-52; accountant Ga. Hwy. Dept., Atlanta, 1952-56; chief probation officer, Marietta, Ga., 1956-69, area probation supr., 1969—; admitted to Ga. bar, 1958; since practiced in Marietta. Part-time instr. sociology Marietta Center, U. Ga., 1964. Apptd. lt. col. gov.'s staff, 1967. Served with USNR, 1944-46. Mem. Am., Ga., Cobb bar assns., Nat. Council on Crime and Delinquency, Ga. Probation and Parole Assn., So. States Corrections Assn. Clubs: Civitan, Marietta Art. Author: Modern Bow Hunting, 1958; also monographs numerous articles in profl. jours., mags. Home: 606 Lee St Smyrna GA 30080 Office: Jud Bldg Marietta GA 30060

GRONER, FRANK S(HELBY), hosp. adminstr.; b. Stamford, Tex., Sept. 25, 1911; s. Frank S. and Laura (Wyatt) G.; B.A., Baylor U., 1934; LL.D., Tex. Bapt. Coll., 1946, Union U., 1952, Baylor U., 1969;; m. Daisy Amanda McFearin, Dec. 12, 1936. Dean sch. bus. Coll. of Marshall (Tex.), 1934-36; asst. adminstr. So. Bapt. Hosp., New Orleans, 1936-43, adminstr., 1943-46; adminstr. Bapt. Meml. Hosp., Memphis, 1946—. Cons. USPHS; cons. Div. Hosp. and Med. Facilities, also Bur. Family Services on Med. Matters, U.S. Dept. Health, Edn. and Welfare; exec. dir. Health, Edn. and Research Found. Mem. Surgeon Gen.'s adv. com. on Nat. Health Survey. Bd. govs., exec. com. Blue Cross; bd. dirs. A.R.C., Am. Cancer Soc. Memphis Community Chest. Dollar-a-Year Man, Washington, 1942-45. Recipient Justin Ford Kimball award, 1964, Distinguished service award Am. Hosp. Assn., 1966, Memphis and Shelby County Med. Soc. Distinguished Service award, 1967, gold medal Am. Coll. Hosp. Adminstrs., 1968. Mem. Am. (pres. chmn. council hosp. planning and plant operation, chmn. hosp. architects qualifications, trustee, past pres.) La (past pres.), Tenn. (past pres,) hosp. assns., Southeastern Hosp. Conf. (past pres.), Southwide Bapt. Hosp. Assn. (past pres.), So. Inst. Hosp. Adminstrs. (dir.), Am. Coll. Hosp. Administrs. (pres., dir.), Internat. Hosp. Fedn. (del.) Baptist. Home: 649 Sweetbriar Rd Memphis TN 38117 Office: 899 Madison Av Memphis TN 38103

GRONER, PAT NEFF, hosp. adminstr.; b. Dallas, Dec. 21, 1920; s. Frank Shelby and Laura (Wyatt) G.; A.B., Baylor U., 1941; m. Louise Mary Rugg, May 5, 1944; children—Josephine Louise, Frank Shelby III. Pilot, Colonial Airlines (now Eastern Airlines), N.Y.C., 1946-47; asst. adminstr. Mary Fletcher Hosp., Burlington, Vt., 1947-48; adminstr. Barre (Vt.) City Hosp., 1948-50; adminstr. Baptist Hosp., Pensacola, Fla., 1950-67, exec. dir., 1967—. Dir. Mutual Fed. Savs. & Loan Assn. Pres. Hosp. Research and Devel. Inst.; exec. com. Blue Cross of Fla.; bd. dirs. U. W. Fla. Found. Served with USNR, 1941-42; USMC, 1942-45. Recipient Liberty Bell award Soc. Bar for 1st Jud. Circuit State of Fla., Good Govt. award Pensacola Jr. C. of C., award of merit Fla. Hosp. Edn. and Research Found. Fellow Am. Coll. Hosp. Adminstrs. (bd. regents 1966-70); mem. Am. (trustee 1967-70), Fla. (past pres.), Southeastern (past pres.), hosp. assns. Rotarian (pres. 1966-67). Home: 3420 Dunwody Dr Pensacola FL 32503 Office: 1000 W Moreno St Pensacola FL 32501

GRONLUND, ROBERT BERNARD, univ. exec.; b. Duluth, Minn., May 2, 1926; s. Bernard and Lena J. (Manske) G.; student Ia. State Coll., 1943-44, Duluth Jr. Coll., 1944-47; U. Minn., 1946-47; B.A., Wartburg Coll., 1949; B.D., Wartburg Sem., 1953; postgrad. U. So. Cal., 1954-59; m. Dorothy M. Dahlstrom, June 2, 1951; children—Gaye, Robin, Gregg, Jamie. Ordained to ministry Luth. Ch., 1953; pastor Newport Harbor Luth. Ch., Newport, Cal., 1953-56; campus pastor Los Angeles City Coll., 1956-59; asst. to pres. Cal. Luth. Coll., Thousand Oaks, 1959-62; exec. dir. Am. Luth. Ch. Found., Mpls., 1962-63; v.p. devel. and pub. relations Capital U., Columbus, O., 1963-69, U. Tampa (Fla.), 1969—. Cons. fund raising and pub. relations to colls. and other charitable orgns.; lectr. various colls., Sec., treas. Tampa Bay Art Center, 1970-71, pres., 1971-72. Regent Augustana Acad., 1968-71. Served with AUS, 1944-46. Decorated Bronze Star. Mem. Am. Pub. Relations Assn., Pub. Relations Soc. Am. (chpt. v.p. 1972). Republican. Rotarian. Clubs: University. Yacht and Country (Tampa). Contbr. articles to mags. Home: 2808 Samara Dr Tampa FL 33618

GROOM, THEODORE RICHARD, lawyer; b. Wichita, Kan., June 14, 1934; s. John Fuller and Carrie (Leggitt) G.; A.B., Bucknell U., 1956; LL.B., cum laude, Harvard, 1960; m. Virginia Woodard Miller, June 19, 1956; children—Catherine Martin, John Fuller, Theodore Warren. Admitted to Va. bar, 1960, D.C. bar, 1961; law clk. to chief judge U.S. Dist. Ct., Balt., Md., 1960-61; asso. firm Hedrick & Lane, Washington, 1961-67, mem., 1968—. Chmn., Citizens Police Com., Arlington, 1966; vice chmn. legislation com. Adminstrn. Justice, Washington, 1967-70; chmn. Arlington Fiscal Affairs Adv. Com., 1971, Criminal Justice Adv. Com., 1971, Arlington Criminal Justice Adv. Commn., 1972. Bd. dirs., finance chmn. Alcoholic Rehab., Inc., Arlington, 1966-69; chmn. Arlington Health and Welfare Council, 1969-70, No. Va. Recreation Authority, 1969-71; mem. Arlington Task Force on Drug Abuse. Finance chmn. various individual polit. campaigns, 1967. Served from lt. to capt., AUS, 1956-57, 60-61. Mem. Am. Va., D.C. bar assns., Phi Gamma Delta, Phi Sigma Alpha. Methodist (dir.). Contbr. articles to legal publs. Home: 4901 N 35th Rd Arlington VA 22207 Office: 1001 Connecticut Av Washington DC 20036

GROOMS, HARLAN HOBART, dist. judge; b. Jeffersonville, Ky., Nov. 7, 1900; LL.B., U. Ky.; m. Angeline M. Grooms; children—Harlan Hobart, Ellen Elizabeth, John Franklin, Angeline. Admitted to Ky. and Ala. bars; practiced in Birmingham, Ala., 1926—; former mem. Spain, Gillon, Grooms & Young; U.S. dist. judge, No. Dist. of Ala., 1953—. Trustee Samford U., Birmingham Baptist Hosp. Mem. Am. Bar Assn., Ala. State Bar, Phi Alpha Delta, Omicron Delta Kappa, Pi Kappa Alpha. Baptist. Club: Civitan. Home: 2625 Crest Rd Birmingham AL 35223 Office: Box 34 Birmingham AL 35221

GROSECLOSE, FRANK SNIDER, stock broker; b. Houston, June 4, 1935; s. Frank Edwin and Katherine (Snider) G.; B.B.A., So. Meth. U., 1956; m. Carol Jean Conkle, July 14, 1964; children—Laura Jean, Christine Michelle. Trader, mgr. underwriting dept. E.F. Hutton & Co., Dallas, 1958-65; v.p., mgr. Godnick & Son, Inc., Dallas, 1965-71, Filer, Schmidt & Co., Dallas, 1971—; tchr. corporate seminars. Served with USAF, 1958-64. Mem. Dallas Assn. Security Dealers (pres. 1972), Delta Sigma Pi, Sigma Alpha Epsilon. Home: 3409 Centenary St Dallas TX 75225 Office: First National Bank Bldg Dallas TX 75202

GROSS, HARRY W., educator; b. East Berlin, Pa., Mar. 9, 1896; student West Chester State Normal Sch., 1915-17; B.S., N.Y. U., 1929; M.A., Columbia, 1933; m. Alfarata M. Dilks, June 18, 1921; children— Robert Wilbert, Vera Miriam (Mrs. Schenk). Prin. elementary sch., Greenport, N.Y., 1924-24; prin. Central High Sch., Valley Stream, N.Y., 1924-41; dist. supt. schs., Sole Supervisory Dist., Nassau County, N.Y., 1941-67. Cons. on narcotic edn. to suprs., Hempstead, N.Y.; Mem. adv. council C.W. Post Coll., Brookville, N.Y. Trustee L.I. Ednl. Television Council. Served to maj. U.S. Army, World Wars I and II. Recipient Hofstra U. award for significant contbns. to edn. on L.I., 1967. Mem. Nat. Assn. County and Intermediate Supts. Schs. (past pres.), N.Y. State Dist. Supts. Schs. (past pres.) N.Y. State Ret. Tchrs. Assn. pres. L.I. Zone 1968), L.I. Agrl. Soc. (dir.). Home: 6015 19th St N St Petersburg FL 33714

GROSS, JOHN ARTHUR, architect; b. N.Y.C., Oct. 13, 1937; s. Oliver Twist and Katherin Virginia (Boyle) G.; B.Arch., Okla. State U., 1963; m. Montgomery Louise Hopper, June 1, 1971. Design architect Leo A. Daly Co., Omaha, Neb., 1963-65, James O. Marshall, Lawton, Okla., 1965-66; pvt. practice architecture, McAlester, Okla., 1967—. Archtl. adviser Model Cities of McAlester, 1969-71; archtl. works include McAlester Pub. Library, Howard Smith Ford Showroom. Mem. A.I.A., Democrat. Episcopalian. Lion. Home: 317 E Adams St McAlester OK 74501

GROSS, JOHN C(HARLES), broker, industrialist; b. N.Y.C., Apr. 2, 1904; s. Edward H. and Anna Catharine (Muelhaus) G.; student pub. schs. N.Y.C.; m. Helen Victoria Newman, Sept. 26, 1926; 1 dau., Jean Anne. Pres., treas., dir. John C. Gross, Inc.; treas., dir. Gen. Automation of Del., Gen. Automation of Fla.; pres., treas., dir. Yacht Club Island. Corp.; pres., treas. Ponce de Leon Corp., Artifacts Recovery Corp. reorganized, merged various companies. Mem. Com. of 100 of New Smyrna Beach; mem. Edgewater (Fla.) Planning Bd.; chmn. S.E. Volusia Area Devel. Council. Mem. Nat. Assn. Security Dealers, New Smyrna Beach C. of C. Lutheran (council). Rotarian. Home: 404 N Riverside Dr Edgewater FL 32032 Office: 316 Canal St New Smyrna Beach FL 32069

GROSS, JOHN HENRY, physician; b. Fairy Hill, Can., Nov. 18, 1910; came to U.S. 1949, naturalized 1954; s. Phillip and Eva (Armbruster) G.; B.S., U. Sask., 1935; M.D., U. Man., Winnipeg, 1940; m. Margaret MacDonald, July 31, 1937 (dec. Sept. 1969); 1 son, David Ian, m. 2d, Jimmie N. Gunter, Nov. 26, 1970. Staff physician Sask. Anti-TB League, Fort San, Sask., 1940-49; resident Matson Meml. Hosp., Milwaukie, Ore., 1948; staff physician and asst. chief Battey State Hosp., Rome, Ga., 1949-57, chief of all white treatment wards and asst. to supt., 1957-64, dir. outpatient services dept., co-ordinator med. services, 1964-70, clin. dir. div. Tb Control Service Tb Br. State Ga., 1970-71. Charter mem. bd. dirs. Boy's Club of Rome. Served as maj. M.C., AUS, 1950-52; lt. col. Res. Licentiate Med. Council Canada. Fellow Am. Coll. Chest Physicians; mem. Am. Thoracic Soc. (past pres. Ga. chpt.), Coll. Physicians and Surgeons of Sask., Am., Ga. med. assns., Floyd County Med. Soc. Contbr. articles to profl. jours. Home: 10 Elizabeth St Rome GA 30161

GROSSBART, EMILE LEO, indsl. exec.; b. Memphis, Oct. 24, 1914; s. Jacob J. and Pearl (Bluestein) G.; student pub. schs.; m. Zelda Getsin, May 16, 1968; children—Richard Martin Lebovitz, Dale Lebovitz (Mrs. Royal D. Zell), Paul Allen Lebovitz, Gail E. (Mrs. Terry R. Scharf). Owner, So. Wiping Cloth Co., Memphis, 1941—; pres. Mechanics Laundry Service, Memphis, 1968—. Pres., Leo N. Levi Nat. Arthritis Hosp., Hot Springs, Ark. Bd. dirs. B'nai B'rith Home & Hosp. for Aged. Mem. Nat. Assn. Wiping Cloth Mfrs. (pres. 1957-59), Sales Exec. Club (pres. 1967), Pi Sigma Epsilon. Jewish religion. Mason (32 deg., Shriner); B'nai B'rith (pres. 1962). Home: 5419 Gwynne Rd Memphis TN 38117 Office: 352 N Front St Memphis TN 38103

GROSSEL-ROSSI, MARION NICHOLAS, lawyer; b. New Orleans, June 22, 1931; s. Arthur and Helen G. (Troyanovich) G-R; B.S., Tulane U., 1955, LL.B., 1962. Geologist, Forest Oil Corp., Lafayette, La., 1955-59; admitted to La. bar, 1962; with firm Jackson & Hess, New Orleans, 1962-63; partner firm Leach & Grossel-Rossi, New Orleans, 1963-68, Leach, Grossel-Rossi & Paysse, 1968—; sec.-treas. Elisan Corp., New Orleans. Bd. govs. Southeastern Admiralty Law Inst. Mem. Am., La. bar assns., Maritime Law Assn. U.S., Am. Judicature Soc., New Orleans Assn. Def. Counsel, La. Hist. Soc., Upper Audubon Assn. (pres. 1971-72), Audubon Soc., Nat. Rifle Assn., Internat. Oceanographic Found., La. Bromeliad Soc., Def. Research Inst., Am. Arbitration Assn. (panel arbitrators), La. Assn. Def. Counsel. Clubs: Essex, Sports Car of America (pres. Delta region 1965), South Louisiana Gun, Delta Rifle and Pistol. Home: 282 Audubon St New Orleans LA 70118 Office: 1 Shell Sq New Orleans LA 70130

GROSSER, ELMER JOSEPH, ednl. adminstr.; b. Dayton, Ky., Aug. 31, 1922; s. Albert Joseph and Rose Mary (Wiegand) G.; B.A., St. Gregory Sem., 1943; postgrad. Mt. St. Mary Sem., 1943-46; M.A., U. Toronto, 1949, Ph.D., 1953. Ordained priest Roman Catholic Ch., 1946; missionary, N.D., 1947; dir. Newman Club, U. Ky., Lexington, 1947-49; prof. philosophy Holy Cross Sem., Lacrosse, Wis., 1954-56; founder Sem. St. Pius X, Erlanger, Ky., 1955, rector, 1955-71, pres., 1971—; pastor Ch. Blessed Sacrament, Fort Mitchell, Ky., 1971—. Domestic prelate, 1956; consultor Diocese Covington, 1958. Address: 2415 Dixie Hwy Ft Mitchell KY 41017

GROSSKREUTZ, DORIS C., physician, educator; b. Moline, Ill., 1918; M.D., U. Ill., 1942. Intern Wis. Gen. Hosp., Madison, 1942-43; resident anesthesiology Hartford (Conn.) Hosp., 1949-51; mem. staff gen. practice Protestant Deaconess Hosp., Evansville, Ind. and St. Mary's Hosp., Evansville, 1943-49; mem. staff anesthesiolgy Grace-New Haven Community Hosp., 1951-54, N.C. Meml. Hosp., 1954-56, 59; chief dept. anesthesiology VA Hosp., Durham, N.C., 1956-57, San Antonio Tb Hosp., 1968—; clin. instr. anesthesiology Yale, 1951-54; asst. prof. U. N.C., 1954-57, asso. prof., 1959-62; clin. prof. anesthesiology South Tex. Med. Sch., 1965-68. Diplomate Am. Bd. Anesthesiology. Fellow Am. Coll. Anesthesiologists; mem. A.M.A., Am. Soc. Anesthesiology, Internat. Anesthesiology Research Soc. Address: Box 23340 San Antonio TX 78223*

GROSSMAN, HARRY, lawyer; b. N.Y.C., Oct. 30, 1911; s. Isaac and Anna (Hoffman) G.; B.S., N.Y. U., 1933; LL.B., Columbia, 1936; m. Barbara J. Solomon, Aug. 9, 1942 (div.); 1 dau., Patricia Joyce; m. 2d Anne E. Rafsky, Aug. 6, 1950; children Sandra Kay, Ilene Hope. Admitted to N.Y. BAR, 1937, D.C. bar, 1948; dep. collector Internal Revenue, 1937-40; partner Grossman & Grossman, N.Y.C., 1950-63, Grossman, Grossman & Feigen, N.Y.C., and Washington 1964-68, Grossman, Freigen & Rossetti, 1968-69; counsel Automobile Driving Schs. Assn., Inc., 1949-54, Eastern Dry Cleaning and Laundry Machinery Distbrs. Assn. Inc., 1961-64, Tri-State Machinery Distbrs. Council, 1964-67, Westchester Asso. Stationers, Inc., 1967-68; lectr. Columbia. Practicing Law Inst., Delehanty Inst., Collegiate Inst. Pres., Atlantic Beach Property Owners Assn., 1954-55; past chmn. campaign Nat. Found. Infantile Paralysis. Trustee Harry and Jane Fischel Found. Served from 2d lt. to maj. AUS, 1942-46; lt. col. Res. Decorated Commendation medal; recipient N.Y. Conspicuous Service award, 1946. Mem. Am., N.Y. bar assns., Assn. Bar City N.Y., N.Y. County Lawyers Assn., Fed. Bar Assn. N.Y., N.J., Conn., Am. Acad. Polit. and Social Scis., N.Y. Soc. Assn. Execs., Res. Officers Assn., Mil. Order World Wars, Jewish War Vets., Am. Legion, Grand Street Boys' Assn., Zeta Beta Tau. Democrat. Mem. B'nai B'rith; Elk. Club: Alpine Country. Contbr. articles to periodicals. Home: 25 Sutton Pl S New York City NY 10022 Office: 551 Fifth Av New York City NY 10017 also Davis Bldg Washington DC 20006

GROSSMAN, LAURENCE ABRAHAM, physician; b. Nashville, Tenn., Sept. 21, 1916; s. Henry and Etta (Rothstein) G.; B.A., Vanderbilt U., 1938; M.D., 1941; m. Dorothy Ruth Huffine, Oct. 17, 1942; children—Diana Gail (Mrs. Robert L. Officer), Linda Marie, Susanne, J. Anne. Intern, Vanderbilt U. Hosp., Nashville, 1941-42, resident, 1946-47, now staff; practice medicine, specializing in internal medicine and cardiology, Nashville, 1947—; mem. staff St. Thomas, Bapt. hosps.; clin. prof. medicine Vanderbilt U., Meharry Med. Coll., 1960—; med. dir. Am. Health Profiles, 1971—. Served from 1st lt. to maj. AUS, 1942-45. Diplomate Am. Bd. Internal Medicine. Fellow A.C.P., Am. Coll. Chest Physicians, Am. Coll. Cardiology; mem. Nashville Acad. Medicine, Tenn, Med. Assn. (dist. councillor 1959-63), Tenn. Soc. Internal Medicine (pres. 1957-58), Middle Tenn. (pres. 1956-57), Tenn. (pres. 1965-66) heart assns. Home: 4300 Lillywood Rd Nashville TN 37205 Office: 1816 Hayes St Nashville TN 37203

GROSSMAN, MAURICE SIDNEY, physician; b. Corpus Christi, Tex., June 1, 1927; s. Edward and Sarah (Mushlin) G.; B.A., U. Tex., 1948, M.D., 1952; m. Lois Ruth Rosen, May 20, 1957; children—Carla, Daryl, Sandor. Intern medicine, asst. resident internal medicine St. Louis City Hosp., 1953-54; sr. resident internal medicine New Eng. Center Hosp., Boston, 1954-55; chief fellow gastroenterology Lahey Clinic, Boston, 1955-56; mem. staff New Eng. Bapt. Hosp., also New Eng. Deaconess Hosp., Boston, 1955-56; pvt. practice internal medicine and gastroenterology, Corpus Christi, 1957—; chief dept. medicine Spohn Hosp.; mem. staff Meml. Hosp.; lectr. med. groups. Served to maj., AUS Res., 1965-61; served with USNR, 1945-46. Diplomate Am. Bd. Internal Medicine. Fellow A.C.P., Am. Coll. Gastroenterology; mem. A.M.A., So. Med. Assn., Am. Soc. Internal Medicine, Am. Gastroenterol. Assn. (asso.), Tex. Acad. Internal Medicine, Corpus Christi Acad. Internal Medicine (pres. 1969), Sigma Alpha Mu, Alpha Epsilon Delta. Jewish religion. Contbr. articles profl. jours. Home: 321 Bayshore Dr Corpus Christi TX 78412 Office: 1001 Louisiana Pkwy Corpus Christic TX 74804

GROSSMAN, MAX R., pub. affairs cons. editor; b. Odessa, Russia, April 21, 1904; s. Abraham and Celia (Tocman) A.; B.B.A., Boston U., 1926, M.B.A., 1930, Ed.M., Sch. Edn., 1929; Harvard, 1935; m. Manya Kaufman, Mar. 26, 1931; children—Lysbeth R., Michael Baruch. Reporter, Pawtucket (R.I.) Times, 1926-28; feature writer Boston Sunday Post, 1929-43; news commentator sta. WEEI, Boston, 1938-40; instr. journalism, Boston U., 1929-31, asst. prof., 1931-35, asso. prof., 1935-39, prof. and head dept., 1939-47; provost Brandeis U., 1947-50; mem. Civic Edn. Project, Cambridge, 1950-51; pub. affairs officer USIA, Frankfurt am Main, Germany, 1951-57, Washington, 1957-61; cultural attache Am. Embassy, Quito, Ecuador, 1961-62; cultural affairs officer, Am. Embassy, London, Eng., 1964-68; forum editor for Voice of Am., USIA, 1962-64, 68-71; pub. affairs cons., 1971—; Washington editor Finance mag., 1971—. Writers sect. OWI, 1944-45; sect. chief journalism Biarritz American (France), 1945-46; mng. editor Biarritz Daily Banner, 1945-46; roving corr. The Stars and Stripes (Germany), 1946; lectr. various Brit. univs. and pub. schs. Mem. Fulbright Commn., Quito and London. Mem. Am. Assn. Tchrs. Journalism, English Speaking Union, Am. Assn. Schs. and Depts. of Journalism (pres. 1944-45), Am. Assn. U. Profs., Beta Gamma Sigma, Kappa Tau Alpha (nat. pres. 1944-45), Kappa Omega Sigma. Mason (32 deg.). Clubs: Mass. Press Association; Nat. Press (Washington); Overseas Press (N.Y.C.); Frankfurt Press (Germany); Savile (London). Contbr. articles to mags., newspapers. Address: 603 G St SW Washington DC 20024

GROSSMANN, WILLIAM, physician, pres. Va. Med. Assn. Address: 111 Morton Av Petersburg VA 23805*

GROSVENOR, GILBERT MELVILLE, magazine editor; b. Washington, May 5, 1931; s. Melville Bell and Helen (Rowland) G.; grad. Deerfield Acad., 1950; B.A., Yale, 1954; m. Donna C. Kerkam, June 16, 1961. With Nat. Geolg. Soc., 1954—, trustee, v.p., 1966—, asso. editor, 1967—; adv. bd. Riggs Nat. Bank, Washington. Bd. dirs. D.C. Soc. for Crippled Children, Alexander Graham Bell Assn. for Deaf; trustee Meridian House Found., Ford's Theatre Soc., African Wildlife Leadership Found., Mt. Vernon Jr. Coll. Served with AUS, 1954-56. Mem. Soc. Am. Geographers, Newcomen Soc. Clubs:

Alfalfa, Yale (sec.), Nat. Press, Overseas Writers, Metropolitan (Washington); Explorers (N.Y.C.); Chevy Chase (Md.). Home: 4226 50th St NW Washington DC 20016 Office: Nat Geographic Soc 17th and M Sts NW Washington DC 20036

GROSVENOR, MELVILLE BELL, editor; b. Washington, Nov. 26, 1901; s. Gilbert Hovey and Elsie May (Bell) G.; B.S., U.S. Naval Acad., 1923; Sc.D. U. Miami (Fla.), 1954; LL.D., George Washington U., 1959; Litt.D., Boston U., 1970; m. Helen North Rowland, Jan. 4, 1924;children—Helen Rowland (Mrs. Richard Lemmerman), Alexander Graham Bell, Gilbert Melville; m. 2d, Anne E. Revis, Aug. 12, 1950 children—Edwin Stuart, Sara Anne. Asst. chief illustrations div. Nat. Geographic mag., 1924-35, asst. editor, 1935-54, asso. editor, 1954-57, editor, 1957-67, editor in chief, 1967—; dir. Riggs Nat. Bank, Chesapeake & Potomac Telephone Co. Trustee Nat. Geographic Soc., v.p., 1954-57, pres., editor, 1957-67, chmn. bd., 1967—. Trustee U. Miami, George Washington U., Jackson Hole Preserve, Inc. Decorated Mil. Order of Christ (Portugal); commendatore del ordine al Merito della Republica Italiana; recipient Nat. Park Service Conservation award, Horace Albright Conservation award, Eisenhower medal People to People, Inc., 1970. Clubs: Cosmos, Metropolitan, National Press, Chevy Chase, Overseas Writers, Gibson Island, Bath, Club of Am. Author numerous articles in Nat. Geographic Mag. Editor-in-chief: America's Wonderlands—The National Parks; The Wild Animals of North America; America's Historylands; Men, Ships and the Sea; Great Adventures; Birds of North America, Vol. I, Song and Garden, Vol. II, Water, Prey and Game, Wondrous World of Fishes; National Geographic Atlas of World; Indians of the Americas; Man's Best Friend; This England; Life in Bible Times; Greece and Rome: Builders of World; Age of Chivalry. Home: 5510 Grosvenor Lane Bethesda MD 20014 Office: Nat Geog Soc 17th and M Sts NW Washington DC 20036

GROTE, CARL AUGUST, JR., physician; b. Huntsville, Ala., Oct. 19, 1928; s. Carl August and Willie (Barrier) G.; AB., Vanderbilt U., 1950, M.D., 1954; m. Carole Buzbee, Mar. 26, 1964; children—Mary Eleanor, Carl August, Jane Elizabeth, Charles David. Intern Butterworth Hosp., Grand Rapids, Mich., 1954-55; resident H.P. Long Hosp., Pineville, La., 1957-58; practice gen. medicine, Huntsville, 1958—; mem. exec. com. staff Huntsville Hosp., 1966—, also pres. staff, 1969—. Mem. Madison County Bd. Health and Bd. Censors, 1967-70, chmn., 1971—. Bd. dirs. Ala. Polit. Action Com. Served to capt. M.C., AUS, 1955-57. Diplomate Am. Bd. Family Practice. Mem. Am. Acad. Gen. Practice (Ala. bd. dirs.), Med. Assn. Ala. (Coll. Counselors), A.M.A. Editors Ala. Family Physician Jour., 1967-69. Home: 1807 Mt. Brook St Huntsville AL 35801 Office: 700 Green St SE Huntsville AL 35801

GROTEFEND, MARY EMERY, nursing educator, sociologist; b. Wetmore, Kan., Dec. 1, 1910; d. Edward Henry Herbert and Lucy (Ward) Emery; R.N., Bethany Hosp. Sch. Nursing 1931; B.A., Baker U., 1934; M.S., Catholic U. Am., 1944; postgrad. U. Md., 1948-51; Ph.D. in Sociology, Am. U., 1966; m. Ralph L. Grotefend, July 1, 1937 (dec. Mar. 1963); 1 son, Edward Emery. Sci. instr. Jameson Hosp. Sch. Nursing, New Castle, Pa., 1934-35, Columbia Hosp. Sch. Nursing. Milw., 1935-37; ednl. dir. Burge Hosp. Sch. Nursing, Springfield, Mo., 1938-40; sci. instr., asst. dir. Sch. Nursing and Nursing Service. W. Balt. Gen. Hos., 1941-47; social sci. instr., asst. prof. pub. health nursing U. Md., College Park and Balt., 1947-65, asso. prof. pub. health nursing, 1965-68; project dir. Facilitation of Student Learning through Meaninful Use of Community Resources, also asso. prof. Med. Coll. Ga., Augusta, 1968-71; asso. prof., chmn. nursing div. South Ga. Coll., Douglas, 1971—. Chmn. social sci. com. Md. Bd. Examiners of Nurses, 1946-47. Mem. Am., Md. (sec. dist. 2, 1946-48), (mem. at large exec. com. pub. health sect. 1958-60), Mo. (pres. dist. 4, 1940) nurses assns., Nat., Md. (chmn. membership com. 1945-47) leagues for nursing, Am. Sociol. Assn., Am. Assn. U. Profs., Am. Assn. U. Women, Mental Health Assn., Am. Pub. Health Assn., Women's Soc. Christian Service (pres. 1969-71), League Women Voters, Zeta Tau Alpha, Sigma Theta Tau (organizer, counselor Pi chpt., faculty adviser 1957-60). Methodist (local bd. stewards 1956-59, chmn. commn. on missions 1956-60). Clubs: Augusta Kennel, Dalmatian of America. Contbr. articles profl. jours. Home: Green Acre Farms PO Box 1022 Douglas GA 31533

GROUPE, VINCENT, biologist; b. Phila., Sept. 13, 1918; s. Andrew V. and Georgia (Patterson) G.; B.A., Wesleyan U., 1939; Ph.D., U. Pa., 1942; m. Gerry Finley Nash, Mar. 30, 1942; children—David Vincent, Lawrence Nash. Research asst. Children's Hosp., Phila., 1941-42; bacteriologist E. R. Squibb & Sons, New Brunswick, N.J., 1942-44; research asso. Squibb Inst. Med. Research, New Brunswick, 1944-47; asso. prof. Storrs (Conn.) Agrl. Expt. Sta., 1947-49; asso. prof. microbiology Rutgers U., New Brunswick, N.J., 1949-54, prof. virology, 1954-68, vis. prof., 1968-70; v.p. Life Scis., Inc., St. Petersburg, Fla., 1968—. Cons., Nat. Cancer Inst., Bethesda, Md., Carter-Wallace Labs., Cranbury, N.J. Trustee Princeton Group Arts, New Life Found., The Science Center. Recipient citation for Outstanding Achievement as Tchr. and Scholar Wesleyan U., 1959. Fellow Am. Acad. Microbiology, N.Y. Acad. Medicine, N.Y. Acad. Scis., A.A.A.S.; mem. C. of C., Commerce Club, Com. of 100, Pinellas Mfrs. Assn., Am. Assn. Cancer Research, Soc. Exptl. Biology and Medicine, Am. Assn. Immunologists. Research in cancer viruses, virus chemotherapy. Home: 444 Bath Club Blvd N St Petersburg FL 33708 Office: 2900 72d St N St Petersburg Fl 33710

GROVE, BERTRAM EDWARD, headmaster; b. Cleve., Mar. 12, 1916; s. Edward and Marie (Dorward) G.; B.S., Northwestern U., 1938, M.A., 1950; Ed.D., Western New Eng. Coll., 1966; m. Dorothy Marie Black, Oct. 14, 1939; children—James Leland, Janet Lynore. Scientist, Chgo. Natural History Mus., 1940-44; dir. studies, guidance councilor, dir. audiovisual edn. Lake Forest (Ill.) Acad., 1944-52; dean, mem. exec. staff Morgan Park Mil. Acad., Chgo., 1952-56; asst. headmaster Elgin (Ill.) Acad., 1956-58; asst. prof. Elgin Community Coll., 1956-58; headmaster Carteret Sch., West Orange, N.J., 1958-60; headmaster, pres. Webster (Mass.) Acad., 1960-68; headmaster Golden Hills Acad., Ocala, Fla., 1968-69; headmaster, pres. Graham-Eckes Sch., Palm Beach, 1969-71. Spl. officer Ill. Dept. Conservation, 1946; chmn. fund raising campaign Lake Forest March of Dimes, 1946; mem. Mayor's Com. on Juvenile Delinquency, Chgo., 1955; mem. Gov.'s Adv. Com. Youth Service Bd. Mass., 1962-69; mem. Tchr. Edn. Adv. Council, Fla., 1969; mem. ednl. adv. com. Inst. Am. Strategy; lt. col., aide de camp to gov. Ga., 1967. Chief judge Lake Forest Election Bd., 1950-52; adminstrv. asst. Republican Nat. Conv., Chgo., 1952; Rep. candidate congressman, 1956; Rep. candidate Sch. Com., Webster, 1967. Mem. adv. bd. L'Ecole En Famille, Liege, Belgium; mem. Norton Gallery and Sch. Art. Decorated French and British govts. Mem. N.E.A., Air Force Assn., Mil. Order World Wars, A.A.A.S., Inland Bird Banding Assn., Nat. Assn. Biology Tchrs., Assn. for Edn. by Radio, New Eng. Assn. Colls. and Secondary Schs., Nat., Mass. assns. ind. schs., Nat. Assn. Sch. Adminstrs., Mass. Secondary Sch. Prins. Assn., Council Basic Edn., Fraternal Order Police, Res. Officers Assn. (regional v.p. 1955), C. of C. (bd. dirs., New Eng. Assn. Coll. Admissions Counselors, Mass. Police Assn., Ancient Order of Deep, Am. Legion, English Speaking Union, Ret. Officers Assn., Internat. Platform Assn., Exec. and Profl. Hall of Fame (chmn.), S.A.R., Order of Lafayette, Sigma Xi, Sigma Alpha Epsilon, Beta Beta Beta, Sigma Gamma Epsilon. Presbyn. Clubs: Army and Navy (Chgo.); Gezira Sporting (Cairo, Egypt); Officers (Ft. Sheridan, Ill.); Golden Hills Turf and Golf (Ocala); Beach (Palm Beach). Address: 401 Executive Center Dr West Palm Beach FL 33401

GROVE, ERNEST WILSON, economist; b. New Kensington, Pa., June 14, 1910; s. Edward Thomas and Adelaide (Wilson) G.; A.B., U. Cal. at Berkeley, 1932, Ph.D., 1948; m. Esther Elizabeth Krewson, Mar. 8, 1947; children—Kathryn Frances, Daniel Edward. Agrl. economist Bur. Agrl. Econs., U.S. Dept. Agr., 1936-41, 46-53, head farm income estimates sect. Agrl. Econs. Div., editor The Farm Income Situation, Washington, 1954-60; staff economist Agrl. Stabilization and Conservation Service, 1960—. Chmn. Citizens Com. for Sch. Improvement Arlington, Va., 1961-62; mem. Arlington Pub. Utilities Commn., 1963-64; chmn., 1964. Served from 2d lt. to lt. col. Control Div., Hdqrs. Army Service Forces, AUS, 1942-45. Decorated Legion of Merit. Fellow A.A.A.S.; mem. Am. Econ. Assn., Am. Agrl. Econs. Assn., Am. Statis. Assn., Conf. on Research in Income and Wealth, Internat. Conf. Agrl. Economists, Nat. Economists Club, Internat. Platform Assn., Phi Beta Kappa, Delta Sigma Rho, Omicron Delta Epsilon. Author jour. articles. Home: 5429 S 5th St Arlington VA 22204 Office: Dept of Agr Washington DC 20250

GROVE, JAMES ROBERT, welding equipment co. exec.; b. Larned, Kan., May 1, 1931; s. James and Marie (Purcell) G.; B.S. in Mech. Engring., Kan. State U., 1954; m. Beverly Ann Jones, May 31, 1952; children— Holice K., Jay Robert, Jeffery Jones, James Andrew. Sales engr. Union Carbide Corp., Kansas City, Mo., 1954-55, Amarillo, Tex., 1955-57, Houston, 1957-60, mgr., Houston, 1960-63; v.p. Indsl. Welding Equipment Co. and Indsl. Welding Equipment Co. Rentals, Inc., Houston, 1963-67; pres. Alloy Weld Supply Co., 1967—, Indsl. Welding Equipment Co., Inc., So. Welding Supply, Indsl. Welding Equipment Co. Rentals, Inc., (all Houston), 1969—. Vice pres. Reilco Corp., Houston, 1969—. Mem. Pi Tu Sigma, Phi Delta Theta. Presbyn. (deacon 1960, elder 1962—). Rotarian (mem. com. 1969—). Club: Brae Burn Country (Houston). Home: 343 Knipp Forest Houston TX 77024 Office: 8350 Moseley St Houston TX 77034

GROVE, JAMES RONALD, county agrl. agt.; b. Fishersville, Va., Aug. 17, 1938; s. G. Grayson and Mary (Vint) G.; B.S. with honors in Animal Sci., Va. Poly. Inst., 1959; m. Dorothy Lee Stoneburner, June 6, 1964. Asst. county agt. Prince William County, Manassas, Va., 1959-62, Shenandoah County, Woodstock, Va., 1962-65; county extension agrl. agt., Madison County, Madison, Va., 1965—. Sec. Charlottesville Area Jr. Beef Show, 1968. Served with AUS, 1966. Mem. Va. County Agts. Assn. (asst. sec.-treas. 1965, state dir. 1970—), Madison County Jr. C. of C. (v.p. 1970), Epsilon Sigma Phi. Lutheran (sec. 1969—). Club: Ruritan (Brightwood, Va.). Home: Route 1 Box 189 Madison VA 22727 Office: PO Box 10 Madison VA 22727

GROVES, DAVID UPDEGRAFF, pub. relations exec.; b. Lexington, Mo., Nov. 10, 1926; s. William Lester and Adelaide Rebecca (Updegraff) G.; B.A., U. Md., 1950; M.A., Johns Hopkins, 1951; m. Nancy Jane Bustamante, June 23, 1951; children—Nancy Alice, Patricia Rebecca. Cartoonist, writer syndicated newspaper feature Spotlight on Bus., Stars and Stripes and Washington Post, 1946-51; mgmt. and pub. relations cons., indsl. relations cons. U.S., Guatemala, and Cuba, 1951-60; gen. mgr. Relaciones Publicas Intermericanas S.A., Mexico City, Mexico, 1960—; Mexico rep. Klein & Saks, Inc., Washington. Dir., pres. pub. relations com. Fundacion Mexicana para el Desarrollo; dir., treas., pres. exec. and finance com. Fomento Educacional; dir. Patrimex Cath. Sch. Bd. Served with AUS, 1944-46. Mem. Am. C. of C. of Mexico (chmn. communications adv. com. 1971-72), Pub. Relations Soc. Am., Internat. Assn. Bus. Communicators, Am. Philatelic Soc. Roman Catholic. Clubs: Club de Golf La Hacienda, University (Mexico City). Home: Monte Athos 246 Mexico 10 DE Mexico Office: Copenhague 4 Despacho 3 Mexico 6 DF Mexico

GROVES, DONALD GEORGE, sci. adminstr.; b. Syracuse, N.Y., Aug. 24, 1920; s. Perry Edward and Marguerite (Grass) G.; B.S., Syracuse U., 1939, M.S., 1949; m. Barbara L. Matticks, Mar. 19, 1949. Mech. designer Hudson Motor Car Co., Detroit, 1941-43; elec. designer, systems engr. Gen. Electric Co., 1954-61; staff engr., sci. staff adminstr. Nat. Acad. Sci., 1961—. Mem. bd. mgmt. Washington YMCA. Served to lt. comdr. USNR, 1943-46, 51-54. Recipient Freedoms Found. medal award, 1970; Am. Republics fellowship award, 1950. Fellow Washington Acad. Scis.; mem. Internat. Oceanographic Found., Am. Soc. Naval Engrs., Marine Tech. Soc., Profl. Div. Armed Forces Writers Assn., Mil. Order World Wars. Clubs: Washington Athletic (pres. 1969-70), Pentagon Athletic. Contbr. numerous articles to profl. jours., book. Home: Town House 601 19th St NW Washington DC 20006 Office: 2101 Constitution Av Washington DC 20418.

GROVES, JAMES MARTIN, county ofcl.; b. Elkton, Ky., June 24, 1934; s. Michael Newton and Viola (Blake) G.; A.B., Transylvania U., 1956; student Austin Peay U., 1954, U. Ky., 1958-59. Adminstrv. aide Congressman Frank W. Burke, Washington, 1960; dep. clk. Todd County Circuit Ct., Elkton, Ky., 1961-63, clk., 1963—. Mem. Ky. State Democratic Exec. Com., 1968-72; sec. Todd County Democratic Com., 1968-72. Bd. dirs. Western Ky. State Fair, 1968—, Milliken Meml. Community House, Elkton, Ky., 1969—. Served with AUS, 1956-58. Named Outstanding Young Man, Todd County, 1968. Mem. Ky. Assn. Circuit Ct. Clks. (pres. 1967), Todd County Jr. C. of C. (charter pres. 1967), Kappa Alpha. Mem. Disciples of Christ Ch. Rotarian (pres. 1965-66). Home: Goebel Av Elkton KY 42220 Office: Todd County Ct House Elkton KY 42220

GROVES, SIDNEY KEPLER, elec. engr.; b. Rome, Ind., Jan. 26, 1917; s. Sidney Kepler and Dessa (Ramsey) G.; B.S. with distinction, Purdue U., 1937 m. Virginia Leonore Lehman, June 14, 1941; 1 dau., Anne Leonore. Tchr. sci. and mathematics Cannelton (Ind.) High Sch., 1937-42; factory engr. Ken-Rad and Gen. Elec. Co., Tell City, Ind., 1942-51; sect. engr. Gen. Elec. Co., 1951-56; specialist process engring., 1956-60, sr. engr. product design, Owensboro, Ky., 1960—. Registered profl. engr., Ind., Ky. Mem. Nat., Ky. socs. profl. engrs., I.E.E.E., Nat. Rifle Assn., Sigma Pi Sigma. Republican. Home: 1612 Ford Av Owensboro KY 42301 Office: 316 E 9th St Owensboro KY 42301*

GROVES, SIGRID MARCZOCH, editor; b. Osnabruck, Germany, Jan. 24, 1937; d. Fritz and Erna (Haselroth) Marczoch; student Alliance Francaise, Paris, 1958-60, West London Coll. Commerce, 1960-61; m. Philp E. Groves, Dec. 24, 1968. Came to U.S., 1961, naturalized, 1966. Asst. editor The Pharmacologist, Bethesda, Md., 1962-64, Profl. Engr. mag., Washington, 1964-68; editor Nat. Candy Wholesaler mag., Washington, 1968—. Mem. Vols. for Internat. Tech. Assistance, Washington, 1967—, sec., 1967-68. Mem. Soc. Nat. Assn. Publs. Home: 2127 California St NW Washington DC 20008 Office: 1430 K St NW Washington DC 20008

GROVES, WILLIAM E., actuary; b. Pollock, La., Aug. 11, 1906; s. Clyde Olan and Sallie (Walters) G.; A.B., La. State U., 1928, M.S., 1933; M.A., U. Mich., 1937; m. Gladys Rhodes, Sept. 1, 1928; children—Barbara, William Clyde, Eugene Rhodes. Cons. actuary, New Orleans, 1938—; v.p. Gallery Circle Theater, 1954—. Sec.-treas. bd. trustees Tchrs. Retirement Fund of New Orleans. Sec., mgr. Dist. Attys. Retirement System of La. Mem. Conf. Actuaries in Pub. Practice (v.p. 1959-60, 63-64, pres. 1965-66), Nat. Assn. State Retirement Adminstrs. (sec.-treas. 1957-60), Nat. Acad. Actuaries (bd. dirs. 1966—), Dist. Attys. Assn. La. (sec.). Co-author: Louisiana Painters and Paintings. Home: 6422 Cartier Dr New Orleans LA 70122 Office: 506 Frenchmen St New Orleans LA 70116

GROWALD, MARTIN CHANDLER, architect; b. Salem, Mass., Aug. 21, 1930; s. Henry Kurt and Edith (Chandler) G.; B.S. in Architecture, U. Va., 1954; M.A., Harvard, 1955; m. Monika Bange, Oct. 6, 1962; children—Olaf Martin, Chandler Kurt. Instr. architecture N.C. State Coll., Raleigh, 1955-56, U. Mich., Ann Arbor, 1957-58; designer Skidmore, Owings & Merrill, N.Y.C., Chgo., San Francisco, Portland, Ore., 1958-63, participating asso., 1963-66, asso. partner, 1966-72; partner firm Growald/Schutts Architects, Inc., Ft. Worth, 1972—. Vis. archtl. critic Sch. Architecture, U. Va., Charlottesville, 1966; prof. archtl. design U. Tex. at Arlington, 1972—. Served with AUS, C.E., 1956-57. Recipient Sparks Meml. medal Chi Phi, 1952, 53, 54, Alpha Rho Chi medal, 1954. Mem. A.I.A., Archtl. League N.Y. (exec. com. 1967—, chmn. membership com., sec.), Chi Phi. Club: Harvard of New York. Patentee shell form structure. Sr. designer Chase Manhattan Bank, N.Y.C. 1958-60, Royall Nat. Bank, Tex., 1961, Pennsylvania Av. Commn., Washington, 1962, Main Place, Dallas, 1963, Ford Motor Credit Co. Bldg., Dearborn, Mich., 1965, Mt. Sinai Med. Sch. Lab., N.Y.C., 1966, Blue Hill Office Park, Orangetown, N.Y., 1968, Olympic Tower, N.Y., 1972, Dept. Housing and Urban Devel. Operation Break-Through, Weehawken, N.J., 1972. Home: 2705 Simondale St Fort Worth TX 76109 Office: 515 Fort Worth Nat Bank Bldg Fort Worth TX 76102

GRUB, PHILLIP DONALD, cons., educator; b. Medical Lake, Wash., Aug. 8, 1931; s. Carl Dreyer and Barbara R.M. (Johnson) G.; B.A. in Econs. and Bus. Edn. with highest honors, Eastern Wash. State U., 1953; M.B.A., George Washington U., 1960, Ph.D., 1964. Individual practice accounting, auditing, Spokane, Wash., 1953-54; chmn. dept. bus. and econs. Twisp (Wash.) High Sch., 1956-58; chmn. dept. bus. Mead (Wash.) High Sch., 1959-60; vis. prof. bus. and econs. Eastern Wash. State U., Cheney, 1960-62; asso. prof. bus. adminstrn., dir. programs in internat. bus. George Washington U., 1963-70, chmn. dept. bus. adminstrn., 1968-71; distinguished vis. prof. E.S.S.E.C., Paris, France, 1970, Helsinki (Finland) Sch. Econs., 1971; dir. Ohio World Trade Center, 1972—; vis. prof. internat. bus., dir. programs internat. bus. Cleve. State U., 1972—. Chmn. bd. Indotrin, Inc.; v.p. Multinat. Marketing. Cons. internat. bus. problems and exec. devel. to numerous multi-nation firms, govt. agys., U.S. and fgn.; mem. Pres.'s. Export Expansion Council, Md.-D.C. region, 1970. Served with AUS, 1954-56; PTO. Mem. Am. Mgmt. Assn., Assn. Internat. Execs., Am. Econ. Assn., Am. Assn. U. Profs., Assn. Edn. Internat. Bus., Soc. Internat. Devel., Acad. Mgmt., Alpha Kappa Psi. Co-author: American-East European Trade, 1969; Executive Leadership-the Art of Successfully Managing Resources, 1969; International Marketing in Perspective, 1971; The Multinational Firmin Transition, 1972. Contbr. articles to profl. jours. Home: 815 S 18th St Arlington VA 22202 Office: George Washington U Washington DC 20006

GRUBBS, CHESTER LEE, broadcasting engr., physicist; b. Ft. Worth, Oct. 13, 1923; s. Lee Vanner and Christine (Nelson) G.; B.A., Tex. Christian U., 1950; m. Ada Murie Webber, May 31, 1947; children—Carolyn Lee, Van Alan. Chief engr. Bluebonnet Broadcasting Co., KCNC/KJIM, Ft. Worth, 1950-58, Trinity Broadcasting Co., 1958-62; dir. engring. KTOW/KJEM, Oklahoma City, 1959-62; v.p., dir., chief engr. Trinity Broadcasting Co., Ft. Worth, 1963-64; dir. engring. KTOK Radio, Inc., Oklahoma City, 1964—, v.p., 1971—. Served with AUS, 1943-46. Decorated Bronze Star. Mem. Am. Inst. Physics, Am. Phys. Soc., I.E.E.E., Soc. Broadcast Engrs. Baptist (deacon). Lion (pres.). Home: 5701 NW 82d St Oklahoma City OK 73132 Office: 1800 W Main St Oklahoma City OK 73101

GRUBBS, JAMES BRYAN, stock broker; b. Greensboro, N.C., Nov. 5, 1910; s. O. L. and Alice Estelle (White) G.; grad. high sch.; m. Ellen Elizabeth Rollins, Nov. 23, 1935; children—James Bryan, Elizabeth G. (Mrs. James G. McCurry), Nancy Rollins. With Fenner & Beane, Greensboro, 1928, 31; account exec. E.A. Pierce &Co., Columbia, S.C., 1934-38, br. mgr., 1938-57; br. mgr. Merrill, Lynch, Pierce & Beane, Houston, 1957-59; v.p. Merrill, Lynch, Pierce, Fenner & Smith, Inc., Houston, 1959-67, dir., 1967—, regional dir. S.W. Region, 1972—. Treas. S.C. Tb Assn., 1940-42; chmn. Houston Grand Opera Drive, 1965. Served to 1st lt. USMCR, World War II. Mem. Houston C. of C. Republican. Presbyn. Clubs: Houston Country (dir.), Ramada (Houston). Home: 6122 Riverview Way Houston TX 77002 Office: First City Nat Bank Bldg Houston TX 77002

GRUBEN, JOHN HENRY, JR., ins. co. exec.; b. Terrell, Tex., Apr. 17, 1909; s. John Henry and Jennie Cecil (Scott) G.; student Tex. A. and M. U., 1928-30; student journalism, Columbia, 1932, Sorbonne, U. Paris (France), 1944; m. Dorothy Barbara Walton, Feb. 11, 1933; 1 dau., Barbara Antoinette (Mrs. Edwin Conway Barker). With Am. Nat. Ins. Co., Galveston, Tex., 1934—, v.p., 1971—, writer, editor Star Bull., 1946—, co. conv. histories, 1946—. Pres. Galveston Little Theatre, 1950-52. Served with AUS, 1944-46; ETO. Decorated Meritorious Service citation (France); recipient Journalism award Freedom's Found., Galveston, 1954, 55, 56, 57; Nat. Editors award Life Insurers Conf., Galveston, 1956, 57; also many leadership awards. Mem. Tex., Harrison County hist. assns., East Tex. Hist. Soc., Galveston Hist. Found. Methodist (ordained minister 1954). Clubs: Galveston Rifle; Gun (pres. Galveston 1958-59). Author: Fabulous Colonel Buck, Home: 5210 Av U Galveston TX 77550 Office: Am Nat Ins Co Moody Av at Market St Galveston TX 77550

GRUENDER, CARL DAVID, educator; b. Cleve., May 24, 1927; s. Charles Frederick and Charlotte (Freiman) G.; B.A., Antioch Coll., 1951; M.A., U. Chgo., 1953; Ph.D., U. Wis., 1957; m. Anne Sherwood, Mar. 26, 1955; children—Reesha, Martha, Elizabeth. Instr. to asst. prof. philosophy Kan. State U., 1957-63; asst. prof. philosophy Case Inst. Tech., 1963-67; asso. prof. to prof. philosophy Fla. State U., 1967—. Served as sgt., USAAF, 1945-46. Mem. Am. Philos. Assn., Philosophy of Sci. Soc., A.A.A.S., Am. Assn. Univ. Profs. Asso. editor of Social Theory and Practice, 1968—. Contbr. articles to profl. jours. Office: Florida State University Tallahassee FL 32306

GRUIS, EDWARD GEORGE, lawyer; b. Chgo., Jan. 20, 1924; s. Edward George and Helen (Bruce) G.; B.S., Purdue U., 1949, M.S., 1951; Dr. en Droit, U. Lyon (France), 1950; J.D. with honors, George Washington U., 1954, LL.M., 1955; postgrad. Georgetown Law Sch., 1960; m. Rosemary Nottingham, Apr. 3, 1948; children—Leslie Nottingham, Tracy Nottingham. Admitted to D.C. bar, 1954, Ind. bar, 1954, also U.S. Supreme Ct. bar; trial atty. antitrust div. U.S.

Dept. of Justice, Washington, 1954-59; private practice law, Washington, 1959; trial atty. FTC, Washington, 1960-70; dep. gen. counsel FMC, Washington, 1970—. Pres. Capitol Hill Restoration Soc., 1957, 58, 67; gen. counsel Nat. Conf. State Socs., 1966-68, 3d v.p., 1969-70, Bd. dirs., treas. Indiana Soc, Washington, 1966-71; bd. dirs., vice chmn. Christ Child Settlement House, Washington, 1968-70. Served with AUS, 1943-46. Mem. Am., Fed., Ind. bar assns., Lambda Chi Alpha, Delta Theta Phi. Republican. Episcopalian. Home: 326 2d St SE Washington DC 20003 Office: FMC Washington DC 20573

GRUMBLES, LELAND CREED, educator, veterinarian; b. Star City, Ark., Sept. 21, 1921; s. James Rufus and Martha (Baker) G.; student Lamar State Coll., Beaumont, Tex., 1940; D.V.M., Tex. A. and M. U., 1945, M.S., 1957; postgrad. R.I. State U., 1947; m. Helen Beatrice Battle, Sept. 18, 1943; children—Paula Ruth, Jane Sallie. Individual practice vet. medicine, 1945-46; asst. prof. R.I. State U., 1946-48, La. State U., 1948-49; mem. faculty Tex. A. and M. U., 1949-53, 55—, prof., 1957—, head dept. vet. microbiology, 1967—. Cons., pres. Animal Disease Research Workers So. States, 1965. Served with USAF, 1953-55. Recipient Faculty award service and achievement Southwestern Veterinarian, 1957. Mem. Am. Coll. Vet. Microbiologists (v.p. 1967), Am. Assn. Avian Pathologists (chmn. 1967), Am., Tex. (award 1967) vet. med. assn. Baptist. Lion. Research infectious diseases animals. Editor Avian Diseases, 1967—. Home: Route 4 Box 616 Bryan TX 77801 Office: Tex A and M U Coll Station TX 77843

GRUND, CLARENCE B., JR., elec. engr.; b. Portland, Ore., July 31, 1925; s. Clarence B. and Frances (Eckert) G.; B.E.E., Ala. Poly. Inst., 1951, M.E.E., 1952; m. Marilyn Grace Hornsby, May 2, 1948. Engr. system planning Ala. Power Co., Birmingham, 1953-58; engr. rate dept. So. Services, Inc., Birmingham, 1958-63; supr. research rate dept., 1964-67, asst. mgr. rate dept., 1967-69, mgr. rate dept., 1969—; instr. Ala. Poly. Inst., 1951-52, extension center U. Ala., 1952. Pres., Rocky Ridge Vol. Fire Dept., 1957-58, bd. dirs., 1956-62. Served with USAAF, World War II. Registered profl. engr., Ala., Miss. Mem. I.E.E.E., Nat. Soc. Profl. Engrs., Birmingham Soc. Engrs., Newcomen Soc. N.Am., Internat. Platform Assn., Am. Legion, Phi Kappa Phi, Tau Beta Pi, Eta Kappa Nu. Contbr. articles profl. jours. Home: 3421 Cruzan Dr Birmingham AL 35243 Office: Southern Services Inc 64 Perimeter Center E PO Box 720071 Atlanta GA 30346

GRUNER, VIRGINIA SHAW (MRS. GEORGE JOHN GRUNER), club woman; b. Chgo., Feb. 19, 1912; d. Neil John and Rose (Tenwick) Shaw; grad. Chgo. Tchrs. Coll., 1931; B.S., Northwestern U., 1932; m. George John Gruner, Nov. 6, 1935 (dec.); children—Valerie Dale, Diane Rae. Tchr., Parker Practice Sch. of Chgo., Chgo. Tchrs. Coll., 1935-40. Active Girl Scouts Am., 1949-53; v.p. Factotums, Scarsdale (N.Y.) Woman's Club. 1953. Recipient Civic Achievement award City of Chgo. Mem. Internat. Platform Assn., High Mus. Art Members Guild, Pi Lambda Theta, Cui Bono, Alpha Omicron Pi. Republican. Presbyn. Clubs: Scarsdale Golf (chmn. women's golf assn. 1954-56), American Yacht (Rye, N.Y.), Indian Harbor Yacht (Greenwich, Conn.), Coral Ridge Country (Ft. Lauderdale, Fla.). Home: 140 Maison Pl Cross Creek NW Atlanta GA 30327

GRYMES, WILLIAM LLOYD, physician; b. Memphis, Nov. 10, 1928; s. Eldridge Phipps and Sarah (Woods) G.; B.S., Murray State Coll., 1950; postgrad U. Wis., 1950-51, U. N.D., 1951-52; M.S. in Anatomy, U. Tenn., 1958, M.D., 1957; m. Jane Cary Herbert, Aug. 10, 1958; children—Cathy, Dan, Bill. Intern, Nashville Gen. Hosp., 1957-58; practice of medicine, Lewisburg, Tenn., 1958-63, Mount Airy, N.C., 1964—; mem. staff Northern Hosp. of Surry County, Mount Airy, N.C., chief staff 1972—. Mem. Am., N.C., Surry County med. assns., Nat. Rifle Assn., Trout Unlimited, Bass and Salt Water Fly Rodders of Am. Home: 274 Herring St Mount Airy NC 27030 Office: 731 Worth St Mount Airy NC 27030

GUAY, RICHARD FRANCOIS, govt. ofcl.; b. Detroit, Apr. 3, 1937; s. Edmond Francois and Marguerite (Monfette) G.; student Wayne State U., 1957-58, Colo. State Coll., 1960, Georgetown U. 1963-64; m. Miriam Regina McKernan, May 17, 1963; children—Monique, Paul, John, Catherine. With govt. D.C., 1959-60; with Nat. Machine Tool Builders, Washington, 1961-62; chief data processing Export Import Bank Washington, 1962-64; exec. sec. Nat. Tool, Die & Precision Machining Assn., Rochester, N.Y., 1964-66; nat. tng. dir. Inst. Scrap Iron & Steel, Washington, 1966-69; chief nat. contracts on the job tng. U.S. Dept. Labor, Washington, 1969-70; dir. manpower devel. staff Environmental Protection Agy., Washington, 1970—. Mem. subcom. on profl., sci. and tech. manpower Nat. Manpower Adv. Com.; mem. Nat. Camp Area Manpower Planning System, Dept. Labor. Pres., Guay-Horgan Inc., Washington; officer Happy Hour Investment Club. Home: 5404 Galena Pl NW Washington DC 20016 Office: Washington DC 20006

GUBERMAN, REUBEN, editor; b. N.Y.C., Aug. 21, 1926; s. Leon and Clara (Tobolsky) G.; student Bklyn. Coll., 1943-45; m. Tamara Frances Sherman, Feb. 21, 1960; children—Leon, Ira, Nanette. Free lance writer children's cartoons, English dialogue motion pictures, actor, dir., Miami, Fla., 1948-68; personality radio shows, Miami, 1965-68; editor Convenience Store Jour., also Non-Foods Merchandising, Atlanta, 1968—. Mem. B'nai B'rith Youth Orgn. Bd., Miami, 1967. Mem. Am. Soc. Bus. Press Editors. Jewish religion. Author: 52 Retail Promotions, 1968. Contbr. articles to bus. mags. Home: 2695 Terratim Lane Decatur GA 30034 Office: Convenience Store Jour United Pub Co 735 Spring St NW Atlanta GA 30308

GUBERN, CARLOS SANTIAGO, physician; b. Barcelona, Spain, Aug. 16, 1901; s. Juan and Rosario (Puig) G.; M.D., Sch. Medicine, Barcelona, Spain, 1924; m. Antonia Barraso, July 2, 1934; children—Montserrat (Mrs. Felipe A. Garcia). Intern, Clinic Hosp., Barcelona, 1924, 25, 26; resident St. Cruz and St. Pablo Hosp., Barcelona, 1926-27; resident Hosp. Hotel Dieu, Paris, France, 1927-28, Peck Carson Meml. Hosp., Bklyn., 1944-45; practice medicine, Barcelona, 1931-36; chief obstetrics and gynecology Fajarde Dist. Hosp., P.R., 1948-51; practice medicine specializing in obstetrics and gynecology, Dr. Gubern's Hosp., Fajardo, P.R., 1951—. Counsu nof Spain in Lille France, Mazagan, French Morroco, 1936-39. Mem. P.R. Med. Assos., Hosp. Asso. P.R. Rotarian, Odd Fellow. Home: E16 Calle 5 Fajardo Sta Isidra PR 00648 Office: 110 Antonie R Barcelo Fajardo PR 00648

GUCKENHEIMER, LUDWIG, govt. ofcl.; b. Darmstadt, Germany, Apr. 19, 1911; s. Maximillian Moritz and Sofie (Hirsch) G.; student U. Frankfurt, 1928-29, U. Heidelberg, 1929-31, Rechts Referendar, U. Giessen, 1932; postgrad. Northwestern U., 1935-36; M.S.W., Tulane U., 1941; m. Gertrude Goldschmidt, Sept. 29, 1939; children—Anna Maria (Mrs. B. Howard Rappaport), Elizabeth Hanna (Mrs. William Lee), John Mark, Sam Robert. Came to U.S., 1933, naturalized, 1939. Clk., cashier, salesman Armour & Co., Chgo., 1934-37; counselor Elmwood Home for Boys, Springfield, Pa., 1938, Orthodox Jewish Home for Children, Cleve., 1938-39; clk. Neisner Bros., 1939; research analyst New Orleans Council Social Agys., 1941; with La. Dept. Pub. Welfare, Baton Rouge, 1941-64, successively caseworker, case supr., social analyst, 1941-52, dir. Div. Spl. Services, 1953-64; regional adminstrv. and fiscal specialist Bur. Family Services, U.S. Dept. Health Edn. and Welfare, Dallas, 1964-67, asst. acting chief div. state adminstrv. and fiscal standards, Assistance Payments Adminstrn., Social and Rehab. Service, Washington, 1967-70, chief, 1970—. Spl. lectr. La. State U. Sch. Social Welfare, 1962-64. Mem. Troop com. Boy Scouts Am., 1957-68, dist. com., 1960-64; 2d v.p. Baton Rouge council Camp Fire Girls, 1961; past sec. La. Orgns. State Legislation. Recipient George Freeman award La. Conf. Social Welfare, 1962. Mem. Nat., La. (treas. 1960-64) confs. social welfare, Nat. Assn. Social Workers (past chmn. local chpt., past sec.), Am. Pub. Welfare Assn., La. Mental Health Assn., Nat. Rehab. Assn., Am. Acad. Polit. and Social Scis., Nat., La., Baton Rouge assns. retarded children, Nat. Conf. on Social Welfare, La. Council for Handicapped, Systems and Procedures Assn., Am. Soc. Pub. Adminstrn., Am. Mgmt. Assn., Data Processing mgmt. Assn. Contbr. articles to profl. jours. Home: 5901 Jarvis Lane Bethesda MD 20014 Office: Assistance Payments Adminstrn Social and Rehab Service to US Dept Health Edn and Welfare Washington DC 20201

GUDE, ALBERT VALDEMAR, physician; b. Atlanta, Oct. 15, 1922; s. Albert Valdemar and Helen (O'Brien) G.; A.B., Emory U., 1942; M.D., Johns Hopkins, 1946; m. Donna Rae Currier, Dec. 22, 1945; children—Helen and Anne (twins), Margaret, Donna Doris. Intern Union Meml Hosp., Balt., 1946-47; resident Lawson VA Hosp., Chamblee, Ga., 1949-51, Emory U. Hosp., Atlanta, 1950-51; practice medicine specializing in anesthesiology, Atlanta, 1951—; mem. staff Piedmont Hosp., Atlanta. Mem. Soc. St. Vincent de Paul, 1962-64. Served to lt. (j.g.) USNR, 1947-49. Diplomate Am. Bd. Anesthesiology. Mem. A.M.A., Am. Soc. Anesthesiologists, Johns Hopkins Alumni Assn. (past pres. Ga. br.), Phi Beta Kappa, Chi Phi. Roman Catholic. Club: Piedmont Driving. Address: 4968 Carol Lane NW Atlanta GA 30327

GUDGEN, RAYMOND EARL, JR., telephone co. ofcl.; b. Quincy, Ill., June 26, 1917; s. Raymond Earl and Ethel Lee (Mason) G.; B.S. in Indsl. Engring., U. Ala., 1951; postgrad. Ia. State U., 1966; m. Ernestine Elizabeth Sargent, Feb. 14, 1940; 1 son, Ronald Earl. Asst. chem. lab. Lehigh Portland Cement Co., 1935; prodn. worker Lamson & Session Co., 1939-40; lineman So. Bell Tel. & Tel. Co., Birmingham, Ala., 1940-41, cable splicer helper, 1941-46, cable splicer, 1946-50, jr. engr., 1951, outside plant engr., 1951-66, project engr., 1966-68; project engr. South Central Bell Tel. Co., Birmingham, 1968—. Served with U.S. Navy, 1935-39, 42-45; PTO. Registered profl. engr., Ala., Ga. Mem. Inst. Indsl. Engrs., Nat., Ala. socs. profl. engrs., St. Pats Engr. Soc., Telephone Pioneers Am. (pres. Mobile, Ala. council 1964-65), Alpha Pi Mu. Home: 4832 Clairmont Av Birmingham AL 35222 Office: South Central Bell Telephone Co PO Box 2662 Birmingham AL 35202

GUDNASON, HALLDOR VICTOR, physician; b. Reykjavik, Iceland, July 16, 1932; s. Gudni Emil and Kristin (Ingibsartar) K.; student Menntaskoli Reykjavik, 1950-54; M.D., U. Iceland Med. Sch., 1954; m. Drofn Markusdottir, Sept. 4, 1952; children—Haukur Markus, Ingi Valdimar, Gudbjorg Helga, Kristin Halldora. Came to U.S., 1965. Rotating intern U. Hosp. Iceland, 1962-63, St. Joseph Hosp., Chgo., 1965-66; resident anesthesiology U. Va. Hosp., Charlottesville, 1966-69; gen. practice medicine, Olafsfsordur, Iceland, 1963-65; staff physician Rehab. Center for Rheumatic Patients, Hveragerdi, Iceland, 1965; pvt. practice medicine specializing in anesthesiology, Falls Church, Va., 1969—; mem. staff, chief dept. anesthesiology Culpeper (Va.) Meml. Hosp., 1971—; mem. staff Fairfax Hosp., Falls Church, Fauquier Hosp. Recipient NIH Grant, 1969. Mem. Iceland, Va., Fairfax County med. socs., A.M.A., Am., Va. socs. anesthesiologists. Lutheran. Address: 8917 Lynnhurst Dr Fairfax VA 22030

GUENTER, JOSEPH MARTIN, educator, physicist; b. North Little Rock, Ark., Mar. 21, 1938; s. Bernard Henry and Mary (Martin) G.; B.A., Hendrix Coll., 1960; M.S., U. Ark., 1965. Instr. natural sci. U. Ark. at Monticello, 1962-65, asst. prof. Nat. Sci., 1965-66, head dept. physics, 1966—, head dept. phys. sci., 1970—. Vis. scientist Ark. Acad. Sci.; adviser Upsilon chpt. Sigma Tau Gamma; mem. adv. bd. S.E. Ark. Arts and Sci. Center; chmn. College Heights Credit Union. Mem. A.A.A.S., Am. Assn. U. Profs., Ark. Acad. Sci., Am. Assn. Physics Tchrs., Am. Phys. Soc., Am. Geophys. Union Am. Am. Optical Soc., Nat. Trust for Historic Preservation, Health Physics Soc., Am. Astron. Soc., Sigma Pi Sigma. Presbyn. (deacon, past chmn. bd., treas.). Home: 204 W Bolling Monticello AR 71655

GUENTHER, GEORGE CARPENTER, govt. ofcl.; b. Reading, Pa., Aug. 27, 1931; s. John H. and Eleanor (Carpenter) G.; A.B. in Psychology, Amherst Coll., 1952; m. Kathleen Lance Coyle, Oct. 20, 1962; children—George Carpenter, Todd C., John B. Pres. John H. Guenther Hosiery Co., Reading, 1955-67; dep. sec. Pa. Dept. Labor and Industry, 1967-69; dir. Bur. Labor Standards, Dept. Labor, 1969-71, asst. sec. labor for occupational safety and health, 1971—. Bd. dirs. Nat. Safety Council; chmn. Fed. Safety Council. Served with USN, 1952-55. Mem. Am. Soc. Safety Engrs. Home: 5508 Wilson Lane Bethesda MD 20014 Office: Dept of Labor Washington DC 20210

GUENTHER, LOUIS CHARLES, univ. adminstr.; b. Pitts., Jan. 23, 1905; s. Herman Julius and Emma (King) G.; B.A., Southwestern Coll., 1934; M.A., U. Pitts., 1938, Ph.D., 1958; m. Joanne VanDerLyke Bouterse, Sept. 2, 1938; 1 dau., Barbara (Mrs. Byron Douglas Hill). Registrar Howard Coll., Birmingham, Ala., 1938-43, Mary Washington Coll., U. Va., Fredericksburg, 1943-59; dir. admissions Wake Forest U., Winston-Salem, N.C., 1959-60; registrar Fla. Presbyn. Coll., St. Petersburg, 1960-67; registrar Samford U., Birmingham, Ala., 1967—. Mem. Am., So., Ala. assns. collegiate registrars and admissions officers, Ala. Edn. Assn., Pi Gamma Mu, Alpha Phi Omega, Phi Eta Sigma, Kappa Phi Kappa. Baptist. Home: 4164 Winston Way Birmingham AL 35213

GUERRA, HUMBERTO RUBEN, dentist; b. Mission, Tex., Dec. 19, 1929; s. Cipriano F. and Bertha (Pena) G.; B.S. in Pharmacy Loyola U. of South, 1955, D.D.S., 1962; m. Gail Coons, Aug. 22, 1965; children—Stephen, Thomas, Karen, Gregory. Asst. mgr. Walgreens, New Orleans, 1957-62; pvt. practice dentistry, New Orleans, 1962—. Prof. pharmacology Loyola U., New Orleans, 1966—; pres., dir. Aero-Dent, Inc., New Orleans, 1971—. Served with AUS, 1955-57. Mem. Am., New Orleans, La. dental assns., Acad. Gen. Dentistry. Inventor spl. dental spray Detex. Home: 4800 Marque Dr New Orleans LA 70126 Office: 8339 Chef Menteur Hwy New Orleans LA 70127

GUERRERO, JOAQUIN C., govt. ofcl.; b. Agana, Guam, Dec. 8, 1920; s. Joaquin and Luisa L. (Castro) G.; B.S., Ind. U., 1958, M.S., 1959, M.B.A., 1961. Immigrant insp. Govt. of Guam, Agana, 1951, adminstrv. officer, 1952-53, chief adminstrn., 1963, asst. to dir. finance, 1961-64, dir. finance, 1965-68, dir. revenue and taxation, 1968, dir. Bur. Budget and Mgmt. Research, 1969—. Guam del. South Pacific Commn.; dir. for Guam, Office Emergency Preparedness. Chmn. Guam chpt. A.R.C., 1968-69. Served to 1st lt. Guam Militia. Mem. Municipal Finance Officers Assn., Fed. Govt. Accountants Assn. Rotarian. Clubs: Hawaiian Golf; Windward Hills Golf. Home: PO Box 2228 Agana Guam 96910 Office: Office of Governor Govt of Guam Agana Guam 96910

GUERRERO, MANUEL FLORES LEON, former gov. Guam; b. Agana, Guam, Oct. 25, 1914; s. Jose L.G. Leon and Maria Lujan (Flores) G.; ed. in Guam; LL.D., W. Va. Inst. Tech., 1968; L.H.D., Colo. State Coll., 1968; m. Delfina T. Tuncap, Oct. 18, 1934; children—Alfredo, Lolita (Mrs. Charles J. Huxel, Jr.), Rudolpho, Evelyna (Mrs. Floyd Bonner), Teresita (Mrs. Paul DeDominico), Manuel Flores Leon Guerrero, Patricia. With Guam Govt., 1930-48, 50-69, asst. sec. Guam, 1956-60, adminstrv. staff officer 6th Guam Legislature, 1960-61, sec. of Guam, 1961-63, gov. of Guam, 1963-69. Bd. dirs., v.p. Guam Comml. Corp., 1946-48, fiscal adviser, controller, 1948-49. Mem. Guam Congress Ho. of Assembly, 1948-50, chmn. finance com., 1948-50; mem. 1st Guam Legislature, 1950-52, chmn. rules and land transfer bd. coms., 1950-52. Mem. U.S. delegation 4th S. Pacific Conf., New Caledonia, 1963; U.S. observer S. Pacific Conf., 1962; alternate U.S. commr. to S. Pacific Commn., 1961, permanent U.S. commr., 1964—. Capt., Guam Militia. Mason (Shriner). Home: PO Box 223 Agana GU 96910

GUERRY, J. H., state ofcl. Exec. dir. Fla. Jud. Adminstrv. Commn., Tallahassee. Address: Box 1654 Supreme Ct Bldg Tallahassee FL 32304*

GUESS, GORDON BLUE, banker; b. Princeton, Ky., June 18, 1936; s. Neil Gordon and Virginia (Blue) G.; B.A., Vanderbilt U., 1958; m. Mary Carole Naber, Aug. 8, 1970. Trainee, Louisville Trust Co., 1961, programmer, 1962-64, mgr. data processing div., 1965-69, asst. v.p. money mgmt. and investment div., 1969—; asst. mgr. computer dept. Fla. Nat. Bank of Jacksonville, 1965; dir. Peoples Bank, Marion. Co-founder, dir. The Ky. Republican, 1964; vice chmn. Young Rep. Clubs Ky., 1966; nat. committeeman Young Rep. Nat. Fedn., 1969-71; mem. Louisville-Jefferson County Rep. Exec. Com., 1970-71; mem. Rep. State Central Com., 1970-71; chmn. Ky. 3d Dist. Young Reps., 1970-71. Served to capt. AUS, 1959-60, 61-62. Mem. Am. Inst. Banking, Systems and Procedures Assn., Jr. C. of C., U. Louisville Assos., Delta Kappa Epsilon. Methodist. Clubs: Louisville Quarterback, Lincoln (Louisville, Ky.). Home: 5828 Prince William St Louisville KY 40207 Office: 200 S 5th St Louisville KY 40202

GUEST, M(AURICE) MASON, scientist, educator; b. Fredonia, N.Y., July 30, 1906; s. Maurice S. and Daisy (Mason) G.; A.B., U. Mich., 1930; Ph.D., Columbia, 1941; m. Alice Rhoda Avery, Aug. 16, 1936; children— Avery Mason, John Andrew. Field asst. U.S. Dept. Agr. Bur. of Entomology, 1930-31; sci. tchr. Sherman (N.Y.) High Sch., 1931-36; instr. physiology Columbia, 1936-40, research asso., 1940-42; asso. prof. physiology Wayne U. Coll. Medicine, 1946-51; prof., chmn. dept. physiology U. Tex. Med. Br., Galveston, 1951—. Served to maj. USAAF, 1942-46. Mem. Am. Physiol. Soc., A.A.A.S., Am. Assn. U. Profs., Soc. for Exptl. Biology and Medicine, Internat. Hematol. Soc. Contbr. articles to profl. jours. Home: 1409 Harbor View Dr Galveston TX 77550

GUIBERTEAU, JAMES JOSEPH, dentist; b. Houston, Sept. 10, 1934; s. Milton Joseph and Dorothy (Porter) G.; B.S., Tex. A. and M. U., 1956, postgrad., 1957-58; D.D.S., U. Tex., 1962; m. Naurene Alece Hall, June 2, 1957; children—James Joseph, Peggy Jean, John Joseph. Grad. teaching asst. Tex. A. and M. U., 1957-58; pvt. practice dentistry, Houston, 1964—; staff dentist VA Hosp., Houston, 1967; dental dir. Richmond State Sch., Tex. Dept. Mental Health and Mental Retardation, 1968—; mem. med. staff Meml. Baptist Hosp. System, Houston, 1966—; clin. instr. Sch. Dental Hygiene, Wharton County Jr. Coll., 1970—. Welbelos leader, Eagle Scout adviser Sam Houston Area council Boy Scouts Am., 1967—; mem. Candlelight Plaza Civic Club, 1967—. Served to capt. Dental Corps., AUS, 1962-64. Recipient certificates of recognition Sam Houston Area council Boy Scouts Am., 1967. Mem. Am., Tex. dental assns., Houston Dist. Dental Soc., Assn. Mil. Surgeons of U.S., Tex. Acad. Pub. Health and Instl. Dentists (exec. sec. 1972—), So. Assn. for Instl. Dentists, U. Tex. Dental Br. Alumni Assn., Tex. A. and M. U. Former Students Assn. Episcopalian. Mason. Home: 1002 Bethlehem Houston TX 77018 Office: 2100 Preston Richmond TX 77469

GUIDRY, LOUIS CHARLES, lawyer; b. New Orleans, July 24, 1896; s. Louis C. and Marie DeBlanc (DeLacroix) G.; J.D., Loyola U., 1922; m. Winifred Hollies, Sept. 19, 1923; children—Frederick Hollies, Frances Winifred. Admitted to La. bar, 1922, U.S. Supreme Ct., 1946, asso. Dart, Kernan, & Dart, 1922; mem. firm Dart, Guidry & Dart, and predecessor firms, 1942-60. Lectr. civil code and taxation Loyola U. South, 1929-31; judge adv. La. dept. Am. Legion, 1930-31; mem. group com. on proposed Internat. Safety-at-Sea Conf.; spl. counsel Inland Waterways Corp., 1943-45; mem. spl. probate adv. com. La. State Law Inst., 1960. Organizer, mem. New Orleans Meml. Day Assn., 1929; pres. Met. New Orleans Safety Council, 1958-59. Mem. Am. Bar Assn., Am. Legion (past post comdr.). Home: 1205 St Charles Av New Orleans LA 70130 Office: Nat Bank Commerce Bldg New Orleans LA 70112

GUILBEAU, HUGH FRANCIS, dentist; b. Branch, La., Mar. 29, 1918; s. Robert Eaton and Corrine Marie (Junca) G.; student U. S.W. La., 1935-36; D.D.S., Loyola U., 1940; m. Connie Hoffpauir, July 19, 1941; children— Hugh Francis, Jr., Catherine (Mrs. Phillip J. Denoncourt, Jr.). Pvt. practice dentistry, Iota, La., 1940-41, Jennings, La., 1945—. Sec., treas., dir. Am. Legion Hosp., Jennings, 1952—. Treas. Jennings Youth Center, 1969. Bd. dirs. Boy's Village, 1940-50. Served with AUS, 1941-45; ETO. Mem. Am. Legion (post treas. 1946—), Assn. Commerce (bd. dirs. 1948-51), 7th Dist. Dental Soc., Am., La. dental assns., V.F.W., Delta Sigma Delta, Alpha Sigma Chi. Roman Catholic. Kiwanian (pres. 1949, lt. gov. 1956), Elk. Clubs: Jeff Davis Country (sec. 1961-62), Golf (both Jennings, La.). Home: 815 Church St Jennings LA 70546 Office: 213 W Plaquemine St Jennings LA 70546

GUILLAUME, BERNARD GEORGE, realtor; b. Guernsey, Channel Island, July 11, 1910; s. Stephen Osmond and Jessie May (LePage) G.; student LaSalle Extension U., 1940, Loyola U., Chgo., 1941, Northwestern U., 1942; m. Ethylle Marie Perkins, Aug. 27, 1938; 1 son, Stephen B. Owner, mgr. Ebb Tide Motel, Treasure Island, Fla., 1954-70; controller Pickard, Inc., Antioch, Ill., 1945-54; real estate broker Guillaume Realty Co., Seminole, Fla., 1958—. Mem. City Commn., Treasure Island, 1960-70; mem. Pinellas County Planning Council, 1964-71, chmn. council, 1968; mem. Pinellas County Charter Commn., 1971—. Mem. Gulf Beach-Seminole Bd. Realtors (pres. 1968, v.p., dir. 1969—). Republican. Methodist. Mason (32 deg.). Home: 11120 54th Av N St Petersburg FL 33708 Office: 6701 Seminole Blvd Seminole FL 33542

GUILLEN, LUIS E., lawyer; b. El Salvador, Feb. 6, 1909; LL.D., U. El Salvador; LL.B., N.Y. Law Sch., 1956. Admitted to El Salvador bar, 1935, N.Y. bar, 1957, U.S. Supreme Ct. bar, 1961. Prof. internat. pvt. law U. El Salvador, 1939-44; prof. comml. law Inst. Comml. Scis., El Salvador, 1939-44; now mem. firm Curtis, Mallet-Prevost, Colt & Mosle, Washington. Del. UN, 1948. Justice Income Tax Appellate Ct., El Salvador, 1941-44; pres. Ct. Accounts, El Salvador, 1945-48. Mem. Am. Bar Assn. Address: Curtis Mallet-Prevost Colt & Mosle 1523 L St NW Washington DC 20005*

GUILLIAMS, GEORGE CORNELIOUS, ednl. supr.; b. Rocky Mount, Va., Feb. 22, 1922; s. Thomas Cornelious and Callie Ruth (Agee) G.; B.S., Va. Poly. Inst., 1942, M.S., 1950; m. Mabel Elnora Conner, Sept. 14, 1943; children—Steven Morris, Sue Ellen (Mrs. Robert Warren Thacker). Tchr. vocational agr. Auburn High Sch., Riner, Va., 1942-66; gen. supr. Montgomery County Schs., Christianburg, Va., 1966-67, county supr. vocational edn., 1967—; supr. student tchrs. Va. Poly. Inst., Riner, 1942-66. Organized Livestock Registry Assn. Va., 1956. Treas. Community Action Agy., 1968-70; mem. Montgomery County Pub. Service Authority, 1970—, vice chmn., 1970-72. Bd. dirs. Montgomery County Tb Assn. Mem. Nat., Va., Montgomery County (v.p. 1963-65) edn. assns., Blue Ridge Vocational Agr. Tchrs. (treas. 1960-68), Va. Assn. Future Farmers Am. (hon.), Young Homemakers Va. (hon.). Methodist. Pioneer in planning of water system for Riner area. Home: Route 3 Box 648 Riner VA 24149 Office: 200 Junkin St Christianburg VA 24073

GUILLIAMS, MABEL ELNORA CONNER (MRS. GEORGE C. GUILLIAMS), former corp. exec.; b. Saltville, Va.; d. Noah Adolphas and Abbiegail (Vest) Conner; student pub. schs.; m. George C. Guilliams, Sept. 22, 1943; children—Steven Morris, Sue Ellen (Mrs. Thacker). Payroll supr. Blue Ridge Mfg. Co., Christiansburg, Va., 1939-45; treas. Montgomery Pub. Corp., Christiansburg, 1959-71; sec.-treas. Messenger Realty Corp., 1967-71, Tri-City Printing Corp., 1967-71. Chmn. fund dr. Am. Cancer Soc., 1962-64, A.R.C., 1960-64, bd. dirs., 1961-62. Democrat. Methodist (treas. ch. 1953-61, 70—, financial sec. 1966—). Grange. Home: Route 3 Box 648 Riner VA 24149

GUILLIOT, ROY, dentist; b. Youngsville, La., Jan. 18, 1918; s. Jerry J. and Olive (LeBlanc) G.; student La. State U., 1936-38; D.D.S., Loyola U., New Orleans, 1942; m. Joyce Margaret Blanchet, Dec. 27, 1941; children—Roy, Paul Jerome, Anita Joyce, John Albert. Pvt. practice dentistry, Lafayette, La., 1942-46; mem. staffs Lady of Lourdes, Lafayette Gen. hosps. Trustee, Lafayette Gen. Hosp. Served with USNR, 1942-46. Mem. Acad. Gen. Dentistry, Health Manpower Com. La., Acadiana Health Planning Council, Am., La., 3d Dist. dental assns., Lafayette Dental Soc. (pres. 1959). Roman Catholic. K.C. (4 degree). Clubs: Oak Bourne Country, Serra. Home: 1621 Myrtle Place Lafayette LA 70501 Office: 430 Jefferson St Lafayette LA 70501

GUILLORY, TROY TILLMAN, bank exec.; b. Sikes, La., Mar. 27, 1920; s. Gill Gilbert and Grace Mae (Burks) G.; student La. State U., 1938-39; B.S., Omaha U., 1960; M.B.A., George Washington U., 1961; postgrad. Indsl. Coll. Armed Forces, 1960-61; m. Mary Joe Standley, Dec. 20, 1941; children—Troy Tillman, Jr., Barbara (Mrs. Noel Mulhearn), Mary Margaret. Commd. ensign U.S. Navy, 1941, advanced to capt., 1961, ret., 1968; with Central Savs. Bank & Trust Co., Monroe, La., 1968—, sr. v.p., 1969—. Crusade chmn. Am. Cancer Soc., 1968-69, pres. 1970-71. Decorated D.F.C., Air medals (2). Mason, Lion. Home: 417 Lakeshore Dr Monroe LA 71201 Office: Central Bank PO Box 5020 Monroe LA 71201

GUILLOT, ROBERT MILLER, ins. co. exec.; b. Headland, Ala., Jan. 2, 1922; s. Clarence Miller and Ruth (Lindsey) G.; B.S., Auburn U., 1943; LL.B., U. Ala., 1948; m. Patty Shirley, Sept. 1, 1947; children—Patti Ann, Robert Miller, Shirley Lynne. Admitted to Ala. bar, 1948; practice in Dothan, 1948-51; sr. v.p., sec. Vulcan Life Ins. Co., Birmingham, Ala., 1952-66; pres. Am. Educators Life Ins. Co., Birmingham, 1966—. Mayor of Vestavia Hills, Ala., 1960—. Trustee, Troy State U. Served with AUS, 1942-45. Decorated Bronze Star. C.L.U., 1966. Mem. Assn. Ala. Life Ins. Cos. (pres.) Ala. League Municipalities (pres. elect), Nat. Assn. Life Underwriters, Am. Soc. Chartered Life Underwriters. Baptist. Mason. Club: Vestavia Hills Arts Council, Inc. Home: 2100 Longleaf Circle Vestavia Hills AL 35216 Office: 2910 Linden Av Birmingham AL 35209

GUIN, J(UNIUS) FOY, JR., lawyer; b. Russellville, Ala., Feb. 2, 1924; s. Junius Foy and Ruby (Pace) G.; student Ga. Inst. Tech., 1940-41; J.D., U. Ala., 1947; LL.D., Magic Valley Christian Coll., 1963; m. Dorace Jean Caldwell, July 18, 1945; children—Janet Elizabeth Smith, Judith Ann Mullican, Junius Foy III, David Jonathan. Admitted to Ala. bar, 1948; practiced in Russellville, Ala., 1948—; sr. partner Guin, Guin, Bouldin & Porch, Russellville, Ala., 1948—; pres. Abstract Trust Co., Inc.; sec. Iuka TV Cable Co., Inc., Haleyville TV Cable Co., Inc.; dir., gen. counsel First Nat. Bank Russellville, Franklin Fed. Savs. & Loan Assn. Russellville. Mem. adv. com. civil practice and procedure Supreme Ct. Ala., 1971—; chmn. Ala. Jud. Commn., 1972—; active World Peace Through Law Center. Chmn. Russellville City Planning Com., 1954-57; county chmn. Republican party, 1954-58, 71—, state finance chmn., 1972—; candidate for U.S. Senator from Ala., 1954. Served to 1st lt., inf., AUS, 1943-46. Mem. Am. Radio Relay League, Am. Counsel Assn., Assn. Ins. Attys., Am. (mem. spl. com. on residential real estate transactions 1972—), Ala. (com. chmn. 1965—), Franklin County bar assns., Ala. Law Inst. (dir. 1969—), Am. Trial Lawyers Assn., Ala. Defense Lawyers Assn., Ala. Plaintiffs Lawyers Assn., Farrah Law soc. Ala. State Bar (commr. 1965—, 2d v.p. 1969-70), Farrah Order jurispudence, Phi Beta Kappa, Delta Chi. Mem. Ch. of Christ (elder 1969—). Rotarian. Home: 2005 Wilson Av NW Russellville AL 35653 Office: 500 N Jackson St PO Box 940 Russellville AL 35653

GUINN, GEORGE EARL, coll. pres.; b. Mossville, Miss., Aug. 21, 1912; s. David Howard and Martha Inez (Easterling) G.; A.B., La. Coll., 1937; student Southwestern Bapt. Theol. Sem., 1938-39; Th.M., New Orleans Bapt. Theol. Sem., 1942, Th.D., 1944; D.D., Mercer U. (Ga.), 1961; LL.D., William Jewel Coll., 1970; m. Gail Holmes, July 13, 1937 (dec. 1969); 1 dau., Peggy Elaine (Mrs. Herschel Wood Crump); m. 2d, Neva Norsworthy DeMoss, June 12, 1970. Ordained to ministry Bapt. Church, 1933; pastor First Ch., Sterlington, La., 1937-41, Jennings, La., 1941-45, Bossier City, La., 1945-48; head dept. homiletics Southwestern Bapt. Theol. Sem., Fort Worth, 1948-51; pres. La Coll., Pineville, 1951—. Trustee Acadia Bapt. Acad., Eunice, La., 1941-48, Baton Rouge Gen. Hosp., 1944-45. Chmn. La. Bd. Instns., 1956-58; v.p. La. Found. Pvt. Colls., 1953-54, pres. 1954-55, 60-61, 64-65, 67-68; v.p. La. Coll. Conf., 1953-54; mem. edn. commn. So. Bapt. Conv., 1952-58, 68—; mem. commn. on colls. and univs. So. Assn. Colls. and Schs., 1961-67, 68—, pres. 1970-71. Mem. Pi Kappa Delta. Mason. Rotarian. Co-author So. Bapt. Preaching, 1959. Home: 1127 College Dr Pineville LA 71360

GUITTARD, CLARENCE ALWIN, appeals ct. judge; b. Waco, Tex., Mar. 17, 1917; s. Francis Gevrier and Mamie (Welhauen) G.; student U. Colo., 1937; A.B., Baylor, 1940, L.B., 1940; postgrad. U. Tex., 1941; m. Mary Lou Kee, Aug. 30, 1940; children—Charles F., John R., Mary Louise. Admitted to Tex. bar, 1940; asso. firm Lloyd & Lloyd, Alice, Tex., 1940-41, briefing atty. Tex. Supreme Ct., 1941-43; partner firm Burford, Ryburn & Ford, Dallas, 1943-61; judge 14th Dist. Ct., County, Dallas County, Dallas, 1961-71; asso. justice Ct. Civil Appeals 5th Supreme Jud. Dist., Dallas, 1971—. Lectr., Insts. Eminent Domain, Southwestern Legal Found., 1957—. Mem. Dallas County Democratic Exec. Com., 1956-61, Tex. Dem. Exec. Com., 1960-61. Bd. dirs. Dallas Theatre Center. Served with AUS, 1943-44. Mem. Am., Dallas bar assns., State Bar Tex. (inst. lectr. eminent domain and appellate practice), Am. Judicature Soc. Methodist. Club: Northwood. Contbr. articles to legal publs. Home: 6306 Desco Dr Dallas TX 75225 Office: Ct Civil Appeals Dallas County Courthouse 600 Commerce St Dallas TX 75202

GULLATT, E(NNIS) MURRAY, oil corp. exec.; b. Ada, Okla., Jan. 14, 1935; s. Ennis Murray and Flora Mae (Rainbolt) G.; B.S., Okla. U., 1957, M.S., 1958; M.B.A., Stanford, 1960; m. Nancy Bronaugh, July 23, 1955; children—John Michael, Deborah Leigh. Staff petroleum engr. Delhi-Taylor Oil Corp., Dallas, 1960-63; petroleum engr. Whitney Engring. Co., Tulsa, 1963; chief engr. Livingston Oil Co., Tulsa, 1963-65, v.p., 1965-67; exec. v.p. LVO Corp., Tulsa, 1967-71, pres., 1971—, also dir. Mem. bd. mgmt. Downtown YMCA, 1969-72; bd. dirs. Tulsa Sci. Found., 1968-71. Mem. Ind. Petroleum Assn. Am., Soc. Petroleum Engrs., Am. Petroleum Inst., Pi Epsilon Tau. Methodist. Home: 5809 E 63d St Tulsa OK 74136 Office: PO Box 2848 522 S Boston St Tulsa OK 74101

GULLETT, B. B., lawyer; b. Manchester, Tenn., Dec. 9, 1905; A.B., Cumberland U., 1927, L.B., 1927; postgrad. Vanderbilt U., 1928-29. Admitted to Tenn. bar, 1927; chief clk. Tenn. Senate, 1939-41; spl. asst. to atty. gen. State of Tenn., 1941-54; now mem. firm Gullett, Steele, Sanford, Robinson & Merritt, Nashville. Mem. Jud. Conf. 6th Circuit. Mem. Am. Judicature Soc., Nashville (pres. 1959-60), Tenn. (pres. 1967-68), Am. (ho. of dels. 1968—) bar assns. Address: Gullett Steele Sanford Robinson & Merritt 23d Floor Life and Casualty Tower Nashville TN 37219*

GULLEY, WILLARD QUENTIN, plastics co. exec.; b. Bulls Gap, Tenn., July 27, 1918; s. William Calvin and Etta Elizabeth (Berry) G.; B.S. in Chem. Engring., U. Tenn., 1943; m. Mazelle Holleman, Oct. 9, 1940; children—John Quentin, Jean Elizabeth. Engr. E.I. duPont de Nemours, 1942-46; v.p. Carolina Indsl. Plastics, Mt. Airy, N.C., 1946-52; sec.-treas. to pres., treas., dir. Vinylex Corp., Knoxville, Tenn., 1952—; dir. Extron Corp., Vinylex Corp. of Fla., Vinylex Corp. of Tex., Formall Plastics. Knox County Rep. finance chmn. for Gov. Winfield Dunn, 1970; mem. Gov.'s Study Com. for Econ. Devel., 1971-72. Baptist. Home: Cove Point Lane Concord TN 37720 Office: 3600 Pleasant Ridge Rd Knoxville TN 37921

GULLIVER, HAROLD STRONG, author; b. New Haven, July 30, 1893; s. Henry Strong and Harriet (Evans) G.; A.B., Yale, 1916; M.A., Columbia, 1921; Ph.D., Yale, 1930; m. Augusta Rentz, June 16, 1934; children— Harold Strong, William Bradford. Tutor, Robert Coll., Constantinople, 1916-17, 20-21; lectr. Columbia, 1921-22; instr. Yale, 1922-29; prof., head dept. English Valdosta State Coll., 1929-61; vis. prof. English Peabody Coll. summers, 1931, 32; vis. prof. U. Ga., summers 1935-38; vis. prof. German, Emory U. at Valdosta, 1948-53; vis. Fulbright prof. Damascus U., Syria, 1961-62; vis. prof. Heidelberg Coll., Tiffin, O., 1965-66, Ga. Christian Sch., 1968-69. Served to 1st. lt. U.S. Army, 1917-19; A.E.F. Mem. Modern Lang. Assn., Am. Assn. U. Profs. (past pres.), Am. Legion (past comdr.), Phi Beta Kappa. Democrat. Episcopalian. Clubs: Rotary, Executives (past pres.), Southern Pines Dinner (pres. 1965-66). Author: Thackeray's Literary Apprenticeship, 1934; Out of the Bog and Other Poems, 1938. Address: 216 W Alden Av Valdosta GA 31603

GUM, COLEMAN PREWITT, JR., dentist; b. Knoxville, Tenn., Apr. 12, 1935; s. Coleman Prewitt and Sara (Gallaher) G.; B.A., Centre Coll., 1957; D.M.D., U. Louisville, 1961; m. Lucy Lee Sharp, Nov. 1, 1957; children—Michael, Mitchell, Martha. Pvt. practice dentistry, Danville, Ky., 1968—, Pres. Boyle County Cancer Soc., 1968-70. Served with AUS, 1961-68. Kiwanian. Home: 522 Boone Trail Danville KY 40422 Office: 131 N 4th St Danville KY 40422

GUMB, DANA FREDERIC, microwave equipment mfg. co. exec.; b. N.Y.C., Nov. 24, 1924; s. Irving Turple and Elizabeth (Keller) G.; B.S. in Elec. Engring., 1946; M.S., Ga. Tech. U., 1949; m. Margaret Love Smith, Apr. 3, 1948; children—Edwin Smith, Dana F., Irving T. Engr. Hazeltine Engring. Co., N.Y.C., 1949-52; sr. engr. Melpar Co., Alexandria, Va., 1952-55, project engr., 1955-58; lab. dir. AGA Corp., Alexandria, 1958-60, Airtronics Inc., Bethesda, 1960-62; pres. Vega Precision Labs., Vienna, W.Va., 1963—, also chmn. bd. Served with USNR, 1943-49. Mem. I.E.E.E., Am. Ordnance Assn., Air Force Assn., Pi Mu Epsilon, Phi Gamma Delta. Home: 7401 Dulany Dr McLean VA 22101 Office: 800 Follin Lane Vienna VA 22180

GUNDERSON, FLORENCE O'BRIEN (MRS. GILBERT C. GUNDERSON), housemother, ret. exec.; b. Milw., July 29, 1899; d. Thomas C. and Flora H. (Hansen) O'Brien; student U. N.D., 1918-19, Dickinson State Coll., 1925-26; m. Gilbert C. Gunderson, July 2, 1922 (dec. July 1956); children—Constance (Mrs. C. H. Totten), Gilbert C., Betty (Mrs. Thomas P. Meehan), Judy (Mrs. Thomas G. McGowan), Thomas E. Tchr. pub. schs., 1918-40; with Maccabees Life Ins. Co., 1941-66, N.D. comdr., 1952-56, gen. agt. for N.D., Dickinson, 1960-66, dist. mgr., 1942-66, nat. del., 1948-52; dept. head S & L Store, Dickinson, 1956-64; housemother Kappa Delta, N.D. State U., 1968-70, U. Tulsa, 1970—. Active A.R.C., Am. Cancer Soc., United Fund drives, 1932-36. Mem. Am. Legion Aux., V.F.W. Aux., Catholic Daus. Am. (grand regent 1942-44, sec. 1938-41, dist. dep. 1948-58, nat. del. 1954), Beta Sigma Phi (dir. supplementary information Rho chpt. 1945-55). Roman Catholic. Clubs: Zonta Internat. (sec. 1955-56), Housemothers of N.D. State U.; University Womens (Tulsa). Address: 3134 E 5 Pl Tulsa OK 74104

GUNN, LEWIS BURWELL, banker; b. Richmond, Va., Aug. 20, 1905; s. Randolph Wellford and Alla (Jones) G.; student bus. adminstrn. U. Richmond, 1929-30; grad. Am. Inst. Banking, 1929; m. Dorothy Ryce, Apr. 14, 1934; children—Margaret V. (Mrs. James B. Farinholt, Jr.) (dec.), Lewis Burwell. With State-Planters Bank of Commerce & Trusts, Richmond, 1922-71, clk. asst. trust officer, trust officer, 1922-42, v.p. and trust officer charge trust dept. 1942-61, dir., 1945-71, exec. v.p., 1961-63, vice chmn. bd., 1963-70; vice chmn. bd. United Va. Bankshares, Inc., 1963-70, dir., 1963—; dir. Publishers Envelope Co., Chesapeake Corp. Va., Mut. Assurance Soc. Va. Mem. investment com. Richmond Instructive Vis. Nurses Assn. to 1971. Bd. dirs. Collegiate Schs., Richmond, Richmond Eye Hosp., Richmond Meml. Hosp., Ellis-Olsson-Chesapeake Found., West Point, Va. Mem. Phi Kappa Sigma. Home: 1808 Monument Av Richmond VA 23220 Office: 900 E Main St Richmond VA 23219

GUNN, WILLIAM SCHUYLER, investment co. exec.; b. Harvey, Ill., July 1, 1931; s. Harry E. and Irma (Zatkalik) G.; B.A., Beloit Coll., 1953; M.P.A., U. Kan., 1955; m. Diana Gaile Metts, June 12, 1954; children—Jeffrey, Susan, Karen. Adminstrv. asst., City of Janesville, Wis., 1954-55; asst. city mgr., Pompano Beach, Fla., 1957-60; account exec. Lee Higginson, Boca Raton, Fla., 1960-63; v.p., Walston & Co., Inc., Boca Raton, Fla., 1963—. Mem. Civil Service Bd., 1962-64; treas., dir. Internat. Found. Gifted Children, 1968-72. Bd. dirs., pres. United Fund, Boca Raton, Fla. Served with USN. Mem. Boca Raton C. of C. (pres., dir. 1963-67), Sigma Pi, Pi Sigma Alpha. Unitarian-Universalist (pres., treas. 1962-68). Kiwanian. Home: 360 E Alexander Palm Rd Boca Raton FL 33432 Office: 514-16 Via de Palmas Boca Raton FL 33432

GUNTER, JERRY MARSHALL, orthodontist; b. Gastonia, N.C., Mar. 27, 1938; s. Daniel Cornelius and Flake Harriet (Gilbert) G.; B.S., U. N.C., 1960, D.D.S., 1963; orthodontic certificate Northwestern U., 1968; m. Roberta Lou Kent, July 19, 1969. Orthodontist, Gastonia, N.C., 1968—. Bd. dirs. Am. Cancer Soc., Gastonia, N.C., 1969—. Served with USAF, 1963-66. Mem. N.C., Gastonia dental socs., Am. Dental Assn., So. Soc. Orthodontists, Am. Assn. Orthodontists, Wesleyan. Methodist. Rotarian. Home: 2912 Whitson Rd Gastonia NC 28052 Office: 224 New Hope Rd Gastonia NC 28052

GUNTER, WILLIAM D., JR., state senator; b. Jacksonville, Fla., July 16, 1934; s. William D. and Ruth (Senterfitt) G.; B.S.A. with high honors, U. Fla., 1956; postgrad. U. Ga., 1957-58; m. Leslie Letitia Peaden (dec.); children—Bartlett David, Joel Stephen. Tchr., Orange County, Fla., 1958-59; ins. agt. State Farm Ins. Co., 1959-61, agy. mgr., 1961—; mem. Fla. Senate, 1966—. Mem. Orlando (Fla.) Rehab. and Devel. Adv. Com., 1966. Bd. dirs. Central Fla. Fair. Served with AUS, 1956-58. Mem. Central Fla. Assn. Life Underwriters, Gen. Agts. and Mgrs. Assn., U. Fla. Alumni Assn. (past v.p.). Democrat. Baptist. Home: 3206 Inverness Ct Orlando FL 32806 Office: PO Box 14001 Orlando FL 32807*

GUPTA, VENU GOPAL, educator; b. Hoshiarpur, Punjab, India, Apr. 3, 1934 (came to U.S. 1966).; s. Ram Dass Gupta and Ram Piari (Aggarwal) G.; B.A. with honors, Punjab U., 1953, M.A., 1955, M. Ed. (Gold medalist), 1959; 0B.Ed., Delhi U., 1958; postgrad. (Dean's Spl. Grad. Studies award) U. Alta. (Can.), 1963-66; m. Sunita Aggarwal, Nov. 29, 1961; children—Sunil, Sanjiv. Lectr. Coll. Punjab and Kurukshetra U. (India), 1955-56, 59-63; grad. teaching and research asst. U. Alta., 1964-66; asst. prof. psychology Wis. State U. at Stevens Point, 1966-68; asst. prof. psychology, ednl. psychology and guidance, Eastern Ky. U., Richmond, 1968—. Recipient certificate for Distinguished Service to Teaching Profession, 1970; named Outstanding Educator Am., 1971. Mem. Am. Ednl. Research Assn., A.A.A.S., Am. Personnel and Guidance Assn., Assn. Counselor Edn. and Supervision, Internat. Council Edn. for Teaching, Am. Oriental Soc., Internat. Congress Orientalists, Am. Assn. U. Profs. Home: 926 Vickers Village Eastern Ky U Richmond KY 40475

GUPTA, VISHNU DAS, educator; b. Kalyanpur, India, Nov. 6, 1931; (came to U.S., 1959, naturalized, 1971); s. Anant Ram and Devki Devi (Aggarwal) G.; B.S., Panjab U., 1953, M.S., 1957; M.S., U. Tex., 1961; Ph.D., U. Ga., 1967; m. Kanta Kumari Goel, Sept. 2, 1957; children—Alka, Varun. Head quality control dept. Schlicksup Drug Co., Peoria, Ill., 1961-63; dir. labs. Kapco Inc., Kalamazoo, Mich., 1965-66; asst. prof. U. Houston, 1967-71, asso. prof. pharmaceutics, 1971—. Cons. pharm. analysis Harris County Hosp. Dist., Houston, 1970—. Recipient First Prize, Lunsford-Richardson Pharmacy Research Awards Competition, 1967. Mem. Am. Assn. U. Profs., Indian, Am., Tex. pharm. assns., Am., Tex. socs. hosp. pharmacists, Sigma Xi, Rho Chi, Kappa Psi. Home: 4903 Trail Lake Houston TX 77045 Office: Pharmacy Dept U Houston Houston TX 77004

GURAM, MALKIAT SINGH, ednl. adminstr.; b. Ludhiana, Punjab, India, Jan. 4, 1928; s. Tara Singh and Bishan (Kaur) G.; B.S., Punjab U., 1948, M.S., 1955; Ph.D., Ohio State U., 1967; m. Malbinder Kaur, Aug. 15, 1950; children—Apjinder, Servjinder, Mukhvinder. Came to U.S., 1964, naturalized, 1969. Lectr. Khalsa Coll., Amritsar, Punjab, 1948-49; lectr. Punjab Agrl. Coll., Ludhiana, 1953-56, prof. zoology and entomology, 1962-64; asst. entomologist Punjab Agrl. Dept., Chandigarh, 1956-60; prof., head dept. biology Voorhees Coll., Denmark, S.C., 1967-68, chmn. div. natural scis. and math., acad. dean, 1968—. Mem. A.A.A.S., Am. Inst. Biol. Scis., N.E.A., Entomol. Soc. Am., Am. Conf. Acad. Deans, Nat. Assn. Coll. Deans and Registrars, S.C. Edn. Assn., Alpha Kappa Mu. Contbr. articles on pesticide residues in plant and animal tissue to profl. jours. Address: Voorhees Coll Denmark SC 29042

GURLEY, MAX LYNN, dentist; b. Sardis, Tenn., Aug. 29, 1931; s. Alton Isom and Allie (Scott) G.; B.S., Middle Tenn. State Coll., 1958; D.D.S., U. Tenn., 1961; m. Sarah Kate Conrad, Apr. 3, 1954; children— Sarah Alisa, Cynthia Lynn, Lydia Annette, Amy Elizabeth, Timothy Isom. Dental intern Hillsborough County Hosp., Tampa, Fla., 1961-62; pvt. practice dentistry, 1962—. Served with USAF, 1951-55. Mem. Am., West Coast dental assns., Hillsborough County Dental Soc., Brewster Research Clinic, Internat. Assn. Orthodontics. Democrat. Baptist. Club: Cigar City Gun. Home: 11508 Carrollwood Dr Tampa FL 33618 Office: 10552 Florida Av Tampa FL 33612

GURNEY, EDWARD JOHN, U.S. senator; b. Portland, Me., Jan. 12, 1914; s. Edward J. and Nellie (Kennedy) G.; B.S., Colby Coll., 1935; LL.B., Harvard, 1938; LL.M., Duke, 1948; m. Natalie Ahlborn, Aug. 1, 1941; children—Jill, Sarah. Admitted to N.Y. bar, 1939, Fla. bar, 1949; practice in N.Y.C., 1938-41, Winter Park, Fla., 1948—; mem. 88th-90th Congresses from 5th Fla. Dist.; U.S. senator from Fla., 1968—. City commr., Winter Park, 1952-58, mayor 1961-62. Served to lt. col. AUS, 1941-46; ETO. Decorated Silver Star, Purple Heart. Mem. Am., Fla., N.Y. State bar assns., Am. Legion, V.F.W., Res. Officers Assn., Alpha Tau Omega. Republican. Conglist. Elk, Rotarian. Office: Senate Office Bldg Washington DC 20510

GURTLER, MARTIN MATHIAS, II, civil engr.; b. New Orleans, May 3, 1916; s. Martin Mathias and Louisa Benedicta (Rieth) G.; B.S. in Civil Engring., Tulane U., 1937; m. Audrey May Salzer, Apr. 15, 1944; children—Martin Mathias III, Linda Anna, Friedrich W. L., Michael K. A. Indsl. engr. Engring. Splty. & Mfg. Co., New Orleans, 1937-39; chief engr. LeMieux Bros., Inc., foresters and piledriving contractors, 1939-41; constrn. engr. Doullut & Ewin, Inc., civil engrs., gen. contractors, 1944-46; v.p. Bernard & Byrd, Inc., gen. contractors, 1946-51; pres. Gurtler, Hebert & Co., Inc., civil engrs., gen. contractors, New Orleans, 1951—; pres., dir. Am. Thrift & Finance Plan, Inc.; partner K.W. Salzer & Co., City Park Av. Floral Co. Bd. dirs. New Orleans Opera House Assn.; bd. dirs., mem. exec. com. Information Council of Americas; trustee Geneal. Research Soc. New Orleans, Mem. La. Engring. Soc., Nat. Soc. Profl. Engrs., Nat. Geneal. Soc., Swiss Am. Soc. New Orleans, France-Amerique de la Louisiane, Tau Beta Pi. Roman Catholic. Clubs: Round Table, International House, Paul Morphy (New Orleans); Metairie (La.) Country; City (Baton Rouge). Home: 1320 Second St New Orleans LA 70130 Office: 1539 Pleasure St New Orleans LA 70130

GUSDON, JOHN PAUL, JR., educator; b. Cleve., Feb. 13, 1931; s. John Paul and Pauline (Malencek) G.; B.A., U. Va., 1952, M.D., 1959; m. Marcelle Deiber, Aug. 1, 1956; children—Marguerite, John Phillip, Veronique. Intern Western Res. U. Sch. Medicine (now Case Western Res. U.), Cleve., 1959-60, resident, 1960-64, postdoctoral fellow, 1964-66, mem. faculty, 1966-67; mem. faculty Bowman Gray Sch. Medicine, Winston-Salem, N.C., 1967—, asso. prof. obstetrics and gynecology and microbiology, 1970—. Served with USN, 1952-55. Recipient research awards Cleve. Soc. Obstetrics and Gynecology, 1961, N.Am. Postgrad. Soc., 1965, South Atlantic Assn. Obstetrics and Gynecology, 1968, Found. Prize award Am. Assn. Obstetrics and Gynecology, 1971, Horsley Meml. award U. Va., 1971. Mem. A.A.A.S., Am. Coll. Obstetrics and Gynecology, Am. Assn. Immunologists, Soc. for Gynecol. Investigation. Roman Catholic. Contbr. articles to profl. jours. Home: 3240 Nottingham Rd Winston-Salem NC 27104

GUSEMAN, JOHN LEE, city ofcl.; b. Boise, Ida., July 5, 1910; s. Staley Lee and Villa Elizabeth (Clevidence) G.; student Fed. Bur. Investigation Nat. Acad., 1953, Municipal Police Adminstrn., Internat. City Mgrs. Assn., 1957; m. Helen Woods, Jan. 7, 1933; children—Robert, Patricia (Mrs. William L. Pelfrey). Chief police, Harlingen, Tex., 1952-58; asst. chief police, Bryan, Tex., 1961, police chief, 1961; dir. police Victoria, Tex., 1961-72; program specialist Office Traffic Safety Adminstrn., Tex. Dept. Community Affairs, 1972—. Instr. Police Acad., San Antonio, 1947-51, Victoria Police Acad., 1962-71; guest instr. Tex. A. and M. U., 1953-63, Victoria Coll., 1970-71. Commr. Tex. Urban Devel. Commn., 1970-71, vice chmn. law enforcement com., 1970-71. Bd. dirs. Tex. Inst. Children and Youth, 1957-58, FBI Nat. Acad. Assos. Tex., 1953-71. Served with USNR, 1941. Mem. Tex. Assembly on State and Urban Crisis, Internat. Assn. Chief Police, Tex. Police Assn. (dir. 1962-63), Internat. Assn. Identification (div. pres. 1958-59). Mason (Shriner), Rotarian. Club: Toastmaster (pres. 1955-56) (Harlingen, Tex.). Home: 2012 E Misteltoe St Victoria TX 77901 Office: PO Box 2268 Victoria TX 77901

GUSSMAN, HERBERT, oil producer; b. N.Y.C., Aug. 25, 1911; s. Samuel and Lottie (Simon) G.; A.B., Cornell U., 1933; m. Roseline Nadel, Apr. 14, 1935; children—Ellen J. (Mrs. Stephen Adelson), Barbara (Mrs. Stephan J. Heyman). With Reserve Drilling Co., Tulsa, 1940—, chmn. bd., 1950—; dir. M.P. R.R. Co., 1956—, Tulsa Fed. Savs. & Loan Assn., Mississippi River Corp. Exec. v.p. Tulsa Philharmonic Soc., Inc. Mem. Tulsa C. of C. (dir.), Phi Mu Alpha. Home: 4644 S Zunis Av Tulsa OK Office: 1st Nat Bank Bldg Tulsa OK

GUSTAFSON, JOEL KARL, lawyer; b. New Haven, May 24, 1937; s. J. Arthur and Jane (Thompson) G.; A.B., Lafayette Coll., 1960; LL.B., Tulane U., 1963; m. Judyth H. Field, Sept. 2, 1961; children—Kimberly Ann, Scott Evan, Stacey Lynn. Admitted to Fla. bar, 1964; prosecuting atty. City of Ft. Lauderdale, Fla., 1964-67; atty. Ft. Lauderdale (Fla.) Bd. of Adjustment, 1964-67, Ft. Lauderdale Planning and Zoning Bd., 1964-67; practiced in Ft. Lauderdale, Fla., 1964—; mem. firm Gustafson, Caldwell & Stephens, 1968—; mem. Fla. Ho. of Reps., 1967—. Mem. Broward County Narcotics Guidance Council, Fla. Law Revision Commn.; mem. Nat. Hwy. Safety Adv. Com., 1971—. Recipient award for meritorious pub. service, 1969. Mem. Am., Fla., Broward bar assns., Kappa Sigma, Fraternal Order of Police Assos. Republican. Presbyn. Home: 1636 SE 12th Ct Fort Lauderdale FL 33316 Office: Internat Bldg 2455 E Sunrise Blvd Fort Lauderdale FL 33304

GUSTAFSON, JOHN CONRAD, design engr.; b. N.Y.C., Dec. 13, 1936; s. Axel Conrad and Hedvig (Lorentson) G.; student Upsala Coll., 1955-56; B.S., U. Conn., 1960; m. Helen Elaine Parson, Aug. 16, 1958; children— Carl William, Carolyn Elaine, John David. Mech. engr., asst. project engr. Kearfott div. Gen. Precision, Inc., 1960-62; aerospace technologist NASA, 1962—. Mem. Am. Soc. M.E., Nat. Soc. Profl. Engrs., Sigma Pi Sigma. Lutheran. Home: 883 Cascade Dr Newport News VA 23602 Office: NASA Hampton VA 23365

GUSTAFSON, ROBERT KOVITZ, educator; b. San Diego, Feb. 6, 1929; s. Charles and Hazel Charlotte (Kovitz) G.; B.A., U. Cal. at Los Angeles, 1951; M.Divinity, Union Theol. Sem., 1956, Th.M., 1957, Th.D., 1964; m. Helen Leonia Sherrill, June 23, 1953; children—Glenn Louis, Sheryl MacLean. Ordained to ministry Presbyn. Ch., 1956; pub. relations Columbia Broadcasting System, Hollywood, Cal., 1947-51; minister Montpelier Presbyn. Ch., Wagram, N.C., 1957-58; asso. prof. Bible Flora MacDonald Coll., 1958-60; asso. prof. religion St. Andrews Presbyn. Coll., Laurinburg, N.C., 1961-68; dean Southeastern Community Coll., Whiteville, N.C., 1968-69; prof. philosophy and religion, chmn. dept. Pembroke (N.C.) State U., 1969—. Instl. rep. to U. N.C. Faculty Assembly, 1972, to Commn. Undergrad. Curricula Reform, 1972—. Chmn. Community Betterment Com., Scotland County, 1965-67; leadership tng. chmn. Cape Fear council Boy Scouts Am., 1968-71. Bd. dirs. Tri County Community Action Program, 1965-68; sr. asso. Danforth Found., 1964—. Served to lt. AUS, 1951-53. Mem. Am. Acad. Religion, Am. Soc. Ch. History, Sigma Chi. Contbr. articles to profl. jours. Home: Frederick Av Laurinburg NC 28352 Office: Pembroke State U Pembroke NC 28372

GUSTE, WILLIAM JOSEPH, govt. ofcl.; b. New Orleans, May 26, 1922; s. William Joseph and Marie Louise (Alciatore) G.; B.A., Loyola U., New Orleans, 1942, LL.B., 1943; m. Dorothy Elizabeth Schutten, Apr. 7, 1948; children—William Joseph III, Bernard Randolph, Marie Louise, Melanie Ann, Valerie Eve, Althea Maria, Elizabeth Therese, James Patrick, Anne Duchesne. Admitted to La. bar, 1943; now mem. firm Guste, Barnett & Columb, New Orleans; mem. La. Senate, from 1968; now atty. gen. State of La. Pres. Met. New Orleans Crime Commn., 1956; mem. Parish of Orleans Juvenile Ct. Adv. Com., 1952-66; mem. Com. Law Enforcement and Adminstrn. Justice, 1969-70. Del. Democratic nat. conv., 1968. Mem. bd. adminstrs. La. Charity Hosp., New Orleans, 1962-66; bd. dirs. Cancer Assn. Greater New Orleans, United Cancer Council; chmn. bd. lay regents Xavier U.; past pres. Assn. Catholic Charities. Mem. New Orleans, La., Am. bar assns. Roman Catholic. Home: 4 Richmond Pl New Orleans LA 70115 Office: 1624 Nat Bank Commerce Bldg New Orleans LA 70112*

GUTERMUTH, CLINTON RAYMOND, conservationist, naturalist; b. Fort Wayne, Ind., Aug. 16, 1900; s. Henry Christian and Alice Virtue (Zion) G.; student Notre Dame, 1918-19; grad. Am. Inst. Banking, 1927, post grad. work, 1927-28; D.Sc., U. Ida., 1972; m. Ila Bessie Horm, Mar. 4, 1922. Asst. cashier St. Joseph Valley Bank, Elkhart, Ind., 1922-34; dir. div. of edn., Ind. Dept. of Conservation, Indianapolis, 1934-40, dir. div. fish and game, 1940-42; Ind. rent dir. O.P.A., Indpls., 1942-45; exec. sec. Am. Wildlife Inst., Washington, 1945-46; v.p. Wildlife Mgmt. Inst. 1946-71. Sec., trustee N.A. Wildlife Found., Inc., 1946—; v.p., trustee Stronghold, Inc.; former chmn., hon. mem. Natural Resources Council Am.; treas., dir. World Wildlife Fund (U.S.); trustee, mem. exec. council World Wildlife Fund (Internat.); exec. com. Am. Com. Internat. Wildlife Protection, Citizens Com. for Natural Resources. Recipient Leopold medal Wildlife Soc., 1957; Albright medal Am. Scenic and Historic Preservation Soc., 1971. Fellow A.A.A.S.; mem. Fishing Hall of Fame, Nat. Rifle Assn. (life mem., 1st v.p., dir. 1963), Izaak Walton League Am., Outdoor Writers Assn. Am., Wildlife Soc. (trustee), Am. Forestry Assn. (life mem.), Am. Soc. Range Mgmt., Nat. Audubon Soc., Nat. Parks Assn., Wilderness Soc., Am. Fisheries Soc., Internat. Assn. Game, Fish and Conservation Commrs., Soil Conservation Soc., (life mem.), Arctic Inst. N. Am., Zool. Soc. (N.Y.), Mason (32 deg., K.T.). Clubs: Cosmos, Nat. Press (Washington); Explorers, Boone & Crockett, Camp Fire (N.Y.C.): (hon.) Booneville (Ind.) Press. Elkhart (Ind.) Conservation. Miami (Fla.) Sailfish. Tanana Valley (Alaska) Sportsmen's. Author: Where to Go in Indiana, Official Lake Guide, 1938; Quips and Queries page on natural history, Outdoor Indiana, 1934-42; W.M.I. bi-weekly Outdoor News Bull, 1947-50; co-author: The Fisherman's Encyclopedia; The Standard Book of Fishing. Author articles on natural resource restoration. Home: 4801 Connecticut Av NW Washington DC 20008 Office: Wire Bldg Washington DC 20005

GUTH, DONALD JOHN, corp. exec.; b. Manning, Ia., Mar. 24, 1916; s. T. R. and Laura (Guth) McCann; student Capital City Comml. Coll., 1934, Am. Inst. Bus., 1935, Harvard, 1952; m. Josephine C. Lindsey, Mar. 16, 1934; 1 son, Donald D. Clk., Mut. Benefit Life Ins. Co., Des Moines, 1934-35; accountant Ford Motor Co., Des Moines, 1935-42; comptroller, treas., chief financial officer Solar Aircraft Co., Des Moines, N.Y.C., San Diego, 1942-61; controller, chief accounting officer Collins Radio Co., Dallas, 1961-68; vice pres. GF Industries, Inc., Dallas, 1969—; v.p., sec.-treas. Varo, Inc., Garland, Tex., 1972—; v.p., dir. Gen. Earth Minerals Corp., Dallas, 1969—; pres., dir. GFI Minerals Fund Mgmt. Corp., Dallas, 1969—; asst. treas. So. States Molded Foam Products, Dallas, 1969—; mem. exec. com., dir. Computerized Natural Resources, Natchez, Miss., 1969—; dir. Mid-Continent-Marine Drilling, Inc., Natchez, U., 1950-51. Pres., Taxpayers Assn., Des Moines and San Diego. Served with Ia. State Guard, 1942-45. Recipient Remington Rand trophy as pres. Nat. Assn. Accountants, 1948. Mem. Financial Execs. Inst. (nat. dir., past pres. Dallas and Ia. chpts., past nat. v.p.), Nat. Assn. Accountants (past nat. v.p., mem. nat. exec. com., past pres. Des Moines chpt., council continuing ednl. policies 1965-68), Am. Accounting Assn. Home: 7832 Royal Lane Apt 212 Dallas TX 75230 Office: 2203 Walnut St Garland TX 75040

GUTHE, ALFRED KIDDER, anthropologist, educator; b. Detroit, Apr. 30, 1920; s. Carl Eugen and Grace Ethel (McDonald) G.; student U. N.C., 1937-39; A.B., U. Mich., 1941, Ph.D., 1956; M.A., U. Chgo., 1948; m. Lois Frances Kuhlman, Sept. 2, 1944; children—Carol Jean, Nancy Lee, Janet Tate, Philip Bruce, Martin Eugene, Donald Edward. Jr. anthropologist, then curator anthropology Rochester (N.Y.) Mus. Arts and Scis., 1949-61; lectr. anthropology U. Rochester, 1949-61; prof. anthropology U. Tenn., 1961—, head dept., 1961-71, dir. Frank H. McClung Mus., 1961—, archaeol. research Northeastern U.S. Served with USNR, 1942-45. Fellow Am. Anthrop. Assn.; mem. Soc. Am. Archaeology, Tenn. Assn. of Mus. (pres. 1963-65), Sigma Xi. Unitarian. Kiwanian. Editor Tenn. Archaeologist, 1961—; asst. editor (N.E.) Am. Antiquity, 1952-61, (N.E.) Abstracts of New World Archaeology, 1959-62. Contbr. articles to profl. publs. Home: 8008 Chesterfield Dr Knoxville TN 37919

GUTHRIE, KENNETH BERNARD, newspaper editor; b. Jasper, Ala., Aug. 9, 1931; s. Elliott Bernard and Esther (Blevins) G.; B.S. with honors in Journalism, U. Fla., 1953; m. Rita Locy, Aug. 8, 1958; children—Richard Bernard, Susan Yvonne. Editor, Jasper (Ala.) Mountain Eagle, 1955-56; reporter Palatka (Fla.) Daily News, 1956-57, editor, 1960-61; reporter Daytona Beach (Fla.) News-Jour., New Smyrna Beach bur., 1957-58, Palatka bur., 1958-60; state editor Pensacola (Fla.) News-Jour., 1961-65; state editor Orlando (Fla.) Sentinel-Star, 1966-69; editor Osceola (Fla.) Sun., 1969-70, editor, pub., 1970—, dir., 1969—. Served with AUS, 1953-55. Home: 708 Robert St Kissimmee FL 32741 Office: 700 W Vine St Kissimmee FL 32741

GUTHRIE, NORMAN EUGENE, state ofcl.; b. Salisbury, N.C., Oct. 16, 1930; s. Thomas Ralph and Gene Irene (Deal) G.; B.C.E., N.C. State U., 1957; m. Joyce Elizabeth Teal, Sept. 6, 1956; 1 dau., Deborah Anne. Design engr. Fraioli-Blum-Yesselman, Cons. Engrs., Norfolk, Va., 1957-58; project engr. HSM & M, Architects and Engrs., Roanoke, Va., 1958-63; chief civil engrs. property control div. N.C. Dept. Adminstrn., Raleigh, 1963—. Served with AUS, 1952-54. Mem. Nat. Soc. Profl. Engrs., Am. Soc. C.E. Home: 4100 Spruce Dr Raleigh NC 27609 Office: NC Dept Adminstrn 116 W Jones St Raleigh NC 27602

GUTHRIE, W(ILLIAM) NELSON, clergyman; b. Walker County, Ala., Aug. 5, 1903; s. William Eual and Alice (Adkins) G.; student Birmingham So. Coll., 1921-26; spl. student Emory U.; D.D., Athens Coll., 1942; m. Jessie Lucille Welch, Nov. 5, 1927; children—Carolyn Jayne, William Nelson. Ordained to ministry Meth. Ch., 1929; pastor Meth. churches Tarrant, Ala., 1928-32, Birmingham, Ala., 1933-35, 45-49, Albertville, 1936-38, Sheffield, 1938-40, Tuscaloosa Dist., 1941-45, Decatur (Ala.) Central Meth. Ch., 1949-50; exec. sec., supt. Meth. homes, 1951-57; exec. sec. Meth. Home for Aging, Birmingham, 1957-59; exec. sec. Superannaute Homes, Birmingham, 1959—. Mem. Mayor's Com. Settle Racial Troubles, 1943. Mem. Gen. Conf. Meth. Ch., 1956, 60, 64, 66, 68, Jurisdictional Conf., 1944, 48, 56, 60, 64, 67, 68; chmn. pensions com. No. Ala. Conf. Meth. Ch., 1968-72; mem. bishop's spl. com. on pensions; mem. Tri-Conf. Com. on Merger, dir. Area IV Conf. Council. Trustee Huntington Coll. Clubs: Civitan, Lions, Rotary, Kiwanis. Pioneered establishment homes for ret. Meth. ministers' widows. Address: 2048 Kentucky Av Birmingham AL 35216

GUTIERREZ, ARIEL ELOY, real estate co. exec.; b. Havana, Cuba, Dec. 14, 1943; s. Enrique and Ana Maria (Rodriguez) G.; came to U.S., 1961, naturalized, 1965; student Fairleigh Dickinson U., 1961-63; B.S. in C.E., Ga. Tech. U., 1965, M.S. in C.E., 1966 div.; children—Ana Christina, Ana Victoria. Partner, E. H. Gutierrez & Assos., A.I.A., San Juan, P.R., 1967-71; pres. EHG Enterprises, Inc., San Juan, P.R., 1969, also dir; dir. Mut. Savs. Bank P.R. Bd. dirs. Jr. Achievement. Served to 1st lt. AUS, 1966. Registered profl. engr., P.R. Mem. Internat. Acad. Profl. Bus. Execs. Am. Soc. C.E., P.R. Soc. Profl. Engrs., C. of C., Better Bus. Bur., Bankers Club P.R. Clubs: Caribe Hilton-Swimming and Tennis (San Juan); N.Y. Athletic (N.Y.C.). Home: Torre del Mar Condominium Apts 1806 Av Ashford San Juan PR 00907 Office: PO Box 13171 Santurce PR 00908

GUTIERREZ, ENRIQUE HIRAM, architect; b. Havana, Cuba, May 20, 1901; s. Enrique and Ana Maria (Rodriguez) G.; architect, U. Havana, 1955; m. Marta Saavedra, Sept. 26 1952; children—Ana Teresa, Fernando. Partner, Alvarez & Gutierrez, Havana, Cuba, 1952-55; partner, head archtl. dept. Saenz, Cancio, Martin, Alvarez & Gutierrez, Havana, Cuba, 1955-59, 1960-63; asst. prof. design U. Havana, 1957-59; prin. partner E. H. Gutierrez & Assos., San Juan, P.R., 1963—; chmn. bd. EHG Enterprises, Inc., 1969—; dir. Brickell Bank, Miami, Hon. consul Costa Rica in San Juan, P.R., 1970—. Dir. Democratic Com. P.R., 1969—. Bd. dirs. St. John's Sch. Recipient Nat. award Colegio Nacional de Arquitectos de Cuba, 1960; Golden Plate award Am. Acad. Achievement, 1972. Mem. A.I.A., Casino de P.R., Colegio de Ingenieros, Arquitectos yAgrimensores de P.R. Clubs: Nautico (San Juan, P.R.); N.Y. Athletic (N.Y.C.); Cay Cay (Bahamas); Ocean Reef (Cayo Largo, Fla.). Home: 1362 Magdalena St San Juan PR 00907 Office: Box 13171 Santurce PR 00908

GUTIERREZ, JOSE SANTOS, agrl. exec.; b. Alamos, Sonora, Mexico, June 12, 1916; s. Alberto and Argelia Garcia Gutierrez; grad. Heriberto Aja, 1934; m. Elsa Luken, Oct. 29, 1942; children—Elsa (Mrs. Hector Amavizca), Jose Santos, Lupita, Juan Alberto, Javier, Monica. Accountant in bank, 1934-40; pres. Gutierrez Hermanos S.A., Hermosilla, Mexico, 1947—, Industrias Avicolas, S.A., Hermosilla, 1947—, Molinos Mezquital del Oro, Hermosilla, 1966—, Lacteos de Sonora, S.A., Hermosilla, Incubardoras Mezquital del Oro, Hermosilla, Frigorifica y Empacadora, S.A., Mezquital del Oro, Hermosillo. Gen. treas. State of Sonora, Mexico, 1955-58. Trustee U. Sonora. Clubs: Old Pueblo (Tucson); Casino de Hermosillo. Home: 700 Alatoree St Hermosillo Sonora Mexico Office: PO Box 138 Hermosillo Sonora Mexico

GUTIERREZ-PELAEZ, FRANCISCO ALBERTO, physician; b. Pinar del Rio, Cuba, Aug. 7, 1918; s. Francisco Gutierrez Fonte and Vicenta Pelaez Mila; M.D., Havana U. Med. Sch., 1943; m. Maria E. Rissett Mazorra Vega, Aug. 22, 1943; children—Juan Francisco, Jorge Martin, Alberto Lejandro, Maria Eugenia. Intern, U. Havana, 1944-45, surgical resident, 1945-46; asso. gynecology Havana U., 1946-50; anesthesiologist Havana Municipal Maternity Hosp., 1950-61; dir. Anesthesia Institute de Cirugia Cardiovascular ydel torax, Havana, 1961-62; clin. asso. anesthesiology Boston City Hosp., 1962-63; asst. prof. surgery, anesthesia U. W. Va., 1963-68; asso. prof. U. Ala., Birmingham, 1968—. Cons. VA. Hosp., Tuskegee, VA Hosp., Birmingham. Diplomate Am. Soc. Anesthesiologists. Fellow Am. Coll. Anesthesiologists. Home: 3512 S Woodridge Rd Birmingham AL 35223

GUTIERREZ ZORRILLA, FELIPE, lawyer; b. Monterrey, Nuevo Leon, Mexico, Aug. 21, 1923; LL.B., Nat. U. Mexico, 1948; postgrad. N.Y.U. Admitted to Mexican bar, 1948; now mem. firm De La Garza, Gutierrez Zorrilla y Asociado. Mem. Mexican Ho. of Reps., 1967-70. Mem. Nuevo Leon, Mexican, Inter-Am. bar assns. Address: Suite 606 Condominio Acero Monterrey Zaragoza 1000 Sur Monterrey Nuevo Leon Mexico*

GUYTON, JOSEPH WARREN, cons. engr.; b. Vicksburg, Miss., Mar. 24, 1933; s. Joseph Owen and Alice Irene (Potts) G.; B.S., U. Ill., 1955, M.S., 1957; m. Carolyn Ann Owens, Dec. 29, 1956; children—Mark Owen, Paul Warren, Timothy Lee. Transp. planning engr. Harland Bartholomew & Assos., St. Louis, 1959-60, resident engr., Fayetteville, N.C., 1960-61, transp. planning engr., Memphis, 1962-63, asso. partner, Memphis, 1964-70, partner 1971—. Tchr., guest lectr. U. Ill., 1955—, U. Miss., 1963—, U. Tenn., 1965—, Memphis State U., 1967—, U. Ala., 1968-69. Served with C.E., AUS, 1957-59; ETO. Recipient C. C. Wiley Traveling award hwy. enging. U. Ill., 1955. Registered profl. engr., Fla., Ill., Ind., Ky., O., Mich., Tenn. Mem. Am. Soc. C.E., Hwy. Research Bd., Soc. Am. Mil. Engrs., Inst. Traffic Engrs., Chi Epsilon, Alpha Kappa Lambda. Presbyn. (chmn. bd. deacons). Memphis Athletic. Home: 2085 Firefly Cove Memphis TN 38138 Office: 188 Jefferson Av Memphis TN 38103

GUYTON, PERCY LOVE, economist; b. Kosciusko, Miss., Sept. 29, 1905; s. Thomas Percy and Annie D. (Love) G.; B.S., Miss. State U., 1927; M.B.A., Northwestern U., 1932; postgrad. U. Ill., 1933, U. Ia., 1942; Ph.D., Duke, 1952; m. Margaret Heath Ames, June 26, 1930; children—Jean Love (Mrs. Albert Sidney Newton), Ames Lee. Asst. to gen. mgr. Potts-Oliver Co., Kosciusko, 1922-25; instr., asst. prof. history and econs. Miss. State U., 1928-36; grad. asst. Duke, 1936-38, Duke-Brookings fellow, 1938-39; head dept. econs. and bus. adminstrn. Simpson Coll., 1939-43; with Miss. Dist. and Atlanta Regional OPA, 1943-45; interim instr. econs. Northwestern U., 1945-46; head dept. econs. and bus. adminstrn. King Coll., Bristol, Tenn., 1946-54; prof. econs. Memphis State U., 1954-60; dir. materials devel. Joint Council on Econ. Edn., 1960-66; chmn. div. bus. adminstrn., dir. Center for Econ. Edn., Jacksonville (Fla.) U., 1966—; cons. to econ. edn. project So. States Work Conf., 1961-65; adviser Jacksonville Indsl. Manpower Center, 1969-70; treas. Fla. Council Econ. Edn., 1970—. Dir. University Heights Civic Club, Memphis, 1958-60; pres. Memphis Campus Christian Life Bd., 1958-60; chmn. program com., chmn. br. council, pres. Friendship Club, Grand Central YMCA, 1964-66. Recipient Distinguished Service awards N.Y.C. Grand Central YMCA, 1966, Kiwanis Club, N.Y.C., 1966. Mem. Am., So. econ. assns., Alpha Kappa Psi. Democrat. Presbyn. (elder). Club: St. Johns Dinner (Jacksonville). Co-editor: Economic Education Experiences of Enterprising Teachers, 1962-65; Our Growing America, 1963; Teachers Guide to Economics in the Business Education Curriculum, 1963; Teachers Guide to DEEP, 1964; Suggestions for aBasic Economics Library, 1965; Money and You, 1967. Home: 931 Overlook Dr Jacksonville FL 32211

GUYTON, ROBERT POOL, banker; b. Blue Mountain, Miss., Mar. 31, 1937; s. Albert J. and Birma Elizabeth (Pool) G.; B.B.A., U. Miss., 1958; M.B.A., Harvard, 1966; m. Katherine Cole Taylor, June 15, 1960; children—Robert Pool, Randall Taylor. With Deposit Guaranty Nat. Bank, Jackson, Miss., 1960-71, asst. cashier, 1963-66, asst. to pres., 1966-69, sr. v.p., 1969, exec. v.p., 1969-71; pres., dir. Nat. Bank Ga., Atlanta, 1971—. Dir. Miss. Chem. Co., First Miss. Corp., First Nat. Bank New Albany. Bd. dirs. Miss. Econ. Council, 1968-71, treas., 1970; bd. dirs. Miss. Indsl. & Spl. Service, Inc., Miss. Art Assn., Miss. Opera Assn., Miss. Council Econ. Edn.; trustee Blue Mountain Coll. Served to 1st lt. AUS, 1958-60. Named Outstanding Young Man of Year Miss. Jr. C. of C., 1968. Mem. Jackson C. of C., Am. Bankers Assn., U. Miss. Alumni Assn. (exec. com. 1970-71), Omicron Delta Kappa, Sigma Chi. Baptist (chmn. bd. 1969). Clubs: Country (bd. govs. 1970-71), Capital City Petroleum, Patio (Jackson). Home: 700 Montana Rd NW Atlanta GA 30327 Office: Box 1234 Atlanta GA 30301

GUYTON, WALTER RANDOLPH, coll. dean; b. York, Ala., Mar. 21, 1933; s. James Robert and Mamye (Jordan) G.; B.S., Livingston U., 1953; M.A., U. Ala., 1958, Edn.D., 1966; m. Glenda Keith, July 8, 1961; 1 dau., Elizabeth Anne. Tchr. Demopolis (Ala.) City Schs., 1954-59; adminstr. U. Ala., Tuscaloosa, 1959-67; acad. dean Carson-Newman Coll., Jefferson City, Tenn., 1967—. Participant Danfort Inst. Coll. Devel., 1969-71, Am. Council Edn.-Adminstrs. Inst., 1969-70. Mem. Jason Soc., Coll. Community Council, Kappa Delta Pi, Phi Delta Kappa, Alpha Tau Omega, Rho Alpha Tau, Omicron Delta Kappa, Phi Eta Sigma, Phi Sigma Tau, Phi Alpha Theta. Baptist. Lion, Kiwanian. Home: 1212 Leon Dr Jefferson City TN 37760

GUZMAN-ACOSTA, MANUEL, orthopedic surgeon; b. Mayaguez, P.R., June 24, 1922; s. Manuel Guzman Rodriguez and Soledad Acosta Velarde; A.B., U. Pa., 1943; M.D., Boston U., 1946; m. Awilda Valiente Jimmenez, Feb. 5, 1949; children—Manuel, Eduardo, Jose-Julian. Rotating intern Bayamon Dist. Hosp., P.R., 1946-47, surg. resident, 1947-48; surg. resident St. Joseph's Hosp., Lexington, Ky., 1950-51; orthopedic resident St. Vincent's Hosp., S.I., N.Y., 1951-52, St. Luke's Hosp., N.Y.C., 1952-54; chief orthopedic surgeon Hosp. Mimiya, Santurce, P.R., Profl. Hosp., 1960—; asso. attending orthopedic surgeon Presbyn. Hosp. Santurce, 1960—, asst. clin. prof. orthopedic surgery U. P.R. Sch. Medicine, 1960—; orthopedic surgeon VA Center, San Juan. Hon. cons. Ramey AFB, Aguadilla, P.R., 1959—; cons. P.R. State Ins. Fund, P.R. Indsl. Commn., Retirement Bd., Govt. P.R. Employees Assn. Served to capt. M.C., AUS, 1949-50. Diplomate Am. Bd. Orthopedic Surgery. Mem. Am. Acad. Orthopedic Surgeons, A.C.S., A.M.A., P.R. Med. Assn. Home: Himalya St 231 Monterrey Devel Rio Piedras PR 00926 Office: Mimiya Hosp Jose de Diego 303 Santura PR 00909

GWALTNEY, MARION LEWIS, lawyer; b. Dothan, Ala., Jan. 3, 1918; s. Alvin W. and Bernice (Warrick) G.; student in bus. adminstrn., U. Ala., 1937-39, LL.B., 1942; m. Mary Estelle Creel, Sept. 14, 1946; children—Marion Lewis, Kathy Creel. Admitted to Ala. bar, 1942; atty. Chief Atty.'s Office, VA, Ala., 1945-46; asso. Maurice F. Bishop, Birmingham, Ala., 1947-52; asst. U.S. atty. for No. Dist. of Ala., 1952-57; with firm Levine and Fulford, Birmingham, Ala., 1957-70, partner, 1958-69; practice law, Birmingham, 1970; exec. dir. Legal Aid Soc. Jefferson County, Ala., Birmingham,

1970—. Faculty, Cumberland Sch. Law, Samford U., Birmingham, 1970—. Served with USAAF, 1942-45; ETO. Mem. Ala., Birmingham bar assns. Home: 571 Shades Crest Rd Birmingham AL 35226 Office: 504-B Jefferson County Courthouse Birmingham AL 35226

GWALTNEY, STANLEY LANE, farmer; b. Isle of Wight County, Va., Sept. 13, 1908; s. Stanley Lee and Vivian F. (Lane) G.; ed. pub. schs., Smithdeal Bus. Coll.; m. Marguerite S. Walden, June 11, 1932; children—Dorothy, William A., Margaret Ann, Nancy (Mrs. William P. Gillett), Edith (Mrs. William A. Bell), Linda K. Owner saw mill, 1933-63; farmer, Smithfield, Va., 1929—. Dir. Bank of Smithfield, Prescription Fetz, Old Dominion Investors Trust, Inc., Dairyman, Inc. Mem. Dem. Com.; mem. Isle of Wight Sch. Bd., 1938-50; mem. Isle of Wight County Bd. Suprs., 1966-68. Mem. Norfolk Coop. Milk Producers Assn. Club: Windsor Ruritan (pres.) Home: Route 2 Box 99 Windsor VA 23487

GWATHMEY, EDWARD SMITH, aircraft co. exec.; b. Norfolk, Va., Nov. 4, 1909; s. George Tayloe and Margaret Cabell (Smith) G.; B.S., U. Va., 1930, M.S., 1932; Ph.D., 1937; postgrad. Columbia, 1933-36; m. Berwyn Neal Heise, July 11, 1944; children—James Tayloe, Anne Temple (Mrs. Maxwell Perrotta). Instr. physics Coll. City N.Y., 1933-37; dir. research Specialties, Inc., Syosset, N.Y., 1945-48; v.p. new devels. Feed Products, Groveland, Fla., 1948-51; dir. research Specialties, Inc., Charlottesville, Va., 1951-64; dir. engring. and research Automated Specialties, div. Teledyne, Inc., Charlottesville, 1965-69; gen. mgr. Teledyne Avonics div. Teledyne, Inc., Charlottesville, 1969—. Served to comdr. USNR, 1937-45. Fellow Am. Inst. Aeros. and Astronautics; mem. A.A.A.S., Raven Soc. Clubs: Colonade, Boarshead (Charlottesville). Home: Flordon Dr Charlottesville VA 22901 Office: Box 888 Charlottesville VA 22902

GWIN, JOHN DURDEN, govt. ofcl.; b. Tchula, Miss., Apr. 15, 1906; s. Walter Keirn and Mary (Wolfe) G.; B.A., Davidson Coll., 1928. With Nat. City Co., N.Y.C., 1928-30, Harris, Forbes & Co., N.Y.C., 1930-31, R.H. Macy & Co., N.Y.C., 1931-32, various banks, 1932-36; with U.S. Treasury Dept., 1936—, spl. asst. to comptroller of currency, Washington, 1965-66, acting dep. comptroller, 1966-67, dep. comptroller of currency, 1967—. Mem. Fed. Exec. Bd., Atlanta, 1963-65; instr. Interagy. Sch. for Examiners, Washington, 1958-62. Recipient Meritorious Service award Treasury Dept., 1969. Mem. Phi Gamma Delta. Presbyn. Lion (past sec.). Clubs: Capital City (Atlanta); University (Washington); Army Navy Country (Arlington, Va.). Home: 2301 E St NW Washington DC 20037 Office: Main Treasury Bldg Pennsylvania Av and 15th Washington DC 20220

HAACK, DAVID ARNO, geologist; b. St. Louis, Dec. 21, 1931; s. Arno John and Florence (Reppert) H.; A.B., Washington U., St. Louis, 1954, M.A., 1955; m. Katherine Ann Vanston, June 6, 1953; children— William James, Robert David. Teaching asst. Washington U., 1954-55; geologist, dist. devel. supr. Texaco, Inc., Corpus Christi, Tex., 1957-67, div. staff geologist, well log analyst, devel. supr., Houston, 1967-69; dist. geologist Clark Oil Producing Co., Corpus Christi, 1969-71; chief geologist Normandy Oil and Gas Co., Corpus Christi, 1971-72; exploration geologist Mitchell Energy Boy Scouts Am., Houston, 1967-69. Served to 1st lt. AUS, & Devel. Corp., Houston, 1972—. Com. chmn. 1955-57. Mem. Am. Assn. Petroleum Geologists, Houston, Corpus Christi geol. socs., Sigma Xi, Tau Kappa Epsilon. Clubs: Imperial Point Civic (exec. bd. 1967-69), Alief Band Boosters (v.p. 1968-69) (Houston). Home: 12003 Chessington Dr Houston TX 77071 Office: Mitchell Energy & Devel Corp 3900 One Shell Plaza Houston TX 77002

HAAS, CHARLES DAVID, dentist; b. N.Y.C., Jan. 3, 1941; s. Milton Harold and Elizabeth Ester (Newman) H.; A.B., Boston U., 1962; D.M.D., Tufts U., 1966; m. Sheila Carole Greenberg, July 26, 1964; children—Andrew Scott, Gary Adam. Dental health coordinator Migrant Health Program, Commonwealth of Mass., 1965; intern Montefiore Hosp. and Med. Center, N.Y.C., 1966-67; individual practice dentistry, Miami Beach, Fla., 1969—. Served to capt. U.S. Army, 1967-69. Mem. Internat. Assn. Dental Research, Royal Soc. Health (London), Am. Dental Assn., Alpha Epsilon Pi, Alpha Omega. Author: (with others) Year Book of Dentistry, 1969. Home: 100 Kings Point Dr North Miami Beach FL 33160 Office: 1688 Meridian Av Miami Beach FL 33139

HAAS, JOSEPH BROOKS, architect; b.Savannah, Ga., Feb. 28, 1922; s. Morton Van Buren and Elizabeth (Frances) H.; B.S. in Archtl. Engring., Ga. Tech. U., 1943; m. Harriet Farwell, Jan. 20, 1947; children— Bruce Farwell, Robert Van Buren, Elizabeth Anne. Draftsman, 1946-47; pvt. practice architecture, Jacksonville, Fla., 1947—; partner firm Haas & Reed Architects, Inc.; prin. works include Jacksonville U. Library, Auditorium, Gymnasium, 1951-55, Frawer Meml. Hosp., Macclenny, Fla., 1957, Columbia High Sch., Lake City, Fla., 1958, Research Lab. USOA, Olustee, Fla., Capehart Housing Project, San Juan, P.R., Stillwell Jr. High Sch., Jacksonville, 1963, VA Hosp., Gainesville, 1964; Butler Sr. High Sch., 1966, Jacksonville Service Centers, 1968, Grandfather Mountain Golf and Country Club Resort Devel., Linville, N.C., 1970, lo-story motel, Jacksonville Beach, 1971, Sugar Mountain Ski Resort, 1970; cons. to sch. bds. Served with AUS, 1943-46; ETO. Mem. AIA (charter mem. Jacksonville chpt.), Fla. Assn. Architects, Fla. Planning and Zoning Assn., Ch. Archtl. Guild, Soc. Am. Mil. Engrs., Sigma Chi. Episcopalian. Clubs: Florida Yacht, River (Jacksonville). Home: 4305 Venetia Blvd Jacksonville FL 32210 Office: 1045 Riverside Av Jacksonville FL 32204

HAAS, MICHAEL ELISHA, retail trade exec.; b. Kiln, Miss., Feb. 1, 1898; s. Elisha Nicholas and Alice Norton (Herlihy) H.; B.S., St. Stanislaus Coll., 1914; postgrad. Tulane U., 1918; m. Violet Mae Brown, Dec. 27, 1930; 1 son, Steve. Pres., Haas Stores, Slidell, La., 1947—; sec.treas. Slidell Growth, Inc., 1967—; exec. v.p., dir. First Fed. Savs. and Loan Assn., 1966—; dir. Bank of Slidell. Bd. dirs. St. Tammany Parish dept. Pub. Welfare, Mem. Greater Slidell C. of C. (bd. dirs. 1963-66, treas. 1963-65). K.C., Lion (bd. dirs. 1963-64). Home: Slidell LA 70458 Office: 2149 Carey St Slidell LA 70458

HAAS, THELMA ROBERTS SUMNER(MRS. CHARLES ELMER HAAS), ednl. adminstr.; b. Dade City, Fla., Feb. 28, 1910; d. Jefferson Davis and Mittie (Roberts) Sumner; B.A., Fla. State U., 1931; postgrad. Duke, summers 1935-36; M.Ed. in Personnel Services, U. Fla., 1963; m. Charles Elmer Haas, June 11, 1938; children—Donald Victor, Edith Douglas (Mrs. Stanley W. Hill). Tchr. English and history Benjamin Franklin Jr. High Sch., Tampa, Fla., 1931-34, Andrew Jackson Sr. High Sch., Jacksonville, Fla., 1939-45; tchr. English, H. B. Plant Sr. High Sch., Tampa, 1934-38; tchr. sci. and health North Shore Elementary-Jr. High Sch., Jacksonville, 1954-57; tchr. history Andrew Jackson Sr. High Sch., Jacksonville, 1957-61, guidance counselor, 1961-69, dean girls, 1970—; dean of girls Oceanway Jr. High Sch., Jacksonville, 1969-70. Sec. Marigold Circle Garden Club, 1953-54, v.p., 1954-55; mem. Civic Music Assn., Friends of Pub. Library, Jacksonville, Fedn. Garden Clubs, 1952-56. Mem. N.E.A., Fla. Edn. Assn., Am. Personnel and Guidance Assn., Fla. Deans and Counselors Assn., Am. Assn. U. Women (pres. Tampa br. 1936-38, pres. Jacksonville br. 1939-40, Fla. treas. 1936-37), Mortar Bd., Delta Kappa Gamma (chpt. pres. 1966-68, chmn. coordinating council 1968-70), Alpha Chi Alpha, Pi Lambda Theta, Kappa Delta Pi (corr. sec. 1968-70), Phi Mu. Democrat. Baptist. Home: 332 W 69th St Jacksonville FL 32208 Office: Andrew Jackson Sr High Sch 3816 Main St Jacksonville FL 32206

HABEGGER, JAMES HOWARD, physician; b. Indpls., July 30, 1931; s. Myron Lester and Elizabeth Case (Largent) H.; B.S., Ind. U., 1953; M.B.A., Ohio State U., 1956; M.D., McGill U., 1964; m. Phinetta Jane Copeland, Apr. 4, 1952; 1 dau., Etta Ellen. With standards dept. Warner Bur. Div. Bd., Warner Corp., Muncie, Ind., 1953-54; job study engr. Proctor and Gamble Co., Cin., 1956-59; intern Tampa (Fla.) Gen. Hosp., 1964-65; pvt. practice medicine, Rockledge, Fla., 1966—; mem. staff Wuesthoff Hosp.; pres., dir. Rockledge Pharmacy, Inc., Rockledge Med. Arts Bldg., Inc. Served with USAF, 1954-56. Mem. Am., Fla., Indsl. med. assns., Brevard County Med. Soc., Am. Acad. Family Practice. Democrat. Mem. Disciples of Christ Ch. Mason. Home: 815 Rockledge Dr Rockledge FL 32955 Office: 9 Orange Av Rockledge FL 32955

HABER, PAUL ADRIAN LIFE, physician; b. N.Y.C., Feb. 14, 1920; s. Benjamin Walter and Gussie Esther (Schnur) H.; B.A., U. Tex., 1941; M.A., Columbia, 1942; M.D., U. Tex., 1949; M.S., George Washington U., 1968; m. Mary Agatha Crolley, Oct. 25, 1959; 1 son, Peter William. Research chemist Calco Chem. Co., Bound Brook, N.J., 1942-43; intern, Los Angeles County Gen. Hosp., 1949-50; resident VA Hosp., Los Angeles, 1950-52; practice medicine, specializing in internal medicine, Long Beach, Cal., 1952-53; dir. extended care VA Central Office, Washington, 1963-70, dep. asst. chief med. dir., 1970—; asst. clin. prof. medicine U. Cal. at Los Angeles, 1959-63, George Washington U., Washington, 1965-72. Mem. Los Angeles County Council on Aging, 1960-63. Served with M.C., USAF, 1953-55. Decorated Air Force Commendation medal; recipient exceptional service medal VA, 1967, commendation medal, 1955. Fellow A.C.P., Am. Geriatrics Soc.; mem. Phi Beta Kappa. Home: 7501 Honeywell Lane Bethesda MD 20014 Office: 810 Vermont St Washington DC 20420

HABERER, PHILLIP COWSERT, civic worker; b. Dimmitt, Tex., Nov. 8, 1924; s. Roy Earl and Ruth (Cowsert) H.; grad. high sch.; m. Nora Jean Wilson, Jan. 1, 1947; children—Daniel Ray, Sharla Sue, Kleta Kay. Farmer, Earth, Tex., since 1952—; dir. Dimmitt Agrl. Industries, Inc. (Tex.); dir. Earth Co-op Gin (Tex.), 1971—. Chmn. drive A.R.C., Earth, 1969—. Trustee Earth Meml. Cemetery, 1965-70, pres., 1970-72. Served with AUS, 1944-46. Mem. Castro County Farm Bur. (dir. 1954-56), Earth C. of C. (dir. 1965), Agrl. Stblzn. and Conservation Community (Castro county community committeeman 1960-62, Lamb County, 1970—). Baptist. Lion (pres. 1971-72). Home: Box 17 Earth TX 79031

HABERER, WALTER JOSEPH, JR., county ofcl.; b. Dayton, O., Feb. 4, 1914; s. Walter Joseph and Eva (Smith) H.; student U.S. Army War Coll., 1959, Army Mgmt. Sch., 1962; B.S. in Elec. Engring., U. Dayton, 1935; m. Marcella Dickason, June 3, 1938; children—Marsha (Mrs. Shannon Holsinger), Monica (Mrs. John F. Blaine), Walter Joseph III. Commd. 2d lt. U.S. Army, 1940, advanced through grades to col., 1955; exec. officer VII Corps Arty., Germany, 1953-56; with Joint Chiefs of Staff, 1961-63; chief provincial affairs MACV, Vietnam, 1963-64; div. chief Def. Intelligence Agy., 1964-65; ret., 1965; exec. dir. Reservoirs Regional Planning Commn., Chatham, Va., 1967-68; exec. sec. Campbell County, Va., 1968—. Bd. dirs. Piedmont Tb Assn. Decorated Legion of Merit, Bronze Star (2); Spl. Breast Order Yuuh Hui (China); others. Mem. Assn. Virginia County Adminstrs., Internat. City Mgmt. Assn., Am. Legion, Ruritan. Home: Route 1 Box 452 Rustburg VA 24588 Office: Courthouse Rustburg VA 24588

HABERMAN, CAROL R. (MRS. RUDY A. HABERMAN), lawyer, city ofcl.; J.D., St. Mary's Sch. Law, 1957; M.Social Service, Our Lady of Lake Coll.; m. Rudy A. Haberman; 2 sons. Admitted to Tex. bar, 1957, since practiced in San Antonio; mem. San Antonio City Council, 1970—. Project. dir. Marshall St. Sr. Center, 1968—; mem. Tex. Commn. on Status of Women. Recipient Matrix award Theta Sigma Phi Journalism Group, Distinguished Service award for improvement of services rendered to elderly; named one of San Antonio's Outstanding Women, Express and News. Mem. State Bar Tex. (family law council), San Antonio Bar Assn. (program chmn. 1969-70), Altrusa Internat. (gov. dist. 9), Tex. Fedn. Bus. and Profl. Women's Clubs. Home: 327 Nottingham Pl San Antonio TX 78209 Office: 522 Milan Bldg San Antonio TX 78205

HACK, FREDERICK COURTLAND, land devel. co. exec.; b. Walthourville, Ga., Feb. 16, 1914; s. George Byron and Ethel (Davis) H.; m. Will Davis Stebbins, Mar. 28, 1942; children—Martha Avary, Frederick Courtland, Orion Byron. With Family Land Mgmt., Hinesville, Ga., 1931-38, Ga. Hwy. Dept., 1938-41, land acquisition and div. cartography U.S. Dept. Agr., Washington, 1941-46; lumber operator, Hinesville, 1946-49; exec. v.p., gen. mgr. The Hilton Head Co. (merged with Island Devel. Corp. and Port Royal Plantation, Inc. 1971), Hilton Head Island, S.C., 1950-61, pres., 1961—; pres. Island Devel. Corp., Hilton Head Island, 1960-71; chmn. bd. Port Royal Plantation, Inc., Hilton Head Island, 1967-71; co-trustee Honey Horn Plantation Properties, Hilton Head Island, 1957—; adv. dir. Bank of Beaufort (S.C.), 1967—; dir., mem. exec. com. Oxford First Corp., Phila., 1972—. Mem. Toll Bridge Authority, James F. Byrnes Crossing, Hilton Head Island, 1955-62; vice chmn. Beaufort County Bd. Commrs., 1952-62. Bd. dirs. Am. Cancer Soc., Beaufort County; adv. dir. Presbyn Home, Summerville, S.C., 1968—. Mem. Midway Soc. (bd. selectman 1970—). Presbyn. (elder 1956—, commr. 105th gen. assembly 1965). Lion. Address: Honey Horn Plantation Hilton Head Island SC 29928

HACKENDAHL, RICHARD HUGHES, assn. exec.; b. Milw., Nov. 30, 1923; s. Paul Carl and Florence (Hughes) H.; student Yale U., 1944-45; student Milw. Sch. Engring., 1941;; m. Janice C. Moore, Nov. 1970. Mgr., Conn. Gen. Life Ins. Co., Conn., Cal., 1946-51; regional mgr. Bekins Van Lines Co., Los Angeles, Washington, 1951-62; dir. Nat. Clean-Up, Paint-Up, Fix-Up Bur., Washington, 1962-71; gen. mgr. Am. C. of C. Execs., Washington, 1971—. Adviser White House Speakers Bur.; chmn. sub-com. urban problems Nat. Hwy. Beautification Com.; adviser Pres.'s Council on Environmental Quality; mem. adv. council environment Dept. Health, Edn. and Welfare. Mem. Cal. Republican Central Com., 1958-60. Served with USMCR, 1941-45. Kiwanian (past dir., past v.p.). Home: 3268 Sydenham St Fairfax VA 22030 Office: 1133 15th St NW Washington DC 20005

HACKER, WILLIAM JOE, JR., educator; b. Ada, Okla., May 26, 1930; s. William Joe and Doris M. (Whipman) H.; B.A., Harding Coll., 1955, M.A., 1958; M.R.E., Southwestern Theol. Sem., 1961, D.R.E., 1966; m. Joan Benson, Dec. 13, 1951; children—Timothy, Denise, Carol, Catherine. Ordained to ministry Ch. of Christ, 1951; minster Ch. of Christ, Searcy, Ark., 1955-61; mem. faculty Harding Coll., Searcy, 1961—, prof. Bible and philosophy, chmn. Bible dept., 1961—, dir. internat. studies program, 1972—. Pres. Internat. Service, Inc., Memphis, 1971—. Adminstr. Ezell Mission Fund, Searcy, 1970—. Rockefellow Bros. grantee, 1963-65. Mem. Am. Acad. Religion, Religious Edn. Assn., Alpha Chi. Author: Bible School Directors Handbook, 1962; Vacation Bible School Handbook, 1962; Study in Motivation, Training and Experience Background among Missionaries Church of Christ, 1968-69, 1970. Home: 17 Harding Dr Searcy AR 72143 Office: Box 615 Harding Coll Searcy AR 72143

HACKERMAN, NORMAN, univ. pres., chemist; b. Balt., Mar. 2, 1912; s. Jacob and Anna (Raffel) H.; A.B., Johns Hopkins, 1932, Ph.D., 1935; m. Gene Allison Coulbourn, Aug. 25, 1940; children—Patricia Gale, Stephen, Sally, Katherine. Asst. prof. Loyola Coll., Balt., 1935-39; research chemist for Colloid Corp., 1936-40; chemist U.S. Coast Guard, S.I. 1939-41; asst. prof. Va. Poly. Inst., Blacksburg, 1941-43; research chemist Kellex Corp., 1944; asst. prof. chemistry U. Tex., 1945-46, asso. prof., 1946-50, prof., 1950-70, chmn. dept., 1952-61, dir. corrosion research lab., 1948-61, dean research and sponsored programs, 1960-61, v.p., provost, 1961-63, vice chancellor acad. affairs, 1963-67, pres., 1967-70; prof. chemistry Rice U., Houston, 1970—, pres., 1970—. Chmn. Gordon Corrosion Research Conf., 1950; cons. in corrosion, 1946—; chmn. Inter Soc. Corrosion Com., 1956-58; chmn. Gordon Research Conf. on Chemistry, 1959; mem. nat. sci. bd. NSF, 1968—. Recipient Whitney award Nat. Assn. Corrosion Engrs., 1956; Joseph J. Mattiello Meml. lectr. Fedn. for Socs. of Paint Tech., 1964. Fellow N.Y. Acad. Sci.; mem. Am. Chem. Soc. (bd. editors, 1956-62, exec. com. colloid div. 1955-58, 1965 S.W. Regional award), Electrochem. Soc. (pres. 1957-58, Palladium medal 1965), Faraday Soc., A.A.A.S., Nat. Corrosion Engrs. (dir. 1952-55, chmn. com. on edn. Corrosion Research Council 1957—, Argonne Univs. Assn. (chmn. bd. trustees 1969—), Nat. Acad. Scis., Am. Philos. Assn., Sigma Xi, Phi Lambda Upsilon, Alpha Chi Sigma, Phi Kappa Phi. Tech. editor Jour. Electrochem. Soc., 1950-69, editor, 1969—; mem. editorial bd., mem. adv. edn. bd. Corrosion Sci., 1969—; mem. editorial bd. Catalysis Revs.; interim editor Electrochem. Tech., 1965-68. Home: President's House Rice Univ PO Box 1892 Houston TX 77001

HACKES, PETER SIDNEY, radio-TV news corr.; b. N.Y.C., June 2, 1924; s. John R. and Ruth (Misch) H.; B.A., Grinnell Coll., 1948; M.A., U. Ia., 1949; Litt.D., Grinnell Coll.; m. Mary Ellen Propper, Mar. 30, 1954; children—Pamela Townsend, Carole Austin, Peter Quinn. With radio sta. WELM, Elmira, N.Y., 1946-47, WSUI and KXIC, Iowa City, 1948-49, WAKR, Akron, O., 1949-50, WHAS, Louisville, 1950-52; Washington corr. CBS, 1952-55; Washington corr. NBC, 1955—, Def. Dept. corr., 1956-67, anchorman NBC World News Roundup, 1957-61, also reporter spl. activities NASA, State Dept., White House, U.S. Congress, polit. convs., elections, Chilean earthquake, Hungarian revolt airlift, others. Served to lt. (j.g.) USNR, World War II. Mem. Radio-TV Corrs. Assn., Sigma Delta Chi. Clubs: National Space (past gov.), Nat. Press (Washington). Office: 4001 Nebraska Av NW Washington DC 20016

HACKETT, CHARLES S., architect; b. Roslyn, N.Y., May 7, 1907; student N.Y.U., Beaux Arts Inst. Design, N.Y.C.; m. Geraldine Harris. With various engring. and archtl. firms., N.Y.; owner, operator constrn. co., Westchester County, N.Y., 4 years; supt. constrn. Colonial Williamsburg (Va.), from 1946, later dir. bldg. constrn. and maintenance, coordinator constrn. and maintenance, asst. v.p. for constrn. and maintenance, 1959-64, dir. div. architecture, constrn. and maintenance, 1964—, v.p., 1964—. City rep. to Williamsburg Planning Dist. Commn., also mem. utilities com.; chmn. Williamsburg Library Bldg. Com.; mem. adv. bd. Head Start Program; mem. Williamsburg-James City-County Courthouse Bldg. Com.; active Williamsburg Fire Dept., pres. 1954-55. Mem. Williamsburg City Council, 1968—, vice mayor, 1970—. Bd. dirs. United Community Funds and Councils of Va. Served with Corps Engrs., AUS, World War II. Episcopalian. Mason, Rotarian (past pres. Williamsburg). Club: German. Office: Colonial Williamsburg Goodwin Bldg Wiliamsburg VA 23185

HACKETT, CHARLES WILSON, JR., educator; b. Austin, Tex., Oct. 26, 1921; s. Charles Wilson and Jean (Hunter) H.; B.A., U. Tex., 1942, M.B.A., 1948; D.B.A., U. Wash., 1955; m. Ruby E. Bloomquist, July 25, 1953; children—Jean Elizabeth, Ruth Christina. Instr., Air Activities Tex., Corsicana, 1942-44, Schreiner Inst., Kerrville, Tex., 1946; mgmt. engr. Gulf Oil Corp., Port Arthur, Tex., 1948-50; instr., research bus. adminstr. U. Wash., Seattle, 1950-55; asst. prof. bus. orgn. Ohio State U., Columbus, 1955-56; industry financial analyst, credit rep. U.S. Steel Corp., Pitts., 1956-64; asst. dist. credit mgr., Houston, 1964-66; asst. prof. finance U. Tex. at Austin, 1966-69, asso. prof., 1969—. Trustee St. Andrew's Episcopal Sch., Austin. Served with USAAF, 1944-46. Recipient Exec. award Dartmouth Coll. Grad. Sch. Credit and Financial Mgmt., 1964. Mem. Am. Finance Assn., Acad. Mgmt., Phi Beta Kappa, Beta Gamma Sigma, Phi Kappa Sigma, Alpha Kappa Psi, Sigma Iota Epsilon, Pi Sigma Alpha, Sigma Delta Pi, Phi Eta Sigma. Episcopalian. Author: A Techno-Fundamental Portfolio Management Simulation with Computer Applications, 1967. Home: 102 W 33d St Austin TX 78705 Office: Dept Finance U Tex Austin TX 78712

HACKETT, WILLIAM THOMAS, JR., assn. exec.; b. Port Gibson, Miss., Dec. 17, 1924; s. William Thomas and Lois (Hightower) H.; student Ga. Sch. Tech., 1943; A.B., Mercer U., 1949; m. Mary Frances Aultman, Dec. 3, 1944; children—William Thomas III, Michael A., Neil M. With Waterways Expt. Sta., Vicksburg, Miss., 1948-49, Forest (Miss.). C. of C., 1949-51, Canton (Miss.) C. of C., 1953-56, Madison Woodworking Co., Canton, 1956-59, Jones & Yandell Mfg. Co., Canton, 1959-60, Meridian (Miss.) C. of C., 1960-61; exec. v.p. Miss. Agrl. and Indsl. Bd., Jackson, 1961-64; exec. dir. La. Dept. Commerce and Industry, Baton Rouge, 1964-72; exec. v.p. Shreveport (La.) C. of C., 1971—. Served with USNR, 1943-46, 51-53. Mem. Am., So. indsl. devel. councils. Nat., So. assns. state devel. agys. Home: 10039 Smitherman Dr Shreveport LA 71105 Office: Box 74 Shreveport LA

HACKL, ALPHONS J., publisher, printer; b. Warman, Can., Mar. 31, 1917; s. John J. and Anna (Moser) H.; grad. Handelsschule, Salzburg, Austria, 1934; student Nat. U., 1937-38, Corcoran Sch. Art, 1938-40, U. Chgo., 1941; B.A., Sussex Coll. Tech.; m. Muriel J. Forster, Feb. 2, 1946; 1 son, John Raymond. Apprentice, Funder & Mueller, printers, Salzburg, Austria, 1934-36; advt. dept. Hecht Co., Washington, 1936-39; advt. exec. Kronstadt Advt. Agy., 1939-40; owner Colortone Press, Washington, 1946—; pres. Colortone Typographic Div., Inc., 1953—; publisher, founder Acropolis Book, Ltd., Washington. Bd. dirs. Friends Non-Profit Housing, Inc.; mem. adv. bd. Montgomery Coll.; mem. adv. council Small Bus. Adminstrn.; vice chmn. bd. Accuracy in Media, Inc.; chmn. printing and publishing adv. bd. Washington Tech. Inst. Served from pvt. to capt. AUS, 1940-45. Decorated Bronze Star. Recipient George Washington Honor medal Freedoms Found. Fellow Corcoran Art Gallery, Pub. Relations Soc. Am., Printing Industry Am., Nat. Assn. Photo-Lithographers, U.S. C. of C., Mem. Soc. of Friends. Clubs: Capital Hill, Nat. Press (Washington). Contbr. articles in field to publs. Patentee of programmed instrn. device. Home: 3077 Cleveland Av NW Washington DC 20008 Office: 2400 17th St Washington DC 20009

HACKMAN, JEANNE FRANCES LEIGHTON (MRS. JOHN EDWARD HACKMAN), assn. exec.; b. Austin, Minn., July 1, 1940; d. Charles William and Margaret (Fisch) Leighton; student U. Minn., 1961-62; B.S., Coll. St. Teresa, 1962; postgrad. Niagara U., 1964-65; m. John Edward Hackman, Aug. 28, 1964; children— Jennifer, Jonathan Leighton. Research, Proctor & Gamble Co., 1962-64; asst. dir. Diary Council of Niagara Frontier, 1964-66; program dir. Lexington (Ky.) Dairy Council, 1966-69; exec. dir. Dairy Council Ky. and So. Ind., Inc., Louisville, 1969—. Pres., Gov.'s Commn. on Nutrition, 1972—. Mem. Agys. Exec. Club in Blue Grass (sec.-treas. 1967-68, pres. 1969), Farm, Press, Radio Assn. Ky. (sec.-treas. 1966—, 1st v.p.) Am., Ky. home econs. assns., Am. Pub. Health Assn., Blue Grass Dietetics Assn., Dairy Tech. Soc., Womans Aux.-Student Am. Med. Assn., Teresan Alumni, Nutrition Club Louisville, Cin. Home Economists in Bus. Clubs: Interns and Residents Wives (pres. 1972—), Zonta (pres. Lexington 1969-71). Home: 2452 Heather Way Lexington KY 40503 Office: 3344 Newburg Louisville KY 40218

HACKNEY, BURTON, state ofcl. Commr. pub. welfare, Tex. Home: 4004 Sierra Dr Austin TX 78731 Office: Pub Welfare Dept John H Reagan Bldg Austin TX 78701

HACKNEY, JAMES ACRA, III, motor vechicle co. exec.; b. Washington, N.C., Sept. 27, 1939; s. James Acra and Margaret Dunston (Hodges) H.; B.S. in M.E., 1961, B.S. in Indsl. Engring., 1962; m. Constance Garrenton, June 5, 1961; children—Kenneth Ross, Jane Mather. Chief engr. J.A. Hackney & Sons, Inc., Washington, N.C., 1961-63, asst. gen. mgr., 1963-65, exec. v.p., gen. mgr., 1965-70, pres., corporate gen. mgr., 1970—; dir. Wachovia Bank &Trust Co. Pres. Coastal Plain Devel. Assn., 1969; chmn. bus. adv. com. Beaufort Tech. Inst., 1969—; chmn. Beauhywaty dist. East Carolina Council Boy Scouts Am., 1970—. Mem. zoning bd. adjustment, Washington, N.C., 1965-66; mem. zoning and planning commn., Washington, 1966—. Served to 1st lt. Ordnance Corps, AUS, 1963-65. Recipient Distinguished Service award Jr. C. of C., Washington, 1970; named N.C. Small Businessman Man of Yr., Small Bus. Adminstrn., 1971; Young Engr. of Yr., Profl. Engrs. N.C., 1970-71; Nat. Young Engr. of Yr., Nat. Soc. Profl. Engrs., 1971. Registered profl. engr., N.C., Kan. Mem. Truck Body and Equipment Assn. (dir. 1970—), Beverage Body Mfrs. Assn. (pres. 1969-70), Am. Inst. Indsl. Engrs. (pres. Eastern N.C. chpt. 1967-68), Profl. Engrs. N.C. (pres. Eastern N.C. chpt. 1971-72), N.C. Soc. Engrs., Washington C. of C. (v.p. 1971-72, pres. 1972-73). Methodist (bd. stewards 1965-68, 70—). Clubs: Yacht and Country (Washington, N.C.); Brook Valley Country (Greenville, N.C.). Home: Macswoods Route 4 Box 554 Washington NC 27889 Office: 400 Hackney Av Washington NC 27889

HACKNEY, RUFUS RUDOLPH, JR., educator; b. Durham, N.C., July 26, 1934; s. Rufus Rudolph and Olivia (Drennon) H.; B.A., U. N.C., 1956, M.Ed., 1957, Ph.D., 1970; m. Betty Duncum, Sept. 1, 1954; children—David Michael, Grace Elizabeth. Dir. intramurals U. N.C., 1955-57; dir. sports program-basketball and tennis coach N. Ga. Coll., Dahlonega, 1957-61; chmn. dept. phys. edn., dir. athletics St. Andrews Coll., Laurenburg, N.C., 1961-71; v.p. student affairs Francis Marion Coll., Florence, S.C., 1971—; cons. phys. edn. bldgs. and facilities. Vice pres. Coll. Conf. Phys. Edn., 1968-69; mem. Gov.'s Conf. on Edn. in N.C., 1967; mem. Nat. Com. on Intramural Sports, Washington, 1967. Bd. dirs. Am. Cancer Soc. Recipient Outstanding Pres. award Dixie Intercollegiate Athletic Conf., 1964; named Coach of Year in Tennis, Ga. Intercollegiate Athletic Conf., 1958-60, Coach of Year in Soccer, Nat. Assn. Intercollegiate Athletics, 1968. Mem. A.A.H.P.E.R., N.C. Assn. Health, Phys. Edn. and Recreation (past sect. chmn.), Nat. Assn. Coll. Dirs. Athletics, Nat. Coll. Phys. Edn. Assn. for Men, Nat. Intramural Assn., Nat. Assn. Intercollegiate Athletics, Am. Assn. U. Profs., Laurinburg Jr. C. of C. (1st v.p.), Phi Delta Kappa. Baptist. Lion, Rotarian. Club: Scotch Meadows Country (dir.) (Laurinburg). Home: 1315 Third Loop Rd Florence SC 29501

HADAWI, SAM, author; b. Jerusalem, Mar. 6, 1904 (came to U.S. 1952); s. Elias and Sarah Bertha (Yaaqub) H.; ed. privately; m. Nora Badr, June 25, 1931 (dec.); children—Nabil, Aida (Mrs. Roy Karaoglan). Ofcl. Palestine Govt., 1920-48, ofcl. land valuer, insp. assessments, 1935-48; dir. inland land revenue Jordan Govt., 1949-52; land specialist UN, N.Y.C., 1952-55; adviser Iraq Mission to UN, N.Y.C., 1955-58; dir. pub. relations Arab States Delegations Office, adviser to Yemen Mission to UN, N.Y.C., 1959-60; dir. Arab Information Center, Dallas, 1960-65; dir. Inst. Palestine Studies, Beirut, Lebanon, 1965-67. Expert Palestine land and polit. affairs; lectr., writer Palestine land and polit. affairs. Decorated Mem. Brit. Empire for Outstanding Service in Palestine Govt., 1943. Episcopalian. Author numerous books including Palestine: Loss of a Heritage, 1963; Bitter Harvest, 1967; Palestine in Focus, 1968; Palestine Occupied, 1969; Village Statistics, 1970; (with Robert John) The Palestine Diary, 1914-1948, 1970. Home: 191 Classen Dr Dallas TX 75218 also 46 Granlea Rd Willowdale Ontario Canada

HADDEN, ROBY, U.S. dist. atty. for eastern Tex. Address: US Dist Atty's Office Tyler TX 75702

HADDICAN, JAMES, Sunday editor Times-Picayune, New Orleans. Address: 2124 Daniels Rd Gretna LA 70053 Office: 3800 Howard Av New Orleans LA 70140*

HADDOCK, R(EYBURN) PHILIP, lawyer; b. Astoria, Ore., Jan. 8, 1919; s. Walter Hill and Jamie (Wilson) H.; A.B., Coll. William and Mary, 1942, student law sch., 1945-46, J.D., Stetson U., 1947; m. Doris Helen Hussell, June 12, 1948; 1 son, Randolph Reyburn. Admitted to Fla. bar, 1947, since practiced in Lakeland; atty. City of Mulberry, 1950-61; municipal judge, Lakeland, Fla., 1963-64. Trustee Polk County Law Library; bd. dirs. Polk County Blood Center, pres., 1962—; bd. dirs. Fla. Assn. Blood Banks, Lakeland Boys Club. Chmn. Polk County Draft Bd. Served as sgt. inf. AUS, 1942-45. Decorated Bronze Star medal. Mem. Am., Fla., 10th Jud. Circuit (pres. 1957-58), Lakeland (pres. 1960) bar assns., Acad. Fla. Trial Lawyers, Am. Trial Lawyers Assn., Lake Region Audubon Soc. (dir.), C. of C. (pres. 1962), Stetson Alumni Assn. (past pres. Polk County chpt.), Am. Legion, V.F.M., 36th Div. Assn., Phi Alpha Delta Kappa Alpha. Republican. Methodist (bd. stewards; pres. bd. trustee Fla. Conf. 1966-68). Kiwanian (pres. 1957), Mason (32 deg.). Home: 2734 Fairmount Av Lakeland FL 30803 Office: 601 E Lime St Lakeland FL 33802

HADEN, CHARLES MCINTYRE, lawyer; b. Timpson, Tex., Aug. 6, 1923; s. Charles Clinton and Cecil (McIntyre) H.; B.A., Rice U., 1949; LL.B., U. Tex., 1949; m. Cynthia Suzanne Tracy, Dec. 20, 1944; children—Sharon Dianne (Mrs. Gordon Anthony Gabbert, Jr.), Susan Carol, Charles McIntyre. Admitted to Tex. bar, 1949; legal counsel and spl. rep. to pres. Trans-Tex. Airways, 1949; law clk. U.S. Dist. Ct., So. Dist. Tex., 1950; asst. dist. atty. Harris County, Houston, 1950-52; trial lawyer Fulbright, Crooker, Freeman & Bates, Houston, 1952-63; partner Fulbright, Crooker, Freeman, Bates & Jaworski, Houston, 1963-70, Brown & Haden, Houston, 1970—. Mayor, City Hunter's Creek Village, Tex., 1956-58. Chmn., Republican Party Harris County, Houston, 1964; del. Rep. Nat. Conv., 1964. Served as lt. (j.g.) USNR, World War II. Mem. Am., Houston bar assns., Am., Tex. (dir.) trial lawyers assns., State Bar Tex., Nat. Assn. R.R. Trial Counsel, Houston C. of C. (vice-chmn. govtl. affairs com.). Presbyn. (elder). Club: Memorial Drive Country. Contbr. articles to profl. jours. Home: 10709 Old Coach Lane Houston TX 77024 Office: 2d Floor 609 Fannin St Houston TX 77002

HADGOPOULOS, GEORGE JOHN, educator; b. Lamia, Greece June 29, 1935; s. Ioannis G. and Maria (Tsipnis) H.; B.A., with distinction, Am. U. (Beirut, Lebanon), 1962; M.A., Emory U., 1964; A.B.D., N.Y. U., 1967; m. Saralyn DeHaven Poole, Nov. 23, 1963; 1 son, John George DeHaven. Rep., Case Farm Machinery, Lamia, Greece, 1952-53; interpreter CARE, Inc., Greece, 1954-55; instr. Lamiaki Sch. Mcht. Marine Mechanics, Lamia, 1955-57, Inst. Fgn. Langs., Lamia, 1956-57; instr. English mil. terminology Greek Army Officers, Greece, 1955-59; grad. teaching asst. Emory U., Atlanta, 1962-64; asst. prof. English, Slippery Rock (Pa.) State Coll., 1967-69; mem. faculty Tidewater Center, George Washington U., Virginia Beach, 1972—. Served with Greek Army, 1957-59. Fellow Inst. Linguists (London, Eng.), mem. Modern Lang. Assn. Am., Linguistic Soc. Am., Nat. Hist. Soc., Internat. Platform Assn., Nat. Council Tchrs. English, Archaeol. Inst. Am. Address: PO Box 5582 Bayside Sta Virginia Beach VA 23455

HADGOPOULOS, SARALYN POOLE (MRS. GEORGE JOHN HADGOPOULOS), educator; b. Atlanta, Aug. 31, 1931; d. George Grady Poole and Sarah (Wimberly) Shaw; student Vassar Coll., 1949-51, Sorbonne, Paris, 1951, U. Ga., 1952; B.S., Columbia, 1955; M.A., N.Y. U., 1961; Ph.D., Emory U., 1965; m. George John Hadgopoulos, Nov. 23, 1963; 1 son, John George de Haven. Promotion asst. TV Programs Am., N.Y.C., 1955-56; asst. to fashion and beauty editor Am. Weekly Mag., N.Y.C., 1956-57; tchr. Miami Edison Sr. High Sch., Fla., 1958-60; asso. prof. English, Slippery Rock (Pa.) State Coll., 1967-69; instr. Navy Amphibious Sch., George Washington U., Little Creek, Va., 1972—. Mem. Inst. Linguists London (Eng.), Modern Lang. Assn. Am., Internat. Platform Assn., Nat. Council Tchrs. English, Archaeol. Inst. Am. Home: 2309 Treasure Island Dr Virginia Beach VA 23455

HADLER, JACQUES BAUER, naval architect; b. Arndt, N.D., June 27, 1918; s. Bernhard Herman and Mable Lyle (Jacques) H.; B.S., U.S. Naval Acad., 1941; M.S., Mass. Inst. Tech., 1947; m. Caryl Loggins, Feb. 21, 1942; children—Jacques Bauer, James, Stephen, Susan. Commd. ensign U.S. Navy, 1941, advanced through grades to lt. comdr., 1945; engring. duties various naval shore establishments; ret., 1949; head full-scale trial br. David Taylor Model Basin, Washington, 1949-51, head surface ship powering br., 1951-53, head ship powering div., 1953-70; acting head advance ship concepts Naval Ship Research and Devel. Center, Bethesda, Md., 1965-66, head spl. study group, 1968, head ship dynamics div., 1970—; cons. naval architect to pvt. shipbuilding co., 1960—. Recipient Letter of Commendation, Chief Bur. Ships, 1944, Joseph Linard award Soc. Naval Architects and Marine Engrs., 1966, U.S. Navy Meritorious Civilian Service award, 1969. Mem. Soc. Naval Architects and Marine Engrs. (com. chmn.), Royal Inst. Naval Architects (Eng.), Japanese Soc. Naval Architects and Marine Engrs., Internat. Towing Tank Conf. (com. chmn.), Am. Towing Tank Conf., Sigma Xi. Contbr. articles to profl. jours. Patentee in field. Home: 6425 Dahlonega Rd Washington DC 20016 Office: Bethesda MD 20034

HADLEY, DONALD BOYD, public relations cons.; b. Grinnell, Ia., Dec. 24, 1903; s. Elam Jessup and Minnie Mae (Boyd) H.; A.B., Grinnell Coll., 1925; postgrad. U. Wis., 1927-28; m. Ayo Oma Rice, June 7, 1930; Children—Donald Henry. Asst. state editor Des Moines Register-Tribune, 1925-26; night editor Des Moines Bur., A.P., 1926-27; U. Wis. campus corr. Milw. Jour. and copy desk of Wis. State Jour., 1927-28; mng. editor Capitol Hill Beacon, Oklahoma City, 1928-31; bus. editor, editor Washington facts and figures, Washington Star, 1936-56, financial editor, daily columnist, 1950-69; now pub. relations cons. Mem. Newcomen Soc. Am., Am. Inst. Banking (life; outstanding service award Washington chpt.), Washington Soc. Investment Analysts, Sigma Delta Chi. Republican. Conglist. Mason. Club: Exchequer. Home: 9409 Woodland Dr Silver Spring MD 20910

HADLEY, ELEANOR MARTHA, economist; b. Seattle, July 17, 1916; d. Homer More and Margaret (Floyd) Hadley; B.A., Mills Coll., 1938; M.A., Radcliffe-Harvard, 1943, Ph.D., 1949. Research analyst O.S.S., Washington, 1943-44; economist, commodities div. Dept. of State, Washington, 1944-46; econ. analyst Govt. Sect., Gen. Hdqrs.-Supreme Comdr. for Allied Powers, Tokyo, Japan, 1946-47; economist Pres. Truman's Commn. on Migratory Labor, Washington, 1950-51, U.S. Senate Com. on Labor and Pub. Welfare, Washington, 1951-52; rep. Nat. Consumers League, Washington, 1952-53, Nat. Assn. Social Workers, Washington, 1953-56; asso. prof. econs., dean class 1962 Smith Coll., Northampton, Mass., 1956-65; economist U.S. Tariff Commn., Washington, 1967—; professorial lectr. Dept. Econs., George Washington U., 1972. Vice chmn., dir. Nat. Consumers League, 1954—. Recipient Fulbright research scholar, 1962-63. Mem. Am. Econ. Assn., Assn. for Asian Studies. Author: Anti-Trust in Japan, 1970. Home: 5040 Klingle St NW Washington DC 20016 Office: 7th and E Sts NW Washington DC 20436

HAEDICKE, THOMAS ARTHUR, physician; b. Bisbee, Ariz., July 10, 1917; s. George Ernest and Lou (Dysinger) II.; student Port Huron Jr. Coll., 1935-37; B.S., Wayne U., 1939, M.D., 1943; m. Jean Gramling, Apr. 5, 1947; children—George Joseph, Anne Chandler. Rotating intern Harper Hosp., Detroit, 1943-44; commd. 1st lt. U.S. Army 1944, advanced through grades to col., 1966; med. service Lawson Gen. Hosp., Atlanta, 1944-45, Walter Reed Gen. Hosp., 1945-50; spl. lectr. tropical medicine Georgetown U., 1946-48; spl. lectr. pharmacology George Washington U., 1947-48; chief med. sect. area med. office VA, 1952-55; instr. medicine Emory U., 1953-55; internist and gastroenterologist Med. Service VA Center, Jackson, Miss., 1955-60; med. service VA Center, Montgomery, Ala., 1960-70; dep. chief profl. div. Med. Services Adminstrn., Ala. Dept. Pub. Health, Montgomery, 1970-72, med. dir. Med. Services Adminstrn., 1972—; clin. instr. medicine U. Miss., 1955-60; clin. asst. prof. dept. pub. health and epidemiology U. Ala. in Birmingham, Med. Center, 1970—. Diplomate Am. Bd. Internal Medicine. Fellow A.C.P.; mem. A.M.A., Central Med. Soc. Methodist (steward). Mason. Author articles in med. jours. Home: Route 1 Box 16-C Pike Road AL 36064 Office: Med Services Adminstrn 304 Dexter Av Montgomery AL 36104

HAERING, GEORGE, govt. ofcl.; b. Rangoon, Burma, Oct. 7, 1930; s. George John and Olga (Perret) H.; A.B., Princeton, 1952; student Am. U., 1955-59; m. Lois Larson, Dec. 13, 1952; children—Kathryn, Kristin, George. Budget examiner Budget Bur., Washington, 1955-59; team leader Mass. Inst. Tech. Operations Evaluation Group, Washington, Far East, also Hawaii, 1960-67; asst. for spl. analysis Office Chief of Naval Operations, Washington, 1967—. Served to lt. (j.g.) USNR, 1952-55. Mem. A.A.A.S., Operations Research Soc. Am. Home: 114 59 Washington Plaza W Reston VA 22070

HAEUSSERMANN, WALTER, aero. devel. engr.; b. Kuenzelsau, Germany, Mar. 2, 1914; s. Otto and Margarete (Henn) H.; B.S., Inst. Tech., Stuttgart, Germany, 1935; M.S., Inst. Tech., Darmstadt, Germany, 1938, Dr. Ing., 1944; m. Ruth Knos, Mar. 24, 1940. Came to U.S., 1948, naturalized, 1954. Research and devel. engr. German Rocket Research Center, Peenemuende, Germany, also Inst. Applied Physics, Darmstadt, 1939-45; scientist Inst. Tech., lectr. Coll. Engring., Darmstadt, 1946-47; supr., aero. devel. engr. Guided Missile Research and Devel., Ft. Bliss, Tex., 1948-50; supr. aero. devel. engr. Ordnance Missile Lab., Redstone Arsenal, Ala., 1950-56; supervising phys. scientist, devel. operations div. Army Ballistic Missile Agy., Guidance and Control Lab., 1956-58, aero. research admistr., dir. guidance and control lab., 1958-60; dir. astronics lab. George C. Marshall Space Flight Center, NASA, Huntsville, Ala., 1960-69, dir. Central System Engring., 1969-72, asso. dir. for sci., 1972—. Mem. grad. faculty elec. engring. Auburn (Ala.) U. Fellow Am. Astronautical Soc.; mem. Am. Inst. Aeros. and Astronautics, Rocket City Astro. Assn., Inst. Navigation, Sigma Xi. Home: 1607 Sandlin Av SE Huntsville AL 35812 Office: S and E Dir George C Marshall Space Flight Center NASA Huntsville AL 35812

HAFER, JAMES STANLEY, govt. ofcl.; b. Twin Falls, Ida., Sept. 20, 1918; s. Carl L. and Emma (Tarr) H.; B.A., Shepherd Coll., 1950; M.A., Am. U., 1953; m. Rachel Virginia Jennings, June 15, 1947; children— Timothy, Jan, Louise, Karl, Anna Lise. Asso. prof. polit. sci. Shepherd Coll., Shepherdstown, W.Va., 1956-67, chief, plans and programs br., spl. facilities div. Office of Emergency Preparedness, Exec. Office Pres., Washington, 1967-68, dep. chief, 1968—. Cons. W.Va. Office Emergency Planning, Charleston, 1964-67; adj. prof. Sch. Gen. Studies, U. Va., 1967—; mem. W.Va. Gov's Civil Def. Adv. Council, 1965-70; mem. exec. com. Eastern W.Va. Research and Devel. Center, Shepherd Coll., 1960-65. Served with AUS, 1941-46, to lt. col., 1950-53; ETO, Korea. Decorated Bronze Star. Mem. Am. Assn. U. Profs., A.A.A.S. Home: 210 German St Shepherdstown WV 25443 Office: Exec Office Bldg Annex 17th and F Sts Washington DC 20504

HAFFER, LOUIS PAUL, lawyer, assn. exec.; b. Boston, May 19, 1914; s. George and Laura (Yager) H.; LL.B. cum laude, Boston U., 1937; m. Hilda Elizabeth Thompson, Aug. 8, 1941; children—Laura S. (Mrs. J.P. Demombynes), Douglas P. Admitted to Mass. bar, 1937, U.S. Supreme Ct. bar, 1945, D.C. bar, 1949; sec. to justices Mass. Supreme Jud. Ct., 1937-39; atty. Wage and Hour Adminstrn., 1939-42, FDA, 1942; trial atty. Dept. Justice, 1942-48; practiced in Washington, 1948—; exec. v.p., counsel Air Freight Forwarders Assn., Washington, 1956—. Lectr., Catholic U. Sch. Law, 1955-64, Am. Inst. Banking, 1953-54. Mem. consumer adv. bd. CAB, 1970-72. Recipient John Ordronaux prize Boston U., 1937. Mem. Am. Bar Assn. (anti-trust com., adminstrv. law com.). Democrat. Editor-in-chief Boston U. Law Rev., 1937. Home: 4711 MacArthur Blvd NW Washington DC 20007 Office: 1730 Rhode Island Av NW Washington DC 20036

HAFFNER, GEORGE LESLIE, optometrist; b. Pittsfield, Mass., Oct. 8, 1932; s. Harold Richard and Maude (Barnum) H.; A.A., U. Fla., 1953; B.S., So. Coll. Optometry, 1958, Dr. Optometry, 1958; m. Marjorie Newsom, Dec. 30, 1956; children—Marjorie Gail, April Charlene, Kimberlee Anne, George Leslie. Practice optometry, Tampa, Fla., 1959—. Sec., dir. Vision Care, Inc. of Fla., 1969—; mem. Fla. Health Manpower Council, 1969—; mem. profl. staff Easter Seal Soc. Crippled Children, 1967-69; mem. adv. staff optometric assistance course Hillsborough County Sch. System, 1971—. Chmn. optometry div. United Fund, 1966, 70-71. Served to capt. AUS, 1954-56. Recipient Distinguished Service award Key Club Internat., 1967. Fellow Am. Acad. Optometry; mem. Am. (mem. career guidance com. 1972-73, Outstanding Service pin 1970), Fla. (trustee 1971-73, chmn. career guidance 1965—) optometric assns., Hillsborough Soc. Optometrists (pres. 1964-66). Democrat. Methodist (lay speaker). Mason (32 deg.), Kiwanian. Home: 408 Lakewood Av Tampa FL 33612 Office: 4515 S Manhattan Av Tampa FL 33611

HAFNER, E. R., exec. dir. Fla. Assn. County Commrs. Address: Box 549 Tallahassee FL 32302*

HAGAN, G. ELLIOTT, congressman; b. Sylvania, Ga., May 24, 1916; student U. Ga.; m. Frances Bryant; children—G. Elliott, Charles Franklin, Frances Bryant. Engaged in life insurance, estate planning; sec.-treas., dep. dir. Ga. Bd. Workmen's Compensation, 1946; Ga. mem. Nat. Council State Govts.; past mem. Ga. Ho. of Reps., Ga. Senate; mem. 87th-92d Congresses 1st Dist. of Ga. Dist.; dir. OPS, 1951-52, dep. Regional dir. Atlanta office, 1953. Bd. dirs. Grace Home; trustee Tift Coll. Served with Signal Corps, AUS, World War II. Mem. Am. Legion, Farm Bur., Ga. Press Assn. (bd. mgrs.). Democrat. Baptist. Mason (Shriner), Elk, Rotarian. Home: Sylvania GA 30467 also 4887 N 35th St Arlington VA 22207 Office: House Office Bldg Washington DC 20515

HAGAN, HELEN, librarian, educator; b. Sylvania, Ga., Mar. 15, 1909; d. Charles Elliott and Annie Helen (Pfeiffer) Hagan; B.A., Ga. State Coll. for Women, 1930; B.S. in L.S., George Peabody Coll., 1933; M.S. in L.S., Columbia, 1941. Circulation-reference librarian Ga. State Coll. Women, 1930-36; librarian Judson Coll., 1936-41; librarian, asso. prof. library sci. Coker Coll., 1941-54; vis. lectr. library sci. Appalachian State Tchrs. Coll., summers 1949-50, Emory U., summer 1947, 52; asst. prof., asst. dir. div. librarianship Emory U., 1954-64; librarian U. N.C. at Wilmington, 1964—. Mem. Am., N.C., Southeastern library assns., Spl. Libraries Assn., Am. Assn. U. Women, Delta Kappa Gamma. Home: Oleander Ct Wilmington NC 28401

HAGEMAN, ELMER LAVERNE, ret. union ofcl.; b. Ford, Kan., May 13, 1905; s. Oscar Y. and Rella (Imel) H.; m. Evelyn T. Kelly, Apr. 5, 1941; 1 dau., Helen. Morse operator, printer operator, telegraph technician Western Union, 1921-46; regional pres. Western Union div. Comml. Telegraphers Union, Eastern region, 1947-53, nat. pres. Western Union div., 1953-71, internat. pres. United Telegrapher Workers, AFL-CIO, 1963-71. Home: 4205 4th St S Arlington VA 22204

HAGEMEYER, JESSE KALPER, business exec.; b. Meridian, Miss., July 29, 1908; s. John William and Jessie (Kaiper) H.; student pub. schs., Meridian; m. Juanita Hasty, July 29, 1928; children—Jack W., Juanita C. (Mrs. James R. Bolton), Jesse Kaiper. Mgr. radio and refrigeration dept. Motor Supply Co., 1936-40; owner Radio Supply Co., Meridian, 1940-54; owner J. K. Hagemeyer Co., radio and TV distbr., Meridian, 1954—, Radio Supply Bldg., Hagemeyer Bldg. Vice pres. Lamar Sch. Found. Mem. United Comml. Travelors Am. Mason (32 deg., K.T.), Lion (dist. gov. 1966-67). Home: 4506 Royal Rd Meridian MS 39301 Office: 1115 25th Av Meridian MS 39301

HAGEN, VERNON DONOHUE, ednl. adminstr.; b. nr. Waycross, Ga., Jan. 27, 1936; s. Robert Fulton and Emma Lou (Hall) H.; student Berry Coll., 1954-56; B.S., U. Ga., 1958, M.Ed., 1964, postgrad., 1967-68; m. Edith Lane Murphy, June 21, 1959; children—Kim Hugh, Karen Leigh, Kenda Lynn. Tchr., Fairmont (Ga.) High Sch., 1958-61; tchr. Hiram (Ga.) High Sch., 1961-67; prin. Hiram Elementary Sch., 1967—. Councilman, Post 2, Powder Springs, Ga., 1969-71. Named Star Tchr. Hiram High Sch. and Paulding County, 1967. Mem. N.E.A., Ga. Assn. Edn., Ga. Elementary Sch. Prins., Nat. Assn. Elementary Sch. Prins., Paulding County Edn. Assn. (pres.),

Paulding County Prins. Assn. (pres.), Phi Kappa Phi. Baptist. Club: Civitan (treas.). Home: 4003 LaFayette Dr Powder Springs GA 30073 Office: Seaboard Av Hiram GA 30141

HAGENS, LOYCE DAWSON, psychologist, educator; b. Henderson, Tex., May 31, 1920; d. Edwin H. and Ada (Hollingsworth) Dawson; student McMurry Coll., 1937-38; B.S., U. Tex., 1941, M. Ed., 1950, Ph.D., 1965; m. Jerome F. Mc Gehearty, July 15, 1948 (div. Oct. 1958); children—Michael Jerome, Patrick Fabian; m. 2d, R.C. Hagens, July 24, 1971. Dir. recreation, Houston, 1941; dir. religious edn. Tyler St. Meth. Ch., Dallas, 1945; psychometrist Ind. Sch. Dist., Austin, 1947-48, counselor, 1948-49; counselor Ind. Sch. Dist., Corpus Christi, Tex., 1954-60; counseling supr. ednl. psychology U. Tex., 1960-63; coordinator demonstration centers child behavior cons. Interprofl. Relations Commn. on Pupil Personnel Services, Austin, Tex., 1963-66; asst. prof. ednl. psychology S.W. Tex. State Coll., San Marcos, 1965-66; prof. psychology, dir. guidance service U. Corpus Christi, 1966-—; dir. Nat. Def. Edn. Act Counseling and Guidance Inst. and Edn. Professions Devel. Act project, Corpus Christi, summers 1967-69; lectr. in field. Bd. dirs. Parents without Partners, Corpus Christi, 1969-71, Coastal Bend Mental Health Assn., Corpus Christi, 1969-71, Family Counseling Service, 1970-71, Inst. Child Devel., 1969-—. Mem. Am., Southwest, Tex. psychol. assns., Am. Tex. personnel and guidance assns., Am Coll. Personnel Assn., Assn. Counselor Educators and Suprs., Assn. Measurement and Evaluation in Guidance. Editor, columnist Elementary Guidance and Counseling Jour.; asst. editor TPGA Jour. Contbr. articles profl. jours. Home: 313 Meldo Park Corpus Christi TX 78411

HAGER, ALICE ROGERS, author, writer; b. Peoria, Ill.; d. Harry James and Caroline Augusta (Sammis) Rogers; A.B. Leland Stanford U., 1915; postgrad. U. Cal., 1917; m. John Manfred Hager, Aug. 3, 1916 (div. 1942); children—Carolyn, Helen. Spl. agt. Bur. Labor Statistics, U.S. Dept. Labor, 1918; reporter Los Angeles Herald, 1923-24; chief of pub. information Women's Bur., U.S. Dept. Labor, 1927-29; spl. writer N.Y. Times, Washington Star and other newspapers and mags., 1929-34; reporter on aviation North Am. Newspaper Alliance, 1934-40; chief pub. information, CAB, 1940-42; war corr. China, Burma, India theatre, Skyways Mag., 1944, Washington editor, 1942-47; pub. affairs officer Am. Embassy, Brussels, 1948-52; area officer USIA, 1952-57. Decorated Order of Southern Cross (Brazil), Order of Merit of Santos Dumont (Brazil); recipient Avon Gold medal for war correspondence, 1945. Fellow Am. Geog. Soc.; mem. Am. Acad. Polit. Sci., Childrens Book Guild, Delta Delta Delta. Episcopalian. Clubs: Overseas Press, Women's National Press (pres. 1946-47). Author: books including Brazil, Giant to the South, 1945; Wings for the Dragon, 1945; Janice. Air Line Hostess, 1947; The Canvas Castle (Julia Ellsworth Ford Found. award, 1948), 1948; Washington, City of Destiny (with Jackie Martin), 1948; Dateline-Paris, 1954; Wonderful Ice Cream Cart, 1955; Washington Secretary, 1958; Love's Golden Circle, 1962; Cathy Whitney: President's Daughter, 1966. Address: Carillon House 2500 Wisconsin Av NW Washington DC 20007

HAGER, JOHN STEWART, lawyer; b. Owensboro, Ky., Apr. 3, 1927; s. Lawrence White and Augusta (Brown) H.; grad. Phillips Exeter Acad., Exeter, Mass., 1945; A.B., Princeton, 1950; J.D., U. Mich., 1954; m. Marjorie McManus, Apr. 4, 1953; children—Laura Susan, Sarah Marjorie, John Stewart, Bruce William. Admitted to Ky. bar, 1954; asso. firm Byron, Sandidge, Holbrook, Owensboro, 1954-60; partner firm Sandidge, Holbrook, Craig & Hager, Owensboro, 1960-—; pres., dir. Owensboro Pub. Co.; dir. radio sta. WOMI, Owensboro, Owensboro Nat. Bank, 1969-71. Chmn. Commn. Missions Meth. Ch., 1960-63, chmn. work area ecumenical affairs, 1969-70, ex-officio mem. Council Ministries, 1969-70. Bd. dirs. Family Y Bd., Jr. Achievement. Served with USNR, 1945-46. Mem. Ky. (chmn. sect. taxation 1965-66), Daviess County bar assns. Home: 1920 Eaton Av Owensboro KY 42301 Office: 100 St Ann Bldg Owensboro KY 42301

HAGER, LAWRENCE WHITE, newspaper pub.; b. Louisville, Ky., May 28, 1890; s. Samuel Wilber and Bessie Woods (White) H.; A.B., Centre Coll., Danville, Ky., 1909, A.M., 1910; Litt.D., Ky. Wesleyan Coll., 1965; m. Martha Augusta Brown, June 25, 1921; children—Lawrence White, John Stewart. With Owensboro (Ky.) Inquirer, 1910-—, Owensboro Messenger since Jan. 2, 1929, now editor and pres. of both; apptd. postmaster Owensboro, 1935, reapptd. 1939, resigned, Feb. 28, 1941; pres. Owensboro Broadcasting Co., 1938-—. Pres. Ky. Press Assn., 1933, Ky. Postmasters Assn., 1935-36; nat. chmn. Am. Legion Publicity Com., which launched The Nat. Legionnaire, weekly newspaper, 1935. Chmn. County War Finance Com., 1942-45. Mem. Am. Legion Publs. Commn., 1939-50, vice chmn., 1949-50. Del. Dem. Nat. Conv., 1956. Trustee Centre Coll., 1949-50; bd. dirs., chmn. finance com. Ky. Wesleyan Coll., 1951-56. Served as officer F.A., U.S. Army, in Argonne offensive, World War I. Charter mem. C. of C. (dir.). Democrat. Methodist. Mason (K.T.). Clubs: Owensboro Investigators, Rotary (pres. 1922; dist. gov. 1938-39); Filson (Louisville). Home: 1844 Griffith Av Owensboro KY 42301 Office: 1401 Frederica St Owensboro KY 42301

HAGGARD, CURTIS ANDREW, dentist; b. Brooklyn, Ala., July 6, 1913; s. William Andrew and Estelle (Avinger) H.; B.S., U. Fal., 1936; D.M.D., U. Louisville, 1941; m. Marjorie Tumlin, Sept. 2, 1937; children— Patricia (Mrs. Darrel J. Mase, Jr.), William Andrew. Practice dentistry, Miami, Fla., 1941-55, Coral Gables, 1957-—. Dir. Bank Coral Gables. Cons. Ritter Dental Mfg. Co., Rochester, N.Y., 1960-—; mem. adv. com. U. Fla. Dental Sch., Gainesville, 1962-—. Chmn. Fla. State Racing Commn., 1953-55. Served as maj., Dental Corps, USAF, 1955-57. Named Dentist of Year Fla. Dental Assn., 1970. Mem. Am. (1st v.p., 1954-55), Fla. dental assns., E. Coast Dist. Dental Soc., Am. Acad. Restorative Dentistry, Nat. Assn. Racing Commrs. (treas., 1953-54), Pi Kappa Alpha. Democrat. Presbyn. Mason (Shriner, Jester), Kiwanian (pres.). Club: Riviera Country. Home: 4301 Santa Maria St Coral Gables FL 33146 Office: 385 Alhambra Circle Coral Gables FL 33134

HAGGARD, JACK OLIFF, dentist; b. Alma, Ga., May 9,, 1925; s. Jack Oliff and Laura Elizabeth (Folger) H.; B.S. in Bus. Adminstrn., U. Tenn., 1949, D.D.S., 1958, M.S. in Orthodontics, 1969; m. Martha Ann Isbell, July 9, 1945; children—Deborah Jean, Denise Folger, Melissa Ann. Pub. health dentist Hillsborough County Health Dept., Tampa, Fla., 1959; gen. practice dentistry, Tampa, 1959-67; practice orthodontics, Tampa, 1969-—. Served with USAAF, 1942-45. Mem. Hillsborough County, West Coast dist. dental socs., Am. Dental Assn., Am. Assn. Orthodontists, Psi Omega, Omicron Kappa Upsilon. Episcopalian (vestryman 1964-67). Home: 4711 Laurel Rd Tampa FL 33609 Office: 1947 W Buffalo St Tampa FL 33607 also 8305 W Hillsborough Tampa FL

HAGGARD, THEODORE MERRILL, ednl. adminstr.; b. Bowling Green, Ky., Apr. 8, 1926; s. Gerstle Merrill and Violet Estelle (Marsh) H.; A.B., U. Ky., 1949, M.A., 1950; B.D., Emory U., 1959, Ph.D., 1971; m. Ann Elizabeth Sageser, Aug. 21, 1949; children—Elizabeth Ann, Kathryn Louise, Melissa Merrill. Prin., Am. Inst., Cochabamba, Bolivia, South Am., 1951-55; ordained deacon United Methodist Ch., N.Ga. Methodist Conf., 1958, elder, 1959; pastor Wesley Chapel Meth. Ch., Decatur, Ga., 1956-58, Salem Meth. Ch., Covington, Ga., 1958-60, Silvertown Ch., Thomaston, Ga., 1960-62, Bethesda Meth. Ch., Lawrenceville, Ga., 1962-65, Palmetto (Ga.) Meth. Ch., 1965-66; dean Reinhardt Coll., Waleska Ga., 1966-72; dir. devel. Pfeiffer Coll., Misenheimer, N.C., 1972-—. Served with USNR, 1944-46. Mem. Am. Soc. Ch. History, Am. Acad. Religion, Soc. Scientific Study of Religion. Rotarian. Home: Pfeiffer College Wisenheimer NC 28109 Office: Dir Devel Pfeiffer Coll Drawer 915 Misenheimer NC 28109

HAGGERTY, JAMES JOSEPH, writer; b. Orange, N.J., Feb. 1, 1920; s. James Joseph and Anna (Morahan) H.; student pub. schs.; m. Marian Smith Mitten, Nov. 20, 1962; children—Karin, James Joseph, Brian (by previous marriage). Reporter Orange (N.J.) Daily Courier, 1938-40; mil. editor Am. Aviation Publs., 1948-53; aviation editor Collier's, 1953-56; free lance writer on sci. and aerospace subjects, 1956-—; editor Aerospace Year Book, 1957-—; aerospace cons. Served with USAAF, 1942-48. Decorated D.F.C., Air medal with clusters. Mem. Aviation Space Writers Assn. (past pres.), Nat. Press Club, A.A.A.S., Air Force Assn. Clubs: Bethesda Country; Touchdown (Washington). Author: First of the Spacemen, 1960; Spacecraft, 1961; Flight, 1964; The U.S. Air Force: A Pictorial History in Art, 1965; Spacecraft II, 1965; Food and Nutrition, 1966; Apollo Lunar Landing, 1969. Address: 502 H St SW Washington DC 20024

HAGLER, JOHN CARROLL, III, iron works exec.; b. Augusta, Ga., Feb. 14, 1923; s. John Carroll and Susan (Barrett) H.; B.S., U. Ga. 1946; m. Mary Anne Tyler, Oct. 16, 1948; children—Mary Anne, John Carroll IV, Richard Belton, Katharine Waterman, Elizabeth Tyler. Chmn. bd. Ga. Iron Works Co., 1947-—; chmn. bd. GIW Industries, Inc., pres., treas. H & T Brass & Aluminum Foundry, Inc., Evans, Ga., 1965-—, Winfield Hills, Inc., Augusta, Ga., 1967-—; exec. v.p. Paga Molds, Inc., Augusta, Greenville, Pa., 1961-—; v.p., dir. Broad Oaks, Inc., Augusta, 1967-—; dir. Ga.-Carolina Brick and Tile Co. Mem. Augusta Aviation Commn., 1962-—. Trustee, pres. Historic Augusta, Inc.; bd. dirs. Augusta Museum, Richmond County Hist. Soc., Augusta Art Assn. Served with A.C., AUS, 1943-45. Mem. Am. Foundrymen's Soc., Am. Inst. Mining, Metall. and Patroleum Engrs., Am. Soc. for Testing and Materials. Am. Soc. for Metals, Asso. Industries Ga., Nat. Assn. Mfgrs., Aircraft Owners and Pilots Assn., Nat. Pilots Assn., Nat. Rifle Assn., Quiet Birdmen, Ducks Unltd. (chmn. Augusta area), Sigma Alpha Epsilon. Republican. Roman Catholic. Rotarian. Clubs: Augusta Country, The Pinnacle. Home: 999 Highland Av Augusta GA 30904 Office: PO Box 626 Grovetown GA 30813

HAHN, GILBERT, JR., lawyer; b. Washington, Sept. 12, 1921; s. Gilbert and Hortense (King) H.; A.B., Princeton, 1943; LL.B., Yale, 1948; m. Margot Hess, June 29, 1950; children—Gilbert III, Amanda B., Polly K. Admitted to D.C. bar, 1948, Md. bar, 1958, U.S. Supreme Ct. bar, 1954; partner firm Amram, Hahn & Sandground, 1954-—. Dir. Wm. Hahn & Co., 1950-71, U.S. Shoe Corp., 1970-—. Alternate del. Republican Nat. Conv., 1952; pres. Washington Young Rep. Club. 1949; chmn. D.C. Rep. Com., 1968-69; chmn. D.C. City Council, 1969-72; mem. Nat. Rep. Finance Com., 1964-68. Pres., bd. dirs. Washington Hosp. Center, 1966-69, Washington Hosp. Center Research Found., 1964-66. Served to 1st lt. AUS, 1942-46; ETO. Decorated Purple Heart. Mem. D.C., Md., U.S. Supreme Ct. bar assns. Clubs: Cannon; Corby Court; Federal City. Address: 3022 University Terrace NW Washington DC 20016

HAHN, MARJORIE FLAACKE (MRS. GEORGE CHRISTIAN HAHN), educator, civic worker; b. N.Y.C., Sept. 13, 1903; d. Henry C. and Katherine (Schwartz) Flaacke; B.S., N.Y. U., 1928, M.A., 1931; m. George Christian Hahn, Aug. 13, 1938; 1 son. William George. Faculty, N.J., State Tchrs. Coll., Newark, 1922-38; personnel work Charleston (S.C.) Navy Yard testing and selecting women for def. work, 1942; employees' relations specialist U.S. Army Letterkenny Ordnance Depot, Chambersburg, Pa., 1943-44. Treas., Georgians for Quality Public Edn., 1969-70. Trustee Youth Mus. Savannah, 1954-—, pres. bd. 1954-57, treas., pres. 1964-65; bd. dirs. Chatham County chpt. Infantile Paralysis, 1951-61; trustee Savannah Sci. Mus. Recipient Savannah Outstanding Citizen award, 1962; Sch. Bell award Chatham Edn. Assn., 1967. Mem. Am. Assn. U. Women (nat., state bd. dirs., nat., state legislative chmn., state pres. 1961-63), Pi Lambda Theta. Home: 110 Harris St Savannah GA 31401

HAHN, RAYBURN EDGAR, accountant; b. Wilson, Tex., Aug. 9, 1925; s. John Ludwig and Lillie (Umlang) H.; B.A., Tex. Tech. Coll., 1949, M.B.A., 1954; m. Elizabeth Anne Vanhala, Nov. 28, 1953; children— Pamela, Rayburn, Tanya, Melissa. Govt. auditor, 1951-53, 54-55; accountant Chance Vaught Aircraft, 1956-59; partner Craven & Millican, C.P.A.'s 1959-71, Alford, Meroney & Co., C.P.A.'s, 1971-—; part-time instr. accounting So. Meth. U., 1956-66. Br. sec. Aid Assn. for Lutherans, 1960-70. Bd. dirs. Tex. dist. Luth. Ch.-Mo. Synod. Served with USNR, 1943-46; to 1st lt. USAF, 1951-53. C.P.A., Tex. Mem. Am. Inst. C.P.A.'s, Tex. Soc. C.P.A.'s, Petroleum Accountants Soc., Luth. Vets. of Japan (pres. 1967-69). Home: 2012 W Colorado Blvd Dallas TX 75208 Office: 3500 1st Nat Bank Bldg Dallas TX 75202

HAHN, T MARSHALL, JR., coll. pres.; b. Lexington, Ky., Dec. 2, 1926; s. Thomas Marshall and Mary Elizabeth (Boston) H.; B.S. in Physics, U. Ky., 1945; Ph.D., Mass. Inst. Tech., 1950; m. Margaret Louise Lee, Dec. 27, 1948; children—William Marshall, Elizabeth Lee, Anne Dillon. Teaching asst. U. Ky., 1944-45; physicist U.S. Naval Ordnance Lab., 1946-47; research asst. Mass. Inst. Tech., 1947-50; asso. prof. U. Ky., 1950-52, prof., dir. grad. studies physics, also dir. Nuclear Accelerator Labs., 1952-54; prof. physics, head dept. Va. Poly. Inst. and State U., 1954-59, pres., 1962-—; dean arts and scis. Kan. State U., 1959-62; physicist N. Am. Phillips Co., summer 1945; staff mem. div. indsl. coop. Mass. Inst. Tech., summer 1950; research participant Oak Ridge Nat. Lab., summer 1951; cons. Reynolds Metals Co., 1958-59, Leeds and Northrup Co., 1958, AEC, 1959; dir. The Lane Co., 1st Nat. Exchange Bank Va., Dominion Bank Shares Corp., Roanoke Electric Steel Corp., Shenandoah Life Ins. Co. Chmn. Va. Met. Areas Study Commn., 1966-68. Served with USNR, 1945-46. Fellow Am. Phys. Soc.; mem. A.A.A.S., Am. Assn. Physics Tchrs., Phi Beta Kappa, Sigma Xi, Omicron Delta Kappa, Sigma Pi Sigma, Pi Mu Epsilon. Methodist. Rotarian. Home: Rainbow Ridge Blacksburg VA 24060

HAIG, ALEXANDER MEIGS, JR., army officer, govt. ofcl.; b. Phila., Dec. 2, 1924; s. Alexander Meigs and Regina Anne (Murphy) H.; student U. Notre Dame, 1943; B.S., U.S. Mil. Acad., 1947; M.A., Georgetown U., 1961; grad. Naval War Coll., 1960, Army War Coll., 1966; m. Patricia Antoinette Fox, May 24, 1950; children—Alexander P., Brian F., Barbara E. Commd. 2d lt. U.S. Army, 1947, advanced through grades to brig. gen., 1969; staff officer Office Dept. Chief of Staff for Operations, Dept. of Army, 1962-64; mil. asst. to Sec. of Army, 1964; dep. spl. asst. to Sec. and Dep. Sec. of Def., 1964-65; bn. and brigade comdr. 1st Inf. Div., Vietnam, 1966-67; regtl. comdr., dep. comdt. U.S. Mil. Acad., 1967-69; mil. asst. to Asst. to the Pres. for Nat. Security Affairs, 1969-70; dep. asst. to the Pres. for Nat. Security Affairs, Washington, 1970-—. Decorated D.S.C., Silver Star with oak leaf cluster, Legion of Merit with 2 oak leaf clusters, D.F.C. with 2 oak leaf clusters, Bronze Star with oak leaf cluster, Air medal with 27 oak leaf clusters, Army Commendation medal, Purple Heart (U.S.); Nat. Order 5th Class, Cross of Gallantry with gold palm (Vietnam). Mem. Soc. of 1st Div. (v.p.). Home: 4622N 38th St Arlington VA 22207 Office: The White House Washington DC 20500

HAILE, WILLIAM FERGUSON, dentist; b. San Marcos, Tex., Feb. 24, 1902; s. Milton Fanin and Margaret (Crews) H.; student U. Tex., Baylor U.; D.D.S., West Tex. Dental Coll. (now Dental Sch., U. Tex.), 1930; m. Ethel Meier, Mar. 10, 1928; 1 dau., Josephine (Mrs. Nations) (dec.). Practice gen. dentistry, Austin, 1930-—. Recipient Certificate Appreciation, for service to Selective Service System Pres. Franklin Roosevelt, 1945, from Pres. Harry Truman, 1947. Mem. Austin Dental Soc. (past pres.), Tex. (life; recipient Good Fellowship award 1963), Am. dental assns. Club: Civitan (Austin). Office: 500 W 15th St Austin TX 78701 Home: 501 Honeycomb St Austin TX 78701

HAILEY, JOHN PHILLIP, foam mfg. co. exec.; b. Scooba, Miss., Nov. 11, 1924; s. Thomas D. and Christine (West.) H.; student, Ohio State U., 1946-48, U. Tampa, 1943-44; m. 1 son, Mark Steven (dec.). Field rep. Goodyear Tire & Rubber Co., Akron, O., 1951-53; br. mgr. Merry Weather Foam Latex Co., Akron, 1953-55; dir. sales Dryden Rubber Co., Keokuk, Ia., 1955-58; pres. Phillips-Foscue Corp., High Point, N.C., 1958-—. Served with M.C., AUS, 1943-46. Mem. N.C. Wildlife Fedn., Young Presidents Orgn. Clubs: Willow Creek Country; String and Splinter; Southern Furniture (High Point, N.C.). Home: PO Box 669 High Point NC 27261 Office: PO Box 1306 High Point NC 27261

HAIMAN, ROBERT, newspaper co. exec.; m. Elizabeth Royce Greenlaw; 1 son, Robert Greenlaw. Mng. editor Times, St. Petersburg, Fla.; dir. Times Pub. Co. Mem. A.P. Mng. Editors Assn. (dir.). Presbyn. (deacon). Kiwanian. Clubs: Bath, Racquet, University. Home: 3275 Walnut St NE St Petersburg FL 33731 Office: Times PO Box 1121 St Petersburg FL 33731

HAINES, KENNETH A., govt. ofcl.; b. Pendleton, Ind., Mar. 27, 1907; s. Oscar William and Lena Blanche (Hileman) H.; B.S., Purdue U., 1929; M.S., Ohio State U., 1931; m. Helen Elizabeth Evans, June 28, 1936; children—Kenneth Hileman, Thomas Richard. With Ohio State Experiment Station, 1929-30; with U.S. Dept. Agr., 1933-—. entomologist, Bur. Entomology and Plant Quarantine, N.J., 1933-39, N.Y.C., 1939-40, Washington, 1940-48, Pa., 1948-49, Mass., 1949-51;, asst. dir., 1951-54; asst. dir. program appraisal and internal audit Agrl. Research Service, Washington, 1954-58; asso. dir. internat. programs div. Agrl. Research Service, Hyattsville, Md., 1959-—. U.S. mem. bd. dirs. Inter-Am. Inst. Agrl. Scis., 1962-—; mem. U.S. delegations Food and Agrl. Orgn. of U.N., 1961-65, 67, 69, 71. First aid chmn. Spokane (Wash.) council Boy Scouts Am., 1944-47; treas. P.T.A., Arlington, Va., 1953-62; mem. joint bd. sci. edn. Greater Washington area, 1954-—, vice chmn., 1971-—. Mem. Entomol. Soc. Am., Entomol. Soc. Washington (program chmn. 1954), Washington Acad. Scis., A.A.A.S., Phi Sigma Kappa, Gamma Alpha. Mason. Home: 3542 N Delaware St Arlington VA 22207 Office: U S Dept Agriculture Agrl Research Service Room 648 Fed Center Bldg Hyattsville MD 20782

HAINS, FRANK WOODRUFF, JR., newspaperman; b. Parkersburg, W.Va., July 7, 1926; s. Frank Woodruff and Earlena (Meyer) H.; A.B., Marietta Coll., 1951. Announcer, WPAR, Parkersburg, 1947-51; asst. mgr. WVIM, Vicksburg, Miss., 1951-54; spl. programmer WQBC, Vicksburg, 1954-55; amusements editor, lit. editor, columnist Jackson (Miss.) Daily News, 1955-—. Guest dir. U. So. Miss., summer 1961-68, Belhaven Coll., 1962; guest dir. Vicksburg Little Theatre, 1967, U. Miss., 1969; set designer Millsaps Coll., 1963, 70, Miss. Coll., 1963, Belhaven Coll., Jackson Opera Guild, 1965. Vice pres., founding mem. bd., designer New Stage Theatre, Jackson, Miss., 1966-—; bd. dirs. Millsaps Coll. Arts and Lecture Series. Served with AUS, 1945-46. Recipient Nat. Pop Warner Conf. award for service to youth, 1958; Rust Coll. Shield, 1970; Distinguished Service award Miss. Authority Ednl. TV, 1971. Mem. Jackson Little Theatre (mem. staff of dirs. 1955-—, v.p. 1956-65). One man theatrical photography show Jackson Art Gallery, 1960; dir. Miss. Arts Festival, 1965; writer, producer, dir. ednl. Miss. Ednl. TV program A Season of Dreams, winner 1st pl. award So. Ednl. Communications Assn. competition, 1971, Ohio State award, 1972. Office: 311 Pearl St Jackson MS 39201

HAIR, JOHN STACEY, dentist; b. Fayetteville, N.C., Dec. 21, 1921; s. Lill Gaston and Burline (Downing) H.; student Mars Hill Jr. Coll., 1939-40, Wake Forest Coll., 1940-41; D.D.S., Med. Coll. Va., 1945; m. Mary Grace Silvertsen, Aug. 18, 1941; children—Sarah (Mrs. John Thomas Shipman III), John Stacey. Gen. practice dentistry, Fayetteville, 1945-—. Chmn. Cumberland County Jury Commn., 1968-—. Served to capt. USAF, 1950-52, lt. col. Res., 1952-—. Mem. N.C. Dental Soc., Am. Dental Assn., Exchange Club (bd. dirs. 1971-—), Cumberland County Dental Soc. (pres. 1947-48). Democrat. Baptist. Moose, K.P. Clubs: Green Valley Country, Carrousel. Home: 2718 Morgantown Rd Fayetteville NC 28304 Office: 308 Green St Fayetteville NC 28301

HAIRE, JOHN DANIEL, oil co. exec.; b. Mt. Sterling, Ill., Jan. 26, 1897; s. Sylvester and Flora (Homberg) H.; m. Marie Finnegan, Apr. 5, 1926; 1 son, John Daniel, Jr. Agt. Sinclair Oil, Chgo., 1918-26; mgr. Akron Oil Co., 1926-30; asst. mgr. nat. accounts Shell Oil, St. Louis, 1937-39; with Delta Oil Co., 1939-—, now exec. officer, vice chmn.; vice chmn., chief exec. officer Realty Investments, Inc., Petersburg, Va., City Point Oil Terminal Co., Hopewell, Va., Delta Realty Co., Petersburg, Colonial Oil Co., Colonial Heights, Va., Delta Materials, Hopewell Delta Properties; v.p. Willow Oaks Farms, Hickory Hill Farms. Dir. Appomatox Basin Indsl. Devel. Corp. With Richmond-Petersburg Turnpike Authority, Petersburg, Va., 1965-—, bd. dirs., 1971-—, vice chmn., 1971-—. Served with USNR, 1918. Recipient many awards including Outstanding Citizens award Petersburg B'nai B'rith. Mem. Petersburg C. of C. (dir. 1969-72), Petersburg U.S.O. (dir. 1945), Nat. Council U.S.O., Hopewell C. of C., Nat. Oil Marketers Assn., Va. Oil Men's Assn., Va. Oil Jobbers Assn., U.S. Army Assn. (chpt. pres. 1961-62). Rotarian. Clubs: Country (Petersburg, Va.); Fort Lee Officers' and Golf (Va.). Home: 1801 Westover Petersburg VA 23803 Office: 801 Bollingbrook Petersburg VA 23803

HAISE, FRED WALLACE, JR., astronaut; b. Biloxi, Miss., Nov. 14, 1933; s. Fred Wallace and Lucille (Blacksher) H.; A.A., Perkinston Jr. Coll., 1952; B.S. in Aero Engring., U. Okla., 1959; D.Sc. (hon.), Western Mich. U., 1970; m. Mary Griffin Grant, June 4, 1954; children—Mary Margaret, Frederick Thomas, Stephen William, Thomas Jesse. Naval aviation cadet U.S. Navy, 1952-54; fighter pilot U.S. Marine Corps, 1954-56, Air N.G., Okla., Ohio, 1957-63; capt. U.S. Air Force, 1961-62; research pilot NASA Lewis Research Center, Cleve., 1959-63, NASA Flight Research Center, Edwards AFB, Cal., 1963-66; astronaut NASA Manned Spacecraft Center, Houston, 1966-—, lunar module pilot Apollo 13, Apr. 1970. Active Indian Guides YMCA, Lancaster, Cal. 1965-—. Recipient AB Honts trophy USAF Aerospace Research Pilot Sch., Edwards AFB, 1964; Presdl. Medal of Freedom, 1970; City of Houston Medal for valor, 1970; Jeff Davis award, Biloxi, Miss., 1970; Gold medal City N.Y.,

1970; Distinguished Civilian Service medal State of Miss., 1970. Mem. Soc. Exptl. Test Pilots, Phi Theta Kappa, Tau Beta Pi, Sigma Gamma Tau. Office: Code (CB) NASA Manned Spacecraft Center Houston TX 77058

HAITHCOCK, WILLIE MERLE, ret. supt. schs.; b. Estelline, Tex., Jan. 30, 1901; d. Francis Marion and Salina Arris (Duncan) Trapp; B.S., W. Tex. State Tchrs. Coll., 1941; postgrad. U. Tex., 1943-44; M.Ed., Tex. Technol. Coll., 1951; m. Riley Columbus Haithcock, July 5, 1928; 1 dau., Carolyn (Mrs. William Randolph Hale). Tchr. elementary sch., Tex., 1918-20; tchr. English, history high schs., Tex., 1920-46; county sch. supt. Hale County Schs., Plainview, Tex., 1947-70. Mem. Hale County Tchrs. Assn. (pres.), Nat. Assn. County Intermediate Unit Supts. (dir.), Tex. Assn. County Supts. (sec.), C. of C. (women's com.), Delta Kappa Gamma (chpt. pres., state v.p.). Clubs: Plainview Women's (mem. bd.), As You Like It Study (pres.), Altrusa (pres., dir. Plainview). Baptist. Mem. Order Eastern Star. Home: 1205 Houston St Plainview TX 79072 Office: County Courthouse Plainview Tx 79072

HAKKARINEN, WILLIAM, govt. engr.; b. Negaunee, Mich., July 11, 1913; s. Charles and Elizabeth (Hyytinen) H.; A.B. in physics cum laude, No. Mich. U., 1939; m. Vilma Helen Pynnonen, Aug. 9, 1940; children—William David, Richard Kyle, Charles Stanley, Ida Marie. Tchr. high sch., Baraga, Mich., 1939-42; engr. Nat. Bur. Standards, 1942-61, project leader, 1961-66; chief engr. Naval Weapons Quality Assurance Office, Washington, 1966—. Mem. I.E.E.E., A.A.A.S., U.S. Naval Inst., Marine Tech. Soc. Patentee in field. Home: 910 Somerset Pl Hyattsville MD 20783 Office: Washington Navy Yard Washington DC 20090

HALBERT, SEYMOUR PUTTERMAN, research physician; b. Phila., Mar. 20, 1917; s. Morris and Fanny (Ellman) H.; student Bklyn. Coll., 1933-35; B.A., U. N.C., 1937; M.D., Johns Hopkins, 1941; m. Martha Swanson, Nov. 7,1965; children—Lynn, Alan, Bruce. Intern, L.I. Coll. Hosp., 1941-42; research asso. U. Pa. Med. Sch., 1942-45; asst. prof. exptl. medicine U. N.C., 1946-49; asst. prof. microbiology Columbia U. Coll. Physicians and Surgeons, 1949-52, asso. prof. microbiology and ophthalmology research, 1952-61, prof. ophthalmology research, 1961-65; prof. pediatrics U. Miami (Fla.) Med. Sch., 1965—. Cons. NIH, 1963—; dir. immunology Cordis Labs., 1963—. Served as asst. surgeon USPHS, 1945-46. Guggenheim fellow, Helen Hay Whitney fellow, 1956-57. Mem. Am. Soc. Bacteriologists, Am. Assn. for Immunologists, N.Y. Acad. Scis., Harvey Soc., A.A.A.S., Assn. for Research in Ophthalmology, Brit. Soc. for Immunology, N.Y. Acad. Medicine, Biochem. Soc., Am. Chem. Soc., Collegium Internat. Allergologicum. Home: 12450 Rock Garden Lane Miami FL 33156 Office: 1475 NW 12th Av Miami FL 33136

HALBOUTY, MANAH ROBERT, air force officer; physician; b. Beaumont, Tex., Apr. 28, 1914; s. Tom C. and Sodia (Monolley) H.; M.D., Tulane U., 1937; grad. Sch. Aviation Medicine, 1940, Med-Field Service Sch., 1941, Army Air Staff Command and Gen. Staff Sch., 1944;; m. Gracye Collinsworth, Mar. 23, 1940; 1 son, Michel Robert William. Intern St. Paul's Hosp., Dallas, 1937-38, resident internal medicine, 1938-39; house doctor Mo.-Kan.-Tex. R.R. Hosp., Denison, Tex., 1939-40; commd. 1st lt., M.C., U.S. Army Air Force, 1940, advanced through ranks to col., 1951; aviation examiner, sr. flight surgeon chief flight surgeon and med. aircraft observor; research aviation medicine Mayo Clinic, 1941; asst. chief med. processing center SAACC, Tex., 1942; hosp. comdr., Ohio and Fla., 1943-44; troop carrier wing surgeon, Italy, Germany, 1945-46, comdr. hosps., wing and base surgeon, N.Y. State, Alaska, Ariz., Tex., 1956-57; div. surgeon 43d Air Div., comdr. 8th Tactical Hosp., also 6160th USAF Hosp., Itazuke AFB, Japan, 1957-60; chief flight surgeon, div. surgeon 819th Air Div., dir. base med. services hosp. and 819th Med. Group, Comdr. Dyess AFB, Abilene, Tex., 1960-66, also chief preventive medicine and comdr. USAF Hosp.; USAF surgeon gen.'s staff med. rep. on USAF Phys. Rev. Council, Hdqrs. USAF Mil. Personnel Center, Randolph AFB, Tex., 1966—; sr. med. officer USAF Phys. Evaluation Bd., USAF Mil. Personnel Center, 1966-68; practicing med.clinician Randolph AFB Hosp. Decorated Legion of Merit, 2d Army and 3 Air Force Commendation medals, Gold Flight Surgeon's Wings with citation from Comdg. Gen. Chinese Nationalist Air Force. Mem. A.M.A., Assn. Mil. Surgeon's U.S., Aerospace Med. Assn. U.S., Am. Acad. Gen. Practice, Civil Aviation Med. Assn., Japanese-Am. Med. Assn. (founder), Assn. U.S. Flight Surgeons. Contbr. articles to mil. and profl. med. jours. Home: 46 Outer Octagon Rancolph AFB TX 78148 Office: USAFMPC (AFPMA-PRC), Randolph AFB TX 78148

HALBOUTY, MICHEL THOMAS, geologist, petroleum engr., ind. producer, operator; b. Beaumont. Tex., June 21, 1909; s. Tom Christian and Sodia (Monnelly) H.; B.S., Tex. A. and M. Coll., 1930. M.S., 1931, Profl. Degree in Geol. Engring., 1956; E.D., Mont. Coll. Mineral Sci. and Tech., 1966;; m. Fay Renfro, June 22, 1945. Geologist, petroleum engr. Yount-Lee Oil Co., Beaumont, Tex., 1931-33, chief geologist, petroleum engr., 1933-35; v.p., gen. mgr., chief geologist and petroleum engr. Glenn H. McCarthy, Inc., Houston, 1935-37; owner firm of cons. geologists and petroleum engrs. in Houston, 1937—; discoverer numerous oil fields La. and Tex.; pioneer independent to discover gas field Alaska. Chmn. bd. North Side State Bank, Houston, First Nat. Bank, West Side Nat. Bank (both San Angelo, Tex.), First Nat. Bank, Paris, Tex., First Nat. Bank, Deport; dir. Bank of Tex., Houston. Served as lt. col. AUS, 1942-45. Mem. many tech. and sci. socs. Episcopalian. Clubs: Houston, Petroleum, River Oaks Country (Houston); Eldorado Country (Palm Desert, Cal.); Dallas Petroleum; New Orleans Petroleum; Broadmoor Golf (Colorado Springs, Colo.); Cosmos (Washington). Author: Petrographic and Physical Characteristics of Sand from Seven Gulf Coast Producing Horizons, 1937; Salt Domes—Gulf Region, United States and Mexico, 1967; co-author: Spindletop, 1952, The Last Boom, 1972; also numerous tech. and sci. papers on geology and petroleum engring. Home: 3630 Willowick Rd Houston TX 77019 Office: 5111 Westheimer Rd Houston TX 77027

HALBROOK, WILLIAM MARCUS, state ofcl.; b. Zion, Ark., May 9, 1926; s. Dalton Clyde and Vera O. (Haywood) H.; B.S., U. Ark., 1948; LL.B., Ark. Law Sch., 1952; m. Marilyn R. Perkins, Apr. 18, 1970; 1 dau., Emily, Lynne. Research statistician, asst. dir. Ark. Legislative Council, 1949-53, dir. research dept., exec. sec., 1953—. Mem. bd. mgrs. Council State Govts., 1963-64; v.p. Nat. Legislative Conf., 1962-63, pres., 1963-64. Mem. Am., Ark. bar assns. Democrat. Baptist. Home: 7404 L St Little Rock AR 72207 Office: State Capitol Bldg Little Rock AR 72201

HALBROOKS, NORMAN EARL, physician; b. Bryan, Tex., Nov. 18, 1924; s. William Everett and Myrtle Pauline (Mathis) H.; B.S. (Julia Ball Lee fellow 1941), Tex. A. and M.U., 1946; M.A., M.D., (Gail Borden fellow 1954) U. Tex., 1954; m. Carolyn Sue Miller, July 13, 1952; children—Anne Elizabeth, Ronald Frederick, Mary Pauline, Carol Margaret, Laura Sue, Gary Norman. Intern John Sealy Hosp., Galveston, Tex., 1954-55, resident 1955-57, now mem. staff; practice medicine specializing in anesthesiology, Tyler, Tex., 1957—; pres. Anesthesiologists of Tyler & Assos., 1971—; mem. staffs Med. Center, Mother Frances Hosp., Glenwood Gen. Hosp., Eastern Tex. Chest Hosp., Tyler, Nan Travis Hosp., Jacksonville, Parkland Hosp., Dallas. Trustee U. Tex. Med. Branch, pres., 1971-72; pres. East Tex. Symphony, 1967—. Served with USNR, 1942-46. Fellow Royal Coll. Health of England; mem. Am., Tex. med. assns., Smith County Med. Soc. (sec. 1971—), Am., Tex. socs. anesthesiologists, So. Med. Soc., Mu Delta. Mason. Home: 4411 Old Bullard Rd Tyler TX 75701 Office: 916 Hospital Dr Tyler TX 75701

HALBROOKS, WILLIAM JACKSON, aerospace engr.; b. Birmingham, Ala., July 21, 1931; s. William Barnet and Melba (Bailey) H.; B.S., Auburn U., 1952; m. Sallie Boyce Barlow, Aug. 24, 1952; children—Martin William, Robert Jackson, Brenda Alwyn, William David. Exptl. engr. Allison div. Gen. Motors, 1957-58; test engr. missile div. Chrysler Corp., Redstone Arsenal, Ala., 1958-59; test engr. with test div. Marshall Space Flight Center, NASA, 1959-61, aerospace engr. on div. staff test lab., 1961-65, project engr. in F-1 engine office indsl. operations, 1965-67, chief engring. support br. F-1 engine project, program mgmt., 1967-70, engine program office spl. missions, space shuttle engine, 1970—. Active Boy Scouts Am. Served to lt. USNR, 1952-56. Recipient Wood badge Boy Scouts Am., 1970; Sustained Superior Performance award Marshall Space Flight Center, 1970. Registered profl. engr., Ala. Mem. Am. Inst. Aeros. and Astronautics (mem. liquid rocket tech. com. 1971—), Phi Kappa Tau. Baptist. Contbr. articles to profl. jours. Home: 606 Hillmont St NW Huntsville AL 35805 Office: Redstone Arsenal AL

HALDEMAN, HARRY R. (BOB), govt. ofcl.; b. Los Angeles, Oct. 27, 1926; s. Harry F. and Katherine (Robbins) H.; student U. Redlands, 1944-45, U. So. Cal., 1945-46; B.S. in Bus. Adminstrn. U. Cal. at Los Angeles, 1948; m. Jo Horton, Feb. 19, 1949; children—Susan Ward, Harry Horton, Peter Robbins, Ann Kurtz. Account exec. J. Walter Thompson Co., Los Angeles, N.Y.C., 1949-59, v.p., mgr. Los Angeles office, 1960-68; asst. to Pres. of U.S., Washington, 1969—; dir. Haledman, Inc., Los Angeles. Chief staff Nixon presdl. campaign, 1968. Bd. regents U. Cal., 1965-67, 68-69; trustee Cal. Inst. Arts, 1961—, chmn. bd., 1968. Served with USNR, 1944-46. Mem. Beta Theta Pi, Pi Delta Epsilon. Office: The White House Washington DC 20500

HALDERMAN, JOHN W(ILLIAM), lawyer; b. Astoria, Ore., Dec. 5, 1907; s. Charles Walker and Bertha Emily (Hobson) H.; B.S., U. Ore., 1933, LL.B., 1931; postgrad. Princeton, 1936-37, Nat. War Coll., 1950-51; m. Elenor B. Lonergan, Feb. 4, 1938; 1 son, Charles Reed. Admitted to Ore. bar, 1931 and practiced in Ore., 1931-36; asst. to legal adviser Dept. State, 1937-42, Internat. Orgn. Affairs, 1942-50, 59-60; served in Am. diplomatic missions at Bonn, Berlin, Casablanca, Colombo, 1959-59; with Rule of Law Research Center, Sch. of Law, Duke U., Durham, N.C., 1960—. Served in AUS, 1943-45. Mem. secretariat U.N. Com. of Jurists, Washington, 1945; sec. com. on Internat. Ct. Justice, U.N. Conf. on Internat. Orgn., San Francisco, 1945. Adviser U.S. delegation U.N. Prep. Commn., London, 1945, 1st session U.N. Gen. Assembly, London, 1946, 9th Internat. Conf. of Am. States, Bogota, 1948, U.N. Palestine Conciliation Commn., 1949. Mem. Phi Beta Kappa, Phi Delta Phi. Author: The United Nations and the Rule of Law. Contbr. legal periodicals. Home: 2216 Elmwood Av Durham NC 27707

HALE, CHARLES HERBERT, forester; b. Hobgood, N.C., Mar. 28, 1915; s. George Herbert and Annie Lane (Thigpen) H.; C.E., N.C. State Coll., 1937; m. Margaret Quinn Coates, July 10, 1952; children—Geneva Quinn, Charles Herbert. Forester, True Temper Corp., Plymouth, N.C., 1937-40, Am. Package Corp., Murfreesboro, N.C., 1946-65, Ga. Pacific Corp., Scotland Neck, N.C., 1965—. Mem. Good Neighbor Council, Halifax County, N.C., 1969-70. Democratic precinct chmn., 1965-70. Trustee, sec. Our Community Hosp., Scotland Neck. Served with AUS, 1941-46; ETO. Mem. Soc. Am. Foresters, Am. Congress on Surveying and Mapping, Am. Legion, Am., N.C. forestry assns., N.C. Soc. Surveyors, N.C. Lumber Mfg. Assn., Halifax County Hist. Assn., Lambda Chi Alpha. Episcopalian (vestryman). Mason (Shriner). Clubs: Scotfield Country, Holly Oak Gun (Scotland Neck, N.C.). Home: 1918 Clarksville Dr Scotland Neck NC 27874 Office: 711 Vance St Murfreesboro NC

HALE, DOUGLAS VAN, mech. engr., state legislator; b. Birmingham, Ala., Jan. 1, 1942; s. Willard Douglas and Marion Wilamina (Meeter) H.; B.S. in Mech. Engring., Auburn U., 1964; M.S. in Nuclear Engring (AEC fellow), Mass. Inst. Tech., 1965; now student Cumberland Sch. Law; m. Joanne Tyus, June 29, 1963; 1 dau., Holly Anne. Mech. engr. Lockheed Co., Huntsville, Ala., 1965-71; systems engr. Computer Scis. Corp., Huntsville, Ala., 1971-72; mem. Ala. Ho. of Reps., 1970-74. Dir. Huntsville Indsl. Expansion Com., 1970—. Active numerous civic orgns. Mem. County Exec. Com. Republican Party, 1966—, State Exec. Com., 1971—. Mem. Huntsville Jr. C. of C., Tau Beta Pi, Pi Tau Sigma, Pi Mu Epsilon, Phi Delta Kappa, Phi Kappa Phi, Pi Kappa Alpha. Baptist (deacon). Home: 2105 Clubview Ct NW Huntsville AL 35810

HALE, ELLIS FLEMING, cons. engr.; b. Rome, Ga., Feb. 10, 1907; s. Bernard and Mary Louisa (Fleming) H.; B.S., Emory U., 1927, M.S., 1928; postgrad. Johns Hopkins, 1928-29; m. Elizabeth Hand, Apr. 30, 1931; 1 dau., Nancy Elizabeth (Mrs. William E. Johnson). Prodn. supt. Celanese Fibers Co., Rome, Ga., 1929-68; staff dir. Ga. div. Am. Cancer Soc., 1968-70; cons. engr., Rome, 1970—; Dir. Rome Bank & Trust Co. Exec. Dir. Ga. Adv. Com. on Edn., 1970—; Pres. Riverside Fed. Credit Union, 1955-68. Pres. United Fund, Rome, 1967. Mem. bd. edn. Rome City Schs., 1949-57, chmn., 1954-57. Trustee Darlington Sch. for Boys. Mem. Rome-Floyd C. of C. (pres. 1963). Presbyn. (elder). Rotarian. (pres. 1959-60). Home: 212 E 9th St Rome GA 30161 Office: 307 E 3d Av Rome GA 30161

HALE, MARGIE NORNHAUSSER, chem. co. exec.; b. Carlsbad, N.M., Oct 20, 1921; d. Muryl Marshall and Lena Florence (Witthauer) N.; B.S. U. Texas, 1942, M.S. Purdue U., 1948; m. Cecil Harrison Hale, May 6, 1945; children—Bryan M., Connie M., Chris A. Analytical chemist Esso Labs., Standard Oil Devel. Baton Rouge, 1942-46, patent contact, 1948-49, research chem. 1949-50, teaching asst. Purdue U., 1946-48; owner Southwestern Analytical Chems. Austin, Tex., 1950-65; v.p. Southwestern Analytical Chems., Inc. Austin, 1965—. Mem. Am. Chem. Soc., A.A.A.S., Sigma Xi., Methodist (steward 1960-70). Contbr. articles to prof. jours. Home: 1300 Windsor Rd Austin TX 78703 Office: 821 E Woodward Austin TX 78704

HALE, MASON ELLSWORTH, JR., museum curator; b. Winsted, Conn., Sept. 23, 1928; s. Mason Ellsworth and Lillian (Swanson) H.; B.S., Yale, 1950; M.A., U. Wis., 1951, Ph.D., 1953;; m. Beatrice Wilde, Apr. 19, 1952; children—Janet Arlene, Sandra Louise, Robert Allan. Asst. prof. biology U. Wichita 1953-55, W.Va. U., 1955-57; asso. curator div. cryptogams, dept. botany Mus. Natural History, Smithsonian Instn., 1957-62, curator, 1962—, chmn., 1968—; field exploration Arctic Can., 1950, Mexico, 1960, Pacific area, 1964-65; spl. research taxonomy and chemistry lichenized fungi. Mem. Am. Soc. Plant Taxonomists (editorial bd.), Am. Biological Soc., Swedish Bot. Soc., Japan Am. Soc., Phi Beta Kappa, Sigma XI. Author: Lichen Handbook, 1961; Biology of Lichens, 1967; How to Know the Lichens, 1969. Address: Smithsonian Instn Washington DC 20560

HALE, NANCY, author; b. Boston, Mass., May 6, 1908; d. Philip L. and Lilian (Westcott) Hale; grad. Winsor Sch., Boston, 1926; student Sch. of Boston Mus. Fine Arts, 1927-28; studied in father's studio number of yrs.; m. Fredson Bowers, Mar. 16, 1942; children—(by former marriage)—Mark Hardin, William Wertenbaker. Asst. editor, Vogue, 1928-32, Vanity Fair, 1933-34; news reporter N.Y. Times, 1935; advisor to advt. agy., 1930-35; lectr. short story Bread Loaf Writers Conf., 1957-65. Recipient O. Henry prize for short-short story, 1933; Benjamin Franklin spl. citation for short story, 1958; Henry H. Bellaman award for lit., 1969. Clubs: Cosmopolitan (N.Y.C.). Author: The Young Die Good, 1932; Never Any More, 1934; The Earliest Dreams, 1936; The Prodigal Women, 1942; Between the Dark and the Daylight, 1943; The Sign of Jonah, 1950; The Empress's Ring, 1955; Heaven and Hardpan Farm, 1957; A New England Girlhood, 1958; Dear Beast, 1959; The Pattern of Perfection (short stories), 1960; The Realities of Fiction (essays), 1962; Black Summer, 1963; New England Discovery (anthology), 1963; The Life In The Studio, 1969; Secrets, 1971. Author short stories which have appeared in over 40 anthologies, including the Foley and O. Henry collections. Contbr. to New Yorker, Harper's Bazaar, Harper's. Home: Route 8 Charlottesville VA 22901

HALE, RUSSELL WILLIAM, economist, govt. ofcl.; b. Syracuse, N.Y., Apr. 17, 1909; s. Harry William and Viola (Lape) H.; student Syracuse U., 1928-29, McGill U., 1929-30; m. Sue Evelyn Galloway, Mar. 21, 1952; 1 son, William Franklin. Buyer John Wanamaker, N.Y.C., 1931-36; merchandise mgr. Joslin Dry Goods Co. (dept. store), Denver, 1936-41; regional price exec. (N.Y., N.J., Pa., Md., Del., D.C.), OPA, 1942-47; dir. trade and services Gen. Hdqrs., SCAP, Tokyo, Japan, 1947-52; cons. to chmn. NSRB, 1952; adviser on Far East trade to dep. dir. Mut. Def. Assistance Control, FOA, 1952-55; asst. dept. dir. ICA for Mut. Def. Assistance Control, 1955-57, asst. dep. adminstr. State Dept., Mut. Def. Assistance Control, 1958-61, asst. exec. sec. Nat. Aeros. and Space Council, Office of Pres., Washington, 1961—. Mem. Sigma Chi. Home: 1500 Arlington Blvd Arlington VA 22209 Office: Exec. Office of Pres Washington DC 20502

HALE, SHADRACH PAYNE, real estate lawyer; b. Trenton, Ga., Jan. 13, 1912; s. Shadrach Jerome and Clara (Street) H.; LL.B., Chattanooga Coll. Law, 1931, LL.M., 1934; m. Margaret Virginia Ashworth, Apr. 16, 1937; children—S. Jerome II, Patricia Elaine (Mrs. Herbert William Sams, Jr.). Admitted to Ga. bar, 1931, Tenn. bar, 1936; mem. firm Hale & Hale, Trenton, 1931-36; mem. firm McClure, McClure & Hale (formerly McClure & McClure), Chattanooga, 1936-41, Hale & Ellis, 1941—; sec. Milligan-Reynolds Guaranty Title Agy., Inc., 1941—, dir., 1944—. Mem. Am., Tenn., Chattanooga bar assns., Chattanooga Bd. Realtors (asso.), Home Builders Assn. Chattanooga (asso.), Sigma Delta Kappa. Methodist. Elk, Kiwanian. Clubs: Valleybrook Golf and Country, Lakeshore Country, Mountain City. Home: Goldpoint Circle Hixson TN 37343 Office: 722 Cherry Chattanooga TN 37402

HALE, WILLIAM HENRI, univ. pres.; b. Krebs, Okla., Aug. 8, 1914; s. George and Carrie (Holmes) H.; B.S., Langston (Okla.) U., 1940; M.A., U. Wis., 1941; Ph.D., U. Chgo., 1949; L.H.D., Okla. Sch. Religion, Langston, 1964; m. Larzette Golden, May 24, 1940; children— Pauline (Mrs. James Jackson), Janis, Gina. Research asst. sociology Fisk U., 1941-42; acting registrar Langston U., 1942-43; registrar Bethune-Cookman Coll., 1942-44, dean-registrar, 1944-46, acting pres., summer 1946; prof. social sci., chmn. dept. Clark Coll., Atlanta, 1948-60; pres. Langston U., 1960—; vis. summer prof. Atlanta U., 1947, 50-52, 55, 59-60, State Tchrs. Coll., Montgomery, Ala., 1948, Hampton Inst., 1949. Nat. adviser pre-alumni group mem. instns. United Negro Coll. Fund, 1958-60; treas. Atlanta Interracial Work Camp, 1956, Atlanta PanHellenic Council, 1958-60; dir. youth activities Atlanta br. N.A.A.C.P., 1949-51; mem. Okla. State Commn. on Human Rights; bd. dirs. Atlanta Assn. Mental Health, 1958; mem. Okla. Small Bus. Adv. Council, Okla. Curriculum Improvement Commn.; mem. com. edn. center planning Oklahoma City Pub. Schs.; mem. Gov.'s Com. Phys. Fitness; mem. commn. on colls. and univs. North Central Assn. Colleges and Secondary Schs.; mem. exec. com. of council of pres.'s Nat. Assn. Land-Grant Colls. and State Univs.; mem. adv. com. U.S. Coast Guard Acad. Named Mason of the Year, 1964. Mem. Am. Sociol. Soc., Assn. Higher Edn, Am. Assn. Sch. Admisntrs., N.E.A., Nat. Conf. Christians and Jews, Alpha Phi Alpha (nat. dir. ednl. activities 1957-58, nat. pres. 1961—), Alpha Kappa Delta, Kappa Delta Pi, Phi Delta Kappa. Address: Langston Univ Langston OK 73050

HALE, WILLIAM JOHN, physician; b. Oklahoma City, Nov. 20, 1938; s. Ival Jennings and Gertha Irene (Wright) H.; B.S., Central State Coll., Edmond, Okla., 1959; M.D., U. Okla.; m. Sandra Lea Martin, Oct. 20, 1961; children—Christi, Bill, Shelly, Mike. Intern USPHS Hosp. and Charity Hosp.; resident USPHS Hosp., 1964-65; gen. practice medicine, Oklahoma City, 1966—; mem. staff Bapt. Meml., Deaconess, Drs. Gen., Mercy, hosps., Oklahoma City. Served with USPHS. Mem. Am. Acad. Gen. Practice, Am., Okla. med. assns., Oklahoma City, Okla. chambers commerce, Alpha Lambda Chi, Alpha Omega Alpha. Mason. Home: 9108 Autumn Rd Oklahoma City OK 73111 Office: 2733 W Britton Rd Oklahoma City OK 73121

HALEY, GEORGE W., ofcl. Transp. Dept.; b. Henning, Tenn., Aug. 28, 1925; B.A., Morehouse Coll.; m. Doris Moxley; children—David, Anne. Individual practice law, Kan., 1952-55; asst. city atty., Kansas City, Kan., 1955-65; gen. counsel, dir. Cursader Life Ins. Co.; pres., dir. Mid-Central Mortgage and Investment Co., Inc.; gen. counsel Douglass State Bank Kansas City, Kan.; apptd. chief counsel Urban Mass Transp. Adminstrn., Transp. Dept., Washington, 1969—. Vice pres. Project Equality, Kansas City. Mem. Kan. Senate, 1964-68, chmn. pub. utilities com., vice chmn. pub. welfare com., mem. Legis. Council. Served with USAAF, 1943-46. Recipient price nat. competition A.S.C.A.P., 1952; delivered centennial toast to Kan. later reprinted in Congl. Record, 1961; featured in Reader's Digest article The Man Who Wouldn't Quit, 1963. Mem. Am., Nat., Wyandotte County, Kansas City (sec.) bar assns., Bar Assn. State Kan., Alpha Phi Alpha. Home: 1805 Parkside Dr Washingtin DC 20012 Office: 4419 C St SE Washington DC 20003

HALEY, HERBERT PRESTON, bottling co. exec.; b. Albany, Ga., May 27, 1912; s. William Banks and Vernon (Shelley) H.; B.S. in Mech. Engring., Ga. Sch. Tech., 1933; M.S. in Mech. Engring., Mass. Inst. Tech., 1935, Sc.D., 1938; m.2Helen Marian Peacock, Mar. 6, 1953; 1 dau., Stella LeVan. Vice pres. Albany (Ga.) Coca-Cola Bottling Co., 1938-50, pres., 1950—; chmn. 1st State Bank & Trust Co., Albany, Ga.; now pres.; chmn. 1st State Bank of Cordele (Ga.), Fort Gaines Banking Co. (Ga.), 1956—; dir. Fulton Nat. Bank, Atlanta. Past pres. Dougherty County Bd. Edn. Trustee Wesleyan Coll., Macon, Ga., Albany YMCA. Served to lt. comdr. USNR, 1942-46. Mem. C. of C. (dir.). Methodist (trustee). Rotarian (past pres. Albany club). Home: 1204 Pinecrest Dr Albany GA 31705 Office: PO Box 47 925 Pine Av Albany GA 31701

HALEY, JAMES ANDREW, congressman; b. Jacksonville, Ala., Jan. 4, 1899; s. Andrew Jackson and Mary Lee (Stevenson) H.; student U. Ala., 1919-20; m. Aubrey B. Ringling. Accountant, Sarasota, Fla., 1925-33; gen. mgr. John Ringling estate, 1933-43; 1st v.p. Ringling Circus, 1943-45, pres., 1946-48; pres., dir. Ringling Bros. Barnum & Bailey Circus, Sarasota, 1943-48; mem. Fla. Ho. of Reps., 1948-52; mem. 83d-92d Congresses from 7th Fla. Dist. Chmn. Sarasota Democratic Exec. Com., 1935-52. Served with U.S. Army, World War I. Mem. S.A.R., Am. Legion, 40 and 8, V.F.W. Democrat. Methodist. Mason, Elk. Clubs: Sarasota Yacht, Sun and Surf. Home: 4211 S Shade Av Sarasota FL 33581 Office: Longworth Bldg Washington DC 20515

HALEY, JAMES OLIVER, circuit ct. judge; b. Crystal Springs, Miss., June 17, 1912; s. James O. and Belle (Barlow) H.; student, Howard Coll., 1932-34; LL.B., Birmingham Law Sch., 1938; m. Mildred Ellis, Feb. 24, 1938; children—Jane (Mrs. Ronald H. Dykes), James E., John W. Admitted to Ala. bar, 1936; practice law with firm Lange, Simpson, Robinson & Somerville, Birmingham, 1934-68, asso. lawyer, 1936-40, partner, 1941-68; judge circuit ct., Birmingham, 1968—. Law mem. Birmingham City Appeal Bd., 1962-68. Bd. dirs. Birmingham Met. YMCA, 1955-72. Served with USNR, 1944-46. Fellow Am. Coll. Trial Lawyers; mem. Birmingham Bar Assn. (pres. 1963), Ala. State Bar (chmn. practice and procedure sect. 1966-67), Nat. Assn. Ins. Counselors, Am. Assn. R.R. Trial Lawyers. Home: 1405 Panorama Dr Birmingham AL 35216 Office: 716 N 21st St Birmingham AL 35216

HALEY, JOHN HARVEY, lawyer; b. Hot Springs, Ark., May 29, 1931; s. Harvey H. and Anne (Tanner) H.; A.B., Emory U., 1952; LL.B., U. Ark., 1955; m. Maria Luisa Mabilangan, Sept. 11, 1971; children (by previous marriage)—John Stuart, Susan Downs, David Costen. Admitted to Ark. bar, 1955; law clk. Ark. Supreme Ct., 1955-56; asso. Rose, Meek, House, Barron, Nash & Williamson, Little Rock, 1956-58, partner, 1959-70; partner firm Haley, Young, Bogard & Gitchel, 1971—. Mem. Ark. Bd. Law Examiners, 1959-65, chmn., 1961-64. Chmn., Election Research Council, 1964-68; pres. Morgan Owens Found. Deaf Coll. Students, 1962-67; chmn. State Bd. of Correction, 1968-72. Bd. dirs. Ark. Council on Human Relations, 1972—. Mem. Am., Ark., Pulaski County bar assns., Sigma Chi. Presbyn. Home: Pine Burro Hwy 10 Little Rock AR 72207 Office: 1690 Worthen Bank Bldg Little Rock AR 72201

HALEY, JULIUS C., govt. ofcl. Architect Dept. Navy, Washington. Address: 216 Whittier St NW Washington DC 20012*

HALEY, POPE ALLEN, editor; b. Elberton, Ga., Mar. 19, 1908; s. George Walton and Sarah (Arnold) H.; A.B., magna cum laude, U. Ga., 1929;; m. Joy Elizabeth Bailey, Nov. 30, 1937; 1 dau., Melissa Arnold. Reporter, U.S. Daily, Washington, 1929-31; reporter, editor A. P., Richmond Va., 1931-36, Washington, 1936-46; nat. news editor Pathfinder News Mag., Washington, 1946-50, pub. relations, 1950-58; asst. Sunday editor Nashville Tennessean, 1958-62; asso. editor editorial page. Fla. Times-Union, Jacksonville, 1962—, occasional contbr. reviews serious music. War corr., 1943. Mem. Nat. Conf. Editorial Writers, Nat. Press Club, Sigma Delta Chi. Methodist.Home: 2560 Oak St Jacksonville FL 32204 Office: 1 Riverside Av Jacksonville FL 32202

HALEY, WILLIAM HALE, JR., bank dir.; b. Paris, Tex., June 15, 1930; s. William H. and Mabel E. (Beard) H.; B.S., Tex. A. and M. U., 1951; m. Cherilyn Smith, June 22, 1951; children—William Hale III, Steven C., Leslie Elizabeth. Territorial mgr. Nutrena Mills, Inc., Wichita Falls, Tex., 1953-54; staff mgr. Prudential Ins. Co., Houston, 1954-60; asso. gen. agt. Mut. Benefit Life Ins. Co., Houston, 1960—; pres. Bus. Plans, Inc., Houston, 1960-70, Source Life Ins. Co., Houston, 1972—; prin. William H. Haley Jr. & Assos., Houston, 1967—; chmn. bd. 1st State Bank, Willis, Tex., 1968—, 1st Nat. Bank Raymondville, Tex., 1969—; Lott (Tex.) State Bank, 1967—, co-chmn. bd. 1st State Bank, Alamo, Tex., 1970—; vice chmn. bd. Union State Bank, Carrizo Springs, Tex., dir. Fannin Bank, Houston, Universal Land Title Co., Conroe, Tex., Brazosport Bank Commerce, Freeport, Tex., Elgin Nat. Bank, Elgin, Tex., chmn. bd. Houston Investment Realty Trust, 1971, Benefit Security Life Ins. Co., Houston, 1971—; Am. Capital Corp., 1971—. Served to 1st lt. USAF, 1951-53. C.L.U. Mem. Am. Soc. C.L.U.'s, Houston Assn. Life Underwriters, Assn. Former Students Tex. A. and M. U. Clubs: Aggie, Touchdown, Million Dollar Round Table, 1962, 63, 65. Home: 33 E Shady Lane Houston TX 77042 Office: Post Oak Tower Houston TX 77027

HALEY, WILLIAM ROBERT, govt. ofcl.; b. Heflin, Ala., Mar. 22, 1912; s. Andrew Duke and Bessie (Coggin) H.; student pub. schs.; m. Sarah Lee Jones, Mar. 29, 1936; children—William R., Sara Ann. Sect. labor So. Ry. Co., Heflin, Ala., 1934-38; machinist Monasanto Chem. Co., Anniston, Ala., 1938-44; plumber W. R. Haley, Heflin, Ala., 1944-60; clk. U.S. Post Office, Heflin, Ala., 1960—; exec. dir. Heflin Housing Authority, 1959—. Capt., sec.-treas. Cleburne County Rescue Squad, 1960—; capt. Heflin City Fire Dept. Baptist. Mason, Lion. Home: 301 Brockford Rd Heflin AL 36264

HALFACRE, ROBERT GORDON, educator; b. Newberry, S.C., June 22, 1941; s. Edwin Harvey and Lela Mae (Ruff) H.; B.S., Clemson U., 1963, M.S., 1965; Ph.D., Va. Poly. Inst. and State U., 1968; m. Mary Carolyn Folk, Jan. 24, 1963; children—Angela Carolyn, Gordon Robert. Asst. prof. dept. horticultural sci. N.C. State U., Raleigh, 1968-71, asso. prof., 1971—. Recipient research award Sigma Xi, 1968, Julian C. Miller research award Am. Soc. Hort. Sci., 1968, Charles Carter Newman award Clemson U., 1963, outstanding tchr. award N.C. State U., 1970. Mem. Blue Key, Sigma Xi, Phi Kappa Phi, Alpha Zeta, Phi Sigma, Pi Alpha Xi, Gamma Sigma Delta. Lutheran. Author: Carolina Landscape Plants, 1971; Keep 'Em Growing, 1972. Home: 3416 Malibu Dr Raleigh NC 27607

HALFACRE, WILLIAM RALPH, city ofcl.; b. Jackson, Mich., Aug. 30, 1930; s. William Jefferson and Rettie (Gregory) H.; student U. Mich., 1954; B.S., Mich. State U., 1959, postgrad., 1959—; m. Monica Joyce Miller, Feb. 16, 1952; children—Judith Michelle, Heather Karin. Supr. planning Housing Authority city Little Rock, 1959-61; dir. city planning N. Little Rock, 1961-62; dir. state planning, asst. exec. dir. Ark. Planning Commn., Little Rock, 1962-69; dir. City Demonstration Agy., City of North Little Rock, 1969-70; asst. dir. for city and regional planning Lincoln Trail Area Devel. Dist., Elizabethtown, Ky., 1970—. Served to lt. col. Ark. wing, Civil Air Patrol, 1964—. Served with USNR, 1948-52. Mem. Am. Inst. Planners, Triangle. Lutheran. Home: 1239 Greenview Dr Radcliff KY 40160 Office: 50 Public Sq Elizabethtown KY 42701

HALFHILL, CURTIS SELBY, civil engr.; b. Corydon, Ia., May 23, 1915; s. Clyde Peter and Grace Winifred (Ayres) H.; B.S., Ia. State U., 1946; m. Maude H. Hamlett, Oct. 18, 1945 (dec. Feb., 1968). With Walter Hook & Assos., architects, engrs., Charlotte, N.C., 1946-47; with J.N. Pease Assos., architects, engrs., planners, Charlotte, N.C., 1947—, head structural engring. dept., 1951—. Mem. Charlotte Bldg. Standards Bd., 1964-67, chmn., 1967; chmn. Charlotte Mecklenburg Architects and Engrs. Liason Com., 1970—. Served to lt. col. AUS, 1941-45. Decorated Silver Star medal. Fellow Am. Soc. Civil Engrs., Profl. Engrs. N.C. (chmn. scholarship com. 1969—), Nat. Soc. Profl. Engrs., N.C. Soc. Engrs., Am. Concrete Inst., Prestressed Concrete Inst. Club: Optimist. Home: 4535 Bradbury Dr Charlotte NC 28209 Office: 2925 E Independence Blvd Charlotte NC 28205

HALL, ALICE ELIZABETH CLAY (MRS. VERNON ADDISON HALL), poet, artist; b. Marysville, Va.; d. William and Gertrude (Butler) Clay; student Salem Acad. and Coll., 1913-15, Blackstone Coll. for Girls, 1915-19, Longwood Coll., 1919-20, Randolph Macon Coll., 1920-21, William and Mary Coll., 1921-23; m. Vernon Addison Hall, Oct. 22, 1924; 1 dau., Cynthia Jane (Mrs. George Irving Urbach); 1 foster-dau., Pamela Elaine (Mrs. Douglas George Bresler, Jr.). Exhibited in group shows at River Art Show, Conv. Hdqrs. Tex. Fed. Womens Clubs (both San Antonio). Recipient certificate of commendation Ivan Franko Meml. competition, London, Eng., 1966. Fellow Intercontinental Biog. Assn.; mem. Assn. Research and Enlightenment, Avalon World Arts Acad., Poetry Soc. Tex. (counsellor-at-large), San Antonio Art League, World Poetry Soc. Intercontinental, Poetry Soc. Va. (various positions), Internat. Platform Assn., Tex. Fine Art Assn., Council Internat. Relations, Nat. Soc. Arts and Letters. Author: April Hunger, 1958; Chaliced Atoms, 1972; numerous poems. Home: 109 Saddletree Rd San Antonio TX 78231

HALL, BENJAMIN FRANKLIN, educator; b. Wilmington, N.C., Feb. 26, 1908; s. John and Katherine Boger (Hoke) H.; A.B., Davidson Coll., 1929; B.D., Union Theol. Sem. Va., 1932, Th.M., 1933, Th.D., 1936; D.D. (hon.), Westminister Coll. Mo., 1942; m. Adelaide Peiffer, Oct. 10, 1933; children—John Tannahill, Michal Hoke, Frank Peiffer. Ordained to ministry Presbyn. Ch., 1932; minister Morehead City and Wildwood (N.C.) Presbyn. chruches, 1933-37; minister Central Presbyn. Ch., St. Louis, 1938-48, Pearsall Meml. Presbyn. Ch., Wilmington, N.C., 1949—; prof. philosophy Wilmington Coll., 1963-69; chmn. dept. philosophy and religion U. N.C. at Wilmington, 1969—. Columnist Wilmington Star, 1954—; pres. St. Louis Ch. Fedn., 1946, Mo. Council Churches, 1947. Charter mem., Lower Cape Fear Hist. Soc., 1957—, pres., 1958-60; pres. Wilmington Community Council, 1957, New Hanover Council on Alcoholism, 1961—. Trustee Westminster Coll., Fulton, Mo., 1940-48, Louisville Presbyn. Theol. Sem., 1942-48, Flora Macdonald Coll., Red Springs, N.C., 1949-61, St. Andrews Coll., Laurinburg, N.C., 1955-66, Davidson (N.C.) Coll., 1956-71. Recipient Keever award for Community Service Exchange Clubs of Wilmington. Mem. Am. Assn. U. Profs., Phi Beta Kappa, Sigma Upsilon, Pi Kappa Phi. Democrat. Author: This Company of New Men, 1965. Contbr. articles to mags. Home: 2819 Chestnut St Wilington NC 28401

HALL, BENNY, govt. ofcl. Dir. Bur. Vet. Medicine, Dept. Health, Edn. and Welfare, Rockville, Md. Address: Health Services and Mental Health Adminstrn Dept Health Edn andWelfare 5600 Fishers Lane Rockville MD 20852*

HALL, BILLY MIKE, dentist; b. Oklahoma City, June 29, 1925; s. Cleveland G. and Bertha M. (Cassidy) H.; B.S., East Central State Coll., 1946-47; D.D.S., Kansas City Sch. Dentistry, 1947-51; m. Elizabeth Ann Huddleston, Feb. 7, 1944; children—Patrick M., Jerry C., Jeffrey L. Individual practice dentistry, Oklahoma City, 1951—. Bd. dirs. Young Men's Club, 1954-70, 2d v.p., 1968-69; pres. dental div. United Appeal, Oklahoma City, 1964. Bd. dirs. B. Mike Hall Trust, Oklahoma City. Served with M.C., AUS, 1943-46. Home: 3220 NW 35th Pl Oklahoma City OK 73112 Office: 2408 N Geraldine St Oklahoma City OK 73107

HALL, CHARLES HENRY, JR., transp. co. exec.; b. New Bern, N.C., Mar. 8, 1911; s. Charles Henry and Mary Macon (Berry) H.; ed. Craven and Pamlicca Tech. Inst., 1967-68; m. Virginia Lecompte Smith, June 7, 1938; children—Virginia V., Jessie (Mrs. Joel Gardner). Driver Barbour Boats, New Bern, N.C., 1927-30; with Seashore Transp. Co., New Bern, 1930—, mgr., 1946—, v.p., 1946—, also dir. Mem. New Bern Airport Authority, 1948—. Mem. Nat. (mem. safety com. 1969—), N.C. (dir. 1970-73; pres. 1961-62) bus. assns., New Bern C. of C. (dir. 1971-74), U.S. Power Squadrn (instr. 1959-69). Home: 1815 Rhem Av New Bern NC 28560 Office: PO Box 1229 New Bern NC 28560

HALL, CLARENCE WINDLEY, judge; b. Newport, N.C., May 3, 1904; s. James S. and Bettie (Garner) H.; A.B., U. N.C., 1926, J.D., 1928; m. Inez Abernethy, Apr. 27, 1940; children—Ramsey Windley (dec.), Beatrice Avery. Admitted to N.C. bar, 1927; practiced in Durham, N.C., 1928-53; judge Superior Ct. N.C., Durham, N.C., 1953—. Served to col. Judge Advocate Gen. Corps, AUS, 1942-46. Mem. Am., N.C. bar assns. Democrat. Methodist. Home: 1402 Ward St Durham NC 27707

HALL, DAVID, gov. Okla.; b. Oklahoma City, Oct. 20, 1930; B.A., U. Okla., 1952; LL.B., U. Tulsa, 1959. Admitted to Okla. bar, 1959, U.S. Supreme Ct. bar, 1965; asst. dist. atty., Tulsa County, Okla., 1959-62, dist. atty., 1962-67; mem. firm Hall & Williams, Tulsa; gov. Okla., 1971—. Lectr. U. Okla. Sch. of Law, 1965-66; lectr. U. Tulsa Sch. of Law, 1963-65, adj. prof., 1969—. Served with USAF. Mem. Am. (adv. com. Nat. Criminal Def. Manual 1966—), Fed., Okla. (chmn. criminal law sect. 1964-65), Tulsa County (exec. com. 1963-65) bar assns., Bar Assn. D.C., Phi Beta Kappa, Phi Alpha Delta. Office: State Capital Bldg Oklahoma City OK

HALL, ESTHER JANE WOOD (MRS. JULIAN KENNIS HALL), educator; b. Gadsden, Ala., Sept. 18, 1911; d. Henry William and Emma Virginia (Crowe) Wood; B.S., Samford U., Birmingham, Ala., 1939; M.S., U. Tex., 1953, Ph.D., 1957; m. Julian Kennis Hall, Jan. 13, 1949; 1 dau., Virginia Ann. Pharmacist, Fairview Pharmacy, Birmingham, 1929-39; prodn. control mgr., statistician Warren-Teed Products Co., Columbus, O., 1939-44; label cons., dir., asst. prodn. control mgr. S.E. Massengill Co., Bristol, Tenn., 1944-46; asst. prof. Howard Coll., Birmingham, 1946-47; asst. prof. Coll. Pharmacy, U. Tex., Austin, 1947-61, asso. prof., 1961—; distinguished lectr. history Mercer U., 1964; cons. Am. Pub. Health Assn., Washington, 1961; spl. research Walgreen Co., Chgo., 1960; dir. Tex. Prescription Survey, Abbott Labs., Chgo.; chmn. surveys Tex. Pharm. Assn., 1965-69, Gosselin Rx Surveys, Dedham, Mass., 1961-70, chmn. med. market research, 1970-71. Chmn. manpower com. The Pharm. Found., U. Tex. Coll. Pharmacy, 1956—. Faculty fellow Am. Found. for Pharm. Edn., 1953-57; recipient Lederle Lab. faculty award, 1961, 64; participant Pharmacy Industry Forum, Princeton, 1959, Pharmacy Adminstrv. Seminar, Walgreen Co., Chgo., 1953, 60, 68. Del., participant Pan Am. Congress Pharmacy and Biochemistry, 1957. Fellow A.A.A.S.; faculty fellow Am. Coll. Apothecaries (chmn. com. on edn., mem. hosp. com.); mem. Am. Assn. Colls. of Pharmacy (chmn. sect. of tchrs. of pharmacy adminstrn., mem. com. on curriculum; mem. com. visual aids 1967-68), Am. Pub. Health Assn., Am. Assn. Indsl. Engrs., Nat. Assn. Retail Druggists, Am. Soc. Hosp. Pharmacists, Friends History Pharmacy Med. Coll. Va., Am. Coll. Apothecaries (sec. Tex. 1967-69), Am. (sec. hist. sect.; state historian Texas 1965-67), Tex. (com. edn. and research 1970-71), Austin, Capital Area pharm. assns., Am. Inst. History of Pharmacy (council), Royal Soc. Health (London, Eng.), Rho Chi, Kappa Epsilon (grand council editor, Tex. sec:), Sigma Iota Epsilon, Phi Mu (adviser). Episcopalian. Club: University (Austin). Author: (with A. H. Chute) The Pharmacist in Retail Distribution, 1953, 55, 60; Teachers Guide, 1960; Study Guide for Pharmaceutical Jurisprudence, 1951, 56, 59, 61, 67; (with Henry M. Burlage) Pharmaceutical Abstracts, 1959-68; also various manuals. Contributor to American Professional Pharmacist, Am. Jour. Pharmacy Edn., Prac. Edition, Am. Pharm. Assn. Jour., So. Pharm. Jour., Tex. Druggist, Tex. Jour. Pharmacy, Tex. Pharmacy, Am. Druggist, Drug Standards, Dissertation Abstracts, Jour. Am. Hosp. Assn., Texas Pharmacy, Pa. Med. Jour., 1959—. Contbr. articles and tech. papers to profl. jours. Home: The Westgate 1122 Colorado St Austin TX 78701

HALL, GEORGE LEONARD, JR., ednl. adminstr.; b. Leaksville, N.C., Nov. 7, 1932; s. George L. and Ella Mecks (Hall) H.; A.B., Elon Coll., 1957; M.A., East Carolina U., 1969; postgrad. U. N.C., 1968, U. S.C., 1968, William and Mary Coll., 1969; Ph.D. in Edn., Fla. State Coll., 1972; m. Nadine Flinchum, Mar. 31, 1956; children—Pamela, George Leonard III, Mollie Sue. Editor, Stoneville Press, 1955-56; prin. Hoffman High Sch., 1967, Clio (S.C.) High Sch., 1968, Windsor (Va.) High Sch., 1969—. Served with USAF, 1950-53. Mem. N.E.A., Nat. Assn. Secondary Sch. Prins. (mem. nat. sch. com., state curriculum com.), Va. Edn. Assn. (dist. sec. 1970-73), V.F.W., D.A.V. Mem. Knights of the Blue Nose. Clubs: Ruritan (pres. Rockingham County Club 1953-65) (Leaksville, N.C.); Isle of Wight Investor's (pres. 1970-72) (Windsor Va.). Home: PO Box 220 Windsor VA 23487 Office: 248 Church St Windsor VA 23487

HALL, HARVEY, physicist; b. Butte, Mont., Aug. 18, 1904; s. Horace Mark and Helen L. (Kirkendall) H.; A.B., Occidental Coll., 1927; postgrad. Cal. Inst. Tech., 1927-28; M.A., U. Cal. at Berkeley, 1930, Ph.D., 1931; m. Mary Emily Allen, Sept. 17, 1934; children—William Harvey, John Howland, Mary Suzanne. Instr. Columbia, 1931-34; lectr. N.Y.U., 1934-36; became instr. Coll. City N.Y., 1936, asst. prof. until 1949; asso. prof. U. So. Cal., 1949-51; dir. operational research div. Office Naval Research, Washington, 1951-57; prof., head physics dept. Fla. State U., 1957-62; with U. Cal. Radiation Lab., 1960; chief scientist Advanced Mission Program, NASA, Washington, 1961—. Mem. geophys. scis. com. Research and Devel. Bd., Def. Dept., 1947-49; spl. sub.-com. on upper atmosphere NACA, 1949-50. Served from lt. comdr. to comdr. USNR, 1942-46. Recipient Navy Civilian Service award, 1958; commendation from Sec. of Navy, 45, 60. Fellow Am. Phys. Soc.; sr. mem. I.E.E.E., Phi Beta Kappa, Sigma Xi. Club: Cosmos (Washington). Home: 7001 Leewood Forest Dr Springfield VA 22151 Office: Advanced Missions Program NASA Washington DC 20546

HALL, HOWARD RALPH, JR., dentist; b. Cin., May 1, 1919; s. Howard Ralph and Juanita (Coleman); B.S., Wilberforce U., 1943; D.D.S., Meharry Med. Coll. Sch. Dentistry, 1947; m. Dorothy Lillian Johns, Oct. 2, 1948; children—Lillian (Mrs. Lawrence Hawkins, Jr.), Howard Ralph III, Juanita R. Intern Del. State Bd. Health, 1947-48, Cin. Bd. Health Dental Dept., 1948-68; pvt. practice dentistry, Covington, Ky., 1943—; dir. Covington Model City Dental Program, 1970—. Mem. com. mgmt. Melrose Br. YMCA, 1969-70. Bd. dirs. Cin. chpt. A.R.C., 1971-72. Served with Dental Corps USNR, 1949-52. Decorated Bronze Star medal. Mem. Ohio Valley (pres. 1960-61), North Eastern dental socs., Nat. Dental Assn. (asst. publicity chmn. 1970—, mem. house dels. 1968—), Am. Dental Assn., Kappa Alpha Psi. Club: Fenwick (Cin.). Home: 3969 Zinsle St Cincinnati OH 45213 Office: Coppin Bldg Covington KY 41011

HALL, J. FLOYD, educator; b. Langdale, Ala., Aug. 11, 1925; s. William Clyde and Eunice (Colley) H.; student U. Tenn., 1944, B.S., Auburn U., 1948, M.S., 1951, Ed.D., 1957; m. Martha Bell Snider, Mar. 20, 1947; children—Michael Benton, Reginald Snider. Tchr. sci. Sr. High Sch., Lanett, Ala., 1948-51; asst. prin. elementary Jr. High Sch., Fairfax, Ala., 1951-52; supt.-prin. schs., Fairfax, Ala., 1952-58; supt. Ramey AFB Schs., P.R., 1958-60; asst. Evanston (Ill.) Twp. High Schs., 1960-67; supt. Oak Park (Ill.) and River Forest High Sch., 1967-70; supt. Greenville County (S.C.) Sch. Dist., 1970—; ednl. cons. on sch. orgn. Bloomington (Ill.) City Sch. Bd., 1965-66; visited and evaluated schs. for children mil. personnel, Germany, 1966. Active Boy Scouts Am. Served with USAAF, 1943-45. Named Young Man Of The Year in Chambers County, Ala., 1955. Recipient John Hay fellowship at Colo. Coll., 1963; Silver Beaver award from Boy Scouts of Am., 1965. Mem. Nat. Assn. Secondary Sch. Prins. (life), N.E.A., Assn. Supervision and Curriculum Devel., Am. Assn. Sch. Adminstrs. Baptist (deacon). Rotarian (past pres. Oak Park club). Contbr. articles in field to profl. jours. Home: 100 Hunting Hollow Greenville SC 29607 Office: Box 5575 Station B Greenville SC 29607

HALL, JAMES BENEDICT, JR., pedodontist; b. Macon, Ga., July 22, 1941; s. James Benedict and Betty Jane (Favors) H.; B.A., Mercer U., 1963; D.D.S., Northwestern U. Dental Sch., 1967; M.S. in Pediatric dentistry Northwestern U., 1969; m. Beverly Louise Cross, Aug. 22, 1964; children—Jennifer Elaine, Allison Elizabeth. Dental researcher Research Inst. Am. Dental Assn., 1967-69; pvt. practice pedodontics, Evanston, Ill., intermittently, 1967-69; pvt. practice pedodontics, Atlanta, 1971—. Served with AUS, 1969-71. Decorated Army Commendation medal; recipient Certificate Merit for outstanding interest and proficiency in dentistry for children Am. Soc. Dentistry for Children, 1969, numerous certificates appreciation for presentations at profl. meetings. Mem. Am., Ga. dental assns., Am. Acad. Pedodontics, No. Dist., 5th Dist. dental socs., Am. Soc. Dentistry for Children, Ga. Soc. Pediatric Dentistry, Alpha Tau Omega, Delta Sigma Delta (award 1966). Republican. Methodist. Office: 5675 Peachtree Dunwoody Rd Atlanta GA 30342

HALL, JAMES DONALD, JR., assn. exec.; b. Tifton, Ga., July 8, 1933; s. James Donald and Drury Eudeara (Fuller) H.; B.B.A., U. Ga., 1965; m. Frances Marion Jones, Aug. 20, 1960; children—James Donald III, Mary Foute, Catherine McDuffie. Salesman, Todd div. Burroughs Corp., Atlanta, 1958-63; mgmt. trainee Jefferson Mills (Ga.), 1964-65; indsl. developer, asst. dir. Ga. Dept. Industry and Trade, Atlanta, 1965-68; dir. Brunswick-Golden Isles C. of C., Brunswick, Ga., 1968—. Mem. vocational and tech. adv. com. Glynn County Pub. Schs., 1969—; mem. Gov.'s Govt. Reorgn. Program, 1971—. Mem. Glynn County Water and Sewerage Commn., 1971—. Served with AUS, 1953-55. Mem. Ga. C. of C. Execs. Assn. (dir. 1970—), Ga. Indsl. Developers Assn. (dir. 1970—), Ga. (chmn. econ. devel. com. 1967), Capital Hills (pres. 1967-68) jr. chambers commerce, Phi Delta Theta. Baptist. Home: 103 Wymberly Rd St Simons GA 31522 Office: 2000 Glynn Av Brunswick GA 31520

HALL, JAMES WILLIAM, JR., press assn. exec.; b. Montgomery, Ala., Dec. 23, 1931; s. James William and Hazel (Kemp) H.; student Huntington Coll., 1950; B.A., U. Ala., 1958, M.A., 1968; postgrad. Tulane U., 1964; m. Martha Faye George, Aug. 31, 1958. Gen. assignment reporter Montgomery Advertiser, 1956-57; with So. Bell Telephone Co., New Orleans, 1958-66, directory compilation mgr., 1963-64, pub. relations mgr., 1965-66; sec., mgr. Ala. Press Assn., University, 1966—. Lectr. journalism dept. U. Ala., Tuscaloosa, 1966—; pres. Quest. Inc., Tuscaloosa, 1968-71; v.p. Ala. News Service, Tuscaloosa, 1969-71. Mem. Ala. Safety Coordinating Com., 1968—, Ala. Farm-City Week Com., 1970—; 2d v.p. New Orleans Floral Trail, 1966. Sec. Ala. Press Assn. Journalism Found., 1968—. Served with USAF, 1951-54. Named Outstanding Indsl. Editor, Greater New Orleans Area United Fund, 1966; Hon. Blind Man Ala. Sch. for Deaf and Blind, 1967; Distinguished Alumnus, U. Ala. Dept. Journalism, 1972. Mem. Ala. Council Assn. Execs., Am. Soc. Assn.

Execs., Phi Beta Kappa, Omicron Delta Kappa, Chi Phi, Sigma Delta Chi (pres. 1970), Newspaper Assn. Mgrs. Presbyn. Clubs: Indian Hills Country, Birmingham Press. Mason. Editor Ala. Pub., 1966—. Home: 11 Windsor Dr Tuscaloosa AL 35401 Office: Manly Hall University AL 35401

HALL, JOHN BRADY, univ. adminstr.; b. Dothan, Ala., Apr. 7, 1921; s. James R. and Cora B. (Carter) H.; B.S., Ala. State Coll., 1947; postgrad. Northwestern U., 1948; M.A., N.Y. U., 1959; m. Lillie Waddle, Aug. 15, 1946; children—Carolyne G. (Mrs. Johnnie Simmons), John Brady. Tchr. art, coach Trenholm High Sch., Tuscumbia, Ala., 1947-49, Dunbar-Abrams High Sch., Bessemer, Ala., 1949-61; supr. art Jefferson County Schs., Birmingham, Ala., 1961-67; dir. cultural activities Tuskegee Inst. Summer Program, 1962; head art dept. Ala. State U., Montgomery, 1967—. Dir. spl. project Traveling Students Art Exhibit, State Ala., Ala. State Council Arts and Humanities, 1971-72. Project coordinator Roosevelt Civic League, Bessemer, Ala., 1955-56. Served with AUS, 1943-46. Recipient Achievement award for meritorious services to youth Jefferson County Council P.T.A., 1965, Man of Year award Birmingham chpt. Alpha Phi Alpha, 1966. Mem. Nat. (state dir. higher edn. 1971—), Ala. (pres. 1970-72) art edn. assns., Alpha Phi Alpha. Mason. Club: Athletic Boosters' (corr. sec. 1970—). (Montgomery, Ala.). Home: 1004 Faculty Circle Montgomery AL 36101

HALL, JOHN COX, mortgage banker; b. Carrollton, Ala., Oct. 27, 1905; s. Origin Garrett and Clara Love (Cox) H.; B.S., Ga. Sch. Tech., 1926; m. Elizabeth Denson Mackey, Oct. 22, 1930; 1 son, John Cox. With Jemison Co., Birmingham, Ala., 1926-32; with mortgage dept. Met. Life Ins. Co., 1932-37; with Realty Mortgage Co., Birmingham, 1937-46; with Cobbs, Allen & Hall Mortgage Co., Inc., Birmingham, 1946—, pres., 1950-64, chmn., pres., 1964—. Mem. Birmingham C. of C. (dir. finance div.), Mortgage Bankers Assn. Am. (pres. 1957-58, Distinguished Service award 1952), Birmingham Real Estate Bd. (pres. 1948), Ala. Real Estate Assn. (pres. 1949), Nat. Assn. Real Estate Bds. (dir. 1949), Birmingham Mortgage Bankers Assn. (pres. 1941, 49), Sigma Alpha Epsilon, Delta Sigma Pi. Episcopalian. Clubs: Birmingham Country, Down Town, Birmingham Monday Morning Quarterback, The Club, Redstone, Mountain Brook County, Relay House. Home: 3316 Country Club Rd Mountain Brook Birmingham AL 35213 Office: 2119 6th Av N Birmingham AL 35203

HALL, JOHN GREGORY, librarian; b. Sherman, Tex., July 28, 1936; s. John Clayton and Gladys Maudie (Gregory) H.; B.A., So. Meth. U., 1958; M.L.S., U. Tex., 1960. Reference librarian Dallas Pub. Library, 1960; reference librarian Austin Coll., Sherman, Tex., 1962-67, coll. librarian, 1968-70; reference librarian Borough Barnet, London, Eng., 1967-68; vol. Peace Corps, Meshed (Iran) U., 1970-72; documents librarian So. Meth. U., Dallas, 1972—. Served with AUS, 1960-62. Mem. Tex. Library Assn., Phi Beta Kappa. Democrat. Methodist. Home: Lantern Yard Ravenna TX 75476 Office: Fondren Library Southern Methodist U Dallas TX 75222

HALL, JOHN RANDOLPH, JR., physician; b. Napton, Mo., June 20, 1913; s. John Randolph and Ferda (Roberts) H.; A.B., Central Mo. Meth. Coll., 1935; B.S. in Medicine, U. Neb., 1938; M.D., Washington U., St. Louis, 1939; M.S. in Pharmacology, U. Chgo., 1949; M. Pub. Health, Johns Hopkins, 1954; m. Josephine Miles, Nov. 24, 1938; children—John Randolph III, Sarah (Mrs. William Thompson Garcelon), M. Bruce, Rogers. Commd. lt. M.C., U.S. Army, 1934, advanced through ranks to col., 1946, retired, 1964; intern St. Louis City Hosp., 1939-40; partner Kelsey-Seybold Clinic, Houston, 1964-69, chief occupational medicine, 1964-69; pres. Space Center Med. Assos., Houston, 1969—; mem. staffs Space Center Meml., Meml. Baptist, Methodist, St. Lukes, Galveston County Meml. hosps.; acting dean, organizer Sch. Pub. Health, U. Tex., Houston, 1968-69, adj. prof., 1969—. Bd. dirs. Houston Community Welfare Assn., 1964-70, mem. exec. com., 1968-70; bd. dirs. Family Service Centers, Houston, 1971—. Decorated Silver Star, Legion of Merit, Bronze Star medal (3), Air medal, Purple Heart; recipient Andreas Vesalius medal Augsburg Fortbilding, Augsburg, Germany, 1969. Diplomate Am. Bd. Preventive Medicine. Fellow A.C.P., Am. Coll. Preventive Medicine, Indsl. Med. Assn., Am. Pub. Health Assn.; mem. Assn. Mil. Surgeons U.S., A.M.A., Tex. Med. Assn., Harris County Med. Soc., C. of C. Clear Lake (dir. 1971—), C. of C. Dickinson, Nu Simga Nu. Mason (32 deg., K.T., Shriner). Clubs: Doctors (Houston); Clear Lake Country (Tex.). Contbr. to publs. in field. Home: 309 Ivy Lane Dickinson TX 77539 Office: Space Center Med Assos 907 Bay Area Blvd Houston TX 77058

HALL, JOHN RAYMOND, govt. ofcl.; b. Fall River, Mass., June 6, 1912; s. Robert Alfred and Lena (Kenney) H.; Ph.B., Brown U., 1934; M.A., Am. U., 1953; m. Elizabeth Florence Lord, May 29, 1946; children— John Raymond, Judith Elizabeth. Tchr., Swansea, Mass., 1936-42; civilian ocean transp. specialist to chief naval operations, U.S. Navy, 1946-49, Mil. Sea Transp. Service, 1949-51, 53-54; operations research analyst Air Force, Wiesbaden, Germany, 1954-57, Oklahoma City, 1957-60, Syracuse, N.Y., 1960-62; with weapons system evaluation group Inst. Def. Analyses, 1962-63; with Arms Control Disarmament Agy., 1963-66; spl. asst. for systems analysis Bur. Health Manpower, USPHS, Arlington, Va., 1967-68; exec. sec. health care systems study sect. USPHS, Nat. Center Health Services Research and Devel., Dept. Health, Edn. and Welfare, Arlington, 1968—. Pres. Tchrs. Club, Swansea, 1939; pres. P.T.A. U. Okla. Sch., 1959-60. Served to comdr. USNR, 1942-46, 51-53. Mem. Operations Research Soc. Am. (chmn. health applications sect., asst. editor health newsletter), Inst. Mgmt. Sci., A.A.A.S., Res. Officers Assn. Am. (pres. Tinker chpt.). Home: 5733 N 27th St Arlington VA 22207 Office: NCHSRD 5600 Fishers Lane Rockville MD 20852

HALL, JOSIAH CALVIN, educator; b. Mentone, Ala., Sept. 22, 1909; s. Josiah Calvin and Mary Walter (Collins) H.; A.B., U. Fal., 1931; M.A., N.Y.U., 1936; Ed.D., Fla. State U., 1955; m. Ella Faye Price, Nov. 16, 1942; children—Joe and Ed (twins), Mary and Martha (twins), Elizabeth. Prin., tchr., coach Leon High Sch., Tallahassee, 1932-35; supervising prin. Carrabelle (Fla.) Schs., 1935-36; dir. tchr. edn. and certification, cons. health and phys. edn. Fla. Dept. Edn., Tallahassee, 1937-42, dir. div. instrn., 1946-48; dir. instrn. Dade County Pub. Schs., Miami, Fla., 1948-49, asst. supt., 1949-53, asso. supt., 1953-56, supt., 1957-68; prof. edn. U. Miami, Coral Gables, 1968—. Fla. chmn. March of Dimes, 1953; unit v.p. United Fund Campaign, 1967; mem. exec. bd. South Fla. council Boy Scouts Am. Bd. dirs. Dade County Tb Assn., Dade County chpt. A.R.C., Mus. Sci. and Natural History Miami. Served from lt. (j.g.) to lt. comdr. USNR, 1942-46. Mem. Am. Assn. Supervision and Curriculum Devel., Nat. (life), Fla. (chmn. dept. health, phys. edn. and recreation 1939-40, chmn. program, action and resolutions com., pres. 1964-65) edn. assns., A.A.H.P.E.R. (dir. So. div. 1939-42), Everglades Nat. Park Commn., Nat. Conf. Christians and Jews (sec. Fla. region 1955), P.T.A. (life), U.S. (nat. chmn. youth welfare com.), Fla. (pres. 1940-41, continuing ednl. council) jr. chambers commerce, Am. Legion, U. Fla. Alumni Assn. (v.p.), Fla. State U. Alumni Assn. (dir. 1955), Blue Key, Kappa Delta Pi, Sigma Delta Psi, Pi Kappa Alpha. Kiwanian (pres. Coral Gables 1962). Home: 500 Hardee Rd Coral Gables FL 33144

HALL, LELA MOORE, social worker; b. Sylva, N.C., Mar. 10, 1926; d. David McKee and Edith (Moore) Hall; A.B., U. N.C., 1948; M.S., Tulane U., 1953. Casework asst. Macon County Welfare Dept., Franklin, N.C., 1948-51; caseworker Haywood County Welfare Dept., Waynesville, N.C., summer 1952; child welfare worker Mecklenburg County Welfare Dept., Charlotte, N.C., 1953-54, sr. casework supr., 1954-56; dir. Harnett County Welfare Dept., Lillington, N.C., 1956-62, New Hanover County Welfare Dept., Wilmington, N.C., 1962—; chmn. State Child Welfare Com., 1966. Mem. project com. New Hanover County (N.C.) Fund Project, 1964; mem. Lower Cape Fear Juvenile Detention Com., Task Force on Research and Demonstration for Aged. Bd. dirs. New Hanover County Tb Assn., New Hanover County Cancer Soc., Community Council Wilmington, Services to the Aging, Half-Way House, Head start, Tech. Action Panel, Child Devel. Center, Inc.; dist. chmn. N.C. Mother Assn. of Am. Mothers Com., Inc., 1965-67; bd. dirs. sec. Opportunities, Inc.; admission and budget com. of New Hanover County United Fund, 1966—; mem. Census Tract com.; bd. dirs. New Hanover County Workshop. Mem. N.C. Caseworkers Assn. (pres. 1955-56), Nat. Assn. Social Work (pres. Charlotte chpt. 1956), N.C. (dir. 1962), N.D. dirs. assns., Am. Pub. Welfare Assn. (mem. com. on aged 1959-61, com. services for children and youth 1963-64), Acad. Certified Social Workers. Democrat. Methodist. Clubs: Wilmington Executive; National Beta. Home: 903 Schloss St Wrightsville Beach NC 28480 Office: New Hanover County Dept Social Services 1020 Rankin St Wilmington NC 28401

HALL, LELAND FRANK, engring. co. exec.; b. Corning, N.Y., Sept. 23, 1924; s. Edward Earl and Edna Augusta (Christen) H.; B.S., N.C. State U., 1950, postgrad., 1967; m. Geraldine Elizabeth Shunk, Aug. 9, 1944; 1 dau., Carla Elaine. Project mgr., mech. installations Rowe-Goodin-Jones, Durham, N.C., 1950-57, profl. mech. engr. Piatt & Davis & T.C. Cooke, Durham, 1957-62; research mech. engr. Chemstrand Research Center, Research Trangle Park, N.C., 1962-68; v.p. John D. Latimer & Asso., Durham, 1968—. Instr. Durham Tech. Inst., 1967-69. Dir. intelligence sect. Durham City-County Civil Def., 1966-67. Served with USAAF, 1943-46. Registered profl. engr., 17 states. Mem. Am. Soc. M.E., Am. Soc. Heating, Refrigerating and Air-Conditioning Engrs., Nat. Soc. Profl. Engrs., Profl. Engrs. N. C. (dir. 1964), N. C. Soc. Engrs., N. C. Assn. Professions, Durham Engrs. Club (sec. treas. 1962-65, dir. 1960-64). Presbyn. (deacon 1968-69). Patentee in field. Home: 3608 Hope Valley Rd Durham NC 27707 Office: PO Box 177 Durham NC 27702

HALL, MARIAN DRAKE, econ. analyst; b. Bklyn., Aug. 5, 1916; d. Edgar Albert and Salena (Mangold) Hall; student Barnard Coll., 1934-36, U. So. Cal., 1940-41; A.B., Bklyn. Coll., 1940. Field employee War Dept., 1942-44; with Dept. Commerce, Washington, 1944-50, bus. asst. in indsl. projects unit, 1944-46, bus. specialist in drugs and pharm. div., 1947-50; bus. economist, div. productivity and tech. devels. Dept. Labor, 1951-53; research analyst NSF, Washington, 1953-57; econ. analyst Legislative Reference Service, Library of Congress, Washington, 1957—. Mem. Am. Assn. U. Women, P.E.O., Phi Beta Kappa. Mem. staff which produced Funds for Research in Med. Schs., 1953-54; Expenditures for Research and Development in the United States, 1953. Contbr. articles on econ. and pub. adminstrn. to publs. Home: 4607 Connecticut Av NW Washington DC 20008 Office: Library of Congress Washington DC 20025

HALL, MARY FRANCES, camp exec.; b. Jacksonville, Fla., Jan. 9, 1925; d. Joseph Dow and Margaret (Jones) Hall; B.S., Fla. State U., 1946; M.A., U. Ia., 1949, Ph.D., 1958. Tchr., Mainland High Sch., Daytona Beach, Fla., 1946-48; instr., asst. prof. Fla. State U., Tallahassee, 1949-61, asso. prof. phys. edn., 1961-69; research asst. U. Ia., 1958; owner, dir. Camp Illahee, Brevard, N.C., 1969—. Mem. Am. Camping Assn. (dir. 1959-63, sec. 1965-67, sect. pres. 1951-52), A.A.H.P.E.R., Fla. Assn. Health, Phys. Edn. and Recreation, Nat., Fla. assns. phys. edn. for coll. Women, Phi Delta Pi. Author: (with others) Physical Education. Office: Camp Illahee Brevard NC 28712

HALL, MICHAEL GRAYSON, physician; b. Havana, Fla., Nov. 9, 1938; s. Raimond Baldwin and Lillie Mae (Odom) H.; A.B., Asbury Coll., 1960; M.D., U. Louisville, 1965; m. Marjorie Jane Lloyd, Aug. 18, 1962; children—Sandra Mae, Michael Grayson. Intern Lakeland (Fla.) Gen. Hosp., 1965-66; gen. practice medicine Brooksville, Fla., 1968—; mem. staff Lykes Meml. Hosp., Brooksville. Served with USAF, 1966-68. Mem. Tri-County Med. Soc., Fla. Med. Assn., A.M.A. Home: 221 Alpine Circle Brooksville FL 33512 Office: 621 W Jefferson St Brooksville FL 33512

HALL, MILES LEWIS, JR., lawyer; b. Ft. Lauderdale, Fla., Aug. 14, 1923; s. Miles Lewis and Mary Frances (Dawson) H.; A.B., Princeton, 1947; LL.B., Harvard, 1950; m. Muriel M. Fisher, Nov. 4, 1950; children—Miles Lewis III, Don Thomas. Admitted to Fla. bar, 1951, since practiced in Miami; partner Hall & Hedrick, 1953—; admitted to U.S. Supreme Ct. bar, 1959. Mem. nominating com. Dade County Met. Ct., 1969-72; chmn. nominating council Dist. Ct. Appeals., 3d Dist. Fla., 1972—. vice pres. Orange Bowl Com., 1961-63, pres., 1964-65, dir., 1966—; vice chmn. Fla. Council of 100, 1961-62, mem., 1971-72; exec. bd. S. Fla. council Boy Scouts Am., 1966-67; vice chmn., dir. Dade County chpt. A.R.C., 1961-62, chmn., 1963-64, dir., 1967—, nat. fund cons., 1963, 66-68; mem. adv. bd. Salvation Army, 1968—; bd. dirs. Coral Gables War Meml. Youth Center, 1967—, v.p., 1968-69, pres., 1969-72; mem. citizens bd. U. Miami, 1961-66; pres. Ransom Sch. Parents Assn., 1966; chmn. S. Fla. Gov.'s Scholarship Ball, 1966. Served to 2d lt. USAAF, 1943-45. Mem. Am. (Fla. co-chmn. membership com., sect. corp. banking and bus. law), Dade County (dir. 1964-65, v.p. 1966-67, pres. 1967-68) bar assns., Fla. Bar, Am. Judicature Soc., Miami-Dade County C. of C. (v.p. 1962-64, dir. 1966-68), Harvard Law Sch. Assn. Fla. (dir. 1964-66), Alpha Tau Omega. Methodist (steward). Kiwanian, Clubs: Princeton Southern Fla. (past pres., dir.); Harvard of Miami; Cottage; The Miami. Author: Titles, Ejectment and Election of Remedies, Vol. VIII, Fla. Law and Practice, 1958. Home: 2907 Alhambra Circle Coral Gables FL 33134 Office: 150 SE 2d St Miami FL 33131

HALL, NANCY JOHNSON (MRS. CLARIS G. HALL), state ofcl.; b. Prescott, Ark., Oct. 5, 1904; d. George Sim and Minnie (Bryan) Johnson; grad. high sch., Little Rock; m. Claris G. Hall, Oct. 5, 1929; 1 dau., Nancy Anne (Mrs. R. Robert Bailey). Head stenographer Ark. Hwy. Dept., 1925-30; asst. sec. state State of Ark., Little Rock, 1937-61, sec. state, 1961-63, treas., 1963—. Mem. bd. Employees Retirement System, Hwy. Retirement System, Tchr. Retirement System, Ark. Bd. Finance (sec.), Ark. Rural Endowment Fund, Inc. (sec.-treas.). Mem. Womens C. of C., U.D.C., Daus. of 1812, Bus. and Profl. Womens Club. Democrat. Presbyn. Club: Zonta. Home: 4206 Woodlawn St Little Rock AR 72205 Office: Dept Treasury State Capitol Little Rock AR 72201

HALL, PALMER L., coll. adminstr.; b. McDowell, Ky., May 3, 1910; s. James Emory and Minda (Moore) H.; student Alice Lloyd Jr. Coll., 1928-29; A.B., Tusculum Coll., 1931; postgrad. Coll. Law U. Ky., 1936-39, M.A., 1952, Ed.D., 1955; m. Oval Geneva Bingham, Sept. 20, 1940; 1 dau., Pamalea (Mrs. George Carlos Hill). With Floyd County (Ky.) Sch. System, 1926-52, asst. supt., 1945-46, supt., 1946-52; dean coll. W.Va. Inst. Tech., Montgomery, 1955-57; dir. grad. study Morehead (Ky.) State U., 1957-66, coordinator grad. study Coll. Edn., 1966—. Served with 42d Inf. Div., AUS, 1943-45; POW, 1945. Mem. Floyd County Hall of Fame, 1956—. Mem. N.E.A., Ky. Edn. Assn. (pres. higher edn., 1970-71), Phi Delta Kappa. Methodist. Clubs: Morehead Mens, Ky. Long Rifles. Home: 503 N Wilson Av Morehead KY 40351

HALL, PAUL EZRA, energy cons.; b. Vernon, Tex., July 2, 1913; s. Anderson Wade and Nan (Townsend) H.; B.S., Tex. Tech. Coll., 1935; postgrad. U. Tex., 1941-42, 45; m. Nettie Fay Brown, Aug. 3, 1939; children—Nan Elizabeth, Marianne. Project engr. Stearns-Roger Mfg. Co., 1941-46, Humble Oil and Refining Co., 1937-41, Austin Bridge Co., 1935-37; chief engr. Fish Engring. Corp., Houston, 1946-50; pvt. practice as cons. engr., Bellaire, Tex., 1950-53; v.p. sales Wyatt C. Hedrick Engring. Corp., Houston, 1953-54, adminstrv. v.p., 1954-57; v.p., project mgr. Goliad Corp., Calgary, Alta., Can., 1957-58, mgr. devel., Houston, 1958-61; mgr. natural gas div. Oasis Oil Co., joint venture Continental Oil Co., Tripoli, Libya, 1961-65; project mgr. Continental Oil Co., Tripoli, 1965-66, project coordinator, Madrid, Spain, 1966-67, rep. ad hoc task force, Ponca City, Okla., 1967-68; project mgr. King Resources Internat., Denver, 1968-69; mgr. coordinating and planning Imperial-Am. Mgmt. Co., Houston, 1968-69; partner Hinson & Hall, Houston, 1969-72; v.p., sec.-treas. Hinson, Hall & Smith, Houston, 1971-72; pvt. practice as energy cons., 1972—. Pres. Bellaire Good Govt. League, 1954-55. Mem. Natural Gas Men Houston. Methodist (steward 1959-60). Home: 4409 Willowbend Blvd Houston TX 77035 Office: The Main Bldg Houston TX 77002

HALL, RAY COWAN, advt. co. exec.; b. Searcy, Ark., July 22, 1940; s. Maurice M. and Pansy Lucille (Cowan) H.; B.A., U. Okla., 1962, M.A., 1965; m. Jan Susan Cooper, Nov. 27, 1965; children—Lauren Elise, Julie Steele. Pub. information officer State Okla., Oklahoma City, 1964-65; with Southwestern Bell Telephone, various locations, 1965-71; asso. Neal Spelce Assos. advt./pub. relations, Austin, Tex., 1971—. Exec. v.p. Austin Symphony Orch. Soc., 1970-72; vice commodore Austin Aqua Festival, 1970-72. Recipient Gold medal addy awards, Austin Advt. Club, 1970, 71, Nat. Bronze award Mut. Advt. Agy. Network, 1971. Mem. Pub. Relations Soc. Am., Tex. Pub. Relations Assn., Austin Ad Club, C. of C., Sigma Delta Chi, Delta Tau Delta. Baptist. Clubs: Headliners, Westwood Country, Lost Creek Golf. Home: 4004 Edgemont Dr Austin TX 78731 Office: PO Box 1905 Austin TX 78767

HALL, ROBERT BRUCE, bishop; b. Wheeling, W. Va., Jan. 27, 1921; s. Kent Bruce and Mary Ellen (Hazlett) H.; B.A., Trinity Coll., Hartford, Conn., 1943, D.D., 1967; S.T.B., Episcopal Theol. Sem., Cambridge, Mass., 1949; D.D., Seabury Western Theol. Sem. 1966, Va. Theol. Sem., 1967, Kenyon Coll., 1969; m. Dorothy Varner Glass, Jan. 26, 1949; children—Ellen Lynn, Kent Bruce II, Elizabeth Hazlett, Anne Louise, Susan Glass. Ordained to ministry Episcopal Ch., 1949; asso. minister, Huntington, W. Va., 1949-53; rector, Huntington, 1953-58, Chgo., 1958-66; bishop coadjutor Episcopal Diocese Va., Richmond, 1966—. Mem. corp. Seabury Western Theol. Sem., 1964—; trustee Va. Theol. Sem., 1967—, St. Paul's Coll., Lawrenceville, Va., 1968—, Blue Ridge Sch., Dyke, Va., 1968—, United Charities, Chgo., 1965-66. Served with AUS, 1943-46. Fellow Coll. of Preachers, Delta Phi, Pi Gamma Mu. Clubs: Racquet (Chgo.); Rotunda (Richmond, Va.). Home: 11 River Rd Richmond VA 23226 Office: 110 W Franklin St Richmond VA 23220

HALL, ROBERT JOSEPH, physician; b. Buffalo, June 4, 1926; s. Joseph Mathew and Florence C. (Kirst) H.; student Canisius Coll., 1943-45; M.D., U. Buffalo, 1948; m. Dorothy Nowak, Aug. 28, 1948; children— Thomas, Kathleen, Mary Jeanne, Michael, Steven. Commd. lt. U.S. Army, 1948, advanced through ranks to col., 1966, retired, 1969; intern Mercy Hosp., Buffalo, 1948-49; resident Walter Reed Gen. Hosp., Washington, 1949-52; chief cardiology Brooke Gen. Hosp., San Antonio, 1961-66, Walter Reed Gen. Hosp., Washington, 1966-69; med. dir. Tex. Heart Inst., Houston, 1969—; cons. cardiology to Surgeon Gen. U.S. Army, also VA Hosp., Houston; clin. prof. medicine Baylor U. Coll. Medicine, 1969—. Mem. Pres.'s Panel on Heart Disease, 1972. Decorated Commendation Ribbon (2), Legion of Merit. Diplomate Am. Bd. Internal Medicine, subsplty. bd. cardiovascular disease. Fellow A.C.P., Am. Coll. Cardiology (gov. Tex.); mem. A.M.A., Am. Heart Assn. (fellow council clin. cardiology). Contbr. articles to profl. jours. Home: 5504 Sturbridge St Houston TX 77027 Office: Texas Heart Inst PO Box 20269 Houston TX 77025

HALL, RONALD GLENN, power co. exec.; b. Thomaston, Ga., Nov. 26, 1943; s. Robert Glenn and Mary Nelle (Walton) H.; B.Indsl. Engring., Auburn U., 1966; m. Judith Carolyn Meek, Dec. 19, 1965; children—Thomas Glenn, Cynthia Paige. Sales engr. Ga. Power Co., Carrollton, 1967-69, Rome, 1969—. State chmn. Brace-A-Child Coffee Day Campaign, Ga. Easter Seal Soc., 1971. Recipient Kay Man award Rome Jr. C. of C., 1971. Mem. Ga. Assn. Realtors, Inc., Home Builders Assn. Rome and Floyd County (mem. exec. com. 1970—), Rome Jr. C. of C. (state dir. 1971-72). Methodist (mem. commn. on social affairs 1970—). Home: 24 Kenwood Dr Rome GA 20161 Office: 800 Broad St Rome GA 30161

HALL, STANDISH, finance, trusteeships and warehousing exec.; b. Chgo., Sept. 30, 1891; s. Harry Newbury and Anne (Russell) H.; grad. Hotchkiss Sch., 1912; A.B., Harvard, 1916; m. Helen Brooks, June 5, 1920 (dec. Dec. 1961); children—Brooks, Wolcott (died in service AAF, 1944), Bradford; m. 2d, Margaret Bailey Echols, Dec. 12, 1962. With W. R. Grace & Co., Peru, 1916-17; with credit dept. Union Trust Co., Chgo., 1919-20, mgr. new bus. dept., 1920-21, advt. dir., 1921-22, asst. sec., 1922-23; v.p., dir. Union Nat. Bank, Wichita, 1923-28; v.p., dir. Guarantee Title & Trust Co., 1928-29, pres., dir., 1929-30; pres., dir. Yellow Van & Storage Co., 1931-52, Met. Warehouse Co., 1931—; operator Standish Hall Co., gen. ins. and investment, 1930—; trustee ct. apptd. oil royalty syndicates. Trustee Gerontol. Research Found., St. Louis. Dir. civil def. State of Kan., 1950-54; pres. Nat. Assn. State Civil Def. Dirs., 1951-52. Served from seaman to ensign, USNR, 1917-19, comdr., 1941-46. Awarded Commendation medal. Mem. Kan. Hist. Soc. (dir.), Wichita Art Assn. (trustee), Wichita Civic Music Assn. (trustee). Republican. Episcopalian. Clubs: University (Chgo.); Army and Navy (Washington). Home and office: Apartado Postal 418 Cuernavaca Morelos Mexico

HALL, SUE MARION, educator; b. Omaha; d. Frederick Meredith and Rosamond Helen (Peterson) Hall; B.S., U. Neb., 1930; M.S., U. So. Cal. 1937; Ph.D., Ohio State U., 1948. Tchr. phys. edn. Minne Lusa Sch., Omaha, 1930-32. North Jr. and Central High Sch., Sioux City, Ia., 1932-37; instr. phys. edn. U. Minn., Mpls., 1937-38; phys. edn. supr. various schs., Falls City, Neb., 1939-40; prof., dept. health, phys. edn. and recreation, U. Louisville, 1940—; del. Internat. Congress Phys. Edn. and Sports for Girls and Women, 1949, 61; dist. coordinator Ky. Life Sports Project, 1967-69, chmn. past president's com., 1971—; chmn. phys. edn. for coll. women com. Profl. Prep. Project Conf., 1969-71. Recipient 25 year service plaque U. Louisville, 1966; named Del. White House Conf. on Children, 1950. Chmn. Louisville-Jefferson County Sch. Health Council, 1951-53; mem. Ky. Council on Edn., 1958—. Mem. A.A.H.P.E.R. (So. dist. pres. 1961-62, nat. membership dir. for. Ky. hon. Ky. col., 1958-60, honor award 1959), Ky. Assn. Health, Phys. Edn. and Recreation (pres. 1950), honor award 1955, Mustaine award 1962, Sue Hall Day award 1955, 50th Anniversary certificate of achievement 1960), Am. Assn. U. Women (br. pres. 1953-55). Nat., So. assns. phys. edn. for coll. women, Mortar Bd., Falls City Womens Golf Assn. Alpha Delta Psi (hon.), Delta Kappa Gamma, Gamma Phi Beta. Clubs: Louisville Arts, Plantation Swim, Beckham Bird. Home: 1518 Herr Lane Louisville KY 40222

HALL, WILLIAM LLOYD, surgeon; b. Wichita Falls, Tex., Aug. 25, 1925; s. Lloyd Lorenso and Frankie (Hodges) H.; M.D., Southwestern med. Coll., 1947; student N. Tex. State U., 1942-44; m. Ann Carolyn Short, July 11, 1947; children—Marc William, Michael Steven, Lisa Merenith, Jay Jonathan; m. 2d, Ann Lee Gilley Gunn, Feb. 26, 1971; 1 dau., Jennifer Gunn. Intern George Washington U. Hosp., 1947-48; resident Gt. Lakes Naval Hosp., 1948-49, Baylor U. Hosp., 1953-56; practice medicine specializing in surgery, Dallas, 1956—; mem. staff Meth. Hosp.; chief of surgery Kessler Hosp., 1961-62. Served at lt. M.C., USN, 1948-53, Diplomate Am. Bd. Surgery. Mem. Am., Tex. med. assns., Dallas County Med. Soc. Rotarian. Home: 4509 S Crown Knoll Circle Dallas TX 75232 Office: 122 W Colorado Dallas TX 75208

HALL, WILLIAM STONE, physician, mental health ofcl.; b. Wagener, S.C., May 1, 1915; s. Henry F. and Mary (Gantt) H.; M.D., Med. Coll. S.C., 1937; student Sch. Mil. Neuropsychiatry, 1944, Columbia 1947, U. Chgo., 1959; m. Oxena Elizabeth Gunter, June 29, 1940; children—William Stone, Carol Lynn, Richard F. Intern Columbia (S.C.) Hosp., 1937-38; mem. staff S.C. State Hosp., Columbia, 1938—, supt., 1952-69, supt. Pineland State Tng. Sch. and Hosp., 1953-66. Palmetto State Hosp., 1963-66; commr. mental health S.C. Dept. Mental Health, 1963—; clin. prof. phychiatry Med. Coll. S.C., 1957—. Area chief S.C. Civil Def., 1959—; mem. Pres.'s Task Force on Mentally Handicapped, 1970; chmn. planning com. Surgeon Gen's Conf. State and Territorial Mental Health Authorities, 1971, 72; mem. State-Wide Master Planning Com. on Nursing Edn., 1971—; cons. nat. adv. mental health council Nat. Inst. Mental Health, 1972—. Bd. dirs. Richland and Lexington counties United Community Services, 1960—; trustee United Fund Torch Dr.; mem. adv. bd. Remotivation Technique Orgn., 1972—. Served as maj. M.C., AUS, 1942-46. Recipient Distinguished Service plaque S.C. Mental Health Assn., 1960, Distinguished Service award as outstanding state employee S.C. Employees' Assn., 1967; Distinguished Pub. Service award S.C. dept. Am. Legion, 1970; Distinguished Service award S.C. Hosp. Assn., 1972; Organizational award S.C. Vocational Rehab. Assn., 1969; center intensive treatment research and edn. at Columbia, S.C. named William S. Hall Psychiat. Inst. 1964. Diplomate Am. Bd. Neurology and Psychiatry. Fellow Am. Psychiat. Assn. (life; pres. S.C. dist. br. 1957, mem. com. certification in adminstrv. psychiatry 1972), Am. Coll. Psychiatrists (charter); mem. Southeastern Soc. Neurology and Psychiatry (pres. 1955), Columbia Med. Soc. (pres. 1958), A.M.A. (com. on nursing 1966—), Assn. Med. Supts. Mental Hosps. (pres. 1964-65, Meritorious Service award 1971), Nat. Assn. State Mental Health Program Dirs. (pres. 1969-71), Am. Hosp. Assn. (chmn. governing council psychiat. hosp. sect.), S.C. Employees Assn. (dir., v.p. 1971-73). Baptist (deacon). Rotarian. Mem. editorial bd. Staff mag. Home: 1427 Summerville Av Columbia SC 29201 Office: 2414 Bull St Columbia SC 29202

HALLADAY, DANIEL WHITNEY, univ. pres.; b. Santa Ana, Cal., Oct. 13, 1920; s. Harlow Monroe and Marion (Winans) H; B.A., Pomona Coll., 1942; M.A., Claremont Grad. Sch., 1947; postgrad. U. So. Cal., 1949; Ed.D., Columbia, 1955; m. Elaine Owings, Aug. 21, 1941 (dec.); children—Whitney Sue (Mrs. Ernest Whitelaw), Steven Owings; m. 2d, Cherie Longeway, May 19, 1972. Athletic coach Pomona Coll., 1946-47; asso. prof. phys. edn. and health U. Fla., 1947-51; lectr. health edn. Columbia, 1953-54, asst. provost Tchrs. Coll., 1954-55; prof. edn. and dean of students U. Ark., 1955-66; pres. East Texas State U., Commerce, 1966-72; pres. Tex. A. and I. U. at Corpus Christi, 1972—. Mem. spl. adv. com. to commr. higher edn. State of Tex.; adv. com. on formulas for sr. colls. and univs., coordinating bd. Tex. Coll. and Univ. System; chmn. Fedn. N. Tex. Area Univs., 1970, Interuniv. Council N. Tex. Area, 1971, Sulphur River Municipal Water Dist. Bd.; mem. Nat. Commn. on Future State Coll. and Univs., 1970-72. Bd. dirs. Netseo Trails council Boy Scouts Am.; bd. visitors U.S. Mil. Acad. Served to capt. AUS, 1942-46, from capt. AUS, 1951-53; lt. col. Res. Decorated Silver Star, Bronze Star to maj. with two clusters, Commendation medal, Purple Heart with cluster. Mem. Am., Ark. (pres.) personnel and guidance assns., Am., Ark. (pres.) coll. personnel assns., Southwest Assn. Student Personnel Adminstrs. (pres.), Council of Pres.'s of State Sr. Colls. (pres. 1967-68), Am. Assn. State Colls. and Univs. (com. on policies and purposes, com. on student affairs), Tex. Assn. Colls. and Univs. (chmn. commn. on ednl. policy), Northwest Ark. Res. Officers Assn., Fayetteville (dir. 1959-63, v.p.), U.S. (edn. and manpower devel. com.), East Texas (dir.), Commerce (dir.) chambers commerce, Kappa Delta Pi, Phi Delta Kappa. Methodist. Kiwanian. Home: 6440 Everhart St Apt 3B Corpus Christi TX 78413

HALLAM, H. CHARLES, JR., govt. ofcl Librarian U.S. Supreme Ct., Washington. Address: U S Supreme Ct Bldg 1 1st St NS Washington DC 20543*

HALLE, KAY (KATHARINE) MURPHY, author; b. Cleve.; d. Samuel Horatio and Blanche (Murphy) Halle; student Smith Coll., Cleve. Inst. Music. Broadcaster WGAR, Cleve.; music commentator Cleve. Symphony Orch., 1938-40; feature writer Cleve. Press, Cleve. Plain Dealer. Chmn. garden com. Blair House, Washington; co-chmn. fine arts com. Womans Nat. Democratic Club, Washington. Bd. dirs. Washington Opera Soc. Served with OSS, World War II. Author: Irrepressible Churchill; Winston Churchill, on America and Britain; Randolph Churchill, the Grand Original. Contbr. chpt. to The Teacher and the Books. Home: 300 Dent Pl NW Washington DC 20007

HALLE, MARGARET JANE ABRAHAMSON (MRS. AUSTIN ARTHUR HALLE, JR.), opthalmologist; b. Cin., Apr. 10, 1921; d. Ira Arthur and Fay (Levy) Abrahamson; B.S., U. Cin., 1943, M.D., 1946; postgrad. U. Ill., 1949-52; m. Austin Arthur Halle, Jr., Apr. 25, 1952; children—Austin Arthur III, Jean Fay. Intern, Grasslands Hosp., Valhalla, N.Y., 1946-47; resident Ill. Eye and Ear Infirmary, Chgo., 1949-52; practice medicine, specializing in ophthalmology, Memphis, 1952—; asst. prof. ophthalmology U. Tenn. Sch. Medicine, 1953—; courtesy staff LeBonheur Children's Hosp., St. Joseph's Hosp; cons. staff Bapt. Meml. Hosp.; attending staff Meth. Hosp. Mem. bd. Pub. Affairs Forum, 1953-64. Fellow Am. Acad. Ophthalmology and Otolaryngology; mem. Assn. Am. Physicians and Surgeons, Memphis and Shelby County Med. Soc., Memphis Soc. Ophthalmology, Am. Assn. Ophthalmology, Pan Am. Med. Assn., Contact Lens Assn. Ophthalmologists. Home: 4605 Minden Rd Memphis TN 38117 Office: 3364 Poplar Av Memphis TN 38111

HALLETT, DAVID KENNETH, govt. ofcl.; b. Zanesville, O., Oct. 17, 1932; s. Homer Carl and Mildred Livana (Conaway) H.; B.S., Ohio State U., 1954; postgrad. Syracuse U., 1971-72; m. Carol Elizabeth Schulze, June 13, 1953; children—Bruce Alan, Mark Edward. Developer standards for livestock and meat U.S. Dept. Agr., Washington, 1960-65, dir. Fed. Meat Grading Service Programs, 1966—. Mem. Am. Soc. Animal Sci., Am. Meat Sci. Assn., Am. Soc. Pub. Adminstrn. Author: (with others) Introduction to Livestock Production. Home: 6438 Tucker Av McLean VA 22101 Office: 14th and Independence St NW Washington DC 20250

HALLEY, HARRY L(EE) S(TUART), judge; b. Antlers, Okla., Sept. 5, 1894; s. John Henry and Annie Howard (Stuart) H.; A.B., U. Okla., 1915, LL.B., 1917; m. Fredrica Probst, Sept. 6, 1923; 1 dau., Matilda Ann (Mrs. J. R. Rummage). Admitted to Okla. bar June 1916, practiced in Tulsa, 1918-49; asst. city atty., 1922-28, dist. judge Tulsa and Pawnee Counties, Tulsa, 1931-47; justice Supreme Ct. State Okla., 1949—, vice chief justice 1952, 63-65, chief justice, 1953-55, 65-66, supernumerary judge, 1967—. Served with the U.S. Army 1917-18, disch. as capt., Inf.; entered U.S. Army as lt. col., 1942; served N. Africa, Italy, France, 1943-45; disch. to res. as col., Inf., 1945. Mem. Am., Okla., Tulsa County bar assns., Am. Legion, Am. Judicature Soc., Res. Officers Assn., Mil. Order World Wars, Ret. Officers Assn., V.F.W., C. of C., YMCA, Order of the Coif, Phi Delta Phi, Sigma Chi. Democrat. Methodist (steward). Mason, K.P. Club: High Twleve. Office: PO Box 53302 State Capitol Oklahoma City OK 73105

HALLIBURTON, JULIAN DOUGLAS, banker; b. Macon, Ga., Dec. 15, 1918; s. Thomas Henley and Lizzielou (Douglas) H.; B.A. summa cum laude U. Ga., 1940; m. Martha Ruth Howard, Sept. 22, 1945; children—Julian Douglas, Anne Howard, David Henley, Jane Douglas. Admitted to Ga. bar, 1951; clk. trust dept. C & S Nat. Bank, Macon, 1946-49; asst. trust officer Fulton Nat. Bank, Atlanta, 1950-54; agt. N.Y. Life Ins. Co., 1954; v.p., copy chief Purse Co., Chattanooga, 1954-58; trust officer Bank of Melbourne & Trust Co. (Fla.), 1958-59; asso. trust officer Exchange Nat. Bank, Tampa, Fla., 1959-66; v.p., trust officer Dania Bank (Fla.), 1966-71; v.p., trust officer Key Biscayne Bank and Trust Co. (Fla.), 1971—; grad. asst., instr. U. Ga., 1945-46; spl. adviser to bd. dirs. Charles McArthur Dairies, Inc., N.O. McArthur, Inc., B.B. McArthur, Inc., C.M. McArthur, Inc. Charter mem., treas. Estate Planning Council, Tampa, 1960-62; dir., treas. Community Coordinating Council, 1962-64; mem. aging com. Family Service Assn., 1963-64; mem. study com. Tampa Community Trust Found., 1964—; chmn. Bay Area com. on Inst. for Retired Persons, Tampa and St. Petersburg, 1965; pres. Dania Indsl. Devel., Inc., 1967-68; chmn. pension com. City of Dania, 1967-68. Bd. dirs. Tampa Med. Research Found., 1963—; mem. founders group Vanguard Sch., Ft. Lauderdale, 1969. Served from 2d lt. to maj. Q.M.C., AUS, 1940-45. Mem. Am., Ga. bar assns., Fla. Bankers Assn., Internat. Platform Assn., Dania C. of C. (chmn. indsl. com. 1967-68, award for outstanding community service 1968), Blue Key, Kappa Alpha, Phi Beta Kappa, Phi Kappa Phi, Omicron Delta Kappa. Democrat. Methodist. Author: Georgia Democratic Party, 1948; Modern Trust Services, 1956. Contbr. articles to profl. jours. Home: 1487 NE 60th St Fort Lauderdale FL 33308 Office: Key Biscayne Bank & Trust Co Key Biscayne FL 33149

HALLMAN, ELEANOR HANCOCK (MRS. ROBERT R. HALLMAN), civic and religious worker; b. Warm Springs, Ga.; d. Royan Thomas and Addie (Simmons) Hancock; student U. Ga. 1927-28; m. Robert R. Hallman, Apr. 15, 1926; 1 son, Robert Richard. Sec.-treas., dir. Hallman Bros. Constrn. Co., 1972—. Volunteer A.R.C., Ga. Bapt. Hosp., 1966—, chmn. vols., 1972; bd. dirs. Warren Meml. Boys' Club Am., 1965—; bd. dirs. Home Mission Bd., So. Bapt. Conv., 1965—, chmn. Christian Social Ministries com., 1965—, adminstrv. com., 1968—, 2d v.p. bd., 1968—; mem. exec. com. Womans Missionary Union, Atlanta Bapt. Assn., 1952—, dist. sec., 1953-56, v.p., 1956-60, pres., 1960-64, treas. youth orgn., 1966—; trustee Atlanta Bapt. Coll., 1971—. Mem. Northside Library Assn., Met. Atlanta Better Films Council, Atlanta Symphony Guild, Women in Constrn. Atlanta, Ga. Fedn. Womens Clubs. Clubs: Atlanta Womans, Atlanta Music. Home: 1040 Lindridge Dr NE Atlanta GA 30324

HALLMAN, GRADY LAMAR, JR., physician; b. Tyler, Tex., Oct, 25, 1930; s. Grady Lamar and Mildred (Kennedy) H.; B.A., U. Tex., 1950; M.D., Baylor U., 1954; m. Martha Suit, June 7, 1953; children—Daniel S., David L., Charles H. Intern, Chgo. Wesley Meml. Hosp., 1954-55; resident Baylor U. Coll. Medicine Hosps., 1955-56, 58-62; practice medicine specializing in surgery, Houston, 1962—; mem. staff St. Luke's, Tex. Children's, Meth. hosps.; instr. dept. surgery Baylor U. Coll. Medicine, 1962-63, asst. prof,, 1963-67, asso. prof., 1967-69, clin. asso. prof., 1969—. Served with M.C., AUS, 1956-58. Diplomate Am. Bd. Surgery; Am. Bd. Thoracic Surgery. Fellow A.C.S., Am, Coll. Cardiology, Am. Coll, Chest Physicians; mem. Soc. U. Surgeons, Am. Assn, for Thoracic Surgery, Soc. Thoracic Surgeons, Internat. Cardiovascular Soc., Soc. for Vascular Surgery, A.M.A., Internat. Soc. Surgery, Am. Geriatric Soc., Southwestern Surg. Congress, Tex., Houston surg. socs., Pan-Am. Med. Assn., Royal Soc. Health, So., So. Thoracic surg. assns., Internat. Soc. Surgery. Author: Surgical Treatment of Congenital Heart Disease, 1966. Home: 3443 Inwood St Houston TX 77019 Office: 6621 Fannin PO Box 20345 Houston TX 77025

HALLMAN, ROBERT RICHARD, dentist; b. Atlanta, Dec. 6, 1936; s. Robert Rant and Eleanor Kathleen (Hancock) H.; A.A., Mars Hill Coll., 1956; D.D.S., Emory U., 1961; m. Mary Tolbert Bryant, July 24, 1971. Individual practice dentistry, Atlanta, 1963—. Alternate del. Atlanta div. to Easter Seal Soc., 1971. Served with USNR, 1961-63; mem. Res. Named Kiwanian of Yr., Buckhead Kiwanis Club, Atlanta, 1971. Mem. Am., Ga. dental assns., No. Dist., 5th Dist. dental socs., Acad. Gen. Dentistry. Baptist (deacon 1969—). Kiwanian (dir. 1970-72). Home: 3460 Buford Hwy NE Atlanta GA 30329 Office: 1843 Peachtree Rd NE Atlanta GA 30309

HALLORAN, RICHARD COLBY, newspaper corr.; b. Washington, Mar. 2, 1930; s. Paul James and Catherine (Lenihan) H.; A.B. with distinction, Dartmouth, 1951; M.A., U. Mich., 1957; m. Carol Prins, June 21, 1958 children—Christopher Paul, Laura Colby, Catherine Anne. Staff writer, then asst. fgn. editor Business Week mag., 1957-61; Tokyo (Japan) bur. chief McGraw-Hill World News, 1962-64; mem. staff Washington Post, 1965-69, bur. chief, Tokyo, 1966-68, Washington corr., 1968-69; gen. corr. N.Y. Times, Washington, 1969-72, bur. chief, Tokyo, 1972—. Served to 1st lt. AUS, 1952-55. Ford Found. fellow Columbia, 1964-65. Recipient citation for interpretation foreign affairs Overseas Press Club, 1969. Clubs: Washington Press; Foreign Correspondents (Tokyo). Author: Japan, Images and Realities, 1969; Conflict and Compromise: The Dynamics of American Foreign Policy, 1972. Home: 5809 Wiltshire Dr Washington DC 20016 Office: Asahi Shimbun 2-3 Yurakucho Chiyoda-ku Tokyo Japan

HALLUM, GYDA ALMIRA, psychologist; b. Foxhome, Minn.; d. John O. and Emma (Smerud) Hallum; B.A., Trinity U., 1951, M.A., 1955; M.S., Tex. Arts and Industries Coll., 1958; Ph.D., (U.S. Dept. Health, Edn., and Welfare, fellow) U. Tex., 1962. Caseworker, psychometrist Children's Service Bur., San Antonio, 1948-51; spl. investigator Harris County Probation Dept., Houston, 1951-52; supr. med. and psychiat. social service, acting clin. psychologist U.S. Naval Hosp., Corpus Christi, Tex., 1954-57; spl. services tchr., Harlingen (Tex.) Ind. Sch. Dist., 1958-59; chief clin. psychologist El Paso (Tex.) Child Guidance Center, 1962-63; asst. prof. Tex. Western Coll., U. Tex., El Paso, 1964, asso. prof., 1965, lectr., Extension Div., 1964; research psychologist Abilene (Tex.) State Sch., 1965-66; program coordinator Austin (Tex.) State Sch., 1966-67; chief psychologist Gulf Bend Diagnostic Clinic, Victoria, 1967-70. Private practice, Victoria 1970—; practice psychology, Corpus Christi, El Paso, Abilene, Austin, 1955—. Cons., Pre-Sch. for Deaf and Hearing Handicapped, El Paso, 1963-65, Canutillo (Tex.) Ind. Sch. Dist., 1964-65, W. Tex. Rehab. Center, Abilene, 1965-66, Region III Edn. Service Center, 1971—. Recipient Best Poem of Year award Avalon Mag., 1947, 1st prize Nat. Pen-Women's Contest, 1946, 2d prize Corpus Christi Art Show, 1955. Mem. Am., Southwestern, Tex. psychol. assns., Internat. Assn. Cross Cultural Psychology, Alpha Chi. Writer poetry, 1945-50, pageant, Saga of Spring Grover, 1947. Contbr. articles to profl. jours. Home: Route 5 Box 118C Austin TX 78704 Office: 2701 N Azalea Victoria TX 77901

HALLWORTH, GERALD, educatior. Asso. prof. polit. sci., chmn. dept. pub. justice St. Mary's U., San Antonio. Address: St Mary's U 2700 Cincinnati St San Antonio TX 78284*

HALMOS, EUGENE ERWIN, JR., editor; b. N.Y.C., Aug. 24, 1916; s. Eugene Erwin and Rose (Gyory) H.; student Coll. City N.Y., 1931-33; m. Elizabeth Ann Cummings, Feb. 14, 1938. With newspapers, North Platte, Neb., Twin Falls, Ida., Salt Lake City, N.Y.C., 1933-38; news editor McGraw-Hill Pub. Co., 1939-41, mng. editor, 1946-54, sr. editor Engrng. News Record, 1954-58; Washington editor Progressive Architecture, Civil Engrng. and others, 1958—. Cons. AEC, 1971-72, Nat. Acad. Scis., 1970—. Vice pres. Montgomery County chpt. Md. Municipal League, 1970-71, pres., 1971-72. Pres. commrs., mayor Town of Poolesville, Md., 1963—. Served with USAAF, 1942-45; ETO. Decorated Purple Heart, Air medal. Mem. Am. Soc. C.E., Road Gang, Assn. Petroleum Writers, Constrn. Writers Assn. (pres. 1957-58; Silver Hardhat award Constrn. Writers Assn., 1969). Presbyn. (elder 1958—). Elk. Club: Nat. Press. Home: PO Box 132 Poolesville MD 20837 Office: 601 13th St NW Washington DC 20005

HALPERN, KATHERINE SPENCER (MRS. ABRAHAM HALPERN), educator; b. Reading, Mass.; d. Carl Mason and Bertha (Beaudry) Spencer; B.A., Vassar Coll., 1935; M.A., U. Chgo., 1944, Ph.D., 1952; m. Abraham Halpern, in 1968. Social Science Research Council fellow 1941; consultant to A.R.C., Alaska, 1942-44; social sci. analyst OWI, Washington, 1944-46; research asst., dept. social relations Harvard, 1946-50, asso. dir. Community Health Project, 1953-57; asst. prof. N.Y. Sch. Social Work, Columbia, 1950-52; asso. prof. Boston U. Sch. of Social Work, 1954-64, prof., 1964-70, lectr. dept. sociology and anthropology, 1960-70; prof. anthropology Am. U., Washington, 1970—; research associate in social anthropology at McLean Hosp., 1958-65; research asso. dept. psychiatry Harvard 1960-65; cons. div. Indian Health USPHS, 1964-71. Fellow Am. Anthropology Assn.; mem. Soc. for Applied Anthropology, Nat. Assn. Social Workers, Phi Beta Kappa, Sigma Xi. Author: Reflections of Social Life in the Navaho Origin Myth (U. N.M. Publs. in Anthropology No. 3), 1947; Mythology and Values, an Analysis of Navaho Chantway Myths (Memoir of the Am. Folklore Soc. No. 48), 1957. Home: 4100 W St NW Washington DC 20007

HALPERT, SYLVIA SIDRANSKY (MRS. HAROLD P. HALPERT), social worker, educator; b. N.Y.C., Feb. 16, 1914; d. Morris and Elizabeth (Katz) Sidransky; B.A., Bklyn. Coll., 1937; M.S., Cath. U. Am., 1945, Dr. Social Welfare, 1965; certificate psychiatry Washington Sch. Psychiatry, 1949; m. Harold P. Halpert, Apr. 27, 1937. Psychiat. social worker Washington Inst. of Mental Hygiene and Hillcrest Children's Center, Washington, 1945-62; asst. prof. research Howard U. Sch. Social Work, Washington, 1965-68; psychiat. social worker Marriage and Family Inst., Washington, 1966—; pvt. practice psychiat. social work, Washington, 1950—. Cons. Head Start Program, 1968—; mem. prof. adv. bd. D.C. Inst. Mental Hygiene, 1968—. Recipient Nat. Inst. Mental Health fellowship, 1962-64. Fellow Am. Orthopsychiat. Assn.; mem. Council on Social Work Edn., Acad. Certified Social Workers, Nat. Assn. Social Workers, Am. Sociol. Assn. Address: 4606 Bayard Blvd Washington DC 20016

HALSEY, ASHLEY, JR., assn. exec., museum dir.; b. Charleston, S.C.; m. 5 children. Mgr. editorial promotion Saturday Evening Post, 1945-48, asso. editor, spl. features editor, 1949-62; prof., adminstr. U. S.C., 1963-66; dir. publs. Nat. Rifle Assn., editor Am. Rifleman, dir. Firearms Mus., Washington, 1966—; lectr., cons. antique arms. Served with USNR, World War II. Fellow Co. Mil. Historians; mem. S.A.R., Sons Confederate Vets. (past nat. officer), Am. Soc. Arms Collectors. Address: Nat Rifle and Firearms Museum 1600 Rhode Island Av NW Washington DC 20036*

HALSEY, WILLIAM MELTON, artist, educator; b. Charleston, S.C., Mar. 13, 1915; s. Ashley and Eleanor (Loeb) H.; student U. S.C., 1932-34, Sch. Boston Mus. Fine Arts, 1935-39; m. Corrie P. McCallum, June 5, 1939; children—Eleanor Paige (Mrs. Laird Slade), David Ashley, Louise McCallum. Exhibited in one-man shows including U. S.C., Columbia, 1962, Gibbes Art Gallery, Charleston, 1963, Va. Poly. Inst., 1964, Savannah Art Assn., Ga., 1965, Columbia Mus., S.C., 1966, Greenville Mus., S.C., 1966, exhibited in group shows including Ringling Mus., Sarasota, Fla., 1963, Hunter Gallery, Chattanooga, 1965, Mint Mus., Charlotte, 1966; retrospective exhbn. S.C. museums, 1972-73; executed murals at Balt. Hebrew Congregation Temple, 1952, Sears Roebuck Bldg., Charleston, 1954; dir. art sch. Telfair Acad. Art, Savannah, Ga., 1942-43, Gibbes Art Gallery, Charleston, 1945-53; instr. painting and drawing Charleston Art Sch., 1953-65; instr. art Coll. Charleston (S.C.), 1966-72, asst. prof. art, 1972—; instr. Newberry (S.C.) Coll., 1968-70. Paige fellow, 1939-41; Pepsi Cola fellow, 1948-49; Hughes fellow, 1950-52. Mem. Guild S.C. Artist, Carolina Art Assn., Charleston Artists Guild. Author (with Corrie McCallum) A Travel Sketch Book, 1971, also articles in field. Address: 38 State St Charleston SC 29401

HALTIWANGER, GEORGE ALBERT, dentist; b. Hamlet, N.C., Feb. 28, 1929; s. William Leonard and Hazel (McCullough) H.; student U. N.C., 1947-49; D.D.S., Emory U. Sch. Dentistry, 1953; m. Jean Jenkins, Aug. 3, 1952; children—Jean Elizabeth, Beverly Carol, Albert Jerkins. Pvt. practice dentistry, Rockingham, N.C., 1955—. Dist. com. chmn. Richmond County Boy Scouts Am., 1960-65. Bd. trustees Richmond County Sch. Served with USAF, 1953-55. Mem. Am. Dental Assn., N.C. Dental Soc., Richmond County Dental Soc. (pres. 1965-70), Rockingham (dir. 1967-69, v.p. 1969-70), Rockingham Jr. (dir., sec. 1956-60) chambers of commerce. Lutheran (ch. councilman 1967-70). Club: Civitan (dir. 1961-65) (Rockingham, N.C.). Home: 1336Carolina Dr Rockingham NC 28379 Office: 208 E Franklin St Rockingham NC 28379

HALTOM, THOMAS BRANSON, physician; b. Nashville, Jan. 16, 1920; s. William Coleman and Katie Pool (Foster) H.; B.A., Vanderbilt U., 1939, M.D., 1942; m. Martha Anne O'Connor, Apr. 12, 1947; children—Helen F. (Mrs. Charles Ousley), Katherine A., Barbara A., Mary L. Intern, Grady Meml. Hosp., Atlanta, 1942-43, asst. resident medicine, 1946-47; asst. resident medicine Thayer VA

Hosp., Nashville, 1947-48, sr. resident medicine, 1948-49, tng. diseases of chest, 1949-54, asst. chief Tb service, 1949-54; practice medicine, specializing in internal medicine, Nashville, 1954—; cons. VA Hosp., Nashville; faculty Vanderbilt U., Nashville, 1948—, asst. prof. clin. medicine, 1961—. Served with AUS, 1943-46. Diplomate Am. Bd. Internal Medicine. Fellow Am. Coll. Chest Physicians; mem. A.C.P., A.M.A., Am., Nashville socs. internal medicine, Tenn. Thoracic Soc. (sec.-treas. 1969-71, pres. 1971—), Nashville Acad. Medicine, Davidson County Anti-Tb Assn. (pres. 1969-71. Contbr. articles in field to profl. jours. Home: 728 Darden Pl Nashville TN 37205 Office: 2122 West End Av Nashville TN 37203

HAM, CLARENCE EDWARD, supt. schs.; b. Wink, Tex., Dec. 27, 1936; s. Clarence Joseph and Edwina Olive (Brantley) H.; student Baylor U., 1955-56, B.A., 1959; student Tex. Technol. U., 1956-58, M.Ed., 1965; NSF fellow N.M. State U., 1963; Ph.D. (NDEA Title IV Grad. fellow 1966-69), Tex. U., 1969; m. Joyce Suzella Travis, Apr. 20, 1962; 1 dau., Patricia Lynn. Tchr. Perrin (Tex.) Ind. Sch. Dist., 1960-62, Cotton Center (Tex.) Ind. Sch. Dist., 1962-66; bus. mgr. Orange (Tex.) Ind. Sch. Dist., 1967; supt. Orange County Sch. Dist., 1967-68, Bay City (Tex.) Ind. Sch. Dist., 1969—. Bd. dirs. Matagorda County Econ. Action Com., 1969—, Wharton-Matagorda County Child Welfare Bd., 1971—. Mem. N.E.A., Tex. State Tchrs. Assn., Nat., Tex. assns. sch. adminstrs., Tex. Assn. Curriculum Devel., Phi Delta Kappa. Baptist. Rotarian. Home: 2909 Del Monte Av Bay City TX 77414 Office: 1301 Live Oak St Bay City TX 77414

HAM, GOLDIE SUTTLE (MRS. GORDON BELL HANSON), ret. physician; b. Atlanta, Sept. 29, 1896; d. Eugene Gatewood and Edna (Bell) Ham; B.A., Agnes Scott Coll., 1919; M.D., Tulane U., 1923; m. Gordon Bell Hanson, Nov. 11, 1932 (dec. Apr. 1968); children—Ann Louise (Mrs. Ernest Anthony Merklein, Jr.), Elizabeth Bell (Mrs. Wolfgang Christian Durr). Intern, Charity Hosp., New Orleans, 1923-24; resident St. Joseph Hosp., Houston, 1924-26; practice medicine, specializing in obstetrics and gynecology, Houston, 1924—; mem. obstet. teaching staff Jefferson Davis Charity Hosp.; mem. staff St. Joseph, Meth., St. Luke's, Herman hosps. Clin. instr. obstetrics Baylor U. Med. Sch., 1943-60, mem. cons. staff, 1960—. Mem. Houston Bd. Health, 1937-38; mem. bd. Sheltering Arms, 1964-66, 68-71. Diplomate Am. Bd. Obstetrics and Gynecology. Mem. A.M.A., Am. Coll. Obstetricians and Gynecologists, Tex. Med. Assn., Mortar Bd., Alpha Omega Alpha, Alpha Delta Pi. Republican. Presbyn. Home: 2929 Buffalo Speedway Lamar Tower Houston TX 77006

HAM, TIBOR, physician; b. Rakos Palota, Hungary, June 8, 1914 (came to U.S. 1951, naturalized 1956); s. Janos and Marget (Papp) H.; M.D., U. Pazmany, Budapest, Hungary, 1938; m. Margaret Diener, Feb. 28, 1943; children—Andrew, Tibor, Eugene, Christine, Christopher. Asst. physician City Hosp., Budapest, 1939-41, dep. chief physician, 1941-45; intern Doctor's Hosp., Washington, 1951-52, mem. staff, 1953—; gen. practice medicine, Budapest, 1939-48, Vienna, Va., 1953—; owner Vienna Med. Clinic, 1953—; mem. staff Fairfax (Va.) Hosp., N.Va. Doctor's Hosp., Arlington, 1959—, Jefferson Hosp., Alexandria, Va., 1967—. Pres. Bernard Notes, Vienna, 1957; dir. AM Growth Investment Co., Washington. Pres. Am-Hungarian Cultural Center, Washington, 1966—. Lord lt. Province of Sopron, Hungary, 1945-46; majority whip Hungarian Parliament, 1946-47. Leader Youth Resistance Group, Hungary, World War II. Decorated Achievement in Underground Activities award Hungarian Govt., 1945. Fellow Royal Soc. Health (Eng.); mem. Am. Acad. Gen. Practice, A.M.A., Fairfax, Arlington med. socs., Piarist Alumnea Soc. (N.Y.C.). Home: 7016 Green Oak Dr McLean VA 22101 Office: 135 Center St Vienna VA 22180

HAMADY, DAN R., govt. ofcl.; b. Baakline, Lebanon, Feb. 11, 1915; s. Ralph H. and Yamma (Kasim) H.; (parents Am. citizens); brought to U.S., 1920, naturalized, 1927; student Am. U., Beirut, Lebanon, 1930-35; m. June Milam, Dec. 14, 1957; children—Walter, Susan. Owner hardware store, Flint, Mich., 1944-55; asst. adminstr. Housing and Home Finance Agy., Dept. Housing and Urban Devel., Washington, 1955-63; U.S. rep., mem. exec. com. Internat. Council Bldg. Research Studies and Documentation, Rotterdam, Holland, 1959-62; chmn. U.S. delegation UN Econ. Commn. for Europe Housing Com., 1955-63; v.p. W. Evans Buchanan Cos., builders, developers and real estate investments, 1963; internat. bus. and indsl. cons., 1963-66; dep. chief Office Bus. Devel., U.S. Dept. Commerce, Washington, 1966-71; dir. multi-family div. U.S. Dept. Housing and Urban Devel., 1971—, also dir. unsubsidized insured mortgage programs FHA; pres., mng. dir. Eucomar Investment & Loan Soc., Geneva, Switzerland, 1964-65. Former mem. Michigan Retail Hardware Assn., Flint Jr. C. of C., Flint C. of C. Mason (32 deg., Shriner), Elk (chmn. house com. Flint), Kiwanian (past pres.). Home: 4101 Cathedral Av NW Washington DC 20016

HAMAKER, RAYMOND WEAVER, physicist; b. Harrisburg, Pa., Jan. 13, 1934; s. Raymond Glass and Harriet (Weaver) H.; student Gettysburg Coll., 1952; B.S. in Elec. Engring., Pa. State U., 1956, M.S. in Elec. Engring., 1959, postgrad., 1964—, Ph.D. in Solid State Sci., 1968; m. Emily Bell Flegal, June 16, 1958; children—Karen Clare, Raymond Alan, Clare Rene, Mark Horace. Jr. engr. AC Spark Plug, Milw., 1956-57; asso. physicist Martin Co., Balt., 1959; staff physicist IBM, Owego, N.Y., 1959-64; research asso. Materials Research Lab., University Park, Pa., 1963-68; adv. physicist IBM, Lexington, Ky., 1968-70, Manassas, Va., 1970—. Chmn. Pa. State Alumni Fund, Owego, N.Y., 1961. Recipient Outstanding Invention award IBM, 1963. Mem. Am. Physics Soc., Am. Ceramics Soc., I.E.E.E., Sigma Xi. Republican. Mem. Evang. Ref. Ch. Invented tunnel diode and process, 1962; semicoductor device and process, 1963. Home: 4408 Shari Ct Catharpin VA 22018

HAMBLEN, LAPSLEY WALKER, JR., lawyer; b. Chattanooga, Dec. 25, 1926; s. Lapsley Walker and Libbie (Shipley) H.; B.A., U. Va., 1949, LL.B., 1953; m. Martha O'Hagan Murdock, Apr. 15, 1950 (div. Oct. 1970); children—Lapsley Walker III, Allen Murdock, William Shipley; m. 2d, Claudia R. Terrell, Mar. 20, 1971. Admitted to W. Va. bar, 1954, Ohio bar, 1955, Va. bar, 1957; law asso. Spilman, Thomas, Battle & Klostermeyer, Charleston, W. Va., 1953-54; asso. Smith, Schnacke & Compton, Dayton, O., 1954-55; trial atty. Office Chief Counsel, Internal Revenue Service, Atlanta, 1955; atty.-adviser to judge Tax Ct. U.S., 1955-56; partner Caskie, Frost, Davidson & Hobbs, 1957-69, Caskie, Frost, Davidson, Hobbs & Hamblen, 1969—. Dir. Staunton Foods, Inc.; organizer, dir. Jefferson Nat. Bank, Lynchburg, Va.; co-dir. U. Va. Ann. Conf. Fed. Taxation, 1970—. Served with USNR, 1945-46. Mem. Am., Fed., Va., Lynchburg bar assns., Va. State Bar, U. Va. Alumni Assn., Greater Lynchburg C. of C. (pres., dir. 1971-72), Raven Soc., Order of Coif, Omicron Delta Kappa. Contbr. articles to profl. jours. Home: 3708 Manton Dr Lynchburg VA 24503 Office: 2306 Atherholt Rd Lynchburg VA 24501

HAMBLEY, WILLIAM ARTHUR, JR., govt. ofcl.; b. Creighton Mine, Ont., Can., July 16, 1925 (parents Am. citizens); s. William Arthur and Almira (Bullock) H.; B.S., U. Wis., 1950; M.A., U. Minn., 1953, postgrad., 1957-66; m. Sharon Lee Robinson, Sept. 10, 1965; 1 dau., Gwyneth Ellen. Indsl. engr. Proctor & Gamble Co., Cin., 1952-53; research asst. Office Sec. Def., Washington, 1953-54; comml. officer, asst. attache Am. embassy, Seoul, Korea, 1954-55; intelligence officer CIA, Washington, 1955-56; staff asst. Sen. Patrick V. McNamara, Washington, 1956-57; mgmt. analyst mgmt. office Govt. D.C., 1957; teaching asst., instr. polit. sci. U. Minn., Mpls., 1957-60; instr. Macalester Coll., St. Paul, 1960; adminstrv. fellow Bur. Student Loans and Scholarships, U. Minn., 1961-62, asst. to v.p. for ednl. relationships and devel., 1962-63, research asso. dean Coll. Med. Scis., 1965-66; asst. prof. No. Mich. U., Marquette, 1963-64; mgmt. intern Office Chief Staff Army, Washington, 1966-67; dir. mgmt. improvement and work simplification programs Army Work Simplification Program, Office Army Comptroller, Washington, 1967—, editor Army Mgmt. Practices Letter, 1967—, Armed Forces Comptroller mag., 1970—. Chmn. 2d ward Democratic Com. Mpls., 1958-59; mem. 3d Congl. Dist. Exec. Com., 1958-61, Central Com. Hennepin County, 1958-62; del. Minn. Conv., 1960, 62. Served with AUS, 1943-46. Citizenship Clearinghouse Nat. fellow, 1961-62; Tozer fellow, 1963. Recipient North Star award U. Minn., 1959. Mem. Am. Polit. Sci. Assn., Am. Soc. Zero Defects (nat. dir.), Am. Soc. Pub. Adminstrn., Assn. U.S. Army, Mil. Police Assn., Am. Vets. Com., Alpha Tau Omega, Theta Tau. Democrat. Unitarian. Home: 2514 Pinoak Lane Reston VA 22070 Office: Office Comptroller Army Washington DC 20310

HAMBLIN, ROBERT LEE, clergyman; b. Hamilton, O., June 29, 1928; s. Millard Fillmore and Rhoda (Muncy) H.; B.A., Union U., 1950, B.D., Southwestern Bapt. Theol. Sem., 1954, Th.D., 1959; m. Mary Ruth Miller, Aug. 27, 1948; children—Bobbie Ruth, Karis Jan, Mary Carole. Ordained to ministry Bapt. Ch., 1947; pastor Elliston Av. Bapt. Ch., Memphis, 1956-58, Harrisburg Bapt. Ch., Tupelo, Miss., 1958—. Mem. bd. Miss. Bapt. Conv., 1967—, pres. exec. com., 1969, pres. bd., 1970-72; vice chmn. exec. com. Brotherhood Commn., 1969. Bd. dirs. Lee United Neighbors; trustee Clarke Meml. Coll., Newton, Miss., 1962-67. Kiwanian (pres. 1965). Author: Studies in Galatians, 1972. Home: 210 Hancock Dr Tupelo MS 38801 Office: 1800 W Main St Tupelo MS 38801

HAMBRICK, THERA OLLIS, librarian; b. Lowndes County, Ga.; d. John Tapley and Ruth (Mc-Millan) Hambrick; B.A., Ga. State Woman's Coll., 1942; B.S. in L.S., La. State U., 1947; postgrad. Fla. State U., 1960-61. Tchr. St. George (Ga.) High Sch., 1936-39, Echols County High Sch., Statenville, Ga., 1939-42; librarian Gulf High Sch., New Port Richey, Fla., 1942-43, The Bolles Sch., Jacksonville, Fla., 1943-46; asst. librarian Valdosta (Ga.) Coll., 1946-61, librarian, 1961—. Mem. Mental Health Assn., Southeastern, Ga. library assns., Ga. Assn. Educators. Democrat. Baptist. Home: Route 1 Box 120 Hahira GA 31632 Office: Valdosta GA 31601

HAMBY, DAME SCOTT, educator; b. Macon, Ga., July 8, 1920; s. G. T. and Emma (Scott) H.; B.S., Auburn U., 1946; m. Edna Estelle Johnson, Jan. 20, 1943; children—Michael, Barbara. With Goodyear Tire & Rubber Co., Atco, Ga., 1937-42, Celanese Corp. Am., 1943-45, B.F. Goodrich Co., 1947-48; prof. Sch. Textiles, N.C. State U., Raleigh, 1948-65, head dept. textile tech., 1965-70, dir. textiles extension and continuing edn., 1970—. Dir. Tuscarora Mills, Oakboro Mills. Cons. to numerous textile cos.; mem. field testing com., adv. bd. q.m. research and devel. Nat. Acad. Scis., 1964-70. Recipient Distinguished Service award, textile div. Am. Soc. Quality Control, 1966. Fellow Textile Inst., Am. Soc. Quality Control (chmn. publs. com. textile div. 1957-60), A.A.A.S.; mem. Am. Assn. Textile Technologists (vice chmn. Piedmont sect. 1960-61), Am. Standards Assn. (chmn. com. internat. standardization of textile testing 1961-66), Am. Soc. Testing and materials (chmn. com. D-13, 1966-72, dir. 1967), Sigma Xi, Phi Kappa Phi, Sigma Tau Sigma. Author: Handbook of Textile Testing and Quality Control, 1960. Editor: The American Cotton Handbook, vols. 1 and 2, 1965. Home: 319 Golf Course Dr Raleigh NC 27610

HAMEL, JOSEPH DONAT, clergyman; b, Rumford, Me., Aug. 9, 1923; s. Donat Henry and Ethel (Kennison) H.; B.S., Ashland Coll., 1949, D.D., 1972; M.R.E., Ashland Theol. Sem., 1951; m. Jean Marie Rowsey, Aug. 7, 1949; children—Joan, John, Janet. Ordained to ministry Brethren Ch., 1950; pastor Lanark (Ill.) Brethren Ch., 1951-53, Large City Brethren Ch., South Bend, Ind., 1953-60; pastor Sarasota (Fla.) Brethren Ch., 1960—; tchr. Sarasota County Schs., 1960—; moderator Brethren Ch., Ill., Ia. 1953-54, Ind., 1958-59, nat. moderator, 1960-61. Chaplain, Civil Air Patrol, 1960—; state fire chaplain Fla., 1962—; aux. dep. sheriff Sarasota County, 1961—; mem. exec. bd. P.T.A. County Council. Bd. dirs. Project Alert. Served with AUS, 1943-46. Recipient Freedom award Sertoma Clubs, 1964; named Citizen of Year, City of Sarasota, 1964. Mem. Am. Legion, V.F.W., D.A.V., Fla. Firemen's Assn. (life). Club: Bay View Optimist. Home: 605 Caruso Pl Sarasota FL 33577 Office: 150 N Shade Av Sarasota FL 33577

HAMER, JAN, educator, chemist; b. Gombong, Indonesia, May 2, 1927; s. Gerard Pieter and Wijke (de Boer) H.; Candidaat, U. Leiden (The Netherlands), 1948, doctorandus, 1955, doctorate, 1956; m. Millicent May, Mar. 10, 1956; children—Elizabeth May, Hilary Halsey. Research asso. Tulane U., New Orleans, 1956-57, asso. prof., 1960-65, asso. prof. chemistry, 1965—; asso. prof., chmn. dept. chemistry Dillard U., New Orleans, 1958-60. Dir. Applied Research Corp., New Orleans; cons. So. Regional Research Lab., U.S. Dept. Agr.; chmn. Organic Discussion Group, New Orleans, 1965-66. Served to 1st lt. Royal Netherlands Army, 1949-51. Mem. A.A.A.S., Am. Assn. U. Profs., Chem. Soc. (London), Royal Netherlands, Am. (sect. exec. com. 1965—) chem. socs., Sigma Xi, Alpha Chi Sigma. Club: Round Table Home: 299 Walnut St New Orleans LA 70118

HAMER, WALTER J(AY), chemist; b. Altoona, Pa., Nov. 5, 1907; s. Jess James and Naomi Gertrude (Roland) H.; B.S., Juniata Coll., 1929, Sc.D., 1966; Ph.D., Yale, 1932; m. Alma Robinson, Mar. 19, 1941; 1 dau., Margaret Jay. Postdoctoral research fellow phys. chemistry Yale, 1932-34; research asso. phys. chemistry Mass. Inst. Tech., 1934-35; chemist Nat. Bur. Standards, 1935-50, chief electro-chemistry sect., 1950-70, dir. electrolyte center, cons. electrochemistry, 1970—; research chemist nat. def. research com. OSRD and Manhattan Project, 1943-44; cons. Dept. Def., 1951-53; lectr. Georgetown U., 1947-50, Cath. U. Am., 1944-45, Grad. Sch. Dept. Agr., 1940-49, Grad. Sch. Nat. Bur. Standards, 1944-45, 52-53. Mem. commn. electro-chemistry Internat. Union Pure and Applied Chemistry, 1957-65; U.S. tech. adviser primary batteries Internat. Electrotech. Commn., 1950-68; adv. council electrochemistry lab. U. Pa., 1962. Recipient Certificate of Merit, OSRD, 1945, Manhattan Project, 1945; Exceptional Service Gold medal Dept. Commerce 1965. Fellow I.E.E.E., N.Y. Washington acads. scis., A.A.A.S., Am. Inst. Chemists; mem. Electrochem. Soc. (pres. 1963-64), Am. Chem. Soc., Am. Phys. Soc., Am. Standards Assn. (chmn. dry cell com. 1950-68), Sigma Xi, Alpha Chi Sigma. Club: Cosmos (Washington). Editor: The Structure of Electrolytic Solutions, 1959. Compiler: Electrochemical Constants, 1953. Home: 3028 Dogwood St NW Washington DC 20015 Office: Nat Bur Standards Washington DC 20234

HAMES, LUTHER CLAUDE, JR., judge; b. Marietta, Ga., Nov. 18, 1917; s. Luther C. and Patience (Owen) H.; LL.B., Woodrow Wilson Coll. of Law, Atlanta, 1938; m. Kathryn Johnson, May 6, 1942; children— Dorothy Kay Coker, Lucia Ann (Mrs. Phillips), Patricia Lee. Admitted to Ga. bar, 1939; pvt. practice 1939-68; judge superior ct., spl. asst. atty. gen. Ga., 1965; dir. Comml. Bank Cobb County. City councilman; mayor protem, City of Marietta, Ga., 1948-50; solicitor gen., 1953-67; chmn. Marietta Housing Authority, 1950-59; sec., treas. Cobb County Democratic Exec. Com., 1948-60; mem. contest com. Ga. State Conv., 1954. Served from 2d lt. to capt. AUS, 1942-45. Mem. C. of C. (past pres.), Solicitors Gen. Assn. of Ga. (pres. 1956), Am., Ga., Cobb County (pres. 1964-65) bar assns., Council of Trial Judges, Sigma Delta Kappa. Democrat. Baptist. Mason. Home: RFD 4 Old Trace Rd Marietta GA 30060 Office: Cobb Judicial Bldg Marietta GA 30060

HAMIL, DAVID ALEXANDER, govt. ofcl.; b. Dec. 3, 1908; s. James Newton and Ada (Walker) H.; A.B., Hastings Coll., 1930; m. Genevieve Robinson, Dec. 24, 1933; children—JoAnn (Mrs. Donald A. Ostwald), Donald William, Jack Robinson. With Hamil Bros. Inc., Hamil Bros. Land Co., 1932—; mem. Gen. Assembly Colo., also speaker; dir. Colo. Dept. of Instns., 1963-69; adminstr. Rural Electrification Adminstrn., Washington, 1956-61, 69—. Trustee Northeast Jr. Coll., Sterling, Colo., Hastings (Neb.) Coll., United Presbyn. Found. Recipient 4-H Alumni award. Mason, Elk, Rotarian. Home: 2000 S Eads St Arlington VA 22202 Office: S Agr Bldg Washington DC 20250

HAMILL, WALTER, JR., accountant; b. Lumberton, N.C., Feb. 26, 1933; s. Walter Franklin and Mabel (Braswell) H.; B.S., U. Va., 1958; postgrad. Old Dominion U., 1958-59; m. Valerie Brooks McConnell, Mar. 5, 1955; 1 dau., Margaret Brooks. Mem. staff Craver, Green & Co., Norfolk, Va., 1959-66, partner, 1966-70; partner Hamill, Grissom and Co., C.P.A.'s, Norfolk, 1970—. Bd. dirs. Jr. Achievement Norfolk, Norfolk Community Concert, Girls Club Norfolk, Cape Henry Sch. Served with AUS, 1954-56. Mem. Am. Inst. C.P.A.'s, Va. Soc. C.P.A.'s (edn. com., dir. Tidewater chpt.), Alpha Tau Omega. Episcoplian (dir. vestry). Club: Sertoma of Norfolk.Home: 1400 Graydon Pl Norfolk VA 23507 Office: Bank Virginia Bldg Norfolk VA 23510

HAMILL, WILLARD DEARING, investment broker; b. Roanoke, Va., Mar. 9, 1932; s. Willard Robert and Helen (Hogan) H.; B.S., Va. Polytech. Inst., 1958; m. Jeanette Martin. Seasonal park ranger Blue Ridge Pkwy., Roanoke, Va., summers 1957-58; investment broker Cash, Shoaf & Co., Inc., 1958—, sec., 1960—, pres., treas., 1971—. Served with AUS, 1953. Decorated Bronze Star. Mem. Nat. (trustee), Va. (pres.) christmas tree growers assns., Alpha Kappa Psi. Presbyn. Club: Sertoma. Home: 3121 King St NE Roanoke VA 24012 Office: 7 W Campbell Av Roanoke VA 24011

HAMILTON, BRUCE ROSS, lawyer; b. Frankfort, Ky., Sept. 2, 1930; s. Reynolds G. and Mary Ross (Rogers) H.; student Eastern State Coll., 1948-50, U. Ky., 1950-51; B.S., U. Louisville, 1951, J.D., 1953; m. Hilda Ann King, Nov. 29, 1958; children—Virginia, Sandra, Laura. Admitted to Ky. bar, 1954; practiced in LaGrange, Ky., 1956—; city atty., LaGrange 1958-65; county atty. Oldham County, Ky., 1966-72; commonwealth atty. 12th Judicial Dist. Ky., 1972—; sr. partner firm Hamilton & Pike. Dir. Crestwood State Bank. Bd. dirs. Mallory-Taylor Hosp., 1958-66, Econ. Opportunity Devel. Com., 1966-68. Served with AUS, 1954-56. Mem. Am., Ky., Oldham County (pres. 1960) bar assns., Am. Judicature Soc., Am. Assn. Trial Attys., Ky. Assn. Trial Lawyers, Nat. Dist. Attys. Assn., Ky. County Attys. Assn., Oldham County Jr. C. of C. (pres. 1958; Outstanding Young Man award 1958). Mem. Christian Ch. Democrat. Mason, Kiwanian (pres. 1962). Club: Oldham County Country (dir.). Home: 118 Sunset Dr LaGrange KY 40031 Office: 114 E Main St LaGrange KY 40031

HAMILTON, CHARLES GRANVILLE, clergyman; b. Homestead, Pa., July 18, 1905; s. Augustus William and Mary Catherine (Frey) H.; A.B., Berea Coll., 1925; B.D., Columbia Sem., 1928, M. Div., 1971; D.D., Ministerial Coll., 1941; M.A., U. Miss., 1947; Ph.D., Vanderbilt U., 1958; postgrad. U. S.C., Butler U., Columbia, Emory U., Ind. U., Miss. State U., Temple U., Tulane U., U. Wis., others; m. Mary Elizabeth Casey, May 23, 1939. Ordained to ministry Episcopal Ch., 1929; rector Mid-South field, 1928—; chaplain, prof. religious edn. Okolona Coll., 1933-40, prof. Wood, Furman, Memphis State, Vanderbilt and other univs., 1942—; Danforth fellowships, 1955-60; fellowships St. Augustine's, Canterbury, England, 1961, Ford, 1962, Truman Library, 1963, Bell Telephone 1964, Am. Philos. Soc., 1969; minister Quiet Hour radio broadcast, 1942—; commentator The World Goes On, 1934—; pres., v.p., sec. Miss. Council for Christian Social Action, 1938—; v.p., dir. Rural Fellowship, 1955-63; sec., dir., pres. Crossroads Fellowship, 1964—; columnist Aberdeen (Miss.) Examiner, 1933-47. Del. Province of Sewanee, 1935, 36, 38, 39, 53, 54; sr. reporter Episcopal Convs., 1937—, World Council Chs., 1963. Mem. Miss. Ho. of Reps., 1940-44, floor leader, 1942; del. Democratic Nat. Convs. 1940, 48, 52, 56, 60, 64, 68, 72, mem. credentials com. 1952; chmn. Miss. Vols. for Stevenson, 1952, 56, for Humphrey, 1968; pres., sec., sponsor Young Democrats, 1944-60; mem. White House Traffic Safety Commn., Tenn. Constn. Conv. Commn. Bd. dirs. Family Protection League. Served as 1st lt., chaplain AUS, 1940-42. Named Miss. Minister of Year, 1953; recipient research award Acad. Sci., 1955; Ky. col. Mem. Am., So., Miss. hist. socs., Am., So. polit. sci. socs., Eugene Field Soc., Soc. Sacred Songwriters, Sons Confederate Vets. (chaplain gen.), Order Stars and Bars (chaplain gen.), New Orleans Civil War Roundtable (sec.), Pi Sigma Alpha, Phi Kappa Phi. Author many works, 1936—, including: Within Whose Memories Abide, 1935; South, 1935; There Came One Running, 1937; Mississippi I Love You, 1941; These United States, 1942; The Prophet in Wartime, 1947; Negro Education in Mississippi, 1952; Lincoln and the Know Nothings, 1954; 48 in '48, 1956; Democratic America, 8th edit., 1969; You Can't Steal First Base, 1971; also booklets. Editor: Brave Voyage, 1936; Lyric Monroe, 1937; Basic Relationships of Science, 1939; Those Precious Years, 1941; Preaching is Flame, 1961; Singing Spirit, 1962; Moments of Meditation, 1963; Music of Eternity, 1964; Grass on the Mountains, 1966; God of the Years, 1968; Our Yesterdays (Mary C. Hamilton), 1969; Christianity in 52 Words, 1970; Life is Benediction, 1971. Contbr. Poems of Justice, Master of Men, Poems for Life, others. Editor Jour. Miss. History, 1941-52. Editor: Crossroads, 1957—, Churchman, 1958—. Home: S Meridian at Monroe St Aberdeen MS 39370

HAMILTON, EUGENE LEVERETT, newspaperman; b. Staunton, Ind., Aug. 13, 1917; s. Leverett John and Floy Mae (Stout) H.; grad. high sch.; m. Mary Frances Hammons, July 31, 1942; children—Mary Alice, Betty Jean. Clk., Houser Bros. Grocery, Jasonville, Ind., 1937-39; tank wagon salesman Shell Oil Co., Clearwater, Fla., 1939-40; advt. exec. Myers Dept. Store, Clearwater, 1945-47; advt. exec. Clearwater Sun, 1947-51; advt. mgr. Tuscaloosa (Ala.) News, 1951-53, bus. mgr., 1953, v.p., 1954—, gen. mgr., 1966-70, cons., adviser, 1970—. Active United Fund, YMCA, Tuscaloosa Citizens Sch. Com., Warrior Tombigbee Waterways Devel. Assn. Served with AUS, 1941-45; PTO. Mem. Am. Legion, Tuscaloosa C. of C. Presbyn. Kiwanian. Club: Tuscaloosa Country. Home and office: 25 Lakeshore Dr Tuscaloosa AL 35401

HAMILTON, EUGENE NOLAN, judge; b. Memphis, Aug. 24, 1933; s. Thomas E. and Barbara (Blakey) H.; B.A., U. Ill., 1955, LL.B., 1959; m. Virginia David, June 16, 1956; children—Barbara Jane, John Steven, James Poole, Eric Eugene, David Nolan, Rachel Olivette. Admitted to Ill. bar, 1959; sr. trial atty. U.S. Dept. Justice, Washington, 1961-70, asso. judge Superior Ct. D.C., Washington, 1970—. Bd. dirs. Bethany House, Rockville, Md. Served with Judge Adv. Gen. Corps, AUS, 1959-61. Mem. Am. Bar Assn., Phi Delta Phi. Home: 15305 Sweetridge Rd Silver Spring MD 20904 Office: 613 G St NW Washington DC 20001

HAMILTON, FRANCES, educator; b. Farmington, Mo., Jan. 17, 1916; d. Roscoe Franklin and Zora (Nations) Hamilton; B.S., S.W. Mo. state Coll., 1940; M.A., Columbia, 1948. Tchr. pub. schs., Mo., 1937-45; supr. student teaching Md. State Tchrs. Coll., Frostburg, 1945-47; tchr. Montgomery County, Md., 1947-48; supr. elementary schs. Howard County, Md., 1948-51; asso. sec. Assn. Childhood Edn. Internat., 1951-52, exec. sec., 1952-59; ednl. program specialist U.S. Office Edn., Dept. Health, Edn. and Welfare, 1959—; part-time instr. edn. U. Va. Chmn. Nat. Adv. Com. Exchange of Tchrs., 1956-57; sec.-treas. Youth Conservation Clearing House, 1954—; sec. U.S. Nat. Com. on Childhood Edn., 1955-57, 59-61; mem. Office Edn. Adv. Com. of Nat. Orgns., 1955-59, co-chmn., 1958-59; chmn. Women's Joint Congl. Com., 1956-58; del. White House Conf. on Edn., 1955; tech. cons. White House Conf. on Children and Youth, 1960. Mem. Assn. Childhood Edn. Internat., World Orgn. Early Childhood Edn., D.C. Council Adminstrv. Women (exec. com., pres. 1968-69), Nat. Council Adminstrv. Women in Edn. (pres. 1971—), N.E.A., Am. Assn. U. Women, Assn. Supervision and Curriculum Devel., John Dewey Soc., Am. Assn. Sch. Adminstrs., World Edn. Fellowship, Kappa Kappa Iota, Delta Kappa Gamma. Clubs: Internat. (Washington); Quota. Home: 4200 Cathedral Av NW Washington DC 20016 Office: US Office Edn Dept Health Edn and Welfare Washington DC 20202

HAMILTON, HARVEY, JR., lawyer; b. Morehead City, N.C., Aug. 7, 1921; s. Harvey and Pearl (Cooper) H.; B.S. in Commerce, U. N.C., 1941, LL.B., 1944; m. Betty Jeanne Blair, Dec. 20, 1951; children—Holly Jeanne, Cynthia Blair. Admitted to N.C. bar, 1944; practiced in Morehead City, 1947—; with Guy T. Caswell, Atty., Charlotte, N.C., 1944-46; mem. firm Sims, Hasty & Hamilton, Attys., Charlotte, 1946-47. Mem. Carteret County (N.C.) Bd. Edn., 1965—. Chmn., Morehead City Democratic Precinct Com., 1949—. Mem. Am., N.C., Carteret County, 3d Jud. Dist. bar assns., N.C. State Bar, Morehead City C. of C., Am. Trial Lawyers Assn., N.C. Acad. of Trial Lawyers, Am. Judicature Soc. Methodist. Moose, Mason (Shriner), Elk. Home: 3116 Evans St Morehead City NC 28557 Office: First Citizens Bank Bldg Morehead City NC 28557

HAMILTON, HOLMAN, historian, educator; b. Ft. Wayne, Ind., May 30, 1910; s. Dr. Allen and Helen (Knight) H.; A.B., Williams Coll., 1932; Ph.D., U. Ky., 1954; L.H.D., Franklin Coll., Ind., 1966; m. Suzanne W. Bowerfind, Oct. 7, 1939; 1 dau., Susan C. Reporter, Ft. Wayne Journal-Gazette, 1932-34; editorial writer, 1935-42, 46, 47-50; asst. prof. history U. Ky., Lexington, 1954-57, asso. prof., 1957-65, prof., 1965—, Hallam prof., 1969—; Guggenheim fellow, 1946; Fulbright prof. U. Chile, Santiago, 1966. Trustee Lincoln Meml. U., 1957-63. Served from pvt. to maj. AUS, 1942-46. Recipient Pelzer prize Miss. Valley Hist. Assn., 1954; faculty research award U. Ky., 1965, Great Tchr. award, 1968. Mem Am., So. hist. assns., Orgn. Am. Historians, Soc. Am. Historians, Ind., Ky. hist. socs. Clubs: Nat. Press (Washington); Book Thieves, Idle Hour (Lexington); Williams (N.Y.C.). Author: Zachary Taylor: Soldier of the Republic, 1941; Zachary Taylor: Soldier in the White House, 1951; White House Images and Realities, 1958; Prologue to Conflict, 1964. Co-author: The Democratic Experience, 1963, rev. edit., 1968. Contbr. to Dictionary of American History, 1940; Major Crises in American History, 1962. Co-editor: Indianapolis in the Gay Nineties, 1964. Editor: Three American Frontiers, 1968. Home: 220 Barrow Rd Lexington KY 40502

HAMILTON, HUBERT EARL (BERT), JR., educator; b. Liberty, S.C., July 19, 1907; s. Hubert Earl and Cynthia (Riddle) H.; A.B., The Citadel, 1932; M.A., Peabody Coll., 1934, Ed.D., 1954; m. Carolyn Dudney, July 29, 1949; children—Hubert Earl III, Bruce Dudney. Tchr., Walhalla (S.C.) High Sch., 1932-33, pub. schs., Atlanta, 1935-53; prin. Vinceland Sch., Easley, S.C., 1933-34; prof. edn., chmn. dept. Mercer U., 1953—, McCommon prof., 1956—. Alderman, Macon, 1959-63, 67-70; senator Ga. Gen. Assembly, 1970—. Served to maj. AUS, 1941-46; ETO; now lt. col. Res. ret. Mem. Greater Macon C. of C., Am. Assn. U. Profs., Nat., Ga. edn. assns., Assn. Student Teaching, So., Ga. councils tchr. edn., Middle Ga. Hist. Soc., Friends of Library, Ga. Conservancy, Macon Music Club, V.F.W., Am. Legion, Phi Delta Kappa, Kappa Delta Pi, Pi Gamma Mu, Kappa Phi Kappa. Mem. Christian Ch. Moose, Eagle. Club: Macon Exchange. Home: 464 W Buford Rd Macon GA 31204

HAMILTON, RAY V., broker; b. Eden, Ia., Aug. 11, 1904; s. Albert J. and Sarah Margaret (Cox) H.; student U. Ia., 1926-29; m. Susanne Fjelstad, Apr. 5, 1931. Gen. mgr. St. Louis Star-Times Radio Stas., 1933-40; account exec. NBC, 1940-42; dir. English lang. propaganda U.S. Dept. State, 1942-44; exec. v.p. Asso. Broadcasters, San Francisco, Los Angles, Seattle, 1944-46; chmn. bd., pres., owner Hamilton-Landis & Assos., Inc., brokers, Chgo., Dallas, Washington, San Francisco, 1946—; pres., dir. Blackburn-Hamilton Investment Corp., Blackburn-Hamilton Co., Inc., Broadcast Realty Co., Tulsa Industries, Inc., others; chmn. Round The World Shops, Inc. Clubs: Press, Broadcasters of Washington, University, Georgetown (Washington); Press (San Francisco); Circumnavigator; Chicago Athletic. Author (with others) Advertising for the High School Journalist. World traveler. Home: 4740 Connecticut Av NW Washington DC 20008 also Carlton Towers St Petersburg FL 33701 Office: 1100 Connecticut Av NW Washington DC 20036 also John Hancock Apts Chicago IL 60611

HAMILTON, ROBERT SMITH, railroad exec.; b. Benton, Ill., Feb. 7, 1919; s. Earl Raymond and Lela (Smith) H.; B.S. in Indsl. Engring., Ill. Inst. Tech., 1949; m. Mabel Matilda Ayers, Nov. 13, 1941. With Electro-Motive div. Gen. Motors Corp., 1949-52, Arthur Young & Co., 1952-54, N.Y.C. R.R., 1959-60; with So. Ry. Co., 1954-58, 60—, v.p. charge marketing, 1962-70, exec. v.p. marketing and planning, 1970—; dir. Control of Ga. R.R., C.N.O. & T.P. Ry., A.G.S. R.R., G.S. & F.R. Ry., Carolina & Northwestern Ry. Co., Fruit Growers Express Co.; pres. So. Region Distbn. Services, Inc., Central of Ga. Motor Transport. Served with AUS, 1943-45. Mem. Newcomen Soc. N. Am., Washington Soc. Engrs., Tau Beta Pi. Clubs: Internat., City Tavern Assn., Metropolitan (Washington); Fairfax Rod and Gun; Annapolis Yacht. Home: 4201 Cathedral Av NW Washington DC 20016 Office: Southern Railway Co 920 15th St NW Washington DC 20005

HAMILTON, ROBERT WILLIAM, ret. state justice; b. Nashville, Ark., Mar. 24, 1899; s. Charles Putnam and Eddie (Lassiter) H.; student Alexander Coll., 1916-18; B.A., U. Tex., 1924, law student, 1925-27; m. Lois Rogers, May 4, 1929; children—Robert William, Emily, Ann. Admitted to Tex. bar, 1927; practiced in Midland, 1935-50; county atty. Martin County, 1929-33; dist. atty., Tex., 1933-35; dist. judge, Midland and Ector counties, 1950-53; chief justice 8th Ct. of Civil Appeals, 1953; asso. justice Supreme Ct. of Tex., 1959-71. Mem. sch. bd., Midland Tex., 1945-51. Democratic chmn. for Smith County, 1927-28, Midland County, 1937-38. Served as pvt. U.S. Army, World War I. Mem. Am., El Paso, Midland bar assns., State Bar Tex. Episcoplaian. Home: 600 W 10th St Austin TX 78701

HAMILTON, RODNEY CARROLL, SR., city ofcl.; b. Fort Worth, Mar. 24, 1932; s. Carroll Alexander and Myrtle Adeline (Mills) H.; student U. Southwestern La., 1954-56; m. Barbara Jane Webb, May 31, 1952; children—Rodney Carroll, Rhonda, Danna, Jeffrey, Carroll. Salesman, field mgr. Fuller Brush Co., Lafayette, La., 1948-53; rep. Fidelity Union Life Ins. Co., Lafayette, 1955-56; accountant, City of Lafayette, 1956-57; sales rep. Libby, McNeil and Libby, S.W. La., 1959-61; salesman radio sta. KXKW, Lafayette, 1962-65, KLFY TV, Lafayette, 1965-68; trustee pub. property, Lafayette, 1969—; pres. Northside Inc., 1963, 64. Bd. dirs. Lafayette Parish Council Govts., 1970-71. Served with USMCR, 1950-52. Decorated Purple Heart. Mem. Am. Pub. Works Assn., Am. Water Works Assn., Am. Pub. Power Assn., D.A.V., Am. Legion. Democrat. Baptist. Clubs: Beavers (dir. 1966-72). Home: 110 Martin Oaks Dr Lafayette LA 70501 Office: 733 Jefferson St Lafayette LA 70501

HAMILTON, THOMAS EARLE, educator; b. Savannah, Ga., June 10, 1905; s. Homer Francis and Catherine (Langford) H.; A.B., So. Meth. U., 1927, M.A., 1929; Ph.D., U. Tex., 1940; m. Juanita Vivian Adams, Aug. 2, 1933; children—Earle Hartwell, Charles Lee, Helen Catherine (Mrs. Paul A. Anthony). Instr., Garland (Tex.) High Sch., 1927-29, Highland Park High Sch., Dallas, 1929-37; instr. Tex. Tech. U., Lubbock, 1940-43, asst. prof., 1943-45, asso. prof., 1945-55, prof. Spanish and classics, 1955-71, prof. emeritus, 1971—; vis. prof. Spanish, Tex. Women's U., Saltillo, Mex., summer 1945; vis. prof. Spanish and classics Austin Coll., 1962-63. Mem. Modern Lang. Assn., Tex. Fgn. Lang. Assn. (pres. 1958, hon. life mem.), Am. Assn. Tchrs. Spanish and Portuguese, Assn. Coll. Honor Socs. (chmn. com. on standards and definitions), Eta Sigma Phi, Sigma Delta Pi (nat. v.p. 1950-59, nat. pres. 1959—). Methodist. Editor, S. Central Modern Lang. Assn. Bull., 1954-56, asso. editor, 1965-67; founder, 1st editor Tex. Fgn. Lang. Assn. Bull., 1953-57. Contbr. articles to profl. jours. Home: Route 1 Box 596 Kingsland TX 78639

HAMITER, JOHN CECIL, hosp. administr.; b. Carrollton, Ala., Aug. 28, 1919; s. John Tyler and Emma (Corder) H.; B.S., U. Ala., 1952; M.H.A., U. Minn., 1954; m. Miriam Elise Doughty, Dec. 27, 1947; children—John Cecil, Margaret Ann, Miriam Anita. Administrv. resident Jefferson Hillman Hosp. (now U. Hosp.), Birmingham, Ala., 1953-54; asst. adminstr. Carraway Meth. Hosp., Birmingham, 1954-57; adminstr. Bapt. Meml. Hosp., Gadsden, Ala., 1957-69, pres., 1969—; administr. Etowah-Cherokee-DeKalb Counties Mental Health Center, 1967—. First v.p., dir. E. Gadsden Bank; dir. Rainbow Med. Equipment Co.; v.p., dir. So. Hosp. Adminstrv., Planning and Ednl. (SHAPE) Services, Inc.; Vis. faculty Sch. Hosp. Services Adminstrn., U. Ala. Bd. dirs. Etowah County chpt. A.R.C.; chmn. bd. dirs. Gadsden-Etowah Area Redevel. Commn.; mem. Gadsden Indsl. Devel. Bd.; chmn. bd. Etowah County Dept. Pensions and Security; bd. dirs. Blue Cross-Blue Shield Ala. Mem. adv. bd. Gadsden State Jr. Coll., Gadsden State Tech. Trade Sch., Ida V. Moffett Sch. Nursing, Birmingham, Lurleen B. Wallace Sch. Nursing, Jacksonville State U. Served with AUS, 1940-45. Fellow Am. Coll. Hosp. Adminstrs. (regent Ala.); mem. Ala. Assn. Hosp. Execs. (pres. 1967-70), Ala. Assn. Pub. Welfare Bds,, Birmingham Regional Hosp. Council (pres. 1957), N.E. Ala. Hosp. Council (pres. 1966), N.E. Ala. Health Planning Assn. (dir.), Am., Protestant, Ala. (pres. 1964), Baptist hosp. assns., Gadsden C. of C. Home: 1428 Monte Vista Dr Gadsden AL 35901 Office: 1007 Goodyear Av Gadsden AL 35903

HAMLET, JAMES F., army officer. Commd. officer U.S. Army, advanced through grades to brig. gen., 1971; comdr. 1st Cavalry 11th div. group, Vietnam. Address: 5409 Rosecroft Blvd Oxon Hill MD 20021*

HAMLIN, OMER, JR., med. librarian; b. Tollesboro, Ky., July 16, 1930; s. Omer and Anna Will (Teager) H.; A.B., Milligan Coll., 1956; postgrad. Lexington Theol. Sem., 1957-58, Morehead State U., summer 1958; M.S. in L.S., U. Ky., 1959; m. Evon Thompson, Aug. 1, 1959; children—David Omer, Stephen Alan. Head librarian Milligan Coll., 1959-62; serials librarian U. Ky. Med. Library, Lexington, 1962, reference and circulation librarian, 1962, asst. med. librarian, 1963, acting med. librarian, 1963, dir. med. library, 1963-70, dir. Med. Center Library and Communication Systems, 1970—. Named Outstanding Spl. Librarian Ky., 1965. Mem. A.L.A., Med. (pres. So. group 1965-66), Ky. (pres. 1968), Lexington library assns., Health Sci. Communication Assn. Home: 3405 Westridge Circle Lexington KY 40502

HAMLIN, WALTER BERGEN, justice La. Supreme Ct.; b. New Orleans, Mar. 13, 1898; s. Charles Hector and Henrietta Mary (Bergen) H.; student Soule Coll., New Orleans, 1914-16; LL.B., Loyola U., New Orleans, 1919; m. Stella Malynn, Apr. 3, 1923. Admitted to La. bar, 1919; gen. practice, New Orleans, 1919-48; judge Civil Dist. Ct., Orleans Parish, 1948-58; asst. city atty. New Orleans, 1943-46; asso. justice Supreme Ct. of La., 1958—. Democratic candidate for atty. gen., La., 1932, Served with U.S. Army, World War I; with USNR, 1935-42. Home: 2735 Palmer Av New Orleans LA 70118 Office: 301 Loyola Av New Orleans LA 70112

HAMMER, JANE ROSS (MRS. PHILIP HAMMER), philosopher, educator, violinist; b. Charlotte, N.C., Apr. 9, 1916; d. Otho Bescent and Lucy (Harris) Ross; B.A., U. N.C., 1936, M.A., 1937; m. Philip G. Hammer, Aug. 27, 1937; children—Philip G., Thomas Ross, Michael Levering. Tchr. Spelman Coll., Atlanta, 1946-58; violinist; mem. Atlanta Symphony, 1947-52; charter mem. N.C. Symphony and mem. Symphony Quartet. Sec. Ga. Council Human Relations 1960-61; pres. Margaret Mitchell Sch. P.T.A., 1960-61; mem. bd. Trinity Sch., 1960-61; del. U. N.C. inauguration of Wallace Alston as Pres. Agnes Scott Coll., 1951; gen. chmn. Orgns. Assisting Schs. Sept., Atlanta, 1961; program dir. Overseas Edn. Fund, League Women Voters U.S., 1962-63, trustee of Edn. Fund, 1966-69, chmn. inner city project, 1966-69, 1st v.p., D.C., 1964-65, mem. spl. research com., 1970—; bd. overseers Dag Hammarskjold Coll., Columbia, Md. Mem. Woman's Nat. Democratic Club. Mem. Ga. Philos. Assn., So. Soc. Philosophy of Religion, So. Soc. Philosophy and Psychology, League Women Voters (mem. Ga. bd. 1954-61), Friday Morning Music Club (trustee Found.), Phi Beta Kappa, Chi Omega. Presbyn. Club: Bethesda Country. Co-author manual Voting is People Power, 1967. Editor: Logic for Living (H.H. Williams), 1951. Home: 5152 Manning Pl NW Washington DC 20016

HAMMER, PHILIP GIBBON, urban economist; b. Phila., Sept. 18, 1914; s. John Levering and Emma (Gibbon) H.; A.B., U. N.C., 1936; student Grad. Sch. Arts and Scis., Harvard, 1936-37, Littauer Sch. Pub. Adminstrn., 1938-39; m. Jane Amelia Ross, Aug. 27, 1937; children—Philip, Thomas Ross, Michael Levering. With Dept. Agr., 1939-42, State Dept., 1942; asst. to dir.-gen. UNRRA, 1942-45; pres. South Assos., Atlanta, 1945-47; econ. cons. Joseph K. Heyman Co., Atlanta, 1947-50; dir. Atlanta Met. Planning Commn., 1950-53, Fund for Advancement Edn., 1953; pres. Hammer and Co. Assos., now Hammer, Greene, Siler Assos., 1954—. Mem. Atlanta Met. Planning Commn., 1956-58; v.p. Potomac Inst., Washington, 1967—; chmn. Nat. Capital Planning Commn., 1968—; mem. President's Task Force on Suburban Problems, 1967-68; mem. D.C. Bicentennial Commn., 1972—; mem. cons. council Conservation Found., 1971—, bd. dirs., 1972—. Bd. dirs. Atlanta Urban League, 1958-61, Atlanta C. of C., 1958-60, So. Regional Council, 1956-58. Mem. Am. Soc. Planning Ofcls. (bd. dirs. 1964-67, pres. 1968-69), Delta Psi. Clubs: Commerce (Atlanta); University (Washington); Bethesda (Md.) Country. Home: 5152 Manning Pl NW Washington DC 20016 Office: 1140 Connecticut Av NW Washington DC 20036

HAMMERSCHMIDT, JOHN PAUL, congressman; b. Harrison, Ark., May 4, 1922; s. Arthur Paul and Junie (Taylor) H.; student The Citadel, 1938-39, U. Ark., 1940-41, Okla. State U., 1945-46; m. Virginia Sharp, Oct. 11, 1948; 1 son, John Arthur. With Hammerschmidt Lumber Co., Harrison, 1946—, pres., 1959—; dir. Harrison Fed. Savs. & Loan Assn., First Nat. Bank Harrison; mem. Harrison City Council, 1948, 60, 62; mem. 90th-92d Congresses, 3d Dist. Ark. Chmn. Ark. Republican Com., 1964-66; mem. Rep. Nat. Finance Com., 1960-64. Served as pilot USAAF, World War II; CBI. Decorated Air medal with 4 oak leaf clusters, D.F.C. with 3 oak leaf clusters. Mem. Ark. Lumber Dealers Assn. (past pres.), Southwestern Lumbermens Assn. (past pres. Kansas City), Harrison C. of C. (named Man of Yr. 1965), Am. Legion, V.F.W. Presbyn. (elder). (deacon). Mason (32 deg., Shriner), Elk, Rotarian (past pres. Harrison). Home: 1710 Kent St Arlington VA 22209 Office: Cannon House Office Bldg Washington DC 20515

HAMMES, JOHN ANTHONY, educator; b. Sault Ste. Marie, Mich., Nov. 1, 1924; s. Roman Burchart and Daisy (Martin) H.; B.A., Duquesne U., 1948; M.A., Cath. U., 1950; Ph.D., Pa. State U., 1953; m. Dorothy Janelle Perkins, Feb. 22, 1964; children—John, Paul, Penny. Research asso. Human Resources Research Office, Washington, 1953-56; asst. prof. U. Ga., 1956-62, asso. prof., 1962-68, prof. psychology, 1968—, dir. Civil Def. Research, 1962—, asso. head dept. psychology, 1969—. Mem. Athens-Clarke County Shelter Plan Steering Com., 1965-66. Served with USNR, 1943-46. Mem. Am. Psychol. Assn., Contemporary Authors, Cardinal Newman Hon. Soc., Sigma Xi, Psi Chi. Home: 235 Davis Estates Rd Athens GA 30601

HAMMET, BAN HAY, coll. publ. dir.; b. Allendale, S.C., Feb. 13, 1922; s. Benjamin Joseph and Nelleen (Hay) H.; B.A., Presbyn. Coll., 1943; postgrad. Columbia, 1946; B.J., U. Mo., 1948; m. Florence Jane Jenkins, Apr. 29, 1949; children—Ben Hay, Jr., Lewis Jenkins, Errol Scott. Southeastern night editor Internat. News Service, Atlanta, 1948; bur. mgr., 1948-49; dir. alumni and pub. relations, dir. publs., editor coll. mag. Presbyn. Coll., Clinton, S.C., 1949—. Served with AUS, 1943-46. Recipient Outstanding Service award Presbyn. Coll. Bd. Visitors, 1966, Alumni Gold P Presbyn. Coll. Alumni Assn., 1971, Alumni Giving Incentive award U.S. Steel Found., 1967. Mem. Am. Coll. Pub. Relations Assn., Am. Alumni Council, Pub. Relations Soc. Am. (chpt. sec. treas. 1970—), Blue Key, Kappa Tau Alpha. Presbyn. (deacon 1967-71). Kiwanian (pres. 1964). Home: 110 E Maple St Clinton SC 29325 Office: Presbyn Coll S Broad St Clinton SC 29325

HAMMETT, ARTHUR BENJAMIN JOHN, banker; b. nr. Marysville, Kan., Nov. 23, 1900; s. Benjamin J. and Rena Mae (Neal) H.; student mil. and pvt. schs.; m. Alice Neeley, July 19, 1925 (div. July 1935); children—Jo Ann (Mrs. Morgan Huff), Jacqueline Lee (Mrs. S. J. Gaylord, Jr.); m. 2d, Mary Sterne Vandenberge, Oct. 20, 1952; step-children—Mary Gladys (Mrs. Lamar Bevil), Thomas L. Sterne. With Exchange Bank of Schmidt & Koester, Marysville, Kan., 1917-20; with legal dept. Belt Rwy. Chgo., 1920-23; with Fulsom Wheeler & Co., investment bankers, Kansas City, Mo., 1922-25; exec. mfg. div. Marshall Field & Co., N.Y.C., 1932-37; pres. Village Bus. Center, Inc., 1953—, A.B.J. Hammett Investment Banking Co., 1953—, Victoria Profl. Office Bldg. Corp. (Tex.), 1955—, Kimberlite Diamind Mining Co.; pub. Victoria Mirror Newspaper, 1958—; chmn. bd. Comml. Nat. Bank, Victoria, 1963—. Active in civic affairs. Served to comdr. naval aviation USNR, 1942-46. Commd. adm. Tex. Navy, 1958. Mem. Tex. Mfrs. Assn., So. Tex. C. of C., V.F.W., Petroleum Club, Mason (32 1/2, Shriner), Elk. Clubs: Victoria Country, Beverley Hills (Cal.); Albany (London, Eng.); Yachting of Am. (charter). Author: Texas Prison Story: Miracle Within the Walls; The Rise and Fall of a Golden Empire—The History of Gold; Merrily We Spend and Spend; the Empresario. Designed and constructed complete new modern city for Victoria, Tex. Home: 701 N Washington St Victoria TX 37393 Office: Village Office Bldg Victoria TX 37393 also Commercial National Bank Victoria TX 37393

HAMMETT, CECIL EDGAR, cons. engr.; b. Marysville, Kan., Apr. 6, 1906; s. Edgar Allen and Mary Eva (Barnes) H.; B.S. in Elec. Engring., Kan. State Coll., 1929; M.S. in Elec. Engring., U. Neb., 1932; postgrad. Armour Inst., 1937-38, U. Mich., 1939-40; m. Ruth Hildaguard Avery, Sept. 11, 1929; children—Robert Edgar, Carolyn Virginia (Mrs. Johnnie Hartsfield). Grad. student Westinghouse Co., East Pittsburg, Pa., 1929; instr. U. Neb., Lincoln, 1929-33, Armour Inst. Tech., Chgo., 1934-39; chief mech. research, sr. research engr. E. I. duPont de Nemours & Co., Inc., Wilmington, Del., 1946-49; prof. engring. drawing and machine design, head dept. Auburn (Ala.) U., 1949-52; project engr. guided missiles U.S. Army Missile Command, Redstone Arsenal, Ala., 1952-67, chief requirements and policy office U.S. Army Metrology and Calibration Center, 1967-72; cons. engr., 1972—. Radiol. def. officer Huntsville/Madison County (Ala.) Civil Def., 1956-62. Served with AUS, 1940-46, maj. Res. ret. Registered profl. engr., Ala. Fellow Am. Soc. M.E.; mem. Engrs. in Govt. Service (gov. 1967), Soc. Rheology, Army Ordnance Assn., Assn. U.S. Army, Res. Officers Assn., Nat., Ala. (pres. 1965-66) socs. profl. engrs. Home: PO Box 1069 Auburn AL 36830

HAMMETT, LAMAR GIBBS, banker; b. Gt. Falls, S.C., Feb. 27, 1937; s. Horace Greeley and Lorene (Woody) H.; B.S., U. S.C., 1959; postgrad. Sch. Banking of South, La. State U., 1971—; m. Mary Dian Shaylor, Apr. 16, 1960; children—Edward Gibbs, Leslie Jane. Field rep. Appliance Buyers Credit Corp., Columbia, S.C., 1959-61; v.p. S.C. Nat. Bank, Bamberg, 1961—. Treas. Bamberg County Tricentennial Com., 1969-70. Bd. dirs. Bamberg Midget Football Program, 1968—, coach, 1967—; state bd. dirs. S.C. Heart Assn., 1967—. Served with AUS, 1959. Recipient Meritorious Service award Am. Heart Assn., 1968, Outstanding Service award Bamberg Area C. of C., 1968, Distinguished Service award Bamberg Jr. C. of C., 1970. Mem. Am. Inst. Banking (local treas. 1969—), Bank Adminstrn. Inst., Bamberg Area C. of C. (dir. 1970, pres. 1970). Baptist (trustee 1970—). Lion (dir. 1968-70). Home: 502 Pine St Bamberg SC 29003 Office: 212 W Railroad Av Bamberg SC 29003

HAMMOCK, DONALD WAYNE, glass co. exec.; b. Port Arthur, Tex., Jan. 8, 1939; s. Oren and Una Mae (Forque) H.; student U. Houston, 1958-59; m. Alice Joan Taylor, Apr. 4, 1959; 1 son, Kenneth Wayne. Asst. mgr. Obrien's Super Market, 1956-57; with Northshore Glass & Mirror, Inc., Conroe, Tex., 1957—, v.p., 1959—. Mem. Conroe City Council, 1969—. Bd. dirs. Conroe chpt. A.R.C.,

1962-—, United Fund, Conroe, 1964-—, Montgomery County (Tex.) council Boy Scouts Am., 1965-—. Mem. Montgomery County C. of C. (2d v.p. 1968, 1st v.p. 1969, pres. 1971-72, dir. 1964-—). Mason (32 deg., Shriner), Rotarian (pres. Conroe club 1966-67, dir. 1961-68; dist. gov.'s aid 1968-69, dist. gov. 1971-72; award 1964, 65, 66. Club: Embassy (pres. Conroe 1964-65). Home: 1108 Cowan St Conroe TX 77301 Office: PO Box 343 Conroe TX 77301

HAMMOCK, JOHN COWLING, ret. naval officer; b. Monticello, Ark., Oct. 15, 1903; s. Ernest G. and Letie F. (Cowling) H.; B.S., U.S. Naval Acad., 1925. Commd. ensign U.S. Navy, 1925, advanced through grades to capt., 1944; supervised tng. for amphibious warfare; adminstr. mil. govt. of Pacific Islands, navy sea transp. to No. and Western Europe; mem. faculty U.S. Naval Acad., 1937-39; ret., 1956. Mayor of Dermott, Ark., 1967-71. Decorated Cross of Mil. Service, U.D.C., 1962. Mem. Ark. Hist. Assn. (past pres.), Internat. Platform Assn., Am. Legion, Chicot County Hist. Soc. (past pres.), Dermott C. of C. (pres. 1972-—), Ark. Geneal. Soc. (dir.), Ret. Officers Assn., Naval Acad. Alumni Assn. Democrat. Presbyn. Mason, Rotarian (past pres.). Author: With Honor Untarnished: Story of the First Arkansas Regiment, C.S.A., 1961. Home: 506 S Pecan St Dermott AR 71638

HAMMOND, ARTHUR BARKSDALE, retail furniture exec.; b. Graycourt, S.C., Nov. 5, 1921; s. Arthur Wasmansky and Elizabeth (Barksdale) H.; B.S., Wofford Coll., 1942; m. Ann Goolsby, June 3, 1943; children—Arthur Cullen, Robert Wesley. With Hammond-Brown Jennings & Co., Spartanburg, S.C., 1942, salesman, 1945-49, dir., 1949-52, sec., 1952-59, v.p., 1959-66, sr. v.p., 1966-—; dir., treas. Eagle Furniture Co., Anderson, S.C., 1969-—. Chmn., Spartanburg Housing Authority, 1966-—. Bd. dirs. Vis. Nurses Assn., 1963-68. Served to 2d lt. AUS, 1942-43; to capt. USAAF, 1943-45; col. USAF Res. Decorated Air medal with 3 oak leaf clusters, D.F.C. Mem. So. (pres. 1963-64), Nat. (dir. 1964) retail furniture assns., C. of C. (dir. 1965-69), Pi Kappa Phi, Scabbard and Blade, Pi Gamma Mu. Methodist. Mason. Club: Sertoma. Home: 1530 Barberry Lane Spartanburg SC 29302 Office: PO Box 1050 Spartanburg SC 29301

HAMMOND, CHARLES, JR., economist; b. Canton, Ill., Nov. 14, 1927; s. Charles Brown and Laura Marguerite (Bohannon) H.; B.A. cum laude (Van B. Eyerly scholar), U. Ill., 1949, M.A., 1954, Ph.D., 1958 Grad. asst. U. Ill., 1955-57; lectr. econs. Muskingum Coll., New Concord, O., 1957-58; lectr. U. Md., overseas branch, Heidelberg, Germany, 1958-60; internat. economist Dept. Commerce, Washington, 1960-66; economist Export-Import Bank of U.S., 1966-—. Served with AUS, 1951-53. Mem. Am. Econ. Assn., Capitol Hill Restoration Soc. Contbr. articles to profl. pubs. Home: 111 10th St SE Washington DC 20003 Office: Export-Import Bank 811 Vermont Av NW Washington DC 20571

HAMMOND, JOHN PAYNE, petroleum cons.; b. Okmulgee, Okla., Apr. 19, 1913; s. John Whitten and Grace (Payne) H.; B.S., U. Tulsa, 1936; m. Katharine R. Rees, May 17, 1937; children—Grace (Mrs. Stanley Betzer, Jr.), Patricia Kay (Mrs. Bryan S. Watt), Sara Jo. With Amerada Petroleum Corp. (merger with Hess Oil & Chem. Corp. 1969), Tulsa, 1941-71, asst. gen. prodn. supt., 1951-60, v.p., 1960-62, sr. v.p., 1962-67, exec. v.p., 1967-71, dir., 1963-71; pres. Amerada div. Amerada Hess Corp., 1969-71; petroleum cons., 1971-—; dir. Apache Exploration Corp., 1st Nat. Bank & Trust Co. of Tulsa. Bd. dirs. Goodwill Industries, Tulsa. Mem. Am. Inst. Mining, Metall. and Petroleum Engrs. (past v.p., dir.), Soc. Petroleum Engrs. (past pres.), Am. Petroleum Inst., Mid-Continent Oil and Gas Assn., Phi Epsilon Tau, Tau Beta Pi. Presbyn. (elder). Clubs: Southern Hills Country, Petroleum (Tulsa). Home: 2706 S Birmingham Pl Tulsa OK 74114 Office: PO Box 2902 Tulsa OK 74101

HAMNER, JAMES EDWARD, III, pathologist, dentist, govt. ofcl.; b. Memphis, July 29, 1932; s. James Edward and Violeg Louise (Plows) H.; B.S., U. Tenn., 1954, D.D.S., 1955; M.S. in Exptl. Pathology, Med. Coll. Va., 1964; Ph.D. in Gen. Pathology, Georgetown U., 1971; m. Joan Gaston Wentzell, Feb. 16, 1957; children—James Edward IV, H. Wentzell. Mem. staff USPHS Hosp., Balt., 1959-61; resident dept. gen. pathology Med. Coll. Va., Richmond, 1961-62; resident in oral pathology Nat. Inst. Dental Research, Bethesda, Md., 1962-64, Armed Forces Inst. Pathology, Washington, 1964-65; sr. investigator Nat. Inst. Dental Research, NIH, 1965-68, chief sect. oncology, 1968-—, chief Nat. Inst. Dental Research unit S.W. Found. for Research and Edn., San Antonio, 1968-—. Project officer Tata Inst. Fundamental Research, Bombay, India, 1966, vis. prof., 1969; cons. oral cancer WHO, 1969; clin. asso. prof. dept. pathology U. Tex. Sch. Medicine, San Antonio, 1969-—; cons. in oral pathology Bexar County Hosp., San Antonio, 1969-—; sci. cons., lectr. Wilford Hall Hosp., Lackland AFB, Brooke Sch. Aerospace Medicine, San Antonio, 1969-—; vis. faculty in ecology Tex. Mil. Inst., San Antonio, 1971-—; mem. nat. adv. bd. for biomaterials Clemson U., 1971-—. Served to lt. USNR, 1955-59. Diplomate Am. Bd. Oral Pathology. Fellow Am. Acad. Oral Pathology; mem. Am. Dental Assn., Am. Cancer Soc., Internat. Assn. for Dental Research, A.A.A.S., Soc. Exptl. Medicine and Surgery in Primates, Am. Acad. Implant Dentistry, Washington, San Antonio socs. pathologists, Rocky Mountain Dental Study Club. Episcopalian (sr. warden). Author: (with F.S. Mehta and J.J. Pindborg) Oral Cancer and Precancerous Conditions in India, 1972. Mem. editorial bd. Med. Primatology, 1971-—. Contbr. numerous articles and abstracts to profl. jours., chpts. to books. Home: 5192 Albemarle St Washington DC 20016 also 122 E Terra Alta St Apt 15 San Antonio TX 78209 Office: Nat Insts Health Bldg 10 Room 5N-216 Bethesda MD 20014

HAMNER, LEWIS HERSCHEL, JR., lawyer; b. Camp Hill, Ala., Feb. 21, 1928; s. Lewis H. and Lillian (Rodgers) H.; LL.B., U. Ala., 1950; m. Marion Pinnell, Nov. 17, 1950; children—Lewis H. III, Jodie Pinnell, Lee Rodgers. Admitted to Ala. bar, 1950; pvt. practice law, Camp Hill, Ala., 1950, Roanoke, Ala., 1952-—. Exec. dir. Roanoke (Ala.) Housing Authority, 1955-—. Recorder, Municipal Ct. Judge, Roanoke, 1960-68; chmn. Roanoke Bd. Edn., 1965-—. Served with Judge Advocate Gens. Corps, AUS, 1950-52. Mem. Am., Ala. bar assns., Am. Trial Lawyers Assn., Am. Legion, V.F.W., Delta Chi, Phi Alpha Delta. Lion. Home: 452 Bullock St Roanoke AL 36274 Office: 29 Main St Roanoke AL 36274

HAMNER, REGINALD TURNER, assn. exec.; b. Tuscaloosa, Ala., June 4, 1939; s. Raiford Samuel and Ellie Wells (Turner) H.; B.S., U. Ala., 1961, LL.B., 1965; m. Anne Ellen Young, Nov. 8, 1969; 1 son, Patrick Turner. Admitted to Ala. bar, 1965; law clk. Supreme Ct. Ala., Montgomery, 1965; dir. legal-legislative affairs Med. Assn. Ala., Montgomery, 1968-69; exec. sec. Ala. State Bar, Montgomery, 1969-—. Bd. dirs. Montgomery County Mental Health Assn., Montgomery County Leukemia Soc. Served with Judge Adv. Gen., USAF, 1966-68; capt. Res. Mem. Am., Fed. bar assns., Ala. State Bar, Am. Judicature Soc., Nat. Assn. Bar Execs., Phi Alpha Delta, Alpha Epsilon Delta, Delta Tau Delta. Democrat. Episcopalian. Kiwanian. Editor Ala. State Bar Found. Bull., 1969-—. Home: 3362 Wilmington Rd Montgomery AL 36105 Office: 415 Dexter Av Montgomery AL 36103

HAMPTON, AMBROSE GONZALES, newspaper exec.; b. Columbia, S.C., May 17, 1900; s. Frank and Gertrude (Gonzales) H.; B.S., The Citadel, 1921, C.E., 1928, LL.D., 1965; postgrad. N.C. State U., 1939, 51; m. Henriette duBose Dargan, Oct. 10, 1923; children—Henriette Dargan (Mrs. Ben Rankin Morris), Ambrose Gonzales, Resident engr. bridge constrn. S.C. Hwy. Dept., 1921-32; dist. engr. Forest Service Eastern S.C., 1932-36, engr. hwy. and bridge constrn. U.S. Bur. Pub. Rds. in N.C., Raleigh, 1936-42, dist. engr. access rds. to mil. posts in N.C., 1942-45, dist. engr. charge design, 1945-55; from asst. to pres. to chmn. exec. com., publisher State-Record Co., Columbia, S.C., 1955-—; chmn. exec. com. Bestway Express, State Printing Co., State Telecasting, Inc.; chmn. exec. com., publisher Columbia Newspapers, Inc., Gulf Pub. Co.; dir. S.C. Nat. Bank. Commr. Richland County Hist. Preservation Commn.; past pres., bd. dirs. United Community Services; v.p., trustee Historic Columbia Found.; past dir. Columbia Music Festival Assn.; bd. dirs. S.C. Indsl. Devel. Corp., Carolina Eastern State U. Served with U.S. Army, 1918. Mem. Am. Soc. C.E., Columbia C. of C. (past dir.), Sigma Delta Chi. Episcopalian (past vestryman, past sr. warden). Clubs: Kosmos, Forest Lake, Palmetto, St. Cecelia. Home: 5020 Garners Ferry Rd Columbia SC 29209 Office: PO Box 1333 Columbia SC 29202

HAMPTON, JAMES WILBURN, physician, educator, researcher; b. Durant, Okla., Sept. 15, 1931; s. Hollis Eugene and Ouida (Mackey) H.; student Southeastern State Coll., Durant, Okla., 1950; B.A., U. Okla., 1952, M.D., 1956; m. Carol C. McDonald, Feb. 22, 1958; children—Jaime Jennifer, Clayton C., Diana E., Neal M. Intern, Univ. Hosps., Oklahoma City, 1956-57; resident Univ. Hosps. and VA Hosp., Oklahoma City, 1957-59; research trainee U. Okla. Sch. Medicine, Oklahoma City, 1959-61, clin. asst. medicine, 1960-61, instr. medicine, 1961-62, asst. prof., 1962-67, asso. prof. medicine, 1967-71, prof. medicine, head hematology-oncology sect., 1971-—; mem., head hematology lab. Okla. Med. Research Found., 1972-—; vis. research asso. dept. pathology U. N.C. Sch. Medicine, Chapel Hill, 1966-67; vis. prof. dept. blood coagulation research Karolinska Inst. Stockholm, Sweden, 1967; mem. staff VA Hosp., Central State Hosp. Cons. hematology Tinker AFB Hosp., 1965-—; asso. coordinator Med. Edn. for Nat. Def. Program Okla., 1963-68. Pres. Okla. chpt. Nat. Hemophilia Found., 1965-66, nat. trustee, 1964-65. Recipient Career Devel. award Nat. Heart Inst., 1966-—; Honors Achievement award Angiology Research Found., 1968. Fellow A.C.P.; mem. Am. Physiol. Soc., Am. Genetic Assn., Am. Coll. Angiology, A.C.P., Am. Hematological Soc., A.A.A.S., Am. Psychosomatic Soc., Am. Fedn. Clin. Research (councilor midwestern sect. 1965-68, chmn. 1969-70), So. Soc. for Clin. Investigation, Internat. Soc. on Hemostasis and Thrombosis, Central Soc. for Clin. Research, N.Y. Acad. Sci., Alpha Omega Alpha (chpt. historian 1964-—), Sigma Xi (pres. local chpt. 1972-73), Sigma Tau Delta, Phi Alpha Theta. Democrat. Episcopalian. Clubs: Oklahoma City Golf and Country, Faculty House. Contbr. articles to sci. jours. Research in hematology and oncology. Office: Okla Med Research Found 825 NE 13th St Oklahoma City OK 73104

HAMPTON, LEE ROYAL, JR., dentist; b. Ocala, Fla., Aug. 27, 1923; s. Lee Royal and Effie Carrie (Mitchell) H.; B.S., Fla. A. and M. U., 1949; D.D.S., Howard U., 1953; m. Miriam Patricia Campbell, Nov. 6, 1945; children—Lee Royal III, Kerry LaRue, Ronald Mitchell, Gwendolyn Alice. Pvt. practice dentistry, Ocala, Fla., 1954-—; pres. L.R.H. Co. Ocala, Inc., 1954-—. Mem. staff Munroe Meml. Hosp., 1963. Trustee, chmn. bd. Hampton Jr. Coll. Served from 2nd lt. to 1st lt. AUS, 1943-46. Mem. Fla. Med., Dental and Pharm. Assn. (pres. 1971-—), N.A.A.C.P. (treas. Marion County br. 1961-—), Ocala Marion County C. of C., Nat. Guardsmen Club, Alpha Phi Alpha. Mason. Home: 2646 SW Broadway Ocala FL 32670 Office: 124 SW Broadway St Ocala FL 32670

HAMPTON, MARION HENRY, automotive parts and supply exec.; b. Lavon, Tex., Jan. 4, 1900; s. Mikel T. and Lula (Newell) H.; aircraft engines degree, diploma Okla. U., 1945; m. Yuwana Russell, 1968; 1 son (by previous marriage), Donald Henry. Agt., Express Depot, Ardmore, Okla., 1921-22; supt. Okla. County Hwy., Oklahoma City, 1935-39; pres., founder H & H Auto Supply Co., Inc., Oklahoma City, 1946-—, Save Auto Stores, Inc., 1961-—. Democrat. Baptist (deacon). Home: PO Box 1296 Del Rio TX 78840

HAMRICK, J. NAT, lawyer, business exec.; b. Rutherfordton, N.C., Nov. 21, 1912; s. Fred D. and Natalie Rose (Harris) H.; B.A., U. S.C., 1936; LL.B., U. N.C., 1939; m. Jenice Brown, July 14, 1936; children—J. Nat, Herman, Jenice. Practice of law, 1939-—; pres. Rutherford County Transit Co., 1942-—. County chmn. Nat. Found. Infantile Paralysis, 1940-48. Mem. Am., N.C. bar assns., N.C. Bus. Assn. (pres. 1946-48), Phi Delta Phi, Pi Kappa Alpha. Presbyn. Club: Rutherford County (past pres.). Author articles. Home: Mountain St Rutherfordton NC 28139 Office: Main St Rutherfordton NC 28139

HAMRICK, JOSEPH THOMAS, research co. exec.; b. Carrollton, Ga., Mar. 20, 1921; s. James Mayfield and Mattie Almon (Gaston) H.; B. Mech. Engring., Ga. Inst. Tech., 1946, M.S., 1948; m. Dorothy Elizabeth Jones, June 19, 1948; children—Jane Elizabeth, Nancy Ann, Thomas Mayfield. Aeronautical research scientist, NASA Lewis Lab., Cleve., 1948-55; chief research engr. TRW Inc., Euclid, O. 1955-61; pres. Aerospace Research Corp., Roanoke, Va. 1961-—, also dir. Served to 1st lt. AUS, 1943-46. Mem. Am. Soc. M.E. (chmn. controls and aux. 1970-72), Pi Tau Sigma. Republican. Unitarian (pres. congregation 1967, 68). Contbr. articles to profl. jours. Patentee in field. Home: 6364 JAE Valley Rd SE Roanoke VA 24014 Office: 5454 JAE Valley Rd SE Roanoke VA 24014

HAMRICK, REBECCA HOLLOWELL (MRS. ALGER VASON HAMRICK, JR.), educator, club woman; b. Edenton, N.C., Apr. 17, 1920; d. Charles T. and Annie (Gordon) Hollowell; student Mars Hill Coll., 1938; A.B. in English, U. N.C., 1940, M.Ed. in English, 1959; m. Alger Vason Hamrick, Jr., June 14, 1941; children— Alger Vason III, Charles Gregory. Tchr., Taylorsville (N.C.) High Sch., 1940-41, Shelby (N.C.) High Sch., 1957-—. Office mgr., traffic mgr. Coop. Mills, Inc., Statesville, N.C., 1942-46; office mgr., accountant A. V. Hamrick & Co., Shelby, 1949-57. Active Mac Dowell Music Club, Statesville, 1942-48; pres. Jr. Service League, Statesville, 1945, Shelby Jr. Mother's Club, 1957; v.p. Shelby Inter-City Music Council, 1956; active Dogwood Garden Club, Shelby, Shelby Music Club, P.T.A., Shelby; bd. dirs. N.C. Baptist Bus. Women's Club; mem. Statesville Woman's Club, 1943-47. Mem. N.C. Edn. Assn. (v.p. Shelby unit), Nat., N.C. (pres. English tchrs. Southwestern dist.) councils English tchrs., Am. Assn. U. Women (pres. Shelby 1958-60, N.C. elementary secondary edn. chmn. N.C. div. 1960-61, sec. N.C. div. 1961-64, S. Atlantic regional sec.-treas. 1965-—, pres. N.C. div. 1971-—), Bapt. Bus. Women of Kings Mountain Assn. (pres. 1958-59), Alpha Delta Kappa (v.p. 1969-70, pres. 1970-—), Beta Sigma Phi (pres. Statesville 1944). Democrat. Baptist (tchr. adult class, choir soloist). Home: 847 W Marion St Shelby NC Office: Shelby High Sch Dixon Blvd Shelby NC

HANCOCK, HORACE HOLLOWAY, newspaper exec.; b. Tampa, Fla., Aug. 5, 1924; s. Horace B. and Juanita (Johnston) H.; student pub. schs.; m. Margaret Vogel, Dec. 4, 1943; children—Lynda Lee, Carole Elaine, Richard Douglas, Cynthia Diane. State circulation mgr. Fla. Times-Union, Jacksonville, 1949-54; circulation mgr. Tampa Times, 1954-58, Lakeland (Fla.) Ledger, 1958-63, Tampa Tribune, 1963-64, Atlanta Times, 1964-65; gen. mgr. Hunstville (Ala.) News, 1965-66; exec. v.p. Courier News Corp., 1966-69, pres., 1969-—; pub. Plant City (Fla.) Courier, 1966-—, Brandon (Fla.) News, 1966-—, Palmetto (Fla.) Press, 1966-—. State dir. Little Boys Baseball, 1963-64; pres. Babe Ruth Baseball, 1963-64; mem. Plant City Library Bd., Chamber Edn. Com.; bd. dirs. Blood Bank; v.p. United Fund; bd. dirs. S. Fla. Bapt. Hosp. Served with USN, 1942-45. Named Citizen of Yr., Plant City. Mem. Internat., So. (pres. 1965-66, dir. 1967-68) circulation mgrs. assns., Plant City C. of C. (pres. 1968). Baptist (deacon). Kiwanian. Home: 122 W Beacon Rd Lakeland FL 33803 Office: 101 N Thomas St PO Box K Plant City FL 33566

HANCOCK, JAMES HARVEY, civil engr.; b. N.Y.C., Aug. 31, 1911; s. Daniel Harrison and Sabra Caroline (Short) H.; B.S. in Civil Engring., Auburn U., 1938; m. Lillias Louise Christie, May 26, 1938; children— Sabra (Mrs. Philip Spinolo, Jr.), Sarah Jean (Mrs. Larry Stephens), Caroline (Mrs. Frank Casey, III), Marian, Dan, Imrie. Structural engr. third locks project, sea level studies Panama Canal, 1941-48; cons. engr., civil, structural engr. James H. Hancock Cons. Engr., Memphis, 1948-—. Active Boy Scouts Am. Served with AUS, 1933-34. Registered profl. engr., Tenn., Mo., Ky., Ark., Ala., Miss. Mem. Am. Soc. C.E. Baptist. Home and office: 6323 Limewood St Memphis TN 38128

HANCOCK, JOHANNA BERTHA, speech and hearing therapist; b. Louisville, June 1, 1935; d. James Duffy and Marie (Seelbach) Hancock; student Coll. of Notre Dame, Md., 1953-54, Loyola U. of Los Angeles, summer 1956; B.S. in Speech, Marquette U., 1957; M.A. in Speech Pathology, Cath. U. Am., 1959; postgrad. Western Res. U., summer 1957, M.Md., spring 1958, George Washington U., fall 1958; M.A. in Psychology, U. Louisville, 1967. Speech pathologist and audiologist, Louisville, 1959-—; part-time therapist Rehab. Center, Inc., Louisville, 1957, United Cerebral Palsy of Greater Louisville, 1959-60, Louisville Deaf-Oral Sch., 1959; instr. dept. speech and communications Bellarmine Coll., Louisville, 1959-61, chmn. dept., 1961-62. Cons. therapist Cleft Palate Clinic, Ky. Commn. for Handicapped Children (vol.). Bd. dirs. Jefferson County Med. Soc. Woman's Aux.; mem. Younger Woman's Club of Louisville, Spinsters Cotillion. Recipient certificate appreciation A.R.C.; Distinguished Alumni Achievement award in speech therapy Marquette U., 1966. Mem. Am. (certificates of competence in speech pathology and audiology), Ky. (exec. council), Louisville speech and hearing assns., Internat. Council for Exceptional Children, Speech Assn. Am., Alexander Graham Bell Assn. for Parents and Tchrs. of Deaf, Am. Assn. U. Profs., Am. Hearing Assn., Am. Acad. Pvt. Practitioners in Speech Pathology and Audiology, Psi Chi, Tau Kappa Alpha (hon.), Sigma Alpha Eta (hon.). Mem. Jr. Circle of Queen's Daus. Author publs. in field. Home: 80 Valley Rd Louisville KY 40204 Office: Med Arts Bldg 1169 Eastern Pkwy Louisville KY 40217

HANCOCK, LUCILE R. MUSSELMAN (MRS. WILLIAM S. HANCOCK), banker; b. Waynoka, Okla., Oct. 13, 1915; d. Mahlon M. and Mamie (McGee) Musselman; student Northwestern State Coll., summer 1935, Fla. State Coll. for Women, 1935-36; A.B., Fla. So. Coll., 1939; m. William S. Hancock, May 15, 1966; 1 stepdau., Sandra (Mrs. James B. Wilmot). Head bookkeeper Pasco Packing Co., Dade City, Fla., 1939-44; supr. bookkeeper Bank of Pasco County, Dade City, 1946-65, asst. cashier, auditor, 1960-—. Treas., Cancer Cursade East Pasco County, Dade City, 1967-—. Served with WAVES, 1944-46. Mem. Nat. Assn. Bank Women, Delta Zeta. Methodist. Home: Route 3 Box 330 Dade City FL 33525 Office: PO Box 127 Corner Meridian and 7th Sts Dade City FL 33525

HANCOCK, LYNN DALE, dentist; b. Devils Lake, N.D., Aug. 10, 1906; s. Arthur James and Charlotte (Smith) H.; D.D.S., U. Minn., 1931; postgrad. U. Ky., 1960, U. Md., 1963; m. Wilma Ann Isker, May 25, 1934. Pvt. practice dentistry, Mpls., 1932-41, Hettinger, N.D., 1946-53; commd. capt. Dental Corps, U.S. Army, 1941, discharged, 1946, recalled to active duty, 1953, advanced through ranks to col., 1962, retired, 1966; oral surgeon Osaka (Japan) Army Hosp., 1956-57; oral surgeon, oral diagnostician Tokyo (Japan) Army Hosp., 1957-58; chief dental clinic, Camp Drake, Japan, 1958-59; post dental surgeon, Camp Breckinridge, Ky., 1960; chief dependent and hosp. dental clinics, Ft. Knox, Ky., 1960-61; dep. post dental surgeon, Ft. Polk, La., 1961, post dental surgeon, 1962, 64-66; dental surgeon UN, U.S. Armed Forces and 8th U.S. Army, Korea, 1963-64; test adminstr., student counsellor U.S. Army Ednl. Center, Ft. Polk, La., 1966-72; dir. health services Vernon Parish Schs., Leesville, La., 1967-—; owner (with wife) Candles by Hancock, wholesale and retail candles, Leesville, 1967-—. Mem. La. Oral Health Com., 1970-—, La. Regional Med. Program, 1970-—. Mem. city council City of Hettinger (N.D.), 1946-48. Decorated Army Commendation medal. Fellow Internat. Coll. Dentists; mem. Am. (life), La. (life) dental assns., Psi Omega. Mason, Sojourners. Club: Retired Officers' (pres. 1967-68) (Ft. Polk, La.). Home: Route 6 Box 40 Leesville LA 71446 Office: 201 Belview Rd Leesville LA 71446

HANCOCK, ROBERT THURSTON, chem. engr.; b. Alexcity, Ala., Mar. 13, 1919; s. Virgal A. and LaVell (Salter) H.; B.S. in Chem. Engring., Auburn U., 1942; postgrad. U.S. Army Officer Candidate Sch., 1944-45, U. Ala., 1948-50; m. Helen Estes, June 8, 1963. Chem. engr. process equipment C.W.S., Huntsville (Ala.) Arsenal, 1942-44; with U.S. Bur. Mines, 1948-51; cons. engr., 1951-57, 61-63; with So. Research Inst., 1957-61; chem. engr. U.S. Army Missile Command, Redstone Arsenal, Ala., 1963-—. Dir. Hancock's Jewelry, Bessemer, Ala. Served with CIC, AUS, 1945-47. Mem. Am. Chem. Engring. Soc., Soc. Profl. Engrs. Lion. Club: Civitan. Patentee in high burning rate propellants. Home: 6309 Davies Av Huntsville AL 35806 Office: US Army Missile Command Redstone Arsenal AL 35809

HAND, JOHN ANTHON, banker; b. Rome, Ga., Nov. 18, 1901; s. Thomas Oscar and Berta (Maddox) H.; grad., Sch. Banking, Rutgers U.; student Harvard; m. Eula Elizabeth Gibson, Nov. 1, 1930; children— Barbara Elizabeth, John Anthon. Asst. nat. bank examiner 6th Fed. Reserve Dist., 1924-28; auditor Am. Traders Nat. Bank, Birmingham, Ala., 1928-30; comptroller First Nat. Bank of Birmingham, 1930-38, v.p., 1934-53, exec. v.p., 1953-56, pres., 1956-68, chmn. bd., 1968-—, also dir., dir. Ala. Power Co., Protective Life Ins. Co. of Birmingham. Bd. dirs. Community Chest. Methodist. Rotarian. Club: Birmingham Country. Home: 3822 Cove Dr Birmingham AL 35213 Office: First Nat Bank Birmingham AL 35203

HANDLER, FRANCES CLARK (MRS. FRANK STEVENSON HANDLER), educator, writer, assn. exec.; b. Maplewood, N.H., Feb. 28; d. Frank J. and Marie (Jamia) Clark; B.S. in Bus. Machine Teaching, Boston U., B.B.S. in Accounting, A.B. in Banking and Finance; Litt. D., Internat. Research Socs., U. Asia, Pakistan, 1968; m. Frank Stevenson Handler, Sept. 21, 1946. Instr. accounting Burroughs Sch., Boston, later collaborating writer poetry books, hist. novels, autobiographies, children's books. Lectr. on women's vocations Barry Coll., Miami, Fla., 1965-—; founder, nat. dir. Fla. Nat. Poetry Day Com., 1965-—. Named hon. poet laureate UN Day, Philippines, 1967; recipient over 100 awards and prizes, including King Journalism award, 1972. C.P.A., Mass. Mem. United Poets Laureate Internat. (award, 1967, membership chmn. 1968-—), World (internat. dir.), Fla. (founder, sec., treas. 1965—, editor, pub. Flamingo 1969), Nev. (hon. life) poetry socs., Fla. Arts Council, Ia. Poetry Day Assn. (hon. life). Nat. League Am. Pen Women (treas. Coral Gables, Fla. br. 1963—), Hotel Accountants Assn. (pres. 1947-51). Author: Reina Mercedes, 1956; Canberra, 1957. Contbr. to Ency. of Jazz, 1955, Selected Poems, 1969-71, Memorial Award Books, 1966-71. Editor, designer International Hall of Fame Poets, 4 books, 1969-72, Governor's Book, 1971-72, 9 Muses I and 9 Muses II, 1971. Home: 1110 N Venetian Dr Miami Beach FL 33139

HANDLER, HENRY, govt. ofcl.; b. Newark, July 5, 1911; s. Morris and Sadie (Kaufer) H.; M.E., Stevens. Inst. Tech., 1935; postgrad. Rutgers U., 1938-40; m. Janet Mills Roberts, June 7, 1944; children—Gwendoline Roberts, Henry Morris. Guided missile coordinator Naval Aviation Ordnance Test Sta., Va., 1948-50; with Office Chief Ordnance, Dept. Army, Washington, 1950-62, chief anti-aircraft fire control unit, 1950-56, guided missile coordinator, 1956-59, mech. engr., 1959-60, spl. asst. tech. relations, 1960-62; tech. relations adviser to comdg. gen. U.S. Army Materiel Command, Washington, 1962-72; tech.-mil. adviser Inst. Environmental Scis. Bd. dirs. Inst. Navigation. Served to lt. col. AUS, 1942-46, Decorated Legion of Merit. Recipient certificate of appreciation Soc. Automotive Engrs., 1961, Bronze medallion Am. Ordnance Assn., 1962, certificate of merit Nat. Security Indsl. Assn., 1966, Meritorious Civilian Service award with bronze leaf cluster U.S. Army Materiel Command, 1968. Mem. Am. Ordnance Assn. (nat. dir. 1954-70), Armed Forces Mgmt. Assn. (regional v.p. 1963-70, v.p. programs Nat. Capital chpt. 1967-72, hon. life mem.), Assn. U.S. Army (v.p. George Washington chpt. 1958-72), Soc. Mfg. Engrs., Armed Forces Communications and Electronics Assn., Am. Prodn. and Inventory Control Soc., Am. Inst. Aeros. and Astronautics, Internat. Soc. Terrain Vehicle Systems, Soc. Automotive Engrs. Home: 3504 Perry St Fairfax VA 22030 Office: US Army Materiel Command Bldg T-7 Washington DC 20315

HANDLER, PHILIP, educator; b. N.Y.C., Aug. 13, 1917; s. Jacob and Lena (Heisen) H.; B.S., Coll. City, N.Y., 1936; Ph.D., U. Ill. 1939; D.Sc. (hon.), Case-Western Res. U., Carnegie-Mellon U., Colo. State U., U. N.C., N.Y. Med. Coll., Yeshiva U., Hebrew U. Jerusalem, Temple U., Nova U., U. Wis.; LL.D., Emory U.; m. Lucille P. Marcus, Dec. 6, 1939; children—Mark, Eric Paul. Instr., Duke, 1939-40, asso., 1940-41, asst. prof. physiology, 1941-44, asso. prof. biochemistry and nutrition, 1944-49, prof., 1949—, chmn. dept., 1950-69, James B. Duke prof. biochemistry, 1961—, dir. AEC fellowship tng. program, 1948-53; pres. Nat. Acad. Scis., Washington, 1969—; Distinguished prof. med. scis. George Washington U., 1970—. Cons. USPHS, AEC, NRC, VA; chmn. biochem. study sect. NIH, 1956-59; mem. Nat. Adv. Com. Research Facilities and resources, 1963-67; mem. Nat. Adv. Health Council USPHS, 1959-62; mem. biology and medicine research facilities panel NSF, 1958-61; mem. divisional com. for biology and medicine NSF, 1960-62, Mem. Nat. Sci. Bd., NSF, 1962—, vice chmn., 1964-66, chmn., 1966-70; mem. Pres.'s Sci. Adv. Com., 1964-68, 69—; chmn. com. radiation & aging NIH-U.S. AEC, 1959-62. Dir. E.R. Squibb, Inc., 1967-69. Trustee Found. Advanced Edn. Med. Scis., Cold Spring Harbor Lab. Quantitatives Biology Rockefeller U., Nutrition Found., Hebrew U., Sci. Council Smithsonian Instn.; mem. sci. adv. bd. Scripps Metabolic Clinic, U. Notre Dame, U. Va., Kettering Inst., Johns Hopkins Inst. for Cancer Research. Mem. Unitarian Service Com., Med. Mission to Japan, 1951. Recipient N.C. award Gov. N.C.; Townsend Harris medal Coll. City N.Y.; Distinguished Achievement in Sci. medal A.M.A.; Illini Achievement award U. Ill. Alumni Assn. W.O. Atwater lectr. U.S. Dept. Agr.; Bicentennial lectr. Coll. City N.Y.; Ann. Distinguished lectr. Albany Med. Coll., Cushing Soc., Pa. State Med. Soc., Welch Found., Am. Iron and Steel Inst., Stevens Inst. Tech. Benjamin Franklin fellow Royal Soc. Arts and Scis. Mem. Am. Soc. Biol. Chemists (sec. 1953-57, councilor 1958-61, pres. 1962-63), Am. Acad. Arts. and Scis., Am. Philos. Soc., Fedn. Am. Socs. for Exptl. Biology (exec. com. 1959-66, chmn. bd. 1964-65). Am. Inst. Nutrition, A.A.A.S., Soc. Exptl. Biology and Medicine (pres. S.E. sect. 1953-54), Am. Chem. Soc., N.Y. Acad. Scis. (Chas. B. Mayer award), Nat. Acad. Scis., Sigma Xi; hon. fgn. mem. Swiss, German acads. scis. Club: Cosmos (Washington). Author: Principles of Biochemistry (textbook); also tech. publs. Editor: Biology and the Future of Man; The Life Sciences. Mem. editorial com. Jour. Theoretical Biology 1961-67, Jour. Comparative Biochemistry and Physiology, 1962-65; bd. publs. Jour. Biol. Chemistry, 1965-71; editorial bd. Law and Contemporary Problems, 1967-69; editor Geriatrics, 1957-65. Home: 2700 Virginia Av Washington DC 20037

HANDMAKER, STUART ALLEN, lawyer; b. Louisville, May 27, 1930; s. Sidney David and Ethel Gertrude (Baron) H.; A.B., Stanford, 1952, J.D., 1953; m. Muriel Beton, Aug. 30, 1953; children—Ellen, David, William, Robert. Admitted to Ky. bar, 1953; practiced in Louisville, 1956—; mem. firm Handmaker, Weber & Meyer, attys.-at-law, Louisville, 1956—; sec., dir. Union Trust, Inc., Executone Systems Co. Pres. U.S.O., Jewish Welfare Bd. Armed Services Com., 1961; nat. chmn. leadership devel. Council Jewish Fedn. and Welfare Funds, 1963; pres. Art Center Assn., Inc., Louisville Sch. Art, 1970—. Served with AUS, 1953-56. Mem. Am., Ky., Louisville bar assns., Order of Coif, Phi Beta Kappa, Phi Alpha Delta. Democrat. Jewish religion. Mem. B'nai B'rith. Club: Standard Country (Louisville). Home: Glenview KY 40025 Office: Citizens Plaza Louisville KY 40202

HANEMAN, VINCENT SIERING, JR., cons. engr., educator; b. Orange N.J., Feb. 19, 1924; s. Vincent Siering and Helen (Harris) H.; S.B., Mass. Inst. Tech., 1947; M.S. in Aero. Engring., U. Mich., 1950, Ph.D., 1956; m. Adelaide Russell, Oct. 3, 1961; children—Vincent Siering III, Charles Frederick. Asst. head flight research Project Meteor, Mass. Inst. Tech., 1947-49; project head automatic wind tunnel data reduction U. Mich., 1949-51; head analogue computer research Wright Air Devel. Center, O., 1951-52; asso. prof., asst. dept. head aero. engring. Air Force Inst. Tech., Wright Patterson AFB, O., 1955-59; chief spl. projects div. guidance and control directorate Air Force Ballistic Missile Div., 1959-60; pres., sr. asso. Haneman Assos., Richardson, Tex., 1960-66, 67—; chmn. bd. Haneman Assos., Inc., Richardson, 1961—, exec. v.p., Stillwater, Okla., 1966-67; prof. mech. engring., dir. engring. research, asso. dean engring. Okla. State U., 1966-72; dean engring. Auburn (Ala.) U., 1972—; constrn. flight engr. Simulator project U. Mich., 1952-55; cons. Gen. Electric Co., Gen. Dynamics, Space Tech. Labs., Chance Vought Corp., Ling-Temco-Vought, others. Mem. Army Sci. Adv. Panel, 1967—. Served to 1st lt. USAAF, 1943-45; MTO; to maj. USAF, 1951-60; now brig. gen. Res. Decorated D.F.C. with oak leaf cluster, Air medal with 7 oak leaf clusters, Air Force Commendation medal. Registered profl. engr., Ohio, Okla., Tex. Asso. fellow Am. Inst. Aeros. and Astronautics; mem. Am. Soc. for Engring. Edn. (past sec. mech. div., nat. chmn. aero div., past mem. gen. council, mem. exec. com. engring. research council), Am. Astronautical Soc. (sr.), Am. Helicopter Soc., I.E.E.E., Sigma Xi, Tau Beta Pi, Sigma Tau, Pi Epsilon Gamma, Sigma Nu. Presbyn. (deacon). Contbr. articles on instrumentation, control and guidance, aircraft performance to tech. jours. Home: 1324 N Washington Stillwater OK 74074 Office: Haneman Assos Inc 1324 N Washington Stillwater OK also Auburn Univ Auburn AL 36830

HANES, FRANK BORDEN, author; b. Winston-Salem, N.C., Jan. 21, 1920; s. Robert March and Mildred (Borden) H.; grad. Woodberry Forest Sch. (Va.), 1938; B.A., U. N.C., 1942; m. Barbara Mildred Lasater, Dec. 3, 1942; children—Frank Borden, Nancy (Mrs. Sydnor Montgomery White), Robin March. Columnist, feature writer, reporter, copy editor Winston-Salem Jour. & Sentinel, 1946-49; vice chmn., dir. Mchts. Devel. Co., shopping center, Winston-Salem, 1964—; dir. Chatham Mfg. Co., Elkin, Hanes Dye & Finishing Co., Winston-Salem. Chmn. Com. for Endowed Professorships, U. N.C., 1965-67, Friends of U. N.C. Library, 1966-68, Old Salem, Inc., 1968-70; pres. Winston-Salem Operetta Assn., 1949-50, Winston-Salem Arts Council, 1955-56. Trustee Morehead Found., Chapel Hill, N.C., John W. and Anna Hodgin Hanes Found.; bd. visitors U. N.C. Press. Served with USNR, 1942-45. Recipient first Roanoke Chowan award for poetry N.C. Literary and Hist. Assn., 1953, Sir Walter Raleigh award for fiction, 1961, award Winston-Salem Arts Council, 1957. Mem. P.E.N., N.C. Writers' Conf. (chmn. 1951-52), Order of Gimghoul (pres. 1940-41), Order of Minotaur (pres. 1941-42), Sigma Alpha Epsilon. Rotarian. Clubs: Old Town (Winston-Salem, N.C.); Roaring Gap (N.C.), Cane River (Pensacola, N.C.); Rainbow Springs (Macon County, N.C.). Author: Abel Anders, 1951; The Bat Brothers, 1953; The Fleet Rabble, 1961; Journey's Journal, 1958; Jackknife John, 1964. Home: 2020 Buena Vista Rd Winston-Salem NC 27104

HANES, GORDON, hosiery mfr.; b. Winston-Salem, N.C., Mar. 3, 1916; s. James Gordon and Emmie Holt (Drewry) H.; grad. Woodberry Forest Sch., 1928-33; A.B., Yale, 1937; student Pace Inst., 1937-39; m. Helen Greever Copenhaver, Aug. 30, 1941; children—James Gordon, III, Eldridge C., Margaret Drewry. With Hanes Hosiery, Winston-Salem, 1939-41, sec., 1946-48, v.p., 1948-53, exec. v.p., 1953-57, now chmn.; became pres., chief exec. officer Hanes Corp., 1966, now chmn. bd., dir.; dir. Security Life & Trust Co. Trustee Woodberry Forest Sch.; mem. alumni bd. Yale U. Served as adminstrv. officer Naval Insp. of Ordnance, 1941-45. Mem. Color Assn. U.S., Inc., Nat. Assn. Hosiery Mfrs. (past chmn. bd.). Address: PO Box 1413 Winston-Salem NC

HANES, JOHN CHISMAN, lawyer; b. Pine Hall, N.C., May 26, 1909; s. John Lewis and Eliza Pescud (Chisman) H.; A.B., Duke, 1930, LL.B., 1933; student Harvard Law Sch., 1930-31; m. Laura L. Reeves, May 4, 1940; 1 son, John Chisman. Admitted to N.C. bar, 1933, D.C. bar, 1947; gen. practice law, Raleigh, N.C., 1933-34; mem. legal div. R.F.C., 1934-36, 37-42; asst. to chmn. Atty. Gen's. Adv. Com. on Crime, Dept. Justice, 1936-37; spl. asst. to exec. dir. Office of Def. Plants, R.F.C., 1945-46; practice law, Washington, 1946—. Chmn. nat. council Duke, 1967-68; trustee Episcopal Theol. Sem. Va.; bd. dirs. Alexandria Hosp., St. Stephen's Episcopal Sch. for Boys, Alexandria. Served to maj. USAAF, 1942-45. Mem. Am. (mem. council adminstrv. law sect. 1966-69), D.C., N.C. bar assns., Am. Judicature Soc., Nat. Legal Aid and Defender Assn., Newcomen Soc. Eng., Am. Arbitration Assn. (nat. panel arbitrators), Phi Delta Theta, Phi Delta Phi, Omicron Delta Kappa. Episcopalian. Clubs: Army-Navy, National Lawyers (Washington); Belle Haven Country (Alexandria, Va.). Contbr. articles to profl. jours. Home: 1319 Bishop Lane Alexandria VA 22302 Office: Ring Bldg Washington DC 20036

HANES, LEIGH B., JR., U.S. atty.; b. Roanoke, Va., Apr. 4, 1918; s. Leigh Buckner and Lillian Lee (Thompson) H.; B.A. cum laude, Hampden-Sydney Coll., 1940; LL.B., U. Md., 1948; m. Frances H. Hilton, Nov. 1, 1945; children—Katherine Whitney (Mrs. Mark E. Feldmann), Leigh Thompson, David Hilton. Admitted to Va. bar, 1951, Supreme Ct. bar, 1970; spl. agt. FBI, 1943-49; partner firm Hanes & Hanes, Roanoke, 1951-56; asst. U.S. atty., Roanoke, 1956-59; clk. U.S. Dist. Ct., Western dist. Va., Roanoke, 1960-69; U.S. atty., 1969—. Tchr., Va. Western Community Coll., 1967-69; lectr. Am. Inst. Banking, Roanoke, 1951-56. City councilman, vice mayor, Roanoke, 1953-56. Served with AUS, 1944-46. Mem. Am., Fed., Roanoke bar assns., Am. Judicature Soc., Va. State Bar, Omicron Delta Kappa, Kappa Alpha, Tau Kappa Alpha, Chi Beta Phi, Sigma Upsilon. Republican. Presbyn. (elder). Mason (Shriner). Home: 2814 S Jefferson St Roanoke VA 24014 Office: 222 Federal Bldg Roanoke VA 24008*

HANES, R. PHILIP, JR., textile dyeing co. exec.; b. Winston-Salem, N.C., Feb. 25, 1926; s. Ralph Philip and Dewitt (Chatham) H.; grad. Woodberry Forest Sch. 1944; student U. N.C., 1944-46; B.A., Yale, 1949; m. Joan Audrey Humpstone, Jan. 14, 1950. Vice pres. Hanes Dye & Finishing Co., Winston-Salem, 1962-63, exec. v.p., 1963-65, pres., 1965-68, chmn. bd., 1968—. Mem. adv. com. Kennedy Center for Performing Arts, Washington, 1962-65; mem. N.C. Recreation Commn., 1962-65; bd. dirs. Moravian Music Found., Winston-Salem, 1963-65; vice chmn. Winston-Salem Community Center Fund Drive, 1957, Salem Coll. Arts Center Drive, 1962-63, N.C. Sch. for Arts Drive, 1964-65; vice chmn. Winston-Salem Total Devel. Commn. 1960-62; Bd. dirs. Forsyth Econ. Devel. Corp., 1969-71, Winston-Salem Symphony, 1956-66, Winston-Salem Arts Council Endowment Fund, Film Friends; trustee Sparta Hosp., 1956, Elkin Hosp., Chatham Meml. Hosp., 1956, Salem Coll., 1961-64; trustee, mem. exec. com. N.C. Sch. for Arts; bd. visitors Barter Theatre, State Theatre Va., 1967—, 1966—; bd. dirs. Winterhur, 1972—; chmn. com. music sch. Yale U. Council. Served to lt. USNR, 1950-52. Recipient Arts Council award, 1960; named Young Man of Yr., N.C., Winston-Salem Jaycees, 1958; Gov.'s award for preservation natural areas, 1969. Asso. fellow Jonathan Edwards Coll., Yale U., 1971—. Life fellow Royal Soc. Arts; mem. Boston Mycol. Soc., Arts Councils Am. (pres. 1964-66), Nat. Council on Arts (mem. adv. music panel 1970-72), Tri-States (pres. 1959-61), N.C. (chmn. 1964-67), Winston-Salem (v.p. 1963-64) arts councils, N.C. Arts Soc., N.Y. Classical Guitar Soc., Wilderness Soc., Newcomen Soc. N. Am., Asso. Artists N.C., Ducks Unltd., Sierra Club, N.C. Collectors, Trout Unltd., ANTA, Young Pres. Orgn. (arts dean 1967, 70), Am. Crafts Council (nat. adv. com. 1970—), Jargon Soc. (pres. 1968—), Am. Assn. Museums, Am. Symphony Orch. League (dir. 1958-61), Nat. Audubon Soc. (dir. 1972—), Delta Kappa Epsilon. Methodist (steward 1960). Rotarian. Clubs: Piedmont, Appalachian Trail (nat. adv. com. 1970—) (Greensboro, N.C.); Currituck (Jarvisburg, N.C.); Cane River (Burnsville, N.C.); Yale (N.Y.C.); Twin City, Old Town (Winston-Salem); Roaring Gap (N.C.). Home: Box 749 Winston-Salem NC 27102 Office: Buxton St Winston-Salem NC 27102

HANES, THOM FITZHUGH, banker; b. Washington, May 3, 1936; s. Stanley Bartlett and Helen Lee (Crippen) H.; B.A., Hampden-Sydney Coll., 1958; m. Elizabeth Dean Barnes, Mar. 10, 1965; 1 dau., Ashley Elizabeth. Dep. clk. county and circuit ct. Circuit Ct. Fairfax County, Va., 1960-61; teller Nat. Bank Fairfax (Va.), 1961-63; teller, Citizens Nat. Bank, Herndon, Va., 1963-65, asst. cashier, 1965-69, v.p., 1969—, also dir. Sec.-treas. Sully Hist. Found., 1966—; sec.-treas., dir. Sully Found., Ltd., 1971—. Del. Fairfax Democratic Central Com., 1963. Mem. Herndon Jr. C. of C. (state dir. 1964, pres. 1965). Rotarian. Home: 303 Van Buren St Herndon VA 22070 Office: 40 Station St Herndon VA 22070

HANEY, JAMES WESLEY, bldg. contractor; b. Beaumont, Tex., July 31, 1931; s. William Clyde and Clara Neches (Vanover) H.; student Lamar Jr. Coll., 1948-49; B.S., Tex. A. and M. Coll., 1953; m. Frances Evelyn Thompson, Aug. 19, 1961; children—James Beaumont, Scott Thompson, Brett Wesley. Purchasing agt. Herman Weber, Inc., Beaumont, Tex., 1955-57; estimator T.D. Howe Constrn. Co., Inc., Houston, 1957-59, Gene Murphree, Inc., Houston, 1959-60; constrn. mgr. Gen. Apt. Co., Atlanta, 1960-70; pres. bldg. contractor Haney Constrn. Co., Inc., Atlanta, 1970—. Mem. phys. edn. com. YMCA, 1966-70. Served to 1st lt. USAF, 1953-55. Named Home Builder of Yr. Home Builders Assn. Met. Atlanta, 1969. Mem. Nat. Assn. Home Builders (nat. dir. 1968-71), Atlanta Apt. Assn. (pres. 1967-68), Home Builders Assn. Met. Atlanta (pres. 1970-71). Home: 8990 River Run Atlanta GA 30338 Office: 1401 W Paces Ferry Rd NW Atlanta GA 30327

HANFT, RUTH S. SAMUELS (MRS. HERBERT HANFT), govt. ofcl.; b. N.Y.C., July 12, 1929; d. Max Joseph and Ehtel ((Schechter) Samuels; B.S., Cornell U., 1949; M.A., Hunter Coll., 1963; m. Herbert Hanft, June 17, 1951; children— Marjorie Jane, Jonathan Mark. Cons. Urban Med. Econs. Project, Hunter Coll., N.Y.C. and D.C. Dept. of Health, 1962-63; health economist Office of Research and Statistics, Social Security Adminstrn., Washington, 1964-66; chief grants mgmt., health div. Office of Econ. Opportunity, Washington, 1966-68; sr. health analyst Office of Asst. Sec. Planning and Evaluation, Dept. Health, Edn. and Welfare, Washington, 1968—, spl. asst. to asst. sec. health, 1971-72; sr. research asso. Nat. Inst. Medicine, Nat. Acad. Scis. Fellow Am. Pub. Health Assn.; mem. Royal Soc. Health. Jewish religion. Contbr. articles to profl. jours. Home: 1412 Ivanhoe St Alexandria VA 22304 Office: 2101 Constitution Av NW Washington DC 20201

HANGER, BOB GRANT, pub. relations exec.; b. Huntington, W.Va., May 18, 1934; s. Theodore Otis and Percie Lee (Tucker) H.; student Marshall U., 1951, U. Va., 1962-64; m. Ruth Ann Suiter, Nov. 24, 1960 children—Pamela Diane, Robert, Connie Sue, Robbie Lee, Rhonda Lynn, Roni Lea. Broadcaster, exec. WINA radio-TV, Charlottesville, Va., 1960—; sales and pub. relations exec. Charlottesville Broadcasting Corp., 1960—; group talent mgr. Bee-Gee Enterprises, Charlottesville, 1961—; nat. sales mgr. Bee-Gee Prodns., Charlottesville, 1961—; pres. Bee-Gee Records Div., 1963—, Music Div., 1962—; cons. Dogwood Festival, 1962-65, Hillbilly Pub. Co., 1964—; dir. Bee-Gee Prodns. Talent Agy., Cottonhill Pub. Co. Cons. Cherry River Festival, Richwood, W.Va., 1969—. Nat. sec. U. Hard Knocks, Inc., 1965-68. Mem. East Coast Talent Soc. (dir. 1964—), Va. Soc. Country and Folk Music, Nat. Assn. Broadcasters, Am. Soc. Notaries. Republican. Presbyn. Kiwanian (dir. 1963—). Club: Ruritan (pub. relations dir. Earlysville 1972). Home: 4010 Tompkins Dr Charlottesville VA 22901 Office: Jefferson Village Route 4 Charlottesville VA 22901

HANHAUSEN, FERNANDO, lawyer; b. Mexico City, 1921; ed. French prep. sch. Admitted to Mexican bar, 1944; now mem. firm Hardin, Hess, Santos Galindo & Hanhausen, Mexico City. Address: Hardin Hess Santos Galindo & Hanhausen Cale Lopez No 1 Mexico DF Mexico*

HANKINS, FRANK DALE, librarian; b. Harlingen, Tex., Mar. 1, 1922; s. Archie Bonner and Mary Alma (Taylor) H.; B.J., U. Tex. at Austin, 1949, M.L.S., 1951; m. Margaret Frances Bragg, Sept. 1, 1950. Librarian, Montavilla br. library, Library Assn. Portland, Ore., 1951-52; librarian Parsons (Kan.) Pub. Library, 1952-55; asst. librarian Wichita (Kan.) City Library, 1955-58; librarian Del Mar Coll., Corpus Christi, Tex., 1958—. Bd. dirs. OPUS Inc. conservation, Corpus Christi, 1968—. Served with M.C., AUS, 1942-46. Mem. Tex. (pres., 1966-67; chmn. intellectual freedom com. 1963-65), Am., Southwestern library assns., Tex. Jr. Coll. Tchrs. Assn. (chmn. library sect. 1962-63), Tex. Assn. Ednl. Technology. Democrat. Methodist. Home: 721 Crestview St Corpus Christi TX 78412

HANKINSON, JOHN CRIMMINS, JR., banker; b. Waynesboro, Ga. Oct. 14, 1933; s. John Crimmins and Sara (Blount) H.; B.S., Clemson U., 1955; grad. Sch. Banking of South, La. State U., 1964, S.C. Bankers Sch., 1965; m. Shirley Davis Aug. 16, 1955; children—Mona Lane, Ann Crimmins. Mgmt. trainee S.C. Nat. Bank, Greenville, 1957-59, adminstrv. asst., Sumter, 1959-60, asst. cashier, Cheraw, 1960-63, asst. v.p., sr. officer, Bennettsville, 1963-67, v.p. internat. banking div., Columbia, 1967-71, v.p. adminstrn. nat. banking div., 1971—. Pres., Bennettsville Parking and Devel. Co., 1965-67. Chmn. Pee Dee Area chpt. Nat. Found. March Dimes, 1966-67; chmn. S.C. edn. funds crusade S.C. div. Am. Cancer Soc., 1969-70, treas. S.C. div., 1970-72; vice chmn. S.C. Regional Export Expansion Council, 1969-73. Served with AUS, 1956. Presbyn. Home: 3147 Travis Ct Columbia SC 29204 Office: 1241 Main St Columbia SC 29202

HANN, JOHN ROBERT, oral surgeon, army officer; b. Maryville, Mo., Nov. 3, 1933; s. John Ramsy and Wilda (Jones) H.; B.A., Baker U., 1955; D.D.S., U. Kansas City, 1959; postgrad. Georgetown U., 1966-67; m. Dorothy Lou Kochan, June 8, 1956; children—John Michael, Karen Lea. Dental intern Womack Army Hosp., Ft. Bragg, N.C., 1959-60; commd. 2d lt. U.S. Army, 1958, advanced through grades to lt. col., 1968; dental officer, Ft. Lawton, Wash., 1960-62, Hawaii, 1962-66; resident oral surgery Inst. Dental Research Walter Reed Army Med. Center, Washington, 1966-67, Womack Army Hosp., 1967-69; oral surgeon, chief dept. dentistry 121th Evacuation Hosp., Korea, 1969-70; oral surgeon, chief dept. dentistry, Ft. Gordon, Ga., 1970—; cons. in field. Diplomate Am. Bd. Oral Surgery. Mem. Am. Dental Assn., Am. Soc. Oral Surgeons, Omicron Kappa Upsilon, Xi Psi. Home: 3103 Shelley Ct Augusta GA 30904 Office: Dental Activities MEDDAC Fort Gordon GA 30905

HANNA, THOMAS LOUIS, educator; b. Waco, Tex., Nov. 21, 1928; s. John Dwight and Winifred (Beaumier) H.; B.A., Tex. Christian U., 1949; B.D., U. Chgo.,1954, Ph.D., 1958; m. Susan Taff, May 10, 1951; children—Mary Alice, Michael John, Wendell France. Dir., Jean de Beauvais Student Refugee Club, U. Paris, 1951-52; dir. boys div. Notre Maison Orphanage, Brussels, Belgium, 1952-53; asso. prof., chmn. dept. philosophy Hollins (Va.) Coll., 1958-64, dir. overseas study program, Paris, 1961-62; writer-in-residence Duke, 1964-65; prof., chmn. dept. philosophy U. Fla., Gainesville, 1965—. Am. Council Learned Socs. fellow, 1968-69. Mem. Am. Philos. Assn., Internat. Assn. for Humanistic Psychology, Modern Lang. Assn. Author: The Thought and Art of Albert Camus, 1958; The Bergsonian Heritage, 1963; The Lyrical Existentialists, 1963; Bodies in Revolt, 1970. Home: 518 NE 4th Av Gainesville FL 32601

HANNAH, JOHN ALFRED, govt. ofcl.; b. Grand Rapids, Mich., Oct. 9, 1902; s. Wilfred Steele and Mary Ellen (Malone) H.; student Grand Rapids Jr. Coll., 1919-21, U. Mich., 1921-22; B.S., Mich. State U., 1923, D.Agr. (hon.), 1941; LL.D., U. Mich., 1944; HH.D., U. Ryukyus, 1952; L.H.D., U. Fla., 1953, U. Md., 1966, U. Americas, 1970; D.Sc., Mich. Tech. U., 1953, U. Nigeria, 1961, Tri-State Coll., 1967; LL.D., U. R.I., 1954, Central Mich. U., 1955, Albion Coll., 1957, Colo. State U., 1963, Alma Coll., 1964, U. Me., 1965, Ariz. State U., 1966, Howard U., 1966, Western Mich. U., 1967, Oakland U., 1969, U. Notre Dame, 1970, U. Akron, 1970; A.A., Northwood Inst., 1963; Litt.D., No. Mich. Coll., 1957, Grand Valley State Coll., 1968, Ohio U., 1969, Hope Coll., 1970; Hon. Prof. School of Business,

Sao Paulo, Brazil, 1960; 1966; m. Sarah May Shaw, June 22, 1938; children—Mary Elisabeth, Robert W., Thomas A., David H. Extension specialist poultry husbandry Mich. State U., 1923-33, sec. bd. trustees, 1933-41, pres. univ., 1941-69; adminstr. U.S. AID, Washington, 1969—; mng. agt. Fed Hatchery Co-ordinating Com., Kansas City, Mo., 1933-35; asst. sec. of def. for manpower and personnel Dept. Def., 1953-54. Chmn. bd. Overseas Pvt. Investment Corp., 1970. Mem. Nat. 4-H Service com.; del. Mich. Contl. Conv., 1961-62. Bd. dirs. Mich. United Fund, 1955—, Am. Council Edn., Nutrition Found.; mem. ednl. policies commn. N.E.A.-Am. Assn. Sch. Adminstrs.; U.S. del. World's Poultry congresses, 1930, 33, 36, 48; chmn. U.S. Civil Rights Commn., 1957-69; mem. Internat. Devel. Adv. Bd., Point IV, 1950-52; past chmn. U.S. sect. Permanent Joint Bd. on Def., Can.-U.S.; trustee Inter-Am. Social Devel. Inst., 1970. Recipient Medal of Freedom, 1954. Mem. Assn. State Univs. and Land-Grant Colls. (past pres., past chmn. exec. com.), Found. European Ednl. Centers, Electoral Coll. Hall of Fame, Newcomen Soc., Detroit Com. Fgn. Relations, Atlantic Council, Edn. and World Affairs Assn. (orignal trustee; dir.), Pres.'s Profl. Assn., Phi Eta Sigma, Alpha Pi Omega, Phi Kappa Phi, Sigma Delta Chi, Pi Kappa Delta, Alpha Zeta. Mason, Rotarian. Clubs: Lansing (Mich.) Country; University (N.Y.C.); Cosmos (Washington); Detroit, Detroit Athletic, Economic, University (Detroit). Author numerous tech. bulletins. Home: The Colonnade 2801 New Mexico Av NW Washington DC 20007 Office: USAID Washington DC 20523

HANNAH, MARGERY E., govt. research engr.; b. Lewiston, Ida., Mar. 11, 1911; d. William J. and Phoebe (John) Hanna; B.A., Williamette U,, 1932; M.S. in Edn., U, Ida., 1938, postgrad, U. Wash., summers 1938-39, tng. program NASA. Tchr., 1933-39; computer Langley Research Lab. NASA, Langley Field, Va., 1930-43, mathematician, 1943-51, aero, research scientist, 1951-56, aero. research engr., 1956-58; aero. research engr. NASA, Langley AFB, Va,, 1958-61, aerospace technologist, 1961-62, aerospace engr., 1962—. Recipient alumni citation for outstanding achievement Williamette U., 1968. Mem. Am. Assn. U. Women (dir. Hampton Va. 1952-57, 59-61, pres. 1955-57, 1st v.p. Va. div. 1968—), Sci. Research Soc. Am. Methodist. Author govt. tech. papers. Home: 138 Yeardley Dr Newport News VA 23502 Office: NASA Langley Research Center Langley AFB VA 23365

HANNAN, PHILIP MATTHEW, archbishop; b. Washington, May 20, 1913; s. Patrick F. and Lillian Louise (Keefe) H.; student St. Charles Coll., 1931-33; A.B., Cath. U., 1935, M.A., 1936, J.C.D., 1949; student North Am. Coll., 1936-40; S.T.B., S.T.L., Gregorian U., Rome, 1940. Ordained priest Roman Catholic Ch., 1939; clerical appointment St. Thomas Aquinas Ch., Balt., 1940-42; student Cath. U., 1946-49, vice chancellor, 1948-51, chancellor, 1951-62, vicar gen., 1960-65; archbishop of New Orleans, 1965—; adminstr. St. Patrick's Ch., Washington 1951-56, pastor, 1956-65; aux. bishop Archdiocese of Washington, 1956-65; editor-in-chief Cath. Standard, 1951-65. Mem. administrv. bd. U.S. Cath. Conf., chmn. dept. communications. Mem. White House Conf. on Children and Youth. Trustee Cath. U. Am., United Fund New Orleans. Served as chaplain USAAF, 1942-46. Address: 7887 Walmsley Av New Orleans LA 70125

HANNAY, ALLEN BURROUGHS, dist. judge; b. Hempstead, Tex. Feb. 14, 1892; s. Robert Edwards and Katherine Donaldson (Allen) H.; student Tex. A. and M. Coll., 1907-09, LL.B., U. Tex., 1931; m. Frances Edna Johnson, July 16, 1918; children—Helen Johnson (Mrs. Ralph C. Dixon), Allen Burroughs. Admitted to Tex. bar June 10, 1913; practiced in Hempstead and Houston, Tex., 1913-30; judge Waller County, 1915-17; apptd. dist. judge 113th Dist. of Tex., 1930; U.S. dist judge So. Dist. Tex., Houston, 1942—. Dir. Lorain Coal & Dock Co., Columbus, O. Served in USAF, 1917-18. Mem. Am., Houston, Fed., Galveston bar assns., State Bar Tex., Delta Sigma Phi. Mason (32 deg. Shriner), Elk (past pres. Tex.). Clubs: Houston A and M, River Oaks County (Houston). Home: 4001 Ella Lee Lane Houston TX 77027 Office: Federal and US Courts Bldg Houston TX 77002

HANNIFIN, JERRY BERNARD, mag. correspondent; b. Boise, Ida., Apr. 5, 1917; s. John B. and Isabella (Munn) H.; B.A., U. Cal. at Berkeley, 1943; m. Rieck Kerber, June 24, 1963; 1 dau., Consuelo (Mrs. Donald Scardino). Reporter, Boise (Ida.) Capitol News, 1938-39; United Press staff corr. West Coast, Mexico Central Am., 1939-46; corr. Time, Inc., Washington, 1947—, chief of bur., U.S., Latin Am., Europe, 1947-69. Past pub. mem. adv. com. Daniel and Florence Guggenheim Found. for Air Safety. Mem. Aviation-Space Writers Assn. (v.p. 1956—), Nat. Aviation Club (v.p. 1967-69), Soc. Air Safety Investigators, Assn. des Amis de Musee de l'Air (France). Roman Catholic. Home: 1500 Massachusetts Av NW Washington DC 20005 Office: 888 16th St NW Washington DC 20006

HANNON, RAYMOND EDWARD, computer co. exec.; b. Youngstown, O., Oct. 25, 1935; s. John Michael and Opal Lorena (Reitz) H.; B.Sc., McGill U., 1955. Research asst. Canadian Pacific Ry., Montreal, 1955-59; asst. pub. Calgary Albertan, 1959-61; pub. relations officer Burroughs Corp., Pasadena, Cal., 1961-63; dir. communication C-E-I-R, Inc., Washington, 1963-66; v.p. Univ. Computing Co., Dallas, 1966—. Mem. Pub. Relations Soc. Am., Nat. Assn. Passenger Traffic Officers, Nat. Assn. R.R. Passengers. Home: 4716 Westchester Mall Dallas TX 75219 Office: UCC Tower 7200 Stemmons Freeway Dallas TX 75247

HANOR, EUGENE BERTRAM, artist; b. Hot Springs, Ark., Oct. 26, 1905; s. Sebastian Montague and Jennie Bell (Cook) H.; student Chgo. Acad. Art, 1925-27, Chgo. Art Inst., 1930-31, Am. Acad. Art, 1935; m. Muriel Louise Tourssen, Mar. 23, 1932; children—Jeffrey S., John B. Illustrator, Chgo. Studio, 1928-29; illustrator, art editor Dog World Mag., Chgo., 1930-35; illustrator Am. Research Corp., 1935-40; illustrator, art dir., buyer Buchen Advt., Inc., Chgo., 1940-68; one-man shows at So. Artists Galleries, Hot Springs, Ark., Ark. State Festival of Arts, 1972; exhibited in group shows at Chgo. Daily News, So. Artists Assn., Ark. Art Center Little Rock (Ark. Pub. Library); represented in numerous pvt. collections. Art dir., bd. dirs. So. Artists Galleries, Hot Springs, Ark., 1969-71. Recipient 1st awards Ark. State Festival Arts, 1969, 70, 71; 1st award S.E. Ark. Arts & Sci. Center, 1970. Mem. Jamestowne Soc,, S.A.R., So. Artists Assn., Mid-So. Water Colorists. Address: 101 Terryland Dr Hot Springs AR 71901

HANRY, CAROLYN KAY OWENS (MRS. ROBERT EARL HANRY), banker; b. El Dorado, Ark., Dec. 8, 1947; d. Clinton Willie and Maurice (Pepper) Ayers; student pub. schs.; m. Robert Earl Hanry, June 31, 1966; children—Lesia Kay, Kimberly Carol. With Union State Bank, Junction City, Ark., 1965—, asst. cashier, 1966-68, cashier, 1968—. Baptist. Home: 707 S Main St Junction City AR 71749 Office: Box F Junction City AR 71749

HANS, IRLINE COEN (MRS. CLIFFORD J. HANS), oil producing co. exec.; b. Sunflower County, Miss. June 7, 1919; d. Claudius C. and Mary Ann (Hooker) Coen; student Copiah-Lincoln Jr. Coll., 1938-39, Blue Mountain Coll., 1939-40; m. Clifford J. Hans., Oct. 18, 1957. Sec., Nat. Def. Office, Tupelo, Miss. 1941; bookkeeper Crippled Children's Service, sec. Vocational Ednl. Dept., Miss. Dept. Edn., Jackson, 1941, sec. high sch. supr., 1942; sec. Vaughey & Vaughey Ind. Oil Producers, 1942-47, tax accountant, 1944-47, office mgmt., personnel supr., 1947-57, exec. sec. to mgmt., 1957—; participating partner, exec. sec. Vaughey, Blackburn & Vaughey Pipeline Co., 1958—; sec.-treas. Sonora Devel. Corp., 1959—, also dir. Comml. inst. Nat. Youth Adminstrn., Tupelo, 1941. Dist. chmn. Oil Industry Information Com., 1957-58; state chmn. for women Natural Gas and Oil Resources Com., 1955-56. Mem. U.D.C., Exec. Secs., Inc. (charter mem. Jackson, dir. 1957). Methodist. Clubs: Jackson Country, Desk and Derrick (pres. 1951-52). Home: 1565 E Meadowbrook Rd Jackson MS 39211 Office: PO Box 4268 4001 Northview Dr Jackson MS 39216

HANSEN, ALICE MCBRIDE, med. librarian; b. Pitts., June 6, 1898; d. Homer James and Victoria (Vaughan) McBride; A.B., Vassar Coll., 1919; B.L.S., Columbia, 1920; Ed.M., Harvard, 1932; m. Robert Arthur Hansen, Oct. 13, 1923; 1 son, Wilbur Vaughan. Cataloger for Columbia U. Library, 1922-24; current periodicals asst. N.Y. Pub. Library, 1922-24; tchr., librarian Irwin (Pa.) High Sch., 1925-27, Munhall High Sch., 1927-28; librarian Slippery Rock State Tchrs. Coll., Pa., 1928-42. Pa. Coll. Women, 1942-51, Rollins Coll., 1951-69; med. librarian Winter Park (Fla.) Meml. Hosp., 1969—. Mem. Am., Fla., Southeastern library assns., Fla. Med. Librarians, Pi Gamma Mu, Sigma Tau Delta. Methodist. Clubs: Vassar of Central Florida; Zonta, Central Florida Harvard. Home: 1551 Lasbury Av Winter Park FL 32789

HANSEN, CHAN FREDRIC, computer co. exec.; b. Salt Lake City, Jan. 28, 1932; s. Conrad John Zahl and Rose Elvina (Christensen) H.; B.S. in E.E., U. Utah, 1958; M.S. in E.E., Seattle U., 1961; m. Shirley Jensen, Nov. 25, 1954; children—Barry Dean, Scott Fredric. Engr., Boeing Co., Seattle, 1958-64, supr., Huntsville, Ala., 1964-70; br. mgr. Boeing Computer Services, Huntsville, Ala., 1970—. Served with USAF, 1950-53. Recipient Manned Flight Awareness award Boeing Corp.-NASA. Registered profl. engr., Ala. Mem. Boeing Mgmt. Assn. (v.p. 1971). Club: Burningtree Country (Decatur, Ala.). Home: 710 Esslinger Rd Huntsville AL 35802 Office: PO Box 1680 Huntsville AL 35807

HANSEN, DONALD VERNON, govt. ofcl.; b. Seattle, Jan. 18, 1931; s. Vernon Arthur and Dolores (Wahl) H.; B.S., U. Wash., 1954, M.S., 1961, Ph.D., 1964; m. Eva Busemann, Aug. 23, 1958; children—Peter, Norman, Christa. Engr., Boeing Airplane Co., Seattle, 1956-57; tchr. Seattle Pub. Schs., 1957-58; research asst. prof. U. Wash. at Seattle, 1964-65; writer Earth Sci. Curriculum Project, Boulder, Colo., 1965-66; oceanographer Environmental Sci. Services Adminstrn., U.S. Dept. Commerce, Silver Spring, Md., 1966-67, Miami, Fla., 1967-70, dir. Phys. Oceanographic Lab., Atlantic Oceanographic and Meteorol. Labs., Nat. Oceanic and Atmospheric Adminstrn., Miami, 1970—; adj. prof. U. Miami, 1970—. Served with AUS, 1954-56. Mem. Am. Soc. Limnology and Oceanography, Am. Geophys. Union, Sigma Xi. Asso. editor Jour. Geophys. Research, 1966-68. Home: 5900 SW 104th St Miami FL 33150 Office: US Dept Commerce 15 Rickenbacker Causeway Miami FL 33130

HANSEN, HOBART GARFIELD, hosp. dir.; b. Hancock, N.Y., Aug. 10, 1923; s. Hobart Garfield and Dorothy (Nielsen) H.; A.B., Columbia, 1945, M.A., 1946; M.D., U. Va., 1957; m. Archer Ellis, Sept. 3, 1949; children—Christian Stowe, Margaret Ellis. Intern research psychology N.Y. State Psychiat. Inst. and Hosp., 1945-46; intern clin. psychology N.Y. State Dept. Mental Hygiene, 1946-47; clin. psychologist Elmira (N.Y.) Reception Center and Elmira Reformatory, 1947-51; chief psychologist Western State Hosp., Staunton, Va., 1951-53; med. intern Va. Hosp., 1957-58; staff physician Western State Hosp., 1958-60; resident psychiatry St. Elizabeth's Hosp., Washington, 1960-63; clin. dir. Western State Hosp., 1963-65, asst. supt., 1965-67, supt., 1967—; clin. instr. psychiatry U. Va. Sch. Medicine, 1965-69, asst. prof., 1969—. Mem. Am. Psychiat. Assn., A.M.A., Am. Hosp. Assn., Assn. Med. Supts. Mental Hosps. Home: 148 Fallon St Staunton VA 24401 Office: 301 Greenville Av VA 24401

HANSEN, NILES MAURICE, educator; b. Louisville, Jan. 2, 1937; s. Kristian and Alma (Jensen) H.; B.A., Centre Coll. Ky., 1958; M.A., Ind. U., 1959, Ph.D., 1963; m. Josephine Drescher, Aug. 22, 1959; children— Karen, Eric, Laura. Mem. research staff Center for Regional Econs., Ghent (Belgium) U., 1961-62; asst. prof. econs. U. Tex. at Austin, 1963-65, prof. econs., dir. center for econ. devel., 1969—; prof. econs. U. Ky. at Lexington, 1967-69; dir. research project Dept. Labor and Econ. Devel. Adminstrn., Dept. Commerce, 1967—. NSF fellow U. Paris (France), 1965-66. Mem. Am., So. econ. assns., Assn. Comparative Econs., Regional Sci. Assn., Assn. French Speaking Regional Economists. Author: French Regional Planning, 1968; France in the Modern World, 1969; Rural Poverty and the Urban Crisis, 1970; Intermediate-Size Cities as Growth Centers, 1971; Growth Centers and Regional Devel., 1972. Contbr. profl. jours. Home: 4003 Tablerook Dr Austin TX 78731 Office: Dept Econs U Tex Austin TX 78712

HANSEN, NILS ERLING, cons. engr.; b. New Orleans, July 28, 1931; s. Hans Trygve and Hanna (Hansen) H.; B.S., Tulane U., 1953; m. Johanna Reinetta Wristers, May 13, 1960; children—Norman Trygve, Helen Reinetta, Jon Erling. Chief engr. T. Hansen Constrn., Inc. New Orleans, 1956-62; design engr. Prescott Follett & Assos., New Orleans, 1962-66; prin. N. E. Hansen & Assos., Cons. Engrs., New Orleans, 1966-70; chief engr. Petro-Marine Engring., Inc., 1970—; pres. T. Hansen Constrn., Inc., New Orleans, 1962—. Chmn. bd. trustees Norwegian Seamen's Mission, New Orleans. Served to lt.(j.g.) USCG, 1953-56; comdr. Res. Decorated St. Olav's medal (Norway); recipient Achievement medal U.S. Coast Guard, 1970. Mem. Am. Soc. C.E., Mil. Order World Wars, U.S. Naval Inst., U.S. Coast Guard Officers Assn., Norseman's League, Sons of Norway, Soc. Tulane Engrs., La. Engring. Soc., Res. Officers Assn. (pres. 1969-71). Home: 6707 Canal Blvd New Orleans LA 70124 Office: 1141 Whitney Av Gretna LA 70053

HANSING, FRANK DETLEFF, govt. ofcl.; b. Bonfield, Ill., Nov. 25, 1919; s. John Henry and Anna (Krueger) H.; student Ill. State U., 1937-40; B.S., U. Ill., 1941, M.S., 1947, Ph.D., 1954; m. Frances B. Koch, Apr. 25, 1943; children—Kenneth E., David F. Tchr. high sch. Hinckley, Ill., 1941-42; with U.S. Dept. Agr., Va. Poly. Inst., 1948-55, U. Del., 1955-56, Agr. Research Service, Washington, 1956-62; with NASA Hdqrs., Washington, 1962—, chief tng. div. Office Grants and Research Contracts, 1962-68, dir. sustaining univ. program Office Univ. Affairs, 1968-71, dir. Office Univ. Affairs, 1971—. Active Boy Scouts Am., 1955-65. Served with USNR, 1942-46. Recipient Scouters Key, 1961. Mem. Gamma Sigma Delta. Methodist. Contbr. profl. jours. Home: 9701 Cedar Lane Bethesda MD 20014 Office: Office of Univ Affairs NASA Hdqrs Washington DC 20546

HANSON, CLARENCE BLOODWORTH, JR., publisher; b. Augusta, Ga., Nov. 7, 1908; s. Clarence Bloodworth and Harriet (Pinkham) H.; student Richmond Acad., Augusta, Ga., 1921-25, B.S., U. Va., 1930; m. Elizabeth Fontaine Fletcher, Sept. 9, 1929; 1 son, Victor Henry II. Advt. dept. Indpls. Star, 1929-30; with advt. dept. Birmingham (Ala.) News, 1930-34, nat. advt. mgr., 1934-37, asst. advt. dir., 1937-42, pub., 1945; pres., dir., mem. exec. com. The Birmingham News Co. (pubs. Birmingham News, Huntsville Times, Agent, Birmingham Post-Herald); v.p., dir. Mercury Express, Inc.; dir., mem. exec. com. First Nat. Bank Birmingham, Ala. Bancorp., Hayes Internat. Corp.; chmn. exec. com., dir. Royal Crown Cola Co. Bd. dirs. Birmingham Mus. of Art; trustee Alabama Mus. Natural History, Eye Found. Hosp. Served as maj. AC, AUS, 1942-45. Mem. Asso. Press (v.p. 1953-56), Am., So. (pres. 1950) newspaper pubs. assns., Ala. Press Assn. (pres. 1951), Phi Gamma Delta. Episcopalian. Clubs: Mountain Brook County, Birmingham Country, Relay House (Birmingham); Grolier (N.Y.C.). Home: 4055 Old Leeds Rd Mountain Brook Birmingham AL 35213 Office: 2200 4th Av N Birmingham AL 35203

HANSON, GARNER BLANTON, hotel co. exec.; b. Edmonson County, Ky., Jan. 17, 1924; s. Carl Irvin and Agnes S. (Doyle) H.; student Syracuse U., 1943, U. Ill., 1944; B.S., Bowling Green Coll. Commerce (now Western Ky. U.), 1949; m. Jacquetta Jackman, Dec. 26, 1955; 1 dau., Julie Leigh. Account clk. Hermitage Hotel, Nashville, 1942; with Nat. Park Concessions, Inc., 1946—, office mgr. accounting dept., 1949-53, mgr. Rock Harbor Lodge, Isle Royale Nat. Park, Mich., 1953-54, mgr. Blue Ridge Pkwy. operations, 1954, Mt. McKinley Nat. Park Hotel, Mt. McKinley, Alaska, 1955-58, pres., gen. mgr. Nat. Park Concessions, Inc., 1958—; dir. Park City State Bank (Ky.); dir., sec., treas. Park City Civil Improvement Corp., 1964—. Trustee Ky. Travel Council. Served with USAAF, 1943-45. Mem. Hotel Greeters (pres. Ky. chpt. 1956-57, pres. Mid-So. Regional chpt. 1956-57), Ky. (dir., treas. 1964—, pres. 1961-63, legislative chmn. 1968—), Am. (quality invironment com. 1966—, exec. bd. 1966-67, Merit award 1967) hotel and motel assns., Ky. (mem. rep.), Cave City (mem. rep.), Bowling Green (mem. rep.), Glasgow (mem. rep.) chambers commerce, Conf. Nat. Park Concessioners (mem. exec. com.), Soc. Ky. Cols. Mason (Shriner), Lion. Home: Route 2 Park City KY 42160 Office: Mammoth Cave KY 42259

HANSON, VICTOR HENRY, II, newspaper exec.; b. Augusta Ga., Aug. 17, 1930; s. Clarence Bloodworth, Jr, and Elizabeth (Fletcher) H.; grad. Choate Sch., 1949; student U. Va., 1949-51; B.A., U. Ala., 1954; m. Elizabeth Stallworth, Dec. 29, 1953; children—Clarence Bloodworth III, Victor Hanson III, Elizabeth Mickel. Mary Fletcher, Robert Stallworth. With The Birmingham (Ala.) News, 1946-54, 57—, mem. advt. dept., 1958-59, asst. to pub., 1959-53, gen. mgr. 1963—; with advt. and prodn. dept. WAPI-TV, Birmingham, 1954-55; v.p. Birmingham News Co., 1960—; dir. City Fed. Savs. and Loan Assn. Pres., Ala. High Sch. Fine Arts. Bd. dirs. A.R.C., Jefferson County United Appeal. Served as 1st lt. USAAF, 1955-57. Mem. C. of C., Kappa Alpha. Presbyn. Rotarian. Clubs: Birmingham Country, Downtown, Mountain Brook, The Club, Relay House (Birmingham). Home: 3557 River Bend Rd Birmingham AL 35243 Office: 2200 4th Av N Birmingham AL 35223

HANST, KENNETH FREDERICK, JR., life ins. exec.; b. Woodbury, N.J., May 16, 1920; s. Kenneth Frederick and Kathleen (Elliott) H.; B.S., U.S. Mil. Acad., 1942; m. Barbara Lois Gnau, Dec. 19, 1942; children—Kenneth Frederick III, Susan E. With Army Mut. Aid Assn., Arlington, Va., 1947—, exec. v.p., 1957-71, pres., 1971—. Bd. dirs. Army Distaff Found., West Point Alumni Found. Served with AUS, 1942-47; CBI. Decorated Bronze Star (2). C.L.U. Mem. West Point Soc. D.C. (pres. 1963-64, Benjamin F. Castle award 1967), Chartered Life Underwriters (chpt. pres. 1964-65), Nat. Assn. Uniformed Services (dir.), D.C. Life underwriters, Assn. Grads. U.S. Mil. Acad. (trustee). Home: 5597 Seminary Rd 610 Falls Church VA 22041 Office: Fort Myer Arlington VA 22211

HAPP, STAFFORD COLEMAN, geologist; b. Sparrow Bush, N.Y., Sept. 16, 1905; s. Conrad and Hattie A. (Coleman) H.; A.B. (cum laude), Marietta Coll., 1931; student Wesleyan U., 1926-27; Ph.D., Columbia U., 1939; m. Inez Ellen Hale, Dec. 26, 1935; 1 dau., Ellen (Mrs. Kenneth W. Hill). Head stream and valley sedimentation research Soil Conservation Service, Washington, 1935-43; head geology soils sect. Army Engrs., Ocala, Fla., 1943-44; head geology and underground investigations Army Engrs., Kansas City, Mo., 1944-55; chief geologic reports and information sect. AEC, Grand Junction (Colo.) Office 1955-56, asst. chief geologic br., 1957-58, chief prodn. services br., 1959-64; research geologist U.S. Geol. Survey, 1964-65; research geologist Agrl. Research Service, Oxford, Miss., 1965—. Fellow Geol. Soc. Am. (chmn. engring. div. 1960); mem. Am. Inst. Mining, Metall. and Petroleum Engrs., A.A.A.S., Am. Geophys. Union, Am. Soc. C.E., Phi Beta Kappa, Sigma Xi. Contbr. to profl. jours. Office: USDA Sedimentation Lab PO Box 30 Oxford MS 38655

HAPPEL, RALPH, ret. hist. researcher; b. Fredericksburg, Va.. Apr. 12, 1911; s. John and Margaret (Reiser) H.; B.S., 1932, M.S., 1934; m. Martha Louise Williams, Jan. 1, 1940. With Nat. Park Service, Fredericksburg, Va., 1936-72, hist. research, interpreter. Bd. dirs. Historic Fredericksburg Found.; bd. dirs., v.p. Fredericksburg Cemetery Co. Mem. Soc. for Preservation Va. Antiquities, Confederate Meml. Lit. Soc., others. Presbyn. Home: Fredericksburg VA 22401

HARADEN, ROBERT CHESTER, govt. ofcl.; b. Bar Harbor, Me., June 10, 1922; s. Shirley E. and Sylvia (Brewer) H.; B.S. in Civil Engring., U. Me., 1949; m. Adelaide Alice Cleaves, Apr. 27, 1946; children—Carl, Stephen, Peter. Civil engr. Me. State Park System, 1949-55, Nat. Park Service, Phila., 1955-58; chief park engr. Rocky Mountain Nat. Park, Estes Park, Colo., 1958-64, Sequoia-Kings Canyon Nat. Park, Three Rivers, Cal., 1964-66; asst. supt. Grant Teton Nat. Park, Moose, Wyo., 1967-68; supt. Natchez Trace Parkbay, Tupelo, Miss., 1968—. Served with USNR, 1943-46. Registered profl. engr., Colo., Me. Mem. Wilderness Soc., Nature Conservancy. Rotarian

HARBERT, BILL LEBOLD, constrn. co. exec.; b. Indianola, Miss., July 21, 1923; s. John Murdock and Mae (Schooling) H.; B.S., Auburn U., 1946; grad. Advanced Mgmt. Program, Harvard, 1966; m. Mary Joyce Patrick, June 28, 1952; children—Anne, Elizabeth, Bill LeBold. Exec. v.p., dir. Harbert Constrn. Corp., Birmingham, Ala., 1948—, Montin-Harbert Pipeline Co., Oklahoma City, 1959—, Harbert & Cargile Co., Birmingham, 1952—; v.p., dir. Harbert-Distral Co., Birmingham, 1968—, Carrez Internat., Inc., 1968—. Co-chmn., trustee Laborers Central and So. States Pension Fund, 1968—. Mem. sch. bd. Vestavia Hills Sch., 1968—. Trustee Constrn. Advancement Program of Ala. Served with inf. AUS, 1945. Mem. Pipeline Contractors Assn. (dir. 1968—). Methodist (mem. bd. 1972—). Club: Vestavia Country (pres. 1971) (Birmingham, Ala.). Home: 205 Vestavia Circle Birmingham AL 35216 Office: 2900 Cahaba Rd PO Box 1297 Birmingham AL 35201

HARBIN, WAYNE DEWITT, mfg. co. exec.; b. Donna, Tex., Apr. 29, 1925; s. Jesse Matthew and Lela (Betts) H.; B.B.A., U. Tex., 1948; Advanced Mgmt. Program, Harvard Grad. Sch. Bus., 1962; m. Elinor Victoria Tolish, Apr. 17, 1946; children—Kenneth Wayne, Richard Wayne. Mgr., Arthur Young & Co., C.P.A.'S, N.Y.C., 1949-58, managing partner, Houston, 1958-68; pres., chmn. bd. Marathon Mfg. Co., fabricated metal products, Houston, 1968—; vice chmn. bd. Crutcher Resources Corp., Houston; dir. Service Corp. Internat., Houston. Adv. council U. Tex. Bus. Sch.; mem. pres.'s corp. com.

Baylor U., Waco, Tex. Served with USNR, 1942-46. Mem. Tex., N.Y. socs. C.P.A.'s, Am. Inst. C.P.A's. Mason. Clubs: River Oaks Country, Houston, Coronado, (all Houston). Home: 3994 Inverness St Houston TX 77019 Office: 801 Houston Natural Gas Bldg Houston TX 77002

HARBOUR, MACK DAVE, hosp. adminstr.; b. Viola, Ark., June 5, 1937; s. Roy D. and Nova (Snelgrooes) H.; B.A., U. Ark., 1958, M.Ed., 1959, postgrad., 1960-62; postgrad. Ark. State U., 1966-67; m. Greta E. Martin, Jan. 31, 1958; children—Mark, Rebecca, Sarah. Tchr. Vila and Newark (Ark.) High Schs., 1958-60; sch. adminstr. Viola High Sch., 1960-62; adminstr. Fulton County Hosp., Salem, Ark., 1962-65, Community Meth. Hosp., Paragould, Ark., 1965—. Chmn. Parks and Recreation Commn. and Housing Authority, Paragould, Ark., 1968—; pres. Greene County Community Fund, Inc., 1968; chmn. Osage dist. Boy Scouts Am. Bd. dirs. Ark. Arthritis Found. Mem. Am., Ark. (dir.) hosp. assns., C. of C. (pres. elect 1969), Am. Coll. Hosp. Adminstrs., Blue Key. Baptist (deacon). Mason, Kiwanian. Contbr. articles to profl. jours. Home: 316 N 4th St Paragould AR 72450 Office: 900 W Kings Hwy Paragould AR 72450

HARBY, SAMUEL FARKAS, educator; b. Sumter, S.C., Mar. 3, 1908; s. Jackson M. and Freddie (Farkas) H.; B.A., U. Wash., 1929; M.A., Columbia, 1931, Ph.D., 1938; m. Mary Elizabeth White, Dec. 20, 1933; children—Rebecca (Mrs. Fred Tran), Melinda (Mrs. Gerald Lubensky); m. 2d, Mary Lourita Adams, June 10, 1964. Instr. phys. edn. and hygiene U. Wash. at Seattle, 1928-30, Columbia, 1930-33; prin. Montezuma Sch. for Boys, Los Gatos, Cal., 1933-34; edn. adviser, dist. supr. Civilian Conservation Corps, N.Y. State, 1934-38; asst. prof. edn. Antioch Coll., Yellow Springs, O., 1938-41; information specialist, film officer Surgeon General's Office, USPHS, 1941-42; asso. in research and prodn. Ency. Brit. Films, Inc., 1945-46; cons., research and tng. specialist USPHS, 1946-49, 52-55; asso. prof. edn. Pa. State U., 1949-52; prof. edn. U. Miami, Coral Gables, Fla., 1955—, dir. audio-visual, 1955-61. Vice pres. Washington Film Council, 1948-49; chmn. Fed. Visual Aids Workshop, Washington, 1953-54. Pres., Pine Ridge Civic Assn., Dade County, Fla., 1966-67, dir., 1967-69; pres. Greater Miami Council Internat. Visitors, 1965-66, dir., 1960—. Served to comdr. USNR, 1942-45; ETO, PTO. Mem. Am. Assn. U. Profs. (pres. U. Miami chpt. 1963-64, 70-71, dir. 1964-71), Phi Beta Kappa, Kappa Delta Pi, Omicron Delta Kappa. Author: Tumbling for Teachers and Students, 1931; CCC-The American Folk School, 1939; Tumbling Manual, 1939. Contbr. numerous articles profl. jours. and popular mags. Writer, producer, supr. numerous tng. films U.S. Govt., 1942-55. Research in loop-films, mental practice, audience-response systems in teaching. Home: 5200 SW 82d Av Miami FL 33155

HARDAWAY, ERNEST, II, dentist; b. Columbus, Ga., Mar. 3, 1934; s. Ernest and Virginia Laura (Hill) H.; B.S., Howard U., 1957, D.D.S., 1966, postgrad. (Louise Ball fellow), 1968-69, 71, certificate in oral surgery, 1972; postgrad. Johns Hopkins, 1972—. Instr. dept. oral surgery Howard U., Washington, 1967-68; staff oral surgery dept. Freedmen's Hosp., Washington, from 1967, now chief resident; staff oral surgeon Group Health Assn., Washington, 1967-71; project dir. Health Maintenance Orgn. for D.C., 1970-71; exec. asst. to dir. human resources, exec. office D.C., Govt., 1971; preceptor George Washington U. Grad. Sch. Health Care Adminstrn., Washington, 1971—; treas., dir. Dental Health Service Corp. D.C., 1971—; pres. H.A.P., Inc., Washington. Minority affairs adviser U.S. Naval Acad., 1969; mem. exec. com. Dental Health Service Corp. and Blue Cross of Washington, 1970—; pres. Concerned Citizens for Better Health Care, 1969—; mem. Mayor's Com. on Dental Health Task Force, 1970-71; mem. planning staff, health services and hosp. devel. adv. council United Planning Orgn., 1971; cons. in health affairs to chmn., profl. staff mem. U.S. Ho. of Reps. Ways and Means Com., 1972; mem. health adv. bd. Nat. Urban Coalition, 1972—. Served to lt. comdr. USNR. Recipient Global Community Health fellowship Dept. Health, Edn. and Welfare, 1971-73. Mem. Am., Nat. dental assns., Royal Soc. Health, Nat. Assn. State Dental Cons., Am. Assn. U. Profs., Maimonides Dental Soc., Am. Pub. Health Assn., Chi Delta Mu. Kiwanian (dir. 1971). Club: Northern Virginia Racquet (Fairfax, Va.). Home: 300 M St SW Washington DC 20024 Office: Freedmen's Hosp Dept Oral Surgery 6th and Bryant Sts NW Washington DC 20001

HARDEE, HOWARD DAVIS, physician; b. Fernandina, Fla., Oct. 20, 1922; s. John Richardson and Ella (Davis) H.; B.S., Fla. So. Coll., 1942; B.S., Tulane U., 1943, M.D., 1946; student Hartford (Conn.) Sem. Found., 1948-49, Prince Leopold Inst. Tropical Medicine, Antwerp, Belgium, 1949-50; m. Ruth Piper, Jan. 24, 1952; children—Dorothy Ann, Ruth Ann. Intern Charlotte (N.C.) Meml. Hosp., 1946-47; resident Tampa (Fla.) Gen. Hosp., 1947-48; med. dir. Meth. Mission, Kapanga, Belgian Congo, Africa, 1950-52, Hillsborough County Welfare Bd., Tampa, 1953-54; gen. practice medicine, Tampa, 1954—. Served as 2d lt. AUS, World War II. Diplomate Nat. Bd. Med. Examiners, Mem. A.M.A., World, Fla., Hillsborough County med. assns., Am. Acad. Gen. Practice, Am. Geriatric Soc. Home: 2823 Samara Dr Carrollwood Tampa FL 33618 Office: 4809 Central Av Tampa FL 33604

HARDEN, ARTHUR GARDNER, hosp. adminstr.; b. Norfolk, Va., Mar. 28, 1927; s. Ernest Richard and Hilda Reid (Gardner) H.; B.A., U. Va., 1949, M.D., 1953; m. Elizabeth Kearny Wilson, June 23, 1951; children— Rebecca Stratton, Joseph Reid, David Gardner. Intern, Cornell Med. Center, N.Y.C., 1953-54, asst. resident internal medicine, 1954-55, resident chest disease and cardiology, 1957-58; fellow physiology, allergy and arthritis U. Va., Charlottesville, 1958-61; pvt. practice medicine, Winchester, Va., 1961-62; med. dir. Western State Hosp., Staunton, Va., 1962-69, asst. supt., 1969—; mem. staff King's Daus.' Hosp., Staunton; clin. asst. prof. internal medicine U. Va., Charlottesville, 1970—. Served with USNR, 1955-57; now lt. comdr. Res. ret. Mem. A.C.P., Am. Soc. Internal Medicine, Neuropsychiat. Soc., Soc. Internal Medicine, Am. Psychiat. Assn., Am. Heart Assn., A.M.A., Med. Soc. Va., Augusta County Med. Soc., Alpha Omega Alpha, Omicron Delta Kappa. Home: 212 Hendren Av Staunton VA 24401 Office: 301 Greenville Av Staunton VA 24401

HARDEN, JOHN WILLIAM, textile mill exec.; b. Graham, N.C. Aug. 22, 1903; s. Peter Ray and Nettie Cayce (Abbott) H.; A.B., U. N.C., 1927; m. Josephine Holt, June 13, 1928 (dec. Dec. 15, 1951); children—Glenn Abbott (Mrs. Fred Springer-Miller), John William; m. 2d, Sarah Plexico, Oct, 5, 1953; children—Holmes Plexico and Mark Michael (twins), Jonathan Holder. Circulation mgr., advt. mgr. Burlington (N.C.) Daily Times-News, 1922, also editor Graham news dept.; classified advt. mgr. Raleigh News and Observer, 1923; with U. N.C. News Bur., 1923-28; reporter, columnist Charlotte (N.C.) News, 1928-37; news editor Salisbury Evening Post, 1937-44, Greensboro Daily News, 1944; pvt. sec. to Gov. R. Gregg Cherry, 1945-48; co-mgr. campaign for U.S. Senator William B. Umstead, 1948; dir. pub. relations Burlington Industries, 1948-58, asst. v.p., 1948, v.p. 1949-58; pub. relations counsellor, cons. John Harden Assos., Greensboro, 1958—; asst. to pres. Cannon Mills Co., Kannapolis, N.C., 1971—; v.p. Rowan Printing Co., Salisbury, N.C.; pres., treas. Cochran, Harden and Stuart; sec.-treas. Stuart Studio, Inc. Mem. Greensboro exec. bd. Boy Scouts Am. Bd. dirs. Carolina Motor Club, Excellence Fund, Inc. of U. N.C. at Greensboro, N.C. Bus. Found., Inc., trustee, mem. exec. com. Penick Home for Aging; mem., vice chmn. bd. visitors Guilford Coll. Mem. Greensboro C. of C. (dir., pres.), N.C. Soc. Preservation Antiquities, Antiquities Soc. (dir.), N.C. Press Assn. Gen. Alumni Assn. U. N.C. (pres. 1955), Pub. Relations Soc. Am. (N.C. chmn. eligibility com.). Democrat. Episcopalian (chmn. 1958 every mem. canvass; vestryman, sr. warden). Clubs: Merchants and Manufacturers, Rotary (local pres., dir.; dist. gov.), Greensboro Country; Grandfather Golf and Country (dir., chmn. exec. com.); Grandfather Mountain Lake (dir.). Author: Alamance County: Economic and Social, 1928; The Devil's Tramping Ground and Other North Carolina Mystery Stories, 1949; Tar Heel Ghosts, 1954; North Carolina Roads and Their Builders, 1966. Contbr. articles to trade publs. Home: 2700 Twin Lakes Dr Greensboro NC 27407 Office: 100 East Lake Dr Greensboro NC 27420 also Cannon Mills Co Kannapolis NC 28081

HARDEN, JUNIUS HOLT, elec. engr.; b. Graham, N.C., Sept. 3, 1915; s. Peter Ray and Nettie (Abbott) H.; B.S., N.C. State U., 1938; m. Mary Alice Helms, Apr. 28, 1946; children—Steven Helms, Sarah Kay. Electricians helper N.C. State Coll. Service, 1935-39; electrician Golden Belt Mfg. Co., Durham, N.C., 1939; equipment installer Western Electric Co., Inc., Atlanta, 1939-43, quality control engr., Burlington, N.C., 1946-1949, quality control sect. chief, 1949-52, engr., 1952-56, engr. planning, 1956-59, sr. engr., 1959—. Bd. dirs. Providence Meml. Assn. Served to lt., USNR, World War II; PTO, CBI. Registered profl. engr., N.C. Mem. Nat. Soc. Profl. Engrs., N.C. Soc. Engrs., Telephone Pioneers Am. Methodist (chmn. commn. on edn.). Clubs: Burlington-Graham Engineers (past pres., dir.), Rotary (dir. 1965-66). Home: 430 Ward St Graham NC 27253 Office: 204 Graham-Hopedale Rd Burlington NC 27215

HARDEN, ROSS ULLMAN, lawyer; b. Rockford, Ala., Apr. 20, 1909; s. James Elzie and Eunice (Ward) H.; A.B., Mercer U., 1929, LL.B., 1931; m. Annie Mandell Bates, Dec. 12, 1938; children—Sydney (Mrs. Anthony Smith Wynne), Annette (Mrs. Joseph Daniel, Jr.). Admitted to Ga. bar, 1931; practiced in Cairo, 1933-35, Waynesboro, 1947—; law clk. Supreme Ct. Ga., Atlanta, 1936-42; asst. atty. gen. State of Ga., Atlanta, 1943-44, 45-47; solicitor State Ct. Burke County, 1965—. Mem. Burke County Democratic Exec. Com., 1950—, chmn., 1961—. Served with USMCR, 1944-45. Mem. Am. Judicature Soc., State Bar Assn. Ga., Blue Key, Pi Kappa Phi, Phi Alpha Delta. Baptist. Home: 901 Waters St Waynesboro GA 30830 Office: 221 E 6TH St Waynesboro GA 30830

HARDEN, SARAH PLEXICO (MRS. JOHN WILLIAM HARDEN), actress, personal presentation counselor; b. Salisbury, N.C., Apr. 27, 1925; d. S. Holmes and Thelma (Kerr) Plexico; student Catawba Coll, 1936-41, Greensboro Coll., 1942-44, Boston U., 1945; B.A., Emerson Coll., 1946, M.A., 1946; m. John William Harden, Oct. 5, 1953; children—Holmes Plexico and Mark Michael (twins), Jonathan Holder. Actress stage plays including The Late George Apley, 1947, For Love or Money, 1949, also plays in New Eng., N.Y.C. and the South, 1946-52; appeared on TV programs including Kraft Theatre, Man Against Crime; lectr., tchr. John Robert Powers, N.Y.C., Atlanta, Kansas City, 1950; lectr. Plexico Series Personal Presentation, Greensboro N.C., 1952—, mdse. cons. Mdse. Group, Inc., N.Y.C., 1954—. Mem. N.C. Gov's. Exec. Mansion Fine Arts Com. Mem N.C. Lit. and Hist. Assn., Hist. Book Club N.C., Inc. (sec. 1954-61, membership chmn. 1961), Greensboro Friends of Library (pres. 1955, dir. 1953-60). Episcopalian (1st v.p. women's aux. 1961-63). Clubs: Greensboro Country, O. Henry Study (pres. 1959) (Greensboro); Grandfather Mountain Golf and Country. Home: 2700 Twin Lakes Dr Greensboro NC 27407

HARDER, ARCHIE DANA, ins. co. exec.; b. Marion, Ind., May 18, 1902; A.B., U. Okla With Southwestern Life Ins. Co., Dallas, 1925—, dir., 1954—, formerly chmn. bd. Mem. Am. Life Conv., Financial Execs. Inst., Am. Bankers Assn., Ins. Accounting and Statis. Assn. Home: 3701 Turtle Creek Blvd Dallas TX 75219 Office: PO Box 2699 Dallas TX 75221

HARDESTY, CECIL DONALD, supt. schs.; b. Kensington, Kan., Aug. 24, 1907; s. Don and Viola (May) H.; A.B., Kan. Wesleyan U., 1928; M.A., U. So. Cal., 1932, Ed.D., 1933; m. Sunshine Barnhart, Dec. 22, 1928; children—Jeanne (Mrs. Howard Pitts), Donna (Mrs. Thomas Smith). Tchr. high sch., Lost Spring, Wyo., 1928-29; supt. high sch., Calhan, Colo., 1929-31; supt. elementary sch. dist., Westminster, Cal., 1933-35; bus. mgr. Beverly Hills (Cal.) Unified Sch. Dist., 1935-39; supt. Montebello (Cal.) Unified Sch. Dist., 1939-46; supt. San Jose (Cal.) City Schs., 1947-50; supt. schs., San Diego County, Cal., 1950-69; supt. schs., Duval County, Jacksonville, Fla., 1969—. Chmn. Cal. Commn. on Pub. Sch. Adminstrn., 1954-57. Bd. dirs. YMCA, San Jose and San Diego, San Diego Hall Sci. and Industry Corp., Gator Bowl Assn. Served as lt. USNR, 1943-46. Recipient Am. Educators medal Freedoms Found. at Valley Forge, 1962; Golden Plate award Acad. Achievement, 1962. Mem. Cal. Assn. Sch. Adminstrs. (pres.1953), N.E.A. (pres. nat. county and rural areas supts. div. 1961), Jacksonville C. of C., Am. Legion, Phi Delta Kappa. Kiwanian (pres. San Diego). Contbr. articles ednl. publs. Office: Courthouse 330 E Bay St Jacksonville FL 32202

HARDESTY, JERRY WARREN, county agrl. agt.; b. nr. Elizabeth City, N.C., Aug. 2, 1935; s. Benjamon T. and Lena Pearl (Cannor) H.; B.S., N.C. State U., 1957, M.A., 1970; m. Mary Ann Jones, Sept. 4, 1955; children—Sheryl, Donna, Randal. Tchr., Great Bridge High Sch., Chesapeake, Va., 1957-58; asst. farm agt. Currituck County, N.C., 1958-63, county extension chmn., 1963—. Sec., Currituck Resources Council, 1963-65; chmn. Currituck Planning Bd., 1966—; mem. Congress Nat. Rivers. Mem. N.C. County Agt. Assn. (pres., dist. 1971-72), N.C. Farm Markets Assn. (dir. 1971—). Baptist. Club: Ruritan (dist. gov. 1964-65; chmn. planning bd. 1966—). Address: Currituck NC 27929

HARDIE, VIRGINIA SMITH (MRS. NEWTON GARY HARDIE), psychologist, educator; b. nr. Sycamore, Ga., June 12, 1907; d. Wilbur Riddick and Pearl (Fields) Smith; student Agnes Scott Coll., 1925-27; A.B., LaGrange Coll. 1929; M.A., U. Ga., 1933; postgrad. Columbia U. and N.Y. U., 1948-49, U. N.C., 1951; Ed.D., U. Colo., 1955; m. Newton Gary Hardie, Apr. 14, 1936 (dec. Nov. 1958). Tchr. Columbus (Ga.) High Sch., 1935-40, Atlanta and Fulton County high schs., 1940-43; supr., coordinator counseling and rehab. U.S. Army Hosp. Service, 1943-48; owner, dir. pvt. counseling offices N.Y.C. and Augusta, Ga., 1948-54; dir. counseling and placement Atlanta and Fulton County Schs., Atlanta, 1948-50; dir. guidance Richmond County Schs., Augusta, 1950-54; counselor trainer Colo. Dept. Vocational Edn., Denver, 1954-55; acting asst. prof. edn. U. Colo., 1954-55; prof. gerontology adult continuing edn. center Clemson (S.C.) Coll. 1957, 58; asso. prof. ednl. psychology U. Tenn., 1959-62; counseling psychologist, dir. counseling Clemson U., 1962—; vis. prof. various univs. and colls; vocational cons.; psychol. cons. Dir. S.C. Nat. Bank. Bd. dirs. Presbyn. Coll., Clinton, S.C. Recipient Colo. Bus. and Profl. Women fellowship grant, 1954. Mem. Am., S.C. (tri-county pres. 1963-64) personnel and guidance assns., Am., Southeastern, S.C. psychol. assns., S.C. Mental Health Assn. (pres.-elect, mem. exec. bd.), Am. Assn. U. Profs., Am. Assn. U. Women (pres. Columbus 1937-38, 1st v.p. Ga. chpt. 1940-41, 1st v.p. Clemson chpt. 1955-56), Bus. and Profl. Women, League Women Voters, Pi Lambda Theta, Kappa Delta Pi, Kappa Alpha Theta (chpt. pres. 1928-29). Author: Women at Work. Club: Altrusa. Contbr. articles profl. jours. Home: PO Box 86 Pendleton SC 29670

HARDIN, DALE WAYNE, govt. ofcl.; b. Peoria, Ill., Sept. 9, 1922; s. James P. and Lucille Center; H.; student Bradley U., 1941, 46-47; A.A., A.B., George Washington U., 1949, J.D., 1951; m. Virginia Phillips, Apr. 21, 1946; children—Bradley James, Rebecca May. Admitted to Va. and D.C. bars, 1951; pvt. practice, 1951; spl. agt. FBI, 1951-54; legislative atty., Congl. liaison officer ICC, 1954-63; sec., counsel Transp. Assn. Am., 1959; mgr. transp. and communication dept. U.S. C. of C., 1963-66; v.p. Overmeyer Co., Washington, 1966-67; spl. counsel Am. Trucking Assn., 1967; commr. ICC, 1967—, vice chmn, 1970—; mem. council of Adminstrv. Conf. U.S., 1971—. Served with USMCR, 1942-46. Mem. Fed., Va., D.C. bar assns., Soc. Former FBI Agts., Phi Delta Phi. Clubs; Congressional Country, Nat. Lawyers (Washington). Bus. sec. George Washington Law Rev., 1950. Home: 1011 Emerald Dr Alexandria VA 22308 Office: Interstate Commerce Commn Washington DC 20423

HARDIN, EDWARD REEL, lawyer; b. Wadesboro, N.C., Sept. 26, 1936; s. Paul and Dorothy Elizabeth (Reel) H.; A.B., Duke U., 1958, LL.B., 1960, J.D., 1970; m. Elizabeth McAshan Crawford, July 1, 1967. Admitted to N.C. bar, 1960; asso. James B. Lovelace, atty., High Point, N.C., 1961-62; partner Lovelace, Hardin & Bain, High Point, 1962—; officer, dir. numerous corporations; sec. So. Film Extruders, Inc., High Point, 1966—; v.p. Cardinal Industries, Inc., High Point, 1969—; pvt. real estate developer, High Point, 1961—. Mem. Gov.'s com. Constitutional Amendments, 1968-69; active A.R.C., Salvation Army Boys Club, United Appeal. Pres., Young Democrats Club, 1962-63, active many campaigns. Bd. dirs., pres. Youth Unltd., 1970-72. Served to capt. U.S. Army Res., 1961-69. Mem. Am. Bar Assn. (del. 1967-69), N.C. Bar Assn. (chmn. young lawyers sect. 1968-69), High Point Community Concert Assn. (pres. 1965-68), High Point C. of C. (hon. life mem.; dir. 1966—; pres.-elect 1973), High Point Arts Council. Rotarian (dir. 1964-65). Home: 1018 Wellington St High Point NC 27262 Office: 111 Hayden Place High Point NC 27260

HARDIN, GEORGE CECIL, JR., petroleum co. exec.; b. Oakwood, Tex., Oct. 6, 1920; s. George Cecil and Pearl (Moore) H.; B.S. in Geology and Petroleum Engring., Tex. A. and M. U., 1941; Ph.D. in Geology (Van Hise fellow 1941), U. Wis., 1942; m. Virginia Howard, Nov. 21, 1942; children—George Howard, Susan. Mining engr. Victory Fluorspar Mine, Cave in Rock, Ill., 1942; geologist U.S. Geol. Survey, 1942-45, party chief, 1944-45; geologist Carter Gragg Oil Co., Palestine, Tex., 1945-46; geologist, petroleum engr. M. T. Halbouty Cons. Firm, Houston, 1946-51; exploration and prodn. mgr. M.T. Halbouty Oil and Gas Interests, Houston, 1951-59, gen. mgr., 1959-61; exec. v.p. Halbouty Alaska Oil Co., 1957-61, dir., 1957—; pres. Ada Exco, v.p. Ada Oil Exploration Co., 1970-71; pres. Ashland Exploration Co., 1971—; sr. v.p. Ashland Oil, Inc., 1971—; partner Hardin and Hardin, cons. geologists, Houston, 1961-64; mgr. oil and gas exploration Kerr-McGee Oil Ind., Inc., 1964-65; v.p. N.Am. Oil & Gas Exploration, 1965-67, v.p. oil, gas and minerals exploration, 1967-68, group v.p. exploration, 1968; v.p. Kerr-McGee Argentina, 1967-68, Kerr-McGee Can., Ltd., 1967-68, Kerr-McGee Australia, Ltd., 1967-68; pres., chief exec. officer Royal Resources Corp., Houston, 1968—; dir. Continental Bank & Trust Co., Houston, 1956—, mem. exec. com., 1956-62, chmn. auditing com., 1962—; dir. North Side State Bank, Houston; owner Poverty Ridge Farm, Okla. City, 1966—. Registered profl. engr., Tex., Okla. Fellow Geol. Soc. Am., A.A.A.S.; mem. Houston Geol. Soc. (pres. 1961-62), Soc. Econ. Paleontologists and Mineralogists, New Orleans, South Tex. geol. socs., Gulf Coast Assn. Geol. Socs. (pres. 1959), Am. Assn. Petroleum Geologists (sec.-treas. 1964-66; chmn. house dels. 1971-72), Assn. Mexicana de Geologos Petroleros, Soc. Exploration Geophysicists Am. Inst. Profl. Geologists. Clubs: Petroleum (dir. 1956-58), Terra (dir. 1958-59); Brazos River Hunting and Fishing (dir. 1961-64) (West Columbia, Tex.). Author articles in field. Home: 204 Arborway Houston TX 77027 Office: PO Box 1503 Houston TX 77002

HARDIN, HILLIARD FRANCES, microbiologist; b. Columbia, S.C., Dec. 12, 1917; d. Lawrence Legare and Addria (Chreitzberg) Hardin; A.B., Duke, 1939, M.A., 1949, Ph.D., 1953. Microbiologist, Atomic Bomb Casualty Commn., Hiroshima, Japan, 1950-51; instr. U. Ark., 1953-57; research asso. Duke Med. Center, 1957-62, instr., 1962-63; supervisory microbiologist USPHS, 1963; chief mycology tng. unit Communicable Disease Center, Atlanta, 1963-68; chief microbiology lab. VA Hosp., Little Rock, 1968—; asso. prof. microbiology U. Ark. Med. Center, 1968—. Served with WAVES, USNR, 1942-45. Mem. Am. Thoraic Soc., N.Y. Acad. Sci., Med. Mycology Soc. Am., Sigma Xi, Pi Beta Phi. Home: Quapaw Towers Little Rock AR 72202 Office: Microbiology Lab VA Hosp, 300 E Roosevelt Rd Little Rock AR 72206

HARDIN, JAMES N., lawyer; b. Greeneville, Tenn., June 4, 1903; s. Neal H. and Nina (Cox) H.; A.B., Maryville Coll., 1924; LL.B., Harvard, 1927; m. Ina Anderson, June 19, 1937; children—James Neal, George Timothy. Admitted to Tenn. bar, 1926, pvt. practice, Greeneville, 1927-39, 1946—; sec. to Gov. of Tenn., 1939-43. Mem. Tenn. State Legislature, 1953-54; pres. Greene County Agrl. Fair, 1949-66; mayor City of Greeneville, 1964-68, 70—. Chmn. bd. Kingswood Sch.; pres. Tenn. Assn. of Fairs, 1965-66. Served as capt. to lt. col. AUS, 1943-46. Mem. Vets. Fgn. Wars (past dep. comdr.; past judge advocate gen.), Pi Kappa Delta. Methodist. Elk, Moose. Kiwanian (lt. gov. 1963). Author: New York to Oberplan. Home: 108 McKee St Greeneville TN 37743 Office: First Nat Bank Bldg Greeneville TN 37743 also Town Hall Greeneville TN 37743

HARDIN, MILTON AVERY, financial exec.; b. Eldorado, Okla., Feb. 15, 1933; s. Joseph Milton and Myra (Reeves) H.; B.S., Fort Hays Kan. State Coll., 1959; postgrad. U. N.M., 1964, Oklahoma City U., 1967, Okla. U., 1970; m. June Dorothea Bussart, Feb. 20, 1960; 1son, Stacey Milton. Jr. accountant Poos & Monroe, C.P.A.'s, Great Bend, Kan., 1957-60; self employed as C.P.A., Hutchinson, 1960-61; controller Chandler Constrn. Co., Sterling, Colo., 1961-63; accountant Homestake-Sapin Partners, Grants, N.M., 1963-65; controller J.J. Cook Constrn., Inc., Oklahoma City, 1965-66; controller, v.p. Yarbro Constrn., Inc., Oklahoma City, 1966-68; treas., controller Sequoyah Enterprises, Inc., Oklahoma City, 1968-70, also dir.; treas., controller World Market Centers, Inc., Tulsa, Tulsa, 1971—. Instr. Adela Hale Bus. Career Sch., Hutchinson, Kan., 1960-61. C.P.A., Kan., Colo., Okla. Republican. Methodist. Installed 1st fully automated dept. store with complete perpetual inventory, 1971. Home: 2445 NW 35th St Oklahoma City OK 73112 Office: 3907 N Tulsa St Oklahoma City OK 73112

HARDIN, PAUL, JR., ret. bishop; b. Joanna, S.C., Nov. 7, 1903; s. Paul and Harriet (Wannamaker) H.; A.B., Wofford Coll, 1924, D.D., 1950, B.D., Emory U., 1927; D.D., Birmingham-So. Coll., 1950; m. Dorothy Elizabeth Reel, Oct. 18, 1927; children—Betsy Reel (Mrs. Arthur Utley, Jr.), Paul III, Edward Reel. Ordained to ministry Methodist Ch., 1927; pastor in N.C., 1927-49, First Meth. Ch., Birmingham, Ala. 1949-60; bishop, Columbia, S.C., 1960-72. Del. gen. and jurisdictional confs. Meth. Ch. 1960; trustee, mem. exec.

com. Lake Junaluska Assembly; pres. Council World Service and Finance, United Meth. Ch., 1968-72; pres. Council of Bishops, United Meth. Ch., 1971-72. Trustee, v.p., mem. exec. com. Emory U. Home: Box 338 18 Oxford Rd Lake Junaluska NC 28745

HARDIN, SIDNEY LANIER, lawyer, lectr., commentator; b. Prairie Hill, Tex., Nov. 16, 1894; s. Lee P. and Clementine (Mitchell) H.; grad. Sam Houston State Coll., 1914; student U. Tex., summers 1914-19; Columbia U. seminar, 1920; U. Cal. at Berkeley, seminars, 1921-22, U. Tex. Law Sch., summer 1929; m. Lucille Mason, Oct. 12, 1935 (dec.); children—Sidney Lee, Margaret Francis, John C.; m. 2d, Lucile Hill. Supt. city schs., Mission, Tex., 1917-32; admitted to Tex. bar, 1930; dist. atty., Edinburg, Tex., 1932-35; pvt. practice law, Edinburg, 1935-—; city atty., Edinburg, 1950-54, radio commentator covering Southwestern States, 1940-—; lectr., after-dinner speaker, 1924-—. Polit. speaker nat. campaigns, 1940-— mem. speakers staff of Lifeline Seminars, N.C., Washington. Bd. dirs. Pan-Am. Cancer Found., San Antonio. Recipient Congress of Freedom Liberty award Alcalde of San Antonio (hon. mayor for life), 1963; Silver medal award S.A.R.; George Washington Honor Medal award Freedoms Found., 1970. Mem. Inter-Am. Bar Assn., State Bar Tex., Internat. Platform Assn., U.S. C. of C. Democrat. Baptist. Rotarian (gov. 47th dist., hon. life mem.). Home: 121 Austin Blvd Edinburg TX 75839 Offfce: First State Bank Bldg Edinburg TX 78539

HARDING, HENRY KNOWLES, architect; b. Dedham, Mass., Dec. 20, 1904; s. Charles Lewis and Harriet Appleton (Knowles) H.; grad. St. Georges Sch., 1924; B.S., Princeton, 1928; B. Architecture, U. Pa., 1930; postgrad. Fontainbleu Sch., Paris, 1930, N.Y.U., 1935; m. Lynn Saul, Oct. 17, 1953; children—Florence Harding, Priscilla, Katherine, Susan, Henry Knowles. Owner, Henry K. Harding, architect, Palm Beach, Fla., 1936-—. Mem. town council, Ocean Ridge, Fla., 1960, mem. zoning and planning bd., 1967. Served to lt. comdr. USNR, 1941-44. Club: Ivy (Princeton). Home: Dolphin Rd Ocean Ridge FL 33444 Office: 318 Royal Poinciana Plaza Palm Beach FL 33480

HARDISON, OSBORNE BENNETT, JR., educator; b. San Diego, Oct. 22, 1928; s. Osborne Bennett and Ruth (Morgan) H.; B.A., U. N.C., 1949, M.A.. in English Lit., 1950; Ph.D., U. Wis., 1956; Litt. D., Rollins Coll., 1970; m. Marifrances Fitzgibbon, Dec. 23, 1950; children—Charity Ruth, Sarah Frances, Laura Fitzgibbon, Agnes Margaret, Osborne Bennett, Mathew Fitzgibbon. Teaching asst. U. Wis., 1950-53; instr. English, U. Tenn., Knoxville, 1954-56, Princeton, 1956-57; mem. faculty U. N.C. at Chapel Hill, 1957-60, prof. English and comparative lit., 1967-69; dir. Folger Shakespeare Library, Washington, 1969-—. Chmn. Southeastern Inst. Medieval and Renaissance Studies, 1965, co-chmn., 1966. Trustee U. Detroit. Fulbright fellow, Rome, Italy, 1953-54; Folger Library fellow, summer 1958; Guggenheim fellow, 1963-64; recipient Haskins medal Medieval Acad. Am., 1967. Mem. Modern Lang. Assn. (exec. council 1968-71), Renaissance Soc. Am., (exec. council 1969-70), Phi Beta Kappa. Author: Lyrics and Elegies, 1958; Modern Continental Literacy Criticism, 1962; The Enduring Monument, 1962; English Literary Criticism: The Renaissance, 1964; Christian Rite and Christian Drama in the Middle Ages, 1965; Practical Rhetoric, 1966; Aristotle's Poetics for Students of Literature, 1968; Toward Freedom and Dignity, 1972. Editor: (with others) The Encyclopedia of Poetry and Poems, 1965; Medieval and Renaissance Studies, 1966; The Quest for Imagination, 1971; Film Scripts 1-4, 1972. Editor Studies in Philology, 1966-69; also series editor for book pubs. Home: 18 3d St SE Washington DC 20003 Office: Folger Shakespeare Library 2d and E Capitol St SE Washington DC 20005

HARDLEY, GARY KAYE, social work exec.; b. Pontiac, Mich., Dec. 30, 1931; s. Walter Arnold and Virginia (Gaynor) H.; B.S., Wheaton Coll., 1956; M.S.W., Fla. State U., 1960; postgrad. Miss. So. U., 1960-61, Fla. State U., 1966, U. Va., 1970-—; m. Wilma Elizabeth Culpepper, Aug. 8, 1939; children—Kay Marie, William Arnold, Brenda June, David Jonathan, Gary Paul. Tchr. Buckley (Mich.) High Sch., 1956-57; mgr. Clark Oil & Refining Co., Glen Ellyn, Ill., 1957-58; psychiat. social worker VA Center, Gulfport, Miss., 1960-61; casework supr. Evang. Child Welfare Agy., Chgo., 1961-64; dir. social service Woodstock (Ill.) Children's Home, 1964-65; field work instr. Fla. State U., 1965-67; exec. dir., marriage counselor Community Counseling Center Inc., Columbus, Ga., 1967-70; exec. dir., marriage and family counselor Family Service, City of Charlottesville, Va., 1970-—; instr. devel. program academically retarded Columbus Coll., 1968-70; instr. marriage and family Madison Coll., Harrisonburg, Va. Mem. exec. com. The Well; pres. Attention Homes, Inc.; mem. adv. bd. Youth Counseling Service. Mem. Am. Assn. Marriage Counselors, Acad. Certified Social Workers, Nat. Council Family Relations, Child Study Assn. Am., Am. Assn. Sex Educators and Counselors, Council Social Work Edn. Home: 1035 Locust Av Charlottesville VA 22901 Office: 307 E Market St Charlottesville VA 22901

HARDWICK, CHARLES VINCENT, judge; b. Kinsale, Va., Sept. 1, 1910; s. Vincent Branson and Willie (Unruh) H.; student U. Va., 1929-32; LL.B., George Washington U., 1937; m. Mary Elizabeth McBirney, July 3, 1937; children—Charles Vincent, Ann McBirney. Admitted to Va. bar, 1937; practice law, Tappahannock, Va., 1937-58; judge, county, juvenile and domestic relations cts., Essex, Richmond and Westmoreland counties, Tappahannock, 1958-72; judge 11th Regional Juvenile and Domestic Relations Ct., 1972-—. Served to 2d lt. inf. AUS, 1945. Mem. Va., No. Neck bar assns., Delta Upsilon. Democrat. Methodist. Lion. Club: Ruritan. Home: Hwy 17 Tappahahnock VA 22560 Office: 215 Queen St Tappahannock VA 22560

HARDWICK, GALLY JEFF, JR., architect; b. Little Rock, Oct. 25, 1922; s. Gally Jeff and Charlotte Elizabeth (Barber) H.; student Ark. Poly. Coll., 1940-42, U. Ark., 1942, 46-47; m. Flo E. Parchman, May 15, 1944; children—Jeff Norman, John C. Draftsman, Breggeman-Swaim & Allen, architects, Little Rock, 1947-50; sr. draftsman Swaim & Allen, architects, 1950-55; office mgr. br. office, North Little Rock, Ark., 1955-59; asso., Swaim-Allen-Wellborn & Assos., architects, Little Rock, 1959-—. Mem. Spl. Com. on Edn., North Little Rock, Ark., 1966-67. Served to maj. USAAF, 1943-46; ETO, PTO. Mem. A.I.A., Constrn. Specifications Inst. (dir. Little Rock chpt. 1967-70), Little Rock, North Little Rock chambers commerce. Democrat. Baptist (mem. planning com. 1970-71). Clubs: Optomist (dir. 1956-57) North Hills Country (both North Little Rock, Ark.). Prin. archtl. works include Park Hill Bapt. Ch., North Little Rock, Ark., addition to St. Vincent Infirmary, Little Rock. Home: 923 E H Av North Little Rock AR 72116 Office: 215 Louisiana St Little Rock AR 72201

HARDWICK, JOHN HAROLD, banker; b. Stanton, Ky., Jan. 12, 1910; s. John Hudson and Ella (Grigsby) H.; A.B., Washington and Lee U., 1931; M.B.A., Harvard, 1933; m. June Lankford Warden, May 21, 1938; children—John Harold, Robert Duncan, Wayne Clay. With Guaranty Trust Co., N.Y.C., 1933-34; with Louisville Trust Co., 1934-—, pres., 1962-—, chmn. bd., 1967-—, also dir.; dir. Porter Paint Co., Commonwealth Life Ins. Co., Elkhorn Ins. Co., Blue Cross Hosp. Plan. Bd. dirs. Lexington Theol. Sem., Bellarmine Coll. Mem. Ky. Bankers Assn., Assn. Res. City Bankers, Louisville C. of C., Phi Beta kappa, Phi Delta Theta, Omicron Delta Kappa. Republican. Mem. Christian Ch. Home: 2531 Tophill Rd Louisville KY 40206 Office: Louisville Trust Co One Riverfront Plaza Louisville KY 40201

HARDY, FLORENCE C.(MRS. WILLIAM G. HARDY), city ofcl.; b. Pawtucket, R.I.; d. William E. and Mary Baker (Burns) Calland; student Brown U., 1919, U. Fla., 1958; m. William Guthrie Hardy, Jan. 8, 1920; children—Abigail Walker (Mrs. Paul Rust), William Guthrie. Statistician Providence Dist. Nursing Assn., 1915-25; asst. sec. C. of C., Fort Lauderdale, Fla., 1925-26; sec. to pres. First Nat. Bank, 1927-28; asst. acting city mgr. Fort Lauderdale, Fla., 1928-—, acting personnel dir., 1946-51, exec. asst. to commn., 1955, city auditor, 1937-39, clk., 1957-63, ret., 1963. Mem. Ft. Lauderdale City Charter Com., 1964-66. Trustee Stranahan Found. Fund. Named Woman of Yr., Bus. and Profl. Woman's Club, 1954; recipient Distinguished Service award Rotary Club, 1959. Kiwanis Club, 1966; Rosicrucian award, 1963; Florence C. Hardy Park dedicated, 1963. Mem. Ft. Lauderdale Hist. Soc. (a founder, pres., acting dir.). Episcopalian. Club: Zonta. Home: 325 SE 9th Av Fort Lauderdale FL 33301 Office: 850 NE 12th Av Extension Holiday Park Fort Lauderdale Fl 33304

HARDY, FRANK LEWIS, constrn. co. exec.; b. Columbus, Ind., July 30, 1910; s. Frank Lewis and Eunice (Kirk) H.; B.S., Auburn U., 1933; m. Margaret Wood, July 30, 1935; children—Mary Margaret (Mrs. David Phillips), Susan Henderson. Jr. engr. West Point Foundry & Machine Co., 1933-34; engring.-contracting trainee York Corp., Pa., 1934-36, zone mgr., Birmingham, Ala., 1936-39; v.p. Rushton Equipment Co., 1940-52; pres., chmn. Hardy Corp., Birmingham, 1953-— and affiliates Marwood Corp. and Marsue Realty Co., Inc.; dir. Central Bank & Trust Co., Birmingham, Diversified Foundries, Inc., Birmingham, Thomas Foundries, Inc.; Birmingham, Pollution Control Walther Co. Am. Soc. Heating, Refrigeration and Air Conditioning Engrs., Blue Key, Omicron Delta Kappa, Phi Delta Theta. Clubs: Birmingham Country, Mountain Brook Country (Birmingham). Home: 45 Ridge Dr Birmingham AL 35213 Office: Hardy Corp 430 12th St S Birmingham AL 35233

HARDY, GEORGE FRANCIS, JR., hosp. adminstr.; b. Boston, Aug. 29, 1913; s. George Francis and Ida May (Kenney) H.; B.B.A., Bentley Coll., 1937; m. Eileen Corwin, June 13, 1943; 1 son, David. Pub. accountant Scovell Wellington Co., Boston, 1930-38; office mgr. Sawyer Constrn. Co., 1938-48; asso. adminstr. Good Samaritan Hosp., West Palm Beach, Fla., 1948-67; adminstr. Coral Ridge Psychiat. Hosp., Ft. Lauderdale, Fla., 1967-—. Sec.-treas. Broward County area Planning Council, Ft. Lauderdlae, 1971-—. Served with AUS, 1942-44. Fellow Am. Coll. Hosp. Adminstrs.; mem. Am. Hosp. Assn. Home: 1900 S Ocean Blvd Pompano Beach FL 33062 Office: 4545 N Federal Hwy Fort Lauderdale FL 33308

HARDY, HARVEY LOUCHARD, lawyer; b. Dallas, Dec. 2, 1914; s. Nat L. and Winifred (Fouraker) H.; student San Antonio Coll., 1932-33; m. E. Vivian Bedell, Feb. 14, 1948; children—Victoria Elizabeth, Alice Anne. Admitted to Tex. bar, 1936; since practiced San Antonio; 1st asst. dist. atty. Bexar County, Tex., 1947-51; city atty. San Antonio, 1952-53, Castle Hills, 1959-—, Leon Valley, 1967-—. Served as 1st lt. Inf., AUS, 1941-45. Decorated Bronze Star with cluster. Fellow State Bar Tex.; mem. Am., San Antonio bar assns., Am. Judicature Soc. Methodist. Home: 215 Atwater St San Antonio TX 78213 Office: GPM Life Bldg San Antonio TX 78216

HARDY, JACK, advt. exec., past state senator; b. nr. Jefferson, Ga., Apr. 21, 1916; s. Charles Edward and Ada (Tolbert) H.; B.S., U. Ga., 1940; m. Eleanor Harris, May 25, 1935; children—Joel C., Daniel Allen. Controller, Le Tourneau Co. of Ga., 1940-46, Dittler Bros. Inc., 1948-52; pres. Cleaners Control Systems, Inc., 1946-48; exec. v.p. Burke Dowling Adam, Inc., 1952-—; pres. Star Oil Co., Inc., 1963-—, Interstate Marketing Corp., 1965-—; v.p. Batton, Barton, Durstine & Ostorne, Inc., 1964-—; state senator, Ga., 1969-72; pres. Transland Corp., Atlanta, 1972-—. Home: 450 Grenock Circle NW Atlanta GA 30328 Office: 120 Copeland Rd NE Atlanta GA 30342

HARDY, PAUL CURTIS, architect; b. Littleton, N.C. June 17, 1916; s. Joseph Benjamin and Sarah Matilda (Ward) H.; grad. high sch.; m. Ellen Mae Barnes, Nov. 3, 1937; 1 son, Paul Curtis. Prin. asso. J.N. Pease Assos., Charlotte, N.C., 1944-—, constrn. adminstr., 1963-69, dir. support operations, 1969-71, hosp. planner, 1971-—, certified fallout shelter analyst, 1961-—. Mem. A.I.A. (chmn. office procedures com. N.C. chpt. 1965; 67, 70-71, bd. dirs. 1972-—, mem. nat. specifications com. 1966-67, mem. nat. adminstrv. office practice com. 1968-70). Co-author specification work sheets A.I.A., 1963-67. Home: 901 Wimbledon Dr Charlotte NC 28209 Office: PO Box 12725 Charlotte NC 28205

HARDY, RICHARD E., educator; b. Victoria, Va., Oct. 11, 1938; B.S., Va. Poly. Inst. and State U., 1960; M.S. in Rehab. Counseling, Va. Commonwealth U., 1962; advanced certificate counseling U. Md., 1964; Ed.D., 1966; m. Lectr., mem. faculty So. Ill. U., Carbondale, 1964-68; mem. faculty dept. psychology U. S.C., 1968; asso. prof. Va. Commonwealth U., Richmond, 1968-69, asso. prof., chmn. dept. rehab. counseling, 1969-—; cons. Dept. Health, Edn. and Welfare, others. Rehab. counselor Va. Commn. Visually Handicapped, 1961-63; chief psychologist, supr. profl. tng. S.C. Dept. Vocational Rehab., Columbia. Mem. Richmond's Comprehensive Health Planning com.; mem. Va. Gov.'s Com. Problems Aging, Com. Employment Handicapped. Mem. Am. Correctional Assn., Am. Coll. Personnel Assn., Am. Personnel and Guidance Assn., Am. Psychol. Assn., Am. Rehab. Counselor Assn., Assn. Counselor Edn. and Supervision, Council Rehab. Counselor Educators, Nat. Employment Counselors' Assn., Nat. Rehab. Assn., Nat. Rehab. Counseling Assn., Nat. Vocational Guidance Assn., Va. Assn. Workers for Blind, Assn. Vol. Action Scholars, Vocational Evaluation and Work Adjustment Assn. Author: The Unfit Majority: A Study of Selective Service Rejectees, 1967; Vocational Rehabilitation: Profession and Process, 1972; Social and Rehabilitation Services for the Blind, 1973. Editor (with J.G. Cull) Drug Dependence and Rehabilitation, 1972; (with J.G. Cull) Foundations in Correctional Systems and Criminal Behavior, 1972; Introduction to Correctional Rehabilitation, 1972. Contbr. articles to profl. jours. Address: 104 W Franklin St Apt 611 Richmond VA 23220

HARDY, ROBERT CARLISLE, financial cons., broker; b. Buffalo, Nov. 8, 1904; s. Robert C. and Alicia (Carlisle) H.; B.S., Dartmouth, 1925; J.D., Columbia, 1928; m. Hilda Carswell Hardy, May 12, 1956. Admitted to N.Y. bar, 1928; mem. firm Wilkie, Owen, Farr, Gallagher & Walton, 1937-49; financial cons., 1949-58; pres., dir. Hardy, Hardy & Assos., Inc., 1958-—, also chmn. bd.; mem. Phila.-Balt.-Wash. Stock Exchange; asso. mem. Boston Stock Exchange, Pitts. Stock Exchange, 1959-—; mem. Montreal Stock Exchange, 1961-—, Cin. Stock Exchange, 1969-—; dir. James T. White & Co. Mem. Whitfield-Ballentine Zoning Commn. Mem. Sarasota C. of C., Whitfield-Ballantine Manor Estates Assn., So. Srs. Golf Assn., Am., N.Y., N.Y.C., N.Y. County bar assns., Delta Tau Delta, Phi Delta Phi. Clubs: Sara Bay Country, Sarasota Yacht, Ivy League, Dartmouth of Sarasota, Field, 200, World Seniors. Home: 1130 Whitfield Av Sarasota FL 33580 Office: 3640 S Tamiami Trail PO Box 15447 Sarasota FL 33579

HARE, (STEPHEN) HOPKINS, artist; b. N.Y.C., Dec. 1, 1921; s. Clarence Hopkins and Ethel (Anyon) H.; adopted by Channing Hare, 1970; grad. Kent Sch., 1940; student Yale, 1940-42. Exhibited one man shows, 1947-—, Margaret Brown Gallery, Boston, Grand Central Moderns, N.Y.C., Worth Av. Gallery, Palm Beach, Fla., Palm Beach Galleries; permanent collections exhibited Boston Mus. Fine Arts, Toledo Mus. Art, Houston Mus. Art., IBM Collection Am. Art, Norton Gallery Art, West Palm Beach, Fla.; nat. mus. collections include Met. Mus., N.Y.C., Whitney Mus., Phila., Carnegie Inst. Tech., Pitts., U. Ill., Detroit Inst., John Herron Mus., Indpls., Corcoran Gallery, Washington. Served with AUS, 1942-44. Club: Bath and Tennis (Palm Beach). Address: 220 Worth Av Palm Beach FL 33480

HARE, ROY ALLEN, physician; b. Sanford, N.C., Apr. 2, 1921; s. Simpson Turner and Halsie (Holleman) H.; B.S., Wake Forest Coll., 1942; M.D., Bowman Gray Sch. Medicine, 1945; m. Myrtle Frances Brandon, June 20, 1945; children—Joyce (Mrs. Lowell Hugh Mallard), Roy Allen, George Brandon, Ellen Penny. Intern Hartford (Conn.) Hosp., 1945-46; resident in internal medicine Bapt. Hosp., Winston-Salem, N.C., 1949-51; practice medicine specializing in internal medicine, Durham, N.C., 1951-—; mem. staff Watts Hosp., Durham, 1951-—; cons. N.C. Meml. Hosp., Chapel Hill, 1956-—. Served with USAF, 1947-49. Mem. A.C.P., N.C., Durham-Orange County med. socs., U.S. Power Squardon. Baptist. Kiwanian. Club: Hope Valley Country (Durham). Home: 3828 Somerset Dr Durham NC 27707 Office: 731 Broad St Durham NC 27705

HARGIS, BILLY JAMES, clergyman, coll. pres.; b. Texarkana, Tex., Aug. 3, 1925; s. Jimmie Earsel and Laura Lucille (Fowler) H.; student Ozark Bible Coll., 1943-45; B.A., Pikes Peak Bible Sem., 1957; Th.B., Burton Coll., 1958; LL.D., Bob Jones U., 1961; m. Betty Jane Secrest, Dec. 21, 1951; children—Bonnie Jane, Billy James II, Becky Jean, Brenda Jo. Ordained to ministry Christian Ch., 1943; pastor First Christian Ch., Sallisaw, Okla., 1944-46, Granby, Mo., 1946-47, Sapulpa, Okla., 1947-50, Ch. of Christian Crusade, Tulsa, 1966-70; pres. Christian Echoes Nat. Ministry, Inc. (Christian Crusade), Tulsa, 1948-70; pres. Am. Christian Coll., Tulsa, 1970-—. Speaker, Christian Crusade network radio broadcasts, 1949-—; pub. Christian Crusade Monthly mag., 1948-—, Weekly Crusader, 1960-—; pres. bd. Sch. of Christian Crusade, 1967-—. Vice pres. Internat. Com. for Def. Christian Culture, West Germany, Austria, Portugal, Spain, 1964-—. Author books including: Communist America—Must It Be, 1960; Communism—The Total Lie, 1961; Facts About Communism and Churches, 1962; The Real Extremists—The Far Left, 1964; Distortion By Design, 1965. Recorded albums. Home: 6641 E 60th Pl Tulsa OK 74145

HARGRAVE, GEORGE HERBERT, med. service co. exec.; b. Meridian, Miss., Jan. 26, 1943; s. George Herbert and Clara Bell (Gibson) H.; student Temple Jr. Coll., 1961-63; m. Sammie Kay Dupre, June 20, 1964; children— George, Kim, Cindy. Adminstr., Parkview Nursing Home, Waco, Tex., 1960-64; pres., adminstr. Twin Oaks Retirement Center, Inc., Waco, 1964-68; v.p. Nat. Living Centers, Inc., Houston, 1968-—. Mem. Central Tex. chpt. Tex. nursing Home Assn. (pres. 1961-65). Mason. Home: 5831 W Bellfort St Houston TX 77035 Office: 3003 W Alabama St Houston TX 77006

HARGRAVE, WILLIAM LOFTIN, bishop; b. Wilson N.C., Nov. 10, 1903; s. Benjamin Worthington and Frances (Daniel) H.; LL.B., Atlanta Law Sch., 1924; B.D., Va. Theol. Sem., 1932, D.D., 1962; S.T.M., U. of South, 1952, D.D., 1962; m. Minnie Frances Whittington, Feb. 13, 1939; children—Frances, Elizabeth, Sarah, William. Admitted to Ga. bar, 1925; asst. trust officer Miami Bank & Trust Co. (Fla.), 1924-26; asso. firm Shutts & Bowen, Miami, 1926-27; ordained to ministry Episcopalian Ch., 1932; rector in Cocoa, Fla., 1932-43, Ft. Pierce, Fla., 1943-45, Holy Comforter Ch., Miami, 1945-48, Holy Communion Ch., Charleston, S.C., 1948-53; exec. sec. Diocese of South Fla., Winter Park, 1953-61, bishop 1961-69; bishop Diocese of S.W. Fla., St. Petersburg, 1969-—. Pres. Wuesthoff Hosp. Cocoa, Fla., 1941-43, Porter Mil. Acad. Charleston, 1952. Pres. Fla. Council Chs., 1957-58, Fla. Migrant Ministry, 1963-66; mem. gen. bd. Nat. Council Chs. Christ, 1964-69. Clubs: Rotary (pres. Cocoa 1937); Orlando (Fla.) Country; St. Petersburg Yacht. Home: 1701 Brightwaters Blvd NE St Petersburg FL 33704 Office: Box 20827 St Petersburg FL 33742

HARGRAVES, J. ARCHIE, clergyman, univ. pres.; b. Greensboro, N.C., Aug. 2, 1916; s. Archie and Geneva (McCollum) H.; B.S., Agrl. and Tech. Coll. N.C., 1940; B.D., Union Theol. Sem., 1948; postgrad. Columbia, 1948-51; certificate regional and city planning, Mass. Inst. Tech., 1961; L.H.D., Lewis and Clark Coll., 1967; Dr. Religion, Chgo. Theol. Sem., 1968; m. Inez Boger, Nov. 5, 1942; 1 dau., Janet Delmanda. Dir. pub. relations Agrl. and Tech. Coll., Greensboro, N.C., 1938-41; asst. information specialist OPA, Washington, 1941-42; advt. rep. N.Y. Amsterdam News, N.Y.C., 1942-43; ordained to ministry; minister East Harlem Protestant Parish, N.Y.C., 1948-51, West Side Christian Parish, Chgo., 1952-56, Lawndale Presbyn. Ch., Chgo., 1954-56, Nazarene Conglist. Ch., Bklyn., 1956-61; sec. for Urban Ch., United Ch. Bd. for Homeland Ministries, N.Y.C., 1961-64; dir. mission devel. Urban Tng. Center for Christian Mission, Chgo., 1964-71; pres. Shaw U., Raleigh, 1971-—. Chaplain dept. correction, N.Y.C., 1958-64; lectr. social problems Bibl. Sem. N.Y., N.Y.C., 1959-61, Inst. Social and Religious Studies, Jewish Theol. Sem. Am., N.Y.C., 1961-63; clin. instr. Chgo. Theol. Sem., 1964-68, prof. urban mission Chgo. Theol. Sem., 1968-71. Pres. Bedford Stuyvesant (N.Y.) Area Project, 1956-60; dir. tng. Bklyn. Coordinating Council for Youth, 1958-60; v.p. Bklyn. Protestant Council, 1959-60; mem. program bd. div. Christian life and mission, Nat. Council Chs. Christ U.S.A., N.Y.C., 1960-—; mem. agenda com. Chgo. Freedom Movement, 1966-71; pres., chmn. West Side Orgn., Chgo., 1964-71; mem. staff The Black Consortium, 1968-—. Bd. dirs. Chgo. City Missionary Soc., Am. Civil Liberties Union. Served to 2d lt. AUS, 1943-46. Recipient Alumni award Agrl. and Tech. Coll. N.C., 1963. Mem. Religious Research Assn., Nat. Assn. for Community Devel. Author: Stop Pussyfooting Through a Revolution, 1964. Home: Shaw Univ Raleigh NC 27602

HARGRAVES, WILLIAM DAVID, pub. co. exec.; b. Chickasha, Okla., June 6, 1910; s. William David and Martha Armilda (McDowell) H.; grad. high sch.; m. Clyda Louise McLain, Aug. 30, 1929; 1 dau., Conita Anne (Mrs. Howard Bradford). Printer, The Landmark (now Gazette), Rush Springs, Okla., 1920-27, Duncan (Okla.) Banner, 1927; printer, operator Altus Times-Democrat, 1927, Hollis, Okla., 1927-28; printer, machinist Lawton Pub. Co., Inc. (Okla.), 1928-39, supt., prodn. mgr., 1939-—, mem. trust com., 1958-—. Mem. So. Newspaper Pub. Assn. (chmn. western div. 1960, exec. com. 1939-—), Izaak Walton League, Internat. Typographical Union (pres. 1929-31). Methodist (active fund drives). Home: 1131 Elm St Lawton OK 73501 Office: 102 S 3d St Lawton OK 73501

HARGREAVES, MARY WILMA MASSEY (MRS. HERBERT WALTER HARGREAVES), editor, educator; b. Erie, Pa., Mar. 1, 1914; d. Albert Edward and Bess (Childs) Massey; A.B., Bucknell U., 1935; M.A., Radcliffe Coll., 1936, Ph.D., 1951; fellow Brookings Instn., 1939-40; m. Herbert Walter Hargreaves, Aug. 24, 1940. Research editor Harvard Grad. Sch. Bus. Adminstrn., 1937-39; asso.

editor Papers of Henry Clay, U. Ky., Lexington, 1952-—, asst. prof. history, 1964-69, asso. prof., 1969-—. Mem. Am. Assn. U. Women (chpt. pres. 1957-59, state dir. 1957-64, 66-71), Am. Assn. U. Profs., Am., So. hist. assns., Orgn. Am. Historians, Agrl. History Soc., Phi Beta Kappa (chpt. sec. 1964-70, pres. 1970-71), Phi Alpha Theta, Sigma Tau Delta. Author: Dry Farming in the Northern Great Plains, 1957. Contbr. articles to profl. jours. Home: 237 Cassidy Av Lexington KY 40502 Office: Office Tower U Ky Lexington KY 40506

HARGRODER, CHARLES MERLIN, polit. writer; b. Franklin, La., Sept. 5, 1926; ed. La. State U., 1943-47. With Baton Rouge Morning Advocate, 1947-50, Monroe (La.) Morning World, 1952-53; exec. asst. to gov. of La., 1953-56; pub. relations sec. to Congressman Hale Boggs, 1956-57; regional rep. Inter-Industry Hwy. Safety Com., 1957-58; polit. writer New Orleans Times-Picayune, 1959-—. Served to sgt. AUS, 1950-52. Mem. Sigma Delta Chi. Office: PO Box 44122 Capitol Sta Baton Rouge LA 70804

HARKEY, PAUL, lawyer; b. Idabel, Okla., Mar. 4, 1920; s. John Paul and Jessie (Elliott) H.; B.A., Southeastern State Coll., 1950; J.D. U. Okla., 1961; m. Lucille Roy, June 1, 1942; children—Cheryl Annette, Roy Lee, John Paul. Admitted to Okla. bar, 1948; practice law, Idabel, 1948-55; atty. DeLeuw Cather Engrs., 1955-59; atty. Okla. Hwy. Dept., 1959-64; hearing examiner U.S. Dept. Health, Edn. and Welfare, Dallas, 1964-—. Mem. Okla. Legislature, 1946-54; chmn. So. regional edn. bd. Council on Mental Health and Tng., 1955-59. Served with USNR, 1940-46; ETO, PTO; capt. Res. Named to Okla. Med. Scis. Hall of Fame, 1958. Mem. Am. Judicature Soc., Am., Fed., Dallas, Okla. bar assns., State Bar Tex., Am. Soc. Trial lawyers, Nat. Conf. Trial Examiners, Order of Coif, Phi Delta Phi. Mason (Shriner). Home: Box 22122 Dallas TX 75222 Office: 1512 Commerce St Dallas TX 75202

HARKINS, HERSCHEL SPRINGFIELD, lawyer, state rep.; b. Asheville, N.C., Mar. 22, 1917; s. Thomas J. and Roxy (Seevers) H.; student Davidson Coll., 1933-35; A.B., U. N.C., 1938, LL.B., 1940; m. Mary Anne Koonce, Dec. 23, 1968; children—(by previous marriage) Jane (Mrs. Larry M. Cairnes), Spring, Hope. Admitted to N.C. bar, 1940; practiced in Asheville, 1940-—; mem. firm Harkins, Van Winkle and Walton, 1940-49, Herschel S. Harkins, 1949-—; mem. N.C. Ho. of Reps., 1967-—. Mem. N.C. Cts. Commn., 1969-71; chmn. Army Adv. Com. 1949-54; mem. N.C. Local Govt. Study Commn., 1967-71, N.C. Child Care Study Commn., 1967-69. Pres., Asheville Community Theater, 1949. Pres. Buncombe County Young Democratic Club, 1963. Bd. dirs., sec. Victoria Hosp., 1952-54; bd. govs. Sports Car Club of Am., 1964, 66-67. Served to maj. USAAF, 1942-46. Decorated D.F.C., Air medal with twelve oak leaf clusters, Silver Star medal. Mem. Am., N.C., Buncombe County (v.p. 1954) bar assns., Am. Judicature Soc., Asheville C. of C., Phi Delta Theta. Democrat. Episcopalian. Mason (32 deg.). Clubs: Asheville Country, Mountain City (sec. 1954). Home: 5 Griffing Blvd Asheville NC 28804 Office: PO Box 7266 Asheville NC 28807

HARKINS, RALPH DOUGLAS, govt. ofcl.; b. Ponca City, Okla., Apr. 29, 1939; s. Floyd L. and Wilma (Mieir) H.; B.S., Central State Coll., Edmond, Okla., 1962; M.S., U. Okla., 1964, Ph.D., 1967; m. Judy M. Mosley, Aug. 12, 1960; children—Linda, Joe, Karen. Computer programmer U. Okla., 1962-63; math. statistician Fed. Water Pollution Control Adminstrn., Ada, Okla., 1965-67, chief pollution surveillance br., 1967-71; chief tech. and adminstrv. data support br. Environmental Protection Agy., Dallas, 1971-72; mgr. region VI facility Environmental Protection Agy., Ada, 1972-—. Served with USMC, 1959-65. Mem. Am. Statis. Assn., Biometric Soc. Home: Route 3 Ada OK 74820 Office: PO Box 159 Ada OK 74820

HARKINS, WILLIAM G., librarian; b. Macon, Miss., Mar. 28, 1911; s. Samuel Walter and Mattie (Dillard) H.; A.B., U. Ala., 1932; B.S. in L.S., U. Ill., 1933; M.A. in L.S., U. Mich., 1940; postgrad. U. Chgo., 1948-50, Rutgers U., 1958; m. Nina Elizabeth Markette, May 27, 1936 (dec. 1969); m. 2d, Jean Barrett Foerster, Nov. 25, 1969; 1 son, Barrett Jonathan Foerster. Med. librarian, cataloger U. Miss., 1933-36, asst. librarian, 1937; asst. reclassification U. Mich., 1936-37; asst. librarian U. Ala., 1937-40; librarian U. Miami, 1940-51, Coll. William and Mary, 1951-57; asso. dir. libraries U. Fla., 1957-62, U. of South, 1962-—. Served with USAAF, 1942-46. Mem. A.L.A., Tenn., Southeastern library assns., Assn. Coll. Research Libraries, Phi Sigma Kappa. Methodist. Home: Sewanee TN 37375

HARLAN, JAMES CLARKE, banker; b. Charlottesville, Va., May 1, 1928; s. John Frederick and Myrtle (Clarke) H.; B.A., U. Va., 1950, M.A., in Polit. Sci., 1952; certificate Stonier Grad. Sch. Banking, Rutgers U., 1964; m. Betty Anne Blakey, Apr. 16, 1955; children—James Clarke, Sally Blakey. With State-Planters Bank (name changed to United Va. Bank 1971), Richmond, Va., 1954-—, v.p., 1965-71, sr. v.p., 1971-—. Lectr. banking courses Univ. Coll., U. Richmond, 1959-—; instr. Va.-Md. Bankers Sch., Charlottesville, 1964-—, Stonier Grad. Sch. Banking, Rutgers U., 1970-—. Served to 1st lt. AUS, 1952-54; capt. Res. ret. Mem. Am. Inst. Banking, Robert Morris Assos., Delta Upsilon. Presbyn. Clubs: Farmington Country (Charlottesville); Richmond Host Lions (v.p.). Home: 8705 Shadow Lane Richmond VA 23229 Office: 9th and Main Sts Richmond VA 23219

HARLAN, JOHN FREDERICK, JR., hosp. adminstr.; b. Charlottesville, Va., Dec. 18, 1925; s. John Frederick and Myrtle (Clarke) H.; B.A., U. Va., 1950; grad. Med. Coll. Va. Sch. Hosp. Adminstrn., 1952; m. Dorothy Reedy Koontz, Sept. 6, 1950; children—Patricia Ann, John Frederick III, Dorothy Karol and Barbara Ellen (twins), Douglas Allen. Adminstrv. asst. U. Va. Hosp., Charlottesville, 1952-54, asst. dir., 1954-58, asso. dir., 1958-65, dir., 1965-—. Chmn. Community Drive Nat. Found. Infantile Paralysis, 1958; mem. Charlottesville Sch. Bd., 1963-66. Mem. Albemarle Democratic Com., 1956-60. Pres. U. Va. Hosp. Employees Credit Union; bd. dirs. United Givers Fund, U. Va. Student Aid Found., Blue Cross/Blue Shield of Va. Served with AUS, 1944-46. Decorated Bronze Star medal; recipient Key Man award Jaycees, 1959. Mem. Med. Coll. Va. Sch. Hosp. Adminstrn. Alumni Assn. (dir.), U. Va. Alumni Assn., Albemarle County Med. Soc., Charlottesville-Albemarle Jr. C. of C. (past pres.), Va. Hosp. Assn. (pres. elect). Lion (past pres.). Home: 1628 Keith Valley Rd Charlottesville VA 22901 Office: U Va Hosp Charlottesville VA 22901

HARLAN, JOHN MARSHALL, asso. justice U.S. Supreme Ct.; b. Chgo., May 20, 1899; s. John Maynard and Elizabeth Palmer (Flagg) H.; A.B., Princeton, 1920; B.A., M.A. (Rhodes Scholar), Balliol Coll, Oxford U., 1923, hon. fellow, 1955; LL.B., N.Y. Law Sch., 1924, LL.D., 1955; LL.D., Columbia, Brandels U., Oberlin Coll., Evansville Coll, Princeton U. Mich., 1959, Northwestern U., 1960, U. Pa., 1963; m. Ethel Andrews, Nov. 10, 1928; 1 dau. Eve (Mrs. Frank Dillingham). Admitted to N.Y. State bar, 1925; asst. U.S. atty. So. Dist. N.Y., 1925-27; spl. asst. atty. gen., N.Y., 1928-30, 51-53; mem. firm Root, Ballantine, Harlan, Bushby & Palmer, N.Y.C., 1931-54; judge U.S. Ct. of Appeals, 2d Circuit, 1954-55; asso. justice Supreme Ct. of U.S., 1955-—. Chief counsel, gen. counsel, N.Y. State Crime Commn. 1951-53. Served as col. USAAF, 1943-45; chief operations analysis sect. 8th Air Force, Eng. Decorated Legion of Merit, Croix de Guerre (France), Croix de Guerre (Belgium). Mem. Am., N.Y. State bar assns., Bar Assn. City N.Y., N.Y. County Lawyers Assn. Clubs: Century Assn., University (N.Y.C.); Country (Fairfield, Conn.), Ivy (Princeton, N.J.). Home: 1677 31st NW Washington DC 20007 also Weston CT 06880 Office: US Supreme Ct Washington DC 20543

HARLAN, MONAS OSCAR, educator, tenor; b. New Castle, Pa., Feb. 19, 1912; s. Benjamin Victor and Edith (Cunningham) H.; student Westminster Coll., 1931-33, 36-38, B. Pub. Sch. Music, 1938; postgrad. (scholar) Juilliard Grad. Sch. Music, 1939-42; Mus.M., U. So. Cal., 1950; m. Vivianne Elaine Hodge, Dec. 28, 1962; stepchildren—Laura (Mrs. Eran Buckley), Maribeth Turner, Janis Turner, Charles Turner. Ch. soloist various chs., 1931-—, soloist First Ch. Christ Scientist, Shreveport, La., 1959-—; mem. faculty U. Louisville, 1953-56, Mont. State U., 1956-59, Centenary Coll., Shreveport, 1959-—; world premiers include Volpone, 1953, The Transposed Heads, 1954, Double Trouble, 1954, Sch. for Wives, 1955, Nora, 1967; soloist Los Angeles Philharmonic Orch., 1949, San Francisco Symphony, 1950, Radio Free Europe, 1958, choral groups, Europe, 1956-60; also performer in numerous operas and recitals; dir. Centenary Coll. Opera Workshop, 1964-—; judge Met. Opera Auditions, 1962-—, voice festivals and talent contests. Served to 1st lt. AUS, 1942-46; PTO. Decorated Bronze Star. Mem. Nat. Assn. Tchrs. of Singing, La. Music Tchrs. Assn. (chmn. voice sect. 1961-65), Pi Kappa Lambda. Home: 141 Atkins St Shreveport LA 71104

HARLAN, ROSS EDGAR, utility co. exec.; b. Poteau, Okla., July 11, 1919; s. Edgar L. and Leola (Carter) H.; student Southeastern State Coll., Durant, Okla., 1937-38, Eastern Okla. A. and M. Coll., 1938-39; B.S., Okla. State U., 1941; m. Margaret Burns, May 31, 1942; children—Raymond Carter, Rosemary, Marvin Allen, Scott Lee. Bus. instr. Poteau (Okla.) Jr. Coll., 1946; with Okla. Gas & Electric Co., 1946-—, v.p., Oklahoma City, 1964-—. Bd. dirs. Oklahoma City area Campfire Girls, Okla. Council Econ. Edn., Variety Health Center, Oklahoma City. Served to lt. col. USAAF, 1941-46. Recipient George Washington Honor medal Freedoms Found., Valley Forge, Pa., 1969. Mem. Oklahoma City C. of C., Beta Gamma Sigma. Methodist. Kiwanian. Club: Beason (Oklahoma City). Author: Strikes, 1947. Home: 2639 Eagle Lane Oklahoma City OK 73127 Office: 321 N Harvey St Oklahoma City OK 73101

HARLAN, VERNON ELIJAH, farm implement co. exec.; b. Batesville, Miss., Nov. 14, 1904; s. Luther Montgomery and Jessie Lawrence (Legge) H.; student Warren Bus. Coll., 1929, LaSalle Extension U., 1932; m. Sarah Elizabeth Watson, Oct. 15, 1933; children—Dowell Brooks, Carolyn Drew (Mrs. Cecil Knight Province, Jr.). Prodn. clk. Bradley Lumber Co., Warren, Ark., 1923-29; payroll clk. Lee Wilson & Co., Wilson, 1929-32; office mgr. Keiser Supply Co., Keiser, 1932-37, Lee Wilson & Co., Victoria, 1937-40; treas. Missco, Inc., Osceola, 1940-—, Missco Implement Co., Inc., Monette, 1951-—; Missco Implement Co. of Blytheville, Inc., 1941-—; registered rep. Consumer-Investor Planning Corp., St. Louis, 1960-71. Treas. Osceola chpt. A.R.C., 1942-45. Mem. C. of C. Osceola. Baptist (treas. 1953-66, sec. bd. deacons 1971-—). Mason. Home: 404 E Johnson Av Osceola AR 72370 Office: 501 S Walnut St Osceola AR 72370

HARLAND, JOHN HERDMAN, pub. co. exec.; b. Bessbrook, N. Ireland, Jan. 22, 1885; s. John and Emma Gaynor (Wells) H.; came to U.S., 1901, naturalized, 1912; student pub. schs.; m. Wilhelmina Drummond, Oct. 18, 1922; 1 dau., Miriam (Mrs. John A. Conant). With H. Midwood Sons, wholesale grocers, Providence, R.I., 1901-05, Austin Nichols Co. Grocers, N.Y.C., 1905-06, Foote & Davies Co., printers, Atlanta, Ga., 1907-23; pres. John H. Harland Co., printing co., Atlanta, Ga., 1923-69, chmn. bd., 1969-—. Bd. dirs. Atlanta Boys Club. Recipient outstanding achievement award Boys Clubs of Am., 1963. Episcopalian. Mason, Kiwanian. Club: Atlanta Athletic, Commerce. Home: 1027 Oxford Rd Atlanta GA 30306 Office: 655 Lambert Dr NE Atlanta GA 30324

HARLEY, WILLIAM GARDNER, assn. exec.; b. Madison, Wis., Oct. 9, 1911; s. Joel Alva and Elizabeth (Gardner) H.; B.A., U. Wis., 1935, M.A., 1940, LL.D. (hon.), 1972; m. Jewell Bunnell, June 15, 1940; children—Cynthia (Mrs. Kenwood Foster), Linda (Mrs. John Settle), Gratia, Gail (dec.). Instr. dept. radio-television edn. and staff Sta. WHA, U. Wis., 1936-42, asst. prof., 1942-53, asso. prof., 1953-57, prof., 1957-60; chief announcer Wis. Broadcasting System, 1935-40, program dir., 1940-44, acting dir., 1944-46; program coordinator Ford-Nat. Assn. Ednl. Broadcasters Adult Edn. Radio Project, 1950-52; pres. Nat. Assn. Ednl. Broadcasters, Washington, 1960-—; mem. nat. industry adv. com. FCC, 1960-—; del. Internat. Conf. on Schs. Broadcastings, Rome, 1961, Tokyo, 1964, Paris, 1967; bd. dirs. U.S.-Japan Television Program Exchange Center, 1964-68; v.p. Joint Council Ednl. Telecommunications, 1960-—; pres. Ednl. Media Council, 1966-68; chmn. screening com. for Radio-TV Fulbright Scholarships, 1966-—; mem. U.S. Nat. Commn. UNESCO, 1962-68, 70-—; chmn. Mass Communications Com., 1967-68; del. UNESCO Conf. Use Space Broadcasting, Paris, 1971, Internat. Broadcasting Unions Conf. Communications Satellites, 1972. Cons. Rothschild Found., AID, Com. for Econ. Devel., USPHS. Recipient Distinguished Citizen award Creighton U., 1965, Distinguished Alumnus award Wis. Alumni Assn. of Washington, 1966. Mem. Nat. Assn. Ednl. Broadcasters, Am. Assn. Sch. Adminstrs., Broadcast Pioneers, Nat. Broadcasters Club, Phi Eta Sigma, Beta Theta Pi. Club: Congressional, International, Cosmos, Broadcasters (Washington). Contbr. articles profl. jours. Home: 5301 Boxwood Ct Washington DC 20016 Office: 1346 Connecticut Av Washington DC 20036

HARLOW, JAMES GINDLING, JR., utility exec.; b. Oklahoma City, May 29, 1934; s. James Gindling and Adalene (Rae) H.; B.S., U. Okla., 1957, postgrad., 1959-61; m. Jane Marriott Bienfang, Jan. 30, 1957; children— James Gindling III, David Ralph. Research analyst Okla. Gas and Electric Co., Oklahoma City, 1961-63, div. auditor, 1963-65, adminstrv. asst., 1965-66, asst. treas., 1966-68, treas., 1968-69, sec.-treas., 1969-70, v.p., treas., 1970-72, exec. v.p., treas., 1972-—, also dir.; dir. Fidelity Bank N.A., Village Bank, Oklahoma City. Treas., Oklahoma County Red Cross, 1969; vice chmn. Frontiers of Sci. Found., Inc., 1970-—. Bd. dirs. Salvation Army, Community Council Central Okla., Jr. Achievement; bd. visitors U. Okla. Coll. Bus. Served with USNR, 1957-59. Mem. Okla. Soc. Security Analysts. Clubs: Petroleum, Economic, Oklahoma City Golf and Country, Men's Dinner, Whitehall (Oklahoma City). Home: 1713 Pennington Way Oklahoma City OK 73116 Office: PO Box 321 Oklahoma City OK 73101

HARM, MARVIN PAUL, educator; b. Bertrand, Neb., Nov. 17, 1932; s. Vernon G. and Emma L.J. (Koch) H.; B.A., Sacramento State Coll., 1965; M.S. in Library Sci., Fla. State U., 1966; postgrad. U. Ga., 1968-69; m. Jewel Dean Rains, July 9, 1954; children—Lyndean, Steven Paul, Jeanine, Ruthanne. Head librarian Albany (Ga.) Jr. Coll., 1966-70; asst. prof. library adminstrn. and ednl. media Emory U., Atlanta, 1970-—. Served to capt. USAF, 1953-60. Mem. S. Ga. Acad. Librarians (chmn. 1967-68), Am., Southeastern Ga. library assns., Assn. Ednl. Communications and Technology, Assn. Am. Library Schs., Nat. Assn. Ednl. Broadcasters, Beta Phi Mu. Lutheran. Initiator, editor Plan weekly, Albany Jr. Coll., 1966-67. Home: 3405 Breton Circle NE Atlanta GA 30319

HARM, RAY, artist; b. Randolph County, W. Va.;, 1926; student Cooper Sch. Comml. Art, Cleve.; hon. doctorate Centre Coll., 1967, Pikeville, Coll., 1968, Davis and Elkins Coll, 1969; m. Mildred Anne Atkins, Aug. 12, 1969. Cowhand, horse wrangler, rodeo rider Western U.S.; staff artist Cleve. Audubon Soc.; wildlife artist; conservation lectr.; writer, illustrator Louisville Times; former artist-in-resident U. Ky. Cons. C.E. Buckley wildlife sanctuary, Versailles, Ky. Mem. Nat., Louisville, Buckley Hills Audubon Socs. Author: The Ray Harm Nature Sketchbook. Home: Chenoa KY 40925

HARMAN, ALEXANDER M(ARRS), judge; b. War, W.Va., Feb. 7, 1921; s. Alexander M. and Rose Sinclair (Brown) H.; student Concord Coll., 1938-41; LL.B., Washington and Lee U., 1944, Nat. Coll. State Trial Judges, 1965. Admitted to Va. bar. 1943; partner Gilmer, Wysor & Gilmer, 1947-52, Gilmer Harman & Sadler, 1952-64; judge 21st Jud. Circuit, 1964-69; justice Supreme Ct. Appeals Va., 1969-—. Town atty., 1944-46; substitute trial justice, 1945-47. Chmn. Pulaski County Development Authority, 1962-64; chmn. bd. zoning appeals, 1958-64. Chmn. State Bd. Elections of Va., 1955-64; chmn. Pulaski County Dem. Com. 1960-64; mem. finance com. Dem. State Central Com. 1956-64; sec. 19th Dist. Dem. Senatorial Com., 1956-64; mem. Va. Commn. Constnl. Revision, 1968; chmn. Battle for Gov. Com. for Pulaski County, 1949. Pres. New River Valley Indsl. Found., Inc., 1963-—, bd. dirs., 1961-64. Mem. Am., Va. (v.p. 1949-51), Pulaski County bar assns., Phi Delta Phi, Omicron Delta Kappa, Pi Kappa Alpha. Mason, Elk (Va. pres. 1963-64). Home: 1303 Prospect Av Pulaski VA 24301 Office: Municipal Bldg Pulaski VA also Supreme Ct Appeals Bldg Richmond VA 23219

HARMAN, JAMES WILLIAM, JR., lawyer; b. Richmond, Va., Sept. 29, 1922; s. James William and Coralie (Laird) H.; student Lynchburg Coll., 1940-41; B.S. in Bus. Adminstrn., Washington and Lee U., 1947, LL.B., 1949; m. Evelyn R. Herring, Mar. 29, 1949; children—James William III, Jonathan H. Partner Harman & Burgess Co., Tazewell, Va., 1946-—; admitted to Va. bar, 1949; since practiced law in Tazewell; partner Harman & Harman 1949-70; sr. partner Harman & Campbell, 1970-—; atty. Town of Tazewell, 1956-61; commonwealth's atty. Tazewell County, 1952-56; sec., treas., dir. Coal Creek Coal Co., Tazewell, 1951-—; partner Edwards & Harman, Welch, W.Va., 1959-—; gen. counsel S.W. Va. Nat. Bank, Bluefield, 1963-—. Recorder Town of Tazewell, 1949-51, mayor, 1961-67. Pres., bd. dirs. Tazewell Community Hosp., 1968-—. Served with AUS, 1943-46. Mem. Am., Va. (dist. com. 1957-60, chmn. 1960), Tazewell County (pres. 1960-61) bar assns., Phi Beta Kappa, Omicron Delta Kappa, Phi Delta Phi. Republican. Episcopalian. Rotarian (pres. Tazewell club 1962-63). Club: University (Bluefield). Home: 724 Fairgrounds Rd Tazewell VA 24651 Office: 116 W Main St Tazewell VA 24651

HARMAN, WILLIAM BOYS, JR., lawyer; b. Newport News, Va., June 5, 1930; s. William Boys and Helen (Conner) H.; A.B., Coll. William and Mary, 1951, B.C.L., 1956; LL.M., Georgetown U., 1960; m. Claudia Carrington Richmond, Dec. 21, 1952; children—Susan Carol, Thomas Scott, Ann Carrington. Tax atty. Gen. Motors Corp., Detroit, 1956-58; atty. Office of Chief Counsel, Internal Revenue Service, Washington, 1958-59; atty. Office of Tax Legislative Counsel, U.S. Treasury Dept., Washington, 1959-61; atty. Cummings & Sellers, Washington, 1961-62; asso. gen. counsel Am. Life Conv., Washington, 1962-67, gen. counsel, 1968. Sec.-treas., bd. dirs. Arthur W. Radford Charitable Found. Served with USCGR, 1952-54. Mem. Am., Fed. bar assns., Va. State Bar, Bar Assn. D.C., Assn. of Life Ins. Counsel, Am. Law Inst., S.A.R., William and Mary Law Sch. Assn., Phi Beta Kappa, Phi Alpha Delta, Sigma Alpha Epsilon. Clubs: Washington Golf and Country, University, Nat. Lawyers, Metropolitan. Home: 4905 N 35th Rd Arlington VA 22207 Office: 1701 K St NW Washington DC 20006

HARMON, ALFRED EUGENE, physician; b. Crowley, La., Oct. 13, 1942; s. Warren Walter and Rita Lucille (Burgin) H.; B.S., U. So. La., 1965; M.D., La. State U., 1967 children—Alfred Eugene II, Stephen Kindred, Christine Marie, Mary Catherine. Intern Charity Hosp., New Orleans, 1967-68; resident Lafayette (La.) Charity Hosp., 1968-69; practice medicine specializing in family medicine, Crowley, 1969-—. Mem. Crowley Jr. C. of C., Acadia Parish Med. Soc. (sec.-treas., 1971), Phi Beta Phi. Home: 325 E 8th St Crowley LA 70526 Office: PO Box 920 Crowley LA 70526

HARMON, CHARLES CALVIN, supt. schs.; b. LaJunta, Colo., Mar. 14, 1920; s. Charles George and Elizabeth (Foreman) H.; B.S., U. Tex., 1950, M.Ed., 1953; Ph.D., East Tex. State U. of Commerce, 1969; m. Bonnie Grace Harmon, Apr. 25, 1942; children—Winona, Charles Calvin II, Marsha (Mrs. Karl Harman), Kathleen, Nathan, Beverly, Sterling. Prin., Hart (Tex.) Elementary Sch., 1950-51; prin., coach Kelton (Tex.) Independent Sch. Dist., 1951-52, supt. schs., 1952-55; supt. schs. Vega (Tex.) Ind. Sch. Dist., 1955-61; Nat. Defense Edn. Act. Inst. fellow U. Tex., 1961-62; supt. schs., Hawkins, Tex., 1962-—. Chmn. exec. council East Tex. Sch. Study Council, 1971-72; mem. exec. council Region VII Service Center, 1970-71; mem. exec. dist. Region VII council Boy Scouts Am., 1962-72. Served with AUS, 1941-45; PTO Decorated Bronze Star with palm. Mem. N.E.A., Am. Assn. Sch. Adminstrs., Tex. Tchrs. Assn. (county pres. 1964-65, Congress of Parents and Tchrs., Phi Delta Kappa. Methodist (chmn. finance com. 1965-72). Lion (pres. 1964-65), Kiwanian (pres. 1957-58). Club: Quarterback, University of Texas T Assn. Home: 715 Raymer St Hawkins TX 75765 Office: Drawer L Hawkins TX 75765

HARMON, GEORGE MARION, educator; b. Memphis, Aug. 12, 1934; s. George Marion and Madie (Pink) H.; B.A. with distinction, Southwestern U. at Memphis, 1956; M.B.A., Emory U., 1957; D. Bus. Adminstrn., Harvard, 1963; m. Bessie Will Porter, Dec. 27, 1958; children— Nancy Ruth, Mary Katherine, Elizabeth Tucker, George Marion III. Market research analyst Continental Oil Co., Houston, 1957; research asso. Harvard, 1960-63; asst. prof. Syracuse (N.Y.) U., 1963-66; sr. asso. Planning Research Corp., Washington, 1966-67; prof. econs. and bus. adminstrn. Southwestern at Memphis, 1967-—, chmn. dept., 1968-—, dir. continuing edn. in econs., 1967-—; asso. Logistics Research, Inc., Columbia, Mo., 1970-—. Dir. Ramcon, Inc., Memphis; v.p., treas, Allen Industries, Inc., Memphis, 1972-—, also dir.; dir. Audio-Visual Systems, Inc., Memphis, 1972-—; cons. in field. Mem. Memphis-Shelby County Consolidation Com., 1971; pres. Scenic Hills Action Club, 1970-—. Mem. bd. edn. Fayetteville-Manlius Consol. Sch. Dist., 1965-66. Served with AUS, 1957-59. Mem. Financial Execs. Inst., Am., So. econ. assns., C. of C. (mem. research policy com. 1968-—), Phi Beta Kappa, Omicron Delta Kappa, Beta Gamma Sigma. Kiwanian. Club: Scenic Hills Recreation (dir. 1970-73; chmn. bd. 1971-—) (Memphis). Author: Transportation: The Nation's Lifelines, 1968, Contbr. articles to profl. jours. Home: 3256 Ancroft Cove Memphis TN 38128

HARMON, HUBBARD WILTON, supt. schs.; b. nr. Tyler, Tex., May 10, 1915; s. Hubbard Jefferson and Emma Evrona (Mullican) H.; B.S., Sam Houston State U., 1940; M.Ed., East Tex. State U., 1958; m. Pearl C. Key, Nov. 28, 1936; children—Brenda (Mrs. William E. Baker), Charles Wilton, James Gary. Coach, tchr. pub. schs., Golden,

Tex., 1940-42, Consol. Steel Schs., Orange, 1942-45; prin. high sch., Whitehouse, 1945-47; supt. schs., Golden, 1947-56, Alba-Golden, 1956-62, Dell City, 1962-68, Socorro Ind. Sch. Dist., El Paso, 1968-—. Mem. Am., Tex. assns sch. adminstrs., N.E.A., Tex. Tchrs. Assn. Lion (1st v.p. 1970-71), Mason (K.T., Shriner). Home: 15099 Homestead St El Paso TX 79927 Office: 10150 Alameda El Paso TX 79927

HARMON, LOREN FOSTER, art dealer; b. Judsonia, Ark., Nov. 5, 1912; s. Alfred Roscoe and Mae (Foster) H.; student Ind. U., 1930-32, Ohio U., 1932-33; B.A., State U. Ia., 1935, M.A., 1936; m. Martha Foster, July 25, 1943. Dir. Univ. and Exptl. Theatre, Ind. U., Bloomington, 1936-42; pub. relations mgr. WKBN Broadcasting Corp., Youngstown, O., 1943-48; owner, dir. Pine Shores Park, Sarasota, Fla., 1950-54 v.p., dir. Players, Sarasota, 1955-57; pub. relations dir. Ringling Mus. Art, 1958-59; dir. Oehlschlaeger Galleries, Sarasota, Fla,, 1961-70; v.p. Vandium Tool Co., Athens, O., 1962-69; owner, dir. Harmon Gallery, Naples, Fla., 1964-—. Adviser, Baker Center Collection Am. Art, Ohio U. Bd. dirs. Ringling Mus. Mems. Council, 1957-—; corp. mem. Naples Community Hosp., 1966-—. Recipient Certificate of Merit, Ohio U., 1970. Mem. Am. Ednl. Theatre Assn. (founder), Am. Fedn. Arts, Sarasota Art Assn. (pres. 1959-60), Fla. League Arts, St. Armands Assn. (pres. 1957-58). Methodist. Clubs: Sarasota Yacht, University. Home: 117 S Polk Dr Lido Sarasota FL 33577 Office: Harmon Gallery 1258 3d St S Naples FL 33940 also PO Box 6187 Sarasota FL 33578

HARMON, ROGER Q., JR., physician; b. Texarkana, Tex., Aug. 31, 1919; s. Roger O. and Clyde Madiline (Perry) H.; student Texarkana Coll., 1939, N. Tex. State U., 1940-41, Kings Coll., Cambridge, England, 1942, Centenary Coll., 1945; grad. La. State U., 1946; M.D., U. Tex., 1951; m. Alma Faye Hall, June 21, 1947; 1 dau., Kay Madelon. Intern, Confederate Meml. Hosp., Shreveport, La., 1951-52; practice medicine specializing in gen. practice, Marshall, Tex., 1952-—; mem. staff Meml. Hosp., v.p., 1954, chief med staff, 1972; pres. Pinecrest Med. Center, 1954-—; city health officer City of Marshall, 1952-64. Bd. dirs. Cancer Found., 1953. Served with USAAF, 1941-45. Mem. E. Tex. Show Horse Assn. (bd. dirs. 1965-68), C. of C., Tex. Cammelia Soc. (pres. 1964-65), Marshall Cammelia Soc. (pres. 1959-60), Sigma Alpha Epsilon, Delta Sigma, Theta Kappa Psi. Club: Long Island Ocelot (pres. southwestern br. 1970-—). Home: 606 Lansdowne St Marshall TX 75670 Office: 401 E Pinecrest Dr Marshall TX 75670

HARMS, HAROLD HARVEY, physician; b. Cordell, Okla., Sept. 16, 1916; s. John Henry and Margaret Ruth (Kliewar) H.; B.A., Bethel Coll., 1939; B.S., U. Okla. Sch. Medicine, 1939, M.D., 1941; m. Ruth Maydell James, June 7, 1941; children—Karen Marie (Mrs. Wayne Foster), Linda Jayne (Mrs. Dwight A. Lee), Mary Frances. Intern U. Neb. Hosp., Omaha, 1941; resident Shurly Hosp., Detroit, 1946-47, Wayne County Gen. Hosp., 1947-49; ophthalmologist Green Clinic, Ruston, La., 1949-—; mem. staff Lincoln Gen. Hosp., Ruston. Clin. instr. ophthalmology La. State U. Sch. Medicine, Shreveport, 1971-—. Served from 1st lt. to maj. M.C. AUS, 1942-45. Decorated Bronze Star medal. Diplomate Am. Bd. Ophthalmologists. Fellow Am. Acad. Ophthalmology and Otorhinolarynology, La.-Miss. Opthal. and Otol., PanAm. Ophthalmology Soc. A.C.S., mem. North Central Parishes, La. State Med. Soc., A.M.A., Assn. Research Ophthalmologists, Soc. Cryosurgery. Methodist. Kiwanian (pres. 1955). Home: 407 Pinecrest Dr Ruston LA 71270 Office: Green Clinic Ruston LA 71270

HARMS, LOUISE IVIE (MRS. WILLARD DANIEL HARMS), librarian; b. Birmingham, Ala., June 25, 1924; d. Henry J. and Lola (Hicks) Ivie; B.S., U. Ala., 1944; B.S. in L.S., George Peabody Coll. for Tchrs., 1946; m. Willard Daniel Harms, Oct. 17, 1955; children—Dennis Leon, Daniel Lee, Willard Daniel. Asst. librarian Coll. Edn. Library, U. Ala., 1944-45; night reference asst. George Peabody Coll. Tchrs., Nashville, 1945-46; cataloger Allegheny Coll. Library, Meadville, Pa., 1946-47; 1st asst. cataloging dept. U. Ark. Library, Fayetteville, 1947; head cataloger Coll. Edn. Library, U. Ala., 1948-51; spl. services librarian U.S. Army, Europe, 1951-55, library adminstr. spl. activities div., 1958-63; tchr. English, Sweetwater (Tenn.) High Sch., 1963-64; asst. librarian Merner-Pfeiffer Library, Tenn. Wesleyan Coll., Athens, 1964-65, head librarian, 1965-—. Mem. A.L.A., Southeastern, Tenn. library assns., N.E.A., Am. Assn. U. Profs., Alpha Beta Alpha. Presbyn. Home: 20 Hickory Lane Sweetwater TN 37874 Office: Tenn Wesleyan Coll Athens TN 37303

HARMS, PAUL GEORGE, air force officer; b. Fairbury, Ill., Nov. 21, 1941; s. Roy Amos and Mabel Irene (Bayston) H.; B.S., U. Ill., 1963, M.S., 1965; PH.D., Purdue U., 1969; m. Lois Ellen Kyburz, Jan. 23, 1966; 1 son, Konrad Paul. Research and teaching asst. U. Ill., Urbana, 1963-65, Purdue U., Lafayette, Ind., 1965-68; commd. lt. USAF, 1968, advanced through ranks to capt., 1971; staff research physiologist U.S. Air Force Sch. Aerospace Medicine, Brooks AFB, Tex., 1968-—. Recipient David Ross fellowship Purdue U. Research Found., 1966. Mem. Soc. for Study of Reprodn. (charter), Aerospace Med. Assn., Am. Soc. Animal Sci., A.A.A.S., Farm House. Republican. Baptist. Contbr. articles to profl. jours. Home: 642 Funston Pl San Antonio TX 78209 Office: USAF Sch Aerospace Medicine SMPR Brooks AFB TX 78235

HARMS, ROBERT HENRY, educator; b. Dover, Ark., Sept. 27, 1923; s. Charles W. and Stella (Moore) H.; B.S., U. Ark., 1953, M.S., 1954; Ph.D. (Ralston Purina fellow), Tex. A. and M. U., 1956; m. Catherine McAllister, Apr. 4, 1944 (dec. Nov. 1962); children—Carolyn (Mrs. Elwin R. Thrasher, Jr.), Robert Henry; m.2d, Mary Bryan, June 22, 1966. Asst. prof. U. Tenn., Nashville, 1955-57, asso. prof., 1957; asso. prof. U. Fla., Gainesville, 1957-62, prof., 1962-63, chmn. dept. poultry sci. Inst. Food and Agrl. Sci., 1963-—. Served with AUS, 1945-46. Recipient Jr. Faculty award Fla. chpt. Gamma Sigma Delta, 1962; Am. Feed Mfrs. Assn. award, 1966. Mem. Am. Inst. Nutrition, Soc. Exptl. Biology and Medicine, Poultry Sci. Assn., World Poultry Sci. Assn., Sigma Xi, Alpha Zeta, Gamma Sigma Delta. Home: 1421 NW 28th St Gainesville FL 32601

HARNED, HENRY H., assn. exec. Exec. dir. Ky. Bar Assn., Frankfort. Address: 243 State Capitol Frankfort KY 40601*

HARNER, CHARLES EMORY, editor; b. N.Y.C., Aug. 27, 1901; s. Lloyd Charles and Anna (Webster) H.; A.B., U. Ill., 1923; m. Zofia Wasilewska, July 27, 1935; 1 son, Michael James. Reporter, Hinsdale (Ill.) Doings, 1917-19, Ill. State Jour., Springfield, 1923-24, Chgo. Tribune, 1924-25, Champaign (Ill.) News-Gazette, 1925-28; editor A.P., Chgo., Washington, S.Am., N.Y.C., 1928-41; pub. relations counselor N.W. Ayer & Son, Hill & Knowlton, N.Y.C., 1944-48; dir. pub. relations Nat. Retail Mchts. Assn., N.Y.C., 1944-48; owner, operator advt. agy., Oceanside, Cal., 1948-52; pub. affairs officer Am. embassies, San Salvador, El Salvador, 1952-56, La Paz, Bolivia, 1956-60, Caracas, Venezuela, 1960-64; asso. editor Fla. Trend Mag., Tampa, 1965-—. Served from capt. to maj. USAAF, 1942-44. Mem. Tau Kappa Epsilon, Sigma Delta Chi. Episcopalian. Mason (32 deg.) Home: 669 Avenida de Mayo Sarasota FL 33581 Office: Box 2350 Tampa FL 33601

HARPER, CHARLES FLOYD, architect; b. Bonham, Tex., Nov. 15, 1929; s. Charles Floyd and Donna Gertrude (Coonrod) H.; B.Arch., Tex. Tech. U., 1955; m. Catherine Elysabethe Fonville, July 1, 1955; children— Charles Martin, Jon Mark. Apprentice architect Harris & Killebrew, architects and engrs., Wichita Falls, Tex., 1955-57; chief designer Butler-Kimmel Co., architects and engrs., Lubbock, Tex., 1957-61; asso. James R. Killebrew & Assos., architects and engrs., Wichita Falls, Tex., 1961-62; partner Harper, Martin & Assos., architects, engrs., Wichita Falls, 1962-69; prin. architect Charles Harper & Assos., architects, programmers, planners, Wichita Falls, Tex., 1969-—. Pres., Concern, 1969-70; treas. Concerned Ams. for Responsible Edn., 1971; chmn. Wichita Falls Common Cause. Bd. dirs. Southside Girls' Club, 1962, Golden Cross Found., Mem. A.I.A. (pres. Wichita Falls chpt. 1967), Human Resources Council, Tex. Soc. Architects (v.p. 1972), Tech. Execs. Assn. (dir. Wichita Falls 1964-72, pres. 1972), Guild Religious Architects. Democrat (del. state conv. 1972). Methodist (dist. treas. 1970-71). Mason (Shriner). Club: Red Raider (Wichita Falls). Prin. archtl. works include Classroom/Office Bldg. Tex. Tech. U., Evans Elementary Sch., Bonham, Tex., Bethania Hosp., Wichita Falls, Univ. United Meth. Ch., Wichita Falls, Augustan Apts., Vernon, Tex. Home: 4632 Sierra Madre Dr Wichita Falls TX 76310 Office: 4724 Old Jacksboro Hwy Wichita Falls TX 76302

HARPER, CLYDE WALLACE, physician; b. Greer, S.C., July 23, 1929; s. Clyde Austin and Cecil Stella (Mayfield) H.; student Wofford Coll., 1946-48; A.B., Duke, 1950; M.D., Med. Coll. S.C., 1956; m. Paula Dew, July 23, 1965; children—Susan Elizabeth, Sarah Dew. Intern St. Louis (Mo.) City Hosp., 1956-57; resident, Med. Center Hosp., Charleston, S.C., 1957-60; fellow in clin. hematology Emory U. Sch. Med., 1960-61; practice medicine specializing in internal medicine, Greenville, S.C., 1961-—; sr. asso. in medicine Greenville (S.C.) Gen. Hosp.; cons. medicine Shriner's Hosp. for Crippled Children, Greenville. Mem. council assos. Wofford Coll., Spartanburg, S.C., 1970-—. Diplomate Am. Bd. Internal Medicine. Mem. A.C.P., A.M.A., S.C. Med. Assn., Greenville County Med. Soc. Methodist. Club: Greenville Country. Home: 2 Petiver Lane Greenville SC 29605 Office: 24 Vardry St Greenville SC 29601

HARPER, EDWARD J., clergyman. Ordained priest Roman Catholic ch., 1939; consecrated bishop, 1960, now bishop St. Thomas (V.I.). Address: Box 1825 St Thomas VI 00801*

HARPER, EDWIN LELAND, govt. ofcl.; b. Belleville, Ill., Nov. 13, 1941; s. Horace Edwin and Evelyn Ruth (Wright) H.; B.A. with honors Principia Coll., 1963; Ph.D., U. Va., 1968; m. Lucy Davis, Aug. 21, 1965; 1 dau., Elizabeth Allen. Lectr. dept. polit. sci. Rutgers U., New Brunswick, N.J., 1966-68; spl. asst. to dir. Resources Planning Staff, Bur. of the Budget, Washington, 1968-69; sr. cons. Arthur D. Little, Inc., Washington, 1969; spl. asst. to Pres. U.S., 1969-—; asst. dir. Domestic Council, White House, 1970-—. Participant, UN World Population Conf., Belgrade, 1965; Mem. foreign affairs com. Nat. Fedn. Youth Republicans, 1961-62. Recipient travel and study grant Ford Found., 1965, Nat. Defense fellowship, 1963. Mem. Am. Soc. Pub. Adminstrn., Am. Polit. Sci. Assn., So. Polit. Sci. Assn., Raven Soc., Omicron Delta Kappa. Home: 2701 Connecticut Av NW Washington DC 20008 also 9200 Litzsinger Rd St Louis Mo 63144Office: The White House Washington DC 20500

HARPER, GEORGE LEWIS, judge; b. Crawfordville, Fla., Apr. 8, 1925; s. Joseph A. and Ora E. (Allen) H.; student Fla. State U., 1946-48; LL.B., U. Fla., 1952; m. Naomi R. Enfinger, June 27, 1951; children— George L., William R., Kenneth E., Larry. Admitted to Fla. bar, 1952; practiced in Tallahassee, 1952-56; county and juvenile judge Wakulla County, Crawfordville, Fla., 1957-—. Served with AUS, 1943-46. Mem. State County Judges Assn., Nat., Fla. juvenile judges assns., V.F.W., Am. Legion. Democrat. Mason (Shriner). Home and office: Crawfordville FL 32327

HARPER, GEORGE MILLS, educator; b. Linn Creek, Mo., Nov. 5, 1914; s. Avery and Grace (Shipman) H.; A.B., Culver-Stockton Coll., 1940; M.A., U. Fla., 1947; postgrad. U. Cal. at Berkeley, 1947-48; Ph.D., U. N.C., 1951; m. Mary Jane Hughes, June 15, 1944; children— Margaret Mills, Ann Christian. From instr. to prof., also chmn. English dept. U. N.C., 1950-66, asso. dean arts and scis., 1955-60; prof., chmn. English dept. U. Fla., 1966-69; dean Coll. Arts and Scis., Va. Poly. Inst., 1969-70; prof., chmn. dept. English, Fla. State U., 1970-—. Cons. U.S. Office Edn., 1967, 68, 69. Bd. govs. Chapel Hill (N.C.) Pub. Library, 1958-64, Chapel Hill United Fund, 1964-66. Served with USNR, 1942-46; ETO. Mem. Modern Lang. Assn., Nat. Council Tchrs. English, Coll. English Assn., Lambda Chi Alpha. Democrat. Methodist. Author: The Neoplatonism of William Blake, 1961; Yeats's Quest for Eden, 1966; Thomas Taylor: Selected Writings, 1968. Contbr. articles profl. publs. Home: 407 Plantation Rd Tallahassee FL 32303

HARPER, JAMES COLQUITT, oil field service co. exec.; b. Shreveport, La., Mar. 11, 1931; s. George Colquitt and Ruth (Shannon) H.; B.S., La. Tech. U., 1953; m. Jerry Viola Jackson, Feb. 22, 1952; children—Jerry Douglas Rayburn, Pamela, Jamie Michelle, Sandra Lynn, Rebecca Ann. Petroleum engr. Humble Oil & Refining Co., New Orleans, 1953-59; mgr. drilling and prodn. J. Ray McDermott &Co., Inc., Houston, 1959-66; v.p., gen. mgr. Dresser Offshore Services, Inc., oil field services, Houston, 1966-71; owner, pres. Services Equipment & Engring., Conroe, Tex., 1971-—. Cons. engr. Mem. Am. Assn. Oilwell Drilling Contractors (dir.), Am. Inst. Mining Engrs, Am. Petroleum Inst. Mason (Shriner). Clubs: Conroe Country, Conroe; Lamplighter (bd. dirs. 1969-70) (New Orleans). Patentee in field. Address: Route 5 Box 350A Conroe TX 77301

HARPER, JAMES CUNNINGHAM, band dir.; b. Lenoir, N.C., Feb. 17, 1893; s. George Finley and Frances (Cunningham) H.; student Culver Naval Sch.; B.S., Davidson Coll., 1915, L.H.D., 1965; M.A., U. N.C., 1916; grad. student Duke, 1928, Lenoir Rhyne Coll., 1930, Columbia, 1932; m. Charlotte Critz, Mar. 19, 1927 (dec.); children—Lucy (Mrs. L.A. Grier, Jr.), James Cunningham, George F., Charlotte C. (Mrs. George E. Stone). Band dir. Lenoir (N.C.) High Sch., 1924-58, emeritus, 1958-—; v.p., dir. Fairfield Chair Co., Lenoir, N.C.; tchr. summer sch. Appalachian State Tchrs. Coll., 1955, Davidson Coll. Bd. trustees Caldwell Meml. Hosp. Served O.T.C., 1917, commd. 2d lt., promoted capt., 1918, S.A.T.C., 1918-19. Mem. Am. (pres. 1955, chmn. bd. dirs. 1956), N.C. (pres. 1943-44) bandmasters assns., Am. Sch. Band Dirs. Assn., Music Educators Nat. Conf. (hon. life mem. N.C. assn.), C. of C., Am. Legion (chaplain 1950), Phi Mu Alpha Sinfina Soc., Phi Beta Mu. Presbyn. (elder). Club: Lenoir Country. Contbr. articles to sch. mags. and jours. Home: 203 Norwood St Lenoir NC 28645

HARPER, JAMES SHIELDS, retail trade, real estate exec.; b. Clover, S.C., Jan. 16, 1923; s. Carl Brown and Nannie (Dickson) H.; grad. pub. high sch.; m. Edna Marie Wilson, June 14, 1947; children—Susan (Mrs. John D. Hornaday), James Shields. Loan, br. mgr. Comml. Credit Corp., Fayetteville, and Durham, N.C., 1946-49; partner Vann Motor Finance Co., Fayetteville, 1949-55; partner Highland Lumber Co., Fayetteville, 1949-55, sec., 1955-69; pres. Brookwood Water Corp., Fayetteville, 1963-—; v.p. Mobile Home Sales Corp., Fayetteville, 1962-—; sec. Handy Pantry, Inc., Fayetteville, 1970-—, and others. Chmn. bd. trustees Cape Fear Valley Hosp., Fayetteville, 1966; sec. bd. trustees Cumberland County Hosp. System Inc., Fayetteville, 1967-—. Presbyn. (elder). Kiwanian. Club: Highland Country (Fayetteville). Home and office: 2306 Raeford Rd Fayetteville NC 28305

HARPER, JOHN PRESTON, judge; b. Portsmouth, Va., Jan. 12, 1921; s. Wilson B. and Bertie (Turner) H.; A.B., Coll. William and Mary, 1941; J.D., U. Va., 1946; m. Dorothy Leigh Hogshire, Oct. 10, 1942; children—John Preston, Penelope Anne. Admitted to Va. bar, 1942; gen. practice Norfolk, Va., 1946-68; gen. counsel Norfolk, Balt. & Carolina Line, Inc., 1960-68, sec., 1965-68; asst. U.S. atty. Eastern Dist. Va., 1947-51; judge Civil Justice Ct., 1968-69, Ct. Law and Chancery, 1969-—. Mem. Ho. of Dels., Gen. Assembly Va., 1955-60 Mem. alumni bd. Coll. William and Mary, 1958-60, bd. visitors, 1960-68, vice rector, 1966-68. Served with USNR, 1942-46; capt. Res. Mem. Am. Judicature Soc., Pi Kappa Alpha. Presbyn. Clubs: Virginia, Norfolk Yacht and Country. Home: 1501 Eleanor Ct Norfolk VA 23508 Office: 100 St Pauls Blvd Norfolk VA 23510

HARPER, MONTER BLAINE, banker; b. Frenchton, W. Va., June 4, 1920; s. Monter Arnol and Lola Anna (Cutright) H.; student Benjamin Franklin U., 1940-43, Carolinas Sch. Banking, U. N.C., 1946-52; m. Mary Elizabeth Shaw, June 14, 1945; children—Mary Lou (Mrs. James Franklin Lowery, Jr.), Anna Katherine, Sarah Helen. Asst. cashier Central Nat. Bank, Buckhannon, W.Va., 1937-40; files analyst FBI, Washington, 1940-43; with the Carolina Bank, Sanford, N.C., 1946-—, exec. v.p., 1965-—, also dir. Instr. Carolinas Sch. Banking, 1971-72; cons. Personnel Commn., Bank Adminstrn. Inst., 1969-72. Chmn., Indsl. Devel. Com., Sanford, 1964-70. Served with AUS, 1943-46. Recipient Order of Long Leaf Pine, by Gov. N.C., 1971, distinguished service award Sanford Lions Club, 1970. Mason (Shriner), Elk, Moose. Mem. C. of C. (pres. 1969-70); (distinguished citizen award 1969). Presbyn. Home: Route 3 Box 735 Sanford NC 27330 Office: P O Drawer 2100 Sanford NC 27330

HARPER, ROBERT ANDREWS, govt. ofcl.; b. Jenkinsberg, Ga., Oct. 11, 1925; s. James Bernard and Dasilee (Nutt) H.; student Emory U., 1943-44; B.S., U. Ga., 1948; m. Frances Whelchel McWhirter, Sept. 4, 1948; children—Frances Ruth, Martha Ann, Robert Andrews, James Hubert. Forester Hercules Powder Co., Starke, Fla., 1948; with U.S. Forest Service, 1949-—, forester Chattahoochee Nat. Forest, 1949-51, Yazoo-Little Tallahassee Flood Prevention Project, 1951-53; asst. dist. ranger Apalachicola Nat. Forest, 1953-55, Kisatchee Nat. Forest, 1955, dist. ranger Francis Marion Nat. Forest, 1955-58, personnel officer, Atlanta, 1958-60, recreation staff officer Nat. Forests in Fla., 1960-69, Chattahoochee-Oconee, Gainesville, Ga., 1969-—. Mem. Fla. Resource Use Edn. Com., 1967-69; pres. Nat. Forest Credit Union Tallahassee, 1967-68, Fla. Inst. Park Personnel, 1969. Mem. troop com. Boy Scouts Am., Tallahassee, 1965-69. Mem. adv. com. Lake City (Fla.) Jr. Coll., 1966-69. Served with USNR, 1943-45. Mem. Nat. Recreation Park Assn. (mem. dist. adv. com. 1967-69, mem. nat. council 1969), Soc. Am. Foresters. Home: Route 12 Skylark Pl Gainesville GA 30501 Office: Box 1437 Gainesville GA 30501

HARPER, SPENCER EARL, JR., lawyer; b. Little Rock, Oct. 17, 1933; s. Spencer Earl and Eleanor (Rieder) H.; B.A., U. Louisville, 1955, J.D. cum laude, 1957; m. Clarice Carol Sharpe, July 1, 1955; children—Spencer Earl III, Grafton Sharpe. Admitted to Ky. bar, 1958; practiced in Louisville, 1961-—; partner firm Grafton, Ferguson, Fleischer & Harper, 1961-—. Trustee, Louisville Law Alumni Found. Served to capt., Judge Adv. Gen. Corps, USAF, 1958-61. Mem. Am., Fed., Ky., Louisville bar assns., Am. Judicature Soc., Arnold Air Soc., Phi Kappa Phi, Pi Kappa Phi, Delta Theta Phi, Omicron Delta Kappa. Democrat. Presbyn. Clubs: Pendennis, Tavern, Jefferson. Home: 3309 Green Hill Lane Mockingbird Valley Rd Louisville KY 40207 Office: 310 W Liberty St Louisville KY 40202

HARPER, THOMAS, lawyer, mem. Democratic Nat. Com.; b. Greenwood, Ark., Nov. 23, 1908; s. Robert Atlas and Merton (Othella) H.; student U. Ill., 1927-28; m. Vivien W. Tatum, Jan. 16, 1939 (dec. June 1966); children—Thomas, Granville T., Blake W., Kay Nelson. Admitted to Ark. bar, 1930; practice in Greenwood, 1930-39, Ft. Smith, 1939-—. Sec., v.p., dir., gen. counsel Ark.-Best Freight System, Inc., v.p., gen. counsel Ark. Best Corp.; dir. gen. counsel City Nat. Bank. Chmn. Ark. Dem. Com., 1954-64; del. Dem. nat. convs., 1956, 60, 64, chmn. delegation, 1960, 64; mem. Dem. Nat. Com. for Ark., 1964-72. Bd. dirs. Ft. Smith Boys Club. Served to lt. (j.g.) USNR, 1944-45. Mem. Am. Coll. Trial Lawyers, Am., Ark., Sebastian County bar assns., Motor Carrier Lawyers Assn. Methodist. Home: 5001 S Cliff Dr Fort Smith AR 72901 Office: Kelley Bldg Fort Smith AR 72901

HARPER, WALTER W., devel. cons.; b. Leggett, N.C., 1919; B.S. in Civil Engring., N.C. State U., 1948. Joined N.C. Div. Commerce and Industry, 1948, head div. from 1957; now devel. cons., Greensboro, N.C. Address: 1512 Kirkpatrick Pl Greensboro NC 27408*

HARPSTER, JAMES ERVING, lawyer; b. Milw., Dec. 24, 1923; s. Philo E. and Pauline (Daanen) H.; Ph.B., Marquette U., 1950, LL.B., 1952. Admitted to Tenn. bar, 1953, Wis. bar, 1952; dir. information services, Nat. Cotton Council Am., Memphis, 1952-55; dir. pub. relations, Christian Bros. Coll., 1956; mgr. govt. affairs dept. Memphis C. of C., 1956-62; exec. v.p. Rep. Assn. Memphis and Shelby County, 1962-64; private practice of law, Memphis, 1964-67; partner Rickey, Shankman, Blanchard, Agee & Harpster, and predecessor firm, Memphis, 1967-—. Mem. Shelby County Tax Assessor's Adv. Com., 1960-61; editor, asst. counsel Memphis and Shelby County Charter Comm., 1962; mem. Shelby County Election Commn., 1968-70; mem. Tenn. State Bd. Elections, 1970-—, sec., 1971-—. A founder Lions Inst. for Visually Handicapped Children, 1954, chmn. E. H. Crump Meml. Football Game for Blind, 1956; pres. Siena Student Aid Found., 1960; bd. dirs. Memphis Pub. Affairs Forum; mem. Civic Research Com., Inc., Citizens Assn. Memphis and Shelby County. Republican candidate Tenn. Gen. Assembly, 1964; v.p. Nat. Council Republican Workshops, 1967-69; pres. Rep. Workshop Shelby County, 1967, 71, Rep. Assn. Memphis and Shelby County, 1966-67. Served as sgt. USAAF, 1942-46. Mem. Am., Tenn., Wis. bar assns., Navy League U.S., Am. Conservative Union, Cardinal Mindszenty Found., Am. Legion. Roman Catholic. Lion (dir. Memphis 1955-62). Clubs: Executives, Press, Toastmasters (Memphis). Home: 3032 E Glengarry Rd Memphis TN 38128 Office: Suite 3500 100 North Main Bldg Memphis TN 38103

HARR, KARL GOTTLIEB, JR., lawyer, assn. exec.; b. South Orange, N.J., Aug. 3, 1922; s. Karl Gottlieb and Mildred (Reid) H.; A.B., Princeton, 1943; LL.B., Yale, 1948; D.Phil. (Rhodes scholar), Oxford U., 1950; m. Patricia Stratton Adams, Oct. 11, 1947; children—Timothy Adams, Karl Gottlieb III, Catherine Anne, Amy. Admitted to N.Y. bar, 1951; asso. Sullivan & Cromwell, N.Y.C., 1950-54; spl. asst. to under-sec. state for adminstrn., staff dir. sec. state's pub. com. on personnel, 1954-55; dir. spl. project Richardson Found., 1955; dep. asst. sec. def. Nat. Security Council Affairs and Plans, alternate def. mem. Nat. Security Council Planning Bd., 1956-57; spl. asst. to Pres. of U.S., vice chmn. Operations

Coordinating Bd., adviser Nat. Security Council Planning Bd., 1958-61; counsel to Rogers, Hoge, Hills, N.Y.C., 1961-63; pres. Aerospace Industries Assn. Am., Inc., Washington, 1963—; dir. Union Trust Co., Washington. Chmn. Council Def. and Space Industry Assns., 1964; chmn. internat. coordinating council Aerospace Industries Assn.; chmn. Nat. Aero. Noise Abatement Council, 1964; bd. dirs. Expt. in Internat. Living, Outward Bound. Alumni trustee Princeton U. Served with AUS, 1943-46. Mem. Am. Bar Assn., Phi Beta Kappa, Phi Delta Phi. Home: 6 W Kirke St Chevy Chase MD 20015 Office: 1725 Desales St Washington DC 20036

HARRA, CHARLES CLAYTON, edn. adminstr.; b. Greensboro, N.C., June 20, 1924; s. Charles Emmanuel and Shirley (Clayton) H.; B.A., Rollins Coll., 1949; m. Marilyn Bennett Hoffman, Sept. 23, 1952 (div. July 1964); 1 dau., Virginia Bennet. Controller Ringling Museum Art, Sarasota (Fla.) 1959-65; bus. mgr. New Coll., Sarasota, 1965—. Served with USAAF, 1943-45, 51-53. Decorated Air medal with silver cluster. Home: PO Box 1898 Sarasota FL 33579

HARRAR, HELEN JOANNE, librarian; b. Seattle, May 9, 1935; d. Ellwood Scott, Jr. and Marion (Green) Harrar; B.A., Oberlin Coll., 1957; M.L.S., Rutgers U., 1960, Ph.D., 1962. Student asst. Duke U. Library, summers 1951-55, Oberlin Coll. Library, 1953-57; asst. Duke U., Library, 1957-58; research asst., then instr. library service Grad. Sch. Library Service, Rutgers U., 1958-60, research asso., 1960-61; research asst., then asst. to dir. Columbia Univ. Library, 1961-63; librarian, prof. library sci. Winthrop Coll., Rock Hill, S.C., 1963-70; asso. dir. libraries U. Ga., 1971—. Mem. adv. com. library research and tng. projects U.S. Office Edn., 1968-71; cons. various libraries. Mem. Am., S.C., N.C., Ga., Southeastern library assns., Am. Assn. U. Women, Am. Soc. Information Sci., Delta Kappa Gamma. Beta Phi Mu. Editor, Southeastern Librarian, 1972—. Home: 620 Hill St Athens GA 30601

HARRAWOOD, PAUL, univ. dean; b. Akin, Ill., Aug. 28, 1928; s. Raymond E. and Verdie Alma (Galbraith) H.; B.S., U. Mo. at Rolla, 1951, M.S., 1956; Ph.D. (NSF fellow), N.C. State U., 1967; m. June Anne Harris, Nov. 28, 1953; 1 dau., Laura Anne. Instr. civil engring. U. Mo. at Rolla, 1954-56; asst. prof. civil engring. Duke, 1956-67, asst. dean engring., 1961-62; asso. prof. civil engring. Vanderbilt U., Nashville, 1967-70, prof., 1970—, asso. dean engring., 1967—, acting dean engring., 1970-71; test engr. McDonnel Aircraft Corp., 1957; constrn. mgmt. engr. U.S. Army C.E., 1958. Served with USNR, 1951-54. Mem. Am. Soc. C.E., Soc. Am. Mil. Engrs., Am. Soc. Engring. Edn., Am. Assn. Higher Edn., A.A.A.S., Sigma Xi, Tau Beta Pi, Chi Epsilon. Home: 5314 Camelot Ct Brentwood TN 37027 Office: Vanderbilt U Box 1607 Sta B Nashville TN 37203

HARRELL, CHARLES HOPKINS, coll. adminstr.; b. Snow Hill, N.C., May 1, 1932; s. William and Fannie (Young) H.; B.S., E. Carolina U., 1955; postgrad., U. Ky., 1964; m. Faye Watson, May 22, 1955; children—Kelly, Rene, Charles Jr. Auditor, N.C. Revenue Dept., 1955-59, Burlington Industries, Greensboro, N.C., 1959-63; bus. mgr., treas. Mount Olive (N.C.) Coll., 1963—. Bd. dirs. F.W.B. Childrens Home, 1968-69, pres. alumni assn., 1968-69. Commr., Mount Olive Housing Authority, 1969—. Recipient Outstanding Young Man of Year award, 1965; Founders award A.R.C., 1967. Mem. N.C. Financial Aid Adminstrs., So. Assn. Coll. and Univ. Bus. Officers, Assn. Sch. Bus. Officers, Internat. (senator, life mem.), U.S. (nat. dir. 1968), N.C. (v.p. 1967, state project chmn. 1968-69), Mount Olive jr. chambers commerce, Mount Olive C. of C. (sec. 1972-73, pres., dir.). Mason (Shriner), Woodman of World. Clubs: Trojan (treas.), Goldsboro (N.C.) Country. Home: 110 College Circle Mount Olive NC 28365 Office: 209 Breazeale Av Mount Olive NC 28365

HARRELL, JAMES ANDREW, dentist; b. Elkin, N.C., July 14, 1922; s. Roy Brannock and Mattie Reid (Doughton) H.; student U. N.C., 1939-42; D.D.S., Va. Commonwealth U., 1945; m. Idabel Jane Gibbs, June 19, 1945; children—James Andrew, Deborah (Mrs. Robert Lee Kirkham III), Gavin Gibbs, Stephen Westall. Pvt. practice dentistry, Elkin, N.C., 1945—; V.P. Dillon and Norman, Inc., 1969—; dir. Yadkin Valley Bank and Trust Co., United Savs. and Loan Assn. Commr., City of Elkin, 1961-67, mayor, 1967—. Bd. dirs. YMCA, pres. 1962; bd. dirs. Hugh Chatham Meml. Hosp., United Fund, pres. 1964; pres. N.C. Dental Found., 1971—. Served with AUS, 1943-45, USNR, 1945-46, 52-54. Decorated Fauchard medal; named Man of Year, Kiwanis Club, Elkin, 1968. Fellow Internat. Coll. Dentists, mem. Blue Ridge (pres. 1968), N.C. (pres.-elect 1972—), Second Dist. (pres. 1960-61) dental socs., Pierre Fouchard Acad., Omicron Kappa Upsilon. Democrat. Methodist (chmn. bd., lay leader). Kiwanian (pres. 1963). Home: 430 Hawthorne Rd Elkin NC 28621 Office: 128 W Main St Elkin NC 28621

HARRELL, MORRIS, lawyer; b. Grandview, Tex., Apr. 16, 1920; B.B.A., Baylor, U., 1942, LL.B., 1942. Admitted to Tex. bar, 1942, U.S. Dist. Ct. bar, 1946, U.S. Supreme Ct. bar, 1959; asst. U.S. atty. No. Dist. Tex., 1947-51; now practice law, Dallas. Research fellow, trustee Southwestern Legal Found. Fellow Am. Coll. Trial Lawyers, Tex., Am. bar founds.; mem. Dallas (pres. 1962), Am. bar assns., State Bar Tex. (chmn. bd. 1968-69; pres. 1970-71). Address: 4200 Republic Bank Bldg Dallas TX 75201*

HARRELL, ROGER LEON, educator; b. Clovis, N.M., Nov. 25, 1935; s. Joel Reagan and Dorothy (Poe) H.; B.S., Eastern N.M. U., 1956, M.A., 1959, Ed.M., 1963; Ed.D., U.N.M., 1967; m. Mary Rose, July 26, 1957; children—John Roger, Kelli Julienne, Elizabeth Jill. Tchr. pub. schs., Clovis, 1956-58, Modesto, Cal., 1958-64; dir. curriculum and instrn. Santa Fe Pub. Schs., 1964-65; asst. prof. Tex. A. and M. U., College Station, 1965-67, asso. prof., 1968-69; career fellow U.S. Office Edn., Washington, 1966-67; consortium dir. ESC Group F, Edn. Professions Devel., El Paso, Tex., 1969-72; asso. prof. ednl. adminstrn. U. Tex. at El Paso, 1969-72; dir. curriculum and fellowship programs, Monrovia, Cal., 1971—. Mem. N.E.A., Assn. Supervision and Curriculum Devel., Mem. Ch. of Christ. Rotarian. Home: 619 W Hillcrest St Monrovia CA 91016

HARRELL, ROY ALVIN, JR., govt. ofcl.; b. Fort Worth, Jan. 9, 1936; s. Roy Alvin and Lucile (Ingham) H.; B.A., U. Tex., 1957; M. Internat. Service, Am. U., 1960; m. Charlotte Elizabeth Purcell, Feb. 11, 1967; 1 dau., Carol Elizabeth. Translator, Library Congress, Washington, 1958-60; intelligence analyst Dept. State, Washington, 1960-62; program operations analyst Am. embassy, Conakry, Guinea, 1962-65; econ. support officer AID, Dept. State, Washington, 1965-67; attache for econ. affairs Am. embassy, Ft. Lamy, Tehad, Africa, 1967-70; chief budget dir. Office Planning for Internat. Security Affairs, Dept. State, Washington, 1970—. Recipient Outstanding Service award U.S. Govt., 1965. Mem. Pi Delta Phi, Sigma Delta Pi, Alpha Phi Omega, Phi Sigma Alpha. Methodist. Mason, Rotarian. Contbr. profl. and religious jours. Home: Drawer B Ozona TX 76943 Office: Dept State Washington DC

HARRELSON, WILLIAM LOUIS, state ofcl.; b. Mullins, S.C., July 25, 1913; s. Maxey Clarence and Dora (Page) H.; student The Citadel 1931-32; LL.B., U. S.C., 1937; m. Grace Hough, Mar. 29, 1956; children— Cynthia Page, William Louis. Admitted to S.C. bar; farmer Mullins, 1932—; dir. Davis Nat. Bank, Mullins and Marion Broadcasting Co., Mullins. Mem. S.C. Ho. of Reps., 1941-42, State Senate, 1953-55; commr. agr. State of S.C., 1956—. Chmn., S.C. Marketing Commn.; ex-officio mem. S.C. Dairy Commn. Served with USCGR, 1942. Mem. S.C. Crop Improvement Assn., Farm Bureau, Nat. (bd. dirs.), So. (past pres.) assns. state depts. agr., Blue Key, Phi Delta Phi, Gamma Sigma Delta. Democrat. Presbyn. (elder). Mason. Clubs: Pineland Country, Mullins Cotillion. Contbr. articles to Names in S.C. publ. Home: 306 Wine St Mullins SC 29574 Office: Wade Hampton Bldg Columbia SC 29202

HARRER, GUSTAVE ADOLPHUS, librarian; b. Durham, N.C., Dec. 30, 1924; s. Gustave Adolphus and Florence Caroline (Wagner) H.; A.B., U. N.C., 1948, M.A., 1950, Ph.D. in Germanic Langs., 1953; M.S. in L.S., U. Ill., 1954; m. Elizabeth Varnado, Sept. 3, 1948; children— Elizabeth Ida, Kathryn Florence, Hugh, Thomas. Asst. prof. German and Latin, Millsaps Coll., 1949-51; asst. order librarian, 1955-57; chief acquisition librarian Stanford Libraries, 1957-58, asst. dir. for central services, 1958-60; dir. libraries and museums Boston U., 1960-68; chmn. dept. library sci., dir. libraries U. Fla. at Gainesville, 1968—. Served with AUS, 1943-45. Faculty fellow Fund for Advancement Edn., 1951-52; Katherine L. Sharp fellow U. Ill. Library Sch., 1953-54; fellow Carnegie Project Advanced Library Adminstrn., Rutgers U., 1958. Mem. A.L.A. Contbr. articles to profl. jours. Home: 4129 NW 36th Terrace Gainesville FL 32601 Office: Research Library U Fla Gainesville FL 32601

HARRIETT, ALBERT LEE, social worker; b. New Bern, N.C., Nov. 25, 1932; s. James Macon and Georgia (Lee) H.; B.A., U. N.C., 1958, M.S.W., 1960; m. Phyllis Norine Sherman, Sept. 18, 1960; children—Gregory Lee, Susan Dianne. Clin. social worker VA Hosp., Salem, Va., 1960-62; psychiat. social worker Roanoke (Va.) Gudiance Center, 1962-65; casework supr. Family Service Assn., Roanoke, 1965-66; exec. dir. Family Service-Travelers Aid Roanoake Valley, 1966-70; psychiat. social work cons. Mountain Empire Guidance Center, Radford, Va., part time 1966-69; therapist Edgemeade of Va., Rocky Mount, 1968-70; exec. dir. Family Service Soc., New Orleans, 1970—. Mem. Nat. Assn. Social Workers, Acad. Certified Social Workers. Home: 2126 St Nick St New Orleans LA 70114 Office: 535 Gravier St New Orleans LA 70130

HARRIGAN, ANTHONY HART, editor, author; b. N.Y.C., Oct. 27, 1925; s. Anthony H. and Elise (Hutson) H.; m. Elizabeth Ravenel, Aug. 16, 1950; children—Anthony Hart III, Elliott McPherson, Elizabeth Chardon, Mary Ravenel. Asso. editor The News and Courier, Charleston, S.C., 1958—, asst. editor, 1968-70; exec. v.p. So. States Indsl. Council, Nashville, 1970—; bd. dirs. Ednl. Found.; mem. nat. strategy com. Am. Security Council; lectr. U.S. Nat. War Coll., other mil. and acad. orgns. Chgo. Episcopalian. Author: The Editor and The Republic, 1954; Red Star Over Africa, 1964; Defense Against Total Attack, The New Republic, 1965; One Against The Mob, 1966; A Guide to the War in Vietnam, 1967. Contbr. Am. and European scholarly and mil. jours. Home: 54 Legare St Charleston SC 29401 Office: Stahlman Bldg Nashville TN 37201

HARRIMAN, EDWARD EUGENE, govt. ofcl.; b. Berwick, Me., June 14, 1921; s. Kirk Eugene and Annie (McKay) H.; B.S. in Mech. Engring., U. N.H., 1944; postgrad. student Cath. U. Am., 1947-56; M.S., U. N.H., 1950; M.S. in Indsl. Mgmt. (Sloan fellow), Mass. Inst. Tech., 1957; m. Jean C. Buescher, June 11, 1949; children—Linda Lee, Robert Kirk. Engr. research and devel. labs., Ft. Belvoir, Va., 1946-50; engr. research and devel. div. Bur. Ordnance, U.S. Navy Dept., 1950-58; sci. adviser to dir. guided missiles, exec. sec. to sci. adv. com. Office Sec. Def., 1958-59; chief satellite br., advanced research projects agy. Office Sec. Def., 1959-61; dir. Office Research and Engring., P.O. Dept., 1961-66; dir. tech. services Housing and Urban Devel., 1966-67; dir. policy devel. Dept. Health, Edn., Welfare, 1967—. Active civic orgns. Served with C.E., AUS, 1943-46. Recipient Superior Accomplishment award U.S. Govt., 1956. Registered profl. engr., Me., D.C. Mem. Assn. Engrs. and Scis. Bur. Ordnance, Am. Rocket Soc., Am. Soc. M.E., Citizens' Assn. Wellington Heights. Home: 7613 Holiday Dr Wellington Heights Alexandria VA 22308 Office: Dept Health Edn Welfare Washington DC 20202

HARRINGTON, ALFRED DAVID, JR., accountant; b. Miami, Fla., Feb. 25, 1929; s. Alfred David and Caroline (Truluck) H.; B.S., U. Fla., 1951; m. Anne V. Sulm, Dec. 19, 1953; children—Marilyn Anne, Brian David. Partner Ring, Mahony & Arner, C.P.A.'s, Miami, 1951-52, Ft. Lauderdale, Fla., 1954-69; partner Lybrand, Ross Bros. & Montgomery, Ft. Lauderdale, 1969—. Campaign chmn., Broward County Tb and Health Assn., Inc., 1961-62, dir., 1963—; treas. Broward Community Coll. Found., Inc. Served from 2d lt. to 1st lt., AUS, 1952-54. Mem. Am., Fla. insts. C.P.A.'s, Estate Planning Council of Broward County, Delta Tau Delta. Democrat. Home: 1700 SE 10th St Fort Lauderdale FL 33316 Office: 1 Financial Plaza Suite 2500 Fort Lauderdale FL 33394

HARRINGTON, CHARLES WRIGHT, librarian; b. Miami, Fla., July 29, 1923; s. Frederick H. and Ina (Hamilton) H.; B.A., U. N.C., 1944; M.A., U. N.M., 1953; postgrad. Tulane U., 1953-60; M.S. in L.S., La. State U., 1961. Librarian trainee Queens Borough Pub. Library, N.Y.C., 1961-62; dir. activities Instituto Guatemalteco Americano U.S. Binational Center, Guatemala City, Guatemala, 1947-49; adminstrv. dir. Instituto Cultural Dominico-American, Ciudad Trujillo, Dominican Republic, 1949-51; head librarian Centenary Coll., Shreveport, La., 1963—. Library cons. U. Minn.-Ford Found. Cooperative project with U. Concepcion (Chile), 1967-69. Served with USNR, 1943-46. Mem. A.L.A., La. Library Assn. Episcopalian. Home: 7441/2 Delaware St Shreveport LA 71106

HARRINGTON, EVANS, educator, author; b. Ala.; student Miss. Coll.; Ph.D., U. Miss. Prof. Am. lit. and creative writing U. Miss.; Faulkner scholar. Recipient Henry Bellaman award creative writing. Bread Loaf Writers Sch. fellow. Author: The Prisoners (novel); Faulkner's Mississippi; Land into Legend (film). Editor University of Mississippi Studies in English. Contbr. short stories to mags. Address: U Miss University MS 38677*

HARRINGTON, JAMES LOYD, city ofcl.; b. Nederland, Tex., July 5, 1938; s. Oren Joseph and Lena Evelyn (Jefferson) H.; student Tex. Firemen's Tng. Sch. Tex. A. and M. u., 1967; m. Gloria Sue Lester, June 11, 1955; children—Samuel Pierce, Christopher Todd. Fireman, Nederland Fire Dept., 1951-58, asst. chief, 1958-65; chief Port Neches (Tex.) Fire Dept., 1965—. Instr. Ann. Tex. Firemen's Tng. Sch., Tex. A. and M. U., 1965-71, Lamar U. Firemen's Tng. Sch., 1970-71. Co-chmn. Port Neches (Tex.) Fall Festival, 1971. Served with AUS, 1961-63. Recipient Fire Chief of the Year award Sabine-Neches Chief's Assn., 1969. Mem. Tex. Fire Chief's Assn., S.E. Tex. Fire Marshal's Assn., Sabine-Neches Chief's Assn. (pres. 1972-73; Fire Chief of Year award 1969). Lion. Home: 2634 Hampton Lane Port Neches TX 77651 Office: 1209 Merriman St Port Neches TX 77651

HARRINGTON, LEONARD RILEY, social worker; b. Miami, Fla., Aug. 22, 1939; s. Irving and Margaret (Allison) H.; B.A. cum laude, U. Miami, 1961; M.S.W., Tulane U., 1963. Social worker VA Hosp., New Orleans, 1964—, Protestant Home for Babies, New Orleans, 1964—; instr. field work La. State U. Sch. Social Welfare, Baton Rouge, 1968—; clin. social worker Southeastern Alcoholism Clinic, New Orleans, 1969—; caseworker Orleans Parish Dept. Pub. Welfare, 1964, Charity Hosp. of La., New Orleans, 1963. Mem. Nat. Assn. Social Workers, Council on Social Work Edn., Nat. Conf. on Social Welfare. Episcopalian. Home: 1208 Bourbon St New Orleans LA 70116 Office: 1601 Perdido St New Orleans LA 70140

HARRINGTON, LISLE RICHARD, supt. schs.; b. Fairmont, Okla., May 24, 1910; s. Foster Harold and Anna Marie (Facks) H.; B.S., Okla State U., 1934, M.S., 1946; m. Vadora E. Woods, Aug. 20, 1935; 1 son, Richard Darrell. Tchr., asst. coach Jet (Okla.) Pub. Sch., 1935; coach, tchr. Bixby (Okla.) Pub. Sch., 1936-38; tchr., coach Inola (Okla.) Pub. Sch., 1938-42, supt. schs., 1942-54; prin. Verdigris Pub. Sch., Claremore, Okla., 1954-63; supt. schs., Rogers County, Claremore, 1963—. Bd. dirs. Northeast Okla. Econ. Devel. Dist. Mem. Am. Assn. Sch. Adminstrs., N.E.A., Nat. Rural edn. assns., Elks Nat. Found., County Supt. Assns. Okla. County Officers Assn. (state treas. 1971-72, dist. pres. 1971-72), County Schoolmasters. Elk (exalted ruler 1956-57). Home: 203 Falletti St Claremore OK 74017 Office: Box 6 Claremore OK 74017

HARRIS, AL, coll. pres.; b. Altus, Okla., Dec. 15, 1909; s. Francis M. and Aggie (Fourmentin) H.; B.S., Southwestern State Coll., Weatherford, Okla., 1931, B.A., 1934; M.A., George Peabody Tchrs. Coll., 1938; Ed.D., Okla. State U., 1955; m. Joe de Bob Dickerson, June 26, 1938; 1 dau., Ruth. Tchr. sci. and math. Custer (Okla.) schs., 1931-33, supt. schs., 1933-39; supt. schs., Watonga, Okla., 1939-47. Clinton, Okla., 1947-60; pres. Southwestern State Coll., 1960—. Pres. Okla. Tchr. Edn. and Certification Commn., 1954-55; mem. Okla. Commn. Improvement Ednl. Adminstrn., 1951-60, Okla. Curriculum Improvement Commn., 1960—. Mem. Nat., Okla. edn. assns., Am., Okla. assns. sch. adminstrs., Clinton C. of C. (dir. 1950), Phi Delta Kappa. Methodist. Mason, Rotarian (pres. Clinton 1948-49). Home: 815 N Custer St Weatherford OK 73096

HARRIS, BEVERLY, women's editor Houston Chronicle. Address: 512-20 Travis St Houston TX 77002*

HARRIS, BILLY JACKSON, investment co. exec.; b. Salisbury, N.C., Feb. 20, 1941; s. William Jackson and Annie Frances (Tallant) H.; B.S., Clemson U., 1962; postgrad. U. Fla., 1965-67; M.S., U. N.C., 1971; m. Barbara Sue McSwain, Mar. 2, 1960; children—Katherine Teresa, Julia Marie, Brian Jackson. Sr. design engr. Pratt & Whitney Aircraft, West Palm Beach, Fla., 1962-67; asst. mgr. corporate research Gilbarco, Inc., subsidiary Standard Oil Co. N.J., Greensboro, N.C., 1967-71; mgr. corporate finance McDaniel Lewis & Co., Greensboro, N.C., 1971—. Served to 1st lt., Ordnance Corps, AUS, 1963-65. Registered profl. engr., N.C. Mem. Am. Soc. M.E., I.E.E.E., Greensboro Jr. C. of C. (project chmn. 1969). Methodist (chmn. worship commn. 1966-67). Elk. Patentee in field. Home: 3102 Round Hill Rd Greensboro NC 27408 Office: 925 W Market St Greensboro NC 27402

HARRIS, BYRON LEWIS, bank exec.; b. Atlanta, Dec. 23, 1937; s. Byron Paul and Dena (Lewis) H.; B.A., Vanderbilt U., 1959; postgrad. Sch. Banking of South, 1968; m. Ann Frederick Pegram, Nov. 28, 1969; children—John B. Lyle, Martha Lyle, Jay Lyle (step-children), Byron Lewis. With First Nat. Bank Atlanta, 1959—, comml. trainee, 1959-64, asst. cashier, 1964-68, asst. v.p., 1968-69, v.p., 1969—. Program chmn. Leadership Atlanta, 1969-70, chmn., 1970-71; div. chmn. United Appeal, 1970—, mem. budget com., 1971—. Bd. dirs. Met. Atlanta Council Alcohol and Drugs, 1971-73, Atlanta Florence Crittenden Services Inc., 1971-74. Mem. Atlanta C. of C, (subcom. vice chmn. 1970), Phi Delta Theta. Kiwanian (dir. 1969-71, pres., 1971-72). Club: Capital City (Atlanta). Home: 517 Arden At Argonne NW Atlanta GA 30305 Office: First Nat Bank Atlanta PO Box 4148 Atlanta GA 30302

HARRIS, BYRON P., accountant; b. Atlantic City, Jan. 11, 1904; s. Harry G. and Hattie W. Harris; ed. pub. schs. of Atlantic City, LaSalle Extension course, 1925; m. Dena Lewis, June 1, 1929; children—Arthur F.M., Byron L. Accountant Shaner & Knauer, Atlantic City, 1920-25; partner Arthur F. Morton & Co., accountants, 1927-55; partner in charge A. M. Pullen & Co., public accountants, 1955—; lectr. on tax forums. Mem. budget exec. com. Community Services, 1958—, admissions com., 1964; treas., mem. exec. com. Atlanta Art Assn., 1960-64. Bd. dirs. Atlanta Symphony Orch., 1958—, High Museum of Art; trustee Ga. Tax Research Found., 1961-66. C.P.A., Ga., N.C., Va., Pa., N.Y. Mem. Am. Inst. C.P.A.'s (former chmn. social security com., mem. estate planning com. 1958-60, fed. taxation com. 1961-65, mem. council 1969—), Nat. Assn. Accountants, Ga. Soc. C.P.A.'s (past pres., chmn. estate planning com. 1960-62, trustee 1938—), Ga. (chmn. taxation and spending council 1960, area adviser 1956—; nat. affairs com. 1963—), Atlanta (pub. finance and taxation com. 1961, chmn. 1963) chambers commerce, Atlanta Estate Planning Council (pres. 1966), Asso. Industries Ga. (finance com), S.A.R. Episcopalian (vestryman). Clubs: Peachtree, Commerce, Kiwanis (past treas.), Chattahoochee Country, Capital City. Home: 1820 W Paces Ferry Rd NW Atlanta GA 30327 Office: 1230 Candler Bldg Atlanta GA 30303

HARRIS, CARLETON, state justice; b. Pine Bluff, Ark., Dec. 31, 1909; s. Frank A. and Ada (Rodgers) H.; student Union U., Jackson, Tenn., 1929-31; LL.B., Cumberland U., 1932; LL.D., Ouachita Bapt. Coll., 1960; m. Marjorie Wilson, Apr. 20, 1934; 1 son, Eugene Starke. Admitted to Ark. bar, 1932; practice in Pine Bluff 1932-48; pros. atty., Pine Bluff, 1947-48; judge 4th Chancery Dist. Ark., 1949-56; chief justice Ark. Supreme Ct., 1957—. Pres. Ark. Jud. Council, 1955. Mem. Ark. Ho. of Reps., 1933-38. Mem. nat. council Boy Scouts Am.; past dir. Pine Bluff Pub. Library, Pine Bluff Community Chest; disaster relief chmn. Jefferson County A.R.C., 1943—; past v.p. Jefferson County Men of Chs.; mem. exec. com. So. Bapt. Conv., 1967—. Mem. Am., Ark., Jefferson County (pres. 1942) bar assns., Central States Shrine Assn. (past pres.), Nat. Conf. Chief Justices (chmn. 1966-67). Democrat. Baptist. Mason (past grand lodge orator: Shriner, past potentate), Lion (pres. Pine Bluff 1936). Home: 2005 Laurel St Pine Bluff AR 71601 also Plaza Towers Apts Little Rock AR 72201 Office: Justice Bldg Little Rock AR 72201

HARRIS, CHARLES, union exec.; b. Sulligent, Ala., Feb. 15, 1926; s. Charles and Annie Mae (Holliday) H.; student U. Ala., 1947; m. Doris Eleanor Ketring, Feb. 14, 1948; children—Blake James, Blaine Charles, Blair Howard. Profl. baseball player various teams including Phila. Athletics, 1948-51; profl. baseball mgr., West Palm Beach, Fla., 1951-52, Cleve. Indians, 1952-53; bus. mgr. Internat. Brotherhood Elec. Workers, West Palm Beach, 1956-63; pres. Fla. State Elec. Workers, West Palm Beach, 1962-63, Fla. AFL-CIO, Miami, 1963—. Bd. dirs. Variety Childrens Hosp., Miami. Served with USNR, 1944-46, Democrat. Baptist. Elk. Home: 4730 Maine St Lake Worth FL 33460 Office: 1400 36th St Miami FL 33142

HARRIS, CHARLES EDGAR, wholesale grocery co. exec.; b. Englewood, Tenn., Nov. 6, 1915; s. Charles Leonard and Minnie (Borin) H.; m. Dorothy Wilson, Aug. 20, 1938; children—Charles Edgar, William John. With H.T. Hackney Co., Knoxville, Tenn., 1948—, treas., 1958—, v.p., 1964-71, pres., chief adminstrn. officer, 1971—, also dir.; pres., dir. Appalachian Realty Corp., Knoxville,

Park Oil Co., Alcoa, Tenn., Knoxoil Co., Knoxville, Carolina Oil and Gas Co., Bryson City, N.C., Valley Oil Co., Athens, Tenn.; v.p., dir. Hackney Carolina Co., Murphy, N.C., Hackney Harlan Co., Harlan, Ky., Haywood Wholesale Grocery Co., Waynesville, N.C., Maryville Wholesale Grocery Co. (Tenn.), Brink's, Inc., Knoxville, Testoil Co., Harlan, Ky.; chmn. bd., dir. Central State Oil Co., Mid State Investment Corp. (both McMinnville, Tenn.). Mem. exec. bd. Great Smoky Mountain council Boy Scouts Am., 1956-57; bd. dirs. Met. YMCA, Knoxville. Mem. Knoxville Wholesale Credit Assn. (dir. 1955-58, pres. 1956-57). Baptist (deacon 1957—). Rotarian. Home: 7709 Westland Dr Knoxville TN 37919 Office: Fidelity Bldg Knoxville TN 37902

HARRIS, EWING JACKSON, lawyer; b. Sylvia, Tenn., Mar. 17, 1901; s. John Clifton and Sarah Frances (Walker) H.; ed. pub. schs. Tenn. and Detroit; LL.B., Cumberland U., 1928; m. Lena Sue Hartman, Mar. 28, 1931; children—Frances Ann Harris (Mrs. Frank Avent), Marjorie Sue Harris (Mrs. Dean Lucht), Ewlene Harris. Admitted to Tenn. bar, 1928 and practiced in Bolivar, 1932—; city atty., Bolivar, 1942—; county atty. Hardeman County, 1942-70; dir. Bank of Bolivar. Pres. State Bd. of Elections, 1949-53, Tenn. Democratic Exec. Com. 1949-51, 1953-55; mem. Tenn. State Senate, 1937-39; del. Tenn. Constl. Conv., 1965. Fellow Am. Coll. Probate Counsel; mem. Am., Tenn. (bd. govs. 1959-62, mem. spl. joint com. on ct. modernization), Hardeman County bar assns., Am. Judicature Soc., C. of C. (pres.1958), Phi Beta Gamma. Democrat. Methodist (trustee). Mason, Elk, Rotarian. Clubs: West Tenn. Executives (v.p.). Home: 332 Sycamore St Bolivar TN 38008 Office: Bank of Bolivar Bldg Box 148 Bolivar TN 38008

HARRIS, FRANK MAURICE, lawyer; b. St. Petersburg, Fla., Oct. 16, 1902; s. William B. and Mamie (McMullen) H.; J.D., U. Fla., 1925; m. Frances B. Coryell, Aug. 16, 1927; children—Frank Maurice, Richard C., Jeannine (Mrs. John L. Green, Jr.), Marilyn H. (Mrs. Robinson), Carolyn H. (Mrs. Richard W. Nelson). Admitted to Fla. bar, 1924; sr. mem. Harris, Clark, Green, Piper & Robinson, St. Petersburg, 1963—. Dir. Union Trust Nat. Bank of St. Petersburg. Chmn. Fla. Bd. Control, 1949-53. Mem. Blue Key, Delta Chi, Delta Theta Phi. Presbyn. Mason (Shriner), Elk. Home: 1650 Beach Dr NE St Petersburg FL 33704 Office: W Coast Title Bldg 30 6th St N St Petersburg FL 33731

HARRIS, FRED ROY, lawyer, U.S. senator; b. Walters, Okla., Nov. 13, 1930; s. Fred Byron and Addie Alene (Person) H.; B.A., U. Okla., 1952, LL.B. with distinction, 1954; m. LaDonna Vita Crawford; children—Kathryn Cornell, Byron Baldwin, Laura Loretta. Mem. Okla. Senate, 1956-64; U.S. senator from Okla., 1964—, chmn. senate subcom. on govt. research, mem. govt. operations com., finance com., chmn. select com. on small bus.; mem. Pres.' Nat. Adv. Commn. Civil Disorders. Chmn. Democratic Nat. Com., 1969-70. Named Outstanding Young Man of Okla., Jr. C. of C., 1959, One of Ten Outstanding Young Men of 1965, U.S. Jr. C. of C. Mem. Great Plains Hist. Soc. (dir.), Lawton C. of C., Order of Coif, Phi Beta Kappa. Baptist. Mason (Shriner), Rotarian. Author: Alarms and Hopes, 1968; Now is the Time: A New Populist Call to Action, 1971; The New Populism, 1973. Home: 1104 Waverly Way McLean VA 22101 Office: Old Senate Office Bldg Washington DC 20510

HARRIS, FREDERICK ARTHUR, soils engr.; b. McAlister, Okla., July 9, 1912; s. William Thomas and Florence Blanche (Dunton) H.; B.S., U. Fla., 1935; m. Mary Elizabeth Gieselbreth, Oct. 17, 1934; children— Frederick Arthur, Richard, Mary Frances, Juanita. Soils technician U.S. Waterways Expt. Sta., Vicksburg, Miss., 1935-40; sr. lab. engr. Tex. Hwy. Dept., Houston, 1945-56, cons. soils engr., Houston, 1956-59; constrn. supervision and promotion various firms, 1959-61; soils engr. So. Inspection Service, Inc., Houston, 1961—. Served with AUS, 1940-45; ETO. Fellow Am. Soc. C.E.; mem. Tex. Soc. Profl. Engrs. Inventor Harris ring soil density apparatus, Transmatic tri-axial compression soil test cell. Home: 1601 Hollyhurst St Houston TX 77027 Office: 8400 Westglen St Houston TX 77042

HARRIS, HAROLD FLOYD, judge; b. Rogers, Tex., Aug. 30, 1929; s. Claude Leo and Lois (Rawls) H.; B.S. in Elec. Engring., Tex. A. and M., 1955, M.S. in Elec. Engring., 1956; J.D., U. Tex., 1970; m. Benigna Ann Durst, Feb. 23, 1951; children—Donald Blake, Benigna Susan. Design engr. Tex. Instruments, Dallas, 1956-57, project mgr., 1957-61, tng. control dept., 1962, mgr. components optics br., 1963-68; admitted to Tex. bar, 1970; pvt. practice law, 1970-71; county judge Bell County, Tex., 1971—. Cubmaster Boy Scouts Am., 1963-64; football coach YMCA, 1965—. Served with USNR, 1950-54. Mem. Tex., Bell-Mills-Lavipassas bar assns., Tex. Soc. Profl. Engrs., Internat. Platform Assn., Tex. Aggie Band Assn., Eta Kappa Nu. Mem. Ch. Christ (deacon). Home: 2210 N 9th St Temple TX 76501 Office: Bell County Courthouse Belton TX 76513

HARRIS, HARWELL HAMILTON, architect, educator; b. Redlands, Cal., July 2, 1903; s. Frederick Thomas and May Julia (Hamilton) H.; student Pomona Coll., 1921-23, Otis Art Inst., 1923-25; m. Jean Murray Bangs, Feb. 23, 1937. Sculptor 1926-29; practice architecture with Richard Neutra, 1929-32; pvt. practice, 1933—, Los Angeles, 1933-51, Austin, Tex., 1951-56; prin. Harris & Sherwood, Ft. Worth, 1956-57; architect with office in Dallas, 1958-62; lectr. U. So. Cal., 1945, 1946; vis. critic Columbia, 1943, Yale, 1950, 52; design cons. to Nat. Orange Show, 1950-56; grad. design critic Columbia, 1960-61, dir. sch. architecture U. Tex. 1951-55; prof. architecture N.C. State U., 1962—. Prin. works Lowe House, 1934, Fellowship Park House, 1935, Havens House, 1941, Birtcher House, 1942, Johnson House, 1947, English House, 1950, Chadwick Sch., 1951, Tex. State Fair House, 1954, J. Lee Johnson House, 1956. Am. Embassy, Helsinki, 1957, Havens Meml. Plaza, Berkeley, Cal., 1961, Greenwood Mausoleum, Ft. Worth, 1960, Treanor House, 1959, St. Giles Presbyn. Ch., 1969, others; prin. projects: the Segmental House for Revere Copper & Brass Co., 1942, Pottenger Hosp., 1946, Palos Verdes Coll., 1947, Homestyle Found. House for S. West, 1956. Recipient 1st prize Pitts. Glass Inst., 1937, 1938. Fellow A.I.A.; mem. Congres Internationaux d'Architecture Moderne (sec. Am. chpt. 1932, chpt. for relief and postwar planning, 1944), Tau Sigma Delta. Home: 124 Cox Av Raleigh NC 27607 Office: 122 Cox Av Raleigh NC also Sch Design NC State Univ Raleigh NC 27605

HARRIS, HENRY HITER, JR., banker; b. Richmond, Va., Aug. 16, 1922; s. H. Hiter and Mary L. (Murdoch) H.; grad. Woodberry Forest Sch., 1941; A.B., Princeton, 1945; postgrad. N.Y.U., 1946-47; m. Elizabeth Spalding Trueheart, Apr. 16, 1955;children—Mary Lawrence and Elizabeth Robinson (twins), Henry Hiter III. Credit analyst Chem. Bank N.Y. Trust Co., N.Y.C., 1946-51; asst. treas., asst. v.p. Chase Manhattan Bank, 1951-55; v.p. Colonial-Am. Nat. Bank, Roanoke, Va., 1955-59; v.p. So. Bank & Trust Co., Richmond, 1959-60, pres., dir., 1961—, chmn. bd., 1967—; chmn. bd., pres. So. Bankshares, Inc., Richmond, 1970—. Mem. Va. State Commn. Local Debt, 1962—. Mem. Richmond City Sch. Bd., 1966-70. Trustee Mary Baldwin Coll., Staunton, Va., chmn. finance com., 1968—; trustee Va.-Md. Bankers Schs., U. Richmond, mem. exec. com., 1969—; bd. dirs. Central Va. Ednl. TV Corp., 1964—, exec. com., 1968—, v.p., 1971—; bd. dirs. Va. Indsl. Devel. Corp., 1961—; bd. dirs. Crippled Children's Hosp., 1962—, chmn. finance com., 1967—; bd. dirs. Children's Home Soc. Va., 1960—, pres., 1966-68; bd. dirs. Richmond Meml. Hosp., 1961—; mem. adv. bd. Council Ind. Colls. Va., 1971—; trustee Richmond Poly. Inst. Found., 1971—. Served as 1st lt. USAAF, 1943-45. Mem. Soc. Va. Creepers, Soc. Colonial Wars, Va. Hist. Soc., Richmond Hundred. Presbyn. (elder). Clubs: Commonwealth (past dir.), Country of Virginia (dir.), Forum (Richmond); University (N.Y.C.). Home: 4206 Sulgrave Rd Richmond VA 23221 Office: PO Box 12205 Richmond VA 23241

HARRIS, HORATIO PRESTON, dentist; b. Savannah, Ga., Sept. 25, 1925; s. Horatio Preston and Faustine Althia (Williams) H.; B.S., Howard U., 1951, D.D.S., 1956; m. Barbara Elaine Monroe, Sept. 16, 1950; children—Gary Preston, Patricia Lynn, Michael Monroe, Conrad Wayne, Nancy Elaine (dec.), David Matthew, Cathy Colleen, Robert Horatio, Roxanne Denise. IBM specialist VA, Washington, 1949; intern oral surgery St. Elizabeth Hosp., 1956-57; individual practice dentistry, Washington, 1957—; dental officer Bur. Dental Health, 1963-65; instr. Howard U., 1966-67, asst. prof., 1967-71; mem. courtesy staff oral surgery Freedman's Hosp. Served with USNR, 1943-46. Mem. Am., Nat., D.C. dental assns., R.T. Freeman Soc., Omega Psi Phi. Home and office: 1400 Franklin St NE Washington DC 20018

HARRIS, HOYT CLARK, physician; b. Sparta, Tenn., May 27, 1920; s. Bob Floyd and Otie Mae (Poore) H.; student David Lipscomb Coll., 1940; LL.B., Middle Tenn. State U., 1943; M.D., U. Tenn., 1946; m. Beverly Jolet, June 20, 1946 (dec. 1967); children—Linda Ellen (Mrs. John E. Hinds), Hoyt Clark, Stephen Jolet. Rotating intern Baroness-Erlanger Hosp., Chattanooga; resident surgery Bapt. Meml. Hosp., Memphis; practice medicine specializing in gen. surgery, Lewisburg, Tenn., 1957—; mem. staff Gordon, Taylor hosps., Lewisburg. Dir. First Nat. Bank Lewisburg. Served with M.C., AUS, World War II. Diplomate Am. Bd. Abdominal Surgery. Fellow Am. Coll. Angiology; mem. Am. Soc. Abdominal Surgeons, Am., Tenn., Middle Tenn. med. assns., Marshall County Med. Soc., Lewisburg C. of C. Republican. Mem. Ch. of Christ (Sunday sch. tchr.), Mason (Shriner). Home: 334 Oakwood Dr Lewisburg TN 37091 Office: Med Arts Clinic 3d Av North Lewisburg TN 37091

HARRIS, HUNTINGTON, business exec.; b. N.Y.C. May 15, 1914; s. Hayden Bartlett and Lina (Small) H.; student U. Chgo., 1931-37; B.S., Am. U., 1939; Ph.D., Columbia, 1950; m. Mary Winifred Hutchison, Oct. 9, 1944; children—Susan Valeria (Mrs. Philip E. Smith), Henry John Hayden. Expert witness Dept. Justice, 1940-41; pres. press Intelligence, Inc., 1946-66; chmn. bd. Farrington Mfg. Co., 1959-63, Adrema, Ltd., 1961-64; now engaged in investments; dir. Quadri-Science, Inc., Harris Trust and Savs. Bank, Chgo., Peoples Nat. Bank, Leesburg, Va. Truste, pres. Asheville (N.C.) Sch.; trustee Syracuse U., Brookings Instn., Washington. Served from capt. to col. OSS, 1941-46. Decorated Medal for Freedom; Ouissam Alouite (Morocco), Fellow Royal Soc. Arts London. Episcopalian. Clubs: University (Washington and N.Y.C.); Chicago; Nat. Press, Metropolitan (Washington). Home: RFD 1 Leesburg VA 22075 Office: 1028 Connecticut Av NW Washington DC 20036

HARRIS, JACK, broadcasting ofcl. Pres., gen. mgr. KPRC-TV, Houston. Address: 3014 S Post Oak Rd Houston TX 77027*

HARRIS, JAMES BRANTLEY, extension personnel dir.; b. Marietta, Ga., Oct. 7, 1940; s. James Robert and Floy (Spratlin) H.; B.S., U. Ga., 1962, M.S., 1964; Ed.D., Cornell U., 1970; m. Emily Anne Byrd, Jan. 18, 1964; children—Cynthia Byrd, James Brantley. Research asst. U. Ga., 1962-64; NSF fellow U. P.R., summer 1962; asst. county extension agt. Walker County, Ga., 1964-65; extension tng. specialist and instr. extension edn. U. Ga., Athens, 1965-71, extension personnel devel. coordinator, asst. prof., 1971—. Mem. Adult Edn. Assn. U.S.A., Ga. Adult Edn. Council, Nat. Mem. Ga. Adult Edn. Council, Nat. Assn. County Agrl. Extension Agts., Phi Delta Kappa, Xi Sigma Pi, Alpha Zeta, Gamma Sigma Delta. Lion. Contbr. articles in field profl. jours. Home: Route 3 Spinks Rd Athens GA 30601 Office: Cooperative Extension Service U Ga Athens GA 30601

HARRIS, JAMES DOUGLAS, JR., lawyer; b. Tallassee, Ala., Feb. 12, 1943; s. James Douglas and Edna Marie (Flournoy) H.; A.B., U. Ala., 1960, J.D., 1964; m. Sara Jean Brooks, May 7, 1966; children—Jennifer Brooks, James Douglas III, Stewart, Katherine. Admitted to Ala. bar, 1967, U.S. Supreme Ct., 1971; mem. firm Harris & Harris, Montgomery, Ala., 1967—. Active United Appeal. Mem. Ala. Ho. of Reps., 1970—. Bd. dirs. YMCA Youth Legislature. Served with AUS, 1967-69. Decorated Bronze Star medal. Mem. Am. Legion, V.F.W., Jr. C. of C., Phi Alpha Delta, Sigma Chi. Democrat. Baptist. Home: 301 Eagerton Rd Montgomery AL 36111 Office: Union Bank Bldg Montgomery AL 36104

HARRIS, JAMES GORDON, clergyman; b. Little Rock, Ark., Oct. 27, 1913; s. James Gordon and Ellen (McManaway) Ill.; B.A., La. Bapt. Coll., 1935; Th.M., M.R.E., Southwestern-Bapt. Theol. Sem., 1939; D.D., Ouachita Bapt. U., 1956; m. Tunis Johns, Jan. 10, 1939; children—Gordon, John, Jane. Ordained to ministry Bapt. Ch., 1933; pastor First Bapt. Ch., Bunkie, La., 1940-45, Calvary Bapt. Ch., Birmingham, Ala.,1945-48, Beech St. Bapt. Ch., Texarkana, Ark., 1948-54, University Bapt. Ch., Ft. Worth, 1954—; preacher Columbia Ch. of Air, CBS Radio, 1955, Christmas Services, NBC Radio, 1963. Mem. Radio and TV Commn. So. Bapt. Conv., 1953-59, mem. Fgn. Mssion Bd., 1971—; mem. Christian life commn. Bapt. Gen. Conv. Tex., 1959-66, 69—, v.p., 1965-66, 71-72, mem. exec. bd., 1964-72, chmn., 1969-71; moderator Tarrant Bapt. Assn., 1962-63; pres. Gen. Ministers Assn., Ft. Worth, 1963-65, Bapt. Pastor's Conf., Ft. Worth, 1967-68. Mem. Mayors Com. on Human Relations, Ft. Worth, 1965. Bd. dirs. Ft. Worth United Fund, 1960-69. Trustee Baylor U., 1965—. Rotarian. Home: 3712 Somerset Lane Fort Worth TX 76109 Office: 2720 Wabash St Fort Worth TX 76109

HARRIS, JESSIE G. (MRS. HUBERT LAMAR HARRIS), ednl. adminstr.; b. Athens, Ga., May 12, 1909; d. Wiley Jackson and Dora (Hilley) Ginn; B.B.A., U. Ga., 1956; A.B., Ga. State Coll., 1960; m. Hubert Lamar Harris, Nov. 25, 1930; children—Mary Ann Harris (Mrs. William Wallace Holley), Hubert Lamar, Dorothy Elizabeth (Mrs. Ronald Zazworsky), Martha Susan (Mrs. R.R. McCue, Jr.). Various secretarial positions, ins. and law offices, 1923-30; sec. div. of gen. extension U. Ga., 1930-35, asst. dir. div. gen. extension, 1935-47; asst. compilations survey Univ. System, Ga., 1949-50, adminstrv. asst. to regents, 1951-63, asst. exec. sec., 1963-67, asso. exec. sec., 1967—. Asst. exec. dir. State Scholarship Commn., 1965-66. Mem. Am. Assn. U. Women (chmn. study group 1964-66, treas. 1972-74), Crimson Key Honor Soc., Mortar Board, Phi Chi Theta, Delta Mu Delta, Psi Chi. Club: Atlanta Writers. Home: 765 Douglas Rd NE Atlanta GA 30342 Office: 244 Washington St NW Atlanta GA 30334

HARRIS, JOHN B., JR., exec. v.p. Greenwood Mills. Address: Greenwood Mills Greenwood SC 29646*

HARRIS, JOHN BLACK, chem. and food co. exec.; b. Bklyn., Apr. 17, 1918; s. John Black and Helen (Woodman) H.; A.B., Bard Coll., 1939; postgrad. econs. Columbia, 1939-42; m. Elizabeth Moody, Nov. 29, 1941; children—Pamela Preston, Lee Woodman, Holly Stetson, John Black. Financial, research staff Chase Nat. Bank, 1939-42, fgn. credit depts., 1946-50; asst. to treas. W. R. Grace & Co., N.Y.C., 1950-51, asst. to pres., 1951-52, asst. project mgr. chem. devel., 1951-52, dir. personnel, 1953-55, v.p. mgmt. orgn. and planning 1955-56, v.p., gen. mgr. operations West Coast S.A., G.A., 1956-60; dir. indsl. operations, chmn. diversification com. United Fruit Co., Boston, 1960-63, v.p., 1961-64, pres. Liana, Inc. subsidiary, 1960-63, v.p. United Fruit and Food Corp. subsidiary, 1960-64; v.p. gen. devel. div. W.R. Grace & Co., 1964-68, v.p. Frozen Foods div., 1970—. Trustee, treas. Bard Coll., 1946-49. Served as maj. USAAF, 1942-46. Home: 122 Asbury St St Simons Island GA 31522 Address: Box 667 St Simons Island GA 31522

HARRIS, JOHN BRAME, public accountant; b. Durham, N.C., May 10, 1919; s. Boyd White and Alma (Evans) H.; B.C.S., U. N.C., 1940; m. Ewing Elizabeth Schleeter, Dec. 6, 1951; 1 dau., Janice Ewing. Office mgr. Raleigh Nehi Bottling Co., 1940-41; sr. accountant J. Beverly Redford, C.P.A., 1941-50; partner Redford & Harris, 1951-56; owner J. B. Harris, C.P.A., Durham, 1956-68; partner Harris, Bailey, Self and Anderson, C.P.A.'s, 1968-69, Harris, Bailey, Self & Harris, 1970—; dir., sec.-treas. First Fed. Savs. & Loan Co.; treas., dir. Willowhaven, Inc., 1956—; pres., dir. Marjan, Inc., 1956—; treas., dir. Superior Mech. Contractors, Inc., 1959-70, Vistas, Inc., 1960-70, Aviation & Land Devel. Co., 1961—, Joint Properties, Inc., 1962—. Mem. budget com. Community Chest, 1953-54; chmn. budget com. Durham United Fund, 1955-57. C.P.A., N.C. Mem. United Comml. Travelers, N.C. Assn. C.P.A.'s, Am. Inst. Accountants, Am. Numis. Assn. Presbyn. (deacon). Elk, Mason (K.T., Shriner). Clubs: Willowhaven Country (pres. 1965), Sertoma (treas., dir. 1949-55). Home: Holly Lane Willowhaven Durham NC 27705 Office: First Fed Bldg Durham NC 27701

HARRIS, JOHN HARPER, supt. schs.; b. Peoria, Ill., Oct. 30, 1910; s. Lewis P. and Esther (Yutt) H.; B.S., Bradley U., 1935; M.A., Columbia, 1940, Ed.D., 1948; postgrad. U. Ia., 1935-36, U. Ill., 1941-42, Harvard, 1958, Drake U., 1963; L.H.D., Coll. Medicine and Surgery, Des Moines, 1961; LL.D., Simpson Coll., Dr. Pub. Adminstrn., Parsons Coll., 1964; m. Vera Justus, Aug. 10, 1938; 1 son, John J. Tchr., Peoria, 1935-41, elementary prin., 1941-43, asst. supt. schs., 1943-53; supt. schs., Downers Grove, Ill., 1953-57, Des Moines, 1957-64; dir. met. pub. schs. Nashville-Davidson (Tenn.) County, 1964—; summer lectr. Bradley U., 1949, 50, U. Wyo., 1953, U. Miss., 1954, U. Colo., 1956, Drake U., 1961, 62, E. Carolina State Coll., 1963, 64. Dir. Greater Ia. Ins. Co., Des Moines. Mem. exec. bd. Tall Corn council Boy Scouts Am., 1959-64; mem. Child Welfare Bd., 1961—; adviser to gov. Ia. Ednl. TV Bd., 1962-64. Bd. dirs. Coll. Osteopathic Medicine and Surgery, Jr. Achievement. Fullbright fellow in France, Finland, 1960. Mem. Am., Tenn. assns. sch. adminstrs., N.E.A., Tenn., Nashville edn. assns., Air Force Assn., Ia. Research Assn. (mem. bd.), Nashville C. of C., Phi Delta Kappa. Rotarian. Home: 6596 Jocelyn Hollow Dr Nashville TN 37204 Office: 2601 Bransford Av Nashville TN 37204

HARRIS, JOHN WOODS, banker; b. Galveston, Tex., Sept. 23, 1893; s. John Woods and Minnie (Hutchings) H.; LL.B., U.Va., 1920; m. Eugenia Davis, June 14, 1917; children—Eugenia (Mrs. Archibald Rowland Campbell, Jr.), Anne (Mrs. Donald C. Miller), Joan (Mrs. Alvin N. Kelso), Florence (Mrs. Marshall McDonald, Jr.) (dec.). Admitted Tex. bar, 1920; practiced as atty., mng. agt. oil, farm, ranch properties in Tex., 1922—; dir. Hutchings Sealy Nat. Bank, 1930-58; chmn. exec. com., chmn. bd. First Hutchings Sealy Nat. Bank, Galveston, 1960—; pres. Hutchings Joint Stock Assn., 1936—; dir. Galveston Corp., Cotton Concentration Co., Gulf Transfer Co., Tex. Fibreglas Products, Inc., Galveston. Vice pres., chmn. land com. The Sealy and Smith Found. for John Sealy Hosp.; pres. bd. Rosenberg Library, Galveston Orphans Home. Served as aviator USN, 1918. Mem. Sons of Republic of Tex., Am. Legion, Delta Kappa Epsilon. Episcopalian. Clubs: Galveston Artillery; Farmington Country (Charlottesville, Va.). Home: 2603 Av O Galveston TX 77550 Office: US Nat Bank Bldg Galveston TX 77550

HARRIS, LA DONNA CRAWFORD (MRS. FRED R. HARRIS), civic worker; b. nr. Temple, Okla., Feb. 15, 1931; d. William and Lily (Tabbytite) Crawford; student pub. schs; m. Fred R. Harris, Apr. 8, 1949; children—Kathryn, Byron, Laura. Mem. Joint Commn. on Mental Health; hon. pres., founder Oklahomans for Indian Opportunity; mem. Comanche Indian Tribe; founder, pres. Americans for Indian Opportunity. Mem. policy council Nat. Women's Polit. Caucus. Bd. dirs. Common Cause, Center for Community Change, Americans for Democratic Action, Nat. Urban League, Nat. Urban Coalition, Frontlash; trustee Antioch Coll.; bd. visitors U. Okla. Address: 1104 Waverly Way McLean VA 22101

HARRIS, LOUIS CARL, newspaper editor; b. Montgomery, Ala., Feb. 20, 1912; s. Augustus J. and Florence (Hirsch) H.; student pub. schs.; m. Margaret M. Brown, Aug. 9, 1944; children—Jeffrey Peden, Louis Carl, William McCollough. Carrier, Montgomery Advertiser, 1931-32; asst. circulation mgr. Augusta (Ga.) Chronicle, 1932-34, reporter, telegraph editor, 1934-38; reporter Pontiac (Mich.) Daily Press, 1938-40, telegraph editor, 1946-47; news editor Columbus (Ga.) Ledger, 1947—; news editor Augusta Chronicle and Herald, 1947—, editor, 1959—; v.p. Augusta Chronicle and Herald; v.p. Southeastern Newspapers Corp., 1966—. Dir. Richmond Assos., Inc. Bd. dirs. Augusta United Fund, 1952-58. Served to capt. USAAF, 1940-45. Decorated Bronze Star medal; Nieman travel fellow, Japan, 1956. Mem. Ga. Asso. Press News Council (pres. 1950, 52), Am. Soc. Newspaper Editors, Augusta C. of C. (v.p.), Ga. Press Assn. (pres. 1967-68). Presbyn. (deacon). Kiwanian (dir. Augusta 1950). Home: 618 Oberlin Rd Augusta GA Office: 725 Broad St Augusta GA 30901

HARRIS, LOUIS CECIL, lawyer; b. Roba, Ala., July 3, 1906; s. Henry Jackson and Anne Laurie (Swint) H.; LL.B., Chattanooga Coll. Law, 1929, LL.M., 1930; m. Ella M. Brown, June 10, 1932; children—Louis Cecil, Helen (Mrs. James C. Dale, III). Admitted to practice Tenn. bar, 1929, U.S. Dist. Ct. bar, 1931, U.S. Supreme Ct bar, 1956, U.S. Ct. Appeals bar, 1957, U.S. Ct. Mil. Appeals bar, 1956; practiced in Chattanooga, 1929—; sr. mem. firm Harris, Moon & Meacham, 1967—. Mem. adv. commn. Tenn. Supreme Ct., 1965—. Pres. Chattanooga Council Community Forces, 1958-61; pres. Chattanooga Travelers Aid Assn., 1957-58; v.p. region 4 Nat. Travelers Aid Assn., 1957-61. Bd. dirs. United Fund Greater Chattanooga, 1962—; vice chmn. adv. bd. Chattanooga Hamilton County Health Dept., 1971—. Served as lt. col. AUS, 1942-46. Named Outstanding Optimist Chattanooga Optimist Club, 1944. Fellow Internat. Soc. Barristers; mem. Internat. Assn. Ins. Council, Am., Tenn., Chattanooga bar assns., Am. Judicature Soc., Delta Theta Phi. Presbyn. (tchr. Louis Harris Bible class 1947—; del. commr. to Gen. Assembly Columbus, O., 1958; elder 1938—; clk ch. 1971—). Kiwanian (pres. Chattanooga 1966; lt. gov. div. 3 Ky.-Tenn. dist. internat. 1971-72). Clubs: Mountain City (sec. 1966-67, 68-69), Chattanooga Golf and Country (v.p. 1957-58). Home: 1504 Sunset Rd Chattanooga TN 37405 Office: 1217 Hamilton Nat Bank Bldg Chattanooga TN 37402

HARRIS, LOUIS PAUL, state ofcl.; b. Cin., Oct. 18, 1924; s. Morris and Bess (Libbert) H.; student U. Cin., 1946-48; m. Peggy Lou Leeper, Aug. 10, 1952; 1 dau., Michele. News editor radio sta. WCNH,

Quincy, Fla., 1948-49, radio sta. WTAL, Tallahassee, 1950-56; travel editor Fla. State News Bur., Fla. Dept. Commerce, Tallahassee, 1956-63, mgr. Fla. Welcome Stas., 1963-68, asst. bur. chief marketing and tourism, 1969-71, acting bur. chief, 1971—, state coordinator N.Y. World's Fair, Fla. Pavilion, 1964. Served with USAAF, 1942-46; PTO. Recipient award Midwest Travel Writers, 1960, 64. Mem. Capital Press Corps (charter). Home: 1113 Wisteria Dr Tallahassee FL 32303 Office: 107 W Gaines St Tallahassee FL 32304

HARRIS, LUMAN, baseball mgr.; b. Birmingham, Ala., Jan. 17, 1915; s. Chalmer Lee and Lula Jane (Taylor) H.; grad. high sch.; m. Margaret Reynolds, Feb. 15, 1936; children—Pat (Mrs. Charles M. Renta), Phil, Johnny. Began profl. career as pitcher Atlanta club, 1938; pitcher Phila. Athletics, 1941-46, Washington Senators, 1947, Buffalo, 1948-49, Balt., 1950; coach Chgo. White Sox, 1951-55; coach Balt. Orioles, 1955-61, mgr. 1961; became head coach Houston Astros, 1961, mgr., 1964; now mgr. Atlanta Braves, Inc., mgr. Caracas (Venezuela) Baseball club, 1958, San Juan (P.R.) Club, Winter 1961. Served with USNR. Home: 810 Piedmont St Sugar Land TX 77478

HARRIS, LUTHER DELBERT, supt. schs.; b. Searcy, Ark., Sept. 1, 1918; s. James Elbert and Mary Ella (Henderson) H.; B.A., Harding Coll., 1940; M.A., Geroge Peabody Coll., 1949; Ed.S., U. Ark., 1970; m. Reedie Bridges, Mar. 3, 1940; children—Luther Delbert, Jr., Ruth (Mrs. Ronald MacDonald). Prin., coach Alpin (Ark.) Pub. Schs., 1940-41, Judsonia (Ark.) Pub. Schs., 1941-43; supt. schs., Kensett, Ark., 1943-51; prin. Paris (Ark.) High Sch., 1951-61, Blytheville (Ark.) Sch. Dist., 1961-63, dir. instrn. 1963-65, asst. supt. instrn., 1965-70, supt. schs., 1970—. Served with USNR, 1944-46. Mem. Ark. Assn. Supervision and Curriculum Devel. (pres. 1968-69), Ark. Edn. Assn. (dir. 1957-58), Ark. Dept. Edn. (chmn. adv. council 1969-71), Paris C. of C. (pres. 1960). Methodist (sec. ofcl. bd. 1954—, lay speaker 1954-72). Kiwanian (pres. 1960). Club: Key (sponsor 1951-70) (Paris, Blytheville). Home: 732 Adams St Blytheville AR 72315 Office: 614 Chickasawba St Blytheville AR 72315

HARRIS, MARSHALL S., state legislator; b. Detroit, Feb. 2, 1932; s. David Harris and Dorothy (Karol) H.; B.S., Harvard, 1953, LL.B., 1956; m. Harriet I. Lipton; children—Steven Matthew, Jennifer Lisa, Andrew David. Practice law, partner firm Harris & Robinson, 1960, Harris & Sirkin, Miami, Fla., 1966—; now mem. Fla. Ho. of Reps. chmn. Appropriations com. Vice pres. Jewish Occupational Council, Greater Miami Jewish Fedn., Jewish Vocational Service; active YM-YWHA, United Fund Dade County, Am. Jewish Com. Served with AUS, 1956-58. Mem. Dade County, Fla., Am. bar assns., Jewish War Vets. Mem. B'nai B'rith. Home: 4725 Pine Dr Miami FL 33143 Office: 12th Floor Dade Fed Bldg 101 E Flagler St Miami FL 33131

HARRIS, NANCY EDWARDS (MRS. FOLEY WHITE HARRIS), nurse, civic worker, club woman; b. nr. Fredericksburg, Va., July 15, 1918; d. John Frederick and Mary Maude (Frank) Edwards; R.N., Capitol City Sch. Nursing, 1939; B.S.N.E. Cath. U. Am., 1951, postgrad., 1951; m. Foley White Harris, June 13, 1946; children—Charles Edward, Dale Louis. Night supt. D.C. Gen. Hosp., Washington, 1942-44, asst. dir. nursing service, 1944-46, clin. supr. psychiat. div., 1951-52, night supr., 1970—; asst. registrar D.C. Grad. Nurses Assn., Washington, 1946-47; staff nurse Fed. Employees Health div. USPHS, Washington, 1947-48; nursing staff Alexandria (Va.) Hosp., 1969-70. Mem. Brookeville-Seminary Valley Citizens Assn., Alexandria, Va., 1961—, 1st v.p. Patrick Henry Sch. P.T.A., 1964-66; rec. sec. John Adams Middle Sch. P.T.A., Alexandria, 1967-68; den mother Cub Scouts, Washington, 1960-62, Alexandria, 1963-65. Mem. D.A.R. (chpt. treas. 1964-66), Nat. Soc. Daus. of 1812 (state treas. 1961-64, rec. sec. 1964-67, nat. chmn. reciprocity 1964-67), U.D.C. (chpt. 3d v.p., div. rec. sec. 1965-67), Children of Am. Revolution (sr. state treas. 1964-69, sr. nat. registrar 1965-67, sr. nat. rec. sec. 1968-70, hon. sr. nat. v.p. 1970-73), Nat. Officers Club, No. Neck Hist. Soc. Lutheran. Home: 4705 Surry Place Alexandria VA 22304 Office: DC Gen Hosp 19th and Massachusetts Av SE Washington DC 20003

HARRIS, OREN, judge, ex-congressman; b. Belton, Ark., Dec. 20, 1903; s. Homer and Bettie (Bullock) H.; A.B., Henderson State Coll., Arkadelphia, Ark., 1929; LL.B., Cumberland U., 1930; m. Ruth Ross, May 9, 1935; children—Carolyn Marie, James Edward. Admitted to Ark. bar, 1930; admitted to U.S. Supreme Ct. Bar, 1943; dep. pros. atty. Union County, Ark., 1933-36; pros. atty. 13th Judicial Circuit, 1936-40; mem. 77th to 82d Congresses (1941-53) 7th Ark. Dist., 83-89th Congresses (1953-66) 4th Ark. Dist.; chmn. com. on Interstate and Fgn. Commerce Ho. of Reps.; fed. judge U.S. Dist. Ct., Eastern and Western Dist. Ark., 1966—. Mem. Am., Ark. bar assns., Sigma Alpha Epsilon. Democrat. Baptist. Mason (32 deg., Shriner, K.C.C.H.), K.P., Lion (dist. gov. Ark. 1939-40). Home: 1110 W Main El Dorado AR 71730 Office: Fed Bldg El Dorado AR 71730

HARRIS, PHILIP LESLIE, cons. nutrition; b. Detroit, May 7, 1910; s. David Charles and Agnes (McCullough) H.; B.S., Alma Coll., 1931; M.S., Pa. State U., 1932, Ph.D., 1934; m. Flora Ellen Lau, Aug. 24, 1933; children—David Alan, Gordon Lau, Philip Scott. With United Fruit Co., N.Y.C., 1935-37; instr. in physiol. chemistry and nutrition U. S.C. Med. Coll., Charleston, 1937-40; dir. biochem. research Distillation Products, Inc., Rochester, N.Y., 1940-62; dir. div. nutrition Fed. Drug Adminstrn., Dept. Health, Edn. and Welfare, Washington, 1963-69; cons. in nutrition, 1969—; staff officer Nat. Acad. Scis., Washington, 1970—. Research and teaching asso. in physiology U. Rochester Med. Sch., 1942-62. Diplomate Am. Bd. Nutrition. Mem. Am. Chem. Soc., Am. Inst. Nutrition, Am. Soc. Biol. Chemists, Inst. Food Technologists, Soc. Toxicology, Sigma Xi. Mem. editorial bds. Jour. Nutrition, 1956-60, Fedn. Proceedings, 1958—. Research and numerous publs. in vitamin and mineral metabolism, foods and nutrition, analytical methods. Home: 3122 Birch St NW Washington DC 20015

HARRIS, POLLY ADAIR ELSTEIN (MRS, PAUL HARRIS), pub. relations exec.; b. Kansas City, Mo., Dec. 18, 1924; d. Mordy A. and Lyllian (Harris) Elstein; A.A., Kansas City Jr. Coll., 1943; B.S. in Psychology, U. Mo. at Kansas City, 1945; m. Paul Harris, Mar. 31, 1949. Mem. bus. staff U. Mo., Kansas City, 1945-49; radio broadcaster, writer El Paso, Tex., 1950-55; writer, accountant exec., pub. relations dir. Mithoff Advt., 1956-68; pub. relations dir. Empire Aircraft; dir. Harris & Harris Pub. Relations Fashion, hairstyle TV commentator, 1958—; publicity dir. El Paso-Southwestern Sun Carnival, 1959—; speaker on Civic Theater; dir. Press Club Gridiron Show; mus. comedy dir. El Paso Theater Downtown; dir. hist. pageants State Nat. Bank. Recipient Feature Writing award Tex. Press Women; awards Voice of Am.; named Woman of Yr., El Paso Herald-Post, 1971-72. Mem. El Paso Advt. Club (pres. 1972—, dir., Achievement award 1959, 60, 61, Outstanding Mem. award 1964), Internat. Platform Assn. Clubs: Press (dir.), Empire (dir.), Bullfight (El Paso). Office: 2810 Montana El Paso TX 79903

HARRIS, REUBEN EARLE, pub. service adminstr.; b. Memphis, Mar. 17, 1921; s. Reuben A. and Louise (Farmer) H.; B.S., U. Tenn., 1948, M.S., 1957; m. Mary Evelyn Caldwell, Dec. 28, 1942; children—Mary Harris (Mrs. Phillip Wayne Lynn), Elizabeth Anne, Phyllis Elaine, Matthew Caldwell. Design engr. Monsanto Chem. Corp., Oak Ridge, 1946-47; mech. engr. Phillips Petroleum Co., Bartlesville, Okla., 1947-51; project engr. Union Carbide Nuclear Corp., Oak Ridge, 1951-56; design engr. Boeing Airplane Co., Wichita, Kan.- 1956-58; reactor engr. U.S. AEC, Washington, 1958-63; dir. Center Indsl. Services, U. Tenn., Nashville, 1963—. Vice mayor, Brentwood, Tenn., 1971. Served to 1st lt. USAAF, 1944-46. Registered profl. engr., Tenn., Kan. Mem. Brentwood C. of C. (pres. 1971), Order of Engr., Tau Beta Pi, Phi Kappa Phi, Am. Soc. Qual. Control. Home: 503 Arnold Rd Brentwood TN 37027 Office: 323 McLemore St Nashville TN 37203

HARRIS, RICHARD BURL, lawyer; b. Wister, Okla., May 1, 1926; s. Claib and Lehmon (Baldwin) H.; B.A., East Central State Coll., Ada, Okla., 1949; LL.B., U. Okla., 1955; m. Janis Willey, July 5, 1949; children—Richard Burl, Dawn Carole. Admitted to Okla. bar, 1955; practice law, Ada, Okla., 1955—. U.S. commr., 1965-67; atty. Ada City, 1967-69; atty. Stratford City, 1968—. Chmn., Christmas Seals, drive chmn. Ada Community Chest, 1961, pres., 1962. Mem. Pontotoc County Democratic Central Com. Trustee East Central State Coll. Found., Ada; trustee First Methodist Ch. of Ada Found., sec. 1970. Served with USNR, 1944-46, 50-52; PTO. Recipient spl. service award Community Chest, 1961, 62, 64. Mem. Am., Okla., Pototoc County (pres. 1956) bar assns., Okla. Assn. Def. Counsel (v.p. 1967), Ada C. of C., E. Central State Coll. Alumni Assn. (pres. 1970-71). Methodist. Home: 414 W Kings Rd Ada OK 74820 Office: PO Box 817 Townsend Bldg Ada OK 74820

HARRIS, RICHARD WARWICK, librarian; b. LaPorte, Ind., Jan. 22, 1919; s. Clarence Eugene and Winnie Louise (Brown) H.; B.A., North Central Coll. at Naperville, Ill., 1940; M.L.S., U. N.C., 1966; m. Carolyn Louise Simmons, Nov. 27, 1968; 1 dau., Laura Kathryn. Commd. USAAF, 1940, advanced through grades to maj. USAF, 1960; C.B.I., 1942-43; with hdqrs. Air Weather Service, 1945; instr. meteorology, 1947-51; with Far East Air Force, 1951-53, 19th Air Force, 1962-64; serials librarian Med. Center Library Duke U., Durham, N.C., 1966-67; sci. librarian Tex. A. and M. U., College Station, 1967-69; library dir. Tex. State Tech. Inst., Waco, 1959-72; dir. Learning Resources Center Chattanooga State Tech. Inst., 1972—. Cons., RocketDyne, McGregory, Tex., 1968. Decorated Air medal. Mem. A.L.A., Beta Phi Mu. Home: 1323 Comet Trail Hixson TN 37343

HARRIS, ROBERT HARDING, aerospace exec.; b. Montgomery, Ala., Oct. 31, 1920; s. Augustus Jackson and Florence (Hirch) H.; B.Aero. Engring., Auburn U., 1947; postgrad., Union Coll., 1948, Emory U., 1962-63; m. Zuma Jeanette Williams, Aug. 30, 1946; children— Susan Elaine (Mrs. Franklin Mills Lindsey), Margaret Ann, Robert Harding, Nancy Jeanette. With Gen. Electric Co., 1947—, guided missile engr., Schenectady, N.Y., 1947, application engr., aviation, 1948-49, rectifier, motor specialist, Atlanta, 1950, sales engr., 1951-55, mgr. Atlanta territory, aviation and def., 1956-59, regional def. rep., 1960-61, mgr. Atlanta dist. operation, def. programs div., 1962-69, mgr. Eastern region operation, aerospace programs relations div., 1969—. Served to capt. USAAF, 1942-45. Decorated D.F.C., Air medal. Mem. Am. Inst. Aero and Astronautics, Am. Helicopter Soc., Aviation Hall of Fame, Air Force Hist. Found., Air Force Assn. (chpt. pres. 1965), Elfun Soc. (pres. 1960), Atlanta C. of C. (chmn. aviation com.), Tau Beta Pi, Pi Tau Sigma, Omicron Delta Kappa, Sigma Nu. Methodist. Rotarian (v.p.). Clubs: Aviation Executives (Miami, Fla.); Cherokee Town and Country (Atlanta). Home: 4147 Paran Pines Dr NW Atlanta GA 30327 Office: Suite 417 1800 Peachtree Rd NW Atlanta GA 30309

HARRIS, ROBERT RAY, city ofcl.; b. Smithfield, N.C., Oct. 8, 1932; s. Milton David and Inez (McVickers) H.; B.A., Elon Coll., 1957; student U. N.C., 1955; m. Dorothy Jane Elder, July 26, 1956; children— Richard Robert, Ronald Ray, Robin Ryan. Town mgr., Siler City, N.C., 1957-60; exec. staff mem. N.C. League Municipalities, 1960-67; city mgr., Sanford, N.C., 1967—. Dist. vice chmn. Boy Scouts of Am., 1967-72. Mem. Gov.'s Commn. N.G. Affairs. Bd. dirs. Sanford Advancement Center. Served with USMC, 1950-54. Mem. N.C., Internat. city mgrs. assns., N.C. City and County Mgrs. Assn., Am. Legion, Nat. Guard Assn. Rotarian, Elks. Home: McCracken Heights Sanford NC 27330 Office: PO Box 338 Sanford NC 27330

HARRIS, RODGER SHERMAN, librarian; b. Milw., Jan. 24, 1932; s. John Coman and Laura (Rodgers) H.; B.S., U. Wis., 1953, M.S., 1955; M.L.S., U. Okla., 1971; m. Kathryn Astrid Mygdal, Dec. 21, 1956; children—Laura Margaret, Tod Sherman. Jr. geologist Shell Oil Co., Hobbs, Las Vegas, N.M., Midland, Sweetwater, Tex., Houston, 1956-57; prodn. geologist Shell Devel. Co., Houston, 1958; geologist Shell Oil Co., Midland, Tex., 1959-70; geology and zoology librarian U. N.C. at Chapel Hill, 1970-72, personnel librarian and adminstrv. asst. to head cataloger L. R. Wilson Library, 1972—. Pres. Midland Civic Concerts Assn., 1964-67; pres. Friends of Midland County Pub. Library, 1966, treas., 1963-65, 67, mem. county library bd., 1969-70, chmn. 1970; bd. dirs. YMCA, Midland, 1969-70. Mem. W. Tex. Geol. Soc. (chmn. library com. 1969-70), Beta Phi Mu. Home: 316 Ridgecrest Dr Chapel Hill NC 27514

HARRIS, RUFUS CARROLLTON, univ. pres.; b. Monroe, Ga., 1897; s. Virgil Vascar and Jessie (Green) H.; grad. Gordon Inst., Barnesville, Ga., 1915; A.B., Mercer U., 1917, LL.D., 1931, LL.B., Yale, 1923, J.D., 1924; LL.D., U. Ala., 1941; William Jewell Coll., 1943; Litt.D., Birmingham So. U., 1950, U. Miami, 1958; D.C.L., U. Hawaii, 1952; LL.D., U. Me., 1953, U. Chattanooga, 1953, Northwestern U., 1958, La. State U., 1960, Tulane U., 1965; prof. honoris causa, U. Pueblo, 1956; m. Mary Louise Walker, June 23, 1918; children—Rufus Carrollton, Joseph Henry Walker, Louie Kontz. Prof. law Mercer U. Law Sch., 1923-27, dean, 1925-27; dean, prof. law Tulane U., 1927-37, pres. 1937-60; pres. Mercer U., Macon, Ga., 1960—; dir. U.S. Fed. Res. Bank, Atlanta, 1938-56, chmn. bd. dirs., 1954-56. Pres. So. Assn. Colls. and Secondary Schs., 1958, chmn. com. on Latin Am. relations; mem. higher edn. adv. com. Edn. Commn. of States; mem. commn. acad. affairs Am. Council on Edn.; pres. Council So. Univs., 1956-57, So. U. Conf., 1941-43; mem. adv. com. VA, Washington, 1943-69, chmn. 1958. Trustee, Eisenhower Exchange Fellowships, Inc., 1953—, bd. dirs. Carnegie Found. for Advancement of Teaching, 1945—, chmn. 1955; bd. mem. Lane Bryant Awards Com.; edn. commn. So. Bapt. Conv. Served as 1st lt. inf. U.S. Army, 1917-19; France. Decorated French Legion of Honor, 1953, Most Excellent Order of British Empire, 1970. Mem. Am., La., Ga., New Orleans bar assns., Nat. Planning Assn. (trustee; chmn. com. on So. devel.), Assn., Am. Law Schs. (sec. 1931-35, pres. 1935). Order of Coif, Phi Beta Kappa, Omicron Delta Kappa, Phi Delta Theta. Baptist. Democrat. Mason. Clubs: Boston, Recess, Round Table, New Orleans Country, Capital City, Commerce (Atlanta); Century Association (N.Y.C.). Home: 1309 Adams St Macon GA 31201

HARRIS, RUSSEL CLEMONS, JR., constrn. co. exec.; b. Waycross, Ga., Apr. 7, 1937; s. Russel Clemons and Ruth May (Joyner) H.; B.S., Ga. Inst. Tech., 1959; m. Rena Hoyt Clark, Oct. 29, 1960; children—Sally Burney, Rena Clark. Vice-pres. W. S. Clark & Sons, Tarboro, N.C., 1962—; pres. Harris Industries, Inc., Tarboro, N.C., 1964—, R & S Enterprises, Inc., Tarboro, 1968—, Tarboro Inn, 1971—. Mem. Tarboro Edgecombe Devel. Com., Coastal Plains Devel. Commn. Bd. dirs. Wesleyan Coll. Found. Served with USMCR. Mem. Nat. Fertilizer Solutions Assn. (dir.), Ind. Mfrs. Com., Merchants Assn. Episcopalian (jr. warden 1968-69). Home: St Andrews Extension Tarboro NC 27886 Office: 495 W St James St Tarboro NC 27886

HARRIS, STANLEY SUTHERLAND, judge; b. Washington, Oct. 19, 1927; s. Stanley Raymond and Elizabeth (Sutherland) H.; student Va. Poly Inst., 1945; B.S., U. Va., 1951, J.D., 1953; m. Rebecca L. Ashley, Aug. 1, 1964; children—Scott Sutherland, Todd A., Mark A. Admitted to D.C. bar, 1953; asso. Hogan & Hartson, Washington, 1953-64, partner, 1964-70; judge D.C. Superior Ct., 1971-72, D.C. Ct. of Appeals, 1972—. Dir. Allen Weather Corp., 1963-68, Newfound Corp., 1969-70. Gen. counsel, dir. Landon Alumni Assn., 1962-70; trustee Landon Sch. Corp., 1965-68. Served with AUS, 1945-47. Mem. Am. (vice chmn. gas, electric and nuclear energy com. 1966-67, vice chmn. adminstrv. practice and specialization in the law com. 1968-70, vice chmn. communications com. 1969-70), FCC (sec. 1964-66, exec. com. 1966-69) bar assns., Bar Assn. D.C. (chmn. ann. conv. com. 1969-70, bd. dirs. 1970-72), Raven Soc., Phi Kappa Sigma, Phi Delta Phi, Pi Delta Epsilon. Republican. Clubs: Metropolitan, Barristers (sec. 1969-70), Chevy Chase (Washington), Home: 9621 Weathered Oak Ct Bethesda MD 20034 Office: DC Superior Ct Washington DC 20001

HARRIS, STEVEN EARL, city ofcl., civil engr.; b. Mayking, Ky., May 30, 1933; s. Spence Edward and Sadie Elizabeth (Hoolbrook) H.; B.S. in C.E., U. Ky., 1957; m. Patricia A. Tucker, Dec. 27, 1953; children—Steven Earl, James Edward. Constrn. engr. Verville Constrn. Co., 1953-63; city engr., Maysville, Ky., 1963—. Registered profl. engr., Ky. Mason, Lion. Mem. Christian Ch. (mem. ch. bd. 1962—). Home: Main St Tollesboro KY 41189 Office: 1008 Forest Av Maysville KY 41056

HARRIS, SUSIE MARGARET MCMILLAN, librarian; b. Gainesville, Ga., Apr. 24, 1911; d. Henry Newton and Jane Florence (Dunagan) McMillan; A.B., Piedmont Coll., 1937; B.S. in L.S., George Peabody Coll. for Tchrs., 1945, M.S. in L.S., 1950; m. Elbert Clifton Harris, Sept. 8, 1929 (div. Mar. 1965). Tchr. pub. schs., Ga., 1929-44; head librarian N. Ga. Coll., Dahlonega, 1945—. Chmn. bd. Lumpkin County Library, 1950-60; mem. acad. com. on libraries Ga. U. System. Mem. Am., Southeastern (sect. chmn. 1957-59), Ga. library assns., Ga. Edn. Assn., Dahlonega Bapt. Women's Missionary Soc. (pres. 1964-66), Kappa Delta Pi. Baptist. Clubs: Women of North Ga. (pres. 1970-71), College; Dahlonega Woman's. Contbr. articles profl. jours. Home: 910 Park St Dahlonega GA 30533 Office: Box 96 N Ga Coll Dahlonega GA 30533

HARRIS, THOMAS ALBERT, ret. army officer; b. South Bend, Ind., Apr. 5, 1917; s. Jay Albert and Agnes Lucy (Lundy) H.; B.S. in M.E., Purdue U., 1940; M.B.A., U. Mich., 1964; m. Cornelia Anne Moore, Jan. 7, 1942; children—Martha Anne, Frances Gayle. Commd. 2d lt, U.S. Army 1940, advanced through grades to lt. col., 1951; comdr. Arty. Bns., Redstone Missile Group; prof. mil. sci., head dept. U. Mich., 1961-64; asso. prof. mil. sci. Eastern Ky. U., 1965-68; 1st prof. mil. sci., head dept. Morehead (Ky.) State U., 1968-70; plant personnel tng., safety adminstr. Grinnell Corp., Princeton, Ky., 1970—. Pres. United Givers Fund, Princeton, Ky. Decorated Bronze Star medal with oak leaf cluster; Meritorious Service medal U.S. Army. Mem. Assn. U.S. Army, Nat. Rifle Assn., Pi Kappa Phi, Delta Sigma Pi. Home: PO Box 492 Princeton KY 42445

HARRIS, THOMAS EVERETT, lawyer, labor union ofcl.; b. Little Rock, May 25, 1912; s. Marvin and Ina (Thomas) H.; B.A., U. Ark., 1932; LL.B., Columbia, 1935; m. Lucille Hassell, 1935 (div. 1944); children—Marvin Bryan, Ruffin Kirby; m. 2d, Margaret Samson, Aug. 14, 1944; 1 son, Thomas Everett. Admitted to N.Y., D.C. bars; law clk. to Justice Stone, 1935-36; asso. firm Covington & Burling, Washington, 1936-37; with Dept. Justice, 1937-41, assigned Office Solicitor Gen., 1939-41; asso. gen. counsel FCC, 1941-42, OPA, 1942-43; with Bd. Econ. Warfare, 1943; asso. firm Cahill, Gordon, Zachry & Parlin, N.Y.C., 1943-45; with U.S. Mil. Govt. in Germany, 1945-46; partner firm Alvord & Alvord, Washington, 1946-47, spl. asst. to atty. gen., alien property div. Dept. Justice, 1947-48; asso. gen. counsel CIO, 1948-55, AFL-CIO, 1955—. Mem. Nat. Labor Mgmt. Panel, 1963-67. Democrat. Home: 1201 Key Dr Alexandria VA 22302 Office: 815 16th St NW Washington DC 20006

HARRIS, VINCENT MADELEY, bishop; b. Conroe, Tex., Oct. 14, 1913; s. George Malcolm and Margaret (Madeley) H.; student St. Mary's Sem., La Porte, Tex., 1932-34, Pontifical N.Am. Coll., Rome, Italy, 1934-39; S,T.B., Pontifical Gregorian U., Rome, 1936, J.C.B., 1939; J.C.L., Cath. U. Am., 1940. Ordained priest Roman Catholic Ch., 1938; prof. St. Mary's Sem., La Porte, Tex., 1940-51; sec.-treas. St. Mary's Sem., Houston, 1952-66; chancellor Diocese of Galveston-Houston, 1948-66, diocesan consultor, 1950-66; 1st bishop of Beaumont, Tex., 1966-71; coadjutor bishop, Austin, 1971, 2d bishop, Austin, 1971—. Made domestic prelate with title Rt. Rev. Msgr., 1956. Decorated Knight Commdr. with Star, Equestrian Order of Holy Sepulchre of Jerusalem. Mem. Alumni Assn. N.Am. Coll, in Rome. K.C. (Tex, chaplain 1967-69). Home: 4007 Balcones Dr Austin TX 78731 Office: 1600 N Congress Av Austin TX 78701

HARRIS, VIRGINIA MARY (MRS. EARL D. HARRIS), Democratic nat. committeewoman; b. Newark, Aug. 27, 1922; d. William Charles and Mary A. (Busteed) Happel; ed. Drake Jr. Coll.; m. Earl Donovan Harris, Jan. 29, 1943; children— Donovan, Craig L. Vice pres. Citizens Adv. Bd., Monmouth County, N.J., 1957-61; spl. asst. to exec. dir. Nat. Capital Housing Authority, Washington, 1963-68; coordinator neighborhood and spl. projects Mrs. Lyndon Johnson's Com. for More Beautiful Nat. Capital, 1966-68; Dem. nat. committeewoman for C.Z., 1968—. Home: PO Box 115 Fort Clayton Canal Zone

HARRIS, WALTER PRESTON, physician; b. Beech Grove, Ark., Jan. 4, 1921; s. Elmer Henderson and Alice (Cothern) H.; B.S., Ark. State Coll., 1943; M.D., U. Ark., 1950; m. Louise Woodrum, Feb. 4, 1950; children—Tommy Dean, Mary Alice, Patricia Gail. Intern, Ark. Bapt. Hosp., Little Rock, 1950-51; gen. practice medicine, Danville, 1951—; chief staff Yell County Hosp., 1954-70. Served with AUS, 1943-46; ETO. Mem. A.M.A., Am. Assn. R.R. Surgeons, Res. Officers Assn., Ark., Pope-Yell County med. socs. Home: 1321 Main St Danville AR 72833 Office: Dan Ark Village Danville AR 72833

HARRIS, WILLIAM HENRY, newspaper publisher; b. Laurel, Miss., May 24, 1925; s. Edgar G. and Beulah (Ligon) H.; B.S., Miss. State U., 1948; m. Wanda Marie West, Dec. 10, 1947; children—Beulah Marie (Mrs. Harry Luke, Jr.), William Henry, Carol Elizabeth, Edgar West. With Daily Times Leader, West Point, Miss., 1945—, editor, pub., 1952—; pub. Starkville (Miss.) Daily News, 1960—; dir. Clay County Fed. Savs. & Loan Assn., West Point, Miss. Pres., Miss. Econ. Council, 1969-70. Commr., Golden Triangle Regional Airport, 1966—. Served with USAAF, 1943-45. Mem. Miss. Press Assn. (past pres.), So. Newspaper Pub. Assn., Sigma Chi.

Baptist (deacon). Rotarian (past pres.). Home: 948 E Main St West Point MS 39773 Office: 227 Court St West Point MS 39773

HARRIS, WILLIAM MADISON, banker; b. Farmville, Va., Feb. 28, 1932; s. William Madison and Ann (Thackston) H.; B.S., Coll. William and Mary, 1953; m. Marion Leonie Burks, July 27, 1957; children—Ann Holladay, William Claiborne, Elizabeth Madison, John Spencer Randolph. Dist. traffic supr., traffic engr., traffic supr.-personnel Chesapeake & Potomac Telephone Co. of Va., Richmond, Norfolk, Lynchburg, 1953-63; personnel dir. Central Nat. Bank of Richmond, 1963-71; v.p. personnel Planters Nat. Bank, Rocky Mount, N.C., 1971—; lectr. U. Richmond, 1965-71. Co-chmn. United Givers Fund, 1961-68. Mem. Henrico County Republican Com., 1964-66. Mem. exec. bd. Va. Coll. Placement Assn., 1968-69; bd. dirs. Richmond Senior Center, 1970-71. Served as lt. USNR, 1953-56. Mem. Am. Soc. Personnel Adminstrn. (past pres. Richmond), S.R. (sec. Va. chpt. 1970-71), Richmond C. of C., Sigma Epsilon Pi, Kappa Alpha, Republican. Presbyn. (elder). Clubs: Cosmopolitan (pres. 1958) (Lynchburg); Fishing Bay Yacht (commodore 1970) (Deltaville, Va.); Benvenue Country (Rocky Mount). Home: 210 Gravely Dr Rocky Mount NC 27801 Office: 131 N Church St Rocky Mount NC 27801

HARRIS, WILLIAM OVERTON, JR., physician; b. Norfolk, Va., Sept. 27, 1933; s. William Overton and Thelma (Dalton) H.; A.B., Va. Mil. Inst., 1955 M.D., Med. Coll. Va., 1959; m. Sally Ann Lauck, June 7, 1958; children—Grayson Lauck, William Overton III. Intern medicine Med. Coll. Va., 1959-60, resident medicine, 1962-65; spl. fellow neurology Mayo Clinic, 1965-67; practice medicine specializing in neurology, Richmond, Va., 1967-69, Newport News, Va., also Hampton, 1969—, asst. prof. neurology Med. Coll. Va., Richmond, 1967-69, clin. asst. prof. neurology, 1969—; neurologist, Hampton Roads Neurol. Center, Newport News, Va., 1969—; neurology cons. Kecoughtan VA Hosp.; mem. staff Riverside Hosp., Newport News, Va., Dixie Hosp., Hampton, Va., Mary Immaculate Hosp., Hampton, Va. Bd. dirs. Peninsula Multiple Sclerosis Soc., Peninsula Muscular Dystrophy Soc. Served as capt. USAF, 1960-62. Recipient Henry W. Woltman award Mayo Clinic, 1968. Diplomate Am. Bd. Internal Medicine, Am. Bd. Neurology and Psychiatry. Mem. Am. Acad. Neurology, A.C.P., A.M.A., So. Med. Assn., Va. Med. Soc., Peninsula Acad. Medicine, Newport News Med. Soc. Home: 20 Beverly Hills Dr Newport News VA 23606 Office: 11 Bruton Av Newport News VA 23606

HARRISON, ALBERT EDWIN, telephone co. exec.; b. Hartwell, Ga., Jan. 18, 1918; s. Paul Pride and May (Patton) H.; B.S., Ga. Inst. Tech., 1940; m. Marian Jane Smith, June 7, 1947; children—John M., Marianne R., Douglas P. Technician Radio Sta. WRDW, Augusta, Ga., 1935-39; elec. engr. Pacific Tel. & Tel. Co., Los Angeles, 1946-55; regional mgr. sales Lenkurt Electric Co., San Carlos, Cal., 1956-58; pres., owner Ellijay Telephone Co. (Ga.), 1958—, Community Television Co., Ellijay, 1968—. Sec., dir. Gilmer County Indsl. Devel. Corp., 1960—; chmn. Municipal-County Planning Commn., Gilmer County, Ga., 1965—, Gilmer County Indsl. Devel. Authority, 1968—. Served to maj. Signal Corps, AUS, 1940-46. Mem. I.E.E.E. Lion (pres. 1964-65, dep. dist. gov. 1967-68). Home: Boardtown Rd Ellijay GA 30540 Office: 36 Dalton St Ellijay GA 30540

HARRISON, ANN WICKER (MRS. BEN HARRISON), counselor; b. High Point, N.C., Apr. 28, 1929; d. Worth and Ella (Pender) Wicker; student Salem Coll., Winston-Salem, N.C., 1946-47; B.S., East Carolina U., 1951, M.A., 1959; m. Ben Harrison, May 28, 1948; children—Ben, Katherine Pender, Martha Ann, James Nathaniel. Dir. Christian edn., vocational counselor St. Paul's Episcopal Ch., Greenville, N.C., 1960-65; ednl. worker Pitt County Alcohol Information Center, Greenville, 1965-67; counselor Elmhurst Elementary Sch., Greenville, 1967-70, dir. guidance Research Project, 1968-70; dir. elementary guidance services Greenville City Schs., 1970—, coordinator programs for exceptional children, 1971—. Sec. Diocesan Dept. Christian Edn. Mem. Greenville Service League, 1955-60; v.p. Parents League, 1960-62; mem. adv. bd. Mental Health Assn. Mem. Am. Personnel and Guidance Assn., Classroom Tchrs Assn., N.E.A., N.C. Edn. Assn. Club: Greenville Country. Home: 1717 Circle Dr Greenville NC 27835 Office: Greenville City Schs W 5th St Greenville NC 27835

HARRISON, BILL, gypsum co. exec.; b. Oklahoma City, Okla., Oct. 2, 1930; s. Josiah James and Rose (Cantrell) H.; B.S.A., Okla. State U., 1955; m. Betty Ann Frey, June 2, 1950; children—Charles William, Robert Theadore, David Bishop, John Josiah. Salesman Harrison Gypsum, Inc., Lindsay, Okla., 1955-62, pres., 1962—; pres. Nat. Interstate Life Ins. Co., LIC Corp., No. Rivers Ltd. dir. First Am. Bank, Purcell, Okla. Mem. Lindsay City Council, 1959-62; chmn. McClain County Soil Conservation Bd., Okla., 1967—. Served to lt., USAF, 1950-52. Mem. Delta Tau Delta. Methodist. (chmn. bd. 1965-67). Rotarian, Elk. Address: Box 336 Lindsay OK 73052

HARRISON, C. BENNETT, banker; b. Memphis, May 10, 1918; s. Caldwell and Nell (Fuqua) H.; B.S., Davidson Coll., 1940; student Vanderbilt U. Grad. Sch., 1940-41; m. Hunter Wright, Sept. 16, 1950; children—C. Bennett, James. With credit dept. Chem. Bank N.Y. Trust Co., 1946; v.p. First Nat. Bank, Miami, Fla., 1948-65; chmn. bd. Union Planters Nat. Bank, Memphis, 1965—, also dir.; dir. Fed. Co., Holiday Inns Am. Active Shelby United Neighbors. Trustee So. Coll. Optometry, William R. Moore Sch. Tech. Served to maj., inf. AUS, 1941-46. Decorated Bronze Star. Mem. Robert Morris Assos. (bd. dirs.), Assn. Res. City Bankers, Sigma Alpha Epsilon, Omicron Delta Kappa, Scabbard and Blade. Home: 155 Grove Dale Memphis TN 38117 Office: 67 Madison Av Memphis TN 38103

HARRISON, CLARK EDWARD, real estate co. exec.; b. Decatur, Ga., Sept. 24, 1924; s. Clark Edward and Ima Mae (Roemer) H.; student U. Ga., 1941-43, St. Johns U., Collegeville, Minn., 1943-44; A.B. in Journalism, Emory U., 1948; postgrad. Yale U. Law Sch., 1948-49; m. Emily Frances Guess, June 21, 1947; children—Tom Clark, Robert Guess. With Harrison-Draughon Sch. Commerce, 1949-51, Am. Hosp. Supply Corp., 1951-52, Harrison Sales Co., 1952-56; county commr., 1957-60; with Clark Harrison & Co., Inc., realtors, Decatur, 1961—. Chmn., DeKalb County Bd. Commrs., 1969-72. Served with AUS, 1943-46. Decorated Purple Heart. Baptist. Home: 9 Charter Sq Decatur GA 30030 Office: Court House Decatur GA 30030

HARRISON, DAMON WILSON, state ofcl.; b. Aurora, Ky., Apr. 27, 1918; s. Wilson Bryan and Edith (Morris) H.; A.B., Western Ky. U., 1939; postgrad. U. Ky., 1939-41; m. Annie Pierce Steger, Mar. 5, 1966; children— Wendy (Mrs. W. Ron Helton), Bryan Louis, Damon Wilson. Research supr. U.S. Employment Service, Frankfort, Ky., Louisville, 1941-42, 46-48; research dir. Ky. Dept. Econ. Security, 1948-57; dir. research and indsl. devel. Louisville C. of C., 1957-60; research and planning dir. Ky. Dept. Commerce, Frankfort, 1960-71, acting commr. commerce, 1971—. Served with USMCR, 1942-46. Decorated Purple Heart. Democrat. Presbyn. Home: Apt 12 216 Briarcliff Frankfort KY 40601 Office: Bush Bldg Frankfort KY 40601

HARRISON, EDWIN D(AVIES), corp. exec.; b. Evadale, Ark., Jan. 8, 1916; s. William Franklin and Anna Elizabeth (Williams) H.; B.S., U.S. Naval Acad., 1939; M.S., Va. Poly. Inst., 1948; Ph.D., Purdue U., 1952, D. Eng. (hon.), 1962; D. Sc., Jacksonville U., 1960; D. Eng. (hon.), U. Toledo, 1961; m. Dorothy Estelle Manyon, May 25, 1940; children—Robert W., Richard M. Instr. physics and chemistry Randles Prep. Sch., 1939-42; asst. prof. Va. Poly. Inst., 1946-50, asst. dean engring. and architecture, 1952-55; dean Coll. Engring. U. Toledo, 1955-57; pres. Ga. Inst. Tech., Atlanta, Ga., 1957-69; research Purdue Research Found., Va. Engring. Expt. Sta.; exec. v.p. tech. services J.P. Stevens & Co., Inc., N.Y.C., 1969—, also dir.; dir. Gen. Electric Co., 1962-69. Bd. visitors U.S. Mil. Acad., 1961-63, Air U., 1962-65, U.S. Naval Acad., 1965-70. Served with USNR, 1942-46; capt. Res. Registered profl. mech. engr., Va.; registered profl. engr., Ga. Mem. Am. Soc. Engring. Edn., Am. Soc. M.E., Sigma Xi, Tau Beta Pi, Pi Tau Sigma, Phi Kappa Phi, Omicron Delta Kappa. Presbyn. Home: 1984 Ferncliff Rd Charlotte NC 28211

HARRISON, EMMETT CARROLL, credit bur. exec.; b. nr. Calvary, Ga., Aug. 19, 1931; s. Hadley Thomas and Mae (Johnson) H.; B.S., Fla. State U., 1958; student Southeastern Mgmt. Inst., U. N.C., 1958-65; m. Catherine Arrington, June 3, 1956 (div.); children—Emmett C., Thomas Hadley. Asst. mgr. Midland Finance Co., Tallahassee, 1954-55; pres., treas. Credit Bur. of Tallahassee, Inc., 1955—; pres. Ha-La Corp., 1964—. Instr. financial mgmt. Southeastern Mgmt. Inst., U. N.C., 1964—, Midwest Mgmt. Inst., U. Kan., 1966—. Trustee Southeastern Mgmt. Inst., U. N.C., 1961-63. Served with AUS, 1952-54. Mem. Asso. Credit Burs. Am. (dir. 1965-66, 67—), Asso. Credit Burs. Fla. (pres. 1964-66, treas. 1966—), Asso. Credit Burs. S.E. (pres. 1965—, dir. 1962-65), State Fla. Consumers Council, Tallahassee C. of C. Methodist. Rotarian. Home: 2104 Ridgetop St Tallahassee FL 32303 Office: 322 Madison St Tallahassee FL 32301

HARRISON, G.B., broadcasting exec. Sta. and gen. mgr. KOFM-FM, Oklahoma City. Address: 1200 NE Britton Rd Oklahoma City OK 73114*

HARRISON, GILBERT NEWTON, lawyer; b. Brownwood, Tex., Dec. 25, 1909; s. Gilbert Newton and Belle (Grinnan) H.; B.A., U. Mich., 1931, J.D., 1933; m. Joyce Manwaring, Dec. 3, 1955; children—Sarah, Penelope, Gilbert Nicholas. Admitted to Tex. bar, 1933, since practiced in Brownwood; city atty., 1948—. Dir. First Nat. Bank, Brownwood. Trustee Hall Bros. Found. Served to capt. AUS, 1942-46. Mem. Tex. Bar Assn., Sigma Chi. Episcopalian. Home: 803 Center Av Brownwood TX 76801 Office: First Nat Office Bldg Brownwood TX 79801

HARRISON, GRESHAM HUGHEL, lawyer; b. Johnson County, Ga., June 19, 1924; s. James W. and Geneva (Jordan) H.; J.D., Mercer U., 1954; m. Leslie Powell, Aug. 27, 1943; 1 son, Samuel Hughel. Admitted to Ga. bar, 1955; with State of Ga. Dept. of Law, 1954-63; asst. atty. gen. State of Ga., 1956-63; sr. partner Harrison & Garner, Lawrenceville. Sec., dir. Gwinnett Comml. Bank, Lawrenceville; judge Recorder's Ct., Gwinnett, Ga. Pres. cystic fibrosis Ga. chpt. NCFR Found., 1963-69; mem. Gwinnett County Research and Devel. Bd. Served with USNR, 1943-45; ETO; as Momm 1/c, 1951-52. Mem. Am., Ga., Gwinett County (pres. 1967-68) bar assns., Am. Legion (post comdr.), Gwinett C. of C. Presbyn. (elder). Kiwanian. Home: 331 Perry St SW Lawrenceville GA 30245 Office: 151 Pike St NE PO Box 88 Lawrenceville GA 30245

HARRISON, GWEN WYCHE, ednl. adminstr.; b. Waco, Tex., Nov. 27, 1932; d. John Adams and Ruth (Dunken) Harrison, Jr.; B.A. in Psychology, So. Meth. U., 1956; M.S. in Student Personnel Adminstrn., Ind. U., 1969. Asst. to dean women So. Meth. U., Dallas, 1964-68; asso. head counselor residence halls counseling and activities, Ind. U., Bloomington, 1968-69; univ. ednl. asst., area coordinator student personnel div. U. Conn., Storrs 1969—. Mem. Nat., Tex., Conn. assns. women deans and counselors, Am. Personnel and Guidance Assn., Am. Coll. Personnel Assn., Nat. Assn. Student Personnel Adminstrs., Pi Delta Phi, Delta Zeta. Presbyn.Office: Buckley Hall U Conn Storrs CT 06268

HARRISON, HASTINGS, coll. ofcl.; b. Leonard, Tex., Nov. 20, 1894; s. James Johnson and Savannah Elizabeth (Dial) H.; student Trinity U. Normals, Waxahachie, Tex. (now at San Antonio), summers 1915-16, Litt.D., 1935; m. Fay Farmer, Dec. 14, 1919; children—Jo Fay (Mrs. John Kirby Godbey, Sr.), Hubert James. Tchr. social studies pub. schs., Dawson, Tex., 1915-17; asso. gen. sec. YMCA, Corsicana, Tex., 1917-18, gen. sec., 1919-24, Beaumont, 1924-30, gen. sec., Tulsa, 1930-39, cons. gen. sec., 1939-40; southwestern dir. Nat. Conf. Christians and Jews, 1939-44, nat. 1st v.p., southwestern dir., 1944-59; cons. to chancellor So. Meth. U., 1959—. Chmn. Tulsa Juvenile Ct. Bd., 1933-36; dir. Tulsa Boys Home, 1930-40. Pres. Jefferson-Orange Co., Texas Social Service Council, 1928-29. Served as pvt. 34th div. U.S. Army, A.E.F., 1918-19. Recipient Estelle Manton Alumni Service award Trinity U., 1955; nat. citation Nat. Conf. Christians and Jews, 1959; dedicated Harrison Instrumental and Choral Bldg., So. Meth. U., 1967; named to Waxahachie (Tex.) High Sch. Hall of Fame, 1967. Mem. S.A.R., Am. Legion, V.F.W. Methodist. Mason (32 deg.), Rotarian (bd. dirs. Beaumont 1927; sec. Dallas 1962-63). Clubs: Dallas Athletic, Dallas Athletic Country. Author: Gordon Carr, 1935; Liberty—The Language of America, 1939; An Abridged History of the Daniel Bluford Harrison Family, 1951; Martin Dial and Related Families, 1959. Home: 4316 W Potomac St Dallas TX 75205

HARRISON, JOHN ALBERT, computer co. exec.; b. Louisville, May 9, 1943; s. Albert and Mary Agnes (Travis) H.; student Purdue U., 1961-63; B.A., U. Louisville, 1965; m. Jacqueline Kay Collins, Aug. 8, 1970. Sales rep. Fetter Printing Co., Louisville, 1965-66; prodn. foreman Nat. Southwire Aluminum, Hawesville, Ky., 1969-70; self-employed as land surveyor, 1969—; br. mgr. Honeywell Inc., Atlanta, 1970—. Served with AUS, 1966-69. Decorated Purple Heart. Democrat. Presbyn. Home: 514 Baltimore Av Lilburn GA 30247 Office: 500 Plasters Av Atlanta GA 30324

HARRISON, JOHN RAYMOND, newspaper exec.; b. Des Moines, June 8, 1933; s. Alfred and Dorothy (Stout) Cohen; grad. Phillips Exeter Acad., 1951; A.B., Harvard, 1955, postgrad. Bus. Sch., 1955-56; m. Lois Cowles, June 24, 1955; children—Gardner Mark, Kent Alfred, John Patrick, Lois Eleanor. Vice pres., dir. Lakeland (Fla.) Ledger, 1963, pres., 1966—; pres. dir. Ft. Pierce (Fla.) News Tribune, 1960; pres., dir., Gainesville (Fla.) Sun, 1963—, also pub.; v.p. Indian River Land Investments, Inc., Ft. Pierce, 1961—; pres. Ocala (Fla.) Star-Banner, 1969—. Bd. dirs. Ft. Pierce-St. Lucie County Indsl. Devel. Council, 1959-62, Ft. Pierce Meml. Hosp., 1959-62, Lincoln Park Child Care Center, 1959-62, Gainesville United Fund, 1965, Boys Club, Gainesville, 1965; chmn. bd. dirs. Ft. Pierce Art Gallery, 1965. Recipient Pulitzer prize for editorial writing, 1965. Mem. Sigma Delta Chi. Rotarian. Clubs: Lone Palm Golf, Lakeland Yacht and Country (Lakeland); Gainesville Golf and Country; Pelican Yacht (Ft. Pierce). Home: 2311 Nevada Rd Gainesville FL 32601 Office: Box 408 Lakeland FL 33802

HARRISON, JOSEPH WELLMAN, research economist; b. Washington, Jan. 11, 1929; s. Ralph H. and Bernice (Pirkey) H.; B.A., U. Va., 1952, M.A., 1958, Ph.D., 1964; m. Virginia B. Barnes, Dec. 1, 1953; children— Leigh M., Bruce B. Research economist Va. Dept. Hwys., Charlottesvillle, 1956-59, U. Miss., University, 1959-60; economist, programmer Amerad Corp., Charlottesville, 1961-62; economist Nat. Resources Evaluation Center, Office Emergency Planning, Washington, 1962-63; economist Gen. Electric Co., Syracuse, N.Y., 1964-67, Washington, 1967-72; mem. tech. staff Gen. Research Corp., Arlington, Va., 1972—. Mem. Am. Econs. Assn., Am. Acad. Polit. and Social Sci., Delta Sigma Pi. Office: Gen Research Corp 1501 Wilson Blvd 600 Arlington VA 22209

HARRISON, REESE LENWOOD, JR., lawyer, govt. ofcl.; b. San Antonio, Jan. 5, 1938; s. Reese Lenwood and Ruth (Fischer) H.; B.B.A., Baylor U., 1959, M.S., 1965; J.D., So. Meth. U., 1962; m. Judith Karen Scott, Oct. 9, 1964. Admitted to Tex. bar, 1962; practiced in San Antonio, 1962—; mem. firm Oppenheimer, Rosenberg, Kelleher & Wheatley, 1972; chief criminal sect., asst. U.S. atty., San Antonio, 1964—. Sec. Tex. DeMolay Found., 1961—. Served with USAF, 1963-64. Mem. Soc. Govt. Economists (dir. 1971-72). Inter-Am., Fed. (pres. San Antonio chpt. 1971-72), Am., San Antonio (vice-chmn. criminal law com. 1971-72) bar assns., State Bar Tex. Mason (Shriner). Club: Town (San Antonio). Home: 11630 Sandman St San Antonio TX 78216 Office: PO Box 477 San Antonio TX 78292

HARRISON, RICHARD DONALD, food co. exec.; b. Salt Lake City, May 19, 1923; s. William Z. and Mary Frances (Sappington) H.; B.A., Stanford, 1946; LL.B., U. Mich., 1949; m. Marilyn Fleming, Aug. 30, 1953; children—Amy Virginia, Leslie Lynn, Julie Fleming, Susan Elizabeth, Alyse Carric, Richard Donald. Admitted to D.C. bar, 1950, Mich. bar, 1950, Utah bar, 1950, Wash. bar, 1952, also U.S. Supreme Ct. bar; spl. asst. to atty. tax div. appellate sect. Dept. Justice, 1950-52; pvt. practice, Seattle, 1952-54; wth Fleming Co., Topeka, 1954—, v.p., 1957-60, dir. planning, 1963-64, pres., 1964—, also chief exec. officer, dir.; dir. First Nat. Bank, Mid-Continent Life Ins., Oklahoma City, Quaker Oats. Bd. dirs. Okla. Christian Coll., Sci. and Arts Found., YMCA. Mem. Nat. Am. Wholesale Grocers Assn. (bd. govs.), Oklahoma City C. of C. (dir.), Ind. Grocers Alliance (chmn. bd.), Sigma Chi, Phi Delta Phi. Presbyn. Clubs: River (Kansas City, Mo.); Beacon, Oklahoma City Golf and Country (Oklahoma City). Home: 1508 Guilford Lane Oklahoma City OK 73120 Office: 3545 NW 58th St Oklahoma City OK 73112

HARRISON, RICHARD REX, dentist; b. Wewoka, Okla., Mar 27, 1922; s. Thomas Franklin and Perney Ethel (Williams) H.; B.A., U. Okla., 1944; D.D.S., Baylor U., 1946; m. Eunice Spurgin Knapp, Sept. 14, 1951. Practice gen. dentistry, Wewoka, Okla., 1946-49, Comanche, 1949-51, Oklahoma City, 1953—. Served to capt. U.S. Army. Mem. Am., Oklahoma, Oklahoma County dental assns., Okla. Gem and Mineral Soc., Okla. Ornithological Soc., Nat. Audubon Soc., Nat. Woodcarvers Assn. Baptist. Mason. Home: 4113 NW 21st Terrace Oklahoma City OK 73107 Office: 3416 NW 23d St Oklahoma City OK 73107

HARRISON, W. EARL, banker; b. Ellis County, Tex.; s. Robert E. and Lucretia (Vestal) H.; law degree under pvt. tutorship, 1936; grad. Rutgers U. Sch. Banking, 1939; m. Minnie Louise Howell, June 1, 1926; 1 son, William Earl. Admitted to Tex. bar, 1935; with First Nat. Bank Waco, Tex., 1926—, pres., 1965-70, also dir.; dir. Waco Hardware Co., Golden Triangle Corp., Baylor Stadium Corp., Baylor Bear Club. Bd. dirs. Tex. Good Roads Assn.; trustee Baylor U.; mem. Baylor U. Council for Instl. Devel.; trustee McLennan Community Coll.; past pres., dir. Waco YMCA, Waco Library. Served to lt. USNR, World War II. Mason (Shriner); Lion (past pres., dir. Waco). Club: Ridgewood Country (Waco). Home: 3111 Austin Av Waco TX 76710 Office: 811 Washington Av Waco TX 76701

HARRISON, WILLIS EDWARD, dentist; b. Reydon, Okla., Nov. 7, 1938; s. Bruce E. and Laura Pearl (Sanford) H.; B.S., W. Tex. State U., 1957-61; D.D.S., U. Tex., 1961-65; m. Mary Ann Brown, Nov. 30, 1955; children—Monte Ray, Julie Ann, Willis Ward. Pvt. practice dentistry, Canyon, Tex., 1967—. Mem. Canyon (Tex.) City Commn., 1970—. Bd. dirs. High Plains Eye-Bank, Randall County Cancer Soc. Served with Dental Corps, AUS, 1965-67. Mem. Am. Dental Assn., Panhandle Dist. Dental Soc., Canyon C. of C. (v.p. 1969), Sigma Nu. Methodist (mem. bd. finance 1969-71). Lion. Home: 2500 11th Av Canyon TX 79015 Office: 1419 7th Av Canyon TX 79015

HARRON, MARION JANET, judge; b. San Francisco, Sept 3, 1903; d. Charles Merrill and Minnie Jane (Little) Harron; A.B., U. Cal., 1924, J.D., 1926. Teaching fellow U. Cal., 1924-26; staff Cal. Minimum Wage Commn., 1925; admitted to Cal. bar, 1926, U.S. Supreme Ct. bar, 1938; dir. Survey of Labor Laws in N.Y. State, Nat. Indsl. Conf. Bd., N.Y.C., 1926-27; mem. faculty Inst. of Law, Johns Hopkins U., 1928; gen. practice of law, 1929-33; asst. counsel NRA, Washington, D.C., 1933-35; regional custodian of rehab. corps. Resettlement Adminstrn., Berkeley, Cal., 1936; judge Tax Ct. U.S., formerly U.S. Bd. Tax Appeals, 1936—. Mem. Fed. Bar Assn., Bar Assn. San Francisco, Internat. Fedn. Women Lawyers, Nat. Lawyers Club, Am. Assn. U. Women, Nat. Assn. Women Lawyers, Phi Beta Kappa, Delta Sigma Rho, Phi Delta Delta. Democrat. Conglist. Author: Current Research in Law (1928-29), 1929. Address: Tax Court US Washington DC 20044

HARRY, ROBERT LEE, A.R.C. exec.; b. Sharon, Pa., Mar, 27, 1918; s. Fred L. and Lorena (Heile) H.; student Pa. State U. Extension, 1939-40, A.R.C. Mgmt. Development Sch., 1955, pub. relations Am. U., 1958; m. Donna M. Smith, Sept. 27, 1941; children—Dianne, Robert. With Pa. Dept. Unemployment Compensation, 1937-38, Pa. Dept. Pub. Assistance, 1939-41; with A.R.C., 1942—, dir. fund raising Eastern area, 1955-57, asst. dir. nat. fund raising, 1957-59, nat. dir. fund raising, 1959—. Home: 2000 Basset St Alexandria VA 22308 Office: Am Nat Red Cross 17th and E Sts Washington DC 20002

HARSDORFF, WILSON F., newspaper editor; b. Woodsboro, Tex., July 3, 1925; s. Dave Christian and Margaret (McKenzie) H.; B.A., Tex. Arts and Industry U., 1949; m. Jo Katherine Becker, Oct. 9, 1952; children—Mark, Lori, Joey. With Kingsville (Tex.) Record, 1949-50; reporter Corpus Christi (Tex.) Caller, 1950-54; reporter Times Picayune, New Orleans, 1954-58, night city editor, 1958-65, city editor, 1965—. Served with USNR, 1942-45, 50-52. Club: New Orleans Press (pres. 1965-66). Home: 1140 Tensas St Harvey LA 70058 Office: 3800 Howard Av New Orleans LA 70140

HARSH, HAROLD CURTIS, mfg. co. exec.; b. Harlem Springs, O., Mar. 10, 1910; s. William C. and Emma Elizabeth (Hanna) H.; student Wooster Coll., 1927-29; B.A., Ohio State U., 1931; M.S., Mass. Inst. Tech., 1934; m. Evelyn Smith, Jan. 16, 1939; children— Priscilla (Mrs. Robert J. Smith), Robert Arthur. Supr. Ansco div. Gen. Aniline & Film Corp., Binghamton, N.Y., 1934-39, supr. new emulsions, 1939-43, mgr. color products devel. lab., 1943-46, mgr. chem. devel. dept., 1946-49, quality control mgr., 1949-52; prodn. mgr. Ansco div. Gen. Aniline & Film Corp., Binghamton, N.Y., 1952-55, mgr. operations, 1955-60, gen. mgr., 1960-62, dir. mfg., 1962; v.p.

operations Kalvar Corp., New Orleans, 1962-64, pres., chief exec. officer, 1964—; also dir. Kalvar Corp./Kal Graphic, Inc.; dir. Data Processing Center, Inc., New Orleans, So. Microfilm Corp., Metairie, La.; chmn. bd. Metro Kalvar, Inc., Darien, Conn., COM IV, Inc., Bloomfield, Conn. Vice pres. Susquehanna Valley Home, Binghamton, 1958; pres. Binghamton Boys' Club, 1958. Bd. dirs. Boys Club Greater New Orleans, 1970—; bd. dirs., exec. com. Sheltered Workshop for Disabled, Inc., Binghamton, 1960; Boss of Year award Nat. Secs. Assn., 1972. Recipient Army Dept. citation, 1951, medallion Boys' Club, 1959. Fellow Photog. Soc. Am., Soc. Motion Picture and TV Engrs., Am. Inst. Chemists; mem. Am. Chem. Soc., Nat. Microfilm Assn., Soc. Photog. Scientists and Engrs., New Orleans C. of C., La. Mfrs. Assn., Soc. Advancement Mgmt. (recipient Profl. Mgr. citation award, 1961), Chemists Club. Clubs: International House, Timberlane Country. Patentee in field. Home: 2011 State St New Orleans LA 70118 Office: 907-909 S Broad St New Orleans LA 70125

HARSHBARGER, JOHN CARL, JR., scientist; b. Weyers Cave, Va., May 9, 1936; s. John Carl and Alma (Baker) H.; B.A., Bridgewater Coll., 1957; M.S., Va. Poly. Inst. 1959; Ph.D., Rutgers U., 1962. NSF research asso. Insect Pathology Lab. U.S. Dept. Agr., Beltsville, Md., 1962-64; asst. research pathobiologist U. Cal. at Irvine, 1964-67; dir. Registry of Tumors in Lower Animals, Smithsonian Instn., Washington, 1967—. Mem. A.A.A.S., Am. Assn. for Cancer Research, Soc. Invertebrate Pathology, Entomol. Soc. Am., Sigma Xi, Phi Sigma. Contbr. articles to sci. jours. Home: 2026 Columbia Pike Arlington VA 22204 Office: Smithsonian Instn MNH Washington DC 20560

HART, ALAN ETHREL, supt. schs.; b. nr. Branford, Fla., Nov. 9, 1908; s. John Allen and Mollie (Poore) H.; B.A. in Edn., U. Fla., 1935, M.A. Edn., 1946; postgrad. Fla. State U., 1950; m. Clarice Gillis, Jan. 24, 1943. Prin., tchr. rural schs. Dixie and Lafayette counties, Fla., 1925-35; tchr. Mayo (Fla.) High Sch., 1929-30; tchr., asst. prin. Taylor County, Fla., 1935-42, supr. instrn., 1946-63; supt. schs. Taylor County, Perry, Fla., 1963—. Bd. dirs. Fla. Tb. and Respiratory Disease Assn. Served with USAF, 1942-46; now lt. col. Res. ret. Mem. Fla. Assn. Dist. Sch. Supts. (pres. 1970-71), Fla. Assn. Suprs. Instrn. (pres. 1951-52), Phi Eta Sigma, Kappa Delta Pi, Theta Chi. Methodist. Mason (Shriner), Kiwanian. Home: 604 E Bay St Perry FL 32347 Office: Court House PO Box 509 Perry FL 32247

HART, ALLIE CARROLL, state ofcl.; b. Madison, Ga.; d. Joseph Martin and Maud (Atkinson) Hart; A.B., Brenau Coll.; M.A., U. Ga. Former serials cataloger U. Ga. Libraries; asst. archivist Ga. Dept. Archives and History, Atlanta, 1957-64, dir., 1964—, dir. Ann. Archives Inst., 1967-71. Mem. Ga. Council for Environmental Quality, 1969. R.J. Reynolds Found. coastal research grantee. Mem. Soc. Am. Archivists (state and local records com. 1966-68), Am. Records Mgmt. Assn. (dir., sec. Atlanta chpt. 1966-70), Ga. League Hist. Socs. (v.p., pres. 1968-71), Ga. Hist. Soc. (curator 1966—), Atlanta Audubon Soc., Phi Beta Kappa, Alpha Delta. Democrat. Methodist. Club: Soroptimist. Home: 18 Peachtree Circle NE Atlanta GA 30309 Office: Ga Dept of Archives and History 330 Capitol Av SE Atlanta GA 30334

HART, CARL ORLANDO, aerospace engr.; b. Enid, Okla., Dec. 9, 1904; s. Caius O. and Anna (Musgrave) H.; student Okla. State U., 1923-26; B.S. in Aerospace Engring., Okla. U., 1961, M.S., 1965; m. Norma Putman, May 19, 1926; children—Orlando Joe, Rudy J. Field engr. MacCray Refrigeration Co., 1937-42; gen. engr. U.S. Air Force, Tinker AFB, Okla., 1943-50, supervisory gen. engr. 1950-56, chief product engring. div., 1956-61, chief propulsion engring. br., 1961-66, chief aero. tchr. indsl. and middle mgmt. U.S. Air Force, 1959-66, chief aero. systems br., 1966-68, chief value engring. br., 1968-71, chief engring. planning br., 1971—; partner Cons. Engring. Service, Hart-Henderson, Okla., 1952—. Recipient Sustained Superior award U.S. Air Force, 1965. Registered profl. engr., Okla. Mem. Nat., Okla. socs. profl. engrs., I.E.E.E. (vice chmn. 1960). Democrat. Methodist (chmn. bd. trustees). Mason. (K.T.). Patentee in field. Home: 8113 Victoria Dr Oklahoma City OK 73159 Office: Tinker AFB OK 73145

HART, CARL RAYMOND, civil engr.; b. Rio Vista, Tex., Mar. 27, 1905; s. John Chitwood and Leila (Sandusky) Hart; student John Tarlton Jr. A. and M. U., 1924-26; B.S., Tex. Tech. U., 1931; m. Ruth Smith, Aug. 6, 1930; children—Carl Raymond, Robert Franklin. With engring. dept. Santa Fe R.R., Temple, Tex., 1927-28; with Tex. Hwy. Dept., Lubbock, 1932—, supervising resident engr., 1970—. Registered profl. engr., Tex. Mem. Tex., Am. socs. profl. engrs., Tex. Pub. Employees Assn. Mem. Ch. of Christ. Mason. Home: 2332 19th St Lubbock TX 79401 Office: Box 771 Lubbock TX 79408

HART, ELMER FRANKLIN, coll. adminstr.; b. Lexington, Ky., Aug. 11, 1944; s. Elmer Bayse and Nada (Amburgey) H.; B.S. in Civil Engring., Va. Poly. Inst. and State U., 1967, M.S. in Civil Engring., 1968; postgrad. U. Mo., 1969, W. Va. U., 1971; m. Carol Sue Morgan, Dec. 22, 1966; children—Tonya Morgan, Angie Caroline. Engrs. aide TVA, Chattanooga, 1963-66; asst. prof. Bluefield (W.Va.) State Coll., 1967-72, dir. pre-engring., 1968-69, asst. dir. div. tech., 1969-72, registrar, dir. admissions, 1970-71, dir. financial aid, 1971—, pres. faculty council, 1969-70. Cons. engr. Chinquipin Devel. Corp., Mudfork Devel. Corp., Lakeview Devel. Corp., Mudfork Coal Co., 1968—. Sec.-treas. Tazewell County Republican Club, 1970—. Bd. dirs. Learning Resources Computer Network, W.Va. Ednl. Computer Network. Recipient Distinguished Service award Kiwanis Club, 1969, NSF fellowship U. Mo., 1969. Registered profl. engr., Va. Mem. Nat. Soc. Profl. Engrs. (chpt. v.p.), Am. Soc. C.E., Am. Tech. Edn. Assn., Am. Soc. Engring. Edn., W.Va. Land Surveyors Assn., W.Va. Assn. Admissions Officers, Va. Poly. Inst. and State U. Alumni Assn., Tau Beta Pi, Chi Epsilon, Kappa Theta Epsilon. Kiwanian (pres. Bluefield 1972—). Club: Richwood Golf (Bluefield). Home: Route 3 Box 296 Bluefield VA 24605 Office: Bluefield State Coll Bluefield WV 24701

HART, GEORGE LUZERNE, JR., U.S. judge; b. Roanoke Va., July 14, 1905; s. George Luzerne and Lavela (Slicer) H.; A.B., Va. Mil. Inst., 1927; LL.B., Harvard, 1930; m. Louise Neller, Oct. 12, 1935; 1 son, George Luzerne III. Admitted to D.C. bar, 1930, Va. bar, 1936; mem. firm Lambert & Hart, 1930-40, Lambert, Hart & Northrop, 1946-58; judge U.S. Dist. Ct. for D.C., 1958—. Home: 3901 Jenifer St NW Washington DC 20015 Office: US Courthouse Washington DC

HART, HENLEY EDWARD, city ofcl.; b. Atlanta, Apr. 5, 1924; s. Charles E. and Arrie May (Bingham) H.; student bus. adminstrn. Carroll Lynn Bus. Coll., 1947-51; m. Frances Baugh, Oct. 10, 1941; children—Charles W., James T. Foreman Celanese Corp. Am., 1946-48; salesman Kirkland Motor Co., 1948-51; dir. pub. works, City of Rome, Ga., 1968—. Served with AUS, 1942-46. Mem. Water Pollution Assn., (dir. 1971—), Fed. Pollution Assn., Pub. Works Assn., Am. Water Works Assn., Ga. Water Pollution Control Assn. Home: 11 Chief Vann Dr Rome GA 30161 Office: Box 1433 Rome GA 30161

HART, HERBERT CARLTON, psychologist; b. Ironton, O., Mar. 2, 1026; s. William Carl and Gertrude (Layne) H.; B.A., U. Fla., 1954, M.A., 1956, Ph.D., 1959; m. Frances Lee Lloyd, Jan. 2, 1947; children—Jan C., Melissa A., Julie M. Staff psychologist Bryce Hosp., Tuscaloosa, Ala., 1959-61; acting chief psychologist VA Hosp., Tuscaloosa, 1961-63, asst. chief, Marion, Ind., 1963-65; asst. prof. extension div. U. Ind., 1963-65; chief psychologist VA regional office, Columbia, S.C., 1965-68, also asst. prof. U. S.C., Columbia; sr. field assessment officer Peace Corps, Escondido, Cal., 1968; chief psychologist VA Center, Jackson, Miss., 1968-70; clin. asst. prof. Med. Sch., U. Miss., Jackson, 1968-70; cons. U. So. Miss., Hattiesburg, 1968—, U. Hosp., Jackson, 1968-70; chief psychology service VA Hosp., Richmond, Va., 1970—. Dir. New Stage Summer Film Festival, Jackson, 1969. Served with AUS, 1944-46, 48-52. Mem. S.C. Aero. Assn., Am., Southeastern, Miss., Va., Richmond psychol. assns. Publications in video tape, drug addiction, alcohol abuse. Home: 5526 Jamson Rd Richmond VA 23234 Office: McGuire VA Hosp Richmond VA 23219

HART, KYLE MCNUTT, ins. co. exec.; b. Knoxville, Tenn., Jan. 23, 1925; s. Cowan McNutt and Hazel (Brown) H.; B.S., U. Tenn., 1952; m. Carol Diana Davies, Dec. 5, 1947; children—David Kyle, Diana Jean. Treas., dir. Allied Life, Charlotte, N.C., 1954-58; sr. v.p., dir. Lincoln Am. Life, Memphis, 1958-64; founder-chmn. bd. dirs., pres. Nat. Savs. Life Ins. Co., Murfreesboro, Tenn., 1964—; dir. Royal Pubs., Inc., Real-Time Computers, Inc., University Parks, Inc., Nat. Savs. Corp. Chmn., Washington County Heart Fund, 1960; mem. meml. com. Carroll Reece Meml. Library, E. Tenn. State U., 1960—. Served with USAAF, 1942-46. Mem. Am. Inst. C.P.A.'s, Tenn. Soc. C.P.A.'s, Beta Alpha Psi. Clubs: Stones River Country, Ponte Vedro, Kingwood. Home: 1019 Houston Dr Murfreesboro TN 37130 Office: 231 SE Broad St Murfreesboro TN 37130

HART, LUCIUS LANE, state ofcl.; b. Norfield, Miss., May 20, 1913; s. J. L. and Mattie A. (Albritton) H.; student Copiah-Lincoln Jr. Coll., 1931-32, Clarke Meml. Coll., 1932-33, Washington and Jefferson Coll., 1943-44; m. Mary Varnado, Dec. 31, 1939; children—Mary Lane (Mrs. John Reed), Ross Varnado. Dist. mgr. Nat. Reemployment Service, 1933-37; supr. Miss. Unemployment Compensation Com., 1937-41; supr. USES, 1941-46; chief programs and methods Miss. Employment Security Commn., 1946-57; dir. Miss. Employment Service, Jackson, 1957—. Mem. State Agr. Coordinating Council, Prodn. Adv. Com. on Miss. Agr.; co-chmn. Placement and Services Com. on Vocational Rehab. Served with C.E., AUS, 1943-46. Decorated Legion of Merit; recipient Merit award Miss. chpt. Internat. Assn. Personnel Employment Security, 1947, Sertoma Gem award. Mem. Interstate Conf. Employment Security Agys. (chmn. farm placement com. 1953-58, chmn. adminstrv. grants com. 1960-61), Am. Legion, V.F.W., Internat. Assn. Personnel Employment Security (past pres. Miss. chpt.). Baptist. Mason. Club: Sertoma (local pres.). Home: 1475 Wooddell Dr Jackson MS 39212 Office: 1520 W Capitol St Jackson MS 39205

HART, STANLEY MARVIN, constrn. exec.; b. N.Y.C., Feb. 26, 1924; s. Sidney Sheppard and Shirley (Horvitz) H.; B.S., Miss. State U., 1943; m. Justine Hatry, Dec. 2, 1945; children—Richard Lawrence, Jules Sheppard. With concrete research lab. U.S. Army C.E., 1946-47; pres. Hart-McCowan Found. Co., Inc., Jackson, Miss., 1947—; cons. civil engr. Pres. Jackson Jewish Welfare Fund, 1958-60; active Boy Scouts Am.; dir. Hinds County March of Dimes, 1956; chmn. Hinds County chpt. Nat. Found. Infantile Paralysis, 1957-58; active United Givers. Trustee B'nai B'rith Home and Hosp. for Aged, Memphis, Leo N. Levi Meml. Hosp., Hot Springs, Ark., Jewish Children's Home Service, New Orleans. Served with C.E., AUS, 1943-46; ETO; maj. Res. ret. Decorated Bronze Star Medal, Purple Heart; recipient award for contbns. to Jewish community, B'nai B'rith, 1971. Registered profl. engr., Miss., La. Mem. Nat., Miss. socs. profl. engrs., Am. Soc. C.E., Assn. Gen. Contractors, Nat. Home Builders Assn., Sales Exec. Club, Jackson C. of C., Miss. Mfrs. Assn., Nat. Rifle Assn., Am. Legion, Res. Officers Assn., Sigma Alpha Mu. Jewish religion (1st v.p. congregation). Mason (32 deg.); mem. B'nai B'rith (bd. govs. 1971-74). Home: 2121 Eastover Dr Jackson MS 39211 Office: PO Box 9867 3008 W Northside Dr Jackson MS 39206

HART, WILLIAM T., govt. ofcl. Spl. adviser trade agreements U.S. Tariff Commn., Washington. Address: US Tariff Commn E St between 7th and 8th Sts Washington DC 20436

HART, WINSTON SCOTT, journalist, author; b. Farmville, Va., Nov. 10, 1902; s. James Littleton and Clara (Jenkins) H.; student pub. schs.; m. Virginia LaValle Taylor, May 22, 1937 (div. 1959); children—Martha Scott (Mrs. Robert Ryland Harlan), Jonathan. Reporter, Richmond (Va.) News-Leader, 1924-25, Roanoke (Va.) Times, 1925-31, Richmond Times-Dispatch, 1931-36; columnist Washington Post, 1937-43; staff corr. Time mag., 1943-45; speech writer Dem. Nat. Com., 1945-46; chief Washington bur., contbr. articles Coronet-Esquire mag., 1946, Changing Times mag., 1946-50. CIA, 1950-54, Nat. Geog. Soc., 1955-58; became chief historian Civil War Centennial Commn., 1959; free-lance writer. Mem. N.Y. So. Soc. Democrat. Episcopalian. Club: Nat. Press (Washington). Author: The Moon is Waning, 1939; Eight April Days, 1949; Stony Lonesome, 1954; Route Obscure and Lonely; 1967; Washington at War 1941-45, 1970. Co-author: The Symbol and the Sword, 1962. Contbr. Dateline: Washington, 1949; Battle of the Civil War (pictorial presentation). Address: 2807 Connecticut Av NW Washington DC 20008

HARTE, EDWARD H(OLMEAD), newspaper pub.; b. Pilot Grove, Mo., Dec. 5, 1922; s. Houston and Isabel (McCutcheon) H.; B.A., Dartmouth, 1947; m. Janet Frey, Feb. 8, 1947; children—Christopher, Elizabeth, William Julia. With Kansas City Star, 1948-50; editor, co-owner Synder (Tex.) Daily News, 1950-52; pres. San Angelo (Tex.) Standard-Times, 1952-56; v.p. Corpus Christi Caller Times, 1956-62, pub., pres., 1962—. Home: 222 Ohio St Corpus Christi TX 78404 Office: 820 Lower Broadway Corpus Christi TX 78403

HARTE, HOUSTON HARRIMAN, newspaper-TV exec.; b. San Angelo, Tex., Feb. 15, 1927; s. Houston and Caroline Isabel (McCutcheon) H.; B.A., Washington and Lee U., 1950; m. Carolyn Esther Hardig, June 17, 1950; children—Houston Ritchie, David Harriman, Sarah Elizabeth. Partner, Snyder (Tex.) Daily News, 1950-52, editor, 1952-54; with Des Moines Register and Tribune, 1954-56; pres. San Angelo (Tex.) Standard, Inc., 1956-62; v.p. Express Pub. Co., San Antonio, 1962-66, pres., 1966-72; chmn. bd. Harte-Hanks Newspapers, Inc. Pres. San Angelo Symphony, 1960; v.p. Concho Valley council Boy Scouts Am., 1960-62. Bd. visitors USAF Acad., 1965-69; bd. regents East Tex. State U., 1970—. Served with USNR, 1945-46. Democrat. Presbyn. Rotarian. Home: 2207 Camelback St San Antonio TX 78209 Office: PO Box 2171 San Antonio TX 78206

HARTER, JOHN SPENCER, physician; b. Kokomo, Ind., Nov. 30, 1903; s. Arthur and Frances (Lung) H.; student U. Wis., 1922-25; M.D., Washington U., St. Louis, 1928; postgrad. pathology U. Minn., 1928-29; m. Margaret Burton, June 16, 1928; 1 son, John Burton. Intern Barnes Hosp., St. Louis, 1928-30; surg. intern Strong Meml. Hosp., Rochester, N.Y., Lamoille fellow surg. research Harvard, 1931-33; house officer surgery Mass. Gen. Hosp., 1933-35; 1930-31; fellow, asst. thoracic surgery, Lahey Clinic, 1935-36; chief thoracic surgery, Miss. State Sanatorium, Sanatorium, 1936-45; practice medicine specializing in thoracic surgery, Louisville, 1945—; mem. staff U. Louisville Med. Sch., 1945—, clin. prof. thoracic surgery, 1962—. Diplomate Am. Bd. Surgery, Am. Bd. Thoracic Surgery. Mem. Jefferson County, Am., Ky. (pres. 1971-72) med. assns., Am. Assn. Thoracic Surgery, The Thoracic Soc., Am. Coll. Chest Physicians, Internat. Soc. Surgery, Soc. Thoracic Surgeons, Central Surg. Assn., So. Thoracic Surg. Assn. (pres. 1957-58), A.A.A.S. Presbyn. Rotarian. Club: Big Spring Country (Louisville). Home: 1410 Castlewood Av Louisville KY 40204 Office: 1226 Med Arts Bldg 1169 Eastern Pkwy Louisville KY 40217

HARTER, NEWMAN WENDELL, dentist; b. Ulmers, S.C., Aug. 11, 1923; s. Newman and Lucy Marie (Kinard) H.; B.S., The Citadel, 1947; D.D.S., Emory U., 1947; m. Dorothy Virginia Wright, June 2, 1944; children— Newman Wendell, Mark Richard. Gen. practice dentistry, Hampton, S.C., 1947—. Served with AUS, 1943-44. Chmn. financial drive Coastal Empire council Boy Scouts Am., 1955-56; pres. P.T.A., 1964. Mem. Coastal Dist. Dental Soc. (pres., 1953-54), Am. Legion (past comdr.). Mason (Shriner), Lion. Home: PO Box 487 Hampton SC 29924 Office: 200 Elm St E Hampton SC 29924

HARTFELDER, HERBERT EDWARD, food exec.; b. Kansas City, Kan., Jan. 8, 1914; s. George and Christine (Rollwagen) H.; ed. Kansas City Jr. Coll., Dallas Coll. of So. Meth. U.; m. Ruby Akins, May 7, 1939; children—Jack Fryar, Patricia Anne (Mrs. Richard A. Haberman), Orra Christine (Mrs. Charles Simpson), Mary Lee (Mrs. Altus E. Wilder III). With Oak Farms Dairies, 1936—, sec., treas., v.p., 1936-46, pres., 1953—; dir. Southland Corp., 1956—, exec. v.p., 1961-68, pres., 1968—; pres. Midwest Dairies. Velda Dairies, Embassy Dairies, Cooper Farms Dairies, Cabell's Dairies, Delvale Ice Cream Co., Spreckles-Russell Dairies, The Hathco, Inc.; chmn. bd. Hamp Properties, Allhart Corp.; dir. Oak Cliff Bank & Trust Co. Bd. dirs. Milk Industry Found. Mem. Nat. Assn. Accountants (pres. Dallas 1945), Dairy Products Inst. Tex. (pres. 1953), Nat. Dairy Council (dir., v.p.), Internat. Assn. Ice Cream Mfrs. (dir., mem. exec. com.), So. Assn. Ice Cream Mfrs. (pres.), Newcomen Soc. Methodist. Clubs: Petroleum, Dallas Athletic, Dallas, Northwood Country. Home: 9300 Hathaway St Dallas TX 75220 Office: 2828 N Haskell St Dallas TX 75226

HARTLEY, HAROLD W., ins. co. exec.; b., 1923; B.A., Hamline U.; m. Analyst, Minn. Mut. Life Ins. Co., 1949-55; sr. analyst Investors Diversified Services Inc., 1955-61; sr. analyst Republic Nat. Bank, 1961-65; securities officer Southwestern Life Ins. Co., Dallas, 1965-67, 2d v.p. securities, 1967-69, v.p., treas., 1969-70, sr. v.p. finance, 1970—. Served with USCGR, 1943-46. Home: PO Box 2699 Dallas TX 75221

HARTLEY, MARGARET LOHLKER, editor; b. St. Paul, July 28, 1909; d. William Arnold Lohlker and Edna (Hughes) Lohlker; B.A., Pomona Coll., 1930; m. Roland English Hartley, Oct. 14, 1942 (div. Jan. 1944). Editorial asst. So. Meth. U. Press., Dallas, 1947-49, mng. editor, 1949-61, editor, 1961—, asso. dir., 1971—; asst. editor S.W. Review, Dallas, 1947-61, mng. editor, 1961-63, editor, 1965—. Mem. Tex. Inst. Letters, Phi Beta Kappa. Episcopalian. Home: 3500 Granada Av Dallas TX 75205 Office: So Meth U Press Dallas TX 75222

HARTLEY, VIRGIL AGAN, editor; b. Miami, Fla., Dec. 20, 1931; s. John Frederick and Thelma Naniska (Dasher) H.; B.A., Emory U., 1954; m. Nancy Elizabeth Smathers, Sept. 18, 1954; children—Elizabeth Anne, John Charles. Editor, Emory Mag., Atlanta, 1964—. Served with U.S. Army, 1956-59. Mem. Chi Phi. Office: Gatewood House Emory U Atlanta GA 30322

HARTMAN, WALTER MICHAEL, corrosion engr.; b. McKeesport, Pa., Aug. 26, 1925; s. Arthur Henry and Hettie Carpenter (Michael) H.; B.S, U. Pitts., 1949; postgrad. U. Tex., 1956, Hahnemann Med. Coll., 1957-59 children—Cathy, Carol, Cynthia, Sandra. Corrosion engr. A.V. Smith Engring. Co., Narberth, Pa., 1960-66, mgr. so. operations, Charlotte, N.C., 1966—. Served with USNR, 1943-46. Registered profl. engr., Pa., Del., Va., N.C., S.C., Ga., Ala. Mem. Nat. Soc. Profl. Engrs., Am. Water Works Assn., Nat. Assn. Corrosion Engrs., Profl. Engrs. N.C., N.C. Assn. Professions, U.S. Power Squadron, Charlotte Engrs. Club. Presbyn. Club: Ski Bees (Charlotte, N.C.). Mailing address: 3807 Frontenac Av Charlotte NC 28203 Office: PO Box 3272 Charlotte NC 28203

HARTMAN, WILLIAM ISLES, univ. adminstr.; b. Boston, June 29, 1918; s. Nicholas and Nellie (McKay) H.; B.S., Okla. State U., 1950, M.S., 1951; postgrad. Harvard, 1954, U. Okla., 1958; m. Edythe Locke, Oct. 14, 1944; children—William Warren, Holly Isles, Edwin Brian. Dir. occupational safety and health tng. project U. Okla., Norman, 1955—, dir. safety and supervisory training, 1963—. Chmn. Nat. Task Force System Safety Com., 1971; mem. coll. sect. Nat. Com. Fleet Supervisors Tng., 1965—. Served with USNR, 1940-45. Decorated Air medal (2). Recipient leadership award Nat. Com. Fleet Suprs., 1968. Mem. Am. Assn. Oilwell Drilling Contractors (mem. edn. com. 1970-72), Am. Soc. Safety Engrs. (pres. 1965-66), Oilwell Drilling Contractors Assn. Australia. Home: 1404 Lincoln St Norman OK 73069

HARTMANN, PAUL ELLSWORTH, bus. exec., former naval officer; b. officer b. Ashland, Mass., Sept. 13, 1914; s. Max and Margaret (Daly) H.; student Bowdoin Coll., 1931-33; B.S., U.S. Naval Acad., 1937; m. Margaret Philips Moore, Aug. 3, 1940; children—Robin P., Margaret P. (Mrs. Larry L. Coy), Mary E. (Mrs. Robert E. Money), Martha D., Paul K. Commd. ensign U.S. Navy, 1937, designated aviator, 1940, advanced through grades to rear adm., 1964; operations officer 7th Fleet, 1959-60; comdr. U.S.S. Antietam, 1960-61; operations officer Atlantic Fleet, 1961-63; comdr. Fleet Air, Western Pacific, 1963-66, Carrier Div. 20, 1966-67; dir. logistics plans div. Navy Dept., 1967-68; asst. vice chief naval operations Office Dir. Naval Adminstrn., 1968-70, ret.; pres. Global Enterprises, Arlington, Va., 1970—. Decorated Bronze Star medal (3); Third Order of Rising Sun (Japan). Mem. Naval Inst., Naval Hist. Soc., Theta Delta Chi. Home: 1701 N Albemarle St McLean VA 22101 Office: 1815 Ft Myer Dr Arlington VA 22209

HARTSFIELD, HENRY WARREN, JR., astronaut; b. Birmingham, Ala., Nov. 21, 1933; s. Henry Warren and Alice Norma (Sorrell) H.; B.S., Auburn U., 1954; postgrad. Duke U., 1954-55, Air Force Inst. Tech., 1960-61; M.S., U. Tenn., 1970; m. Judy Frances Massey, June 30, 1957; children—Judy, Keely. Commd. U.S. Air Force, 1955, advanced through grades to lt. col.; grad. Aerospace Research Pilot Sch., 1965; astronaut Dept. Def. Manned Orbiting Lab. Program, 1966-69, Manned Spacecraft Center, NASA, Houston, 1969—. Recipient Meritorious Service medal. Office: Code CB NASA-Manned Spacecraft Center Houston TX 77058

HARTSFIELD, OSCAR WINFRED, nursing home adminstr.; b. Tallahassee, July 26, 1922; s. Oscar Vanbrunt and Annie Mae (Alcorn) H.; student Sch. Continuing Edn. U. Fla., Gainesville, 1964, 65; m. Blanche Emogene Lett, June 28, 1942; children—Oscar Winfred, Gloria Jean (Mrs. Robert M. Barrington). Nursing home adminstr. Tallahassee Convalescent Home, Inc., 1959—, pres., chmn. bd., 1959—; nursing home cons., 1967—; health care adviser,

1969-—. Mem. Fla. Consumer Council, 1967-—; mem. Gov.'s Conf. on Aging, 1968-70; life mem. Fla. Council on Aging; mem. Fla. Nursing Home Council, 1969-—; vice chmn. Fla. Bd. Examiners Nursing Home Adminstrs., 1971-72. Bd. govs. Nat. Assn. Bds. for Nursing Home Adminstrs., 1971-72; Served with USNR, 1943-46. Fellow Am. Coll. Nursing Home Adminstrs.; mem. Am., Fla. (dir. 1968-69, trustee 1971-—; legislative chmn. 1967-69, legislative mem. 1970-72; chmn. nominating com. 1972) nursing home assns., Fla. Sheriff's Assn. Democrat. Baptist (deacon 1952; tchr. Sunday sch. 1955-64, supt. 1954-55). Mason. Home: 1102 Lothian Dr Tallahassee FL 32303 Office: 2510 Miccosukee Rd Tallahassee FL 32303

HARTSFIELD, WAYNE, state ofcl. Mem. Ark. Bd. Edn., Little Rock. Address: Education Bldg Little Rock AR 72203

HARTSON, MAURICE JOHN, JR., ins. agt.; b. New Orleans, Jan. 20, 1906; s. Maurice J. and Marguerite (Calongne) H.; grad. Loyola U. of South, 1922-26; m. Elizabeth Freret, June 6, 1929; children—Liseanne (Mrs. J. Parham Werlein), Maurice J. III, Elizabeth. In ins. bus., 1924-—; pres. M.J. Hartson, Inc., New Orleans, 1937-—; dir. Lafayette Ins. Co.; dir., v.p. Columbia Homestead Assn. Past chmn. New Orleans Fire Prevention Bd.; past pres. New Orleans Community Chest; pres. United Fund Greater New Orleans, 1962-63; pres. adv. com. Convent of Good Shepherd; pres. St. Marys Boys Orphan's Asylum; chmn. Civic Affairs Com.; pres. New Orleans Area Health Planning Council. Bd. dirs. St. Mary's Dominican Coll., New Orleans Speech and Hearing Center. Mem. Nat. Assn. Ins. Agts. (dir., mem. exec. com.), War of 1812 Soc., Blue Key (elected hon. mem. 1963), Sigma Alpha Epsilon. Catholic. Most loyal gander Blue Goose. Clubs: Pickwick (past pres.); Serra (pres. New Orleans; dist. gov.); Stratford, New Orleans Country, Southern Yacht. Home: 1528 Webster St New Orleans LA 70118 Office: 332 Carondelet St New Orleans LA 70130

HARTZ, WILLIAM ROGERS, ins. exec.; b. Richmond, Va., Apr. 23, 1936; s. Arthur Paul and Mary Frances (Rogers) H.; B.A., U. Va. 1958. Vice pres. A. Paul Hartz, Inc., Waverly, Va., 1963-—. Chmn. County Cancer Crusade, Waverly, Va., 1964; area chmn. Va. Heart Assn., 1965-66; mem. Gov.'s Com. on Employment of Handicapped, 1968; mem. Nat. Citizens Com. Broadcasting, 1968-—. Mayor, Town of Waverly, 1970-—. Bd. dirs. Va. Soc. for Prevention of Blindness, 1968-—; chmn. trustee Nat. Coordinating Council on Drug Abuse Edn. and Information, 1969-71; bd. dirs. Va. Mental Health Assn., 1969-—; charter trustee Vol. Rescue Squad, 1964-65. Served to lt. AUS, 1958-62. Recipient Mem. U.S. (v.p., dir. 1968-69), Va. (pres. 1967-68, chmn. bd. 1968-69) jr. chambers commerce, Kappa Alpha. Democrat. Methodist (bd. stewards). Mason. Club: Downtown. Home: Coppahaunk Av Waverly VA 23890 Office: North St Waverly VA 23890

HARTZOG, GEORGE BENJAMIN, JR., govt. ofcl.; b. Colleton County, S.C., Mar. 17, 1920; s. George Benjamin and Mazell (Steedly) H; student Wofford Coll., Spartanburg, S.C., 1937; B.S. in Bus. Adminstrn., Am. U., 1953; m. Helen Carlson, June 28, 1947; children—George, Nancy, Edward. With Bur. Land Mgmt. and Nat. Park Service, Dept. Interior, 1946-62; exec. dir. Downtown St. Louis, Inc., 1962-63; asso. dir. Nat. Park Service, 1963-64, dir., 1964-—; trustee John F. Kennedy Center Performing Arts, mem. exec. com.; admitted to S.C. bar, 1942, Mo. bar, 1963, also Supreme Ct. U.S., 1949, U.S. Dist. Ct. D.C., 1970. Mem. Zoning Commn. D.C., Nat. Capital Planning Commn. Trustee, chmn. property mgmt. com. Nat. Trust Historic Preservation; chmn. Com. Preservation White House; exec. dir. Pres. Adv. Council Historic Preservation; sec. Nat. Park Found; bd. dirs. White House Hist. Assn. Mem. Nat. Recreation and Park Assn. (trustee), Washington Nat. Monument Soc. (sec.). Home: 1643 Chain Bridge Rd McLean VA 22101 Office: Interior Bldg Washington DC 20240

HARVARD, CLEMENTS ELIOT, ednl. adminstr.; b. Savannah, Ga., Aug. 11, 1937; s. Lucius Clyde and Florine (Wilson) H.; B.S., Ga. So. Coll., 1961, M.Ed., 1965; m. Alice Jane Hardy, June 18, 1961; children—Paul Eliot, Gilbert John. Tchr. social sci., prin. Clyo Elementary Sch., Effingham County Schs., Ga., 1961-65; prin. Royston Elementary Sch., (Ga.), 1965-67; prin. East Side Elementary Sch., Thomasville, 1967-69, prin. Thomasville Middle Sch., 1969-71, dir. quarter curriculum activities, Thomasville City Schs., 1971-72; prin. Waynesboro (Ga.) High Sch., 1972-—. Served with USMCR, 1956. Mem. Kappa Phi Kappa. Methodist. (chmn. council ministries 1969). Republican. Kiwanian (pres. elect 1971). Home: PO Box 677 Waynesboro GA 30830

HARVEY, ARTHUR, oil exec.; b. Edom, Tex., Sept. 26, 1895; s. John Arthur and Mary Ann (Williams) H.; student pub. schs. Minden, Tex.; m. Sylva Vogelsong, July 9, 1929; children—Inez Elizabeth, Arthur Herbert, Sylva Ann. Postal clk., spl. agt., intelligence unit Bur. Internal Revenue, Treasury Dept., 1920-39; owner Tex-Harvey Oil Co., 1939-—, now operating in Tex., crude oil producer; pres., sole stockholder Harvey Park Co., Denver; owner Tex.-Harvey Water Co., Hidland, Tex. Discoverer of Tonti Oil Field, Marion, Ill., Angus Oil Field, Navarro County, Tex., East Long Lake Oil Field, Anderson County, Tex., Tex-Harvey Oil Field, Midland and Glasscock Counties, Tex. Mem. Res. Officers Assn. U.S. Baptist. Club: Denver Athletic. Home: 334 Peerman Pl Corpus Christi TX 78411

HARVEY, ARTHUR EDWIN, JR., value engring. mgr.; b. Brewton, Ala., May 7, 1918; s. Arthur Edwin and Ruby M. (Britton) H.; B.S., Auburn U., 1940, M.S., 1946; m. Mae-Parish Singletary, June 7, 1942; children—Judy-Parish (Mrs. Forrest Robert Spiva), Janet-Corrine, Arthur Edwin III, James Britton, Deborah-Ann (Mrs. Rick Lynn Coates). Devel. engr. Pitts. Plate Glass, Barberton, O., 1947-50; project engr. Govt. Labs., Akron, 1950; statis. chem. engr. Thiokol Chem. Corp., Huntsville, Ala., 1951-53; chief equipment and facilities, research and engr. labs. Redstone Arsenal (Ala.), 1953-56; chief engr. services Army Ballistic Missile Agy., 1956-58, dep. chief quality assurance, 1958-59, chief value analysis, 1959-62, value engring. mgr. Army Missile Command, 1962-—; pres. Harvey Enterprises, chem. engring. cons., Ala. Waterways, Inc.; cons. Main Battle Tank for Value Engring., 1967; lectr., producer value engring. movies. Served to capt. with AUS, 1940-45. Decorated Bronze Star with oak leaf cluster, Purple Heart; recipient First Place trophy for two movie prodns. Indsl. Mgmt. Soc., 1966, 68. Fellow Soc. Am. Value Engrs. (past chpt. pres., internat. meritorious award 1966, fellow award 1967, life mem. award 1970, pres.'s spl. award 1971, spl. value engr. award Redstone chpt. 1969); mem. Army Materiel Command Value Engring. Mgrs. Council, Ala. Soc. Profl. Engrs. (value engr. year award 1969), Am. Inst. Chem. Engrs., Soc. for Advancement of Mgmt., Am. Soc. Quality Control, Assn. U.S. Army, Am. Ordnance Assn., Electronic Industries Assn., Sales and Marketing Execs. Assn., Tennessee Valley Geneal. Soc., Huntsville C. of C., Ret. Officers Assn., Alpha Phi Omega (pres.), Phi Lambda Upsilon. Lutheran. Elk. Clubs: Redstone Yacht (dir.), Redstone Officers. Contbr. articles to profl. jours. Home: 12001 Rockcliff Dr NW Huntsville AL 35810 Office: US Army Missile Command Redstone Arsenal AL 35809

HARVEY, GEORGE, JR., physician; b. Canton, Miss., Nov. 9, 1912; s. George and Patty (Person) H.; B.A., Vanderbilt U., 1935, M.D., 1938; m. Rosa Marion Fox, Apr. 2, 1941; children—Rosa Marion (Mrs. Perry Carroll), George III, Mary Lucinda. Intern and asst. resident in internal medicine Balt. City Hosps., 1938-39; fellow in internal medicine Mayo Clinic, Rochester, Minn., 1940, 41, 46, 47; pvt. practice internal medicine Jackson, Miss., 1948-54, Jackson, Tenn., 1954-—. Dir. The Jackson Sun, local newspaper, 1957-—; pres., dir. Sun Pub. Co. Trustee Union U. Served from lt. to maj. Med. R.C., 1942-46. Diplomate Am. Bd. Internal Medicine. Fellow A.C.P.; mem. Am., Tenn., So. med. assns., Am. Coll. Chest Physicians, V.F.W., Am. Legion, Beta Theta Pi, Phi Chi. Baptist. Home: 36 Northwood Jackson TN 38301 Office: 700 W Forest St Jackson TN 38301

HARVEY, JAMES DOUGLAS, hosp. adminstr.; b. Yankton, S.D., Jan. 19, 1929; s. Guy Hazelton and Edythe (Canon) H.; B.A., U. S.D., 1950; M.H.A., U. Minn., 1952; m. Inadoll Cruickshank, Sept. 9, 1950; children— Stuart James, Barbara Beth, Scot Wallace. Asst. adminstr. Hillcrest Med. Center, Tulsa, 1955-61, adminstr., 1961-—; instr. hosp. adminstrn. Okla. Baptist U., 1959-60; vis. lectr. Washington U., St. Louis, 1963-—. Served with Med. Service Corps, USAF, 1952-54; Korea. Fellow Am. Coll. Hosp. Adminstrs. (council regents 1964-—); mem. Am. (chmn. com. personnel 1965-66), Okla. (treas. 1958-59, 60-61, pres. 1961-62, 63-64) hosp. assns., Tulsa Hosp. Council (pres. 1961-62), Tulsa Exec. Assn., Midwest Hosp. Assn. (pres. 1970-71), Beta Theta Pi. Episcopalian. Mason (32 deg., Shriner), Rotarian (pres. Will Rogers club 1962). Home: 2207 Terwilleger Tulsa OK 74114 Office: 1120 S Utica Av Tulsa OK 74104

HARVEY, JAMES HALBERT, dir. import/export affairs Tex. Indsl. Commn., Austin. Address: Sam Houston State Office Bldg Austin TX 78711*

HARVEY, JASPER ELLIOTT, educator; b. Sweetwater, Tex., July 15, 1924; s. Wiley James and Julia Mae (Nolen) H,; B.A., U. Tex., 1950, M.Ed., 1952, Ph.D., 1960; m. Kathryn McDaniel, Nov. 27, 1947; children— Laurel, Leigh. Dir. spl. edn., Texas City, Tex., 1952-53; tchr. spl. edn. pub. schs., Austin, Tex., 1953-54; dir. Variety Sch. for Exceptional Children, Las Vegas, 1954-57; lectr. spl. edn. U. Tex., Austin, summers 1954, 58, 59, research asso. Dept. Ednl. Psychology, 1957-59; asst. prof. edn. U. Ala., Tuscaloosa, 1959-60, asso. prof., 1960-63, prof. spl. edn., 1963-69, chmn. dept. spl. edn., 1959-69; prof., chmn. dept. spl. edn. U, Tex., Austin, 1969-—. Cons. Ala. Com. on Edn. of Exceptional Children and Youth, 1959-69, Ala. Planning Project for Mental Retardation, 1963-69; mem. exec. com. Ala. Gov.'s Adv. Com. on Statewide Planning for Vocational Rehab., 1966-69, interim com. Reorgn. of Ala. Dept. Edn., 1967-69; mem. adv. bd. Handicapped Children Project, So. Regional Edn. Bd., 1964-68; mem. adv. bd. on mental retardation Ala. Bd. Mental Health, 1967-69; mem. med.-profl. adv. and evaluation bd. United Cerebral Palsy of Ala., 1961-69, chmn., 1966-69; governing bd. Council for Exceptional Children, Arlington, Va., 1967-69, 71-73, also chmn. legislative com., Ala. gov.'s apointee to White House Conf. on Mental Retardation, 1963; mem. spl. edn. adv. com. United Cerebral Palsy Research and Ednl. Found., N.Y.C., 1964-—. research asso. U.S. Office Edn. Research Project 1972, U. Tex., 1957-59; dir. United Cerebral Palsy-Ala. Dept. Edn. Project to Provide Tchr. Tng. for Tchrs. of Exceptional Children, 1961-64; dir. Vocational Rehab. Adminstrn.; project dir. staff tng. for exemplary early childhood centers project Bur. Edn. for Handicapped, U.S. Office Edn., 1969-—, field reader, 1966-—. Served with M.C., AUS, 1944-46; PTO. Mem. Am. Assn. on Mental Deficiency (Ala. rep. 1966-69), Am. Psychol. Assn., Am. Speech and Hearing Assn., Am. Acad. for Cerebral Palsy of the A.M.A. Episcopalian. Contbr. articles to profl. jours. Address: Sutton Hall U Tex Austin TX 78712 also PO Box 691 Sweetwater TX 79556

HARVEY, ROBERT, lawyer, state senator; b. Swifton, Ark., May 22, 1914; s. W.R. and Lula (Shaver) H.; A.B., LL.B., Vanderbilt U. Former dep. pros. atty.; former mem, Ark. Ho. of Reps.; mem. Ark. Senate. Dir. Mcht.'s Planter's Bank Newport, Ark. Chmn. Ark. Legislative Council, 1965-67; mem. Ark. Constl. Study Commn., Ark. Constl. Conv.; state treas. Ark. Democratic Com. Served with AUS World War II. Mem. Jackson County Farm Bur. (pres.). Methodist. Lion. Address: Swifton AR 72471 also Legislative Bldg Little Rock AR 72201

HARVEY, ROBERT WILSON, editor; b. Washington, Mar. 18, 1920; s. Robert Porter and Margaret (Wilson) H.; B.A., Dartmouth, 1941; postgrad. U. Stockholm (Sweden), 1946-47; m. Barbara Ann Landon, Sept. 3, 1941; children—Michael L., Martha E., Sara M. Reporter, Washington Post, 1941-43; asst. mng. editor Nation, N.Y.C., 1945-46; free-lance writer, Stockholm, 1946-47; asst. mng. editor Reporter, Washington, 1948; staff editor Changing Times, Kiplinger Mag., Washington, 1948-51, asst. mng. editor, 1951-58, mng. editor, 1958-64, editor, 1964-—; dir. Kiplinger Washington Editors, Inc. Bd. dirs. D.C. Heart Assn., 1964-68; bd. govs. D.C. Amateur Athletics Union, 1962-64. Served with USMCR, 1943-45; PTO. Episcopalian. Clubs: Dartmouth of Washington, Nat. Press, Washington Golf and Country, International. Home: 4513 N 40th St Arlington VA 22207 Office: 1729 H St NW Washington DC 20006

HARVEY, ROY SEARS, oil well service co. exec.; b. Wisdom, Mo., Nov. 3, 1920; s. Roland Roy and Ruth Anna (Sears) H.; B.S., Kan. State U., 1948; m. Eleanor Lucille Striegel, Sept. 4, 1949; children—Vance, Kala, Shane. Jr. clerk Stanolind Oil and Gas Co. (name now changed to Amoco Prodn. Co.), Hobbs, N.M., 1948-51; clk., Famariss Oil & Refining Co., Hobbs, N.M., 1951-53; sec.-treas., office mgr. X-Pert Well Service, Inc., Hobbs, N.M., 1953-69; sec-treas. D.C. Well Service, Inc., Denver City, Tex., 1969-—. Chmn. Hobbs (N.M.) Water Bd., 1968-69. Served with USAAF, 1942-46. Mem. Assn. Oil Well Servicing Contractors (chmn. safety com. 1970-—), Pi Kappa Alpha. Republican. Presbyn. (elder 1967-70). Mason (Shriner), Elk, Kiwanian, Lion. Home: 522 E Permian St Hobbs NM 88240 Office: Box 1449 Denver City TX 79323

HARVEY, W. BRANTLEY, lawyer; b. Hampton, S.C., June 5, 1893; B.S., U. S.C., 1922, LL.B., 1922. Admitted to S.C. bar, 1922; now mem. firm Harvey, Harvey & Battey, Beaufort, S.C. Mem. S.C. Ho. of Reps., 1924-28, S.C. Senate, 1929-52. Trustee U. S.C., 1941-42, Winthrop Coll., 1941-42. Mem. Beaufort, S.C. (pres. 1952-53) bar assns. Address: 1001 Craven St Beaufort SC 29902

HARVEY, WILLIAM BARTLETT, pub.; b. Pitts., Aug. 27, 1914; s. Walter B. and Aurelia (Bartlett) H.; A.B., U. Pitts., 1936; m. Dorothy Colvin, Aug. 14, 1943; children—Walter B. II, George C., Claudia. Mng. editor Macmillan Co., 1948-55; asst. dir. U. Chgo. Press, 1955-58; dir. N.Y. U. Press, 1958-67, U. Fla. Press, Gainesville, 1967-—; chmn. bd. Am. Univ. Press Services, Inc., 1971-72. Served from pvt. to capt. F.A., AUS; 4 campaigns ETO. Decorated Bronze Star, Purple Heart with oak leaf cluster, 1941-45. Mem. Assn. Am. U. Presses (pres. 1971-72), Delta Tau Delta, Omicron Delta Kappa. Home: 2911 NW 13th Ct Gainesville FL 32601 Office: 15 NW 15th St Gainesville FL 32601

HARVEY, WILLIAM BRANTLEY, JR., lawyer, state legislator; b. Walterboro, S.C., Aug. 14, 1930; s. William Brantley and Thelma (Lightsey) H.; A.B., in Polit. Sci. (2d honor grad.), The Citadel, 1951; J.D. magna cum laude, U. S.C., 1955; m. Helen Coggeshall, Dec. 30, 1952; children—Eilen L., William Brantley III, Helen C., Margaret D., Warren C. Admitted to S.C. bar; practiced in Beaufort, S.C., 1955-—; sr. partner firm Harvey, Battey, Macloskie & Bethea; mem. S.C. Ho. of Reps. from Beaufort County, 1958-—, chmn. rules com., mem. constl. revision com. Dir. Peoples Bank, Tidewater Investment & Devel. Corp. Served to lt. AUS, 1952-54. Mem. Am., S.C., Beaufort County bar assns., Phi Beta Kappa, Kappa Alpha, Phi Delta Phi. Democrat. Presbyn. (elder; tchr. Sunday sch.). Home: 121 N Hermitage Rd Beaufort SC 29902 Office: PO Box 1107 1001 Craven St Beaufort SC 29902

HARVISON, CLIFFORD JAMES, assn. exec.; b. Phila., Apr. 4, 1939; s. James Elmer and Lellis Camilla (Kallenbach) H.; B.A., Duquesne U., 1961; m. Sondra Masemer, July 2, 1966; 1 son, John Devon. With CIA, 1963-65; mng. dir. Nat. Tank Truck Carriers, Inc., Washington, 1972-—. Served to 2d lt. AUS, 1961-63. Mem. Nat. Assn. Expn. Mgrs., Internat. Assn. Approved Basketball Ofcls. Club: Toastmasters (exec. v.p. 1970-72) (Washington). Home: 6154 Kellogg Dr McLean VA 22101 Office: 1616 P St NW Washington DC 20036

HARWARD, STEPHEN CANNADA, univ. treas.; b. Durham, N.C., May 7, 1922; s. James Louis and Geneva (Cannada) H.; grad. Duke, 1943; m. Cora Lynn Young, Apr. 7, 1947; children—James T., Timothy R. Accountant, R. L. Steele & Co., C.P.A.'s, Raleigh, N.C., 1947-48, S.C. Harward, C.P.A., Durham, N.C., 1948-56; controller Duke U., Durham, N.C., 1956-70, asst. sec., asst. treas., 1970-72, treas., 1972-—. Mem. Bd. of Edn., Durham, 1967-—; bd. dirs. Durham United Fund, 1969. Served with USAAF, 1943-45. Mem. Am. Inst. C.P.A.'s, N.C. Assn. C.P.A.'s. Kiwanian (pres. 1968). Home: 2502 Sevier St Durham NC 27705 Office: Allen Bldg Duke U Durham NC 27706

HARWELL, HELON BALDWIN (MRS. JOHN EARL HARWELL), educator; b. Center, Tex., Jan. 6, 1921; d. Aaron F. and Bernice (Gibson) Baldwin; B.S., Stephen F. Austin State Coll., 1948; M.R.E., S.W. Bapt. Theol. Sem., 1949, D.R.E., 1955; M.A., N.E. Mo. State Tchrs. Coll., 1962; Ph.D., E. Tex. State U., 1967; m. John Earl Harwell, Aug. 22, 1953. Instr., Tex. Christian U., Ft. Worth, 1950-52; tchr. St. Joseph Acad., Tucson, 1953-54; asst. prof. psychology E. Tex. Bapt. Coll., Marshall, 1954-56, 62-65; asso. prof. childhood edn. New Orleans Bapt. Theol. Sem., 1956-61; prof. elementary edn. S.W. Bapt. Coll., Bolivar, Mo., 1965-67; asso. prof. edn. Nicholls State U., Thibodaux, La., 1967-—. Cons. kindergarten edn. workshops. Mem. Assn. Childhood Edn. Internat., Assn. Student Teaching, La. Tchrs. Assn., Alpha Chi. Contbr. kindergarten resource book, also articles to profl. and religious jours. Home: Route 1 Box 220 Supercharge Dr Thibodaux LA 70301

HARWELL, JACK UPCHURCH, editor; b. Mobile, Ala., Oct. 18, 1932; s. Hoyt Horace and Minnie Eleanor (Upchurch) H.; B.S., Samford U., 1953; m. Blanche Virginia Beard, Dec. 21, 1954; children—Ronald Horace, Donald Ray. Pub. relations specialist U.S. Air Force, 1956; asso. editor Christian Index newsmag. Ga. Bapt. Conv., Atlanta, 1957-66, editor, 1966-—. Adviser, Americans United for Separation Ch. and State, 1966-71. Bd. dirs. Ga. Council on Alcohol Problems. Served with AUS, 1953-55. Recipient Spl. Citation for outstanding achievement in mass communications Samford U., Birmingham, Ala., 1967. Mem. Atlanta Press Club. Baptist (deacon 1958-—). Author: Bulldozer Revolution, 1965; (with Louie D. Newton) Fifty Golden Years, 1959; An Old Friend With New Credentials, 1972. Home: 3159 Beech Dr East Point GA 30344 Office: 291 Peachtree St NE Atlanta GA 30303

HARWELL, NORMAN LESLIE, constrn. co. exec.; b. San Antonio, Aug. 18, 1922; s. John Leslie and Orma (King) H.; grad. vocational and tech. high sch., 1938; m. Joyce Lowe Wilson, Aug. 17, 1968; children—(by previous marriage) Sharon Ann (Mrs. Cordell Hull), N. Wayne, Michelle, Yvonne; stepchildren—Rebecca and Kimberly Wilson. With Alamo Iron Works, San Antonio, 1939-41; partner Harwell & Harwell, contractors, San Antonio, 1946-57, owner, 1957-—; pres. Norman Harwell Assos., Inc., contractors, 1959-—; founder NHA, Inc., tech-date co., 1966-—, chmn. bd., 1968-70; founder John Yantis Co., 1962-—, sec.-treas., 1962-—; dir. Main Bank & Trust Co., 900 N. Main Co., Computer Knowledge Corp. Served with USNR, 1942-46. Decorated Air medal. Mem. Builders Exchange Tex. (pres. 1955-61), San Antonio Home Builders Assn., San Antonio C. of C. (bd. dirs. 1959-61). Mason (Shriner), Lion (pres. 1960). Home: 114 Chattington Court San Antonio TX 78213 Office: P O Box 18286 San Antonio TX 78218

HARWOOD, JAMES EDWARD, tobacco products mfg. exec.; b. Nashville, Nov. 2, 1902; s. James Eugene and Katharine (Murray) H.; LL.B., U. Memphis, 1927; m. Katharine D. Butler, Feb. 27, 1933; children—James Edward III, Katharine B. With Am. Snuff Co., Memphis, 1924-—, v.p., 1949-59, exec. v.p., 1959-—, also dir.; dir. Taylor Bros. Tobacco Co., Hot-Shot Quality Products Co., Blevins Popcorn Co., Harvell-Kilgore Corp. Mem. Delta Theta Phi. Roman Catholic. Clubs: Memphis Country (past pres.), Memphis Hunt and Polo. Home: 2875 Arawata Lane Memphis TN 38111 Office: 701 N Main St Memphis TN 38103

HARWOOD, JOHN ELLIS, state ofcl.; b. Asheville, N.C., Jan. 7, 1916; s. John Ellis and Gertrude Franklin (Clash) H.; student Coll. William and Mary, 1932-35; m. Nathalie Hubbard, June 26, 1937 (dec. May 28, 1961); children—Nathalie Dean (Mrs. Robert Colby Perkins), Gertrude Clash (Mrs. Richard C. Stevens); m. 2d, Mary Lancaster Hubbard, Nov. 3, 1965. With survey party mapping Jamestown Island, Nat. Park Service, 1935; draftsman and design engr. Va. Dept. Hwys., Richmond, 1935-54, asst. location and design engr., 1954-58, location and design engr., 1958-64, asst. chief engr., 1964, dir. programming and planning, 1964-65, dep. commr., chief engr., 1965-—. Served with AUS, World War II. Mem. Am. Soc. C.E., Am. Assn. State Hwy. Ofcls., (mem. engring. policy com.), Am. Rd. Builders' Assn. (past dir.). Episcopalian. Home: 4805 Rodney Rd Richmond VA 23230 Office: 1221 E Broad St Richmond VA 23219

HARWOOD, ROBERT BERNARD, state justice; b. Eutaw, Ala., June 4, 1902; s. Bernard and Helene (Braune) H.; A.B., LL.B., U. Ala.; LL.M., Harvard; m. Mary Lee Leach, Sept. 11, 1926; children—Eve Minturn, Robert Bernard. Admitted to Ala. bar; mem. firm Harwood & McQueen, Tuscaloosa, 1926-27; pvt. practice law, 1927-32; asst. U.S. atty. for No. Dist. Ala., 1933-35; asso. prof. law U. Ala., 1935-36, prof., 1936-37, asst. to dean, 1937; atty. gen. State of Ala., 1945; judge Ct. Appeals, 1945-63; now asso. justice Supreme Ct. Ala. Commr., Uniform State Laws, 1940. Mem. Ala. Ho. of Reps., 1927-31. Served from capt. to maj., AUS, 1942-45. Mem. Am., Ala. bar assns., Delta Kappa Epsilon, Phi Delta Phi, Omicron Delta Kappa. Democrat. Episcopalian. Club: Montgomery Country. Author books. Contbr. articles to law jours. Home: 36 Haardt Dr Montgomery AL 36105 Office: Judicial Bldg Montgomery AL 36102

HARWOOD, ROBERT BERNARD, JR., lawyer; b. Tuscaloosa, Ala., Oct. 17, 1939; s. Robert B. and Mary Lee (Leach) H.; student U. of South, 1958-59; B.S. in Commerce and Bus. Adminstrn., U. Ala., 1962, LL.D., 1963; m. Belle Walter, July 30, 1959; children—Robert Bernard III, Richard Scott. Admitted to Ala. bar, 1963; practice law, Tuscaloosa, Ala., 1963-—; mem. firm Rosen, Wright & Harwood,

1967—. Legal cons. Ala. Cons. and Devel. Co., Inc., 1970—; spl. asst. atty. gen. State of Ala., 1969—. Mem. Tuscaloosa County Civil Service Bd., 1969-70; mem. exec. bd. Black Warrior council Boy Scouts Am., 1969—. Mem. Am., Ala., Ala. State, Tuscaloosa County bar assns., Farrah Order of Jurisprudence, Farrah Law Soc., Alpha Tau Omega. Methodist (mem. ch. bd. 1969-70). Home: 79 Riverdale St Tuscaloosa AL 35401 Office: 1020- 25th Av Tuscaloosa AL 35401

HARWOOD, ROBERT HEWETT, plantation exec.; b. Trenton, Tenn., Mar. 1, 1920; s. Robert Hewett and Evelyn Hope (Wade) H.; B.S., U.S. Naval Acad., 1942; M.S., U.S. Naval Post Grad. Sch., 1946; student Indsl. Coll. Armed Forces, 1964-65; M.S., George Washington U., 1965; m. Zenobia Frith Pratt, Apr. 4, 1943; children—Mary Buie, Evelyn Hope (Mrs. William R. Liebke), Robert Henry. Commd. ensign USN, 1941, advanced through grades to capt., 1961; comdg. officer submarine, 1946-54; nuclear submarine div. comdr., 1957-61; submarine attack squadron comdr., 1965-66; comdr. Naval Ordnance Plant, Chgo., 1962-64; ret., 1968; v.p. Frithland Plantation, Inc., Bunkie, La., 1966—; dir. Turner Lumber Co. (LeMoyen, La.); lectr. La. Dept. Pub. Safety. Mem. tech. com. La. Criminal Justice Information System and Nat. Crime Information Center, 1970-71; active Boy Scouts Am., Cub Scouts. Decorated Silver Star, Bronze Star medal. Mem. Am. Soc. Tool and Mining Engrs., U.S. Naval Acad. Alumni Assn., Indsl. Coll. Armed Forces Assn., Tau Kappa Omega. Democrat. Episcopalian. Clubs: Avoyelles Country. Home: Frithland Plantation Box 643 Bunkie LA 71322 Office: 6271 Boone Dr., Baton Rouge LA 70808

HARWOOD, THOMAS PERKINS, JR., state ofcl.; b. Green Bank, W.Va., Jan. 22, 1929; s. Thomas Perkins and Mary (Moomau) H.; B.A., Va. Mil. Inst., 1950; LL.B., U. Va., 1956; m. Mary Virginia Ambrose, June 30, 1956; children—Sally Christian, Thomas Perkins III, Leland Hunter. Admitted to Va. bar, 1956; asso., partner Lane, Paul & Rudd, attys.-at-law, Richmond, Va., 1956-60; dep. commr. Indsl. Commn. of Va., Richmond, 1960-64, commr., 1964—. Served to 1st lt. inf. AUS, 1950-53. Decorated Purple Heart. Mem. So. Assn. Workmen's Compensation Adminstrs. (pres. 1967-68), Am., Va., Richmond bar assns., Am. Judicature Soc., Am. Legion, Kappa Alpha, Sigma Nu Phi, Omicron Delta Kappa. Democrat. Presbyn. (elder 1962—, trustee 1963—). Home: 2736 Kenbury Rd Richmond VA 23225 Office: PO Box 1794 Richmond VA 23214

HASKETT, JAMES NORPHLETT, govt. ofcl.; b. Claremont, Va., Oct. 24, 1930; s. Willie Lloyd H. and Mary Elizabeth (Emory) H.; B.A. in History, U. Richmond, 1957; postgrad. Longwood Coll., 1959-62; m. Sherrie Anne Elliot, July. 12, 1958; children—James Bruce, Michael Craig, Laura Kimberly. Ins. agt. John Hancock Mut. Life Ins. Co., Richmond, Va., 1957-58; with Nat. Park Service, 1958—, park historian Petersburg (Va.) Nat. Mil. Park, 1958-59, Appomattox Courthouse (Va.) Nat. Hist. Park, 1959-62, Manassas (Va.) Nat. Battlefield Park, 1962-63, Ft. Smith (Ark.) Nat. Hist. Site, 1963-66; supt. Ft. McHenry Nat. Monument and Historic Shrine, Balt., 1966-68; chief interpretation and visitor services Colonial Hist. Park, Yorktown, Va., 1968—. Served with AUS, 1951-53. Recipient J. Tyler Ellison award U. Richmond, 1957. Mem. Am. Assn. for State and Local History (toastmaster 1965—, pres. 1970, exec. v.p. 1970), Phi Alpha Theta, Pi Sigma Alpha, Pi Kappa Alpha. Home: Somerwell House Yorktown VA 23490 Office: Colonial Nat Hist Park Yorktown VA 23490

HASS, CHARLES GLEN, educator; b. Mansfield, O., Mar. 7, 1915; s. Charles William and Ethel Vernice (Newlon) H.; B.A. (Edith Boughton Denious scholar 1933-37), U. Denver, 1937; M.A., Stanford, 1946; Ed.D., Columbia, 1953; m. Margaret Mary Walters, June 12, 1940; 1 son, Rolland Glen. Tchr. pub. schs., Denver, 1937-42; elementary sch. prin., Battle Creek, Mich., 1949-50; asst. supt. schs., Arlington, Va., 1950-58; prof. edn. U. Fla., Gainesville, 1958—. Vis. prof. U. Denver, 1942, N.Y. U., 1958-61, U. Colo., 1961, U. Utah, 1961. Served to capt. AUS, 1942-46. Mem. John Dewey Soc. (nat. pres. 1967-69), Soc. Prof. Edn. (nat. pres. 1971-72), Assn. Supervision and Curriculum Devel. (nat. bd. dirs. and nat. exec. bd., 1956-62, 72-76). Club: Torch. Author and editor: Readings in Curriculum, 2d edit., 1970, Readings in Secondary Teaching, 1970, Readings in Elementary Teaching, 1971. Editor and co-author: Leadership for Improving Instruction, 1960, Author: In Service Education Today, 1957. Home: 1116 N W 61 Terrace Gainesville FL 32601

HASS, CHARLES JOHN WILLIAM, instrument co. exec.; b. Fond du Lac, Wis., Aug. 19, 1934; s. Bernard Albert and M. Elizabeth (Diener) H.; B.B.A. in Indsl. Mgmt. and Engring., U. Wis., 1959; m. Barbara Jane Demyen, 1964. Engring. asst. Giddings & Lewis Machine Tool Co., Fond du Lac, 1953-54; asst. to pres. Hass Instrument Corp., Washington, 1956-59, v.p., 1959-62, pres., chmn. bd., 1963—; sec., dir. C. &K. Enterprises, Washington, 1961-62. Trustee Takoma Acad., Shenandoah Valley Acad., Potomac Conf. Corp., Hadley Meml. Hosp.; chmn. bd. H.J. Detweiler Sch. Served with AUS, 1954-56. Mem. Am. Soc. Tool and Mfg. Engrs., Soc. for Advancement of Mgmt., Am. Ordnance Assn., Air Force Assn., Alpha Kappa Psi. Rotarian. Club: Tantallon Country. Contbr. articles to profl. jours. Home: 2100 Brooks Dr Washington DC 20028 Office: 6711 Old Branch Av Washington DC 20031

HASSE, WARREN LOUIS, broadcasting exec.; b. Mauston, Wis., Oct. 15, 1923; s. Louis A. and Bertha (Hasse) H.; student U. Wis., 1941; m. Romelle Helen Johnson, Jan. 31, 1944; children—John Louis, Mary Sue. Classified advt. mgr. Portage (Wis.) Daily Register, 1947-48; sports editor Pampa (Tex.) News, 1948-50, mng. editor, 1950-52; co-owner Radio Sta. KPDN, 1952-60, owner, gen. mgr. 1960—. Chmn. Gray County March of Dimes Campaign, 1955, United Fund Campaign, 1957; mem. Boy Scout Council; mem. Pampa (Tex.) Sch. Bd., 1968—, sec., 1969, pres., 1971-72; treas. Top O' Tex. Rodeo Assn., 1967—. Bd. dirs. A.R.C., United Fund, Top O' Tex. Found.; trustee Pampa Sch., 1968—, pres., 1971-72. Served from aviation cadet to 1st lt., bombardier-navigator USAAF, 1941-45; ETO. Decorated D.F.C., Air medal with 4 oak leaf clusters. Recipient Outstanding Young Man award Jaycees of Pampa, 1957; named Sportscaster of Yr., Panhandle Sports Hall of Fame, 1965; Adult Leader of Yr., 1966; West Texan of Yr., Lambda Chi Alpha, 1969. Mem. C. of C. (pres. 1958-59). Presbyn. Clubs: Knife and Fork; Kiwanis (dist. lt. gov. 1958; dist. pub. relations chmn. 1961-62), Pampa Country. Home: 1704 Christine St Pampa TX 79065 Office: Radio Sta KPDN Pampa TX 79065

HASSELL, MORRIS WILLIAM, lawyer; b. Jacksonville, Tex., Aug. 9, 1916; s. Alonzo Seldon and Cora (Rainey) H.; A.A., Lon Morris Coll., 1936; LL.B., U. Tex., 1942; m. Mauriete Watson, Sept. 3, 1944; children—Morris William, Charles Robert. Tchr. Cherokee County Pub. Schs., 1937-38; admitted to Tex. bar, 1942; pvt. practice since 1946, mem. firm Norman, Rounsaville Hassell; sec. The S.W. Title and Guaranty Co. of Tex.; dir. First State Bank of Rusk; chmn. bd. Swift Oil Co.; sec. H & I Oil Co., I, H & I, Inc. County atty. Cherokee County, Tex., 1943-46; mayor of Rusk, 1959-63. Scoutmaster, Boy Scouts Am., 1944-45; Dem. nominee for County atty., 1942 and 1944; v.p. Jr. Bar of Tex., 1944. Mem. state adv. com. Wesley Found., Austin, Tex.; bd. devel. Lon Morris Coll. Mem C. of C. (pres.), Am., E. Tex. (dir. 1964-65) bar assns., State Bar Tex. (dir.; chmn. gen. practice sect. 1967-68, chmn. profl. ethics com. 1970—). Methodist (steward). Odd Fellow, Mason, Kiwanian (dist. lt. gov.). Office: First State Bank Bldg Rusk TX 75785

HASSELL, (ANDREW) PIERSON, JR., govt. ofcl.; b. Takamatsu, Japan, May 2, 1916 (parents Am. citizens); s. Andrew Pierson and Barbara (Savage) H.; B.S. in Physics and Math., Davidson 1936; grad. Fed. Exec. Inst., 1968; m. Mary Harrison Benson, June 22, 1940; children—Mary Benson (Mrs. Don Stuart Whisonant), Barbara Amelia (Mrs. Richard Thomas Duemler). With Agrl. Stblzn. and Conservation Service, U.S. Dept. Agr., 1936—, div. chief state office, Raleigh, N.C., 1949-61, state exec. dir., 1961-66, dep. dir. budget div., Washington, 1966-68, dir., 1968—; dir. Budget Commodity Credit Corp., Washington, 1968—. Recipient Superior Service award U.S. Dept. Agr., 1961. Mem. Orgn. Profl. Employees U.S. Dept. Agr., Nat. Agrl. Stblzn. and Conservation Service County Employees Assn., Sigma Phi Epsilon. Democrat. Presbyn. (elder). Home: 1327 Rand Dr Raleigh NC 27608 also Hunting Towers Alexandria VA 22314 Office: 6605 South Agr Bldg 14th and Independence Av Washington DC 20250

HASSKARL, ROBERT ALBERT, museum dir.; b. Brenham, Tex., July 24, 1929; s. Robert Albert and Willie (Knolle) H.; B.S., U. Tex., 1956; M.Ed., Sam Houston State Coll., 1957; D.Ed., U. Okla., 1963; m. Eula Faye Richardson, Apr. 30, 1956; children—James Robert, Leif Robert. Prof. history Blinn Coll., 1957-61; lectr. social sci. U. Okla., 1961-63; prof. edn. East Central State Coll., 1964-66, dir. Upward Bound Program, 1966—, coordinator Upward Bound and Spl. Services, 1971—, museum dir., 1964—. Served with USAF, 1948-55. Decorated Air medal. Mem. Phi Alpha Theta, Phi Delta Kappa, Kappa Delta Pi. Author: Brenham, Texas 1844-1958 Guide to Heraldry, 1959; Knolle Family of Texas, 1959. Home: Rt 4 Box 268 Ada OK 74820 Office: East Central State Coll Museum Ada OK 74820

HASSKARL, WALTER FREDERICK, JR., physician; b. Brenham, Tex., July 6, 1917; s. Walter Frederick and Dora (Roberts) H; B.A., U. Tex., 1939, M.D., 1942; M.S., U. Minn., 1949; m. Carolyn Joan Boyle, Aug. 6, 1947; children—Joan, Ann, Lee, John. Intern, Phila. Gen. Hosp., 1943, M. and S. Hosp., San Antonio, 1945; resident State Sanitorium, 1944; practice medicine, specializing in gen. surgery, Brenham, Tex., 1949—; surgical fellow Mayo Clinic, Rochester, Minn., 1945-48, 1st asst., 1948-49; pres. Brenham Clinic Assn., 1965-72; chief surgery St. Jude Hosp., Brenham; mem. staffs Bohne Meml. Hosp., Brenham, Lee Meml. Hosp., Giddings, Grimes County Hosp., Navasota, Goodnight Meml. Hosp., Caldwell; dir. devel. bd. U. Tex. Med. Sch., 1970—. Dir. Farmers Nat. Bank, Brenham, Tex. Mayor, City of Brenham, Tex., 1968-72. Served with USAF, 1953-55. Mem. Am., Tex. med. assns., Tex. Surgical Soc., Brenham C. of C. (pres. 1963), Alumni Assn. U. Tex. (rep. 1961-64), U. Tex. Cowboys, Mayo Clinic 1963-69, Alumni Assn. (bd. dirs. 1971—), Kappa Sigma, Alpha Kappa Kappa. Elk. Clubs: Champions Golf (Houston); Brenham (Tex.) Country. Home: 1907 Tison St Brenham TX 77833 Office: Academy and Baylor Sts Brenham TX 77833

HASSLACHER, ROBERT NEIL, govt. ofcl.; b. South Amboy, N.J., Jan. 19, 1931; s. George John and Lillian Beatrice (Brown) H.; student Hiram Coll., 1949-50; B.B.A., Baylor U., 1961; postgrad. U. Tenn., 1968-69; m. Barbara Jeannine Farmer, Jan. 1, 1955; children—Neil Ross, Eric John. Gen. mgr. Marlin (Tex.) C. of C., 1961-63; marketing rep. H.J. Heinz, Dallas, 1963-65; regional economist U.S. Army C.E., Galveston, Tex., 1965-66; regional economist Nat. Resource Analysis Center, Leesburg, Va., 1966-68; industry economist U.S. Bur. Mines, Knoxville, Tenn., 1968-70; dir. econs. U.S. Dept. Housing and Urban Devel., Birmingham, Ala., 1970—. Chmn., Falls County, Tex. Parole Bd., 1961-63; exec. officer Mil. Police Co. Tex. State Guard Res., 1961-66. Served with USAF, 1950-54. Mem. Am. Econ. Assn., Soc. Govt. Economists, Ala. Social Scis. Adv. Com. Author: Impact of Sulfur Emission Controls on Fuel Marketing Patterns, 1970; The Phosphate Industry in the Southeastern U.S. and Its Relationship to World Mineral Fertilizer Demand, 1969; course U.S. Civil Service Commn., 1971. Home: 3443 Meadow Woods Dr Birmingham AL 35216 Office: 15 S 20th St Birmingham AL 35233

HASTINGS, GEORGE E., govt. ofcl. Dir. region 3 Office Emergency Preparedness, Denton, Tex. Address: Office Emergency Preparedness Denton Fed Center Denton TX 76201

HASTINGS, ROLF, lawyer; b. Kristiansand, South Norway, Nov. 22, 1912; came to U.S., 1940, naturalized, 1944; s. Albert Simonsen and Edvarda (Hille) H.; student Johns Hopkins, 1946-47; J.D., U. Miami (Fla.), 1950. Admitted to Fla. bar, 1950; practiced in Coral Gables, 1950-54; asso. firm Keen, O'Kelley & Spitz, Tallahassee, 1954-64, partner, 1964—. Pres., dir. Runnymede, Inc., Tallahassee, Gwynndale, Inc., real estate developers, Tallahassee, 1943-45. Bd. dirs. So. Scholarship and Research Found., Inc. Served with AUS, 1943-45; ETO. Mem. Am., Tallahassee bar assns., Fla. bar, Am. Judicature Soc., Delta Theta Phi. Lutheran. Elk, Moose. Home: Old Bainbridge Rd Tallahassee FL 32302 Office: PO Box 3153 Tallahassee FL 32302

HASTY, FREDERICK GRIER, orthodontist; b. Carthage, N.C., Apr. 29, 1932; s. Wade Hampton and Lora (Johnson) H.; B.S., High Point Coll., 1954; D.D.S., U. N.C., 1958, M.S., 1962; m. Josephine Tilley, Sept. 4, 1954; children—Michael Alan, David Hampton, Robert Grier. Pvt. orthodontic practice, Fayetteville, N.C., 1963—; cons. Ft. Bragg Dental Clinic, 1963-65, Pope AFB Dental Clinic, 1969—. Mem. Mayors Council Pub. Relations, 1969-70. Bd. dirs. YMCA, Fayetteville, 1966-68, Indsl. Devel. Corp., Fayetteville, 1967-69. Served with AUS, 1958-61. Diplomate Am. Bd. Orthodontics. Mem. Am. Dental Assn., Am. So. assns. orthodontists, N.C., 4th Dist. (pres. 1972-73) dental socs., Orthodontic Research Study Club (charter pres.). Club: Exchange (charter pres.). Dist. editor N.C. Dental Jour., 1968-70. Home: 2836 Skye Dr Fayetteville NC 28303 Office: 3401 Melrose Rd Fayetteville NC 28304

HASTY, GERALD RICHARD, army officer; b. Pekin, Ill., Apr. 12, 1926; s. Leslie Parke and Bernice Arthene (Brown) H.; B.S., Bradley U., 1952; M.B.A., 1954; postgrad. Harvard, 1961; M.A., Am. U., 1962; Ph.D., Northwestern U., 1963; LL.B., Blackstone Sch. Law, 1968; postgrad. summers U. Toledo, 1958, U. Me., 1963, State U. N.Y. at Buffalo, 1963, Armed Forces Staff Coll., 1968, Air War Coll., 1965; m. Betty Anne Osmundson, June 23, 1951; children—Grant Rutledge, Mark Osmund, Deborah Anne. Commd. 2d lt. U.S. Army, 1954, advanced through grades to lt. col., 1966; chief Q.M. Supply div. 7th Logistical Command, Korea, 1961-62; comdg. officer 34th Supply and Service Bn., Vietnam, 1966, also dir. adminstrn. 58th Field Depot; exec. asst. joint logistics rev. bd. Office Sec. Def., Washington, 1969-70; comdg. officer Charleston (S.C.) Army Depot, 1970—; asst. prof. pub. adminstrn. George Washington U., Washington, 1964-65, 67, asso. prof., 1968-69; vis. prof. polit. sci. Bapt. Coll., Charleston, 1970—; tchr., lectr., various colls., U.S. Korea, Vietnam. Counselor, Boy Scouts Am., 1968—; mem. citizen's adv. and action council to gov. Coastal Carolina Community Pre-release Center, S.C. Dept. Corrections. Bd. dirs. Charleston Safety Council. Served AUS, 1944-50. Decorated Legion of Merit with oak leaf cluster, Purple Heart with oak leaf cluster. Mem. Charleston Trident C. of C., La. Societe Francaise deBienfaisance de Charleston, Navy League, Fed. Exec. Assn. (com. on govt.-wide policy areas), Armed Forces Mgmt. Assn., S.C. Law Enforcement Officers Assn., Nat. Def. Transp. Assn., Pi Sigma Alpha, Tau Kappa Epsilon. Lutheran. Mason (32 deg., Shriner), Kiwanian. Home: 8316 Wagonwheel Rd Alexandria VA 22309 also Quarters 1 Army Depot Charleston SC 29401 Office: Office of Comdr Army Depot Charleston SC 29401

HATCH, AMY BONNIE BELTZ (MRS. JOHN MANNING HATCH), educator, corp. exec.; b. Detroit, Sept. 4, 1940; d. Charles Robert and Amy (Ferguson) Beltz; student U. Mich., 1958-60; B.A., Am. U., 1962; postgrad. Wayne State U., 1963; m. John Manning Hatch, Dec. 29, 1962; children—Charles Worth, Robert Manning, Thomas Ferguson. Tchr., Washington and Lee, Arlington, Va., 1962-63; dir., v.p. Beltemp Corp., Grosse Pointe, Mich., 1968—; dir. Greenbrook Creative Day Sch., Fairfax, Va., v.p., dir. Greenbrook Corp., Fairfax, 1969—, Internat. Salvage Corp.; Sec., dir. N. Am. Investment Corp. Mem. No. Va. Pvt. Sch. Assn. Republican. Presbyn. Club: Greenbriar Womens. Home: 1334 Merrie Ridge Rd McLean VA 22101 also 500 Lakeland Av Groose Pointe MI 48230 Office: PO Box 132 Oakton VA 22124

HATCH, RUTH DELAR STREETER (MRS. DOUGLAS LORENZO HATCH), educator, writer; b. Elko, Nev.; d. Oscar J. and Jessie De (DeLar) Streeter; student Dominican Coll., San Rafael, Cal., 1921-24; A.B., U. Nev., 1928; postgrad. George Washington U., 1932-34, Colo. Coll., Cath. U.; m. Douglas Lorenzo Hatch, July 19, 1929 (dec. July 1962); children—Douglas Lorenzo, Ruth DeLar (Mrs. Vadim Vinogradov), Annette (Mrs. Matthew N. Norton). Actress, Salt Lake City Stock Co., 1927; tchr. dramatics and English, Austin High Sch., 1928-29; research Library of Congress, 1929-34; free-lance writer Europe, 1949; Washington editor Palm Beach Life mag., 1955; tchr. Fairfax County Schs., 1958; mgmt. self owner real estate investments, 1940—; Washington rep. Film News mag., 1964—; Washington partner Sugar City Musical, 1964—; v.p. Ranch Estates, Inc.; chmn. bd. Millstone Farm Summer Day Camp and Riding Sch.; free-lance writer for NANA, sci. writer. First sec., founder Fairfax County Library Bd., 1934—; mem. woman's bd. George Washington U. Hosp.; dir. mgr. United China Gift Shoppe for United China Relief, 1940. Sloan fellow in advance sci. writing project Sch. Journalism, Columbia U., 1967-68. Mem. Nat. Assn. Sci. Writers, N.Y. Acad. Scis., A.A.A.S., Nev. State Soc., Delta Delta Delta, Phi Kappa Phi. Clubs: 1925 F. St., Sulgrave, National Lawyers (Washington); Am. Newspaper Women's Club, Tail-Waggers (bd. dirs.); Overseas Press (N.Y.C.). Author Lobby, a capital game, 1954; Alice in Mergerland. Home: Millstone Farm Burke VA 22015 Office: 2027 O St NW Washington DC 20007

HATCHER, CLIFF CICERO, III, security dealer exec.; b. Atlanta, Mar. 2, 1923; s. Cliff Cicero and Elizabeth Horton (Lochridge) H.; LL.B., Emory U., 1948; m. Elizabeth Heath Coleman, Feb. 8, 1952; children—Cliff Coleman, Elizabeth Hollis. Vice-pres., dir., mgr. municipal bond dept. Furman Co., Greenville, S.C., 1957—. Financial cons., City of Greenville, North Charleston Consol. Pub. Service Dist., 1966—. Mem. ad hoc com. Greenville County Planning Commn., 1964—; dir. S.C. Municipal Council, 1963-69. Served with USAAF, 1942-45, USAF, 1951-57, now lt. col. Res. ret. Decorated D.F.C., Air medal with three oak leaf clusters. Mem. Investment Bankers Assn. (chmn. elect. so. group legislative com. 1972), Greenville C. of C. (mem. finance com. 1968-71), Sigma Alpha Epsilon. Episcopalian. Clubs: Poinsett, Greenville Country. Home: 217 Rock Creek Dr Greenville SC 29605 Office: Daniel Bldg Greenville SC 29602

HATCHER, HERSCHEL FISHER, JR., dentist; b. Moultrie, Ga., Oct. 19, 1922; s. Herschel Fisher and Annie Ruth (Seagroves) H.; student North Ga. Coll., 1939-40, Mercer U., 1946; B.S., Stetson U., 1948; D.D.S., Emory U., 1953; postgrad. U. N.C., 1956, 60; m. Martha Lois Roberts, July 29, 1945; children—Brenda Lynn, Herschel Fisher III. Individual practice dentistry, Decatur, Ga., 1953—; instr. pedodontics Emory U., Atlanta, 1953-58, asso. prof., 1957-58. Served with USAAF, 1942-46. Mem. Am., Ga. dental assns., No. Dist. (treas. 1959-60), 5th Dist. (exec. council 1964-67) dental socs., Psi Omega, Beta Beta Beta, Gamma Sigma Epsilon. Methodist. Lion (v.p. 1955). Home: 628 Park Lane Decatur GA 30033 Office: 250 E Ponce de Leon Av Decatur GA 30030

HATCHER, MILDRED (OBERA), educator; b. Murray, Ky.; d. William Thomas and Lorena (Taylor) Hatcher, Jr.; B.S. with high distinction, Murray State Coll., 1927; M.A. George Peabody Coll. Tchrs., 1930, postgrad., summers 1932, 48; postgrad. Vanderbilt U., 1930, U. Wis., summer 1947, Ind. U., summer 1964; D. Litt., P.E. U., London, Eng., 1967. Asst. prin., head English dept. Hardin (Ky.) High Sch., 1927-29; tchr. math. city pub. schs., Paducah, Ky., 1930-34; tchr. English, Paducah Tilghman High Sch., 1934-48; critic tchr. Murray State Coll., summer 1946; asst. and asso. prof. English, Austin Peay State Coll., Clarksville, Tenn., 1948-60; asst. prof. English, Murray State Coll., 1960-61; asso. prof., 1961—. Commd. Ky. Col., 1967. Mem. Nat., Ky. edn. assns., Conf. Coll. Composition and Communication, Nat. Council Tchrs. English (del. 1958-59, spl. pub. relations rep. golden anniversary 1960, dir. 1959—, judge ann. writing awards 1961-68, mem. spl. pub. relations com. 1963-69), Ky. Hist. Soc., Am. Studies Assn., Ky. (v.p. 1970, pres. 1971-72), Tenn. (v.p. 1957, pres. 1958-60) folklore socs., Middle Tenn. English Assn. (v.p. 1959-62, liaison officer 1959—), U.D.C. (pres. 1955-56), D.A.R. (chpt. regent 1953-54), Murray State U. Alumni Assn. (v.p. 1945-46), Marquis Library Soc. (adv. bd. 1969), Chi Alpha Pi, Kappa Delta Pi, Delta Kappa Gamma. Baptist. Clubs: Nat. Writers; Woman's. Contbr. articles and poems to profl. jours. Poems included in ann. Nat. Poetry Anthology, 1953-60. Home: 1305 Olive Blvd Murray KY 42071

HATCHETT, META RUTH, educator; b. nr. Durant, Okla., Oct, 20, 1905; d. Jesse Mercer and Meta Belle (Yarborough) Hatchett; B.A., U. Okla., 1926, M.A., 1940, postgrad., 1952-53; B.S., Southeastern State Coll., 1927; postgrad. Okla. State U., 1954, 57. In pvt. bus., 1927-36; chmn. dept. English, Atoka (Okla.) High Sch., 1936-43, Durant (Okla.) High Sch., 1943-46; asst. prof. English, Southeastern State Coll., Durant, 1946-71, prof. emeritus, 1971—. Owner, operator farm, Durant, 1945—. Named Tchr. of Year, Southeastern State Coll. Faculty, 1967-68. Mem. Modern Lang. Assn., Coll. English Assn., Nat. Council Tchrs. English, Okla. Edn. Assn., Am. Assn. U. Profs., Am. Assn. U. Women (pres. Durant 1952-54), D.A.R., Delta Kappa Gamma, Phi Alpha Theta, Theta Sigma Phi, Pi Kappa Delta. Democrat. Baptist. Home: Box 334 Star Route Durant OK 74701

HATFIELD, CECIL CURTIS, physician, banker; b. Saltville, Va., Aug. 19, 1908; s. James Abram and Sarah (Osborne) H.; B.S., Roanoke Coll., 1930; M.D., Med. Coll. Va., 1934; m. Laura Margaret Horne, Oct. 7, 1939; 1 son, James Andrew. Intern St. Vincent's Hosp., Erie, Pa., 1934-35; practice medicine, Saltville, Va., 1936; indsl. physician Olin Mathieson, Saltville, 1936-66; dir. 1st Nat. Bank, Saltville, Va., 1949—, pres., 1963—. Various positions Boy Scouts of Am., 1930—; pres., Saltville Rescue Squad, 1958-60; Vice pres., YMCA, 1960—, dir. So. dist., 1968-70; bd. dirs. Highland Community Coll., 1970—. Democrat. Methodist. Mason, Kiwanian (lt. gov. 1960). Address: Drawer C C Saltville VA 24370

HATFIELD, DONALD GENE, educator, artist; b. Detroit, May 23, 1932; s. Floyd L. and Helen R. (Nehmer) H.; A.A., Northwestern Mich. Coll., 1958; B.A., Mich. State U., 1960, M.A. 1961; M.F.A., U. Wis., 1962; m. Marilyn Ann Grindstuen, Sept. 10, 1960; children—Suzanne, John, Kathleen. Tchr. art, elementary art supr. Auburndale (Wis.) High Sch., 1962-64; asst. prof. art Auburn (Ala.) U., 1964-71, asso. prof., 1971—; exhibited in group shows at numerous state and nat. exhbns.; one-man shows Wis. State Coll., La Crosse, 1963, Auburn U., 1967, Columbus (Ga.) Mus. Arts and Crafts, 1968, Birmingham (Ala.) Mus. Arts and Crafts, 1968, Savannah (Ga.) Art Assn., 1962, Birmingham So. Coll., 1970, Montgomery Mus. Art, 1970, LaGrange (Ga.) Coll., 1971; two-man show Montgomery (Ala.) Museum Art, 1969. Served with USN, 1952-56. Recipient purchase award Annual Exhbn. of Wis. Art, Milw. Art Center, 1964, La Crosse (Wis.) State Coll., 1963; numerous others. Mem. Internat. Platform Assn., V.F.W., Ala. Art League (pres. 1970-73), Birmingham Art Assn. Presbyn. Elk. Home: 550 Forest Park Circle Auburn AL 36830

HATFIELD, GENE EDWIN, cons. engring. co. exec.; b. West Point, Ky., Dec. 29, 1928; s. Walter Ned and Ressie (Hart) H.; B.S. in Civil Engring., U. Ky., 1954; m. Mildred Ann Murphy, Aug. 22, 1952; children— Michael Edwin, Walter Harrison, William Arch. Resident engr. Ky. Dept. Hwys., 1954-57; design engr. Nichols Engring. Co., Union City, Tenn., 1957-61; v.p. Edward T. Hannan & Assos., Inc., Paducah, Ky., 1962-70, dir. 1966-70, dir., Evansville, Ind., 1967-70; pres., chmn. bd. Community Program Cons., Inc., Paducah, 1971—; dir. South/West Planning Assos., Bryan, Tex. Mem. Fulton (Ky.) Ind. Bd. Edn., 1960—, vice chmn., 1964-66, chmn., 1966—; exec. dir. Fulton Municipal Housing Commn., 1959-61; mem. Fulton Planning Commn., 1956-59; mem. Fulton Urban Renewal and Community Devel. Agy., 1969-71. Served to maj. mil. assistance and adv. group AUS, Japan, 1961-62. Registered profl. engr., Ky.; registered land surveyor. Mem. Am. Water Works Assn., Water Pollution Control Fedn., Nat., Ky. socs. profl. engrs., Ky. Hist. Soc., Ky. Sch. Bds. Assn., Sigma Nu. Mem. Christian Ch. (ofcl. bd. 1955—, chmn. 1965-67, vice chmn. 1967-70, bd. elders 1960—). Home: 103 Henderson Dr S Fulton KY 42041 Office: 700 Jefferson St Paducah KY 42001

HATFIELD, JACK KENTON, lawyer; b. Medford, Okla., Jan. 26, 1922; s. Loate L. and Cora (Walsh) H.; B.S., Phillips U., 1947, A.B., 1953; J.D., Oklahoma City U., 1954; m. Dorothy Ann Keltner, Dec. 5, 1943; children—Susan Kathryn (Mrs. Michael F. Dean), Sally Ann (Mrs. William Frohnapfel). Admitted to Okla. bar, 1954; practice accounting and law, Enid, 1954-58; chief br. budget and finance Dept. Interior, Southwestern Power Adminstrn., Tulsa, 1958-67, dep. asst. adminstr. for adminstrn., 1967-69, chief div. mgmt. services, 1969-70, chief div. financial mgmt., 1970-71, chief div. adminstrv. mgmt., 1971—. Organizer, dir. Profl. Mens Assn. Kansas City, Inc., Profl. Mens Assn, Okla., Inc.; dir. Griffin Producing Co., Calumet Ranch Co. Organizer, trustee Garfield County Cerebral Palsy Clinic for Speech and Hearing. Served with AUS, 1943-46. C.P.A. Mem. Am. Inst. C.P.A.'s, Okla. Soc. C.P.A.'s Am., Okla., Tulsa County bar assns. Republican. Methodist. Home: 2976 E 75th St Tulsa OK 74136 Office: NBT Bldg Tulsa OK 74103

HATHAWAY, AMOS TOWNSEND, naval officer, educator; b. Pueblo, Colo., Dec. 5, 1913; s. James Amos and Nina (North) H.; B.S., U.S. Naval Acad., 1935; postgrad. U.S. Naval War Coll., 1947-48; M.A. in Teaching, Duke, 1965-66; m. Marianne Langdon Train, June 10, 1937; children—Joan Langdon, Marianne Train, Melinda North, Barbara Spencer, Sarah Townsend. Commd. ensign U.S. Navy, 1935, advanced through grades to capt., 1954; exec. officer, navigator destroyer minesweeper Zane, Guadalcanal, 1942; command destroyer Heermann, Battle off Samar, 1944; mem. faculty U.S. Naval Acad., 1945-47, U.S. Naval War Coll., 1951-53; mem. war staff Gen. MacArthur, Korea, 1948-50, writer theater logistic plan Inchon Landing, 1950; exec. officer cruiser St. Paul, 1950-51; command Destroyer Div. 92, 1953-54, command attack transport Okanogan, 1958-59; command cruiser Rochester, 1959-60; mem. joint staff Joint Chiefs of Staff, 1961-63, dir. logistic plans Office Chief of Naval Operations, 1963-65, ret., 1965; asst. prof. math. The Citadel, Charleston, S.C., 1966—. Decorated Navy Cross, Legion of Merit (2), Bronze Star (2), Mem. Math. Assn. Am., U.S. Naval Acad. Alumni Assn., U.S. Naval Acad. Athletic Assn. (dir. 1945-47), U.S. Naval Inst., Kappa Delta Pi. Club: Army Navy Country (Arlington, Va.). Home: 11 Sayle Rd Charleston SC 29407

HATTAL, ALVIN MORTON, pub. relations exec., govt. ofcl.; b. N.Y.C., Sept. 15, 1926; s. Henry and Frances Beatrice (Berlin) H.; student Cornell U., 1944, N.Y.U., 1950; m. Rita Miller, June 12, 1949; children—Gary, Daniel. Mng. editor Geyer-McAllister Publs., Inc., N.Y.C., 1951-55; mng. editor Sponsor Mag., N.Y.C., 1955-56; asso. editor Am. Builder Mag., N.Y.C., 1956-59; mgr. news and information depts. Nat. Forest Products Assn., Washington, 1960-64; pub. relations dir. Am. Inst. Steel Constrn., Inc., N.Y.C., 1964-65; asst. exec. dir. Nat. Assn. Small Bus. Investment Cos., Washington, 1965-67; v.p., gen. mgr. Padilla, Sarjeant, Sullivan & Speer, Inc., N.Y.C., 1968-69; asst. to dir. pub. affairs div. Internal Revenue Service, Washington, 1969—. Mem. Fed. Editors Assn. (pres.), Govt. Information Orgn. (treas.), Pub. Relations Soc. Am. (dir. Washington chpt. 1966), Club: Nat. Press. Author column Washington Focus, Pub. Relations Jour., 1967—. Home: 8608 Victory Lane Potomac MD 20854 Office: 1111 Constitution Av NW Washington DC 20224

HATTEN, JAMES ROBERT, dentist; b. Columbia, Miss., Jan. 26, 1927; s. Abb Louis and Johnny Mary (McCorkle) H.; student Holmes Jr. Coll., 1947-49, Miss. Coll., 1949-50; D.D.S., Emory U., 1954; m. Marianne Lobdell, Aug. 2, 1952; children—Cynthia Lela, Kathryn Lynn, James Andrew, Richard Lobdell. Pvt. practice dentistry, Jackson, Miss., 1954—; dental staff University Med. Center, dir. dept. dental hygiene, 1970-71; pres. University Aviation, Inc., 1969—. Adv. Charles Sullivan campaign for Gov., 1969. Served with USAAF, 1945-46. Decorated Army Commendation Medal. Mem. Am. Dental Assn., University Flying Assn. (pres. 1970-71), Xi Psi Phi. Presbyn. (chmn. bldg. commn. 1966). Clubs: Civitan (pres. 1961-62), Capitol Gun. Home: 1112 Meadowbrook Rd Jackson MS 39206 Office: 344 B N Mart Plaza Jackson MS 39206

HATTON, JULIAN RAY, agrl. products co. exec.; b. Brutus, Ky., Jan. 9, 1931; s. Joseph Leon and Lois (Crippen) H.; B.S., U. Fla., 1952; m. Betty Joan Barwick, Jan. 6, 1953; children—J. Ray II, Henry B., Leslie Joan, Shelley Jean. Supr. pest control U. Fla., 1951-52; field foreman Joe Hatton & Sons, Pahokee, Fla., 1952-54; pres. Hatton Bros., Inc., 1954-72; v.p. Palm Beach Sugar Corp., 1962—. Mem. Sch. Improvement Com., Pahokee, Fla., 1967-71; mem. Fla. State com. Agr. and Soil Conservation Service, U.S. Dept. Agr. Mem. Entomol. Soc. Am., Alpha Zeta, Lambda Chi Alpha. Republican. Methodist. Elk, Lion (pres. AUS, 1946-48. Mem. Am., Tex. med. assns., 1968-69). Home: 2927 Bacom Point Rd Pahokee FL 33476 Office: Drawer 558 Pahokee FL 33476

HAUBERG, ROBERT ENGELBRECHT, U.S. dist. atty.; b. Brookhaven, Miss., Nov. 20, 1910; s. Frederick and Wilhelmina (Mortensen) H.; student Millsaps Coll., 1928-30; LL.B., Jackson (Miss.) Sch. of Law, 1932; m. Robbie Mae Bowen, Dec. 11, 1940; 1 son, Robert Engelbrecht. Admitted to Miss. bar, 1932, since practiced in Jackson; prof. law Jackson Sch. Law, 1933-64, registrar, vice-dean and dean, 1938-54; asst. city pros. atty., Jackson, 1932-37; asst. U.S. atty., 1944-54; U.S. dist. atty. for So. Dist. Miss., 1954—. Treas. Hinds County chpt. A.R.C., 1937-46; dir. Miss. Assn. on Crime and Delinquency, 1941; mem. Jackson Juvenile Council; mem. Council Social Agys., 1940-44. Mem. Miss. Senate from 12th senatorial dist., 1940-44. Mem. Am., Miss., Hinds County, Fed. bar assns., Jackson Jr. C. of C. (charter mem.; pres. 1935), Alpha Omega, Sigma Delta Kappa. Methodist. Club: Knife and Fork (Jackson). Home: 1045 Claiborne St Jackson MS 39209 Office: PO Box 2091 Post Office Bldg Jackson MS 39205

HAUGAARD, WILLIAM PAUL, educator; b. Bklyn., Jan. 19, 1929; s. William Edward and Bess (Holdzkom) H.; grad. Horace Mann Sch. for Boys, N.Y.C., 1946; A.B. magna cum laude, Princeton U., 1951; S.T.B., Gen. Theol. Sem., 1954, Th.D., 1962; m. Janet McKee Butler, June 19, 1954; children—Margaret McKee, Mary Butler. Ordained to ministry Protestant Episcopal Ch. as deacon, 1954, priest, 1954; vicar St. James Ch., Brewster, Wash., and Ch. of the Transfiguration, Twisp, Wash., 1954-58; fellow, tutor Gen. Theol. Sem., N.Y.C., 1958-62; asso. prof. ch. history Seminario Episcopal del Caribe, 1962-71, prof., 1971—, acting dean, 1962-63, 68-69, dean, 1969—. Staff mem. Group Life Labs. Dept. Christian Edn., Episcopal Ch., 1956-58; additional mem. Dept. Christian Edn., Nat. Council, Episcopal Ch., 1958-59. Recipient the Daily Princetonian award, Princeton U., 1949, Rockerfeller Doctoral fellowship, 1960-62, Episcopal Ch. Found. fellowship, 1966. Mem. Am. Hist. Assn., Am. Soc. Ch. History, Renaissance Soc. Am, Phi Beta Kappa. Author: Elizabeth and the English Reformation, 1968. Editorial bd. Historical Mag. of the Protestant Episcopal Ch., 1970—. Contbr. articles to religious and hist. pubs. Address: Apartado 757 Carolina PR 00630

HAUN, ELOISE CLYMER (MRS. JACOB HAUN, JR.), physician; b. Phila. Sept. 30, 1936; d. Harvie Maris and Louise (Skerdlant) Clymer; B.A., Bryn Mawr Coll., 1958; M.D., Med. Coll. Va., 1962; m. Jacob Haun, June 11, 1960; children—Jacob III, Harvie Clymer, Frank Hollingsworth. Intern surgery Med. Coll. Ga., 1962-63; resident pediatrics Columbia (S.C.) Hosp. of Richland County, 1963-66; resident in child psychiatry, Med. Coll. Va., Richmond, 1971—; practice medicine specializing in pediatrics, Columbia, S.C., 1966-68; house physician St. Mary's Hosp., Richmond, Va., 1968-71; mem. staff St. Mary's Hosp., Richmond Meml. Hosp., Med. Coll. Va. Hosp. Med. dir. Project Headstart, Lexington and Richland Counties, S.C., 1966-68. Mem. women's com. Richmond (Va.) Symphony, 1969—. Named Outstanding Young Woman Nat. Publs. Am., 1965. Diplomate Am. Bd. Pediatrics. Mem. Richmond Acad. Medicine; Richmond Pediatric Soc. Home: 1408 Wilmington Va Richmond VA 23227 Office: Dept Psychiatry Med Coll Va Richmond VA 23219

HAUPT, FREDERICK, III, assn. exec.; b. Louisville, Sept. 12, 1921; s. Fred L. and Marguerite (McConnell) H.; A.B., U. Louisville, 1946; postgrad. Harvard, 1946-47; m. Martha A. Montague, Mar. 31, 1949; 1 child, Frederick Christian. Pub.'s rep. Appleton-Century-Croft and Alfred A. Knopf, Inc., N.Y.C., 1947-52; mem. staff N.Y. Times, N.Y.C., 1952-53; pub. relations cons., Washington, 1953-61; pub. relations dir. Opera Soc. Washington, 1957-61; press attache Am. embassy, Bonn, Germany, 1961-62; information officer, attache U.S. Mission, Berlin, Germany, 1962-65; information officer, consul AID, Karachi, Pakistan, 1965-67; news editor Voice of Am., Rhodes, Greece, 1967; dir. pub. affairs Nat. Trust Historic Preservation, Washington, 1968—. Served with Armed Forces, 1942-46. Decorated Knight's Cross, Order Merit (Germany). Democrat. Home: 3629 Fulton St NW Washington DC 20007 Office: Nat Trust Historic Preservation 740-748 Jackson Pl NW Washington DC 20006

HAUSER, HARRIS MILTON, physician; b. Galveston, Tex., Oct. 20, 1932; s. Abe and Florence (Paysee) H.; student U. Tex., 1949-51, U. Houston, 1950-53; M.D., Baylor U., 1955; M.S., U. Minn., 1960; m. Jaclyn Lee Reader, Feb. 12, 1953 (div. 1970); children—Terri Lynn, Karen Louise, John Bradley, Ann Katherine, Heather Joan; m. 2d, Mary Barbara Harris, Sept. 16, 1970. Intern Methodist Hosp., Houston, 1955-56; fellow neurology and psychiatry Mayo Found., Rochester, Minn., 1956-60; chief closed psychiatry Brooke Army Hosp., Ft. Sam Houston, San Antonio, Tex., 1960-61, asst. chief neurology, 1961-62; cons. neurology Kelsey-Seybold Clinic, Houston, 1962-66; gen. practice neurology and psychiatry Hauser Clinic, Houston, 1962-70; clin. asst. prof. neurology and psychiatry U. Tex. Med. Br., Galveston, 1963—; asst. prof. neurology Baylor U. Coll. Med., Houston, 1966—; dir. EEG Labs., 1963—; mem. staff Meml. Baptist Hosp. Systems, Heights hosps. (all Houston). Recipient H. V. Jones award Mayo Found., 1960; Award of Merit, Am. Legion, 1962. Mem. A.M.A., Am. Psychol. Assn., A.C.P., Am. Acad. Neurology, Central Neuropsychiat. Assn., Am., So. (pres. 1970) EEG socs., Alpha Omega Alpha. Contbr. articles in field profl. jours. Home: 2600 Bellefontaine Houston TX 77025 Office: Shamrock Profl Bldg Houston TX 77025

HAUTZIG, LUDWIG, hotel exec.; b. Vienna, Austria, May 31, 1920; s. Joseph and Rose (Haber) H.; B.S., Lausanne, Switzerland, 1938; m. Rosina A. Lubrano, Dec. 8, 1961; 1 dau., Anna Maria. Asst. front office mgr. Grosvenor Hotel, London, Eng., 1938; kitchen apprentice Hotel Intourist, Moscow, Russia, 1939; asst. mgr. Talati House Hotel, Tientsin, China, 1939-41, Imperial Hotel, Tientsin, China, 1941-42; mgr. Hotel de Wagon Lits de Pekin, Peking, 1942-43; regional mgr. Hong Kong, Shanghai Hotels Corp., 1943-45; mgr. Royal Dutch Airlines Hotels, Singapore, Crown Colony, Jakarta, Indonesia, 1945-51; dir. Thai Tourist Govt. Project, Erawan Hotel, Bangkok, Thailand, 1951-53; cons. Oberoi Hotels, India, Great Eastern Hotel, Calcutta, Metropole Hotel, Karachi, 1953-55, Zamora Properties, Inc., Bay View Hotel, Grand Hotel, Philippines, 1955-58; adminstrv. asst. to the pres. Jack Tar Hotels, Galveston, Tex., 1958-62; adminstrv. asst. Drake Hotels, Chgo., 1962-63; v.p., gen. mgr. Sheraton-Tampa Motor Hotel, Tampa, Fla., 1963—; vice chmn., chmn. ITT Sheraton Inns Nat. Council, 1969-71. Mem. adv. bd. Hillsborough Jr. Coll., 1972; mem. St. Joseph Hosp. Devel. Council, 1972; active Pan Am. Commn., Boys Clubs Am. Mem. adv. bd. Salvation Army; bd. dirs. Nat. Safety Council. Recipient Mgmt. of Year award Sheraton Hotel, 1968, 69, 72. Mem. Am., Fla. (dir. 1963-71) hotel and motel assns., Sales and Marketing Execs., Fla. Com. 100, Fla. Restaurant Assn. (mem. bd. 1964—). Merchants Assn. Greater Tampa (dir. 1964—), Tampa Hotel and Motor Motels (pres. 1966), Greater Tampa C. of C. (bd. govs. 1964—). Mason (Shriner), Rotarian. Club: Palma Ceia Golf and Country, Tower (Tampa, Fla.); Executive (Chgo.). Office: 515 E Cass St Tampa FL 33602

HAVEE, JUSTIN PAUL, airline co. ofcl.; b. Stamford, Conn., Aug. 19, 1915; s. Edward and Kathryn C. (Nollett) H.; B.B.A., cum laude, U. Ill., 1938; M.B.A., U. Miami, 1970. Technician, So. Bell. Tel. &Tel., Miami, Fla., 1936-38; engr. Western Electric Co., Miami, 1939-42; engr. Pan Am. World Airways, Inc., Miami, 1946-48, purchasing agt., 1942-46, 48—. Chmn. United Fund, Miami. Mem. Assn. Am. Museums, Am. Assn. State and Local History, Fla. Anthrop. Soc., Fla. Hist. Soc., Hist. Assn. So. Fla. (exec. sec. 1942-66), Everglades Natural History Assn., Air Force Assn., Purchasing Mgmt. Assn. Fla., Nat. Assn. Purchasing Mgmt., Greater Miami C. of C., Opera Guild of Miami. Elk. Clubs: Wings, Management, Aviation Executives (Miami). Home: 3513 SW 25th Terrace Miami FL 33133 Office: Pan Am Bldg Miami FL 33159

HAVERFIELD, ROBERT METCALFE, state senator; b. Cadiz, O., Oct. 26, 1918; s. J. Craig and Elizabeth (Metcalfe) H.; student Ohio State U., 1939-42; B.B.A., U. Miami, then LL.B., 1947; m. Shirley O'Connor; children—Betty Ann, Carol Lee, Hill O'Connor. Admitted to Fla. bar; sr. partner firm Aronovitz & Haveerfield, Miami, Fla., 1957—; mem. Fla. Senate, 1969—. Legal aid atty. Dade County, Fla., 1949-51; asst. city atty., Miami, 1951-56; mem. Dade County Commn., 1958-60. Served with AUS, 1942-44. Trustee Eastridge Lutheran Sr. Citizen's Retirement Village. Mem. Am., Dade County, Fla. bar assns., Am. Judicature Soc., Greater Miami Aviation Assn. Kiwanian. Home: 1701 SW 62d Av Miami FL 33156 Office: 1117 City Nat Bank Bldg Miami FL 33130

HAVILAND, VIRGINIA, librarian; b. Rochester, N.Y., May 21, 1911; d. William J. and Bertha M. (Esten) Haviland; B.A., Cornell U., 1933. With Boston Pub. Library, 1934-63, successively children's librarian, br. librarian, 1934-52, reader's adviser for children 1952-63; lectr. in library services to children Simmons Coll. Sch. Library Service, 1957-63; chief librarian Children's Book Sect., Library of Congress, 1963—; profl. reviewer of children's books and asso. editor Horn Book Mag., 1952—. Chmn. Newbery-Caldecott award com., 1953-54; judge N.Y. Herald Tribune Spring Book Festival awards, 1955, 57, 68; mem. jury Hans Christian Andersen internat. children's book award, 1959-68, pres. jury, 1970—; mem. jury Nat. Book award for children's lit., 1969. Del from U.S.A. to conf. of Internat. Bd. on Books for Young People, Vienna, Austria, 1955, Florence, Italy, 1958, Luxembourg, 1960, Hamburg, 1962, Madrid, 1964, Ljubljana, 1966, Amriswil, Switzerland, 1968, Bologna, 1970, Nice, 1972, Internat. Fedn. Library Assns., Belgium, 1955, Sweden, 1960, Switzerland, 1961, Scotland, 1962, Bulgaria, 1963, Italy, 1964, Finland, 1965, Netherlands, 1966, Toronto, 1967, Germany, 1968, Denmark, 1969, USSR, 1970, Liverpool, Eng., 1971, Hungary, 1972, working congress children's librarians in Scheveningen, Holland, 1959. Mem. A.L.A. (chmn. children's services div. 1954-55), Pi Lambda Theta. Author: The Travelouge Storybook of the Nineteenth Century, 1950; William Penn, Founder and Friend, 1952; Favorite Fairy Tales Told in England, 1959; Favorite Fairy Tales Told in Germany, 1959; Favorite Fairy Tales Told in France, 1959. Compiler: 100 Best Books for Children, 1956; Favorite Fairy Tales Told in Russia, 1961; Favorite Fairy Tales Told in Norway, 1961; Favorite Fairy Tales Told in Ireland, 1961; Favorite Fairy Tales Told in Scotland, 1963; Favorite Fairy Tales Told in Spain, 1963; Favorite Fairy Tales Told in Poland, 1963; Ruth Sawyer, 1965; Favorite Fairy Tales Told in Italy, 1965; Favorite Fairy Tales Told in Czechoslovakia, 1966; Favorite Fairy Tales Told in Sweden, 1966; Favorite Fairy Tales Told in Japan, 1968; Favorite Fairy Tales Told in Greece, 1969; (with William Jay Smith) Children and Poetry, 1970; Favorite Fairy Tales Told in Denmark, 1971; A Fairy Tale Treasury, 1972. Editor: Children's Lit.: A Guide to Reference Sources, 1967, 1st Supplement, 1972. Books in Search of Children, 1969. Home: Harbour Sq 520 N St SW Washington DC 20024 Office: Library of Congress Washington DC 20540

HAVIRD, CYRIL OLIVER, govt. ofcl.; b. Newberry, S.C., Nov. 27, 1923; s. Henry David and Georgia Fant (Hair) H.; student Newberry Coll., 1941-42; B.A., U. S.C., 1949, M. Ed., 1950; m. Frances Ann Dent, Mar. 21, 1951; children—David Clyde, Suzanne, Cyril Oliver. Athletic dir. Springs Mills, Lancaster, S.C., 1949-53; tchr., coach North (S.C.) High Sch., 1953-55, Eau Claire High Sch., Columbia, S.C., 1955-63; prin. Wright Jr. High Sch., 1963-65; supt. schs. Richland Sch. Dist. 2, 1965-71; exec. dir. Richland County Housing Authority, 1972—. Served with AUS, 1943-46. Mem. Nat., S.C., Richland County edn. assns., Am. Assn. Sch. Adminstrs., S.C. Assn. Sch. Supts. (dir. 1970-72; exec. com. 1959-60), Greater Columbia C. of C., Am. Legion (comdr. Eau Claire 1959-60). Lion (pres. 1965). Club: Rockbridge (Columbia). Home: 4740 Arcadia Rd Columbia SC 29206 Office: PO Box J 1973 Columbia SC 29201

HAWES, CHARLES FOREST, physician; b. Rose Hill, N.C., May 5, 1907; s. Charlie Bunyan and Mary Emma (Dickson) H.; B.S., Wake Forest Coll., 1930; M.B., Northwestern U., 1932, M.D., 1933; m. Mary Emma Stewart, June 27, 1932; children—Charles Forest, Bettie (Mrs. Ernst Wilheim Meyer), Emma (Mrs. Newland Kay Crocker), David Hills. Intern, Milwaukee County Gen. Hosp., Wauwatosa, Wis., 1932-33; practice medicine, specializing in gen. practice, Rose Hill, N.C., 1933—; owner, adminstr. Obstetrical Clinic, 1952—; mem. staff Duplin County Hosp., Kenansville, N.C. Mem. County Bd. Health, 1965—. Mayor, Rose Hill, N.C., 1934-38; mem. local sch. bd., 1938—, chmn. bd., 1945—. Named Local Man of Yr., V.F.W., 1954. Mem. A.M.A., N.C., Duplin County (pres. 1940, 52, 68) med. socs. Democrat. Baptist. Home: 303 E Ridge St Rose Hill NC 28458 Office: 201 S Marshall St Rose Hill NC 28458

HAWES, FOREMAN MCCONNELL, ret. jr. coll. pres.; b. Richmond County, Ga., Sept. 18, 1899; s. John Baptist and Daisy Lane (McCord) H.; A.B., Mercer U., 1922; M.S., Emory U., 1929; postgrad. U. Wis., Columbia; m. Lilla Kennerly Mills May 29, 1936. Instr. Locust Grove Inst., 1923-28; instr. Emory U., 1928-29; instr. Ga. Inst. Tech., 1929-35; instr. Armstrong Jr. Coll., Savannah, Ga., from 1936, dean of students, 1941-42, pres. 1943-64. Fellow Ga. Acad. Sci.; mem. Sigma Alpha Epsilon, Alpha Chi Sigma. Rotarian. Club: Oglethorpe (Savannah). Home: 1134 E 49th St Savannah GA 31404

HAWES, JEAN ELIZABETH HERMES, artist; b. N.Y.C., Nov. 21, 1914; d. Jacob William and Dora (Neinstead) Hermes; student Goucher Coll., 1932-33, Packard Bus. Sch., 1934, Carmel Sch. Art, Monterrey Jr. Coll., 1947-48, Am. U., 1962-63, Corcoran Sch. Art, 1963-64; m. Philip Robert Hawes, June 18, 1938 (dec. Oct. 1956); children—Philip Robert, Ann Adele Hermes (Mrs. Stephen A. Bard), Howard Hermes (dec.). Executed mosaics Ebb Tide, Jamestowne Village Office, Alexandria, Va., 1966, Pueblo (3d award ceramic sculpture), Norfolk (Va.) Mus., 1966; became tchr. painting Jamestowne Village Art Group, 1966; now tchr. Hodges Gallerie, Ltd.; Alexandria, Va.; designer posters D.C. chpt. A.R.C., 1965-69. Recipient various letters commendation, including one for Art Pony and art edn. outline George Washington High Sch., Alexandria, Va., 1966. Mem. Nat. League Am. Pen Women (treas. Alexandria br. 1962-64, Va. art chmn. 1966-68, coordinator state shows 1967). Research in native clays Va., Md. for use in sculpture. Home: 1591A N Van Dorn St Alexandria VA 22304

HAWES, LILLA KENNERLY MILLS (MRS. FOREMAN MCCONNELL HAWES), librarian, hist. soc. exec.; b. Camden, S.C., Feb. 1, 1908; d. Laurens Tenney and Margaret (Johnstone) Mills; A.B., Agnes Scott Coll., 1928; B.S. in L.S., George Peabody Coll. for Tchrs., 1939; certificate preservation and adminstrn. archives Am. U., 1948; m. Foreman McConnell Hawes, May 29, 1936. Sec. chemistry dept. Ga. Inst. Tech., 1930-36; gen. asst. Savannah (Ga.) Pub. Library, 1937-40, reference asst., 1941-43, br. librarian, 1943-48; dir. Ga. Hist. Soc., Savannah, 1948—. Sec. Savannah-Chatham County Historic Site and Monument Commn., 1955-66. Bd. dirs. Youth Mus. Savannah, Inc., 1954-66, rec. sec., 1954-56, corr. sec., 1962-64; bd. dirs. Historic Savannah Found., Inc., 1955-62. Recipient award of merit Lachlan McIntosh chpt. D.A.R., 1956; award of merit Historic

Savannah Found., 1966. Mem. Ga., Southeastern library assns., Soc. Am. Archivists, Am. Assn. for State and Local History, So. Hist. Assn., Ga. Hist. Soc., Savannah Hist. Research Assn. (pres. 1946-48), Am. Assn. U. Women (sec. Ga. chpt. 1943-45), Telfair Acad. Arts and Scis., League Women Voters, Nat. Soc. Colonial Dames Am. in State Ga., Victorian Soc. Savannah, Pi Gamma Mu, Delta Kappa Gamma. Presbyn. Editor: Collections of the Georgia Historical Society, Vols. X-XIV, 1952-64; Lachlan McIntosh Papers in the U. Ga. Libraries, 1968. Home: 1134 E 49th St Savannah GA 31404 Office: 501 Whitaker St Savannah GA 31401

HAWES, PEYTON SAMUEL, JR., state govt. ofcl.; b. Elberton, Ga., June 27, 1937; s. Peyton Samuel and Virginia (Smith) H; B.A., U. N.C., 1960; LL.B., U. Va., 1963; m. Mary Gregory, June 10, 1961; children— David Cooper, Gregory Battle, Elizabeth Claiborne, Peyton Samuel III (dec.). Admitted to Ga. bar, 1964; asst. atty. gen. Dept. Law, Atlanta, 1964-66; atty. Jones, Bird & Howell, Atlanta, 1966-71, Cofer, Beauchamp & Hawes, 1971—; mem. Ga. Ho. of Reps., 1969—; Mem. reorgn. com. Ga. Democratic party, 1969; mem. exec. com. Dem. Com. Ga., 1970—. Mem., Am., Ga., Atlanta bar assns., Lawyers Club of Atlanta, Sigma Alpha Epsilon, Phi Alpha Delta. Episcopalian. Home: 78 Broad St NW Atlanta GA 30303

HAWES, RUSSELL ALOYSIUS, city ofcl.; b. Alexandria, Va., Feb. 10, 1905; s. Abner Lodge and Annie (Butler) H.; attended FBI Nat. Acad., 1937; m. Vernell Mevelton Shackelford, Dec. 25, 1929. Engr. Mut. Ice Co., 1923-27, Alexandria Gas Co., 1927-31; joined Alexandria Police Service, 1931, chief, 1952—. Trustee, Alexandria YMCA. Mem. Va. Assn. Chiefs of Police (pres. 1964), FBI Nat. Police Acad. Assos. (pres. Va. chpt., 1965). Methodist. Mason (32 deg., Shriner, K.T.), Lion (pres. Alexandria 1958). Home: 822 S Pitt St Alexandria VA 22314 Office: Police Service 400 N Pitt St Alexandria VA 22314

HAWK, ROBERT MARTIN, assn. exec.; b. Plainfield, N.J., July 11, 1938; s. Kenneth Martin and Marianne Virginia (Concilio) H.; B.A., Am. U., 1962; postgrad. Pace Coll., 1966-67; m. Verna Marie Carlson, July 25, 1964; 1 dau., Shirley Ann. Editorial asso. Traffic World Mag., Washington, 1960-63; pub. relations rep. Pa. R.R., N.Y.C., 1963-66; rail dev. rep. Port of N.Y. Authority, N.Y.C., 1966-67; transp. com. exec., communications com. exec. U.S. C. of C., Washington, 1967—. Bd. dirs. Greenbriar Civic Assn., Fairfax, Va., 1971-72. Served to 1st. lt. AUS, 1961. Mem. Pub. Relations Soc. Am. Club: Nat. Press. Home: 4213 Marble Lane Fairfax VA 22030 Office: 1615 H St NW Washington DC 20006

HAWKINS, CHARLES ALLEN, JR., elec. engr.; b. Greenville, S.C., Mar. 1, 1937; s. Charles Allen and Sarah (Matthews) H.; B.S. in E.E., Clemson U., 1959; M.S. in Bus. Adminstrn., U. Rochester, 1970; m. Sarah Jennings, Sept. 29, 1959; children—Richard Brian, Sandra Lynn. Design engr. J.E. Sirrine Co., Greenville, S.C., 1962-63; tech. adviser, mgr. U.S. Army Security Agy., Arlington, Va., 1963—. Served with AUS, 1959-62. Decorated Army Commendation medal; recipient Defense Edn. Program fellowship, 1968. Registered profl. engr., Ala. Mem. Armed Forces Communications and Electronics Assn., Assn. Old Crows (chmn. nominating com. 1970-71), Jr. C. of C. Baptist. Club: Admirals (N.Y.C.). Home: 415 Orleans Circle Vienna VA 22180 Office: Arlington Hall Station VA 22212

HAWKINS, CHARLES FRANCIS, lawyer; b. N.Y.C., May 27, 1927; B.A. magna cum laude, Williams Coll., 1950; LL.B. magna cum laude, Harvard, 1953. Admitted to N.Y.C. bar, 1960, Tex. bar, 1961, U.S. Supreme Ct. bar, 1971; now practice law, Dallas. Fellow Southwestern Legal Found.; mem. Dallas, Am. bar assns., Phi Beta Kappa. Editor Harvard Law Rev., 1951-53. Contbr. articles to legal jours. Address: 1137 Frito-Lay Tower Dallas TX 75235

HAWKINS, DAVID ROLLO, psychiatrist, educator; b. Springfield, Mass., Sept. 22, 1923; s. James Alexander and Janet (Rollo) H.; B.A., Amherst Coll., 1945; M.D., U. Rochester (N.Y.), 1946; m. Elizabeth G. Wilson, June 8, 1946; children—David Rollo, Robert Wilson, John Bruce, William Alexander. Intern Strong Meml. Hosp., Rochester, N.Y., 1946-48; Commonwealth Fund fellow in psychiatry and medicine U. Rochester, 1950-52; instr. psychiatry U. N.C. Sch. Medicine, 1952-53, asst. prof., 1953-57, asso. prof. psychiatry, 1957-62, prof., 1962-67, dir. curriculum review and revision, 1965-67; prof., chmn. dept. psychiatry U. Va. Sch. Medicine, 1967—, asso. dean, 1969-70; psychiatrist-in-chief U. Va. Hosp., 1967—; asso. attending physician N.C. Meml. Hosp., Chapel Hill, N.C., 1952-62, attending physician, 1962-67; cons. Watts Hosp., Durham, 1952-67, VA Hosp., Fayetteville, North Carolina, 1956-67, Eastern State Hosp., Williamsburg, Va., 1971—; spl. research fellow Inst. Psychiatry, U. London, 1963-64; cons. VA Hosp., Salem, Va., 1969—, mem. deans com., 1971—. Mem. small grants com. Nat. Inst. Mental Health, 1958-62; mem. nursing research study sect. NIH, 1965-67; mem. Gov.'s Commn. Mental, Indigent and Geriatric Patients, 1968—; mem. research evaluation com. Va. Dept. Mental Hygiene and Hosps., 1971—, chmn., 1972—; mem. behavioral sci. test com. Nat. Bd. Med. Examiners, 1970—. Served as capt. M.C., AUS, 1948-50. Fellow Am. Coll. Psychoanalysts (charter); mem. Am. Psychosomatic Soc. (mem. council 1959), A.M.A., Group for Advancement Psychiatry (chmn. com. med. edn.), Am. Psychiat. Assn., Royal Soc. Medicine (London), Assn. Am. Med. Colls., Am. Psychoanalytic Assn., Am. Coll. Psychiatrists, Am. Acad. Psychoanalysis, A.A.A.S., Group Analytic Soc. (London), So. Profs. Psychiatry, Washington Psychoanalytic Soc., Am. Assn. U. Profs., Soc. for Neurosci., Am. Assn. Chmn. Depts. Psychiatry (sec.-treas. 1971—), Assn. Psychophysiol. Study Sleep, Phi Beta Kappa, Alpha Omega Alpha. Review editor: Psychosomatic Medicine, 1958-70, asso. editor, 1970—. Office: U Va Sch Medicine Dept Psychiatry Charlottesville VA 22901

HAWKINS, DON ANDREW, banker; b. Birmingham, Ala., Sept. 30, 1917; s. Robert Llewelyn and Katie (Davis) H.; student pub. schs.; m. Mary Lou Eads, Sept. 20, 1938; children—Donald Lelias, Robert Larry, Brenda Lou, Janet Lynn. Clk., Fed. Res. Bank, 1938-40; chief accountant, office mgr. Glidden Co., Atlanta, 1940-44, PPG Industries, Birmingham, 1946-69; v.p. Nat. Bank of Commerce, Birmingham, 1969—. Mem. Birmingham City Council, 1963—; chmn. Community Relations, 1963—; pres. Birmingham Park and Recreation Bd., 1966—. Del. Democratic Nat. Conv., 1968. Served with USNR, 1944-46. Mem. Painting and Decorating Contractors of Am. (chpt. pres. 1960), Ala. Credit Execs., Am. Rhododendron Soc., Arlington Hist. Soc. Methodist. Mason (Shriner, Lion. Clubs: Crestwood Civic, Birmingham Paint. Home: 5609 9th Av S Birmingham AL 35212 Office: 2101 1st Av N Birmingham AL 35203

HAWKINS, E. STANLEY, city ofcl. fire chief Tulsa, Okla. Home: 824 E 54th St Tulsa OK 74126 Office: 411 S Frankfort Tulsa OK 74120

HAWKINS, ELINOR DIXON (MRS. CARROLL WOODARD HAWKINS), librarian; b. Masontown, W.Va., Sept. 25, 1927; d. Thomas Fitchie and Susan (Reed) Dixon; A.B., Fairmont State Coll., 1949; B.S. in L.S., U. N.C., 1950; m. Carroll Woodard Hawkins, June 24, 1951; 1 son, John Carroll. Children's librarian Enoch Pratt Free Library, Balt., 1950-51; head circulation dept. Greensboro (N.C.) Pub. Library, 1951-56; librarian Craven-Pamlico Library Service, New Bern, N.C., 1958-62, Craven-Pamlico-Carteret Regional Library, 1962—; storyteller children's TV program Tele-Story Time, 1952-58, 63—. Bd. dirs. Craven County Community Concert Assn. Mem. N.C. Assn. Retarded Children, N.C. Library Assn., New Bern Hist. Soc. Baptist. Club: Pilot (pres. 1957-58, v.p. 1962-63). Home: PO Box 57 Cove City NC 28523 Office: 400 Johnson St New Bern NC 28560

HAWKINS, ELMER JOHN, physician; b. Jayton, Tex., July 8, 1922; s. Elmer and Arlis (Cunningham) H.; B.S., McMurry Coll., 1942;M.D., Baylor U., 1945; m. Gabie Smallwood, June 19, 1943; children—Lou Ann (Mrs. C. Richard Bullock), James Earl, Sharon Kay, Jonathan Lewis. Intern, Meth. Hosp., Madison, Wis., 1945-46. practice gen. medicine, Roby, Tex., 1948-49, Hamlin (Tex.) Hosp. & Clinic, 1949-72, Stamford (Tex.) Clinic, 1972—; mem. staffs West Tex. Hosp., Hendricks Hosp., Abilene, Tex., Stamford Meml. Hosp. Served to capt. AUS, 1946-48. Mem. Am., Tex. med. assns., Taylor-Jones County Med. Soc. Methodist. Club: Petroleum (Abilene). Home: PO Box 23 Stamford TX 79553 Office: Stamford Clinic Stamford TX 79553

HAWKINS, ERNEST, football coach E. Tex. State U. Address: Athletic Dept E Tex State U Commerce TX 75428*

HAWKINS, FRANK, mech. engr.; b. Mountain View, Okla., Aug. 24, 1916; s. Berton Frank and Dycie (Imhoff) H.; B.S., U. Okla., 1940; m. Elizabeth Snoddy, Dec. 26, 1941; children—Frank Robert, Mary Dale (Mrs. John Reginald Cook), William Thomas, Donald Haisten. With Phillips Petroleum Co., Houston, 1945-71, mech. and maintenance supt., 1945-63, asst. plant mgr., 1963-64, plant supt., 1964-71; owner, mgr. Frank Hawkins Engring. and Sales, Houston, 1971—. Del., Tex. Democratic Conv., 1961, 62. Bd. dirs. Water Dist. Tex. Served from 2d lt. to lt. col., Ordnance Dept., AUS, 1940-45. Registered profl. engr., Okla., Tex. Mem. Nat. Soc. Profl. Engrs., Am. Soc. M.E. (past chmn. Panhandle sect.). Methodist. Mason (Shriner. Patentee in field. Home: 394 Connaught Way Houston TX 77015 Office: Northshore Profl Bldg 13435 East Freeway Houston TX 77015

HAWKINS, HAROLD LESLIE, educator; b. Armada, Mich., July 28, 1921; s. Clifford Loren and Grace (Cudworth) H.; B.S., Mich. State Normal Coll., 1951; M.A., U. Mich., 1953; certificate advanced study Harvard, 1957, Ed.D., 1958; m. Barbara Joan Benner, June 2, 1951; children— Kathryn Ann, David Leslie. Supt. schs. Kimball Unit, Port Huron, Mich., and Jefferson Sch., Mt. Clemens, Mich., 1948-56, Marine City, East China Twp. Sch. Dist.,Mich., 1957-62, 16th Air Force Dept. Def., Spain, 1962-64, Olean, N.Y., 1964-67; profl. endl. adminstrn., head dept. Tex. A. and M. U., College Station, 1967—. Mem. joint com. Region IV Edn. Service Center, Huntsville, Tex., 1970—. Mem. adv. bd. The School Law Newsletter, 1971—. Mem. Tex. Assn. Secondary Sch. Prins. (university liaison com. 1970—), Assn.Sch. Bus. Assn. U.S. and Can. (univ. contacts research com. 1971—), Nat. Assn. Secondary Sch. Prins. (nat. adv. bd. 1971—). Author: Texas School Law and Board Authority, 1970. Home: 3406 Spring Lane Bryan TX 77801 Office: Tex A and M U College Station TX 77840

HAWKINS, LAMAR TRAVIS, constrn. co. exec.; b. Oneonta, Ala., Oct. 16, 1938; s. Claude Travis and Audrey Louise (Harp) H.; B.S. in Civil Engring., Auburn U., 1963; m. Margie Elaine Thomason, Sept. 3, 1960; children—Pam, Patti, Steve. Project engr. bridge constrn. Blount County Engring. Dept., 1956-59, project engr., 1961-62; project engr. W.S. Fowler Constrn. Co., Oneonta, Ala., 1963-66; gen. supt. Pawnee Constrn. Co., Birmingham, Ala., 1966-69, v.p., 1969—. Mem. Am. Soc. C.E. Baptist. Lion. Home: 1101 Edwards Lake Rd Birmingham AL 35215 Office: PO Box 6257 Birmingham AL 35217

HAWKINS, MARY ELIZABETH GARDNER, home economist, educator; b. Suffolk, Va., Aug. 19, 1945; d. Thomas Allen and Helen (Williams) Gardner; B.S. in Home Econs. Edn., Madison Coll., 1967; postgrad. in early childhood edn., U. Va., 1968, Va. Commonwealth U., 1970; m. Joel David Hawkins, Oct. 19, 1969. Home service rep. Va. Electric and Power Co., Charlottesville, 1967-69; tchr. Chesterfield County (Va.) Schs., 1969—. Mem. Am. Home Econs. Assn., Va. Home Econs. Assn. (dist. program chmn. 1968-69), Va. Home Economists in Bus., Pi Omicron Tau. Club: Soroptimist of Charlottesville (rec. sec. 1969—, del. regional conv. 1969, nat. conv. 1969). Home: 1425 Oakhurst Lane Richmond VA 23225 Office: Falling Creek Elementary Sch Hopkins Rd Richmond VA 23225

HAWKINS, MERRILL MORRIS, coll. dean; b. Maben, Miss., Mar. 19, 1914; s. Edgar Preston and Viola (Monts) H.; student Wood Jr. Coll., 1934-36; B.S., Miss. State U., 1944, M.S., 1950; Ed.D., U. Miss., 1960; m. Carrie Lee Brabham, Dec. 21, 1946; children—Jane Hawkins, Merrill Morris. Supt. schs., Centreville, Miss., 1953-56; critic tchr. Univ. High Sch., U. Miss., 1956-57; instr. edn. U. Miss., 1956-57; asst. supt. schs., Vicksburg, Miss., 1957-60, supt., 1960-65; prof. dept. elementary and secondary edn. Miss. State U., State College, 1965-66, asst. dean Coll. Edn., 1966-68, asso. dean Coll. Edn., 1968-70, dean Coll. Edn., 1970—. Served with AUS, 1941-43. Mem. Am., (past pres.) Miss. assns. sch. adminstrs., Council Ednl. Facility Planners, Miss. Edn. Assn., Starkville C. of C., Blue Key, Omicron Delta Kappa, Phi Kappa Phi, Phi Delta Kappa, Kappa Delta Pi, Methodist. Mason; mem. Order Eastern Star, Rotarian. Home: Tally Ho Dr Starkville MS 39759 Office: PO Box 5365 Mississippi State MS 39762

HAWKINS, PAULA FICKES (MRS. WALTER EUGENE HAWKINS), mem. Republican Nat. Com.; b. Salt Lake City; d. Paul B. and Leoan (Staley) Fickes; student Utah State U.; m. Walter Eugene Hawkins, Sept. 5, 1947; children—Genean, Kevin Brent, Kelley Ann. Pres., Something Great, Maitland, Fla.; dir. First Nat. Bank, Maitland. Precinct committeewoman Orange County Rep. Com., 1965—; speakers chmn. Fla. Rep. Exec. Com., 1967—; mem. Fla. Rep. Nat. Conv., 1968, 76 Nat. Fedn. Rep. Women, 1965—; bd. dirs. Fla. Fedn. Rep. Women, 1968—; mem. Rep. Nat. Com. for Fla., 1968—; mem. adv. council Young Rep. Nat. Fedn., 1971—; chmn. host com. Rep. Nat. Conv., 1972, mem. rules com., 1972. Mem. Maitland Civic Center, 1965—; charter mem. bd. dirs. Fla. Ams. Constl. Action Com., of 100, 1966—, sec.-treas., 1966; mem. Central Fla. Mus. Speakers Bur., 1967; mem. Gov. of Fla. Commn. Status Women, 1968-71; co-chmn. Orange County March of Dimes, 1970-71. Recipient citation for service Fla. Rep. Com., 1966-67; Above and Beyond award as outstanding woman in Fla., politics 1968; nominated Orange County Woman of Year, Maitland Womans Club, 1969. Mem. Maitland C. of C. (chmn. congl. action com. 1967-68). Mem. Ch. of Jesus Christ of Latter-day Saints (pres. Relief Soc., Orlando Stake 1964-64, tchr. Sunday sch. 1964—). Clubs: Winter Park (Fla.) Racquet; Maitland Woman's Home: 241 Dommerich Dr Maitland FL 32751 Office: PO Box 91 Maitland FL 32751

HAWKINS, REGINALD ARMISTICE, dentist, clergyman; b. Beaufort, N.C., Nov. 11, 1923; s. Charles C. and Lorena (Smith) H.; B.S., Johnson C. Smith U., 1948, B.D., 1956, LL.D., 1962; D.D.S., Howard U., 1948; m. Catherine Elizabeth Richardson, Sept. 8, 1945; children—Pauletta, Reginald Armistice, Wayne, Lorena. Practice dentistry, Charlotte, N.C., 1948—; ordained to ministry Presbyn. Ch., 1956; pastor, evangelist social edn. and action. Chmn., Southeastern Regional Investment Corp., Parker Heights Ltd., Charlotte; vice chmn. Eastern N.C. Devel. Corp., 1967—. Civil rights leader, 1948—. Mem. Black Econ. Devel. Council, Small Bus. Adminstrn., 1968. Candidate for gov. N.C., 1968, 72; del. Democratic Nat. Conv., 1968; precinct chmn. N.C. Dem. Com., 1954-65; mem. Dem. Nat. Speakers Bur., 1960-64. Trustee N.C. Central U., Durham, 1961-66; mem. N.C. Good Neighbor Council, 1963-65. Served to 1st lt. Dental Corps, AUS, 1951-53. Recipient Distinguished Service award Alpha Kappa Alpha, 1969. Mem. Am., N.C. dental assns., Old North State (citation of merit 1968), Nat. dental socs., Acad. Gen. Dentistry, Internat. Platform Assn., N.A.A.C.P., Beta Kappa Chi, Kappa Alpha Psi. Home: 1703 Madison Av Charlotte NC 28208 Office: 1218 Beatties Ford Rd Charlotte NC 28208

HAWKINS, RICHARD CLIFTON, C. of C. exec.; b. Sycamore, O., Feb. 15, 1915; s. Howard C. and Prudence (Meck) H.; D.D., Eastern Pilgrim Coll., 1958; m. Helen Louise Pinner, Feb. 12, 1939; children—Richard J., Judith Ann. Pastor Pilgrim Holiness Ch., Newberry, Mich., 1939-41, Pontiac, Mich., 1941-46, youth dir. Mich. dist., 1943-46, supt., 1946-54, sec. ch. extension, 1954-66; chmn. bd. Owosso Coll., 1948-54, 1960-66; chmn. Ch. Extension Loan Fund Dirs., 1954-66; chmn. Pilgrim Manor Nursing Home Dirs., 1963-66; sec.-treas. Mid-Am. Enterprises, Inc.; former Miss. rep. U.S. C. of C., dist. mgr. Louisville Dist., 1971—. Mem. Nat. Assn. Evangelicals, Nat. Holiness Assn. Club: Lantern. Address: 8902 Shelbyville Rd Louisville KY 40222

HAWKINS, WILLIAM BLEDSOE, JR., lawyer, state legislator; b. Lynchburg, Va., Aug. 27, 1911; s. William Bledsoe and Nellie W. (Rangeley) H.; A.B., Davidson Coll., 1932; LL.B., U. S.C., 1936; m. Sari N. Hestle, Dec. 1, 1945; children—Diana, William, Melissa. Admitted to S.C. bar, 1935; partner firm Hawkins & Bethea, 1935-41, 46-57, Hawkins & McInnis, Dillon, S.C., 1969—; pvt. practice 1957-69; mem. S.C. Ho. of Reps., 1967—. Dir., 1st Citizens Bank & Trust Co. Mem. adv. bd. St. Eugene Hosp.; mem. area council Boy Scouts Am. Mem. Dillon County Devel. Bd., 1965-66; chmn. Dillon County Democratic Com., 1948-54, S.C. Dem. Exec. Com., 1954—; del. state conv., 1950, 52, 54, 56, 58; fed. election commr., 1938—. Trustee Dunbar Meml. Library. Served as 2d lt. to lt. col., USAAF, 1941-46. Mem. Am., S.C. bar assns., Dillon County Hist. Soc., Dillon County C. of C. (dir. 1963—), Am. Legion, Res. Officers Assn. (pres. 1948-49), Fish and Game Assn. (pres. 1948), Phi Delta Phi, Phi Delta Theta. Presbyn. (chmn. deacons, trustee, elder). Mason. Clubs: Dillon County Country (pres. 1967), Rotary (pres.), Lions pres. 1937-39), Modern Woodmen (comdr, 1938-39). Home: 310 Johnson Dr Dillon SC 29536 Office: 302 W Harrison St Dillon SC 29536

HAWKS, BETTY KIGER (MRS. ARNOLD WAYNE HAWKS), journalist; b. Alexandria, Va.; d. John Jacob and Leslie (Lee) Kiger; student Longwood Coll., 1941-43; B.A., U. N.C., 1945; m. Arnold Wayne Hawks, Nov. 4, 1950 (dec. Apr. 1968); children—John Kiger, Anthony Wayne, Timothy Roderick. Claims adjuster Liberty Mut. Ins. Co., Boston, 1945-46; asst. dir. Alexandria (Va.) Tb Assn., 1946-48; social worker Alexandria Dept. Pub. Welfare, 1948-51; free lance writer, area newspapers, 1950-61; pub. information dir. Alexandria chpt. A.R.C., 1962-70; womens editor The Journal, 1968—; advt. columnist, saleswoman Jour. Newspapers, 1965—. Dir. Alexandria Jr. Assembly, 1969—. Publicity dir. Little Theatre, Alexandria, 1968-69; asst. editor Rambling Thru Alexandria, 1969-71. Mem. Alexandria Community Welfare Council, 1955-60; chmn. Alexandria Christmas Bur., 1958-69; publicity chmn. Twig, Jr. Aux. Hosp., 1958-62. Mem. Alexandria Hosp. Corp., 1966—. Mem. Va. Press Women, Alpha Sigma Alpha, Nat. Capital Garden Club Fedn. (corr. sec. 1958-60). Episcopalian. Club: River Port Garden (pres. 1957-59). Home: 6033 Grove Dr Alexandria VA 22307 Office: 331 N Fairfax St Alexandria VA 22314

HAWKS, BYRON LOVEJOY, physician; b. N.Y.C., Nov. 23, 1909; s. Everett Merle and Maria (Granger) H.; B.S., Duke, 1935; M.D., N.Y. U., 1939; m. Nan Crawford Hawks, June 21, 1941; children—Everett M., Thomas Reid, Flora F. Intern Bklyn. Hosp., 1939-41; resident obstetrics and gynecology Woman's Hosp., N.Y.C., 1941-42; asso. prof. obstetrics and gynecology U. Ark. Sch. Medicine, Little Rock, 1962-70, prof., 1970—; dir. Ark. Maternity Infant Care Project, 1965—. Served to capt. USN. Diplomate Am. Bd. Obstetrics and Gynecology. Fellow Am. Coll. Obstetrics and Gynecology; mem. A.M.A. Contbr. articles to profl. jours. Home: 105 N Plaza Dr Little Rock AR 72205 Office: U Ark Med Center Little Rock AR 72201

HAWSEY, LAWRENCE SHELTON, 4-H agt.; b. Evergreen, Ala., Jan. 22, 1937; s. Alma Carlton and Eunic Mae (Calvert) H.; B.S., Auburn U., 1959, M.Ed., 1966; m. Virginia Ann Crews, July 20, 1963; children—Patricia Michelle, Kenneth Byron. Vocational edn. tchr. Meml. High Sch., Apopka, Fla., 1960-64; 4-H agt. Auburn U. Extension Service, Wetumpka, Ala., 1965-72, Opelika, Ala., 1972—. Gen. chmn. Wetumpka Area Family Life Conf., 1968—; div. chmn. Montgomery Area United Appeal, 1971—. Recipient Outstanding 4-H Agt. Ala. award, 1972. Mem. Ala. Assn. County Agr. Agts. (Extension Pub. Information award 1968), Nat. Assn. County Agr. Agts., Kappa Delta Pi. Methodist (ch. lay leader 1972). Lion. Home: 711 E Magnolia Av Auburn AL 36830 Office: Federal Bldg Opelika AL 36801

HAWTHORNE, JESSE J., athletic dir. E. Tex. State U. Address: Athletic Dept E Tex State U Commerce TX 75428*

HAWTHORNE, JOHN DAVID, retail hardware mcht.; b. Abingdon, Va., Apr. 30, 1923; s. Arthur Hopkins and Beulah (Crenshaw) H.; student King Coll., 1940-42, Wittenberg Coll., 1943, U. Richmond, 1946-47; m. Dorothy Jane Montgomery, May 28, 1955; children—David Malcom, Mary Elizabeth, Nancy. With George E. Failing Supply Co., 1947-49; partner Mut. Warehouse Inc., Enid, Okla., 1950-57, owner, 1957-58; partner Walker Truck Lines, Enid, 1955-57, owner, 1957-60; with Montgomery Oil Co., Enid, 1959-63; owner Rude & Co. Hardware, Enid, 1963—. Mem. Met. Area Planning Commn., Enid, 1963-67; Enid rep. Okla. Soc. Crippled Children, 1954—. Served to 1st lt. USAAF, 1943-45. Decorated Air medal with five oak leaf clusters. Mem. Okla. Assn. Realtors, Nat. Assn. Real Estate Bds., Enid Bd. Realtors, Air Force Assn., Kappa Sigma. Presbyn. (elder 1966-69). Rotarian (sec.-treas. 1964-69). Home: 425 N Oakwood Rd Enid OK 73701

HAWVER, CARL FULLERTON, financial assn. exec.; b. Fredericksburg, O., Apr. 29, 1914; s. Harley H. and Carrie (Fullerton) H.; student Adrian Coll., 1930-33; B.S., Bowling Green State U., 1937, M.A., 1939; postgrad. Fresno State Coll., 1948-49; Ph.D., Am. U., 1963; m. Frances Jewell Renick, Apr. 15, 1935; children—Karl Derek, Dennis Arthur, Karen Joyce. Tchr. Lake Twp. High Sch., Walbridge, O., 1937-41, Napoleon (O.) High Sch., 1941-43, 46-48, Fresno (Cal.) High Sch., 1948-50; adminstv. asst. to mem. U.S. Ho. of Reps., 1950-54, Nat. Republican Congl. Com., 1954-56; aide to U.S. sec. agr., Washington, 1956-57; dir. ednl. relations Nat. Consumer Finance Assn., Washington, 1957-61, exec. v.p., chief exec. officer, 1961—. Dir. Washington U.S.O., 1965—, Nat. U.S.O., 1968—; chmn. bd. govs. Marquette U. Consumer Credit Insts., 1962-64; chmn. exec. com. Nat. Consumer Credit Conf., 1962-65; founder, dir. Nat. Found. for Econ. Edn. for Clergy, 1958-64, 67—, chmn. bd., 1971—; mem. Nat. Council Trends and Perspective, 1966-69, Nat. Council on Consumer Issues, 1967—. Served with USNR, 1943-46. Mem. Pub. Relations Soc. Am. (pres. Washington chpt. 1967, mem. nat. assembly 1967-70, nat. dir. 1970—), Am. Soc. Assn. Execs. (Washington pres. 1967-68, nat. dir. 1968-71), U.S. C. of C. (nat. chmn. assn. sect.), Nat. Council Family Relations, Bur. Rehab., Sigma Alpha Epsilon, Republican. Presbyn. (elder). Club: Cosmos. Author: The Congressman's Conception of His Role, 1963; (with James A. Peterson and Roy A. Burkhart) Money and Your Marriage, 1963. Contbr. articles to profl. jours. Home: 8100 Kerry Lane Chevy Chase MD 20015 Office: 1000 16th St NW Washington DC 20036

HAY, CHARLES KENDALL, mfg. exec.; b. DeQueen, Ark., Oct. 2, 1917; s. William Edward and Maggie Vera (Morris) H.; grad. South Tex. Sch. Commerce, 1940; student U. Houston, 1940-42; m. Lois Joyce Holcombe, July 8, 1939; children—Charles Kendall, Joyce Annette (Mrs. Dean Davis). With Hughes Tool Co., Houston, 1935—, supr., foreman, gen. foreman, process engr., dept. mgr., sales mgr., 1935-69, mgr. mfg. engring., 1969—. Instr., U. Houston, 1945-48. Handicrafts dir. Boy Scouts Am., 1949-51, scout commr., 1951-53. Recipient Engring. '72 Merit award San Fernando Valley Engring. Council. Hon. fellow Instn. Prodn. Engrs. (London, Eng.); mem. Soc. Mfg. Engrs. (nat. treas. 1967-68, nat. v.p. 1968-71, nat. pres. 1972-73), Am. Gear Mfg. Assn., Am. Ordnance Assn., Houston C. of C. Methodist. Mason (32 deg.). Club: Hughes (past pres.), Hughes 25 Year (past pres.). Home: 13102 S Wayside Dr Houston TX 77048 Office: PO Box 2539 Houston TX 77001

HAY, RICHARD CARMAN, physician; b. Queens, L.I., N.Y., June 9, 1921; s. Richard Carman and Frances (Woodbury) H.; B.S., U. Vt., 1944, M.D., 1946; m. Martha Jean Fambrough, Mar. 2, 1957; children—Richard C., William W., Anne H., Sandra L., Bradford T., Holly K. Intern Bishop De Goesbriand Hosp., Burlington, Vt., 1946-47, resident, 1947-48; resident Hitchcock Hosp., Hanover Vt., 1950-51; practice medicine specializing in anesthesiology, Houston, 1954—; mem. staff Meml. Bapt. Hosp.; asst. anesthesiologist Worchester (Mass.) Meml. Hosp., 1953-54; asst. prof. anesthesiology U. Tex., Houston, 1954-61. Mem. Am., Tex. State socs. anesthesiology, Harris County Med. Soc. Home: 11811 Cobblestone St Houston TX 77024 Office: 1717 N Loop West Houston TX 77008

HAYDEN, JULIUS JOHN, JR., coll. pres.; b. Pass Christian, Miss., May 19, 1920; s. Julius John and Forrest (Spring) H.; A.A., Perkinston Jr. Coll., 1940; B.S., Miss. State U., 1949, M.S., 1950; Ed.D., U. So. Miss., 1966; m. Lillian R. Aschbacher, Apr. 23, 1943; children—Julius John III, Glover Richard, Susie Stafford. Tchr., coach Lee Road Sch., St. Tammany Parish, La., 1949-50; instr. history Perkinston (Miss.) Jr. Coll., 1950-52, dean, 1952-53, pres., 1953-62; pres. Miss. Gulf Coast Jr. Coll., Perkinston, 1962—. Mem. projects com. Mississippians for Ednl. TV, 1972—, Miss. Jr. Coll. Commn., 1971—. Served with USAF, 1940-41, USCGR, 1941-45. Mem. So. Assn. Colls. and Schs. (trustee 1971—), Sons of Confederacy, Miss. Coast Power Boat Squadron, Phi Theta Kappa (dir. 1971—). Rotarian. Home: Perkinston MS 39573

HAYES, BASCOM BEATTY, educator; b. Bardwell, Tex., Jan. 8, 1908; s. James Ernest and Ethel Olive (Driskell) H.; A.B., Trinity U., 1927; M.A., U. Mo., 1935; Ed.D., U. Tex., 1954; m. Donna Loyless, Dec. 23, 1930; 1 son, Barry. Tchr., Burleson (Tex.) High Sch., 1927-29; prin. Everman (Tex.) High Sch., 1929-31, Edna High Sch., 1931-33; supt. schs., Edna, Tex., 1933-50; asst. commr. Tex. State Dept. Edn., 1950-57; supt. schs., Brazosport, Tex., 1957-60; prof. ednl. adminstrn. U. Tex., Austin, 1960-72. Endl. cons. Mem. Am., Tex. assns. sch. adminstrs., Tex. Assn. Coll. Tchrs., N.E.A. (life mem.), Phi Delta Kappa. Baptist (deacon 1938—). Mason. Author: How School Boards Function, 1955. Home: 2719 Mount Laurel Lane Austin TX 78703

HAYES, CHARLES PATTON, JR., physician; b. Schenectady, Apr. 25, 1934; s. Charles Patton and Susan Elizabeth (Hearn) H.; student Duke U., 1952-55; M.D., Duke U. Med. Sch., 1959; m. Jo Moore Smithwick, Apr. 4, 1959; children—Barrie Elizabeth, Charles Gregory. Intern, Duke U. Med. Center, Durham, N.C.; nephrology fellow, 1962-64, mem. faculty, 1964-69, asso., 1964-66, asst. prof., 1966-69; resident internal medicine U. Tex. Med. Br. at Galveston, 1960-62; pvt. practice medicine specializing in internal medicine and nephrology, Riverside Clinic, Jacksonville, Fla., 1969—; mem. staffs Riverside and Univ. hosps., Jacksonville; asso. clin. prof. U. Fla. Med. Sch., 1971—; cons. Kidney Disease Control Branch Pub. Health Service, 1965-68; chmn. Kidney Adv. Bd., Fla., 1971—; mem. Fla. Med. Found. Peer Review Com., 1971—; mem. med. adv. bd. Fla. Kidney Found., 19—. Diplomate Am. Bd. Internal Medicine. Fellow A.C.P., Am. Heart Assn.; mem. A.M.A., Am. Soc. Nephrology, Am. Soc. Artificial Internal Organs, Fla. Kidney Found., Nat. Kidney Found., S.E. Dialysis and Transplantation Assn. (council. Clubs: Timuguana Country, Ponte Vedra. Home: 4754 Long Bow St Jacksonville FL 32210 Office: 2005 Riverside Av Jacksonville FL 32204

HAYES, HORACE HAYWOOD, ednl. adminstr.; b. Blue Springs, Miss., Dec. 10, 1926; s. William Alexander and Aurelia (McClure) H.; student Bob Jones Coll., 1943-45, Erskine Coll., 1946-47; B.S., Middle Tenn. State U., 1951; M.Ed. U. Cahttanooga, 1961; Ed.S., U. Ga., 1963; m. Carolyn Morris Hayes, June 28, 1952; children—William Alexander II, Phillip Morris, Jeri Carol. With Lincoln County Bd. Edn., Fayetteville, Tenn., 1947-50; with Whitfield County Bd. Edn., Dalton, Ga., 1951—, tchr. Dawnville Sch., 1951-62, prin., 1962—. Mem. Nat., Ga., Whitfield (pres. 1964) edn. assns., Local Prins. Assn. (pres. 1966-67), Ga. Elementary Prins. Assn. (v.p. 1967-68), Phi Delta Kappa. Methodist (steward 1964—). Club: Ruritan. Address: Route 4 Dalton GA 30720

HAYES, JOHN COLEMAN, JR., cons. engring. co. exec.; b. Nashville, Apr. 23, 1937; s. John Coleman and Reba (Walker) H.; B.Engring. in Civil Engring., Vanderbilt U., 1959; J.D., YWCA Night Law Sch., Nashville, 1965; m. Juanita Rae Haynie, Dec. 20, 1958; children—Holly, Lisa, John Coleman. Admitted to Tenn. bar, 1965; state airport engr. Tenn. Aero. Commn., Nashville, 1959-64; founding prin., owner firm John Coleman Hayes, Jr. & Assos., Nashville, 1964—; dir. Interstate Systems, Inc., Nashville; sec. Panelling Center Am., Inc., Nashville. Registered profl. engr., Tenn. Mem. Cons. Engrs. Tenn. Assn. (past pres.), Tenn. (sec. treas.), Nat. (mem. civil engring. council) socs. profl. engrs., Tenn. Bar Assn., Barristers Club Nashville. Presbyn. Mason (Shriner). Home: 779 Greeley Dr Nashville TN 37205 Office: 2109 Abbott Martin Rd Nashville TN 37215

HAYES, JOHN DANIEL, naval officer, historian; b. N.Y.C., Jan. 23, 1902; s. John Sullivan and Margaret (Hurley) H.; B.S., U.S. Naval Acad., 1924; M.S., U. Cal. at Berkeley, 1933; postgrad. Indsl. Coll. Armed Forces, 1949-50, Georgetown U., 1953-56; m. Nellie Mae Quinn, Jan. 15, 1949; children—(by previous marriage) David Breingan Hayes, Jean Berdot Hayes. Commd. ensign USN, 1924, advanced through grades to rear adm.; with Amphibious Force, PTO, 1942-44, planning officer 7th Amphibious Force, 1944-46, comdr. Service Squadron 1, Pacific Fleet, 1950-51; faculty Indsl. Coll. Armed Forces, Washington, 1951-54, ret., 1954; editor Shipmate mag., Annapolis, Md., 1956-64. Decorated Purple Heart. Mem. Am. Mil. Inst. (pres. 1955-58), U.S. Naval Inst., Tex. Hist. Assn., Naval Hist. Found., Orgn. Am. Historians. Author: (with Vincent J. Esposito) Concise History of World War I, 1964, Concise History of World War II, 1964. Editor: Samuel Francis DuPont, A Selection From His Civil War Letters, 3 vols., 1969; contbg. editor Ency. Americana, 1958-72, Naval Review, 1966-72). Address: PO Box 2667 Texas City TX 77590

HAYES, JOHN EDWARD ROLLINS, textile co. exec.; b. Chick Springs, S.C., June 18, 1927; s. Clifford Barron and Dorothy (Lawson) H.; grad. Asheville Sch. Boys, 1954; B.S., U. Va., 1960; m. Mary Love Cates, May 12, 1962; children—John Edward Rollins II, Robert Cates, Clifford Barron, Mary Love Cates. Pres. Hayes Textiles, Inc., Spartanburg, S.C., 1959—. Served with USNR, 1954-55. Mem. Beta Theta Phi. Home: 1040 Woodburn Rd Spartanburg SC 29302 Office: 1078 Union Rd Spartanburg SC 29302

HAYES, KYLE, lawyer; b. Purlear, N.C., Oct. 4, 1905; s. Charles Clayton and Ida (Huffman) H.; LL.B., Wake Forest Coll., 1931; m. Margaret Smithey, Nov. 10, 1932. Admitted to N.C. bar, 1930; also U.S. Supreme Ct. bar; sr. mem. firm Hayes & Hayes, North Wilkesboro, 1935—. Owner retail furniture, hardware stores; pres. The Northwestern Finance Co., North Wilkesboro. Mem. bar candidate com. 23d Jud. Dist. N.C. Republican candidate for U.S. Ho. of Reps., 1936, for lt. gov. N.C., 1946, gov., 1956, U.S. Senate, 1960. Trustee Wilkes Community Coll., Wilkesboro; adv. bd. Gardner-Webb Coll., Boiling Springs, N.C. Served with USMCR, 1942-44. Mem. Am., N.C. (gov.) bar assns., Am. Judicature Soc., Jud. Conf. 4th Circuit, Am. Trial Lawyers Assn., Practising Law Inst., Def. Research Inst. Baptist (deacon). Mason (Shriner), Elk, Moose, Kiwanian, K.P. Club: Oakwoods Country (North Wilkesboro, N.C.). Home: 604 E Main St Wilkesboro NC 28697 Office: 309 9th St North Wilkesboro NC 28659

HAYES, ORRILL WILLIAM, personnel training co. exec.; b. N.Y.C., Mar. 31, 1918; s. Anthony V. and Bertha G. (Hayes) Seferovic; student, McIntosh Coll. Bus., 1937-39; m. Elizabeth Ann Goffinet, July 6, 1968; children—Christina L., Celeste L. Profl. baseball gen. mgr. Buffalo Internat. League, 1946-52; v.p. Am. Desk Mfg. Co., 1953-59, Continental Belton Mfg. Co., 1960-63; pres. Hayes Assos., Amarillo, Tex., 1959—. Lectr. Tex. State Police Acad., 1952-61, Braniff Internat. Airways Sch., 1957-61. Maj.-aide-de-camp Gov's. staff, N.H., 1940; mem. N.H. Ho. of Reps., 1940-41; Republican nominee for lt. gov. Tex., 1962, for U.S. Congress, 1964. Adv. council U. Plano, 1972—. Served to capt. USAAF, 1942-46. Recipient Profl. Baseball Exec. of Year award The Sporting News, 1951, Good Sportsmanship award U.S. Baseball Congress, 1938; decorated Sovereign Order -Knight of Malta, Late King Peter II, 1967. Author: Your Memory, Speedway To Success, 1959. Home: 6108 Hanson Rd Amarillo TX 79106

HAYES, RALPH EUGENE, writer; b. Columbus, Ind., Sept. 3, 1927; s. Ralph Emmons and Ruth Virginia (Lister) H.; B.A., U. Mich., 1951, J.D., 1954; m. Donna June Ford, July 21, 1951. Writer many short stories pub. in various lit., mystery, and men's mags., including Alfred Hitchcock's Mystery Mag., Knight, Today, others. Served with USAAF, 1945-47. Mem. State Bar Mich., Grand Rapids Bar Assn., East African Wildlife Soc., African Wildlife Leadership Found., East Martello Hist. Soc., Key West Old Island Restoration Found. Author novels, including: The Visiting Moon, 1971; One Springtime in Venice, 1967; The Secret of Sulphur Creek, 1970; The Wayward August of Virgie Tate, 1967; Hunter's Moon, 1971; The Soul Stealers, 1971. Short stories pub. in lit. textbooks, lit. anthologies. Address: 826 Eaton St Key West FL 33040

HAYES, RAY HOGAN, hosp. supt., psychiatrist; b. Elizabethtown, Ky., Oct. 14, 1919; s. John Howard and Wilma (Hogan) H.; B.S., Georgetown U., 1946, M.D., 1950 widower; children—Kristen Suzanne, Armand Christopher. Intern Providence Hosp., Washington, 1950-51; resident chest diseases Glenn Dale Tb Hosp., 1951-54; resident chest diseases Springfield State Hosp., Sykesville, Md., 1954-55, resident psychiatry, 1954-55; resident psychiatry U. Louisville Sch. Medicine, 1955-57; dist. psychiatrist Eastern region Ky. Dept. Mental Health, 1957-61; chief psychiat. service USPHS Hosp., Lexington, Ky., 1961-62, clin. dir., 1962-65; supt. Central State Hospital., Louisville, 1965—; instr. psychiatry U. Louisville Sch. Medicine, 1957-62, clin. asst. prof. psychiatry, 1965—; adj. prof. pastoral care Coll. of Bible Lexington, 1957-62; instr., then clin. asst. prof. psychiatry U. Ky. Sch. Medicine, 1961-65. Diplomate Am.Bd. Psychiatry and Neurology. Mem. A.M.A., Am. Pub. Health Assn., Am., Ky. psychiat. assns., Am. Group Psychotherapy Assn., Tri-State Group Psychotherapy Assn., A.A.A.S., Assn. Med. Supts. Mental Hosps. Contbr. profl. jours. Home: 2108 Lakeland Rd Louisville KY 40223 Office: Central State Hosp Louisville KY 40223

HAYES, ROBERT DEMING, educator; b. Lexington, Ky., Mar. 11, 1925; s. Roy Bagley and Esther (Brigman) H.; B.S., U. Ky., 1948, M.S., 1950; M.S., Ga. Inst. Tech., 1957, Ph.D., 1964; m. Nancy Ellen Taylor, Aug. 30, 1947; children—William T., Katherine D., Carol E., Jennifer D. Grad. asst. U. Ky., 1947-50; field engr. Western Electric Co., Winston-Salem, N.C., 1950-54; asst. research engr. Ga. Inst. Tech., Atlanta, 1954-55, research engr., 1955-64, asso. head radar br., 1965-66, asst. prof. 1958-64, asso. prof. elec. engring., 1964-66, prof., 1968—; prin. engr. Radiation, Inc., Melbourne, Fla., 1966-68. Adj. prof. Fla. Inst. Tech., 1966-68; cons. engr., 1963—; cons. Lockheed Ga. Co., U.S. Army, Pure Food, Inc., Radiation, Inc. Mem. Cobb County Planning and Zoning Commn., 1964-66, chmn., 1969—; mem. com. Boy Scouts Am., 1954-62. Served with USAAF, 1943-46. Mem. I.E.E.E. (v.p. 1960), Cobb County C. of C., Sigma Xi, Phi Kappa Tau, Sigma Pi Sigma, Eta Kappa Nu. Presbyn. Kiwanian. Home: 605 Chestnut Hill Rd Marietta GA 30060 Office: Ga Inst Tech Atlanta GA 30332

HAYES, THOMAS JARRELL, JR., pipeline co. exec.; b. Whitehall, Tex., Sept. 28, 1939; s. Thomas Jarrell and Ruby Vida (Welch) H.; B.B.A., Tex. A. and I. U., 1962; m. Peggy Anne Carpenter, Mar. 14, 1959; children— Brian, Kelvin. Sales engring. coordinator Cameron Iron Works, Inc., Houston, 1962-67; v.p., gen. mgr. Anbeck Co., Houston, also v.p., officer Keltron Corp., 1967-71; v.p. Zapata Pipeline Tech., Inc., Houston, 1971—. Mem. Pipeliners Club. Home: 1910 Mapleton St Houston TX 77043 Office: 11500 Kilburn St Houston TX 77055

HAYMAN, LOUIS DEMARO, JR., physician; b. Weldon, N.C., Apr. 10, 1920; s. Louis DeMaro and Bess (Widenhouse) H.; B.S. in Medicine, U. N.C., 1942; M.D., C.M., McGill U., 1943; m. Carol Deane Bessent, Aug. 30, 1945; children—Richard Louis, Susan (Mrs. Mark Williams). Rotating intern Med. Coll. Va., Richmond, 1943-44, Firestone Rubber Plantation, Liberia, 1944-45; resident in medicine VA Hosp., Oteen, N.C., 1947-49, Swannanoa, N.C., 1949-51; practice medicine specializing in internal medicine, Florence, S.C., 1951-55, also subspecializing in cardiology, Jacksonville, N.C., 1955—; dir. coronary care unit Onslow Meml. Hosp., Jacksonville, 1965—. Served with M.C., AUS, 1945-47; ETO. Named Community Man of Year, Jacksonville Jr. C. of C., 1962. Diplomate Am. Bd. Internal Medicine. Fellow A.C.P., Am. Coll. Cardiology (asso.); Am. Soc. Internal Medicine, Am., So. Med. assns., N.J. State Med. Soc. Contbr. articles to med. jours. Home: 406 Carmen Av Jacksonville NC 28540 Office: 617 College St Jacksonville NC 28540

HAYMES, BENJAMIN FRANKLIN, dentist; b. Claremore, Okla., Oct. 2, 1917; s. John David and Mamie Ethel (Matthews) H.; student Tulsa U., 1935-36; D.D.S., U. Mo., 1941; m. Bonnie Katherine Petrisco, Apr. 20, 1969. Sec. engring. dept. Phillips Petroleum Co., 1936-42; commd. officer U.S. Navy, 1942, advanced through grades to comdr., 1969; sr. dental officer U.S.S. Grand Canyon and U.S.S. Leyte; oral surgeon U.S. Naval Hosp., Guantanamo, Cuba, Memphis, Bainbridge, Md.; stationed Naval Air Sta.,Pensacola, Fla. Mem. Am., Kan., Okla., Mo. dental assns. Kiwanian. Club: Tulsa University Glee (Tulsa). Home: Box 4336 Warrington FL 32507 Office: 400 Navy Blvd Warrington FL 32507

HAYNES, ABNER, business exec.; b. Denton, Tex., Sept. 19, 1938; B.A., North Tex. State U., 1960; m. Helen Herron, Mar. 27, 1963; children— Byron, Abner, David. Running back, pass receiver, kickoff and punt return specialist Dallas Texans, 1960-62, Kansas City Chiefs, 1963-64, Denver Broncos, 1965-66, Miami Dolphins, 1967, N.Y. Jets, 1967; marketing specialist Lone Star Brewery, 1961, Fant Milling Co., 1962, Pepsi-Cola, 1963-64; loan officer, community affairs rep. Continental Indsl. Bank, Denver, 1965-66; mgr. employee relations, asst. v.p. urban affairs and employee relations Zale Corp., Dallas, 1968—. Bd. dirs. Youth Guidance Commn. of YMCA, S.W. Ednl. Devel. Labs. Mem. North Tex. State U. Alumni Assn. (dir.), Nat. Assn. Marketing Developers (dir.). Home: 5907 Sumatra Lane Dallas TX 75241 Office: 3000 Diamond Park Dr Dallas TX 75247

HAYNES, CHARLES GUTHRIE, govt. ofcl.; b. Kansas City, Mo., Feb. 24, 1920; s. Howard and Catherine (Guthrie) H.; B.C.S., Southeastern U., 1941, M.C.S., 1946; m. Jessie Irene Smith, Oct. 27, 1941; children— Judith W. (Mrs. John T. Miller), Mary Catherine (Mrs. Albert M. Warfield), Margaret Ann (Mrs. Ronald Ryan), Charles Guthrie, Stephen Jay. Accountant, Spicer and Rees, C.P.A.'s, Washington, 1939-41; spl. agt. FBI, 1941-52, 53-55, 57; staff, later dir. surveys and investigations Appropriations com. U.S. Ho. of Reps., 1952-53, 55-57; dir. internal audit Dept. Health, Edn. and Welfare, 1957-60; dir. fgn. assistance investigations Dept. of State, 1960-61; dir. inspections NASA, Washington, 1961-69; dir. hdqrs. adminstrn. NASA, 1969-70; dep. auditor gen. AID, 1970-72; insp.-gen. Dept. Housing and Urban Devel., Washington, 1972—. Chmn. bd., pres. Guthrie Properties, Inc. C.P.A., D.C. Mem. Am. Inst. C.P.A.'s, Internat. Assn. Chiefs of Police, Assn. Fed. Investigators, Soc. Former Spl. Agts. FBI, Fed. Govt. Accountants Assn. Home: 10200 Brookmoor Dr Silver Spring MD 20901 Office: Dept Housing and Urban Development 7th and D Sts SW Washington DC 20410

HAYNES, CLIFFORD RUDOLPH, physician, surgeon; b. Trinidad, Tex., June 9, 1927; s.Lewis C. and Willie Mae (Stogner) H.; B.A., U. Tex., 1949, M.D., 1951. Intern, Hermann Hosp., Houston, 1951-52; pvt. practice, Malakoff, Tex., 1952—; staff Kilman Hosp., 1952-60; staff, owner, adminstr. Haynes Hosp., 1960—; staff Henderson County Meml. Hosp.; sch. and athletic physician Malakoff Ind. Sch. Dist. Mem.-at-large Circle Ten council Boy Scouts Am. Councilman, City of Malakoff, 1955-60, mayor pro-tem, 1957, 58, 59. Mem. chancellor's council U. Tex., 1966—. Served from pvt. to sgt., AUS, 1945-46. Mem. A.M.A., So. Tex., 11th Dist., Henderson County (pres. 1955) med. socs., Am., Tex. heart assns., Tex. Soc Athletic Team Physicians, Ex-Students Assn. U. Tex. (life), Assn. Am. Physicians and Surgeons, Internat. Platform Assn., Phi Rho Sigma. Democrat. Baptist (deacon, trustee). Rotarian (pres. 1956-57, 58-59). Home: 107 Woodland St Malakoff TX 75148 Office: Haynes Hosp Malakoff TX 75148

HAYNES, DOUGLAS MARTIN, physician, univ. dean; b. N.Y.C., Jan. 25, 1922; s. Daniel Hagood and Courtenay (Collins) H.; student Allhallows Sch., Rousdon, Devon, Eng., 1935-38; B.A., B.S., So. Methodist U., 1943; M.D. Southwestern Med. Coll., 1946; m. Elizabeth Burwell Johnson, June 17, 1961; children—Douglas Marshall, Lewis D. Intern in pathology Parkland Meml. Hosp., Dallas, 1946-47, resident obstetrics and gynecology, 1949-52; chief pathology 4th med. lab., Heidelberg, Germany, AUS, 1947-49; asst. prof. Southwestern Med. Sch., U. Tex., 1952-55; asso. prof. U. Louisville, 1955-57, prof., chmn. dept., 1957-69, interim dean Sch. Medicine, 1969-70, dean, 1970-72, prof., 1972—. Diplomate Am. Bd. Obstetrics and Gynecology (asso. examiner). Fellow A.C.S., Am. Assn. Obstetricians and Gynecologists; mem. A.M.A., So. Med. Assn., Central Assn. Obstetricians and Gynecologists, Am. Coll. Obstetricians and Gynecologists, Phi Beta Kappa, Alpha Omega Alpha, Phi Chi, Delta Chi. Democrat. Presbyn. Editor: Medical Complications During Pregnancy, 1969. Contbr. articles to profl. jours. Home: 5204 Tomahawk Rd Louisville KY 40207

HAYNES, GEORGE WILLIAM, judge; b. Pelahatchie, Miss., Feb. 19, 1917; s. Charles McCaslin and Alzie (Vaughn) H.; student Millsaps Coll., 1934-35; LL.B., Jackson Sch. Law, 1951; m. Dorothy Currie, Oct. 7, 1940; 1 son, George William. Admitted to Miss. bar, 1951; practiced in Utica, 1955-66; chancery judge 5th Chancery Ct. Dist. of Miss., 1966—. Served with USMC, 1935-39, to capt. USMCR, 1942-47. Decorated Silver Star medal, Purple Heart. Mem. Am., Miss., Hinds County bar assns. Methodist. Address: Utica MS 39175

HAYNES, HUGH WILLIS, banker; b. Villa Rica, Ga., Apr. 1, 1911; s. Henry Willis and Tallalah (Riggs) H.; student Emory U., 1931; m. Mattalyn, July 17, 1940; children—Jonathan, Julie. Credit mgr. Sears Robeuck & Co., Atlanta, 1936-47; v.p. Nat. Bank of Ga., Atlanta, 1947—; dir. Edwards Baking Co., Atlanta. Bd. dirs. So. Union Conf. Seventh Day Adventists. Mem. DeKalb County C. of C. Seventh Day Adventist (ch. bd. 1972—). Club: Civitan (Atlanta). Home: 1955 Wellborn Rd Lithonia GA 30058 Office: 34 Peachtree St Atlanta GA 30301

HAYNES, J.K., assn. exec. Exec. sec. La. Edn. Assn., Baton Rouge. Address: Box 1767 Baton Rouge LA 70821*

HAYNES, KIT HILL, assn. exec.; b. Murfreesboro, Tenn., Sept. 18, 1911; s. Christopher Hill and Minnie Mae (Hardcastle) H.; A.B., Vanderbilt U., 1933; postgrad. U.S. Dept. Agr. Grad. Sch., 1944-46; m. Barbara Barker Askew, Sept. 9, 1939. Editor, Clarksville (Tenn.) Star, 1933-34; sports editor, reporter Murfreesboro Daily News-Jour., 1934-36, editor, 1938-39; farm editor Nashville Banner, 1936-38; makeup editor, copy reader Nashville Tennessean, 1939-42; information specialist U.S. Dept. Agr., Washington, Washington, 1942-46, mem. nat. adv, com. on information, 1954, adv. com. pub. relations, 1961, chmn. sub-com., 1961; dir. information Tenn. Farm Bur. Fedn., Columbia, 1946-48, Nat. Council Farmer Coops., Washington, 1948-67; asst. legislative dir. Am. Farm Bur. Fedn., Washington, 1967—. Mem. bd. cons. Farm Film Found., Washington, 1948—; mem. ECA Study Mission to Europe, 1952. Mem. Pub. Relations Soc. Am., Agrl. Relations Council, Tenn. (treas. 1950), Ky. state socs. Presbyn. (deacon 1962-64). Clubs: Nat. Press, University, Vanderbilt (Washington). Home: 5513 Montgomery St Chevy Chase MD 20015 Office: 425 13th St NW Washington DC 20004

HAYNES, LEONARD L., JR., educator; b. Austin, Tex., Mar. 16, 1923; s. Leonard L. and Thelma (Watkins) H.; A.B., Huston Tillotson Coll., 1942; B.D., Gammon Theol. Sem., 1945; Th.D., Boston U., 1948; m. Leila Davenport, Nov. 21, 1945; children—Leonard L. III, Walter Lafayette, Angeline Thelma, Leila Anne. Ordained to ministry Methodist Ch., 1948; pastor Wesley United Meth. Ch., Baton Rouge, 1960—; dean students, prof. philosophy Philander Smith Coll., Little Rock, 1948-52; dir. humanities Ark. State Coll., Pine Bluff, 1952-54; dean of coll. Claflin Coll., Orangeburg, S.C., 1952-57; pres. Morristown Jr. Coll., 1957-59; prof. philosophy and edn. Wiley Coll. Marshall, Tex., 1959-60, So. U., Baton Rouge, 1963—. Mem. Human Relations Council, Baton Rouge, 1967. Recipient Distinguished Alumnus award Boston U. Sch. Theology, 1971. Mem. Ministerial Assn. Baton Rouge, Alpha Kappa Mu, Omega Psi Phi, Mason. Author: The Negro Community within American Protestantism, 1619-1844, 1952. Home: 1798 77th St Baton Rouge LA 70821

HAYNES, RICHARD DUVAL, lawyer; b. Oklahoma City, Mar. 2, 1931; s. Marvin Floyd and Helen (Hays) H.; A.B., U. Okla., 1953; J.D., Washington and Lee U., 1958; m. Norine Castle, Nov. 8, 1958; children—Ellen Elizabeth, Caroline Lillie. Admitted to Okla. bar, 1958, Tex. bar, 1962; practiced in Dallas, 1961—; mem. firm Rainey, Flynn &Welch, 1958-61, Ethan B. Stroud, 1962-64, Haynes & Boone, Dallas, 1964—; counsel Electro-Sci. Investors, Inc., Dallas, 1961-62. Lectr. So. Methodist U., 1966-68, 70-73. Bd. dirs. Dallas Civic Opera Co., 1966-71. Served to 1st lt. USAF, 1955-57. Mem. Am., Okla., Dallas bar assns., State Bar Tex. Republican. Contbr. articles to profl. jours. Home: 3509 Princeton Av Dallas TX 75205 Office: 2900 LTV Tower Dallas TX 75201

HAYNIE, HUGH, editorial cartoonist; b. Reedville, Va., Feb., 1927; s. Raymond Lee and Margaret Virginia (Smith) H.; A.B., Coll. William and Mary, 1950; L.H.D., U. Louisville, 1968; m. Lois Ann Cooper, Dec. 5, 1953; 1 son, Hugh Smith. Cartoonist, Richmond (Va.) Times-Dispatch, 1950-53, Greensboro (N.C.) Daily News, 1953-55, 56-58, Atlanta Jour., 1955-56; with Louisville Courier Jour., 1958—, now editorial cartoonist; syndicated by Los Angeles Times, 1964—. Dir. Haynie Products, Inc., Balt. Served to lt. USCGR, 1944-46, 51-52; PTO, Recipient Headliner award, 1966; Freedoms Found. award, 1966, Pulitzer prize; named One of 10 Outstanding Young Men, U.S. Jr. C. of C., 1962. Mem. Soc. Alumni Coll. William and Mary (dir.), Phi Beta Kappa, Omicron Delta Kappa, Pi Kappa Alpha, Democrat. Episcopalian. Club: Windmill Point Yacht (Foxwells, Va.). Home: Indian Hills Trail and Tribal Rd Louisville KY 40207 Office: Courier Jour 525 W Broadway Louisville KY 40202

HAYNIE, ROBERT LOWREY, civil engr.; b. Collierville, Tenn., Dec. 15, 1939; s. Henning Lowrey and Edna Willise (Thomas) H.; B.S., Union U., 1961; B.S. in Civil Engring., Miss. State U., 1962; postgrad. Samford U., 1970-71; m. Becky Lee Maness, June 10, 1962; children—Vivian Lynn, Mark Lowrey. Mgmt. trainee South Central Bell Telephone Co., Nashville, 1962-64; cons. engr. Harland Bartholomew and Assos., Birmingham, Ala., 1964-72; cons. engr. Wooten, Smith & Weiss, Memphis, 1972—. Served with AUS, 1963. Mem. Am. Soc. C.E., Nat. Soc. Profl. Engrs., Am. Pub. Works Assn., Inst. Traffic Engrs., Am. Soc. Planning Ofcls., Tau Beta Pi. Republican. Baptist. Home: 6710 Aberfoyle Cove Memphis TN 38138 Office: 2600 Poplar Av Memphis TN 38112

HAYNIE, THOMAS POWELL, III, physician, educator; b. Hearne, Tex., Aug. 9, 1932; s. Thomas Powell and Sue (Cummings) H.; student U. of South, 1949-51, U. Tex,, 1951-52; M.D., Baylor U., 1956; m. Bette Maxine Hutchins, Mar. 10, 1956; children—David Powell, Amy Cummings, Sue Cummings. Intern, resident U. Mich. Med. Sch., 1956-60, instr., 1960-62, asst. prof., 1962; practice medicine, specializing in nuclear and internal medicine, Houston, 1965—; mem. staff M. D. Anderson Hosp.; asst. prof. medicine U. Tex. Med. Br., 1962-65; asso. prof. medicine U. Tex.-M. D. Anderson Inst., Houston, 1965—; chief sect. nuclear medicine U. Tex.-M. D. Anderson Hosp. and Tumor Inst., Houston, 1967—; asso. grad faculty U. Tex. Grad. Sch. Biomed. Scis., Houston, 1969—; cons. Wilford Hall U.S. Air Force Hosp., Lackland AFB, Tex., 1967—; cons preventive med. div. Space Flight Biotech. Splty. Teams NASA, Manned Space Center, Houston, 1968— Tech expert IAEA Casablanca, Morocco, 1964; mem. adv. panel on radio pharmaceuticals Am. Hosp. Formulary Service, 1970—. Fellow A.C.P.; mem. A.M.A., Soc. Nuclear Medicine, Am. Thyroid Assn. Home: 18626 Barbuda Lane Houston TX 77058 Office: 6723 Bertner St Houston TX 77025

HAYNSWORTH, CLEMENT FURMAN, JR., federal judge; b. Greenville, S.C., Oct. 30, 1912; s. Clement Furman and Elsie (Hall) H.; student Darlington Sch. Rome, Ga.; A.B. summa cum laude, Furman U., 1933, LL.D., 1964; LL.B., Harvard, 1936; m. Dorothy Merry, Nov. 25, 1946. Admitted to S.C. bar 1936; asso. firm Haynsworth & Haynsworth (later Haynsworth, Perry, Bryant, Marion & Johnstone), 1936-40, partner 1940-46, exec. partner 1947-57; alternate mem. Regional Wage Stblzn. Bd., 1950-51; judge U.S. Ct. of Appeals for 4th Circuit, 1957—, chief judge, 1964—. Past pres. Greenville Community Chest; adv. council Furman U.; former dir. United Fund of Greenville. Served with USNR, 1942-45. Mem. Am., S.C., Greenville bar assns., Am. Law Inst., Am. Judicature Soc. (dir.). Episcopalian. Clubs: Poinsett (Greenville); Commonwealth (Richmond, Va.). Home: 415 Crescent Av Greenville SC 29605 Office: Fed Bldg Greenville SC 29603

HAYS, DONALD OSBORNE, govt. ofcl.; b. New Braintree, Mass., June 5, 1907; s. Edward Christopher and Grace Theresa Osborne (Hays) Luethi; grad. Mt. Hermon Prep. Sch., 1925; student Middlebury Coll., 1925-27; B.A., U. Colo., 1929; M.A., Columbia, 1937, postgrad. 1942; postgrad. Am. U., 1951; m. Mary Katherine Jackson Oliver, Aug. 30, 1937. Tchr. English, head dept. English, pub. schs., Colo., Pa., 1929-38; head English dept., sr. master Woodmere (L.I.) Acad., 1938-42; mgmt. analyst, asst. dir., mgmt. and planning staff Spl. Services, VA, 1946-51; asst. dir. budget and mgmt. div. NPA, 1951-53; asst. dist. commr. for adminstrn. Internal Revenue Service, Balt., 1953, asst. regional commr. for adminstrn., Boston, 1953-54, Phila., 1954-57; asst. to dir. Bur. Fgn. Commerce, Dept. Commerce, Washington, 1957-61, now the Bur. Internat. Commerce, 1961-63; dir. overseas personnel div. Office Fgn. Comml. Services, Dept. Commerce, 1963-68, dir. performance evaluation div., 1968—. Dept. Commerce mem. 13th and 16th Fgn. Service Officer Selection Bd., Dept. State, 1959, 62; dep. examiner Bd. Fgn. Service Examiners, Dept. State, Washington, 1960—. Served from lt. (j.g.) to lt. comdr., USNR, 1942-46; mem. staff Comdr. Fourth Fleet, Recife, Brazil, 1943-44 contact negotiator, electronics div. Bur. Ships, also staff Navy Manpower Survey Bd., 1944-46, Mem. Cum Laude Soc., S.A.R. (pres. D.C. soc. 1971), Alpha Sigma Phi, Kappa Phi Kappa. Episcopalian (jr. warden). Clubs: Metropolitan, Dacor (Washington). Home: 4000 Massachusetts Av NW Washington DC 20016 Office: Dept of Commerce Washington DC 20230

HAYS, GRANVIL LEE, dentist; b. Tonkawa, Okla., Dec. 15, 1940; s. Donald Ray and Eleanor Aileen (Jones) H.; Asso. Sci., No. Okla. Coll., 1961; D.D.S., U. Mo., Kansas City, 1965; m. Adelheid Erna Heise, Aug. 8, 1964; children—Larissa, Brandon. Resident mgr. Univ. Residence Center, U. Mo., Kansas City, 1964-66; pvt. practice dentistry, Kansas City, 1965-66; commd. capt. U.S. Army, 1966, advanced to maj., 1969; gen. practice dentistry, Ft. Meade, Md., 1966-68; prosthodontist 39th Med. Dental Rep. of Vietnam, 1968-69; student officer advance course Ft. Houston, Tex., 1969; dental officer U.S. Army Hosp., U.S. Mil. Acad., West Point, N.Y., 1970—. Decorated Army Commendation medal. Mem. Am. Dental Assn., Army Athletic Assn., Alumni Assn. U. Mo. at Kansas City, Delta Sigma Delta. Home: Box 993 Guymon OK 73942 also 4156 Lancaster Av Newburg NY 12550 Office: U S Army Hosp US Mil Acad West Point NY 10996

HAYS, JAMES DEFORD, fedn. exec.; b. Huntsville, Ala., Aug. 20, 1909; s. James Elgie and Rena (DeFord) H.; B.S., U. Ala., 1931; m. Annie Wade Street, Sept. 8, 1928; children—Martha DeFord Enfinger, James R., John Wade. Mem. staff Ala. Geol. Survey, Tuscaloosa, 1931-33; mem. staff U.S. Forest Service, Black Warrior Nat. Forest, Moulton, Ala., 1933-34; project supt. TVA Forest Nursery, Muscle Shoals, Ala., 1934-37; owner, operator Haysland Farms, Huntsville, 1937—; pres. Ala. Farm Bur. Fedn., Montgomery, Ala., 1961—, AFB Mut. Casualty Ins. Co., Montgomery, 1961—; chmn. bd. Am. Nat. Bank, Huntsville, Ala., 1967-69; pres. Huntsville Indsl. Assos., Inc., 1967-70; dir. State Nat. Bank, Decatur, Ala.; dir. Am. Farm Bur. Fedn., Chgo. Bd. dirs., vice chmn. 4-H Found., 1965—; dir. Ala. Space Sci. Exhibit Commn., 1965—; mem. adv. council Ala. Community & Tech. Services, 1966—, Ala.-Guatemala Partners of Alliance, 1967—; pres. Huntsville Real Estate Investment Trust, 1970—; mem. Ala. Agri-Bus. Council, 1971; Ala.-U.S. Dept. Agr. Rural Devel. Council, 1971—, Com. for Increased Funding for Vocational Edn. in Ala., 1971—; mem. plant protection bd. Dept. Agr., 1971—; chmn. Ala. Resource Devel. Com., Montgomery, 1971—. Mem. Ala. C. of C. (agri-bus. com. 1970—), U. Ala. at Huntsville Assos., Newcomen Soc., Gamma Sigma Delta, Gamma Alpha, Pi Kappa Alpha. Mem. Ch. of Christ. Rotarian (pres. 1959). Home: 300 Haysland Rd Huntsville AL 35802 Office: PO Box 11000 Montgomery AL 36111

HAYS, ROBERT WILLIAM, educator; b. Atlanta, Oct. 17, 1925; s. Calvin Samuel and Elizabeth (Green) H.; student Duke, 1943-44; A.B., Presbyn. Coll., 1947; M.Ed., Emory U., 1957; m. Rebecca Guy Copeland, June 15, 1950; children—Michael Stephen, David, William. Comml. mgr. Sta. WSFT, Thomaston, Ga., 1947-48, Sta. WLBG, Laurens-Clinton, S.C., 1948; co-owner Clinton Plastic Co. (S.C.), 1948-49; instr. So. Tech. Inst., 1950-51, asst. prof., 1952-57, head dept. English, 1953—, asso. prof., 1958-60, prof., 1960—; supr. tng. course devel. Lockheed Aircraft Corp., Marietta, Ga., 1951-52. Communications cons. Served from apprentice seaman to lt. (j.g.), USNR, 1943-46. Recipient 2d place nat. Arthur Williston award for contbns. to lit. of engring. tech., 1967. Mem. Soc. for Tech. Communications, Am. Bus. Communications Assn. Author: Pacific Parodies, 1947; Principles of Technical Writing, 1965; Practically Speaking in Business, Industry and Government, 1969; Guide to Technical Writing, 1970; also numerous articles pub. in profl. and trade jours. Research on tech. communication ednl. methodology. Home: 130 Benson Dr Marietta GA 30060

HAYSLETT, DAN DEFOREST, broadcasting exec.; b. Chgo., Feb. 3, 1919; s. Dan DeForest and May (Sheehan) H.; student Northwestern U., 1937-38, DePaul U., 1938-39, Harvard, 1966; m. Mary Belle Weaver, Jan. 9, 1943; children—Dan DeForest, Richard Randolph. Mgr., Allen C. Kaye Martin Prodns., Chgo., 1945-46; owner, operator Muzak Corp., Waco, Tex., New Orleans, Oklahoma City, 1946-50; gen. and comml. mgr. Radio Sta. WACO, 1952-54; operations mgr. Stas. KFDA-AM and KFDA-TV, Amarillo, Tex., 1954-57; mgr. Dallas sales office KFJZ-TV, Ft. Worth, 1957; mgr. Radio Sta. KIXL, Dallas, 1957-64; partner, owner Strauss Broadcasting Co., Radio Stas. KCEE AM/FM Tucson, KIXL AM/FM, WGKA AM/FM, Atlanta, 1964-70, pres., 1970-72; pres. Dan Hayslett & Assos., broadcast broker and cons., 1972—. Served as capt. USAAF, 1941-45, USAF, 1950-52. Decorated Air medal. Mem. Assn. Broadcasting Execs. Tex. (past pres.), Sales and Marketing Execs. (v.p.), Nat. Assn. Broadcasters, Nat. Assn. Broadcasters, Record Industry Assn. Am., Dallas Advt. League. Home: 10607 Boedeker St Dallas TX 75230 Office: 1401 S Akard St Dallas TX 75215

HAYSLIP, MARCIA KAY SAMPSON, artist, interior designer; b. Houston; d. James Willard and Dorothy (Compton) Sampson; student U. Tex. 1956-58, Flint Inst. of Arts, 1966-68; m. William L. Hayslip, Oct. 26, 1956 (div. Jan. 1966); children—Mark Lane, Craig Compton, Wendell Grant, Andrea Leigh. Interior designer Marcia Hayslip Ltd., Houston, 1957—. Artist, 1966—; one-man show, 1967; art tchr., Houston, 1968—. Vol. com. chmn. fund raising drives Contemporary Art Mus., Houston Symphony, Mus. Fine Arts, Heritage Soc. 1962-64. Mem. Zool. Soc. Home: 241 Bylane St Houston TX 77024 Office: 1721 S Post Oak St Houston TX 77027

HAYWARD, OLGA LORETTA HINES (MRS. SAMUEL E. HAYWARD), librarian; b. Alexandria, La.; d. Samuel James and Lillie (George) Hines; A.B., Dillard U., 1941; B.S. in L.S., Atlanta U., 1944; M.A., U. Mich., 1959; m. Samuel E. Hayward, July 12, 1945; children—Anne Elizabeth, Olga Patricia. Tchr., Marksville (La.) High Schs., 1941-42; head librarian Grambling (La.) Coll., 1944-46; br. librarian br. nine New Orleans Pub. Library System, 1947-48; reference librarian, asso. prof. So. U., Baton Rouge, 1948—. Active Girl Scouts U.S.A. Bd. dirs. La. Diocese Episcopal Community Services. Mem. Am., La. library assns., Nat. Assn. Coll. Women, Am. Assn. U. Profs. Episcopalian. Author: Graduate Theses of Southern University 1959-71; Publication Number One, also other bibliographies. Home: 1632 Harding Blvd Baton Rouge LA 70807

HAYWOOD, WILLIAM THOMAS, coll. exec.; b. Columbia, Tenn., May 25, 1928; s. William Thomas and Frances (Stone) H.; student Millsaps Coll., 1945-46, Bowling Green Bus. U., 1948-49; B.B.A., U. Miss., 1951; postgrad. Tulane U., 1958-60; LL.D., Atlanta Law Sch., 1969; m. Sylvia Anne Graham, Nov. 25, 1954; children—William Thomas, Sylvia Annette, Robert Alton, Susan Lynne. Bus. mgr., instr. accounting and econs. East Central Jr. Coll., 1951-58; purchasing agt. Tulane U., 1958-59, chief accountant, 1959-60; bus. mgr., instr. econs. Mercer U., Macon, Ga., 1960-67, sec. corp., 1960—, v.p. for bus. and finance, 1967—; instr. econs. Miss. State U., 1954-56. Cons. Ford Found. N.Y.C., 1963-64; sec. Walter F. George Sch. Law Found., Macon, 1963—. Trustee, v.p. Common Fund Non-Profit Instns., 1969—. Served with USNR, 1946-48. Mem. So. (pres. 1968-69), Nat. (dir., 1969—, (pres. 1972-73) assns. coll. and univ. bus. officers, Nat. Assn. Edn. Buyers (pres. 1967-68), So. Assn. Colls. and Schs. (policies and functions com.), Beta Alpha Psi, Delta Sigma Pi, Lambda Chi Alpha. Elk. Club: Idle Hour Golf and Country (Macon). Contbr. articles to profl. publs. Home: 1546 Linden Av Macon GA 31207

HAZAM, LOUIS JOSEPH, TV producer; b. Norwich, Conn., Jan. 3, 1911; s. George John and Afifi (Habeeb) H.; B.A. in Journalism, Columbia, 1933; m. Ruby Gene Hymer, Oct. 30, 1939; children—Nancy Lynn, Chad Thomas. Script writer U.S. Dept. Interior, 1938-45; freelance writer for radio and TV, 1945-59; TV producer, writer NBC News, Washington, 1959—. Mem. bd. Council Internat. Nontheatrical Events, Washington. Recipient Christopher award, 1960; George Foster Peabody award, 1961; Bronze award Venice Film Festival, 1962, 1st place for documentary, 1963; Golden Gate award San Francisco Internat. Film Festival, 1963, 64, 66, 71. Mem. Nat. Acad. Television Arts and Scis. (Emmy award 1961-62), Radio and Television Corrs. Assn., Writers Guild. Club: Nat. Press (Wasington). Producer, writer: Way of the Cross, 1960; Vincent Van Gogh, 1961; US, 1962; River Nile, 1963; Shakespeare: Soul of an Age, 1963; Greece: The Golden Age, 1964; Michelangelo, The Last Giant (Part I), 1965, (Part II), 1966; The National Gallery of Art, 1967; The Art Game, 1968; Sahara, La Caravane Du Sel, 1969; Venice Be Damned, 1971. Office: 4001 Nebraska Av NW Washington DC 20016

HAZARD, JAMES OVINGTON, JR., elec. engr.; b. nr. Doylestown, Pa., May 7, 1918; s. James Ovington and Emma (Backus) H.; B.S., Tenn. Polytech. Inst., 1943; m. Rosemary Jensen, Aug. 11, 1943; children—James O. III, Robert F. Elec. engr. Norfolk (Va.) Navy Yard, 1943-44; field engr. Manhattan project, Tenn. Eastman Co., Oak Ridge, 1944-46; plant engr. Rohm & Haas Co., Knoxville, Tenn., 1946-49; design engr. TVA, 1949-55; project engr., engr. operation supr. AEDC, ARO, Inc., Arnold Air Force Sta., Tenn., 1955—, Mem. Nat., Tenn. (state dir. 1963-66) socs. profl. engrs. Presbyn. Mason. Home: 214 Jackson Circle Tullahoma TN 37388 Office: ARO Inc Arnold Air Force Station TN 37389

HAZELRIGG, HAROLD THEODORE, pub. relations exec.; b. Oklahoma City, Apr. 22, 1923; s. Harold T. and Talma (Groves) H.; grad. Riverside Mil. Acad., 1940; B.A., Okla. State U., 1947; m. Bonnie Sue Moore, Jan. 31, 1947; children—Richard Dean, Nancy Kate; m. Lucile S. Langton, Jan. 28, 1966; children—James V. Scruggs, William S. Langton. News editor The Citizen, 1947-48; pub. relations dir. Sam Houston area council Boy Scouts Am., 1948-50; program dir. Sta. KCOH, Houston, 1950-51; advt. dir. Graybar Electric Co., 1951-53; pub. relations counselor Kemp & Hazelrigg, Houston, 1953-61; pres. Hal Hazelrigg, Inc., 1961-65; dir. pub. relations and advt. Brown & Root, Inc and asso. cos., 1965-72; pub. relations counselor Hazelrigg & Whitmore, Houston, 1972—. Dir. Houston Community Council, 1958-61; mem. exec. com. Family and Child Welfare, 1957-61; mem. exec. com. Houston Crime Commn., 1956-61, 65, 67. Spl. counsel to Com. 75, U. Tex., 1958-59; dir. Vol Community Services, 1957-61. Vice pres. dir., U. Houston Alumni Inter-fraternity Council, 1958-59. Trustee, Merit Shop Found., Ltd. Served with A.S.T.P., 14th Armored Div., AUS, World II. Mem. Am. Arab Soc. (dir.), Pub. Relations Soc. Am. (past pres., dir. Houston chpt., nat. assemblyman), Assn. Petroleum Writers, Asso. Builders and Contractors (nat. sec.), Okla. State U. Alumni Assn. (past pres.), Tex. Good Roads Assn. (past dir.), S.A.R., Houston C. of C., Blue Key, Sigma Delta Chi, Sigma Phi Epsilon. Episcopalian. Clubs: Warwick, World Trade, Houston, Rivers Plantation Country, University, Plaza. Home: 17323 Rolling Creek Houston TX 77090 Office: PO Box 3 Houston TX 77001

HEAD, PHILIP WAYNE, physician; b. Fort Smith, Ark., July 6, 1937; s. Herbert Haskell and Lessie Lee (Phillips) H.; B.S., Northeastern State Coll., Okla., 1960; M.D., Okla. U., 1964; m. Alethea Irene Tucker, June 1, 1958; children—Lori Andrea, Alissa Lynette. Intern St. Joseph's Hosp., Wichita, Kan., 1964-65; pvt. practice medicine, Carnegie, Okla., 1965-72, Miami, Okla., 1972—. Pres. Carnegie Health Service, Inc., Head's Hand Weapons. Fellow Am. Geriatrics Soc.; mem. A.M.A., Am. Acad. Family Practice, So., Mid South, Okla. med. assns., Okla. Acad. Gen. Practice, Royal Soc. Health (London), Am. Coll. Emergency Physicians, Miami Jr. C. of C. Mason (Shriner), Kiwanian (pres. 1965-71. Home: 1400 15th St NE Miami OK 74354 Office: 201 W Central St Miami OK 74354

HEAD, ROBERT GRADY, pub. co. exec.; b. Memphis, Tenn., Jan. 7, 1942; s. Robert Grady and Nell Louise (Langham) H.; student Oberlin Coll., 1959-60, U. Guanajuanto (Mexico), summer, 1962, Tulane U., 1962-63, U. Dublin (Ireland), 1964-65. Editor, Nola Express, New Orleans, 1968—. Author: Sancticity; (with Darlene Fife) After Word Comes Weird, 1969. Address: Box 2342 New Orleans LA 70116 Home: 1212 Royal St New Orleans LA 70116

HEADLEY, ANNE RENOUF (MRS. JOHN MILES HEADLEY), environmental planner; b. N.Y.C., Apr. 3, 1937; d. Henry Charles and Helen (Donovan) Renouf; grad. Emma Willard Sch., 1954; A.B., Bernard Coll., 1959; M.A., Yale, 1962, Ph.D., 1966; postgrad. Duke Law Sch., 1971—; m. John Miles Headley, July 27, 1965. Asst. prof. dept. polit. sci. U. N.C., Chapel Hill, 1966-71; legal asso., 1971-72; environmental planner. Sr. faculty fellow U.S. Dept. State, 1967; sr. staff mem., vis. research scholar Carnegie Endowment for Internat. Peace, 1968-69; mem. Nat. Adv. Council on Grad. Edn., 1970—. Mem. Nat. Com. for the Sanger Meml., 1969—. Woodrow Wilson fellow, 1958. Mem. Am. Polit. Sci. Assn., Am. Acad. Cons., Am. Soc. Internat. Law, Internat. Studies Assn., The Innovation Group, Tech. and Communication, Phi Beta Kappa. Democrat. Home: 603 Laurel Hill Rd Chapel Hill NC 27514

HEADLEY, JESSE MELVIN, banker; b. Clanton, Ala., Oct. 8, 1928; s. Lee and Maggie Louize (Keith) H.; grad. high sch.; m. Mary Eunice Thompson, Apr. 9, 1950; children—Belinda (Mrs. Roy R. Price), Gary Melvin. With 1st Nat. Bank, Clanton, 1952—, cashier, 1957, v.p., 1970—. Served with AUS, 1946-48. Lion. Home: Lay Dam Rd Clanton AL 35045 Office: 501 2d Av N Clanton AL 35045

HEALD, ROBERT L., lawyer; b. Sioux City, Ia., Jan. 22, 1917; A.B. cum laude, Miami, U., Oxford, O., 1939; M.A., Western Res. U. (now Case Western Res. U.), 1940; J.D., Georgetown U., 1947. Admitted to D.C. bar, 1946, U.S. Supreme Ct. bar, 1949, Md. bar, 1952; spl. agt. FBI, 1941-46; clk. U.S. Ct. Appeals judge, Washington, 1946-47; cons. U.S. Joint Congl. Com. Atomic Energy, 1949-50; asst. counsel U.S. Senate com. fgn. relations, 1950; chief atty. Nat. Assn. Radio and TV Broadcasters, 1955-57; now mem. firm Fletcher, Heald, Rowell, Kenehan & Hildreth, Washington. Mem. Bar Assn. D.C., Am., Fed. Communications (pres. 1968-69) bar assns., Phi Beta Kappa. Address: 1225 Connecticut Av NW Washington DC 20036

HEALY, GEORGE WILLIAM, JR., editor; b. Natchez, Miss., Sept. 22, 1905; s. George William and Rosa Lee (Longmire) H.; A.B., U. Miss., 1926; m. Margaret Hoy Alford, Sept. 22, 1927; children—George William 3d, Floyd Alford (dec.). Corr., A.P. and several newspapers while at coll.; reporter Knoxville (Tenn.) Sentinel, 1926; with Times-Picayune, New Orleans, 1926—, as reporter, then city editor, 1931, mng. editor, 1936, editor, 1952-64, mng. editor Times-Picayune and New Orleans States, exec. editor, 1964-69, editor Times-Picayune, 1969—; treas. Times-Picayune Pub. co., 1939; v.p., 1942—, dir., 1948—; dir. A.P., 1957-66, v.p., 1965-66; lectr. (part time) Tulane U., 1946-52; dir. domestic branch. OWI, on leave from Times-Picayune, 1944; cons. on domestic problems, OWI, 1945. Mem. nat. council U.S.O., 1963—; chmn. New Orleans chpt. A.R.C., 1956-58. Trustee Jefferson Mil. Coll., 1950-62, Am. Heritage Found.; dir. Advt. Council, Inc., 1954-60. Decorated caballere Order de Cristobal Colon (Dominican Republic) 1946; Order Leopold II (Belgium), 1956; Star of Solidarity (Italy). Mem. A.P. Mng. Editors Assn. (chmn. 1943-46), Am. Soc. Newspaper Editors (pres. 1958-59), Inter Am. Press Assn. (dir. 1950-58), S.A.R. (pres. La Soc. 1951), Navy League U.S. (nat. historian 1967-71), Internat. House (v.p. 1964-67). Sigma Nu, Sigma Delta Chi (pres. 1946). Democrat.

Methodist. Mason. Clubs: Recess (pres. 1947-48). Southern Yacht (past gov.), Boston, Louisiana (New Orleans); Nat. Press (Washington); Circumnavigators (N.Y.C.); Mt. Kenya Safari (East Africa). Pass Christian (Miss.) Yacht. Home: 2110 State St New Orleans LA 70118 Office: 3800 Howard Av New Orleans LA 70140

HEALY, PATRICK, cons.; b. Los Angeles, Apr. 30, 1910; s. Patrick and Mary (Sedwick) H.; A.B., Amherst Coll., 1932, LL.D. (hon.), 1972; postgrad. Syracuse U., 1932-33; m. Ruth Potter Snagg, May 26, 1934 (dec. Jan. 1955); 1 son, Patrick IV; m. 2d. Martha Ann Dumke, June 3, 1957; children—Edmund, Nancy Lee. Field cons. League Va. Municipalities, 1933-34; exec. dir. N.C. League Municipalities, 1934-42; editor-pub. Southern City, 1937-42; owner-mgr. Pepsi-Cola Bottling Co., Ogden, Utah, 1946-55; chmn. Utah Tax Commn., 1950-54; exec. v.p. Nat. League of Cities, Washington, D.C., 1954-72; editor Nation's Cities, 1963-72; pres. Am. Inst. for Municipal Research, Edn. and Tng., Inc., 1958-72, League Cities-Conf. Mayors, 1967-72; sec. Urban Studies, Inc., 1960—; v.p., pres. U.S. sect. Internat. Union Local Authorities, 1971—; dir. Pub. Tech., Inc., 1970-72, Unicon Parking Structures, Inc., 1971—. U.S. del. Internat. Congress Local Authorities, Rome, 1955, The Hague, 1957, Berlin, 1959, Tel Aviv, 1960, Brussels, 1963, Stockholm, 1965, Inter-Am. Municipal Congress, San Juan, 1954, Panama, 1956, Rio de Janeiro, 1958, San Diego, 1960, Punta del Este, 1962, Caracas, 1966; v.p. Internat. Union Local Authorities, The Hague, 1971—; trustee Pub. Adminstrn. Service, Chgo., 1955-72; mem. U.S. Census Adv. Com. on State and Local Govt. Statistics, 1956-72; mem. dept. urban transp. planning Hwy. Research bd. Nat. Acad. Scis., 1962-72; adv. council on police tng. Internat. Assn. Chiefs of Police, 1964-72; mem. Pres.'s Com. on Employment of Handicapped, 1963-72, Pres.'s Nat. Adv. Council on Extension and Continuing Edn., 1966-69. Chmn. Weber County (Utah) Republican Central Com., 1946-50, chmn. 1st Utah Congl. Dist. Rep. Com., 1946-50; del. Rep. Nat. Conv., 1948; candidate for mayor of Ogden, 1947. Mem. adv. council Internat. Eye Found.; bd. dirs. Govtl. Affairs Inst., Washington, 1969—. Served to lt. comdr. USNR, World War II; comdr. Res. Recipient Order of Municipal Merit, Inter-American Municipal Orgn., 1968; Exceptional Govtl. Leadership award Internat. Inst. Municipal Clks., 1970; Distinguished Pub. Service award U.S. Conf. Mayors, 1972. Mem. U.S. C. of C. (co-chmn. nat. urban leadership adv. council 1968-72), Am. Soc. Pub. Adminstrn., Internat. City Mgmt. Assn. (hon.), Am. Soc. Assn. Execs., Internat. Municipal Parking Congress, Nat. Trust for Historic Preservation, Psi Upsilon. Episcopalian. Mason (Shriner). Clubs: Weber (Ogden); Chevy Chase, International, Nat. Capital Trap and Skeet, Army and Navy, Nat. Press (Washington). Author reports. Mem. editorial bd. Jour. Law and Edn., 1971—. Home: 2500 Calvert St NW Washington DC 20008 Office: 1620 I St NW Washington DC 20006

HEALY, ROBERT EDWARD, advt. exec.; b. Bklyn., Aug. 15, 1904; s. Walter F. and Florence E. (Davis) H.; grad. Dwight Prep. Sch., N.Y.C., 1924; student Pace Inst., N.Y.C., 1924-26; D.S.C. (hon.), Pace Coll., 1961; m. Lilie Rose, Aug. 3, 1927; children—Lilie Jane, Patricia Anne, Robert E. (dec.); m. 2d, Wayne Clark, Jan. 11, 1957; children—Edward W., James D. Salesman, T.J. Adikes, Jamaica, N.Y., 1926, Hoover Co., 1927-28; asst. to v.p. charge sales promotion Johns-Manville Co., 1929-33; mgr. prodn. sect. advt. dept. Colgate-Palmolive Co., Jersey City, 1934-36, asst. advt. mgr. 1936-39, brand advt. mgr., 1939-42, gen. advt. mgr., 1942-46, v.p. charge advt., 1946-52; v.p., treas., dir., mem. exec. com. McCann-Erickson, Inc., 1952-53, v.p., gen. mgr., dir., mem. exec. com., 1953-54, gen. mgr. N.Y. office, 1954, exec. v.p., 1955-58, vice chmn. bd., 1958-60, chmn. bd., 1960-62, mem. finance com., 1957-61; chmn. bd. McCann-Erickson Corp. (Internat.), 1956-58; pres. Interpublic, S.A., Geneva, Switzerland, 1962-65; exec. v.p. Interpublic Group Cos., Inc., 1965-67, pres., 1967-71, chief exec. officer, 1967-71, chmn. bd., mem. finance com., 1968—. Mem. adv. council Pace Coll. Clubs: N.Y. Athletic; Rod and Reel (Miami Beach); Ocean Reef; Confrerie de la Chaine des Rotisseurs; Paris American. Home: 1111 Crandon Blvd Key Biscayne FL 33149 Office: 1271 Av of Americas New York City NY 10020

HEARD, (GEORGE) ALEXANDER, univ. chancellor; b. Savannah, Ga., Mar. 14, 1917; s. Richard Willis and Virginia Lord (Nisbet) H.; A.B., U. N.C., 1938, LL.D., 1968; M.A., Columbia U. 1948, Ph.D., 1951, LL.D., 1965; m. Laura Jean Keller, June 17, 1949; children—Stephen Keller, Christopher Cadek, Francis Muir, Cornelia Lord. With Depts. Interior, War and State, U.S. Govt. Service, 1939-43; research asso. Bur. Pub. Adminstrn., U. Ala., 1946-49; asso. prof. polit. sci. U. N.C., 1950-51, prof. polit. sci., 1952-63, dean Grad. Sch., 1958-63; chancellor, prof. polit. sci. Vanderbilt U., Nashville, 1963—. Ford research prof. govt. Harvard, 1957-58. Dir., Time, Inc., 1968—. Bd. dirs. Citizens Research Found., 1958-71, pres., 1968-71; trustee Ford Found., 1967—, chmn., 1972—; chmn. President's Commn. on Campus Costs, 1961-62; mem. U.S. Adv. Commn. Intergovtl. Relations, 1967-69; spl. adviser to Pres. on campus affairs, 1970. Served from ensign to lt. USNR, 1943-46. Mem. Internat., Am. (exec. council 1956-58, v.p. 1962-63), So. (exec. council 1951-54, pres. 1961-62) polit. sci. assns.; Phi Beta Kappa, Sigma Alpha Epsilon, Pi Sigma Alpha. Democrat. Episcopalian. Clubs: Belle Meade Country (Nashville); Century (N.Y.C.); Cosmos (Washington). Author: A Two-Party South 1952; Southern Politics in State and Nation (asst. to V. O. Key, Jr.), 1949; Southern Primaries and Elections (with Donald S. Strong), 1950; The Costs of Democracy, 1960, rev. edit., 1962; The Lost Years in Graduate Education, 1963. Contbr. to periodicals. Office: Kirkland Hall Vanderbilt University Nashville TN 37240

HEARD, LUTHER MARTIN, JR., real estate broker; b. Elberton, Ga., Apr. 17, 1906; s. Luther Martin and Mamie (Latimer) H.; B.S., Clemson Coll., 1928; m. Miriam Dean, Nov. 9, 1933; children—Miriam Dean (Mrs. William K. Stoddard), Anne Latimer (Mrs. John W. Stokes, Jr.), Margaret McGee (Mrs. George Rea Walker, Jr.). Tchr. math. Laurens (S.C.) High Sch., 1929; salesman J. M. Tull Metal & Supply Co., Atlanta, 1930; adjustor Comml. Credit Co., Birmingham, Ala., 1931, with credit dept., Atlanta, 1932, indsl. mgr., 1933-35, mgr., Mobile, Ala., 1935; sec.-treas. McGee Dean Cotton Co., Leland, Miss., 1936-39; partner-mgr. Porter & Heard, Leland, 1940-52; owner-mgr. Heard & Co., Leland, 1945-51, Martin Heard, Realtor, Leland, 1951—. Miss. levee commr., 1956—, pres. bd. commrs., 1965—; exec. com. Lower Miss. Valley Flood Control Assn., 1965—; vice chmn. Delta Council Flood Control com., 1965—. Served to capt., CAC, AUS, 1942-44. Baptist (deacon). Rotarian (pres. Leland 1970-71). Home: 310 Deer Creek Dr SW Leland MS 38756 Office: 209 Broad St Leland MS 38756

HEARIN, ROBERT MATLOCK, banker; b. Demopolis, Ala., Dec. 9, 1916; s. Jesse Bethea and Johnnie (Kennedy) H.; B.A., U. Ala., 1939; m. Annie Laurie Swain, June 27, 1940; children—Annie Laurie, Robert Matlock. Land man United Gas Co., 1939-53, mgr. transmission and prodn. facilities Miss., Ala., Fla., 1953-56; vice chmn. First Nat. Bank of Jackson, Miss., 1956-58, pres., 1958-69, chmn. bd., chief exec. officer, 1969—; pres. First Capital Corp., dir. Miss. Power & Light Co., Lamar Life Ins. Co., First Miss. Corp., Miss. Valley Title Ins. Co., Amerada Hess Corp., S. Central Bell Telephone Co.; chmn. bd. Intersystems, Inc. Chmn., Miss. Arts Center. Bd. dirs. Piney Woods Sch. Mem. Mid-Continent Oil and Gas Assn., Sigma Alpha Epsilon. Home: 139 Woodland Dr Jackson MS 39216 Office: PO Box 291 Jackson MS 39205

HEARIN, W.J., pres., publisher Mobile (Ala.) Press-Register. Address: 304 Government St Mobile AL 36630

HEARN, JAMES WOODROW, clergyman; b. McIntyre, La., Mar. 7, 1931; s. John Elton and Alta (Fordham) H.; B.A., La. Poly. Inst., 1952; S.T.B., Boston U., 1955, Th.D., 1965; m. Elizabeth Anne Connaughton, Aug. 25, 1952; children—John Mark, Paul Woodrow, Diana Elizabeth, Bruce Charles. Ordained to ministry Methodist Ch., 1953; pastor Center Point Meth. Ch., Jonesboro, La., 1950-52, Wellington Community Meth. Ch., Medford, Mass., 1953-56, Davidson Meml. Meth. Ch., Lafayette, La., 1956-60; asso. pastor First Meth. Ch., Shreveport, La., 1960-64; pastor Elysian Fields Meth. Ch., New Orleans, 1964-66; exec. dir. Ft. Worth Area Council Chs., 1966-69; dir. program council La. Ann. Conf., United Meth. Ch., Shreveport, 1969—. Chmn. bd. Christian Social Concerns, La. Conf., Meth. Ch., 1964-68; mem. com. on research and planning and jurisdiction council South Central jurisdiction United Meth. Ch., 1969—; mem. Bishop's Linkage Group as personal rep. at Nat. Div. Missions, 1969—; chmn. Nat. Fellowship Program Council Dirs., 1971—. Mem. community relations com., Fort Worth, 1966-67; mem. cabinet Tarrant County United Fund, 1968; mem. exec. com. Longhorn council Boy Scouts Am., 1968-69. Recipient Distinguished Service award Tex. Safety Council, 1967, 68. Rotarian. Clubs: Ridglea Country (Ft. Worth); East Ridge Country (Shreveport). Home: 316 S Wickford Circle Shreveport LA 71105 Office: 100 E Kings Hwy Shreveport LA 71104

HEARON, SHELBY REED (MRS. ROBERT J. HEARON, JR.), writer; b. Marion, Ky., Jan. 18, 1931; d. Charles Boogher and Evelyn Shelby (Roberts) Reed; B.A. with honors, U. Tex., 1953; m. Robert J. Hearon, Jr., June 15, 1953; children—Anne Shelby, Robert Reed. Bookkeeper, Washington and Austin, Tex., 1953-59; free lance writer, pub. in McCall's, Redbook, 1966—. Pres. Planned Parenthood Bd., Austin, 1959-61. Mem. Authors Guild, Authors League Am., English Speaking Union, Jr. League Austin (pres. 1969-70), Pi Beta Phi. Democrat. Methodist. Author: Armadillo In The Grass, 1968; Small Expectations, 1970. Home: 4601 Cat Mountain Dr Austin TX 78731

HEARST, JOSEPH FRANCIS, journalist; b. St. Joseph, Mo., Nov. 27, 1901; s. Loren Andrew and Frances (Dunn) H.; grad. high sch.; m. Susan E. Gogerty, Feb. 6, 1932. Former reporter St. Joseph News Press, Kansas City (Mo.) Star, Internat. News Service, United Press; mem. staff Chgo. Tribune, 1943—, corr. Washington bur. Chgo. Tribune Press Service, 1944—. Mem. White House Corrs. Assn. Roman Catholic. Club: Nat. Press (Washington) Home: 4301 Columbia Pike Arlington VA 22204 Office: 1750 Pennsylvania Av NW Washington DC 20006

HEARTZ, FREDERICK RICHARD, cons. civil engr.; b. Exeter, N.H., May 12, 1921; s. Harold Francis and Catherine Mary (McEnhill) H.; B.S., U. N.H., 1944; M.S., Mo. Sch. Mines and Metallurgy, 1949; m. Barbara Louise Goodrich, June 19, 1944; 1 son, William Thomas. Asso. prof. S.D. State Coll., Brookings, 1949-57; sr. v.p. Tanner, Thomsom, D'alli & Heartz, Inc., Melbourne, Fla., 1957-61; pres. Heartz Engring. & Testing Co., Inc., Palm Bay, Fla., 1961—; lead engr. Radiation, Inc., Palm Bay, 1967-70. Instr. civil engring. Mo. Sch. Mines and Metallurgy, S.D. State Coll. Registered profl. engr., Fla., S.D. Mem. Fla. Engring. Soc., Nat. Soc. Profl. Engrs., Am. Soc. C.E., Am. Soc. Mil. Engrs., Am. Concrete Inst., Palm Bay C. of C. (v.p. 1965). Rotarian. Club: Melbourne Yacht. Home: 225 Worth Ct Palm Bay FL 32905 Office: PO Box 67 Palm Bay FL 32905

HEATH, CHARLES RAYMOND, hosp. adminstr.; b. Duck Hill, Miss., Aug. 11, 1924; s. John Arthur and Zelma Irene (Greer) H.; D.V.M., Tex. A. and M. U., 1947; postgrad. U. Ala., 1969-70; m. Esther Maudine Riley, May 8, 1949; children—Susan (Mrs. James Ronald Robertson), Charles Raymond, Cynthia Irene. Pvt. practice vet. medicine, Winona, Miss., 1947-67; adminstr. Tyler Holmes Meml. Hosp., Winona, 1967—. Owner Registered Angus Ranch, 1952-72. Pres. North Delta Hosp. Council, 1970. Served with USAAF, 1942. USPHS Tng. grantee for health services adminstr. devel. program, 1969-70. Mem. Am. Vet. Med. Assn., Am., Miss. hosp. assns. Baptist (deacon 1958-72). Rotarian. Home: 431 Tyler Holmes St Winona MS 38967 Office: 1 Tyler Holmes St Winona MS 38967

HEATH, FRANK BRADFORD, dentist; b. Houston, Dec. 11, 1938; s. Robert Bradford and Maudie (Sweeney) H.; B.S., Sam Houston State U., 1961; D.D.S., U. Tex., 1965; m. Heide Jutta Marianne Schmidt, Aug. 20, 1965; children—Dirk Alan, Shannon Erika. Practice gen. dentistry, Houston, 1967—. Served with AUS, 1965-67. Mem. Houston Dist. Dental Soc., Xi Psi Phi, Delta Tau Delta. Methodist. Home: 12610 Mile Dr Houston TX 77040 Office: 12315 Jones Rd Houston TX 77040

HEATH, JAMES EDWARD, state ofcl.; b. El Paso, Tex., Oct. 26, 1938; s. Wayne Edward and Leah (Gibson) H.; B.B.A., Baylor U., 1962; m. Linda McCormick; children—Kellie Noel, Kimberly Kay. Mgr., Iowa Park C. of C., 1964; staff exec. Wichita Falls C. of C., 1964-65; mgr. Snyder Tex. C. of C., 1965-66; sr. indsl. devel. cons. Tex. Indsl. Commn., Austin, 1966-70, dir. indsl. prospect devel., 1970—. Mem. Tex. Indsl. Devel. Council, So. Indsl. Devel. Council. Served with USNR. Mem. U.S. Jr. C. of C., Tex. C. of C. Mgrs. Assn. Democrat. Mem. Ch. of Christ (deacon). Lion. Home: 1906 Sunny Brook St Austin TX 78723 Office: Tex Indsl Commn Capital Sta Box 12728 Austin TX 78711

HEATH, LESLIE ARTHUR, public accountant; b. Phila., Dec. 11, 1903; s. Albanus M. and Annie (Houpt) H.; student N.C. State Coll., 1951-52, Walton Sch. Commerce, 1921-27; LL.B., Am. Extension Sch. Law, 1949; student Exec. Program U. N.C., 1954-55; m. 2d, Margaret V. Biggers, April 11, 1955; children (by previous marriage)—Betty (Mrs. E. S. Shannonhouse), Leslie (dec.), James B., Murray A. Accountant Wolf & Co., 1921-26; resident mgr. Peat, Marwick, Mitchell & Co., 1926-42; prin. auditor RFC, 1942-44; v.p. finance Queen City Coach Co., 1944-52; pvt. practice as C.P.A., Charlotte, N.C., 1952-69; partner Heath and Myers, Charlotte 1969—. Sometime instr. U. N.C., Duke, Queens Coll.; past pres. N.C. State Bd. C.P.A. Examiners, Charlotte Exec. Program. C.P.A., N.C., Pa. Mem. A.I.M. (asso.), Am. Accounting Assn., N.C. (past pres.), Charlotte Area (pres.) assns. C.P.A.'s, Am. Inst. C.P.A.'s (com. profl. ethics), Rosicrucian. Episcopalian. Mason (Shriner), Home: 1333 Queens Rd Charlotte NC 28207 Office: 1229 Greenwood Cliff Charlotte NC 28204

HEATH, WILLIAM SCHLEY, bottling co. exec.; b. Cartersville, Ga., Dec. 7, 1914; s. Alfred Taylor and Ann D. (Howell) H.; B.S., Ga. Inst. Tech., 1936; m. Marian Elizabeth Bradford, May 21, 1946; children— Dorothy Caroline (Mrs. John Bristow Jackson). With Carolina Coca-Cola Bottling Co., Sumter, S.C., 1936—, dir., 1950—, sec., 1956—, treas., 1959—. Chmn. United Fund drive, 1954, Shaw-Sumter Community Council, 1956-68, City-County Health Dept. Bd., 1957-60, S.C. Hwy. Safety Commn., 1962, City-County Devel. Bd., 1966-68. Bd. dirs. YMCA. Served from 2d lt. to lt. col., Arty., 1940-45. Decorated Bronze Star medal. Mem. Kappa Sigma. Elk, Rotarian. Home: 72 Paisley Park Sumter SC 29150 Office: 712 E Liberty St Sumter SC 29150

HEBERT, ACHILLE CHARLES, elec. engr., educator; b. Boley, Okla., Aug. 2, 1910; s. William Edward and Blanche Julia Ann (Leon) H.; B.S. in Elec. Engring., Kan. State U., 1933; M.S., Okla. State U., Stillwater, 1965; m. Barbara Jane Copeland, Oct. 19, 1942; children—Carole Eloise (Mrs. Summers), Achille Charles II, Michael Rand. Asst. engr. State Hosp., Taft, Okla., 1934-37; chief engr. State Hosp., also Deaf, Blind and Orphans Inst., Taft, 1937; supt. bldgs. and grounds Langston U., 1937-38; tchr. engring., Langston U., 1938-47, surplus property procurement officer, mgr. Vets. Housing Project, 1947-61, dir. phys. plant operation, 1952—, dir. div. tech. and vocational edn. Langston U., 1962-66; head dept. applied physics James Connally Campus of Tex. State Tech. Inst., Waco, 1966—. Served as 1st lt. AUS, 1943-45; comdg. officer Service Co., 377th Inf. Res., 1954-59; capt. Res., 1955—. Mem. I.E.E.E., N.E.A., Okla. Edn. Assn., Am. Vocational Assn., Am. Soc. Tech. Edn., Okla. Indsl. Arts Assn., Okla. (bd.), Tex. tech. socs., Midstate Minutemen Okla., Am. Platform Assn., Am. Tech. Edn. Assn., Am. Legion, Alpha Phi Alpha, Iota Lambda Sigma, Phi Delta Kappa. Roman Catholic. Contbr. articles to Jour. Tech., Okla. Indsl. Arts News.Address: 312 Stead Dr Waco TX 76705

HEBERT, ADAM OTIS, JR., state ofcl.; b. Abbeville, La., Sept. 22, 1930; s. Adam Otis and Etta (Babineaux) H.; B.A., U. Southwestern La., 1952; M.Ed., La. State U., 1958, M.A., 1959; m. Elsie Stallworth, Aug. 7, 1965; stepchildren—Richard Stallworth, Darryl Stallworth. Tchr., Erath (La.) High Sch., 1952, 54-57, Port Allen (La.) High Sch., 1963; instr. Southeastern La. Coll., Hammond, 1959; grad. asst. La. State U., Baton Rouge, 1959-63; asst. prof. history Nicholls State Coll., Thibodaux, La., 1963-66; archivist Catholic Diocese, Baton Rouge, 1964-66; dir. La. Archives and Records, Baton Rouge, 1966—. Chmn. La. Hist. Preservation and Cultural Commn., 1968-70. Served with AUS, 1952-54. Mem. Soc. Am. Archivist, So., La. (sec.-treas.), Attakdpas hist. assns. Editor: (with Harry T. Williams) Louisiana in the Civil War: A Chronology, 1959—; Louisiana History, 1962-63. Contbr. articles to profl. jours. Home: 370 Nassau Dr Baton Rouge LA 70815 Office: PO Box 44222 Capitol Sta Baton Rouge LA 70804

HEBERT, CHARLES EDWARD, JR., dentist; b. New Roads, La., Mar. 11, 1918; s. Charles Edward and Marie (Hymel) H.; student La. State U., 1934-35; D.D.S., Loyola U., New Orleans, 1940; m. Gertrude Alford, Oct. 15, 1942; children—Charles E., Marilyn (Mrs. Richard Hebert), Lucillel (Mrs. Larry McCaskill), Mary Katherine, James A., Louis A. Practice gen. dentistry, New Roads, 1940—. Prin. livestock farm, New Roads, 1956—. Mem. Pointe Coupee Parish Sch. Bd., 1946-66. Served with USNR, 1942-46. Mem. Am. (trustee), La. (del. to Am. Dental Assn. 1961-69), 6th Dist. (past bd. dirs., past pres.) dental Assns., Pierre Fauchard Acad., Am. Legion, Am., Internat. colls. dentists, Omicron Kappa Upsilon, Delta Sigma Delta. Roman Catholic (mem. lay council). Lion, K.C. Club: False River Country. Home: 206 Richey St New Roads LA 70760 Office: 206 Richey St New Roads LA 70760

HEBERT, F. EDWARD, congressman, former editor; b. New Orleans, Oct. 12, 1901; s. Felix Joseph and Lea (Naquin) H.; student Tulane U., 1920-24; m. Gladys Bofill, Aug. 1, 1934; 1 dau., Dawn Marie. Sports reporter New Orleans Times-Picayune, 1919-20, asst. sports editor, 1920-25; asst. sports editor New Orleans States, 1925-26, polit. editor and columnist, 1929-37, city editor, 1937-40, when paper broke La. Scandals, 1939, resulting in overthrow of Huey Long Political machine (paper subsequently awarded Delta Sigma Chi plaque for courage in journalism); dir. publicity, Loyola U., New Orleans, 1926-29; dir. Central Savings & Loan Assn.; mem. 77th-92d congresses from 1st La. Dist., chmn. armed services com., 1971—. Pres., Young Men's Bus. Club of New Orleans, 1932. Mem. Delta Sigma Phi (nat. v.p. 1937-49). Democrat. Roman Catholic. Author: I Went, I saw, I Heard. Home: 5367 Canal Blvd New Orleans LA 70124 Office: House Office Bldg Washington DC 20515

HEBERT, GEORGE N., oil co. exec.; b. Lake Charles, La., May 24, 1921; s. George W. and Ethel (Landry) H.; student U. Southwestern La., 1938-40; m. Elva Kiplinger, Nov. 8, 1941; 1 dau., Dianne (Mrs. Cyrus Miller, Jr.). Clk., La. dist. office Shell Oil Co., Iowa, La., 1939-41; salesman Kelly, Weber & Co., Lake Charles, La., 1941-43; mechanic M.W. Kellog Co., Lake Charles, 1943-44; various supervisory positions Cities Service Refining Corp., Lake Charles, 1944-50, editor Citiesentinel, 1950-61; Petroleum Chem., Inc. exchanger Cities Service Lake Charles Operations, 1961-62, asst. mgr. pub. relations, 1962-63, mgr. pub. relations, 1963-67; mgr. pub. relations Cities Service Oil Co., Tulsa, 1967—. Lectr. journalism U. Tulsa, 1971—. Recipient awards Freedoms Found.; annually 1951-62; award for best editorial Soc. Indsl. Editors, 1956, spl. award for origination and implementation of opinion research program Okla. Petroleum Council, 1971. Mem. Assn. Petroleum Writers, Am. Petroleum Inst. (pub. relations adv. com. 1967—), Pub. Relations Soc. Am. (Tulsa pres. 1970—), Okla Petroleum Council (chmn. pub. relations com. 1971—), Tulsa C. of C. (chmn. pub. relations com. 1969). Clubs: Tulsa Petroleum; Press. Home: 611 W 15th St Tulsa OK 74127 Office: PO Box 300 Tulsa OK 74102

HECHT, M(ORTON) ROBERT, investment exec.; b. Galveston, Tex., Dec. 16, 1934; s. Edmund M. and Mae (Leitner) H.; student U. Tex., 1950-52, U. Houston, 1952-55, Baylor U., 1955-57; m. Shirley Miller, Dec. 29, 1956; children—Michael Robert, Kathryn Ann. Partner, Hecht Ins. Agy., Houston, 1957—; pres. Keystone Homes, Inc., Houston, 1958—; exec. v.p. Mortgage Co. of Am., Houston, 1965—; chmn. bd., dir. MCA Financial Corp., Del., 1968—, Peden Industries, Inc., Nev., 1969—; dir. Am. Mchts. Life Ins. Co., Citizens Bank, Houston, Oak Forest Bank, Houston. Gen. chmn. Appeal for Human Relations, Houston, 1969, Houston United Jewish Campaign, 1971, 72. Bd. dirs. Jewish Family Service, Jewish Community Council, Am. Jewish Com. Mem. Phi Epsilon Pi. Jewish religion. Mason (32 deg.). Club: Westwood Country (gov.). Home: 514 Timberwilde St Houston TX 77024 Office: 1 Shell Plaza Houston TX 77002

HECK, CARL EDWARD, JR., cons. civil engr.; b. Houma, La., Jan. 24, 1942; s. Carl Edward and Verna Mae (Talbot) H.; B.S. in Civil Engring., La. State U., 1964, J.D., 1968; m. Amelia Margaret Clement, Sept. 4, 1965; children—Carl Edward III, Timothy Clement, Michael, Braden. Admitted to La. bar, 1968; v.p. Carl Heck Engrs., Inc., cons. civil engrs., Houma, La., 1968—; partner Heck Realty Ltd., Houma, 1971—; v.p. Waubun Devel. Co., Thibodeux, La. Registered profl. engr., La. Mem. Am. Soc. C.E., La. Engring. Soc., La. Land Surveyors Assn., Nat. Soc. Profl. Engrs., La., Terrebonne bar assns., Houma C. of C., Sigma Tau Sigma, Phi Alpha Delta, Kappa Sigma. Club: Houma Kiwanis (dir. since 1970—). Contbr. law rev. articles. Home: 203 Malibou Blvd Houma LA 70360 Office: 511 School St Houma LA 70360

HEDBERG, LLOYD EUGENE, govt. ofcl.; b. St. Paul, Apr. 13, 1915; s. Jonas Gustav and Eugenia (Westerlund) H.; B.A., U. Minn., 1937; M.A., Georgetown U., 1945; postgrad. U. Md., 1962; m. Nancy

Irene DeLong, May 20, 1967. Adminstrv. officer Office of Emergency Mgmt., Exec. Office of Pres., 1942-44; exec. dir. Civilian Mil. Edn. Fund, 1945-47; spl. asst. Office Sec. of Air Force, 1948-50, 52-54; advisor to dir. tng. Dept. Air Force, 1950-52; research dir. Office Asst. Sec. of Def., Washington, 1954-57, staff dir. Res. Forces Policy Bd., 1957-70; adviser to auditor gen. AID, Washington, 1970-71; spl. asst. Office Asst. Sec. Transp. (Adminstrn.), Transp. Dept., Washington, 1971—. Editorial cons. to Operations & Policy Research, Inc., Washington, 1958—. Bd. dirs. Am. Peace Soc., Washington, 1965—, treas., 1967—; sec., bd. dirs. Helen Dwight Reid Ednl. Found., 1965—, trustee, 1962—; corp. mem. Coop. Research Inst., San Francisco, 1961—. Mem. Am. Polit. Sci. Assn., Am. Soc. for Pub. Adminstrn., Pi Sigma Alpha, Phi Alpha Theta. Home: 8830 Piney Branch Rd Silver Spring MD 20903 Office: Office of the Sec of Transportation Nassif Bldg Washington DC 20590

HEDERMAN, R.M., JR., publisher Jackson (Miss.) Clarion-Ledger and Daily News. Home: 1320 Belvoir Pl Jackson MS 39202 Office: 311 E Pearl St Jackson MS 39201*

HEDERMAN, THOMAS MARTIN, JR., newspaper editor; b. Jackson, Miss., May 23, 1911; s. Thomas Martin and Pearl (Smith) H.; B.A., Miss. Coll., 1932, LL.D., 1967; postgrad. Columbia, 1932-33; m. Bernice Flowers, May 11, 1938; children—Thomas Martin III (dec. USAF), Bernice (Mrs. Richard W. Hussey). Asso. editor Clarion-Ledger, Jackson, 1948, editor, co-pub., 1948—; v.p. Miss. Pubs. Corp.; pres. Capitol Broadcasting Co., owners WJTV and WSLI; chmn. bd. Magnolia Fed. Savs. & Loan Assn., Jackson. Pres. bd. trustees Miss. Coll. Exec. com. Miss. Research and Devel. Commn. Named Outstanding Alumnus of Year, Miss. Coll.; recipient Silver Em award Miss. Scholastic Press Assn. and Miss. Journalism Assn., 1970. Mem. Miss. Press Assn. (pres.), Am. Soc. Newspaper Editors, So. Newspaper Pubs. Assn, (dir. 1947-49). Home: 1331 Belvoir Pl Jackson MS 39202 Office: 311 E Pearl St Jackson MS 39201

HEDERMAN, ZACH TAYLOR, publishing co. exec.; b. Jackson, Miss., Feb. 5, 1913; s. Robert M. and Jennie Belle (Taylor) H.; B.S., Miss. Coll., 1935; B.S. Indsl. Mgmt., Carnegie Mellon U., 1938; m. Margaret Love, July 3, 1943; children—Carol Love, Zach T., Margaret Ann. Partner, Hederman Bros., Jackson, 1938—; v.p. Miss. Pub. Corp., Jackson, 1938—, Hattiesburg Am. Pub. Co. (Miss.), 1961—, Madison County Herald, Canton, Miss., 1965—; dir. Magnolia Fed. Savs. & Loan Assn. Past pres. Jackson YMCA. Chmn. bd. Miss. Bapt. Hosp. Served to capt. AUS, 1942-45. Mem. Capitol City Petroleum Club, Printing Industry Am. (past dir.), So. Graphic Arts Assn. (past dir.), Jackson C. of C. (past pres). Baptist (deacon, past chmn.). Kiwanian (past pres. Jackson). Club: Jackson Country. Home: 1311 Riverside Dr Jackson MS 39202 Office: Pearl at Congress Sts Jackson MS 39205

HEDGEPATH, LESLIE EUGENE, physician; b. Chillicothe, O., Dec. 16, 1922; s. Leslie Oliver and Florence Elizabeth (Gamble) H.; M.D., Howard U., 1947; m. Ruth Harris, June 28, 1949; children—Leslie Eugene, Gregory. Intern Harlem Hosp., N.Y.C., 1947-48, admitting physician, 1948-49; asst. resident in medicine Freedmen's Hosp., Washington, 1953-54, chief resident in medicine, 1954-55; practice medicine specializing in internal medicine, Washington, 1959—; instr. medicine Howard U., Washington, 1955-56, 59—, instr. physiology, 1959-64; asst. chief med. service VA Hosp., Pitts., 1956-58, chief med. service, 1958-59; attending physician Freedmen's Hosp., Howard U. Med. Service-D.C. Gen. Hosp., 1959—; sr. attending physician Washington Hosp. Center, 1961—. Served with M.C., AUS, World War II, 1949-52. Decorated Silver Star, Bronze Star with oak leaf cluster; recipient Service award Howard U., 1968. Mem. A.C.P., Am. (com. pvt. practice 1972—), Nat. med. assns., Med. Soc. D.C. (bd. credentials 1962-64; exec. bd. 1971—), Am. Soc. Internal Medicine, Kappa Pi. Club: Pigskin (Washington). Research in hemodynamic and angiocardiographic observations in adults with persistent left superior vena cava draining into the coronary sinus, congenital cardio-vascular anomalies in adults, incidence and significance of bacteriuria in female diabetics. Home: 1432 Iris St NW Washington DC 20012 Office: 106 Irving St NW Washington DC 20010

HEDGEPETH, T. HARVEY, lawyer; b. Monticello, Miss., Apr. 12, 1906; student Cumberland U., then LL.B., 1927. Admitted to Miss. bar, 1934, U.S. Supreme Ct. bar, 1934; asst. gen. counsel Fed. Land Bank New Orleans, 1934-43, acting gen. counsel, 1943-44; now mem. firm Hedgepeth and Hedgepeth, Jackson, Miss. Mem. Hinds County, Am. (mem. com. coop. corp. law 1946-51) bar assns., Miss. State Bar. Address: 1501-1510 Depost Guaranty Bank Bldg Jackson MS 39205

HEDIN, PAUL ARTHUR, chemist; b. Maple Plain, Minn., July 9, 1926; s. Arthur E. and Esther (Nelson) H.; B.S., U. Minn., 1950, M.S., 1953, Ph.D. (Tozer fellow), 1958; m. Anne Johns, June 21, 1951; children— Deborah, Mark, Holly, Stuart, Rebecca, Dale. Chemist U.S. Army Food and Container Inst., Chgo., 1958-62; head chem. investigations Boll Weevil Research Lab., U.S. Dept. Agr., State College, Miss., 1962—. Adj. prof. chemistry, biochemistry Miss. State U., 1963—. Served with AUS, 1953-55. Cotton, Inc. research asso., 1971-72. Mem. Am. Chem. Soc. (chmn. Miss. 1970-71), Entomol. Soc. Am., Bot. Soc. Am., Sigma Xi, Phi Lambda Upsilon. Baptist. Patentee in field. Contbr. to profl. jours. Home: Rte 3 Box 375 Starkville MS 39759 Office: Box 5367 State College MS 39762

HEDMEG, ANDREW, state ofcl.; b. Bratislava, Czechoslovakia; s. John and Susan (Hutnik) H.; came to U.S., 1912, naturalized, 1922; A.B., Ohio State U., 1931, M.D., 1936; M.P.H., Johns Hopkins, 1941; m. Jennie Katonak, May 21, 1932; 1 dau., Andra (Mrs. Francis Ledet). County health officer Miss. Bd. Health, 1937-52; dir. div. preventative medicine, and dir. div. local health services La. Bd. Health, New Orleans, 1952-66, pres., state health officer, 1966—. Clin. prof. pub. health adminstrn. La. State U. Sch. Medicine, 1953—; adj. prof. Tulane U. Sch. Tropical Medicine and pub. health, New Orleans, 1953—. Served with AUS, 1942-46. Recipient C.B. White Meml. award La. Pub. Health Assn., 1964, Outstanding Service award So. br. Am. Pub. Health Assn., 1966. Diplomate Am. Bd. Preventive Medicine. Fellow Am. Pub. Health Assn. (life); mem. La., Orleans Parish med. socs., Brit. Royal Soc. Health. Home: 900 Robert E Lee Blvd New Orleans LA 70124 Office: PO Box 60630 New Orleans LA 70160

HEDRICK, FLOYD DUDLEY, vending and food service co. exec.; b. Lynchburg, Va., Jan. 19, 1927; s. Silas Dudley and Alice (Stowe) H.; grad. Va. Comml. Coll., 1948; grad. Advanced Mgmt. Program, Harvard U., 1971; m. Rachel Conelia Childress, May 27, 1950; children—Susan Kaye, Alice Rae. Purchasing agt., supt. stores Trailways, Inc., 1947-65; v.p. purchasing Macke Co., Washington, 1966—, pres. subsidiary Atlantic Supply Co., Hyattsville, Md., 1967—. Pres. Lynchburg chpt. Fed. and State Credit Unions, 1956-57. Served with USNR, 1944-46, 50-52. Mem. Am. Mgmt. Assn. (mem. purchasing planning council 1969—), Nat. Assn. Purchasing Mgmt. (v.p. 1972—, chmn. food industry group 1970-71), Purchasing Mgmt. Assn. Washington (pres. 1969-70), Izaak Walton League (v.p. Lynchburg 1957). Mason (32 deg). Author: Purchasing Management in the Smaller Company, 1971. Home: 5404 Clifton St Springfield VA 22151 Office: 1 Macke Circle Cheverly MD 20781

HEDRICK, JERALD WILLIAM, educator; b. Kingsville, Tex., Sept. 12, 1931; s. James Oscar and Alta (Hardy) H.; B.S. in Secondary Edn., Tex. A. and I. U., 1961; postgrad. in Indsl. Edn., Tex. A. and M, 1964—; m. Joanne Schmidt, Aug. 15, 1953; children—Jerald William, Joseph Charles, James Oscar III, Jennifer Joanne Amanda. Automotive parts mgr. Chrysler Corp., Corpus Christi, Tex., 1950-57; tchr. Corpus Christi Ind. Sch. Dist., 1961-62; prof. Tex. Arts and Industries U. Kingsville, 1965—; mem. Tex. Arts and Industries U. Upward Bound faculty, summers 1967—. Chmn. Indsl. Arts Resource Com., regions I, II, and XX Tex., 1968—; mem. indsl. arts curriculum study and research project Tex. Edn. Agy. Mem. Tex. Tchrs. Assn., Nat., Tex. (sponsor 1971-72, named outstanding indsl. arts tchr. from Coastal Bend) Coastal Bend indsl. arts assns., Tex. Assn. Coll. Tchrs., Am., Tex. councils indsl. arts tchr. edn., Nat. Assn. Indsl. Tchr. Edn., Tex. Audio-Visual Edn. Assn., Iota Lambda Sigma (past historian Chi chpt.), Alpha Chi. Methodist. Home: 730 W Av A Kingsville TX 78363

HEDRICK, ROBERT K., financial analyst; b. Stockton, Cal., Oct. 1, 1929; s. David Dennis and Mable (Hollingsworth) H.; B.B.A., Tex. A. and M. Coll., 1951; M.B.A., So. Methodist U., 1964; LL.B., LaSalle Extension U., 1965; m. Christina Marie Davie, Feb. 1, 1961; 1 dau., Christina Roberta. Accountant, Kernaghan & Harvey, C.P.A.'s, 1958-61; pub. accountant Bright, Shinn & Strange, C.P.A.'s, Dallas, 1961-63, controller M.P. Crum Co., Dallas, 1963; investment co. examiner Small Bus. Adminstrn., Dallas, 1964-67; financial analyst, asst. v.p. First Nat. Bank, Dallas, 1967—. Served to lt. USNR, 1951-56. Recipient Silver medal S.A.R., 1946. C.P.A., Tex. Mem. Am. Inst. C.P.A.'s, Tex. Bar, Dallas Assn. Investment Analysts, Inst. Chartered Financial Analysts, Am. Legion (past post comdr.). Mason. Home: 7615 Lovers Lane E Dallas TX 75225 Office: First Nat Bank Bldg Dallas TX 75222

HEEBE, FREDERICK JACOB REGAN, U.S. dist. judge; b. Gretna, La., Aug. 25, 1922; s. Bernhardt and Marguerite (Reagan) H.; B.A., Tulane U., 1943, L.B., 1949; m. Willie Dee Barnes, Aug. 29, 1947; children— Frederick Riley, Adrea Dee. Admitted to La. bar, 1949; practiced in Gretna, 1949-60; dist. judge div. B, 24th Jud. Dist. Ct., Jefferson Parish, La., 1961-66; U.S. dist. judge Eastern Dist. La., 1966—. Charter mem. Community Welfare Council Jefferson Parish, 1957—; chmn. Jefferson Parish Bd. Pub. Welfare, 1953-55. Mem. Jefferson Parish Council, 1958-60, vice chmn., 1958-60. Bd. dirs. Social Welfare Planning Council New Orleans, New Orleans Regional Mental Center and Clinic, West Bank Assn. for Retarded. Served to capt., inf., AUS, World War II. Decorated Purple Heart. Bronze Star. Mem. Am., La., New Orleans Fed. bar assns., Am. Judicature Soc., Phi Beta Kappa. Home: 1407 Whitney Av Gretna LA 70053 Office: 400 Royal St New Orleans LA 70130

HEFFERNAN, JOHN WILLIAM, journalist; b. Stockbridge, Eng., Oct. 21, 1910; s. John and Alice Ann (Edwards) H.; student Clark's Coll., Putney, Eng., 1926; m. Lea Arney, Aug. 6, 1938; m. 2d, Edith Curry, Dec. 10, 1948; 1 stepson, Anthony E. Heffernan. Came to U.S., 1946. Editorial asst. Central News Ltd., London, Eng., 1929-34; sub-editor Press Assn., London, 1934-36, sports reporter, 1936-39, news desk editor, 1939-41; with Reuters, 1946—, chief corr. at UN, 1952-57, chief corr. in Washington, 1957—. Pres. UN Corr. Assn., 1956. Served to maj. Brit. Army, 1941-46; CBI. Decorated officer Order Brit. Empire, comdr. Order Brit. Empire. Clubs: Nat. Press (gov. 1964—), International (Washington); Overseas Press (N.Y.C.). Home: 2852 Arizona Av NW Washington DC 20016 Office: Nat Press Bldg Washington DC 20004

HEFFERNAN, JOSEPH ANTHONY, JR., physician; b. Savannah, Ga., Oct. 2, 1928; s. Joseph Anthony and Louise (Jeffrey) H.; B.S., U. Ga., 1951; M.D., Med. Coll. Ga., 1955; m. Jean Ann Stalvey, July 22, 1950; children—Nancy, Joseph, Mark, John, Gregory. Intern, Mercy Hosp., Buffalo, 1955-56; gen. practice medicine, Savannah, 1956—; chief med. cons. City of Savannah, 1966—; cons., lectr. drug abuse mgmt. in region. Mem. Savannah Mayor's Council on Drug Abuse, 1968-72. Served with USNR, 1946-48. Mem. A.M.A., Am. Acad. Family Practice, Med. Assn. Ga., Ga. Med. Soc. Clubs: Savannah Yacht, Forest City Gun. Home: 5706 Sweetbriar Circle Savannah GA 31406 Office: 20 Med Arts Center Savannah GA 31405

HEFFNER, GEORGE PAUL, physician; b. Wapakoneta, O., Feb. 10, 1909; s. Edward Frederic and Ida Orel (Collins) H.; A.B. cum laude, Harvard, 1930, M.D., 1934; m. Eileen Mae Van Giesen, Nov. 20, 1942; children—Judith Ann, Carol Sue, Mary Kay. Intern, Lankenau Hosp., Phila., 1934-36; practice medicine specializing in internal medicine, Charleston, W. Va., 1936-70, Fort Lauderdale, Fla., 1963—; attending physician dept. internal medicine Charleston (W.Va.) Gen. Hosp., 1941-63. Founder, pres. W. Va. Diabetes Assn., 1953; established free camp for diabetic children in W. Va., 1950; founded Charleston Lay Soc. for Diabetics, 1952; clin. asso. prof. U. Miami Med. Sch., Dept Endocrinology; attending staff Holy Cross Hosp., Beach Hosp., Fort Lauderdale, Fla. Fellow Am. Coll. Physicians; mem. A.M.A., Am. (bd. dirs. 1971—), Fla. diabetes assns. Methodist. Kiwanian, Elk. Club: Harvard (Broward County, Fla.) (v.p. 1965-71). Contbr. articles to profl. jours. Home: 1220 S E 3d Terrace Pompano Beach FL 33060 Office: 4602 N Federal Hwy Fort Lauderdale FL 33308

HEFFNER, HUBERT CROUSE, govt. ofcl.; b. Maiden, N.C., Feb. 22, 1901; s. Sylvanus Lafayette and Lily (Crouse) H.; A.B. in Lang. and Lit. with honors, N.C., 1921, M.A., 1922; student U. Chgo., 1930-34, 1944 (autumn); L.H.D. Ill. Wesleyan U., 1964; m. Ruth Penny, Apr. 8, 1922; 1 son, Hubert Heffner, Jr., Instr. English and dir. dramatics U. Wyo., 1922-23; instr. English, div. dramatics U. Ariz., 1923-26; asst. prof. English and asso. dir. The Carolina Playmakers, U.N.C., 1926-30; prof. dramatic lit. Northwestern U., 1930-39; prof. dramatic lit., exec. head dept. speech and drama Stanford U., 1939-54; acting prof. U. Colo., 1950; Rockefeller grant in aid for research and study in France and Eng., 1951-52; Folger Shakespeare Library grant in aid 1952; Fulbright award, 1954-55; prof. speech, theatre, and dramatic lit. Ind. U. 1954-61, Distinguished Service prof. dramatic lit., 1961-70; dep. dir. office Sci. and Tech., Exec Office Pres., Washington, 1970—; vis. prof. summers Northwestern U., 1930, Stanford, 1937, U. Cal., 1939, Cornell, 1948, U. Colo., 1950, 65, U. Denver, 1962; Carnegie vis. prof. drama U. Hawaii, 1958, U. Bristol, 1954-55. Commd. capt., Spl. Res., AUS, 1943; grad. Sch. of Mil. Govt., U. Va., 1943; inactive status in charge of mil. govt. instrn. Civil Affairs Tng. Sch., Stanford, 1943-44; research project Provost Marshal Gen's. Office, 1944; head Theatre and Radio Arts Branch, chief Fine Arts sect. Biarritz Am. U., 1945-46. Fellow Am. Edn. Theatre Assn. (pres. 1949; editor Jour. 1955-56); mem. Am. Assn. U. Profs., Speech Assn. Am., Modern Lang. Assn., Nat. Theatre Conf., ANTA bd. dirs. 1953-56, 60—). Author numerous publs. Editor: Davy Crockett and Other Plays (with Isaac Goldberg), 1940. Asso. editor Quarterly Jour. of Speech, 1947-50; dir. number of theatrical prodns. for U. Wyo., U. Ariz., The Carolina Playmakers, Northwestern U. and Stanford U. Office: Office Sci and Tech Executive Office Bldg Washington DC 20506

HEFFNER, RICHARD LOUIS, packaging co. exec.; b. St. Louis, Apr. 9, 1933; s. Edward Louis and Esther (Herter) H.; A.B., Columbia, 1955; M.B.A. cum laude, U. Tenn., 1965; m. Charlotte Anne Maclellan, Sept. 2, 1961; children—Richard Louis, Thomas Maclellan. Asst. advt. mgr. Richardson-Merrell, Inc., N.Y.C., 1957-60; new products market mgr. Chattem Drug & Chem. Co., 1960-64; v.p. marketing, corp. planning Dorsey Corp., Chattanooga, 1964-69, v.p., asst. sec., 1970—; dep. adminstr. Bus. and Def. Services Adminstrn., Dept. Commerce, Washington, 1969-70, mem. nat. marketing adv. com., 1971—; pres., chief exec. officer, dir. Chattanooga Glass Co., subsidiary Dorsey Corp., 1970—; trustee Glass Container Industry Research Corp. U.S., 1971—. Mem. Nat. Def. Exec. Res., 1969—; vice chmn. Regional Export Expansion Council, 1971—. Mem. allocations com. Chattanooga United Fund, 1961—; bd. dirs. Chattanooga Tb and Respiratory Diseases Assn., 1962—, pres., 1969-70; v.p. Chattanooga Allied Arts Fund, 1969-70; bd. dirs. Chattanooga Family Service Agy., Chattanooga Travelers Aid Soc., 1968-69, Jr. Achievement, 1971—. Served to lt. USNR 1955-57. Mem. N.A.M. (marketing com. 1967-70), Nat. Alliance Businessmen (metro chmn. 1970-71), Young Presidents' Orgn., Chattanooga C. of C. (dir.), Sigma Alpha Epsilon. Presbyn. Rotarian. Clubs: Chattanooga Tennis; Kenwood Country (Washington). Fairyland Country (Lookout Mountain). Home: 721 E Brow Rd Lookout Mountain TN 37350 Office: Alton Park Chattanooga TN 37410

HEFLIN, AUBREY NEWBILL, banker; b. Fredericksburg, Va., Sept. 21, 1912; s. Joseph Granville and Addie Garnett (Newbill) H.; B.A., U. Richmond, 1933; LL.B., U. Va., 1936; grad. Stonier Grad. Sch. of Banking, Rutgers U., 1951; m. Ellen Virginia Simmerman, May 28, 1939; children—Ellen H. (Mrs. George W. Ramsey), Joseph Granville. Admitted to Va. bar, 1936; asso. atty. Parrish, Butcher & Parrish, Richmond, Va., 1936-40; with Fed. Res. Bank of Richmond, 1941—, pres., 1968—. Trustee U. Richmond, Union Theol. Sem. Va. Served to lt. (j.g.) USNR, 1942-45. Mem. Am., Va., Richmond City bar assns., Lambda Chi Alpha. Presbyn. Club: Country of Va. (Richmond). Home: 6161 River Rd Richmond VA 23226 Office: 9th and Franklin Sts Richmond VA 23261

HEFNER, JOE DENSON, ins. agy. exec.; b. Atlanta, Tex., Sept. 20, 1930; s. Byron Denson and Marcele (Johnson) H.; B.A., N. Tex. State U., 1954; m. Cecile Cariker, apr. 30, 1954; children—Jerri Lynn, Julie Cecile, Debra Jo. Div. mgr. Continental Oil Co., Ft. Worth, 1954-63; pres. J.D. Hefner Assos., ins., Dallas, 1964—; chmn. bd. Nat. Trust Corp., financial planners, Dallas, 1971—; dir. Commonwealth Nat. Bank, Dallas. Vice pres. Tex. div. Am. Cancer Soc., 1971—. Served to capt. 49th Armored Div., AUS, 1961-63. Mem. Million Dollar Round Table (life), Nat., Dallas (dir. 1970—) assns. life underwriters, Assn. for Advanced Life Underwriters, Internat. Assn. Financial Counsellors, Nat. Assn. Securities Dealers, Dallas Estate Council. Contbr. articles to profl. jours. Home: 7116 Stefani Dr Dallas TX 75225 Office: 4525 Lemmon Av Dallas TX 75219

HEGSTROM, WILLIAM JEAN, ednl. adminstr.; b. Macomb, Ill., Oct. 21, 1923; s. Carl William and Thelma (Canavit) H.; student Western Ill. U., 1941-42; B. Sc., Rutgers U., 1949, Ed.M. 1952; M.A. Teaching, Purdue U., 1964; postgrad. U. Fla., 1961, Fla. Atlantic U., 1965-68; Ed.D., U. Miami, 1971; m. Grace Ann Paladino, May 3, 1944; children—Elizabeth Louise (Mrs. Edward Cook), William Jean II, Jean. Tchr. jr. high sch., South Plainfield, N.J., 1949-52, high sch., Bernardsville, N.J. 1952-54, Oak St. Sch., Bernard's Twp., N.J., 1954-55, high sch., Summit, N.J., 1955-58, jr. high sch., Delray Beach, Fla, 1958-65; chmn. math. dept. John I. Leonard High Sch., Lake Worth, Fla., 1965-68, dir. Palm Beach County research project, 1966-68; adj. prof. Fla. Atlantic U., 1965-69, asso. prof., 1969-70; counselor coordinator John Leonard Adult Center, Lake Worth, 1965-68; supr. research and evaluation Palm Beach County Sch. Bd., West Palm Beach, Fla., 1970—. Served with USAAF, 1942-46. Mem. Am. Assn. U. Profs., N.E.A., Nat. Council Tchrs. Math., Math. Assn. Am., Fla. Edn. Assn., Fla. Council Tchrs. Math., Am. Ednl. Research Assn., Assn. Supervision and Curriculum Devel., Phi Delta Kappa. Contbr. articles to profl. jours. Home: 231 Seacrest Circle Delray Beach FL 33444 Office: School Board of Palm Beach County West Palm Beach FL 33104

HEGYELI, ANDREW FRANCIS, scientist; b. Kispest, Hungary, Jan. 28, 1920; s. Zoltan and Erzsebet (Szollosy) H.; D.V.M., U. Palatinus Josephus, Budapest, Hungary, 1944, Ph.D. in Anatomy, 1944; m. Ruth Johnsson Hegyeli, 1966. Came to U.S., 1957, naturalized, 1962. Bacteriologist, Phylaxia Inst., Budapest, 1944-45; head vet. med. dept. Servita Pharm. Co., Budapest, 1945-48; ind. investigator biochemistry Richter Pharm. Co., Budapest, 1948-50; asso. head biochemistry dept. Research Inst. for Pharm. Industry, Budapest, 1950-56; ind. investigator Inst. for Muscle Research, Marine Biol. Lab., Woods Hole, Mass., 1957-65; sr. pathologist Battelle Meml. Inst., Columbus, O., 1965-69; chief biomed. evaluation div. U.S. Army Med. Biomech. Research Lab., Walter Reed Army Med. Center, Frederick, Md., 1969—. Guest lectr.; corp. mem. Marine Biol. Lab., Woods Hole, Mass. Served with Hungarian Cav., 1940-44. Recipient U. Palatinus Josephus award, 1940; Hungary State award for blood research, 1948; Inst. Pharm. Industry awards, 1950, 52-54, 56. Fellow A.A.A.S.; mem. Am. Vet. Med. Assn., Am. Chem. Soc., Am. Inst. Biol. Sci., N.Y. Acad. Sci. Contbr. articles to profl. jours. Home: 10824 Middleboro Dr Damascus MD 20750 Office: US Army Med Biomech Research Lab Ft Detrick Bldg 568 Frederick MD 21701

HEIDBRINK, VIRGIL EUGENE, paper co. exec.; b. Ireton, Ia., Dec. 4, 1925; s. Edward H. and Luella (Dittmer) H.; A.B., U.S.D., 1949; B.F.T., Am. Inst. Fgn. Trade, 1950; postgrad. Hunter Coll., 1952-53, Coll. City N.Y., 1953-54, N.Y. U. Grad. Sch. Bus., 1954-56. Export asst. fgn. trade, various firms, N.Y.C., 1951-56; with Hammermill Paper Co., Erie, Pa., 1956, Chgo., 1956-57, dist. sales mgr. S.W. ty., Dallas, 1958—. Del. Tex. Republican Conv., 1964, 70, 72. Served with Med. Dept., AUS, 1944-46, 50-51. Decorated Bronze Star. Mem. Dallas Advt. League, Phi Beta Kappa. Lutheran. Club: Toastmasters (pres. 1965, dist. gov, 1968-69). Home: 2623 Hudnall St Dallas TX 75235 Office: 6434 Maple Av Suite 405 Dallas TX 75235

HEIDORN, DONALD RICHARD, ednl. adminstr.; b. South Solon, O., Feb. 24, 1933; s. William Earl and Myrtle Ruth (Frederick) H.; B.S., Florence State U., 1960; M.A., U. Ala., 1964; m. Lucy Marie Ryan, Apr. 16, 1957; 1 son, David Earl. Tchr., coach Carbon Hill (Ala.) Bd. Edn., 1960-62; tchr., coach Muscle Shoals, (Ala.) Bd. Edn., 1962-64, coach, asst. prin., 1964-67, prin. high sch., 1967-70, supt. edn., 1970—. Bd. dirs. Jr. Achievement, YMCA, Sheffield-Tuscumbia Credit Union. Served with USNR, 1952-56. Mem. Am., Ala. assns. sch. adminstrs., N.E.A., Ala., Muscle Shoals edn. assns., So. Assn. Colls. and Schs., Florence State U. (pres. 1968), U. Ala. alumni assns., Muscle Shoals Bus. and Profl. Assn. (pres. 1971), Kappa Phi Kappa. Methodist. Lion (1st v.p. 1971). Club: Sportsmans (pres. 1968) (Florence State U.). Home: 1510 Fordway Muscle Shoals AL 35660 Office: Avalon Av Muscle Shoals AL 35660

HEIFNER, RICHARD GLENN, economist; b. Greenfield, Ia., Jan. 9, 1934; s. George Clifford and Tillie (Thrailkill) H.; B.S. Ia. State U., 1956; Ph.D., 1963; m. Marjorie Ellen Martin, Nov. 22, 1960; children—Steven, Catherine, John. Research asso. Ia. State U., 1960-62, asst. to asso. prof. Mich. State U., 1963-69, leader, Grades and Standards Research Group, Econ. Research Service, U.S. Dept.

Agr., Washington, 1969—. Served with AUS, 1956-58. Mem. Am. Agrl. Econ. Assn., Am. Econ. Assn., Am. Statis. Assn. Home: 3817 Whitman Rd Annandale VA 22003 Office: 500 SW 12th St Washington DC 20250

HEILMAN, EARL BRUCE, univ. pres.; b. La Grange, Ky., July 16, 1926; s. Earl Bernard and Nellie (Sanders) H.; diploma Campbellsville Jr. Coll., 1948; B.S., Peabody Coll., 1950, M.A., 1951, Ph.D., 1961; postgrad. U. Tenn., 1951-52, U. Omaha, summers 1953, 55, U. Ky., summers 1954, 56; LL.D., Wake Forest U., 1967; H.H.D., Campbell Coll., 1971; m. Betty June Dobbins, Aug. 27, 1948; children—Bobbie Lynn, Nancy Jo, Terry Lee, Sandra June, Timothy Bruce. Instr. bus. Peabody Coll., Nashville, 1950-51, bursar, 1957-60, adminstrv. v.p., 1963-66; instr. accounting Belmont Coll., Nashville, 1951-52; auditor Albert Maloney Co., Nashville, 1951-52; asst. prof. accounting, bus. mgr. Ky. Wesleyan Coll., Owensboro, 1952-54; treas. Georgetown (Ky.) Coll., 1954-57; treas. housing project City of Louisville, 1955-57; coordinator higher edn. and spl. schs. State of Tenn., Nashville, 1960-61; v.p. dean Ky. So. Coll., Louisville, 1961-63; pres. Meredith Coll., Raleigh, N.C., 1966-71, U. Richmond (Va.), 1971—. Dir., Central Nat. Bank. Cons. instl. studies in edn. and adminstrn., 1954—; dir., cons. long range planning confs. Fund for Advancement Edn., 1960— cons. Acad. Ednl. Devel., 1966—. Mem. steering com. Baptist Ednl. Study Task. Bd. advisers Bapt. Hosp. Sch. Nursing, 1959-60, 64—; mem. adv. bd. Richmond Ballet; bd. dirs. Bill Wilkerson Speech, Hearing Center, Richmond Symphony, United Givers Fund. Served with USMCR, 1944-47. Recipient Merit award Owensboro Jr. C. of C., 1953, Service award Agrl. and Industry U. Nashville, 1961. Mem. Nat. Fedn. Bus. Officers, Nat. Fedn. Bus. Officers Cons. Service, So. Assn. Colls. for Women (pres. 1970), Tenn. Edn. Assn., Ky. Ednl. Buyers Assn., Ky. Assn. Acad. Deans, Peabody Alumni Assn. (exec. com.), Nat., So. assns. colls. and univs. bus. officers, N.C. Assn. Colls. and Univs. (pres.-elect), Internat. Platform Assn., Richmond C. of C. (dir.), Phi Beta Kappa, Pi Omega Pi, Kappa Phi Kappa, Kappa Delta Pi, Omicron Delta Kappa, Beta Gamma Sigma, Delta Pi Epsilon. Democrat. Baptist (deacon). Rotarian. Club: Downtown (Richmond). Author: (with others) Sixty College Study, 1954. Contbr. articles to profl. publs. Developer accounting and reporting program for Tenn. state colls. and univs. Home: 8832-E Three Chopt Rd Richmond VA 23229

HEIMLICH, FREDERICK JUNIOR, psychologist; b. Lafayette, Ind., Sept. 29, 1921; s. Fred J. and Esther (Lewis) H.; B.S., Purdue U., 1948, M.S., 1950, Ph.D., 1952; m. Mary M. Ryan, June 21, 1947; children—Michael E., David A., Christopher P., Barbara E.; m. 2d, Margaret Ann Becker, June 22, 1968; 1 dau., Laura R. Asst. chief psychology service VA Hosp., Marion, Ind., 1952-54; chief psychologist Beatty Hosp., Westville, Ind., 1954-57; chief psychologist Orange County Guidance Clinic, Orlando, Fla., 1957-61; pvt. practice psychology, Orlando, 1958-68; dir. adult services Brevard County Mental Health Center, Rockledge, Fla., 1968—. Served with USCGR, 1942-46. Mem. Am., Fla. psychol. assns. Home: 1716 Golfview Dr Rockledge FL 32955 Office: 1770 Cedar St Rockledge FL 32955

HEIMLICH, SETH SCHAFER, ednl. adminstr.; b. Florence, S.C., Sept. 24, 1938; s. Chester S. and Bernice (Schafer) H.; A.S., Marion Inst., 1957; B.S., Clemson U., 1959, M.S., 1970; m. Doreen (Feibusch), May 24, 1968; 1 dau., Larissa Andrea. Commd. 2d lt. Med. Service Corps, U.S. Army, 1959, advanced through ranks to capt., 1965; dir. adult edn., Pickens County Six Mile, (S.C.), 1970—. Bd. dirs. Pickens County Literacy Assn.; del. to S.C. White House Conf. on Aging. Mem. Alpha Kappa Chi. Address: Box 57 Six Mile SC 29682

HEINL, ROBERT DEBS, JR., ret. marine corps officer, writer; b. N.Y.C., Aug. 12, 1916; s. Robert Debs and Helen (Corbin) H.; grad. St. Abans Sch., Washington, 1933, A.B. with Orations (cum laude), Yale, 1937; m. Nancy Gordon Wright, Sept 23, 1939; children—Pamela Gordon (Mrs. John R. Burdick), Michael Charles Corbin. Commd. 2d lt. USMC, 1937, advanced through grades to col.; service at Pearl Harbor, 1941, Wake Island relief expn., 1941, South Pacific, 1942; Iwo Jima, 1945, occupation of Japan, 1945, North China, 1946; dir. marine corps history, 1946-49; comdr. East Coast Islands, also served with 1st Marine div., 1952-53; later chief military assistance adv. group and U.S. Naval Mission, Port-au-Prince, Haiti, 1958-63; ret. 1964; cons. to U.S. Navy on long-range gun systems, 1967-68; def. corr. Detroit News, 1968—; contbg. editor Jour. of Armed Forces, 1969—. Mem. Inst. for Strategic Studies. Decorated Legion of Merit with combat V, Bronze Star medal with combat V; recipient Alfred Thayer Mahan award, 1968; award of merit U.S. Naval Inst., 1968. Episcopalian. Clubs: Army and Navy; Carabao; N.Y. Yacht, Yale (N.Y.C.); American (London); Mory's; Nat. Press. Author: The Defense of Wake, 1947, Marines at Midway, 1948; The Marshalls: Increasing the Tempo, 1953; The Marine Officer's Guide, 1956, 3d edit., 1967; Soldiers of the Sea, 1962; Dictionary of Military and Naval Quotations, 1966; Victory at High Tide, 1967; Handbook for Marine NCO'S, 1970. Contbr. to Ency. Brit., Dictionary Am. Biography, Nat. Geog., Am. Heritage, Atlantic Monthly, Reporter, New Republic, Washington Post, and profl. jours. Home: 2400 California St NW Washington DC 20008 Office: 511 Nat Press Bldg Washington DC 20004

HEISKELL, JOHN NETHERLAND, editor; b. Rogersville, Tenn., Nov. 2, 1872; s. Carrick White and Eliza Ayre (Netherland) H.; A.B., U. Tenn., 1893; Litt.D., Little Rock Coll., 1929; LL.D., Ark. Coll., 1934, U. Ark., 1938, Colby Coll., 1958; m. Wilhelmina Mann, June 28, 1910; children—Mrs. George Whitfield Cook, Mrs. Hugh B. Patterson, Jr. Editor, Ark. Gazette, 1902—; chmn. bd. Gazette Pub. Co. U.S. senator from Ark. apptd. Gov. Donaghey, Jan. 6 - Jan. 29, 1913. Pres. bd. trustees Little Rock Public Library. Former chmn. Little Rock City Planning Commn.; former mem. State Planning Bd.; 2d v.p. Asso. Press, 1926-27. Recipient citation A.L.A., 1957; medal and citation Syracuse U. Sch. Journalism, 1958; annual award Columbia Sch. Journalism, 1958; Lovejoy award Colby Coll., 1958; U. Mo. Sch. of Journalism Distinguished Service medal, 1962; John Peter Zenger award dept. journalism U. Ariz; citation and plaque Sigma Delta Chi, 1966. Fellow Sigma Delta Chi; mem. Sigma Alpha Epsilon. Democrat. Clubs: Country of Little Rock, Top of the Rock, Little Rock. Home: 6015 Greenwood Rd Little Rock AR 72207 Office: Ark Gazette 112 W 3d St Little Rock AR 72203

HEIT, RAYMOND ANTHONY, civil engr.; b. Norfolk, Va., Sept. 12, 1936; s. Lawrence Henry and Cecelia Helen (Klauke) H.; B.S., U. Cin., 1959; m. Helen Carlee Langford, Oct. 25, 1969; 1 son, Christopher Carl. Staff engr. Factory Mut., Cleve., 1959-62; village engr. Village of Cuyahoga Heights, O., 1963-65; project engr. Union Carbide Co., Houston, 1966-68; individual practice as cons. engr., Houston, 1969—; instr. strength of materials Tex. A. and M. Maritime Acad., Galveston, 1968—. Registered profl. engr., Tex., Ohio. Mem. Am. Soc. C.E., Tex. Soc. Profl. Engrs., Houston Engring. Soc. Club: Houston Ski. Home: 1724 Wroxton St Houston TX 77005 Office: 4141 SW Freeway Houston TX 77027

HEJTMANCIK, MILTON RUDOLPH, physician, educator; b. Caldwell Tex., Sept. 27, 1919; s. Rudolph Joseph and Millie (Jurcak) H.; B.A., U. Tex., 1939, M.D., 1943;; m. Myrtle Lou Erwin, Aug. 21, 1943; children—Kelly Erwin, Milton Rudolph, Peggy Lou. Resident internal medicine U. Tex., 1946-49, instr. internal medicine 1949-51, asst. prof. internal medicine, 1951-54, asso. prof. internal medicine, 1954-65, prof. internal medicine, 1965—, dir. heart clinic, 1949—, dir. heart station, 1965—; chief staff John Sealy Hosp., 1957-58. Served from 1st lt. to capt., M.C., AUS, 1944-46, ETO. Diplomate in cardiovascular diseases Am. Bd. Internal Medicine. Fellow A.C.P., Am. College Chest Physicians, Am. Coll. Cardiology; mem. Am. (fellow council clinical cardiology), Tex. (chmn, cardiac clinics com. 1956—, v.p., 1958), Galveston Dist. (pres. 1956) heart assns., A.M.A., Am. Fedn. Clin. Research, A.A.A.S., Tex. Acad. Internal Medicine, Phi Beta Kappa, Sigma XI, Alpha Omega Alpha, Mu Delta. Contbr. numerous papers on cardiovascular disease to profl. jours. Home: 118 Marlin St Galveston TX 77550 Office: 816 Strand St Galveston TX 77550

HELD, MARGARET J. DUNKLEY, realtor; b. Washington, Sept. 11, 1911; d. Randolph Lee and Susie (Engelke) Jennings; student Am. U., 1946, Southeastern U., 1944-47; m. Charles W. Dunkley, Aug. 30, 1937 (dec. July 1954); m. 2d, Emil G. Held, Aug. 20, 1955. Real estate broker, Md., D.C., Va., 1936—; owner, pres. Margaret J. Dunkley Realtor, Bethesda, Md., owner, dir. Margaret J. Dunkley, interior designers, 1953—, Margaret J. Dunkley Ins. Agy., Inc., 1961—; v.p. Fed. Supply Co., Inc., Washington, 1955-70, pres., gen. mgr., 1970—. Mem. women's fitness bd. YMCA, Bethesda; trustee Montgomery County Crippled Childrens Soc., 1956-58; mem. com. United Givers Fund, 1961—; active woman's Aux. for Cancer Research, Womans Aux. Washington Bible Coll.; past realtor chmn. Montgomery County Heart Assn. Named Realtor of Year, Montgomery County, 1956, 57. Mem. Montgomery County Bd. Realtors (pres. 1954-55), Bethesda-Chevy Chase C. of C. (v.p. 1956, 58), Montgomery County C. of C. (past v.p.), Nat. Assn. Real Estate Bds. (past pres. Md. women's council), Nat. Inst. Brokers (gov. 1957-59), Md. Real Estate Assn. (gov. 1957-60), Internat. Real Estate Fedn. (del. to internat. congress Geneva, Switzerland, Vienna, Austria, 1954). Clubs: Congressional Country (Bethesda); Mid-Ocean (Bermuda). Home: 8613 Fenway Dr Bethesda MD 20034 Office: 7613 Wisconsin Av Bethesda MD 20034 also Federal Supply Co Inc 1108 K St NW Washington DC 20005

HELLEMS, HARPER KEITH, physician, educator; b. Sinks Grove, W.Va., Mar. 16, 1920; s. Harvey Kem and Nilah Irene (Eppline) H.; M.D., U. Va., 1943; m. Anne Alexia Wheatley, Feb. 12, 1939; children—Harper Keith, Eric Wheatley. Intern, Montreal (Que., Can.) Gen. Hosp., 1944-45; research fellow, asst. in medicine Peter Bent Brigham Hosp., Boston, 1946-49, sr. asst. resident in medicine, 1949-50; asst. resident in medicine West Roxbury (Mass.) VA Hosp., 1948-49; teaching fellow in medicine Harvard Med. Sch., Boston, 1949-50; asst. prof. medicine Wayne State U., Detroit, 1950-55, asso. prof., 1955-59, prof., 1959-60; prof. medicine, dir. div. cardiovascular diseases N.J. Coll. Medicine, Jersey City, 1960-65; prof., chmn. dept. medicine U. Miss. Sch. Medicine, Jackson, 1965—. Served to lt. (j.g.), M.C., USNR, 1944-46. Fellow A.C.P., Am. Coll. Cardiology; mem. Am. Soc. for Clin. Investigation, Am. Physiol. Soc., Assn. Univ. Cardiologists, Am. Heart Assn., Am. Clin. and Climatol. Assn., Assn. Am. Physicians, Central Soc. for Clin. Research (council 1960-63), Sigma Xi, Alpha Omega Alpha. Contbr. numerous articles to med. publs. Home: 5365 Suffolk Dr Jackson MS 39211 Office: 2500 N State St Jackson MS 39216

HELLER, FRANK ALBERT, JR., city ofcl.; b. Louisville, Nov. 6, 1931; s. Frank Albert and Adeline E. (Traband) H.; B.S., U. Louisville, 1953; m. Sue Ann Baker, July 18, 1953; children—Rank Albert III, Susan, Lee. Sr. accountant E.A. Bowden, C.P.A., Louisville, 1955-62; self-employed accountant, Louisville, 1962-68; gen. partner Cecil & Heller, C.P.A.'s, Louisville, 1968—; budget officer, asst. dir. finance, acting chief accountant Dept. Pub. Finance, City of Louisville, 1962-67, dir. finance, 1967—. Bd. mgrs. St. Matthews YMCA; bd. dirs. Louisville Meml. Hosp. Served with USNR, 1953-55; now lt. comdr. Res. C.P.A., Ky. Mem. Am. Inst. C.P.A.'s, Ky. Soc. C.P.A.'s (chmn. com. local govtl. accounting and auditing 1969-70), Nat. Municipal Finance Officers Assn., Municipal Finance Officers Assn. Ky. (state chmn. 1970—), Nat. League Cities (mem. com. on revenue and finance 1969-71), Nat. Assn. Accountants, Navy League U.S. (Louisville sec. 1969), Municipal Treas. Assn. U.S., Shelby County Fish and Game Protective Assn., Louisville Police Officers Assn. (hon.), Frat. Order Police (hon.). Home: 1127 Ridge Line Dr Louisville KY 40207 Office: City Hall Annex Louisville KY 40202 also 3415 Bardstown Rd Louisville KY 40218

HELLER, PEARL BAILIE (MRS. RAYMOND J. HELLER), manpower cons.; b. Turtle Creek, Pa., Aug. 12, 1918; d. John Langfitt and Hannah (Boord) Bailie; B.S., Columbia, 1949, M.A., 1950; R.N., Mt. Sinai Hosp., N.Y.C., 1943; m. Raymond J. Heller, Apr. 9, 1955. Supr. surg. wards Mt. Sinai Hosp., 1946-48; rehab. counselor Queensboro (N.Y.) Tb and Health Assn., 1950-54; program dir. Hartman Area Neighborhood Centers Assn., Houston, 1954-63, asst. to city program dir., 1963-67; now pvt. practice as manpower cons., program specialist. Mem. Nat. Assn. U. Women, Nat. Assn. Social Workers, Acad. Certified Social Workers. Author: An Outreach Demonstration, 1967; (with Malcolm S. Host) Creative Administration: Key to Successful Day Care, 1971. Home: 310 Stratford St Houston TX 77006

HELLIWELL, PAUL LIONEL EDWARD, lawyer; b. Bklyn., Sept. 17, 1914; s. L. H. and Nola C. (Harless) H.; A.B., U. Fla., 1937, J.D., 1939; m. Marjoria Mueller, Aug. 8, 1942; 1 dau., Anne Elizabeth. Admitted to Fla. bar, 1939, since practiced in Miami, specializing in corp. and ins. law, sr. partner firm Helliwell, Melrose, DeWolf; sr. v.p., gen. counsel Am. Bankers Ins. Co. of Fla., 1947-70, sec., gen. counsel, 1970—; sec., gen. counsel Am. Bankers Life Assurance Co. of Fla., 1952-70, chmn. bd., gen. counsel, 1970—; pres. Helliwell, Melrose & DeWolf Chartered; dir. 1st Nat. Bank of Homestead (Fla.), Palm Beach Mail Bank; chmn. bd. Bank of Cutler Ridge, 1965—, Bank of Perrine, 1962—; pres. Fla. Shares, Inc., 1959—. Co-dir. Miami study team Nat. Comm. Causes and Prevention Violence, 1968-69; mem. Fla. Council of 100, 1971—. Vice chmn. bd. trustees Miami Art Center, 1964—. State chmn. Fla. Citizens for Eisenhower, 1952, 56; del. Rep. Nat. Conv., 1952, 56. Served as col. M.I. and OSS, AUS, 1941-46, mem. Res., 1946—. Decorated Legion of Merit with oak leaf cluster; Order Cloud and Banner (Chinese); comdr. Order of White Elephant (Thailand). Mem. Am., Fla., Dade County bar assns., Bar Assn. City N.Y., Fedn. Ins. Counsel, Orange County Bar Assn., Chi Phi, Phi Alpha Delta. Clubs: Bankers, Miami; River (Jacksonville, Fla.); Kings Bay Yacht; University (Orlando). Home: 9800 SW 62d Ct Miami FL 33156 Office: 600 Brickell Av Miami FL 33131 also 100 S Orange Av Orlando FL 32801

HELLMAN, GLENN ERNEST, sch. supt.; b. Muenster, Tex., Mar. 25, 1933; s. Arthur Bernard and Pauline (Otto) H.; B.S. in Agr., East Tex. State U., 1955; M.Ed., in Adminstrn., North Tex. State U., 1961; m. Elizabeth Rose Zimmerer, Feb. 17, 1955; children—Dwayne, Glenna, Sandra, Brian, Gina, Jeffery. Vocational agr. instr. Muester (Tex.) Pub. Sch., 1955-59, prin., 1959-63; supt. Lindsay (Tex.) Ind. Sch. Dist., 1963—. Mem. Am., Tex. assns. sch. adminstrs., N.E.A., Tex. State Tchrs. Assn. K.C. Home: 102 E 1st St Lindsay TX 76250 Office: Lindsay TX 76250

HELLMAN, RICHARD, economist, educator; b. N.Y.C., Oct. 5, 1913; s. Abraham and Sarah (Levine) H.; A.B., Columbia, 1934, Ph.D., 1967; m. Violet Grace Zeitlin, 1936; children—Peter, Elizabeth, Caroline. Economist, Dept. Commerce, 1951-67, FPC, 1941-49, Small Bus. Adminstrn., 1967 (all Washington); dir. econ. planning and research U.S. Small Bus. Adminstrn., Washington, 1967-70; adj. prof. Am. U., Washington, 1968-70; vis. prof. econs. U. R.I., Kingston, 1970-71, prof., dir. Research Center in Bus. and Econs., 1971—; pres. U.S. Hosp. Air Conditioning Engrs. Inc., 1954—; dir. DISC Inc., Washington. Mem. Underwriters Labs., Inc., also on burglary council, 1970—. Pres., Washington Modern Dance Soc., 1964—. Mem. Bd. Jewish Edn., Washington area, 1968-70. Served with USNR, 1943-47. Fulbright award, Paris, 1951-52; Fed. Exec. fellow Brookings Inst., 1965-66. Mem. Am. Econ. Assn., Am. Soc. Heating, Refrigerating and Air Conditioning. Author: Crime Against Small Business, 1969; Government Competition in Electric Utility Industry, 1972. Editor: R.I. Bus. Quar., 1971—. Home: 6505 Waterway Dr Falls Church VA 22044 Office: Econs Dept U RI Kingston RI 02881

HELM, DURY LANE, oil and gas broker, evangelist; b. Clifton, Tex., Nov. 22, 1896; s. Willis Sparks and Ellen (Lane) H.; B.S., Tex. A. and M. Coll., 1916; m. Ardella Rebecca Jones, Aug. 3, 1922 Lay leader, deacon, evangelist Ch. of Christ, 1917—; psychic psychologist; dir. polit. and pub. affairs Clara Driscoll, 1938-44; active state and nat. legislation affecting conservation and devel. natural resources, 1932-58; adviser to current state and nat. govt. ofcls., officials, 1935—. Mem. Farm Debt Adjustment Com., 1933-34; exec. asst. to dir, Tex. office OPA, 1941-43. Democratic county chmn., 1934-38; del. Dem. Nat. Conv,, 1936; mem. Nat. Dem. Club Am. Trustee Elizabeth H. Gillespie Estate, 1958- ; mgr., owner W. S. Helm Estate, 1960-65; adminstr. Joseph L. Helm Estate, 1960—; trustee Willie Helm Estate, 1969—. Served from 2d lt. to 1st lt., U.S. Army, World War I. Life mem. D.A.V. Perfected a device to trace oil and gas structures. Home: Bosque County Clifton TX 76634 Office: PO Box 391 Clifton TX 76634

HELM, HUGH BARNETT, govt. ofcl.; b. Bowling Green, Ky., Dec. 27, 1914; s. Hugh Barnett and Ermine (Cox) H.; B.A., Vanderbilt U., 1935, postgrad. law sch., 1936-37, 52-53, Stanford, 1953-56; m. Vivian Loreen Downing, June 5, 1943; children—Beverly, Hugh B. III, Nathaniel Henry. Admitted to Ky. bar, 1938, Tenn. bar, 1938, U.S. Supreme Ct. bar, 1942; atty. Trade Practice Conf., FTC, Washington, 1938-42; asso. counsel U.S. Internat. Prosecution Sect. G.H.Q., SCAP, Tokyo, Japan, 1946; practiced in Nashville, 1946-53; bond specialist Swett & Crawford, San Francisco, 1956-57; resident mgr. Totten & Co., San Francisco, 1958, v.p. gen. mgr., 1959-60; sr. trial atty. Bur. Restraint of Trade, FTC, Washington, 1961-66, chief div. of adv. opinions, 1966—, acting dir. Bur. Industry Guidance, 1969-70, atty. adviser FTC Bur. Consumer Claims, fed. hearing examiner Bur. Hearing and Appeals, Social Security Adminstrn., Dept. Health, Edn. and Welfare, Chattanooga, 1971—. Pres. Surety Claims Assn. No. Cal., 1957-58. Mem. Tenn. Ho. of Reps., 1949-50. Served with Inf., USAAF, 1941-45; served to capt. AUS, 1950-52. Decorated Bronze Star, Combat Infantry Badge. Mem. Am., Ky., Tenn. bar assns., Am. Acad. Polit. and Social Sci., Am. Judicature Soc., Am. Acad. Polit. Sci., Pi Sigma Alpha, Tau Kappa Alpha. Club: Commonwealth (San Francisco). Presbyn. (deacon). Home: Rockintop Forest Park Dr Signal Mountain TN 37377 Office: Bureau Hearings and Appeals Social Security Adminstrn Dept Health Education and Welfare Chattanooga TN 37402

HELM, JAYE CROCKETT, supt. schs.; b. Mertzon, Tex., Nov. 21, 1916; s. John Cornelius and Cynthia Beatrice (Sanders) H.; student Tarleton State Coll., 1934; B.S., North Tex. U., Denton, 1937, M.S., 1951; postgrad. Tex. A. and M. U.; m. Ruth LaVerne Isham, Sept. 14, 1940; children—Janis Kaye, Jimmy Jaye. High sch. prin., tchr. Newburg Consol. Sch. Dist., Comanche County, Tex., 1937-39; asst. county sch. supt., Comanche County, 1939-41, supt. schs., 1945-49; tchr. Brownwood (Tex.) Schs., 1941; supt. schs., DeLeon, Tex., 1949-54; supt. schs., Stephenville, Tex., 1954—. Chmn. United Fund, Stephenville, 1960. Served with USAAF, 1942-45. Recipient Distinguished Service award Jr. C. of C., 1965. Mem. N.E.A. (life), P.T.A., (life), Am., Tex. assns. sch. adminstrs., So. Assn. Secondary Schs. (chmn. Ft. Worth Dist.), Mid-Tex. (pres.), Tex. (mem. exec. com.) tchrs. assns., Stephenville C. of C. (past pres.). Democrat. Mem. Ch. of Christ (deacon). Mason, Lion. Home: 854 W McNeil St Stephenville TX 76401 Office: Box 453 Stephenville TX 76401

HELM, THOMAS WILLIAM, III, author; b. St. Augustine, Fla., May 3, 1919; s. Thomas William and Grace (Spencer) H.; student Birmingham So. Coll., 1946-47; m. Dorothy Loraine Hunter, Sept. 30, 1943. Radio announcer WRNL, Richmond, Va., 1942, WDLP, Panama City, Fla., 1943-44; reporter Birmingham (Ala.) Age-Herald, 1945; forest ranger Ala. Dept. Forestry, 1946; asst. editor Progressive Farmer mag., Birmingham, 1946-54; free-lance mag. writer 1945-54; free lance writer, 1955—; editor Dunedin (Fla.) Times, 1972—. Tchr. creative writing Pinellas County Adult Edn, Center, Clearwater (Fla.) High Sch., 1962-63, U. So. Fla., Tampa. Served with USN, 1938-42. Mem. V.F.W., Authors Guild. Author: The Sea Lark, 1955; Treasure Hunting Around the World, 1960; Shark. 1961; Monsters of the Deep, 1962; Ordeal by Sea, 1963; The Everglades, 1963; Hurricane Coming, 1964; A World of Snakes; Hurricanes: Weather at Its Worst, 1967; The Frank Murphy Story, 1968; Fishing Southern Salt Waters, 1972. Editor: Seminole Courier, 1970—. Home: 123 Valencia Dr Dunedin FL 33528

HELMERS, GORDON BERT, dentist; b. Gresham, Neb., Sept. 1, 1936; s. Albert Ferdnand and Merle (Moore) H.; student Fullerton Jr. Coll., 1955-57; A.B., U. Cal. at San Francisco, 1957-61; D.D.S., U. Ala., 1965, M.S.D. in Orthodontics, 1967; m. Jo Ella Robinson, June 23, 1962; children—John Byron, Kristen Lee. Asst. prof. orthodontics U. N.C. Dental Sch., Chapel Hill, 1967-69; practice dentistry, specializing in orthodontics, Spartanburg, S.C., 1969—. Served with Dental Corps, AUS, 1962-64. NIH teaching fellow, 1965-67. Recipient 4th place award Am. Assn. Orthodontics research contest, 1969. Mem. S.C. Dental Assn., Am. Dental Assn., Am. Assn. Orthodontics, So. Soc. Orthodontics, S.C. Soc. Dentistry for Children. Inventor dental devices. Home: 132 Fernbrook Circle Spartanburg SC 29302 Office: 610 Montgomery Bldg N Church St Spartanburg SC 29301

HELMS, RICHARD MCGARRAH, govt. ofcl.; b. St. Davids, Pa., Mar. 30, 1913; s. Herman H. and Marion (McGarrah) H.; B.A., Williams Coll., 1935; m. Julia Bretzman Shields, Sept. 8, 1939 (div. 1968); 1 son, Dennis J.; m. 2d, Cynthia McKelvie, 1968. Staff corr. in Europe, U.P., 1935-37; mem. staff Indpls. Times Pub. Co., 1937-42; with CIA, 1947—, dep. dir., 1965-66, dir., 1966—. Served with OSS, USNR, 1942-46; ETO. Recipient Career Service award Nat. Civil Service League, 1965. Clubs: Chevy Chase (Md.); Alfalfa (Washington); Rolling Rock (Ligonier, Pa.). Office: Central Intelligence Agy Washington DC 20505

HELSABECK, WYAT, librarian; b. Troy, N.C., June 26, 1921; s. Wyatt Wilson and Lula (Henry) H.; student Pfeiffer Coll., 1939-42; A.B. in English, U. N.C., 1949, postgrad., 1950-54; postgrad. Fla. State U., 1963. Student mgr. U. N.C. Stores, Chapel Hill, 1953-57;

desk clk. Carolina Inn, Chapel Hill, 1958-59; reference librarian Pub. Library Charlotte and Mecklenburg County (N.C.), 1964—. Mgr. fall-out sect. Civil Def., Charlotte, N.C., 1965—. Served with AAC, 1942-46. Mem. Mecklenburg (pres.), N.C., Southeastern, Am. library assns., Phi Beta Kappa. Author: Poems Written in an Army Hospital, 1943. Editor Library Newsletter, Charlotte Pub. Library, 1966—. Home: 1121 Myrtle Av Charlotte NC 28203 Office: 310 N Tryon St Charlotte NC 28202

HELSTROM, HERBERT ALGOT, aerospace engr.; b. Chgo., Sept. 18, 1916; s. Herbert Algot and Bertha Mathilda (Hard) H.; B.S. in Mech. Engring., Purdue U., 1938; M.B.A. in Engring. Mgmt., Tex. Christian U., 1962; postgrad. North Tex. State U., 1966—; m. Norma Eugenia Anderson, Oct. 6, 1939; children—Carol Jeanne, Wade Richard, Herbert Algot III. Tunnel constrn. engr. Chgo. San. Dist., 1938-39; equipment research engr. Montgomery Ward and Co., Chgo., 1939-40; structures engr. Gen. Dynamics Co., San Diego, 1940-42, Ft. Worth, 1942-44, design engr., 1944-50; design project engr. Vought Aeros. Co., LTV Aerospace Corp., Dallas, 1950-51, lead designer landing gear unit, 1951-53, supr. surfaces design group, 1953-55, asst. chief design, 1955-57, chief engring. adminstrn. and procedures, 1957-59, chief adminstrv. engr., 1959-61, mgr. engring. adminstrn. dept., 1961-64, product design mgr., 1964-67, dir. facilities, 1967-69, dir. mgmt. systems and controls, 1969-71, dir. ground transp. programs, 1971—. Mem. Naval Air Systems Effectiveness Adv. Bd., 1965-70. Mem. Dallas Citizens Traffic Commn. Registered profl. engr., Tex. Mem. Soc. Automotive Engrs. (tech. bd. Tex. sect. 1965-67, dir. 1967-69, chmn. aerospace council 1970—), Am. Mgmt. Assn., Conf. Bd., Omicron Delta Epsilon, Sigma Iota Epsilon. Presbyn. Mason (Shriner). Clubs: Engineers, Brookhaven Country (Dallas); Tanglewood Hills Country (Pottsboro, Tex.). Contbr. articles to profl. publs. Patentee in field. Home: 4426 Laren Lane Dallas TX 75234 Office: Dept 2-18000 PO Box 5907 Dallas TX 75222

HELTON, JOHN WILLIAM, dentist; b. Colorado City, Tex., Nov. 10, 1908; s. James Monroe and Lilly Mae (Childers) H.; student U. Tex., 1926-28; D.D.S., Baylor U., 1933; postgrad. U. Pa., 1948-49; m. Nancy Maxene Travis, Nov. 9, 1936; 1 son, John William. Resident oral surgery Episcopal Hosp., Phila., 1949-50; resident anesthesia Robert B. Green Hosp., San Antonio, 1954; practice dentistry specializing in oral surgery, Jacksonville, Tex., 1933-40, San Antonio, 1954—; chief oral surgery Bapt. Meml. Hosp. Systems, 1958—; mem. staff Santa Rosa, Meth. hosps. Chief oral surgery service, dir. oral tng., clin. prof. oral surgery service U. Tex., Robert B. Green Hosp., U. Tex. Med. Sch., 1954-67; cons. oral surgery VA Hosp., Kerrville, Tex., 1958—. Served to lt. col. U.S. Army, 1940-54. Decorated Legion Merit, Bronze Star medal. Diplomate Am. Bd. Oral Surgery. Fellow Am. Coll. Dentists; mem. Am. Dental Assn., Am. Soc. Oral Surgeons, Southwest Soc. Oral Surgeons (pres. 1972—). Baptist (deacon 1950—). Mason. Home: 226 W Fair Oaks Place San Antonio TX 78209 Office: 235 E Hildebrand Av San Antonio TX 78212

HELTON, THOMAS HOWARD, govt. ofcl.; b. Milton County, Ga., May 16, 1929; s. Henry A. and Lena Mae (Nunn) H.; grad. Abraham Baldwin Agrl. Coll., Tifton, Ga., 1946-48; B.S., U. Ga., 1950, M.S., 1956; m. Katie Lee Strickland Helton, July 20, 1957. Asst. county extension agt. U. Ga., Jasper County, 1950-51, Burke County, 1952-53, De Kalb County, 1953-58, asso. county agt., 1958-60, county agt.-chmn., 1960—. Active Am. Cancer Soc., A.R.C., Ga. Heart Assn. Served to capt. AUS, 1950-53. Mem. Nat. (distinguished service award), Ga. (distinguished service award) county agts. assns., Internat. Platform Assn., Ga., Nat. farm bur. fedns., U. Ga. Alumni Soc., Alpha Gamma Rho. Baptist. Home: 1470 N Peachtree St Norcross GA 30071 Office: 101 Old Courthouse Ct Sq Decatur GA 30030

HELVENSTON, BRANTLY WALKER, III, ins. agy. exec.; b. Live Oak, Fla., Sept. 2, 1928; s. Brantly Walker and Mary Perry (DaMon) H.; student U. Fla., 1945-46; B.S., Fla. State U., 1949; m. Laura Harriett Cantrell, Dec. 20, 1952; children—Laura Damon, Harriett Darrow, Brantly Walker IV. Mem. firm B.W. Helvenston & Sons, Live Oak, Fla., 1949—, partner, 1962—; dir. 1st Comml. Bank, Live Oak. Tchr. ins. course Suwannee Hamilton County area Vocational Sch., 1962—. Civic mediator Tchrs. Strike, 1968; mem. Live Oak Zoning Commn., 1960, chmn., 1969-72; mem. Gov's adv. com., Suwannee County, 1971—. Chmn. Suwannee County Democratic exec. com., 1970—. Acad. admissions counselor Sewanee Acad., 1971—; bd. dirs. Children's Home Soc. Fla., 1965-68. Served with AUS, 1950-52. Named Outstanding Young Man Suwannee County Jr. C. of C., 1959. Mem. Suwannee County C. of C. (v.p. 1971-72), Am. Legion, Suwannee Little Theatre (pres. 1954), Suwannee Concert Assn. (v.p. 1957); Alpha Tau Omega. Democrat. Episcopalian (vestryman 1966, sr. warden 1969). Mason, Kiwanian (pres. 1968). Club: Suwannee Country (sec. 1960-62). Home: 600 Pine St Live Oak FL 32060 Office: 109 E Howard St Box 818 Live Oak FL 32060

HELWIG, ELSON BOWMAN, physician; b. Pierceton, Ind., Mar. 5, 1907; s. Llewellyn and Grace (Bowman) H.; B.S., Ind. U., 1930, M.D., 1932; m. Mildred Stoelting, Apr. 20, 1933; children—Alan S., Warren B., Ann (Mrs. Thomas Gordon). Rotating intern Indpls. City Hosp., 1932-33, resident pathology, 1933-34; asst. resident pathology Inst. Pathology, Western Res. U., 1934-35, resident pathology Cleve. City Hosp., 1935-36; asst. pathologist New Eng. Deaconess Hosp., Boston, 1936-39; mem. faculty Washington U. Sch. Medicine, St. Louis, 1939-46, asst. prof. pathology, 1946; sr. pathologist, chief skin and gastro-intestinal pathology br. Armed Forces Inst. Pathology, Washington, 1946—, chief department of pathology, 1955—, asso. dir. for consultation, 1967—; profl. lectr. George Washington U. Sch. Medicine, 1947-64, clin. prof., 1964—; vis. profl. dermatol. pathology Temple U. Sch. Medicine, 1958—, cons. skin and cancer hosp. of univ., 1959—; cons. Walter Reed Army Hosp., 1953—, WHO, 1965—. Mem Armed Forces Epidemiological Bd., 1968—. Served to col., M.C., AUS, 1942-45; PTO. Recipient Meritorious Civilian Service award Dept. Army, Exceptional Civilian Service award, 1964; Distinguished Civilian Service award Dept. Def., 1965; President's award for Distinguished Fed. Civilian Service, 1966. Mem. Coll. Am. Pathologists, Am. Soc. Clin. Pathologists, Internat. Assn. Pathologists, Am. Assn. Pathologists and Bacteriologists, A.M.A., Mass. Med. Soc., Washington Pathology Soc., Washington Dermatol. Soc., Am. Acad. Dermatology, Assn. Mil. Dermatologists, Am. Soc. Dermatopathology (pres. 1964-65), Assn. Mil. Surgeons, Histochem. Soc., Out-Pathology Soc., Pacific Dermatol. Assn., Soc. Columbiana de Patologica, French Soc. Dermatology and Syphiology (fgn. corr.). Contbr. numerous articles to profl. publs. Identified and classified adnexal tumors of skin; established relationship between Bowen's disease and internal cancer; identified cloacogenic carcinoma of anus, anatomic and histochem. Office: Armed Forces Inst Pathology Washington DC 20305

HELZNER, MANUEL LOUIS, econ. research orgn. exec.; b. Lynn, Mass., Oct. 17, 1928; s. Samuel and Bessie (Portnoy) H.; B.A., George Washington U., 1950, M.A., 1954; m. Charlotte R. Fertel, Sept. 3, 1950; children—Rochelle M., Robyn A., David E. Economist U.S. Post Office Dept., 1954-55, 59-62; asso. economist Nat. Planning Assn., Washington, 1954-59, dep. dir., 1966-69, project dir., 1969—; fiscal economist U.S. Bur. Budget, 1962-66. Mem. Am. Econ. Assn., Am. Statis. Assn. Author: (with Gerhard Colm) Public Finance: Needs, Sources and Utilization, 1961; (with Gerhard Colm, Theodore Geiger) The Economy of the American People, 1961. Home: 1817 Franwall Av Silver Spring MD 20902 Office: Nat Planning Assn 1666 Connecticut Av Washington DC 20009

HEMBREE, HUGH LAWSON, III, holding co. exec.; b. Ft. Smith, Ark., Nov. 16, 1931; s. Raymond N. and Cladys (Newman) H.; B.S. in Bus. Adminstrn., U. Ark., 1953, LL.B., 1958; m. Sara Janelle Young, Sept. 1, 1956; children—Hugh Lawson IV, Raymond Scott. In middle mgmt. Ark.-Best Freight System, Inc., Ft. Smith, 1958-61, dir., 1960—, dir. finance 1961-65, v.p., 1965—; pres., dir. Ark.-Best Corp., Ft. Smith, 1966—; pres. Hembree Farms, Inc., Ft. Smith, 1962—; chmn. exec. com., dir. Nat. Bank of Commerce, Dallas; chmn. 1st Bankers Real Estate Trust, 1968; dir. Am. Found. Life Ins. Co., Comml. Nat. Bank, Universal Ins. Co. (all Little Rock), Riverside Furniture Corp., Mid-Am. Industries, S.W. Die Casting (all Ft. Smith), Robertson Distbn. Systems, Inc., Houston. Pres., Westark Area council Boy Scouts Am., 1966-67, mem. nat. council, mem. regional exec. bd., 1967—, chmn. regional sustaining membership com.; treas. Endowment Trust Fund, U. Ark., bd. dirs., mem. dean's adv. com. Sch. Bus.; chmn. bd. devel. St. Edward Community Med. Center, 1972—. Sec., Ft. Smith-Sebastian County Joint Planning Commn., 1964—; mem. Ark. Legislative Tax Study Commn., 1969; pres. Sebastian County Mental Health Assn., 1964. Justice of peace Sebastian County, 1959—; mem. Ark. Democratic Central Com., 1968—. Bd. dirs. Jr. Achievement of Ft. Smith, Coalition for Rural Am., 1971, Ark. Council on Econ. Edn., 1964—; trustee Ft. Smith Children's Mus.; chmn. bd. trustees St. Edwards Community Hosp., 1970—. Served to 1st lt. USAF, 1953-55. Recipient Silver Beaver award Boy Scouts Am., 1969, Distinguished Service award Ft. Smith Jr. C. of C., 1965, Leadership award State of Ark., 1970; named Ark. Outstanding Young Man of Year, 1965. Mem. Nat. Assn. Devel. Orgns. (chmn. adv. com.), Ark. (v.p. 1969—), Ft. Smith (pres., dir.) chambers commerce, Young Pres.'s Orgn., U. Ark. Alumni Assn. (dir., bldg. com.), Am. Trucking Assn. (nat. accounting and finance council), N.A.M. (nat. dir. 1971), Ark. Arts Center, Scabbard and Blade, Delta Theta Phi, Sigma Alpha Upsilon. Episcopalian (vestryman, co-chmn. ch. finance com.). Clubs: Chapperell, Lancers, Economic (Dallas); Town, Ft. Smith Hardscrabble Country (Ft. Smith); Capital (Little Rock); N.Y. Athletic; Presidents (dir.) (Hendrix Coll., Conway, Ark.). Home: 3220 Park Av Fort Smith AR 72901 Office: 1000 S 21st St Fort Smith AR 72901

HEMNESS, RAY LESLIE, hosp. adminstr.; b. Milltown, Wis., Oct. 28, 1926; s. Louis H. and Maria (Ruud) H.; B.C.S., Strayer Coll., 1948; m. Peggy Ann Sims, Feb. 14, 1947; 1 dau., Deborah Kay. Treas., Standard Engring. Co., Washington, 1956-61; asst. adminstr. No. Va. Doctors Hosp., Arlington, 1961-62, adminstr., dir., 1962—, sec., 1970—; sec. Va. Doctors Properties, Arlington, 1969—; dir. Seven Corners Med. Bldgs., Inc., Falls Church, Va., 1962-71. Chpt. chmn. A.R.C., Arlington, 1967-70, now bd. dirs. Bd. dirs. No. Va. Heart Assn., Instrs., Internat. Underwater Explorers Soc. Mason (32 deg.), Rotarian. Home: 3027 Hazelton St Falls Church VA 22044 Office: 601 S Carlyn Springs Rd Arlington VA 22204

HEMPHILL, CALVIN RALPH, sch. adminstr.; b. Seattle, Mar. 4, 1925; s. Ralph and Jane (Skea) H.; student U. Cal. at Los Angeles, 1946-49; B.A., Claremont Mens Coll., 1951; postgrad. U. Ams. (Mex.), 1951-52; m. Lilia Fernandez, Oct. 10, 1953; children—Arturo, Vivian, Ralph II, Eric. Supr., Hemphill Schs., Mexico, D.F., Mexico, 1951-64, exec. dir. Hemphill Schs., Los Angeles, 1964—; pres. Continental-Tech. Corp., Republic of Panama, 1955—; pres. Sistemas Universales S.A., Mexico, 1972. Pres. Nat. Home Study Council, Washington, 1972—. Co-chmn. United Fund, Mexico D.F., Mex., 1964. Bd. dirs. Sister City Assn., Beverly Hills, Cal.; mem. adv. com. So. Cal. Inst. Internat. Edn.; bd. affiliates Claremont Men's Coll. Served with USNR, 1943-46. Mem. Young Pres.' Orgn. Mason (Shriner). Clubs: Chapultepec Golf; Los Angeles Country; White Friars; University of Mexico. Home: Durango 355-6 Piso Mexico 7 DF Mexico

HEMPHILL, JAMES ARTHUR, plastic co. exec.; b. Pickens, Miss., Oct. 3, 1923; s. E.A. and Helen (Simpson) H.; student Holmes Jr. Coll., 1941-43, U. Ala., 1945-46; m. Rachel A. Roberson, July 14, 1944; children— William Lee, James Arthur, Mary Susan, Helen Catherine. Owner, Hemphill Electric Co., Kosciusko, Miss., 1947-56; prodn. mgr. Vickers, Inc., Jackson, Miss., 1956-60; pres. R & H Mfg. Co., Jackson, 1960-63; v.p., gen. mgr. Gulf Plastics Inc., Jackson, 1963-71; adviser, cons. Briarwood Products, Jackson, 1968-71; plastics cons. Piper Industries, Memphis, 1971-72, pres. plastic div., 1972—; plastic cons. Lott Enterprises, Jackson, 1971—. Served with AUS, 1943-44; ETO. Mem. Soc. Plastic Engrs., Jackson C. of C., Miss. Mfrs. Assn. Home: 5425 Charter Oak Jackson MS 39211 Office: 1320 Boling St Jackson MS 39206

HEMPHILL, ROBERT WITHERSPOON, judge, ex-congressman; b. Chester S.C., May 10, 1915; s. John McLure and Helen (Witherspoon) H.; A.B., U. S.C., 1936, LL.B. 1938; m. Forrest Isabelle Anderson, June 29, 1942; children—Forrest Richardson, Harriet Witherspoon, Robert Witherspoon. Admitted to S.C. bar, 1938; asso. firm Hemphill & Hemphill. Chester, 1938-64; solicitor 6th S.C. Jud. Circuit, 1950-56; mem. 85th-88th congresses from 5th S.C. Dist.; now U.S. dist. judge for Eastern and Western S.C. mem. S.C. Ho. of Reps., 1947-48. Served with USAAF, 1941-45; mem. USAF Res. Mem. Am., S.C., Chester County bar assns., Am. Law Inst., S.C. Farm Bur., S.C. Wildlife Assn., Am. Legion, 40 and 8, Am. Judicature Soc. Democrat. Presbyn. K.P., Elk, Moose. Clubs: Army and Navy (Washington); Palmetto (Columbia, S.C.); Carolina Yacht (asso.) (Charleston, S.C.) Home: 167 York St Chester SC 29706 Office: Ct House Columbia SC 29201

HEMPHILL, WILLIAM LEE, dairy exec.; b. Greensboro, N.C., Oct. 4, 1921; s. Ross and Nell (Bean) H.; B.S., Bowling Green U., 1948; postgrad. U. N.C., 1967; m. Joan Thatcher, Sept. 20, 1945; children—William Lee II, Ross Frank. Partner, Lindsay, Squires and Everett, C.P.A.'s, Greensboro, N.C., 1948-58; chief financial and adminstrn. officer United Dairies, Inc., and predecessor co., Greensboro, 1958-72, exec. v.p., 1972—; treas. First Mortgage Ins. Co., Greensboro, 1963—. Cons. corp. orgn. and finance; chmn., Gov.'s Adv. Council Vocational Edn., 1969-71; commr. N.C. Milk Commn., 1971—. Pres. bd. Greensboro Community Council, 1966-68; v.p. Greensboro United Community Services, 1968-69. Served with USAAF, 1942-46. Mem. Financial Execs. Inst., Am. Inst. C.P.A.'s, Am. Inst. Mgmt. Democrat. Episcopalian. Home: 508 Audubon Dr Greensboro NC 27410 Office: 3939 W Market St Greensboro NC 27402

HEMRY, JEROME ELDON, lawyer; b. Kirksville, Mo., July 22, 1905; s. U. S. G. and Rose M. (Plumb) H.; A.B., Oklahoma City U., 1926; LL.B., U. Okla., 1928; LL.M., Harvard, 1929; m. Martha L. Langston, Aug. 1, 1934; children—Jerome Louis, Kenneth Marshall. Admitted to Okla. bar, 1928; partner Hemry & Hemry, Oklahoma City, since 1931; prof. law Central Okla. Sch. Law, 1931-41; dean, prof. law Langston U., 1948-49; dir., counsel Am. Gen. Life Ins. Co. Okla.; pres., gen. counsel Gen. Constrn. Corp., 1941-45; legislative counsel Okla. Chain Store Assn., 1941-44. Bd. dirs. Family and Children's Service, 1939-56. Mem. Okla. Assn. Mun. Attys. (pres. 1956-57), Am., Okla. bar assns., Order of Coif, Phi Delta Phi, Lambda Chi Alpha. Methodist (pres., counsel trustees Bd. Conf. Claimant's Okla. Ann. Conf., treas. S. dist. Oklahoma City). Clubs: Lions, Men's Dinner (Oklahoma City). Author articles in legal jours. Home: 2255 NW 55th St Oklahoma City OK 73112 Office: 1355 First Nat Bldg Oklahoma City OK 73102

HEMSTREET, ARTHUR C., govt. ofcl.; b. Troy, N.Y., 1912; ed. Hamilton Coll., Whartor Sch. Finance U. Pa. Vice pres., treas. Fed. Nat. Mortgage Assn., Washington. Home: 440 East West Hwy Bethesda MD 20014 Office: Fed Nat Mortgage Assn 1133 15th St NW Washington DC 20005*

HENCK, FRED WILLIAM, editor; b. Latrobe, Pa., May 10, 1921; s. Fred W. and Elsie (Adam) H.; student Ohio U., 1937-39; m. Bettye M. Hinchcliff, June 23, 1944; children—Kathryn Elizabeth, Joanne Susan, William Oliver. Editor, Independent Syndicate, Washington, 1939-40, Asso. Editors, Washington, 1940-41, Army Times, Washington, 1941; asso. editor Telecommunications Reports, Washington, 1941-48, mng. editor, 1948-52, exec. editor, 1952-64, editor, 1964—; pres., dir. Telecommunications Pub. Co., Washington, 1964—; editor Washington bur. Telephone Engr. &Mgmt., 1946—. Mem. Arlington County (Va.) Pub. Utilities Commn., 1964—. Served with USAAF, 1942-46. Decorated Bronze Star. Mem. Ind. Newsletter Assn. (pres. 1967). Clubs: International, Nat. Press. Home: 2407 N Quebec St Arlington VA 22207 Office: Nat Press Bldg Washington DC 20004

HENCKEL, GEORGE, JR., city mgr. San Antonio, Tex. Address: City Hall Military Plaza San Antonio TX 78205*

HENDERSON, ARTHUR FLOYD, printing co. exec.; b. Atlanta, Mar. 17, 1934; s. William Dewey and Alice (Aldora) H.; student Ga. State Coll., 1968-69; m. Mary Ruth Porter, Nov. 26, 1954; children—Donna, Kay, Cindy, Arthur Floyd. With Darby Printing Co., Atlanta, 1955—, salesman, 1964-66, operations supr., 1966-68, v.p., gen. mgr., 1968—. Served with USAF, 1951-55. Named Most Outstanding Apprentice Printer in Atlanta, 1958. Democrat. Baptist. Club: Craftsman. Home: 2599 Kings Park Circle Decatur GA 30034 Office: 715 W Whitehall St SW Atlanta GA 30310

HENDERSON, CHARLES MURRAY, prison ofcl.; b. Del Rio, Tenn., Aug. 21, 1920; s. Charles M. and Judith (Huff) H.; B.S., Carson Newman Coll., 1954; LL.B., John R. Neal Coll., 1942; M.S., U. Tenn., 1956; postgrad. Vanderbilt U., 1956-57; m. Marie Antoinette Hurst, Jan. 13, 1948; children—Marie Jeanne, Thomas Gerald. Chief psychiatric social worker Central State Hosp., Nashville, 1956-58; dir. social services Ark. State Hosp., Little Rock, 1958-61; asso. warden Men's Reformatory, Anamosa, Ia., 1961-65; warden Tenn. State Penitentiary, Nashville, 1965-68, La. State Penitentiary, Angola, 1968—. Asso. prof. Little Rock U., 1959-60; instr. Ia. Peace Officers Acad., Iowa City, 1963-64. Mem. Ark. Govs. Commn. on Aging, 1960; mem. bd. Ia. Council on Crime and Delinquency, 1964-65. Served with AUS, 1942-48. Mem. Nat. Council on Alcoholism, Am. Correctional Assn., Nat. Assn. Social Workers, V.F.W. Elks.Home: PO Box 66 Angola LA 70712 Office: La State Penitentiary Angola LA 70712

HENDERSON, DAVID NEWTON, congressman; b. Hubert, N.C., Apr. 16, 1921; s. Isaac Newton and Virginia (Boney) H.; B.S., Davidson Coll., 1942; LL.B., U. N.C., 1949; m. Mary Wellons Knowles. Dec. 11, 1942; children— David Bruce, Wiley Bryant, Wimbric Boney. Admitted to N.C. bar, 1949; practiced in Wallace until 1960; asst. gen. counsel com. edn. and labor Ho. of Reps., 1951-52; solicitor Duplin County Gen. Ct., 1953-57, judge, 1957-59; mem. 88th-92d congresses from 3d Dist. N.C. Served to maj. USAAF, 1942-46. Mem Am. Legion, V.F.W. Democrat. Presbyn. Mason, Lion. Home: 503 E Murphy St Wallace NC 28466 Office: House Office Bldg Washington DC 20515

HENDERSON, DOUGLAS BOYD, lawyer; b. Pitts., Sept. 21, 1935; s. Arthur G. and Mildred E. (Rickenbach) H.; B.S., Pa. State U., 1957; J.D. with honors, George Washington U., 1963; m. Olivia Lauer, July 6, 1957; children—Scotland Weaver, Keith Arthur, Heather Alice. Salesman, Arthur G. Henderson, Akron, O., 1957-59; patent agt. Swift and Co., Washington, 1959-62; admitted to Va. bar, 1962, D.C. bar, 1963; law clk. U.S. Ct, of Claims, Washington, 1962-63; practiced in Washington, 1963—; atty. Irons, Birch, Swindler and McKie, 1963-65; mem. firm Finnegan and Henderson, Washington, 1965-69, Finnegan, Henderson and Farabow, 1969-72, Finnegan, Henderson, Farabow and Garrett, 1972—. Mem. Sleepy Hollow Run Civil Anns., Annandale, Va., 1965—. Mem. Fed., Am., Va. bar assns., Bar Assn. D.C., Am. Patent Law Assn., Patent Office Soc. Phi Gamma Delta, Delta Theta Phi. Methodist. Clubs: University, Touchdown (Washington); Rehobeth Beach (Del.) Country. Home: 6715 Wemberly Way McLean VA 22101 Office: 1775 K St NW Washington DC 20006

HENDERSON, EDMUND MCKEILL, physician; b. Bridgetown, Va., Apr. 16, 1915; s. Upshur Kerr and Bessie Trower (Roberts) H.; M.D., U. Va., 1942; m. Mary Lawton Mathews, June 18, 1945; children—Edmund M., James Lamar, Elizabeth T., Thomas L. Intern, U.S. Naval Hosp., Parris Island, S.C., 1942-43; resident U.S. Naval Hosp., Phila.; gen. practice medicine, Nassawadox, Va., 1949—; pres. staff, chief obstetrics Northampton-Accomac Meml. Hosp. Served with M.C., USN, 1942-49. Mem. Med. Soc. Va., A.M.A., Northampton County Med. Soc. (pres. 1955-56, 71-72). Episcopalian (treas. 1962-67). Address: Nassawadox VA 23413

HENDERSON, FRANK PAUL, ceramic industry cons.; b. Bluff City, Kan., Aug. 28, 1905; s. James Melvin and Josephine (Sharp) H.; student Southwestern Coll., 1922-25, Kan. State Agr. U., 1925-26; m. Della Kate Bailey, Feb. 7, 1947; children—Robert, David. Chemist, Empire Refining Co., Ponca, Okla., 1925-26; engr. U.S. Bur. of Rds., Vancouver, Wash., 1926-27; asst. ceramic engr. Cal. Clay Products Co., South Gate, 1927-29; plant supt. So. Co., San Antonio, 1929-33; engr. Ladrillera Monterrey (Mex.), 1933-34; constrn. engr. Ferro Corp., Cleve., 1936-38, 45-51; supt. Camark Pottery Co., Camden, Ark., 1938-42; cons. ceramic industry, Tyler, Tex., 1959—. Served with AUS, 1942-45. Mem. Am. Ceramic Soc., Nat. Inst. Ceramic Engrs., Am. Soc. for Testing and Materials. Address: 1701 McDonald Rd Tyler TX 75701

HENDERSON, GEORGE HALL, lumber co. exec.; b. Corrigan, Tex., Mar. 10, 1897; s. Julius Leonidas and Sarah Josephine Flavilla (Neyland) H.; student pub. schs.; m. Maurine Canon, Sept. 17, 1929; children—Mildred Louise (Mrs. Fred Edward Grinstead), George Hall. Gen. mgr. Angelina Hardwood Co., Ewing, 1923-45, v.p., 1945—; pres. Angelina Hardwood Lumber Co., Lufkin, 1945—; dir. First Bank & Trust, Lufkin, Home Savs. & Loan Assn. Past pres., trustee sch. bd. Lufkin Ind. Sch. Dist. Trustee Meml. Hosp. Mem. Nat. Hardwood Lumber Assn. (pres. 1946-48), Hardwood Mfrs. Inst. (pres. 1931-33), Southwestern Hardwood Club (pres. 1927-31), Angelina County C. of C. (past pres.). Methodist (trustee). Club:

Lufkin (past pres., mem. bd.). Home: 906 Markus St Lufkin TX 75901 Office: 1312 Wilson St Lufkin TX 75901

HENDERSON, GEORGE ROBERT, librarian; b. Ft. Worth, May 7, 1918; s. George R. and Jessie (Mitchell) H.; Mus.B. (Theodore Presser music scholar), Tex. Wesleyan Coll., 1940; Mus.M., North Tex. State U., 1949; B.L.S., Pratt Inst., 1948; m. Frances O'Neal, June 30, 1941. Tchr. music, pub. schs., Farmersville, Tex., Ft. Worth, 1941-42; music cataloger N.Y. Pub. Library, N.Y.C., 1947-48; chief music div. Pub. Library, Washington, 1948-53; fine arts librarian Tex. Christian U., Ft. Worth, 1953-54, Dallas Pub. Library, 1954—. Instr. sch. music So. Methodist U., 1966-67. Served with AUS, 1942-45. Mem. Music Library Assn. (sec. 1950-53), Dallas Print and Drawing Soc. (pres. 1965-67), Internat. Assn. Music Libraries, Internat. Fedn. Libraries Assn., Tex. Library Assn. (chmn. fine arts roundtable 1964-65), Dallas (hon.), Nat., Tex. fedn. music clubs. Home: 4511 Livingston Av Dallas TX 75205 Office: Fine Arts Dept Dallas Pub Library Dallas TX 75201

HENDERSON, HAROLD ALPHEUS, economist; b. Leoma, Tenn., May 6, 1924; s. Talmadge Pressley and Vesta (Stout) H.; B.S., U. Tenn., 1947, M.S., 1951; Ph.D., Purdue U., 1963; m. Joanna Elizabeth McCammon, June 5, 1947; children—James Harold, Elizabeth Ann. Spl. instr. Knox County, Tenn., 1947-49; asst. prof. Auburn U., 1952-54; agrl. economist U.S. Dept. Agr., 1954-63; adviser Mysore U. Agrl. Scis., Bangalore, India, 1964-66; agrl. economist TVA, Muscle Shoals, Ala., 1963-64, 66—. Tchr., Purdue U., 1956-57, Grad. Sch., U. Tenn., 1957-63. Commr., Lauderdale (Ala.) dist. council Boy Scouts Am. Bd. dirs., treas. Shoals Area Youth for Christ. Served to capt. USMCR, 1944-46, 51-52. Mem. Internat. Assn. Agrl. Economists, Indian Soc. Agrl. Economists, Am., Farm econ. assns., Tenn. Soc. Farm Mgrs. (dir. 1964), Knoxville Econs. Club (v.p. 1963), Gideons Internat. Baptist (deacon). Clubs: Exchange (Florence, Ala.). Contbr. articles to profl. jours. Home: 722 W Lakeside St Florence AL 35630 Office: Agrl Resource Devel Br TVA Muscle Shoals AL 35660

HENDERSON, HAROLD RAINS, engring. exec.; b. Marshall, Tex., Jan. 24, 1907; s. William D. and Dora (Strickland) H.; B.S. in Civil and Irrigation Engring., Colo. State U., 1929; m. Rose Henning, Dec. 31, 1928; children—Harold William, Robert Henning. Constrn. engr. Mo. Hwy. Dept. 1929-30, Mo. Portland Cement Co., Independence, 1930-31; project engr. Tex. Hwy. Dept., 1932-34; engr. Harrison County, Tex., 1935-42; gen. supt. McKinney Constrn. Co., Marshall, 1942-47; v.p. H. R. Henderson & Co., Marshall, 1947-58; pres. Turnbull, Inc., Marshall, 1958-70, Turnbull Corp., 1965-71, also dir.; pres. Eastex Metal Fabricators, Inc., 1970—, EnDeCo, Inc., Marshall, 1971—; pres., dir. Pure Metals, Ltd., Geneva, Switzerland, 1962-69; cons. to City of Marshall, Harrison County, Tex., Govt. Iran for aluminum prodn. Mem. Marshall Indsl. Found., Greater Marshall Indsl. Found. Registered profl. engr., Tex. Fellow Am. Soc. C.E.; mem. Marshall C. of C. Home: 2107 N Franklin St Marshall TX 75670 Office: PO Box 329 Marshall TX 75670

HENDERSON, JAMES ALVIN, civil engr.; b. Clinton, Tenn., Jan. 2, 1929; s. Hence Hicks and Georgia (Rhyne) H.; B.S. in Agrl. Engring., U. Tenn., 1951; M.B.A., Ala. A. and M. U., 1972; m. Hedy Fay Conner, Feb. 23, 1952; children—Stuart Alvin, Karen Fay. Constrn. mgmt. engr. Clark Hill Dam, Clarks Hill, S.C., 1951-54, Kings Bay Army Terminal, St. Marys, Ga., 1955-57, Hartwell (Ga.) Dam, 1958-63, Miss. Test Facility, Bay St. Louis, 1963-66, civil engr. Anti Ballistic Missile Program, Mobile, Ala., 1966-67, Huntsville, Ala., 1967—. Served with USNR, 1948-49. Registered profl. engr., Ga. Mem. Assn. U.S. Army. Baptist (deacon, tchr. Sunday sch.). Home: 815 Mira Vista Dr Huntsville AL 35802 Office: Anti Ballistic Missile Program Wynn Dr Research Park Huntsville AL 35807

HENDERSON, JAMES B., ret. gas pipeline co. exec.; b. Amarillo, Tex., June 13, 1909; s. James E. and Belle Vida (McBride) H.; LL.B., U. Okla., 1932; m. Laura Jane Brookins, Feb. 28, 1931; children—James B., Mary Jane. Admitted to Okla. bar, 1932; practiced in Okla., Kan., 1932-34; asso. firm Phillips, Tramme, Estes, Edwards and Orn, Ft. Worth, 1934-37; legal dept. Ark. Nat. Gas Corp., 1937-49; v.p., gen counsel Transcontinental Gas Pipe Line Corp., 1949-61, exec. v.p., 1961-67, pres., 1967-72, chief exec. officer, 1968-72, also dir. Mem. Am., Tex., Okla. bar assns., Tex. Mfrs. Assn. (dir.), So. Gas Assn. (dir.), Phi Delta Phi. Home: Lake L B J Marble Falls TX

HENDERSON, JAMES FREEMAN, architect; b. Macon, Ga., May 30, 1927; s. Shelton LaFayette and Nora Lillian (Watson) H.; student Middle Ga. Coll., 1948; certificate So. Tech. Inst., 1950; m. Betty Beck, July 8, 1950; children—Julie Pamela, Betty Jill, James Freeman. Draftsman Dennis and Dennis Architects, Macon, 1949-60; prin. Henderson & Bray Architects, Macon, 1960-65; prin. Dunwody, Dunwody, Henderson and Bray Architects, Macon, 1965-68; asso. Dennis and Dennis Architects, Macon, 1968—. Chmn. Jones County Planning and Zoning Bd., 1969-70; chmn. Jones County Beautification Com., 1970—. Served with USNR, 1945-46. Mem. A.I.A., Constrn. Specifications Inst., Phi Delta Theta. Methodist (trustee 1968—). Home: Route 6 Henderson Rd Macon GA 31201 Office: 1101 So Trust Bldg Macon GA 31201

HENDERSON, JAMES HENRY, dentist; b. Henderson, N.C., Jan. 29, 1925; s. James and Sarah Elizabeth (Evans) H.; B.S., Hampton Inst., 1948; D.D.S., Meharry Med. Coll., 1953; m. Mabel Joyce White, July 21, 1956; children—Eryn Janyce, Edythe Jeannelle, James Henry. Intern VA Hosp., Tuskegee, Ala., 1955-56; dentist La. Dept. Hosps., 1956-59; individual practice dentistry, New Iberia, La., 1957—; mem. staff Iberia Parish Hosp., Dauterive Hosp., Found. Hosp., Franklin, La.; mem. vis. staff New Orleans Charity Hosp. Dir. Bacmonila, Inc., John A. Andrews Meml. Clinics, Tuskegee. Founder Community Progress League, 1960, pres., 1960-63; chmn., parade marshall La. Sugar Cane Festival and Fair, 1962-66; chmn. Iberia Parish Tb. Assn., 1962; pres. br. N.A.A.C.P., 1964-70, state bd., 1965-70, state treas., 1969-70; mem. La. Commn. on Human Relations, Rights and Responsibilities, 1965-70; coach Little League Baseball, 1972. Bd. dirs. Pee Wee Football League, New Iberia. Served with AUS, 1943-46; with Dental Corps, U.S. Army, 1952-55. Recipient award of achievement Omega Psi Phi, 1962, award of merit La. Beauticians Assn., 1968. Mem. Am. (diplomate nat. bd.), Nat., Chgo., Pelican State dental assns., Alpha Phi Alpha, Beta Kappa Chi. Baptist (trustee). Mason (Shriner). Club: Royal Vanders Social (New Iberia). Home: 400 S Curtis St New Iberia LA 70560 Office: 403 W Pershing St New Iberia LA 70560

HENDERSON, JAMES (MARVIN), advt. exec.; b. Atlanta, Mar. 28, 1921; s. Isaac Harmon and Ruth (Ashley) H.; student Furman U., 1939-40, Clemson Coll., 1940-42, N.Y.U., nights, 1943-44; B.S., U. Denver, 1946; grad. Advanced Mgmt. Program, Harvard, 1956; m. Donna Fern Baade, Apr. 28, 1945; children—Linda Dee, James Marvin, Deborah Fanchon. Sales supr. Gen. Foods Corp., N.Y.C., 1942-44; account exec. Curt Freiberger Advt. Agy., Denver, 1944-46; pres. Henderson Advt. Agy., Inc., Greenville, S.C. and Atlanta, 1946—; dir. Citizens & So. Nat. Bank, 1st Fed. Savs. & Loan, Greenville, S.C. spl. asst. to postmaster gen., 1969-70. Pres. Greenville Heart Assn., 1953-54; mem. Greenville Youth Commn., 1953-54; pres., dir. Greenville Mental Hygiene Clinic, 1954-57; bd. dirs. United Fund, 1954-55, pres., 1958. Chmn. Eisenhower campaign Greenville County, 1952; Republican candidate for lt. gov. S.C., 1970; chmn. S.C. Com. for Reelection of Pres., 1972. Chmn. Greenville County Found., 1968. Served with AUS, World War II. Named Young Man of Year, Greenville, 1954; Salesman of Yr., 1969. Mem. S.C. (past dir.), Greenville (past pres.) jr. chambers commerce, Greater Greenville C. of C. (past pres.), Young Pres.'s Orgn. (chmn. S.E. chpt.), Greenville Advt. Council (past pres.), Am. Assn. Advt. Agys. (nat. dir.). Methodist (steward, finance com.). Kiwanian (past dir.). Home: Route 7 Hickory Lane Greenville SC 29609 Office: 55 S Pleasantburg Dr Greenville SC 29607

HENDERSON, JOHN BROWN, economist; b. Glasgow, Scotland, Jan. 3, 1918; s. John Brown and Mary (Kerr) H.; M.A., U. St. Andrews (Scotland), 1939; student King's Coll., Cambridge (Eng.) U., 1939-40; Ph.D., Harvard, 1956; m. Joanna Baxter, Sept. 10, 1954; children—Mary Joanna, Margaret Brown, Elizabeth Campbell, John Stalker Kerr. Came to U.S., 1950, naturalized, 1956. Lectr. polit. economy U. St. Andrews, 1946-52; vis. prof. Union Coll., Schenectady, 1950-51; tutor econs. Harvard, 1954-56; economist Fed. Res. Bank of N.Y., 1956-60; Andrew Wells Robertson prof. econs. Allegheny Coll., Meadville, Pa., 1960-66; internat. economist Joint Econ. Com., U.S. Congress, 1966-68; dep. asst. sec. for econ. affairs U.S. Dept. Commerce, 1968-70; dir. econ. studies div. Bur. Labor Statistics U.S. Dept. Labor, Washington, 1970-72; chief econ. div. Congl. Research Service, 1972—. Mem. Meadville Charter Commn., 1965. Served to flight lt. RAF, 1941-46. Mem. Am. Econ. Soc., Soc. Internat. Devel. Home: 4119 N 27th Rd Arlington VA 22207 Office Library of Congress Washington DC 20540

HENDERSON, KAYE NEIL, civil engr., bus. exec.; b. Birmingham, Ala., June 10, 1933; s. Ernest Martin and Mary (Head) H.; B.S., Va. Mil. Inst., 1954; B.A. with honors, U. South Fla., 1967; m. Betty Jane Belanus, June 26, 1954; children—David Scott, Alan Douglas, Helen Kaye. Mgmt. trainee Gen. Electric Co., Schenectady, 1954; sales engr. Fla. Prestressed Concrete, Tampa, 1956-57; field engr. Portland Cement Assn., Tampa, 1957-63; gen. mgr. residential and comml. sales Tampa Electric Co., 1963-66; v.p. Watson & Co., architects and engrs., Tampa, 1966-69; v.p. Reynolds, Smith & Hills, architects, engrs. and planners, Jacksonville, Fla., 1969—. Vice chmn. Temple Terrace Planning and Zoning Bd., 1962-67. Pres. Guidance Center Hillsborough County, 1969. Mem. Duval County Republican Exec. Com. Bd. dirs. Salvation Army Home and Hosp. Council, 1964-69. Mem. found U. South Fla. Served to 1st lt. USAF, 1954-56. Recipient Service awards Greater Tampa C. of C., 1964-66; named Outstanding Young Man of Tampa Jr. C. of C., 1965; Outstanding Young Man of Am., U.S. Jr. C. of C., 1967. Registered profl. engr., Fla. Mem. Fla. Engring. Soc., Phi Kappa Phi. Republican. Episcopalian. Clubs: Ye Mystic Revellers, Timuguana Country, University (Jacksonville). Home: 4606 Yacht Club Rd Jacksonville FL 32210 Office: 4019 Blvd Center Dr Jacksonville FL 32207

HENDERSON, LEE GIBBONS, ednl. adminstr.; b. Miami, June 4, 1923; s. Ulysses Virgil and Mildred (Gibbons) H.; student Palm Beach Jr. Coll., 1940-42, U. Mo., 1942-43; B.S., U. Fla., 1947, M.A., 1950, Ed.D., 1954; m. Betty McIntosh, Dec. 17, 1950; children—Craig Lee, Preston McIntosh. Gen. ins. agt. Lewis E. Cook Agcy., Miami, 1947-49; dean boys Pensacola (Fla.) High Sch., 1950-52, asst. prin. and curriculum dir., 1954-55; supr. curriculum Brevard County, Fla., 1955-57; asst. dir. div. community jr. colls. Fla. Dept. Edn., Tallahassee, 1957-66, exec. dir. div. community colls., 1966-67, dir., 1968—. Cons. on community colls., states of Ark., 1964, S.C., 1966, Va., 1968; mem. So. Regional Edn. Bd. Mem. Fla. Council of 100. Mem. Am. Assn. Higher Edn., Council State Dirs. Two-Year Colls. (chmn. 1971-72), N.E.A., Am. Assn. Community and Jr. Colls. (dir. 1972—), Fla. Edn. Assn., Delta Tau Delta, Phi Kappa Phi, Phi Delta Kappa, Kappa Delta Pi. Presbyn. Kiwanian. Home: 2225 Armistead Rd Tallahassee FL 32303 Office: Knott Bldg Tallahassee FL 32304

HENDERSON, LOUIS CLIFTON, ins. co. exec.; b. Harlan, Ky., July 21, 1937; s. Louis Clifton and Aileen (Richmond) H.; B.S., U. Ark., 1960; m. Sharon Elizabeth Ward, Jan. 24, 1959; children—Lisa Ward, Ann Richmond. Staff accountant Price Waterhouse & Co., Houston, 1959-61; treas. Investors Preferred Life Ins. Co., 1961-68; exec. v.p. adminstrn. Am. Preferred Life Ins. Co., Birmingham, Ala., 1965-68, exec. v.p., treas. 1968—, also dir.; asst. to pres., treas. Tidelands Capital Corp., New Orleans, 1967—, also dir.; dir. Tidelands Life Ins. Co., New Orleans. Served with Finance Corps, USAF, 1960. C.P.A., Tex. Mem. Am. Inst. C.P.A.'s, Beta Gamma Sigma, Sigma Alpha Epsilon. Presbyn. Rotarian. Home: 3032 Westmoreland Dr Birmingham AL 35223 Office: 1900 Crestwood Blvd Birmingham AL 35210

HENDERSON, PHILIP S., psychologist; b. N.Y.C., Oct. 3, 1910; s. Herman and Molly (Winston) H.; B.S., City Coll. N.Y., 1930; M.A., Columbia, 1932; Ph.D., U. Tenn., 1950; postgrad. Pomona Coll., 1943, N.Y. Psychoanalytic Inst., 1937, Emory U., 1947; m. Norma Jean Edsel, July 1, 1950; children—Victor Warren, Helen Kay. Psychology intern Elmira Reformatory, 1932-33; psychology externe N.Y. Child Guidance, 1934; psychologist Sing Sing Prison, 1935-38; head psychologist Woodbourne Inst. Defective Delinquents, 1934-46; chief psychologist VA Hosp., Murfreesboro, Tenn., 1946-48, Knoxville, Tenn., 1948-49, Tuscaloosa, Ala., 1949-50, Ft. Roots, Ark., 1951-58, Augusta, Ga., 1958—. Tchr. N.Y. U., 1936-37, Pasadena Coll., 1944, U. Tenn., 1948-50. Served with AUS, 1941-45. Diplomate Am. Bd. Profl. Psychology. Mem. Am., Ga. psychol. assns. Home: 1403 Habersham Dr Augusta GA 30904 Office: VA Hosp Lenwood Wrightsboro Rd Augusta GA 30904

HENDERSON, THOMAS HOWARD, univ. pres.; b. Newport News, Va., Jan. 31, 1910; s. Rev. Hamilton M. and Mamie J. (Hamlette) H.; B.S., Va. Union U., 1928; A.M., U. Chgo., 1938, Ph.D., 1946; m. Kate R. Gilpin, Feb. 1, 1936; 1 dau., Tommyzee. Tchr. chemistry Armstrong High Sch., Richmond, Va., 1928-41; dean of coll. Va. Union U., Richmond, 1941-60, pres., 1960—. Mem. Richmond Sch. Bd. Mem. Richmond Urban League, Phi Delta Kappa, Alpha Phi Alpha, Sigma Pi Phi, Alpha Kappa Mu. Home: 1500 N Lombardy St Richmond VA 23220

HENDERSON, WALLACE W., dir. Fla. Planning and Budget Commn. Address: State Capitol Tallahassee FL 32304*

HENDERSON, WARREN S, state senator; b. Exeter, N.H., Nov. 14, 1927; B.A., Denison U., 1951; m. Polly Ann Schurr; children—Warren C., Susan D., Wendy L. Investment, financial exec.; now mem. Fla. Senate. Mem. Sarasota County (Fla.) Planning and Zoning Commn., 1957-58; chmn. Manatee/Sarasota Airport Authority, 1961-63; chmn. West Coast Inland Nav. Dist., 1962-63; mem. Fla. Bicentennial Commn. Del. Republican nat. conv., 1968; mem. Fla. Rep. com., 1970—. Served with USNR, World War II. Mem. C. of C., Phi Delta Theta. Presbyn. Elk, Mason. Address: PO Box 1358 Venice FL 33595

HENDERSON, WILLIAM HAROLD, rehab. inst. exec.; b. Ft. Dodge, Ia., Jan. 4, 1925; s. Harold Alexander and Benice Gertrude (Bonney) H.; student Humbold State Coll., Cal., 1946-47; B.S. in Zoology, Gustavus Adolphus Coll., 1949; m. Mary M. Hamren, Dec. 18, 1949; 1 son, Paul. Teaching asst. dept. zoology U. Cal. at Los Angeles, 1949-50, asst. research engr. Biotech. Lab. dept. engring., 1956-59; asso. in zoology U. Cal. at Davis, 1950; orthopedic appliance technician Cal. Rehab. Center, Santa Monica, 1953-55, Rancho Los Amigos Hosp., Downey, Cal., 1955-56; asso. staff specialist biomechanics lab. U. Cal. at San Francisco, 1959-67; sr. field rep. Joint Commn. on Accreditation Hosps. assigned to Commn. on Accreditation Rehab. Facilities, 1967-69; exec. dir. Dallas Rehab. Inst., 1969—; tech. assistance cons. Rehab. Services Adminstrn., Dept. Health, Edn. and Welfare, 1969—; cons. Mgmt. Services Assos., Austin, Tex., 1970—; regional survey cons. Commn. on Accreditation of Rehab. Facilities, 1971—; clin. instr. dept. phys. medicine and rehab. Southwestern Med. Sch., U. Tex., Dallas, 1969—, clin. instr. Sch. Allied Health Professions, 1970—; mem. Developmental Disabilities Planning and Adv. Council Tex., 1971—. Mem. profl. adv. com. Dallas Assn. for Retarded Children, 1970—; mem. Citizens Adv. Commn. for Vocational Rehab. Planning, Tex. Legislative Council, 1970—; mem. Interagy. Task Force to develop State Plan for Developmental Disabilities Act, 1971. Trustee Laguna Salada Union Sch. Dist., San Mateo County, Cal., 1964-65. Served with AUS, 1943-45; PTO. Mem. Nat. Rehab. Assn., Nat. Rifle Assn., Tex. Muzzle Loaders Assn., Internat. Assn. Rehab. Facilities (program chmn. 2d Ann. Conf. 1971), Dallas Area Rehab. Assn. (pres. elect), Sigma Xi. Contbr. articles to profl. jours. Home: 3130 Golfing Green Ct Farmers Branch TX 75234 Office: 7850 Brook Hollow Rd Dallas TX 75235

HENDON, ROBERT CARAWAY, transp. and mfg. co. exec.; b. Shelbyville, Tenn., Jan. 13, 1912; s. William Oscar and Anna Bertha (Caraway) H.; B.A. in Journalism, U. Mont., 1931, J.D., 1934; m. Ruth Perham, Apr. 23, 1936; children—Robert Caraway, Elizabeth Anne (Mrs. MacDonald Dunbar, Jr.). Admitted to Mont., Tenn. bars, 1934; gen. law practice, 1934-35; spl. agt., spl. agt. in charge FBI, 1935-39; inspr., adminstrv. asst. to dir., 1939-47; exec. rep. to pres. Ry. Express Agy. (name changed to REA Express), 1947, various exec. positions, 1947-50, v.p. personnel, 1953-55, v.p. operations, 1955-64, v.p. industry affairs, 1964-68; v.p. Consol. Freightways, Inc., 1968—; asst. to pres., dir. personnel Mathieson Chem. Corp., 1950-52; dir. REA Leasing Corp., 1961-68, pres., 1964-67, vice chmn. 1967-68; pres., dir. REA Express Seven Arts Transvision Inc., 1965-68, TOFC Leasing Corp., 1966-68; dir., chmn. exec. com. Fast Service Shipping Terminals, 1961-68; dir., mem. exec. com., chmn. audit com. Manhattan Life Ins. Co. Bd. dirs. Nat. Safety Council, chmn. nat. safety awards com., 1960-68; trustee, exec. com. U. Mont. Found., pres., 1966-68; bd. mgrs., vice chmn. Grand Central YMCA, 1958-68; trustee Center for Environmental and Resource Analysis. Recipient Distinguished Service award U. Mont., 1967. Mem. Newcomen Soc. N.Am., Transp. Assn. Am. (mem. policy implementation and facilitation coms.), Phi Sigma Kappa, Sigma Delta Chi. Episcopalian (past vestryman, warden). Clubs: University (Larchmont, N.Y.); Union League, Deadline (N.Y.C.). Author: Frontiers in Labor-Management Relations, 1956; Seniority; First In, Last Out, 1958; also articles. Home: 1128 Kensington Rd McLean VA 22101 Office: Suite 403 World Center Bldg 918 16th St NW Washington DC 20006

HENDRICK, ALFORD GANDEY, physician; b. Franklin, Ga., Feb. 14, 1902; s. Alford Gandey and Josie Lenora (Daniel) H.; M.D., Emory U., 1930; postgrad. Johns Hopkins, 1936-37; m. Mildred Deadwyler, Sept. 7, 1951. Intern Henry Grady Hosp., Atlanta, 1930; commr. health Sylvester and Worth counties Ga. Pub. Health Dept., 1937-41; gen. practice medicine, Perry, Ga., 1941—; mem. staff Perry Houston County Hosp., 1969—, chief staff, 1971-72; med. adviser Oaks Nursing Home, Marshallville, Ga., New Perry Nursing Home, Ga. Ch. Home Mem. Houston County Bd. Health, 1944—; med. adviser, examiner Houston County Coroner's Office, 1941—; med. mem. Houston County Selective Service Bd., 1942—; med. examiner local N.G. unit, 1944-69. Served with USPHS, 1931-36. Named Man of Yr., Perry Kiwanis Club, 1958, Exchange Club, Perry, 1970. Mem. Am., So., Ga., Peach med. assns., Democrat. Methodist. Mason (32 deg., Shriner), Kiwanian. Home: 1106 1st St Perry GA 31060 Office: 1100 Swift St Perry GA 31069

HENDRICKS, CHARLES MARVIN, JR., physician; b. Greenville, S.C., Jan. 31, 1926; s. Charles Marvin and Elizabeth (Cochran) H.; student Furman U., 1942-44; M.D., U. S.C., 1948; m. Norma Elizabeth Rutter, Apr. 22, 1949; 1son, Charles Marvin III. Intern, U.S. Naval Hosp., Portsmouth, Va., 1948-50; Charity Hosp., New Orleans, 1954-56; practice medicine specializing in internal medicine, Fort Lauderdale, Fla., 1956-61; chief med. service VA Center, Dublin, Ga., 1961—, head cons. teaching program in assn. with Med. Coll. Ga., 1965—. Served with M.C., USN, 1948-54. Fellow Am. Coll. Physicians; mem. A.M.A., Phi Chi. Presbyn. Rotarian. Club: Dublin (Ga.) Country. Address: VA Center Dublin GA 31021

HENDRICKS, DONALD DUANE, librarian; b. Flint, Mich., Nov. 3, 1931; s. Edgar F. and Grace L. (Roska) H.; A.B.,U. Mich., A.M. in L.S., 1955; Ph.D., U. Ill., 1966; m. Mary Jean Elrich, Feb. 17, 1951; children— Philip, Scott, Randall. With Detroit Public Library, 1955-57; head librarian Owosso (Mich.) Pub. Library, 1957-60, Millikin U., 1960-63; dir. libraries Sam Houston State U., 1966—; cons. in field. Grantee U.S. Office Edn., 1966. Mem. Am., Tex. library assns., Bibliog. Soc. (London, Eng.), Bibliog. Soc. Am., Huntsville C. of C. Kiwanian (pres. 1968-69). Author monographs, articles. Co-Author: Resources of Texas Libraries, 1968. Home: 2117 Roundabout Rd Huntsville TX 77340

HENDRICKS, ERNEST LEROY, govt. ofcl.; b. St. Augustine, Fla., Oct. 8, 1909; s. Ernest Jackson and Alice (Carlton) H.; B.S. in Civil Engring., U. Fla., 1931; m. Idena Marguerite Bridges, June 14, 1934; children—Ernest LeRoy, Lauralee (Mrs. Ray Nelson Cooley, Jr.), Mary Hope (Mrs. James Edwin Bacon, Jr.). Surface water investigations U.S. Geol. Survey, Fla., Ga., La., 1935-52, staff engr. Ga., 1952-56, chief research sect. gen. hydrology br., Washington, 1956-60, chief surface water br., 1960-63, asso. chief water resources div., Washington, 1963-66, chief hydrologist, 1966—. Fellow Am. Soc. C.E.; mem. Am. Geophys. Union, A.A.A.S., Geol. Soc. Am. Club: Cosmos. Home: 2900 N Edison St Arlington VA 22207 Office: Gen Services Adminstrn Bldg Washington DC 20242

HENDRICKS, OTTIS ERLE, supt. schs.; b. Dubach, La., May 20, 1921; s. Ottis Erle and Sadie Valentine (Miller) H.; B.S., La. Inst. Tech., 1942; M.S., Mexico City Coll., 1949; M.S., Tex. A. and I. U., 1951; postgrad. U. Tex., 1958, Baylor U., 1965; m. Marion Francis Watson, Sept. 27, 1942; children—Lillian, Judy (Mrs. R. J. Henderson), Linda Sue (Mrs. Robert Prewitt), Lynette. Coach, Vernon Parish Schs., Leesville, La., 1943-46; coach, prin. Am. Sch. Found., 1946-49; prin., Weslaco (Tex.) Jr. High Sch., 1949-50, Brooks County High Sch., Falfurrias, Tex., 1950-54, Pharr-San Juan-Alamo High Sch., 1954-58; asst. supt. Pharr-San Juan-Alamo Schs., 1958-62; asst. supt. Harlingen (Tex.) Schs., 1962-64; supt., Corsicana (Tex.) Pub. Schs., 1964-66, New Braunfels (Tex.) Ind. Schs., 1966—. Mem. N.E.A., Tex. State Tchrs. Assn. (dist. pres. 1970-71), Tex. Assn. Sch.

Adminstrs. (v.p. 1971-72), New Braunfels C. of C. (life). Methodist. Mason, Elk, Rotarian. Home: 300 Oak Tree Lane New Braunfels TX 78130 Office: 431 W Mill St New Braunfels TX 78130

HENDRICKSON, ELLWOOD ROBERT, engring. co. exec.; b. York, Pa., Nov. 4, 1921; s. Elwood Harkins and Myrtle (Hollinger) H.; B.S., Pa. State U., 1942; M.S., U. Wis., 1948, Ph.D., 1950; m. Cecelia Marie Berry, June 25, 1946; 1 dau., Lynda (Mrs. Garland Cox). San. engr. Oficina Tecnica Stubbins, Caracas, Venezuela, 1946-47; instr. U. Wis., 1949-50; asso. prof. U. Fla., 1950-58, prof., 1958-66, dir. research, 1964-66, now adj. prof.; v.p. Resources Research, Inc., Falls Church, Va., 1966-68; pres. Environmental Engring., Inc., Gainesville, Fla., 1968—; dir. Poly Con Corp., Ramsey, N.J., Reynolds, Smith and Hills, Architects-Engrs.-Planners, Inc., Jacksonville; spl. cons. USPHS, 1954—. Chms. Fla. Air Pollution Control Commn., 1958-66; chmn. Gordon Research Conf., 1967. Served from 2d lt. to capt. C.E., AUS, 1942-46. Recipient award for distinguished service Fla. Engring. Soc., 1968. Registered profl. engr., Fla. Diplomate Am. Bd. Indsl. Hygiene, Am. Acad. Environmental Engrs. Mem. Am. Soc. C.E. (past sect. pres.), Am. Pub. Health Assn., Nat. Soc. Profl. Engr. (dir.), Fla. Engring. Soc. (past pres.), Air Pollution Control Assn. (past pres.), Am. Soc. Testing Materials, Am. Indsl. Hygiene Assn., Water Pollution Control Fedn., T.A.P.P.I. Clubs: Gainesville Golf and Country, Tampa Yacht and Country. Author: (with H.D. Townsend) Register of Air Pollution Analysis, 1958, also others. Contbr. articles to profl. jours. Home: 2044 NW 7th Pl Gainesville FL 32601 Office: 2324 SW 34th St Gainesville FL 32601

HENDRICKSON, JEROME ORLAND, assn. exec., lawyer; b. Eau Claire, Wis., July 25, 1918; s. Harold and Clara (Halvorson) H.; student Wis. State Coll., 1936-39; J.D., U. Wis., 1942; m. Helen Phoebe Harty, Dec. 27, 1948; children—Jaime Ann, Jerome Orland. Admitted to Wis. bar, 1942, U.S. Supreme Ct. bar, 1956; pvt. practice, Eau Claire, 1946; sales and advt. mgr. Coca-Cola Bottling Co., Inc., Eau Claire, 1947-48; exec. sec. Eau Claire Community Chest, 1948-49; in charge dist. office Am. Petroleum Inst., Kansas City, Mo., 1950-53, Chgo., 1953-55; exec. dir. Nat. Assn. Plumbing-Heating-Cooling Contractors, 1955-64; exec. v.p. Cast Iron Soil Pipe Inst., Washington, 1964—; sec. Joint Apprentice Text, Inc., 1955-64. Treas. Wis. Community Chest, 1948-49. Treas. All-Industry Plumbing and Heating Modernization Com., 1956-57; co-sec. Joint Industry Program Com., 1958-64; sec. Nat. Conf. Plumbing-Heating-Cooling Industry, 1962—; chmn. nat. conf. Plumbing-Heating-Cooling Conf., 1967-69. Served from ensign to lt. USNR, 1943-46. Mem. Am., Wis. bar assns., Am. Soc. Assn. Execs., U. Wis. Alumni Assn., Wis. Law Alumni Assn. (pres. 1970—), Bldg. Ofcls. Conf. Am., Internat. Assn. Plumbing and Mech. Ofcls., Wis. State Soc. Washington (pres. 1966-68), Am. Soc. San. Engring., Gamma Eta Gamma (pres. Upsilon chpt. 1941-42). Episcopalian. Mason (32 deg., Shriner). Clubs: Washington Golf and Country; International (Washington). Home: 4621 33d St N Arlington VA 22207 Office: 2029 K St Washington DC 20006

HENDRIX, CLYDE, JR., banker; b. Decatur, Ala., Sept. 9, 1906; s. Clyde and Estelle (Yarbrough) H.; B.S., Auburn U., 1927; M.S., Columbia, 1929; m. Carolyn Fussell, June 4, 1934. Asst. nat. bank examiner, 1929-35; asst. supervising examiner FDIC, 1933-34; nat. bank examiner 1936-42; with Hibernia Nat. Bank, New Orleans, 1946—, exec. v.p., 1965, pres., 1965—, also dir. Bd. dirs. Better Bus. Bur. New Orleans, 1963-67; trustee United Fund New Orleans, 1966-67; bd. dirs. New Orleans council Boy Scouts Am., 1964-66, Police Found. Greater New Orleans, 1962-67. Served to lt. comdr. USNR, 1942-45. Mem. C. of C. Greater New Orleans Area (bd. dirs. 1965-67, treas. 1966-67). Assn. Res. City Bankers, Phi Kappa Alpha, Alpha Kappa Psi, Blue Key, Scabbard and Blade. Clubs: Internat. House (bd. dirs. 1966-67), New Orleans Country, Matairie Country, Pickwick, Louisiana. Plimsoll (New Orleans). Home: 220 Sycamore Dr Metairie LA 70005 Office: Hibernia Nat Bank Carondelet and Gravier Sts New Orleans LA 70112

HENDRIX, HAROLD BRINDLEY, elec. and mech. engr.; b. Cullman, Ala., Mar. 24, 1908; s. Columbus N. and Nancy (Reid) H.; B.S. in Elec. Engring., U. Ala., 1931, B.S. in Mech. Engring., 1933; m. Willida Gossett, Dec. 31, 1938; children—Brindley B., John B. Specification engr. Standard Co., Linden, N.J., 1936-40; elec. and mech. engr. TVA, Knoxville, 1940-42, asst. dir., chief of procurement, Chattanooga, 1954—; mem. faculty U. Chattanooga Evening Coll.; mem. purchasing adv. com. City of Chattanooga. Served to lt. col. C.E., AUS, 1942-46. Registered profl. engr., Tenn. Mem. I.E.E.E., Tenn. Soc. Profl. Engrs. Baptist. Patentee in field. Home: 3774 Queens Rd Chattanooga TN 37416 Office: Lupton Bldg Chattanooga TN 37401

HENDRY, JAMES B., internat. orgn. exec. Head agrl. econs. sect. Internat. Bank Reconstrn. and Devel., Washington. Author: The Small World of Khanh Hau. Address: 1818 H St NW Washington DC 20433*

HENDRY, JAMES E., lawyer, automobile club exec.; b. Perry, Fla., Nov. 7, 1912; s. Wesley Alonzo and Mae (Weaver) H.; student St. Petersburg Jr. Coll., 1930-32; J.D., U. Fla., 1935; m. Frances Swope, June 25, 1948; children—James E., Jayne L., Thomas S., John W., David F. Vice pres. Hendry Lumber Co., 1935-42, sec., treas., 1946-60; partner, mgr. Hendry Bldg. Co., 1946-60; practice law as James E. Hendry, atty., 1961—; pres. Gulf Housing Corp., 1946; sec.-mgr. St. Petersburg A.A.A. Motor Club, 1962-67, exec. v.p., gen. mgr., 1967—; v.p. Club Ins. Agy., Inc., 1962—; adv. bd. Farmer's Nat. Life Ins. Co. Admitted to Supreme Ct. bar. Mem. City Planning and Zoning Bd., 1948-57, Pinellas County Sch. Bd., 1957-66; mem. Pinellas Co. Airport Com., 1952. Mem. citizens adv. com. St. Petersburg Jr. Coll., 1948-68, bd. govs., 1938-48, chmn. dist. bd. trustees; pres. bd. dirs. YMCA, 1951; mem. Mound Park Hosp. Bd., 1951-52; mem. bd. Pinellas County chpt. Am. Cancer Soc., chmn. Cancer Drive, 1962; mem. Civil Def. Council; pres. Fla. Sch. Bd. Assn., 1964; sec.-treas. Southeastern Conf. AAA Motor Clubs, 1964, v.p., 1965, pres., 1966, treas. Eastern Conf. AAA Motor Clubs, 1970-71, vice chmn., 1972-73; exec. com. Continuing Ednl. Council Fla., 1964; mem. Nat. Com. Support Pub. Schs., 1964; mem. Pinellas Com. of 100, St. Petersburg Traffic and Safety Com., State Community Coll. Council. Pres., St. Petersburg Jr. Coll. Found. Lt. comdr. USCG Res. Mem. Am., St. Petersburg bar assns., Fla. Bar, Am. Judicature Soc., Fla. C. of C., Fla. Travel Council, Nat. Assn. Home Builders (past dir.), Contractors and Builders Assn. of Pinellas County (pres. 1953), Fla. Home Builders Assn. (v.p. 1955), Phi Delta Theta, Phi Alpha Delta. Democrat. Methodist. Kiwanian (pres. St. Petersburg 1951). Clubs: St. Petersburg Yacht, Quarterback, Commerce. Home: 409 Snell Isle Blvd Petersburg FL 33704 Office: 1211 1st Av N St Petersburg FL 33705

HENDRY, NORMAN C., judge; b. Adel, Ga., Jan. 20, 1905; s. Andrew Alexander and Hennie Lou (Hurst) H.; student So. Fla. Coll. Law, U. Miami Law Sch.; m. Elsie May Davison, Jan. 11, 1926. Admitted to Fla. bar, 1932, since practiced in Miami; judge Civil Ct. of Dade County, 1940; now judge 3d Dist. Ct. of Appeal, Miami. Mem. Am., Dade County bar assns., Fla. Bar, Am. Judicature Soc., S.A.R., Com. of 100, Phi Alpha Delta. Democrat. Methodist. Mason (Shriner), Elk. Clubs: Exchange, Century, Flamingo. Address: 1350 NW 12th Av Miami FL 33136

HENICAN, CASWELL ELLIS, lawyer; b. New Orleans, Feb. 10, 1905; s. Joseph Patrick and Alice (Boning) H.; LL.B., Tulane U., 1926; m. Elizabeth Cleveland, June 18, 1930; children—Alice (Mrs. Claude V. Perrier, Jr.), Caswell Ellis, Margaret (Mrs. F. Gordon Wilson, Jr.), Dorothy (Mrs. Charles E. Heidingsfelder), Joseph Patrick III. Admitted to La. bar, 1926, since practiced in New Orleans; asso. firm Lemle, Moreno & Lemle, 1926-33; sr. partner firm Henican, Carriere & Cleveland, 1933-40, Henican, James & Cleveland, 1940—. Chmn. La. Bd. Pub. Welfare, 1940-47; pres. New Orleans Community Chest, 1940, Council Social Agys., 1939, Asso. Catholic Charities New Orleans, 1938, Archidiocesian Vocation Devel. Commn. Chmn. adv. bd. Mercy Hosp., Retreat House of Cenacle for Women. Decorated Knight of St. Gregory, Order of St. Louis King of France; recipient medal as most outstanding young man New Orleans Jr. C. of C., 1940, F. Edward Hebert award as most outstanding alumnus of Jesuit High Sch., 1960. Mem. Am., La., New Orleans (pres. 1958) bar assns., Soc. Hosp. Attys. Club: Serra (chpt. pres. 1960). Home: 1831 Octavia St New Orleans LA 70115 Office: 4440 One Shell Sq New Orleans LA 70139

HENINGTON, DAVID MEAD, librarian; b. El Dorado, Ark., Aug. 16, 1929; s. Bud Henry and Lucile (Scranton) H.; B.A. in History, U. Houston, 1951; M.S. in L.S., Columbia, 1956; m. Barbara Gibson, June 2, 1956; children—Mark David, Gibson Mead, Paul Billins. Young adult librarian Bklyn. Pub. Library, 1956-58; head lit. and history dept. Dallas Pub. Library, 1958, asst. dir., 1962-67; dir. Waco (Tex.) Pub. Library, 1958-62, Houston Pub. Library, 1967—. Served with USAF, 1951-55. Rotarian. Home: 6225 San Felipe Rd Houston TX 77027 Office: 500 McKinney St Houston TX 77002

HENIZE, KARL GORDON, astronomer, astronaut; b. Cin., Oct. 17, 1926; s. Fred R. and Mabel (Redmon) H.; student Dennison U., 1944-45; B.A., U. Va., 1947, M.A., 1948; Ph.D., U. Mich., 1954; m. Caroline Weber, June 27, 1953; children—Kurt Gordon, Marcia Lynn, Skye Karen, Vance Karl. Observer, U. Mich. Lamont-Hussey Obs., Bloemfontein, South Africa, 1948-51; Carnegie postdoctoral fellow Mt. Wilson Obs., Pasadena, Cal., 1954-56; sr. astronomer charge Photog. Satellite Tracking Stas., Smithsonian Astrophys. Obs., Cambridge, 1956-59; asso. prof. dept. astronomy Northwestern U., 1959-64, prof., 1964-67, on leave of absence, 1967-72; scientist-astronaut NASA, 1967—, mem. astronomy subcom. NASA Space Sci. Steering Com., 1965-68; jet pilot tng. Vance AFB, Enid, Okla., 1968-69; support crew mem. Apollo 15 Mission, 1970-71. Guest observer Mt. Stromlo Obs., Canberra, Australia, 1961-62; cons. Ency. Brit. Films, 1959-67. Trustee, Adler Planetarium, 1971—. Served with USNR, 1944-46; lt. comdr. Ret. Res. Mem. Am. (vis prof. 1958-64), Royal, Pacific astron. socs., Internat. Astron. Union, A.A.A.S., Phi Beta Kappa, Sigma Xi. Home: 18630 Point Lookout Dr Houston TX 77058 Office: Astronaut Office NASA Manned Spacecraft Center Houston TX 77058

HENLE, PETER, govt. ofcl.; b. N.Y.C., Feb. 12, 1919; s. James and Marjorie (Jacobson) H.; B.A., Swarthmore Coll., 1940; M.A., Am. U., 1947; m. Theda Ostrander, Aug. 25, 1941; children—Michael Gilman, James Marston, Paul Jacobson. Economist, AFL, 1946-55; asst. research dir. AFL and CIO, 1955-61; dep. asso. commr. Bur. Labor Statistics, U.S. Dept. Labor, Washington, 1961-66, chief economist, 1966-71; Fed. Exec. fellow Brookings Instn., 1971-72; sr. specialist Congl. Reference Service, Library of Congress, 1972—. Served to maj. AUS, USAAF, 1941-45. Mem. Indsl. Relations Research Assn. (past mem. exec. bd.), Am. Econ. Assn., Am. Statis. Assn. Contbr. articles to profl. jours. Home: 3219 N Wakefield St Arlington VA 22207 Office: Library of Congress Washington DC 20540

HENLEY, JAMES WALTON, ret. bishop; b. Cleveland, Tenn., July 14, 1901; s. Charles Walton and Teressa Dowthett (Johnston) H.; B.A., Emory U., 1923, D.D., 1946; B.D., Yale, 1926; postgrad., U. Edinburgh (Scotland), 1929-30; m. Huldah Jo Chapin, Dec. 31, 1931 (dec. Oct. 1968); children—James Walton, Chapin; m. 2d, Margaret Ward Hollis, June 20, 1970. Ordained to ministry Methodist Ch., 1926, consecrated bishop, 1960; pastor in Spring City, Tenn., 1926-27, Crossville, Tenn., 1927-28, Harriman, Tenn., 1928-29, Morristown, Tenn., 1930-31, Knoxville, Tenn., 1932-37, Chattanooga, 1937-44, West Edn. Meth. Ch., Nashville, 1944-60; bishop of Jacksonville Area, 1960-64; Fla. Area, 1964-72. Mem. gen. bd. edn. Meth. Ch., 1960-72; mem. program council United Meth. Ch., 1968-72. Trustee Scarritt Coll. Christian Workers, Fla. So. Coll., Bethune Cookman Coll., Wesleyan Coll., Macon, Ga.; bd. govs. Wesley Theol. Sem. Mem. Meth. World Council (Am. sect.), Omicron Delta Kappa, Kappa Alpha. Author: Sermons on Our Lord's Prayer, 1952; His Twelve Apostles, 1958; Jesus Christ is Lord, 1961. Home: 2205 Cleveland Heights Blvd Lakeland FL 33803

HENLEY, J(ESSE) SMITH, U.S. dist. judge; b. St. Joe, Ark., May 18, 1917; s. Ben H. and Jessie (Smith) H.; LL.B., U. Ark., 1941; m. Dorothy E. Ingram, Sept. 30, 1938; children—Jane Karen and Wordna Sharon (twins). Admitted to Ark. bar, 1941, practiced in Harrison, 1941-54; asso. gen. counsel FCC, Washington, 1954-56; dir. Office Adminstrv. Procedure, Dept. Justice, Washington, 1956-58; U.S. dist. judge Eastern and Western dists. Ark., 1959—, now chief judge Eastern dist. Ark. Mem. Am., Ark. bar assns. Presbyn.Home: 11780 Rivercrest St Little Rock AR 72207 Office: US Ct House Little Rock AR 72201

HENLEY, JOE RAMA, dentist; b. Greeneville, Tenn., Nov. 7, 1942; s. Orval Rama and Minnie Maude (Mathes) H.; student E. Tenn. State U., 1961-62; D.D.S., U. Tenn., 1966, M.S., 1970 Linda Anne Fletcher, Mar. 14, 1964; children—Wynne Michele, Todd Fletcher, Kendall Paige. Extern Knox County Health Dept., 1966; pvt. practice orthodontics, Kingsport, Tenn., 1970—; mem. staff Holston Valley Community Hosp. Served to capt. USAF, 1966-68. Mem. Tenn. Dental Assn., Kingsport, 1st Dist. dental socs., Am., So. assns. orthodontics, Sigma Phi Epsilon, Psi Omega. Republican. Mem. Christian Ch. Moose, Eagle. Club: Metropolitan Dinner (Kingsport). Home: 910 Glade Mill Dr Kingsport TN 37663 Office: 1209 Wilcox Dr Kingsport TN 37660

HENLEY, VERNARD WILLIAM, banker; b. Richmond, Va., Aug. 11, 1929; s. Walter Abraham and Mary Ellen (Crump) H.; B.S., Va. State Coll., 1951; m. Pheriby Christine Gibson, June 14, 1958; children—Vernard William, Wade Gibson, Adrienne Christine. Teller, cashier Mechanics and Farmers Bank, Durham, N.C., 1951-52, 54-58; v.p. Consol. Bank & Trust Co., Richmond, 1958—, also dir. Vice chmn. adv. com. Vol. Service Bur., 1964-69; chmn. adv. bd. Salvation Army Boys Club, 1965-69; asst. treas. Richmond chpt. A.R.C., 1968-69; dist. commr. Robert E. Lee council Boy Scouts Am., 1964-69. Bd. dirs. Richmond Community Hosp., Inst. for Bus. and Community Devel., 1966-69, Richmond Met. Authority, 1966-69. Served to 1st lt. AUS, 1952-54. Decorated Bronze Star medal. Recipient Order of Merit, Boy Scouts Am., 1967, Man and Boy award Boys Club, 1969. Mem. Am. Inst. Banking, Bank Adminstrn. Inst., Richmond C. of C., Alpha Phi Alpha. Baptist. Home: 1709-C Colorado Av Richmond VA 23220 Office: 329 N 1st St Richmond VA 23240

HENLEY, WALLACE BOYNTON, journalist, govt. ofcl.; b. Birmingham, Ala., Dec. 5, 1941; s. Wallace Boynton and Wilfred (Vasser) H.; B.A., Samford U., 1964; postgrad. Southwestern Bapt. Theol. Sem., 1964-65; m. Mary Irene Lambert, Sept. 4, 1961; children—Mary Lauri, Travis Wallace. Ordained to ministry Baptist Ch., 1962; minister to youth Central Park Bapt. Ch., Birmingham, 1963; minister of youth edn. Travis Av. Bapt. Ch., Ft. Worth, 1964-66; pastor Antioch Bapt. Ch., Nuremberg, West Germany, 1966; dir. pub. relations Mobile (Ala.) Coll., 1966-68; religion editor, editorial writer Birmingham News, 1968-70; asst. dir. Cabinet Com. on Edn., Washington, 1970-71; staff asst. to Pres. of U.S., 1971—. Host panel show Know Your News, Ala. Ednl. TV network, 1968-69. Recipient gold Certificate for creative journalism Birmingham News, 1968, R. S. Reynolds award for outstanding religion coverage Presbyn. Ch. in U.S., 1969. Mem. Sigma Delta Chi. Club: Birmingham Press. Home: 5403 Ellzey Dr Fairfax VA 22030 Office: The White House Washington DC

HENNAGE, JOSEPH HOWARD, publishing, printing co. exec.; b. Washington, Jan. 2, 1921; s. Joseph Howard and Helen (Cook) H.; student pub. schs., Washington; m. June Elizabeth Stedman, Sept. 29, 1947. Organizer, pres. Hennage Creative Printers, Washington, 1945—, Jonage Investment Corp., Washington, 1958—; pres., founder Highland House Pubs., Washington, 1969—; mem. adv. bd. Am. Security & Trust Co., Washington; dir. Graphic Arts Mut. Ins. Co., United Ins. Co. Ltd., Hamilton Bermuda. Mem. fine arts com. U.S. Dept. State; dir. at large Met. Washington Bd. Trade, 1972; chmn. joint govt.-industry study group Govt. Printing Office, 1972; chmn. Americana com. Nat. Archives, 1972. Trustee Am. Cancer Soc.; exec. com. Washington Conv. and Visitors Bur.; bd. dirs. Boys Club Washington, 1949—, recipient award for distinguished service 1951, Alumni award, 1959; mem. council for Sch. Govt. and Bus. Adminstrn. George Washington U., chmn. Printing Mgmt. Edn. Trust Fund, 1971—. Served with USNR, 1942-45. Recipient Potomacland Ambassador, Washington Bd. Trade, 1963; Freedom Found. award, 1969; Distinguished Service award U.S. Pub. Printers, 1972; citation Brit. Fedn. Master Printers, 1971. Mem. Master Printers Am. (pres. 1967-69, man of yr. award 1969), Printing Industries Am. (chmn. bd. 1969-70, v.p. pub. relations 1971-72, Graphic Arts Man of Year 1971), Printing Industry Washington (pres. 1964-65, distinguished service award 1969), Creative Printers Am. (pres. 1963-64), Master Printers Washington (pres. 1960-61), Optimists Internat. (distinguished gov. 1957-58). Methodist (dir. 1966-70). Clubs: Nat. Capitol Optimist (pres. 1953-54), Metropolitan, City Tavern of Georgetown (Washington); Columbia Country (Chevy Chase, Md.); Farmington Country (Charlottesville, Va.). Home: 6211 Highland Dr Chevy Chase MD 20015 Office: 814 H St NW Washington DC 20001

HENNECY, JAMES HOWELL, govt. buyer; b. Marion, S.C., Mar. 10, 1913; s. Gabriel Marion and Annie Laurie (Boatwright) H.; student Mercer U. 1948-51; J.D., Walter F. George Sch. Law, 1953; m. Bobbie Helen Bobo, Dec. 28, 1963; 1 dau., Ardith Erin. Plant cashier Bordens Milk Co., Macon, Ga., 1953-55; contract specialist Dept. Air Force, Robins AFB, 1955-58, contract negotiator, 1964—; law librarian, instr. in law Walter F. George Sch. Law, Mercer U., Macon, 1958-63. Active Boy Scouts Am.; spokesman Macon Citizens for Better Hwy. Planning, 1959-62. Adviser, Young Democrats Club, 1960-63. Served with AUS, 1942-45; ETO, MTO. Mem. V.F.W., Young Americans for Freedom (asso.), Marion (S.C.) Jr. C. of C. (charter), Am. Ordnance Assn., Am. Legion, Internat. Platform Assn., Alpha Tau Omega, Delta Theta Phi, Alpha Psi Omega. Baptist (deacon). Lion. Club: Toastmaster (local pres. 1965, dist. edn. chmn. 1959-60). Home: 1347-B Adams St Macon GA 31201 Office: Directorate Procurement and Prodn WRAMA Robins AFB GA 31093

HENNESSEY, THOMAS EDGAR, banker; b. Anadarko, Okla., Oct. 3, 1923; s. Martin Francis and Eva Nevada (Kelly) H.; student St. John's Minor Sem., 1941-42, St. John's Major Sem., San Antonio, 1942-46; J.D., St. Mary's U., San Antonio, 1950; m. Rosemary Elizabeth Mushall, Aug. 7, 1954; children—Richard Kevin, Thomas Allen, Stephen Joseph, Laura Kathleen. Head teller, gen. ledger bookkeeper Harlandale State Bank, San Antonio, 1951-55; admitted to Tex. bar, 1951; practiced in San Antonio, 1951-56; partner Hennessey &Hennessey, 1951-56; v.p., trust officer Bexar County Nat. Bank, San Antonio, 1956—. Treas. cub pact 360 Boy Scouts Am., 1967-70; sec., bd. dirs. San Antonio Estate Planners Council. Mem. Am. Bankers Assn. (past com. chmn.), San Antonio Bar Assn., Am. Inst. Banking. Roman Catholic. Club: Fathers of Central Catholic High School, (San Antonio). Home: 403 Kate Schenck Av San Antonio TX 78223 Office: 325 N St Mary's St San Antonio TX 78291

HENNESSY, JOHN J., lawyer; b. Savannah, Ga., Dec 20, 1905; s. James W. and Lucy (Downing) H.; A.B. magna cum laude, U. Ga.; postgrad. Harvard; J.D., Georgetown Law Sch., LL.M. with highest distinction. Admitted to Ga. bar, 1931, since practiced in Savannah; mem. firm Hennessy & Hennessy, 1942-65; spl. hearing officer Dept. Justice, 1948-67. Grand marshall Armed Forces Day parade, 1970. Served from lt. to lt. comdr. USCGR, 1942-46; capt. Res., 1961—. Mem. Am., Ga., Savannah bar assns., Harvard Law Sch. Assn., Georgetown U., U. Ga. alumni socs., Am. Legion, Mil. Order World Wars, V.F.W. (past post comdr., dist. judge adv.), Res. Officers Assn. (past state pres.), Navy League, Phi Beta Kappa, Phi Kappa Phi, Delta Theta Phi. Elk (hon. life, past exalted ruler), Eagle. Mem. editorial staff Georgetown U. Law Jour., 1930-31. Home: 233 E 52d St Savannah GA 31405 Office: PO Box 1114 Savannah GA 31402

HENNESSY, LAWRENCE JEREMIAH, gen. contracting exec.; b. St. Petersburg, Fla., June 9, 1922; s. Aeneas P. and Madeleine (Kelly) H.; student St. Petersburg Jr. Coll., 1941-42, U. Fla., 1942-43; m. Elizabeth O'Brien, Nov. 25, 1948; children—Sharon Elizabeth (Mrs. Patrick Callahan), Timothy Kelly, Mary Susan, Michael Kelly, Jeremiah Kelly. With A.P. Hennessy & Sons, Inc., St. Petersburg, Fla., 1946—, pres., gen. mgr., 1950—, dir. Franklin Fed. Savs. & Loan Assn., St. Petersburg, First Comml. Bank St. Petersburg, Northside Community Bank, St. Petersburg, Community Banks Fla. Mem. contractors exam. bd. City of St. Petersburg, 1954-60, chmn., 1956-60, mem. city bldg. code com., 1955-60; mem. constrn. adv. bd. Pinellas County, 1961-68. Mem. exec. com. Pinellas area council Boy Scouts Am., 1959-66; mem. bd. United Fund, 1964-67. Pilot commr. Port of St. Petersburg, 1964. Served to 1st lt. C.E., AUS, 1943-46. Named to Gulf Marine Racing Hall of Fame, 1971. Mem. St. Petersburg C. of C. (gov. 1969-72), Asso. Gen. Contractors Am. (pres. Fla. West Coast chpt. 1957), Am. Power Boat Assn. (cruiser racing commn. 1969-72, Region 5 cruiser racing chmn. 1971—), St. Petersburg Power Squadron, Phi Delta Theta. Democrat. Roman Catholic. Kiwanian. Clubs: St. Petersburg (pres. 1963), St. Petersburg Yacht (vice commodore 1971-72). Home: 5440 Joe's Creek Dr St Petersburg FL 33709 Office: 2300 22d St N St Petersburg FL 33713

HENNING, RUDOLF ERNST, coll. dean; b. Hamburg, Germany, Aug. 3, 1923 (came to U.S. 1939); s. Ernest P. and Emmy (Rosenfeld) H.; B.S., Columbia, 1943, M.S., 1947, D.Eng. Sci. (Sperry Gyroscope fellow 1949-50) 1954; m. Patricia Ann Miklas, Sept. 30, 1961;

children—Patricia, Emerson Irwin. With Sperry Gyroscope Co., Great Neck, N.Y., 1947-58, head engring. sect., 1954-57, head engring. dept., 1957-58; with Sperry Microwave Electronics div. Sperry Rand Corp., Clearwater, Fla., 1958-70, chief engr., 1961-70; instr. elec. engring., asst. dean Coll. Engring., U. So. Fla., Tampa, 1970-71, asso. prof., asst. dean Coll. Engring. 1971—. Head engring. sci. dept. Naval Electronics Lab. Center, San Diego, 1971. Mem. devel. council Morton Plant Hosp., Clearwater, Fla., 1970—; chmn. Pinellas County Commn. on Higher Edn., 1958-63. Served with AUS, 1944-46. Fellow I.E.E.E. (chmn. nat. symposium, microwave theory and techniques group, 1968—; mem. Armed Forces Communications and Electronics Assn., Sigma Xi, Tau Beta Pi. Patentee in field. Home: 400 Ponce de Leon Blvd Clearwater FL 33516

HENNINGS, LEROY, JR., librarian; b. Mt. Kisco, N.Y., Aug. 17, 1936; s. LeRoy and Gretchen (Butcher) H.; A.B., U. Miami, 1960; M.S. in Library Sci., Fla. State U., 1968. Sch. librarian, tchr. geography Glades County sch. system, Moore Haven, Fla., 1961-62; librarian U. Miami Engring. and Physics Library, Coral Gables, Fla., 1962-63; librarian Miami-Dade Jr. Coll., 1964-65; librarian gen. reference and bus., sci. and tech. depts. Miami (Fla.) Pub. Library, 1966-68; librarian interlibrary loan dept. Fla. State U., Tallahassee, 1968; dir. Martin County Pub. Library, Stuart, Fla., 1968—. Mem. Am., Fla. library assns., Kappa Alpha. Democrat. Methodist. Home: 6 Gardner Lane Jensen Beach FL 33457 Office: 701 E Ocean Blvd Stuart FL 33474

HENRY, AARON EDD, Democratic nat. committeeman; b. Coahoma County, Miss., July 2, 1922; s. Edd and Mattie (Logan) H.; B.S., Xavier U., 1950; m. Noelle Michael, June 10, 1950; 1 dau., Rebecca. Sec., Miss. Pharm. Soc., 1955—. Vice chmn. Ams. for Black Aged, 1972. Del. Dem. Nat. Conv., 1968; chmn. Miss. Dem. Com., 1968—; mem. Democratic Nat. Com., 1972—; chmn. Miss. Dem. Exec. Com.; state campaign mgr. Presdl. campaign, 1972. Bd. dirs. Rural Housing Alliance, Washington, Rural Am. Alliance, Ky. State Ho., Mound Bayou (Miss.) Community Hosp., Miss. Council Human Relations; nat. bd. dirs. So. Christian Leadership Conf., So. Regional Conf. Served with AUS, 1943-46; PTO. Recipient Rosa Parks award So. Christian Leadership Conf., Outstanding Citizen's award Office Econ. Opportunity. Mem. Nat. Pharm. Assn. (pres. 1963), N.A.A.C.P. (nat. dir., pres. Miss. Conf.), Coahoma County C. of C., Am. Legion, V.F.W., Omega Psi Phi. Methodist. Home: 636 Page St Clarksdale MS 38614*

HENRY, DAVID PROBASCO, hosp. adminstr.; b. Arlington, Mass., Jan. 1, 1910; s. David Patterson and Ruth (Wilbert) H.; A.B., U. N.C., 1937; postgrad. Duke, 1956-58, Columbia, 1966; m. Lola Lee Harward, Feb. 15, 1942; children—Patricia Ann Noah (Mrs. Harley Harry Jones), David Patterson II, Lee Elizabeth (Mrs. Dale Martin Chodorow). Mgr., Durham Rd. Dairy, Chapel Hill, N.C., 1937-55; adminstrv. asst., coordinator continued care research Duke U. Med. Center, Durham, N.C., 1958-64; hosp. cons. U.S. commr. welfare Dept. Health, Edn. and Welfare, Washington, 1964-66; adminstr., hosp. adminstr. Central Prison, N.C. Dept. Correction, Raleigh, 1966-70, dir. health affairs, 1970—. Mem. N.C. Hosp. Assn., S.A.R., Nat. Council on Crime and Delinquency, Am. Correctional Assn., Sigma Chi. Democrat. Presbyn. Mason. Home: 14 Williams Cr Chapel Hill NC 27514 Office: 831 W Morgan St Raleigh NC 27603

HENRY, GENE PATRICK, dir. investigation Tariff Commn.; b. Dundee, Ill., Nov. 16, 1920; s. Harry DeWitte and Edith Cora (Allensworth) H.; B.A., Hamline U., 1942; postgrad. Georgetown U., 1946-47; m. Eleanor Gwenn Kufus May 28, 1943; children—Philip Michael, David Kufus. Economist, Tariff Commn., Washington, 1943-47, 48-69, dir. investigation, 1970—; economist CIA, 1947-48, House Select Com. on Fgn. Aid, 1947. Served with USNR, 1943-46. Mem. Am. Econ. Assn. Methodist. Home: 10914 New Hampshire Av Silver Spring MD 20903 Office: US Tariff Commission 8th and E St NW Washington DC 20436

HENRY, HARVEY BENART, physician; b. Waco, Tex., Aug. 27, 1899; s. Fred and Pauline (Mueller) H.; M.D., U. Tex., 1922, B.S., 1929; m. Mary Erkle Pitts, Dec. 21, 1920; children—Harvey Benart, Mary Erkle (Mrs. Dennis Frangias), Susan Elizabeth (Mrs. Robert Kealhofer). intern, John Sealy Hosp., Galveston, Tex., 1922; practice medicine, specializing in eye, ear, nose and throat, Luling, Tex., 1922-40, Austin, Tex., 1940-60, William Clinic, Woodward, Okla., 1961, Denton, Tex., 1962-64; chief eye, ear, nose and throat VA Hosp., Alexandria, La., 1964-70; pvt. practice, Pineville, La., 1970—; dir. chronic diseases Central La. State Hosp., 1971—. City health officer, Luling, 1922-44; chmn. Caldwell County (Tex.) Certified Med. Milk Commn., 1932-44. Active Boy Scouts Am., Nat. council rep., 20 years. Served with U.S. Army, 1918. Recipient Silver Beaver award Boy Scouts Am., 1940. Mem. Am., La., Parish med. assns., Am. Legion. Methodist (steward 1944-58). Mason (32 deg., K.T., Shriner), Kiwanian. Home: 609 Lallah St Pineville LA 71360

HENRY, JACK HOPKINS, orthopedic surgeon; b. Lubbock, Tex., Apr. 20, 1937; s. Wells Blackburn and Mattie Allene (Hopkins) H.; B.A. in Chemistry, Tex. Tech. U., 1960; M.D., U. Tex., 1964; m. Jane Hopkins Underwood, June 10, 1965; 1 son, David Blackburn. Intern, Ben Taub Hosp., Houston, 1964-65; resident gen. surgery U. Pa. Hosp., 1965-66; resident orthopedic surgery Columbia-Presbyn. Med. Center, N.Y.C., 1966-69, sr. Annie C. Kane fellow hip surgery, 1971-72; practice, medicine, specializing in orthopedic surgery, San Antonio, Tex., 1972—; mem. staff Methodist, Baptist, Santa Rosa, Nix Meml. hosps. Nat. v.p. student A.M.A., 1963-64. Served to maj. USAF, 1969-71. Carl Berg travelling fellow, 1972. Diplomate Am. Bd. Orthopedic Surgery. Mem. Phi Gamma Delta, Nu Sigma Nu. Presbyn. Address: 1303 McCullough Av San Antonio TX 78212

HENRY, JOHN CASE, financial cons.; b. Wickford, R.I., Nov. 4, 1905; s. William J. and Mariette (Porter) H.; Ph.B., Brown U., 1927; m. Elizabeth Baltz; children—Alan Pemberton, Caroline Hazard. With Providence Jour., 1927-34, Washington corr., 1933-34; with Evening Star, Washington, 1934-71, Sunday editor, 1946-53, editorial writer, 1953-63, bus. news editor, 1963-71; cons. U.S. Price Commn., 1971-72. Served from capt. to col. USAAF, 1942-46. Decorated Bronze Star medal. Mem. Overseas writers, White House Corr. Assn. (past pres.), Soc. Am. Bus. Writers (bd. govs., pres. 1970). Clubs: Nat. Press, Nat. Aviation, International (Washington); Columbia Country (Chevy Chase, Md.); City Tavern Assn. (Georgetown, D.C.). Home: 4000 Cathedral Av NW Washington DC 20016 Office: 2000 M St NW Washington DC 20508

HENRY, JOHN JAMES, physicist; b. White Pine, Tenn., Feb. 12, 1929; s. Herbert Holloway and Clara (Spurgeon) H.; student U. Fla., 1946-48; B.S., Lincoln Meml. U., 1954; m. Audrey Duffield, Sept. 14, 1954: children—Mark Stephen, Claudia Alexandra, John James. Instrument technician Carbide & Carbon Chem. Co., Oak Ridge, 1954-56; asso. physicist Union Carbide Corp., Oak Ridge, 1956-61, physicist nuclear div., 1961—. Instr. transistor circuit theory Oak Ridge Adult Edn. Program, 1962-65. Scoutmaster, Boy Scouts Am., Oak Ridge, 1960-62; tympanist Oak Ridge Symphony Orch., 1965—, publicity chmn., 1966-67, v.p., 1968-69. Served with USMCR, 1949-52. Mem. Instrument Soc. Am. (sr.), A.A.A.S., I.E.E.E. Episcopalian. Patentee in field. Home: 105 Audubon Rd Oak Ridge TN 37830 Office: Y12 Plant Oak Ridge TN 37830

HENRY, JOSEPH RAYMOND, physician; b. New Albany, Miss., June 3, 1913; s. George Willis and Retta (Parker) H.; B.A., Miss. Coll., 1934; M.D., U. Tenn., 1939; m. Mary Souter Winders, Sept. 11, 1949. Intern Grace Hosp., Detroit, 1939-40; resident Brooke Army Hosp., San Antonio, 1947-50; commd. 1st lt. U.S. Army, 1939, advanced through grades to col., 1956; chief surg. service Scott AFB (Ill.) Hosp., 1950-52; comdr. George AFB Hosp., Cal., 1953-56, chief surgery 1953-56; chief profl. services USAF Hosp., Tachikawa, Japan, 1956-59; comdr. USAF Hosp., Keesler AFB, Miss., 1960-64; comdr. USAF Hosp. Wiesbaden, Germany, 1964-67, Keesler AFB, Miss., 1967-69; mem. staff Union County Gen. Hosp., Tippah County Gen. Hosp. Decorated Legion of Merit with two oak leaf clusters, Soldier's Medal, Bronze Star, Air medal (Army); recipient Miss. Magnolia medal. Diplomate Am. Bd. Surgery. Fellow A.C.S.; Internat. Coll. Surgeons; mem. A.M.A., Aerospace Med. Assn., Air Force Clin. Surgeons Soc., Air Force Flight Surgeons Soc. Baptist. Home: 1089 Hwy 30 W New Albany MS 38652 Office: 110 Colter Dr New Albany MS 38652

HENRY, JOSEPH WARD, lawyer; b. Lynnville, Tenn., Sept. 20, 1916; s. Joseph Walter and Annie Louise (Ward) H.; student Middle Tenn. State U., 1935-37; LL.B., Cumberland U. Law Sch., 1937-38; postgrad. Washington Coll. Law, 1939-40; m. Marjorie Royster Clark, June 28, 1943; children—Joseph Ward, Robert Clark. Admitted to Tenn. bar, 1940; practice law, Pulaski, Tenn., 1941—. City atty., Pulaski, 1947-53; mem. Tenn. Ho. of Reps., 1949; adj. gen., Tenn., 1953-59; chmn. Democratic Exec. Com., Giles County, Tenn., 1967-71. Bd. dirs. Cumberland Heights Found., Nashville. Served with AUS, 1941-46. Decorated Bronze Star. Mem. Am. Legion (comdr. post 1947-48; comdr. dist. 1948-49), Tenn. (pres. 1970-71), Am. bar assns., Tenn. Trial Lawyers Assn. (pres. 1964-66), Am. Judicature Soc. (dir. 1971—), Am. Trial Lawyers Assn. Methodist. Elk. Home: 313 Rose St Pulaski TN 38472 Office: 119 S 1st St Pulaski TN 38478

HENRY, MATTHEW GEORGE, bishop; b. Chapel Hill, N.C., Oct., 25, 1910; s. George Kenneth Grant and Mary Elizabeth (Harding) H.; A.B., U. N.C., 1931; B.D., Va. Theol. Sem., 1935, D.D., 1949; D.D., U. of South, 1948; m. Cornelia Catharine Sprinkle, June 30, 1937; children—Anna Catharine, George K., Matthew G., Elizabeth H. Teaching fellow in chemistry U. N.C., 1931-32; ordained to ministry Protestant Episcopal Ch., 1935; temporarily in charge St. Phillip's Ch., Durham, also St. Paul's Ch., Winston-Salem, N.C., 1935; in charge Christ Ch., Walnut Grove, St. Phillip's Ch., Germanton, Messiah Ch., Mayodan, and Emmanual Ch., Stoneville, N.C., 1936; rector Calvary Parish, Tarboro, N.C., 1936-43, Christ Ch., Charlotte, N.C., 1943-48; bishop Diocese of Western N.C., Asheville, 1948—. Pres. N.C. Council Chs., 1964-67. Trustee St. Augustine's Coll., Raleigh, N.C., Patterson Sch., U. of South. Mem. Phi Beta Kappa, Alpha Chi Sigma, Delta Upsilon. Home: 9 Crowningway Dr Asheville NC 28804 Office: PO Box 368 Black Mountain NC 28711

HENRY, MAURICE KENT, newspaper cons.; b. Daleville, Va., Jan. 27, 1916; s. Jerry Maurice and Virgie (Wickline) H.; B.A., Bridewater Coll., 1936; M.A., George Peabody Coll., 1939; m. Helen Kincaid, Dec. 29, 1939; 1 dau., Kay (Mrs. James Ballard). Tchr., prin. pub. schs., Covington, Va., 1936-42; with Middlesboro (Ky.) Daily News, Citizens News Co., 1947-70, pub., 1951-70; sec. Radio Sta. WMIK, Middlesboro, 1951—; pres. Tri-State Poster Advt. Co., Middlesboro, 1959—; asso. George C. Cooper Assos., newspaper consultants. Chmn., Pine Mountain Health Council, 1966-69, Community Chest, 1956; chmn. Middlesboro Indsl. Commn., 1961-65. Dir. publicity Ky. Republican Com., also Senator John Sherman Cooper, 1960. Chmn. bd. trustees Appalachian Regional Hosps., 1967-69, bd. dirs., 1962—; bd. dirs. Ky. Indsl. Finance Authority, Ky. Travel Council; chmn. bd. Southeastern Ky. Regional Health Demonstration, 1966-70. Served to lt. comdr. USNR, 1943-45. Mem. Ky. Press Assn. (past pres., Outstanding mem. 1962), Middlesboro C. of C. (past pres.), Sigma Delta Chi. Episcopalian. Home: Dorchester Av Middlesboro KY 40965 Office: Sta WMIK N 19th St Middlesboro KY 40965

HENRY, NORMAN H., JR., dist. ct. judge. Judge 3d appellate dist. ct., Miami, Fla. Home: 1821 SW 12th St Miami FL 33135 Office: 1350 NW 12th St Miami FL 33135*

HENRY, ROBERT FILLMORE, bus. exec.; b. Trinity, Ala.; s. W. G. and Mary (Davis) H.; B.Ph., Emory U., 1926, student, Lamar Sch. Law, 1927; LL.D., Birmingham So. Coll., 1966; m. Annie Mae Branch, Oct. 14, 1932; children—Robert Fillmore, Anne (Mrs. J. Wallace Tidmore). Formerly pres. Birmingham So. Coll.; chmn. Robert F. Henry Tile Co., Inc., Montgomery, Ala.; dir. Nat. Waterways Conf., Inc., Union Bank & Trust Co., Ala. Gas Corp., Allied Life Ins. Co. Hon. consul of Thailand. Pres. Coosa, Ala. Rivers Improvement Assn. Trustee Robert F. Henry Found.; mem. 3d U.S. Army Adv. Com.; past pres. United Appeal Montgomery, Montgomery Symphony Orch. Assn. Recipient Patriotic Civilian Service award, Dept. Army, 1963. Mem. Birmingham-So. Coll. Alumni Assn. (chmn. exec. com. of bd. trustees, past pres.), English Speaking Union (past pres. Montgomery chpt.), Mem. U.S., Ala. (dir.), Montgomery (dir., past pres.) chambers commerce, So. Tile, Marble and Terrazo Contractors Assn., Tile Contractors Assn. Am. Inc., Ala. Hist. Soc., Newcomen Soc. N. Am., Pi Kappa Alpha, Phi Delta Phi, Omicron Delta Kappa. Methodist (past chmn. bd. trustees). Clubs: Montgomery Country, Beauvoir, Crescent Lake Country, Kiwanis (past pres. Montgomery chpt.). Home: 3211 Le Bron Av Montgomery AL 36106 Office: 919 Bell St Montgomery AL 36104

HENRY, ROBERT WILLIAM, bank exec.; b. Conway, Ark., Aug. 22, 1928; s. J. Wendell and Amma (Reeves) H.; A.B., Hendrix Coll., 1950; J.D., U. Ark., 1953; m. Barbara Jean Blackburn, June 10, 1951; children—Frank Wendell, Robert William, Clifford Joseph, Margaret Jeanne. Admitted to Ark. bar, 1953, U.S. Dist. Cts., 1953; partner Henry & Henry, Conway, 1953-58; individual practice, Conway, 1958-71; partner Henry & Henry, Conway, 1971—; dir. 1st Nat. Bank Conway, 1961—; tchr. bus. law Hendrix Coll., Conway, 1971—; city atty., Conway, 1955—. Bd. dirs. Faulkner County Day Sch., Conway, 1971—. Mem. Am., Ark., Faulkner County bar assns., Delta Theta Phi. Democrat. Methodist. Rotarian. Home: 7 Randolph Pl Conway AR 72032 Office: 1004 Front St Conway AR 72032

HENSGEN, SISTER CAROLEEN, supt. schs.; b. St. Louis, Nov. 18, 1914; d. Jules Francis and Louise (Meyer) Hensgen; student Notre Dame Coll., St. Louis, 1932-36, Quincy Coll., 1933-40; A.B., St. Louis U., 1944, M.A., 1948; postgrad. Loyola U., New Orleans, 1956, Marquette U., 1956, Georgetown U., 1962, Loretto Heights Coll., 1963, N.Y. U, 1965, Tex. A. and M., 1967, U. Utah, 1968. Joined Order Sch. Sisters Notre Dame, 1932, tchr. elementary grades, St. Francis, Quincy, Ill., 1933-40, Cathedral Sch., Belleville, Ill., 1940-42, St. Alphonsus, St. Louis, 1942-44; tchr. Latin and English Rosati-Kain High Sch., St. Louis, 1944-48; prin. Notre Dame High Sch., St. Louis, 1948-50, St. Paul High Sch., Highland, Ill., 1950-51, St. John Jr. High Sch., Burlington, Ia., 1951-56, Redemptorist High Sch., New Orleans, 1956-62, Redemptorist Sr. High Sch., Baton Rouge, 1962-67; supr. 13 elementary schs. Diocese Baton Rouge, 1962-67; supt. schs. Diocese Dallas-Ft. Worth, Dallas, 1967—. Dir. Head Start for Baton Rouge, summer 1966; rep. Title IV to Title III Cultural Program to S.Am., summer 1967. Mem. Human Relations Group Baton Rouge, 1962-67; mem. planning com. United Givers, 1967; chmn. Head Start Program, 1968-71. Bd. dirs. Community Advancement, Inc., Baton Rouge, 1966-67, War on Poverty, 1968-71, Dallas Day Care Centers, 1971—, Assn. for Prevention Blindness, 1971—; bd. dirs., mem. exec. com. S.W. Ednl. Devel. Lab. for La. and Tex. Title IV, 1967. Spl. grantee for implementation civil rights under Title III, summer 1965. Mem. Nat. Assn. Secondary Sch. Prins., La. Prins. Assn., Nat. Cath. Edn. Assn. (adv. bd. 1969—), So. Assn. Colls. and Schs., So. Assn. Ind. Schs., Assn. Supervision and Curriculum Devel., Supts. Assn. U.S. Cath. Conf. Home: Route Box 4 Irving TX 75062 Office: 3915 Lemmon Av Dallas TX 75219

HENSHEL, WALTER MARCUS, pub. relations exec.; b. Chgo., May 12, 1904; s. Leo M. and Eva (Davidson) H.; B.S. in Econs., U. Ill., 1925; m. Beatrice Bach, Mar. 1, 1928; 1 son, Richard Lee; m. 2d, Pauline Goodman Steinberg, June 8, 1955; 1 stepson, Meredith Henshel. Publicity dir. Dallas-Interstate Circuit, Inc., 1931-43; publicity dir. Braniff Airways, Inc., Dallas, 1944-47, dir. pub. relations, 1947-54, v.p. pub. relations, 1954—. Bd. dirs. Tex. Mental Health Assn., Dallas Mental Health Assn. Mem. Pub. Relations Soc. Am., Air Transport Assn. (mem. pub. relations com.), Internat. Air Transport Assn. (pub. relations Com.). Newcomen Soc. Home: 4822 Dorset Rd Dallas TX 75235 Office: Braniff Airways Bldg Exchange Park Dallas TX 75235

HENSLEY, LARRY DONALD, dentist; b. Radford, Va., Oct. 6, 1941; s. Paul Grant and Vivian (Cregar) H.; B.S., Hampden-Sydney Coll., 1964; D.D.S., Med. Coll. Va., 1968; m. Emily Anne Turner, June 15, 1968; 1 dau., Mary Lynnette. Intern U.S. Naval Hosp., Portsmouth, Va., 1968-69; practice dentistry, La Crosse, Va., 1971—. Served with USNR, 1968-71. Recipient essay award Nat. Safety Council, 1960. Mem. Am. Acad. Dentistry, Am. Sch. Health Assn., Am. Soc. Dentistry for Children, La Crosse and South Hill C. of C., Phi Beta Kappa, Chi Beta Phi (nat. historian 1964-68), Sigma Zeta. Republican. Baptist. Home: 506 Chaptico Rd South Hill VA 23970 Office: Box 97 La Crosse VA 23950

HENSLEY, MARBLE JOHN, SR., cons. engr.; b. Ball Ground, Ga., Nov. 6, 1922; s. Paul and Ober (Penland) H.; B.C.E., Ga. Inst. Tech., 1949; m. Ruth Collins, Sept. 11, 1948; children—Carol and Sandra (twins), Kathlyn, Marble John. Loftsman, Bell Aircraft, 1942-44; field engr. Paul Hensley, 1946-48; design engr. Ga. Hwy. Dept., 1949; asst. traffic engr. City of Atlanta, 1950-54; dir. traffic and planning City of Chattanooga, 1954-58, city coordinator, 1958-63; pres. Hensley-Schmidt Inc., cons. engrs., 1963—. Mem. Nat. Adv. Com. on Uniform Traffic Control Devices; dir. Cons. Engring. Council. Served from apprentice seaman to aviation metalsmith 3d class USNR, 1944-46. Mem. Inst. Traffic Engrs. (pres. So. sect. 1961-62, dir., nat. dir. 1965, nat. sec.-treas. 1966, tech. v.p. 1967, adminstrv. v.p. 1968, pres. 1969), Am. Soc. C.E., Nat. Soc. Profl. Engrs., Am. Soc. Planning Ofcls., Cons. Engrs. Council, Cons. Engrs. of Tenn. (pres. 1971). Democrat. Presbyn. (elder). Kiwanian. Club: Chattanooga Automobile (dir. 1955-62). Home: 1504 Dalewood Dr Chattanooga TN 37411 Office: Am Nat Bank Bldg Chattanooga TN 37402

HENSON, E. G., mng. editor Jacksonville (Fla.) Jour. Address: care Jacksonville Jour 1 Riverside Av Jacksonville FL 32202*

HENTGES, JAMES FRANKLIN, JR., educator; b. Perry, Okla., Feb. 6, 1925; s. James Franklin and Edna Lillian (Golliver) H.; B.S., Okla. A. and M. U., 1948; M.S., U. Wis., 1950, Ph.D., 1952; m. Iris Lavaun McGill, Mar. 10, 1946; children—Douglas Eric, Eric James, Kurt William. Instr. U. Wis., 1951-52; asst. prof. animal scis. U. Fla., 1952-56, asso. prof., 1956-66, prof., 1966—; cons. to Cuban, Venezuelan and Costa Rican govts. Served with inf. AUS, also with USAAF, 1943-46. Decorated Bronze Star. Mem. Am. Inst. Nutrition, Am. Soc. Animal Sci., Am. Soc. Range Mgmt., Sigma Xi, Phi Kappa Phi, Phi Eta Sigma, Alpha Zeta. Presbyn. Contbr. articles to profl. jours., chpts. in books. Home: 550 N W 55th St Gainesville FL 32601

HEPTING, EDWIN ALBERT, JR., constrn. co. exec.; b. New Orleans, Feb. 24, 1929; s. Edwin Albert and Edna Mae (Delery) H.; student LaSalle Extension U., 1954; Delgado Coll., 1968; m. Paula Geraldine Junot, Mar. 4, 1950; children—Carolyn Anne (Mrs. Gary Gerard Hornosky), Pamela Anne, Sheila Anne, Kris Albert. With Gulf Oil Corp., Gretna, La., 1947-52; accountant, salesman George Engine Co., Harvey, La., 1952-59; accountant H.B. Fowler & Co., Harvey, 1960-61; office and sales mgr. Hunt Engine & Equipment Co., Harvey, 1961-64; gen. mgr. Watts Constrn. Co., Inc., Marrero, La., 1964—, also sec.-treas., dir.; sec.-treas., dir. B & E, Inc., Barge Maintenance, Inc., Oilfield Fabricators, Inc. Mem. So. States Indsl. Council. K.C., Old Hooks. Clubs: Woodland West Country, Woodland West Swim and Raquet (Harvey, La.). Home: 2684 Vulcan St Harvey LA 70058 Office: Route 1 Box 637 Marrero LA 70072

HERALD, WILLIAM GLENWOOD, dentist; b. Canon City, Colo., May 30, 1924; s. William Vern and Louella (Ware) H.; B.S., Okla. State U., 1950; D.D.S., U. Mo. at Kansas City, 1952; m. Leona Mae Underwood, June 9, 1944. Practice dentistry, Stillwater, Okla., 1952—. Served with AUS, 1943-46. Mem. Am., Okla. dental assns., Internat. Assn. Orthodontics, Am. Soc. Dentistry for Children, Fedn. Dentaire Internationale. Mason (32 deg.), Lion. Home: P O Box 608 Stillwater OK 74074 Office: 718 S Walnut Stillwater OK 74074

HERBERT, CHARLES WESTCOTT, physician; b. Hendersonville, N.C., Aug. 28, 1931; s. James Manning and Nell Brooks (Westcott) H.; B.S., The Citadel, 1957; M.D., Bowman Gray Sch. Medicine, 1961; m. Sylvia Deanne Goode, Sept. 10, 1955; children—Charles Westcott, Lisa, Eugene, Brett. Intern, resident Meml. Hosp. Chatham County, Savannah, Ga., 1961-63; pvt. practice medicine, West Palm Beach Fla., 1964—; med. dir. Palm Beach County Occupational Health Dept.; town physician, Palm Beach. Aviation med. examiner FAA Crash Investigator; spl. dep. Palm Beach County. Past pres. bd. Link Found.; bd. dirs. Alcohol-Drug Abuse Council of Palm Beach County; exec. bd. dirs. Doctors Hosp., Lake Worth, Fla. Served with AUS, 1951-54. Decorated Combat Inf. Badge, Combat Med. Badge. Mem. A.M.A., Fla., Palm Beach County med. socs., Flying Physicians Assn., Internat. Platform Assn., Fraternal Order Police Assns. Home: 501 N Country Club St Atlantis FL 33460 Office: 3420 Forest Hill Blvd West Palm Beach FL 33406

HERBERT, GEORGE RICHARD, research exec.; b. Grand Rapids, Mich., Oct. 3, 1922; s. George Richard and Violet (Wilton) H.; student Mich. State U., 1940-42; B.S., U.S. Naval Acad., 1945; D.Sc., N.C. State U., 1967; m. Lois Anne Watkins, Aug. 11, 1945; children—Gordon, Patricia, Alison, Douglas, Margaret. Line officer USN, 1945-47; instr. elec. engring. Mich. State U., 1947-48; asst. to dir. Stanford Research Inst., 1948-50, mgr. bus. operations, 1950-55, exec. asso. dir., 1955-56, asst. sec., 1950-56; treas. Am. & Foreign Power Co., Inc., N.Y.C., 1956-59; pres. Research Triangle Inst., 1959—. Mem. N.C. Bd. of Space and Tech. Mem. N.C. Gov.'s Sci. Adv. Com., tech. adv. bd. U.S. Dept. Commerce, 1964-69, N.C. Atomic Energy Adv. Com. Bd. dirs. Oak Ridge Asso. Univs., 1971—. Mem. Sigma

Alpha Epsilon. Home: 46 Beverly Dr Durham NC 27707 Office: Box 12194 Research Triangle Park NC 27709

HERBERT, IRA WALLACE, educator; b. Hope, Ark., June 28, 1913; s. Joseph M. and Ethyl (Tatman) H.; B.S., Ouachita Coll., 1935; M.S., La. State U., 1937; Ed.D., Okla. State U., 1955; m. Lois Maureen Allen, Aug. 6, 1940; children—Allen Joseph, Wallace (dec.), Cecile Marie. Chmn. math. dept. Shenandoah Coll., Dayton, Va., 1938-39, Ranger (Tex.) Jr. Coll., 1940-42; prof. math. La. Poly. Inst., Ruston, 1942-—, chmn. astronomy com., 1962-—, dir. planetarium, 1969-—, Mem. Am. Assn. U. Profs. (chpt. pres. 1964, 66), Ruston Men's Camellia Soc. (sec. 1964-—). Home: 623 W Alabama St Ruston LA 71270

HERBERT, LEO, govt. ofcl.; b. Douglas, Ariz., Mar. 7, 1912; s. Kumen Ohni and Urilla (Whipple) H.; B.S., Brigham Young U., 1939; M.B.A., La. State U., 1941, Ph.D., 1944; m. Ruth Parker, June 29, 1937; children—Franklin Wayne, Dahnelle Kay (Mrs. Roger Overly), Judith Ellen (Mrs. Cary Spencer). Supr. pub. funds State of La., Baton Rouge, 1952, asst. state auditor State Auditors Office, 1952-56; dir. office of staff mgmt., dep. dir. for staff devel. Office Policy and Spl. Studies, U.S. Gen. Accounting Office, Washington, 1956-68, dir. office of personnel mgmt., 1968-—; prof. accounting, head dept. bus. adminstrn. La. Polytech. Inst., 1947-52; asso. prof. accounting Brigham Young U., 1946-47; asst. prof., instr., grad. asst. La. State U., 1940-46. Mem. Fed. Govt. Accountants Assn. (chmn. edn. com. 1969-70), Am. Accounting Assn. (v.p. 1964), Am., D.C. insts. C.P.A.'s, Va. Soc. C.P.A.'s, Soc. Personnel Adminstrn., Nat. Assn. State Auditors, Comptrollers and Treasurers, Am. Soc. Pub. Adminstrn. Contbr. articles to profl. jours. Home: 5228 N 32d St Arlington VA 22207 Office: 441 G St NW Washington DC 20548

HERBICH, JOHN BRONISLAW, educator; b. Warsaw, Poland, Sept. 1, 1922 (came to U.S. 1953, naturalized 1962); s. Henry Pawel and Jadwiga Eleonora (Lopienski) H.; B.Sc., U. Edinburgh, Scotland, 1949; M.S. in C.E., U. Minn., 1957; Ph.D., Pa. State U., 1963; postgrad. U. Cal. at Berkeley, 1964, Utah State U., 1966; m. Margaret Pauline Boylan, Jan. 27, 1951; children—Ann (dec.), Barbara K., Gregory J., Patricia J. Field engr. John Laing & Son, London, Eng., 1948; research engr. U. Delft, The Netherlands, 1949-50; intermediate engr. Aluminum Co. Can., Ltd., 1950-53; research fellow U. Minn., 1953-57; asst. prof. Lehigh U., 1957-60, asso. prof., 1960-65, prof., 1965-67; prof. civil engring., head coastal and ocean engring., head hydraulic engring. and fluid mechanics div., dir. Center for Dredging Studies, Tex. A. and M. U., College Station, 1967-—; on leave as UN project mgr. Central Waterpower Research Sta., Govt. of India, Khadakwasla, Poona, 1972-—; dir. Ocean Pollution Control, Inc., Dallas; pres. Cons. and Research Services, Inc., Bryan, Tex. Pres. P.T.A. Hamilton Sch., Bethlehem, Pa., 1965-66. Served with Brit. Army, 1940-45. Recipient Karl Emil Hilgard Hydraulic Prize, Am. Soc. C.E., 1965-66; NSF Faculty-Sci. fellow, 1963-64. Registered profl. engr., Tex. Mem. Internat. Assn. Hydraulic Research, World Dredging Assn., Am. Soc. Engring. Edn., Am. Soc. C.E., Am. Soc. Oceanography, Sigma Xi, Phi Kappa Phi, Chi Epsilon. Patentee in field. Home: 764 S Rosemary Dr Bryan TX 77801 Office: Civil Engring Dept Tex A and M U College Station TX 77843

HERBLOCK, cartoonist, see Block, Herbert Lawrence

HERCHENROEDER, JOHN, editor; b. Louisville, May 20, 1908; s. John F. and Louise J. (Ernwein) H.; student U. Louisville, 1930; m. Elsie V. Middleton, June 5, 1948 (dec. Nov. 1971). With Courier-Jour., Louisville, 1926-—, city editor 1945-65, asst. to exec. editor Courier-Jour. and Louisville Times, 1965-—. Active Old Ky. Home Dist. council Boy Scouts Am., 1940. Mem. Christian Ch. Home: 106 Southampton Rd Louisville KY 40223 Office: 525 W Broadway Louisville KY 40202

HERD, CHARLES F., assn. exec. Exec. v.p. Louisville (Ky.) C. of C. Address: Louisville C of C 300 W Liberty St Louisville KY 40202*

HEREFORD, JOHN DONALD, public accountant; b. New Market, Ala., Apr. 10, 1906; s. John Donald and Texanna (Petty) H.; B.S. in Commerce and Bus. Adminstrn., U. Ala., 1929; m. Lorence Watts, May 16, 1936; children—Susan Jane (Mrs. Willmore M. Dameron, III), Pamela. (Mrs. Maurice C. Hendrick). Staff accountant Lybrand, Ross Bros. & Montgomery, N.Y.C., 1929-47; asst. treas. May McEwen Kaiser Co., Burlington, N.C., 1948; comptroller So. Pool operations Geo. H. McFadden & Bros., Memphis, 1949; asst. comptroller Robbins Mills, Inc., Clarksville, Va., 1950-53; pvt. practice C.P.A., Clarksville, 1953-—. Mem. Am. Inst. C.P.A.'s, N.Y. State, Va. socs. C.P.A.'s Phi Beta Kappa, Beta Gamma Sigma. Presbyn. (elder). Lion (dep. dist. gov. 1963-64). Address: Clarksville VA 23927

HERHOLD, WAYNE, hosp. adminstr.; b. Mpls., Aug. 4, 1929; B.A., Cornell Coll., Mt. Vernon, Ia., 1951; M.H.A., U. Mich., 1957; m. 4 children. Adminstrv. resident Henry Rood Hosp., Detroit; asst. dir. William Beaumont Hosp., Royal Oak, Mich., 1957-61; asso. dir. Rockford (Ill.) Meml. Hosp., 1961-65; exec. dir. Hosp. Planning Council Kanawha Valley, Charleston, W. Va., 1965-67; asst. dir. U. Wis. Med. Center, Madison, 1967-69, asso. dir., 1969-70; dir. Shands Teaching Hosp. and Clinics U. Fla., Gainesville, 1970-—, also asso. prof., asso. dir. Grad. Program Health and Hosp. Adminstrn. Mem. W. Va. Gov.'s Task Force on Health, 1966-67; mem. tech. adv. com. W. Va. Commn. Aging, 1967; mem. corporate bd. Health Planning Council, Madison. Served with USNR, 1952-55. Mem. Am. Coll. Hosp. Adminstrn., Am., Fla. hosp. assns., Phi Kappa Phi. Address: Shands Teaching Hosp U Fla Gainesville FL 33601

HERIN, WILLIAM ABNER, judge; b. Macon, Ga., May 14, 1908; s. William Abner and Caroline (Davenport) H.; A.B., U. Fla., 1930, J.D., 1933; m. Frances Elizabeth Christian, Aug. 2, 1952. Admitted to Fla. bar, 1933; asso. firm Hudson & Cason, Miami, 1933-48; judge 11th Jud. Circuit, Miami, Fla., 1949-—. Sec. to Congressman J. Mark Wilcox, 4th Dist., Miami, 1936-38; legislative counsel Dade County del. Fla. Legislature, 1939, 41; legal adviser U.S. Dept. State in Far East, 1947. Pres. Nat. Conf. Met. Cts., 1969-70. Mem. adv. bd. So. Fla. council Boy Scouts Am. Bd. dirs. Met. Miami YMCA; trustee Boys' Clubs Greater Miami; bd. visitors Inst. for Ct. Mgmt., 1970-—. Capt. USNR Res., Ret. Mem. Am. Law Inst., Am. Judicature Soc., Am., Dade County bar assns., Fla. Bar, S.A.R., Newcomen Soc., So. Fla. Hist. Soc., Inst. Jud. Adminstrn., Phi Beta Kappa. Methodist. Author: Trial Jurors' Handbook, 1952; Standard Grand Jury Charge, 1955; Aviation Activities of the late J. Mark Wilcox, 1955; Local Court Rules, 1957; also articles in profl. revs. Home: 470 NE 51st St Miami FL 33137 Office: Dade County Courthouse Miami FL 33130

HERLONG, ALBERT SYDNEY, JR., govt. ofcl.; ex-congressman; b. Manistee, Ala., Feb. 14, 1909; s. Albert Sydney and Cora Violetta (Knight) H.; LL.B., U. Fla., 1930; m. Mary Alice Youmans, Dec. 26, 1930; children—Mary Alice (Mrs. A.G. Pattillo, Jr.), Margaret (Mrs. James H. Mayfield), Dorothy (Mrs. Charles Hay), Sydney (Mrs. Jed. J. Johnson, Jr.). Admitted to Fla. bar, 1930; practiced in Lake County, Fla., 1930-49; county judge, Lake County, 1937-49; mem. 81st-89th congresses from 5th Dist. of Fla., 90th Congress from 4th Dist. of Fla.; commr. SEC, Washington, 1969-—. Served as capt., judge adv. gen. dept., AUS, 1941. Mem. Fla. County Judges Assn., (pres. 1943-44), Alumni Assn. U. Fla. (pres. 1947-48), Fla. State Baseball League (pres., 1947-48), Pi Kappa Phi. Democrat. Methodist. Home: 1009 Shore Acres Dr Leesburg FL 32748 Office: 500 N Capitol St Washington DC 20549

HERMAN, DANIEL JACQUES, educator; b. Brussels, Belgium, Oct. 22, 1931; s. Octave Simeon and Jane Lelia (Massar) H.; came to U.S., 1951, naturalized, 1954; B.A., U. R.I., 1960; B.A., U. Louvain (Belgium), 1961; M.A., Northwestern U., 1966, Ph.D., 1968; m. Anne Bohlke, Oct. 22, 1965; 1 dau., Nicole. Asst. prof. philosophy Ithaca (N.Y.) Coll., 1967-69; asst. prof. philosophy U. W. Fla., Pensacola, 1969-—. Served with USMC, 1952-55. Mem. Am., Fla. philos. assns. Home: 7910 Le Jeune Dr Pensacola FL 32504

HERMAN, LAURENCE TRUE, newspaper exec.; b. Chgo., Feb. 25, 1913; s. Earl Leslie and Florence (Grund) H.; A.B., Dartmouth, 1934; m. Florence Thomas Dingle, Oct. 28, 1939; children—Laurence True, Deborah Anne, Florence, Katherine. Space buyer Neisser Meyerhoff Advt. Agy., 1934; space sales Herald-Examiner, Chgo., 1935; with advt. dept. Marshall Fields, 1935; sales promotion mgr., retail advt. mgr. Chgo. Daily News, 1936-54; exec. dir. Waxed Paper Inst., Waxed Paper Merchandising Council, Chgo., 1955-57; advt. dir. Detroit News, 1958-65; v.p. sales & marketing, dir. Times Pub. Co., St. Petersburg (Fla.) Times, Evening Ind., Congl. Quar., Editorial Research Reports, Washington, 1967-—; co-owner Mr. Steak Pontiac, Inc., Pontiac, Mich., Mr. Steak BSM, Inc., Westland, Mich., 1966-—; dir. Newspaper Preprint Corp. Chmn. policy com. Met. Sunday Newspapers, 1961-—. Mem. Ill. District 108 Sch. Bd., 1952-58; dir. budget Highland Park Community Fund, 1946-47; vice chmn. Chgo. Community Fund, 1948-49; chmn. A.R.C., Highland Park, 1951-52, div. chmn., Chgo., 1953-55; organizer, bd. dirs. Highland Park Civic Assn., 1954-58; chmn. bd. dirs. Mich. Career Inst., Detroit, 1965-—. Mem. Am. Newspaper Pubs. Assn. (plans bd., bur. advt.), St. Petersburg C. of C. (gov., pres.), Delta Kappa Epsilon. Presbyn. Clubs: Pinellas County Com. of 100, Commerce of Pinella County; St. Petersburg Sales and Marketing Execs., St. Petersburg Yacht, Treasure Island Yacht and Tennis. Home: 454 First St NW Tierra Verde FL 33715 Office: 490 First Av S St Petersburg FL 33701

HERMAN, RICHARD L., ofcl. State Dept.; b. Neb., Aug. 6, 1920; m. Margaret Martin. U.S. commr. Internat. Boundary Commn.-U.S.-Can., Dept. State, Washington, 1969-—. Served to capt. AUS, 1942-45. Office: Internat Boundary Commn Room 3810 441 G St NW Washington DC 20548

HERMAN, WILLIAM ROSS, restaurant exec.; b. Taylorsville, N.C., Nov. 25, 1921; s. Lawrence E. and Effie I. (Crouch) H.; grad. high sch.; m. Eleanor Barnes Crocken (div.); children—Larry, Nathan. Mgr., Mid-Atlantic Area, Nat. Toddle House Corp., Greensboro, N.C., 1938-63; founder Hermies, Inc., Florence, S.C., 1963, pres., 1963-—. Bd. dirs. Florence Symphony Orch., Florence County Mental Health Assn. Served with AUS, 1943-44. Lutheran. Lion, Elk. Home: 1321 Clarendon Av Florence SC 29501 Office: P O Box 832 Florence SC 29501

HERMANSON, DEAN E(DWIN), mech. engr.; b. Sioux City, Ia., Feb. 23, 1927; s. Edwin H. and Hattie (Johnson) H.; student Morningside Coll., 1947-48; B.S. in Gen. Engring., Ia. State U., 1950; m. Mary Ann Timm, Sept. 13, 1953; children—Kent Edwin, Susan Jo. Indsl. engr. Aluminum Co. Am., Vernon, Cal., 1950-51, Wincharger Corp. subsidiary Zenith Radio Corp., Sioux City, Ia., 1951-53; engring. supr. U.S. Industries, Huntington Park, Cal., also Longview, Tex., 1953-63; chief engr. Continental Emsco div. Youngstown Sheet & Tube, Garland, Tex., 1963-—. Instr. metallurgy Letourneau Coll., Longview, Tex., 1961-62. Served with USAAF, 1945-46. Registered profl. entr., Tex. Mem. Am. Petroleum Inst. (citation for service 1968), Am. Soc. M.E. (chmn. petroleum br. N. Central Tex. 1970-71), Am. Inst. M.E., Am. Mgmt. Assn., Nat. Assn. Corrosion Engrs. Patentee in field. Home: 1114 Elizabeth Lane Richardson TX 75080 Office: Box 248 Garland TX 75040

HERNANDEZ, ARMANDO H., banker. Pres. Bank of Commerce, Mexico. Address: Venustiano Carranzo No 44 PO Box 9 Bis Mexico City 1 Mexico*

HERNANDEZ-COLON, RAFAEL, govt. ofcl.; b. Ponce, P.R., Oct. 24, 1936; s. Rafael Hernandez-Matos and Dorinda (Colon-Clavell) H.; A.B., Johns Hopkins U., 1956; LL.B., U. P.R., 1959; m. Lila Mayoral, Oct. 24, 1959; children—Rafael, Jose Alfredo, Dora Mercedes, Juan Eugenio. Admitted to P.R. bar, 1959; practiced in Ponce, 1959-65, 67-69; mem. firm Hernandez Colon & Bauza, 1967-69; asso. pub. service commr. Puerto Rico, 1960-62; atty. gen. P.R., 1965-67; mem., pres. P.R. Senate, 1969-—. Lectr. civil proc. Catholic U. P.R. Law Sch., 1961-65. Mem. Nat. council Boy Scouts Am., Ponce, 1967-—. Mem. Democratic Nat. Com., 1968-—. Bd. dirs. Colegio Ponceno de Varones, Ponce. Named one of Ten Distinguished Young Men of P.R., Jr. C of C. Rio Piedras, 1967. Mem. Interam., P.R. bar assns., Acad. Polit. Sci., Am. Acad. Polit. Sci., Acad. Law and Sci., Am. Acad. Polit. and Social Sci., Valley Forge Mil. Acad. Alumni Assn. (dir.), Phi Beta Kappa, Phi Eta Mu. Home: One Sol St San Juan PR 00904 Office: Senate Commonwealth of PR San Juan PR 00904

HERNANDEZ-MATOS, RAFAEL, justice P.R. Supreme Ct.; b. Cabo Rojo, P.R., Oct. 24, 1902; s. Pablo and Enriqueta (Matos) Hernandez; LL.B., U. P.R., 1926; m. Dorinda B. Colon, Oct. 24,1934; children—Rafael, Jose Angel, Cesar-Ariel, Gladys. Admitted to P.R. bar, 1926, practiced in Ponce until 1957; asso. Justice Supreme Ct. P.R. 1957-—. Home: 434 Lloren St Floral Park Hato Rey PR 00919 Office: PR Supreme Ct Box 2392 San Juan PR 00903

HERNANDEZ-RIVERA, NICOLAS, economist, educator; b. Aquadilla, P.R., Sept. 10, 1929; s. Angel and Providencia (Rivera-Quinones) Hernandez-Hernandez; B.A. cum laude, U. P.R., 1957; M.A., Rutgers U., 1963 Ph.D., 1965; m. Juvencia Ayala-Morales, Mar. 29, 1958; children— Maritza, Ariel, Gynna. Lectr. econs. U. P.R., Mayaguez, 1957-60, asst. prof., 1966-68, asso. prof. econs., 1968-—, counselor to chancellor, 1966-68; teaching asst. Rutgers U., 1962-64; head Econs. and Planning Office, P.R. Dept. Commerce, Santurce, 1965-66; counselor to sec. commerce, counselor P.R. Legislature, counselor to Gov. P.R., 1965-66. Served with inf., U.S. Army, 1950-53. Mem. Am. Econs. Assn. Popular Democrat. Roman Catholic. Lion. Home: 222 Barbosa Moca PR 00716 Office: Econs Dept Arts and Scis Faculty Coll Agr Mayaguez PR 00708

HERNANZ, HIPOLITO, JR., broadcaster; b. Buenos Aires, Argentina, June 14, 1938; s. Hipolito and Agueda Luisa (Calvino) H.; came to U.S., 1957; student Boston U., 1957-58, Georgetown U., 1958-63; m. Linda Joyce Johnson, July 22, 1961; 1 son, Eric Stetson. Econ. research asst. Orgn. Am. States, Washington, 1963; econs. and labor analyst U.S. Information Agy., Voice of Am., 1964-67; v.p., gen. mgr. CSG Corp., Washington, 1964-67; bus. mgr. WETA/TV and FM, Washington, 1968-—. Latin Am. cons. for CTW (N.Y.C.); dir. Representation Unltd., (Washington); composer for the piano. Mem. Nat. Acad. TV Arts and Scis. Author: Fifteen Short Poems, 1972. Home: 1110 Fidler Lane Silver Spring MD 20910 Office: WETA 2000 L St NW Washington DC 20036

HERNDON, BOOTON, author; b. Charlottesville, Va., Dec. 9, 1915; s. Booton and Bertie (Wood) H.; student U. Mo., 1934-38; m. Bernadette Dorrity, Aug. 5, 1949; children—Booton III, John, Sue. Newspaper reporter, editor, New Orleans, 1939-42; free-lance writer, 1945-—. Pres., Charlottesville YMCA, 1966. Mem. Charlottesville Democratic Com., 1964-—. Served to 1st lt. AUS, 1943-45. Mem. Soc. Mag. Writers, D.A.V., N.A.A.C.P., Kappa Sigma. Clubs: N.Y. Athletic; Farmington Country. Author: 17 books including Young Men Can Change The World, 1965; Ford, 1969; The Great Land, 1971; Satisfaction Guaranteed, 1972. Editor: Rickenbacker, 1967. Contbr. numerous articles to various mags. Home: 2422 Jefferson Park Av Charlottesville VA 22903

HERNDON, JOHN GLENN, civil engr.; b. Elberton, Ga., June 1, 1925; s. Dillard Claude and Flora Ella (Herndon) H.; student Mercer U., 1943; La. State Northwestern Coll., Natchitoches, 1944; B.S. in Agrl. Engring., U. Ga., 1948; m. Willie Rivenburg, Dec. 8, 1950 (div. 1971); 1 stepdau., Cassie Elizabeth (Mrs. Geofrey Kruse); children—Martha Celeste, John Glenn. Served with USNR, 1943-45; joined U.S. Navy, 1948, aviator, 1948-60; jr. profl. engr. U.S. Dept. Agr., Houma, La., 1948, civil engr. Soil Conservation Service, Athens, Ga., 1961-62; tchr. Elbert County (Ga.) High Sch., 1960-61; tchr. sci., math., driver safety edn., 1962-65; civil engr. U.S. Corps Engrs., Savannah, Ga., 1966-—; helicopter pilot. Soc. Am. Mil. Engrs. Methodist (steward, mem. ofcl. bd.). Co-author: Aircraft T-34, 1955. Home: 107 W Jones St Savannah GA 31401 Office: 200 E St Julian St Savannah GA 31401

HERNDON, MICHAEL NEIL, lawyer; b. Ione, Ga., Dec. 3, 1939; s. Harry Eston and Irma Lee (McMillan) H.; student Washington and Lee U., 1958-62, U. Mexico, 1959; J.D., U. Ga., 1965; m. Jane Elizabeth Dykes, Feb. 11, 1972. Admitted to Ga. bar, 1965; practiced in Thomasville, 1967-—. Mem. Ga. Senate, 1971-—. Served with AUS, 1965-67. Mem. Am., Thomas County (pres. 1969) bar assns., State Bar Ga., Am. Judicature Soc., Internat. Platform Assn., L.Q.C. Lamar Soc., Pi Kappa Phi, Phi Delta Phi. Democrat. Elk. Club: Glen Arven Country (Thomasville); Atlanta City. Home: 205 Seward St Thomasville GA 31792 Office: PO Box 1507 Thomasville GA 31792

HERNDON, WILLIAM BANKS, lumber mfg. co. exec.; b. Atlanta, Apr. 6, 1921; s. Oma Ernest and Kate (Banks) H.; student U. Ala., 1939-40, Tex. Technol. Coll., 1941-42; m. Martha Charma Walker, Mar. 10, 1945; children—William Banks, Robert Walker, Oma Lewis, Alan Maier. With Walker-Williams Lumber Co., Hatchechubbee, Ala., 1946-—, gen. mgr., 1952-63, pres., 1963-—; pres. Atlanta Forest Products, Inc., Union City, Ga., 1968-71; dir. 1st Fed. Savs. & Loan Assn., Phenix City, Ala. Mem. Ala. Water Improvement Commn., 1968-71, Ala. Forestry Commn., 1969-71. Trustee, Brookstone Sch., Columbus, Ga., 1969-—. Served to 1st lt., Signal Corps, AUS, 1942-45. Mem. C. of C. (pres. 1969, dir.), Am. Wood Preservers Inst. (pres. 1972-73), Ala. Forest Products Assn. (pres. 1967). Methodist. Rotarian. Home: PO Box 113 Hatchechubbee AL 36858 Office: PO Box 7 Hatchechubbee Al 36858

HERRERO, BLAS C., U.S. dist. atty. for P.R. Address: San Juan PR 00904*

HERRING, CHARLES F(ERGUSON), lawyer, state senator; b. McGregor, Tex., June 1, 1914; s. Luther L. and Minnie (Townsend) H.; LL.B., U. Tex., 1938; LL.D., St. Edwards U., 1957; m. Doris Wallace, Sept. 4, 1935; children—Doris Carol, Cecelia Ann, Charles Ferguson, Antonia Minette. Admitted to Tex. bar, 1938; farmer McLennan Co., Tex., 1931-33; asso. firm Looney & Clark, Austin, 1938-41, 46-48; county atty., Travis County, Tex., 1941-42; area atty., OPA, 1942-43; sec. to Congressman Lyndon Johnson, Washington, 1943; parliamentarian Tex. Senate, 1951; now partner law firm Small, Herring, Werkenthin & Craig; U.S. atty. Western Dist. of Tex., 1951-55; chmn. bd. First Fed. Savs. & Loan Assn., Austin; mem. Tex. Senate 1956-—. Mem. Tex. Ethics Commn., Tex. Civil Jud. Council. Served at lt. (j.g.) USNR, Pacific, 1943-45. Mem. Am. Bar Assn., State Bar Tex., Tex. Fine Arts Assn., Sigma Nu. K.C. (dep. grand knight, 4 deg.). Home: 3105 Bowman Rd Austin TX 78703 Office: Perry Brooks Bldg Austin TX 78701

HERRING, DOUGLAS ASHLEY, banker; b. Morton, Miss., Aug. 19, 1936; s. William Eastman and Pauline Virginia (Murphy) H.; student East Central Jr. Coll. at Decatur (Miss.), 1956; m. Mozelle Williams, Dec. 22, 1956; children—Kimberly Leigh, Todd Ashley. Audit clk. 1st Nat. Bank, Jackson, Miss., 1956-60; sr. examiner Miss. State Banking Dept., Jackson, 1960-63; exec. v.p. Security State Bank, Starkville, Miss., 1963-—, also dir.; dir. Herschede Hall Clock Co., Inc., Starkville, Briarwood Lamp Co., Inc., Starkville. Chmn. Oktibbeha County Community Fund, 1963. Bd. dirs. Oktibbeha County Indsl. Found., 1971. Named Outstanding Young Man of Miss. Jr. C. of C., 1968. Mem. Miss. Bankers Assn. (exec. com. 1971), Oktibbeha County C. of C. (pres. 1969). Methodist. Lion. Home: Route 1 Box 11 Starkville MS 39759 Office: PO Box 131 Starkville MS 39759

HERRING, GROVER CLEVELAND, lawyer; b. Nocatee, Fla., Dec. 9, 1925; s. Joseph I. and Martha (Selph) H.; LL.B., U. Fla., 1950; m. Dorothy L. Blinn, Apr. 17, 1947; children—Stanley T., Kenneth Lee. Admitted to Fla. bar, 1950; asso. firm Haskins & Bryant, Sebring, 1950-52; practiced in West Palm Beach, Fla., 1952-60, 1964-—, mem. firm Blakeslee, Herring & Bie, and predecessor firm, 1953-60, Warwick, Paul & Herring, 1964-70, Herring & Evans, 1970-—; atty. City of West Palm1960-63, City of Atlantis, 1959-61, Town of Ocean Ridge, 1953-61, 1964-63, Village of Royal Palm Beach, 1964-—, Town of South Palm Beach (Fla.), 1966-—; spl. master-in-chancery 15th Jud. Circuit in and for Palm Beach County, 1953-54; judge ad litem Municipal Ct., West Palm Beach, 1954-55. Field rep. Lawyers Title Guaranty Fund, 1955-60, 64-—; dir. Lawyers Title Services, Inc., West Palm Beach. Active PTA, Family Service Agy., Palm Beach County Mental Health Assn.; chmn. profl. sect. A.R.C., 1960; mem. Charter Revision Com. West Palm Beach, 1960-65, Palm Beach County Resources Devel. Bd., 1959-—; appointed mem. Governmental Study Commn. by Fla. Legislature. Bd. dirs. Community Chest. Mem. Democratic Exec. Com., 1965-70. Served with USNR, 1944-46. Mem. Am., Palm Beach County (treas. 1960), John Marshall bar assns., Fla. Bar, Am. Judicature Soc., Lawyer's Title Guaranty Fund East Coast Estate Planning Council, Nat. Inst. Municipal Law Officers, Law-Sci. Acad., Am. Trial Lawyers Assn. (asso. editor 1960-—), Lawyers Lit. Club, Nat. Municipal League, U. Fla. Law Center Assn., World Peace Through Law Center, Fla. Sheriff's Assn. (hon.), U. Fla. Alumni Assn., V.F.W., Am. Legion, West Palm Beach C. of C., Civic Music Assn., Palm Beach County Hist. Soc. (pres. 1969-72) New Eng. Hist. Geneal. Soc. Boston. Mason (32 deg.), Elk, Moose. Clubs: West Palm Beach Country (hon.); Airways (N.Y.C.); History Book (Stamford, Conn.). Contbr. legal articles to profl. revs. Home: 3515 Australian Av West Palm Beach FL 33407 Office: Citizens Bldg West Palm Beach FL 33401

HERRING, NEWMAN LYNN, farmer; b. Kuttawa, Ky., Aug. 13, 1916; s. O. B. and May (Waters) H.; student Valpariso Tech. Sch., 1936-37; m. Rhea Sadler, Mar. 10, 1938; children—James Michael, David N. Farm mgr., owner farm, Eddyville, Ky., 1959—. Chmn., Lyon County Housing Commn., 1957—, Lyon County Water Commn., 1968—. Named Master Conservationist of Lyon County, 1970; recipient Commendable Community Service plaque Woodmen of World Life Ins. Soc., 1971. Mem. Lyon County Farm Bur. (dir., past pres.). Democrat. Baptist (deacon). Home: Route 2 Eddyville KY 42038 Office: PO Box 278 Eddyville KY 42038

HERRING, ROBERT RAY, utility co. exec.; b. Childress, Tex., Feb. 11, 1921; s. Lonnie Ray and Clara (Wolford) H.; B.A., Tex. A. and M. Coll., 1941; m. Sylvia Carmen Grant, Oct. 27, 1945; children—Sylvia Diane, Robert Ray, Randolph W. Vice pres. Fish Engring. Corp., 1950-52; pres. Fish Service Corp., 1952-58; pres. Valley Gas Prodn., Inc., 1958-63; v.p., gen. mgr. Houston Pipe Line Co., 1963-67; sr. v.p. Houston Natural Gas Corp., 1965-67, pres., chief exec. officer, 1967—; dir. Tex. Commerce Bank, Proler Steel Corp., First Continental Mortgage Co. Pres., Tex. Heart Inst.; mem. exec. com. Med. Research Found. Tex.; v.p. Houston Symphony Soc. Trustee U. Houston Found., Ray C. Fish Found., Rice U.; bd. dirs. Salvation Army, Energy Research and Edn. Found. Mem. Houston C. of C. (past pres.), Am. Gas Assn. (dir.), Tex. Mid-Continent Oil and Gas Assn. (dir.), Inst. Gas Tech. (trustee), Inc. Petroleum Assn. Am. Home: 3195 Inwood Dr Houston TX 77019 Office: PO Box 1188 Houston TX 77001

HERRMANN, ALOIS, wholesale trade exec.; b. Bischofstein, Germany, Feb. 6, 1914; s. Franz and Mathilde (Dombrowski) H.; B.A. and M.A., Heeresverwaltungsakademie, Munich, Germany; m. Gerda Edith Polkehn, July 7, 1951; children—Eleanor, Gabrielle B. Came to U.S., 1957, naturalized, 1964. Trainee comml. banking Bischofsburg, Germany, 1933-35; prisoner of war in Russia, 1945-49; head import control dept. Vereinsbank, Hamburg, Germany, 1950-56; with Mount Vernon Bank, Alexandria, Va., 1957-58; with Interarms, importer, Alexandria, 1958—, asst. treas., 1964-67, sec., 1967-70, v.p., 1970—; sec. Colonial Enterprises, 1965—. Tchr. French and German, U.S. Army, C.E., Fort Belvoir, Va., 1960-70; mem. faculty George Washington U., U. Va., 1959—, asso. in German, 1963—. Mem. West Springfield Civic Assn., Nat. Symphony Assn., Atlantic Fellowship Found., sec. bd. Colonial Hist. Found., Alexandria, 1966—. Served to capt. Germany Army, 1935-36, 39-45. Decorated Eisernes Kreuz, Kriegsverdienstkreuz 1. Klasse. Episcopalian. Clubs: Springfield (Va.) Golf and Country, Charnita (Pa.) Golf and Country, High Knob Country (Front Royal, Va.). Home: 7806 Glenister Dr Springfield VA 22152 Office: 10 Prince St Alexandria VA 22313

HERRMANN, EDWARD J., bishop; b. Balt., Nov. 6, 1913; s. Walter E. and Jennie (Doyle) H.; A.B., Mt. St. Mary's Coll. and Sem., Emmitsburg, Md., 1947. Ordained priest Roman Catholic Ch., 1947; asst. Our Lady of Victory Parish, 1947-60, pastor, 1968—; pastor St. Mary's Ch., Washington, 1960-68; asst. chancellor Archdiocese of Washington, 1951-62, vice chancellor, 1962-64, consultor, 1964—, vicar gen., 1966, chancellor, 1966—; aux. bishop Washington, titular bishop of Lamzella, 1966—. Home: 4835 MacArthur Blvd NW Washington DC 20007 Office: 1721 Rhode Island Av NW Washington DC 20036

HERRMANN, GEORGE HENRY CHRISTIAN, IV, physician; b. Fort Wayne, Ind., July 25, 1928; s. George Rudolph and Anna Harriet (Williams) H.; B.S., Sul Ross State U., Alpine, Tex., 1947; M.D., U. Tex., Galveston, 1950; m. Gloria Ladelle Jones, June 4, 1950; children—Harriet Ann, George Rudolph V. Intern, U. Mich. Hosp., 1950-51; resident John Sealy Hosp., Galveston, Tex., 1951-52, U.S. Army, 1952-54; chief indsl. medicine Kelly AFB, 1954-55; pvt. practice medicine, Castroville, Tex., 1955-56, Del Rio, Tex., 1956—. Cons., Dow Chem. Co. (La Dominicia Mine), 1968—; fed. jail physician, Del Rio; Val Verde County health officer, 1959-64; city health officer, Del Rio, 1964-69. Pres. Val Verde County Sch. Bd., 1968-70; mem. Val Verde County Airport Bd., 1960-70. Served to 1st lt., M.C. AUS, 1952-54. Mem. A.M.A., Tex. Med. Assn. (councillor), 5th Dist., 9 Counties (past pres.) med. socs. Mason. Home: 105 Austin Ct Del Rio TX 78840 Office: 710 Bedell Av Del Rio TX 78840

HERRMANN, GEORGE R., physician; b. Ft. Wayne, Ind., 1894; B.S., U. Mich., 1916, M.S., 1918, M.D., 1918, Ph.D., 1922. Med. house officer Peter Bent Brigham Hosp., Boston, 1918-19; asst. resident Robert Abbot Barnes Hosp., St. Louis, 1919-20, resident, 1920-21; vis. physician, dir. cardiology lab. Charity Hosp., New Orleans, 1925-31; mem. pathology staff U. Mich., 1916-18, instr. internal medicine, 1921-24, asst. prof., 1925; asst. in medicine Washington U., St. Louis, 1920-21; asst. prof. medicine Tulane U., New Orleans, 1925-28, asso. prof. 1928-31; prof. clin. medicine U. Tex., Galveston, 1931-39, prof. medicine, 1939-65, Ashbel Smith prof. medicine, 1965—, dir. Cardiovascular Research Lab., 1939—; cons. in field. Mem. NRC Com. Essential Drugs, 1942. Served with chem. warfare service U.S. Army, 1918. Recipient Distinguished Service award A.M.A., 1971. Diplomate Am. Bd. Internal Medicine, with supsplty. cardiovascular medicine. Fellow A.C.P., Am. Coll. Chest Physicians, A.A.A.S., Am. Coll. Cardiology; mem. So. Med. Assn., A.M.A., Assn. Am. Physicians, Am. Clin. and Clinmatological Assn., Am. Soc. Clin. Investigation, Am. Soc. Exptl. Pathology, Soc. Exptl. Biology and Medicine, Am. Heart Assn. Address: Dept Internal Medicine U Tex Galveston TX 77550*

HERRON, JOHN TATE, physician, state ofcl.; b. Lonoke, Ark., 1910; M.D., U. Ark., 1936; M.P.H., Harvard, 1949. Intern Scott & White Hosp., 1936-38; exec. sec., also health officer Ark. State Bd. Health, Little Rock; prof. medicine U. Ark. Diplomate Am. Bd. Preventive Medicine. Fellow Am. Pub. Health Assn. Office: 4815 W Markham St Little Rock AR 72201

HERSCHELL, WILSON JAMES, sch. adminstr.; b. Tonawanda, N.Y., Feb. 25, 1922; s. James Wilson and Bessie (Mowitz) H.; B.S., Ga. So. Coll., 1949; M.S., N.C. State U., 1956; m. Mary Helen Drew, June 25, 1944; 1 son, James Wilson. Tchr. indsl. arts, Pinehurst, N.C., 1949-52, Albany (Ga.) High Sch., 1952-62; prin. Dougherty High Sch., Albany, 1962-67, Westover High Sch., Albany, 1967—. Served with USNR, 1942-45. Mem. Ga. Assn. Educators, N.E.A., Nat. Assn. Secondary Sch. Prins., Ga. Assn. Sch. Prins., Dougherty County Edn. Assn. (past pres.), 2d Dist. Prins. Assn. (past pres.), Am. Legion. Methodist (ofcl bd.). Rotarian. Home: 1909 E Lakeridge Dr Albany GA 31705 Office: 2600 Patridge Lane Albany GA 31705

HERSH, SEYMOUR M., journalist; A.B., U. Chgo., 1958. Formerly police reporter Chgo. News Bur., U.P.I., A.P., Chgo. and Washington; now free-lance reporter. Recipient Pulitzer prize in journalism for internat. reporting, George Polk Meml. award, Sigma Delta Chi award, Worth Bingham prize, U. Chgo. Pub. Service award. Author: Chemical and Biological Warfare: America's Hidden Arsenal, 1968; My Lai 4, A Report on the Massacre and Its Aftermath. Address: 2118 Cortland Pl NW Washington DC 20008*

HERSHEY, LEWIS BLAINE, army officer; b. Steuben County, Ind., Sept. 12, 1893; s. Latta Freleigh and Rosetta (Richardson) H.; B.S., Tri-State Coll., Angola, Ind., 1912, B.Pd., A.B., 1914; student Ind. U., 1917; attended Field Arty. Sch., Fort Sill, Okla., 1922-23; Command and Gen. Staff Sch., 1931-33, Army War Coll., 1933-34, U., Hawaii, 1935-36; LL.D., (hon.), Tri-State Coll., Ohio State U., Oglethorpe U., Norwich U., Albright Coll., LaFayette Coll., Columbia U., Ind. U.; m. Ellen Dygert, Nov. 29, 1917; children—Kathryn Elizabeth (Mrs.A. Alvis Layne, Jr.), Gilbert Richardson, George Frederick, Ellen Margaret (Mrs. Sam L. Barth), Tchr. twp. sch. Jamestown Twp., Steuben, Ind., 1910; high sch. prin., Flint, Ind., 1914-16; successively pvt., cpl., sgt., 2d lt., 1st lt., Ind. N.G., 1911-16; commd. 1st lt. U.S. Army, 1916, and advanced through grades to gen.; asst. prof. mil. sci. and tactics Ohio State U., 1923-27; asst. G-4, Hawaiian Dept., 1934-36; mem. War Dept. Gen. Staff, 1936-40; sec. and exec. officer, Joint Army and Navy Selective Service Com., 1936-40; promoted to brig. gen. Oct. 1940, in recognition of work in preparing plans for Selective Service System; appointed dept. dir. Selective Service System, Dec. 19, 1940, dir. July 31, 1941; promoted to major gen., Apr. 1942; retired phys. disability, Dec. 31, 1946; assigned dir. Selective Service (active duty), Jan. 1, 1947; apptd. dir. Office of Selective Service Records, Mar. 31, 1947-48; promoted to lt. gen., 1956; apptd. dir. Selective Service by Pres. Truman, 1948; now adviser to Pres. on manpower moblzn., 1970. Chmn. Montgomery County chpt. A.R.C., 1952-58; past pres. Nat. Capital area council Boy Scouts Am. Trustee Tri State Coll., Angola, D.S.M. from Army and Navy; D.S.M. of Am. Legion, 1946 also N.G. Assn. of U.S., 1954; Distinguished Service award Mil. Chaplains U.S., 1957; George Washington medal Freedoms Found., 1958; Bernard Baruch award V.F.W., 1966; Silver Beaver award Boy Scouts, 1961, Silver Antelope award, 1963, Silver Buffalo, 1966. Republican. Mason. Author: Selective Service in Peacetime; Selective Service in Wartime; Selective Service as the Tide of War Turns; Selective Service in Victory; also mag. articles. Home: 5500 Lambeth Rd Bethesda MD 20014 Office: The White House Washington DC 20500

HERSHMAN, JACOB EARL, govt. ofcl.; b. Mechanicsburg, Pa., Nov. 7, 1913; s. John R. and Fairy (Pfaltzgraff) H.; B.S., Elizabethtown (Pa.) Coll., 1936; M.Ed., U. Md., 1949, D.Ed., 1956; m. Alberta Garns, Jan. 2, 1942; children—Joan Elaine, John Garns, Lucie Ann. Regional display supr. Montgomery Ward Co., 1939-42; tchr. high sch., Washington, Md., 1945-56; curriculum specialist South Hagerstown (Md.) High Sch., 1956-57; prin. Hancock (Md.) High Sch., 1957-61; dean Elizabethtown Coll., 1961-66; program specialist Bur. Higher Edn., Office Edn., 1966-67, higher edn. specialist div. coll. facilities, 1967—, now chief Instnl. Eligibility Unit. Active Boy Scouts, Community Chest, A.R.C. fund drives. Bd. dirs. Hancock Free Library. Served as sgt. AUS, 1942-45. Mem. N.E.A., Md., Washington County tchrs. assns., Nat., Md. assns. secondary sch. prins., Nat. Biology Tchrs. Assn., Md. History Tchrs. Assn., Eastern Assn. Coll. Deans, Pa. Assn. Acad. Deans, Phi Delta Kappa. Rotarian. Home: 6735 Tower Dr Alexandria VA 22306 Office: Div Coll Facilities US Office Edn GSA Bldg 7th and D Sts SW Washington DC 20405

HERVEY, FRED TAYLOR, food co. exec.; b. El Paso, Tex., July 28, 1909; s. Taylor Master and Sarah Gertrude (Crossett) H.; ed. pub. schs., El Paso children—Helen Shirleen (Mrs. John A. Gillett, Jr.), Fred Taylor, Evelyn Diane. Chmn. bd. Circle K Corp., El Paso, 1951—; chmn. bd. Am. Bank of Commerce, Coaches of Am., Inc., Financial Computer Services, Inc.; pres. Central Ariz. Broadcasting Co., Rio Grande Broadcasting Co., Fred Hervey, Inc., O.A. Corp., S.W. Drive-Ins. Finance chmn., dir. Rio Grande council Girl Scouts Am., 1970-72. Mayor, El Paso, 1951-54; El Paso County Republican finance chmn., 1968—; mem. State Rep. Exec. Com., 1970—; dist. Rep. committeeman, 1970—. Chmn. bd. devel. U. Tex., El Paso; bd. dirs. St. Joseph Hosp. Served with USNR, 1943-45. Mem. El Paso C. of C. (dir.). Home: 937 Rim Rd El Paso TX 79902 Office: 1001 E Yandell St El Paso TX 79902

HERVEY, JAMES BYRON, savs. and loan exec.; b. Greenville, Tex., June 2, 1920; s. Oney S and M. Elizabeth (Jarrett) H.; B.S., Tex. A. and M. U., 1942; m. Nedra Louise Scott, July 3, 1946; children—R. Scott, James Dickson, Robert Ray. Pres., Community Savs. and Loan Assn., College Station, Tex., 1966—; pres. The Normandy Corp., Brownwood, Tex., 1970—; dir. Univ. Nat. Bank, Edge-Rite Corp; Pres. A & M. Consol. Sch. Bd. Trustees, 1960-63; Mayor, City of College Station, 1971—. Served with USAAF, 1942-46. Mem. Assn. Mayors (2d v.p. 1971-72), Tex. Municipal League. Democrat. Home: 1201 Winding Rd College Station TX 77840 Office: Drawer 2800 College Station TX 77840

HERZIK, GUS RALPH, JR., state ofcl.; b. Engle, Tex., Oct. 23, 1913; s. Gus and Adel (Nesrsta) H.; B.S. in Civil Enging., Tex. A. and M. U., 1934, M.S., 1936, C.E., 1942; S.M., Harvard, 1938; m. Frances Katherine Brunner, July 3, 1946; children—Steven Ralph, Kaye Adele. Instr. civil engring. Tex. A. and M. U., College Station, 1934-36; instrumentman Tex. Hwy. Dept., 1936-37; with Tex. Dept. Health, Austin, 1937—, chief engr., 1940-59, chief environmental sanitation services, 1959-67, dep. commr. environmental health, 1967—. Cons., U. Tex., 1962-69, USPHS, 1963-67. Bd. dirs. Tex. Water Research Council, 1959—, Tex. Water and Sanitation Research Found.; mem. council pub. health cons. Nat. Sanitation Found, 1966-67. Served to lt. col. AUS, 1942-45. Mem. Nat. Soc. Profl. Engrs., Am. Water Works Assn., Water Pollution Control Fedn., Tex. Pub. Health Assn., Am. Acad. Environmental Engrs. (inter soc. bd.), Conf. State San. Engrs., Tau Beta Pi, Delta Omega. Co-author: Manual for Water Works Operators, 1969, Manual for Wastewater Operations, 1971. Home: Route 7 Box 632 Austin TX 78703 Office: 1100 W 49th St Austin TX 78756

HERZOG, WILLIAM THEODORE, pub. health adminstr.; b. Peoria, Ill., Aug. 22, 1933; s. Charles E. and Helen (Martin) H.; B.A., Knox Coll., 1955; M.S. in Pub. Health, U. N.C., 1958; m. Sandra Lou Reimers, Sept. 3, 1955; children—Lee Ann, Thomas Eric. Health edn. asso. pub. health edn. Peoria (Ill.) City Health Dept., 1956-57, Allegheny County Health Dept., Pitts., 1958-59; research asso. Sch. Pub. Health, U. N.C., Chapel Hill, 1959-61, asst. dir. Continued Edn. Service, asst. prof. health edn., asst. prof. pub. health adminstrn., 1964-69, dir. continuing edn. health scis. div. health affairs, 1969—; sr. operations analyst Research Triangle Inst., Durham, N.C., 1962-64, now cons. Served to 1st lt. AUS, 1956. Mem. Am. Pub. Health Assn., Assn. Schs. Allied Health Professions, Acad. Health Adminstrs., N.C. Assn. Health Educators (pres. 1961), Delta Omega. Contbr. articles to profl. jours. Home: 302 Hemlock Lane Chapel Hill NC 27514

HESS, LAURIE FLOYD, engring. cons. exec.; b. Washington, Aug. 21, 1901; s. James Albert and Blanche (Hess) H.; B.S., George Washington U., 1935; m. Ada King Swigart, Nov. 24, 1928; children—Carol Margaret (Mrs. Walter H. Keim), Patricia Ann (Mrs. David Jernigan). Asso. structural engr. U.S. Treasury Dept., Washington, 1930-40; commd. 2d lt. U.S. Army, 1940, advanced through grades to lt. col., 1953; theatre logistician Hdqrs. European Command, Heidelberg, Germany, 1950-52; chief, troop planning sect. Army Map Service, Washington 1952-58; pres. Combined Cons. Services, Washington, 1961-66, Resources Engring., Inc., Washington, 1966—, Resources Engring. Panama, S.A. Mem. Nat. Soc. Profl. Engrs. Am. Soc. C.E. (chmn. emergency assistance com.), Am. Soc. Testing and Materials, Soc. Mil. Engrs., Permanent Internat. Soc. Navigational Congresses. Home: 3807 Kanawha St NW Washington DC 20015 Office: 1701 16th St NW Washington DC 20009

HESS, WALTER C., former coll. pres, biochemist; b. Phila., July 19, 1899; s. Edward and Theresa (Cohen) H.; B.S., U. Pa., 1920; Ph.D., George Washington U., 1930; m. Jeanette Samuel, June 11, 1922; 1son, Walter C. Chemist, USPHS, 1926-31; mem. faculty Georgetown U., 1931-68, prof. biochemistry, chmn. dept. Med. and Dental Sch., 1946-68, asso. dean, 1960-64, v.p. for grants and contracts, 1964-68, emeritus, 1968—; pres. Dunbarton Coll., Washington, 1968-70. Adv. com. U.S. commr. edn., 1945-47. Exec. com. D.C. Community Chest, 1939-40. Served with U.S. Army, 1917-18. Mem. Am. Soc. Biol. Chemists, Soc. Exptl. Biology and Medicine (chmn. D.C. sect. 1945), Internat. Assn. Dental Research, Am. Chem. Soc., Washington Acad. Sci., D.A.V., (dept. comdr. 1939-41), Phi Beta Kappa, Sigma Xi. Home: 3607 Chesapeake St NW Washington DC 20008

HESTER, ELMO CLEVELAND, JR., editor; b. Cuthbert, Ga., Sept. 19, 1924; s. Elmo Cleveland and Frances L. (Miller) H.; B.S., U. Ga., 1947; student N.C. State Coll., 1943-44, U. Ky., 1944; m. Mary Carole Black, Dec. 26, 1947; children—Rebecca Lynn, Donna Marie, Linda Susan. Farm and state news editor Columbus (Ga.) Enquirer, 1948-49; farm editor Atlanta Jour., 1949-55; editor Va. Poultryman, also Southeastern Poultryman, 1955-57, Ga. Farmer, 1957-62; coordinator coop. services Ga. Dept. Agr., 1962-65; editor Ga. Farmer, also S.C. Farmer-Grower, Atlanta, 1965—, pub., owner, 1971—; editor So. Hog Producer, DelMarVa Farmer, N.C. Grower, 1970. Served with AUS, 1943-45, 50-52; MTO, Korea; lt. col. Res. Recipient various writing and reporting activities awards. Mem. Am. Agrl. Editors Assn., Res. Officers Assn. (Ga. pub. relations dir. 1969-72, nat. pub. relations com. 1970-71), Assn. U.S. Army, Ga. Agribus. Council (sec. and dir. 1966-67), Alumni Assn. Coll. Agrl. U. Ga. (sec.-treas, 1961-67, dir. 1960-61), Sigma Delta Chi, Omicron Delta Kappa, Alpha Zeta, Blue Key, Scabbard and Blade. Home: 665 Willivee Dr Decatur GA 30033 Office: 476 Plasamour Dr Atlanta GA 30324

HESTER, THOMAS ARGUS, JR., planter, agrl. conservationist; b. Mathiston, Miss., May 19, 1907; s. Tom A. and Julia Ann Victoria (Sealy) H.; B.S. in Agrl. Engring., Miss. State U., 1931, spl. study, summer 1967; spl. study U. N.H., summer 1957, U. Ga., summer 1961; m. Eleanor Ellis, Jan. 1, 1933; children—Thomas Argus III, John W. Soil conservationist Bolivar County Dept. Agr., Miss., 1935-36, Carroll County, Carrollton, 1936-37, Clay County, West Point, 1937-42, Covington County, Collins, 1942, Jones County, Laurel, 1942, George County, Lucedale, 1943-44, Franklin County, Headville, 1944-48, Tallahatchie County, Sumner, Dept. of Agr., Soil Conservation Service, P.R., 1942-43, Bolivar County, Shelby, 1948—; owner, operator Last Jump-Off Plantation, Shelby, 1935—; dir., pres. Hester Engring. Services, Inc. Cons. area solutions to regional problems Progressive Farmer, Delta Farm Press, 1948—; mem. Delta council soil conservation com., Agrl. com. Boliva County Farm Bur., 1948; farm planner, appraiser, estates cons. Recipient regional award Miss. Wild Life Fedn., 1962, state award outstanding work conservation U.S. Dept. Agr., 1963. Mem. C. of C. Am. Soc. Agrl. Engrs., Miss. Soc. Farm Mgrs. Appraisers (v.p.), Miss. State Alumni Assn., Conservation League of Beulah, Donelson Point, Island 66, Nat. Rifle Assn., Soil Conservation Soc. Am. Baptist (supt. Sunday sch.). Rotarian (pres. Shelby). Club: DeSoto Lake Hunting and Fishing (pres.) (Shelby, Miss.). Co-author series articles on land levelling. Spl. work in conservation planting and planning, wildlife improvement, fishing area improvement, wildlife feeding crops. Patentee in field. Home: Honey Bayou Rd Last Jump-Off Plantation Shelby MS 38774 Office: Shelby MS 38774

HESTER, MRS. THOMAS ARGUS, JR. (ELLEN ORR), author; b. Ackerman, Miss., July 18, 1907; d. William Ahas and Mamie (Hames) Ellis; B.A., Miss. Woman's Coll., 1929; student U. Mo., 1931; m. Thomas Argus Hester, Jr., Jan. 1, 1933; children—Thomas Arugs III, John William. Free-lance writer, 1931—; news and soc. corrs. Bolivar Comml., Cleveland, Miss.; columnist Delta Farm Press, Clarksdale, Miss., 1949—, Bolivar Comml.; co-owner with husband Last Jump-Off Plantation; v.p.; sec. Hester Engring. Services, Inc.; cultural Spanish English tchr. Dist. III, 1966—. Mem. Vol. Program Community Enrichment. Winner 2d, columnist, Miss. Press Assn., 1962, 3d, 1963, 3d, Nat. League Am. Pen Women, 1963, state and nat. awards Press Womens Assn., 1965, 1st place, Miss. Press Women Awards, 1966-71. Mem. Miss. Press Women, Nat. League Am. Pen Women, Nat. Press Womens Assn., Miss. Folklore Soc. (lectr.), Theta Sigma Phi. Democrat. Baptist. Club: Shelby Woman's. Author, co-editor; Delta Decameron, 1955; contbg. author short story New Voices; American Writing Today. 1955; contbr. Miss. Folklore mag., Delta Rev., Nat. Tech. mag. Home: Box 242 Honey Bayou Rd Shelby MS 38774

HEWETSON, HENRY WELDON, educator; b. Toronto, Ont., Can., Mar. 10, 1904 (came to U.S. 1948); s. Henry Charles and Kathleen Maud (Weldon) H.; B.A., U. Toronto, 1924; M.A., U. B.C., 1925; Ph.D., U. Chgo., 1951; m. Frances Mary Chambers, Sept. 14, 1929; 1 dau., Nancy (Mrs. Phillip F. Cooke). With Mich. State U., 1928-29, U. Alta., 1929-48; with Mary Washington Coll. of U. Va., 1948—, now prof. econs. Mem. Am., Canadian econs. assns., Omicron Delta Epsilon. Contbr. articles to profl. jours. Home: 1428 Royston St Fredericksburg VA 22401

HEWGLEY, JAMES MARION, JR., former mayor of Tulsa; b. Gallatin, Tenn., Nov. 7, 1916; s. James Marion and Margaret (Corbett) H.; B.A., U. Okla., 1938; married; 4 sons, 2 daus. Mayor, City of Tulsa, 1966-70. Chmn. Alcoholic Beverage Control Bd., Oklahoma City, 1961-64. Vice-pres. Bd. Regents Okla. Coll. Liberal Arts, Chicasha, 1965-66; trustee Children's Med. Center, 1964—; bds. dirs. Tulsa A.R.C., 1964-66, Tulsa Opera, 1962-66; pres. bd. trustees Holland Hall Sch., Tulsa, 1960-65. Served to 1st lt. AUS, 1942-46. Mem. Phi Kappa Psi. Episcopalian. Clubs: Southern Hills Country; Tulsa. Home: 2454 E 30th Tulsa OK 74114 Office: 1207 Philtower Bldg Tulsa OK 74103

HEWINS, KENNETH FITZGERALD, journalist, educator; b. Evansville, Ind., Nov. 16, 1902; s. Dan and Etta (Gardner) H.; B.A., Ind. U., 1925, M.A., 1926; postgrad. U. Miss., 1952; m. Lillian Louise Loge, July 3, 1927 (dec.); children—Marilyn June (Mrs. Leary Leo Wright), Eleanor Joyce (Mrs. Charles F. Robinson). Reporter, Evansville Press, summer 1922; editor-in-chief Ind. Daily Student, 1924; city editor Bloomington (Ind.) Star, 1924; asst. editor Ind. U. Alumnus, 1924-26; alumni editor, mgr. Press Bur. U. Ark., 1926-29; asst. prof. to prof., head journalism dept., dir. publicity La. Tech. U., Ruston, 1929-68; cons. journalistic field, 1968—. Mem. Acacia, Sigma Delta Chi, Sigma Tau Delta. Author: Mississippi Press Laws, 1952. Home: 306 E Arizona Av Ruston LA 71270

HEWITT, PURSER, exec. editor Jackson (Miss.) Clarion-Ledger. Address: 311 Pearl St Jackson MS 39201*

HEYCK, GERTRUDE PAINE DALY (MRS. THEODORE R. HEYCK), club woman; b. Houston, Nov. 30, 1910; d. David and Gertrude (Paine) Daly; student Wellesley Coll., 1929, Pembroke

Coll., 1931-34; B.A., Brown U., 1934; m. Theodore R. Heyck, May 1, 1935; children—Jane Peel (Mrs. Donald H. Gaucher), Theodore Daly. Dir., Union Stock Yards, San Antonio, 1961-64. Sustaining mem. Jr. League, Houston. Mem. Harris County Heritage Soc. Clubs: Brown-Pembroke (v.p.), Houston Country. Home: 1907 Bolsover St Houston TX 77005

HEYD, LOUIS ANTHONY, JR., city ofcl.; b. New Orleans, Nov. 1, 1933; s. Louis A. and Lillian (Pritchard) H.; B.A. in Polit. Sci., Tulane U., 1955, J.D., 1959; m. Joan Marie Meyer, June 25, 1955; children—Theresa Marie, Michael Louis, Julie Ann. Admitted to La. bar, 1959; practiced in New Orleans; asst. dist. atty. Orleans Parish, New Orleans, 1961-62, criminal sheriff, 1966—. Served to lt. USMCR, 1955-57. Mem. Nat. Jail Assn. (pres. 1971-72). Home: 6110 Duplessie St New Orleans LA 70122 Office: 2700 Tulane Av New Orleans LA 70119

HEYNS, ROGER WILLIAM, ednl. assn. exec.; b. Grand Rapids, Mich., Jan. 27, 1918; s. Garrett and Rosa (Klooster) H.; student Hope Coll., 1936-37; A.B., Calvin Coll., 1940; M. Clin. Psychology, U. Mich., 1942, Ph.D., 1948, LL.D., 1967; LL.D., U. San Francisco, 1968; m. Esther Gezon, Sept. 20, 1941; children—Michael, John, Dan. Instr. psychology U. Mich., 1947-48, asst. prof., 1948-55, asso. prof., 1955-57, prof., 1957-65, v.p. acad. affairs, 1965; chancellor U. Cal. at Berkeley, 1965-71; pres. Am. Council Edn., Washington. Dir. Norton Simon, Inc. Mem. ad hoc sci. adv. com. NASA; mem. Nat. Sci. Bd. Bd. trustees Ednl. Testing Service. Served from pvt. to capt., USAAF, 1942-46. Recipient outstanding tchr. award U. Mich., 1952, faculty distinguished service award, 1958. Fellow Am. Psychol. Assn; mem. Phi Beta Kappa, Sigma Xi, Phi Kappa Phi. Office: 1785 Massachusetts Av NW Washington DC 20016

HIBDON, JAMES EDWARD, educator; b. McAlester, Okla., Sept. 1, 1924; s. William Wesley and Minnie Irene (McBride) H.; student Okla. Bapt. U., 1942-43, Syracuse U., 1943; B.A., U. Okla., 1948, M.A., 1949; Ph.D., U. N.C., 1957; m. Mina Mae Gilreath, Aug. 20, 1944; children—Mary Ann, Jennifer Lee. Asst. prof. econs. Ga. State U., 1954-57, asso. prof., 1957-59; asso. prof. Tex. A. and M. U., 1959-61; asso. prof. U. Okla., Norman, 1961-67, prof., 1967—, chmn. econs. dept., 1971—. Trustee annuity bd. So. Bapt. Conv. Served with AUS, 1943-46, 50-51. Mem. Am., So., Midwest econ. assns., Southwestern Social Sci. Assn., Rocky Mountain Social Sci. Assn., Beta Gamma Sigma, Omicron Epsilon. Author: Price and Welfare Theory, 1969. Home: 1501 Leslie Lane Norman OK 73069

HICKEY, THOMAS HAROLD, physician; b. London, Ark., May 14, 1924; s. Mike J. and Anna Mae (Spillers) H.; student Ark. Poly. Coll., 1942-44; B.S., M.D., U. Ark., 1951; m. Ruth Newton, Jan. 28, 1950; children—Ellen (Mrs. Charles Malone), Nancy, Treva. Intern, Ark. Bapt. Med. Center; practice medicine, specializing in gen. practice, Morrilton, Ark., 1952—; physician Hickey White Clinic, Morrilton; mem. staff St. Anthony's Hosp., Morrilton, Conway County Hosp., Morrilton. Mem. Conway County (Ark.) Hosp. Bd., 1952—, Arkansas River Valley Action Bd., 1966—. Mayor, City of Morrilton, 1962-72. Served to staff sgt. AUS, 1943-46. Mem. Am., Ark., Conway County med. assns., Morrilton C. of C. Presbyn. (bd. synod). Mason (32 deg.). Home: 100 S Cherokee St Morrilton AR 72110 Office: 1109 E Broadway Morrilton AR 72110

HICKMAN, BERNARD, athletic dir. U. Louisville. Address: Athletic Dept U Louisville Louisville KY 40208*

HICKMAN, DAVID, artist. Asst. prof. art U. Houston. Home: 8814 Rowan St Houston TX 77036*

HICKMAN, JACK WALTER, educator; b. Indpls., June 3, 1931; s. Walter Frederick and Sally Estella (Hurst) H.; student Wabash Coll., 1948-51; B.S., Ind. U., 1952, M.D., 1955; m. Mary Addison Landers, Jan. 6, 1954; children—William L., Elizabeth H., Anne R. Intern, Indpls. Gen. Hosp., 1955-56, resident internal medicine, 1958-59, Lahey Clinic, Boston, 1956-58; dir. med. edn. Marion County Gen. Hosp., Indpls., 1961-68; asst. prof. internal medicine Ind. U. Sch. Medicine, Indpls., 1963-67, asso. prof., 1967-70, asst. dean, 1968-70; asso. prof. internal medicine, asso. dean U. So. Fla. Coll. Medicine, Tampa, 1970—. Diplomate Am. Bd. Internal Medicine. Fellow Am. Coll. Physicians. Mem. Am., Fla. med. assns., Am. Diabetes Assn., Phi Delta Theta, Nu Sigma Nu. Clubs: Indianapolis Literary, University, Woodstock (Indpls.); Tampa Yacht and Country. Editorial bd. Jour. Ind. State Med. Assn., 1967-70. Home: 58 Martinique Av Tampa FL 33606

HICKMAN, ROY D., mfg. co. exec., assn. exec.; b. Chattanooga, Jan. 27, 1902; B.A., U. N.M., 1925; m. Dorothy Dunkerley; 1 dau., Mary Lynn. Chmn. bd. Ala. Engraving Co., Birmingham, Platemakers, Inc., Birmingham. Past dist. gov. Rotary Internat., past dir., chmn. conv., 1958, internat. pres., Evanston, Ill., 1972-73. Past pres. Ala. Tb Assn.; chmn. adv. bd. United U.C. Appeal, 1971-72. Trustee Brooke Hill Sch. Mem. Birmingham C. of C. (past pres.), Pi Kappa Alpha. Clubs: Downtown, Executives. Presbyn. Address: 3357 Hermitage Rd Birmingham AL 35223*

HICKS, ALICE BROWN (MRS. GEORGE W. HICKS), writer; b. Auburn, Ind., Nov. 24, 1914; d. Harold Charles and Hazel (Swisher) Brown; student DePauw U., 1932-34; m. George W. Hicks, Dec. 21, 1940; children—Mark, Nancy, Jane, Mary, Nina, Lora. Newspaperwoman, Evening Star, Auburn, 1938-40; lectr. Pineywoods Writers Conf., Stephen F. Austin State Coll., Nacogdoches, Tex., 1966, 67. Lit. co-chmn. South Miss. Festival of Arts, 1967-70; adult leader 4-H Club, Pascagoula, Miss., 1956-65. Bd. dirs. Jackson County Fair Assn., 1961-66, pres., 1964-66. Mem. World Poetry Soc., Poetry Soc. Tex., Cow Belles of Mobile Country, Writers Unlimited of Pasagoula (pres. 1967). Delta Zeta. Author (under name Betty Brown Hicks): I Sing My Amazement, 1968; Lyrics from Cor Meum, 1969. Home: 1510 Jackson Av PO Box 208 Pascagoula MS 39567 Office: PO Box 208 Pascagoula MS 39567

HICKS, ARINGIA ADDAMSON, extension agt.; b. Kilgore, Tex., Oct. 11, 1902; s. Middie and Nancy Marlo (Robinson) H.; B.S., Tuskegee Inst., 1927; postgrad. U. Va., 1963-64, Agrl. Tech. Coll., Greensboro, N.C., 1962-65; m. Willie Jureal Withers, Oct. 19, 1932; 1 dau., Marian Edythe (Mrs. James Anthony Colston). Agrl. extension agt., Clarke County, Ala., 1929-49, Franklin County, Va., 1950—. Dir. Franklin County Fed. Credit Union, 1969—. Vice-pres. Franklin County council P.T.A., 1968-70; mem. Franklin County Vocational Adv. Bd., 1969—, Planning Dist. Commn., 1972—. Bd. dirs. Franklin County Office Econ. Opportunity, United Fund, Roanoke Area Tb and Respiratory Disease Assn., Franklin Meml. Hosp., Comprehensive Health Planning Council of West Piedmont. Mem. Extension Agts. Assn. (sec.-treas. 1970—), Franklin County Assn. Chs. (sec. 1969—), Franklin County C. of C. (dir. 1967—), Epsilon Sigma Phi. Baptist. Mason. Home: 213 Patterson Av Rocky Mount VA 24151 Office: PO Box 26 Rocky Mount VA 24151

HICKS, DAVID SMITH, city ofcl.; b. Van Buren, Ark., May 6, 1930; s. Oscar and Treva (Smith) H.; A.A., West Ark. Jr. Coll., 1957; m. Glenna Fay Brooks, Mar. 21, 1954; children—Pamela, Lisa, David Brooks, With Okla. Gas & Electric Co., 1954-66; dir. Ft. Smith (Ark.) Housing Authority, 1966—. Chmn. housing sub-com. City Citizens Adv. Com., 1968—. Bd. dirs. James S. Beckman Sr. Citizen Center, Ft. Smith. Served with AUS, 1951-53. Mem. Housing and Renewal Ofcls. (state chpt. pres. 1969—), United Comml. Travelers, Assn. U.S. Army (chpt. sec.-treas. 1967—), Ft. Worth C. of C. Home: 3401 Wirsing St Fort Smith AR 72901 Office: 2100 N 31st St Fort Smith AR 72901

HICKS, DOUGLAS BRECKENRIDGE, broadcasting exec.; b. Dewey County, Okla., Oct. 29, 1907; s. William Absalom and Ora Naomi (Newton) H.; A.B., Baylor U., 1929; m. Evelyne Louise Johnson, Oct. 7, 1939. Reporter, staff writer, city editor Houston Press, 1929-41; pub. relations dir. Houston C. of C. 1941-42; sr. account exec., asst. mgr. Max H. Jacobs Pub. Relations Agy., Houston, 1946-51; pub. relations rep. with Tenneco, Inc., Houston, 1951-52, pub. relations mgr., 1952-63, asst. dir. pub. relations and advt., 1963-68; partner Vets. Broadcasting Co., Houston, 1948-62; v.p. Tex. Coast Broadcasters, Inc., Tex. Coast Broadcasters of Beaumont, Inc., 1962-68, chmn. bd., 1969—. Councilman, Bunker Hill Village, 1963-69. Served from lt. to lt. comdr. USNR, 1942-46; PTO. Mem. Pub. Relations Soc. Am., Assn. Petroleum Writers, Tex. Mid-Continent Oil and Gas Assn., Houston C. of C. Baptist. Clubs: Press (Houston); Pine Forest Country, Panorama Country, Tennwood. Home: 46 Ivy Ct Conroe TX 77301 Office: 4701 Caroline St Houston TX 77002

HICKS, ELDER BARNEY, clergyman; b. Wichita, Kan., July 11, 1907; s. Daniel H. and Carrie (Smith) H.; A.B., Washburn U., 1951; Th.B., Central Baptist Sem., 1934, D.D. (hon.), 1940; D.D., Monrovia Coll. & Indsl. Inst., Monrovia, Liberia, West Africa, 1961; m. Effie Mae Hayes, Mar. 9, 1927 (dec. 1960); children—Rose Marie (Mrs. Dewey Sanderson), Milton T., James Edward, E. Barney; m. 2d Roena S. Starks, Oct. 10, 1961. Ordained to ministry, Bapt. Ch., 1934, pastor in Paxico, Kan., 1934-36, Holton and Horton, Kan., 1936-37, Duluth, Minn., 1937-42; exec. sec., missionary Bapt. Conv. of Kan., 1945-56; dir. Bapt. Ednl. Centers of Am. Bapt. Home Mission Socs., 1956-63, asso. dir community witness program, div. ch. missions, 1963-67, program asso. for inner city work, 1967-69, asst. sec. dir. parish devel., 1969-71; regional exec. minister Am. Bapt. Chs. of South, Atlanta, 1971—. Served from 1st lt. to capt., as chaplain, AUS, 1942-45. Mem. N.A.A.C.P. Office: Suite 936 Citizens Trust Bldg 75 Piedmont Av NE Atlanta GA 30303

HICKS, GEORGE WARREN, physician; b. Berrien County, Mich., Oct. 6, 1916; s. Carl M. and Ruth (Lundy) H.; B.S., U. Mich., 1938, M.D., 1950; m. Alice Louise Brown, Dec. 21, 1940; children—Mark Carl, Nancy Dell (Mrs. Lloyd Nelson), Jane Eileen (Mrs. Thomas J. Walker), Mary Elizabeth, Nine Louise (Mrs. Fletcher Burchette), Lora Lee. San. engr. Chgo. Pump Co., 1939-42; intern Bronson Methodist Hosp., Kalamazoo, Mich., 1950-51; gen. practice medicine, Pascagoula, Miss., 1951—; mem. active staff Singing River Hosp., 1952-72, mem. cons. staff, 1972—, chief of staff, 1956, 69. Past treas. Miss. Festival of Arts Found. Served as maj. AUS, 1942-46; PTO. Mem. Am. Acad. Family Practice, Am. Legion (life), V.F.W. (life), Santa Gertrudis Breeders Internat., Ala., Miss. cattlemen's assns. Home: 1510 Jackson Av Pascagoula MS 39567 Office: PO Box 208 1510 Jackson Av Pascagoula MS 39567

HICKS, GORDON T., banker; b. Sycamore, Ill.; B.S.B., Miami U., Oxford, O., 1942. Formerly with Bank Am., San Francisco; then exec. v.p. U.S. Jr. C. of C.; now v.p. bus. devel. met. div. Nat. Bank Tulsa. Chmn. Tulsa Park and Recreation Bd., 1956-60; mem. adv. bd. Salvation Army, 1956-60; now mem. Capital Program Rev. com. City of Tulsa; v.p. Indian Nations council Boy Scouts Am. Trustee, mem. exec. com. Gilcrease Inst., Tulsa, 1958-66, bd. dirs., 1967—, v.p. bd., 1969-71, pres., 1971—; chmn. bd. trustees Okla. Osteo. Hosp. Address: Nat Bank Tulsa PO Box 2300 Tulsa OK 74103

HICKS, HENRY STACEY, engring. co. exec.; b. Comanche, Tex., Feb. 21, 1919; s. Newton Sanford and Susan Ann (Pennland) H.; m. Verdell Marshall, May 16, 1941; children—Stacia (Mrs. Jerry Cowan), Shirley (Mrs. Jack Gregory), Sandra (Mrs. Ted Rushing), Linda. Resident engr., dist. engr. H. N. Roberts & Assos., Littlefield, Tex., 1944-47; asst. chief engr., chief engr. H. N. Roberts & Assos., Lubbock, 1947-49; pres. gen. mgr. Hicks & Ragland, Lubbock, 1950—; pres. Midwest Reprodn. Co., Inc., Hicks & Ragland Engrs., Inc.; pres. Teltronics, Inc.; dir. Ionate Corp. Am., Inc. Mem. Am. Inst. Aeros. and Astronautics. Democrat. Methodist. Mason (32 deg., Shriner). Home: 3216 53d St Lubbock TX 79410 Office: Hicks & Ragland 40th and Av U Lubbock TX 79410

HICKS, JOHN LOUIS, JR., elec. products mfg. co. exec.; b. Hustonville, Ky., July 1, 1922; s. John Louis and Ann Blanche (Barnett) H.; B.S., U. Ky., 1948; m. Flora Baker, Oct. 1, 1948; children—John Louis III, Lucy Beth. With Clarke Stewart Wood, gen. contracting, Lexington, Ky., 1948-52; pres., owner Allen Hicks Elec. Engring. Corp., Lexington, 1952—. Active Boy Scouts Am., 1963-66. Served to capt. AUS, 1942-46. Registered prof. engr., Ky. Mem. Nat., Kan. socs. profl. engrs., Blue Grass Profl. Engrs., Blue Grass Sportsman's League, Civil War Round Table. Mem. Disciples of Christ Ch. (deacon 1957-60). Clubs: Lexington Country, Iroquois Hunt. Home: Rural Route 4 Combs Ferry Rd Winchester KY 40391 Office: 206 S Limestone St Lexington KY 40508

HICKS, MASON SPILLER, architect; b. Bluefield, W. Va., Nov. 8, 1921; s. William Bane and Mary (Baylor) H.; B.S., W.Va. Wesleyan Coll., 1943; meteorology certificate Mass. Inst. Tech., 1943, M.Arch., 1950; B.Arch., Va. Poly. Inst., 1949; m. Grace Irene Brown, Aug. 24, 1943; children—Jan Engel, Daniel Mason, Sue Baylor. Archtl. asso. James M. Webb, Chapel Hill, N.C., 1949-53; partner Dan MacMillan (architect & assos.), 1953-58, MacMillan, Hicks, MacMillan, 1958-60; partner Hicks, Willis, architects, 1965-67, Mason S. Hicks, architects, Fayetteville, N.C., 1960-65, 67—. Mem. Fayetteville Planning Bd., 1959-67, Mayor's Community Rehab. Com., 1966-68, Cumberland County Joint Planning Bd., 1967—; v.p. Southeastern Econ. Devel. Commn., Coastal Plains Region, 1967-68, chmn., 1968-70. Served to capt. with AUS, 1942-46; ETO. Recipient N.C. Design award, Fayetteville, 1966. Mem. A.I.A. Democrat. Presbyn. (deacon). Rotarian (pres. 1969-70), Home: 1415 Summit Av Fayetteville NC 28305 Office: 827 Arsenal Av Fayetteville NC 28305

HICKS, VERNON JOHNSON, architect; b. N.Y.C., Aug. 24, 1930; s. Marshall MacLemore and Cora Johnson (Sapp) H.; student San Diego Jr. Coll., 1958-60; B.Arch., La. State U., 1965; m. Elizabeth Lee Schulken, June 5, 1954; children—Elizabeth Ann, Teresa Dawn, Mary Ellan. Archtl. designer-draftsman W. Conway Washburn, architect, Baton Rouge, 1963-64; chief draftsman-designer Lionel H. Abshire, architect, Baton Rouge, 1965; designer-project architect Leslie N. Boney, architect, Wilmington, N.C., 1965-71; pvt. practice, Wilmington, 1972—. Served to 1st lt. USMC, 1950-60. Mem. A.I.A., Navy League. Lutheran. Kiwanian. Club: Hanover Seaside (Wrightsville Beach, N.C.). Prin. archtl. works include Isothermal Community Coll., Spindale, N.C., Lenoir Community Coll., Kinston, N.C., Moore and Sanford Halls, U. N.C., Charlotte, Air Terminal Bldg., Elizabeth City, N.C., Presant Warehouse Facility, Phoenix, N.C. Home: 1814 Grace St Wilmington NC 28401 Office: One Ten Orange St Wilmington NC 28401

HICKS, WILLIAM NATHAN, physician; b. Fort Worth, Tex., Apr. 10, 1937; s. Lewis Binus and Callie Elizabeth (Spiceland) H.; B.A., U. Tex., 1959, M.D., 1963; m. Sandra Jane Nicholas, June 13, 1959; children— Laura Catherine, Andrew Nathan, Julia Anne. Intern, Meml. Hosp., Corpus Christi, Tex., 1963-64; practice medicine, Garland, Tex., 1966—; sec. med. staff Garland Clinic and Hosp.; v.p. med. staff Meml. Hosp. of Garland. Served with USNR, 1964-66. Mem. Am., Tex. med. assns., Dallas County Med. Soc., Am. Acad. Family Physicians, Am. Coll. Emergency Physicians, Theta Kappa Psi. Ex-students. Mason. Home: 3909 Dixie St Garland TX 75042 Office: 1002 Marion St Garland TX 75042

HICKS, WILLIAM TROTTER, economist; b. Enterprise, Miss., Mar. 15, 1907; s. William Wooten and Matilda (Trotter) H.; B.S. and M.S., U. Fla., 1928; Ph.D., Northwestern U., 1937; postgrad. Harvard, 1955-56; m. Za-Ida Moore, June 15, 1930; children—William Trotter, Colquitt Keeling, Beverly Ann (Mrs. Edward West Mullen). Asst. prof. econs. and marketing U. Fla., 1928-37; economist U.S. Depts. Commerce and Agr., chief mil. requirements div. War Food Adminstrn., 1937-47; prof., dir. bur. bus. research U. Ga., 1947-50; chmn. dept. econs., bus. adminstrn. U. Miss., 1950-66; regional supervisory economist U.S. Army Corps Engrs., Vicksburg, Miss., 1966—; chief econs. br. Mississippi River Commn., 1966—. Recipient Distinguished Service award Alpha Kappa Psi, 1939, Ford Found. fellow, 1956. Mem. Am., So. econs. assns., Permanent Internat. Assn. Nav. Congresses (Belgium), Soc. Am. Mil. Engrs. (post v.p. 1969-71). Episcopalian (vestryman). Home: 43 Chapel Hills Vicksburg MS 39180 Office: Box 80 US Army Corps Engineers Vicksburg MS 39180

HIERONYMUS, CLARA BOOTH WIGGINS (MRS. SENATOR C. HIERONYMUS), newspaper writer; b. Drew, Miss., July 25, 1913; d. Bruce Charles and Maude (Watson) Wiggins; B.A. cum laude, U. Tulsa, 1932; M.S.W., U. Okla., 1936; m. Senator Cleo Hieronymus, Apr. 24, 1937; children—Bruce Lee, Jane (Mrs. David H. Piller). Employment counselor YWCA, Tulsa, 1936-37; employment interviewer, labor market analyst State and Fed. Employment Service, Tulsa, 1937-50; instr. sociology U. Tulsa, 1938-50; book reviewer radio sta. KFMJ, Tulsa, 1942; art and drama critic, home furnishings editor The Tennessean, Nashville, 1956; freelance writer; speaker for clubs. Pres., Samaritans, 1967-69. Recipient Dorothy Dawe award Am. Furniture Mart, 1960, 63, 65, 69. Dallas Furniture Market award, 1965; named Woman of Year in Communications, Bus. and Profl. Women of Nashville, 1966. Mem. Assn. du Theatre pour les Enfants et Jeunesse, Internat. Assn. Children's Theatre, Nat. Hemophilia Soc., Nat. Arthritis Found., Nashville Childrens Theater, Cheekwood Fine Arts Center, Theta Sigma Phi. Democrat. Methodist. Club: Centennial (Nashville). Author: (with Barbara Izard) Requiem for a Nun; On Stage and Off, 1970. Home: 2200 Hemingway Dr Nashville TN 37215 Office: 1100 Broad St Nashville TN 37202

HIGDON, WILFORD DAIN, educator; b. Quinlin, Tex., Jan. 28, 1917; s. John H. and Sally (O'Kelley) H.; B.A., U. Tex., 1939, M.A., 1948; postgrad. Trinity U., 1952-53; m. Ida Jean Douglass, Jan. 1, 1943; children—James Noel, Albert Dain, Janice Jean. Cons. to Mexican Dept. Agr., U.S. Dept. Agr., Cuidad Anahuac, N.L., 1939-40, pear psylla control, Spokane, Wash., 1940-41; asst. prof. sci. Trinity U., San Antonio, 1947-49; grass research Twin Oaks Ranch, Dinero, Tex., 1949-51; tchr. sci., prin. San Antonio Ind. Sch. Dist., 1951—. Owner, operator Camp Jada for Girls, Fischer, Tex., 1972—. Bd. dirs. Alamo Dist. Sci. Fair, Inc., San Antonio, 1955—, fair dir., 1958-59. treas., 1960-61, v.p., 1961-62. Served with AUS, 1942-45. Mem. Adminstrs. and Suprs. Assn., Tex. Tchrs. Assn., Am. Legion (post comdr. 1965-67). Baptist. Mason, Rotarian (dir. San Antonio, sec. 1961-62, pres. 1962-63, gov. Dist. 584, 1972-73). Ecol. research on grass. Home: 127 W Josephine St San Antonio TX 78212

HIGGINBOTHAM, FRED CASWELL, JR., oil co. exec.; b. Dallas, Oct. 19, 1919; s. Fred Caswell and Etta R. (Anderson) H.; B.B.A., So. Methodist U., 1942; student Northwestern U., 1942-43; postgrad. Harvard Advanced Bus. Sch., 1970; m. Jean McLachlan, Mar. 23, 1945; children—Virginia Ann, Gary Jon. Agt., Internal Revenue Service, 1946-51; with Gen. Am. Oil Co., of Tex., Dallas, 1951—, asst. treas., controller, 1954-59, v.p., controller, 1959-66, v.p., treas., 1966-70, sr. v.p., treas., 1970—, also dir., mem. exec. com.; exec. v.p., dir. Meadows Bldg. Corp., 1954—; v.p., asst. sec., dir. Gen. Am. Oils, Ltd. 1953—; v.p., dir., mem. exec. com. Premier Petrochem. Co.; dir., mem. exec. com. Stockton, Whatley, Davin & Co. C.P.A., Tex. Mem. Controllers Inst. Petroleum Accountants Soc. Dallas (pres. 1959-60), Phi Delta Theta (pres. So. Meth. U. chpt. 1941), Beta Gamma Sigma. Clubs: Texas (dir.), Petroleum, Dallas Athletic (Dallas). Home: 6533 Greenwich Lane Dallas TX 75230 Office: Meadows Bldg Dallas TX 75206

HIGGINBOTHAM, RALPH DANIEL, printer; b. Flatrock, Ala., July 13, 1916; s. Emory Lawrence and Josie Ella (Atkins) H.; student Anniston (Ala.) Bus. Coll., 1934; m. Dorothy Lee Burnham, Feb. 20, 1937; children—Linda Diane, Ralph Daniel, Nancy Jo. Newspaper carrier Anniston Star, 1928-33, asst. circulation mgr., 1933-35, apprentice printer, 1935-41, journeyman printer, 1941-44; printer, linotype operator Strong Printing Co., Birmingham, Ala., 1944-45; printer Birmingham Post, 1945-46; owner Stephens Printing Co., Anniston, 1946—, Sawyer Printing Co., Anniston, 1950—, Moore printing Co., 1962— (all now Higginbotham, Inc.); pres. Calhoun Pub. Co., Jacksonville, Ala., 1963—; pub. Jacksonville News, 1963—. Vice pres. Anniston Cerebral Palsy unit, 1966-67, pres., 1967-68; mem. Anniston Bd. Edn., 1959—, pres., 1962-63, 66—, pres. Anniston Com. Better Schs., 1964-65; pres. Calhoun County Drys, 1962-63; mem. exec. com. Calhoun County Baptist Assn.; 1957-61; pres. Calhoun County Baptist Brotherhood Assn., 1959-61; dir. Ala. Coalition Better Edn., Inc., 1968-70; mem. Ala. Vocational Adv. Com., 1969-71. Bd. trustees Judson Coll., 1968—. Named Man of Year, Anniston Star, 1970. Mem. Anniston C. of C. (dir. 1957-59, 61-62, 64-65, 67-68, 70-71, v.p. 1967), Ala. Assn. Sch. Bds. (dir., 1961—, pres. 1966-70), Nat. Sch. Bds. Assn. (del. 1964-70), United Comml. Travelers. Democrat. Baptist (chmn. bd. deacons 1966-68). Mason, Gideon. Clubs: Exchange (pres. 1956-57), Anniston Country. Home: 336 Wildwood Rd Anniston AL 36201 Office: 1116 Moore Av Anniston AL 36201

HIGGINS, CARLISLE WALLACE, justice; b. Ennice, N.C., Oct. 17, 1889; s. Martin Alexander and Jennie (Bledsoe) H.; A.B., U. N.C., 1912, LL.D., 1914; m. Myrtle Bryant, Nov. 26, 1916; children—Carlisle W., Mary Cecile. Admitted to N.C. bar, 1914; solicitor 11th Jud. Dist. of N.C., 1931-34; U.S. atty. Middle Dist. of N.C., 1934-47; now asso. justice Supreme Ct. N.C. Mem. N.C. Ho. of Reps., 1924-26, N.C. Senate, 1928-30. Asst. and acting chief of counsel internat. prosecution sect. SCAP Hdqrs., Tokyo, Japan, 1945-47. Served in U.S. Army, World War I. Mem. N.C. Bar Assn., Am. Legion. Democrat. Mason. Club: Sir Walter Gun. Office: Supreme Court Bldg Raleigh NC 27601

HIGGINS, JAMES BENTON, JR., educator, coll. ofcl.; b. Maypearl, Tex., Jan. 10, 1920; s. James Benton and Wilma (Burford) H.; B.A., Trinity U., 1941; M.Ed., U. Houston, 1951; m. Ioma Blocker, May 3, 1944; 1 son, James Benton III. Profl. football player Chgo. Cardinals, 1941; football coach Port Arthur (Tex.) High Sch.,

1946-48; line coach Lamar State Coll., Beaumont, Tex., 1949-52, head football coach, 1953-63, dir. athletics, head dept. health and phys. edn., prof., 1963—. Served to capt. USMCR, 1942-46; col. Res. Mem. Am. Assn. U. Profs., Am. Football Coaches Assn. (Regional Coach of Year award 1962), Beaumont C. of C., Young Mens Bus. League. Kiwanian. Contbr. articles to profl. athletic coaching mags. Organizer Southland Athletic Conf. Home: 250 Giles St Beaumont TX 77704

HIGGINS, LAWRENCE ERNEST, social work exec.; b. New Orleans, Oct. 2, 1907; s. Lawrence Ambrose and Marie (Jaunet) H.; B.S., Tulane U., 1928; student La. U. Sch. Social Welfare, 1931, certificate of social work, 1955; m. Carolyn Belle Cresap, Oct. 20, 1933; children— Kathleen, Laureen. Welfare visitor dept. pub. welfare, New Orleans, 1937-42; asst., acting commr. La. State Bd. Pub. Welfare, 1942-48, commr., 1948-50; exec. sec. La. Youth Commn., 1950—. Mem. ten-man survey team, Internat. Refugee Orgn., Geneva, Switzerland and U.S. State Dept. to work on welfare and displaced persons problems in Germany and Austria, 1950; adminstr. Interstate Crime Compact, 1948-50; mem. La. State Bd. of Parole, 1945-48; Sec.-treas. Juvenile Ct. Commn., 1948-50; mem. state com. on planning for White House Conf. on Children and Youth, also chmn. pub. welfare sect., vice chmn. La. State adv. com., 1960, del. 1960 conf., cons. 1960 conf. staff; dir. Nat. Council State Coms. Children and Youth, 1957-62, pres. So. States Probation and Parole Conf., 1960-61; coordinator Nat. Council Juvenile Ct. Judges Spl. Tng. Project; sec.-treas. La. Displaced Persons Commn.; pres. La. P.T.A.; adv. com. Nat. Soc. Crippled Children and Adults; chmn. La. State Inter deptl. Com.; cons. Family Ct. East Baton Rouge Parish, La. Council for Evaluation Center Exceptional Children; adv. com. on edn. exceptional children, State Dept. Edn.; spl. adviser President's Com. on Juvenile Delinquency and Youth Crime; cons. on juvenile delinquency Nat. Conf. of Governors; mem. Nat. Conf. of Juvenile Agencies; dir. La. Conf. Social Welfare (past pres.), Family Service Society Baton Rouge; pres. La. Conf. Correctional workers with Juveniles; nat. com. to develop standards for police service in handling juveniles, U.S. Children's Bur.; mem. nat. com. appointed by Nat. Probation and Parole Assn. for developing revised standards for juvenile cts., vice chmn. profl. council; secretary So. States Probation and Parole Assn.; director La. Council Handicapped Children; exec. com. La. Conf. Retarded Children; chmn. profl. council Nat. Council Crime and Delinquency; mem. state com. White House Conf. Children and Youth, 1970, Nat. Joint Commn. Correctional Manpower and Tng.; field cons. Nat. Survey Corrections for President's Crime Commn., 1967; mem. La. Commn. Law Enforcement and Adminstrn. Criminal justice. Lectr. Tulane U., La. State U. Mem. Nat. Assn. Social Workers, Internat., La. juvenile officer's assns., Am. Public Welfare Assn. (nat. com. on protective services for children), Nat. Conf. Social Work Am. Acad. Polit. and Social Scis., Nat. Adult Edn. Assn., Acad. Certified Social Workers, Alpha Chi Sigma, Sigma Pi. K.C. Author articles in field. Home: 3410 Hyacinth Av Baton Rouge LA 70808 Office: State Office Bldg 150 Riverside Mall Baton Rouge LA 70801

HIGGS, CYRUS HENRY, JR., psychiatrist; b. Greenville, Miss., Apr. 25, 1927; s. Cyrus Henry and Jessie Inez (Hightower) H.; B.A., U. Miss., 1955, med. certificate, 1953; M.D., U. Tenn., 1954; m. Edna Juanita Dye, July 6, 1957; children—Emily Cheryl, Cyrus Henry, David Allen. Intern, Baptist Meml. Hosp., Memphis, 1955; staff physician Miss. State Hosp., Whitfield, 1956-58; resident medicine City of Memphis Hosp., Kennedy VA Hosp., 1958-61; resident psychiatry VA Hosp., North Little Rock, Ark., 1961-64, staff psychiatrist, 1964-67; staff psychiatrist Tenn. Psychiat. Hosp. and Inst., Memphis, 1967—; instr. psychiatry U. Tenn., 1967—. Served with USNR, 1945-46. Mem. A.M.A., Am., Mid-Continent psychiat. assns., Shelby County, Memphis med. socs., Alpha Kappa Kappa. Methodist. Home: 1413 Briarwood Dr Memphis TN 38111 Office: 865 Poplar Av Memphis TN 38105

HIGHLEYMAN, DALY, business exec.; b. St. Louis, May 20, 1905; s. Locke Tiffin and Katherine (Daly) H.; grad. Pomfret Sch., 1925; student Yale, 1926-27; m. Doris DeGarmo, June 4, 1954; children—Peter Thacher, Patricia Daly. Jr. exec. de Saint Phalle & Co., N.Y.C., 1928-29; sec., treas. Tamiami Trail Land Co., Miami, Fla., 1930-38; pres. Fidelity Mortgage & Guarantee Co., Miami, 1930-32, asst, supr. cost reduction sect, indsl. engring. Consol. Vultee Aircraft Corp., San Diego, 1941-46, pres. Tikada Holding Co., 1953-55; v.p. Avenger Yachts, Inc., 1965-67, pres., 1967-69; pres. Datif Investment Corp., 1969—, Tikada Mgmt. Corp., 1969—. Active Coconut Grove Civic Club. Mem. Hist. Assn. So. Fla., Marine Hist. Assn., Internat. Oceanographic Found., Council for Internat. Visitors of Greater Miami. Clubs: Coral Reef Yacht (commodore 1963-64) (Coconut Grove, Fla.); San Diego Yacht; Yale (Miami). Home: 3737 El Prado Coconut Grove FL 33133 Office: 132 Madeira Av Coral Gables FL 33134

HIGHT, WILLIAM BLANNIE, JR., educator; b. Henderson, N.C., Aug. 27, 1926; s. William B. and Mary (Powell) H.; A.B., U. N.C., 1948, M.Ed., 1959, Ph.D., 1962 children—Christopher T., Eric J. Tchr., coach Vance County and Alamance County (N.C.), 1948-57; tchr. Burlington, N.C., 1957-59; dir. guidance Burlington City Schs., 1960-62, prin., 1961-62; asso. prof. edn., dir. student counseling center Davidson (N.C.) Coll., 1962—, dir. summer liberal arts program for tchrs., 1967—. Recipient Ford Found. fellow for travel and study in Europe, 1955-56. Mem. Kappa Sigma, Phi Delta Kappa. Home: 125 Crescent Dr Davidson NC 28036

HIGHTOWER, DAVID PETERSON, psychoanalyst; b. York, Ala., Nov. 15, 1912; s. Council Berry and Georgie (Mellown) H.; B.S., Birmingham So. U., 1933; M.D., Tulane U., 1937. Intern, Hillman Hosp., 1937-39, chief resident medicine, 1939-40; commd. lt. (j.g.) M.C., U.S. Navy, 1940, advanced through grades to capt., 1955; clin. instr. Georgetown U., 1947-60; dir. mental hygiene unit U.S. Naval Acad., 1952-60; ret., 1960; psychoanalyst Washington Psychoanalytic Inst., 1947—; practice medicine, specializing in psychotherapy, York, 1960—; cons. in psychotherapy East Miss. State Hosp., 1968—; clin. asso. div. continuing med. edn. U. Ala. Sch. Medicine, 1970—. Mem. Am., Ala., Sumter County med. assns., York C. of C. (past dir.), Kappa Alpha, Theta Kappa Psi, Beta Beta Beta, Kappa Phi Kappa. Methodist. Rotarian. Home: 401 5th Av York AL 36925 Office: 720 4th Av York AL 36925

HIGHTOWER, JESS M., mfg. co. exec.; b. Kirksville, Mo., Feb. 9, 1922; s. Jesse Moss and Grace (Renfrow) H.; B.A., U. Tulsa, 1950, postgrad., 1951-52; m. Bette Jean Blackburn, Feb. 21, 1943; children—Jere Jean, Jess Vince, Jami Jean. Pres. Herb-O-Tone Medicine Co., Tulsa, 1946-48; free lance writer, 1949-50; reporter Tulsa Daily World, 1950-51; with McDonnell Douglas Corp., Tulsa, 1951—, mgr. external relations, editor div. publs., 1957—, mgr. pub. relations Douglas Aircrft Southeastern plants Melbourne, Ark. and St. Stephen, S.C., 1969—. Guest lectr. U. Okla., 1969, U. Tulsa, 1970-71. Mem. Okla. Air Pollution Council, 1967—, exec. com. Gov's Link Com., 1970—, Indian Nations Area council Boy Scouts Am., 1968—; vice chmn. pub. relations com. Ark. Basin Devel. Assn., 1969—; chmn. housing com. Mayor's Com. Tulsa Model Cities Program, 1966-67. Trustee Children's Med. Center, Tulsa, 1969-75, Tulsa Charity Horse Show, 1965—, Tulsa Met. Zoo, 1971—. Served with AUS, 1943-45. Decorated Bronze Star medal. Mem. U. Tulsa Alumni Assn. (trustee, 1965—), Nat. Mgmt. Assn., Pub. Relations Soc. Am. (bd. dirs., 1964-67), UN Assn. (bd. dirs., 1969—). Episcopalian. Mason. Clubs: Oaks Country, Tulsa Press. Author articles, stories in mags., 1961—(some with pseudonym Jim Grant). Author, producer, director movie Course of Action for Okla. Retarded Childrens Assn., 1957. Home: 5345 E 22d Pl Tulsa OK 74114 Office: 2000 N Memorial Dr Tulsa OK 74115

HIGLEY, BRUCE WADSWORTH, orthodontist; b. Iowa City, Dec. 1, 1928; s. Lester Bodine and Harriet (Wadsworth) H.; D.D.S., State U. Ia., 1952, M.S., 1953; student Grinnell Coll., 1946-48, orthodontic certificate, 1953; m. Mary Victoria Eckey, Aug. 24, 1949; m. 2d, Marta Beatriz Velasco, Sept. 23, 1966. Research, instr. Ia. Dental U., 1952-53; practice dentistry, specializing in orthodontics, South Miami, Fla., 1955—. Owner, chmn. bd., M.B.H. Enterprises, Inc., Miami, Fla., 1960—. Vice chmn. dist. council Boy Scouts Am., 1959-62; mem. personnel bd., South Miami, 1959. Served as 1st lt., Dental Corps, AUS, 1953-55. Mem. Fla. Orthodontic Soc., So., Miami socs. orthodontists, Am. Assn. Orthodontists, Fla., Am. socs. dentistry for children, Fla., Fla. East Coast, Miami dental socs., Am., South Dade dental assns., English Royal Acad., U. Kansas City Seminar, Jr. Cof C. (past dir.), C. of C. (past dir., past sec., past treas.), Fedn. Dentaire Internat., Psi Omega, Omicron Kappa Upsilon. Presbyn. (deacon). Clubs: Rotary (pres. 1961-62), Coral Reef Yacht, Coral Gables Country, Kings Bay Yacht and Country, Royal Palm Tennis, Snapper Creek Lakes, Executive (all greater Miami). Elk. Home: 10705 Snapper Creek Rd Miami FL 33156 Office: 7210 Red Rd South Miami FL 33143

HILDEBIDLE, RALPH GEORGE, gas turbine engine mfg. co. exec.; b. Great Falls, Mont., Oct. 18, 1919; s. Ralph David and Lavera Mae (Marvel) H.; student Ball State U., 1937-40; m. Nancy Conrad Harnsberger, Mar. 4, 1971; children—David Edgar, Judith Ann (Mrs. Edward J. Shaw), Daniel Thomas. Process engr. Gen. Motors Corp., Buick Motor Co., Flint, Mich., 1941-42, Chgo., 1942-43; prodn. foreman Chevrolet Motor div., Flint, Mich., 1946-53, supt. mfg., 1953-68; gen. supt. mfg. Avco Corp., Charleston, S.C., 1969-70, dir. mfg., 1970, dir. operations, 1971—. Troop leader Tall Pine council Boy Scouts Am., 1953-54. Served with USNR, 1943-46. Recipient Order of the Gear award Gen. Motors Corp., 1953. Mem. Soc. Mfg. Engrs. (chmn. Charleston chpt. 1970-71), Am. Mgmt. Assn., Indsl. Mgmt. Club. Elk, Kiwanian. Author: Requisites for a Man, 1967. Home: 1926 Maybank Hwy Charleston SC 29412 Office: Leeds Av PO Box 10048 Charleston SC 29411

HILDEBRAND, FRANK, govt. ofcl.; b. Winston-Salem, N.C., Feb. 5, 1929; s. Franklin and Mildred (Brown) H.; B.A., Tulane U., 1950; m. Joyce Bruff, May 31, 1952. Editor, asso. pub. Jennings (La.) Daily News, 1952-57; bus. editor Baytown (Tex.) Sun, 1957-58; travel editor, bus. news writer Houston Post, 1958-60; feature writer Dallas Morning News, 1960-62; exec. dir. Tex. Tourist Devel. Agy., Austin, 1963—. Nat. sec., dir. Discover Am. Travel Orgns.; state liaison officer U.S. Travel Service; chmn. Tex. Travel Trails Com.; dir. Tex. Travel Counselors Conf.; chmn. Conquistadores Trail Com. Mem. sea grant adv. council Tex. A. and M. U.; commr. Tex. Film Commn. Served with AUS, 1950-52. Named U.S. Travel Dir. of Year, 1971. Club: Lakeway Yacht (Austin). Episcopalian. Mason (32 deg.). Home: 432 Ridgewood Rd Austin TX 78746 Office: Reagan State Office Bldg Austin TX 78711

HILDEEN, CATHERINE ARDELLE RIGGS (MRS. ROGER GUSTAV HILDEEN), bus. exec.; b. Mpls., Jan. 14, 1921; d. Herbert Samuel and Ardelle (Wells) Riggs; B.A., U. Minn., 1942; postgrad. U. Chgo., 1944; m. Roger Gustav Hildeen, July 1, 1944. Researchist with Continental Ill. Nat. Bank, Chgo., 1942-47; personnel mgr. Wieboldt Stores, Chgo., 1947-51; v.p. personnel Greenbelt Consumer Services, Silver Springs, Md., 1952—. Mem. Am. Soc. Personnel Adminstrn. (nat. sec. 1972—), Supermarket Inst. (mem. personnel com. 1966), Washington Personnel Assn. (pres. 1967-68). Home: 7510 June St Springfield VA 22150 Office: 8547 Piney Branch Rd Silver Springs MD 20901

HILDRETH, PHILIP ELWIN, educator, univ. dean; b. Marlboro, N.H., Jan. 14, 1923; s. Lewis George and Mary (Adams) H.; A.B., Dartmouth, 1947; M.A., U. Cal. at Berkeley, 1951, Ph.D., 1955; m. Gretchen Meredith Swanson, Apr. 19, 1952; children—Bradley Edward, Pamela Eden, Todd Randall. Research biologist Lawrence Radiation Lab., U. Cal. at Berkeley, 1951-56, 59-67; asst. prof. biology Long Beach (Cal.) State Coll., 1956-59; distinguished prof. biology, chmn. dept. U. N.C., Charlotte, 1967—, chmn. div. math. and natural scis., 1968-70, dean Coll. Sci. and Math., 1970—. Served with USNR, 1944-46. Mem. Genetics Soc. Am., Am. Soc. Zoologists, Assn. Southeastern Biologists, A.A.A.S., Am. Inst. Biol. Scis., Sigma Xi. Contbr. numerous articles to sci. jours. Home: 1100 Circlewood Dr Charlotte NC 28211

HILEMAN, MELVIN J., banker; b. Wheeling, W.Va., May 6, 1929; s. Bert Norman and Mary J. (Lyda) H.; grad. Am. Inst. Banking, 1956, Stonier Grad. Sch. Banking, 1965; m. Elizabeth Ann Watson, June 10, 1950; children—Victoria L., Scott W. With Washington Loan & Trust Co. (consol. with Riggs Nat. Bank 1954), 1947—, served in all banking depts., beginning as note teller, successively, asst. mgr., asst. cashier, asst. mgr., asst. v.p., asst. mgr., 1962-64, asst. v.p., mgr S.E. office, 1964-66, v.p., mgr., 1966—. Active Community Chest drives 1951-54; sect. capt. Am. Cancer Soc., Washington, 1965; active Boy Scouts Am. Trustee Morris Cafritz Meml. Hosp.; bd. advisers Inst. Family and Marriage Relations, Inc. Mem. Met. Washington Bd. Trade, Nat. Capital Active Club (sec.-treas. 1951-52), U.S. Navy League (asst. treas.), Naval Sea Cadet Corps (asst. treas.). Lion (dir.). Home: 6434 Burwell St Springfield VA 22150 Office: 1750 Pennsylvania Av NW Washington DC 20006

HILGERT, RONALD JOSEPH, economist; b. St. Paul, Aug. 5, 1934; s. John Frank and Mary (Grabowenski) H.; B.S., U. Minn., 1956; postgrad. Am. U., 1960-62; m. Cecelia Helwig, Nov. 4, 1967. Statistician, Bur. Labor Statistics, U.S. Dept. Labor, Washington, 1959-66; program officer U.S. Dept. Commerce, Econ. Devel. Adminstrn., Washington, 1966; economist CAB, Washington, 1967—. Served with AUS, 1956-58. Recipient hon. award for sustained meritorious performance CAB, 1968, Spl. Achievement award, 1971. Mem. Am. Econ. Assn., Am. Statis. Assn. Home: 1100 22d St NW Washington DC 20037 Office: 1825 Connecticut Av Washington DC 20428

HILL, A(LFRED) GARRETT, cons. chemist, educator; b. West Point, Miss., June 21, 1906; s. Asa Edwin and Bettie Alberta (Garrett) H.; B.A., Baylor U., 1926. M.A., 1926; Ph.D., Yale, 1932; m. Lois Jenkins, Dec. 25, 1935. Head sci. dept. Burleson Coll., 1926 28; instr. Baylor U., 1928-29; with Bound Brook (N.J.) plant Am. Cyanamid Co., 1932-63, research chemist, subsequently devel. chemist, 1939-44, chief chemist intermediates dept., 1944-46, asst. mgr. control and devel. dept., 1946-47, tech. dir. intermediates and rubber chems., 1947-55, resident tech. dir., 1955-57, mgr. pharms. mfg. dept., 1957-58, asst. plant mgr., 1958-59, plant mgr., 1959-62, asst. to gen. mgr. Organic Chems. Div., 1962-63; dir. County Bank and Trust Co., Somerset 1960-63; chmn. div. natural sci. Mobile (Ala.) Coll., 1963-67, prof. chemistry, 1963—; v.p. Gulf Coast Inst. Research and Tech., Mobile, 1967—; mem. tech. adv. com. Tex. Air Control Bd., 1972—; staff cons. Gulf States Pollution Control, Inc., Tex., Jacksonville, 1970—; ind. cons. chemist, tech. and adminstrn. Vice chmn. Com. Aid to Edn., Mobile, 1967-69. Pres. Warren Twp. Bd. Edn., 1949-50; v.p. Somerset County Vocational Bd. Edn., 1961-63; bd. dirs. Civil Def. and Disaster Control, Warren Twp., N.J., 1950-54, 57-59; active A.R.C., bd. dirs. Plainfield (N.J.) chpt., 1956-63; trustee Warren Twp. Community Fund. 1961-63; pres. Jarratt Cemetery Assn., 1971—. Fellow Am. Inst. Chemists, Ala. Acad. Sci. (v.p. 1966-67), mem. Am. Chem. Soc., (nat. councilor 1966—), Am. Inst. Chem. Engrs., (dir. Mobile 1967), Mobile Hist. Soc., Warren Twp. Civic Assn. (pres. 1946-47), Sigma Xi, Alpha Chi Sigma. Republican. Baptist. Mason (32 deg., Shriner), Rotarian (pres. Jacksonville 1972-73). Contbr. articles on chems. sci. jours. Patentee chems. Home: Beaucore Route 6 Jacksonville TX 75766

HILL, BRYCE DALE, sch. adminstr.; b. Seminole, Okla., Mar. 5, 1930; s. Charles Daniel and Ollie (Nichols) H.; B.S., East Central State Coll., 1952, M.Teaching, 1957; postgrad. U. Okla. 1959-70; profl. adminstrs. certificate, 1969; m. Wilma Dean Carter, Aug. 16, 1956; 1 son, Bryce Anthony. Tchr. pub. schs., New Lima, Okla., 1952-56, supt. pub. schs., 1956—; owner New Lima Gas Co., 1958—. Chmn. bd. dirs. Seminole County chpt. A.R.C.; v.p. bd. dirs. Redland Community Action Program. Chmn. Seminole County Democratic Central Com., 1962-64, 70-72. Mem. N.E.A., Okla. Edn. Assn., Am., Okla. assns. sch. adminstrs., Seminole County Tchrs. Assn. (pres. 1964, 71-72), Seminole County Sch. Adminstrs. Assn. (chmn. 1969-70), Seminole County Schoolmasters Club (pres. 1963-69), Seminole Hist. Soc. (v.p.). Baptist. Home: Box 97 New Lima OK 74858

HILL, CAESAR GRANT, statistician; b. Savannah, Ga., Sept. 18, 1926; s. Raymond A. and Mary (Grant) H.; A.B., Morehouse Coll., 1949; postgrad. Atlanta U., 1950-51; m. Wanda Jean Clemens, Aug. 14, 1955; children—Stephen, Gary. Instr. math. Voorhees Coll., 1949-53; pub. relationist Citizens for Eisenhower Congress Com., Washington, 1953-54; statistician Bur. Census 1954—, chief area sample surveys br., 1965-66, chief retail programs implementation br., 1966—; dir. 1970 Decennial Census Dist. Office, Compton, Cal., Jan.-July 1970, chief wholesale census br., 1970-72, spl. asst. to dep. adminstr. social and econ. statistics adminstrn., 1972—, dir. Census Fed. Credit Union, 1962-64. Mem. auditing com. Episcopal Diocese, Washington, 1967—; sec.-treas. com. Boy Scouts of Am., Washington, 1960-63. Served with Corps Engrs., AUS, 1944-46. Mem. Am. Statis. Assn., Am. Marketing Assn., Census Bur. Welfare and Recreation Assn. (v.p. 1957-61). Alpha Phi Alpha. Episcopalian. Home: 1766 41st Pl SE Washington DC 20020 Office: Bur of Census Washington DC 20233

HILL, CARLOS ERASMUS, JR., mech. engr.; b. Louisville, Miss., July 4, 1932; s. Carlos E. and Pauline Avis (Sellers) H.; B.S., Miss. State U., 1957; m. Maureen C. Starr, May 7, 1960; children—Lauren Caryl, Tripp. Maintenance engr. Monsanto Co., Pensacola, Fla., 1957-60, project engr., 1960-64; pres., gen. mgr. Hill Engring. Co., 1964—. Served with C.E., AUS, 1951-53. Registered profl. engr., Ala., Miss., La. Mem. Am. Soc. M. E., Indsl. Mgmt. Assn., Mfg. Agts. Nat. Assn., Fla. Engring. Soc., Material Handling Equipment Dealers Assn. Republican. Episcopalian. Club: Pensacola Country, Industrial Toastmasters (pres. 1962) (Pensacola). Home: 230 Clematis St Pensacola FL 32503 Office: P O Box 2517 Pensacola FL 32503

HILL, CAROLYN GREGG (MRS. VICTOR G. HILL, JR.), lawyer; b. Boston, June 4, 1936; d. David A., II and Virginia (Thompson) Gregg; B.A., Wellesley Coll., 1958; J.D., Oklahoma City U., 1969; m. Richard Howland Rawls, June 15, 1957 (dec.); children—Margaret Gregg, Richard Gregg; m. 2d, Victor G. Hill, Jr., May 6, 1967; 1 son, Victor Gerald III. Treas., dir. Cardast Corp., Wilton, N.H., 1958-62; customers broker N.Y. Stock Exchange, 1962-64; atty. Kerr-McGee Corp., Oklahoma City, 1969—. Finance adviser Swift Water council Girl Scouts U.S.A., Manchester, N.H., 1960-62; pres. Wilton Youth Center, 1961-63. Del. to N.H. Republican Conv., 1960, 62, 64; pres. Southegan Women's Rep. Club, 1961-62. Mem. Am., Okla. bar assns., Colonial Dames, Okla. Art Center. Republican. Clubs: Old English Sheepdog of Am., Appalachian Mountain; Oklahoma City Golf and Country. Home: 1606 Camden Way Oklahoma City OK 73116 Office: Kerr-McGee Bldg Oklahoma City OK 73102

HILL, CECIL JAMES, lawyer; b. Asheville, N.C., Nov. 20, 1919; s. Burton H. and Vallie (Staton) H.; A.A., Mars Hill Coll., 1941; B.S., U. N.C., 1943, J.D., 1945; m. Elizabeth T. Richardson, Dec. 15, 1945; children—Elisabeth Hartsfield, James Harrison. With W. Bowen Henderson, C.P.A., Asheville, 1941-43; admitted to N.C. bar, 1945; since practiced in Brevard; mem. firm Ramsey, Hill, Smart, 1959—. Dir. First Union Nat. Bank of N.C., Brevard. Chmn. Brevard Housing Authority. Vice pres. Brevard Music Festival Assn., 1949. Bd. dirs. Moorehead Sch. for Blind, 1965—; chmn. bd. dirs. Gov. Morehead Sch. Mem. Transylvania County Bar Assn. (pres. 1950-51), Brevard C. of C. (pres. 1957), Delta Sigma Pi. Democrat. Baptist. Mason (32 deg.), Lion (pres. 1949). Home: Woodside Dr Brevard NC 28712 Office: Legal Bldg Brevard NC 28712

HILL, CHARLES LEE, librarian; b. Houston, Tex., Nov. 15, 1910; s. Charles Samuel and Ola (McPherson) H.; B.S., Stephen F. Austin U., 1933; M. Music Edn., North Tex. State U., 1948, postgrad., 1951, N.Y. U., 1948-49, U. Houston, 1954-55; library sci. state certificate Sam Houston State U., 1961. Bandmaster, Stephen F. Austin U., 1933-34; high sch. band dir., Troup, Tex., 1934-35, Overton, 1935-42; saxaphone, clarinet instrumentalist Ted Johnson Dance Band, 1946-48; asso. prof. music Sam Houston State U., 1948-53; high sch. band dir., pub. sch. music tchr., Lovelady, Tex., 1953-59; tchr. instrumental music and pub. sch. music North Forest Ind. Sch. Dist., Houston, 1959-66, sch. librarian, 1966—. Composer and arranger of band and stage band music. Served with AUS, 1942-45. Recipient certificate of recognition Tex. Bandmaster's Assn., 1971. Mem. A.S.C.A.P., Tex. Bandmaster's Assn., Tex. Music Educator's Assn., Tex. Library Assn. Democrat. Methodist. Lion (pres. 1958-59, 71-72). Composer and arranger RRV, 1942, Gremlin Ball, 1944, Prairie Jump, 1948, Band Folio, 1952, Space City, U.S.A., 1962. Contbr. articles to music pubs. Home: 5802 Tidwell St Houston TX 77016 Office: 10750 Homestead St Houston TX 77016

HILL, CHESTER, state ofcl. Dir. Ednl. TV Tenn. Dept. Edn., Nashville. Address: 3147 Stafford Dr Nashville TN 37214*

HILL, CLARENCE LEWIS, ins. co. exec.; b. Winston-Salem, N.C., Mar. 1, 1914; s. George Washington and Mamie (Ennis) H.; B.S., W.Va. State Coll., 1935; m. Barbara Dowell, Jan. 10, 1940; children—Clarence Lewis, Talmadge L., Louise. Owner service sta., 1935-39; agt. Winston Mut. Life Ins. Co., 1929-41, office clk., 1941-53, sec., 1953—, also v.p., 1967—. Mem. adv. council Winston-Salem Civil Dev. Bd. dirs. Winston-Salem Urban League; past bd. dirs. United Fund of Forsyth County (N.C.). Mem. Kappa Alpha Psi. Democrat. Baptist (trustee). Club: Social Promoters. Home: 1101 Cameron Av

Winston-Salem NC 27101 Office: PO Box 998 Winston-Salem NC 27602

HILL, CLAUD JUSTIN, assn. exec.; b. Boonesville, Ark., Aug. 3,, 1923; s. Carl Justin and Clara (Elkins) H.; A.A., Little Rock U., 1950; m Dortha Lyon, Mar. 18, 1951 children—Wayne Justin, Kenneth Erwin. Mgr. Lido Cafeteria, Little Rock, 1950-59; dir. Ark. Restaurant Assn., 1960; dep. exec. dir. Okla. Restaurant Assn., Oklahoma City, 1960-—, exec. dir., 1965-—; dir. Oklahoma Egg Council. Mem. Okla. Gov.'s Com. on Tourism. Served with AUS, 1943-46. Mem. Internat. Soc. Restaurant Assn. Execs. (past pres.), Am., Okla. (dir.) socs. assn. execs Am. Mgmt. Assn. Baptist. Mason Okla. (32 deg.). Home: 1923 Barryton Rd Oklahoma City OK 73120 Office: 2207 N Broadway Oklahoma City OK 73103

HILL, CLYDE BROOKS, univ. adminstr.; b. Fulton, Ky., Apr. 27, 1921; s. Clyde B. and Lela (Lucas) H.; B.S. in Civil Engring., U. Ky., 1946; m. Miriam Anne Krayer, Aug. 18, 1942; children—Fred B., David L., Connie R. Constrn. supt. Don W. Hill Constrn. Co., Fulton, 1947-51; engring. field supr. Giffel & Vallet Engrs., Portsmouth, O., 1951-54; prodn. engr. Goodyear Atomic Corp., Portsmouth, 1954-55; chief engr. Pullora, Bowen & Watson, Tampa, Fla., 1955-58; asst. dean adminstrn. U. South Fla., Tampa, 1958-—. Mem. Hillsborough County Planning Commn., 1965-—, chmn., 1968-—; mem. Temple Terrace (Fla.) Zoning Bd. Adjustment, 1965-—, chmn., 1966-68. Served to capt. USAAF, 1942-46; ETO. Mem. Am. Soc. C.E., Soc. Univ. Planners, Assn. Phys. Plant Adminstrs. Univ. and Colls. (pres. 1971-72), S.E. Regional Assn. Phys. Plant Adminstrs. Univs. and Colls. (pres. 1962-63). Presbyn. (deacon 1964-66). Rotarian. Home: 411 Island Rd Temple Terrace FL 33617

HILL, DOUGLASS ORVILLE, physician; b. Oaklette, Va., Oct. 4, 1922; s. Edgar Garlicke and Clarius Verlinda (Newcombe) H.; B.S., Randolph-Macon Coll., 1944; M.D., Med. Coll. Va., 1947; m. Roberta Elaine Wildman, June 21, 1952; children—Douglass Orville, Geoffrey Lee, Mark Randolph. Intern Norfolk (Va.) Gen. Hosp., 1947-48, resident, 1948-49, McGuire VA Hosp., Richmond, Va., 1949-51; pvt. practice internal medicine, Winchester, Va., 1951-—; mem. staff Winchester Meml. Hosp.; cons. staff Morgan County Meml. Hosp., Berkeley Springs, W.Va., Shenandoah Meml. Hosp., Woodstock, Va. Med. examiner Winchester-Frederick County, 1959-—. Bd. dirs. Northwestern Workshop. Fellow Am. Geriatrics Assn., Am. Coll. Angiology, Am. Coll. Chest Physicians (asso.); mem. A.C.P. (life), Am., Va. (exec. com. 1970-—) socs. internal medicine, Am. Thoracic Soc., Winchester C. of C., Izaak Walton League, Med. Assn. Valley Va. (pres. 1971-72), A.M.A., Med. Soc. Va., Med. Soc. No. Va., So. Med. Assn., Nat. Guard Assn., Res. Officers Assn., Kappa Alpha, Phi Chi, Omicron Delta Kappa. Democrat. Methodist (trustee 1972-—). Lion. Club: Winchester Country. Home: 143 Hawthorne Dr Winchester VA 22601 Office: 137 W Boscawen St Winchester VA 22601

HILL, EARL EDWARD, supt. schs.; b. Kansas, Okla., June 9, 1923; s. Earl A. and Bessie Mae (Williams) H.; B.S., Okla. State U., 1948, M.S., 1955; m. Edith Jane Boyles, July 23, 1941; children—Twila (Mrs. David Ingle), Earl Edward, Donna (Mrs. Lee Sorum), Ricky Noel. With Lockheed Aircraft Co., Burbank, Cal., 1941-44; tchr., Vale, Okla., 1947-48, Lone Wolf, Okla., 1948-50, Dewey, Okla., 1950-54, Red Rock, Okla., 1954-56, Dover, Okla., 1956-59, Hennessee, Okla., 1959-60, Oaks, Okla., 1960-67; supt. schs., Salina, Okla., 1967-—. Democratic Precinct Chmn., Salina, 1970-72. Bd. dirs. Resource Conservation and Devel., Northeastern Okla. Community Devel. Corp. Served with USNR, 1943-44. Mem. Okla. Edn. Assn. (human relations com. 1970-71). Mason, Lion (pres. 1971-72). Home: General Delivery Salina OK 74365 Office: Box 98 Salina OK 74365

HILL, EDWARD P., appeals ct. judge; b., 1904; grad. U. Louisville Law Sch. Admitted to bar, 1927; now judge appeals ct., Frankfort, Ky. Address: New Capitol Bldg Frankfort KY 40601*

HILL, EDWIN HOLLIS, JR., wholesale co. exec.; b. Miami, Nov. 21, 1932; s. Edwin Hollis and Lillian Dorothy (Hampton) H.; student Rollins Coll., 1950-51; B.A., U. Miami at Coral Gables, 1954; m. Phyllis Hilburn, Feb. 19, 1964; children—Alan Dale, Edwin Hollis III, John Hampton, Wendy Pace. With Hill Brothers, Inc., Miami, Fla., 1957-—, pres., chmn. bd., 1965-69, chmn. bd., 1969-—; dir. Coral TV, Miami, Peoples Nat. Bank, Miami, Peoples Hialeah Bank (Fla.), and others. Mem. adv. bd. Salvation Army, 1965-71; active United Fund Dade County, 1969-—, Orange Bowl Com., 1965-—; mem. bd. Miami Crime Commn., 1971-—. Bd. dirs. A.R.C., 1969-71, Miami Heart Inst., 1965-—, Big Brothers, 1965-—, Jr. Achievement, 1968-—, Nat. Conf. Christians and Jews, 1971-—. Served to capt. USAF, 1954-57. Mem. Miami C. of C., Young Pres.'s Orgn., Econ. Soc. Conglist. Clubs: Coral Reef Yacht (Miami, Fla.); Biscayne Bay Yacht, Key Largo Anglers, Jockey, Rod and Reel, University (Miami). Home: 6955 Sunrise Terrace Coral Gables FL 33133 Office: PO Box 765 Miami FL 33152

HILL, EVERETT WENTWORTH, writer; b. Russell, Kan., Jan. 10, 1884; s. John Harris and Frances Emily (Wentworth) H.; student Cascadilla Prep. Sch., Ithaca, N.Y., 1903; B.S. in Econs., Wharton Sch. Finance and Commerce, U. Pa., 1907; m. Ethel Laing, June 3, 1908 (dec.); 1 dau., Ethel; m. 2d, Cleo Riley. With Standard Oil Co., 1907-08; settled at Shawnee, Okla., in ice mfg., 1908; settled at Oklahoma City, 1922; moved to Indian Bluff Farm, James River Ozarks, 1941; moved to Lakeshore Gardens, Flathead Lake, Polson, Mont., 1945; moved to Springfield, Mo., 1963; mgr. extensive farm lands. Mem. Nat. Boys and Girls Week com.; mem. internat. bd. dirs. Waterton-Glacier Internat. Peace Park Assn. Mem. Kan. Ind. Oil and Gas Assn., Am. Acad. Polit. and Social Sci., Nat. Econ. League, Phi Kappa Sigma. Democrat. Episcopalian. Mason (32 deg., Shriner), Rotarian (internat. pres. 1924-25). Clubs: Polson (hon.); Oklahoma City. Author: Toward the Sun; Light Across the Valley; He Who Seeks Gold; also writer verse, essays, philos. articles, short stories. Bd. counselors Sunshine mag. adv. staff. Speaker before Rotary clubs in N.Am., other countries. Address: 2525 NW 62d St Apt 207 Oklahoma City OK 73112

HILL, FRED GENE, psychiat. social worker; b. Port Arthur, Tex., Dec. 17, 1933; s. Fred G. and Mary (Culp) H.; student Tex. A. and M. U., 1952-53; B.A., Baylor U., 1956; postgrad. Southwestern Theol. Sem., 1956-57, Esalen Inst., S.W. Center for Human Potential, 1968-69; M.S. in Social Work, Tex. U., 1960; children—Frederick, Sonya, Scott, Angela (dec. 1970). With Kilgore Children's Psychiat. Center and Hosp., 1960-67, sr. psychiat. social worker, 1963-67; pvt. practice as marriage and family therapist, Amarillo, Tex., 1967-—. Exec. sec. Catholic Family Service, Amarillo, part-time 1965-68; cons. various local welfare and social agys. Mem. Nat. Assn. Social Workers (chpt. pres. 1965), Acad. Certified Social Workers, Tex. Social Welfare Assn. (chpt. pres. 1964), Am. Assn. Marriage and Family Counselors, Conf. for Advancement Pvt. Practice in Social Work, Tex. Soc. for Clin. Social Work, Am. Assn. Psychiat. Clinics for Children (sec. Southwestern region 1963), Nat. Assn. Mental Health (nat. staff council 1962-64). Presbyn. Office: 903 Bank of Southwest Bldg Amarillo TX 79109

HILL, GEORGE B(ARKER), newspaperman; b. Sulphur Springs, Tex., July 9, 1915; s. John B. and Grace (Summers) H.; student Ardmore Bus. Coll., 1931-32, Ardmore Night Law Sch., 1932-33, Okla. Baptist U., 1933-34; m. Margaret Ellen Culbertson, Sept. 19, 1943; children—John Carl, Judy (dec.), Mary (dec.). Reporter, Ardmore Democrat, 1935; news editor Aransas Pass (Tex.) Progress, 1936; feature writer Ard (Okla.) Ardmoreite, 1936; news editor Madill (Okla.) Record, 1937-38, 39, 45, Ada (Okla.) Bull., 1938; pub. Tishomingo Capital-Democrat, 1940-41, 46-49, Coalgate (Okla.) Record-Register, 1949-—, pub. Coalgate Pub. Co.; pres. Evans Pub. Co.; adv. dir. Atkinson Enterprises; adv. bd. TUSC. Chmn. adv. com. Sch. Journalism, Okla. State U., 1960-62. Chmn. legal pub. com. OPA, 1952-54, chmn. editorial bd., 1966-67; pres. S.E. Okla. Water Rights Assn., 1967-69; sec., treas. Okla. Water, Inc., 1970-—. Del. Democratic Nat. Conv., 1964. Served from pvt. to staff sgt. AUS, 1941-45. Recipient 52 awards Okla. Press Newspaper contests, 1946-—, also 2 sweepstakes; named publisher's Aux. Nat. Editor of Week, 1954. Mem. Okla. Press Assn. (dir., 1950-58, pres. 1957), C. of C. (pres. 1968). Democrat. Baptist. Mason (chmn. pub. relations grand lodge 1966-67, 70-—), Odd Fellow, Redman. Home: 505 S Byrd St Coalgate OK 74538 Office: Main St Coalgate OK 74538

HILL, HAROLD NELSON, JR., lawyer; b. Houston, Apr. 26, 1930; s. Harold N. and Emolyn (Geeslin) H.; B.S., Washington and Lee U., 1952; LL.B., Emory U., 1957; m. Jane Fell, Aug. 16, 1952; children—Ward Nelson, Douglas Allyn, Nancy Pierce. Admitted to Ga. bar, 1957, since practiced in Atlanta; asso. firm Gambrell, Harland, Russell & Moye, 1957-65, partner, 1965-66; asst. atty. gen. State of Ga., Atlanta, 1966-68, exec. asst. atty. gen., 1968-—. Part-time instr. Emory U. Sch. Law, 1960-—. Served with Ordnance Corps, AUS, 1952-54. Mem. State Bar Ga. (chmn. jurisprudence com. younger lawyers sect. 1966-67), Am., Ga., Atlanta (police-community relations com. 1967) bar assns., Am. Judicature Soc. Club: Atlanta Lawyers. Home: 455 Forest Valley Rd NE Atlanta GA 30342 Office: Judicial Bldg Atlanta GA 30334

HILL, ISAAC WILLIAM, newspaper editor; b. Opelika, Ala., Aug. 8, 1908; s. Isaac W. and Laura (Jones) H.; student George Washington U., 1925-26; A.B., Washington and Lee U., 1929; m. Catherine H. Dawson, June 25, 1932 children—Catherine R., Joyce E. Reporter-editor Mobile Press, 1929-30; deskman Washington Evening Star, 1930-37, city editor, 1937-49, news editor, 1949-54, asst. mng. editor, 1954-62, mng. editor, 1962-68, asso. editor, 1968-—. Lectr. newspaper personnel Am. Press Inst., Columbia, 1955-—; Kilgore journalism counselor De Pauw U., 1970. Mem. Am. Soc. Newspaper Editors, A.P. Mng. Editors Assn. (pres. 1967), Newspaper Comics Council, Inc., Lambda Chi Alpha, Pi Delta Epsilon, Sigma Delta Chi. Clubs: International, Nat. Press, Chevy Chase (Washington). Co-author: Mirror of War, 1961. Contbr. short stories to popular mags. Home: 3203 Leland St Chevy Chase MD 20015 Office: 225 Virginia Av Washington DC 20003

HILL, JAMES MARK, physician; b. Water Valley, Miss., Oct. 7, 1918; s. Martin Luther and Lillian (Addington) H.; B.A., U. Miss., 1940, M.A., 1942, B.S., 1945; M.D., Jefferson Med. Coll., 1948. Intern resident Bapt. Hosp., Memphis, 1949-54; prison physician Miss. State Penitentiary, Parchman, 1950; practice medicine specializing in surgery, Memphis, 1954-—; mem. staff Bapt. Meml. Hosp.; instr. anatomy U. Miss., 1943-45, prof. surg. anatomy, 1950-55. Mem. adv. bd. Peoples Protective Life Ins. Co. Served with USNR, 1945, served to lt M.C., 1955-57. Fellow A.C.S.; mem. A.M.A., So. Med. Assn., Tenn., Memphis and Shelby County med. socs., Memphis Surg. Soc., Phi Chi. Mason (32 deg., K.T., Shriner). Home: 1222 Dovecrest Memphis TN 38128 Office: 899 Madison Av Memphis TN 38103

HILL, JANE MARGARET, editor; b. Youngstown, O., May 25, 1919; d. Joseph Hamilton and Edith (Lowry) Hill; B.S. with distinction in Edn., Ohio State U., 1940, M.A., 1948. Tchr., Claridon Twp. Sch., Marion County, O., 1940-42, Upper Sandusky (O.) High Sch., 1942-43, Washington Pub. Schs., 1943-61; asst. dir. dept. math. Washington Pub. Schs., 1961-64; exec. dir. Pi Lambda Theta, Washington, 1964-70; mng. editor the Arithmetic Tchr., 1970-—. Content cons. ednl. TV series Sets and Systems, 1963-—; content cons. T.V. program on Brookline (Mass.) math project, summer 1967; vis. faculty George Washington U., 1956-57, U. Va., 1956-57, Montclair (N.J.) State Coll., summer, 1959, 61, Colo. State Coll. summer, 1959, 61, U. Coll., U. Md., 1961-—. Mem. N.E.A. (life), Nat. Council Tchrs. Math., Math. Assn. Am., Central Assn. Sci. and Math. Tchrs., A.A.A.S., (co-author math bibliography), Am. Assn. U. Women, Pi Lambda Theta (nat. treas.), Phi Delta Gamma, Alpha Delta Kappa, Delta Kappa Gamma. Home: 3051 Harrison St NW Washington DC 20015 Office: 1201 16th St NW Washington DC 20006

HILL, JOHN DANIEL, III, electronics engr.; b. Little Rock, Oct. 14, 1930; s. John Daniel and Dorothy (Reid) H.; student Little Rock Jr. Coll., 1948-50; B.S., U. Ark., 1954; postgrad. So. Methodist U., 1956-59; m. Bamma Lee Allred, Sept. 15, 1950; children—Debra Diane, John Clayton, Christopher Steven. Electronics engr. RCA, Camden, N.J., 1954-55; automatic controls engr. Reynolds Metals Co., Jones Mill, Ark., 1955-56; research and devel. electronics engr. Collins Radio Co., Dallas, 1956-57, research and devel. proj. engr., 1957-60, research and devel. group head, 1960-65, head research and devel. dept., 1965-67, asst. dir. research and devel., 1967-69, div. dir. computer hardware research and devel., 1969-70; gen. mgr. SCI Electronics Co., Houston, 1970-—. Served with USAF, 1950-52. Mem. I.E.E.E., Assn. for Computing Machinery. Methodist. Contbr. articles to profl. jours. Patentee in field. Home: 2022 Oceanview St Seabrook TX 77586 Office: SCI Electronics Co 8330 Broadway Houston TX 77017

HILL, JOHN WILLIAM, ednl. cons.; b. Warrior, Ala., July 16, 1923; s. Arthur Lee and Hester (Blackburn) H.; B.S., U. Ala., 1953, M.A., 1955, Ed.D., 1968; m. Zelma Elizabeth Jones, Apr. 2, 1952; 1 dau., Miriam Jane. Counselor, adminstr. Jefferson County Bd. Edn., Birmingham, Ala., 1955-68; asso. prof., cons. Troy (Ala.) State U., 1968-70; cons. Ala. Dept. Edn., Montgomery, 1969-—. Mem. City Zoning and Planning Bd., Gardendale, Ala., 1962-63. Served with USAAF, 1942-45. Mem. Ala. Media Assn., Ala. Guidance Assn., Ala. Edn. Assn., Ala. Assn. Sch. Adminstrs., Kappa Phi Kappa, Phi Delta Kappa. Republican. Methodist. Lion (chpt. vice chmn. 1963-64). Home: 602 Milan Court Montgomery AL 36109 Office: 416 State Office Bldg Montgomery AL 36104

HILL, L. DONALD, educator; b. St. Louis, Oct. 31, 1931; s. Lester Samuel and Pearl Pearl (Long) H.; A.B., Trevecca Coll., Nashville, 1957; M.A., (Long) H. Peabody Coll., 1958; m. Jean Allender, June 23, 1951; 1 son, Mark LeScott. Editor, Free Will. Baptist Sunday Sch. Bd., Nashville, 1957-58; tchr. Nashville schs., 1958-59; prof. Bryan Coll., Dayton, Tenn., 1959-66, exec. registrar, 1971-—; supt. Rhea County schs., Dayton 1966-69; dir. continuing edn. Cleveland (Tenn.) State Coll., 1969-71. Minister of music 1st Bapt. Ch., Dayton. Active March of Dimes, Boy Scouts Am.; committeeman S.E. Tenn. Exceptional Children Found. Served with AUS, 1952-54. Mem. Nat., Tenn. edn. assns., Assn. Childhood Edn. Internat., Assn. Higher Edn., Nat. Soc. for Study Edn., Phi Delta Kappa. Democrat. Baptist. Home: Edgewater Estates Dayton TN 37321

HILL, LEO H., lawyer; b. Greenville, S.C., May 26, 1927; student Furman U.; B.A., Erskine Coll., 1949; J.D., U. S.C., 1952; m. Grace Lucile Garrison, 1952; children—Lillian, Howard, Gary. Admitted to S.C. bar, 1952; partner firm Hill, James, Long, Fore & Wyatt, Greenville; atty. City of Greer (S.C.), 1963-—. Mem. Jud. Conf. 4th Circuit Ct. Appeals; chmn. com. that established Legal Aid Agy. Greenville County, also Pub. Defender Office Greenville County. Mem. Am., Greenville County (chmn. com. econs. of bar 1959), S.C. (circuit v.p. 1961-62, chmn. com. on continuing legal edn. 1961-62, com. insts., sems., symposiums, 1962-63, v.p., 1966-67, mem. exec. com. 1964-70, pres. 1968-69), bar assns., Am., S.C. trial lawyers assns., S.C. Assn. City Attys., Nat. Conf. Bar Presidents, Nat. Inst. Municipal Law Officers, S.C. Def. Lawyers Assn., Am. Judicature Soc., Phi Delta Phi. Home: 208 Arundel Rd Greenville SC 29607 Office: 100 Williams St at Pettigru Greenville SC 29601

HILL, MAX LLOYD, JR., realtor; b. Belleville, Ill., Aug. 15, 1927; s. Max L. and Leora (Jacobs) H.; student Purdue U., 1944-47; B.S., U.S. Naval Acad., 1951; postgrad. Harvard Law Sch., 1955-56; m. Jane Olivia Evatt, June 23, 1951; children—Larkin Payne, Max Lloyd III, Naomi Evatt. Sales engr. indsl. equipment Indsl. Welding Supplies, Inc., 1957-59; real estate salesman Simmons Realty Co., Inc., Charleston, S.C., 1959-63; pres. Max L. Hill Co., Inc., realtors, Charleston, 1963-—. Lectr., S.C. Realtor's Inst., 1967-—, U. S.C. Sch. Gen. Studies and Extension, 1962-—. Pres., Greater Charleston YMCA, 1965-67; mem. Charleston Planning and Zoning Commn., 1969; sec. Charleston County Bd. Assessment Control, 1972. Bd. dirs. Edn. Found., S.C. Assn. Realtors. Served with AUS, 1945-46, USNR, 1946; to 1st lt. USAF, 1951-55. Mem. S.C. Assn. Realtors (dir.), Greater Charleston Bd. Realtors (pres. 1970), Phi Gamma Delta. Methodist (ofcl. bd. 1964-—). Mason. Club: Carolina Yacht. Home: 96 Ashley Av Charleston SC 29401 Office: 33 Broad St Charleston SC 29401

HILL, POLLY KNIPP (MRS. GEORGE S. HILL), etcher, artist; b. Ithaca, N.Y., Apr. 2, 1900; d. Charles Tobias and Frances (Knause) Knipp; student Chesterton Br. Perse Sch., Cambridge, Eng., pub. schs., Urbana, Ill., U. Ill., 1918-20; B. Painting U. Syracuse, 1923; m. George Snow Hill, Nov. 16, 1925 (Dec. Feb. 1969); 1 son, George Jonathan. Forty one-man shows of etchings in N.Y.C., Boston, Nat. Mus., Washington, Syracuse, Detroit, St. Louis, Louisville, Dallas, Miami Beach, 1930-—, also Bradenton and Naples, Fla., Highlands, N.C.; has exhibited in group shows in most nat. print shows, 1930-—; represented in permanent collection Library of Congress, Pennell Collection Met. Mus., Syracuse Mus., Speed Mus., Louisville, Shillard-Smith Collection, Bellaire, Fla., Nat. Bezalel Mus., Israel, Ind. U., Bloomington, Hudson Library, Highlands, N.C., N.Y.C. Pub. Library; work represented in Fine Prints of the Year, 1930, 32, 33, Contemporary Am. Prints, 1931, Prize Prints of the 20th Century, 1950; also works as water colorist, portrait drawings. Nathan I. Bijur prize, Bklyn. Soc. Etchers, several prizes Fla. Fedn. Art, Clearwater Mus., Fla., The Gulf Coast Group, So. States Art League, Am. Artists group prize for etching Soc. Am. Ethcers; hon. mention The Phila. Sketch Club, 1956; awards Nantahala Art Show, 1966, 67, 68. Mem. Soc. Am. Graphic Artists, Prairie Printmakers, The St. Petersburg (Fla.) Art Center, St. Petersburg Museum of Fine Arts, Ringling Mus. (Sarasota), Civic Music Assn. St. Petersburg, Am. Assn. U. Women, Panhellenic, Kappa Pi, Phi Kappa Phi, Kappa Kappa Gamma. Episcopalian. Commn. etching Suwannee River, 1962, gift print for Print Makers Soc. Cal. Home: 2233 Green Way S St Petersburg FL 33712 also Hicks Rd Highlands NC 28741

HILL, RAYMOND MATHEW, supt. schs.; b. Bessemer, Mich., July 5, 1923; s. John Albert and Julia Elizabeth (Sarri) H.; student Gogebic Jr. Coll., 1946-48; B.S., U. Ga., 1950, M.Ed., 1954, postgrad., 1954-60; m. J. Eudene Cook, June 29, 1945; children—Paula (Mrs. Phillip O. Brock), Pamela. Tchr., coach Oglethorpe County Bd. Edn., Lexington, Ga., 1950-56; tchr. Cartersville (Ga.) Sch. Bd., 1956, coach, 1956-58, asst. prin., 1956-58, curriculum dir., 1958-61, prin., 1961-65, supt. schs., 1965-—. Asst. dir. Gov's. Honors Program, summer 1964. Mem. program com. Ga. YMCA, 1965-67. Served with AUS, 1943-46. Recipient Service award YMCA, 1968. Mem. N.E.A., Ga. Assn. Sch. Supts., Ga. Sch. Bds. Assn., Ga. Assn. Educators, Cartersville Edn. Assn. (dir. 1961), Cartersville-Bartow County C. of C., Kappa Delta Pi. Clubs: Country. Civitan (pres. 1963) (Cartersville). Home: 196 Etowah Dr Cartersville GA 30120 Office: 1 Erwin St Cartersville GA 30120

HILL, RICHARD HARRISON, lawyer, historian; b. New Castle, Ky., Nov. 15, 1887; s. Benjamin Franklin and Edmonia West (Samuell) H.; student Centre Coll. Ky., 1905-06; A.B., Princeton, 1909; J.D., Harvard, 1912; m. Mary Jo Lazarus Gheens, Aug. 3, 1966. Admitted to Ky. bar, 1912; practiced in Louisville, 1912-17, 21-34; judge Jefferson Circuit Ct., Chancery br., 1926-27; asst. to atty. gen. U.S., Dept. Justice, Washington, 1934-41; dir. law City of Louisville, 1941-43, 44-46; ret., 1946; dir., sec. Filson Club (hist. soc.), Louisville, 1947-—, pres., 1972-—. Farmer, Henry County, 1942-—. Active Community Chest, A.R.C. drives. 1912-46; Sec., trustee Louisville Childrens Free Hosp., 1928-34. Served to maj. Judge Adv. Gen. Corps, U.S. Army, 1917-20, to lt. col. Mil. Govt., AUS, 1943-44. Mem. Am., Ky., Louisville bar assns., Ky. Soc. Colonial Wars, Ky. S.A.R., Phi Delta Theta. Democrat. Unitarian. Clubs: Pendennis, Country, River Valley, Law, Conversation, Wranglers. Editor: Filson Club History Quar., 1946-72. Home: 6100 Longview Lane Louisville KY 40222 Office: 118 W Breckinridge St Louisville KY 40203

HILL, VICTOR, dentist; b. St. George, S.C., Oct. 18, 1926; s. John Heaton and Cora Louise (Brownlee) H.; B.S., U. S.C., 1952; D.M.D., U. Ala., 1964; m. Junelle Ferguson, Jan. 20, 1949; children— Victor Lamont, Debra Junelle. Pvt. practice gen. dentistry, Orangeburg, S.C., 1964-—. S.C. state chmn. for Nat. Childrens Dental Health Week, 1970; mem. staff Orangeburg Regional Hosp., chief dental staff, 1971. Served with USMCR, 1946-48. Mem. Am., S.C., Coastal Dist. (v.p. 1971, pres. elect 1972) dental socs. Baptist. Club: Orangeburg Country. Home: 226 Hillsboro Rd Orangeburg SC 29115 Office: 1291 Boulevard N E Orangeburg SC 29115

HILL, WILLIAM BAPTIST, museum ofcl.; b. Birmingham, Ala., Mar. 2, 1909; s. William Henderson and Lucy R. (Baptist) H.; B.S., U. Va., also LL.B. Formerly practiced law, Memphis and Boydton, Va.; founder, dir. Roanoke River Mus., Clarksville, Va., 1959-—. Trustee Roanoke River Mus., Prestwould Found., Boyd Family Meml. Found. Mem. Am. Soc. Ethnohistory, Am. Anthrop. Assn., Va. Hist. Soc., Assn. Preservation Va. Antiquities (past trustee), Archeol. Soc. Va. Democrat. Author: Land by the Roanoke, 1957; The Boyds of Boydton, 1967; The Indians of Axacan and the The Spanish Martyrs, The Beginnings of Virginia, 1970. Address: Prestwould House Clarksville VA 23927

HILL, WILLIAM CLYDE, constrn. co. exec.; b. Chgo., Jan. 26, 1920; s. Clyde William and Elizabeth Mary (Doyle) H.; B.C.E., U. Dayton, 1940; m. Gloria M. Emmanuelli, Aug. 29, 1942; children—Gloria Elizabeth, Edward Charles. Surveyor, Greeley-Howard, Norlin, Chgo., 1940; san. engr. Chgo. Pump Co.,

1940-41, 45-47; civil engr. Earl K. Burton, Inc., San Juan, P.R., 1947—, v.p., 1957—, treas., 1965—. Served with AUS, 1941-46. Registered profl. engr., Ill., P.R. Mem. Am. Soc. Civil Engrs. (sect. pres. 1952), P.R. Assn. Engrs. Architects and Surveyors, Mil. Order of World Wars (chpt. comdr. 1959), Res. Officers Assn. (dept. pres. 1957, nat. v.p. 1958), Soc. Am. Mil. Engrs., Assn. of the U.S. Army. Roman Catholic. Club: Serra International (dist. gov. 1967-69). Home: 7W Palma Sola St Garden Hills Guaynabo PR 00619 Office: Gen P O Box 1367 San Juan PR 00936

HILL, WILLIAM FARRIS, state ofcl.; b. Manatee, Fla., Jan 24, 1927; s. William Farris and Hester (Odum) H.; A.B., Emory U., 1951; M.D., U. Tenn., 1956; M.P.H., U. Cal., 1961; m. Elizabeth Colleen Howard, Aug 27, 1947; children—William Farris III, Rebecca Lynn. Intern, Greenville (S.C.) Gen. Hosp., 1956-57; dir. Highlands-Glades-Hendry County Health Dept., Sebring, 1957-67, Polk County Health Dept., Winter Haven, Fla., 1967—. Served with USNR, 1944-46, 50-51. Mem. Am., Fla. (pres. 1972) pub. health assns., A.M.A., Fla. Med. Assn., Fla. Assn. County Health Officers. Home: 138 Lake Ring Dr Winter Haven FL 33880 Office: PO Box 1480 Winter Haven FL 33880

HILL, WILLIAM LEON, advt. exec.; b. Greensburg, Pa., Sept. 4, 1932; s. Leon McDonald and Hanna (Schaffer) H.; Asst. B.A., Amarillo Coll., 1952; B.F.A., Kansas City Art Inst., 1956; m. Rae Ellen Warren, Mar. 3, 1956; children—Shaun Elise, Tamara, Warren Schaffer, Christian Canady. With Mel Richman & Assos., 1958; asst. art dir. DeGarmo Advt., N.Y., 1958; with Bloom Advt., Dallas, 1956-58, 59—, creative dir., 1963—, sr. v.p., 1965—. Exhibited in group shows including Dallas-Ft. Worth Art Dirs. Club, 1959-68, Am. Film Festival, N.Y.C., 1966-67, Internat. Film Festival N.Y.C., 1965, Dallas Ad League, 1965-68, USIA Overseas Exhibit. Judge various Southwestern advt. and coll. exhibits. Active various community drives. Served with USNR, 1950-58. Recipient various awards; named Art Dir. of Year, Dallas-Ft. Worth Soc. Visual Communications, 1968. Mem. Dallas-Ft. Worth Art Dirs. Club (1st v.p. 1967-68, editor Push Pin). Episcopalian. Home: 300 Sutton Pl Richardson TX 75080 Office: 3000 Diamond Park Dallas TX 75222

HILLARD, JAMES MILTON, librarian; b. Nortonville, Ky., Sept. 27, 1920; s. Cornelius and Leona L. (Hicks) H.; B.A. with high honors, Ohio U., 1947; M.S. in L.S. with honors, U. Ill., 1948; m. Ella Louise Winzenried, Dec. 23, 1944; children—James Randolph, Jerrold Manley. Asst. librarian Free Pub. Library, Summit, N.J., 1948-50; city librarian Carnegie City Library, Ft. Smith, Ark., 1950-52; dir. Curtis Meml. Library, Meriden, Conn., 1952-55; asso. librarian U.S. Mil. Acad., W. Point, N.Y., 1955-57; librarian The Citadel, Charleston, S.C., 1957—. Served with AUS, 1942-46. Mem. Am., Southeastern, S.C. (sec. 1960; treas. 1965—) library assns., Am. Assn. U. Profs. Methodist. Club: Optimist. Contbr. profl. jours. Address: The Citadel Charleston SC 29409

HILLEARY, WILLIAM, textile co. exec.; b. Grand View, Tenn., Sept. 26, 1892; s. Harry Caspar and Mary LeGrand (Thompson) H.; LL.B., Cumberland U., 1914; B.C.S., YMCA Sch. Commerce, Cin., 1926; m. Sarah Neil, Apr. 16, 1932; 1 son, W. Campbell. Successively tchr., high sch. prin., county supt. schs. Rhea County, Tenn., 1917-18; owner, operator ins. bus., Dayton, Tenn., 1920-21; admitted to Tenn. bar, 1921, asso. editor Ins. Salesman mag., 1921; bus. mgr. Diamond Life Bull., Cin., 1922-28; organizer, mgr. So. Silk Mills, Spring City, Tenn., 1928-33, pres., 1933-72, also dir. Mem. local SSS bd., 1940-65. Mem. Rhea County Sch. Bd., 1921-23; justice of peace Rhea County, 1934-46. Served to 1st lt. U.S. Army, World War I. Presbyn. (elder, Sunday sch. supt.). Mason (Shriner), Kiwanian (Man of Year award Spring City 1940). Author: Life Insurance and Taxation, 1925. Home: 3d St and Rhea Av Spring City TN 37381 Office: So Silk Mills Hwy 27 Spring City TN 37381

HILLENBRAND, BERNARD FRANCIS, assn. exec.; b. Syracuse, N.Y., May 11, 1925; s. Leonard L. and Anne (Green) H.; B.A., Syracuse U., 1949; M.A., Maxwell Sch. Pub. Adminstrn., 1950; m. Elizabeth M. Dwyer, July 9, 1955; children—Betsy, John, Susan, Laura. Adminstrv. analyst Budget dept. State of Wis., Madison, 1951-52; dep. dir. Am. Municipal Assn. (now Nat. League Cities), Washington, 1955-57; exec. dir. Nat. Assn. of Counties, Washington, 1957—. Mem. steering com., adv. bd. Keep America Beautiful, 1962—; mem. adv. com. Census of Govts. U.S. Bur. Census, 1965—; mem. Pres.'s Commn. on Employment of Handicapped, 1966—. Bd. dirs. Met. Manpower Study Washington Center for Met. Studies; bd. dirs. Nat. Assn. Regional Councils. Served with inf. AUS, World War II. Decorated Purple Heart. Mem. U.S. C. of C. (mem. crime com.), Nat. Safety Council. Home: 5104 Moorland Lane Bethesda MD 20014 Office: 1001 Connecticut Av NW Washington DC 20036

HILLEY, LEWIS MOORE, educator; b. Waco, Tex., May 21, 1914; s. John Gordon and Janie (Moor) H.; student Washington and Lee U., 1944, Phillipine Inst., 1945, U. Okla., 1951; A.B., Baylor U., 1940; M.Ed., U. Tex., 1947, Ed.D., 1955; m. Jean Peevey, Oct. 9, 1942; children—Michael Lewis, Gregory Alan, Gordon Mark. Coach and tchr., Sabinal, Tex., 1940-41; phys. tng. dir. U.S. Air Corps, Maxwell Field, Ala., 1941-42; dir. Austin Athletic Club, coach Tex. Sch. for Deaf, Austin, 1946-48; tennis profl. Caswell Tennis Center, Austin, 1948-51, Morgan's Point (Tex.) Yacht and Tennis Club, 1971—; dir. intramurals, prof. Lamar State Coll. Tech., Beaumont, 1951-62, dir. athletics, 1955-62, chmn. dept. health and phys. edn., recreation, 1963-65; program chmn. health, phys. edn. and recreation U. South Fla., Tampa, 1963-65; chmn. dept. health, phys. edn. and recreation U. South Ala., Mobile, 1965-70; dir. athletics, chmn. dept. health, phys. edn. and recreation Mary Hardin-Baylor Coll., Belton, Tex., 1971—. Cons. Baldwin County (Ala.) Phys. Edn. Workshop, 1968-69; pres. Beaumont Greater Phys. Fitness Assn., 1958-59; chmn. Greater Mobile Fitness Council, 1965; recreational cons. Gt. Western Real Estate Corp., Morgan's Point, Tex., 1971—. Recipient Leadership award Beaumont C. of C., 1963. Served to capt. USAAF, 1941-46; PTO. Fellow A.A.H.P.E.R. (chmn. men's athletic sect. So. dist. 1968-69, rep. to U.S. Collegiate Sports Council 1968—); mem. Fla., Ala. Coll. (pres. 1968-69), Ala. assns. for health, phys. edn. and recreation, Am. Assn. U. Profs., U.S. Lawn Tennis Assn., U.S. Profl. Lawn Tennis Assn., Fla. Drive Edn. Assn., S.W. Football and Basketball Ofcls. Assn. Home: 65 Oakmont Circle Morgan's Point Route 1 Belton TX 76513

HILLIARD, JOHN ROY, JR., educator; b. Irving, Tex., Feb. 7, 1924; s. John Roy and Nora Ruth (Hendrix) H.; B.A., Trinity U., 1947; M.A., U. Colo., 1951; Ph.D., U. Tex., 1959; m. Evelyn Joyce Herzog, Dec. 25, 1951; children—James Ronald, Richard Alan. Instr. biology and sci. Tivy High Sch., Kerrville, Tex., 1944-45; instr. biology Trinity U., 1948-51; asso. prof., head dept. biology McMurry Coll., 1951-54; teaching asst. U. Tex., 1954-55; prof., head dept. biology McMurry Coll., 1957-68; asso. prof. biology Sam Houston State U., 1968-70, prof., 1970—, dir. dept., 1972—. Bd. dirs. Community Day Care Assn. of Huntsville, Inc., 1969-70; v.p. Christian Orgn. Missionary Endeavor, 1971. Served as sgt., AUS, 1945-46. Fellow Tex. Acad. Scis.; mem. A.A.A.S., Am. Inst. Biol. Scis., Entomol. Soc. Am., Entomol. Soc., Ecological soc. Am., Southwestern Assn. Naturalists, Sigma Xi. Methodist. Research on systematics, biology and ecology of orthoptera. Home: Rt 2 Box 276-2 Huntsville TX 77340

HILLIER, JAMES C., head Inst. Animal Sci. and Industry, Okla. State U. Address: Inst Animal Sci and Industry Okla State U Stillwater OK 74074*

HILLIS, CHARLES LEWIS, physician; b. Vidette, Ga., Jan. 13, 1931; s. Jake Lewis and Mamie (Kelly) H.; A.B., Emory U., 1951, B.D., 1954, M.D., 1967; m. Varese Chambless, June 14, 1953; children—Charles Lewis, Kelly, Mark. Ordained to ministry Methodist Ch., 1954; pastor, Bronwood, Ga., 1951-54, Odum, Ga., 1954-56, Reynolds, Ga., 1956-60; St. Mary's, Ga., 1960-62; intern, Floyd Hosp., Rome, Ga., 1967-68; practice gen. medicine, Lafayette, Ga., 1968—; mem. staff Tri-County Hosp., Ft. Oglethorpe, Ga., sec. staff, 1972-74; pres., Drs. Clinic Lafayette, Inc., 1971-72. Coroner, Walker County, Ga., 1969-73. Mem. A.M.A., Med. Assn. Ga., Tri County Med. Soc., Delta Tau Delta. Republican. Methodist. Mason, Elk, Kiwanian (pres. 1962). Club: Optimist (Lafayette). Home: 14 Sunset Dr LaFayette GA 30728 Office: Box 846 N Main St LaFayette GA 30728

HILLIS, JOHN BUSSEY, librarian; b. Des Moines, Feb. 24, 1932; s. Cyrus Bussey and Hazel (Maphet) H.; student U. N.M., 1950-52; B.A., Drake U., 1954; M.S. in L.S. (fellow 1958-60), Cath. U. Am., 1961; m. Anne Mary Kilmer, Dec. 29, 1960; children—David Bussey, Stephen Kenton, Jennifer Lea. Reference asst. Mullen Library, Cath. U. Am., 1960; reference librarian Hdqrs., Arlington County (Va.) Library System, 1961-62; dir. Glencarlyn Br. Library, Arlington, 1962-63; asst. city librarian West Palm Beach (Fla.) Pub. Library, 1963-71, city librarian, 1971—. Served with U.S. Army, 1954-56. Mem. Am., Fla. library assns., Audubon Soc., Mensa, Phi Kappa Tau. Republican. Home: 1424 Lake Bass Dr Lake Worth FL 33460 Office: Flagler Park West Palm Beach FL 33401

HILLS, MRS. A.S., broadcasting exec. Pres., WKAQ, San Juan, P.R. Address: GPO Box 4668 San Juan PR 00936*

HILLS, ARGENTINA S., publishing co. exec. Publisher El Mondo, San Juan, P.R. Address: El Mondo 383 Roosevelt St San Juan PR 00907*

HILLS, JOHN MOORE, educator; b. Oak Park, Ill., Mar. 15, 1910; s. Edward Rowland and Mary (Moore) H.; B.S., Lafayette Coll., 1931; Ph.D., U. Chgo., 1934; m. Sally Ward, Dec. 11, 1934; children—Edward Eyerly, Joseph Ward, Susan Moore (Mrs. Glen H. Lambertson). Geologist, Amerada Petroleum Corp., Midland, Tex., 1934-41; cons. geologist Penn, Hills & Turner, Midland, Tex., 1941—; prof. geology U. Tex., El Paso, 1967—. Vis. lectr. U. Tex., Austin, 1959-60. Mem., chmn. Midland Planning Commn., 1949-53, city councilman, 1953-55. Fellow Geol. Soc. Am., A.A.A.S.; mem. West Tex. Geol. Soc. (pres. 1950), Soc. Petroleum Engrs., Am. Geophys. Union, Soc. Econ. Paleontologists and Mineralogists, Am. Assn. Petroleum Geologists, Am. Inst. Profl. Geologists, Nat. Assn. Geology Tchrs., Phi Beta Kappa, Sigma Xi. Presbyn. Clubs: Midland Country, El Paso (Tex.). Home: 818 Kerbey Av El Paso TX 79902 Office: Box 418 Midland TX 79701 also Dept Geology U Tex El Paso TX 79968

HILLS, LEE, newspaperman; b. Granville, N.D., May 28, 1906; s. Lewis Amos and Lulu Mae (Loomis) H.; student Brigham Young U., 1924-25, U. Mo., 1927-29; grad. Oklahoma City U. Sch. Law, 1934; Sc.D. in Bus. Adminstrn., Cleary Coll., 1958; L.H.D., U. Utah, 1969; LL.D., Eastern Mich. U., 1969; m. Eileen Whitman, June 4, 1948 (dec. 1961); 1 son (by previous marriage), Ronald Lee, 1 stepdau., Toni Terry (Mrs. Carl Griffith); m. 2d, Tina S. Ramos, Oct. 31, 1963. News reporter News-Advocate, Price, Utah, 1924-25, editor, 1926; reporter Oklahoma City Times, 1929-32; polit. writer Okla. News, 1932-35, editor, 1938-39; reporter, copyreader Cleve. Press, 1935-36, news editor, 1940-42; chief editorial writer, asso. editor Indpls. Times, 1936-37; asso. editor Memphis Press-Scimitar, 1939-40; mng. editor Miami (Fla.) Herald, 1942-51, exec. editor, 1951-66, asso. pub., 1966-70, pub., 1970—; exec. editor Detroit Free Press, 1951-69, pub., 1963—, pres., 1967—; exec. editor Knight Newspapers, Inc., 1959—, exec. v.p., 1966-67, pres., 1967—, chmn. exec. com., 1969—; admitted to Okla. bar, 1935. Awarded Maria Moors Cabot gold medal for distinguished contbn. to Inter-Am. relations Columbia U., 1946, Pulitzer prize in journalism, 1956. Pres. Detroit Arts Commn.; trustee Founders Soc. Detroit Inst. Arts, Washington Journalism Center. Mem. Internat. Press. Inst., Mich. Press Assn., Inter-Am. Press Assn. (pres. 1967-68; dir.), Am. Soc. Newspaper Editors (pres. 1962-63), Am. Newspaper Pubs. Assn., A.P. Mng. Editors Assn. (past pres.), Fla. A.P. Assn. (past pres.), United Found. (dir.), Sigma Delta Chi (past pres.). Clubs: Nat. Press; Detroit Athletic, Detroit, Hundred, Grosse Pointe (Detroit); Miami, Bath and Surf (Miami). Home: 4450 Banyan Lane Miami FL 33137 also Sheraton-Cadillac Hotel Detroit MI 48226 Office: Miami Herald Miami FL 33101 also Detroit Free Press Detroit MI 48231

HIMES, LUTHER ROBERT, JR., city ofcl.; b. Fort Worth, Oct. 26, 1924; s. Luther Robert and Carrie Belle (Lewis) H.; Asso. Sci., North Tex. Agrl. Coll., 1943, postgrad., 1945-47; m. Lajuana Wilson, Mar. 18, 1948; children—Cathey Lynn (Mrs. James L. Robertson), Luther Robert III, Terry Lee. With Fort Worth Fire Dept., 1947—, driver fire fighting div., 1955-59, lt. fire fighting, 1959-64, capt. tng. officer, 1964-68, dist. chief, asst. fire marshall, 1968-69, fire chief, 1969—. Tchr. Tex. A. and M. U., 1964-68. Pres. Meadowbrook Little League, 1969. Served with USAAF, 1943-45. Decorated Air medal with five oak leaf clusters. Mem. Petroleum Club, West Tex., Fort Worth chambers commerce. Home: 2501 McGee St Fort Worth TX 76112 Office: 1000 Throckmorton St Fort Worth TX 76102

HIMMELSBACH, CLIFTON KECK, univ. dean; b. Phila., Mar. 17, 1907; s. Adam Jones and Blanche Gertrude (Keck) H.; M.D., U. Va., 1931; fellow pharmacology, Western Res. U., 1933; m. Virginia Thurmond Martin, Nov. 28, 1928 (dec. 1959); 1 son, Robert Peale; m. 2d, Kathryn Kilgour Kilian, June 15, 1961; 1 stepdau., Nina Louise Kilian. Intern USPHS Hosp., New Orleans, 1931-32; commd. USPHS, 1932, med. dir., 1949; clin. research drug addiction Ft. Leavenworth, Kan., Pondville, Mass., Lexington, Ky., 1933-44; clin. dir. USPHS Hosp., Lexington, 1938-39, dir. research, 1940-44; with NIH, Bethesda, Md., 1944-45; regional med. cons. Office Vocational Rehab., Kansas City, Mo., and Chgo., 1945-47; med. officer charge USPHS outpatient clinic, Washington, 1948-53; asst. chief, then chief div. hosps., USPHS, 1953-57; dir. spl. programs, div. research grants NIH, 1957-59, asso. dir. clin. center, 1959-65; asso. dean (research) Georgetown U. Sch.'s of Medicine and Dentistry, Washington, 1965—, prof. community medicine and internat. health, 1966—, adminstr. sponsored programs, 1970—. Chmn. com. infections hosps. Am. Hosp. Assn., 1961-70, mem. council on planning, 1969—. Recipient USPHS Meritorious Service award. Fellow A.C.P.; mem. Council Med. Adminstrs. (pres. 1961), S.A.R., Sigma Xi, Phi Beta Pi. Author articles pharmacology, drug addiction, hosp. infections. Home: 3731 Harrison St NW Washington DC 20015

HINCHEE, FRED LEE, hosp. adminstr.; b. Haileyville, Okla., Nov. 11, 1919; s. Jonah and Augusta Henry (Wiggs) H.; student U. Cal. at Santa Barbara, summer 1944; B.S. in Bus., U. Okla., 1948; M.S. in Hosp. Adminstrn., Northwestern U., 1958; m. Yvonne Dee Lindsay, June 15, 1958; 1 dau., Ellen Rachel. Registrar asst. Houston VA Hosp., 1945-55; credit asst. Chgo. Wesley Meml. Hosp., 1956-57; adminstrv. resident Hillcrest Med. Center, Tulsa, 1957-58; adminstr. Shawnee (Okla.) Municipal Hosp., 1958-63, Mission Hill Meml. Hosp., Shawnee, 1963—. Bd. dirs., past v.p., past pres. Pottawatomie County Mental Health Assn. Served to 1st lt. USAAF, 1943-44. Mem. Am. Mgmt. Assn., Am., Okla. (chmn. central dist. 1970) hosp. assns., Am. Coll. Hosp. Administrs. Democrat. Methodist. Kiwanian (chmn. vocational guidance Shawnee 1961). Contbr. articles to profl. jours. Home: 1609 N Oklahoma St Shawnee OK 74801 Office: 1900 Gordon Cooper Dr Shawnee OK 74801

HINDS, CHARLES FRANKLIN, librarian; b. Henderson, Ky., Oct. 31, 1923; s. Charles Fretwell and Ruth Alice (Carson) H.; A.B., U. Ky., 1950, M.A., 1958, M.S. in L.S., 1968, postgrad., 1968—; postgrad. U. Louisville, 1950-52, 54-56, Am. U., 1961; m. Doris May Rooney, June 8, 1946; children—Joseph, James. Account and rate clk., auditor freight accounts L & N R.R., Louisville, 1941-53; tchr. Male High Sch., Louisville, 1953-56; dir. Ky. Hist. Soc., Frankfort, 1956-59; state historian, Ky., 1956-59; field rep. U. Ky. Libraries, Lexington, 1959-60; state archivist, records adminstr. State Archives and Records Commn., Frankfort, 1960-67; head librarian Murray (Ky.) U., 1967—. Lectr., U. Ky., 1960-67; instr. Ky. State Coll., 1966-67, asso. prof. Murray State U., 1967—. Sec., mgr. Ky. Hist. Markers Program, 1956-62; chmn. State Records Control Bd., 1956-58; mem. State Archives and Records Commn., 1958-60, sec., 1960-62; mem. Civil War Centennial Commn., 1958-65. Served with AUS, 1941-45. Decorated Bronze Star medal. Mem. Ky. Tennis Assn. (pres. 1967-68), S.A.R. (pres. Ky. chpt. 1969-70), Soc. Am. Archivists (chmn. state archives com. 1965, 66), Phi Beta Kappa, Phi Alpha Theta, Beta Phi Mu. Democrat. Episcopalian (vestryman 1967-68). Rotarian. Clubs: Optimist (1st v.p. 1963), Toastmasters (pres. 1964-65, lt. gov. So. div. dist. 11 1968-69). Editor: Register, state hist. quar., 1956-59; Checklist of Ky. State Publs., 1963-67. Home: RFD 4 Murray KY 42071

HINDS, JACKSON CEIVERS, lawyer, utility co. exec.; b. Brownsville, Tex., Aug. 28, 1921; s. Jackson Ceivers and Tallulah G. (Raffo) H.; B.B.A., U. Tex., 1942, LL.B., 1948; postgrad. indsl. adminstrn., Harvard, 1943, M.B.A., 1947; m. Artie Lee Page, June 18, 1946; children—Stephen Randolph, Page Aline, Denise Jacqueline. Admitted to Tex. bar, 1948, since practiced in Houston; with firm Fulbright, Crooker, Freeman. Bates & Jaworski, 1948-56; gen. counsel Houston Natural Gas Corp. and subsidiaries, 1956-69, sr. v.p., dir., 1962-67, exec. v.p., dir., 1967-69; pres. United Gas, Inc., Houston, 1969—; dir. Med. Center Bank, Main Bank Houston, Univ. Savs. & Loan Assn. (all Houston). Pres. Houston Housing Devel. Corp., 1968—; chmn. Houston Mayor's Adv. Com. on Housing, 1967—. Served to lt. USNR, 1942-46. Decorated Bronze Star medal. Mem. Am., Tex., Houston bar assns., Fed. Power Communications Bar Assn., Am., So. gas assns. Home: 2437 Brentwood Dr Houston TX 77019 Office: PO Box 2628 Houston TX 77001

HINES, CARL RICHARD, city ofcl.; b. Louisville, Mar. 23, 1931; s. Fred Richard and Ruth Lory (Johnson) H.; student U. Ill., 1949-50, U. Louisville, 1954-60, 60-62; m. Teresa M. Churchill, Mar. 5, 1960; children—Carl Richard, Keith, Cheryl, Cory. Staff mgr. Mammoth Ins. Co., 1963-65, dist. mgr., 1965-70; city dir. Housing Opportunity Centers, Inc., Louisville, 1970-72, exec. dir., 1972—. Exec. sec. Louisville Community Action Commn., 1969-70; mem. Louisville Bd. Edn., 1968-69, vice chmn., 1970, chmn., 1971; vice chmn. Louisville Chestnut St. YMCA. Served with USAF, 1951-53. Decorated Air medal, D.F.C. Optimist. Club: Just Mens. Home: 635 Southwestern Pkwy Louisville KY 40211 Office: 1111 W Broadway Louisville KY 40202

HINES, HOWARD H(ARRY), social scientist; b. Iowa City, June 30, 1922; s. Harry Matlock and Leona (Fisher) H.; B.A., U. Ia., 1942, A.M., Harvard, 1948, Ph.D., 1950. Tchr. econs. U. Ia., 1947, Bowdoin Coll., 1948, Harvard, 1948-50; from asst. prof. to prof. econs. Ia. State U., 1950-62; program dir. for econs. NSF, 1962-64, div. dir. for social scis., 1964—; acting asst. prof. bus. adminstrn. U. Cal. at Berkeley, 1955-56. Served with AUS, 1943-46. Mem. Am., Midwest (1st v.p. 1957-58) econ. assns., Royal Econ. Soc., Phi Beta Kappa, Delta Sigma Rho, Order of Artus. Office: Nat Science Found 1800 G St NW Washington DC 20550

HINES, MERRILL ODOM, surgeon, med. adminstr.; b. Jackson, Miss., Nov. 17, 1909; s. Hulon Hunter and Ava Ione (Odom) H.; B.S., Millsaps Coll., 1931; M.D. (Commonwealth fellow from Miss.), Tulane U., 1936; m. Margaret McLaurin Davis, Aug. 24, 1937; children—Margaret Anne, Merrill Odom. Intern Baroness Erlanger Hosp., Chattanooga, 1936-37, resident, 1937-38, chief resident surgery, 1938-39; staff surgeon Tylertown (Miss.) Hosp., 1939-42; mem. staff Alton Ochsner Med. Found., New Orleans, 1944—, head dept. proctology, 1946-61; head dept. proctology Ochsner Found. Hosp., 1947-62, pres. staff, 1946-47; asst. med. dir. Ochsner Clinic, 1954-60, mem. bd. mgmt., 1960—, med. dir., 1960—; sr. vis. surgeon Charity Hosp., New Orleans, 1956—; courtesy staff Sara Mayo Hosp., New Orleans, 1954—; sr. asso. surgery Touro Infirmary, New Orleans, 1953-64; courtesy staff Flint-Goodridge Hosp., New Orleans, 1949—; asst. prof. clin. surgery Tulane Med. Sch., 1949-62, asso. prof. clin. surgery, 1962-64, prof. clin. surgery, 1964—; cons. Ill. Central Hosp., New Orleans, 1958-70; cons. group practice of medicine Dept. Health, Edn. and Welfare, 1966-70; mem. Govt. Health Ins. Benefits Adv. Council, 1968-72; mem. nat. adv. drug com. FDA, Dept. Health, Edn. and Welfare, 1972—. Bd. dirs. Am. Cancer Soc. Greater New Orleans, 1957—, sec., 1957-58; v.p., 1959-60, pres., 1961-62, mem. exec. com., 1962—; mem. La. Bd. Nurse Examiners, 1962-66; co-chmn. health com. New Orleans C. of C., 1959-65; mem. Adv. Bd. Med. Spltys., 1962-72, mem. exec. com., 1968-70. Trustee Alton Ochsner Med. Found., sec.-treas., 1966-70, pres., 1970—. Served to capt. M.C., AUS, 1942-44. Diplomate Am. Bd. Proctology (bd. 1956—), Am. Bd. Colon and Rectal Surgery (v.p. 1960-61, pres. 1961-63). Fellow A.C.S. (gov. 1967—); mem. Am. (chmn. sect.), Orleans Parish, La. med. socs., Am. (pres. 1961-62), Mid West, Southeastern (pres. 1954) proctologic socs., New Orleans (treas. 1945), Southeastern, La., Alton Ochsner surg. socs., Alumni Alton Ochsner Med. Found. Fellows Assn. (1st pres. 1954-56), New Orleans Grad. Med. Assembly. Democrat. Methodist (chmn. ofcl. bd. 1957-59). Clubs: Louisiana, Round Table, International House (New Orleans). Mem. editorial bd. Jour. Diseases Colon and Rectum, 1957—. Home: 1634 Robert St New Orleans LA 70115 Office: 1514 Jefferson St New Orleans LA 70121

HINES, NEAL OLDFIELD, assn. exec., author; b. Crawfordsville, Ind., Nov 22, 1908; s. Linnaeus Neal and Bertha (Wiggs) H.; B.A., Ind. U., 1930; M.S., Northwestern U., 1941; m. Martha Perry, Sept. 17, 1946; children—Melissa, Martha Anne, Nancy. With newspapers in Ind., Wis., 1930-40; mem. journalism faculty U. Cal. at Berkeley, 1946-48; dir. publs., univ. relations, asst. to pres. U. Wash., Seattle, 1948-63; dir. information services Nat. Assn. Coll. and Univ. Bus. Officers, Washington, 1963—. Mem. AEC-U. Wash. Radiobiol.

Surveys, Bikini, Eniwetok, 1949, 56, Christmas Island, 1962. Served with USAAF, 1942-46. Mem. Phi Kappa Psi, Sigma Delta Chi. Republican. Methodist. Author: Proving Ground, An Account of the Radiobiological Studies in the Pacific, 1946-61, 1962; Atoms, Nature and Man, 1966; also articles, reports. Home: 136 Hesketh St Chevy Chase MD 20015 Office: 1 Dupont Circle Washington DC 20036

HINES, RENE, civil engr.; b. Cordell, Okla., July 4, 1912; s. David Claude and Emily Elizabeth (Craig) H.; student Okla. State U., 1929-32; m. Marjorie Marie Reich, Dec. 25, 1936; children—Peter Craig (dec.), John David. With Okla. State Hwy. Dept., 1932-—, div. engr., Clinton, Okla., 1964-—. Registered profl. engr., Okla. Mem. Nat., Okla. (chmn. Whichita Mt. chpt. 1963) socs. profl. engrs. Presbyn. (deacon 1969-—). Home: Box 574 Clinton OK 73601 Office: Box 118 Clinton OK 73601

HINKEL, HELEN MARY RYKOWSKI (MRS. JOSEPH LOYD HINKEL), librarian; b. Dayton, O., Oct. 28, 1911; d. John and Regina (Perzanowska) Rykowski; student U. Cal., at Berkeley, 1949, Mary Hardin Baylor Coll., 1959; m. Joseph Loyd Hinkel, Dec. 1, 1934; 1 son, Vossler Sigmund. Reference asst. Fort Meade, Md., 1950-51; library asst. Ft. Lewis, Wash., 1952-53, Fort Hood, Tex., 1957-58; head librarian Killeen Pub. Library, Killeen, 1959-70, library dir., 1970-—. Mem. Bell County Council on Alcoholism. Mem. C. of C., Am., Tex. library assns., Tex. Municipal League Librarians Assn., Tex., Killeen friends of the library, Nat. Council Cath. Women, Am. Bus. Women's Assn. (program chmn. 1969-70), Civil Air Patrol, Tex. Geneal. Soc., Internat. Soc. for Heraldry and Family Trees, Bell County Hist. Soc. Clubs: Killeen Garden, Killeen Area Music (reporter, historian). Home: 3200 Lake Ann Killeen TX 76541 Office: 711 North Gray Killeen TX 76541

HINKEL, JAMES EDWARD, city mgr.; b. Mt. Vernon, N.Y., July 1, 1920; s. Emory E. and Margaret (Ambrose) H.; B.E.E., N.C. State Coll., 1951; m. Thelma Morgan, Apr. 6, 1946; children—Laura Jeanne, David Michael, John Edward, Donald Charles. Cons. engr. B.O. Vannort Engrs., Inc., 1951-55; dir. utilities City of Monroe (N.C.), 1955-58, city mgr., 1958-—. Pres. Monroe Little League; dir. Piedmont Cities Assn. Served with USAAF, 1942-45. Registered profl. engr., N.C. Mem. I.E.E.E., Am. Pub. Works Assn., Am. Gas Assn., Nat. Soc. Profl. Engrs., Profl. Engrs. N.C., Carolian Govtl. Purchasing Assn. Rotarian (asst. sec.). Home: 305 Bay St Monroe NC 28110 Office: Box 4 Monroe NC 28110

HINN, HAROLD JOSEPH, grain co. exec.; b. Plainview Tex., Sept. 11, 1910; s. Albert George and Annie Lochie (Mayhugh) H.; student U. Wis., 1927-30, U. Tex., 1930-31; m. Evelyn Caughron, Sept. 8, 1951; children -Albert George, Carl Robert. With Harvest Queen Mill & Elevator Co., 1933-—, chmn. bd., 1940-50, pres., chief exec. officer, 1950-—; pres. Metall. Resources, Inc., 1960-—, Gibraltar Minerals Co., 1955-—, Internat. Metal Processing Corp., 1965-—, pres. Global Enterprises., Inc. 1969-—, Food Equipment, Inc., 1968-—, Power, Inc., 1970-—, Gen. Physics, Inc., 1971-—; dir. Nat. Data Communications, Inc., Whitehall Electronics Corp., Citizens Nat. Bank, Lubbock, Tex., Preston State Bank, Dallas. Bd. dirs. Tex. Technol. U., Lubbock, 1957-69; a founder, chmn. trustee High Plains Research Found., Plainview, Tex., 1956-—; trustee Tex. 4-H Youth Devel. Found. 1964-—. Home: 5915 Desco Dr Dallas TX 75225 Office: Republic Nat Bank Tower Dallas TX 75221

HINSCH, WILLIAM PAUL, ins. co. exec.; b. Bklyn., July 15, 1910; s. Henry Theodore and Elinor (Kuhn) H.; grad. high sch.; m. Eva Lee Harralson, Feb. 7, 1947; children—Patricia Ann, Melissa Ann. Asst. mgr. actuarial dept. Southland Life Ins. Co., Dallas, 1930-47; actuary, asst. sec., dir. So. States Life, Houston, 1947-49; with Am. Security Life Ins. Co. (formerly Am. Hosp. & Life Ins. Co.), San Antonio, 1949-—, vice chmn. bd., chmn. exec. com., 1972-—, mem. exec. com., 1959-—, mem. investment com., 1959-—. Mem. Interim Senate Ins. Study Com. Tex., 1970; mem. Hosps.-Ins.-Physicians Joint Adv. Com. Tex., 1955-—; mem. adv. com. policy approval guidelines for health ins. Tex. Bd. Ins., 1970-—; mem. Pres.'s Com. Employment of Handicapped, 1970, Gov.'s Com. Employment Handicapped, 1970. Bd. mgrs. Bexar County Hosp. Dist., San Antonio, 1971-—. Served with AUS, 1943-45. Mem. Tex. Life Conv. (bd. dirs. 1969-70), San Antonio C. of C. (vice chmn. med. devel. com. 1971, mem. health services task force 1972, publs. adv. com. 1972), Conf. Actuaries in Public Practice, Actuaries Club Southwest (exec. com. 1953-54, 57-58), Am. Acad. Actuaries, Ins. Soc. U. Tex. (hon.), Health Ins. Assn. Am., Tex. Health Ins. Assn. (bd. dirs. 1958-—, pres. 1958), Health Ins. Council. Methodist. Home: PO Box 2341 San Antonio TX 78298 Office: PO Box 2341 San Antonio TX 78298

HINSHAW, LERNER BRADY, physiologist; b. San Diego, June 9, 1921; s. Lerner A. and Ruth A. (Brady) H.; B.A., U. So. Cal., 1949, M.S., 1952, M.A., 1953, Ph.D., 1955; postgrad. U. Minn., 1955-61; m. Alice E. Larson, June 28, 1946; children—Mark L., Carol J., Roger W., Paul B. Instr., asst, prof. U. Minn. Med. Sch., 1955-61; research physiologist Civil Aeromed. Research Inst., FAA, Oklahoma City, 1961-65; physiologist prof. physiology VA Hosp., U. Okla. Med. Center, Oklahoma City, 1965-—; prof. Oklahoma City U., 1965-—. Served from pvt. to capt., with C.E., AUS, 1942-46. Mem. Am. Physiol. Soc., Western Clin. Soc., A.A.A.S., Am. Soc. Nephrology, Soc. Exptl. Biol. Medicine, Am. Soc. Pharm. Exptl. Therapeutics, Am. Heart Assn. (mem. council on circulation), Sigma Xi. Presbyn. Contbr. articles in field to profl. jours. Home: 401 Merkle Dr Norman OK 73069 Office: 921 NE 13th St Oklahoma City OK 73104

HINSON, RUSSELL CORTEZ, judge; b. Moss, Tenn., Feb. 12, 1926; s. H.B. and Jewell (Yates) H.; B.S., Tenn. Poly. Inst., 1948; LL.B., Vanderbilt U., 1951; m. Earlyne Reed, May 9, 1947; 1 dau., Marjorie Jane. Admitted to Tenn. bar, 1951; practiced in Nashville, 1951-52, Chattanooga, 1959-63; claims adjustor, claims mgr. U.S. Fidelity & Guaranty Co., 1952-59; mem. firm Wood & Wheat, Chattanooga, 1959-63; judge Gen. Sessions Ct., Hamilton County, Tenn., 1963-68, Criminal Ct., 6th Jud. Circuit, Chattanooga, 1968-—. Trustee, Greater Chattanooga Children's Home. Mem. Tenn. (various coms.), Chattanooga (various coms.) bar assns., Am. Legion, V.F.W. Elk, Toastmaster (pres. Chattanooga, 1967, area gov., 1968). Club: Chattanooga Civitan (dir. 1966-69). Home: 3417 Audubon Dr Chattanooga TN 37411 Office: Hamilton County Courthouse Chattanooga TN 37402

HINTON, C. SNOW, mcht., mayor; b. Tuscaloosa, Ala., Dec. 10, 1918; s. Clarence S. and Mae (Auxford) H.; student U. Ala., 1937-40; m. Marilyn Morgan, Oct. 26, 1946; children—Margaret (Mrs. John Gary Hogue). Pat. Owner Diamond Sundry, Inc., Tuscaloosa, 1946-—; mayor City of Tuscaloosa, 1969-—; dir. City Nat. Bank, Tuscaloosa. City commr., Tuscaloosa, 1967-—. Served with AUS, 1941-46. Mem. C. of C. Baptist. Mason (Shriner), Rotarian. Home: 28 The Downs Tuscaloosa AL 35401 Office: City Hall Tuscaloosa AL 35401

HIPKENS, THEODORE PETTY, health care adminstr.; b. Syracuse, N.Y., Dec. 14, 1913; s. Ernest F. and Fanny (Petty) H.; B.S., N.Y. State Coll. Forestry, 1937; postgrad. Syracuse U., 1937-38; m. Norma E. Hitchings, May 26, 1939; children&Robert, Anne, Henry. Tchr. high sch., N.Y., 1939-41; civilian instr. U.S. Army Air Force, Maxwell Field, 1941-42; rehab. exec. VA, Bath, N.Y., 1946-51; rehab. adminstr. United Mineworkers Welfare and Retirement Fund, Pitts., 1954-57; exec. dir. Home for Crippled Children, Pitts., 1957-66, sr. cons., 1966-—; pres. Appalachian Regional Hosps., Lexington, Ky., 1966-—. Bd. dirs. Commn. on Accreditation Rehab. Facilities; commr. Commn. on Edn. for Health Adminstrn. Served with USMCR, 1942-46, 51-54. Decorated Bronze Star. Fellow Am. Pub. Health Assn.; mem. Internat. Assn. Rehab. Facilities (dir.). Unitarian-Universalist. Home: 141 Elm St Versailles KY 40383 Office: Jordan Bldg Lexington KY 40503

HIPP, HOWELL EDSEL, sch. adminstr.; b. Saluda, S.C., Mar. 2, 1925; s. Wilbert Airel and Willie Mae (Fulmer) H.; A.B., Wofford Coll., 1949; M. Edn., Furman U., 1956; postgrad. U. Ga., summers 1963-66; m. June Annise Cloyd, Jan. 1, 1950; children—Rodney, Stanley. Prin., Inman (S.C.) Elementary Sch., 1950-54, prin. high sch., 1954-55; prin. Chapman High Sch., Inman, 1956-58, Inman Jr. High Sch., 1955-56; dir. instrn. Dist. One Schs., Spartanburg County, S.C., 1958-68, supt. schs., 1968-—. Cons. S.C. Migrant Edn., 1970-—; mem. S.C. Testbook Com., 1967-69; counselor Epworth Children's Home, 1949-50; mem. Spartanburg County White House Conf. on Children and Youth, 1970; mem. S.C. Com. for Funding under Title 6, Elementary Sch. Edn. Act, 1970-—; chmn. edn. Spartanburg County United Fund, 1967. Bd. dirs. Charles Lee Center for Handicapped Children, Spartanburg County Speech and Hearing Clinic, Spartanburg County Tech. Edn. Center. Served with USNR, 1943-46. Mem. Spartanburg County Supts. Assn. (chmn., 1971-72), S.C. Instrnl. TV Adv. Council (chmn. 1971-72, regional chmn. 1967-—), Nat., S.C., Spartanburg County (pres. 1955-56) edn. assns., Am., S.C. assns. sch. adminstrs. Methodist (chmn. bd. 1971-72, lay speaker 1970-—). Rotarian. Home: 25 W Miller St Inman SC 29349 Office: Box 218 Campobello SC 29322

HIRSCH, ARNOLD HARRY, public utility cons.; b. Phila., Dec. 25, 1895; s. Julius and Fanny (Krouse) H.; C.E. with honors, U. Pa., 1918; postgrad. Temple Law Sch., 1924-26; m. Ann B. Fieldstone, Apr. 9, 1916; children—Walter, Edwin P. Admitted to Pa. bar, 1928, U.S. Supreme Ct. bar, 1944; sales engr., indsl. rep. Phila. Electric Co., 1920-30; practice engring., law as pub. utility cons. to regulatory commns., municipalities, indsl. consumers in U.S. and Can., 1930-—; rate expert, chief pub. utilities OPA, Washington, 1943-47. Hon. citizen New Orleans; hon. col. gov.'s staff State of La. Mem. Am., Fed., Phila. bar assns., Am. Judicature Soc. Mason (life). Club: Nat. Lawyers (founder) (Washington). Author tech. articles on rate-making. Home: 4501 Connecticut Av Washington DC 20008 Office: Nat Press Bldg Washington DC 20004

HIRSCHFELD, GENE WOLFE, educator; b. N.Y.C., Apr. 21, 1917; s. Herman Marcus and Esther (Orange) H.; B.A., N.Y. U., 1937, D.D.S., 1940; M.S., Old Dominion Coll., 1968; m. Mary Chenman, Sept. 23, 1943; children—Esther (Mrs. Nathaniel Cohen), Richard, JoAnn. Intern oral surgery Cumberland Hosp., 1940-41; pvt. practice dentistry, Norfolk, Va., 1945-66; dir. schs. of dental hygiene and assisting Old Dominion U., Norfolk, 1966-—, prof. dental hygiene, 1967-—. Mem. dental inst. com. Greater Norfolk area, 1967-—; mem. statewide com. on curriculum for dental aux. edn. Va. Bd. Higher Edn., 1967-—; cons. health careers Norfolk city schs., 1971-—, S.E. Va. Planning Commn., 1971-—; mem. Norfolk City Health subcom., 1968-—; mem. health services div. Norfolk Model City neighborhood project, 1968-69; mem. Norfolk City Citizens' Com. on Voluntarism and Urban Life Project, 1970-71. Served with AUS, 1942-45. Fellow Internat. Coll. Dentists, Va. Dental Assn. (mem. edn. com. 1967-—); mem. Am. Legion, Jewish War Vets., Nat. Conf. Christians and Jews. Jewish religion (dir. temple 1946-—). Mem. B'nai B'rith. Home: 7320 Glenroie Av Norfolk VA 23505 Office: Tech Bldg Old Dominion Univ Norfolk VA 23508

HIRSCHMAN, MAX ABRAHAM, govt. ofcl.; b. Hudson, N.Y., Nov. 9, 1916; s. Paul Carmen and Yetta (Kranz) H.; B.S. cum laude, Coll. City N.Y., 1938, M.S., 1940; J.D., George Washington U., 1947, LL.M., 1948; J.S.D., Guam Law Sch., 1950; m. Jean M. Goldman, Sept. 15, 1949; children—Edward, Gale Phyllis, Alfred. Admitted to D.C. bar, 1947. Guam bar, 1951; practiced in D.C., 1947-49, Guam, 1950-51; chief operations analysis office Hdqrs. Alaskan Command, Elmendorf AFB, Alaska, 1961-63; dir. cost and econ. analysis div. U.S. Dept. Navy, Washington, 1963-66; br. mgr. systems analysis div. Naval Facilities Engring. Command, Washington, 1966-69; supervising operations research analyst Office Planning and Research, Bur. Customs, Washington, 1969-—. Cons. Inter-Am. Devel. Assos., Inc., 1951-60; lectr. econs. Catholic U., 1949; U. Alaska, 1961-63. Mem. Operations Research Soc. Am., Washington Operations Research Council, Chapel Square Civic Assn. Democrat. Jewish religion. Home: 4605 Holborn Av Annandale VA 22003 Office: Office of Planning and Research Bureau of Customs Washington DC 20036

HIRSHEY, CHARLES EDWARD, educator; b. Conneaut, O., Sept. 4, 1913; s. Nicholas J. and Emelia (Koski) H.; A.B., Findlay Coll., 1936; M.Ed., U. Pitts., 1939, Ed.D., 1960; m. Marjorie J. Cameron, 1937; children— Shirley, Charles. Tchr., coach Conneaut Schs., 1936-47, pub. schs., Fla., 1947-57; supt. schs. Eglin AFB, 1957-62, Kenston Sch. Dist., Chagrin Falls, O., 1962-64, Franklin (Pa.) Schs., 1964-66; prof. Clarion State Coll., 1966-67; prof., head dept. edn. The Citadel, 1967-—; cons. Named to Findlay Coll. Athletic Hall of Fame, 1971. Mem. N.E.A., Am. Assn. Sch. Adminstrs., S.C. Edn. Assn., Assn. Tchr. Educators, Phi Delta Kappa, Alpha Kappa Delta. Mason (Shriner). Home: Box 744 Charleston SC 29402

HIRST, JOHN MENDEL, med. entomologist, educator; b. Indiana, Pa., Sept. 8, 1908; s. Charles Francis and Edith (Herpel) H.; B.S., Bethany Coll., 1932; M.S., U. Pitts., 1938, Ph.D., 1941; m. Hazel Catherine Rogers, Feb. 3, 1933; children—Robert Charles, Betty Sue (Mrs. Charles E. Beauchamp). Commd. lt. U.S. Navy, 1942, advanced through grades to capt., 1962; entomolgist Disease Vector Control Center, Jacksonville, Fla., 1947-52, Alameda, Cal., 1952-57, med. entomologist Pacific area Preventive Medicine Unit, Pearl Harbor, Hawaii, 1957-59, head preventive medicine div. Naval Med. Sch., Nat. Naval Med. Center, Bethesda, Md., 1959-65, chief entomology div. Naval Med. Field Research Lab., Camp Lejeune, N.C., 1965-70; tchr. sci. Platts Acad., Winter Park, Fla., 1971-—. Mem. Fla. Anti-Mosquito Assn. (pres. 1958), Am. (pres. 1958), N.C. (pres. 1969) mosquito control assns. Home and Office: 906 Golfside Dr Winter Park FL 32789

HIRST, JULIAN F., city ofcl. City mgr., Roanoke, Va. Office: City Hall Roanoke VA 24011*

HIRT, AL, musician; b. New Orleans, Nov. 7, 1922; s. Alois and Linda (Guepet) H.; student Loyola U., New Orleans, also Cin. Conservatory Music; m. Mary Patureau, Aug. 13, 1942; children—Mary Lee, Gretchen, Rebecca, Bridgid, Rachel, Stephen, Jennifer, Jefferson Davis. Profl. trumpet player, 1940-—; part owner Pier 600, night club, New Orleans, 1961-64; owner Al Hirt, night club, New Orleans, 1964- —; appeared Basin St. East, N.Y.C., Eden Roc Hotel, Miami, Fla., Greek Theatre, Los Angeles, Carter Barron Theatre, Washington, Pres. Kennedy's Inaugural Ball, Starlight Theatre, Kansas City, Mo., Riviera Hotel, Las Vegas, Palmer House, Chgo. and others; TV appearances on Dinah Shore, Ed Sullivan, Andy Williams, Jimmy Dean, Perry Como shows and others; appeared in movies World by Night, Lovers Must Learn, has made many recs., Honey in the Horn, Java entitled him to gold record; part owner New Orleans Saints Football Team. Served with AUS, 1942-46. Office: 801 American Bank Bldg New Orleans LA 70130 also 7540 Canal Blvd New Orleans LA

HISLOP, RICHARD WALTER, supt. schs.; b. Gilmanton, N.H., Aug. 25, 1923; s. Robert Willis and Bertha Mae (Ellis) H.; B. Edn., Plymouth State Coll., 1951, M.Ed., 1962; D. Ed., U. Va., 1969; m. Marjorie Phelon, May 14, 1955; children—Claire, Walter, Wendy Sue, Mark. Supt. schs. N.H. Supervisory Union # 7, Colebrook, 1966-68; dir. U. Va. Sch. Gen. Studies, 1968-69; div. supt. Bristol (Va.) City Schs., 1969-—. Advisor, cons. Office Edn. div. Health Edn. and Welfare, Phila., 1971-—. Search pilot Civil Air Patrol, 1967-—. Bd. dirs. Bristol Assn. Retarded Children. Served with AUS, 1943-46. DuPont scholar, 1964-65; recipient Outstanding Service award Bristor Assn. for Retarded Children, 1971. Mem. Am., Va. assns. sch. adminstrs., Nat., Va. edn. assns., Va. Congress Parent-Tchrs. Assns. (life), Bristol C. of C. (planning and devel. bd. 1969-—), Phi Delta Kappa, Kappa Delta Pi. Methodist (adminstrv. bd. 1969-—). Kiwanian (edn. officer 1969-—). Home: 33 Duff Lane Bristol VA 24201 Office: Oak St Bristol VA 24201

HITCHCOCK, JAMES, clergyman, educator. Ordained as priest Roman Catholic Ch., now monsignor; supt. schs. Diocese of Nashville. Address: 2015 West End Av Nashville TN 37203*

HITT, CLIFFORD LEE, banker; b. Jane Lew, W.Va., Jan. 8, 1931; s. Clifford B. and Evelyn B. (Mowery) H.; student Miami pub. schs.; m. Charlene Burke, June 2, 1952; children—Sherrie Leigh, Bruce Lee. Asst. cashier 1st Nat. Bank of Miami (Fla.), 1955-62; exec. v.p. 1st Nat. Bank of San Angelo (Tex.), 1962-—. Served with USAF, 1951-54. Baptist. Club: West San Angelo Optimist (past pres., dir.). Home: 4101 Mercedes St San Angelo TX 76901 Office: Box 4031 San Angelo TX 76901

HITT, DAVID H., univ. med. center adminstr.; b. Ala.; M.S. in Commerce and Bus. Adminstrn., U. Ala., M. Hosp. Adminstrn., U. Minn. Hosp. adminstr., 1947-—; with Baylor U. Med. Center, 1952-—, successively various bus. positions, now co-chief mgmt. Pres. Dallas Hosp. Council, 1959. Fellow Am. Coll. Hosp. Adminstrn. (past regent), Am. Pub. Health Assn.; mem. Am. Hosp. Assn. (chmn. Council Financing), Alumni Assn. U. Minn. Program Hosp. Adminstrn. (past pres.). Club: Exchange (pres. 1957) (East Dallas). Contbr. numerous articles to profl. jours. Home: 7231 Twin Tree Lane Dallas TX 75214 Office: Baylor U Med Center Dallas TX 75219*

HITT, DICK, columnist Dallas Times-Herald. Address: 1101 Pacific St Dallas TX 75202*

HITT, EDWIN EARL, physician; b. Red Springs, Tex., Aug. 6, 1939; s. Preston Edwin and Josephine (Long) H.; A.A., Tyler (Tex.) Jr. Coll., 1959; student Eastern N.M. U., 1959-61; M.D., Tulane U., 1965; m. Patty Sue Kidd, Apr. 15, 1967; 1 dau., Felicia Dawn. Intern, Meth. Hosp., Dallas, 1965-66; gen. practice medicine, Dallas, 1968-—; mem. staff Dallas Meth. Hosp. Served with AUS, 1966-68. Named Outstanding Intern of Year, Meth. Hosp. Dallas, 1966. Mem. A.M.A., Tex., Dallas County med. socs., Silver Key, Phi Theta Kappa, Alpha Omega Alpha. Club: Oak Cliff Country (Dallas). Home: 6430 Autumn Woods Trail Dallas TX 75232 Office: 301 Westcliff Professional Bldg Dallas TX 75224

HITT, HOMER LEE, univ. chancellor; b. Comanchee, Tex., Apr. 22, 1916; s. Allen and Sammie (Daniel) H.; student Edinburg Jr. Coll., 1932-33; B.S., La. State U., 1935, M.A., 1937; Ph.D., Harvard, 1941; m. Douglas Grace Callari, Aug. 2, 1939; children—Dian (Mrs. James O. Sanders, III), Louvin (Mrs. Robert J. Skinner). Social scientist Bur. Agrl. Econs., U.S. Dept. Agr. 1939-41; asst. prof. sociology, asst., rural sociologist La. State U., Baton Rouge, 1941-44, asso. prof., asso. rural sociologist, 1945-47, prof. sociology, rural sociologist, head depts. sociology and rural sociology, 1947-—, acting dean grad. sch., 1952, clin. prof. preventive medicine Sch. Medicine, La. State U., 1953-54, asso. dean grad. sch., 1954-57, dean La. State U. in New Orleans, 1957-59, v.p. in charge, 1959-63, chancellor, 1963-—. Lectr. founds. social sci. Atlanta U., 1950. Chmn., Gov.'s Council on Mental Health Tng. and Research, 1957 -—, Dir. La. Health Council; chmn. budget com. Baton Rouge Community Chest. Bd. dirs. New Orleans Philharmonic Symphony Soc.; pres. bd. trustees WYES-TV Ednl. TV Found; council trustees Gulf South Research Inst. Served as ensign USNR, 1944-45. Recipient Robert Treat Paine Meml. award Harvard, 1937-38, Headline of Year award New Orleans Press Club, AFL-CIO. Grant-in-Aid, Social Sci. Research Council 1942. Mem. Am., Rural So. (pres. 1956-57) sociol. socs., Assn. So. Agrl. Workers (chmn. agrl. econs. and rural social. sect. 1953-54), Union Internat. pour L'Etude Sci. de la Population, Sociol. Research Assn., Population Assn. Am., Am. Acad. Polit. and Social Sci. La. State U. New Orleans Alumni Assn. (hon. life), Lambda Chi Alpha, Omicron Delta Kappa, Phi Kappa Phi, Pi Gamma Mu. Rotarian (past pres.). Clubs: Plimsoll, Round Table. Episcopalian. Author: (with A. L. Bertrand) Social Aspects of Hospital Planning in Louisiana, 1947; (with T. Lynn Smith) People of Louisiana, 1952. Editor. Rural Sociology 1952-53. Contbr. articles to sci. jours. Home: 6301 Paris Av New Orleans LA 70122

HIXSON, JACK ANDREW, journalist; b. Newport, Tenn., Jan. 1, 1923; s. Clarence Rupert (Jack) and Gypsy (Acton) H.; B.S., U. Tenn., 1949; postgrad. U. Mo., 1949-50. Instr. journalism Okla. Sch. Tech., Okmulgee, 1950-51; news editor Newport (Tenn.) Plain Talk, 1952-61; exec. dir. Newport Housing Authority, 1961-71; writer, photographer Cocke County Banner, Newport, 1971-—. Sec. Newport Regional Planning Commn., 1967-69. Served with AUS, 1943-45. Mem. C. of C. (dir. 1960-63). Baptist. Clubs: Smoky Mountain Country, Gatlinburg Ski, Rotary (charter pres. 1958, sec. 1966-—). Home: 1014 Jones Circle Newport TN 37821 Office: 312-14 Broadway Newport TN 37821

HO, SHUI, operations research analyst; b. Macao, Sept. 16, 1931; s. Tak Fai and Way-Chor (Fung) H.; B.E., U. Adelaide (Australia), 1955; S.M., Mass. Inst. Tech., 1957, Sc.D., 1963; m. Kean-Yue Chung, Feb. 14, 1959; 1 son, Vincent B. Engr. trainee Snowy Mountain Hydro-Electric Authority, Australia, summer 1953; structural engr. Engring. and Water Supply Dept., Adelaide, 1954-55; research asst. Mass. Inst. Tech., Cambridge, 1955-57, research asst. 1960-61; sr. draftsman Jackson & Moreland, Engrs., Inc., Boston, summer 1956, designer, 1957-58, jr. engr., 1958-60; tech. staff Mitre Corp., Bedford, Mass., 1962-66; profl. staff Center for Naval Analyses, Arlington, Va., 1966-—. Adj. prof. civil engring. Howard U., Washington, 1967-—. Mem. Operations Research Soc. Am., Am. Soc. C.E., Am. Soc. Engring. Edn., A.A.A.S., Inst. Engrs. Australia, Sigma Xi. Lutheran. Home: 9114 Ashmeade Dr Fairfax VA 22030 Office: 1401 Wilson Blvd Arlington VA 22209

HOADE, ETHEL ESTHER, govt. ofcl.; b. Phila., Apr. 18, 1911; d. Michael Charles and Ethel (Addy) Hoade; B.S. Simmons Coll., 1938; M.S. in Social Work, U. Tenn., 1959. Visitor, Mothers Assistance Fund, Phila., 1935-36; social worker Hahnemann Med. Coll. and

Hosp., 1938-40, dir. spcial service, 1940-42; case supr. Am. Nat. Red Cross, Lawson Gen. Hosp., Atlanta, 1943, hosp. field supr. S.E. area, 1943-45, ednl. cons., 1945-46, dept. dir., 1946-47, dir. Southeastern area, 1947-54; med. social cons. Fulton County Dept. Pub. Welfare, Atlanta, 1955-58; chief med. services specialist Bur. Family Services, Dept. Health, Edn. and Welfare, Washington, 1959, formerly acting chief program devel. br., med. services adminstrn. Social and Rehabilitative Services, asst. dir. program planning and devel. div., 1965-70, spl. asst. to asso. commr. med. services adminstrn., 1970—. Mem. Am. Pub. Health Assn., Am. Pub. Welfare Assn., Nat. Assn. Social Workers., Acad. Certified Social Workers. Contbr. articles to profl. jours. Home: 6101 Walhounding Rd Glen Echo Heights MD 20016 Office: 330 Independence Av Washington DC 20201

HOAGLAND, JIMMIE LEE, journalist; b. Rock Hill, S.C., Jan. 22, 1940; s. Mrs. James L. Estes; A.B. cum laude (S.C. Press Assn. scholar; J. Rin McKissick journalism scholar; Beauford Watts Ball journalism scholar; Burlington Indsl. Found. scholar), 1961; postgrad. (Rotary Found. fellow) U. Aix-en-Provence (France), 1961-62; m. Gretchen Hoagland, Oct. 10, 1970. Reporter Evening Herald, Rock Hill, summers 1958-60; copy editor N.Y. Times, Paris, France, 1964-66; city reporter Washington Post, 1966-68, African corr., hdqrs. Nairobi, Kenya, 1969—. Served with USAF, 1961-64. Recipient Pulitzer prize internat. reporting, 1971. Ford Found. fellow Columbia Grad. Sch. Journalism, 1968-69. Author: The Divided House; Civilizations in Conflict, 1972. Address: care Washington Post PO Box 7866 Nairobi Kenya*

HOBART, THOMAS FITZHUGH, civil engr., educator; b. Birmingham, Ala., Mar. 5, 1906; s. Lewis Alonzo and Frances (Fitzhugh) H.; B.S., Auburn U., 1927, C.E., 1944; m. Marion Johnson, Aug. 25, 1934; children— Elizabeth (Mrs. Fred Goad, Jr.), Thomas Fitzhugh. Field engr. Gulf States Steel Co., 1929-32; asst. div. engr. Ala. Hwy. Dept., 1932-46; v.p., gen. mgr. So. Amiesite Asphalt Co., Inc., North Birmingham, Ala., 1946-71; lectr. civil engring. dept. Auburn (Ala.) U., 1971—; dir. Vulcan Life & Accident Ins. Co. Mem. Auburn Alumni Assn. (past pres.), Am. Soc. C.E. (past pres. Ala. sect.), Asso. Gen. Contractors Am. (past pres., dir. Ala. br.), Ala. (past pres. contractors div.), Am. (past v.p. So. dist.) road builders assns. Home: 309 Kimberly Dr Auburn AL 36830

HOBBS, BILLY SEWELL, ednl. adminstr., mayor; b. Columbia, Tenn., Dec. 22, 1934; s. Wilburn S. and Ethel (Fox) H.; B.A., George Peabody Coll., 1956, M.A., 1957, LL.D., Burton Coll. and Sem., 1965; m. Jaska R. Moore, Sept. 5, 1953; children—Jeffrey Moore, Joseph Sewell, James Franklin. Tchr., Spring Hill (Tenn.) High Sch., 1956-58; prin. White House (Tenn.) High Sch., 1958—; mayor City of White House, 1971—. Magistrate, Sumner County Ct., 1972—. Mem. Tenn. Edn. Assn., Nat. Soc. for Study Edn., Kappa Phi Kappa, Phi Delta Kappa. Democrat. Baptist. Mason (32 deg., Shriner), Lion. Home: East Side Dr White House TN 37188

HOBBS, GARDNER J., ednl. adminstr.; b. Wrens, Ga., Oct. 7, 1932; s. Newman and Arlena (Robinson) H.; B.S., Savannah State Coll., 1957; M.A., Fish U., 1966; postgrad. Atlanta U., 1968-70; m. Gladys W. Whigham, Apr. 10, 1960. Sci. tchr., coach, Hancock County, Ga., 1957-59, Jefferson County High Sch., 1959-67; prin., Avera, Ga., 1968-69; prin. Wrens (Ga.) High Sch., 1969—; pres., dir. Twin Lakes, Inc. Research fellow Ia. State U., 1968. Served with AUS, 1953-54. Mem. N.A.A.C.P., N.E.A., Ga. Assn. Educators, Nat. Sci. Tchrs. Assn., Jefferson County Tchrs. Assn. (pres. 1968-70), Kappa Alpha Psi. Mason. Club: Century. Home: PO Box 526 Wrens GA 30833 Office: Wrens High Sch Griffith St Wrens GA 30833

HOBBS, NED PETER, optometrist; b. Worden, Ill., Dec. 26, 1921; s. Kermit Ludolph and Marie (Massa) H.; Dr. Optometry, Ill. Coll. Optometry, 1947; postgrad. U. S.C.; m. Kathryn Louise Stonecypher, Sept. 16, 1941; children—Steven Craig, Karen Susan, Michael Jeffrey. Pvt. practice optometry, Darlington, S.C., 1947—. Pres.-elect S.C. Bd. Examiners Optometry, 1958-63; county commr. of Darlington County, 1964—; coroner Darlington County, 1969—. Dir. All Risks Ins. Co. Mem. med. adv. bd. Darlington County chpt. Polio Found., 1960-63; internat. chmn. equivalent standards com. Internat. Assn. Bds. Examiners Optometry; pres. S.C. Bd. Examiners of Optometrists and Opticians; pres. Pee Dee Perpetual Care Cemetery Assn. Mem. Darlington City Council, 1950-52. Served from pvt. to capt., Med. Adminstrv. Corps, AUS, World War II; PTO. Named Citizen of Yr., Kiwanis Civic Club, 1950, Optometrist of South, So. Optometrist Jour., 1952, Optometrist of Year in S.C., 1966. Fellow Am. Acad. Optometry (pres. S.C. chpt. 1959-63); mem. Am., S.C. (pres. 1953-54) optometric assns., So. Council Optometrists (pres. 1958-59), Southeastern Optometry Congress (past sec.), Pee Dee Optometric Assn. (pres., optometrist of Year 1970), V.F.W., Am. Legion, Darlington C. of C., Royal Soc. Health, Optometric Extension Program, Am. Optometric Found. Baptist. Mason (Shriner), Elk, Lion (pres. 1949-50 Outstanding Lion of Year, Darlington 1950), Toastmaster (v.p. Darlington). Home: 420 James St Darlington SC 29532 Office: 161 Cashua St Darlington SC 29532

HOBBS, OLIVER KERMIT, farm equipment mfg. exec.; b. Hobbsville, N.C., Sept. 21, 1918; s. Ephriam J. and Sallie (Brown) H.; student pub. schs., Hobbsville; m. Frances Allsbrook Piland, June 14, 1941; children—Oliver Kermit, Cynthia Russell. Service rep. Sadler Music Co., Suffork, Va., 1939-42; service mgr. A.E. Sadler Co., Suffolk, 1945-49; gen. mgr. Shotton's Farm Service, Suffolk, 1949-58; dir. research and engring. Benthall Machine Co. Inc., Suffolk, 1958-63, dir., 1959-63; organizer, partner Hobbs Engring. Co., 1963-70; pres. Hobbs-Adams Engring. Co., 1970—. Cons. agrl. mech. devices, 1956—. Served with USNR, 1942-45; ETO. Recipient Horace Hayden Meml. trophy, 1954. Mem. Va. Farm Equipment Assn., Aircraft Owners and Pilots Assn., Woodmen of World, Suffolk-Nansemond C. of C., Suffolk-Nansemond Hist. Soc., Va. Mfrs. Assn., Internat. Platform Assn. Baptist. Clubs: Ruritan (Suffolk), Kings Fork (pres. Suffolk 1959). Patentee automotive and agrl. field. Designer mech. sampling devices, peanut harvesting equipment, automatic control devices, power transmission equipment. Home: 120 Elm St Suffolk VA 23434 Office: PO Box 1306 Suffolk VA 23434

HOBBS, RICHARD WHITE, lawyer; b. West Eminence, Mo., July 24, 1912; s. James Richard and Mary Ellen (White) H.; LL.B., J.D., Northwestern Coll. Law, 1940; LL.B., Ark. Law Sch., 1942; m. Louise Ann Redus, July 5, 1942. Admitted to Ark. bar, 1942; practiced in Hot Springs, 1946—; partner Hobbs & Longinotti, 1970—; lectr. Law Sci. Acad. Am., Law Sci. Found. Am. Chief dep. pros. atty. 18th Judicial Dist. Ark., 1949-52. Served to capt. USAAF, 1942-46. Decorated Bronze Star medal with 7 oak leaf clusters. Mem. Am. Bar Assn., Am., Ark. trial lawyers assns., Am. Judicature Soc. Episcopalian. Club: Exchange (past pres., past dist. dir.) (Hot Springs). Home: 115 Shelby St Hot Springs AR 71901 Office: Thompson Bldg Hot Springs AR 71901

HOBBY, DIANA POTEAT STALLINGS (MRS. WILLIAM PETTUS HOBBY, JR.), newspaper editor; b. N.Y.C., Apr. 22, 1931; d. Laurence and Helen (Poteat) Stallings; B.A., Radcliffe Coll., 1952; M.A. Georgetown U., 1955; m. William Pettus Hobby, Jr., Sept. 11, 1954; children—Laura, Paul, Andrew. Book editor Houston Post, 1957—. Home: 1506 South Blvd Houston TX 77006 Office: 2410 Polk Av Houston TX 77001

HOBBY, OVETA CULP (MRS. WILLIAM P. HOBBY), newspaper publisher; b. Killeen, Tex., Jan. 19, 1905; d. I.W. and Emma (Hoover) Culp; student Mary Hardin Baylor Coll., H.H.D., 1956; L.H.D., Bard Coll., 1950, Lafayette Coll., 1954; LL.D., Baylor U., Sam Houston State Tchrs. Coll., U. Chattanooga, 1943, Bryant Coll., Ohio Wesleyan U., 1953, Columbia, Smith Coll., Middlebury Coll., 1954, U. Pa., Colby Coll., 1955, Fairleigh Dickinson, Western Coll., 1956; D. Litt., Colo. Women's Coll., 1947, C.W. Post Coll., 1962; m. William P. Hobby, Feb. 23, 1931; children—William, Jessica (Mrs. Henry E. Catto, Jr.). Parliamentarian Tex. Ho. of Reps., 1926-31, incomplete terms 1939, 41, joined Houston Post as research editor, 1931, successively lit. editor, asst. editor, v.p., exec. v.p., exec. v.p. and editor, 1931-52, editor and pub., 1952-53, pres. editor, 1955-65, chmn. bd., editor, 1965—; dir. Gen. Foods Corp., sta. KPRC, KPRC-TV; chief women's interest sect. War Dept. Bur. Pub. Relations, 1941-42; apptd. dir. WAAC, 1942; commd. col. AUS, dir. WAC, 1943-45; fed. security adminstr., 1953; sec. Dept. Health, Edn. and Welfare, 1953-55; trustee Mut. Ins. Co. N.Y. Gov. A.R.C., 1950-55; nat. vice chmn. Am. Cancer Soc. campaign, 1949; pres. So. Newspaper Pubs. Assn., 1949; mem. Am. Design Awards com.; mem. nat. com. Am. Mus. Immigration, 1956; dir. nat. bd. United Cerberal Palsy. Mem. nat. adv. com. Citizens for Eisenhower, 1956; sponsor Clark Sch. for Deaf; mem. Coll. Commn. Diocese of Tex., 1956; trustee Rice U., Eisenhower Birthplace Meml. Park; mem. President's coms. on Employment Physically Handicapped, Civilian Nat. Honors; trustee Am. Assembly, 1957—, Eisenhower Exchange Fellowships; bd. dirs. Houston Symphony Soc.; mem. S.W. adv. bd Inst. Internat. Edn.; mem. Com. of 75, U. Tex., 1958 —, mem. So. regional com. Marshall Scholarships, 1957—; mem. Carnegie Commn. of Ednl. TV; mem. Rockfeller Bros. Fund Spl. Studies Project; adv. bd. George C. Marshall Research Found., 1960—; nat. council Eleanor Roosevelt Meml. Found.; bd. dirs. Com. for Econ. Devel.; mem. nat. bd. devel. Sam Rayburn Found.; mem. Crusade for Freedom, Inc., 1958—, Bus. Com. for Arts, Inc., 1967 —, Nat. Met. Opera; bd. dirs. Corp. for Pub. Broadcasting, Tex., 1968-72, Heart Assn.; vis. com. Grad. Sch., Edn., Harvard, 1961-67; trustee Soc. Rehab. Facially Disfigured, People to People; ch. mem. Acad. of Tex., 1969—. Recipient Distinguished Service Medal, 1944; Philippine Mil. Merit medal, 1947; Honor Award for Distinguished Service in Journalism, U. Mo., 1950; Pub. of Yr. award Headliners Club, 1960; Living History award Research Inst. Am., 1960, Honor award Nat. Jewish Hosp., 1962; award for advancement and diffusion of knowledge and understanding Carnegie Corp., 1967. Mem. Gamma Alpha Chi (hon. vice chmn.). Episcopalian. Clubs: Headliners; Houston, Bayou, Ramada, Junior League (Houston). Author: Mr. Chairman (parliamentary law textbook); also syndicated column same title. Home: Houston TX 77001 Office: Houston Post 2410 Polk Av Houston TX 77001

HOBBY, WILLIAM PETTUS, newspaper editor; b. Houston, Jan. 19, 1932; s. William Pettus and Oveta (Culp) H.; B.A., Rice U., 1953; m. Diana Poteat Stallings, Sept. 11, 1954; children—Laura Poteat, Paul William, Andrew Purefoy, Katherine Pettus. Asst. sec.-treas. Houston Post, 1957-59, asso. editor, 1959-60, mng. editor, 1960-63, exec. editor, 1963—, exec. v.p. Houston Post Co., 1963-65, pres. 1965—; vice chmn. Channel Two TV Co., KPRC Radio Co., 1970—. Parliamentarian, Tex. Senate, 1959; nominated for lt. gov. Tex., 1972. Bd. dirs. Child Guidance Center Houston, 1957-63, pres., 1960-62. Served to lt. (j.g.) USNR, 1953-57. Mem. Am. Soc. Newspaper Editors, Tex. Hunter and Jumper Assn. (dir. 1953—, pres. 1959-61), U.S. Equestrian Team, Inc. (v.p. 1959-60), Houston C. of C. (dir.). Home: PO Box 326 Houston TX 77001 Office: 4747 Southwest Freeway Houston TX 77001

HOBSON, T. FRANK, JR., judge; b. St. Petersburg, Fla., Dec. 2, 1928; s. Tolbert Francis and Mabel (Miller) H.; student Wake Forest Coll., 1946-47, U.S. Naval Acad., 1947-48; A.B., John B. Stetson U., 1951, LL.B., 1952;; m. Janet Louise Funk, Oct. 29, 1949 (div. May, 1959); children—Margot Kim, Melissa Catherine; m. 2d, Janet Susan Rothermel; children—Keller Frances, T. Frank III, Thomas Carroll, Susan Elizabeth. Asst. atty. gen. State of Fla., 1952; gen. counsel Haven Ins. Co., 1954-58; practiced in St. Petersburg, 1954-60; dep. commr. for Fla. Indsl. Commn., 1959-60; circuit judge, St. Petersburg, 1960-64; partner firm Meros, Hobson & Wilkinson, 1964-65; judge 2d Dist. Ct. of Appeal, 1965—, chief judge, 1969—. Dir. v.p. Haven Ins. Co. 1956-58. Trustee Julia and Dick Pope Found., Inc. Served to capt. USMCR, 1952-54. Mem. Fla. Bar, Am., St. Petersburg bar assns. Democrat. Baptist. Home: 4180 Narvarez Way S St Petersburg FL 33712 Office: Dist Ct Appeal 2d Dist Memorial Blvd Lakeland FL 33801

HOCHMAN, ROBERT FRANCIS, educator; b. Chgo., May 1, 1928; s. Francis and Anna (Holak) H.; B.S. in Metallurgy, U. Notre Dame, 1950, M.S., 1954, Ph.D., 1959; m. Carolyn Bennett, June 22, 1960; 1 son, Robert Francis. Instr., U. Notre Dame, 1957-58, Mich. State Extension Service, Benton Harbor, 1957-58; asst. prof. Ga. Inst. Tech., Atlanta, 1959-62, asso. prof. metallurgy Sch. Chem. Engring., 1962-68, prof., 1968—; dir. research stress corrosion Advanced Research Project Agy., Dept. Def. 1966-71, asso. dir. metallurgy, 1971—, Advanced Research Project Agy. Dept. Agy. Tng. grantee in dental materials, 1963—; cons. Zimmer Mfg. Co., Warsaw, Ind., 1957—, Lockheed-Ga. Co., Marietta, Ga., 1964—. Chmn., editor procs. Forum for Nat. Commn. on Materials Policy, 1972. Pres., Confraternity Christian Doctrine program Holy Spirit Parish, Atlanta, 1967-69. Served with AUS, 1951-52; Korea. Decorated D.S.M.; NSF grantee to attend internat. conf. metallic corrosion, Moscow, USSR, 1966. Mem. Nat. Assn. Corrosion Engrs. (chmn. nat. edn. com. 1963-67, dir. 1963-68), Am. Soc. Metals (mem. edn. com. 1962-65; chmn. So. metal conf. 1961, 69), Am. Soc. Testing Materials, Soc. for Non-Destructive Testing, Nat. Inst. Dental Research, Sigma Xi. Club: Atlanta Notre Dame (pres. 1961-63, dir. 1963—). Editor: (with E. Muller and B. Ralph) Field Ion Microscopy in Physical Metallurgy and Corrosion. Contbr. articles to profl. jours. Patentee in field. Research in phys. metallurgy, med. materials, fundamentals of corrosion, metal deterioration. Home: 3186 River Heights Dr Smyrna GA 30080

HOCKERSMITH, FORREST DAVITTE, govt. ofcl.; b. Nashville, Sept. 19, 1906; s. Thomas Milton and Melissa (Davitte) H.; B.S. in Civil Engring., Ga. Inst. Tech., 1932; m. Bessie Florence Sisk, Feb. 9, 1935; children— Thomas Edward, Joseph Davitte, Teresa Ann. With W. Horace Williams Co., Inc., Tavares, Fla., 1926-27, Ga. Hwy. Bd., 1928-32, Spur Distbg. Co., 1932-34; asst. sci. aide U.S. Coast and Geodetic Survey, 1934-35; sr. constrn. engr. WPA, 1935-43; asst. dir. indsl. projects div. FEA, 1943-46; asst. dir. material div. Office Housing Expediter, 1946-47; cons. engr., Washington, 1947-48; with Dept. Commerce, 1948—, acting and dep. adminstr. Bus. and Def. Services Adminstrn., 1965-66, dep. adminstr., 1966—. Mem. com. mgmt. Fairfax County (Va.) YM-69, acting and dep. adminstr., 1969—. Mem. com. mgmt. Fairfax County (Va.) YMCA, 1958-61, mem. fund drive com., 1960-61. Recipient Silver medal Dept. Commerce, 1961, Gold medal, 1967. Methodist (chmn. ofcl. bd. 1958-61). Home: 4209 Penner Lane Fairfax VA 22030 Office: Dept of Commerce 14th and Constitution Av NW Washington DC 20230

HOCOTT, JOE BILL, chem. engr., educator; b. nr. Big Flat, Ark., Sept. 19, 1921; s. Jeiks Edmonds and Frances Clara (Berry) H.; B.S., U. Ark., 1945; M.S., Okla. State U., 1951. Insp., Maumelle Ordnance Works, U.S. Army Ordnance Dept., Little Rock, 1942-43; head sci. dept. Joe T. Robinson High Sch., Little Rock, 1945-46; instr. chemistry U. Tulsa, 1946-47; teaching fellow Okla. A. and M. Coll., Stillwater, 1947-49; research chem. engr. Deep Rock Petroleum Corp., Cushing, Okla., 1950, Kerr-McGee Oil Corp., Stillwater, 1951; chem. engr. cons. Joe Bill Hocott, Little Rock, 1952-55, 63—; med. technician U. Ark. Med. Center, Little Rock, 1955-56, research asso., 1956-57, instr. internal medicine, 1957-62; head chemistry dept. Little Rock Central High Sch., 1963-66; head sci. dept. Met. Vocational-Tech. High Sch., Little Rock, 1967—. Asst. scoutmaster Boy Scouts Am., 1945-46, troop committeeman, 1945-46, 57-58, neighborhood commr., 1969-70. Bd. dirs. Ark. Jr. Sci. and Humanities Symposium, 1965-72, asst. dir., 1972. Mem. Am. Inst. Chem. Engrs., Nat. Soc. Profl. Engrs., Ark., Ark. Jr. (dist. dir. 1966—) acads. sci., Sigma Xi, Phi Lambda Upsilon, Unitarian. Home: 1010 Rice St Little Rock AR 72202 Office: 7701 Scott Hamilton Dr Little Rock AR 72206

HODES, RICHARD, state ofcl. Chmn. Fla. Health and Rehab. Service, Tampa. Address: 305 Morgan St Tampa FL 33602*

HODGE, LESTER CLARK, JR., orthodontist; b. Gainesville, Fla., Aug. 3, 1936; s. L. C. and Anne (Gocek) H.; student U. Fla., 1954-57; D.D.S., Emory U., 1961, M.S., 1965; m. Betty Jo Hunter Mar. 25, 1958; children—Lester Clark III, Shannon Lee. Pvt. practice orthodontics, Gainesville, 1965—. Vice-chmn. United Fund campaign, Gainesville, 1968, chmn., 1970, also bd. dirs. Mem. Gainesville Plan Bd., 1967-70; mem. North Central Planning Council, 1968—. Served to capt., Dental Corps, AUS, 1961-63. Recipient Distinguished Service award Jr. C. of C., 1969. Mem. Am. Orthondontic Soc., Am. Dental Assn., Sigma Chi, Xi Psi Phi. Home: Callison Rd Gainesville FL 32601 Office: 3500 SW 2d Av Gainesville FL 32601

HODGELL, MURLIN RAY, univ. dean; b. Mankato, Kan., Jan. 6, 1924; s. Ray Darias and Lora (Overman) H.; student Washburn U., 1943, U. Ia., 1944; B.S., Kan. State U., 1949; M.S., U. Ill., 1952; Ph.D., Cornell U., 1959; m. Bille Ro Jean Seward, July 20, 1947; children—Janet, Kristen, Kevin. Extension architect Kan. State U., 1949-50; asst. prof. agrl. engring. U. Ill., 1950-55; mem. housing research staff Cornell U., 1955-56; asso. prof. architecture Kan. State U., 1957-63; chmn. dept. city and regional planning Rutgers U., 1963-64; dir. Sch. Architecture U. Neb., 1964-69; dean Coll. Environmental design U. Okla., Norman, 1969—. Cons. Hodgell Assos. in Architecture, Planning, Engring., 1960-69, Rockefeller Found., 1967-68. City planning dir., Manhattan, Kan., 1957, planning commr., 1958-63; chmn. Riley County, Kan., Nat. Found. and March of Dimes, 1960-62. Served to lt. (j.g.) USNR, 1943-46. Named Man of Year, Manhattan Jr. C. of C., 1959, Kan. Outstanding Young Man of Year, Jr. C. of C., 1960; recipient Distinguished Community Service award Lane-Bryant Found., 1960. Registered profl. engr., Kan. Mem. Am. Inst. Planners, A.I.A., Am. Soc. C.E., Tau Sigma Delta, Sigma Tau. Author: Contemporary Farmhouses, 1956; Zoning, 1958. Home: 712 Lindsay Av Norman OK 73069

HODGENS, PAUL MORTON, SR., hosp. adminstr.; b. Albertville, Ala., Dec. 18, 1925; s. John C. and Fannie V. (Morton) H.; diploma Snead Jr. Coll., 1946-47; B.S. in Sci., Jacksonville State Coll., 1948; postgrad. Auburn U.; m. Mary Grace Wilson, July 5, 1944; children—Lisa Grace, Paul Morton, John Bart. Med technologist Anniston (Ala.) Meml. Hosp., 1947-58; insp. Ala Bd. Health, Oneonta, 1948-50; chief lab. technologist Sand Mountain Infirmary, Albertville, 1950-56, x-ray technician, 1953-56, purchasing agt., 1954-56; adminstr. Boaz (Ala.)-Albertville Hosp., 1956—. Trustee Albertville Schs. Served with USNR, 1944-45. Mem. Am. Coll. Hosp. Adminstrs., Ala. Hosp. Assn. (trustee), N.E. Ala. Hosp. Council (res. 1958-60). Home: 311 Nixon St Albertville AL 35950 Office: PO Box 338 Boaz AL 35957

HODGES, CECIL MOYE, banker; b. Oconee, Ga., Oct. 27, 1897; s. Charlie Marshall and Berta Louise (Moye) H.; student Ga.-Ala. Bus. Coll., 1917-18; m. Mattie Louise Smith, Oct. 23, 1924; children—Mary Patsy (Mrs. Thomas Aaron Hutcheson), Rosa Ann (Mrs. Donovan Dewitt Kinnett), Cecil Moye. Founded Cecil Hodges Lumber Co., Sandersville, Ga., 1919, pres., 1919-71; pres. Cecil Farms, Inc., Sandersville, 1961, Washington Land & Timber, Inc., Sandersville, 1965; dir. George D. Warthen Bank, Sandersville. Mem. Forestry Commn. Washington County, Ga., 1960—. Mem. Central Ga. council Boy Scouts Am., Macon, 1952—. Bd. dirs. Hodges Found. Recipient award Central Ga. council Boy Scouts Am., 1954, citation Washington County Forestry Commn., 1963. Mem. Christian Ch. (elder). Mason (33 deg., Shriner), Lion (past pres. Sandersville). Home: PO Box 70 Oconee GA 31067 Office: PO Drawer B Sandersville GA 31082

HODGES, EDWARD GREY, JR., TV prodn. co. exec.; b. Miami, Fla., Dec. 11, 1937; s. Edward Grey and Shirley Louise (Varner) H.; B.S. in Indsl. Mgmt., Ga. Inst. Tech., 1960; certificate in exec. mgmt. N.Y. U., 1969; m. Eugenia Williams Morrison, Sept. 17, 1960; children—Christopher Grey, Jeffrey Howard, Michael Patrick. Partner, Diehl Assos., Inc., editorial cons. for mags., Atlanta, 1962-63; So. editor Miller Freeman Publs., Atlanta, 1963-64, mng. editor, N.Y.C., 1964-65; mgr. publs. Previews div. Reeves Telecom Corp., N.Y.C., 1965-66, marketing mgr. Prodn. Services dir., 1966-67, v.p. marketing, 1967-68, sr. v.p. Prodn. Services div., 1968-70; mng. dir. Jefferson Prodns., Charlotte, N.C., 1971—. Served as 1st lt. USMCR, 1960-62. Mem. Videotape Prodn. Assn. (charter; treas. 1969—), Nat. Indsl. TV Assn. (standards com. 1970—). Presbyn. (deacon 1968—). Home: 4242 Chevington Rd Charlotte NC 28211 Office: Jefferson Productions 1 Julian Price Pl Charlotte NC 28208

HODGES, HENRY AMBROSE, ret. coll. adminstr.; b. Marquez, Tex., Dec. 30, 1903; s. Henry and Eula (Grayson) H.; B.A., U. Tex., 1926, M.A., 1927; postgrad. U. Chgo., 1945-46, U. Wis., 1935-36; LL.D., Howard Payne U., 1963; m. Ella Fay Gregg, Aug. 30, 1930; 1 son, Henry Robert. Tchr. rural schs. Tex., 1921-22; instr. Victoria Jr. Coll., 1927-28, Westmoorland Coll., San Antonio, 1928-29; prin. Marquez High Sch., 1929-30; instr. Edinburg (Tex.) Jr. Coll., 1930-34, asso. dir., 1934-48, acting pres., 1942-45; dean Edinburg Regional Coll., 1948-60; dean Pan Am. Coll., Edinburg, 1960-65, acad. v.p., 1965-70. Dir., Rio Farms, Inc. Vice chmn. com. on pub. edn., schs. and colls. Am. Cancer Soc., 1967—. Fellow Tex. Acad. Sci.; mem. Am. Assn. Higher Edn., Tex. Assn. Colls., Tex. Tchrs. Assn., Alpha Chi. Baptist. Mason (Shriner). Rotarian (dist. gov. dist. 593, 1972-73). Home: 1307 S 13th St Box 296 Edinburg TX 78539

HODGES, JOHN GRADY, circuit judge; b. Atlanta, Aug. 29, 1911; s. Joseph Harper and Alice (Parlin) H.; student Emory U., 1930-32; J.D., Georgetown U., 1938; m. Mary Ruth Betts, Aug. 18, 1950; children—John Grady, Robert Collier, Jane Betts. Admitted to Fla. bar, 1939; practiced in Tallahassee, 1939-41, Tampa, 1941-60; asst. U.S. atty. So. Dist. Fla., 1946-47; gen. counsel Fla. Beverage Dept., 1954-60; judge 13th Jud. Circuit Fla., Tampa, 1960-69, presiding judge, 1969-71. Chmn. explorer post program Boy Scouts Am.,

1965—, vice chmn. Bay Ridge council, 1964—. Bd. dirs. Travellers Aid, Police Athletic League. Served to comdr. USNR, 1942-46. Mem. Am., Fla., Hills County bar assns., Am. Legion. Episcopalian. Kiwanian (dir.), Elk (presiding justice). Clubs: University, Gasparilla Krew, Merrymakers, Palma Ceia Golf and Country. Home: 1626 Sunset Dr Tampa FL 33609 Office: County Court House Tampa FL 33602

HODGES, LORENTZ RYAN, JR., architect, engr.; b. Charleston, W.Va., Apr. 18, 1930; s. Lorentz Ryan and Mary Lavinia (Cabell) H.; B.S., Ga. Inst. Tech., 1957, B.Arch., 1958; m. Mary Susanne Fant, June 30, 1962; children—Lorentz Ryan III, Mary Elizabeth, James Fant. With Toombs-Amisano & Wells, Atlanta, 1958-61, Irving-Bowman & Assos., Charleston, W.Va., 1961-65, Washington, 1965-67; individual practice architecture, Alexandria, Va., 1967—. Active Belle Haven Civic Assn. Bd. dirs. Alexandria Boys Club, Mt. Vernon Recreation Assn. Served with USNR, 1951. Mem. A.I.A., Constrn. Specifications Inst., Va. Profls., Soc. Archtl. Historians. Club: Alexandria Optimist (dir.). Home: 1817 Edgehill Dr Alexandria VA 22307 Office: 116 Royal St Alexandria VA 22314

HODGES, PRICILLA DAWNE BERRY (MRS. JAMES W. HODGES), retail store exec.; b. Leaksville, N.C., Feb. 28, 1940; d. Willie Albert and Flora Hannah (Bryant) Berry; student Tri-City Night Sch., 1955-56; B.A., Western Carolina Coll., 1960; m. James W. Hodges, Aug. 26, 1960; children—Otis Albert, Helen Marie. Pvt. sec. Style-Knits, Inc., 1964-67; part owner Peg-to-pre Knits, Greensboro, N.C., 1967-68, Hodges Knits, Inc., Greensboro, N.C., 1968—; owner, Enterprise Fabrics, Greensboro, since 1968—. Tchr. piano and voice, Greensboro, 1961—. Mem. Am. Bus. Women's Assn. Presbyn. Club: Sedgefield Swim and Rachet (Greensboro). Home: 5803 High Point Rd Greensboro NC 27407 Office: Box 5052 Greensboro NC 27407

HODGES, RALPH B., judge; b. Anadarko, Okla., Aug. 4, 1930; s. Dewey E. and Pearl (Emenlisen) H.; B.A., Okla. Baptist U., 1952; LL.B., U. Okla., 1954; m. LaVerne M. Crain, Dec. 23, 1951; children— Chari Lynn, Mark B., Randall R. Admitted to Okla. bar, 1954; practice law, Durant, Okla., 1954-56; dist. atty., Bryan County, Okla., 1957-58; dist. judge Jud. Dist. 19, 1959-65; asso. justice Okla. Supreme Ct., Oklahoma City, 1965—. Mem. Durant Jr. C. of C. (past pres.). So. Legal Inst. (past pres.). Baptist. (chmn. bd. deacons). Mason (32 deg.), Odd Fellow, Kiwanian (past pres. Durant, Okla.). Home: 6101 N State St Oklahoma City OK 73105 Office: State Capitol Bldg Oklahoma City OK 73105

HODGES, RANDOLPH, state ofcl. Dir. Fla. bd. conservation, Tallahassee. Address: 107 W Gaines St Tallahassee FL 33611*

HODGIN, WILLIAM KENDRICK, county agrl. agt.; b. Santa Rita, N.M., Mar 27, 1923; s. William DeForrest and Herrise (Kendrick) H.; B.S. Tex. A. and M. U., 1948; m. Myra Nell Anders, Apr. 28, 1951; children—Wade K. Norris W. Ranch asst. mgr. Floyd Gage ranch, Chihuahua, Mexico, 1940-41; asst. county agr. agt. Fort Bend County, Richmond, Tex., 1948-51; county agr. agt. Goliad County, Goliad, Tex., 1951-52; farm mgr. C & M Ranch Co., Artesia, N.M., 1952-53; county agrl. agt. McMullen County, Tilden, Tex., 1954—. Served with AUS, 1943-46. Mem. Nat., Tex. (dist. dir. 1962-64) county agrl. agts. assns., Epsilon Sigma Phi (dist. dir. 1962-64). Mason, Lion (past pres.). Author: McMullen County Program; Production Guidelines for McMullen County. Home: PO Box 215 Tilden TX 78072

HODGSON, DALE LEROY, elec. engr.; b. Duluth, Minn., Mar. 16, 1925; s. Fred Basil and Isla (Worthing) Reamer; student Marquette U., 1943-44; B.S. in Elec. Engring., Purdue U., 1946; m. Sarah Leonora LaRowe, July 14, 1946; children—Elida Juana, Irene Belle. Sr. design engr. McDonnel Aircraft Corp., St. Louis, 1946-51; supr. engring. liaison with LTV Vought Aeros., Dallas, 1951-70, chief design liaison, 1970—. Served with USNR, 1943-46. Registered profl. engr., Mo. Mem. I.E.E.E., Nat. Geog. Soc., Acad. Polit. Sci., Dallas Civic Opera Guild. Democrat. Methodist. Club: LTV Supervisors (Dallas). Home: 703 McKay Dr Arlington TX 76010 Office: LTV Vought Aero Dallas TX 75222

HODGSON, JAMES BARKER, JR., operations analyst, systems engr.; b. Cedar Rapids, Ia., July 29, 1920; s. James Barker and Etta (Evans) H.; B.A., Coe Coll., 1942; postgrad. U. Zurich (Switzerland), 1947-50, Georgia-Augusta U. (Goettingen, Germany), 1950-52; m. Gertrud Berninger, 1946; children—Adam, Michael, Lawrence, Christopher, Anne. Historian, Office of Chief Mil. History, Washington, 1953-55; operations analyst Tech. Operations, Inc., Washington, 1955-58; project engr. Melpar, Inc., Falls Church, Va., 1958-61; operations research scientist System Devel. Corp., Falls Church, 1961-65; cons. operations research and systems engring., Washington, 1965-68; pres. Ability Devel. Services, Inc., Washington, 1968—; gen. mgr., dir. Hobar, Inc., Washington, 1971—. Mem. exec. bd. Capitol Hill Community Council, 1964—; vice chmn. adv. com. S.E. Neighborhood Devel., 1965; pres. Capitol Hill Restoration Soc., 1964-66; bd. mgrs. Christ Child Settlement House, 1962-65. Served to maj. AUS, 1942-47. Mem. Am. Hist. Assn., Mediaeval Acad. Am., Operations Research Council, Operations Research Soc. Am., Inst. Mgmt. Scis., Phi Mu Alpha Sinfonia. Roman Catholic. Home: 506 A St SE Washington DC 20003 Office: Suite 300 1707 H St NW Washington DC 20006

HODGSON, JAMES DAY, sec. of labor; b. Dawson, Minn., Dec. 3, 1915; s. Fred Arthur and Casaraha (Day) H.; A.B., U. Minn., 1938, postgrad., 1940; postgrad. U. Cal. at Los Angeles, 1947-48; hon. doctorate Temple U., 1971; m. Maria Denend, Aug. 24, 1943; children—Nancy (Mrs. Richard J. Nachman), Frederic. Supr. youth employment Minn. Dept. Employment, 1940-41; with Lockheed Aircraft Corp., 1941-69, corporate v.p. indsl. relations, 1968-69; under sec. of labor, Washington, 1969-70, sec. of labor, 1970—. Mem. Cabinet Com. on Econ. Policy, President's Productivity Commn., Nat. Cost-of-Living Council. Mem. exec. com. Mayor Los Angeles Labor-Mgmt. Com., 1962-69; cons. Cal. Com. Automation and Manpower, 1965-67. Served to lt. USNR, 1943-46. Author articles. Home: 2801 New Mexico Av NW Washington DC 20007 Office: Dept Labor 14th and Constitution Av Washington DC 20210

HOEFER, F.A., Dutch diplomat. Consul-gen. from Netherlands, Houston. Address: Consulate Gen of Netherlands World Trade Bldg Houston TX 77002*

HOEHLER, FRED K., JR., educator; A.M., U. Chgo., 1947. Formerly asst. dir. dept. social security AFL-CIO; mem. faculty Mich. State U., East Lansing, 1956—, now prof., asso. dir. Sch. Labor Relations; vis. prof. pub. adminstrn. U. P.R.; vis. asst. prof., acting head Labor Edn. Service Pa. State U.; developer programs for officers labor unions Brookings Instn.; cons. in field. Recipient U. Chgo. Pub. Service citation. Address: 2311 Connecticut Av NW Washington DC 20008*

HOEHNE, WALTER ELMER, govt. ofcl.; b. Des Peres, Mo., Oct. 20, 1927; s. Henry and Theodora (Weiss) H.; A.A., U. Cal. at Los Angeles, 1950, B.A., 1951, postgrad., 1965-66; postgrad. U. Md., 1959; m. Bonnie Catherine Brenot, Sept. 27, 1952; children—Laura Lee, William Alan, David Christopher. Observer, meterologist U.S. Weather Bur., San Francisco, 1951-52, St. Louis, 1952-53, Omaha, 1953-54; atmospheric physicist U.S. Naval Research Lab., Washington, 1954-62, Pacific Missile Range, Point Mugu, Cal., 1962-67; chief functional experimentation and test br. Sterling (Va.) Research and Devel. Center, U.S. Weather Bur., 1967—. Served with USNR, 1945-46. Mem. Am. Meteorol. Soc. Lutheran. Home: 10836 Charles Dr Fairfax VA 22030 Office: RR 1 Sterling VA 22170

HOERMANN, SIEGFRIED ARMIN, statistician; b. Highland Park, Ill., Sept. 27, 1921; s. William and Maria (Harz) H.; B.A., U. Ia., 1943; postgrad. U. Chgo., 1946-49; m. Sheila S. Boyd, Oct. 17, 1953; children— Hillary T., Siegfried Armin II. With U.S. Bur. of Census, 1950-55, 63-66, asst. acting div. chief demographic operations, 1963-66; chief farm population sect. U.S. Dept. Agr., 1955-57; statis. adviser to Iranian Govt., 1957-62; div. dir. health resources statistics Nat. Center Health Statistics, Washington, 1966—. Sec. sub-com. U.S. Nat. Com. on Health and Vital Statistics, 1967—. Pres., New Alexandria Citizens Assn., 1969-70. Served to lst lt. USAAF, 1943-46. Mem. Population Assn. Am., Am. Statis. Assn., Am. Pub. Health Assn., Internat. Union for Sci. Study Population, Phi Beta Kappa, Delta Phi Alpha. Author: (with Bogue, Shryock) Streams of Migration, 1957; (with Bowles, Rohrer) Population of the Northeast 1900-1950, 1960; (with others) Health Manpower, 1968, Hospital Discharge Data, 1970. Home: 6406 16th St Alexandria VA 22307 Office: 330 C St SW Washington DC 20201

HOFF, CLAYTON HENRY, educator; b. Chgo., Feb. 1, 1926; s. Henry C. and Alicia (Koke) H.; B.A., McGill U., 1950; M.A., Washington U., St. Louis, 1951; m. Evelyn Abbey; 1 son, Gregory. Instr. English, Bloomfield Coll., N.J., also Brevard Coll., N.C., 1954-58; asso. prof. English, Pembroke (N.C.) State Coll., 1958-62; asst. prof. English, Ga. So. Coll., Statesboro, also Ga. Center for Continuing Edn., Athens, 1962—. Served with USNR, 1943-46. Mem. Ogeechee Camellia Soc., Ga. Edn. Assn., South Atlantic Modern Lang. Assn. Lutheran. Contbr. articles to profl. jours. Home: 402 Marvin Av Statesboro GA 30458

HOFFMAN, EDGAR PETER, banker; b. Oklahoma City, Mar. 8, 1920; s. Roy and Estelle (Conklin) H.; grad. Hotchkiss Sch., 1939; B.A., Yale, 1943; m. Marion Briscoe, Mar. 18, 1942 (div. Mar. 1967); children— Susan (Mrs. Arthur Wheelock), Edgar Peter, Marion (Mrs. Thomas White), Kent Briscoe; m. 2d, Jane Van Cleef Corbyn, January 17, 1968. Exec. v.p. First Nat. Bank, Oklahoma City, 1946—. City councilman, Nichols Hills, 1959-64, mayor, 1962-64; chmn. Okla. Indsl. Finance Authority, 1965—. Treas., mem. exec. com. United Fund; chmn. bd. dirs. Oklahoma County chpt. A.R.C.; bd. dirs. Community Council Oklahoma City; mem. exec. com. Okla. Med. Research Found.; v.p. bd. trustees Casady Sch. Served to capt. F.A., AUS, 1943-46; PTO. Decorated Bronze Star medal. Home: 5505 N Brookline St Oklahoma City OK 73112 Office: 120 N Robinson St Oklahoma City OK 73125

HOFFMAN, FRANKLIN GORDON, physician; b. Newark, Aug. 16, 1913; s. Joseph and Sadie (Gordon) H.; B.S., Rutgers U., 1935; M.S., U. Cin., 1938, M.D., 1942; m. Gabrielle M. Danielle Delannoy, Aug. 8, 1946. Intern Cin. Gen. Hosp., 1942-43; resident in cardiology VA Hosp., Indpls., 1952-54; practice medicine specializing in cardiology, Nashville, 1955-56, Los Angeles, 1956-57, Columbia, S.C., 1957-60, Lake City, Fla., 1960-62, Louisville, 1962—; asst. chief, chief med. service, chief cardiology USAF Hosp. Sampson AFB, N.Y., 1954-55; asst. cardiology VA Hosp., Nashville, 1956; asst. chief med. service VA Hosp., Sepulveda, Cal., 1958; chief med. service VA Hosp., Sepulveda, Cal., 1958; chief med. service VA Hosp., Dayton, O., 1959-60; chief cardiology VA Hosp., Louisville, 1960—; cons. cardiology Jewish Hosp., Louisville, 1970—; instr. histology U. Cin., 1938-40; instr. medicine Vanderbilt U., 1956-57; clin. instr. medicine U. Cal. at Los Angeles, 1957-58; asst. prof. medicine Ohio State U., 1960; clin. asst. prof. medicine U. Louisville, 1962—. Served to lt. col., USAF, 1942-55. Recipient S. Vander Poole prize Rutgers U., New Brunswick, N.J., 1935. Diplomate Pan Am. Med. Assn. Fellow A.C.P., Am. Coll. Cardiology; mem. N.Y. Acad. Scis., A.M.A., Am. Heart Assn., Am. Diabetes Assn., Med. Soc. U.S.A. and Mexico, Louisville Soc. Internists. Club: Jefferson (Louisville). Contbr. articles to profl. jours. Home: 207 Blankenbaker Lane Louisville KY 40207 Office: VA Hosp Zorn Av Louisville KY 40202

HOFFMAN, IRWIN, orch. condr.; b. N.Y.C., Nov. 26, 1924; s. Harry and Augusta (Cohen) H.; student Juilliard Sch. Music, 1942-43, 45-48; m. Esther Glazer, Feb. 21, 1946; children—Joel H., Gary, Toby, Deborah. Condr. Phila. Orch., Robin Hood Dell summer 1942; teaching fellow Juilliard Sch. Music, 1948; condr. Bronx (N.Y.) Symphony, 1948-52, Yonkers (N.Y.) Philharmonic, 1950-52, Westchester (N.Y.) Chamber Orch., 1950-52, for Martha Craham Dance Co., 1949-50; condr., mus. dir. Vancouver (B.C., Can.) Symphony Orch., 1952-64; asso. condr. Chgo. Symphony, 1964-68, acting music dir., 1968-69; prin. condr. Grant Park Symphony, 1964-68; condr. St. Louis Little Symphony, summers 1959-64; music dir. Fla. Gulf Coast Symphony, 1968—; lectr. condr. U.B.C., State Coll. Wash., 1958; guest condr. Toronto, Vancouver, Chgo., Israel Philharmonic, 1960, Dallas Symphony, 1962, Brazil, 1962, St. Louis Symphony Orch., 1963, Manchester BBC Orch., 1968-69, Strasbourg Radio Orch., 1968, Brussels Radio Orch., 1969, Orchestre Nat. Paris, 1970, Orchestre Philharmonique, 1971, New Philharmonia London, 1971; protege Serge Koussevitzky, Tanglewood, Mass., 1948-50. Served with AUS, 1943-45. Composer two string quartets, violin sonata, others. Collector autograph music manuscripts, mus. memorabilia. Home: 1901 Brightwaters NE St Petersburg FL 37704 Office: Box 2131 St Petersburg FL 33704

HOFFMAN, JULIUS, physician, educator; b. Bronx, N.Y., Feb. 4, 1921; s. Samuel and Ida (Kaplan) H.; B.A., N.Y. U., 1941, M.D., 1944; M.A., Ohio State U., 1958, M.Med. Sci., 1962; M.S., So. Ill. U., 1972; m. Ray Naomi Lockoff, June 6, 1943; children—Paul Lewis, Deborah Ann, Robert Jon. Intern, resident, fellow neurology Kings County Hosp., N.Y.C., 1944-46, 48-49; fellow psychiatry Menninger Found. Sch. Psychiatry, 1949-51; resident pediatrics Childrens Hosp., Columbus, O., 1961-62; fellow pediatric neurology Nat. Inst. Neurol. Diseases, 1961-62; asst. prof. psychiatry Ohio State U. Coll. Medicine, 1951-53, asso. prof. Sch. Social Work, 1951-63; asso. prof. neurology and pediatrics Georgetown U., Washington, 1963-65; prof. pediatrics Howard U., 1964—; lectr. dept. psychiatry George Washington U.; lectr. Found. Advancement in Edn. in Sci., NIH, 1971—; mem. staff D.C. Gen., Childrens, Freedmens, Sibley hosps., Washington Hosp. Center. Cons. spl. asst. on mental retardation to Pres., 1963, NIH div. research facilities and resources, 1964, USPHS Neurol. and Sensory Disease Service, 1965, Civil Service Commn.; chief psychiatry Group Health Assn. Washington. Bd. dirs. Hughlings Jackson Found. for Neurol. Research. Served to capt. M.C., AUS, 1946-48. Diplomate Nat. Bd. Med. Examiners, Am. Bd. Psychiatry and Neurology, Am. Bd. Pediatrics. Fellow Am. Acad. Neurology, Am. Psychiat. Assn., Am. Acad. Pediatrics, A.A.A.S.; mem. A.M.A., Am. Assn. on Mental Deficiency, Caducean, Phi Beta Kappa, Sigma Xi, Beta Lambda Sigma, Mu Chi Sigma. Home: 7805 Green Twig Rd Bethesda MD 20034 Office: 3000 Connecticut Av NW Washington DC 20008

HOFFMAN, PHILIP (GUTHRIE), univ. pres.; b. Kobe, Japan, Aug. 6, 1915 (parents Am. citizens); s. Benjamin Philip and Florence (Guthrie) H.; student George Washington U., 1936-37; A.B., Pacific Union Coll., 1938; M.A., U. So. Cal., 1942; Ph.D., Ohio State U., 1948; H.H.D., Jacksonville U., 1962 LL.D., U. of Ams., 1965, U. Akron, 1971; H.L.D., Pikeville Coll., 1969; m. Mary Elizabeth Harding, Aug. 31, 1939; children—Philip Guthrie, Mary Victoria, Ruth Ann, Jeanne. Credit mgr. Harding Sanitarium, Worthington, O., 1938-40; instr. history Ohio State U., 1946-49; asst. prof. history U. Ala., 1949-51, asso. prof., 1951-53, dir. arts and scis. extension services, 1949-53; vice dean. asso. prof. history gen. extension div. Ore. System Higher Edn., 1953-55, dean, prof., 1955-56; dean faculty, prof. history Portland State Coll., 1956-57; v.p., dean faculties, prof. history U. Houston, 1957-61, pres., 1961—. Mem. bd. S.W. World Affairs Council Houston (pres. 1964-66), Houston Grand Opera Assn., Houston Mus. Natural Sci., Houston Research Inst., Inc., Houston Symphony Soc., Assn. Urban Univs. (pres. 1965-66), Am. Council on Edn.; mem. exec. council commn. on colls. So. Assn. Colls., 1965—, Nat. Commn. on Accrediting, 1965—; mem. Houston Com. Fgn. Relations. Served from ensign to lt. (j.g.), USNR, 1943-45. Mem. Am. Hist. Assn., Am. Assn. U. Profs., Philos. Soc. Tex., Kappa Delta Pi, Phi Kappa Phi, Phi Alpha Theta (nat. pres. 1952-54) Omicron Delta Kappa. Rotarian. Clubs: Houston, University, Petroleum (Houston); River Oaks Country; Astrodome. Contbr. articles to profl. jours. Home: 427 Brown Saddle Houston TX 77027

HOFFMAN, WALTER EDWARD, U.S. dist. judge; b. Jersey City, July 18, 1907; s. Walter and Ella Adele (Sharp) H.; B.S. in Econs., U. Pa., 1928; postgrad. Coll. of William and Mary, 1928-29; LL.B., Washington and Lee U., 1931, LL.D. (hon.), 1970; m. Evelyn Virginia Watkins, Apr. 6, 1939 (dec.); children—Carole Lee, Walter Edward; m. 2d, Helen C. Ballard, Nov. 6, 1971. Admitted to Va. bar, 1931, practiced in Norfolk, Va., 1931-35; partner firm Breeden & Hoffman, 1935-54; instr. to asst. prof. Coll. of William and Mary, 1933-42; referee in bankruptcy Norfolk div. Eastern Dist. of Va., 1942-44; U.S. dist. judge Eastern Dist. of Va., 1954-62, chief judge, 1962—. Mem. Jud. Conf. of U.S., 1964-70; chmn. Jud. Conf. Com. on Adminstrn. of Probation System, 1966-71; bd. dirs. Fed. Judicial Center, Center, 1972—; chmn. spl. Com. on Habeas Corpus, 1971—; mem. State-Fed. Jud. Council of Va., 1971—; mem. adv. com. on criminal rules Supreme Ct. Del. Republican Nat. Conv., 1952. Trustee Randolph-Macon Coll. Mem. Am., Va. (v.p. 1948-49), Norfolk, Portsmouth (pres. 1948-49) bar assns. Methodist (dist. lay leader 1949-53). Mason (Shriner). Club: Cosmopolitan (pres. 1953). Home: 5737 Shenandoah Av Norfolk VA 23509 Office: Federal Bldg Norfolk VA 23510

HOFFMAN, WILLIAM, educator, author; b. Charleston, W.Va., May 16, 1925; s. Henry William and Julia (Beckley) H.; B.A., Hampden-Sydney Coll., 1949; postgrad. Washington and Lee U., 1949-50. State U. Ia., 1950-51; m. Alice Sue Richardson, Apr. 17, 1957; children—Ruth Beckley, Margaret Kay. Prof. English, Hampden-Sydney (Va.) Coll., 1952-59, 1966—; author novels, short stories; playright; pres. Patrick Henry Acad., Charlotte Court House, Va., 1966—; dir. Elk Grocery Co., Charleston, Elk Storage and Warehouse Co., Charleston, Kay Co., Charleston. Served with AUS, 1943-46; ETO. Mem. Authors Guild, Phi Beta Kappa, Omicron Delta Kappa, Pi Delta Epsilon, Sigma Chi, Sigma Upsilon. Presbyn. (deacon). Clubs: Farmington Hunt; Charlotte Country (gov., past pres.) (Charlotte, Va.). Author: The Trumpet Unblown, 1955; Days in the Yellow Leaf, 1958; A Place for My Head, 1960; The Dark Mountains, 1962; Yancey's War, 1966; A walk to the River, 1970. Playwright: The Love Touch, 1967. Home: PO Box 241 Charlotte Court House VA 23923

HOFHEINZ, ROY MARK, profl. baseball exec.; b. Beaumont, Tex., Apr. 10, 1912; s. Frederick Joseph and Nonie (Planchard) H.; student Rice Inst., 1928-29, U. Houston, 1929-30; LL.B., Houston Law Sch., 1933; m. Irene Cafcalas, July 19, 1933; children—Roy Mark, James Frederick, Dene. Admitted to Tex. bar, 1932; mem. Tex. Legislature, 1934-36; judge, Harris County, 1936-44; chmn. bd. Tex. Radio Corp., sta. KTHT, Houston, Pilot Broadcasting Corp., sta. WILD, Birmingham, 1951—; partner Houston Slag Materials Co., 1946—; v.p. Houston Consol. TV Co.; chmn. bd. Houston Astros Baseball Club; chmn. bd., pres. Houston Stars Soccer Club. Past mayor of Houston. Mem. Am. Bar Assn., Am. Arbitration Assn., Sons of Hermann. Elk, Optomist, Eagle. Clubs: Pine Forest Country, Lakeside; Houston Yacht, Briar (Houston). Home: 2400 Yorktown Dr Houston TX 77027 Office: Houston Baseball Club The Astrodome Houston TX 77025

HOGAN, BEN MILES, JR., contractor; b. Helena, Ark., July 11, 1928; s. Ben Miles and Alyne (Russell) H.; student Hill Sch., Pottstown, Pa., 1945-46; B.C.E., Stanford, 1950; m. Magalene Ingram, Aug. 8, 1959; children—Ben Miles III, Magalene Ingram, Dan Phillips. Partner, Ben M. Hogan Co., 1950-64; pres. Ben M. Hogan Co., Inc., Little Rock, 1964—; dir. First Nat. Bank Little Rock, Capital Savs. & Loan, Little Rock. Commr., Ark. Game and Fish Commn., 1964-65. Bd. dirs. Quapaw council Boy Scouts Am. Mem. Asso. Gen. Contractors Ark. (past pres., chmn. hwy. div. 1971), Nat. Asphalt Paving Assn. (bd. dirs. 1968—). Democrat. Methodist. Mason (32 deg.). Clubs: Little Rock Country, Pleasant Valley Country. Home: 48 River Ridge Rd Little Rock AR 72207 Office: 1100 Fairpoint St Little Rock AR 72203

HOGAN, DANIEL WISE, banker; b. Modesto, Ill., Oct. 24, 1867; s. Daniel Wise and Arminda Jane (Turner) H.; grad. Northwestern Normal Sch., and Business Inst., Stanberry, Mo., 1889; m. Anna S. Harvey, Dec. 25, 1891 (died Oct. 14, 1939); children—Clark Harvey, Daniel Wise; m. 2d, Faye B. Locker, Apr. 20, 1946. Bank clk., 1890-92, organized First Nat. Bank of Yukon, Okla., 1892; organized City Nat. Bank, Muskogee, Okla., 1904, cashier Am. Nat. Bank, Oklahoma City, 1907-11; pres. City Nat. Bank & Trust Co., Oklahoma City, 1911—; v.p., dir. City Nat. Bank, Sayre, Okla.; past pres. Oklahoma City Clearing House Assn. Chmn. nat. bd. field advisers for Okla., Small Bus. Adminstrn., Washington. Mem. Taxpayers Research Inst. (past pres.), C. of C. (life dir.), Okla. Bankers Assn. (charter mem., past pres., 1st treas.), Oklahoma State Fair Assn. (exec. council), Motion Picture Panel of Arbitrators, Okla. Future Farmers of Am. and 4-H Club (hon.), Collegiate Engrs., Knights of St. Patrick Assn., Newcomen Soc. Eng., Beta Gamma Sigma (hon. mem.). Methodist. Clubs: Capitol City Gun (pres.), Men's Dinner (charter mem.); Sirloin, Lotus (Oklahoma City); Beacon of Okla., City Golf and Country. Home: 300 NW 16th St Oklahoma City OK 73103 Office: Oklahoma City OK 73103

HOGAN, ERNEST LYNN, ins. exec.; b. Davy, W.Va., Apr. 10, 1913; s. Ernest Lynn and Edna (Harris) H.; ed. Oxford Bus. Coll.; m. Mildred Shepard, Jan. 18, 1936; 1 dau., Dorothy Washington (Mrs. James D. Sheker). With Peoples Life Ins. Co., Washington, 1935—, exec. v.p., 1968-70, pres., 1970—, dir., 1965—; dir. Capital Holding Corp. Mem. Life Ins. Agy. Mgmt. Assn. (dir.), Life Underwriters Tng. Council (treas.), Va. Life Underwriters Assn. (past v.p.). Club: Loudoun County Golf and Country (Purcelleville, Va.). Home: Rt 1 Box 134 Purcelleville VA 22132 Office: 601 New Hampshire Av NW Washington DC 20037

HOGAN, MILTON EARL, banker; b. Durham, N.C., Feb. 5, 1919; s. Milton Earl and Carrie Lee (Pickard) H.; B.S., U. N.C., 1939; m. Mary Edith Horsfield, Aug. 14, 1943; children—Alice (Mrs. Arthur J. Slayton), Richard Horsfield. Clk. Planters Nat. Bank, 1939-41; examiner for U.S. Controller of currency, 1941-48; v.p., trust officer N.C. Nat. Bank, 1948-62; v.p. B.C. Remedy Co., 1962-67; v.p., sr. trust officer Bank of N.C., N.A., Jacksonville, 1967—; sec. Bancshares of N.C., Inc.; dir. Marine Broadcasting Co., City Fuel & Tire, Crump Oil Co.; lectr. Carolina Coastal Coll. Dir. Campbell Coll. Estate Planning Council; mem. N.C. Order Long Leaf Pine; active N.C. Heart Assn., N.C., Cancer Assn., Durham Mental Health Assn. Treas. Onslow Dental Found., Callie Bingham Found. Served to 1st lt., AUS, 1942-46; PTO. Mem. Am. (trust sec.), N.C. (trust sec.) bankers assns., Carolina Playmakers, Alpha Tau Omega, Delta Sigma Phi. Episcopalian. Club: Jacksonville Country. Editor: Attorney's Handbook, 1971. Home: 111 Courtland Dr Jacksonville NC 28540 Office: New River Shopping Center Jacksonville NC 28540

HOGAN, ROBERT LEO, computer leasing co. exec.; b. Johnson City, N.Y., May 27, 1935; s. Paul William and Anna (Sejan) H.; student Pensacola Jr. Coll., 1957, Coll. Great Falls, 1965-67; m. Claire McGowan, Feb. 20, 1954; children—Elaine, Mark, Gail. Sr. educator computer dept. Univac Corp., Washington, 1965-67, account mgr. NASA Manned Spacecraft Center, Houston, 1967-68; regional mgr. U. Computing Co., Washington, 1968-69, Computer Leasing Co., Arlington, Va., 1969—. Vice-pres. Young Republican Coub, Coll. Great Falls (Mont.), 1966-67; precinct capt. Fairfax County Rep. Com., Fairfax, Va., 1969. Served with USAF, 1952-65. Mem. Assn. Computer Machinery, Alpha Phi Omega. Roman Catholic. Home: 3166 Musket Ct Fairfax VA 22030 Office: 11480 Sunset Hills Rd Reston VA 22070

HOGAN, ROBERT STEADHAM, physician; b. Birmingham, Ala., Nov. 3, 1922; s. Marion Elias and Kathleen (Steadham) H.; student Ala. Poly. Inst., 1941-43; B.S., U. Ala., 1947; M.D., Med. Coll. Ala., 1951; m. Alice Katherine Hardin, June 6, 1949; children—Robert Steadham, Nelle Lindsay, Richard Hardin, James Baker. Intern, Univ. Hosp., Birmingham, 1951-52, resident, 1952-54, chief resident, 1955-56; NIH trainee arthritis, Bethesda, Md., 1954-55; practice medicine specializing in internal medicine, Birmingham, 1956-70, specializing in rheumatology, Birmingham, 1970—; mem. staff Univ., Bapt., St. Vincent's hosps.; clin. asso. prof. medicine Ala. Sch. Medicine, 1964—; med. dir. Am. Educators Life Ins. Co., 1968—; cons. VA Hosp., 1960—. Mem. State Bd. Examiners Nursing Home Adminstrs., 1970—. Bd. dirs. Ala. chpt. Arthritis and Rheumatism Found. Served to 1st lt. USAAF, 1942-45; prisoner of war, Germany. Decorated Purple Heart, Air medal with oak leaf clusters. Diplomate Am. Bd. Internal Medicine. Fellow A.C.P.; mem. A.A.A.S., Am. Rheumatism Assn., A.M.A., Am., Ala., Birmingham socs. internal medicine, Ala., Jefferson County med. socs., Birmingham C. of C., Kappa Alpha, Phi Chi, Alpha Omega Alpha, Omicron Delta Kappa, Phi Chi. Unitarian-Universalist. Rotarian. Club: Country (Birmingham, Ala.). Home: 2926 Canterbury Rd Birmingham AL 35223 Office: Med Arts Bldg 1023 20th St S Birmingham AL 35205

HOGARTH, CHARLES PINCKNEY, coll. pres.; b. Brunson, S.C., Nov. 14, 1911; s. Charles Pickney and Maude (Griner) H.; B.S. Clemonson Coll., 1932; B.D., Yale, 1935, M.A., 1941; Ph.D., Peabody Coll., 1947; m. Nancy Harris, Dec. 14, 1940 children—Nancy (Mrs. Hal McClanahan), Charles. Sec. Christian Assn., student counselor Pa. State Coll., 1935-37; asst. to pres., dir. pub. relations Lander Coll., Greenwood. S.C., 1939-41; dir. publ. relations, bus. mgr., tchr. Detroit Country Day Sch., 1941-42; dean Ward-Belmont Coll., Nashville, 1942-47; registrar Fla. State U., 1947-49; v.p., prof. psychology Gulf Park Coll., Gulfport, Miss., 1949-50, pres., 1950-52; pres. Miss. State Coll. for Women, Columbus, 1952—. Lectr., Europe, summer 1934; research asso. Am. Council Edn., Harvard, 1938. Dir. area council Boy Scouts Am., Columbus Community Chest. Mem. Columbus C. of C., N.E.A., Miss. Assn. Sch. Adminstrs., So. Assn. Colls. for Women (past pres.), Miss. Assn. Colls. (past pres.), Jr.-Sr. Coll. Conf. Miss. (past pres.), So. U. Conf. (pres.), Am. Assn. State Colls. and Univs. (state rep.), Newcomen Soc. N.A., Pub. Instns. Higher Learning in So. States (past pres.), Miss. Edn. Assn., Pres.'s Council of State Instns. of Higher Learning in Miss. (past pres.). Am. Assn. Sch. Adminstrs., A.I.M. (past mem. pres.'s council), Phi Theta Kappa, Pi Tau Chi, Chi Psi, Pi Kappa Delta, Phi Kappa Phi, Phi Delta Kappa. Methodist. Mason. Clubs: Columbus Country, Rotary (dir.). Author: Policy Making in Colleges Related to the Methodist Church, 1949; Crisis in Higher Education, 1957; also articles in ednl. publs. Home: 1217 2d Av S Columbus MS 37901

HOGG, ASTOR, state ofcl.; b. Roxana, Ky., Nov. 13, 1901; s. George and Mahala (Combs) H.; LL.B., U. Ky., 1924; m. Gertrude Lewis, June 29, 1927; children—Stanley, Janelle Hogg Pope. Admitted to Ky. bar, 1924, also U.S. Supreme Ct. bar; practice of law, Whitesburg, 1924-35, Harlan, 1941-51; county atty. Letcher County, Ky., 1930-34; trial atty. FTC, Washington, 1935-37; spl. asst. to atty. gen. of U.S., Washington, 1937-39; commonwealth's atty. 26th Jud. Dist. Ky., 1942-45, circuit judge, 1951-55; judge, Ct. Appeals of Ky., Frankfort, 1955-57; chief asst. atty. gen. Dept. Hwys., 1957-60; administrative dir. Cts. of Ky., 1960-71, now spl. circuit judge; spl. counsel firm Creech, Hogg & Johnson, Ashland, Ky. Mayor of Whitesburg, 1927-28. Del. Dem. Nat. Conv., 1928. Mem. Am., Ky. bar assns., Am. Judicature Soc., Phi Alpha Delta. Baptist. Rotarian (pres.); Kiwanian (Harlan). Club: Filson (Louisville). Home: 200 Paul Sawyier Frankfort KY 40601 Office: State Capitol Bldg Frankfort KY 40601 Died Aug. 5, 1972

HOGGARD, HORATIO CORNICK, III, engr.; b. Norfolk, Va., Mar. 18, 1923; s. Horatio Cornick and Helen Lisle (Scott) H.; B.S. in Indsl. Engring., Va. Poly. Inst., 1949; grad. U.S. Army Engr. Sch., Command and Gen. Staff Coll.; m. Betty Wrenn Bevan, Apr. 16, 1955; 1 son, Horatio Cornick IV. Elec. and indsl. engr. Bur. Standards, Washington, 1949-50; asso. prof. mil. sci. and tactics City Coll. N.Y., 1952-53; civil engr. Tidewater Constrn. Co., Ga., Va., 1954; civil engr. City of Norfolk, 1954-64, bldg. ofcl., 1964-69, zoning adminstr., 1969— dockmaster, 1964-69; cons. Norfolk Redevel. and Housing Authority, 1955-58; instr. Norfolk State Evening Coll., 1967—. Mem. engring. staff Civil Def., Norfolk; chmn. Bd. Elec. Exams; sec. Bd. Zoning Appeals, Bd. Adjustment and Appeals, Bd. Plumbing Code Appeals, Permanent Bldg. Code Com., Regional Code Com. Pres., dir. Johnny Davis Meml. Found., Inc.; asst. scoutmaster troop 32 Boy Scouts Am., 1968—. Served to staff sgt. USAAC, 1943-46; served to 1st lt. C.E., AUS, 1950-54; lt. col. Res. Mem. Am. Soc. Mil. Engrs., Va. Water Pollution Control Assn., C. of C., So. Bldg. Code Congress, Internat. Conf. Bldg. Ofcls., Bldg. Ofcls. Conf. Am., Va. Bldg Ofcls. Conf., Am. Soc. Testing Materials (dir. Middle Atlantic dist. coms. E-5, E-6, C-20), Va. Municipal League, Nat. Fire Prevention Assn., Am. Legion (post comdr.), Res. Officers Assn., Va. Poly. Inst. Alumni Assn., James River Retriever Club, Golden Retriever Club Am., Tidewater Kennel Club, Hampton Roads Obedience Tng. Club, Potomac Valley Golden Retriever Club. Episcopalian (vestryman 1968—). Rotarian. Club: Mallory Country. Home: 1128 Graydon Av Norfolk VA 23507 Office: City Hall Norfolk VA 23510

HOGGE, ERNEST A., physicist; b. Morehead, Ky., Nov. 7, 1911; s. James W. and Lyda (Christian) H.; B.S., Morehead State Coll., 1931; M.S., U. Ky., 1934; Ph.D., Ohio State U., 1940; m. May Ward, Sept. 7, 1935 (dec. 1972); children—Joseph Ernest, William Clayborne. Asst. prof. phys. chemistry U. Ga., 1940-41; research chemist Hercules Powder Co., Wilmington, Del., 1941-45, B.F. Goodrich Co., Akron, O., 1946-48; phys. chemist, physicist Naval Ordnance Lab., White Oak, Md., 1948-56; physicist U.S. Navy Mine Def. Lab., Panama City, Fla., 1956—. Fellow A.A.A.S., Am. Inst. Chemists; mem. Am. Chem. Soc., Am. Geophys. Union, Research and Engring. Soc. Am., Sigma Xi, Sigma Pi Sigma. Home: 1002 2d Plaza Panama City FL 32401 Office: Naval Coastal Systems Lab (P704) Panama City FL 32402

HOGNESS, JOHN RUSTEN, educator; b. Oakland, Cal., June 27, 1922; s. Thorfin R. and Phoebe (Swenson) H.; student Haverford Coll., 1939-42; B.S., U. Chgo., 1943, M.D., 1946; m. Katharine Ruenauver, Dec. 19, 1944; children—Erik, Susan, Karen, David, Jody. Intern, Presbyn. Hosp., N.Y.C., 1946-47, asst. resident, 1949-50; chief resident King County Hosp., Seattle, 1950-51; asst. U. Wash. Sch. Medicine, 1950-52, Am. Heart Assn. research fellow, 1951-52, clin. asso., 1952-54, clin. instr., 1954-56, clin. asst. prof., 1956-58, asst. prof., 1958-60, asso. prof., 1960-64, prof., 1964—, med. dir. U. Wash. Hosp., 1958-63, asst. dean, 1959-61, asso. dean, 1961-64, dean medicine, chmn. bd. health scis., 1964-69, exec. v.p. of univ., 1969—, dir. Health Scis. Center, 1970—. Mem. adv. com. for environmental scis. NSF; mem. adv. com. NIH; mem. adv. com. to dir. health services and mental health adminstrn.; mem. commr's. adv. com. on exempt orgns. Internal Revenue Service. Trustee China Med. Bd. Diplomate Am. Bd. Internal Medicine. Mem. A.M.A., A.C.P., Alpha Omega Alpha. Home: 6820 51st NE Seattle WA 98115

HOGUE, MALCOLM CULTBARTSON, farm machinery and supply co. exec.; b. Weiner, Ark., May 7, 1912; s. Lewis and Maggie (Tees) H.; student accounting Ark. State U., 1931-32; m. Mildred Gilmore, Aug. 5, 1940; children— Lou Ann (Mrs. Aubry Looney), Malcolm Gilmore, Kathy (Mrs. Ronnie Hatcher), Lewis. Distbr., Hogue Wholesale Oil Co., 1933-72; owner, Hogue Farm Supply Distbr., Weiner, Ark., 1950—; farmer, Hogues Farm, Weiner, 1951-72; dir. Bank Weiner. Trustee U. Phillips, Enid, Okla. Served with USAAF, 1942-45. Mem. Am. Legion (comdr. 1946-72). Mem. Christian Ch. (elder 1962—, trustee 1964—). Lion. Home: 302 W 3d St Weiner AR 72479 Office: 91 Van Buren St Weiner AR 72479

HOGUE, TRUDEAU J., JR., elec. engr.; b. Baton Rouge, July 24, 1917; s. Trudeau J. and Ethel (Hart) H.; B.S., La. State U., 1940; m. Lois Gayle Akers, June 18, 1943; one son, Trudeau J., III. Jr. engr. South Central Bell Telephone Co,, 1940-41, engr., 1946-52, program planning engr., 1952-53, exchange plant engr., 1953—, dist. engr., Baton Rouge, 1958-59, div. staff engrs., Baton Rouge, 1959-70, state outside plant engr., New Orleans, 1970—. Mem. exec. bd. Istrouma area council Boy Scouts Am. Served from 2d lt. to maj., AUS, 1942-45. Assn. U.S. Army, I.E.E.E., La. Engring. Soc. (pres.), Nat. Soc. Profl. Engrs. Democrat. Roman Catholic. Kiwanian. Club: Sherwood Forest Country. Home: 9833 N Parkview Dr Baton Rouge LA 70815 Office: 1215 Prytania St New Orleans LA 70140

HOHOS, JOSEPH ANDREW, electronics co. exec.; b. Tarentum, Pa., May 15, 1922; s. Louis and Anna (Kavacky) H.; B.S., U. Pitts., 1943; m. Carol Ruth Jones, May 12, 1947; children—Joseph, Richard, Carol, Lois. Engr., sr. engr. Philco Corp., Phila., 1943-50; sr. engr., project engr., sect. head Melpar, Inc., Falls Church, Va., 1950-59; chief mech. engr., dir. corp. planning Scope, Inc., Falls Church, 1959-62, dir. engring. adminstrn., 1964-66, v.p. planning and control, 1966-70, dir., v.p. operations, sec., asst. clk., 1961—; v.p. finance, sec.-treas. Scope Electronics, Inc., Reston, Va., 1970, asst. to pres., sec., 1971—. Bd. dirs. Lake Barcroft Community Assn., 1962-64. Mem. I.E.E.E., Pi Tau Sigma, Sigma Tau. Patentee in field. Home: 3413 Mansfield Rd Falls Church VA 22041 Office: 1860 Michael Faraday Dr Reston VA 22070

HOLCOMB, CHARLIE CALVIN, supt. schs.; b. Ledey, Okla., Oct. 17, 1912; s. Charles Augusta and Elmer (Williams); A.B., Southwestern State Coll., 1935; M.Ed., Okla. U., 1950, Ed.D., 1963; m. Vinita Corene Ward, Mar. 12, 1937; children—Charlotte (Mrs. Jimmie Newberry), Sandra Jeanne. Tchr. schs. Custer & Roger Mills counties, Okla., 1931-33; coach, prin. Trail (Okla.) Schs., 1934-37; tchr. Rhea Sch., Okla., 1937-38; prin. supt. Putnam (Okla.) Schs., 1938-48; supt. Lone Wolf (Okla.) Schs., 1952-57, Burns Flat (Okla.) Schs., 1948-52, 1957-70; supt. Western Okla. Vocational Tech. Sch., Burns Flat, 1970—. Dir. Dill State Bank, Washita County Indsl. Corp. Dist. chmn. Lions Okla. Individual Opportunity for Achievement Boys Ranch, 1964-65; mem. Washita County Health Bd., 1966—. Sec. treas. Midwestern Okla. Indsl. Found., 1966—; bd. dirs. Okla. Lions Eye Bank. Mem. Okla. (bd. dirs. 1964-66), County Oklahoma edn. assns., County Schoolmasters (pres. 1963-64), N.E.A., Am., Okla. assns. sch. adminstrs., Comparative Edn. Soc., Phi Delta Kappa. Democrat. Baptist. Lion (pres. 1963-64, dist. gov. 1969-70), Mason (32 deg.); mem. Order Eastern Star. Club: Burns Flat Sports. Home: 202 Bryan Av Burns Flat OK 73624 Office: PO Box 149 Burns Flat OK 73624

HOLCOMB, DAVID WALLACE, JR., interior decorator; b. Winston-Salem, N.C., Nov. 26, 1937; s. David Wallace and Margaret Elizabeth (Houchins) H.; student U. N.C., 1956-58; B.F.A., Va. Commonwealth U., 1963. Partner, Holcomb & Carpenter Interiors, interior design firm, Winston-Salem, 1964—. Bd. dirs. Little Theatre, Winston-Salem, Art Gallery Originals, Forsyth County Heart Assn., 1968-70. Served with AUS, 1964. Recipient hon. fellowship Forsyth County Heart Assn., 1969. Mem. Am. Inst. Interior Designers (v.p. dist. chpt. 1968-70). Contbr. articles to profl. pubs., and popular mags. Home: 2441 Reynolds Dr NW Winston Salem NC 27104 Office: 735 Summit St Winston-Salem NC 27102

HOLCOMB, ELAINE PARKS (MRS. LUTHER J. HOLCOMB), sociologist, writer; b. Dallas, Nov. 22, 1916; d. Joseph Floyd and Lucy (Largent) Parks; student Randolph-Macon Woman's Coll., 1934-35, B.A., Baylor U., 1938; M.A., So. Meth. U., 1956; m. Luther J. Holcomb, Sept. 6, 1938; children—Henry, Jan (Mrs. Larry W. Flowers). With new accounts dept. Riggs Nat. Bank, Washington, 1970-71. Mem. White House Conf. on Children and Youth, 1960; pres., United Ch. Women of 1958-59, pres. United Ch. Women of Tex., 1962-65; mem. nat. nominating com. of Ch. Women United of Nat. Council Chs., 1967-71; mem. women's planning com. Japan Internat. Christian U. Found.; bd. mgrs. Nat. United Ch. Women, Nat. Council of Chs., 1962-65; mem. exec. com. United Ch. Women of Nat. Capitol Area, 1965-68, Women's div. Washington Nat. Conf. Christian and Jews, 1965-67; ofcl. rep. to Council Nat. Orgns. for Children and Youth, 1965; adminstrv. dir. Pastoral Inst., Washington, 1968-70. Mem. bd. Girl's Found. Dallas Fedn. Women's Clubs. Recipient Brotherhood medallion Nat. Conf. Christians and Jews, 1965, Mem. Am. Assn. U. Women, Kappa Alpha Theta. Baptist. Contbr. articles to profl. jours. Home: Harbour Sq 540 N St SW Apt S604 Washington DC 20024

HOLCOMB, LUTHER JENKINS, govt. ofcl.; b. Yazoo City, Miss., Dec. 19, 1911; s. Thomas Luther and Willie (Jenkins) H.; student U. Okla., 1931-35; So. Baptist Theol. Sem., Louisville, 1936-38; D.D., Howard Payne Coll., 1957; m. Elaine Parks, Sept. 6, 1938; children—Henry, Jan (Mrs. Larry Wayne Flowers). Ordained to ministry Bapt. Ch., 1940; leader in youth meetings in 20 states, Nashville, 1938-39; pastor 1st Ch., Durant, Okla., 1940-42, Temple and Luther Rice Meml. Chs., Washington, 1942-46, Lakewood Ch., Dallas, 1946-58; exec. dir. Greater Dallas Council Chs., 1958-65; vice chmn. Equal Employment Opportunity Com., Washington, 1965—. Vis. instr. dept. religion So. Methodist U., 1944; spl. religious emphasis missions for Air Force in Far East, 1953, 62, Arctic, 1956, Central Am., 1958; ofcl. adviser 53d session UNESCO, Geneva, Switzerland, 1972. Commr. Dallas Housing Authority, 1955-65; chmn. Tex. Adv. Com. to U.S. Civil Rights Com., 1963-65; dir. Council on World Affairs, 1955-65, sec.-treas. 1961-63, v.p. 1963-65. Bd. dirs Community Chest, Dallas, 1951-53, Child Guidance Clinic, 1955-62, Timberlawn Found., 1960-67, Sr. Citizens Found., 1968—. Mem. Washington Fedn. Chs. (sec. 1943-46, exec. com. 1943-46), Tex. State Soc. in Washington (pres. 1972), Delta Upsilon. Home: Harbour Sq 540 N St SW Apt S604 Washington DC 20024 Office: 1800 G St NW Washington DC 20506

HOLDER, HAROLD HENRY, JR., oil co. exec.; b. Pickens, S.C., Jan. 28, 1921; s. Harold Edgar and Flora Ann (Parson) H.; student Bowling Green U., 1937, Wofford Coll., 1940-43, Strayer Coll., 1941; Biarritz Am. U., 1946; m. Helen Lucile Gilstrap, Dec. 9, 1965; 1 dau., Dora. Gen. mgr. Holder Bros., 1937-40; sec.-treas. Red Diamond Oil Co., Pickens, S.C., 1946-57, pres., 1957-65; pres. Holder and Holder, 1957-65; sec.-treas. Red Diamond Oil, Inc., Pickens, S.C., 1965-70, pres., 1971—. Asst. coach football Pickens (S.C.) High Sch., 1948-58. Served with AUS, 1943-46. Baptist. Mason (Shriner). Home: Box 38 Pickens SC 29671 Office: Box 443 Pickens SC 29671

HOLDER, HARRELL LEE, supt. schs.; b. Scranton, Tex., Feb. 4, 1932; s. Truett Harrell and Alta Ruth (Sprawls) H.; A.A., Howard County Jr. Coll., 1951; B.A., Tex. Tech. Coll., 1953, M.Ed., 1959; m. Martha Sue McGuire, June 8, 1957; children—Robert Harrell, William Barton. Tchr., Denver City, Tex., 1956-64; supt., Three Way Ind. Sch. Dist., Maple, Tex., 1964-67, Southside Ind. Sch. Dist., San Antonio, 1967-70, Bishop (Tex.) Consol. Sch. Dist., 1970—. Bd. dirs. Coastal Bend Youth City, Driscoll, Tex. Served with AUS, 1953-55. Mem. N.E.A., Am. Legion, Am., Tex. assns. sch. adminstrs., Tex. State Tchrs. Assn. Mason, Lion. Home: 507 10th St Bishop TX 78343 Office: Box 788 Bishop TX 78343

HOLDER, HOWARD RANDOLPH, broadcasting corp. exec.; b. Moline, Ill., Nov. 14, 1916; s. James William and Charlotte (Brega) H.; B.A. Augustana Coll., 1939; m. Clementi Lacey-Baker, Feb. 21, 1942; children—Janice (Mrs. Earl Collins), Susan (Mrs. Charles A. Rudolph), Marjory E., Howard Randolph. With WHBF, Rock Island, Ill., Part-time 1939-41, WOC, Davenport, Ia., 1945-47, WINN, Louisville, 1947, WRFC, Athens, Ga., 1948-56, WGAU, Athens, 1956—; pres. Clarke Broadcasting Corp., Athens, 1956—, Mid-West Broadcasting Corp., Griffin, Ga.; v.p. Washington Properties, Inc., Rome, Ga.; dir. Citizens & So. Nat. Bank Athens. Chmn., Salvation Army adv. bd,, 1962-63, Parks and Recreation Bd., 1952-62; mem. bd. Athens-Clarke County A.R.C., Georgians for Safer Hwys.; chmn. region IV Am. Cancer Soc., 1968; mem. lay adv. bd. St. Marys Hosp.; chmn. Cherokee dist. Boy Scouts Am., 1966,67, mem. exec. bd. N.E. Ga. area Council. Mem. Athens Crime Prevention Com.; mem. bd. Area Emergency Planning Com. Mem. 10th Dist. Democratic Exec. Com. Served with AUS, 1941-46; ETO. Named Boss of year, Athens Jr. C. of C., 1959; Ga. Broadcaster of Year, 1962; Employer of Yr., Athens Bus. and Profl. Women, 1969, Athens Citizen of Year, Athens Woman's Club, Athens Rotary legislative com.), Ga. (pres. 1961), assns. broadcasters, Ga. Club, 1971. Mem. Res. Officers Assn. (pres. Athens 1962), Nat. (nat. A.P. Broadcasters (pres. 1963), Internat. Platform Assn., Athens Area C. of C. (pres. 1970), Golden Quill, Sigma Delta Chi, Alpha Delta Sigma, Di Gamma Kappa (Ga. Pioneer Broadcaster of Year). Clubs: Gridiron, Rotary (pres. 1957-58, Found. com. chmn.; dist. gov. 1969-70), Touchdown (pres. Athens 1963-64). Home: 383 W View Dr Athens GA 30601 Office: 850 Bobbin Mill Rd Athens GA 30604

HOLDERNESS, HAYWOOD DAIL, telephone co. exec.; b. Tarboro, N.C., July 30, 1909; s. George A. and Harriet (Howard) H.; A.B., U.N.C., 1931; M.A., U. Pa. Wharton Sch. Finance, 1933; m. Nancy Burton Braswell, Mar. 19, 1938; children—Haywood Dail, James B., Zelle B. (Mrs. John C. Jester III), Nancy duVal (Mrs. Thomas S. Reams), Russell B. With Carolina Tel. & Tel. Co., Tarboro, 1933—, sec., treas., 1937-57, v.p., 1945-57, pres., 1957—, also dir., mem. exec. com.; dir. United Utilities, Inc., Kansas City, Mo., Rocky Mount Investment Co. (N.C.), Sero Corp., Rocky Mount, Fed. Res. Bank Richmond. Past chmn. Tarboro United Fund. Trustee Union Theol. Sem., Richmond, St. Andrews Presbyn. Coll. Recipient Silver Beaver award Boy Scouts Am.; Distinguished Citizens award Gov. N.C., 1967. Mem. U.S. (pres. 1966-67), N.C. (past pres.) ind. telephone assns., U. N.C. Alumni Assn. (pres. 1960-61). Presbyn. (elder). Rotarian (past pres. Tarboro). Home: 805 S Howard Circle Tarboro NC 27886 Office: Carolina Tel & Tel Co Tarboro NC 27886

HOLLADAY, CARLTON EDWIN, judge; b. Carrollton, Va., Nov. 10, 1902; s. Walter Jackson and Bettie (Fulgham) H.; A.B., Coll. William and Mary, 1924; m. Mary Sue Davis, June 27, 1931. Admitted to Va. bar, 1925, practiced in Va., 1925-58; judge 3d Jud. Circuit Va., 1958—; past v.p., dir. Bank of Sussex & Surry. Past mem. adv. bd., appeal agt. SSS; Dollar a Year speaker War Finance Com., 1943-44; past mem. bd. dirs., pres. 1934 Ruritan Nat.; trustee Va. Methodist Children's Home, 1962-66. Mem. Am., Va. bar assns., Nat. Conf. State Trial Judges, William and Mary Law Sch. Assn. (past pres.), Tidewater Automobile Assn. (dir.), Phi Beta Kappa, Omicron Delta Kappa, Sigma Pi. Methodist (mem. ofcl. bd., lay leader, supt. Ch. Sch.). Mason (Shriner). Club: Wakefield Sportsmen's. Home: Wakefield VA 23888

HOLLADAY, CHARLES EDWIN, supt. schs.; b. Newton, Miss., July 12, 1918; s. Clarence O. and Gladys (Bounds) H.; B.A., Miss. Coll., 1946; M.A., Peabody Coll., 1949; Ed.D., U. Miss., 1969; m. Bess Edward, May 25, 1939; children—Charles E., Stephen E. Tchr., Duncan (Miss.) Pub. Schs., 1941-43, Enochs Jr. High Sch., Jackson, Miss., 1946-49; asst. prin. Central High Sch., Jackson, 1949-53, prin., 1953-58; supt. schs., Tupelo, Miss., 1958—. Exec. sec. N.E. Miss. TV Council, 1961—; chmn. Miss. Accrediting Commn., 1963-65; ednl. auditor Fed. project; developer ednl. mgmt. tng. program for adminstrs. N.E. Miss. Trustee Blue Mountain (Miss.) Coll. Served with USAAF, 1942-46. Recipient merit award for outstanding ednl. program Miss. Econ. Council, 1966. Mem. N.E.A. (Pace Maker award for Miss. 1965), Miss. (past pres. adult edn. div.), Tupelo edn. assns., Miss. Secondary Sch. Prins. Assn. (past pres.), Am., Miss. assns. sch. adminstrs., Mental Health Assn. Baptist (deacon). Rotarian (past dir.). Home: 626 Magnolia Dr Tupelo MS 33801 Office: PO Box 557 Tupelo MS 33801

HOLLADAY, DURAND ALLEN, lawyer, mortgage firm exec.; b. Montgomery, Ala., Mar. 15, 1925; s. Will Lee and Ruby (Allen) H.; B.S. in Aero. Engring., Ga. Inst. Tech., 1945; J.D., U. Miami, 1949;

m. Mary Blanche Faver, Oct. 14, 1945; children—William Marshall, Patricia Lynn. Admitted to Fla. bar, 1949; practiced in Miami, Fla., 1949-65; mem. firm Holladay, Swann & Gardner and predecessor firm; gen. counsel Mortgage Consultants, Coral Gables, Fla., 1962-65, pres., 1965-72, chmn. bd., 1972-—; trustee, sec. Continental Mortgage Investors, Boston, 1966-—, mng. trustee, 1972-—; sr. v.p., dir. Continental Investment Corp., Boston, 1968-—; pres. Diversified Advisers, Inc., Coral Gables; chmn. bd. trustees, mng. trustee Diversified Mortgage Investors; dir. Investors Mortgage Ins. Corp., Boston. Trustee, U. Miami, Baptist Hosp. Served with USNR, 1945-46. Mem. Am. Bar Assn., Fla. Bar, Phi Alpha Delta, Pi Kappa Alha. Baptist (Sunday sch. bd. 1963-69). Mason. Club: Nat. Exchange (regional v.p. 1962-63, state pres. 1959-60). Home: 4430 Santa Maria Coral Gables FL 33146 Office: 5915 Ponce de Leon Coral Gables FL 33146

HOLLADAY, JAMES FRANKLIN, wire mill exec.; b. Birmingham, Ala., Apr. 5, 1922; s. Allen A. and Mary (Campbell) H.; B.S., Ga. Inst. Tech., 1950; m. Anna Wedsworth, July 17, 1948; children—James F., David Allen, Cinthia Ann. Plant engr. Erwin Mills, Inc., Stonewall, Miss., 1950-52; plant engr. Southwire Co., Carrolton, Ga., 1952-63, v.p., 1963-—, bd. dirs., 1957-—. Chmn., Elec. Bd., Carrollton, 1958-—; dist. gov. Lions Internat. Dist. 18-E Ga., 1963-64; pres. Carrollton Jr. High P.T.A., 1967-68. Served to 1st lt. Inf. AUS, 1942-46. Named Plant Engr. of Year S.E. U.S., 1966. Mem. Ga. Past Dist. Govs. Assn. (pres. 1966-67), I.E.E.E., Am. Inst. Plant Engrs. (internat. sec.). Baptist (deacon). Clubs: Dixie Management (v.p. 1963-—), West Ga. Executive (Carrollton, Ga.). Home: 305 Kramer St Carrollton GA 30117 Office: Southwire Co Fertilla St Carrollton GA 30117

HOLLADAY, JAMES WILLIAM, dentist; b. Montpelier, Ky., June 3, 1921; s. Joe Douglas and Bessie (Young) H.; student Lindsey Wilson Coll., 1946-48, U. Ky., 1948-49; D.D.S., U. Louisville, 1953; m. Claudette Imogene Marcum, Oct. 27, 1962. Pvt. dental practice, Russell Springs, Ky., 1953-54, Columbia, 1954-—; staff Adair County Meml. Hosp. Mem. Adair County Bd. Health, 1960-64, Ky. Bd. Dental Examiners, 1965-— (pres. 1967-68). Bd. dirs., sec.-treas. Summit Manor Nursing Home, 1967-71. Served with Signal Corps, AUS, 1942-43. Mem. Am., Ky. (exec. bd. 1961-63, 68-—) dental assns., S. Central Ky. Dist. Dental Soc. (pres. 1963-64, sec.-treas. 1964-65). Columbia-Adair County C. of C. (pres. 1966), Delta Sigma Delta, Omicron Delta Kappa, Sigma Delta, Omicron Kappa Upsilon, Phi Kappa Phi, Phi Delta. Democrat. Baptist. Clubs: Lions, Pinewood Country. Office: 209 Burkesville St Columbia KY 42728

HOLLAHAN, GEORGE LOVETT, JR., state senator; b. Pitts., May 1, 1919; s. George Lovett and Margaret (Ames) H.; B.S. in Bus. Adminstrn., U. Miami, 1942, LL.B., 1949; m. Anne Thompson; children—Kathleen Ames, George Lovett III, Linley Anne, Michael Scott. Admitted to Fla. bar; practice law, Miami; mem. Fla. senate, 1963-—, chmn. Com. Govt. Reorgn. and Efficiency, Formerly municipal judge, South Miami, Fla.; asst. state atty., Fla., 1953-54; mem. Fla. Ho. of Reps., 1956-62. Served with USNR, World War II; PTO. Mem. Municipal Judges Assn. Dade County (past v.p.), Dade County, Fla., Am. bar assns., V.F.W. Episcopalian. Rotarian, Eagle, Elk, Moose. Home: 5409 Riviera Dr Coral Galbes FL 33146 Office: 7211 SW 62d Av Suite 208 South Miami FL 33143*

HOLLAND, BEN HANSON, concrete products co. exec.; b. nr. Manassas, Ga., July 4, 1913; s. Walter Deal and Mary (Jackson) H.; student Ga. So. Coll., 1932-34; m. Frances Wright, July 18, 1942; children—Ben Hanson II, Rachael Ann (Mrs. Russell W. Branch, Jr.), Jerry W., Mary Rebecca. Clerk, Hardaway Contracting Col, Columbus, Ga., 1936-41; head bookkeeper R.H. Wright & Son, 1941-42; office mgr., sec., treas. Concrete Industries, Inc., Albany, Ga., 1945-—, also dir.; treas. Concrete Service and Trucking Co., Albany. Treas. Sowega Youth Home, Albany, 1967-68, pres., 1969. Served with AUS, 1942-45. Decorated Bronze Star medal. Mem. Am. Legion. Baptist (chmn. bd. deacons 1968). Elk. Home: Route 5 Box 423 Dawson Rd Albany GA 31701 Office: 110 Baldwin Dr Albany GA 31705

HOLLAND, BOBBY WENDELL, dentist; b. Liberty, Tex., Apr. 6, 1935; s. William Wesley and Hazel (Martin) H.; B.A., U. Tex., 1958, D.D.S., 1964; m. Merle Stokes, June 29, 1963; children—Guy Wesley, Beth Ann, Mark Wendell. Practice dentistry, Houston, 1964-69, Ft. Worth, 1969-—. Ofcl. weather watcher Channel 5, WBAP, Ft. Worth-Dallas. Bd. dirs. Ridglea Country Club Estates Homeowner's and Civic Club, Ft. Worth Westside YMCA. Mem. Am., Tex., Houston Dist., Fort Worth dental assns., Psi Omega. Baptist (deacon). Club: Briarmeadow Civic. Home: 6912 Benito Ct Fort Worth TX 76126 Office: 2120 Ridgmar Blvd Fort Worth TX 76116

HOLLAND, EARL DEAN, city ofcl.; b. Pilot Point, Tex., Jan. 6, 1944; s. Sterling Mayfield and Ruby Ann (Cox) H.; student Tarrant County (Tex.) Jr. Coll., 1969-71; m. Frances Darleen Moore, June 15, 1962; 1 dau., Dana. With fire dept. City of North Richland Hills, Tex., 1965-—, fire chief, 1971-—. Adv. bd. fire tech. program Tarrant County Jr. Coll., 1970. Mem. Internat. Assn. Fire Chiefs, Tex. Police Assn., Tarrant County, N.E. Tarrant County (v.p. 1970) fire fighters assns. Mason (Shriner). Home: 7504 Lola Dr Fort Worth TX 76118 Office: 4101 Morgan Circle Fort Worth TX 76118

HOLLAND, JACK, ednl. adminstr.; b. Mansfield, Tex., Sept. 9, 1911; s. Fred Darwin and Martha Mae (Harris) H.; B.B.A., U. Tex., 1936, M.B.A., 1952; m. Angela Beatrice King, June 18, 1938; children—Barbara, Darwin, Jeffrey. Employment supr. Consol. Vultee Aircraft Corp., 1943-46; asst. dean of men U. Tex. 1946-48, dean of men, 1948-60, asst. prof. mgmt., 1958-60, dir. univ. personnel office, 1960-64, dean of students, 1964-68, system adviser for student affairs, 1968-—. Bd. dirs. Texas Soc. Crippled Children, 1954-57, 63-66, pres. Travis County, 1951-53; bd. dirs., treas. Tex. Assn. Retarded Children, 1967-69; bd. dirs. exec. com. United Cerebral Palsy Tex. 1952-57, v.p. 1953-58, exec. v.p. 1957-58; bd. dirs. United Cerebral Palsy Travis County, 1953-58; United Cerebral Palsy Regional Conv. Com., 1956; pres. Austin Council Retarded Children, 1949-50, exec. com., 1950-56, bd. dirs. 1958-60; active Boy Scouts Am. Mem. Am. Personnel and Guidance Assn., Inc., 1955-58; 60-62, Tex. Personnel and Mgmt. Assn. (state adv. bd.), Austin Personnel Assn. (pres. 1963-65), Tex. Assn. Student Personnel Adminstrs. (pres. 1954), Am. Soc. Pub. Adminstrs. (pres. Austin chpt. 1965-66), Sigma Iota Epsilon, Alpha Phi Omega (life), Omicron Delta Kappa. Mason, Kiwanian. Home: 1801 Northwood Rd Austin TX 78703

HOLLAND, JAMES RICKS, govt. ofcl.; b. Savannah, Ga., Aug. 3, 1929; s. Francis Ross and Eleanor (Struck) H.; student Armstrong Jr. Coll., 1948-49; A.B. in Journalism, U. Ga., 1954; m. Paula Helene Shepard, Feb. 14, 1959; children—Kristine, Carey, Jamie. Reporter, weekly newspaper, 1953-54; with Internat. News Service, N.Y.C., Detroit, Birmingham, Ala., and Atlanta, 1954-58; with U.P.I., N.Y.C., 1958-59, J. Walter Thompson, N.Y.C., 1959-61; with John Hancock Mut. Life Ins. Co., Boston, 1961-70, 2d v.p. advt. and pub. relations, 1966-70; spl. asst. to postmaster gen. for pub. information, Washington, 1970-71, asst. postmaster for communications and pub. affairs, 1971-—. Served with USAF, 1950-52. Mem. Pub. Relations Soc. Am., Sigma Delta Chi. Home: 105 Summerfield Rd Chevy Chase MD 20015 Office: US Postal Service 12th and Pennsylvania Av Washington DC 20260

HOLLAND, LEWIS GERALD, security broker; b. Atlanta, Feb. 17, 1936; s. Julius Kurt and Carolyn W. (Weinstock) H.; B.S., U. N.C., 1958; m. Marjorie Altshool, June 7, 1961; children—Richard L., Lewis G., Lynn Paula. With E. F. Hutton, Atlanta, 1959-63; with Robinson-Humphrey, Atlanta, 1963-—, v.p., 1969-71, sr. v.p., 1971-—, also dir. Div. chmn. young leadership group United Jewish Appeal, 1967; mem. com. United Appeal, 1972-—; mem. Leadership Atlanta, 1971-—. Bd. dirs. Arbour Acad. Served with USAF, 1959-60, 61-62. Mem. Northside Jr. C. of C. (dir. 1962, v.p., 1963, pres. 1964), Izaak Walton League (pres. 1972), Ga. Securities Dealers, Zeta Beta Tau. Republican. Jewish religion (chmn. budget and finance coms., temple). Mason. Clubs: Circle R, Commerce, Standard Town & Country (Atlanta). Home: 315 Eppington Dr N W Atlanta GA 30327 Office: 2 Peachtree St N W Atlanta GA 30303

HOLLAND, SAMUEL HYMAN, lawyer; b. Lutzin, Latvia, July 1, 1892; s. Zalman I. and Chaye D. (Lev) H.; came to U.S., 1909, naturalized, 1915; LL.B., John Marshall Law Sch., 1915; postgrad. U. Chgo., 1915, Nat. Autonomous U. Mexico, 1959-62; m. Tillie Perlman, Aug. 8, 1920; children—Joshua Zalman, Miriam Filler, Ruth Waddell, Judith King. Admitted to Ill. bar, 1915; practiced in Chgo., 1915-58, Mexico City, Mexico, 1959-62, Washington, 1962-—; mem. firm Holland & Shuckter, Chgo., 1930-47. Bd. dirs. Jewish Welfare Fund Chgo., 1938-53; mem. Chgo. Com. on Human Relations, 1945-58. Mem. Am. Assn. State and Local History, Am. Jewish Hist. Soc., Chgo. Bar Assn., Jewish Hist. Soc. Greater Washington (exec. v.p. 1965-—). Home: 1314 Massachusetts Av NW Washington DC 20005 Office: 1330 Massachusetts Av NW Washington DC 20005

HOLLAND, SPESSARD LINDSEY, lawyer, former U.S. senator; b. Bartow, Fla., July 10, 1892; s. Benjamin Franklin and Fannie Virginia (Spessard) H.; Ph.B., Emory U., 1912, LL.D., 1943; LL.B., U. Fla., 1916, D.C.L., 1953; LL.D., Rollins Coll., Fla. So. Coll., 1941, Fla. State U., 1956; H.H.D., U. Tampa, 1956; LL.D., U. Miami, 1962, Stetson U., 1970; m. Mary Agnes Groover, Feb. 8, 1919; children—Spessard Lindsey, Mary Groover, William Benjamin, Ivanhoe. Tchr. high sch. Warrentown, Ga., 1912-14; tchr. sub-freshman dept. U. Fla., 1914-16; admitted to Fla. bar, 1916, since practiced in Bartow; pros. atty., Polk County, Fla., 1919-20, county judge, 1921-29; mem. Fla. Senate, 1932-40; gov. State of Fla., 1941-45; apptd. by gov. of Fla. to succeed late Charles O. Andrews in U.S. Senate, Sept. 25, 1946; U.S. senator from Fla., 1946-71. Served to capt., C.A.C., U.S. Army, World War I; 24th Squadron Air Corps, in France. Awarded Distinguished Service Cross, 1918. Trustee Emory U., Fla. So. Coll., Lakeland, 1932-35, 60-—, Fla. Presbyn. Coll., St. Petersburg. Mem. Fla. Bar, Am., Bartow bar assns., U. Fla. Alumni Assn. (exec. council 1922-—; pres. 1931), Am. Legion, V.F.W., S.A.R., Phi Beta Kappa, Phi Kappa Phi, Alpha Tau Omega, Phi Delta Phi. Democrat. Methodist. Mason (33 deg., Shriner), Elk, Kiwanian. Home: 1005 S Broadway Bartow FL 33830

HOLLAND, WILLIAM MEREDITH, lawyer; b. Live Oak, Fla., Feb. 6, 1922; s. Isaac and Annie E. (Williams) H.; B.A., Fla. A. and M. Coll., 1947; LL.B., Boston U., 1951; m. Mamie Smith, June 3, 1948; children— William Meredith, Maurice. Admitted to Fla. bar, 1951; since practiced in West Palm Beach. Served with AUS, 1943-46. Mem. Council Human Relations, Am. Civil Liberties Union; cooperating atty. N.A.A.C.P. Legal Def. Fund. Mem. Am., Palm Beach County bar assns., Am. Judicature Soc., Phi Beta Sigma. Episcopalian. Home: 520 17th St West Palm Beach FL 33401 Office: 613 3d St West Palm Beach FL 33401

HOLLANDER, RICHARD ISAAC, editor; b. N.Y.C., Apr. 6, 1912; s. Herman and Bertha (Gichner) H.; student Georgetown U., Washington, 1928-30, George Washington U., 1931; m. Helen Cornelia Eskesen, Mar. 7, 1953. Editorial staff Washington Daily News, 1929-—, editor, 1966-—; engaged as lectr., inst. langs. and linguistics Sch. Fgn. Service, Georgetown U., also George Washington U. Decorated Order Brit. Empire, 1945. Compiler: History of the Psychological Warfare Division, Supreme Headquarters Allied Expeditionary Forces, 1945. Home: 3502 Macomb St N W Washington DC 20016 Office: 1013 13th St NW Washington DC 20005

HOLLARS, GARLAND MIDDLETON, supt. schs.; b. Duke, Okla., Sept. 23, 1927; s. Walter Lee and Dezzie Venora (Middleton) H.; B.S., Southwestern State Coll., Weatherford, Okla., 1952; M.Ed., Okla. U., 1954, Ed.D., 1969; m. Norma Jean Tankersley, Aug. 12, 1947; children—Gary, Mark, Luann, Sherol. Tchr. math and sci. pub. schs., Snyder, Okla., 1949-54; supt. schs., Indiahoma, Okla., 1956-60, Wilson, Okla., 1960-61, Dover, Okla., 1961-65, Cyril, Okla., 1965-72, Noble, Okla., 1972-—. Cons. non-graded orgn. elementary schs., area sch. dists. Finance dir. Stumbling Bear Council Boy Scouts Am., 1970, sustaining mem., 1971-—. Served with USAAF, 1946-47. Recipient Appreciation certificate Black Beaver council Boy Scouts Am., 1970. Mem. Okla. Assn. Sch. Adminstrs., Am. Assn. Sch. Adminstrs., Okla. Sch. Bus. Ofcls. Assn., Okla. Edn. Assn., N.E.A., Phi Delta Kappa. Rotarian. Home: 7 Cartwright Dr Noble OK 73068 Office: PO Box 624 Noble OK 73068

HOLLENBACH, LOUIS JACOB, III, former county judge; b. Louisville, Feb. 23, 1940; s. Louis Jacob and Marie (O'Meara) H.; B.A., U. Notre Dame, 1962; LL.B., J.D., U. Louisville, 1965; m. Carroll DeHart, Oct. 17, 1959; children—Louis Jacob IV, John Phillip, Caroline DeHart. Admitted to Ky. bar, 1965, since practiced in Louisville; mem. firm Marshall, Cochran, Heyburn & Wells, 1963-67, Segal Isenberg, Sales & Stewart, 1967-68, Hendricks, Belknap & Hollenbach, 1968-70; Jefferson County judge, Louisville, 1970-—; chmn. Jefferson County Legislature, also chief county exec. Mem. Am., Ky., Louisville bar assns., Ky. Trial Lawyers Assn., Nat. Assn. Counties (dir., chmn. pollution com.), Louisville Jr. C. of C. (legal counsel 1968). Home: 3303 Natchez Av Louisville KY 40206

HOLLENSHEAD, CLYDE WILLYS, natural gas co. exec.; b. Ruple, La., Apr. 2, 1914; s. Thomas Franklin and Kathryn (Miller) H.; B.S. in Civil Engring., La. Poly. Inst., 1935; postgrad. Mid South Exec. Devel. Program, 1960-63, Advanced Mgmt. Program, Harvard, 1967; m. Armenta Scott, Aug. 10, 1963; children—Thomas C., Richard E. With United Gas Pipe Line Co. and predecessor co., Houston, 1935-—, sr. v.p. engring. and operations, 1969-—, also dir.; sr. v.p., dir. United Offshore Co., Shreveport, La., 1967-—; pres. Sea Robin Pipeline Co., Pennzoil Offshore Transmission Co.; dir. Pennzoil Pipeline Co., Houston. Mem. Citizens Action Program, Houston, 1967-—; mem. exec. bd. Norwela council Boy Scouts Am., 1955-—; mem. Met. Planning Commn., Shreveport, 1963-69. Mem. Am. Petroleum Inst., Ind. Natural Gas Assn. Am., La. Engring. Soc., La. Bd. Profl. Engrs., Mid Continent Oil and Gas Assn., Nat. Soc. Profl. Engrs., Houston, Shreveport petroleum clubs, Am., So. gas assns. Club: Shreveport. Home: 211 Blue Willow Dr Houston TX 77042 Office: 1500 Southwest Tower Houston TX 77002

HOLLERS, HARDY, judge; b. Clarendon, Tex., May 20, 1901; s. James Lemuel and Mattie (Mays) H.; student Southwestern U., 1918-19; LL.B., U. Tex., 1927, J.D., 1927; m. Mildred Bernice Calk, Apr. 18, 1921; children—Hardy Warren, Richard Van, James Carlyle. Admitted to Tex. bar, 1927, since practiced in Austin; asst. county atty., Travis County, 1928-29; asst. dist. atty., Travis County, 1933-34; spl. dist. judge, Travis County, 1935-—. Trial counsel maj. war criminals, Nuremberg, Germany, 1945. Pres., Modern Indsl. Developers, Inc. Gen. chmn. Greater Austin Assn., 1968-—. Served from maj. to col. AUS, 1941-46; ETO. Decorated Legion of Merit (U.S.); Croix de Guerre with palm (France). Fellow Tex. Bar Found.; mem. Nat. Res. Officers Assn., Am. Legion (past post comdr.), Am., Tex. (past dir.), Travis County bar assns. Methodist. Mason. Home: 2710 Townes Lane Austin TX 78703 Office: Perry Brooks Bldg Austin TX 78701

HOLLEY, CHARLES RICHARD, circuit judge; b. Jacksonville, Fla., Nov. 11, 1924; s. Clyde Cecil and Louise (Roberts) H.; A.B., Duke, 1948; LL.B., U. Fla., 1950, J.S.D., 1950; m. Erlynne Douglas, July 13, 1972; children by previous marriages—Natalie Blanche, Cary Martin, Anita Louise (Mrs. Eugene Raborg), Charles Richard, Jr. Admitted to Fla. bar, 1950; estate planning officer Union Trust Co., St. Petersburg, 1950-53; practice law, St. Petersburg, 1954-67; mem. firms Askew, Wehle, Earle, Goldner & Holley, 1954-59, Charles R. Holley, 1959-68; circuit judge Sixth Jud. Circuit of Fla., Clearwater, 1968-—. Mem. Fla. Ho. of Reps., 1960-64; Republican candidate for gov. Fla., 1964. Served with USNR, 1942-46. Mem. Fla. Bar Assn. Home: 485B S Paula Dr Dunedin FL 33528 Office: Pinellas County Ct House Clearwater FL 33516

HOLLEY, EDWARD GAILON, librarian; b. Pulaski, Tenn., Nov. 26, 1927; s. Abe Brown and Maxie Elizabeth (Bass) H.; B.A. magna cum laude, David Lipscomb Coll., Nashville, 1949; M.A., George Peabody Coll., 1951; Ph.D., U. Ill., 1961; m. Robbie Lee Gault, June 19, 1954; children—Gailon Boyd, Edward Jens, Amy Lin, Beth Alison, Holley. Asst. librarian David Lipscomb Coll., 1949-51; mem. staff U. Ill., 1951-62, librarian edn., philosophy and psychology library, 1957-62; dir. libraries U. Houston, 1962-71; dean Sch. L.S., U. N.C., 1971-—. Served to lt. (s.g.) USNR, 1953-56. Mem. Am. (Scarecrow Press award 1964), Southeastern, Tex. library assns., Assn. Coll. and Research Librarians (editor Monographs 1969-72), Phi Kappa Phi, Kappa Delta Pi, Beta Phi Mu. Democrat. Mem. Ch. of Christ. Author: Charles Evans, American Bibliographer, 1963; Raking the Historical Coals, 1967; (with Don Hendricks) Resources of Texas Libraries, 1968; also articles. Home: 1508 Ephesus Ch Rd Chapel Hill NC 27514

HOLLEY, J(AMES) ANDREW, educator; b. Clay, Miss., Dec. 29, 1898; s. Andrew and Pamelia (Hale) H.; A.B., U. Colo., 1923; M.A., Columbia, 1928, Ed.D., 1947; m. Moreta Burnett, June 14, 1924 (died Mar. 2, 1936); children—William Andrew, Wanda Jean (Mrs. Roy Fish), Helen Jane (Mrs. Helen LeBar); m. 2d Edith Johnson, June 5, 1937. Tchr. rural schs., Okla., 1916-17, prin. village schs., 1919-21; supt. schs., Luther, Okla., 1923-26; asst. high sch. insp., Okla., 1926-29; chief high sch. insp. Okla. State Dept. Edn., 1929-32, 33-36, dir. curriculum, 1936-39; spl. summer lectr. and instr. Central State Coll., Edmond, Okla., 1926, Okla. A. and M. Coll., 1930, U. Okla., 1931-32, 34-36; dep. adminstr. Nat. Youth Adminstrn., 1939-40; prof., head dept. bus. edn. Okla. State U., 1940-51, became dean sch. edn., dir. summer sessions, 1951, now emeritus; asso. ednl. adminstrn. (Columbia), 1946-47; asso. dir. Nat. Council Accreditation Tchr. Edn., 1964-70; ednl. cons., 1970-—. Formerly chmn. child edn. sect. Nat. Safety Congress; active N. Central Assn. Colls. and Secondary Schs., 1929-64, chmn. Okla com., 1929-32, 33-39, chmn. com. on secondary schs., 1936-38, hon. mem., 1963-—; chmn. Okla. Com. Tchr. Edn. and Certification, 1953-55; mem. Nat. Commn.Accrediting Bus. Schs., 1952-65. Served with USN, 1917-18; comdr. (ret.) USNR. Fellow A.A.A.S.; mem. Am. Assn. Sch. Adminstrs., N.E.A., Okla. Edn. Assn., Am. Ednl. Research Assn., Internat. Platform Assn., Delta Sigma Rho. Phi Delta Kappa, Phi Kappa Phi, Delta Pi Epsilon, Sigma Alpha Epsilon, Tawse. Democrat. Baptist. Rotarian. Author articles; co-author books and surveys. Address: 1718 W 4th Av Stillwater OK 74074

HOLLEY, MAX DEAN, elec. engr., govt. ofcl.; b. Altus, Okla., June 24, 1933; s. Elza Monroe and Beulah (Carter) H.; B.S., Okla. State U., 1955; postgrad. U. Ala., 1956-59, Case Inst. Tech., 1962, U. Houston, 1963-64; m. Lee McBride, July 31, 1959; children— Kandy Lee, Dawn Michele. Distbn. engr. Pub. Service Co., Duncan, Okla., 1955-56; engring. evaluation team leader Corporal Missile, Army Rocket and Guided Missile Agcy., Ft. Bliss, Tex., 1956-58; chief electronics sect. Nike Project Office, Huntsville, Ala., 1958-63; mgr. Apollo Guidance and Nav. Devel. Office, Manned Spacecraft Center, NASA, Houston, 1963-—. Served to 1st lt. Ordnance Corps, AUS, 1956-58. Recipient Superior Performance award NASA, 1967, Superior Achievement award, 1969. Registered profl. engr., Okla. Mem. Eta Kappa Nu. Unitarian. Home: 206 Wyndwood Dr Seabrook TX 77586 Office: NASA, Manned Spacecraft Center Rd 1 Houston TX 77058

HOLLEY, PHILIP WILEY, govt. ofcl.; b. Lake Charles, La., Feb. 26, 1932; A.A., Texarkana Coll., 1955; B.B.A., U. Tex., 1958; grad. N.Y. Inst. Finance, 1963; M.B.A., N. Tex. State U., 1968; m. Leilah Onys Nix, Dec. 28, 1956; children—Candace Ann, Cynthia Kay. Quality control staff Gen. Tire & Rubber Co., Waco, Tex., 1958-59; statistician Tex. Elect. Service Co., Fort Worth, 1959-62; adminstrv. asst. City Fort Worth, 1962-67; budget officer HUD, Fort Worth, 1967-—. Instr. accounting Tarrant County Jr. Coll., Fort Worth, 1968-—. Served with USAF, 1951-53. Mem. Mcpl. Finance Officers Assn., Internat. City Mgrs. Assn., Tex. Tchrs. Assn., Pi Sigma Alpha. Home: 2912 Hunter St Fort Worth TX 76112 Office: HUD 814 Taylor St Fort Worth TX 76112

HOLLEY, ROBERT LEON, physician; b. Coffeeville, Miss., Sept. 26, 1915; s. Robert Leon and Clara (Aston) H.; A.B., U. Miss., 1935, B.S., 1938, med. certificate, 1938; M.D., Tulane U., 1940; m. Jeanne Lowry, June 11, 1952. Asst. univ. physician, instr. physiology U. Miss. Sch. Medicine, 1940-42; practice medicine, Macon, Miss., 1947-49, Oxford, Miss., 1949-—; asso. medicine U. Miss. Sch. Medicine, 1953-55; adminstr. Oxford Hosp., Inc., 1956-63; pres. med. staff Oxford-Lafayette County Hosp., 1965, 70. Served with inf. AUS, 1942-45. Decorated Bronze Star. Mem. Am. Acad. Family Physicians, Am., Miss. med. assns., N. Miss. Med. Soc., Delta Kappa Epsilon. Episcopalian. Home: 201 Park Dr Oxford MS 38655 Office: 2200 S Lamar Oxford MS 38655

HOLLEY, RUDOLPH EUGENE, lawyer, state senator; b. Aiken, S.C., Feb. 15, 1926; s. Norton Hansford and Harriett (Holley) H.; B.B.A., U. Ga., 1949, LL.B. magna cum laude, 1958; m. Louise Herman Brittingham, Sept. 19, 1953; children—Robert Eugene, Phillip Gerard, Stephen Thomas, Anna Louise, Eugene Norton. Admitted to Ga. bar, 1957; practiced in Augusta, Ga., 1958-—; mem. firm Congdon and Leonard, 1958, Congdon and Holley, 1959-66, Sanders, Hester and Holley, 1967-—; mem. Ga. State Senate, 1965-—, Democratic majority leader, 1971-—; dep. asst. atty. gen., Ga., 1964-65. Dir. West Lake Devel. Co., Medi-Center of Augusta, Met. Land & Investment Co. (all Augusta). Trustee Hillcrest Meml.

Park Perpetual Care Trust. Served with USAAF, 1943-45, to capt. USAF, 1949-55. Decorated D.F.C. Mem. Phi Beta Kappa, Chi Psi, Phi Kappa Phi, C. of C. Democrat. Baptist. Club: Sertoma. Editor: Ga. Bar Jour., 1957-58. Home: 2715 Walton Way Augusta GA 30904 Office: Commerce Bldg Augusta GA 30902

HOLLINGS, ERNEST F(REDERICK), U.S. senator, lawyer; b. Charleston, S.C., Jan. 1, 1922; s. Adolph G. and Wilhelmine D. (Meyer) H.; B.A., The Citadel, 1942; LL.B. U. S.C., 1947; children—Michael Milhous, Helen Hayne, Patricia Salley, Ernest Frederick, III. Admitted to S.C. bar, 1947; mem. S.C. Ho. of Reps., 1948-54, speaker pro tem, 1950-54; lt. gov. of S.C., 1955-59; gov. of S.C., 1959-63; practiced in Charleston, 1963-—; U.S. senator from S.C., 1966-—. Mem. Hoover Commn. on Intelligence Activities, 1954-55; mem. President's Adv. Commn. on Intergovtl. Relations, 1959-63. Mem. exec. council Lutheran Ch. Am. Trustee Newberry Coll. Named One of 10 Outstanding Young Men, U.S. Jr. C. of C., 1954. Mem. Assn. Citadel Men, Hibernian Soc., Phi Delta Phi. Democrat. Lutheran. Club: Sertoma (Charleston). Home: 120 S Battery Charleston SC 29407 Office: 141 East Bay St Charleston SC 29401 also US Senate Washington DC 20510

HOLLINGS, ROBERT M., lawyer; b. Charleston, S.C., 1915; A.B., Coll. Charleston, 1936; LL.B., Harvard, 1939. Admitted to S.C. bar, 1939, D.C. bar, 1940; now practice law, Charleston. Vice pres. So. Fed. Tax Inst., 1968-69, pres., 1969-70, chmn. bd., 1970-—. Chmn. Charleston Planning and Zoning Com., 1950-—; mem. Charleston Regional Planning Com. Alderman, Charleston. Mem. Charleston, S.C., Am. bar Assns. Address: 39 Broad St Charleston SC 29402*

HOLLINGSWORTH, ALBERT FREEMAN, supt. schs.; b. Lake, Miss., Sept. 5, 1923; s. Albert A. and JoAnna (Gay) H.; B.S., U. So. Miss., 1948, M.A., 1950; m. Fannie Mae McDonald, July 4, 1943; children—Patricia Ann (Mrs. Alan Lowe), Torrey Freeman. Prin., Lexie High Sch., 1946-51; bus. positions, 1951-58; prin., Lake (Miss.) High Sch., 1959-67; county supt. edn., Scott County, Miss., 1967-—. Trustee East Central Jr. Coll. Served with USMCR, World War II; PTO. Mem. Am. Assn. Sch. Adminstrs., Miss., Scott County tchrs. assns. Baptist (deacon 1971-—). Mason (Shriner), Kiwanian. Home: Route 1 Box 22 Lake MS 39092 Office: Ct House Forest MS 39074

HOLLINGSWORTH, BOBBY J., mathematician; b. Sunset, Tex. Aug. 17, 1927; s. Ralph E. and Georgia (Davis) H.; B.S. in Civil Engring., La. Poly. Inst., 1949; M.S., Okla. A. and M. Coll., 1951; Ph.D., Kan. U., 1955; m. Bettie Rea Fox, June 8, 1953; children—Rebecca Rea, Lee Ann. With United Gas Corp., Shreveport, La., 1955-68, research mathematician, 1955-61, operations research asso., 1961-63, corporate planning asso., 1963-65, corporate devel. analyst, 1966-68, exec. asst. corporate finance, 1968-71; mgr. financial analysis Pennzoil United, Inc., Houston, 1971-—. Instr. math. evening div. Centenary Coll., 1959-65, La. Poly. at Barksdale AFB, 1965-68. Served with USNR, 1945-46. Mem. Am. Gas Assn. (research com. on transient flow 1962-—), Am. Math. Soc., Soc. Indsl. and Applied Math., Canadian Math. Congress, Lambda Chi Alpha, Phi Kappa Phi. Democrat. Methodist. Home: 5339 Tilbury Houston TX 77027 Office: Southwest Tower Houston TX 77002

HOLLINGSWORTH, CECIL JAMES, hosp. adminstr.; b. Chickasha, Okla., July 5, 1908; s. William Columbus and Addie (Phillips) H.; grad. high sch.; m. Clarice Keith, May 25, 1929; 1 son, William K. Asst. cashier First Nat. Bank, 1926-30, asst. receiver comptroller of currency, 1930-35; bus. mgr. W. Tex. Hosp., Lubbock, 1935-36, adminstr., 1936-—; pres SPD Service, Inc., Lubbock, 1965-—; dir. S. Plains Drugs, Inc. Mem. State Health Adv. Com. for Comprehensive Health Planning, 1969-—; commr. Hub Home Housing Authority, 1960-63; vice chmn. Community Planning council, 1963-65. Trustee Blue Cross-Blue Shield of Tex. Mem. N.W. Tex. (past pres.), Tex. (past pres.) hosp. assns. Baptist. Kiwanian (dir.). Home: 3611 46th St Lubbock TX 79413 Office: 1302 Main St Lubbock TX 79401

HOLLINGSWORTH, ROBERT EDMUND, editor; b. Monroe, La., June 30, 1926; s. Oswald Murray and Ora (Redfearn) H.; student U. Tex., Austin, 1946-49; m. Ann Elizabeth Prather, July 9, 1949; 1 dau., Lynn. Reporter, Dallas Times Herald, 1949-55; polit. editor, 1955-61, city editor, 1961-63, chief Washington Bur., 1963-65, mng. editor, 1965-71, corporate adminstrv. asst. to pub. and pres., 1971-—. Mem. adv. bd. journalism edn. U. Tex. System; mem. scholarship selection com. St. Johns Coll., Santa Fe. Served with USNR, 1944-46. Mem. S.W. Journalism Forum, Am. Polit. Sci. Assn., Headliners, Sigma Delta Chi. Home: 4920 Mill Creek Rd Dallas TX 75234 Office: Herald Sq Dallas TX 75202

HOLLINS, ARTHUR, III, accountant; b. Lake Charles, La., Aug. 14, 1930; s. Arthur and Mary (Muth) H.; B.S., Washington and Lee U., 1951; m. Gloria Guerry, May 5, 1951; children—Elizabeth, Paula. Pres., Hollins Ins. Agy., Inc., Lake Charles, 1954-65; partner Hollins &Schram, C.P.A.'s, Lake Charles, 1956-—; chmn. 1st Nat. Bank, Lake Charles, 1967-—. Instr., McNeese State Coll., 1955-56. Mem. Lake Charles Draft Bd., 1967-—; pres. Lake Charles Civic Symphony, 1968-69. Trustee Lake Charles Cemetery Assn. Served with AUS, 1951-53. Mem. La. Soc. C.P.A.'s (trial bd. 1965-71), C. of C., Phi Kappa Psi. Episcopalian. Kiwanian. Home: 1510 11th St Lake Charles LA 70601 Office: 616 Broad St Lake Charles LA 70601

HOLLIS, LOYE YVORNE, educator; b. Bonham, Tex., July 28, 1933; s. Herman Lester and Ruby (Nicewarner) H.; student Paris Jr. Coll., 1950-51, E. Tex. State U., 1951-52; B.S., Tex. Tech. Inst., 1954, M.Ed., 1959, E.Ed., 1964; m. Carolyn Huggins, Sept. 14, 1957; 1 dau., Tanya Rene. Elementary sch. tchr., Gail, Tex., 1956-57, Odessa, Tex., 1957-59, prin., 1959-63; teaching fellow Tex. Tech. Inst., Lubbock, 1963-64; asst. prof. U. Houston, 1964-66, asst. prof., chmn. dept. elementary edn., 1966-67, asso. prof., 1967-—, chmn. dept. curriculum and instrn., 1967-70, asso. dean Coll. Edn., 1970-—. Math. cons., dir. in-service program Harris County (Tex.) schs., 1964-—; condr. math. workshops Mich. State U. East Lansing, 1966-67, U. Houston, 1965-—; demonstration tchr., cons. for math. films on teaching strategies South Park Ind. Sch. dist., Beaumont, Tex., 1966-—. Served with AUS, 1954-56. Mem. N.E.A., Tex. State Tchrs. Assn., Tex. (dir.), Houston assns. supervision and curriculum devel., Assn. Supervision and Curriculum Devel., Am. Edn. Research Assn., Nat. Council Tchrs. Math., Sigma Alpha Epsilon, Phi Delta Kappa, Kappa Delta Phi. Methodist (lay leader). Optimist (pres. Odessa, Tex. 1962-63). Contbr. numerous articles to profl. jours. Home: 6122 Rutherglenn Houston TX 77035

HOLLIS, WALTER JESSE, physician; b. Bossier City, La., Mar. 17, 1921; s. Charles Basil and Evie (Barber) H.; M.D., La. State U., 1945; m. Hazel Loree West, Dec. 22, 1945; children—Walter Jesse, Clara Jean, Mary Evelyn. Intern Charity Hosp. La., Shreveport, 1945-46, asst. resident, 1946-47, asso. resident, 1947-48, vis. physician, 1948-51; asst. in medicine Sch. Medicine, La. State U., 1948, mem. faculty, 1953-—, prof. medicine, 1965-—; practice gen. medicine, Bossier City and Shreveport, 1948-51; cardiologist Charity Hosp. La., New Orleans, 1956-64, sr. vis. physician Charity Hosp. New Orleans, 1963-—. Med. examiner, cons. La. Dept. Pub. Welfare, New Orleans, 1960-—; cons. S.E. La. Hosp., Mandeville, 1953-59, electrocardiagram heart sta. Hotel Dieu Hosp., New Orleans, 1971-—. Served to capt. M.C., USAF, 1951-53. Diplomate Am. Bd. Internal Medicine. Fellow A.C.P.; mem. La. Med. Soc., Orleans Parish, La. med. socs., Phi Chi, Alpha Omega Alpha. Baptist. Contbr. to profl. jours. Home: 761 Glouster Pl Gretna LA 70053 Office: 1542 Tulane Av New Orleans LA 70112

HOLLIS, WILLIAM SLATER, educator, lawyer; b. Little Rock, Feb. 11, 1930; s. William T. and Ida Sue (Johnson) H.; B.S. in Bus. Adminstrn., U. Ark., 1952, J.D., 1969; M.A. in Econs., Memphis State U., 1962; Ph.D. in Econs., U. Miss.; m. Nancy Gant, Sept. 4, 1955; children—Laura Lynn, John Pete, Leslie Carol, Mark Bruce. Faculty, Delta State Coll., 1958; admitted to Ark. bar, 1958, Fed. bar, 1959, Tenn. bar, 1965, U.S. Supreme Ct. bar, 1970; practiced in Memphis, Tenn., 1959, 61-—; faculty The Citadel, 1960; asso. prof. law, econs. Memphis State U., 1961-—. Participant, Nat. Def. Strategy Seminar, Nat. War Coll., Washington, 1967. Mem. new govt. structure commn. Shelby County (Tenn.) Govt., 1969; pres. Taxpayers, Inc., 1968-—; mem. nat. exec. com. Citizens for Decent Lit., 1968. Served with USAF, 1952-55; now lt. col. U.S. Army Res. Fellow Found. for Econ. Edn.; mem. Am., So. econ. assns., Am. Assn. U. Profs., Am. Legion, V.F.W., Mil. Order World Wars. Baptist. Mason. Author: The Economic Costs of Alcoholic Beverages to Governments and Taxpayers, 1971. Office: PO Box 80876 Memphis TN 38111

HOLLOMAN, HASKELL ANDREW, ret. judge, rancher; b. Frederick, Okla., Nov. 12, 1907; s. Andrew Harvey and Dora (Prophit) H.; student Okla. State U., 1926-27, U. Okla. Coll. Law., 1935-38; m. Cornelia Louise Lewis, May 23, 1940. Admitted to Okla. bar, 1938; county atty. Frederick, Okla., 1939-41; atty. for state examiner and inspector, Oklahoma City, 1941-42; asst. atty. gen. Okla., 1946; county atty. Frederick, 1946-47, county judge, 1947-49, 52-69; spl. dist. judge Southwestern Okla. Dist., 1969-71. Dir. Tex.-Okla. Fair Assn., Tillman County Mental Health Assn.; dir., past pres. Tillman County Farmers Union Assn. Served from lt. (j.g.) to lt. comdr. USN, 1942-46. Mem. Okla. Assn. County Judges (past pres., Am. Judicature Soc., Am. Legion, Okla., Caddo County, Tillman County (past pres.) bar assns., Okla. Jud. Conf., Frederick C. of C., Okla.-Texas (director), Okla. (dir.) polled hereford assns., Tex.-Okla. (dir.), Red River Valley (pres.), Big Pasture (dir.), Shortgrass (dir.) hereford assns., Southwestern Okla. Cattlemen's Assn. (dir.), Tillman County League of Young Democrats (past pres.), V.F.W. Democrat. Methodist. Kiwanian. Club: Frederick Golf and Country. Home: 412 N 12th St Frederick OK 73542

HOLLOMAN, JEFF JOE, physician; b. Frederick, Okla., Mar. 5, 1922; s. Andrew H. and Dora (Prophit) H.; B.S., Okla. State U., 1947; M.D., Harvard, 1951; m. Wilma Hamm, June 2, 1943; children—Lucinda, Lorraine, Andrew, Joseph. Intern U.S. Navy Hosp., Oceanside, Cal., 1951-52, resident, 1952-53; pvt. practice medicine specializing in family practice, Savannah, Ga., 1953-—; mem. staff Candler Gen. Hosp., Meml. Med. Center, Ga. Infirmary (all Savannah). Diplomate Am. Bd. Family Practice. Fellow Am. Acad. Gen. Practice; mem. 1st Dist. Med. Soc. (pres., 1965-66), Ga. Med. Soc. (trustee, 1971-72), Exchange Club. Presbyn. (elder). Home: 1216 Brightwood Dr Savannah GA 31406 Office: 313 E Hall St Savannah GA 31401

HOLLOWAY, GEORGE REECE, tobacco co. exec.; b. Tazewell, Va., Apr. 25, 1922; s. Henry Franklin and Elizabeth (Johnson) H.; B.S., U. Ky., 1949; m. Mary Jean Michler, Nov. 9, 1946; children—Leslie Elaine, Laura Lee, Roger Wayne, Patricia Jean. Plant supt. Southwestern Tobacco Co., Lexington, Ky., 1950-56; buyer Universal Leaf Tobacco Co., Richmond, Va., 1956-58, prodn. supr., 1958-59; v.p., gen. mgr. Simcoe Leaf Tobacco Co., Ltd. (Ont., Can.), 1959-62, pres., mng. dir., 1962-—. Served with USAAF, 1941-46, USAF, 1951-52. Mem. Hamilton Officers Assn. Clubs: Norfolk Country (Simcoe); Commonwealth, Executive, Deep Run Hunt (Richmond); LaSalle Hunting and Fishing (St. Alexis DesMonts, Que., Can.). Home: 8901 Tresco Rd Richmond VA 23229 Office: 2d and Hunt Sts Simcoe Ontario Canada

HOLLOWAY, LEONARD LEVEINE, found. exec.; b. Ada, Okla., Mar. 23, 1923; s. Leonard L. and Mamie (Burroughs) H.; B.A., Okla. Baptist U., 1948; M.A., U. Okla., 1949, M.S., 1950, D.D. (hon.), 1958; m. Betty Gould Holloway, May 29, 1944; children—Sheila Kay, Jamie Lynn. Mem. faculty Tex. Women's U., 1950-51, Wayland Coll., 1951-52, dir. pub. relations Baptist Gen. Conv., Tex., 1953-59; v.p. H.E. Butt Found., 1959-61, mem. exec. staff, 1970-—; v.p., prof. New Orleans Bapt. Theol. Sem., also So. Bapt. Theol. Sem., 1961-66; pres. Mary Hardin-Baylor Coll., 1966-68, U. Corpus Christi, 1968-70; part-time pub. relations and mgmt. cons., 1958-66. Bd. dirs., past pres. Bapt. Pub. Relations Assn.; edn. tng. dir. local Civil Def.; community relations adviser Peace Corps; mem. President's Com. Refugee Placement. Chmn. bd. dirs. local A.R.C., Conf. Southwest Founds.; bd. dirs. Internat. Christian Leadership. Served with USAAF, 1941-45, 52-53; lt. col. Res. Decorated D.F.C., Air medal with clusters. Mem. Am. Assn. Ind. Coll. and Univ. Presidents, Tex. Assn. Colls. and Univs. (mem. edni. policies commn.), Assn. Bapt. Colls. Author: Encounter with God, 1972; also booklets, articles. Home: 33 Townhouse Lane Corpus Christi TX 78412

HOLLOWAY, RUSSELL BENJAMIN, lawyer; b. Kiefer, Okla., Mar. 19, 1920; s. Mark Holmes and Flora (Lunsford) H.; student Okla. State U., 1938-40; B.S., U. Ark., 1942; LL.B., U. Okla., 1947; m. Bette Lou, Oct. 29, 1944; children—Russell B., Danny and Dave (twins), Bart; m. 2d, Nadine Norton, August 25, 1967 (div.). Admitted to Okla. bar, 1947; chief trial asst. Oklahoma County county atty., 1948-49; mem. firm Rhodes, Hieronymus, Holloway & Wilson, Oklahoma City and Tulsa, 1948-—. Mem. adv. bd. Mercy Hosp., 1959-—; active Boy Scouts. Trustee Reding Trust. Served to capt. AUS, 1942-47. Mem. Am., Okla., Oklahoma City bar assns. Democrat. Mem. Christian Ch. Blue Goose. Home: 5502A Woodbrier Dr Oklahoma City OK 73122 Office: Rhodes Hieronymus Holloway and Wilson 1st Nat Bldg Oklahoma City OK 73102

HOLLOWAY, TERESA FLOYD BRAGUNIER (MRS. JOHN CALVIN HOLLOWAY), author; b. Apalachicola, Fla., Jan. 17, 1906; d. David Ralph and Mordina (Floyd) Bragunier; grad. Fla. State Coll. Women, 1925; postgrad. U. Fla., 1930; m. John Calvin Holloway, Oct. 21, 1926: 1 son, John (dec.). Office mgr., publicity writer Fla. C. of C., Jacksonville, 1928-35; polit. campaign office mgr., speech writer, W. Palm Beach, Fla., 1935-36; owner, operator wholesale mfg. bus., Jacksonville, 1936-43; attache Fla. Senate, 1947-67; campaign coordinator, Jasper Fla., 1968-—; instr. creative writing Fla. Jr. Coll., Jacksonville, 1966-67, Jacksonville U., 1969-71; lectr. Cons. to pres. Fla. Tech. U., 1965-66; spl. corr. documentary scripts WFGA-TV, Jacksonville, 1955-—. Mem. Friends of Library, 1960-—. Recipient various certificates of recognition Gov. P.R., 1933, SSS, 1948, Pres Harry Truman, 1951, U. Fla. Journalism Conf., 1959, Fla. Jr. Coll., 1966, Jacksonville U., Sears Found. Regional award for writing, 26 Intramural awards for writing and photography, Outstanding Literary Contribution award Nat. League Am. Penwomen, 1966. Mem. Nat. League Am. Penwomen (past pres. Jacksonville br., editor Southeastern region 1964-68), Mystery Writers Am. Author numerous novels including Girl In Studio B, 1967; Murder at Auction, 1961; Lady Lawyer, 1964; Nurse on Dark Island, 1969; Nurse to Remember, 1970; Nurse Transplanted, 1971; Campaign for Pam, 1971; Nurse Paige's Triumph, 1972. Contbr. articles, columns, newspaper features. Home and office: 4349 Irvington Av Jacksonville FL 32210

HOLLOWAY, VERNON CARLYLE, state legislator; b. Richmond, Va., Sept. 5, 1919; s. Samuel Lee and Maude Estelle (Powell) H.; ed. Va. Mech. Inst., U. Miami; m. Roberta Mae Galbraith, July 28, 1960; children—Jean Estelle, Vernon Carlyle, Lee Anthony. Pres., founder Interstate Electric Co., Miami, Fla., 1949-—; mem. Fla. Ho. of Reps., 1966-—. Mem. Dade County (Fla.) Mediation Bd., 1957-66, Dade County Bd. Rules and Appeals, 1964. Mem. Nat. Elec. Contractors Assn. (past pres. chpt.), Fla. State Elec. Masters Assn. (past pres.), Fla. Electric Council (past pres.), I.E.E.E. Rotarian, Mason (Shriner). Address: 6444 NE 4-th Av Miami FL 33138*

HOLLOWAY, WILLIAM VERNON, univ. adminstr.; b. Weimer, Tex., Oct. 18, 1903; s. John William and Ethel (Carlton) H.; B.A., Southwestern U., 1925; M.A., U. Wis., 1928; Ph.D., U. Wash., 1932; m. Mary Catherine Bowen, Oct. 31, 1925; children—William Bowen, Catherine Carlton. Asst., then asso. prof. polit. sci. U. Ala., 1928-36; asso. prof. polit. sci. Tulane U., 1936-46; asso. prof., then prof. polit. sci. U. Tulsa, 1946-56; prof. pub. adminstrn. Fla. State U., 1956-58; dean Grad. Sch., U. Tulsa, 1958-—, v.p. univ., 1959-—. Chief classification div. New Orleans Civil Service Commn., 1943-46; cons. Stanolind Oil and Gas Co., Tulsa, summers 1952-54; mem. Tulsa County Excise Bd. and Bd. Equalization, 1961-65. Mem. Am. Polit. Sci. Assn., Southwestern Social Sci. Assn., Pi Kappa Alpha, Pi Gamma Mu, Phi Eta Sigma. Author: State and Local Government in the U.S., 1951. Co-author: American Government, 1959; Study Guide in American Government, 1959. Home: 214 E 27th Pl Tulsa OK 74114

HOLLOWELL, WILLIE B., hosp. adminstr.; b. Huntingdon, Tenn., June 29, 1915; s. William Esco and Beulah (Morris) H.; student Bethel Coll., 1933-35, U. Tenn. Night Coll., 1955-59; m. Kate Elizabeth Orr, June, 1936 (div. May 1954); children—Roger, Jan (Mrs. Charles Collins), Mary; m. 2d, Anna Ruth Hill, May 4, 1959. Office mgr. Texaco Oil Co., Trenton, Tenn., 1946-50; owner Hollowell Sausage Co., Trenton, Tenn., 1950-55; bus. mgr. Campbell Clinic and Hosp., Memphis, 1955-61; bus. mgr. Bleecker Clinic, Memphis, 1961-69; adminstr. Carroll County Gen. Hosp., Huntingdon, 1969-—. Served with USNR, 1945-46. Mem. Tenn. Hosp. Assn., W. Tenn. Hosp. Council. Republican. Baptist. Mason. Home: RFD 1 Westport TN 38387 Office: 625 High St Huntingdon TN 38344

HOLLY, HOWARD, govt. ofcl.; b. Burgaw, N.C., Oct. 24, 1922; s. David Frank and Agnes (Ward) H.; grad. Campbell Coll., 1940; m. Elizabeth Page, June 11, 1967. Bookkeeper, Kramer's Dept. Store, Wallace, N.C., 1943-61; auditor Pender County, Burgaw, N.C., 1962-—, county tax supr., 1962-—, clk. County Bd. Commrs., 1962-—. Mem. Pender County Bd. of Edn., 1955-61, chmn. bd. 1960-61; mayor pro-tem, commr., Burgaw, N.C., 1951-54. Trustee Campbell Coll., 1968-72; bd. govs. N.C. Advancement Sch., Winston-Salem, 1967-70; trustee Cape Fear Tech. Inst., Wilmington, N.C., 1963-—; past pres. Pender Fair Assn.; exec. com. gen. bd. N.C. Bapt. State Conv., moderator Wilmington Bapt. Assn., 1969-71. Mem. N.C. Assn. County Accountants (1st v.p.), N.C. Assn. Agrl. Fairs (past pres.). Baptist (deacon). Mason, Rotarian. Home: PO Box 4 Burgaw NC 28425 Office: County Courthouse Burgaw NC 28425

HOLMAN, C(LARENCE) HUGH, educator, writer; b. Cross Anchor, S.C., Feb. 24, 1914; s. David Marion and Jessie Pearl (Davis) H.; B.S., Presbyn. Coll., 1936, A.B., 1938, Litt.D., 1963; Ph.D., U. N.C., 1949; L.H.D. (hon.), Clemson U., 1969; m. Verna Virginia McLeod, Sept. 1, 1938; children—Margaret McLeod, David Marion. Dir. pub. relations Presbyn. Coll., 1936-39, dir. radio, 1939-41, instr. English, 1941-45, acad. dean, 1945-46; instr. English, U. N.C., 1946-49, asst. prof., 1949-51, asso. prof., 1951-56, prof., 1956-59, Kenan prof. English, 1959-—, chmn. div. humanities, 1959-62, chmn. dept. English, 1958-62, Kenan prof. on research leave, 1957, chmn. of Coll. Arts and Scis., 1954-55, dean Grad. Sch., 1963-66, provost, 1966-68. State publicity dir. S.C. Council Nat. Defense, 1942-44. Academic coordinator 2199th BU, USAAF, 1943-45. Guggenheim fellowship, 1967-68. Mem. N.C. Univ. Press (chmn. bd. govs.), Coll. English Assn., S. Atlantic Modern Lang. Assn., Modern Lang. Assn. Am., Am. Studies Assn., Nat. Council Tchrs. English, Alpha Sigma Phi, Phi Beta Kappa. Democrat. Presbyn. Author 5 detective novels, 1942-47 (with others) The Development of American Criticism, 1955; (with W. F. Thrall and A. Hibbard) A Handbook to Literature, 3d edit., 1970; (with others) The Southerner as American, 1960, Southern Writers Appraisals in Our Time, 1964, Seven Modern American Novelists, 1964; Thomas Wolfe, 1960; John P. Marquand, 1965; The Am. Novel Through Henry James, A Bibliography, 1966; Three Modes of Modern Southern Fiction, 1966; Roots of Southern Writing, 1972; articles in field. Editor: Short Novels of Thomas Wolfe, 1961; The Yemassee, 1961; The World of Thomas Wolfe, 1962; The Thomas Wolfe Reader, 1962; Simms's View and Reviews, 1962; Garretson Chronicle (G.W. Brace), 1964; Of Time and the River (Thomas Wolfe), 1965; co-editor: The Letters of Thomas Wolfe to His Mother, 1968, Southern Writing, 1585-1920, 1970. Collaborator: Annual Rev. Am. Lit. Scholarship, 1963-65, Fifteen Modern American Authors, 1969, Fifteen American Authors Before 1900, 1971. Home: 109 Pine Lane Chapel Hill NC 27514

HOLMAN, JAMES MARVIN, lawyer, judge; b. Dover, Ark., Jan. 17, 1929; s. William T. and Maude (Trotter) H.; B.S., Ark. Poly. Coll., 1955; J.D., U. Ark., 1959; m. Carol Joyce Barns, May 28, 1960; children— Andrea Lynn, James Michael, Kimberly Kay. Admitted to Ark. bar, 1959; practice law, Clarksville, Ark., 1959-—; municipal judge, Clarksville, 1969-—. Mem. Clarksville Bd. Edn., 1966-71, pres. bd., 1970. Served with AUS, 1951-53; Korea. Mem. Am., Ark. bar assns. Rotarian (pres. 1969-70). Home: 206 Rogers St Clarksville AR 72830 Office: 205 Sevier St Clarksville AR 72830

HOLMAN, (CLYDE) JOE, mfg. and oil exec.; b. Omaha, Dec. 7, 1930; s. Clyde Wilson and Eunice (Springer) H.; LL.B. magna cum laude, Woodrow Wilson Coll., 1966; m. Mary Jo Langley, Jan. 7, 1960; children—Gregory Joe, Pamela Sue (Mrs. Rick Abney), Patrick Vaughn, Glede Holman. Area sales engr. Milwhite Mud Sales Co., New Orleans, 1953-55; sales mgr. Reed Engring., New Orleans, 1955-56; spl. rep. Mayronne Mud & Chem. Co., New Orleans, 1956-59; gen. mgr. Riverside Oil Co., New Orleans, Tulsa, 1956-59; dir. indsl. sales Hammons Products Co., Stockton, Mo., 1959-—, agt.; owner, operator Holman Oil Co.; oil producer, Okla.; dir. Oil Patch, Inc., Oklahoma City, Ridgemore Properties, Atlanta. Served with USNR. Mem. Internat. Platform Assn., Sigma Delta Kappa. Baptist. Mason (32 deg., Shriner), Elk. Home: 1508 Woodland Dr Okmulgee OK 74447 Office: PO Box 819 Okmulgee OK 74447

HOLMAN, WILLIAM ROGER, librarian; b. Oklahoma City, Sept. 7, 1927; B.A., U. Okla., 1949; M.S. in Library Sci., U. Ill., 1950; m. Barbara Louise Switzer, Sept. 1, 1945; children—David, Roger, Gregory. With circulation dept. U. Kan. Library, 1950-51; head librarian Pan Am. Coll., 1951-55, Rosenberg Library, Galveston, Tex., 1955-57; dir. San Antonio Pub. Library, 1957-60; city librarian San

Francisco Pub. Library, 1960-67; dir. acad. programs Humanities Research Center, U. Tex., Austin, 1967—. Mem. Am. (chmn. friends of libraries com. 1957-59, mem.. council 1966—), Tex. (chmn. legislative com. 1951-52, pub. libraries sect. 1957-58), Southwestern (chmn. pub. libraries div.) library assns. Author: Library Publications, 1965. Home: 3412 Foothill Terrace Austin TX 78731 Office: Box 8254 U Tex Austin TX 78712

HOLMAN, WOODROW WILSON, sch. supt.; b. Dierks, Ark., Aug. 9, 1912; s. Lyman Christian and Paralee (Price) H.; student U. Ark., 1930-31; B.S., Ark. State Tchrs. Coll., Conway, 1938; postgrad. Southeastern State Tchrs. Coll., Durant, Okla., summer 1941; M.S., Okla. State U., 1952; m. Lois Dee Mantooth, Aug. 25, 1936; 1 dau., Sally Anne (Mrs. Marvin Wayne Crusoe). With Idabel (Okla.) Sch. System, 1940—, prin. high sch., 1950-55, supt. sch. ind. dist. No. 5, 1955—. Mem. C. of C. (bd. dirs., 1955), Okla. Edn. Assn. (v.p., 1953-54). Presbyn. (elder). Mason, Lion. Home: 511 S Av G Idabel OK 74745 Office: 100 NE Av D Idable OK 74745

HOLMANN, ANNE SHARPE (MRS. E. J. HOLMANN), wholesale drug exec., bottling exec., civic worker; b. Bainbridge, Ga., Nov. 7, 1900; d. John Greenleaf and Anne Elizabeth (Sharpe) Garrett; student Salem Acad. and Coll., 1916-19; A.B., Vanderbilt U., 1922; m. Joseph Lee Brown, June 13, 1923 (dec. Apr. 4, 1931); children—Anne Poindexter (Mrs. Reginald Heber Helvenston, Jr.), Joseph Lee, John Garrett, Stephen Glenmore; m. 2d, Ernest McClelland Archer, June 22, 1933 (dec. Jan. 10, 1951); m. 3d, Edward Jacob Holmann, Mar. 29, 1952. Former sec. Jonesboro (Ark.) Coca Cola Bottling Co., also Statesboro (Ga.) Coca Cola Bottling Co., pres., treas. (both companies), 1951—; former v.p. Archer Drug Co., Little Rock, now pres., treas.; mem. bd. Davis Wholesale Drug Co., Shreveport, La. Bd. dirs. City Beautiful Commn.; patron mem. Musical Coterie; bd. dirs. Little Rock Progress Up; mem. health subcom. Little Rock Model Cities Orgn. Chosen Little Rock Woman of Week, Jan. 1948, Jan. 1949; Little Rock Citizen of Week, Feb. 1949; Ark. Woman Year, 1948; Elizabeth Wyman Alumnae award Alpha Omicron Pi, 1951. Mem. Am. Assn. U. Women (former v.p., pres. Ark. div., past legislative chmn. Little Rock br.), YMCA, Nat. Cathedral Assn. (former state chmn.), Women's, Little Rock chambers commerce, Bus. and Profl. Women's Club, Ark. Drug Travelers, U.D.C., D.A.R., Dames Ct. of Honor (past pres.), Daus. Am. Colonists (v.p.), Daus. Colonial Wars, Colonial Dames Am., Delta Kappa Gamma, Alpha Omicron Pi. Methodist (steward). Clubs: Fine Arts of Ark. (past pres.), Little Rock Garden (past pres.), Womans City, Altrusa, Aesthetic, Little Rock Country. Home: 3518 Hill Rd Little Rock AR 72203 Office: 107 E Markham St Little Rock AR 72203

HOLMBERG, ALBERT WILLIAM, JR., publishing co. exec.; b. Orange, N.J., Sept. 18, 1923; s. Albert William and Margaret (Flanagan) H.; B.S. in Bus. Adminstrn., Lehigh U., 1947; m. Dorothy McCollum, Oct. 27, 1945; children—Jeanne (Mrs. Fletcher J. Johnson, Jr.), Margaret D. (Mrs. Roy D. Duckworth III), Ellen T. With N.Y. Times, 1947-70, circulation mgr., 1964-70; pres., gen. mgr. Chattanooga Times, 1970—; pres., dir. Times Pub. Co. Mem. No. Valley Regional High Sch. Bd., Demarest, N.J., 1958-62. Trustee Huguonot Meml. Ch., Pelham, N.Y., 1967-70. Served to 1st lt. USAAF, World War II. Clubs: Rotary, Mountain City (Chattanooga). Home: 611 E Brow Rd Lookout Mountain TN 37350 Office: 117 E 10th St Chattanooga TN 37401

HOLMBERG, RUTH SULZBERGER, printing co. exec.; b. N.Y.C., Mar. 12, 1921; d. Arthur Hays and Iphigene (Ochs) Sulzberger; A.B., Smith Coll., 1943; m. Ben Hale Golden, June 1, 1946 (div. Mar. 1965); children— Stephen A.O., Michael D., Lynn Iphigene, Arthur Sulzberger; m. 2d, A. William Holmberg, Jr., May 26, 1972. Reporter, N.Y. Times, summers 1939-45, dir. N.Y. Times Co., 1961—; music critic Chattanooga Times, 1946-57, dir. spl. activities, 1956—; asst. sec. Times Printing Co., 1950-60, v.p., 1956-65, pres., 1965-70, chmn. bd., 1970-72, pub., 1965—; pres., pub. Chattanooga Post, 1966-70. Pres. Chattanooga Symphony, 1959-61; dir. Chattanooga Times Found., Inc.; trustee U. Chattanooga. Served in ETO with A.R.C., 1943-45. Sustaining mem. Jr. League. Home: 919 Scenic Hwy Lookout Mountain TN 37350 Office: 117 E 10th St Chattanooga TN 37402

HOLMES, A. BARON, III, lawyer; b. Hendersonville, N.C., Oct. 20, 1905; B.A., U. N.C., 1927, LL.B., 1930. Admitted to S.C. bar, 1930, N.C. bar, 1930; now mem. firm Holmes & Thomson, Charleston, S.C. Pres. Legal Aid Soc., 1963-66. Served to lt. comdr. USNR, World War II. Mem. Charleston County, S.C., Am. bar assns., Am. Judicature Soc., Nat. Assn. R.R. Trial Counsel, Phi Delta Phi. Lion (pres. 1967-68). Address: People's Office Bldg 18 Broad St Charleston SC 29402*

HOLMES, ANN HITCHCOCK, journalist; b. El Paso, Tex., Apr. 25, 1922; d. Frederick E. and Joy (Crutchfield) Holmes; student Whitworth Coll., 1940; Mus.D., So. Coll. Fine Arts, 1954. With Houston Chronicle, 1942—, fine arts editor, 1948—. Founder-mem. Municipal Art Commn., Houston, 1966—; mem. fine arts adv. com. U. Tex., Austin, 1968—. Recipient Ogden Reid Found. award for study of arts in Europe, 1953, Ford Found. award, 1965. Guggenheim fellow, 1960-61. Home: 10807 Beinhorn Rd Houston TX 77002 Office: Houston Chronicle 512-20 Travis St Houston TX 77002

HOLMES, CHARLES DAVID, supt. schs.; b. Mt. Calm, Tex., June 4, 1912; s. Charlie Blair H.; B.S., Abilene Christian Coll., 1935; M.E., Tex. Tech. Coll., 1950; postgrad. Tex. A. and M. U., 1961; m. Christine Young, May 18, 1936. Prin., coach Truscott (Tex.) High Sch., 1935-37; coach Bishop (Tex.) High Sch., 1937-38; with sch. system, Friona, Tex., 1938-47, prin. elementary sch., 1940-42, supt., 1945-47; supt. schs. Stratford, Tex., 1947-52; indsl. supt., Vanderbilt, Tex., 1952-64; supt. schs. Calhoun County Ind. Sch. Dist., Port Lavaca, Tex., 1964—. Cons. Tex. A. and M. U., 1952-58; mem. adv. bd. Abilene (Tex.) Christian Coll. Served with USCGR, 1942-45. Mem. C. of C. (bd. dirs., 1970—), Am. Assn. Sch. Adminstrs., Tex. Tchrs. Assn., Tex. Sch. Adminstrs. Home: 506 Brook Hollow St Port Lavaca TX 77979 Office: Drawer DD Port Lavaca TX 77979

HOLMES, CHARLES EVERETT, lawyer, banker; b. Wellington, Kan., Dec. 21, 1931; s. Charles Everett and Elizabeth (Bergin) H.; B.A., Wichita U., 1953; LL.B., Okla. U., 1961; m. Lynn Lacy, Jan. 2, 1954; children—Ann Lacy, Charles Everett III, Rebecca. Trainee, Halliburton Oil Well Cementing Co., Great Bend, Kan., 1956-58; admitted to Okla. bar, 1961; practiced in Tulsa, 1961—; mem. firm Rogers, Bell & Robinson, 1969-71; v.p., trust officer Nat. Bank of Tulsa, 1971—; sec. Sinclair Oil & Gas Co., Sinclair Can. Oil Co., Mesa Pipeline Co., Border Pipe Line Co., Sinclair Transp. Co., Ltd. Del. Okla. Council Cath. Diocese, 1966—; chmn. Cath. Parish Governing Body, 1968—. Served with USAF, 1954-56, 61-62. Mem. Am., Okla., Tulsa County bar assns. Home: 3824 E 60th St Tulsa OK 74135 Office: Nat Bank of Tulsa Bldg Tulsa OK 74103

HOLMES, CHARLES WILMORE, health ofcl.; b. Bloomfield, N.J., Feb. 7, 1913; s. Howard H. and Florence (Canfield) H.; A.B., Elon Coll., 1936; M.P.H., U.N.C., 1958; student N.Y.U., 1938; m. Edythe E. Holmes, 1936; children—Leigh, Carolyn, Richard, Edward. Sanitarian, Collier County Health Dept., Naples, Fla., 1952-60; environmental health dir. Sarasota County Health Dept., Sarasota, Fla., 1960-66, acting engring. sect. dir., 1966-68, adminstrv. health program analyst, 1968—. Mem. Well Drilling Bd., Sarasota County, Fla., 1962-67, Plumbing Bd., 1958-62. Pres. Fla. Environmental Health Dirs. Conf., 1966. Mem. Nat. Assn. Sanitarians, Gulf Coast Health Conf. (chmn. 1971-72). Home: 740 Canal Rd Sarasota FL 33581 Office: 1938 Laurel St Sarasota FL 33577

HOLMES, DEAN LEE, physician; b. Sandersville, Ga., Jan. 12, 1936; s. Edward Alonza and Margaret (Davis) H.; A.B., Emory U., 1958; M.D., Med. Coll. Ga., 1962; m. Barbara Jean Avant, Aug. 20, 1957; children—Keith Dean, Barbara Andrea, Shannon Rene. Intern Spartanburg (S.C.) Gen. Hosp., 1962-63; practice medicine, Sandersville, Ga., 1963—; mem. staff Meml. Hosp. of Washington County, chief staff, 1970. Mem. Med. Assn. of Ga., Washington County Med. Soc. (pres. 1970). Baptist. Rotarian. Home: 712 Lahnel Dr Sandersville GA 31082 Office: 524 Sparta Rd Sandersville GA 31082

HOLMES, JACK DAVID LAZARUS, educator; b. Long Branch, N.J., July 4, 1930; s. John Daniel Lazarus and Waltrude Helen (Hendrickson) Holmes; B.A. cum laude, Fla. State U., 1952; M.A., U. Fla., 1953; postgrad. Universidad Nacional Autonoma de Mexico, 1954; Ph.D., U. Tex. at Austin, 1959;; m. Anne Elizabeth Anthony, Sept. 6, 1952 (div. Dec. 1965); children—David H., Jack Forrest, Ann M.; m. 2d, Martha Rachel Austin, Feb. 11, 1966 (div. June 1967); m. 3d, Gayle Jeanette Pannell, July, 1967 (div. 1970); 1 son, Daniel; m. 4th, Stephanie Pasneker, Apr. 10, 1971. Instr. history Memphis State U., 1956-58; asst. prof. McNeese State Coll., Lake Charles, La., 1959-61; lectr. U. Md. at Constantina, Spain, 1962; asso. prof. U. Ala. in Brimingham, 1963-68, prof., 1968—. Reading clk. Fla. Ho. of Reps., 1955; reporter-photographer Memphis Press-Scimitar, 1957-58; cons. U.S. Parks Service, 1962, Pensacola (Fla.) Hist. Commn., 1969-70. Served with inf., AUS, 1951. Charles W. Hackett fellow, 1959; Fulbright fellow, 1961-62; Assn. State and Local History grant, 1966; U. Ala. grants, 1964, 66, 68; Mexican Govt. grant, 1954. Mem. Tenn. Squires, Am. Assn. U. Profs., Orgn. Am. Historians, So. Hist. Assn., La. Hist. Assn., Miss, Fla. hist. socs., Ala. Acad. Sci., Phi Beta Kappa, Phi Kappa Phi, Sigma Delta Pi, Phi Alpha Theta, Pi Kappa Phi. Author: Documentos ineditos para la historia de la Luisiana, 1963; Gayoso, 1965; Honor and Fidelity, 1965; Jose de Evia, 1968; Francis Baily's Journal, 1969; New Orleans: Facts and Legends, 1970; Luis de Onis Memoria, 1969; Guide to Spanish Louisiana, 1970. Home: 520 S 22d Av Birmingham AL 35205

HOLMES, JACK THOMAS, marketing advt. and pub. relations co. exec.; b. Fort Worth, Mar. 30, 1915; s. Thomas W. and Margaret (Morse) H.; B.J., U. Tex., 1938; m. Janice Aliwy Nicholson, Jan. 11, 1 dau., Niki Lynn. Mail order buyer/supr. Montgomery Ward, 1939-41; regional sales mgr. WBAP-R-TV, 1948-50, ZIV TV, 1950-51; v.p., co-owner Advt. Agcy., 1951-52; pres., owner Jack T. Holmes & Assos. Advt., Inc., Fort Worth, 1952—; owner Research Assos., Fort Worth, 1955—, Art Assos., Fort Worth, 1955—, Put. Relations Assos., Fort Worth, 1955—. Served to 1st lt., AUS, 1942-45. Mem. Nat. Fedn. Advt. Agcys. (pres. 1958). Downtown Fort Worth Assn. (dir. 1963-67), S.W. Hort. Soc. (pres. 1959), Tex. Pub. Relations Assn. (dir. 1959), Tex. Camellia Soc. (pres. 1970), Confrerie St. Etienne, Confrerie du Guillion. Clubs: Colonial Country Club, Shady Oaks Country Club, Fort Worth Club. Home: 2806 6th Av Fort Worth TX 76110 Office: 2800 W Lancaster St Fort Worth TX 76101

HOLMES, THOMAS JOSEPH, clergyman; b. Sandersville, Ga., June 1, 1917; s. Emmett Lee and Kate (Averett) Holmes; A.B., Mercer U., 1939, D.D., 1965; and B.D., Southeastern Baptist Theol. Sem., Wake Forest, N.C., 1956; m. Grace Bryan, June 4, 1940; children—Lila Katherine (Mrs. Edward Simmons), Thomas Joseph. Ordained to ministry Bapt. Ch., 1936; pastor First Bapt. Ch., Hogansville, Ga., 1942-43; asso. dept. evangelism Ga. Bapt. Conv., 1944; pastor First Bapt. Ch., Manchester, Ga., 1945-51, Lakewood Heights Bapt. Ch., Atlanta, 1951-52, First Bapt. Ch., Franklinton, N.C., 1952-54, First Bapt. Ch., College Park, Ga., 1954-57, Northside Drive Bapt. Ch., Atlanta, 1957-60; dir. univ. devel. and alumni relations, asst. prof. Christianity, Mercer U., 1960-65; pastor Tattnall Sq. Ch., Macon, Ga., 1965-66, asst. to pres. Mercer Univ., 1966—. Mem. exec. com. Ga. Bapt. Conv., 1946-51, mem. endowment com., 1955-58, mem. Home Mission Bd., 1956-60; Active in A.R.C., Community Chest. Dir. bldg. fund campaign Mercer U. So. Sch. Pharmacy, Atlanta. Served as 1st lt. Ga. State Guard, 1942-43. Recipient Author of Yr. award in non-fiction Dixie Council Authors and Pubs., 1970. Mem. Nat. Soc. Fund Raisers (pres. Ga. chpt. 1970), Am. Coll. Pub. Relations Assn., Chi Alpha Omega. Author: Ashes for Breakfast, 1969. Address: 4883 Roswell Rd NE Atlanta GA 30342

HOLMES, WILL STANDLEE, realtor; b. Higgins, Tex., July 6, 1930; s. W. Tom and Clara (Gassaway) H.; student N. Tex. State U., 1947-49; m. Barbara Lanier, Sept. 21, 1951; children—William L., Lou Ann, Jennifer. Sec.-treas., gen. mgr. Mid-State Milling Corp., Alexandria, La., 1954-61; real estate appraiser Stephens Agy., Inc., Alexandria, 1961-64; self employed as real estate broker, appraiser, Lufkin, Tex., 1964—. Contract appraiser Tex. Hwy. Dept., 1966—, Trinity River Authority Tex., 1965—, Sabine River Authorities of Tex. and La., 1962—. Served to 1st lt. USAF, 1950-54. Mem. Soc. Real Estate Appraisers (sr.), Tex. Assn. Realtors, Lufkin Bd. Realtors (pres. 1969), Tex. Soc. Rural Appraisers. Methodist (chmn. bd. 1959-60). Kiwanian. Home: 1420 Sleepy Hollow Dr Lufkin TX 75901 Office: 1422 S 1st St Lufkin TX 75901

HOLMQUEST, DONALD LEE, astronaut; b. Dallas, Apr. 7, 1939; s. Sidney Browder and Lillie Mae (Waite) H.; B.S. in Elec. Engring., So. Meth. U., 1962; M.D., Baylor U., 1967, Ph.D. in Physiology, 1968; m. Charlotte Ann Blaha, July 15, 1961; 1 dau., Hilary Catharine. Student engr. Ling-Temco-Vought, Dallas, 1958-61; electronics engr. Tex. Instruments, Inc., Dallas, 1962; intern Methodist Hosp., Houston, 1967-68; pilot tng. USAF, Williams AFB, Ariz., 1968-69; scientist-astronaut NASA, Houston, 1967—; research asso. Mass. Inst. Tech., 1968-70; asst. prof. radioiogy and physiology Baylor Coll. Medicine, 1970—. Mem. I.E.E.E., Aerospace Med. Assn., Assn. Advancement Med. Instrumentation, Am. Fighter Pilots Assn., Sigma Xi, Alpha Omega Alpha, Sigma Tau. Contbr. med. jours. Home: 4019 Elderwood Seabrook TX 77586 Office: Manned Spacecraft Center Houston TX 77058

HOLMSTROM, FRITZ MILTON GILBERT, anesthesiologist; b. Jamestown, N.Y., Feb. 15, 1923; s. Fritz Emanuel and Hildur Maria (Johnson) H.; student Brown U., 1940-42; M.D., Harvard, 1949, M.P.H., 1955; m. Anne Marguerite Mullikin, June 24, 1948; children—Anne M. (Mrs. Morton W. Baird), Fritz R. Intern, Del. Hosp., 1949-50; gen. practice medicine, Arlington, Va., 1952-54; resident dept. anesthesiology Bexar County Hosp., San Antonio, 1969—; asst. prof. anesthesiology U. Tex. Med. Sch., San Antonio, 1971—. Served with AUS, 1942-45, USAF, 1950-52, 54-69. Decorated Legion of Merit. Fellow Am. Coll. Preventive Medicine, A.C.P., Am. Coll. Anesthesiologists; mem. A.M.A., Aerospace Med. Assn. Home: 1321 Wiltshire Av San Antonio TX 78209 Office: 7703 Floyd Curl Dr San Antonio TX 78229

HOLODNAK, HELEN BARBARA, clin. psychologist; b. N.Y.C., Apr. 11, 1912; d. Casimir and Anna (Stadnyk) Holodnak; B.A., Washington Square Coll., N.Y.U., 1936; M.A., 1939. Chief psychologist Inst. for Crippled and Disabled, N.Y.C., 1939-49; cons. psychologist N.J., Crippled Children Comm., Trenton, N.J., 1944-45; instr. spl. edn. Tchrs. Coll. Columbia, 1945-52; vis. asst. prof. spl. edn. San Francisco State Coll., 1950, 1952-53, vis. asso. prof. spl. edn., 1954-56; exec. dir. United Cerebral Palsy Assn. of San Francisco Pre-Nursery Program, Children's Hosp., 1952-54; dir. rehab. project, vocational counsellor Cal. Tb and Health Assn., San Francisco, 1955-56; rehab. cons. Nat. Multiple Sclerosis Soc., N.Y.C., 1957-58, dir. rehab. services Kings County chpt., Bklyn., 1957-60, cons., 1965-66; adminstr. world commn. on research in rehab. Internat. Soc. for Rehab. Disabled, 1960-62; research asso. Miriam Home for Exceptional children, Montreal, Can., 1963; cons. on services and programming for mil. personnel Nat. Assn. Retarded Children, N.Y.C., 1963-64; dir. psychol. services Community Mental Health Retardation Center, Wichita Falls, Tex., 1970-71. Fellow Am. Assn. Mental Deficiency; mem. Am., Eastern psychol. assns., N.Y. Acad. Scis., Soc. for Projective Techniques, Altrusa Internat. (bd. dirs. 1971-72), Nat. Rehab. Assn., Council Exceptional Children, UN Assn. U.S.A., Internat. Council Psychologists, Kappa Delta Pi, Pi Lambda Theta. Home: 4633 Dexter St Fort Worth TX 76107

HOLSHOUSER, JAMES EUBERT, JR., lawyer; b. Boone, N.C., Oct. 8, 1934; s. James Eubert and Virginia (Dayvault) H.; B.S., Davidson Coll., 1956; LL.B., U. N.C., 1960. Admitted to N.C. bar; practice law. Mem. N.C. Ho. of Reps., 1963-72; chmn. N.C. Republican Com., 1968-72; Rep. candidate for gov. N.C., 1972. Mem. Boone Jr. C. of C., Phi Delta Theta, Phi Alpha Delta. Presbyn. (deacon, treas.). Address: PO Box 328 Boone NC 28607

HOLSTUN, GORDON ROBINSON, educator; b. Waverly, Ala., May 28, 1910; s. P. Reese and Annie L. (Robinson H.; B.S., Ala. Poly. Inst., 1931, M.S., 1940; m. Cora Louise Hooten, Oct. 14, 1932; 1 dau., Beverly Louise. Tchr. R. E. Lee Inst., 1931-38, head social sci. dept., also athletic dir., 1936-37; prin. Lee Jr. High Sch., 1939-40; supt. Upson County (Ga.) Schs., 1941-70, Thomaston (Ga.) Pub. Schs., 1948-70; asso. prof. edn. Tift Coll., Forsyth, Ga., 1970—. Trustee Tift Coll., 1954-58, vice chmn., 1958. Mem. Ga. Edn. Assn. (dir.), State Supts, and Bd. Mems. Assn. (past pres.), Ga. Assn. County Sch. Supts., (past pres.), Ga. Assn. Sch. Adminstrs. (pres. 1960, dir.), Ga. Accrediting Commn. (vice chmn. 1960), Internat. Platform Com., Nat. Soc. Study of Edn., S.A.R., Phi Delta Kappa. Baptist (deacon). Mason (Shriner), Woodman of World. Clubs: Lions (past dist. gov., counselor), National Beta (Ga. chmn. 1969— dir.). Home: 411 S Green St Thomaston GA 30286 Office: Tift College Forsyth GA 31029

HOLT, DON S., textile mfg. exec.; b. Graham, N.C., Mar. 7, 1908; s. Seymour S. and Glenna (Shaw) H.; A.B., U. N.C., 1929; m. Margaret McConnell, 1932. Exec. v.p. Travora Mfg. Co., 1938-49; dir. Nat. Bank of Alamance, 1939-50; v.p. Cannon Mills Co., 1951-60, exec. v.p., 1960-61, pres., 1962—, chmn. bd., 1971—; chmn. bd. subsidiary Cannon Mills, Inc., N.Y.C.; dir. Cabarrus Bank & Trust Co., Social Circle Cotton Mill (Ga.), Imperial Cotton Mills, Eatonton, Ga. Mem. U.S. bd. Anglo-Am. Textile Mission to Japan, 1950; dir. N.C. Textile Mfrs. Assn., 1952. Served as lt. comdr. USNR, 1942-45. Mem. Am. Textile Mfrs. Inst. (exec. com., dir.), Phi Psi. Methodist. Office: Cannon Mills Co Kannapolis NC 28081

HOLT, HAMILTON TATUM, JR., mfg. co. exec.; b. Tampa, Fla., Apr. 20, 1925; s. Hamilton Tatum and Melva (Clark) H.; A.B., U. Ga., 1947, M.B.A., Stanford, 1949; m. Susan Phister, Sept. 20, 1948; children— Susan W., Hamilton T. III, Lisa C.; m. 2d, Georgia Pelham, Jan. 24, 1970. Vice pres., dir. Kickernick, Inc., Mpls., 1954-57; asso. McKinsey & Co., San Francisco, 1958-60; partner, co-founder Strong, Wishart & Holt, San Francisco, 1960-64; v.p. HITCO, Gardena, Cal., 1965-67, pres., dir., 1967-70; chmn. bd. Clark Memls., Inc., Macon, 1963—; pres. All-Tech Industries, Inc., Miami Lakes, Fla., 1970—. Served to lt. USNR, 1943-46, 52-53. Home: 2412 Laguna Dr Fort Lauderdale FL 33316 Office: 14000 NW 57th Ct Miami Lakes FL 33014

HOLT, JOSEPH FRANK, justice. Asso. justice Ark. Supreme Ct., Little Rock. Address: Fed Office Bldg Little Rock AR 72201*

HOLT, RALPH MANNING, JR., hosiery mill exec.; b. Burlington, N.C., Sept. 7, 1931; s. Ralph Manning and Margaret (McElwee) H.; B.S., Davidson Coll., 1953; student Harvard Bus. Sch., 1956-57; m. Eda Luciana Contiguglia, June 3, 1957; children—Ralph Manning III, Margaret Berrena, John Anthony, Michael McElwee. With Holt Hosiery Mills, Inc., Burlington, 1957—, v.p., 1958-66, treas., 1959-66, exec. v.p., 1966-67, pres., 1967—; v.p., treas. Holt Hosiery Corp., N.Y.C., 1959-69; dir. Bush Unversal, Inc., HMW Ind., Inc., Lancaster, Pa. Div. leader Burlington United Fund, 1960-61. Trustee, chmn. Meml. Hosp., Burlington; bd. visitors Davidson Coll. Served to lt. (j.g.) USNR, 1953-55. Mem. Beta Theta Pi. Club: N.Y. Athletic. Home: Mays Lake PO Box 819 Burlington NC 27215 Office: Box 1757 Burlington NC 27215

HOLTER, WILLIAM HUDSON, mathematician, actor; b. Lock Haven, Pa., Nov. 30, 1929; s. Willard Clyde and Josephine (Tibbins) H.; B.S. magna cum laude, Franklin and Marshall Coll., 1952; M.A., Am. U., 1960; m. Margaret Lawrence, Nov. 24, 1961. Mathematician, sr. scientist, head applied math. computer analysis sect. Atlantic Research Corp., Alexandria, Va., 1953-66; project scientist Booz-Allen Applied Research, Inc., Bethesda, Md., 1966-70; tech. staff Mitre Corp., McLean, Va., 1970—. Actor summer stock, 1953—; actor appearing in Uniquecorn Revue, Washington, 1961-62, A Political Party, N.Y.C., 1963. Treas. Waterford Players, 1967—; bd. dirs. Waterford (Va.) Found., 1966—; gov. bd. dirs. Alexandria Little Theatre, 1957; actor dinner theater circuit, Washington, 1968—. Mem. Operations Research Soc. Am., Internat. Platform Assn., Math. Assn. Am., Soc. Indsl. Applied Math., Am. Inst. Aeros. and Astronautics, Am. Ordnance Assn., Phi Beta Kappa. Home: Box 146 Waterford VA 22190 also 523 Queen St Alexandria VA 22314 Office: Mitre Corp McLean VA 22101

HOLTON, ABNER LINWOOD, JR., gov. of Va.; b. Big Stone Gap, Va., Sept. 21, 1923; s. Abner Linwood and Edith (VanGorder) H.; B.A., Washington and Lee U., 1944, LL.D., 1971; LL.B., Harvard, 1949; grad. Sr. Res. Officers Course, Naval War Coll., 1965; LL.D., Va. State Coll., 1971; m. Virginia Harrison Rogers, Jan. 10, 1953; children— Virginia Tayloe, Anne Bright, Abner Linwood III, Dwight Carter. Admitted to Va. bar, 1949; mem. firms Hunter, Fox & Holton, Roanoke, Va., 1949-53, Eggleston, Holton, Butler & Glenn, Roanoke, 1954-69; gov. Commonwealth of Va., Richmond, 1970—. Chmn. So. Growth Policies Bd., 1972. Chmn. Roanoke City Republican Com., 1952-54; vice chmn Va. Rep. Central Com., 1960-69; del. Rep. Nat. Conv., 1960, 68; state campaign mgr. for H. Clyde Pearson, candidate for gov., 1961; Rep. candidate for gov., 1965; regional coordinator Nixon for Pres. Com., 1967-68; chmn. policy com. Rep. Govs.' Assn., 1971, vice chmn. assn., 1971—. Bd. dirs. Roanoke Fine Arts Center, 1965. Served with USNR, World War II; capt. Res.; mem. Nat. Naval Res. Policy Bd., 1961-63. Mem. Am., Va. (v.p. 1965-66), Roanoke (dir.) bar assns., Washington and Lee Alumni Assn. (pres. Roanoke chpt. 1964), Roanoke C. of C. (pres. Backbone Club 1964), Omicron Delta Kappa. Republican. Presbyn. (elder 1954-57, tchr. Sunday sch. 1952-69). Clubs: Country of Va., Downtown (Richmond); Shenandoah (Roanoke). Home: Governor's Mansion Richmond VA 23219 Office: Office of the Governor of Virginia Richmond VA 23219

HOLWAY, JAMES COLIN, steel co. exec.; b. Youngstown, O., Nov. 14, 1927; s. Robert G. and Marie W. (Kane) H.; B.S., Ohio State U., 1950; M.B.A., Pa. State U., 1952; m. Patricia Ann Touscany, Aug. 31, 1957; children—Moira Ann, Colin, Brent Patrick, Jamison McAndrew. Sales trainee U.S. Steel Corp., 1951-55; salesman Republic Steel Corp., Cleve. and Detroit, 1955-58; dist. sales mgr. Tenn. Products & Chem. Corp., Detroit, 1958-60; dist. sales mgr. Nat. Steel Corp., Charlotte, N.C., 1960-72; pres. Southeastern Steel Rolling Mills, Charlotte, 1972—. Served with USNR, 1945-46. Mem. Am. Inst. Mining, Metall. and Petroleum Engrs. (asso.), Internat. Platform Assn. Clubs: Country of Detroit (Grosse Pointe, Mich.); University (Detroit); Charlotte (N.C.) Athletic, Charlotte City, Charlotte Country. Home: 2312 Pembroke Charlotte NC 28207 Office: Suite 1711 Johnston Bldg Charlotte NC 28202

HOLWAY, WILLIAM REA, cons. engr.; b. Sandwich, Mass., Apr. 29, 1893; s. Jerome Richardson and Ella (Ellis) H.; student Dartmouth, 1910-12; B.S. in San. Engring., Mass. Inst. Tech., 1912-15; m. Frances Hope Kerr, July 28, 1916; children—Donald Kerr, Charlotte (Mrs. Ralph Meagher), William Nye; m. 2d, Helen Annette Thayer, Mar. 31, 1970. Asst. engr. City of Providence, R.I., 1915-17; engr. water plant, Tulsa, 1918-20; owner, pres. W. R. Holway & Assos., cons. engring., Tulsa, 1920—. Recipient Outstanding Achievement award Mass. Inst. Tech. Alumni Assn., 1957. Mem. Am. Inst. Cons. Engrs., Am. Soc. C. E., Am. Soc. M. E., Am. Water Works Assn. Unitarian (pres. 1922-23). Mason (32 deg.). Author: History of the Grand River Dam Authority, 1968. Home: 2472 E 22d St Tulsa OK 74114 Office: 1850 S Boulder St Tulsa OK 74119

HOLZMAN, IRVING MURRAY, anesthetist; b. Knoxville, Tenn., Oct. 21, 1936; s. Jacob Leroy and Tessie (Levine) H.; B.A., Vanderbilt U., 1958; grad. Pensacola Jr. Coll. Sch. Nursing, 1960, Mayo Clinic Sch. Anesthesia, 1962. Staff anesthetist U. Fla. Med. Center, Gainesville, 1962-65; asst. chief anesthesia dept. Meml. Hosp., Panama City, Fla., 1965—, dir. Sch. Anesthesia, 1968—. Unit chmn. United Fund, 1971. Mem. Am., Fla. (trustee 1965-66, pres. 1968-70) assns. nurse anesthesists, Southeastern Assembly Nurse Anesthetists (trustee 1968-70), Jr. C. of C. (dir. 1968-69, chaplain 1969-70). Home: PO Box 2472 Panama City FL 32401 Office: 600 N MacArthur Av Panama City FL 32401

HOMER, LEWIS HOLMAN, JR., real estate broker; b. Andover, Mass., June 4, 1915; s. Lewis Holman and Edith (Whittemore) H.; student La Salle Extension U.; m. Jean Rees, Mar. 8, 1941; children—Lewis Holman III, John Whittemore. Owner Homer Realty, Clearwater, Fla.; pres. Homer Properties, Inc.; dir. Clearwater Fed. Savs. & Loan Assn. Mem. Clearwater Zoning Bd., 1949-55, Clearwater Planning Bd., 1955-57, Pinellas County Indsl. Council, 1955; chmn. Clearwater Indsl. Devel. Com., 1955-57; mem. Pinellas County Bd. Commrs.; mayor City of Clearwater, 1957-58; mem, Pinellas County Library Bd.; dir. Bayview Gardens Housing, Inc.; treas. Bayview Gardens Housing, Congregational House. Served with USAAF, 1943-45. Member Clearwater Bd. Realtors (pres. 1954-55), Clearwater C. of C. (pres. 1961). Am. Legion (comdr. 1947). Clubs: Clearwater Yacht, Carlouel Yacht. Home: 719 Mandalay Rd Clearwater Beach FL 33515 Office: 1212 Cleveland St Clearwater FL 33515

HOMER, PORTER WYMAN, county ofcl.; b. Oxford, N.Y., Apr. 7, 1923; s. Willis Heald and Grace Katherine (Wyman) H.; B.A., U. Conn., 1948; postgrad. Syracuse U., 1948-49; m. Laura Magdalen McHale, Nov. 10, 1949; children—Katherine, Peter, Gregory, Andrew, Pierce. Dir. research, budget, Kansas City, Mo., 1949-55; city mgr., Tucson, 1955-62; city mgr., Rochester, N.Y., 1962-65; county mgr., Dade County, Miami, Fla., 1965—. Adv. com. urban devel. Dept. Health, Edn. and Welfare. Served with inf. AUS, 1943-46; ETO. Mem. Internat. City Mgrs. Assn. (v.p., chmn. goals com.), Am. Soc. Pub. Adminstrn., Nat. Assn. County Ofcls., Municipal Finance Officers Assn., Nat. League Cities (chmn. personnel policy com.), L.P. Cookingham Alumni Assn. (past pres.). Home: 11710 SW 67th Ct Miami FL 33156 Office: County Ct House Miami FL 33101

HONEYCUTT, LEX EDWARD, city ofcl.; b. Gold Hill, N.C., Nov. 26, 1924; s. Charles Edward and Mary Kathleen (Hahn) H.; B.S. in Civil Engring., Duke, 1950; m. Katherine Elizabeth Barringer, June 4, 1947; children—Len Edward, Lex Edward II. Asst. dir. pub. works, City of Salisbury, N.C., 1950-55; dir. pub. works, city engr., City of Thomasville, N.C., 1955-60, City of Wilson, N.C., 1960-70, City of Lenoir, N.C., 1970—. Mem. bd. alderman, Town of Rockwell, N.C., 1953-55; mem. N.C. Air Control Adv. Council, 1967—; mem. Solid Waste Commn., 1970—. Served with AUS, 1944-46; ETO. Registered profl. engr., N.C. Mem. Am. Pub. Works Assn. (dir. N.C. sect. 1964-65, pres. 1967), Am. Water Works Assn. (trustee N.C. sect. 1969-70). Presbyn. Home: 301 Olive Av Lenoir NC 28645 Office: 206 S Main St Lenoir NC 28645

HONEYCUTT, WALLACE BLAIR, dentist; b. Gastonia, N.C., June 28, 1934; s. Worth Daniel and Anna Belle (Wallace) H.; A.A., Brevard Jr. Coll., 1954; B.S., U. NC., 1960, D.D.S., 1964; m. Patricia Marilyn Greene, Dec. 22, 1956; children—Stephany, Whitney, Kristin, Matthew. Practice dentistry, Statesville, N.C., 1964—. Co-chmn. Cancer Crusade, 1967. Served to 1st lt. AUS, 1955-58. Mem. Iredell County Dental Soc. (pres., 1971). Kiwanian, Elk. Club: Statesville Country. Home: 308 Augusta Dr Statesville NC 28677 Office: 110 Stockton St Statesville NC 28677

HONHOLT, EDITH, newspaper editor; b. Charlotte, Mich., Mar. 3, 1928; d. Herman J. and Lillian klebe (Bradley) Honholt; B.A., Cornell Coll., Mount Vernon, Ia., 1951. Sec., researcher, editorial asst. New Yorker Mag., N.Y.C., 1953-57; TV editor, TV mag. editor, editoral asst., women's reporter, women's editor Houston Post, 1957-70, asso. editor Tempo, Sunday rotogrovure Mag., 1970-71, spl. makeup editor Houston Post, 1957—. Mem. Theta Sigma Phi. Episcopalian. Home: 5529 Beverly Hill Houston TX 77027 Office: 4747 Southwest Freeway Houston TX 77001

HOOD, ANDREW MCCAUGHRIN, judge; b. Anderson, S.C., Oct. 13, 1900; s. John Kyle and Sarah (Kennedy) H.; A.B., Erskine Coll., 1921; LL.B., Georgetown U., 1924; m. Mildred Booth, Dec. 20, 1951; 1 son, Peter Andrew. Admitted to D.C. bar, 1924; practiced in Washington, 1924-42; judge D.C. Ct. of Appeals, 1942-62, chief judge, 1962—. Home: 2237 46th St NW Washington DC 20007 Office: 400 F St NW Washington DC 20001

HOOD, BILL JIM, supt. schs.; b. Brownwood, Tex., July 25, 1925; s. W. A. and Margaret (Johnson) H.; B.A., Hardin-Simmons U., 1949, M.Ed., 1952; postgrad. Sul Ross State Coll., summers 1958-61, Abilene Christian Coll., summer 1954, Tex. Tech. U., 1969; m. Mary Carolyn Clark, Jan. 29, 1950; children—William Leslie, James Bruce, Steven Clark. Tchr. English high sch., Sterling City, Tex. 1951-53; tchr. English high sch. Rankin, Tex., 1953-57, jr. high prin., 1957-58, high sch. prin., 1958-63, supt., 1963-67; supt. schs., Snyder, Tex., 1967—. Dist. com. chmn. Boy Scouts Am., 1965-67, dist. chmn., 1968—. Served with USNR, 1943-46. Mem. Tex. Tchrs. Assn. (pres. Rankin local unit 1956-57, dist. IV 1967-68), N.E.A., Tex. Assn. Sch. Adminstrs., Assn. Sch. Adminstrs. Baptist (mem. Christian edn, commn. Bapt. Gen. Conv. Tex.). Mason, Lion (pres. Rankin 1963, 64). Home: 3001 34th St Snyder TX 79549

HOOD, EVANS CARROL, supt. schs.; b. Sweetwater, Tex., Mar. 10, 1929; s. Marvin and Mary (Gentry) H.; B.S., N.Tex. State U., 1950; M.A., Hardin-Simmons U., 1952; postgrad. Colo. State Coll., summers 1961-62; Ph.D., E.Tex. State U., 1965; m. Bettie Horn, July 21, 1950; children—Marc C., Kathryne Ann. Jr. high sch. tchr., Olden, Tex., 1950-52; jr. high sch. prin., Spur, Tex., 1952-53; elementary sch. tchr., Odessa, Tex., 1953-56, elementary sch. prin., 1956-65; instr. Evening Coll., Odessa, 1958-65; dir. personnel, Odessa, 1965-66; supt. schs., Palestine, Tex., 1966—. Served with USMCR, 1946-48. Mem. Tex. Tchrs. Assn., Am., Tex. assns. sch. adminstrs., Palestine C. of C., Phi Delta Kappa. Rotarian. Home: Box 248 Palestine TX 75801 Office: Box 440 Palestine TX 75801

HOOD, FRED, educator; b. Harrodsburg, Ky.; grad. Georgetown (Ky.) Coll., 1960; Ph.D., Princeton, 1970. Formerly asst. prof. history Georgetown Coll., now asso. prof. Nat. Endowment for Humanities grantee for publ. dissertation. Address: Georgetown Coll Georgetown KY 40324*

HOOD, GORDON HUBBARD, lawyer; b. Cin., May 2, 1928; s. William Glazier and Alice (Hood) H.; A.B., Dartmouth, 1950; LL.B., U. Cin., 1953; m. Jo Ann E. Zeidler, May 26, 1951; children—Gordon Hubbard, Kathleen J., Bradford M., Denise A. Admitted to Ohio bar, 1953, Ky. bar, 1954; practiced law, Cin., 1953, Covington, Ky., 1954—; mem. firms Heckerman & Hood, 1959. Vice chmn. Bd. Edn., Beechwood Sch. Dist., Ft. Mitchell, Ky., 1959—; chmn. Ky. Council on Pub. Higher Edn. Mem. adv. bd. Booth Meml. Hosp., Covington, 1963—, Hanover Coll., Ind.; bd. dirs. No. Ky. YMCA, 1964—. Home: 226 Ft Mitchell Av Ft Mitchell KY 41011 Office: 2400 Central Trust Tower Cincinnati OH 45202 also 1st Nat Bank Bldg Covington KY 41011

HOOD, GRAHAM, museum ofcl. Formerly asso. curator Garvan Collection, Yale; then curator Am. art Detroit Inst. Arts; curator Colonial Williamsburg (Va.), 1971—; lectr. in field. Address: Colonial Williamsburg Found Williamsburg VA 23185*

HOOD, JOHN THOMAS, JR., judge; b. Hazelhurst, Miss., Aug. 16, 1909; s. John Thomas and Minnie (Stewart) H.; B.A., La. State U., 1931, J.D., 1933;; m. Alvina Ruth Good, Sept. 10, 1938; children—Susan Janet, John Stewart. Admitted to La. bar, 1933; practiced in Jennings, La., 1933-46; dist. judge La. 14th Jud. Dist., Lake Charles, 1946-60; judge Ct. Appeals, La. 3d Circuit, Lake Charles, 1960—; past sec. La. Conf. Ct. of Appeal Judges. Past pres. YMCA, Lake Charles. Served to maj. AUS, 1942-46. Decorated Legion of Merit. Mem. Am., La., S.W. La. bar assns., Am. Judicature Soc., Inst. Jud. Adminstrn., La. Law Inst., La. Dist. Judges Assn. (past pres.), Appellate Judges Conf., Greater Lake Charles C. of C., Am. Legion, V.F.W., Lake Charles Power Squadron, La. Outdoor Drama Assn., La. State U. Alumni Fedn. (past pres.), La. State U. Law Sch. Alumni Assn. (past pres.), Lambda Chi Alpha, Gamma Eta Gamma (past chancellor), Order of Coif, Scribes. Presbyn. (elder). Mason, Kiwanian (past lt. gov.). Club: Lake Charles Country. Contbr. profl. jours. Home: 1008 8th St Lake Charles LA 70601 Office: PO Box 3000 Lake Charles LA 70601

HOOD, WILLIS TED, dentist; b. Mt. Hermon, Ky., Apr. 25, 1934; s. Prentise and Anna (Brown) H.; student Western Ky. State U., 1952-54, 58-60; D.M.D., U. Louisville, 1964; m. Aileen Clay, Aug. 20, 1960; children—Melody, Maria, Edward Mitchell. Practice dentistry, Mt. Sterling, Ky., 1964—. Cons. Area Comprehensive Health Planning Council; mem. Montgomery County Bd. Health. Served with USNR, 1954-58. Mem. Am., Ky., Blue Grass dental assns., Am. Acad. Gen. Dentistry, Am. Analgesia Soc. Republican. Rotarian (dir. 1968—). Baptist (deacon). Home: PO Box 443 Mt Sterling KY 40353 Office: 30 N Main St Mt Sterling KY 40353

HOOK, ARTHUR BENJAMIN, physicist; b. Arlington, S.D., July 27, 1926; s. Benjamin Mandred and Rena (Waldron) H.; B.S., S.D. State U., 1951, M.S., 1952; postgrad. U. Wis., 1954; Ph.D., Georgetown U., 1964; m. Ruth Arlene Gottschalk, Aug. 17, 1952; children—Lynn Rene, David Arthur, Laureen Moselle. Lectr. physics and math. Lawrence U., Appleton, Wis., 1954; asst. prof. physics and math. Ripon Coll., Ripon, Wis., 1955; physicist research br. Bur. of Engraving and Printing, Washington, 1956-58; chief plasma rediation segment Basic Research Lab., Ft. Belvoir, Va., 1958-62; chief laser research br. Night Vision Lab., Ft. Belvoir, Va., 1962-68; chief combat support operations div. Inst. Land Combat, U.S. Army Combat Devels. Command, Ft. Belvoir, 1968-72. Served with USAAF, 1946-48, lt., 1951. Mem. Am. Assn. Physics Tchrs., Optical Soc. Am., Astron. Soc. Am., A.A.A.S., Am. Inst. Physics, Am. Assn. Physicists in Medicine, Soc. for Neurosci., Sigma Pi Sigma, Sigma Xi. Presbyn. Home: 7424 Clifton Rd Clifton VA 22024

HOOKER, H. LESTER, JR., coll. dir. Dir. Coll. William and Mary, Williamsburg, Va., 1972—, also athletic dir. Address: Coll William and Mary Williamsburg VA 23185

HOOKS, G. EUGENE, educator; b. Goldsboro, N.C., May 15, 1927; s. Louis Gaylor and Selma (Pittman) H.; B.S., Wake Forest U., 1950; M.Ed., U. N.C., 1952; Ed.D., Peabody Coll., 1956; m. Jean Knott, Apr. 9, 1951; children—David Eugene, Dennis Jesse, Michael Louis. Asso. prof. phys. edn. Wake Forest U., N.C., 1956-64, athletic dir., 1964—. Served with USNR, 1945-46. Rotarian. Author: Application of Weight Training to Athletics. Home: 2005 Faculty Dr Winston-Salem NC 27109

HOOKS, GENE, athletic dir. Wake Forest U. Address: Wake Forest U Athletic Dept Winston-Salem NC 27106

HOOKS, LANCE GILBERT, govt. ofcl.; b. Mt. Vernon, Ark., Sept. 16, 1906; s. Edward Charles and Nancy (Thompson) H.; student Washington U., 1925-27, U. Chgo., 1930-32, Northwestern U., 1933; m. Altha Floreetha Hazlewood, Sept. 6, 1932; 1 son, Daryl Lance. Marketing and information specialist U.S. Dept. Agr., St. Louis, 1925-28, Chgo., 1928-35, 40-45, San Antonio, 1935-40, Washington, 1945-64; marketinc cons. U.S. State Dept., Ministries Agr. in Brazil, Peru, Colombia, Republic of Panama, Guyana, Barbados, Vietnam, 1964-72. Cons. FAO, UN, Peru, 1969. Internat. Devel. Service Barbados, 1970. Served with AUS, 1943. Recipient Merit awards U.S. Dept. Agr., 1963, 68, 69; Superior Service award U.S. Dept. Agr. and Alpha Kappa Psi, 1968. Mem. Am. Assn. Agrl. Coll. Editors, Pub. Relations Soc. Am., Nat. Press Club. Mason (32 deg., Shriner). Home: 408 S George Mason Dr Arlington VA 22204 Office: Agrl Marketing Service US Dept Agr 14th and Independence Av NW Washington DC 20250

HOOLE, WILLIAM HAROLD, ednl. adminstr.; b. Blackdiamond, Wash., Mar. 26, 1913; s. William Henry and Etta (Moore) H.; A.B., Wooster Coll., 1936; M.A., N.Y. State Coll. Tchrs., 1937; M.Ed., U. S.C., 1948; m. Sara Babb Armstrong, Dec. 29, 1938; 1 son, William Harold. Tchr. math. and social studies high sch., Surrency, Ga., 1937-39, Deckerville, Mich., 1939-41; supt. schs. Society Hill, S.C., 1941-53, Cordova, S.C., 1953-72; dir. programs for exceptional children Lake Greenwood Project, Ninety Six, S.C., 1972—. Extension instr. U. S.C., Columbia, 1945-51; chmn. county sch. surveys S.C. State Finance Commn., 1950-52. Mem. S.C. Edn. Assn. (state chmn. citizenship com., 1949-52, rural life and edn. com., 1955-58), Orangeburg County Edn. Assn. (pres. 1965-66), Orangeburg County Tech. Edn. Commn., Am., S.C. assns. sch. adminstrs., Assn. Supr. and Curriculum Devel., So. Assn. Colls. and Schs. (state com., 1964-66). Methodist. Lion (pres.). Home and office: Route 3 Ninety Six SC 29666

HOOPE, ELLSWORTH WILLIAM, city ofcl.; b. Marilla, N.Y., Nov. 22, 1917; s. Edward William and Clara (Richter) H.; student U. Buffalo, 1938-40; m. Gwen Sahli, June 17, 1939; children—William, Cheryl (Mrs. Andrew R. Haslett), Toby Sue. Teller, Citizens Nat. Bank, Lancaster, N.Y., 1937-42; property accountant, dir., purchasing agt. Curtiss Wright Corp., Camp Curtissaire, Cheektowaga, N.Y., 1942-47; sales rep. Lily Tulip Cup Corp., N.Y.C., 1947-50; owner Cayuga Supply Co., 1950-56; purchasing agt. City of Pompano Beach, Fla., 1956-63, personnel dir., 1960-61, city mgr., 1963-70; city mgr., Eustice, Fla., 1970—. Exec. dir. Teen Club, Lancaster, N.Y., 1942-44; pres. Lancaster P.T.A., 1954-55; chmn. Eustice Cancer Crusade, 1971; gov's. del. Nat. Rivers and Harbors Congress, 1969. Bd. govs. Broward County (Fla.) United Fund. Recipient Outstanding Service award Kiwanis Club, 1963-65; named Pompano Beach Boss of the Year, Nat. Secretarial Assn. Internat., 1965. Mem. Assn. Basketball Ofcls., Internat., Fla. dir. 1969) city mgrs. assns., Fla. Police Chiefs' Assn., Lake County League of Municipalities (sec.-treas. 1972), Pompano Beach Navy League (dir. 1967-68), Pompano Beach Men's Golf Assn. Presbyn. Kiwanian. Home: 1421 Tedford Av Eustis FL 32726 Office: 10 N Gtove St Eustis FL 32726

HOOPER, BUDDY WILLIAM, coll. adminstr.; b. Phila., Jan. 31, 1946; s. William and Theresa (Roberts) H.; B.S., Fort Valley State Coll., 1968, M.S., 1969; postgrad. U. Wis., 1971-72. Dir. pub. relations and devel. Paul Quinn Coll., Waco, Tex., 1969-70; dir. devel. Prairie View (Tex.) A. and M. Coll., 1970—. Asst. dir., cons. Model Cities Youth Program, Waco, Tex., 1970; com. mem. Boy Scouts Am., 1970-71; active YMCA. Recipient Young Man of the Year award Alpha Phi Alpha, 1970. Mem. N.E.A., Pub. Relations Soc. Am., Am. Assn. Alumni Council, Tex. Edn. Agy., Internat. Acad. Forensic Psychology, Am. Coll. Pub. Relations Soc., Alpha Phi Omega. Home: 2513 Brentwood Ct Decature GA 30032 Office: PO 2622 Prairie View A and M Coll Prairie View TX 77445

HOOPER, C. L., sch. supt., Raleigh, N.C. Address: 601 Devereux St Raleigh NC 27605*

HOOPER, FRANK ARTHUR, fed. judge; b. Americus, Ga., Apr. 21, 1895; s. Frank Arthur and Helena (Callaway) H. Sr.; student Ga. Inst. Tech., LL.B., LL.D., Atlanta Law Sch.; LL.D., Mercer U.; m. Carolyn Newton, June 29, 1926; children—Frank A., Charles N., Ellis C. Admitted to Ga. bar, 1916; sec. to judge Ga. Ct. Appeals, 1917; pvt. practice, Atlanta, 1919-43; judge Ga. Ct. Appeals, 1933; instr. Atlanta Law Sch., 1934-43; asst. city atty., Atlanta, 1940-43; judge Superior Ct., Atlanta Jud. Circuit, 1943-49; U.S. dist. judge No. Dist. Ga., 1949—, sr. judge, 1967—. Rep., Ga. Legislature, 1925-28. Lt. (j.g.), USNRF, 1919. Mem. Am. Legion, Ga.-Tech. Nat. Alumni Assn. (pres. 1945-47), Sigma Alpha Epsilon. Democrat. Baptist. Mason (32 deg., Shriner). Club: Kiwanis. Home: 3303 Habersham Rd NW Atlanta GA 30305 Office: US Courts Northern Dist of Ga Atlanta GA 30301

HOOPER, JAMES FULLERTON, III, farmer, polit. worker; b. Selma, Ala., Sept. 2, 1915; s. James Fullerton and Kathleen (Walker) H.; B.S. in textile engring., Auburn U., 1938; m. Virginia Reid Fite, Jan. 29, 1942; children—Cynthia Marriman (Mrs. Ralph Edward Rood), James Fullerton IV, Pleasant Fite. With various orchs. Music Corp. Am., 1938-41; farmer, owner Columbus Canning Co., Columbus, Miss., 1946-57; farming, owner Hooper Dairy, Columbus, 1957—. Bd. dirs. Lowndes County Farm Bur., 1960-63. Chmn. state candidates com. Miss. Republican State Execs. and Central Com., 1963—; chmn. Lowndes County Rep. Com. 1967—; mem. Miss. Rep. Exec. Com., 1962—; v.p. Tombig-bee Valley Authority. Trustee Miss. Kidney Found., 1969—. Served to maj. USAF, 1941-46. Mem. C. of C. (chmn. resources com. 1949-52), Miss. Rivers and Harbors Assn. (pres. 1961-62; mem. bd. rivers and harbors 1962—), Lowndes County Hist. Soc. Presbyn. Clubs: Magowa Gun and Hunt; Columbus Country; Lowndes County Chowder and Marching Soc. Home: 800 8th St N Columbus MS 39701 Office: Old Plymouth Rd Hwy 45 Columbus MS 39701

HOOPER, VIRGINIA FITE, mem. Republican Nat. Com.; b. Byhalia, Miss., Sept. 23, 1917; d. Pleasant LaFayette and Nell Estelle (Brooks) Fite; B.S. in Econs., U. Ala., 1940; m. James Fullerton Hooper III, Jan. 29, 1943; children—Cynthia Merriman, James Fullerton IV, Pleasant Fite. Vice chmn. Miss. Rep. Party, 1960-62; mem. Rep. Nat. Com. for Miss., 1962—, mem. exec. com., 1969—. Adv. bd. So. Debutante Assn.; pres. Lowndes County Garden Council, 1952-54; mem. Columbus City Beautification Com., also mem. Lowndes County Kidney Found.; v.p. Columbus Swim Assn., 1968-69. Meml. gifts chmn. Lowndes County Heart Assn., 1967—. Named Outstanding Alumna for Miss., Chi Omega, 1968; Miss. G.O.P. Woman of Yr., 1968; Lady of Yr., Lowndes County chapt. Beta Sigma Phi, 1972. Mem. Nat. Assn. Jr. Auxs., (pres. 1949-50), Columbus C. of C. (chmn. merit awards), D.A.R., U.D.C., Nat. Assn. Parliamentarians, Am. Legion Aux., Lowndes County Hist. Soc., Lowndes County, Columbus assns. preservation antiquities, Delta Beta Sigma (v.p. 1937), Chi Omega (pres. chpt. 1940). Presbyn. (v.p. Women of Ch. 1967, 68, chmn. community services 1968, 69). Mem. Order Eastern Star. Clubs: Columbus Country, Lowndes County Chowder and Marching Soc. (Columbus); Magowa Gun (Lowndes County, Miss.); Cherokee Garden. Address: 800 8th St N Columbus MS 39701

HOOPER, WILFORD CLYDE, JR., dentist, educator; b. Houston, July 15, 1927; s. Wilford Clyde and Hilda (Gallia) H.; B.S., U. Houston, 1949; D.D.S., U. Tex., 1954; m. Mary Louise Jones, June 9, 1950; children— Donald Paul, David Clyde. Mem. faculty dental br. U. Tex., Houston, 1954—, asst. prof. endodontics, 1967, now asso. prof.; practice dentistry, specializing in endodontics, Houston, 1964—. Cons. M.D. Anderson Hosp., Houston, 1972—. Served with USNR, 1945-47 Mem. Houston Dist., Tex., Am. dental socs., Southwest Soc. Endodontists (pres.), Omicron Kappa Upsilon, Xi Psi Phi. Methodist (steward). Home: 6706 Redding St Houston TX 77036 Office: 135 Hermann Profl Bldg 6440 Fannin Houston TX 77025

HOOPER-SPEAR, EMILY FRANCIS, interior designer; b. Hamilton, Ont., Can., Sept. 3, 1891; d. Francis William and Mary Evelyn (Twizell) Hooper; B.A., Columbia, 1920; m. Alexander Spear, July 26, 1920. Advt. rep. Furniture World, N.Y.C., 1920-23; account exec. Blumenthal Bros., N.Y.C., 1923-35, Hyman & Co., N.Y.C., 1935-39, Fellows Davis, N.Y.C., 1939-42, all mems. N.Y. Stock Exchange; pvt. practice as interior designer, Miami, Fla. Mem. Nat. Soc. Interior Designers, Designers and Decorators Guild Miami, Miami Shores C. of C., Internat. Platform Assn. Clubs: Da La Casserole (Paris, France); La Gorce Country (Miami Beach, Fla.); Miami Shores Country, Jockey (Miami). Home: 10659 NE 10th Pl Miami FL 33138

HOORNSTRA, EDWARD H., bus. exec.; b. Sault Ste. Maire, Mich., 1921; Pres. Pic-N-Pac Food stores, 1952-65; v.p. operations Li'l Gen. Stores, Inc., 1965-66, pres., 1966-69; v.p. operations Gen. Host Corp., 1969-70, pres., dir., 1970—; pres., dir. ESEM Corp. West Fla., Fil-A-Sak, Inc., Pik-N-Pak South La., Inc.; dir. Comml. Bank Tampa, Tropicana Pools, Inc. Mason (Shriner). Home: 1761 Long Bow Lane Clearwater FL 33516 Office: 245 Park Av New York City NY 10017

HOOTEN, WILLIAM JARVIS, ret. newspaper editor; b. Chocowinity, N.C., Sept. 5, 1900; s. William Thomas and Martha (Jarvis) H.; student St. Paul's Sch., Beaufort, N.C., 1906-11, Belhaven Sch., Belhaven, N.C., 1911-15; m. Grace Bull, June 17, 1922; children—William Pearce, Grace, Charles Carlton. Comml. and railroad telegrapher, 1916-18. Asso. Press, 1918-27; reporter El Paso Herald, 1927-29, city editor, 1929-31; city editor El Paso Times, 1931, mng. editor, 1931-40, editor, 1940-56. v.p., editor, 1956-70. Bd. dirs. Roderick Found. Mason (33 deg., Shriner). Rotarian. Home: 3611 Clifton Av El Paso TX 79903

HOOVER, JIMMIE HARTMAN, librarian; b. Board Camp, Ark., Nov. 5, 1930; s. James Thomas and Alice Victoria (Peters) H.; student Coll. Ozarks, 1948-49; B.A., Ark. Poly. Coll., 1952; M.S., La. State U., 1958; m. Lillian Elaine Fitzgerald, Jan. 2, 1959. With La. State U. Library, Baton Rouge and New Orleans, 1958—, head order dept., Baton Rouge, 1965-67, head govt. documents dept., 1968—. Served with Security Service, USAF, 1952-56. Mem. La. (bus. mgr. bulletin, 1964-65), Am., Southwestern library assns., Spl. Libraries Assn. (nat. govt. information service com., 1969-71), Am. Legion. Author: (with J. Norman Heard) Bookman's Guide to Americana, 6th ed., 1970. Editor Spl. Libraries Assn. Ark., Miss. and La. chap. Bulletin, 1970, La. Library Assn. Coll. Sect. Bulletin, 1968—. Home: 1815 Myrtledale Av Baton Rouge LA 70808

HOOVER, THOMAS BREM, educator, clergyman; b. Paw Creek, N.C., Feb. 27, 1914; s. Thomas Brem and Leona Jane (Henderson) H.; A.A., Lees-McRae Coll., 1934; B.A., Davidson Coll., 1936; B.D., Columbia Theol. Sem., 1940, M. Div., 1971; Ph.D., U. Edinburgh, 1951; m. Catherine Brandon Bagwell, Feb. 6, 1954; children—Kenneth Haywood, Thomas Henderson, Robina Ellen. Ordained to ministry Presbyn. Ch. in U.S., 1940; minister Presbyn. Ch., Nashville and Columbia, S.C., 1940-55, United Presbyn. Ch., Newport Beach, Cal., 1958—; prof. Upper Ia. U., Fayette, 1956-58; prof. div. internat. edn. Chapman Coll., Orange, Cal., 1966-67; prof., dept. chmn. religion and philosophy Barber-Scotia Coll., Concord, N.C., 1969—. Tchr. Presbyn. Pan-Am. Sch., Kingsville, Tex., 1936-37; asso. headmaster Blue Ridge Sch. for Boys, Hendersonville, N.C., 1951-52; guest prof. Seawise U., 1966-67. Vice pres. MAN Assos., Inc., 1971—. Served as capt. AUS, 1943-46. Recipient Danforth Found. award for philos. study, 1958. Mem. Jr. C. of C. (mem. com. 1946-47), N.C. Assn. Religion Tchrs., Catawba Presbytery. Democrat. Club: Torch (Tampa, Fla.). Home: 637 Forest St NW Concord NC 28025 Office: 206 Berry Hall Barber-Scotia Coll Concord NC 28025

HOOVER, WENDAL EUGENE, supt. schs.; b. Coyville, Kan., Apr. 12, 1928; s. Kermit William and Jennie Lee (Callahan) H.; student Pittsburgh (Kan.) State Tchrs. Coll., 1948-50; B.S., Tex. Christian U., 1952, M.E., 1955; m. Glenda Kay Barton, Aug. 23, 1952; children—Lana Kay, Keith Wendal, Lisa Ann. Tchr. high sch., Springtown, Tex., 1952-53; prin. elementary sch., Azle, Tex., 1953-61, supt. schs., 1961—. Served with USMC, 1946-48. Mem. Tex. Tchrs. Assn., C. of C., Tex. Assn. Sch. Adminstrs., Am. Assn. Sch. Adminstrs., Phi Delta Kappa. Lion. Home: 1017 Lakeview St Azle TX 76020 Office: 300 Roe St Azle TX 76020

HOPE, JAMES FRANKLIN, civil engr.; b. Toledo, Aug. 2, 1917; s. George Thomas and Alice (Martin) H.; B.S. magna cum laude in Civil Engring., U. Toledo, 1939; m. Virginia Lee Mountoy, June 10, 1944; children—James Franklin, Virginia Lee BeVille. Field engr., asst. supt. constrn. Art Metal Constrn. Co., Jamestown, N.Y., 1939-40; asst. to chief engr. Doyle & Russell, Wise Constrn. Co., Richmond, Va., 1940-41, exec. engr. constrn., Norfolk, Va., 1941-43; pres. Reid & Hope, Inc., Suffolk, Va., 1946—. Dir. Old Dominion council Boy Scouts Am.; mem. bd. Suffolk Community Chest, campaign chmn., 1961-62, pres., 1962-63. Mem. Suffolk City Council, 1963—, vice mayor, 1965-66, mayor, 1966—; mem. Southeastern Virginia Regional Planning Commn., vice chmn., 1965-67, chmn., 1967-69. Served to lt. USNR, 1943-46. Registered profl. engr., Va., Ohio. Mem. Soc. Am. Mil. Engrs., Nat., Va. socs. profl. engrs., Asso. Gen. Contractors Am. (pres. Va. 1959), Eastern Va. Assn. Contractors, Va. State C. of C., Tau Beta Pi, Phi Kappa Phi, Pi Mu Epsilon, Sigma Rho Tau, U. Toledo Honor Soc. Methodist (trustee). Lion (pres. 1961-62). Home: 704 Jones St Suffolk VA 23435 Office: Route 642 Wilroy Rd Suffolk VA 23435

HOPE, WALTER BARRINGTON, univ. lectr.; b. Aruba, Antilles, Aug. 4, 1934; s. Aaron and Gladys Elizabeth (Gillis) H.; came to U.S., 1957; gen. certificates edn. Queen's Coll., 1951, 53; B.A. cum laude, Howard U., 1960; M.A., Cath. U., 1962, postgrad. 1964-67, 68—; m. Beryl Kathlyn Johnson, Sept. 30, 1961; children—Walter Barrington, Lee, Juan. Instr. social sci. and geography Howard U., Washington, 1961-67, acting head dept. geology and geography, 1968-69, chmn. dept. geology and geography, 1970—. Lectr. D.C. Tchrs. Coll., 1965, Guyana Peace Corps Program, 1966. Keyman, Combined Fed. Campaign, 1963—. Ford Found. fellow, 1968, NSF grantee, 1969, Howard U. fellow, 1970. Fellow Am., Royal geog. socs.; mem. Am. Econ. Assn., Am. Forestry Assn., Assn. Am. Geographers, Nat. Council Geog. Edn., Assn. Social and Behavioral Scientists, Nat. Planning Assn., Phi Alpha Theta, Pi Gamma Mu. Home: 1319 44th Pl SE Washington DC 20019

HOPKINS, AMY LONGCOPE (MRS. EDWIN BUTCHER HOPKINS), civic worker; b. Lampasas, Tex., Sept. 5, 1887; d. Edmund McLeod and Madeleine (Beall) Longcope; m. Edwin Butcher Hopkins, June 20, 1913; children—Amy (Mrs. Duke Selig), Jane (Mrs. Jack Munger), Louise (Mrs. Harris Underwood), Madeleine (Mrs. James K. Wade), Edwin Butcher. Past trustee Dallas Mus. Fine Arts, Dallas Symphony Soc.; bd. dirs. Dallas Civic Opera Assn., Arts Found., Found. for Humanities and Scis. of So. Methodist U., Found. for Arts of Tex. Tech U., Dallas Civic Opera. Mem. Colonial Dames Am., Daus. Barons of Runnemede, Daus. of 1812, Daus. Republic of Tex., Dau. Founders Patriots Am., Order Crown, Dallas Council on World Affairs, Magna Charta Dames, Plantagenet Soc. Episcopalian. Clubs: Brook Hollow Golf, Dallas Petroleum, Public Affairs Luncheon, (Dallas). Home: Park Towers 3310 Fairmount Dallas TX 75201

HOPKINS, BURTRAM COLLVER, II, architect; b. Indpls., Aug. 19, 1936; s. Burtram Wilcox and Anita Letitia (Heyland) H.; student Ia. State U., 1954-57; B.Arch., U. Okla., 1960; M.S., Columbia, 1963; m. Susan Jane Key, Apr. 2, 1960; children—Mark Collver, Julie Ann. Architect, Woodward, Cape & Assos., 1963-69; partner, Woodward, Cape & Partners, 1969-70; officer, Envirodynamics, Inc., Dallas, 1970, pres., 1970—; dir. Southwestern Dynamics, Inc. Mem. Urban Design Task Force, advisers Dallas Dept. Urban Devel., 1969-71. Mem. A.I.A., Am. Soc. Planning Ofcls., Urban Land Inst., Phi Delta Theta. Home: 7214 Wild Valley Dallas TX 75231 Office: 1 Lemmon Park N McKinney Av at Blackburn Dallas TX 75204

HOPKINS, ELLIE, editor, writer; b. Meridian, Miss., May 26, 1909; s. Jack W. and Elizabeth (Swanner) H.; student E. Tex. Bapt. Coll., 1927-29; m. Nina Hall, Apr. 8, 1933; children—Mary Beth (Mrs. James Quillen), Jack Hall. Proofreader, reporter Marshall (Tex.) News Messenger, 1928-29; news editor Jefferson (Tex.) Jour., 1930; with Longview (Tex.) Daily News and Longview Morning Jour., 1930—, editor-in-chief, 1945—, v.p., 1967—; editor Texas Oil Jour., 1945—; dir. Lone Star Steel Co., Dallas. Mem. bd. lectrs. Freedoms Found., Valley Forge, Pa., 1963-65; mem. pub. relations adv. bd. Bapt. Gen. Conv. Tex., 1958-60. A founding sponsor, mem. first bd. dirs. Longview (Tex.) YMCA, 1954- 55; bd. dirs. LeTourneau Coll., Longview, 1959-65, Recipient George Washington Honor medal for editorials Freedoms Found., 1952, 53, 54, 55, 56, 62, 63, 69; Press award for religious news writing Tex. Bapt. Conv., 1957; Sam C. Holloway Meml. award N. and E. Tex. Press Assn., 1969. Mem. Tex. Press Assn. (pres. 1970-71), Assn. Petroleum Writers (past dir.), N. and E. Tex. Press Assn. (pres. 1966-67). Baptist (deacon). Rotarian (pres. Longview 1953-54). Home: 1603 Hillmont Av Longview TX 75601 Office: 314 E Methvin St Longview TX 75601

HOPKINS, ERNEST LOYD, physician; b. Birmingham, Ala., Aug. 14, 1930; s. Clay and Ada (Fields) H.; B.S., Morehouse Coll., 1952; M.D., Howard U., 1957; L.H.D., Monrovia Coll., 1962; m. Lillie B. Blanks, Apr. 24, 1959; children—Ernest C., Loyd Byron, William E. Intern, Freedmen's Hosp., Washington, 1957-58, resident, 1958-62. resident Western Res. U., Cleve., 1961-62, asst. prof. obstetrics, gynecology and physiology Howard U. Coll. Medicine, 1965-69, asso. prof. obstetrics and gynecology, 1969—, dir. audio visual aids sect., 1967—. Attending physician Providence Hosp., Cafitz Meml. Hosp., Washington Hosp. Center, Hadley Meml. Hosp., Columbia Hosp. for Women, Freedmen's Hosp. Patron, Met. Police Boys' Clubs, 1965—, Mt. Pleasant Civic Assn. Knight, Humane Order of Star of African Redemption Republic of Liberia, 1962. USPHS spl. fellow, Western Res. U. Cleve., Universidad de la Republica, Uruguay, 1963-65. Diplomate Am. Bd. Obstetrics and Gynecology. Mem. A.M.A., Nat. Med. Assn., Am. Coll. Obstetricians and Gynecologists, Am. Fertility Soc., Am. Heart Assn., A.A.A.S., Med. Soc. D.C. (exec. com, obstetrics and gynecology sect. 1966—). Home: 9351 Mellenbrook Rd Columbia MD 21043 Office: 1413 K St NW Washington DC 20005

HOPKINS, GEORGE MATHEWS MARKS, patent lawyer; b. Houston, June 9, 1923; s. C. Allen and Agnes Cary (Marks) H.; B.S. in Chem. Engring., Ala. Poly. Inst., 1944; student Ga. Sch. Tech., 1943-44; J.D., U. Ala., 1949; postgrad. George Washington U., 1949-50; m. Betty Miller McLean, Aug. 21, 1954; children—Laura McLean, Edith Cary. Admitted to Ala. bar, 1949, Ga. bar, 1954; asso. atty. A. Yates Dowell, 1949-50, Edw. T. Newton, 1950-62; asst. dir. research, legal counsel Auburn Research Found., 1954-55; partner Newton, Hopkins, Jones & Ormsby, 1962-67, Newton, Hopkins & Ormsby, 1967—. Sec.-treas. Tufted Patterns, Inc., 1959-62; exec. v.p., sec., treas. Fabulous Fabrics, Inc., 1960-62; chmn. bd. Southeastern Carpet Mills, Inc.; pres. Entertainment Investors, Inc., 1967-70, GNG Corp.; dir. Drawer Systems, Inc., Xepel Inc. Served as lt., submarine service, 1944-46, 50-51. Registered profl. engr., Ga., U.S., Can. Mem. Am., Ga., Atlanta bar assns., Nat. Soc. Profl. Engrs., Am. Judicature Soc., Phi Delta Phi, Sigma Alpha Epsilon. Episcopalian. Clubs: Cherokee Town and Country, Atlanta City. Home: 765 Old Post Rd NW Atlanta GA 30303 Office: Equitable Bldg 100 Peachtree St NE Atlanta GA 30303

HOPKINS, GEORGE WALTER, JR., accountant; b. Lindale, Ga., Oct. 13, 1928; s. George Walter and Fannie Lou (Davis) H.; B.A., Mercer U., 1949; m. Doris Josephine Poole, Sept. 16, 1951; children—Jana Elise, Derek Kyle. Accountant, Harvey H. Hunt Co., C.P.A.'s, Rome, Ga., 1949; accountant Ernest J. Rudert, C.P.A., Rome, 1949-50, pub. accountant, 1957—; accountant Rudert & Nash, C.P.A.'s, 1953-57. Dir. Ednl. Found. of Ga. Soc. C.P.A.'s Inc., 1965-66. Served to 2d lt. USAF, 1950-53. C.P.A., Ga. Mem. Am. Inst. C.P.A.'s, Ga. Soc. C.P.A.'s (pres. 1965-66, chpt. v.p., trustee 1965-66), Travelers Protective Assn. Am., Air Force Assn., Kappa Sigma, Phi Eta Sigma, Alpha Phi Omega, Kappa Phi Kappa. Baptist. Clubs: Lin Valley Country (dir. 1962-64, 65-68); Callier Springs Country. Home: 9 Saddle Mountain Rd Rome GA 30161 Office: PO Box 589 1st Nat Bank Bldg Rome GA 30161

HOPKINS, HENRY TYLER, mus. ofcl.; b. Idaho Falls, Ida., Aug. 14, 1928; s. Talcott Thompson and Zoe O. (Erbe) H.; student Coll. Idaho, 1946-49; B.A., Art Inst. Chgo., 1952, M.A., 1955; postgrad. U. Cal. at Los Angeles, 1958-61; m. JoAnne Bybee, Sept. 1, 1954 (div. Oct. 1969); children—Victoria Ann, John Thomas, Christopher Tyler. Asst. curator Los Angeles County Mus. Art, 1961, head edn., 1963-66, curator exhbns. and pubs., 1967-68; dir. Fort Worth Art Center Mus., 1968—, Sun Valley Creative Arts Center, Sun Valley, Ida., 1970—. Instr. art history Tex. Christian U., Fort Worth, 1968—; cons. art program Northwood Inst., Dallas, 1969—; mem. vis. com. fine arts U. Okla., 1971—, Tex. Christian U., 1971—; dir. U.S. representation 35th Venice Bienalle, Venice, Italy, 1970; dir. art presentation Festival of Two Worlds, Spoleto, Italy, 1970. Served with AUS, 1952-54. Mem. Am. Assn. Art Mus. Dirs., Coll. Art Assn., Internat. Animated Film Soc. Contbr. articles to profl. pubs. Home: 5524 Byers St Fort Worth TX 76107 Office: 1309 Montgomery St Fort Worth TX 76107

HOPKINS, ROBERT HOWELL, JR., mortgage banker; b. Dallas, June 29, 1931; s. Robert H. and Pauline (Richardson) H.; B.B.A., Tex. Christian U., 1952; postgrad. Harvard Grad. Sch. Bus., 1952-53; m. Joanne Schneider, Aug. 16, 1952; children—Robert Howell III, Matthew William, Paula. Pres., Nat. Mortgage Corp. Am., Dallas, 1967—. Past pres. Christian Chs. N.M. Mem. Dallas Mortgage Bankers Assn., Tex. Christian U. Letterman's Assn. Home: C6 118 Joyce Way Dallas TX 75225 Office: Box 8046 Dallas TX 75205

HOPKINS, SEWELL HEPBURN, educator; b. Gloucester, Va., Mar. 24, 1906; s. Nicholas Snowden and Selina (Hepburn) H.; B.S., William and Mary Coll., 1927; M.A., U. Ill., 1929, Ph.D., 1933; student Johns Hopkins, 1927-28; m. Pauline Cole, 1929; children—Thomas Johns, Nicholas Arthur. Research asst. U. Ill., Urbana, 1928-33; instr. Danville Jr. Coll., Ill., 1933-35; instr., asst. prof., asso. prof. Tex. A. & M. Coll., College Station, 1935-45, prof. biology, 1947-72, prof. emeritus, 1972—; asso. biologist Va. Fisheries Lab., Yorktown, Va., 1945-46; project dir. Research Found., 1947-50. Mem. A.A.A.S., Am. Inst. Biol. Sci., Am. Soc. Parasitologists, Ecol. Soc., Am. Soc. Limnology and Oceanography, Phi Beta Kappa, Sigma Xi. Contbr. numerous articles in field to profl. jours. Home: 709 Garden Acres Bryan TX 77801 Office: College Station TX 77843

HOPKINS, TERRY WAYNE, dentist; b. Wewoka, Okla., Feb. 4, 1940; s. Hubert Wayne and Edra Mable (Franklin) H.; B.A., Okla. Bapt. U., 1963; D.D.S., U. Mo., 1967; m. Margaret Helen Bryan, Dec. 19, 1959; children—Gregory Wayne, Jon Eric, David Mathew. Practice dentistry, Prague, Okla., 1967-69, Shawnee, Okla., 1969—. Vice pres. BCJ Corp., Shawnee, 1970—; cons. Redlands Community Action, Chandler, Okla., 1968—. Coach, Little League, Shawnee, 1971-72. Mem. Central Dist. Dental Soc. (sec.-treas. 1971-72), Okla. (ho. of dels. 1970—), Am. dental assns. Baptist (deacon). Rotarian, Elk. Home: 1901 Dougherty Dr Shawnee OK 74801 Office: 1414 N Kennedy St Shawnee OK 74801

HOPKINS, THERON COLE, shipping co. exec.; b. Carmel, N.Y., Jan. 30, 1905; s. Chauncey A. and Antoinette (Barrett) H.; student N.Y.U., 1921-22; m. Margaret Ellsworth, May 20, 1939. Asst. mgr. Cunard S.S. Co., N.Y.C., 1922-28; v.p. Funch, Edye & Co., N.Y.C., 1929-41; dep. dir. Brit. Ministry War Transport, 1941-46; asst. to pres. Cosmopolitan Shipping Co., N.Y.C., 1947-56; exec. v.p. U.S. Nav. Co., 1956—. Mem. Am. Arbitration Assn., St. George Soc. N.Y., Am. Asiatic Soc. (gov.). Clubs: Richmond County Country, Dowtown Athletic, Whitehall Lunch (N.Y.C.). Home: 2623 Seville Blvd Apt 312 Clearwater FL 33516 Office: 17 Battery Pl New York City NY 10004

HOPKINS, WILLIAM BENJAMIN, JR., Democratic nat. committeeman; b. Richmond, Va., Apr. 16, 1922; student Roanoke Coll.; A.B., Washington and Lee U.; LL.B., U. Va.; m. Virginia George. Lawyer, Roanoke, Va.; mem. Va. Senate, 1960—; Dem. nat. committeeman from Va., 1968—. Del., Dem. Nat. Conv., 1968. Served with USMCR. Mem. Am. Legion, V.F.W., D.A.V. Episcopalian. Address: 1102 Oakwood Dr SW Roanoke VA 24015

HOPLA, CLUFF EARL, med. zoologist; b. Mapleton, Utah, Dec. 28, 1917; s. David S. and Lilly (Erickson) H.; student Brigham Young U., 1936-41, 46-47; B.S., U. Utah, 1942; M.S., Tulane U., 1947; Ph.D., U. Kan., 1950; m. Moyra Ullock, Dec. 12, 1941; children—Richard E., Dan M., Anna Kristine. Med. entomologist USPHS, 1950; postdoctorate fellow U. Kan., 1950-51; asst. prof. zoology and pub. health U. Okla., 1951-56, asso. prof. zoology, 1956-63, prof., chmn. dept. zoology, 1963—, George Lynn Cross Research prof., 1969. Cons. Okla. Dept. Health, 1956—, NIH, 1967—. Mem. Council on Research Oklahoma City Zoo; explorer adviser Last Frontier council Boy Scouts Am. Served to lt. comdr. USNR, 1942-46. Fellow Okla. Acad. Scis.; mem. Entomol. Soc. Am. (vice-chmn. sect., chmn. 1960-62, program chmn. 1968—). Contbr. articles in field. Home: 1123 Berry Circle Norman OK 73069

HOPPER, COLUMBUS BURWELL, educator; b. Forest City, N.C., Dec. 22, 1931; s. Walter M. and Ellen (Bland) H.; B.A., Furman U., 1954; M.A., U. N.C., 1957; postgrad. U. Chgo., 1959-60; Ph.D., Fla. State U., 1964; m. Patricia Ann Benoy, Nov. 6, 1954; children—Christopher Brian, Arthur Walter. Asst. prof. sociology U. Miss., Oxford, 1957-64, asso. prof., 1965-68, prof., 1968—; asso. prof. sociology S.E. Mo. State Coll., Cape Girardeau, 1964. Cons. in research methods LeFlore County Sch. System, Greenwood, Miss., 1967-68; mem. com. on corrections Miss. Crime Commn., Jackson, 1967—. Served with AUS, 1954-56. Mem. Am., So. sociol. socs., Fla. Correctional Assn., Alpha Kappa Delta. Republican. Baptist. Author: Sex in Prison, 1969. Contbr. articles to profl. jours. Research on conjugal visiting in prison. Home: 1303 S 11th St Oxford MS 38655

HOPPING, WADE LEE, lawyer; b. Dayton, O., Aug. 12, 1931; s. Paul W. and Mildred L. (Flinta) H.; B.A., LL.B., Ohio State U., 1953; m. Mary Munroe, June 6, 1971; children—Stephen Wade, Kiff, Judson Stuart, Mary Beth, Henry Lee. Admitted to Ohio bar, 1955, Fla. bar, 1958; partner firm Adams and Hopping, Columbus, 1957-58; Fla. Supreme Ct. research asst., 1958-60, 62-64; asso. M.F. Baugher, Palm Beach, Fla., 1960-61; dir. continuing legal edn. Fla. Bar, 1964-67; legislative asst. to Fla. Gov., 1966-68; justice Supreme Ct. Fla., 1968-69; partner firm Mahoney, Hadlow, Chambers and Adams, Jacksonville, Fla., 1969—. Chmn., Fla. Law Revision Council. Bd. dirs. Children's Home Soc., Jacksonville Univ. Council. Served to 2d lt. AUS, 1955-57. Mem. Fla. Bar, Am. Bar Assns. Republican. Episcopalian. Kiwanian. Author: Re Attorney Client Relationship, 1963, 70. Office: Tallahassee Bank Bldg Tallahassee FL 32301

HOPPS, HOWARD BERTRAM, lawyer, lectr.; b. nr. Caney, Kan., Feb. 18, 1887; s. John Jacob and Laura J. (Garrett) H.; B.O., Epworth U. (now Oklahoma City U.), 1909; m. Freda C. Andreen, Aug. 12, 1917; children— Dorothy Jeanne (Mrs. George E. Millard), Howard Bertram. With transp. dept. Panama Canal, 1905-07; admitted to Okla. bar 1909; asst. county atty., Oklahoma County, 1916-17; pres. Am. Assn. Ret. Persons, 1967—, also contbr. column to local chpt. monthly. Chmn. 5th dist. Okla. Republican. party. Lectr. on leisure, retirement. Served with 5th div., U.S. Army, World War I; AEF. Recipient Teddy Roosevelt medal for service on Panama Canal, 1907. Mem. Okla., Ark., Mo. archeol. socs., C. of C., Am. Legion (post comdr., 1919-20, chmn. nat. finance com., 1920). Mason (32 deg.). Club: Oklahoma City Golf and Country. Author: Friend, 1967. Home: 7321 Waverly St Oklahoma City OK 73120 Office: First Nat Bldg Oklahoma City OK 73102

HOPPS, WALTER, mus. dir. Dir. Pasadena (Cal.) Art Mus., 1964-67; formerly dir. Washington Gallery Modern Art; now dir. Corcoran Gallery of Art, Washington. Address: 17th and New York Av NW Washington DC 20006

HORADAM, WEYMAN WILSON, banker; b. Yeakum, Tex., May 25, 1916; s. Frank A. and Verna (Willemin) H.; B.B.A., U. Tex., 1941; m. Lucile Simonton, July 12, 1952; children—Diana Louise, William Warren. With RFC, Houston, 1946-52; with Bank of Southwest, N.A., Houston, 1952—, sr. v.p., mgr. personal banking div., 1966—; dir. Nat. Bankamericard. Served as capt. USAAF, 1942-46. Mem. Robert Morris Assos., Houston C. of C., Beta Gamma Sigma, Beta Alpha Psi. Home: 5642 Sylmar St Houston TX 77036 Office: 900 Main St Houston TX 77001

HORAN, WILLIAM DAVID, educator; b. Jackson, Miss., July 1, 1933; s. Leo and Kathryn B. (Gallaspy) H.; B.A., Tulane U., 1955; M.A., La. State U., 1957, Ph.D., 1963. Prof., chmn. fgn. langs. La. State U., Alexandria, 1960-63; prof., chmn. romance langs. Millsaps Coll., Jackson, Miss., 1963-67; prof., chmn. fgn. langs. St. Mary's Dominican Coll., New Orleans, 1967—. Host, Brussels Worlds Fair, 1958; lectr. Russian Loyola U., 1972; mem. acad. adv. bd. Council Devel. French in La. Recipient award French Govt., 1953, Louis Bush medal Tulane U., 1954. Mem. Modern Lang. Assn., Athenee Louisianais, Phi Sigma Iota, Sigma Delta Pi, Delta Phi Alpha, Pi Delta Phi, Dobro Slovo, Alpha Mu Gamma. Episcopalian. Author: The Poems of Bonifacio Calvo, A Critical Edition, 1966. Home: 1916 Dauphine St New Orleans LA 70116

HORDEN, HAROLD MILTON, physician; b. Middletown, Conn., Aug. 18, 1931; s. Milton Joseph and Agnes (Pasner) H.; B.A., U. Conn., 1953; postgrad., U. Richmond, 1957-58; M.D., Med. Coll. Va.,

1962; m. Constance Wray Loving, Aug. 20, 1955; children—Mary Kimball, James Todd. Intern, Norfolk Gen. Hosp., 1962-63; resident in gen. practice, 1963-64; practice medicine specializing in family medicine, Norfolk, Va., 1964—; mem. staffs De Paul, Norfolk Gen., Kings Daus. Childrens, Leigh Meml. hosps. (all Norfolk); dir. dept. family practice, DePaul Hosp., Norfolk, 1970—. Served to lt., USNR, 1953-57. Diplomate Am. Bd. Family Practice. Mem. Va. Acad. Family Practice (chmn. com. 1969-72). Episcopalian. Home: 6801 Meadowlawn Dr Norfolk VA 23518 Office: 9615 Granby St Norfolk VA 23503

HORECKY, PAUL LOUIS, librarian, govt. ofcl.; b. Trutnov, Czechoslovakia, Sept. 8, 1913; s. Bedrich and Elsa (Weinerova) H.; LL.D., U. Prague, 1936; M.A. (Charles Smith scholar), Harvard, 1951; m. Emily M. Ivey, Dec. 12, 1949; 1 son, Frederick John. Gen. law practice Prague, 1936-37; trial atty. U.S. Office of Chief of Counsel, Nuremberg, Germany, 1947-49; researcher Harvard U. Russian Research Center, Cambridge, 1949-51; Slavic and East European specialist Library of Congress, Washington, 1951-58, asst. chief Slavic and Central European div., 1958-71, chief, 1972—. Mem. subcom. on East-Central and S.E. European studies and Joint Com. on Eastern Europe, Am. Council Learned Socs.-Social Sci. Research Council, 1968—; chmn. research and library resources adv. com. Am. Council Learned Socs., 1970—. Served to capt. Brit. Armed Forces, 1944-47. Mem. Am. Polit. Sci. Assn., Am. Assn. for Advancement Slavic Studies (mem. com. on bibliography and documentation 1970—), A.L.A. Clubs: Cosmos, Harvard (Washington). Author: Libraries and Bibliographic Centers in the Soviet Union, 1959. Editor, contbr. Basic Russian Publications, 1962; Russia and the Soviet Union, 1965; East Central Europe, 1969; Southeastern Europe, 1969; other monographs. Contbr. to Ency. Americana, profl. jours. Home: 2207 Paul Spring Rd Alexandria VA 22307 Office: Library of Congress Washington DC 20540

HORGAN, ANDREW BOTHWELL, III, assn. ofcl.; b. Orange, N.J., Apr. 5, 1940; s. Andrew Bothwell and Helen Marion (Leith) H.; B.A. (Acad. scholar), Seton Hall U., 1962; student (Proctor fellow) Georgetown U. Law Sch., 1962-63; m. Kathleen Theresa Arata, Sept. 19, 1970. Editorial asst. Newark Star Ledger, 1960-62; spl. asst. Nat. Adv. Commn. Civil Disorders, Washington, 1967-68; dir. information and fed. aids services Nat. League of Cities-U.S. Conf. of Mayors, Washington, 1968—. Exec. sec. Municipal Intergovtl. Coordinators Assn., 1970—; mem. local govt. adv. bd. to Pres.'s Fed. Task Force on Grant Simplification, 1970-72; adviser to Pres.'s Council Youth Opportunity, 1969-70; dir. Nat. Summer Youth Transp. Program, 1969, 70. Served to capt. CIC, AUS, 1963-67. Mem. Res. Officers Assn., Phi Beta Sigma, Phi Kappa Theta. Editor, publisher manual and bulletin Fed. Aids to Local Govt., 1970—. Home: 207 10th St SE Washington DC 20003 Office: 1612 K St NW Washington DC 20006

HORGAN, ROBERT JOSEPH, educator, ednl. adminstr.; b. Elgin, Ill., Feb. 6, 1924; s. Patrick Donald and Margaret (McCarthy) H.; B.A., U. N.D., 1949, M.A., 1950; Ph.D., U. Notre Dame, 1959; m. Patricia Ann Jeffrey, June 1, 1950; children—Mark Patrick, Gregory Paul, Jeffrey Paul. Mem. faculty Clarke Coll., 1954-67, asso. prof. polit. sci., 1959-67; asso. prof. polit. sci. U. Richmond (Va.), 1967—, dir. Urban Center, 1967—. Asso. prof. polit. sci. Kalamazoo Coll., summer, 1966. Mem. City Council, Dubuque, Ia., 1962-66; mayor, Dubuque, 1964, 65. Served with AUS, 1943-46. Recipient Excellence award Am. Security Council, 1967. Mem. Am., So. polit. sci. assns., Am. Soc. Pub. Adminstrn., Pi Sigma Alpha. Home: 6116 Westower Dr Richmond VA 23225

HORN, THOMAS DARROUGH, educator; b. Iowa City, Ia., June 26, 1918; s. Ernest and Madeline (Darrough) H.; B.A., State U. Ia., 1940, M.A., 1946, Ph.D., 1947; postgrad. U. Cambridge, Eng., 1945; m. Grace Ellen Adams, Aug. 2, 1941; 1 dau., Diane. Tchr. pub. schs., Denver, 1940-42, River Forest, Ill., 1942-43; asst. prof. U. No. Ia., 1947-51; vis. lectr. U. Pitts., summer 1949, Harvard, summer 1959, U. Mich., 1963; asso. prof. curriculum and instrn. Coll. Edn., U. Tex., Austin, 1951-59, prof., 1959—, chmn. dept. curriculum and instruction, 1962—, dir. bi-cultural project Research and Devel. Center, Coll. Edn., 1965-67, dir. lang. research project, San Antonio, 1967-68, dir. lang. research project, 1968—. Served from pvt. to sgt. 78th Inf. Div., AUS, 1943-46, ETO; capt. USAF Res., 1950-55. Mem. Am. Ednl. Research Assn., Assn. Student Teaching (exec. bd. 1953-59, pres. 1957-58), Tex. Assn. for Student Teaching (pres. 1952-53), Internat. Reading Assn., Nat. Conf. on Research in English (exec. bd. 1957-60, nat. pres. 1958-59), Nat. Council Tchrs. English (dir. elementary sect. 1965-68). N.E.A., Nat. Soc. Study Edn., Tex. Tchrs. Assn., Phi Delta Kappa, Phi Gamma Delta. Contbr. articles to profl. jours. Co-author, cons. spelling and reading textbooks, instructional films. Editor research monographs, book. Home: 5302 Ridge Oak Dr Austin TX 78731

HORN, WILLIAM ANTHONY, mathematician; b. Cin., Feb. 19, 1937; s. Anthony Charles and Mildred (Weak) H.; B.S., U. Cin., 1959, M.A., 1961; Ph.D., U. Md., 1967. Instr., Xavier U., Cin., 1961-62; research fellow Research Inst. for Advanced Study, Balt., 1963-64; analyst Inst. for Def. Analyses, Arlington, Va., 1964-66; mathematician Nat. Bur. Standards, Washington, 1967—. NSF fellow, 1959-60, 60-61, 62-63. Mem. Am. Math. Soc., Math. Assn. Am. Soc. Indsl. and Applied Math. Club: 20-30 (pres. 1967-68). Home: 611 N Pegram St Alexandria VA 22304 Office: Nat Bur Standards Washington DC 20234

HORNAK, ANN, librarian; b. College Station, Tex., June 3, 1922; d. Josef and Anna (Drozd) Hornak; B.A., U. Tex., 1944; B.S. in L.S., U. Ill., 1945; M.Ed., U. Houston, 1956. Children's librarian Schenectady Pub. Library, 1945-47, Pasadena (Cal.) Pub. Library, 1947-49; supr. juvenile div. Houston Pub. Library, 1949-57, asst. dir., 1957—. Mem. Tex. Library Assn. (chmn. pub library div. 1963-64, rep.-at-large 1967—), Houston Library Club (pres. 1967-68), Kappa Delta Pi. Home: 1831 W Main St Houston TX 77006 Office: 500 McKinney Av Houston TX 77002

HORNBACK, RAYMOND RICE, univ. adminstr.; b. Greenville, Ky., July 19, 1934; s. Raymond C. and Daisy N. (Rice) H.; A.B., U. Ky., 1956, M.A., 1962; Ed.D., Ind. U., 1968; m. Betty J. Collins, July 28, 1966; children—Katherine Jeanelle, Raymond Rice. Staff writer Asso. Press, 1955; dir. publicity and publs. Morehead (Ky.) State U., 1956-59, dir. pub. relations, 1959-62, asst. to pres., 1962-68, v.p. for u. affairs, 1968—, asso. prof. higher edn., 1968—. Served with AUS, 1963. Mem. Am. Coll. Pub. Relations Assn. (program chmn. S.E. dist. 1973, pub. affairs com. 1972—), Phi Kappa Tau (long range planning com. 1971—), Phi Delta Kappa, Sigma Delta Chi. Democrat. Methodist. Clubs: Optimist (pres. 1965, dist. lt. gov.). Author: Policy Boards of Public State-Supported Institutions of Higher Education, 1968. Home: 107 E 5th St Morehead KY 40351

HORNE, ALEXANDER, newspaper editor; b. Warsaw, Poland, Nov. 9, 1932; B.A., Williams Coll., 1954; m. 5 children. With Berkshire Eagle, Pittsfield, Mass., 1955-56; asst. city editor Washington Post, 1958-60, local reporter, 1960, asst. editor Potomac, 1960-62, asst. world editor, 1962-65, day nat. editor, 1965-69, nat. reporter, 1969-70, dep. nat. editor, 1970-71, editor Outlook, 1971—. Served with AUS, 1956-58. Home: 7214 Rebecca Dr Alexandria VA 22307 Office: Washington Post 1150 15th St NW Washington DC 20005*

HORNE, ARTHUR EARLE, physician; b. Memphis, Dec. 19, 1923; s. Reuben Orlando and Erin Mildred (Banks) H.; B.S., Tenn. Agrl. and Indsl. State U., 1947; M.D., Meharry Med. Coll., 1951; m. Martha Louise Pipes, Dec. 19, 1946; children—Arthur Earle II, Muriel (Mrs. Hill), Janet Faye, Anthony Carl. Intern, Lincoln Hosp., Durham, N.C., 1951-52; resident Bapt. Meml. Hosp., preceptorship, Memphis, 1968; practice medicine, specializing in family practice, Memphis, 1952—; mem. active staff Collins Chapel, E. H. Crump, Bapt. hosps. (all Memphis); dir. Memphis Corp., Dental & Med. Corp. Mem. adv. bd. Mutual Fed. Savs. & Loan, 1958-72; mem. planning com. Regional Med. Program, 1971-72. Bd. dirs. Boys Club Am. Served with AUS, 1944-46; ETO. Mem. N.A.A.C.P. (life), Nat. Med. Assn. (state del. 1965-68), A.M.A., Mid-South, Tenn., Vol. State (pres. 1967) med. assns., Memphis, Shelby County, Bluff City (pres. 1966) med. socs., Bus. and Profl. Investment Club, Alpha Phi Alpha. Clubs: Top Hat and Tails, Tri-State Sportsmen, 19th Holers Golf (Memphis). Home: 1974 S Parkway E Memphis TN 38114 Office: 975 Thomas St Memphis TN 38107

HORNE, LINWOOD TYLER, clergyman; b. Norfolk, Va., Apr. 17, 1922; s. Jennings Tyler and Mattie Gertrude (Sawyer) H.; B.A., U. Richmond, 1943; B.D., So. Bapt. Theol. Sem., 1947, Th.M., 1948, Th.D., 1958; m. Helon May Wallace, Aug. 18, 1945; children—Linwood Tyler, Janice May, Karen Elaine, Wallace Jennings. Ordained to ministry Bapt. Ch., 1948; asst. pastor 2d Bapt. Ch., Richmond, 1944-45; pastor Brownstown Ch. (Ind.), 1949-52, Walnut Hill Ch., Petersburg, Va., 1952-63, 1st Bapt. Ch., Radford, 1963-70; dir. for ch. relations and Sch. Christian Studies, U. Richmond, 1970—. Clergy counselor Southside (Va.) Family Counseling Service, 1957-63; pres. Southside Area Mental Health Assn., 1958-60. Trustee Religious Herald. Mem. So. Bapt. Conv. (mem. com. on bds. 1968-69), Bapt. Gen. Assn. Va. (1st v.p. 1967-68), Radford Ministerial Assn. (pres. 1966), Omicron Delta Kappa, Pi Delta Epsilon, Phi Gamma Delta. Author: History of the Petersburg Baptist Association in Virginia, 1906-56, 1956. Home: 6821 Westcott Dr Richmond VA 23225 Office: Ryland Hall U Richmond Richmond VA 23173

HORNE, MALLORY ELI, state senator, community devel. exec.; b. Tavares, Fla., Apr. 17, 1925; s. Cleveland Reid and Clifford (Parnell) H.; student Fla. State U., 1948; LL.B., U. Fla., 1950; m. Anne Veronica Livingston, Mar. 15, 1945; children—Mallory Eli, David Albert. Admitted to Fla. bar, 1950; chmn. bd. chief exec. officer, Killearn Properties, Inc., Tallahassee, 1964—; dir. Tallahassee Bank and Trust Co., Tallahassee Bank North; mem. Fla. Senate, 1966—; pres. designate, 1972-74. Mem. Fla. Ho. of Reps., 1954-65, speaker 1962-64. Bd. dirs. pres. Tallahassee Meml. Hosp. 1965-67. Served to capt. USAAF, 1942-45. Recipient Good Govt. award Fla. Jr. C. of C., 1961; named Most Outstanding House Mem., St. Petersburg Times, 1963, Most Outstanding Senator, 1972. Mem. Fla. Bar (pres. jr. sect. 1954-55), Fla. State U. Alumni Assn., (pres. 1967). Mason, Elk. Club: Tallahassee Exchange (pres.). Home: 2410 Killarney Way Tallahassee FL 32303 Office: Suite 200 Tallahassee Bank Bldg Tallahassee FL 23201

HORNER, CHARLES EDWARD, surgeon; b. Pekin, Ill., Aug. 31, 1912; s. Robert C. and Clara (Bird) H.; B.S., Antioch Coll., 1934; M.D., Georgetown Med. Sch., 1942; m. Katherine Howe Farrington, Dec. 31, 1951. Mech. engr. Superior Engine Div., Nat. Supply Corp., Springfield, O., 1934-37; clin. instr. surgery Georgetown Med. Sch., 1950-51; pvt. practice surgery Washington, 1950-59, sr. surgeon USPHS, 1959-62, medical dir., 1962—; asso. chief surg. services, USPHS Hosp., S.I., 1960-62; chief surg. service, USPHS Hosp., Savannah, Ga., 1962-66; chief surgery USPHS out-patient clinic, Washington, 1966-71; dep. med. dir. Bur. Employees Compensation, U.S. Dept. Labor, Washington, 1971—. Served from 1st lt. to maj. M.C., AUS, 1943-46, ETO. Diplomate Am. Bd. Surgery. Fellow A.C.S.; mem. A.M.A., Assn. Mil. Surgeons U.S. Club: Army and Navy. Home: 4000 Massachusetts Av NW Washington DC 20016 Office: Bur Employees Compensation US Dept Labor 711 14th St Washington DC 20201

HORNER, FENTRESS THOMPSON, judge; b. Troy, N.C., Sept. 16, 1902; s. Kenneth C. and Luola (Arnette) H.; student Campbell Coll., 1923, Wake Forest Coll., 1924-25; m. Mary Frances Sawyer, June 15, 1929. Admitted to N.C. bar, 1925; practice law Elizabeth City, 1925—; mem. firm Worth & Horner; judge Pastuotank County (N.C.) Recorder's Ct., Elizabeth City, 1938-42, 46-66; chief judge Dist. Ct., 1966—. Mem. adv. bd. Albemarle Mental Health Clinic, Elizabeth City, 1958, Salvation Army, 1942; pres. Elizabeth City Boys Club, 1969. Alternate del. Dem. Nat. Conv., 1956. Served from lt. to lt. comdr., USNR, 1942-46. Mem. Am. Legion, V.F.W. Democrat. Episcopalian. Elk, Improved. Order of Red Men, Kiwanian. Home: 1116 E Williams Circle Elizabeth City NC 27909 Office: Elizabeth City Courthouse Elizabeth City NC 27909

HORNER, GARNETT DENTON, newspaperman; b. Chattanooga, Mar. 22, 1909; s. Charles A. and Elizabeth (Denton) H.; student U. Chattanooga, 1927-30; m. Leota Still Stivers, Sept. 4, 1948. Reporter, Chattanooga News, 1927-31; asst. bur. mgr., night mgr. United Press, Atlanta, bur. mgr., Birmingham, Ala., night mgr., N.Y.C., Washington, 1931-37; reporter Washington Star, 1937—, White House corr., 1954—; press attache to Robert D. Murphy, polit. adviser Allied Force Hdqrs. Mediterranean, 1943-44. Mem. White House Corrs. Assn. (pres. 1959-61, sec. 1961—. Club: Nat. Press (Washington). Home: 4811 Albermarle St NW Washington DC 20016 Office: 225 Virginia Av SE Washington DC 20003

HORNSBY, HATTIE B. (MRS. WALTER S. HORNSBY), real estate executive; b. Augusta, Ga.; d. Charles Andrew and Hattie (Pritchard) Dryscoll; student pub. schs., Haines Normal and Indsl. Inst.; m. Walter Spurgeon Hornsby, June 25, 1930 (dec.); children—Charlotte (Mrs. John David Watkins), Jean Lenore, Harriett Waltina. Owner, Hornsby-McCoy Realty Co., Augusta, 1926—. Mem. Ga. Council Human Relations. Mem. N.A.A.C.P., UN Assn. U.S.A., Augusta C. of C. Baptist. Clubs: Women's Civic, Links, Inc. Home: 1518 Twiggs St Augusta GA 30901 Office: 1129 Gwinnett St Augusta GA 30901

HORNSBY, J(AMES) RUSSELL, lawyer; b. Manchester, Ky., July 2, 1924; s. Benjamin Franklin and Lillie (Weiss) H.; student Center Coll., 1947; LL.B., John B. Stetson U., 1950 div.; children—Lawrence H., James Russell, Kevin Lee, Tonya Lisa, Brandon. Admitted to Fla. bar, 1950; gen. practice Orlando, 1950—; 1st vice chmn. Cape Kennedy Coll. Bus and Technology, 1964-65. Served with USMCR, 1943-45. Mem. Internat. Acad. Sci. and Law, Acad. Fla. Trial Lawyers, Am., Orange County bar assns., Delta Theta Phi, Delta Mu. Clubs: Rolling Hills Country, Executive, Industrialists Key, Optimists, Lake Beresford Yacht. Home: 1001 Esplanade Way Casselberry FL 32707 Office: 311 N Rosalind Av Orlando FL 32801

HORSLEY, THOMAS MARTIN, physician; b. Lovingston, Va., May 15, 1921; s. Thomas Martin and Ruby Temple (Harris) H.; B.S. summa cum laude, Hampden-Sydney Coll., 1942; M.D., Johns Hopkins, 1945; m. Kathleen Brady Keith, Mar. 20, 1948; children—Brian Douglas, Anne Elizabeth. Intern Ch. Home Hosp., Balt., 1945-46; resident McGuire Vets. Hosp., Richmond, Va., 1948-51; practice internal medicine, Elizabeth City, N.C., 1951—; chief internal medicine Albemarle Hosp., Elizabeth City, 1956-57, 62, 65, 68, 71, pres. med. staff, 1959-60. Pres. Albemarle Med. Corp., 1971-72, Colonial Village Inc., 1971-72. Served to capt., M.C., AUS, 1946-48. Mem. A.C.P., Pasquotank, Camden, Currituck, Dare Counties Med. Soc. (pres. 1957-58), 1st Dist. N.C. Med. Soc., Med. Soc. N.C., A.M.A., Am., N.C. socs. internal medicine, Elizabeth City C. of C. Methodist (trustee). Kiwanian. Home: 2000 Rivershore Rd Elizabeth City NC 27909 Office: 1142 N Road St Elizabeth City NC 27909

HORSTMYER, KENNETH LEROY, consumer products co. exec.; b. Scotia, N.Y., Nov. 13, 1921; s. Albert William and Elizabeth May (Buhrmaster) H.; B.S. in Bus. Adminstrn., Miami U., Oxford, O., 1947; grad. bus. program Columbia, 1958; m. Madeleine Slaughter, Apr. 14, 1950; children—Kendra Sally, Linda Cheryl, Jeffrey Lee, Andrew William. Dir. new market devel. Union Carbide Corp., N.Y.C., 1960-63; exec. v.p. Quality Cts. Motels, Inc., Daytona Beach, Fla., 1963-66; pvt. bus. cons., 1966-67; pres. frozen foods div. W.R. Grace & Co., N.Y.C., 1967-70; group v.p. operations Burger King Corp., Miami, Fla., 1970—. Served with USNR, 1943-47. Mem. Am. Mgmt. Assn., Am. Marketing Assn. Home: 613 Ocean Dr Key Biscayne FL 33149 Office: 7360 N Kendall Rd Miami FL 33156

HORTEN, CARL FRANK, textile mfg. co. exec.; b. Fort Lauderdale, Fla., Aug. 19, 1914; s. Joseph Frederick and Phyllis (Gregory) H.; B.S., Geneva Coll., 1936; M.B.A., Harvard, 1938; grad. exec. program, U. N.C., 1959; m. Alice Jeannette Yereance, June 8, 1940; children—Bruce Carl, Lynn Alice, Heather Belle. Sales corr. L. Sonneborn Sons, 1938-40; asst. controller Nashua Mfg. Co., 1940-47; controller Textron So., Inc., 1947-49; with Springs Mills, Inc., Ft. Mill S.C., 1949—, v.p., 1964-66, treas., 1967—, exec. v.p., 1966—, also dir.; chmn. bd. Lancaster Internat. Sales Corp.; dir. Carolina Carpet Co., P.T. Daralon Textile Mfg. Corp. of Indonesia. Served to lt. (j.g.) USNR, 1943-46. Home: PO Box 396 Fort Mill SC 29715 Office: Springs Mills Inc Fort Mill SC 29715

HORTON, DAVID, educator; b. St. Louis County, Mo., Mar. 13, 1914; s. Daniel Edgar and Lisabel (Luke) H.; A.B., Washington U., St. Louis, 1935, A.M., 1936; Ph.D., Harvard, 1948; m. Janet Louise Glamore, Jan. 31, 1943; children—Barbara Ellen (Mrs. William A. Jones), David Lamont, Elizabeth Anne (Mrs. Ben S. DeVan), Douglas Glamore. Instr. Wright Jr. Coll., Chgo. City Jr. Colls., 1939-42; with WPB, 1942-45, Civilian Prodn. Adminstrn., 1945-47; mem. faculty Westminster Coll., Fulton, Mo., 1947-66, prof. polit. sci., head dept., 1950-66; prof., chmn. dept. polit. sci. U. So. Ala. at Mobile, 1966—. Cons. to various govt. agys. Pres. Daniel Boone Regional Pub. Library, Columbia, Mo., 1960-61. Recipient Award for Meritorious Achievement, Mo. Library Assn., 1961. Mem. Am., So. polit. sci. assns., Am. Judicature Soc., Phi Beta Kappa, Pi Sigma Alpha, Omicron Delta Kappa. Author: (with others) Introduction to Social Science, I-II, 1942; Import Policies and Programs of the War Production Board, 1947. Editor: Freedom and Equality: Addresses by Harry S. Truman, 1960. Home: 4721 St Dominic Pl Mobile AL 36609

HORTON, FINAS WADE, supt. schs.; b. Fairfield, Tex., Feb. 8, 1921; s. Issac Fred and Velma Estelle (Lambert) H.; student Tex. Christian U., 1944-45; B.A., U. Tex., 1948, M.A., 1950, postgrad. 1953-56; m. Ferdel Speilman, June 23, 1946; children—Marcia (Mrs. Darryl Smith), Velma (Mrs. Karl Rivers), Rosemary. Classroom tchr. Odessa Pub. Schs., 1948-51, Austin Pub. Schs., 1952-53; asst. county supt. schs. Travis County Schs., Austin, Tex., 1953-62, county sch. supt., 1963—. Bd. dirs. Neighborhood Youth Corps, Travis County. Served with USNR, 1941-46, 51-52. Recipient Scholarship, Kellogg Edn. Adminstrn., 1952. Democrat. Baptist (deacon 1960—). Kiwanian. Club: Civitan (treas. 1961-63) (Austin). Home: 1308 Harriet Ct Austin TX 78756 Office: PO Box 1748 Austin TX 78767

HORTON, FRANK BARRETT, III, air force officer; b. Wilmington, Del., Oct.29, 1940; s. Frank Barrett and Margaret Mary (Parmelee) H.; B.S., U.S. Mil. Acad., 1962; M.P.A., Harvard, 1966, Ph.D., 1969; m. Patricia Sue Gimon, June 23, 1962. Commd. 2d lt. USAF, 1962, advanced through grades to capt., 1966; computer programmer, systems analyst Offutt AFB, Neb., 1962-65; instr. dept. polit. sci. USAF Acad., Colo., 1968-70; staff analyst Directorate Tactical Analysis, Hdqrs. 7th Air Force, Vietnam, 1970-71; asst. prof., exec. officer dept. polit. sci. USAF Acad., 1971-72, asso. prof., 1972—. Cons., UN Inst. Tng. and Research, 1968, DCS-Plans and Operations, USAF, 1968-70, 71—, Nat. Security Council, 1969-70, Rand Corp., 1969-70. Named Outstanding Young Man Am., 1970. Mem. Am. Polit. Sci. Assn., Am. Acad. Polit. and Social Sci., Internat. Inst. for Strategic Studies, Air Force Assn., Assn. Grads. U.S. Mil. Acad., Army Athletic Assn., Air Force Athletic Assn., Internat. Studies Assn., Council Religion and Internat. Affairs, Fgn. Service Inst., Center for Study Dem. Instns. Episcopalian. Clubs: Toastmasters (dist. lt. gov.), Sierra. Home: 106 W Alamo St Brenham TX 77833 also 1637 Woodmen Rd Colorado Springs CO 80918 Office: Dept Polit Sci USAF Academy CO 80840

HORTON, GRANVILLE EUGENE, physician; b. Jean, Tex., July 2, 1927; s. James Granville and Etna (Boyle) H.; B.A., Tex. Technol. Coll., 1950; M.D., U. Tex., 1954; m. Mildred Helen Veale, June 13, 1953; children—Robert Herman Newlin, Linda Kay, Kevin Bruce, Carson Scott. Intern, Detroit Receiving Hosp., 1954-55; tng. in radioactive isotope techniques Oak Ridge Inst. Nuclear Studies, 1958; pvt. practice medicine Weslaco, Tex., 1955-56, Outlar-Blair Clinic, Wharton, 1956—; part-time research asso. radioisotope dept. Methodist Hosp., Houston, 1961-66; mem. med. adv. com. and sec. med. staff Caney Valley Meml. Hosp., Wharton, Tex.; clin. dir. Wharton County Tb Assn. Bd. dirs. Wharton County div. Am. Cancer Soc., pres., 1960-61; dist. dir. 8th dist. Tex., Citizens com. for Hoover Report, 1957-58. Served with USNR, 1946-47. Diplomate Am. Bd. Nuclear Medicine. Fellow Am. Coll. Angiology; mem. Wharton C. of C. (dir., v.p. 1960-61), Am., Tex. (ho. of dels. 1959-61) med. assns., Am. Nuclear Soc., Phi Chi. Republican. Episcopalian. Elk. Contbr. articles to med. publs. Home: 425 Croom Dr Wharton TX 77488 Office: 3027 N Richmond Rd Wharton TX 77488

HORTON, HAMILTON COWLES, JR., lawyer; b. Winston-Salem, N.C., Aug. 6, 1931; s. Hamilton Cowles and Virginia Lee (Wiggins) H.; summer student U. Grenoble (France), 1950, U. Salzburg (Austria), 1952; A.B., U. N.C., 1953, LL.B., 1956; m. Evelyn Hanes Moore, Feb. 16, 1963; 1dau., Rosalie Hanes. Admitted to N.C. bar, 1956; asso. Craige, Brawley, Lucas & Hendrix, Winston-Salem, 1960-62, partner Craige & Brawley (formerly Craige, Brawley, Lucas & Horton), 1963—. Mem. N.C. Ho. of Reps., 1969-71, N.C. Senate, 1971—. Mem. Gov.'s Commn. to Study Uniform Consumer Credit Code, Legislative Com. on Environmental Problems. Bd. dirs. Friends of Salem College Library, Ft. Defiance Restoration. trustee N.C. Symphony Soc. Served to lt. (j.g.) USNR, 1956-60; lt. Res. Mem. Am., N.C., Forsyth County bar assns., N.C. Lit. and Hist. Soc. (dir. 1971-72), Phi Beta Kappa, Phi Delta Phi, Beta Theta Pi. Republican. Mem. Moravian Ch. (elder, del. N.C. Council Chs.). Clubs: Rotary,

Torch, Old Town. Home: 10 Stump tree Lane Winston-Salem NC Office: Pepper Bldg Winston-Salem NC 27102

HORTON, JAMES ALPHONZO, govt. ofcl.; b. Morehead City, N.C., Apr. 1, 1924; s. Curtis Henry and Ada (Becton) H.; B.S., Lincoln U., 1949; postgrad. U. Minn., 1950; m. Dorothy Monson, Jan. 6, 1954; children—Bartt, Mitchell, Stuart, Curtis. Writer, editor U.S. Dept. Agr., Washington, 1962-64, editor agrl. marketing mag., 1964-69; information chief Nat. Inst. Mental Health, Dept. Health, Edn. and Welfare, 1969-70; spl. asst. to dir. Office of Minority Bus. Enterprise, U.S. Dept. Commerce, 1970—. Named profl. agrl. worker Profl. Agr. Workers Assn., 1966. Home: 8817 Lanier Dr Silver Spring MD 20910 Office: OMBE US Dept Commerce Washington DC 20230

HORTON, JEAROLD POWELL, hosp. adminstr.; b. Albertville, Ala., June 30, 1930; s. William Jesse and Sally (McLendon) H.; B.S., Jacksonville (Ala.) State U., 1958; m. Bobbie June Carter, Oct. 26, 1953; children—Steven Jeffrey, Tracy Dianne. Intern med. tech. Holy Name of Jesus Hosp., Gadsden, Ala., 1957-58; chief med. technologist City Hosp., Guntersville, Ala., 1958-63, Guntersville (Ala.) Hosp., 1963-64; adminstr. Guntersville (Ala.) Hosp., 1964—. Served with USAF, 1948-52. Mem. Am., Ala. hosp. assns., Am. Coll. Hosp. Adminstrs., Am. Soc. Clin. Pathologists. Republican. Methodist. Home: Auxiliary Route 4 Guntersville AL 35976 Office: 2067 Dunlap Av Guntersville AL 35976

HORTON, J(OSEPH) REX, broadcasting engr.; b. Greeneville, Tenn., Dec. 20, 1908; s. Adolphus Bryan and Rebecca (Marshall) H.; grad. Am. Sch., 1936, Nat. Radio Inst., 1940; m. Mary Charlotte Felix, July 28, 1933; children—Joseph Rex, Robert Earl, Charlotte Anne. With A. B. Horton, bldg. constrn., Knoxville, Tenn., 1928-32; retail service sta. mgr., 1933; retail salesman Pure Oil Co., 1934-35; sta. mgr. Retail Service Orgn., Phoenix, 1936-37; route salesman Radio Sales & Service, Knoxville, 1938-42; chief engr. WBIR-AM-FM-TV, Knoxville, 1943—. Home: 1715 North Hills Blvd Knoxville TN 37917 Office: 1513 Hutchison Av Knoxville TN 37917

HORTON, JULIUS BROYLES, assn. exec.; b. Chickamauga, Ga., Nov. 24, 1888; s. James Richards and Ophelia C. (Simmons) H.; grad. Chattanooga Inst. Tech., 1912; L.H.D., Newberry Coll., 1953; m. Jessie Clarkson, Dec. 25, 1916; children—Mary Latimer (Mrs. John Hunter Glass), Sallie McKelvy (Mrs. James Wilson Hunter). With YMCA, 1909—, edn. dir. Knoxville, 1909-14, Louisville, 1915-16, Pitts., 1916-19; gen. sec., Columbia, S.C., 1920—, mem. nat. council, 1926-30, del constnl. conv., Buffalo, 1924, mem. faculty Silver Bay YMCA Sch., conf. speaker Golden Anniversary Employed Officers Conf., 1942. Del., Gen. Conf. Meth. Ch., 1934, United Conf. Meth. Chs., 1939, Gen. Conf., 1938, World Sunday Sch. Conf., 1938, Jurisdictional Conf., 1940, mem. gen. bd. publ., 1940-44, del. World Religious Conf., 1942; mem. bd. Christian edn. Upper S.C. Conf., 1920-44; chmn. Conf. Bd. Evangelism, 1944-48; mem. Bd. on Location New Chs., 1946—; mem. ofcl. bd. Washington St. Meth. Ch.; mem., chmn. Miss. Appeal Bd. Selective Service, 1948—. Recipient Appreciation certificate Pres. U.S., 1958, Meritorious Service certificate N.Am. Nat. Assn. Secs., 1959, Christian Workers diploma Gen. Bd. Christian Edn. Meth. Ch., 1938. Rotarian. Home: 1722 Crestwood St Columbia SC 29205 Office: 1420 Sumter St Columbia SC 29201

HORTON, LARNIE GLENN, coll. pres.; b. Pittsboro, N.C., Oct. 23, 1935; s. John and Sadie Beatrice (Perry) H.; A.B. cum laude, Morris Brown Coll., 1960, B.D., 1967; postgrad. (Rockefeller fellow) Duke, 1967, (Woodrow Wilson fellow), U. N.C., 1961; m. Katrena Lee Baldwin, June 10, 1962; children—Larnie Glenn, Langston Garvey. Pastor chs. Saxaphaw, N.C., 1960-64; pastor Emmanuel A.M.E. Ch., Durham, N.C., 1964-66; acad. dean Kittrell (N.C.) Coll., 1961-62, pres., 1966—. Cons. Am. Assn. Jr. Colls.; mem. research adv. com. N.C. Commn. on Higher Edn. Facilities; mem. Black Studies adv. com. U. Cal. at Los Angeles. Chmn., Henderson-Vance County Community Council. Trustee Vance Tech. Inst.; bd. dirs. Nat. Lab. for Higher Edn., Soul City Found. Served with AUS, 1952-54. Recipient Civic Achievement award Morris Brown Coll. Nat. Alumni Assn. Mem. N.A.A.C.P., Mchts. Assn. Chapel Hill, Henderson C. of C., Alpha Phi Alpha. Home: P O Box 218 Kittrell NC 27544

HORTON, ODELL, coll. pres.; b. Whiteville, Tenn., May 13, 1929; grad. Morehouse Coll., 1951; LL.B., Howard U., 1956; L.H.D., Miss. Indsl. Coll.; m. Evie Horton; children—Odell, Christopher. Practice law, Memphis, 1957-62; asst. U.S. atty. western dist. Tenn., 1962-67; dir. Div. Hosps. and Health Services City of Memphis, 1968; judge Shelby County (Tenn.) Criminal Ct., from 1968; now pres. LeMoyne-Owen Coll., Memphis. Past bd. dirs. Family Service Memphis; bd. mgmt. Methodist Hosp., Memphis. Served with USMC. Mem. Am. Bar Assn., N.A.A.C.P. Recipient L.M. Gravel Meml. Health award Interagy. Health com. Mid-South Med. Center Council, 1969; Distinguished Alumni award Howard U., 1969. Mem. M.E. Ch. Address: LeMoyce-Owen Coll Memphis TN 38126*

HORTON, THOMAS MANNING, orthodontist; b. Pendleton, S.C., Aug. 12, 1922; s. Childs Clinton and Frances Grace (Hughes) H.; B.S., Clemson U., 1942; D.D.S., Emory U., 1946; m. Dorothy Jeanette Sterne, Apr. 26, 1944; children—Thomas Manning, Amanda Caron. Practice orthodontics, Spartenburg, S.C., 1948-49; pvt. practice dentistry specializing in orthodontics, Columbus, Ga., 1950—; pres. Profl. Assn., Columbus, 1969—; pres. Dental Support Services, Inc., 1970—. Bd. trustees Brookstone Sch, Columbus Coll. Found.; bd. dirs. United Givers, YMCA. Served to capt., Dental Corps, USAF, 1946-48. Fellow Am. Coll. Dentists, Ga. Dental Assn. (hon.); mem. Am., Ga. dental assns., So., Begg socs. orthodontics, Am. Assn. Orthodontics, Psi Omego. Episcopalian. Mason, Rotarian. Clubs: Big Eddy, Green Island (both Columbus), Piedmont (Spartanburg, S.C.). Home: 6698 Waterford Court Columbus GA 31904 Office: 1200 Wynnton Rd Columbus GA 31906

HORTON, WILLIAM LAMAR, educator; b. Rock Hill, S.C., Aug. 26, 1935; s. Luther Burns and Ruth (Stogner) H.; Mus.B., Furman U., 1956; M.Sacred Music, So. Bapt. Theol. Sem., 1958, D.Mus. Arts, 1970; postdoctoral study U. Mich., 1968; m. Peggy Ann Small, June 16, 1958; children—Richard Lamar, Ronald William, Randall Alan. Minister music First Bapt. Ch., Taylors, S.C., 1954-56, Broadway Bapt. Ch., Louisville, 1956-58, First Bapt. Ch., Douglas, Ga., 1958-59; instr. music U. Ga., 1958-59, So. Bapt. Theol. Sem., Louisville, 1959-62; prof. music, chmn. dept. ch. music Ouachita Bapt. U., Arkadelphia, Ark., 1963-68; prof. music Okla. Bapt. U., Shawnee, 1968—; minister music Univ. Bapt. Ch., Shawnee, 1968—. Clinician, adjudicator music festivals throughout S. and S.W., baritone soloist various musicals, oratorios, other prodns. Mem. Music Tchrs. Nat. Assn. (exec. com. S.W. dist. 1968—), Nat. Assn. Tchrs. of Singing, Okla. Music Tchrs. Assn. (3 v.p. 1970—), A.S.C.A.P., So. Bach. Ch. Mus. Conf., Phi Mu Alpha Sinfonia (Okla. province gov. 1968—). Mason, Rotarian. Author: Introduction to Singing, 1968. Composer: Song of the Lamb, 1958, Salvation to Our God, 1962, How Excellent is Thy Name, 1962, Praise Ye The Lord, 1963. Contbr. articles to profl. jours. Home: 18 Mojave Dr Shawnee OK 74801

HORWARD, DONALD DAVID, educator; b. Pitts., Jan. 9, 1933; s. Frank J. and Selena U. (Hartman) H.; A.B., Waynesburg Coll., 1955; M.A., Ohio U., 1956; Ph.D., U. Minn., 1962; m. Annabel Lee Vanscyoc, July 19, 1958. Faculty adviser U. Minn., Mpls., 1958-61; instr. history Fla. State U., Tallahassee, 1961-63, asst. prof., 1963-66, asso. prof., 1966—, asst. to chmn. dept. history, 1964-67, asso. chmn., 1967-69, acting chmn., 1969-70, chmn., 1970—. Com. mem. Interuniv. Consortium on Revolutionary Europe. Research grantee The Calouste Gulbenkian Found., Lisbon, Portugal, 1967—; Woodrow Wilson Found. grantee, 1960; Tozer Found. grantee, Minn., 1960; Greater U. Minn. grantee, 1960. Mem. Am. Hist. Assn., French Hist. Soc., Soc. for Army Hist. Research, Institut Napoleon, Societe Belge d'Etudes Napoleonienne, Societe d'Histoire Moderne, Societe du Chateau Imperial de Pont-de-Briques (Am. rep. com. of honor 1966—), Royal Arty. Inst., Royal Arty. Hist. Soc. (hon. mem.). Author: The Battle of Bussaco: Massena vs. Wellington, 1965; Guide to the French Revolution-Napoleon Collection at Florida State University, 1972. Home: 2101 Great Oak Dr Tallahassee FL 32303

HORWITZ, ABRAHAM, physician, orgn. exec. Dir. Pan Am. San. Bur., Washington. Address: Pan Am Health Orgn 525 23d St NW Washington DC 20037*

HOSKA, LUKAS ERNEST, JR., educator; b. Tacoma, May 9, 1913; s. Lukas Ernest and Marion (Pratt) H.; student Whitman Coll., 1932-33; B.S., U.S. Mil. Acad., 1937; M.S. in Pub. Administrn., Syracuse U., 1949; M.A. in Internat. Affairs, George Washington U., 1963; M.A., U. Md., 1951, Ph.D., 1966; m. Florence Elizabeth Knettle, July 25, 1939; children—Conrad Louis, Elizabeth Anne (Mrs. James Sterling Jones), Lukas Ernest III, Stephen Marion. Commd. 2d lt. arty., U.S. Army, 1937, advanced through grades to col., 1945; gen. staff officer various locations, 1948-56, 63-67; army fellow Harvard, 1959-60; instr. Nat. War Coll., 1960-63; ret., 1967; asso. prof. Prince George's Community Coll., 1967-68; asso. prof. polit. sci. Indsl. Coll. Armed Forces, Washington, 1968—. Active Boy Scouts Am. Decorated D.S.M., Silver Star with oak leaf cluster, Legion of Merit, Bronze Star medal with oak leaf cluster, Air medal, Purple Heart, Army Commendation medal with oak leaf cluster. Mem. Acad. Polit. Sci., Am. Acad. Polit. and Social Sci., Am. Assn. U. Profs., Am. Polit. Sci. Assn., Indsl. Relations Research Assn., Am. Soc. Pub. Adminstrn., Phi Kappa Phi, Phi Alpha Theta, Pi Sigma Alpha. Home: 1293 Delaware Av SW Washington DC 20024 Office: Indsl Coll Armed Forces Fort Lesley J McNair Washington DC 20315

HOSKINS, NADINE CAMPBELL (MRS. CARL LOWRY HOSKINS), artist; b. Atlanta, July 28, 1912; d. Clinton Rice and Esther (Hartley) Campbell; student Highland Park Jr. Coll., 1930-32, Detroit U., 1935, U. Miami, Coral Gables, Fla., 1949-50; m. Carl Lowry Hoskins, June 29, 1935; 1 dau., Karen Gail (Mrs. Teal Traina). Exhibited Victor Hammer Gallery, N.Y.C., Raymond Burr Galleries, Beverly Hills, Cal., The Gallery, Ft. Lauderdale, Fla., Petoskey, Mich.; represented in permanent collections Joe and Emily Lowe Mus., U. Miami Mus. Recipient art awards Design Derby, 1963, Huston purchase award prize Lowe Mus., 1962, 1st fiction award Nat. League Am. Pen Women, 1951. Mem. Nat. Home Fashion League, Beaux Arts-Lowe Mus. (hon.), Theatre Arts League, Miami Ballet Soc. Clubs: Palm Bay, Jockey, Coral Gables Country. Contbr. short stories to McCalls, True, various newspapers.Home: 803 Coral Way Coral Gables FL 33134 Studio: 3490 Main Hwy Coconut Grove Miami FL 33133

HOSKINS, ROBERT NATHAN, r.r. co. exec.; b. Keota, Ia., Feb. 23, 1917; s. Frank A. and Ora E. (Wayman) H.; student U. Mo., 1934-37; B.S., Ia. State U., 1939; m. Julia L. Jones, July 19, 1946; children—Nancy Carol, Mary Susan, Julia Ann, Robert Nathan. Towerman, Sam A. Baker State Forest, Mo. Conservation Commn., 1939, sr. forester, 1940-41; extension forester Fla. Forest Service, 1941-45; indsl. forester Seaboard Air Line R.R. Co. (name changed to Seaboard Coast Line R.R. Co. 1967), Richmond, Va., 1945-46, gen. forestry agt., 1956-64, gen. indsl. and forestry agt., 1964-65, gen. mgr. indsl. devel., 1965-68, asst. v.p. containerization and spl. projects, 1968-69, asst. v.p. forestry and spl. projects, 1969—. Mem. core com. Keep Fla. Green, 1946-50, Keep N.C. Green, 1947-49; mem. Gov.'s Adv. Com. on Forestry Va. Economy, 1950-53; mem. adv. com. on forestry program in agrl. edn. Va., N.C., S.C., Ga., Fla., Ala., 1950-65; mem. adv. com. vocational edn. Va. State Bd. Edn., 1950-60; mem. profl. adv. group indsl. devel. Commonwealth Va., 1967-68; mem. staff of resources Future, 1949-50; adviser on forestry edn. So. Regional Edn. Bd., 1957-58; southeastern regional chmn. sponsoring com. Nat. Future Farmers Am. Found., 1969-72; mem. nat. adv. com. to sec. agr. on state and pvt. forestry, 1970-72. Named Norfolk's Outstanding Young Man, Norfolk Jr. C. of C., 1951, recipient certificate of merit, 1952; recipient Distinguished Service award S.C. Agrl. Tchrs., 1953, Alumni Merit award Chgo. Alumni Assn., Ia. State U., 1954, Key to City, Mayor of Cin., 1960, Mayor of Phila., 1961, Merit award Fla. Vocational Agrl. Assn., 1965, Appreciation award Va. Agrl. Tchrs. Assn., 1967, Distinguished Service award S.C. Future Farmers Am. Assn., 1968, Spl. award for distinguished service to sponsoring com. Nat. Future Farmers Am., 1971. Mem. Am. (Merit award 1954, awards chmn. 1949-54), Ga. (liaison and coordinating com. 1955-56), N.C. (reforestation com. 1951-52), Ala., Fla. forestry assns., Va. Forests, Fla. Forest and Park Assn., Soc. Am. Foresters, Ry. Tie Assn. (chmn. conservation com. 1956-58), Forest Farmers Assn. (ednl. com. 1957-58), Am. Vocational Assn. (award merit 1958), U.S. (mem. agribus. and rural affairs com. 1972), Fla. State (forestry com. 1952-53), Va. State (indsl. devel. com. 1965-68), Richmond chambers commerce. Methodist (finance com. 1962-63). Elk. Clubs: Va. Press (Richmond), Soc. of Va., Hermitage Country. Author: (with M.D. Mobley) Forestry in the South, 1956. Editor SCL Forestry Bull., 1945-65. Contbr. articles to profl. jours. Home: 7605 Cornwall Rd Richmond VA 23229 Office: 3600 W Broad St Richmond VA 23230 also PO Box 27581 Richmond VA 23261

HOSS, RALPH HALAND, govt. ofcl.; b. Pawhuska, Okla., Apr. 6, 1927; s. Ralph W. and Irene (Price) H.; student Baylor U., 1944, Tex. A. and M. Coll., 1945, Tulsa U., 1950-52; m. Fern Burdine, Feb. 17, 1950; children—Kurt David, Walter Kris. With U.S. Army C.E., 1947—, civil engr., Tulsa, 1951-52, Roswell, N.M., 1954-57, Eufaula, Okla., 1960-65, materials engr., Wichita Falls, Tex., 1952, Altus, Okla., 1953, asst. resident engr., Amarillo, Tex., 1957-60, Broken Bow, Okla., 1965-66, resident engr., Muskogee, Okla., 1967-70, chief reservoir br., Tulsa, 1970—. Served with AUS, 1944-46. Recipient Superior Performance award Army C.E., 1959, Outstanding Constrn. Office award, 1968, 69. Registered profl. engr., Okla. Mem. Soc. Am. Mil. Engrs., Nat., Okla. socs. profl. engrs. Home: Box 666 Eufaula OK 74432 Office: US Army CE PO Box 61 Tulsa OK 74102

HOST, MALCOLM STUART, social service exec.; b. Milw., June 26, 1926; s. Ambrose A. and Esther (Zarwell) H.; A.B., Wittenberg Coll., 1950; M.A., Ind. U., 1952; m. Donna J. Thorne, Apr. 26, 1953; children—Jeffery, Steven, Cheryl. Casework dir. Luth. Child Welfare Assn., Indpls., 1952-55; exec. dir. Day Nursery Assn., Indpls., 1955-57, Day Care Assn., Houston, 1958-69, Neighborhood Centers -Day Care Assn., Houston, 1969—. Lectr., U. Houston, 1964—; cons. U.S. Children's Bur., 1963. Project Headstart, 1965-68; chmn. Tex. Day Care Adv. Com., 1967—. Served with AUS, 1944-46. Mem. So. Assn. on Children under Six (pres. 1962), Child Devel. and Day Care Council Am. (v.p. 1960-69). Author: (with others) Day Care Administration, 1971. Home: 7806 DeMoss St Houston TX 77036 Office: 9 Chelsea Pl Houston TX 77006

HOTCHKISS, WILLIAM S., physician; b. Waco, Tex., 1915; M.D., U. Tex., 1939. Intern Henry Ford Hosp., Detroit, 1940-41, surg. resident, 1947-49, resident thoracic surgery, 1949-51; sr. asst. surgeon U.S. Marine Hosp., Norfolk, Va., 1942-45, U.S. Marine Hosp., Boston, 1945-47; resident thoracic surgery McKinney (Tex.) VA Hosp., 1951; now practice medicine specializing in thoracic surgery. Served with USPHS, 1941-46. Diplomate Am. Bd. Surgery, Am. Bd. Thoracic Surgery. Fellow Am. Coll. Chest Physicians; mem. A.M.A., Med. Soc. Va. (pres. elect). Address: Med Tower 400 Gresham Dr Norfolk VA 23507*

HOUCK, CATHERINE MAGILL (MRS. WILLIAM C. HOUCK), librarian; b. Washington, Oct. 9, 1907; d. Charles H. and Annette E. (Paige) Magill; B.A., George Washington U., 1930; B.L.S., Columbia, 1939; m. William C. Houck, Oct. 17, 1928. With D.C. Pub. Library, Washington, 1930—, personnel officer, 1942-54, adminstrv. asst., budget officer, 1954-57, asso. dir., 1957—. Bd. dirs. Legal Aid Soc. Recipient Govt. employees incentive award, Sustained Superior Performance rating, 1957, Outstanding Performance ratings, 1962, 64. Mem. A.L.A., Delta Zeta. Club: Zonta (past pres., Washington). Author: (with Harry N. Peterson) Access to the D.C. Public Library, 1963, Distribution and Characteristics of D.C. Public Library Agencies, 1964. Home: 2732 Rittenhouse St NW Washington DC 20015 Office: 499 Pennsylvania Av NW Washington DC 20001

HOUCK, FRANK SCANLAND, scientist; b. Phila., Aug. 27, 1930; s. Ivan Deweese and Catherine (Cabeen) H.; B.S., Dickinson Coll., 1952; M.A., Columbia, 1957, Ph.D., 1959; m. Dorothy Fales, June 26, 1955; children—Catherine, Margaret, Dorothy. Operations analyst U.S. Navy, Operations Evaluation Group, 1957-63; chief analysis br., field operations div. U.S. Arms Control and Disarmament Agy., Washington, 1963-68, chief nuclear br., 1968—. Recipient Meritorious Honor award U.S. Govt., 1968. Mem. Operations Research Soc. Am., Sigma Xi, Phi Beta Kappa, Phi Lambda Upsilon, Kappa Sigma. Home: 401 E Columbia St Falls Church VA 22046 Office: US Arms Control and Disarmament Agy State Dept Washington DC 20451

HOUGHTON, JAMES AUBREY, city mgr.; b. Portsmouth, Va., Aug. 28, 1925; s. Carl Clifford and Viola (Deans) H.; Chem.E., Va. Poly. Inst., 1946; m. Jean Warren, June 5, 1948; children—Nancy Rhea, Betty Jean. City purchasing agt., Portsmouth, 1951-52, adminstrv. asst. to city mgr., 1952-56; city mgr., South Boston, Va., 1956—. Mem. Internat. City Mgrs. Assn., Am. Soc. Pub. Adminstrn., Halifax County C. of C. (past pres.). Presbyn. (deacon). Lion (past pres. South Boston). Home: 2100 Westmoreland St South Boston VA 24592 Office: City Hall 436 Main St South Boston VA 24592

HOUGLAND, HUBBARD, dentist; b. Indpls., Jan. 10, 1937; s. George E. and Bernice M. (Ridlen) H.; B.A., Vanderbilt U., 1959; M.S. in Dentistry, U. Neb., 1967; D.D.S., Ind. U., 1963; m. Marjorie Lucas, Sept. 20, 1964. Pvt. practice pedodontics, San Antonio, Tex., 1967—; mem. staff Santa Rosa Hosp., San Antonio. Served with USAF, 1963-65. Home: 6718 Callahan St No 406 San Antonio TX 78229 Office: 3111 San Pedro St San Antonio TX 78212

HOUNTHA, PATSY SIMS (MRS. LAWRENCE GEORGE HOUNTHA), newspaperwoman; b. Beaumont, Tex., Feb. 14, 1938; d. Robert Ray and Edna (Shanks) Sims; B.A. in Journalism, Tulane U., 1960; m. Lawrence George Hountha, Nov. 25, 1960. Mem. staff New Orleans States-Item, 1958—, women's editor, 1969—. Recipient Catherine O'Brien award, 1964; award for best sports story ann. New Orleans Press Club Awards, 1969. Mem. Theta Sigma Phi. Club: New Orleans Press. Home: 772 Fairfield Av Gretna LA 70053 Office: 3800 Howard Av New Orleans LA 70140

HOUSE, GEORGE ROBERT, JR., city ofcl.; b. Durham, N.C., Aug. 6, 1928; s. George Robert and Beatrice (Deahl) H.; B.A., U. N.C., 1954, certificate municipal adminstrn., 1956; m. Myra Virginia Bland, June 24, 1951; children—George Robert III, Bettye Jo. Asst. city mgr. Durham, 1954-56; city mgr., Emporia, Va., 1956-60; city mgr., Bedord, Va., 1960-61, county mgr., Forsyth County, N.C., Winston-Salem, 1961-69; city mgr., Chesapeake, Va., 1969-71, Norfolk, Va., 1971—. Served to 1st lt. USAF, 1951-53; England. Nat. Assn. County Adminstrs. (pres., 1969-70; dir., 1969-70), Nat. Assn. County Ofcls. (dir., 1970-71), Internat. City Mgmt. Assn., Nat. Municipal League. Home: 5740 Shendoah Av Norfolk VA 23509 Office: City Hall Norfolk VA 23501

HOUSE, WALTER CHARLES, clergyman; b. Louisville, Ky., Feb. 22, 1913; s. Walter D. and Florence I. (Patterson) H.; student Georgetown Coll., 1945; Moody Bible Inst., 1938, So. Bapt. Sem., 1938; m. Artic E. Colvin, Nov. 5, 1933; dau., Priscilla Ann. Furniture salesman to 1938; ordained to Baptist ministry, 1940; pastor Mt. Pleasant Ch., Canaan, Ind., 1940-46; asso. pastor First Ch., Madison, Ind., 1948-49; pastor Liberty Bapt. Ch., Prospect, Ky., 1949-50; real estate broker; exec. dir. Temperance League Ky., 1950-65; acting exec. dir. Temperance League of Washington, 1961-62; chaplain Life Ins. Co. Ky., 1957-64, exec. asst. to pres., 1967-69, now mem. adv. bd. dirs.; chaplain, asst. to pres. Life of Ky. Financial Corp., Louisville, 1970-71; cons., asst. mgr. Independent Postal System Am., Cin., 1971—; mem. adv. bd. dirs. Ky. Industries Trust Co., Louisville. Former State Field Rep. Ind. Temperance League and United Dry Forces Ind.; adv. com. State Div. Alcoholism State Health Dept., 1961; v.p. Nat. Found. for Hwy. Safety, Hartford, Conn., 1944; chmn. area panel OPA, Madison, Ind., 1952-58; chmn. Gov's adv. com. on child welfare, 1955-59; del. White House Conf. on Children and Youth, 1960; rep. to White House Conf. on Traffic Safety, 1958-59; lobbyist for Ky. Dry Forces to State Legislature; exec. chmn. So. Indiana Christian Citizenship League, 1945-48; mem. Ky. Com. of Partners for Alliance for Progress for Sister State in S. Am., Ecuador, 1966. Vice chmn. Louisville and Jefferson County Council on Alcoholism, 1963-64, v.p, Am. Council on Alcohol Problems. Mem. Am. Bus. Men's Research Found. Hon. col. Ky. State Police, 1955. Mem. Ky. Police Officers Assn., Christians Citizens Internat., Nat. Temperance League (1st vice chmn. exec. com.; chmn. adminstrv. com., chmn. legislative com.), Adult Edn. Assn. Chgo., Ky., Ind. sheriffs assns., Friends of Ky. State Fair, Inc. (v.p.). Clubs: Rotary, Nat. Travel. Commd. Ky. Col. Home: 6605 Moorhaven Dr Louisville KY 40218 Office: 965 N Bend Rd Cincinnati OH 45224

HOUSER, JOHN EDWARD, lawyer; b. Richmond, Va., Dec. 24, 1928; s. Aubrey Alphin and Winnifred (Savage) H.; B.S., U. Va., 1959, LL.B., 1959; m. Rives Pollard; children—Allen Rives Cabell Lybrook, Andrew Murray Lybrook II. Admitted to Fla. and Federal bars, 1959, U.S. Supreme Ct. bars, 1970; gen. practice Jacksonville, Fla., 1959—; dir. Wm. P. Poythress & Co., Richmond, Neal F. Tyler & Sons, Jacksonville. Served with AUS, 1953-57. Mem. Internat. Assn. Indsl. Accident Bds. and Commns., Maritime Law Assn. U.S., Jacksonville, Atlanta claimsmen assns., Am., Jacksonville bar assns., Fla. Bar, Fla. Def. Counsel Assn., Am. Judicature Assn., Am. Arbitration Assn., Nat. Trust for Historic Preservation, Fla. Inst. Pub. Affairs, Navy

League, Jacksonville Assn. Def. Counsel, Def. Research Inst., Jacksonville Univ. Council, Jacksonville Symphony Assn., Fla., Jacksonville hist. socs., Cummer Gallery of Art, Jacksonville C. of C., English-Speaking Union (dir. 1970—, v.p. 1971—), Theta Delta Chi, Sigma Nu Phi. Clubs: River, Fla. Yacht; Deerwood, Ponte Vedra River, Exchange, German, Ye Mystic Revellers, University. Home: 4741 Algonquin Jacksonville FL 32210 Office: Fla Nat Bank Bldg Jacksonville FL 32202

HOUSER, JOHN WESLEY, JR., dentist; b. Orangeburg, S.C., July 10, 1918; s. John Wesley and Eva (Hollins) H.; B.S., Claflin Coll., 1940; postgrad. Atlanta U., 1941-43; D.D.S., Meharry Med. Coll., 1946; m. Louise Kelley, Sept. 18, 1943; children—John Wesley III, George. Practice dentistry, Rome, Ga., 1946—; mem. staff Floyd Hosp.; asso. dentist Battey State Hosp., Floyd County Health Services, 1950-71. Owner, pres. Brentwood Med.-Care Nursing Home, Inc., 1964—. Ga. bd. dirs. Am. Cancer Soc., 1950-58; bd. dirs. Girls Club, 1967—. Mem. City Planning Commn., 1968—. Served with AUS. Named Ga. Dentist of Year, Omega Psi Phi, 1960, Pres's award Nat. Dental Assn., 1961, Dentist of Year, 1963; recipient Service Plaque Am. Cancer Soc., 1964. Fellow Coll. Nursing Home Adminstrs; mem. Ga. Dental Soc. (pres. 1954), John A. Andrew Clin. Soc. (pres., 1963), Nat. Dental Assn. (zone v.p., 1959-64), C. of C., Phi Beta Sigma. Baptist (deacon). Mason. Home: 121 Jackson St Rome GA 30161 Office: 1006 E 1st St Rome GA 30161

HOUSTON, DANIEL COLLIER, architect; b. Montgomery, Ala., May 21, 1923; s. Walter Howell and Caroline (Ramer) H.; B.Arch., Auburn U., 1951; m. Dorothy Lamar Smith, May 11, 1945; children—Daniel Collier, Walter Lamar. Owner Houston Assos., Architects, Albany, Ga., 1953—. Mem. State Art Commn., 1954-59. Served with Canadian Army, 1940-41, Brit. Army, 1941-42, AUS, 1942-45. Certified Nat. Council Archtl. Registration Bds. Mem. A.I.A. (dir.), Am. Legion. Elk, Lion. Address: Route 2 Box 646-A Blue Springs Rd Albany GA 31701

HOUSTON, DAVID LIPSCOMB, city ofcl.; b. Wichita Falls, Tex., June 4, 1921; s. David Lipscomb and Katherine (Blackburn) H.; B.S. in Mech. Engring., U. Tex., 1950, M.S. in Community and Regional Planning, 1970; m. Maude Cardwell, July 18, 1945 (div. Jan. 1956); children—Franklin C., Ronald D. Electric designer electric dept. City of Austin (Tex.), 1950-52, design engr. water dept., 1953-54, planning engr. planning dept., 1955-66; city planner cons. Tex. State Dept. Health, 1966-69, chief environmental devel. program, 1970—. Served with AUS, 1942-45; ETO; lt. col. Res. Registered profl. engr., Tex. Mem. Nat., Tex. socs. profl. engrs., Am. Inst. Planners, City Planners Assn. Tex., Am. Soc. Pub. Adminstrn., Internat. Folk Dance Assn., Am. Soc. Planning Ofcls. Mem. P.E. Ch. Mason (Shriner). Home: 1306 Arcadia St Austin TX 78757 Office: 1100 W 49th St Austin TX 78756

HOUSTON, JAMES GORMAN, JR., lawyer; b. Eufaula, Ala., Mar. 11, 1933; s. James Gorman and Mildred (Vance) H.; B.S., Auburn U., 1954; LL.B., J.D., U. Ala., 1956; m. Marthur Martin, Dec. 3, 1955; children—Mildred Vance, James Gorman III. Admitted to Ala. bar; law clk. Chief Justice Ala. Supreme Ct., Montgomery, 1956-57; gen. practice law, Eufaula, 1960—; atty. Barbour County, Citizens Bank; dir. Citizens Bank Eufaula. Atty., Indsl. Devel. Bd. Eufaula, Barbour County Hosp. Assn., 1961-69. Chmn. Barbour County chpt. A.R.C., 1960-64; mem. Waterworks and Sewer Bd. Eufaula, 1968—. Alderman, mayor pro-tem City of Eufaula, 1964—. Served to 1st lt., Judge Adv. Gen. Dept., USAF, 1957-60. Mem. Am., Barbour County (pres.) bar assns., Eufaula C. of C. (dir. 1961-66), Farrah Order Jurisprudence, Omicron Delta Kappa, Phi Delta Phi. Rotarian, Kiwanian. Club: Eufaula Country (pres.). Bd. editors Ala. Law Rev. Home: Country Club Rd Eufaula AL 36027 Office: 201 E Broad St Eufaula AL 36027

HOUSTON, WALTER RAY, banker; b. Andalusia, Ala., June 13, 1911; s. Walter Howell and Callie (Ramer) H.; student pub. schs.; m. Clara Ruth Alexander, June 15, 1930; children—Warner Ray, Carol Ruth (Mrs. Kenneth L. Makant, Jr.), Beverly Clair (Mrs. James R. Eddens). Night mgr. Postal Telegraph & Cable Co., Montgomery, Ala., 1930-35; office mgr. Universal Credit Co., 1935-36; sales mgmt. trainee Sears, Roebuck & Co., Montgomery and Albany, Ga., 1936-42 with Bank of Albany, 1942-59, successively asst. cashier, cashier, v.p., exec. v.p., dir.; exec. v.p. Bank of Fulton County, East Point, Ga., 1959-60, pres., chmn. bd., 1960—; dir., mem. finance com. Kennesaw Life & Accident Ins. Co., Bankers Fire & Marine Ins. Co., appraiser for various companies, 1946-59. Mem. gov.'s staff and financial com. Commr. Housing Authority, City of Albany, 1947-58. Bd. dirs. Atlanta Girls Club, Atlanta area council Boy Scouts Am.; trustee, chmn. finance com. Fulton-DeKalb Hosp. Authority; governing bd. Woodward Acad., College Park; trustee Wesley Homes, Inc., Epworth Towers. Served with USNR, 1943-45. Mem. Ga., South Fulton, East Point (past pres.) chambers commerce, 40 and 8, Am. Legion (past comdr., past Ga. vice comdr.), Am., Ind., Ga. (pres. 1968-69) bankers assns., Ga. Hosp. Assn. Methodist (trustee Atlanta S.W. dist.). Mason (Shriner), Elk, Kiwanian (past pres.). Clubs: Atlanta Athletic, Atlanta Tarpon; Lakeside Country (dir., past pres.). Home: 2998 Pineywood Dr East Point GA 30344 Office: Bank of Fulton County East Point GA 30344

HOUTHAKKER, HENDRIK SAMUEL, educator, govt. ofcl.; b. Amsterdam, Netherlands, Dec. 31, 1924; s. Bernard and Marion (Lichtenstein) H.; D.Econs., U. Amsterdam, 1949; m. Anna-Teresa Tymieniecka, Sept. 8, 1955; children—Louis, Isabella, Jan Nicolas. Came to U.S., 1951, naturalized, 1966. Mem. research staff dept. applied econs. U. Cambridge (Eng.), 1949-51; research staff Cowles Commn. Research Econs., U. Chgo., 1952-53; from acting asso. prof. to prof. econs. Stanford, 1954-60; prof. econs. Harvard, 1960—; sr. staff economist Council Econ. Advisers, 1967-68, now mem. council; vis. prof. U. Tokyo, 1955, Mass. Inst. Tech., 1957-58, Harvard, 1958-59, Stanford, 1962. Cons. U.S. Treasury Dept., 1961—. Fellow Econometric Soc. (council 1961-63, pres. 1967), Am. Statis. Assn.; mem. Am. Econ. Assn. (John Bates Clark medal 1963), Internat. Statis. Inst. Author: (with S. J. Prais) The Analysis of Family Budgets, 1955; (with Lester D. Taylor) Consumer Demand in the United States, 1929-70, 1966; also articles. Asso. editor Econometrica, 1953-60. Home: 348 Payson Rd Belmont MA 02178 Office: Executive Office Bldg Washington DC 20506*

HOUTMAN, JACQUES, condr. Condr. Richmond (Va.) Symphony. Address: 112 E Franklin St Richmond VA 23219*

HOUTZ, DUANE TALBOTT, hosp. adminstr.; b. Kansas City, Mo., Apr. 28, 1933; B.S., U. Kan., 1955; M. H.A., Washington U., St. Louis, 1960; m. Margaret McNiel; children—Jamie Denice, Erik Siegfried. Adminstrv. resident Orange Meml. Hosp., Orlando, Fla., 1959-60, adminstrv. asst., 1960; asst. dir. teaching hosp. and clinics J. Hillis Miller Health Center U Fla., Gainesville, 1961-65, asst. prof. Center Health and Hosp. Adminstrn., 1964-65; adminstr. Highland Av.Bapt. Hosp., Birmingham, Ala., from 1965; now exec. v.p. Baptist Med. Center-Montclair, Birmingham. Pres. Birmingham Regional Hosp. Council, 1972. Served with USAF, 1955-58. Fellow Am. Coll. Hosp. Adminstrs.; mem. Ala. Hosp. Assn. (chmn. research and edn. found. liaison com.), Am. Protestant Hosp. Assn., Am. Mgmt. Assn., Emergency Med. Service Com., Ala. Assn. Hosp. Exec., Ala. Pub. Health Assn., Greater Birmingham Safety League Phi Delta Theta. Kiwanian (v.p.). Contbr. articles to profl. jours. Address: Bapt Med Center 800 Montclair Rd Birmingham AL 35213

HOVEY, LESTER EUGENE, accountant; b. La Porte, Tex., May 16, 1933; s. John Williard and Clara (Sharp) H.; student Southwestern U., 1951-52; B.B.A. cum laude, U. Tex., 1957, M.Profl. Accounting, 1961; m. Claudia Janet Meiners, June 20, 1954; children—Sheryl Susan, Sandra Kay, Richard Eugene. Audit and tax accountant Arthur Andersen & Co., Houston, 1958-60; in practice as Eugene Hovey, C.P.A., La Porte, 1961—; tchr. accountant San Jacinto Coll., part-time 1961-63. Dir. La Porte Neighborhood Center, 1961-62. Served with AUS, 1954-56. C.P.A., Tex., Mem. Am. Inst. C.P.A.'s, C. of C. Methodist. Home: 606 S 1st St La Porte TX 77571 Office: 902 W Main St La Porte TX 77571

HOWARD, BARROLS AUGUSTUS, JR., scientist; b. Moorewood, Okla., July 15, 1914; s. B.A. and Augusta (Blair) H.; B.S., Southwestern State Tchrs. Coll., 1937; postgrad. Ohio State U., 1943-44, U. Ia., 1956-66; m. Cynthia M. Webber, Nov. 14, 1942; children—Cynthia Sue (Mrs. Kenneth Campbell), David Alan. Jr. project engr. Tenn. Eastman, Oak Ridge, 1944-45; project engr., engring. analyst Bendix Aviation, Davenport, Ia., 1955-58; phys. sci. adminstr. U.S. Army Weapons Command, 1958-66; sci. staff asst., operations research analyst U.S. Naval Weapons Lab., Dohlgren, Va., 1966—. Tchr. U. Ia., 1966. St. Ambrose Coll., Davenport, Ia., 1956-58, Palmer Jr. Coll., 1965-66. Served with C.E., AUS, 1941-45. Mem. Am. Phys. Soc., Am. Chem. Soc., A.A.A.S., Ia. Acad. Sci., Am. Soc. M.E. Home: 1801 Genther Lane Fredericksburg VA 22401 Office: US Naval Weapons Lab Dohlgren VA 22448

HOWARD, BERNARD EUFINGER, mathematician, educator; b. Ludlow, Vt., Sept. 22, 1920; s. Charles Rawson and Ethel (Kearney) H.; student Middlebury Coll., 1938-40; B.S., Mass. Inst. Tech., 1944; M.S., U. Ill., 1947, Ph.D., 1951; m. Ruth Belknap, Mar. 29, 1942. Mem. staff Radiation Lab., Mass. Inst. Tech., 1942-45; asst. math. dept. U. Ill., 1945-50; sr. mathematician Inst. for Air Weapons Research, U. Chgo., 1951, asst. to dir., 1951-54, asst. to dir. Inst. for Systems Research, 1954-56, asso. dir., 1956-60, asso. dir. Labs. for Applied Scis., 1958-60; prof. math. U. Miami, Coral Gables, Fla., 1960—, dir. sci. computing center, 1961-64. Exec. sec. Air Force Adv. Bd. on Simulation, 1951-54; cons. Systems Research Labs., Inc., Dayton, O., 1963—, acting dir. math. scis. div., 1965; cons. Variety Childrens Research Found., 1964-66, Fla. Power & Light Co., 1968—, Shaw & Assos., 1969—. Vice pres. Pine Ridge Civic Assn., 1968—. Bd. dirs. Blue Lake Assn., 1969—. Mem. Am. Math. Soc., Soc. for Indsl. and Applied Math. (treas. S.E. sect. 1964), Am. Phys. Soc., Am. Assn. U. Profs., A.A.A.S., Assn. for Computing Machinery (chpt. chmn. 1969-70), I.E.E.E., Simulation Councils, Sigma Xi, Phi Kappa Phi, Pi Mu Epsilon, Alpha Sigma Phi. Home: 7320 Miller Dr Miami FL 33155 Office: U Miami Coral Gables FL 33124

HOWARD, DALE EUGENE, hosp. adminstr.; b. Grand Junction, Ia., Jan. 24, 1922; s. Virgil R. and Celene (Williams) H.; Certificate in hosp. adminstrn. Ga. State Coll., 1959; m. Fabian Lee Lavender, Dec. 27, 1959; children—Celene Renee, Shannon Lee. Lab. technologist Bethesda Hosp., Ft. Dodge, Ia., 1946-52; chief x-ray lab. technologist Immanuel-St. Joseph Hosp., Mankato, Minn., 1952-54, Pipestone (Minn.) Meml. Hosp., 1955-56, Hancock Meml. Hosp., Britt, Ia., 1956-58; adminstrv. asst. Macon (Ga.) Hosp., 1959-60; asst. adminstr. Polk Gen. Hosp., Bartow, Fla., 1961-63; adminstr. Citrus County Hosp., Inverness, Fla., 1963-65, Tarpon Springs (Fla.) Gen. Hosp., 1965—. Mem. Am. Coll. Hosp. Adminstrs., Phi Epsilon Rho. Episcopalian. Home: 621 Bayshore St Tarpon Springs FL 33589 Office: 1395 S Pinellas St Tarpon Springs FL 33589

HOWARD, JASPER SMITH, mcht.; b. Monroe, La., Nov. 24, 1932; s. Verna E. and Ruth Moryne (Jackson) H.; B.B.A., Abilene (Tex.) Christian Coll., 1954; m. Peggy Nell Bobo, Jan. 16, 1955; children—Leslie, Ann, Jonathan, Sara. Pres., Howard-Gibco Corp., Texarkana, Tex., 1959—; gen. mgr., pres. Howard Discount Centers; pres. Howard Ins. & Investment Co.; sec.-treas. Central Printers & Pubs., Monroe; dir. Comml. Nat. Bank, Texarkana, Mid-South Devel. Co., Monroe. Bd. dirs. Caddo area council Boy Scouts Am., Abilene Christian Coll., Howard Found.; mem. adv. bd. Harding Coll., Searcy, Ark., York Coll. Served with AUS, 1955-56. Mem. Texarkana C. of C. (dir.). Mem. Ch. of Christ (deacon). Home: Route 5 Box 11 Texarkana TX 75501 Office: Summerhill Park Rd Texarkana TX 75501

HOWARD, JOHN GARFIELD, savs. and loan exec.; b. Pineville, Ky., Nov. 11, 1935; s. Durham W. and Katherine (Morgan) H.; student U. Louisville, 1953-54, Lincoln Meml. U., 1954-55; m. Janice R. Haws, Nov. 29, 1958; children—John David, Jasper Alan. Salesman, Howard Ins. Agy., Pineville, 1958-60; teller 1st Fed. Savs. & Loan Assn., Pineville, 1961, cashier, 1962-63, asst. sec., 1964, sec., asst. mgr., 1965—, also dir.; chmn. Bell County Library Constrn. Corp.; dir. Pineville Municipal Properties Corp. City councilman, Pineville, 1970—. Pres., Pineville Indsl. Found., 1969—; bd. dirs., adv. bd. Ky. Mountain Laurel Festival, 1968—; bd. dirs. Middlesboro-Bell County Airport Bd., 1966—, Middlesboro-Bell County chpt. A.R.C., 1969-70. Served with AUS, 1955-58. Mem. C. of C. (pres. 1969). Presbyn. Kiwanian (pres. 1969-70). Home: 205 Summit Dr Pineville KY 40977 Office: Virginia Av at Oak St Pineville KY 40977

HOWARD, JOHN JOLLEY, clergyman; b. Emerson, Ga., May 10, 1909; s. Wilson Nathan and Bernadina (Jolley) H.; A.B., U. Miami, 1934; Lic. Theo. Va. Episcopal Sem., 1951; m. Mary Meade Southall, July 31, 1941; children—Elizabeth Meade (Mrs. Allan Joseph Bomberger), Mary Meade (Mrs. Kenneth J. Lee). Dist. mgr. Standard Duplicating Machine Co., Roanoke, Va., 1947-49; ordained deacon Episcopal Ch., 1951, priest, 1952; rector St. Mary's Ch., Bluefield, 1951-53, St. Luke's Ch., Blackstone, Va., 1953-57; rector Emmanuel Ch., Hampton, Va., 1957-72, rector emeritus, 1972—. Chmn. armed forces commn. Diocese of So. Va., 1955-63, mem. bd. promotion and missions, 1962-63; pres. Va. Ch. Assn., 1959-66. Bd. dirs. Peninsula Boys Club, 1959-63. Served to major AUS, 1942-46; lt. col. Res. ret. Mem. Mil. Order World Wars, Am. Legion (past dept. comdr., past nat. chaplain). Mason (32 deg., Shriner), Rotarian, Lion (hon.). Home: 408 N Nansemond St Richmond VA 23221

HOWARD, JOHN ZOLLIE, editor; b. Gainesboro, Tenn., Dec. 20, 1897; s. John W. and Lizzie (Van Hooser) H.; B.A., U. Tenn., 1924; m. Jessie Magill, Oct. 28, 1920; children—Joseph E., William Edwin. Instr. U. Tenn., 1924-25; reporter, Sunday editor, city editor Knoxville News-Sentinel, 1925-40; mng. editor Memphis Press-Scimitar, 1940-64, asso. editor and editor editorial page, 1964—. Treas., The Goodfellows of Memphis, Inc. Presbyn. Home: 896 Robin Hood Lane Memphis TN 38111 Office: 495 Union Av Memphis TN 38101

HOWARD, LARRY BRUCE, state ofcl.; b. Seattle, Apr. 1, 1928; s. Walter Joseph and Anita (Schnitzlein) H.; B.S., U. Mont., 1950; Ph.D., U. Minn., 1956; postgrad. Emory U., 1956-58; m. Elaine Annette Ungherini, Sept. 20, 1952; children—Randy, Rick, Laure, Lisa. Asst. dir. Ga. Crime Lab., Atlanta, 1956-59, dir., 1969—. Mem. faculty criminology Ga. State U., 1967, mem. faculty anatomy Emory U., 1971—, Ga. Police Acad., 1966—. Mem. Ga. Sci. and Tech. Commn., 1969-72; mem. Atlanta YMCA Athletic Council, 1958-59. Served with AUS, 1945-46. Mem. Am. Acad. Forensic Scis., A.A.A.S., So. Assn. Forensic Scientists, Atlanta Instrument Soc., Sigma Phi Epsilon. Home: 3106 Lanier Dr NE Atlanta GA 30319 Office: PO Box 1456 Atlanta GA 30301

HOWARD, MICHAEL, theater dir.; ed. Neighborhood Playhouse Sch. of Theatre. Actor play Country Girl, N.Y.C.; dir. plays Third Best Sport, The Trouble Makers, Land Beyond the River; dir. revivals of Finian's Rainbow, Mr. Roberts; dir. Misalliance, Am. Conservatory Theatre; actor, dir. more than 100 TV plays; artistic dir. Alliance Theatre, Atlanta, dir. plays Marat/Sade, King Arthur, Romeo and Juliet, Twelfth Night, Major Barbara, Threepenny Opera, Much Ado About Nothing, Long Day's Journey into Night, others. Address: 15 16th St NE Atlanta GA 30309

HOWARD, MILO BARRETT, JR., state ofcl.; b. Montgomery, Ala., Oct. 21, 1933; s. Milo Barrett and Josepha (Key) H.; B.A., Auburn U., 1955, M.A., 1960 Archivist, Ala. Dept. Archives and History, Montgomery, 1958-64, asst. dir., 1964-67, dir., 1967—; instr. U. Ala., 1964-68; research lectr. Auburn U., 1968—. Chmn. Ala. Hist. Commn., 1966—; sec. Ala. Acad. Honor, 1969—; chmn. State Capitol Preservation Commn., State Records Commn.; mem. Ala. Art Commn., Ala. Sesquicentennial Commn. historiographer Episcopal Diocese Ala., 1969—. Bd. dirs. Montgomery Historic Devel. Commn., Landmarks Found. of Montgomery. Served to 1st lt., M.I., AUS, 1955-57. Recipient Distinguished Service award Montgomery Jr. C. of C., 1967. Mem. Ala. Hist. Assn. (treas., past pres.), Ala. Archeol. Soc. (dir.). Author: (with Robert R. Rea) The Memoire Justificatif of the Chevalier Montaut de Monberout, 1965. Contbr. articles to profl. jours. Home: 802 Felder Av Montgomery AL 36106 Office: Archives and History Dept Montgomery AL 36104

HOWARD, MOSES WILKERSON, physician; b. Harlan, Ky., Aug. 25, 1909; s. George Turner and Nancy (Smith) H.; A.B., U. Ky., 1931; M.D., U. Louisville, 1933; m. Dorris Cole, Mar. 30, 1940; children—Nancy Ellen (Mrs. Charles Manis), Perry Cole, Mary Pamelia, Jo-Anna. Intern, Bellevue Hosp., N.Y.C., 1935-36; resident Boston City Hosp., 1936-37; physician TVA, 1937-38; ship physician S.S. Delvale, 1938; practice medicine specializing in urology, Knoxville, Tenn., 1946-66, Naples, Fla., 1966—; mem. staff Naples Community Hosp. Served to lt. col. M.C., AUS, 1941-46. Diplomate Am. Bd. Urology. Fellow A.C.S.; mem. A.M.A., S.E. Surg. Congress, Phi Chi, Delta Tau Delta. Home: 561 Palm Circle E E Naples FL 33940 Office: 837 4th Av N Naples FL 33940

HOWARD, PATRICK MCCOLLOGH, mining engr.; b. Welch, W.Va., Nov. 8, 1938; s. Clifford Peter and Harriet (Hoge) H.; student Pikeville Coll., 1956-57; U. Ky., 1957-59; m. Mary Elizabeth Cook, Apr. 8, 1960; children—Marjorie Marie, Patrick McCollough. Jr. designer Electric Elevator div. Dover Corp., Cin., 1959-61; chief engr. Kentland-Elkhorn Coal Corp., Pikeville, Ky., 1961-70, Feds Creek Coal Co., 1962-70; dir. engring. Ky. div. Pittston Co., 1970-71, gen. mgr. Buchanan County Mines Rapoca Resources, 1970—. Owner Mine Tech. Service, Phyllis, Ky., 1965—, Howard Homes Co., Phyllis, Ky., 1967—. Scoutmaster Boy Scouts Am. Served with inf. AUS, 1955. Mem. Nat., Ky. (chpt. pres.) socs. profl. engrs., Am. Inst. Mining, Metall. and Petroleum Engrs., Big Sandy Elkhorn Mining Inst. Republican. Presbyn. Club: Willow Brook Country. Home: PO Box 228 Grundy VA 24614 Office: Conaway VA 24611

HOWARD, RHEA, newspaper pub.; b. Wichita Falls, Tex., July 25, 1892; s. Ed and Jettie Lee (Malony) H.; student Trinity U., Waxahachie, Tex., 1910-11, Eastman Coll., Poughkeepsie, N.Y., 1912; m. Kathleen Benson, Oct, 22, 1913; 1 dau., Anna Katherine (Mrs. James B. Barnett). With The Times Publishing Co. (Wichita Daily Times and Wichita Falls Record News) 1913—, pres., 1948—; v.p. and dir. Wichita Water Irrigation Dist.; dir. Burlington Ry. Bd. dirs. Wichita Falls United Fund, Texas Law Enforcement Found. Mem. Texas State Democratic Exec. Com. Named Pub. of Yr. by Headliners Club, 1960. Mem. Am. Soc. Newspaper Editors, N. Tex. Oil and Gas Assn. (dir.), Am., So. newspaper pubs. assns., C. of C. (dir.), Asso. Press, Tex. Council Higher Edn. (charter; exec. com.), Sigma Delta Chi. Democrat. Presbyn. Club: President's. Home: 2105 Berkley Dr Wichita Falls TX 76307 Office: Times Publishing Co 1301 Lamar Wichita Falls TX 76307

HOWARD, RICHARD FOSTER, museum dir.; b. Plainfield, N.J., July 26, 1902; s. Lawrence Riggs and Nina Margaret (Kellogg) H.; B.S., Harvard, 1924, grad. student, 1929-31; grad. student Cornell, summer, 1930, Inst. Human Relations, Yale, 1931; m. Anne Okeson, Sept. 3, 1925; 1 dau., Margaret Anne; m. 2d, Frances Flanders, Dec. 17, 1932; m. 3d, Helen Boswell, Oct. 14, 1943; 1 son, James Boswell; m. 4th, Ethel Dunnam Booker, Feb. 28, 1970. Tchr. The Hill Sch., Pottstown, Pa., 1924-26, Arnold Sch., Pitts., 1926-27, Chestnut Hill Acad., Phila., 1927-29; staff psychologist Pa. Mus. Art. 1932-35; dir. Dallas Mus. Fine Arts, 1935-42; lctr. art So. Meth. U., 1936-42; instr. art Hockaday Jr. Coll., Dallas, 1937-39; dir. Des Moines Art Center, 1948-49, Birmingham Mus. Art, 1950—. Commd. capt. F.A., AUS, 1942, advanced to lt. col., 1944, comdg. officer 787th F.A. Bn. in Germany: chief monuments, fine arts and archives sect. OMG US, 1946-48; col. res., 1954. Mem. Am. Fedn. Art, Am. Assn. Museums Western Assn. Art. Mus. Dirs., Mil. Order Loyal Legion U.S., Am. Numis. Soc., Sigma Alpha Epsilon. Conglist. Contbr. art jours. Home: 3920 9th Court S Birmingham AL 35222 Office: Birmingham Museum Art Oscar Wells Meml Bldg Birmingham AL 35203

HOWARD, RICHARD RALSTON, physician; b. Arkansas City, Kan., May 19, 1918; s. Harry D. and Dorothy (Ralston) H.; B.S., Northwestern U., 1940, B.M., 1943, M.D., 1943; postgrad. sch. medicine U. Pa., 1948; fellowship internal medicine, cardiology, Mass. Gen. Hosp., 1950; m. Ione Zulma Mayer, Sept. 14, 1946; 1 son, Richard Ralston II. Physician, cons. Snyder-Jones Clinic, Winfield, Kan., 1946-53; pvt. practice internal medicine Slidell, La., 1953—; pres. med. staff Slidell Meml. Hosp., 1963. Served from lt. (j.g.) to lt. USNR, 1944-46. Fellow Seminars on Hypnosis Found.; mem. A.M.A., St. Tammany Parish Med. Soc. (pres. 1962), N.Y. Acad. Sci., Am. Soc. Clin. Hypnosis, C. of C. (v.p. 1962, mem. bd.), Am. Soc. Internal Medicine, Assn. Am. Physicians and Surgeons, Nu Sigma Nu, Phi Delta Theta. Mason (32 deg.). Club: Pinewood Country (bd.). Author articles in field. Home: Chateau Beaux Chenes Bonfouca LA 70458 Office: Howard Clinic 1544 Front St Slidell LA 70458

HOWARD, ROBERT JAMES, discount store exec.; b. Hot Springs, Ark., Apr. 20, 1945; s. William L. and LaRue E. (Jones) H.; grad. high sch.; m. Linda S. Crowell, Aug. 14, 1966, children—Stacy E., Robert Chad. Accountant, Garelick, Bradley & Heller, C.P.A.'s, 1967-68; accountant, Howard Bros. Discount Stores, Inc., Monroe, La., 1968, sec.-treas., 1969—; pres. J. Howard, Ltd., Monroe, 1970—. Mem. devel. council Harding Coll., Searcy, Ark., 1970. Mem. Ch. of Christ. Kiwanian. Home: 2113 Maywood St Monroe LA 71201 Office: 3030 Aurora St Monroe LA 71201

HOWARD, ROBERT PALMER, med. educator; b. Iowa City, Nov. 4, 1912; s. Campbell Palmer and Ottilie F. (Wright) H.; B.A., McGill U., 1932, M.D., C.M., 1937, M.Sc., 1947; m. Muriel Isabel Hearn, June 18, 1943; children—Campbell P., Caroline (Mrs. Charles E. Mast). Intern, fellow, asst. resident Johns Hopkins Hosp. and U., Balt., 1937-40; fellow Royal Victoria Hosp., Mont., Que., 1945-46; research fellow Mass. Gen. Hosp., Boston, 1947; asst., medicine and metabolism depts. Montreal (Que., Can.) Gen. Hosp., 1947-51; mem. faculty U. Okla., 1951—, prof. history of medicine, 1966—, adj. prof. history, 1970—. Mem. then head endocrinology sect. Okla. Med. Research Found., Oklahoma City, 1951-58, asso. head cardiovascular sect., 1958-66. Served with M.C., Canadian Army, 1940-45. Josiah Macy Jr. Found. fellow, Tulane, 1967-68; USPHS fellow, 1968-69. Fellow A.C.P.; mem. Royal Coll. Physicians, Endocrine Soc., Am. Fedn. Clin. Research, Central Soc. Clin. Research, Arteriosclerosis Council, Am. Heart Assn., A.M.A., Am., Western, Okla., Oral hist. assns., Midwest Junto, Okla. Westerners, Sigma Xi, Alpha Omega Alpha. Episcopalian. Contbr. profl. jours. Home: 2524 Somerset Pl Oklahoma City OK 73116

HOWARD, WILLIAM EDWARD HARDING, educator; b. Athens, Ga., Oct. 1, 1924; s. James Paul and Annie (Carithers) H.; B.S., W.Va. State Coll., 1945; M.A. (Fulbright fellow), U. Glasgow (Scotland), 1950; M.S.Sc., Inst. Social Studies, The Hague, 1953; Ph.D., Free U. Amsterdam, 1955. Cons., Ministry of Edn., Govt. of Ethiopia, 1946-49, 50-52; prof. polit. sci. Fla. A. and M. U., Tallahassee, 1956—. Mem. Fla. Inter-U. Com. on Internat. Programs, 1965; dir. research Fla. Voters League, 1964—; cons. Gov.'s Commn. Quality Edn. Fla., 1967—; adv. council Am. Forum Internat. Study, 1972—, group leader comparative East African socs. program, 1972—. Mem. Am. Assn. U. Profs. (exec. com. 1965—), UN Assn. U.S.A. (exec. com. 1962—), Am., So. polit. sci. assns., A.A.A.S., Am. Soc. African Culture, Assn. Social Sci. Tchrs., Phi Delta Kappa, Pi Gamma Mu, Alpha Phi Alpha. Democrat. Baptist. Author: Public Administration in Ethiopia, 1956. Home: 543 Okaloosa St Tallahassee FL 32304

HOWARD, WILLIAM LEE, govt. ofcl.; b. Atlanta, June 15, 1924; s. Lee Groves and Ruby Louise (Copeland) H.; B.E.E., Ga. Inst. Tech., 1949; m. Anne Elizabeth Kling, Nov. 4, 1951; children—Andrew Clark, Elizabeth Lee, Carolyn Sue. Engr., design and operation of hydroelectric U.S. Army C.E., Allatoona Dam, Ga., 1950-52, 53-54, 54-56, Clarkhill Dam., S.C., 1952-53, Lookout Point and Dalles Dam, Ore., 1954; asst. powerhouse supt., aerospace engr. design and devel. control system for control space vehicles Redstone, Jupiter, Saturn, NASA, Marshall Space Flight Center, Ala., 1956—. Chmn. troop com. TVA council Boy Scouts Am., 1965. Served to capt. USNR, 1941-45; PTO; Capt. Res. Registered profl. engr., Ala. Mem. Res. Officers Assn. U.S. (state pres. 1970-71), Naval Res. Assn., Res. Officers Assn. U.S., U.S. Power Squadron. Home: 125 Wingate St Huntsville AL 35801 Office: NASA Marshall Space Flight Center AL 35812

HOWARD, WILLIAM M., educator. Formerly mem. faculties various schs., Ida., Tex., Wis., Fla.; now prof. finance and ins. U. Fla., Gainesville; pres. W.M. Howard, Inc.; cons. in field. Mem. Am. Risk and Ins. Assn., Actuarial Soc. Author books. Contbr. articles to profl. jours. Address: Box 14321 Univ Station Gainesville FL 32601*

HOWARD, WILLIE ABBAY, state ofcl.; b. Tunica, Miss., June 5, 1891; d. William G. and George Anne Elizabeth (Irwin) Abbay; student U. Miss., summer 1933; m. Thomas Percy Howard, Oct. 12, 1920 (dec.); children—Thomas Percy (dec.), GeorgeAnne Irwin (Mrs. Robert Peel Sayle), Elizabeth Irwin (Mrs. Cooper Yerger Robinson). Partner, Howard Plantation, Lake Cormorant, Miss., 1922-55, owner, operator, 1955—, Commr. Yazoo-Miss. Delta Levee Bd., 1955—, Welfare dir. DeSoto County, Miss., 1932-36, DeSoto and Tate counties, 1933-34; organizer, instr. Gulf div. A.R.C., 1917-18; co-organizer, trustee DeSoto County Library Bd., 1946—; co-organizer Citizens Library Movement, DeSoto County, Miss., 1947, first Regional Library Miss., 1950, trustee, 1950-63; pres. Miss. Citizen's Library Movement, 1950-52; del. nat. conv. Nat. Rivers and Harbors Congress, Washington, 1964. Trustee Northwest Jr. Coll., Senatobia, Miss., 1943—. Mem. Miss. Fedn. Women's Clubs (state rec. sec. 1920-22), English-Speaking Union, Memphis Execs., Lower Miss. Valley Flood Control Assn. (v.p. 1961, 71) D.A.R., Colonial Dames 17th Century. Presbyn. Clubs: Memphis Country, Memphis Woman's (pres. 1968-69), Tunica County woman's (founder 1914, pres. 1916, 1921, 28-29, trustee 1915—). Editor: DeSoto County C.L.M. Handbook, 1946. Address: Howard Plantation Lake Cormorant MS 38641

HOWE, ARTHUR G., lawyer; b. Charleston, S.C., Aug. 12, 1927; student The Citadel; LL.B., U. S.C., 1950; Admitted to S. C. bar, 1950; asst. U.S. atty., 1953-60; circuit solicitor Charleston and Berkley County (S.C.), 1964-68; now practice law, Charleston. Mem. Charleston County, S.C. bar assns. Address: 57 Broad St Charleston SC 29402*

HOWE, WILLIAM EMERSON WHITE, physicist; b. Hartford, Conn., June 5, 1920; s. Edmund Grant and Eleanor Louise (White) H.; A.B., Yale, 1941; cetificate U. Ala., 1942; M.S., Georgetown U., 1957; postgrad. Nat. War Coll., 1963; m. Mary Louise Hixon, Nov. 27, 1942; children— William Clay, Eleanor Cameron, Robert Collins. Asst. instr. U. Ala., 1942; electronic sci. Naval Research Lab., Washington, 1942-49; electronic engr. and electronic cons. chief of Naval Operations, 1949-64; sr. sci. adviser Dept. of Army, 1964—. Served to ensign USNR, 1944-45. Recipient Distinguished Civilian Service medal Dept. of Navy, 1964. Mem. Armed Forces Communication and Elec. Assn., Am. Geophys. Union A.A.A.S., Am. Phys. Soc., Am. Ordnance Assn., I.E.E.E., Phi Gamma Delta. Democrat Episcopalian. Home: 4940 Lowell St NW Washington DC 20016 Office: Pentagon Washington DC 20301

HOWELL, EDGAR MCPHERSON, museum curator; b. Richmond, Va., July 16, 1915; s. George Cook and Anne (McPherson) H.; B.A., Princeton, 1938; m. Winfred Harriet Harward, July 17, 1942; children—Harriet Vandergrift, Edgar McPherson, Charles Jarrett McPherson. Historian, Office Chief Mil. History, Dept. Army, 1949-56; curator div. mil. history, chmn. dept. nat. and mil. history U.S. Nat. Museum, Smithsonian Instn., 1956—. Served to maj., F.A., U.S. Army, 1940-49. Author: The Soviet Partisan Movement, 1941-44, 1956; (with J. D. Campbell) American Military Insignia, 1800-1851, 1963; (with D. E. Kloster) United States Army Headgear to 1854, 1968. Editor: Uniform Regulations for the Army of the United States, 1861, 1961. Episcopalian. Home: 307 Poplar Dr Falls Church VA 20046 Office: Smithsonian Instn Washington DC 20025

HOWELL, GEORGE WASHINGTON, lawyer, corp. exec.; b. Fairfield, Ala., Jan. 11, 1927; s. George Washington and Margaret (Hamric) H.; student Emory U., 1944-45, U. S.C., 1945-46; B.S. in Math., U. Ala., 1948, J.D., 1951; m. Joan Cotty White, Sept. 4, 1954; children—Jeffrey Page, Jennifer Margaret. Admitted to Ala. bar, 1951, Miss. bar, 1962; atty. U.S. Steel Corp., Fairfield, Ala., 1951-57; atty. Ingalls Shipbldg. Corp. (now div. Litton Industries, Inc.), Pascagoula, Miss., 1957-60, counsel, 1960-61, sec., 1961-68, gen. atty., 1961-65, gen. counsel, 1965—, v.p., 1965—; v.p., gen. counsel marine group Litton Industries, Inc., 1968—; pres. Litton Industries Leasing Corp. Served to ensign USNR; 1944-47; comdr. Res. Mem. Am., Miss., Ala. bar assns., Shipbuilders Council Am. (chmn. legal com. 1963-69), Miss. Mfrs. Assn. (dir. 1969—, chmn. taxation com. 1964-67), Blue Key, Miss. Econ. Council (dir., chmn. employer-employee relations com. 1969—), Omicron Delta Kappa, Pi Mu Epsilon, Pi Kappa Alpha, Presbyn. Clubs: Hickory Hill Country, Longfellow House. Home: 1100 Eastwood Rd Pascagoula MS 39567 Office: PO Box 149 Pascagoula MS 39567

HOWELL, HENRY EVANS, JR., lt. gov. Va.; b. Norfolk, Va., Sept. 5, 1920; student Coll. William and Mary; LL.B., U. Va.; m. Elzabeth McCarty; children—Mark, Henry, Susan. Admitted to Va. bar; lt. gov., Va., 1971—. Mem. Va. Ho. of Dels., 1960-66, Va. Senate, 1966-71; Democratic candidate gov. Va., 1969. Mem. Va. Trial Lawyers Assn., Nofolk C. of C., Izaak Walton League, Hampton Roads Fgn. Commerce Club, Hampton Rds. Maritime Assn. Episcopalian. Clubs: Mace, Propeller. Address: State Capitol Capitol Sq Richmond VA 23219*

HOWELL, HUGH HAWKINS, JR., lawyer; b. Atlanta, Aug. 18, 1920; s. Hugh and Ethleen (Horne) H.; student Riverside Mil. Acad., Boys High Sch., Atlanta, Emory U.; A.B., U. Ga., 1942; LL.B., John Marshall Law Sch., 1947, LL.M., 1958, J.D., 1959, LL.D., 1960; m. Dorris Callahan; children—Hugh Howell III, James Finn. Admitted to Ga. bar; sr. partner firm Howell & Bobet. Dir. Spring Lakes Apts., Inc., Bolton Estates, High Point Apts. Active Atlanta A.R.C., Community Chest, Legal Aid Soc., mem. Ga. Vets. Service Bd. Trustee John Marshall U. Served as capt. USNR, World War II. Mem. Atlanta Legal Aid Soc., Judge Advs. Assn. (nat. pres. 1968), Am. Judicature Soc., Fed. (v.p. 5th U.S. Circuit), Am., Ga., Atlanta bar assns., Atlanta Hist. Soc., Am. Legion, Navy League (nat. dir.), Naval Res. Assn. (nat. v.p.), S.A.R., S.C.V. (comdr.), Naval Hist. Found., Old Guard of Gate City Guard (comdt.), Phi Delta Theta, Sigma Delta Kappa. Mason (32 deg., Shriner). Clubs: Athletic, Ansley Golf, Old War Horse Lawyers, Men's Garden (dir.), Veteran Luncheon, Lawyers. Home: 2811 Ridgewood Rd NW Atlanta GA 30327 Office: 1505 Rock Springs Circle NE Atlanta GA 30306

HOWELL, JAMES DUANE, editor; b. Post, Tex., July 27, 1930; s. Lonnie Dexter and Fleda (Gilliam) H.; grad. in agr. Tex. Technol. U., 1951, B.A. in Journalism, 1953; m. Ava Geraldine Honea, Sept. 30, 1956; children—Cynthia Ann, Lisa Beth, James Lonnie. Farm reporter Abilene (Tex.) Reporter News, 1953-57, Lubbock (Tex.) Avalanche-Jour., 1957—; Tex.-Okla. editor Cotton Farming mag., 1964-69; free-lance agrl. writing. Mem. Stock Show com., Tex. Farm Market Builder Tour Europe 1965. Recipient hon. State Farmer degree Future Farmers Am., 1955, Meritorious Agrl. Press award Houston Bank Coops., 1963, Distinguished Service award Vocational Agr. Tchrs. Assn. Tex., 1965. Mem. Newspaper Farm Editors Assn., Newspaper Farm Editors Am. (South and West v.p. 1969), Tex. Agrl. Workers Assn., Comml. Agriculturists Council, Sigma Delta Chi. Democrat. Baptist. Home: 3803 26th St Lubbock TX 79410 Office: 710 Av J Lubbock TX 79408

HOWELL, JAMES GOFF, assn. exec.; b. Delavan, Wis., Feb. 4, 1916; s. Dorsey G. and Rispah (Goff) H.; student Yankton (S.D.) Coll., 1932-34; J.D., U. Neb., 1938; m. Anna Louise Van Horn, Oct. 10, 1946; children—Particia Louise (Mrs. Jon H. Knickerbocker), Deborah Lynne, Constance Diane. Admitted to Neb. bar, 1938; practiced in Albion, 1938-40; spl. agt. FBI, Richmond, N.Y.C., Detroit, Omaha, 1940-46; v.p. Mountain States Employers Council, Denver, 1946-67; pres. New Orleans S.S. Assn., 1967—; dir. Internat. Trade Mart. Mem. Nat. Def. Exec. Res.; chmn. indsl. relations group Nat. Indsl. Council. Mem. Beta Theta Pi, Phi Delta Phi. Republican. Conglist. Clubs: University (Denver); Metairie (La.) Country; Plimsoll, Pickwick (New Orleans). Home: 4821 Cleveland Pl Metairie LA 70003 Office: 219 Carondelet St New Orleans LA 70130

HOWELL, JOHN B., JR., librarian; b. Greer, S.C., Oct. 25, 1925; s. John B. and Alleyne (Richbourg) H.; B.A., Furman U., 1945; B.A., in L.S., Emory U., 1946; M.S., U. Ill., 1954. Acquisitions librarian Emory U., Atlanta, 1946-51; asst. librarian Furman U., Greenville, S.C., 1951-52, Clemson (S.C.) U., 1954-58; circulation librarian U. Ga., Athens, 1958-60; librarian Miss. Coll., Clinton, 1960—. Mem. Miss. (treas. 1966-67, pres. 1970), Southeastern library assns., A.L.A. Baptist. Editor: The S.C. Librarian, 1956-58, Miss. Library News, 1972. State reporter The Southeastern Librarian, 1967—. Home: 118 Fairmont St Clinton MS 39056 Office: Box 47 Clinton MS 39056

HOWELL, MABLE GREY, lawyer; b. Hillsboro, Tex., Feb. 10, 1910; d. Robert Edward and Josephine (Glover) H.; B.A., U. Tex., 1930; LL.B. with honor, Baylor U., 1933. Admitted to Tex. bar, 1933, pvt. practice, Waco, 1933-38, 41-46; asst. city atty., City of Waco, 1938-41; asso. atty. Pioneer Savs. Assn., Waco, 1946-51; asso. Helm, Jones, McDermott & Pletcher, Houston, 1951-61; pvt. practice, 1961—; substitute judge Corp. Ct. City Houston; spl. justice Ct. of Civil Appeals for 10th Supreme Ct. of Tex.; lectr. law U. Houston Coll. Law, 1963. Pres. United Cerebral Palsy Assn., Inc., 1959, rep. dir. nat. and southwestern region, 1959-61, v.p. United Cerebral Palsy Tex. Inc., 1961. Mem. State Bar Tex., Am., Houston (chmn. women's sect. 1959) bar assns., Bus. Women's Assn., Soroptimist Fedn. of Americas, Am. Assn. U. Women. Episcopalian. Club: Soroptimist (pres. 1958-59, dir. 1960). Home: 38 Bash Pl Houston TX 77027 Office: Sterling Bldg Houston TX 77002

HOWELL, MACK RUSSELL, forester, surveyor; b. Whittier, N.C., Apr. 28, 1931; s. William Harley and Myrtle (Varner) H.; grad. Nat. Sch. Forestry and Conservation, 1960; m. Willa Dean Teague, Oct. 26, 1951; children—William Russell, Mildred Dean, Harriet Evelyn. With U.S. Forest Service, 1951-53; area supr. land acquisition-surveys, forestry dept. Champion Papers, Inc., Murphy, N.C., 1953-62; cons. in forestry and surveying, boundary and topog. surveys, site locations, ct. surveys, Bryson City, N.C., 1962—. Mem. Am. Congress Surveying and Mapping, Soc. Am. Foresters, N.C. Forestry Assn. Presbyn. Mason. Home: PO Box 228 Bryson City NC 28713 Office: Depot St Bryson City NC 28713

HOWELL, OSCAR DEVIER, JR, judge; b. Tampa, Fla., Nov. 22, 1913; s. Oscar Devier and Nellie (Hemphill) H.; LL.B., U. Fla., 1937; m. Margaret E. Weber, Sept. 20, 1940; children—Margaret Ellen, Robert S., Jeanne E. Admitted to Fla. bar, 1937; practiced in Tampa, Fla., 1937-40, 45-54; judge Juvenile Ct., Hillsborough County, Tampa, Fla., 1954—. Served from 1st lt. to lt. col. F.A., AUS, 1940-45. Mem. Fla. State, Hillsborough County (pres. 1954) bar assns., Nat., Fla. State counsel of juvenile ct. judges. Presbyn. (elder). Home: 209 S Woodlynne St Tampa FL 33609 Office: Court House Annex Tampa FL 33602

HOWELL, ROBERT MACARTHUR, educator; b. Sumter, S.C., Apr. 4, 1940; s. Alfred Wayne 1958-61; D.D.S., Med. Coll. Va., 1965; M.S.D., Ind. U., 1967; m. Linda Claire Rowell, July 15, 1961; children—Seana Elizabeth, Paul Ian. Instr. oral pathology U. Ky. Dental Sch., Lexington, 1967-70; asst. prof. oral pathology Va. Commonwealth U.-Med. Coll. Va. Dental Sch., Richmond, from 1970; now with Med. Coll. Ga. USPHS postdoctoral fellow, 1965-66. Diplomate Am. Bd. Oral Pathology. Fellow Am. Acad. Oral Pathology; mem. Sigma Zeta, Omicron Kappa Upsilon, Delta Sigma Delta. Lutheran. Home: 504 Arnlee Way Augusta GA 30904 Office: Sch Dentistry Dept Oral Pathology Med Coll Ga Augusta GA 30902

HOWELL, WILLIAM DONALD, lawyer; b. Big Rock, Tenn., Mar. 8, 1925; s. Oliver L. and Ethleen (Taylor) H.; B.A., Vanderbilt U., 1948, LL.B., 1950; m. Louise Burrell, June 4, 1950; children—Karen, Harriet. Admitted to Tenn. bar, 1950; gen. practice law, Dover, Tenn., 1950—; mem. firm Howell & Howell, Dover; chmn. bd. dirs. Dover-Peoples Bank & Trust Co. Del. Tenn. State Constl. Conv., 1953; mem. Tenn. Ho. of Reps., 1955, Tenn. Senate, 1957—. Served to lt. (j.g.), USNR, 1943-46. Mem. Tenn. Bar Assn., Phi Delta Phi. Address: Dover TN 37058

HOWERTON, JOEL DOAN, assn. exec.; b. Iuka, Miss., Nov. 11, 1892; s. George Taylor and Lula (Doan) H.; student E. Central State Coll., Okla., 1910-12; diploma Memphis State U., 1913; B.S. with honors, Miss. State U., 1915; postgrad.; m. Peggy Jackman, Sept. 6, 1918. Tchr., Lamar County (Miss.) Agrl. High Sch., Purvis, 1915-16; county agrl. agt. U.S. Dept. Agr., Adams County, Natchez, 1916-19, Lauderdale County, Meridian, Miss., 1919-61; pub. relations and spl. assignments officer E. Miss. Electric Power Assn., Meridian, 1962—. Mem. Lauderdale County 4-H Adv. Council, 1930—; chmn. rural area devel. com. 1962—, Lauderdale County Coordinating Council, 1935—, mem. tech. action panel, 1965—. Recipient awards including Distinguished Service award Nat. Assn. County Agrl. Agts., 1955. Mem. Miss. State U. Alumni Assn. (county pres. 1961, dist. pres. 1962, chpt. chmn. scholarship com. 1963—), County Farm Bur. (organizer), Meridian C. of C. Episcopalian. Mason (Shriner), Lion. Clubs: Meridian Downtown, Northwood Country. Home: 1839 Country Club Blvd Meridian MS 39301 Office: E Miss Electric Power Assn Meridian MS 39301

HOWIE, HENRY SANFORD, JR., children's agy. exec.; b. Abbeville, S.C., Oct. 10, 1927; s. Sanford and Anna (Biggers) H.; B.A., Presbyn. Coll., 1950; postgrad. U. Ark., 1953, Furman U., 1954, Winthrop Coll., 1955-56; M.S.W., U. N.C., 1965; m. Betty Jane Shirley, Dec. 20, 1949; children—Lynda Elizabeth, Anna Shirley, Genevieve Sharpe, Henry Sanford III, Robert Marcus. Coach, prin., Norway, S.C., 1949-50; trainee Deering Milliken, 1951-52; sch. prin., Rock Hill (S.C.) Pub. schs., 1952-57; exec. dir. Episcopal Ch. Home for Children, York, S.C., 1957—. Del., White House Conf. on Children, 1970. Bd. mem. S.C. Social Welfare Forum, 1967—, S.C. Com. on Children and Youth, 1966—; chmn. S.C. Com. on Childhood Mental Illness, 1971—; v.p. York County Council on Alcoholism, 1971-72; del. dir. S.C. Mental Health Assn.; chmn. regional adv. com. S.C. Dept. Pub. Welfare. Bd. dirs. Tri-County Mental Health Center; trustee Group Child Care Cons. Services. Served with USNR, 1945-46. Mem. Nat. Assn. Social Workers, Acad. Certified Social Workers, Southeastern Child Care Assn. (pres. 1966-67), York County Mental Health Assn. (pres. 1968), Pi Kappa Phi (pres. Beta chpt. 1948). Episcopalian (sr. warden 1965-67, vestryman 1955-58). Rotarian (pres. York 1964). Clubs: Springlake Country (York), Crustbreakers (pres. 1966-67). Address: Episcopal Ch Home for Children York SC 29745

HOWISON, JAMES FICKLEN, III, govt. ofcl.; b. Richmond, Va., Apr. 18, 1934; s. James Ficklin, Jr. and Edna Mildred (Russell) H.; B.S., Va. Poly. Inst., 1961; m. Lynda Ann Wilder, July 2, 1971; children— Jennifer Michelle, Cheryl Janine, Vicki Lynn. Gen. engr. U.S. Naval Missile Center, Point Mugu, Cal., 1961-64; systems engr., commodity mgr. U.S. Army Missile Command, Huntsville, Ala., 1964—. Served with U.S. Army, 1954-57. Registered profl. engr., Ala. Patentee in field. Home: 1510 Wells Av Huntsville AL 35801

HOWSE, ROXY SOLON, civil engr.; b. Nashville, Dec. 10, 1937; s. Philip M. and Mary (Pursley) H.; B.S. in Civil Engring., Tenn. Tech. U., 1964; m. Jeanette Williams, Sept. 3, 1959; children—Ronald Solon, Ryan Shannon. Engr. technician State of Ill., 1959-61; co. engr. John L. Burns, Inc., Nashville, 1961-64; asst. county engr. Hillsborough County (Fla.), 1964-67; city engr., Melbourne, Fla., 1967-69; county engr., pub. works adminstr. Orange County (Fla.), 1969-72; chief engr. Major Realty Corp., Orlando, Fla., 1972—. Mem. Am. Soc. C.E. (sec. Cape Canaveral br. 1968-69), Am. Pub. Works Assn., Am. Water Works Assn., Fla. Engring. Soc. (treas. Tampa chpt. 1967), Nat. Soc. Profl. Engrs. Mason (Shriner). Home: 5251 Lima Pl Orlando FL 32807 Office: 118 W Kaley St Orlando FL 32803

HOY, DOUGLAS STUART, dentist; b. Urbana, Ill., Mar. 28, 1939; s. Harry Eugene and Eldora Christina (Larsen) H.; student U. Okla., 1957-60; D.D.S., U. Neb., 1964; m. Laurelyn Sue Buller, June 15, 1964. Resident oral surgery U. Okla. Med. Center, 1964-67; individual practice oral surgery, Norman, Okla., 1967—; mem. staff Norman Municipal Hosp., S.W. Clinic Hosp., Lawton, Okla., Comanche County Meml. Hosp., Lawton, Valley View Hosp., Ada, Okla.; clin. asst. prof. oral surgery U. Okla. Health Center; cons. Griffith State Meml. Hosp., Norman, USPHS Indian Hosp., Lawton. Mem. Am., Okla. dental assns., Cleveland County Dental Soc. (past pres.), Am. (past del.), Okla. (past pres.) socs. oral surgeons. Lion. Home: 2215 W Iowa St Norman OK 73069 Office: 700 Asp St Norman OK 73069

HOYT, AUSTIN, U.S. judge; b. Beacon, N.Y., Apr. 26, 1915; s. Ferdinand Augustus and Beatrice (Watson) H.; student U. Ala., 1933-34, St. John's U., 1934-35; LL.B., U. Va., 1938; m. Margaret Llewellyn Carter, Nov. 11, 1939; children—John Carter, Julia Vail, Dale Llewellyn. Admitted to D.C. bar, 1939, N.Y. bar, 1940, Colo. bar, 1949; atty. REA, 1938-40; pvt. practice, Beacon, 1940-42; spl. asst. U.S. atty. gen., 1942-49; asst. chief compromise sect., tax div. Dept. Justice, 1946-49; mem. firm Ziegler & Hoyt, Colorado Springs, Colo., 1949-54, Hoyt & Gallagher, 1954-59; judge dist. ct. 4th Jud. Dist. Colo., 1959-61; judge U.S. Tax Ct., 1962—. Pres. Colorado Springs Symphony Assn., 1958-60, Colorado Springs Sch. for Girls, 1961-62. Served to lt. (s.g.) USNR, 1943-46. Mem. Am., Colo. bar assns., Am. Judicature Soc., Bar Assn. D.C., U. Va. Law Sch. Alumni Assn. (mem. council 1965-68, pres. Washington chpt. 1966-67, mem. exec. com. 1965—), Soc. Mayflower Descs., Order of Coif, Phi Delta Theta, Phi Alpha Delta. Mem. editorial bd. Va. Law Rev., 1937-38. Home: Prospect Hill Tidewater Trail Fredericksburg VA 22401 Office: US Tax Court Washington DC 20044

HOYT, HOMER, real estate economist; b. St. Joseph, Mo., June 14, 1896; s. Homer and Elizabeth (Vath) H.; A.B., M.A., U. Kan., 1913; J.D., U. Chgo., 1918, Ph.D., 1933; student George Washington U., 1918-19; m. Gertrude O'Neill, Aug. 13, 1941; 1 son, Michael Robert. Instr. econs. Beloit Coll., 1917-18; economist War Trade Bd., Washington, 1918-19; prof. econs. U. Del., 1919-20; economist Am. Tel. & Tel., N.Y.C., 1920-21; asso. prof. U. N.C., 1921-23; instr. debating U. Chgo., 1923-24; asso. prof. U. Mo., 1924-25; real estate analyst Homer Hoyt Assos., Chgo., 1925-33; prin. economist FHA, Washington, 1933-41; dir. research Chgo. Plan Commn., 1941-43; dir. econ. studies Regional Plan Assn., N.Y.C., 1943-46; pres. Homer Hoyt Assos., Washington, 1946—. Chmn. bd., dir. Homer Hoyt Inst. Recipient Urban Affairs award Lambda Alpha, 1971. Mem. Am. Inst. Real Estate Appraisers (George L. Schmutz 1st prize 1964), Am.

Econ. Assn., Lambda Alpha. Author: One Hundred Years of Land Values in Chicago, 1933; Structure and Growth of Residential Neighborhoods in American Cities, 1939; (with Arthur M. Weimer) Real Estate, 1939, 46, 54, 60, 66, 72; People, Profits, Places, A Blueprint for Retailing, 1969; According to Hoyt, 1970. Address: 2939 Van Ness St NW Washington DC 20008

HSU, TING CHEN, economist; b. Shanghai, China, Dec. 2, 1921; s. Tse Chien and Lan Ying (Tsong) H.; B.S., U. Mo., 1950, M.A., 1953; postgrad. U. Mich., 1954-56; m. Sylvia Martin, Nov. 29, 1953. Came to U.S., 1945, naturalized, 1960. Research asst. Alfred Politz, Inc., N.Y.C., 1957-58; econ. cons. P.R. Planning Bd., Santurce, P.R., 1958-59; research supr. W.R. Simmons & Assos. Research Inc., N.Y.C., 1959-60; sr. research analyst Girl Scouts U.S.A., N.Y.C., 1960-63; cons. P.R. Treasury Dept., San Juan, 1963-69, exec. dir., 1970, chief economist, 1971-—. Lectr. Inter Am. U. P.R., Hato Rey, 1967-—. Mem. men's adv. com. Caribe Girl Scout Council, 1967-—, chmn., 1971-—. Served to capt. Chinese Nationalist Army, 1943-46. Mem. Am. Econ. Assn., Tax with Representation, Financial Mgmt. Assn., Internat. Studies Assn., Alpha Pi Zeta. Club: Cosmopolitan (pres. 1951-52) (Columbia, Mo.). Home: 710 Fernandez Juncos Av Santurce PR 00907 Office: PR Treasury Dept San Juan PR 00905

HUBBARD, CARROLL, JR., lawyer; b. Murray, Ky., July 7, 1937; s. Carroll and Beth (Shelton) H.; grad. Georgetown Coll., 1959, U. Louisville Law Sch., 1962; m. Joyce Lynn Hall, Aug. 20, 1966. Admitted to Ky. bar, 1962; partner Hubbard, Weisenberger & Null, Mayfield, Ky., 1969-—. State senator, 1st Dist, of Ky., 1967-—. Home: 410 Macedonia Rd Mayfield KY 42066 Office: 118 W Broadway Mayfield KY 42066

HUBBARD, GEORGE THOMPSON, clergyman; b. Rochester, N.Y., Mar. 24, 1905; s. George Marquis and Sarah Jane (Thompson) H.; A.B. cum laude, Tusculum Coll., Greeneville, Tenn., 1932; B.D., Louisville Presbyn. Theol. Sem., 1936; m. Dorothy Elizabeth Ramsey, Dec. 22, 1933; children—Sarah Kathryn (Mrs. Roy Edward Lancaster), Harriet Lucille (Mrs. Norman Gerren), George Thompson. Ordained to ministry Presbyn. Ch., 1936; pastor rural mountain chs. East Tenn., 1928-32, Main St. Presbyn. Ch., Petersburg, Ind., 1933-37, Beecher Presbyn. Ch., Lawrenceburg, Ind., 1937-41, East End Presbyn. Ch., Ottumwa, Ia., 1941-43, rural chs., Kingsport, Tenn., 1943-44, Russell St. (now Eastminster) Presbyn. Ch., Nashville, 1944-52, Westminster Presbyn. Ch., Decatur, Ala., 1952-60, First Presbyn. Ch., Calvert City, Ky., 1960-68; adminstr. Rose Anna Hughes Presbyn. Home, Inc., Louisville, 1968-70. Chmn. stewardship and promotion com. Mid-South Synod, 1944-49, moderator, 1953-54; commr. Gen. Assembly Presbyn. Ch. in U.S.A., 1937, 49, 56; sec., pres. Nashville Pastors Assn., 1949-50, Decatur Pastors Assn., 1954-55. Mem. bd. United Fund Drive, Decatur, 1959-60; mem. Marshall County Library Bd., 1965-68, chmn. 1967-68; mem. Gov.'s Citizens Com. for Barkley Boys' Camp, 1964-68; chmn. Calvert City Library Bd., 1963-68. Bd. dirs. Louisville Presbyn. Theol. Sem., 1949-60; mem. permanent judicial commn. United Presbyn. Ch. in U.S.A., 1961-67, clk. permanent jud. commn., 1962-67; moderator Synod of Ky., 1965-67; stated clk. Nashville Presbytery, 1948-52, Huntsville Presbytery, 1952-60, Western Ky. Presbytery, 1961-68. Lion. Address: 107 Lind St McMinnville TN 37110

HUBBARD, GEORGE WENDELL, supt. schs.; b. Albany, Okla., Feb. 19, 1927; s. Monterey R. and Helen Nancy (Capshaw) H.; B.S., Southeastern State Coll., 1947; M.S., Okla. State U., 1950; Ed.D., U. Okla., 1958; m. Marjorie Del Stewart, Aug. 6, 1950; 1 son, George Wendell. Prin., tchr. Albany (Okla.) High Sch., 1945-46; tchr., McAlester (Okla.) High Sch., 1947-50, Capitol Hill High Sch., Oklahoma City, 1950-55; asst. prin. Harding High Sch., Oklahoma City, 1955-59; supt. schs. Washington dist., Kansas City, Kan., 1959-67; supt. schs., Sherman, Tex., 1967-—. Rotarian. Home: 1702 Shields St Sherman TX 75090 Office: PO Box 1156 Sherman TX 75090

HUBBARD, JOHN BARRY, banker; b. Sweetwater, Tex., Mar. 16, 1917; s. John Howard and Shirley (McCarty) H.; B.B.A., U. Tex., 1939, LL.B., 1940; m. Virginia Marie Olsen, Dec. 10, 1943; children—Carol Ann (Mrs. Sam Houston Lane III), Virginia Sue, Jean Ellen, John Barry. With FBI U.S. Dept. Justice, 1940-53; exec. v.p., trust officer Ft. Worth Nat. Bank, 1953-—; faculty Southwestern Grad. Sch. Banking So. Meth. U. Treas., bd. dirs. Longhorn council Boy Scouts Am., Girls Service League. Mem. Tex., Tarrant County bar assns., Tex. Bankers Assn. (past pres. trust sect.). Mem. Christian Ch. Home: 6491 Woodstock Rd Fort Worth TX 76116 Office: 800 Main St Fort Worth TX 76102

HUBBARD, JOHN ROWLEY, dentist; b. Gaffney, S.C., Sept. 2, 1934; s. Corbett Cecil and Nannie (Rowley) H.; B.S., Furman U., 1956; D,D.S., Med, Coll. Va., 1960; m. Martha Jean Gilreath, Apr. 19, 1957; children—Nancy Lee, Douglas Gilreath. Pvt. practice dentistry, Gaffney, 1962-—; v.p. Cherokee Petroleum Co., Gaffney, 1967-69. Chmn. United Fund Campaign, Gaffney, 1968; mem. bd. govs. Coll.-Community Theatre Gaffney, 1969-—; adv. bd. local chpt. Am. Cancer Soc.; mem. S.C. Appalachian Region Health Planning and Policy Com. County mgr. Republican senatorial campaign, 1966, 68; del. to S.C. Rep. conv., 1966. Served with USNR, 1960-62. Recipient Spoke award U.S. Jr. C. of C., 1963; Citizenship award Community Chest, 1968. Mem. Am., S.C. (mem. ho. of dels. 1968-71, chmn. vets. adv. and mil. affairs com. 1971-72), Piedmont Dist. dental assns., Acad. Gen. Dentistry (charter mem. S.C. 1970), Navy Res. Assn., Sigma Alpha Epsilon, Xi Psi Phi, Chi Beta Phi, Alpha Epsilon Delta. Presbyn. (deacon). Home: College Park Route 7 Gaffney SC 29340 Office: 302 W Birnie St Gaffney SC 29340

HUBBARD, JULIA SHEPHARD (MRS. FORD HUBBARD), civic worker; b. Colorado City, Tex.; d. James Leftwich and Julia (Josey) Shephard; B.A., M.A., U. Tex.; m. Ford Hubbard; 1 son, Ford. Corr. sec. Jr. League, Houston, 1945-46, placement chmn, 1946-48, pres., 1948-49; bd. dirs. women's com. Houston Symphony Soc., 1940-48; v.p. Houston Little Theatre, 1949-50, pres., 1950-51; bd. dirs. Houston Vol. Community Service, 1946-49; chmn. conservation and Americanism com. D.A.R., Houston, 1958-60, res. sec., 1960-61, del. to state and nat. confs., 1957-68, state vice chmn. Am. music, 1962-63, state chmn. nat. def., 1964-—, speakers staff com., 1968-—, also state regent, mem. nat. officers club; chmn. leader com. Bd. Internat. Edn., Houston, 1959-61, del. nat. conf., San Francisco, 1960, rec. sec. Tex. State Bd. D.A.R.; precinct chmn. Freedom in Action, Houston, 1960, spl. rep. Cal., 1961; v.p. Harris County council Girl Scouts U.S.A., 1949-51; pres. River Oaks Women's Assn.; entertainment com. Houston Symphony Soc. Bd. dirs. Hermann Hosp., Houston, 1948-49. Mem. English-Speaking Union (chmn. speakers com.), Magna Charta Dames, Houston Mus. Fine Arts. San Francisco Opera Guild, Harris County Heritage Soc., Zeta Tau Alpha. Clubs: Houston, Racket (Houston); River Oaks County (pres. Womens Assn.); Bolero. Home: 2425 Pine Valley St Houston TX 77019

HUBBARD, LAFAYETTE RONALD, author, explorer; b. Tilden, Neb., Mar. 13, 1911; s. H. R. and Ledora May (Waterbury) H.; student Swavely Prep. Sch., 1929, Woodward Prep. Sch., 1930; B.S. in Civil Engring., George Washington U., 1934; postgrad. Princeton Sch. Govt., 1945; Ph.D., Sequoia U., 1950; m. Mary Sue Whipp; children—Lafayette Ronald, Catherine May, Diana, Quentin, Suzette, Arthur Ronald. Writer aviation and travel articles, 1930-—; writer of novels, 1936-—; explorer, 1934-—; comdr. Caribbean Motion Picture Expdn. and W. I. Minerals Expdn., 1935. Alaskan Radio-Exptl. Expdn., 1940; writer for 90 nat. mags., Hollywood studios and radio; licensed comml. glider pilot, master of motor vessels, master of sailing vessels (all oceans), radio operator. Mem. 163d Inf., Mont. N.G., 1927-28, 20th Marines, Marine Corps Res., 1930-31; served as lt. USNR, 1941-46; comdg. escort vessels and navigator in all theaters, Fellow Oceanographic Found. Founder of Scientology. Clubs: Explorers' (New York City); Capital Yacht. Author: Buckskin Brigade, Final Blackout. Rebellion; Dianetics: Modern Science of Mental Health; and 20 other volumes on Dianetics and Scientology; also motion pictures, mag. fiction, two texts on psychology. Home: Washington DC Office: 1812 19th St NW Washington DC 20009

HUBBARD, RAY, broadcasting exec. Formerly nat. TV program mgr., exec. producer for pub. affairs Westinghouse Broadcasting co.; with Post-Newsweek Stations, Washington, 1969-—, now v.p. programming, prodn.; film producer, represented in permanent collections Modern Art Film Library, N.Y.C., Eastman HOuse, Rochester, N.Y., Library Congress, U. Cal. at Berkeley. Recipient awards for TV programs including Dupont award, George Foster Peabody award, Emmy award. Address: Post-Newsweek Stations 4001 Brandywine ST NW Washington DC 20016*

HUBBARD, ROBERT ALBERT, cons. transp. engr.; b. Rice, Va., Sept. 11, 1932; s. Harvey Johnson and Louise (Bradshaw) H.; B.S., Va. Mil. Inst., 1954; certificate Bur. Hwy. Traffic, Yale, 1955; m. Ann Glenn, Sept. 4, 1951; children—Robert Albert, Harvey Bradshaw, Susan Glenn. Hwy. engr. Va. Dept. Hwys., Richmond, 1954-57, dist. traffic engr., Bristol, 1957-59, asso. traffic engr., Richmond, 1959-60; prin. asso., asso. engr. Wilbur Smith & Assos., Columbia, S.C., 1960-65, prin. asso., office mgr., 1965-67, dir. computation research and devel., 1968-70, v.p., dir. internat. operations, 1970-—, dir. Freeman, Fox, Wilbur Smith & Assos., London, Eng. Dir. program tech. confs. and lectures Ministry Pub. Works, Madrid, Spain, 1964. Served to 1st lt. U.S. Army, 1955-57. Named Outstanding Young Man Am., 1966. Registered profl. engr., S.C., Ky., La., Va. Mem. Am. Soc. C.E., Nat. Soc. Profl. Engrs., Inst. Traffic Engrs., Am. Rd. Builders Assn., Instn. Civil Engrs. (London), Engrs. Club Richmond. Baptist. Clubs: Va. Military Institute Alumni, Sportsmens (Lexington); Richland Sertoma (Columbia).Home: 3735 Oakleaf Rd Columbia SC 29206 Office: 4500 Jackson Blvd Columbia SC 29209

HUBBARD, SAMUEL FRED, supt. schs.; b. Eoline, Ala., Sept. 8, 1930; s. Harper Albert and Veda Elizabeth (Hubbard) H.; B.S., U. Ala., 1958, M.A., 1960; m. Sallie Daniel Edwards, Sept. 26, 1958; children—Freda Evelyn, Kenneth Fred. With Bibb County Bd. Edn., Centreville, Ala., 1958-63; prin. Perry County Bd. Edn., Marion, Ala., 1963-65; supt., Marion (Ala.) City Bd. Edn., 1965-—. Chpt. chmn. A.R.C., 1970-72. Coll., mil. staff Gov. George C. Wallace, Ala., 1964-—. Served with USN, 1951-55. Recipient Distinguished Service award Marion Jr. C. of C., 1966. Mem. Am. Assn. Sch. Adminstrs., Ala. Dept. Elementary Sch. Prins. (state membership chmn. 1970-72), Ala. Edn. Assn. Methodist (ch. sch. supt. 1968-71). Club: Civitan (gov. Ala. central dist. 1966-67, sec.-treas. 1971-72, honor key, Past Gov.'s award 1964; Marion Civitan of Year 1969). Home: School Dr Marion AL 36756 Office: Box 960 Monroe St Marion AL 36756

HUBBELL, FLOYD EUGENE, retail clothier; b. Galveston, Tex., Feb. 10, 1923; s. Francis E. and Garna (Ward) H.; student S.W. Tex. State Tchrs. Coll., 1946-47, Sam Houston State Tchrs. Coll., 1947; B.B.A., Baylor U., 1950; m. Margaret Fraser, Sept. 1, 1946; children—Allan, David, Richard, John, Ruth, Steven, Shiles. Dept. mgr., asst. mgr., mgr. J.C. Penney Co., Waco, Tex., 1950-54, Odessa, Tex., 1954-57, Midland, Tex., 1957-59, Lubbock, Tex., 1959-62, Abilene, Tex., 1962-65; owner, mgr. Hubbell's Men's Shop, Rosenberg, Tex., 1965-—. Chmn. Youth Com., 1969; chmn. Easter Seals, 1969. City councilman, Rosenberg, 1968-—. Served with AUS, 1943-46; PTO. Recipient Distinguished Service award Rosenberg Rotary, 1969. Mem. Rosenberg C. of C. (dir.). Baptist (deacon). Rotarian, Kiwanian. Home: 1310 Rice St Rosenberg TX 77471 Office: 5028 Av H Rosenberg TX 77471

HUBBERT, FORD WILLIAM, JR., profl. assn. editor; b. Madill, Okla., Aug. 8, 1942; s. Ford William and Jeanette Lorena (Smith) H.; B.A., Okla. City U., 1965; M.L.A., So. Meth. U., 1972; m. Ernestine Cantu, Sept. 4, 1965; children—Anne Marie, Julie Anne. Writer, office pub. information Oklahoma City U., 1965; editor, promotion writer, reporter Okla. Pub. Co., 1965-67; editor The Skeet Shooting Review, Nat. Skeet Shooting Assn., Dallas, 1967-—. Nat. Skeet Shooting Assn. grantee, 1970-72. Mem. Nat. Skeeting Shooting Assn. (com. promotion and devel. collegiate shooting 1970-—, mem. Hall of Fame selection com. 1970-—), Outdoor Writers Assn. Am. Republican. Mem. Ch. of the Nazarene (bd. dirs. ch. 1967-—). Clubs: Dallas Gun; Garland Public Shooting Range (Garland, Tex.). Home: 1729 Indian School Rd Garland TX 75040 Office: 2608 Inwood Rd Dallas TX 75235

HUBER, PAUL SPEER, JR., newspaper pub.; b. Norfolk, Va., Mar. 14, 1921; s. Paul Speer and Elizabeth (Lingamfelter) H.; grad. Woodberry Forest Sch.; student U. N.C.; m. Sarah Jane Booth, Sept. 17, 1948; children—Paul Speer III, Peter McPherson. With Landmark Communications, Inc., 1947-—, now pres. and dir.; pres. Virginian-Pilot; dir. WTAR Radio Corp., Norfolk Savs. & Loan. Scaboard Citizens Nat. Bank. Bd. dirs. Leigh Meml. Hosp. v.p. United Communities Fund. Home: 1415 Daniel Av Norfolk VA 23505 Office: 150 W. Brambleton Av Norfolk, VA 23510

HUBER, WOLFGANG KARL, physician, educator; b. Freiburg/Breisgau, Germany, June 10, 1927; s. Richard J. and Kaete (Goetz)H.; student U. Heidelberg, 1946; M.D., U. Frankfurt/Main, 1957; m. Gudrun Lydia Beeck, June 28, 1958; 1 son, Christian Michael. Came to U.S., 1957, naturalized, 1962. Rotating intern St. Vincent Charity Hosp., Cleve., 1957-58; neuropsychiat. tng. U. Hosps., Frankfurt/Main, 1956-57, Central State Griffin Meml. Hosp., Norman, Okla., 1958-59, VA Hosp., Oklahoma City, 1959, Mental Health Clinic, Oklahoma City, 1960-61; asst. clin. dir., chief dept. neuropsychiatry Central State Griffin Meml. Hosp., Norman, Okla., 1962-67; dir. Mental Health Center, Norman, 1967-—; instr., clin. cons. U. Okla. Sch. Medicine, 1963-68, asst. prof. research medicine, 1968-—, research asso. exptl. therapeutics unit, dept. medicine, 1964-—; clin. cons. 2792d USAF Hosp., Tinker AFB, Okla., Okla. State Penitentiary Hosp. asst. clin. prof. psychiatry and behavioral scis. U. Okla., 1971-—, research psychiatrist, div. clin. pharmacol., dept. medicine. Fellow Am. Psychiat. Assn. (v.p. Okla.); mem. World Fedn. Mental Health (U.S. com.), Acad. Religion and Mental Health, A.A.A.S., A.M.A., Okla. Med. Soc., Mil-Continent Psychiat. Assn., World Psychiat. Assn., N.Y. Acad. Scis. Contbr. articles to profl. jours. Home: Route 4 Norman OK 73069 Office: PO Box 151 Norman OK 73069

HUBERT, JOSEPH ARTHUR, lawyer; b. Northport, N.Y., Mar. 22, 1930; s. Joseph F. and Adelyn (Condon) H.; A.B., Centre Coll., 1951; LL.D., U. Miami, Coral Gables, Fla., 1956; m. Theresa Ailene Mackey, Sept. 5, 1953; children—Nancy, Lisa, James, Robert, Jean Marie. Admitted to Fla. bar, 1956; partner firm Watson, Hubert & Davis, Fort Lauderdale, Fla., 1956-—; dir. Lawyers Title Services, Inc., Broward County 1964-—. Pres., Community Service Council, 1965, Econ. Opportunity Coordinating Group Broward County, 1965; pres. United Fund of Broward County, 1967. Served with CIC, AUS, Korea, Japan, 1951-53. Mem. Am., Broward County (pres. 1969) bar assns., Fla. Bar, Execs. Assn. Ft. Lauderdale. Kiwanian. Home: 1759 SE 10th St Fort Lauderdale FL 33316 Office: 3600 N Federal Hwy Fort Lauderdale FL 33308

HUCKABAY, GARY CLAYTON, bank exec.; b. Mountain Park, Okla., Jan. 3, 1938; s. Thomas Clayton and Areta (Wilburn) H.; B.S. in E.E., U. Okla., 1961; m. Deanna Erwin, June 4, 1960; children—Shawn Lettice, Clayton Todd, Wade Barrett. Vice pres., cashier First Nat. Bank, Snyder, Okla., 1961-69; pres. First Mustang (Okla.) State Bank, 1969-—, also dir.; dir. Bank of the Wichitas, Snyder, Okla., S.W. State Bank, Sentinel, Okla., Exchange Nat. Bank, Del City, Okla. Mem. exec. com. Boy Scouts Am., Lawton, Okla., 1967-69. Mem. Snyder C. of C. (v.p., dir. 1962-63), Engring. Club (treas. 1959-60), Student Senate (treas. 1959-60), Kappa Sigma (v.p. 1959), Omicron Delta Kappa, Sigma Tau. Democrat. Methodist. Rotarian (pres. 1966-67), Elk. Home: 15416 Lake Park Dr Mustang OK 73064 Office: First Mustang State Bank Mustang OK 73064

HUCKABEE, HARLOW MAXWELL, lawyer, govt. ofcl.; b. Wichita Falls, Tex., Jan. 22, 1918; s. Edwin Cleveland and Gladys Idella (Bonney) H.; A.B., Harvard, 1948; LL.B., Georgetown U., 1951; m. Gloria Charlotte Comstock, Jan. 10, 1942; children—Bonney M., David C., Stephen M. Br. office cashier Columbian Nat. Life Ins. Co., Boston, 1935-40; admitted to D.C. bar, 1952; atty. FH, Washington, 1955-56; trial atty. Criminal sect. tax div. U.S. Dept. Justice, Washington, 1956-63, trial atty., organized crime and racketeering sect., criminal div. 1967-68, trial atty., criminal sect., tax div., 1968-—; atty. office Chief Counsel, Internal Revenue Service, Treasury Dept., Washington, 1963-67; Justice Dept. rep. on internal revenue commr.'s com. on psychiat. defenses in tax fraud cases, 1970-—. Mem. standing com. problems connected with mental exam. of accused in criminal cases before trial Jud. Conf. D.C. Circuit 1960-65. Served from pvt. to maj., AUS, 1940-45, 48-55; lt. col. Res. Decorated Bronze Star with oak leaf cluster. Mem. Nat. Council on Crime and Delinquency, Am. Correctional Service Fedn., Bur. Rehab. Nat. Capitol Area. Fed. Bar Assn. Methodist. Home: 3648 N Monroe St Arlington VA 22207 Office: US Dept Justice Washington DC 20530

HUCKABEE, MARTHA CAROLYN, pharmacist; b. Uniontown, Ala., Oct. 13, 1926; d. Thomas Fendley and Carolyn (Blakeney) Huckabee; B.S., Ala. Poly. Inst., 1947. Pharmacist, Jones Drug Co., Anniston, Ala., 1948-49, Bradford Drug Co., 1949-65; owner, pharmacist Huckabee Drugs, Uniontown, 1965-—. Instr. first aid A.R.C., 1960-—; dir. med. services Civil Def., Perry County, 1961-—; hon. dep. sheriff Perry County,1962-—. Bd. dirs. Uniontown Community Chest. Mem. Uniontown Mchts. Assn., Nat. Assn. Retail Druggists, Am., Ala. (Perry county dir.), Perry County (pres.) pharm. assns., Nat. C. of C., D.A.R., Auburn, Auburn Pharmacy alumni assns. Republican, Baptist. Mem. Order Eastern Star. Home: 101 Front St Uniontown AL 36786 Office: 300 N Water St Uniontown AL 36786

HUCKABEE, TOMMIE JACK, architect; b. Bonham, Tex., Apr. 8, 1936; s. Clyde Martin and Pauline Nina (Chaffin) H.; student Tex. Tech. U., 1954-56; diploma architecture Canadian Inst. Sci. and Tech., 1960; m. Sylvia Wingo, Dec. 30, 1960; children—Timothy Michael, Phyllis, Christopher Martin. Draftsman, Butler-Kimmel, architects, Lubbock, Tex., 1956-58; designer-draftsman Hermann Riherd & Assos., architects, Lubbock, Tex., 1960-68; prin., Riherd & Huckabee, architects, Lubbock, Andrews, Tex., 1968-—. Archtl. cons. Andrews Indsl. Found., 1968-71. Chmn. indsl. constrn. com. Andrews Indsl. Devel. Team, 1970-71. Registered architect. Served with USMCR, 1958-59. Registered architect Nat. Council Archtl. Registration Bds. Mem. A.I.A., Tex. Soc. Architects, Andrews County C. of C. (dir. 1964-67). Democrat. Methodist (mem. bd. trustees 1963-67). Prin. archtl. works include Ward County Library, Wentworth Mfg. Co., W. Tex. Telephone Co., Monahan Jr. High Sch., Main Post Office, Commerce Tex., Greenwood High Sch., Denver City Jr. High Sch., Stanton Jr. High Sch. Home: 203 Mesquite Lane Andrews TX 79714 Office: PO Box 1451 Andrews TX 79714

HUDDLE, DONALD LEROY, educator; b. Los Angeles, Jan. 1,, 1933; s. Roy Lee and Elaine (Armstrong) H.; B.S., U. Cal., Los Angeles, M.A., 1960; Ph.D., Vanderbilt U., 1964; student Los Angeles City Coll., 1956; m. Germaine Burchard, Aug. 20, 1959; children—Clarissa Anne, Gerard Ellis, Richard Lee, Roy Lee. Instr. Vanderbilt U., 1963-64; asst. prof. Rice U., Houston, 1964-66, asso. prof. econs., 1967-69, dir. grad. studies, 1968-69, prof., chmn. dept. econs., 1969-72; vis. research scholar Yale, 1966-67. Cons. AID, Washington, 1966-67. Precinct rep. Democratic Party, Houston. Served to 1st lt. USAF, 1952-56. Recipient Nat. Def. Edn. fellowship in econ. devel., 1960-63. Mem. Am. Econ. Assn., Am. Assn. U. Profs. (regional rep. 1966), Royal Econ. Soc., Am. Civil Liberties Union. Unitarian-Universalist. Mem. editorial bd. So. Econ. Jour., 1970-—.‡

HUDDLESTON, JAMES EDGAR, ret. social worker; b. Washington, Jan. 30, 1924; s. James Edgar and Edith (Bouis) H.; A.B., George Washington U., 1945; M.S., Columbia, 1947; m. Margaret Elizabeth Lynn, June 25, 1949; children—William Lynn, Donald James, Nancy Anne. Caseworker, Community Service Soc., N.Y., 1947-48; dist. sec. Health Council Greater N.Y., 1948-50; research asst. Community Welfare Council Milwaukee County, Wis., 1950-52; community orgn. cons. N.J. Bd. Child Welfare, Trenton, 1952-59; dep. dir. Burlington County Welfare Bd., Mt. Holly, N.J., 1959-63, dir., 1963-68; family and child welfare specialist, social and rehab. service U.S. Dept. Health, Edn. and Welfare, Washington, 1968-70, acting dir. child and family services div. Community Services Adminstrn., 1970-72. Pres. Burlington County Mental Health Bd., 1962, 63, 67; sec. Hosp. and Pub. Health Adv. Council Burlington County, 1965-67; active Boy Scouts Am., 1966-—. Mem. Nat. Assn. Social Workers (chpt. pres. 1957-59, mem. nat. com. on inquiry, 1964-66), Am. Pub. Welfare Assn., Phi Beta Kappa, Omicron Delta Kappa. Presbyn. Home: 2528 N Upland St Arlington VA 22207 Office: 330 C St SW Washington DC 20201

HUDDLESTON, JOSEPH RUSSELL, lawyer; b. Glasgow, Ky., Feb. 5, 1937; s. Paul Russell and Frances (Martin) H.; A.B., Princeton, 1959; LL.B., U. Va., 1962; m. Heidi Lynn Wood, Sept, 12, 1959; children—Johanna Lynn, Lisa Diane, Kristina Lee. Admitted to Ky. bar, 1962; practiced in Bowling Green, Ky., 1962-—; mem. firm Huddleston & Huddleston; dir. Nehi-Royal Crown Bottling and Distbg. Co., Houk Ins., Inc., Hart Stone Co. Mem. Ky. Crime Commn., 1972-—; mem. Adv. Com. Criminal Law Revision, 1969-71. Bd. dirs. Princeton U. Fund, 1958-59. Mem. Am., Ky. (ho. dels.), Bowling Green (pres.) bar assns., Am. Trial Lawyers Assn. (dir. Ky. chpt.), Phi Alpha Delta. Clubs: Cap and Gown (Princeton); Port Oliver Yacht; Bowling Green Country. Home: 3150 Smallhouse Rd

Bowling Green KY 42101 Office: 1032 College St Bowling Green KY 42101

HUDDLESTON, WALTER DARLINGTON, broadcast exec.; b. nr. Burkesville, Ky., Apr. 15, 1926; s. Walter Franklin and Lottie (Russell) H.; A.B., U. Ky., 1949; m. Martha Jean Pearce, Dec. 20, 1947; children—Stephen Pearce, Philip Dee. Program-sports dir. WKCT, Bowling Green, Ky., 1949-52; gen. mgr. WIEL, Elizabethtown, Ky., 1952—; dir. 1st Fed. Savings & Loan Assn., Elizabethtown, Ky., Citizens Security Nat., Inc., Owensboro, Ky., Radio Sta. WLBN, Lebanon, Ky. Mem. Ky. State Senate, 1966—, majority leader, 1970—. Democratic Caucus chmn., 1968; Democratic nominee for U.S. senator, 1972. Served with AUS, 1944-46. Mem. C. of C. (pres. 1959), Ky. Broadcasters Assn. (pres. 1958). Methodist. Club: Pendennis (Louisville). Home: Seminole Rd Elizabethtown KY 42701 Office: Leitchfield Rd Elizabethtown KY 42701

HUDDLESTON, WILLIAM ENNIS, physician; b. Batesville, Ark., Aug. 25, 1928; s. William McKinley and Edna Cecil (Ennis) H.; student Ark. Coll., 1946-48, Ark. State Tchrs. Coll., 1948-49; B.S. in Medicine, M.D., U. Ark., 1953; m. Pauline Maxine Coffman, Sept. 7, 1953; children—Thomas Kevin, Linda Marchand, Kelly Ennis. Intern, Mo. Meth. Hosp., St. Joseph, 1953-54; practice medicine, specializing in family practice, Iowa Park, Tex., 1956-57, Bridgeport, Tex., 1957—; mem. staff Bridgeport Hosp. Mem. Bridgeport City Council, 1960-72. Served with USAF, 1953-56. Diplomate Am. Bd. Family Practice. Fellow Am. Acad. Family Practice (charter), Am. Acad. Family Physicians (charter); mem. Am., Tex. med. assns., So. Med. Soc. Mason. Methodist (trustee 1962-72). Home: 26 Robinhood Lane Bridgeport TX 76026 Office: 1301 Halsell St Bridgeport TX 76026

HUDGINS, CARL THOMAS, lawyer; b. DeKalb Co., Ga., June 18, 1891; s. John H. and Mattie Mobley (Kittredge) H.; LL.B., Atlanta Law Sch., 1915;; m. Edna McDaniel, Sept. 21, 1921. Practice of law, 1915—; attorney for City of Chamblee, Ga., 1926-64. Mem. lower house Ga. Gen. Assembly, 1933-35. Mem. Georgia, Stone Mountain Circuit (past pres.), Decatur (past pres.) bar assns., Atlanta, DeKalb Co. (past pres.) hist. socs., Sons and Daus. of Pilgrims, Sons Confederate Vets., Old War Horse Lawyers Club, Atlanta Lawyers Club. Methodist. Mason. Club: Fort Barrington (v.p.). Home: 118 Erie Av Decatur GA 30031 Office: PO Box 1403 Decatur GA 30031

HUDGINS, CATHERINE HARDING (MRS. ROBERT SCOTT HUDGINS, IV), business exec.; b. Raleigh, N.C., June 25, 1913; d. William Thomas and Mary Alice (Timberlake) Harding; B.S., N.C. State Coll., 1929-33; grad. tchr. N.C. Sch. for Deaf, 1933-34; m. Robert Scott Hudgins, IV, Aug. 20, 1938; children—Catherine Harding, Deborah Ghiselin, Robert Scott V. Tchr., N.C. Sch. for Deaf, Morganton, 1934-36; sec. Dr. A. S. Oliver, Raleigh, 1937; tchr. N.J. Sch. for Deaf, Trenton, 1937-39; sec. Robert S. Hudgins Co., Charlotte, N.C., 1949-60, v.p., sec., treas., 1960—, also dir. Mem. Jr. Service League, Easton, Pa., 1939; project chmn. ladies aux. Profl. Engrs. N.C., 1954-55, pres., 1956-57; pres. Christian High Sch. P.T.A., 1963; program chmn. Charlotte Opera Assn., 1959-61, sec., 1961-63; sec. bd. Hezekiah Alexander House Restoration, 1949-52. Mem. N.C. Hist. Assn., English Speaking Union, Mint Museum Arts (pres. drama guild 1967-69), Daus. of Am. Colonists, D.A.R. (chpt. regent 1957-59, N.C. program chmn. 1961-63; N.C. sr. pres. Children Am. Revolution 1963-66, nat. bd. mgmt. 1963—; nat. vice chmn. Southeastern region, 1965-68, sr. nat. corr. sec. 1966-68, sr. nat. 1st v.p. 1968-70, sr. nat. pres., 1970-72, nat. chmn. for D.A.R., 1970-72), Internat. Platform Assn. Presbyn. (past chmn. home missions, annuities and relief Women of Ch., past pres. Sunday Sch. class). Club: Carmel Country (Charlotte). Home: 1514 Wendover Rd Charlotte NC 28211 Office: PO Box 17217 Charlotte NC 28211

HUDGINS, CURTIS RANDOLPH, JR., investment banker; b. Norfolk, Va., July 15, 1924; s. Curtis Randolph and Lillian Mabel (Smith) H.; B.A., Hampden-Sydney Coll., 1947; postgrad. U. Pa. Wharton Sch., 1948, Rutgers U. Grad. Sch. Banking, 1955, U. Va. Grad. Sch. Basic Advanced Mgmt., 1966; m. Anna Robertson Taylor Black, Nov. 4, 1950; children—Jane Barron, Curtis Randolph III, Anna Brooke, William Alexander. With trust dept. Nat. Bank Commerce, Norfolk, 1947-51, asst. trust officer, 1953-56; reg. rep. Wheat & Co., investment bankers, Norfolk, 1956-59, mgr. Norfolk office, 1960-69, partner, 1963-66, v.p., dir., 1966—. Pres. Jr. Achievement of Tidewater, 1972-73, Tidewater Westminister Homes, 1968-70; adv. bd. Salvation Army. Trustee Hampden-Sydney Coll., Leigh Meml. Hosp., Norfolk. Served to lt. USNR, 1945-46, 51-53. Mem. Financial Analysts Soc. Richmond (Va.), Chi Phi. Democrat. Presbyn. (elder 1961-71, moderator Norfolk Presbytery 1968). Clubs: Sertoma (v.p. 1951), Kiwanis (dir. 1968-69), Norfolk Yacht and Country, Harbor, Virginia (all in Norfolk). Home: 7634 North Shore Rd Norfolk VA 23505 Office: 3 Main Plaza E Norfolk VA 23510

HUDGINS, MARY DENGLER, writer; b. Hot Springs Nat. Park, Ark., Nov. 24, 1901; d. Jackson Wharton and Ida (Dengler) Hudgins; B.A., U. Ark., 1924, student Rice Sch. of Spoken Word, 1925, U. Chgo., 1940, U. Wis., 1941, Emory U., 1952. Tchr., Waldo (Ark.) High Sch., 1924-25; free-lance writer, 1925-39, 60—; librarian Hot Springs Pub. Library, 1939-43; med. and gen. librarian Army and Navy Gen. Hosp., Hot Springs, 1943-59; writer articles (specializing in Ark. topics) pub. in ency., hist., lit., profl. and popular publs. Dir., Hot Springs Writer's Workshop, 1960-61; incorporator, dir. Fine Arts Council, Hot Springs, 1960—; local historian YWCA, Hot Springs; active Hot Springs Little Theater, 1928-34. Mem. Ark. Hist. Assn. (mem. bd. 1963-71, v.p. 1972), Garland County Hist. Soc. (pres. 1962-63), Ark. (sec. spl. libraries div. 1959-60, reporter to S.W. div. A.L.A. 1955), Med. library assns., Ark. Folklore Assn. (1st v.p. 1958-59), Am. Assn. U. Women (Ark. 1st v.p. 1929-30), pres. Hot Springs br. 1927, Ark. fellowship chairman, 1959-61, Arkansas Geneal. Soc. (mem. bd.), D.A.R. Presbyn. (historian). Clubs: Hot Springs Music, Fortnightly, Sabina (pres. 1935), Current Book (pres. Hot Springs 1952, 64), Altrusa Internat. Address: 1030 Park Av Hot Springs National Park AR 71901

HUDGINS, WILLIAM HENRY, lawyer; b. Chase City, Va., Nov. 19, 1915; s. Edward Wren and Lucy (Morton) H.; B.A. in Journalism, Washington & Lee U., 1938; J.D., U. Va., 1941; postgrad. Fgn. service Inst., Washington, 1947. Admitted to Va. bar, 1953; vice consul Am. embassy, Santiago, Chile, 1947-48; atty. Office Judge Adv. Gen. of Navy and White House aide, 1949-50; aide flag lt. to Comdr.-in-Chief Eastern Atlantic & Mediterranean, London, Eng., 1950-51; sr. aide to comdr.-in-chief S. Europe, NATO, Naples, Italy, 1951-53; apptd. to spl. assignments as aide to supreme NATO comdr. (Gen. Eisenhower) and to King Paul of Greece, 1952-53; atty., Chase City, Va., 1953-70; co-owner, partner Marine Transport Assos., Inc., N.Y.C., 1971—; world traveller and lectr. on fgn. affairs. Commd. midshipman USNR, 1940, advanced through grades to comdr., 1953. Decorated Commendatore de Italia (Italy). Commandeur de l'Ordre du Ouissam Alaouite Cherifien (France). Mem. Assn. Preservation Va. Antiquities, Nat. Trust for Historic Preservation, Soc. Colonial Wars, S.A.R., Soc. Descs. of Original Knights of the Garter, Magna Carta Barons, Roanoke River Art Assn., Phi Alpha Delta, Sigma Delta Chi, Omicron Delta Kappa, Beta Theta Pi. Episcopalian (vestryman 1964-65, gen. chmn. bicentennial commemoration 1966). Club: University (Washington). Home: MacCallum More 500 Walker St Chase City VA 23924

HUDSON, CLYDE MILTON, judge; b. Stratford, Tex., Dec. 3, 1929; s. Eugene Henry and Edna (Dovel) H.; B.A., Tex. Tech., 1951; LL.B., Tex. U., 1954; m. Mary LaVonne Riley, July 14, 1957; children—Martha Elizabeth, Michael Eugene. Admitted to Tex. bar, 1954; county judge Sherman County, Stratford, Tex., 1955-59; staff atty. Tex. State Hwy. Dept., Amarillo, Tex., 1959-65; practiced in Amarillo, 1965-66; city judge, Amarillo, 1966—. Mem. Delta Theta Phi. Home: 3413 Kingston St Amarillo TX 79109 Office: 610 S Buchanan St Amarillo TX 79101

HUDSON, DONALD PAUL, dentist; b. Jonesboro, Ark., Dec. 14, 1940; s. Homer U. and Edna Inez (Drope) H.; B.S., Ark. State U., 1961; D.D.S., U. Tenn., 1964; m. Zelma Lavern Dorton, Nov. 8, 1968; 1 dau., Donna. Practice of dentistry, Jonesboro, Ark., 1964—; mem. faculty periodontal dept. U. Tenn. Coll. Dentistry, part-time 1968. Mem. Am., Ark. dental assns., Northeast Ark. Dental Soc., Psi Omega, Lambda Chi Alpha, Omicron Kappa Upsilon. Baptist. Home: Route 3 Box 837 Jonesboro AR 72401 Office: 2822 E Nettleton Jonesboro AR 72401

HUDSON, EDWARD RANDALL, JR, lawyer; b. Ft. Worth, July 24, 1934; s. Edward R. and Josephine (Smith) H.; B.A., U. Tex., 1955; LL.B., Harvard, 1958; m. Ann Frasher, Sept. 19, 1959; children—Randall, Frasher. Admitted to Tex. bar, 1958, since practiced in Ft. Worth. Pres. Ft. Worth Art Assn., 1965—; mem. Tex. Commn. Arts and Humanities. Trustee Mary Couts Burnett Trust; bd. dirs. Festival of Two Worlds, Spoleto, Italy, Ft. Worth Opera Assn., Northwood Inst. Contemporary Arts Council, Ft. Worth Zool. Assn., William E. Scott, Ft. Worth; exec. com. Streams and Valleys, Ft. Worth. Mem. Phi Beta Kappa. Roman Catholic. Home: 55 Westover Terrace Fort Worth TX 76107 Office: First Nat Bank Bldg Fort Worth TX 76102

HUDSON, FOSTER LEON, mech. engr.; b. Ethridge, Tenn., Oct. 2, 1921; s. Ola Marvin and Mayme (Escue) H.; B.S., Tenn. Poly. Inst., 1949; m. Nella Jane Sills, Mar. 19, 1949; children—William Escue, Randall Lee, Charles Brent and Claudia Lynne (twins). Draftsman, Massman, Metcalfe & Hamilton, Center Hill Dam, Tenn., 1949-50; mech. engr. C.E., U.S. Army, Nashville, 1950—. Served with USAAF, 1943-45. Home: 2350 Dennywood Dr Nashville TN 37214 Office: PO Box 1070 Nashville TN 37202

HUDSON, HUBERT R., lawyer; b. Oklahoma City, July 31, 1928; s. Hubert R. and Dorothy (Hoffman) H.; grad. Culver Mil. Acad., 1945; B.A. with highest honors, Williams Coll., 1949; LL.B., U. Tex., 1952; m. Sarah Gibbs Pell, June 25, 1949 (div. Sept. 1955); children—William Parke Custis, Sarah Gibbs; m. Nancy Paxton Moody, Dec. 4, 1959 (div. Mar. 1968). Admitted to Tex. bar, 1952; pvt. practice law Brownsville, Tex. Mem. Tex. Senate, 1956-63; chmn. State of Tex. Investments Com. Chmn. bd. S. Tex. Lumber Co., Cicero-Smith Lumber Cos., Deco-Unicel, Mex., Aspern J. Theatrical Prodns. Broadway, Automatic Insect Control Corp., Brownsville; dir. Beaver Creek Industries, Inc., Atlanta, Dalto Electronics, Norwood, N.J., El Centro Supermarkets, Brownsville, Boca Chica Leasing Co., also Brownsville Savs. & Loan, Seaport Service & Supply, High Plains Natural Gas Dallas; dir., mem. exec. com., mem. trust com. First Nat. Bank, Brownsville. Part time prof. history and constnl. law Tex. S.M. Coll.; mem. Com. of 75 for reevaluation U. Tex. Dir. Texas Citizens Com., 1955-59; trustee United Fund, Brownsville, 1954-56; chmn. founding of Good Neighbor Settlement House, 1953—; dir. Valley council Boy Scouts Am., 1954-58; pres. Charro Days, Brownsville, 1954-55, chmn. Rio Grande Valley Festival of Music. Commr. City of Brownsville Water Bd., 1956—; trustee Greater Brownsville Commn. (pres. 1969—). Chmn. finance com. Tex. Southmost Coll., 1956-58; sr. trustee Hudson Found., 1956-59; dir. U. Tex. Found. Sch. Business, Grand Opera Com. Rio Grande Valley; trustee Camille Playhouse, U. Tex. Sch. Architecture, Episcopal Day School, Texas Mil. Inst.; chmn. Day Sch. Found.; bd. dirs. San Antonio Symphony Soc.; patron Rio Grande Valley Zool. Soc. Recipient Outstanding Community Award Service medal Nat. Jr. C. of C., 1954, 56. Mem. Am. Bar Assn., Bar Assn. Tex., S. Tex. Heritage Soc. (trustee), Rio Grande Valley C. of C. (pres. 1960), Phi Beta Kappa, Phi Alpha Delta. Democrat. Episcopalian (vestry; dir. diocese evaluation com.). Clubs: Austin (Austin, Tex.); Piping Rock (N.Y.C.). Author: The Roosevelt Corollary, 1949. Home: Casa Poinciana Brownsville TX 78520 Office: First Nat Bank Bldg Brownsville TX 78520

HUDSON, JAMES PAUL, museum dir.; b. Canon City, Colo.; s. James Spencer and Julia Darce (Lopez) H.; B.A., Stanford, 1931, M.A., 1933; m. Ethel Sandys Jackson, May 4, 1936; 1 son, David Spencer. Mus. curator Nat. Park Service, Yosemite Nat. Park, 1934, Muir Woods Nat. Monument, 1935, Washington, 1936, George Washington Birthplace Nat. Monument, 1937, U.S. Dept. Interior Mus., 1938-40, Morristown (N.J.) Nat. Hist. Park, 1940-43, 45-47, regional office, Richmond, Va., 1947-54, Jamestown (Va.) Mus., 1954—; head curator Colonial Nat. Hist. Park; lectr. in field. Fellow Corning (N.Y.) Mus. of Glass, 1959; dir. tng. course for hostesses and guides Stratford Hall, Va., 1959—. Bd. dirs. James River Museum Conf. Mem. Va., No. Neck of Va. hist. socs., Am. Assn. Museums, Assn. for Preservation Va. Antiquities (dir. Williamsburg br. 1960-63, exec. sec. Jamestown com., dir.), Williamsburg Archeol. Soc. (pres.), S.A.R. (chaplain Williamsburg chpt.), Archeol. Soc. Va. (dir.). Episcopalian (vestryman of church). Kiwanian. Author: A Pictorial History of Jamestown, 1957; Early Jamestown Commodities and Industries, 1957; (with John L. Cotter) New Discoveries at Jamestown, 1957; Early Jamestown House and Buildings, 1964; This Was Green Spring, 1969. Contbr. articles on colonial period cultural objects to profl. publs. Research on 17th century glass, Eng., 1964. Home: 708 Powell St Williamsburg VA 23185 Office: Jamestown Museum Jamestown VA 23081

HUDSON, JESSE TUCKER, JR., financial exec.; b. Roanoke, Va., Sept. 25, 1920; s. Jesse Tucker and Bernice (Ragland) H.; B.A., U. Va., 1946; m. Bertha Browning Wood, June 9, 1944; children—Greg Hudson, David, Amy Jean. Staff asso. T. Coleman Andrews & Co., Richmond, Va., 1948-51; sr. accountant A. M. Pullen & Co., 1915-54; asst. controller Miller & Rhoads, Inc., 1954-59; comptroller, asst. treas., vice chancellor finance U. Pitts., 1959-64; v.p. finance, treas. Colonial Stores, Inc., Atlanta, 1964-70; v.p. finance and adminstrn. David Food Service, Inc., Atlanta, 1970-71; v.p. finance S.E. Banking Corp., Miami, Fla., 1971—. Served from 2d lt. to maj., AUS; maj. Res. Mem. Financial Execs. Inst., Am. Econ. Assn., Am. Mgmt. Assn., Nat. Assn. Accountants, Miami C. of C. Home: 735 Coronado Av Miami FL 33143 Office: 100 S Biscayne Blvd Miami FL 33131

HUDSON, JOHN ALLEN, librarian; b. Beaumont, Tex., May 14, 1927; s. Walter Byron and Bessie Gertrude (Aman) H.; B.A., U. Tex., 1951, M.A., 1954; M.L.S., Case Western Res. U., 1957; m. Genevieve Lynch, Jan. 3, 1948. Librarian I U. Tex., 1951-53, Librarian II, 1953-55; dir. extension Tex. State Library, 1955-56; univ. librarian U. Tex. at Arlington, 1957—. Library cons. So. Assn. Colls. and Univs., 1963-72. Trustee Arlington Pub. Library. Served with USNR, 1945-46. Mem. Am., S.W., Tex. library assns., Am. Hist. Assn., Council Tex. Coll. and U. Librarians (pres. 1969—), Interuniv. Council (chmn. library com. 1970—), Phi Beta Mu. Author: All But the People, 1969. Editor Tex. Libraries, 1955-56, Tex. Library Jour., 1956. Contbr. articles to profl. jours. Home: 1409 Juanita Dr Arlington TX 76013

HUDSON, JOSEPH WILLIS, ins. co. exec.; b. Woodruff, S.C., Feb. 3, 1934; s. Joseph Taylor and Martha Jane (Willis) H.; student U. N.C., 1952-55; m. Elsa Garrow Perlitz, Sept. 1, 1955; children—Elsa Garrow, Joseph Willis. Salesman, Hudson & Co., Inc., Spartanburg, S.C., 1955-59, pres., 1959-72, dir., 1959—; founder, pres. Willis Brinkman, Ins., Spartanburg, 1960-67; founder Nat. Bank Commerce, Spartanburg, S.C., 1968, chmn. bd., 1968-70 (merged First Citizens Bank & Trust Co. 1970), now dir. First Citizens Bank & Trust Co., Columbia, S.C., dir. Red Fox Properties, Tryon, N.C. Mem. Small Bus. Adminstrn. Adv. Council for S.C., 1969-70. Trustee Ducks Unlimited. Served with AUS, 1957-59. Mem. Sigma Chi. Clubs: Springdale Hall (Camden, S.C.); African Safari of New York (N.Y.C.). Home: 30 Lake Forest Dr Spartanburg SC 29302 Office: 450 E Henry St Spartanburg SC 29302

HUDSON, LARRY GILBERT, supt. schs.; b. Emerson, Ark., Feb. 27, 1933; s. John Ward and Eva Lee (McMahen) H.; B.S., So. State Coll., 1958; M.Ed., U. Ark., 1964; m. Marjorie Ann Wilbanks, July 11, 1955; children—Jody Lynn, Gina Ann. Coach, supt. Garland (Ark.) Pub. Schs., 1958-66; supt. schs. Lewisville (Ark.) Pub. Schs., 1966—. Served with AUS, 1953-55. Mem. Am. Legion, Am. Assn. Sch. Adminstrs., Ark. Edn. Assn. Baptist. Rotarian. Home: PO Box 1 Lewisville AR 71845 Office: PO Box 400 Lewisville AR 71845

HUDSON, MORLEY ALVIN, mfg. exec.; b. San Antonio, Mar. 31, 1917; s. Oscar Alvin and Ruth (Morley) H.; B.S. in Mech. Engring., Ga. Inst. Tech., 1938; m. Lucy North, Nov. 11, 1944; children—Nancy Lucile, Lucy N., Courtney Morley. Advt. engr. Allis-Chalmers Mfg. Co., West Allis, Wis., 1938-40; safety engr. Am. Surety Co., Dallas, 1940-41; chief corrosion engr. Mobil Oil Co., Beaumont, Tex., 1942-45; dist. mgr. Eggelhof Engrs., Inc., Shreveport, La., 1946-52; pres., gen. mgr. Hudson-Rush Co., Inc., Shreveport, 1952—; v.p. McElroy Metal Mill, Inc., Bossier City, La., 1962—. Pres. Community Council, Shreveport, 1965; Vice chmn. La. Gov.'s Com. on Employment of Handicapped, 1964-69. Mem. La. Ho. of Reps., 1964-68, minority leader, 1964-68; La. vice chmn. Republican party, 1969; Rep. candidate for lt. gov., 1971-72. Served with AUS, 1941-42. Named Handicapped Louisianan of Yr. Gov.'s Commn. on Employment of Handicapped, 1964. Mem. Shreveport C. of C. (dir. 1969—), Am. Soc. M.E.'s, Omicron Delta Kappa, Tau Beta Pi, Sigma Nu, Phi Kappa Phi. Presbyn. (elder). Home: 4609 Gilbert Dr Shreveport LA 71106 Office: 819 Kings Hwy Shreveport LA 71104

HUDSON, WILLIAM RONALD, educator; b. Temple, Tex., May 16, 1933; s. C.W. and Nannie Dale (Skinner) H.; B.S. in Civil Engring., Tex. A. and M. Coll., 1954, M.S. in Civil Engring., 1955; Ph.D. in Civil Engring., U. Tex., 1965; m. Martha Ann Collins, July 29, 1958; children—Stuart William, Alan David, Paul Collin. Civil engr. S.J. Buchanan & Assos., Bryan, Tex., 1957-58; research engr. Tex. Hwy. Dept., Austin, 1957-58; asst. prof. engring. U. Tex., from 1963, then asso. prof., now prof.; cons. in field. Mem. Austin Fed. Safety Council, 1963-65; mem. Planning Commn., Street and Rd. Safety Commn., Rollingwood, 1969. Recipient Ann. Hwy. Research Bd. award, 1964, James R. Cross medal, 1968. Registered profl. engr. Mem. Am. Soc. C.E., Tex. Soc. Profl. Engrs., Nat. Acad. Sci., Sigma Xi, Phi Kappa Phi, Chi Epsilon. Episcopalian. Club: Capitol City A and M. Office: U Tex Austin TX 78712

HUDSPETH, BENNIE HIXIE, supt. schs.; b. Ore City, Tex., Oct. 3, 1908; s. James Harvey and Sarah Cathryn (Loyd) H.; B.S., East Tex. State U., 1935; M.A., George Peabody Coll., 1941; m. Ruby Louella Williamson, Aug. 30, 1931; children—Benjamin Harold, George Robert, John Harvey, William Henry. Prin. high sch., New Diana, Tex., 1930-32, Grice, Tex., 1932-33, Union Grove, 1933-40; supt. schs., Spring Hill, Tex., 1940-42, McLeod, 1942-45, Atlanta, Tex., 1945-60; right of way agt. Tex. Hwy. Dept. 1960-63; supt. schs., Hallsville, Tex., 1963—. Pres., United Fund, Hallsville, 1965-68; mem. Caddo council Boy Scouts Am., 1950-55; chmn. area Polio Found., Atlanta, Tex., 1946-50; mem. Gov.'s Indsl. Found., Tex., 1971—. Named Man of the Year, Hallsville C. of C., 1971. Mem. Tex. Tchrs. Assn. (pres. 1945-47), Tex., Am. assns. sch. adminstrs., Tex. Music Educators of Univ. Interscholastic League (dir. 1955-56), C. of C. (dir. 1946-49). Methodist (pres. men's class 1970-71). Mason, Lion, Rotarian (pres. 1954-55). Club: Knife and Fork (Longview, Tex.). Home: 508 Tullie Dr Longview TX 75601 Office: Box 247 Hallsville TX 75650

HUDSPETH, WILLIAM ROY, JR., chem. co. exec.; b. Winston-Salem, N.C., Mar. 21, 1923; s. William Roy and Lee (Wilcox) H.; student Wake Forext Coll., 1942, U. Wis., 1943; B.S., U. N.C., 1948, postgrad., 1948; m. Nancy Webber, Dec. 22, 1944; children—William Broughton, Patricia Lee, Nancy Ann. Control engr. Western Electric Winston-Salem, N.C., 1948-49; research engr. Asheville Minerals Research Lab., 1949-51; plant chemist Foote Mineral Co., Kings Mountain, N.C., 1951-52, metall. engr., 1952-54, mill supt., 1954-56, plant supt., Sunbright, Va., 1956-58, gen. supt. 1958, asst. mgr., 1958-59, plant mgr., Cold River, N.H., 1959-60, mgr. spl. project, Exton, Pa., 1960-62, gen. mgr. comml. devel., 1962-65, asst. v.p. marketing, 1965—; asst. to pres. McCall Pattern Co., 1967, v.p. mfg., 1968-71; v.p., gen. mgr. chems. Chattem Drug and Chem. Co. (Tenn.), 1971—. Mem. research adv. bd. N.C. State U., 1956—; mem. Easttown Library Bd., 1964—; mem. council bd. Boy Scouts Am., 1958—. Bd. dirs. Johnson Recreational Park Bd., 1959—; trustee Holston Valley Hosp. Served with USAAF, 1942-44. Mem. Am. Inst. Chem. Engrs. (career guidance bd.), Am. Inst. Mining, Metall. and Petroleum Engrs., Am. Ceramic Soc., Am. Chem. Soc., N.H. Edn. Assn., Am. Legion, Jr. C. of C., Alpha Chi Sigma, Phi Kappa Sigma. Republican. Methodist. Lion, Rotarian. Club: Waynesborough Country. Inventor mica recovery process, mineral analytical technique. Home: 137 Valleybrook Circle Hixson TN 37343 Office: 1715 W 38th St Chattanooga TN 37409

HUERKAMP, FREDERICK JOHN, orgn. exec.; b. Cin., Aug. 9, 1929; s. Frederick James and Clair S. (Schmidt) H.; student Miami U., 1947-49; B.S., Xavier U., 1951, M.B.A., 1964; m. Elizabeth Ann Brewer, July 3, 1965; 1dau., Natalie Ann. Securities portfolio analyst First Nat. Bank, Cin., 1955-56; sales rep. Hill-Rom Co., Batesville, Ind., 1956-63; adminstrv. resident Duval Med. Center, Jacksonville, Fla., 1964; exec. sec. Health Planning Council Jacksonville Area, Inc., 1964—. Bd. dirs. Jacksonville Hosp. Council, 1964—; v.p. Jacksonville Area Research Assn., 1967. Mem. adv. com. bd. CAMPS, 1967-68; mem. adv. com. Office Econ. Opportunity, 1967—. Bd. dirs. Jacksonville Hosp. Ednl. Program, Jacksonville U. Sch. Nursing Tech. Adv. Com. Served with USAF, 1951-55. Mem. Am. Hosp. Assn., Am. Pub. Health Assn., Hosp. Information Council, Sigma Alpha. Presbyn. Home: 1590 Geraldine Dr Jacksonville FL 32204 Office: 118 W Adams St PO Box 629 Jacksonville FL 32202

HUESTIS, CHARLES BENJAMIN, ednl. adminstr.; b. Seattle, Jan. 27, 1920; s. Claude Erwin and Eloise Marie (Pettit) H.; student Griffin Murphy Coll., Seattle, 1938-39, U. Cal. at Berkeley, 1946; m. Kathryn Alice Porter, Mar. 1, 1942; children—Stephen Porter, Jeffrey Charles, Robin Rebecca. With Seattle First Nat. Bank, 1941; accountant Rheem Mfg. Co., Richmond, Cal., 1946-51, chief accountant aircraft div., Downey, Cal., 1951-54, comptroller company, 1954-56; v.p. treas. Hall-Scott, Inc., Berkeley, Cal., 1956; exec. v.p. dir. treas. 1956-57; adminstrv. cons. Overseas Nat. Airways, Oakland, Cal., 1957-58; controller El Sequndo div. Hughes Aircraft Co., 1958-59, Tucson div., 1959, treas., dir. finance co., 1959-66, chmn. finance com., 1959-66, v.p., 1962-66, v.p., treas., dir. Am. Mt. Everest Expdn., 1963, Inc., Santa Monica, Cal., 1962-67; v.p. bus. and finance Duke U., Durham, N.C. 1966—. Dir. Technomics, Inc., Falls Church, Va., Durham Investment Corp. Bd. dirs. Santa Barbara (Cal.) Research Center, 1959-66; bd. dirs., mem. exec. com. Research Triangle Found., Research Triangle Park, N.C.; trustee Research Triangle Inst. Mem. Archaeol. Inst. Am. Clubs: Explorer, Sierra (treas. 1969—, dir. 1970—). Home: 1803 Woodburn Rd Durham NC 27705 Office: Duke U Charlotte NC 27706

HUETER, HANS HERBERT, govt. ofcl.; b. Bern, Switzerland, Mar. 21, 1906; s. Otto Carl and Katharina (Schelowsky) H.; M.E., Tech. Coll., Mittweide, Germany, 1927; D.Sc. (hon.), Adelphi Coll., 1959; m. Ruth Lieselotte Jeremias, Feb. 5, 1938; children—Eike, Uwe, Wendula. Came to U.S., 1945; naturalized, 1955. Design and test engr. various plants, Germany, 1927-32; project engr. rocket research Soc. for Space Travel, Berlin, 1932-34; project engr. aircraft guidance and control equipment Siemens, 1935-37; chief test engr., then project dir. for ground support systems German Missile Devel. Center, Peenemunde, 1937-45; tech. advisor Army Ordnance, White Sands Proving Grounds, 1945-47, chief flight test engr. Guided Missile Devel. Group, Fort Bliss, Tex. and Huntsville, Ala., 1947-51; dir. systems support equipment Army Ballistic Missile Agy., Huntsville, 1951-60; project dir. Centaur and Agena missile systems, NASA, Marshall Space Flight Center, 1960-62, dir. spl. assignments office, 1963, dep. dir. indsl. operation, 1964-69, dir. safety, 1969—. Recipient Dept. of Army award for Exceptional Civilian Service, 1959; Exceptional Service medal NASA, 1969. Mem. Am. Inst. Aeronautics and Astronautics, Assn. U.S. Army. Lutheran. Home: 1409 Locust Dr SE Huntsville AL 35801 Office: George C Marshall Space Flight Center Huntsville AL Died Sept. 6, 1970

HUEY, GEORGE PHILIP, JR., city ofcl.; b. Graham, Tex., Apr. 4, 1931; s. George Philip and Homerette (Whatley) R.; B.S. in Floriculture, Tex. A. and M. U., 1953. With Gen. Dynamics Corp., Ft. Worth, 1956-57; floriculturist Dallas Park Dept., 1957-60, supr. park dept., 1960-62, gen. supt., 1962-66, supt. of parks, 1966—. Served to 1st lt. AUS, 1953-56. Mem. Am. Inst. Park Execs., Def. Supply Assn., S.A.R. (sec.-treas. 1961-63, v.p. 1963-64), Former Students Assn. Tex. A. and M. U., Tex. Turfgrass Assn. (pres. 1968-69). Presbyn. Home: 6330 E University St Dallas TX 75214 Office: 3203 Junius St Dallas TX 75226

HUEY, MARY EVELYN BLAGG (MRS. GRIFFIN BURNS HUEY), univ. dean; b. Wills Point, Tex., Jan. 19, 1922; d. Henry Hurst and Evelyn (Manning) Blagg; B.S., Tex. Woman's U., 1942, M.A., 1943; M.A., U. Ky., 1947; Ph.D., Duke, 1954; m. Dr. Griffin B. Huey, Aug. 21, 1954; 1 son, Henry Griffin. Instr. English, Tex. Woman's U., 1943-45; asst. dir. Bur. Pub. Administrn., U. Miss., 1946-47; instr. govt. N. Tex. State U., 1947-51, asst. prof., 1954-63, asso. prof., 1963-66, prof., 1966-71; prof. govt., dean Grad. Sch., Tex. Woman's U., Denton, 1971—; dir. Joint U. Center for Community Services, 1966-67. Conferee, Oak Ridge Inst. Nuclear Studies Conf., summer 1965; mem council Regional Archives U.S., 1971—; mem. adv. council Nat. Archives, 1971—. Mem. bd. adjustment Planning and Zoning Commn. Denton, chmn., 1963-68; regional citizen mem. North Central Texas Council of Govts., 1968-71, bd. dirs., 1970-71; sec. Denton County Planning Council, 1969; bd. dirs. N. Central Tex. Health Planning Council, 1969. Vice chmn. Denton County Republican Com., 1960-63; mem. state steering com. Women for Nixon, 1968. Mem. Am. Assn. U. Women (local exec. bd. 1955-56, 61-62, 64-68, pres. Denton br. 1962-63), Am. Polit. Sci. Assn., Am. Soc. Pub. Administrn. (mem. council N. Tex. Chpt. 1966-71, pres. 1969-70, mem. nat. conf. com. 1972), Southwestern Social Sci. Assn., Tex. Assn. Coll. Tchrs. (sec.-treas. local chpt. 1958-59), Women's Aux. to Tex. Dental Assn. (dist. pres., mem. state exec. bd. 1956-61, state parliamentarian, 1958-59, state revisions chmn. 1960-61), Council Grad. Schs. U.S. (summer conf. grad. deans 1972, com. for non-degree programs 1972-73), Assn. U. Profs., So. Polit. Sci. Assn., Southwestern Polit. Sci. Assn., League Women Voters, D.A.R. (rec. sec. Benjamin Lyon chpt. 1967-68, regent 1970—, sr. pres. Children Am. Revolution 1968-70), Colonial Dames XVIII Century, Daus. Republic Tex., Nat. Geneal. Soc., Pi Sigma Alpha, Delta Kappa Gamma. Presbyn. (ruling elder). Clubs: Denton County Republican Women's (charter pres. 1955-56), Ariel (parliamentarian 1956-59, chmn. lit. dept. 1971—). Author: The Legislative Process: A Handbook for Mississippi Legislators, 1947; Texas Constitutional Revision: The Legislative Branch, 1962; also book rev. and articles profl. jours.; co-author: Clarksville: A Fiscal Study, 1947. Home: 2801 Longfellow Lane Denton TX 76201

HUFF, CALVIN RALPH, mayor; b. Burlingame, Kan., Nov. 4, 1902; s. Ralph Whitney and Lottie (Higginson) H.; grad. Tex. A. and M. Coll., 1925; m. Adele Johnson, July 7, 1940; children—Martha Kaye (Mrs. Fenn), Janice (Mrs. Smith). Mayor, City of Raymondville, Tex., 1946-47, 59—; real estate dealer. Kiwanian. Home: 362 E Van Eaton St Raymondville TX 78580 Office: 228 S 7th St Raymondville TX 78580

HUFF, HENRY BLAIR, lawyer; b. Louisville, Aug. 30, 1924; s. Joseph B. and Mattie (Ireland) H.; B.S., LL.B., Wake Forest Coll., 1949; M.A., U. Louisville, 1958; m. Mary Anderson May 24, 1969. Admitted to N.C. bar, 1949, Ky. bar, 1954; law practice, Lenoir, N.C., 1949-54, Louisville, 1954—. OLCO, Inc. Chmn. bd. trustees City of Brownsboro Village, 1958-65; trustee Cleark Creek Bapt. Sch., 1967; exec. bd. Louisville area Council Chs., 1962—, pres., 1967—; mem. exec. bd. Ky. Bapt. Conv., chmn. finance com., 1971. Served with C.E., AUS, 1943-46. Mem. Am., Ky., Louisville bar assns., Am. Judicature Soc. Home: 170 West Wind Rd Louisville KY 40202 Office: 310 W Liberty St Louisville KY 40202

HUFF, JOHN SEATON, advt. agy. exec.; b. Louisville, Feb. 28, 1903; s. John Andrew and Ophelia (Seaton) H.; student Centre Coll., 1920; B.S., U. Pa., 1924; m. Margaret Aline Phillips, Sept. 27, 1928; children—Nancy Elizabeth (Mrs. Gordon Lee Hathaway), Margaret Montague (Mrs. Jesse Malin Matlack). Vice pres. Thomas E. Basham Co., Louisville, 1924-31, Gardner Advt. Co., Louisville, 1931-35; founder, pres. Farson & Huff Advt., Louisville, 1935—; pres. Braitling Engraving Co., Louisville, 1942—. Mem. Civil War Centennial Commn., 1965—. Mem. Bd. dirs. Derby Festival Assn., 1954—; trustee Lincoln Meml. U., Harrogate, Tenn., 1969—; founder, pres. Jr. Achievement Kentuckiana, 1963—. Mem. Nat. Athletic Inst., Rural Library Assn., Ky. Hist. Soc., Ky. Louisville chambers commerce, Asso. Industries Ky., Sigma Phi Epsilon. Republican. Mem. Ch. of Christ. Scientist. Mason. Clubs: Pendennis, Optimist. Home: 5737 Watterson Trail Louisville KY 40291

HUFF, MAXWELL ERNEST, physician; b. nr. Covington, Ky., Nov. 22, 1935; s. Ernest and Edrie (Sexton) H.; M.D., U. Tenn., 1959; m. Beatrice Kesterson, Jan. 17, 1959; children—Maxwell Ernest II, Warren Keith, Avery Carlton, Alison Christine. Intern, Erlanger Hosp., Chattanooga, 1960; gen. practice Oneida, Tenn., 1961—; med. examiner, Scott County, 1962—; mem. Scott County Bd. of Health, 1964—; chief-of-staff Scott County Hosp., 1965, bd. dirs. Mem. Democratic Exec. Com., 1967-68. Recipient Physician's Recognition award A.M.A., 1970. Diplomate Am. Bd. Family Practice. Mem. Scott County Med. Soc. (past pres.), C. of C. Baptist. Mason, Kiwanian. Home: Hwy US 27 Oneida TN 37841 Office: 157 Cross St Oneida TN 37841

HUFF, THOMAS EUGENE, supt. schs.; b. Village Mills, Tex., July 23, 1926; s. Thomas Sullivan and Nannie Selman (Millican) H.; B.S., East Tex. Bapt. Coll., 1950; M.Ed., U. Houston, 1954; postgrad. Tex. A. and M. U., 1972; m. Jimmie C. Mosier, Sept. 2, 1947; 1 son, Charles Thomas. Classroom tchr., West Orange (Tex.) schs., 1940-55, elementary prin., 1955-59, prin., High Sch., 1959-63; supt. West Orange Cove Sch. Dist., Orange, Tex., 1963—. Mem. Exec. council Boy Scouts Am., 1968—; mem. adv. bd. Salvation Army, 1968-71; mem. Orange Council on Alcoholism, 1968—; active A.R.C., United Fund. Served with AUS, 1944-46. Mem. Am., Tex. assns. sch. adminstrs., N.E.A., Tex. State Tchrs. Assn., Phi Delta Kappa. Rotarian. Home: 2301 Hilton St Orange TX 77630 Office: 501 15th St Orange TX 77630

HUFFARD, JOHN CLOYD, metal products co. exec.; b. N.Y.C., Oct. 31, 1936; s. Cloyd Hudson and Mary Agnus (Gwyn) H.; B.S., Washington and Lee U., 1958; m. Jane Evans Lineberger, Oct. 29, 1966; children—John Cloyd, Gwyn Evans. Salesman Union Carbide Corp., 1960; with Southwire Co., Carrollton, Ga., 1961—, adminstrv. asst., 1965-67, financial v.p., 1967—; dir., treas. Empreza Productos de Aluminio, Lorena, Brazil, 1962-65; treas. Nat. Southwire Aluminum Co., 1968, Wire Wynd, 1970. Trustee Oak Mountain Acad. Served to 1st lt. AUS, 1958-60. Mem. Sigma Nu. Presbyn. (deacon 1970-72). Rotarian. Home: 119 Hillcrest Dr Carrollton GA 30117 Office: PO Box 1000 Carrollton GA 30117

HUFFER, MARY A. (MRS. JOHN W. HUFFER), librarian; b. S.I., N.Y., Sept. 7, 1930; d. Thomas P. and Mary (Collins) Hanagan; A.B., Trinity Coll., 1952; postgrad. Georgetown U. Law Sch., 1952-55, Catholic U. Grad. Sch. Arts and Scis., 1955; m. John W. Huffer, Sept. 3, 1954; children—Mary Agnes, Kathleen Theresa. Loan desk librarian Smithsonian Instn., Washington, 1954-56, reference librarian, 1956-58, bur. librarian, 1958-60, asst. chief reference and circulation librarian, 1960-62, chief reference and circulation librarian, 1962-64, acting head librarian, 1964-65, acting dir. libraries, 1965-67, asst. dir. libraries, 1967-72; dir. office Library Services, U.S. Dept. Interior, 1972—. Mem. Fed. Library Com., chmn. task force on acquisition of library materials and correlation fed. library resources; vice chmn. librarians tech. adv. com. Met. Council Govts., Washington. Mem. Spl. Libraries Assn. (pres. Washington chpt. 1969-70), Am., D.C. (pres. 1971-72) library assns., Am. Soc. Information Scis., A.A.A.S., Am. Polit. Sci. Assn., Am. Mus. Assn., Nat. Microfilm Assn., Geosci. Information Soc., Kappa Beta Pi. Roman Catholic. Home: 6327 Hardwood Dr Lanham MD 20801 Office: Dept of Interior 18th and C Sts NW Washington DC 20240

HUFFINES, HILMAN HOWARD, county agrl. agt.; b. Hilham, Tenn., Oct. 16, 1919; s. Theodore Thurston and Maudie (Flatt) H.; B.S., U. Tenn., 1949, M.S., 1972; div.; children—Gwenell (Mrs. Delane Streeter), Beryl, Dwaine Howard. Asst. county agrl. agt., Morgan County, Tenn., 1949-51; county agrl. agt., Lewis County, 1951-53, Scott County, 1953—. Served with U.S. Army AC, 1942-46. Decorated D.F.C., Air Medal. Named Tenn. Tree Farmer. Mem. Am. Farm Bur., County Agts. Assn., Block and Bridle, Epsilon Sigma Phi. Kiwanian (local pres. 1961). Author: The Making of a Man and Other Poems, 1970. Home: PO Drawer H Oneida TN 37841 Office: Fed Office Bldg Oneida TN 37841

HUFFMAN, JOSEPH GRANT, state ofcl.; b. Petersburg, W.Va., June 5, 1933; s. Richard A. and Carmen (Hiser) H.; B.A. in Secondary Edn., Shepherd Coll., 1957; M.S. in Rehab. Counseling, W.Va. U., 1965; m. Elaine Sheppard, Dec. 27, 1958; children—Jalane Adaire, Jayma Lynn. Tchr., coach pub. high schs., W.Va., 1957-59, Fla., 1959-61; social case worker W.Va. Dept. Welfare, Petersburg, 1961-62; counselor field office Div. Vocational Rehab., Martinsburg, W.Va., 1962-63, Weston (W.Va.) State Hosp., 1965, sr. counselor, 1966, unit supr., 1966-67; program supr. Va. Dept. Vocational Rehab., Western State Hosp., Staunton, 1967—. Served with Signal Corps, AUS, 1953-55. Mem. Nat. Rehab. Assn., Nat. Rehab. Counseling Assn. Mem. United Brethern Ch. Mason. Home: 910 Selma Blvd Staunton VA 24401 Office: Rehab Unit Western State Hosp New Site Staunton VA 24401

HUFFMAN, RUFUS CHARLES, educator; b. Bullock County, Ala., Feb. 5, 1927; s. Nathan Luther and Mary Liza (Gambles) H.; B.S., Ala. State U., 1952, Ed.M., 1966; postgrad. N.Y.U., 1968; m. Callie Iola Harris, July 28, 1948; children—Rufus Charles, Henry Nathaniel. Tchr., prin. Russel County Bd. Edn., 1947-49, Autauga County Bd. Edn., Prattville, Ala., 1951-53, Bullock County Bd. Edn., Union Springs, Ala., 1953-56, 1963-67, Randolph County Bd. Edn., Cuthbert, Ga., 1956-63; coordinator, treas., mgr. Seasha Fed. Credit Union, Tuskeegee Institute, Ala., 1968-70; edn. field dir. spl. contribution fund N.A.A.C.P., Tuskeegee Institute, 1970—. Tchr., coach, prin., cons. Neighborhood Health Centers. Vice pres. Bullock County Improvement Orgn.; chmn. Bullock County Coordinating Com.; pres. Union Springs br. N.A.A.C.P.; v.p. Bullock County Adv. Council, Office Ecn. Opportunity. Named Tchr. of the Year, Bullock County, 1963-64; Ford Found. Leadership Devel. fellow. Mem. N.E.A., Bullock County Tchrs. Assn. (pres.), Bullock County Athletic Assn. (pres.). Baptist (deacon). Elk. Home: 223 Underwood Av Union Springs AL 36089 Office: Scott and Calloway Sts Tuskegee Institute AL 36088

HUFSCHMIDT, MAYNARD MICHAEL, educator; b. Catawba, Wis., Sept. 28, 1912; s. John Jacob and Emma (von Arx) Hufschmid; B.S., U. Ill., 1939; M.P.A., Harvard, 1955, D.P.A., 1964; m. Elizabeth L. Leake, July 5, 1941; children—Emily Ann, Mark Andrew. Planning editor Ill. State Planning Commn., Chgo., 1939-41; engr. U.S. Nat. Resources Planning Bd., Washington, 1941-43; budget examiner U.S. Bur. of Budget, Washington, 1943-49; program staff mem. Office of Sec., U.S. Dept. Interior, Washington, 1949-54; research asso. Harvard water program Harvard U., Cambridge, Mass., 1955-61, dir. research, 1961-65; prof. city and regional planning and environmental scis. and engring. U. N.C., Chapel Hill, 1965—. Cons. to various govt. agys. Recipient Clemens Herschel award Boston Soc. Civil Engrs., 1959. NSF Sr. Postdoctoral Research fellow, 1970-71. Mem. Am. Soc. Pub. Adminstrn., Regional Sci. Assn. (v.p. 1969), Elisha Mitchell Sci. Soc., Sigma Xi, Tau Beta Pi. Club: Cosmos. Author: (with others) Design of Water-Resource Systems, 1962; (with M.B. Fiering) Simulation Techniques for Design of Water-Resource Systems, 1966. Author, editor: Regional Planning: Challenge and Prospects, 1969. Home: 912 Kings Mill Rd Chapel Hill NC 27514

HUGE, ROBERT RUSSELL, indsl. editor; b. Cleve., Sept. 23, 1938; s. Russell Martin and Jeannette Elizabeth (Warner) H.; B.A., Ohio U., 1961; m. Patricia Lehr Hall, Nov. 24, 1961; children—Margery Elizabeth, Elizabeth Hall. Editorial asst. Newspaper Enterprise Assn., Cleve., 1961-62, editor, 1962-65; writer Ashland Oil, Inc. (Ky.), 1965-66, editor Ashland Dealer, 1966-70, editor Ashland News, 1966—, editor Valvoline World, 1970, editor publs., 1971—. Recipient award of merit Internat. Assn. Bus. Communicators, 1965, award of excellence, 1966. Episcopalian (sec. vestry 1971—). Contbr. poems and stories to profl. pubs. Home: 824 Edgwood Av Ashland KY 41101 Office: PO Box 391 Ashland KY 41101

HUGER, JAMES ERMINE, coll. bus. exec.; b. Tampa, Fla., Jan. 4, 1918; s. Thomas Albert and Rosetta (Williams) H.; student Bethune-Cookman Coll., 1937-39, LL.D., 1972; student W.Va. State Coll., 1939-41, U. Mich., 1950-51; m. Phannye Brinson, Aug. 23, 1941; children—James Ermine, Thomas Albert II, John Leland. Asso. treas. Bethune-Cookman Coll., Daytona Beach, Fla., 1941-42, adminstrv. asst. to pres., 1957-61, bus. mgr., 1961—; gen. sec. Alpha Phi Alpha Fraternity, Inc., 1951-57. Mem. selection com. Dollars for Scholars, 1968-71; mem. State Commn. on Aging, 1966—; mem. Regional Adv. Com. on Pub. Health, Atlanta, 1968—; mem. Gov.'s. Com. on Community Affairs, 1969—; mem. City Commn. Daytona Beach, 1965-71; mem. Fla. Probation and Parole Commn., 1969—; mem. Environmental Control Com., 1970-71. Pres. Mental Health Assn. Volusia County; v.p. Boys Club Am.; bd. dirs. Salvation Army; trustee Tb. and Respiratory Disease Assn. Served with USMCR, 1942-46. Recipient Charles W. Green award for outstanding service to humanity, 1961, Westside Bus. and Profl. Assn. award for outstanding service as civil servant, 1967, Meritorious award Eastern Regional Conf. Alpha Phi Alpha, 1957, Citizen of Year award on This Is Your Life Program, 1969, Bethune-Cookman Coll. award as Adminstr. of Year, 1970, Distinguished Service award for contbn. to civic affairs Zeta Phi Beta, 1970, Fla. Morticians Assn. award of honor, 1970, Distinguished Service award Social Engrs., 1968, award of achievement N.A.A.C.P., 1968, award of appreciation State of Fla., 1968, Fla. Voters League Meritorious Community Service award, 1970, James E. and Florence Davis award as outstanding adminstr. of year, 1970; named Man of Year, Alpha Phi Alpha, 1967. Mem. N.A.A.C.P. (life), Am. Legion, Assn. for Study Negro Life and History, Social Engrs., West Side Bus. and Profl. Assn., Daytona Beach C. of C., Alpha Phi Alpha. Methodist. Mason (Shriner), Elk. Home: 935 Sycamore St Daytona Beach FL 32014 Office: Bethune-Cookman Coll Daytona Beach FL 32015

HUGER, KILLIAN LOEW, JR., diversified industry exec.; b. New Orleans, Sept. 7, 1928; s. Killian Loew and Miriam Deare (Hopkins) H.; B. Comml. Sci., Tulane U., 1953; m. Eugenie Penick Jones, Oct. 24, 1953; children—Sally Polk, Eugenie Elizabeth, Deborah Hopkins, Caroline Merrick, Miriam Hopkins, James Middleton. With Celotex Corp., New Orleans, 1952-54, New Orleans Pub. Service, 1949-52, Avondale Shipyard, 1954—, Beer & Co., 1954—; pres. Huger Constrn. Co., Inc., 1954—; pres. Charlotte Devel. Co., Inc., 1955—; pres. Central Marine Service, Inc., 1962—; v.p. Canal Barge Co., 1964—; pres., dir. Interstate Fed. Savings and Loan Assn., 1971— (all New Orleans). Mem. Tulane U. Annual Giving Com., 1965-68; active United Fund, 1968-69, Heart Fund, 1968. Trustee Metairie Park Country Day Sch.; v.p. Joseph M. and Eugenie P. Jones Found., 1968. Served with USNR, 1946-48. Mem. New Orleans C. of C., Internat. House, Clubs: Petroleum, Plimsoll, Boston, Southern Yacht (New Orleans). Home: 1112 State St New Orleans LA 70118 Office: 1200 Hibernia Bank Bldg New Orleans LA 70112

HUGGINS, FRED LEON, probate judge; b. nr. Coffeeville, Ala., Sept. 27, 1935; s. Eddie E. and Nora (Brown) H.; grad. high sch.; m. Gloria Newsom, Feb. 15, 1957; children—Carl Eddie, Steven Leon, Molly Frances. With radio sta. WHOD, Jackson, Ala., 1956-66, pres., gen. mgr., 1963-66; publisher The South Alabamian, weekly newspaper, 1966-69; dir. pub. relations Mchts. Bank, 1969-70; judge probate Court, Grove Hill, Clarke County, Ala., 1971—. Vice-pres. Jackson Little League, 1970-71; vice chmn. State of Ala. Hank Williams Meml. Commn., 1968—. Chmn. bd. trustees Jackson Schs., 1969-70. Bd. dirs. Clarke County chpt. A.R.C. Baptist (vice-chmn. bd. deacons 1971—). Democrat, Mason, Rotarian (pres. 1963). Home: 2029 Katherine Av Jackson AL 36545 Office: Courthouse Grove Hill AL 36451

HUGGINS, LAWRENCE CHANDLER, civil engr.; b. Istachatta, Fla., Feb. 22, 1913; s. Ira Francis and Effie Lee (Langford) H.; B.S., U. Fla., 1934; m. Helen Summers, Dec. 24, 1935; children—Loretta Coleen (Mrs. John T. Smith), Frank Augustus, Jr. civil engr. U.S. Forest Service, 1934-38; design engr. Smith & Gillespie, engrs., Jacksonville, Fla., 1938-45; staff engr. Burlington Industries, Greensboro, N.C., 1947-62; design engr. Eastern Engring. Corp., Atlanta, 1962-65; v.p. Patterson & Dewar, engrs., Decatur, 1965-67; individual practice profl. civil engring. Decatur, Ga., 1967-69; prin. engr. Catalytic, Inc., engrs., Charlotte, N.C., 1969—. Served with USNR, 1943-46. Registered profl. engr. Ga., N.C. Mem. Nat., Ga. socs. profl. engrs., Am. Water Works Assn., Water Pollution Control Fedn. Baptist. Home: 15 Beaufort St Greenville SC 29607 Office: 700 N Pleasantburg Dr Greenville SC 29607

HUGHES, ALBERT EVERETT, food mfg. co. exec.; b. Covington, Ky., May 13, 1913; s. Allen Porter and Marie (Holland) H.; student Tulane U., 1938-40; m. Nell Riley Salter, Dec. 22, 1935; children—Albert Everett, Martha Ellen (Mrs. Stephen Geer Stoneburn). Mem. accounting, auditing depts. Fed. Land Bank of New Orleans, 1932-43; sec.-treas. Fed. Land Bank Assn. of Jeff Davis and Simpson Counties, Miss., 1943-44; sec. Iberia Sugar Cooperative, New Iberia, La., 1946—. Mem. indsl. com. New Iberia (La.) C. of C., 1960-62, mem. pollution control com., 1969-70. Served with USAAF, 1943-46. Mem. Am. Soc. Sugar Cane Technologists, Am. Sugar Cane League, La. Sugar Producers Assn. (v.p. 1964-66, pres. 1966-68), La. Council Farmer Cooperatives (dir. 1963-65), Nat. Soc. Accountants for Cooperatives, Iberia Parish Farm Bur. Office: PO Box 1389 New Iberia LA 70560 Home: 16 Bluehaven Dr New Iberia LA 70560

HUGHES, CHARLES DAVID, food service equipment co. exec.; b. Mineral, Ark., Dec. 31, 1938; s. Charles and Arla Lorene (Helms) H.; B.S. in Bus. Adminstrn., U. Ark., 1960; m. Julia Mae Rumph, Sept. 30, 1960; children—Charles David, Anne Elizabeth, Alice Lorene. Zone credit rep. Internat. Harvester Co., Little Rock, 1961-63; v.p. Dixie Equipment Co., Little Rock, 1963—. Active Boy Scouts Am. Served with AUS, 1960-61. Mem. A.I.M. (pres.'s council 1971—), Sales and Marketing Execs., Ark. Restaurant Assn., Sigma Nu Alumni Assn. (dir. Eta Xi chpt. 1964—), Holy Souls Mens Club, Blue Key, Alpha Kappa Psi, Sigma Nu. Democrat. Roman Catholic. K.C. Clubs: Capitol, Pleasant Valley Country, Top of the Rock (Little Rock). Home: 5307 Southwood Rd Little Rock AR 72205 Office: Dixie Equipment Co 7th and Collins Sts Little Rock AR 72203

HUGHES, CHARLES WILLIAM, banker; b. Danville, Ky., Mar. 31, 1910; s. Charles W. and Edith (Galloway) H.; B.A., Vanderbilt U. LL.D., Bethel Coll., 1969; m. Emily Ann Thomas, Aug. 31, 1934; children—Thomas, Robert, William. tchr., Columbia Mil. Acad., 1935-40; with Hermitage Securities Co., Nashville, 1945-49; exec. sec. bd. finance Cumberland Presbyn. Ch., Memphis, 1949-50; with

Valley Fidelity Bank and Trust Co., Knoxville, Tenn., 1951—, sr. v.p., 1960-69, pres., 1969-71, vice chmn., 1971—; lectr. Sch. Consumer Banking, U. Va., 1962-71. Bd. dirs. United Fund, 1956-62. Served to lt. comdr. USNR, 1941-45. Recipient Presdl. Commendation. Mem. Knoxville C. of C. (dir. 1959-63). Home: 303 Mayflower Rd Knoxville TN 37920 Office: Clinch and Market Sts Knoxville TN 37901

HUGHES, DAVID JAMES, physician; b. Charleston, S.C., Jan. 15, 1924; s. John W. and Blanche (Houser) H.; B.S., The Citadel, 1943; M.D., Emory U., 1947; m. Ann C. McCurdy, Dec. 21, 1945; children—Judy L., Janice L., Jay. Intern Grady Meml. Hosp. Atlanta, 1947-48, resident 1948-50; pvt. practice internal medicine, Atlanta, 1953—; mem. staff Emory U., Ga. Baptist, Grady Meml. Hosps., St. Joseph's Infirmary; asst. prof. clin. medicine Emory U. Sch. Medicine, 1957-65, clin. asso. prof. medicine, 1965—. Served to capt., M.C., AUS, 1950-53. Mem. Am., Ga., Fulton County med. assns., So. Med. Soc., Am., Ga. heart assns., Emory U. Alumni Assn. (pres. 1967-68). Home: 918 Oakdale Rd NE Atlanta GA 30307 Office: Decatur North Profl Bldg Decatur GA 30030

HUGHES, ED, profl. football coach. Head coach Houston Oilers. Address: Houston Oilers 6910 Fannin St Houston TX 77025*

HUGHES, FRANKLIN FLETCHER, govt. ofcl.; b. Meridian, Miss., May 24, 1921; s. Fletcher Franklin and Florrie Leona (Pogue) H.; student Meridian Jr. Coll., 1939-41; B.S., Miss. State U., 1948, M.S., 1970; m. Mary Frances Ford, June 2, 1950; children—Benford F., Maretta A. On-farm tng. instr. County Dept. Edn., Meridian, 1948-50; asst. county agt., 4-H leader Miss. Agrl. Extension, State College and Pascagoula, Miss., 1950-54, asso. county agt., Covington County, 1954-58; county leader Jefferson Davis County, Prentiss, Miss., 1959-64, 65—. Pres. Jefferson Davis Council on Aging, 1971—; instl. rep. Comalada dist., Pine Burr council Boy Scouts Am., 1963-70. Pres. Co-ordinating Council Jefferson Davis County, 1965; mem. inter-alumni council State Instns. Higher Learning, 1965—. Served to sgt. AUS, 1942-46. Mem. Jefferson Davis County Livestock Assn. (sec.-treas. 1959—), Miss. County Agts. Assn. (dir.), Miss. Assn. County Agrl. Agts., Nat. Assn. County Agts., Am. Forestry Assn., Nat. Rifle Assn., Nat. Geog. Soc., Epsilon Sigma Phi. Baptist (deacon 1952—, Sunday sch. supt. 1961-64, 66-68). Mason, Rotarian (pres. 1968-69). Home: Box 687 Prentiss MS 39476 Office: PO Box H Prentiss MS 39476

HUGHES, GEORGE FARANT, JR., safety engr.; b. Roanoke, Va., June 22, 1923; s. George Farant and Pattie (Shafer) H.; B.S., Va. Mil. Inst., 1948; m. Frances Miriam Perdue, July 1, 1950. With roadway maintenance dept. N. & W. Ry. Co., Roanoke, Va., 1948, with Liberty Mut. Ins. Co., Roanoke, Balt., 1949-61, asst. div. mgr., Pitts., 1962-63; safety supr. Westinghouse Electric Corp., Balt., 1963-64; supr. safety and accident prevention, Buffalo, 1965-67; safety dir. U.S. Naval Weapons Sta., Yorktown, Va., 1967—. Served with AUS, 1943-46, 50-52. Decorated Bronze Star with oak leaf cluster, Purple Heart. Registered profl. engr., Va.; certified safety profl. Mem. Am. Soc. Safety Engrs., Western N.Y. Safety Conf. (dir. 1966-67), Nat. Soc. Profl. Engr., Am. Soc. Mil. Engrs. Lion. Home: 520 Randolph St Williamsburg VA 23185 Office: US Naval Weapons Sta Yorktown VA 23491

HUGHES, HAROLD DANIEL, elec. engr.; b. Haileyville, Okla., May 5, 1902; s. Daniel John and Florence (Davis) H.; B.S. in Elec. Engring., U. Okla., 1925; m. Ruby Lucille Harper, May 18, 1935; children—Patricia Ann (Mrs. Thomas Ballard Foster), Paula Kay (Mrs. Charles Strader Goree, Jr.). Elec. engr. Okla. Gas & Electric Co., Oklahoma City, 1925-40; staff projects U.S. Dept. Def., 1940-47; elec. engr. Pan Am. Petroleum Corp., Tulsa, 1947-67, Williams Bros. Co., Tulsa, 1967-69; individual practice cons. engring., Tulsa, 1969-70, Williams Bros. Engring. Co., Tulsa, 1970—. Registered profl. engr., Okla. Mem. I.E.E.E., Illuminating Engring. Soc., Nat. Soc. Profl. Engrs. Mason. Home: 3102 E 2d St Tulsa OK 74104

HUGHES, ISRAEL HARDING, JR., city ofcl.; b. Greensboro, N.C., June 5, 1923; s. Israel Harding Sr. and Josephine (Bowen) H.; A.B., U. N.C., 1944; M.Pub. Adminstrn., U. Mich., 1948; m. Dorothy Jean Curtis, Aug. 1, 1953; children—Jean, Thomas Harding, David, Jo Lynn. City planning asst., Flint, Mich., 1948-49; adminstrv. asst. to city mgr., Winston-Salem, N.C., 1949-51, budget dir., 1951-58; city mgr., Aiken, S.C., 1958-63, Durham, N.C., 1963—. Served with USNR, 1943-46, lt. comdr. Res. (ret.). Mem. Internat. City Mgmt. Assn. Episcopalian. Rotarian. Office: City Hall Durham NC 27701

HUGHES, JAMES DONALD, air force officer; b. Balmville, N.Y., July 7, 1922; s. Edward A. and Alice Frances (Cooney) H.; B.S., U.S. Mil. Acad., 1946; grad. Flying Sch., Stewart Field, N.Y., 1946; M.S. in Internat. Affairs, George Washington U., 1966; grad. Nat. War Coll., 1966; m. Mary Elizabeth Masterson, June 4, 1946; children—Donna, Michael, Karen, Robert. Various assignments, U.S., 1946-55; assignment officer, assignment div. dir. mil. personnel Hdqrs. USAF, 1957-61; aide to v.p. of U.S., 1961-62; evaluation officer Hdqrs. 31st Tactical Fighter Wing, George AFB, Cal., 1961; squadron operations officer 306th TACFRON, George AFB, 1961; then wing plans officer Hdqrs. 31st Tactical Fighter Wing, George AFB, comdr. 31st CAMRON, George AFB, 1962; air liaison officer Hdqrs. 2d ADVON, Tan Son Nhut, Vietnam, 1962, asst. operations officer, Hdqrs. 2d Air Div., 1962-63, chief spl. operations br. Hdqrs. 2d Air Div., 1963; personnel staff officer dept. personnel planning Hdqrs. USAF, 1963, asst. exec., 1963-65; dep. for test and evaluation, 4525th Fighter Weapons Wing, Bellis AFB, Nev., 1966, vice comdr., 1966-68; dir. safety Hdqrs. USAFE, Linsdey AS, Germany, 1968; mil. asst. to President Nixon, 1969—. Decorated Air medal with 9 oak leaf clusters, D.F.C. with oak leaf cluster, Bronze Star, Purple Heart, various area and unit medals. Home: Quarters 58-B Westover Av Bolling AFB Washington DC 20332 Office: The White House Washington DC 20500

HUGHES, JOHN THOMAS, educator; b. Selma, N.C., July 5, 1919; s. John Thomas and Anne (Hood) H.; B.S., Wake Forest Coll., 1940; D.D.S., U. Md., 1947; M.P.H., U. N.C., 1958, D.P.H., 1963; m. Elizabeth Smith Disney, Nov. 1, 1947; children—John Thomas, Robert Fred. Tchr., Wilson County Sch., N.C., 1940-42; pvt. practice dentistry, Pittsboro, N.C., 1947-55; pub. health dentist N.C. State Bd. Health, 1955-57, asst. dir., 1960-66, research coor., 1963-66; asso. prof. dept. health adminstrn. Sch. Pub. Health, U. N.C., Chapel Hill, 1966-71, prof., 1971—, asso. prof. dept. dental ecology Sch. Dentistry, 1967—. Supr. residents N.C. Bd. Health, 1966-72; dist. com. Occoneechee council Boy Scouts Am., 1960-72; mem. Chatham County (N.C.) Morehead Scholarship Selection Com., 1959-72, chmn., 1960-71; sec.-treas. Pittsboro (N.C.) Swimming Assn., 1960-63; pres. Pittsboro PTA, 1958-62. Chmn. Pittsboro Planning Bd., 1970-72. Exec. bd. N.C. Council on Food and Nutrition. Served with AUS, 1942-44. Diplomate Am. Bd. Dental Pub. Health. Fellow Am. Coll. Dentists, Am. Pub. Health Assn.; mem. Am. Dental Assn., N.C. (com. chmn. 1960-65), 3d Dist. dental socs., Am. Pub. Health Assn., N.C. Pub. Health Assn. (chmn. 1958-72). Author: Family Patterns of Dental Disease, 1963, (with John T. Fulton) Life Cycle of Human Teeth, 1964, Natural History of Dental Disease (with John T. Fulton), 1965. Editorial bd.: The Health Bulletin, 1962-65. Home: PO Box 237 Pittsboro NC 27312 Office: Room 260 School of Public Health Dept of Health Adminstrn University of North Carolina Chapel Hill NC 27514

HUGHES, KENNETH JERRY, banker; b. Nacogdoches, Tex., Dec. 10, 1933; s. Lee Dulon and Ella Pauline (McLain) H.; B.S. in Speech, Stephen F. Austin U., 1954; m. Nell Johnson, May 30, 1953; children—Kenton Alan, Sherlyn Ann. Cashier, Mchts. Nat. Bank, Port Arthur, Tex., 1956-62; pres. Dallas County State Bank, Carrollton, Tex., 1962—, also dir.; dir. Carrollton Acceptance; owner Intercontinental Travel Agts., Carrollton. Precinct committeeman Republican party, 1964-66. Bd. dirs. Carrollton Hosp. Authority, treas., 1968—. Served with USNR, 1954-56. Recipient Spl. Service award City of Carrollton, 1966, Outstanding Citizen award Greater N.W. C. of C., 1968; named Outstanding Young Businessman Carollton Jr. C. of C., 1964. Mem. Carrollton (pres. 1966-68), Greater N.W. (pres. 1969, dir. 1968—) chambers commerce. Baptist (mem. ch. coms.). Elk. Clubs: Carrollton Lions (pres. 1966-67), Carrollton Rotary (dir. 1969—), Camelot Country (pres., chmn. since 1971—). Home: 1802 Northcrest St Carrollton TX 75006 Office: PO Box 38 Carrollton TX 75006

HUGHES, MAURY, JR., cons. engr.; b. Dallas, Jan. 17, 1923; s. Maury and Ann Louise (Higgins) H.; B.S., Rice Inst., 1948; m. Phoebe Foster, Apr. 23, 1949; children—Phoebe Jane, Carrie Annette, Maury III. With Leo L. Landauer & Assos., Dallas, 1948-72, resident engr., Little Rock, 1950-61, v.p., Dallas, 1955-72; resident engr. Zumwalt & Vinther, Austin, Tex., 1972—. Scoutmaster, Boy Scouts Am., 1950-58, 61-63. Served to lt. (j.g.) USNR, 1953-55. Mem. Am. Soc. Heating, Air Conditioning and Refrigeration Engrs., Illuminating Engring. Soc., Cons. Engrs. Council Tex. (chpt. pres. 1969-70). Home: 1507 The High Rd Austin TX 78711 Office: Scarborough Bldg Austin TX 78711

HUGHES, SISTER M INNOCENT, hosp. adminstr.; b. Bedford, Pa.; B.S., Carnegie Inst. Tech. Adminstr. Mercy Hosp., Pitts., 1944-50; adminstr., v.p., treas. chief exec. officer Holy Cross Hosp., Fort Lauderdale, Fla., 1959—. Mem. Am. Coll. Hosp. Adminstrs. Address: Holy Cross Hosp PO Box 23460 Fort Lauderdale FL 33307

HUGHES, ROYCE WILLIAM, educator, clergyman; b. Hallettsville, Tex., June 11, 1924; s. William David and Sophie (Marak) H.; B.S., St. Edward's U., Austin, 1950; M.A., U. Notre Dame, 1960; S.T.L., Lateran U., Rome, Italy, 1964; B.Th., U. St. Thomas, Rome, 1962, S.T.D., 1965 Ordained priest Roman Catholic Ch., 1964; tchr. pub. schs., Salt Lake City, 1954-58; instr. U. Notre Dame, 1959-60; asst. prof. Villanova U., 1965-69; rector Holy Trinity Ch., Jarrell, Tex., 1969—. Superior, Inst. of the Cenacle in U.S. Served with USNR, 1944-46. Contbr. articles in field to profl. jours. Address: Holy Trinity Ch Jarrell TX 76537

HUGHES, SARAH TILGHMAN, judge; b. Balt., Aug. 2, 1896; d. James Cooke and Elizabeth (Haughton) Tilghman; A.B., Goucher Coll., 1917; LL.D., 1950; LL.B., George Washington U., 1922; LL.D., So. Meth. U., 1967, Ind. State U., 1967, Ia. Wesleyan Coll., 1969; m. George E. Hughes, Mar. 13, 1922. Tchr. Salem Acad. and Coll., Winston-Salem, N.C., 1917-19; police woman Met. Police Dept. Washington, 1919-22; admitted to Tex. bar, 1922, and practiced in Dallas, 1922-35; judge 14th Dist. Ct. of Tex., 1935-61; judge U.S. Dist. Ct., No. Dist. Tex., 1961—; instr. law So. Meth. U., 1942-43. State rep. Tex. Legislature, 1931-35. Active Nat. Fedn. Bus. and Profl. Women's Clubs, 1931—, 1st v.p., 1948-50, pres., 1950-52. Trustee Goucher Coll.; mem. bd. trustees Bishop Coll. mem. nat. commn. UNESCO. Mem. State Bar Tex., Am., Dallas bar assns., Am. Judicature Soc., Nat. Assn. Women Lawyers, Am. Assn. U. Women, Phi Beta Kappa, Delta Sigma Rho, Kappa Beta Pi, Delta Gamma, Delta Kappa Gamma (hon.). Dem. Epis. Clubs: Bus. and Professional Women's (v.p. Internat. Fed. 1953-59). Home: 3816 Normandy St Dallas TX 75205 Office: Fed Bldg 1100 Commerce St Dallas TX 75201

HUGHES, VERLON ELLIS, dentist; b. Mize, Miss., Jan. 22, 1936; s. Chester Lee and Nettie (Mangum) H.; B.S., U. So. Miss., 1956; D.D.S., U. Tenn., 1961; postgrad. Dewey Sch. Orthodontia, 1963; m. Patricia Carole Reddoch, Nov. 27, 1957; children—Lisa Carole, Cathy Lynn. Private practice dentistry, Raleigh, Miss., 1961—, Bay Springs, 1964—; mem. staff Jasper County Gen. Hosp., Bay Springs, Smith County Gen. Hosp., Raleigh. Bd. dirs. Smith County Cancer Soc., 1967—. Mem. U. So. Miss. Alumni Assn. (chpt. pres. 1963), Dean Soc., Pi Kappa Pi, Kappa Mu Epsilon, Xi Psi Phi. Baptist (deacon). Address: Hwy 35 S Raleigh MS 39153

HUGHES, VESTER THOMAS, JR., lawyer; b. San Angelo, Tex., May 24, 1928; s. Vester Thomas and Mary Ellen (Tisdale) H.; student Baylor U., 1945-46; B.A. with distinction, Rice U., 1949; LL.B. cum laude, Harvard, 1952. Admitted to Tex. State bar, 1952; law clk. U.S. Supreme Ct., 1952; asso. firm Robertson, Jackson, Payne, Lancaster & Walker (name later changed to Jackson, Walker, Winstead, Cantwell & Miller), Dallas, 1955—, partner, 1958—; dir. Exell Cattle Co. LX Cattle Co., Post Co., Stewart Engring. Co., Campbell Taggart, Inc.; vis. prof. law So. Methodist U. Grad. Sch. Tax counsel Dallas Community Chest Trust Fund. Bd. dirs. Byrd Found., Larry and Jane Harlan Found., Troy Post Found., Found. for Christian Cummunication, Goodwill Industries Dallas; trustee Dallas Bapt. Coll.; trustee, exec. com. Scottish Rite Hosp. for Crippled Children; bd. overseers vis. com. Harvard Law Sch., 1969—. Served to lt. AUS, 1952-55. Mem. Am. Bar Assn. (mem. council sect. taxation 1969—), Am. Law Inst. (mem. council 1966—), Phi Beta Kappa, Sigma Xi. Baptist. Mason (32 deg.); mem. Order Eastern Star. Home: 1222 Commerce St Dallas TX 75202 Office: First Nat Bank Bldg Dallas TX 75202

HUGHES, WILLIAM CASWELL, physician; b. Evington, Va., Apr. 23, 1918; s. Earl Byrd and Loulie Gaither (Porter) H.; B.A., Lynchburg Coll., 1939; postgrad. U. Louisville, 1945-47; M.D., U. Cin., 1951; m. Florence Elizabeth Holtman, Feb. 14, 1946; children—William Caswell (dec.), Mary Katherine. Sch. prin., tchr., Pittsylvania County, Va., 1939-41; intern, Med. Coll. Va., 1951-52; practice gen. medicine, Franklin County, Boones Mill, Va., 1952—; mem. staffs Franklin Meml. Hosp., pres. med. staff, 1971—, Roanoke Meml. Hosp.; v.p. Blue Ridge Firestone, Inc., Rocky Mount, Va., 1971—. Served to maj. USAF, 1941-45. Decorated D.F.C., Air medal, Purple Heart. Mem. Soc. Gen. Practice, Am. Assn. Gen. Practice, Roanoke Acad. Medicine, Va. Med. Soc., A.M.A., Alpha Omega Alpha. Methodist. Club: Willow Creek Country. Home: Route 5 Box 34 Rocky Mount VA 24151 Office: Boones Mill VA 24065

HUGHES, WILLIAM PULASKI, fgn. service officer; b. Lytle, Tex., Sept. 16, 1911; s. Harry Davis and Clarkie Lee (Riley) H.; B.B.A., Baylor U., 1934; M.B.A., Harvard, 1938, grad. Advanced Mgmt. Program, 1950; m. Elizabeth Oswald, June 18, 1937; children—Clark, Joe Kelly, Craig. Comptroller, Gallaudet Coll., 1938-41; underwriting supr. FHA, 1941-42; staff Office of Coordinator Inter-Am. Affairs, Honduras and Brazil, Dept. of State, 1942-44, analyst Dept. of State, 1945-47; attache, Mexico City, 1947-49; exec. dir., bur. inter-Am. affairs, 1949-51; mem. Mexico-U.S. Internat. Boundary and Water Commn., 1951-54; dir. Office Fgn. Bldgs., directed design and constrn. 42 embassies and consulates, including London, New Delhi, Oslo, Lima, The Hague, Athens, Accra, Leopoldville, Lagos, 1954-61; dir. U.S. operations mission to Bolivia, 1961-63; consul gen. Ciudad Juarez, Mexico, 1963—. Home: Ijamsville MD Office: American Consulate General Ciudad Juarez Chihuahua Mexico

HUGHES, WILLIAM THOMAS, labor counselor; b. Florence, Mo., Oct. 14, 1889; s. O.W. and Ella (Phillips) H.; student Okla. Normal Inst., 1913-16; m. Margaret Dameron, Dec. 22, 1942; children (by previous marriage)-Herbert, Wray, Hazel. Tchr. pub. schs., 1909-16, 19-20; with U.S. Postal Service, 1916-24; engaged in ins. bus., 1924-40; owner, pub. newspaper, 1921-24, 45-48; successively state fire marshal, field auditor, tag and title ofcl. State Tax Commn., State of Okla., 1955-62, state labor commr., Oklahoma City, 1962-67; owner, operator Money Adjustment Service. Trustee Govt. Employees Retirement Fund. Mem. AFL Internat. Assn. Govt. Labor Ofcls., Internat. Platform Assn. Democrat. Mem. Christian Ch. Rotarian, K.P. Home: Star Route Durant OK 74701 Office: 1123 Linwood St Oklahoma City OK 73106

HUGHSTON, HAROLD VAUGHAN, lawyer; b. Tuscumbia, Ala., Aug. 15, 1915; s. Hubert H. and Lutie (Vaughan) H.; LL.B., U. Ala., 1940; m. Lucy C. Allison, Sept. 19, 1948; children—Caroline, Lucy Ann, Harold Vaughan, James D. Admitted to Ala. bar, 1940; practiced in Tuscumbia, 1940-42, 46-47, 55—; mem. firm Kirk, Rather and Hughston, 1955—; judge Colbert Law and Equity Ct., Tuscumbia, 1947-48; circuit judge 11th and 31st Ala. Jud. Circuits, 1948-55. Dir. 1st Nat. Bank, Tuscumbia, Sheffield Fed. Savs. & Loan Assn. (Ala.), New Southland Life Ins. Co.; v.p., dir. Nat. Telephone of Ala. Solicitor, Colbert County, Ala., 1947, now atty., city atty., Tuscumbia, 1965—; atty. Colbert County Bd. Edn., 1964—; mem. City Bd. Edn., also chmn.; atty. Colbert County Commn. Served to capt. Judge Adv. Gen. Corps, AUS, 1942-46. Mem. Ala., 31st Jud. (pres. 1970-71), Colbert County bar assns., Nat. Alumni Assn. U. Ala. (pres. 1970-71), Farah Law Soc., V.F.W., Am. Legion, Kappa Alpha, Phi Delta Phi, Alpha Beta Housing Corp. (pres. 1964—). Presbyn. (elder, trustee). Kiwanian (dist. gov. 1955). Home: 805 E 4th St Tuscumbia AL 35674 Office: Old State Nat Bank Bldg Tuscumbia AL 35674

HUGIN, ADOLPH CHARLES, lawyer, engr., inventor; b. Washington, Mar. 28, 1907; s. Charles and Eugenie (Vigny) H.; B.S. in Elec. Engring., George Washington U., 1928; M.S. in Elec. Engring., Mass. Inst. Tech., 1930; J.D., Georgetown U., 1934; LL.M., Harvard, 1947; S.J.D., Catholic U. Am., 1949. Examiner, U.S. Patent Office, 1928; engr. Gen. Electric Co., Lynn, Mass., 1928-30, patent investigator, Washington, 1930-33, patent atty., Washington and Schenectady, 1933-46; engr. Gen. Electric Co., Schenectady, 1942-45; practiced in Cambridge, Mass.; 1946-47; vis. prof. law Catholic U. Am., 1949-55; pvt. practice law, cons. engr. Washington, 1947—. Bd. dirs. St. Margaret's Fed. Credit Union, 1963-67, 1st v.p., 1965-67. Mem. Schenectady com. Boy Scouts Am., 1940-42; charter mem., 1st bd. mgrs. Schenectady Catholic Youth League, 1935-38, hon. life mem. 1946; chmn. St. Margaret's Bldg. Fund, 1954; lector St. Margaret's Parish, 1966-68, lector-commentator St. Michael's Parish, 1969—; mem. St. Margaret's Parish Council, 1969-71. Registered profl. elec. and mech. engr., D.C.; registered patent atty. U.S. Patent Office. Mem. Holy Name Soc. (parish pres. 1950-52, pres. Prince Georges County sect. 1953, pres. Washington archdiocesan union 1953-55), St. Vincent de Paul Soc. (parish conf. pres. 1965—, pres. county particular council 1959-61, rep. Prince George County on Washington Archdiocesan Central Council Soc. 1961-62), St. Margaret's Parish Con-fraternity of Christian Doctrine (pres. 1960-61), Council of Catholic Men (pres. so. county deanery 1956-58, 65-68), Men's Retreat League (exec. bd. Washington, 1954-58, St. Margaret's Retreat Group capt. 1965-68), Nocturnal Adoration Soc., John Carroll Soc., Am. Bar Assn., Am. Patent Law Assn., Delta Theta Phi. Club: Catholic Men's First Friday. Author: Trade Regulatory Arrangements and the Antitrust Laws, 1949; also articles in field of patents, copyrights, antitrust, radio and air law. Editor-in-chief Bull. Am. Patent Law Assn., 1949-54. Patentee in field dynamoelectric machines, dynamometers, insulation micrometers, ecology and pollution control, mus. instruments, others. Home: 7602 Boulder St North Springfield VA 22151 Office: Nat Press Bldg Washington DC 20004

HUGULEY, GEORGE MURPHY, textile plant mgr.; b. West Point, Ga., Oct. 26, 1912; s. William Gaines and Corinne Stewart (Murphy) H.; student Ga. Inst. Tech., 1935; m. Jean Linn, Jan. 1, 1935; children—George Gilreath, Rebecca Jean (Mrs. David James Felkel). With Dixie Mills, LaGrange, Ga., 1934-37; asst. supt. Scottdale Mills, (Ga.), 1937-39; supt. Bonham Cotton Mills (Tex.), 1939-46, Pelzer (S.C.) upper plant Kendall Mills, 1946-50; supt. Clinton Mills (S.C.), 1950-63, plant mgr., 1963—. Trustee Laurens County Dist. 56, 1951-69, sec. bd., 1963-69. Mem. Clinton C. of C., Phi Psi. Club: Clinton Lions (past dir.), Lakeside Country of Clinton (pres. 1957). Home: 309 Spruce St Clinton SC 29325 Office: 600 Academy St Clinton SC 29325

HUIE, WILLIAM BRADFORD, author; b. Hartselle, Ala., Nov. 13, 1910; s. John Bradford and Margaret Lois (Brindley) H.; A.B., U. Ala., 1930; m. Ruth Puckett, Oct. 27, 1934. Mem. Phi Beta Kappa. Author: Mud on the Stars, 1942; The Fight for Air Power, 1942; Can Do: The Story of the Seabees, 1944; From Omaha to Okinawa, 1945; The Case Against the Admirals, 1946; The Revolt of Mamie Stover, 1951; the Execution of Private Slovik, 1954; The Crime of Ruby McCollum, 1956; Wolf Whistle, 1959; The Americanization of Emily, 1959; The Hero of Iwo Jima, 1960; Hotel Mamie Stover, 1963; The Hiroshima Pilot, 1964; Three Lives for Mississippi, 1965; The Klansman, 1967. Author numerous mag. articles and stories. Home: Hartselle AL 35046

HUISMAN, GARY BRANT, librarian; b. Grand Haven, Mich., Apr. 8, 1940; s. Henry J. and Jennie (Hoebeke) H.; A.B., Calvin Coll., 1963; postgrad. U. Mich., summer 1964, M.S.L., Western Mich. U., 1966. Librarian, Covenant Coll., Lookout Mountain, Tenn., 1966—. Mem. A.L.A., Assn. Coll. and Research Libraries, Assn. for Advancement Christian Scholarship. Home: 404 Carter Dr Lookout Mountain TN 37350

HULCHER, WENDELL ELLSWORTH, govt. ofcl.; b. Girard, Ill., Nov. 3, 1922; s. Elmer Ellsworth and Vena (Thompson) H.; M.B.A., Harvard, 1950; m. Violet Marie Bell, Nov. 27, 1946; children—Karen Marie (Mrs. Standfest), Larry Ellsworth, Randall Kent, Philipp Lynn. Mgmt. cons. asso. McKinsey & Co. Washington, 1952-54; mgr. various marketing and product planning depts. Lincoln-Mercury div. Ford Motor Co., Dearborn, Mich., 1954-66; mayor, Ann Arbor, Mich., 1965-69; dep. dir. Office Intergovt. Relations, Exec. Office of Pres., Washington, 1969—. Mgmt. cons., 1966-69. Mem. World Service and Finance Com., Detroit Conf. Meth. Ch., 1964-69. Mem. City Council, Ann Arbor, 1960-64; mem. Gov.'s Spl. Commn. on Urban Problems, 1966-68. Trustee Ann Arbor Area Found. Served to maj. USAAF, 1941-46, USAF, 1950-52. Decorated D.F.C., Air medal with 3 clusters. Mem. Harvard Bus. Sch. Assn. Republican. Methodist. Home: 9028 Marseille Dr Potomac MD 20854 Office: Exec Office Bldg 17th and Pennsylvania Av NW Washington DC 20006

HULEN, ALFRED CLAYTON, research inst. exec.; b. Mexico, Mo., Jan. 25, 1904; s. Edward Kennan and Blanche (Gillespie) H.; student U. Mo., 1921-22; m. Margaret Worner, Sept. 30, 1931; children—Kennan, Margaret (Mrs. Bobby Ray Huggins), Clayton, Martha (Mrs. Kevin H. McKenna). Mem. accounting staff Mo. Power & Light Co., Mexico, 1923-40, sr. accounting and fiscal officer, 1941-46; comptroller Slick Airways, Inc., 1946-48; accountant, bus. mgr. Earl F. Slick, 1948-50; controller, asst. treas. Southwest Research Inst., San Antonio, 1950-55, treas., 1955-61, sec.-treas., 1961-69, v.p. finance, sec., 1970—; sec.-treas. Southwest Patents, Inc., San Antonio; dir., asst. sec.-treas. Sci. Indsl. Park, San Antonio. Mem. Am. Mgmt. Assn., Nat. Assn. Accountants, Tex. Good Roads Assn., San Antonio C. of C., Baptist. Optimist (life), Modern Woodman of Am. Home: 8401 N New Braunfels St San Antonio TX 78209 Office: 8500 Culebra Rd San Antonio TX 78284

HULKA, JAROSLAV FABIAN, physician; b. N.Y.C., Sept. 29, 1930; s. Jaroslav Hugo and Milada (Touskova) H.; B.A., Harvard, 1952; M.D., Columbia, 1956; m. Barbara E. Sorenson, Nov. 13, 1954; children—Carol Ann, Gregory Fabian, Bryan Herbert. Intern, Roosevelt Hosp., N.Y.C., 1956-57; resident Sloane Hosp. for Women, Columbia-Presbyn. Med. Center, N.Y.C., 1957-60; Josiah Macy, Jr. fellow Columbia-Presbyn. Med. Center, 1960-61; practice medicine specializing in obstetrics and gynecology, 1961—; asst. prof. obstetrics and gynecology U. Pitts. Sch. Med., 1961-66, asso. mem. grad. faculty, 1962-66, acting chmn. dept. obstetrics and gynecology, 1963-64; asso. prof. dept. obstetrics and gynecology Sch. Medicine, U. N.C., Chapel Hill, 1967—, asso. prof. dept. maternal and child health, 1967—, asso. dir. Carolina Population Center, 1967—. Diplomate Am. Bd. Obstetrics and Gynecology. Fellow Am. Coll. Obstetricians and Gynecologists; mem. Soc. for Gynecol. Investigation, Assn. Profs. Obstetrics and Gynecology, Am. Fertility Soc., A.A.A.S., A.M.A. Home: 2317 Honeysuckle Rd Chapel Hill NC 27514 Office: Obstet and Gynecol Dept Meml Hosp Chapel Hill NC 27514

HULL, BEN LEROY, physician; b. New Florence, Pa., Nov. 20, 1895; s. Ben Covode and Sadie (Decker) H.; A.B., U. Pa., 1921, M.D., 1925, M.Med.Sci., 1940; postgrad. Mass. Gen. Hosp., Boston, Reconstrn. Hosp., N.Y.C., 1933-34; m. Helen Hauk Stevens, June 27, 1926; children—Suzanne E., Jess Stevens. Intern, Ancon (C.Z.) Hosp., 1925-26; practice medicine, specializing in orthopaedic surgery, Altoona, Pa., 1926-58; chief orthopaedic surgery Gorgas Hosp., C.Z., 1958-63; orthopedist dept. medicine and surgery VA Regional Office, St. Petersburg, Fla., 1963—. Med. adviser Polio Found., Blair County, Pa., 1941-58. Served with U.S. Army, 1917-19. Diplomate Am. Bd. Orthopaedic Surgery. Fellow Am. Acad. Orthopaedic Surgery, A.C.S., Internat. Coll. Surgeons; mem. A.M.A., Pa. Med. Soc., Am. Assn. Ry. Surgeons. Home: 3704 El Centro St St Petersburg Beach FL 33706 Office: VA Regional Office St Petersburg FL 33706

HULL, DAVID CARLOCK, petrochem. co. exec.; b. Marion, Va., Dec. 15, 1908; s. Wythe M. and Clyde (Carlock) H.; B.S., Emory and Henry Coll., Emory, Va., 1930, D.Sc., 1969; M.S., U. Tenn., 1931; m. Nola C. Murray, Sept. 17, 1933; children—Betty Jane (Mrs. Earl Roberts, Jr.), David Carlock, Jr. Chemist, supt. acetic anhydride dept., supt. acid div., prodn. mgr. Clinton Engring. Works, Tenn. Eastman Co., Kingsport, 1931-50; mgr., v.p. Tex. Eastman Co. div. Eastman Kodak Co., Longview, 1950-63, pres., 1963—; pres., dir. First Fed. Savs. & Loan Assn.; dir. First Nat. Bank, Longview, Bd. dirs. Longview YMCA; bd. mgrs. Good Shepard Hosp.; mem. Engring. Found., U. Tex., Austin. Mem. Tex. Mfrs. Assn. (dir.), Am. Chem. Soc., Am. Inst. Chem. Engrs. Methodist. Patentee in field. Home: 1104 Yates Dr Longview TX 75601 Office: PO Box 7444 Longview TX 75601

HULL, DOYLE EDWIN, banker; b. Hawthorne, Cal., May 18, 1933; s. James Everett and Sadie Ellen (Lucas) H.; B.S. in Bus. Adminstrn. cum laude, N.E. Mo. State Tchrs. Coll., 1957; postgrad. Rutgers U. Stonier Grad. Sch. Banking, 1967-69; m. Camilla Suzanne Oestreich, June 9, 1962; children—Patricia Lynn, Doyle Edwin, David Brian. With Va. Nat. Bank and predecessor, Norfolk, 1957—, sr. v.p., mgr. mortgage loan operations, 1964—; dir. Mortgage Investment Corp., Richmond, Va., exec. v.p., 1969—. Mem. Norfolk Model City Commn., 1971—. Bd. dirs. Tidewater Assn. Home Builders Scholarship Found., Tidewater Community Colls. Served with USMCR, 1951-54. Mem. Norfolk C. of C. Methodist. Mason. Club: Harbor (Norfolk). Home: 7615 Nancy Dr Norfolk VA 23518 Office: Virginia National Bank 1 Commercial Pl Norfolk VA 23510

HULL, JAMES MONTGOMERY, clergyman, ch. assn. adminstr.; b. Kirksville, Mo., Mar. 9, 1926; s. Thomas Noel and Edna (Montgomery) H.; A.B., U. Mo., 1948; B.D., Mo. Sch. Religion Grad. Sem., 1956; postgrad. George Washington U.; m. Mary Virginia Mathieson, Dec. 22, 1946; children—Mary Christine, Constance Ann, James Montgomery, Thomas Lewis. Ordained to ministry Christian Ch., 1948; pastor chs. in Montgomery City, Mo., 1945-47, Clifton Heights, St. Louis, 1948-49, Fayette, Mo., 1950-57, Sullivan, Ill., 1957-60; adminstr. Emily E. Flinn Home, Marion, Ind., 1960-68, Fla. Christian Home, Jacksonville, Fla., 1968—. Mem. state bd. Mo. Assn. Christian Chs., 1955-57, Ill. Disciples of Christ, 1957-60. Fellow Am. Coll. Nursing Home Adminstrs.; mem. Am., Fla. assns. homes for aging, Am., Fla. nursing home assns., Ind. Assn. Philanthropic Homes for Aged (sec. 1961-63), Disciples Christ Hist. Soc., Soc. Desc. Colonial Clergy (life). Rotarian. Club: Mississinewa Camera. Home: 3524 Corby St Jacksonville FL 32205 Office: Fla Christian Home 1071 Edgwood Av Jacksonville FL 32205

HULSEY, MARK, JR., lawyer; b. Jacksonville, Fla., Sept. 25, 1922; B.A., U. Fla., 1943, J.D., 1948. Admitted to Fla. bar, 1948, U.S. Supreme Ct. bar, 1966; asst. U.S. atty., So. dist. Fla., 1952-53. Mem. Am., Jacksonville (pres. 1962) bar assns., Fla. Bar (gov. 1964-68, pres. 1969-70), Acad. Fla. Trial Lawyers, Phi Delta Phi. Address: PO Box 1086 Jacksonville FL 32201*

HULSEY, PAUL DOUGLAS, police chief; b. Beeville, Tex., Sept. 22, 1934; s. Paul Salis and Nancy Pauline (Wisenbaker) H.; A.A., Tex. Southmost Coll., 1959; postgrad. Tex. A. and I. U., 1966, Sam Houston State U., 1971; m. Mary Jo Alsobrook, May 25, 1957; children— Douglas, Steve, Daniel, Tamara. Patrolman, Police Dept., Harlingen, Tex., 1955-56, Plainview, 1960-63, Hale County Sheriff's Dept., 1963-64; with Kingsville (Tex.) Police Dept., 1965—, police chief, 1968-72; chief police, Amarillo, Tex., 1972—. Team capt. United Fund, Kingsville, 1969. Served with AUS, 1952-55. Decorated Purple Heart; recipient distinguished service and outstanding citizen award Jr. C. of C., 1960. Mem. F.B.I. Acad. Assos. Tex., Tex. Police Chiefs Assn. (exec. bd. 1970-72). Office: Chief Police Police Dept Amarillo TX 79101

HULTMAN, CHARLES WILLIAM, educator; b. Oelwein, Ia., Apr. 6, 1930; s. John William and Alma (Loeb) H.; B.A., Upper Ia. U., 1952; M.A., Drake U., 1957; Ph.D., U. Ia., 1960; m. Irene Oliver, June 7, 1957; children— Susan, Gregory. Asst. prof. U. Ky., Lexington, 1960-64, prof. econs., 1967—, chmn. dept. econs., 1969-71, asso. dir. Center for Developmental Change, 1971—; vis. asso. prof. U. Cal., 1964-65. Served with AUS, 1952-55. Fulbright lectr. Ireland, 1967-68. Mem. Am., So., Midwest econ. assns. Lutheran. Author: International Finance, 1963; American Business and the Common Market, 1964; Problems of Economic Development, 1967; Ireland in the World Economy, 1969; (with M. Wasserman, R. Ware) International Economics, 1969. Home: 3341 Crown Crest Lexington KY 40502

HUMANN, WALTER JOHANN, aerospace co. exec.; b. Dallas, May 30, 1937; s. Walter Christoph and Lois (Smith) H.; B.S. in Physics, Mass. Inst. Tech., 1959; M.B.A., Harvard, 1961; postgrad. U. Okla., 1961-62; J.D. (LL.B.), S.M.U.; m. Beatrice Read, July 31, 1959; children—Walter John, David Andrew, Lisa Kathleen. Admitted to Tex. bar, 1966; gen. mgr. consumer products div. Dorsett Electronics, Inc., Norman, Okla., 1962-63; engr. project mgmt. staff Ling-Temco-Vought, Inc., Dallas, 1963-67; partner G.O.F. & Co., 1964-67; sec., asst. treas. LTV Aerospace Corp., Dallas, 1967-70, v.p., sec., gen. counsel, 1970-72, corporate v.p. coml. group, 1972—; sec. Computer Tech. former subsidiary LTV Aerospace Corp., 1968-70, bd. chmn. LTV Recreation Devel., Inc., LTV Edn. Systems, Inc., Internat. Technovation, Inc. Dir. Oak Cliff Savs. & Loan Assn., United Nat. Bank of Dallas. Asst. to nat. postmaster-gen. and White House fellow, 1966-67; nat. chmn. Citizens for a Postal Corp.; vice chmn. Dallas Task Force on Edn.; mem. sec. labor's adv. bd. employment security, 1968-70; chmn. Skyline Adv. Bd. Apptd. to President's commn. on White House Fellows, 1968-69. Served as 1st lt. AUS, 1961-62. Recipient Outstanding Young Man of Dallas award Dallas Jaycees, 1969; named One of Five Outstanding Young Texans, Texas Jaycees, 1970; One of Ten Outstanding Young Men of Am., U.S. Jaycees, 1970. Mem. White House Fellows Assn. (pres. 1968-69), Am., Tex., Dallas bar assns., Dallas C. of C. (vice chmn. bd. dirs. 1972—), Dallas 40, Idlewild, Sigma Xi, Sigma Alpha Epsilon. Episcopalian. Clubs: Dallas Forum, Dervish, Press (Dallas). Home: 3131 Lovers Lane Dallas TX 75225 Office: LTV Aerospace Corp PO Box 5003 Dallas TX 75222

HUMBER, ROBERT LEE, lawyer; b. Greenville, N.C., May 30, 1898; s. Robert Lee and Lena Clyde (Davis) H.; A.B., Wake Forest Coll., 1918, LL.B., 1921, LL.D., 1949; M.A., Harvard, 1926; B. Litt., Oxford (Eng.) U.; Rhodes scholar from N.C., 1923; Am. field service fellow U. Paris, 1926-28; LL.D., U. N.C., 1958; H.H.D., Duke U., 1967; m. Lucie Berthier, Oct. 16, 1929; children—Marcel Berthier, John Leslie. Admitted to N.C. bar, 1920; tutor dept. govt. history and econs. Harvard, 1919-20; lawyer and bus. exec., Paris, France, 1930-40. Founded at Davis Island, N.C., Dec. 1940, Movement for World Fedn. whose prins. and objectives were embodied in a resolution, approving World Fedn., that has been passed by 16 State Legislatures of U.S. Rep. So Council on Internat. Relations, San Francisco Conf., 1945, Vice pres. United World Federalists, 1947-50, mem. Nat. Exec. Council, 1947-49, pres. N.C. br., 1961-64, co-founder, 1947; v.p. N.C. Baptist Conv. 1947. Trustee Meredith Coll., 1947-50, Wake Forest Coll., 1951-54, 59-60, pres. bd., chmn. exec. com., 1960, life trustee, 1970—. Chmn., N.C. Art Commn., 1951-61; mem. N.C. State Arts Council (chmn. 1964-67); mem. Edenton Hist. Commn., pres., 1962—, bd. dirs. Coastal Plains Planning and Devel. Commn., 1962—, chmn. 1962-64; chmn. bd. trustees N.C. Mus. Art, 1961—; mem. N.C. Conservatory Commn., 1962-63, N.C. Capital Planning and Heritage Sq. Commn., 1962-65, Gov.'s Study Com. in Vocational Rehab. 1967—, N.C. Mus. of Art Bldg. Commn., 1967—, Pitt County Devel. Commn., 1959—; bd. dirs. Pitt County chpt. A.R.C., 1957—; mem. N.C. Mus. Art Found., 1963—. Alternate del. Democratic Nat. Conv., 1956; mem. N.C. Senate, 1959, 61, 63. Bd. dirs., mem. exec. com. N.C. State Symphony; mem. Tryon Palace Commn.; trustee Pitt Indsl. Edn. Center (chmn. 1961-64), Pitt Tech. Inst. (chmn. 1964—). Served as 2d lt., F.A., U.S. Army, 1918. Awarded World Govt. News medal for most outstanding service by an individual to World Fedn., 1948, Am. War Dads Prize for greatest single contbr. toward World Peace, 1948; Salmagundi medal for enduring service to art on state and nat. level, 1966; Peace award Am. Freedom Assn., 1967. Mem. N.C. Art Soc. (dir. 1945—, chmn. exec. com. 1949-61, pres. 1955-61), N.C. Lit. and Hist. Assn. (pres. 1950), Roanoke Island Hist. Assn. (chmn. 1955-59), Pitt County Hist. Soc. (pres. 1964-68), Community Coll. Trustees Assn. (pres. 1968—), Am. Legion, Epsilon Pi Tau, Omicron Delta Kappa, Sigma Phi Epsilon, Phi Beta Kappa, Phi Delta Phi. Democrat. Baptist. Rotarian. Clubs: Watauga (Raleigh); Salmagundi, Harvard, Century (N.Y.C.). Author of resolution: The Declaration of the Federation of the World. Home: 117 W 5th St Greenville NC 27834

HUME, DAVID, lawyer; b. Eagle Pass, Tex., Oct. 2, 1915; s. David E. and Lupita (James) H.; B.A., U. Tex., 1937; student Temple U. Sch. Law, 1939-41; LL.B. with honors, So. Meth. U., 1946; m. F. Arlee Eaton, Aug. 28, 1943 (div. 1964); children—David III, Stephen; m. 2d, Margaret Williams; one dau., Marge Ann. Admitted to the Texas State bar, 1946, and D.C., bars 1954, U.S. Supreme Ct., 1948, also court Mil. Justice, FCC, ICC; trial atty. U.S. Dept. Justice, 1947, spl. asst. to atty. gen. U.S., 1948; with firm Steptoe & Johnson, Washington, 1954-58; mem. firm Hume & Stewart, Washington, 1958-65; mem. firm Hume & Hume, Eagle Pass, Tex., 1965—. Rep. Am. Bar Assn., 12th Inter-Am. Bar Assn. conv., Bogota, Columbia, 1961. Mem. Md. Bd. Natural Resources. Chmn. Democratic Com. So. Md., 1958, treas., 1958-60; mem. Dem. Nat. Adv. Council, 1958-60; candidate for Gov. Md., 1962. Bd. dirs. Balt. Civic Opera. Served with Submarine Service, USNR, World War 11, Korean War; capt. Res. Decorated Bronze Star. Mem. Am., Inter-Am., Md., Border bar assns., Nat. Trial Lawyers Assn. (v.p.), Tex. Criminal Def. Lawyers Assn., Judge Adv. Assn., Am. Vets. Com., Am. Legion, Navy League, S.A.R., Md. Hist. Soc., Izaak Walton League, Sigma Chi, Phi Delta Phi. Clubs: Terrapin (University of Maryland); Jefferson Island (St. Mary's County, Md.); Marlboro Hunt (Prince George's County, Md.); Taylor's Landing Rod and Gun (Washington County, Md.); Hawthorne Country (Charles County, Md.). Author numerous articles on conservation, govt. and agrarian reform, Latin Am. Home: Eagle Pass TX 78852 Office: Quarry and Madison Sts Eagle Pass TX 78852

HUME, PAUL CHANDLER, music editor; b. Chgo., Dec. 13, 1915; s. Robert Woolsey and Katherine English (Rockwell) H.; ed. U. Chgo., 1937; Mus.D., Thiel Coll., 1969; m. Ruth Fox, Dec. 29, 1949; children—Paul, Michael, Ann, Peter. Music editor Washington Post, 1947—; prof. music, dir. glee club Georgetown U., 1950; organist and baritone, 1936—; solo, oratorio and opera appearances in Chgo. and Washington, 1936—. Mem. Am. Assn. U. Profs., Music Critics Assn. (exec. com. 1962-63). Author: Catholic Church Music, 1956; (with Mrs. Hume) The Lion of Poland, 1962, The King of Song, 1964. Co-editor: Hymnal of Christian Unity, 1964. Home: 3625 Tilden St NW Washington DC 20008 Office: 1515 L St NW Washington DC 20005

HUMELSINE, CARLISLE HUBBARD, pres. found.; b. Hagerstown, Md., Mar. 12, 1915; s. Charles Ellsworth and Anna Barbara (McNamee) H.; A.B., U. Md., 1937; LL.D., Coll. William and Mary, 1963, Hampden-Sydney Coll., 1970; m. Mary Miller Speake, Aug. 16, 1941; children—Mary Carlisle (Mrs. Thomas K. Norment), Barbara Anne (Mrs. Roger Harmon). Editor pubs., spl. asst. to pres. U. Md., 1937-41; dir. personnel Colonial Williamsburg, 1945-46, now pres. The Colonial Williamsburg Found.; dir. Office Departmental Administrn., U.S. Dept State, 1946-47, exec. sec., 1947-50, dep. under sec. state, 1950; spl. asst. to sec. state at meeting Council Fgn. Ministers, London, Nov.-Dec. 1947. Dir. Grand Teton Lodge Co., Caneel Bay Plantation, Chesapeake & Potomac Telehone Co., United Va. Bankshares, Inc., dir., mem. exec. com. N.Y. Life Ins. Co.; dir. Garfinckel, Brooks Bros., Miller & Rhoads. Adv. cons. George C. Marshall Research Library, Papers of George Washington, Robert E. Lee Meml. Found. Former chmn., Va. Bd. Conservation and Econ. Devel.; mem. bd., chmn. study com., finance com. Mariners' Mus.; past pres. Va. Mus. Fine Arts; mem. bd. Jamestown Corp.; mem. bd., mem. exec. com., mem. officers nominating com., awards com. Nat. Trust for Historic Preservation; former chmn. Am. Revolution Bicentennial Comm.; bd. dirs. Sleepy Hollow Restorations, Jamestown Found. Served from lt. to col. AUS, 1941-45; asst. mil. sec. to chief staff, mem. mil. secretariat U.S. Army, Que., Malta, Yalta, Pottsdam confs. Decorated D.S.M., Bronze Star. Mem. Am. Antiquarian Soc. (mem. bd.), Alpha Tau Omega, Omicron Delta Kappa, Pi Delta Epsilon. Democrat. Episcopalian. Clubs: F Street (Washington); Commonwealth, Forum (Richmond). Home: Coke-Garrett House Williamsburg VA 23185 Office: The Colonial Williamsburg Found Williamsburg VA 23185

HUMES, JAMES CALHOUN, lawyer; b. Williamsport, Pa., Oct. 31, 1934; s. Samuel Hamilton and Elenor (Graham) H.; student Hill Sch., Pottstown, Pa., 1947-52, Stowe Sch., Buckinghamshire, Eng., 1952-53, Williams Coll., 1953-55; A.B., George Washington U., 1959, LL.B., 1962; m. Dianne Stuart, July 25, 1957; children—Mary Stuart, Rachel Bailey. Admitted to Pa. bar, 1963; practiced in Williamsport, 1963-67; counsel Greater Phila. C. of C., 1966-67; exec. dir. Phila. Bar Assn., 1967-69; spl. asst. to the Pres., policy planning sect., Washington, 1969-70; dir. Office of Policy and Plans, U.S. Dept. State, 1971—. Mem. Pa. Ho. of Reps., 1962-64. Trustee Pa. Hist. Found.; bd. dirs. Phila. Assn. Retarded Children, Pa. Council on Alcoholism. Mem. S.R., Hist. Soc. Pa., St. Andrew's Soc. Phila., English-Speaking Union, Am., Pa., Phila. bar assns., War 1812 Soc. Republican. Presbyn. Author: Sweet Dream-Tales of a River City. Contbr. articles to mags. Home: 2227 49th St NW Washington DC 20007 Office: US Dept of State Washington DC 20520

HUMPHREY, BURWELL W., hosp. adminstr. Dir. Emory U. Hosp., Atlanta. Address: Emory U Hosp 1364 Clifton Rd NE Atlanta GA 30307*

HUMPHREYS, ALLISON, asso. justice Tenn. Supreme Ct. Address: Supreme Ct Bldg Nashville TN 37201*

HUMPHREYS, CECIL CLARENCE, univ. pres.; b. Paris, Tenn., May 17, 1914; s. Robert Lee and Cecil Clara (Huggins) H.; B.S., M.A., U. Tenn.; Ph.D., N.Y.U., 1957; LL.D., Southwestern at Memphis, 1966; m. Florence Van Natta, Jan. 22, 1949; children—Robert Hunter, Cecil Clarence. Mem. faculty Memphis State U., 1937-41, 47—, dir. Grad. Sch., 1959-60, pres. 1960—; spl. agt. FBI, 1942-44, 46-47. Dir. Union Planters Nat. Bank. Mem. bd. Mid-South Med. Center Council. Commr. Goodwyn Inst. Served to lt. (j.g.) USNR, 1944-46. Mem. Memphis Area C. of C. (dir.), Am. Legion, Mil. Order World Wars, Sigma Chi. Rotarian (dir. Memphis). Club: University (Memphis). Home: 4035 Grandview Memphis TN 38111

HUMPHREYS, EDWIN WARD, tobacco co. exec.; b. Henderson, Ky., July 17, 1910; s. Llewelyn and Vashti (Ward) H.; B.S. in Metall. Engring., U. Ky., 1932; m. Susan Gaines Grover, Sept. 22, 1934; children— Eleanor (Mrs. Robert E. Milward), Edwina (Mrs. Audry W. Simmons, Jr.). Foreman in tobacco processing and maintenance, Lexington, Ky. and Wilson, N.C., 1934-37; tobacco buyer, 1938-45; with Universal Leaf Tobacco Co., and subsidiaries, 1956—, v.p. charge operations, 1955-65, sr. v.p., 1966—, also dir.; v.p. subsidiary Southwestern Tobacco Co.; dir. Greeneville Redrying Co., Southwestern Tobacco Co., Rudolph Hach Co. Recipient Centennial Alumni award U. Ky., 1965. Mem. Tobacco Assn. U.S. (pres. 1951-53, bd. dirs.), Phi Delta Theta. Presbyn. (elder). Clubs: Jiggers; Idle Hour Country (Lexington); Country of Va., Commonwealth, Rotunda (Richmond). Home: RFD 3 Georgetown KY 40324 Office: 201 S 3d St Richmond VA 23219

HUMPHREYS, GRUNDY WEST, leather goods co. exec.; b. Huntsville, Ark., June 1, 1889; s. John Patterson and Clementine (Bradshaw) H.; student N. Tex. State U.; m. Ruth Abrams, July 20, 1920; 1 dau., Elaine (Mrs. J.R. Floyd). Tchr. pub. schs., Tex., 1908-18; organizer Justin Leather Goods Co., Nocona, Tex., 1919, pres., gen. mgr., chmn. bd., 1955—. Mem. City Council, Nocona, 1931-37. Recipient Distinguished Citizen award, 1965. Mem. Nocona C. of C. (pres.). Home: 410 Sherman St Nocona TX 76255 Office: 105 Clay St Nocona TX 76255

HUMPHREYS, HOMER ALEXANDER, educator; b. nr. Waynesboro, Va., Feb. 7, 1902; s. Lewis Greenberry and Annie (Sampson) H.; B.A., Bridgewater Coll., 1928; M.A., U. Va., 1941, research fellow, 1943-44; m. Ruth Elizabeth Gilbert, Sept. 1, 1926; children—Faye (Mrs. Hezekiah Sadler), Joye (Mrs. James Malcolm Hart Harris, Jr.), Anne (Mrs. Richard Edward Talman), Homer Alexander, Jane (dec.), Kaye (Mrs. Ralph Franklin Jones, Jr.). Instr. Moyock (N.C.) High Sch., 1928-29; prin. Darlington Heights (Va.) High Sch., 1929-33, Green Bay (Va.) High Sch., 1934-44; supervising prin. West Point (Va.) High Sch., 1944-65; gen. supr. instrn. Williamsburg-James City County Schools, 1965-67; dir. aviation edn. Mont. State U., Missoula, also Eastern Coll. Edn., Billings, Mont., summers 1954, 55, U. Va., Charlottesville, summers 1956-71; instr. Coll. William and Mary Extension, 1963-68. Coordinator, Civil Def., King William County and Town of West Point, 1950-61. Served from 2d lt. to lt. col. USAF, Civil Air Patrol, 1945—; dir. aviation edn. Va. Wing, Civil Air Patrol, 1956-65. Mem. N.E.A. (past 1st zone v.p. dept. audio-visual instrn.), Va. High Sch. League (chmn. 1955-57), King William-King and Queen Edn. Assn. (pres. 1956-58), Phi Delta Kappa. Kiwanian (pres. West Point 1949, lt. gov. capital dist. div. four 1956). Author: A History of Education in Prince Edward County, Va., 1941; column Wings Over Va., 1956-62; also numerous articles, reports and surveys. Home: 110 Oxford Circle Williamsburg VA 23185

HUMPHREYS, RAYMOND V, orgn. exec.; b. Huntington, W.Va., May 3, 1911; s. Edward and Zelda (Henson) H. Editor, pub. The Chronicle, Huntington, 1930-35; exec. sec. to mayor, Huntington, 1935-36; exec. sec. W. Va. Republican Finance Com., 1937-38; pres. Asso. Underwriters, 1938-42, Raymond V. Humphreys Assos., 1946-51; mem. West Virginia Ho. Delegates, 1951-52; cons. to Congressman Will E. Neal, Washington, 1953; v.p. Trail-Craft Corp., 1955-57; exec. v.p. Nat. Sales Corp., 1955-57; field rep. Nat. Rep. Congl. Com., Washington, 1957-60, dir. edn. and tng., 1960-63; dir. edn. and training Rep. Nat. Com., 1963-69; mng. partner Raymond V. Humphreys Assos., polit. mgmt. consultants, 1969—; author, developer Moblzn. Rep. Enterprise program. Republican candidate for Ho. of Reps. for 4th Dist. W. Va., 1936-38. Served from pvt. to maj., AUS, 1942-46; maj. AUS, 1951-52. Mem. Nat. (dir. 1950-51). W. Va. (pres. 1948-49) mut. ins. agts. assns. Baptist. Author: Republican Mobilization Training School Handbook, 1960. Contbr. articles to profl. publs. Home: Bull Run Battlefield Haymarket VA 22069 also Lonesome Cedar Farm Hurricane WV Office: Hotel Congressional Washington DC 20003

HUMPHRIES, EUGENE ELMORE, SR., motor freight co. exec.; b. Gaffney, S.C., Apr. 6, 1917, 1917; s. Walter Valley and Eugenia (Peeler) H.; B.A., Furman U., 1939; m. Lillian Rita Maffett, Feb. 19, 1939; 1 son, Eugene Elmore. With So. Bell Telephone and Telegraph Co., Greenville, S.C., 1939-48; traffic rep. Johnson Motor Lines, Inc., Greenville, S.C., 1948-50, dist. sales mgr., 1950-51, Carolina sales mgr., 1951-53, so. sales mgr., 1954-55, gen. sales mgr., Charlotte, 1955-61, v.p. sales, 1961-64, v.p. operations and sales, 1964-69, sr. v.p. operations and sales, 1969—. Mem. regional export expansion council Dept. Commerce, 1960-71. Mem. Am. Transportation Assn., Inc., Nat. Sales Council (bd. dirs., N.C. Sales Council (chmn. 1958-59), Sales Exec. Club, N.C. Motor Carriers Assn., N.C. World Trade Assn., Navy League U.S. Republican. Baptist. Mason (Shriner). Rotarian. Clubs: West Charlotte Rotary, Myers Park Country (Charlotte); Sertoma, Exchange (v.p. 1947-48) (Greenville). Home: 3808 Pomfret Lane Charlotte NC 28211 Office: 2426 N Graham St Charlotte NC 28206

HUMRICKHOUSE, GEORGE RANDOLPH, lawyer; b. Boydton, Va., Dec. 27, 1909; s. John Johnson and Mary Elizabeth (Pleasants) H.; B.S., U. Va., 1933, LL.B., 1933; m. Margaret Page Thompson, Apr. 3, 1941; children—Mary Frances, George Randolph. Admitted to Va. bar, 1933; asso. Hutcheson and Hutcheson, Boydton, 1933-42; asst. U.S. atty. Eastern dist. Va., 1942-47, U.S. atty., 1947-51; partner Williams, Mullen, and Christian and predecessor firms, Richmond, Va., 1951—. Chancellor, Episcopal Diocese Va., 1958—, dep. to Gen. Conv. Diocese Va. and So. Va., 1946—. Bd. dirs. Friends of Library, Richmond. Mem. Am., Va., Richmond bar assns. Democrat. Mason, Kiwanian. Home: 4504 Seminary Av Richmond VA 23227 Office: United Va Bank Bldg Richmond VA 23219

HUNG, WELLINGTON, physician; b. Detroit, Aug. 26, 1932; s. Ching Chong and Florence (Loo) H.; B.S., Am. U., 1953; M.D., George Washington U., 1957; m. Blanche Wong, Aug. 28, 1955; children—Kathleen Gail, Wayne, Elaine Denise, Deborah Lynn. Intern, Washington Hosp. Center, 1957-58; resident Children's Hosp. of D.C., Washington,, 1958-60, endocrinologist, 1962—; fellow Johns Hopkins, 1960-62; chief sect. endocrinology Research Found. of Children's Hosp.; prof. child health and devel. George Washington U.; cons. Washington Hosp. Center, Providence Hosp., Holy Cross Hosp. Silver Spring, Md., DeWitt Army Hosp., Ft. Belvoir, Va. Am. Acad. Pediatrics grantee, 1962. Fellow Am. Acad. Pediatrics, Am. Coll. Nutrition, A.C.P.; mem. Endocrine Soc., Soc. Pediatric Research, Am. Thyroid Assn., Am. Diabetes Assn., Am. Fedn. Clin. Research, Soc. Nuclear Medicine. Editor: Adolescent Endocrinology, 1970. Contbr. articles profl. jours. Home: 8902 Maxwell Dr Potomac MD 20854 Office: 2125 13th St NW Washington DC 20009

HUNGATE, JOSEPH IRVIN, JR., educator; b. Killarney, W.Va., Apr. 30, 1921; s. Joseph Irvin and Nellie (Lickliter) H.; A.B. cum laude, Concord Coll., 1948; M.A., U. Chgo., 1950; Ph.D., U. Tex., 1963; postgrad. St. Louis U., 1948-49; m. Betty Lou Hatzenbuehler, Sept. 11, 1948; children—Ann Elisabeth, Joseph Irvin III, Sue Carol. Disaster rep. Chgo. chpt. A.R.C., 1950; chief psychiat. social work service Valley Forge Army Hosp., Phoenixville, Pa., 1951; psychiat. caseworker Fitzsimons Army Hosp., Denver, 1952-53; chief med. social work service Ft. Jackson, S.C., 1953-55; class dir., social work specialist program Army Med. Sch., San Antonio, 1955-58; asso. prof. social work U. Tex., 1959-68; dean and prof. social work Grad. Sch. Social Work, U. S.C., Columbia, 1968—. Teaching cons. Austin State Hosp., 1963-68, William S. Hall Psychiat. Inst., 1972; spl. cons. Tech. Tng. div. Bur. Family Services, Dept. Health Edn. and Welfare, Washington, 1962-65; mem. profl. adv. com. S.C. Mental Health Assn.; chmn. S.C. Gov.'s Com. on Criminal Adminstrn. and Juvenile Delinquency; mem. S.C. Gov.'s Health and Welfare Council. Served to 1st lt. USAAF, 1942-45, capt. M.S.C., AUS, 1950-58. Decorated Air medal with 3 oak leaf clusters, Purple Heart. Mem. Nat. Assn. Social Workers, Acad. Certified Social Workers, Council on Social Work Edn., Am. Assn. U. Profs., S.C. Welfare Forum. Author: A Guide for Training Public Welfare Administrators, 1965; articles in profl. jours. Home: 3433 Willow Ridge Rd Columbia SC 29206

HUNLEY, CLAY CHARLTON, dentist; b. Donaldsonville, La., Nov. 30, 1932; s. Henry Martin and Mary Ann (Schaff) H.; student Loyola U., New Orleans, 1951-53, Centenary Coll., 1952; D.D.S., Loyola U. Sch. Dentistry, New Orleans, 1957; m. Anita Marie LeBreton, Jan. 20, 1958; children—Adrienne Elizabeth, Charlton Dewitt. Intern, Charity Hosp., New Orleans, 1957-58, resident, 1958-60; practice dentistry specializing in oral surgery, New Orleans, 1960—; v.p., sec. Drs. Kuebel and Hunley, Inc., 1971—; sr. staff Touro Infirmary Hosp.; active staff Eye Ear Nose and Throat Hosp., Hote Dieu Hosp., Mercy Hosp., New Orleans. Mem. New Orleans Mus. Fine Arts. Mem. Am., Southeastern, La. (sec. 1970-72) socs. oral surgeons, Am., La., New Orleans (sec. 1968-69) dental assns., S.A.R., New Orleans C. of C. Club: Southern Yacht (New Orleans, La.). Home: 3617 Ridgeway Dr Metairie LA 70002 Office: 1636 Louisiana Av New Orleans LA 70002

HUNSUCKER, WILLIAM JAMES, accountant; b. Darlington, S.C., Mar. 26, 1930; s. Rober Knox and Leila (Caribo) H.; B.S. in Accounting, U. S.C., 1958; m. Elizabeth Beck, Aug. 25, 1956; children—Joan Elizabeth, Debra Jean. Pub. accountant W. J. Hunsucker, C.P.A., Hartsville, S.C., 1958-62; comptroller Williams Trucking Service, Inc., Hartsville, 1962-67; resident partner Leach, Calkins & Scott, C.P.A.'s, 1967; Lybrand, Ross Bros. & Montgomery, C.P.A.'s, Hartsville, S.C., 1967-71; sec.-treas., dir. 1st Fed. Savs. & Loan Assn., Hartsville, 1971—. Treas., Hartsville Area Council for Retarded Children. Bd. dirs. Byrnes Scholars aux. to James F. Byrnes Found., 1964-65, pres., 1965-66; bd. dirs., treas. James F. Byrnes Found., 1970—. Served with USAF, 1950-54. Mem. Greater Hartsville C. of C. (dir. 1969-72, pres. 1972). Club: Civitan (treas. 1961-62). Home: 215 Richardson Circle E Hartsville SC 29550 Office: 328 S 5th St Box 429 Hartsville SC 29550

HUNT, ANDREW W., lumber co. exec.; b. Nacogdoches, Tex., Sept. 30, 1909; s. Andrew W. and Lula (Crawford) H.; A.B., Baylor U., 1931, M.A., 1933; Ph.D., U. Tex., 1941; m. Elizabeth Mullen, Sept. 5, 1941; children—Lacy H., Andrew W., William Crawford. Adminstr., tchr. Tex. Pub. Sch., 1931-39; prof. psychology and edn. McMurry Coll., 1949-55; Harris County psychologist, 1955-64; v.p. J. S. Hunt Lumber Co., Lacy H. Hunt Lumber Co., Nacogdoches, Tex.; dir. Meyerland State Bank, Houston, 1966—. Lectr., cons. Child Welfare Groups. Mem. Tex. Commn. on Edn. Bd. dirs. Houston Community Council. Mem. Tex. Social Welfare Assn., Nat. Assn. Probation and Parole, Nat. Council Tests and Measurements, Nat. Assn. Sch. Adminstrs., Nat. Assn. for Student Teaching (research com.), Assn. Future Tchrs. Am. (Tex. sponsor), Mental Hygiene Soc., Elementary Prins. and Suprs., N.E.A., Tex. Soc. S.A.R., Sons Rep. Tex. (pres. San Jacinto chpt.), Sam Houston Meml. Assn. (v.p.), English Speaking Union, Phi Delta Kappa, Kappa Delta Pi, Alpha Psi Omega. Lion, Rotarian (pres. 1969-70). Club: Warwick. Author articles ednl. jours. Home: 5154 Jackwood Houston TX 77035 Office: Commercial Bank Bldg Nacogdoches TX 75961

HUNT, DONALD WAYNE, orthodontist; b. nr. Gaffney, S.C., Jan. 11, 1940; s. Wayne Brackett and Eunice Elizabeth (Allen) H.; student Presbyn. Coll., 1958-59, U. S.C., 1960-63; D.D.S., Med. Coll. Va., 1967, postgrad. orthodontics, 1967-69; m. Susan Kelly Anderson, Aug. 13, 1963; children—Smyre Anderson, Donald Wayne, Clayton Brackett. Practice dentistry specializing in orthodontics, Greenville, S.C., 1969—. Bd. dirs. Med. Coll. at Va. Orthodontic Found. Mem. Am. Dental Assn., Am., So. (asso.) socs. orthodontists, Omicron Kappa Upsilon, Psi Omega, Sigma Chi. Club: Greenville Country. Home: 185 Chapman Rd Greenville SC 29605 Office: 16 Rushmore Dr Greenville SC 29607

HUNT, EARL GLADSTONE, JR., bishop, coll. pres.; b. Johnson City, Tenn., Sept. 14, 1918; s. Earl Gladstone and Tommie Mae (DeVault) H.; B.S., E. Tenn. State U., 1941; B.D., Emory U., 1946; D.D., Tusculum Coll., 1956, Duke 1969; LL.D., U. Chattanooga, 1957; D.C.L. (hon.), Emory and Henry Coll., 1965; m. Mary Ann Kyker, June 15, 1943; 1 son, Earl Stephen. Ordained to ministry Methodist Ch., 1944; pastor Sardis Meth. Ch., Atlanta, 1942-44; asso. pastor Broad Street Meth. Ch., Kingsport, Tenn., 1944-45; pastor Wesley Meml. Meth. Ch., Chattanooga, 1945-50, First Meth. Ch., Morristown, Tenn., 1950-56; pres. Emory and Henry Coll., 1956-64; resident bishop The Charlotte Area, Meth. Ch., 1964—. President Inst. Homiletical Studies, 1966—. Participant Meth. series Protestant Hour, nationwide broadcast, 1956; mem. Meth. Gen. Bd. Edn., 1956-68; del. Meth. Gen. Conf., 1956, 60, 64, S.E. Jurisdictional Conf., 1952, 56, 60, 64. Board fellows Interpreters' House, Inc. Trustee Brevard Coll., Emory U., Greensboro Coll., High Point Coll., Pfeiffer Coll., Lake Junaluska Meth. Assembly, Bennett College; bd. mgrs. Charlotte Meth. Home; chmn. gen. com. on family life United Meth. Ch.; mem. Com. One Hundred, Emory U. Named young man of Year, Morristown Jr. C. of C., 1952. Mem. Pi Kappa Delta. Home: 3912 Beresford Rd Charlotte NC 28211 Office: Cole Bldg 207 Hawthorne Lane Charlotte NC 28204

HUNT, EDWIN CHAMBERS, farmer; b. nr. Wake Forest, N.C., May 8, 1899; s. Richard Parthenia and Nonie Eva (Allen) H.; student Mars Hill Coll., 1919-20; m. Nellie Gray Fuller, June 7, 1924; children—Ellen (Mrs. Thomas O. Chewning), Edwin Chambers, Mary (Mrs. Max Smith), William T. Postal clk., Wake Forest, N.C., 1945-68; farm owner, Wake Forest, 1925—; sec. Wake Electric Membership Corp., 1940-72; dir. Wake Electric and Tar Heel Electric Membership Assn., Inc. Mem. N.C. Farm Bur., Civitan. Baptist (deacon). Address: Rt 2 Box 10 Wake Forest NC 27587

HUNT, JACOB TATE, educator; b. Sweetwater, Tenn., Aug. 22, 1916; s. Samuel Lon and Grace (Beals) H.; A.B., Maryville Coll., 1938; M.S., U. Tenn., 1941; Ph.D., U. Cal. at Berkeley, 1950; postgrad. U. Ill., 1956-57; m. Harriet Elizabeth Durnell, June 17, 1944; 1 son, Steven Craig. Tchr. pub. schs., Tenn., 1938-40, Wash., 1940-42; instr. U. Cal. at Berkeley, 1946-48; vis. prof., 1963; asst. prof. Western Res. U., Cleve., 1948-51; asst. prof. ednl. psychology U. N.C., 1951-56, asso. prof., 1956-57; asso. prof. spl. edn. U. Ariz., 1957-60, prof., chmn. dept. spl. edn., 1960-64; prof., chmn. spl. edn. U. Wash., 1964-68; prof., chmn. spl. edn. U. Ga., 1968—; vis. prof. U. Colo., 1960, 62, U. Ill., 1957—. Bd. dirs. Pima County (Ariz.) Assn. Mental Health, 1958-63; adviser Cerebral Palsy Assn., Am., 1958-60. Served with USNR, 1942-45. Ford Found. fellow, 1956-57. Mem. Am. Ednl. Research Assn., Am. Psychol. Assn., Am. Assn. Mental Deficiency, Council Exceptional Children, Internat. Reading Assn. Editor: High Sch. jour. 1952-56, Am. Ednl. Research Assn. Newsletter, 1959-64. Rev. of Ednl. Research, 1964-69; asso. editor Exceptional Children, 1966—; editorial bd. Internat. Jour. Edn., 1967—, Jour. Spl. Edn., 1968—, Scientia Paedagogica Experimentalis, 1966—. Home: 105 Chinquapin Way Athens GA 30601

HUNT, JAMES MATHEWS, architect; b. Elberton, Ga., Aug. 2, 1915; s. Looney H. and Annie Lee (Gaines) Hunt; student Ala. Poly. Inst., 1937; B.S., Clemson U., 1938; m. Mary Elizabeth Jenkins, Sept. 13, 1947; children—James Mathews, Annie Elizabeth, Howard Jenkins. Archtl. designer Housing Authority Architects City of Charleston, S.C., 1939-40, archtl. aide to Housing Authority City of Charleston, S.C., 1940-42, 46-47; archtl. aide Liberty Granite Co., Elberton, Ga., 1947-48; self-employed as architect, Elberton, Ga., 1948-; dir. Elberton Devel. Co., Inc. Chmn. Gov's Commn. on State Bldg. Constrn. and Financing, 1971; mem. State Bd. Examination Qualification and Registration Architects, 1971-76. Lt. col. Aide de Camp Gov. Marvin Griffin, 1955-59, Gov. S. Ernest Vandiver, 1959-62; admiral Ga. Navy, 1971-74. Mem. Democratic, exec. com. Ga., 1971-72. Served to 1st lt., C.E., AUS, 1942-46; PTO. Recipient Appreciation awards Producer's Council, Atlanta chpt., 1967, Ga. Assn. A.I.A., 1968, North Ga. chpt. A.I.A., 1969; mem. Family of Year Ga. Federated Women's Club, 1970. Mem. A.I.A. (pres. Ga. 1968, pres. N. Ga. 1969, mem. nat. housing com. 1971, 72), V.F.W., Am. Legion, Soc. Am. Mil. Engrs. Baptist (deacon 1948—). Rotarian. Clubs: Country (Elberton, Ga.); Carolina Yacht (Charleston, S.C.). Prin. archtl. works include Marriott Motor Hotel, Atlanta, 100 pub. housing projects, S.C., Ga. Home: 136 Parkwood Dr Elberton GA 30635 Office: PO Drawer 808 16 Chestnut St Elberton GA 30635

HUNT, JOE BYRON, state ofcl.; b. Mammoth Spring, Ark., Jan. 23, 1907; s. John Fisher and Iuka (Woodall) H.; student Okla. U., 1927-28; m. Anna Maude Dial, Oct. 8, 1935; 1 dau., Jo Ann. Ins. agt., Edna, Tex. until 1942; mgr. rating dept. Okla. Ins. Bd., 1942-54, pres., 1955—; commr. Okla. Ins. Dept., Oklahoma City, 1955—. Chief ins. man Chickasaw Nation of Indians, 1960—. Mem. Okla. Burial Bd., 1955—; state dir. Firemens Relief and Pension Fund, Policeman's Pension and Retirement System, Motor Vehicle Assigned Risk Plan, 1955—; mem. Okla. Hwy. Safety Coordinating Com.; hon. lt. gov., Okla., 1960—. Dist. vice chmn. Last Frontier council Boy Scouts Am., asst. on exec. com. Oklahoma City United Fund, 1959. Mem. Seminole (Okla.) City Council, 1935. Bd. dirs. Jane Brooks Sch. for Deaf; trustee Okla. Fire Fighter Museum. Recipient Oscar, Iota Nu Sigma, 1957; Citation for Meritorious Service, Employment for Physically Handicapped, 1957; Distinguished Service award Gov.'s Com. on Employment of Handicapped, 1970; Distinguished Service award Okla. Rehab. Assn., 1970; named Boss of Yr., Galatea chpt. Am. Bus. Women's Assn., 1971-72. Mem. Nat. Assn. Ins. Commrs. (fed. liaison com., zone 5 chmn. 1960-66), Profl. Fire Ins. Soc., Internat. Assn. Fire Chiefs, Okla. Retired Firemen's Assn. (hon. life), Fedn. Ins. Council, Am. Assn. U. Tchrs. Ins., Oklahoma City C. of C. Presbyn. (past pres., trustee). Lion (charter). Home: 4309 NW June St Oklahoma City OK 73112 Office: Will Rogers Meml Bldg State Capital Complex Oklahoma City OK 73105

HUNT, JOHN CONWAY, govt. ofcl.; b. Bethesda, Md., Mar. 9, 1912; s. Henry J. and Rosamond (Warder) H.; grad. Am. Inst. Banking, 1936; LL.B., Southeastern U., Washington, 1941; postgrad. Armed Forces Indsl. Coll., 1946, Am. U., 1956-58; m. Margaret Lansdowne, Nov. 8, 1941; children—Conway, Betsy, Robyn, Patricia, Julia. Asst. mgr. S.W. br. Am. Security & Trust Co., Washington, 1930-41; commd. lt. (j.g.) U.S. Navy, 1942, advanced through grades to comdr., 1950, naval aviator Atlantic Fleet, 1942-45, mem. staff Office Naval Material, Ins. and Contracting Office, 1947-51, comdg. officer Mil. Sea Transp. Office, Inchon, Korea, 1952-53; ret., 1967; admitted to Md. bar, 1950, also D.C. bar, U.S. Supreme Ct. bar; practiced in Rockville, Bethesda and Chevy Chase, Md., 1954-58; atty. Fed. Maritime Commn., Washington, 1963—. D.C. real estate assessor, 1958-62; bd. dirs. Fed. Maritime Credit Union. Pres. Ft. Sumner Citizens Assn., 1967. Mem. Md. Bar Assn., U.S. Naval Inst., Assn. Assessing Officers, Navy League, Soc. Residential Appraisers, Am. Inst. Real Estate Appraisers, Am. Legion. Episcopalian. Clubs: Aztec 1847 (nat. pres. 1966), Chevy Chase Country. Contbr. articles hist. jours. Home: 5225 Westpath Way Washington DC 20016 Office: Fed Maritime Commn 1405 Eye St Washington DC 20573

HUNT, JOSEPH THOMAS, dentist; b. nr. Louisburg, N.C., June 21, 1923; s. Joseph Baldy and Annie Aileen (Edwards) H.; student Louisburg Jr. Coll., 1940-41, Wake Forest U., 1941-43; D.D.S., Med. Coll. Va., 1946; m. Dora Perrle Webster, Jan. 24, 1945; children—Joseph Thomas, Garry D., Timothy W., Debby G., Stephanie M. Practice dentistry, Henderson, N.C., 1947-50, 53—; pres. Pentose Devel. Corp., Henderson, N.C., 1971—; dir. People's Bank and Trust Co. Bd. dirs. N.C. Dental Found., 1951. Served with AUS, 1943-44, USAF, 1951-53. Mem. Am. Dental Assn., N.C., 4th Dist. dental socs., N.C. Soc. Anesthesiology, Pierre Fauchard Acad., Psi Omega. Elk. Home: 1835 Summit Rd Henderson NC 27536 Office: 519 S Chestnut St Henderson NC 27536

HUNT, JOSEPH VICTOR, govt. ofcl.; b. Phila., July 21, 1905; s. James Francis and Alice (Malone) H.; B.S., St. Joseph's Coll., 1932, LL.D., 1969; A.M., U. Pa., 1941; LL.D., Gallaudet Coll., 1969; m. Dolores Consilia Hede, Oct. 19, 1935; children—Rosemary Dolores, Joseph Michael, Dolores, Cecilia. Asst. dir. Anthracite Industries research in operations of local govt., Schuykill and Northumberland counties, Pa., 1932-36; chmn. dept. bus. adminstrn. St. Joseph's Coll., Phila., 1936-41; sr. bus. economist OPA, Washington, 1941-42; chief div. adminstrv. mgmt. Bur. Old-Age and Survivors Ins., Social Security Bd. (now Social Security Adminstrn., Dept. of Health, Edn. and Welfare), Washington, 1942-43; asso. commr. Vocational Rehab. Adminstrn., Dept. Health, Edn. and Welfare, 1943-67, commr. Rehab. Services Adminstrn., 1967-69, dep. commr. Community Services Adminstrn., 1970—. Recipient Christophers Nat. award, 1953; Superior Service award, Dept. Health, Edn. and Welfare, 1958, Distinguished Service award, 1961; Pres.'s award Nat. Rehab. Assn., 1966, Nat. award Goodwill Industries Am., 1968; named Washington Alumnus of Year, St. Joseph's Coll., 1962. Mem. Am. Assn. Workers for Blind, Internat. Soc. Rehab. of Disabled, Nat. Rehab. Assn., Am. Pub. Welfare Assn., John Carroll Soc., Nat. Soc. Sci. Honor Soc., Pi Gamma Mu. Roman Cath. Club: Nat. Press (Washington). Home: 109 N George Mason Dr Arlington VA 22203 Office: Community Services Adminstrn 330 C St SW Washington DC 20201

HUNT, RUSSELL FRANK, lawyer, banker; b. Wagoner, Okla., Apr. 27, 1909; s. W.T. and Martha (Rose) H.; student U. Okla., 1928-29; LL.B., Cumberland U., 1931; m. Margaret Kerr, Mar. 30, 1932; 1 son, Russell Kerr. Admitted to Okla. bar, 1931, since practiced in Tulsa; v.p. First Nat. Bank & Trust Co. of Tulsa, 1950-55, exec. v.p., 1955-66, vice chmn., 1966—; dir. Am. Gen. Life Ins. Co. Okla. Chmn. Okla. Ordnance Works Authority; mem. Tulsa Urban Renewal Authority. Bd. Dirs. Tulsa Community Chest. Mem. Tulsa C. of C. (past pres., dir.), Res. City Bankers Assn. Clubs: Southern Hills (past pres., dir.), Tulsa (past dir.) (Tulsa). Home: 2916 S Yorktown St Tulsa OK 74114 Office: Box 1 Tulsa OK 74102

HUNT, THOMAS WEBB, music educator; b. Mammoth Spring, Ark., Sept. 28, 1929; s. Thomas Hubert and Ethel (Webb) H.; B.Mus., Ouachita Bapt. U., 1950; student Julliard Sch. Music, 1946, Memphis State U., 1950; M. Mus., N. Tex. State U., 1957, Ph.D., 1967; m. Martha Laverne Hill, July 22, 1951; 1 dau., Melana Claire. Tchr., Osceola (Ark.) High Sch., 1950-52, 54-56; choral dir. First Bapt. Ch., 1954-56; fellow N. Tex. State U., 1957-60; organist First Bapt. Ch., Denton, Tex., 1957-61; mem. faculty Okla. Coll. for Women, 1961-63; organist First Bapt. Ch., Chickasha, Okla., 1962-63; faculty Southwestern Bapt. Theol. Sem., 1963—; faculty Spanish Bapt. Sem., Barcelona, Spain, 1969-70; organist Gambrell St. Bapt. Ch., 1963-67; dir. Ft. Worth Euterpean Piano Quartets, 1966-68; concerts and lectures, U.S., Europe, Orient. Served with AUS, 1952-54. Mem. Am., Internat. musicological socs., Am. Guild Organists, Nat. Guild of Piano Tchrs., Soc. for Ethnomusicology, Hymn Soc. Am., Ft. Worth League Composers, So. Bapt. Ch. Music Conf., Phi Mu Alpha, Pi Kappa Lambda, Alpha Chi. Author music: Gentle Guide, 1961; Voluntary on Old Hundredth, 1963; Tonal Materials in the Organ Works of Messiaen, 1957; The Dictionaire de musique of Jean-Jacques Rousseau, 1967; also articles in field. Home: 3617 Walton St Fort Worth TX 76133

HUNTER, ALLAN OAKLEY, mortgage assn. exec., lawyer; b. Los Angeles, June 15, 1916; s. Henry Allan and Janet (Oakley) H.; A.B., Fresno State Coll., 1937; J.D., U. Cal. at Berkeley, 1940; m. Loberta Geene Taylor, Jan. 15, 1949; children—Genella (Mrs. Harold Williamson), Janet Oakley, John Henry, Allan Oakley. Admitted to Cal. bar, 1940; spl. agt. FBI, 1940-44; practiced in Cal., 1946-50, 58-69; gen. counsel HHFA, Washington, 1955-57; pres., dir. Fed. Nat. Mortgage Assn., Washington, 1970—. Chmn. Cal. Commn. Housing and Community Devel., 1967-69; mem. U.S. Ho. of Reps. from 12th Cal. dist., 1951-54. Bd. councillors U. So. Cal. Center Urban Affairs, 1969—. Served with USNR, 1944-46. Mem. State Bar Cal., Am., Fed. bar assns., Phi Delta Phi, Sigma Chi. Clubs: Congressional Country, Metropolitan (Washington). Home: 4937 Crescent St Chevy Chase MD 20016 Office: Fed Nat Mortgage Assn 1133 15th St NW Washington DC 20005

HUNTER, CHARLES EDWIN, mfrs. rep.; b. Oklahoma City, Nov. 8, 1910; s. Charles Edwin and Gertrude (Buchanan) H.; diploma Christian Bros. Coll., 1931; student Memphis State U., 1932-33; m. Marguerite Catledge, May 29, 1954; children—Charles Edwin, Timothy, Kipling, Holly. Salesman Standard Coffee Co., New Orleans, 1933-35, stock clk. Orgill Bros., Memphis, 1935-36; athletic dir. Memphis Park Commn., 1936-37; adjustor Gen. Contract Purchase Corp., 1938-39, unit mgr., 1940-41; salesman Tommy Tucker Co., 1946-47; pvt. bus. as mfrs. rep., Conyers, Ga., 1947—. Served from pvt. to pfc., USMCR, 1942-45. Home: RFD 3 Box 30 McCalla Rd Conyers GA 30207 Office: PO Box 250 Conyers GA 30207

HUNTER, DEAN DWIGHT, JR., city ofcl.; b. Ft. Worth, Sept. 5, 1926; s. Dean D. and Ollie (Sears) H.; B.S., Ohio State U., 1950; M. Govtl. Adminstrn., U. Pa., 1959; m. Pauline Lane, June 15, 1957; children—Jane Ellen, Jan Caroline, Jill Marie, Dean Jon. Asst. to city mgr., Corpus Christi, Tex., 1958-59; mgr. City of Mountlake Terrace, Wash., 1959-66; city mgr., Frankfort, Ky., 1966-68; asst. chief adminstrv. officer, New Orleans, 1968—. Commr., Snohomish County Airport, 1961-66. Served to maj. USAF, 1945, 50-53; mem. Res. Presbyn. Home: 2139 Valentine Ct New Orleans LA 70114 Office: City Hall New Orleans LA 70112

HUNTER, EDGAR HAYES, architect, educator; b. Hanover, N.H., Aug. 1, 1914; s. Edgar Hayes and Edna (Hill) H.; A.B., Dartmouth Coll, 1938, M.A., 1955; M.Arch., Harvard, 1941; m. Margaret Greenough King, May 8, 1943; children—Christopher King, Margaret Greenough. Instr. naval architecture Mass. Inst. Tech., 1941-42; pvt. practice architecture-planning E.H. and M.K. Hunter, Raleigh, N.C., 1945-66, 69—; prof. architecture Dartmouth Coll, 1946-66. v.p. Lyles, Bissett, Carlisle & Wolff, Colombia, S.C.,

1966-69, dir. Raleigh office, 1966-69; v.p. Cricket Corp., 1970—. Exhibited in Munich 1958, Traveling Exhibit to U.S. Colls. and Mus., 1963-66. Mem. Hanover Town Planning Commn., 1964-66. Trustee Bridgton Acad. (Me.) 1960-64; bd. dirs. Raleigh Chamber Music Soc. Recipient Progressive Architecture awards, 1946, 47; 2d pl. N.H. State Office Bldg. competition, 1950. Mem. A.I.A., N.C. Archtl. Soc. (chmn. pub. ins. 1969—), N.C. Land Use Congress, Newcomen Soc. Mem. Ch. Christ. Archtl. works include: Out Patient Clinic, N.H. State Hosp., Toll Collectors Sta. and canopies, Everett and Spaulding Turnpikes, N.H., Luth. Chapel and Parsonage, Hanover, N.H., Auditorium-music bldg. and sci. bldg., Colby Jr. Coll., New London, N.H. Stratton mountain site planning, Vt., Loon Mountain Ski Area, Lincoln, N.H., Dormitory Conn. Coll. for women, New London, Conn., classroom bldg. and dormitories Bridgton Acad. (Me.), campus plans N.C. Central U., Sims (Cal.) Acad. Works pub. in numerous Am. and fgn. mags. and books. Home: 1108 Manchester Dr Raleigh NC 27609 Office: 4224 Six Forks Rd Raleigh NC 27609

HUNTER, EDWARD, editor, author, analyst; b. N.Y.C., July 2, 1902; s. Edward and Rose (Weiss) H.; self ed.; m. Tatiana Pestrikoff, June 30, 1932 (div. May 1961); children—Robert, Tate Ann. Reporter, news editor various newspapers, including New Orleans Item, N.Y. Post, N.Y. American, Phila. Bull., San Francisco Bull.; reporter Paris edit. Chgo. Tribune, 1924-25; news editor Japan Advertiser, Tokyo, 1927, editor Hankow (China) Herald, 1928-29, Peking Leader, 1929-30; covered Japanese conquest of Manchuria, Spanish Civil War, Italian conquest of Ethiopia, Internat. News Service, 1931-36; pioneered in revealing brainwashing, putting word into written language; staff cons. various govt. agys. including Senate Internal Security Subcom.; editor monthly publication Tactics, 1964—. Cons. psychol. warfare USAF, 1953-54. Served as propoganda warfare specialist AUS, with morale operations sect., OSS, Asia, World War II. Author: Brain-Washing in Red China, 1951, rev. edit., 1971; Brainwashing: The Story of Men Who Defied It, 1956, rev., retitled: Brainwashing: From Pavlov to Powers, 1960; The Story of Mary Liu, 1957; The Black Book on Red China, 1958; The Past Present: A Year in Afghanistan, 1959; In Many Voices: Our Fabulous Foreign-Language Press, 1960; Attack by Mail: A Textbook on Communist Tactics, 1964; Tactics for 1964; Tactics for 1965; Tactics for 1966; Tactics for 1967; Tactics for 1968; Tactics for 1969; Tactics for 1970; Tactics for 1971. Contbr. articles on psychol. warfare, polit. extremism numerous mags. Clubs: Overseas Press, Silurians. Address: 4114 N 4th St Arlington VA 22203

HUNTER, EDWIN D, mng. editor Houston Post. Home: 2425 Sage Rd Houston TX 77027 Office: 2410 Polk Av Houston TX 77001*

HUNTER, EDWIN FORD, JR., U.S. judge; b. Alexandria, La., Feb. 18, 1911; s. Edwin Ford and Amelia (French) H.; student La. State U., 1930-33; LL.B., George Washington U., 1938; m. Shirley Kidd, Nov. 9, 1941; children—Edwin Kidd, Janin, Kelley. Admitted to La. bar, 1938, mem. Smith, Hunter, Risinger & Shuey, Shreveport, 1940-53. Mem. La. State Legislature, 1948-52; exec. counsel Gov. La., 1952; mem. La. State Mineral Bd., 1952; judge U.S. Dist. Ct., Western Dist. La. Served as lt. USNR, 1942-45. Mem. Am. Bar Assn. (La. state chmn. jr. bar sect. 1945), Am. Legion (post comdr. 1945, judge adv. Dept. La. 1948), Sigma Chi. Roman Catholic. Home: 1000 Bayou Oaks Lane Lake Charles LA 70601 Office: PO Box 1337 Lake Charles LA 70601

HUNTER, GORDON COBLE, banker; b. nr. Greensboro, N.C., July 29, 1894; s. Samuel G. and Lalah Vance (Coble) H.; student U. N.C., 1915-17; m. Ethel Gray Wilson, Jan. 26, 1918; children—Rebecca Vance (Mrs. V. Paul Vittur), Rachel Gray (Mrs. George J. Cushwa). With Am. Exchange Nat. Bank, Greensboro, 1919-31; bank examiner FDIC, 1933; exec. v.p. Peoples Bank, Roxboro, N.C., 1933-57, pres., 1957—, chmn. bd., 1960—; chmn. bd. First Union Nat Bank, Roxboro; dir. Radio Sta. WRXO, Morris Telephone Co., Reinforced Plastic Container Corp., Roxboro Devel. Corp. Treas., bd. dirs. Town of Roxboro, 1934-60. Person County chmn. A.R.C., 1937-38, U.S.O Drive, 1943-44; N.C. chmn. Nat. Found. 4-H Club, 1955-57; an organizer, bd. dirs. Person County Meml. Hosp.; mem. N.C. Bd. Conservation and Devel., N.C. Forestry Adv. Com. Served from private to 2d lt. inf. U.S. Army, 1917-18. Named Citizen of Year, Person County, 1956; recipient citation for 25 yr. devoted service Nat. Found.; Certificate of Appreciation in recognition 25 yrs. leadership for sales U.S. Savs. Bonds, U.S. Dept. Treasury. Mem. Am. (nat. research council 1955-57, exec. com. 1946-49, regional v.p. 1958-60, N.C. legislation com. 1960-62), N.C. (pres. 1945-46) bankers assns., Roxboro C. of C. (1st pres. 1935), Am. Legion (past comdr. Lester Blackwell post), 40 and 8. Methodist (steward). Rotarian (past pres. Roxboro). Home: 115 Academy St Roxboro NC 27573 Office: 203 N Main St Roxboro NC 27573

HUNTER, JAMES ALSTON, physician; b. Ross, Tex., Nov. 20, 1915; S. James Alston and Ellanor (Kirkpatrick) H.; A.B., Baylor U., 1936; M.D., U. Tex., 1940; m. Lucy Elizabeth Eaton, July 23, 1939; children—Andrea 0Ann; Ronald D. Strong), Kirk Patrick, James Eaton, Lucy Ann; m. 2d, Margaret Elizabeth Ziegert, May 20, 1966; children—Mary Margaret, William Allen. Rotating intern John Sealy Hosp., Galveston, Tex. 1940-41; surg. resident USPHS Hosp., Detroit, Wayne State U., 1947-49; med. officer Coast Guard Icebreaker Northwind, Byrd-Navy Antarctic Expdn., 1946-47; adminstr. USPHS Hosps. Vineyard Haven, Mass., Balt., Detroit, Springfield, Mo., Alaska Native Hosp., Anchorage, 1950-62; sr. med. officer Coast Guard Tng. Center, Cape May, N.J., 1962-67; ret., 1967; staff psychiatrist Rusk (Tex.) State Hosp., 1967—, also dir. maximum security unit. Mem. devel. council Baylor U. Fellow Royal Soc. Health (Eng.); mem. Am. Coll. Hosp. Adminstrs. A.A.A.S., Assn. Mil. Surgeons, A.M.A., Tex. Med. Assn., Cherokee County Med. Soc. (pres. 1972), Alpha Epsilon Delta, Nu Sigma Nu. Democrat. Disciple of Christ. Rotarian, Mason. Home: 108 S Main St Rusk TX 75785 Office: Rusk State Hosp Rusk TX 75785

HUNTER, JAMES CHARLES, oil co. exec.; b. Kansas City, Mo., Jan. 28, 1931; s. James Madison and Zelma Allene (Jefferson) H.; B.A., William Jewell Coll., 1952; postgrad. U. Mo., 1957-61 Region advt. rep. Cities Service Oil Co., Kansas City, Mo., 1955-61, div. advt. and promotion mgr., 1962-64, marketing pub. relations mgr., Tulsa, 1964-67, asst. mgr. pub. relations, 1967-69, program mgr. pub. relations, 1969-72; mgr. pub. relations Southeast, Cities Service Co., Atlanta, 1972—. Lectr., Am. Mgmt. Assn., N.Y.C., 1970, Chgo., 1971; mem. pub. relations adv. com. Fla. Phosphate Council; mem. communications com. Fertilizer Inst., Am. Mining Congress. Mem. pub. relations com. Goodwill Industries Atlanta. Bd. govs. William Jewell Coll. Alumni Assn. Served with AUS, 1952-54. Mem. Kansas City (Mo.) Advt. Roundtable, Assn. Petroleum Writers, Pub. Relations Soc. Am., Am. Petroleum Inst. (So. region adv. com. on pub. relations), Atlanta C. of C., Lambda Chi Alpha, Pi Kappa Delta. Methodist. Club: Atlanta Press. Home: 111 Adrian Pl Cross Creek Pkwy NW Atlanta GA 30327 Office: 3445 Peachtree Rd NE Atlanta GA 30326

HUNTER, JEHU CALLIS, biologist; b. Washington, Mar. 11, 1922; s. Jehu Louis and Alice (Callis) H.; B.S. cum laude, Howard U., 1943; m. Frances Henrietta Simons, Aug. 16, 1966; children—Joyce Alessandra (Mrs. Harry Stanton, Jr.), Maria Alice, Roberto Jehu (by previous marriage). Grad. asst. zoology Howard U., 1947-48; research technician Nat. Cancer Inst., NIH, Bethesda, Md., 1949-51, biologist, 1953-62, research biologist, 1962-65, sci. adminstr. Nat. Inst. Child Health and Human Devel., 1965-69, asst. dir. for planning, 1969—. Served with AUS, 1943-47, 51-52. Decorated Bronze Star. Travel grantee to Attend 8th Internat. Cancer Congress, 1962. Mem. Am. Soc. for Cell Biology, A.A.A.S., Royal Soc. Medicine, Soc. Developmental Biology. Contbr. articles to profl. jours. Research in cell physiology. Home: 7822 16th St NW Washington DC 20012 Office: NIH Bethesda MD 20014

HUNTER, JOHN ANDERSON, ret. univ. pres.; b. Donner, La., Apr. 23, 1914; s. John A. and Minnie Lee (Steinwinder) H.; B.S., Davidson Coll., 1934; M.A., La. State U., 1947, Ph.D., 1949; m. Doris G. Paine, June 13, 1937; children—David M., John Anderson. Tchr., coach Gulf Coast Mil. Acad., 1934-37, comdt., 1941-43; geophys. work Stanolind Oil and Gas, 1937-39; ednl. adviser Civilian Conservation Corps, 1939-41; dir. classified personnel La. State U., 1947-49, asso. prof. edn., 1951-59, prof., 1959—, registrar, 1951-56, dean jr. div., 1956-59, dean of student services, 1959-62, pres., 1962-72, pres. emeritus, 1972—; supr. research La. Dept. Edn., 1949-51. Mem. Nat. Citizens Com. for Community Relations; mem. adv. com. Pub. Health Service Hosp., 1966-69; mem. La. Fulbright Scholarship Com.; mem. So. Regional Edn. Bd., 1962—, mem. exec. com., 1962—; mem. Commn. on Higher Ednl. Opportunity in South, 1966—; mem. adv. council on state depts. edn. U.S. Office Edn., 1968-70. Adv. bd. Our Lady of Lake Hosp.; bd. govs. Photog. Art and Sci. Found., Inc. Served as lt. (j.g.) USNR, 1943-46. Decorated Order of Vasco de Balboa (Panama); Order of Ruben Dario (Nicaragua); recipient hon. state farmer degree, 1962; hon. 4-H Key award, 1963. Mem. So. Assn. Collegiate Registrars (past pres.), La. Assn. Collegiate Registrars and Admissions Officers (hon.), La. Sch. Bds. Assn. (planning com.), So. Assn. Colls. Secondary Schs. (sec. of exec. council of commn. on colls. and univs.). Am. Assn. Collegiate Registrars Admissions Officers, Nat., La. edn. assns., So. Assn. Land-Grant Colleges and State Univs. (pres. 1964-65), Am. Legion (past local comdr.), La. Hist. Assn., Am. Radio Relay League, Southeastern Conf. (v.p. 1966, 67), La. Registrars Assn. (past pres.), La. Tchrs. Assn., Vis. Tchrs. Assn. La., So. Assn. Colls. and Schs. (pres. 1963-64, trustee 1962-65), S.A.R., Alpha Sigma Lambda, Phi Kappa Phi, Kappa Delta Pi, Phi Delta Kappa, Kappa Phi Kappa, Phi Eta Sigma, Omicron Delta Kappa, Sigma Phi Epsilon, Gamma Beta Phi (mem. state council 1964—). Episcopalian. Mason (Shriner, 33 deg.). Clubs: Internat. House (bd. dirs. 1963-65). Pickwick; Camelot (gov. 1967—) (Baton Rouge). Contbr. to publs. in field. Home: 718 Kenilworth Pkwy Baton Rouge LA 70808

HUNTER, MARJORIE ROSE, newspaper corr.; b. Bethany, W.Va., June 2, 1922; d. Joshua Allen and Minnie (Gilliland) Hunter; A.B., Elon Coll., 1942. Reporter News and Observer, Raleigh, N.C. 1942-48, Houston Press, 1949; reporter, polit. corr. Winston-Salem (N.C.) Jour., 1950-61; mem. Washington bur. N.Y. Times, 1961—. Mem. N.C. Soc., Washington Press Club, White House Corrs. Assn. Corcoran Gallery Art, Episcopalian. Home: 3517 R St NW Washington DC 20007 Office: 1920 L St Washington DC 20036

HUNTER, MARY JANE BURNS (MRS. JOSEPH LAWTON HUNTER), journalist; b. Atlanta, Oct. 31, 1919; d. Cecil Olney and Mary (Cheves) Burns; student U. Ga., 1935-36, High Mus. Sch. Art, Atlanta, 1937; m. Joseph Lawton Hunter, Oct. 8, 1944; children—Mollie, Ellen. Landscape designer, horticulturist, Fort Lauderdale, Fla., 1960-65, Freeport, Grand Bahama I., 1965-66; writer, garden columns Freeport News, 1966-68, mem. editorial staff, 1968-70, editor weekly entertainment supplement, 1968-70; women's editor Cape Coral (Fla.) Breeze, 1970—. Corr. various travel publs., Bahamas, 1969—. Recipient 2d Pl. Feature Writing award Weekly div. Better Newspaper Contest, Fla. Press Assn., 1970. Mem. Internat. Platform Assn. Contbr. articles to publs. Home: 4902 Sorrento Ct Cape Coral FL 33904 Office: Cape Coral Breeze Box 846 Cape Coral FL 33904

HUNTER, OAKLEY, govt. ofcl. Pres. Fed. Nat. Mortgage Assn., Washington. Home: 4937 Crescent St Chevy Chase MD 20015 Office: 1133 15th St NW Washington DC 20005

HUNTER, ORA ANDERSON (MRS. STILL HUNTER), educator; b. Bay Springs, Miss., Aug. 4, 1905; d. Sidney Hugh and Sue (Daniel) Anderson; B.A., U. Ala., 1925, M.A., 1957, advanced profl. diploma, 1961; postgrad. Columbia, 1926; m. Still Hunter, Aug. 25, 1929 (dec. 1952); children—Mary Elizabeth (Mrs. Thomas Hartley Murray), Still. Chmn. English dept. Carbon Hill (Ala.) High Sch., 1927-30; chmn. social studies dept. Walker County High Sch., Jasper, Ala., 1945—, guidance counselor, 1951—; instr. English lit. and composition Walker Jr. Coll. Counselor freshmen, U. Ala., Tuscaloosa, summer 1959. Pres., P.T.A., Jasper, 1943-45, Thursday Study Club, Jasper, 1937-38; chmn. family finance Ala. Fedn. Women's Clubs, 1938. Named Woman of Month, Mountain Eagle, 1953, Tchr. of Year of Walker County. Mem. Nat., Ala. edn. assns., Assn. Classroom Tchrs., Am. Personnel and Guidance Assn. (asso.), Nat. Vocational Guidance Assn. (asso.), U. Ala. Guidance Inst., Walker County Tchrs. Assn. (pres. 1964-65), D.A.R. (regent chpt. 1954-58), Phi Beta Kappa, Kappa Delta Pi, Delta Kappa Gamma (treas. Jasper 1957-58). Democrat. Baptist. Mem. Order Eastern Star (worthy matron Jasper 1944). Home: 1403 3d Av Jasper AL 35501 Office: Walker County High Sch Highland Av Jasper AL 35501

HUNTLEY, ROBERT E.R., univ. pres.; b. Winston Salem, N.C.; B.A., Washington and Lee U., also LL.B., LL.M., Harvard. Formerly practiced law, Alexandria, Va.; mem. faculty Washington and Lee U., 1958—, formerly prof. law, dean law sch., pres. univ., 1968—. Mem. Va. Bd. Edn., 1970—. Mem. Order Coif, Phi Beta Kappa, Omicron Delta Kappa. Address: Washington and Lee U Lexington VA 24450*

HUNTON, RICHARD EDWIN, physician; b. Boonville, Ind., Dec. 23, 1924; s. Edwin Chandler and Nellie Cecicia (Wright) H.; A.A., George Washington U., 1947, A.B., 1949, M.D., 1952; m. Agnes Katherine Setser, Aug. 22, 1953; children—Jennifer Leigh, Richard Edwin. Instrument maker U.S. Naval Observatory, Washington, 1942-44; intern Gallinger Municipal Hosp., Washington, 1952-53; resident Spartanburg (S.C.) Gen. Hosp., 1953-54; practice gen. medicine limited to women, Scurry Clinic, Greenwood, S.C., 1954—; mem. staff Self Meml. Hosp., Greenwood, S.C. bd. dirs. Greenwood County Mental Health Assn., Greenwood County chpt. A.R.C., Greenwood County Tb. Assn. Served with AUS, 1944-45. Decorated Purple Heart. Mem. Am., S.C. med. assns., Am. Acad. Gen. Practice, Phi Beta Kappa, Phi Eta Sigma. Baptist. Club: Christian Business Men's Committee. Author: Formula for Fitness, 1966. Home: 112 Wendover Rd Greenwood SC 29646 Office: Scurry Clinic Greenwood SC 29646

HUPP, EUGENE WESLEY, educator; b. Bloomfield, Neb., Feb. 23, 1933; s. William S. and Alice (Josiassen) H.; student Norfolk Jr. Coll., 1950-51; B.S., U. Neb., 1954, M.S. 1956; Ph.D., Mich. State U., 1958; m. Phyllis Glover, June 22, 1957; children—Stephen, Michael, Alice. NSF predoctoral fellow Mich. State U., East Lansing, 1956-57, grad. research asst., 1957-58; asst. scientist Agrl. Research Lab., Oak Ridge, Tenn., 1958-60, asso. scientist, 1960-62; asso. prof. Tex. A. and M. U., College Station, 1962-65; asso. prof. biology Tex. Woman's U., Denton, 1965-69; prof., 1969—. Served with USNR, 1953-55. Fellow Tex. Acad. Sci.; mem. Radiation Research Soc., Soc. for Study Reprodn., Am. Soc. Animal Sci., Am. Soc. for Lab. Animal Sci. Home: 909 Edgewood PL Denton TX 76201

HURLEY, CLAY BOHANNAN, hosp. adminstr; b. Birmingham, Ala., July 25, 1931; s. John L. and Bettie (Clay) H.; B.S., Florence State Coll., 1962; m. Marion Louise Black, July 10, 1958. Adminstrv. asst. Colbert County Hosp., Sheffield, Ala., 1960-62; adminstr. Cullman (Ala.) Hosp., 1962-67; cons. Applied Mgmt. Controls Co., 1967-69; adminstr. George H. Lanier Meml. Hosp., Langdale, Ala., 1969—. Served with USNR, 1950-54. Mem. Am. Coll. Hosp. Adminstrs., Ala. Hosp. Assn., N. Ala. Hosp. Council, Beta Beta Beta, Phi Kappa Alpha. Episcopalian (trustee). Home: 1406 N 8th Av Lanett AL 36863 Office: 4800 48th St Langdale AL 36864

HURLEY, ELIZABETH ANN, educator; b. Ft. Worth, Nov. 20, 1912; d. Frank Evans and Lillie B. (Bailey) Hurley; B.S., Tex. Woman's U., 1934, M.A., 1952; postgrad. Columbia, summer 1938, (Wall St. Jour. fellow), U. Minn., summer 1967, (Newspaper Fund fellow), Tex. Tech. U., summer 1969. Mem. staffs Lufkin (Tex.) Daily News, 1934-41, A.P., Austin, Tex., 1941; mng. editor Marshall (Tex.) News-Messenger, 1941-45, Denton (Tex.) Record-Chronicle, 1945-49; instr. journalism Tex. Woman's U., 1951-53; tchr. journalism, adviser weekly sch. newspaper and yearbook Pampa (Tex.) High Sch., 1953—. Vice pres. Denton Record-Chronicle, 1946-49; participant, speaker various confs., publs. workshops. Recipient Gold Key award Columbia Scholastic Press Assn., 1964; named Outstanding High Sch. Journalism Tchr. Tex. Interscholastic League Press Conf., U., Tex., 1964. Edith Fox King award ILPC, 1970; Pioneer award Nat. Scholastic Press Assn., 1970. Mem. Tex. Assn. Journalism Dirs. (pres. 1963, state dir., rep. nat. assns. 1964-65), Tex. (faculty chmn. 1963, 1968), West Tex. (faculty pres. 1959) high sch. press assns., Journalism Edn. Assn. (medal of merit 1969), S.W. Council Student Publs. (pres. 1970), N.E.A., Tex. State Tchrs. Assn., Tex. Classroom Tchrs. Assn., Theta Sigma Phi, Delta Kappa Gamma. Presbyn. Contbr. articles to newspapers, mags. Home: 319 N Somerville St Pampa TX 79065 Office: Pampa High School 111 E Harvester St Pampa TX 79065

HURLEY, FRANK THOMAS, JR., realtor; b. Washington, Oct. 18, 1924; s. Frank Thomas and Lucille (Trent) H.; A.A., St. Petersburg Jr. Coll., 1948; B.A., U. Fla., 1950. Reporter St Petersburg (Fla.) Evening Independent, 1948-53; editor Arcadia (Cal.) Tribune, 1956-57; reporter Los angeles Herald Express, 1957; v.p. Frank T. Hurley Assos., Inc. Realtors, 1958-64, pres., 1964—. Mem. St. Petersburg Beach Bd. Commrs., 1965-69; candidate Fla. Ho. of Reps., 1966; chmn. Pinellas County Traffic Safety Council, 1968-69. Pres. Pass-A-Grille Community Assn., 1963, Gulf Beach Bd. Realtors, 1969; mem. St. Petersburg Museum Fine Arts. Served with USAAF, 1943-46. Mem. Fla. Assn. Realtors (dist. v.p. 1971), Vina del Mar Island Assn., Am. Legion, Sigma Delta Chi, Sigma Tau Delta. Home: 2808 Sunset Way St Petersburg Beach FL 33741 Office: 2506 Pass-A-Grille Way St Petersburg Beach FL 33706

HURLEY, JAMES FRANKLIN, III, newspaper editor, publisher; b. Salisbury, N.C., July 22, 1931; s.; Woodberry Forest Sch., 1949; B.A. in Journalism, U. N.C., 1953; postgrad. Am. Press Inst., Columbia U., 1962, 66; m. Frances Geraldine Trammell, June 11, 1958. Reporter, Salisbury (N.C.) Post, 1955-62, editor, 1962—; pub. Cooleemee Jour.; pres. Davie County Pub. Co., Holmes Investment Co., Salisbury, Post Pub. Co., Salisbury; dir. Western N.C. Pub. Co., Lincolnton, Wachovia Bank & Trust Co., Salisbury. Bd. dirs. United Fund, YMCA; chmn. Lincoln Park Swimming Pool Drive, 1963, Rowan County Morehead Scholarship Selection Com., 1966—. Served with 3d Inf. Div., AUS, 1953-55. Named Young Man of Year, Jr. C. of C., 1962; editorial writing 1st prize N.C. Press Assn. newswriting competition, 1960-62, 67, Sports 1st prize, 1962. Mem. N.C. Assn. Afternoon Newspapers (pres. 1966), Salisbury-Rowan C. of C. (pres. 1962), Am. Legion, Salisbury-Rowan Mchts. Assn. (bd. dirs.), Phi Beta Kappa, Zeta Psi. Democrat. Presbyn. (chmn. bd. deacons). Elk. Club: Salisbury Country (dir.). Home: 219 W Corriher Av Salisbury NC 28144 Office: Salisbury Evening Post W Innes St Salisbury NC 28144

HURLEY, JEREMIAH JOSEPH, accountant; b. Washington, Aug. 28, 1923; s. Jeremiah John and Annie (McInerney) H.; B.C.S., Columbus U., 1947, M.C.S., 1948, C.P.A., 1950. Asst. bookkeeper George I. Borger Real Estate, Washington, 1941-42; jr. accountant William Claybaugh & Co., Washington, 1942-43, staff accountant, 1946-50, sr. accountant, 1950-52, asso. mem., 1952; prof. accountancy Columbus U., 1951-52; asso. mem. S. Frank Levy & Co., 1953-61, partner, 1962—. Served as staff sgt. Office of Fiscal Dir., Finance Corps, U.S. Army, ETO, 1943-46. Mem. Am. Inst. C.P.A.'s, Holy Name Soc., Gonzaga Alumni Assn., Assn. Practicing C.P.A.'s, Columbus U. Alumni Assn., Chi Sigma Mu. Club: Rehoboth (Del.) Beach Country. Home: 5036 Weaver Terrace NW Washington DC 20016 Office: 700 10th St NW Washington DC 20001

HURLEY, WILLIAM MARVIN, assn. exec.; b. Hector, Ark., Apr. 19, 1906; s. James Henry and Onie (Turnbow) H.; student Ark. Poly. Coll., 1925-28; B.A., U. Ark., 1929, M.A., 1930; m. Marjorie Sue Caldwell, June 17, 1934; children—James Franklin, Gerald Marvin. Instr. journalism, editor Ark. Alumnus, U. Ark., 1929-35; publicity mgr. Tulsa, C. of C., 1935-37, indsl. mgr., asst. gen. mgr., 1938-41; exec. v.p. U.S. Jr. C. of C., St. Louis, 1937-38; gen. mgr. Lincoln (Neb.), C. of C., 1941-43; asst. gen. mgr. Houston, C. of C., 1945-50, exec. v.p., 1951—. Bd. dirs. Houston Symphony Soc., Houston Livestock Show, Jr. Achievement Houston, Houston Port Bur. Served as lt. col, C.E., AUS, 1943-45. Decorated Legion of Merit (U.S.); Royal Order of Vasa (Sweden); cavalier Order Leopold II (Belgium); recipient distinguished alumnus citation U. Ark., 1955; Freedoms Found. award, 1953, 55, 56, 62, 65, 67, 68, 69; named to Hall of Distinction Ark. Tech., 1965. Mem. U.S. C. of C. (past chmn. regents Insts. Orgn. Mgmt., edn. com.), Am. C. of C. Execs. (pres. 1958), So. Assn. C. of C. Execs. (pres. 1954), Nat. Inst. Comml. and Trade Orgn. Execs. (pres. 1954), Southwestern C. of C. Inst. (pres. 1952), Tex. C. of C. Mgrs. Assn. (pres. 1963-64), Am. Soc. Oceanography (dir.), Nat. Space Hall Fame (exec. v.p.), Lambda Chi Alpha, Kappa Tau Alpha. Democrat. Methodist (past chmn. ofcl. bd.). Clubs: Houston, Lakeside Country, Kiwanis (past pres.). Author: Chamber of Commerce Administration, 1942; Chamber of Commerce Management, 1960; Decisive Years for Houston, 1966. Editor: Am. C. of C. Execs. Jour., 1962. Home: 914 Wild Valley Rd Houston TX 77027 Office: Houston Chamber of Commerce Box 53600 Houston TX 77052

HURSEY, RUDOLPH JULIAN, dentist; b. Lakeland, Fla., July 31, 1927; s. Rudolph Julian and Margaret Francis (Griggs) H.; B.S., Wofford Coll., 1950; D.D.S., Georgetown U., 1954; m. Jean Moore, June 24, 1948, children—Mary (Mrs. James Edwin Stanton), Susan Melinda, Laura Jean. Dental intern Childrens Hosp., Washington, 1954-55; practice dentistry specializing in pedodontics, Spartanburg, S.C., 1955—. Mem. Mayor's Adv. Council, Spartanburg, S.C., 1968—; mem. Broad River Tb. Assn., 1967—. Served with USNR, 1945-47. Mem. Am. Dental Assn., S.C., Piedmont Dist., Spartanburg County (pres. 1958) dental socs., Southeastern Soc. Pedodontics (sec.

1971), S.C. Soc. Dentistry for Children (pres. 1963), S.C. Assn. Pedodontists (pres. 1969-71), Delta Sigma Delta. Methodist (financial sec. adminstrv. bd. 1967). Club: Spartanburg Country. Home: 1310 Pinecrest Rd Spartanburg SC 29302 Office: 444 Kennedy St Spartanburg SC 29302

HURSON, DANIEL LAWRENCE, ins. co. exec.; b. Washington, Apr. 26, 1920; s. Daniel and Ellen (Gerrity) H.; B.S., Georgetown U., 1942; M.B.A., Harvard Bus. Sch., 1947; m. Mary J. Adams, July 27, 1946; children—Daniel, John, Matthew, Frederick. Planning asst. Acacia Mut. Life Ins. Co., Washington, 1947-51, adminstrv. asst. to exec. v.p., 1951-55, asst. to exec. v.p., 1955-56, asst. to pres., 1956, 2d v.p., 1956-62, v.p., gen. comptroller, 1962-65, exec. v.p., 1965-67, pres., 1967-69, chmn. bd., pres., 1969—; dir., mem. exec. com. Nat. Savs. & Trust Co., Washington; dir. Potomac Electric Power Co., Washington. Mem. Met. Washington Bd. Trade, 1955. Trustee, Fed. City Council and Downtown Progress, Davis Meml. Goodwill Industries. Served with USAF, World War II. Decorated D.F.C., Air medal. Life Office Mgmt. Assn. Inst. fellow, 1956. Mem. Am. Mgmt. Assn., Life Office Mgmt. Assn. (dir.), Pres.'s Assn., Friendly Sons St. Patrick. Rotarian (dir.). Clubs: Columbia Country, Burning Tree, Internat., Harvard Business School (Washington). Home: 9623 W Bexhill Dr Kensington MD 20795 9623 W Bexhill Dr Kensington MD 20795 Office: 51 Louisiane Av NW Washington DC 20001

HURST, FANNIE MAE FANT (MRS. JOHN H. HURST), biologist, educator; b. Waco, Tex.; d. Bennett B. and Fannie (Green) Fant; B.A. cum laude, Baylor U., 1948, M.A. with honors, 1950; Ph.D., Purdue U., 1955; postgrad. (NSF fellow) U. Okla. History Sci. Inst., 1961; m. John H. Hurst, June 8, 1932; 1 dau., Pauline Carol (Mrs. Allen Clark Cullens). Instr. biology Baylor U., Waco, Tex., 1948-49, 52-53, asst. prof., 1953-59, asso. prof., 1959-68, prof., 1968—; instr. Purdue U., Lafayette, Ind., 1949-52. Vis. scientist Tex. Acad. Sci., 1963—; counselor Tex. Jr. Acad. Sci., 1964—. Past dir., past mem. edn. com. McLennan County chpt. Am. Cancer Soc. Fellow Tex. Acad. Sci.; mem. A.A.A.S., Bot. Soc. Am., Internat. Assn. Plant Taxonomists, Internat. Soc. Plant Morphologists, Nat. Assn. Biology Tchrs. (coll. membership chmn. for Tex.), North Tex. Biol. Soc. (v.p. 1959-60, pres. 1968-69), Southwestern Assn. Naturalists, Am. Assn. U. Profs., Am. Inst. Biol. Scis., Am. Assn. U. Women (higher edn. com. Waco br. 1960-63), Ft. House Soc. Historic Preservation, Sigma Xi (sec. Baylor club), Alpha Chi, Beta Beta Beta, Sigma Delta Epsilon. Democrat. book revs. to Bios. Research on endodermis of smilax, nutritional studies of aspergillus, phylogeny of liliales. Home: 400 Rice Av Waco TX 76708

HURST, JAMES KENNETH, oil investment co. exec.; b. Port Arthur, Tex., Nov. 26, 1936; s. Ben Morris and Jewel C. (Jackson) H.; B.B.A., Lamar U., 1962; m. Julia Armstrong; children—Julianne, Charles, Curtis, Deborah, Mike. Sr. auditor Peat Marwick Mitchell & Co., Houston, 1962-67; partner, Dillashaw, Hurst & Co., C.P.A.'s, 1967-70; treas., controller Kirby Petroleum Co., 1966-70; v.p. Skyline Employment Service, 1970; exec. v.p. Goldston Oil Corp., 1970-71; bus. mgr. Kenneth Franzheim, II, Houston, 1971—; dir. Farmers State Bank. Mem. Financial Execs. Inst., Houston Power Squadron, Am. Inst. C.P.A.'s, Tex. Soc. C.P.A.'s, Am. Mgmt. Assn., Nat. Assn. Accountants, Blue Key, Sigma Phi Epsilon. Clubs: Exchange, Racquet. Home: 3720 Olympia St Houston TX 77019 Office: 2040 Post Oak Tower Houston TX 77027

HURST, JOHN WILLIS, cardiologist; b. Cooper, Ky., Oct. 21, 1920; s. John M. and Verna (Bell) H.; B.S., U. Ga., 1941; M.D., Med. Coll. Ga., 1944; m. Nelie Wiley, Dec. 20, 1942; children—John, Steve, Phil. Intern, U. Hosp. Med. Coll. Ga., 1944-45, asst. resident, 1945-46; cardiac fellow Mass. Gen. Hosp., 1947-49; practice medicine, specializing in cardiology, Atlanta, 1949—; teaching, research fellow cardiology Sch. Medicine Harvard, 1948-49; fellow cardiology Sch. Medicine Emory U., Atlanta, 1950-51, instr., 1951-53, asso. in medicine, 1953-56, asst. prof., 1956-57, prof., chmn. dept. medicine, 1957—, dir. Postgrad. Teaching Program, 1956—; regional cons. cardiology VA Hosp., Atlanta, 1951—; chief of medicine Grady Meml. Hosp., Atlanta, 1957—. Mem. Presidents Com. on Heart Diseases, Cancer and Stroke, 1965—. Served to capt. AUS, 1946-47; to comdr. USNR, 1954-55. Diplomate Am. Bd. Internal Medicine, Am. Bd. Cardiovascular Disease. Fellow A.C.P., Am. Coll. Cardiology; mem. A.M.A., Ga., Fulton County med. assns., Am., Ga. (past pres.) heart assns., Am. Fedn. Clin. Research, Assn. Profs. Medicine, Assn. Am. Phyician, Assn. U. Cardiologists, So. Soc. Clin. Research, Am. Clin. and Climatological Assn., Alpha Omega Alpha. Author: (with G.C. Woodson) Atlas of Spatial Vector Electrocardiography, 1952; Cardiac Resuscitation, 1960; (with R. Bruce Logue) The Heart, 1966. Editor: (with N. K. Wenger) Electrocardiographic Interpretation, 1963; The Heart, 1966. Mem. editorial bd. Am. Heart Jour., 1964—. Contbr. articles to med. jours. Home: 45 Blackland Rd NW Atlanta GA 30305 Office: 69 Butler St SE Atlanta GA 30303

HURST, KENNETH, accounting co. exec.; b. Medford, Okla., July 22, 1907; s. William A. and Letha (Hughes) H.; student Phillips U., 1925-27, 1929; B.S., Okla. State U., 1932, M.S., 1933; m. Gertrude B. Nugent, Sept. 19, 1926; 1 dau., Patricia Ann (Mrs. G. Carroll Fisher). Auditor Income Tax div. Okla. Tax Commn., Oklahoma City, 1935-39, asst. dir., 1939-42, dir., 1942-45; partner firm Williams, Hurst & Groth, C.P.A.'S, Oklahoma City, 1945-61; partner firm Arthur Young & Co., CPA's, Oklahoma City, 1961-65; mng. partner, adminstrv. partner Hurst, Thomas & Co., Oklahoma City, 1965—. Mem. Okla. Bd. Accounting, 1951-59, chmn., 1955-59. Vice-chmn. Okla. Gov.'s tax adv. com., 1967-71. Bd. govs., mem. investment com. Okla. State U. Devel. Found. Mem. Okla. City Council Chs. (vice-chmn. 1952-53), Okla. Soc. C.P.A.'s (pres. 1948-49), Am. Inst. C.P.A.'s (mem. council 1945-50, 1958-60), So. States Conf. C.P.A.'s (pres. 1958-59), Acctg. (chmn. 1955-59). Mem. Christian Ch. (chmn. gen. bd. 1959-60). Author: Major Differences in Federal and Oklahoma Income Tax Laws, 1957, rev. edits., 1963, 64, 66, 1970; editor The Oklahoma CPA, 1961-71. Home: 5908 N Barnes St Oklahoma City OK 73112 Office: 1250 First National Center Oklahoma City OK 73102

HURST, VICTOR, univ. adminstr.; b. Rutherford, N.J., May 6, 1915; s. Albert Edward and Sarah (Schaefer) H.; B.S., Rutgers U., 1938, M.S., 1940; Ph.D., U. Mo., 1948; m. Henrietta A. Goerler, Nov. 28, 1942; children—William T., Ann V., Ruth M., Ellen R. Asso. prof. dairy sci. Clemson (S.C.) U., 1948-59, prof., 1959-62, alumni prof., 1962-65, dean grad. sch., 1965-66, dean univ., also v.p. acad. affairs, 1966—. Active Boy Scouts Am. Served with USCGR, 1942-46. Mem. Sigma Xi, Alpha Zeta, Gamma Sigma Delta, Phi Kappa Phi, Delta Upsilon, Alpha Epsilon Delta. Home: 210 Grove Dr Clemson SC 29631

HURT, CHARLES D., lawyer; b. Macon, Ga., Jan. 21, 1903; B. Ph., Emory U., 1925, LL.B., 1927. Admitted to Ga. bar 1927; now mem. firm Hurt, Hill and Richardson, Atlanta. Mem. Atlanta, Am. bar assns., State Bar Ga., Internat. Assn. Ins. Counsel, Fedn. Ins. Counsel, Am. Judicature Soc., Phi Delta Phi, Omicron Delta Kappa. Address: Hurt Hill and Richardson 614 William-Oliver B ldg Atlanta GA 30303*

HURT, FLOYD KINZER, physician; b. Marion, Va., Oct.9, 1910; s. William Whitfield and Zula Caroline (Kinzer) H.; B.S., Emory and Henry Coll., 1929; M.D., U. Va., 1935; m. Veronna Inez Griffin, Sept. 3, 1937; children—Robbie Jean (Mrs. Francis H. Mitchell Jr.), Martha Caroline (Mrs. Hewell Wynne.). Intern Duval County Hosp., Jacksonville, 1935-37; resident Duke Hosp., Durham, N.C., 1938-39; practice medicine specializing in radiology, Jacksonville, 1940—; chief dept. radiology, St. Vincent's Hosp., 1950, Riverside Hosp., 1960, also Duval Med. Center. Pres. Duval County chpt. Am. Cancer Soc., 1951. Bd. dirs. Jacksonville Art Mus. Served with M.C., AUS, 1942-45. Diplomate Am. Bd. Radiology. Fellow Am. Coll. Radiology; mem. Duval County Med. Soc. (treas. 1960), Fla. Med. Assn. (sec. 1963-71; treas. 1963-70; pres. 1970-71), Fla. Blue Shield (dir. 1954-63), S.C.V. Phi Chi. Methodist. Rotarian. Club: Timuquana Country (Jacksonville). Home: 3305 St Johns Av Jacksonville FL 32205 Office: 460 St James Bldg Jacksonville FL 32202

HURT, FRANK BENJAMIN, educator; b. Ferrum, Va., Oct. 22, 1899; s. John Kempleton and Lelia (Angle) H.; A.B., Washington and Lee U., 1923; M.A., U. Va., 1925; A.M. Princeton, 1926; grad. study Johns Hopkins, 1929-30; additional study Harvard, summers 1938-40; m. Mary Ann Wescott, June 3, 1943. Teaching fellow, University N.C., 1926-27; Instr., Ferrum Jr. Coll., 1927-29; asso. prof. polit. sci., Western Md. Coll., 1930-65, prof. emeritus, 1965—, head div. polit. sci., 1949; head div. social sci. Ferrum (Va.) Jr. Coll., 1965—, prof. emeritus, 1970—; lectr. sch. spl. and continuation studies U. Md., 1950-65; instr. summers Hun Sch., Princeton, 1927-32. Dir. First Nat. Bank. Mem. Am. Polit. Sci. Assn., Am. Hist. Assn., Am. Acad. Polit. and Social Sci., Nat. Collegiate Fgn. Lang. Soc., Franklin County Hist. Soc. (pres. 1969-70), Am. Assn. U. Profs., Pi Gamma Mu. Democrat. Methodist. Lion (pres. Ferrum 1968). Address: Ferrum Jr Coll Ferrum VA 24088

HURT, HARRY, oil co. exec.; b. Dallas, Feb. 20, 1899; s. Harry Aldenhoff and Margaret (Sweet) H.; B.S., Va. Mil. Inst., 1919; postgrad. Columbia, 1920; m. Margaret Regina Bitting, June 12, 1950; children—Harry III, Margaret Dorothy, William Richard, Dorothy Margaret. Began career as trainee, The Tex. Co.; partner Callery & Hurt Co., Houston, 19-; gen. partner Hurt Oil Co., Ltd., Houston, 1952—; dir. Capital Nat. Bank of Houston. Served with USNR, World War II. Mem. Am. Petroleum Inst., Mid-Continent Oil and Gas Assn., Am. Wildcatters (charter mem.), Houston C. of C (mem. steering com. Aviation com.). Clubs: Houston Country, River Oaks, Ramada (Houston); Racquet and Tennis (N.Y.C.); Seminole (Palm Beach, Fla.) Home: 2198 Troon Rd Houston TX 77019 Office: 1510 First City Nat Bank Bldg Houston TX 77002

HUSKINS, J. FRANK, state supreme ct. justice; b. Burnsville, N.C., Feb. 10, 1911; s. Joseph Erwin and Mary Etta (Peterson) H.; student Mars Hill Jr. Coll., 1927-29; A.B., U. N.C., 1930, postgrad. Sch. Law, 1930-32; m. Ruth Houck McNeill, Oct. 20, 1963; stepchildren—Robert Glenn McNeill, Ruth Elizabeth (Mrs. Melvin Webb II). Chmn., N.C. Indsl. Commn., 1949-55; judge N.C. Superior Ct., 1955-65; dir. adminstrv. office Cts. of N.C., 1965-68; asso. justice N.C. Supreme Ct., Raleigh, 1968—. Mayor, Burnsville, 1939-42; mem. N.C. Ho. of Reps., 1947-51. Served to lt. comdr. USNR, 1942-46. Mem. N.C. State Bar, N.C., Wake County bar assns., Am. Judicature Soc., Nat. Conf. Ct. Adminstrv. Officers, Am. Legion. Club: Raleigh Executives. Home: 3204 Beaufort St Raleigh NC 27609 Office: 307 Justice Bldg Raleigh NC 27601

HUSSEY, ROBERT JONES, cotton co. exec.; b. Memphis, Sept. 25, 1904; s. Clarence Wellington and Neva (Jones) H.; student Columbia Mil. Acad., 1922; LL.B., U. Ala., 1926; m. Kathleen Conant, Nov. 10, 1931; children—Robert Jones, Richard W., Edwin C. Pres., owner C.W.Hussey & Co., Memphis, 1935—; v.p. Growers Equipment Co. Pres. Memphis Cotton Exchange. Chmn. bd. trustees Presbyn. Day Sch.; trustee Memphis U. Sch., Hussey Found. Mem. Alpha Tau Omega. Presbyn. (elder). Home: 4185 Gwynne Rd Memphis TN 38103 Office: 110 S Front St Memphis TN 38103

HUSSEY, WILLIAM DAVIS, trade assn. exec.; b. Boston, July 20, 1933; s. Simeon A. and Marjorie (Rice) H.; B.S., Fla. So. Coll., 1958; student U. Fla., 1951-53; m. Elizabeth Ann Hatton, Sept. 10, 1960; children—William Davis, Jeffrey Rice. With Fla. Savs. & Loan League, Orlando, 1958—, sec., 1961—, exec. v.p., 1962—; dir. Fla. Informanagement Services, Inc., Orlando. Served with AUS, 1953-55. Mem. Fla. Soc. Assn. Execs. (pres., dir.), Savs. Assn. Trade Execs., Am. Soc. Assn. Execs., U. Fla. Alumni, Fla. State, Orlando Chambers Commerce, Sigma Alpha Epsilon, Pi Delta Epsilon. Clubs: Kiwanis, University, Tallahassee Country, Country (Orlando). Home: 1200 W Audubon Pl Orlando FL 32804 Office: 109 E Church St Orlando FL 32802 also PO Box 2246 Orlando FL 32802

HUSSMAN, WALTER E., newspaper publisher, broadcaster; b. Bland, Mo., July 20, 1906; s. Walter J. and Anna (Vaughn) H.; student U. Mo., 1929-32; m. Betty M. Palmer, Dec. 24, 1931; children—Gayle (Mrs. Richard S. Arnold), Marilyn (Mrs. James M. Augur), Walter E. With Palmer Newspapers, Camden, Ark., 1933—, mgr. bus., advt., 1947-57, asst. pub., 1947—, pres., owner 1970—; pres. Marigayle Realty Co., Camden, 1970—, Palma Media Group S.A., Acapulco, Mexico, 1970—. Mem. Ark. Judiciary Commn., 1965-67; chmn. Ark. Citizens Judicial Council, 1967-68. Served to maj. AUS, 1942-45. Recipient Gavel award, Certificate Merit, Am. Bar Assn., 1969. Mem. Ark., Camden (past pres.) chambers commerce Ark., So., Tex. Daily (past pres.) newspaper assns., Nat. Overseas press clubs, Inter-Am. Press Assn., Am., Soc. Newspaper Editors, Nat. Broadcasters Club, Am. Judicature Soc., Sigma Delta Chi, Pi Kappa Alpha. Presbyn. (trustee). Clubs: Camden Country, The Shreveport (La.), Shreveport Country.Home: 1890 Marigayle Lane Camden AR 71701 Office: 113Madison St Camden AR 71701

HUSTED, WALTER, magazine editor; b. Bklyn., Feb. 7, 1906; student Columbia, 1922-23, N.Y.U., 1923-25; m. Margaret Denton, July 30, 1927; 1 dau., Myra. Reporter, Bklyn. Eagle, 1925-26, Des Moines Register, 1926-29, A.P., 1929-31; copy reader N.Y. World-Telegram, 1931-34; night editor N. Am. Newspaper Alliance, 1934-40; gen. news editor U.S. News & World Report, 1940—. Mem. Am. Inst. Graphic Arts, Early Am. Industries Assn. Club: Nat. Press (Washington). Home: 6021 Franconia Rd Alexandria VA 22310 Office: 2300 N St NW Washington DC 20037

HUSTON, LUTHER ALLISON, author, journalist; b. Paulina, Ia., Nov. 18, 1888; s. Luther Allen and Alice (Noble) H.; student U. So. Cal., 1908-11; m. Dora Lee Carey, Feb. 15, 1929; 1 dau., Ann Noble. Reporter, Bellingham (Wash.) Herald, 1912-14, Seattle Times, 1914-17; reporter, bur. mgr., fgn. corr., news editor, sales mgr. Internat. News Service, 1917-34; city editor Washington Post, 1934-35; bur. mgr., staff corr. Washington Bur., N.Y. Times, 1935-57; dir. pub. information Dept. Justice, Washington, 1957-61, asst. to dir. Am. Bar Assn., Washington, 1961-63; with Ernest Wittenberg Assos., pub. relations, 1964-65; Washington corr., editor and pub., 1966—. Recipient Wells key Sigma Delta Chi, 1949, George Polk Meml. award, 1954. Fellow Sigma Delta Chi (nat. pres. 1947-48). Episcopalian. Club: Nat. Press (gov. 1952-57, chmn. 1957). Author: Pathway to Judgment, A Study of Earl Warren, 1966; The Department of Justice, 1967. Home: 4000 Tunlaw Rd NW Washington DC 20007 Office: Nat Press Bldg Washington DC 20004

HUSTVEDT, ERLING HALVOR, mgmt. engr., polit. scientist; b. Washington, Dec. 11, 1919; s. Olaf Mandt and Irene (Cooper) H.; B.S., Mass. Inst. Tech., 1941; M.A. Tufts U., 1947; student George Washington U., 1959-64; m. Jane Elizabeth Parker, July 16, 1960; children—Eric, Elin (Mrs. Thomas Edward Bull), Scott, Dana, Nancy, Kent. Cons. indsl. engr., Portland, 1947-53, San Francisco, 1953-57; tchr. Menlo Sch., Menlo Park, Cal., 1957, St. Albans Sch., Washington, 1957-59; teaching fellow George Washington U., Washington, 1959-61; operations research analyst Nat. Bur. Standards, Washington, 1966-71; dep. dir. Federalism Seventy-Six, 1971—. Mem. ednl. council Mass. Inst. Tech., 1965—; trustee Alfred D. Cooper Fund, 1966—. Served as capt. Office Chief of Naval Operations, USNR, active duty 1942-45. Mem. Soc. for Advancement Mgmt. (chpt. v.p. 1952), Naval Res. Assn. (nat. v.p. 1965, nat. historian 1970—), Am. Polit. Sci. Assn., Operations Research Soc. Am., Am. Soc. for Information Scis., Phi Beta Epsilon, Mil. Order of Carabao. Club: City of Portland (Ore.), Aircraft Owners and Pilots Assn. Home: 5105 Philip Rd Annandale VA 22003 Office: Federalism Seventy-Six 1776 Massachusetts Av NW Washington DC 20236

HUTCHERSON, HUBERT ARNOLD, supt. schs.; b. Buena Vista, Ga., Apr. 16, 1928; s. Lorenza and Lila Faye (Whitley) H.; A.B., Mercer U., 1950; M.Ed., U. Ga., 1954 Tchr. Vidalia (Ga.) High Sch., 1950-55, R.E. Lee Inst., Thomaston, Ga., 1955-60; prin. Monroe Elementary Sch., Forsyth, Ga., 1960-64, Mary Persons High Sch., Forsyth, 1964-69, Perry (Ga.) High Sch., 1969-71; asst. supt. instrn. Houston County Bd. Edn., Perry, 1971—. Dir. Upper Ocmulgee Econ. Opportunity Commn., 1966-69. Named Tchr. of Year Monroe County by C. of C., 1969. Mem. N.E.A., P.T.A. (life), Nat. Assn. Secondary Sch. Prins., Ga. Assn. Sch. Adminstrs. (dir., 1967-68), Kappa Delta Pi. Episcoplaian. Kiwanian, Elk, Moose. Home: 1104 Kenwood Dr Perry GA 31069 Office: 1211 Washington St Perry GA 31069

HUTCHERSON, WILLIAM POWELL, gynecologist; b. College Grove, Tenn., Nov. 20, 1918; s. Lemuel Ransom and Willie Eva (Maxwell) H.; B.S., Tenn. Tech. U., 1940; M.D., U. Tenn., 1944; m. Harmon Harding Lee, Feb. 19, 1966; 1 dau. (by previous marriage), Jain Foster. Intern, Meth. Hosp., Memphis, 1944; resident Cook County Hosp., Chgo., 1947-50; practice medicine, specializing in obstretrics and gynecology, Chattanooga, 1950—; chmn. dept. obstetrics and gynecology Meml. Hosp., 1960-67; chmn. dept. obstetrics and gynecology Barness Erlanger Hosp. 1968-72, attending physician, gynecologist, 1968—. Served to capt. M.C., AUS, 1945-46. Diplomate Am. Bd. Obstetrics and Gynecology. Fellow Am. Coll. Obstetricians and Gynecologists, A.C.S.; mem. Central Assn. Obstetrics and Gynecology. Republican. Contbr. articles to profl. jours. Home: 910 Avon Pl Chattanooga TN 37405 Office: Med Towers Bldg 1000 E 3d St Chattanooga TN 34703

HUTCHESON, JAMES BYRON, physician; b. Roanoke, Va., July 17, 1922; s. James Byron and Kathleen (Marmon) H.; A.B., Emory and Henry Coll., 1943; M.D., U. Va., 1946; m. Judith Anne Baldwin, Dec. 27, 1950; children—Mary Lee, Nancy Reed, Jill Marmon, James Byron IV (dec.), Holly. Intern Med. Coll. Va., Richmond, 1946-47; intern, N.Y. Hosp., 1949-50, asst. resident, 1951-52, resident pathologist, 1951-52; pathologist, dir. labs. Lewis-Gale Hosp., Roanoke, 1952-55; pathologist, chief anat. pathology Baylor U. Med. Center, 1955-59; instr. pathology Cornell Med. Sch., N.Y.C., 1952-53; asso. prof. Baylor U. Grad. Research Inst., Dallas, 1955-59; asso. prof. Baylor U. Sch. Dentistry, Dallas, 1955-59; clin. asst. prof. U. Tex., Southwestern Med. Sch., Dallas, 1955-59; pathologist, chief anat. pathology Tampa Gen. Hosp., 1959—, dir. pathology, 1962—, vice chief of staff, 1968-69; dir. pathology U. Community Hosp., 1962-69; pres. Drs. Hutcheson, Moseley, Marham, Ruffolo & Hooper, Tampa, 1961—, Pathol. Assos., Tampa, 1969—; clin. prof. pathology U. South Fla., 1971—. Dir. N.J. Life Ins. Co., Davis Blvd. Corp., 1st Nat. Bank, Plant City, Fla., 1963-69. Bd. dirs. Am. Cancer Soc., pres. Hillsborough County unit, 1968-69. Served as lt. (j.g.) USNR, 1947-49. Recipient Research grant Am. Cancer Soc., 1951-53, Mead Johnson Research grant, 1962, USPHS research grants, 1962, 67-70. Diplomate Am. Bd. Pathology. Fellow A.C.P., Coll. Am. Pathologists; mem. Am., So. med. assns., Fla., Hillsborough County med. socs., Am. Soc. Clin. Pathologists, Am. Assn. Blood Banks, Soc. Exptl. Biology and Medicine, Fla. Soc. Pathologists, Intersoc. Cytology Council, Am. Assn. Pathologists and Bacteriologists, Am. Soc. Cytology, Fla. West Coast Pathology Assn. (pres. 1968—). Clubs: Torch, University. Contbr. articles to med. jours. Home: 3609 Beach Dr Tampa FL 33609 Office: Tampa Gen Hosp Davis Island Tampa FL 33606 also 1 Davis Blvd Davis Islands Tampa FL 33606

HUTCHESON, JOHN YOUNG, lawyer; b. Mecklenburg, Va., July 7, 1896; s. Herbert Farrar and Mary H. (Young) H.; legal edn. U. of Va., 1927; student William and Mary Coll. Admitted to Va. bar 1928, since practiced at Boydton. Mem. Am., Va. bar assns., Kappa Sigma. Address: Boydton VA 23917

HUTCHESON, SAMUEL LEWIS, constrn. and investment co. owner; b. Phila., July 17, 1930; s. Samuel Lewis and Jean (Crow) H.; student Choate Sch., 1944-46, McCallie Sch., 1946-49, Ga. Inst. Tech., 1949-52 children—Samuel Lewis III, Laura Susan, James Olan, Henry Lee. Formerly v.p., dir. Peerless Woolen Mills, N.Y.C.; v.p. Burlington Industries, N.Y.C., 1952-59; v.p., dir. Olan Mills, Inc., photography studios, Dallas, 1959-63, 67-70, now cons.; operator investment and constrn. firm Hutcheson-Lee, Inc., Dallas, 1963-67; owner S.L.H. Assos., Inc., Dallas, 1970—, also dir.; dir. Rossville Devel., Inc., Sumter Farm & Stock, Inc., First Assos., Inc., First Bank and Trust of Richardson, Pioneer Stor & Lok, Inc., L.O.G. Devel.; chmn. bd. Patjanella Ranch, Inc., Hutcheson-Ingram Devel. Co., Hutcheson-Richards Enterprises, Inc., Mallard Prodn. Co., Hutcheson England, Inc. Bd. dirs. Dallas Civic Opera, 1971—. Served with USNR. Mem. Camp Fire Club Am., Phi Delta Theta. Methodist (bd. govs. 1965-66). Club: Dallas Gun. Home: 10624 Ravenscroft St Dallas TX 75230 Office: 2930 Turtle Creek Plaza Dallas TX 75219

HUTCHINGS, GEORGE ERNEST, hosp. adminstr.; b. Griffin, Ga., Jan. 20, 1915; s. Clarence Pierce and Ruby Russell (Collins) H.; B.A., Mercer U., 1937; m. Mary Lou Joiner, May 11, 1946; 1 dau., Elizabeth Russell (Mrs. Richard Stratigos). With Coleman Meadows Pate, wholesale drug co., Macon, Ga., 1935-43; asst. adminstr. Homer D. Cobb Meml. Hosp., Phenix City, Ala., 1967-69; adminstr. Marion Meml. Hosp., Buena Vista, Ga., 1969-72; adminstr. Gilman Hosp., also St. Marys Convalescent Home, 1972—. Served to col. U.S. Army, 1943-66. Mem. Am. Acad. Med. Adminstrs., Assn. U.S. Army, Officers Assn., Am. Coll. Nursing Home Adminstrs. Methodist (music dir. 1964—, lay leader 1965—). Lion. Club: Civitan. Home: 2101 Monaco Dr Columbus GA 31903 Office: 805 Dilworth St St Marys GA 31558

HUTCHINS, CHARLES ANTHONY, social worker; b. Forrest City, N.C., Aug. 7, 1931; s. John Samuel and Carolyn (McKenzie) H.; B.A., Furman U., 1957; M.S.W., Fla. State U., 1959; post-grad. work,

U. of Wash., 1968-69, Certificate community Mental Health; m. Eva Grey Martin, June 27, 1953; children—Anna Camille, Ralph Edwin, John Paul. Ednl. asst. Northside Meth. Ch., Greeneville, S.C., 1955-57; caseworker Family Service Assn., Greenville, 1957-58; caseworker Holston Methodist Children's Home, Greeneville, Tenn., 1959-61, dir. social service dept., 1961-69, dir. children's services, 1969-72, asso. exec. dir., 1972-—; v.p. Tenn. Conf. of Social Workers, 1963-—; cons. social work. Chmn. personnel com. Cherokee Guidance Center.; del. gen. conf. United Meth. Ch., 1968, 70, 72, del. Southeast jurisdiction conf., 1964, 68, 72. Alderman, City of Greenville, Tenn., 1964-66; Election commr. Greene County, 1968-70. Served with AUS, 1949-52. Decorated Purple Heart, Bronze Star, Combat Infantryman's badge. Named Social Worker of Yr., Knox area chpt. Nat. Assn. Social Workers, 1970; Mem. Nat. Assn. Social Workers, Acad. Certified Social Workers, Am. Group Psychotherapy Assn., V.F.W., D.A.V., Am. Legion. Methodist. Mason (32 deg., Shriner). Home: Holston Dr Box 188 Greenville TN 37743

HUTCHINS, DERRELE CAMDEN, agriculturist; b. Greenville, S.C., Aug. 12, 1926; s. J. Sam and Carolyn (McKenzie) H.; B.S., Clemson U. 1951, postgrad., 1952, 53, 56, 57, 59; m. Betty Lucille Sloan, Aug. 12, 1949; children—Derrele Camden, David Michael, Barbara Gale, Daniel Sloan. Vets. farm tng. instr. Oconee pub. schs., 1947-48; tchr. vocational agr. Oconee County pub. schs., 1951-54; asst. county agt. Clemson U. Extension Service, Spartanburg, S.C., 1954-57, extension marketing specialist, Columbia 1957-65, marketing information specialist, 1965-68, dir. information filter center, 1965-70, asso. extension specialist marketing, 1968-70; agr. specialist marketing S.C. Dept. Agr., Columbia, 1970-—. Adviser, cons., exec. sec., dir. pub. relations S.C. Fresh Fruit and Vegetable Assn., 1959-—, coordinator scholarship fund, 1963-—; marketing cons. S.C. Peach Council and Promotion Bd., 1970-—. Master Cleveland Grange, 1952-54, Green Pond Grange, 1955-56; organizer Springdale (S.C.) Community Scouters, 1964, pres., 1964-70; mem. Richland-Lexington County Coordinating Council, 1965-66. Served with USNR, 1944-46. Mem. Epsilon Sigma Phi. Methodist (chmn. ecumenical affairs, 1969-72, supt. ch. sch. 1959-64). Mason. Home: 2201 Platt Springs Rd West Columbia SC 29169 Office: PO Box 11280 Columbia SC 29211

HUTCHINSON, CONRAD, JR., educator; b. Bloomsburg, Pa., Oct. 25, 1919; s. Conrad and Helen M. (Parks) H.; B.S., Tuskegee Inst., 1940; M.S., Vandercook Coll. Music, Chgo., 1960; postgrad. U. Cin., New Eng. Conservatory, Boston; m. Rose Onealia Middleton, May 21, 1940; children—Conrad III, David E., Ann E., R. Keith. Bandmaster Mobile County Tng. Sch., 1940; band dir. Lincoln-Grant High Sch., Covington, Ky., 1941-52; bandmaster Grambling Coll., 1952-—; staff organist sta. WSAI, Cin., 1947-52, also condr. pit bands in Cin. Theatres, 1947-52; cons. and adjudicator in 14 states. Active Boy Scouts Am. Served with AUS, 1944-46. Mem. Coll. Band Dirs. Nat. Assn. Compositions: Black & Gold March, 1959; In A Rhapsodic Mood, 1957; Fight, 1956; Overture for Band, 1967. Home: Box 623 Grambling LA 71245

HUTCHINSON, RICHARD GLENN, physician; b. LaGrange, Ga., Aug. 18, 1933; s. Richard and Margaret Ann (Jordan) H.; B.A., Emory U., 1951-55; M.D., Med. Coll. Ga., 1959; m. Celeste Clanton, June 20, 1959; children— Richard Glenn, Wendell Clanton. Intern, Bapt. Hosp., Nashville, 1959-60; resident internal medicine Med. Coll. Ga. Hosps., Augusta, 1960-63; Ga. Heart Assn. cardiology fellow, 1963-64; staff physician VA Hosp., Jackson, Miss., 1966-67; instr. medicine U. Miss. Med. Sch., Jackson, 1967-69, asst. prof., attending physician, 1969-—, also dir. univ. coronary drug research clinic. Served to capt. USAF, 1964-66. James Bruce Traveling scholar A.C.P., 1970; Miss. Heart Assn. Research grantee, 1971-72. Fellow Am. Coll. Angiology, Internat. Coll. Angiology; mem. A.C.P., Am. Fedn. Clin. Research, Am. Heart Assn., Am. Coll. Chest Physicians, Miss. Heart Assn., Jackson Acad. Medicine. Methodist (mem. adminstrv. bd. 1971, chmn. commn. missions 1971). Contbr. articles to prof. pubs. Home: 1840 Springridge Dr Jackson MS 39211 Office: 2500 N State St Jackson MS 39216

HUTCHISON, JOHN ATKINS, electric utility co. exec.; b. Baird, Tex., Mar. 6, 1911; s. John A. and Ruth Emma (Brown) H.; student Hardin-Simmons U., 1927-28, Tex. A. and M. U., 1928-30; B.S., Cal. Inst. Tech., 1932; m. M. Eleanor Jones, Dec. 23, 1936; children—Eleanor Elaine (Mrs. Robert W. Hampton), John A. III, David S. Distbn. engr. West Tex. Utilities Co., Abilene, 1936-54, asst. supt. prodn. and enging., 1955-60, chief engr., 1960-—, v.p., 1965-—, also dir.; dir. States Gen. Life Ins. Co. Served to capt. AUS, 1941-44. Fellow I.E.E.E.; mem. Tex. Profl. Engrs. Soc., Abilene Petroleum Club, West Central Tex. Oil and Gas Assn., Tex. Water Conservation Assn. Clubs: Abilene Country, Exchange. Home: 2114 Shoreline Circle Abilene TX 79602 Office: PO Box 841 Abilene TX 79604

HUTCHISON, RALPH OSWALD, mfg. co. exec.; b. Frazier, Ky., Oct. 3, 1923; s. Wendell Blackburn and Hulda (Colditz) H.; B.Chem. Engring., U. Louisville, 1946; Nuclear-Metall. Engr., Oak Ridge Inst. Nuclear Studies, 1950; m. Pauline Mosby, July 12, 1946; children—Ronald L., Roger N., Mark W., Philip L., Stephen C. Chief materials project engr. AEC, Augusta, Ga., 1951-54; corporate staff specialist Lockheed Aircraft Co., Marietta, Ga., 1954-55; plant mgr. nuclear facilities plant Babcock, Wilcox Co., Lynchburg, Va., 1955-56; with Am. Machine & Foundry Co., 1956-61, exec. sec. bd. mgmt., N.Y.C., exec. asst. to chief exec., Washington, 1958-61, dir. electronic comml. devel., Washington, 1960-61; with Ling-Temco-Vought, Inc., Dallas, 1961-66, asst. to exec. v.p. and pres., Dallas, 1961-65, chief exec. Friedrich Co. div., 1963-64, exec. v.p., gen. mgr. univ. sound div., Oklahoma City, 1965-66; dir., chmn. exec. com. Gt. S.W. Warehouses Corp. subsidiary, v.p. Gt. S.W. Corp., Dallas, Ft. Worth, 1966-69, pres. GSC Devel. Corp., Atlanta, 1969-—; exec. v.p. Gt. Southwest Corp., 1970-—; chief exec. Lakeway Land Co., Austin, Tex., 1971-—; exec. v.p. Internat. City Corp., Atlanta, 1971-72. Instr. chem. engring. U. Tenn. Extension, 1950-51. Served to lt. USNR, 1943-46. Presbyn. Patentee hafnium stabilized stainless steel; developed process for obtaining hafnium metal in quantity. Home: 376 Blanton Rd NW Atlanta GA 30342 Office: First Nat Bank Bldg Atlanta GA 30303

HUTCHISON, WILLIAM JELIER, physician; b. Chgo., May 21, 1923; s. Roy M. and Mary (Jelier) H.; B.S., Northwestern U., 1943, M.D., 1946; m. Helen Jane Weider, Apr. 5, 1947; children—Thomas William, James Richard, Jean Elizabeth, Susan Louise. Intern, Cook County Hosp., Chgo., 1946-47; resident Southwestern Med. Sch., U. Tex., 1949-52, instr. anatomy, 1950-51; chief orthopedic surgery VA Hosp., Augusta, Ga., 1952; instr. Med. Coll. Ga., 1952; practice medicine, specializing in orthopedic surgery, Tallahassee, 1953-—; chief staff Tallahassee Meml. Hosp., 1968-69; sr. surgeon Dist. VI Fla. Crippled Childrens Commn., 1953-71; orthopedic cons. Dept. Justice. Pres. Comprehensive Health Planning Council Big Bend Area, 1969-71. Pres., St. Marks Devel. Corp., St. Marks, Fla. Bd. dirs. Easter Seal Soc., Healthways of Tallahassee; pres. Fla. Easter Seal Soc. for Crippled Children and Adults, 1970-72; pres. Easter Seal Rehab. Center, Tallahassee, 1966-67. Served with USNR, 1943-45, 47-49. Diplomate Am. Bd. Orthopedic Surgery. Fellow Am. Acad. Orthopedic Surgeons; mem. Fla. Orthopedic Soc. (pres. 1966-67), Fla. Med. Assn., Phi Beta Pi. Research in bone physiology. Home: 2113 Trescott Dr Tallahassee FL 32303 Office: 1214 Magnolia Dr Tallahassee FL 32303

HUTSELL, JAMES KENDALL, newspaper editor; b. Columbia, Mo., Dec. 3, 1907; s. John Hedges and Eulah (Keene) H.; B.J., U. Mo., 1929, postgrad., 1930-32. News desk Des Moines Tribune, 1929-30; editor Columbia (Mo.) Herald-Statesman, 1935-37; columnist Mo. Press Assn., Columbia, Mo., 1937-39; news editor Hattiesburg (Miss.) Am., 1942-43; news desk New Orleans States, 1943-45; telegraph editor Asheville (N.C.) Times, 1945-48, Pensacola (Fla.) Journ., 1948-54; editor Ala. Courier, Athens, Ala., 1956-57; telegraph editor Huntsville (Ala.) Times, 1957-61, asso. editor, 1961-—. Dir. publicity Mo. State Fair, Sedalia, Mo., 1939-41. Served as civilian in pub. relations with AUS, 1941-42. Mem. Huntsville Lit. Assn., Huntsville Hist. Soc., U. Mo. Alumni Assn., Sigma Delta Chi, Kappa Tau Alpha. Club: The Press (Huntsville Alabama). Author: History of the Missouri Press Association, 1931; A Stylebook for Newspaper Editors and the Law of the Press, 1951; also, articles in profl., lit., gardening, hist. mags. Home: Harvest Hill RFD 1 Box 311 Harvest AL 35749 Office: 2317 Memorial Pkwy SW Huntsville AL 35805

HUTTO, TERRELL DON, correctional adminstr.; b. Sinton, Tex., June 8, 1935; s. Terrell Sanford and Winnie (Custer) H.; student Tarleton State Coll., 1953-54, U. Tex., 1954, Gainesville Jr. Coll., 1955, Paris Jr. Coll., 1955-56; B.S., E. Tex. State Coll., 1958; postgrad. So. Meth. U., 1958-59, George Washington U., 1960-61, Am. U., 1963-64, Sam Houston State Coll., 1966-67; m. Nancy Sue Moore, June 10, 1960; children—Jennifer Marie, Shelley Anne, Robyn Suzanne. Tchr., Sidney Lanier Intermediate Sch., Fairfax County, Va., 1962-64; custodial officer Tex. Dept. Corrections, Otey, 1964-65, asst. warden Pre-Release Center, 1965, asst. warden Ferguson, 1965-67, warden Ramsey Units, 1967-71; commr. Ark. Dept. Corrections, Little Rock, 1971-—. Served with AUS, 1960-62. Mem. So. States Corrections Assn., Assn. State Correctional Adminstrs. Am. Correctional Assn. Democrat. Methodist. Rotarian, Elk. Address: State Capitol Little Rock AR 72201

HYATT, DONALD MCINTOSH, shipbuilder, mayor; b. Waynesville, N.C., June 7, 1909; s. William Arthur and Evelyn (McIntosh) H.; student Duke, 1928-32; m. Julia May, July 29, 1933; 1 son, Donald McIntosh. Asst. to dir. personnel and indsl. relations Newport News Shipbuilding & Dry Dock Co. (Va.); mayor, Newport News, 1962-—. Bd. dirs. War Meml. Mus. Methodist. Mason (Shriner, Jester), Lion. Home: 54 Main St Newport News VA 23601 Office: 4101Washington Av Newport News VA 23607

HYATT, FRANCIS MARION, city ofcl.; b. Marietta, Okla., Feb. 21, 1905; s. Frank W. and Gertrude (Sholly) H.; student Ia. Wesleyan Coll., 1924-25; m. Alice Louise Waterman, June 17, 1934; children—Philip W., James Robert. Owner, operator radio sales and service co., Ottumwa, Ia., 1926-40; announcer, mgr. Sta. WJHO, Opelika, Ala., 1940-51; announcer Sta. WAUD, Auburn, Ala., 1951-60; exec. dir. Opelika Housing Authority, 1951-—. Instr. shelter mgmt. Opelika Civil Def., 1963-—. Chmn. Opelika Park and Recreation Bd., 1947-52, Lee County chpt. A.R.C., 1961-64, Opelika Library Bd., 1942-46; chmn. Lee County Welfare Bd., 1958-—, Ala. pres., 1963-64; chmn. Birmingham Regional Blood Bank, A.R.C., 1967-71; mem. adv. com. Region 6 Combined Service Territory, Birmingham Area A.R.C., 1965-71; chmn. Ala. div. adv. com. A.R.C., 1971-—. Recipient Outstanding Citizen award Opelika Jr. C. of C., 1962. Mem. Ala. Assn. Housing Authorities (pres.), C. of C. (v.p. 1952), Sigma Phi Epsilon. Methodist (chmn. ofcl. bd. 1961-63). Rotarian (pres. Opelika 1945-46). Home: 1004 Fitzpatrick Av Opelika AL 36801 Office: 316 Pleasant Dr Opelika AL 36801

HYDE, C.J., city ofcl. Police chief, Louisville. Address: Police Hdqrs Louisville KY 40202*

HYDE, DEWITT S., judge; b. Washington, Mar. 21, 1909; s. Burr Hamilton and Ethel (Holland) H.; J.D., George Washington U., 1935; m. Mildred Sullivan. Admitted to D.C. bar; law clk. FCA, 1933-38; partner firm Hilland & Hyde, 1938-59; judge D.C. Ct. Gen. Sessions, 1959-71; judge Superior Ct. D.C., 1971-— prof. law Benjamin Franklin U., 1946-52, 60-—. Mem. 83d to 85th Congresses from Md. Chmn. Bd. dirs. Christ Ch. Child Center, 1961-—. Served to lt. comdr. USNR, 1943-46. Mem. Am., D.C. bar Assns., The Barristers, George Washington U. Alumni Assn. Republican. Club: Columbia Country. Home: 5606 McLean Dr Bethesda MD 20014 Office: Superior Ct DC 4th and E Sts NW Washington DC 20001*

HYDE, EDWIN, dept. store exec.; b. Charleston, S.C., June 15, 1905; s. Tristram Tupper and Minnie (Black) H.; student Furman U., Greenville, S.C., 1923-24; LL.D., Washington and Lee U., 1971; m. Camilla Price Alsop, Dec. 4, 1930; 1 dau., Camilla (Mrs. Carlton P. Moffatt, Jr.). Vice pres. The Bank of Va., Richmond, 1931-44; exec. v.p. Peoples Nat. Bank, Charlottesville, Va., 1944-46; v.p. Miller & Rhoads, Richmond, 1946-47, exec. v.p., 1947-53, pres., dir., 1953-68, chmn. bd., 1968-—; vice chmn., chmn. finance com. Garfinckel, Brooks Bros., Miller & Rhoads, Inc., Washington, 1967-—; pres. Sixth St. Enterprises; dir., mem. exec. com. Va. Indsl. Devel. Corp.; dir. Central Va. Ednl. TV Corp.; dir., mem. exec. com. Shenandoah Life Ins. Co., United Va. Bank, Frederick Atkins, Inc. Mem. mchts. council N.Y. U.; Council of Naval Affairs, Nat. Citizens Com. for Community Relations; corp. patron Va. Mus. Fine Arts; dir. Central Richmond Assn. Trustee, pres. Miller & Rhoads Found.; trustee Richmond Meml. Hosp.; trustee, mem. finance com. retirement system A.R.C.; bd. dirs. Va. Found. for Independent Colls., Ind. Coll. Funds Am.; pres. bd. trustees U. Va. Grad. Sch. Bus. Sponsors. Mem. Soc. Colonial Wars in Va., Sons of the Revolution, St. Cecelia Soc., Newcomen Soc. Episcopalian. Clubs: Commonwealth, Country of Virginia, German (Richmond). Home: 209 Lock Lane Richmond VA 23226 Office: 517 E Broad St Richmond VA 23261

HYDE, FLOYD H., govt. ofcl.; b. Fresno, Cal., 1921; J.D., U. So. Cal. Admitted to Cal. bar, 1950; practiced in Fresno, 1950-65; mayor, Fresno, 1965-69; asst. sec. for community devel. Dept. Housing and Urban Devel., 1969-71, asst. sec. for community devel., 1971-—. Sr. Mem. Fresno Citizens' Com. for Community Improvement, 1962-63; mem. Fresno Community Council; past v.p. Nat. League Cities; mem. nat. adv. bd. U.S. Conf. Mayors; founding mem. Nat. Urban Coalition. Bd. dirs. YMCA, 1960-61. Served to capt. USMCR, World War II; PTO. Office: Dept Housing and Urban Devel Washington DC 20410

HYDE, JAMES SYLVESTER, JR., lawyer; b. Chattanooga, June 17, 1926; s. James Sylvester and Althea (Baker) H.; student North Ga. Mil. Coll., 1944; B.A., U. Chattanooga, 1950; LL.B., U. Tenn., 1951, J.D., 1968; m. Opal M. England, Nov 14, 1947; children—Delisa, Lieda, Nada, Eldon. Lab. foreman E. I. Dupont, 1951-54; claim rep. State Farm Mutual, 1955-59; ins. adjuster Pritchett Co., 1959-61; admitted to Tenn. and Fed. bar, 1962; gen. practice, Chattanooga, 1962-—. Served with AUS, 1944-46. Mem. Soil Conservation Soc. Am. (sec.-treas.), Phi Delta Phi. Baptist. Club: Chattanooga Geology. Lectr. anthropology. Home: 8440 Chambers Chattanooga TN 37421 Office: Pioneer Bank Chattanooga TN 37402

HYDE, ORRIE EUGENE, elec. supply co. exec.; b. Olla, La., Dec. 2, 1927; s. Orrie Eugene and Ethyl (Brockner) H.; student La. State U., 1944-46; m. Helen Ruth Evans, Sept. 24, 1948; children—Bernia Susan (Mrs. Charles E. White, Jr.), Ted Evans. Wtih Evans Elec. Supply, Inc., Baton Rouge, 1947-— sales mgr., 1954-56, v.p., 1956-—; rodeo producer Gonzales, La., 1948-57; dir. Home Builders Assn. Greater Baton Rouge. Served with AUS 1946-47. Mem. Sales and Marketing Execs. Baton Rouge (pres. 1968-69), Sales and Marketing Execs. Internat. (internat. dir.). Democrat. Methodist. Home: 1757 Pollard Pky Baton Rouge LA 70808 Office: 1060 Nicholson Dr Baton Rouge LA 70821

HYDEN, ABNER ANGLIN, coll. adminstr.; b. Thornton, Tex., Dec. 11, 1920; s. J. J. and Sarah (De Hart) H.; B.A., Wayland Baptist Coll., 1949; B.D., Southwest Bapt. Theol. Sem., 1953, M.R.E., 1953, D.R.E., 1960; m. Marjorie Lee Barnett, Nov. 25, 1947. Ordained to ministry Baptist Ch., 1948; dir. religious edn., high sch. counselor, tchr. Buckner Orphans Home, Dallas, 1949-56; with Mary Hardin-Baylor Coll., Belton, Tex., 1956-68, dir. student personnel services, asst. prof. psychology and religion, 1956-60, dean coll., prof. ednl. psychology and religion, 1960-68; dir. personnel Baylor U., Waco, 1968-72, asst. to pres., dir. acad. advisement, 1972-—. Mem. acad. com. Tex. Edn. Agy. for Tex. Wesleyan Coll., Ft. Worth, 1963; chmn. com. Mary Hardin-Baylor for evaluation for So. Assn. Colls. and Univs., 1960. Served with Signal Corps, AUS, 1942-45; ETO. Recipient Distinguished Alumnus award, Wayland Bapt. Coll., 1963; Certificate of Achievement for outstanding service Def. Atomic Support Agy., Sandia Base, 1964. Mem. Internat. Platform Assn., So. Counselors Personnel Assn., Central Tex. Dinner Assn. (pres. 1964-65), Phi Delta Kappa. Rotarian. Address: Union Bldg Box 363 Baylor U Waco TX 76703

HYDER, CHARLES MONROE, ednl. adminstr.; b. Hickory, N.C., Jan. 3, 1926; s. Adrian Alvin and Violet Irene (Cline) H.; B.S. magna cum laude, Appalachian State U., 1951, M.A., 1955; Ed.D., Duke U., 1968; m. Ruth Wilene Kiser, Feb. 24, 1950; 1 son, Charles Michael. Tchr., adminstr. Charlotte-Mecklenburg Schs., Charlotte, N.C., 1952-66; grad. asst. Duke U., Durham, N.C., 1966-68; asso. prof. edn., dir. elementary edn. U. Tenn., Chattanooga, 1968-71, dir. human services program, 1971-—, prof. edn., 1972-—. Vis. prof. U. Ga., West Ga. State U., 1969. Dir. Model Cities Bd. Training Program, Chattanooga, 1969; dir. U. Tenn. Parent-Child Center Evaluation Team, 1970-—; cons. sch. systems, Tenn., Ga. Served with USNR, 1943-47, 51-52. Recipient Ivy award U. Tenn., 1971, grant U. Chattanooga Found., 1970. Mem. Kappa Delta Pi, Phi Delta Kappa, Pi Gamma Mu. Methodist. Democrat. Home: 4200 Rogers Rd Chattanooga TN 37411

HYLL, JULIA ANN HUGHES (MRS. RICHARD H. HYLL), mortician; b. Marion, O., Oct. 28, 1930; d. Merle H. and Katherine (Hecker) Hughes; B.S., Bowling Green State U., 1952; degree in embalming cum laude, Cin. Coll. Embalming, 1953; m. Richard H. Hyll, Aug. 29, 1953; children—Sharon Lee, Mark Louis. Histological technician Chgo. Lying-in Hosp., 1954-55; funeral dir. Hughes-Hyll Mortuary, Marion, 1956-67, sec. bd. dirs., 1958-67; co-owner Richard Hyll Funeral Home, St. Croix, V.I., 1967-—. Charter mem. Jr. Federated Women Marion County, Marion, 1954, pres., 1959-60; chmn. art. dept. Marion County Fedn. Women's Clubs, 1960-61, chmn. Am. home dept., 1965-66; pres.-elect sun and shade unit Marion Garden Club; flower show judge for Nat. Council, 1965-—. Named Mrs. Marion, 1961. Mem. Marion Assn. U. Women (pres. 1961-62), Alpha Arrangers (pres. 1964-66) I,e Mecure Fed. Club, Croix Art Guild, St. Croix Garden Club, St. Croix Diving Assn. (v.p. 1971), Beta Beta Beta. Methodist (organizer Evelyn Kendall Circle 1959). Clubs: Altrusa, Alpha Arrangers (v.p.) (Marion). Address: Box 989 Christiansted St Croix VI 00820

HYMAN, ALBERT LEWIS, physician; b. New Orleans, Nov. 10, 1923; s. David and Mary (Newstadt) H.; B.S., La. State U., 1943; M.D., 1945; postgrad. University of Cin., U. Paris, and University of London; m. Neil Steiner, March 27, 1964; one son, Albert Arthur. Intern, Charity Hospital, 1945-46; resident Cin. Gen. Hosp., 1946-47, Charity Hosp., 1947-49; instr. medicine La. State U., 1950-56, asst. prof. medicine, 1956-57, Tulane U., 1957-59, asso. prof., 1959-63; asso. prof. surgery Tulane Med. Sch., 1963-70, prof. research surgery in cardiology, 1970-—; dir. Cardiac Catheterization Lab., 1957-—; sr. vis. physician Charity Hosp., 1959-63, Touro Hosp., Touro Infirmary, Hotel Dieu; chief cardiology Sara Mayo Hosp.; cons. in cardiology to USPHS, New Orlans Crippled Children's Hosp., St. Tammany Parish Hosp., Covington, La. area VA; electrocardiographer Metairie Hosp., 1959-64, Sara Mayo Hosp., Touro Infirmary, St. Tammany Hosp.; cons. cardiovascular disease New Orleans VA Hosp.; cons. cardiology Baton Rouge Gen. Hosp. Diplomate Am. Bd. Internal Medicine. Fellow A.C.P., Am. Coll. Chest Physicians, Am. Coll. Cardiology, Am. Fedn. Clin. Research; mem. Am. Heart Assn. (fellow and regional rep. council clin. cardiology), So. Soc. Clin. Investigation, So. Med. Soc., Am. Physiol. Soc., N.Y. Acad. Scis. Home: 5550 Jacquelyn Ct New Orleans LA 70124 Office: 3629 Prythania St New Orleans LA 70115

HYNDMAN, JAMES BENJAMIN, microbiologist; b. Jeffersonville, Ind., June 25, 1914; s. Arthur Warwick and Elsie (Swartz) H.; student Tulane U., 1931-33, Springhill Coll., 1933-34; A.B., U. Ala., 1935; M.S., Duke, 1938; m. Ruth Ella Wright, Oct. 12, 1940; 1 son, James B. Asst. bacteriologist State of Ala., 1937; dir. labs. Meml. Hosp., Andalusia, Ala., 1938; bacteriologist, biochemist Minear Labs., San Antonio, 1938-39; city chemist San Antonio, 1939-40; state sorologist Tex. State Health Dept., 1941-42; bacteriologist FDA, Fed. Security Agy, 1942-53; bacteriologist U.S. Dept. Health Edn. and Welfare, 1953-62; supervisory microbiologist FDA, Health Edn. and Welfare Dept., Dallas, 1962-—. Fellow Am. Pub. Health Assn.; mem. Am. Soc. for Microbiology, Tex. Pub. Health Assn., Am. Acad. Microbiology, Assn. Ofcl. Analytical Chemists, Am. Chem. Soc. Contbr. articles to profl. jours. Home: 7015 Wake Forest Dr Dallas TX 75214 Office: 3032 Byran St Dallas TX 75204

HYSON, CHARLES DAVID, economist; b. Hampstead, Md., Dec. 29, 1915; s. Harry Perry and Rose (Miller) H.; A.B., St. John's Coll., Annapolis, 1937; M.S., U. Md., 1939; M.A., Harvard, 1942, Ph.D., 1943; m. Winifred Chandler Prince, Sept. 7, 1946; children—David Prince, Pamela Chandler, Christopher Perry. Agri. economist FCA, 1939-40; staff Surplus Marketing Adminstrn., Washington, 1940-41; resident tutor, then sr. tutor Harvard, 1942-49, research asso., 1943-44, resident cons. Grad. Sch. Pub. Adminstrn., 1943-49, instr. econs., 1946-48, asso. dir. marketing research program, 1948-49; regional economist, then chief prices and cost of living br. U.S. Bur. Labor Statistics, 1944-46; indsl. economist Fed. Res. Bank Boston, 1946-48; asst. econ. commr. ECA Mission to Norway, Oslo, 1949-50; trade specialist, staff spl. rep. in Europe, Paris, 1950, spl. asst. to chief of mission ECA, Mut. Security Agy., Lisbon, Portugal, 1950-52; dep. dir. U.S. Operations Mission to Portugal, Mut. Security Agy., FOA, ICA, 1952-55; spl. rep. to Portugal, ICA, 1955-57, chief Western Europe div., Washington 1957-59, chief European div., 1959-60; Nat. War Coll., 1960-61; counselor of embassy for econ. affairs Am. Embassy, Lisbon, 1955-57; dep. asst. dir. for exec. staffing AID, Washington, 1961-62; adviser for econ. affairs Office Material Resources, AID, 1962-63, spl. asst. for econs. and trade, 1963-—.

Dep. nat. export expansion coordinator, dep. exec. dir. Cabinet Com. Export Expansion, 1964. Mem. internat. secretariat and econ. adv. conf. on Human Skills in Decade Devel., San Juan, P.R., 1962; mem. trade com. for White House Conf. on Internat. Cooperation, 1965. Decorated Order of Merit (Portugal); recipient Spl. Commendation and Meritorious Service award, Superior Honor award U.S. Govt. Mem. Am. Fgn. Service Assn., Royal Econ. Soc., Am. Acad. Polit. and Social Sci., Am. Econ. Assn., Am. Agrl. Econs. Assn., Sigma Alpha Epsilon. Clubs: Harvard (Washington); Keene Valley (N.Y.) Country; Internat. (Washington); Edgemoor (Bethesda). Contbr. articles econ. jours. Home: 7407 Honeywell Lane Bethesda MD 20014 Office: Dept of State Washington DC 20523

I'ANSON, LAWRENCE WARREN, state judge; b. Portsmouth, Va., Apr. 21, 1907; s. James Thornton and Emma (Warren) I'A.; A.B., Coll. William and Mary, 1928, LL.D., 1964; LL.B., U. Va., 1931; m. May Frances Tuttle, Aug. 5, 1933; children—Lawrence Warren, May F. Ramsey. Admitted to Va. bar, 1931; practiced in Portsmouth, 1931-41; commonwealth's atty., Portsmouth, 1938-41; judge Ct. of Hustings, 1941-58; judge Supreme Ct. of Va., 1958—. Mem. jud. council, 1948—; chmn. com. that prepared Handbook for Jurors used in all cts. of record in Va. Mem. Council of Higher Edn. of Va., 1956-59. Pres. Beazley Found., Inc., Found. Boys Acad.; chmn. bd. trustees Frederick Mil. Acad. Named First Citizen Portsmouth, 1946; recipient William and Mary Alumni medallion. Mem. Va. State Bar Assn. (chmn. jud. sect. 1949), Am. Judicature Soc. (dir.), Phi Beta Kappa, Pi Kappa Alpha, Omicron Delta Kappa, Order of Coif, Phi Alpha Delta, Democrat. Baptist. Mason (past dist. dept. Va.; Shriner). Clubs: Kiwanis (past pres. Portsmouth); Harbor (Norfolk, Va.); Commonwealth (Richmond). Home: 214 West Rd Portsmouth VA 23707 Office: Citizens Trust Bldg Portsmouth VA 23704 also Supreme Court Bldg Richmond VA 23219

ICE, NOEL VICTOR, physician; b. Cleve., Feb. 4, 1928; s. Noel Carlysle and Zelma Elizabeth (Jockisch) I.; student Edinburg Jr. Coll., 1944-45; M.D., Tulane U., 1950; m. Minnie Lee Smith, Mar. 10, 1950; children—Noel Carlysle II, Geoffrey, John, James. Intern, U.S. Naval Hosp., San Diego, 1950-51; gen. practice medicine, McAllen, Tex., 1951-52, 55-58; resident anesthesiology Scott & White Hosp., Temple, Tex., 1958-60; pvt. practice medicine, specializing in anesthesiology, Ft. Worth, 1960—; dir. anesthesia St. Joseph Hosp., Ft. Worth. Zone coordinator Army Mil. Affiliate Radio System, 1967-71, asst. state dir. Tex., 1972—. Served to lt. comdr. USNR, 1952-55. Mem. Tex. Med. Assn., Am., Tex. socs. anesthesiologists, Internat. Anesthesia Research Soc. Mason. Home: 4009 Glenwood Dr Fort Worth TX 76109 Office: 800 5th Av Fort Worth TX 76104

IDDINS, MILDRED, librarian; b. Fountain City, Tenn., Sept. 14, 1915; d. Joseph Franklin and Lucy Ann (Chandler) Iddins; A.B., Carson-Newman Coll., 1936; B.S., Peabody Coll., 1941. Tchr., Bell House, Knoxville, Tenn., 1936-37; tchr.-librarian Roane County High Sch., Kingston, Tenn., 1937-41; librarian Dandridge (Tenn.) High Sch., 1941-43; army librarian Ft. Oglethorpe, Ga., 1943-44; librarian Carson-Newman Coll., Jefferson City, Tenn., 1944—. Mem. Am., Southeastern, Tenn. library assns., Assn. Univ. Women. Clubs: Monday Literary, Modern Book. Home: 403 Russell St Jefferson City TN 37760 Office: Library Carson-Newman Coll Jefferson City TN 37760

IDE, JOHN MCDONALD, engring cons.; b. Mt. Vernon, N.Y., Aug. 17, 1907; s. Herbert Chandler and Harriet (McDonald) I.; B.A., Pomona Coll., 1927, D.Sc., 1965; M.S., Harvard, 1929, D.Sc., 1931; m. Margaret R. Martin, July 11, 1929; children—Margot (Mrs. Christopher S. Andrews), Katherine (Mrs. R. L. Curl), Cynthia (Mrs. Peter Rockwell). Instr. physics Harvard U., 1931-36; geophysicist Shell Oil Co., Houston, 1936-41; physicist, sect. head Naval Research Lab., Washington, 1941-45; tech. dir. U.S. Navy Underwater Sound Lab., New London, Conn., 1945-59; dep. asst. dir. Def. Research and Engring. Advanced Research Projects, Dept. Def., Washington, 1959-61; dir. Supreme Allied Comdr. Atlantic Anti-Submarine Warfare Research Center, NATO, La Spezia, Italy, 1961-64; dir. div. engring. NSF, Washington, 1964-71; cons. to Nat. Sci. Bd. NSF, Washington, 1971—. Fellow I.E.E.E.; mem. Phi Beta Kappa, Tau Beta Pi. Patentee in field. Contbr. articles in field to profl. jours. Home: 426 S Fairfax St Alexandria VA 22314 Office: 1800 G St NW Washington DC 20550

IDE, ROY WILLIAM, III, lawyer; b. Geneva, Ill., Apr. 23, 1940; s. Roy William and Jenny Logan (Coleman) I.; B.A. cum laude, Washington and Lee U., 1962; LL.B., U. Va., 1965; M.B.A., Ga. State U., 1972; m. Gayle Marie Oliver, Jan. 27, 1967; children—Oliver Logan, Jennifer Nava. Law clk. U.S. 5th Circuit Ct. Appeals, Atlanta, 1965-66; admitted to Ga. bar, 1966; asso. firm King & Spalding, Atlanta, 1966-71; partner firm Huie & Harland, Atlanta, 1971—. Pres. Ga. Indigents Legal Services, Inc., 1970-72; bd. dirs., mem. exec. com. Nat. Legal Aid and Defender Assn.; bd. dirs. Atlanta Legal Aid Soc., Ga. Legal Services Program, Youngmen's Roundtable. Mem. Am. Bar Assn. (nat. dir. young lawyers sect. 1971-72), State Bar Ga. (exec. council younger lawyers sect. 1970-72, sec. 1972). Club: Lawyers (Atlanta). Home: 3216 Roberta Dr NW Atlanta GA 30327 Office: 822 Fulton Fed Bldg Atlanta GA 30303

IDYLL, CLARENCE PURVIS, biologist; b. Edmonton, Alta., Can., Feb. 10, 1916; s. Albert Charles and Annabelle (Purvis) I.; B.A., U.B.C., 1938, M.A., 1940; Ph.D., U. Wash., 1951; m. Marion Janet Daniels, June 28, 1941; children—Marilyn Judith (Mrs. Richard Dana Hamly), Janice Leah, Jacqueline Margaret. Biologist, Internat. Pacific Salmon Fisheries Commn., New Westminster, B.C., 1941-48; asst. prof. zoology U. Miami, Fla., 1948-50, asst. prof. marine biology, 1950-53, asso. prof. marine biology, 1953-56, prof., 1956-72, chmn. Fishery Scis. div. Inst. Marine Scis., 1953-72, chmn. Gulf and Caribbean Fisheries Inst., 1958-72; sr. research adviser FAO, Rome, Italy, 1972—. Vice pres. Friends of Chamber Music, Miami, Fla., 1960—. Mem. Nat. Acad. Scis., Am. Inst. Fishery Research Biologists, Am. Fisheries Soc., Am. Soc. Ichthyologists and Herpetologists, Fla. Acad. Sci., Sigma Xi, Phi Sigma, Beta Beta Beta, Omicron Delta Kappa. Contbr. articles in field to profl. jours. Author: Abyss: The Deep Sea and The Creatures That Live In It, 1964; Exploring The Ocean World: A History of Oceanography, 1969; The Sea Against Hunger, 1970. Home: 716 Tibidabo Av Coral Gables FL 33143 also Via Pasteur 33 Rome Italy Office: FAO Via delle Terme di Caracalla Rome Italy

IGO, DONALD JAMES, economist; b. Plymouth, Mass., June 28, 1926; s. James Edward and Mary (Cavicchioli) I.; A.B. in Econs. cum laude, Harvard, 1950; M.A., Am. U., 1958; student U.S. Dept. Agr. Grad. Sch., 1967-70; m. Doris Therese Grandmont, Oct. 6, 1951; children—Susan, James, Joseph, Karen. Economist, Ceir, Inc., Arlington, Va., 1955-57; research analyst Melpar, Inc., Alexandria, Va., 1957-58; economist Analytic Services, Inc., Alexandria, 1958-61; economist, cost engr. RAND Corp., Bethesda, Md., 1961-62; economist, chief econ. impact group Research Analysis Corp., McLean, Va., 1962-68; economist U.S. Dept. Transp., Washington, 1968—. Mem. program com. Monticello Woods-York Manor Civic Assn., 1967. Served with USNR, 1946-48. Mem. Am. Econ. Assn. Club: Harvard (Washington). Author: (with others) Economic Impact Analysis: A Military Procurement Final Demand Vector, 1967. Contbg. author: Northeast Corridor Transportation Report, 1970, Recommendations for Northeast Corridor Transportation, 1971. Home: 6209 Cloud Dr Springfield VA 22150 Office: 400 7th St SW Washington DC 20590

IGO, FRANCES VIRGINIA KERBOW (MRS. GALEN H. IGO), accountant; b. nr. Clarksville, Tex.; d. Russell Park and Blewett (Barnes) Kerbow; B.A., U. Tex., 1925, M.A., 1932; B.B.A., U. Houston, 1957; m. Galen Haggard Igo, July 3, 1933 (dec. Apr. 1946); 1 dau., Frances Virginia. Tchr. Spanish and math., Mason, Alvin and San Angelo, Tex., 1925-32; sr. accountant Roy H. Reece, 1946-66. Parliamentarian, 2d vice chmn. United Ch. Women of Houston. Named Woman of the Year, Am. Bus. Women's Assn., 1963. Mem. Am. Soc. Women Accountants (dir.), Coll. Women of Houston, Descs. of Mayflower. D.A.R., Daus. Republic Tex., Magna Charta Dames, Descs. Plymouth Colony, Alpha Xi Delta. Democrat. Presbyn. Mem. Order of Eastern Star, Order of the Rainbow for Girls (mother adviser 1964; mem. Grand Cross of Color). Home: 7400 Erath Houston TX 77023 Office: Bank of the Southwest Bldg Houston TX 77002

IKARD, FRANK NEVILLE, petroleum assn. exec.; b. Henrietta, Tex., Jan. 30, 1913; s. Lewis and Ena (Neville) I.; A.B., U. Tex., 1936, LL.B., 1936; m. Jean Hunter, Oct. 15, 1940 (dec. Apr. 1970); children— Frank Neville, William Forsyth; m. 2d, Jayne Brumley, July 22, 1972. Admitted to Tex. bar, 1936; mem. firm Bullington, Humphrey & Humphrey, Wichita Falls, 1937-47; judge 30th Jud. Dist. Ct., Wichita Falls, 1947-52; mem. 81st to 86th congresses from 13th Tex. dist.; exec. v.p. Am. Petroleum Inst., Washington, 1963, pres., N.Y.C., 1963-70, pres., Washington, 1970—; dir. VLN Corp., N.Y.C., Union Trust Co., Washington. Mem. natural gas adv. council Fed. Power Commn., 1964-70; mem. adv. bd. Center for Strategic Studies, Washington, 1966-69; mem. Nat. Petroleum Council, 1964-60; mem. Pres.'s Nat. Adv. Com. on Hwy. Beautification, 1966-68, Pres.'s Nat. Citizens Commn. on Internat. Cooperation, 1965-68; mem. Pres.'s Industry-Govt. Spl. Task Force on Travel, 1966-68; mem. U.S. nat. conf. World Energy Congress, 1967-69, World Petroleum Congresses, 1963-70. Trustee John F. Kennedy Center for Performing Arts, Washington; vice chmn. bd. regents U. Tex. at Austin. Served with AUS, 1942-45. Mem. Am. Bar Assn., State Bar of Tex., Ind. Petroleum Assn. Am., Japan-Am. Soc. Episcopalian. Mason. Clubs: Burning Tree (Chevy Chase, Md.); City (Dallas); Carleton, City Tavern Assn., Internat., Metropolitan (Washington); Hemisphere, 28, University (N.Y.C.). Home: Shoreham West 2500 Calvert St NW Washington DC 20008 Office: 1801 K St NW Washington DC 20006

IKENBERRY, HENRY CEPHAS, JR., lawyer; b. Cloverdale, Va., March 23, 1920; s. Henry Cephas and Bessie (Peters) I.; B.A., Bridgewater Coll., 1947; J.D., U. Va., 1947; m. Margaret Sangster Henry, July 3, 1943; children—Anna Catherine (Mrs. Fawell), Mary Margaret. Admitted to Va. bar, 1947, W.Va. and D.C. bars, 1948; asso. Steptoe & Johnson, Washington, 1947-49, 50-53, partner, 1953—; asst. counsel Gen. Aniline & Film Co., N.Y.C., 1949-50. Mem. com. on unauthorized practice D.C. Ct. Appeals, 1972—. Served ensign to lt. comdr. USNR, 1941-46, commanded anti-submarine vessels, participated Atlantic, Philippine, Okinawa campaigns. Mem. Am., Va. bar assns., Bar Assn. D.C. (chmn. comml. and bus. law com. 1969-72), Raven Soc., Am. Legion, Newcomen Soc. in N.Am., Order of Coif, Phi Delta Phi, Tau Kappa Alpha. Presbyn. (ruling elder 1970-72). Clubs: Metropolitan (Washington); Chevy Chase (Md.); Farmington Country. Home: 3725 Cardiff Rd Chevy Chase MD 20015 Office: 1250 Connecticut Av Washington DC 20036

IKENBERRY, JESSE EMMERT, educator; b. Daleville, Va., Jan. 30, 1907; s. John William and Ida (Barnhart) I.; A.B., Bridgewater Coll., 1928; M.A., Cornell U., 1932, Ph.D., 1937; m. Anna Katherine Maxwell, June 4, 1930; children—Lynn David, Jean Katherine. Instr. math. and phys. sci., dir. residence for boys Daleville Acad., Va., 1928-30; instr. math., dean men Bridgewater Coll., Va., 1930-32, asst. prof., dean of men, 1932-35; asst. prof. math. Franklin and Marshall Coll., 1937-45; prof. math. Madison Coll., Harrisonburg, Va., 1945—, head dept. math., 1945-69, dir. div. natural scis., 1952-69, dir. summer session, 1964-66; acting dean Madison Coll., 1965-66, dean sch. natural scis., 1969—. Mem. Am. Math. Soc., Math. Assn. Am., Nat. Council Tchrs. Math., Va. Acad. Sci., A.A.A.S., Tau Kappa Alpha, Sigma Xi. Mem. United Ch. of Christ. Home: 310 W View St Harrisonburg VA 22801

ILDERTON, ROBERT BLAIR, govt. ofcl.; b. Phila., Dec. 16, 1930; s. Blair McKenzie and Laura (Fife) I.; B.S., U. Md., 1951; M.S George Washington U., 1970; m. Marie Barbara Schmuck, Mar. 15, 1967; children—Thomas Robert, Laura Fife. Auditor Price, Waterhouse & Co. N.Y.C., 1951-52; supervisory auditor U.S. Army Audit Agcy., Europe, Chgo., 1954-62, program mgr., Washington, 1962-65; program mgr. advanced audit techniques br. Def. Contract Audit Agcy., Alexandria, Va., 1965-67, chief, 1967—. Served to 2d lt. AUS, 1952-54. C.P.A., Md., Mem. Am. Inst. C.P.A.'s, Am. Statis. Assn. Fed. Govt. Accountants Assn. Author: (with Thomas McCarthy) Sampling Techniques and Regression Analysis for Accounting and Auditing Information, A Practical Approach, 1967. Home: 9003 Volunteer Dr Alexandria VA 22309 Office: Cameron Sta Alexandria VA 22314

ILER, ARTHUR TRIPLETT, judge; b. Rockport, Ky., Mar. 3, 1900; s. William Perry and Nellie (Young) I.; student Western Ky. State Coll., 1917-19; LL.B., Columbus U., 1934; m. Kathryn Wallace, June 19, 1927; children—Richard W., William Perry II. With Washington Herald, Washington News, 1930-33; with FHA, D.C., Ky., 1934-40; admitted to Ky. bar, 1935; practiced in Louisville, 1940-41; asst. atty. gen. Ky., 1941-43; atty. Muhlenberg County, 1954-56; circuit judge 45th Jud. Dist. Ky., Greenville, 1956—; farmer, horse raiser, 1950—. Pres., Muhlenberg County Fair Bd., 1948-58. Bd. dirs. Travelers Protective Assn. Served with inf. U.S. Army, 1918. Named Man of Year, Central City C. of C., 1958. Mem. Am. Legion (post comdr.), 40 and 8, Ky. Thoroughbred Assn., Sigma Delta Kappa. Presbyn. (elder). Clubs: All States Society (past pres. Washington); Rotary (past pres. Central City, Ky.). Home: 1004 Broad St Central City KY 42330 Office: Court House Greenville KY 42345

ILLE, BERNARD GLENN, ins. co. exec.; b. Ponca City, Okla., Feb. 8, 1927; s. Frank L. and Marie (Cornwell) I.; B.S., Okla. U.; m. Mary Lou Allen, Aug. 23, 1952; children—Meredith, Leslie, Frank. Agt. Phoenix Mut. Life Ins. Co., Oklahoma City, 1953-55; gen. agt. Farmers & Bankers Life Ins. Co., Oklahoma City, 1955-56; various positions United Founders LIfe Ins. Co., Oklahoma City, 1956-66, pres., 1966-70, chmn. bd., pres., 1970—, also dir.; pres., chmn. bd., dir. Reis Corp., Oklahoma City; dir. Founders Bank & Trust, Oklahoma City; chmn. bd., dir. United Founders Life Ins. Co. Ill., Chgo.; dir. Modern Security Life, Springfield, Mo., LSB Industries, Inc., Landmark Land, Inc. (both Oklahoma City), Gen. Life of Tenn. Ins. Co., Columbia. Trustee John Galvin Meml. Scholarship Fund. Served with USCGR, 1945-46. C.L.U. Mem. Nat. Football Found. Hall of Fame (chpt. pres. 1966—), Young Presidents Orgn., Kappa Alpha Alumni Assn. (past pres.). Club: Quail Creek Golf and Country. Home: 3117 Elmwood St Oklahoma City OK 73116 Office: 5900 Mosteller Dr Oklahoma City OK 73112

ILLICH, IVAN, philosopher; b. Vienna, Austria, Sept. 4, 1926; s. Petar and Ellen (Regenstreif) I.; Lic.U. Philos., Gregorian U., Rome, 1945, Lic.U. Theology, 1950; Dr. Fac. Phil., U. Salzburg, 1951. Ordained priest Roman Cath. Ch.; parish priest among Puerto Ricans, N.Y.C., 1951-56; v.p. U. Santa Maria, Ponce, P.R., 1956-60; ind. author, 1960—; researcher Center for Intercultural Documentation, Cuernavaca, Mexico, 1961—, pres. bd., 1963-68. Mem. Council Higher Edn., Commonwealth P.R., 1959-61. Author: Celebration of Awareness, 1970; Deschooling Society, 1971. Contbr. to various jours. and mags. Home: Casa Blanca Rancho Tetela APDO 479 Cuernavaca Morelos Mexico

IMBURG, IRVING JEROME, dentist; b. Richmond, Va., July 7, 1924; s. Samuel and Nettie (Meyers) I.; student Med. Coll. Va., 1942-43, Washington U. at St. Louis, 1943-44; D.D.S., Med. Coll. Va., 1948; m. Clare Cardozo, Dec. 21, 1948; children—Catherine (Mrs. Richard M. Kaplan), Susan, Nancy Elizabeth. Gen. practice dentistry, Richmond, Va., 1948-50, Falls Church, Va., 1952— founder William Byrd Free Dental Clinic, Richmond, 1948; mem. courtesy staff Alexandria (Va.) Hosp.; pres. Drs. Imburg, Rudin &Coleman & Rock, Ltd., Falls Church, 1971—. Pres. MacArthur Sch. P.T.A., Alexandria, 1965, Howard Middle Sch. P.T.A., Alexandria, 1966; v.p. T.C. Williams High Sch. P.T.A., Alexandria, 1968-69. Served with AUS, 1943-44, to capt. USAF, 1950-52. Fellow Internat. Coll. Dentists; mem. No. Va. (pres.-elect), Fairfax (past pres.) dental assns., Commonwealth Dental Study Club (co-founder 1963, past pres.), Va. Dental Assn. (continuing edn. com. 1970—, ho. of dels. 1972-73), D.C. Dental Soc., Am. Dental Assn., Alpha Sigma Chi. Jewish religion (trustee congregation). Editor No. Va. Dental Newsletter, 1966-67. Home: 1230 Kingston Pl Alexandria VA 22302 Office: 6319 Castle Pl Falls Church VA 22044

IMEL, ARTHUR BLAINE, architect; b. Blackwell, Okla., Dec. 30, 1921; student Okla. Mil. Acad., 1939-41; B.Arch. (A.I.A. award student), U. Okla., 1950. Draftsman, U. Okla. and Wichita, Kan., 1949-50; past mem. firm Buchner & Imel; pvt. practice A. Blaine Imel, architect; now mem. firm Stanfield, Imel & Walton, Tulsa; prin. works include Tradewinds Motor Hotel and Restaurant (award Am. Restaurant Soc., 1960), Tulsa, Key Club and Banquet Hall, Tulsa, 1961, Perkins High Sch., 1955, Admiral State Bank, 1961, Robert Fulton Elementary Sch., 1960, fellowship hall and classes Yale Av. Presbyn. Ch., 1960. Tech. adviser, mem. design bd. Civic Center, Tulsa; mem. Mayor's Street Light Com. Served to maj. USMCR, 1942-45. Mem. A.I.A. (chpt. dir. 1957-60), Tulsa C. of C. (planning com. 1955). Author: Esempi, 1952. Asst. editor Perspective Mag. Address: 3816 S Erie St Tulsa OK 74135*

IMHOFF, JOHN LEONARD, educator; b. Balt., Feb. 9, 1923; s. John and Elizabeth (Franz) I.; student Johns Hopkins, 1941; B.S., Duke, 1945; M.S., U. Minn., 1947; Ph.D., Okla. State, 1971; m. Lois Rebecca Johnson, Mar. 20, 1948; children—John Edwin, Karen Elizabeth, Carl Henning. Facilities design engr. Crosse & Blackwell, Ltd., Balt., 1940; head engring. metal treatment Rustless Iron & Steel Corp., Balt., 1941-43; asst. prof. indsl. engring. U. Minn., 1947-51; prof., head indsl. engring. U. Ark., Fayetteville, 1953—. Mgmt., engring. cons. Army Ordnance Mgmt. Tng. Div., 1949—; Ph.D. planning group So. Regional Edn. Bd., 1963—. Chmn. engring. sect. Boys Club Fund Raising Program, Fayetteville, 1964-65; dist. chmn., council mem. Boy Scouts Am. Served with USNR, 1943-46. Recipient Outstanding Educator award U. Ark., 1964. AEC fellow U. Cal. at Berkeley, 1958, Argonne Nat. Lab., 1959; NSF Sci. Faculty fellow Stanford, 1960-61. Registered profl. engr., Minn., Ark. Mem. Am. Inst. Indsl. Engrs. (past v.p., dir.), Am. Soc. Engring. Edn. (dir., past chmn. Mo.-Ark. sect.), A.A.A.S., Am. Statis. Assn., Nat. Soc. Profl. Engrs., Internat. Mgmt. Soc. for Educators, Indsl. Engring. Acad. Dept. Chmn. (chmn. nat. council), Phi Beta Kappa, Omicron Delta Kappa, Tau Beta Pi, Alpha Pi Mu (past nat. pres.). Methodist. Author: (with H.F. Dennett) Descriptive Geometry and Graphical Mathematics, 1962; (with O.W. Gatchell) Engineering Computations, 1964. Home: 224 Cleburn St Fayetteville AR 72701

IMLER, ALLISON E(LLWOOD), radiol., oncologist; b. Altoona, Pa., Nov. 15, 1910; s. Thomas H. and Lydia E. I.; B.S., U. Pitts., 1933, M.D., Hahnemann Med. Coll. Phila., 1937; m. Elwys Fawl, Feb. 19, 1946; children—Teresa Carol, Thomas Allison, Stephen, Daniel. Intern, Hahnemann Hosp., Phila., 1937-38; resident in cancer Jeanes Hosp. of Phila., 1938-41; pvt. practice medicine, specializing in radiology and oncology, Birmingham, Ala., 1947—; group practice Lloyd Noland Hosp. and Clinic, Fairfield, Ala.; asso. prof. radiology, dir. univ. tumor clinic Med. Coll. Ala., 1946-47, asso. prof. oncology, 1949-50; cons. staff Brookwood Hosp., Homewood, Birmingham. Served as maj. M.C., AUS, Walter Reed Gen. Hosp., Washington, 1941-42, Torney Gen. Hosp., Palm Springs, Cal., 1942-44, Letterman Gen. Hosp., San Francisco, 1944-46. Diplomate Am. Bd. Radiology, therapeutic radiology, 1941, radiology, 1944. Fellow Am. Coll. Radiology, Am., Internat. colls. surgeons, Southeastern Surg. Congress; mem. Radio. Soc. N.A., Jefferson County Med. Soc., So., Ala. med. assns., Ala., Pa. radiol. socs., A.M.A., Am. Roentgen. Ray Soc. Contbr. med. jours. Home: 1912 Shades Crest Rd Birmingham AL 35216 Office: Lloyd Noland Hosp Fairfield AL 35064

IMM, VAL DELLA, writer; b. Mankato, Minn., Mar. 11, 1930; d. Val M. and Gertrude (Fehlandt) I.; student Bethany Lutheran Coll., Mankato State Coll. Fashion editor Tex. Fashion Mfg. Assn., 1959-60; soc. editor, columnist Dallas Times Herald, 1960—. Bd. dirs. Soc. for Abandoned and Neglected Children, Spl. Care Sch. Handicapped Children. Recipient Southwestern Journalism Found. award, 1968; Tex. U.P.I. award, 1968; award in field Interpretive Writing, 1968. Mem. Dallas Council on World Affairs. Clubs: Dallas Gun, Lakewood (Dallas). Lutheran. Home: Maple Terrace 3005 Maple Ave Dallas TX 75201 Office: Dallas Times Herald Dallas TX 75202

IMMASCHE, FRANCIS WILLIAM, econ. adviser, farmer; b. Saffordville, Kan., Oct. 21, 1907; s. William George and Margaret (Lyles) ImM.; B.S., Kan. State U., 1929; M.A., U. Chgo., 1933. Livestock economist Armour & Co., Chgo., 1930-31, Fed. Farm Bd., Washington, 1931-33; asst. chief, econ. and credit research div., FCA, Washington, 1933-42; dep. dir. livestock and dairy div. U.S. Dept. Agr., Washington, 1947-65, adviser on livestock and wool situation, including Australia and New Zealand, 1971—; pres. Goldpoint Mining Co. (Nev.), 1941—; farmer, Chase County, Kan. Pres. Meml. Lawn Cemeteries Assn., Emporia, Kan., 1959-70. Served from 1st lt. to col. USAF, 1942-47; now col. USAF ret. Mem. Sigma Alpha Epsilon, Alpha Zeta, Alpha Kappa Psi. Clubs: Congressional Country (Washington); Saddle and Sirloin (Chgo.); Indian Wells Country (Palm Springs). Home: 3133 Connecticut Av Washington DC 20008 also Strong City KS 66869

INGERSOLL, ROBERT ELLIS, orthopedic surgeon; b. Boston, Feb. 21, 1915; s. Frank and Helen (Brown) I.; B.A., Dartmouth, 1936; M.D., U. Rochester, 1939; m. Marjorie Smith, Aug. 30, 1962. Intern, Cambridge City Hosp., 1940-41; resident N.Y. Reconstrn. Home, 1941-43, N.Y. Orthopedic Hosp., 1943-45, Boston City Hosp.,

1945-46; practice medicine specializing in orthopedic surgery, N.Y.C., White Stone, L.I., N.Y., 1947, Boston, 1947-62, Malden, Mass., 1958-62, Hollywood, Fla., 1962—; chief surgery Dr.'s Hosp., Hollywood, 1967, chief staff, 1969-71; mem. staffs Meml. Hosp., Hollywood, Golden Isles Hosp., Hallandale; instr. orthopedic surgery Columbia, 1944-47; instr. orthopedic surgery, trauma Tufts U. Med. Sch., 1947-62. Fellow A.C.S.; mem. Internat. Coll. Surgeons, Mass. Com. Fractures and Traumas, Mass. Soc. Examining Physicians, Mass. Med. Soc., Am. Acad. Orthopedic Surgery, A.M.A., Am. Fracture Assn., Am. Geriatrics Assn., Miami, Boston orthopedic socs., Latin-Am., Fla. orthopedic assns., Fla., So., Pan Am. med. assns., Pan Pacific Surg. Assn., Com. of 100, Phi Gamma Delta. Mason (Jester, Shriner). Elk, Rotarian. Office: 3711 Garfield St Hollywood FL 33021

INGRAHAM, JOE MCDONALD, judge; b. Pawnee County, Okla., July 5, 1903; s. Millard F. and Emma (Patton) I.; LL.B., Nat. U., 1927; m. Laura Munson, Oct. 29, 1954. Admitted to D.C. bar, 1927, Okla. bar, 1927, Tex. bar, 1928; practiced in Stroud, Okla., 1927-28, Ft. Worth, 1928-35, Houston 1935-54; judge U.S. Dist. Ct., So. Dist. Tex., 1954-69, U.S. Ct. Appeals, 5th Circuit, 1969—. Served as officer USAAF, 1942-46. Recipient Good Citizenship award Tex. Soc. S.A.R., 1958. Mem. Am., Houston bar assns., Tex. State Bar, S.A.R. (pres. Tex. 1937-38), Am. Judicature Soc., Am. Legion. Republican. Presbyn. Home: 1605 Banks St Houston TX 77006 Office: US Court House Houston TX 77002

INGRAM, ALVIN JOHN, physician; b. Jackson, Tenn., Mar. 31, 1914; s. Alvin Hill and Margaret (Gallagher) I.; B.S., U. Tenn., 1939, M.D., 1939, M.S. in Orthopedic Surgery, 1947; m. Catherine Davis, Feb. 7, 1943; children—Mildred (Mrs. Dyer), Cathy (Mrs. Doyle), Peggy (Mrs. Tagg). Intern Univ. Hosp., Ann Arbor, Mich., 1939-40, asst. resident surgery, 1940-41; fellow orthopedic surgery Campbell Clinic, Memphis, 1941-42, 46-47, mem. staff, 1947—, dep. chief hosp. staff, 1968-69, chief staff clinic, 1970—; practice medicine, specializing in orthopaedic surgery, Memphis, 1947—; med. dir. Crippled Children's Hosp., 1948-61, chief staff, 1961-71; med. dir. Les Passes Cerebral Palsy Treatment Center, 1953-56; mem. adv. com. Memphis and West Tenn. chpt. Nat. Found., 1947-57, chmn., 1947-55; med. adv. com. Shrine Sch. Crippled Children, 1947-56; mem. adv. bd. Variety Club Convalescent Hosp., 1952-56; asso. prof. orthopaedic surgery U. Tenn. Coll. Medicine, 1960-71, prof., 1971—, chmn. dept., 1971—; mem. staff Bapt. Meml. Hosp., chmn. dept. orthopedic surgery, 1969-71, mem. exec. com. med. staff, 1969-70, pres. med. staff, 1973; mem. staff St. Joseph Hosp., LeBonheur Children's Hosp. (trustee 1969-72); cons. staff Methodist Hosp. Program chmn. 2d Tenn. Conf. Handicapped Children, 1958; chmn. med. div. United Fund Shelby County, 1961, mem. budget com., 1963-65; dir. at large Nat. Assn. Blue Shield Plans, 1965-70; mem. Gov. of Tenn.'s Adv. Bd. Crippled Children's Service, 1961—, chmn., 1971—. Bd. dirs. Front Street Theatre, Memphis, 1963-64. Served to maj., M.C., AUS, 1942-46. Diplomate Am. Bd. Orthopaedic Surgery. Mem. Am. Acad. Orthopaedic Surgeons (chmn. program com. 1954), Am. Orthopaedic Assn. (chmn. program com., pres. elect 1972), Central Orthopaedic Club (charter), Tenn. (pres. 1963-64), Clin. orthopaedic socs., Willis C. Campbell Club (pres. 1967), Internat. Soc. Orthopaedics and Traumatology, Am. Acad. Cerebral Palsy (chmn. program com. 1955, publs. com. 1957, exec. com. 1958, pres. 1958-59) A.C.S., Am. (sec.-treas. 1968-70, trustee 1964-70), So., Tenn. med. assns., Memphis and Shelby County Med. Soc. (pres. 1962, bd. censors 1963-65, ho. of dels. 1965-72), Nat. Acad. Scis.-Inst. Medicine (membership com. 1971-73, mem. council 1971-74), U.S. C. of C. Methodist (ofcl. bd. 1952—, pres. 1971-72, gen. chmn. every mem. canvass 1955-57, 63, pres. men's club 1958, sec. stewardship 1964-65). Contbr. to books. Home: 3876 Central Av Memphis TN 38111 Office: Campbell Clinic 869 Madison Av Memphis TN 38103

INGRAM, ANNE G., educator; b. Carrollton, Ga.; d. Irvine Sullivan and Martha (Munroe) Ingram; student W. Ga. Coll., 1941-43; A.B., U. N.C., 1944; M.A., U. Ga., 1948; Ed.D., Columbia, 1962; postgrad. U. Oslo (Norway), 1965. Instr., La. Poly. Inst., Ruston, 1950-51; asst. prof., U. Miss., Oxford, 1951-54, Western Ill. U., Macomb, 1960-61, George Washington U., 1961-62; asso. prof. U. Md., College Park, 1962—. Mem. Am. Assn. U. Profs., A.A.H.P.E.R., Nat. Assn. Women Deans and Counselors, Internat. Assn. Sport Psychology, Am. Sociol. Assn., Alpha Delta Pi. Author: (with James H. Humphrey) Introduction to Pnysical Education for College Students, 1969; Moving with Music—A Syllabus for Teaching Dance and Rythms, 1969. Contbr. articles to profl. jours. Home: 114 Hillcrest Dr Carrollton GA 30117 Office: Cole Bldg U Md College Park MD 20740

INGRAM, CHARLES DEAN, librarian; b. Lawton, Okla., Dec. 29, 1928; s. Jim Cisney and Nan (Shelton) I.; student Oklahoma City U., 1946-49; B.F.A., U. Okla., 1951, M.L.S., 1963. Library asst. Oklahoma City Libraries, 1948-53, chief prodn. asst., 1954-59; asst. acquisitions librarian U. Okla., 1962-63; asst. librarian for pub. services U. Okla. Med. Center Library, 1963-65; documents librarian Oklahoma City U. Library, 1965-68, acquisitions librarian, 1968—. Mem. Okla. Library Assn. (chmn. coll. and univ. div. 1968, chmn. constn. and bylaws com. 1971, chmn. auditing com. 1972), Midwest City Art Guild (pres. 1969—), Beta Phi Mu. Democrat. Presbyn. Home: 225 Leonard Lane Midwest City OK 73110 Office: 25th and Florida Sts Oklahoma City OK 73106

INGRAM, DEAN, banker; b. Non, Okla., Jan. 11, 1940; s. Milburn Cisney and Velma Viola (Russell) I.; B.S., Southwestern State Coll., 1962; certificate Am. Inst. Banking; 1 dau., Tammy Gay. Prodn. accountant Apco Oil Corp., Oklahoma City, 1962-63; auditor First Nat. Bank and Trust Co., Oklahoma City, 1963—. Mem. membership com. Oklahoma City YMCA, 1966-68. Mem. Bank Adminstrn. Inst. (dir. Oklahoma City). Home: 1437 NW 48th St Oklahoma City OK 73107 Office: 120 N Robinson St Oklahoma City OK 73125

INGRAM, EDITH JACQUELINE, judge; b. nr. Sparta, Ga., Jan. 16, 1942; d. Robert T. and Katherine (Hunt) Ingram; B.S. in Edn., Fort Valley (Ga.) State Coll., 1963. Store mgr. High's Dairy Products, Washington, summers 1956-63; tchr. Moore Elementary Sch., Griffin, Ga., 1963-67; tchr. Hancock Central Elementary Sch., Sparta, Ga., 1967-68; judge Ct. of Ordinary, Sparta, 1969—. Sec., Hancock County Democratic Club, 1967—; mem. Ga. Dem. Exec. Com. Bd. dirs. Nat. Domestic Workers Union of Am.; 2d v.p. Ga. Council on Human Relations, Sheriff's Retirement Assn. Ga., Ordinaries Retirement Ga.; sec. Hancock County Com. for Social and Econ. Devel., Oconee Area Minority Adv. Com., Labor Dept.; bd. dirs. East Central Com. for Opportunity. Mem. N.A.A.C.P., Fort Valley State Coll. Alumni Assn., Delta Sigma Theta. Baptist. Club: Hancock Womens. Home: 718 New St Sparta GA 31087 Office: PO Box 151 Sparta GA 31087

INGRAM, EVERETT JEFFERSON, banker; b. Ashland, Ala., Aug. 9, 1911; s. Francis Jefferson and Evelyn (Johnson) I.; B.S., Samford U., 1935; student U. Ala., 1941; m. Kay Hammett Ingram, Oct. 28, 1936; children— Carol Kay (Mrs. William H. Matthews), Lee J. Statistician accountant, supr. Birmingham (Ala.) Bd. Edn., 1935-42; successively spl. agt., asst. personnel officer, insp., spl. agt. in charge, exec. asst. to dir. FBI, Washington, 1942-65; v.p. Hamilton Nat. Bank, Knoxville, Tenn., 1966—. Bd. dirs. Knox County chpt. A.R.C., The Arthritis Found., Jr. Achievement, Better Bus. Bur., Downtown Knoxville Assn. Mem. Pi Kappa Phi, Pi Gamma Mu. Baptist. Rotarian. Clubs: City Club of Knoxville, Cherokee Country. Home: 1540 Agawela Av Knoxville TN 37919 Office: 531 S Gay St Knoxville TN 37902

INGRAM, HUGH BEDIEL, state ofcl.; b. Jacksonville, Fla., Dec. 29, 1922; s. Hugh Bediel and Carrie A. (Mills) I.; B.A., U. Fla., 1950, M.Ed., 1953; m. Elizabeth Caroline Koch, July 29, 1944; children—David Hugh, Jonathan Edward. English and math. tchr. Bradford High Sch., Starke, Fla., 1950-52; prin. Lawtey Jr. High Sch., Lawtey, Fla., 1952-59; supervising prin. Bradford High Sch., Starke, 1959-62; dir. profl. rights and responsibilities Fla. Edn. Assn., Tallahassee, 1962-68, exec. sec.-treas. dept. second sch. prins., 1966-67; exec. dir. Fla. Profl. Practices Commn., Tallahassee, 1968—. Served to 1st lt. AUS, 1943-46. Mem. Nat., Fla. edn. assns., Fla. Dept. Secondary Sch. Prins., Nat. Assn. Secondary Sch. Prins., Fla. N.G. Officers Assn., N.G. Officers Assn. Am., Phi Delta Kappa. Home: 1724 Dora Dr Tallahassee FL 32303 Office: Tallahassee Bank & Trust Bldg Tallahassee FL 32301

INGRAM, JOHN WILSON, corp. exec.; b. Varadam, Miss., Nov. 13, 1919; s. William Russell and Ruby Corrine (McMurray) I.; grad. Prabody High Sch., Trenton, Tenn., 1937; m. Helen Clara Yoakum, Jan. 20, 1951. With Great Atlantic & Pacific Tea Co., 1938-48; with Fischer Lime and Cement Co., North Little Rock, Ark., 1948—, v.p., mgr., 1964-72, sr. v.p., 1972—; mem. nat. adv. council Armstrong Cork Co., 1962, 70. Pres. City Chain Store Council, 1941-42. Recipient Distinguished Sales award Memphis Sales Mgrs. Club, 1950. Mem. Assn. Bldg. Distbrs. Ark. (past pres.), Ark. Home Builders Assn. (life mem. Spike Club), Ark., Little Rock, North Little Rock chambers commerce, Nat. Bldg. Material Distbrs. Assn., Ark. Lumbermans Assn., S.W. Lumber Assn. Baptist. Mason (Shriner). Club: North Hills Country (Sylvan Hills, North Little Rock). Home: 4809 Hickory St North Little Rock AR 72116 Office: 1650 E Washington St North Little Rock AR 72119

INGRAM, LAWRENCE WARREN, pub. relations cons.; b. Mt. Moriah, Mo., June 19, 1921; s. Earl Russell and Ella (Phillips) I.; student U. Minn., 1939-40; A.A., George Washington U., 1947; B.J., U. Tex., Austin, 1949; m. Irene Isabel Farrell, Oct. 11, 1942. With Adj. Gen.'s Office, U.S. War Dept., 1940-42; staff mem. President's Commn. on Higher Edn. 1946-47; reporter to mng. editor Temple (Tex.) Daily Telegram, 1949-56; reporter, asst. city editor, television editor, editorial writer Denver Post, 1956-61; from exec. editor to editor Temple Telegram, 1961-72; pub. relations cons., 1972—. Chmn. bd. dirs. Temple U.S.O. Council, 1965-66; bd. dirs. Bell County Soc. for Crippled Children; pres. Temple Lions Crippled Childrens Found. Served with OSS, AUS, 1942-45. Mem. Temple C. of C. (past dir.). Methodist. Club: Temple Country (past dir.). Home: 312 E Munroe Av Temple TX 76501 Office: First National Bank Bldg Temple TX 76501

INGRAM, LEE RONALD, dentist; b. Long Beach, Cal., Jan. 7, 1937; s. Carl Lee and Martha Margaret (Herring) I.; student Fullerton Jr. Coll., 1956-57; B.S., Northwestern State Coll., Alva, Okla., 1962; postgrad. Tex. Christian U., summer, 1963; D.D.S., U. Mo., 1969; m. Dianne Jeanette Schmitz, Jan. 6, 1969; children—Carla Lynn, Monica Lea. Practice dentistry, Spearman, Tex., 1969—; mem. staff Hansford County Hosp., Spearman. Sec., Hansford County Credit Bur., Spearman, 1969-71. NSF grantee, 1963. Mem. N.E.A., Panhandle Dist. Dental Soc., Tex., Kan., Am. dental assns., Central Dist. Dental Soc., U. Mo. at Kansas City Alumni Assn., Jr. C. of C., Spearman C. of C., Xi Psi Phi. Home: 1118 S Barkley St Spearman TX 79081 Office: 712 S Roland St Spearman TX 79081

INGRAM, ROBERT A., physician; b. Dallas, June 6, 1922; s. Henry Lee and Bernice (Benedict) I.; B.A., Rice Inst., 1947; M.D., U. Tex., 1951; m. Dorace McGill, Sept. 7, 1946; 1 dau., Ruth Elizabeth. Intern, Baptist Meml. Hosp., San Antonio, Tex., 1951-52; practice gen. medicine, Orange, Tex., 1952—; mem. staff Orange (Tex.) Meml. Hosp. Served with USNR, 1944-46. Diplomate Am. Bd. Family Practice. Mem. Am. Acad. Gen. Practice, Am., Tex. med. assns., Internat. Platform Assn., Mensa. Home: 1906 Link Orange TX 77630 Office: 908 12th St Orange TX 77630

INGRAM, ROBERT COLEMAN, dentist; b. Charlotte Court House, Va., Aug. 29, 1903; s. John Henry and Martha (Priddy) I.; student Hampden-Sydney Coll., 1919-21; D.D.S., Med. Coll. Va., 1926; m. Mildred H. Cotton, June 11, 1928 (dec. 1968); 1 dau., Barbara Coleman (Mrs. Thomas Joel Hall). Pvt. practice dentistry, New Bern, N.C., 1927-32; resident D.C. Hosp., Laurel, Md., 1932-40; pvt. practice dentistry, Laurel, 1946-47; chief dental service VA Hosp., Shreveport, La., 1951-55; chief dental service VA Hosp., Atlanta, 1955-64, dir. oral surgery residency program, 1955-64, chmn. VA med. research, 1963; mem. faculty Emory U., 1956-64; free lance writer, 1964—. Mem. Gov.'s Natural Resources Com., State Fla., 1966-68. Served as col. USAAF, 1940-46. Fellow Am. Coll. Dentists; mem. Am. Dental Assn., A.A.A.S., Internat. Platform Assn., Kappa Sigma, Xi Psi Phi. Episcopalian (lay reader 1927-32). Rotarian, Lion. Author: Doctors in Retirement. Contbr. articles to profl. jours. Home: 205 Route A1A Apt 605 Satellite Beach FL 32937 Office: 205 Alabama St Satellite Beach FL 32937

INGRAM, SAM HARRIS, coll. pres.; b. Acton, Tenn., Jan. 31, 1928; s. John Q. and Lois (Abernathy) I.; B.S., Bethel Coll., 1951; M.A., Memphis State U., 1953, Ed.D., U. Tenn., 1959; m. Betty Ann White, July 14, 1950; children—Sam W., Glenn D. Elementary tchr., elementary prin., secondary prin. McNairy County Schs., Selmer, Tenn., 1949-57; asso. dir. curriculum Tenn. Dept. Edn., Nashville, 1959, 61; asso. prof. edn. Memphis State U., 1961, 62; chmn. edn. dept. Middle Tenn. State U., Murfreesboro, 1962-67, dean sch. edn., 1967-69; pres. Motlow State Community Coll., 1969—. Served with USMCR, 1946-47. Home: 205 Lake Circle Dr Tullahoma TN 37388

INGRAM, VIRGINIA BURROW HOWELL (MRS. WILLIAM THOMAS INGRAM), librarian; b. nr. Rutherford, Tenn., June 7, 1912; d. John William and Bertie (Lankford) Howell; B.A., Bethel Coll., 1936; M.A., Peabody Coll. Tchrs., 1956; m. William Thomas Ingram, Jr., Aug. 2, 1933; children—William Thomas III, John Howell. Librarian McKenzie (Tenn.) High Sch., 1952-65; librarian Frazer High Sch., Memphis, 1965-66; asst. cataloger Memphis U. Library, 1966—. Mem. N.E.A., Tenn., W. Tenn., Memphis edn. assns., A.L.A., Tenn. Library Assn., Delta Kappa Gamma, Pi Gamma Mu. Presbyn. Home: 210 N Avalon St Memphis TN 38112 Office: Memphis U Library Memphis TN 38111

INLOW, ROBERT FRANCIS, investment co. exec.; b. Oklahoma City, Okla., Nov. 19, 1936; s. Robert Frost and Evelyn (Milburn) I.; B.B.A., North Tex. State U., 1959; student So. Meth. U., 1965-68; m. Julie Scott Barnes, June 13, 1964; 1 son, Robert Julian. Investment banker First Nat. Bank in Dallas, 1962-64; with Hinton Mortgage & Investment Co., Dallas, Houston also Albuquerque, 1964—, sr. v.p., mgr. income property financing and devel., Dallas, 1969—. Mem. Dallas United Fund Bur. Served to capt. USAF, 1959-68. Mem. Dallas Mortgage Bankers Young Mens Assn. (pres. 1967), Delta Sigma Pi. Baptist. Home: 9934 Knoll Krest Dr Dallas TX 75238 Office: 4111 N Central Expressway Dallas TX 75204

INMAN, HARRY A., lawyer; b. Rochester, N.Y., Aug. 2, 1924; A.B., Harvard, 1948; LL.B., U. Va., 1951. Admitted to N.Y. bar, 1952, D.C. bar, 1953; partner firm Patton, Blow, Verrill, Brand & Boggs, Washington, Ortiz, Ramos & Inman, Mexico City, Mexico. Mem. Am. (chmn. sect. internat. and comparative law 1971—), Fed. (mem. conf. com. Inst. on Legal aspects of European Community), Inter-Am. (mem. council) bar assns., Bar. Assn. D.C., Am. Soc. Internat. Law. Author: Legal and Economic Aspects of Incorporation in Mexico, 1966. Office: Ortiz Ramos & Inman Morelos 98-103 Mexico City Mexico also 1200 17th St NWWashington DC*

INMAN, LESLIE LAUDER, lawyer; b. Little Rock, June 1, 1927; s. Frederick I. and Edith (Hooper) I.; student U. Tenn., 1946-47; B.A., Tulane U., 1950, LL.B., 1952; m. Freda Jean Jolly, Sept. 12, 1948; children—Paul Lauder, Leslie Karen, John Hooper. Admitted to La. bar, 1952, since practiced in New Orleans; partner Kullman, Lang, Inman & Bee, 1952—; asst. prof. labor law Coll. Law, Tulane U., 1970—. Served with USNR, 1945-46. Mem. Am. Bar Assn., Am. Judicature Soc., Omicron Delta Kappa. Republican. Presbyn. Editor-in-chief Tulane Law Rev., 1952. Home: 5710 Garfield St New Orleans LA 70115 Office: 615 Howard Av New Orleans LA 70130

INNIS, JOHN JAMES, surgeon; b. Hillsboro, Tex. Mar. 6, 1920;; s. John Edward and Eula Vita (Renshaw) I.; B.S. Southwestern La. Inst., 1943; M.D., Baylor U., 1949; postgrad. Tulane U., 1955-58; m. Gladys Lucille Griffin, June 27, 1949; children—John James, Sharion Denise, m.2d, Macye Ruth Steele children—William Eric, Grace Elaine. Chemist Down Chem. Co., Freeport, Tex., 1942-45; intern Charity Hosp., New Orleans, 1949-50; gen. practice medicine, Fairfield, Tex., 1952-55; asst. in orthopedic surgery Tulane U., 1955-58; practice medicine, specializing in orthopedic surgery. Fort Worth, 1958—; men, staff All Saints, Harris, St. Joseph, Peter Smith hosps. (all Ft. Worth); ednl. dir. chief orthopedics Fort Worth Childrens Hosp. Served as officer M.C., AUS, 1950-52. Decorated Bronze Star. Diplomate Am. Bd. Orthopedic Surgeons. Mem. Tex. Med. Assn., Tarrant County Med. Soc., A.M.A., Internat. Coll. Surgeons. Author films, articles orthopedic field. Home: 4401 Inwood St Fort Worth TX 76109 Office: 1401 8th Av Fort Worth TX 76104

INNIS, ROBERT TERRANCE, mech. engr.; b. Port Lavaca, Tex., Dec. 7, 1926; s. Homer Clarence and Eunice (Shofner) I.; B.M.E., U. Tex., 1951; grad. Advanced Mgmt. Program, Harvard U., 1960; m. Palma Payne, June 2, 1951; children—Terry, Robin, Dana, Seth, Mathew, Peter. Design engr. lightning arresters Westinghouse Corp., Pitts., 1951-56, design engr. power reclosers, 1956-59, engring. sect. mgr. lightning arresters, 1959-61, engring. sect. mgr. capacitor equipments, Ellettsville, Ind., 1961-69, engring. mgr. comml. and indsl. air conditioning div., Staunton, Va., 1969—; mem. nat. profl. coms. on arresters, capacitors, air conditioning devices. Mem. Town Planning & Ordinance Bd., Ellettsville, Ind., 1964-67; pres. Ellettsville Little League, 1966-67; chmn. Ellettsville Park Bd., 1968-69. Served with AUS, 1945-47. Methodist (tchr. Sunday sch. 1961-72, chmn. ofcl. bd. 1966-67, chmn. bldg. com. 1967-69). Patentee lightning arresters, reclosers, power capacitors, air conditioning system. Home: 322 Rainbow Dr Staunton VA 24401 Office: Box 2510 Staunton VA 24401

INNIS, WALTER DEANE, ret. naval officer, govt. ofcl.; b. Rushville, Ind., Mar. 6, 1909; s. John W. and Olive (Glass) I.; B.S., U.S. Naval Acad., 1932; grad. Naval War Coll., 1948; m. Pauline B. Coleman, Aug. 1, 1959. Commd. ensign USN, 1932, advanced through grades to rear adm.; designated naval aviator, 1936; served in Atlantic Neutrality Patrol, 1941, Mediterranean area, 1942, Aleutians, 1942-43, S.W. Pacific, Saipan, 1944, Iwo Jima, Okinawa, Japan, 1945, Korea and Formosa Strait, 1950-51; exec. officer Naval Air Sta., Dutch Harbor, Alaska, 1943; comdg. officer U.S.S. Bering Strait, 1944-45, exec. officer U.S.S. Philippine Sea, 1950-51; comdg. officer Naval Air Sta., Corpus Christi, Tex., 1946; attended Naval War Coll., 1947-48; faculty Naval War Coll., 1948-50; mem. staff sec. def., Washington, 1954-56, mem. U.S. delegation Austrian state treaty, Vienna, 1955, mem. staff U.S. ambassador to NATO, Paris, France, 1956-57; mem. spl. mission from Pres. Eisenhower to Marshall Tito, Yugoslavia, 1955, mem. operations coordinating bd., Washington, 1954-56; cons. Argentine Govt., Buenos Aires, 1959-60; Washington cons. The MITRE Corp., Bedford, Mass., 1962-64; systems analyst Navy Dept., 1964—. Decorated Legion of Merit, Bronze Star. Mem. Operations Research Soc. Am., Naval Hist. Found., Navy League U.S., Naval Acad. Found., Netherlands-Am. Found., English-Speaking Union, Naval Acad. Alumni Assn., Ind. Soc., Nat. Audubon Soc., Ret. Officers Assn. Republican. Presbyn. Clubs: Gibson Island (Md.); Gibson Island Yacht Squadron; Army-Navy (Washington); Explorers. Author spl. studies for Navy Dept. and Naval War Coll., MITRE Corp. Home: Watergate West 2700 Virginia Av NW Washington DC 20037 also Skippers Row Gibson Island MD 21056 Office: Bldg 196 Washington Navy Yard Washington DC 20390

INSCH, WILLIAM E., physician. Recipient Distinguished Performance award Ciba-Geigy Corp. Address: 2971 Good Hope Rd Winston-Salem NC 27106

INZER, WILLIAM HENRY, asso. justice Miss. Supreme Ct.; b. Pontotoc, Miss., Jan. 5, 1906; s. James William and Lou Delia (Caldwell) I.; LL.B., U. Miss., 1931; m. Charline Lawrence, Mar. 10, 1939; 1 son, William Henry. Admitted to Miss. bar, 1931; practiced in Pontotoc, 1931-40; county atty., Pontotoc, 1936-40; judge Circuit Ct., 1st Jud. Circuit, 1940-43; chancellor Chancery Ct., judge Youth Ct. Div., 1st Dist., 1943; now asso. justice Miss. Supreme Ct., Jackson. Served to maj. AUS, World War II. Democrat. Presbyn. Address: Judicial Bldg Jackson MS 39201

IRBY, WILSON, ry. exec.; b. El Dorado, Ark., Sept. 5, 1914; s. Arlie Jerry and Sallie (Mason) I.; B.S., Ouachita Baptist U., 1937; m. Ruth Eloise Garrett, Feb. 21, 1947; children—Dennis Wilson, John Arleigh. Clk. El Dorado & Wesson Ry., El Dorado, Ark., 1937-47, agt., 1947-72, traffic mgr., 1951-72, gen. auditor, sec.-treas., 1953—, also dir. Mem. El Dorado City Council, 1966-72. Served with AUS, 1942-46. Decorated Royal Order Scotland; hon. Legion of Honor, Order De Molay. Mem. Ark. Passenger and Freight Assn., El Dorado C. of C., Ark. Municipal League. Democrat. Methodist. Mason (32 deg., Shriner). Home: 508 E Block St El Dorado AR 71730 Office: PO Box 46 El Dorado AR 71730

IRELAND, LLOYD KENNETH, JR., govt. ofcl.; b. Tampa, Fla., Aug. 10, 1912; s. Lloyd Kenneth and Josephine Adalaide (Timberlake) I.; grad. Lively Bus. Sch., 1932; m. Margaret Alice Holt, Apr. 27, 1940; children—Patricia (Mrs. Edward McClendon), Lloyd Kenneth III, Beverly (Mrs. Milton Cox). Chief auditor, Fla. Emergency Relief Adminstrn., Tallahassee, 1932-36; cost accountant Ebersbach Constrn. Co., Tampa, 1936-40; chief accountant State Bd. of Adminstrn., Tallahassee, 1941-58; chief fiscal analyst Fla. Senate, Tallahassee, 1958-71; sec. of adminstrn. Dept. of Adminstrn.,

Tallahassee, 1971—. Mem. Fla. Council of 100, Tampa, 1971-72; mem. supervisory bd. Gov. Council on Criminal Justice, Tallahassee, Fla., 1971-72, Comprehensive Health Planning Council, Tallahassee, 1971-72. Served with USNR, 1943-46. Recipient Resolution of Appreciation award Fla. Senate, 1967; Resolution of Appreciation, Fla. Ho. of Reps., 1968. Mem. Leon County Farm Bur. Democrat. Presbyn. Lion (Tallahassee). Home: PO Box 645 Tallahassee FL 32302 Office: The Capitol Tallahassee FL 32304

IRISH, EDWIN FURBER, dentist; b. Wolfeboro, N.H., Dec. 16, 1925; s. Robert Jasper and Miriam (Furber) I.; B.A., Am. U., 1950; D.D.S., Med. Coll. Va., 1953; m. Marjorie Elizabeth Birdsall, Dec. 20, 1949; children—Stephen Birdsall, Robin, Diane. Staff dentist VA Hosp., Syracuse, N.Y., 1953-55; resident in prosthodontics VA Center, Milw., 1955-57; asst. chief dental service VA Hosp., Washington, 1957-64; chief dental service VA hosp., Richmond, Va., 1964-71; asst. dir. dental requirements service VA, Washington, 1971—; asst. prof. denture prosthodontics Med. Coll. at Va., 1965-71. Pres. Falling Creek Jr. High Sch. PTA, 1967-68; treas. Green Acres Civic Assn., 1960. Served with AUS, 1944-46, 1961-62. Diplomate Am. Bd. Prosthodontics. Fellow Am. Coll. Prosthodontists; mem. Richmond Dental Soc. (bd. dirs. 1968-71) Va. Dental Assn. (state insts. com. 1969-70), Am. Dental Assn., Alpha Tau Omega, Delta Sigma Delta, Omicron Kappa Upsilon. Methodist (mem. ofcl. bd. 1965-71). Home: 14704 Essington Rd Rockville MD 20853 Office: VA 810 Vermont Av NW Washington DC 20420

IRONS, CARY FREDERICK, physician; b. Pickaway, W.Va., Feb. 3, 1913; s. Cary F. and Sallie (Gibson) I.; A.B., Washington and Lee U., 1933; M.D., Med. Coll. Va., 1941; m. Malene Grant, June 10, 1939; children—Thomas Grant, Ben Gibson, Cary Frederick. Pvt. practice medicine, Greenville, 1945—; coll. physician East Carolina Coll., 1947—, dir. student health service, 1967—; sec. Med. Arts Clinic, 1950-61, v.p., 1961—. Pres. med. staff Pitt County Meml. Hosp., 1959-60; mem. N.C. Bd. Nurse Registration and Nursing Edn. Served from lt. to capt. M.C., AUS, 1942-45. Decorated Bronze Star. Diplomate Am. Bd. Family Practice. Fellow Am. Geriatrics Soc.; mem. N.C., Pitt County med. socs., A.M.A., Am. Acad. Gen. Practice. Democrat. Methodist. Rotarian (pres. elect). Home: 1104 W Rock Spring Rd Greenville NC 27834 Office: Infirmary East Carolina U Greenville NC 27834

IRONS, WILLIAM FRANCIS, air conditioning co. exec.; b. Sanborn, Ia., Feb. 20, 1927; s. Francis William and Edna (Allen) I.; B.S., U. N.D., 1951; P.E., U. N.D., 1958; m. Iva Mae Bendt, Mar. 9, 1947; children— Kathy (Mrs. Earl B. Houser), Amy Lisa, Tammy Frances; guardian to Michael Allen Damon. With Westinghouse Elec. Corp., 1951—, gen. mgr. central residential air conditioning, Norman, Okla., 1971— Staunton, Va., 1967-71. Vice pres. exec. council Boy Scouts Am., 1970-71; mem. vis. com. Coll. Bus. Adminstrn. Okla. U., 1971—. Served with USNR, World War II. Mem. Nat. Soc. Profl. Engr., Operations Research Sos. Am., Air-Conditioning Refrigeration, Inst., Nat. Assn. Accountants. Republican. Methodist. Mason. Home: 456 Thorton St Norman OK 73069 Office: Box 2510 Staunton VA 24407

IRVIN, FREDRIC BRINKER, coll. pres.; b. Mt. Pleasant, Pa., Oct. 13, 1913; s. Frederick Swisher and Bessie (Brinker) I.; B.A., Temple U., 1936, LL.D., 1957; M.A., U. Pitts., 1942, Ph.D., 1947; L.H.D., Thiel Coll., 1960; m. Ruth McElhaney, Dec. 23, 1939; children— Sara (Mrs. John H. Shields), Mary Jane (Mrs. John Pethick), Joseph Frederick. Tchr. high sch., P.R., 1937-38, Bellevue High Sch., Pitts., 1938-42; asst. registrar, instr. Temple U., Phila., 1942-47; v.p. Andhra Christian Coll., Guntur, India, 1947-52; pres. Thiel Coll., Greenville, Pa., 1952-60; cultural attache, Berlin, Germany, 1960-63, Bonn, Germany, 1963-66, Rawalpindi, Pakistan, 1966-68; pub. affairs officer U.S. consulate, Hamburg, Germany, 1968-70; chief outplacement and counseling services USIA, Washington, 1970-71; pres. Newberry Coll. (S.C.), 1971—. Served with AUS, 1943-45. Lutheran. Address: 2104 Luther St Newberry SC 29108

IRVIN, J(OHN) LEA, ret. engr.; b. Victoria, Tex., Oct. 6, 1897; s. Thomas S. and Leila (Ragland) I.; student pub. schs., Internat. Corr. Schs., Advanced Mgmt. program Harvard; m. Dorothy Vivyan Walker, Jan. 17, 1926; 1 dau., Pat C. (Mrs. E. L. Raulston). Design and constrn. West Texas Gulf Pipe Line Co., 1917-20, machine shop foreman, 1920-22, machine shop supt., 1922-24, asst. chief engr., 1924-29, asst. gen. supt., 1929-47, supt. pipe lines, 1947-49, mgr., 1949-52, became gen. mgr. all pipe lines, U.S. and Can., 1952, now pres. and dir.; pres., dir. Gulf Refining Co.; v.p., dir. Four Corners Pipe Line Co.; dir. Lurel Pipe Line Co. Registered profl. engr. Tex., La. Mason (32 deg., Shriner). Clubs: Engineers, Petroleum. Home: 6418 Auden Houston TX 77005 Office: PO Drawer 2100 Houston TX 77001

IRVIN, THOMAS T., state ofcl.; b. Hall County, Ga., July 14, 1929; s. C.T. and Gladys (Hogan) I.; ed. pub. schs., White County, Ga; m. Edna Bernice Frady, June 1, 1947; children—James Thomas, Johnny Mark, David Lewis, Londa Lynn, Lisa Ann. Engaged in lumber bus., 1946—, real estate bus., 1950—; mem. Ga. Ho. of Reps. from Habersham County, 1967, asst. adminstrv. floor leader, 1967; exec. sec. to gov. Ga., 1967-68; commr. agr. State of Ga., 1969—. Past bd. dirs., v.p., pres. Ga. Sch. Bds. Assn.; past bd. dirs. Ga. Jr. C. of C. Baptist (deacon). Mason (Shriner). Home Route 1 Mount Airy GA 30563 Office: 19 Hunter St SW Atlanta GA 30334

IRWIN, DAVID HENRY, educator; b. Tennessee Ridge, Tenn., Sept. 9, 1924; s. William H. and Clevie (Agy) I.; B.A., U. Tenn., 1948, M.S., 1949, postgrad., 1954-55; postgrad. U. Wash., 1957-58. Instr., U. Tenn., Knoxville, 1962-64; asst. prof. Murray (Ky.) State Univ., 1964-65, acting chmn. div. geography, 1965-67, asso. prof., 1966—, faculty sponsor Geography Club, 1964-67, Gamma Theta Upsilon, 1966-69. Served with AUS, 1942-45; USN, 1950-54. Decorated Purple Heart. Mem. Nat. Council Geog. Edn., Assn. Am. Geographers, Ky. Acad. Sci. (chmn. geography sect. 1972-73), Am. Geog. Soc. Address: Box 1054 Murray State Coll Murray KY 42071

IRWIN, JAMES ELLIS, lawyer; b. Memphis, May 1, 1920; s. Robert L. and Ethel (Farris) I.; LL.B., U. Memphis, 1940, LL.B. (hon.), Memphis State U., 1946; postgrad. U. Tenn., 1946-47; m. Nada Saskor, Apr. 29, 1946; 1 dau., Gwyneth Anne. Admitted to Tenn. bar, 1940; partner Blount & Irwin, 1947-52, Irwin & Dunlap, 1953-65; sr. partner Irwin, Owens, Gillock, Calton & Lyne; corporate counsel Pepper & Tanner, Inc., First Am. Bank of Memphis. Chmn., Shelby County Democratic Exec. Com., 1962—, del. nat. conv., 1964-68; Dem. candidate for U.S. Ho. of Reps., 1968. Appeal agt. Draft Bd. 104, 1957-71. Served to lt (j.g.) USCGR, 1941-46. Mem. Am., Tenn., Memphis and Shelby County bar assns., Memphis Trial Lawyers' Assn. (pres.), Delta Theta Phi. Clubs: Colonial Country, Winterhaven Country. Home: 3496 McCorkle Memphis TN 38116 Office: 100 N Main Bldg Memphis TN 38103

IRWIN, LEO HOWARD, judge; b. Stratford, N.C., Aug. 1, 1917; s. W. Carl and Mallie (Wilson) I.; student U. N.C., 1935-38; A.B., George Washington U., 1940; LL.B., Georgetown U., 1947; m. Doris Mickelson children—Sandra Lee, Lisa Ann, Patrice Camille, Leo Howard, Lori Denice. Admitted to N.C. and D.C. bars, 1947, also U.S. Supreme Ct.; with various govt. agencies, 1938-48, atty. Gen. Counsel's Office, CAB, 1947-48; mem. profl. staff, minority counsel com. ways and means Ho. of Reps.,1949-55; chief counsel; 1955-68; judge U.S. Tax Ct. 1968—; guest German Govt. on econ. study tour, 1964, Swedish and Danish govts., 1964; adj. prof. Georgetown U. Law Center Grad. Sch., nights, 1962-63. Active local Boy Scouts Am. Served as officer USNR. 1942-46. Mem. Fed. Bar Assn. Home: 5508 24th Av SE Washington DC 20031 Office: US Tax Ct Washington DC 20044

IRWIN, PAT, justice; b. Leedey, Okla., June 12, 1921; s. Marvin J. and Ollie D. (Newton) I.; student Southwestern State Coll., 1939-41; LL.B., U. Okla., 1949; m. Margaret Boggs, Aug. 18, 1950; children—William, Margaret. Admitted to Okla. bar, 1949; county atty., Dewey County, 1949-50; pvt. practice law, 1950-58; sec. to commrs. land office State Sch. Land Commn., State Okla., 1955-58; justice State Supreme Ct. Okla., 1959—, chief justice, 1969-70. Mem. Okla. State Senate, 1950-54. Served as capt. USMC, 1942-46; PTO. Mem. Am. Legion, Delta Theta Phi. Democrat. Mason. Home: 1325 Andover Ct Oklahoma City OK 73120 Office: State Capitol Bldg Oklahoma City OK 73102

ISAAC, JOSEPH ELIAS, theatre exhibitor; b. Zahle, Lebanon, Apr. 12, 1898; s. Elias Isaac and Rose (Aziz) I.; student pub. schs.; m. Alene Thomas, June 13, 1925; children—Joseph, Alfred, Samuel, Mary Jo, Barbara Alene, Rigdon, Victoria. Pres. Cumberland Amusement Co., Inc. Theatre Chain (9) Theatres, 1928—, Guaranty Deposit Bank Cumberland, Ky., 1936—. Chmn. City Planning and Zone Commn. Served as lt., U.S. Army, 1918-19. Mem. Ky. Assn. Theatre Owners (dir.), Am. Legion. Mason (Shriner, 32 deg.). Home: Isaac and Main Sts Cumberland KY 40823 also 601 University Blvd Daytona Beach FL 32018

ISLEY, MAX, architect; b. Yanceyville, N.C., June 8, 1929; s. Charles Henry and Media (Ward) I.; student U. Okla., 1947-49; B.Arch., N.C. State U., 1957; M.Arch., Harvard, 1959; m. Elizabeth Jane Skinner, Jan. 16, 1955; children—Alexander Max, Malcolm Ward, Nathan Charles, Duncan Walter. Faculty, Sch. Architecture, Mont. State Coll., 1957-58; with O. Berg & Assos., Architects, Bozeman, Mont., 1959-60; architect John D. Latimer & Assos., Architects, Durham, N.C., 1960-69; partner in charge Durham office Smart, Woodall, Isley & Assos., Inc., architects and planners, Durham, Raleigh, Greenville, 1969—. Served with CIC, U.S. Army, 1952-54. Mem. A.I.A., Durham Council Architects (pres.). Home: 5327 Yardley Terrace Durham NC 27707 Office: 602 W Chapel Hill St Durham NC 27702

ISRAEL, FIROOZ, structural engr.; b. Tehran, Iran, Sept. 13, 1941; s. Hay and Helen (Sadga) I.; B.S. with honors, Am. Coll. (Iran), 1963; M.S. in structural engring., Ga. Inst. Tech., 1964; m. Gisele Cohen, Mar. 21, 1965; 1 son, Daniel F. Came to U.S., 1963, naturalized, 1968. Research engr. Ga. Tech. Engring. Expt. Sta., Atlanta, 1964; structural engr. Vogt-Ivers & Assos., Atlanta, 1964-69; head structural dept. Lockwood Greene, Inc., Atlanta, 1969—. Chmn. Young Engrs. Com. Ga., 1972-73. Registered profl. engr., Ga., Ohio, N.C., Va., Tex., Ky. Mem. Am. Soc. C.E., Nat., Ga. (dir. Atlanta chpt.) socs. profl. engrs., Am. Concrete Inst., Profl. Soc. for Nuclear Def., Met. Assn. Urban Designers and Environmental Planners. Jewish religion. Editor Ga. Profl. Engr., 1969-70. Home: 2339-A Briarcliff Rd NE Atlanta GA 30329 Office: 1776 Peachtree St NW Atlanta GA 30309

ISRAEL, LARRY HERBERT, broadcasting co. exec.; b. McKeesport, Pa., Nov. 4, 1919; s. Nathan and Sophia (Eliashof) I.; B.J., U. Mo., 1948; m. Audrey Westerman, Oct. 14, 1951; children—Susan, Howard. Vice pres., gen. mgr. sta. WENS-TV, Pitts., also gen. mgr. KMGM, Mpls., 1953-57; gen. mgr. sta. WJZ-TV, Balt., 1957-59; v.p., gen. mgr. Television Advt. Reps., 1959-61, pres., 1961-63, also dir.; exec. v.p. Westinghouse Broadcasting Co., 1963-66, dir., 1966-68; pres. Westinghouse Broadcasting Sta. Group, 1966-68; chmn. bd., chief exec. officer Post-Newsweek Stas., Inc., 1968—; v.p., dir. Washington Post Co., 1968—. Mem. Newcomen Soc., Mo. Soc. N.Y., Kappa Tau Alpha, Sigma Delta Chi. Home: 22 Stanmore Ct Potomac MD 20854 Office: Broadcast House 40th and Brandywine Sts NW Washington DC 20016

IUELE, JOHN, condr.; b. Italy; came to U.S., 1928; grad. Mich. State U., 1941, Julliard Sch. Music, 1944. Tchr. instrumental music pub. schs., camps, colls.; trumpet player Detroit Symphony, N.Y. Symphony, Boston Symphony, City Center Opera Orch., Radio City Music Hall Orch., Atlanta Symphony, N.Y. Philharmonic; asst. condr. N.Y.C. Symphony, Atlanta Symphony; organizer, condr. Atlanta Civic Orch., Atlanta Civic Ballet Co.; guest condr. Lansing (Mich.) Symphony, Brevard Music Center Orch., N.C.; condr. Winston-Salem (N.C.) Symphony, 1952—. Home: 2211 Buena Vista Rd Winston-Salem NC 27104 Office: 610 Coliseum Dr Winston-Salem NC 27104

IVER, WILLIAM HENRY, dentist; b. Port Chester, N.Y., June 22, 1917; s. Alex R. and Beulah (Levy) E.; student U. Wis., 1936-38; D.D.S. cum laude, Georgetown U., 1942; m. Raye Bennett, Mar. 23, 1967; children—Robert Drew, Randolph, Carole. Pvt. practice dentistry, Miami Beach, Fla., 1945—. Bd. dirs. Lincoln Small Bus. Investment Corp.; mem. bd. Ka-Line Mfg. div. Sun Engring. Corp. Served to lt. comdr. USNR, 1942-45. Mem. Am., Fla., East Coast, Miami Beach dental assns. Home: Maison Grande 6039 Collins Av Miami Beach FL 33140 Office: 605 Lincoln Rd Miami Beach FL 33139

IVES, GEORGE SKINNER, chmn. Nat. Mediation Bd.; b. Bklyn., Jan. 10, 1922; s. Irving McNeil and Elizabeth (Skinner) I.; grad. Taft Sch., 1940; A.B., Dartmouth, 1943; LL.B., Cornell U., 1949; m. Barbara K. Turner, Aug. 14, 1948;&9cElizabeth Turner, Nancy McNeil. Admitted to N.Y. bar, 1949, D.C. bar, 1959; legal asst. to chmn. NLRB, 1949-50; asso. Simpson, Thatcher & Bartlett, N.Y.C., 1950-53; adminstrv. asst., legal counsel to Senator Irving M. Ives of N.Y., Washington, 1953-58; practice law and labor arbitration, 1959-69; chmn. Nat. Mediation Bd., 1970—. Served to lt. USNR, 1943-46. Mem. Am., N.Y., D.C. bar assns., Nat. Acad. Arbitrators, Am. Arbitration Assn. Home: 5969 Searl Terrace Washington DC 20016 Office: Nat Mediation Bd 1230 16th St NW Washington DC 20572

IVESTER, WILLIAM JAMES, lawyer; b. Sayre, Okla., Sept. 13, 1921; s. James Alford and Johnnie (Turner) I.; B.A., U. Okla., 1943, LL.B., 1949; m. Eleanor Louise Thompson, Nov. 26, 1947; children—Allison Ann, James Eric. Admitted to Okla. bar, 1948; practice law, Altus, Okla., 1948—; partner firm Ivester and Braddock, 1963—. Dir. First State Bank Altus. Asst. county atty. Jackson County, Okla., 1948-49; mem. Okla. Ho. of Reps., 1950-54; city atty. City of Altus, 1953—. Served to lt. USNR, 1943-46. Mem. Am., Okla., Jackson County (pres. 1950) bar assns., Okla. Municipal Attys. Assn. (dir. 1958-60), Western Trail Hist. Soc. (v.p. 1968—), Phi Delta Phi. Democrat. Methodist. Mason, Elk, Lion (pres. Altus club 1960-61). Home: 1812 Hudson Dr Altus OK 73521 Office: 501 N Hudson St Altus OK 73521

IVESTER, ZOE ANN, social worker; b. Sayre, Okla., Jan. 8, 1927; d. William Lando and Golda (Hodgson) I.; B.S. Okla. State U., 1948; M.S.W., U. Denver, 1956; student Okla. Coll. Women, 1944-45. Caseworker Okla. State Welfare Dept., child welfare supr., field rep., 1948-51, 1963—; caseworker Am. Red. Cross, Kan., 1951-54; caseworker Kan. Childrens Service League, 1955-59; child welfare supr. Nev. State Welfare Dept., 1959-62, also dist. dir. Mem. Nat. Assn. Social Workers, D.A.R. Methodist. Mem. Order Eastern Star. Home: Box 57 Sayre OK 73662 Office: Beckham County Dept Welfare Sayre OK 73662

IVEY, MONTERIA, SR., govt. ofcl. Dep. exec. dir. Nat. Capital Housing Authority, Washington. Office: 1170 12th St NW Washington DC 20430*

IVEY, ROBERT GENE, librarian; b. DeQuincy, La., Aug. 27, 1940; s. Evans Oslyn and Vicy Yvonne (Young) I.; B.A., McNeese State U., Lake Charles, La., 1963; postgrad. Southwestern Baptist Theol. Sem., 1964-65.; m. Tchr., Westlake (La.) High Sch., 1963-64; librarian, tchr. Deweyville (Tex.) Ind. Sch. Dist., 1965-69; librarian La. Correctional and Indsl. Sch., DeQuincy, 1969—. Mem. exec. bd. S.W. La. Library Regional Planning System, 1971—. Mem. La. (chmn. adult edn. com.), Calcasieu (v.p. 1971-72) library assns., Lake Charles Community Concert Assn. Democrat. Baptist. Club: DeQuincy Optimist (chmn. nominating and inter club coms. 1971-72). Author article. Home: 317 Yoakum Av DeQuincy LA 70633 Office: PO Box 1056 DeQuincy LA 70633

IVIE, CLAUDE MOORE, state ofcl.; b. Cornelia, Ga., Feb. 26, 1920; s. Claude Moore and Maude (Stephens) I.; A.B., Piedmont Coll., 1939; M.Ed., U. Ga., 1948; Ed.D., Fla. State U., 1953; m. Virginia Little, Aug. 2, 1947; children—Stephen L., William J., Virginia A. Tchr., prin. Maysville (Ga.) High Sch., 1939-41; prin. Rentz, Ochlochnee, Moultrie high sch., Moultrie, Ga., 1947-50; prin. lab. sch., dir. student teaching Troy, (Ala.) State Coll., 1952-55; asst. supt. for instrn. Meridian (Miss.) Pub. Schs., 1955-64; dir. div. curriculum State Dept. Edn., Ga., 1964—. Ga. sales rep. Row Peterson & Co., 1945-47. Served with USNR, 1941-45. Decorated Air medal with oak leaf cluster. Mem. N.E.A., Ga. Edn. Assn., Assn. Supr. Curriculum Devel. Contbr. to edn. jours. Home: 2328 Shasta Way Atlanta GA 30329 Office: State Dept. Edn Atlanta GA 30334

IVIE, JOHN MARK, psychiatrist; b. Memphis, Feb. 17, 1933; s. James M. and Gladys (Brooks) I.; M.D., Memphis State U., 1955-59; M.D., U. Tenn., 1962; m. Shirley Marie Gilliland, Dec. 30, 1955 (div. Feb. 1966); 1 dau., Marianne. Intern, St. Joseph Hosp., Memphis, 1962-63; resident U. Tenn. dept. psychiatry, Memphis, 1963-66; staff psychiatrist Tenn. Psychiat. Hosp. and Inst., Memphis, 1966-67; pvt. practice psychiatry, 1967—; cons. Ark. Div. Vocational Rehab. Served with USAF, 1950-55. Mem. A.M.A., Tenn., Memphis, Shelby County med. assns., Am. Psychiat. Assn., Lambda Chi Alpha, Phi Rho Sigma, Chi Beta Phi. Home: 881 S Perkins Av Memphis TN 38117 Office: 5050 Poplar Av White Station Tower Memphis TN 38117

IVY, ROBERT ADAMS, hosp. adminstr.; b. Muldon, Miss., Nov. 8, 1916; s. Robert Adams, and Loretta (Lilley) I.; B.S., Millsaps Coll., 1939; postgrad. U.N.C., 1941-42; m. Frances Heard Ledyard, Oct. 23, 1942; 1 son, Robert Adams. Adminstr., v.p. Doster Hosp. and Clinic, Columbus, Miss., 1944-69; administr. Lowndes Gen. Hosp., Columbus, 1970—. Dir. Miss. Blue Cross. Bd. dirs., sec.-treas. Stephen D. Lee Found. Fellow Am. Coll. Hosp. Adminstrs. (1st Miss. regent, pres., dist. gov. 1967-72); mem. Miss. Hosp. Assn. (past pres., dir., speaker ho. dels.), Southeastern Hosp. Conf. (past pres.), Columbus C. of C., Columbus Pilgrimage Assn. (pres.), Kappa Alpha. Methodist (steward). Rotarian (past pres.). Home: 1206 N 7th St Columbus MS 39701 Office: 2520 N 5th St Columbus MS 39701

IZZARD, WESLEY SHERMAN, editor; b. Chgo., Apr. 19, 1900; s. Arthur John and Cora May (Sherman) I.; A.B., U. Ill., 1923; m. Helen Elizabeth Easterday, Feb. 3, 1922; children—Wesley Robert, Marilyn Ann. Reporter, Kansas City Jour., 1919, copy desk chief, 1923-24; mng. editor Amarillo (Tex.) Globe, 1924-26, mng. editor Amarillo Globe and Daily News (combined), 1926-35; prodn. mgr. Radio Sta. KGNC, Amarillo, 1935-38; editor-in-chief Globe-news, 1943-51; editor, pub. Daily News, 1951—; sec., Plains Radio Broadcasting Co., Amarillo, 1937—; news commentator radio sta. KGNC, 1935-61, gen. mgr. KGNC radio and TV sta., 1954-66. Mem. Am. Soc. Newspaper Editors, Delta Alpha Epsilon, Sigma Delta Chi. Home: 2605 Hughes St Amarillo TX 79109 Office: Globe-News Pub Co Amarillo TX 79101

JABLONSKI, T. HENRY, ednl. adminstr.; b. Wilmington, Del., Jan. 9, 1915; s. Frank W. and Wladysawa (Wilchinska) J.; B.S., Trenton State Coll., 1938; m. Laura Marian Depue, Nov. 7, 1936; children—Thaddeus Henry, Alice (Mrs. Thayer Smith), Frank, Alfred, Jon, Kathryn, Laura, Richard. Indsl. arts instr. Merchantville (N.J.) High Sch., 1939-43; Radnor High Sch., Pa., 1943-45; asst. exec. dir. Pa. Soc. for Crippled Children, 1945-52; pres. Washington Coll. Acad., Washington College, Tenn., 1952—. Pres., Washington County Soc. for Crippled Children, 1958-60. Active Boy Scouts Am. Presbyn. Mason, Rotarian. Home: Washington College TN 37681

JACHIMCZYK, JOSEPH ALEXANDER, physician, lawyer; b. Bridgeport, Conn., Sept. 15, 1923; s. Michael A. and Mary M. (Wozny) J.; M.D., U. Tenn., 1948; LL.B., Boston Coll. Law Sch., 1958; m. Loretta T. Slomski, June 17, 1950; children—Jane, Michael, Peggy, Mary. Intern, Queen's Hosp., Honolulu, 1948-49; resident pathology Hamot Hosp., Erie, Pa., 1949. Norwalk (Conn.) Hosp., 1949-50, City Hosp., Cleve., 1950-53; asst. med. examiner State of Md., Balt., 1953; teaching fellow Harvard Dept. Legal Medicine, Boston, 1954-57; sr. surgeon USPHS, Boston, 1954-56; forensic pathologist, chief med. examiner Harris County, Houston, 1957—; admitted to Tex. bar, 1959. Served with AUS, 1943-45. Fellow Coll. Am. Pathologists, Am. Soc. Clin. Pathologists; mem. Am. Acad. Forensic Scis., Internat. Acad. Pathology, U.S. Mil. Surgeons Assn., Am., Houston bar assns., Tex., Harris County med. socs.Home: 3403 Bradford Pl Houston TX 77025 Office: County Courthouse Houston TX 77002

JACK, WILLIAM HARRY, lawyer; b. Kaufman, Tex., Dec. 13, 1899; s. William Harry and Kosci (Snow) J.; LL.B., U. Tex., 1922, A.B., 1923; m. Marian Price, Nov. 27, 1928 (dec.); children—Robert W., Patricia Allen (Mrs. J.W. Porter, Jr.), Marian E. Jenkins; m. 2d, Josephine Hunley Dillon, Aug. 16, 1969. Admitted to Tex. bar, 1922; partner Jack & Jack, attorneys, Corsicana, Texas, 1923-26; mem. Saner, Jack, Sallinger & Nichols, Dallas, 1926—. Dir. Booth, Inc. Pres., dir. Blanche Mary Taxis Found.; dir. past pres. Child's Guidance Clinic; vice chmn. bd. trustees Southwestern Legal Found. Served as pvt. U.S. Army, 1918, maj. USAAF, 1942-44; lt. col. U.S. Army Res. Fellow Am. Bar Found., Southwestern Legal Found, Am. Coll. Probate Counsel (pres. 1963-64); mem. State Bar Tex. (past dir., v.p.), Dallas (pres. 1951), Am. (ho. of dels.) bar assns., Phi Beta Kappa, Phi Delta Phi, Sigma Delta Chi. Democrat. Presbyn. (elder; bd. Christian edn. Presbyn. Ch. U.S.). Mason (Shriner). Clubs: National Exchange (past v.p.; pres.), Dallas Country, Dallas, Chaparral. Home: Terrace House 3131 Maple Av Dallas TX 75201 Office: Republic Nat Bank Bldg Dallas TX 75201

JACKS, CLIVE FRANKLIN, JR., educator; b. Atlanta, Mar. 16, 1932; s. Clive Franklin and Elizabeth Catherine (George) J.; A.B., Emory U., 1952; B.D., Columbia Theol. Sem., 1955; Th.D., Union Theol. Sem., 1966; m. Ann Elizabeth Mulvey, June 11, 1966; 1 son, Timothy Franklin. Vis. lectr. Bangor (Me.) Theol. Sem., 1962-64; asst. prof. Spelman Coll. Atlanta, 1965-69; asso. prof. religion Queens Coll., Charlotte, N.C., 1969—; ordained to ministry Presbyn. Ch., 1955. Mem. Am. Assn. U. Profs., Soc. Bibl. Literature, Am. Assn. Religion. Home and Office: 1029 Sewickley Dr Charlotte NC 28209

JACKS, HORACE LEONARD, banker; b. Waco, Tex., June 17, 1924; s. Thomas L. and Mollie (Gibson) J.; student So. Meth. U., 1958-60; m. Mary Louise Branch, Mar. 2, 1946; children—George Michael, Mary Lynette. Bookkeeper First Nat. Bank, Waco, 1942; bookkeeper First Nat. Bank, Dallas, 1946-54, asst. cashier, 1954-56, asst. v.p., 1956-62, v.p., 1962—; pres., dir. ARM, Inc., 1966-67. Bd. dirs. Children, Inc. Served with USNR, 1943-46. Mem. Systems and Procedures Assn. (pres. Dallas 1964-65). Home: 908 Oak Park Dr Dallas TX 75232 Office: 1401 Elm St Dallas TX 75222

JACKSON, ALLEN KEITH, coll. pres.; b. Rocky Ford, Colo., July 22, 1932; s. Monford L. and Leliah Jean (Hipp) J.; B.A., U. Denver, 1954; Fulbright fellow, Cambridge (Eng.) U., 1955; Th.M. (Elizabeth Iliff Warren fellow 1958), Iliff Sch. Theology, Denver, 1958; Ph.D. (Honor fellow 1959), Emory U., 1960; m. Barbara May Hollard, June 13, 1954; children—Cary Vincent, Deborah Kay and Edward Keith (twins), Frederick James. Methodist student minister, Erie, Colo., 1955-58; ordained elder Methodist Ch., 1958; instr. sociology Emory U., 1958-60; chaplain, asst. prof. religion and sociology Morningside Coll., Sioux City, Ia., 1960-62, dean of coll., 1962-68; pres. Huntingdon Coll., Montgomery, Ala., 1968—. Pres., Montgomery United Appeal, 1972-73. Mem. adv. bd. St. Margaret's Hosp. Mem. Ala. Assn. Independent Colls. (pres. 1969-71), Phi Beta Kappa, Omicron Delta Kappa, Beta Theta Pi. Methodist (ofcl. bd.). Rotarian. Contbr. profl. jours. Home: 1393 Woodley Rd Montgomery AL 36106

JACKSON, ALVIN ROSS, physician; b. Waxahachie, Tex., May 12, 1897; s. Robert Andrew and Ava (Stewart) J.; A.B., U. Okla., 1924, B.A., 1928, M.D., 1930; m. Prenda Hermosa Tidwell, Sept. 2, 1925; children—Elizabeth Ann (Mrs. James K. Dewbre). Intern, St. Anthony's Hosp., 1930-31; pvt. practice medicine, Oklahoma City, 1930-71; ret., 1971; dir. Okla. Nat. Bank; med. examiner, dir. Mid-Am. Investors Life Ins. Co.; pres. Capitol Hill Gen. Hosp. Bd. dirs. Capitol Hill YMCA. Served with U.S. Navy, 1918-20. Mem. A.M.A., Okla., Oklahoma County med. socs., Alpha Tau Omega. Club: Capitol Hill Lions (past pres.). Home: 613 SW 30th St Oklahoma City OK 73109

JACKSON, AMOS EVERETT, lawyer; b. nr. Gainesville, Ga., Jan. 8, 1909; s. Wiley Edward and Cora (Thompson) J.; student pub. schs.; m. Gertrude Edythe Rose, Aug. 15, 1930; children—Judith D. (Mrs. Robert D. Joines), Michael E. Admitted to Fla. bar, 1946; accounting clk. Fla. Motor Lines, Inc., Orlando, Jacksonville, 1927-37; office mgr. Milam, McIlvaine & Milam, attys., Jacksonville, 1937-39; asst. trust officer First Nat. Bank, Palm Beach, Fla., 1940-42; accountant C. W. Fisher, C.P.A., West Palm Beach, Fla., 1944-46; treas. Gulf Atlantic Transp. Co., Jacksonville, 1946; gen. practice, West Palm Beach, 1947-50, Palm Beach, 1950—. Former chmn. Palm Beach County Devel. Bd.; past chmn. Palm Beach Zoning Comm., 1968—. Trustee Mount Ida Jr. Coll., Newton Centre, Mass. Served with USNR, 1942. Mem. Fla. Bar, Am., Palm Beach County bar assns. Home: 1233 N Ocean Way Palm Beach FL 33480 Office: 230 Royal Palm Way Palm Beach FL 33480

JACKSON, BETTY RUTH, architect, structural engr.; b. Pawhuska, Okla., Jan. 5, 1927; d. Fred Hildreth and Ruth (Daniels) Jackson; B.S. in Archtl. Engring., U. Okla., 1949, M.C.E., 1950 With Hudgins, Thompson, Ball & Assos., Inc., architects, engrs., planners, Oklahoma City, 1948—, draftsman, 1948, 49, jr. engr., 1950-54, jr. architect, 1950-57, structural engr., project architect, 1957—. Registered profl. engr., Okla.; licensed architect, Okla. Mem. A.I.A., Nat. Okla. socs. profl. engrs., Norman Bus. and Profl. Women (past pres.; chmn. state com.). Episcopalian. Club: Altrusa (past pres. Norman club). Prin. archtl. works include Will Rogers World Airport Terminal, 1966, FAA Aero. Center, 1957 (both Oklahoma City), Amarillo (Tex.) Airport Terminal, 1970. Home: 643 Okmulgee St Norman OK 73069 Office: Hudgins Thompson Ball & Assos 1411 Classen Blvd Oklahoma City OK 73106

JACKSON, BLYDEN, educator; b. Paducah, Ky., Oct. 12, 1910; s. George Washington and Julia Estelle (Reid) J.; A.B., Wilberforce U., 1930; A.M., U. Mich., 1938, Ph.D. (Rosenwald fellow 1947-49), 1952; m. Roberta Bowles, Aug. 2, 1958. Tchr. English, Louisville pub. schs., 1934-45; asst., then asso. prof. English, Fisk U., 1945-54; prof. English, head dept. So. U., 1954-62, dean Grad. Sch., 1962-69; prof. English, U. N.C., Chapel Hill, 1969—; spl. research criticism Negro lit. Mem. Coll. Lang. Assn. (pres. 1957-59), Modern Lang. Assn., Nat. Council Tchrs. English (Distinguished lectr. 1970-71, chmn. coll. sect. 1971—), Coll. English Assn., Speech Assn. Am., La. Edn. Assn., Alpha Phi Alpha. Contbr. articles to profl. jours. Asso. editor CLA Bull., 1959—; mem. editorial adv. bd. So. Lit. Jour. Home: 102 Laurel Hill Rd Chapel Hill NC 27514

JACKSON, BURL THURSTON, accountant, lawyer; b. Waldo, Ark., May 19, 1907; s. John Andrew and Ethel (Thrailkill) J.; H.A., LaSalle Extension U., Chgo., 1932; LL.B., Ark. Law Sch., 1941; student N.Y.U. Inst. on Fed. Taxation, 1951, 58; m. Lelia Gordon, Aug. 6, 1930. Bookkeeper Am. Grocer Co., Little Rock, 1928-31; bookkeeper, mgr., asst. to pres., legal and tax counsel Comml. Warehouse Co., Inc., 1931-51, now sec.-treas., dir., legal counsel; sec.-treas., dir. legal counsel Merchants Transfer Warehouse Co., Inc.; sec.-treas. Porter Foods, Inc.; admitted to Ark. bar, 1941; practice accounting and tax law, 1951—. Ark. chmn. Membership Com. Tax Inst. Trustee Little Rock Boys Club Athletic Field. C.P.A., Ark., La. Mem. S.W. Warehouse and Transfermen's Assn. (v.p. Ark. 1951-52), Ark. Soc. C.P.A.'s Am. Inst. Accountants, Am., Ark. bar assns., Am. Assn. Atty.-C.P.A.'s, Am. Arbitration Assn. (nat. panel arbitrators). Baptist (chmn. bd. deacons). Kiwanian. Home: 1312 S Tyler St Little Rock AR 72204 Office: 1800 E Roosevelt Rd Little Rock AR 72206

JACKSON, CHARLES, state ofcl. Exec. dir. Dept. Bus. Regulation, State of Fla., Tallahassee. Office: 304 Carlton Bldg Tallahassee FL 32304*

JACKSON, CHARLES WAYNE, coll. adminstr.; b. Carlisle, Ark., June 23, 1929; s. Terrell and Margaret (Sanders) J.; A.B., Hendrix Coll., 1952; M.Ed., U. Ark., 1958, Ed.D., 1966; grad. Inst. Ednl. Mgmt., Harvard, 1972; m. Marette McCauley, July 1, 1950; children—Charles Wayne, Retta Cauley, Shelia Lucyle. Tchr., pub. schs., Wright, Ark., 1950-54; prin. pub. schs., Augusta, Ark., 1954-59; supt. pub. schs., Swifton, Ark., 1959-63; asso. editor Ark. Sch. Bds. Assn. publs. U. Ark., Fayetteville, 1964-65; v.p. adminstrn. S. State Coll., Magnolia, Ark., 1965—. Chmn. A.R.C., Augusta, 1955. Bd. dirs. Magnolia Boys Club. Mem. Am. Assn. Higher Edn., Ark. Edn. Assn. (v.p. higher edn. 1972-73), N.E. Ark. Schoolmasters Club (pres. 1960), Phi Delta Kappa (historian 1964), Kappa Delta Pi. Methodist (chmn. ofcl. bd. 1961). Rotarian. Home: 201 Reeves Terrace Magnolia AR 71753 Office: So State Coll Magnolia AR 71753

JACKSON, CLAYTON LEROY, ins. exec.; b. Owen Sound, Ont., Can., Aug. 25, 1917; s. Chester C. and Edna (Green) J.; B.A., U. Toronto, 1949; m. Eula E. Gardner, Aug. 20, 1946; children—Heather, Alan. Came to U.S., 1955. Asst. actuary Mut. Life of Can., Waterloo, Ont., 1953-55; asst. actuary United Life and Accident Ins. Co., Concord, N.H., 1955, actuary, 1955-69, v.p., 1958-65, sr. v.p., 1965-69, also dir.; v.p., actuary Am. Nat. Ins. Co., Galveston, Tex., 1969-70, sr. v.p., actuary, 1970—. Served with Canadian Army, 1943-46. Fellow Canadian Inst. Actuaries, Soc. Actuaries, Life Office Mgmt. Assn.; mem. Actuaries Club S.W., Am. Acad. Actuaries, Internat. Actuarial Assn., Am. Risk and Ins. Assn. Conglist. Office: 1 Moody Plaza Galveston TX 77550

JACKSON, DELLA ROSETTA HAYDEN, civic worker, educator; b. Mill Spring, N.C., Mar. 2, 1905; d. Robert Twitty and Amanda (Petty) Hayden; B.A., Johnson C. Smith U., 1948; M.A., N.C. Coll., 1956; m. G. Franklin Davenport, Sept. 28, 1930 (dec. Jan. 1936); children—Evelyn Frances (Mrs. Alonzo David Petty), Amanda Elizabeth (Mrs. Lourn Clinton Gray), Robert Franklin; m. 2d, Clarence Eugene Jackson, Oct. 30, 1943 (dec. Mar. 1951); children—Mae Carolyn (Mrs. Joseph Williams, Jr.), Clarence Stinson. Tchr., Stony Knoll Sch., Polk County, N.C., 1927-30, Tryon Sch., 1930-31, Pea Ridge Sch., 1932-39, Union Grove Sch., 1939-48, Edmund Embury Sch., 1949-51, Cobb Elementary Sch., Tryon, N.C., 1951-65; tchr. adult edn. Isothermal Community Coll., Mill Spring, N.C., 1971—; librarian Stony Knoll Community Library, 1937—, also chmn. bd. trustees; spl. edn. tchr. Polk Central High Sch., Mill Spring, 1966-69. Mem. Central Highlands Health Council, 1968-70; 2d v.p. Polk County Homemakers Council; sec.-treas. Polk County Community Devel. Council; leader, 4-H Club; v.p. Polk County Child Devel. Council, 1971—, Eastern Appalachian Children's Council, 1971—; chmn. Polk County Child Care Com., 1971—. Bd. dirs. Isothermal Health Council, sec., 1972—; bd. dirs. Polk County Mental Health Council, St. Luke Hosp. Aux., Regional Health Council Eastern Appalachia. Named Mother of Year, Afro, 1948, Mother of Year, Homemakers Council Polk County and Western Dist. N.C., 1971; recipient certificate service N.C. Recreation Soc., 1962, certificate leadership for service Western N.C. Community Devel. Program Asheville Agrl. Devel. Council, 1962. Mem. League Women Voters (dir. 1970—), Stony Knoll Recreation Soc. Club: Stony Knoll Community (pres. 1959-62). Home: Box 95 Mill Spring NC 28756

JACKSON, DOROTHY LOUISA GREENLEE (MRS. FRED KNOX JACKSON), ct. reporter; b. Hamburg, Ia., Feb. 19, 1911; d. Henry Oliver and Mattie (Landreth) Greenlee; student pub. schs.; m. Fred Knox Jackson, Oct. 3, 1944. Asst. county ct. reporter, Auburn, Neb., 1927-29; sec. local atty., 1927-29; sec. Berksons, Kansas City, Mo., 1929-33; corr. A.A.A., Washington, 1933-36; sec. Intelligence Unit, Kansas City, St. Louis, 1936-40; free-lance ct., conv. reporter, St. Louis, 1940-44; free-lance ct. reporter, Prattville, Ala., 1948—; contract reporter Ala. Pub. Service Commn., Montgomery. Co-owner, operator Prattville (Ala.) Quick Freeze, 1948-63; owner Quiet Acre, Cottonwood, Ala. Chmn., Autauga County Operation Santa Claus, State Christmas Card, Bryce Mental Hosp., Tuscaloosa, Ala., 1963-70. Mem. Nat. League Am. Pen Women (br. pres. 1964-68, state v.p. 1970-71, state pres. 1972—), Birmingham Opera Guild, Ala. Writers Conclave, Montgomery Press and Authors Club (pres. 1971-72), Ala. Shorthand Reporters Assn., Montgomery Assn. Legal Secs., Nat. Shorthand Reporters Assn., Internat. Platform Assn. Club: Autauga County Bus. and Profl. Women's (named County Woman of Achievement 1971). Author: Fallen Leaves, 1968; Poody, Story of a Cat-Nothing But a Cat, 1970. Home: 856 Gillespie St Prattville AL 36067 Office: 132 Adams Av Montgomery AL 36104

JACKSON, E(DWARD) FRANKLIN, clergyman; b. Pensacola, Fla., July 19, 1911; s. Charles Wesley and Phebe (Hart) J.; student Fla. A. and M. Coll., 1932, Tuskegee Inst., 1935; D.D., Livingstone Coll.-Hood Sem., 1948; m. Mildred Elizabeth Dodson, Sept. 1, 1937; children—Edward Franklin, Cameron Wesley, Gloria Jean, Darryl Joseph. Ordained to ministry A.M.E. Zion Ch., 1934; pastor Burnt Corn Circuit, Evergreen, Ala., 1934-36, Brakebill Chapel, 1937, Price Meml., Cleveland, Tenn., 1937-40, Harris Chapel, Chattanooga, 1940-42, St. Paul, Johnson City, Tenn., 1942-43, St. Lukes Ch, Buffalo, 1943-52, John Wesley A.M.E. Zion Ch., Washington 1952—. Pres. N.A.A.C.P., Washington 1959-64; v.p. citizens adv. com. to Civil Rights Commn., 1962—. Vice pres. Central Democratic Com., D.C., 1960-64; Dem. nat. committeeman for D.C., 1964-68; mem. Nat. Dem. Speaker Bur., 1960—. Named Afro Am. Man of Year, 1957. Mem. Omega Psi Phi. Mason (32 deg., Shriner). Author: The Full Grown Minister, 1949; My Church, 1952. Home: 1736 Webster St NW Washington DC 20011 Office: 1514 14th St NW Washington DC 20005

JACKSON, ELMO LOUIS, economist, price analyst, b. 1913; B.S., Fla. U., 1935; A.M., Harvard, 1937, Ph.D., 1942; m. Corinne Reginna Klemm, Jan. 31, 1948. Econ. cons., def. counsel, U.S. vs. Am. Tobacco Co. et al, 1940-41; engaged research and writing on consumption of tobacco products from 1900-40; tobacco tax cons. U.S. Treasury, 1942; tobacco price economist OPA, 1942; economist U.S. Dept. Agr., 1938-40; instr. econs. Harvard, 1945-46; asso. prof. econs. and statistics U. Fla., 1946-56, prof. econs., 1956—; leader study research group at Vanderbilt U. to examine econ. problems in marketing prin. types of tobacco leaf, 1950-51; vis. prof. Old Dominion Coll., 1967-68. Served as 2d lt. to maj. F.A., AUS, 1942-46; overseas. Mem. Am., So. econ. assns. Author: The Pricing of Cigarette Tobaccos, 1955. Home: 1515 NW 14th Av Gainesville FL 32601

JACKSON, FLOYD LOUIS, judge; b. Alvord, Tex., Apr. 13, 1902; s. John Washington and Laura May (Parson) J.; LL.B., U. Okla., 1927; m. Geneva Morrison, Sept. 7, 1931. Admitted to Okla. bar, 1927; practicing atty., 1927-42; dist. judge, Cotton and Comanche counties, Okla., 1947-54; justice Okla. Supreme Ct., 1955—, chief justice, 1967-68. Served with AUS, 1942-46; lt. col. ret. Named to Okla. Hall of Fame, 1968. Home: Lawton, Okla. Office: State Capitol Bldg Oklahoma City OK

JACKSON, FRED CAMERON, lawyer; b. Clarks, La., Sept. 6, 1929; s. Leonard L. and Mabel (Allen) J.; B.A., La. State U., 1950, J.D., 1956; m. Anne Purnell Smith, Sept. 10, 1955; children—Nanette Davis, Jefferson Purnell, Martie Anne, Fred Cameron, James Alexander. Admitted to La. bar, 1956; practiced in St. Francisville, La.; mem. firm Kilbourne, Dart & Jackson, St. Francisville, 1960; asst. dist. atty. 20th Jud. Dist. La., 1964-72. Served with AUS, 1950-53. Mem. Am., La. bar assns., Nat. Dist. Attys. Assn., Am. Legion, V.F.W., Scabbard and Blade, Kappa Sigma. Mason (Shriner). Club: West Feliciana Civic (past pres. St. Francisville). Home: PO Drawer 489 Saint Francisville LA 70775

JACKSON, GEORGE LINTON, judge; b. Gray, Ga., Oct. 31, 1923; s. Joseph Benjamin and Lillie P. (Mobley) J.; student Middle Ga. Coll., 1943; A.B., Mercer U., 1945, LL.B., 1948; m. Sarah Folds, Aug. 4, 1956 children—Estelle, George Linton. Admitted to Ga. bar, 1947; practiced in Gray, Ga., 1948-68; mem. Ga. Ho. of Reps., 1951-57; mem. Ga. Senate, 1957-59; county atty. Jones County, 1955-59, 65-68; judge Superior Ct. Ocmulgee Circuit, 1968—. Lion Home: PO Box 183 Gray GA 31032

JACKSON, JAMES OLIVER, life ins. co. exec.; b. Denison, Tex., July 17, 1920; s. Oliver Ivans and Josephine (Moore) J.; B.S., Abilene Christian Coll., 1942; M.S., North Tex. State U., 1953; m. Biddie M. Rowland, Dec. 14, 1944; children—Sara Anderson (Mrs. Robert H. Anderson), Rolanda, Lola. Prof. health, phys. edn., track and field, football coach Abilene Christian Coll., 1946-63; agt. Rep. Nat. Life Ins. Co., 1955-60; agt., agy. mgr. Am. Founders Life Ins. Co., 1960-65, v.p., 1965-68, sr. v.p., dir. sales, 1968—; pres. Abbott Athletics, Inc. Active United Fund; chmn. research com. Abilene Christian Coll. Nat. Devel. Council, 1970-72. Served to capt. USAAF, 1942-46. Named Outstanding Alumnus Abilene Christian Coll., 1960. Mem. Nat., Tex. assns. life underwriters, Nat. Track Coach's Assn. (pres. 1961), Life Ins. Agy. Mgmt. Assn. (mem. mgmt. devel. com. 1970-72). Mem. Ch. of Christ (elder 1970—). Kiwanian. Home: 6600 Mesa Dr Austin TX 78731 Office: PO Box 2068 Austin TX 78767

JACKSON, JERRY LEE, rubber co. exec.; b. Nashville, Aug. 9, 1939; s. Robert Lee and Pauline (Jones) J.; B.S., U. Tenn., 1962; m. Crilla Aleece Wolfe, Dec. 30, 1967; children—Jerry Lee, Angela Michelle. Coop. student Colonial Rubber Works, Inc., Dyersburg, Tenn., 1959-62, chief chemist, 1962-68, v.p., tech. service dir., 1968—. Chmn. Dyer County (Tenn.) Republican Com., 1969-71; state chmn. Tenn. Young Rep. Fedn., 1971—. Recipient Outstanding Local Young Rep. Chmn. award Tenn. Young Rep. Fedn., 1967. Mem. Am. Chem. Soc. (chmn. local arrangement com. rubber div. 1971), So. Rubber Group (chmn. 1969-70), U. Tenn. Alumni Assn. (pres. Dyer County chpt. 1968-69). Moose, Kiwanian. Home: 1836 William Cody St Dyersburg TN 38024 Office: 150 S Connell Av Dyersburg TN 38024

JACKSON, JOHN WINGFIELD, lawyer; b. Washington, Dec. 30, 1905; s. E. Hilton and Ann (Wingfield) J.; B.S. in Econs., U. Pa., 1928; LL.B. with distinction, George Washington U. Law Sch., 1932; m. Eleanor Murdoch Lind, Jan. 14, 1935; children—John Wingfield, Margaret (Mrs. Jerry R. Russom), Beverley Anne L. (Mrs. James J. Johnston, Jr.). Admitted to D.C. bar, 1931, Va. bar, 1941; individual practice law, Washington, 1933, 41-61, Va., 1941—; investigator Dept. Interior, PWA, 1933-36; asst. U.S. Atty., D.C., 1936-41; sometime spl. asst. to atty. gen. U.S., 1952-54. Cons., OSS, 1945; adj. prof. law George Washington U. Law Sch., 1947—; substitute judge Juvenile and Domestic Relations Ct. Arlington County, Va., 1966—. Former mem. bd. dirs. Washington Criminal Justice Assn., Arlington chpt. A.R.C. Mem. No. Va. Estate Planning Council (pres. 1966-67), Nat. Assn. Estate Planning Councils (dir. 1966-70), Order of Coif, Phi Delta Phi. Club: Metropolitan. Home: 4844 N Rock Spring Rd Arlington VA 22207 Office: 1400 N Uhle St Arlington VA 22201

JACKSON, JULIAN ELLIS, corp. pres.; b. Perry, Fla., Oct. 24, 1913; s. Eddie H. and Eva M. (Reid) J.; grad. Andrew Jackson High Sch., Jacksonville, Fla., 1931; m. Laurana H. Filson, Oct. 6, 1956; children— Julian Ellis, Eddie King, Robert Allen, Victor Pharis, Julian Ellis IV, Lester Mitchell. With Great Atlantic & Pacific Stores, 1931-43; pres. Jax Meat Co., 1943-58, Jackson's Minit Markets, Inc., 1958-69, Julian Jackson Investment Co., 1955—, Lil'Champ Food Stores, 1971—; co-owner Jackson-Cowart Realty Co., 1955—; dir. Fla. Nat. Bank, Jacksonville, Fla. Nat. Bank, Arlington. Past pres. United Cerebral Palsy, Jacksonville; chmn. Jacksonville Boxing Commn., 1952—; pres. Gator Bowl Assn., 1957, Fla. Baseball League, 1958-60. Bd. dirs. Palmdale Med. Center. Named Super Market Man of Year, 1960. Mem. Fla. Ind. Super Market Assn. (pres. 1950-59), Fraternal Order Police. Mason (Shriner). Clubs: River, University, Sportsman (Jacksonville); Elinor Village (Daytona Beach, Fla.). Home: 1005 Rio St Johns Dr Jacksonville FL 32211 Office: 5165 Beach Blvd Jacksonville FL 32207

JACKSON, KERN CHANDLER, educator; b. Kansas City, Mo., Oct. 13, 1920; s. Chandler Cheshire and Maude (Kern) J.; B.S., Mich. Technol. U., 1947, M.S., 1950; Ph.D., U. Wis., 1951; m. Emily C. Dillon, June 14, 1944 (div. Nov. 1969); children—Kern Chandler II, Ross D., Bruce R., Paul D.; m. 2d, Barbara Garvey Seagrave, Mar. 29, 1970. Mem. faculty U. Me., 1950-52, U. Ark. at Fayetteville, 1952—, prof. geology, 1961—. Geologist Me. Geol. Survey, 1951-52, Ark. Geol. Commn., 1965-69; cons. Humble Oil & Refining Co., Houston, 1954-59. Served to lt. USNR, 1940-46. Decorated Purple Heart. Mem. A.A.A.S., Am. Assn. Petroleum Geologists, Geol. Soc. Am., Mineral. Soc. Am., Sigma Xi. Author: Textbook of Lithology, 1970. Home: 235 Baxter St Fayetteville AR 72701

JACKSON, LILA MONTEZ, bank dir.; b. nr. Paris, Tenn., Nov. 23, 1908; d. Charles Mother and Olive Vera (Barton) Brockwell; student pub. schs. Henry County, Tenn.; m. Thomas Albert McDaniel, Mar. 8, 1925; 1 dau., Carol (Mrs. Ancil Ray McDuffee); m. 2d, Alonzo Costello Jackson, Oct. 28, 1967. Co-owner, asst. mgr. McDaniels Dept. Stores, various locations, Tenn., 1930-54; co-owner, office mgr. R.E.A. Jackson Bldg., Apts. and Offices, Paris, 1955-61; co-owner, mgr. comml. and residential properties, Paris, 1961—; co-owner, operator Greystone Hotel, Paris, 1965—; dir. 1st Trust & Sav. Bank, Paris, 1965—. Host radio program Happenings in Our Community, WTRR, Paris, 1970—. Bd. dirs. Sr. Citizens Assn., Tenn. TB and Respiratory Disease Assn. Mem. Retail Mcht. Assn., C.of C. (co-chmn. tourist and recreation com. 1969-70), Quota Internat., Inc. (named Paris Woman of Yr. 1970), Bus. and Profl. Women's Assn. (bd. dirs., 1970), Internat. Platform Assn. Baptist. Club: Blossomway Garden. Home: Jackson Manor Paris TN 38242 Office: 301 W Washington St Paris TN 38242

JACKSON, LUKE, dentist; b. Recovery, Ga., Sept. 17, 1919; s. John Barnabus and Malissie (Jones) J.; B.S., Ga. State Coll., 1942; student Atlanta U., 1945-46; D.D.S., Meharry Med. Coll., 1951; m. Lillian L. Henderson, June, 1953 (div. Nov. 1957); children— Charles L., Wayne D.; m. 2d, Shirley Ann Head, Aug. 21, 1959; children—Shirlee Barnetta and Shirlene Elizabeth (twins). Instr. prosthetic dentistry Meharry Med. Coll., 1951-53; pvt. practice dentistry, Chattanooga, Tenn., 1953—. Chmn. bus. div. Chattanooga Council for Community Action, 1963-68; mem. Bi-racial Mayors Com., 1963; mem. bd. mgmt. Henry br. YMCA, 1965-70. Served with USNR, World War II. Diplomate Nat. Bd. Dental Examiners (pres. Pan-Tenn. 1957-59), Tenn. Dental Assn., George W. Hubbard Dental Soc. (pres. 1951—). Baptist (trustee 1955—, coordinator bldg. council 1970-71). Home: 5124 Lantana Lane Chattanooga TN 37416 Office: 752 E 9th St Chattanooga TN 37403

JACKSON, MAYNARD HOLBROOK, JR., lawyer, city ofcl.; b. Mar. 23, 1938; A.B Morehouse Coll.; J.D., N.C. Central U. Admitted to bar, 1965; sr. partner firm Jackson, Patterson & Parks; vice mayor, pres. bd. aldermen Atlanta 1970—. Address: 40 Marietta St NW Atlanta GA 30303

JACKSON, MILES MERRILL, JR., librarian; b. Richmond, Va., Apr. 28, 1929; s. Miles Merrill and Thelma Eugertha (Manning) J.; student U. N.M., 1949-50; B.A. in English, Va. Union U., 1955; M.S. in L.S., Drexel Inst. Tech., 1956; postgrad. Ind. U., 1961; m. Bernice Olivia Roane, Jan. 7, 1954; children—Miles Merrill III, Marsha,

Muriel, Melia. Br. librarian Free Library of Phila., 1955-58; acting librarian C. P. Huntington Meml. Library, Hampton (Va.) Inst., 1958-59, librarian, 1959-63, asst. prof. library sci., 1958-62; territorial librarian Am. Samoa, 1962-64; chief librarian Trevor Arnett Library, Atlanta U., 1964-—, also lectr. Sch. Library Sci., Fulbright lectr. U. Tehran, Iran, 1968, 69. Sec. Unitarian Fellowship of Peninsula, 1961-62. Bd. dirs. We Shall Overcome Fund, Martin L. King Jr. Meml. Library. Served with USNR, 1945-48. Research grantee Am. Philos. Soc., 1966. Mem. Am., Va. (chmn. coll. and univ. sect. 1961-62) library assns., Adult Edn. Assn. U.S., Charles Sumner Lit. Soc. (pres. 1961-62), Coll. Lang. Assn. (hon. mention poetry 1954, 2d prize award short story 1955), Unitarian Fellowship of Pen (sec. 1962). Democrat. Editor: A Bibliography of Materials on Negro History and Culture for Young People, 1968. Contbr. articles prof. jours. Book reviewer Library Jour. Home: 626 Beckwith St SW Atlanta GA 30314 Office: Tervor Arnett Library Atlanta U Atlanta GA 30314

JACKSON, NYLE M., govt. ofcl.; b. Bradleyville, Mo., Mar. 27, 1914; s. James Richard and Emma (Huntsman) J.; B.A., Westminster Coll., Fulton, Mo., 1935; m. Elaine Hutcheson, Sept. 4, 1938. Advt. mgr. for daily and weekly newspapers, Seymour, Ind., 1938-41; exec. sec. to Rep. Earl Wilson of Ind. 1941-53; adminstr. asst. to Sen. William E. Jenner of Ind., 1953-59; spl. staff mem. for Sen. Homer E. Capehart of Ind., 1959; legislative asst. to Sen. Thruston B. Morton, chmn. Republican Nat. Com., 1959; exec. asst. to postmaster gen., 1959-61, asst. to exec. asst., 1961-63; asst. dir. customer relations div. Post Office Dept., Washington, 1963-68, exec. asst. to asst. post-master gen., 1969 asst. to spl. counsel to Pres., 1969-70; mng. dir. ICC, 1970-—. Del.-observer Intergovtl. Commn. European Migration, 1957. Asst. sgt. at arms Rep. Nat. Conv., 1956. Served to lt. USNR, World War II. Mem. Am. Legion, V.F.W., Congl. Secs. Club, Orgn. Cabinet Assts., Senate Assts. Group, Mil. Order of Carabao. Club: Capitol Hill (Washington). Baptist. Home: 4429 35th St NW Washington DC 20008 Office: Interstate Commerce Commn. Washington DC 20423

JACKSON, PRINCE ALBERT, JR., coll. pres.; b. Savannah, Ga., Mar. 17, 1925; s. Prince Albert and Julia (Robinson) J.; B.S., Savannah State Coll., 1949; M.S., N.Y. U., 1950; postgrad. U. Kan., 1961-62, NSF fellow Harvard, 1962-63; Ph.D., Boston Coll., 1966; m. Marilyn Striggles, Dec. 22, 1950; children—Prince Albert III, Rodney Mark, Julia Lucia, Anthony Brian. Tchr. sci., math. William James High Sch., Statesboro, Ga., 1950-55; faculty Savannah State Coll., 1955-—, asso. prof. math., physics, 1966-71, chmn. natural sci. div., dir. instl. self study, 1969-71, pres., 1971-—. Athletic dir. St. Pius X High Sch., Savannah, 1955-64; teaching fellow, vis. instr. Boston Coll., 1964-66; cons. sci., math. Vice pres. Bd. Pub. Edn. Savannah and Chatham County, 1971-—; mem. edn. com. U.S. Cath. Conf., 1971-—; mem. So. Regional Edn. Bd., 1971-—; mem. Chatham-Savannah Charter Study Com. Bd. mgrs. W. Broad St. YMCA, Savannah, 1962; vice chmn. St. Pius X Ednl. Council, Savannah, 1967-—; mem. exec. com. N.A.A.C.P., Savannah, 1968-—; adviser Community Devel. Corp., Savannah, 1969; bd. dirs. Ga. Heart Assn., Goodwill Industries, A.R.C., Boy Scouts Am. Served with USNR, 1942-46. Recipient Outstanding leadership and Service award Savannah State Coll. Nat. Alumni Assn., 1967. Mem. A.A.A.S., Am. Assn. U. Profs., N.E.A., Ga. Tchrs. Edn. Assn., Nat. Sci. Tchrs. Assn., Nat. Council Tchrs. Math., Am. Edn. Research Assn., Nat. Council on Measurement in Edn. Nat. Inst. Sci., Savannah Area C. of C. (dir.), Phi Alpha (Man of Year 1960, 67, So. Region Man of Year 1967), Phi Delta Kappa, Alpha Phi Omega. Roman Catholic (pres. Holy Name soc. 1969-—, mem. pastoral council 1967-—). Home: 1215 E Duffy St Savannah GA 31404

JACKSON, RANDALL C(ALVIN), lawyer; b. Baird, Tex., Mar. 21, 1919; s. Rupert and Anna (Faust) J.; J.D., U. Tex., 1946; B.B.A., 1941; m. Betty S. Johnson, June 18, 1955; 1 son, Randall Calvin. Admitted to Tex. bar, 1946, practiced in Abilene, 1962-—; sr. partner firm Jackson & Jackson, 1949-—. Vice pres., dir. 1st Nat. Bank, Baird; dir. T. S. Lankford & Sons Co.; dir., gen. counsel Bank of Commerce, Abilene. Mem. Tex. Securities Bd., 1966-69; chmn. Abilene Spl. Housing Study Com. Pres. bd. dirs. Boys Ranch, Abilene; former chmn. bd. regents Tex. Woman's U., 1961-66; past finance chmn. Chisolm Trail council Boy Scouts Am. Del., Dem. Nat. Conv., 1960, 64; mem. Tex. Dem. Exec. Com., 1960-64. Enlisted USAC, 1942, disch. capt., 1946, assigned Exec. Office Statis. Control Unit, Guam. Fellow Am. Coll. Probate Counsel; mem. Southwestern Legal Found., Tex. Bar Found. (charter mem.), Indsl. Found. Abilene, State Bar Tex. Am., Callahan-Taylor County (dir.) bar assns., Am. Judicature Soc., Am. Hereford Assn., Tex. Hereford Assn., Nat. Cattlemen's Assn., Am. Legion (past comdr.), Abilene C. of C. Methodist (chmn., dist. trustee). Mason (32 deg., Shriner). Clubs: Headliners (Austin, Tex.); Abilene Country (Abilene). Home: 1406 Tanglewood Dr Abilene TX 79605 Office: Bank of Commerce Bldg Abilene TX 79602

JACKSON, ROBERT MANSON, editor; b. Alamogordo, N.M., Jan. 21, 1907; s. Robert Mallory and Margaret (Mason) J.; B.J., U. of Mo., 1928; m. Helen Dowty, Nov. 17, 1936; 1 son, Robert Manson III. Mem. staff San Angelo (Tex.) Standard-Times, 1928-31; clerk to R. E. Thomason, M.C., 1931-33; asst. librarian U.S. Senate, 1933-34; sec. to Senator Tom Connally, 1934-38; staff writer Washington bur. A.P., 1938-41; mng. editor Corpus Christi (Tex.) Times, 1941-45, editor Caller-Times, 1945-—. Recipient Honor award distinguished service in journalism U. Mo., 1966. Mem. Am. Soc. of Newspaper Editors. Presbyn. Club: National Press (Washington). Home: 314 Laurel Dr Corpus Christi TX 78404 Office: Caller-Times Box 9136 Corpus Christi TX 78408

JACKSON, R(OY) GRAHAM, architect; b. Sherman, Tex., July 1, 1913; s. Watt J. Jackson and Lilly Thompson (Graham) J.; B.S. in Architecture, Rice U., 1935; m. Violet Stephen Lawrence, May 1, 1971. Pvt. practice architect R. Graham Jackson, Architect, Houston, 1936-46; mem. firm. Jackson & Dill, architects, Houston, 1946-53, Wirtz, Calhoun, Tungate & Jackson, architects, 1953-65, Calhoun, Tungate & Jackson, architects, 1965-—. Asst. prof. architecture U. Houston, 1947-53; vis. lectr. Rice U. Mem. Houston Symphony Soc., Friends of Bayou Bend. Founding com. Houston Bapt. Coll., 1958-60. Fellow Constrn. Specifications Inst., A.I.A.; mem. Houston C. of C. Baptist. (deacon 1944-—). Club: The Houston. Prin. archtl. works include Willford Hall Hosp., Lackland AFB, Tex., 1955, 59; (with other firms) Manned Spacecraft Center, Houston, 1961, Fort Hood Army Hosp., 1963, VA Hosp., Temple, Tex., 1966. Home: 716 Chimney Rock St Houston TX 77027 Office: 2506 Richton St Houston TX 77006

JACKSON, RUTH BERTHA LAVENDER (MRS. HOWARD JAMES JACKSON), civic worker; b. Seney, Mich., Oct. 19, 1914; d. Edward John and Bertha (Knuth) Lavender; A.B., U. Mich., 1937, postgrad., 1958-63; postgrad. U. Ga., Va. Poly. Inst.; m. Howard James Jackson, June 29, 1939; 1 son, James Howard. Tchr., Newberry (Mich.) High Sch., 1937-39, Rutland (O.) High Sch., 1942-43; exec. sec. Valley Day Sch., Charleston, W. Va., 1950-52; tchr. courses landscape design W. Va. State Coll., 1967-—. Sec., Kanawha County Planning and Zoning Commn., 1959-70; pres. League Women Voters W. Va., 1963-70; mem. Gov.'s Commn. on Status Women, 1963-70; Nat. Com. for Support Pub. Schs., 1963-70, Citizens Air Pollution Control Council, 1965-70; chmn. Vol. Service Bur., 1965-66; mem. Gov.'s Task Force on Surface Mining, 1966, Citizens Adv. Commn. W. Va. Legislature, 1967-70, State Adv. Com. on Mental Health, 1966-70; co-chmn. State Citizens for Constl. Conv., 1967-70; adv. mem. Charleston Municipal Planning Commn., 1967-70; mem. recreation planning com. Action for Appalachian Youth-Community Devel., 1967; mem. womans com. Charleston Symphony Orch.; mem. W. Va. Planning Assn. Bd. dirs. Sunrise Found., Community Council Kanawha Valley; trustee United Fund Kanawha Valley; incorporator W. Va. Cleanup, Inc. Recipient citation for Lane-Bryant Community Achievement Awards, 1967; named Top Clubwoman of Year Charleston Gazette-Mail, 1961. Mem. U.S. Figure Skating Assn. (nat. vice chmn. program devel.), Charleston Rose Soc., Nat. Council State Garden Clubs, Phi Beta Kappa, Phi Kappa Phi, Pi Lambda Theta. Clubs: Charleston Figure Skating, West Virginia Garden (chmn., sec.-treas. judges council); Essex Skating (N.J.). Contbr. articles to profl. publs. Home: 701 Leawood Dr Greensboro NC 27410

JACKSON, SHERMAN KEITH, state ofcl.; b. Holton, Kan., Sept. 7, 1907; s. William Barton and Musa (Townsend) J.; student Park Coll., 1925-26, 27-28; B.S. in Civil Engring., Kan. State U., 1930; post-grad. State U., Ia., 1935-37; m. Mary Olive Speer, Nov. 25, 1937; children—Sherman Keith, Betty (Mrs. Thomas Burke), Mary Melanie. Jr. engr. Ill. Hwy. Dept., 1930-31; with water resources div. U.S. Geol. Survey, 1931-66, div. chief, Rocky Mountain region, Denver, 1957-66; dir. Ark. Soil and Water Conservation Commn., Little Rock, 1967-—. Fellow Am. Soc, C.E. Home: 4801 N Hills Blvd North Little Rock AR 72116 Office: State Capitol Little Rock AR 72201

JACKSON, THEODORE KING, lawyer; b. Mobile, Ala., Dec. 27, 1910; s. Theodore King and Lollie Belle (Gould) J.; student Lawrenceville Sch., 1926-30; J.D., U. Ala., 1935; m. Louise Mason Hempstead, Aug. 2, 1937; children—Theodore King III, Robert Hempstead. Admitted to Ala. bar, 1935; partner Armbrecht, Jackson & DeMouy and predecessor firms, Mobile, 1935-—. Pres., Jacksoco Oil Co., 1965-—; dir. Ala. Dry Dock & Shipbldg. Co. Pres., Sr. Bowl Assn., 1969-—. Bd. dirs. Boys Clubs Mobile; pres., trustee Mobile Arts and Sports Assn., 1969-—; trustee Mobile Opera Guild, Univ. Mil. Sch. Served as comdr. USNR, 1941-46. Mem. Am., Ala., Mobile bar assns., Am. Judicature Soc., Am. Soc. Internat. Law, Maritime Law Assn. U.S. (1st v.p. 1958-60), Ind. Petroleum Assn. (v.p., dir. 1959-—), Mid-Continent Oil and Gas Assn. (v.p., dir. 1965-—), Comite Maritime International (titulary mem.). Episcopalian (vestryman 1960). Rotarian. Clubs: Propeller, Country (Mobile). Home: 2205 Springhill Av Mobile AL 36607 Office: Mchts Nat Bank Bldg Mobile AL 36601

JACKSON, WALTER DUNAWAY, dentist; b. El Dorado Springs, Mo., Aug. 22, 1917; s. Walter John and Ferol (Dunaway) J.; B.S., S.W. Mo. State Coll., 1940; D.D.S., Kansas City U., 1950; m. Norma Louise Lovan, Nov. 18, 1942; children—Alan Scott, Thomas Farrell, Jay Norman. Practice dentistry, Miami, Okla., 1950-—; mem. staff Miami Bapt. Hosp. Served with USNR, 1942-46. Mem. Pierre Fauchard Acad., Am., Okla., Dist. dental assns., Am. Legion, V.F.W. Mason, Rotarian. Home: 420 Bay St Miami OK 74354 Office: Robinson Bldg Miami OK 74354

JACKSON, WILL WOODWARD, ins. co. exec.; b. Waynesboro, Tenn., Apr. 20, 1890; s. George Washington and Marhta Mollie (Craig) J.; A.B., Southwestern U., Georgetown, Tex., 1916, Litt.D., 1940; M.A., U. Tex., 1928; postgrad. Yale, 1929-30; m. Ruth Goddard, Aug. 20, 1919; children—Leila Craig, Will Woodward. Supt. pub. schs., Normangee, Tex., 1916-17; sec. Student YMCA of Ark., 1919-21; pres. Wesleyan Inst., San Antonio, 1921-29, Westmoorland Coll., 1930-36, U. San Antonio, 1936-42; v.p., dir. pub. relations Trinity U., 1942-46; formerly adminstrv. v.p. Am. Hosp. Life Ins. Co. (became Am. Hosp. and Life), San Antonio, now sr. v.p. Regional exec. USO, 1942-46; mem. Air Force Community Council. Mem. Tex. Bd. Edn., 1950-59, chmn., 1959-69; mem. exec. com. jurisdictional conf. Meth. Ch., lay del. world-wide confs. Chmn. bd. dirs. San Antonio Heart Assn., 1954-61, Tex. Heart Assn., 1961; bd. dirs. YMCA, Nat. Travelers Aid Assn., A.R.C., Tex. Council Econ. Edn., S.W. Ednl. Research Lab.; pres. Community Welfare Council, San Antonio, 1964-66; bd. govs. St. Mary's U.; mem. bd. devel. Southwestern Meth. U. Served with F.A., U.S. Army, 1917-19. Recipient Distinguished Alumnus award Southwestern U., 1961; Ann. Conf. award Christians and Jews, for contbn. to human relations, 1962. Mem. San Antonio Council Chs. (pres.), C. of C. (bd. dirs.), Am. Sociol. Soc., Am. Acad. Polit. and Social Scis., Alpha Chi. Methodist. Mason, Rotarian (dist. gov. 1943). Home: 2136 W Summit St San Antonio TX 78201 Office: American Hospital and Life Bldg San Antonio TX 78205

JACKSON, WILLIAM NEIL, agr. co. exec.; b. Stratford, Tex., Jan. 26, 1928; s. Harry Thomas and Effie Elizabeth (Webb) J.; B.S., W. Tex. State U., 1949; m. Theresa Keeney, Jan. 8, 1955; children—Patti, Kim. Rancher, cattle buyer, 1953-67; pres. Stratford Feedyards, Inc., 1967-—; v.p. Stratford of Tex., Inc., Houston, 1969-—; dir. 1st State Bank, Stratford. Pres. Stratford Sch. Bd., 1963-66. Served with AUS, 1951-53. Mem. Christian Ch. Home: 1020 N Maple St Stratford TX 79084 Office: First State Bank Bldg Stratford TX 79084

JACOB, CAROL G., physician; b. Hamburg, Germany, Mar. 27, 1921; d. Leo and Claire (Lewisohn) Jacob; R.N., Johns Hopkins Hosp. Sch. Nursing, 1946; B.S., Johns Hopkins, 1950; M.A., U. Chgo., 1951; postgrad. Roosevelt U., 1955-57; M.D. cum laude Woman's Med. Coll. Pa., 1961. Came to U.S., 1940, naturalized, 1945. Head nurse surg. pediatrics Johns Hopkins Hosp., Balt., 1946-48; head nurse med. pediatrics State U. Ia. Clinics, Iowa City, 1948-50, U. Chgo. Clinics, 1951-53; head nurse psychiat. nursing Psychosomatic and Psychiat. Inst. Research and Tng., Michael Reese Hosp., Chgo., 1953-55; supr. psychiat. nursing St. Luke's Hosp., Chgo., 1955-57; rotating intern Montefiore Hosp., Pitts., 1961-62; resident teaching fellow psychiatry U. Pitts. Sch. Medicine and Western Psychiat. Inst. and Clinic, Pitts., 1962-63; staff psychiatrist VA Hosp., Pitts., 1963-64; resident psychiatry Sheppard and Enoch Pratt Hosp., Towson, Md., 1964-65, St. Elizabeth's Hosp., Washington, 1965-67; practice of medicine, specializing in psychiatry, Washington, 1967-—; candidate Washington Psychoanalytic Inst., 1968-—. Cons. psychiatrist Group Health Assn., Washington, 1968-—. Mem. A.M.A., Am. Psychiat. Assn., Washington Psychiat. Soc., Med. Soc. D.C., Mortar Bd. Alpha Omega Alpha. Jewish religion. Address: 309 N St SW Washington DC 20024

JACOB, GEORGE RICHARD, lawyer; b. Norfolk, Va., Oct. 1, 1900 George R. and Sarah Wilkins (Dalby) J.; student Tex. A. and M. Coll., 1916; B.A., U. Va., 1919, LL.B., 1921; m. Cornelia Frances Jordan, Jan. 29, 1931; children—Arlene (Mrs. James William Singleton), George Richard. Admitted to Va. bar, 1921, Ga. bar, 1921; practiced in Talbotton, Ga., 1933-—. Dir. The Utelwico, Inc., Talbotton. Sec., Ga. bar, 1963-—; mem. Ga. Jud. Selection Commn., 1972-—. Chmn. Talbot County chpt. A.R.C., 1942-—. Mem. Am., Ga. (sec. 1961-—), Chattahoochee Jud. Circuit (past pres.) bar assns., Am. Judicature Soc., Old War Horse Lawyers Club, Lawyers Club (past pres. Columbus, Ga.), English-Speaking Union, Phi Gamma Delta. Episcopalian (jr. warden). Address: Talbotton GA 31827

JACOB, HENRY JUDSON, ednl. adminstr.; b. Carpenter, Miss., Sept. 29, 1904; s. James Henry and Mary Josephine (Anderson) J.; B.A., Miss. Coll., 1929; M.A., George Peabody Coll., 1946; Ph.D., La., State U., 1952; m. Nell Slay, Aug. 11, 1940; 1 dau., Marynell. Educator, coach, ednl. adminstr. Miss. high schs., 1929-46; faculty Delta State Coll., Cleveland, Miss., 1946-—, prof. edn., 1955-—, chmn. div. edn. and psychology, 1958-—, dir. grad. studies, 1965-—. Mem. Miss. Edn. Assn., Nat., Miss. (pres. 1967) assns. student teaching, Am. Fern Soc., Nat. Wildlife Fedn., Phi Delta Kappa, Kappa Delta Pi. Baptist. Mason (Shriner), Kiwanian (local pres. 1965) Home: 906 S Court St Cleveland MS 38732

JACOB, JOHN EDWARD, social worker; b. Trout, La., Dec. 16, 1934; s. Emory and Claudia (Sadler) J.; B.A., Howard U., 1957, M.S.W., 1963; m. Barbara Singleton, Mar. 28, 1959; 1 dau., Sheryl Rene. With Dept. Pub. Welfare, Balt., 1960-65, sr. case worker, 1963, case supr., 1963-65; with Washington Urban League, various brs., 1965-—, asso. dir. adminstrn., Washington, 1967-68, acting exec. dir., 1968-—. Lectr., Howard U. Sch. Social Work, Washington, 1968-69, dir. field work student unit, 1967-68; mem. adv. council Washington Tech. Inst., 1968-69. Mem. Washington Health and Welfare Council, 1969; mem. Mayor's Com. on Crime and Delinquency; chmn. Mayor's Subcom. on Job Availability and Tng. Served to 2d lt., inf. AUS, 1957-58. Mem. Nat. Assn. Social Workers (v.p.), Acad. Certified Social Workers, Nat. Council on Social Welfare, Kappa Alpha Psi. Democrat. Episcopalian. Home: 4821 16th St NE Washington DC 20019 Office: 1424 16th St NW Washington DC 20036

JACOBEEN, FRANK HENRY, JR., geologist; b. Rivervale, N.J., Apr. 10, 1926; s. Frank Henry and Gertrude (Vander Wyden) J.; B.A., Princeton, 1949; m. Marion Therese Chupka, Apr. 14, 1951; children—Diana, Bruce, Brian, David. Geologist USN Hydrographic Survey, Washington, 1950-51, Shell Oil Co., Kan., 1951, Wichita Falls, Tex., 1951-55, Evansville, Ind., 1955-58, Pitts., 1958-66; geologist Washington Gas Light Co., 1966-—. Served with USNR, 1943-46. Mem. Am. Inst. Profl. Geologists, Am. Assn. Petroleum Geologists, Geol. Soc. Am., Va. Acad. Sci., Pitts. Geol. Soc., Geol. Soc. Washington. Lutheran. Home: 8709 Piccadilly Pl Springfield VA 22151 Office: 6801 Industrial Rd Springfield VA 22151

JACOBS, ALBERT JERRY, supt. schs.; b. Beaver County, Okla., Dec. 24, 1924; s. Albert Leroy and Viola (Adams) J.; B.S., W. Tex. State Coll., 1948, M. Adminstrv. Edn., 1951; m. Wilma Jean Miller, Sept. 7, 1948; children—Sharlette Jean, Edward Leroy. Tchr., coach Canyon (Tex.) Ind. Sch. Dist., 1948; prin. Texline (Tex.) Ind. Sch. Dist., 1949-52; supt. schs. Channing (Tex.) Ind. Sch. Dist., 1952-56; supt. schs. Lefors (Tex.) Ind. Sch. Dist., 1956-62, Edna (Tex.) Ind. School Dist., 1962-67, Canyon (Tex.) Ind. Sch. Dist., 1967-—. Dir. Lefors Community Credit Union; dir., past pres. Gulf Bend Center for Handicapped Children. Served with AUS, 1943-46. Mem. N.E.A. (life), Tex. Adminstrs. Assn., Tex. (life), Dallam-Hartley (past pres.), Gray-Roberts (past pres.) tchrs. assns., Panhandle Assn. Sch. Supts. (past pres.), Am. Assn. Sch. Adminstrs., Lower Guadalupe Supts. Assn. (pres.), Canyon C. of C., Red Red Rose, Phi Delta Kappa. Methodist. Mason. Lion (pres. Lefors 1959-60, dist. zone chmn.), Rotarian. Home: 6 Country Club Dr Canyon TX 79015 Office: 910 11th St Canyon TX 79015

JACOBS, ARTHUR HOWARD, dentist; b. Bklyn., June 6, 1941; s. Milton and Ruth (Freilich) J.; A.B. in Chemistry, Lafayette Coll., 1962; D.M.D., U. Pa., 1966; m. Joyce Linda Belgene, Nov. 23, 1963; children—Jodi Lynn, Jamie Lee. Asso., George S. Pankey, dentist, St. Cloud, Fla., 1968; pvt. practice dentistry, Orlando, Fla., 1968-—. Tchr., cons. dental asst. program Fla. So. Coll. 1967-—. Served to capt. Dental Corps, USAF, 1966-68. Mem. Am., Fla., Orange County dental assns., Am. Soc. Preventive Dentistry, Internat. Inst. Hypnosis, Am. Analgesia Soc., Am. Profl. Practice Assn. Jewish religion (bd. dirs. temple 1970-71, v.p. temple men's club 1970-71). Home: 1012 Marabon Av Orlando FL 32806 Office: 4853 S Orange Av Orlando FL 32806

JACOBS, EUGENE ROBERT, physician; b. N.Y.C., Sept. 22, 1929; s. Kalman Monroe and Sylvia (Hurwitz) J.; B.A. cum laude, Syracuse U., 1951; M.D., State U. N.Y. at Syracuse, 1955; m. Carol Ruth Levine, July 1, 1951; children—Lori Ellen, Susan Robin. Intern Temple U. Hosp., 1955-56, resident radiology, 1956-59; chief radiology U.S. Army Hosp., Ft. Jay, N.Y., 1959-61; dir. radiology Nat. Orthopaedic and Rehab. Hosp., Arlington, Va., 1961-—; mem. No. Va. Orthopaedic and Allied Specialties Clinic, Alexandria, 1965-—. Mem. Alexandria Sanitation Authority, 1967-—. Served to capt. AUS, 1959-61. Diplomate Am. Bd. Radiology. Mem. Alexandria Med. Soc., Med. Soc. Va., Am., So. med. assns., Am. Coll. Radiology, A.C.P., Va. Water Pollution Control Assn., Phi Delta Epsilon. Home: 1307 Kingston Av Alexandria VA 22302 Office: 2500 N Van Dorn St Alexandria VA 22302

JACOBS, FREDERIC WEIL, foundry exec.; b. Indpls., Oct. 25, 1917; s. Frederic Burnham and Mina (Price) J.; B.S., Case Inst. Tech., 1939; m. Honora Mary Masters, Jan. 17, 1942; children—Frederic C., Gary N., Philip J. Metallurgist, Lake City Malleable Co., Cleve., 1939-41, chief metallurgist, Ashtabula, O., 1944-48, asst. plant mgr., 1948-50; prodn. mgr. Columbus Malleable Iron Co., 1941-44; chief metallurgist Tex. Foundries, Inc., Lufkin, Tex., 1950-57, tech. dir., 1957-—. Bd. dirs. Angelina County Tb Soc.; bd. dirs. Salvation Army, Lufkin, chmn. bd., 1972. Mem. Am. Foundrymen's Soc. (exec. com. 1961-—), Malleable Founders Soc. (chmn. research and tech. com. 1968-70), Tex. Soc. Profl. Engrs. (state dir. 1962-65, chpt. chmn. 1961), Alpha Delta, Phi Kappa Tau. Methodist (chmn. commn. on edn. 1969-71, chmn. council on ministries 1971-—). Kiwanian (dir. 1971-—). Club: Exchange (v.p. 1968). Home: 1112 Wildbriar Dr Lufkin TX 75901 Office: PO Box 1608 Lufkin TX 75901

JACOBS, HOWARD, columnist New Orleans Times-Picayune. Home: 2116 State St New Orleans LA 70118 Office: 3800 Howard Av New Orleans LA 70140*

JACOBS, JOHN CLAYTON, JR., lawyer, corp. exec.; b. Guymon, Okla., June 27, 1917; s. John C. and Patience (Goodlander) J.; B.S. in Chem. Engring., Ga. Inst. Tech., 1939; LL.B., Yale, 1948; m. Elinor M. Blanchard, June 20, 1942; children—Ann Clayton, Elizabeth Pelham. Admitted to Tex. bar, 1949; process engr. Standard Oil of La., Baton Rouge, 1939-44; supervisory engr. Creole Petroleum Corp., Caracas, Venezuela, 1944-46; atty. firm Heldt & O'Boyle, Dallas, 1948-51; pvt. practice law, Dallas, 1951-53; exec. v.p., dir. Wilcox Trend Gatherine System, Inc., Dallas, 1953-55; v.p. Tex. Eastern Transmission Corp., Houston, 1955-66, sr. v.p., 1966-—. Chmn. bd. Tex. Bill of Rights Found., 1972-—. Mem. Am. Inst. Chem. Engrs., Am. Inst. Mining, Metall. and Petroleum Engrs., Am. Bar Assn., Beta Theta Pi, Omicron Delta Kappa, Phi Kappa Phi. Episcopalian. Clubs: Ramada, Bankers, Hurlingham. Author: (with Leeston and Crichton) The Dynamic Natural Gas Industry, 1963. Home: 4627 Banning St Houston TX 77027 Office: PO Box 2521 Houston TX 77001

JACOBS, JOHN KEDZIE, editor; b. New Paltz, N.Y., Apr. 5, 1918; s. Edward Clarence and Bertha (Deyo) J.; B.A., Antioch Coll., Yellow Springs, O., 1940; student Columbia Law Sch., 1946-47; m. Catherine

Altschuller, Jan. 10, 1952; children—John Kedzie, Eleanor, Lucia, Katherine. Writer, Am. Inst. Pub. Opinion, Princeton, N.J., 1940-43; with USIA, 1948—, editor Amerika, chief regional projects office, Vienna, Austria, 1970—. Served to capt. USAAF, World War II. Home: 7704 Tauxemont Rd Alexandria VA Office: Vienna care State Dept Washington DC 20521

JACOBS, MYLON CECIL, JR., oilfield co. exec.; b. Tulsa, Apr. 25, 1936; s. Mylon Cecil and Freda (Davis) J.; student Okla. U., 1955-59; m. Karen Joyce Seacat, Sept. 12, 1968; children—Mark, Michael Douglas, Mylon Cecil III, Melissa. Salesman, Western Supply Co., Tulsa, 1959-63; pres., dir. Mylon C. Jacobs Supply Co., Tulsa, 1963—; pres., dir. Southeastern Kan. Gas Co. Trustee Jacobs Industries. Mem. So. Gas Assn. Republican. Methodist. Club: Southern Hills Country. Home: 3419 E 75th Pl Tulsa OK 74136 Office: 4252 S 74 E Av Tulsa OK 74101

JACOBSEN, HUGH NEWELL, architect; b. Grand Rapids, Mich., Mar. 11, 1929; s. John E. and Lucy (Newell) J.; B.Arch., Yale, 1955; B.A., U. Md., 1951; certificate Archtl. Assn., Sch. Architecture, London, 1954; m. Robin Kearney, Dec. 27, 1952; children—John E., Matthew C., Simon T. With Phillip Johnson, New Canaan, Conn., 1955, Paul Schweikher, New Haven, 1955, Keyes, Lethbridge & Condon, Washington, 1957-58; pvt. archtl. practice, Washington, 1958—. Guest lectr. Nat. Conf. Archtl. Rev. Landmarks and Historic Dists., Ball State U., Howard U., Corcoran Gallery Art, Brandeis U. Alumni Assn., Am. Assn. U. Women; vis. prof. arts and humanities U. Cairo (Egypt), 1970; John F. Kennedy Meml. fellow and lectr. Govt. New Zealand, 1971. Mem. bd. assos. Gettysburg Coll., 1970—; mem. Com. 100 Fed. City; mem. Washington Planning and Housing Assn.; mem. judging panel 1970 Koppers Archtl. Student Design Competition; mem. creative and visual arts adv. panel Open House U.S.A. com. Am. Revolution Bicentennial Commn. Trustee Washington Theatre Club, 1965—, Washington Gallery Modern Art; mem. Georgetown Planning Council; mem. exec. com. bd. govs. Corcoran Gallery Art, 1969—. Served to 1st lt. USAF, 1955-57. Recipient Archtl. Record award house design, 1964, 65, 66, 67, 68, 69, 70, 71, interiors design, 1970, 71, apt. design, 1971; award A.I.A. Potomac Valley chpt., 1962, 64, 66, 68; A.I.A. award homes for better living, 1965, 66, 67, 68 (3), 69; award A.I.A. N.Y. chpt., 1964 (2), 67; award of merit Washington Bd. Trade, 1962, 64, 66 (3), 69 (3), 71 (2); Honor award A.I.A., 1969; award No. Va. sect. A.I.A., 1969; Masonry Inst., 1961; A.I.A. Middle Atlantic Honor award, 1969 (2); award A.I.A. Middle Atlantic Regional Conf., 1969 (2), 1971; award Bethesda-Chevy Chase C. of C., 1971. Fellow A.I.A. (exec. com. Washington, met. chpt. 1964-67; mem. nat. design com., subcom. arts and graphics com. inst. hdqrs., awards program code task force, 1970 honor awards jury; dir. 1972—, mem. com. on design, pub. relations com.); mem. Smithsonian Instn. Luncheon Group, Archtl. and Art Alumni Assn. Yale U. (mem. exec. com.). Club: Cosmos (Washington). Editor: A Guide to the Architecture of Washington, D.C. Contbr. articles to mags. including New Republic, House and Garden; articles on urban design to Washington Post. Home: 1352 28th St NW Washington DC 20007 Office: 1427 27th St NW Washington DC 20007

JACOBSEN, JAKE, lawyer; b. Atlantic City, July 21, 1919; student Coll. South Jersey; LL.B., U. Tex., 1948; postgrad. in law Temple U. Admitted to Tex. bar, 1948; briefing clk. Tex. Supreme Ct., 1948-49; exec. asst. atty.-gen. Tex., 1949-53; adminstrv. asst. to U.S. Senator Price Daniel, 1953-56; exec. asst. to Gov. Daniel of Tex., 1956-69; mem. firm Jacobsen and Long, Austin, Tex.; legislative counsel to Pres. U.S., 1965-67. Mem. State Bar Tex., Am. Bar Assn. Address: Jacobsen and Long 208 Westgate Bldg Austin TX 78701*

JACOBSEN, LEIF YNGVE, physician; b. Bergen, Norway, Oct. 8, 1902; came to U.S. 1925, naturalized 1932; s. Jonas Jacob and Wilhelmina (Thomsen) J.; A.B., Columbia, 1928; M.D., Cornell U., 1932; m. Marie Pope Heiberg, Aug. 4, 1928; children—Greta Thomson, Leif Yngve, Karen Smith. Intern Orange Meml. Hosp., 1932-33; resident Princeton Hosp., 1933-34; practice internal medicine, Douglaston, N.Y., 1934-66; cons. health service UN, 1966-69; emergency room physician Naples (Fla.) Community Hosp., 1970—; instr. Cornell U. Med. Coll., 1934-56; attending physician medicine North Shore Hosp., Manhasset, N.Y., 1954-66. Served from capt. to lt. col. M.C., AUS, 1942-45. Diplomate Am. Bd. Internal Medicine. Fellow A.C.P. Clubs: Marco Island Country, Sailing (Marco Island, Fla.). Home: 870 Chestnut St Marco Island FL 33937 Office: Naples Community Hosp Naples FL 33940

JACOBSON, BERNARD, lawyer; b. Hartford, Conn., Feb. 27, 1930; s. Samuel Barnard and Lillian (Canter) J.; A.B., Amherst Coll., 1951; LL.B., Columbia, 1954; m. Florence Ellen Greenberg, Oct. 7, 1956; children—Daniel, Alice, Nancy. Admitted to Conn. bar, 1955, Fla. bar, 1957; practiced in Miami, 1957—; mem. firm Fine, Jacobson, Block & Semet, Miami, 1968—; gen. partner Mortgage Investment Services, Ltd., 1968-70; v.p., sec., dir. Mortgage Investment Services, Inc., 1970—; trustee Republic Mortgage Investors, 1968—, sec., 1969—. Chmn. Dade County Citizens Adv. Com. on Community Improvement, 1969-70. Alumni adviser on admissions Amherst Coll., 1964—. Lectr. law U. Miami, 1965-66. Served with CIC, AUS, 1955-57. Mem. Am., Fla., Dade County bar assns., Phi Delta Phi. Home: 90 N Prospect Dr Coral Gables FL 33133 Office: Dade Fed Bldg Miami FL 33131 also 2401 Douglas Rd Miami FL 33134

JACOBSON, DAVID, rabbi; b. Cin., Dec. 2, 1909; s. Abraham and Rebecca (Sereinsky) J.; A.B., U. Cin., 1931; rabbi, Hebrew Union Coll., 1934, D.D. (hon.), 1959; Ph.D., St. Catherine's Coll., U. Cambridge (Eng.), 1936; LL.D., Our Lady of Lake Coll., 1964; m. Helen Gugenheim, Nov. 6, 1938; children—Elizabeth Ann, Dorothy Jean (Mrs. Sam Miller). Instr., Hebrew Union Coll., 1933-34; rabbi W. Central Liberal Congregation, London, Eng., 1934-36, Indpls. Hebrew Congregation, 1936-38, Temple Beth-El, San Antonio, 1938—. Pres., Kallah of Tex. Rabbis, 1950-51; chmn. health com. and rabbinical tenure and security com. Central Conf. Am. Rabbis, pres. S.W. region 1969-70; mem. Rabbinical Placement Commn., Tex. Ethics Com.; mem. com. on welfare reform Tex. Senate, 1970; arbitrator San Antonio Typographical Union 172; founder U. Ind. Hillel Found., 1938; pres. San Antonio Soc. Crippled Children and Adults, 1963-66; pres. Goodwill Industries San Antonio, 1956-60, also mem. bd.; mem. bd. Goodwill Industries Am., 1965—; pres. Bexar County chpt. Nat. Tb Assn., 1955-57; founder Community Welfare Council San Antonio, 1944, pres., 1951-53; pres. Tex. Social Welfare Assn., 1967-69; life mem., exec. com. Tex. United Community Services, Inc., 1970—, U.S.O. Nat. Council, 1968—; commr. Housing Authority San Antonio, 1954-58; v.p. S.W. region Am. Jewish Com. Bd. dirs. Our Lady of Lake Coll., Nat. Jewish Welfare Bd., 1964-72, Nat. Council Crime and Delinquency; bd. govs., overseer Hebrew Union Coll. Jewish Inst. Religion, 1966-69; bd. dirs. S.W. Texas Meth. Hosp., San Antonio Med. Found., Alamo council Boy Scouts Am., Children's Hosp. Found., Keystone Sch., San Antonio, Am. Social Health Assn., Nat. Assn. State-wide Health and Welfare, Cath. Youth Orgn.; pres. San Antonio Area Found., 1965—, San Antonio Manpower Devel. Council, 1968—. Served as chaplain USNR, 1944-46. Recipient Silver Beaver award Boy Scouts Am., 1958, Aristotle-Aquinas award Cath. Coll. Found. S.A., 1959, Golden Deeds award Exchange Club San Antonio, 1959; Keystone award Boys Clubs Am., 1962; Edgar J. Helms award Goodwill Industries Am., 1972; named outstanding Jew, Nat. Conf. Christians and Jews, 1961, Outstanding Citizen of Year, Sembradores de Amistad, 1971. Mem. Tex. P.T.A. (hon. life), Soc. Bibl. Lit., San Antonio Ministers Assn., Nat. Conf. Social Welfare (bd. 1967-69), Sigma Alpha Mu, Pi Tau Pi. Rotarian. Clubs: Torch (past pres.), Argyle (San Antonio). Author: Social Background of the Old Testament, 1942; The Synagogue Through the Ages, 1958; also articles. Home: 207 Beechwood Lane San Antonio TX 78216 Office: 211 Belknap Pl San Antonio TX 78212

JACOBSON, HELEN G. (MRS. DAVID JACOBSON), civic worker; b. San Antonio, Apr. 24, 1908; d. Jac Elton and Rosetta (Dreyfus) Gugenheim; B.A., Hollins Coll., 1928; m. David Jacobson, Nov. 6, 1938; children—Elizabeth Ann, Dorothy Jean (Mrs. Sam Miller). News, spl. events staff NBC, N.Y.C., 1933-38. First v.p. San Antonio, Bexar County council Girl Scouts U.S.A., 1957-63; Tex. state rep. UNICEF, 1964-69, bd. dirs. U.S. Com. UNICEF; chmn. Mayor's Commn. on Status of Women. Bd. dirs. Tex.-Okla. Fedn. Temple Sisterhoods, Temple Beth-El Sisterhood; bd. dirs. Community Guidance Center, chmn. bd., 1960-63; bd. dirs. Sunshine Cottage Sch. for Deaf Children, chmn. bd., 1952-54; pres. bd. trustees San Antonio Pub. Library, 1957-61; nat. trustee Nat. Council on Crime and Delinquency, 1964-70, now bd. mem. Tex. council; trustee San Antonio Mus. Assn.; trustee Nat. Assembly Social Policy and Devel., sec., 1969—; bd. dirs. Community Welfare Council, pres., 1968-70; bd. dirs. Tex. United Community Services; bd. dirs. Foster Grandparents Bexar County, pres., 1968-69, v.p., 1970—; bd. dirs. San Antonio Urban Coalition; mem. gov.'s steering com., del. 1970 White House Conf. on Children and Youth. Recipient Headliner award for civic work San Antonio chpt. Theta Sigma Phi, 1958; named Vol. Woman of Year, Express-News, 1959; honored San Antonio chpt. Nat. Conf. Christians and Jews, 1970. Mem. San Antonio Women's Fedn., Tex. Fedn. Women's Clubs (past bd. mem. Alamo dist.), Nat. Council Jewish Women, Symphony Soc. (women's com.). Club: Argyle. Home: 207 Beechwood Lane San Antonio TX 78216

JACOBSON, JOHN HOWARD, JR., coll. dean; b. Evanston, Ill., Nov. 6, 1933; s. John Howard and Grace Katharine (Whitney) J.; B.A. magna cum laude, Swarthmore Coll., 1954; M.A., Yale, 1956, Ph.D., 1957; m. Jeanne G. McKee, Aug. 15, 1954; children—John Edward, Jean Katharine, Jennie Grace, James George. Instr., then asst. prof. philosophy Hamilton Coll., Clinton, N.Y., 1957-63; mem. faculty Fla. Presbyn. Coll., St. Petersburg, 1963—, asso. prof., 1964-67, dean coll., prof., v.p. acad. affairs, 1967—. Mem. Am. Council Edn. (commn. acad. affairs). Presbyn. (elder). Club: Exchange (West St. Petersburg). Author: (with John Blyth) Logic: A Programmed Text, 1963. Home: 5819 3d St S St Petersburg FL 33705

JACOBSON, LEONARD I, educator, psychologist; b. Bklyn., Aug. 9, 1940; s. Louis H. and Violet (Natkin) J.; A.B. cum laude (N.Y. State Regents scholar), City U. N.Y., 1961; Ph.D., State U. N.Y., Buffalo, 1966. Research psychologist Children's Hosp., Buffalo, 1965-66; asst. prof. psychology U. Miami, Coral Gables, Fla., 1966-71, asso. prof. psychology, 1971—, adj. asst. prof. Guidance Center, 1969-70; cons. Sunland Tng. Center at Miami, Opa-Locka, 1969—; clin. psychology cons. Community Mental Health Services Clinic, Miami, 1968—; cons. BKR exptl. project Sunland Tng. Center, Miami, 1970, Camarillo (Cal.) State Hosp., 1970. USPHS clin. fellow, 1962-63, research grantee NSF, 1966-68, Nat. Inst. Mental Health, 1967-68, NIH, 1968, Soc. for Psychol. Study Social Issues, 1969, NASA, 1969—. Mem. Am., Southeastern, Western, Fla. psychol. assns., Am. Assn. U. Profs., Fla. Conf. U. Profs., A.A.A.S., Assn. for Advancement of Behavior Therapy, Am. Assn. on Mental Deficiency, Soc. for Research in Child Devel., Am. Ednl. Research Assn., Psychonomic Soc., Sigma Xi, Psi Chi. Republican. Contbr. articles to profl. publs. Home: 6273 Sunset Dr South Miami FL 33143 Office: Dept Psychology U Miami Coral Gables FL 33124

JACOBSON, PAULINE BINKLEY (MRS. ALVIN H. JACOBSON), ret. advt. exec.; b. Winston-Salem, N.C., July 5, 1911; d. Olesta Arthur and Ida (Reich) Binkley; R.N., Bapt. Hosp. Sch. Nursing, Winston-Salem, 1932; m. Alvin H. Jacobson, Aug. 18, 1943 (dec. Sept. 1966). Pvt. duty nurse, Winston-Salem, 1932-35; obstet. nurse Columbia Hosp., Washington, 1935-37; staff nurse W.W. Hastings Hosp., Tahlequah, Okla., 1937-39; head nurse Indian Hosp., Fort Hall, Ida., 1939-42; sec-treas. Avin H. Jacobson Advt. Agy., Norfolk, Va., 1955-66; sec., media dir. Seamark Communicating Arts Cons. 1966-72. Served to 1st lt. Nurse Corps, AUS, 1942-46. Mem. N.C. Bapt. Hosp. Alumni Assn., Norfolk Mus. Home: 330 W Brambleton Av Norfolk VA 23510 Office: 3d and Front Sts Norfolk VA 23510

JACOBSON, RALPH WILLIAM, dentist; b. Bronx, N.Y., May 21, 1939; s. Irving and Jean (Linial) J.; student Emory U., 1957-59; D.D.S., U. Md., 1963; m. Phyllis Kay Weiner, Feb. 28, 1960; children—Michael Scott, Laurie Ann. Pvt. practice dentistry, Miami, Fla., 1965—; mem. staff Variety Children's Hosp., Miami, 1965—. Served to capt. Dental Corps, USAF, 1963-65. Fellow Gorgas Odontological Soc.; mem. Am. Dental Assn., E. Coast Dist., S. Dade County dental socs., Alpha Omega. Contbr. articles to Dental Students Mag. Home: 7345 SW 123d Terrace Miami FL 33156 Office: 9230 Bird Rd Miami FL 33165

JACQUES, WILFRED JAMES, JR., marketing co. exec.; b. Chatham, Ont., Can., May 5, 1932; s. Wilfred James and Almeda (Buie) J.; student U. Ga., 1950-51; B.A., U. Western Ont., 1956; LL.B., U. Ga., 1956; LL.M., N.Y. U., 1964; m. Mary Aleece Strickland, Mar. 7, 1958; 1 son, Wilfred James III. Admitted to Ga. bar, 1957; with Deen and Jacques attys. at law, Alma, Ga., 1957-63; with Straus Duparquet Inc., House Counsel, N.Y.C., 1964-65; with Harrell Internat. Inc. & Subsidiaries, Jacksonville, Fla., 1965—, now sr. v.p., dir. Home: 15 Maria Pl Ponte Vedra Beach FL 32082 Office: 4161 Carmichael Av Jacksonville FL

JACUNSKI, EDWARD W., engr.; b. Marion, Ill., June 22, 1912; s. Zenon and Cecilia (Jorkie) J.; B.S., U.S. Mil. Acad., 1938; M.A. in Engring., U. Fla., 1951; m. Mary Louise Guiteras, June, 1938; children— George J., Jinx (Mrs. D.T. Travis), Janice (Mrs. E.J. Corcoran). Commd. 2d lt. U.S. Army, 1938, advanced through grades to lt. col., resigned, 1954; asst. dean Coll. Engring., U. Fla., 1951—. Mem. Am. Soc. Engring. Edn., West Point Assn. Graduates, various engring. socs. Rotarian (com. dir.). Research, contbr. profl. publs. Home: 2718 SW 3d St Gainesville FL 32101

JADLOW, JOSEPH MARTIN, JR., educator; b. Nevada, Mo., Oct. 27, 1942; s. Joseph Martin and Polly (Yancey) J.; B.A., Central Mo. State Coll., 1964, M.A., 1965; Ph.D., U. Va., 1970; m. Janice Lynn Wickstead, Aug. 30, 1969. Interim asst. prof. econ. U. Va., summer 1968; asst. prof. econ. Okla. State U., 1968—; cons. govtl. agys. on econs. of U.S. ethical drug industry. Thomas Jefferson fellowship, 1965-66; Earhart fellowship, 1966-67; duPont fellowship, 1967-68. Mem. Am., So., Midwest econ. assns. Republican. Methodist. Contbr. articles to profl. jours. Research on the econs. of the ethical drug industry. Home: 18 Canyon Rim Dr Stillwater OK 74074 Office: Dept. Economics Coll Bus Admistrn Okla State U Stillwater OK 74074

JAFFE, EUGENE LEONARD, economist; b. N.Y.C., Apr. 10, 1929; s. Jack and Rose (Keller) J.; B.S., Purdue U., 1955; M.B.A., U. City N.Y., 1965; m. Eleanor F. Weisberg, Nov. 1955, (div. Sept. 1969); 1 dau., Maris R. Sr. economist N.Y. State Div. Internat. Commerce, N.Y.C., 1963-65; fgn. service res. officer U.S. Dept. State, Saigon, Vietnam, 1966-68; economist U.S. Dept. Def., Arlington, Va., 1968—; macro-economist U.S. Army Logistics Mgmt. Centre, Ft. Lee, Va. Served with AUS, 1950-52. Mem. Am. Econ. Assn. Home: Box 745 Chester VA 23831

JAFFE, JEROME HERBERT, physician; b. Phila., July 6, 1933; s. Louis and Cecelia (Chairnoff) J.; A.B. in Psychology, Temple U., 1954, M.A. in Exptl. Psychology, 1956, M.D., 1958; m. Faith Kessel, June 22, 1958; children—Miriam Ann, Celia Pam, Ari Benjamin. Rotating intern USPHS Hosp., S.I., 1958-59; resident psychiatry USPHS Hosp., Lexington, Ky., 1959-60, mem. psychiat. staff, 1960-61; postdoctoral fellow Interdisciplinary program Albert Einstein Coll. Medicine, 1961-62, asst. prof. psychiatry and pharmacology, 1964-66, vis. asst. prof., 1966-71; postdoctoral fellow, resident psychiatry Albert Einstein Coll. Medicine and Bronx Municipal Hosp. Center, 1962-64; asst. prof. psychiatry U. Chgo., 1966-69, asso. prof., 1969-71; dir. Drug Abuse program, Ill. Dept. Mental Health, Chgo., 1967-71; dir. Spl. Action Office for Drug Abuse Prevention, Exec. Office of Pres., and spl. cons. to Pres. for narcotics and dangerous drugs, Washington, 1971—. Mem. rev. com. Center Studies Narcotics and Dangerous Drugs Nat. Inst. Mental Health, 1966-71; cons. N.Y. State Narcotic Addiction Control Commn., 1966-68; mem. tech. adv. bd. Nat. Coordinating Council Drug Abuse Edn. and Information, 1969-71; mem. adv. com. Drug Abuse Tng. Center, Cal. State Coll. at Hayward, 1970-71; cons. Bur. Drugs Adv. Panel Systems, Dept. Health, Edn. and Welfare, 1970-71; spl. cons., tech. adviser Expert Com. Drug Dependence WHO, Geneva, Switzerland, 1970; cons. Joint Information Service Am. Psychiat. Assn. and Nat. Assn. Mental Health Project on Current Methods for Treatment of Addiction, 1970-71. USPHS postdoctoral fellow in pharmacology, 1961-64; recipient USPHS research career devel. award, 1964-66, 67-70. Mem. Am. Psychiat. Assn. (mem. task force alcoholism 1970-71), Am. Soc. Pharmacology and Exptl. Therapeutics (mem. com. div. clin. pharmacology 1970—), World Psychiat. Assn. (sec. sect. drug dependence 1969-71), Ill. State Med. Soc. (mem. com. narcotics and dangerous drugs). Contbr. articles to profl. jours. Office: The White House Washington DC 20500

JAFFE, THEODORE, govt. ofcl.; b. Providence, Aug. 24, 1910; s. David and Ette (Cipkin) J.; Ph.B., Brown U., 1932; LL.B., Harvard, 1935. Admitted to Mass. bar, 1935, R.I. bar, 1936, D.C. bar, 1948; practiced in Providence, 1935—; mem. firm Higgins, Cavanaugh & Cooney; commr. U.S. Fgn. Claims Settlement Commn., Washington 1961—. Served with AUS, 1942-45. Mem. Am., R.I. bar assns., Bar Assn. D.C. Home: 2727 29th St NW Washington DC 20008 Office: 1111 20th St NW Washington DC 20579

JAGGERS, CHARLES STANLEY, supt. schs.; b. Mt. Pleasant, Tex., Oct. 29, 1932; s. Worth and Loretta (Redfern) J.; B.S., E.Tex. State U., 1956, M.Ed., 1961; m. Kay Louwayne Branum, Jan. 1955; children—Patricia Lou, Chuck Bradley, Janna Ruth. Football coach, Anna, Tex., 1956, Frisco High Sch., 1957-63; athletic dir. Bridgeport (Tex.) High Sch., 1963-66; prin. high sch., Bridgeport, 1966-68; supt. schs., Wheeler, Tex., 1968-70; supt. schs., Quanah, Tex., 1971—. Served with USNR, 1951-53. Lion. Home: PO Box 65 Quanah TX 79252 Office: PO Box 150 Quanah TX 79252

JAGIELLO, WALTER EDWARD, mus. pub.; b. Chgo., Aug. 1, 1930; s. John Joseph and Katharine (Mirek) J.; ed. Holy Innocents Sch., Chgo., 1937-45; m. Jeanette Kozak, Mar. 17, 1972; children by previous marriage—Edward, Julieann, James. Founder Jay-Jay Record Co., Chgo., 1952, pres., 1971—; entertainer as Lil Wally, 1945—; pres. Jay Jay Pub. Co., 1955—, Walters Music Co., 1966—, Lil Wally Music Prodns., 1960—, Splty. Distbn. Co., Inc., 1969—; drummer, vocalist, band leader. Bd. dirs. Panair. Named to Polka Hall of Fame, Songwriters Hall of Fame. Mem. Internat. Polka Assn., Nat. Acad. Rec. Arts and Scis. Composer over 1500 mus. compositions; rec. 120 albums and 310 singles. Address: 910 Bay Drive Miami Beach FL 33141 Office: 1959 71st St Miami Beach FL 33141

JAKOB, WERNER LEONARD, entomologist; b. Wurzburg, Germany, Apr. 11, 1926; s. John Philip and Minna Barbara (Gerhardt) J.; came to U.S., 1929, naturalized, 1939; postgrad. Princeton, 1944-45; B.A., Duke, 1947; M.S. (Ethyl Corp. fellow), Rutgers U., 1952; m. Eleanor Craig, May 11, 1948; children—Craig P., John A., Duane E. Foreman, T L Ranch, Hillside, Ariz., 1956-61; quarantine insp. Ariz. Commn. Agr. and Horticulture, Phoenix, 1961; research entomologist Tech. Devel. Lab., USPHS, Savannah, Ga., 1962—. Dir. Triangle Soil Conservation Dist., Yavapai County, Ariz., 1959-60. Served with USNR, 1944-45. Mem. Am. Mosquito Control Assn., Entomol. Soc. Am., Sigma Chi. Contbr. articles to profl. jours. Home: 2237 Armstrong Dr Savannah GA 31404 Office: PO Box 2167 Savannah GA 31402

JAMES, ADVERGUS DELL, JR., coll. adminstr.; b. Garden City, Kan., Sept. 24, 1944; s. Advergus Dell and Helen Gertrude (Lee) J.; B.S., Langston (Okla.) U., 1966 M.S., Okla. State U., 1969. Asst. registrar Langston U., 1966-68, instr. bus. dept., dir. admissions and records, 1969-70; grad. asst. Okla. State U., 1968-69; asst. prof. bus. dept., dir. student financial aid Prairie View (Tex.) A. and M. Coll., 1970—. Mem. Am., Okla. assns. collegiate registrars and admissions officers, Nat. Bus. Edn. Assn., Am. Vocational Assn., Higher Edn. Alumni Council, Langston U., Okla. State U. alumni assns., N.A.A.C.P., Nat. Assn. Student Financial Aid Adminstrs., Phi Beta Lambda, Alpha Phi, Phi Delta Kappa, Kappa Delta Pi. Mason (32 deg.); mem. Order Rising Star. Address: Drawer C Prairie View TX 77445

JAMES, ALLIX BLEDSOE, univ. pres.; b. Marshall, Tex., Dec. 17, 1922; A.B., Va. Union U., 1944, B.D., 1946; Th.M., Union Theol. Sem., 1949, Th.D., 1957; m. 2 children. Instr. religion Va. Union U., Richmond, 1947-50, dean students, 1950-56, dean Sch. Theology, 1957-70, v.p., 1960-70, pres., 1970—. Chmn. Richmond City Planning Commn., 1969—; pres. council theol. edn. Am. Bapt. Conv., 1969—; pres. Am. Assn. Theol. Schs., 1970—. Co-author: The Continuing Quest, 1970; Calling a Baptist Pastor, 1968. Address: Va Union Univ 1500 N Lombardy St Richmond VA 23173*

JAMES, BENJAMIN ESCOTT, accountant; b. Edwardsville, Pa., Aug. 18, 1895; s. Benjamin Reese and Catherine (Escott) J.; B.S. in Econ., U. Pa., 1921; m. Lola M. White, Apr. 29, 1923; children—Patricia Jane (Mrs. R.G. Bullock Jr.), Benjamin Escott Jr. Accountant, John W. Gunby, Jacksonville, Fla., 1922-26; owner, operator firm Benjamin E. James, C.P.A., Jacksonville, 1926-46; sr. partner firm James & Harris, Jacksonville, 1946—, dir. Petroleum Carrier Corp., Jones Bros. Co., Jacksonville. Mem. Fla. Bd. Accountancy, 1965-69, chmn. 1968-69. Mem. adv. bd. Boys Home Assn., Jacksonville, 1935-45, Big Bros. Assn., 1935-40. Served with U.S. Army, 1917-19; ETO. C.P.A., Fla. Mem. So. States Accountants Conf. (pres. 1945), Fla. (pres. 1931), Am. insts. C.P.A.'s, Nat. Assn. State Bds. Accountancy, Am. Accountants Assn., Am. Legion, Sigma Nu, Beta Alpha Psi (hon.). Episcopalian (vestryman). Clubs: Meninak (pres. 1940), Timuquana Country, Seminole, Fla. Yacht, St. John's Dinner, Ye Mystic Revelers (all Jacksonville). Home: 1560 Lancaster Terrace Jacksonville FL 32204 Office: Fla Nat Bank Bldg Jacksonville FL 32202

JAMES, BOBBY EUGENE, state bar ofcl.; b. Kannapolis, N.C., May 6, 1930; s. Robert Conley and Myrtle Ulayia (Hallman) J.; student Wingate Jr. Coll., 1953-55; B.S., Wake Forest U., 1957, J.D. cum laude, 1959; m. Ruby Lee Ledbetter, Apr. 18, 1952; children—Randolph Michael, Cynthia Dee, Lisa Courtney. Admitted to N.C. bar, 1959, practiced in High Point until 1961; atty. N.C. State Bar, Raleigh, 1961-67, sec.-treas., 1967—, also sec.-treas. N.C. Bd. Law. Served with USAF, 1948-53. Mem. Am., N.C. bar assns., Am. Soc. Assn. Execs., Phi Theta Kappa. Democrat. Baptist. Home: 4713 Terry St Raleigh NC 27609 Office: Box 25850 Raleigh NC 27611

JAMES, CARL DAVID, educator; b. Webster County, Miss., Dec. 23, 1939; s. Carl Bradford and Mary Ellen (Denton) J.; diploma Holmes Jr. Coll., 1959; B.S.E., Delta State Coll., 1961; M.Ed., U. Miss., 1968; m. Anita Mann, May 2, 1964; children—Carla Janell, David Lewis. Tchr., East Clayton Elementary Sch., Ellenwood, Ga.; asst. prin. Lee St. Elementary Sch., Jonesboro, Ga., now prin. Mem. Nat., Ga., Clayton County edn. assns., Clayton County Dept. Elementary Sch. Prins. Kiwanian (bd. dirs. Jonesboro). Address: 178 Lee St Jonesboro GA 30236

JAMES, EARL DANIEL, mayor of Montgomery, Ala.; b. Florala, Ala., Aug. 10, 1914; s. Walter Home and Atha (Daniel) J.; B.S., Ala. Poly. Inst.; m. Dorothy Goggans; children—Walter Thomas, Kathleen Sue. Former tchr., athletic instr. Montgomery Pub. Schs., former athletic dir.; former asso. city commr. City of Montgomery, now mayor. Served with USAAF, World War II. Mem. Phi Delta Kappa. Methodist. Optomist. Home: 26 Oak Forest Dr Montgomery AL 36109 Office: Office of the Mayor Montgomery AL 36102

JAMES, GEORGE EDWARD, JR., ins. co. exec.; b. Richmond, Va., Jan. 27, 1921; s. George Edward and Ruthe Mae (Brightwell) J.; jr. accounting degree Va. So. Coll., 1947; m. Patricia Ann Howery, Nov. 29, 1969; children—Edward Derekson, Brenda Leigh, Amy Page. Financial clk. mortgage loans Jefferson Standard Life Ins. Co., Greensboro, N.C., 1947-49; successively salesman, asst. field mgr., supt. agys., tng. dir. Shenandoah Life Ins. Co., Roanoke, Va., 1949-62, asso. mgr. field, 1962-63, regional supt. agys., 1966-67, dir. manpower devel., 1967-68, asst. v.p. agys., 1968, 2d v.p. marketing, 1968—; v.p. agys. Estate Life Ins. Co., Roanoke, 1963-65; pres. Am. Standard Life Ins. Co., Poplar Bluff, Mo., 1966; v.p. Shenandoah Equity Services, Roanoke, 1971—, prin., tng. cons., 1969—. Asst. dist. commr. Blue Ridge council Boy Scouts Am., 1964-65. Served to 3d class petty officer USNR, World War II; PTO. C.L.U. Mem. Roanoke C. of C., Am. Soc. Life Underwriters, Nat. Assn. Life Underwriters. Baptist (deacon 1960—, supt. Sunday sch. 1960-68). Club: Raleigh Court Lions (pres. 1965). Home: 1406 Haydon St Salem VA 24153 Office: 2301 Brambleton Av Roanoke VA 24015

JAMES, GRACE MARILLYN, physician; b. Charleston, W.Va., Aug. 12, 1923; d. Edward Lawrence and Stella Grace (Shaw) J.; B.A., W.Va. State Coll., 1944; M.D., Meharry Med. Coll., Nashville, 1950 div.; 1 son, David Marshall. Gen. rotating intern Harlem Hosp., N.Y.C., 1950-51, resident pediatrics, 1951-52; resident pediatrics Vanderbilt Clinic, Babies Hosp., Columbia Presbyn. Med. Center, N.Y.C., 1952-53; traineeship in child psychiatry Nat. Inst. Mental Health, Creedmoor State Hosp., Queens Village, N.Y., 1964-65; tng. fellow Care of Handicapped Children, Childrens Evaluation and Rehab. Clinic, Albert Einstein Coll. Medicine, Yeshiva U. at Jacobi Hosp., 1966; camp physician Camp Woodlands, Phoencia, N.Y., 1952; practice medicine, specializing in pediatrics, Louisville, 1953-64, 67—; child health physician Louisville and Jefferson County Dept. Health, 1953-55, pub. sch. physician, 1962-63; mem. staff West End Day Care Center; mem. attending staff Childrens Hosp., Louisville; asst. vis. psychiatrist, full-time staff child psychiatry Kings County Hosp. Center, Bklyn., 1965-66; dir. diagnostic and evaluation div. Frankfort (Ky.) State Hosp., 1966; dir. Diagnostic and Evaluation Service, div. mental retardation Dept. Mental Health, Frankfort, 1966-67; instr. child health U. Louisville Sch. Medicine, Louisville Gen. Hosp., 1953-62, asst. clin. prof. pediatrics, 1962—; asst. clin. prof. pediatrics Meharry Med. Coll., Nashville, 1970; clin. pediatrician Kosair Crippled Childrens Hosp., Ky. Commn. for Handicapped Children, 1968—; pres. West Louisville Med. Center, 1972—; mem. active staff Red Cross Hosp., Childrens Hosp., Louisville; mem. courtesy staff Jewish Hosp., St. Josephs Hosp., St. Anthonys Hosp., Meth. Evang. Hosp., Nortons Hosp., Louisville, Geo. W. Hubbard Hosp., Nashville; pres. med. staff Red Cross Hosp., 1963; mem. Action Research team, U. Louisville. Chmn. instns. and agys. com. Louisville Human Relations Com., 1961-64; chmn. com. on sch. dropouts Louisville Urban League, 1963; Community Council mem. Family Service Orgn., 1958-62; mem. housing adv. com. Dept. Housing Inspection, City of Louisville, 1970—; mem. health and welfare council United Way, Louisville, 1971—; mem. steering liaison com. Health Maintenance Orgn., Louisville, 1971—. Bd. dirs. Louisville br. N.A.A.C.P., 1953-55, West End Day Care Center, 1960-63. Diplomate Am. Bd. Pediatrics. Fellow Am. Acad. Pediatrics (mem. community health com. 1971—), Am. Assn. Mental Deficiency; mem. A.M.A., Nat. (vice chmn. sect. on pediatrics 1962-66), Ky. med. assns., Jefferson County (alternate del. 1959-60), Falls City (sec. 1960-64, chmn. community health services 1971—) med. socs., Ky., Louisville pediatrics socs., Delta Sigma Theta. Home: 684 S 44th St Louisville KY 40211 Office: 4221 W Broadway Louisville KY 40211

JAMES, GRAY, bank exec., city ofcl.; b. Tulsa, Sept. 16, 1909; s. James Henry and Nora (Holmes) G.; grad. high sch.; m. Evelyn Winona Jones, May 30, 1936; children—James Paul, Donald Earl. Retail mcht., Kan., 1940-49; with Gro-Feed-Seed, Augusta, Kan., 1945—; dir. First State Bank, Alamo, Tex., 1967—; mayor, Alamo, Tex., 1969—. Mem. C. of C. Lion (pres. 1954-55, 62-63). Home: 1221 Whiway 83 Alamo TX 78516 Office: PO Box 695 Alamo TX 78516

JAMES, HIBBARD GARRETT, communications exec.; b. Cin., Dec. 16, 1922; s. Edward M. and Elizabeth Cheyney (Garrett) J.; S.B., Harvard, 1945; postgrad. Columbia Tchrs. Coll., 1954, Springfield Coll., 1955-56; m. Betty Miles, March 30, 1963. Faculty, New Eng. Conservatory Music, 1945-46, Tilton Acad,, 1946-47; pub. relations dir. Wichita Community Chest, 1948-51, Indpls. Community Chest, 1951-53, YMCA of Greater N.Y., 1953-58, nat. capital area United Givers Fund, 1958-69; communications dir. Washington Cathedral (D.C.), 1969—; producer Overview, WRC-TV, 1970—. Vis. lectr. pub. relations N. Va. Community Coll., 1966—. Mem. pub. relations Councils Am., 1952-66; mem. broadcast and film commn. Nat. Council Chs., 1969—. Chmn. bd. trustees Cheyney (Pa.) Burying Ground, 1963—. Mem. Pub. Relations Soc. Am., Washington Shakespeare Soc. (dir.). Mem. Soc. of Friends. Clubs: Players (N.Y.C.); Nat. Broadcasters, Nat. Press (Washington). Author: Poesie, 1943; German Opera in Boston, 1945. Music critic various publs., 1954-60; book reviewer Washington Evening Star, 1963—; archtl. critic Washington Daily News, 1967—. Home: 521 5th St Washington DC 20003 Office: Washington Cathedral Mount St Alban Washington DC 20016

JAMES, JESSE, state ofcl.; b. Milam County, Tex., Oct. 10, 1904; s. John A. and Della (Story) J.; student bus. coll., Somerville Law Sch.; m. Zana Bell; 1 dau., Doris Marie. With drug and merc. co., Cameron, Tex., 1927-35; chief clk. Tex. Treasury Dept., Austin, 1937-41, state treas., 1941—. Mem. Tex. Ho. of Reps., 1933-37. Mem. State Banking Bd., State Depository Bd., State Bond Bd., Automatic Tax Bd., State Tax Bd., Bd. of County and Dist. Rd. Indebtedness; pres. Nat. Assn. State Auditors, Controllers and Treasurers U.S., 1952. Hon. mem. Future Farmers Am. Lion, Mason (Shriner). Home: 3601 Taylors Dr Austin TX 78703 Office: State Capitol Bldg PO Box 12404 Capitol Sta Austin TX 78711

JAMES, JOSEPH B., educator; b. Clearwater, Fla., July 17, 1912; s. L. P. and Ilah J. (Miles) J.; A.B.E., U. Fla., 1934, A.M., 1935; Ph.D., U. Ill., 1939; m. Jacquelyn McWhite, June 8, 1937; children— Glenn Joseph, William Bruce. Instr. gen. extension div. U. Fla., 1935-36; asst. and fellow U. Ill., 1936-39; head dept. history and polit. sci. Williamsport Dickinson Jr. Coll., 1939-40; Union Coll., Ky., 1940-43; dean of faculty William Woods Coll., 1943-45; head dept. social studies Miss. State Coll. for Women, 1945-58; dean of coll. Wesleyan Coll., Macon, Ga., 1958-71, Callaway prof. polit. sci., 1971—; vis. prof. summer sessions U. Fla., U. Miss., Florence (Ala.) State Tchrs. Coll., Middle Tenn. State Coll. Mem. So. Polit. Sci. Assn., So. Hist. Assn., Assn. Coll. Honor Socs. (council mem.), Phi Beta Kappa (past pres. Middle Ga. Grad. Assn.), Phi Kappa Phi, Kappa Delta Pi, Kappa Phi Kappa, Pi Gamma Mu (nat. pres. emeritus). Methodist (adminstrv. bd.). Rotarian. Author: The Framing of the Fourteenth Amendment, 1956, rev. edit., 1965. Contbr. to scholarly Jours. and reference publs. Home: 3450 Osborne Pl Macon GA 31204

JAMES, JOSEPH SHEPPARD, state ofcl.; b. Gum Spring, Va., May 25, 1902; s. Richard Gregory and Lillie (Sale) J.; student Va. Mechanics Inst.; m. Virginia Lambeth, June 27, 1925; children—Joseph Sheppard, Beverly (Mrs. Willard Travell Weeks). Asst. auditor pub. accounts State of Va., Richmond, 1944-67, auditor pub. accounts, 1967—. Instr. accounting Va. Mechanics Inst., 1934-51. C.P.A., Va. Home: 3850 Brook Rd Richmond VA 23227 Office: Blanton Bldg Richmond VA 23219

JAMES, JULIUS VAIDEN, clergyman; b. Grove Hill, Ala., Sept. 29, 1916; s. Thomas P. and Lena (Cox) J.; A.B., Howard Coll., 1938; Th.M. So. Bapt. Theol. Sem., 1941; m. Frances Newton Nov. 12, 1941; 1 dau., Linda Carolyn. Ordained to ministry Bapt. Ch., 1933; pastor 1st Bapt. Ch., Glencoe, Ala., 1941-45; supt. missions, Gadsden, Ala., 1945-48; pastor Calvary Bapt. Ch., Gadsden, 1948-53; supt. missions, Columbus, Ga., 1953-57; dir. juvenile rehab. Bapt. Home Mission Bd., Atlanta, 1959-63; supt. missions, Chattanooga, 1963—; trustee Am. Bapt. Sem., Nashville. Mem. religious sect. United Fund, Chattanooga, 1969. Named Hon. Texan, Gov., 1960. Mason. Pioneer work in setting up nationwide denominational work dealing with juvenile delinquency, 1957. Home: 3407 Audubon Dr Chattanooga TN 37411 Office: 1022 McCallie Av Chattanooga TN 37403

JAMES, M(ALOY) C(OWAN), mfg. co. exec.; b. Star, N.C., Jan. 4, 1886; s. William Henry and Annie Florence (Usher) J.; student Mars Hill Coll., 1902-07; m. Della May Pierce, June 29, 1911; children—Guy Masten, Maloy Cowan. Various positions, 1909-36; founder pres. The James Hosiery Mills, Inc., Greeneville, Tenn., 1936—. Presbyn. Mason (32 deg., Shriner). Club: Cherokee Country (Knoxville, Tenn.). Home: 501 W Main St Greeneville TN 37743 Office: 110 Elm St Greeneville TN 37743

JAMES, MALOY COWAN, JR., textile co. exec.; b. Winston-Salem, N.C., May 14, 1922; s. Maloy Cowan and Della May (Pierce) J.; student U. Tenn., 1938-40; m. Anna Lou Witt, Oct. 25, 1949. Treas., James Hosiery Mills, Greeneville, Tenn., 1934-62; owner, pres. James Knitting Co., Inc., Greeneville, 1962—. Served with AUS, 1943. Mem. U.S. (sectional affairs com. 1969—), Tenn. (v.p. 1958, 67-68, pres. 1959, 69) golf assns., Am. Legion, Pi Kappa Alpha. Presbyn. Elk, Moose. Clubs: Link Hills (pres. 1954-58; dir. 1954-65) (Greeneville); Cherokee (Knoxville, Tenn.); Ponte Vedra (Fla.). Home: 101 Monument Av Greeneville TN 37743 Office: 1000 W Irish St Greeneville TN 37743

JAMES, MARSHALL ORR, ednl. adminstr., clergyman; b. Anderson, S.C., Feb. 25, 1929; s. Jesse Alvin and Flora Louise (Shore) J.; B.S., Furman U., 1949; M.S., La. State U., 1951; B.A., Oxford U., Eng., 1956, M.A., 1959; S.T.B., Gen. Theol. Sem., 1957, Millsaps Coll., 1965; m. Winifred Griffith Wills, Nov. 17, 1957; children—Frederick Martin St. John, David Marshall, Jonathan Andrew. Ordained to ministry Protestant Episcopal Ch. as deacon, 1956, priest, 1958; pastor chs., Greer, S.C., 1957-59, Clemson, S.C., 1959-63; chaplain Clemson Coll., 1959-63, prof. philosophy, 1960-63; headmaster St. Andrew's Episcopal Sch., Jackson, Miss., 1965-71; canon St. Andrews Cathedral, Jackson; dir. religion dept. St. Martin's Protestant Episcopal Sch., Metairie, La., 1971—. Active various community drives. Served with AUS, 1951-54. Mem. Phi Kappa Phi. Rotarian. Home: 401 Haring Rd Metairie LA 70003 Office: 5309 Airline Hwy Metairie LA 70003

JAMES, NORMA WHITENER (MRS. JOHN WARREN JAMES), civic worker; b. Lincolnton, N.C., Feb. 14, 1903; d. John Roadman and Hattie (Hull) Whitener; student U. Fla., 1925; m. John Warren James, Sept. 13, 1937 (dec. Dec. 1943). Mem. Broward Hosp. Auxiliary, 1950-55, Opera Guild, 1952-59, Civic Music Assn., 1956-58; chmn. Broward County unit Am. Cancer Soc., 1950-51, hon. life mem. bd. dirs. Mem. Internat. Platform Assn., Nova U. Assn. (charter mem. Ft. Lauderdale). Clubs: Golden Hills Turf and Country, Lauderdale Yacht. Home: PO Box 38 Fort McCoy FL 32637

JAMES, PHILIP WAYNE, assn. exec.; b. Dallas, Sept. 11, 1934; s. Dalton L. and Minnie R. (Caldwell) J.; B.S., Tex. Tech. U., 1953, M.S., 1957; m. Peggy J. Welling, May 31, 1971. Field sec. Tex. Tech Ex-Students Assn., 1957-60, exec. dir., 1960—; sec.-treas. Tex. Tech Loyalty Fund, 1960—. Instr. mass communications dept. Tex. Tech U., 1971. Bd. dirs. Tex. Tech U. Found. Recipient Regional and nat. awards in alumni activities Am. Alumni Council. Mem. Am. Alumni Council (dir. 1969-72), Internat. Platform Assn., Sigma Delta Chi, Phi Delta Kappa, Alpha Phi Omega. Mason (Shriner), Rotarian. Clubs: Tex. Tech Century, Red Raider (Lubbock); Dallas Press. Editor Tex. Techsan, 1960-72. Home: 3002 60th St Lubbock TX 79413 Office: Tex Tech U Lubbock TX 79409

JAMES, ROBERT BERNARD, educator; b. Houston, Oct. 26, 1942; s. Patrick Henry and Edith (Keating) J.; B.S., St. Edward's U., 1963; D.D.S., U. Tex., 1967, certificate pedodontics, 1971; m. Carol Germaine Collins, June 12, 1965; children—Jeffrey, Brian, Stephanie. Asst. prof. pedodontics U. Tex. Dental br., Houston, 1971—; dir. Jr. League Out-Patient Dept., Tex. Children's Hosp. Dental Clinic, Houston, 1971—. Served with USAF, 1967-69. Mem. Am., Tex. dental assns., Houston Dist. Dental Soc., Am. Soc. Dentistry for Children, Reserve Officers Assn., Delta Sigma Delta. Roman Catholic. Home: 10803 McClearen Houston TX 77035 Office: 6516 John Freeman St Houston TX 77025

JAMES, ROBERT LEIGH, author, banker, lawyer; b. Worthington, O., July 29, 1918; s. Frank and Jessie (Brummitt) J.; student Ind. U., 1937-39, U. Cal., Los Angeles, 1938; A.B., U. Chgo., 1941, J.D., 1947; m. Genevieve Palmer Capouch, Oct. 4, 1943; 1 dau., Alexandra Mary. U.S. Fgn. Service officer, 1947-50; admitted to Ill. bar, 1947, also D.C., Cal. bars; atty. Bank of Am., 1951-52; land and legal rep. Western hemisphere Cal. Exploration Co., 1952-58; v.p. Moa Bay Mining Co., Nicaro Nickel Co., Island Exploration Co., 1958-60; v.p., Washington rep. Bank of Am. N.T. and S.A., San Francisco, 1960—. Served to lt. comdr. USNR, 1941-46. Mem. Wash. Inst. Fgn. Affairs, U.S. C. of C. (mem. internat. com.), Theta Chi. Clubs: The Nineteen Twenty-five F Street, City Tavern Assn., Chevy Chase, Internat. (Washington); University (N.Y.C.). Author: The Chameleon File, 1967; The Capitol Hill Affair, 1968; The Push-Button Spy, 1970; Penelope's Zoo, 1971; Janus, 1973. Home: 4301 Bradley Lane Chevy Chase MD 20015 Office: 1800 K St NW Washington DC 20005

JAMES, S.H., clergyman, city ofcl.; b. Pledger, Tex.; grad. Tenn. State Coll.; S.T.M., Andover Theol. Sch.; postgrad. Boston U., Harvard; D.D., Selma U.; LL.D., Bishop Coll.; married; 3 children. Ordained to ministry Baptist Ch.; pastor 2d Bapt. Ch., San Antonio; formerly instr. religion, dean of men Bishop Coll., Dallas; now mem. San Antonio City Council. Moderator La Grange Bapt. Dist. Assn. Tex.; pres. southwestern region Progressive Nat. Conv. Former mem. San Antonio Planning and Zoning Commn. Bd. dirs. central br. San Antonio YMCA, United Fund, Community Welfare Council. Contbg. editor David C. Cook Pub. Co., Elgin, Ill. Home: 430 N Pine St San Antonio TX 78202*

JAMES, SIDNEY JULIUS, educator; b. Columbia, Miss., June 25, 1935; s. Odell James and Vivian Nelson (Martin) J.; B.S., Alcorn A. and M. Coll., Lorman, Miss., 1958; student Ind. U., summer 1961, U. So. Miss., Hattiesburg; m. Margie Jaunit Pope, Aug. 12, 1962; 1 dau., Kenja Darnee. Mem. faculty Prentiss (Miss.) Jr. Coll., 1960—, dean students, dir. student financial aid, 1967—. Part-owner V&O Restaurant, Columbia, J&J Package Store, Columbia. Mem. Columbia City Planning Commn. Bd. dirs. Marion County chpt. A.R.C., Marion chpt. N.A.A.C.P. Named Coach of Year, So. Intercollegiate Conf., 1966. Mem. N.E.A., So. Assn. Student Financial Aid Adminstrs., So. Coll. Personnel Assn., Kay Frat. Methodist (chmn. trustees). Mason. Club: Marion County Civic (bd. dirs.). Home: 1200 Maxwell St Columbia MS 39429 Office: Prentiss Inst Prentiss MS 39474

JAMES, SIDNEY LORRAINE, ednl. TV exec.; b. St. Louis, Aug. 6, 1906; s. William Henry and Katherine (Wiese) J.; student Washington U.; m. Agnes McCarthy, Oct. 21, 1932; children—Christopher, Timothy, Mary, Sidney. Mem. editorial staff St. Louis Post-Dispatch, 1928-36; nat. affairs writer Time mag., 1936-38; chief Time, Inc., Chgo., 1938-41, chief Western editorial operations. 1941-46; asst. mng. editor Life mag., 1946-54; mng. editor Sports Illustrated, N.Y.C., 1954-60, pub., 1960-65; v.p. corp. mgmt. Time, Inc., N.Y.C., 1965-67, v.p., Washington, 1967-70; chmn. bd. Greater Washington Ednl. Telecommunications Assn., Channel 26, 1970—; chmn. bd. Nat. Pub. Affairs Center for TV, 1970—. Mem. President's Adv. Com. Youth Fitness; lay trustee Trinity Coll. Mem. Def. Orientation Association. Clubs: American Yacht, Apawamis (Rye, N.Y.); New York Racquet and Tennis; Burning Tree; 1925 F Street, International, U.S. Seniors Golf Assn. (Washington). Home: 2101 Connecticut Av NW Washington DC 20008 Office: WETA 2100 L St NW Washington DC 20036

JAMES, W. ERVIN, lawyer; b. Montgomery, Ala., Jan. 29, 1911; LL.B., George Washington U., 1941. Admitted to Ala. bar, 1941, D.C. bar, 1941, Tex. bar, 1955; asst. to sec. of commerce, 1939-41; asst. to gen. counsel FCC, 1946. Served to lt. USNR, World War II. Mem. Am., Houston (pres. 1969-70) bar assns., Fed. Communications Bar Assn., State Bar Tex.Address: 1107 S Coast Bldg Houston TX 77002*

JAMESON, DEXTER CLAIR, JR., educator; b. Pembroke, Ky., Aug. 27, 1927; s. Dexter Clair and Eva M. (Oliver) J.; B.S. in Civil Engring., U. Tenn., 1952, M.S., 1963; m. Robin L. Abrams, Aug. 25, 1951; children—Joy, Stephen. With TVA, Boone Dam, 1952, Union Carbide Nuclear Co., Oak Ridge, 1954-56; instr. U. Tenn., Knoxville, 1957-59, asst. prof., 1959-67, asso. prof. civil engring., 1967—. Served with USN, 1945-48, AUS, 1952-54. Registered profl. engr., Tenn. Mem. Am. (dir. ednl. div. 1971—), Tenn. (named distinguished prof. 1967) road builders assns., Nat., Tenn. socs. profl. engrs., Am. Soc. C.E., Am. Soc. Engring. Edn., Chi Epsilon (councillor So. Dist., also mem. supreme council 1970—, exec. sec. 1972—). Home: Blacks Ferry Rd Route 18 Knoxville TN 37921

JAMESON, ROBERT CAREY, hosp. adminstr.; b. Coleman, Tex., Feb. 10, 1918; s. Emmett Clarence and Lettie (Davis) J.; student John Tarleton Agrl. Coll., 1939-40; m. Helen Mae Stone, Dec. 10, 1942; children— Daniel V., Frances Lorraine. Asst. v.p., dir. Coleman (Tex.) Bank, 1950-68; adminstr. Overall-Morris Meml. Hosp., Coleman, Tex., 1968—. Served to lt. col. AUS, 1940-46. Mem. Coleman C. of C. (dir. 1965-67, pres. 1967). Baptist (supt. Sunday sch. 1950-59, deacon 1950—). Kiwanian (dir. 1960, pres. 1963). Home: 1215 Austin St Coleman TX 76834 Office: 310 Pecos St Coleman TX 76834

JAMIESON, JOHN RODNEY, govt. ofcl.; b. Madison, Wis., July 10, 1923; s. John Rodney and Marion (Brown) J.; B.S. in Mech. Engring., U. Wis., 1947; M.S., U. Minn., 1948; m. Ruth Kumlien, Jan. 17; 1952 children— Peter K. Sundstrom, Mary M. Sundstrom, Ruth Elizabeth. Research asso., instr. U. Ill., Urbana, 1949-52; engr. Honeywell, Inc., Mpls., 1952-65; commr. hwys. State of Minn., St. Paul, 1965-67, Fed. Hwy. Adminstrn., Dept. Transp., Washington, 1967—. Served with USAAF, 1943-45. Decorated Air medal, D.F.C. Mem. Am. Soc. M.E., Am. Soc. Heating Refrigeration and Air Conditioning Engrs. Home: 713 6th St SW Washington DC 20024 Office: Dept Transp Fed Hwy Adminstrn Washington DC 20591

JAMISON, JOHN AMBLER, circuit judge; b. Florence, S.C., May 14, 1916; s. John Wilson and Elizabeth (Fleming); LL.B., Cumberland U., 1941; postgrad. George Washington U., 1943-44; grad. Indsl. Coll. Armed Forces, 1962; J.D., Samford U., 1969; m. Mildred Holley, Sept. 22, 1945. Admitted to S.C. bar, 1941, Va. bar 1942, U.S. Supreme Ct. bar, 1945; atty. Va. Div. Motor Vehicles, Richmond, 1947-54; practice law, Fredericksburg, 1954-72; asso. judge County Cts. Stafford and King George Counties, Va., Municipal Ct., Fredericksburg, 1956-72; judge 39th Va. Jud. Circuit, 1972—. Dir., counsel Nat. Bank of Fredericksburg, 1968-72. Mem. adv. com. Gov.'s Hwy. Safety Commn., 1956-58; pres. Fredericksburg Rescue Squad, 1960-62, now hon. life mem. Chmn. bd. Fredericksburg Area Mental Hygiene Clinic, 1962-63; bd. dirs. Rappahannock Area Devel. Commn., 1960-66. Served from ensign to comdr. USNR, 1941-46; comdg. officer Richmond Naval Res. Div., 1948-54; naval aide to gov. of Va., 1954—. Recipient award S.C. Confederate War Centennial Commn. Mem. Am., S.C., Va., 39th Va. Jud. Circuit (pres. 1959-60, 69-70) bar assns., Va. Trial Lawyers Assn., Am. Judicature Soc., Res. Officers Assn. U.S., Am. Legion (post comdr. 1951-52), Blue Key, Sigma Delta Kappa. Episcopalian (vestryman, lay reader). Mason (32 deg., Shriner, Jester), Kiwanian (dir.). Address: PO Drawer 29 Fredericksburg VA 22401

JANASKE, PAUL C(ARLYLE), information scientist; b. Shamokin, Pa., July 28, 1920; s. Michael Edward and Pearl Anna (Paul) J.; B.S., Dickinson Coll., 1942; M.S. in L.S., Columbia, 1949; m. Virginia May Lightner, Nov. 4, 1945 children—Paul Carlyle, Stephen Charles. Head service dept., instr. Sch. Library Sci., Kent (O.) State U. Library, 1949-51; with U.S. Govt., 1951-60; asst. dir. biol. scis. communication project Am. Inst. Biol. Scis., 1960-63; exec. dir. Am. Documentation Inst., 1963-64, Fed. Clearinghouse for Sci. and Tech. Information, 1964-67, div. library programs U.S. Office Edn., Washington, 1967-—. Lectr. dept. library sci. Catholic U. Am., 1966-—. Served with USNR, 1942-46. Mem. Phi Kappa Sigma. Methodist. Editor: Information Handling and Science Information, 1962; Automation and Scientific Communication, 1963. Home: 4508 N Dittmar Rd Arlington VA 22207 Office: US Office of Education 7th and D Sts SW Washington DC 20202

JANEWAY, RAY CURTIS, librarian; b. Siloam Springs, Ark., March 14, 1916; s. Charles Newton and Blanche (Moore) J.; A.B., U. Kan., 1938; B.L.S., U. Ill., 1941, M.S., 1944; m. Bonnie Ethel Fenstemaker, July 22, 1935; children—Gerald Ray, Bonnie Joyce (dec.). Library asst. U. Kan., 1938-40, asst. dir. libraries, 1946-49; library asst. U. Ill., 1941-44; librarian Bradley U., 1944-46. Tex. Tech. Coll. 1949-—. Summer tchr. Grad. Library Sch., U. Tex., Austin. Mem. Tex. (pres. 1959-60), S.W. library assns., Tex. Assn. Coll. Tchrs. (pres. 1968-69). Rotarian. Home: 3207 45th St Lubbock TX 79413

JANEWAY, RICHARD, coll. dean; b. Los Angeles, Feb. 12, 1933; s. VanZandt and Grace Eleanor (Bell) J.; A.B., Colgate U., 1954; M.D., U. Pa., 1958; m. Katherine Esmond Pillsbury, Dec. 23, 1955; children— Susan Kent, David VanZandt, Elizabeth Anne. Intern Hosp. U. Pa., 1958-59; resident N.C. Bapt. Hosp., Winston-Salem, 1963-66; practice medicine specializing in neurology, Winston-Salem, 1966-—; mem. faculty Bowman Gray Sch. Medicine, Wake Forest U., Winston-Salem, 1966-—, prof. neurology, 1971-—, dir. cerebral vascular research center, 1969-71, dean sch., 1971-—. Cons. neurology VA Hosp., Salisbury, N.C., 1969; mem. spl. task force on arteriosclerosis Nat. Heart and Lung Inst., 1971-—; joint com. for stroke facilities, 1969-72; chmn. policy com. Winston-Salem/Forsythe County Bd. Edn., 1970-—. Served to capt., USAF, 1959-63. USPHS fellow, 1956; Markle scholar, 1968-—. Fellow A.C.P.; mem. Am. Neurol. Assn., N.Y. Acad. Sci., Am. Heart Assn., Assn. Am. Med. Colls., Phi Beta Kappa, Alpha Omega Alpha. Rotarian. Home: 2815 Country Club Rd Winston-Salem NC 27104

JANSSEN, JAMES HAJO, metallurgist; b. Pekin, Ill., Sept. 21, 1909; s. Gerhardt U. and Alpha (Norris) J.; B.S., U. Ill., 1931; Ph.D., U, Chgo,, 1934; m. Beatrice R. Atteberry, Aug. 18, 1962; children— Shirley Ann (Mrs. Robert A. McDonald.). Wire mill metallurgist Keystone Steel & Wire Co., Peoria, Ill., 1934-40; ferrous metallurgist Western Cartridge Co., East Alton, Ill., 1940-43; chief metallurgist Colo. Fuel & Iron Co., Buffalo, 1945-47, asst. chief metallurgist Eastern div., Buffalo, 1947-50; chief metallurgist Pratt & Letchworth Foundry, Buffalo, 1950-55, Ft. Pitt Steel Foundry, McKeesport, Pa., 1955-56, Keokuk Steel Castings (Ia), 1956-59; corp. cons., chief metallurgist Halliburton Services, Duncan, Okla., 1959-—; pres. Janssen & Assos., Inc., metall. engring. consultants, Duncan. Served with AUS, 1943-45. Registered profl. engr., Okla. Mem. Am. Soc. for Metals, Nat. Soc. Corrosion Engrs. Mason (Shriner). Office: 2206 Chisholm Dr Duncan OK 73533

JANSSEN, MELVIN RUSSEL, economist; b. Minonk, Ill., Oct. 12, 1921; s. John Evers and Greta Johanna (Cassens) J.; B.S., U. Ill., 1943, M.S., 1948; M.P.A. (Ferguson fellow), Harvard, 1948, A.M. (Ferguson fellow), 1949, Ph.D., 1953; m. Marianna Kilian, Aug. 4, 1943; children—Elaine (Mrs. Frederick C. Cue), Paul M., Joanne F., Lee K. Research asst. U. Ill., 1946-48; agrl. economist U.S. Dept. Agr., Lafayette, Ind., 1949-64, leader No. and Western Area, Washington, 1964-65, asst. dir. field coordination Econ. Research Service, Washington, 1965-—; asst. prof. agrl. econs. Purdue U., 1961-64. Chmn. Sch. Reorgn. Adv. Com., Lafayette, 1959-64. Served with AUS, 1943-46. Decorated Air medal with oak leaf cluster. Mem. Am. Econ. Assn., Am., Western, So. agrl. econ. assns. Mem. United Ch. of Christ. Home: 6063 N 6th St Arlington VA 22203 Office: Econ Devel Div Econ Research Service Dept Agr Washington DC 20250

JANUARY, MAX LEE, real estate co. exec.; b. Oklahoma City, Apr. 2, 1943; s. Marvin Lawrence and Norma Lee (Cole) J.; B.S. in Agr., Okla. State U., 1967; postgrad. Okla. U., 1967; m. Susan Kathleen Martin, Nov. 16, 1962; children—Mari Lee, Mark Levi, John Lawrence, April Ann. Staff appraiser Okla. Hwy. Dept., 1967-68; loan officer, appraiser Stillwater Savs. & Loan Assn. (Okla.), 1968-71; owner Watova Mercantile, real estate appraisal, sales, devel. and farming, Nowata, Okla., 1971-—. Guest lectr. Okla. State U., 1969-70. Mem. Stillwater Homebuilders Assn. (past sec.), Okla. Soc. Farm Mgrs. and Rural Appraisers (past sec., treas.). Baptist. Home and Office: Route 2 Nowata OK 74048

JANZEN, JERRY LEE, engring. exec.; b. Enid, Okla., Oct, 28, 1936; s. Abe H. and Vivian (Bradley) J.; student Phillips U., 1954-56; B.S., Okla. State U., 1960, M.S., 1963; m. Mary Ann Johnson, Dec. 3, 1960; children—Sherry Lynn, Terry Kay. Lead engr. Western Electric Co., 1960-64; project engr. FAA, 1964-67; prin. Arthur Young & Co., Oklahoma City, 1967-—. Vis. asst. prof. Okla. State U., 1964. Registered profl. engr., Okla. Mem. Am, Inst. Indsl. Engrs. (chpt. pres. 1969-—), Nat., Okla. Socs. profl. engrs., Am. Prodn. and Inventory Control Soc., Bank Adminstrn. Inst. Club: Engineers. Contbr. articles to profl. publs. Home: 3713 NW 68th St Oklahoma City OK 73116 Office: Liberty Tower Oklahoma City OK 73102

JARMAN, JOHN, congressman; b. Sallisaw, Okla., July 17, 1915; s. John H. and Lou Neal (Jones) J.; student Westminster Presbyn. Coll., Fulton, Mo., 1932-34; A.B., Yale, 1937; LL.B., Harvard, 1941; m. Ruth Virginia Bewley, Feb. 25, 1942 (dec. 1964); children—Jay, Susan, Stephan; m. 2d, Marylin Grant, Feb. 10, 1968. Admitted to Okla. bar, 1941, since practiced Oklahoma City. Mem. ho. of reps. Okla. State Legislature, 1947; mem. state senate, 1949; mem. 82d-92d Congresses, 5th Okla. Dist. Served with AUS, 1942-45. Home: 1805 Huntington Oklahoma City OK 73116 Office: Rayburn House Office Bldg Washington DC 20515

JARMAN, JULIAN A., physician; b. Eatonton, Ga., 1909; M.D., Med. Coll. Ga., 1934. Intern, Trinity Hosp., Bklyn., 1934-35; sr. intern Queens Gen. Hosp., Jamaica, N.Y., 1935-36, asst. resident in surgery, 1936-37; resident in surgery Mt. Sinai Hosp., N.Y.C., 1937-38, asst. pathologist, 1938-39, asst. and research fellow, 1939-40, asst. surg. pathologist, 1939-40, clin. asst. surgeon, 1940-41; commd. in U.S. Army, 1941, advanced through grades to col.; ret., 1962; med. adviser Fulton-DeKalb Hosp. Authority, 1962-65; chief staff VA Hosp. Atlanta, 1965-69, dir., 1969-—. Decorated Bronze Star medal. Diplomate Am. Bd. Surgery. Office: VA Hosp 1670 Clairmont Rd NE Box 29457 Atlanta GA 30329

JARMAN, THOMAS RODES, JR., banker; b. Charlottesville, Va., Nov. 19, 1929; s. Thomas Rodes and Augusta (Firth) J.; student U. Va., 1948-51; B.B.A., U. Richmond, 1957; m. Paula Knickerbocker, June 19, 1955 (div. Oct. 30, 1966); children—James Cardwell, Kenneth Mills. Salesman, Addressograph-Miltigraph Corp., Richmond, Va., 1957-59; with United Virginia Bank State Planters (name changed by transfer to holding co. to United Virginia Bankshares Inc.), Richmond, Va., 1959-—, comml. marketing services officer, 1967-—. Served with AUS, 1952-54. Mem. Pub. Relations Soc. Am., Richmond Pub. Relations Assn. (membership chmn. 1970-71). Clubs: Country Club of Virginia, Deep Run Hunt, Farmington, Country. Home: 7 Country Squire Lane Richmond VA 23229 Office: 900 E Main St Richmond VA 23219

JARMAN, WALTON MAXEY, bus. exec.; b. Nashville, May 10, 1904; s. J. F. and Eugenia (Maxey) J.; ed. Mass. Inst. Tech.; m. Sarah Anderson, Oct. 10, 1928; children—Franklin, Anne, Eugenia. Sec.-treas. Jarman Shoe Co., 1925-32, pres., 1932-33; pres. Gen. Shoe Corp. (corp. name changed to GENESCO, Inc., 1959), Nashville, 1933-47, chmn., 1947-—; dir. S.H. Kress Co., H & M Rayne, Ltd. (London); trustee Greenfield Real Estate Investment Trust, Mut. Life Ins. Co. N.Y. Mem. Tenn. Tax Commn., 1949. Trustee, Moody Bible Inst., Nat. Jewish Hosp., Denver; bd. dirs. Freedoms Found.; v.p. So. Baptist Conv., 1959. Mem. Commodity Exchange, Nat. Boot and Shoe Mfrs. Assn. (dir.), Dirs. Inst., Am. Bible Soc. (v.p.), Eta Mu Pi, Pi Delta Epsilon, Theta Delta Chi, Theta Tau. Republican. Clubs: Capital Hill (Washington); Bellemeade Country, Blue Grass Country; Union League, Metropolitan (N.Y.C.). Author: Businessman Looks at the Bible. Editor: O Taste and See. Home: 3610 Woodlawn Dr Nashville TN 37215 Office: Box 941 Nashville TN 37202

JARRELL, CECIL PALMER, JR., dentist; b. Monroe, La., Jan. 8, 1936; s. Cecil Palmer and Mary (McClanahan) J.; student Westminster Choir Coll., 1954-55, La. State U., 1955-58, Northeast U., 1959-61, Loyola U. Dental Sch., New Orleans, 1961-66; m. Beverly Ann Bonebreak, Dec. 31, 1967; children—Elizabeth Ann, Kathryn Suzanne, Cecil Palmer III. Oral Surgeon Charity Hosp., New Orleans, 1966-68; individual practice dentistry, Monroe, La., 1971-—; mem. staff St. Francis Hosp., 1971-—, Glenwood Hosp., 1971-—. Served to capt. AUS, 1968-71. Mem. Am., La., Fifth Dist. Dental assns., Am. Assn. Hosp. Dentists, S.A.R., Sigma Alpha Epsilon, Xi Psi Phi. Episcopalian. Rotarian. Home: 608 Orleans St Monroe LA 71201 Office: 701 Walnut St Monroe LA 71201

JARRELL, WILBURN ERIC, physician; b. Floyd, Va., Mar. 14, 1926; s. Benjamin Alex and Mary Alma (Hancock) J.; B.A. in Psychology, U. Va., 1950, M.D., 1954; m. Jewel Beatrice Davis, Aug. 22, 1953; children— Wilburn Eric, Jr., Beverly Jewel, Davis Hancock, Susan Beatrice. Intern, U. Va. Hosp., 1954-55; pvt. gen. practice medicine, Ararat, Va., 1955-58, Mt. Airy, N.C., 1958-—; mem. staff No. Surry Hosp., Mt. Airy med. examiner Surry County, N.C., 1971-—; chief obstetric services No. Surry Hosp., Mt. Airy, N.C., 1971-—. Served with USNR, 1944-46; PTO. Democrat. Methodist. Kiwanian, Elk, Mason. Club: Cotillion (Mt. Airy). Home: 1001 Wilburn Rd Mt Airy NC 27030 Office: 2007 Salem Rd Mt Airy NC 27030

JARRETT, THOMAS DUNBAR, univ. pres.; b. Union City, Tenn., Aug. 30, 1912; s. William Robert and Annie Sybil (Thomas) J.; A.B., Knoxville Coll., 1933; A.M., Fisk U., 1937; Ph.D., U. Chgo., 1947; m. Annabelle Madeline Gunter, Aug. 22, 1939; 1 dau., Paula Lynn. Tchr., Central High Sch., Paris, Tenn., 1933-37; asst. prof. English, Knoxville Coll., 1937-40; asso. prof. English, Louisville Municipal Coll., 1941-43; prof. English, Atlanta U., 1955-67, acting dean Sch. Art and Scis., 1957-61, dean Grad. Sch., 1961-67, pres., 1968-—. Ford Found. fellowship lectr., Eng., 1953; mem. Mayor's Com. on Adult Education, Atlanta, 1962-64; cons. Dept. Health Edn. and Welfare Prospective Tchrs. Fellowship Program, 1966-68; adv. com. Nat. Def. Lang. Devel. Program, 1966-68, Ga. Sci. and Tech. Commn., 1969-—. Served to lt. inf. AUS, 1943-46. Fellow Gen. Edn. Bd., 1939-40; Carnegie grant for research, 1951-52. Mem. Nat. Council Tchrs. English (dir. 1963-—; chmn. nominating com. 1962, commn. on English 1968-—), Nat. Assn. Deans and Registrars (pres. 1968-69), Coll. Lang. Assn., Council Grad. Schs., U.S., Nat. Assn. Collegiate Deans and Registrars (v.p.), Kappa Boule, Sigma Pi Phi, Alpha Phi Alpha. Editor Language and Literature, 1959-64. Book and poetry editor Phylon, 1948-—. Contbr. to English Jour., monthly, 1959-64. Contbr. numerous articles profl. publs. Home: 691 Beckwith St SW Atlanta GA 30314

JARROTT, THELMA HATCHER (MRS. ARCH ADAMS JARROTT, JR.), bus. exec.; b. Marshall, Tex.; d. Edwin Lawrence and Minnie (Jennings) Hatcher; student East Tex. Bapt. Coll., 1929-31, N.Y. Sch. Design, 1944; A.A., Coll. Marshall; m. Cary McClure Abney, Jr., July 14, 1936 (dec.); m. 2d, Arch Adams Jarrott, Jr., June 12, 1946 (dec. Oct. 1963). Sec. to pres. Coll. Marshall, 1930-31; legal sec. Caven & Caen Attys., 1931-32; asst. sec. to mgr. Marshall C. of C., 1932-33; chief clk. County Agts. Office, 1933-34; bank sec., bookkeeper, teller State Nat. Bank, Marshall, 1934-43; sec. to officers Marshall Nat. Bank, 1945; owner Abney Ins. Agy., Marshall, 1945-47; sec. to gen. foreman Tex. & Pacific Ry. Co., 1948-49; sec.-treas. Sollberger Engring. Co., 1949-51; credit mgr. Hansons Paint & Glass Co., 1951-59; exec. dir. Marshall-Harrison County Assn. for Mental Health, 1961-62; social work State Dept. Pub. Welfare, Marshall, 1962-65, with quality control div., 1965-—; owner Thelma H. Jarrott, Investments, 1961-—. Mem. Gov.'s Commn. on Status of Women, 1970; organizer, 1st chmn. Harrison County Commn. on Status Women, 1971-—. Bd. dirs. Marshall Harrison County Assn. Mental Health, 1962-—; mem. Lyndon B. Johnson State Park Adv. Com., 1968-69. Mem. Harrison County Hist. Soc., Tex. Social Welfare Assn., Tex. Pub. Employees Assn., Am. Pub. Welfare Assn., Tex. Fedn. Bus. and Profl. Women's Clubs (past pres., award by bd. dirs. 1967), Pilot Club, Marshall Bus. and Profl. Women's Club (woman of achievement award 1968, Living Meml. award 1969), Harrison County Conservation Soc. (charter mem.). Mem. Order Eastern Star (past matron). Baptist. Democrat. Home: 200 Brownrigg Marshall TX 75670 Office: PO Box 484 and State Welfare Office Old Courthouse Marshall TX 75670

JARVIS, CHARLES WALTON, dentist; b. Waxahachie, Tex., Feb. 17, 1923; s. John Pelham and Betty (Douglass) J.; student U. Houston, 1948-49, Tex. A. and M. U., 1940; B.S., U.S. Naval Acad., 1944; D.D.S., U. Tex., 1953; m. Maxine Spiller, Jan. 26, 1946; 1 dau., Pam (Mrs. John Chester Foster). Pvt. practice dentistry, San Marcos, Tex., 1953-—; pub. speaker, 1960-—; pub., human relations lectr. Dentral br. U. Tex., 1961-—. Served with USN, 1941-44, 1946-48. Mem. Omicron Kappa Upsilon. Mem. Christian Ch. Kiwanian (pres. 1960). Recorded speeches: Prescription for the Happy Life, 1970; This Won't Hurt—Much, 1971. Home: 107 Rogers Ridge San Marcos TX 78666 Office: PO Box 1094 San Marcos TX 78666

JARVIS, HAROLD SIMS, banker; b. Chattanooga, Nov. 21, 1930; s. Storm Harold and Evelyn Leftwich (Sims) J.; B.A., U. Ala., 1952; LL.B., Woodrow Wilson Coll. Law, 1958; postgrad. Grad. Sch. Banking, Rutgers U., 1959; m. Joan Church, Aug. 28, 1954 (div. Mar. 31, 1969); 1 son, Harold Sims. Mem. trust dept. Birmingham Trust Nat. Bank (Ala.), 1952-54; comptroller currency, nat. bank examiner U.S. Treasury Dept., Atlanta, 1954-55; mem. trust dept. 1st Nat. Bank, Atlanta, 1955-59; admitted to Ga. bar, 1958; sr. trust officer Citizen & So. Nat. Bank S.C., Greenville, 1959-67, v.p., head urban affairs devel. dept., Columbia, 1967-—. Instr. estate planning Furman U., Greenville, 1963-64. Mem. finance com. Greenville County Found., 1965-66; mem. legacy com. S.C. chpt. Am. Cancer Soc., 1967; treas. Hosp. Bldg. Fund-Raising Compaign, Greenville, 1968-69; mem. adv. com. local commemorative events S.C. Tricentennial Commn., 1970-—; mem. adv. council comprehensive health planning State Bd. Health, 1970-—. Bd. dirs. Tamassee (S.C.) D.A.R. Schs., 1963-69, Community Council, Greenville, 1968-69, S.C. Wildlife Fedn., 1968-—; mem. adv. bd. Juvenile-Domestic Relations Ct., Richland County, 1970-—; trustee Columbia Indsl. Edn. Center, 1970-—; adv. trustee Action Found., 1969-—. Mem. Am., Ga. bar assns., Ala. Alumni Assn. (pres. 1967-—). Home: 1757 Tall Pines Circle Columbia SC 29205 Office: 1801 Main St Columbia SC 29204

JASPER, JOSEPH JAMES, judge; b. Wheeling, W.Va., July 16, 1927; s. James M. and Adele (George) J.; A.B., U. Ala., 1953, LL.B., 1954; m. Beatrice Imogene Lancaster, Sept. 2, 1954; children—Mary Ann, Debra Faye, Joseph Norman, Lisa Elizabeth. Admitted to Ala. bar, 1954; gen. practice law, 1954-65; elected judge Trussville (Ala.) Recorders Ct., 1958-63; judge Birmingham (Ala.) Recorders Ct., 1963-65, presiding judge, 1965-69; circuit judge 10th Jud. Circuit Ala., 1969-—. Mem. Inner Club Safety Com., Mayor's Traffic Safety Coordinating Com. Served with USNR, 1945-46, 50-52. Recipient Erskine Ramsay Civic award, 1970. Mem. Am., Ala., Birmingham bar assns., Ala. circuit judges assn., Amvets, V.F.W., Fraternal Order Police, Sigma Delta Kappa. Roman Catholic. Eagle, K.P., Knight of Khorrassan. Home: 315 Lawson Rd Birmingham AL 35215 Office: Jefferson County Court House Birmingham AL 35203

JAWORSKI, LEON, lawyer; b. Waco, Tex., Sept. 19, 1905; s. Joseph and Marie (Mira) J.; LL.B., Baylor U., 1925, LL.D., 1960; LL.M., George Washington U., 1926; m. Jeannette Adam, May 23, 1931 children—Joan, Claire, Joseph III. Admitted to Tex. bar, 1925; asso. firm Fulbright, Crooker, Freeman & Bates, Houston, also Washington, 1931-34, partner, 1934-51; sr. partner Fulbright, Crooker & Jaworski, Houston, 1951-—; spl. asst. U.S. atty. gen., 1962-65; spl. counsel atty. gen. Tex., 1963-65, 72; dir., mem. exec. com. Bank of S.W., Intercontinental Nat. Bank, Village Nat. Bank. Anderson, Clayton & Co., Gulf Printing Co., Gulf Pub. Co., Coastal States Gas Producing Co. (all Houston). Mem. Pres.'s Commn. on Law Enforcement and Adminstrn. of Justice; U.S. mem. Permanent (Internat.) Ct. of Arbitration, The Hague; chmn. Gov.'s Com. on Pub. Sch. Edn.; mem. Commn. on Marine Sci., Engring. and Resources, 1967-69, Pres.'s Commn. on Causes and Prevention of Violence 1968-69. Trustee Houston Legal Found.; bd. dirs. A.R.C., chpt. chmn., 1954-55; trustee United Fund, 1958-—; trustee, mem. exec. com. Southwestern Legal Found., chmn. bd. trustees, 1968-—; chmn. joint adminstrv. com. Tex. Med. Center, Baylor Coll. Medicine; pres. Baylor Med. Found.; trustee M.D. Anderson Found. Served as col. AUS, 1942-46, chief war crimes trial sect. Judge Adv. Gen. Dept., ETO. Fellow Am. Coll. Trial Lawyers (regent 1958-66, pres. 1961-62), Am. Bar Found.; mem. Nat. Conf. Christians and Jews (protestant chmn., mem. nat. bd.), State Bar Tex. (pres. 1962-63), Am. Law Inst., Am., Houston (pres. 1949) bar assns., Tex. Civil Jud. Council (pres. 1950-52), C. of C. (pres. 1960), Order of Coif, Phi Delta Phi. Presbyn. Clubs: Houston, Houston Country, Rotary (pres. 1955-56); Coronado, Headliners; Warwick. Author: After Fifteen Years, 1961. Home: 3665 Ella Lee Lane Houston TX 77027 Office: Bank of Southwest Bldg Travis and Walker Houston TX 77002

JAY, EDWARD GEORGE, JR., entomologist; b. Atlanta, Mar. 23, 1932; s. Edward George and Reba Allene (Davis) J.; B.S.A., U. Fla., 1958, M.S.A., 1961; Ph.D., U. Ga., 1970; m. Letitia Warren Little, June 10, 1954; children—Cheryl Diane, Douglas Edward. Med. entomologist U.S. Dept. Agr. Orlando, Fla., 1958-61, stored products entomologist, Savannah, 1961-—. Adj. prof. entomology U. Ga., Athens, 1970-—. Scoutmaster Boy Scouts Am. Tomo-Chi-Chi Council, 1968-71, com. chmn., 1971-—. Served with USN, 1951-55. Mem. Entomol. Soc. Am., Ga. Entomol. Soc., Ecol. Soc. Am., British Ecol. Soc., Am. Soc. Mammalogists, Sigma Xi. Home: 404 Sharondale Rd Savannah GA 31406 Office: PO Box 5125 Savannah GA 31403

JAY, JAMES ALBERT, ins. co. exec.; b. Superior, Wis., Aug. 24, 1916; s. Clarence William and Louie (Davies) J.; student pub. schs., Mpls.; m. Margie Hoffpauir, Dec. 23, 1941; 1 son, James A. Franchise with The Stauffer System of Cal., 1946-49; Ala. dist. mgr. Guaranty Savs. Life Ins. Co., Montgomery, Ala., 1949-51, state mgr. La., 1951-—, dir., 1952-—, La. gen. agent, 1964-—; La. gen agt. Gen. United Life Ins. Co. of Des Moines, 1969-—. Com. chmn. Attakapas council Boy Scouts Am., Alexandria, La., 1955, council commr., 1961-62, commr. Manchac dist., 1967-—. Served as cpl. USMC, 1942-45, PTO. Decorated Purple Heart. Mem. Baton Rouge Life Underwriters Assn., C. of C., Internat. Platform Assn. Methodist. Elk. Home: 5919 Clematis Dr Baton Rouge LA 70808 Office: 3404 Convention St Baton Rouge LA 70806

JAYCOX, WARREN CECIL, lawyer; b. East Fishkill, N.Y., Aug. 26, 1899; s. Charles Wilbur and Mabel (Horton) J.; LL.B. magna cum laude, Boston U., 1919. Admitted to Mass. bar, 1921; asso. with law firm Ropes, Gray, Best, Coolidge and Rugg, Boston, 1925-42; legislative atty. CAB, Washington 1946-65; mem. law firm Schleit & Jaycox, 1966-—. Served as pvt. U.S. Army, 1918; served from capt. to lt. col. USAAF, 1942-46; col. Res. Mem. Am., Fed. bar assns., Judge Adv. Gens. Assn., S.A.R. Presbyn. Mason. Club: University (Washington). Home: 3133 Connecticut Av NW Washington DC 20008 Office: 1028 Connecticut Av NW Washington DC 20036 also 214 West St Duxbury MA 02332

JAYSON, LESTER SAMUEL, govt. ofcl.; b. N.Y.C., Oct. 25, 1915; s. Morris and Mary (Gardner) J.; B.S.S. with spl. honors in History and Govt., Coll. City N.Y., 1936; J.D., Harvard, 1939; m. Evelyn Lederer, Feb. 6, 1943; children—Diane Frankie, Jill Karen. Admitted to N.Y. bar, 1940, U.S. Supreme Ct. bar; asso. firm Oseas & Pepper, N.Y.C., 1939-40, firm Marshal, Bratter, & Seligson, N.Y.C., 1940-42; spl. asst. to atty. gen. U.S., Washington, 1942-50; trial atty. Dept. Justice, Washington, 1951-56, chief torts sect., civil div., 1957-60; sr. specialist in Am. pub. law and chief Am. law div. Congl. Research Service, Library of Congress, Washington, 1960-62, dep. dir., 1962-66, dir., 1966-—. Wilton Park fellow, Brit. Fgn. Office, 1965. Mem. Am., Fed. (chmn. tort law com. 1967-68) bar assns., Pi Sigma Alpha. Author: Handling Federal Tort Claims: Judicial and Adminstrative Remedies, 1964, 68, 69, 70. Supervising editor: The Constitution of the U.S.A.-Analysis and Interpretation, 1964. Home: 7512 Newmarket Dr Bethesda MD 20034 Office: Library of Congress 10 1st St SW Washington DC 20540

JEANES, JOE WESLEY, profl. engr.; b. Houston July 9, 1927; s. John H. and Violet (Reitz) J.; B.S., U. Houston, 1949; m. Billie Frances Jowell, Apr. 6, 1946 children—Pamela Sue, Kathryn Kim, William H. Engr., Southwestern Labs., Houston, 1950-56, mgr., Beaumont, Tex., 1956-58, asst. dist. mgr., Gulf Coast dist., Houston, 1958-67, dist. mgr., Houston, 1967-—, also dir. Served with USNR, 1943-46. Mem. Am. Soc. C.E., Am. Concrete Inst., U. Houston Grad. Engrs. Assn., Houston Engrs. and Sci. Soc., Nat., Tex. (chpt. pres. elect 1971-72) socs. profl. engrs. Episcopalian. Club: Brae Burn Country. Home: 7903 Braesview Lane Houston TX 77071 Office: PO Box 8768 Houston TX 77009

JEFFARES, DONALD JACKSON, cons.; b. McDonough, Ga., Mar. 16, 1936; s. Arthur and Ruby (Jackson) T.; B.Ceramic Engring., Ga., Inst. Tech., 1959; m. Susan Hull, Aug. 7, 1956; children—Lori Susan, Donna Allyson, Donald Jackson. With Ferro Corp., Tyler, Tex., 1959-66; with Fla. Tile Industries, Lakeland, Fla., 1966-70, v.p. mfg., 1967-69, v.p., gen. mgr. tile div., 1969-70; cons., 1970—. Bd. dirs. Fla. Midland Corp., Lakeland. Mem. Am. Ceramic Soc., Methodist (mem. adminstrv. bd., chmn. finance com.). Rotarian. Home: Rt 1 Box 336 Lakeland FL 33803 Office: 1526 Commercial Park Dr Lakeland FL 33802

JEFFE, HULDAH CHERRY, artist; b. Dallas; d. Max Milton and Gertrude (Morgan) Cherry; grad. Miss Hockaday Sch., Dallas; studies art in Italy, France; student Grand Central Sch. Arts, N.Y. City; pupil Robert Brackman; m. Gen. Ephraim Franklin Jeffe, Dec. 29, 1945. Designed series of covers for Brides Mag., 1945-46; paintings reproduced in Mademoiselle, Vogue, Harper's Bazaar, Town and Country; prints works reproduced annually by N.Y. Graphic Soc.; paintings reproduced by Hallmark on greeting cards; represented in permanent collection Ga. Mus. Art; paintings in art displays arranged by Bonwit Teller, Dorothy Gray, Coty, Revlon, Saks-Fifth Av.; New designs of Huldah Girls for ceramic figurines by Hummelwerks, Bavaria, West Germany. W. Gaebel Co., West Germany, Awarded hon. mention Salon des Artistes Francais, Paris, France, 1948. Address: 680 S County Rd Palm Beach FL 33480

JEFFERS, LEROY, lawyer; b. Ferris, Tex., Oct. 15, 1909; LL.B., U. Tex., 1932. Admitted to Tex. bar, 1932; mem. firm Vinson, Elkins, Searls, Connally & & Smith, Houston. Chmn. bd. regents U. Tex.; pres. Houston Smith, Houston. Chmn. bd. regents U. Tex.; pres. Houston Legal Found.; bd. regents S. Tex. Sch. Law; trustee Episcopal Theol. Sem. S.W.; past chmn. bd. dirs. Tex. Bill of Rights Found. Fellow Am. Coll. Trial Lawyers; mem. State Bar Tex. (pres. elect 1972-73), Am. (chmn. sect. of antitrust), Houston (past pres.) bar assns., Order of Coif; Chancellors, Delta Theta Phi. Address: Vinson Elkins Searls & Connally 1st City Nat Bank Bldg. Houston, TX 77002

JEFFERS, THEBAUD, city ofcl.; b. Roxboro, N.C., July 5, 1911; s. George Washington and Leona Hortense (Humphrey) J.; A.B., Johnson C. Smith U., Charlotte, N.C., 1931; postgrad. Cornell U., 1936-37; M.A., U. So. Cal., 1940; m. Maude Marion Mitchell, Dec. 24, 1935. Tchr. English and French, Reid Sch., Belmont, N.C., 1932-37; prin. Highland Jr.-Sr. High Sch., Gastonia, N.C., 1940-68; asst. prof. edn. N.C. Central U., Durham, summers 1959-62. Mem. Gastonia City Council, 1963-69, mayor pro tem, 1969—. Pres. Excelsior Credit Union, 1945-57, Gaston Community Action, 1970, N.C. Educators Credit Union, 1970; sec. bd. dirs. Gaston Community Hosp., 1960-67. Recipient Silver Beaver award Boy Scouts Am., 1946; named Omega Man of Year, Gastonia, 1957. Mem. N.E.A. (life), P.T.A. (life), Omega Psi Phi. Mason, Elk. Home: 204 W Walnut Av Gastonia NC 28052 Office: Gaston County Schs Gastonia NC 28052

JEFFERSON, BEN ROBERT, oil investments exec.; b. Stamford, Tex., Nov. 7, 1933; s. Ephriam Dent and Ethel (Owens) J.; B.S., Tex. Technol. U. 1956; J.D., Baylor U., 1968; m. Imogene Hays, May 16, 1951; 1 son, Edward Du Wayne. Geophysicist, So. Geophys. Co,, Ft., Worth, 1952-53; geologist Pan Am. Petroleum Corp. (now Amoco Prodn. Co.), Ft. Worth, 1957-65; admitted to Tex. bar, 1968; trust officer Frost Nat. Bank, San Antonio, 1968-69; asst. v.p., fund mgr. Prudential Funds, Inc., Dallas, 1969—. Mem. Am. Bar Assn., Tex. State Bar, Am. Assn. Petroleum Geologists, Dallas Geol. Soc., Sigma Gamma Epsilon, Delta Theta Phi. Home: 3322 High Vista Dr Dallas TX 75234 Office: 1960 One Main Pl Dallas TX 75250

JEFFORDS, JOE SAM, state ofcl.; b. Lamar, S.C., Sept. 2, 1912; s. Samuel Joseph and Bessie Irene (Boykin) J.; B.S. in Civil Engring., Clemson U., 1936; m. Mary Emma Colclough, June 18, 1938; children— Samuel Joseph II, Ben Colough. With S.C. Hwy. Dept., 1936-42, W.C. Olsen Cons. Engrs., Raleigh, N.C., 1942-43, McClean Contracting Co., Balt., 1943-45; with S.C. Hwy. Dept., 1945—, dist. engr., 1967—. Mem. design and drafting adv. com. Orangeburg-Calhoun Tech. Ednl. Center, 1968—. Mem. S.C. Soc. Engrs. Methodist (ofcl. bd. 1960-66; trustee 1969—). Lion (v.p. 1st Orangeburg 1969). Home: 337 Pinehill St Orangeburg SC 29115 Office: PO Box 1086 Orangeburg SC 29115

JEFFRESS, CARL O., newspaper publisher; b. Greensboro, N.C., 1915; grad. U. N.C., 1938. Publisher, dir. Greensboro News Co., Pub. Greensboro News and Record; dir. First Union Nat. Bank. Pres., dir. Wesley Long Community Hosp. Home: 820 Country Club Dr Greensboro NC 27408 Office: 200-04 N Davie St Greensboro NC 27402*

JEFFREYS, ALVIS WALDO, JR., psychologist; b. South Hill, Va., Mar. 13, 1923; s. Alvis Waldo and Connie (Dodson) J.; student Hampden-Sydney Coll., 1941-43; B.A., U. Va., 1948; M.A., Mich. State U., 1950; Ph.D., U. Houston, 1953; m. Virginia Ogilvie, June 28, 1948; children—Jay C., Jan S. Instr. U. Tex. Med. Sch., 1950-52; asst. prof. Commonwealth U., Richmond, Va., 1953-54; chief psychologist Western State Hosp., Staunton, 1954—, dir. alcoholic unit, 1954—. Pres. Appalachian Dulcimer Corp., Staunton, Va., 1962—. Served with USNR, 1943-45. Home: 232 W Frederick St Staunton VA 24401 Office: Western State Hosp Staunton VA 24401

JEFFRIES, ALEXANDER HARDIE, JR., architect; b. Richmond, Va., Dec. 28, 1937; s. Alexander Hardie and Georgia Bryan (Grinnan) J.; grad. Hill Sch., Pottstown, Pa., 1956; student Hampden-Sydney Coll., 1956-57; B.Arch., U. Pa., 1961; m. Roberta Fleming Rust, Nov. 15, 1969. With Weihe, Black & Jeffries, Architects (and predecessor), Washington, 1961—, partner, 1968—. Mem. A.I.A. (corporate mem.). Contbr. design of Crystal City, Arlington, Va.; office bldgs. in Washington; Skyline Center, Fairfax County, Va. Home: 1722 Hoban Rd NW Washington DC 20007 Office: 1101 17th St NW Washington DC 20036

JEFFRIES, RICHARD MANNING, JR., lawyer; b. Walterboro, S.C., Oct. 30, 1919; s. Richard Manning and Annie S. (Savage) J.; A.B., U. S.C., 1942, LL.B., 1947; m. Emily Brown, Aug. 22, 1942; children—Richard Allan, Emily McBurney. Admitted to S.C. bar, 1947; partner Brown, Jeffries & Mazursky, Barnwell, S.C., 1947—. Pres. Barnwell Industries, Inc., 1950—. Chmn. S.C. Ednl. TV Commn., 1957—; county chmn. A.R.C., Barnwell, 1955-56. Sec., treas. Barnwell County exec. com. Democratic party, 1950—. Bd. visitors Presbyn. Coll., Clinton, S.C. Served to lt. USNR, 1942-45. Mem. Am. Legion (past comdr.). Presbyn. (deacon). Lion (past pres.). Home: 1906 Main St Barnwell SC 29812 Office: Bankers Trust Bldg Barnwell SC 29812

JEKO, LESLIE JEWEL, accountant; b. Port Arthur, Tex., Mar. 1, 1930; s. Jewel Edward and Hazel (Heard) J.; B.B.S., Trinity U., 1954; B.B.A., U. Tex., 1957; m. 2d, Parr Davidson, Dec. 24, 1950; children— Catherine Parr, Cynthia Lea. Auditor, Ernst & Ernst, Houston, 1957-60; asst. controller David C. Bintliff Interests, Houston, 1961-62; div. auditor Pure Oil Co., Houston, 1962-64; pvt. practice accounting, Houston, 1964—; sec., dir. W.W. Properties, Inc., Houston, 1970—. Served with USAF, 1950-54. Mem. Am. Inst. C.P.A.'s, Tex., Houston socs. C.P.A.'s, Petroleum Accountants Soc. Houston. Baptist. Mason. Home: 7718 Bellaire Blvd Houston TX 77036 Office: 3926 W Main St Houston TX 77027

JELKS, FREEMAN NAPIER, securities co. exec.; b. Hawkinsville, Ga., Mar. 15, 1903; s. Nathaniel Augustus and Lila Jeanette (Napier) J.; student U. Va., 1920-21; LL.B., U. Ga., 1925; m. Retta Fannin Conly, Oct. 30, 1928; children—Freeman Napler, Jr., Retta (Mrs. Allen I. Vance). Salesman Citizens & So. Co., Savannah, Ga., 1926-33; with Johnson, Lane, Space, Smith & Co., Inc., Savannah, 1933-72, v.p., 1933—. Mem. Phi Delta Theta, Phi Delta Phi. Baptist (deacon 1927-30). Clubs: Chatham, Oglethorpe, Golf (pres. 1944-45) (Savannah). Home: 28 E 56th St Savannah GA 31405 Office: 101 E Bay St Savannah GA 31401

JEMISON, FRANK ZIMMERMAN, financial, motor hotel, real estate exec.; b. Memphis, July 10, 1920; s. William Dearing and Blanche (Zimmerman) J.; B.S., Miss. State U., 1941; m. Peggy Boyce, Apr. 10, 1947; children— Frank Zimmerman, Marguerite Bailey, David Marshall. Exec. v.p. W.D. Jemison & Sons, Inc. subsidiary AMCON Internat., Inc., Memphis, 1945-55, pres., 1955—; chmn. bd., treas., dir. AMCON Internat., Inc., 1968—; chmn. bd., dir. Modern Diversified Industries, Valdosta, Ga.; exec. v.p., dir. Winter Garden Freezer Co.; dir. Tenn. Foods, Inc., United Foods, Inc. Bd. dirs. Edn. For Freedom, Atlanta; mem. pres.'s council Southwestern U. Memphis; trustee, treas. Memphis U. Sch. Mem. Chief Execs. Forum. Presbyn. (elder). Rotarian. Clubs: University, Memphis Country. Home: 1054 Aubudon Dr Memphis TN 38117 Office: AMCON International Inc 2731 Nonconnah Blvd S PO Box 30303 Memphis TN 38130

JEMISON, T.J., gen. sec. Nat. Baptist Conv. U.S. Address: 915 Spain St Baton Rouge LA 70802*

JEMISON, WILLIAM DEARING, JR., hotel chain exec; b. Memphis, July 3, 1918; s. William D. and Blanche (Zimmerman) J.; student Southwestern U., 1937-38; B.S. in Bus. Adminstrn., Miss. State U., 1940; postgrad. U. Tenn., 1947; m. Eva Lee Williams, Nov. 12, 1947; children— Blanche Lee, William Dearing, Ethel Gay. With W.D. Jemison & Sons, 1953-56, exec. v.p., 1956-63; pres. Mid-Continent Corp., 1963; now pres. AMCON Internat., Inc. and predecessor cos., Memphis. Mem. exec. com. Future Memphis, 1963—; pres. Porter Leath Children's Center, 1960—. Served to maj. USAAF, 1942-46. Mem. Home Builders Assn. (past pres.), Nat. Assn. Home Builders (dir. 1953-60), Memphis C. of C. (dir.), Kappa Alpha. Clubs: University, Chickasaw Country (Memphis). Home: 47 Avon St Memphis TN 38117 Office: 2731 Nonconnah Blvd Memphis TN 38131

JENKINS, ADAM, JR., coll. bus. mgr.; b. North Carrollton, Miss., Sept. 9, 1942; s. Adam and Annie (Hill) J.; B.S., Alcorn A. and M. Coll., 1967; student U. Omaha, summer 1968; Miss. State U., 1968-69; m. Margaraee Gordon, June 10, 1962; children—Veronica, Randolph, Darryl. Cashier Utica (Miss) Jr. Coll., 1967-68, bus. mgr., 1969—; cons. Natchez Jr. Coll. Mem. Miss. Jr. Coll. Bus. Mgrs. Assn., Nat. Assn. Colls. and U. Bus. Officers, N.E.A., Miss. Teachers Assn., N.A.A.C.P., Phi Beta Sigma (sec.-treas. 1971-72). Home: North Carrollton MS Office: Utica Jr Coll Utica MS 39175

JENKINS, ARTHUR WARREN, state ofcl.; b. Ava, Mo., Sept. 23, 1921; s. Robert Fulton and Daisy (Shelton) J.; student pub. schs., Coffeyville, Kan.; m. Martha Levenia Williams, Oct. 26, 1946; 1 dau., Sharon Kay; m. 2d, Victoria Hamilton, June 26, 1970; children—Lisa, Kristi, Scott. Dockman, checker Chief Freight Lines, Tulsa, 1940-41, asst. terminal mgr., 1946-47; owner, mgr. B and BLines, Tulsa, 1947-49, partner, 1950-51; pres. Rocket Freight Lines Co., Tulsa, 1952-66, chmn. bd., 1966—; chmn. bd. Tuloma Rigging, Inc., 1966—; pres. Accounts Finance Corp., 1965—; now exec. asst. to gov. Okla. Bd. dirs. Southwestern Motor Freight Bur., 1961-63.; chmn. Shortline Carrier Conf., Inc., 1966-67. Served with USAAF, 1941-45. Decorated D.F.C., Air medal with four oak leaf clusters. Mem. Okla. Class A Short Lines Motor Carriers Assn. (pres. 1953, 55), Tulsa Motor Carriers Assn. (pres. 1952), Regular Route Motor Common Carrier Assn. Okla. (chmn., dir.). Mem. Disciples of Christ Ch. (dir. 1959-60). Mason (32 deg., Shriner), Elk. Club: Cosmopolitan (pres. Tulsa 1960, internat. v.p. 1962-63). Home: 3245 Hickory Stick Rd Oklahoma City OK 73120 Office: State Capitol Bldg Oklahoma City OK

JENKINS, CHARLES RODERICK, physician; b. Ellisville, Miss., Nov. 20, 1912; A.B., U. Ala., 1932; M.D., Tulane U., 1936. Intern, Highland Sanitarium, New Orleans, 1936-37; resident Lutheran Hosp., Balt., 1938-39, Akins (S.C.) Hosp., 1939-40, Brooks Gen. Hosp., San Antonio, 1945; pvt. practice medicine, specializing in gen. practice, Ellisville, 1937-45, Laurel, Miss., 1945—. Served with M.C., AUS, 1940-45. Mem. A.M.A., Miss. Med. Assn. (pres.), Jones County, South Miss. med. socs., Am. Acad. Family Practice, Southeastern Surg. Congress. Office: The Medical Center 535 5th Av Laurel MS 39440

JENKINS, CLARA BARNES, educator; b. Franklinton, N.C.; d. Walter and Stella (Griffin) Barnes; B.S., Winston-Salem State U., 1939; M.A., N.C. Central U., 1947; Ed.D., U. Pitts., 1965; postgrad. N.Y. U., 1947-48, U. N.C., N.C. Agrl. and Tech. State U.; m. Hugh Morris Jenkins, Dec. 24, 1949 (div. Feb. 1955). Faculty Fayetteville State U., 1945-53, Rust Coll., Holly Spring, Miss., 1953-58; asst. prof. Shaw U., 1958-65; now prof. edn St. Paul's Coll., Lawrenceville, Va.;vis. prof. edn. Friendship Jr. Coll., Rock Hill, S.C., summer 1947, N.C. Agr. and Tech. State U., summers 1966-71. United Negro Coll. Fund Faculty fellow, 1963-64; grant recipient Am. Bapt. Conv., Valley Forge, Pa., 1963-64. Mem. Am. Assn. U. Profs., Nat. Soc. for Study Edn., N.E.A., Am. Assn. U. Women, Am. Hist. Assn., Va. Edn. Assn., Am. Acad. Polit. and Social Sci., A.A.A.S., Internat. Platform Assn., Doctoral Assn. Educators, Assn. Tchr. Educators, Marquis Biog. Library Soc., Am. Assn. for Higher Edn., Acad. Polit. Sci., Am. Psychol. Assn., History of Edn. Soc., Phi Eta Kappa, Zeta Phi Beta. Episcopalian. Home: 920 Bridges St Henderson NC 27536 Office: St Pauls Coll Lawrenceville VA 23868

JENKINS, DONALD, banker; b. Milw., Jan. 22, 1919; s. Lee C. and Mathilda (Thielecke) J.; student Columbia, 1940-41; m. Gloria J. Killans, Apr. 15, 1945; children—Victoria G. (Mrs. Guy Bowers), Michael S., Roseanna L., Roberta M. Asst. to treas. Bank of Commerce, N.Y.C., 1945-46; v.p., treas. Community State Bank, Albany, N.Y., 1947-62; (also dir.); v.p., sec. Financial Gen. Bankshares Inc., Washington, 1962—; dir. Bank of Buffalo, Chesapeake Nat. Bank (Towson, Md.), Peoples Nat. Bank (Leesburg, Va,), Valley Nat. Bank (Harrisonburg, Va.), Financial Gen. Bankshares Inc. (Washington), Morris Plan Corp. (N.Y.C.). Mem. Va., Consumer bankers assns. Lion. Club: Farmington Country (Va.). Home: 9022 Hamilton Dr Fairfax VA 22030 Office: Financial General Bankshares Inc 1701 Pennsylvania Av NW Washington DC 20006

JENKINS, ERBY LEE, lawyer; b. Raccoon Valley, Tenn., Sept. 19, 1907; s. Marion Lockwood and Bertha Alma (Smith) J.; student Racoon Valley Acad., U. Tenn.; LL.B., Cumberland U., 1931; m. Neil Hubbs, Apr. 26, 1929; 1 son, Ray Lee. Admitted to Tenn. bar, 1931, since practiced in Knoxville; mem. firm Jenkins & Jenkins; spl. justice Supreme Ct. Tenn., 1965, 69. Chmn., Knox County Republican Exec. Com., 1942-48, 50-58; mem. Tenn. Rep. Exec. Com., 1956—, chmn., 1962—. Fellow Am. Bar Found., Am. Coll. Trial Lawyers (sec.), Internat. Acad. Trial Lawyers; mem. Am. (state del., bd. govs.), Internat. bar assns., Bar Assn. Tenn. (pres. 1959-60), Phi Delta Phi. Home: 4608 Tazewell Pike Knoxville TN 37918 Office: Bank Knoxville Bldg Knoxville TN 37902

JENKINS, HERBERT T., city ofcl. Police chief Atlanta. Office: Police Dept 165 Decatur St SE Atlanta GA 30303

JENKINS, JAMES, clergyman. Ordained to ministry United Methodist Ch. Supt., Memphis conf. United Meth. Ch. Office: PO Box 314 533 College St Brownsville TN*

JENKINS, JOHN HOLMES, III, publisher; b. Beaumont, Tex., Mar. 22, 1940; s. J. Holmes and Sue (Chalmers) J.; grad. U. Tex., 1963; m. Maureen Vera Mooney, June 5, 1962; 1 son, John Holmes IV. Pub., The Pemberton Press, Austin, 1962—, Southwestern Art Jour., 1965—, Jenkins Book Pub. Co., Inc., 1968—; pres. Country Store Gallery, Inc., 1963—, The Jenkins Co., 1962—, Fine Arts Corp., 1969—, India, Inc., 1969—. Bd. dirs. Collectors Inst. Served with AUS, 1966. Fellow Tex. State Hist. Assn.; charter mem. Western History Assn.; mem. Appraisers Assn. Am., Delta Tau Delta. Author: Recollections of Early Texas, 1958; Neither The Fanatics Nor the Fainthearted, 1963; Honest Bob and the Texas Congress, 1964; Jenkins Land Guide to the City of Austin, 1964; Cracker Barrel Chronicles, 1965; Patriotic Songs and Poems of Early Texas, 1966; Aubudon's Southwest, 1967; The Texas Navy, 1967; The Life of Frank Hamer, 1968. Home: Cromwell Hill Austin TX 78703 Office: Box 2085 Austin TX 78767

JENKINS, LEEMAN LEROY, ednl adminstr.; b. Baldwin, Fla., Mar. 26, 1930; s. Wilbur Kirley and Selata (Williams) J.; student U. Tampa, 1952-53; B.S., Fla. So. Coll., 1956; M.Ed., U. Ga., 1959, student, 1960-63; student U. Va., summer 1964, Auburn U., 1965; Ed.D., Atlanta U., 1971; m. Frances Linda Owen, June 12, 1954; children—Mark, Todd, Gay. Football coach, Waycross, Ga., 1956-58; bldg. prin., Waycross Ga., 1959-60; asst. prin. Southwest DeKalb High Sch., 1960-61, prin., 1961-62; prin. Gordon High Sch., DeKalb County, 1962-66; exec. v.p. Fran Tarkenton Inc., Atlanta, 1966-67; sales mgr. Josten's, Atlanta, 1967-69; supt. Bremen (Ga.) Pub. Schs., 1969—. Mem. Ga. State Bd. Edn., 1967-69. Served with USNR, 1948-52. Mem. Nine County Metro-Atlanta High Sch. Prins. Assn. (sec. 1964-65, pres. 1965-66), Phi Delta Kappa. Baptist. Kiwanian. Home: 615 Poplar St Bremen GA 30110 Office: Lamar County Bd Edn 204 Gordon Rd Barnesville GA 30204

JENKINS, LEO WARREN, coll. pres.; b. Succasunna, N.J., May 28, 1913; s. Warren Maylon and Cecelia (McPeek) J.; B.S., Rutgers U., 1935; M.A., Columbia, 1937; grad. study Duke, summer 1937; Ed.D., N.Y.U., 1941; m. Lillian Olga Jacobsen, Oct. 11, 1942; children—James, Jeffrey, Patricia, Sallie, Jack, Suzanne. Tchr. English and social studies Pleasantville (N.J.) High Sch., 1935-37; tchr. history, dean boys Somerville (N.J.) High Sch., 1937-41; supr. practice tchrs., faculty mem. Montclair (N.J.) State Tchrs. Coll., 1945-46; asst. higher edn. N.J. Dept. Edn., Trenton, 1946-47; dean instrn., dir. summer sch. E. Carolina Coll., Greenville, N.C., 1947-59, v.p., 1959-60, pres., 1960—. Dir., Wachovia Bank & Trust Co., Carolina Tel. & Tel. Mem. Gov.'s Com. for Pub. Schs., Gov.'s Commn. on Edn. Beyond High Sch., Gov.'s Commn. on Financial Aid, N.C. Commn. for Internat. Trade, N.C. Adv. Com. Ednl. Administrn.; cons. N.C. Edn. Commn.; adviser to dir. div. spl. edn. N.C. Dept. Edn. Resource-Use Edn. Commn.; ednl. chmn. N.C. Congress Parents and Teachers; mem. N.C. Sch. Survey Panel; mem. com. on allied health professions, nat. commn. on accrediting Am. Assn. State Colls. and Univs.; mem. State Atomic Energy Adv. Com.; chmn. Council Presidents State Instns. Higher Edn. Chmn. Pitt County Polio Campaign, 1950, Pitt County Red Cross Fund Campaign;. Bd. dirs. N.C. League for Crippled Children, Louisburg Coll., N.C. Zool. Authority, N.C. Repertory theater; del. White House Conf. Edn.; del. Uniting Meth. Conf., Southeastern Jurisdictional Conf. Served as capt. USMC, Guadalcanal, Guam, Iwo Jima, 1942-46; capt. Res. Decorated Bronze Star medal (2), Presidential Unit citation. Mem. N.E.A., Am. Assn. Sch. Administrs., Newcomen Soc. N. Am., Am. Legion, N.C. Assn. Acad. Deans (pres.), Kappa Delta Pi, Phi Delta Kappa, Lambda Chi Alpha, Phi Mu Alpha, Alpha Phi Omega. Methodist, (steward). Clubs: Kiwanis (dir., past pres.), Executives (dir. Pitt County). Home: 605 E 5th St Greenville NC 27834

JENKINS, LLOYD THEODORE, chemist; b. Lead, S.D., Feb. 2, 1919; s. Alfred and Ramona (Snyder) J.; B.S., Colo. State Coll., 1949; M.S., U. Okla., 1951; m. Wylodine Reeves, Sept. 1, 1944; children—Richard, Linda, Thomas. Research chemist polymers Union Carbide Co., Texas City, Tex., 1951-54, Chemstrand Co., Decatur, Ala., 1954-58; mgr. patent liaison Chemstrand Research Center, Raleigh, N.C., 1958-70, supr. product technology, Pensacola, Fla., 1970—. Mem. Cary Planning and Zoning Commn., 1963—. Served with USAAF, 1941-46. Decorated Air medal, D.F.C. Mem. Am. Chem. Soc. Research and devel. on polymers, polymer evaluation, synthetic fibers, fiber evaluation. Home: 3540 Alpha Pl Pensacola FL 32503 Office: Chemstrand Technical Center Pensacola FL 32802

JENKINS, MARION T., physician; b. Hughes Springs, Tex., 1917; M.D., U. Tex., 1940. Intern, U. Kan. Hosp., Kansas City, 1940-41; asst. resident internal medicine John Sealy Hosp., Galveston, Tex., 1941-42; resident in surgery Parkland Meml. Hosp., Dallas, 1946-47; asst. resident anesthesiology Mass. Gen. Hosp., Boston, 1947-48; dir. anesthesiology Children's Med. Center, Presbyn. Hosp.; cons. anesthesiology VA Hosp., Lisbon, Tex., Baylor U. Med. Center, Dallas, Meth. Hosp., St. Paul Hosp.; McDermott prof., chmn. dept. anesthesiology U. Tex. Southwestern Med. Sch. at Dallas. Fellow Royal Coll. Surgeons; mem. A.M.A., Am. Soc. Anesthesiologists (pres.), Am. Coll. Allergists, Am. Urol. Assn., Internat. Anesthesia Research Soc., Australian Soc. Anesthesiologists. Office: Southwestern Med Sch Univ Tex Dallas TX 75235*

JENKINS, R. LEE, diversified co. exec.; b. Beggs, Okla., 1929; A.B., U. Okla., 1952, LL.B., 1956; LL.M., N.Y. U., 1959. Admitted to Okla. bar, 1956; asso. firm Allende & Brea, 1959-60; exec. v.p., gen. counsel White Eagle Internat., Inc., 1960-65; v.p. corporate devel., dir. Plough, Inc., Memphis, 1965—; dir. Schering Corp. Served to capt. USMCR, 1952-54. Home: 6998 Poplar St Germantown TN 38083 Office: 3022 Jackson Av Memphis TN 38122*

JENKINS, ROBERT DARRELL, state ofcl.; b. Potecasi, N.C., July 11, 1929; s. Arthur Thomas and Martha (Draper) J.; B.S., N.C. State U., 1951; m. Anne Hodge Beale, June 1, 1952; children—Robert Darrell, David Thomas. Vocational agr. tchr. Hobbsville, N.C., 1953-54, Jackson, N.C., 1954-61; marketing specialist N.C. Dept. Agr., 1961-64; food industries specialist and regional rep. N.C. Dept Conservation and Devel., 1964-66, asso. exec., 1966—. Served with AUS, 1951-53. Decorated Bronze Star. Mem. Kappa Phi Kappa, Alpha Gamma Rho. Democrat. Baptist. Mason. Home: 528 Cooper Rd Raleigh NC 27610 Office: 505 Oberlin Rd Raleigh NC 27605

JENKINS, THOMAS EVERTS, ofcl. NSF; b. Scranton, Pa., Apr. 21, 1924; s. William Arthur and Thelma Marie (Atwell) J.; student Lincoln U., 1940-43; A.B. in Pub. Adminstrn., U. Cal. at Berkeley, 1947, postgrad., 1947-48; postgrad. Am. U., 1950-52; m. Carrie L. Moore, Nov. 27, 1963; children—Maria, Thomas, Carolyn, Jacqueline, Brent. Analyst, budget officer Naval Research Lab., Washington, 1951-55, dep. comtroller, bus. mgr. Project Vanguard, 1955-58; adminstrv. officer Goddard Flight Center NASA, Greenbelt, Md., 1958-59. program mgmt. officer space flight programs, Washington, 1959-61, asst. dir. mgmt. reports, 1961-63, dir. program reports div., 1963-68, asst. dir. Apollo Project, 1968-69; dep. asst. dir. adminstrn. NSF, 1969—. Served with USNR, 1943-46. Recipient Superior Civilian Service award Dept. Navy, 1960, Exceptional Service medal NASA, 1969. Mem. Am. Mgmt. Assn., Soc. Advancement Mgmt., Am. Soc. Pub. Adminstrn., A.A.A.S. Home: 2847 Hillcrest Dr SE Washington DC 20020 Office: NSF 1800 G St NW Washington DC 20550

JENKINS, THOMAS MILLER, coll. pres.; b. Hot Springs, Va, Apr. 23, 1925; s. Beaufort Z. and Pauline (Beale) J.; B.A. summa cum laude, W.Va. State Coll., 1946; LL.B. cum laude, Boston U., 1950; m. Evelyn Mildred Keys, Sept. 15, 1950; 1 son, Thomas Miller III. Admitted to Mass. bar, 1950, Tex. bar, 1951; dep. research dir. Mass. Re-Codification Commn., Boston, 1949-51; law librarian, asst. prof. law Tex. So. U., 1951-53; dean, prof. law Fla. A. and M. U., 1953-65; pres. Albany (Ga.) State Coll., 1965—. Faculty adviser Fla. Bar com. municipal law, traffic cts. and safety, memls., also Communist tactics, strategy and objectives, 1958-65; mem. com. legal edn. and admissions to bar Fla. Supreme Ct., 1958-65; mem. Ga. Adult Edn. Council, 1967—, Ga. Assn. Coll., 1966—; exec. com. Nat. Bar Assn., 1959—, world peace through law com., 1961 ; spl. cons. wage and hour pub. contracts div. Dept. Labor, 1963—. Sec., trustee Fla. A. and M. Hosp., 1963-65; bd. dirs. legal edn. Southwest Bar Assn., 1958-65, United Fund Dougherty County, 1968—, Ga. Planning Commn., 1968—; v.p., bd. dirs. Albany Urban League, 1968—; v.p. Chehaw council Boy Scouts Am., 1968—. Recipient citations Kappa Alpha Psi, Tallahassee Bus. League, Chehaw Council Boy Scouts Am., Southwest Bar Assn., English High Sch., Boston, W.Va. State Coll., Boston U.; recipient plaque Nat. Assn. Colored Women's Clubs, 1966. Albany Ministers Wives, 1967. Contbr. profl. jours. Home: 129 Peyton Pl SW Atlanta GA 30311

JENKINS, WILLIAM LEWIS, lawyer, govt. ofcl.; b. Detroit, Nov. 29, 1936; s. Lewis C. and Maud (Wilson) J.; B.S., Tenn. Tech. Inst.; J.D., U. Tenn.; m. Mary Kathryn Myers, June 12, 1959; children—Rebecca, Georgeanne, Lewis, Douglas. Admitted to Tenn. bar, 1962; practice law, Rogersville 1962—; partner firm Hyder, Jenkins & Boyd, 1962-70; mem. Tenn. Ho. of Reps. from Hancock County, 1962—, speaker, 1969—; commr. conservation State of Tenn., 1971—. Served with AUS, 1959-60. Home: Arnold Rd Brentwood TN 37027

JENKS, GEORGE FRANCIS, newspaper exec.; b. Detroit, Oct. 19, 1908; s. Frank H. and Julia (Pennington) J.; A.B., Colo. Coll., 1929; m. Louise McMahon, July 19, 1937; children—Judith P., George M., Frank M., Ann B. Staff, Wood County News, Bowling Green, O., 1930-32; successively reporter, legislative corr., asst. to publisher Toledo Blade, 1933-38, chief Washington Bur., 1958—. Mem. Sigma Delta Chi. Clubs: Nat. Press (Washington); Press of Ohio. Home: 5315 Carvel Rd Washington DC 20016 Office: Nat Press Bldg Washington DC 20004

JENKS, WILFRED, internat. labor organ. exec. Dir. gen. ILO, Washington. Address: 666 11th St NW Washington DC 20001*

JENKS, WILLIAM ALEXANDER, historian, educator; b. Jacksonville, Fla., Jan. 20, 1918; s. Thomas William and Marjorie (Garvie) J.; B.A., Washington and Lee U., 1939; M.A., Columbia, 1940, Ph.D., 1949; m. Dorothy Jane Irving, Dec. 26, 1949; children—Margaret Elaine, Thomas William II. Faculty, Washington and Lee U., Lexington, Va., 1946—, asso. prof., 1951-56, prof., 1956—; vis. asst. prof. U. Va., 1950-52; vis. prof. Duke, summer 1963, U. Md., summer 1966, Va. Mil. Inst., spring 1967. Served with OSS, AUS, 1942-45. Faculty fellow Fund for Advancement Edn., 1954-55; recipient Fulbright research award, Austria, 1955; Social Sci. Research Council faculty fellow, 1961-62; fellow Am. Council Learned Socs., 1967-68. Mem. Am. Hist. Assn., Phi Beta Kappa, Omicron Delta Kappa, Sigma Nu. Democrat. Presbyn. Author: The Austrian Electoral Reform of 1907, 1950; Vienna and the Young Hitler, 1960; Austria under the Iron Ring, 1879-1893, 1965. Home: 617 Marshall St Lexington VA 24450

JENNINGS, AMY REBECCA, librarian; b. Murfreesboro, Tenn., May 17, 1907; d. E. Bertram and Lillian Lee (Jordan) Jennings; student Middle Tenn. State Tchrs. Coll., 1929-33; A.B., Cumberland U., 1940; B.S. in L.S., George Peabody Coll. Tchrs., 1942. Tchr., prin. pub. schs. Wilson County, Tenn., 1927-39; librarian city sch. systems, Tenn., Miss., 1939-42; reference librarian Law Library, Social Security Bd., Washington, 1943, Law Library, U.S. Dept. Agr., Washington, 1943-44; chief librarian NLRB, Washington, 1944-47; chief librarian FTC, Washington, 1947-72, librarian, adviser to exec. dir. for adminstrn., 1972—. Trustee Falls Church (Va.) Pub. Library. Mem. Law Librarians' Soc. D.C. (sec. 1946-48), Spl. Libraries Assn. (Washington chpt. chmn. legislative reference sect. 1946-48), D.A.R., Nat. Trust Historic Preservation. Episcopalian. Contbr. articles to profl. jours. Home: 417 Poplar Dr Falls Church VA 22046 Office: FTC Pennsylvania Av at 6th St NW Washington DC 20004

JENNINGS, ARTHUR HOWARD, agrl. exec.; b. Tulia, Tex., May 14, 1909; s. Richard Otto and Nora (Johnson) J.; B.S., West Tex. State U., 1933; m. Anna Myrtle Duke, Nov. 30, 1933; children—Linda (Mrs. James Brent Joy), Eldon Ray. Tchr. Y-L Sch., Muleshoe, Tex., 1933-34; tchr. Salem Sch., Tulia, Tex., 1934-35; tchr. Stone Sch., Canyon, Tex., 1935-39; farmer nr. Tulia, Tex., 1941—; dir. Houston Elevator, 1959—, Tulia Feed Lot, 1963—, Houston Fertilizer Supply 1959—; owner farm Yuma, Ariz. and Tulia, 1962—. Bd. dirs. Lubbock Christian Coll. Democrat. Mem. Central Ch. Christ (elder 1958—). Home and Office: Rt 1 Tulia TX 79088

JENNINGS, FEENAN DEE, ofcl. NSF; b. Los Angeles, Aug. 11, 1923; s. John Thomas and Rhesa Lorrain (Owens) J.; A.A. Compton Jr. Coll., 1948; B.S. in Chem. Engring., N.M. A. and M.U., 1950; postgrad. Scripps Instn. Oceanography, U. Cal., 1950-51, 53-55, U. Cal. at Los Angeles, 1951-52; m. Marylou Forman, Dec. 26, 1965; children— David, Lorraine. Sr. engr. Scripps Instn. Oceanography, 1955-58; oceanographer Geophysics br. Office Naval Research, 1958-66. dir. ocean sci. and tech. div., 1966-70; head office internat. decade ocean exploration NSF, Washington, 1970—. Served with USNR, 1942-46. Recipient Meritorious Civilian award Dept. Navy, 1960; Superior Ser. award, 1966; Mil. Oceanography award, 1970. Home: 10016 Taylor Av Oxon Hill MD 20022 Office: 1800 G St NW Washington DC 20550

JENNINGS, FRANK CLAY, author, publisher, printing co. exec.; b. Garrard County, Ky., June 30, 1913; s. Hamlet Manford and Jane (Reynolds) J.; student pub., pvt. schs. Ky.; m. Helen Maurine Music, Aug. 24, 1940. Area finance officer Fed. Works Agy., Ky., 1935-41; chief wage adminstr. War Dept., Ft. Knox, 1942-46; free lance writer, 1947-49; asso. editor Thoroughbred Record, 1950-51, mng. editor, 1952-54, exec. dir. Thoroughbred Record, Inc., gen. mgr. Thoroughbred Press, Inc., 1955—, treas., 1957—; dir. v.p., treas. Record Pub. Co., Inc., 1963—. Mem. Lexington Kennel Club, Throughbred Club Am., Thoroughbred Farm Mgrs. Club: Blue Grass Sportsmens' League. Home: 1715 Courtney Av Lexington KY 40502 Office: PO Box 580 Lexington KY 40505

JENNINGS, HENRY SMITH, JR., physician; b. Cordele, Ga., May 22, 1922; s. Henry Smith and Lillian (Cannon) J.; B.S., Emory U., 1942, M.D., 1945; m. Elizabeth Pruett Martin, Sept. 28, 1943; children—Elizabeth M., Henry Smith III. Intern Grady Meml. Hosp., Atlanta, 1945-46; resident Lawson VA Hosp., 1948-50, Emory U. Hosp., 1950-51; mem. staff Emory U. Clinic, 1951-53; partner Jennings, Stribling, Poole and Butts, Gainesville, Ga., 1953-71; partner Northeast Ga. Diagnostic Clinic, Gainesville, Ga., 1971—; instr. medicine Emory U. Sch. Medicine; dist. med. cons. Vocational Rehab. div. State Dept. Edn. Dir. Gainesville Nat. Bank. Commr. Gainesville Housing Authority, 1965; mem. Chattahoochee Dist. com. Boy Scouts Am., 1957-59. Bd. dirs. Ga. Med. Care Found. Served to capt. M.C., AUS, 1946-48. Diplomate Am. Bd. Internal Med. Mem. Ga. Heart Assn. (pres. 1966-67), Ga. Soc. Internal Medicine (pres. 1961-62), Med. Assn. Ga. (v.p. 1964-66), A.M.A., Hall County Med. Soc. (pres. 1961-62), A.C.P., So. Med. Assn., Sigma Alpha Epsilon, Phi Chi. Methodist (chmn. adminstrv. bd. 1968-70). Clubs: Chattahoochee Country, Kingwood Country; Atlanta City. Home: 1304 Springdale Rd NE Gainesville GA 30501 Office: 1114 Vine St NE Gainesville GA 30501

JENNINGS, HOWARD WILLIAM, II, optometrist; b. Rochester, N.Y., Oct. 30, 1925; s. Howard W. and Nellie (Smith) J.; A.B., U. Rochester, 1949; B.S. in Optometry, Ohio State U., 1952; m. Rita Mary Thomas, Dec. 30, 1954; 1 son, Howard William III. Pvt. practice optometry, Boynton Beach, Fla., 1955—; naval architect. Founder, pres. Fla. Vision Found., Inc., 1961. Served with AUS, 1944-46. Decorated Purple Heart. Recipient Editors award Optometric Weekly, 1966. Diplomate Nat. Bd. Optometry. Mem. Am., Fla. (exec. com.), Fla. East Coast (pres. 1965-66) optometric assns., U.S. Naval Inst., Alpha Kappa Kappa, Sigma Chi. Episcopalian. Lion (past v.p. Boynton Beach), Rotarian. Office: 435 NW 2d St Boynton Beach FL 33435

JENNINGS, JAMES WILSON, dentist; b. Danville, Va., Oct. 2, 1914; s. John Leonard and Helene (Hall) J.; student U. Richmond, 1934-35, U. Ala., 1935-38; D.D.S., Emory U., 1942; m. Mary Lee Patton, Aug. 31, 1940; children—James Wilson, Bickford Patton. Gen. practice dentistry, Danville, 1946—. Mem. Va. Bd. Health, 1963-70; plan rep. Va. Dental Service, 1970—. Pres. bd. dirs. YMCA Bldg. Fund Drive, 1953, 64, chmn., 1964; charter mem., v.p., pres., chmn. bldg. procurement Danville Mus. Fine Arts, 1961—. Pres. Danville Art Assn., 1949; v.p., bd. dirs. Danville Pittsylvania Cancer Soc., Wayles Harrison Cancer Soc.; bd. dirs. Roman Eagle Nursing Home, A.R.C.; trustee Va. Museum Fine Arts, 1972-77. Served to capt., Dental Corps, AUS, 1942-46; PTO. Mem. Am., Piedmont (mem. exec. com.) dental assns., Danville Dental Soc. (past pres.), Phi Gamma Delta, Delta Sigma Delta. Episcopalian (past vestryman). Clubs: Danville Golf, Young Mens, Garden (Danville). Polit. cartoonist Comml. Appeal Weekly Newspaper, 1953-55. Author scripts Stratford Coll. May Festivals, 1962-65, Dental Health TV Show, 1972. Home: 291 Dogwood Dr Danville VA 24541 Office: 753 Main St Danville VA 24541

JENNINGS, JOHN MELVILLE, assn. exec.; b. Toano, Va., Oct. 22, 1918; s. John Melville and Grace Armistead (Davis) J.; B.A., Coll. William and Mary, 1938, LL.D., 1968; M.A., Am. U., 1948. Curator manuscripts and rare books Coll. William and Mary, 1939-43, 46-47; librarian Va. Hist. Soc., Richmond, 1948-51, dir., 1953—. Vice chmn. Va. Historic Landmarks Commn.; adv. bd. Assn. Preservation Va. Antiquities; cons. Robert E. Lee Meml. Found.; mem. publs. adv. com. Winterthur Mus., adv. bd. Nat. Cathedral Rare Book Library. Served with USNR, 1944-46, 51-53. Fellow Soc. Am. Archivists; mem. Bibliog. Soc. Am., Am. Hist. Assn., Mass. Hist. Soc., Am. Antiquarian Soc. Home: 204 N Granby St Richmond VA 23220 Office: PO Box 7311 Richmond VA 23221

JENNINGS, KNOX GILMORE, social worker; b. Bessemer, Ala., Jan. 29, 1939; s. Charles and Willie Mae (Gilmore) J.; student Rollins Coll., 1956-58; B.A., U. Ala., 1960; M.S.W., Fla. State U., 1964; m. Carolyn Kitchens, Dec. 28, 1962; children—Lisa Kitchens, Karen Lynne. Caseworker Jefferson County Dept. Pensions and Security. 1960-62; casework supr., 1964-66; casework supr. Mercy Home, 1966-67; tng. supr. Dept. Pensions and Security, Birmingham, Ala., 1967-69. supr. div. Juvenile Delinquency Service, 1969-71, projects and grants coordinator Dept. Pensions and Security, 1971—. Mem. Nat. Assn. Social Workers, Acad. Certified Social Workers‡

JENNINGS, LEWELLYN A., banker; b. Birch Tree, Mo., Dec. 1, 1906; s. Horace and Laura (Bodle) J.; student pub. schs. Silver Creek, N.Y.; m. Virginia Lee Campbell, June 28, 1941. With Silver Creek (N.Y.) Nat. Bank, 1924-29; asst. nat. bank examiner Office Comptroller of Currency, 2d Fed. Res. Dist., N.Y.C., 1929-35, nat. bank examiner, N.Y., N.J., Conn., 1935-37, examiner fgn. brs. nat. banks, Europe, S.A. and Caribbean area, 1937-39, asst. chief nat. bank examiner, Washington, 1941-50, 3d dep. comptroller, 1950-51, 2d dep. comptroller, 1951-52, 1st dep. comptroller of the currency, Feb. 1952-60, on loan to Govt. of Haiti to make surveys and examinations of Central Bank, Republic of Haiti, part-time, 1938, 41, Guam and Samoa, for U.S. Navy Dept., 1948; sr. v.p., exec. com. Republic Nat. Bank of Dallas 1960-61, exec. v.p. for adminstrn., 1961-63; chmn. bd., chief exec. officer Riggs Nat. Bank, Washington, 1963—; dir. Met. Life Ins. Co., Potomac Electric Co., Chesapeake and Potomac Telephone Co., Garfinkel, Brooks Bros., Miller & Rhodes. Trustee George Washington U.; bd. dirs. D.C. chpt A.R.C. Served from pvt. to capt. AUS, 1942-46, mil. govt. officer, ETO, 1944-46. Decorated Legion of Merit. Mem. Assn. Res. City Bankers, Nat. Civil Service League (dir.), Transp. Assn. Am. (dir.) Washington Inst. Fgn. Affairs, Met. Washington Bd. Trade (dir.), Fed. City Council (chmn.). Mason. Clubs: Congressional Country. Alfalfa, Burning Tree, Metropolitan, Internat. (Washington). Home: 16 Farmington Ct Chevy Chase MD 20015 Office: Riggs Nat Bank Washington DC 20013

JENNINGS, RUFUS EDWARD, sch. prin.; b. Saluda, S.C., Jan. 8, 1909; s. John D. and Martha (Chapman) J.; B.A., Newberry Coll., 1933; M.Ed., U. S.C., 1948; m. Virginia Timmerman, Dec. 22, 1936. Jr. high sch. prin., athletic coach Edgefield (S.C.) High Sch., 1933-41; asst. prin., coach Tarpon Springs (Fla.) High Sch., 1941-44, prin., 1949-51; athletic dir., coach Plant City (Fla.) High Sch., 1945-49; supervising prin. Arcadia City (Fla.) Sch., 1951-57; asst. prin. Boone High Sch., Orlando, Fla., 1957-58; prin. Colonial High Sch., Orlando, 1958-71, Parker Elementary Sch., Edgefield, S.C., 1971—. Served with U.S. Mcht. Marine, 1944-45. Mem. Orange County Secondary Principals Organization (pres. 1963), Metro Conf. (pres. 1964-65), Fla. High Sch. (dist. dir. Dist. VII 1966-67) athletic assns., P.T.A. Fla. Clubs: Lions, Kiwanis (dir. 1953). Home: Martintown Rd Clarks Hill SC 29821 Office: Rt 1 Box 223-E Edgefield SC 29824

JENNINGS, TROY SETH, agronomist; b. Calico Rock, Ark., Oct. 6, 1912; s. Roland E. and Phoebie L. (Thompson) J.; B.S.A., U. Ark., 1936; m. Josephine F. Dritt, Dec. 25, 1936; children—Frances (Mrs. Robert Vigna), Juliet (Mrs. Larry Black), Elizabeth (Mrs. Graham Henderson), Troy Joe, William Roland, Mary Dritt. With A.A.A., Harrison, Ark., 1936-37, county adminstrv. officer, Clinton, Ark., 1938-42, Danville, Ark., 1943; asst. county agt., Morrilton, Ark., 1944; county agt. Jasper, Ark., 1945, Ozark, Ark., 1946-47, Piggott, Ark., 1948-55, Wynne, Ark., 1955—. Recipient Nat. County Agts. Assn., Distinguished Service award, 1954. Mem. Ark. County Agts. Assn. (bd. dirs. 1954-55). Mem. Christian Ch. (elder; chmn. bd. 1965-72). Rotarian (rural urban chmn. 1963-64). Home: 814 Terry St Wynne AR 72396 Office: County Court House Wynne AR 72396

JENNINGS, VANCE SHELBY, educator; b. Oklahoma City, Aug. 10, 1925; s. Reedy Vance and Bess (Cudd) J.; B. Mus., Eastman Sch. Music, Rochester, N.Y., 1950; performer's certificate in clarinet, 1950; M.Ed., U. Miss., 1952; m. Chris Boyd, Nov. 26, 1969; 1 dau., Terri Lorene. Instr. woodwinds, asst. dir. bands U. Miss., 1950-53; asst. prof. clarinet and saxophone Wichita State U., 1953-67; asst. prof. music U. South Fla., Tampa, 1967—. Solo clarinetist Wichita Symphony Orch., 1953-67, Fla. Gulf Coast Symphony, Tampa-St. Petersburg, 1968-70. Served with AUS, 1943-46; lt. col. Res. Mem. Nat. Assn. Coll. Wind and Percussion Instrs. (nat. pres. 1964-66), Music Educators Nat. Conf., Scabbard and Blade, Phi Mu Alpha Sinfonia, Kappa Kappa Psi, Phi Delta Kappa, Kappa Delta Pi, Pi Kappa Alpha. Mason. Contbr. articles to profl. publs. Home: PO Box 16155 Temple Terrace FL 33617

JENNINGS, VIRGIL LESLIE, physician; b. Joplin, Mo., June 10, 1911; s. John Lilburn and Pearl Katherine (Brannock) J.; student Tulsa U., 1929-30; D.O., Kansas City Coll. Osteo. Medicine, 1940; M.D., Kansas City U., 1941, D.P.H., 1942; m. Natalie Bailey, July 4, 1968; children—Jerrie Jo, Wright. Intern Robert B. Green Hosp., San Antonio, 1943-44, resident, 1944-46; practice medicine, specializing in surgery, Fort Worth, 1946-55, gen. practice, 1955—; mem. staff Hurst (Tex.) Gen. Hosp., Ft. Worth Osteo. Hosp.; builder, prin. owner, chief staff Hurst (Tex.) Gen. Hosp., 1962-68; asso. prof. occupational medicine Tex. Coll. Osteopathic Medicine; dir. Fort Worth Osteo. Hosp., 1947-52, pres., 1946-47; pres. Fort Worth Coll. Emotional Cons., 1971—. Organizing dir. First State Bank, Bedford, Tex. Fellow Am. Coll. Gen. Practitioners; founding fellow Internat. Acad. Preventive Medicine (sec.); mem. Am. Coll. Practology, Am. Coll. Preventive Medicine (treas.), Hurst-Euless-Bedford C. of C. (pres. 1965-66). Methodist. Mason (Shriner), Lion (organizing dir. Organ and Eye Bank, 1970-72). Home: 2043 W Lotus St Fort Worth TX 76111 Office: 3312 E Belknap St Fort Worth TX 76111

JENNINGS, WALTER STANLEY, physician; b. nr. Norfolk, Va., Apr. 22, 1926; s. Walter Edward and Edna (Davis) J.; A.A., Coll. William and Mary, Norfolk div., 1946; student U. Va., 1946-47; M.D., Med. Coll. Va., 1951; m. Emily Estelle Doughty, July 27, 1947; children— Stanley, Jennifer, Elizabeth Helon. Intern, Norfolk Gen. Hosp., 1951-52; practice medicine, Hickory, Va., 1952, South Norfolk, 1952—; mem. staff Leigh Meml., Norfolk Gen. hosps. Pres. Harstan Corp. Served with USAAF, 1944-45. Mem. A.M.A., Norfolk County, So. med. socs., Theta Kappa Psi. Home: 1160 Virginia Av Chesapeake VA 22046 Office: 1446 Chesapeake Av South Norfolk Chesapeake VA 22324

JENSEN, ALVIN CARL, ednl. adminstr.; b. North Lake, Wis., Apr. 15, 1921; s. Frank Roy and Amelia (Nelson) J.; B.Ed., Wis. State U., 1958; M.A., George Washington U., 1960, Ed.D., 1967; m. Marilyn Ann Sorenson, Oct. 6, 1954; children—Allyn Mary, Peter Stuart. Commd. 2d lt. U.S. Army, 1942, advanced through grades to col.; mem. staff Joint Chiefs of Staff, 1963-67, office asst. Sec. Defense, 1967-70; ret., 1970; asso. dean, dir. credit programs Coll. Gen. Studies, George Washington U., 1970—, faculty adviser to Alpha Alpha chpt. Alpha Sigma Lambda, 1971—. Committeeman Arlington County troop council Boy Scouts Am., 1970—. Mem. Am. Assn. Sch. Adminstrs., Am. Assn. U. Profs., Am. Assn. Higher Edn., Phi Delta Kappa (editor newsletter 1960-70, 2d v.p. 1971). Presbyn. (ruling elder session 1967-69, 71—). Clubs: University, Ft. Meyer Officers. Home: 3188 Key Blvd Arlington VA 22201 Office: 2003 G NW Washington DC 20006

JENSEN, GILBERT WALTER, pump co. exec.; b. Rockford, Ill., Mar. 19, 1926; s. Jens C. and Anna Belle (Crowe) J.; B.S. in Mech. Engring., Ill. Inst. Tech., 1951; m. Ruby Eileene Jones, Sept. 22, 1945; children— Arnold Eric, Steven Craig, Karen Kristine. Asso., Am. Gas Assn. Research Lab., Cleve., 1951-52; research engr. George D. Roper Corp., Rockford, 1952-57; chief engr. Avon Mfg. Co., Rockford, 1957-59; with Roper Pump Co., Commerce, Ga., 1959—, pres., 1968—. Instr. tank truck sch. Purdue U., 1962-63. Pres. P.T.A., Loves Park, Ill., 1958-59, 70—. Bd. dirs. Petroleum Equipment Inst. Served with USMCR, 1942-46. Mem. Assn. Indsl. Advertisers (dir. 1969-70), Hydraulic Inst. (chmn. rotary sect. 1969-70), Commerce C. of C. (bd. dirs. 1970—), Am. Legion. Presbyn. Kiwanian. Clubs: Athens (Ga.) Country; Kingwood Country, Sky Valley Ski (Clayton, Ga.). Patentee in field. Home: 265 Lakeland Dr Athens GA 30601 Office: Box 269 Commerce GA 30529

JENSEN, LARRY DON, automotive implement and appliance co. exec.; b. Enid, Okla., Oct. 31, 1934; s. Alfred C. and Avarella O. (Sturgeon) J.; student So. Meth. U., 1953-54; B.A., Okla. U., 1957; m. Sue Ann Schultz, Sept. 14, 1957; children—Donald Jeffrey, Susan Ann. Gen. sales mgr., sec.-treas. Jensen's, Inc., Fairview, Okla., 1962—. Served with U.S. Army, 1957-60. Selected as one of 4 Men in N.Am. to serve on Nat. J.I. Case Dealer Council, 1971, 72, 1 of 2 Men to rep. Pontiac Dealers at 8 State Meeting, 1970, 71. Mem. Fairview C. of C. (pres., dir.), Methodist Men (pres.), Beta Theta Pi. Mason, Lion. Home: 602 N 11th St Fairview OK 73737 Office: 218 S Main St Fairview OK 73737

JENSEN, MALCOLM W., govt. ofcl. Dir., Bur. Product Safety, Washington. Home: 11812 Seven Locks Rd Alexandria VA 22301*

JENSEN, TOM, state legislator, chem. corp. exec.; b. Knoxville, Tenn., Oct. 28, 1934; s. Irving Oscal and Christine (Scarbrough) J.; B.S. U. Tenn., 1952-59; m. Carolyn Frances Carter, June 17, 1960; children—Lucinda Anne, Thomas Carter. Founded Jensen Corp., Knoxville 1958, purchased Tripure Water Co., 1960, co-founder Delta Cleaning Contractors Inc., 1965—, Gen. Chem. Corp., 1967; pres. Delta Devel. Corp., 1965; chmn. bd. So. Automatic Sprinkler Corp.; pres., bd. mem. Jensen Corp., Delta Devel. Corp., Gen. Chem. Corp.; owner Indsl. Leasing Co.; mem. Tenn. Ho. of Reps., 1967—, majority whip, 1969-70, minority leader, 1971—, chmn. spl. joint com. on state-fed. relations. Mem. Gov.'s Adv. Com. on Ins. Vice pres. Knoxville Community Forum, 1966; commr. Edn. Commn. of States; chmn. natural resources com. Nat. Legislative Conf.; del. White House Conf. on Aging, 1971; bd. advisers Carson Newman Coll., Knoxville YWCA. Bd. dirs. United Cerebral Palsy; trustee Children's Mus. Knoxville. Recipient Outstanding Community Service, Knoxville Jr. C. of C., 1963, Nat. Govtl. Affairs Award, 1965; named Outstanding Young Man Knoxville, 1970. Mem. Am. Bottled Water Assn., Nat. Assn. Ind. Businessmen, Nat. Soc. State Legislators (v.p.), Nat. Conf. State Legislative Leaders, Tenn. Jr. C. of C. (v.p. 1966, sec.

treas. 1967), Knoxville C. of C. Republican (mem. Knox County Exec. com.). Club: Sertoma (charter mem.). Home: 2323 Juniper Dr Knoxville TN 37912 Office: War Memorial Bldg Nashville TN 37219

JENSON, MYRON MAGNUS, pipeline co. exec.; b. Fairy, Tex., July 15, 1924; s. Jesse Justin and Helen (Rohne) J.; B.S., Tex. A. and M. Coll., 1949; m. Alma Jack Busch, June 12, 1949; children—Myron Michael, Frank Justin, Charles Eugene. Jr. engr. Tex. Eastern Transmission Corp., Baytown, 1950-54, asst. engr., Shreveport, La., 1954-59, dist. engr., Cuero, Tex., 1959-71, operations supr., Baytown, 1971—. Cubmaster Boy Scouts Am., 1960-64. Served with USNR, 1942-47. Mem. Tex. Soc. Profl. Engrs. Lutheran. Lion. Home: 2103 Pinemont St Baytown TX 77520 Office: PO Box 426 Baytown TX 77520

JENTZ, GAYLORD ADAIR, educator, author; b. Beloit, Wis., Aug 7, 1931; s. Merlyn Adair and Delva (Mullen) J.; B.A., U. Wis., 1953, J.D., 1957, M.B.A., 1958; m. JoAnn Mary Hornung, Aug. 6, 1955; children— Katherine Ann, Gary Adair, Loretta Ann, Rory Adair. Admitted to Wis. bar, 1957; pvt. practice law, Madison, 1957-58; from instr. to asso. prof. Bus. law U. Okla., 1958-65; vis. instr. to vis. prof. U. Wis. Law Sch. summers 1957-65; asso. prof. to prof. U. Tex., 1965-68, prof., 1968—, chmn. gen. bus. dept., 1968—. Served with AUS, 1953-55. Recipient Outstanding Tchr.'s award, Tex. U. Coll. Bus., 1967. Mem. Am. Arbitration Assn. (nat. panel 1966—), Am. (pres. 1971-72), So. (pres. 1967) bus. law assns., Tex. Assn. Coll. Tchrs. (pres. Austin chpt. 1967-68, exec. com. 1969-70, state pres. 1971-72, Jack G. Taylor Teaching Excellence award 1971), Wis. Bar Assn. Author: (with others) Business Law Text and Cases, 2d edit., 1968; Tex. Uniform Comml. Code, 1967, rev. edit., 1972. Contbr. articles to profl. jours. Asso. editor Social Sci. Quarterly, 1966—; editorial staff Am. Bus. Law Jour., 1967-69, editor-in-chief, 1969—. Home: 4106 North Hills Dr Austin TX 78731

JENTZSCH, RICHARD ALVIN, orthodontist; b. Chgo., Dec. 4, 1892; s. Richard and Ella (Zuerkel) J.; D.D.S., U. Ill., 1926, M.S., 1931; m. Adeline M. Hayek, Nov. 8, 1934 (dec. 1958); m. 2d, Pauline R. Jones, Mar. 9, 1964. Faculty, U. Ill., 1926-36; practice dentistry specializing in orthodontics, 1926—, now ret. Mayor, Village of Wood Dale, Ill., 1943-47. Served with U.S. Army, 1918-19. Mem. Ill., Chgo. (past v.p.) dental socs., Am. Dental Assn., Chgo. Assn. Orthodontists, USCG Aux., Navy League U.S., Omicron Kappa Upsilon, Tau Kappa Epsilon. Home: 450 Bow Line Bend Naples FL 33940

JENZANO, ANTHONY FRANCIS, planetarium dir.; b. Phila. May 20, 1919; s. Joseph and Theresa (Monzo) J.; grad. Marine Elec. Sch., Phila., 1942, USN Gun Fire Control Sch., 1943, USN Advanced Gun Fire Control Sch., 1943, Capitol Radio Engring. Inst., 1951; m. Myrtle E. Packer, Nov. 12, 1941; children—Anthony Francis, Carol. Head technician Fels Planetarium, Phila., 1946-49; chief technician Morehead Planetarium, University of N.C., 1949-51, manager planetarium, art galleries and sci. exhibit areas, 1951-60; planetarium director, 1960—; engaged in complete dismantlement and reassembly Zeiss Planetarium instruments, Fels, 1948, Morehead 1949, 59, 69 (model VI). U.S, adviser to architect and contractors for London (Eng.) Planetarium, 1956-57; cons. Buhl Planetarium console, 1957, Atlanta Planetarium, 1967. Dir. Celestial Tng. Program for U.S. Mercury, Gemini, Apollo and Skylab astronauts, 1960—; state dir. N.C. Sci. Fairs, 1961-63. Instnl, rep. Boy Scouts Am. Served with USNR, 1943-45. Mem. Am. Assn. Museums, U.S. Maj. Planetarium Ofcls. Group, N.C. Acad. Scis., Am. Astron. Soc. (asso.), Phi Omega. Home: 37 Oakwood Dr Chapel Hill NC 27514 Office: Morehead Planetarium Chapel Hill NC 27514

JEREMIAH, WILLIAM EDWARD, city clk.; b. Youngstown, O., Dec. 30, 1917; s. William and Florence C. (Edwards) J.; student Hiram Coll., 1936-37; B.S. in Metall. Engring., Case Inst. Tech., 1941; m. Mildred A. Levy, July 26, 1941; children—William L., Richard E., Dianne Lynn, Renee L., Phyllis J. Commd. comdr. U.S. Navy, 1941; ret., 1968; city clk., Dunedin, Fla., 1970—. Decorated Navy Commendation medal. Mem. Tech. Assn., Am. Soc. Planning Ofcls., Internat. Inst. Municipal Clks. Home: 2347 Watrous Dr Dunedin FL 33528 Office: 750 Milwaukee Av Dunedin FL 33528

JERMAN, ALBERT CHARLES, dentist; b. Bristol, Conn., Nov. 12, 1935; s. Frank Michael and Estelle (Wilson) J.; B.A., Yale, 1957; D.D.S., U. Neb., 1961; m. Grace Jacobson, Jan. 25, 1963; children—Rachel Estelle, Eric Anton. Comms. 1st lt., U.S. Air Force, 1961, advanced through grades to maj., 1968; chief exptl. dentistry sect. Dental Scis. br. U.S. Air Force Sch. Aerospace Medicine, Brooks AFB, Tex., 1967—, also lectr.; lectr. U.S. Air Force Med. Service Sch., Wilford Hall Med. Center. Fellow Am. Coll. Dentists; mem. Am. Dental Assn., Internat. Assn. Dental Research, Am. Acad. Oral Pathology, Am. Soc. Forensic Odontology, A.A.A.S. Unitarian. Developed dental restorative material which resists decay. Contbr. articles forensic odontology to med., dental jours. Home: 206 Driftwind St San Antonio TX 78239 Office: USAF Sch Aerospace Medicine Brooks AFB TX 78235

JERNIGAN, IRVING CURTIS, JR., economist; b. Portsmouth, Va., Sept. 12, 1943; s. Irving Curtis and Clara (MacKenzie) J.; B.A., Washington and Lee U., 1965; M.A., Ind. U., 1967; student Nat. Law Center The George Washington U., 1971—. Economist Antitrust div. U.S. Dept. Justice, Washington, 1967—. Recipient U.S. Dept. Justice Spl. Achievement award, 1971. Mem. Am. Econ. Assn. Research competitive effects of conglomerate mergers. Home: 1110 E St SE Washington DC 20003 Office: Antitrust div US Dept Justice Washington DC 20530

JERNIGAN, JAMES COFFEY, univ. pres.; b. nr. Van Alstyne, Tex., Dec. 20, 1914; s. Austin Wallace and Blanche (Coffey) J.; B.S., N. Tex. State Tchrs. Coll., 1937, M.S., 1939; postgrad. U. Tex., summers 1941-42; Ph.D., U. Chgo., 1949; m. Frances Williams, June 28, 1940; children—James William, Laura Frances. Tchr., Rosamond Chapel Sch., 1934-36; tchr., prin. Whitewright (Tex.) High Sch., 1936-39; supt. Pilot Point (Tex.) Pub. Schs., 1939-41; dep. state supt. Tex. Dept. Edn., 1941-42; dean student life Tex. A & I U., 1946-47, dir. student personnel, 1949-50, dean coll., 1950-62, pres., 1962-72; chancellor Tex. A & I U. System covering campuses Kingsville, Laredo, Corpus Christi and Weslaco, 1972—; conducted guidance workshop So. Meth. U., summer 1950. Served to capt. inf. AUS, 1942-46; ETO. Recipient Distinguished Service award Tex. Assn. State Sr. Coll. and Univ. Bus. Officers, 1971. Mem. Tex. Tchrs. Assn., Tex. Assn. Colls. and Univs. (pres. 1962-63). Mem. Christian Ch. (elder). Kiwanian (past pres.). Home: President's Home Kingsville TX

JERNIGAN, JESS EARL, oil and gas co. exec.; b. Paris, Tex., Jan. 14, 1913; s. Frank W. and Maude H. (Harry) J.; B.S. in C.E., Okla. State U., 1937; m. Rose Marie Wells, Sept. 7, 1937; children—Robert Mark, Janet Kay (Mrs. John D. Bradley), Stephen Alan, James Bradford. Petroleum engr. Pan Am. Petroleum Oklahoma City, 1937-46; cons. engr. petroleum Oklahoma City, 1947-50; partner Jernigan & Morgan Oil Co., Oklahoma City, 1950-70, pres. Jernigan-Morgan Transmission Co., Oklahoma City, 1950-70, Pacific Oil & Gas Co., Oklahoma City, 1970—. Mason. Club: Oklahoma City Golf and Country. Home: 1903 Bedford Dr Oklahoma City OK 73116 Office: Colcord Bldg Oklahoma City OK 73102

JERNIGAN, SARA STAFF, educator; b. Lakewood, O.; d. Otto Karl and Elsie (Walther) Staff; B.S., Stetson U., 1935; M.A., 1937; m. Harvey Jordon Jernigan, Dec. 16, 1942. Dir. dept. phys. edn. women Stetson U., DeLand, Fla., 1937-65, prof., 1942—. Chmn. bd. dirs. Nat. Inst. Girls Sports, 1963-69; chmn. women's bd. U.S. Olympic Devel. Com., 1960-68, mem.-at-large U.S. Olympic Devel. Com., 1964-68; mem. bd. consultants U.S. Olympic Com., 1969-73; lectr. Internat. Olympic Acad., Olympia, Greece, 1965, 66, 70, 72, hon. life mem., 1969; U.S. State Dept. grant to teach in Greece, 1966. Recipient Woman of Year award Central Fla. So. Assn. Phys. Edn. Coll. Women, 1963. Fellow Am. Coll. Sports Medicine; mem. A.A.H.P.E.R. (v.p. 1961-62, chmn. div. for girls and women's sports 1961-62, internat. relations So. dist.; Dist. Honor award 1962, Nat. Honor Fellow award 1971), Fla. Assn. Health, Phys. Edn. and Recreation (v.p. phys. edn. 1958-59, v.p. recreation 1963-64; Honor award 1958), Am. Recreation Soc., Internat. Recreation Assn., Nat. (bd. dirs. 1958-61), So. (pres. 1958-61, chmn. internat. relations com. 1968-71) assns. phys. edn. coll. women, Country Dance Soc. Am., U.S. Lawn Tennis Assn., Internat. Assn. Phys. Edn. and Sports Girls and Women (del. internat. congress London, 1957, Cologne, Germany, 1965, Tokyo, 1969), Am. Assn. U. Profs., Am. Assn. U. Women, Ikebana Internat., Nat. League Am. Pen Women, Mortar Board (honor circle), Delta Delta Delta, Kappa Delta Pi, Delta Kappa Gamma. Club: Internat. Relations (pres.) (Volusie County). Sr. author: Playtime: World Recreation Handbook, 1972. Contbr. to profl. publs. Home: 623 N Cherokee Av DeLand FL 32720

JERNIGAN, WILLIAM WADE, JR., librarian; b. Savannah, Ga., Mar. 4, 1935; s. William Wade and Hettie (Smith) J.; A.B., Trevecca Nazarene Coll., 1957; B.D., Nazarene Sem., 1960; M.A., George Peabody Coll., 1961; Ed.D., U. Tulsa, 1972; m. Juanita Orndoff, Dec. 19, 1956; children—Julie, Lisa. Asst. librarian Trevecca Nazarene Coll., 1965; dir. libraries Oral Roberts U., 1965-67, dir. learning resources and libraries, 1967-71, dir. extended sessions, 1969-71, v.p. learning resources and instrn., 1971—; cons. instructional tech. and ednl. media; cons. Tulsa Jr. Coll. Mem. Friends of the Library, Am. Assn. Higher Edn., Okla. Library Assn., Nat. Assn. Summer Sessions, Assn. Ednl. Communications and Tech. Democrat. Nazarene (tchr. Sunday Sch. 1950—). Author: Preparing Software for Modern Media in Higher Education, 1970; An Investigation of the Use of the Dial Access Information Retrieval System at Oral Roberts University for the Teaching of First Semester Freshman English, 1972. Home: 2683 E 75th St Tulsa OK 74105 Office: 7777 S Lewis Av Tulsa OK 74105

JERVEY, HAROLD EDWARD, ret. govt. ofcl.; b. Charleston, S.C., Sept. 22, 1894; s. Joseph Edward and Jessie (Balentine) J.; student, Coll. Charleston, 1910-14, Med. Coll. State of S.C., 1914-16; m. Stella White, Oct. 16, 1916; children—Harold Edward, Herbert V., William T. Tchr., High Sch. Charleston, 1916-25; pub. accountant, Jacksonville, Fla., 1926-30; internal auditor S.C. Hwy. Dept., 1930-42, dir. Motor Vehicle Div., 1935-36; asst. state auditor, Columbia, S.C., 1942-69. Treas. Heathwood Hall Episcopal Sch., 1951—. Trustee Protestant Episcopal Diocese of Upper S.C. Bd. dirs. Columbia Art Assn., Columbia Mus. Art, treas. 1953-58. Recipient Silver Beaver award, Boy Scouts Am., 1944. Mem Soc. of the Cincinnati. Episcopalian (vestryman, warden). Home: 2906 Duncan Columbia SC 29205 Office: Wade Hampton Office Bldg Columbia SC 29202

JERVEY, HAROLD EDWARD, JR., physician; b. Charleston, S.C., Dec. 3, 1920; s. Harold Edward and Stella (White) J.; B.S., U. S.C., 1941; M.D., Med. Coll. S.C., 1949; m. Lillian Pearce Hair, July 13, 1946; children—Nancy, Harold Edward III, Margaret Pearce, Harriet Beacham, Helen White, Charles Stewart, Lillian Pearce. Intern Greenville (S.C.) Gen. Hosp., 1949-50, Baptist Gen. Hosp., Columbia, S.C., 1951-54; gen. practice, Columbia, 1951—; mem. staff Columbia, Bapt. and Providence hosps. Mem. S.C. Bd. Med. Examiners, 1953—, sec., 1955-58; pres. Fedn. State Med. Bds., 1960, sec., editor bull., 1961. Treas., 1962—; mem. Adv. Bd. Med. Specialists, 1959—. Served to lt. comdr. USNR, 1941-45. Decorated Bronze Star. Mem. Am. Acad. Gen. Practice (S.C. del. 1956-60), A.M.A., Columbia C. of C., Soc. Cincinnati, Kappa Sigma. Episcopalian. Clubs: Sertoma Internat.; Carolina Yacht (Charleston); Columbia Sailing, Forest Lake Country (Columbia). Home: 798 Kawana Rd Columbia SC 29205 Office: 1515 Bull St Columbia SC 29201

JESSNER, LUCIE NEY, psychiatrist; b. Frankfurt am Main, Germany, Sept. 15, 1896; d. Emanuel and Rose (Lowenhaar) Ney; Ph.D., Frankfurt (Germany) U., 1924; M.D., U. Koenigsberg (Germany), 1926; m. Frederick Jessner, 1928 (dec.); stepchildren—Anne, Mrs. Eva Sampson. Intern, Charite Berlin, Germany, 1926-27; asst. psychiatry U. Koenigsberg, 1928-33; psychiatrist Sanatorium Muenchenbuchsee. Switzerland, 1933-37; res. psychiatrist McLean Hosp., Waverly, Mass., Baldpate, Georgetown, Mass., 1938-41; acting dir. Habit Clinic for Child Guidance, Boston, asst. psychiatrist Mass. service for children Mass. Gen. Hosp., 1947-55; prof. psychiatry Sch. Medicine, U. N.C., 1955-63; prof. Psychiatry Georgetown U. Med. Center, Washington, 1963—; instr. psychiatry Harvard, 1944—, also clin. asso. Harvard Med. Sch. Psychiat. Inst. Mem. A.M.A., N.E. Med. Soc., Boston Psychoanalytic Soc., Boston Psychiat. and Mental Soc. Author: (with Gerald Ryan) Shock Treatment in Psychiatry, 1941; (with Eleanor Pavenstedt) Dynamic Psychopathology In Childhood, 1959. Address: Georgetown U Hosp 3800 Reservoir Rd NW Washington DC 20007

JESSUP, HARVEY MICHAEL, educator, adminstr.; b. N.Y.C., July 4, 1925; s. William F. and Elizabeth (Harvey) J.; B.S., N.Y. U., 1948, M.A., 1950, Ph.D., 1967; m. Dorothy Lynch, Dec. 27, 1952; children— Deborah, Dolores. Dir. athletics, phys. edn. Power Meml. High Sch., 1947-49; dir. athletics Western Conn, State Coll., Danbury, 1949-61; faculty Tulane U., New Orleans, 1961—, exec. asst. dir. athletics, 1961—, prof. phys. edn., 1961—, head dept. phys. edn., 1968—. Vis. prof. N.Y. U., N.Y.C., 1948-60. Mem. Joint U.S. Olympic Devel. Com., 1967—. Served with USNR. 1943-46. Recipient Founders Day award N.Y. U., 1967. Mem. A.A.H.P.E.R. (v.p. 1966-69, mem. jour. editorial bd. 1967-70), Am. Assn. Higher Edn., N.E.A., Nat. Assn. Basketball Coaches, Omicron Delta Kappa, Phi Epsilon Kappa, Kappa Phi Kappa. Author (with others): Physical Activities for the Mentally Retarded, 1968. Home: 4117 Page Dr Metairie LA 70003 Office: Div Athletics Tulane U New Orleans LA 70118

JESSUP, JOE LEE, mgmt. cons., educator; b. Cordele, Ga., June 23, 1913; s. Horace Andrew and Elizabeth (Wilson) J.; B.S., U. Ala., 1936; M.B.A., Harvard Grad. Sch. Bus. Administrn., 1941; LL.D., Chung-Ang U., Seoul, Korea, 1964; m. Genevieve Quirk Galloway, Aug. 29, 1946; 1 dau., Gail Elizabeth. Sales rep. Proctor & Gamble, 1937-40; liaison officer bur. pub. relations U.S. War Dept., 1941; spl. asst. and exec. asst. Far Eastern div. and office exports Bd. Econ. Welfare, 1942-43; exec. officer office deptl. adminstrn. Dept. State, 1946; exec. sec. adminstr.'s adv. council War Assets Adminstrn., 1946-48; v.p. sales Airkem Capitol & Service Co., 1948-49; pres. Jessup & Co., 1957—; dir. Hunter Assos. Labs., Inc., Fairfax, Va., 1965-69; asso. prof. bus. administrn. George Washington U., 1949, prof., 1952, asst. dean Sch. Gov., 1951-60. Dir. Giant Food, Inc., Washington, 1971—, Internat. Careers Inst., Inc., Los Angeles, 1972—. Coordinator resources mgmt. program U.S. Air Force, 1951-60; regional chmn. Harvard Bus. Sch. Fund, 1960—. Del. 10th Internat. Mgmt. Conf., Sao Paulo, Brazil, 1954, 11th, Paris, France, 1957, 12th, Sydney and Melbourne, Australia, 1960, 13th, N.Y.C., 1963, 14th, Rotterdam, Holland, 1966, 15th, Tokyo, Japan, 1970. Served from 2d lt. to lt. col. AUS, 1941-46. Decorated Bronze Star; recipient certificate of appreciation Sec. of Air Force, 1957. Mem. Acad. Mgmt., Am. Mgmt. Assn., Soc. Advancement Mgmt., Alpha Kappa Psi. Clubs: Harvard (N.Y.C.); Harvard Business School (v.p. programs 1960—), Congressional Country, International (Washington). Home: 8539 W Howell Rd Bethesda MD 20034 Office: 5454 Wisconsin Av Chery Chase MD 20015

JESSUP, PERCY WELLS, JR., dentist; b. Lumberton, N.C., Sept. 12, 1941; s. Percy Wells and Merle (Savage) H.; B.S. in Chemistry, U. N.C., 1963, D.D.S., 1967; m. Martha C. Phillips July 19, 1970; 1 son, Lance Wells. Practice dentistry, Fayetteville, N.C., 1969—. Served to capt. Dental Corps, AUS, 1967-69. Mem. Am. Dental Assn., Am. Acad. Gen. Dentistry, Am. Assn. Dentists, Am. Soc. Preventive Dentistry, Am. Soc. Dentistry for Children, Internat. Soc. Gen. Semantics. Presbyn. Club: Toastmasters (pres. Cape Fear club 1971—; gov. area 10 since 1971). Home: 74 Briarwood Arms Fayetteville NC 28306 Office: 1647 Owen Dr Fayetteville NC 28304

JETT, JOHN LYNDELL, monument co. exec.; b. Sparta, Tenn., Dec. 12, 1936; s. Charles O. and Charlie Mae (Jarvis) J.; B.S., Tenn. Tech. U., 1958; m. Annelle Bockman, Aug. 17, 1958; 1 son, John Lyndell. Mgmt. trainee, then asst. br. plant mgr. Davis Cabinet Co., Nashville, 1958-59; with Sparta Monumental Works, Inc., 1959—, v.p., mgr., 1965—; pres., chmn. bd. Sparta Electric System, Sparta Water & Sewer Highland Cemtery Corp., Sparta, 1966—; dir. Mem. bd. aldermen City of Sparta, 1969—. Bd. dirs. Sparta Little League. Methodist. Mason. Club: Civitan (v.p. Sparta 1966-67) Home: Route 8 Sparta TN 38583 Office: Cookeville Rd Sparta TN 38583

JETT, LOIS MARIE, lawyer; b. Dayton, Tex.; d. Willis Warren and Laura (Frazier) Jett; B.B.A., U. Tex., 1951, J.D., 1960; postgrad. Loyola U., New Orleans, 1964-65. With Humble Oil & Refining Co., 1951-56, 60—, land records analyst land dept., New Orleans, 1961-66, asso. landman, land dept., 1966-69, now sr. land records analyst in landowner's relations dept., Houston; admitted to Tex. bar, 1959, La. bar, 1965; practiced in Houston and Liberty, Tex., 1960-61. Mem. Am., La., Houston bar assns., State Bar Tex., Am. Judicature Soc., Am. Assn. U. Women, Am. Assn. Petroleum Landmen, Houston Petroleum Landmens Assn., Daus. Republic Tex., Sigma Iota Epsilon, Kappa Beta Pi, Beta Beta Alpha. Club: Humble (past officer) (Houston). Home: 3601 Allen Pkwy Houston TX 77019 Office: PO Box 2305 Houston TX 77001

JETTON, ALLEN CARPENTER, banker; b. Union Grove, Ala., Dec. 31, 1908; s. David Mitchell and Alice Elmira (Carpenter) J.; B.S., Jacksonville (Ala.) State Tchrs. Coll., 1930; m. Rosalie Black, Dec. 11, 1931. Tchr. schs., Marshall County (Ala.) 1926-30, prin., 1931-43; agt. Liberty Nat. Life Ins. Co., Albertville, Ala., 1943-48; bookkeeper Forrester & Dickerson Furniture Co., Guntersville, Ala., 1948-52; with Citizens Bank of Guntersville 1952—, pres., 1966-68, chmn. bd., 1968—; dir. Val Monte Shores, Inc., 1966—; v.p. Citizens Realty Co., 1965— (both Guntersville). Dir. Guntersville Electric Bd., 1970—. Mem. Ala. Bankers Assn. Baptist. Clubs: Civitan (sec.-treas. 1967), Val Monte Country (Guntersville). Home: 13 Ringold St Gundersville AL 35976 Office: 370 Broad St Guntersville AL 35976

JETTON, CLYDE THOMAS, educator; b. St James, Ark., Oct. 23, 1918; s. William Thomas and Laura Ellen (Greenway) J.; B.A., Northeastern State Coll., 1939; M.A., Okla. State U., 1940; Ph.D., Tex. Technol. Coll., 1955; m. Dorothy Marie Chasteen, Nov. 30, 1944; 1 son, Ronald Clyde. Tchr. elementary sch., Locust Grove, Okla., 1940; psychometrist Hardin-Simmons U., 1947-49; counselor VA, 1949-51, Sweetwater (Tex.) Pub. Schs., 1951-54; prof. edn. Hardin-Simmons U., Abilene, Texas, 1955—, grad. dean, 1965—; vis. prof. Colo. State U., 1957-59, George Peabody Coll., 1963; cons. mental retardation, psychol. testing, counseling. Served to maj. AUS, 1940-47. Decorated Bronze Star Medal, Purple Heart. Mem. Am. Personnel and Guidance Assn., N.E.A., Tex. Tchrs. Assn., So. Assn. Counselor Educators and Suprs. Nat. Vocational Guidance Assn., Phi Delta Kappa. Baptist. Club: Civitan (sec. 1963, dir. 1962—). Home: 720 Amherst Dr Abilene TX 79601

JEWELL, ROBERT BURNETT, engring. exec.; b. Binghampton, N.Y., Mar. 20, 1906; s. Howard Clinton and Anne (Burnett) J.; B.S. in Civil Engring., Lehigh U., 1928; m. Helen Louise Pflug, May 18, 1935; children—Robert William, Linda Louise. Asst. engr. Friestedt Found. Co., N.Y., 1928-30; asst. engr. Port of N.Y. Authority, 1930-39; with Mason & Hanger Co., 1939-43, field engr. Rays Hill Tunnel, 1939-40; chief draftsman Radford Ordnance Works, 1940-41; asst. chief engr. design Badger Ordnance Works, 1942; resident engr. constrn. Bklyn.-Battery Tunnel, 1942-43; job mgr. hemp mill constrn., Polo, Ill., 1943; with Silas Mason Co., 1943-55; asst. prodn. supt. operation La. Ordnance Plant, 1943-46, chief engr. design of facilities U.S. AEC, Ia. Ordnance Plant, 1947-48; project mgr. constrn. Fort Randall Dam Outlet Works Tunnels, 1948-50, AEC Pantex Ordnance Plant, 1951-52; project mgr. engring. services AEC Nev. Test Site, 1951-53; chief engr., co. rep. Harvey Canal Tunnel, 1953-55; v.p. Mason & Hanger-Silas Mason Co., Inc., 1955—, v.p., chief engr., 1959-64, v.p. for operations, 1964—, also dir. Registered profl. engr., N.Y., Ky. Fellow Am. Soc. C.E.; mem. Am. Concrete Inst., Am. Inst. Aeros. and Astronautics, Nat. Soc. Profl. Engrs., Am. Ordnance Assn., The Moles, The Beavers, Tau Beta Pi. Presbyn. Clubs: Engineers (N.Y.), Lexington Country. Home: 1036 The Lane Lexington KY 40504 Office: 200 E Main St Lexington KY 40507

JEWELL, WILLIAM HORACE, lawyer; b. Hope, Ark., Dec. 16, 1919; s. Albert T. and Eliza (Winn) J.; LL.B., U. Ark., 1944; m. Irma Murphy, Sept. 18, 1944; children—Anne (Mrs. Louis H. Edrington), Judy (Mrs. F.M. Freeman), Becky, Joe, John. Admitted to Ark. bar, 1944; practice law, Little Rock, 1944—; partner House, Holmes & Jewell, Little Rock, 1944—; dir. S.W. Hotels, Inc., Arlington Hotel Co., Majestic Hotel Co., River Ridge Devel. Corp., Cedar Hill Corp. Mem. Am., Ark., Pulaski County bar assns., Am. Judicature Soc. Home: 306 Fairfax St Little Rock AR 72205 Office: Tower Bldg Little Rock AR 72201

JEWETT, WILLIAM AMORY, coll. adminstr.; b. Gardner, Mass., Oct. 1, 1919; s. Everett Porter and Mae Virginia (Crowley) J.; grad. Mt. Hermon Sch., 1937; A.B., Brown U., 1941, postgrad., 1946-47; m. Alva Althea Pearson, June 14, 1942; 1 dau., Linda (Mrs. Harry M. Wales). Placement officer, asst. to pres., registrar Brown U., 1945-51; civilian adminstrv. officer U.S. Army, Washington, Munich, Germany and Taipei, Taiwan, 1952-65; v.p. mgmt. Melmar Corp., Perrine, Fla., 1966-69; v.p. financial affairs Mt. Vernon Coll., Washington, 1969—. Trustee Nat. Soc. Prevention Blindness. Served to lt. comdr. USNR, 1945. Mem. Nat. Assn. Coll. and Univ. Officers, Assn. Financial Aid Adminstrs., So. Assn. Coll. Bus. Officers. Home: 1911 Kenbar Ct McLean VA 22101 Office: 2100 Foxhall Rd Washington DC 20007

JILES, CHARLES WILLIAM, educator; b. Vienna, La., Aug. 11, 1927; s. Robert Algin and Selma (Willis) J.; B.S. in Elec. Engring., La. Poly. Inst., 1949, B.A. in Math., 1949; M.S. in Elec. Engring., Okla. State U., 1950, Ph.D., 1955; m. Opal Earl Baber, Aug. 27, 1950; children—David Lee, Linda Sue, Ruth Ann, Darrell Wayne. Instr. elec. engring. Okla. State U., 1949-55; specialist design Gen. Dynamics Corp., Ft. Worth, 1955-60; prof. elec. engring., nat. cons. automatic controls U. Tex. at Arlington, 1960—; pres., Arlington Engring. Asso., Inc., 1960-66. City councilman Benbrook, Tex., 1957-60; pres. Tarrant County Joint Bds. Christian Chs., 1962-64. Registered Profl. Engr., Tex., Okla. Mem. Am. Astroautics Soc., I.E.E.E., Am. Soc. Engring. Edn., Sigma Xi, Tau Beta Pi, Phi Kappa Phi, Eta Kappa Nu, Sigma Pi Sigma. Kiwanian (past chmn. support of chs. com. chmn. internat. relations). Author: (with S.F. Crumb) Transients in Linear Systems. Home: 620 Westview Terrace Arlington TX 76013

JIMENEZ-TORRES, CARLOS FEDERICO, physician; b. Aquada, P.R., Oct. 19, 1921; s. Carlos and Pura (Torres) Jimenez; student U. P.R., 1936-39; M.D., George Washington U., 1943; postgrad. in radiology U. Pa., 1948-49; m. Domitila Ferrer, June 18, 1949; children—Lorraine, Carlos Federico, Luis Javier, Pura Elaine, Janet Arlene. Intern, Fajardo Dist. Hosp., 1943-44; resident Presbyn. Hosp., Phila., 1949-51; physician VA Center and Hosp., San Juan, P.R., 1946-48; practice medicine, specializing in radiology, Ponce, P.R., 1952—; instr. radiology U. Pa. Sch. Medicine, 1950-51; lectr. radiology U. P.R. Sch. Medicine, 1952—; cons. in radiology Ponce Med. Center. Bd. dirs., past treas. Liceo Ponceno. Served with AUS, 1944-46. Diplomate Am. Bd. Radiology. Mem. Am., Pan Am., P.R. med. assns., Am. Coll. Radiology, P.R., Inter-Am. radiol. socs., Am. Legion, USCG Aux., U.S. Power Squadron. Roman Catholic. K.C., Lion (past dist. zone chmn., past pres. Ponce). Club: Ponce Yacht (dir.). Home: 16 Universidad St Ponce PR 00731 Office: Lorraine Bldg Ponce PR 00731

JIMERSON, WILA, govt. ofcl. Supr. modern fgn. langs. Ark. Dept. Edn. Office: Education Bldg Little Rock AR 72203*

JINKS, ROBERT LARRY, newspaper editor; b. Mt. Pleasant, Tex., Jan. 26, 1929; s. Leon Carlton and Mary (Cunnyngham) J.; B.Journalism, U. Mo., 1950; M.S., Columbia, 1956; m. Claire Van Ravesteyn; children—Laura Beth, Daniel Carlton. News editor Muskogee (Okla.) Times-Democrat, 1950-51; reporter Greensboro (N.C.) Daily News, 1953-55; reporter, city editor Charlotte (N.C.) Observer, 1956-60; mem. staff Miami (Fla.) Herald, 1960—, mng. editor, 1966-72, exec. editor, 1972—. Bd. dirs. Dade County chpt. and nat. A.R.C. Served with AUS, 1951-53. Named to 50th anniversary honors list Columbia Grad. Sch. Journalism, 1963. Unitarian. Home: 1229 Andora Av Coral Gables FL 33146 Office: 1 Herald Plaza Miami FL 33101

JOANOS, JAMES EMANUEL, judge; b. Tallahassee, June 28, 1934; s. Emanuel George and Theologia (Patragas) J.; B.S., Fla. State U., 1956; LL.B., Yale, 1962; m. Betty Lou Whittle, May 25, 1957; children—Julia Lee, Janet Theologia, James Emanuel. Admitted to Fla. bar, 1962; research asst. Fla. 1st Dist. Ct. Appeals, Tallahassee, 1962-63; mem. firm Dye & Joanos, 1963-68, Joanos, Parsons & Hayes, 1969-71; judge Leon County Felony Ct. Record, 1971—; v.p. Capital Sq. Bldg., Inc., Tallahassee, 1968—. Served with USAF, 1956-59. Recipient Distinguished Service award Tallahassee Jr. C. of C., 1967; Fla. State U. Gold Key outstanding alumnus award, 1967. Mem. Fla., Tallahassee bar assns., Tallahassee (pres. 1964-65), Fla. (v.p. 1965-66) jr. chambers commerce, Fla. State U. Alumni Assn. (pres.), Gold Key, Omicron Delta Kappa, Phi Delta Phi, Sigma Chi, Pi Sigma Alpha. Episcopalian. Mason (Shriner), Elk. Home: 2001 Seminole Dr Tallahassee FL 32301 Office: Leon County Courthouse Tallahassee FL 32302

JOBE, EUCLID RAY, ednl. cons.; b. Chalybeate, Miss., June 25, 1898; s. Lewis Harmon and Alice (Ray) J.; B.A., U. Miss., 1918, M.A., 1935; Ph.D., George Peabody Coll. for Tchrs., 1948; LL.D., William Carey Coll., 1965; m. Martha McKnight, June 22, 1922. Prin., Natchez (Miss.) High Sch., 1921-22; supt. Hazlehurst (Miss.) High Sch., 1922-35; state high sch. supr., Miss., 1936-45; ednl. officer U.S Office Edn., 1946; exec. sec., dir., trustee State Instns. of Higher Learning of Miss., 1945-68; edn. cons., commn. on Christian edn. Miss. Bapt. Conv. Bd., Jackson, 1969—. Sec., Miss. Textbook Commn., 1934-36; chmn. Miss. Commn. on Coll. Accrediation, 1950—; exec. sec. Miss. High Sch. Accrediting Commn., 1936-45; exec. com. Miss. Research and Devel. Council; mem. Miss. Interagy. Commn. on Mental Health cons. dir. Assn. Governing Bds. State Univs. Served with U.S. Army, 1918. Mem. Assn. Higher Edn., Nat., Miss. ednl. assns., Asso. Consultants in Edn., Nat. Assn. Secondary Sch. Prins. (pres.), Miss. Assn. Colls. (pres.), Newcomen Soc., Phi Delta Kappa, Kappa Phi Kappa, Kappa Delta Pi, Pi Gamma Mu. Mason, Rotarian. Home: 3934 Old Canton Lane Jackson MS 39206

JOELSON, MARK R., lawyer; b. Paris, France, Oct. 23, 1934; B.A. cum laude, Harvard, 1955, LL.B. cum laude, 1958; Diploma in Law (Fulbright scholar), Oxford U. (Eng.), 1962. Admitted to D.C. bar, 1958, U.S. Supreme Ct. bar, 1963; Since practiced in Washington; atty. Dept. Justice, 1959-63; mem. firm Arent, Fox, Kintner, Plotkin & Kahn. Mem. Fed. Bar Assn. (chmn. council antitrust and trade regulation 1969-71, mem. council on internat. law and fgn. trade). Office: Federal Bar Bldg Washington DC 20006*

JOERNS, JACK CHASE, aerospace engr., govt. ofcl.; b. Chgo., July 9, 1917; s. Arnold and Estelle (Chase) J.; student Northwestern Mil. and Naval Acad., 1933-35, Ill. Inst. Tech., 1935-36; B.S. in Aero. Engring, St. Louis U., 1940; postgrad. Tex. Christian U., 1955-57; m. Rita Mary Phipps, Oct. 21, 1944; m. 2d, Susan Jones Clements, Feb. 14, 1967; 1 son, Dana Beowulf Christian. Sr. engr. Gen. Dynamics Corp., Ft. Worth, 1948-56; engr. Puget Sound Naval Shipyard, Bremerton, Wash., 1957-58, Bell Helicopter Co., Ft. Worth, 1958-62; sci. specialist Edgerton, Germeshausen & Grier, Las Vegas, Nev., 1962-63; aerospace engr. NASA Manned Spacecraft Center, Houston, 1964—. Bd. dirs. U.S. Parachute Assn., Monterey, Cal. Served to flight lt. RAF, 1941-45. Mem. Am. Inst. Aeros. and Astronautics, Soc. Automotive Engrs., Am. Ordnance Assn., Nat. Geog. Soc. (mem. Vilcabamba Expdn. 1963), Exptl. Aircraft Assn. Republican. Presbyn. Elk. Clubs: OX-5 (Pitts.). Home: 18410 King's Lynn Houston TX 77058 Office: NASA Manned Spacecraft Center Houston TX 77001

JOFFE, SEYMOUR, data transmission co. exec.; b. Bklyn., Nov. 8, 1929; s. Nathan and Esther (Bass) J.; B.A., Bklyn. Coll., 1951; postgrad. N.Y. U., 1951; m. Phyllis Cushing Probitsky, Aug. 28, 1955; children—Sandra Lee, Norman Elliot, Michel Matthew, Robin Arthur. Systems programmer Univac div. Sperry Rand Corp., N.Y.C., 1955-62, salesman, Houston, 1962-67; v.p. University Computing Co., Dallas, 1967-71; sr. v.p., chief marketing officer Data Transmission Co., Vienna, Va., 1971—. Bd. dirs. Dallas Soc. Crippled Children, 1969. Served to lt. USNR, 1952-55. Named Outstanding Man in Sales Mgmt., Houston Sales Assn., 1962. Mem. Am. Mgmt. Assn., Assn. Computer Machinery, Electronic Industries Assn. Home: 6224 Lakeview Dr Falls Church VA 22041 Office: 8130 Boone Blvd Vienna VA 22180

JOFFRE, ANTHONY ROCH, dentist; b. Savannah, Ga., Nov. 8, 1919; s. Rocco and Mary Concetta (Fasciola) J.; B.A., La. State U., 1940; D.D.S., Loyola U., New Orleans, 1943; m. Eleanor I. Tesone, June 19, 1948; children—Denise, John Anthony, Anne. Practice dentistry, Miami, Fla., 1946—. Chmn., Restorative Dentistry group, 1955-72. Bd. dirs. Dade County Dental Research Clinic; v.p., bd. dirs. Med. Service Bur., Inc., Miami, 1972—; bd. dirs. Dental Clinic Centro Hispene Cathohia, 1960-72. Adminstrv. bd. Mercy Hosp., Miami, Biscayne Coll. Served to capt. AUS, 1943-46. Mem. Am., Fla. dental assns., Miami, East Coast, South Dade County dental socs., Acad. Gen. Dentistry (chpt. pres. 1972-73), Fedn. Dentaire Internat., Pierre Fauchard Acad. Democrat. Roman Catholic. K.C. (4 deg.). Club: Serra (trustee 1970-72) (Miami, Fla.). Home: 173 Shore Dr S Miami FL 33133 Office: 733-36 Alfred I du Pont Bldg Miami FL 33131

JOFTES, SAUL EUGENE, assn. exec.; b. N.Y.C., Nov. 1, 1914; s. Yoineh and Manya (Rodier) J.; Adj in Arts, Harvard, 1941; M.A., Boston U., 1941; J.D., Northeastern U., 1936, LL.M., 1938; postgrad. Harvard Law Sch., 1939; m. Miriam Minna Uretsky, Feb. 22, 1938. Lectr., Boston U., 1940-44, Law Sch., 1944-46; lectr. govt. Harvard, Cambridge, Mass., 1946-47; edn. dir. Anti-Defamation League B'Nai B'rith, Boston, 1947-48, dir. European office, Paris, France, 1948-52, dir. Latin Am. office, Santiago, Chile, 1953, dir. internat. affairs, Washington, 1953-67, sec.-gen. internat. council, 1959-67, research dir., 1967-68; dir. gen. World Confedn. Nat. Jewish Orgns., Washington, 1969—. Non-govtl. rep. at UN, Coordinating Bd. Jewish Orgns., 1949-67; observer for B'nai B'rith at Nurenberg Trials, Germany, 1949. Mem. nat. bd. sponsors Inst. Am. Strategy; nat. voter adv. bd. Am. Security Council. Mem. Am. Soc. Internat. Law, Harvard Law Sch. Assn., Harvard Club N.Y.C. Mem. B'nai B'rith. Home: 6410 Cross Woods Dr Falls Church VA 22044

JOHANOS, DONALD, orch. condr.; b. Cedar Rapids, Ia., Feb. 10, 1928; s. Gregory Hedges and Doris (Nelson) J.; Mus.B., Eastman Sch. Music, 1950, Mus.M., 1952; D.F.A. (hon.), Coe Coll., 1962; m. Thelma Trimble, Aug. 27, 1950; children—Jennifer Claire, Thea Christine, Gregory Bruce (dec.), Andrew Mark, Eve Marie. Mus. dir. Altoona (Pa.) Symphony, 1953-56, Johnstown (Pa.) Symphony, 1955-56; asso. condr. Dallas Symphony Orch., 1957-61, resident condr. 1961-62, mus. dir., 1962—; guest condr. Phila. Orch., Amsterdam Concertgebouw Orch., Pitts Symphony, Rochester Philharmonic, New Orleans Philharmonic, Denver Symphony, Vancouver Symphony, Netherlands Radio Philharmonic, Swiss Radio Orch., Mpls. Symphony; tchr. Pa. State U., 1953-55, So. Methodist U., 1958-62, Hockaday Sch., 1962-65. Advanced study grantee Am. Symphony Orch. League and Rockefeller Found., 1955-58. Mem. Am. Fedn. Musicians, Internat. Congress of Strings (dir.). Office: Dallas Symphony Orchestra PO Box 8472 Dallas TX 78405

JOHANSEN, CAREY, dentist; b. Wei, India, Aug. 17, 1913 (parents Am. citizens); s. Thorvald S. and Anna T. (Ommundsen) J.; B.A., U. Minn., 1935, D.D.S., 1938; D.D.S., U. Pa., 1939; m. Marion Teresa Hebron, July 19, 1941; children—Robert Carey, Sharon (Mrs. James Bath), Stephen Paul, Deborah Ann. Practice dentistry, Englewood, N.J., 1939-42; dentist VA Hosp., Richmond, Va., 1947—. Served with Dental Corps, USAAF, 1942-46. Mem. Am. Dental Assn. Republican. Baptist. Home: 8957 Rustic Rd Richmond VA 23235 Office: VA Hosp Richmond VA 23219

JOHN, DAVID RUSSELL, JR., financial cons.; b. N.Y.C., Sept. 8, 1937; s. David Russell and Elizabeth (Dumbris) J.; B.S., U. Pa., 1959; m. Carolyn Beer, Nov. 24, 1962; children—Jennifer Lynn, David Russell III. Exec. trainee Mfrs. Trust Co., N.Y.C., 1959-60; v.p. Fla. Capital Corp., Palm Beach, 1960-68; v.p. finance, dir. Cinecom Corp., N.Y.C., 1968-69; chmn. bd. Indsl. Electronics Assos., Inc., Palm Beach, 1969-71; chmn. bd., pres. Beefy King Internat., Inc., 1970-71; chmn. bd., pres Southeastern Consultants, Inc., West Palm Beach, Fla., 1971—. Mem. Fla. N.G., 1960-66. Mem. Sigma Nu. Home: 242 List Rd Palm Beach FL 33480 Office: Harvey Bldg West Palm Beach FL 33401

JOHN, LEWIS GEORGE, coll. dean; b. Waco, Tex., Nov. 25, 1936; s. Lewis Hervin and Margaret Elizabeth (Reese) J.; B.A., Washington and Lee U., 1958; postgrad. (Fulbright scholar) U. Edinburgh (Scotland), 1958-59; M.P.A. (Woodrow Wilson fellow), Princeton, 1961; postgrad. Syracuse U. (H. Lehman fellow), 1966-68; m. Annette Louise Church, June 3, 1961; children—Andrew, Christopher. Exec. trainee Office Sec. Def., Washington, summers 1960, 61; dir. student financial aid and placement Washington and Lee U., Lexington, Va., 1963-66, 68-69, dean students, asst. prof. politics, 1969—. Sec. Rockbridge Area Drug Council, 1970—. Served to lt. AUS, 1961-63. Mem. Am. Soc. Pub. Adminstrn., Am. Polit. Sci. Assn., Am. Econ. Assn., Nat. Assn. Student Personnel Adminstrs., Va. Assn. Student Personnel Adminstrs. (sec.-treas. 1970-71), So. Coll. Personnel Assn., Phi Beta Kappa, Omicron Delta Kappa, Omicron Delta Epsilon. Kiwanian. Home: 8 Edmondson Av Lexington VA 24450

JOHNS, BENJAMIN RILEY, JR., architect; b. Richmond, Va., July 14, 1921; s. Benjamin Riley and Marie Blanche (Williams) J.; B.S. in Archtl. Engring., N.C. State Coll., 1948; m. Geraldine Charlotte Price, Sept. 10, 1945; children—Benjamin Riley III, Pamela P. Draftsman, E. Tucker Carlton, architect, Richmond, 1940, 41, 46-48, architect, 1948-54; draftsman Dept. Conservation and Devel., N.C. Dept. State Parks, summer 1942; propr. Ben R. Johns, Jr., architect, Richmond, 1954—. Sec., E. View Corp., Richmond, Va., 1970-71. Mem. Richmond Bd. Zoning Appeals, 1955-60, 62—, chmn. 1967-69; mem. Richmond City Council, 1960-62, Richmond Planning Commn., 1960-62. Served with AUS, 1942-45; lt. col. Res. Mem. A.I.A. (corporate mem.; pres. Richmond sect. Va. chpt. 1959-60), Va. Citizens Planning Assn., Constrn. Specifications Inst. (corporate mem.), Va. Assn. Professions, Richmond C. of C., Richmond First Club (pres. 1959-60), N.C. State Alumni Assn. (pres Richmond 1958, 59), Central Richmond Assn. (dir. 1960-62), USCG Aux. (flotilla comdr. 1971), Am. Legion, Navy League. Methodist. Mason (K.T.). Clubs: Windmill Point Yacht (Foxwells, Va.); Downtown of Richmond (pres. 1963-64). Home: 4530 W Seminary Av Richmond VA 23227 Office: One N 5th St Richmond VA 23219

JOHNS, JAY JOSE, physician; b. Round Rock, Tex., Oct. 30, 1900; s. George Washington and Claudia Genoma (Nelson) J.; B.S., U. Tex., 1924, M.D., 1924; m. Catherine Hildegarde Davison, Sept. 17, 1924; children—Mary Victor (Mrs. John J. Kane), Hildegarde (Mrs. J.H. Stjepcevich). Intern, Taylor Sanitorium, 1924-25; practice medicine specializing in gen. practice and surgery, Taylor, Tex., 1924—; founder The Johns Clinic, 1946—; founder The Johns Hosp., 1948, chief staff, 1955—; dir. City Nat. Bank. Trustee Johns Community Hosp., chmn. fund drive, 1971—. Named Taylor Citizen of the Year, C. of C., 1968. Fellow A.C.S.; mem. Am., Tex. (v.p. 1968) med. assns., Southwestern Surg. Congress (founding mem.), Seventh Dist. Med. Soc. (councilor 1959-68). Home: 717 Huff St Taylor TX 76574 Office: 720 W 6th St Taylor TX 76574

JOHNS, RICHARD ALTON, JR., pub. co. exec.; b. Tyler, Tex., July 17, 1929; s. Richard Alton and Annie Sarah (Hill) J.; A.A., Tyler Jr. Coll., 1948; B.A., N. Tex. State U., 1950; m. Joan Turner, Nov. 8, 1958; children—Richard Andrew, Janis. Fashion artist Kline's Dept. Store, Tyler, 1950; engring. illustrations editor Gen. Dynamics Corp., Fort Worth, 1951-61; artist, writer, editor Tyler Star Newspaper, 1961—. Fashion artist advt. cons., stores, Tyler. Served with F.A., AUS, 1950-51. Presbyn. Author: Thirteenth Apostle, 1966; Garden of the Okapi, 1968; Return to Heroism, 1969; (play) The Legacy, prod. on TV, 1965. Home: 912 W Camellia St Tyler TX 75701 Office: PO Box 1073 Tyler TX 75701

JOHNSON, A. BRUCE, economist, educator; b. Pensacola, Fla., Apr. 10, 1917; s. Thomas Arthur and Margaret Genevieve (Watson) J.; B.S., U.S. Naval Acad., 1939; postgrad. Harvard, 1944, Naval War Coll., 1954-55, N.Y. Inst. Finance, 1960; M.S., Fla. State U., 1965, Ph.D., 1967; m. Mary Louise Mahoney, Sept. 16, 1950; children—Douglas Bruce, Patricia Genevieve. Draftsman, Newport News Shipbldg. & Dry Dock Co., 1939-40; commd. ensign USN, 1940, advanced through grades to comdr., 1950; hull inspection officer Navy Shipyard, Charleston, S.C., 1940-41; instr. Navy Supply Corps Sch., Harvard, 1941-42; asst. supply officer U.S.S. Long Island, 1942-43, supply officer, 1943-44; comdg. officer Navy Material Redistbn. Center, Corpus Christi, Tex., 1944-45; officer in charge property accounting div. Bur. Supplies and Accounts, Navy Dept., Washington, 1945-48; supply officer U.S.S. Macon, 1948-49; fiscal officer Naval Gun Factory, Washington, 1949-52; supply, fiscal, budget and adminstrv. officer Office Chief Naval Operations, Navy Hydrographic Office, Washington, 1952-54; supply and budget officer Navy sect. Mil. Assistance Adv. Group, Lisbon, Portugal, 1955-57; officer in charge Navy Regional Accounts Office, Cleve., 1957-60; staff supply officer, chief Naval Air Basic Tng., Pensacola, 1960-61; ret., 1961; investment adviser, stock broker, Pensacola, 1961-64; asst. prof. econs. U. W. Fla., Pensacola, 1967-72, asso. prof., 1972—. Mem. Am. Assn. U. Profs., Am., So. econ. assns., Am. Security Council, Ret. Officers Assn., Naval Acad. Alumni Assn., Am. Assn. Security Dealers, Omicron Delta Epsilon, Kappa Delta Pi. Democrat. Roman Catholic. Club: Navy Officers (Pensacola). Contbr. articles profl. jours. Home: 1700 N 10th Av Pensacola FL 32503

JOHNSON, ALCEE LABRANCHE, educator; b. Fernwood, Miss., July 22, 1905; s. Jonas Edward and Bertha (LaBranche) J.; student Alcorn Coll., 1925; A.B., Fisk U., 1927; M.A., Columbia, 1956; postgrad. U. So. Cal., 1962; D. Hum. (hon.), Miss. Bapt. Sem., 1972; m. Thelma M. Wethers, Dec. 25, 1931; children—Joyce (Mrs. James L. Bolden), Al Wethers. Instr., Prentiss (Miss.) Inst. Jr. Coll., 1927-30, dir. instrn., 1931-36, 37-71, pres., 1971—; Miss. state supr. Survey Vocational Edn. and Guidance, Office Edn., Dept. Interior, Washington, 1936-37; 1st v.p., dir. State Mut. Fed. Savs. & Loan Assn.; inst. rep. Heifer Project, Inc. Mem. Miss. Regional Med. Program, Image Commn. Miss. Econ. Council, Phelps-Stokes Fund Conf. Edn. Leaders. Chmn. Western div. Boy Scouts Am., com. mem. JDC Mut. Fed. Credit Union, 1960—; del. White House Conf. on Aging, 1971; mem. Miss. Probation and Parole Bd., 1972—. Mem. Voters League, 1964—. Bd. dirs. So. Miss. Econ. Devel. Dist. So. Interracial Commn. grantee, 1930, Silver Beaver award Boy Scouts Am., 1960. Mem. Am., Miss. (past pres.), 6th Dist. (past pres.) tchrs. assns., N.E.A. (life), N.A.A.C.P. (local coordinator), Jefferson Davis County, Miss. Chambers Commerce, Alpha Phi Alpha, Phi Delta Kappa. Mem. Ch. of Christ (trustee). Mason. Home: PO Box 112 Prentiss MS 39474 Office: Drawer C Prentiss MS 39474

JOHNSON, ANDREW EMERSON, III, headmaster; b. Monterey, Va., July 26, 1931; s. Andrew Emerson and Virginia (Miller) J.; B.S., Hampden-Sydney Coll., 1952, Litt.D., 1969; M.Ed., U. N.C. at Chapel Hill, 1959; Nat. Def. Edn. Act fellow Williams Coll., 1967; m. Rophelia Simpson, Aug. 6, 1955; children—Rebecca, Andrew Emerson IV. Instr. math. Norfolk (Va.) Acad., 1952-56, head math. dept., instr. Bible, 1957-59, asst. headmaster, 1959-61; headmaster North Cross Sch., Roanoke, Va., 1961-69; headmaster Charlotte (N.C.) Country Day Sch., 1969—. Chmn. edn. govt. div. United Fund, 1967; mem. adv. com. Roanoke City Chaplain, 1967-69. Bd. dirs. Community Concert Series, Charlotte, 1971—; trustee Roanoke Fine Arts Center, 1967-69. Mem. Nat. Assn. Prin. Schs. for Girls, Omicron Delta Kappa. Presbyn. Mason, Rotarian. Clubs: Charlotte City, Olde Providence Racquet and Swim. Home: 4420 Darventry Ct Charlotte NC 28211 Office: 1440 Carmel Rd Charlotte NC 28211

JOHNSON, ANDREW JAY, coll. adminstr.; b. Beaumont, Tex., Sept. 27, 1933; s. Andrew Jay and Lois C. (Harper) J.; B.A., U. Tex., 1954; M.A., U. Ind., 1955, Ph.D., 1964; M.A. in L.S., U. Chgo., 1966; m. Betty Holmes, Jan. 30, 1955; children—Laura Kathleen, Letitia. Instr. Schreiner Inst., Kerrville, Tex., 1955-56, admissions counselor, 1956-57; mem. faculty Lamar U., Beaumont, 1958—, prof. history, 1968—, dir. library services, 1967-69, v.p. acad. affairs, 1969—. Lectr. Grad. Sch. Library Sci., U. Tex., Austin, 1967-68; cons. S.W. Ednl. Devel. Lab., Dallas, 1966. Mem. Beaumont Library Commn., 1966-69; pres. Am. Heart Assn., Beaumont, 1971-72; mem. budget com. United Appeals, 1970-73. Trustee All Saints Episcopal Sch., 1966—. So. Fellowships Found. fellow, 1956, 60-61. Mem. S.E. Tex. Social Studies Confs. (dir. 1963-65), Beta Phi Mu, Phi Alpha Theta. Episcopalian. Rotarian. Home: 2093 Central Dr Beaumont TX 77706

JOHNSON, AUBREY PHILLIP, city mgr.; b. Portsmouth, Va., Oct. 3, 1917; s. Aubrey Phillip and Alice (Hutchins) J.; student pub. schs., Portsmouth; m. Mary Lea Duncan, Sept. 9, 1939; children—Mary Sue, Alice B. Teller, Am. Nat. Bank, Portsmouth, 1935-43, purchasing agt. City of Portsmouth, 1945-50, city clk., auditor, 1950-58, city mgr., 1958—. Bd. dirs. Beasley Boys Club. Served to 2d lt. USAAF, 1943-45. Mem. Internat. City Mgrs. Assn. Kiwanian, Elk. Home: 362 Washington St Portsmouth VA 23704 Office: 1 High St Portsmouth VA 23704

JOHNSON, BEN BUTLER, physician; b. Bklyn., May 23, 1920; s. Louis Collins and Jeanne Farrell (Payne) J.; grad. Choate Sch., 1937; A.B., Harvard, 1942, M.D., 1944; m. Barbara Ann Maltby, Dec. 22, 1962; children—Louis Collins, III, Charles Martin, Michael David, Mary Jeanne, Margaret Ann. Intern, N.Y. Hosp., 1944-45; resident Bellevue Hosp., N.Y.C., 1947-49; research fellow medicine Bassett Hosp. and Stanford U., 1949-53; instr., asst. prof. medicine Stanford, 1955-59; practice medicine, specializing in internal medicine and nephrology, Jackson, Miss., 1959—; mem. staff Univ. Hosp.; chief renal and electrolyte div. dept. medicine U. Miss. Med. Center, 1959—; asst. prof. U. Miss., 1959-62. asso. prof. medicine, 1962—; dir. Diabetes Clinic, Stanford U. Hosps., 1956-59. Mem. Miss. Nutrition Council, 1961—, chmn., 1962-64. Bd. dirs. Kidney Found. of Miss., 1964-71, sec.-treas., 1965-71, chmn. med. adv. bd., 1971—; mem. nat. med. adv. council Nat. Kidney Found., 1970—, sec., 1971—. Served to lt. (j.g.) M.C., USNR, 1945-46; served to lt. USNR, 1953-55. Diplomate Am. Bd. Internal Medicine, Nat. Bd. Med. Examiners. Fellow A.C.P.; mem. Am., Internat. socs. nephrology, Endocrine Soc., Am. Diabetes Assn., Am. Soc. Internal Medicine, Am. Fedn. for Clin. Research, Western Soc. for Clin. Research, Am., Miss. heart assns., Soc. Mayflower Descs. (surgeon-gen. Miss. soc. 1971—), Am. Assn. U. Profs. (pres. Miss. conf. 1968-69), Sigma Xi. Contbr. articles to profl. jours. Home: 1540 Kimwood Circle Jackson MS 39211 Office: Univ of Miss Medical Center 2500 N State St Jackson MS 39216

JOHNSON, BENJAMIN FRANKLIN, mining co. exec.; b. Virgie, Ky., June 21, 1931; s. Fon Mayo and Nora (Newsom) J.; B.S., Bowling Green Coll. at Commerce, 1953; m. Betty G. Maynard, July 24, 1950; children—Charles Franklin, Mark Douglas, Paul Sheldon. Jr. accountant Albert B. Maloney & Co., C.P.A.'s, Hopkinville, Ky., 1953-55; pres. Ideal Elkhorn Coal Co., Inc., Pikeville, Ky., 1964-71; treas. Famous Elkhorn Coal Sale, Inc., Pikeville, 1955-69; pres. Bull Creek Mining Corp., Hazard, Ky., 1969—. C.P.A., Tenn. Home and office: PO Box 100 Jeff KY 41751

JOHNSON, BENJAMIN LESTER, lawyer; b. Warrenton, Ga., Aug. 13, 1935; s. W. Norman and Mauree (Anderson) J.; A.B., Mercer U., 1957; J.D., U. Ga., 1961; m. Patricia Joan LeCroy, Aug. 18, 1956; children—Carole Wynne, Russell Norman, Arthur Berry. Admitted to Ga. bar, 1961; surveyor U.S. Dept. Agr., Warrenton, 1952-54; draftsman Greenough-McMahon Engrs., Macon, Ga., 1957-58; atty. Dept. Law, Atlanta, 1961-65; asst. atty. gen., Atlanta, 1962-66; partner Mitchel, Pate & Anderson attys., 1966-71; corporate counsel Atlanta Fed. Savs. & Loan Assn., 1972—. Dir. Can-Car, Inc.; sec. Leasing Internat., Inc. Served to lt. AUS, 1958-60. Recipient award labor law excellence, Lawyers Co-op. Pub. Co., 1961. Mem. Am., Ga., Atlanta bar assns., Atlanta Lawyers Club, Blue Key, Ga. Sport Shooting Assn. (pres.), Nat. Rifle Assn., Delta Theta Phi, Kappa Alpha. Methodist. Clubs: Atlanta City, River Bend Gun. Editor: Banking and Trust Company Laws of Georgia, 1964. Editor, Opinions Atty. Gen., 1958-59, 60-61. Home: 314 Brentwood Dr NE Atlanta GA 30305 Office: Atlanta Fed Savs Bldg Atlanta GA 30303

JOHNSON, BERT W(ILLARD), county mgr.; b. Marinette, Wis., Apr. 1, 1915; s. Lawrence and Hanna (Johnson) J.; Ph.B. in Municipal Adminstrn. and finance, U. Wis., 1939; grad. study U. Chgo., 1941-42; m. Dorothy June Stauffacher, June 22, 1940; children—L. Kirk, June C., Ralph W., Ernest W., Cynthia M. Participant research and field projects, 1939-40; finance dir., Winnetka, Ill., 1940-48; city mgr., Lebanon, Mo., 1948-50, Boulder, Colo., 1950-53, Evanston, Ill., 1953-62; lectr. Northwestern U., 1954-62; county mgr., Arlington, Va., 1962—. U.S. rep. Caribbean Seminar, 1964; cons. to govt. U.S. V.I., 1969; mem. Adv. Council on Intergovtl. Personnel Policy, 1971—. Asso. Northwestern U. One of four city mgrs. selected for study tour Republic West Germany, 1953; named one of top ten city mgrs., 1963. Served with USNR, 1943-46. Mem. Nat. Acad. Pub. Adminstrn., Internat. City Mgrs. Assn. (pres. 1963-64), Ill. City Mgrs. Assn. (past pres.), Am. Soc. Pub. Adminstrn. (nat. council), Nat. League Cities (mem. bd. cons. for com. on parking), Nat. Municipal League, U. Wis. Alumni Assn. Presbyn. Club: Army-Navy Country (Arlington). Home: 3621 38th St N Arlington VA 22207 Office: Ct House Arlington VA 22207

JOHNSON, BRUCE KING, physician, educator; b. Harriman, Tenn., Oct. 24, 1918; s. Samuel King and Laura Monro (Jones) J.; B.S., Birmingham-So. Coll., 1940; M.D., U. Tenn., 1944; m. Leila Newman Wright, Apr. 4, 1942 (dec. Nov. 1957); children—Bruce King, Samuel Paul, Thomas Sterling, Leila Anne; m. 2d, Iris Dudley Thomas, Mar. 14, 1959. Intern, Hillman Hosp. and Norwood Hosp., Birmingham, Ala., 1944-45; resident N.C. Bapt. Hosp.-Bowman Gray Med. Sch., Winston-Salem, 1949-51; sr. resident U. Ala. Hosps., Birmingham, 1951; gen. practice medicine, Flat Creek, Ala., 1945-49, specializing in internal medicine, Birmingham, 1952—; med. dir. Birmingham Med. Group Clinic, 1959-68; mem. staff, bd. dirs. Simon-Williamson Clinic and Norwood Properties, Inc.; mem. active staff U. Ala. Hosps.; mem. active and teaching staff Bapt. Med. Center, Princeton; mem. courtesy staff Bapt. Med. Center, Montclair, St. Vincents Hosp., South Highlands Infirmary; clin. instr. U. Ala., 1952-63, clin. asst. prof. dept. internal medicine, 1963—. Bd. dirs. Vis. Nurse Assn., 1962-69, chmn. med. adv. bd., 1970—. Fellow A.C.P.; mem. Birmingham Soc. Internists, Birmingham Acad. Medicine, Am., Ala. socs. internal medicine, A.M.A., Am. Heart Assn., So., Ala., Jefferson County med. assns., Lambda Chi Alpha, Omicron Delta Kappa, Alpha Kappa Kappa, Alpha Omega Alpha. Methodist (mem. adminstrv. bd.). Home: 3016 Warrington Rd Birmingham AL 35223 Office: 2930 12th Av N Birmingham AL 35234

JOHNSON, CARLETON WARE, editor; b. Springfield, Mo., Feb. 23, 1909; s. Frank Tatham and Katherine (Taylor) J.; A.B., U. Ill., 1930, M.A. 1932; m. Martha Byrd Baker, June 1, 1934; children—Martha Ann, Barbara Ruth. Mem. news staff Tampa (Fla.) Tribune, 1937-42, asst. editor, 1942-58; editor Tampa Times, 1958—. Mem. Fla. Soc. Editors, Nat. Conf. Editorial Writers, Sigma Delta Chi (pres. Fla. West Coast chpt.), Alpha Chi Rho. Presbyn. Mason (33 deg., Shriner, Jester). Club: Palma Ceia Golf (Tampa). Home: 3126 Oaklyn Dr Tampa FL 33609 Office: Tampa Times 505 E Kennedy Blvd Tampa FL 33602

JOHNSON, CECIL C., ins. exec.; b. Mexico, Mo., Oct. 13, 1903; B.S. in Elec. Engring., U. Mo., 1928; M.B.A., U. Denver, 1941; grad. Advanced Mgmt. Program, Harvard, 1956; m. Ola B. Bently, June 15, 1927; 1son, C. Bryce. Chmn. finance com., dir. Phila. Life Ins. Co., 1968—; dir. Tenn. Life Ins. Co., Houston Nat. Bank. Mem. Tau Beta Pi, Eta Kappa Nu. Presbyn. Clubs: Wall Street (N.Y.C.); River Oaks Country, Ramada, Houston. Home: 3726 Inwood Dr Houston TX 77019 Office: PO Box 2511 Houston TX 77001

JOHNSON, CECIL EARL, educator; b. Sweetwater, Tex., Feb. 11, 1924; s. Asberry and Jewel (Headrick) J.; B.A. cum laude, Baylor U., 1949, M.A. with honors, 1950; Ph.D. (univ. fellow) U. Tex., 1954; m. Ruth Wade, Aug. 26, 1950. Asst. prof. Tex. Technol. Coll., Lubbock, 1955-60; prof., chmn. dept. polit. sci. So. Meth. U., Dallas, 1960—. Research asso. East Asian Inst., sr. fellow Research Inst. Communist Affairs, Columbia, N.Y.C., 1966-68. Bd. dirs. Arnold Found., Houston. Served with USAAF, 1943-46. Named Outstanding Prof. So. Meth. U., 1964, 66. Mem. Am. Polit. Sci. Assn., Southwestern Social Sci. Assn., Assn. for Asian Studies, Pi Sigma Alpha, Phi Alpha Theta, Alpha Chi. Democrat. Baptist. Author: The Domestic Policies of the Castro Regime, 1961; Communist China and Latin America, 1959-67, 1970. Home: 914 Wedgewood Way Richardson TX 75080 Office: So Meth University Dallas TX 75222

JOHNSON, CHARLES A., JR., assn. exec.; b. Amory, Miss., Nov. 17, 1911; B.S., Miss. State U., 1932, M.S., 1945. Tchr. sci. Amory High Sch., 1937-41, prin., 1941-45; supt. Canton Pub. Schs., 1945-52, Starkville Pub. Schs., 1952-65; exec. sec., editor jour. Miss. Edn. Assn., 1965—, v.p., 1964. Mem. N.E.A., Am. Assn. Sch. Adminstrs., Phi Delta Kappa. Office: Miss Edn Assn 219 N President St Box 22529 Jackson MS 39205*

JOHNSON, CHARLES EDGAR, educator; b. Rochester, N.Y., July 6, 1919; s. Mason Frank and Ethel (Lyons) J.; B.S., Geneseo Tchrs. Coll., 1946; M.A., U. Cal. at Los Angeles, 1948; M.Ed., U. Ill., 1950, D.Ed., 1951; m. Rita Irene Boyd, July 19, 1963. Tchr., Mount Morris, N.Y., 1946-47; instr. Geneseo (N.Y.) Tchrs. Coll., 1948-49; faculty U. Ill., 1949-51, 55-65; asst. prof. U. Kan., 1952-55; prof. edn. U. Ga., Athens, 1965—, asso. dir. research and devel. center, 1965-67, dir. Ga. Ednl. Models, 1967-70. Ednl. researcher Spencer Press, Chgo., 1958-60, Grolier, Inc., N.Y.C., 1960-62; ednl. editor Holiday Books, Garrard Pub. Co., Champaign, Ill., 1962—; vis. prof. edn. U. P.R., Rio Piedras, 1963-64. Served with AUS, 1941-46. Mem. Am. Edn. Research Assn., N.E.A., Assn. Supervision and Curriculum Devel., Phi Delta Kappa, Kappa Delta Pi. Episcopalian (vestryman 1961-63). Elk. Mason. Contbr. articles to profl. jours. Home: 245 Pine Forest St Athens GA 30601

JOHNSON, CHARLES OWEN, lawyer; b. Monroe, La., Aug. 18, 1926; s. Clifford U. and Laura (Owen) J.; B.A., Tulane U., 1946, J.D., 1969; LL.B., Harvard, 1948; LL.M., Columbia, 1955. Admitted to La. bar, 1949, practiced in Monroe, 1949-50; mem. law editorial staff West Pub. Co., St. Paul, 1953; atty. Office of Chief Counsel, Internal Revenue Service, Washington, 1955—, chief Ct. Appeals br. Tax Ct. Div., 1968—. Served with AUS, 1950-52. Mem. Fed., La. bar assns., Nat. Lawyers Club, Soc. Colonial Wars (dep. sec. D.C. chpt.), S.A.R. (pres. D.C. soc.), Soc. War of 1812 (pres. D.C. soc.), S.C.V., Sons Union Vets., S.R., St. Andrew's Soc. Washington, Royal Soc. St. George, Sons and Daus. of Pilgrims, Huguenot Soc. S.C., Soc. Descs. Jersey Settlers, La. Colonials, Jamestowne Soc., Soc. Descs. Old Plymouth Colony, Order Ams. of Armorial Ancestry, Soc. Descs. Colonial Clergy, Hereditary Order Descs. Colonial Govs. (registrar gen.), Order Founders and Patriots of Am. (genealogist gen.), Order First Families Miss. 1699-1817 (gov. gen. 1967-69), Soc. Cin., Nat., Va. geneal. socs., Miss., Va. hist. socs., Phi Beta Kappa. Mason (Shriner, K.T., 32 deg.); mem. Order Eastern Star. Clubs: Pendennis of New Orleans (charter mem.); Arts of Washington. Author: The Geneology of Several Allied Families, 1961. Home: 1021 Arlington Blvd Arlington VA 22209 Office: Office of Chief Counsel Internal Revenue Service Washington DC 20224

JOHNSON, CHARLTON GRAHAM, agrl. engr.; b. Columbus, Ga., Mar. 21, 1920; s. Charlton Graham and Mattie Elba (Waters) J.; student Ga. Sch. Tech., 1938-39, 46-47, U. Ala., 1965-68; m. Mary Frances Saffold, Jan. 7, 1939; children—Charlton Graham, John Lamar, Mary Martha, Thomas Carson. Sales engr. Centennial Cotton Gin Co., Columbus, Ga., 1948-57; chief engr., 1957-60; engr., Moss Gordin Lint Cleaner Co., Memphis, 1960-61; chief engr. Gordin Unit System, Amite, La., 1961-63, Moss-Gordin Co., Amite, La., 1963-64; design engr. Continental-Moss-Gordin, Prattville, Ala., 1964-68; asst. supt. refinery Riverside Oil Mill, Marks, Miss., 1968-69; chief engr. Pacific Bldgs., Inc., Marks, Miss., 1969—. Registered profl. engr., Ala., Miss. Chmn. Weracoba council Boy Scouts Am., 1960. Served with USNR, 1944-45. Mem. Am. Soc. Agrl. Engrs. Republican. Home: PO Box 298 Marks MS 38646 Office: Pacific Bldgs Inc Covington Rd Marks MS 38646

JOHNSON, CLARENCE E., city ofcl. City mgr., Hampton, Va.. Home: 3 Rhonda Circle Hampton VA 23369

JOHNSON, CLEMENT OLE, profl. engr.; b. Savannah, Ga., Aug. 21, 1901; s. Peter Ole and Minnie (Clement) J.; B.S., Ga. Inst. Tech., 1926; m. Mary Allender, July 30, 1955. Coop. student Central of Ga. Ry. Co., Savannah, 1922-26, chemist, chief chemist, 1926-41, asst. mech. engr., 1946; research and test engr. Seaboard Airline R.R., Jacksonville, Fla., 1946-59; mgr. chem. dept., field engr. R. W. Hunt Co., Chgo., 1959-67; profl. engr. C.O. Johnson, Savannah, 1967—. Served to maj. AUS, 1941-44. Mem. Am. Soc. Testing and Materials, Am. Soc. M.E., Nat. Assn. Ry. Engrs. of Tests, Am. Ry. Engring. Assn. Episcopalian. Elk. Home: 646 E 36th St Savannah GA 31401 Office: 10 E Jones St Savannah GA 31401

JOHNSON, CLIFFORD LEE, JR., hosp. adminstr.; b. Hattiesburg, Miss., May 15, 1928; s. Clifford Lee and Velma (Grimsley) J.; B.S. in Bus. Adminstrn., U. So. Miss., 1952; m. Margaret Moseley, Mar. 8, 1952; children—Clifford Lee III, Beverley Victoria, Margaret Amelia, Kendall Moseley. Asst. adminstr. Forrest County Gen. Hosp., Hattiesburg, 1954-58; adminstr. Jefferson Davis County Hosp., Prentiss, Miss., 1958-67, Grenada County (Miss.) Hosp., Grenada, 1967—. Pres., Grenada County chpt. Am. Cancer Soc., 1969—, Dixie Youth Baseball, Prentiss, 1965-67; charter mem., past pres. Grenada Fine Arts Playhouse. Served with USMCR, 1946-48, AUS, 1952-53. Mem. Am. Coll. Hosp. Adminstrs., award of merit 1969, Am., Miss. (bd. govs. 1966-69) hosp. assns., Southeastern Hosp. Conf., Delta Hosp. Council (pres. 1969), U. So. Miss. Alumni Assn. Distinguished Service award 1966, (chpt. pres. 1969-70, exec. com. 1969—), Grenada County C. of C., Jefferson-Davis County C. of C. Man of Year 1967, (pres. 1966), Kappa Alpha. Democrat. Presbyn. (deacon). Clubs: Grenada Country, Rotary (editor Rotary Radiation). Home: 133 Union St Grenada MS 38901 Office: 960 Avent Dr Grenada MS 38901

JOHNSON, CLIFTON HERMAN, historian-archivist; b. Griffin, Ga., Sept. 13, 1921; s. John and Pearl (Parrish) J.; student U. Conn., 1943-44; B.A., U. N.C., 1948, Ph.D. 1959; M.A. U. Chgo., 1949; postgrad. U. Wis., 1951; m. Rosemary Brunst, Aug. 2, 1960; children— Charles, Robert, Virginia. Tutor, LeMoyne Coll., Memphis, 1950-53, asst. prof., 1953-56, prof., 1960-61, 63-66; asst. prof., East Carolina Coll., 1958-59; asst. librarian and archivist Fisk U., 1961-63; dir., Amistad Research Center, New Orleans, 1966—. Dir., Nat. Com. Against Discrimination in Housing, 1967—. Served with AUS, 1940-45. Mem. So. Hist. Assn., Soc. Am. Archivists, Assn. for Study Negro Life and History, Orgn. Am. Historians, Nat. Assn. Human Rights Workers, Nat. Cath. Conf. for Inter-racial Justice. Author: (with Carroll Barber) The American Negro: A Selected and Annotated Bibliography for High Schools and Junior Colleges, 1968. Editor: God Struck Me Dead: Religious Conversions and Experiences and Autobiographies of Ex-Slaves, 1969. Office: Dillard New Orleans LA 70122

JOHNSON, COLLUS OLIVER, educator; b. Sardis, Tenn., Dec. 7, 1905; s. William Thomas and Laura Lula (McBride) J.; B.S., U. Tenn., 1931, M.S., 1948; Ed.D., George Peabody Coll. for Tchrs., 1960; m. Eugenia Irene Caldwell, Dec. 20, 1942; children—Edwin Thomas, Eugene Caldwell, Colleen Susan. Tchr., prin. elementary and high sch., Hardin County, Tenn., Henderson County, Tenn., 1932-36; tchr., housing mgr., population readjustment rep., agriculturist TVA, Knoxville, 1936-42, 46-48; area edn. coordinator Murray (Ky.) State Coll., 1948-51; asso. prof. edn. West Ga. Coll., Carrollton, 1951—, asso. dir. adult edn., 1951-64, tchr. edn. program, 1951-64, dir. continuing edn., 1964—. Pres. bd. mgrs. Ga. Congress Parents and Tchrs., 1951-67; mem. Carroll Service Council, 1960-65. Served to 1st lt. AUS, 1942-46. Mem. N.E.A., Am., Rural edn. assns., Nat. Assn. Pub. Sch. Adult Educators, Ga. Assn. Educators, Ga. Adult Edn. Council, Ga. Gerontology Soc. (pres. 1969-70), Phi Kappa Delta. Methodist. Kiwanian. Home: 203 Griggin Dr Carrollton GA 30117

JOHNSON, CONE, physician, educator; b. Eastland, Tex., Nov. 20, 1926; s. Earle Clay and Eloise (Trigg) J.; B.S., N.Tex. State U., 1949; M.D., U. Tex., Galveston, 1954; m. Patricia Zeller, Oct. 20, 1956; children—Deborah Lynn, Cynthia Kay, Barbara Ann. Intern, John Sealy Hosp., Galveston, 1954-55; resident medicine U. Tex. Med. Br. Hosps., 1955-58; commd. 1st lt. M.C., U.S. Air Force, 1956, advanced through grades to maj., 1962; ret., 1963; mem. sr. staff Scott-White Clinic, 1963-68; pvt. practice medicine, specializing in respiratory therapy and environmental diseases, Abilene, Tex., 1968-69, 70; asso. Cardiopulmonary Inst., Meth. Hosp., Dallas, 1969-70; clin. asst. prof. medicine U. Tex. Southwestern Med. Sch., Dallas, 1969—; med. dir. respiratory therapy service and pulmonary physiology labs. W. Tex. Med. Center Hosp., Abilene, 1970—; med. dir. respiratory therapy service Abilene State Sch., Tex. Dept. Mental Health and Retardation, 1971—, Simmons Meml. Hosp., Sweetwater, Tex., 1970—, Cox Meml. Hosp., Abilene, 1970—; cons. in pulmonary physiology VA Hosp., Big Spring, Tex., 1968—. Dir. Respiratory Therapy Assos., Abilene. Bd. dirs. W.Tex. Med. Center Research Found., 1968. Served with USNR, 1943-46. Diplomate Am. Bd. Internal Medicine and Pulmonary Diseases. Fellow A.C.P., Am. Coll. Chest Physicians (pres. Tex. chpt.); mem. A.A.A.S., Research Engring Soc. Am., Am. Coll. Sports Medicine, A.M.A., Am. Fedn. Clin. Research, Am. Thoracic Soc., Am. Heart Assn. (dir.), Aero Medics of Tex., Central Tex. Research Soc., Mu Delta (award for outstanding intern 1955). Contbr. articles profl. jours. Home: 770 Sayles Dr Abilene TX 79605 Office: 1026 N 21st St Abilene TX 79601

JOHNSON, DALE WARREN, realtor; b. Trowbridge, Ill., Feb. 17, 1921; s. Edler Elmer and Letha (Tipsword) J.; B.Ed., Eastern Ill. U., 1943; m. Julie Ann Rogers, Oct. 5, 1952; children—Roger Wayne, Craig Robert, Darrell Dale. Dir., Vets. Service Center, New Britain, Conn., 1946-47; salesman Coleman Co., Wichita, Kan., 1948, Phoenix Mut. Life Ins. Co., Hartford, Conn., 1949-50; pres. Johnson & Johnson, Inc., Kensington, Conn., 1951-67; v.p. Rado, Inc., bldg. co.; pres. Johnson Enterprises, Inc., 1953-69, Kingman Corp., Stuart, Fla., Grand Bahama (Freeport, Lucaya) Realty, Inc., 1965-70; owner Dale W. Johnson Co., Berlin, Conn., 1967-70; sec., treas. Kimberly Enterprises, Inc., 1969-70; pres. Dale W. Johnson Realty Corp., Stuart. Sec. Berlin Fair, 1958-64, pres., 1965. Treas., Town of Berlin, Conn., 1950-51; dist. chmn. Republican Town Com., 1962-66. Bd. dirs. New Britain chpt. A.R.C., New Britain Gen. Hosp., Conn. Assn. Real Estate Bds. Served with USNR, 1943-46. Named Realtor of Year, New Britain Bd. Realtors, 1965. Mem. V.F.W., Am. Legion, Berlin Land Owners and Contractors Assn. (pres. 1960-62), Berlin C. of C. (pres. 1954-56). Lutheran (pres. ch. men's club 1959-61). Mason (32 deg.), Lion (pres. Berlin 1965-66). Club: Svea Social (pres. 1952). Home: Stuart Yacht and Country Club 443 Park Pl Stuart FL 33494 Office: Edler Dr PO Box 569 Stuart FL 33494

JOHNSON, DAVE TOBIN, ins. co. exec.; b. Pensacola, Fla., May 2, 1909; s. Joseph I. and Annie (Tobin) J.; grad. parochial schs.; m. Mary Catherine Comforter, Dec. 16, 1937; children—Mary Catherine (Mrs. James R. Thompson), Patricia Ann (Mrs. Gregory Deal), David Tobin Jr. With Fisher-Brown, Inc., Pensacola, 1923—, asst. sec., 1932-39, v.p., 1939-50, exec. v.p., 1950-55, pres., 1955—; pres. Security Finance Co., Friendly Finance Co.; v.p. Muldon Motor Co.; dir. Citizens & Peoples Nat. Bank. Chmn., U. W. Fla. Found., Inc.; mem. adv. bd. Bapt. Hosp. Served with USMCR, 1943-45. Named Boss of Year, Bus. Man of Year, 1963; recipient Kiwanis Cup for Outstanding Civic Achievement, 1963. Mem. Pensacola Fire and Casualty Agts. (past pres.), Nat. (past chmn. nat. advt. com., fidelity, surety com., v.p., mem. exec. com., past pres.), Fla. (past pres.) assns. ins. agts. Democrat. Roman Catholic. Rotarian, Elk, K.C. (4 1/2). Clubs: Pensacola Country, Senio Hills Country, Yacht. Home: 1517 N 19th Av Pensacola FL 32503 Office: Box 711 Pensacola FL 32502

JOHNSON, DAVID FOOTE SELLERS, ins. co. exec.; b. Chattanooga, Feb. 8, 1916; s. Joseph Wilson and Nell (Evans) J.; student Vanderbilt U., 1939; m. Elise Elrod, Apr. 9, 1938; children—Anita Elise (Mrs. William Branch Hamilton), Sarah Beverly (Mrs. DeWitt Malone Shy). With Interstate Life & Accident Ins. Co., Chattanooga, 1936—, pres. Life Co., 1972—; v.p. Fire Co., mem. finance com., 1964—, mem. exec. com., dir. Interstate Corp., 1968—; dir. Invesco, Inc., Chattanooga; mem. exec. com. br. offices Hamilton Nat. Bank, Chattanooga. Pres. Nixon appointee as local chmn. Nat. Alliance Businessmen, 1969-71; pres. Allied Arts Fund, Inc., 1969; mem. adv. com. Salvation Army, 1967; pres. Chattanooga Automobile Club, 1965, bd. dirs. 1965; Bd. dirs., sec. Evans Found., Inc. Chattanooga. Mem. Greater Chattanooga Area C. of C. (pres. 1971), Phi Delta Theta. Mem. Christian Ch. Rotarian. Clubs: Mountain City; Men's Cotillion, Chattanooga Yacht, Yachting of America (Ft. Lauderdale, Fla); Capitol Hill (Washington). Republican. Home: 211 Sylvan Dr Lookout Mountain TN 37350 Office: 540 Mc Callie Av Chattanooga TN 37402

JOHNSON, DAVID FREEMAN, biochemist; b. Nashville, Jan. 28, 1925; s. David Freeman and Coma Mae (Davidson) J.; B.S., Allegheny Coll., 1947, D. Sc., 1972; M.S., Howard U., 1949; Ph.D., Georgetown U., 1957; m. Gloria D. Tapscott, Oct. 24, 1947; children—Toni Y., David G. Instr. Howard U., Washington, 1949-50; research chemist Freedmens Hosp., Washington, 1950-51; research biochemist NIH, Bethesda, Md., 1952—, instr. Grad. Sch., 1960—. Trustee Prince George's Community Coll., Largo, Md., 1969—. Fellow Am. Soc. Exptl. Biology; mem. Am. Chem. Soc., A.A.A.S., Endocrine Soc., Kappa Alpha Psi. Contbr. to profl. jours. Home: 1011 Carrington Av Washington DC 20027 Office: National Institute Health Bethesda MD 20014

JOHNSON, DAVID L(IVINGSTONE), engring. ednl. adminstr.; b. Gustavus, O., Feb. 17, 1915; s. David Charles and Margaret (Delaney) J.; A.B., Berea Coll., 1936; M.A., State U. Ia., 1938, B.S. in Elec. Engring., 1942; M.S., Okla. State U., 1950, Ph.D., 1957; m. Eugenia Gibson McQuarie, Jan. 23, 1954. Instr., U.S. Naval Tng. Sch., Okla. State U., 1942-44; field engr. Airborne Coordinating Group, 1944-45; instr. Spartan Sch. Aeros., Tulsa, 1945-48; asst. prof. Okla. State U., 1948-55; prof., head dept. elec. engring. La. Tech U., Ruston, 1955—. Cons. automatic controls. Registered profl. engr., La., Okla. Mem. A.A.A.S., I.E.E.E., Am. Soc. Engring. Edn., Assn. Computing Machinery, Nat. Soc. Profl. Engrs., Soc. Indsl. and Applied Math., Am. Assn. U. Profs., Am. Documentation Inst., Instrument Soc. Am., Sigma Xi, Eta Kappa Nu, Phi Kappa Phi, Pi Mu Epsilon, Sigma Tau, Tau Beta Pi. Home: 1610 Valley St Ruston LA 71270

JOHNSON, DEWEY E(DWARD), dentist; b. Charleston, S.C., Mar. 19, 1935; s. Dewey Edward and Mabel (Momeier) J.; A.B. in Geology, U. N.C., 1957, D.D.S., 1961. Practice dentistry, Charleston, S.C., 1964—, asso. to Stanley H. Karesh, D.D.S., 1970—. Served to lt. USNR, 1961-63. Mem. Royal Soc. Health, Charleston C. of C. (mem. cruise ship com. 1969), Am. Dental Assn., Charleston Dental Soc., Hibernian Soc., Phi Kappa Sigma, Sigma Gamma Epsilon, Psi Omega. Conglist. Optimist.Home: 142 S Battery Charleston SC 29401 Office: 112 1/2 Ashley Av Charleston SC 29402

JOHNSON, DEWEY MACON, judge; b. Fla., Apr. 6, 1907; s. Alexander Love and Annie Lou (Bassett) J.; LL.B., U. Fla., 1930; m. Margie Kimbrough, May 5, 1945; 1 dau., Sandra (Mrs. Allen Campbell). Admitted to Fla. bar; practiced law 1930-65; judge 1st Dist. Ct. of Appeal, Quincy, Fla., now Tallahassee. Past mem. Fla. Ho. of Reps., Fla. Senate. Office: First Appellate Dist Ct Tallahassee FL 32351

JOHNSON, DONALD MAURICE, orgn. exec.; b. Topeka, Oct. 27, 1922; s. Carl Oscar and Esther Augusta (Anderson) J.; student Northwestern U., 1943-44; A.B., U. Kan., 1948, postgrad., 1948-49; m. Lucille Louise Horn, May 20, 1950; children—Mark Tait, Cheryl Ann. Sales rep. Kan. Blue Cross, Topeka, 1949-50; agt. Nat. Res. Life, Topeka, 1951-53; securities salesman Estes & Co., Topeka, 1950-51; agt., gen. agt. United Am. Life, Denver, 1953-57; agy. v.p. Western Empire Life, Denver, 1957-61; exec. dir. Sigma Phi Epsilon Frat., Richmond, Va., 1961—. Chmn., undergrad. conf. Nat. Interfrat.

Conf., 1965; exec. dir. Sigma Phi Epsilon Ednl. Found., 1961—. Bd. dirs. Nat. Housing Corp. Sigma Phi Epsilon. Served as lt. (j.g.) USNR, 1942-46. Mem. Coll. Frat. Execs. Assn. (exec. com., pres. 1970-71), Am. Soc. Assn. Execs., Am. Mgmt. Assn., Am., Richmond contract bridge leagues, Kan. U. Alumni Assn., Navy League, Richmond C. of C., Am. Alumni Council. Presbyn. Home: 1908 Parma Rd Richmond VA 23229 Office: 5800 Chamberlayne Rd PO Box 1901 Richmond VA 23227

JOHNSON, DONALD ROSS, govt. ofcl.; b. Chgo., Feb. 9, 1920; s. George William and Grace (Roos) F.; B.Sc., U. Ill., 1943; M.Sc., U. Minn., 1950; m. Beryl Lucille Edman, June 15, 1947; children—Gary Ross, Lynn Kay, Lee Ross, Laura Kay. Research asst. entomology U. Minn., St. Paul, 1946-48; asst. entomologist State of Minn., St. Paul, 1948-51; dep. chief malaria eradication program AID, Washington, 1957-64; med. entomologist USPHS, Djakarta, Indonesia, 1951-53, office of internat. health, Washington, 1953-57, chief spl. services Aedes aegypti eradication program, Atlanta, 1964-66; sanitarian dir. malaria program center For Disease Control, USPHS, Atlanta, 1966—. Served to lt. (j.g.) USNR, 1943-46. Mem. A.A.A.S., Am. Mosquito Control Assn. (chmn. Worldwide com.), Entomol. Soc. Am. (chmn. sect. 1958), Indian Soc. Malaria and Other Communicable Diseases. Lutheran. Contbr. articles to publs. Home: 1362 N Decatur Rd NE Atlanta GA 30306 Office: 1600 Clifton Rd Atlanta GA 30333

JOHNSON, EDD WILSON, hosp. adminstr.; b. New Middleton, Tenn., Sept. 23, 1911; s. James Frank and Lydia (Clark) J.; student Air U., 1946, LaSalle Law Sch., 1951; m. Ruby West, July 25, 1941; children— James David, Martha (Mrs. Thomas Stephens), John Daniel. Commd. 2d lt., U.S. Air Force, 1930, advanced through grades to lt. col., 1959; personnel officer, 1945-50, air insp. mgmt. analysis, 1952-56; ret., 1959; adminstr. Miller County Hosp., Calquitt, Ga., 1967-69; adminstr. Worth County Hosp., Sylvester, Ga., 1969—. Chmn. bd. U.S. Civil Service Examiners in Northeast Air Procurement Dist., Boston, 1951. Mem. Am. Legion. V.F.W. Lion, Kiwanian. Home: 102 Elm St Sylvester GA 31791 Office: 307 N Westberry St Sylvester GA 31791

JOHNSON, EDWARD JAMES, govt. ofcl.; b. nr. Wallace, N.C., Apr. 13, 1934; s. John Perry and Alice (Rouse) J.; student Marshall Mars Hill Coll., 1952-54; B.S. in Agrl. Engring., N.C. State U., 1961; m. Ruth Lavada Cooper, Mar. 15, 1957; children—Regina Karen, Perry Lee. Agrl. extension agt. in charge 4-H activities N.C. Extension Service, Onslow County, Jacksonville, N.C., 1961-63; dir. pub. relations and power use Jones-Onslow Electric Membership Corp., Jacksonville, 1963-69; exec. sec. N.C. Apple Growers Assn., Inc., Marion, 1969-71; asst. county supr. Onslow County, Farmers Home Adminstrn., U.S. Dept. Agr., 1971-72, county supr. Brunswick County, 1972—. Dir. Pub. Relations and Power Use for Coops., 1963-69; electrification adviser N.C. Rural Electric Coops., 1963-69; N.C. labor adviser Nat. Council Agrl. Employers; adviser Neuse Area Devel. Assn. Served with USAF, 1955-57. Mem. Nat., N.C. socs. agrl. engrs., N.C. Eextension Workers Assn., N.C. Hort. Council, Nat. Rural Electric Coop. Assn., Asheville Agrl. Devel. Council, Jacksonville-Onslow County C. of C. (chmn. agrl. com. 1965-66), Am. Security Council, McDowell County Farm Bur. (dir. 1971), Grange. Republican. Methodist (steward, adult Sunday Sch. tchr.). Mason, Moose. Home: 402 Brookview Dr Jacksonville NC 28540

JOHNSON, EDWARD WAYNE, real estate exec.; b. Danville, Va., Feb. 20, 1941; s. Hedrick Kessley and Dorothy May (Yeatts) J.; B.S., Va. Poly. Inst., 1963; m. Margie Buettner, Apr. 11, 1964; children—Gina Marline, Angela Dawn. Vice pres. Riverdan Investment Corp., Danville, 1964-66; pres. Hedrick Johnson Devel. Corp., Danville, 1966—. Served with USCGR, 1963-64. Mem. Home Builders Assn. Danville (pres. 1972-73), Va. Homebuilders Assn. (dir., 1969—), Alpha Kappa Psi, Omicron Delta Kappa. Lutheran. Lion, Toastmaster, Optimist. Club: Tuscarora Country. Home: 2057 Woodlake Dr Danville VA 24541 Office: 2321 Riverside Dr Danville VA 24541

JOHNSON, EDWARD WILLIAM, mech. engr.; b. Chgo., May 3, 1909; s. Axel Edward and Hilda (Johansson) J.; B.S., Ill. Inst. Tech., 1934, B.S. in Mech. Engring., 1935; postgrad. Carnegie Inst. Tech., 1936-40, Mass. Inst. Tech., 1943, McGill U., 1950, George Washington, U., 1953-57; m. Irmgard Marie Zeisberg, Mar. 15, 1957; 1 son, Robert David. Jr. mech. engr. Internat. Harvester Co., Chgo., 1934-39; asst. insp. naval material U.S. Navy Dept., Pitts., 1939-40; asso. mech. engr. U.S. Army Ordnance, Balt., 1940-42; mech. engr. asst. chief vehicle devel. U.S. Army C.E., Ft. Belvoir, Va., 1946-47, chief engring. sect. climatic research, 1947-48; environmental engr. Bur. Yards and Docks, Washington, 1948-52, head research programming, 1953-57; mech. engr. U.S. Naval Weapons Lab. Dahlgren, Va. 1957-59; head engring. specifications U.S. Naval Weapons Plant, Washington, 1959-60; sr. engr., asst. chief procurement U.S. Bur. Pub. Rds., 1960-62; asst. chief postal lab., office research engring. U.S. Post Office Dept., Washington, 1962-71; v.p. Basic Testing Labs., Inc., Centreville, Va., 1971—. Served with USNR, 1943-46. Registered profl. engr., D.C. Mem. Am. Soc. M.E., Am. Inst. Aeros. and Astronautics, Nat., D.C., Va. socs. profl. engrs., Am. Ordnance Assn., Am. Polar Soc., Explorers Club, Swedish Hist. Soc. Mason (32 deg., Shriner). Contbr. articles to profl. jours. Home: 6944 Essex Av Springfield VA 22150 Office: Centreville VA 22020

JOHNSON, EDWIN HENNESSY, educator; b. Boulder, Colo., Sept. 21, 1914; s. John Hartwell and Martha Winnifred (Hennessy) J.; B.A., U. Colo., 1936; M.A., U. Mo., 1938; m. Charlotte Marie Kennedy, Dec. 31, 1938. Asst. advt. mgr. A.P. Green Fire Brick Co., Mexico, Mo., 1939; reporter Ft. Morgan (Colo.) Herald, 1940; high sch. tchr., Walsenburg, Colo., 1941; editor Trenton (Mo.) Missourian, 1941-42; asst. prof. journalism S.D. State Coll., 1946-48; head, journalism dept. U. Tulsa, 1948—. Served with USAAF, 1943-46. Mem. Assn. for Edn. Journalism, Pub. Relations Soc. Am. (sec.-treas.), Internat. Council Indsl. Editors, Am. Fedn. Advt., Tulsa Advt. Fedn., Indsl. Editors of Tulsa (dir.), Am. Soc. Journalism Sch. Adminstrs., Am. Acad. Advt., Sigma Delta Chi, Pi Alpha Mu. Methodist. Home: 114 N College St Tulsa OK 74110

JOHNSON, EDWIN WALLACE, lawyer; b. Spartanburg, S.C., July 24, 1904; s. Edwin Wallace and Jesse (Dean) J.; student Wofford Coll., 1923-24, Citadel, 1921-23; LL.B., U.S.C., 1930; m. Eppes Jones, Mar. 3, 1934; children—Wallace Eppes (Mrs. Mabrey W. Vannerson, Jr.), Frances (Mrs. George Brown Sibert, Jr.). Admitted to S.C. bar, 1930, since practiced law Spartanburg; mem. firm Johnson & Smith, 1957—; spl. judge Ct. Common Pleas, 1948, 62. Chmn. spl. com. on redrafting probate ct. law Jd. Council S.C., 1962-65, chmn. spl. com. on redrafting criminal statutes and procedure, 1966—. Vice chmn. S.C. Wildlife Resources Commn., 1952-62, chmn., 1962-65. Mem. S.C. Ho. of Reps., 1944. Named S.C. Conservationist of Year, 1965. Mem. Am., S.C. (pres. 1965-66), Spartanburg County (pres. 1957) bar assns., Am. (S.C. v.p. 1958-60, gov. 1963-65), S.C. (pres. 1958-59) trial lawyers assns., Am. Judicature Soc., Internat. Soc. Barristers. Elk (hon. life). Home: 460 Mockingbird Lane Spartanburg SC 29302 Office: 220 N Church St Spartanburg SC 29301

JOHNSON, ELLWOOD WAGNER, banker; b. St. Louis, Nov. 23, 1904; s. Reno DeOrville and Estelle Elizabeth (Wagner) J.; ed. pub. sch.; m. Anne Long; 1 son, Ellwood Dennis. Formerly with Chino Copper Co., Hurley, N.M.; grove owner, Fla., until 1927; With First Nat. Bank Tampa (Fla.), from 1927, past vice chmn., dir.; v.p., dir. Charter Bankshares Corp., Jacksonville and St. Petersburg, Fla.; exec. v.p. Comml. Bank, Gainesville, Fla.; dir. Comml. Nat. Bank, Pensacole, 1st Nat. Bank, Milton, Fla., Bank of Gulf Breeze (Fla.), Harbor City Nat. Bank, Melbourne, Fla. Mem. Tampa C. of C. Kiwanian. Clubs: University, St. Petersburg Yacht. Home: 920 Beach Dr NE St Petersburg FL 33701 Office: 1st Nat Bank St. Petersburg FL 33701

JOHNSON, ELMER DOUGLAS, librarian; b. Durham, N.C., Aug. 2, 1915; s. Ulysses and Nancy (Smith) J.; A.B., U. N.C., 1936, A.M., 1942, Ph.D., 1951; m. Rosa Shepherd, Nov. 7, 1936; children—Eric S., Lynn D., Elaine C., Giles K. Camp librarian TVA, Guntersville Dam, Ala., 1936-40; circulation supr. U. N.C. Library, 1940-42; librarian, prof. Am. history Limestone Coll., Gaffney, S.C., 1944-53; asso. librarian, prof. library sci. East Carolina Coll., Greenville, N.C., 1953-54; dir. libraries U. Southwestern La., Lafayette, 1954-63; librarian, prof. history Radford (Va.) Coll., 1963—; mng. editor The Radford Rev., 1965—. Research analyst War Dept., Washington, 1942-44. Mem. A.L.A., Bibliography Soc. Am., Phi Beta Kappa, Phi Alpha Theta. Author: Communication, 1955, 3d edit., 1966; Of Time and Thomas Wolfe, a bibliography, 1959; A History of Libraries in the Western World, 1965, 2d edit, 1970; Thomas Wolfe: A Checklist, 1970. Contbr. articles to library jours. Home: 1200 Milton Lane Radford VA 24141

JOHNSON, EMILY WINIFRED, club woman, educator; b. Hamilton, N.C., July 28, 1890; d. George Thomas and Catherine Ann Elizabeth (Powell) Johnson; student Longwood Coll., 1909-11; A.B., George Washington U., 1924; M.A., Tchrs. Coll., Columbia, 1932. Tchr. elementary and high sch., Va., Md., Fla., 1911-17, 20-21, 24-27; clk. Govt. Service War Trade Bd., Treasury Dept., 1917-20, War Dept., 1940-44; coll. tchr., demonstration tchr., supr. Va. and N.C. Tng. Sch., Mary Washington Coll., 1928, Tchr. Tng. Dept. Greene and Ashe Counties, N.C., 1928-32, Western Carolina Tchrs. Coll., Collowhee, N.C., 1932-35; supr. elementary schs., Spring Hope and Penderlea, N.C., Russell County, Va., 1939-40; information specialist, pub. health analyst, editor staff pub. health reports, Pub. Health Service, U.S. Dept. Health, Edn. and Welfare, 1944-60; coordinator Civil War Centennial Lectures, U. Va. No. Center, Arlington, 1960-62; mem. Pan Am. Liaison Com. of Women's Orgn.; staff mem. Golden Anniversary White House Conf. Children and Youth. Mem. assn. and women's com. Nat., Arlington symphonies. Mem. Acad. Polit. Sci., Am. Acad. Polit. and Social Sci., Va. Mus. Fine Arts, U.D.C. (charter, historian, chaplain George Washington Custis Lee chpt.), Civil War Hist. Assn., Va. (life), Arlington hist. socs., George Washington U. Alumni Assn., Armed Forces Writers League, Longwood Coll. Alumni Assn. (pres. Wash. chpt., dir.), Gen., Va. (historian no. dist. 1951-55), Arlington (officer-at-large) fedns. women's clubs, Internat. Platform Assn., Nat. Trust for Hist. Preservation. Mem. Ch. of Resurrection. Clubs: Washington, Columbia University (past pres., past trustee); Women's (pres. 1949-53) (Cherrydale). Home: Goodwin House 4800 Fillmore Av Alexandria VA 22311

JOHNSON, ESTHER FRANCES, labor union exec.; b. Springville, Ia., Dec. 30, 1904; d. Clinton Andrew and Carrie (Gregg) Shanklin; student Coe Coll., Cedar Rapids, Ia., 1922-23; m. Arthur J. Johnson, Oct. 13, 1923; 1 son, Warren Arthur. Sch. tchr. in Ia., 1924; chief clk. Norton AFB, San Bernardino, Cal., 1943-46, Separation Center, Aberdeen Proving Ground, Md., 1946-47; ofcl. hostess V.I.P. Quarters, Hickam Field, Honolulu, 1948-49; supply and distbn. officer Navy Supply Corp., Port Hueneme, Cal., 1950-56; mem. Am. Fedn. Govt. Employees, 1950—, del. nat. convs., 1952—, nat. sec.-treas., 1956—; mem. sec.-treas. conf. AFL-CIO. 1956—. Mem. Commn. Status Employment Women, 1961-63; del. U.S. Traffic Safety Conf., 1958; participant Conf. Employment Physically Handicapped, 1964—. Active Nat. Conf. Christians and Jews, YWCA. Mem. Nat. Orgn. for Women. Home: 3636 16th St NW Washington DC 20010 Office: 400 1st St NW Washington DC 20001

JOHNSON, FRANK MINIS, JR., lawyer, U.S. dist. judge; b. Haleyville, Ala., Oct. 30, 1918; s. Frank M. and Alabama (Long) J.; grad. Gulf Coast Mil. Acad., Gulfport, Miss., 1935, Massey Bus. Coll., Birmingham, 1937; LL.B., U. Ala., 1943; m. Ruth Jenkins, Jan. 14, 1938; 1 son, James Curtis. Admitted to Ala. bar, 1943; pvt. practice in Haleyville and Jasper, 1946—, mem. firm Curtis, Maddox & Johnson, 1946-53; U.S. atty. No. Dist. Ala., 1953-55; U.S. dist. judge Middle Dist. Ala., 1955—, now chief judge. Served as pvt. to capt. inf., AUS, 1943-46. Decorated Purple Heart with oak leaf cluster, Bronze Star. Republican (past mem. state exec. com.). Home: 118 N Haardt Dr Montgomery AL 36105 Office: Fed Bldg Montgomery AL 36102

JOHNSON, FRED W., govt. ofcl. Dist. dir. internal revenue, Little Rock. Address: 700 W Capitol St Little Rock AR 72203*

JOHNSON, FREDERICK DEAN, food co. exec.; b. Shreve, O., Feb. 27, 1911; s. Harry H. and Grace Marcelloa (Cammarn) J.; A.B., Coll. Wooster, 1935; m. Haulwen Elizabeth Richey, June 19, 1937; children—Frederick Dean II, Mary Haulwen, Grace Elizabeth. Dir. research Bama Co., Birmingham, Ala., 1961-65; dir. research Bama Food Products, Borden Foods div. Borden Inc., Houston, 1965—. Bd. dirs, Afton Oaks Civic Club, 1967-70. Mem. Nat. Preservers Assn. (chmn. quality control adv. com. 1969—), Inst. Food Technologists (charter), Am. Chem. Soc., A.A.A.S. Republican. Presbyn. (ruling elder). Home: 4546 Shetland Lane Houston TX 77027 Office: 5501 Clinton Dr Houston TX 77020

JOHNSON, FREDERICK JACKSON, utility exec.; b. Norfolk, Neb., Feb. 11, 1905; s. Oscar J. and Winifred (Leffert) J.; B.S., U. Colo., 1927, E.E., 1933; m. Alice Larimer Connett, Feb. 28, 1929 (dec. Aug. 1960); 1 son, Frederick Kennedy; m. 2d, Laurice Settle Girdler, Dec. 1, 1961. With Henry L. Doherty & Co., 1927-28, St. Joseph Ry., Light, Heat & Power Co., 1928-36; with Honolulu Rapid Transit Co., Ltd., 1937-50, pres., 1950; dir. Louisville Transit Co. (Ky.), 1950—, pres., 1958—; pres., dir. Milw. & Suburban Transport Corp., 1955—; chmn. bd., dir. Indpls. Transit System, Inc., 1956—; dir. Louisville Investment Co., 1958—, pres., 1967—; dir. Mid Empire Corp., 1957—, pres., 1971; dir. Citizens Fidelity Bank & Trust Co., Louisville Cement Co., Speed Industries, C.T. Hertzsch, Inc., Bessemer Cement Co., Miller and Co. Bd. dirs. Louisville chpt. A.R.C., 1954-55; mem. Greater Milw. Com., 1955 . Commr. Louisville Met. Sewer Dist., 1953-55. Registered profl. engr., Hawaii, Ky. Mem. Am. Inst. E.E., Inst. Traffic Engrs., Am. Transit Assn. (pres. 1961-62, dir.), Beta Theta Pi. Clubs: Pendennis (Louisville), Milwaukee, University (Milw.), Harmony Landing Country (Louisville), Columbia (Indpls.); Pacific (Honolulu Hawaii); Balboa (Mazatian Mexico). Home: 1801 Sulgrave Rd Louisville KY 40205 Office: 4212 W Highland Blvd Milwaukee WI 53203

JOHNSON, GEORGE SIMPSON, pub. co. exec.; b. Huntington, N.Y., Nov. 8, 1913; s. Emil G. and Marie (Simpson) J.; student Beckman Sch. Bus. Engring., San Francisco, 1939, Long Beach (Cal.) City Coll., 1947; m. Doris E. Schwartz, Oct. 10, 1932; children—Gary, Darrell, Jenifer (Mrs. Glen Castle). Promotion mgr. Oakland (Cal.) Tribune, 1943; circulation dir. Long Beach Press Telegram, 1946-53; circulation dir. Dallas Times Herald, 1953-60, gen. mgr., 1960-70, sr. v.p., 1970—. Asst. sec. Southwest Sch. Printing, Sam Houston U., 1971-72. Bd. dirs. LIFT program, 1967-72. Mason, Rotarian, Optimist, Lancer. Home: 6990 Walling Lane Dallas TX 75231 Office: 1101 Pacific St Dallas TX 75202

JOHNSON, GEORGE TERRY, dentist; b. Elkin, N.C., Apr. 17, 1939; s. Walter Presley and Carolyn (Maxwell) J.; student Wake Forest U., 1957-60; D.D.S., U. N.C., 1964. Individual practice dentistry, Sparta, N.C., 1964—. Chmn. Am. Flag Display Project, 1970-71; dir. Alleghany County Rescue Squad, 1969—; mem. Morehead Scholarship Com. Alleghany County. Mem. Blue Ridge Dental Soc. (v.p. 1968-69), N.C. Dental Soc., Am. Dental Assn., Delta Sigma Delta. Republican. Baptist (young people's Sunday sch. supt. 1965-67). Lion (program chmn. 1966-69, pres. 1969-70). Home: PO Box 98 Sparta NC 28675 Office: 616 Doctor's St Sparta NC 28675

JOHNSON, GILMER BROOKS, physician; b. Jackson, Miss., Sept. 12, 1916; s. Gilmer Brooks and Lena Leoti (Brown) J.; student Sul Ross State Coll., 1934-35, 46-47; B.S., Northwestern U., 1948, M.D., 1951; m. Avis Elizabeth Palmer, Oct. 9, 1942; children—Carolyn (Mrs. Samuel Neal Braudt), Gilmer Brooks III, David Wallace. Chief warrant officer U.S. Army, 1936-46; intern Baylor U. Med. Center, Dallas, 1951; practice gen. medicine, Plainview, Tex., 1952—; mem. staff Central Plains Gen.Hosp., E. O. Nichols Meml. Hosp. (both Plainview). Decorated Bronze Star. Diplomate Am. Bd. Family Practice. Mem. A.M.A. (Physician's Recognition award 1970), Hale-Briscoe-Swisher-Floyd County Med. Soc. (pres. 1962-63). Baptist (deacon). Home: 205 Yucca Terrace Plainview TX 79072 Office: 814 W 8th St Plainview TX 79072

JOHNSON, GLENN QUINCY, architect; b. Chgo., May 23, 1908; s. John Q. and Emily (Wiezell) J.; B.S. in Archtl. Engring., Crane Coll., Chgo., 1930; postgrad. archtl. design Armour Inst. Tech., 1930-32, Atlier Nelson-Beaux Arts, Chgo., 1933; m. Dorothy Lillian Marie Kaad, June 30, 1934; children—Judith Ann (Mrs. Joseph Francis Corriveau), Gary Quentin. Pvt. practice architecture, Chgo., 1937-41; dir. tooling Douglas Aircraft Co., Chgo., 1941-45; pvt. practice architecture, Park Ridge, Ill., 1945-52, St. Petersburg, Fla., 1952-64; pres. Anderson-Johnson-Henry-Parrish, Architects & Engrs., Inc., St. Petersburg, 1964—. Mem. Nat. Council Archtl. Registration Bd., 1941—. Mem. Blue Ribbon Zoning Com., St. Petersburg, since 1968—. Mem. A.I.A. Republican. Presbyn. (ruling elder 1967—). Lion. Clubs: St. Petersburg Yacht, Exchange, Lakewood Country (St. Petersburg). Major archtl. works include Fla. State Office Bldg., 1971, Pinellas County Jud. Bldg., (FAA 1st award 1972), Azalea Jr. High Sch. (FAA 1st award 1969), St. Petersburg Beach Library (FAA 1st award 1969). Home: 5064 43d St S St Petersburg FL 33711 Office: 10500 Roosevelt Blvd St Petersburg FL 33702

JOHNSON, GORDON OTIS FRASER, mfg. co. exec.; b. Boston, May 1, 1926; s. Richard Newhall and Margaret L. (Paisley) J.; student Mass. Inst. Tech., 1944-45, Tufts Coll., 1945-46; B.A., Stanford, 1948; M.B.A., Harvard, 1950; m. Frances Brigham, Dec. 29, 1951; children— Gordon F.B., Susan Chapman, Brigham Newhall, Christian Paisley Ball. With Econ. Coop. Adminstrn., 1950-52; dir. marketing LogEtronics Inc., Springfield, Va., 1955-67, pres., 1967—, chief exec. officer, 1968—, also dir., 1957—; dir. LogEtronics A.G., Zurich, Switzerland. Served with USNR, 1944-46, 52-54. Mem. Stanford, Mass. Inst. Tech., Harvard alumni clubs, Soc. Photog. Scientists and Engrs. (Recipient Service award 1965; pres. Wash. chpt. 1965-66; program and conf. chmn. Symposia on Unconventional Photographic Systems 1964-67, sr. mem. 1972), Research and Engring. Council Graphic Arts Industry, Tech. Assn. Graphic Arts. Home: 3512 Saylor Pl Alexandria VA 22304 Office: 7001 Loisdale Rd Springfield VA 22150

JOHNSON, HAROLD ANTON, physicist; b. New Orleans, June 14, 1937; s. Harold A. and Marion Colesberry (Wood) J.; B.S., U. Ga., 1960; postgrad. (NSF fellow) Coll. William and Mary, summer, 1961. Tchr. psy. sci., chemistry E. Atlanta High Sch., 1961; physicist Gen. Electric Co., Phila., 1962-63, fgn. sci. and tech. center U.S. Army Materiel Command, Washington, 1965-66, data systems NASA, Kennedy Space Center, Fla., 1966—. Mem. Speaker's Bur., Kennedy Space Center, 1967—. Mem. Am. Phys. Soc., S.A.R. Episcopalian. Home: 1621 Kay Av Brunswick GA 31520 Office: IN-TEL 12 NASA Kennedy Space Center FL 32899

JOHNSON, HARRY LEE, educator; b. Saltville, Va., Apr. 18, 1929; s. Jerry D. and Zella (Henderson) J.; B.A., Emory and Henry Coll., 1952; M.A., U. Va., 1957, Ph.D., 1959; m. Jean D. Youell, Jan. 29, 1955. Mem. faculty U. Ala., 1960-64, prof., 1961-64; asso. prof. U. Tex., 1964-66; prof., head dept. finance U. Tenn., Knoxville, 1966—. Dir. Vol.-State Bank, Knoxville. Corr., So. Econ. Jour., 1962-64; mem. thesis/research library com. Stonier Grad. Sch. Banking, Washington; acad. cons., mem. faculty Tenn. Bankers Assn. Study Conf.; mem. faculty Banking Sch. of South, La. State U., Baton Rouge, 1967—, cons. State Treasurer's Office, Nashville, 1971—. Bd. dirs., treas. Florence Crittenton Agy., Knoxville. Served with AUS, 1952-54. Recipient fellowships Investment Dept. N.Y. Life Ins. Co., 1963, 64; Ayres fellow Stonier Grad. Sch. Banking, 1968. Mem. Financial Mgmt. Assn., Am., Royal, So. econ. assns., Appalachian Finance Assn., So., Am. finance assns., Am. Bankers Assn. (banking edn. com. 1969—), Delta Sigma Pi. Mem. bd. editors So. Jour. Bus., 1966—. Editor: State and Local Tax Problems, 1969; Inflation: 1970 Style, 1970; co-editor: Monetary, 1968. Home: W Topside Rd Knoxville TN 37920

JOHNSON, HAYNES BONNER, journalist; b. N.Y.C., July 9, 1931; s. Malcolm Malone and Ludie (Adams) J.; B.J., U. Mo., 1952; M.S., U. Wis., 1956; m. Julia Ann Erwin, Sept. 21, 1954; children—Katherine Adams, David Malone, Stephen Holmes, Sarah Brooks, Elizabeth Haynes Johnson. Reporter Wilmington (Del.) News-Jour., 1956-57; with Washington Star, 1957-69, nat. affairs corr., 1964-69; nat. affairs corr. Washington Post, 1969—; lectr. colls., univs. Served to 1st lt. AUS, 1952-55. Recipient Pub. Service prize and grand award for reporting Washington Newspaper Guild, 1962, 64, 68, 69, Pulitzer prize for nat. reporting, 1966, Headliners award for nat. reporting, 1968, Sigma Delta Chi award gen. reporting, 1969. Mem. Authors Guild, Phi Gamma Delta. Democrat. Episcopalian. Club; Nat. Press. Author: Dusk at the Mountain, 1963; The Bay of Pigs, 1964; (with Bernard Gwertzman) Fulbright: The Dissenter, 1968. Home: 2316 Valley Dr Alexandria VA 22302 Office: Washington Post 1515 L St NW Washington DC 20005

JOHNSON, HOBART CLAY, lawyer; b. Virgie, Ky., Apr. 23, 1931; s. George Franklin and Vesta (Roberts) J.; A.B., Eastern Ky. U., 1952; LL.B., U. Louisville, 1958; m. Jean Howard, Aug. 14, 1959; children— Benjamin Clay, Amy Ann. Admitted to Ky. bar, 1958; practiced in Pikeville, 1958—; mem. firm Stratton, Johnson & May,

1967—; pres. Gov. Elkhorn Coal Co., Inc., 1967—, also dir.; pres. Mountain Cable Systems, Inc., 1967—; also dir.; sec.-treas. Mormar Mining Co., Inc., 1969—; dir. Citizens Bank of Pikeville, Eastern Ky. Broadcasting Corp., Greater Ky. Broadcasting Corp., Lawrence County Broadcasting Corp., Jellico Broadcasting Corp., Mormar Mining Co., Inc., Blue Grass Augers, Inc., U.S. commr., 1960-62; asst. county atty., Pike County, Ky., 1965-71. Served with USAF, 1952-56. Mem. Am., Ky., Pike County (pres. 1965) bar assns., Delta Theta Phi. Home: Box 295 Virgie KY 41572 Office: Ward Bldg Second St Pikeville KY 41501

JOHNSON, HOWARD ARTHUR, SR., research exec.; b. London, Ind., Dec. 16, 1923; s. Arthur and Ihez (Smiley) J.; A.B., Franklin Coll. Ind., 1949; M.A., Wesleyan U., Conn., 1950; m. Joy Anne Nelson, July 19, 1947; children—Howard A., Kraig N. Physicist U.S. Naval Ordnance Plant, Indpls., 1950-54; operations research analyst Air Proving Ground Command, Eglin AFB, Fla., 1954-58; chief operations analysis 3d Air Force in Eng., 1958; dep. chief operations analysis USAF Europe, Wiesbaden, Germany, 1958-61; dir. operations model evaluation group air force (OMEGA), also sr. mgmt. staff Washington Research Center Tech. Operations, Inc., Washington, 1961-63; sr. staff scientist Spindletop Research, Inc., Lexington, Ky., 1963-66, mgr. comparative effectiveness research div., 1966-67; research dir. Vitro Services div. Vitro Corp. Am., Ft. Walton Beach, Fla., 1967-68; sci. asst. to dir. of test Armament Devel. and Test Center, Eglin AFB, Fla., 1968—. Cons. Supreme Hdgrs. Allied Powers, Europe, 1960-61, USAF, 1964-65, U. Ky. Med. Center, 1967, Gulf South Research Inst., 1968—. Served with USAAF, 1943-45; mem. USAF Res. Decorated Air medal. Mem. Operations Research Soc. Am., Inst. Mgmt. Scis., Am. Statis. Assn., Mil. Operations Research Soc., A.A.A.S., Sigma Xi, Phi Delta Theta. Mason (32 deg., Shriner). Home: 309 Yacht Club Dr NE Fort Walton Beach FL 32548 Office: Hq ADTC (TGY) Eglin AFB FL 32542

JOHNSON, IRA OTIS, JR., precision instrument co. exec.; b. Spencer, Tenn., Mar. 14, 1917; s. Ira Otis and Sallie (Mohon) J.; B.S., U. Tenn., 1940; m. Laurine C. Crawley, Apr. 2, 1938 (div. Feb. 1946); children—Ira Otis III, Melvin C.; m.2d, Darless L. Lane, Feb. 5, 1947; children—Mike Joe, Luke Martin. Tracer, State Hwy. Dept., Nashville, 1936; lab. asst. bridge sect. Am. Lava, Chattanooga, 1938-40: draftsman Fulton Syphon div. Robertshaw Controls Co., Knoxville, Tenn., from 1940, now v.p., gen. mgr., dir. Mem. budget com. United Fund, Knoxville, Tenn., 1970-71. Bd. dirs. Smoky Mountain council Boy Scouts Am., Jr. Achievement, Knoxville. Mem. Am. Soc. M.E., Instrument Soc. Am., Fulton Mgmt. Club, Greater Knoxville C. of C. (v.p. 1970). Mem. Ch. of Christ. Home: 7101 Cheshire Dr Knoxville TN 37919 Office: Box 400 KnoxvilleTN 37901

JOHNSON, IVAN EARL, art educator; b. Denton, Tex., Sept. 23, 1911; s. Ivan E. and Dorothy (Williams) J.; B.S., N. Tex. State U., 1932, B.A., 1933; M.A., Columbia, 1936; Ed.D. (Founders Day award 1960), N.Y.U., 1960; m. Inez Stocker, Oct. 24, 1942; children—Ivan Earl III, Lynn, Joseph, Susan, Jean. Art instr. Southwest Tex. State Coll., San Marcos, 1936-39; design cons. Dept. Agr., 1946-47; dir. art Dallas pub. schs., 1947-52; prof., head dept. art edn. and constructive design Fla. State U., 1952—. Pres. Tallahassee Jr. Museum, 1964-65. Chmn. bd. Tallahassee chpt. A.R.C., 1965-67. Served to lt. comdr. USNR, 1942-46. Mem. Nat. Art Edn. Assn. (v.p. 1953-55, pres. 1955-57, mem. tng. inst. 1969), Western Arts Assn. (pres. 1950-52), Am. Inst. Designers, Kappa Delta Pi, Phi Delta Kappa, Pi Kappa Alpha. Author: (with C. Stafford) Art for Living, 1952, Art for You, 1956; (with G. Hubbard) Instructor Modern Art Portfolio, 1965; (with J. Huasman, others) Report of Commission on Art in Education, 1965. Book editor Arts and Activities mag., 1952—. Mem. editorial bd. Jour. Art Edn., 1962-70. Home: 2304 Charles Ct Tallahassee FL 32303

JOHNSON, JACK DAVIS, educator; b. Westminster, Tex., July 12, 1927; s. Jeff J. and May (Short) J.; B.S., E. Tex. State U., 1949, M.Ed., 1956; postgrad. N. Tex. State U., 1957; m. Modean VanBevers, July 14, 1951; children—Sheila Modean, Tommy J. Tchr., coach pub. sch., Westminster, Tex., 1949-51, 53-55, Clarendon, Tex., 1956-57; prin. Carroll Pub. Schs., Southlake, Tex., 1957-59, supt., 1959—. Served with AUS, 1951-53. Mem. Am. Assn. Sch. Adminstrs. Democrat. Baptist. Mason (32 deg., Shriner). Home: PO Box 838 Southlake TX 76051

JOHNSON, JACK KENT, psychiat. social worker; b. nr. Quaker Gap, N.C., Mar. 30, 1924; s. William Fred and Blannie (Gordon) J.; B.A., Wake Forest Coll., 1950; M.S.W., Tulane U., 1953; m. Marjorie Carolyn Ziglar, Jan. 5, 1946; children—Marjorie Carolyn, Jack Kent II (dec.), Dean Sherrill. Probation counselor juvenile Ct., Winston-Salem, N.C., 1950-51; asst. prof., chief psychiat. social worker dept. psychiatry Bowman Gray Med. Sch., Wake Forest Coll., Winston-Salem, 1954-58, instr. dept. sociology, 1958; chief psychiat. social worker Mental Health Clinic Duval County, Jacksonville, Fla., 1958—; field instr. grad. social work div. Fla. State U., Jacksonville, 1959—; part-time therapist Alcoholic Rehab. Clinic, Jacksonville, 1959—; pvt. practice as therapist, Jacksonville, 1958—. Lectr., Joe Berg Found., Jacksonville, 1961—; lectr. to various civic orgns. and govt. agys. Chmn. personnel com. Alcoholic Rehab. Clinic, Winston-Salem, 1956-58; chmn. Mayor's Research Com. Studying Feasibility Family Cts., Winston-Salem, 1956-57; chmn. edn. com. Mental Health Assn., Jacksonville, 1959-61; lectr., mem. bd. Ann. Mental Health Fair, Jacksonville, 1960—. Served with Signal Corps, AUS, 1943-45. Recipient commendation Joe Berg Found., 1963. Mem. Nat. Assn. Social Workers (chpt. chmn. 1960-61, chmn. profl. practice com. 1962—), Acad. Certified Social Workers. Democrat. Presbyn. Home: 6165 Bartram Rd Jacksonville FL 32216 Office: 2627 Riverside Av Jacksonville FL 32204

JOHNSON, JAMES SYLVESTER, printing co. exec.; b. Andalusia, Ala., Dec. 25, 1939; s. Chester Sylvester and Mary Ethel (Spivey) J.; B.S., Fla. State U., 1963; m. Heather Dianne Hancock, Dec. 29, 1962; 1 dau., Olivia. With Rose Printing Co., Inc., Tallahassee, 1961-63, asst. controller, 1963-67, controller, 1967-71, treas., 1971—. Home: 1813 Sharon Rd Tallahassee FL 32303 Office: 2503 Jackson Bluff Tallahassee FL 32304

JOHNSON, JEROME WALTER, lawyer; b. Port Arthur, Tex., Dec. 26, 1925; s. Sam W. and Edith (Upton) J.; B.A., U. Tex., 1949, LL.B., 1951; m. Madelyn A. Sinclair, Aug. 28, 1949; children—Julia Sinclair, Mary Haise, Sara Madeline, Shannon Elizabeth, Ellen Grey, Amy Ballard, Polly Hall. Admitted to Tex. bar, 1950; Amarillo, Tex.; partner law firm Underwood, Wilson, Sutton, Heare & Berry, Amarillo, 1956—; chmn. bd. Amarex, Inc., Oklahoma City, 1969—; dir. Maywood, Inc., Amarillo. Active in govtl. affairs. Bd. regents State Sr. Colls. Tex., v.p., 1971—. Served to 1st lt. USAF, 1944-46. Mem. Am. Bar. Assn., State Bar Tex. Democrat. Episcopalian. Home: 2802 Harmony St Amarillo TX 79106 Office: PO Box 9158 Amarillo TX 79105

JOHNSON, JERRY A., educator; b. Lubbock, Tex., Sept. 21, 1931; d. Weldon F. and Geraldine (Buckner) Johnson; B.S., Tex. Womans U., 1953; postgrad Washington U. (St. Louis), Radcliffe Coll., 1959-60; M.B.A., Harvard, 1961; Ed.D., Boston U., 1970. Staff occupational therapist USN, Oakland, Cal., 1954-56; dir. occupational therapy Easter Seal Soc., Alton, Ill., 1956, exec. dir., 1957-59; asst. hosp. adminstr, USN, Newport, R.I., 1961-62; legal counsel for party Phys. Evaluation Bd., USN, Chelsea, Mass., 1962-63; asso. prof., chmn. div. occupational therapy Sargent Coll. Allied Health Professions, Boston, 1963-69, acting exec. dir. Rehab. Council, Boston U., 1969-70, prof. occupational therapy, 1970-71; dir. Center for Allied Health Instructional Personnel, U. Fla. at Gainesville, 1971—. Project dir., ednl. cons. Am. Occupational Therapy Assn., Detroit, Chgo., 1966-67, 69-70, mem. exec. bd., 1967—, chmn. task force on social issues, 1971-72, chmn. com. continuing certification, 1972—; ednl. cons. U. Ala., 1968; mem. panel consultants to adv. com. on edn. Allied Health Professions, Council on Med. Edn. A.M.A., 1969—. Mem. med. adv. com. Bay State Soc. for Crippled, 1969—. Mem. Govs. Task Force on Tng. and Manpower in Mental Health, Boston, 1964-66. Recipient Eleanor Clark Slagle Lectureship award 1972. Mem. Mass. Assn. Occupational Therapy, (pres. 1964-66), Nat. Rehab. Assn., Internat. Soc. Rehab. Disabled, World Fedn. Occupational Therapists, Assn. Sch. Allied Health Professions, Harvard Bus. Sch. Assn., Nat. Wildlife Fedn., Common Cause, Smithsonian Instn., Mass. Audubon Soc. Democrat. Episcopalian. Club: Radcliffe College. Contbr. articles to profl. jours. Home: Box 12695 University Sta Gainesville FL 32601

JOHNSON, JESS WALTER, coll. pres.; b. Kansas City, Mo., May 19, 1917; s. Walter O. and Vada (Vanderberg) J.; B.Th., N.W. Christian Coll., Eugene, Ore., 1942; student U. Ore., 1940-41, summer 1945, Union Theol. Sem., N.Y.C., summer 1944; B.D., Christian Theol. Sem., Indpls., 1951; student Butler U., 1947-51; D.D., Milligan Coll., 1959; student LaSalle Extension U., 1966; m. Mary M. Sargent, June 15, 1941;&9cRose Mary (Mrs. Arthur A. Cantrell), Cecil W., Susan Diane, Kevin Lee. Ordained to ministry Christian Ch., 1940; minister in Tillamook, Ore., 1942-47, Frankfort, Ind., 1947-49, Indpls., 1949-51, Portland, Ore., 1951-59, Johnson City, Tenn., 1959-65; v.p. devel. Milligan Coll., 1965-66, exec. v.p., 1966-68, pres., 1968—. Bd. dirs. European Evangelistic Soc., 1952—, Christian Missionary Fellowship, 1950—, Ore. Christian Missionary Soc., 1945, 47, 53, 54; mem. continuation com. N.Am. Christian Conv., 1951-60, chmn. local arrangements com., 1958, v.p., 1959; pres. Christian Missionary Fellowship, 1962-64, N. Area Coordinating Council, 1955; chmn. Johnson City Preaching Mission, 1962, exec. sec., 1965. Vice pres. N. Portland YMCA, 1958; chmn. Johnson City-Washington County chpt. A.R.C., 1967-69; commr. Johnson Housing Authority, 1968-69. Mem. Am. Assn. Ind. Coll. Pres., Soc. Sci. Study Religion, Internat. Platform Assn. Kiwanian. Home: 104 Ridgemont Rd Johnson City TN 37601 Office: Box E Milligan College TN 37682

JOHNSON, JESSIE LARUE, librarian, pianist; b. Sedalia, Mo. Dec. 3, 1908; d. Thomas Henry and Jessie Lee (Harris) Johnson; Asso. Music, Stephens Coll., 1928; Mus.B., So. Meth. U., 1931; B. Pub. Sch. Music, 1933, Mus.M., 1948; certificate library service Columbia, 1947. Instr. piano So. Meth. U., 1931-37; librarian Dallas Ind. Sch. Dist., 1936—. Asst. librarian Children's Library Pretoria Pub. Library, Republic South Africa, 1966-67; program annotator chamber mus. series Dallas Museum Fine Arts, 1956-62. Recipient Mu Phi Epsilon award So. Meth. U., 1931. Served as lt. USNRWR, 1943-46. Mem. Pro Musica (chmn. 1962-64, program chmn. 1950-53, 69-70), Dallas Chamber Music Soc. (bd. dirs. 1954—) Am. Assn. U. Women, Am., Tex. library assns., Dallas Sch. Librarians Club, Stephens Coll. Alumnae Assn., Mu Phi Epsilon. Contbr. articles to profl. jours.; concert reviews newspapers. Methodist. Home: 4524 Belclaire Av Dallas TX 75205 Office: Thomas J Rusk Sch 2929 Inwood Rd Dallas TX 75235

JOHNSON, JOE DAVID, educator; b. Houston, Apr. 2, 1927; s. Carl David and Ruth (Wesley) J.; B.S., N. Tex. State U., 1949; M.Ed., Northwestern State Coll. La., 1960; Ph.D., Baylor U., 1964; m. Doris Clyde Miller, July 3, 1945; children—David Bruce, Kenneth Wayne, Carroll Ray. Ordained to ministry Baptist Ch., 1950; minister various Bapt. chs., Tex., 1946-61; prof. psychology Baylor U., Waco, Tex., 1964—, dir. counseling services, 1967-68, dir. health and counseling services, 1968—. Cons. bus. and Industry, 1964—; cons. U.S. Dept. Health, Edn. and Welfare, 1965—. Served with USNR, 1945-46. Mem. Am., Tex., Central Tex. psychol. assns., Am. Personnel and Guidance Assn., Am. Coll. Personnel Assn., Phi Mu Alpha, Phi Delta Kappa. Mason. Home: Rt 5 Box 76 Waco TX 76705 Office: 1121 S 7th St Waco TX 76703

JOHNSON, JOHN A., communications co. exec.; b. Milw., 1915; A.B., DePauw U., 1937; J.D., U. Chgo., 1940; LL.M,, Harvard, 1946. Admitted to Ill. bar, 1946; atty. Office Gen. Counsel, Burlington & Quincy R.R., 1940-41; with firm Wilson & McIlvaine, 1941-43; asst. Office UN Affairs, Dept. State, Washington, 1946-48; atty. gen. counsel Office Sec. Air Force, 1948-52, gen. counsel Office Air Force, 1952-58; gen. counsel NASA, 1958-63; dir. internat. arrangements Communications Satellite Corp., Washington, 1963-64, v.p. internat., 1964—. Home: 3643 N Nelson St Arlington VA 22207 Office: 950 L'Enfant Plaza S SW Washington DC 20024*

JOHNSON, JOHN ARTHUR, charitable orgn. exec.; b. Chgo., Sept. 29, 1911; s. Andrew John and Clara E. (Dow) J.; B.A., Gustavus Adolphus Coll., St. Peter, Minn., 1936; postgrad. U. Minn., summer 1938, Northwestern U., summer 1939, Purdue U., 1945; m. Audrey England Nelson, Sept. 28, 1940; children—Susan Andrea (Mrs. Paul Harvey Daniel), Scott Bradley. Tchr., Bd. Edn., Duluth, Minn., 1937-42; youth counselor U.S. Employment Service, Duluth, 1942; dir. rehab. for blind Minn. Div. Welfare, 1942-43; personnel adminstr. Honeywell, Inc., Mpls., 1944-54; exec. dir. Columbia Lighthouse for the Blind, Washington, 1954—. Pres. Gen. Council Workshops for Blind; bd. dirs. Nat. Industries for Blind, N.Y.C.; trustee, chmn. standards com., vice chmn. exec. com. Commn. on Accreditation of Rehab. Facilities; mem. adv. bd. Mpls. Soc. for Blind, 1942-54. Recipient Distinguished Alumni award Gustavus Adolphus Coll., 1968. Club: Fairfax (Va.) Country. Home: 619 S Woodstock St Arlington VA 22204 Office: 2021 14th St NW Washington DC 20009

JOHNSON, JOHN EDWARD, dentist; b. Scottsboro, Ala., Nov. 23, 1922; s. Edward Acklin and Johnnie Leah (Armstrong) J.; A.S., St. Bernard Coll., 1942; B.S., U. Chattanooga, 1944; D.D.S., Emory U., 1947; postgrad. U. Mich., 1953, U. N.C., 1967, 68; M.S.D. in Dentistry (USPHS tchr. trainee), U. Ala., 1962, M.S. in Epidemiology (USPHS tchr. trainee), 1964; m. Louise Benefield, June 1, 1963; 1 dau., Linda Leah (dec.). Pvt. practice gen. dentistry, Scottsboro, 1947-50, 54-60; mem. staff Jackson County Hosp., Scottsboro, 1953-60; asst. dir. Bur. Dental Health, Jefferson County Dept. Health, Birmingham, Ala., 1964—; resident dental pub. health Dental Health Center, San Francisco, 1966-67. Instr. dept. community dentistry U. Ala. Sch. Dentistry, Birmingham, 1964—. Served with M.C., AUS, 1943-45; with Dental Corps, USAF, 1951-53. Decorated Fauchard medal. Diplomate Am. Bd. Dental Pub. Health. Mem. Jackson County (Ala.) Dental Assn. (v.p. 1959-60), Birmingham Dist. Dental Soc. (chmn. dental care for home bound 1969—), Ala. Pub. Health Assn. (pres. dental health sect. 1970-71), Am. Dental Assn., Am. Assn. Pub. Health Dentists, Am. Pub. Health Assn., Am. Legion, Psi Omega, Beta Beta Beta, Gamma Sigma Epsilon. Democrat. Baptist (tchr. 1947-60). Contbr. articles to dental jours. Home: 1104 Cresthill Dr Birmingham AL 35213 Office: Bureau of Dental Health Jefferson County Dept of Health PO Box 2646 Birmingham AL 35202

JOHNSON, J(OHN) R(ALPH), agronomist; b. Hull, Ga., Apr. 9, 1912; s. William A. and Dora Ann (Brown) J.; B.S.A., U. Ga., 1933, postgrad., 1950-52; children—Patricia Ann, Martha Carolyn, Rebecca Sue. Agronomist, U.S. Forestry Service, Rolla, Mo., 1934-37; tchr. pub. schs. Ringgold, Ga., 1938-41; agronomist, U. Ga., Athens, 1941-53, head extension agronomy dept., 1954—, prof., 1963—. Recipient Superior Service award U.S. Dept. Agr., 1962; Distinguished Faculty award U. Ga. Coll. of Agr., 1966; Service to Agr. award Gamma Sigma Delta, 1968. Mem. Am. Soc. Agronomy, Crop Sci. Soc. Am., Soil Sci. Soc. Am., Ga. Plant Food Ednl. Soc. (life mem.; exec. sec.; Decennial award 1963), Ga. Soybean Assn. (dir.), Ga. Weed Control Soc. (dir.). Contbr. numerous ednl. bulls. on forage crops, cereals, soil fertility, fertilizers; also articles in profl. jours. Initiated soil fertility and forage programs in Ga. Home: PO Box 5128 Athens GA 30604

JOHNSON, JOSEPH BELTON, dentist; b. Osaka, Va., Feb. 12, 1928; s. George Washington and Roxie Ann (Richmond) J.; B.S. in Civil Engring., Va. Poly. Inst. and State U., 1951; postgrad. Emory and Henry Coll., 1956-57; D.D.S., Va. Commonwealth U., 1962; m. Geraldine Tate, June 2, 1956; 1 dau., Ann Mary. Civil engr. hydraulic engring. div. TVA, Knoxville, 1954-56; gen. children's dentist Va. State Health Dept., Richmond, Nelson County and Henrico County, 1962-63; pvt. practice dentistry, Bon Air, Va., 1963—; pres. Dr. Joseph B. Johnson, Inc. Chmn. Chesterfield County Republican Com., 1969. Served to 1st lt. C.E., AUS, 1951-53. Mem. Am., Va. dental Assns., Richmond Dental Soc., Southside Dental Study Club, Navy League. Mason (Shriner). Club: Salisbury Country (Richmond, Va.). Home: 3830 Wainfleet Dr Richmond VA 23235 Office: 8710 Choctaw Rd Bon Air VA 23235

JOHNSON, JOSEPH E., ednl. adminstr.; b. Vernon, Ala., July 9, 1933; B.A., Birmingham-So. Coll., 1955; M.A., U. Tenn., 1960, Ed.D., 1968; m. Patricia Carole Johnson children—Kent, Kelly. Research asso., instr. polit. sci. U. Tenn., 1958; dir. budget div., dep. commr. finance and adminstrn., exec. asst. to gov. State of Tenn., 1960-63; exec. asst. to pres. U. Tenn., 1963-68, exec. asst. to pres., v.p. instl. research, 1968-70, v.p. devel. and adminstrn., 1970, chancellor med. units, 1970-71, v.p. health affairs, chancellor med. units, 1971—. Served with AUS, 1956-58. Mem. N.E.A., Tenn. Edn. Assn., Am. Coll. Pub. Relations Assn., Assn. Instl. Research, Am. Ednl. Research Assn., Phi Beta Kappa, Omicron Delta Kappa, Phi Kappa Phi. Kiwanian. Mem. Ch. of Christ. Address: 847 Union St Memphis TN 38103*

JOHNSON, JOSEPH EGGLESTON, III, educator, physician; b. Elberton, Ga., Sept. 17, 1930; s. Joseph E. and Marie (Williams) J.; B.A. cum laude, Vanderbilt U., 1951, M.D., 1954; m. Judith Haynes Kemp, Jan. 21, 1956; children—Joseph Eggleston IV, Judith Ann, Julie Marie. Intern, Johns Hopkins Hosp., Balt., 1954-55, resident 1957-61, faculty mem. and staff mem., 1961-66; faculty and staff U. Fla. Teaching Hosp. (J. Hillis Miller Health Center), 1966-72; instr. medicine Johns Hopkins U., 1961-62, asst. prof. medicine, 1962-66, asst. dean for student affairs, 1963-66; asso. prof. medicine U. Fla., 1966-68, prof., 1968-72, chief div. infectious diseases, 1966-72, asso. dean, 1970-72; prof., chmn. dept. medicine Bowman Gray Sch. Medicine, Wake Forest U., 1972—; cons. U.S. Army Biol. Labs., 1966—. Served to lt. USNR, 1956-57. John and Mary R. Markle scholar, 1962; Royal Soc. Medicine travelling fellow, 1970-71. Diplomate Am. Bd. Internal Medicine. Fellow A.C.P. (postgrad. Mead Johnson scholar 1960-61), Royal Soc. Medicine; mem. soc. Exptl. Biology and Medicine, Am. Assn. Immunologists, Am. Acad. Allergy, Am. Clin. and Climatological Assn., So. Soc. Clin. Investigation, Am. Soc. Microbiology, N.Y. Acad. Sci., Am. Fedn. Clin. Research, Infectious Diseases Soc. Am., Phi Beta Kappa, Sigma Alpha Epsilon (chpt. pres. 1950), Phi Chi (chpt. pres. 1953-54), Omicron Delta Kappa, Alpha Omega Alpha. Contbr. to sci. jours. and texts. Home: 3500 Quarterstaff Pl Winston-Salem NC 27104 Office: Bowman Gray Sch Medicine Wake Forest U Wake Forest NC 27587

JOHNSON, JULIAN ERNEST, retail trade exec.; b. Memphis, Jan. 21, 1925; s. Julian Ernest and Hedwig Marie (Streuli) J.; student Miss. State U., 1942-43, U. Miss., 1946-47; m. Merrel Callaway Parker, July 5, 1947; children—Julian Ernest III, Henry Parker, Merrel Callaway. Pres., Johnson Implement Co., Internat. Harvester dealer, Greenwood, Miss., 1954—, also pres. Equipment Center, Internat. Harvester dealer, Blytheville, Ark., 1965—; v.p. Westside Leasing Corp., Greenwood, Miss. 1968—; partner Shoestring Plantation, Greenwood, 1959—; dir. First Nat. Bank Greenwood, Delta Coast, Inc., Greenwood, Whitehaven Corp., Grenada, Miss. Pres. Leflore (Miss.) County Heart Assn., 1965. Mem. Greenwood Planning Commn., 1962-70; dir. Miss. Econ. Council, 1970-71. Bd. dirs. Golden Age Nursing Home, Greenwood. Served with AUS, 1943-45. Mem. Mid-South Farm Equipment Assn. (pres. 1964), Greenwood C. of C. (pres. 1968), Sigma Chi. Republican. Presbyn. (elder 1969—). Elk, Rotarian. Club: Greenwood Country (pres. 1964-65). Home: 605 Robert E Lee St Greenwood MS 38930 Office: Johnson Implement Co Hwy 49-82 W Greenwood MS 38930

JOHNSON, KERMIT ALONZO, univ. pres.; b. Boaz, Ala., Dec. 16, 1911; s. John Arree and Eunice (Pruett) J.; B.S., U. Ala., 1938, M.A., 1944; Ed.D., Columbia U., 1949; m. Golda Watson, Mar. 21, 1932; 1 dau., Judith Kay. Tchr., Cullman (Ala.) County Schs., 1929-36; prin. Garden City (Ala.) Jr. High Sch., 1936-43; prin. Kate Duncan Smith DAR High Sch., Grant, Ala., 1943-45; supt. Tuscaloosa (Ala.) County Schs., 1945-59; asso. supt. Jefferson County Schs., Birmingham, Ala., 1959-61, supt., 1961-68; pres. U. Montevallo (Ala.), 1968—; instr. U. Ala., Tuscaloosa, 1949-59, Birmingham So. Coll., 1960. Participant Fulbright Act, Italy, Netherlands. Mem. Commn. of the States Compact. Bd. dirs. Birmingham Civic Symphony Assn., Boy Scouts Am., Community Chest; chmn. Shelby County March of Dimes. Mem. Ala. Assn. Sch. Adminstrs. (pres. 1951-53), So. Assn. Colls. and Schs. (com. on admission to membership for sr. colls.), Ala. Edn. Assn. (pres. 1963-64), Ala. Congress Parents and Tchrs. (2d v.p. 1958-61), N.E.A. (life), Am. Assn. Sch. Adminstrs. (life mem.). Clubs: Birmingham Executives, Rotary (past pres. Tuscaloosa). Home: Flowerhill Montevallo AL 35115

JOHNSON, L. BARNEY, hosp. adminstr.; b. Winter Haven, Fla., Sept, 9, 1940; s. Ewel Willard and Elizabeth Mary (Baugh) J.; B.A., U. South Fla., 1965; M.H.A., U. Minn., 1967; m. Janice Marie Gunderson, Mar. 4, 1967; 1 son, Leslie Brent. X-ray technologist Baptist Hosp., Plant City, Fla., 1962-65, Watson Clinic, Lakeland, Fla., 1965; asst. adminstr. Winter Haven Hosp.; 1967-68, adminstr., 1968—. Mem. Grievance Bd. City of Winter Haven. Mem. Am. Hosp. Assn., Am. Acad. Med. Adminstrs., Am. Mgmt. Assn., Fla. Hosp; Assn. Kiwanian (bd. dirs. Cypress Gardens. Home: 2101 9th St SE Winter Haven FL 33880 Office: 200 Av F NE Winter Haven FL 33880

JOHNSON, LADY BIRD (CLAUDIA ALTA TAYLOR) (MRS. LYNDON BAINES JOHNSON), b. Karnack, Tex., Dec. 22, 1912; d. Thomas Jefferson Taylor; B.A., U. Tex., 1933, B.Journalism, 1934, LL.D., 1964; LL.D., Tex. Woman's U.; Litt.D., Middlebury Coll.;

L.H.D., Williams Coll.; H.H.D., Southwestern U.; m. Lyndon Baines Johnson, Nov. 17, 1934; children—Lynda Bird (Mrs. Charles S. Robb), Lucy Baines (Mrs. Patrick J. Nugent). Mgr. husband's congl. office, Washington, 1941-42; owner, operator radio-TV sta. KTBC, Austin, Tex., 1942-63, cattle ranches, Tex., 1943-—, also cotton and timberlands, Ala. Former hon. chmn. Nat. Head Start program; hon. chmn. Town Lake Beautification Project; mem. adv. bd. Nat. Parks, Historic Sites, Bldgs. and Monuments. Bd. regents U. Tex., 1971-—, mem. internat. conf. steering com., 1969; trustee Jackson Hole Preserve, Am. Conservation Assn. Recipient Togetherness award Marge Champion, 1958; Humanitarian award B'nai B'rith, 1961; Businesswoman's award Bus. and Profl. Women's Club, 1961; Theta Sigma Phi citation 1962; Distinguished Achievement award Washington Heart Assn., 1962; Industry citation Am. Women in Radio and Television, 1963; Humanitarian citation Vol. Am., 1963; George Foster Peabody award, 1966; Eleanor Roosevelt Golden Candlestick award Women's Nat. Press Club, 1968. Mem. U. Tex. Ex-Students Assn. (life). Episcopalian. Author: A White House Diary, 1970. Address: LBJ Ranch Stonewall TX 78671

JOHNSON, LECTOY TARLINGTON, physician; b. Tyler, Tex., Nov. 28, 1931; s. Lectoy Tarlington and Adele (Delley) J.; B.S., Tex. Coll., 1952; M.D., Howard U., 1956; postgrad. Washington U. Sch. Medicine, 1958-60; m. Helen Collier, Sept. 14, 1958; children—Lectoy Tarlington III, Lynelle Teresa. Intern, Homer G. Phillips Hosp., St. Louis, 1956-57, resident surgeon, 1957-58; resident anesthesiologist Washington U. Sch. Medicine, 1958-59, asst. in anesthesiology, 1959-60; pvt. practice medicine, specializing in anesthesiology, Houston, 1960-—; chmn. dept. anesthesiology St. Joseph's Hosp., Houston, 1969-—, acad. chief, chmn. dept., 1970-—; lectr. anesthesiology U. Tex. Dept. Continuing Edn. Mem. Am. Bd. Anesthesiology, Am. Coll. Anesthesiology, Internat. Anesthesia Research Soc., Kappa Alpha Psi, Chi Delta Mu. Clubs: Houston Diving Assn., Bronze Eagles Flying. Home: 3612 Parkwood St Houston TX 77021 Office: 2000 Crawford St Houston TX 77002

JOHNSON, LEO FRANK, JR., dentist; b. Fort Sill, Okla., May 6, 1943; s. Leo Frank and Dortha Juanita (Case) J.; B.A., Phillips U., 1965; D.D.S., U. Mo., 1969; m. Barbara Ann Morgan, Aug. 22, 1964; children— Berton Case, Stephen Paul. Practice gen. dentistry, Oklahoma City, 1969-—. Mem. Am. Dental Assn., Sertoma Internat, Xi Psi Phi. Mem. Ch. Disciples of Christ (deacon). Democrat. Club: American Brittany. Home: Route 2 Box 66C Tuttle OK 73089 Office: 5700 S Penn St Oklahoma City OK 73119

JOHNSON, LEON DIBRELL, III, utility co. exec.; b. Richmond, Va., May 1, 1917; s. Leon D. and Alice (Faulkner) J., Jr.; B.S. in Elec. Engring., Va. Poly. Inst., 1939; m. Frances Palmore, Oct. 28, 1939; children—Gail (Mrs. John F. Heil), Leon D. IV. Engr., Va. Elec. and Power Co., Richmond, 1939, 45-50, systems planning engrs., 1950-57, chief design engr., 1957-60, dist. mgr., Alexandria, 1960-65, mgr. power supply, 1965-67, mgr. engring. and constrn., 1967-68, v.p., 1968-—. Served from ensign to lt. USNR, 1942-45. Decorated Bronze Star medal. Registered profl. engr., Va. Mem. I.E.E.E., Va., Richmond chambers commerce. Presbyn. Mason. Club: Meadowbrook Country (Richmond). Home: 6411 St George Rd Richmond VA 23234 Office: 701 E Franklin St Richmond VA 23219

JOHNSON, LEROY REGINALD, state senator; b. Atlanta, July 28, 1928; s. Leroy and Elizabeth J.; B.A., Morehouse Coll., 1949; M.A., Atlanta U., 1951; LL.B., N.C. Sch. Law, 1957; m. Cleopatra Whittington; 1 son, Michael V. Tchr. social sci. Atlanta Pub. Sch. System, 1950-54; admitted to Ga. bar, 1957; criminal investigator Solicitor Gen.'s Staff, 1957-61; mem. Ga. senate, 1962-—, chmn. Fulton County delegation. A founder Atlanta Jr. Voters League; mem. exec. com. Atlanta Negro Voters League, Atlanta Com. for Coop. Action; pres. Ga. Assn. Citizens Democratic Clubs. Bd. dirs. Campfire Girls, Inc., West Side br. YMCA. Named one of Atlanta's 5 Outstanding Young Men, Atlanta C. of C., 1963, Citizen of Year, Omega Psi Phi; recipient Freedom award N.A.A.C.P., 1963, Russwurn award Nat. Pubs. Assn., 1962. Mem. Ga., Gate City (v.p.) bar assns., Phi Beta Sigma. Mason. Home: 372 Larchmont Dr NW Atlanta GA 30318 Office: 1014 Gordon St SW Atlanta GA 30310

JOHNSON, LESTER DECHMAN, ret. govt. ofcl.; b. San Jose, Cal., May 15, 1907; s. Andrew Dechman and Mary (Mitchell) J.; A.B., San Jose State Coll., 1929; M.A., Stanford, 1933; m. Faye Lucas, Oct. 12, 1938. Instr., Poly Coll., Oakland, Cal., 1933-35; with U.S. Customs Service, 1935-—, asst. commr., 1964-65, commr. customs, Washington, 1965-69; cons. Treasury Dept., 1969-70. Recipient Exceptional Service award U.S. Treasury Dept., 1966. Club: International (Washington). Home: 6810 Mindello St Coral Gables FL 33146

JOHNSON, LEWIS NOEL, educator; b. Hebbardsville, Ky., May 5, 1918; s. Fred A. and Polly (Bigg) J.; B.S., Western Ky. State U., 1940, M.A., 1956; Ed.D., Peabody Coll., 1961; m. Anna L. Scott, Apr. 10, 1942; children—Joann, Charles. Tchr., prin. schs., Henderson County, Ky., 1946-54; prin. Henderson County High Sch., 1954-61; coordinator Title III ESEA act Ky. Dept. Edn., 1965-68; supt. Henderson County schs., 1968-—. Pres. Petroleum Enterprises, Inc. Mem. Ky. Ho. of Reps., 1961-65. Served to 2d lt. AUS, 1942-46. Decorated Purple Heart. Named Ky. statesman, Ky. col. Mem. Phi Delta Kappa. Mason (Shriner, Jester). Address: PO Box 672 Henderson KY 42420

JOHNSON, LORENZO, food lab. exec.; b. nr. Yazoo City, Miss., Sept. 14, 1908; s. Clint and Mittie (Sanders) J.; B.A., Miss. Coll., 1931; postgrad. U. N.C., 1931-35; m. Beulah Irene Stringer, Apr. 21, 1932; children—Preston Lewis, Carolyn Faye, Jerry Wayne. Asst. tchr. Miss. Coll., 1930-31; head chemistry dept. Copiah-Lincoln Jr. Coll., 1931-35; insp. U.S. FDA, New Orleans, St. Louis, 1935-40, insp. in charge, Dallas, 1941-46; cons. food chemist; 1947-52; owner, dir. Chem. Food Labs., Atlanta, 1953-—; cons. food chemist, 1947-—. Mem. Miss. Coll. Alumni Assn. (dir. Atlanta br.), Inst. Food Technologists. Developer methods for isolation filth from food products, others. Home: 735 Amsterdam Av NE Atlanta GA 30306 Office: 590 Orme Circle NE Atlanta GA 30306 also PO Box 8435 Sta F Atlanta GA 30306

JOHNSON, LOUIS MALCOLM, physician; b. Warrenton, Ga., July 6, 1935; s. Roger and Ruth (Gheesling) J.; B.S., U. Ga., 1960; M.D., U. Tenn., 1963; m. Betty Carolyn Russell, Jan. 12, 1963; children—Mary Colleen, David Roger, Mittie Dianne, Richard Paul. Intern, Athens Gen. Hosp., 1964-65; practice medicine, Warrenton, Ga., 1965-68; asst. depot surgeon U.S. army, Atlanta, 1968; regional med. officer Internal Revenue Ser., Atlanta, 1969; mem. Indsl. Clinic, Atlanta, 1970-—; mem. staff S. Fulton Hosp., Atlanta. Served with AUS, 1954-56. Named Doctor of Day, Ga. Legislature Session, 1971. Mem. Ga. Indsl. Med. Assn. (sec.-treas. 1970-72, pres. elect 1972-73), Med. Assn. Ga., A.M.A., Fulton County Med. Assn., Fulton County Insdl. Med. Assn. Methodist. Home: 939 Andiron Ct Stone Mountain GA 30083 Office: 3450 International Blvd Hapeville GA

JOHNSON, LOYS ALMON, educator; b. Volga, S.D., July 11, 1908; s. Isaac Benhardt and Clara (Johnson) J.; B.S. in Civil Engring., S.D. State U., 1930; M.S. in Civil Engring., U. Wis., 1931; certificate U.S. Naval Postgrad. Sch.; m. Helen St. John Mooney, June 23, 1938; children—Loys Fulton, Eunice Virginia, Claire Elaine (Mrs. Nathaniel P. Baggarly), Dawn Melani. Jr. engr. U.S. Bur. Reclamation, Denver, 1934-36; asst. structural engr. TVA, Knoxville, 1936-41; commd. lt. (j.g.) USN, 1941; with Civil Engr. Corps, 1941-60, various locations abroad, 1941-60, including asst. naval attache U.S. Embassy, London; ret., 1960; prof., chmn. dept. bldg. constrn. U. Fla. at Gainesville, 1960-—. Dir. U. Fla. Campus Credit Union. Registered profl. engr., Tenn. Mem. Am. Soc. C.E., Am. Inst. Constructors (founding dir.), Sigma Lambda Chi. Lutheran. Home: 901 NW 37th Dr Gainesville FL 32601 Office: Dept Bldg Constrn U Fla Gainesville FL 32601

JOHNSON, LUCIUS EUGENE, restaurant co. exec.; b. Mt. Vernon, Ill., Apr. 25, 1904; s. Alva Wright Boswell and Caroline (Wilson) J.; B.A., Va. Mil. Inst., 1925; m. Betty Stout, Oct. 24, 1933; children—Lucius Eugene, Wesley Stout, Betty Lee. Pres., dir. Britling Cafeterias Co. Tenn.; mgr., partner Asso. Caterers and related orgns.; 1941-45; pres., dir. Blue Boar Cafeteria Co., and subsidiaries, Louisville, 1948-—; pres., dir. B & W Cafeteria Co.; chmn. bd. Britling Service Corp.; dir. Liberty Nat. Bank & Trust Co., Louisville. Mem. Louisville Bd. Edn., 1956-63, pres., 1959-60. Bd. dirs. Childrens Hosp., 1938-66, Better Bus. Bur., 1954. Served to capt. AUS, 1943-45; ETO. Named to Restaurant Hall of Fame. Mem. Nat. (dir. 1954-—, pres. 1965-66), Louisville (bd. dirs., past pres.) restaurant assns., Photog. Soc. Am., Ky. (dir. 1966-—), Louisville (bd. dirs., 1955-58, 60-63, pres. 1963) chambers commerce. Presbyn. Mason (Shriner), Rotarian. Clubs: Louisville Country, Pendennis, Filson (Louisville). Home: 547 Primrose Way Louisville KY 40206 Office: 644 S 4th St Louisville KY 40202

JOHNSON, LYNDON BAINES, former Pres. of U.S.; b. Stonewall, Tex., Aug 27, 1908; s. Sam Ealy and Rebekah (Baines) J.; B.S., Southwest Tex. State Tchrs. U., San Marcos, 1930; postgrad. Georgetown Law Sch., 1934; LL.D., Southwestern U., 1943, Howard Payne U., 1957, Brown U., 1959, Bethany Coll., 1959, U. Hawaii, 1961, U. Philippines, 1961, Gallaudet Coll., 1961, East Ky. State Coll., 1961, William Jewell Coll., 1961, Elon Coll., 1962, Southwest Tex. State Tchrs. Coll., 1962, Wayne State U., 1963, Jacksonville U., 1963, McMurray Coll., 1963, U. Md., 1963, Tufts U., 1963, U. Cal. at Los Angeles, 1964, U. Tex., 1964, Swarthmore Coll., 1964, Syracuse U., 1964, Georgetown U., 1964, U. Ky., 1965, Baylor U., 1965, Howard U., 1965, Catholic U., 1965, Princeton, 1966, U. Denver, 1966, Tex. Technol. Coll., 1967, Tex. Christian U., 1968, Thomas More Coll., 1968, St. Francis Coll., N.Y., 1968; D.C.L., Holy Cross Coll., 1964, U. Mich., 1964, U. R.I., 1966; L.H.D., Oklahoma City U., 1960, Yeshiva U., 1961, Fla. Atlantic U., 1964; Litt.D., Glassboro Coll., 1968; D. Litt., St. Mary's Coll., Cal., 1962; D.Polit. Sci., Chulalongkorn U., Thailand, 1966; m. Claudia Alta Taylor (Lady Bird), Nov. 17, 1934; children—Lynda Bird (Mrs. Charles S. Robb), Luci Baines (Mrs. Patrick J. Nugent). Tchr. Houston (Tex.) Pub. Schs., 1930-31; sec. to Congressman Richard M. Kleberg, of Tex., 1931-35; Tex. dir. Nat. Youth Adminstrn., 1935-37; elected to 75th Congress (1937-38) to fill unexpired term of Congressman James B. Buchanan, 10th Tex. Dist.; re-elected to 76th to 80th Congresses (1938-48); U.S. senator, 1949-61, minority leader 83d Congress, majority leader 84th-86th Congresses; v.p. U.S., 1961-63; 36th pres. U.S. (succeeded to Presidency of United States Nov. 22, 1963 on death of Pres. John F. Kennedy); elected President, Nov. 3, 1964, served until Jan. 20, 1969. Past chmn. Pres.'s Com. on Equal Employment Opportunity, Nat. Aeronautics and Space Council, Peace Corps Adv. Council; past mem. Nat. Security Council. Comdr. USNR, active duty, 1941-42. Decorated Silver Star. Democrat. Mem. Christian Ch. Author: My Hope for America, 1964; A Time for Action, 1964; This America, 1966; No Retreat from Tomorrow, 1967; To Heal and to Build, 1968; The Choices We Face, 1968; The Tomorrow; To Heal and to Build; The Choices We Face; The Vantage Point: Perspectives of the Presidency, 1963-69, 1971. Home: LBJ Ranch Stonewall TX 78671

JOHNSON, MALCOLM BLAINE, newspaper editor; b. Wardner, Ida., Feb. 13, 1913; s. James Blaine and Winifred (Ashley) J.; B.S., U. Fla., 1936; m. Dorothy Lucile Burt, Oct. 23, 1937; 1 dau., Donna (Mrs. Sam H. Moorer, Jr.). Reporter, Jacksonville (Fla.) Jour., 1935-36, Daytona Beach (Fla.) Sun Record, 1936; city editor Tallahassee Democrat, 1937, editor, 1954-—; corr. Asso. Press, Tallahassee, 1940-54. Cons., Kiplinger Fla. Letter, 1956-—, World Book Ency., 1964-—. Mem. Fla. Heritage Found. Mem. Tallahassee Hist. Soc. (pres. 1960), Fla. Hist. Soc., Fla. Soc. Newspaper Editors (dir. 1970-—); Am. Soc. Newspaper Editors. Rotarian (pres. 1965). Home: 2933 Meridian Rd Tallahassee FL 32302 Office: 277 N Magnolia Dr Tallahassee FL 32302

JOHNSON, MARVIN GERALD, govt. ofcl.; b. Meridian, Tex., Dec. 6, 1915; s. Martin Robert and Olga (Erickson) J.; A.B., Bethany Nazarene Coll., 1938; postgrad. Okla. Central State Coll., 1939, Tulsa U., 1942; m. Geneva Vondell Ingle, Oct. 27, 1939; children—Gerald Dennis, Larry Eugene, Richard Alan. Civil engr. C.E., U.S. Army, Tulsa, 1939-—, chief relocations br., 1965-—; dir. Tulsa Fed. Employees Credit Union, 1963-—, pres., 1966-67. Committeeman Boy Scouts Am., Tulsa, 1950-56; dir. Burroughs Civic Assn., 1954-56; dir. Lombard Youth Recreation Assn., 1962-66, pres., 1965. Served with USMCR, 1943-46. Decorated Air medal; recipient Superior Performance award U.S. Army, 1959, 66. Registered profl. engr., Okla. Mem. Nat., Okla. socs. profl. engrs. Home: 3721 S Darlington St Tulsa OK 74135 Office: U.S. Corps Engrs 420 S Boulder St Tulsa OK 74101

JOHNSON, NATHANIEL REEVES, JR., telephone co. exec.; b. Cape May County, N.J., July 26, 1920; s. Nathaniel Reeves and Hazel (Hand) J.; B.A., Ursinus Coll., 1941; student Duke U. Law Sch., 1941-42; m. Maybelle F. Larson, Nov. 10, 1944; children—Michael R., Stephen W., Wendy Lynne. Spl. agent FBI, 1942-44, spl. agent, spl. agent-in-charge, 1946-59; asst. v.p. operations So. Bell Tel. & Tel. Co., Atlanta, 1959-65, asst. v.p. personnel, 1965-69, v.p. personnel, 1969-—. Served to ensign USNR, 1944-45. Mem. Ga., Atlanta chambers commerce, Nat. Alliance Businessmen (bus. adv. com.), soc. Former Spl. Agts. FBI (Southeastern regional v.p. 1969-70), Commerce Club, Civitation Club. Presbyn. Club: Athletic (Atlanta). Home: 4980 Jett Rd Atlanta GA 30327 Office: 1701 Hurt Bldg Atlanta GA 30303

JOHNSON, NICHOLAS, govt. ofcl.; b. Iowa City, Sept. 23, 1934; s. Wendell A.L. and Edna (Bockwoldt) J.; B.A., U. Tex., 1956, LL.B., 1958; L.H.D., Winfham Coll., 1971; m. Karen Mary Chapman, 1952; children—Julie, Sherman, Gregory. Admitted to Tex. bar, 1958, D.C. bar, 1963, U.S. Supreme Ct. bar, 1963; law clk. U.S. Circuit Ct. Appeals Judge John R. Brown, 1958-59, to U.S. Supreme Ct. Justice Hugo L. Black, 1959-60; acting asso. prof. law U. Cal. at Berkeley, 1960-63; asso. firm Covington & Burling, Washington, 1963-64; adminstr. Maritime Adminstrn., U.S. Dept. Commerce, Washington, 1964-66; commr. FCC, 1966-—; adj. prof. law Georgetown U., 1971-—. Named One of 10 Outstanding Young Men, U.S. Jr. C. of C., 1967; Pub. Defender award New Republic, 1970. Mem. Am., Fed. bar assns., State Bar Tex., Internat. Soc. Gen. Semantics (dir.), Order of Coif, Phi Beta Kappa, Phi Eta Sigma, Pi Sigma Alpha, Phi Delta Phi. Democrat. Unitarian. Author: How to Talk Back to Your Television Set, 1970; Life Before Death in the Corporate State, 1971. Contbr. to legal and gen. publs.; radio, TV appearances; lectr. Home: 1919 M St NW Washington DC 20554 Office: Fed Communications Commn Washington DC 20554

JOHNSON, NICK GEORGE, san. engr.; b. Langadia, Greece, Aug. 7, 1920; s. George Nick and Mary (Kalotyhou) J.; came to U.S., naturalized, 1929; B.C.E., U. Louisville, 1943; M.S. in Engring., U. Mich., 1950; m. Mary Lee Brown, July 28, 1960; children—Maria, George. Engr. hydraulic design sect. U.S. C.E., Louisville, 1946-47; san. engr. Div. engring., Ky. Dept. Health, Louisville, 1947-53, asst. dir., 1953-59, dir. san. engring. program, Frankfort, 1959-71, dir. san. engring. div., 1971-—. Lectr. san. engring. Served to lt. (j.g.) USNR, 1943-46. Recipient Pub. Speaking award Ky. sect. Am. Soc. C.E., 1943. Mem. Am., Ky. (pres. 1963-64) pub. health assns., Conf. State San. Engrs., Am. Water Works Assn., Assn. Res. Officers USPHS, Theta Tau. Democrat. Mem. Greek Orthodox Ch. Home: 125 Londonderry Dr Lexington KY 40504 Office: 275 E Main St Frankfort KY 40601

JOHNSON, NORMALIE HOLLOWAY, judge; b. Lake Charles, La.; grad. D.C. Tchrs. Coll.; J.D., Georgetown U.; mem; Julius Johnson. Tchr., Taft Jr. High Sch., 1955-63; asst. civil div. Dept; Justice, 1963-67; asst. corp. counsel Govt. D.C., Washington, from 1967, now judge. Democrat. Office: Office Corp Counsel Govt Dist Columbia Washington DC*

JOHNSON, NORMAN AARON, JR., pub. service commr.; b. Philadelphia, Miss., June 8, 1921; s. Norman Aaron and Bobbie (Jasper) J.; B.S., Miss. State U., 1942; m. Mary Grace Stringer, May 16, 1946; children—Norman Aaron III, Amanda. Mcht., farmer; state comdr. Miss. Am. Legion, 1951-52; mayor, Philadelphia, 1953-55; chmn. Miss. Pub. Service Commn., Philadelphia, 1955-—. Pres. Neshoba County Fair Assn., Inc.; chmn. bd. dirs. Miss. chpt. Arthritis Found. Served with USMCR, 1941; with AUS, 1943-45. Mem. Nat. (exec. com.), Southeastern (pres. 1971-72) assns. regulatory utility commrs., Am. Legion, 40 and 8, V.F.W., C. of C., Farm Bur., Sigma Phi Epsilon. Baptist. Mason (Shriner). Home: 506 Peebles St Philadelphia MS 39350 Office: Walter Sillers State Office Bldg Jackson MS 39201

JOHNSON, OLE SIMON, educator; b. Pingree, N.D., Aug. 15, 1917; s. Peter and Caroline (Brevik) J.; B.A., Jamestown Coll., 1940; M.B.A., Northwestern U., 1941; Ph.D., U. Pitts., 1951; m. Ruth Lydia Kitzman, Apr. 20, 1944; 1 son, Ronald Charles. Managerial trainee Montgomery Ward & Co., Chgo., 1940-42; bus. mgr., asst. prof. marketing Jamestown Coll., 1946-49; lectr. marketing U. Pitts., 1949-51; asso. prof., head marketing dept. Ga. State Coll., 1951-53; asso. prof. bus. adminstrn. Mich. State U., 1953-60; prof. marketing Sch. Bus. Adminstrn. Sao Paulo (Brazil), 1954-58; prof., dir. marketing program The American U., Washington, 1960-65; dean, prof. marketing and mgmt. Sch. Bus., Oklahoma City U., 1965-69; dean and prof. marketing Sch. Bus. Adminstrn., Old Dominion U., Norfolk, Va., 1969-—; adv. dir. Shepherd Mall State Bank, Oklahoma City; dir., lectr. several mgmt. seminars, insts., workshops; cons. to trade assns., bus. and industry; bd. dirs. Fed. Statistics Users Conf.; dir. Ann. Washington Conf. on Bus.-Govt. Relations, 1961-65; bd. dirs. Internat. Trade Club of Oklahoma City, 1965-69; chmn. Nat. Census Adv. Com. Served with AUS, 1942-46. Mem. Am. Soc. of Sao Paulo (Brazil) (mem. bd. govs.), Am. C. of C. for Brazil, Am. Marketing Assn. (nat. v.p., nat. bd. dirs., pres. Washington chpt.), Am. Econ. Assn., Am. Acad. Polit. and Social Scis., Soc. Advancement Mgmt., Nat. Assn. Purchasing Agents, Beta Gamma Sigma, Alpha Kappa Psi, Pi Sigma Epsilon. Lutheran. Club: Nat. Economists. Author: The Industrial Store, 1952, contbr. articles in field to profl. jours. Home: 221 Huntsman Rd Norfolk VA 23502 Office: Old Dominion U Norfolk VA 23508

JOHNSON, PAUL NORMAN, optometrist; b. Traverse City, Mich., Mar. 20, 1924; s. Norman Lyman and LaVergne (Beckler) J.; O.D., No. Ill. Coll. Optometry, 1949; m. Phyllis Jean Krock, Sept. 22, 1951. Asso. in practice optometry, Belleville, Ill., 1949-56, Norfolk, Va., 1957-62; pvt. practice optometry, Chesapeake, Va. 1963-—. Served with USMCR, 1943-45. Decorated Purple Heart. Fellow Va. Acad. Optometry; mem., Am. Va. optometric assns., Tidewater Council Optometry, So. Council Optometrists, Am. Legion (post comdr. 1964-65). Lion (pres. 1968-69. Home: 1220 Ginger Crescent Virginia Beach VA 23456 Office: 238 Battlefield Blvd N Chesapeake, VA 23320

JOHNSON, RALPH ALLEN, elec. products co. exec.; b. Reading, Pa., Oct. 10, 1925; s. Ralph Schultz and Sarah Elizabeth (Reider) J.; B.S., U. Fla., 1951; M.B.A., Harvard, 1959; m. Dorothy Anita Spearman, Mar. 24, 1951; children—Mark, Jeffrey, Ann. With Radiation, Inc., Melbourne, Fla., 1951-—, dir. integrated systems support, 1970-—; pres. Fla. Leasing Corp., 1960-62. Pres. Indian River Players, 1952-53; vice chmn. Brevard chpt. A.R.C., 1966-70; chmn. Brevard Econ. Devel. Council, 1968; active Brevard Hosp. Assn. Served with AUS, 1943-46. Decorated Bronze Star medal. Mem. Nat. Council Tech. Services Industries (dir. 1970-—), Am. Mgmt. Assn., I.E.E.E., Phi Kappa Phi. Mem. Reformed Ch. Mason. Club: Eau Gallie Yacht (comdr. 1972) (Indian Harbour Beach, Fla.). Home: 980 Whitmire Dr Melbourne FL 32935 Office: Box 37 Melbourne FL 32935

JOHNSON, RAYMOND EDWARD, publicity dir.; b. McEwen, Tenn., Feb. 27, 1904; s. Edward and Lina (Adams) J.; grad. high sch.; m. Mae Louthan, July 30, 1907; children—Robert Edward, Raymond Eugene. Office boy Nashville Tennessean, 1918-20, sports writer, 1920-25, asst. sports editor, 1926-37, sports editor, 1937-70; publicity dir. Nat. Turf Writers Assn., Churchill Downs, 1971-—; sports editor Eve. Tennessean, 1925-26. Mem. Football Writers Assn. (past pres.). Amateur Softball Assn. Am. (past pres.), Golden Gloves Nat. (past pres.), So. Assn. Baseball Writers (past pres.), Nat. Baseball Writers Assn. Am. (past pres.), Golf Writers Am., Sigma Delta Chi. Democrat. Lutheran. Rotarian, Elk. Home: 1604 17th Av S Nashville TN 37212 Office: 1100 Broadway Nashville TN 37202

JOHNSON, RICHARD CAMPBELL, banker; b. Winter Garden, Fla., Oct. 11, 1928; s. Jesse Wilder and Marjorie (Campbell) J.; B. Landscape Architecture, U. Fla., 1950; m. Betty Jean Kelley, Aug. 10, 1949; 1 son, Richard Kelley. Exec. v.p. Seminole Nurseries (Fla.), 1950-—; dir. Sylvan Abbey Meml. Park, Clearwater, Fla., 1958-—; vice chmn. bd. Bank of Seminole, 1960-—; chmn. bd., pres. First Comml. Bank, St. Petersburg, Fla., 1964-—; vice chmn. First Community Bank, Largo, Fla., 1969-—; chmn. bd. Northside Community Bank, 1972-—, First Bank West Pasco. Chmn. St. Petersburg Zoning Bd. Bd. dirs. local Goodwill Assn., Salvation Army, Boy Scouts Am., Pinellas County United Fund; trustee Pinellas County Community Found. Served to maj. USAF, 1952-54. Mem. Fla. Nurserymen and Growers Assn. (pres. 1966), Fla. Bankers Assn., St. Petersburg Area (pres.), Largo, Clearwater chambers commerce, Pinellas County Com. 100, Kappa Sigma. Methodist. Kiwanian (pres. 1964). Clubs: Pinellas County Commerce; St. Petersburg Yacht. Home: 801 65th St N St Petersburg FL 33710 Office: PO Box 3367 Seminole FL 33540

JOHNSON, RICHARD CARL, educator; b. Chgo., Sept. 2, 1933; s. Carl Helmer and Anne Katherine (Johnson) J.; B.A. in Liberal Arts, U. Chgo., 1954; postgrad. U. So. Cal., 1956-57; B.A. in Philosophy, U. Cal. at Los Angeles, 1958; M.A., U. Colo., 1962; m. Ann Elizabeth Faust, July 3, 1958; children—Eric Richard, Tawny Elizabeth. Asst. to acad. dean U. Colo., Boulder, 1963-65; dean students Tougaloo (Miss.) Coll., 1965-67, asst. prof. philosophy, 1967—, chmn. dept. philosophy and religion, 1969—. Cons. adult basic edn. research project Boston U., 1970. Pres., Jackson Area Council on Human Relations, 1969-71; treas. Am. Civil Liberties Union of Miss., 1971—, mem. exec. com., 1970—; founding bd. mem. Community Coalition for Pub. Schs., 1970—. County and state del. Democratic party, 1963-64. Served with AUS, 1954-56. Mem. Am., Miss. (pres. 1972-73) philos. assns., Southwestern Philos. Soc., Urban League, Am. Assn. U. Profs., Beta Theta Pi. Mem. Ecumenical Ch. Reconciliation. Home: 735 Lawrence Rd Jackson MS 39206 Office: Tougaloo Coll Tougaloo MS 39174

JOHNSON, RICHARD CLAYTON, research physicist; b. Eveleth, Minn., May 9, 1930; s. Elvin and Sadie Abramson) J.; B.S., Ga. Inst. Tech., 1953, M.S., 1958, Ph.D., 1961; m. Sallie Staples Hairston, Aug. 2, 1958 (div. 1971); children—Karen Louise, Diana Elizabeth. With Ga. Inst. Tech., Atlanta, 1952—, instr. physics lab., research asst., 1952-53, research asst., asst. research physicist, asst. prof., research physicist, sr. research physicist, 1956-67, prin. research physicist, 1967—, head radar br. engring. expt. sta., 1963-68, chief electronics div., 1968-71, asst. dir. for systems and techniques, 1971—; cons. industry, fed. govt., 1966—. Served to lt. jg. USNR, 1953-55. Registered profl. engr., Ga. Mem. Am. Phys. Soc., I.E.E.E., Sigma Xi, Tau Beta Pi, Phi Eta Sigma, Phi Kappa Phi, Sigma Pi Sigma, Phi Kappa Sigma. Contbr. articles to profl. jours., chapters to sci. books. Patantee antenna range. Home: 2572-66 Lenox Rd NE Atlanta GA 30324

JOHNSON, RICHARD KEITH, textile co. exec.; b. Camden, Ark., Sept. 16, 1929; s. Chester Forrest and Margaret Leone (Gaught) J.; B.S., La. Tech U., 1952; m. Virginia Catherine Sibille, Jan. 27, 1952; children—Eugene Victor, Richard Keith, Bryan Matthew, Mary Virginia. Jr. accountant United Gas Corp., Shreveport, La., 1952; jr. accountant Firestone Synthetic Rubber & Latex Co., Lake Charles, La., 1952-57, gen. accountant, Orange, Tex., 1957-61; cost analyst Firestone Tire & Rubber Co., Akron, O., 1961-62; with Fireston Synthetic Fibers, Hopewell, Va., 1962—, mgr. accounting, comptroller, 1963—. Mem. Nat. Assn. Accountants (nat. bd. dirs. 1961), Hopewell C. of C. (v.p., bd. dirs.), Kappa Sigma. Club: Jordon Point Country. Home: 3503 W Broadway St Hopewell VA 23860 Office: PO Box 450 Hopewell VA 23860

JOHNSON, ROBERT EDWARD, govt. ofcl.; b. Monson, Mass., Mar. 28, 1905; s. Ernest LeRoy and Ida (Whitcomb) J.; B.A., Clark U., 1928; M.B.A., N.Y.U., 1932; m. Edith Annie McGowan, June 16, 1928; children—Robert Edward, Roger Hutchinson. Statistician, N.Y. Telephone Co., 1928-41; dir. mil. div. WPB, 1942-45; dir. research and adminstrn. Civilian Prodn. Adminstrn., 1945-46; dep. housing expediter Housing Adminstrn., 1947; statistician Am. Tel. & Tel. Co., N.Y.C., 1946-47; chief statistician N.J. Bell Telephone Co., Newark, 1947-49; chief economist, actuary Western Electric Co., N.Y.C., 1949-67; dep. asst. sec. Dept. Air Force, 1967-68; dep. asst. commr. Bur. Labor Statistics, Washington, 1968—. Dir. Help For a Hungry World, Indsl. Devel. Research Council. Fellow Am. Statis. Assn., A.A.A.S.; mem. Am. Econ. Assn., Acad. Actuaries, Nat. Assn. Bus. Economists, Soc. Am. Mil. Engrs., Indsl. Relations Research Assn., Operations Research Soc. Am., Inst. Mgmt. Scis., Conf. Bus. Economists, Econ. Research Round Table, Downtown Econ. Luncheon Group. Author: (with D. N. Morris) Guide To Elementary Statistics, 1954. Home: 5702 37th Av Hyattsville MD 20382 Office: 441 G St NW Washington DC 20212

JOHNSON, ROBERT ERVIN, govt. ofcl.; b. Greenwood, Ark., Nov. 22, 1924; s. George Washington and Lucile (Pettigrew) J.; LL.B., U. Ark., 1946 Admitted to Ark. bar, 1946; partner Johnson & Johnson, Greenwood, Ark., 1946-54; asst. U.S. atty. Western Dist. Ark., Fort Smith, 1954-58, chief asst., 1958—. Dir. Sebastian County Fair, 1947—. Served as 1st lt., JAGC, 1951-52. Decorated Bronze Star medal. Mem. Am., Ark., Sebastian County bar assns., Am. Legion. Methodist. Club: Lions (Greenwood). Home: 3222 S 39th St Fort Smith AR 72903 Office: 6th and Parkers Sts Fort Smith AR 72903

JOHNSON, ROBERT MARTELL, newspaper pub. co. exec.; b. El Paso, Tex., Dec. 22, 1927; s. Frank Denton and Cora (Smith) J.; student San Antonio Jr. Coll., 1946-48; B.J., U. Tex., 1950; m. Jackie Eladean Hale, Jan. 16, 1953; children—Robert Hale, Mark Denton. Reporter, Winnsboro (Tex.) News, 1950; advt. salesman Galveston (Tex.) News-Tribune, 1952-53; advt. salesman Dallas Morning News, 1953-64; asst. to pres. News-Texan, Inc., 1964-65, pres., 1965—, dir., 1972—. Served with inf. AUS, 1950-52. Home: 10110 Mapleridge Dr Dallas TX 75238 Office: 4880 Alpha Rd Farmers Branch TX 75234

JOHNSON, ROBERT MILTON, drainage engr., city ofcl.; b. Putnam, Ala., Jan. 5, 1894; s. Robert Blakely and Elizabeth Anne (Bates) J.; student George Washington U., 1924-25; B.S. in Civil Engring., U. Fla., 1929, M.S. in Engring., 1937, C.E. (hon.), 1931; m. Alda Twilley Elzey, June 28, 1919; children—Robert Milton, James Harrison, William Elzey. Hydraulic research U. Fla., Gainesville, 1934-37; engr. City of Augustine (Fla.), 1937-40; water treatment supr. City of Tampa (Fla.), 1940-45, asst. city engr., 1945—, drainage engr., 1945—. Served to capt. USMC, 1915-21. Registered profl. engr., Fla. Democrat. Baptist. Mason, Woodman of World. Home: 714 S Orleans Av Tampa FL 33606 Office: 404 E Jackson St Tampa FL 33602

JOHNSON, ROBERT PETER, physician; b. Springfield Gardens, N.Y., Sept. 10, 1930; s. Stanley Frances and Viola Josephine (Verinsky) J.; student Palm Beach Jr. Coll., 1948-50; B.S., U. Fla., 1952; M.D., Tulane, 1956; m. Barbara Louise Skipper, Dec. 26, 1965; children—Gordon Raymond, Robert Peter. Intern, Jackson Meml. Hosp., Miami, Fla., 1956-57; univ. physician U. Miami (Fla.), 1960-62 physician, team physician Fla. State U. at Tallahassee, 1962-66, 71—; pvt. practice medicine, Tallahassee, 1966—; mem. staff Tallahassee Meml. Hosp., mem. exec. com., 1971—. Served with M.C., USNR, 1957-60. Fellow Am. Acad. Sports Medicine; mem. Fla. Acad. Gen. Practice (bd. dirs.), Am. Acad. Gen. Practice, A.M.A., Assn. Mil. Surgeons U.S., So. Med. Assn., Fla. Med. Assn. (chmn. ad hoc com. drug abuse), Big Bend TB and Respiratory Disease Assn. (chmn. med. adv. com.), Tri-County Med. Soc. (bd. govs.). Kiwanian (v.p. Tallahassee club 1971). Home: 1006 Lothian Dr Tallahassee FL 32303 Office: 1330 Miccosukee Rd Tallahassee FL 32303

JOHNSON, ROBERT THERON, food co. exec.; b. Rockfield, Ky., July 13, 1923; s. Theron M. and Mattie (Harlan) J.; B.S. in Agr., U. Ky., 1946; student Ohio State U., 1948, U. Louisville, 1953-55; m. Anne N. Colliver, July 30, 1949; children—Vickie Anne, Robert C. With Oscar Ewing Dairy, Louisville, 1949-70, gen. mgr., dir., 1962-70; v.p. Convenient Industries Am., Louisville, 1970—, also dir. Active local Boy Scouts Am. Served with USAAF, 1943-46, USAF, 1951-53. Decorated Air medal. Mem. Dairy Products Assn. Ky. (pres., dir. 1963), Central Dairy Council (past pres., dir.), Tri Cities Dairy Tech. Soc. (past pres.), Inst. Food Technology, Alpha Gamma Rho. Mem. Christian Ch. (deacon). Kiwanian. Club: Plantation Country (Louisville). Home: 7518 Westdale Rd Louisville KY 40222 Office: 981 S 3d St Louisville KY 40201

JOHNSON, ROGER EDWIN, govt. ofcl.; b. Glendale, Cal., Nov. 22, 1906; s. Jonathan Edwin and Jennie (Smith) J.; A.B., U. So. Cal., 1928, LL.B., 1930; m. Louise Thompson, Apr. 18, 1930; children—Jonathan Edwin, Amelia (Mrs. F. Lynn Alexander), Willa Ann. Admitted to Cal. bar; practice law, Whittier, Cal., 1930-43; chief litigation atty, regional office OPA, Los Angeles, 1943-44; asst. v.p. Superior Oil Co., Washington, 1944-61; v.p. Superior Oil Internat., Tripoli, Libya, 1961-63, exec. v.p., gen. counsel, London, Eng., 1963-70; spl. asst. to Pres., Exec. Office Pres., Washington, 1970—. Mem. Cal. State Bar, Pi Kappa Alpha, Phi Alpha Delta, Republican. Mem. Christian Ch. Mason (Shriner). Clubs: Congressional Country, Washington. Home: Apt 1405-E 4201 Cathedral Av NW Washington DC 20016 Office: The White House Washington DC 20500

JOHNSON, ROOSEVELT, JR., orgn. exec.; b. Conroe, Tex., Feb. 22, 1924; s. Roosevelt and Lossie Dee (Mitchell) J.; B.S., Central State Coll., 1949; postgrad. U. N.M., 1950-51, George Williams Coll, 1953-56; m. Juanita Brooks, Oct. 15, 1951; 1 dau., Melonee Danette. Clerk, U.S. Post Office, Dallas, 1950; sec. YMCA, Dallas, 1951-55, exec. sec., Wichita Falls, Tex., 1955-61, exec. dir., Dallas, 1961-69; exec. dir. Dallas Urban League, 1969—. Past chmn. jr. bd. dirs. Gt. Liberty Life Ins. Co., Dallas; chmn. Alpha Merit Group Com., Inc., Dallas; mem. Dallas Safety Commn., 1966—; mem. adv. bd. Youth Opportunity Center, 1967—. Served with USAAF, 1942-45. Mem. Nat. Assn. Inter-group Relations (treas. chpt. 1969—), Assn. YMCA Secs., Alpha Phi Alpha. Methodist. Mason (32 deg.), K.P. Home: 2521 South Blvd Dallas TX 75215 Office: 2606 Forest Av Dallas TX 75215

JOHNSON, ROY EDWARD, educator, musician; b. Kansas City, Mo., May 28, 1923; s. Edward and Mabel (Bloom) J.; B.Music Edn., U. Neb., 1945; M.Music Edn., So. Methodist U., 1958; m. Emma Sue Depwe, June 26, 1948; 1 dau., Susan. Voice tchr. Baylor U., Waco, Tex., 1946-51; minister of music First Meth. Ch., Pampa, Tex., 1951-57, Methodist Ch., Dallas, 1958-67; choral dir. Pearce High Sch., Richardson, Tex., 1967-68, Hillcrest High Sch., Dallas, 1968—; dir. music Ridgewood Park Methodist Ch., Dallas, 1968—. Mus. dir. charity shows, 1958—. Mem. Nat. Fellowship Methodist Musicians (pres. 1965-67), U. Neb. Alumni Assn. (life), Phi Mu Alpha Sinfornia (life). Kiwanian (dir. 1958—). Writer texts anthems: O God of All, Above, Below, 1967; Loud Roar of the Rocket, 1970; O Church of God, Reach Up, Reach Out, 1970; O God, Our Strength and Refuge Sure, 1968; O Men of God, Arise, 1968; Sing Hosanna, 1967; Jesus, Savior, Holy Child, 1970; Rejoice, O Christian Folk, Rejoice, 1970; Jesus, Joy of Every Soul, 1969; Darkness, 1969; A Child's Journey through the Christian Year, 1967. Home: 2255 Springhill Dr Dallas TX 75228 Office: 9024 Hillcrest Av Dallas TX 75230

JOHNSON, RUFUS CLIFTON, JR., city ofcl.; b. Atmore, Ala., Oct. 15, 1923; s. Rufus C. and Annie (Thomas) J.; B.S., Auburn U., 1944; M.S., U. Ala., 1948; m. Jean Roberts, June 25, 1950; children—Emily Elyse, Rufus C. III. Office engr. Polglaze & Basenberg, Engrs., Birmingham, Ala., 1946-47; project engr. Sullivan, Long & Haggerty, Gen. Contractors, Birmingham, Ala., 1948-49, McGowan Constrn. Co., Opelika, Ala., 1949-50; propr. own firm, Douglas, Ga., 1950-60; city mgr., Douglas, 1960—. Served with AUS, 1944-46. Mason (Shriner). Home: 702 E Jefferson St Douglas GA 31533 Office: E Bryan St Douglas GA 31533

JOHNSON, RUSS MARION, banker; b. Durant, Miss., Sept. 11, 1909; s. Edwin Rembert and Margaret Lauda (Comfort) J.; student Millsaps Coll., 1926-27, Rutgers U. Grad. Sch., 1937-41; grad. Am. Inst. Banking; m. Rosalind Gwin Hutton, Apr. 14, 1943; 1 dau., Martha Ryburn (Mrs. Robert Lafayette Stainton). Began banking career, 1927; with Deposit Guaranty Nat. Bank, Jackson, Miss., 1933—, v.p. investments, 1946-53, exec. v.p., dir., from 1953, chmn. exec. com., 1958-69, chmn. bd., chief exec. officer, 1969—, also dir.; with Deposit Guaranty Corp., Jackson, 1933—, chmn. bd., chief exec. officer, 1969—, also dir.; dir. Miss. Power and Light Co., Jackson, Carthage Bank (Miss.). Staff mem. gov. of Miss., 1964-68, 72—. Past pres. Andrew Jackson council Boy Scouts Am., now mem. exec. com. Region V, mem. exec. bd. Andrew Jackson council, mem.-at-large Nat. council; active fund raising for United Givers, various civic, religious and cultural orgns., hosps., ch.-related schs., liberal arts colls.; mem. Miss. Agrl. and Indsl. Bd.; former mem. Miss. Gov.'s Emergency Council; commr. Gen. Assembly, Presbyn. Ch. U.S.A., mem. Bd. Annuities and Relief, chmn. finance com. Bd. dirs. Miss. Econ. Council. Served from pvt. to capt., AUS, 1942-46; ETO. Mem. Am. (past Miss. rep. exec. council, past mem. exec. com. state bank div., mem. govt. borrowing com.), Miss., Ind. (past dir.) bankers assns., Jackson Clearinghouse Assn. (past pres.), Com. for Econ. Devel. (trustee), Newcomen Soc., Am. Legion, Chi Psi. Presbyn. (elder). Lion. Clubs: Jackson Country; Summit (Memphis); Boston (New Orleans). Home: 4323 Brook Dr Jackson MS 39206 Office: 200 E Capitol St Jackson MS 39205

JOHNSON, RUSSELL V., JR., geologist; b. Oklahoma City, Jan. 5, 1925; s. Russell V. and Genevieve (Mott) J.; B.S., U. Okla., 1948; m. Pauline Edwards Love, May 26, 1945; children—Russell V. III, Frank Love. Geologist, Mack Oil Co., Duncan, Okla., 1948-51, Beard Oil Co., Oklahoma City, 1951-55; ind. geologist, oil and gas operator, Oklahoma City, 1955—. Served to ensign USNR, 1943-45. Home: 817 NW 40th St Oklahoma City OK 73118 Office: Cravens Bldg Oklahoma City OK 73102

JOHNSON, SAMUEL HOWARD, hosp. adminstr.; b. Pine Bluff, Ark., Apr. 5, 1925; s. Sam Houston and Nellie (Burdick) J.; B.S., U. Ark., 1950; m. Bonnie Jean Haynes, July 18, 1949; children—Samuel Howard, Charles Brady, Mary Gail. Chief auditor Blaw Knox Constrn. Co., 1949-51; spl. agt. Hardware Mut. Ins. Co., Pine Bluff, 1951-53; adminstrv. asst. Ark. State Hwy. Dept., Little Rock, 1953-55; asst. adminstr. Jefferson Hosp., Pine Bluff, 1955-66; adminstr. Desha County Hosp., Dumas, Ark., 1966—. Served to 2d lt. inf. AUS, 1943-45. Decorated Purple Heart; recipient William G. Follmer award for outstanding service to Am. Assn. Hosp. Accountants, 1966. Fellow Am. Coll. Hosp. Adminstrs.; mem. Hosp. Financial Mgmt. Assn. (past pres. Ark. chpt.), Ark. Hosp. Assn. (past pres. S. Ark. Hosp. Council), Pi Kappa Alpha. Baptist (deacon). Lion. Contbr. articles profl. jours. Home: 129 Adcock St Dumas AR 71639 Office: Desha County Hosp PO Box 126 Dumas AR 71639

JOHNSON, SAMUEL LAWRENCE, clergyman; b. Tyne Dock, Eng., Aug. 16, 1909 came to U.S., 1910, naturalized 1930; s. Samuel and Florence Ann (Woody) J.; B.A., Carleton U., 1930; B.D., Andover Newton Theol. Sch., 1933; D.D., Piedmont Coll., 1958; m. Alice Martha Dundan, Nov. 9, 1935; children—S. Thomas, Denine Ann, Lawrice Kay. Ordained to ministry Conglist. Ch., 1933; minister, Crombie St. Congl. Ch., Salem, Mass., 1933-41, Park Manor Ch., Chgo., 1941-51, Boulevard Congl. Ch., Detroit, 1951-60, 1st Congl. Ch., Kokomo, Ind., 1960-65, Pilgrim Congl. Ch., Birmingham, Ala., 1965—. Bd. dirs. Ministry to U. Ala., Birmingham. Mem. Soc. Bibl. Lit., Nat. Assn. Profs. Hebrew, So. Assn. Marriage Councilors. Mason, Moose, Rotarian. Author: Pig's Brother; The Squirrel's Bank Account. Home: 20 Gaywood St Birmingham AL 35213 Office: 3801 Montclair Rd Birmingham AL 35213

JOHNSON, SHELBY, state ofcl.; b. South, Ky., Nov. 11, 1923; s. James Henderson and Bertha (Hayes) J.; B.S., Western Ky. State Coll., 1950; M.P.H., U. N.C., 1957; m. Doris Zetta Tomes, Dec. 28, 1945; 1 dau., Shelby Sue (Mrs. Jan Carroll Burleson). Tchr. vocational agr. Sunfish (Ky.) High Sch., 1950-54; with Ky. State Dept. Health, Frankfort, Ky., 1954—. Mem. exec. bd. Interstate Milk Shipments Conf., 1965-71, chmn., 1967-71, dir. environmental services program, 1967—. Served with AUS, 1941-45. Recipient Nat. Sanitarians award, 1971. Mem. Ky. Assn. Milk, Food, and Environmental Sanitarians (pres. 1963-64), Central States Assn. Food and Drug Ofcls. (pres. 1959-60, 65-66), Nat. Labeling Com. on Milk and Dairy Products (vice chmn. 1963-69), Assn. Food and Drug Ofcls. So. States (pres. 1970-71), Assn. Food and Drug Ofcls. U.S. (exec. bd. 1972—). Mason (32 deg., Shriner). Home: 519 Menominiee Trail Frankfort KY 40601 Office: 275 E Main St Frankfort KY 40601

JOHNSON, THOMAS, economist; b. Halletsville, Tex., Feb. 12, 1936; s. Louis C. and Gladys (Gilmore) J.; A.A. with high honors, Navarro Jr. Coll., 1955; B.A. with honors, U. Tex., 1957; M.A., Tex. Christian U., 1962; M. Exptl. Statistics, N.C. State U., 1957, Ph.D., 1959; m. Cleta Joy Anderson, Sept. 8, 1956; children— David Eugene, Michael Joseph, Mark Alan. Engr. Gen. Dynamics, Fort Worth, 1957-61; engr. Ling Temco Vought Aeros., 1961-64; analyst Research Triangle Inst., 1964-69; research asso. N.C. State U., 1969; dir. manpower research So. Meth. U., 1970—, chmn. econs., 1971-72. Cons. Research Triangle Inst., 1969-71, Southland Corp., 1969-72, ABT Assos., 1970-71. Recipient Nat. Def. Edn. Act fellowship N.C. State U., 1968-69; NSF grantee N.C. State U., 1969. Mem. Operations Research Soc. Am., Am. Statis. Assn., Econometric Soc., Am., So. econ. assns., Phi Kappa Phi, Phi Theta Kappa, Pi Mu Epsilon. Baptist. Home: 508 S Lois Lane Richardson TX 75080 Office: Dept Econs and Statistics So Meth U Dallas TX 75222

JOHNSON, THOMAS FRANK, economist; b. Lynchburg, Va., Sept. 27, 1920; s. Thomas Frank and Inez (McDaniel) J.; student. Lynchburg Coll., 1939-41; B.A., U. Va., 1943, M.A., 1947, Ph.D., 1949; m. Margaret Ann Emhardt, Dec. 29, 1951; children—Thomas Emhardt, Sarah Lee, William Harrison Johnson. Economist, U.S. Dept. Agr., Washington, 1949-51, U.S. C. of C., 1951-54; asst. commr. FHA, 1954-58; dir. legislative analysis Am. Enterprise Inst. for Public Policy Research, Washington, 1958-59, dir. research, 1960—. Sec.-treas. Inst. Social Sci. Research, Washington. Bd. dirs., pres. Alexandria Hosp. Served to lt. USNR, 1943-45, PTO; lt. comdr. Res. Mem. Am., So., Royal econ. assns., Nat. Tax Assn., Am. Finance Assn., Nat. Assn. Bus. Economists (chpt. pres. 1971). Episcopalian. Club: Cosmos. Author articles in field. Home: 1113 N Gaillard St Alexandria VA 22304 Office: 1150 17th St NW Washington DC 20036

JOHNSON, THOMAS NELSON PAGE, JR., investment banker; b. Farmville, Va., Mar. 2, 1918; s. Thomas Page and Elizabeth Rebecca (Robertson) J.; grad. Woodberry Forest Sch., 1937; B.A., U. Va., 1946; m. Helen Elizabeth Smith, July 7, 1942; children—Mary Parke, Thomas Nelson Page III, Elizabeth Anne, Helen, James. Asst. supt. leaf dept. Export Leaf Tobacco, Richmond, Va., 1944-47; mgr. Eastern Bldg. Supply Co., Norfolk, Va., 1947-50; pres. N. Linkhorn Devel. Corp., 1950-58; account exec.Anderson & Strudwick, 1958-60; sales mgr. Scott and Stringfellow, Richmond, Va., 1960-62; br. mgr. Anderson & Strudwick, Virginia Beach, Va., 1962-63; v.p. Investment Corp. Va., Norfolk, 1963—; dir. Vail Spring Works, Inc., Automotive Exchange, Camp Inns Inc., Va. Ventures, Inc. Trustee, mem. exec. com. Student Aid Found. U. Va. Served as pilot, 1st lt. USAAF, 1941-43. Mem. Raven Soc., Financial Analyst Soc., Soc. Descs. of Signers Declaration of Independence, Bond Club Va., Phi Gamma Delta. Clubs: Princess Anne Country (Virginia Beach, Va.); Country of Va. (Richmond); Farmington Country (Charlottesville); Harbor, Virginia (Norfolk). Home: 221 63d St Virginia Beach VA 23451 Office: United Va Bank Bldg Norfolk VA 23510

JOHNSON, THOR, musician, educator; b. Wisconsin Rapids, Wis., June 10, 1913; s. Rev. Herbert B. and Anna Josephine (Reusswig) J.; A.B., U. N.C., 1934, Mus.D., 1951; Mus. M., U. Mich., 1935; Hon. Mus., Davidson (N.C.) Coll., 1947; Hon. Dr. Mus., Cin. Conservatory Music, 1948, Moravian Coll., 1953, Northwestern U., 1953, Baldwin Wallace Coll., 1956, U. Wis., 1960; LL.D., Beloit Coll.; Dr. Letters, Miami U., 1950; studied under Felix Weingarter, Bruno Walter, Nicolai Malko at Salzburg Mozarteum (Beebe Found. scholarship 1935 for European study), 1936-37; studied conducting under Hermann Abendroth, conservatory of Leipzig; pvt. study in Prague; studied conducting under Dr. Serge Koussevitsky, Berkshire Music Center (scholarships), summers 1940, 41; unmarried. Organizer, condr. orch. of 17 players, Winston-Salem, N.C., age of 13; asst. condr. N.C. State Symphony, 1932-34; condr. U. Mich. Little Symphony, 1934-36, 1938-42. Grand Rapids (Mich.) Symphony Orch. 1940-42, Univ. Musical Soc. (choral union and May festival), Ann Arbor, 1939-42, 47—; asst. prof. music U. Mich., 1937-42; founder and condr. Asheville (N.C.) Mozart Festival, 1937-41; orchestral condr. Julliard Sch. of Music, N.Y.C., 1946-47; permanent condr. Cin. Symphony Orch., 1947-58; mem. music dept. Northwestern U., 1958-64, prof., 1958-64; dir. Interlochen (Mich.) Arts, Acad., 1964-67; music dir. Nashville Symphony Orch., 1967—; condr. Chgo. Little Symphony 1960—; guest condr. N.Y. Philharmonic Smyphony Orch., Phila. Orch., Chgo.Symphony, Boston Symphony Orch., founder-condr. Pennisula Music Festival, Wis., 1953; co-condr. Symphony of the Air, Asia, 1955. Enlisted AUS. 1942; as warrant officer band leader founded 1st soldier symphony orch.; condr. Am. Univ. Symphony Orch., Shrivenham, Eng., on tour of Eng., 1945-46; served in France; disch. June 1946. Recipient Alice B. Ditson prize, 1949; Sachs award, 1950. Mem. Nat. Assn. Am. Composers and Conductors, Am. Fedn. Musicians, Phi Beta Kappa, Phi Kappa Phi, Phi Mu Alpha Sinfornia (recipient 1951 national man of music award), Order of the Golden Fleece. Mem. Moravian Church (Protestant). Address: 823 Cammack Ct Nashville TN 37205

JOHNSON, W. NEIL, JR., ins. co. exec.; b. Corsicana, Tex., 1917; grad. U. Tex., 1939. Exec. v.p. finance, investment officer Southland Life Ins. Co. Home: 7232 Glendora Av Dallas TX 75230 Office: Box 2220 Southland Center Dallas TX 75221

JOHNSON, WALLACE HAROLD, govt. ofcl.; b. Cleve., Oct. 7, 1939; s. Wallace Harold and Esther Emma (Miller) J.; B.A., Ohio U., 1961; postgrad. Rutgers Sch. Law, 1961-62; J.D., U. Toledo, 1965; m. Donna Mae Simpson, June 9, 1962; children—Kimberley, Todd, Victoria. Joined Justice Dept., 1965; chief Organized Crime and Racketeering Strike Force, Miami, Fla., 1968-69; minority counsel Criminal Laws subcom. Senate Jud. Com., Washington, 1969-70; asso. dep. atty. gen. U.S., 1970-72; spl. asst. to the Pres., 1972—. Mem. Am. Bar Assn., Bar Assn. D.C. Republican. Home: 1858 Foxstone Dr Vienna VA 22180 Office: Exec Office Pres White House Washington DC 20500

JOHNSON, WAYNE RAYMOND, physician; b. Duluth, Minn., Nov. 2, 1934; s. Ray Carl and Hildur Elizabeth (Nelson) J.; B.A., Gustavus Adolphus Coll., 1956; B.D., Augustana Theol. Luth. Sem., 1960; M.D., U. Miami, 1968; m. Darlene Marian Cross, Sept. 12, 1959; children— Gwynne, Matthew. Mission developer Luth. Ch. Am., 1960-64; intern Jackson Meml. Hosp., Miami, Fla., 1968; resident physician U. Miami, Jackson Meml. Hosp., 1969-70; pvt. practice medicine, Hollywood, Fla., 1971—; mem. edn. com. Hollywood Meml. Hosp., 1971—; dir. med. edn., dept. family medicine U. Miami Sch. Medicine, 1971, asst. prof., 1971—. Mem. A.M.A., Am., Fla. acads. family physicians, Broward County Med. Assn., Phi Chi. Lutheran (mem. exec. bd. Fla. synod 1970—). Home: 1501 NW 74th Terrace Hollywood FL 33024 Office: 3905 Hollywood Blvd Hollywood FL 33021

JOHNSON, WILEY, lawyer; b. Corsicana, Tex., Mar. 17, 1908; LL.B., So. Meth. U., 1932. Admitted to Tex. bar, 1932; now mem. firm Johnson, Bromberg, Leeds & Riggs, Dallas. Mem. Dallas, Am. bar assns. Address: 1500-211 North Ervay Bldg Dallas TX 75201*

JOHNSON, WILLIAM GARNETT, state ofcl.; b. Providence, Ky., Sept. 30, 1911; s. John Riley and Zita Marguerite (Lucas) J.; student Western Ky. State Coll., 1930-32, U. Ky., 1940-41, George Washington U., 1944-45; m. Elizabeth Hagan Mudd, May 23, 1942; children—William Garnett, Sarah Marguerite (Mrs. John W. Lowery, Jr.). Supr. research and statistics Ky. Unemployment Compensation Commn., Frankfort, 1942-44; chief activities reports unit Bur. Employment Security, Washington, 1944-47; exec. asst. to Ky. commr. econ. security, Frankfort, 1948-55, 55-69, exec. dir. Bur. Employment Security, Dept. Econ. Security, 1969-71; commr. Ky. Dept. Econ. Security, 1955, acting commr., 1971-72, chmn. econ. security task force on mgmt. and orgn., 1972—. Project dir. Asian manpower seminar AID-Internat. Assn. Personnel in Employment Security, 1970-71, project dir. Latin Am. manpower seminar, 1971-72. Mem. Internat. Assn. Personnel in Employment Security (internat. pres. 1956-57), Interstate Conf. Employment Security Agys. (regional v.p. 1971-72, adminstrv. grants com.), Internat. Council for Personnel Devel. in Employment Security, Am. Pub. Welfare Assn., Ky. Welfare Assn., Council for Profl. Advancement, Ky. Hist. Soc. Methodist. Club: Optimist (v.p. East Frankfort 1967-68). Contbr. articles to profl. jours. Home: 401 Hiawatha Trail Frankfort KY 40601 Office: Capitol Annex Office Bldg Frankfort KY 40601

JOHNSON, WILLIAM LEE, lawyer, corp. exec.; b. ville, Tex., Dec. 29, 1911; s. Rufus Edward and Robin (Matlock) J.; A.A., Schreiner Inst., 1930-32; B.B.A., U. Tex., 1934; m. Ruth Hobbs, Jan. 4, 1946; children— Gayl Hyatt, William Hyatt. Sr. accountant Haskins & Sells, 1935-47; asst. treas. Lone Star Steel Co., 1947-48, v.p., asst. treas., 1948-50, v.p., controller, asst. treas., 1950, exec. v.p., 1950-64, v.p., 1964—. Mem. Financial Execs. Inst., N.A.M., Am. Iron and Steel Inst. Episcopalian. Rotarian. Home: 4715 S Lindhurst Dr Dallas TX 75229 Office: 4501 W Mockingbird Lane Dallas TX 75209

JOHNSON, WILLIAM ROYSTER, architect; b. Raleigh, N.C., Aug. 18, 1901; s. Charles Cousins and Maude Eleanor (Harris) J.; student Hampden-Sydney Coll., 1918-21; student U. Va., 1921-25, Art Students League, 1926-27; m. Elizabeth Terry Niedringhaus, Oct. 9, 1959; 1 son, William Royster. Designer, M.S. Wyeth, architect, 1925-26, chief designer, 1927; designer Wyeth & King, architects, 1926, partner, 1932; partner Wyeth, King & Johnson, architects, Palm Beach, Fla., 1944—. Mem. archtl. review commn., Town of Palm Beach. 1971—. Bd. dirs. Palm Beach Art League, 1948-55, pres., 1954-55. Recipient Honorable Mention, Archtl. League N.Y., 1938. Mem. A.I.A., Soc. Four Arts, Palm Beach Art League, Kappa Sigma. Democrat. Episcopalian. Clubs: Bath and Tennis, Everglades (gov. 1970—) (Palm Beach, Fla.). Prin. archtl. works include Vietor Residence, Palm Beach, Fla., Norton Gallery and Sch. of Art, West Palm Beach, Fla., Dining Hall, Mercersburg Acad., Gerard Lambert residence, Manalapan, Fla. Home: 214 Plantation Rd Palm Beach FL 33480 Office: 207 Royal Palm Way Palm Beach FL 33480

JOHNSON, WILLIAM WOODWARD, banker; b. Augusta, Ga., Feb. 16, 1931; s. Dewey H. and Mabel (Woodward) J.; student U. S.C., 1949-53; m. Sarah Pierrine Baker, July 26, 1951; children—Jennifer, Marie, Salley, Jane. With State Bank & Trust Co., Columbia, S.C., 1953—, asst. cashier, 1954-56, asst. v.p., 1956-59, v.p., 1959-60, sr. v.p., 1960-63, exec. v.p., 1963-65, pres., 1965—; pres., dir. Augwood Life & Accident Ins. Co., v.p., dir. Emerald Fire & Casualty Ins. Co.; asst. exec. trustee, asst. sec. State Real Estate Investment Trust. Campaign chmn. United Fund, 1964, mem. exec. bd., 1965—; mem. adv. bd. Salvation Army, 1965—; mem. S.C. Gen. Assembly, 1956-57; mem. S.C. State Ports Authority, 1965—; mem. Richland Tech. Edn. Commn., 1964-65. Treas. Richland County Democratic Party, 1965-66. Bd. dirs. U. S.C. Ednl. Found. Mem. Columbia C. of C. (v.p.), S.C. Young Bankers Assn. (past pres.), S.C. Bankers Assn. Methodist (chmn. ofcl. bd.). Clubs: Pine Tree Hunt, Spring Valley Country, Palmetto. Home: 5011 Quail Lane Columbia SC 29206 Office: 1244 Main St PO Box 448 Columbia SC 29202

JOHNSON, ZACHARY TAYLOR, former coll. pres.; b. Athens, Ga., June 18, 1897; s. John Gilbert and Julia Frances (Snipes) J.; A.B., Asbury Coll., Wilmore, Ky., 1925; A.M., U. Ky., 1926; Ph.D., George Peabody Coll. Tchrs., Nashville, 1929; LL.D., Taylor U., 1942; D.D., Houghton (N.Y.) Coll., 1948; m. Sadie Eloise Mershon, Sept. 11, 1916: children—Walter Henry, Zachary Taylor, Olive Mershon. Minister, 1916-26; tchr. Asbury Coll., 1924-26, Peabody Coll., 1927-29; head of hist. dept. State Tchrs. Coll., Hattiesburg, Miss., 1929-34; minister Wilmore (Ky.) Methodist Ch., 1934-35; exec. v.p. Asbury Coll., Wilmore, Ky., 1935-40, pres., 1940-66. Phi Delta Kappa, Kappa Delta Pi. Democrat. Methodist. Author: Career of Howell Cobb, 1929; Topical Survey of Civilization, 1931; What Is Holiness1935; Sins and Faults, 1939; Methodism and Holiness, 1942; Limiting God, 1947; We Believe, 1957. Contbr. to ednl. and religious jours. Home: Wilmore KY 40390

JOHNSTAD, ERROL, labor union exec.; b. Wis.; student Marquette U., U. Ill., U. Md., U. Tenn.; grad. with honors in math. Washington U., St. Louis; postgrad. propulsion and space engring. U. Mo.; m. Jean Winniger; children—Kristin, Kara, Kurt. Formerly flight test engr., test pilot McDonnell Douglas Co.; then flight engr. Pan Am. World Airways; formerly chmn., contract negogiator Flight Engrs. Internat. Assn., then v.p. chpt., v.p. for internat. affairs, now pres.; mem. gen. bd. AFL-CIO. Served with USAF. Named Airman of Year Gov. Wis. Mem. Alpha Epsilon Delta. Address: Flight Engrs Internat Assn 905 16th St NW Washington DC 20006*

JOHNSTON, CHARLIE GYMANN, ins. co. exec.; b. Lake City, Ark., July 22, 1915; s. James C. and Eva (Coggins) J.; B.S., Ark. State U., 1936; m. Calla Mae Robinson, Apr. 16, 1949 (dec.); 1 dau., Patsy Ruth (Mrs. Richard C. Ivey); 1 stepson, Michael Lee Cruse. With Fidelity Union Life Ins. Co., 1957-62, v.p., 1961-62; v.p. Union Life Ins. Co., Little Rock, 1962-65; pres. Family First Life Ins. Co. of Ark., 1965-66, Universal Am. Life Ins. Co. Ark., 1966-67; exec. v.p. Mil. Assos., Inc., Little Rock, 1967-70; pres. Abel-Johnston Enterprises, Inc., Little Rock, 1970—. Tchr. leadership tng. Dale Carnegie Courses, 1952—. County and probate ct. clk., Jonesboro, Ark., 1941-44; mem. Ark. Ho. of Reps., 1955-58. C.L.U. Mem. Little Rock Sales and Marketing Execs. Assn. (pres. 1970-71). Mason (Shriner). Home: 400 N University St Little Rock AK 72205 Office: Tower Bldg Little Rock AK 72201

JOHNSTON, CURTIS L., state ofcl. Asst. supt. vocational rehab. La. Dept. Edn., Baton Rouge. Address: La Dept Edn PO Box 4406 Baton Rouge LA 70804*

JOHNSTON, DONALD NEWHALL, county ofcl.; b. Sidney, O., Dec. 26, 1918; s. Chester L. and Elizabeth (Newhall) J.; student Miami U., Oxford, O., 1936-40; B.S., Fla. State U., 1952, M.S. in Govt.-Pub. Adminstrn., 1964; m. Isola Nelson, Jan. 17, 1942; children— Kristin Jean, Scott Anthony, Joel Bruce, Erin Beth. With Gen. Machinery Corp., Hamilton, O., 1941-42, Met. Life Ins. Co., Janesville, Wis., 1947-48; entered USAAF as pvt., commd. 2d lt. USAAF, 1942, trans. to USAF, 1947, advanced through grades to lt. col., 1954; asst. prof. air sci., tactics Fla. State U., 1949-53; chief base procurement div. and asst. dir. procurement and prodn. Hdqrs. Air Tng. Command, Randolph AFB, 1959-63, ret., 1963; village mgr. Village Granville (O.), 1965-66; exec. sec. Washington County (Va.), Abingdon, 1966—. Mem. Internat. City Mgrs. Assn., Nat. Assn. County Adminstrs., Va. Assn. Counties (exec. bd.), Va. Assn. County Adminstrs. (pres.), Nat. Municipal League, Am. Legion, V.F.W., Sigma Chi. Methodist. Mason. Home: 143 Stonewall Heights Abingdon VA 24210 Office: County Courthouse Abingdon VA 24210

JOHNSTON, GARVIN H., state ofcl.; b. Marion County, Miss.; grad. Pearl River Jr. Coll.; B.S., Ed.D., U. So. Miss.; M.A., U. Ala.; m. Willene Bullock; 1 dau., Judy Beth (Mrs. Thomas Walley). Successively tchr., prin. and supt. elementary and high sch., supr. high sch. Miss. Dept. Edn.; pres. Pearl River Jr. Coll., Poplarville, Miss., 1953-68; supt. edn. State of Miss., Jackson, 1968—. Chmn. Miss. Bd. Edn., Miss. Jr. Coll. Commn.; mem. Council Chief State Sch. Officers, also rep. other boards; mem. state adv. com. for vocational and tech. edn. Bd. dirs. Miss. Econ. Council, former mem. edn. com. Served with AUS, World War II. Named Citizen of Year, Poplarville, 1967. Mem. Am. Legion, Poplarville Club (past pres.), Miss. Edn. Assn. (past pres.), Miss. Jr. Coll. Assn., Miss. Assn. Colls., Miss. Hist. Soc. Baptist (deacon). Mason, Rotarian. Office: Box 771 501 Sillers SE State Office Bldg Jackson MS 39205

JOHNSTON, HARRY RAYMOND, electric co. exec.; b. Pitts., Dec. 17, 1922; s. Harry Wright and Myrtle Estelle (Bryant) J. With Westinghouse Co., Pitts., also Raleigh, N.C., 1940-43, 45—, traffic mgr., Raleigh, 1956—. Pres., chmn. bd. Wake County Soc. for Prevention of Cruelty to Animals, Raligh, 1968—. Served with AUS, 1943-45. Mem. Triangle Traffic Assn. (dir.). Home: 919 Brookside Dr Raleigh NC 27604 Office: Box 9533 Raleigh NC 27603

JOHNSTON, HENRY POELLNITZ, broadcasting exec.; b. Uniontown, Ala., Jan. 26, 1908; s. Charles P. and Eloise (White) J.; student Culver Mil. Acad., 1923-25; grad. Washington and Lee U., 1929; m. Louise Feagin, Dec. 26, 1946; children—Henry Poellnitz, Margaret Ann. With Kelly Smith, newspaper advt., N.Y.C., 1929-30; nat. advt. dept. Birmingham News-Age Herald, 1930-31, local advt. mgr., 1934-37; pub. Huntsville (Ala.) Times, 1931-34, pres., 1934-56; liaison between Birmingham News-Age Herald and radio sta. WSGN, 1936, v.p. Birmingham News Co., 1936-56; mng. dir. WSGN, 1936-53; pres., mng. dir. Ala. Broadcasting System, 1953-57; chmn. bd. Planters & Mchts. Bank of Uniontown (Ala.); dir. So. Airways; mem. adv. bd. So. div. 1st Nat. Bank, Birmingham. Mem. Jefferson County Personnel Bd.; former mem. adv. com. Voice of Am. Chmn. Interracial Council, 1954-56; chmn. Jefferson County A.R.C., former chmn. regional blood program Jefferson County; v.p., dir. Ala. div., nat. dir. Am. Cancer Soc. Recipient plaque Ala. Broadcasters Assn., 1956. Mem. Nat. Assn. Broadcasters (dir. 1947-49), Ala. Broadcasters Assn. (1st pres.), Soc. Colonial Wars (charter mem. Ala., gov.), S.A.R. (Ala. pres.), S.R. in Ala., Sons of War of 1812, Huguenot Soc., N.C. Soc. Cincinnati, Sales Execs. Club, Omicron Delta Kappa, Alpha Tau Omega, Sigma Delta Chi, Pi Delta Epsilon, Alpha Epsilon Rho. Democrat. Presbyn. Rotarian. Clubs: Down Town, Birmingham Country, Mountain Brook Country, The Club, Quarterback (Birmingham); National Press (Washington); Sales Executives. Author: Little Acorns from the Mighty Oak; Pioneers in Their Own Right; The Gentle Johnstons; William Rufus King and His Kin; Around the World in 42 Days; Me and My Gals. Home: 3123 Overhill Rd Birmingham AL 35223 Office: PO Box 7661 Birmingham AL 35223

JOHNSTON, HUGH BUCKNER, educator, historian; b. Wilson County, N.C., Apr. 11, 1913; s. Hugh Bolden and Ruth (Thomas) J.; A.B., Davidson Coll., 1933; A.M., George Washington U., 1946; m. Elizabeth Aldrich Briggs, Nov. 8, 1941 (div. 1953); children—Hugh Bolden III, Thomas Owen Drakeford; m. 2d, Edna Elizabeth Long, Oct. 23, 1953; 1 son, Hugh Bolden IV. Adminstrv. asst. Am. Nat. Red Cross, Washington, 1941-46; instr. Instituto Chileno-Norteamericano de Cultura, Santiago, Chile, 1947-50; prof. langs. and history Atlantic Christian Coll., Wilson, N.C., 1955—. Historian, Wilson County, 1938—. Mem. Modern Lang. Assn., Soc. War 1812, Am. Assn. Tchrs. Spanish, S.A.R., N.C. State Lit. and Hist. Assn., Carolina Charter Corp., S.C.V., Order First Families of Va., N.C. Soc. Preservation Antiquities, Jamestowne Soc., Am. Assn. U. Profs., Sigma Phi Epsilon. Conservative. Presbyn. Moose. Home: Thomas Farms Wilson NC 27893

JOHNSTON, JAMES ROBERT, elec. engr.; b. Cookeville, Tenn., Feb. 10, 1931; B.S., Tenn. Tech. U., 1954; m. Mattie F. Rodgers, Sept. 18, 1949 (dec. Oct. 1968); children—James E., Mark R.; m. 2d, Dorothy R. Miller, June 26, 1970; step-children—Lee O., Janey A., Peggy Sue Miller. Elec. maintenance dept. head Union Carbide Nuclear div. Oak Ridge Nat. Lab., 1954-66; supt. electric shop Dow Chem. Co., Freeport, Tex., 1966-69, supt. magnesium prodn. plant, 1969—. Registered profl. engr. Tenn., Tex. Mem. Nat., Tex. socs. profl. engrs., I.E.E.E. (sr. mem., sec. subcom. on measurements of dielectrics), Am. Soc. for Testing and Materials. Home: 129 Red Bud St Lake Jackson TX 77566 Office: Dow Chem Co Freeport TX 77541

JOHNSTON, JULIAN ST. CLAIR, elec. engr.; b. Hattiesburg, Miss., July 3, 1924; s. Julian S. and Mabel (Potter) J.; B.E.E., La. State U., 1947; m. Katherine Ann Trowbridge, Feb. 19, 1955; children—Paul Andrew, Lynne Elizabeth, Cynthia Claire, Kathy Ann, Nancy Jean. Office adminstr. C.E., Memphis, 1945; test engr. Gen. Electric Co., Schenectady, 1947, plant engr., Jackson, Miss., 1948-51; sr. elec. engr. Lockheed Aircraft Corp., Marietta, Ga., 1951-66; pvt. practice cons. engr., Smyrna and Atlanta, 1966—. Republican committeeman Cobb County, Ga., 1962—. Served with AUS, 1943-45. Mem. I.E.E.E., Illumination Engring. Soc., Am. Legion, Soc. Am. Mil. Engrs., Tau Beta Pi. Republican. Methodist. Home: 142 Cumberland Dr Smyrna GA 30080

JOHNSTON, LEWIS DUPUY, JR., dentist; b. South Boston, Va., June 23, 1920; s. Lewis Dupuy and Mary Easley (Craddock) J.; B.S., Hampden-Sydney Coll., 1942; D.D.S., Med. Coll. Va., 1950; m. Anne Washington Lee, Jan. 12, 1952; children—Lee, Lewis, Betty. Gen. practice dentistry, South Boston, 1950—. Mem. South Side Regional Planning Commn., 1968—. Mem. City Council, 1958—. Vice pres. Martinsville Convalescent Home. Served to capt. USMCR, 1942-46. Mem. Am. Dental Assn., Piedmont Dental Soc., Am. Acad. Gen. Practice, Acad. Dental Analgesia, Am.Soc. Preventive Dentistry, Kappa Sigma, Delta Sigma Delta. Presbyn. (elder). Home: 1316 South St South Boston VA 24592 Office: 526 Main St South Boston VA 24592

JOHNSTON, MARGUERITE (MRS. CHARLES WYNN BARNES), journalist; b. Birmingham, Ala., Aug. 7, 1917; d. Robert C. and Marguerite (Spradling) Johnston; A.B., Birmingham-So. Coll., 1938; m. Charles Wynn Barnes, Aug. 31, 1946; children— Susan, Patricia, Steven, Polly. Reporter, Birmingham News, 1939-44; Washington corr. Birmingham News, Birmingham Age-Herald and London Daily Mirror, 1945-46; columnist Houston Post, 1947-69, mem. editorial bd., asso. editor, 1969—. Lectr., 1947—; spl. lectr. U. Houston, 1965-66; del. Asian-Am. Women Journalists Conf., Honolulu, 1965; del. 1st World Conf. Women Journalists, Mexico City, 1969. Bd. dirs. Tex. Bill of Rights Found., 1962-64; adv. bd. Houston Council on Alcoholism. Recipient Theta Sigma Phi Headliner award, 1954; certificate of merit Gulf Coast chpt. Am. Soc. Safety Engrs., 1960; Agnese Carter Neims award Planned Parenthood, 1968. Mem. Houston Press Club, Mortar Bd., Phi Beta Kappa. Author: Public Manners, 1957; AHappy Worldly Abode, 1964. Home: 5319 Cherokee St Houston TX 77005 Office: Houston Post Houston TX 77001

JOHNSTON, REED, govt. ofcl. Regional dir. NLRB, Winston-Salem, N.C. Address: 301 N Main St Winston-Salem NC 27101*

JOHNSTON, RICHARD MILLER, ins. agt.; b. Orange, N.J., Dec. 16, 1933; s. Ralph M., Jr. and Virginia (Miller) J.; B.S. in Aero. Engring., U. Md., 1961; m. Lynda Adelle Myers, June 16, 1960; children—Kathryn, Julia, Richard, Meridith. Asso., Lawrence W. Myers Ins. Agy., Lake Worth, Fla., 1961—; sec.-treas. C & J Life, Inc., 1966—. Chmn., United Fund Palm Beach County, 1969—. Served with USAF, 1952-56. Mem. Lake Worth C. of C. (pres.), Phi Sigma Kappa. Conglist. (trustee). Rotarian (pres. 1968—). Home: 1528 N Lakeside Dr Lake Worth FL 33460 Office: 803 Lake Av Lake Worth FL 33460

JOHNSTON, RUPERT BERNARD, economist; b. Shannon, Miss., Jan. 13, 1919; s. John Riley and Lydia (Sanderson) J.; B.S., Miss. State U., 1950, M.S., 1951; Ed.D., Cornell U., 1960; m. Bertie Mae Stevens, Dec. 20, 1940; children—William Riley, Richard Allen, Robert Arthur, Mary Jean. Research asst., acting instr. agrl. econ. dept. Miss. State U., State College, 1951-52, asst. extension economist Miss. Coop. Extension Service, 1952-55, asso. extension economist, 1955-57, leader extension econs. dept., 1957—. Bd. dirs. Wesley Found., Miss. State U. Served with USMC, 1944-46. Mem. Am. Farm Econs. Assn., Nat. Assn. County Agrl. Agts., Miss. Farm Mgrs. and Rural Appraisers Assn., Civitan (dist. gov. 1963), Epsilon Sigma Phi, Alpha Zeta. Home: PO Box 772 State College MS 39762

JOHNSTON, STANLEY DAVID, accountant; b. Birmingham, Ala., Sept. 9, 1935; s. William Farris and Edith (Shepard) J.; B.S., U. Ala., 1957; student U. Md., 1953-54; m. Joan Propst, June 2, 1956; children—Diana Jean, Gregory David. Staff accountant Arthur Andersen & Co., Atlanta, 1957-59; mgr. Downs & Box, Birmingham, Ala., 1960-63; partner Johnston & Raburn, Huntsville, 1963-70, Johnston, Brown &Co., Huntsville, 1970—. Officer, dir. Danmont Corp., Huntsville, 1966—; co-organizer, officer, dir. Mid-America Housing (and successor orgns.), Albertville, Ala., 1963—; officer, dir. Tas-T-O Donuts Am., Inc., Huntsville, 1969—; co-organizer, officer, dir. Am. Data Corp., Huntsville, 1964—. Mem. Huntsville Indsl. Expansion Com., 1968—. Mem. Am. Inst. C.P.A.'s, Ala. Soc. C.P.A.'s, Huntsville C. of C., U. Ala. Alumni Assn. (past v.p.), Beta Gamma Sigma, Kappa Sigma. Presbyn. Home: 2905 Barcody Rd Huntsville AL 35802 Office: 444 State Nat Bank Bldg Hunstville AL 35801

JOHNSTON, STEVE RENWICK, physician; b. Valdosta, Ga., Mar. 5, 1913; s. Sydney Kitrell and Kathryn (Stump) Smith; student U. Fla., 1930-33; M.D., Emory U. Sch. Medicine, 1937; m. Christine P. Johnston; children—(by previous marriage) Venetia (Mrs. William M. Darby), Kathleen. Tchr. biology dept. U. Fla., 1931-33; intern Grady Hosp., Atlanta, 1936-37, Ga. Bapt. Hosp., Atlanta, 1937-38; practice gen. medicine, Okeechobee, Fla., 1938-40, Ft. Pierce, Fla., 1940-54; abdominal surgery, obstetrics, gynecology, Clewiston, Fla., 1954-59, Okeechobee, Fla., 1959—; mem. staff and officer Hendry Gen. Hosp.; chief of staff Okeechobee Gen. Hosp.; pres. elect Okeechobee County Hosp.; chief of staff Ft. Pierce Meml. Hosp. Chmn. cub pack com. Cub Scouts Am., Okeechobee; mem. nat. voter adv. bd. Am. Security Council. Cons. USN Amphibious Tng. Base, Ft. Pierce, 1941-46. Recipient Certificate of Appreciation, Pres. of U.S. for service with SSS; award and scroll as one of South's Outstanding Personalities, 1971. Diplomate Am. Bd. Abdominal Surgery. Fellow Am. Geriatric Soc., Pan Am. Cancer Cytology Soc., Internat. Corr. Soc. Obstetrics-Gynecology, Am. Soc. Abdominal Surgeons, Am., Internat. colls. angiology, Internat. Acad. Law and Sci., Royal Soc. Health; mem. A.M.A., So. Fla. (better govt. com.) med. assns., Okeechobee, St. Lucie, Martin County (v.p. 1948-49, pres. 1951-52, 54-58) med. socs., Nat., Fla. rehab. assns., Am. Brahaman Breeders Assn., Am. Quarter Horse Assn., Am. Palomino Horse Breeders Assn., Fla. Palomino Exhibitors Assn. (1st. v.p., dir.), Internat. Platform Assn., Delta Tau Delta, Phi Chi, Gamma Sigma Epsilon, Alpha Epilson Delta, Phi Eta Sigma. Home: Third St Okeechobee FL 33472 Office: 209 NW 7th St PO Box 1227 Okeechobee FL 33472

JOHNSTON, STUART GOODLOE, JR., lawyer; b. San Antonio, Sept. 8, 1930; s. Stuart Goodloe and Olive Marie (Fleck) J.; J.D., St. Mary's U. at San Antonio, 1956; m. Beverly Jean Kutac, Sept. 22, 1951; children—Stuart, Paul, Stanley, Mark, Morgan, Patrick, Michael. Admitted to Tex. bar, 1956, Okla. bar, 1965; mem. firm Kelso, Locke & King, San Antonio, 1956-59, Stubbeman, McRae, Sealy & Laughlin, Midland, Tex., 1959-64; legal adviser to gen. mgr. Standard Oil of Ohio, Oklahoma City, 1964-68; v.p., gen. counsel Elcor Chem. Corp., Midland, Tex., 1968-70; practice law, Dallas, 1970—. Served with USNR, 1951-54. Home: 12011 Shirestone Lane Dallas TX 75234 Office: 3303 Lee Pky Dallas TX 75219

JOHNSTON, WILLIAM FRANK, dentist; b. Copperhill, Tenn., May 27, 1922; s. Leon and Sarah Helen (Dickens) J.; B.S., Union Coll., 1948; D.D.S., U. Tenn., 1954; m. Elizabeth Norman, Nov. 20, 1943; children— Betsy, Patsy. Individual practice dentistry, Madisonville, Tenn., 1954—. Chmn. Monroe County Health Dept., Madisonville Housing Authority, sec. Madisonville Regional Planning Commn. Bd. dirs. Houston Park, Madisonville Indsl. Commn. Served with AUS, 1943-46. Mem. Am., Tenn. dental assns., Delta Sigma Delta. Presbyn. (trustee, elder). Mason. Home: Philpott St Madisonville TN 37354 Office: Carson St Madisonville TN 37354

JOINER, VERNA JONES (MRS. CHARLES B. JOINER), author; b. Covington, La., Nov. 28, 1896; d. Alexander Spiers and Emma (Spiers) Jones; student Southeastern La. Coll., 1925-26, 51-53; m. Charles B. Joiner, Mar. 29, 1916; children— Charles Ronald, Joyce (Mrs. Herbert L. Baker), Marie (Mrs. G. LaNoyette Mayo), Howell,

Lydia (Mrs. Dalton V. Martin), Tchr, Lumberton (Miss.) Pub. Schs., 1914-17; Ch. of God minister youth, home missions, 1920—; supt. working girls' home, 1925-27; writer column for Youth mag. Warner Press, Anderson, Ind., 1955-68, teen column Sunday Sch. Times and Gospel Herald, Union Gospel Press, Cleve. 1970—; writer youth programs Baptist Publs., Denver, 1971—. Mem. M.M.S. Author: From Papa and Me, 1956; This Home We Build, 1957; Growing Steady, 1959; Five Minutes to Four, 1960, Your Dating Data, 1962; What Teens Say, 1962; When Love Grows Up, 1966. Home: 212 N Chestnut St Hammond LA 70401

JOLLY, ALAN GORDON, advt. exec.; b. Franklin, Ky., Sept. 8, 1930; s. James W. and Rebecca (Henson) J.; A.B., Colgate U., 1950; postgrad. U. Louisville, 1963-66; m. Martha Beverly Logan, Aug. 20, 1950; children—Brent Alan, Beverlee Anne. Radio announcer Bowling Green (Ky.) Broadcasting Co., 1947-50; advt. specialist Gen. Electric Co., Schenectady, Syracuse, N.Y., Bridgeport, Conn., Louisville, 1950-63; v.p., treas., dir. Zimmer-McClaskey-Lewis, Advt., Louisville, 1963—. Served from pvt. to 2d lt. USAF, 1950-53. Mem. Am. Marketing Assn. (chpt. dir. 1968-69), Louisville Advt. Club. Baptist (pub. relations cons.). Home: 8608 Holston Rd Lousville KY 40222 Office: 1469 S 4th St Louisville KY 40201

JONAS, CHARLES RAPER, congressman; b. Lincolnton, N.C., Dec. 9, 1904; s. Charles A. and Rosa (Petrie) J.; A.B., U. N.C., 1925; J.D., 1928; m. Annie Elliott Lee, Aug. 14, 1928; children—Charles Raper, Richard Elliott. Admitted to N.C. bar, 1929; asst. U.S. atty. Western dist. N.C., 1931-33; mem. 83d-87th Congresses, 10th N.C. dist., mem. 88th-93d Congresses, 9th N.C. dist. Mem. N.C. Bd. Law Examiners, 1947-48. Served from capt. to lt. col. Judge Adv. Gen. Corps, U.S. Army, 1940-45. Mem. N.C. Bar Assn. (pres. 1946-47), Order of Coif, Phi Delta Phi, Chi Phi. Republican. Methodist. Clubs: Congressional Country, Capitol Hill (Washington). Home: Lincolnton NC 28092 Office: House Office Bldg Washington DC 20515

JONES, ALAN IVEY, investment co. exec.; b. Shreveport, La., Oct. 20, 1938; s. Joseph Reid and Ruby (Ivey) J.; student Kilgore Jr. Coll., 1957-59; B.S., Tex. Christian U., 1962; postgrad. So. Meth. U., 1967-69; m. Jane Foster Bean, Apr. 21, 1962; children—Juliana, Kathleen Elizabeth. Owner, Alan I. Jones Ins., Dallas, 1962-66; asso. Henry S. Miller Co., Dallas, 1966-69; v.p. M.L. Godwin Investments, Inc., Dallas, 1968-71; pres. Alan I. Jones Investments, Inc., Dallas, 1971—. Served with USNR, 1962, 68. Mem. Sales and Marketing Execs. Dallas, Dallas C. of C., Dallas Better Bus. Bur. Presbyn. (deacon 1967-68). Rotarian (pres. chpt. 1967-68, dist. sec. 1970-71). Home: 5725 Caruth Haven Dallas TX 75206 Office: 4227 Herschel Dallas TX 75219

JONES, ALBERT PEARSON, lawyer; b. Dallas, Tex., July 19, 1907; s. Dr. Bush and Ethel (Hatton) J.; student So. Meth. U., 1924; A.B., U. Tex., 1927, A.M., 1927, LL.B., 1930; m. Annette Lewis, Oct. 3, 1936; children—Dan Pearson, Lewis Avery. Admitted to Tex. bar, 1930, to U.S. Dist. Ct. So. and Eastern Jud. Dists. Tex., U.S. Ct. Appeals 5th Circuit, U.S. Supreme Ct.; assoc. Baker, Botts, Andrews & Wharton, Houston, 1930-43; mem. firm Helm & Jones, Houston 1943-62; prof. law U. Tex., Austin, 1962—; 1st asst. to atty. gen. State of Tex., 1963-64 (on leave). Trustee St. Lukes Hosp., 1949-62, Lulu Bryan Rambaud Charitable Trust, 1947-62. Fellow Am. Coll. Trial Lawyers; mem. State Bar Tex. (pres. 1950-51, dir. 8th congl. dist. 1948-50), Houston, Am. bar assns., Am. Law Inst., Phi Beta Kappa, Phi Delta Phi, Order of Coif. Episcopalian. Clubs: Houston Country; Country (Austin). Home: 4 Niles Rd Austin TX 78703 Office: 2500 Red River St Austin TX 78705

JONES, ALBERT TRELOAR, SR., assn. exec.; b. Taylor, Miss., Feb. 28, 1924; s. William H. and Mary (Treloar) J.; B.B.A., U. Miss., 1953, M.B.A., 1954; m. Mary Ernestine Harmon, Mar. 21, 1948; children—Albert Treloar, Janis Carol. With Mo. Portland Cement Co., 1954-59; gen sales mgr. Miss. Valley Portland Cement Co., Jackson, Miss., 1959-68; exec. dir. Miss. Rd. Builders' Assn., Jackson, 1969—. Served with AUS, 1942-46. Mem. Delta Sigma Pi, Pi Sigma Epsilon. Baptist. Mason (Shriner). Home: 5044 Ashley Dr Jackson MS 39211 Office: 455 N Lamar St Jackson MS 39205

JONES, ALEXANDER WILLIAMSON, lawyer; b. Pensacola, Fla., Nov. 2, 1914; s. Cadwallader and Permelia (Jones) J.; grad. Birmingham So. Coll.; LL.B., U. Ala., 1938; m. Margaret Magruder, June 9, 1945; children— Margaret Magruder, Alexander Williamson, Vannoy Magruder. Admitted to Ala. bar, 1938; partner Pritchard, McCall & Jones, Birmingham, 1939—; dir. City Nat. Bank, Birmingham, Asso. Doctors Health & Life Ins. Co., Thomas Foundaries, Nelson Brantley Glass Co. Pres., bd. dirs. Spastic Aid of Ala., 1971—. Served to lt. USNR, 1951-55. PTO. Mem. Am., Ala., Birmingham bar assns. Kiwanian (dir. 1970-72). Club: Birmingham Monday Morning Quarterback (dir. 1969—). Home: 2617 Abingdon Rd Birmingham AL 35243 Office: 831 Frank Nelson Bldg Birmingham AL 35203

JONES, ALLEN H., educator, editor. Mem. faculty Montgomery Jr. Coll., Rockville, Md.; chmn. bd. editors Community Coll. Press, Washington. Address: Montgomery Jr. Coll Rockville MD 20850*

JONES, ARTHUR HENRY, cons.; b. Phila., Mar. 16, 1902; s. John Henry and Mary (Harrar) J.; A.B., Oberlin Coll., 1929; postgrad. N.Y. Sch. Social Work, 1930, William and Mary Coll., 1940, Northwestern U., 1949-50; m. Gertrude Von Bergen, June 16, 1926; children—Roberta M., Ruth E. (Mrs. Jack Pentes), Clark A. Engraver, Tiffany's, N.Y.C., 1915-21; sec. YMCA, Newark, 1921-25; dir. Emergency Relief, Essex County, N.J., 1929-35; So. rep. Nat. Recreation Assn., N.Y.C., 1935-47; supt. recreation, Charlotte, N.C., 1947-48; sr. v.p. N.C. Nat. Bank, 1948-67; mem. N.C. Gen. Assembly, 1966-68; mem. N.C. Ho. of Reps., Raleigh, 1967-69; cons. Carolina Population Center, U. N.C., Chapel Hill, 1970—; faculty banking schs., N.C., S.C. and Va., Sch. Financial Pub. Relations, Northwestern U., Chgo. Mem. several Gov.'s Commns. N.C., 1950—; mem. Charlotte-Mecklenburg Charter Revision Commn., 1969—. Bd. dirs. United Community Funds and Councils of Am., Greater Charlotte Found. Served with USNR, 1940-42. Democrat. Home: 409 Smith Av Chapel Hill NC 27514

JONES, AVERY SHERRILL, flour mills co. exec.; b. Statesville, N.C., July 18, 1931; s. John Wesley and Gladys A. (Sherrill) J.; B.S., Davidson Coll., 1953; m. Elizabeth Fairly Lucas, June 30, 1956; children—Avery Sherrill, Elizabeth MacKinnon, Margaret Antointte, David Lucas. Br. mgr. Statesville Flour Mills. Co., Kernersville, N.C., 1955-57, office mgr., Statesville, N.C., 1957-60, v.p., dir., 1960-64, asst. sec., treas., asst. gen. mgr., dir., 1964—; v.p. Village Inn Pizza, Wilmington, N.C.; pres., owner Scrogg's Inc.; dir. Northwestern Bank, Statesville; sec.-treas. Interstate Devel. Co. Bd. dirs. Mitchell Coll. Found.; trustee Mitchell Coll.; tactics instr. R.O.T.C., bd. visitors Davidson Coll., Ft. Benning, Ga. Served to 1st lt. Inf. AUS, 1953-55; ETO. Mem. Self-Rising Flour & Corn Meal Program (pres. 1965—), Nat. Soft Wheat Millers Assn. (pres., dir. 1966—), Millers Nat. Fedn. (dir. 1966-67). Rotarian (treas. 1957-58). Home: 1211 Meadow Lane Statesville NC 28677 Office: PO 831 Statesville NC 28677

JONES, BEN WILLIS, coll. pres.; b. Washington, Ga., Apr. 27, 1917; s. Willis Rayden and Ruth (Hinton) J.; B.S., Ga. So. Coll., 1940; M.A., George Peabody Coll. for Tchrs., 1946; Ed.D., U. Tex., 1950; m. Winna Weeks, Dec. 21, 1946; children—Christopher Dan, Kevin Weeks. Prin. Cedar Springs (Ga.) Jr. High Sch., 1939-40, Prospect Jr. High Sch., Montecello, Ga., 1940-42, Rogers & Albert Pike Sch., Ft. Smith, Ark., 1946-47; asst. dir. extension, asso. prof. edn. U. Miss., 1949-52; pres. N.E. Miss. Jr. Coll., 1952-56; pres. Navarro Coll., Corsicana, Tex., 1956—. Mem. steering com. Tex. Program of Nursing Edn. under Kellogg Program; mem. Tex. Gov.'s Com. on Edn. Beyond High Sch.; mem. Bapt. Edn. Study Task, 1966-68. Trustee E. Tex. Bapt. Coll. Served from cadet to maj. USAF, 1942-45. Decorated D.F.C., Air Medal with oak leaf clusters. Mem. Am. Assn. Jr. Colls. (adminstrn. commn. 1959-62, legislation com. 1965-68), Miss. Jr. Coll. Assn. (v.p. 1955-56), Tex. Jr. Coll. Athletic Conf. (pres. 1957, v.p. 1962-63), C. of C., Tex. Jr. Coll. Assn. (pres., finance com. 1963-69), Tex. Jr. Coll. Football Fedn. (pres. 1963-66), Phi Theta Kappa (hon.), Phi Delta Kappa, Kappa Delta Pi, Pi Gamma Mu. Baptist (deacon, vice chmn. deacons 1959-60, 68, chmn. long range planning com. 1970, mem. bldg. com. 1972—). Rotarian. Home: 1007 Bryn Mawr St Corsicana TX 75110

JONES, BILLY RUAL, physician; b. Amarillo, Tex., June 11, 1926; s. Rual and Bess (Crutchfield) J.; B.S., Tufts U., 1946; M.D., Columbia, 1950; m. Elizabeth Anne Corbey, May 3, 1952; children—Deborah Anne, Kevin Timothy, Sharon Elizabeth, Julia Marie, Anne Claire. Intern, Roosevelt Hosp., N.Y.C., 1950-51, resident, 1951-53; resident VA Hosp., Nashville, Tenn., 1956-57; practice medicine, specializing in internal medicine, Amarillo, Tex., 1957—; pres.-elect staff High Plains Bapt. Hosp.; chief staff N.W. Tex. Hosp., chief med. service Bapt. Hosp., N.W. Tex. Hosp., St. Anthony's Hosp. Pres. Potter-Randall County Heart Assn., 1959, 63. Bd. dirs. Potter-Randall County Blood Bank, 1962-66; trustee Dad's Assn., Tex. Tech. U. Served with USNR, 1944-45, 54-56. Mem. A.M.A., Am. Soc. Internal Medicine, A.C.P., Tex. Med. Assn., Tex. Acad. Internal Medicine, Tex. Soc. Internal Medicine, Potter-Randall County Med. Soc. Baptist. Rotarian. Clubs: Tascosa Country (Amarillo, Tex.); Palo Duro (Canyon, Tex.). Home: 2808 Teckla St Amarillo TX 79106 Office: 5211 W 9th St Amarillo TX 79106

JONES, BOBBY LEE, city ofcl.; b. Lundale, W.Va.. Apr. 20, 1933; s. Shirman R. and Sylvia (Lanbert) J.; student St. Johns River Jr. Coll., 1965; m. Barbara Jean Usina, Dec. 15, 1955; children—Theresa Ann, Thomas Lambert. Bobby Lee. Slate picker Logan County Coal Co., Lundale, W.Va., 1950-52; dir. pub. works City of St. Augustine, Fla., 1967—. Regional chmn., sec. Fla. Water and Pollution Control Operators Assn., 1969. Served with USNR, 1952-56. Mem. Am. Water Works Assn., Fla. Pollution Control Assn. Mason (Shriner). Home: 4 Milton St St Augustine FL 32084 Office: PO Drawer 210 40 Hypolita St St Augustine FL 32084

JONES, BOOKER TALIAFERRO, musician, bandleader; b. Memphis, Nov. 12, 1944; s. Booker T. and Lurline (Newell) J.; student Memphis State U., 19xx; B. Mus. Edn., Ind. U., 1966; m. Wilette Gigi Armstrong, Nov. 8, 1963; 1 son, Booker Taliferro III. Staff studio musician, artist, producer Stax Records, Memphis, 1961—; tours colls., univs. and auditoriums, U.S., 1962—, also in France, Eng., Norway, Denmark, Sweden, Scotland and Wales; TV appearances, U.S. and Europe, 1965—; free band concerts for Heart Fund, Memphis Park Commn.; donated free services and royalties to Stay in School project, 1967. Recipient Gold Record Industry Am., 1966; named Leader Number One Nat. Instrumental Combo, Billboard mag., 1968. Mem. Am. Fedn. Musicians, Composers and Lyricists Guild Am., Broadcast Music, Inc., Nat. Acad. Recording Arts and Scis., Kappa Alpha Psi. Composer: Green Onions, 1962; Soul Limbo, 1968; Uptight, 1968. Home: 670 Edith Av Memphis TN 38126 Office: 926 E McLemore Av Memphis TN 38106

JONES, C. LEE, librarian; b. Anderson, Ind., Sept. 21, 1936; s. Clymer and Mary (Stookey) J.; B.A., Carleton Coll., 1959; M.L.S., U. Tex., 1965; m. Peggy Ann Simonton, June 26, 1971; children (by previous marriage)—Robin Dayle, George Cleveland. Indsl. engr. Procter & Gamble, Green Bay, Wis., 1959-63; library intern U. Tex., 1963-64; librarian Austin (Tex.) Natural Sci. Center, 1964; dir. tech. services Trinity U., San Antonio, 1964-67; dir. med. library U. Tex. Med. Br., Galveston, 1967—, vis. lectr. Grad. Sch. Library Sci., 1970. Cons. to Southeast area regional office WHO, 1971, Nat. Library Medicine. Mem. San Antonio com. United Fund, 1965-67; bd. dirs. William Temple Found., Galveston United Fund; mem. adv. and exec. coms. South Central Regional Med. Library, 1969—; pres. Tex. Council Health Sci. Libraries, 1971—. Served with USMCR, 1956-57, AUS, 1959-62. Named Boss of Year, Am. Bus. Women's Assn. Galveston, 1968-69. Mem. Am., Med., Tex., Southwestern library assns., Spl. Libraries Assn., Am. Assn. U. Profs. Rotarian. Mem. editorial bd. Texas Reports on Biology and Medicine, 1968—. Home: 219 Mackerel Av Galveston TX 77550 Office: 9th and Mechanic Sts Galveston TX 77550

JONES, CECIL DERWENT, ret. publisher; b. Thompson Station, Tenn., July 9, 1905; s. James Allen and Cammye Sowell (Evans) J.; student Battle Ground Acad., Franklin, Tenn., Emory U., 1924-26; m. Allie Tucker Yarbrough, July 27, 1929; children—Cecil Derwent, David Sterling. With Methodist Pub. House, Nashville, 1926-70, clk., 1926-27, asst. credit mgr., 1927-30, v.p., 1956-70, ret., 1970; with Abingdon Press 1930-64, salesman, 1930-40, asst. mgr., 1940-56, mgr., 1956-63; v.p. charge publs. div. Methodist Pub. House, Nashville, 1963-64, exec. v.p., 1964-70. Mem. Nat. Council Chs., C. of C., Protestant Ch. Owned Pubs. Assn. (v.p.), Sigma Sigma Chi. Rotarian. Home: 2020 Stonehurst Dr Nashville TN 37215

JONES, CECIL HELLNER, ins. exec.; b. Birmingham, Ala., Feb. 14, 1906; s. Herman and Lilliam (Oldham) J.; A.B., George Washington U., 1931; student Hampden Sydney Coll., 1925-29; m. Virginia Shippey, May 5, 1933; children—Lilliam Oldham (Mrs. Charles D. Joyner); m. 2d, Eileen Barrows, Mar. 25, 1972. Various positions U.S. Govt., 1932-39; legislative rep. Marble Industry, Washington, 1939-40, Knoxville (Tenn.) C. of C. Ind. Devel., Washington, 1940-41; merchandising analyst Coca Cola Co., 1941-45; group rep. John Hancock, Atlanta, 1946-49; regional mgr. Home Life of N.Y., Atlanta, 1949-57, v.p., 1957—, also dir.; dir. Am. Heritage Life Ins. Co., Jacksonville, Fla. Vice-chmn. Duval County Bd. Edn., 1969-71. Served with AUS, 1945-46. Mem. Newcomen Soc. N. Am., Kappa Sigma. Presbyn. Clubs: University, Touchdown, International (Washington); Touchdown, Capital City (Atlanta); Hidden Hills Country. Home: 5000 San Jose Blvd Apt 29 Jacksonville FL 32207 Office: 11 E Forsyth St Jacksonville FL 32202

JONES, CHARLES ALVIS, clergyman, librarian; b. Alexander City, Ala., Aug 7, 1926; s. Ulio I. and Bertha (Smith) J.; A.B., Samford U., 1951; B.D., Southwestern Bapt. Theol. Sem., 1964; M. in Librarianship, Emory U., 1965; postgrad. Troy (Ala.) State Coll., 1955, New Orleans Bapt. Theol. Sem., 1955, N. Tex. State U., 1962, U. Ga., 1971—; m. Hazel Smith, May 23, 1948; children—Margaret Elizabeth, Hazel Pamela. Ordained to ministry Baptist Ch., 1950; pastor Bapt. chs. Covington County, Ala., 1950-52, 55-61, Conecuh County, Ala., 1952-55, 58-60, Sunny South, Ala., 1954-55, Cobb, Tex., 1961-62, Connerville, Okla., 1964; Tate, Ga., 1967-69, Hiawassee, Ga., 1971—; prin. elementary sch. Covington County (Ala.), 1955-57, 58-59, tchr. jr. high sch., 1959-60; tchr. Hawaii Bapt. Acad., Honolulu, 1962-63; librarian, part-time instr. speech and Bible, Reinhardt Coll., Waleska., Ga., 1965-69; librarian Truett McConnell Coll., Cleveland, Ga., 1969-71; instr. div. librarianship Emory U., Atlanta, 1966; instr. library edn. extension center U. Ga., Canton, 1967; instr. library edn. U. Ga., summer 1969, full time, 1971—. Mem. Am., Southeastern, Ga. (chmn. coll. and univ. library sect. 1969-71) library assns., Ga. Edn. Assn., Trident, Beta Phi Mu. Home: Route 1 Villa Rica GA 30180

JONES, CHARLES FRANKLIN, ret. petroleum co. exec., univ. adminstr.; b. Bartlett, Tex., Nov. 23, 1911; s. Charles Edward and Pearl Lee (Keeton) J.; B.S. in Chem. Engring., U. Tex., 1933, M.S. in Chem. Engring., 1934, Ph.D. in Phys. Chemistry, 1937; LL.D. (hon.), Austin Coll., 1965; m. Edith Temple Houston, Apr. 1, 1938; children—Dianne (Mrs. Orson C. Clay), Kenneth Franklin. With Humble Oil and Refining Co., 1937-47, 49-63, mgr. econs. and planning dept., Houston, 1960-62, gen. mgr. central region, Tulsa, 1962-63; asst. to mgr. coordination and econs. dept. Standard Oil Co. (N.J.), 1947-49; pres., dir. Esso Research and Engring. Co., Linden, N.J., 1963-64; exec. v.p. Humble Oil & Refining Co., Houston, 1964, pres., 1964-70, vice chmn. bd., 1970-72, also dir.; dean Coll. Bus. Adminstrn., U. Houston, 1972—; chmn. bd. Fed. Res. Bank of Dallas. Mem. nat. sci. bd. NSF, 1966-72. Pres. Houston Symphony Soc.; mem. exec. com. Tex. Research League. Recipient Distinguished Engring. Grad. award U. Tex., 1964. Registered profl. engr., Tex. Mem. Am. Petroleum Inst., A.A.A.S., Am. Chem. Soc., Soc. Automotive Engrs., Soc. Chem. Industry, Am. Inst. Chem. Engrs., Houston C. of C. (exec. com.), Sigma Xi, Tau Beta Pi, Phi Lambda Upsilon. Presbyn. (elder). Home: 3706 Del Monte St Houston TX 77019

JONES, CHARLIE CROWELL, investment co. exec.; b. Samson, Ala., Oct. 13, 1927; s. Moses Prett and Minnie Mae (Powell) J.; B.A., Baylor U., 1954; m. Helen E. Hollingshead, Sept. 4, 1954; children—Helen Denise, Charles Mark, Andrew Crowell. Adminstrv. v.p. United Services Planning Assn., Ft, Worth, 1965—; sec. United Diversified Corp., 1970—; partner Ind. Research Agy. for Life Ins. Served to lt. USNR, 1954-65; comdr. Res. Mem. Naval Res. Assn. (pres. Ft. Worth), Res. Officers Assn. Baptist. Kiwanian. Club: Ridglea Country (Ft. Worth). Office: 6000 Camp Bowie Blvd Fort Worth TX 76116

JONES, CLARENCE ROLLINS, mech. engr.; b. Ashton, S.C., Nov. 7, 1923; s. Clarence Rollins and Susan (Black) J.; B.S. in Mech. Engring., Clemson A. and M. Coll., 1947, M.S., 1949; m. Eunice Varn Polk, July 26, 1944; children—Susan Varn, Mary Deborah. Instr., Clemson (S.C.) Coll., 1947-49; project engr. Patchen & Zimmerman Engrs., Augusta, Ga., 1950-51; owner, cons. engr., architect Jones Engring. Co., engring., archtl. firm, Augusta, Jones & Assos., architects and engrs., 1951—; founder, sr. partner Jones & Fellers, architects and engrs., Augusta, Columbia, S.C., now pres.; chmn. bd. Mid-South Corp., Augusta; v.p. So. Industries Investment Co., Augusta; dir. Rhodes-Murphy Co., Safety Shelter Corp., Citizens & So. Nat. Bank, Augusta. Vice chmn. Citizens Adv. Com. City of Augusta; mem. emergency resources planning com. State of Ga., 1961—. Served from pvt. to 1st lt. AUS, 1942-47; PTO. Registered profl. engr., 18 states. Mem. Cons. States Engrs. Assn. Ga., Am. Soc. Heating Refrigerating and Air Conditioning Engrs., Am. Soc. M.E., Am. Inst. Cons. Engrs., Soc. Am. Mil. Engrs., Nat. Council State Bds. Engring. Examiners, Nat. (nat. dir., v.p., chmn. liaison com.), Ga. (dir.) socs. profl. engrs., Augusta Com. of 100, Profl. Engrs. in Pvt. Practice, Augusta Mus. Assn., Augusta C. of C., Assn. U.S. Army, Instn. Engrs.-Jamaica. Methodist (bd. stewards). Mason. Clubs: Lions (dir. Augusta 1960—), Augusta Country, Augusta Sailing; Pinnacle; President's, Elks, Ale, Quail and Tale, Ducks Unlimited. Prin. works include design of various comml., indsl. and instnl. facilities throughout U.S., Central Am., S.A. Home: 3445 Walton Way Augusta GA 30904 Office: Mid-South Bldg Augusta GA 30903

JONES, CLAUDE V., lawyer; b. Elizabeth City, N.C., Sept. 23, 1903; LL.B., U. N.C. Admitted to N.C. bar, 1925, U.S. Supreme Ct. bar, 1948; practiced in Durham, N.C., 1925—; atty. City of Durham, 1937—. Mem. Am., N.C. bar assns., N.C. State Bar (pres. 1969—), Delta Theta Phi. Address: Central Carolina Bank Bldg Durham NC 27701

JONES, CRAIG SCOTT, physician; b. Baldwin, Kan., Aug. 7, 1918; s. Pearl West and Elizabeth (Scott) J.; A.B., Baker U., 1939; M.D., U. Kan., 1944; m. Mary Louise Rundell, Mar. 14, 1942; children—Craig Michael, Beth Kathleen (Mrs. Charles Kruchek), Kerry Bruce, Gordon Scott. Intern, Ancker Hosp., St. Paul, 1944; resident internal medicine U. Kan., Kansas City, 1946-49; practice medicine, specializing in internal medicine, Fayetteville, Ark., 1949-50, Tulsa, 1950—; mem. staff Hillcrest Med. Clinic, St. John's Hosp., St. Francis Hosp., Doctor's Hosp. Tulsa); asst. clin. prof. medicine U. Okla., Tulsa, 1971; clin. cardiology fellow St. Joseph's Hosp., Ann Arbor, Mich., 1967. Served with USNR, 1944-46. Fellow A.C.P., Am. Coll. Cardiology; mem. Tulsa County Med. Soc., Okla. Med. Assn., A.M.A., Sigma Phi Epsilon, Phi Beta Pi. Mason. Home: 2813 E 47th Pl Tulsa OK 74105 Office: 1145 S Utica St Suite 202 Tulsa OK 74104

JONES, DANIEL BURR, psychologist; b. Omaha, Aug. 20, 1922; s. Daniel Burr and Flora (Tichnor) J.; B.A., U. Fla., 1943; M.S., Tulane, 1950; Ph.D., U. Mo. at Kansas City, 1965; m. Bettie Garrison, Dec. 9, 1946; children—Daniel T. and Jeffrey B. (twins). Commd. 2d lt. U.S. Army, 1943, advanced through grades to lt. col., 1963; various assignments including South Pacific, Korea, Pentagon, Army Command and Staff Coll.; sr. scientist Operations Research, Inc., Silver Spring, Md., 1963-66; chief human factors engring. Western div. McDonnell Douglas Astronautics Co., Culver City, Cal., 1966-69; chief human engring. Martin Marietta Corp., Orlando, 1969—; lectr. grad. div. Inst. Aerospace Safety and Mgmt., U. So. Cal., Los Angeles, 1967-72, adj. prof. indsl. engring. Fla. Tech. U., 1971-72. Decorated Bronze Star medal. Mem. Am. Acad. Polit. and Social Sci., Human Factors Soc., Assn. Engring. Psychologists, Tulane U. Alumni Assn. (bd. dirs.). Home: Rt 3 Box 936 Orlando FL 32811 Office: Martin Marietta Corp PO Box 5837 Orlando FL 32805

JONES, DAVID HENRY, educator; b. Independence, Mo., Dec. 25, 1930; s. Leon William and Rachel (Demuynck) J.; B.A., U. Mo., 1958; M.A., Harvard, 1960, Ph.D., 1963; m. Virginia A. Lipoma, Dec. 17, 1953. Instr. philosophy U. Kan., Lawrence, 1962-63, asst. prof., 1963-67; prof. Coll. William and Mary, Williamsburg, Va., 1967—. Mem. Am. Civil Liberties Union, 1965—, chmn. Peninsula chpt., 1968, Va. bd. dirs., 1968-70. Served with USNR, 1951-54; Korea. Mem. Am. Philos. Assn., Am. Assn. U. Profs., Va. Philos. Assn. Contbr. profl. jours. Home: 133 Cooley Rd Williamsburg VA 23185

JONES, DAVID HOWELL, univ. press dir.; b. Sept. 16, 1923; B.A., Rice U., 1944; B.S., Juilliard Sch. Music, 1949; m. Carolyn Walker, 1965. Mem. editorial staff Columbia Ency., 1946-50; asst. to exec. editor Columbia U. Press, 1951-55; copy editor, proofreading supr. Columbia Records, 1956-58; chief editor U. Tex. Press, 1958-59; dir., editor Vanderbilt U. Press, Nashville, 1959—. Home: 4505 Harding

Rd Nashville TN 37205 Office: Vanderbilt U Press Nashville TN 37235

JONES, DON HOWARD, civil engr., educator; b. Isabella, Tenn., Feb. 17, 1933; s. William Howard and Cosbie (Brooks) J.; B.S., U. Tenn., 1959, M.S., 1969; m. Martha Ann Burkhart, May 28, 1954; children—Donna Lucy, Rebecca Fay. Clerk, Kaighan & Hughes & Rust Engring. Co's., Oak Ridge, 1953-55; swimming instr., camp counselor YMCA, Knoxville, Tenn., 1951-53; rodman, engring. aid Tenn. Hwy. Dept., Knoxville, 1951-59, resident engr., 1959-63, sr. resident engr., 1963-64, utility relocation engr., 1964-65, regional right-of-way engr., 1965-72; asst. prof. civil engring., asst. dir. Transp. Research Center, U. Tenn., Knoxville, 1972—. Mem. Am. Soc. C.E. (v.p. 1969), Tenn. Soc. Profl. Engrs. (chpt. pres. 1971-72), Am. Soc. Photogrammetry, Chi Epsilon. Home: Sterwart's Ferry Pike Hermitage TN 37076

JONES, DONALD HARL, geologist; b. Crowley, La., Nov. 4, 1926; s. Lara J. and Mary Edwina (Harl) J.; B.A., U. Tenn., 1950; m. Florence G. Sanders, Sept. 1, 1951; children—Kyle D., Greg A. Ind. oil invester, Crowley, La., 1950—; dir. First Nat. Bank, Crowley, La. Active Civil Service Commn., Crowley, La. Served with AUS, 1952. Mem. Ind. Petroleum Assn. Am., Lafayette Geol. Soc., Crowley C. of C. (dir. 1964-66), Am. Legion, Theta Xi. Democrat. Methodist (chmn. bd. 1969-70). Mason (Shriner), Lion. Club: Bayou Bend Country (pres. 1961) (Crowley, La.). Home: 304 W 14th St Crowley LA 70526 Office: PO Box 27 Crowley LA 70526

JONES, DOROTHY MAY, lawyer; b. North Little Rock, Ark., June 26, 1917; d. Elet Sidney and Jeannette Viola (Armstrong) May; LL.B., Ark. Law Sch., 1938; m. Edmund N. Orsini, July 31, 1935 (div. 1966); children—Edmund N., David Armstrong, Merrily Ann; m. 2d, Joseph P. Jones, Jr., Sept. 24, 1966. Admitted to Ark. bar, 1938; practice law with H.B. Stubblefield, Little Rock, 1945-54; exec. dir. Ark. Bar Assn., 1954-66; bus. mgr. Women Lawyer's Jour., 1958-59, editor, 1968-69. Mem. Nat. Assn. Women Lawyers (corr. sec. 1959-60, treas. 1960-61, v.p. 1961-62, pres. 1962-63, past state del., regional dir.), Little Rock Assn. Women Lawyers, Jefferson County Assn. Women Lawyers (v.p. 1971-72), Phi Delta Delta. Episcopalian (mem. altar guild). Club: Zonta. Home: 800 S 4th St Louisville KY 40203

JONES, DYCHE, food chain exec.; b. Tyner, Ky., May 2, 1915; s. Frank Woodson and Bess (Flinchum) J.; student U. Tenn., 1932-33, Union Coll., 1933-34; m. Pauline Chesnut, Jan 22. 1935; 1 son, William Frank. Pres., Dyche Jones Food Stores, London, Ky., 1935—. Pres. London-Laurel County Devel. Assn., 1969-71; treas. Laurel County Homecoming, 1944—, d.c. chmn., 1953-54. Sec. Clearcreek Mountain Preachers Sch., Pineville, 1949-53. Baptist (deacon). Kiwanian (dir., pres. 1953). Home: 607 N Main St London KY 40741 Office: 208 S Broad St London KY 40741

JONES, EARL, coll. pres.; b. Canton, Okla., Aug. 4, 1925; s. Hercel C. and Florence (Hill) J.; B.S., Ore. State U., 1949; M.S., Inter-Am. Inst. of OAS (Turrialba, Costa Rica), 1958; Ed.D., Mont. State U., 1962; m. Eleanor Harriett Vance, July 15, 1952; children—Beverly Anne, Mark Earl, James Richard, Cindy Kay. Tchr. pub. schs., Ontario, Ore., 1949-55; dir. rural programs KSRV, Ontario, 1955-56, KSLM, Salem, Ore., 1956; vocational dir. Arcata (Cal.) Pub. Schs, 1956-57; instr. Inter-Am. Inst., 1957-58, asst. prof., 1960-62; asso. prof. sociology U. Cal. Los Angeles, 1963-66; prof. sociology, edn., asso. dean. Tex. A. and M. U. Coll. Edn., College Station, 1967-71; pres. Incarnate Word Coll., San Antonio, 1971—. Dir. research Caribbean Inst. Sociology, Anthropology, Caracas, Venezuela, 1963-65; chair prof. U. Chile Sch. Law, Santiago, Valparaiso, 1965-66; vis. prof. Royal Danish Acad., Copenhagen; 1955, U. P.R., Mayaguez, 1960, Cath. U., Caracas, 1963-65, U. Pacific, 1966, Cal. State Coll. Los Angeles, Cal. State Coll. San Francisco, 1968. Mem. Gov.'s Coms. on Confluence Tex. Cultures, 1969—, to Reconstruct Tchr. Edn., 1969—; cons. Cabinet Com. on Spanish Speaking Peoples, 1972—. Served with USMCR, 1943-46. Recipient Presdl. citation Republic Guatemala, 1969; Standard Oil Distinguished Teaching award, 1970. Mem. Am. Sociol. Assn., Rural Sociol. Soc., Soc. Comparative Edn., N.E.A., Alpha Zeta, Phi Delta Kappa. Democrat. Roman Catholic. Lion. Author: Rural Youth in the Americas, 1960; Lideracao, 1961; A Study of the Costa Rican Extension Service, 1962; The Cooperative Extension Services of Jamaica, 1962; Supervision en Extension Agricola, 1963; Latin American Literature for Youth, 1968; Some Perspectives on the Americas, 1968; Self-Identification and the Americas, 1970. Home: 320 Park Dr San Antonio TX 78212

JONES, ED, congressman; b. Yorkville, Tenn., Apr. 20, 1912; s. Will Frank and Hortense (Pipkin) J.; B.S. U. Tenn., 1934; postgrad. U. Wis., U. Mo.; D.Litt., Bethel Coll.; m. Llewellyn Wyatt, June 9, 1938; children—Mary Liew (Mrs. Robert S. McGuire), Jennifer Wilson. Insp., Tenn. Dept. Agr., 1934-36; supr. Tenn. Dairy Products Assn., 1936-41; agrl. agt. Ill. Central R.R., West Tenn., 1941-48, Yorkville, Tenn., 1953-69; commr. agr. State Tenn., 1949-52; asso. farm dir. Radio Sta. WMC, Memphis, Tenn., 1952-69. Pres., bd. dirs. Yorkville (Tenn.) Telephone Coop., 1950—; elected to U.S. Ho. Reps. in spl. election 8th Congl. Dist. Tenn., 1970; reelected mem. 92d Congress. State chmn. Farmers for Kennedy-Johnson, 1961. Pres. bd. trustees Bethel Coll., 1950-67. Named Man of Year, Progressive Farmer mag., 1952, Man of Year, Memphis Agrl. Club. Mem. 4-H (state farmer). Presbyn. (elder 1940—). Mason (Shriner), Moose, Elk. Home: Yorkville TN 38389 Office: House Office Bldg Washington DC 20515

JONES, EDMUND RUFFIN, JR., zoologist, educator; b. Charlottesville, Va., Oct. 1, 1905; s. Rev. Edmund Ruffin and Jane Bell (Dabney) J.; B.A., U. Va., 1927, B.S., 1927, M.A., 1928, Ph.D., 1930; m. Helen Purdum Bell, June 11, 1936; children—Helen Bell (Mrs. William Edward Kerby), Frances Dabney (Mrs. Donald Moore Giles). Lectr. biology Dalhousie U., Halifax, N.S., 1930-31; asso. prof. Norfolk Div. of Coll. of William and Mary, 1931-37, prof., 1937-46, chmn. div; natural sci., 1940-46, chmn. faculty, 1941-42, dir. summer session, 1941-44, dir. evening coll. and adult edu., 1942-44; instr. Mt. Lake Biol. Station, 1935, 45, 46, 50, 56, also acting dir., 1945; asso. prof. U. Fla., Gainesville, 1946-47, prof., 1947—, dir. pre-prof. counseling, 1958-69, asst. dean Grad. Sch., 1961-64, asst. dean arts and scis., 1964-70; instr. zoology Marine Biol. Lab., Woods Hole, Mass., 1940, 41; cons. USPHS, 1940-42, Dir. Civilian Def. Tng. Schs. for Norfolk, Va., 1942-44; treas. for Eastern Va. of Young Am. Wants to Help (div. Brit. War Relief Soc.), 1940-42; treas, United Community Fund, Gainesville, 1959-62. Fellow A.A.A.S. (pres. acad. conf. 1962); mem. Am. Soc, Zoologists, Assn. Southeastern Biologists (pres. 1963-64), Soc. Systematic Zoology, Nat. Inst. Dental Research (tng. com. 1962-66, chmn. 1966-67, Am. Microscopic Soc., Corp. of Marine Biol. Lab., Assn. U. Profs., Va., Fla. (pres. 1959) acads. sci., Townsmen's Soc. of Norfolk (past pres.), Phi Beta Kappa, Sigma Xi, Phi Sigma, Phi Delta Theta. Democrat. Episcopalian. Rotarian. Contbr. articles to sci. and tech. publs. Home: Gale Hill Route 3 Box 200 B-1 Gainesville FL 32601

JONES, EDSEL TENSLEY, lawyer; b. Cunard, W.Va., Sept. 24, 1925; s. Ernest Lee and Elsie Christine (Burford) J.; student Concord Coll., Athens, W.Va., 1947-49; B.S., U. Tenn., 1953; M.B.A., U. Ky., 1968, J.D., 1968; m. Robin Hunt Adair, July 13, 1947; children—Mark Henson, Tensley Adair. Indsl. engr. Sylvania Electric Products, Inc., Huntington, W.Va., 1953-57, sr. indsl. engr., Winchester, Ky., 1958-59, supr. indsl. engring., 1959-65; admitted to Ky. bar, 1968; practice law, Winchester, 1968—. Counsel, Winchester Mcpl. Utilities Commn., 1970—. Mayor, Winchester, 1966-70; city atty., Winchester 1972—. Bd. dirs. Clark County Hosp., Winchester, 1966-70. Served with USNR, 1943-45. Registered profl. engr., Ky. Mem. Am., Ky. bar assns., Blue Key, Tau Beta Pi, Phi Kappa Phi, Chi Beta Phi, Kappa Delta Pi, Phi Delta Pi. Mem. Christian Ch. (deacon). Rotarian. Home: 127 Hampton Av Winchester KY 40391 Office: 68 S Main St Winchester KY 40391

JONES, EGBERT MALONE, elec. engr.; b. Memphis, Dec. 16, 1928; s. Egbert Adlai and Willie Wise (Swepston) J.; B.S. in Math., U. of South, Sewanee, Tenn., 1950; E.E., U. Cin., 1955. Process engr. nuclear div. Union Carbide Corp., Paducah, Ky., 1955-65; profl. engr. E.T. Hannan & Assos., cons. engrs., Paducah, Evansville, Ind., 1965-69; profl. engr. Erhart, Eichenbaum, Rauch & Blass, architects and E.K. Riddick, engr., Little Rock, 1969—; elec. cons. Committeeman, Quapaw council Boy Scouts Am., 1971—. Mem. I.E.E.E., Instrument Soc. Am., Nat. Rifle Assn., Nat. Soc. Profl. Engrs. Methodist. Kiwanian. Patentee in field. Home: 10 Nottingham Rd Little Rock AR 72205 Office: Continental Bldg Little Rock AR 72201

JONES, ELIZABETH RIEKE (MRS. WAYNE VAN LEER JONES), club woman; b. Chgo., Oct. 15, 1903; d. Henry Edward and Vina Genevieve (Coulter) Rieke; A.B., Northwestern U., 1925; m. Wayne Van Leer Jones, Jan. 14, 1926; 1 son, Wayne Van Leer, II. Dir. Houston Grand Opera Assn. Mem. Art. Mus. Guild, Assistance League (mem. nat. finance com. 1970-72), U. Women's Alliance (pres. 1951-53, scholarship chmn. 1963—), Houston Geol. Aux. (parliamentarian 1950-51, 60-61, 63-64), Kappa Kappa Gamma, Theta Sigma Phi. Republican. Presbyn. Home: 5672 Longmont Dr Houston TX 77027

JONES, EVERETT RILEY, JR., oil co. exec.; b. Leitchfield, Ky., July 28, 1918; s. Everett Riley and Margie (Hatfield) J.; student Spencerian Comml. Coll., 1936-37, U. Louisville, 1946-47; m. Lois Gibbins, July 15, 1950; children—Stacey Rae, Rande Leigh. Sec.-treas., dir. Lafitte Oil Corp., Louisville, 1947-49; partner Fryer & Hanson Drilling Co., Dallas, 1950-58; pres., dir. Bengal Producing Co., Dallas, 1959—; dir. Dallas County Small Bus. Devel. Center, Inc. Trustee S.W. Engring. Found. Served to capt. USAAF, 1942-45. Decorated D.F.C., Air medal with 4 oak leaf clusters. Episcopalian. Club: Engineers (past pres.) (Dallas). Home: 6231 Desco Dr Dallas TX 75225 Office: Meadows Bldg Dallas TX 75206

JONES, FRANK, univ. athletic dir. Athletic dir. U. Richmond (Va.) Office: Athletic Dept U Richmond Richmond VA 23173*

JONES, FRANKLIN CLINTON, oil co. exec.; b. Oklahoma City, Mar. 30, 1934; s. S.J. and Mildred (Autry) J.; B.S., Okla. U., 1956; m. Berdenia June Wheeler, Jan. 23, 1954 (div. Oct. 4, 1971); children—Deana Kathleen, Jeffery Steven, Gregory Clinton, Jennifer Rene. Geologist, Lone Star Producing Co., San Antonio, 1956-58, Corpus Christi, Tex., 1958-61, dist. geologist, San Antonio, 1961-66, dist. exploration mgr., Oklahoma City, 1966-72, dir. exploration, Dallas, 1972—. Served with AUS, 1950-52. Mem. Am. Assn. Petroleum Geologists, Oklahoma City Geol. Soc., Petroleum Club. Republican. Methodist. Mason. Clubs: Twin Hills Golf and Country (Oklahoma City). Home: 1802 Navajo Pl Irving TX 75060 Office: 301 S Harwood Dallas TX 75201

JONES, FRANKLYN, physician; b. Grenada, BWI, Mar. 18, 1917; s. Cyril B. and Jemina E. (Ross) J.; B.S., Howard U., 1949; M.D., Meharry Med. Coll., 1954; m. Una Gertrude Bonaparte, Aug. 5, 1951; children—Cheryl Gertrude, Franklyn W., Reginald M., Lawrence K. Came to U.S., 1946, naturalized, 1956. Intern Kings County Hosp. Center, Bklyn., 1954-55; practice gen. medicine. Appomattox, Va., 1955-56, Danville, Va., 1956-57, Houston, 1957—; staff Riverside Gen., St. Elizabeth, Bapt. hosps. Dir., Riverside Nat. Bank. Mem. Nat., Am. med. assns., Tex. Harris County med. socs., Am. Acad. Gen. Practice. Home: 3214 Milburn St Houston TX 77021 Office: 4635 Bellfort Blvd Houston TX 77051

JONES, GEORGE HILES, JR., assn. exec.; b. St. Louis, Mar. 17, 1932; s. George H. and Florence (Harris) J; B.A., Birmingham So. Coll., 1954; 1 son, Robert Wolford. Divisional sales mgr. Ebosco Industries, 1954-57; sect. mgr. Ala. Assn. Credit Execs., Birmingham, 1957-63; exec. v.p. Deep South Tire Dealers and Retreaders Assn., Birmingham, 1964—; pres. Assn. Mgmt. Services, Inc. 1969—. Mem. Ala. Gov.'s. Safety Coordinating Com., 1967—. Recipient top award Credit Assn. for Membership, 1958, 59, 60; award Nat. Tire Dealers and Retreaders Assn., 1967, 69. Mem. Nat. Assn. Credit Mgmt. (chmn. secretarial council 1963), Am. Soc. Assn. Execs., Ga. Safety Council, Ala., Ga. hwy. users confs., Ala.-La. Ind. Auto Dealers Assn. (exec. v.p.), Miss. Gasoline Dealers Assn. (exec. v.p.), Ala. Ind. Bus. Assn. (pres.), Ind. Garage Owners La. (adminstr.), Ala. Council Assn. Execs., Alpha Tau Omega. Episcopalian (vestryman 1967-68). Club: West Homewood Civic (pres. 1962) (Homewood, Ala.). Home: PO Box 2835A Birmingham AL 35212 Office: 4500 5th Av S Birmingham AL 35222

JONES, GERALD LEE, realtor; b. Ft. Worth, Jan 23, 1928; s. Oscar Monroe and Cora (Monroe) J.; student Tex. Christian U., 1950-51, U. Tex. at Arlington, 1966-67; m. Emma Lou Bogan, June 17, 1944; 1 son, John Paul. Machinist apprentice Ft. Worth Steel & Machinery, 1943-46; mgr. Hilarity Enterprises, Ft. Worth, 1945-47; machinist Convair, Ft. Worth, 1947-51; machinist-tool and die maker Wilson Specialty Co., Ft. Worth, 1951-56; machinist Petroleum Tool Research, Ft. Worth, 1956-57; machine shop foreman Hydraulics, Inc., 1957-58; machinist Bell Helicopter Co., 1958-59; pres., gen. mgr. C & S Tool & Instrument Co., Inc., Ft. Worth, 1959—; real estate broker, Ft. Worth, 1964—. Democrat. Methodist. Odd Fellow, Mason. Home: 1508 Canterbury Circle Fort Worth TX 76112 Office: 2909 Meaders St Fort Worth TX 76112

JONES, GILMER ANDREW, JR., govt. ofcl.; b. Franklin, N.C., Apr. 19, 1920; s. Gilmer Andrew and Maude (Jacobs) J.; student Brevard Coll., 1936-39, John B. Stetson U., 1947-48; LL.B., U. N.C., 1949; m. Betty Eloise MacCartney, Aug. 2, 1942; children—Marjorie Eloise (Mrs. Louis Marvin Pleasants), Paul Andrew. Chief, wildlife protection div., N.C. Wildlife Resources, Raleigh, 1949-53; admitted to N.C. bar, 1949; practiced in Franklin and Raleigh, N.C., 1953-58; asst. atty. gen., N.C., 1958-63; state budget officer, Dept. Adminstrn., Raleigh, N.C., 1963-72, commr. revenue, 1972— Served with USNR, 1940-45. Mem. N.C. State Bar Assn., Delta Sigma Phi, Phi Alpha Delta. Clubs: Optomist, Lions. Home: 2938 Glenridge Dr Raleigh NC 27604 Office: Revenue Bldg Salisbury St Raleigh NC 27611

JONES, GORDON, banker; b. Atlanta, Jan. 14, 1918; s. Harrison and Kathryn (Gordon) J.; B.S., U. Ga., 1940; m. Ann Creekmore, Oct. 8, 1940; children—Harrison Jones, Caroline (Mrs. Marion H. Allen III), Ann (Mrs. Bussey C. Bonner, Jr.), Kathryn H. With The Fulton Nat. Bank, Atlanta, 1947—, exec. v.p., 1954-58, pres., 1958—, also dir.; dir. Atlanta Gas Light Co., Atlanta Stove Works, Inc., Coastal States Life Ins. Co., Fulton Nat. Corp., Haverty Furniture Cos., Inc. Bd. dirs. U. Ga. Found., Atlanta Arts Assn., Met. Found. Atlanta, Central Atlanta Progress, Inc. Served with USNR, 1941-45. Clubs: Capital City, The Commerce, Piedmont Driving (Atlanta). Home: 660 W Paces Ferry Rd NW Atlanta GA 30327 Office: 55 Marietta St NW Atlanta GA 30303

JONES, GWENDOLA MITCHELL (MRS. JIM ARTHUR JONES), social worker; b. Jacksonville, Fla., Jan. 21, 1936; d. David A. and Merca (Judge) Mitchell; student Hampton Inst., 1952-53; B.S., Tuskegee Inst., 1957; M.A., U. Chgo., 1965; m. Jim Arthur Jones, Apr. 9, 1959; children—Gwendola Evon, Murray Charles. Tchr., Duval County Bd. Pub. Instrn., Jacksonville, 1957-58; social worker Fla. Dept. Pub. Welfare, Jacksonville, 1958-63, state welfare cons., 1965-66, family and childrens supr., 1966-67, orientation tng. supr., 1967-68, casework supr., 1968-70, supr. welfare program, 1970-72; dir. clin. social services div. health Fla. Dept. Health and Rehab. Service, 1972—. Mem. Fair Housing Council, Jacksonville, 1969—; mem. policy adv. bd. Parent Child Center, 1969-70, Summer Head Start, 1969-70; mem. policy adv. bd. Jacksonville Urban Missions, United Meth. Ch., 1967—; mem. agy. adv. com. social work edn. project Univ. Systems Fla., 1972—; mem. Statewide Family Planning Task Force, 1970-71. Mem. Nat. Assn. Social Workers (chpt. sec. 1967-69), Fla. Fedn. Social Workers (v.p. 1968—), Am. Assn. U. Women, Nat. Assn. Beach Social Workers, Nat. Council Negro Women, Womens Soc. Christian Service, Delta Sigma Theta. Democrat. Methodist. Home: 6526 Manhattan Dr Jacksonville FL 32208 Office: PO Box 210 Jacksonville FL 32201

JONES, HALBERT MCNAIR, textile mfr.; b. Laurinburg, N.C., Aug. 13, 1909; s. James A. and Mary (McNair) J.; B.S., U. N.C.; M.B.A., Harvard, 1931; H.H.D. (hon.), N.C. State Coll., 1958; m. Elizabeth Munroe, Apr. 6, 1943; children—Elizabeth M., Mary Ellen, Halbert McNair, James. Pres., treas. Waverly Mills, Inc., 1934-71, chmn. bd., 1971—; v.p., treas. Scotland Mills, Inc., 1939-63; treas. Morgan Jones, Inc., N.Y.C., 1946-63; dir. Wachovia Bank and Trust Co. N.A., Durham Life Ins. Co. Chmn. Laurinburg Sch. Bd., 1953-68, Acting pres., chmn. bd. trustees Flora McDonald Coll., Red Springs, 1948-49; vice chmn. bd. trustees St. Andrews Presbyn. Coll., 1958—. Served as maj. AUS, 1942-46. Mem. Card Yarn Assn. (pres. 1951-52), Am. Cotton Mfrs. Inst. (pres. 1958-59), N.C. Textile Mfrs. Assn. (pres. 1957-58). Presbyn. (elder; moderator N.C. Synod 1969-70). Rotarian (pres. 1946-47). Home: 308 Prince St Laurinburg NC 28352 Office: Waverly Mills Inc Laurinburg NC 28352

JONES, HARRY TUDOR, JR., wholesale fresh food co. exec.; b. Norfolk, Va., Sept. 13, 1920; s. Harry Tudor and Catherine (Roddey) J.; A.B., Va. Mil. Inst., 1943; M.B.A., Wharton Sch., U. Pa., 1947; m. Celetta Powell, Apr. 20, 1946; children—Celetta Randolph, Catherine Roddey, Margaret Powell, Harry T. III, William Powell, Nancy McKay. With W.J. Powell Co., Thomasville, Ga., 1947—, pres., 1968—; dir. Citizens & So. Bank, Thomasville. Trustee Presbyn. Home, Quitman, Ga., 1970—, Thornwell Orphanage, Clinton, S.C., 1970—. Served to 1st lt. AUS, 1943-46. Mem. C. of C. (past v.p.). Rotarian (past pres.). Presbyn. (elder). Home: 333 Glenwood Dr Thomasville GA 31792 Office: PO Box 939 Thomasville GA 31792

JONES, HOMER WALTER, JR., math. statistician; b. N.Y.C., Sept. 3, 1925; s. Homer Walter and Margaret (Campbell) J.; M.E., Stevens Inst. Tech., 1947, M.S., 1950; M.B.A., Am. U., 1959; M.S., George Washington U., 1965, postgrad. in math. statistics, 1965-70; m. Shirley Jean Dabbs, June 15, 1957; children—Laura Gwen, Linda Margaret. Cost estimator Standard Oil Devel. Co., Linden, N.J., 1947-51; product devel. engr. Wallace & Tiernan, Inc., Belleville, N.J., 1957-58; math. statistician U.S. Treasury Dept., Internal Revenue Service, Washington, 1959—. Dir. external affairs D.C. Chess League, 1963-65, dir. tournament, 1965-67, pres., League, 1967-69, exec. dir., 1969—. Treas. Valley Drive Pre-Sch., Inc., Alexandria, Va., 1964. Served with USNR, 1944-45. Mem. Am. Statis. Assn., Inst. Math. Statistics, Nat. Assn. Internal Revenue Employees, U.S. Chess Fedn. (dir., representing Washington 1969-71, Va., 1971—). Republican. Presbyn. (chmn. budget com. 1971, treas. 1971-72). Home: 2503 Taylor Av Alexandria VA 22302 Office: 12th and Constitution Av NW Washington DC 20224

JONES, HOUSTON GWYNNE, state ofcl.; b. Yanceyville, N.C., Jan. 7, 1924; s. Paul Hosier and Lemma (Fowlkes) J.; B.S., Appalachian State Coll., 1949; M.A., Peabody Coll., 1950; postgrad. summers N.Y. U., 1951-52, Am. U., 1957; Ph.D., Duke, 1965. Prof. history Oak Ridge (N.C.) Mil. Inst., 1950-53; vis. prof. history Western Carolina Coll., summer 1955; chmn. div. social scis. W. Ga. Coll., 1955-56; state archivist N.C. Dept. Archives and History, Raleigh, 1956-68, dir. dept., 1968-72; state historian, adminstr. Office Archives and History, Dept. Art, Culture and History, 1972—; adj. prof. history N.C. State U., 1966—. Served with USNR, 1942-46. Recipient Cannon Cup for Historic Preservation, 1971; Distinguished Alumni award Appalachian State U., 1971. Fellow Soc. Am. Archivists (pres. 1968-69); mem. Am., So. hist. assns., Am. Assn. for State and Local History (mem. council 1972—), Nat. Trust for Historic Preservation, Orgn. Am. Historians, N.C. Lit. and Hist. Assn. (sec.-treas. 1969—), Inst. Early Am. History and Culture (mem. council 1970—). Author: Bedford Brown: State Rights Unionist, 1956 (winner R.D.W. Connor award); For History's Sake, 1966 (Waldo Gifford Leland prize); The Records of a Nation, 1969. Editor-in-chief N.C. Hist. Rev., 1968—; mem. editorial bd. William and Mary Quar., 1970—. Address: care NC Dept Art Culture and History Raleigh NC 27611

JONES, HOWARD LEON, educator; b. Phoenixville, Pa., Oct. 20, 1940; s. Walter R. and Marie (McCann) J.; B.S., Millersville (Pa.) State Coll., 1962; M.A., U. Tex., 1964, Ph.D., 1966; m. Renda M. Nowell, Dec. 28, 1963. Project asso., research asso., instr. U. Tex., 1964-66; vis, prof. Okla. State U. summer, 1965; asst. prof. sci. edn. Syracuse U., 1966-68; asso. prof. edn. U. Houston, 1968—, asso. dir. competency-based tchr. edn. program, 1971—; sci. cons. Eastern Regional Inst. for Edn., 1967-69; cons. Exploratory Com. for Assessment of Edn. Progress, Cons. Edn. Testing Service. Fellow A.A.A.S.; mem. Am. Ednl. Research Assn., Nat. Sci. Tchrs. Assn., Nat. Assn. Research in Sci. Teaching, Assn. Supervision and Curriculum Devel., Kappa Delta Pi. Contbr. articles to profl. jours. Home: 12319 Rincon St Houston TX 77077

JONES, HUBERT EUGENE, osteo. physician and surgeon; b. Oakland, Ill., May 8, 1916; s. Clinton and Nora (Kincade) J.; student U. Ill., 1934-35, Kirksville Coll. Osteopathy and Surgery, 1939; m. Phyllis Elinor Creech, May 29, 1937; children—Robert Allan, Paul Lee, Margaret Elizabeth (Mrs. Warren Skelton). Intern Landfather Hosp., Maryville, Mo., 1939-40; pvt. practice. Mena, Ark., 1940-41, Wlster, Okla., 1941-48, Brimingham, Mich., 1948-61, Spiro, Okla., 1961—; chief staff Pontiac (Mich.) Osteo. Hosp., 1957-58, Leflore County Meml. Hosp., Poteau, Okla., 1965-67. Mayor of Spiro, 1969-70. Mem. Am., Okla. (trustee 1970—), Ark., Eastern Okla. (pres. 1969-70) osteo. assns., Am. Acad. Osteopathy, Am. Coll. Endocrinology, Am. Coll. Gen. Practitioners in Osteo. Medicine and Surgery, Am. Soc. Bariatrics, Spiro C. of C. (dir.; recipient outstanding citizen award 1967). Republican. Mason. Lion (pres.). Home: 109 S

Beech St Box 707 Spiro OK 74959 Office: 218 E Broadway Box 70 Spiro OK 74959

JONES, IRVING LEWIS, JR., former hist. restoration co. exec.; b. Renselaer, Ind., Feb. 23, 1903; s. Irving Lewis and Myrtle (Amsler) J.; B.S. in Bus., N.Y. U., 1928; m. Barbara H. Kendall, July 5, 1930; children—Kendall Clark, Cynthia Harvey (Mrs. Dorsey Pleasants), Irving Lewis, III. With Bankers Trust Co., N.Y.C., 1924-25, Chase Manhattan Bank, N.Y.C., 1925-26; mgr. trading dept. Bodell & Co., N.Y.C., 1926-30; tax accountant N.Y. Title and Mortgage Co., 1930-34; with Peat, Marwick & Mitchell, accountants, N.Y.C., 1930-32; treas., comptroller Colonial Williamsburg (Va.), also Williamsburg Restoration, Inc., 1934-68; asst. treas. Jamestown Corp. (Va.). Dir. United Va. Bank. Spl. lectr. Coll. William and Mary, 1950-51. Bd. dirs. Marshall Found., Bruton Parish Ch. Endowment Fund, Community Living Corp.; trustee Community Hosp.; trustee, treas. Va. 350th Anniversary Corp., Jamestown. Mem. Va. C. of C., Financial Execs. Inst., Navy League, Am. Soc. Ins. Mgmt., Richmond Soc. Financial Analysts, Peninsula Execs. Club, Sigma Phi Epsilon (alumni treas.). Episcopalian (treas., trustee, vestryman). Clubs: Rotary (past pres. and treas.), Middle Plantation, Peninsula Executives; German (pres.) (Williamsburg). Home: 335 Burns Lane Williamsburg VA 23185

JONES, J. MACK, civil engr.; b. Temple, Tex., Oct. 25, 1913; s. Jesse Oliver and Ruby (McCulloch) J.; student Temple Jr. Coll., 1931-32, U. Ark., 1936; children—Exa Virginia, Janice. Field engr. Brazos River Dist., Temple, 1936-37; field engr. U.S. Dept. Agr., College Station, Tex., 1937-38; asst. city engr., Corsicana, Tex., 1939-40, city engr., 1940-42; engring. mgr. Limestone County, Grosbeck, Tex., 1947-49; pvt. cons. engr., 1949-62; civil engr. C.E., U.S. Army, Ft. Chaffee, Ark., 1962-64, Laughlin AFB, Tex., 1964-67, airfield pavement engr. Hdqrs. ATC, USAF, 1967—. Speaker water, sewage short course Tex. A. and M. U., College Station, 1939—. Served to capt. USMCR, 1942-47. Recipient Outstanding Performance award U.S. Army, 1963. Registered profl. engr., Tex. Mem. Tex., Nat. socs. profl. engrs., Soc. Am. Mil. Engrs., Tex. Water Utilities Assn., Sigma Phi Epsilon, Theta Tau. Home: PO Box 8572 San Antonio TX 78208 Office: Hq ATC DEMM Randolph AFB TX 78148

JONES, JACK RADFORD, architect; b. Bradenton, Fla., Jan. 31, 1929; s. Berry Smith and Mary Ritchie (Whitehead) J.; A.A., U. Fla., 1948, B.Arch., 1954; postgrad. Fla. State U., 1948; m. June Johns, May 8, 1960; children—Cathye, Charles C., Cheryl, Robin, Adrianne. Foreman, Paul A. Miller-Miller Constrn. Co., Inc., Leesburg, Fla., 1957-59; sec.-treas. Miller Constrn. Co., Inc., Leesburg, 1959-63; self-employed as architect, Leesburg, 1959—. Mem. Leesburg Planning and Zoning Bd., 1961-71, chmn., 1969-70; mem. Lake County Bd. Examiners, 1968—, chmn., 1968-69. Served to lt. USNR, 1954-57. Recipient Home Design award A.I.A., 1967. Mem. A.I.A. (dir. mid-Fla. chpt. 1970), Leesburg Area C. of C. (pres. 1970), Gargoyle. Episcopalian (lay reader 1968—, mem. diocesan liturgical commn. 1970—). Elk, Rotarian. Club: Boat (Leesburg, Fla.). Home: 712 Boylston St Leesburg FL 32748 Office: 613 W Dixie Av Leesburg FL 32748

JONES, JAMES FRED, state supreme ct. justice; b. Mount Ida, Ark., Jan. 12, 1907; s. Ira Seward and Ella (Tyler) J.; LL.B., U. Ark., 1937; m. Walta Lorea Hoback, Sept. 5, 1937; children—James Voland, Vanda (Mrs. Crocker), Lyn. Admitted to Ark. bar; mem. Ark. Ho. of Reps., 1935-39; asst. pros. atty. 18th judicial dist., 1936-38; municipal judge, Little Rock, 1950-51; asso. justice Ark. Supreme Ct., Little Rock, 1967—. Mem. Pulaski, Ark., Am., Interam. bar assns., Am. Judicature Soc., Inst. Judicial Adminstrn. Methodist. Mason. Home: 1208 Silverwood Trail North Little Rock AR 72116 Office: Justice Bldg Little Rock AR 72201*

JONES, JAMES GRADY, physician; b. Pembroke, N.C., Dec. 19, 1933; s. Alton Bruce and Nora (Revels) J.; A.A., Mars Hill Coll., 1953; B.S., Wake Forest Coll., 1955; M.D., Bowman Gray Sch. Medicine, 1959; m. Jerre Roper, June 6, 1959; children—James Grady, Robert Glenn. Intern Grady Meml. Hosp., Atlanta, 1959-60; pvt. practice gen. medicine, Jacksonville, N.C., 1963-65, Jones-Kitchen Clinic, P.A., Jacksonville, 1965—; mem. staff Onswlow Meml. Hosp., chief staff, 1964-65. Commr. edn. com. Regional Med. Program N.C., 1965—; med. examiner Selective Service System, 1962—; chmn. Housing Authority, Jacksonville, 1969—. Trustee Coastal Carolina Community Coll., Jacksonville. Served to lt. USNR, 1960-62. Mem. Am. Acad. Gen. Practice N.C. Acad. Gen. Practice (chmn. com. edn.), N.C. Med. Soc. (v.p.). Baptist. Contbr. articles to jours. Home: 109 Jean Circle Jacksonville NC 28540 Office: 510 College St Jacksonville NC 28540

JONES, JAMES HAROLD, banker; b. Harrison, Ark., Aug. 26, 1930; s. Charlie Mac and Pearl Mary (Wood) J.; B.S. in Bus. Adminstrn., U. Ark., 1952; grad. Southwestern Grad. Sch. Banking, So. Meth. U., 1960; grad. Advanced Management Program, Harvard; m. Peggy Lou Bort, Apr. 2, 1960; children—James Bort, Cliff O., Lee C. With Lakewood State Bank, Dallas, 1953-54; with Republic Nat. Bank of Dallas, 1954-69, v.p., 1960—, sr. v.p., 1963-67, exec. v.p., 1967-69, also chmn. real estate loan com., mem. exec. and sr. loan coms.; pres., dir. Nat. Bank Commerce New Orleans, 1969—; v.p. The Howard Corp., Dallas, Rheims Corp. Chmn., lectr. real estate div. Southwestern Grad. Sch. Banking, 1964-65; faculty mem. Banking Sch. of South, La. State U. Bd. dirs., mem. exec. com., finance com., annuity bd. So. Bapt. Conv. Mem. Am. Bankers Assn. (mem. mortgage finance com.), U. Ark. Alumni Assn. (past dir.), C. of C. Greater New Orleans, Phi Lambda Chi. Clubs: Dallas Athletic Country: New Orleans County, International House. Baptist. Home: 440 Walnut St New Orleans LA 70118 Office: PO Box 60279 New Orleans LA 70160

JONES, JAMES REES, oil co. exec.; b. Britton, S.D., Nov. 26, 1916; s. Buell Fay and Florence (Bockler) J.; B.S. in Accountancy, U. Ill., 1938; m. Betty Jane Preston, May 23, 1943; children—Quentin Buell, Newton James, Preston Lee. Staff, Ernst & Ernest, Detroit, Kalamazoo, 1938-41; with Standard Oil Co. Ind. and subsidiaries, 1948-63, comptroller Amoco Chems. Corp., Chgo., 1956-62, mgr. auditing Standard Oil Co. Ind., Chgo., 1962-63; controller Murphy Oil Corp., El Dorado, Ark., 1963—, also dir.; controller Ocean Drilling & Exploration Co., subsidiary, El Dorado, 1963-66, sec., 1966-69, dir. 1966—, v.p., controller, dir. Deltic Farm & Timber Co., Inc. subsidiary, El Dorado, 1963—. Mem. El Dorado Water Utilities Commn., 1968—. Bd. dirs., past pres. United Fund Campaign, El Dorado. Served to capt. AUS, 1941-46. Mem. Financial Execs. Inst., Am. Petroleum Inst., (corporate accounting com. 1963—, operating com. 1968—), Mid-Continent Oil and Gas Assn., Phi Kappa Psi. Clubs: International (Washington); El Dorado Golf and Country. Home: 2001 W Oak St El Dorado AR 71730 Office: 200 Jefferson Av El Dorado AR 71730

JONES, JENKIN LLOYD, editor, publisher; b. Madison, Wis., Nov. 1, 1911; s. Richard Lloyd and Georgia (Hayden) J.; Ph.B., U. Wis., 1933; m. Juanita Carlson, Nov. 12, 1935; children—Jenkin, David, Georgia. Reporter, columnist Tulsa Tribune, 1933-36, mng. editor, 1936-38, asso. editor. 1938-41, editor, 1941—, also pub.; v.p. Tulsa Tribune Co., 1938—; writer weekly newspaper column syndicated by Gen. Features Corp.; dir. Newspaper Printing Corp. Served as communications officer USNR, 1944-46; PTO; lt. comdr. USNR. Recipient William Allen White award, 1957. Mem. Am. Soc. Newspaper Editors (pres. 1956), U.S. C. of C. (pres. 1969), Phi Gamma Delta, Sigma Delta Chi. Republican. Unitarian. Clubs: Nat. Press, Southern Hills Country. Author: The Changing World. Home: 2272 E 38th St Tulsa OK 74105 Office: Tulsa Tribune Tulsa OK 74103

JONES, JIMMIE, state ofcl.; b. Magnolia, Ark. Mar. 20, 1920; s. Stephen Herbert and Ethel (Stevens) J.; grad. So. State Coll., Ark. Law Sch.; m. Inez Smith, June 18, 1957. Became tax collector Columbia County, 1950; former land commr. State of Ark., Little Rock, auditor, 1957—. Active Boy Scouts Am. Served with AUS, USAAF, World War II; ETO. Decorated D.F.C. with oak leaf cluster, Air medal with oak leaf cluster. Named Magnolia Man of Year, 1955. Mem. V.F.W. (past post comdr.), Am. Legion. Democrat. Methodist. Mason (32 deg. Shriner). Home: Route 5 Box 344 Little Rock AR 72207 Office: State Capitol Bldg Little Rock AR 72201

JONES, JOHN EARLE, electro-mech. engr.; b. Union, S.C., Nov. 23, 1931; s. John Earle and Eleanor (Thomas) J.; B.S., U. S.C., 1953; M.S., Mass. Inst. Tech., 1957; m. Phyllis Ann Hobson, Dec. 11, 1954; children—Margaret Royce, Eleanor Thomas, Elizabeth Anne. Project engr. Gen. Electric Co., Waynesboro, Va., 1957-61; engring. mgr. IBM, Lexington, 1961—. Served from ensign to lt. USN, 1953-56; comdr. Res. Registered profl. engr., Va. Mem. Am. Soc. M.E. (chmn. Eastern N.C.), Tau Beta Pi, Sigma Alpha Epsilon. Republican. Episcopalian (vestryman). Rotarian. Patentee in field. Home: 2412 Tyson St Raleigh NC 27609 Office: IBM Engring Lab Raleigh NC 27611

JONES, JOHN GRAHAM, printing corp. exec.; b. Hubbard, Tex., Feb. 3, 1918; s. Prince Rupert and Alice (Graham) J.; student Baylor U., 1935-40; m. Wilma Marie Richter, Apr. 13, 1941; children—Ronald Graham, Judith Gay (Mrs. David Gary Evans). Salesman, Curry Office Supply, Waco, Tex., 1940-42, mgr., Austin, Tex., 1946-50; mgr., Whitley Co., Austin, 1950—, pres., 1961—. Mem. Better Bus. Bur. Served with AUS, 1942-46. Mem. Printing Industry of Am., Graphic Arts Tech. Found., Printing Industry Austin (past pres.), Austin C. of C. Baptist (deacon). Club: Craftsmans (past pres.). Home: 1512 Forest Trail Austin TX 78703 Office: 301 Brazos St Austin TX 78701

JONES, JOHN LEWIS, music pub.; b. N.Y.C., Jan. 3, 1922; s. George and Caldonia M. (Batts) J.; B.S., N.C. State Tchrs. Coll., 1915; m. Louise F. Fairon, July 26, 1948; children—John Lewis, George W., Paula M. Pres., Elvitrue Rec. Music Pub. Co., Wilmington, N.C. and N.Y.C., 1952—; founder Music Makers Network Am.-Prodns., N.Y.C.; concert pianist. Active N.C. Soc. Civil Liberties. Mem. Am. Fedn. Musicians, Music Pubs. Assn., AFTRA. Baptist. Elk. Home: 306 S 16th St Wilmington NC 28401 Office: 1306 Castle St Wilmington NC 28401

JONES, JOHN MARTIN, III, publisher; b. Sweetwater, Tenn., Dec. 11, 1914; s. Oliver King and Byrd (Browder) J.; grad. Washington and Lee U., 1937; m. Martha Arnold Susong, June 29, 1940; children—John Martin, IV, Alexander Susong, Gregg King, Edith Susong, Sarah Ingles. Advt. mgr. Gilman Paint & Varnish Co., Chattanooga, 1938-42; gen. mgr. Greeneville (Tenn.) Daily Sun, 1946—, editor, pub., 1950—; pres. Greeneville Pub. Co., Newport Pub. Co., Post Athenian Co.; pub. Athens (Tenn.) Daily Post Athenian, Marengo Pub. Co., Monroe Pub. Co.; v.p., dir. Tenn. Electro Minerals Corp., Agrl. Lime Co.; dir. First Nat. Bank, Greeneville, Sweetwater Hosiery Mills, Hamilton Nat. Bank Knoxville, Tenn. Mem. Gt. Smoky Mountain Nat. Park Commn., 1960—, State Armories Commn., Nashville, 1959—, Tenn. Higher Edn. Commn.; chmn. Govs. Emergency Traffic Safety Com., 1963; v.p. Sequoyah council Boy Scouts Am., 1958—; pres. Greene County Indsl. Found., 1950-52. Del., Democratic Nat. Conv., 1956, 60, 64, 68. Alumni bd. Washington and Lee U.; bd. dirs. Greeneville Emergency and Rescue Squad, A.R.C., Greene County Library; trustee Mental Hosp. Bd. Tenn., Tenn. Tb Hosps., Tenn.-Wesleyan Coll., Am. Newspaper Pubs. Assn. Found. Served from 2d lt. to lt. col. AUS, 1942-45. Recipient Pres.'s Cup for outstanding service in field journalism Tenn. Press Assn., 1952. Mem. Tenn. Press Assn. (pres. 1962-63), Alumni Assn. Washington and Lee U. (dir.), Greeneville C. of C. (past pres., Man of Yr. 1950), Nat. Press Club, Am. (dir.), So. (dir.) newspaper pubs. assns. Kappa Sigma. Episcopalian. Elk. Clubs: Gatlinburg (Tenn.) Ski; Link Hills Country, Exchange (Greeneville); City (Knoxville); Cumberland (Nashville). Home: Hilltop Greeneville TN 37743 Office: 200 S Main St Greeneville TN 37743

JONES, JOHN TILFORD, JR., broadcasting exec.; b. Dallas, Dec. 2, 1917; s. John Tilford and Margaret (Wilson) J.; student N.M. Mil. Inst., 1935-38, U. Tex., 1938-40; m. Winifred Ann Small, Oct. 20, 1945; children— Melissa Ann, Jesse Holman II, John Clinton. Pres., Rusk Corp., Radio Sta. KTRH, KLOL, Houston. Served from 2d lt. to capt., U.S. Army, 1940-45; ETO. Presbyn. Office: Gulf Bldg Houston TX 77002

JONES, JOHN WALTER, JR., engineer; b. Miami, Fla., Nov. 23, 1913; s. John Walter and Elinor Burwell (Hickson) J.; student Colo. Sch. Mines, 1933-35; m. Mildred Vivian Puckett, July 20, 1940; children—Elinor Burwell (Mrs. Ralph T. Pyles), Melanie Vivian (Mrs. Byron K. Brown), Ann Spotswood (Mrs. Udy C. Woods, Jr.), Walter Martin, Pamela Sue. Office engr. Biscayne Engring. Co., Miami, 1935-41; asst. airport engr. Pan Am. Airways, 1941-50; propr. J. Walter Jones, Jr. and Assos., South Boston, Va., 1950—; pres. South Boston Devel. Corp., 1967—. Mem. Va. Bd. Exam. and Certification Architects, Profl. Engrs. and Land Surveyors, 1964—, pres., 1968. Fellow Am. Soc. C.E.; mem. Am. Congress Surveying and Mapping, Danville Soc. Engring. and Sci. (pres. 1967), N.C. Soc. Surveyors, Va. Assn. Surveyors (pres. 1962), Kappa Sigma. Mason, Lion. Home: 8 Maplewood Dr South Boston VA 24592 Office: Security Bldg 554 N Main St South Boston VA 24592

JONES, JOSEPH WEST, beverage co. exec.; b. Georgetown, Del., Oct. 9, 1912; s. John Arters and Sallie Emma (West) J.; B.C.S., Beacon Coll., Wilmington, Del., 1932; m. Hattie Johns Bryan, Mar. 3, 1935 (div. 1946); 1 son, Joseph Wayne; m. 2d, Virginia Lee Rhoads, June 14, 1947; children—John Vernon, Terry Lee. With Coca-Cola Co., 1935—, asst. sec., 1956-59, asst. sec.-asst. treas., 1959-61, sec., asst. treas., 1961—. Treas., trustee Trebor Found., Atlanta; trustee Great So. Real Estate Trust, Atlanta; chmn. bd. trustees Lettie Pate Evans Found., Joseph B. Whitehead Found.; mem. governing bd. Woodward Acad., College Park. Clubs: Peachtree Racket, Atlanta Athletic, Phoenix Soc. Atlanta. Home: 3840 Randall Ridge Rd NW Atlanta GA 30327 Office: 310 North Av NW Atlanta GA 30301

JONES, L. BRUCE, music educator; b. Aurora, Ill., Oct. 11, 1905; s. Warren and Anne Wallace (Gehring) J.; B.S., Northeast Mo. State Tchrs. Coll., 1926; Mus. B., U. Ill., 1928; M.A., George Peabody Coll., Nashville, Tenn., 1942; m. Mary Floy Crossgrove, Aug. 29, 1928; children—Robert Bruce, Shirley Louise, Mary Carolyn, Evelyn Denise, Dir. bands and orch. Little Rock (Ark.) Sr. High Sch., 1928-45; supr. instrumental music Little Rock Pub. Schs., 1932-45; chmn. music edn., prof. music La. State U., 1945—, dir. bands, 1945-59, band cons. 1959—; dir. music Immanuel Baptist Ch., Little Rock, 1942-45; concert master Ark. State Symphony, condr., 1942-43; dir. music dept. 1st Bapt. Ch., Baton Rouge, 1945-67; condr. U.S.A. Band & Chorus tour Eastern U.S. and Can., 1966; guest condr. state and nat. clinics, univ. summer sch. music groups. Owner, operator Sandy Creek Farm, cattle and horses, 1952—. Mem. Am. Guild Organists (choir dirs. sect.), Ark. Sch. Band and Orch. Assn. (organizer and 1st pres.), Dixie Band and Orch. Assn. (organizer and 1st pres.). Music Educators Nat. Conf., Nat. Competition Festivals (chmn. region 7), Nat. Sch. Band Assn. (pres. 1940-45), Coll. Band Dirs. Nat. Assn. (pres. 1951-53), Am. Bandmasters Assn., Phi Mu Alpha Sinfonia, Kappa Delta Pi, Phi Delta Kappa. Mason (32 deg.). Author: Building the Instrumental Music Department. Home: 625 Delgado Dr Baton Rouge LA 70808

JONES, L. HALL, mortgage banker, realtor; b. Collierville, Tenn., Mar. 25, 1901; s. Samuel Anderson and Loretta (Hall) J.; m. Louise W. Green, June 20, 1923; children—Mary Louise (Mrs. Thomas Prewitt), L. Hall. Pres., dir. Joyner-Heard Co., Memphis, 1952, Joyner, Heard and Jones, Inc., Memphis, 1952—; sr. partner Joyner, Heard & Jones, realtors, Memphis; pres., dir. Poplar-Highland Plaza, Inc., Memphis, 1953—, Laurelwood Shopping Center, Inc., Memphis, 1961—. Episcopalian. Clubs: Memphis Country, Tenn. Home: 78 E Galloway St Memphis TN 38111 Office: 54 S Prescott St Memphis TN 38111

JONES, LAURENCE CLIFTON, educator; b. St. Joseph, Mo., Nov. 21, 1884; s. John Q. and Lydia (Foster) J.; Ph.B., State U. Ia., 1907, Certificate of Accomplishment, 1947; D. H.L., Cornell Coll., Mt. Vernon, Ia., 1947; M.A. (hon.), Tuskegee Inst.; H.H.D., Bucknell U.; D.D., Pioneer Theol. Seminary, Rockford, Ill., 1955; LL.D., Otterbein Coll., 1965; H.H.D., U. Dubuque, 1969; Ed.D., Lincoln Coll., 1970; m. Grace Morris Allen, June 29, 1912 (dec.); children— Turner Harris, Laurence C. Founded, 1909, and pres. The Piney Woods Country Life Sch., for edn. of boys and girls in Black Belt, Piney Woods, Miss.; started without funds, in open air; property valued (1946) at 500,000, and consisting of 1,700 acres of land, several large school buildings, etc.; also pub., editor The Pine Torch, of Piney Woods, Miss. In charge thrift camp campaign among colored people, Miss., during World War I. Asst. dir. Armenian Relief campaign in Miss.; Negro sec. First United War Work Drive, in Miss.; state exec. com. Negro YMCA work; adv. com. Miss. Fedn. Colored Women's Clubs. Trustee Freedoms Found. Recipient awards Freedom's Found., Founder's Soc. Am.; Silver Buffalo, Boy Scouts Am., 1970. Mem. Miss. Assn. Teachers in Colored Schs., Nat. Negro Press Assn., Nat. Negro Bus. League, Kappa Alpha Psi. Episcopalian. Author: Up Through Difficulties, 1910; Piney Woods and Its Story, 1923; The Spirit of Piney Woods, 1931; The Bottom Rail, 1933; numerous articles regarding race problem. Chautauqua lectr. Home: Piney Woods Sch Piney Woods MS 39148

JONES, LEAH ALBERTA, ret. educator; b. Ridgeland, S.C., Oct. 4, 1903; d. Paul Wesley and Fannie (Malphrus) Jones; B.S., U. Ga., 1947; M.A., George Peabody Coll. for Tchrs., 1951. Tchr. elementary sch. Ridgeland, 1928-51, prin., 1951-69, elementary supr. Jasper County Schs., 1969-71. Sec., S.C. Tchr. Edn. and Profl. Standards Commn., 1966-69. Asso. chmn. Jasper County Centennial Commn., 1961-62; mem. civil def. teaching staff; chmn. Jasper County Tricentennial Schs. Participation Program. Chmn. bd. trustees Frederic R. Pratt Meml. Library, Ridgeland. Named Jasper County Woman Year, 1962-63, 69-70, S.C. Career Woman of Year, 1970. Mem. Jasper County Edn. Assn. (past pres.), Dist. I Elementary Prins. Assn. (past pres.), Ridgeland Bus. and Profl. Women's Club (past pres.), N.E.A. (life), Sr. Citizens Am. (life), Delta Kappa Gamma (life). Mem. Order Eastern Star. Address: Great Swamp Rd Ridgeland SC 29936

JONES, LEE WENDELL, cons. structural engr.; b. Kansas City, May 12, 1929; s. Roy E. and Rachel (Matson) J.; B.S., U. Ill., 1950; m. Iris Ruth Barbier, Mar. 14, 1954; children—Casey Alan, Nancy Lee, Kirk Steven, Clifford Scott, Karl Stewart. Structural engr. Frank A. Busse, Cons. Engr., Memphis, 1950, Walter P. Moore, Cons. Engr., Houston, 1953-66; v.p., dir. Walter P. Moore & Assos., Cons. Engrs., Houston, 1967—. Mem. bd. mgmt. Westland br. YMCA, Houston, 1968-69, chmn. bd., 1969—. Served to 1st lt. C.E., AUS, 1950-52. Profl. engr. La., Tex. Mem. Am. Soc. C.E., Am. Concrete Inst. Methodist. Kiwanian (dir. S.W. Houston 1971—). Club: Civic. Home: 11630 Ashcroft St Houston TX 77035 Office: 2905 Sackett St Houston TX 77006

JONES, LEONARD BONHAM, physician; b. Gregory, Tex., Jan. 18, 1911; s. Charles Von and Ethel Jean (Butler) J.; B.S., Tex. A. and M. Coll., 1932; M.D., U. Tex., 1938; m. Velma Irene Zwilling, June 28, 1941; children—Bonnie (Mrs. David Lee Northcutt), Leana Irene (Mrs. John B. Turbeville, Jr.), Glenda (Mrs. Ronald Lee Detling), Justin Bonham. Intern, resident, Cleve., 1938-41; gen. practice medicine, San Antonio, 1946—; pres. profl. staff S.W. Tex. Meth. Hosp. Served to lt. col., M.C., AUS, 1941-46. Mem. Tex. Acad. Gen. Practice (pres.), Internat. Med. Assembly S.W. Tex. (pres.), Bexar County Med. Soc. (pres.) San Antonio C. of C. (dir.). Presbyn. Mason, Kiwanian. Home: 2151 W Gramercy Pl San Antonio TX 78201 Office: 929 Manor Dr San Antonio TX 78228

JONES, LEROY EARL, constrn. co. exec.; b. Tahoka, Tex., Mar. 1, 1922; s. Leroy Lester and Luna Lavona (Eubanks) J.; student Daniel Baker Coll., 1947-49; m. Viola A. Ory, Sept. 5, 1945; children—Betty Ann, Jerry Wayne. Pres., L. E. Jones Constrn. Co., Brownwood, Tex., 1963—; owner, L. E. Jones, contractor, Brownwood, 1946—; partner, dir. Gulf States Oil Co., 1965—; partner Forked Island Ship Yard, 1971—. Bd. dirs. Cherokee Children's Home. Served with Combat Engrs., AUS, World War II; ETO. Mem. Ch. of Christ (elder 1965—). Home: 4109 Austin Av Brownwood TX 76801 Office: 504 E Lee St Brownwood TX 76801

JONES, LEWIS EARLE, JR., physician; b. Ware Shoals, S.C., Mar. 17, 1932; s. Lewis Earle and Alpha Belle (Cox) J.; B.S., Furman U., 1954; M.D., Med. U. S.C., 1957; m. Dolores Page, Nov. 24, 1955; children— Jimmie, Belle, Kathy, Lewis. Intern, Greenville (S.C.) Gen. Hosp., 1958-59; practice medicine, specializing in family medicine, Greenville, S.C., 1961—; mem. staff Greenville Gen. Hosp., St. Francis Hosp., Greenville. Served with USAF, 1959-61. Mem. A.M.A. Am. Acad. Family Practice, S.C. Med. Assn. Baptist (deacon 1966—). Home: 8 Andrea Lane Greenville SC 29607 Office: 1635 E North St Greenville SC 29607

JONES, LEWIS WADE, sociologist, educator; b. Cuero, Tex., Mar. 13, 1910; s. Wade E. and Lucynthia (McDade) J.; A.B., Fisk U., 1931; postgrad. (Social Sci. Research Council fellow) U. Chgo., 1931-32; M.A. (Rosenwald Fund fellow) Columbia, 1939, Ph.D., 1955; m. Queen E. Shootes, Aug. 13, 1966. Research asst., supr. field studies, instr. sociology dept. social sci. Fisk U., 1932-42; reports analyst domestic br. Bur. Spl. Services, OWI, 1943; editor Informer Papers, 1947-48; asst. prof. sociology, dir. research rural life council, research coordinator, research prof., dir. social sci. research, Tuskegee Inst. (Ala.) Sch. Edn., prof. sociology, dir. research manpower tng. and research project, 1966—. Cons. Opportunities Industrialization

Centers, Bur. Social Sci. Research, Dept. Labor, Women's Bur., Delegacy for Extra-Mural Studies, Oxford U. Mem. race relations dept. United Ch. Christ, 1961-67; past pres. Multi-Racial Corp. Bd. dirs. Nat. Sharecroppers Fund. Highlander Research and Edn. Center, Nat. Com. on Employment of Youth, Nat. Com. for Edn. Migrant Children, Rural Advancement Fund. Served with AUS, 1943-46. Mem. Omega Psi Phi. Democrat. Episcopalian. Author: (With Charles S. Johnson) A Statistical Atlas of Southern Counties; Shifts in the Negro Population of Ala., 1949; (with Adella A. Shields) Health Care Services and Facilities in the Southern Appalachian Region, 1955; (with Dr. Herman H. Long) The Negotiation of Desegregation in Ten Southern Cities, 1965. Asso. editor Negro Yearbook, 1952. Contbr. articles to profl. jours. Home: 310 Bulls Av Tuskegee Institute AL 36088

JONES, LOUIS DAN, lawyer; b. Washington, Mar. 9, 1911; s. Nathan Dan and Ola May (Porterfield) J.; B.S. in Petroleum Engring., U. Okla., 1933; LL.B., George Washington U., 1939. Admitted to D.C. bar, 1939; since practiced in Washington; atty. Ind. Petroleum Assn. Am., 1946-60, gen. counsel, 1960—. Home: 3814 Roberts Lane Arlington VA 22207 Office: 1110 Ring Bldg Washington DC 20036

JONES, MARVIN, judge; b. nr. Valley View, Cooke County, Tex.; s. H. K. and Dosia J.; A.B., Southwestern U., 1905; LL.B., U. Tex., 1907; LL.D., Tex. A. and M. Coll. Admitted to Tex. bar, 1907; practiced at Amarillo; apptd. chmn. bd. legal examiners 7th Supreme Jud. Dist. of Tex., 1913; mem. 65th to 76th Congresses (1917-41), 18th Tex. Dist.; chmn. House Com. on Agr., Dec. 1931-Nov. 20, 1940; judge U.S. Court of Claims, 1940-47, chief justice, 1947-64, sr. judge, 1964—; asst. to Hon. James F. Byrnes 1943; pres. UN Conf. on Food and Agr. 1943; mem. War Moblzn. Com., U.S. food adminstr., 1943-45. Democrat. Mem. Am. Legion, Order of Coif (hon.). Methodist. Mason. Woodman. Elk. Author: How War Food Saved American Lives; Should Uncle Sam Pay—When and Why Home: 2807 Hughes St Amarillo TX also University Club 1135 16th St NW Washington DC 20006

JONES, MARY GARDINER, lawyer, govt. ofcl.; b. N.Y.C., Dec. 10, 1920; d. Charles Herbert and Anna Livingston (Short) Jones; B.A., Wellesley Coll., 1943; J.D., Yale, 1948. Intern tchr. George Sch., Newtown, Pa., 1943-44; research analyst research and analysis br. Internat. Law sect. OSS, Washington, 1944-46; admitted to N.Y. State bar, 1949; asso. firm Donovan, Leisure, Newton and Irvine, N.Y.C., 1948-53; chief trial atty. N.Y. Office, Antitrust div. Dept. of Justice, N.Y.C., 1953-61; asso. firm Webster, Sheffield, Fleischmann, Hitchcock & Chrystie, N.Y.C., 1961-64; commr. FTC, Washington, 1964—. Trustee, Wellesley Coll., 1971-72, Suomi Coll., 1972—, Colgate U., 1972—; mem. exec. com. Yale Law Sch. Assn., 1971—; nat. adv. council Hampshire Coll. Mem. Am. (antitrust sect., subcom. on patents, trademarks and knowhow), Fed. (trade regulation com.) bar assns., Assn. Bar City of N.Y. (internat. law com., trade regulation com.), Am. Arbitration Assn. (past mem. panel of arbitrators), Assn. Consumer Research (adv. council). Contbr. articles to law jours. Home: 3037 West Lane Keys NW Washington DC 20007 Office: FTC 6th and Pennsylvania Av NW Washington DC 20580

JONES, MICHAEL GARY, Democratic nat. committeeman; b. Chattanooga, Oct. 23, 1946; s. Claude M. and Maude (Swanson) J.; A.B.A., Dalton Jr. Coll., 1969; B.A. in Polit. Sci., U. Tenn. at Chattanooga, 1971; m. Jackie O'Neal, June 14, 1969. Ga. youth coordinator campaign Ga. Gov. Jimmy Carter, 1970; vice-chmn. Ga. Dem. com., 1971—; mem. Dem. nat. com., 1972—. Del. White House Conf. Youth. Baptist. Address: 702B Shelly Lane Rossville GA 30741*

JONES, MILNOR, surgeon; b. Athens, Tenn., Mar. 14, 1925; s. Cyril William and Billie (Dodson) J.; B.A., Vanderbilt U., 1945, M.D., 1948; m. Miriam Conner, Aug. 29, 1953; children—Cyril William III, Miriam Conner, Jonathan Milnor, Camille Chambers. Intern, Grady Meml. Hosp., Emory U., Atlanta, 1948, resident surgery, 1949-52, chief resident surgery, 1952-53, instr. surgery, 1952-53; practice medicine, specializing in surgery, Athens, Tenn., 1953—. Dir., mem. exec. com. First Nat. Bank of McMinn County. Vice chmn. Athens Bd. Edn., 1967—. Chmn. bd. trustees Epperson Hosp., Athens, 1970—. Diplomate Am. Bd. Surgery. Fellow A.C.S., Southeastern Surg. Soc.; mem. Chattanooga Acad. Surgeons, A.M.A., So. Med. Assn. Democrat. Episcopalian. Home: 127 Highland Av NE Athens TN 37303 Office: 7 Grove St Athens TN 37303

JONES, MORGAN, JR., banker; b. Abilene, Tex., Sept. 5, 1910; s. Morgan and Jessie Kenan (Wilder) J.; B.S. in M.E., Rice U., 1932; M.A., Wharton Sch. of U. Pa., 1934; m. Mary Elizabeth Whatley, June 3, 1937; children—Harriet Jane, Elizabeth Kenan. Engaged in engring. and sales Hydril Co., Houston, 1934-40; mgmt. duties with div. Morgan Jones Estate, Abilene, Tex., 1940-45; engaged in mgmt. trusts and investments, 1945—; partner Jones & Fulgham, real estate and oil, 1948—; v.p., dir. Southwest Savs. and Loan Assn., Abilene, 1953-68; chmn. bd. Bank of Commerce, Abilene, 1968—; dir. Lone Star Gas Co., Santa Anna Tile Co. Mem. Gov.'s Com. on Pub. Edn., 1966-69; mem. Abilene Sch. Bd., 1951-72, pres., 1956-70; mem. exec. com. Tex. Sch. Bd. Assn., 1957-62; del. White House Conf. Edn., 1955; chmn. Abilene United Fund, 1957-58, bd. dirs., 1955-65; pres. W. Tex. council Girls Scouts U.S.A., 1952-56. Trustee, endowment com. McMurry Coll. Named Outstanding Citizen Abilene, 1958, Outstanding Citizen Contbg. Most to Edn., 1956; recipient Thanks Badge award Girl Scouts Am., 1955. Registered profl. engr., Tex. Mem. Abilene C. of C. (pres. 1956), Rice U. Alumni Assn., Tex. Soc. Profl. Engrs., Tau Beta Pi. Methodist (ofcl. bd.). Home: 3435 S 9th St Abilene TX 79605 Office: PO Box 1320 Abilene TX 79604

JONES, MORTON EDWARD, chemist; b. Alhambra, Ca., Apr. 12, 1928; s. Edward P. and Bonnibel S. (Sanford) J.; B.S., U. Cal. at Berkeley, 1949; Ph.D. in Chemistry, Cal. Inst. Tech., 1953; m. Patricia I. Walker, Mar. 18, 1951; children—Shelley, Steven, Kent, Jay. With Tex. Instruments, Inc., Dallas, 1953—, sr. scientist, 1961-65, dir. Phys. Scis. Research Lab., 1965—. Mem. materials sci. vis. com. U. So. Cal., 1967—; chmn. Solid State Device Research Conf., 1968; vice chmn. Gordon Research Conf. on Chemistry and Mettalurgy of Semicondrs., 1971. Mem. Richardson Park and Recreation Commn., 1966-71; chmn. judging Internat. Sci. Fair, 1966; chmn. judging Dallas Regional Sci. Fair, 1966-69, dir., 1972. Precinct vice chmn. Dallas Republican Com., 1954-62; del. Tex. Rep. Conv., 1964, 68; alternate del. Nat. Rep. Conv., 1968; mem. exec. com. Tex. Rep. Com., 1968—; chmn. Tex. Patronage com. Exec. Office Pres. and Sci. Agys., 1969—. Mem. I.E.E.E. (sr.), Electrochem. Soc. (past vice chmn. semicondrs.), Tex. Acad. Sci., Sigma Xi. Episcopalian. Contbr. articles to tech. jours., chpts. to books. Patentee in field. Home: 619 Northill St Richardson TX 75080 Office: PO Box 5936 MS 145 Dallas TX 75222

JONES, NEWTON BOND, educator; b. Rome, Ga., July 22, 1920; s. Walter Philip and Berta (Simmons) J.; A.B., Emory U., 1941, M.A., 1946; Ph.D., U. Va., 1950; m. Catherine Scott Wing, Nov. 29, 1946; 1 dau., Ellen Cabaniss. Research asst. Va. World War II History Commn., Charlottesville, 1946-47; asso. prof. Presbyn. Coll., Clinton, S.C., 1950-51, prof., chmn. dept. history, 1951-59, 60-62; asso. prof. Furman U., Greenville, S.C., 1959-60, prof. history, 1962—, dir. humanities div., 1969—. Mem. S.C. Archives and History Commn., 1962—; mem. scholarly activities com. S.C. Tricentennial Commn., 1967-70. Served to capt. Q.M.C., AUS, 1942-46. Mem. S.C. Hist. Assn. (pres. 1961-62), Am. Assn. U. Profs. (pres. chpt. 1965-66), Chi Phi. Democrat. Episcopalian. Author: (with others) Pursuits of War, 1948, The Old Dominion, 1964; Records of the Public Treasurers of South Carolina, 1725-1776, 1969. Contbr. articles to profl. jours. Home: 321 Crescent Av Greenville SC 29605 Office: Dept History Furman U Greenville SC 29613

JONES, OLGA ANNA, author, editor; b. Hollansburg, O.; d. Amos and Elizabeth Jane (Harrison) Jones; student Earlham Coll., summers 1908-10; spl. student Ohio State U., 1915-18, 24. Sch. adminstr. Darke County (O.) pub. schs., 1910-15; editorial writer Columbus (O.) Citizen, 1918-22; editor Ohio League Women Voters, 1922-23; asso. dir. Council Social Agencies Columbus, 1923-28; editor Ohio Tchr. mag., dir. Ohio Tchrs. Bur., 1928-31; mem. Pres. Orgn. Employment and Relief, 1931-32; adminstrv. asst. emergency relief div. RFC, 1932-33; dir. sect. Am. Friends Service Com., 1933-35; editor-in-chief U.S. Office Edn., 1935-48, FSA (now Dept. Health, Edn., and Welfare), 1948-50, cons. internat. edn. div., 1958-61; writer, editorial cons., 1950—. Pres. YWCA, Columbus, 1921-23. Mem. Columbus City Council (1st woman) 1922-28. Mem. Ohio State U. Assn., (pres. Washington 1951), N.E.A. (life), Jr. League (hon.), Delta Kappa Gamma, Phi (hon. mem.). Mem. Soc. of Friends. Clubs: Women's Nat. Press, Altrusa (pres. Washington 1936-38). Author: Churches of the Presidents in Washington, 1954; enlarged edit., 1961; What a World for Peace, 1958; also various govt. reports, newspaper and mag. articles. Address: 3133 Connecticut Av NW Washington DC 20008

JONES, OSCAR FREER, JR., lawyer; b. Oglesby, Tex., Oct. 15, 1909; s. Oscar Freer and Margaret G. (Greenwood) J.; student U. Tex., 1926-31, U. Ky., 1929; m. Laila E. Wallace, June 7, 1930 (div.); children—Oscar Freer III, James W., Betsy (Mrs. Wm. K. Kirkgard); m. 2d, Louise Bailey, Feb. 10, 1972. Admitted to Tex. bar, 1933, U.S. Supreme Ct. bar, 1949; practiced in Waco, Tex., 1933-71, Austin, Tex., 1972—; partner firm Sheehy, Jones, Cureton, Westbrook & Lovelace and predecessors, 1936-70; v.p., gen. counsel, dir. Am.-Amicable Life Ins. Co., Waco, 1938-69; asst. dist. atty., Waco, 1970-71; atty. for Tex., Gen. Land Office, Vets. Land Bd., 1971. Past mem., trustee Waco Sch. Bd. Mem. Assn. Life Ins. Counsel, Am. Life Conv. (legal sect.). Episcopalian. Club: Waco Ridgewood Country. Home: 2004 Elton Lane Austin TX 78703 Office: 2825 Hancock Dr Austin TX 78731

JONES, PAUL ISAIAH, supt. schs.; b. Sidney, Tex., June 19, 1913; s. William I. and Lena L. (Hellums) J.; student Tarleton Coll., 1933-35; B.S., Howard Payne Coll., 1947; M.A., W. Tex. U., 1950; postgrad. Tex. Tech. U., 1971; m. Addie Lee Cotten, June 10, 1939; 1 son, William Paul. Bookkeeper shipping Walker-Smith Wholesale, Brownwood, Hobbs, N.M., 1935-37; salesman Tex. News Co., Dallas, 1937-39; tchr. pub. schs., Hasse, Tex., 1940-41; electrician, numerous locations, 1941-45; tchr. pub. schs., Sidney, Tex., 1945-48, supt., 1946-48; tchr. math. high sch., Littlefield, Tex., 1948-49, prin., 1949-65, asst. supt,. 1965-67, supt., 1967—. Chmn. P.T.A., 1957; chmn. Dist. Athletic Conf., 1967-68. Democratic precinct chmn. 1956-62; del. State Dem. Conv., 1960. Mem. County Sch. Adminstrs. (chmn. 1954, 62), Elementary Prins. Assn. (dist. chmn., mem. state exec. bd. 1958), Am., Tex. assns. sch. adminstrs. Rotarian. Home: 224 E 23rd St Littlefield TX 79339 Office: 105 N Lake St Littlefield TX 79339

JONES, RAGON ENTRENKEN, cons. engr.; b. Georgianna, Ala., Oct. 28, 1922; s. James Daniel and Ola Mae (McLain) J.; B.S. in Mech. Engring., U. Ala., 1949; student Alexander Hamilton Bus. Mgmt., 1957; m. Nellie Ruth Simpson, Mar. 15, 1946; children—Lynda Nell, Barry Lee, Daniel Ragon. Engr., draftsman J. B. Converse & Co., Mobile, Ala., A.C. Parker, 1946; city engr. Tuscaloosa, Ala., 1947-49; grad. tng. course Allis-Chalmers Mfg. Co,, Milw., 1949-50; eng. Standard Brass & Mfg. Co., New Orleans, 1951; gen. practice mech. contracting, engring., research, cons., Mobile, 1952-64; cons. engr;, 1964—, faculty Tex. A. and M.U. Mgr;, coach Dixie Little League, Gulfport, Miss., 1967, 68, 69, Dixie Sr. League, 1969, sr. all-star mgr., 1971. Served with USNR, 1942-45. Recipient Gen. Electric award for heat pump devel., 1955. Registered profl. engr., Ala., La., Miss., Tex. Mem. Nat., Miss. socs. profl. engrs. Baptist. Patentee in field. Home: 702 S Coulter Dr Bryan TX 77801 Office: 2800 Texas Av Bryan TX 77801

JONES, RAYMOND LAWRENCE, educator; b. Johnson City, Tenn., Nov. 28, 1924; s. Lawrence and Elizabeth (Pendleton) J.; B.S., East Tenn. State U., 1950; M.S., U. Tenn., 1952; D.Ed., U. Fla., 1960; m. Martha Rebecca Noblitt, June 3, 1950; children—Elizabeth Alace, Rebecca Kathryn, Nancy Lawrence, Rachel Jennifer. Tchr. pub. schs. Knox and Sullivan Counties, Tenn., 1950-54; instr. East Tenn. State U., 1954-57; instr. U. Fla., 1957-61; prof. bus. East Carolina U., Greenville, 1961—; ednl. cons. pub. schs.; dir., cos. personal financial planning seminars; cons. Eastern N.C. Devel. Inst. Served with USAAF, 1943-46. Mem. Am. Bus. Law Assn., Am. Assn. U. Profs. (v.p. East Carolina U. chpt. 1966-68), Phi Delta Kappa, Phi Beta Lambda, Kappa Delta Pi, Pi Omega Pi, Beta Gamma Sigma. Mem. Disciples of Christ Ch. Home: 1708 S Elm St Greenville NC 27834

JONES, RICHARD EARLE, lawyer; b. Jones Mill, Ala., Apr. 5, 1894; s. James Wiley and Mary Frances (Hughes) J.; A.B., U. Ala., 1914, M.A., 1915, LL.B., 1919; m. Lucille Foster, June 10, 1922; children—Richard Earle, Sara Frances. Admitted to Ala. bar 1919; partner Knox, Jones, Woolf & Merrill, Anniston. Dir. 1st Nat. Bank Anniston, Classe Ribbon Co., Inc. Mem. Ala. State Democratic Exec. Com., 1924-40, elector for pres., v.p., 3 terms. Mem. City Bd. Edn., Anniston, 1935-46; chmn. merit system council County Depts. Pub. Welfare, 1947-51. Capt. F. A., AUS, World War I. Mem. Anniston C. of C., Am., Ala., Calhoun County bar assns., Ala. State Bar, Phi Beta Kappa. Baptist. Kiwanian. Home: 1420 Woodstock Av Anniston AL 36201 Office: Comml Nat Bank Bldg Anniston AL 36201

JONES, RICHARD LLOYD, JR., newspaper exec.; b. Nyack, N.Y., Feb., 22, 1909; s. Richard Lloyd and Georgia (Hayden) J.; student Culver Mil. Acad., 1925, Tome Sch., Port Deposit, Md., 1926; Ph.B., U. Wis., 1932; m. Martha Meredeth Corder, Mar. 4, 1933; children—Richard, Dana. Apprentice mech. depts. Tulsa Tribune, 1933-34, with telegraph desk, 1935, display advt. dept., 1935-38, became v.p., bus. mgr., 1938, now pres.; v.p., bus. mgr. Newspaper Printing Corp., 1941-51, pres., 1951; v.p., treas. Hennepin Paper Co., Little Falls, Minn., 1953-56; dir. Brookside State Bank, Tulsa, N.Y. World's Fair 1964-65, Douglas Aircraft Co., A.P. Chmn. Tulsa Airport Authority; dir. state fair, livestock expn., Tulsa. Served as lt. USNR, World War II, comdg. officer gun crew U.S.S. Sharon Victory, U.S.S. Dickinson Victory. Mem. Tulsa C. of C. (dir. 1954—, pres. 1960-61), So. Newspaper Pubs. Assn. (chmn. labor com. 1948-52, pres. 1953-54, chmn. bd. 1954-55), Am. Newspaper Pubs. Assn. (chmn. bd. bur. advt. 1956-58), Aviation Writers' Assn., Phi Gamma Delta. Unitarian. Club: Southern Hills Country (Tulsa). Home: 1754 E 30th St Tulsa OK 74114 Office: Tulsa Tribune 315 S Boulder St Tulsa OK 74110

JONES, ROBERT CUBA, cultural center exec.; b. Gilbara, Oriente, Cuba, May 12, 1902; s. Sylvester and May (Mather) J.; A.B., Earlham Coll., 1923; postgrad. George Williams Coll., 1923-24, U. Chgo., 1923-40; LL.D., Earlham Coll., 1969; m. Ingeborg Hecht, Sept. 15, 1946; 1 dau., Diana May. Dir., Pan Am. Council, Chgo., 1940-42; asso. chief div. labor and social affairs Pan Am. Union, 1942-46, chief, 1946-49; sr. social affairs officer UN, 1949-53; dir. Internat. Cultural Center, Mexico, 1953-71, chmn. bd., 1971—. Mem. Staff Pres.' Commn. on Migratory Labor, 1950-51. Recipient Distinguished Alumni award George Williams Coll. Distinguished Service certificate Western Ill. U. Fellow A.A.A.S., Am. Sociol. Assn.; mem. Am. Polit. Sci. Assn., Am. Econ. Assn., Am. Anthrop. Assn., Soc. Applied Anthropology, Mexican Anthrop. Soc., Mexican Sociol. Assn., Societe des Americanistes de Paris. Author books and articles in field. Home: Chilpancingo 23 Mexico 11 DF Mexico

JONES, ROBERT E., judge, b. 1906; LL.B., Atlanta Law Sch. Admitted to Ga. bar, 1946, since practiced in Atlanta; municipal judge, gen. div. Atlanta Municipal Ct. Address: 165 Decatur St SE Atlanta GA 30303*

JONES, ROBERT E., JR., congressman, lawyer; b. Scottsboro, Ala., June 12, 1912; s. Robert E. and Augusta (Smith) J.; LL.B., U. Ala., 1937; m. Christine Francis, Apr. 9, 1938; 1 son, Robert E. Admitted to Ala. bar, 1937; established law practice with firm, Brewton and Jones, Scottsboro, Ala.; elected judge, Jackson County Ct., 1940, reelected in absentia, 1945; elected to 80th Congress in spl. election to fill vacancy created by John J. Sparkman's election to U.S. Senate; reelected to 81st to 92d Congresses. Served as gunnery officer USN, 1942-46, Atlantic, PTO. Mem. V.F.W., Am. Legion, Kappa Alpha. Home: Scottsboro AL 35768 Office: House Office Bldg Washington DC 20515

JONES, R(OBERT) EUGENE, educator, author; b. Emporia, Kan., July 21, 1924; s. Carl Shem and Edna Elizabeth (Ratcliff) J.; B.S., Kan. State Tchrs. Coll., 1949; M.A., U. Cal. at Berkeley, 1954, postgrad., 1958-59; m. Alice Rose Landham, Aug. 7, 1960; 1 son, Carlin Eugene, 1 stepdau., Elizabeth Ruth Edwards. Coordinator distributive edn. Victoria (Tex.) Pub. Schs., 1949-52; dormitory supr., ednl. counselor Nurnberg (Germany) Am. Dependents Schs., 1954-55; western states mgr. Lang. Master Dept., McGraw-Hill Book Co., San Francisco, 1956-57; research asst., cons. on field service projects, sch. edn. U. Cal., Berkeley, 1957-58; asst. prof. edn., supr. student tchrs. Jacksonville (Ala.) State U., 1959—. Cons. in curriculum and instrn. Pres., Anniston (Ala.) PTA, 1966, Jacksonville Elementary P.T.A., 1971-72; active Boy Scouts Am. Served with USAAF, 1943-45; CBI. Mem. N.E.A., Ala. Edn. Assn., Phi Delta Kappa, Kappa Delta Pi. Kiwanian. Author: Acme Plan of Instruction, 1966. Contbr. articles to profl. jours. Home: 706 7th Av Jacksonville AL 36265

JONES, ROBERT HUBBARD, real estate exec.; b. Charlotte, N.C., May 29, 1928; s. Raymond Allen and Lucille Seymour (Hubbard) J.; B.C.E., Ga. Inst. Tech., 1951; m. Louise McLendon, June 18, 1964; children—Stephen Alan, Darrel Scot; stepchildren—John E. Bailey, Jr., Ralph M. Bailey. Pres., Old S. Investment Co., Atlanta, 1963—; pres. RHJ, Inc., Atlanta, 1961—; pres. All Pro Enterprises, Inc., Atlanta, 1971—, Planned Investment Co., Atlanta, 1969—. Chmn. United Appeal, 1959, Ocean View Meml. Hosp. Fund Drive, 1958. Mem. Ocean Hwy. Assn. (dir., v.p. 1958-59), Myrtle Beach C. of C. (pres. 1958-59). Rotarian. Club: Georgia Tech. 1000 (Atlanta). Home: 3873 Dumbarton Rd NW Atlanta GA 30327 Office: 331 Cleveland Av SW Atlanta GA 30315

JONES, ROBERT L., JR., lawyer; b. Apr. 5, 1922; A.B., Hendrix Coll., 1942; LL.B. with honors, U. Ark., 1948. Admitted to Ark. bar, 1948, since practiced in Fort Smith; spl. asst. U.S. Atty.'s Office, 1950; U.S. commr., 1949-50. Served as 1st lt. AUS, 1950-52. Mem. Am., Ark. (pres. 1969-70), Sebastian County bar assns., Internat. Assn. Ins. Counsel, Phi Alpha Delta. Address: Merchants National Bank Bldg Fort Smith AR 72902

JONES, ROBERT LEE, justice Supreme Ct. Miss.; b. Brookhaven, Miss., Feb. 7, 1898; s. P.Z. and Margaret (Edmanson) J.; student law U. Miss., 1923-24; m. Elizabeth Butterfield, Oct. 28, 1924; children—Elizabeth B. (Mrs. Darwin A. Blanke), Robert E. Ofcl. ct. reporter, 1915-23; admitted to Miss. bar, practiced in Brookhaven, Miss., until 1960; asso. justice Supreme Ct. Miss., Jackson, 1961—. Office: Supreme Court Miss Jackson MS 39201

JONES, ROBERT RUSSELL, cons. engr.; b. Kearney, Neb., Feb. 26, 1922; s. Russell H. and Emma (Braksiek) J.; cadet USCG Acad., 1940-42; B.S. in Engring., U. Mich., 1943; m. Mary Ruth Martin, June 30, 1944; children—Mary Elizabeth, John Russell. Jr. naval architect Md. Drydock Co., Balt., 1943-46; mech. engr. Pub. Bldgs. Adminstrn., Washington, 1946-53, chief mech. estimator, 1958-61, chief mech.-elec. engr., 1961-67; partner Syska & Hennessy cons. engrs., 1967—; asso. Gen. Engring. Assos., Washington, 1953-58. Pres., Tulip Hill Citizens Assn., 1962-63. Registered profl. engr., D.C., Md., Va., N.C., Pa., Cal., Mich. Mem. Nat. Soc. Profl. Engrs., Am. Soc. Heating, Air Conditioning and Refrigeration Engrs., Am. Soc. Plumbing Engrs., Washington Bldg. Congress, Bldg. Mgrs. Assn., Tau Beta Pi. Methodist. Mech. engr. designer 3 U.S. embassies. Home: 1 Bay Tree Lane Washington DC 20016 Office: 1720 Eye St NW Washington DC 20006

JONES, RONALD, mech. engr.; b. Evansville, Ind., Aug. 25, 1924; s. Sylvester H. and Elton (Ashworth) J.; B.S., Purdue U., 1949; m. Betty Jeanne Albright, Feb. 23, 1946; children—Donald Michael, Paula Janeen, Keith Allen, Kevin Bryce. With Phillips Petroleum Co., 1950—, engr., Bartlesville, Okla., 1950-57, materials engr., Odessa, Tex., 1957-64, cons. engr., 1964—. Served with USNR, 1943-46. Registered profl. engr., Okla. Mem. Nat. Assn., Corrosion Engrs. Democrat. Home: 3420 Boulder St Odessa TX 79760 Office: 4th and Washington St Odessa TX 79760

JONES, ROY WINFIELD, ret. educator; b. Shawnee, Okla., Sept. 16, 1905; s. William Winfield and Grace (McCreery) J.; A.B. magna cum laude, Oklahoma City U., 1927; M.S., Kan. State U., 1928; Ph.D., U. Okla., 1937; m. Maurine King, Sept. 1, 1928; children—Neil Winfield, Marian King. Lab. asst. biology Oklahoma City U., 1925-27; research asst. parasitology Kan. State U., 1927-28; high sch. tchr., Alexandria, La., 1928; mem. faculty Central State Coll., Edmond, Okla., 1929-47, dean coll., acting dean men., 1939-47, prof. biology, head dept., 1936-47; prof. zoology, chmn. biol. sci. course Okla. A. and M. Coll., 1947-51; prof. zoology, head dept. Okla. State U., Stillwater, 1951-71, prof. emeritus, 1971—. Chmn. Okla. Com. Improvement Sci. Instrn., 1958-68. Served to lt. comdr. USNR, 1942-45; capt. Res. ret. Collecting Net scholar Marine Biol. Sta., Woods Hole, Mass., 1934. Fellow A.A.A.S., Okla. Acad. Sci. (pres. 1939-40); mem. Am. Biology Tchrs. Assn., Nat. Okla. edn. assns., Am. Soc. Zoologists, Am. Micros. Soc., Soc. Exptl. Biology and Medicine, Nat. Sci. Tchrs. Assn., Am. Inst. Biol. Scis., Am. Legion, Sigma Xi, Phi Kappa Phi, Kappa Delta Pi, Beta Beta Beta, Phi Sigma, Sigma Phi Epsilon, Pi Kappa Delta. Methodist. Lion. Author: (with I.E. Wallen) Biological Science Notebook, 1957; also articles. Home: 2030 W Admiral Rd Stillwater OK 74074

JONES, RUDOLPH, coll. pres.; b. Winton, N.C., June 27, 1910; s. E.R. and Annie (Walden) J.; A.B., Shaw U., 1930; M.A., Cath U. Am., 1947, Ph.D., 1952; m. Mildred O. Parker, Feb. 16, 1935; 1 son, Rudolph Bernard Jones. Prin. Currituck County Tng. Sch., Snowden, N.C., 1931-37; sr. interviewer N.C. Employment Service, Rocky Mount, N.C., 1938-40; student work supr. Nat. Youth Adminstrn., Raleigh, N.C., 1940-42, finance officer master project, Washington, 1942-43; tchr. math. Dunbar High Sch., Washington, 1949-50; tchr., acting dean, then dean Fayetteville Tchrs. Coll., 1952-56, pres., 1956—. Bd. dirs. Fuller Sch. Exceptional Children Fayetteville, Price economist OPS, Washington, 1951-52. Served as seaman 1/c USNR, 1944-45. Mem. Fayetteville Area C. of C. (bd. dirs.), N.E.A., N.C. Coll. Conf., Am. Legion, Alpha Phi Alpha, Pi Gamma Mu. Presbyn. Mason. Address: Fayetteville State Coll Fayetteville NC 28301

JONES, SCRANTON, lawyer, educator; b. Ft. Worth, July 29, 1921; s. Harper and Elizabeth (Boulware) J.; student Tex. Christian U., 1938-40; B.A., U. Tex., 1942, LL.B., 1947; m. Joyce Pegram, Sept. 6, 1947; children—Allison, Julieanne. Admitted to Tex. bar, 1947; since practiced in Ft. Worth; partner Jones & Morris, Attys. Ft. Worth, 1952-68; spl. asst. atty. gen. Tex., Austin, 1962-63; asst. prof. bus. law Tex. Christian U., 1968—; v.p., dir. S. Tex. Water Co., Rosharon; city councilman, mayor pro-tem Ft. Worth, 1963-67. Bd. dirs. Tarrant County Hist. Soc., Council on Alcoholism (pres. Tarrant County Area 1968-69). Served with USNR, 1942-46. Mem. Am., Ft. Worth bar assns., State Bar Tex., Am. Legion. Episcopalian. Mason, Rotarian (dist. gov. 1967-68). Home: 4309 Inwood Rd Fort Worth TX 76110 Office: Tex Christian U Fort Worth TX 76129

JONES, THEODORE CORNELIUS, dentist; b. Jackson, Miss., Sept. 29, 1941; s. George and Mildred (Brent) J.; B.S., Tougaloo Coll., 1962; D.D.S., Howard U., 1966; m. Clintoria Inge, Aug. 9, 1964; children—Dana Lorraine, Vann George-Clinton. Individual practice dentistry, Jackson, 1969—. Dental cons. Friends of Children Miss., Jackson, 1970-71, Jackson Hinds Comprehensive Health Center, 1970-71. Financial sec., bd. dirs. Farish St. br. YMCA, 1970-71; mem. Musica Sacra Singers, 1969-71. Bd. dirs. Theatre Center Miss., 1970—. Served with USAF, 1966-68. Recipient Appreciation award YMCA, 1970; Research fellow Howard U., 1963-64. Mem. Am., Nat. dental assns., Jackson Tougaloo Alumni Club (pres., 1971-72), Alpha Phi Alpha. Democrat. Episcopalian. Home: 1927 Barrett St Jackson MS 39204 Office: 1236 Valley St Jackson MS 39203

JONES, THEODORE LUTRELL, lawyer; b. Tifton, Ga., May 21, 1934; s. Claude Vernon and Lenora (Suggs) J.; student Abraham Baldwin Agrl. Coll., 1951-53; B.S. in Bus. Adminstrn., Northwestern State Coll. La., 1960; LL.B., U. Miss., 1963; LL.M. in Taxation, Georgetown U., 1970; m. Sarah Wonders, Feb. 14, 1966; children—Claude Vernon, Theodore Wonders. Admitted to Miss. bar, 1963; mem. law firm Long & Steeth, Jena, La., 1963-65, Elliott & Naftalin, Washington, 1968-69; asst. collector revenue (tax policy) State of La., Baton Rouge, 1969—; of counsel law firm McCollister, Belcher, McCleary & Fazio, Baton Rouge, 1970—. Adminstrv. asst. U.S. Congressman 8th Dist. La., 1965; spl. asst. to Gov. La., 1966-68. Alternate del. Democratic Nat. Conv., Chgo., 1968. Served with USAF, 1954-58. Mem. Am., Miss. bar assns., Phi Alpha Delta. Mason. Home: 1808 Chopin Baton Rouge LA 70809 Office: American Bank Bldg Baton Rouge LA 70801

JONES, THOMAS FRANKLIN, JR., univ. pres., elec. engr.; b. Henderson, Tenn., July 9, 1916; s. Thomas Franklin and Adye Mae (Moore) J.; B.S., Miss. State Coll., 1939; M.S., Mass. Inst. Tech., 1940, ScD., 1952; LL.D., The Citadel, 1968; D.Eng., Purdue U., 1971; m. Mary Katherine Butterworth, Mar. 9, 1942; children—Thomas, James, Jonathan, Katherine, Andrew. Physicist underwater sound, harbor def. Naval Research Lab., 1941-47; instr. Mass. Inst. Tech., 1947, research asso. guided missiles, analog computation and analysis, 1948-49, asst. prof., 1949-54, asso. prof. charge circuits, electronics and measurement lab., 1954-58; head Purdue U. Sch. Elec. Engring., 1958-62; pres. U. S.C., 1962—. Spl. adviser NSF, 1961-66; mem. Nat. Acad. Scis. Adv. Commn. on Post-Doctoral Study, 1966-69; exec. com. Hwy. Research Bd., 1967-70; mem. Nat. Sci. Bd., 1966—; mem. adv. bd. on ednl. requirements to sec. navy, 1963-66; dir. Engrs. Council Profl. Devel., 1964; chmn. tech. adv. bd. Western Union Telegraph Co., 1966-69. Pres. So. Assn. Land Grant Colls. and State Univs., 1970. Recipient Meritorious Civilian Service award U.S. Navy; named South Carolinian of Year, 1966. Fellow I.E.E.E. (v.p. profl. group on edn.; bd. dirs. 1962, 64-67, mem. exec. com. 1962; editor 1962, mem. editorial bd. 1963-64); mem. Am. Soc. Engring. Edn., Nat. Acad. Engring., Newcomen Soc., Sigma Xi, Phi Eta Sigma, Kappa Mu Epsilon, Tau Beta Pi, Eta Kappa Nu, Theta Xi, Phi Beta Kappa, Phi Mu Alpha. Home: President's Home U.S.C Columbia SC 29208

JONES, THOMAS L., educator; b. Breckinridge County, Ky., Apr. 10, 1931; s. V.A. and Elizabeth (Lambirth) J.; B.S., U. Ky., 1959, LL.B., 1961; LL.M., U. Mich., 1965; m. Shelley Edwards, July 15, 1961. Asst. prof. law U. Ala., Tuscaloosa, 1962-65, asso. prof., 1965-68, prof., 1968—, acting dean Sch. Law, 1970-71. Vis. prof. U. Ky., Lexington, 1965, U. Ill. Coll. Law, 1971-72; Ala. commr. to Nat. Conf. Commrs. on Uniform State Laws, 1967—. Served with USAF, 1951-55. Editor Ala. Will Manual Service, 1965—. Home: 907 Indian Hills Dr Tuscaloosa AL 35401

JONES, THOMAS OSWELL, ofcl. NSF; b. Oshkosh, Wis., May 13, 1908; s. Hugh Edwards and Jane (Davies) J.; B.S., Wis. State U., 1930; Ph.M., U. Wis., 1934, Ph.D., 1937; m. Phyllis Elizabeth Jackson, Aug. 19, 1950; children—Elizabeth Carol, Phyllis Jane. Faculty, Haverford Coll., 1937-56, prof. chemistry, 1954-56; with NSF, Washington, 1956—, div. dir. environmental scis., 1965-69, dep. asst, dir. for nat. and internat. programs, 1969—; asst. to sect. chief Metall. Lab., Chgo., 1944-45, sect. chief info. div., 1945-46; vis. prof. chemistry U. Wis., 1954-55. Decorated Order Al Merito (Chile); recipient Meritorious Ser. medal NSF, 1970. Mem. Am. Chem. Soc., Am. Geophy. Union, A.A.A.S., Phi Beta Kappa, Sigma Xi. Contbr. articles on nuclear scis., isotopes, atomic weights, tracer techniques profl. jours. Home: 7504 Holiday Terrace Bethesda MD 20034 Office: 1800 G St Washington DC 20550

JONES, THOMAS RANDOLPH, dentist; b. Jonesville, Va., Feb. 11, 1939; s. Thomas Everett and Anne Price (Hines) J.; B.S., Lincoln Meml. U., 1960; D.M.D., U. Louisville, 1968; m. Rebecca Susan Perkins, June 25, 1961; children—Susan, Randy, Steve. Pvt. practice dentistry, Jonesville, Va., 1968—. Mem. town council, Jonesville, Va., 1970—. Served to capt. USMCR, 1960-63. Mem. Am., Va. dental assns., S.W. Va. Dental Soc., Jr. C. of C., Psi Omega. Methodist. Odd Fellow, Lion. Address: PO Box 307 Jonesville VA 24263

JONES, VARNAKALE LORENZO, geophysicist, physicist; b. Carthage, Mo., Aug. 8, 1902; s. Harry Lorenzo and Lenore (White) J.; B.A., U. Okla., 1925, M.S., 1927; postgrad. U. Colo., 1927-28, U. Okla., 1931-32. Asst. physics dept. U. Okla., 1925-27, instr. physics, 1931-32; geophysicist Amerade Petroleum Corp., summer 1927; instr. physics, U. Colo., 1927-28; research and devel. cons., Chelsea, Okla., 1928-31; cons. physics and geophysics, Tulsa, exploration control geophysicist Barnsdal Oil [illegible] ulsa), 1936; cons. geophysics, instr. physics, U. Tulsa, 1943-44, head dept. geophysics, 1946-51; geophysicist Standard Oil & Gas, Tulsa, 1944-45; research geophysicist Geophys. Devel. Corp., also geophys. interpreter Frost Geophys. Corp., both Tulsa, 1945-46; chief geophysicist Terrametric Exploration Co., Tulsa, 1951—. Collaborator, Okla. Geol. Survey, sr. author Vertical Magnetic Intensity Map of Okla., 1963-64. Mem. Tulsa Astron. Soc. (pres. 1942-43), Am. Geophys. Union, Seismol. Soc. Am., European Assn. Exploration Geophysics, Soc. Exploration Geophysics (editorial asst. 1959-60), Am. Inst. Physics, Am. Assn. Physics Tchrs., Tulsa, (v.p. 1948-49, editor proc. 1956-57), Oklahoma City geophys. socs., Tulsa, Oklahoma City geol. socs., Sigma Xi, Sigma Pi Sigma, Alpha Sigma Delta, Phi Gamma Kappa. Presbyn. Mason (32 deg., K.T., Shriner). Club: High Twelve (Tulsa). Research and publs. in profl. jours. Home: 1335 E 18th St Tulsa Ok 74120 Office: PO Box 3731 Tulsa OK 74152

JONES, WALTER BEAMON, congressman; b. Fayetteville, N.C., Aug. 19, 1913; s. Walter George and Fannie (Anderson) J.; B.S., N.C. State U., 1934; m. Doris Long, Apr. 26, 1934; children—Dot Dee Moye, Walter Beamon II. Mem. N.C. Gen. Assembly, 1955-59; mem. N.C. Senate, 1965; mem. 89th-92d congresses 1st Dist. N.C. Dir. Security Savs. & Loan Assn., Farmville, N.C. Mayor, Farmville, 1949-53. Former trustee Campbell Coll., U. N.C. Recipient Watchdog of Treasury award Nat. Assn. Businessmen, 1966; named Farmville Man of Year, 1955. Democrat. Baptist (deacon). Mason (32 deg., Shriner), Elk, Rotarian, Moose. Home: May Blvd Farmville NC 27828 Office: Cannon House Office Bldg Washington DC 20515

JONES, WARREN LEROY, judge; b. Gordon, Neb., July 2, 1895; s. Lauren and Katherine (Ballengee) J.; LL.B. cum laude, U. Denver, 1924; LL.D., Stetson U., 1955; Lincoln Diploma Honor, Lincoln Meml. U.; m. Edith Ann Le Prouse, Dec. 23, 1921; 1 dau., Dorothy Lauren (Mrs. Robert P. Shakely). Admitted to Colo. bar, 1924; dep. dist. atty. City and County of Denver, 1924; mem. Jones, Gandy & Wilson, Denver, 1925; admitted to Fla. bar, 1926; asso. Fleming, Hamilton, Diver & Lichliter, Jacksonville, 1926-37; mem. Fleming, Hamilton, Diver & Jones, 1938-41; mem. Fleming, Jones, Scott & Botts, 1942-55, sr. mem., 1948-55; U.S. circuit judge for 5th Circuit, 1955-65, sr. circuit judge, 1965—. Recipient Lincoln Diploma of Honor, Lincoln Meml. U., Harrogate, Tenn. Jud. fellow Am. Coll. Probate Counsel; mem. Maritime Law Assn., Jacksonville C. of C. (pres. 1955), S.A.R., New Orleans Bar Assn., Selden Soc., Order St. Ives, Am. Judicature Soc., Am. Law Inst., Fla. Bar (pres. 1944), Am., Jacksonville (pres. 1939) bar assns., Newcomen Soc., Phi Alpha Delta. Episcopalian. Mason (33 deg., K.T., Shriner), Order DeMolay (supreme council). Clubs: Timuquana Country, Florida Yacht, Seminole, River, University; Civitan (past pres.), Ft. Worth (Tex.); Lawyers (Washington). Collector Lincolniana. Home: 1081 Arbor Lane Jacksonville FL 32207 Office: US Court House Jacksonville FL 32201

JONES, WAYNE VAN LEER, cons. geologist; b. Chgo., June 18, 1902; s. Frank Edgar and Josephine Louella (Van Leer) J.; A.B. Northwestern U. 1923; m. Elizabeth Rieke, Jan 14, 1926; 1 son, Wayne Van Leer II. Accountant, then chief auditor Mission Oil Co., Kansas City, Mo., 1923-28; with F.E. Jones & Son, oil operators, Wichita, Kan., 1928-30; asst. mgr. Exchange Petroleum Co., Shreveport, La. 1930-34; geologist Midcontinent div. Tidewater Asso. Oil Co., Houston, 1934-41, chief geologist, 1941-53; v.p. charge exploration Union Texas Natural Gas Corp. (formerly Union Sulphur & Oil Corp., Union Oil & Gas Corp. of La., merger Allied Chem. Corp., 1962, name now Union Tex. Petroleum div. Allied Chem. Corp.), Houston, 1953-59, sr. v.p., 1959-63, also past v.p. dir. subsidiaries Union Petrolera Venezolana, C.A., Union Petrolera Boliviana, S.A. Unola de Argentina, Ltd., Uno-Tex Petroleum Corp.; cons. geologist, Houston, 1963—. Mem. Am. Commn. on Stratigraphic Nomenclature, 1947-53. Alumni regent Northwestern U., 1965—. Mem. Am. Assn. Petroleum Geologists, Geneal. Soc. N.J., Md., Pa., N.Y. Geneal. and Biog. Soc., Soc. Genealogists (London, Eng.), Houston Geol. Soc., Phi Beta Kappa, Sigma Xi, Sigma Alpha Epsilon. Clubs: Houston, Memorial Drive Country (Houston). Address: 5672 Longmont Dr Houston TX 77027

JONES, WELDON MAXEY, banker; b. Ardmore, Okla., Dec. 8, 1911; s. Fred Buckner and Ella (Burrows) J.; student Phoenix Jr. Coll., 1933-34, U. Ariz., 1931-32; m. Janet Day, Mar. 10, 1940; children—Diana Day (Mrs. Robert L. Wynne), Donald B. Vice pres. Valley Nat. Bank, Phoenix, 1934-55; pres., dir. San Angelo Nat. Bank (Tex.), 1955—. Served to maj. USAAF, 1942-46. Clubs: San Angelo Country, River (San Angelo); Kiva (Phoenix). Home: 725 Park St San Angelo TX 76901 Office: San Angelow Natl Bank San Angelo TX 76901

JONES, WILLIAM BLAKELY, U.S. judge; b. Cedar Rapids, Ia., Mar. 20, 1907; s. James Patrick and Isabel Cecilia (Blakely) J.; A.B., U. Notre Dame, 1929, LL.B., 1931; m. Alice Danicich, Nov. 17, 1937; 1 dau., Barbara. Admitted to Mont. bar, 1931, D.C. bar, 1945, Md. bar, 1954; spl. asst. atty. gen. Mont., 1935-37; practice law Helena, Mont., 1931-37, Washington, 1946-62; atty. Dept. Justice, 1937-43, OPA, 1943; exec. asst. to Am. chmn. Joint British-Am. Patent Interchange Com., 1943-46; judge U.S. Dist. Ct. for D.C., 1962—. Fellow Am. Coll. Trial Lawyers, Am. Bar Found.; mem. Am., D.C. bar assns. Clubs: Lawyers, Nat. Lawyers, Metropolitan (Washington); Columbia Country (Chevy Chase). Home: 5516 Grove St Chevy Chase MD 20015 Office: US Courthouse Washington DC 20001

JONES, WILLIAM ELLIS, univ. adminstr.; B.S., B.A. Asso. dir. phys. planning U. Fla. Home: 1812 NW 11th Rd Gainesville FL 32601 Office: U Fla Gainesville FL 32601*

JONES, WILLIAM LEON, SR., mfg. co. exec.; b. Coffeeville, Ala., May 27, 1912; s. William Sam and Minnie (Clanton) J.; grad. high sch.; m. Sara Frances Price, Nov. 16, 1941; children—William Leon, John Larry, Judy (Mrs. Robert Mathew Free). Parts man Parts Service Corp., Montgomery, Ala., 1933-45; owner Selma Parts Service Co., Inc. (Ala.), 1945-51; chief exec. officer Bush Hog, fabricated metal products co., Selma, 1952—; dir. Citizens Bank & Trust Co., Selma, 1960—. Mem. Ala. C. of C. (bd. dirs. 1968—), Selma C. of C. (bd. dirs. 1966—). Mason (Shriner). Clubs: Selma Country, Civitain (pres. 1957) (Selma). Home: 206 Hooper Dr Selma AL 36701 Office: Box 1039 Selma AL 36701

JONES, WILLIE GERTRUDE CHESS (MRS. Q. L. JONES), educator; b. Greenville, Miss.; d. James and Barbara (Taylor) Chess; B.S., Tenn. A. and I. State Coll., 1942; M.S., Tuskegee Inst., 1951; m. Quintus Leon Jones, Dec. 27, 1961. Tchr. elementary sch., Greenville, 1942-44; supr. Issaquena County, Mayersville, Miss., 1954-59; Y-Teen program dir. State Miss., YWCA, Jackson, 1959-64; project opportunity counselor Rogers High Sch., Canton, Miss., 1966-70; instr. Jackson (Miss.) State Coll., 1970—. Instr. dept. edn. Miss. Valley State Coll., Itta Bena, summers 1952, 53; extension sch. instr. Jackson State Coll., 1953-56. Mem. N.E.A., Am., Miss. personnel and guidance assns., Miss. Jeanes (sec. 1954-57), Miss. State tchrs. assns., Sigma Gamma Rho. Baptist. Home: 1431 Brinkley Dr Jackson MS 39213 Office: Jackson State Coll Jackson MS 39217

JONES, WILLIS WATT, JR., banker; b. Montgomery, Ala., Apr. 17, 1942; s. Willis Watt and Lois Anne (Malone) J.; B.S., U. Ala., 1964; m. Patricia Claire Johnson, Dec. 16, 1967; 1 son, Kelly Fitzpatrick. Nat. bank examiner U.S. Treasury Dept., Montgomery, 1964-68; v.p. First Nat. Bank, Eufaula, Ala., 1968—; dir. Eufaula Realtors, Inc., 1969—. Chmn. Barbour County March of Dimes, 1969; chmn. Lake Eufaula Water Festival, 1971. Bd. dirs. Eufaula Heritage Assn. Recipient Achievement award, Ala. Bankers Assn., 1964. Mem. Kappa Alpha Order, Delta Sigma Pi. Presbyn. Club: Eufaula (Ala.) Country. Home: 316 Azalea Dr Eufaula AL 36027 Office: PO Box 240 Eufaula AL 36027

JONES, WOODROW WILSON, judge; b. Rutherfordton, N.C., Jan. 26, 1914; s. Bernard Bartlett and Karl Jane (Nanney) J.; student Mars Hill Coll., 1932-34, Wake Forest Coll., 1934-37; m. Rachel Elizabeth Phelps, Nov. 21, 1936; children—Woodrow Wilson, Michael Anthony. Admitted to N.C. bar, 1937; solicitor Rutherford County Recorders Ct., 1941-43; mem. N.C. Gen. Assembly, 1947-49; mem. U.S. Ho. of Reps., 1950-56; U.S. dist. judge, Rutherfordton, 1967—, chief judge, 1968—. Dir. Union Trust Co., Shelby, N.C., Citizens Fed. Savs & Loan Assn., Rutherfordton. Chmn. N.C. Democratic Exec. Com., 1958-60. Trustee Gardner-Webb Coll., Boiling Springs, N.C. Served to lt. (j.g.) USNR, 1943-45. Recipient spl. citation for outstanding service Gardner-Webb Coll., 1968. Mem. Am., N.C., Rutherford County bar assns. Baptist. Kiwanian. Home: 1018 N Main St Rutherfordton NC 28139 Office: County Court House Rutherfordton NC 28139

JONG, ING-CHANG, educator; b. Lunpei, Yunlin, Taiwan, Feb. 5, 1938; s. Tzu-Hua and Sue (Liao) J.; B.S., Nat. Taiwan U., 1961; M.S., S.D. Sch. Mines and Tech., 1963; Ph.D., Northwestern U., 1965; m. Louisa Yu-Hsi Liao, Sept. 7, 1966; children—David George, Vida Pearl. Came to U.S., 1962, naturalized, 1972. Research asso. S.D. Sch. Mines and Tech., Rapid City, 1963; research asst. Northwestern U., Evanston, Ill., 1963-65; asst. prof. engring. sci. U. Ark., Fayetteville, 1965-69, asso. prof., 1969—. Served to 2d lt. Taiwan Air Force, 1961-62. NSF grantee, 1967-69, 69-71. Mem. Am. Soc. M. E. (reviewer), Am. Acad. Mechanics, Am. Soc. Engring. Edn., Sigma Xi. Presbyn. (elder). Lion. Contbr. profl. jours. Home: 1723 N Oakland Av Fayetteville AR 72701

JONSON, WILLIAM CRAWFORD, JR., ednl. research adminstr.; b. Greenville, Ky., Jan. 22, 1910; s. William Crawford and Elizabeth (Martin) J.; B.S., U.S. Naval Acad., 1932; m. Frances Wier, Dec. 26, 1937; children— Frances Ann (Mrs. James R. Lloyd), Robert Crawford, Thomas Alexander. Commd. ensign USN, 1932, advanced through grades to rear adm., 1959; ret., 1959; comdg. officer U.S.S. Avocet in Pearl Harbor during Japanese attack, 1941, prof. naval sci. Auburn (Ala.) U., 1956-59; dir. Auburn Research Found., 1959-67; asst. dir. engring. exptl. sta. Auburn U., 1967—. Decorated Bronze Star medal. Mem. Ret. Officers Assn., U.S. Naval Acad. Alumni Assn. Rotarian (treas. 1968-69). Home: PO Box 483 1403 E Glenn Av Auburn AL 36830 Office: Ramsay Hall Auburn U Auburn AL 36830

JONSSON, JOHN ERIK, instrument mfr.; b. N.Y.C., Sept. 6, 1901; s. John Peter and Ellen Charlotte (Palmquist) J.; M.E., Rensselaer Poly. Inst., 1922, D.Eng. (hon.), 1959; D.Sc. (hon.), Hobart and William Smith Colls., 1961, Austin Coll., 1963; LL.D. (hon.), So. Meth. U., 1964, Carnegie-Mellon U., 1972, Skidmore Coll., 1972; D.C.L. (hon.), U. Dallas, 1968; m. Margaret Elizabeth Fonde, Feb. 8, 1923; children—Phillip R., Kenneth A., Margaret Ellen. Engring mfg. and sales Aluminum Co. Am., 1922-27, 29-30; with Tex. Instruments Inc., Dallas 1930—, pres., 1951-58, chmn. bd., 1958-66, hon. chmn. bd., 1966—; dir. Equitable Life Assurance Soc. U.S., Republic Nat. Bank of Dallas. Mem. Am. Revolution Bicentennial Commn. Hon. trustee Dallas Symphony Orch.; bd. dirs., past pres. Dallas County United Fund; chmn. bd. Dallas-Ft. Worth Regional Airport, 1966—; proposer, chmn. planning com. Goals for Dallas, 1966—; mem. vis. com. Sch. Bus. Adminstrn., Harvard U., 1961—; mem. urban transp. adv. council Dept. Transp., 1971—. Mayor Dallas, 1964-71. Trustee Rensselaer Poly. Inst., U. Dallas, Skidmore Coll., Excellence in Edn. Found. (pres.) Am. Assembly; chmn. bd. dirs. Ednl. Facilities Lab., trustee Callier Hearing and Speech Center; chmn. bd. visitors Tulane U., 1970-72; chmn. bd. Lamplighter Sch., Inc., Dallas. Recipient Industrialist award Soc. Indsl. Realtors, 1965; Advancement Research medal Am. Soc. Metals, 1964; Bene Merenti Medal, 1966; Alumnus award Rensselaer Poly. Inst., 1967, Gantt Medal award 1968, Hoover medal, 1970; Chauncey Rose medal Rose-Hulman Inst. Tech., 1972. Mem. Soc. Exploration Geophysicists, Newcomen Soc., Nat. Planning Assn., Conf. Bd. (sr. exec. council), A.I.A. (hon.), Nat. Acad. Engring., Dallas C. of C. (past pres.). Am. Mgmt. Assn. (dir. 1956-64, v.p. 1956-59), Tex. Acad., Tex. Philos. Soc., Dallas Petroleum Club (past pres.). Clubs: Dallas Country (Dallas); Brook Hollow Golf. Home: 4831 Shadywood Lane Dallas TX 75209 Office: Republic Bank Tower Dallas TX 75201

JONSSON, MARGARET ELIZABETH FONDE (MRS. JOHN ERIK JONSSON), civic worker, club woman; b. Mobile, Ala., Sept. 22, 1902; d. Hiram Cornelius and Carrie (Watkins) Fonde; diploma Maryville Poly. Sch. Bus., 1919; M.Litt., Skidmore Coll., 1964; m. John Erik Jonsson, Feb. 8, 1923; children—Philip Raymond, Kenneth Alan, Margaret Ellen. Accounting dept. asst. Aluminum Co. Am., Alcoa, Tenn., 1919-23. Mem. Dallas Woman's Club, 1935—, bd. govs., 1958-63, pres., 1961-62, chmn. adv. bd., 1963-65; mem. Dallas Garden Center, 1959—, pres., 1964-65; bd. dirs. KERA; adv. bd. Dallas Civic Opera, Red Cross Office of Vols.; former mem. women's com. State Fair Tex. Trustee Dallas Mus. Fine Arts, Women's div. State Fair Tex., Marianne Scruggs Garden Club, Standard Study Club. Mem. Woman's Council Dallas County, Woman's Aux. Dallas County Hosp. Dist. (life), Dallas Health and Sci. Mus. (life), Woman's Aux. Nat. Jewish Hosp., Dallas Theater Center, League Women Voters, Dallas Symphony League, Dallas Geol. and Geophys. Aux. Republican. Presbyn. Clubs: Brook Hollow Golf, Country, Chaparral, City, Dallas Press (Dallas); Corinthian Yacht. Home: 4831 Shadywood Lane Dallas TX 75209

JOOR, RUTH HOUSTON (MRS. WILLIAM E. JOOR), civic worker; b. N.Y.C.; d. Hough and Belle (McIntyre) Houston; B.A., Ohio Wesleyan U., M.A., Columbia; m. William E. Joor, Oct. 8, 1938; children—William E. III, Nancy Ruth. Asst. editor Good Housekeeping Mag., 1931-38. Bd. dirs. League Women Voters, Ridgewood, N.J., 1949-52, Houston, 1956-62, pres;, 1959-61; bd. dirs. League Women Voters Tex., 1962-70, pres., 1966-70; pres. bd. dirs. Ridgewood P.T.A., 1951-52; Gov.'s Commn. on Tex. Urban Devel., 1970—. Mem. Alpha Gamma Delta. Methodist. Author: Bermuda Vacation, 1940. Home: 1306 Ben Hur Dr Houston TX 77055

JOPLING, DON WINTER, oil co. exec.; b. Ogden, Ia., Nov. 18, 1907; s. David William and Florence (Wolfe) J.; student Coe Coll., 1929-30, Ia. State U., 1935-38, Colo. U., 1935, U. Tex., 1936; m. Erma Bell Richardson, May 26, 1943; children—Dianne Bell, Laurie Susan, Don David. With bur. pub. rds. Standard Oil N.J., Venezuela, 1938-42; with Exploration Surveys, Inc., Dallas, 1946-62, chmn. bd., pres. Longhorn Prodn. Co., Dallas, 1962-69; chmn. bd., exec. v.p. Dallas Prodn., Inc., Dallas, 1969—; pres. Tex. Interstate Oil & Gas Co., Inc., Dallas, 1969—. Dist. chmn. Circle 10 council Boy Scouts Am., 1969-71. Bd. dirs. Scottish Rite Hosp., Dallas, 1963-67. Served with USNR, 1942-46; PTO. Fellow A.A.A.S.; mem. Am. Assn. Petroleum Geologists, Soc. Exploration Geologists, Am. Inst. Mining Engrs., Soc. Petroleum Engrs., Soc. Econ. Mineralogists and Paleontologists. Mason (Shriner, 32 deg.). Clubs: Corinthian Dallas Yacht (bd. govs.), Dallas Cowboys. Patentee in oil solvents. Home: 4731 S Lindhurst St Dallas TX 75229 Office: Meadows Bldg Milton and Greenville Avs Dallas TX 75206

JORDAN, ADIEL MONCRIEF, clergyman; b. Decatur, Ga., May 30, 1933; s. H. DuPree and Roslyn (Moncrief) J.; student Emory U., 1950-51; A.B., Mercer U., 1954; postgrad. Yale Div. Sch., 1954-56; B.D., So. Baptist Theol. Sem., 1959; postgrad. Princeton Theol. Sem., Union Sem., N.Y.C.; m. Diane Sheffield Owen, June 9, 1956; children—David Moncrief, Joyce Lyn. Ordained to ministry, Bapt. Ch., 1959; asso. pastor Nat. Bapt. Meml. Ch., Washington, 1959-63; pastor Covenant Bapt. Ch., Washington, 1963-69. Signal Mountain (Tenn.) Bapt. Ch., 1969—. Del., Bapt. World Alliance, Tokyo, 1970; mem. instnl. com. Council of Chs., Washington, guest minister Urawa Bapt. Ch., Tokyo, 1970. Bd. dirs. Hillandale Alcohol and Drug Abuse Center; trustee Southeastern Bapt. Theol. Sem., Wake Forest, N.C. Mem. D.C. Bapt. Pastors Conf. (v.p. 1962-63), D.C. Bapt. Conv. (chmn. Christian edn. com. 1965-66), So. Bapt. Conv. (com. on bds.), Hamilton County Bapt. Assn. (chmn. children's home com. 1969—), Signal Mountain Ministerial Assn. (pres. 1971), Clergy Assn. Greater Chattanooga (exec. com). Home: 935 Ridgeway Av Signal Mountain TN 37377 Office: Signal Mountain Bapt Ch Signal Mountain TN 37377

JORDAN, ANNE KNIGHT, civic worker; b. Tampa, Fla., July 8, 1918; d. William Mitchell and Pearl Louise (Brown) Knight; grad. Cortez Peters Bus. Sch., Washington, 1941; B.A., Howard U., 1949, postgrad. 1955; postgrad. Savannah State Coll., 1957, Catholic U. Am., 1958, U. Ga. for Continuing Edn., 1967-68, Armstrong State Coll., 1970-72; m. Carl Rankin Jordan, Jan. 15, 1949; children—Carmen Antoinette, Karen Terez, Harold Kevin. With Social Security Agy., Balt., 1941-42; staff Foster Care Services, Dept. Children's Welfare, govt. of D.C., Washington, 1943; tchr. spl. edn., Savannah, Ga., 1957. Del. Nat. Council Catholic Women, Washington, 1964, Nat. Council Negro Women, Washington, 1969, White House Conf. on Food, Nutrition and Health, Washington, 1969; pub. relations dir. Women in Community Service, Savannah, 1965; chmn. family and parent edn. com. Savannah Deanery Council Cath. Women, 1965; organizer Savannah chpt. Nat. Tots and Teens Inc., 1965, Adopt-A-Family Project for Miss. Delta Poverty Area, 1970. Mem. exec. bd. Savannah chpt. Nat. Found.-March of Dimes, chmn. Mother's March, 1969, del. Leadership Conf., San Diego, 1969; adv. bd. Savannah Speech and Hearing Center, vol. screening program, 1965—. Served with WAC, 1943-46. Mem. Woman's Aux. Nat. Med. Assn. (adminstrv. sec. 1965-68, pres. 1969-70, chmn. exec. bd. 1970-71, organizer Jr. Nat. Med. Assn. 1970), N.A.A.C.P. (life, membership chmn. Savannah br, 1959-60, del. conv. 1959, 60), Woman's Aux. Ga. State Med. Assn. (pres. 1961-62, organizer Future Doctors of Ga. Clubs 1961), Woman's Aux. South Atlantic Med. Soc. (pres. 1956), Sigma Gamma Rho (Sigma of Year 1962). Roman Catholic (pres. guild 1954-56, moderator forum Diocesan Council Cath. Women 1965). Editor: Happy Homemaker Health Book. 1970; mem. adv. bd. New Lady Mag., 1970—. Home: 1627 Mills B Lane Av Savannah GA 31405

JORDAN, ARCHIBALD CURRIE, educator; b. Caldwell, N.C.; s. Archibald Currie and Octavia Graham (Stroud) J.; A.B. Duke U., A.M., Columbia U.; postgrad. Duke U. Law Sch; m. Jane Myers, Sept. 2, 1941; children—Ann Myers, Patsy Jane, Sally Rida, Julie Anna. Gen. Edn. Bd. fellow Columbia U.; admitted to N.C. bar; adviser N.C. Textbook Commn.; asst. prof. English, Duke U. Past pres., chmn. research com. N.C. English Teachers Council; v.p. Coll. English Assn. of N.C., Va. and W.Va. Mem. A.A.A.S., So. Atlantic Modern Lang. Assn., Am. Assn. U. Profs., Am. Dialect Soc., N.C. English Tchrs. Assn., Am., N.C. bar assns., Council for Basic Edn., Phi Delta Kappa, Kappa Delta Pi. Democrat. Presbyn. Author: Essentials of English Composition; College English Tests (forms Aand B); College Handbook of Composition; Fundamentals of College Composition; How to Write Correctly; Everyday Grammar; A Comprehensive Examination in the Fundamentals of Correct English Usage, 1960; The Writer's Manual, 1963, rev. edit., 1967. Address: Box 6006 Duke U Durham N.C. 27708

JORDAN, BENJAMIN EVERETT, U.S. senator; b. Ramseur, N.C., Sept. 8, 1896; s. Henry Harrison and Annie (Elizabeth Sellers) J.; student Rutherford (N.C.) Coll. Prep. Sch., 1912-13, Trinity Coll. (now Duke U.), 1914-15; hon. degree, Duke U., 1940; LL.D., Elon Coll., 1960; m. Katherine McLean, Nov. 29, 1924; children—Benjamin Everett, Rose Ann, John McLean. Worked in jewelry store, and various textile mfrs., 1915-27; organized Seller Mfg. Co., 1927, gen. mgr., sec.-treas., dir., 1927—; gen. mgr., sec.-treas., dir. Jordan Spinning Co., 1939—; pres., treas., gen. mgr., dir. Royal Cotton Mill Co., Wake Forest, N.C., 1945—; sec.-treas. Nat. Processing Co., Burlington, N.C., 1945—; U.S. senator from N.C., 1958—, chmn. com. on rules and adminstrn., chmn. or vice chmn. joint com. on Library of Congress, joint com. on printing, joint congl. com. on inaugural ceremonies, mem. com. on agr. and forestry, com. on pub. works, Senate Office Bldg. Commn., Commn. on Arts and Antiquities; dir. various cos. Mem. N.C. Med. Care Commn.; mem. N.C. Peace Officers Benefit and Retirement Commn.; pres., dir., Alamance County Tb Assn.; dir., Alamance County Red Cross, Cherokee council Boy Scouts Am.; chmn. bd. trustees Alamance County Gen. Hosps. and Tb Sanitoriums. Trustee Duke U., Elon (N.C.) Coll., Am. U.; dir. Cotton Textile Inst. of U.S. Vice pres. Am. Group, Interparliamntary Union. Served with tank corps U.S. Army, 1918-19; with Army of Occupation, Germany, 1919. Recipient Silver Beaver award Boy Scouts Am., 1966. Mem. U.S. Capitol Hist. Soc. (trustee), N.C. Cotton Mfrs. Assn. (dir.), Durene Assn. Am. (v.p.), S.A.R., Omicron Delta Kappa. Democrat. Methodist. Mason, Rotarian (dir. past pres., Burlington). Address: Saxapahaw NC 27340

JORDAN, MRS. CARL R., assn. exec. Nat. pres. Women's Aux. of Nat. Med. Assn. Address: 1627 Mills B Lane Savannah GA 31405*

JORDAN, CASPER LEROY, educator; b. Cleve., Mar. 5, 1924; s. John and Leola (Lloyd) J.; A.B., Case-Western Res. U., 1947; M.S. in Library Sci., Atlanta U., 1951. Chief librarian Wilberforce U., 1951-61, supr. tech. services Nioga Library System, Niagara Falls, N.Y., 1961-67; asst. dir., 1967-68; asst. prof. sch. library service, Atlanta U., 1968—, dir. library planning and devel. U. Center, 1971—; vis. prof. State U. N.Y. at Buffalo, 1963, 65. Mem. COSATI Task Force on Negro Research Libraries; chmn. UNCF Library Steering Com.; vice chmn. adv. com. Martin Luther King, Jr. Meml. Library project. Bd. dirs. Niagara Falls Community Center, 1963-68; mem. Niagara Falls Human Relations Commn., 1965-68; pres. Niagara Falls (N.Y.) br. N.A.A.C.P., 1966-68; chmn. Congress Racial Equality, 1962-65; mem. adv. bd. Salvation Army, Niagara Falls, 1967-68. Mem. N.Y. (pres. 1967), Met. Atlanta (sec. 1971-72) library assns., A.L.A., Assn. Coll. and Research Libraries. Mem. A.M.E. Ch. (trustee). Editor: mag. Free Lance, 1950—. Home: 22 Whitehouse Dr SW Atlanta GA 30314

JORDAN, CHARLES DANIEL, physician; b. Greenville, N.C., Apr. 4, 1914; s. William Daniel and Rosa Ella (Randolph) J.; A.B., East Carolina Tchrs. Coll., 1935; M.A., George Peabody Coll., 1938; postgrad. Duke, 1940-42; M.D., Med. Coll. Va., 1948. Tchr. sci. Elm City (N.C.) High Sch., 1935-38; faculty Ga. State Coll. for Women, Milledge, 1938-40; intern Johnston-Willis Hosp., Richmond, Va., 1948-49; resident obstetrics and gynecology Docts Hosp., Cleve., 1949-50; practice gen. medicine, Bethel, N.C., 1950-69; asst. dir. student health East Carolina U., Greenville, 1969—, also asst. prof. medicine, mem. admissions com. Dir. Home Savs. and Loan Assn., Bethel. Bd. dirs. county and state chpts. Am. Cancer Soc., Pitt County chpt. Eastern Tb and Respiratory Disease Assn. Served with AUS, 1942-44. Mem. Am. Heart Assn., A.M.A., N.C., Pitt County med. socs., Am. Acad. Gen. Practice, So., Seaboard, Tristate med. socs., Am., N.C. Camellia socs., Assn. Am. Physicians and Surgeons. Rotarian. Home: Hammond St Bethel NC 27812 Office: Infirmary East Carolina U Greenville NC 27834

JORDAN, CHESTER HAROLD, architect; b. Dallas, Dec. 29, 1921; s. Chester Arthur and Pearl (Daniel) J.; B.Arch., Tex. A. and M., 1943; postgrad. Princeton U., 1950-51; M.Arch., Harvard, 1961; m. Alice Lee West, Aug. 12, 1950; children—Douglas B., Dirk M., Daniel W. Chief designer Stanley Brown, architect, Dallas, 1947-51; partner Dean & Jordan, architects, 1951-53; asst. prof. Auburn U., Ala., 1953-54; prof. La. State U., Baton Rouge, 1954—. Exec. dir. Capital Region Planning Commn., 1967; mem. E. Baton Rouge Parish Planning Commn., 1962-67, planning bd. United Givers, 1967. Served to 1st lt. AUS, 1943-46. Decorated Silver Star, Bronze Star, Purple Heart. Mem. A.I.A., La. Architects Assn. (dir.). Baptist. Home: 1058 W Lakeview Baton Rouge LA 70810 Office: 101 St Ferdinand Baton Rouge LA 70801

JORDAN, DUPREE, JR., publisher, pub. relations exec., educator, cons.; b. Decatur, Ga., May 14, 1929; s. DuPree and Roslyn (Moncrief) J.; A.B., Mercer U., 1947; postgrad. Crozer Theol. Sem., 1948; M.A. Emory U., 1954; LL.B., Atlanta Law Sch., 1951, LL.D., 1963; Litt.D., Evang. Bible Coll. and Sem., 1970; m. Margaret Virginia Malone, Dec. 28, 1948; children—Margaret, DuPree III, Roslyn, Terri Lee. Ordained to ministry Bapt. Ch., 1945; reporter Macon (Ga.) Telegraph, 1945-47, Chester (Pa.) Times, 1948-49; news dir. WVCH, Chester, 1948-49; asso. dir. Radio-TV Commn., So. Bapt. Conv., 1949-52, acting dir., 1952-53; tchr. Westminister Schs. and Atlanta div. U. Ga., 1953-55; pastor Duluth (Ga.) Bapt. Ch., 1953-54; editor, pub., owner West End Star, Atlanta weekly newspaper, 1955-67; owner, pub. Piedmont Satellite, 1967-68, North DeKalb Record, Chamblee, 1956-64, Tri County Graphic, 1962-64; pres. Jordan Enterprises, Success Publs., Inc., Jordan & Jordan, advt. and pub. relations; dir. Successful Selling Seminars; pres. Ga. Coll. for Leadership Devel.; dir. Clayton and Westbury Devel. Corp., Paramount Enterprises, numerous other corps. Mem. Gov.'s Com. for a World's Fair in Atlanta; mem. Rapid Transit Com. of 100; dir. pub. affairs for So. States Office Econ. Opportunity, 1965-69, spl. asst. to regional dir., 1967-69, nat. religious liaison dir., 1968-69; exec. dir. Assn. Pvt. Colls. and Univs. in Ga., 1970—; mem. cons. staff Gov. Ga., 1962-66, 70—. Bd. dirs. Atlanta Girls Club, Boy Scouts Am., YMCA. Recipient numerous awards from various orgns., including Ga. Press Assn., Nat. Editorial Assn., Sigma Delta Chi, Jr. C. of C.; Distinguished Service award Office Econ. Opportunity, 1967. Mem. Pub. Relations Soc. Am., Nat. Press Club, Nat. Editorial Assn., Ga. Press Assn. (bd. mgrs.), Adminstrv. Mgmt. Soc. (dir. Atlanta chpt.), Am. Mgmt. Assn., Am. Soc. Pub. Adminstrn., Soc. Advancement Mgmt., Am. Soc. Tng. Dirs.; Sales and Marketing Execs. Internat., Sales and Marketing Execs. Atlanta, West End (pres. 1962), Chamblee-Doreville (pres. 1963) businessmen's assns., Ga., DeKalb County, Atlanta chambers commerce, Am., Ga. socs. assn. execs., Soc. Assn. Mgrs., Christian Council Met. Atlanta (pres.), Sigma Delta Chi (dir. Atlanta chpt. 1963). Club: Atlanta City. Home: 1204 Warren Hall Lane NE Atlanta GA 30319 Office: 3330 Peachtree Rd NE Atlanta GA 30326

JORDAN, GILBERT JOHN, educator; b. nr. Art, Tex., Dec. 23, 1902; s. Daniel and Emilie (Willmann) J.; A.B., Southwestern U., 1924; M.A., U. Tex., 1928; postgrad. U. Wis., 1930-33; Ph.D., Ohio State U., 1936; m. Vera Belle Tiller, May 23, 1926; children—Janice Jordan (Mrs. Thomas W. Shefelman), Terry Gilbert. Tchr. pub. schs., Tex., 1922-30; prof. So. Meth. U., Dallas, 1930-68; prof. German dept. fgn. langs. Sam Houston State U., Huntsville, Tex., 1968—. Recipient First Class Merit award Republic, Germany, 1962. Mem. Modern Lang. Assn., Am. Assn. Tchrs. German, Am. Assn. U. Profs., Tex. State Tchrs. Assn. Author: Southwest Goethe Festival, 1949; Four German One-Act Plays, 1951; Verse Translation of Schiller's Wilhelm Tell, 1964. Contbr. articles to profl. jours. Home: 3228 Milton St Dallas TX 75205 Office: Dept Fgn Langs Sam Houston State U Huntsville TX 77340

JORDAN, GRACE HARTLEY EDGINGTON (MRS. LEONARD BECK JORDAN), author; b. Wasco, Ore.; d. Jesse and Martha Ann (Hartley) Edgington; B.A., U. Ore., 1916; m. Leonard Beck Jordan (U.S. Senator Ida.) Dec. 30, 1924; children—Patricia Jean (Mrs. Charles F. Story), Joseph Leonard, Stephen Edgington. Faculty, U. Wash., 1917-20; faculty U. Ore., editor Old Oregon, 1920-24; tchr. pub. schs., Grangeville, Ida., 1943-46; faculty Boise Coll., 1961-62; cons; Creative Writing Workshop Womens Congl. Club, 1963—. Instr. night writing classes Boise YWCA, 1959-62. Mem. League Am. Pen Women, Am. Assn. U. Women, Phi Beta Kappa, Theta Sigma Phi, Pi Beta Phi, Beta Sigma Phi. Republican. Methodist. Author: Home Below Hell's Canyon, 1954; Canyon Boy, 1958; The King's Pines, 1961; Idaho Reader, 1963. Polit. columnist Where Rolls the Potomac, 1963—. Home: 2475 Virginia Av NW Washington DC 20037

JORDAN, HOWARD, JR., univ. adminstr.; b. Beaufort, S.C., Dec. 28, 1916; s. Howard and Julia (Glover) J.; A.B., S.C. State Coll., 1938; spl. student Howard U., 1938-39; Ed.D., N.Y. U., 1956; m. Ruth Menafee, Feb. 14, 1943; 1 dau., Judith Louise. Mem. Faculty, S.C. State Coll., Orangeburg, 1941-63, prof. edn. and psychology, chmn. dept. edn., dean Sch. Edn., 1950-60, dean faculty, 1960-63; pres. Savannah (Ga.) State Coll., 1963-71; vice chancellor-services U. System Ga., Atlanta, 1971—. Mem. Savannah-Chatham County Area Econ. Opportunity Authority; chmn. Orangeburg County Cancer dr., 1948-49, Orangeburg County Crippled Childrens Soc. dr., 1950. Trustee Mather Sch. and Jr. Coll. Served with AUS, 1942-46; ETO. Mem. Am., S.C. psychol. assns., Nat. Soc. Study Edn. Nat. (dept. higher edn.), Palmetto edn. assns., Alpha Phi Alpha, Sigma Pi Phi. Episcopalian (vestryman, sec.). Mason. Address: 2640 Laurens Circle SW Atlanta GA 30311

JORDAN, HUGH DAVID, textile co. exec.; b. N.Y.C., Aug. 12, 1916; s. Hugh and Theresa (Lingenfelser) J.; A.B., Cornell U., 1937; m. Genevieve Whitney Ryther, May 1, 1939. Probation officer Lewis County, N.Y., 1937-42; spl. agt. CIC, 1942-45; accountant, then asst. to pres. and asst. treas. Gould Paper Co. div Continental Can Co., Lyons Falls, N.Y., 1946-55; with Brown Co., Berlin, N.H., 1955-66, gen. mgr. pulp div., 1959-60, v.p., treas. 1960-66, v.p., finance, dir., 1966; with West Point-Pepperell, Inc., West Point, Ga., 1967—, controller, 1967-71, v.p. finance, 1971—. Club: Union League (N.Y.C.). Home: Route 3 Box 249A West Point GA Office: West Point-Pepperell West Point GA 31833

JORDAN, JAMES RALPH, football coach; b. Selma, Ala., Sept. 25, 1910; s. James Harry and Katherine (Darby) J.; B.S., Auburn U., 1932; m. Evelyn Walker, June 11, 1937; children—Susan (Mrs. Thomas Pilgreen), Darby, James Ralph. Head basketball coach, asst. football coach U. Ga., 1946-51; head football coach Auburn (Ala.) U., 1951—. Served with C.E., AUS 1942-45. Decorated Bronze Star, Purple Heart; Nat. Championship coach, 1957; named Coach of Year, Washington Touchdown Club, 1963, Southeastern Conf. Coach of Year, 1953, 57, 63. Mem. Blue Key, Scabbard and Blade, Theta Chi. Home: 185 Woodfield Dr Auburn AL 36830

JORDAN, JOHN WEAVER, state legislator, entrepreneur; b. Danville, Ind., Jan. 4, 1926; s. Paul and Ada Weaver (Christenson) J.; student Butler U., 1946-49. Mem. Fla. Ho. of Reps., 1968—. Bd. dirs. Lions Industries for Blind, Big Bros. Palm Beach County. Served with USAAF, 1944-46. Home: & PO Box 1603 West Palm Beach FL 33401 Office: 711 N Dixie Hwy West Palm Beach FL 33401

JORDAN, JOYE ESCH, museum adminstr.; b. Flinton, Pa.; d. Joseph I. and Mary Catherine (Gates) Esch; ed. Indiana (Pa.) U.; postgrad. Akron U., 1933-34; m. Coy C. Jordan; children—Sara Joan, Jane Lindley. Tchr. pub. schs., Akron, O., 1933-35, Raleigh, N.C., 1943-44; research room cons. N.C. Dept. Archives and History, Raleigh, 1944-45, museums adminstr. N.C. Mus. History, 1945-69, adminstr. div. historic sites and museums, 1969-72, asst. adminstr. office Archives and History, 1972—; chmn. Andrew Johnson Meml. Commn., 1952—. Sec.-treas. N.C. Museums Council, 1953-66. Named Wake County Woman of Yr., 1968. Mem. Am. Assn. Museums (council 1961-65, 1st annual award 1971), Southeastern Museums Conf. (an organizer, sec.-treas. 1951-57 council 1958-61, 68-71, Am. Assn. State and Local History, N.C. Lit. and Hist. Assn., N.C. Art Soc., N.C. Folklore Soc., N.C. Soc. Preservation Antiquities, N.C., Raleigh (pres. 1967) bus. and profl. womans clubs. Democrat. Presbyn. Clubs: Womans, Quota (Raleigh). Home: 1309 Williamson Dr Raleigh NC 27608 Office: 109 E Jones St Raleigh NC 27611

JORDAN, LEMUEL RUSSELL, hosp. exec., educator; b. Smithfield, N.C. Oct. 21, 1924; s. Thomas and Sophronia Lee (Creech) J.; A.A., Mars Hill Coll., 1943; A.B., Amherst Coll., 1947; M.A., Columbia, 1949; postgrad. (Ernest H. Abernathy fellow for research in so. industry 1952-53, Inst. for Research in Social Sci. research fellow 1953-54) U. N.C., 1949-50, 52-54; m. Jean Hildebrand Marrow, Dec. 15, 1951; children—Jean H., Rebecca and Judy. Faculty mem. Sch. Bus. Adminstrn., U. N.C., 1954-55, bus. mgr. Med. Outpatient Clinics, 1955-56; dir. outpatient dept. Duke U., Durham, N.C., 1957-59, asst. prof. hosp. adminstrn., 1957-59; asst. supt. Duke Hosp., 1957-59; dir. teaching hosp. and clinics J. Hillis Miller Health Center at U. Fla., Gainesville, also asso. prof. mgmt. Coll. Bus. Adminstrn., 1959-65, asso. prof. health and hosp. adminstrn. Coll. Health Related Services, 1963-65; pres. Birmingham Baptist Med. Centers, 1965—; asso. prof. health services adminstrn. U. Ala., 1969—; guest lectr. George Washington U., 1969—. Pres. Birmingham Area Manpower Resource Devel. Planning Bd., 1967-70, vice chmn., 1971—; pres. Festival of Arts, 1972; mem. exec. com. Ala. Regional Med. Program Adv. Group, 1968—, sec., 1971—; mem. exec. com. Downtown Action Com., 1972. Served with AUS, 1943-46; from sgt. to 2d lt. USAF, 1950-51; maj. Res. ret. Fellow Am. Coll. Hosp. Adminstrs. (mem. bd. govs.' task force rev. com. 1971—; rep. to accrediting commn. grad. edn. hosp. adminstrn. 1972; testimonials com. 1969—; del. to Nat. Health Forum 1970); mem. Am. Hosp. Assn. (mem. long-range planning manual devel. com. 1970-72, pub. relations rev. com. 1970—), Am. Protestant Hosp. Assn. (trustee, chmn. church, health and welfare relations 1970-71, chmn. council govtl. relations 1972), Birmingham Area C. of C. (chmn. operation native sons and daus., indsl. ambassador, edn. com., v.p. edn. and manpower 1970-72), Ala. Hosp. Assn. (dir., sec.-treas. 1970-71, pres. elect 1972), Birmingham Regional Hosp. Council (dir.), Community Service Council Birmingham and Jefferson County (dir.), Better Bus. Bur. Birmingham (dir. 1967-68, 2d v.p. 1969-70, pres. 1970-72), Theta Xi, Alpha Kappa Psi (div. and dist. councilor Mideast dist. 1953-56, nat. v.p. 1956-59, nat. pres. 1959-61). Baptist. Kiwanian. Home: 4161 Kennesaw Dr Birmingham AL 35213 Office: 3201 4th Av S Birmingham AL 35222

JORDAN, LYNDON KIRKMAN, JR., physician; b. Mount Olive, N.C., Jan. 6, 1935; s. Lyndon Kirkman and Rachael Loucille (Hazelton) J.; B.A., Duke, 1957, M.D., 1961; m. Beverly Hayes Brooks, Aug. 19, 1961; children— Lyndon Kirkman III, Christopher Page, Patrick Brooks. Intern, Watts Hosp., Durham, N.C., 1961-62; staff physician Dorothea Dix Hosp., Raleigh, N.C., 1962; practice gen. medicine, Smithfield, N.C., 1964—; mem. staff Johnston Meml. Hosp., Smithfield, chief staff, 1971. Sponsor, presenter Jordan Citizenship award Mt. Olive Coll., 1959-71. Bd. dirs. Johnson County United Fund, 1966-69. Served with USAF, 1962-64. Named Rotarian of Year, 1969-70. Diplomate Am. Bd. Family Practice (charter). Mem. A.M.A. (Physician Recognition award 1971), 4th Dist. Med. Soc. N.C. (v.p. 1970, pres. 1971), N.C. (del. 1971), Johnson County (sec. 1968) med. socs., Am. Acad. Family Physicians. Home: 1101 Walnut Dr Smithfield NC 27577 Office: 415 N 7th St Smithfield NC 27577

JORDAN, VERNON E., assn. exec.; b. Atlanta, Aug. 15, 1935; grad. DePauw U., 1957; LL.B., Howard U., 1960; m. Shirley M. Yarbrough; 1 dau., Vickee. Law clk. to Donald Hollowell, 1960; field sec. Ga. br. N.A.A.C.P., 1962; then dir. So. Regional Council's voter edn. project; now exec. dir. Nat. Urban League; also exec. dir. United Negro Coll. Fund. Mem. Nat. Adv. Commn. Selective Service, White House conf. To Fulfill These Rights. Home: 966 Casco Lane Lilburn GA 30427 Office: 136 Marietta St NW Atlanta GA 30318*

JORDON, BOBBY GENE, hosp. adminstr.; b. Winnfield, La., Jan. 20, 1943; s. J. C. and Eunice (Pendarvis) J.; B.S., La. Tech. U., 1965; m. Laverne Cockerham, Dec. 27, 1963; children—Laurinda Lynn, Bobby Gene II. Adminstr. Martin Hosp., Winnfield, La., 1966-68; adminstr. Winnfield Gen. Hosp., 1968—, trustee, 1970—. Mem. Am. Assn. Hosp. Accountants, Am. Acad. Med. Adminstrs.; nominee Am. Coll. Hosp. Adminstrs. Baptist (deacon). Club: Winnfield (La.) Country. Home: 103 Cherokee Winnfield LA 71483 Office: 201 Boundary Winnfield LA 71483

JORDRE, WILLIAM STARLING, mech. engr.; b. Mantorville, Minn., June 1, 1906; s. John I. and Anna (Andrist) J.; student Antioch Coll., 1924-28; B.M.E., U. Minn., 1931; m. Hazel E. Olson, Nov. 21, 1931; children— Starling Ann (Mrs. F.W. Kephart, Jr.), Sue H. (Mrs. Laurence J. James), Diane (Mrs. George C. Meyerratken), J. William, JoAnn. Erector, Babcock & Wilcox Co., Barberton, O., 1931-38, dist. erection supt. Cin. office, 1938-43, Chgo. office, 1943-45; exec. v.p., dir. Oberle-Jordre Co., Inc., 1945—; dir. Crestview Lands, Inc. Bd. dirs. Boilermakers Nat. Health and Welfare Fund. Mem. Engring. Soc. Cin., Nat., Ohio, Ky., Ind. socs. profl. engrs., Am. Soc. M.E. Episcopalian. Mason (32 deg.) Home: 1360 East Bend Rd Burlington KY 41005 Office: Tri-State Bldg Cincinnati OH 45202

JORGENSON, JAMES R., lawyer, state ofcl. Mem. Law Rev. Commn. State of Fla. Address: 8235 N Bayshore Dr Miami FL 33138*

JORGENSON, WALLACE JAMES, broadcasting co. exec.; b. Mpls., Oct. 31, 1923; s. Peter and Adelia (Bong) J.; student St. Olaf Coll., 1942-43; A.B., Bowling Green State U., 1944; L.H.D., Lenoir-Rhyne Coll., 1971; m. Solveig Elizabeth Tvedt, Feb. 24, 1945; children—Kristin, Peter, Mark, Lisa, Philip. Staff announcer WCAL, Northfield, Minn., 1941-43; officer in charge Armed Forces Radio Network, Kyushu, Japan, 1945-46; mgr. KTRF, Thief River Falls, Minn., 1946-48; with Jefferson-Pilot Broadcasting Co., Charlotte, N.C., 1948—, v.p., 1966-68, exec. v.p., 1968—; dir. TV Advt. Reps., N.Y.C. Chpt. chmn. A.R.C., 1969-70, bd. dirs., 1970—; dir. Contact Telephone Ministry, 1969-71. Bd. dirs. Charlotte Symphony; chmn. bd. dirs. Lenoir Rhyne Coll., 1971—; bd. dirs., trustee United Community Services. Served to 2d lt. USMCR, 1942-46. Recipient Distinguished Service award Lenoir Rhyne Coll., 1969. Clubs: Charlotte City, Quail Hollow Country (Charlotte). Home: 3210 Eastburn Rd Charlotte NC 28210 Office: 1 Julian Price Pl Charlotte NC 28208

JORGESON, CHARLES MILTON, JR., textile co. exec.; b. Park Ridge, Ill., Apr. 17, 1914; s. Charles Milton and Marjorie Althea (Allen) J.; B.S., Purdue U., 1938; grad. Exec. Program, Carnegie Inst. Tech., 1955; grad. Sch. Indsl. Adminstrn. Cornell U., 1967; m. Sylvia Strickland, Jan. 20, 1971; children—Craig Marshall, Brent Wilson. Indsl. engr. B.F. Goodrich Co., Akron, O., 1941-45; indsl. engr. B.F. Goodrich Co., Miami, Okla., 1945; staff supt. B.F. Goodrich Textile Products, Thomaston, Ga., 1945-67, prodn. supt. 1967-68, gen. mgr., 1968—. Mem.-at-large Nat. council Boy Scouts Am., 1960—, mem. exec. bd. Flint River council 1950—. Chmn. Thomaston Bd. Edn., 1969-70. Bd. dirs. Textile Edn. Found., Inc., 1969—. Mem. Ga. Textile Mfrs. Assn. (dir. 1969—), Phi Kappa Psi. Methodist (adminstrv. bd. 1967—). Contbr. to textbooks for textile industry. Home: 306 Johnston Dr Thomaston GA 30286 Office: 325 Goodrich Av Thomaston GA 30286

JOSEPH, DORRIS GEORGE, coll. dean; b. Palmetto, La., May 9, 1922; s. Charles and Katherine (Jabour) J.; B.S., U. Southwestern La., 1951; M.Ed., La. State U., 1953, Ed.D., 1963; m. Myrtle Spears, Dec. 14, 1941; children—Dennis George, Donna Therese (Mrs. Day), Jeri Lynn (Mrs. Landry). Dir., Vets. Trade Sch., Sunset, La., 1949-51; tchr. Palmetto High Sch., 1951-53; instr. U. Southwestern La., Lafayette, 1953-63; dir. student teaching Nicholls State Coll., Thibodaux, La., 1963-66, dean Coll. Edn., 1966—. Served with USAAF, 1942-45. Mem. La. Tchrs. Assn., Assn. for Tchr. Edn., Confraternity Christian Doctrine, Delta Sigma Phi, Phi Delta Kappa. Lion. Author: A Student's Guide to Louisiana History, 1962; A Teacher's Guide to Louisana History, 1962. Home: 103 Creole Lane Thibodaux LA 70301

JOSEPHSON, JULIAN, educator, engr.; b. Bklyn., Aug. 28, 1934; s. Murray K. and Rhea (Rudd) J.; B.A., N.Y. U., 1955, postgrad. 1956; diploma U. Paris (France), 1959; postgrad. Cath. U. Am., 1967-68; m. Aliza Simha, Apr. 14, 1959; children—Ron, Naomi. With U.S. Naval Oceanographic Office, Washington, 1956-59, 61-69, cartographer, 1961-65; civil engr., Washington, 1965-69; phys. scientist Bur. Mines, 1970-71; instr. chemistry and English, Sch. Marine and Environmental Sci., Fla. Inst. Tech., Jensen Beach, 1971—. Sec. Internat. Buoy Tech. Symposium, 1964. Recipient U.S. Govt. Superior Accomplishment award, 1958, 63; Invention award, 1966, 67, 68, 69, 70. Mem. I.E.E.E., Marine Tech. Soc. (finance chmn. 1965, treas. conf. 1966, founding patron, sec., dir. Cape Canaveral sect. 1971-72). Patentee in field. Contbr. articles to sci. jours. Home: 223 Columbia Dr Cape Canaveral FL 32920 Office: Jensen Beach FL 33457

JOSSI, JACK WILLIAM, oceanographer; b. Portland, Ore., Apr. 4, 1937; s. Jacob and Muriel (Templeman) J.; B.S., Pacific U., 1959; B.S., U. Wash., 1962; M.S., U. Miami (Fla.), 1972 Oceanographer, Bur. Commercial Fisheries, Biol. Lab., Washington, 1962-65; oceanographer Bur. Commercial Fisheries, Tropical Atlantic Biol. Lab., Miami, Fla. 1965—, chief scientist oceanographic expdn., 1966-68, leader marine primary prodn. project, 1967-70; oceanographer Nat. Marine Fisheries Service, Miami, 1970-72, Nat. Oceanic and Atmospheric Adminstrn., Narragansett, R.I., 1972—. Mem. Marine Biol. Assn. U.K., Am. Soc. Limnology and Oceanography, Plankton Soc. Japan, Internat. Oceangraphic Found. Research on ocean's effect on living resources. Home: 4171 Malaga Av Coconut Grove FL 33133 Office: RR-7A Box 522-A Narragansett RI 02882

JOULLIAN, EDWARD CAREY, III, pipeline co. exec.; b. Blackwell, Okla., Aug. 12, 1929; s. Edward G. and Alice (Tallieur) J.; grad. N.M. Mil. Inst., 1949; B.S. in Mech. Engring., Okla. State U., 1951; m. Letitia G. Robertson, Sept. 2, 1950; children—Marion L., Edward C. IV. Natural gas engr. Texas Co., Houston, 1951-52; v.p. Mustang Fuel Corp., Oklahoma City, 1955-60, v.p., 1960-64, pres., chmn. bd., chief exec. officer, 1964—; dir. Am. Fidelity Assurance Co., First Nat. Bank & Trust Co., Oklahoma City, First Okla. Bancorp, Wilson and Co., Inc. Active Boy Scouts Am., A.R.C. Trustee, Casady Sch. Served to 1st lt. AUS, 1952-53. Mem. Nat., Okla. socs. profl. engrs., Natural Gas Processors Assn. (v.p.). Methodist. Rotarian. Home: 7203 Nichols Rd Oklahoma City OK 73120 Office: Box 60466 Oklahoma City OK 73106

JOY, EDWIN DOUGLAS, JR., oral surgeon; b. Bridgeport, Conn., June 15, 1933; s. Edwin Douglas and Bernadette (Fagan) J.; B.A., Yale, 1954; D.D.S., U. Pa., 1958; m. Beverly Edwards, Aug. 29, 1953; children—Edwin Douglas III, David Michael. Intern, Phila. Naval Hosp., 1958-59; resident Med. Coll. Va., 1962-65; practice dentistry specializing in oral surgery, Richmond, Va., 1965-71; mem. staff Norfolk Gen., DePaul hosps., Gen Hosp. Virginia Beach; asst. prof. oral surgery Med. Coll. Va., Richmond, 1965—; dir. dept. dentistry DePaul Hosp., 1967-71. Served to lt. comdr. USNR, 1958-62. Diplomate Am. Bd. Oral Surgery. Mem. Am. Dental Assn., Am. Soc. Oral Surgeons, Va. Soc. Oral Surgeons, Tidewater Dental Study Club, Norfolk C. of C., Omicron Kappa Upsilon, Delta Sigma Delta. Roman Catholic. Lion. Home: 7525 Marilea Rd Richmond VA 23225 Office: Dept of Oral Surgery Medical College of Va Richmond VA 23219

JOYCE, ALBERT JOHN, JR., polit. party ofcl.; b. Ancon, C.Z., Sept. 19, 1932; s. Albert John and Mary Gertrude (Mulrey) J.; B.A., The Citadel, 1954; LL.B., U. S.C., 1960; m. Maria Victoria Faraudo, Dec. 19, 1959; children—Albert John III, Richard Michael. Admitted to C.Z. bar, 1960, since practiced in Balboa; intelligence analyst Dept. Army, U.S. Army Caribbean, 1956-57; acting pub. defender C.Z. Govt., 1966. Vice chmn. C.Z. Regional Democratic Central Com., 1960-62, chmn., 1962—; del. Dem. Nat. Conv., 1968. Served to 1st lt. AUS, 1954-56. Mem. Am., Fed. (3d v.p. C.Z. chpt. 1970), C.Z. (sec. 1965-66, v.p. 1968, pres. 1969) bar assns., Pi Sigma Alpha, Phi Alpha Delta. Acting sports page editor Star and Herald, 1956-57; contbr. sports articles to Panama Am., 1960—. Address: PO Box 615 Balboa Canal Zone*

JOYCE, EVELYN ELIZABETH NORDSTROM (MRS. JOHN THOMAS JOYCE III), granite co. exec.; b. Texarkana, Tex., Mar. 22, 1920; d. Erick Sven and Signe (Johnson) Nordstrom; student U. Okla., 1936-40; m. John Thomas Joyce III, Dec. 27, 1946; children—Gigi Evelyn, John Michael. With Roosevelt Granite Co., Inc., Snyder, Okla., 1940—, v.p., 1945-60; pres., 1960—; pres. Southwestern Granite Supply Co., Snyder, 1957—. Del dist. and state Republican convs., 1968. Mem. Delta Gamma Alumae. Home: Route 1 Box 112 Snyder OK 73566 Office: Box 307 Snyder OK 73566

JOYCE, FRANK, farmer; b. Olive Hill, Tenn., Feb. 24, 1909; s. T.F. and Beulah (Porter) J.; B.S.A., U. Tenn., 1930; m. Anna Louise Beachboard, May 24, 1934; children—Nancy Elizabeth, Alice Ruth, Jean Ann. Asst. farm mgmt. specialist U. Tenn. Agrl. Extension Service, Knoxville, 1930-44; farmer, Winchester, Tenn., 1944—; dir. Tenn. Farmers Mut. Ins. Co., 1948-63; mem. stockholders com. 1st Nat. Bank of Franklin County. Agrl. rep. Tenn. Indsl. and Agrl. Devel. Commn., 1953-59; citizens adv. com. Tenn. Legislative Council Edn. Study, 1956-57; planning com. Tenn. Conf. Edn. Beyond High Sch., 1958. Mem. Middle Tenn. Farmers Inst. (pres. 1951), Tenn. Farm Bur. Fedn. (dir. 1946-62), Franklin County Farm Bur. (pres. 1946-54, dir. 1945—), Franklin Farmers Coop. (dir. 1948-51, 52-54, sec.-treas. 1957-63, pres. 1964-70), Tenn. Rural Health Improvement Assn. (past dir.), Murfreesboro Prodn. Credit Assn. (dir. 1948-54), Franklin County C. of C. (dir. 1958-59), U. Tenn. Alumni Assn. (council 1954-55). Am. Hereford Assn., Alpha Zeta, Phi Kappa Phi. Mem. Church of Christ (former elder). Club: University of Tenn. Block and Bridie (hon.). Monthly contbr. The Progressive Farmer, 1946-61. Address: RFD 1 Winchester TN 37398

JOYNER, HOWARD WARREN, educator; b. Chgo., July 12, 1900; s. Daniel Wright and Alice L. (McKinney) J.; B.F.A., U. Mo., 1927, M.A., 1929; postgrad. Ecole des Beaux Arts, Fontainebleau, France, 1928; M.F.A., Ia. State U., 1941; m. Arista Arnold, July 17, 1934; children—Howard Sajon, David Warren. Asst. prof. Mich. State U., East Lansing, 1927-33; registrar Kansas City Art Inst., 1933-35; head dept. art U. S.D., 1935-37; prof. head art dept. U. Tex., Arlington, 1937—; exhibited in group shows Rockefeller Center, N.Y.C., Detroit Inst. Art, Rosylyn Meml., Omaha, Kansas City Art Inst., Dallas Mus. Fine Arts, others. Recipient Legion of Honor, Order DeMolay. Mem. Ft. Worth (dir.), Arlington art assns., Art Assn. Dallas Mus. of Fine Arts, Phi Mu Alpha, Delta Phi Delta. Episcopalian. Home: 1611 W 2d St Arlington TX 76013

JUDAH, CHARLES BURNET, educator; b. Vincennes, Ind., Feb. 2, 1902; s. Charles Burnet and Edith (Reynalds) J.; A.B., U. Ill., 1925, M.A., 1926, Ph.D., 1929; postgrad. U. London, Eng., 1926-27; m. Dorothea Trautvetter, Sept. 14, 1926; 1 dau., Victoria (Mrs. Irvin Dwayne Longenbadgh). Faculty, N.M. Highlands U., 1931-47; prof. polit. sci. U. M.N., Albuquerque, 1947-67; vis. prof. Tex. A. and I. U., Kingsville, 1967—. Author: Tom Bone, 1942; Christopher Humble, 1956; (with G.M. Smith) The Unchosen, 1962, Life in the North During The Civil War, 1966, Chronicles of the Gringoes, 1968. Home: 704 W Corral St Kingsville TX 78363

JUDICE, C(HARLES) RAYMOND, judge; b. Lafayette, La., July 3, 1929; s. Rene and Letie (Bertrand) J.; student Southwestern La. U., 1946-47; B.B.A. U. Houston, 1956; J.D., S. Tex. Coll. Law, 1961. Admitted to Tex. bar, 1961; mem. firm Judice, Ogg & Merrill, Houston, 1961-63; judge Municipal Ct., Houston, 1963—. Bd. dirs. Houston Cancer Soc., Houston Council on Alcoholism. Served with USAF, 1948-49, 50-51. Recipient gavel award for jud. leadership, 1966, award for best rehab. program N. Am. Judges Assn., 1966, Amicus Curiae award, 1968. Mem. Houston Bar Assn., State Bar Tex. (vice chmn. spl. commn. on cts. of spl. jurisdiction 1969-70, chmn. com. on cts. spl. jurisdiction 1967-68), N. Am. Judges Assn. (chmn. sect. alcoholism and drugs 1967-68; mem. bd. govs. 1969-72, chmn. by-laws com. 1969-70), Tex. Assn. Municipal Judges (pres. 1966-67, dir. 1967—), S. Tex. Coll. Law Alumni Assn. (pres. 1966-67, dir. 1967—), Phi Alpha Delta (dist. justice 1964-66, supreme historian 1966-68, supreme sec. 1968-70, supreme adv. 1970-72, justice Houston alumni chpt. 1968-69). Author: Phi Alpha Delta Law Fraternity: A History, 1969. Home: 2502 Woodhead St Houston TX 77019 Office: Municipal Ct 61 Riesner St Houston TX 77002

JUDKINS, WILLIAM SINCLAIR, carbonated beverage co. exec.; b.Alexandria, Va., Oct. 13, 1919; s. Holland Ball and Esther Dashield (Burke) J.; B.S., U. Va., 1942; m. Catharine Corbin Beverley, Feb. 12, 1944; children—Catharine Corbin. William Beverley. Vice pres. Coca-Cola Bottling Co., Balt., 1952-60, pres., Columbus, O., 1960-62, pres., Chgo., 1963-65; v.p. Coca-Cola Co., Atlanta, 1965—, field mgr. bottler sales, 1967-68, mgr. nat. sales dept., 1968—. Woodberry Forest Sch. Served with USNR, 1942-45. Mem. Beta Theta Pi. Clubs: Pemigewasset Fish and Game (Plymouth, N.H.); Peachtree Golf, Piedmont Driving (Atlanta); Bald Peak Colony (Melvin Village, N.H.), Farmington Country (Charlottesville, Va.). Home: 2268 Woodward Way NW Atlanta GA 30305 Office: 310 North Av NW Atlanta GA 30301

JUENGLING, LEONARD EARL, advt. agy. exec.; b. Bonner Springs, Kan., Apr. 8, 1918; s. Christian Henry and Fannie Eunice (Brown) J.; grad. Kansas City Jr. Coll., 1937; m. Mary Martha Rizk, Sept. 4, 1940; children—Richard Earl and Steven Henry (twins). Advt. mgr. Mid-Continent Airlines, Kansas City, Mo., 1947-50; sales and advt. mgr. Cook Chem. Co., Kansas City, 1950-58; v.p. Simon & Gwyyn, Inc., Memphis, 1959-67, pres., 1967—; pres. Pyramid Prodns., Memphis, 1964—. Mem. Am. Marketing Assn. (bd. dirs., 1st pres.), Memphis Advt. Club (bd. dirs.). Author: Salesman's Guide to Supermarket Selling, 1960. Home: 4704 Normandy Av Memphis TN 38117 Office: 3329 Poplar Av Memphis TN 38111

JUERGENSEN, HANS, educator, poet; b. Upper Sielesia, Germany, Dec. 17, 1919; s. (foster) Hermann A. and Dora (Grossmann) J.; B.A., Upsala Coll., 1942; Ph.D., Johns Hopkins, 1951; Hon. Dr., Boswell Inst., Loyola U. of South, 1970; m. Ilse D. Lobenberg, Oct. 27, 1945; 1 dau., Claudia Jeanne. Came to U.S., 1934, naturalized 1943. Instr. German, U. Kan., 1951-53, Johns Hopkins, summers 1949-53; asst. prof., asso. prof. English, chmn. dept. Quinnipiac Coll., 1953-61; prof. humanities U.S. Fla., 1961—; art critic Tampa Times, 1961-67; one man shows at Studio Gallery, N.Y., Tampa (Fla.) Art Inst. Served with AUS, 1942-45. Fellow Conn. Acad. Arts and Scis., Poetry Soc. Am.; mem. Nat. Fedn. State Poetry Socs. (pres. 1968-70), C. of C., Delta Phi Alpha (hon.). Democrat. Jewish religion. Author: I Feed You From My Cup, 1958; In Need for Names, 1961; Existential Canon, 1965; Florida Montage, 1966; Sermons From The Ammunition Hatch of The Ships of Fools, 1968; From The Divide, 1970; Hebraic Modes, 1972; Points of Departure, 1973. Home: 7815 Pine Hill Dr Tampa FL 33617

JULIA, GILDA, realtor, mem. Republican Nat. Com.; b. San Juan, P.R., Nov. 18, 1927; d. Enrique and Emila (Martinez) Julia; B.S. in Math, U. Va., 1948; div.; children—Maria Emilia, Luis Esteban, Mario Enrique, Maria Luisa, Andres Eduardo, Miguel Antonio, Maria Alexandra. Mem. staff Condominium Enterprises Inc., Castle Enterprises, Inc., San Juan Realty Corp.; City Enterprises, Inc., Center Enterprises, Inc., Caparra Enterprises, Inc., Ceramic Enterprises, Inc., originator 1st condominium apt. bldg. in U.S., 1st condominium office bldg. in U.S., 1st condominium parking garage in U.S., indsl. real estate developer in P.R. Del. Republican Nat. Conv., 1968; mem. Rep. Nat. Com. for P.R., 1968—. Club: Sleepy Hollow Country. Home: Mallorca 37 Hato Rey PR 00917 Office: Box 11605 Santurce PR 00910

JUMPER, KENNETH MARTIN, banker; b. Waco, Tex., Mar. 30, 1929; s. Cecil D. and Jewell D. (Posey) J.; student Central City Coll., Waco, Tex., 1947; m. Nita Lee Webb, Dec. 26, 1969; children—Ronnie Rickey, Kenneth Ray. Teller, Citizens Nat. Bank, Waco, 1947-51; asst. v.p. 1st Nat. Bank, Odessa, Tex., 1951-58; pres. Nat. Bank Odessa, 1959—; also dir.; dir. Am. Energy Co., Odessa, B&S Reconditioning Co., Odessa. Bd. dirs. Salvation Army, 1965—, Odessa Indsl. Found., 1970—. Mem. C. of C. (bd. dirs. 1970-71), Am., Tex. bankers assns. Lutheran. Mason (Shriner), Rotarian. Home: 4218 Kirkwood St Odessa TX 79760 Office: PO Box 634 Odessa TX 79760

JUNG, CLARENCE ROBERT, JR., educator; b. Walnut Ridge, Ark., Aug. 23, 1924; s. Clarence R. and Virginia (Cravens) J.; B.A., DePauw U., 1947; M.A., Ohio State U., 1949, Ph.D., 1953; m. Jeanne Sparks, Dec. 28, 1947; children—David, Dinah, Andrew. Instr. Ohio State U., 1947-53; asst. prof. econ. Coe Coll., 1953-55, asso. prof., chmn. dept., 1955-56; economist Standard Oil Co., Ind., 1956-65; asso. prof. managerial econ. Boston U., 1965-66; prof. econs. U. Richmond (Va.), 1966—, chmn., 1967—; cons. Va. Electric and Power Co., 1966—, Va. Hwy. Users Assn., 1968-69. Served with USAAF, 1943-46. Mem. Am. Assn. U. Profs. Club: Torch. Home: 1612 Princeton Rd Richmond VA 23227

JUNG, DEXTER ADOLPH, JR., dentist; b. Galveston, Tex., Aug. 8, 1921; s. Dexter Adolph and Lucile Elizabeth (Housinger) J.; B.A., Rice U., 1942; D.D.S., U. Tex., 1945; m. Thana Ruth Roberts, June 16, 1946; children—Dexter Adolph III, Robert Loyd. Practice dentistry in McAllen, Tex., 1947—; chief dental staff, McAllen Gen. Hosp., 1971—. Bd. dirs. McAllen chpt. Salvation Army. Served with USNR, 1945-47. Mem. Rio Grande Dental Soc., (pres.), Omicron Kappa Upsilon, Psi Omega. Mem. Seventh Day Adventist Ch. (elder) Home: 1613 Esperanza St McAllen TX 78501 Office: 312 N 10th McAllen TX 78501

JUNG, RODNEY C., physician; b. New Orleans, Oct. 9, 1920; s. Frederick Charles and Clara (Cuevas) J.; B.S. in zoology with honors, Tulane U., 1941, M.D., 1945, M.S. in parasitology, 1950, Ph.D., 1953 Intern Charity Hosp. La., New Orleans 1945-46; dir. Hutchinson Meml. Clinic, 1948; asst. parasitology Tulane U., 1948-50, instr. tropical medicine, 1950-53, asst. prof., 1953-57, asso. prof. tropical medicine 1951-63, prof. tropical medicine, 1963—, head div. tropical medicine, 1960-63; health dir. City of New Orleans, 1963-70; internist-in-charge Ill. Central Hosp., New Orleans, 1956-70; sr. vis. physician Charity Hosp., 1959—; sr. asso. in gastroenterology Touro Infirmary; John and Mary Markie Scholar in med. sci.; area cons. tropical medicine VA, 1959; cons. in tropical medicine USPHS Hosp., 1958; mem. commn. parasitic diseases Armed Forces Epidemiological Bd. Mem. bd. New Orleans Health Planning Council. Diplomate Am. Bd. Internal Medicine. Fellow A.C.P.; mem. Internat. Society Tropical Dermatology, Am. Royal socs. tropical medicine and hygiene, Am. Soc. Parasitologists, La. State, Orleans Parish med. socs., Nat. Rifle Assn., La. Mosquito Control Assn. Am., La. public health assns., Am., La. socs. internal medicine, Am. Ordnance Assn., Delgado Art Assn., Phi Beta Kappa, Sigma Xi, Alpha Omega Alpha. Presbyn. Home: 533 W Marlin Ct Gretna LA 70053 Office: 3600 Chestnut New Orleans LA 70115

JUNGEMANN, EDWARD FREDERICK, airlines exec.; b. Savannah, Ga., Aug. 26, 1918; s. Edward F. and Sara (Masters) J.; grad. Dallas Aviation Sch. and Air Coll., 1938; m. Helen Annette Brown, Aug. 17, 1941; children— Susan Claire, Mary Bothwell, Ann Louise. Flight instr. Strachan Skyways, Savannah, Ga., 1939-41; v.p., gen. mgr. Airflight, Inc., Savannah, 1945-57; pres. Savannah Air Service, Inc., 1958—. Trustee Gen. Aviation Mgmt. Found., Va. Tech. U. Served with A.C., AUS, 1941-45. Mem. Antique Aircraft Assn. Presbyn. Clubs: LaVida Country (Savannah, Ga.), Exchange (Savannah, Ga.). Home: 606 Windsor Rd Savannah GA 31406 Office: Travis Field PO Box 6692 Savannah GA 31405

JUNGERS, RICHARD P(HILIP), educator; b. nr. Random Lake, Wis., Feb. 20, 1914; s. Nickolas J. and Matilda (Krier) J.; B.E., LaCrosse State Coll., 1936; Ph.M., U. Wis., 1946, Ph.D., 1957; m. Edna G. Voigt, Sept. 12, 1942; 1 son, Richard K. Tchr., coach Random Lake (Wis.) High Sch., 1938-41; supervising prin. pub. schs., Glenbeulah, Wis., 1946-51; supt. schs., Random Lake, Wis., 1951-56; prof. edn. Okla. State U., 1957—. Cons. Okla. pub. schs. and ednl. orgns. Served to capt. Signal Corps, AUS, 1941-46. Decorated Bronze Star medal with oak leaf cluster. Mem. Okla. Edn. Assn., Okla. Sch. Adminstrs. Assn., Okla. Sch. Bus. Ofcls. Assn., Okla. Secondary Sch. Prins. Assn. Home: 501 Harned Dr Stillwater OK 74074

JUNGMAN, CLAUDE JACOB, supt. schs.; b. Devine, Tex., Jan. 31, 1922; s. Edwin M. and Helen E. (Schneider) J.; B.S., S.W. Tex. State U., 1948, M.Ed., 1952; postgrad. U. Tex. at Austin, 1961; m. Mary Beth Raymer, July 12, 1951; children—Cynthia, Paul, Susan. Tchr., coach Weslaco (Tex.) Ind. Sch. Dist., 1948-55; tchr., coach, adminstr. Premont (Tex.) Ind. Sch. Dist., 1955-62; secondary prin. Jim Hogg County Ind. Sch. Dist., Hebbronville, Tex., 1962-66, supt., 1967—; secondary prin. Mercedes (Tes.) Ind. Sch. Dist., 1966-67. Pres., Salvation Army; v.p. Am. Cancer Soc. Mem. N.E.A., Tex. Tchrs. Assn., Tex. Assn. Sch. Adminstrs. Lion. Home: 711 Viggie St Hebbronville TX 78361 Office: 910 Wilhelma St Hebbronville TX 78361

JUNIPER, WALTER HOWARD, coll. ofcl.; b. Nelsonville, O., Oct. 25, 1911; s. Charles Walter and Lucena E. (Howard) J;; A.B., B.S., Ohio State U., 1933, A.M., 1934, Ph.D., 1937; postgrad. (Martin Kellogg Fellow in classics), Yale, 1934-35; m. Helen Marjorie Howery, May 25, 1935; 1 dau., Margaret Helen. Instr. classical langs. Ohio State U., 1934-37, instr. English, 1946; instr. French and Latin, dean men Cumberland Coll., Williamsburg, Ky., 1937-38; asst. prof; Latin Baylor U., 1938-41, asst. dean, prof. Latin, 1946-49; dean W. Tex. State U., Canyon, 1949-66, acad. v.p., 1966—. Moderator, Waco Jr. Town Meeting, 1947-49. Served with AUS, 1941-46. Mem. Tex. Assn. for Ednl. Television, N.E.A., So. Conf. Acad. Deans, Am. Assn. U. Profs., Am. Philol. Assn., Tex. Classical Assn. Presbyn. Mason, Rotarian. Author, producer: Jukebox of Yesteryear, 1948-52. Contbr. to profl. jours. Home: 2516 6th Av Canyon TX 79015

JUNKIN, JOHN RICHARD, state legislator; b. Natchez, Miss., Dec. 16, 1896; married. Contractor, planter; mem. Miss. Ho. of Reps., 1944—, now speaker. Mem. Natchez Bd. Suprs., 1928-36. Mem. Am. Legion. Roman Catholic. Address: 311 N Wall St Natchez MS 39120*

JUNKIN, MARION MONTAGUE, artist, educator; b. Chunju, Korea, Aug. 23, 1905 (parents Am. citizens); s. William McCleery and Mary (Leyburn) J.; A.B., Washington and Lee U., 1927, Arts D., 1949; student Art Students League N.Y., 1927-30; studied with Luks, Locke & McCartan, 1930-32; m. Marguerite Eddy, Sept. 16, 1933; children—Michael Eddy, Margo Patricia. Prof. fine arts, asso. dir. Richmond Sch. Arts, Coll. William and Mary, 1933-42; asso. prof., head dept. fine arts Vanderbilt U., 1941-49; prof., head dept. fine arts Washington and Lee U., Lexington, Va., 1949—; exhibited in one man shows at Joseph Luyber Gallery, N.Y.C., 1946, 47, Va. Mus. Fine Arts, 1948; exhibited in group shows at Whitney Mus., 1936,

Corcoran Gallery, 1933, Art Inst. Chgo., 1933, N.Y. Worlds Fair, 1939, Pa. Acad. Fine Arts, 1933, Butler Art Inst., 1943, Carnegie Inst., 1949; fresco paintings in Memphis, Richmond, Roanoke, Va. Mem. Va. Fine Arts Commn., 1939-42. Recipient awards from Va. Mus. Fine Arts, Richmond Acad. Fine Arts, Butler Art Inst., IBM Corp., Brooks Meml. Gallery. Mem. Am. Assn. U. Profs., Omicron Delta Kappa. Episcopalian. Home: 801 Stonewall St Lexington VA 24450

JURISSON, D. B., dentist; b. Mooreland, Okla., Apr. 19, 1923; s. John and Kanard (Germany) J.; student U. Fla., 1942; D.D.S., Baylor U., 1950; m. Rosalie Gwinn, Dec. 18, 1946; children—Virginia (Mrs. Paul Kelley), Cathy Rose. Pub. health dentist, Va., 1950-51; practice dentistry, Christiansburg, Va., 1951—; mem. staff Montgomery County Hosp. Bd. dirs. Community United Fund, 1951-52. Served with USCGR, 1942-45. Mem. Va. Dental Soc., Montgomery County Med. Soc., Psi Omega. Presbyn. (deacon). Kiwanian. Home: 725 W Main St Christiansburg VA 24073 Office: PO Box 91 8 Roanoke St Christiansburg VA 24073

JUST, CAROLYN ROYALL, lawyer; b. Shanghai, China, Sept. 15, 1907; d. Francis Martin and Mary Dunklin (Sullivan) Royall; Ph.B., U. of Chicago, 1934; J.D., De Paul U., 1938; LL.M., George Washington U., 1940; grad. Inter-Am. Acad Comparative Internat. Law. Havana, Cuba, 4th Session, 1949, 5th Session, 1950; 7th Session, 1955, 9th Session, 1957; Certificate, Hague Acad. Internat. Law, 31st Session, 1960; m. Robert Just, Dec. 17, 1925 (dec. Nov. 1943). Violin tchr., 1925-30; chief of staff Concessions Dept., Century of Progress Chicago Exposition, 1933; editorial asst., sec. to Dr. Forest Ray Moulton, permanent sec. A.A.A.S., 1930-38; admitted to D.C. bar, 1938, practiced law at Washington, D.C., 1938; admitted to Ill. bar, 1940; admitted to bar of Supreme Court of U.S., 1941; with U.S. Dept. of Justice, atty. Lands Div., 1938-43; atty. Antitrust Div., 1943-50; atty. Tax Div., 1950—. Mem. D.C. Citizenship (formerly I Am An American) Day Com. (chmn. com. citizen- ship recognition, 1946, gen. sec., 1947-50); mem. Atty. Gen's. Adv. Com. on Citizenship and del. representing Dept. of Justice to nat. confs. on citizenship at Phila., 1946. Washington, 1947, 48, and 1950-55, N.Y.C., 1949. Mem. Am. Bar Assn. (sects. of taxation, antitrust internat. law, chmn. com. on relations with internat. bar orgns; adv. com. on pub. relations 1962-65; mem. com. facilities Law Library Congress 1952-59), Fed. Bar Assn. (formerly asst. editor Fed. Bar Jour.); Nat. Assn. Woman Lawyers, Bar Assn. of D.C., Women's Bar Assn. D.C., Internat. Bar Assn. (charter parton, del. to confs. N.Y.C., 1947, London, England, 1951, Madrid, 1952, Salzburg, 1960, Mexico City, Mexico, 1964; chmn. credentials com. Madrid 1952), Inter-Am. Bar Assn. (delegate to first conference Havana, Cuba, 1941, 3d and 4th confs., Mexico City, 1944, santiago, Chile, 1945, 5th Conf., Lima, Peru, 1947, 6th conf. Detroit, 1949, 8th conf; Sao Paulo, Brazil, 54, 9th conf. Dallas, 1956, 10th conf. Buenos Aires, 1957, 11th conf. Miami 1959, 12th conf, Bogota, Colombia, 1961, 15th conference San Jose Costa Rica 1967; reporter general; council 1945—), Am. Law Inst., Am. Soc. Internat. Law, George Washington U. Alumni Assn., U. Chgo. Alumni Assn., Am. Judicature Soc., Am. Assn. U. Women, Club de las Americas (pres. 1964-65), D.A.R., Internat. Law Assn. (Am. br.), Internat. Fiscal Assn., Pi Gamma Mu, Kappa Beta Pi, Phi Delta Gamma. Mem. George Washington U. Symphony Orch., Gault Chamber Music Players, Amateur Chamber Music Players, Friday Morning Music Club. Home: Harbour Sq 520 N St SW Washington DC 20024 Office: U S Dept of Justice Washington DC 20530

JUSTICE, CORNELIA WINBORNE (MRS. HORACE ALTON JUSTICE), artist, critic; b. Norfolk, Va.; d. Littleton Augustus and Edna (Wade) Winborne; student Coll. William and Mary; m. Horace Alton Justice, Dec. 10, 1943. Exhibited in one man shows Norfolk Mus. Arts, 1959, Cofer's Galleries, Norfolk and Virginia Beach, 1962-64; exhibited in museums Eng. and Scotland, 1964, Cannes, France, 1966, Cognac, France, 1969, Can., 1969; exhibited in numerous group shows throughout country, 1957—, two traveling exhbns., museums and colls. U.S., 1971-72, 75 Am. Women Artists, Florence, also Naples, Italy, 1972; represented in permanent collections La Musee de La Napoule, Cannes, Norfolk Art Mus., Le Musee de la Napoule, Cannes, Alfred Khouri Meml. Instr. advanced painting Norfolk Mus. Arts, 1960-61, Jewish Community Center, Norfolk, 1961-62; art critic Norfolk Virginian-Pilot and Portsmouth Star, 1959-60, Ledger-Dispatch, Norfolk and Beacon, Virginia Beach, 1966-68. Del. Arts Council Tidewater, Va., 1960—; mem. Norfolk Mus. Arts Council, 1959—. Recipient Best in Show awards Internat. Azalea Festival, Norfolk, 1959, Confederacy Competition Outdoor Amphitheater, Virginia Beach, 1959, Internat. Azalea Festival, 1969; 1st hon. mention award Les Semaines Internationales de la Femme, Cannes, 1969. Mem. Tidewater Artists Assn. (past pres.), Nat. Assn. Women Artists, Am. Craftsmens Council, Virginia Beach Art Assn., Norfolk Hist. Soc., Mus. Modern Art, Va. Mus. Fine Arts, Hermitage Found. Mus., Norfolk Mus. Arts, Norfolk Soc. Arts, Internat. Platform Assn., Va. Press Women's Assn., Art Council Tidewater. Art critic Ledger-Star, 1966—. Address: 619 Stockley Gardens Norfolk VA 23507

JUSTICE, WILLIAM S., physician, photographer; b. Lincoln, N.C., May 21, 1900; s. Butler Alexander and Eliza Shipp (Bynum) J.; A.B., U. N.C., 1920, postgrad., 1921-22; M.D., Harvard, 1926. Intern pathology Mass. Gen. Hosp.; intern surgery, then resident surgery Boston City Hosp.; practice medicine specializing in surgery, Asheville, N.C., 1931-69; mem. surg. staff Meml. Mission Hosp., Asheville, 1931-69, chief staff, 1955, 56, emergency room physician, 1969—; mem. staff Biltmore Hosp., Asheville, 1931-55, chief staff, 1951; mem. staff Aston Park Hosp. 1931-69. St. Joseph's Hosp., 1931—. Noted photographer wild flowers N.C. Address: 14 White Oak Rd Asheville NC 28803*

JUSTICE, WILLIAM WAYNE, judge; b. Athens, Tex., Feb. 25, 1920; s. William Davis and Jackie May (Hanson) J.; LL.B., U. Tex., 1942; m. Sue Tom Ellen Rowan, Mar. 16, 1947; 1 dau., Ellen Rowan. Admitted to Tex. bar; practice in Athens, 1946-61, as partner firm Justice & Justice; city atty., Athens 1948-50, 52-58; U.S. atty Eastern Dist. Tex. 1961-68; U.S. dist. judge Eastern Dist. Tex. 1968—. Vice pres. Young Democrats Tex., 1948; adv. council Dem. Nat. Com., 1954; alternate del. Dem. Nat. Conv., 1956; presdl. elector, 1960. Served to 1st lt. F.A., AUS, 1942-46; CBI. Mem. V.F.W. (past post comdr.). Baptist. Rotarian (pres. Athens 1961), Mason (K.T.) Home: 324 W 8th St Tyler TX 75701 Office: Federal Bldg Tyler TX 75701

JUSTIN, ENID, boot co. exec.; b. Nocona, Tex.; d. Herman Joseph and Anna (Allen) Justin; student pub. schs. With H.J. Justin & Sons, Nocona, Tex., 1910-18, pres. Nocona (Tex.) Boot Co., Inc., 1925—. Mem. Nat. Boot and Shoe Assn., Inst. of Mgmt. (pres. council 1965—), Western Apparel and Equipment Mfrs. Assn. (dir.). Mem. Christian Ch. Home: 9th and Mesquite Sts Nocona TX 76255 Office: E Hwy 82 Nocona TX 76255

JYDSTRUP, RONALD ALBERT, assn. exec.; b. Mpls., Feb. 13, 1923; s. Albert E. and Ellen V. (Brandelius) J.; B.B.A., U. Minn., 1948, M.H.A., 1950; m. Lyla Lauraine Johnson, June 24, 1972; children by previous marriage Karen, Jan, Nan, Kathleen, Mary Ellen. Instr. hosp. adminstrn. course U. Minn. also hosp. cons. James A. Hamilton & Asso., Mpls., 1950-53; sec., accounting specialist Am. Hosp. Assn., also spl. lectr. St. Louis U. and U. Minn., 1953-56; dir. N.D. Blue Cross also spl. lectr. U. Minn., 1956-61; sec. Dist. 10 Blue Cross Plans, 1958-61; exec. dir. N.Y. Regional Hosp. Council, Rochester, 1961-67; sec. Hosp. Reviewing and Planning Council, 1961-67; asst. sec. Rochester Hosp. Fund, 1961-67; v.p. Block, McGibony & Assos., health and hosp. consultants, Silver Spring, Md., 1967-70; dir. planning and devel. Group Health Assn., Washington, 1970—. Cons., Dept. Health, Edn. and Welfare, 1970—; vis. lectr. George Washington U. Mem. Fargo United Fund Planning Com., 1959-61; chmn., mem. bd. dirs. Fargo Community Council of Social Agys., 1958-61; pres., dir. Red River Valley council Camp Fire Girls, 1957-61; bd. dirs. Home Care Rochester, Monroe County; mem. N.Y. State Hosp. Rev. and Planning Council's Com.; mem. steering com. health div. Council Social Agys. Rochester, Monroe County; mem. adv. com. on study prepayment plans Columbia U. Hosps.; chmn. council mgrs. com. Hosp. Purchasing Bur., N.Y.C. Bd. dirs. Mpls. War Meml. Blood Bank, 1953, Mental Health Council Rochester and Monroe County. Recipient Silver Key, Mpls. Jr. C. of C., 1953; Sabre Hamilton award U. Minn., 1950. Fellow Royal Soc. for Health; mem. U. Minn. Alumni Assn. (pres., dir. Red River Valley chpt.), Am. Assn. Hosp. Accountants, Am. Hosp. Assn., N.Y. State Hosp. Assn., Beta Alpha Psi. Lutheran. Home: 10607 Weymouth St Bethesda MD 20014 Office: 2121 Pennsylvania Av NW Washington DC 20037

KACHLEIN, GEORGE FREDERICK, JR., lawyer, assn. exec.; b. Tacoma, May 9, 1907; s. George Frederick and Edna June (Burt) K.; A.B., Stanford, 1929; LL.B., Harvard, 1932; m. Retha Hicks, Aug. 30, 1930; 1 son, George Frederick. Admitted to Wash. bar, 1933; asso. firm Bogle, Bogle &Gates, Seattle, 1933-37, partner, 1937-42, 46-65; asst. gen. mgr., asst. sec. Seattle-Tacoma Shipbuilding Corp., 1942-46. Sec. Greater Seattle, Inc., 1952-57, pres., 1958-59; pres. Am. Automobile Assn., 1962-64, exec. v.p., 1965-70, also trustee; v.p. Orgn. Mondiale de Tourisme et del'Automobile. Mem. Pres.'s Nat. Hwy. Safety Adv. Com. Sec. King Neptune VI, 1955-56. Named Seattle's Man of Year, 1963. Mem. Inter-Am. Fedn. Touring and Automobile Clubs (1st v.p.), Am. Wash., Seattle bar assns., C. of C. (trustee 1956-58, 62-64). Clubs: Ranier, Seattle Golf; Thunderbird Country; Wash. Athletic (dir. 1947-53, sec. 50-51); Broadmoor Golf (dir. 1946-52, pres. 1950-51). Home: Shoreham West Washington DC 20006 Office: 1712 G St NW Washington 20006

KACIR, STANLEY, lawyer; b. Temple, Tex., July 10, 1927; s. August and Bettie Marie (Lesikar) K.; B.B.A., U. Tex., 1951, LL.B., 1951; m. Nelta Josephine Collier, Dec. 23, 1950; children—Karl, Kyle, Katherine, Karen, Kent. Admitted to Tex. bar, 1950; pvt. practice with father, Temple, 1951-53; partner firm Kacir, Lesiker and Kacir, Temple, 1953—; judge Corp. Ct., City of Temple, 1953-56; county atty. Bell County, Belton, Tex., 1957-60; dist. atty. 27th Judicial Dist., Belton, 1960—. Served with USNR, 1945-46. Mem. State Bar Tex., Bell, Lampasas, Mills Counties Bar Assn. (past pres.), Central Tex. Police Officers, Am. Judicature Soc., Dist. and County Attys. Assn. Tex., Temple, Belton chambers commerce, V.F.W., Am. Legion. Mason (Shriner); mem. Order Eastern Star. Home: 3209 Pin Oak Dr Temple TX 76501 Office: Bell County Court House Belton TX 76513

KACY, HOWARD WILLIAM, ins. exec.; b. Huntington, Ind., Sept. 19, 1899; s. William J. and Augusta (McNabb) K.; LL.B., Ind. U., 1921; m. Anne Millsaps, Mar. 1, 1924; children—Anne (Mrs. Herbert S. Ainsworth), Howard William. Admitted to Ind. bar, 1921, D.C. bar, 1923; with Acacia Mut. Life Ins. Co., Washington, 1923—, successively asst. counsel, counsel, gen. counsel, v.p., gen. counsel, 1st v.p., exec. v.p., 1923-55, became pres., 1955, dir., 1935—; now chmn., chief exec. officer; dir. Am. Security &Trust Co. Dir. Boys Club Met. Police D.C., Group Hospitalization, Inc., D.C. div. Am. Cancer Soc., D.C. chpt. A.R.C., YMCA, Nat. Capital Area council Boy Scouts Am. Mem. Washington Bd. Trade (dir.), Soc. Friendly Sons St. Patrick (dir., past pres. Washington), Sigma Alpha Epsilon, Phi Delta Phi. Mason (hon. mem. DeMolay Legion of Honor), Rotarian. Clubs: Alfalfa, Metropolitan (Washington); Columbia Country (Chevy Chase, Md.). Home: 1011 N Noyes Dr Silver Spring MD 20910 Office: 51 Louisiana Av Washington DC 20001

KADLECEK, EDWARD JOHN, JR., mgmt. engr.; b. Houston, July 31, 1934; s. Edward John and Louise (Jakubec) K.; B.S. in Mech. Engring., U. Houston, 1958, B.S. in Indsl. Engring., 1961; m. Marilyn Martha Holtman, Nov. 3, 1962; children—Edward John III, Karen Ann, Nancy Lynn. Chief engr. Fed. Steel Corp., Houston, 1964-65; chief maintenance indsl. engring. dept. Structural Metals, Inc., Sequin, Tex., 1965-67; chief programs devel. 3510th C.E. group, USAF, Randolph AFB, Tex., 1967—. Recipient Sustained Superior Performance award Def. Dept., 1968, Outstanding Performance award, 1972. Registered profl. engr., Tex. Mem. Nat. Soc. Profl. Engrs., Am. Inst. Indsl. Engrs., Tex. Profl. Engrs. Soc., Wurst Assn. New Braunfels, Phi Kappa Theta. Eagle. Home: 367 Oakcrest St New Braunfels TX 78130 Office: 3510 CEG Randolph AFB TX 78148

KAELIN, EUGENE FRANCIS, educator; b. St. Louis, Oct. 14, 1926; s. Albert Aloysius and Bertha Emma (Erni) K.; A.B. with distinction, U. Mo., 1949, M.A., 1950; Ph.D., U. Ill., 1954; diplome d'etudes superieures U Bordeaux (France), 1950-51; m. Pierrette Nicole Demartini, Dec. 30, 1952; children—Valerie, Carolyne, Martine. Instr., U. Mo., 1952-53; instr. U. Wis., 1955-57, asst. prof., 1957-61, asso. prof., 1961-65; asso. prof. Fla. State U., 1965-67, prof., 1967—, chmn. dept. philosophy, 1969-72. Mem. nat. adv. bd. Aesthetic Edn. Program, Cemrel, Inc., St. Ann, Mo., 1969—. Served with USMC, 1945-46. Am. Council Learned Socs. fellow, U. Wis., 1960-61; postdoctoral fellow U. Ill., 1954-55. Mem. Am., Fla. philos. assns., Am. Soc. for Aesthetics, Soc. for Phenomenology and Existential Philosophy, Phi Beta Kappa, Phi Eta Sigma. Author: An Existential Aesthetic, 1962; Art and Existence, 1970. Asso. editor Arts in Society, 1959-65. Home: 604 Hillcrest St Tallahassee FL 32303

KAESER, ROBERT SHAW, physicist; b. Pittsfield, Ill., Jan 14, 1928; s. William Heck and Delia (Shaw) K.; A.B., Ill. Coll., 1950; postgrad. U. Ill.; m. Priscilla Livingston Parks, Oct. 12, 1957; 1 son, Steven Walker. Physicist Nat. Bur. Standards, Washington, 1956—. Served with AUS, 1952-54. Mem. Am. Phys. Soc., A.A.A.S., Am. Civil Liberties Union. Democrat. Unitarian. Contbr. articles in field to profl. jours. Inventor glassblower's manostat. Home: 20 Farsta Ct Rockville MD 20850 Office: Nat Bur Standards Washington DC 20234

KAGARISE, RONALD EUGENE, chem. physicist; b. East Freedom, Pa., July 17, 1926; s. Ray Bacon and Ethel (Miller) K.; A.B., Duke, 1948; M.S., Pa. State U., 1949, Ph.D., 1951; m. Barbara A. Saylor, Dec. 24, 1947; children—Thomas Ray, Cynthia Mae, Karl Saylor. Research asso. Pa. State U., 1951-52; head chem. spectroscopy sect. Naval Research Lab., Washington, 1952-66; liaison sci. Office of Naval Research, London, Eng., 1963-64; program dir. phys. chemistry NSF, Washington, 1966-68; Supt., Chemistry Div., Naval Research Lab. 1968—. Served with USNR, 1944-46. Mem. Am. Phys. Soc., Coblentz Soc (bd. mgmt. 1967-70), Am. Chem. Soc., Washington Acad. Scis., Sigma Xi, Sigma Pi Sigma. Contbr. articles to profl. jours. Home: 339 Onondaga Dr Washington DC 20021 Office: Overlook Av SW Washington DC 20390

KAHLER, ELIZABETH SARTOR (MRS. ERVIN NEWTON CHAPMAN), physician; b. Washington, Oct. 20, 1911; d. Armin Adolphus and Lenore Elome (Sartor) Kahler; B.S., George Washington U., 1933, M.A., 1935, M.D. with distinction, 1940; m. Ervin Newton Chapman, Feb. 24, 1942. Intern, Gallinger Municipal Hosp. (now D.C. Gen. Hosp.), 1940-41; resident Children's Hosp., Washington, 1941-42; practice medicine, Washington, 1942—; asso. univ. physician George Washington U., 1942-50; examining physician YWCA, 1942-45; courtesy staff Washington Hosp. Center, Doctor's Hosp., George Washington U. Hosp.; alternate physician to wards of Bd. Pub. Welfare, Dept. Pub. Welfare, Govt. of D.C., 1953—; sch. physician Burdick Vocational High Sch., 1959—. Mem. nat. program com. Camp Fire Girls. Trustee Wilson Coll., Chambersburg, Pa., 1956-66. Mem. Women's Med. Soc. D.C. (pres. 1950-51), Am. Med. Women's Assn. (pres. 1957-58), A.M.A., Med. Soc. of D.C. (chmn. medicine and religion com. 1967-72), D.C. Assn. Mental Health, Am. Heart Assn., Columbian Women George Washington U. (life), George Washington U. Alumnae Soc, (life). Home: 2600 36th St NW Washington DC 20007

KAHLER, MARY ELLIS, librarian; b. Santiago, Chile, Aug. 2, 1919; d. John William and Edna (Doan) Ellis; A.B., Swarthmore Coll., 1940; B.L.S., Drexel Inst. Tech., 1949; M.A., George Washington U., 1953; Ph.D. in History, Am. U., 1968; m. Joseph W. Darlington, Aug. 17, 1940 (dec. 1948); m. 2d, George W. Kahler, Feb. 11, 1950. Library asst. Post Library, Fort Dix, N.J., 1944-48; with Library of Congress, 1949—, asst. chief serial record div., 1953-56, chief, 1957-66, asst, chief of union catalog div., 1966—. Asst. dir. Hispanic Found., 1971—. Mem. A.L.A, (chmn. serials sect. resources and tech. services div. 1959-60, mem. coms., dir. at large 1967-70), Latin Am. Studies Assn. (chmn. com. on scholarly resources 1971—), Spl. Libraries Assn, (local chpt. corr. sec. 1963-64, state rep. A.L.A., Recruitment Network 1966-1968, A.L.A. councilor 1969-72), D.C. Library Assn. (sec. 1964-65), Soc. Am. Archivists, Am. Hist. Assn., Am. Assn. U. Women, Phi Beta Kappa, Phi Alpha Theta. Home: 6395 Lakeview Dr Falls Church VA 22041 Office: Library of Congress Washington DC 20540

KAHN, ELLIS IRVIN, lawyer; b. Charleston, S.C., Jan. 18, 1936; s. Robert and Estelle (Kaminski) K.; A.B., The Citadel, 1958; LL.B., U. S.C., 1961; postgrad. So. Meth. U., 1962-63; m. Janice Weinstein, Aug. 11, 1963; children—Justin, David, Cynthia Anne. Admitted to S.C. bar, 1961; law clk. U.S. Dist. Judge Robert W. Hemphill, Columbia 1964-66; with firm Solomon, Solomon, Kahn & Roberts, Charleston, 1966—. Served to capt. USAF, 1961-64. Mem. Am., S.C. bar assns., Am. (state committeeman), S.C. trial lawyers assns., Phi Delta Phi (chpt. pres. 1960). Democrat. Jewish religion. Mem. B'nai B'rith (pres. 1968-71). Editor: The Brigadier, 1957-58. Home: 316 Confederate Circle Charleston SC 29407 Office: 39 Broad St Charleston SC 29402

KAHN, HANNAH, poet; b. N.Y.C., June 30, 1911; d. David and Sarah (Seigelbaum) Abrahams; m. Frank M. Kahn, Mar. 5, 1941; children—Melvin A., Daniel Lyon, Vivian Dale. Poet, poems pub. in nat. mags., 1938—; song, Stranger, 1956; (poems) Eve's Daughter, 1963; poetry rev. editor Miami (Fla.) Herald, 1958—. Tchr. creative writing Miami Dade Jr. Coll., 1971. Recipient Ralph Chency poetry award, 1946, Jessie Rittenhouse award, 1947, Jane Judge award, 1951, 71, Norfolk prize, 1954, John David Leitch award, 1954, 70, Poetry Soc. of Great Britain and Am. Parsons Sonnent award, 1957; George Washington honor medal Freedoms Found., 1962; 2d prize for ann. award Poetry Soc. Am., 1970. Mem. poetry socs. Am., Va., Ga., Laramore Radar Poetry Group, Theta Sigma Phi, Phi Lambda Phi (hon.). Co-editor: Wind Song (poems), 1969. Home: 40 NE 69th St Miami FL 33138

KAIN, RONALD STUART, editor, writer; b. nr. Helena, Mont., Mar. 5, 1899; s. Henry and Fanny (Clift) K.; M.A., Columbia, 1936; m. Olive McKay, June 29, 1929. Asso. editor Mont. Banker, Great Falls, 1922; reporter Yakima (Wash.) Herald, 1923, Butte (Mont.) Miner, 1923-25; editorial staff N.Y. Herald Tribune, 1926-29; editor for Am. Biography, supplement New Internat. Ency., 1929; asso. editor, 1932-44; fgn. editor New Internat. Year Book, 1929-31; fgn. news editor, N.Y. office, news and features div. Outpost Service Bur., OWI, 1944, Psychol. Warfare Dept., SHAEF, London, 1944-45; chief press sect. Netherlands Unit of OWI in London, 1945, Brussels, 1945, The Hague, 1945 (attached as press officer to psychol. warfare consolidation team 11, Allied mil. mission to Netherlands); chief press and photo sects. USIS, Am. embassy, The Hague, 1945-1946; with State Dept., 1946; free-lance writer and editorial cons., 1946-49; sr. rev. officer Dept. State, 1949-51, chief rev. officer, 1951-54, dep. coordinator, chief rev. officer, 1954-61; dir. internat. surveys staff Office Sec. Dept. Health, Edn. and Welfare, 1961-66; free-lance writer, 1967—; visited Netherlands and Indonesia to study Indonesian revolution during 1947. Mem. English Speaking Union. Unitarian. Club: Cosmos (Washington). Author: Europe: Versailles to Warsaw, 1939. Contbr. articles mags. Home: 3611 N St NW Washington DC 20007

KAISER, GEORGE, farm bur. exec.; b. Elberta, Ala., Nov 27, 1911; s. Paul and Anna (Hollich) K.; student pub. schs.; m. Gertrude Steigerwald, Jan. 26, 1939; children—George P., Gertrude (Mrs. S.D. Denney), Lynda (Mrs. R.P. Krulis), Sidney, Norman. Farmer, Foley, Ala., 1943—; dir. S. Baldwin Bank, Foley. Pres., Baldwin County Farm Bur., 1958—; dir. Ala. Farmer's Market Authority, 1966—, Pesticide Inst. Ala., 1966-69. Bd. dirs. S. Baldwin Hosp., 1954—, pres., 1956-62; trustee St. Benedict Sch., 1964-68. Mem. S.W. Ala. Pecon Assn. (dir. 1961—), Baldwin County Cattlemens Assn. (dir. 1963-67), Foley C. of C. (dir. 1950-58). Rotarian (pres. 1965-66). Roman Catholic. Address: Rt 2 Box 23 Foley AL 36535

KAISER, LEO URBAN, printing and pub. cos. exec.; b. Elyria, O., July 29, 1902; s. Joseph and Agnes (Hauck) K.; student Spencerian Bus. Coll., 1920, Ohio Bus. Coll., 1921; m. Lorene Peine, Apr. 9, 1927; children—Martha (Mrs. William D. Justice), Betsy (Mrs. Robert J. Garlington). Trainee, Am. Multigraph Co., Cleve., 1919-21, factory rep., Houston, 1921-25; founder, owner Premier Printing and Letter Service, Houston, 1925-29, (inc. 1959), pres., 1959—; v.p. Texantics, Unlimited, Houston, 1952—; pres. Premier Advt. Co., Inc. Mem. Mail Advt. Service Assn., Direct Mail Advt. Assn., Houston Advt. Club, Printing Industry Assn., S.W. Mail Producers Guild, Soc. Am. Magicians, Internat. Brotherhood Magicians, Internat. Wine and Food Soc., Les Amis du Vin. Clubs: Warwick, Old Capitol, April 7th, University, Astrodome. Home: 5001 Doliver Dr Houston TX 77027 Office: 2120 McKinney Av Houston TX 77003

KAITZ, HYMAN BENJAMIN, statistician; b. Chelsea, Mass., May 17, 1916; s. Morris and Rebecca (Aptaker) K.; B.A., George Washington U., 1942; M.A., 1950; postgrad. Stanford, 1943; m. Naoni Savan, Dec. 26, 1949; children—Emily, Edward. Statistician, nat. income div. Dept. Commerce, 1946-54; v.p. WCFM Recording Corp., 1952-55; acting chief div. financial and actuarial services U.S. Dept. Labor, 1954-58; asst. chief statistics div. Internat. Bank for Reconstruction and Devel., Washington, 1958; statis. cons., div. manpower and employment statistics Bur. of Labor Statistics, 1959-62, asst. chief, offic econ. growth studies, 1962-63; dir. indsl. growth staff Bus. and Def. Services Asminstrn., U.S. Dept. Commerce,

1963-66; chief div. statis. standards Bur. Labor Statistics, U.S. Dept. Labor, 1966-71, asst. commr. for current employment analysis, 1971—. Served from pvt. to staff sgt. USAAF, 1942-46. Mem. Am. Statis. Assn., Am. Econ. Assn., Royal Statis. Soc., Inst. Math. Statistics, Econometric Soc., Phi Beta Kappa. Author articles in field. Home: 7216 Beechwood Rd Hollin Hills Alexandria VA 22307 Office: GAO Bldg Washington DC 20212

KALB, MARVIN LEONARD, radio and TV corr.; b. U.S., June 9, 1930; s. Max and Bella (Portney) K.; B.S.S., Coll. City N.Y., 1951; M.A., Harvard, 1953, Ph.D. candidate, 1955; m. Madeleine J. Green, June 1, 1958; children—Deborah, Judith. Press attache Am. embassy, Moscow, 1956-57, corr. CBS News, Moscow, 1960-63, diplomatic corr., Washington, 1963—. Served with AUS, 1953-55. Recipient award for best radio analysis Overseas Press Club, 1962, award for best TV analysis, 1965; award for best interpretation of fgn. news on TV, Internat. Cinema Soc., 1967. Mem. Overseas Writers (pres.), State Dept. Corrs. Assn. Clubs: Nat. Press; Harvard (N.Y.C.). Author: Eastern Exposure, 1958; Dragon in the Kremlin, 1961; The Volga, A Political Journey Through Russia, 1967. Roots of Involvement, The U.S. in Asia, 1784-1971, 1971; Introduction to One Day in Life of Ivan Denisovich, 1964. Office: 2020 M St Washington DC 20036

KALBER, FREDERICK ADOLPH, marine research dir.; b. Keene Valley, N.Y., Apr. 24, 1931; s. Frederick A. and Josephine N. (Nickerson) K.; student Franz Theodore Stone Inst. Hydrobiology, Ohio State U., 1951; A.B. in Biology, Alfred U., 1953; M.S. in Marine Biology and Physiology, U. Miami (Fla.), 1955; Ph.D. in Physiol. Chemistry, U. Del., 1962 children—Lynn, Jill, Glenn, Ross. Teaching asst. physiology Alfred U., 1952-53; teaching asst. physiology U. Miami (Fla.), 1953, zoology, 1954, research aide marine biology Marine Lab., 1954, research instr., 1955; instr. biology U. Houston, 1957-58; research asst. fish ecology U. Del., Newark, 1958-61; asst. prof. biology U. Wichita (Kan.), 1961-63; asst. prof. biology Coll. City N.Y., 1963-67; asso. prof. zoology Fla. Atlantic U., Boca Raton, 1967-70, adj. prof., 1970—; dir. research Aquatic Scis., Inc., Boca Raton, 1968—. Doctoral faculty Duke, summers 1965, 66. Mem. NSF rev. bd. pre-doctoral fellowships, 1966, NSF div. undergrad. edn. in sci., 1966, Nat. Acad. Scis. adv. com. Internat. Biol. Program, 1967-68, NSF adv. panel biol. oceanography, 1968; operations dir. Fla. Sci. Talent Search, 1971. Served with AUS, 1955-57, USNR, 1960-66. Mem. A.A.A.S., Am. Soc. Limnology and Oceanography, Am. Soc. Zoologists (comparative physiology div.), Gulf and Caribbean Fisheries Inst., N.Y., Fla. acads. scis., Fla. Found. Future Scientists, Sigma Xi. Editorial com. Handbook of Marine Scis., 1970; editorial bd. Internat. Jour. Aquaculture. Contbr. numerous articles to profl. jours. Patentee microcryoscope and microcryostat. Home: 2890 Churchill Dr Chapel Hill Boynton Beach FL 33435 Office: 2624 NW 2d Av Boca Raton FL 33432

KALE, HERBERT WILLIAM, II, zoologist, ecologist; b. Trenton, N.J., Dec. 24, 1931; s. Samuel Stewart and Julia (Steward) K.; B.S., Rutgers U., 1954; M.S., U. Ga., 1961, Ph.D., 1964; m. Charlotte Ross Jones, July 29, 1961; children—Kathleen Elizabeth, Thomas, John. Teaching and research asst. U. Ga., Athens, 1957-64; ornithologist Encephalitis Research Center, Fla. Bd. Health, Tampa, 1964-66; now vertebrate ecologist Entomological Research Center, Vero Beach, Fla. Served with AUS, 1954-56. Mem. Ecol. Soc. Am., Am. Ornithologists' Union, Wilson, Cooper, Ga. ornithol socs., Nat., Fla. Audubon socs., Carolina Bird Club, Am. Soc. Mammalogists, British Ornithologists' Union, Sigma Xi, Theta Chi, Phi Sigma. Republican. Home: 35 1st Ct SW Vero Beach FL 32960 Office: Entomol Research Center PO Box 502 Vero Beach FL32960

KALLSEN, HENRY ALVIN, educator; b. Jasper, Minn., Mar. 25, 1926; s. Bernhard H. and Irene (Wehrman) K.; B.S., Ia. State U., 1948; M.S., U. Wis., 1952, Ph.D., 1956; m. Harriet Arlene Burger, Sept. 9, 1950; children—Margaret Louise, Laura Ellen, Thomas John, Alice Jean. Asst. engr. Wabash R.R. Co., Moberly, Mo., Montpelier, O., 1948-49; instr., asst. prof. U. Wis., 1949-59; asso. prof. La. Poly. Inst., Ruston, 1959-60, prof., 1960-64, acting head, civil engring. dept., 1962-63; asst. exec. sec. Am. Soc. Engring. Edn., Urbana, Ill., 1964-65; prof. engring. U. Ala., University, 1965—, asst. dean, 1965-72; engr. III, Wis. Hwy Commn., Madison, 1954-55; hwy. engr. Bur. Pub. Rds., Baton Rouge, 1963. Mem. adv. research council La. Dept. Hwys., 1962-64; cons. Bd. Engring. Edn., Commn. on Higher Edn., State Tenn., 1969. Mem. Municipal Planning and Zoning Commn., Ruston, La., 1962-64. Served with USNR, 1944-46. Registered profl. engr., Wis. Mem. Nat., Ala. socs. profl. engrs., Am. Soc. C.E., Am. Soc. Engring. Edn., Sigma Xi, Tau Beta Pi, Phi Kappa Phi, Chi Epsilon. Lutheran. Home: 21 Druid Hills Tuscaloosa AL 35401 Office: Box 1968 University AL 35486

KALLSEN, THEODORE JOHN, educator, univ. dean; b. Jasper, Minn., Mar. 27, 1915; s. Bernhart H. and Irene (Wehrman) K.; B.S., Mankato State Coll., 1936; M.A., U. Ia., 1940, Ph.D., 1949; m. Marvel J. Stordahl, Aug. 27, 1939; children—Carolyn Irene (Mrs. Harold Pate), Tonya Jo. Various teaching positions, Minn., Mo., Ia., 1936-49; asst. prof, integrated studies W.Va. U., Morgantown, 1949-55; prof. English, head dept. Stephen F. Austin State U., Nacogdoches, Tex., 1955-65, prof., dean Sch. Liberal Arts, 1965—. Cons., English curriculum pub. schs.; communications cons, to industries; co-dir. schs., colls., Beaumont region, Tex. Safety Assn., 1965. Served to lt. (j.g.) USNR, 1944-46. Mem. Nat. Council Tchrs. English, Conf. Coll. Composition and Communication (exec. com. 1959-62), Am. Assn. U. Profs., Tex. Conf. Coll. Tchrs. English, Tex. Col. English Assn., Modern Lang. Assn., So. Humanities Conf. Club: Piney Woods Country (dir. Nacogdoches 1958-60). Author: Modern Rhetoric and Usage, 1955; (with D.E. McCoy) Reading and Rhetoric: Order and Idea, 1963; Teachers' Use of Dictating Machines, 1965, Home: 600 Bostwick Lane Nacogdoches TX 75961

KALMAN, JACK RICHMOND, civil engr.; b. Chelsea, Mass., June 6, 1910; s. Max Manuel and Bessie (Richmond) K.; B.S., Mass. Inst. Tech., 1932; M.S., Okla. U., 1957; m. Mabel Dorthy Cottrell, Aug. 30, 1937; children—Jacqueline J. (Mrs. Robert C. Poe), Teresa Ann (Mrs. Douglas B. Brown), Joan Richmond (Mrs. Thomas A. Player), Julie Cottrell. Commd. 2d lt. C.E., U.S. Army, 1940, advanced through grades to lt. col., 1954, planning officer No. area ETO, 1952-54, ret., 1954; engr. city Norman (Okla.), 1954-56; pvt. practice cons. engr., Norman, 1954—; pres. Kalman and Assos., Inc., Precision Testing Labs., Inc. Mem. Nat., Okla. socs. profl. engrs., Soc. Am. Mil. Engrs. Mason (Shriner), Lion. Home: 239 Crestmont St Norman OK 73069 Office: 925 N Flood St Norman OK 73069

KALMANOFF, GEORGE, economist; b. N.Y.C., Sept. 17, 1917; s. Peter and Rebecca (Wassilkowski) K.; B.A. magna cum laude, Coll. City N.Y., 1936, M.S. in Edn., 1938; postgrad. Am. U., 1944-53; m. Jean Paulive, July 4, 1940; children—Barbara (Mrs. Charles Folick), Ellen. Tchr. Spanish, N.Y.C. and Washington, 1936-42; economist OPA, Washington, 1942-44; economist Fgn. Econ. Adminstrn., Dept. of Commerce, Washington, 1944-50; economist UN Econ. Commn. for Latin Am., Washington, 1950-53; econ. adviser Nat. Planning Office, Govt. of Colombia, Bogota, 1953-54, econ. cons., Bogota, 1954-58; asso. dir. Internat. Research Projects, Columbia U. Law Sch., N.Y.C., 1958-65; economist World Bank, Washington, 1965—, now dep. dir. indsl. projects dept. Econ. cons. City of N.Y., 1958-65. Mem. Am. Econ. Assn., Soc. for Internat. Devel., Phi Beta Kappa, Sigma Delta Pi. Author: (with A. O. Hirschman) Investment in Central America, 1956; (with W. G. Friedman) Joint International Business Ventures, 1961; (with W. G. Friedmann and R. Meagher) International Financial Aid, 1966. Home: 5402 Wehawken Rd Washington DC 20016 Office: World Bank 1818 H St NW Washington DC 20433

KALP, MARGARET ELLEN, educator; b. Middletown, N.Y., Apr. 17, 1915; d. William Lawrence and Edith (Phillips) Kalp; B.A., Douglass Coll., 1936; M.A. in L.S., U. Mich., 1942; postgrad. U. Chgo. Library Sch., 1952-53, 56. Reviser, Library Sch., N.J. Coll. for Women, 1936-37; instr.-sec. Hampton Inst. Library Sch., 1937-39; asst. Hunterdon County (N.J.) Pub. Library, 1939-40, Ypsilanti (Mich.) High Sch., 1940-43; librarian Rumson (N.J.) High Sch., 1943-46; librarian Demonstration Sch. libraries, also lectr. library sci. Peabody Coll. for Tchrs., 1946-47, vis. instr., summers 1945-46; asst. prof. U. N.C. Sch. Library Sci., Chapel Hill, 1947-55, asso. prof., 1955—, acting dean, 1964-67. Mem. A.L.A., Southeastern, N.C. library assns., Am. Acad. Polit. and Social Scis., Assn. Am. Library Schs., Am. Assn. U. Profs., Pi Gamma Mu, Beta Phi Mu, Delta Kappa Gamma. Club: Altrusa. Home: PO Box 2624 Chapel Hill NC 27514

KALTER, SEYMOUR SANFORD, virologist; b. N.Y.C., Mar. 19, 1918; s. Aaron H. and Jessie (Schulman) K.; B.S., St. Joseph's Coll., Phila., 1940; M.A., U. Kan., 1943; postgrad. U. Pa., 1943-45; Ph.D., Syracuse U., 1947; m. Gloria V. Verstein, Mar. 3, 1946; children—Susan P., Steven P., Debra I. Asst. instr. bacteriology, U. Kan., 1941-43; research asst. U. Pa., dept. med. bacteriology. 1943-45; from asst. to asso. prof. med. microbiology Upstate Med. Center of N.Y., Syracuse, 1945-56, chief virus diagnositc unit USPHS, CDC, Atlanta, 1956-59, virologist, 1959-60; bacteriologist Syracuse Dept. Health, 1945-56; virologist, microbiology-cellular biology branch Sch. Aviation Med., Brooks AFB, Tex., 1960-63; chmn. dept. microbiology Southwest Found. for Research and Edn., 1963-66, dir. div. of microbiology and infectious diseases, 1966—, also chmn. dept. infectious diseases; adj. prof. dept. biology Trinity U., San Antonio; adj. prof. dept. pediatrics U. Tex., San Antonio; cons. virology Pan Am. San. Bur., Cologne U., Cologne, Germany; cons. WHO, Nat. Cancer Inst. Mem. ad hoc com. classification Simian viruses. Fellow A.A.A.S., Am. Pub. Health Assn.; mem. Am. Acad. Microbiology, Am. Bd. Microbiology, Am. Assn. Immunologists, Soc. Expt. Biology and Medicine, N.Y. Acad. Sci., Am. Soc. Microbiologists, Wildlife Disease Assn., Am. Soc. Tropical Medicine and Hygiene, Royal Soc. Health (Eng.), Am. Assn. Lab. Animal Sci., Am. Soc. Cryobiology, Sigma Xi. Editorial bd. Applied Microbiology, Jour. Med. Primatology, Lab. Animal Sci. Home: 1418 Haskin Dr San Antonio TX 78209 Office: PO Box 28147 San Antonio TX 78284

KALV, FRANCES PALMER DOUGLAS (MRS. GEORGE PAUL KALV), educator; b. Daytona Beach, Fla., Apr. 22, 1917; d. Palmer Louis and Frances E. (Quattlebaum) Douglas; A.B., George Washington U., 1942; M.A., John B. Stetson U., 1951; postgrad. U. Fla., 1953-54; m. George Paul Kalv, Dec. 22, 1942; 1 son, Paul Douglas. Personnel tng. officer Treasury Dept., Washington, 1942-44; tchr. Fullerwood Elementary Sch., St. Augustine, Fla., 1945-46; tchr. English, Ketterlinus High Sch., St. Augustine, 1946-62; guidance counselor St. Augustine High Sch., 1962—. Mem. Am. Assn. U. Women (br. pres. 1969-72), Nat. (dir.), Fla. (pres. 1958-59), St. Johns County (pres. 1956-57) councils tchrs. English, St. Johns County Reading Council (pres. 1962-63), Fla. (pres. area V B 1961-62), St. Johns County edn. assns., Alpha Delta Kappa, Delta Kappa Gamma, Pi Lambda Theta, Kappa Delta Pi, Beta Sigma Phi, Zeta Tau Alpha. Democrat. Baptist. Mem. Order Eastern Star. Home: 9 Venancio St St Augustine FL 32084

KAMENITSA, MAXINE ANNA ELLIOTT, ednl. specialist; b. Neodesha, Kan.; d. William Thomas and Beulah (Morrow) Elliott; B.S., N. Tex. State U., 1950; M.A., Tex. Woman's U., 1958; m. William Thomas Kamenitsa, Sept. 28, 1943; children—Dennis Elliott, Laura Katherine, Cindy Ann. Grad. asst. Tex. Women's U., Denton, 1951-53, dir. pre-sch. demonstration sch., summer 1956; supt.-tchr pre-sch. classes Ft. Worth Children's Mus., 1954-60; instr. child devel. Tex. Christian U., Ft. Worth, 1958-60; tchr. kindergarten, 2nd grade Ft. Worth Ind. Sch. Dist., 1960-68; early childhood specialist S.W. Ednl. Devel. Lab., Austin, 1968—. Mem. N.E.A., Assn. Childhood Edn., Tex. Tchrs. Assn., Ft. Worth Classroom Tchrs. Assn., Nat. Assn. Edn. Young Children (pres.-elect Ft. Worth chpt.), Am. Assn. U. Women, Theta Sigma Phi (chpt. pres. 1945-47, dir. 1966-68), Alpha Delta Kappa. Presbyn. Club: Fort Worth Ski. Author: Parents' Handbook, 1958, 59, 60. Officer Bob Drawing Book, 1958. Co-author: Preschool-Kindergarten Handbook for Teachers, 1967. Home: 2017 David Dr Ft Worth TX 76111 Office: 1815 Cold Springs Rd Ft Worth TX 76111

KAMENSKE, GLORIA LEE CHEEK, psychologist; b. Battle Creek, Mich., Oct. 26, 1931; d. George W. and Edith (Olds) Cheek; A.B., U. Mich., 1953; M.A., Mich. State U., 1955, Ph.D., 1965; m. Bernard H. Kamenske, Dec. 19, 1960. Counselor women's dormitories Mich. State U., East Lansing, 1953-54, statis. teaching asst. psychology dept., 1954-56, research asst. Labor and Indsl. Relations Center, 1956-58; social psychology intern VA Hosp., Ann Arbor, Mich., 1958-59; research psychologist personnel research br. Adj. Gen's Office, Dept. Def., Washington, 1959-60; research asso. tng. methods div. Human Resources Research Office, Washington, 1960-62; manpower research analyst Office of Manpower, Automation and Tng. Dept. Labor, Washington, 1962-63; research asso. Bur. Social Sci. Research, Washington, 1963-65; supervisory research psychologist Social Analysis Nat. Center Health Services Research and Devel., USPHS, 1965-70; social sci. adviser Office of Sec. Health, Edn. and Welfare, 1970—. Cons. Dept. Labor, 1962-63, Union Theol. Sem., 1963-65. Recipient award for service Psi Chi, 1957. Fellow Am. Pub. Health Assn.; mem. D.A.R., Am., Midwestern, Eastern, D.C. psychol. assns., Interamer. Soc. of Psychol., Internat. Council of Psychologists, Internat. Union Sci. Psychology, Am. Acad. Polit. and Social Sci., Am., sociol. assns., Psi Chi. Contbr. numerous articles in field to profl. and trade jours. Home: One Buttonwood Lane Washington DC 20016 Office: Internat Health Ofc of Sec Dept Health Edn and Welfare Washington DC 20201

KAMEROW, MARTIN LAURENCE, accountant; b. Washington, Aug. 25, 1931; s. Jacob A. and Anne (Adler) K.; B.C.S., Benjamin Franklin U., 1951, M.C.S., 1952; m. Corinne Perimeter, Mar. 24, 1951; children—Deborah, Jacqueline, Haskell. Staff accountant various C.P.A. firms, Washington, 1949-52; individual practice accounting, Washington, 1952-59; partner firm Kamerow & Serber, Washington, 1959-63; sr. partner firm Harab, Kamerow & Serber, Washington, 1963—; lectr. Am. U., 1956—; lectr. tax seminars and insts. Mem. nat. council United Synagogue of Am., 1969—, regional treas., 1969—; mem. exec. com. United Jewish Appeal; mem. Zionist Youth Commn.; pres. L.D. Brandeis dist. Zionist Orgn. Am., also mem. nat. bd. dirs. Bd. dirs. World Council Synagogues: v.p., bd. dirs. Jewish Nat. Fund; bd. dirs. United Jewish Appeal D.C. Served with inf. AUS, 1951-53. Recipient Nat. Kidney Found. Service award, 1969. C.P.A., Washington. Mem. Am. Inst. C.P.A.'s, Assn. Practicing C.P.A.'s (pres. 1972—), Inst. C.P.A.'s in Israel, Sigma Alpha Rho. Jewish religion (v.p. temple). Clubs: Nat. Press (Washington), Touchdown (Washington). Author: (with S.A. Kaufman) Consolidated Financial Statements, 1958; (with S. Green) U.S. News and World Reports Book on Income Taxes, 1st edit., 1971, 2d edit., 1972. Home: 405 E Indian Spring Dr Silver Spring MD 20901 Office: 805 15th St NW Washington DC 20005

KAMIN, HENRY, educator, biochemist; b. Warsaw, Poland, Oct. 24, 1920; s. Benjamin and Paula (Mirkowicz) K.; brought to U.S., 1926, naturalized, 1932; B.S., Coll. City N.Y., 1940; Ph.D., Duke, 1948; m. Dorothy Lee Lingle, Oct. 30, 1943. Mem. faculty biochemistry dept. Duke, Durham, N.C., 1940—, research asst., 1940-43, 1946-48, USPHS fellow, 1948-50, instr., asso., 1950-55, asst. prof. 1955-59, asso. prof., 1959-65, prof., 1965—. Prin. scientist VA Hosp., Durham, 1953-68; VA liason mem. biochemistry study sect. NIH, Washington, 1961-65; chmn. basic sci. program rev. com. VA, Washington, 1961-66; mem. biophysics and biochemistry program com. VA, 1969-71; chmn. 3d Internat. Symposium on Flavins and Flavoproteins, Durham, 1969. Served to 1st lt. Sgn. Corps, AUS, 1943-46. Fellow A.A.A.S., Am. Chem. Soc.; mem. Am. Soc. Biol. Chemists. Editor: Flavins and Flavoproteins, 1971. Contbr. numerous articles on mechanism oxidative enzymes, nitrogen metabolism to profl. jours. Home: 2417 Perkins Rd Durham NC 27706

KAMINSKY, BERNARD SHAW, dentist; b. Johnstown, Pa., Dec. 25, 1922; s. Oscar and Rebecca (Nathan) K.; student U. Wis., 1943, Otterbein U., 1948-50; D.D.S, Temple U., 1954; m. Ruby Rosalind Pomerantz, Mar. 21, 1951; 1 dau., Kala Sue. Individual practice gen. dentistry, Fredericksburg, Va., 1954—. Served with 96th Inf. Div., AUS, 1943-45. Decorated Bronze Star medal. Mem. Acad. Gen. Dentistry, John A Kolmer Hon. Med. Soc. Temple U., Am. Dental Assn., Am. Endodontic Soc., V.F.W. (vice comdr. 1956), Alpha Omega, Alpha Epsilon Delta. Jewish religion. Mem. B'nai B'rith. Club: Beth El Men's (Richmond, Va.). Home: 1001 Lomas Ct Richmond VA 23229 Office: 1101 Caroline St Fredericksburg VA 22401

KAMM, ROBERT B., univ. pres.; b. West Union, Ia., Jan. 22, 1919; s. Balthasar and Amelia (Etter) K.; B.A., U. No. Ia., 1940; M.A., U. of Minn., 1946, Ph.D., 1948; m. Maxine Moen, July 10, 1943; children—Susan, Steven. Tchr. Belle Plaine (Ia.) High Sch., 1940-42; research asst., counselor Gen. Coll., U. Minn., 1946-48; dean of students Drake U., 1948-55; dean student personnel services Tex. A. and M. U., 1955-56, dean basic div. and student personnel services, 1956-58; dean coll. arts and scis. Okla. State U., 1958-65, v.p. acad. affairs, 1965-66, pres., 1966—. Mem. regional com. Student Personnel Work for South, 1956; mem. commn. coll. student Am. Council Edn., 1957-60; chmn. Nat. Conf. Acad. Deans, Stillwater, 1961-62; chmn. Mid-Am. State Univs. Assn., 1968-69; pres. Bi-State Mental Health Assn., 1968-70; mem. nat. vocational rehab. and edn. adv. com. VA, 1970—; mem. Pres.'s Commn. on Observance of 25th Anniversary of UN. Bd. visitors Air U., 1967-70. Civilian radio instr. USAAF, 1942-44, coordinator on staff, 1944; naval aviation radar technician USNR, 1944-46. Elected to Okla. Hall of Fame, 1972; recipient Outstanding Achievement award U. Minn., 1971; Alumni Achievement award U. No. Ia., 1970. Fellow Am. Psychol. Assn.; mem. Am. Coll. Personnel Assn. (mem. exec. council 1954-56, pres. 1957), Am. Personnel and Guidance Assn., Nat. Vocational Guidance Assn., So. Coll. Personnel Assn., Nat. Assn. Student Personnel Adminstrn., Assn. Higher Edn., N.E.A. (nat. com. gen. edn. 1961-64), Assn. State Univ. and Land Grant Colls. (chmn. div. arts and scis. 1963-64, co-chmn. home econs. div. 1968-70), Stillwater C. of C. (v.p. 1965-67), Phi Kappa Phi, Omicron Delta Kappa (mem. nat. council 1970—), Kappa Kappa Psi, Phi Delta Kappa, Psi Chi, Kappa Delta Pi, Blue Key, Theta Alpha Phi, Kappa Mu Epsilon, Alpha Phi Omega, Phi Mu Alpha Sinfonia. Methodist. Rotarian (pres. 1962-63). Contbr. edn. profl. jours. Address: 1600 N Monroe St Stillwater OK 74074

KAMPBELL, MILDRED LENORAH NORMAN (MRS. WILLARD PERRY KAMPBELL), religious worker, club woman; b. Little Rock, Dec. 22, 1911; d. Thomas Wade and Hattie (Porter) Norman; student pub. schs., Little Rock; m. Willard Perry Kampbell, Apr. 16, 1930; children—Mary Jane, Helen Ann (Mrs. Waymon Leon Sory), Martha Elizabeth (Mrs. Ben Jay Blazer), Thomas Albert, Willard Perry, Norman Edward, Stephen Allen, William Joseph. Office mgr., state treas. Ark. W.C.T.U., Little Rock, 1951—; sec.-treas. Lulu Markwell W.C.T.U., 1967—. Treas., Vol. Service Club, 1963, 64, 68, pres., 1967; active A.R.C., 1934—; pres. Central High PTA., 1971-72. Named Ark. Merit Mother, 1970. Mem. Woman's Missionary Union (sec. 1962-64), Bus. Women's Social Service Club (pres. 1972-73), Ark. Fedn. Women's Clubs, Ark. Fedn. Garden Clubs, Little Rock Council P.T.A., Bus. and Profl. Woman's Club. Baptist. Clubs: Old Fashioned Garden (pres. 1961-63), Diamond State Grandmother's. Home: 3422 W 10th St Little Rock AR 72204

KAMPHOEFNER, HENRY LEVEKE, univ. dean; b. Des Moines, Ia., May 5, 1907; s. Charles Herman and Mary Amelia (Leveke) K.; B.S. in Architecture, U. Ill., 1930; M.S., Columbia, 1931; D.F.A., Morningside Coll., 1967; m. Mabel C. Franchere, Jan. 5, 1937. Practicing architect, Sioux City, Ia. 1932-36; asso. architect, Rural Resettlement Adminstrn., Washington, 1936-67; prof. architecture, U. Okla., Norman, 1937-48; dean Sch. Design, U. N.C. at Raleigh, N.C., 1948—. Design cons. Chattanooga Housing Authority, 1962—, USN, 1964—. Nat. pres. Collegiate Schs. Architecture, 1964-66. Pres. Raleigh Council Architects, 1952-54. Pres. Raleigh Chamber Music Guild, 1954-56. Fellow A.I.A. Club: Carolina Country (Raleigh). Author: (with others) Cities are Abnormal, 1946; (with others) Churches and Temples, 1953; (with others) The South Builds, 1960. Home: 3060 Granville Dr Raleigh NC 27609

KANATZAR, HOBART DOUGLAS, indsl. engr.; b. San Antonio, Sept. 21, 1919; s. Floyd J. and Mary (Ritchie) K.; B.S. in Indsl. Engring., Okla. State U., 1959; m. Gloria Brunson, Nov. 4, 1944; children—Douglas W., Holliann (Mrs. Ronald M. Dawson), Deelyn. Enlisted USAF, 1940, advanced through grades to maj., 1958, test pilot, Tinker AFB, Okla., 1953, Dobbins AFB, Ga., squadron engring. officer, Elmendorf, Alaska, 1947-49, ret., 1960; engr. mgmt. engring. Kelly AFB, Tex., 1960—. Decorated D.F.C., Air medal. Mem. Nat., Tex. socs. profl. engrs. Pioneer in devel. of estimating equation to forecast manning requirement with projected workload changes. Home: 834 Firefly Dr San Antonio TX 78216 Office: Kelly AFB TX 78241

KANE, HARNETT THOMAS, author, critic; b. New Orleans, Nov. 8, 1910; s. William J. and Anna (Hirt) K.; B.A., Tulane U., New Orleans, 1931, grad. work in sociology, 1932-33; unmarried Reporter, New Orleans Item-Tribune, 1928-43, assignments covered welfare, business, labor, politics; tchr. journalism Loyola U. (New Orleans), 1943-44. Del. of New Orleans Item-Tribune to Cities Investment Trust Found. Safety Seminar, N.Y. City, 1937. Bd. dirs. New Orleans Cultural Attractions Fund. Pres. La. Council for Vieux Carre. Mem. Lyceum Assn. (bd. dirs.), Authors Guild of Am., Soc. of Midland Authors, New Orleans Art Assn., English Speaking Union of New Orleans (v.p.), Chevaliers de Tastevin, France d'Amerique, Athenee Louisianaise, La. Landmarks Soc. (bd. dirs.), Am. Newspaper Guild, Sigma Delta Chi, Theta Nu, Kappa Delta Phi. Recipient Dorothy Dix journalism award, 1930, Ala. Writers' Assn. award for distinguished writing on the South, 1958, Chevalier de Palmes Academiquest award, France, 1958, Guggenheim fellowship for study of So. problems, 1943-44, 44-45. Democrat. Roman Catholic. Club: Arts and Crafts (New Orleans). Author: Louisiana Hayride: The American Rehearsal for Dictatorship, 1941; Bayous of Louisiana, 1943; Deep Delta Country; Plantation Parade—the Grand Manner in Louisiana, 1945; New Orleans Woman, 1946; Natchez on the Mississippi, 1947; Bride of Fortune, 1948; Queen New Orleans, 1949; Pathway to the Stars, 1950; Scandalous Mrs. Blackford, 1951; Gentlemen, Swords and Pistols, 1951; Dear Dorothy Dix (biography with Ella B. Arthur), 1952; The Lady of Arlington, 1953; Spies for the Blue and Gray, 1954; The Smiling Rebebl, 1955; (with Inez Henry) Miracle in the Mountains, 1956; The Gallant Mrs. Stonewall, 1957; The Southern Christmas Book, 1958; The Golden Coast, 1959; The Ursulines, Nuns of Adventure, 1959; Have Pen, Will Autograph, 1959; Gone Art the Days, 1960; The Romantic South, 1961; The Amazing Mrs. Bonaparte, 1963; Young Mark Twain and the Mississippi; published in 1966; also author of several articles pub. in Colliers, Gourmet; Reader's Digest, Am. Mercury, National Geographic and articles and book reviews to newspapers and nat. mags.; also series of articles on leprosy in La. and history of New Orleans and Louisiana. Home: 5919 Freret St New Orleans LA

KANE, JOHN EWING, economist, accountant; b. Quitman, Ark., Apr. 2, 1914; s. Robert Lee and Beulah (Jenkins) K.; B.S., U. Ark., 1936, M.S., 1939; postgrad. U. Minn., 1940; Ph.D., Am. U., 1950; m. Katherine Edna Miller, Sept. 10, 1939; children—Carolyn, Phyllis Anne. Accountant, Lion Oil Co., El Dorado, Ark., 1937-39; instr. U. Ark., Fayetteville, 1939-41, asst. prof., asso. prof., prof., 1946-—, asso. dir. Bur. Bus. and Econ. Research, 1949-50, chmn. dept. gen. bus., 1950-55, chmn. dept. econs., 1966-—, chmn. athletic council, 1966-—, acting v.p. finance, 1967-68; economist U.S. Dept. Commerce, 1942-43; exec. v.p. McIlroy Bank, Fayetteville, 1956-58, bus. and econ. cons., dir. Bd. dirs., faculty Southwestern Grad. Sch. Banking, Dallas; faculty Sch. Banking of South, Baton Rouge, faculty Nat. Assemblies for Bank Dirs. Sec.-treas. N.W. Ark. Regional Airport Authority. Served to lt. comdr. Supply Corps. USNR, 1943-46. Mem. Southwestern Social Sci. Assn. (past pres.), Am. Inst. C.P.A.'s, Ark. Soc. C.P.A.'s, Am. Econ. Assn., Am. Finance Assn., Am. Accounting Assn., So., Midwest econ. assns., Fayetteville C. of C. (past treas.), Alpha Kappa Psi. Methodist (bd. dirs.). Contbr. to Financial Accounting Theory, 1965. Home: 1245 Columbus Blvd Fayetteville AR 72701

KANE, MATTHEW J(OHN), lawyer; b. Guthrie, Okla., July 15, 1910; s. Matthew J. and Kathleen (Reagan) K.; LL.B., U. Okla., 1932; m. Marjorie Kennedy, Sept. 15, 1934; 1 son, Matthew John III. Admitted to Okla. bar. 1932, since practiced in Pawhuska; dir. Nat. Bank Commerce, Pawhuska, Exchange Bank, Skiatook, Okla., Barnsdall State Bank. Mem. Okla. Bd. Bar Examiners, 1938-43; mem. Commn. on Uniform State Laws, 1949-53. Bd. dirs. Loy Found. Served to lt. comdr. USNR, 1943-45. Mem. Am., Okla. bar assns., Sigma Chi, Phi Delta Phi. Democrat. Roman Catholic. Rotarian Home: 115 E 11th St Pawhuska OK 74056 Office: Commerce Bldg Pawhuska OK 74056

KANE, PHILIP FRANCIS, electronics co. exec.; b. London, Eng., Dec. 1, 1920 (came to U.S. 1957, naturalized 1970); s. Cornelius and Frances Rose (Witney) K.; B.Sc., London U., 1948; m. Sybil Dorothy Silk, Oct. 17, 1942; children—Michael, Moira (Mrs. Ronald Edward Gillum). Technician Standard Telephones & Cables, Ltd., London, 1938-48; research chemist Laporte Chems., Ltd., Luton, Eng., 1949-52, chief analyst, 1952-57; supr. research Chemagro Corp., Kansas City, Mo., 1957-59; dir. lab. Tex. Instrument, Inc., Dallas, 1959-—. Fellow Royal Inst. Chemistry (London); mem. Soc. Analytical Chemists (London), Soc. Applied Spectroscopy (pres. North Tex. sect. 1972-—, gen. chmn. nat. meeting 1972-—), Dallas Soc. Analytical Chemists (past chief analyst; award 1967). Author: (with Graydon B. Larrabee) Characterization of Semiconductor Materials, 1971. Editor: (with Graydon B. Larrabee) Characterization of Solid Surfaces, 1972. Home: 1919 Lake Forest Rd Grapevine TX 76051 Office: Tex Instruments Inc PO Box 5936 M/S 147 Dallas TX 75222

KANE, RICHARD FRANCIS, laywer, city ofcl.; b. L.I., N.Y., July 23, 1935; s. James Richard and Rose (Doran) K.; student Pa. State U., 1957-59, U. Fla., 1959, Stetson Coll. Law, 1960; LL.B., Duke, 1963; m. Marilyn Metts, May 9, 1965; children—Karen, Kathy. Admitted to Fla. bar, 1963; asst. U.S. atty., student honors program U.S. Dept. Justice, Raleigh, N.C., 1962; practiced in Daytona Beach, Fla., 1963-—; asst. city prosecutor City Daytona Beach, Fla., 1965-67; municipal judge pro-tem Port Orange, Fla., 1967-68. Instr. Daytona Beach Jr. Coll., 1965-67. Pres. Young Democrats of Volusia County, 1965-66; mayor City Daytona Beach, Fla., 1969-—. Bd. dirs. Child Day Care Center, Inc., Work Orientated Rehab. Center, Inc. Served with USNR, 1953-57. Named Outstanding Young Man of Year Daytona Beach Jr. C. of C., 1970. Mem. Daytona Beach Jr. C. of C. (dir. 1965-66; chmn. better bus. div. 1968), Am., Fla. bar assns. Moose. Home: 457 Tarragona Way Daytona Beach FL 32014 Office: 213 Silver Beach Av Daytona Beach FL 32018

KANTER, JACK CECIL, dentist; b. Norfolk, Va., Nov. 29, 1916; s. Samuel and Rose (Berman) K.; student Coll. William and Mary, Norfolk Div., 1934-35; D.D.S., Med. Coll. Va., 1939; postgrad. Temple U., 1962; m. Henrietta Salsbury, Jan. 16, 1946. Individual practice dentistry, Norfolk, 1939-—; instr. dental assts. Coll. William and Mary, 1952, 54, 57; chief of dentistry DePaul Hosp., 1959-62; mem. staff Norfolk Gen. Hosp.; mem. med. adv. bd. Norfolk Area Med. Authority. Dir. Unico Corp. Mem. adv. bd. Speech and Hearing Center of Old Dominion. Served to lt. comdr., Dental Corps, USNR, 1942-46; ETO. Mem. Am., Va., Va.-Tidewater (past pres.) dental assns., Am. Cleft Palate Assn., Am. Assn. Maxillofacial Prosthetics, Southeastern Acad. Prosthodontics, Fraternal Order Police Assos. (past dir.), Jewish War Vets., Norfolk Firemens Assn., Alpha Omega, Omicron Kappa Upsilon, Sigma Zeta, Sigma Epsilon Pi. Jewish religion (dir. temple). Mason; mem. B'nai B'rith. Contbr. articles to profl. jours. Patentee in field. Home: 7812 Michael Dr Norfolk VA 23505 Office: Wainwright Bldg Norfolk VA 23510

KANTNER, ARTHUR HENRY, banker; b. N.Y.C., Sept. 4, 1918; s. Rudolph Julius and Anna (Westen) K.; student N.Y. State A. and M. Inst., 1936; B.S., Cornell U., 1949, M.S., 1950, Ph.D., 1952; grad. Advanced Mgmt. Program, Harvard, 1971; m. Shelton Valeria Richardson, Dec. 15, 1944; children—Leslie Anne, Neil Arthur, Alyce Marie, Farm laborer, Delhi, N.Y., 1936-38; feed and fertilizer salesman Coop. Grange League Fedn., Ithaca, N.Y., 1938-41; research asst. Coll. Agr., Cornell U., Ithaca, 1947-52; economist Fed. Res. Bank, Atlanta, 1952-58, sr. economist, asst. cashier, asst. v.p., 1959-67, v.p., mgr., New Orleans, 1968-71, sr. v.p., 1971-—. Served to 1st lt. AUS, 1942-46; H. col. Ret. Res. Presbyn. (elder). Home: 81 Dove St New Orleans LA 70124 Office: 525 St Charles Av New Orleans LA 70124

KANTOR, DAVID, librarian; b. Atlanta, Ga., Nov. 2, 1915; s. Sam and Celia (Shafran) K.; B.S., U. Fla., 1938; Licentiate in microbiology Universite Libre de Bruxelles, 1939; B.L.S., Drexel U., 1941; m. Lee Finberg, Nov. 26, 1942. Cataloger U. Fla., 1941-42, chem.-pharmacy librarian, 1942-43; tech. librarian U. S. Army Signal Corps, Ft. Monmouth, N.J., 1943-44; librarian Wash. State Reformatory, 1944-46, 47-49; librarian Farragut Coll., 1946-47; librarian Cal. Dept. Corrections, Folsom Prison, 1949-62; dir. ext. Volusia County Pub. Libraries, Daytona Beach, Fla., 1962-63, dir. libraries Volusia County, 1964-—; cons. instn. libraries Fla. State Library, State Bur. Blind Services, Fla. Mem. Cal. (pres. Golden Empire dist. 1958, dir. 1958), Am. (regional membership com. 1955, hosp. and instns. com. 1956), Fla. (chmn. pub. library sect. 1970-71, v.p., pres. 1972-73) library assns. Author: Survey of Public Library Service in Volusia County, 1964; Survey of Libraries and Library Services in the State Institutions of Florida, 1967. Office: Volusia County Public Libraries City Island Daytona Beach FL 32014

KAPLAN, DAVID L., govt. ofcl.; b. N.Y.C., Feb. 14, 1918; s. Israel and Fannie (Kaples) K.; B.A., N.Y.U., 1939, postgrad., 1939-40; postgrad. Am. U., 1940-45; m. Lillian Schoolman, June 24, 1951; children—Susan B., Leonard S. Statistician, U.S. Census Bur., Washington, 1940-49, chief occupation and industry statistics, 1950-56, census planner, 1957-62, asst. chief population div., 1962-68, coordinator 1970 census population and housing, 1966-—, chief demographic census staff, 1971-—; U.S. rep. working group on population and housing censuses Conf. European Statisticians, Econ. Commn. for Europe, 1963-—. Recipient Gold medal service award U.S. Dept. Commerce, 1971. Fellow Am. Statis. Assn., A.A.A.S.; mem. Population Assn. Am. (past dir.), Washington Statis. Soc. (past pres.). Contbr. articles profl. jours. Home: 204 Belton Rd Silver Spring MD 20901 Office: U.S. Bur of Census Washington DC 20233

KAPLAN, HARRY LELAND, physician; b. Houston, Mar. 7, 1919; s. Rubin and Rose (Fiveshowitz) K.; B.S., So. Methodist U., 1939; M.D., U. Tex., 1942, m. Linda Louise Roberts, Apr. 3, 1965; children—Susan Elaine (Mrs. Fink), Michael Robert. Intern St. Paul's Hosp., Dallas, 1943; resident in internal medicine The John Sealy Hosps., Galveston, Tex., 1944-45, So. Pacific Hosps., Houston, 1947-48; practice medicine, specializing internal medicine and endocrinology, Houston 1948-—; mem. staff Hermann Hosp., Meth. Hosp., Beu Taub Gen. Hosp., Jefferson Davis Hosp., St. Luke's Hosp. (all Houston); chief staff Diagnostic Center Hosp., 1969-—; cons., staff mem. Diagnostic Clin. Houston; clin. asso. prof. internal medicine Coll. Medicine, Baylor U., 1957-—. Served from lt. (j.g.) to lt. M.C. USNR, 1945-46. Asso. A.C.P.; mem. Soc. Nuclear Medicine, Am., Houston socs. internal medicine, Am. Nuclear Soc., Mexican-Am. (founder), Am. Tex. med. assns., Harris County Med. Soc., Am., Houston diabetes assns. Mason (32 deg., Shriner). Author articles profl. jours. Home: 1404 North Blvd Houston TX 77006 Office: Diagnostic Clinic Houston 6448 Fannin St Houston TX 77025

KAPLAN, HARRY LIONEL, printing co. exec.; b. Bklyn., May 13, 1910; s. Bernard J. and Gussie (Harris) K.; grad. high sch.; m. Bess Donsky, Aug. 14, 1934; children—Barbara Jean, Nancy Jane (Mrs. Charles G. Lubar), Leon Jay. Pres. Am. Poster & Printing Co. (name changed to Am. Printing and Lithographing Co.), 1935-69, now chmn. bd.; pres. Am. Graphics, Dallas, 1969-—; pres. Abco, Inc., Am. Legal Printing Co., Inc., Irrigation Age, Inc., Am-Equity Press, Inc.; sec.-treas. Tradetype Dallas, Inc. Pres. Dallas Big Bros., 1948-49, Citizens' Traffic Commn., 1961-63; chmn. Juvenile Driver License Com., 1959-60; mem. Dallas Com. for Good Schs.; active Community Chest, A.R.C., Am. Med. Center, United Jewish Appeal, Nat. Conf. Christians and Jews. Bd. dirs., chmn. juvenile com. Dallas Crime Commn. Mem. Printing Industry Am. (v.p. Dallas chpt. 1965), C. of C. Jewish religion. Mason (33 deg., Shriner), Lion. Home: 6042 Prestonshire Lane Dallas TX 75225 Office: 1600 S Akard St Dallas TX 75215

KAPLAN, MARSHALL ALLEN, economist; b. Chgo., May 21, 1929; s. Benjamin and Rose (Altman) K.; B.S., Ill. Inst. Tech., 1950; M.A., U. Chgo., 1952, Ph.D., 1960; m. Carol M. Green, May 23, 1968; children— Robert, Elizabeth. Research asso. U. Chgo. Center [illegible]rl. Econs., 1953-54; instr. Williams Coll., Williamstown, Mass., [illegible]-56; sr. economist Pres.'s Council Econ. Advisers, Washington, 1956-64; economist Fed. Home Loan Bank Bd., Washington, 1964-—. Lectr., Georgetown U., 1962-66. Mem. Am. Econ. Assn. Author: Demand for Food, 1954. Contbr. articles on housing markets and econ. outlook, savs. and loan market structure to profl. jours. Home: 722 3d St SW Washington DC 20024 Office: Federal Home Loan Bank Board 101 Indiana Av NW Washington DC 20552

KAPLAN, MARVIN IRWIN, dentist; b. Bklyn., Feb. 8, 1937; s. Solomon and Lillian (Warm) K.; B.A., Bklyn. Coll., 1957; D.D.S. (N.Y. Regents medicine and dentistry scholar), N.Y. U., 1961, certificate in orthodontics, 1967; m. Victoria Spring, July 30, 1961; children—Lisa, Robert. Asso., Dr. Angelo Rocco Lombardi, orthodontist, Jersey City, 1967-69; practice dentistry specializing in orthodontics, Newport News, Va., 1969-—. Served as capt. AUS, 1961-63. Mem. Am., Tidewater assns. orthodontists, So., Va. socs. orthodontists, Peninsula Dental Soc., James River Jr. C. of C. (dir. 1971-—), Alpha Omega. Club: Toastmasters (v.p. 1971-72) (Hampton, Va.). Home: 5 Marilea Circle Newport News VA 23606 Office: 13193 Warwick Blvd Newport News VA 23602

KAPLAN, ROBERT, labor union ofcl.; b. Chgo., June 27, 1910; s. Abraham Louis and Sarah (Weitzman) K.; B.S. in Econs., Northwestern U., 1927; m. Grace Liebenson, July 27, 1934. Marketing and research staff Sachs Advt. Agy., Chgo., 1932-34; economist Lord & Thomas, Chgo., 1935-40; research dir. United Mine Workers Am., Washington, 1942-47, statistician, 1968-71, actuary, 1972-—; on loan U.S. Dept. Labor study reducing indsl. accidents, 1942-44. Mem. Conf. Actuaries in Pub. Practice, 1966-—. Served with USN, World War II. Mem. Am. Acad. Actuaries, Am. Econ. Assn., Am. Assn. Aviation. Home: 3601 Wisconsin Av NW Washington DC 20016 Office: 907 15th St NW Washington DC 20005

KAPLAN, STANLEY NORRIS, broadcasting exec.; b. Cleve., Apr. 23, 1926; s. Joseph S. and Tylie (Menitoff) K.; B.A., N. Y. U., 1950, M.A., 1951; postgrad. Harvard Bus. Sch., 1952; 1 dau., Susan; m. Harriet Atlass, Mar. 15, 1964; 1 dau., Leslie Ann. Vice pres. sales Balaban Stas., St. Louis, 1958-60; exec. v.p. Mars Broadcasting Co., Stamford, Conn., 1960-63, WMEX-Radio, Boston, 1963-65; pres. SIS Radio, Inc., Charlotte, N.C., 1965-—. Mem. N.C. Council on Crime and Delinquency, 1969-—; N.C. Zool. Authority, 1969-—. Mem. research com. Radio Advt. Bur., N.Y.C., 1969-—. Chmn. steering com. Mecklenburg (N.C.) Democratic Com., 1968; campaign mgr, lt. gov. N.C., 1968; del. Dem. Nat. Conv., Chgo., 1968. Bd. dirs. Charlotte Area Fund, Boys Town, Opportunities Industrialization Center, Medgar Evers Found. Served with inf. AUS, 1943-45; ETO. Decorated Purple Heart with cluster, Silver Star. Home: 714 Edgehill Rd Charlotte NC 28207 Office: 400 Radio Rd Charlotte NC 28214

KAPLAN, WILLIAM, textile mill exec.; b. Newark, Dec. 7, 1934; s. Sam and Betty (Franklin) K.; B.S., Lowell Technol. Inst., 1956; m. Barbara Esther Weiss, Dec. 31, 1964; children—Deborah Renee, David Joshua. Founder, Wyndmoor Knitting Mills, Inc., Elizabeth, N.J., 1956, pres., 1956-—; founder McGowen Mfg. Co., Inc., Elizabeth, 1958, pres., 1958-—; founder N.C. Spinning Mills, Inc., Lincolnton, N.C., 1963, pres. 1963-—; pres. Houser Spinning Mills, Inc., Cherryville, N.C., 1967-—. Mem. Am. Assn. Chemists and Colorists. Home: 4524 Belknap Rd Charlotte NC 28211 Office: PO Box 818 Lincolnton NC 28092

KAPNER, LEWIS, judge; b. West Palm Beach, Fla., May 21, 1937; s. Irving Michael and Mildred (Pikelny) K.; B.A., U. Fla., 1958; student Harvard, summer 1956, George Washington U., summer 1961; J.D., Stetson U., 1962; postgrad. Fla. Atlantic U., 1970-—; m. Dawn Beth Grossman, Aug. 30, 1964; children—Steven Marshall, Kimberly Anne, Michael Scott, Allison Lori. Admitted to Fla. bar, 1962; asst. county solicitor Palm Beach County, 1962-65; city prosecutor West Palm Beach, 1965-66; partner Kapner & Kapner, 1965-67; legal counsel Palm Beach County Legislative Delegation, 1967; judge Juvenile and Domestic Relations Ct., Palm Beach County, 1967-—, judge Circuit Ct., 1973-—; instr. parliamentary law adult edn. Palm Beach County, 1965; del. White House Conf. on children, 1970; regional chmn. Gov.'s Task Force on Delinquency, 1969-71; mem. Gov.'s Task Force on Drug and Alcohol Abuse, 1969-71. Charter pres. Palm Beach County Young Republicans, 1965; gen. counsel Fla. Young Republicans, 1966-67; candidate Fla. Senate, 1967. Pres. Community Services Council, 1969; pres. Internat. Found. for Gifted Children; v.p. Palm Beach County chpt., mem. nat. exec. com. Am. Jewish Com.; bd. dirs. Fla. Air Acad., Epilepsy Found.; adv. bd. Fla. Ocean Scis. Inst., Buzz Aldren Sci. Mus., Adult Edn. Program, Reading Research Found. Served with USMCR, 1958-65. Recipient Distinguished Service award West Palm Beach Jaycees, 1971; named one of five outstanding young men in Fla., Fla. Jaycees, 1971. Mem. Fla., Palm Beach County (past com. chmn.) bar assns., Nat., Fla. councils juvenile ct. judges, Am. Acad. Trial Lawyers, Mensa, Blue Key, Phi Delta Phi, Phi Alpha Theta, Tau Epsilon Phi. Republican. Jewish religion. Home: 258 Country Club Rd Palm Beach FL 33480 Office: County Courthouse West Palm Beach FL 33402

KAPPUS, KARL DANIEL, biologist; b. Cleve., July 2, 1938; s. Robert D. and Dolores (Zwerman) K.; B.S., Ohio State U., 1960, M.S., 1962, Ph.D., 1964. NRC postdoctoral asso. Army Biol. Labs., Frederick, Md., 1964-66; research asso. Ohio State U., 1967; research entomologist Nat. Communicable Disease Center, Atlanta, 1967-68, research ecologist, 1968-—. Mem. Am. Inst. Biol. Sci., Entomol. Soc. Am., A.A.A.S., Sigma Xi. Home: 454 Superior Av Decatur GA 30030 Office: 1600 Clifton Rd Atlanta GA 30333

KAREM, MARY JANE (MRS. FRED J. KAREM), lawyer; b. Louisville, Oct. 27, 1908; d. Edmund Gibbs and Virginia (Allen) Mansfield; B.A., Catherine Spalding Coll. (formerly Nazareth Coll.), 1931; J.D. magna cum laude, Jefferson 1936; m. Fred J. Karem (dec.); children—Virginia C., James F., Edmund Peter, David Kevin, Jane Catherine. Admitted to Ky. bar, 1949; gen. practice Karem & Karem, attys., Louisville, 1949-—. Committee woman Dem. Party, 1952-—. Bd. counselors, sec. Catherine Spalding Coll.; mem. Louisville and Jefferson County Human Relations Commn. Named Ky. col., Bus. Woman of Year, Louisville Bus. and Profl. Women's Club, 1967; recipient Caritas medal Spalding Coll., 1968. Mem. Nat. Assn. Women Lawyers, Nat. Cath. Theatre Conf., Cath. Theatre Guild of Louisville, Am. Ky., Louisville bar assns., Bellarmine Coll. Athletic Assn., Bellarmine Coll. Parents Assn., Jefferson County (Ky.) Women Lawyers (pres.), Internat. Platform Assn., Catherine Spalding Coll. Alumnae Assn. (pres.), Bellarmine's Womens Council (exec. bd.), English Speaking Union. Clubs: Highland Woman's, Catherine Spalding Coll. Luncheon. Home: 1857 Alfresco Pl Louisville KY 40205 Office: Lincoln Fed Bldg Louisville KY 40202

KARES, PETER, educator; b. Cleve., Aug. 13, 1931; s. Christ and Frances (Kosance) K.; B.S. in Commerce, Ohio U., 1958; M.S., Purdue U., 1961, Ph.D., 1968; m. Gloria M. Kamerer, May 28, 1966; children—Gregory A., Diana E. Lectr., Purdue U., West Lafayette, Ind., 1960-63; asst. prof. State U. N.Y. at Buffalo, 1963-69; asso. prof. dept. finance, Coll. Bus. Adminstrn., U. South Fla., Tampa, 1969-—. Served with USMCR, 1950-52. Mem. Am., Western finance assns., Am. Econ. Assn., Financial Mgmt. Assn. Home: 4704 Travertine Dr Tampa FL 33615

KARESH, COLEMAN, educator; b. Newburgh, N.Y., Jan. 8, 1903; s. David and Lene (Mishkoff) K.; A.B., U. S.C., 1923, LL.B., 1925; m. Anna Weinsel, Oct. 5, 1930 (dec. June 1947); children—Sara (Mrs. Robert Leinkram), Barbara (Mrs. James S. Kriger), Libby (Mrs. Harvey M. Grossman), Miriam (Mrs. Herbert J. Gerber); m. 2d, Alice Freed, Dec. 25, 1949. Admitted to S.C. bar, 1925; practiced with James H. Hammond, Columbia, S.C., until 1937; prof. Law Sch., U. S.C., Columbia, 1937-72, prof. emeritus, 1972-—. Mem. Am., S.C. bar assns., Am. Law Inst., Nat. Conf. Commrs. on Uniform Laws. Jewish religion. Elk; mem. B'nai B'rith. Home: 3000 Amherst Av Columbia SC 29205

KARESH, STANLEY HERBERT, dentist; b. Fall River, Mass., Oct. 30, 1921; s. Alex and Leslie Elinor (Feinberg) K.; D.D.S., U. Md., 1943; m. Charlot Elaine Marks, June 3, 1945; children—Fern (Mrs. Robert Jay Hurst); Gail (Mrs. Stuart Suchin Kassan), Jane. Individual practice dentistry, Charleston, S.C., 1946-—; clin. asso. Coll. Dental Medicine, Med. U. S.C. Bd. dirs. S.C. chpt. Am. Cancer Soc., Am. Soc. Preventative Dentistry. Served to lt. Dental Corps, USNR, 1944-46. Fellow Internat. Coll. Dentists; mem. Am. Dental Assn., Am. Assn. Endodontists, Am. Acad. Dental Practice Adminstrn. (chmn. publs.), Am. Equilibration Soc. Jewish religion. Club: Country of Charleston. Home: 48 Chadwick Dr Charleston SC 29407 Office: 112 1/2 Ashley St Charleston SC 29402

KARLIN, SAMUEL, surgeon; b. Portland, Me., Sept. 7, 1908; s. Myer and Gussie (Rosoff) K.; A.B., Harvard, 1928, M.D., 1932; m. Alece J. Geisenberger, June 27, 1938; children—Robert A., Richard M. Intern, Touro Infirmary, New Orleans, 1933-34, resident, 1934-36, chief surgery, 1959-63; clin. prof. surgery La. State U., New Orleans, 1950-—. Vice chmn. profl. div. New Orleans United Fund, 1963. Trustee Newman Sch., New Orleans. Served to maj. AUS, 1942-46. Decorated Bronze Star. Diplomate Am. Bd. Surgery. Fellow A.C.S., Southeastern Surg. Congress, Surg. Soc. La.; mem. New Orleans Surg. Soc. (pres. 1965). Club: Harvard of La. (pres. 1964-67). Home: 5418 S Miro St New Orleans LA 70125 Office: 3600 Prytania St New Orleans LA 70115

KARMIN, MONROE W., journalist; b. Mineola, N.Y., Sept. 2, 1929; s. Stanley and Phyllis (Appelbaum) K.; m. Mayanne Sherman, Oct. 30, 1955; children—Paul, Betsy. Spl. writer Wall Street Journal, Washington. Recipient Pulitzer prize for nat. reporting, 1967, Sigma Delta award for gen. reporting, 1967. Home: 7011 Beechwood Dr Chevy Chase MD 20015 Office: Nat Press Bldg Washington DC 20004

KARPOFF, EDWARD, govt. ofcl.; b. San Francisco, Feb. 2, 1918; s. Abraham and Esther (Feinberg) K.; B.S., Rutgers U., 1938; M.S., U. Conn., 1940; m. Bella Irma Warhaft, July 26, 1942; children—Peter, Julian. Economist U.S. Dept. Agr., Washington, 1941-—, asst. to asst. adminstr. Fgn. Agrl. Service, 1970-—, mem. U.S. del. to Kennedy Round of Tariff Negotiations, Geneva, Switzerland, 1967. Mem. Am. Agrl. Econ. Assn., Poultry Sci. Assn., World Poultry Sci. Assn., Poultry Hist. Soc., Phi Beta Kappa, Alpha Zeta. Contbr. articles poultry and poultry as an industry to Encyclopedia Americana.

Home: 4906 Bangor Dr Kensington MD 20795 Office: Fgn Agr Service US Dept Agriculture Washington DC 20250

KARR, HARRY A., JR., broadcasting co. exec.; b. Newark, Mar. 9, 1921; s. Harry A. and Katherine (Heine) K.; B.B.S., U. Md., 1947; m. Elaine Ida Kratz, Aug. 5, 1961; 1 dau., Deborah Elaine. Salesman, WRC radio, Washington, 1947-53, sales mgr., 1953-61, sta. mgr., 1961-68, gen. mgr., WRC, WRC-FM, 1968—. Pres., Hamlet Citizens Assn. Chevy Chase, 1966, 67; chmn. United Givers Fund Radio, 1967. Served to 1st lt. USAAF, 1943-45. Decorated Air medal with 5 oak leaf clusters. Mem. U. Md., Montgomery County Md. (bd. dirs.) alumni assns., Chevy Chase C. of C., Washington Bd. Trade, Md.-D.C.-Del. Broadcasters Assn. (dir., Pres. 1970-71). Clubs: Terrapin; Advertising of Washington. Home: 3604 East West Hwy Chevy Chase MD 20015 Office: 4001 Nebraska Av NW Washington DC 20016

KARRAKER, JOHN RICHARD, banker; b. DeSota, Mo., Nov. 14, 1928; s. John Wilson and Mary Olga (Van Hecke) K.; student Brown Bus. Coll., 1947, Northwestern U., 1962, 66, 68; m. Frances Walker Flowers, Dec. 20, 1950; children—Marlo, Wayne, Renee. Trust officer Ga. R.R. Bank & Trust Co., 1952-65; sr. v.p., gen. trust officer Nat. Bank Ga., Atlanta, 1965—; dir. Midville Cotton Warehouse Co. (Ga.), W. R. C. Smith Pub. Co., Atlanta, Pine Mountain (Ga.) Club Chalets, Inc., Fritze Orr Enterprises, Inc., Atlanta. Instr. trusts Ga. Bankers Assn., U. Ga., Athens, 1968—. Citizen mem. Fulton County Employees Pension Fund, 1966-70; crusade chmn. Fulton County Cancer Soc., Inc., 1972. Bd. dirs., mem. finance com. Met. Atlanta Boys' Clubs, Inc.; trustee Frank &William Bone Found., Milledgeville, Ga., Met. Found. Atlanta. Served with AUS, 1948-52. Mem. Am. Inst. Banking, Ga. Bankers Assn. (mem. exec. com. trust div. 1968-72), Atlanta Life Underwriters Assn., Estate Planning Council Atlanta. Roman Catholic. Clubs: Cherokee Town and Country, Commerce (Atlanta). Home: 496 Manor Ridge Dr NW Atlanta GA 30305 Office: 34 Peachtree St Atlanta GA 30301

KARRH, JOHN BARNARD, educator, engr.; b. Ft. Payne, Ala., Oct. 16, 1931; s. James Alvin and Mamie (Barnard) K.; student Auburn U., 1950; B.S. in Civil Engring., U. Ala., 1958; M.S. (Guy F. Atkinson fellow), Stanford, 1959; postgrad. Purdue U., 1963-64; Ph.D. in Civil Engring., U. Ala., 1970; m. Mary Ada Hanchett, Aug. 15, 1964; children—John Barnard, Carolyn Elaine, Kent Hanchett. Stress engr. Hayes Aircraft Corp., Birmingham, Ala., 1958; asst. supt. Sullivan, Long, & Hagerty, gen. contractors, Birmingham, Ala., 1959; dist. engr. Ala. State Hwy. Dept., Birmingham, 1959-63; instr. civil engring. U. Ala., 1966-70; partner J. A. Karrh & Asso. Cons. Engrs., 1964—; asso. prof. civil engring. U. South Ala., Mobile, 1970—. Served with USNR, 1950-54. Named Ala. Rd. Builder's Civil Engring. Honor Grad., U. Ala., 1957. Mem. Am. Soc. C.E., V.F.W., Sigma Xi, Tau Beta Pi, Chi Epsilon, Theta Tau, Phi Eta Sigma. Research and publs. in hwy. bridge dynamics and constrn. materials. Home: 5524 Woodside Dr Mobile AL 36608

KARST, CHARLES EDWARD, lawyer, mayor; b. New Orleans, Sept. 18, 1931; s. Charles and Ethel Marie (Drouin) K.; B.A., Tulane U., 1952; J.D., Loyola U., 1965; m. Judith Ward Steinman, Dec. 27, 1965; children—Alexander Regard, Alicia Barrows. Indsl. engr. Boeing Co., New Orleans, 1963-66; admitted to La. bar, 1965; atty. Ward-Steinman & Karst, New Orleans, 1965-67, Alexandria, La., 1966—. Mayor, City of Alexandria, La., 1969—; v.p. Cenla Mayor's Council, 1971. Served with USAF, 1952-54. Mem. Am. Trial Lawyers Assn., Am., La., Alexandria bar assns., V.F.W., Am. Legion. Roman Catholic. Lion. Home: 2236 Jackson St Alexandria LA 71301 Office: 1128 5th St Alexandria LA 71301

KARTUS, JACK LEE, dept. store exec.; b. Bessemer, Ala., Dec. 1, 1918; s. Harry and Esther (Kaufman) K.; student, U. Ala., 1938-42; m. Miriam Bresler, Jan. 23, 1943; children—Margaret, Lisa, Sallie, Harry. With Outlet Co., Bessemer, 1950—, pres., 1954—; chmn. bd. Kartus, Inc., Selma, 1964—. Bd. dirs. United Appeal, Bessemer. Served to 1st lt. USAAF, 1941-46, USAF, 1950. Mem. C. of C. (v.p. retail div. 1969—). Home: 3139 Pine Ridge Rd Birmingham AL 35213 Office: PO Box 398 Bessemer AL 35020

KARZON, ALLAIRE URBAN (MRS. DAVID T. KARZON), lawyer; b. Newark, July 18, 1925; d. Paul J. and Aurelia (Hemmen) Urban; B.A., Wellesley Coll., 1945; LL.B., Yale, 1947; m. David T. Karzon, May 18, 1946; children—David T., Elizabeth Urban. Admitted to Md. bar, 1948, N.Y. bar, 1952, Tenn. bar, 1969; atty. Office Alien Property Dept. Justice, 1948-49; atty. law dept. RCA, N.Y.C., 1950-52; asso. Hodgson, Russ, Andrews, Woods & Goodyear, Buffalo, 1952-55, partner, 1955-68; v.p., gen. counsel, dir. Performance Systems, Inc., Nashville, 1969-70; partner Neal, Karzon & Harwell, Nashville, 1971-72; dir. law Aladdin Industries, Inc., Nashville, 1972—. Lectr. law Vanderbilt U., 1971—. Pres. bd. mgrs. Vis. Nursing Assn. Buffalo; mem. exec. com. Council Vis. Nurse Assns. N.Y. State; sec., trustee Western N.Y. Ednl. TV, Inc.; bd. dirs., sec. Sr. Citizens Inc., Nashville. Recipient award trust div. N.Y. State Bankers Assn. 1966. Mem. Am., Tenn., Nashville bar assns., Phi Beta Kappa. Presbyn. Club: Nashville Wellesley. Home: 1049 Overton Lea Rd Nashville TN 37220 Office: 703 Murfreesboro Rd Nashville TN 37204

KASE, FRANCIS JOSEPH, govt. ofcl.; b. Most, Austria, Sept. 21, 1910; s. Francis and Alberta (Retovska) K.; came to U.S., 1949, naturalized, 1954; Dr. jur., Charles U., Prague, Czechoslovakia, 1934; D.P.S., Acad. Polit. Sci., Prague, 1934; Ph.D., George Washington U., 1963. Practiced law, Czechoslovakia, 1933-35; govt. ofcl. Land Govt. Bohemia, 1935-45; counsel, div. chief Ministry Fgn. Trade, Czechoslovakia, 1945-48; sec.-treas., research analyst Internat. Peasant Union, Washington, 1951-54; librarian, mem. legal staff U.S. Copyright Office, Library of Congress, Washington, 1956-66; librarian Patent Office Search Center, U.S. Dept. Commerce, 1966-71; law librarian Price Commn., 1971—. Mem. Am. Polit. Sci. Assn., Am. Acad. Polit. and Social Sci., Copyright Office Lawyers' Assn., Pi Gamma Mu. Author: Handbook of Czechoslovak Foreign Trade, 1948; Soviet Theory of People's Democracy, 1963; Copyright in Continental Europe, 1967; Copyright in Czechoslovakia, 1967; People's Democracy, 1968; Foreign Patents, 1972. Contbr. to profl. jours. Research polit. theory, comparative govt. and law, especially Eastern Europe, USSR, Africa, library sci. Home: 5206 Little Falls Dr Bethesda MD 20016 Office: Price Commn Washington DC 20508

KASH, ROBERT WALKER, JR., ret. educator; b. Oak Ridge, Va., Oct. 14, 1917; s. Robert Walker and Eleanor (Coleman) K.; B.S. in Agrl. Engring., Va. Poly. Inst., 1939; m. Janie Morgan, Oct. 18, 1944; children—Robert Morgan, Peyton Walker, Morgan Abbitt. With Soil Conservation Service, U.S. Dept. Agr., Halifax, Va., 1939-40, Va. Poly Inst. Extension Service, 1946-52, 54-72, extension agt. Spotsylvania County, Fredericksburg, Va., 1968-72. Served to col. USMCR, 1940-45, 1952-54. Mem. Va. Assn. Extension Agts. (pres. 1969—). Presbyn. (elder). Home: 7 Fairfax Circle Fredericksburg VA 22401

KASHEF, ABDEL-AZIZ ISMAIL, educator; b. Cairo, Egypt, Feb. 10, 1919 (came to U.S. 1962); s. Ismail Hassan and Fatima Sayed (Abdel-Ghani) K.; B.S., Cairo U., 1940, M.S., 1947; Ph.D., (XR research fellow), Purdue U., 1951; m. Awatef Sidki, Feb. 12, 1948. Irrigation engr. U.A.R. Govt., 1940-45, 48-52; prof. Cairo U., 1945-48, 54-56; prof. Am. U., Beirut, Lebanon, 1956-60, N.C. State U., Raleigh, 1962—. Engring. cons., Egypt, Syria, Saudi Arabia, Lebanon, Nev., Richmond, Va.; cons. High Aswan Dam Authority, 1954-56. Recipient Golden medal Egyptian Govt., 1945. Fellow Am. Soc. C.E., mem. Am. Water Resources Assn. (chief editor Water Resources Bull. 1970—), Nat. Water Well Assn., Am. Geophys. Union, Sigma Xi. Contbr. articles in structures, irrigation, groundwater and soil mechanics to tech. jours. Home: 1104 Currituck St Raleigh NC 27609

KASMAN, FRANKLIN GERALD, dentist; b. Bay City, Tex., Feb. 3, 1941; s. Jake and Helen (Greenberg) K.; D.D.S., U. Tex., 1966; certificate in endodontics, Tufts U., 1970; m. Golda Sue Golub, June 19, 1966; 1 son, Jonathan Alan. Individual practice dentistry, Worcester, Mass., 1968-70, Austin, Tex., 1970—; cons. endodontics USAF; faculty U. Tex. Dental Br. Guest lectr. Elgee Assos. Served with USAF, 1966-68. Decorated Hosp. Commendation medal. Mem. Am. Soc. Dentistry for Children (Achievement award 1966), Zionist Orgn. Am., Tex. Dental Soc., Am. Assn. Endodontics. Jewish religion (dir. Brotherhood). Mem. B'nai B'rith. Home: 6404 Sumac St Austin TX 78731 Office: 311 Med Park Tower Austin TX 78705

KASS, BENNY LEE, lawyer; b. Chgo., Aug 20, 1936; s. Herman and Ethel (Lome) K.; B.S., Northwestern U., 1957; LL.B., U. Mich., 1960; LL.M., George Washington U., 1967; m. Salme Lundstrom, Aug. 30, 1963; children—Gale, Brian. Admitted to D.C. bar, 1960; atty. Maritime Adminstrn., 1960-61; counsel House Information Subcommittee, 1962-65; asst. counsel Senate Adminstrv. Practice Subcom., Washington, 1965-69; pvt. practice law, Washington, 1969—; prof. communication law Am. U.; pub. mem. Nat. Advt. Rev. Bd., 1971—; commr. D.C. Conf. on Uniform State Laws. Chmn. consumer affairs subcom., Mayors Econ. Devel. Com., 1968-70; chmn. Ad Hoc Com. on Consumer Protection, 1965—. Served with USAF, 1961-62. Am. Polit. Sci. Assn. Congl. fellow, 1966. Mem. Am., Fed. bar assns., Am. Polit. Sci. Assn., Sigma Delta Chi. Contbr. articles profl. jours. Home: 3642 Jocelyn St NW Washington DC 20015 Office: Boasberg Kass & Smith 1225 19th St NW Washington DC 20036

KASS, LEON R., scientist. Exec. sec. Com. Life Scis. and Social Policy, Nat. Acad. Sci., Washington. Address: Nat Acad Sci 2101 Constitution Av NW Washington DC 20037*

KASSIN, HAROLD HOWARD, lawyer; b. Bklyn., Dec. 2, 1927; s. Louis and Anna (Gorelick) K.; student Columbia, 1948; J.D., U. Miami, 1951; m. Delores Jean Robey, Nov. 27, 1971. Admitted to Fla. bar, 1951, U.S. Supreme Ct. bar, 1955, also other U.S. and state bars; pvt. practice law, Miami, Fla. Sec., Kassin Investment Corp., Miami Beach, Flagler-Ponce Realty Corp., Miami Beach. Served with AUS, 1946-47. Mem. Am., Fla., Dade County bar assns., Fla. Real Estate Brokers, Nu Beta Epsilon (So. regional chancellor). Democrat. Home: 1921 NE 188th St Sky Lake North Miami Beach FL 33162 Office: Biscayne Bldg 19 W Flagler St Miami FL 33130

KASSIS, RAYMOND, dentist; b. Zahley, Lebanon, Dec. 23, 1937; came to U.S., 1952, naturalized 1961; s. Aziz Habib and Zakia (Shahid) K.; B.S. in Chemistry, Coll. Charleston, 1961; D.D.S., Georgetown U., 1968. Research chemist Charleston Rubber Co. (S.C.), 1962-64; individual practice dentistry, Charleston, 1969—. Recipient S. Keith Johnson Sci. award Pre-med. Club Coll. Charleston, 1961; NSF research grantee, 1960. Mem. Am. Dental Assn., Charleston, Coastal Dist. dental socs., Charleston (Dental) Study Club. Home: 1296 Hwy 171 Charleston SC 29403 Office: 1247 Savannah Hwy Charleston SC 29407

KASTL, FRANK JOHN, elec. engr.; b. Yukon, Okla., Apr. 11, 1918; s. John J. and Fannie (Policky) K.; B.S., Okla. State U., 1941; m. Helen L. Vrana, June 28, 1946; children—David Gene, John F., Steven Lynn, Kathy Sue, Ann Marie. With Southwestern Pub. Service Co., 1946-60; with U.S. Corp. Engrs., 1961; elec. engr. Bechtel Corp., 1962; lead engr. Boeing Aircraft, 1963; sr. facilities engr. Bur. Reclamation, Dept. Interior, 1963-64; project specialist U.S. Air Force, 1965-66, electronic engr., 1967-68; elec. engr. Bur. Indian Affairs, Dept. Interior, Anadarko, Okla., 1969-70; asst. chief engr. engr. VA Hosp., Oklahoma City, 1971—. Served to maj. AUS, 1941-46; ETO. Decorated six Bronze Star medals. Registered profl. engr., Tex., Okla. Home: 1512 Homeland St Norman OK 73069 Office: 921 NE 13th St Oklahoma City OK 73104

KASTNER, HAROLD HENRY, JR., state ofcl.; b. Paola, Fla., Jan. 4, 1928; s. Harold Henry and Essye (Sutton) K.; B.S. in Econs., Fla. State U., 1955, M.S. in Econs., 1958; Ed.D. in Jr. Coll. Adminstrn., U. Fla., 1962; m. Cecilia Ann Franklin, July 30, 1955; children—Kathryn Diane, Susan Claire, Harold Lawrence. Tchr., West Palm Beach (Fla.) High Sch., 1955-57; head social sci. div. St. John's River Jr. Coll., Palatka, Fla., 1958-60; cons. social studies, econs., resource-use edn. Fla. State Dept. Edn., Tallahassee, 1962-65; dean coll. Polk Jr. Coll., Winter Haven, 1965-69, v.p., 1967-69: asst. dir. div. community colls. Fla. Dept. Edn., Tallahassee, 1969—, mem. regulations com., 1971—; project dir. In-Service Tng. Workshops for Community Div. Chmn., Title V Elementary and Secondary Edn. Act, 1972-73; co-dir. Social Work Planning Research Project, Social and Rehab. Services div. Dept. Health, Edn. and Welfare, 1970-72. Adv. com. Southeastern Ednl. Lab., 1966—, Fla. adv. com. Nat. Def. Edn. Act, Title III, 1965—; cons. on disadvantaged So. Regional Edn. Bd., 1969-70, Community Coll.-Univ. Articulation Com., 1971; pres. Instructional Enterprize, Inc., 1969—. Exec. dir., dir. Fla. Council Econ. Edn., 1963-65; cons. Nat. Family Finance Workshop, Madison, Wis., 1964; chmn. social studies com. So. States Work Conf., Daytona Beach, Fla., 1965. Bd. dirs. Fla. State Dept. Edn. Credit Union, 1965. Served with AUS, 1950-53. U.S. Office Edn. research grantee, Kellogg fellow; Am. Legion Merit award and medal. Mem. Am. Econs. Assn., Fla. Council Social Studies, Fla. Tech. Edn. Assn., Nat. Council on Community Services, Am. Assn. Jr. Colls., Fla. Assn. Community Colls., Fla. Soc. Assn. Execs. (chmn. edn. com. 1965), Phi Kappa Phi, Phi Delta Kappa, Alpha Tau Omega. Contbr. numerous articles and dissertations to ednl. jours. Mem. editorial bd. Higher Edn. Collaborative Planning in Higher Edn. for Professions Monograph Series. Home: 1103 Sandhurst Dr Tallahassee FL 32303 Office: Fla Dept Edn Tallahassee FL 32301

KATHAN, WILLIAM KEITH, editor; b. Galveston, Tex., July 2, 1931; s. Kenneth Herbert and Anna Mae Reynolds (Thornton) K.; B.S. in Journalism, So. Methodist U., 1956; m. Sarah Marcella McBryde, June 20, 1958; 1 son, Kenneth James. Corr., United Press, New Orleans, 1956-57; courthouse reporter, gen. assignments Dallas Times Herald, 1957-60; film editor, writer WBAP-TV Tex. News, Fort Worth, 1960-62. editor Life Lines, Life Line Found., Washington, Dallas, 1962—. Served with USAF, 1948-52. Independent. Baptist. Office: 4330 N Central Expressway Dallas TX 75206

KATTEL, G. EDWARD, financial cons.; b. N.Y.C., June 27, 1908; B.C.S., N.Y. U., 1930; m. Dorothea Fleming, June 12, 1930; children—Edward, Richard. With Grace Nat. Bank, N.Y.C., 1951-65, exec. v.p., 1955-65, also dir.; exec. v.p. Marine Midland Grace Trust Co. N.Y., N.Y.C., 1965-69; chmn. Kattel, Inc., Coral Gables, Fla., 1970—; dir. Rotron, Inc., Woodstock, N.Y.; trustee Northwestern Financial Investors, Charlotte, N.C., Hanover Sq. Realty Investors. Mem. Delta Sigma Pi. Mason. Clubs: India House, N.Y. Athletic (N.Y.C.); Miami (Fla.); Key Biscayne Yacht. Home: 615 Ocean Dr Key Biscayne FL 33149 Office: 316 Minorca Av Coral Gables FL 33134

KATTEL, RICHARD L., banker; b. N.Y.C., 1936; grad. Emory U., 1958; postgrad. Harvard. Sch. Bus. Adminstrn.; m. Asst. to pres. Citizens & So. Nat. Bank, Savannah, Ga., 1966-68, exec. v.p. in charge Savannah bank, 1968-71, pres., Atlanta, 1971—; chmn. bd. C & S Community Devel. Corp. v.p., dir. C & S Holding Co. Bd. dirs. Ga. Indsl. Devel. Counsel. Mem. Am. Bankers Assn. (mem. comml. lending com.), Assn. Res. City Bankers, Ga. C. of C. (dir.). Home: 3629 Tuxedo Rd NW Atlanta GA 30305 Office: 35 Broad St NW Atlanta GA 30303

KATTERHENRY, ARNOLD ALLEN, civil engr.; b. New Knoxville, O., June 10, 1906; B.C.E., Ohio State U., 1928; M.S., U. Fla., 1956; m. Ann Sue Derrick, Dec. 22, 1934; children—Arnold Allen, John G. Civil engr. TVA, 1933-46; self-employed as engr., Chattanooga, 1946-48; asst. prof. civil engring. U. Fla., 1948-61; hwy. engr. Fed. Hwy. Adminstrn., Atlanta, 1961—. Registered profl. engr., Ga. Fellow Am. Soc. C.E. (chmn. nat. com. on engring. surveys 1962-66). Elk. Club: Puroga Investment (Atlanta). Home: 4536 E Brookhaven Dr NE Atlanta GA 30319 Office: 900 Peachtree St Atlanta GA 30309

KATTUS, JAMES ROBERT, metallurgist; b. Cin., Aug. 25, 1922; s. Albert A. and Matilda (Gerling) K.; B.S., Purdue U., 1944; m. Josephine Bremer, Mar. 2, 1946; children—Josephine, Robert, Sandra, Laura, Patricia. Research metallurgist Naval Reserach Lab., Washington, 1944-46; chief metallurgist Anderson Electric Corp., Birmingham, Ala., 1947-52; dir. metall. research So. Research Inst., 1952-66; gen. mgr. Bethea Co., Inc., Birmingham, 1966-68; consulting metallurgist, Birmingham, 1968—. Bd. dirs. St. Vincent Sch. of Nursing, Birmingham. Served with USNR, 1943-46. Mem. Am. Soc. for Metals, Am. Soc. for Testing and Materials, Am. Inst. Mining and Metall. Engrs. Contbr. articles to profl. jours. Patentee in field. Home and office: 112 Azalea Rd Birmingham AL 35213

KATZ, KENNETH HAROLD, hotel supply co. exec.; b. San Antonio, Dec. 17, 1943; s. Sam and Sally Meriam (Ambinder) K.; student U. Pa., 1961-64; B.B.A., U. Tex., 1966. Exec. v.p. Better Brands, Inc., wholesale beer distributorship, San Antonio, 1966-69; v.p. marketing Gen. Hotel Supply Co., wholesale and mfr. food service equipment and supplies, San Antonio, 1970-71, exec. v.p., 1971—. Served with AUS, 1964-65. Home: Route 8 Box 229 San Antonio TX 78228 Office: PO Box 158 131 S Cherry St San Antonio TX 78291

KATZ, MORT, psychiat. social worker; b. Bklyn., May 27, 1925; s. Morris and Sophie (Guttman) K.; B.A., Sarah Lawrence Coll., June, 1949; M.S.S.W. Columbia, 1951; m. Ellen Loeb, July 18, 1964. Psychiat. social worker Hillside (N.Y.) Hosp., 1951-53; import agt. B. Sessler Co., N.Y.C., 1953-57; founder Consol. Helicopters, 1959-62; psychiat. social worker Dallas State Mental Health Clinic, 1962-69; pvt. practice family therapy, Dallas, 1969—. Served with AUS, 1943-46; PTO. Fellow Am. Orthopsychiat. Assn.; mem. Family Therapy Assn. of Tex. (pres. 1969-70), Dallas Group Therapy Soc., Acad. Certified Social Workers, Leukemia Soc. Dallas (sec. 1968-69). Author: Marriage Survival Kit, 1972. Home: 4318 Briar Creek Lane Dallas TX 75214 Office: 2930 Turtle Creek Pl Dallas TX 75219

KATZ, S. STANLEY, govt. ofcl.; b. Albany, N.Y., Oct. 21, 1928; s. Jacob and Rose (Cherdack) K.; B.A., Syracuse U., 1954, M.A. in Econs., 1956; Ph.D., Am. U., 1966; m. Cecilia S. Sigalowsky, June 19, 1955; children—Mitchell, Raquel. With U.S. Bur. of Budget, Washington, 1955-59, U.S. AID, Washington, 1957-61; prin. adminstr. OECD, Paris, France, 1962-65; sr. economist Internat. Bank Reconstrn. and Devel., Washington, 1966-67; dir. Office Internat. Investment; Dept. Commerce, Washington, 1967—. Home: 6807 Buttermere Lane Bethesda MD 20034 Office: US Dept Commerce Washington DC 20236

KATZ, STANLEY IVAN, retail trade exec.; b. Detroit, Aug. 2, 1931; s. Harry Leo and Netta (Petchon) K.; student Duke, 1949-51; B.A., Franklin and Marshall Coll., 1953; m. Barbara Hawerth, Aug. 12, 1959 (div. Sept. 1966); children—Kathy Rachael, Elizabeth Sarah. With Hartley's Inc., Miami, Fla., 1956—, buyer sportswear, 1958-68, v.p., 1969—. Served with M.I., AUS, 1953-56. Mem. Pi Lambda Phi. Club: Miami Downtown Optimists (pres. 1960-61). Home: Dinner Key Marina Miami FL 33100 Office: 205 Northside Plaza Miami FL 33147

KATZENTINE, UCOLA COLLIER (MRS. ARTHUR F. KATZENTINE), radio sta. exec.; b. Tonkawa, Okla., Aug 2, 1905; d. Clyde and Lula (Wills) Collier; student Central Mo. State Coll., 1923-25.; m. Arthur Frank Katzentine, June 11, 1928. Vice pres., dir. womens program Sta. WKAT. Miami Beach, Fla., 1937-42, v.p., mng. dir., 1942-46, pres., owner, 1960—. Mem. Sigma Sigma Sigma. Democrat. Roman Catholic. Clubs: Surf (Miami Beach); Palm Bay (Miami, Fla.); Army and Navy (Washington). Home: 4745 Pine Tree Dr Miami Beach FL 33140 Office: 1759 Bay Rd Miami Beach FL 33139

KAUDER, EMIL LEOPOLD FERDINAND CHRISTOPHER, economist; b. Berlin, Germany, June 23, 1901 (came to U.S., 1938, naturalized 1945); s. Hugo and Ernestine (Freifraulein von Feilen) K.; Ph.D., U. Berlin, 1924; m. Helene I. Riegner, July 11, 1943; children—Eunice, Henry Hugh. Expert on custom duties German textile industry, 1928-38; fgn. lang. tchr. Am. prep. schs., 1938-46; prof. econs. various Am. univs. and colls., 1947-68; research worker Hitotsubachi U., Kunitachi, Japan, 1960-61; prof. emeritus, distinguished lectr. U. South Fla., Tampa, 1968—. Served with German Army, 1921. Invited as speaker at centenary of Menger's Principles of Economics, 1971 by U. Vienna and Austrian Republic. Republican. Episcopalian. Author: History of Marginal Utility, 1966. Contbr. articles to profl. jours. Home: 6761 22d Way S St. Petersburg FL 33712

KAUFFELD, NORBERT MARINER, entomologist; b. Trivandrum, Kerala, South India, Jan. 30, 1923; s. Paul Martin and Clara Matlock (Wood) K.; student St. John's Jr. Coll., 1943, S.E. Mo. State Tchrs. Coll., 1943; B.S., Kan. State U., 1949, M.S., 1949; postgrad. Southwestern Coll., 1957; Ph.D., Kan. State U., 1967; m. Mayme Louise Nitschke, Apr. 10, 1945; children—James Mariner, Sharon (Mrs. John Alden Woody), Jon David, Corinne Rose, Clarisse Ann. Millwright, Consol. Flour Co., Winfield, Kan., 1946; rancher, farmer, Winfield, 1949-58; biology and math. instr. Morland Rural High Sch., 1958; biology instr. Junction City Sr. High Sch., 1958-62; chief apiarist State of Kan., 1961-63; instr. agr. Kan. State U., Manhattan, 1962-66; research entomologist U.S. Dept. Agr., U. Wis. at Madison, 1966-67; investigations leader bee breeding investigations, Entomology Research div., La. State U., Baton Rouge, 1967—. Served with USNR, 1943-45. Mem. Entomol. Soc. Am. (chmn. agr. sect. 1970), A.A.A.S., Kan., La. entomol. socs., Bee Research Assn.

Republican. Lutheran. Home: 7240 Antioch Rd Baton Rouge LA 70815

KAUFFMAN, ERLE GALEN, paleontologist-geologist, marine biologist; b. Washington, Feb. 9, 1933; s. Erle B. and Paula V. (Graff) K.; B.S., U. Mich., 1955, M.S., 1956, Ph.D., 1961; m. Carolyn Stinebower, Aug. 25, 1956; children—Donald Erle, Robin Lyn, Erica Jean. Teaching fellow dept. geology U. Mich., 1955-60, instr., 1959-60; asst. curator div. invertebrate paleontology dept. paleobiology Smithsonian Instn., 1961-62, asso. curator, 1963-67, curator, 1967—; lectr. dept. geology George Washington U., 1962-65, adj. prof., 1966—; profl. lectr. Am. Geol. Inst., Smithsonian Soc. Assos., 1963—. Recipient W.A. Tarr award, 1955, E.C. Case award U. Mich., 1961. Mem. Paleontol. Soc., Paleontol. Assn., A.A.A.S., Malacological Soc. London, Internat. Malacological Union, Paleontol. Soc. Washington, Geol. Soc. Washington, Rocky Mountain Assn. Geologists, Sigma Xi, Phi Kappa Phi, Sigma Gamma Epsilon. Contbr. articles profl. jours. Home: 8518 Forest St Annandale VA 22003 Office: E-307 US Nat Mus 10th and Constitution Av NW Washington DC 20560

KAUFFMANN, JOHN HOY, newspaper exec.; b. Washington, Jan. 21, 1925; s. Samuel H. and Miriam (Hoy) K.; grad. Choate Sch., 1943; A.B., Princeton, 1947; m. Laura Allen, July 15, 1946 (div. 1958); children— Bruce Gordon, Louise Miriam, Margaret Ellen, Samuel Hay IV; m. 2d, Patricia Bellinger, Feb. 8, 1958; 1 son, John Hoy II. With Evening Star, Washington, 1949—, successively, asst. advt. mgr., 1952-55, asst. bus. mgr., 1955-57, v.p., bus. mgr., 1957-68, now pres., dir.; dir. Spruce Falls Power and Paper Co., Toronto, Can., Sta. WCIV, Charleston, S.C., Am. Security Corp., Washington, Audit Bur. Circulations, Tal-Star Computer Systems, Inc., Magnavox Co., Peoples Life Ins. Co., Washington Star Syndicate, Inc., N.Y.C., Sta. WMAL, Washington Sta. WLVA, Lynchburg, Va., Am. Finance System, Inc.; v.p., dir. Columbia Planograph Co., Washington. Mem. ANPA Fed. Laws Com. Bd. dirs. A.R.C., Nat. Symphony Orch., Health and Welfare Council, Jr. Achievement of Met. Washington, Washington Better Bus. Bur.; exec. com. Greater Nat. Capital Com., Washington Bd. Trade; trustee Am. Cancer Soc. Trustee Am. U., Washington. Served with USAAF, 1943-45. Decorated Air medal; recipient Community Service award, 1957. Clubs: Metropolitan, Alfalfa (Washington). Home: 620 Boyle Lane McLean VA 22101 Office: Evening Star Washington DC 20003

KAUFHOLZ, KATHRYN ESTHER MARRIOTT (MRS. FERDINAND KAUFHOLZ), designer; b. Marriott, Utah, Sept. 30, 1909; d. Hyrum Williard and Elizabeth Stewart (Morris) Marriott; B.Ed., U. Utah; m. Ferdinand Kaufholz, Nov. 28, 1935; children—Kathryn Ellen (Mrs. Harold Lynn Jewel), Carolyn Marriott (Mrs. David Brooke Taylor), Sharon Stewart (Mrs. Tony Port). Tchr. pub. schs., Utah, 1933-35; exec. sec. Dept. Interior, Washington, 1935-39; advt. mgr. Social List of Washington, 1939-41; pres., dir. Ellen Kaye, Designers, Inc., Washington, 1958-70. Mem. Womens Bd. of Trade, Gt. Books Study Group. Clubs: Bethesda Country, Times (pres. 1956). Home: 5301 Dorset Av Chevy Chase MD 20015 Office: 4713 Wisconsin Av Washington DC 20016

KAUFMAN, HAROLD FREDERICK, educator; b. nr. Greenville, O., May 6, 1911; s. Charles E. and Trecy (Valentine) K.; A.B., U. Mo., 1938, A.M., 1939; Ph.D., Cornell U.; m. Lois Cook, June 8, 1939; 1 son, Harrell Lynn. With U.S. Forest Service, summers 1938, 45; asst. rural sociology Cornell U., 1939-42; instr. U. Mo., 1942-45; asst. prof. U. Ky., 1945-48; chmn. dept. sociology and rural life Miss. State U., State College, 1948-61, prof. sociology, 1948—, dir. Social Sci. Research Center, 1960-69, research prof. sociology, 1969—; seminar participant, Caribbean, 1961, Mexico, 1964, N. Europe, 1968; vis. lectr. Columbia, 1952-53, U. Wis., 1954. Recipient Faculty award for research, 1970; Fulbright research scholar to India, 1961, field research, 64. Fellow Soc. Applied Anthropology, Am. Sociol. Assn.; mem. So. (pres. 1959), Rural (pres. 1962), Indian sociol. socs., European Rural Sociology Soc., Am. Assn. U. Profs. Contbr. numerous monographs, articles to profl. lit. Home: 204 N Nash St Starkville MS 39759 Office: Box 5161 State College MS 39762

KAUFMAN, HERBERT E., physician, ophthalmologist; b. N.Y.C., Sept. 28, 1931; s. Benjamin and Claire (Krinsky) K.; grad. Peddie Sch., Heightstown, N.J., 1948; A.B., Princeton, 1952; M.D. magna cum laude, Harvard, 1956; m. Eleanor Rosenblum, June 30, 1957; children—Stephen, Joshua, Claire. Intern, 1956-57; clin. asso. in both clin. ophthalmology and research NIH, 1957-59; trainee Mass. Eye and Ear Infirmary, Boston, 1959-62, also head Uveitis Lab.; asso. prof., chief ophthalmology U. Fla., Gainesville, 1962-64, prof., chmn. dept. ophthalmology, prof. pharmacology, 1964—, acting dean Coll. Medicine, 1972—. Bd. dirs. N. Fla. Eye Bank; trustee Assn. for Research in Ophthalmology. Named one of the Ten Outstanding Young Men in Am., Jaycees, 1968; recipient Humanitarian award Lions Internat., 1968. Editor, Jour. Investigative Ophthalmology. Contbr. med research papers to profl. jours. Home: 1909 NW 31st Terrace Gainesville FL 32601

KAUFMAN, JACK HAMMER, lawyer; b. San Antonio, Dec. 15, 1925; s. Leon Brown and Karleen Wilma (Hammer) K.; B.B.A., U. Tex., 1950, J.D., 1951; m. Estelle Lieberman, June 18, 1950; children—William Thomas, Karleen Pearl, Nancy Ann. Admitted to Tex. bar, 1951, U.S. Supreme Ct. bar, 1965; asst. dist. atty. Bexar County, San Antonio, 1951-55; practice law, San Antonio, 1955—. Dir., Northside Bank, San Antonio. Councilman, City of San Antonio, 1961-65; trustee San Antonio Waterworks Bd., 1966—, chmn., 1972—. Bd. dirs. Met. YMCA. Served with USAAF, 1944-45. Mem. San Antonio, Tex., Am. bar assns., Zeta Beta Tau. Jewish religion (trustee temple 1955—, pres. 1967-69). Kiwanian. Home: 8104 Countryside Dr San Antonio TX 78209 Office: 900 Alamo National Bldg San Antonio TX 78205

KAUFMAN, WILLIAM HENRY, physician; b. Balt., Jan. 6, 1913; s. Henry and Helen (Boucher) K.; B.A., Johns Hopkins, 1934; M.D., Duke 1937; M.S., U. Va., 1947; m. Beth Pearse, May 27, 1939; children—John Pearse, Elizabeth, Richard Boucher. Intern. asst. resident in medicine Duke U. Hosp., 1937-39; asst. resident in dermatology U. Va. Hosp., 1939-41, resident, fellow in dermatology, 1945-47; pvt. practice dermatology, Roanoke, Va., 1947—; dermatologist community and regional hosps.; vis. dermatologist out-patient dept., clin. asso. prof. dermatology U. Va., 1965—; cons. U.S. Vets. Hosp. Served from 1st lt. to maj. M.C., USAAF, 1941-45, ETO, Panama Canal Zone. Fellow A.C.P., Am. Acad. Dermatology; mem. A.M.A., Med. Soc. Va., So. Med. Assn., Va. (pres. 1965-67), Washington dermatol. socs., Roanoke Acad. Medicine (pres. 1959-60), Sigma Xi. Episcopalian. Clubs: Roanoke Country (Roanoke). Editorial bd. Va. Med. Monthly. Home: 2511 Cornwallis Av Roanoke VA 24014 Office: 127 McClanahan St Roanoke VA 24014

KAUFMANN, ANDERS JOSEPH, architect, educator; b. Tuscaloosa, Ala., Apr. 4, 1934; s. Berwind Petersen and Jessie Thomson (McCulloch) K.; B.Arch., Cornell U., 1956; M.Arch., U. Pa., 1962; m. Peggy Ann Bornman, Apr. 6, 1958; children—Anders Joseph, Kirsten, Jennifer. Designer, draftsman, Mann & Harrover, Architects, Memphis, 1958-61; designer Lyles-Bissett-Carlisle-Wolff, Architects, Columbia, S.C., 1962-63; asso. prof. architecture Clemson U. (S.C.), 1963-72; architect Corkern, Wiggins, Lee, Lominack Architects, Hilton Head Island, S.C., 1972—; cons. architect, 1963-68; practice architecture, Clemson, 1968-70; partner Asso. Design Consultants, Clemson, 1970-72. Active Clemson Little Theatre, Clemson Chorale Soc., Clemson U. Fencing Team. Served with USNR, 1956-58. Mem. A.I.A., Gargoyl Soc., Tau Beta Pi. Episcopalian. (vestryman 1966-69). Home: PO Box 5562 Hilton Head Island SC 29928 Address: Corkern Wiggins Lee Lominack Box 5340 Hilton Head Island SC 29928

KAUFMANN, FRANK SALOMON, paper box co. exec.; b. Mannheim, Germany, Mar. 26, 1911; s. David and Sofie (Hausmann) K.; B.B.A., U. Heidelberg (Germany), 1931, M.B.A., 1932, Dr.Ec., 1933; m. Liese B. Herzog, Dec. 23, 1935; 1 dau., Rita Jane. Came to U.S., 1939, naturalized, 1945. Trained in papermaking and carton mfr. in Germany; mgr., partner Kartonagen Fabrik Kaufmann & Co., Germany, 1935-38; in def. work in U.S., 1939-45; prodn. mgr. Spear Box Co., N.Y.C., 1945-50; sales service and scheduling mgr. Mead Corp. div. Mead Packaging, Inc., Atlanta, 1950-52, dir. purchases and central planning, 1952-59, dir. fgn. market devel., 1960-61; dir. internat. markets Mead S.A. subsidiary Mead Corp., Zug, Switzerland, 1961-63; dir. marketing services Mead Packaging Internat., Inc., 1964-68, asst. v.p. marketing, 1968—; dir. information center Mead Packaging Div., 1969—; asso. prof. Internat. Inst., Ga. State U., 1970—. Mem. Ga. Internat. Trade Assn. (pres.), Zionist Orgn. Am. (dir.), Delta Sigma Pi. Jewish religion. Mem. B'nai B'rith; Mason. Clubs: Progressive, Civitan. Home: 1270 W Peachtree St NW Atlanta GA 30309 Office: Mead Packaging PO Box 4417 Atlanta GA 30302

KAUFMANN, JAMES ARON, physician; b. Detroit, Dec. 15, 1923; s. Adolph and Dena (Lieberman) K.; student Vanderbilt U., 1942-44; M.D., U. Tenn., 1947; m. Jane Monness Lippman, Dec. 27, 1951; children—Nancy Hope, Robert Scott. Intern, Emory U., Grady Meml. Hosp., 1947-48; resident Pratt Diagnostic Hosp., Boston, 1949-50, Louisville Gen. Hosp., 1950-51; practice medicine, specializing in internal medicine, Atlanta, 1952—; mem. staff Grady Meml. Hosp., Crawford W. Long Hosp., St. Joseph Infirmary; clin. research fellow in pharmacology Emory U. Sch. Medicine, 1948-49, instr. medicine, 1952-57, asso. in medicine, 1958—. Mem. gov. bd. Fulton County Heart Council, 1958-64; mem. med. adv. bd. Atlanta Tb Assn., 1953, bd. dirs., 1966—; cons. in medicine South Fulton Hosp., 1963—; U.S. rep. Internat. Com. on Clin. Cardiovascular Disease, Vienna, Austria, 1960; co-dir. med. program Ga. State Legislature, 1970—; bd. dirs. Civic Theater, 1970—; regent Anti-Defamation League, 1968—; patron's soc. Crawford W. Long Meml. Hosp., Atlanta, 1970—; chmn. State Com. on Quackery, 1970—. Exec. com. governing bd., steering com. Fulton County Democratic Party, 1966—. Chmn. bd. trustees Kaufmann Found. Diplomate Am. Bd. Internal Medicine. Fellow A.C.P.; mem. A.M.A., Ga., So., Fulton County (chmn. standing com. on pub. policy and legislative com. 1966—, chmn. council govtl. affairs 1970—) med. assns., Am. Coll. Chest Physicians, Am., Ga. trudeau socs., Am. Ga. heart assns., Am., Ga. diabetes assns., Am. Geriatrics Soc., Am. Coll. Cardiology, Am. Gerontol. Soc., Am. Coll. Angiology, Am. Soc. Internal Medicine, Am. Thoracic Soc. Mem. B'nai B'rith (pres. 1964-65). Contbr. articles to profl. jours. Home: 3635N Stratford Rd NE Atlanta GA 30305 Office: 950 W Peachtree St NW Atlanta GA 30309

KAULBACK, FRANK SANFORD, JR., univ. dean; b. Pitts., May 5 1912; s. Frank Sanford and Elizabeth Flavia (McGuire) K.; B.S., U. Va., 1934, M.A., 1942, Ph.D., 1945; m. Mildred Virginia Van Lear, July 3, 1941; 1 son, Frank Sanford III. Sales dept. Bridgeport Brass Co., 1935-37, Am. Radiator Standard San. Corp., 1937-40; mem. faculty U. Va., 1946—, dean McIntire Sch. Commerce, 1955—; faculty U. Cal., 1947; dir. Nat. Bank & Trust Co., Charlottesville; cons. U.S. Gen. Accounting Office. Cons. OPS, 1951-52. Served as lt. USNR, World War II. Mem. Am. Accounting Assn. (past pres., exec. com. 1969-70), Raven Soc., Beta Gamma Sigma, Alpha Kappa Psi. Rotarian. Clubs: Farmington Country, Colonnade. Home: 215 Montebello Cr Charlottesville VA 22903

KAUZLARICH, JAMES JOSEPH, educator; b. Des Moines, Sept. 27,, 1927; s. Joseph and Mary (Noerror) K.; B.S., State U. Ia., 1950; M.S., Columbia, 1952; Ph.D., Northwestern U., 1958; m. Sally Ann Smith, Sept. 13, 1952; children—Ann Louise, John Howard Susan Mary, Jane Abigail. Engr., Gen. Electric Co., Schenectady, 1952-54; asst. prof. mech. engring. Worcester (Mass.) Poly. Inst., 1958-61; asso. prof. U. Wash., Seattle, 1961-63; prof., chmn. mech. engring. U. Va., Charlottesville, 1963—. Served with USNR, 1945-46. U. Va. Sesquicentennial fellow, vis. researcher Cambridge (Eng.) U., 1970-71. Registered profl. engr., Ia., Mass. Mem. Am. Soc. M.E., Am. Soc. Lubrication Engring., Am. Soc. Engring. Edn., Tau Beta Pi, Pi Tau Sigma, Sigma Xi. Inventor friction welding machine, 1965. Home: 1603 Inglewood Dr Charlottesville VA 22901

KAVANAGH, ARTHUR EDWARD, banker; b. N.Y.C., Feb. 6, 1927; s. Arthur Johnson and Mary (Golik) K.; student Providence Coll., 1947-49; student U. Va., 1949-51, U. Wis., 1960-62; m. Antoinette Theodore, Jan. 31, 1953; children—Virginia, Linda, Constance, Patricia, Dorothy, Kenneth. Auditor asst. First Nat. City Bank N.Y., 1944-55; self-employed as bus. cons. Miami, Fla., 1955-56; v.p., cashier Dania (Fla.) Bank, 1956—. Tchr. Broward County Adult Program, Am. Inst. Banking, 1960—. Chmn. awards com. Gov's. Com. Employment of Handicapped. Bd. dirs. Little League Baseball, So. Fla. dist., 1964-70. Served with AUS, 1944-46. Mem. Am. Inst. Banking, Bank Adminstrn. Inst. (pres. Goldcoast chpt. 1969-70), Broward County Bankers Assn. (chmn. 1969-71), Miami-Dade C. of C. (pres. North Dade Council 1965-66). Republican. Optimist. Home: 6932 Willow Lane Miami Lakes FL 33014 Office: 255 E Dania Beach Blvd Dania FL 33004

KAVANAGH, ROGER PIERCE, JR., constrn. co. exec.; b. Greenwich, Conn., Aug. 27, 1917; s. Roger Pierce and Eleanor (Geffem) K.; student Princeton, 1936-38; m. Jeanette Rusovich, June 5, 1943; children—Basil John, Roger Pierce III. Mgr., N.M. Timber Co., 1938-40; salesman Am. Houses, Inc., N.Y.C., 1945-53; pres. Kavanagh, Smith & Co., Greensboro, N.C., 1953-66; pres., Westminster Co., Greensboro, 1967—; dir. N.C. Nat. Bank. Mem. N.C. Conservation and Devel. Bd., 1960-64; state chmn. Radio Free Europe, 1966. Served with Ordnance Dept., AUS, 1941-45. Decorated Bronze Star. Mem. Nat. Assn. Home Builders, Greensboro C. of C. (past dir.). Home: 605 Sunset Dr Greensboro NC 27408 Office: 200 W Wendover St Greensboro NC 27405

KAVRUCK, SAMUEL, govt. ofcl.; b. N.Y.C., Jan. 20, 1915; s. Meyer and Sophie Kavruck; B.S., Coll. City N.Y., 1937, M.S. in Edn., 1939; A.M., George Washington U., 1950, Ed.D., 1954; m. Angela J. Sherman, May 26, 1940; children—Deborah, Barton. Psychologist city schs., N.Y.C., 1939-41; psychologist, researcher U.S. Civil Service Commn., VA, 1942-59; specialist U.S. Office Edn., 1963—; chief personnel relations FAO, Rome, Italy, 1963-65; professorial lectr. in edn. Am. U., George Washington U. Served with AUS, 1943-46; as capt. USAF, 1949-54. Mem. D.C. Personnel and Guidance Assn. (pres. 1960-61), Am. Psychol. Assn., Nat. Council Measurement in Edn., Am. Assn. U. Profs., Phi Delta Kappa, Psi Chi. Author: Selected References in Test, Measurements and Statistics, 1947; Clinical Psychology in the U.S. Air Force, 1949. Home: 5712 26th St NW Washington DC 20015 Office: Nat Center for Improvement in Ednl Systems US Office Education Washington DC 20202

KAY, TOOMBS HODGES, JR., coll. dean; b. Royston, Ga., Dec. 22, 1929; s. Toombs Hodges and Viola (Wynn) K.; diploma Reinhardt Coll., 1949; A.B., Duke, 1951; B.D., Emory U., 1954; postgrad. Union Theol. Sem., Columbia U., 1954-58; Ph.D., N.Y. U., 1961; m. Sara Elizabeth Beggs, Aug. 25, 1951; children—Elizabeth Ann, Debra Jane, Robert Toombs, Cynthia Jean, Paul Thomas. Ordained to ministry Methodist Ch., 1953; pastor Union City (Ga.) Meth. Ch., 1951-54, Shandaken (N.Y.) Meth. Parish, 1954-55, First Reformed Ch., Jamaica, N.Y., 1956-61; prof., chmn. dept. religion and philosophy LaGrange (Ga.) Coll., 1961-65; dean of instrn. Rehinhardt Coll., Waleska, Ga., 1965-66; acad. dean Tenn. Wesleyan Coll., Athens, 1966—. Mem. Human Relations Council, LaGrange, Ga., 1963-65, Athens, Tenn., 1966—; asst. dist. commr. Boy Scouts Am., 1970—. Bd. dirs. YMCA; hon. trustee Tithers, Inc. Recipient staff award Tenn. Wesleyan Coll., 1970. Mem. Conf. Acad. Deans of So. States, Tenn. P.T.A. (life), Kappa Chi, Kappa Delta Pi. Kiwanian. Home: 18 Robeson St Athens TN 37303

KAY, WILLIAM HAROLD, mobile home transp. co. exec.; b. Anderson, S.C., Feb. 14, 1936; s. Harold and Ella Marie (Whitten) K.; grad. Carolina Sch. Commerce, 1956; m. Mary Edna Holliday, Apr. 22, 1956; children—Sandra Marie, John Sanford, Andrea Leigh. Accountant for atty. specializing in income taxes, 1956-58; accountant, office mgr. Transit Homes, Inc., Greenville, S.C., 1958-61, asst. sec., 1961-63, controller, 1963, treas., 1963-66, sec., 1966-69, adminstrv. v.p., sec.-treas., 1969—; treas. Transit Leasing, Inc., Home Services, Inc., Transit Movers, Inc. Presbyn. Home: Route 1 Midway Rd Anderson SC 29621 Office: PO Box 1628 Haywood Rd Greenville SC 29602

KAYE, ROBERT ADOLPH, govt. ofcl.; b. La Moure, N.D., Aug. 30, 1921; student N.D. Agrl. Coll., 1940-41; A.A., George Washington U., 1947, A.B., 1948, A.M., 1950, D.B.A., 1961; m. Margaret Eck Myklebust, July 22, 1945; children—Robert Michael, Margaret Lynne. Engring. aid Pub. Roads Administrn., Alaska Hwy., 1942-44, Inter-Am. Hwy., Nicaragua, 1944-45; transp. specialist Bur. Pub. Roads, Washington, 1945-57; chief traffic mgmt. br. U.S. AEC, Washington, 1957-70; dir. Bur. Motor Carrier Safety, Fed. Hwy Adminstrn., Dept. Transp., 1970—. Professorial lectr. bus. adminstrn. George Washington U., 1953—; nat. co-chmn. Nat. Transp. Week, 1967. Active Bel-Air Civic Assn. Chmn. bd. dirs. Bur. Pub. Roads Fed. Credit Union, 1954; dir. Asso. Traffic Clubs Am., 1967—. Recipient William A. Jump Meml. Found. award, 1956, superior performance award, AEC, 1959. Mem. Gen. Alumni Assn. George Washington (governing bd. 1968-70), Nat. Def. Transp. Assn., Alpha Kappa Psi, Artus, Delta Nu Alpha. Club: Traffic (pres. 1967-68, dir. 1968-69) (Washington). Contbr. articles to profl. jours. Home: 4420 Stark Pl Annandale VA 22003 Office: DOT Hdqrs Bldg Washington DC 20591

KAYLER, EDWIN MORELAND, indsl. relations exec.; b. Copperhill, Tenn., June 18, 1907; s. Samuel J. and Lorena (Moreland) K.; student U. Tenn., 1926-29, U. Chattanooga, 1941; m. Lora Helen Jones, July 3, 1934; children—James Edwin, Julia Ann (Mrs. Robert Calvin Haynes), Lora Elizabeth. Prodn. mgr., corp. sec. Am. Mfg. Co., Chattanooga, 1936-47; personnel dir. Chattanooga Box & Lumber Co., 1947-68, Gilman Paint & Varnish Co., 1968—. Dir., coordinator Mgmt. Devel. Inst., U. Chattanooga, 1960—; tchr. self improvement subjects McKenzie Sch. and Chattanooga Pub. Schs., 1956—. Mem. Chattanooga Indsl. Personnel Club (chpt. dir. 1967), Soc. for Advancement Mgmt. (v.p. 1971). Baptist. Mason, Lion (pres. Red Bank, Tenn. 1944-45, dist. gov. 1946-47). Home: 4703 Florida Av Chattanooga TN 37409 Office: 216 W 8th St Chattanooga TN 37401

KAYLOR, RICHARD ELLISON, computer software co. exec.; b. Monterey Park, Cal., Feb. 13, 1934; s. George Howard and Marion (Ellison) K.; B.A., Whittier Coll., 1957; computer engring. certificate Mass. Inst. Tech., 1958; postgrad. certificate Harvard Bus. Sch., 1970; m. Nancy Jane Hall, Aug. 25, 1955; children—Scot Richard, Jody Lynn. Computer programmer N. Am. Aviation missile devel. div., Downey, Cal., 1956-57; field engr. Western Electric Def. Systems, div. Ramo Wooldridge, Canoga Park, Cal., 1957-59, mgr. mil. products sect., 1959-63; v.p. Informatics, Inc., Canoga Park, 1966—; pres. Informatics/Computing Tech. Co., River Edge, N.J., 1967. Mem. Assn. Computing Machinery, Franklin Soc. Home: 515 Avon Ct River Vale NJ 07675 Office: 65 Rt 4 River Edge NJ 07661

KAYSER, E.W., JR., businessman, civic leader. Chmn. El Paso (Tex.) Symphony Orch. finance com. Address: 290 E Blanchard St El Paso TX 79902*

KAYSER, OLAF, cement co. exec.; b. Valparaiso, Chile, Sept. 15, 1921; s. Axel G. and Edele (Bentzon) K.; M.S. in Mech. Engring., Royal Poly. Inst., Copenhagen, Denmark, 1946; m. Else Hansen, Oct. 14, 1949; children—Thomas, Joan Eva, Stephen. Came to U.S., 1949, naturalized, 1954. Asst. sales engr. F.L. Smidth & Co., Copenhagen, 1946-49; with Lone Star Industries, 1949—, plant supt. Bonner Springs, Kan., 1958-62, asst. operations mgr., N.Y.C., 1962-63, operations mgr., 1963-64, v.p. mfg., 1964-68, regional v.p., Richmond, Va., 1968—. Home: 8106 Kingston Rd Richmond VA 23229 Office: 5001 W Broad St Richmond VA 23230

KAYSER, PAUL, business exec.; b. Tyler, Tex., Feb. 10, 1887; s. Albert and Mary Louise (Lawrence) K.; A.B., Baylor U., 1909, LL.D., 1953; legal edn. by corr., U. Tex.; LL.D., U. Ariz., 1957; m. Elizabeth Harris Clegg, Sept. 1, 1910; children—Betty and Jean (twins). Prin. high sch., Gatesville, Tex., 1909-11; admitted to Tex. bar, 1913; practiced in Houston, 1913-29; mem. firm Huggins, Kayser & Liddell; founder, pres., chief exec. officer El Paso Natural Gas Co., Houston, 1928-60, chmn., chief exec. officer, 1960-65, hon. chmn., 1965-66; mem. adv. bd. 1st Nat. Bank of San Antonio Tex. Commerce Bank, Houston. Capt., 7th Cav., N.G., World War I. Mem. Ind. Natural Gas Assn. (pres. 1951-52). Episcopalian. Clubs: Houston, River Oaks Country (Houston); University (Chgo.); Recess (N.Y.C.). Contbr. articles to profl. jours. Home: 3260 Del Monte Dr Houston TX 77019 Office: 1006 Main St Houston TX 77002

KAZEN, ABRAHAM, JR., congressman; b. Laredo, Tex., Jan. 17, 1919; student U. Tex., 1937-40, Cumberland Law Sch., Lebanon, Tenn., 1941; m. Consuelo Raymond; children—Abraham III, Mrs. E. C. Dillman, Jr., Christina (Mrs. Ronald K. Attal), Catherine, Jo-Betsy. Admitted to Tex. bar, 1942; mem. firm Raymond, Alvarado & Kazen, Laredo, 1946-55; practiced in Laredo, 1955—; mem. Tex. Ho. of Reps., 1947-52; mem. Tex. Senate, 1952-66, pres. pro tempore, 1959; acting gov. State of Tex., 1959; mem. 91st-92d congresses from 23d Dist. Tex. Past mem. Tex. Legislative Council. Sponsor pre-sch. program for non-English speaking children. Served to capt. USAAF, World War II; NATOUSA; MTO; CBI. Named Man of Year, also Father of Year, Laredo. Mem. Tex., Laredo bar assns., Laredo Internat. Fair and Exposition, Washington's Birthday Celebration

Assn., Am. Legion, U. Tex. Ex-Students Assn. Democrat. K.C. Home: Laredo TX 78040 also 8801 Bradley Blvd Bethesda MD 20034 Office: House Office Bdlg Washington DC 20515

KAZMANN, RAPHAEL GABRIEL, educator; b. Bklyn., Oct. 16, 1916; s. Boris and Elisabeth (Maruchess) K.; B.S., Carnegie Inst. Tech., 1939; m. Mary Caroline Beem, June 27, 1942; children—Elisabeth Paige (Mrs. Craig E. Moore), Hollis Beem, William McKee. Hydraulic engr. U.S. Geol. Survey, Washington, 1940-45, chief hydraulic engr. Ranney Method Water Supplies, Columbus, O., 1946-50; cons., Stuttgart, Ark. 1951-63; asso. prof. La. State U., Baton Rouge, 1963-69, prof. civil engring., 1970—. Fellow Soc. C.E.; mem. A.A.A.S., Am. Inst. Mining Metall. and Petroleum Engrs., Nat. Water Well Assn. Am. Water Works Assn., Soc. Econ. Geologists. Author: Modern Hydrology, 1965, 2d. edit., 1972. Home: 611 College Hill Dr Baton Rouge LA 70808

KEADY, JACK LELAND, newspaper editor; b. Joplin, Mo., Nov. 27, 1914; s. Matthew Norris and Myrtle (Wallace) K.; student La Salle U., 1958-59; m. Alice Louise Mattox, Oct. 4, 1940; 1 son, John Leland. Reporter, Arkansas Democrat Co., Little Rock, 1934-38, sports editor, 1938—. Bd. dirs. Ark. Hall of Fame. Served with AUS, 1942-46 Mem. Nat. Sportscasters-Sportswriters Assn. (Ark. Sportswriter of the Year award, 1966), Nat. Assn. Baseball Writers, Football Writers Assn. Am. Home: 1114 N Harrison St Little Rock AR 72205 Office: Capital Avand Scott St Little Rock AR 72201

KEADY, WILLIAM, U.S. dist. chief judge, Aberdeen, Miss. Address: US Court House Aberdeen MS 39730*

KEANE, MARK EDWARD, assn. exec.; b. Chgo., Sept. 10, 1919; s. Fred J. and Mary E. (Sullivan) K.; B.S. in Pub. Service Engring., Purdue U., 1941; m. Carolyn Mims, Sept. 12, 1942; children—Mark Edward, Daniel, Dennis, Brian, Paul, Mary, Peter, Barry. Intern pub. adminstrn. Nat. Inst. Pub. Affairs, Washington, 1941-42; staff cons. Pub. Adminstrn. Service, Chgo., 1945-48; asst. to city mgr., Wichita, Kansas; 1948-49; city mgr., Shorewood, Wis., 1950-53. Oak Park, Ill., 1953-62, Tucson, 1962-66; dir. land and facilities devel. adminstrn. Dept. Housing and Urban Devel., Washington, 1966-67; exec. dir. Internat. City Mgmt. Assn., Washington, 1967—. Served to maj. AUS, 1942-45. Mem. Nat. Acad. Pub. Adminstrn. Home: 3522 Rittenhouse St Washington DC 20015 Office: 1140 Connecticut Av NW Washington DC 20036

KEARBY, JEROME CLAIBORNE, III, engring. co. cons.; b. Breckenridge, Tex., Sept. 23, 1925; s. Jack and Juanita (Stone) K.; B.S. in Petroleum Engring., Tex. Aand M U., 1951, postgrad., 1952; m. Patricia S. Kearby; children—Teri (Mrs. James Shilling, Jr.), Jerome Claiborne Iv, karen Leigh. Vice pres. S.Am. Enterprises, S.A., Maracaibo, Venezuela, 1952—, v.p. Oilfield Sales & Service, 1952-62, mem. bd. co. owner; pres. Oilfield Internat. Inc., Houston, 1962-70; owner Jerome Kearby & Assos., Houston, 1970—. Served to 1st lt. AUS, 1944-46. Mem. Nomads, Tau Beta Pi, Phi Kappa Phi. Office: 5115 Westheimer St Houston TX 77017

KEARL, WAYNE, communications exec.; b. Edmonton, Can. (came to U.S. 1937); s. Stanley B. and Mabel (Stoddard) K.; student Brigham Young U., 1937-40, Columbia, 1946, U. Utah, 1947-48; m. Dorothy Hatch, May 14, 1941; children—Stanley, Edward, Robert. Announcer, writer, Sta. KOVO, Provo, Utah, 1941-45; promotion mgr., pub. service dir., salesman KSL, Salt Lake City, 1945-52; station mgr., KGMB-TV, Honolulu, 1952-54; comml. mgr. KENS-TV, 1954—, gen. mgr., 1958—. Pres. Express Communications, Inc., 1966—. Mem. bd. Nat. Assn. Broadcasters Code Authority, 1972—. Mem. First Repertory Theater, Com. for Better Environment. Mem. Texas TV Broadcasters (sec.-treas. 1962—), San Antonio C. of C. (bd. dirs. 1971—). Rotary. Home: 216 Arcadia St San Antonio TX 78209 Office: Ave E 4th St San Antonio TX 78205

KEARLEY, ARTHUR JAMES, lawyer; b. Mobile, Ala., Sept. 29, 1900; s. Joseph Dennis and Lula Ann (Bradley) K.; L.L.B., U. Ala., 1923; m. Dorothy Lucille Williams, Oct. 13, 1951. Admitted to Ala. bar, 1923; since practiced in Mobile, Ala.; mem. firm Kearley & McConnell, 1958—. Served with AUS, 1942-43. Mem. Am., Ala., Mobile (pres. 1969—) bar assns., Farrah Law Soc., Phi Delta Phi. Baptist. Mason, Lion (pres. 1944-45). Home: 264 Levert St Mobile AL 36607 Office: Van Antwerp Bldg Mobile AL 36602

KEARNEY, RUSSELL FRANKLIN, JR., dentist; b. Greenwood, Miss., Nov. 6, 1939; s. Russell Franklin and Mary Henrietta (Humphries) K.; B.A., U. Miss., 1961; D.D.S., U. Tenn., 1965; m. Vivia Nell Best, Aug. 19, 1961; children—Karon Elizabeth, Robert Humphries, Mary Lucene. Individual practice dentistry, Memphis, 1966-67, Yazoo City, Miss., 1967—. Mem. Yazoo County Jr. C. of C. (dir. 1968, v.p. 1969), Psi Omega, Sigma Nu. Rotarian. Home: 709 Sunset Dr N Yazoo City MS 39194 Office: PO Box 958 Yazoo City MS 39194

KEATON, ALVIN EUGENE, educator; b. Beckley, W.Va., Nov. 28, 1931; s. Greeley Dee and Faye (Harper) K.; B.S., Marshall U., 1955; M.A., U. Okla., 1966, Ph.D., 1969; m. Mary Laurene Wendler, Jan. 29, 1961. Teaching asst. U. Okla., 1966; mem. faculty Kan. State Coll., Pittsburg, 1967-69, asst. prof. philosophy, 1967-69; asst. prof. sociology, information scis. U. Okla., Norman, 1969—. Served with AUS, 1948-52. Mem. Am., S.W. philos. assns. Author: Mule Skinnerian Approach to Mule Skinning, 1959; The Black Box and Philosophy, 1968; The Philosophical Signifiance Cybernetics, 1969. Editor Southwestern Jour. of Philosophy. Home: 734 S Lahoma St Norman OK 73069

KEATON, JOSIAH LIVINGSTON, tobacco co. exec.; b. Woodville, N.C., Dec. 2, 1908; s. Thomas Calvin and Esther (Jordan) K.; B.S., Wake Forest U., 1930; m. Minnie Ethel Newman, Apr. 30, 1936; 1 son, Philip Newman. Research chemist, R. J. Reynolds Tobacco Co., Winston- Salem, N.C., 1931-61, mgr. standards and quality control div., 1961—. Chmn. commn. controlling Patterson Av. Baptist Mission. Mem. Am. Soc. Quality Control (dir. central N.C. sect.), Tobacco Chemist Conf., Sigma Phi Epsilon. Democrat. Baptist. Club: Winston-Salem Color Photographic. Patentee in field. Home: 2719 Monticello Dr Winston-Salem NC 27106 Office: 401 N Main St Winston-Salem NC 27101

KEATS, CHARLES B., author; b. Bridgeport, Conn., July 21, 1906; s. Abraham and Jeanette (Boges) K.; B.F.A., Syracuse U., 1931; m. Katherine Hamilton Kane, Aug. 21, 1937 (dec.); m. 2d, Kathleen Kenton, Feb. 27, 1967. Artist-writer free lance, N.Y.C., 1931-33; reporter Bridgeport Telegram, 1933-36; city editor Bridgeport City Herald, 1933-39; columnist Bridgeport Times-Star, 1939-41; exec. sec. to gov. Conn., 1947-49; dep. sec. of state for Conn., 1950-53, sec. of state, 1953-55; partner Keats, Allen and Keats, pub. relations, Washington and Hartford, Conn., 1953-65. Chmn. Conn. Employees Merit Award Bd., 1953-55; mem. adv. com. Conn. Civil Def., 1953-55. Publicity dir. Conn. Rep. State Central Com., 1941-50; Republican presdl. elector, 1956. Mem. Authors Guild. Rotarian. Author: Wake Up to Tomorrow; Modigliani; Body of Love; Presidents of the U.S.; Marked Woman: Magnificent Masquerade. Address: 333 Sunset Av Palm Beach FL

KEATS, HAROLD ALAN, corp. exec.; b. Bridgeport, Conn., Oct. 25, 1913; s. Abraham and Jeanette (Boges) C.; student University Sch., Bridgeport, Conn., 1928-31, Washington U., 1932-33; m. Charleen Turner, Dec. 19, 1953; children—Candace, Harold Alan. Owner Harold A. Keats Constrn. Co., Ft. Lauderdale, 1936, Keats S.S. & Tourist Agy.; pres. Indian Citrus Groves, Inc., Fla. Sunshine Groves, Inc., Harold A. Keats Investment Co., Inc., Englewood Mailing Lists, Inc., Rocking K. Cattle Corp., Rocking K Ranch Inc.; partner Keats, Allen & Keats. Nat. vice comdr. Amvets, 1947, nat. comdr., 1948-49. Liaison officer to White House, 1949—; counselor Amvets Nat. Service Found., 1949—, U.S. commr. (succeeding Gen. John J. Pershing) Am. Battle Monuments Commn., 1950-53. Past. nat. chmn. Vets. Democratic Com.; dir. vet.'s div. Nat. Dem. Com. Served with USN, 1942-45; PTO; commd. lt. (s.g.) intelligence Pub. Information, USNR. 1949; temporary active duty in Korea, 1951. Mem. Mil. Order World Wars, Am. Yachtsmen's Assn. (nat. pres.), Knights Round Table Assn. (pres.), Past Nat. Comdrs. Orgn. (nat. chmn.). Mason (32 deg., Shriner). Home: 620 NW 19th St Fort Lauderdale FL 33308 Office: 3034 E Commercial Blvd Fort Lauderdale FL 33308

KEAY, JAMES WILLIAM, banker; b. Manley, Ia., Nov. 16, 1921; s. William J. and Valborg (Biorn) K.; B.A. in Econs., U. Colo., 1947; M.B.A., Northwestern U., 1948; grad. Rutgers U. Grad. Sch. Banking, 1956. Advanced Mgmt. Program, Harvard, 1964; m. Frances Lee Oglesby, Mar. 20, 1954; children—Martha Evelyn, James William, Stuart Enslie. With Republic Nat. Bank, Dallas, 1949—, asst. cashier, 1953, asst. v.p., 1953-56, v.p., 1956-61, sr. v.p., 1961-63, mem. exec. com., 1962—, exec. v.p. loans, 1963-65, exec. v.p. adminstrn., 1965, pres., dir., 1965—; dir. United Fidelity Life Ins. Co., Howard Corp., Gen. Automotive Parts Corp. Bd. dirs. State Fair of Tex., Dallas Assembly, Dallas County United Fund, Inc. Served with AUS, World War II; ETO, MTO. Mem. Assn. Res. City Bankers, Am. Bankers Assn. (econ. policy com.), Pi Gamma Mu. Lutheran (elder). Clubs: Idlewild, Brook Hollow Golf, City, Dallas, Terpsichorean, Preston Trail Golf, Dallas, Dallas Petroleum (Dallas). Office: Republic Nat Bank PO Box 5961 Dallas TX 75222 Home: 13920 Gillon St Dallas TX 75205

KECK, J(ULIAN) WYLLY, engr.; b. Savannah, Ga., Oct. 23, 1899; s. Thomas Peter and Henrietta (Altman) K.; student Baylor U., 1921-24; m. Kathleen Russell, Oct. 15, 1924; children—Julian Wylly, Kathleen (Mrs. Roland T. Ross). Plant engr. Tex. Power & Light Co., Waco, 1920-24, East Tex. Pub. Service Co., Marshall, 1924-25; supt. power plants Fla. Power & Light Co., Miami, 1925-58, v.p., 1958-71, cons., 1971—; cons. engr. J. Wylly Keck & Assos., Atlanta, 1950—, Diamond Power Splty. Corp., Lancaster, O., 1958—. Mem. Fla. Bd. Engring. Examiners, 1940-67, pres., 1942-44, 55-56, 59-63. Recipient Engr. of Year citation S.E. Fla. Engrs., 1955, Distinguished certificate Nat. Council State Bd. Engr. Examiners, 1960. Registered profl. engr., Fla., N.Y. State. Fellow Fla. Engring. Soc. (past pres.), Am. Soc. M.E.; mem. Nat., Fla. socs. profl. engrs., Newcomen Soc. N.Am. Presbyn. Mason (K.T.). Clubs: Biscayne Bay Yacht (Miami); Coral Gables Country. Contbr. numerous engring. articles. Patentee in field. Home: 2520 San Domingo St Coral Gables FL 33134 Office: 4200 W Flagler St Miami FL 33101

KEE, DONALD REX, lawyer, oil co. exec.; b. DeLeon, Tex., Aug. 23, 1926; s. Rex D. and Lela J. (Ross) K.; LL.B. cum laude, Baylor U., 1950, J.D. cum laude, 1969; m. Bettye Joyce Millhollon, Nov. 7, 1946; children—Richard Dow, Bonnie Kim. Admitted to Tex. bar, 1950; practiced in Wichita Falls, 1950-54; 55-57, atty. Clint Murcheson Interests, Dallas, 1955-57; pres., dir. Gulf Coast Leaseholds, Houston, 1958-61; v.p., dir. Talon Petroleum C.A., Caracas, Venezuela, 1965-69. Served with USNR, 1944-46; PTO. Mem. Tex. Bar Assn. Democrat. Baptist. Lion. Home: 2700 SW 15th St Apt 246 Amarillo TX 79102

KEE, WALTER ANDREW, librarian; b. Phila., July 12, 1914; s. Walter Leslie and Regina (Corcoran) K.; B.S., Purdue U., 1949; M.S., Columbia, 1951; m. Genevieve Nolan O'Hair, Dec. 2, 1943; children— Kathleen Leslie (Mrs. Lee O'Ferrall Kise), Sheila Nolan. Instrument maker Brown Instrument div. Mpls.-Honeywell, Phila., 1936-42; engring., phys. scis. librarian N.Y. U., 1950-51; librarian E. I. Dupont de Nemours, Savannah River Lab., Aiken, S.C., 1951-55; head library, documents sect. Martin Co., Balt., 1955-59; librarian U.S. AEC, Washington, 1959-66, tech. utilization officer, 1966-69, chief library br. Hdqrs. Services div., 1969—. Served with USNR, 1942-45. Mem. Spl. Libraries Assn. (chmn. documentation div. 1957-58, chmn. engring. div. 1964-65, chmn. nuclear sci. div. 1969-70), Am. Soc. Information Sci. Episcopalian. Home: 5832 Conway Rd Bethesda MD 20034 Office: USAEC Div Hdqrs Services Washington DC 20545

KEEBLE, SYDNEY FRAZER, JR., life ins. co. exec.; b. Nashville, Sept. 30, 1928; s. Sydney Frazer and Martha (Estes) Lawrence; B.A., Vanderbilt U., 1949, J.D., 1951; m. Sheila Anne Broderick, Aug. 29, 1959; children— Grace Barrett, Patrick Estes, Anne Gray McLaughlin. Admitted to Tenn. bar, Fed. bar, 1951; with Life & Casualty Ins. Co. of Tenn., Nashville, 1951—, atty., 1951-55, ordinary agt., 1955-57, agt., 1958, staff mgr., 1959, dist. mgr., 1960-61, dir. marketing research, 1961-63, asst. v.p., 1963-64, v.p., 1964-70, sr. v.p., 1970—, also dir., mem. exec., finance and sr. mgmt. coms.; dir. First Am. Nat. Bank. Bd. dirs. Nashville Boys' Club; pres. St. Mary's Villa; pres. elect Nashville YMCA; trustee Harpeth Hall Sch., Nashville YMCA Found. Served to 1st lt. AUS, 1952-54. Decorated Bronze Star medal. Mem. Am., Tenn., Nashville bar assns., Nashville Assn. Life Underwriters, Phi Delta Theta, Phi Delta Phi, Omicron Delta Kappa. Clubs: Exchange (pres.), Belle Meade Country (past dir.); Cumberland of Nashville (dir.), Nashville City; Leland (Mich.) Country. Home: Truxton Pl Nashville TN 37205 Office: Life & Casualty Tower Nashville TN 37219

KEEBLER, EUGENE MILLER, coll. dean; b. Eutaw, Ala., Apr. 3, 1923; s. Wesley T. and Sarah (McCaskey) K.; B.S., U. So. Miss., 1945, Ph.D., 1962; B.D., New Orleans Bapt. Theol. Sem., 1949, Th.D., 1953; m. Dorcas Longley, May, 1946; children—Candace, Christina. Ordained to ministry, So. Baptist Ch., 1941; asst. to pres. Clarke Coll., 1951-53; dean-registrar Norman Coll., 1953-62; dean coll. Gardner-Webb Coll., 1962-63; dean coll. La. Coll., 1963-64; v.p. acad. affairs, dean U. Corpus Christi (Tex.), 1964-65; acad. v.p., dean Mobile (Ala.) Coll., 1965—. Mem. Ala. Council Tchr. Edn., Am. Assn. Collegiate Registrars and Admissions Officers, N.E.A., Kappa Delta Pi, Phi Delta Kappa, Phi Theta Kappa. Home: 1001 E Highpoint Dr Mobile AL 36609 Office: PO Box 13220 Mobile AL 36613

KEECH, RICHMOND B., judge; b. Washington, Nov. 28, 1896; s. Leigh R. and Anne L. (Contee) K.; LL.B., Georgetown U., 1922, LL.M., 1923; m. Alice Cashell Berry, Sept. 24, 1957. Engaged in pvt. practice of law, Washington, 1922-25; asst. corp. counsel D.C., 1925-30, people's counsel, 1930-34; law mem. and vice chmn. Pub. Utilities Commn., 1934-40; corp. counsel and as such also served as gen. counsel Pub. Utilities Commn., 1940-45; an adminstrv. asst. Pres. of U.S., 1945-46; judge, U.S. Dist. Ct. for D.C., 1946-66, chief judge, 1966, sr. judge, 1966—. Served in transport service with U.S. Navy, World War I. Mem. Bar Assn. of D.C., Phi Alpha Delta, Am. Legion. Episcopalian (jr. warden). Clubs: The Barristers, Potomac Hunt, Masters of Foxhounds Assn. Am., Rotary, Lawyers, Metropolitan, Chevy Chase, Am. Foxhound (dir.). Home: 12930 Travilah Rd Potomac MD 20854 Office: US Dist Ct for DC Washington DC 20001

KEEFE, LEONARD RAWLINGS, newspaper exec.; b. Norfolk, Va., Jan. 17, 1914; s. George Edward and Fannie (White) K.; student Syracuse U. Grad. Sch. Sales Mgmt. and Marketing, summers 1958-59; advanced mgmt. course Grad. Sch. Bus. Adminstrn., U. Va., 1963; m. Dorothy Evans Branch, May 19, 1952. Copy boy advt. Ledger-Star, Norfolk, 1933-36, salesman retail advt. staff, 1936-51; asst. mgr. gen. advt. Virginian Pilot and Ledger-Star, Norfolk, 1951-60, mgr. gen. advt., 1960-71, dir. spl. projects, 1971—. Served to capt., inf., AUS, 1942-46. Decorated Bronze Star, Combat Infantryman's Badge. Democrat. Methodist. Lion (bd. dirs. 1956-61, 70-71, pres. 1961-62). Club: Norfolk Sports (bd. dirs. 1954-55, 65-66, pres. 1958, scholarship found. chmn. 1958). Home: 211 E 42d St Norfolk VA 23504 Office: 150 W Brambleton Av Norfolk VA 23501

KEEFE, WILLIAM CARROLL, natural gas co. exec.; b. Clinton, Ia., Jan. 18, 1914; s. William J. and Anna B. (Carroll) K.; A.B., U. Notre Dame, 1935; J.D., Harvard, 1938; m. Barbara J. Lilly, Feb. 14, 1942; children—Robert J., Carol A. Admitted to N.Y. state bar, 1940; practiced in N.Y.C., 1940-50; with Panhandle Eastern Pipe Line Co., N.Y.C., 1950—, sec., 1956-65, v.p., 1961-65, financial v.p., 1965-68, pres., Houston, 1968-70, vice chmn. bd., 1970-71, chmn. bd., 1971—; pres., dir. Trunkline Gas Co.; chmn., dir. Century Refining Co., Amadaillo Prodn. Co., Nat. Distillers & Chem. Corp., 20th-Century-Fox Film Corp., Kansas City Life Ins. Co., Nat. Helium Corp. Clubs: Wall Street (N.Y.C.); Siwanoy Country Bronxville); Ramada, Houston Country, Petroleum (Houston). Home: 5413 Sturbridge St Houston TX 77027 Office: 3000 Bissonnet St Houston TX 77005

KEEGAN, ANNA ROSE TEELIN (MRS. NORMAN R. KEEGAN), civic worker; b. Bklyn., Oct. 16, 1933; d. Frank Arthur and Lillian (Lentz) Teelin; B.S., LeMoyne Coll., 1955; M.A., Adelphi Coll., 1957; m. Norman R. Keegan, June 8, 1957; children—Eileen, James, Arthur, Elizabeth. Tchr. Kenwood Jr. High Sch., Balt., 1957-58; tchr., prin. St. Teresa's Sch., Titusville, Fla., 1961-62, tchr., 1964-65. Mem. Juvenile Bd. Merit, 1967-69, 71—; bd. dirs. United Fund, 1969—; mem. met. bd. YMCA, 1968—; chmn. City Library Bd., 1964-65; vice chmn., 1966-68; vice chmn. Brevard County Sch. Bd., 1967—; mem. adv. com. drug abuse Inter-Agy., 1969—. Mem. Am. Assn. U. Women, Fla. Sch. Bds. Assn. Home: 1416 Bell Terrace Titusville FL 32780

KEEGAN, JOSEPH ROGER, statistician; b. N.Y.C., Jan. 20, 1927; s. Roger Joseph and Beatrice (Reape) K.; B.S., L.I. U., 1954; M.Pub. Adminstrn., N.Y.U., 1956, postgrad., 1956-58; postgrad. Am. U., 1963, George Washington U., 1964; m. Patricia Ellen Ford, Dec. 15, 1962. Statistician, N.Y.C. Dept. Health, 1956-59, N.Y. State Div. Employment, N.Y.C., 1959-60, Albany, N.Y., 1960-62; statistician Internal Revenue Service, Washington, 1963—. Served with AUS, 1945-46. Mem. Am. Statis. Assn., Am. Vets. Com., English Speaking Union, Intercollegiate Assn. (v.p. 1959-60). Home: 1346 Northgate Sq Reston VA 22090 Office: 1111 Constitution Av Washington DC 20224

KEELER, W. W., petroleum exec.; b. Dalhart, Tex., Apr. 5, 1908; s. William and Sarah (Carr) K.; student Kan. U., 1926-29, 31-32; LL.D., Coll. Ozarks, Mich. State U.; E.D., Colo. Sch. Mines; H.L.D., Okla. Christian Coll.; m. Sept. 15, 1933; children—William, Bradford Roger, Kenneth Richard. Asst. chemist Phillips Petroleum Co., Bartlesville, Okla., 1929-34, chemist, 1934, control chem., 1934-37, engr., 1937-38, chief chem., 1938-39, night supt. 1939-40 asst. mfg. supt., 1940-41, chief engring. div., 1941, process engr., Apr.-Aug. 1941, chief engr., 1941-43, tech. asst. to v.p., 1943-45, mgr., 1945-47, v.p., 1947-56, exec. v.p., 1956-62, chmn. exec. com., 1962-67, pres., chief exec. officer, 1967-68, chmn., chief exec. officer, 1968—, also dir.; officer subsidiary cos.; dir. 1st Nat. Bank, Bartlesville. Special cons. Sec. Interior, 1961; head delegation U.S. Oil Mem. to Russia, 1960; dir. Dwight Presbyn. Mission; mem. Commn. on Rights, Liberties and Responsibilities of Am. Indian; apptd. prin. chief Cherokee Nation by Pres. of U.S., 1949, elected by tribe, 1971. Recipient Silver Beaver award Boy Scouts Am. Mem. Am. Petroleum Inst. (dir.), Mid-Continent Oil and Gas Assn., Ind. Natural Gas Assn., Nat. Petroleum Refiners Assn. (trustee), Ind. Petroleum Assn. Am. (dir.), Nat. Petroleum Council, Def. Orientation Conf. Assn., C. of C., N.A.M. (chmn. 1970), Sigma Chi, Sigma Tau. Mason (33 deg., Shriner), Legion Honor Order DeMolay. Club: Hillcrest Country. Home: 1118 S Dewey Av Bartlesville OK 74003 Office: Phillips Bldg Bartlesville OK 74003

KEEN, PAUL, govt. ofcl.; b. Trammel, Ky., Sept. 27, 1900; s. Edward Jackson and Lou Etta (Holland) K.; A.A., Bethel Coll., 1921; A.B., Union U., 1922; J.D., U. Ky.; m. Sarah Anne Howell, June 12, 1933; children—Edward Shain, John Paul. Prin. Ozark (Ala.) City High Sch., 1922-23. Dale County High Sch., Ozark, Ala., 1923-24; admitted to Ky. bar, 1926, D.C. bar, 1932; with D.C. Govt., Washington, 1928-69, chief property insp., 1928-42, bus. mgr., Glenn Dale Sanatorium, 1942-50, deputy supt. Dist. Gen. Hosp., 1950-57, exec. asst. Dept. Pub. Health, 1957-64, regulations devel. officer, 1964-69, ret., 1969. Dir., sec. Found. Mentally Retarded Children of Chesapeake dist. Civitan Internat., Inc., 1959-61. Mem. D.C. (life), Am., Fed. (chmn. admissions com. 1970-72) bar assns., Am. Judicature Soc., Met. Washington Bd. Trade, Ky. Soc. of Washington (past pres.), Internat. Platform Assn., Phi Alpha Delta. Baptist. Clubs: Civitan, University Ky. Alumni, Nat. Lawyers, Capitol Hill (Washington); Internat. Town and Country (Fairfax, Va.). Home: 209 W Greenway Blvd Falls Church VA 20046

KEENAN, JOSEPH DANIEL, labor union ofcl.; b. Chgo., Nov. 5, 1896; s. Edward and Mary (Curtin) K.; ed. St. Jarloth's Sch., Chgo.; elec. apprentice course Crane Tech. High Sch., Chgo.; children—John E., Joseph D. Cable splicer Chgo. Telephone Co., 1915-23; supt. elec. constrn. Fed. Electric Co., Chgo., 1921-30; elec. engr. charge Northside treatment plant, Chgo., 1930-37; sec. Chgo. Fedn. Labor, 1937—; dir. WCFL, Chgo., 1937-40; labor adviser to asso. dir. gen. OPM, 1940-41; asso. dir. Labor Prodn. Bd., 1942; vice chmn. labor prodn. WPB, Washington, 1943-45; labor adviser to Gen. Clay, Berlin, Germany, 1945-47; dir. Labor's League for Polit. Edn.; asst. to dir. ODM, 1953—; sec. Elec. Workers Union No. 134; sec.-treas. bldg. and constrn. trades dept. A.F.L., 1950-54; internat. sec. Internat. Brotherhood Elec. Workers, 1954—. Democrat. Roman Catholic. Eagle. Club: Irish Fellowship. Home: 2727 29th St NW Washington DC 20008 Office: 1200 15th St NW Washington DC 20005

KEES, CLIFTON HOMER, corp. exec.; b. Brookhaven, Miss., Oct. 14, 1910; s. I. Clifton and Etta (Moore) K.; B.B.A., Tulane U., 1933; m. Beall Barnes, Oct. 12, 1936; children—Clifton Homer, Martha (Mrs. William P. Orrick). Bond dept. Whitney Nat. Bank, New Orleans, 1937-39; v.p. Brookhaven Bank and Trust Co., Miss., 1940-43; statistician White, Hattier and Sanford, New Orleans, 1946-50; partner Ducournau and Kees, investment bankers, New Orleans, 1950—; v.p., dir. New Orleans Land Co., 1961—. Served from lt. (j.g.) to lt., USNR, 1944-46. Mem. Investment Bankers Assn. Am., La. Bankers Assn., Financial Analysts Soc. New Orleans, New Orleans Bond Club, New Orleans Opera Club. Methodist.Home:

Tchefuncta Club Estates Covington LA 70433 Office: St Charles and Gravier Sts New Orleans LA 70130

KEES, RALPH EMERSON, retail lumber co. exec.; b. Lofton, La., Feb. 14, 1913; s. George Washington and Bertie America (LaCroix) K.; B.A. in Math. with spl. distinction, La. Coll., 1933; m. Rose Elizabeth Baker, Nov. 19, 1936; children—Ralph Emerson, Barbara Sue (Mrs. Dean T. Wallace), Roselyn (Mrs. Enoch F. Nicewarner). House salesman Rapides Grocery Co., Alexandria, La., 1933-35; invoice clk. Roy O. Martin Lumber Co., Inc., Alexandria, 1935-36, traffic and ins. mgr., 1937-48, gen. mgr. retail div., 1948—, also sec., dir., 1950—; dir. Martin Bldg. Materials Co., Inc., Pointe Coupee Lumber Co., Inc., Lake Charles Lumber Co., Inc., Howard Lumber Co., Inc., Teche Acres, Inc., Martin Park, Inc., Superior Lumber & Hardware Co., Inc., Forest-Lawn Meml. Park, Inc. Alderman, City of Pineville, La., 1970—, mayor pro tem, 1971. Trustee, Rapides Gen Hosp., Alexandria. Democrat. Baptist (trustee 1965-70; deacon 1945—; chmn. finance com. 1958-65). Home: 1421 College Dr Pineville LA 71360 Office: 1028 Fenner St Alexandria LA 71301

KEESLING, JAMES EDGAR, educator; b. Indpls., June 26, 1942; s. Fred Edgar and Martha (Grimes) K.; B.S. in Indsl. Engring., U. Miami (Fla.), 1964, M.S., 1966, Ph.D. in Math., 1968; m. Marian Ellen Calley, Jan. 26, 1963; children—James Edgar, Marian Esther, Timothy Carl. Grad. teaching asst. U. Miami (Fla.), 1964-65, NASA fellow math. dept., 1965-67; asst. prof. math. U. Fla., Gainesville, 1967-71, asso. prof., 1971—. Mem. Am. Math. Soc. (reviewer Math. Rev.), Math. Assn. Am., A.A.A.S., Operations Research Soc. Am., Sigma Xi, Tau Beta Pi, Pi Mu Epsilon, Omicron Delta Kappa, Phi Kappa Phi. Presbyn. Contbr. articles profl. jours. Home: 710 NE 6th St Gainesville FL 32601

KEFFER, WALTER FRANCIS, chem. co. exec.; b. Los Angeles, Dec. 3, 1913; s. Walter Griffith and Florence Maybelle (Kidder) K.; B.S. in Chem. Engring., Ia. State U., 1935; m. Barbara Apple, June 7, 1936; children—Eleanor (Mrs. N.J. Thompson), Judith, Lawrence Thomas. Engr. Johns-Mansville, Waukegan, Ill., 1935, Raymond Pulverizer div., 1935-36; with Internat. Filter Co., Chgo., 1936-37; with Tenn. Corp., Copperhill, 1937-70, gen. mgr. 1968-70; v.p. Indsl. Chem. div. Cities Service, Atlanta, 1970—. Served with USAAF, 1941-46. Mem. Am. Inst. Chem. Engrs., Am. Inst. M.E., Alpha Chi Sigma. Republican. Episcopalian. Kiwanian. Club: Cherokee Town and Country (Atlanta). Home: 3364 Chatham Rd NW Atlanta GA 30305 Office: 3445 Peachtree Rd NE Atlanta GA 30326

KEGLEY, GEORGE ANDREW, newspaper editor; b. Wytheville, Va., May 15, 1928; s. Estel Stephen and Ruth (Brown) K.; B.A., Roanoke Coll., 1949; m. Louise Fishburn Fowlkes, May 31, 1958; children—George Andrew, Mary Louise, Robert Parker, Richard Fowlkes. Reporter, Roanoke (Va.) Times, 1949—, bus. writer, 1959-66, bus. editor, 1966—; editor Va. Luth., Roanoke, 1961—. Mem. Va. State Library Bd., 1972—. Bd. dirs. Roanoke City Rescue Mission. Served as pfc. AUS, 1951-53. Mem. Roanoke Hist. Soc. (editor soc. jour.), Va. History Fedn. (dir.), Kappa Alpha. Lutheran. Club: Roanoke German. Home: Tinker Creek Lane Roanoke VA 24019 Office: 201 Campbell Av SW Roanoke VA 24010

KEHLER, BERNAD CLAUD, dentist; b. Shamokin, Pa., Nov. 15, 1916; s. John Garfield and Lucy Rebecca (Reed) K.; student St. Petersburg Jr. Coll., 1934-35; D.D.S., Emory U., 1939; m. Dorothy Mildred MacLawhon, Aug. 21, 1941; children—Bernard Claud, Keith G. Dentist-in-charge Kiwannis Childrens Dental Clinic, West Palm Beach, Fla., 1939-40, Ellory, S.C., 1940; practice dentistry, St. Petersburg, Fla., 1940-42, 46—. Served to maj. USAF, 1942-46. Fellow Am. Coll. Dentists (hon.); mem. Fla. (historian 1960-66), West Coast (pres. 1961-62), Pinellas County (pres. 1951; editor Pinellas County News 1957-59) dental socs. Methodist (supt. sch. 1958; treas. 1956-71, chmn. finance com. 1956-58, vice chmn. bd. trustees 1970-71). Club: Exchange (pres. St. Petersburg 1963-64; Outstanding Exchangite award 1955). Home: 401 Coffee Pot Riviera St Petersburg FL 33704 Office: 285 8th St N St Petersburg FL 33701

KEHOE, CATHARINE ELLEN, pvt. sch. owner, educator; b. New Orleans, Feb. 3, 1929; d. Charles Vincent and Catharine Ann (Roth) Kehoe; B.A., Ursuline Coll., 1949; M.A. with honors, U. So. Miss., 1951. Head dept. health, phys. edn. Ursuline Coll., New Orleans, 1951-53; chmn. dept. health, phys. edn. St. Mary's Dominican Coll., New Orleans, 1953-64; pres. Kehoe Day Camp and Swimming Sch., New Orleans, 1957—; pres., prin., prof. Kehoe Acad., New Orleans, 1962—. Vol. water safety, first aid instr. A.R.C., 1945-70; chmn. New Orleans bd. Nat. Ofcls. Rating Com., 1957-58. Fellow A.A.H.P.E.R.; mem. Am. Assn. U. Profs., Nat., La. assns. secondary sch. prins., Nat., So. assns. phys. edn. coll. women, Internat. Platform Assn., Phi Epsilon Kappa. Home: 9513 Arbor Lane New Orleans LA 70123 Office: Kehoe Acad 10931 Jefferson Hwy New Orleans LA 70123

KEHRER, BETTYE, lawyer, orgn. exec. Formerly head Ford Found. demonstration program Atlanta Municipal Ct.; now exec. dir. Ga. Indigents Legal Services, Inc. and Ga. Legal Services Program Inc., Atlanta. Office: Ga Inigents Legal Services Inc care King & Spalding 2500 Trust & Spalding Co Ga Atlanta GA 30303*

KEIG, EUGENE RAY, physician; b. nr. West Union, Ia., Sept. 8, 1903; s. Harry and Laura (Ray) K.; D.O., Des Moines Still Coll., 1933; L.M., Rotunda Hosp., Dublin, Ireland, 1953; studied U. Vienna, 1959; m. Alice Johnston, Dec. 15, 1926; 1 son, Harry. Resident Rotunda Hosp., Dublin, Ireland, 1938, 53, Geneva (Switzerland) U. Hosp., 1953; pvt. practice obstetrics and gynecology, Mason, W.Va., 1933-50, St. Petersburg, Fla., 1950—; pres. Doctor's Hosp., Inc., St. Petersburg, Fla., 1953—. Mayor of Mason, W.Va., 1938-48. Mem. Sigma Sigma Phi. Mason. Home: 384 15th St N St Petersburg FL 33705 Office: 401 15th St N St Petersburg FL 33705

KEIGER, ROBERT KASON, lawyer; b. Winston-Salem, N.C., June 28, 1934; s. Joseph Lee and Mamie Alberta (Spainhour) K.; B.S. in Accounting, U. N.C., 1956; J.D., Wake Forest Coll., 1960; m. Ann Hayden Williams, Aug. 9, 1969; children—Karol Kimberly, Christopher Kason, Dee Dee Thornton. Salesman, Indera Mills Co., Winston-Salem, 1956-57, dir., 1957—; clk. Oldtown Telephone System, Inc., Winston-Salem, 1957-60, dir., 1957—; admitted to N.C. bar, 1960, since practiced in Winston-Salem. Solicitor, Kernersville (N.C.) Recorders Ct., 1961-68; judge Kernersville Ct., 1968-69; atty. Town of Kernersville, 1961—. Mem. Am., Forsyth County bar assns., Forsyth County Jr. Bar, Phi Alpha Delta. Democrat. Presbyn. Home: 2500 Lullington Dr Winston-Salem NC 27101 Office: Pepper Bldg Winston-Salem NC 27101

KEILEN, JOHN JACOB, rubber co. exec.; b. Pitts., Oct. 24, 1915; s. John Jacob and Mary Jane (Hare) K.; B.S., Carnegie Inst. Tech., 1936, M.S., 1937; Dr. Chem. Engring., Poly. Inst. Bklyn., 1949; m Eleanor Yunker, Aug. 3, 1940. Research engr. W.Va. Pulp & Paper Co., N.Y.C., 1937-41; project leader W.Va. Pulp and Paper, Charleston, S.C., 1941-47, project dir., 1947-53, dir. new product devel., 1953-58; dir. research and devel. Charleston Rubber Co., 1958-66, v.p. research and devel. 1965—, dir., 1969—; pres., dir. Domex Internat., Inc. Fellow Am. Inst. Chemists; mem. Am. Chem. Soc., A.A.A.S., Am. Inst. Chem. Engrs., Am. Nuclear Soc., Am. Soc. Testing Materials, Soc. Plastics Engrs. Club: Charleston Chemical Engineers. Contbr. articles to profl. jours. Patentee in field. Home: 152 Gordon St Charleston SC 29403 Office: Stark Indsl Park Charleston SC 29405

KEILLER, JAMES BRUCE, coll. dean, clergyman; b. Racine, Wis., Nov. 21, 1938; s. James Allen and Grace (Modder) K.; diploma Beulah Heights Coll., 1957; B.A., William Carter Coll., 1963; LL.B., Blackstone Sch. Law, 1964; M.A., Evang. Theol. Sem., 1965, B.D., 1966, Th.D., 1968; m. Darsel Lee Bundy, Feb. 8, 1959; 1 dau., Susanne Elizabeth. Ordained to ministry internat. Pentecostal Assemblies, 1957; pastor Maranatha Temple, Boston, 1957-58, Midland (Mich.) Full Gospel Ch., 1958-64; dean of coll. Beulah Heights Coll., Atlanta, 1964—, trustee, 1964—; nat. dir. youth and Sunday sch. dept. Internatl. Pentecostal Assemblies, 1958-64, dir. world missions, Atlanta, 1964—, youth commn., 1958-64, missions com., 1964—, exec. bd., 1964—, missionary editor Bridegroom's Messenger, 1964—. Named Alumnus of Year, William Carter Coll., 1965. Mem. Woodmen of World, So. Accrediting Assn. Bible Insts., Bible Colls. and Bible Sems. (exec. sec.), greater Atlanta Pentecostal Ministerial Fellowship, Soc. for Pentecostal Studies, Ind. Order Foresters, Am. Acad. Religion, Evang. Theol. Soc. Home: 892 Berne St SE Atlanta GA 30316 Office: 906 Berne St SE Atlanta GA 30316

KEILLER, THOMAS MITCHELL, elec. engr.; b. Galveston, Tex., Mar. 2, 1898; s. William and Jane Julia (McLaughlin) K.; B.A., Rice U., 1920; B.S., Mass. Inst. Tech., 1922; m. Catherine Marie Roeller, June 20, 1925 (dec.). With Houston Electric Co., 1922-24; engr. Stone & Webster, Inc., Houston, 1924-25, Gulf State Utilities Co., Beaumont, Tex., Lake Charles, La., 1925-34, 35-42; engr. El Paso Electric Co., 1934-35; chief elec. engr. Dickson Gun Plant, Houston, 1942-44; planning engr., asst. supt. engring., cons. Houston Lighting & Power Co., 1945-65; cons. elec. engr., Houston, 1965—. Past engring. chmn. Joint Archtl. and Engring. Council Tex. Served with U.S. Army, 1917-19; to lt. comdr. USNR, 1944-46. Decorated Silver Star medal, Army Commendation medal. Registered profl. engr., Tex. Fellow I.E.E.E.; mem. Nat., Tex. socs. profl. engrs., Houston Engring. and Sci. Soc., Theta Xi. Address: 2 Crestwood Dr Houston TX 77007

KEISER, HENRY BRUCE, lawyer, pub.; b. N.Y.C., Oct. 26, 1927; s. Leo and Jessie (Liebeskind) K.; B.A., U. Mich., 1947; LL.B. cum laude, Harvard, 1950; m. Jessie E. Weeks, July 12, 1953; children—Betsy Cordelia, Matthew Roderick. Admitted to N.Y. bar, 1950, D.C. bar, 1955, Fla. bar, 1956, U.S. Supreme Ct. bar, 1954; trial atty. CAB, Washington, 1950-51; head counsel alcoholic beverages sect. OPS, 1951-52; legal asst. to Judge Eugene Black, Tax Ct. U.S., 1953-56; practiced in Washington, 1956—; pres., chmn. bd. Fed. Pubs., Inc., 1959—; chmn. bd. Gene Galasso Assos., Inc., Washington, 1963—, Fed. Constrn. Corp., 1967—. Adv. cabinet Southeastern U., 1965—; cons., AEC, 1965—; professorial lectr. Dept. Agr., 1960—, George Washington U., 1961—, U. San Francisco, 1965-66, Coll. William and Mary, 1966—, Cal. Inst. Tech., 1967—. Served to 1st lt. Judge Adv. Gen. Corps, USAF, 1951-52; maj. Res. Fellow Nat. Contract Mgmt. Assn. (dir. 1966—); mem. Fed. (nat. council 1966—), Am. bar assns., Fla. Bar, Bar Assn. D.C. (dir. 1965-66, chmn. adminstrv. law sect. 1964-65). Jewish religion. Home: 6009 Plainview Rd Bethesda MD 20034 Office: 1725 K St NW Washington DC 20006

KEISTER, THOMAS CLINTON, dentist; b. Tannersville, Va., Mar. 14, 1897; s. Charles Tate and Lilly Gordon (Spraker) K.; D.D.S., Vanderbilt U., 1925; m. Doris L. Hutcherson, Apr. 18, 1936; children—Thomas Clinton, Larry Charles. Mem. staff dental clinics Va. Health Dept., U.S. Pub. Health, 1925-29; gen. practice dentistry, Charlottesville, Va., 1929—; Pres. Component no. 7 of Va., Shenandoah Valley, 1950-51. Mem. Am. Dental Assn., Charlottesville Dental Soc. (pres. 1944-45), English-Speaking Union, Delta Sigma Delta. Elk, Lion (v.p. Charlottesville 1935-36). Clubs: Redland, Farmington Country (Charlottesville). Home: 1803 Blue Ridge Rd Charlottesville VA 22903 Office: 206 E Market St Charlottesville VA 22901

KEITCH, TEDDY BOYD, social worker; b. Omaha, Sept. 22, 1933; s. Harold B. and Crystal (Haynes) K.; B.A., U. Omaha, 1958; M.S.W., U. Neb., 1960; m. Janice Jeanne Wright, June 21, 1959; 1 son, Robert Boyd. Psychiat. case aide Neb. Psychiat. Inst., Omaha, 1958; psychiat. case aide Norfolk (Neb.) State Hosp., 1958, 59; clin. social worker VA Hosp., Omaha, 1960-62; clin. social worker Mental Hygiene Clinic, VA Hosp., Dallas, 1962—. Served with AUS, 1954-56. Mem. Nat. Assn. Social Workers. Methodist. Forester. Home: 2704 Materhorn Dr Dallas TX 75228 Office: 4500 S Lancaster Rd Dallas TX 75216

KEITH, DWIGHT TAYLOR, publisher, coach; b. Argo, Ala., Oct 19, 1900; s. Jefferson Davis and Vianna (Taylor) K.; A.B., U. Ala.; m. Randa Rasco, Aug. 19, 1925; children—Carole Lita (Mrs. Richard Harvin), Dwight Leo. Founder, pub. mag. Coach & Athlete, Atlanta, 1938—; coach high schs., Ala., Miss., Ga., 1923-42; asst. football coach Ga. Inst. Tech., Atlanta, 1942-52, varsity basketball coach, 1943-47, sports publicity dir., 1942-47. Founder, Ga. Prep. Sports Hall of Fame; sec.-trea. Ga. Athletic Hall of Fame. Mem. Ga. Athletic Coaches Assn. (sec., dir. ann. coaching clinic), Am. Football Coaches Assn. (mgr. Coach of the Year clinic Dist. 4), Nat. High Sch. Athletic Coaches Assn. (organizer, exec. sec.), Nat. Football Writers Assn., U.S. Basketball Writers Assn., Atlanta Press Club, Sigma Delta Chi. Presbyn. Mason (Shriner), Kiwanian. Home: 2644 W Wesley Rd NW Atlanta GA 30327 Office: 1421 Mayson St NE Atlanta GA 30324

KEITH, EUGENE VANCE, supt. schs.; b. Afton, Okla., Dec. 30, 1929; s. Lon Frank and Hazel (Mustain) K.; student Northeastern A. and M. Coll., Miami, Okla., 1948-50; B.S., U. Wichita, 1955; M.S., Kan. State Coll., 1961; postgrad. Okla. State U.; m. Mildred Jeannine Laramore, Jan. 6, 1951; children—Sheryl Lynne, Cynthia Maureen, Karen Kay. Tchr., coach Kiowa (Kan.) High Sch., 1955-58, Medicine Lodge (Kan.) High Sch., 1958-60; asst. high sch. prin. Miami (Okla.) High Sch., 1960-63; supt. schs. Medford (Okla.) Pub. Schs., 1963-69; asst. supt. Guymon (Okla.) Pub. Schs., 1969-70, supt., 1970—. Served with AUS, 1951-53. Mem. N.E.A., Am., Okla. assns. sch. adminstrs. Baptist.Rotarian, Lion. Home: 6049 Sunset Dr Guymon OK 73942

KEITH, FREDERICK RULFS, realtor, farmer, mcht.; b. Wilmington, N.C., Dec. 25, 1900; s. Benjamin Franklin and Lillie (Rulfa) K.; student Campbell Coll., N.C. State Coll.; B.S., Ala. Poly. Inst., 1922; Grad. Exec. program U. N.C., 1953-54; m. Grace Butler, Nov. 24, 1927; children—Fred, Mary, Thomas. Pres. St. Pauls Hardware Co., Inc., 1926—, St. Pauls Drug Co., Inc., 1935—. St. Pauls Firestone Home & Auto, Inc., 1945—; v.p., dir. Colonial Freezer Food Locker Plant, 1946—; pres. Keith Realty Co., Inc., 1948—, Keith Farm Co., Inc., 1949—; pres. St. Pauls Bldg. & Loan Assn.; v.p. Carolina Canners, Inc., 1956—; v.p. Cooper Food Stores; dir., mem. loan bd. Scottish Bank, N.C.; dir., chmn. loan bd. First Union Nat. Bank; v.p. Robeson Marketing and Processing Assn., Inc.; dir. Guaranty Sav. and Loan Assn., Fayetteville, N.C., pres. bd. St. Pauls, N.C.; v.p. Advancement, Inc. br, Farmers Home Adminstrn.; state chmn. Agrl. Stblzn. Com. Mayor Town of St. Pauls, 1935-53; pres. Robeson County Municipal Assn., 1951-52, mem. exec. com. N.C. League Municipalities, 1951-53; mem. State Municipal Relations Com., 1951-53; chmn. Robeson County Rural Fire Assn., 1950-56; chmn. N.C. Drought Com. U.S. Dept. Agr., 1954; apptd. state com. man for N.C. of Farmers Home Adminstrn., 1958-59. Chmn. Robeson County Rep. exec. com.; chmn. 7th Congl. Dist., 1956-60; del. Rep. Nat. Conv., 1948, 52, 56, 60, 64. Vice pres. Robeson County Meml. Hosp., 1957-58; trustee Campbell Coll.; chmn. Southeastern Gen. Hosp., 1959. Mem. Farm Bur. (v.p., dir. 1956-57). Lumberton Bd. Realtors, Am. Inst. Banking, A.I.M. (pres.' council), Am. Legion, Cape Fear Bridge Assn. (past pres.), Tau Kappa Epsilon, Republican. Baptist. Mason (32 deg., Shriner), Rotarian (past pres.). Clubs: Pine Crest Country; Robeson County Executive (dir.). Home: 2100 N Elm St Lamberton NC Office: 209 W Broad St St Pauls NC

KEITH, JOHN WILLIAM, furniture mfg. co. exec.; b. Millen, Ga., Apr. 15, 1926; s. Harley H. and Ethel Fay (Watson) K.; student Ind. U., 1944-46; m. Margaret Ellen Showalter, Nov. 30, 1946; children—Alan, John William, Julia. Partner, mgr. Keith Furniture Co., West Palm Beach, Fla., 1949-60; mfr. rep. Flex Steel Industries, Le Brun Bros. Mfg. Co., West Palm Beach, 1960-62; sales mgr. Le Brun Bros., Inc., Greensboro, N.C., 1962-65; sales mgr. Rhyne Co., Marianna, Fla., 1965-68, pres., 1969—. Recipient Design awards Furniture U.S.A., 1969-70, 70-71. Mem. Furniture Club Am., So. Furniture Club, C. of C. (dir. 1970—), Phi Kappa Psi. Republican. Methodist. Rotarian (dir. 1971—). Club: Marianna Country (dir. 1970—). Home: 2405 Caverns Rd Marianna FL 32446 Office: E Lafayette St Marianna FL 32446

KEITH, THOMAS JOSEPH, realtor; b. Lumberton, N.C., May 31, 1941; s. Fred Rulfs and Grace (Butler) K.; student N.C. State U., 1959-61; B.S., Campbell Coll., 1964. Asst. mgr. Keith Farm Co., St. Pauls, N.C., 1964—; sec.-treas. Keith Realty Co., St. Pauls, N.C. 1965—; dir. Robeson County Farm Bur., Lumberton, N.C., Town and Country Bank. Mem. exec. com. County Republican Party, 1964—, chmn., 1968—; sec.-treas. 7th Congl. Dist. Republican Party, 1966—. Mem. New River Grape Growers Assn. (past dir.), Campbell Coll. Alumni Assn. (sec.-treas. 1968), Jr. C. of C. (v.p. 1967), Lumberton Bd. Realtors (pres. 1968), Am. Inst. Real Estate Appraisers, St. Pauls C. of C. Baptist. Club: Pine Crest Country. Home: 2100 N Elni St Lumberton NC 28358 Office: 209 W Broad St St Pauls NC 28384

KEKER, SAMUEL JEREMIAH, pub. co. exec.; b. Pueblo, Colo., Apr. 4, 1917; s. John S. and Helen E. (Economou) K.; B.A., Am. U., 1939; m. Lucy Hearne Spinks, Jan. 4, 1941; children—John Watkins, Samuel Jeremy. With U.S. News & World Report, Inc., Washington, 1946—, formerly circulation gen. mgr, v.p., circulation dir., 1965—, also dir.; dir. Madana Realty Co. Served with USNR, 1942-46, Korea. Club: Nat. Press. Home: 3203 Rolling Rd Chevy Chase MD 20015 Office: 2300 N St NW Washington DC 20037

KELCH, DAVID ERDMAN, utility co. exec.; b. New Orleans, July 19, 1928; s. Raymond Ellsworth and Norma (Erdman) K.; student Coll. Wooster, 1946, Trinidad (Colo.) State Coll., 1948-49; m. Maxine Jones, Oct. 16, 1949; children—Mary Louise, David Carter. Asst. chief accountant Zia Co., Los Alamos, 1951-55; with Tex. Electric Service Co., Ft. Worth, 1955—, sec., asst. treas., 1966—; sec., asst. treas., dir. subsidiary Old Ocean Fuel Co., 1966—. Home: 2101 Yosemite Ct Fort Worth TX 76112 Office: 408 W 7th St Fort Worth TX 76101

KELKER, JAMES JOSEPH ARTHUR, civil engr.; b. Fort Wayne, Ind., May 20, 1906; s. Arthur Dennis and Clara (Kukuk) K.; B.S. in Civil Engring., Purdue U., 1929, P.C.E., 1933; m. Elizabeth McGaughey, June 17, 1932 (dec. May 1954); children—Francis James, Nancy Lee; m. 2d, Elizabeth Houston, Nov. 3, 1961. Engr. to v.p. Ohio Oil Co., Marshall, Ill., 1929-31, engr. Shreveport (La.) div., 1931-41, 46-61; pvt. practice cons. civil engr., Shreveport, 1961—. Scoutmaster, Norwela council Boy Scouts Am., 1951—. Served to col. Arty., AUS, 1941-46; PTO. Recipient Order of Arrow, 1951, Silver Beaver award Boy Scouts Am., 1960. Mem. Am. Legion, Contour, Delta Chi, Chi Epsilon. Rotarian (hon.). Address: 232 E Herndon St Shreveport LA 71101

KELLAM, J.C., broadcasting exec. Pres. KTBC, KTBC-FM, Austin, Tex. Address: PO Box 1209 10th and Brazos Sts Austin TX 78767*

KELLAM, LUCIUS JAMES, JR., oil distbg. co. exec.; b. Belle Haven, Va., Sept. 25, 1911; s. Lucius James and Carrie (Polk) K.; student Trinity Coll., Hartford, Conn., 1931-35; m. Dorothy Douglass, Sept. 12, 1936; children—Dorothy Douglass (Mrs. Hugh L. Patterson), Lucius James, III. Treas., Sturgis Oil Co., Inc., Belle Haven, 1935-38, pres., 1938-46; pres., dir. Kellam Distbg. Co., Inc., Belle Haven, 1946—; pres. Shore Savs. & Loan Corp., Accomac, Va., 1961-70, chmn. bd., 1970—; pres. Kellam Propane Gas Co., Inc., Belle Haven, 1956—; dir. Va. Nat. Bank, Va. Indsl. & Devel. Corp., Peoples Trust Bank; dir. Smith-Douglass Co., Inc., 1954-65. Chmn., Chesapeake Bay Ferry Commn., 1954-60, Chesapeake Bay Bridge & Tunnel Commn., 1960—; mem. Va. Safety Council, Accomack County, 1951—; mem. Delmarva Adv. Council, Salisbury, Md., 1964-70, pres., 1970—. Mem. Accomack County Democratic Central Com., 1947—, State Dem. Finance Com., 1965; del. Dem. Nat. Conv., 1960. Trustee Old Dominion Coll. Ednl. Found., Norfolk, Va., St. James Sch., Hagerstown, Md., Eastern Va. Med. Sch. Found., Broadwater Acad., Exmore, Va., Va. Mus. Fine Arts; trustee, exec. com. Northampton Accomack Meml. Hosp., treas. 1964—, pres., 1967, 68; bd. dirs. Tidewater Automobile Assn., 1941—, v.p., 1964—; bd. dirs. Internat. Bridge, Tunnel and Turnpike Assn., 1962-66, Tidewater Regional Health Planning Council, 1968—; bd. dirs., v.p., Ocean Hwy. Assn., 1954—; bd. dirs., 1st v.p. Va. Travel Council, 1953-66; bd. dirs. Va. Travel Devel. Council, 1967—. Served to lt. USNR, 1943-46. Mem. Delta Psi. Episcopalian. Rotarian (pres. 1939). Clubs: Eastern Shore Yacht and Country (Melfa, Va.); Princess Anne Country (Virginia Beach, Va.); Commonwealth, Downtown (Richmond, Va.); Harbor (Norfolk, Va.); St. Anthony (N.Y.C.). Home: Mt Pleasant Belle Haven VA 23306 Office: Kellam Distbg Co Belle Haven VA 23306

KELLAM, WILLIAM PORTER, librarian; b. McLeansville, N.C., Oct. 9, 1905; s. Henry Davis and Matilda Dee (Wyrick) K.; student Trinity Park Sch., Durham, 1921-22; A.B., Duke U., 1926, A.M., 1929; A.B. in L.S., Emory U., 1931; m. Mary Carrington Umstead, Dec. 27, 1926; children—William Porter (dec.), Mary Umstead (Mrs. Fred H. Mewhinney). Tchr., Mangum Twp. High Sch., Durham County, N.C., 1926-27, prin. Glenn Elementary Sch., 1927-28; asst. Duke U. Library, 1928-29, head circulation dept., 1929-30; edn. librarian U. N.C., 1931, head circulation dept., 1932-34; librarian N.C. State Coll., Raleigh, 1934-39, W.Va. U. Morgantown, 1939-46, U. S.C., 1946-47; asst. librarian U. N.C. 1947-50; dir. libraries U. Ga., 1950—. Bd. dirs. Assn. Coll. and Research Libraries, 1948-49. Pres. W. Va. Library Assn., 1943 45. Chmn. W Va Library Commn. (1941-46). Received Rosenwald scholarship in library work. Mem. A.L.A. (chmn. Oberly Meml. Award com. 1944-48, chmn. membership com. 1955-59), Am. Assn. U. Profs., Ga. (pres. 1955-57), Southeastern (sec.-treas. 1948-50, v.p. 1968-70, pres. 1970-72) library assns. Rotarian. Editor: Southeastern Librarian, 1952-61. Contbr. to library mags. Home: 399 Parkway Dr Athens GA

KELLAWAY, PETER, physiologist, educator; b. Johannesburg, South Africa, Oct. 20, 1920; s. Cecil and Doreen Elizabeth (Joubert) K.; student Haileybury Coll., Melbourn, Australia, 1929-37; B.A., Occidental Coll., 1942, M.A., 1943; Ph.D., McGill U. (Can.), Faculty Medicine, 1947; m. Jo Ann Barbieri, Apr. 26, 1957; children—Judianne, David, Kevin, Christina. Came to U.S., 1937, naturalized, 1947. Demonstrator McGill U., Montreal, Que., Can., 1944, instr., 1945, asst. prof., 1946; asso. prof. physiology Baylor Coll. Medicine, Houston, 1948-61, prof., 1961—; dir. Blue Bird Childrens Clinic for Neurol. Disorder, Meth. Hosp., Houston, 1949-61, dir. sect. neurophysiology, 1949-71, chief dept. physiology, 1972—; chief dept. neurophysiology Tex. Children's Hosp., cons. perinatal com. NIH; cons. Hermann, VA, M.D. Anderson hosps. (all Houston). Dir., Internat. Conf. on Infants, 1962. Mem. adv. bd. Houston Action for Youth, 1966-68. Recipient Sir William Osler medal, Am. Soc. for History Medicine, 1946. Mem. Am. Epilepsy Soc. (pres. 1960, sec.-treas. 1955-59), Am. Neurol. Assn., Am. Physiol. Soc., Am. Acad. Neurology, Houston Neurol. Soc. (v.p. 1957 pres. 1967, chmn. bd. trustees, 1970—), Am. Electro-encephlograph Soc. (treas. 1956, council 1957-59, pres. 1963). Author: Convulsive Disorders of Children, 1959. Editor: Convulsive Disorders, 1958, Neurologic and Electroencephalographic Studies in Infants, 1963; Clinical Electroencephalographic Studies in Children, 1968. Editor Jour. Electroencephalography and Clinican Neurophysiology An Internat. Jour., 1969—. Contbr. numerous articles to sci. jours. Home: 627 E Friar Tuck Lane Houston TX 77024

KELLEAM, JOSEPH EVERIDGE, author; b. Boswell, Okla., Feb. 11, 1913; s. Edwin Avres (M.D.) and Ophelia (Everidge) K.; student Okla. U., 1930-32, Southwestern Coll., 1932-34; B.S., Central Coll., Edmond, Okla., 1936; m. Alta Tolle, Oct. 6, 1934; children—Aljo K. Gregg, Edwina (Mrs. Covington). Employed govt. service 1934-60, successively employed with Treasury Dept., Indian Service, U.S. Engrs., AAF, with pvt. contractors from Washington to Ariz.; formerly contract specialist with USAF at Boeing Airplane Co., Wichita, Kan.; writer specializing on Southwest Americana, oilfields, Indian history and early boom towns. Decorated for hon. service with U.S. Engrs. and Army Air Forces (civilian). Mem. Pi Kappa Phi, Sigma Tau Delta. Author: Blackjack (novel), 1948 (film rights sold to motion picture producer, 1948); Okie Jim and Queen of the Night; Overlords From Space, 1956 (reprinted in German); The Little Men, 1959 (reprinted in Italian); Hunters of Space, 1960 (reprinted in Italian); When the Red King Woke, 1966; (poems) Days Beyond Number, 1971. Contbr. Ford Found., Esquire and other mags. Address: PO Box 156 Garvin OK 74736 also Box 87 Hugo OK 74743

KELLEHER, GRACE JAYNE WALKER (MRS. JOHN EDWARD WALSH), statistician, educator; b. Sarasota, Fla., Aug. 8, 1927; d. Harney Henry and Nella (Yarbrough) Walker; student Am. U., 1946-50, M.A. in Statistics, 1955; B.S. in Pub. Adminstrn. and Mil. Sci., U. Md., 1952, postgrad. in math. econs., 1965-68; postgrad. in econs. So. Methodist U., 1969-71; postgrad. in indsl. engring. U. Tex. at Arlington, 1972—; m. Frank J. Kelleher, 1951 (div. 1968); children—Eileen, Linda; m. 2d, John Edward Walsh, Sept. 18, 1969. Statistician, Dept. Navy, Washington, 1945-50; statistician, logistician Hdqrs. U.S. Air Force, Washington, 1952-63; sr. research staff, econs. and systems analysis Inst. for Def. Analyses, Arlington, Va., 1964-69; lectr. econs. So. Methodist U., Dallas, 1969-70; asst. prof. mgmt. sci. U. Tex. at Arlington, 1970-72; sr. asso. Computer Aid Cos. Inc., Dallas, 1972—. Served to capt. USAF, 1951-52. Recipient Meritorious Civilian Service award USAF, 1957. Fellow A.A.A.S.; mem. Operations Research Soc. Am. (sects. com. 1967-68, long range planning com. 1967-69, A.A.A.S. liaison com. 1970—), Inst. Mgmt. Scis. (vice chmn. Washington chpt. 1968-69), Am. Statis. Assn. Co-author, editor: The Challenge to Systems Analysis: Public Policy and Social Change, 1970. Home: 4151 Shady Bend Dr Dallas TX 75234

KELLER, CHARLES, III, investment banker; b. Ancon, Panama Canal Zone, Apr. 6, 1935; s. Charles and Rosa (Freeman) K.; B.S., Stanford, 1957; M.B.A., Harvard, 1961; m. Jane Carter, June 9, 1958; children—Charlotte, Charles Wade. Resident engr. City and County of San Francisco, 1958-59; data processing analyst New Orleans Public Service, Inc., 1961-63; v.p. Keller Constrn. Corp., New Orleans, 1963-71; asso. corporate finance dept., Kohlmeyer & Co., New Orleans, 1971—; pres. Gen. Enterprises, Inc., New Orleans, 1962—. Bd. dirs. New Orleans Philharmonic Symphony, 1962—, v.p. 1969-72; bd. dirs. New Orleans Speech and Hearing Center, 1963-69, pres., 1969; bd. dirs. Isidore Newman Sch., 1970—, United Fund Greater New Orleans, 1972—. Served with AUS, 1958. Registered profl. engr. Mem. Bur. Govtl. Research, C. of C. of New Orleans, Am. Soc. C.E., Am. Soc. Military Engrs., Nat. Soc. Profl. Engrs., La. Engring. Soc., Internat. House, Phi Beta Kappa, Tau Beta Phi. Democrat. Club: New Orleans Country. Office: 147 Carondelet St New Orleans LA 70130

KELLER, CHRISTOPH, JR., clergyman; b. Bay City, Mich., Dec. 22, 1915; s. Christoph and Margaret Ely (Walter) K.; grad. Lake Forest (Ill.) Acad., 1934; B.A., Washington and Lee U., 1939; student Grad. Sch. Theology, U. South, 1954; certificate spl. work, Gen. Theol. Sem., N.Y.C., 1957; S.T.D. (hon.), Gen. Theol. Sem.; D.D. U. South; m. Caroline P. Murphy, June 22, 1940; children— Caroline, Cornelia, Cynthia, Kathryn, Christoph, Elizabeth. Planter, Alexandria, La., 1940—; pres. Deltic Farm & Timber Co., El Dorado, Ark., 1948-51; exec. v.p. Murphy Corp., El Dorado, 1951-54, dir., 1948—; ordained priest P.E. Ch., 1957; rector, Harrison, Ark., also charge missions in Eureka Springs and Mountain Home, Ark., 1957-61; rector St. Andrews Episcopal Ch., Jackson, Miss., 1962-67; dean St. Andrews Cathedral, Jackson, until 1967; bishop coadjutor Diocese of Ark., 1967-70, diocesan bishop 1970—. Dir. Tallalah State Bank (La.), 1950-51. Bd. trustees Gen. Theol. Sem., P.E. Diocese Ark., 1957-62, mem. exec. council, 1958-60, chmn. dept. promotion, 1958-60, Gen. Theol. Sem., N.Y.; exec., com. P.E. Diocese Miss., 1963-65; dept. Gen. Conv. P.E. Ch., 1958, 61, 64, 67. Pres. La. Aberdeen Angus Breeders Assn., 1947, La. Delta Council, 1950; chmn. United Fund El Dorado, 1952; Mem. Madison Parish (La.) Sch. Bd., 1952-53. Trustee All Saints Jr. Coll., Vicksburg, Miss., 1949-51, Kent Sch., Conn., U. South, Sewanee, Tenn. Served as officer USMCR, World War II. Mem. Pi Kappa Alpha (pres. 1939). Home: 1809 Beechwood Rd Little Rock AR 72207 Office: 300 W 17th St Little Rock AR 72206

KELLER, DOUGLAS DOYLE, dentist; b. Bastrop, La., Apr. 5, 1932; s. Douglas Jewel and Annie L. (Anderson) K.; student La. State U., 1950-52, N.E. La. State Coll., 1953; D.D.S., Loyola U. of New Orleans, 1957; postgrad. U. So. Cal., 1958; m. Martha Florence Brown, May 31, 1953; children—Ann, Nancy, Douglas. Individual practice dentistry, Bastrop, 1959—; mem. staff Morehouse Gen. Hosp., Bastrop, 1959—. Mem. La. State Bd. Dentistry, 1970—. Mem. Morehouse Parish aux. police force, 1967—; organizer, planner Prairie View Acad., Bastrop, 1969-72. Bd. dirs. No. La. Health Planning Council, Council for Dental Care Corp. Served with USNR, 1957-59. Mem. Am., Internat. coll. dentists, Am., La. (dir., also trustee Dental Relief Fund 1967-70), 5th Dist. (pres. 1964) dental assns., Am. Dental Soc. Dentistry for Children, Am. Assn. Dental Examiners, La. Farm Bur., Bastrop C. of C. Baptist (deacon, tchr. 1959-69). Lion. Clubs: Morehouse Country (Bastrop). Home: 1602 Parson Dr Bastrop LA 71220 Office: 312 Durham St Bastrop LA 71220

KELLER, FRANK LEUER, educator; b. Highland Park, Ill., Mar. 27, 1918; s. Ruben C. and Helen (Zahnen) K.; B.A., U. Ill., 1940; postgrad. Northwestern U., 1941; Ph.D., U. Md., 1949; m. Justina Van H. Healy, July 12, 1952; children—Lyndall, Kimberley, Gregory. Asst. prof. Rutgers U., 1949-50; mem. faculty Tulane U., New Orleans, 1950—, prof. econs., 1956—. Vis. prof. U. Cal. at Berkeley, 1964, UN, Chile, 1962-63; cons. to U.S. and fgn. govts.; dir. Gulf Univs. Research Corp., Galveston, Tex. Mem. Met. Crime Commn., New Orleans, 1966—. Bd. dirs. Ursuline Acad., New Orleans. Served to col. AUS, 1941-47. Mem. Am., So. econ. assns., Assn. Am. Geographers, Regional Sci. Assn., Latin Am. Studies Assn., A.A.A.S. Contbr. articles profl. publs.Home: 910 Burdette St New Orleans LA 70118

KELLER, GERALD CHRISTIAN, physician; b. New Orleans, Apr. 24, 1934; s. Dewey Cronelius and Aurelie Mary (Weber) K.; B.S. cum laude in Biology, Loyola U. of South, New Orleans, 1956; M.D., La. State U., 1959; m. Joan Mary Arnold, Dec. 28, 1957; children—Sharon, Chris, John, Jennifer, Jody, Dan, Scott, Roger. Intern, Madigan Army Hosp., Tacoma, Wash., 1959-60; practice gen. medicine, Mandeville, La., 1963—; staff St. Tammany Parish Hosp., 1963—, sec.-treas. 1970—. Clin. instr. dept. gen. practice La. State U. Med. Sch., New Orleans, 1970—. Pres., Our Lady of the Lake Sch. Bd., 1967-69, v.p., 1969-71, chmn. fund drive, 1966—; mem. Olympia Carnival Orgn., 1966—. Alderman, Mandeville, La., 1968-72, mayor pro tem, 1968-72. Served to capt. AUS, 1958-63. Diplomate Am. Bd. Family Practice (charter). Mem. St. Tammany Parish Med. Soc. (pres. 1971—), Mandeville C. of C. K.C. Clubs: Covington (La.) Country; Ponchatrain Yacht, King's of Juno (Mandeville). Home: 2733 North St Mandeville LA 70448 Office: 2810 Florida St Mandeville LA 70448

KELLER, JOHN ESTEN, educator; b. Lexington Ky., Sept. 27, 1917; s. Owen Bullitt and Mary Louise (Welsh) K.; A.B., U. Ky., 1940, M.A., 1942; Ph.D., U. N.C., 1946; m. Dinsmore Davis, Sept. 2, 1942; children—John E., Laura Dinsmore. Instr., U. N.C., 1943-46; asso. prof. U. Tenn., 1947-50; mem. faculty U. N.C., 1950-67, prof., 1957-67; prof., chmn. dept. Spanish and Italian, asso. dean arts and scis. U. Ky., 1967—. Mem. Mediaeval Acad. Am., Modern Lang. Assn., S. Atlantic Modern Lang. Assn. (pres. 1967-68); corr. mem. Consejo Superior de Investigaciones Cientificas Madrid, Spain. Author: Alfonso X, El Sabio, 1967. Editor: (Calila e Digna) Medieval Spanish, 1957; Libro de los Gatos, 1958; Libro de los Enganos 1959; Libro de los Exenplos, 1961. Home: 802 Chinoe Rd Lexington KY 40502

KELLER, OLIVER, JR., state ofcl. Dir. youth services div. Fla. Dept. Health and Rehab., Tallahassee. Address: 311 South Calhoun St Tallahassee FL 32304*

KELLER, PAUL JOSEPH, educator; b. Chgo., Mar. 12, 1904; s. Theodore Christian and Jessie Prince (Smith) K.; B.S. in Elec. Engring., U. Mich., 1927; B.D., McCormick Theol. Sem., 1936; Ph.D., Yale, 1940; D.D., Tusculum Coll., 1969; m. Zita Hargadon, Oct. 15, 1925; children—Paul Joseph, Henry Renault. Surveyer, Ind. and Ill. Coal Corp., 1927-29; engr. Commonwealth Edison Co., Chgo., 1929-30; ordained to ministry Presbyn. Ch., 1936; pastor Congl. Ch., South Dartmouth, Mass., 1941-50, 1st Presbyn. Ch., Deerfield, Ill., 1950-60; prof. philosophy and religion Tusculum Coll., Greeneville, Tenn., 1960—. Pres. bd. dirs. Holston Presbytery, Synod of Mid-South. Served with Mass. State Guard, 1942-45. Nettie E. McCormick fellow for Hebrew excellence McCormick Sem., 1936-38; named Tchr. of Year, Green County, Tenn., 1969. Rotarian. Club: Link Hills Country (Greeneville). Home: Route 9 Greeneville TN 37743 Office: Tusculum Coll Greeneville TN 37743

KELLER, WILLIAM KARL, educator; b. Louisville, Aug. 4, 1906; s. William August and Necia (Hamby) K.; A.B., U. Louisville, 1930, M.D., 1931; m. Elizabeth Trawick, June 13, 1931; children—Elizabeth T., Martha Kendrick (Mrs. Donald E. Janzen). Intern, Louisville Gen. Hosp., 1931-32, resident medicine, 1932-34; resident psychiatry Johns Hopkins Hosp., 1934-35, N.Y. Hosp., 1935-37; Rockefeller fellow neurology, London, Eng., 1937-38; asst. prof. psychiatry U. Louisville, 1938-42, asso. prof., 1942-49, prof., 1949—, chmn. dept. psychiatry, 1964—. Served with M.C., USNR, 1942-45. Recipient Distinguished Alumnus award U. Louisville, 1968. Fellow A.C.P., Am. Coll. Psychiatrists, Am. Psychiat. Assn.; mem. Ky., Jefferson County med. socs., A.M.A., Am. Assn. Automotive Medicine (pres. 1963-64), Central Neuropsychiat. Assn. (pres. 1968-69), Kappa Alpha, Alpha Kappa Kappa, Alpha Omega Alpha. Contbr. articles to profl. jours. Home: 4013 St Ives Ct Louisville KY 40207 Office: Louisville Gen Hosp Louisville KY 40202

KELLETT, WILLIAM HIRAM, JR., educator, designer; b. Bryan, Tex., Oct. 15, 1930; s. William Hiram and Elizabeth (Minsky) K.; A.A., Victoria Coll., 1954; B.Arch., Tex. A. and M. U., 1960, M.Arch., 1967; m. Christiana Maria Binsch, Feb. 2, 1962 (div.); children—Elizabeth Julia, Rene Janine, Kira Lorraine; m. 2d, Ann Robertson Wilkins, Dec. 11, 1971; children—Robert, Patricia. Elec. technician W.E. Kutzschbach Co., Bryan, Tex., 1950-51; engring. technologist Johnston & Davis, Victoria, Tex., 1952-54; mech., elec. systems designer Hall Engring. Co., Bryan, 1955-62; prof. environmental design Tex. A. and M. U., College Station, 1962—; mech. and elec. systems designer Environments, Inc., Bryan, 1962—. Vice chmn. City Charter Com., Bryan, 1969; chmn. Bd. Equalization, 1969-70. Mem. Illuminating Engr. Soc., Am. Assn. U. Profs., Am. Soc. Heating, Refrigeration and Air Conditioning Engrs., Refrigeration Engrs. and Tech. Assn., Phi Theta Kappa, Tau Beta Pi, Tau Sigma Delta. Home: 1000 Esther Blvd Bryan TX 77801 Office: Coll Architecture and Design Tex A and M U College Station TX 77840

KELLEY, ALBERT BENJAMIN, research found. exec.; b. N.Y.C., May 15, 1936; s. Hubert Williams and Anna Alberta (Davis) K.; student Monterey Lang. Inst., 1955, Naganuma Inst., Tokyo, 1957-58, Sophia U., Tokyo, 1957; children—Sumako Chongyol, Hubert Chongsu. Newspaper editor, reporter, Tokyo and Washington, 1957-63; adviser ICC, 1963-66; transp. and communications mgr. U.S. C. of C., 1966-67; dir. Office Pub. Affairs, U.S. Fed. Hwy. Adminstrn., 1967-69; v.p. communications Ins. Inst. for Hwy. Safety, Washington, 1969—. Bd. dirs. Internat. Transp. Research Forum, 1963-65, Nat. Safety Council, 1966-69. Served with AUS, 1954-57. Recipient Golden Eagle award Council Internat. Nontheatrical Events, 1971. Mem. Internat. Assn. Chiefs Police, Democrat. Club: Nat. Press. Author: Pavers and the Paved, 1971. Contbr. articles to profl. jours. Office: Watergate 600 Washington DC 20037

KELLEY, BLAINE, JR., real estate exec.; b. Charlotte, N.C., Jan. 26, 1929; s. Blaine and Margaret (Patterson) Kelley; B.S., Davidson Coll., 1951; m. Sylvia Sanders, July 25, 1959; children—Katharine, Blaine III, Alan S. Br. mgr. Star Paper Tube Co., 1957-61; pres. E-Z Living Homes, Atlanta, 1961-62; v.p., dir. Marthame Sanders & Co., 1962-71; pres., chmn. The Landmarks Group, Inc., Atlanta, 1968—; officer or partner various related real estate and constrn. cos.; dir. Citizens & So. Park Nat. Bank, Atlanta, Austin Kelley Advt., Inc., N.Y.C., Marthame Sanders & Co. Trustee Northside Hosp. Assn. Served to 1st lt., arty. AUS, 1943-56. Presbyn. (elder, chmn. bd. deacons 1969). Home: 400 Glen Arden Atlanta GA 30305 Office: 880 Johnson Ferry Rd NE Atlanta GA 30342

KELLEY, BROWN WILSON, dentist; b. Irvine, Ky., Jan. 2, 1899; s. James S. and Annie (Wilson) K.; student U. Ky., 1917-18; D.D.S., U. Louisville, 1925; m. Lellyn Phillips Durrett, Feb. 16, 1927 (dec.); children—Brown Wilson, James D. Gen. practice dentistry, Louisville, 1925—. Instr. U. Louisville Sch. Dentistry, 1925-37. Served with USN, 1918. Mem. Am., Ky. dental assns., Louisville Dist. Dental Soc., League Ky. Sportsmen (pres. 1934, dir. 1934—), Southend Civic League, Psi Omega, Omicron Kappa Epsilon. Mem. Christian Ch. Clubs: University (sec. 1927), Mercator (Louisville). Home: 100 Ash Av Pewee Valley KY 40056 Office: Fincastle Bldg 325 Broadway Louisville KY 40202

KELLEY, CARLTON WILLIAM, jr. coll. pres.; b. Cullman, Ala., Mar. 19, 1906; s. Monroe Morgan and Louisa Anna (Livingston) K.; B.A., Birmingham So. Coll., 1927; M.A., U. Ala., 1945; L.H.D., Athens Coll.; m. Louella Masterson, Nov. 26, 1937; 1 dau., Ellen Frances. Accountant, Lone Star Cement Co., Birmingham, Ala., 1929-31; tchr. Decatur (Ala.) High Sch., 1931-42; supr. war prodn., also tng. dir. John C. Calhoun Tech. Sch., Decatur, 1942-47; pres. Calhoun Jr. Coll., Decatur, 1947—. Mem. Nat., Ala. edn. assns., Am., Ala. vocational assns., Ala. Assn. Sch. Adminstrs., Am. Assn. Schs., Nat. Assn. Jr. Colls., So. Assn. Secondary Schs., Am. Tech. Edn. Assn., Ala. Commn. for Better Schs., Huntsville, Decatur and Athens chambers commerce, Iota Lambda Sigma, Delta Sigma Phi. Methodist. Lion. Address: Box 427 Decatur AL 35601

KELLEY, CHAPMAN, artist; b. San Antonio, Aug. 26, 1932; s. Ralph Payne and Ruby (Sloane) K.; spl. art student Trinity U., 1948-50; student Pa. Acad. Fine Arts, 1951-55; m. Joan Catherine Wisner, Jan. 8, 1953; children—Cole Chapman II, Kevin Carson. Exhibited numerous one man shows, Dallas, Houston, Austin, Corpus Christi, San Antonio, Longview (all Tex.), Tulsa, N.Y.C., Memphis, New Orleans, San Francisco; exhibited group shows including Ringling Nat. Exhibit, Sarasota, Fla., 1959, Southwestern Print and Drawing Exhibit, 1959, Southwestern Art Invitational, Dallas Mus. Fine Art, 1960, 157th Pa. Acad. Ann., 1962, Former Students Exhibit at Pa. Acad. Fine Arts, 1962, Butler Inst., Youngstown, O., Corcoran Gallery, Washington, 1963, Cummer Gallery Art, 1964, Abilene (Tex.) Fine Arts Mus., 1964, Okla. Art Center, Okla, City, 1964-67; represented in permanent collections Dallas Mus. Fine Arts, Tex. Instruments, Inc., Colorado Springs Fine Arts Center, Mulvane Art Center, Topeka, Okla. Art Center, Witte Meml. Mus., San Antonio, 1st Nat. Bank of Dallas, Tex., numerous other pub. and pvt. collections. Owner, operator Atelier Chapman Kelley, art sch., gallery, frame shop, Dallas; panelist Matrix for Arts Symposium, Center Advanced Studies, U. Ill., 1967; also lectr. Recipient awards including State Fair Tex. Purchase prize 22d Ann. Tex. Painting and Sculpture Exhibit, 1960; S.J. Wallace Truman prize N.A.D.; 1963, Childe Hassam Purchase award Am. Acad. Arts and Letters. William Emlen Cresson European traveling scholar, 1954-55, 1st prize Tex. Painting and Sculpture Exhbn., 1964, 8 State Ann. Painting and Sculpture Exhibit, Okla. Art Center, 1965, Purchase award Nat. Sun Carnival show, El Paso Mus. Home: 5511 Fairfield Dallas TX 75205 Office: 2526 Fairmount St Dallas TX 75201

KELLEY, EOGHAN NEWMAN, architect; b. Sanford, Fla., Oct. 12, 1932; s. Harold H. and Viola (Hage) Kastner; student Marquette U., 1951; student U. Fla., 1951-52, 1956-58; m. Jennifer Castello, June 28, 1958; children—Christopher, Maureen, Kevin, Monica. Practice architecture, Sanford, 1964—. Served with USMCR, 1952-55. Important works include Idyllwilde Elementary Sch., 1970, Teague Middle Sch., Forest City Elementary Sch., Brantley High Sch. Office: 514 Sanford Atlantic Bank Bldg Sanford FL 32771

KELLEY, EVERETT, educator; b. Hamburg, Ark., Mar. 6, 1919; s. Robert Bailey and Sarah Jeanette (Cunningham) K.; B.S., Ark. A. and M. Coll., 1943; M.A., George Peabody Coll., Nashville, 1951; diploma U. Ark., 1964; m. Janie Melvenie Manning, Nov. 6, 1943; children— Sarah Elizabeth, Mary Carol. Prin., Rison Pub. Schs., 1946-49, Gould Pub. Sch., 1949-50; supt. Sherrill Pub. Schs., 1950-51; supt. Van Buren Pub. Schs., 1951-61; supt. Shackover Pub. Schs., 1961-64; supt. Harrison Pub. Schs., 1964—. Served with AUS, 1943-46. Mem. C. of C. (dir.), Ark. Edn. Assn. (dir.), Ark. Sch. Adminstrs., Am. Assn. Sch. Adminstrs., Phi Delta Kappa, Nat., Ark. edn. assns. Lions. Home: 429 Skyline Dr Harrison AR 72601 Office: Sycamore and East South Harrison AR 72601

KELLEY, FORREST MANLEY, JR., architect; b. Gainesville, Fla., Aug. 9, 1914; s. Forrest Manley and Annie Carolyn (Wimberly) K.; B.S., U. Fla., 1936, postgrad., 1937-38; m. Margaret Albine Yates, Dec. 14, 1940; children—Forrest Manley III, Margaret Cynthia (Mrs. C. C. McCorsley), Beverly (Mrs. C. A. Faircloth). Partner, Goin & Kelley, Gainesville, Fla., 1939-41; asso. prof. architecture U. Fla., 1946-51; architect Fla. State Sch., 1951-56, dir. sch. house planning, Dade County, Fla., 1956-58; architect, phys. planning officer State U. System Fla., Tallahassee, 1958—. Served to capt., C.E., AUS, 1942-46. Mem. Assn. U. Architects, A.I.A. Baptist. Prin. archtl. works include Fla. U. System Bldgs. Home: 3519 N Meridian Rd Tallahassee FL 32303 Office: Collins Bldg Tallahassee FL 32304

KELLEY, GRACE WINIFRED COOKNEY (MRS. TRUMAN LEE KELLEY), civic worker; b. London, Eng.; d. William and Annie (Howe) Cookney; student pub. and pvt. schs., Eng.; m. Francis Dufty Madge, June 9, 1921 (div. July 1936); 1 dau., Joyce Winifred (Mrs. Duane Callahan); m. 2d, Truman Lee Kelley, Aug. 4, 1936 (dec.); children—Kalon Lee, Kenneth Truman. Came to U.S., 1922, naturalized, 1937. Sec. Assistance League of Santa Barbara, 1950, projects chmn., 1953—; pres. Fla. Atlantic Music Guild, 1968; 1st v.p. Boca Raton Music Study Club, 1971-72. Mem. Nat. Soc. Arts and Letters (ways and means chmn. 1963, treas. 1965-66, mem. nat. bd.; pres. Santa Barbara 1967-68), Internat. Platform Assn. English Speaking Union (dir.). Republican. Episcopalian. Clubs: Birnam Wood Golf, Boca Raton Golf, Montecito Country, Garden (conservation chmn. 1952). Home: 700 S Ocean Blvd Boca Raton FL 33432

KELLEY, HARVEY LAMAR, chem. co. exec.; b. Baytown, Tex., Sept. 22, 1927; s. William Goble and Thelma (Coker) K.; student Lee Coll., Baytown, 1946-48, Tex. U., 1949-51; m. Gloria Elaine Konecny, Apr. 12, 1952; children—Kerry Lynn, Marla Jan, Patrick Lamar. Mgr. purchasing and stores Diamond Shamrock Chem. Co., Baytown, Tex., 1952—. Councilman dist. 6, Baytown, 1967-71. Bd. dirs. East Harris County Heart Assn. Served with A.C., USNR, 1945-46. Mem. Theta Xi, Delta Sigma Pi. Methodist (chmn. bd.). Home: 3505 Woodcrest St Baytown TX 77520 Office: PO Box 500 Deerpark TX 77536

KELLEY, JOHN DRENAN, sociologist, educator; b. Irasburg, Vt., Oct. 4, 1917; s. Charles Wesley and Grace (Collins) K.; student Concord (N.H.) Coll. Bus., 1935-37; A.B. magna cum laude, Harvard,

1950; M.A., U. Minn., 1957; Ph.D., La. State U., 1961; m. Delores Myrtle Ritter, July 2, 1956. Instr., Laconia (N.H.) Bus. Coll., 1938-40; instr. U. Minn., 1952-53; social sci. analyst USAF, MacDill AFB, Fla., 1956; instr. La. State U., 1959-60; asst. prof. San Fernando Valley State Coll., Northridge, Cal., 1961-63; asso. prof. U. Ga., Athens, 1963—, asso. dept. head, 1965-69; vis. lectr. Fla. State U., 1970; sec. S-61 So. regional research project USDA, 1964-66, chmn., 1966-67, vice chmn., 1967-68; sec. so. rural sociology research com. Farm Found., 1969-71, vice chmn., 1971-72. Active Ga. Easter Seal Soc., Athens-Clarke County Mental Health Soc., Univ. Centers for Rational Alternatives. Mem. Democratic nat. com., 1968—, Ga. Dem. party Forum, 1968—. Served with AUS, 1940-46. Recipient award of merit Fort Dix, N.J., 1945, Metzger award Am. Inst. Cooperation, 1957. Fellow Am. Sociol. Assn., Rural Sociol. Soc. (past com. chmn., mem. exec. council); mem. So. Sociol. Soc., Am. Assn. U. Profs., Ga. Sociol. and Anthrop. Assn., Am. Civil Liberties Union, Menninger Found., Ga. Sheriffs Assn., Alpha Kappa Delta. Contbr. articles profl. jours. Home: 381 Beechwood Dr Athens GA 30601

KELLEY, JOHN TOWNSEND, orthodontist; b. Waco, Tex., Apr. 28, 1915; s. John Townsend and Edna Earle (Ewing) K.; student Baylor U., 1931-34; D.D.S., U. Mo., 1938; m. Margaret A. Stone, Dec. 29, 1936; children—John Townsend III, James E., Margaret (Mrs. Gary Tipton). Gen. practice dentistry, Taylor, Tex., 1938-41, specializing in orthodontics, El Paso, Tex., 1945—; preceptorship in orthodontics Dr. W. T. Chapman, El Paso, 1945-46. Bd. dirs. Southwestern Children's Home, El Paso. Served with AUS, 1941-45. Decorated Bronze Star, Silver Star. Diplomate Am. Bd. Orthodontics. Mem. Am. Dental Assn., Am. Soc. Orthodontists, El Paso Dental Soc. (pres. 1952-53). Episcopalian. Clubs: El Paso Skeet, Coronado Country (El Paso). Home: 4015 Las Vegas St El Paso TX 79902 Office: El Paso Nat Bldg El Paso TX 79901

KELLEY, MELVIN WILLARD, polystyrene container co. exec.; b. Clinton, Ind., Nov. 3, 1933; s. Raymond Willard and Evelyn (Hestella) C.; A.B. in Chemistry, Ind. U., 1961, M.B.A. in Mgmt., 1962; m. Erma Kaywin Kuhns, May 17, 1953; children—Kathryn Elaine, Deborah Lynne. Indsl. engr. prodn. incentives Eli Lilly & Co., Indpls., 1962-65, prodn. coordinator Elanco div., 1965-66, purchasing agt., 1966-68, mgr. purchasing Creative Packaging div., 1968-70, mgr. distbn. services, Roanoke, Va., 1970—. Faculty, Ind. Central Coll., 1963-65, Ind. U., Indpls., 1965-70. Served with AUS, 1954-56; ETO. Mason. Home: 118 Sawyer Dr Salem VA 24153 Office: 4411 Hollins Rd Roanoke VA 24003

KELLEY, MILFORD RAY, accountant; b. Tupelo, Miss., Oct. 18, 1931; s. Ernest B. and Lessie (Smith) K.; B.B.A., U. Miss., 1956; m. Anne Marie Jones, July 15, 1952; children—Ray, Van. Auditor, Crosby Forest Products Co., Picayune, Miss., 1956-62; accountant Milford Ray Kelley, C.P.A., Picayune, 1962—; dir. Bank of Picayune; sec.-treas. Past mem. Picayune Sch. Bd. Served with USAF, 1952-55. Mem. Am. Inst. C.P.A.'s, Miss. Soc. C.P.A.'s, Alpha Tau Omega, Picayune C. of C. (dir. 1969—). Episcopalian. Rotarian (past pres.). Home: 605 Glenwood St Picayune MS 39466 Office: 113 E Canal St Picayune MS 39466

KELLEY, RALPH HOUSTON, lawyer; b. Chattanooga, Sept. 23, 1928; s. Glenn Blair and Louise (Hobson) K.; student U. Md., 1948-49; B.A., U. Chattanooga, 1951; LL.B., Vanderbilt U., 1954; m. Barbara Ann Fahl, June 24, 1960; children—Laura Lee, and Ellen Kay, Karen Lynn. Page boy U.S. Ho. of Reps., 1941-46; admitted to Tenn. bar, 1954; partner firm Kelley, DiRisio & Shattuck, Chattanooga, 1954-69; mayor, Chattanooga, 1963-69; referee in bankruptcy U.S. Dist. Ct. for Eastern Dist. Tenn., 1969—. Faculty English and speech dept. U. Chattanooga Evening Coll., 1954-58. Pres., Hamilton County Young Democratic Club, 1956-60; mem. Tenn. Ho. of Reps. 1959-61. Served with USAAF, 1946-49. Mem. Am., Tenn., Chattanooga bar assns., Am. Judicature Soc., Jr. C. of C., Chattanooga C. of C., Delta Theta Phi, Lambda Chi Alpha. Democrat. Episcopalian. Clubs: Chattanooga Boating (dir., past commodore); Exchange of Chattanooga, Mountain City. Home: 18 Sweetbriar Av Chattanooga TN 37411 Office: Municipal Bldg Chattanooga TN 37402

KELLEY, ROGER TIMOTHY, govt. ofcl.; b. Milw., Jan. 14, 1919; s. John P. and Eleanor C. (Purcell) K.; B.S. in Econs., Holy Cross Coll., 1941; student Grad. Sch. Bus. Adminstrn., Harvard, 1941-42; m. Mary Gertrude Keogh, Oct. 18, 1947; children—Timothy David, Roger John, Peter Aherne, Stephen Michael, Paul Edward, Mary Ellen. With Caterpillar Tractor Co., and subsidiaries, 1946-69, dir. edn. and tng., 1962-64, v.p., 1964-69; asst. sec. def. Manpower and Res. Affairs, Washington, 1969—. Served to lt. USNR, 1942-46; PTO. Mem. Machinery and Allied Products Inst. (indsl. relations council). Club: Country of Peoria (Ill.). Home: 7008 Heatherhill Rd Bethesda MD 20034 Office: Pentagon Washington DC 20301

KELLOGG, ANGEL IVEY (MRS. KARL BRITTAN KELLOGG), club woman; b. Seattle, Nov. 30, 1922; d. Joseph Nettles and Margaret (Armstrong) Ivey; B.S., U. Wash., 1948; m. Karl Brittan Kellogg, Aug. 12, 1955. Dietetic intern N.Y. Hosp., 1949; dietitian Providence Hosp., Seattle, 1953-55. Chmn. local affairs Baton Rouge chpt. League Women Voters, 1955-56, chmn. state affairs, 1956-57, chmn. finance, 1956-57, 1st v.p., 1958-59, bd. dirs. La., 1957-60; bd. dirs. Baton Rouge YWCA, 1957-60, sec. bd. dirs., 1958-59, chmn. pub. relations, 1957-59, chmn. nominating com., 1959-60, mem. adult classes com., 1961—, mem. devel. com., 1961—; capt. United Givers, Baton Rouge, 1962-63, vice chmn., 1964; chmn. layouts for program ads Baton Rouge Civic Symphony Women's Auxiliary, 1957-58, editor newsletter, 1958-59, 1st v.p., 1958-59, pres., 1959-60; bd. dirs. Baton Rouge Civic Symphony Assn., 1957-60; family investigator Goodfellows, 1962-63; vol. Am. Cancer Soc., Baton Rouge, 1963-64, sect. leader; mem. edn. com. La. Commn. Status of Women, 1965-68; chmn. Equal Rights Amendments Com. of Baton Rouge, 1970-71. Precinct committeewoman 45th dist. Seattle Dem. Party, 1954-55. Mem. Baton Rouge Chamber Music Soc., La. Ornithol. Soc., Internat. Platform Assn., Nat. Orgn. Women. Democrat. Methodist. Clubs: Bocage Racquet, Baton Rouge Country (Baton Rouge). Contbr. story mag. Home: 2360 Fairway Dr Baton Rouge LA 70809 2360 Fairway Dr Baton Rouge LA 70809

KELLOGG, GLEN T., san. engr., state ofcl.; b. Geraldine, Mont., May 15, 1915; s. Roecoe J. and Pearl (Yeamans) K.; B.S. in Chemistry, Jamestown Coll., 1937; B.S. in Civil Engring., U. Ia., 1940; M.S. in San. Engring., U. N.C., 1949; m. Martha H. Hoss, Nov. 25, 1942; 1 son, Glen T. Pub. health engr. Miss. Health Dept., Jackson, 1940-41; san. engr. Ft. Belvoir (Va.) Engrs. Bd., 1941-42; with Ark. Health Dept., Little Rock, 1947—, prin. san. engr., 1949-51, asst. dir., 1951-55, chief san. engr., dir. bur. san. engring., 1955—. Mem. Ark. Well Drilling License Com., 1969. Served with AUS, 1942-46. Recipient Henry B. Davis award Am. Soc. San. Engring., 1968; award Ark. Plumbing Contractors, 1968. Registered profl. engr., Ark. Mem. Water Pollution Control Fedn., Nat., Ark. socs. profl. engrs., Am. Water Works Assn. (past chmn. S.W. sec., recipient Fuller award 1963, sec.-treas. 1966-70), Ark. Pub. Health Assn., Fed. Sewage and Indsl. Wastes Assn. (Ark. dir.), Theta Tau. Methodist. Home: 15 Sun Valley Rd Little Rock AR 72205 Office: Ark Health Dept Little Rock AR 72201

KELLY, ANN SHEPARD, med. record librarian; b. Rochester, N.Y., June 27, 1918; d. Raymond Augustine and Monica (Driscoll) Kelly; B.A., U. Rochester, 1938; postgrad. Rochester Gen. Hosp. Sch. Med. Records Librarians, 1939-40. Med. record librarian VA Hosp., Bedford, Mass., 1948-56; chief med. record library br. St. Elizabeths Hosp., Washington, 1957-59; dir. med. record library program VA, 1959-61, chief sci. information coordinator research service, 1962-64; med. record librarian Nat. Center Health Statistics, Dept. Health, Edn. and Welfare, 1964-65, Montefiore Hosp. and Med. Center, Bronx, N.Y., 1965-68, hosp. br. div. health resources Community Health Service, Arlington, Va., 1968—. Mem. Am. Soc. Information Sci. Am. Med. Record Assn., (pres. 1966-67). Contbr. to book. Home: 4201 Lee Hwy Arlington VA 22207 Office: 5600 Fishers Lane Rockville MD 20852

KELLY, BRUCE WILLIAM, govt. ofcl.; b. Clintwood, Va., Oct. 6, 1911; s. Joseph P. and Sylvia (Clarkston) K.; B.S., U. Fla., 1938, M.A., 1950, Ph.D., 1953; m. Faye Lucius, Oct. 22, 1936; children—Josephine (Mrs. John R. Moore), Bruce William. Instr., asso. agrl. economist U. Fla., statistician U.S. Dept. Agr., Washington, 1959-60, chief research and devel., 1960-66, dep. dir., dir. Agrl. Estimates div. Statis. Reporting Service, 1966—; chmn. dept. math. and statistics U.S. Dept. Agr. Grad. Sch. Served from 2d lt. to lt. col., AUS, 1940-48. Decorated Silver Star medal, Purple Heart; recipient Superior Service award U.S. Dept. Agr., 1967. Fellow Am. Statis. Assn.; mem. A.A.A.S., Am. Agrl. Economists Assn., Biometrics Soc., Internat. Platform Assn., Lambda Chi Alpha, Phi Kappa Phi. Club: Cosmos (Washington). Home: 7503 Long Pine Dr Springfield VA 22151 Office: US Dept Agr Washington DC 20250

KELLY, CATHERINE BURTON, judge; b. Washington, Dec. 12, 1917; d. William Francis and Catherine (Burton) Kelly; B.A., Smith Coll., 1939; J.D., George Washington U., 1951 Admitted to D.C. bar, 1951; practiced in Washington; with firm Kelly & Nicolaides, 1951-53; asst. U.S. atty., 1953-57; asso. judge D.C. Ct. Gen. Sessions, 1957-67; asso. judge D.C. Ct. Appeals, 1967—. Recipient George Washington U. Alumni Achievement award, 1965. Mem. Am., D.C., D.C. Womens, Fed. bar assns., Nat. Assn. Women Lawyers, Am. Judicature Soc., Nat. Lawyers Club, Nat. Fedn. Bus. and Profl. Womens Clubs. Kappa Beta Pi. Club: Washington. Home: 4501 Connecticut Av NW Washington DC 20008 Office: 400 F St NW Washington DC 20001

KELLY, HAROLD CLAYTON, supt. schs.; b. Burns, Miss., Sept. 4, 1923; s. E.G. and Eula Mae (Winstead) K.; B.S.E., U. Miss., 1948, M.S. in Sch. Adminstrn. and Supervision, 1951, postgrad. 1960-65, advanced adminstrs. certificate, 1966; postgrad. Peabody Coll. Tchrs., summer 1958; m. Hannah Beeks Pitts, Oct. 27, 1951. Coach, sci. tchr., Batesville, Miss., 1948-49; sci. tchr., high sch. coach Yazoo City (Miss.) Schs., 1949-52, athletic dir., coach, 1952-54, jr. high sch. prin., 1953-54, high sch. prin., 1954-65, asst. supt., 1963-65, supt., 1965—. Mem. sch. evalution com. Miss. Accrediting Com., 1969—. Chmn. govt. and schs. div. United Givers Fund, 1958-62. Served with 5th Army Inf., AUS, 1942-45; ETO. Decorated Purple Heart; named Outstanding Citizen Civitan Club, 1970. Mem. Nat., Miss. (resolutions com. 1969—), Yazoo County edn. assns., Miss. Assn. Sch. Supts., Am. Assn. Sch. Adminstrs., Council Ednl. Facility Planners, Council Pub. Schs. (sec.-treas. 1969—), Yazoo County C. of C., Phi Delta Kappa. Methodist (trustee 1969—, mem. adminstrv. bd. 1961—). Home: 2051 Wildwood Terrace Yazoo City MS 39194 Office: 1133 Calhoun Av Yazoo City MS 39194

KELLY, HARRY CHARLES, ednl. adminstr.; b. Wilkes Barre, Pa., Sept. 3, 1908; s. Thomas A. and Josephine Magdaline (Reilly) K.; B.S. Lehigh U., 1931, M.S., 1933; Ph.D., Mass. Inst. Tech., 1936; LL.D., U. Hokkaido, Japan; m. Irene E. Andes, Dec. 10, 1941; children—Henry C., William T. Teaching fellow Lehigh U., 1931-33; teaching fellow Mass. Inst. Tech., 1933-36, research asso. radiation lab., 1942-46; research engr. Am. Thermos Co., Conn., 1936-37; asst. prof., asso. prof. physics Mont. State Coll., 1937-41; dir. labs St. John's Coll., Md., 1941-42; chief sci. and tech. div., spl. projects unit U.S. Army Occupation, Japan, 1945-50; head sci. sect. Office Naval Research, Chgo., 1950-51; asst. dir. NSF, 1951-62, head div. sci. personnel and edn., 1951-59, asso. dir. ednl. and internat. activities, 1959-62; dean faculty N.C. State U., Raleigh, N.C., 1962-67, provost, 1967—. Mem. Pacific Sci. Bd.; co-chmn. U.S.-Japan Commn. Sci. Cooperation. Recipient commendation for meritorious civilian service U.S. Occupation Forces, 1949. Fellow Am. Acad. Arts and Scis., A.A.A.S.; mem. Phys. Soc. Japan (hon.), Phi Beta Kappa, Sigma Xi. Club: Cosmos (Wash.). Author: A Textbook in Electricity and Magnetism, 1941; also articles profl. publs. Home: 613 Macon Pl Raleigh NC

KELLY, HENRY JERVEY, state ofcl.; b. D'lo, Miss., Nov. 16, 1906; s. Thaddeus Madison and Mabel (Robertson) K.; B.S. in Civil Engring., Ga. Tech. U., 1927; m. Claire Bennett, Mar. 1, 1947; children— Thomas J., Peter B., Nancy C. Engr. firm Stone & Webster, Houston, 1928-29, Humble Oil & Refining Co., Houston, 1930-31, TVA, Knoxville, Tenn., 1932-42; commd. 1st lt. C.E., U.S. Army, 1942, advanced through grades to col., 1945; mem. Gen. staff Gen. Eisenhower, E.T.O., World War II; comdg. officer 2d Engring. Constrn. Group, Korea, 1952-53; logistics staff officer Far Eastern Command Hdqrs., 1953-55; comdg. officer Schenectady Gen. Depot, 1956-58; engr. 12th U.S. Army Corps, Atlanta, 1959-60; dep. engr. South Atlantic div., Atlanta, 1960-62; ret., 1962; asst. dir. Fla. Bd. Conservation, Tallahassee, 1962-69, adminstrv. asst. Fla. Dept. Natural Resources, 1970—. Decorated Bronze Star, Legion Merit; Croix de Guerre with palm (Belgium). Registered profl. engr., Ga. Fellow Am. Soc. C.E.; mem. Pi Kappa Alpha. Methodist. Rotarian. Home: 3203 Enterprise Dr Tallahassee FL 32303 Office: 200 E Gaines St Tallahassee FL 32304

KELLY, JOHN PATRICK, newspaper editor; b. Winston-Salem, N.C., July 16, 1927; s. John Patrick and Emma Gray (Hunter) K.; A.B., U. N.C., 1947; Nieman fellow Harvard, 1958-59; m. Jane Watson, Aug. 29, 1953; children—Jane Megan, John Patrick, Ann Perrin, Kathleen Hayes. Reporter, Winston-Salem Jour., 1947-49, copy desk editor, 1949-51, telegraph editor, 1951-54; Sunday editor Winston-Salem Jour. and Sentinel, 1954-55; mng. editor Raleigh (N.C.) Times, 1955-57; telegraph editor Atlanta Jour., 1957-59, mng. editor, 1960-64; Sunday editor Atlanta Jour. and Constn., 1959-60; exec. news editor Winston-Salem (N.C.) Jour. and Sentinel, 1964—. Chmn. adv. com. course for practicing newsmen U. N.C. Mem. Sigma Delta Chi (pres. Piedmont Found.). Home: 939 Stratford Rd NW Winston-Salem NC 27104 Office: Piedmont Pub Co Winston-Salem NC 27102

KELLY, JOHN PAUL, govt. ofcl.; b. Boston, Dec. 15, 1915; s. Christopher Paul and Gertrude Marie (Kelley) K.; student Holy Cross Coll., 1935-37; grad. Army Command and Gen. Staff Coll., 1953, B.S. in Mil. Sci., U. Md., 1954; postgrad. Merton Coll. Oxford U. (Eng.), 1956; m. Ruth Alene Johnson; children—Karen Paula, Kenneth Joseph, Kathy Sue. Copy boy Boston Post, 1935-37, asst. feature editor, 1937-41, staff reporter, desk editor, 1946-51; commd. 2d lt. U.S. Army, 1942, served to 1946; recalled, 1951, advanced through ranks to col., 1966; officer-in-charge Pacific Stars and Stripes, 1960-63; pub. relations officer, Pentagon, Eng., Europe, Korea, Japan; ret., 1966; dep. chief information Mil. Traffic Mgmt. and Terminal Service Dept. Army, Washington, 1967-68; pub. information officer Nat. Library Medicine, Bethesda, Md., 1968-70; pub. information officer Dept. Housing and Urban Devel., Washington, 1970—. Decorated Legion of Merit. Mem. Pub. Relations Soc. Am., Assn. U.S. Army, Ret. Officers Assn. Lion (dist. pub. relations dir. 1971-72). Clubs: Overseas Press (N.Y.C.); Nat. Press (Washington); London (Eng.) Press. Contbr. articles to mil., profl. jours. Home: 8402 Camden St Alexandria VA 22308 Office: Office Pub Affairs Dept Housing and Urban Devel Room 4182 451 7th St SW Washington DC 20410

KELLY, JOHN PAUL, elec. engr.; b. Louisville, Oct. 1, 1931; s. Joseph Francis and LaDoska (DeJarnett) K.; B.S. in Elec. Engring., U. Ky., 1958; M.S. in Engring. Sci., N.C. State U., 1968; postgrad. Ohio State U., 1966-67, Wake Forest Coll., 1960; m. Edythe Mae Crady, Jan. 21, 1932; children—Byron David, Barry Douglas, Paul Michael, Karla Marshalle. With Western Electric Co., 1958—, contract rep. U.S. Army, 1958-60, staff grad. engr. tng., 1960-64, instr., planning engr. data processing system design Bell Tel. Labs., 1964-67, devel. engr. information systems devel., Greensboro, N.C., 1967-68, system engr., 1968—. Bd. dirs. So. Pilgrim Coll., Kernersville, N.C., sec., 1969—; bd. dirs. United Wesleyan Coll., Allentown, Pa. Republican Party candidate County Commrs., N.C., 1962; vice chmn. Young Reps. N.J., 1966-67. Served as staff sgt. USAF, 1951-55. Recipient Commendations U.S. Army, 1960, 64. Registered profl. engr., N.C. Presbyn. (pres. N.C. Wesleyan men 1969—). Author: Community Development Survey, 1960. Home: 2012 Medhurst Dr Greensboro NC 27410 Office: Dept 5214 Western Electric Co Greensboro NC 27400

KELLY, MARY CLAIRE COLEMAN (MRS. OTIS B. KELLY), coal corp. exec.; b. Lohrville, Ia., Sept. 16, 1916; d. Melvin M. and Virginia (Skeens) Coleman; B.A., Berea Coll., 1962; M.A. U. Ky., 1968, M.S. in L.S., 1967; m. Otis B. Kelly, Apr. 10, 1935 (dec. July 1958); children—Floyd M., Lila Sue (Mrs. Kermit Bentley), Otis B., Lona Gail (Mrs. Franklin Casebolt), Verva Anne (Mrs. Morris Galitz). Pres., Greasy Creek Coal Co., Shelbiana, Ky., 1946-50; v.p. Sutton By-Products Coal Corp., Pikesville, Ky., 1956-58, pres., 1958—; propr. Claire's Book and Gift Shop; research asst. Council of So. Mountains, Berea, Ky.; 1959-60; child welfare worker Wise County Welfare Dept., Wise, Va., 1965; librarian Pikeville Free Pub. Library, 1966, Rowan County Pub. Library, Morehead, Ky., 1967, Louisville Free Pub. Library, 1968. Mem. Am. Assn. U. Women (pres. 1971-72), Pike County Hist. Soc. (pres. 1970-71), Pike County C. of C., Mountain Mental Health and Retardation Assn., Alpha Kappa Delta. Republican. Baptist. Club: Business and Profl. Women's. Home: Box 487 Main St Sta Pikesville KY 41501

KELLY, MATTIE CAROLINE, business woman, educator; b. Vernon, Fla., Mar. 12, 1912; d. William W. and Mary Alice (Russ) May; student Rollins Coll., 1944-46, 48-49; A.B., Fla. State U., 1952, postgrad., 1970-71; postgrad. lit. seminar Columbia, summer 1963; m. Coleman Lee Kelly, Mar. 26, 1932 (div. 1971); children—Carnera Lee, Lila Bernarr, Imogene, Kelly Amos, Carol (Mrs. Robert Charles Adams), Cecelia (Mrs. Stephen William Metz). Tchr. pub. schs., Fla., 1928-33, 37; v.p. Kelly Boat Service, Inc.; sec., treas. Kelly Homes, Inc., Destin, Kelly Enterprises. Mem. coordinating council for arts Okaloosa-Walton Jr. Coll., 1965—, rep. to Fla. Arts Council; mem. Fla. Textbook Selection Council, 1971—; mem. Okaloosa County Hist. Commn., 1972—, chmn. hist. sites com. Mem. Okaloosa County Democratic Com., 1958—; mem. Fla. Dem. Exec. Com. Adv. Bd., 1966—; del. Dem. Nat. Conv., 1968, 72. Bd. dirs. Destin Library, 1956—, Okaloosa County chpt. A.R.C., 1954-60, chmn., 1957-58; adv. bd. diversified coop. tng. Choctawatchee High Sch., 1960—; mem. Legislative Local Govt. Study Commn., Okaloosa County. Recipient award A.R.C., 1960. Mem. Ft. Walton Beach C. of C. (edn. com.), Ft. Walton Beach Woman's Club (chmn. fine arts com. 1957-58), Woman's Club (v.p. 1958-59), Am. Assn. U. Women (mem. legislative com. 1971-72). Mem. Protestant Episcopal Ch. (adminstr., supt. ch. sch. 1956-60, br. chmn. Christian edn. 1955-60, dist. chmn. Christian edn. 1958-61, del. adult conf. 1957, 59, del. religious TV programming workshop 1955-56; v.p. women of ch. 1956-57, 61—, dist. v.p. 1961-64, dist. pres. diocese Fla. 1965—). Author: (poetry) Songs and Sonnets from the Sea. Home: Indian Bayou Destin FL 32541 Office: PO Box 425 Destin FL 32541

KELLY, RICHARD, judge, b. 1924; A.B., Colo. State Coll. Edn.; J.D., U. Fla. Admitted to bar, 1952; judge 6th Circuit Ct., Fla., 1960—. Mem. Am., Fed. bar assns. Address: Courthouse Dade City FL 33525

KELLY, ROBERT FRANCIS, supt. schs.; b. N.Y.C., Sept. 12, 1928; s. Thomas Francis and Martha (Templehof) K.; B.S., N.Y. U., 1953, M.A., 1954; M.A., Columbia Tchrs. Coll., 1958; M.Ed., U. N.C., 1960; Ed.D., U. Tenn., 1965; m. Dorothy E. Boles, June 11, 1952. Tchr., Power Meml. Acad., N.Y.C., 1953; tchr. Horace Mann Sch., N.Y.C., 1954-59; supr., also elementary sch. prin. Norfolk (Va.) city schs., 1960-64; dir. elementary edn. Virginia Beach (Va.) city schs., 1964-66; area adminstr. Fairfax County (Va.) schs., 1966-69; div. supt. Chesterfield County schs., Chesterfield City, Va., 1969—. Bd. dirs. Chesterfield YMCA, Central Va. Ednl. TV. Served with USAAF, 1943-47; PTO. NSF fellow Cornell U., summer 1960, U. N.C., 1960-61, Tex. A. and M. U., summer 1959. Mem. N.E.A., Am. Assn. Sch. Adminstrs. (Va. Acad. leader for Nat. Acad. Sch. Execs. 1970—), Phi Delta Kappa. Optimist (pres. Virginia Beach 1965), Elk, Rotarian (dir. South Richmond-Chesterfield 1971—). Home: 4901 Southmoor Rd Richmond VA 23234 Office: Chesterfield School Administration Bldg Chesterfield City VA 23832

KELLY, ROBERT PERRY, lawyer; b. Hockerville, Okla., Nov. 21, 1926; s. Harry Boon and Verna (Hires) K.; A.B., U. Mo., 1950, LL.B., 1952, J.D., 1969; m. Ella Borden Craig, Aug. 6, 1950; children—Edna Sue, Verna Kay, Henry Boon. Admitted to Okla. bar, 1952, since practiced in Pawhuska; sr. partner Kelly & Gambill, 1965—. Sec., dir. Walters Water Control Co. Pres. Bd. Edn. Ind. Dist. 2, 1964—. Served with USAAF, 1945-47. Mem. Am., Okla., Osage County bar assns., Pawhuska C. of C. (dir. 1959-62). Republican. Presbyn. Kiwanian (lt. gov. Div. 15, chmn. laws, regulations and resolution Tex.-Okla. Dist.). Bd. editors Mo. Law Rev., 1950-52. Home: 315 E 16th St Pawhuska OK 74056 Office: 6th and Kihekah Sts Pawhuska OK 74056

KELLY, THOMAS ALEXANDER, economist; b. Nashville, Nov. 6, 1912; s. Timothy Aloysius and Alice Inez (Scruggs) K.; B.A., Vanderbilt U., 1933, M.A., 1940, Ph.D., 1950; m. Elizabeth Douglass Levine, Feb. 14, 1942; children—Mary E., Sarah J., Timothy A., Ellen D. Instr. econs. Vanderbilt U., 1946-47; asst. prof. bus. adminstrn. Miss. State Coll., 1947-51, asso. prof., 1951-55; chmn. econs. and bus. adminstrn. Roanoke Coll., 1955-59; prof. bus. adminstrn. Lynchburg Coll., 1959-65; economist Va. Div. Indsl. Devel., Richmond, 1965—. Mem. Soc. Advancement Mgmt. (v.p. membership Richmond chpt. 1966-67), So. Econ. Assn. Author: Impact of World War II on the Southeastern U.S., 1951; (with Ben M. Wofford) Mississippi Workers, 1955. Home: 8830 Chippenham Rd Richmond VA 23235 Office: State Office Bldg Richmond VA 23219

KELLY, WILLIAM FREDERICK, constrn. co. exec.; b. New Orleans, Nov. 20, 1912; s. William Frederick and Ada (de Trunillon) K.; student pub. and parochial schs.; m. Eloise Mary Generes, Feb. 15, 1939; children—Carmen Mary (Mrs. Jean-Paul Vandenabeele), Pamela Ann (Mrs. Kenneth Francis Sills), Elizabeth Mary, Micaela Margaret, Allen William, Amelie Eloise. Foreman, Globe Constrn. Co., New Orleans, 1930-35; with W. Horace Williams Co., contractors, New Orleans, 1935-38; owner William F. Kelly Constrn. Co., New Orleans, 1939-50; exec. v.p. Kelly Generes Co., Inc., New Orleans, 1950-60; owner Ebilco, Inc., Avondale, La., 1960—, Kelly Systems, 1965—; pres. Kelven, Inc., 1962—. Mem. Civil Air Patrol. Mem. Asso. Gen. Contractors, Home Builders Assn. Greater New Orleans (pres. 1970), Prestress Concrete Inst., New Orleans C. of C. Democrat. Roman Catholic. Clubs: New Orleans Country, New Orleans Athletic, Covington Country, Lamplighter. Home: 100 Bellaire Dr New Orleans LA 70124 Office: 245 S Jamie Blvd Avondale LA 70094

KELLY, WILLIAM LEO, clin. psychologist; b. Balt., Nov. 11, 1924; s. William L. and Agnes (Higgins) K.; B.A., Loyola U., 1947, M.A., 1952; Ph.D., U. Mainz (Germany), 1961. Asst. prof. philosophy and psychology Georgetown U., Washington, 1961-64; clin. psychologist Psychology Service Bur., Washington, 1961-64; asso. prof. psychology Georgetown U., Washington, 1964-69, prof., 1969—, dir. Psychol. Services Bur., 1964-70. Cons. psychologist Nursing Services, Georgetown U. Hosp., 1965-70. Mem. Am. Psychol. Assn., Internat. Soc. for Study of Symbols (pres. 1969-71), Am. Soc. for Clin. Hypnosis, D.C. Psychol. Assn. Author: Die Neuscholastische und die Empirische Psychologie, 1961; Youth Before God, 1961; Women Before God, 1961; Men Before God, 1963; Readings in the Philosophic of Man, 1967. Home: 37th and O Sts NW Washington DC 20007 Office: Georgetown U Washington DC 20007

KELSO, JOHN HODGSON, govt. ofcl.; b. Iowa City, June 16, 1925; s. Edward Lewis and Eliza (Hodgson) K.; B.A., State U. Ia., 1949, M.A., 1950; m. Marian Louise Towers, Aug. 22, 1948; 1 son, John T. Occupational research analyst Bur. Naval Personnel, Dept. Navy, Washington, 1951-55; orgn. and methods examiner Agr. Research Services, Dept. Agr., Washington, 1955-57; mgmt. analyst mgmt. adv. br. Bur. State Services USPHS, Dept. Health, Edn. and Welfare, Washington, 1957-58, chief survey group, 1958-60, chief mgmt. adv. br., 1960-62, asst. exec. officer, 1962-66, exec. officer, Bethesda, Md., 1966-68; asst. adminstr. mgmt. Health Services and Mental Health Adminstrn., 1968—. Served with AUS, 1943-46. Recipient Superior Service award Dept. Health, Edn. and Welfare, 1969, Distinguished Service award, 1972. Mem. Am. Soc. Pub. Adminstrn., Assn. Mgmt. in Pub. Health, Sigma Alpha Epsilon. Methodist. Home: 2332 N Early St Alexandria VA 22302 Office: 9000 Rockville Pike Bethesda MD 20014

KELSON, KEITH R., govt. ofcl.; b. Wales, Utah, Aug. 11, 1918; B.A. in Zoology, U. Utah, 1939, M.A., 1941, Ph.D., 1949; m. Elaine Kelson; children—James, Carolyn. Teaching asst. U. Utah, 1936-41, instr. zoology, 1946-49; teaching asst. Tex. A. and M. Coll., 1941; postdoctoral research U. Kan., 1949-54; with NSF, Washington, 1954—, dep. asst. dir., then dep. div. dir. div. sci. personnel and edn., 1954-65, dir. div. pre-coll. edn., 1965-66, now acting dep. asst. dir. for edn. Fellow A.A.A.S. (mem. council); mem. Am. Soc. Mammalogists, Wildlife Soc., Soc. Study Evolution, Soc. Systematic Zoologists, Sigma Xi, Phi Sigma. Author: (with E. Raymond Hill) The Mammals of North America (2 Vols.). Contbr. articles to profl. jours. Home: 5311 Baltimore Av Chevy Chase MD 20015 Office: NSF 1800 G St NW Washington DC 20550*

KELTON, DAVID JAMES, aluminum co. exec.; b. Louisville, July 17, 1925; s. David J. and Hilda M. (Weis) K.; B.S., Xavier U., 1950; m. Hilberta C. Miller, June 11, 1949; children—Carol, Kathryn, Diane, Cynthia, Christina. Supr., Ernst & Ernst, C.P.A.'s, Louisville, 1950-60; exec. v.p., treas., dir. Ohio Valley Aluminum Co., Inc., Shelbyville, Ky., 1960—. Served with USNR, 1943-46. C.P.A., Ky. Mem. Ky. State Bd. Accountancy, Ky. Soc. C.P.A.'s. Home: 3430 Pemaquid Rd Louisville KY 40218 Office: Indsl Park Shelbyville KY 40065

KELTON, ELMER STEPHEN, mag. editor; b. Andrews, Tex., Apr. 29, 1926; s. Robert William and Neta Beatrice (Parker) K.; B.A., U. Tex., 1947; m. Anna Lipp, July 3, 1947; children—Gary, Stephen Lee, Kathryn. Agrl. editor San Angelo (Tex.) Standard-Times, 1948-63; editor Sheep and Goat Raiser Mag., San Angelo, 1963-68; asso. editor West Tex. Livestock Weekly, San Angelo, 1968—. Served with AUS, 1944-46. Recipient Spur award Western Writers Am., 1957, 72. Mem. Western Writers Am. (pres. 1962-63), Sigma Delta Chi. Methodist. Elk. Author: The Day the Cowboys Quit, 1971; others. Home: 2460 Oxford St San Angelo TX 76901 Office: 2601 Sherwood Way, San Angelo TX 76901

KEMMERER, WALTER WILLIAM, JR., physician, govt. ofcl.; b. Houston, May 6, 1931; s. Walter William and Helen Martha (Eckerstein) K.; B.S., U. Houston, 1954; M.D., Baylor U., 1959; M.P.H., Harvard, 1964; m. Florence Louise Bozon, Aug. 12, 1952; children—Walter William, Carolyn, Katherine, Marianne, Christopher, Eric. Intern, Jefferson Davis Hosp., Houston, 1959-60; with exptl. medicine sect. NASA Manned Spacecraft Center, Houston, 1964-66, chief biomed. spltys. br., 1966-69, asst. mgr. lunar receiving lab., 1966—, chief preventive medicine div., 1969—; clin. asso. prof. community medicine Baylor U., Waco, Tex; adj. asso. prof. preventive medicine U. Tex. at Houston. Vice-pres., Clear Creek ind. sch. dist. bd. trustees, 1968—. Served with M.C., AUS, 1960-63. Decorated NASA Exceptional Service medal, 1969. Mem. Am. Pub. Health Assn. Home: 1905 E Main St League City TX 77573 Office: Le Marque TX 77568

KEMP, HUBERT O., city ofcl. Police chief, Nashville. Address: City Hall Nashville TN 37201*

KEMP, LAMAR ELLIOTT, lawyer; b. Atlanta, Dec. 5, 1912; s. Thomas Ardell and Rosalie (Elliott) K.; A.B., U. Ga., 1936; LL.B., Atlanta Law Sch., 1946; M.A., U. Md., 1960; m. Willise Carter, Oct. 5, 1940 (dec. Oct. 1961); children—Carolyn Clyde, Barbara Lamar. With advt. dept. Atlanta Constn., 1936-40, 49-50; with pub. relations dept. Atlantic Steel Co., 1940-43; in personnel and pub. relations U.S. Civil Service Commn., Atlanta, 1943-46; admitted to Ga. bar, 1946, U.S. Supreme Ct. bar, 1953, D.C. bar, 1955; information specialist Hdqrs. 7th Army, Atlanta, 1946-47; cons. So. Pub. Relations Inst., Atlanta, 1947-48; atty. Nat. Labor Relations Bd., Atlanta, 1948-49; editor Ga. Petroleum Retailer, Atlanta, 1950; information specialist, historian Hdqrs., Air Force Armament Center, Eglin, AFB, Fla., 1951-52; personnel-pub. relations PRNC Bd. Civil Service Examiners, Washington, 1952-56; adminstrv. and Personnel-pub. relations Hdqrs. AFSC also 459th TCW, Balt. and Washington, 1956-62; information officer Bur. Fed. Credit Unions, U.S. Dept. Health Edn. and Welfare, Washington, 1962-65; lawyer, pub. relations counsel, manpower utilization cons., 1965—; TCA tax counsel, 1972—. Faculty communications law Am. U., 1960-61. Pres., Murray Hill Citizens Assn., 1963-64; v.p. Indian Head Hwy. Area Action Council; 1964-65; co-founder, treas. So. Prince Georges County Congress Civic Assns., 1963-64; founder, pres. Oxon Hill (Md.) Recreation and Cultural Council, 1964-71, v.p., 1971—. Trustee Forest Heights (Md.) Elementary Sch., 1953-56; bd. dirs. Prince Georges Citizens Planning Assn., 1965—. Mem. Am., Fed., Inter-Am. bar assns., Am. Soc. for Internat. Law, Prince Georges County Citizens Polit. Action Assn., Fed. Profl. Assn., Soc. Personnel Adminstrn., Ga. State Soc. Washington (dir. pub. relations 1965—), Internat. Platform Assn., Delta Theta Phi. Democrat. Methodist. Club: Oxon Hill (Md.) Methodist Men's (pres. 1954-56). Home: 8000 Carey Branch Pl Oxon Hill MD 20022

KEMP, LYSANDER SCHAFFER, editor; b. Randolph, Vt., Nov. 13, 1920; s. Lysander Schaffer and Dorothy Burnton (Schontag) K.; B.A., Bates Coll., 1942; M.A., Boston U., 1946. Instr. English, U. Buffalo, 1946-50, asst. prof., 1950-53; writer, Spanish translator, Jocotepec, Mexico, 1953-59, Guadalajara, 1959-65; editor, U. Tex. Press, Austin, 1966—. Served with AUS, 1942-45. Rockefeller Found. grantee, 1960-61. Democrat. Author: The Northern Stranger, 1946; The Conquest, 1971. Translator 8 books. Home: 814 E 30th St Austin TX 78705

KEMP, WILLIAM JAMES, dentist; b. Tulsa, July 17, 1923; s. Johnny Giles and Mary (Blackman) K.; student U. Tex., 1941-43; D.D.S., U. Mo. at Kansas City, 1949; m. Billie Jean Viereck, Nov. 12, 1944; children—William James, Kemberly Kay. Individual practice dentistry, Haskell, Tex., 1949—; chief dental service Haskell County Meml. Hosp., 1949—; mem. staffs Stamford Meml. Hosp., Throckmorton Meml. Hosp., Knox County Meml. Hosp., Aspermont Hosp. Pres. Tex. Bd. Dental Examiners, 1968-69, 72-73. Dist. exec. Chisholm Trail council Boy Scouts Am., 1954—. Bd. dirs. Rice Springs Cave Home for Aged, Haskell, pres., 1964—. Served as aviation cadet AAC, 1943-45. Recipient award Am. Soc. Dentistry for Children, 1944, Silver Beaver award Boy Scouts Am., 1971. Fellow Am. Coll. Dentists; mem. Am. Dental Assn., West Tex. (pres. 1954, sec.-treas. 1964—), 17th Dist. (pres. 1952) dental socs., Am. Acad. Dentistry, Pierre Fauchard Acad., Am. Legion (post comdr. 1955), Haskell C. of C., Haskell Band Booster Club, Omicron Kappa Upsilon (hon.). Methodist (steward 1949—). Mason, Odd Fellow, Lion (pres. Haskell 1954). Home: 910 N Av H Haskell TX 79521 Office: 1404 N 1st St Haskell TX 79521

KEMPNER, HARRIS LEON, business exec.; b. Galveston, Tex., Oct. 6, 1903; s. I. H. and Henrietta (Blum) K.; B.A. cum laude, Harvard, 1924; m. Ruth Alma Levy, Apr. 24, 1939; children—Harris Leon, Marion Lee (killed in action). Chmn. exec. com., dir. Imperial Sugar Co., 1954—, also chmn. Emeritus bd.; chmn. bd. U.S. Nat. Bank, Galveston, Schwaback, Kempner & Perutz, N.Y.C., Dallas, Galveston; trustee H. Kempner, Sugar Land Industries. Mem., past dir. New Orleans Cotton Exchange. Served as comdr. USNR, 1942-45. Decorated Legion of Merit. Mem. Galveston C. of C. (past v.p., dir.), Texas Cotton Assn. (past pres.), Am. Cotton Shippers Assn. (past pres.). Clubs: Artillery, Quarterdeck (Galveston); Harvard (N.Y.C.). Home: 4810 Denver Dr Galveston TX Office: US Nat Bank Bldg Galveston TX

KEMPTER, RUDOLPH HARBISON, JR., govt. ofcl.; b. St. Albans, Vt., Sept. 5, 1922; s. Rudolph Harbison and Marjorie (Prentiss) K.; B.S. in Engring., U. Notre Dame, 1948; postgrad. in bus. adminstrn. U. Cal. at Berkeley, 1949; m. Margaret Ann Gilkinson, Oct. 15, 1950; children— Carlton J., Bryan C., Paul C. Apprentice engr. Grumman Aircraft Engring. Corp., Bethpage, N.Y., 1942-43; test engr. U.S. Navy Indsl. Plant, Pomona, Cal., 1958-62; rocket devel. engr. Aero-jet Gen. Corp., Azusa, Cal., 1954-57; missile system program mgr. Navy Dept., Washington, 1962-66; dep. dir. value engring. Office Sec. Def., Washington, 1966—. Staff lectr. Schs. Engring., George Washington U., 1968—, Va. Poly. Inst., 1969—, Va. Mil. Inst., 1969—; doctoral adviser George Washington U. Grad. Sch. Bus. Adminstrn., 1970—. Served with USNR, 1943-46; PTO; 1950-54; Korea. Recipient certificate commendation Asst. Sec. of Def., 1969; certificate of merit for cost reduction achievement U.S. Navy, 1966. Mem. Soc. Am. Value Engrs. (officer), Sigma Phi. Presbyn. Contbr. numerous articles on tech. mgmt. and value engring. to tech. jours. Home: 1616 Chain Bridge Rd McLean VA 22101 Office: Pentagon Washington DC 20301

KEMPTHORNE, RICHARD LEWIS, constrn. industry exec.; b. Orange, N.J., Jan. 7, 1927; s. James Lewis and Eleanor (McKelvey) K.; Asso. Bus. Adminstrn., Nichols Coll., 1949; B.S., Syracuse U., 1951; m. Alice Clair Prost, Feb. 26, 1949; children—James Lewis III, Ann. Vice pres. Sprayed Insulation Inc., Newark, 1951-53; head Columbia Acoustics & Fireproofing Co., Stanhope, N.J., 1954-56; chief exec., sec.-treas. Fla. Insulation & Fireproofing Co., Miami, 1957-65; pres., dir. Sprayed Fibers, Inc., Miami, 1963-71, Spraydon Overseas Corp., Miami, 1966-71; v.p. Tex. Fireproofing Co., Houston, 1960-63; v.p., dir. Sprayon Research Corp., Ft. Lauderdale, Fla., 1964—; pres., dir. Midwest Sprayon Corp., Miami, 1966-71, pres., dir. Sprayon Internat. Inc., N.Y.C.; acoustical cons. Mem. bd. elections Young Republicans of Miami, 1958—. Pres. Miami Shores Prep. Sch., 1968—. Served with USNR, 1944-46. Mem. Am. Soc. Testing Materials, Nat. Fireprotection Assn., Internat. Assn. Walls and Ceilings Contractors, Amateur Athletic Union. Clubs: Miami Shores Country (pres. swimming assn. 1964-67); Palm-Aire Country. Patentee in field. Address: 5701 Bayview Dr Fort Lauderdale FL 33308

KENAN, FRANK HAWKINS, water co. exec.; b. Atlanta, Aug. 3, 1912; s. Thomas Stephen and Annice Reed (Hawkins) K.; B.S., U. N.C., 1935; m. Elizabeth Price, May 22, 1966; children—Thomas, Owen, Elizabeth, Anne. Pres. Kenan Oil Co., Durham, N.C., 1936—, Kenan Transport Co., Durham, 1942—, West Palm Beach (Fla.) Water Co., 1965—, Flagler System, Palm Beach, Fla., 1971; dir. Central Carolina Bank & Trust Co., Durham. Durham County Commr., 1952-64. Trustee Durham County Hosp. Served to lt. USNR, 1942-45. Kiwanian. Clubs: Hope Valley Country (Durham); Country of N.C. (Pinehurst). Home: 3900 Dover Rd Durham NC 27705 Office: Hillsboro Rd Durham NC 27705

KENDALL, HENRY ELI, state ofcl; b. Shelby, N.C., Aug. 24, 1905; s. Henry E. and Mary (Wiseman) K.; B.S. in Civil Engring., N.C. State Coll., 1926; m. Katharine Kerr, June 21, 1947. Engr., Plumer & Wiseman Co., Danville, Va., 1926-30; asst. office mgr. Dibrell Bros., Shanghai, China, 1930-36; chief operation plants N.C. Sch. Commn., Raleigh, 1937-42; chmn. N.C. Employment Security Commn., Raleigh, 1946—. Mem. Gov.'s Com. Employment Handicapped, 1962—, Com. Aging, 1956—, Com. Refugee Relief, 1957-67, Pres.'s Com. Employment Handicapped, 1957—, Bur. Vet. Re-employment Rights, 1950-66; spl. cons. European manpower conditions U.S. Dept. Labor, 1963; bd. dirs. N.C. Manpower Devel. Corp., State Employees Credit Union; adv. council N.C. Com. Children and Youth; adv. com. State Tech. Services; exec. com. Gov.'s Council Econ. Devel. Served from 1st lt. to lt. col. C.E., AUS, 1942-46. Recipient Outstanding Service commendation Pres.'s Com. Employment Handicapped, 1965, also certificate of appreciation, 1967; Outstanding Service award V.F.W., 1966. Mem. Internat. Assn. Personnel in Employment Securities (recipient merit award 1968), Interstate Conf. Employment Security Agys. (pres. 1953, 62, mem. legislative com. 1969-70, mem. com. conf. constn. and code 1969-70), Raleigh Engrs. Club, N.C. Soc. Engrs., Am. Legion (chmn. N.C. resolutions com. 1956—), V.F.W., N.C. State U. Gen. Alumni Assn. (v.p. 1948, pres. 1949), Phi Kappa Phi, Pi Kappa Alpha, Tau Beta Pi, Theta Tau. Presbyn. Mason, Lion. Home: 2814 Exeter Circle Raleigh NC 27608 Office: Caswell Bldg Jones and McDowell St Raleigh NC 27611

KENDALL, WILLIAM HERSEY, r.r. exec.; b. Somerville, Mass., Mar. 24, 1910; s. Warren C. and Helen (Hodgkins) K.; A.B., Dartmouth, 1932; C.E., Thayer Sch. Civil Engring., 1933; m. Lucile W. Hayworth, Oct. 31, 1935; children—Roberta, William Thomas, James (dec.). Maintenance engr. Pa. R.R., 1933-48; exec. officer A.C.L. R.R., 1948-50, Clinchfield R.R., 1950-54, exec. officer L. & N. R.R., 1954—; v.p., gen. mgr., 1957-59, pres., 1959-72; vice chmn. Seaboard Coast Line Industries, 1972—, also dir., dir. Anaconda Co., N.Y.C., Capital Holding Co., Louisville, Commonwealth Life Ins. Co., Louisville, Hillerich & Bradsby Co., Louisville, Hercules, Inc., Wilmington, Del., Third Nat. Bank of Nashville, Citizens Fidelity Bank & Trust Co., Louisville. Trustee U. Louisville. Bd. dirs. Meth. Hosp. Mem. Am. Soc. Traffic and Transp., Alpha Tau Omega. Clubs: Louisville Country, Pendennis. Home: 6602 Deep Creek Dr Prospect KY 40059 Office: 110 E Market St Louisville KY 40202

KENDERDINE, JAMES MARSHALL, educator; b. Washington, May 12, 1941; s. John Marshall and Su Anne (Carroll) K.; student Duke, 1959-64; B.S., Ind. U., 1965, M.B.A., 1967, D.B.A. (Am. Marketing Assn. fellow, Gen. Electric Research fellow), 1970; m. Nancy Sloan Ingram, Aug. 25, 1964; 1 son, James Adams. Teaching asso. Ind. U. at Bloomington, 1966-69; asst. prof. marketing Okla. U. at Norman, 1969—. Cons. econs. Oklahoma City Urban League, 1970—. Chmn. United Fund, Okla. U., 1970, 71. Mem. Am. Marketing Assn., Am. Mgmt. Assn., Am. Mensa Soc. (pres. central Okla. chpt. 1969-71), U.S. Naval Inst., Theta Chi, Beta Gamma Sigma, Omicron Delta Kappa. Lion. Home: 814 Jona Kay Terrace Norman OK 73069

KENDERDINE, JOHN MARSHALL, mfg. co. exec.; b. Ft. Worth, Dec. 6, 1912; s. Robert Leonard and Caroline (Raab) K.; B.S. in Petroleum Engring., Tex. A. and M. Coll., 1934; grad. Army War Coll., 1953, Advanced Mgmt. Program, Harvard, 1959, Exec. Decision Inst., 1962; m. Su Anne Carroll, Feb. 26, 1937; children—James Marshall, Su Carroll (Mrs. Henry F. Hain III). Petroleum engr. Gulf Oil Corp., 1934-37; br. mgr. Norvell-Wilder Supply Co., Midland, Tex., 1938-41; commd. 1st lt. U.S. Army, 1941, advanced through grades to brig. gen., 1962; mil. logistician in France, Germany and U.S., World War II; spl. asst. to adminstr. War Assets Adminstrn., 1946; mil. staff and command assignments, 1947-60; joint petroleum officer Europe, 1961; exec. dir. supply operations Def. Supply Agy., 1962-65; comdr. Def. Indsl. Supply Center, Phila., 1965-66, Def. Personnel Support Center, Phila., 1966-67; ret., 1967; v.p. spl. tech. Scott Paper Co., Phila., 1967-70; pres. C.F. Adams, Inc., Fort Worth, 1970—. Mem. Phila. Edn. Council. Decorated D.S.M., Legion of Merit, Joint Service Commendation medal, Commendation ribbon with 3 oak leaf clusters. Registered profl. engr., Tex. Mem. Soc. Logistics Engrs., Def. Supply Assn., Assn. U.S. Army, Airline Passengers Assn. (adv. bd.), Phila. C. of C. (dir. 1966). Club: Airways. Contbr. articles on handling and safety of aviation fuels, especially turbine fuels, to profl. jours. Home: 3212 Chapparal Lane Fort Worth TX 76109 Office: Box 253 Fort Worth TX 76101

KENDIG, PERRY FRIDY, coll. pres.; b. Mountville, Pa., July 7, 1910; s. Calvin Miles and Blanche (Fridy) K.; A.B., Franklin and Marshall Coll., 1932; A.M., U. Pa., 1936, Ph.D., 1947; m. Virginia Gantt, Apr. 17, 1947; children—Beth Roberts, John Gantt, William Calvin. Prin. East Drumore Twp. High Sch., Lancaster County, Pa., 1932-34; asst. instr. English, U. Pa., 1936-38; spl. instr. English, Drexel U., 1937-38; from instr. to prof., head dept. English, dean students Muhlenberg Coll., 1938-52; prof. English, Roanoke Coll., 1952—, dean coll., 1952-63, pres., 1963—. Dir. Salem brs. 1st Nat. Exchange Bank Va. Adv. bd. Roanoke YWCA. Served with USNR, 1942-46, lt. comdr. ret. Mem. Modern Lang. Assn. Am., Am. Assn. U. Profs., Va. Soc. Ornithology, Nat. Audubon Soc., Roanoke Valley Bird Club, English-Speaking Union (br. dir.), Roanoke Symphony Soc. (pres. 1966-68, dir.), Newcomen Soc. N.Am., Hawk Mountain Sanctuary Assn., Blue Key, Phi Beta Kappa, Phi Sigma Kappa, Omicron Delta Kappa, Eta Sigma Phi, Alpha Kappa Alpha, Alpha Psi Omega, Tau Kappa Alpha. Lutheran (exec. bd. Va. Synod, Luth. Ch. Am.). Clubs: Commonwealth (Richmond, Va.); University (N.Y.C., Washington); Shenandoah, Phi Beta Kappa of Roanoke Area (past pres.) (Roanoke, Va.); Torch (past pres. Roanoke Valley); Town (Salem, Va.); Faculty of U. Pa. (Phila.). Author: Trinity Reformed Church: an Historical Sketch, 1938; The Poems of St. Columban Translated into English Verse, 1949; Some Notes on a Little Known American Novel: The Prisoners of Niagara or Errors of Edn., 1910 by Jesse Lynch Holman, 1956. Home: 535 Market St Salem VA 24153

KENDREW, A(LBERT) EDWIN, architect; b. Compton County, P.Q., Can., June 24, 1903; s. Albert and Minnie (Bowen) K.; brought to U.S., 1917, naturalized, 1935; student Northeastern U., 1920-22; certificate archtl. constrn., Wentworth Inst., Boston, 1924; student Boston Archtl. Club-Atelier, 1926-29; m. Melinda R. Ide, June 23, 1928; children—Nancy Hale (Mrs. Herbert E. Bell), Lois Rockwood (Mrs. L. A. Caporal). With F. A. Norcross, architect, Boston, 1923-26. Perry, Shaw & Hepburn, architects, Boston, 1926-34; resident architect Colonial Williamsburg (Va.), 1934-43, v.p., 1943-57, sr. v.p., dir. archtl. constrn. and maintenance, 1957-65, sr. v.p., dir. long-range planning, 1965-68; ret.; dir. Strawberry Banke, Inc., Nauvoo Restoration, Inc. Chmn. Williamsburg Planning Commn.; past chmn. Va. Art Commn. Bd. dirs. Chesapeake Bay Maritime Museum. Fellow A.I.A.; mem. Thornton Soc., Nat. Trust for Historic Preservation, Newcomen Soc. Home: 9 Bayberry Lane Williamsburg VA 23185

KENDRICK, AUBREY EARL, JR., furniture mfg. co. exec.; b. Tampa, Fla., June 6, 1934; s. Aubrey Earl and Avis (Bernard) K.; student U.N.C., 1951-53; m. Susan C. Forgette, Sept. 15, 1956; children—Aubrey Earl III, Tracy T., Susan A. Salesman, Sumter Cabinet Co. (S.C.), 1956—; v.p., dir. Newton Mfrs. Co., Hickory, N.C., 1963-65; sec.-treas., dir. Lincoln Hall, Hickory, 1966—; pres., dir. Wood Products Internat. Inc., Charlotte, N.C., 1968—; v.p. D. & J. Maintenance & Supply Inc., Atlanta; dir. Reliable Frame Co., Hickory, 1963-68. Served with AUS, 1953-56.Address: 2701 Pencoyd Lane Charlotte NC 28210

KENNA, EDGAR DOUGLAS, assn. exec.; b. Summit, Miss., Nov. 27, 1894; s. W. B., Sr. and Sarah (Wilson) K.; B.A., Miss. Coll., 1920; LL.B., Cumberland U., 1924; m. Norma Carruth, June 9, 1921; children— Edgar Douglas, Jr., Martha Lynn (Mrs. White). Banker, Jackson, Miss., 1924-32; dir. Miss. Hwy. Dept., Jackson, 1932-45; dir. highway dept., Miss.-Ala. Div. Mid-Continent Oil and Gas Assn., Jackson; now exec. dir. Miss. Council on Aging. Mem. C. of C. Baptist (deacon). Club: Rotary. Home: 3625 Crane Blvd Jackson MS 39216 Office: Dale Bldg Box 5136 Jackson MS 39216

KENNAMER, HAL JACOB, govt. ofcl.; b. Greenbrier, Ark., May 19, 1910; s. Zachary T. and Nancy Adaline (Jordan) K.; B.S., State Coll. Ark., 1941; M.S., U. Ark., 1949; m. Lucille Love, Aug. 25, 1930; children— Joan (Mrs. Charles Lee Dean), William Earl. Tchr. rural schs., Faulkner County, Ark., 1930-38; rural sch. prin. Cross County,

Ark., 1938-40; prin. high sch., Pulaski County, 1943-44, Crossett, Ark., 1944-46; supt. Hamburg, Ark., 1946-48, Paris (Ark.) Schs., 1948-68; program specialist, region 7, U.S. Office Edn., Dallas, 1968—. Mem. Nat., Ark. edn. assns., Am. Assn. Sch. Adminstrs., Phi Delta Kappa, Kappa Delta Pi, Phi Alpha Theta. Democrat. Baptist. Kiwanian. Home: 2612 Monticello Dr Mesquite TX 75149 Office: US Office Edn 1114 Commerce St Dallas TX 75202

KENNAMER, KENNETH ROBERT, newspaper editor; b. Royse City, Tex., Aug. 25, 1931; s. Ovid Arlee and Mary (Shook) K.; student Kilgore Coll., 1948-50; B.A., N. Tex. State U., 1956; m. Joycelyne Hendry, May 4, 1957; children—Alison Diane, Kimberly Ann. Sports writer Longview Jour., 1947-48; athletic publicity dir. Kilgore Coll., 1948-50; reporter Texarkana Gazette, 1950-51, Lubbock Avalanche, 1956-57; reporter San Antonio Express, 1957-59, city editor, 1959-68, asst. mng. editor, 1968-69, mng. editor, 1969—. Instr. journalism St. Mary's U., San Antonio, 1960-62. Served with CIC, AUS, 1952-54. Home: 204 Wisteria St San Antonio TX 78213 Office: San Antonio Express Av E and 3d St San Antonio TX 78206

KENNAMER, LORRIN GARFIELD, JR., coll. dean; b. Abilene, Tex., Dec. 20, 1924; s. Lorrin Garfield and Ruie Lee (Hart) K.; A.B., Eastern Ky. State Coll., Richmond, 1947; M.S., U. Tenn., 1949; Ph.D., George Peabody Coll., 1952; m. Laura Helen Durham, Dec. 22, 1948. Tchr., Oak Ridge High Sch., 1947-49; from instr. to asso. prof., chmn. dept. geography and geology E. Tex. State Coll., Commerce, 1952-56; mem. faculty U. Tex., 1956-67, prof. geography, 1961-67, chmn. dept., 1961-67, asso. dean arts and scis., 1961-67; dean of arts and scis. Tex. Technol. Coll., 1967-70; dean coll. Edn. U. Tex., Austin, 1970— vis. summer prof. U. Vt., 1959, Mich. State U., 1961; vis. prof. U. Wash., summer 1967. Bd. examiners Tex. Edn. Agy., 1964-72; com. exams. Coll. Entrance Exam. Bd., 1965-72. Served to lt (j.g.) USNR, World War II. Hon. life fellow Tex. Acad. Sci. (bd. dirs. 1957-61); mem. Nat. Council Geog. Edn. (exec. bd. 1958-65, sec. 1958-64, 2d v.p. 1965, pres. 1967), Assn. Am. Geographers (exec. council 1962-64), Southwestern Social Sci. Assn. (pres. 1972-73), Am. Geog. Soc., Sigma Xi, Omicron Delta Kappa, Pi Gamma Mu, Phi Delta Kappa, Phi Kappa Phi. Unitarian. Author: (with Bowden and Hoffman) Geography Worktext Series, 1960; (with S. Arbingast) Atlas of Texas, 1963, revised 1967; (with W. Chambers) Texans and Their Land, 1964; (with J. Reese) Texas: Land of Contrast, 1972. Home: 5902 B Mountain Climb Dr Austin TX 78731

KENNEALLY, JOSEPH THOMAS, corp. exec.; b. Mpls., July 31, 1926; s. Joseph Thomas and Olga Loraine (Halverson) K.; B.A. in Econs., U. Minn., 1949, M.A. in Internat. Law and Internat. Econs., 1950; m. Patricia Jane Steele, May 14, 1955; children—Joseph Thomas III, Timothy Dominic, Stephen John, Patricia Jane, Matthew Paul, Michael Terence. With No. Trust Co., Chgo., 1952-54; asst. to sr. partner E.F. Hutton & Co., N.Y.C., 1954-57; v.p. F.W. Richmond & Co., N.Y.C., 1957-59; exec. v.p. Houston Oil Field Material Co., Inc., 1959-60, chmn., chief exec. Internat. Systems & Control Corp., Black, Sivalls & Bryson, Inc.; chmn. J.F. Pritchard & Co. (Del.), Lang Engring. Ltd., Pritchard-Rhodes Ltd.; pres., dir. Oil Equipment Ltd., Calgary, Alta., Can.; gen. partner Kenro & Co., N.Y.C.; dir. Houston Citizens Bank & Trust Co., Adela Ltd., A. G. & P. Ltd. Bd. dirs. Petroleum Equipment Suppliers Assn. Served to capt. AUS, 1944-48, 50-52. Mem. Phi Beta Kappa. Roman Catholic. Home: 2208 Brentwood St Houston TX 77019 Office: 2727 Allen Pkwy Houston TX 77001

KENNEDY, BENNIE EUGENE, supt. schs.; b. Winnsboro, Tex., Dec. 13, 1919; s. William D. and Ruby Mae (Harrison) K.; B.S., Panhandle State Coll., Goodwell, Okla., 1949; M.S., Western State Coll., Gunnison, Colo., 1953; m. Mary A. Johnson, Aug. 9, 1949; children— Deborah, Kim. Football coach Tipton (Okla.) High Sch., 1949-55; jr. and sr. high sch. prin., Tipton, 1955-66; supt. schs., Grandfield, Okla., 1966—. Served with USAAF, 1942-45. Mem. N.E.A., Okla. (S.W. dist. rep. 1964), Tillman County (pres. 1964) edn. assns., Nat., Okla., Tillmann County sch. adminstrs. assns., Grandfield C. of C. (dir.). Methodist. Mason; mem. Order Eastern Star, Kiwanian. Home: 209 E 2d St Grandfield OK 73546

KENNEDY, CLEPHANE ARNOT, univ. pres.; b. N.Y.C., Feb. 20, 1897; d. Frank Clephane and Martha (Smith) Arnot; student Northfield Sem., N.Y.U., George Washington U.; B.C.S., Benjamin Franklin U., 1934; m. John Thomas Kennedy III, 1921 (dec. July 1958); 1 dau., Marthajane. Founding mem. bd. Benjamin Franklin U., 1925, sec., 1943-58, pres., 1958—. Organizer, mem. bd. Friday Morning Music Club Nat. Found., 1946—; mem. Commrs. Adv. Council on Higher Edn. Recipient citation for war service Pres. U.S., 1946. Mem. League Republican Women (v.p. 1947-49), Am. Judicature Soc., Acad. Polit. Sci., Am. Assn. Accounting, Soc. Four Arts (Palm Beach, Fla.), N.E.A. (life), D.C. Council Adminstrv. Women Edn., Am. Assn. Specialized Colls. (charter; trustee). Republican. Presbyn. Clubs: Sesamee Imperial (London); Washington, Univ. Arts (Washington); Soroptimist. Home: Arkenderry 3820 Reno Rd Washington DC 20008 Office: 1100 16th St Washington DC 20006

KENNEDY, CORNELIUS BRYANT, lawyer; b. Evanston, Ill., Apr. 13, 1921; s. Millard Bryant and Myrna (Anderson) K.; A.B., Yale, 1943; J.D., Harvard, 1948; m. Anne Martha Reynolds, June 20, 1959; children—Anne Talbot, Lauren Asher. Admitted to Ill. bar, 1949, D.C. bar, 1965; practiced in Chgo., 1949-54, 55-59, Washington, 1965—; sr. mem. firm Kennedy & Leighton, Washington, 1965—; asst. U.S. atty., Chgo., 1954-55; counsel to minority leader U.S. Senate, Washington, 1959-65. Pub. mem. Adminstrv. Conf. U.S. Past trustee St. Johns Child Devel. Center, Washington. Served with USAAF, 1943-46. Mem. Am. (chmn. adminstrv. conf. com.), Fed., Chgo. bar assns. Clubs: Gibson Island (Md.); F Street, Metropolitan, Capitol Hill (Washington); Adventurers (Chgo.). Contbr. articles in field to profl. jours. Home: 7720 Old Georgetown Pike McLean VA 22101 Office: 888 17th St NW Washington DC 20006

KENNEDY, DAVID M., govt. ofcl., banker; b. Randolph, Utah, July 21, 1905; s. George and Katherine (Johnson) K.; A.B., Weber Coll., Ogden, Utah, 1928; A.M., George Washington U., 1935, LL.B., 1937; grad. Sch. Banking, Rutgers U., 1939; m. Lenora Bingham, Nov. 4, 1925; children—Marilyn, Barbara Ann, Carol Joyce, Patricia Lenore. Mem. of staff bd. govs. Fed. Res. System, 1930-46, serving successfully as tech asst., div. bank operations, economist div. research and statistics, spl. asst. to chmn. bd. govs.; became v.p. bond dept. Continental Ill. Nat. Bank & Trust Co., Chgo., 1946, v.p., 1954-56, dir.-pres., 1956-59, chmn. bd., chief exec. officer, 1959-69; asst. to sec. U.S. Treasury, 1953-54; sec. U.S. Treasury, 1969-71; U.S. ambassador-at-large, mem. cabinet; Council on Internat. Econs. Policy, 1971—; U.S. permanent rep. to NATO, 1972—; dir. Internat. Harvester Corp., Commonwealth Edison Co., Pullman Co., Abbott Labs., ADELA Corp., Swift & Co., U.S. Gypsum Co., Communications Satellite Corp., Nauvoo Restoration, Inc.; trustee Equitable Ia., Savs. & Profit Sharing Pension Fund Sears Roebuck & Co., Employees, chmn. exec. bd. Com. Econ. and Cultural Devel. Chgo.; vice chmn. Chgo. Clearing House Assn. Trustee Presbyn.-St. Luke's Hosp., Chgo., U. Chgo., Brookings Instn., Com. Econ. Devel., George Washington U.; dir. Radio N.Y. Worldwide. Mem. Am. Bankers Assn., Council Latin Am. (trustee), Assn. Res. City Bankers, Com. Econ. Devel. (trustee), Pi Gamma Mu. Mem. Ch. Jesus Christ of Latter-day Saints. Clubs: Bankers University, Union League, Chicago, Mid America, Commercial, Executives (Chgo.); Old Elm Country (Ft. Sheridan, Ill.); Glenview Country. Home: 33 Meadow View Dr Northfield IL 60093 Office: State Dept Washington DC 20220

KENNEDY, DAVID T., mayor; b. Balt., Apr. 7, 1934; s. Howard N. and Nancy (Davies) K.; M. Pub. Adminstrn., Fla. State U.; J.D., U. Miami (Fla.), 1958; m. Lynda de Gibaja, July 10, 1970; 1 son, David T. Pres. Research and Devel. Corp.; mem. Miami City Commr., 1961-71; Miami; mayor, Miami, 1971—. Vol. United Fund, Miami; chmn. Dade County (Fla.) chpt. Nat. Multiple Sclerosis Soc., Speakers Bur. Dade County unit Am. Cancer Soc.; Fla. chmn. Christmas Toy Fund for Mentally Retarded Children in State Instns.; pres. Big Bros. Greater Miami; chmn. Downtown Devel. Authority; mem. Inter-Am. Center Authority, Factory Built Housing Council Fla., Gov.'s Council Criminal Justice; mem. Urban Econ. Policy Com. U.S. Conf. Mayors; mem. investment com. Miami City Employees Retirement System and Plan. Pres. Dade County Young Democrats; Fla. state coordinator Citizens for Kennedy-Johnson com., 1960; asst. to state chmn. Fla. Johnson campaign com., 1964; state finance chmn. campaign Gov. Askew, 1970; city commr., Miami, 1960-70, vice mayor, then acting mayor, 1970. Bd. advisers Fla. State U. Found.; bd. dirs. Haven Sch., St. Luke's Center, Hope Sch.; bd. dirs. Greater Miami Traffic Assn.; trustee, mem. exec. com. Greater Miami Coalition. Recipient C.L. Brown trial award U. Miami; named nat. alumnus of year Fla. State U., 1966; recipient award Fla. South chpt. A.I.A., Latin Polit. Com. for service to Latin community, Exchange Club Miami for work for Haven Sch. Mentally Retarded, others. Mem. Dade County (pres.), Fla. (dir.) leagues cities, Soc. Wig and Robe, Fla. State U. Alumni Assn. (nat. dir.), Omicron Delta Kappa. Mason (Shriner), Moose, Kiwanian. Home: 8510 NE 10th Av Miami FL 33138 Office: 3500 Pan American Dr Miami FL 33133 also Suite 2906 Biscayne Tower 120 Biscayne Blvd North Miami FL 33161

KENNEDY, DONALD CALVIN, communications exec.; b. Beaver, Pa., Mar. 2, 1930; s. C.H. and Bertha (Schroeder) K.; B.S., Geneva Coll., 1953; m. Margaret Graff, Sept. 2, 1950; 1 dau., Rebecca Lynn. Staff announcer WPIC, Sharon, Pa., 1947-48, WBVP, Beaver Falls, Pa., 1948-53; newscaster, childrens personality WSB-TV, Atlanta, 1955-69; mgr., pres., dir. Kenco Music, Inc., 1958-64; mgr. WKLS Radio, Atlanta, 1960—; pres., chmn. Kenco Broadcasting, Inc., Kenco Prodns., Inc. Pres., Muscular Dystrophy Assn. Atlanta. Bd. dirs. Atlanta Humane Soc. Served with AUS, 1953-55. Recipient Honor citation Muscular Dystrophy, 1969; named Young Man of Year, DeKalb County Jr. C. of C., 1963. Mem. Ga. Assn. Broadcasters (dir.), Di Gamma Kappa. Home: 1396 Oak Grove Dr Decatur GA 30033 Office: 1655 Peachtree Rd NE Atlanta GA 30309

KENNEDY, DONALD SIPE, electric utility exec.; b. Rushville, Ind., Jan. 5, 1902; s. Jesse Barnes and Florence (Sipe) K.; student Butler U., 1919-21; A.B., U. Ariz., 1923, LL.D., 1960; LL.D., Oklahoma City U., 1958, Butler U., 1960, Bethany Nazarene Coll., 1967; m. Gertrude Hacker, Aug. 17, 1927; 1 dau., Donna Lee (Mrs. Thomas E. Vogel). Clk., Okla. Gas & Electric Co., 1923, various positions, 1923-28, eastern div. auditor, Muskogee office, 1928-40, asst. treas., main office, 1940-42, treas., v.p. dir., 1942, exec. v.p., 1948, pres., 1949-66, chmn. bd., 1966—; pres. Okla. Industries, Inc., 1952-54; dir. Village Bank of Oklahoma City, M.-K.-T. R.R., Katy Industries. Chmn. U.S. Nat. com. World Power Conf. Pres. Community Chest, 1946-48; civilian aide to sec. army of Okla. Chmn. Okla. State Regents for Higher Edn. Mem. Edison Electric Inst. (pres. 1956-57, dir.), N.A.M. (dir. 1959-62), Oklahoma City C. of C. (pres. 1954), Assn. Edison Illuminating Cos. (pres. 1966), Phi Delta Theta. Episcopalian. Mason (32 1/2). Home: 6616 N Hillcrest St Oklahoma City OK 73116 Office: 321 N Harvey St Oklahoma City OK 73102

KENNEDY, EDWARD JAMES, civil engr.; b. Akron, O., May 22, 1918; s. John Francis and Mary (Appelget) K.; student Balt. Poly Inst., 1931-35; B.S., U. Md., 1938; m. Alice Anne Noon, Jan. 12, 1942; children— Patricia, John F., Joan, Edward James, Bairbre, Robert H. Engr. water resources div. U.S. Geol. Survey, 1938—, dist. engr., Topeka, 1961-67, asst. dist. chief, Lawrence, Kan., 1967, dist. chief, Nashville, 1967-71; floor plain mgmt. hydrologist, Washington, 1971—; water resources cons. Kan. C. of C., 1964-67. Recipient Outstanding award U.S. Geol. Survey, 1959. Registered profl. engr., Kan. Fellow Am. Soc. C.E.; mem. Nat., Tenn. socs. profl. engrs., Engrs. Assn. Nashville, Middle Tenn. Fed. Execs. Assn. (past pres.). Roman Catholic. Home: 11506 Running Cedar Rd Reston VA 22070 Office: Arlington Towers Washington DC 20242

KENNEDY, FRANCES, librarian; b. St. Louis, Dec. 2, 1907; d. William John and Maud (Gilhart) Kennedy; student Oklahoma City U., 1924-26; A.B., U. Okla., 1928; B.L.S., U. Ill., 1931, M.S., 1948. Br. librarian Muskogee (Okla.) Pub. Library, 1928-29; staff State U. Ia., summer 1931; reference librarian Oklahoma City Pub. Library, 1931-47; librarian Oklahoma City U. Library, 1947—, also prof. library sci.; instr. U. Okla. Library Sch., summer 1958, 59. Bd. dirs. Oklahoma County Health Assn., 1956-64. Mem. Am. (council 1956-60, 68-72), Southwestern (bd. dirs., 1955-56, editor 1958-64), Okla. (pres. 1945-47, editor jour., 1954-57, Distinguished Service award 1965) library assns., Am. Assn. U. Women, Alpha Omicron Pi, Beta Phi Mu. Democrat. Episcopalian. Home: 1629 Camden Way Oklahoma City OK 73116

KENNEDY, FRANCIS JOSEPH, educator; b. Scranton, Pa., Mar. 15, 1910; s. Michael Martin and Delia (McManmon) K.; A.B., Catholic U., 1933; M.A., U. Pa., 1936, postgrad., 1937-38, Columbia U., 1938, Yale, 1948, Boston U., 1948, Tulane U., 1951-52, La. State U., 1949, 51, 62-63; m. Lorena Frances Fort, Apr. 20, 1963. Tchr., W. Phila. Cath. Boys High Sch., 1930-34; asst. prof. econs. and social scis. LaSalle Coll., Phila., 1934-38; asso. prof. econs. and social scis. U. Scranton (Pa.), 1938-40; credit and operating mgr. B.F. Goodrich Tire & Rubber Co., Washington, 1941-42; supervising mineral economist U.S. Bur. Mines, Washington, 1942-46; instr. econs. U. Conn., New London, 1946-47; asso. prof. econs. and internat. trade Loyola U. Coll. Bus. Adminstrn., New Orleans, 1947-55; chief statistician U.S. Army Port Embarkation, New Orleans, 1955-56; tchr. DeLaSalle High Sch., New Orleans, 1956-57, Orleans Parish Pub. Schs., 1958-61; tchr. econs., English and sociology, coordinator distributive edn. Thibodaux (La.) High Sch., 1961—. Adviser, Propeller Club, 1947-55, founder, 1947; pub. relations, liaison officer various bus. firms, 1947-55; mem. com. econ. edn. La. Dept. Edn., 1964—; mem. Thibodaux Area Econ. Found. Bd. dirs. Thibodaux Youth Council, 1963—, Playhouse, 1965—. Recipient Outstanding Service awards Nat. Distributive Edn. Club Am., 1965, La. Distributive Edn. Club Am., 1965. Mem. Distributive Edn. Assn. La. (Outstanding Tchr. 1965, pres. 1964-66), Am., Cath., So. econ. assns., N.E.A., La. Tchrs. Assn., Am. Vocational Assn., So. Finance Assn., Nat. Cath. Edn. Assn., Nat. Assn. Distributive Edn. Tchrs. (nat. legislative chmn., v.p. So. region), Thibodaux C. of C. (v.p.), Distributive Edn. Clubs Am., Council Distributive Tchr. Edn., Phi Delta Kappa. Roman Catholic. Rotarian (pres. 1971-72). Author: Vocational Education in LaFourche Parish, 1969-74. Home: 306 Dunboyne Pl Thibodaux LA 70301

KENNEDY, FRANK THOMAS, investment banker; b. Florence, Ala., Sept. 11, 1938; s. William Charles and Frances Jane (Foxworthy) K.; B.S., Stetson U., 1960; m. Waldo Lynn Frierson, Aug. 25, 1961; children—Frank Thomas, Waldo Deborah, Kathryn Lynn. Exec. tng. program Exchange Security Bank Birmingham (Ala.), 1961-63; asst. v.p. Hendrix & Mayes, Birmingham, 1963; v.p. Hendrix, Mohr & Head, Inc., Birmingham, 1963-69; v.p., dir. Hendrix, Mohr & Yardley, Inc., Birmingham, 1969—. Bd. dirs. Shades Valley YMCA, 1969—; mem. YMCA Bus. Mens Club, 1964—. Served to 2d lt. inf. AUS, 1960-61; capt. res. Mem. Birmingham Numismatic Soc., Investment Bankers Assn., Ala. Security Dealers Assn., Pi Kappa Alpha Alumni Assn., Izaak Walton League, Pi Kappa Alpha. Episcopalian. Clubs: Alpha. Birmingham Country, Birmingham Coin (pres. 1968-70), Downtown (dir. 1966-68) (Birmingham); Turtle Point Country (Florence). Home: 4349 Kennesaw Dr Birmingham AL 35213 Office: 2020 First Nat-So Nat Bldg Birmingham AL 35203

KENNEDY, HARVEY JOHN, JR., lawyer; b. Barnesville, Ga., Apr. 9, 1924; s. Harvey John and Marisu (Reeves) K.; grad. Gordon Mil. Coll., 1942; J.D., U. Ga., 1949; m. Jean McRitchie King, Apr. 8, 1950; children— Marisu, Jean Gay. Admitted to Ga. bar, 1948; co. atty., Lamar Co., 1950-52; city atty., Barnesville, Ga., 1953-65; atty. Lamar Elec. Membership Corp.; atty. Lamar County, 1958-60; 65-68; atty., Town of Milner (Ga.), 1963-68. Govt. appeal agt. local bd. 89, 1958—. Trustee Gordon Mil. Coll., 1953-63. Served as 2d lt. to capt., 86th Inf. Div., ETO, PTO, AUS, 1942-46; capt. U.S. Army Judge Advocate Gen. Corps. Res., 1949-52. Decorated Bronze Star medal. Mem. Am. Judicature Soc., Am., Ga. (bd. govs. 1957-58), Flint Circuit (pres. 1961, 64-65) bar assns., Am. Trial Lawyers Assn., Internat. Platform Assn., State Bar Ga., Peace Officers Assn. Ga. (asso.), Am. Acad. Polit. and Social Sci., Ga. Assn. Plaintiffs Trial Attys. (v.p. 1968—), Am. Legion, V.F.W., Chi Phi, Delta Theta Phi. Democrat. Baptist. Mason (32 deg., Shriner), Moose, Rotarian (pres. 1959-60). Home: 392 Spencer St Barnesville GA 30204 Office: 217 Zebulon St Barnesville GA 30204

KENNEDY, J.C., Democratic state chmn. Chmn. Okla. Dem. com. Address: Box 8 Lawton OK 73501*

KENNEDY, JAMES DRAKE, warehouse exec.; b. Chilton, Tex., Aug. 10, 1893; s. David and Eliza Jane (Drake) K.; LL.B., Chattanooga Coll. Law, 1920; postgrad. LaSalle Extension U., 1921; m. Jessie Isabel McKensie, Aug. 26, 1917; children—Mary Kathryn (Mrs. Paul McQuiddy), James Drake. Tchr., Normal Sch., Chillicothe, Mo., 1914-15, Alta Coll., Edmonton, Can., 1915-16, Ramona (Okla.) High Sch., 1916-18; auditor, credit mgr. Chattanooga Roofing & Foundry Co., 1919-22; admitted to Tenn. bar, 1920; practiced in Chattanooga, 1922-24; accountant, Chattanooga, 1922-24; v.p. Cahill Co., Chattanooga, 1925-31, pres., 1931-42; mgr. pvt. properties, Tenn., Tex., 1942-50; pres. Cherokee Warehouses, Inc., Chattanooga, 1950—. Mem. Tenn. Bd. Accountancy, 1923-24. C.P.A., Tenn. Author: They Were Right, 1957. Home: 600 E Brow Rd Lookout Mountain TN 37350 Office: 521 W 31 St Chattanooga TN 37410 also PO Box 1607 Chattanooga TN 37401

KENNEDY, JOHN HINES, physician; b. Washington, Nov. 1, 1925; s. John A. and Viera Miriam (Hines) K.; student Princeton, 1943-45; M.D., Harvard, 1949; m. Barbara Field, Dec. 22, 1947 (dec. Jan. 1971); children—Virginia (Mrs. H.L. Serra), Anne (Mrs. Al F. Ehrbar), Christine Heron, John, Sarah Boudinot, Mark Montgomery, Mary Evelyn, Joan Loomis; m. 2d, Ann White Stockton, Jan. 2, 1972. Intern Mass. Gen. Hosp., 1949-50, asst. resident, 1950-51, 63-64, resident, 1954-55; sr. registrar thoracic unit Frenchay Hosp., Bristol, Eng., 1959-60; clin. asst. in surgery U. Bristol-Bristol Royal Infirmary, 1959-60; dir. div. thoracic surgery Cleve. Met. Gen. Hosp., 1962-69; research asso. Engring. Design Center Case Inst. Tech., 1966-69; asst. prof. thoracic surgery Case Western Res. U., 1962-69; dir. circulatory assist project group NIH, Case Western Res. U., 1967-69, Baylor Coll. Medicine, Houston, 1969-71; dir. Taub Labs. for Mech. Circulatory Support on NIH grant, Baylor Coll. Medicine, 1970—, mem. admissions com., 1971—, prof. surgery Cora and Webb Mading Dept. Surgery, 1969—; adj. prof. biomed. engring. Rice U., Houston, 1969—, mem. com. grad. students Biomed. Engring. Lab., 1970—. Cons. site visitor Program Project grants Nat. Heart and Lung Inst., NIH, 1970. Served to lt. (s.g.) M.C., USNR, 1951-53. Decorated Bronze Star award with Combat V. Diplomate Am. Bd. Surgery, Am. Bd. Thoracic Surgery. Fellow Am. Coll. Cardiology, A.C.S.; mem. Am. Assn. Thoracic Surgery, Am. Assn. U. Profs., Am. Coll. Chest Physicians (mem. com. pulmonary surgery 1961—), Am. Heart Assn. (mem. council cardiovascular surgery 1968—; mem. exec. com. 1970—), Am. Soc. Artificial Internal Organs, Am. Thoracic Soc., Houston Heart Assn. (v.p. 1971), Internat. Cardiovascular Soc., Soc. Thoracic Surgeons, Soc. Cryobiology, Sigma Xi. Author: Support of the Failing Circulation: The Use of the Heart Lung Machine in Clinical Cardiac Failure, 1967; Outline of Thoracic Surgery for Medical Students, 1968. Contbr. articles to profl. jours. Producer, author numerous films in field. Designer suture-holding ring for valvular prosthesis. Home: 2215 Albans Rd Houston TX 77005 Office: Baylor Coll Medicine 1200-Moursand Av Houston TX 77025

KENNEDY, JOHN PAYSON, librarian; b. Atlanta, Jan. 16, 1933; s. John Payson and Frances Jeannette (Law) K.; student Erskine Coll., 1950-52; B.A., Emory U., 1954, M.A. (Univ. fellow), 1959; M.S., U. Ill., 1961; m. Aurelia Turpin, Sept. 14, 1954; children—Catherine Aurelia, Frances Winifred, John Payson, Stewart McRae. Instr. Longwood Coll., Farmville, Va., 1957-59; instr. Hampden-Sydney (Va.) Coll., 1957-59, reference librarian, 1959-60; commerce and sociology librarian U. Ill. Library, Urbana, 1961-63, research asso., 1963-65; data processing librarian Ga. Inst. Tech. Library, Atlanta, 1965—. Vis. lectr. Atlanta U. Library Sch., 1969, Emory U. Div. Librarianship, 1970. Scoutmaster Atlanta area council Boy Scouts Am., 1963—. Served as spl. agt., CIC, AUS, 1954-56. Mem. Ga. Canoeing Assn. (pres. 1968), Phi Beta Kappa. Home: 1308 Valley View Rd Dunwoody GA 30338 Office: Georgia Institute of Technology Library Atlanta GA 30332

KENNEDY, JOHN WESLEY, coll. adminstr.; b. Spencer, N.C., Oct. 9, 1920; s. John Quincy and Willie (Huffman) K.; A.B., Duke, 1942, A.M., 1947; Ph.D., U. N.C. at Chapel Hill, 1951; m. Melva Pearce Dail, Aug. 21, 1942; children—John Wesley, Marcia Frances, Melva Ann. Asst. prof. econs. and bus. adminstrn. U. Fla., 1949-52; asso. prof., then prof. Auburn U., 1952-56; mem. faculty U. N.C. at Greensboro, 1956—, vice chancellor grad. studies prof. econs., 1964—; labor arbitrator, 1954—. Pres. Greesnboro Assn. Retarded Children, 1958-60. Served to lt. USNR, 1942-45. Mem. Am., So. econ. assns., Indsl. Relations and Reserach Assn. Baptist (deacon 1966-71). Author (with others) Economics, Principles and Applications, 8th edit., 1972; A Problem Manual in Economic Theory, 5th edit., 1968; also articles. Home: 2505 Fairway Dr Greensboro NC 27408

KENNEDY, JOSEPH HOWARD, banker; b. Terra Ceia, Fla., Jan. 17, 1929; s. Joseph Howard and Mildred (Perry) K.; B.S. in Bus. Adminstrn., The Citadel, 1952; m. Joyce Ann Hamilton, June 21, 1952; children—Karen, Joseph Howard. With Palmetto Bank and Trust Co. (Fla.), 1956—, pres., 1968—, also dir. Served to 1st lt. USAF, 1951-56. Mem. Am., Fla. bankers assns., Palmetto Jr. C. of C.

(pres. 1963—, dir. 1960-63), Manatee County C. of C. (treas. 1965; pres. 1971-72). Kiwanian. Club: Bradenton Country. Home: 2201 7th St Palmetto FL 33561 Office: 700 8th Av Palmetto FL 33561

KENNEDY, K. DOYLE, constrn. co. exec.; b. Clintwood, Va., June 1, 1932; s. Kermit DeWitt and Tessie Parkis (Colley) K.; B.S. in Civil Engrng., Duke U., 1953; postgrad. Northwestern U., 1956-57, Alexander Hamilton Inst., 1963; m. Mary Margaret Loos, July 30, 1971; children—(by previous marriage)—Beverly, Shirley, Peggy. Engr., U.S. Bur. Reclamation, Sacramento, 1951-52; self employed as surveyor, Durham, N.C., 1952-53; civil engr. Shell Oil Co., Indpls., 1955-57; self employed as cons. engr., Indpls., 1956-57; pres. and gen. mgr., chmn. bd. Kennedy Constrn. Co. of New Smyrna Beach, Fla., 1957—, chmn. bd. Profit Sharing Trust, 1962—; cons. engr., New Smyrna Beach, 1960—. Served with C.E., AUS, 1953-55. Recipient Distinguished Service award, Kiwanis, 1963. Mem. Am. Soc. C.E., New Smyrna Beach C. of C., Daytona Beach, Fla. skin divers assns., Underwater Soc. Am. Baptist (deacon 1959—, mem. ch. council 1959-70). Kiwanian (pres. 1961; dist. chmn. agr. and conservation 1971—). Clubs: Halifax Sport Fishing (v.p. 1968—) (Daytona Beach), New Smyrna Beach Flying (pres. 1968—). Home: 909 Faulkner St New Smyrna Beach FL 32069 Office: PO Box K New Smyrna Beach FL 32069

KENNEDY, ORVILLE ANDERSON, dentist; b. Louisville, Jan. 4, 1898; s. Thomas Worsley and Madge Pet (Willard) K.; Pharm.G., U. Ky., 1921; D.D.S., U. Louisville, 1925; m. Hazel Irene Tutt, Oct. 29, 1936; 1 dau., Georgia (Mrs. William Lynn Higginbotham, Jr.). Individual practice dentistry, Louisville, 1925-42, Cairo, Ga., 1946—; mem. staff Grady County Hosp., Cairo, Ga. Faculty U. Louisville, 1925-27. Served to maj. Dental Corps, AUS, 1942-46. Mem. Am. Legion, Kappa Psi, Delta Sigma Delta, Theta Nu Epsilon, Sigma Pi Upsilon. Home: 1401 7th St NW Cairo GA 31728 Office: 200 1st St SE Cairo GA 31728

KENNEDY, PETER JOSEPH, ins., estate and bus. analyst; b. N.Y.C., Dec. 4, 1912; s. Edward A. and Julia A. (McKernan) K.; B.A., Holy Cross Coll., 1934; M.A., Columbia, 1935, postgrad., 1936-40; m. Gertrude M. Faherty, Apr. 10, 1939; children—Maureen Frances (Mrs. John E. Ormond), Peter Joseph, Christine Marie. Tchr., coach pvt. and pub. schs., N.Y.C., 1935-40; instr. St. John's U., Bklyn., 1940-42; nat. staff U.S.O.-Nat. Catholic Community Service Clubs, 1943-53; asso. Conn. Gen. Life Ins. Co., Washington, 1953—. Pres., Cath. Charities No. Va., 1960. Bd. dirs. nat. capitol area U.S.O. com. Mem. Nat. Assn., Life Underwriters, Am. Soc. C.L.U., Holy Cross Alumni Club (pres. Washington 1959-60), Arlington Council Cath. Men (pres. 1959-60), John Carroll Soc., Internat. Oceanographic Found. Roman Catholic. Clubs: Northern Va. Aquatic; Potomac Polo (Travilah, Md.). Home: 4528 N 2d St Arlington VA 22203 Office: 1250 Connecticut Av NW Washington DC 20036

KENNEDY, PHILIP DALTON, JR., lawyer; b. Statesville, N.C., Mar. 9, 1919; s. Philip Dalton and Elise (Weedon) K.; A.B., Atlantic Christian Coll., 1938; LL.B., U. N.C., 1942. Admitted to N.C. bar, 1944, Fla. bar 1958; practiced Charlotte, N.C., 1945-57, West Hollywood, Fla., 1958—; city atty. City of Miramar, 1958-59, councilman, 1959-65; municipal judge, 1963—. Served from ensign to lt., USNR, 1942-45. Mem. Fla. Bar, N.C., Broward County bar assns., Am. Legion. Presbyn. Asso. editor N.C. Law Rev., 1940-42. Office: 6006 Miramar Pkwy West Hollywood FL 33023

KENNEDY, SABE MCCLAIN, JR., coll. ofcl.; b. Wootton, Colo., May 1, 1923; s. Sabe McClain and Margaret (Heathington) K.; B.A., Tex. Tech. Coll., 1943, M.A., 1946; postgrad. U. Nancy (France), 1945; Ph.D., U. Colo., 1952; m. Mary Frances Peak, Dec. 21, 1946; children—Marta, Lori. With Tex. Tech. Coll., 1946—, successively instr., asst. prof., 1949-53, asso. prof., 1953-57, prof., 1957—, acting asst. dean Coll. Arts and Scis., 1952-53, asst. dean, 1955-59, acting dean, 1959-61, dean, 1961-66, v.p. for academic affairs, 1966—; part-time instr. polit. sci. U. Colo., 1950. Mem. council Deans Arts and Scis. State Univs. and Land Grant Colls. 2d v.p. Tex. Tb Assn. Served from pvt. to 2d lt., AUS, 1943-46; ETO; lt. col. Res. Mem. Assn. Tex. Colls. (chmn. conf. acad. deans 1966-67), So. Conf. Acad. Deans, Internat. Studies Assn., Southwestern Polit. Sci. Assn., Mil. Govt. Assn., S.W. Social Sci. Assn. (chmn. govt. sect. 1953, gen. program chmn. 1958), Res. Officers Assn. (pres. S. Plains chpt. 1953-57), Am., Western polit. sci. assns., W. Tex. Tb assn. (pres. 1968-69), Tex Tb and Respiratory Diseases Assn. (pres. elect), Pi Sigma Alpha, Pi Gamma Mu, Sigma Delta Pi (hon). Mem. Church of Christ. Home: 3705 67th St Lubbock TX 79413

KENNEDY, WADARAN LATAMORE, educator; b. Bison, Okla., Mar. 3, 1905; s. Wilson Green and Millicent (Hicks) K.; B.S., U. Ill., 1927, M.S., 1929; Ph.D., Pa. State U., 1936; m. Lillian Jeffries, June 2, 1948; 1 dau., Yvonne Jeffries. Prof. animal husbandry Va. State Coll., Petersburg, 1927-29; instr. agr. W.Va. State Coll. Inst., 1929-31; prof. dairy sci. N.C. Agr. and Tech. State U., Greensboro, 1936-70, emeritus prof., 1970—. Bd. dirs. Credit Union, 1938—; mem. mgmt. bd. Hayes Taylor YMCA, Greensboro, 1968—. Mem. Am. Dairy Sci. Assn., Am. Soc. Animal Sci., Sigma Xi, Phi Kappa Phi, Gamma Sigma Delta. Democrat. Methodist. Home: 802 Ross Av Greensboro NC 27406

KENNEDY, WALLACE ALBERT, educator, psychologist; b. Monteverde, Fla., Apr. 2, 1929; s. George Leslie and Lucy Elizabeth (Bible) K.; A.B., Fla. State U., 1951, M.A., 1952, Ph.D., 1956; m. Patricia Burghard, June 30, 1950; children—Lois, Wally B., Lucy, Lora. Postdoctoral fellow Harvard, 1956-57; from asst. prof. to prof. psychology Fla. State U., 1957—, dir. clin. tng., 1968—; pvt. practice psychology, Tallahassee, 1959—. Mem. perinatal research com. Nat. Inst. Mental Health. Served with AUS, 1947-48. Diplomate Am. Bd. Examiners Profl. Psychology. Mem. Fla. State Bd. Examiners Psychology (chmn. 1965-67), Am., Southeastern (pres. 1968), Fla. (pres. 1967) psychol. assns., Soc. Research in Child Devel. Research in normative data on Negro intelligence and achievement in Southeastern U.S., motivation of sch. children, psychotherapy of phobias. Home: Route 5 Box 363 K Tallahassee FL 32301

KENNEDY, WALTER (WALLACE), mgmt. cons.; b. Birmingham, Dec. 20, 1898; s. Hughes Benjamin and Katherine (Hausman) K.; LL.B., U. Ala., 1921; student Grad. Sch. of Banking, Rutgers U., 1945-47; m. Myra Belle Pope, Sept. 28, 1926; children—Walter, Ann Carter, Carol Pope. Admitted to Ala. bar, 1921, and practiced in Birmingham, 1921-26; asst. to pres. Birmingham Elec. Co., 1926-29; asst. trust officer First Nat. Bank of Birmingham, 1929-35; trust officer First Nat. Bank of Montgomery, 1935-43, exec. v.p., 1943-48, pres., 1948-64, chmn. bd., 1964-69, hon. chmn. bd., 1969—, also dir.; dir. First Ala. Bancshares, Ala. Power Co. Chmn. bd. regents Grad. Sch. Banking, Rutgers U., 1961-65. Served lt. inf. U.S. Army, 1918-19; lt. col. USAAF, 1942-45; col. USAF ret., 1958. Treas. Community Chest Montgomery, 1947-49, v.p., 1953; v.p. Montgomery Tb Sanitorium, 1948-49; pres. Montgomery Area council Boy Scouts Am., 1937-40; bd. dirs. Montgomery County chpt. A.R.C., v.p., 1952-53. Mem. Am. Amateur Artists Assn., U. Ala. Alumni Assn. (pres. 1949), Am. Bar Assn., Ala. Bankers Assn. (ex-pres.), Am. Bankers Assn. (pres. trust div. 1957-58), Omicron Delta Kappa, Phi Delta Phi, Phi Gamma Delta. Episcopalian. Clubs: Montgomery Country, Rotary (pres. 1963) (Montgomery); Redstone (Birmingham). Author textbooks. Contbr. articles to legal and banking jours. Home: 2092 Myrtlewood Dr Montgomery AL Office: First Nat Bank of Montgomery Montgomery AL

KENNEDY, WILLIAM EDWARD, ret. steel fabricating co. exec.; b. Indpls., Jan. 30, 1895; s. Patrick W. and Mamie (Layne) K.; grad. engrng. Notre Dame U., 1915; m. Frances Crabb, July 16, 1952; children—William E., Mary Ellen (Mrs. John M. Ryan). Pres., Kennedy Tank & Mfg. Co., Indpls., 1927-48, So. Tank & Mfg. Co., Owensboro, Ky., 1946—; owner So. Petroleum Equipment Co., Owensboro, 1959—. Pres. Owensboro-Daviess County Airport Bd., 1951-70; chmn. Selective Service Bd. 20. Bd. dirs. Jr. Achievement, Owensboro, Brescia Coll., Owensboro. Served with A.C., U.S. Army, World War I. Mem. Steel Tank Inst., Nat. Truck Tank and Trailer Tank Inst. (pres. 1952, treas. 1953-62), Am. Inst. Mgmt., Petroleum Equipment Inst., Owensboro-Daviess County C. of C. (pres. 1962), Am. Legion. Roman Catholic. Elk, Rotarian (pres. club 1964), Optimist. Club: Owensboro Country. Home: 1589 Oak Park Dr Owensboro KY 42301 Office: 1501 Haynes Av Owensboro KY 42301

KENNEDY, WILLIAM RICHARD, spectroscopist; b. St. Louis, Aug. 9, 1922; s. William Herschel and Irene (Stege) K.; student Auburn U., 1942-43; B.S., Birmingham So. Coll., 1944; m. Anita Corinne Burns, Mar. 13, 1948; children—Cheryl Lynn, Gwendolyn Marie. Spectroscopist, Am. Cast Iron Pipe Co., Birmingham, Ala., 1944-45, chief spectroscopist, 1945—. Mem. Am. Soc. Testing Materials (com. sec. 1963-67, vice chmn. 1968-72, chmn. 1972—), Soc. for Applied Spectroscopy (sect. pres. 1950-54), So. Assn. Spectrographers. Presbyn. (elder). Home: 341 Orchid Rd Birmingham AL 35215 Office: PO Box 2727 Birmingham AL 35202

KENNER, FREDA, educator; b. Bells, Tenn.; d. Joseph Rodham and Georgia Alice (Kincaid) Kenner; A.B., Union U., 1942; M.A., U. Tenn., 1951 Chmn. speech dept. Messick High Sch., Memphis, 1946—. Trustee Internat. Thespian Soc. Recipient Freedom Found. award, 1959. Mem. Tenn. Speech Assn. (pres. 1951-52), So. Speech Assn. (v.p. 1954-55), Speech Assn. Am. (mem. legislative assembly 1965-67), N.E.A., Tenn. Edn. Assn., Am. Edn. Theatre Assn., Daus. of Founders and Patriots of Am. (state pres. 1967-70), D.A.R., Am. Assn. U. Women, Memphis Symphony Guild, Phi Kappa Phi, Delta Kappa Gamma (state v.p. 1962-64). Methodist. Club: Beta Gamma Book. Contbr. articles to profl. jours. Home: PO Box 102 Bells TN 38006

KENNER, JOANNE (MRS. JOHN CATLETT ALLENSWORTH), physician; b. Abilene, Tex., Apr. 26, 1924; d. Claude William and Elizabeth (Kirby) Kenner; B.A., Hardin-Simmons U., 1947; M.D., Southwestern Med. Sch., 1947; m. John Catlett Allensworth, Oct. 15, 1955. Intern St. Joseph's Hosp., Ft. Worth, 1947-48, rotating resident in gen. surgery, 1948-49; resident physician in obstretrics and gynecology, Harris Hosp., Ft. Worth, 1949-50, Doctor's Hosp., N.Y.C., 1950-51, Woman's Hosp., N.Y.C., 1951-54; practice medicine, specializing in obstretrics and gynecology, Ft. Worth, 1954-55, Mineral Wells, Tex., 1955—; mem. staff Palo Pinto Gen. Hosp., Mineral Wells. Civilian cons. Beach Army Hosp., Ft. Welters, Tex., 1956—; dir., physician Community Family Planning Center, Mineral Wells, 1967—. Diplomate Am. Bd. Obstetrics and Gynecology. Fellow A.C.S., Am. Coll. Obstretrics and Gynecology; mem. Am., Tex. med. assns., Tri-County Med. Soc.; Tex. Soc. Obstetricians and Gynecologists. Home: 2316 NW 4th Av Mineral Wells TX 76067 Office: 208 NW 2d St Mineral Wells TX 76067

KENNEY, HOWARD WASHINGTON, physician; b. Tuskegee Inst., Ala., Oct. 4, 1917; s. John A. and Frieda (Armstrong) K.; B.S., Bates Coll., 1940; M.D., Meharry Med. Coll., 1944; m. Gwendolyn Persley, July 31, 1943; children—Diane Elizabeth, Linda Harper, Phyllis Armstrong, Howard Washington. Intern Syndenham Hosp., N.Y.C., 1944; resident internal medicine Freedmen's Hosp., Washington, 1945-46; fellow internal medicine Howard U. Med. Sch., 1946-47, research fellow cardiovascular disease, 1947-48; staff physician VA Hosp., Tuskegee, 1948-49; pvt. practice, Newark, 1949-51, Tuskegee, 1953-55; mem. staff Tuskegee VA Hosp., 1955-62, hosp. dir., 1959-62, cons., 1953-55; dir. VA Hosp., E. Orange, N.J., 1962-65; med. dir. Tuskegee Inst., 1965-69; regional med. dir. Northeast Region, VA, Washington, 1969—; cons. internal medicine Community Hosp., Newark, 1949-51, John A. Andrew Meml. Hosp., Tuskegee Inst., 1953-55. Mem. NIH Rev. Com. for Div. Regional Programs Heart Disease, Cancer, Stroke and Related Diseases. Chmn. med. adv. com. Macon County chpt. Nat. Found., 1953-55. Mem. Bd. Police Commnrs., E. Orange, 1963-65. Served to capt., M.C., AUS, 1943-44, 51-53. Diplomate Am. Bd. Internal Medicine. Fellow A.C.P.; mem. Am., Nat. med. assns., John A. Andrew Clin. Soc. (pres. 1958, now sec.). Episcoplaian (past vestryman). Author articles in field. Home: 8024 16th St NW Washington DC 20012 Office: Region I Central Office VA Washington DC 20420

KENNEY, JOHN JOSEPH, JR., govt. ofcl.; b. Santa Fe, Apr. 30, 1918; s. John J. and May (Bergere) K.; B.A., U.S. Mil. Acad., 1940; M.A., U. Cal. at Los Angeles, 1948; A.M.P., Harvard, 1965; student Air War Coll., service schs., 1940, 41, 43, 51, 56; m. Josephine Sullivan, Dec. 28, 1940; children—Gloria Suzanne, Richard L., Michael J., Christopher T., Timothy B. Commd. 2d lt. U.S. Army, 1940, advanced through grades to brig. gen., 1966; lt. col. Hdqrs. 9th Army, World War II; instr. Arty. Sch., 1948-51; bn. comdr., Korean War; instr. Armed Forces Staff Coll., 1952-56; sr. U.S. Army rep., Can., 1957-60; Army Gen. staff exec., 1963-66; comdg. gen. I Corps Arty., Korea, 1966-67; asst. comdt. Arty. Sch., 1967-68; Joint Chiefs Staff, Washington, 1968-70; ret., 1970; dir. Okla. postal tng. operations U.S. Postal Service, Norman, Okla., 1970—. Decorated Bronze Stars, Legion of Merit, D.S.M.; Korean Order Merit; Brit. hon. officer Order Brit. Empire, Mem. Sierra Club. Home: 1421 Brookhaven St Norman OK 73069 Office: Dir OPTO PO Box 1400 Norman OK 73069

KENNEY, LAWRENCE LEONARD, city ofcl.; b. Ft. Lauderdale, Fla., Mar. 21, 1920; s. William F. and Anna (Somers) K.; grad. pub. schs., Miami, Fla.; m. Jeannette Ruth Yelverton, Nov. 1, 1941; children— Laurette Diane, Susan Lynn (Mrs. Gerald Maseda), Nora Ruth. With Fla. Nat. Bank, Miami, 1939-41; fireman Miami Fire Dept., 1941-47, lt., 1947-50, capt., 1950-57, chief fire officer, 1957-63, chief, 1963—. Trustee, Firemen's Pension and Relief Fund. Served with USCGR, 1942-45. Mem. Fire Protection Research Internat. (adv. council), Dade County Chief Fire Officers Assn. (pres. 1965), Internat. (dir., exec. com.), Southeastern assns. fire chiefs, Fla. Firemen's Assn. Research in electrocardiogram telemetry. Home: 301 SW 30th Ct Miami FL 33135

KENNY, NICHOLAS NAPOLEON (NICK KENNY), newspaper columnist; b. Astoria, L.I. City, N.Y., Feb. 3, 1895; s. Richard Joseph and Josephine (Duval) K.; student short story and scenario writing Columbia, 1922; m. Kathryn Judge, Oct. 2, 1927; children—Patricia, Joy (Mrs. Robert Kern). Sports writer, writer of column Getting an Earful, rewrite man Bayonne (N.J.) Times, 1920-23; sports editor and rewrite man Boston American, 1923-24; rewrite man N.Y. Journal, 1924-27, N.Y. Daily News, 1927-30; radio columnist N.Y. Daily Mirror, 1930—; writer syndicated column Nick Kenny Speaking (peotry, and news about radio, TV, stage and screen personalities), 1930—; pres. Goldmine Music, Inc., music pubs., 1946—. Decorated by Cardinal Spellman for canteen work, entertaining servicemen, World War II; received awards from Army and Navy depts. for similar work. Served with U.S. Navy, 1911-18; 3rd and 2d mate, Merchant Marine, 1918-20. Mem. Songwriters Protective Assn., Newspaper Guild, Am. Fedn. Radio Artists, Am. Guild of Variety Artists, Profl. Music Men's Contact Assn., Am. Soc. Composers, Authors and Pubs. Roman Catholic. Club: Winged Foot Golf. Writer lyrics of hit songs, including, There's a Gold-mine in the Sky, Love Letters in the Sand, Carelessly, In My Cabin of Dreams, Little Old Cathedral in the Pines, Makebelieve Island, While a Cigarette Was Burning, Beyond the Purple Hills, Scattered Toys, Gone Fishin', It's Funny But It's True, Undertow. Author: Collected Poems of Nick Kenny; Poems to Inspire; others. Lectr. on newspaper bus. and on poetry. Home: 2932 Greenbriar St Sarasota FL

KENNY, ROBERT LEWIS, real estate devel. exec.; b. Spencer, Ia., May 4, 1926; s. James Roy and Grace M. (Lewis) K.; student Baylor U., 1948-50; m. Judith L. Rush, Dec. 1, 1967; children—Colleen Ann, Robin Faye, James Carleton, Dwight Lewis. Vice pres. Travel-Eze Mfg. Co., Spencer, Ia., 1945-47; asst. plant mgr. Stoddard Mfg. Co., Mason City, Ia., 1947-49; civilian flight instr. USAF, Hondo (Tex.) AFB, 1951-58; dir. mem. services Medina Electric Coop., Hondo, 1958-60, Magic Valley Electric Coop., Mercedes, Tex., 1960-71; v.p. Paradise Isle Devel. Corp., 1972—. Mem. Tex. Indsl. Devel. Council., 1968-71; pres. S. Tex. Indsl. Devel. Com., 1970-71; v.p. Medina County Sheriffs Possee, 1955-57; county campaign dir. March of Dimes, 1964; county chmn. Nat. Found., 1965. Adv. bd. Tex. A. and M. U., 1970. Served with USAAF, 1943-45, with USAF, 1950-51. Mem. Tex. Assn. Assessing Officers (asso.), Optomist (v.p. 1957, 71), Rotarian. Home: Mile 9 N and 5 1/2 W Weslaco TX 78596 Office: 405 E Expressway 83 Pharr TX

KENT, BARTIS MILTON, physician; b. Terrell, Tex., June 23, 1925; s. Bartis William and Annie (Smalley) K.; student So. Methodist U., 1942-44; M.D., Baylor U., 1948; m. Ann L. Kiel, July 6, 1954; children—Susan Ruth, Martha Lucille, Bartis Michael. Intern, Jefferson Davis Hosp., Houston, 1948-49; resident pathology Mass. Meml. Hosps., Boston, 1951; resident in internal medicine Baylor U., 1953-56; indsl. physician Humble Oil Co., Houston, 1949-51; instr. dept. medicine U. Ia., 1956-58; staff physician Ia. City VA Hosp., 1956-58; practice medicine specializing in internal medicine, Muskogee, Okla., 1958—; dir. radiosotope service Muskogee (Okla.) Gen. Hosp. Cons. Muskogee (Okla.) VA Hosp. Chmn., Muskogee County chpt. Am. Nat. Red Cross, 1963-65. Served with USAF, 1951-53. Decorated Air medal. Diplomate Am. Bd. Internal Medicine. Mem. A.C.P., Indsl. Med. Assn., Soc. Nuclear Medicine, Am. Fedn. Clin. Research, Am. Heart Assn., Aero Med. Assn., Am., Okla. socs. internal medicine, Muskogee C. of C. Methodist. Mason (Shriner). Home: 800 N 45th St Muskogee OK 74401 Office: 211 S 36th St Muskogee OK 74401

KENT, BRUCE MARTIN, ednl. adminstr.; b. nr. Rocky Mount, Va., Mar. 13, 1915; s. Robert Lee and Rose (Martin)K.; B.S., Coll. William and Mary, 1935, M.Ed., 1952; postgrad. U. Va., 1935-36; m. Clara May Bousman, June 8, 1938; children—Nancy (Mrs. W. H. Young, Jr.), Mary (Mrs. R. Gaines Steer). Prin., Henry Elementary Sch., 1948-51; guidance dir. Franklin County High Sch., 1951-56, asst. prin., 1956-59, prin., 1959-69; gen. supr. Franklin County Pub. Schs., Rocky Mount, 1969—; dir. Bankers Trust Co., Rocky Mount, 1957—, chmn. bd., 1972—. Mem. Ruritan Nat. (dist. gov. 1951), Va. High Sch. League (group bd. chmn., mem. exec. com. 1966-68), Va. Edn. Assn., Nat. Assn. Secondary Sch. Prins. Methodist. Lion. Home: Route 1 Rocky Mount VA 24151

KENT, CARLETON VOLNEY, JR., newspaperman; b. Northfield, Minn., June 13, 1909; s. Carleton Volney and Cecilia (Loizeaux) K.; A.B., U. Kan., 1932; m. Janet Hurd, Oct. 19, 1935; 1 son, Carleton Hurd. Newspaper reporter Lawrence (Kan.) Daily Journal-World, Daily Oklahoman, Okla. City, Kansas City Times, Okla. City Times; with Chicago Times (now Sun-Times), 1939—; war corr., Pacific and European theaters, 1942-4, Washington corr., 1945—. Mem. White House Corrs. Assn. (pres. 1950-51). Clubs: National Press, Overseas Writers (Washington, D.C.); Gridiron; Burning Tree (Bethesda, Md.). Home: 227 N Royal St Alexandria VA 22314 Office: National Press Bldg Washington DC 20004

KENT, JERARD ALLEN, engring. and constrn. co. exec.; b. New Orleans, Mar. 4, 1933; s. John Alva and Hilda (McGovern) K.; Indsl. Engr., Tulane U., 1956; grad. La. State U., 1958; m. Shirley Watson, Apr. 27, 1954; children—Jerard Allen, Paul S., Hope M., Judey A., Deborah A., Jeffrey J., Gregory J. Sr. administrv. engr. Kaiser Aluminum & Chem. Corp., Gramercy, La., 1958-59; v.p. finance Wellman-Lord Inc., Lakeland, Fla., 1959-68, v.p. Planning and diversification, 1969—, also dir.; pres. G-M Indsl. Enterprises, Inc., G-M Properties; Inc., Indsl. Park Utilities, Inc., Eaton Park, Fla.; dir. N.Am. Steel Corp., Lakeland, Hatteras Indsl. Corp., New Bern, N.C., Delta Fabricators Inc., Baton Rouge. Bd. dirs. United Fund, Lakeland, A.R.C., Cath. Charities, Orlando, Fla.; treas. St. Leo (Fla.) Coll., 1969—, also bd. dirs. Served to capt. AUS, 1952-54. Mem. Financial Exec. Inst. (dir.), Nat. Assn. Accountants (dir.). Republican. Roman Catholic (mem. parish council, 1967—). Home: 1609 Clarendon Av Lakeland FL 33803 Office: PO Box 2008 Lakeland FL 33803

KENT, JOEL GILBERT, indsl. engr., govt ofcl.; b. Bklyn., Mar. 13, 1933; s. Sidney Louis and Rose (Levin) K.; B.S., U. Miami, 1958; m. Sandra Snyder, Sept. 3, 1956; children—Daniel Howard, Neil Victor. Broadcast engr. sta. WVCG, Coral Gables, Fla., 1955-56; planning engr., proposal coordinator Dynatronics, Inc., Orlando, Fla., 1958-63; mgr. proposals and advt. Systems Engr. Labs., Ft. Lauderdale, Fla., 1963; sr. engr. writer RCA Service Co., Cocoa Beach, Fla., 1963-64; sr. indsl. engr. Brown Engr. Co., Cocoa Beach, Fla., 1964; Apollo data mgr., installation data mgr. NASA, John F. Kennedy Space Center, Fla., 1964—. Recipient Bunker scholarship Internat. Graphoanalysis Soc., 1969. Mem. Am. Inst. Indsl. Engrs. (dir. Cocoa Beach chpt. 1964-67), Internat. Graphoanalysis Soc., Internat. Platform Assn., Am. Ordnance Assn. (NASA rep. for engring. data mgmt. 1967—), Fla. Graphoanalysts (v.p. 1972—), Inner Circle. Home: 601 Robert Way Satellite Beach FL 32937

KENT, ROSEMARY MAY (MRS. DONALD EAST KENT), pub. health educator; b. Bartlesville, Okla., Jan. 26, 1913; d. William Ernest and Christine (Ruble) May; A.B., Agnes Scott Coll., 1933, M.A., Emory U., 1934; postgrad. (Mary Pemberton Nourse fellow) Vassar Coll., 1945-46; M.P.H., U. N.C., 1946, Ph.D., 1949; m. Donald East Kent, Dec. 25, 1937. Tchr. high sch., Hamilton County, Tenn., 1934-40; health edn. coordinator Norris Area, TVA, 1940-43; health cons. City Pub. Schs., Winston-Salem, N.C., 1943-45; ednl. dir. N.C. div. Am. Cancer Soc., 1947-51; asso. prof. pub. health edn. U. N.C. Sch. Pub. Health, Chapel Hill, 1951-72; prof. health edn. U. Tenn., Knoxville, 1970—. With Nat. Tng. Lab., Bethel, Me., 1967; cons. Headstart Evaluation and Research Center, U. Hawaii, 1968; curriculum cons. USPHS, Indian Health Service, 1969—, WHO Faculty Travel fellow Western Pacific and S.E. Asia, 1956. Fellow Am. Pub. Health Assn., Soc. Pub. Health Educators (charter); mem.

N.C. Pub. Health Assn., N.C. Assn. Health Educators, Assn. Supervision and Curriculum Devel., A.A.A.S., Delta Kappa Gamma, Delta Omega. Contbr. articles to profl. jours. Office: U Tenn 1914 Andy Holt Av Knoxville TN 37916

KENT, SAMUEL DAVIS, dentist; b. Ingram, Va., Aug. 29, 1892; s. Samuel Thomas Anderson and Pattie Cathryn (Davis) K.; student Richmond U., 1911-12; dentistry Med. Coll. Va., 1912-1915; postgrad. Tufts U., 1947-51, Ohio State U., 1947-52; m. Mildred Ann Moir, Oct. 11, 1920; children—Ann (Mrs. Robert J. Boos), Samuel Davis. Practice dentistry, Stuart, Va., 1915-16, Danville, Va., 1917—. VA clinician 5th Internat. Dental Congress, 1936; mem. Va. Bd. Health, 1948-63, v.p., 1948-56. Bd. dirs. Blue Ridge Sanitorium, chmn. 1948-56. Served with Dental Corps, USN, 1918-19. Mem. Va. (pres. 1933-34), Am. dental assns. (Ho. of Dels. 1936). Methodist (steward 1918—). Kiwanian (pres. 1945-46). Club: Danville Danville Golf. Home: 115 Virginia Av Danville VA 24541 Office: Arcade Bldg Danville VA 24541

KENT, WALTER, JR., social worker; b. Savannah, Ga., Feb. 9, 1923; s. Walter and Aurrie (Brown) K.; B.A., Samford U., 1953; M.S., U. Tex., 1964; m. Margaret E. Ward, Dec. 25, 1948. Dir. religious edn. Norwood Bapt. Ch., Birmingham, Ala., 1958-61; social worker Tex. Bapt. Children's Home, Round Rock, 1964-66; psychiat. social worker Austin (Tex.) Child Guidance Center, 1967-68; Austin State Sch., 1968-70; unit dir. Meridell Achievement Center, Austin, 1970—. Mem. Nat. Assn. Social Workers, A.A.A.S. Home: 1910 Pasadena Dr Austin TX 78757

KENWARD, FRANKLIN MONROE, dentist; b. Gary, Ind., Dec. 7, 1919; s. Charles Franklin and Mabel Clair (Monroe) K.; B.S., Ind. U., 1947; D.D.S., cum laude, Loyola U., Chgo., 1952; m. Marcia Hoover, Sept. 4, 1948; children—Scott Franklin, Christopher Floyd. Practice dentistry, Miami, Fla., 1952—; dir. Omega Ins. Agy., Phila. Served with USNR, 1942-45. Fellow Internat. Coll. Dentists; mem. Am., Fla., dental assns., Miami Dental Soc. (pres. 1963-64), Coconut Grove C. of C. (pres. 1965-66), Am. Dental Interfrat. Council (pres. 1968), Blue Key, Omicron Kappa Upsilon, Psi Oemga. Club: Exchange (pres. 1956) (Miami). Editor, Fla. Dental Jour., 1969—. Home: 6090 Killian Dr Miami FL 33156 Office: 3138 Commodore Plaza Miami FL 33133

KENWORTHY, CARROLL H., newspaperman; b. Kokomo, Ind., May. 10, 1904; s. Murray S. and Ida Lenora (Holloway) K.; A.B., Earlham Coll., Richmond, Ind., 1925; student Hartford (Conn.) Sem., 1926; A.M., Columbia, 1927; m. Mary Lowes, Jan. 1, 1932; children—Thomas L., David K. (dec.), Lee Hadley. Reporter Hartford Courant, 1926, Japan Advertiser, Tokyo, 1927-29; corr. for newspapers in U.S. and China from Tokyo, 1927-29; with Washington Bur. of Wall Street Jour., 1929; diplomatic reporter for Washington Bur. of United Press, 1930-40, editor fgn. dept., Washington, D.C., 1941-67. Trustee, Earlham Coll., 1954-63. Mem. Overseas Writers (twice pres.), Nat. Press Club. Home: 1425 44th St Washington DC 20007 Office: Nat Press Bldg Washington DC 20007

KENYON, ALBERT PRENTICE, educator, govt. ofcl.; b. Westerly, R.I., Oct. 13, 1906; s. Albert Prentice and Mabel (Tuckerman) K.; A.B., Milton Coll., 1929; M.A., Columbia, 1936; m. Chloe H. Jenkins, June 4, 1931. Tchr. high sch., Chadwick, Ill., 1929-37, Westerly 1937-42; with Bur. Naval Personnel, Washington, 1943-72, asst. dir. tng. mgmt. div., 1950-60, supervisory edn. and tng. planner, 1960-72; spl. asst. for policy to dir. edn. and tng. Office of Chief of Naval Operations, Washington, 1972—. Lectr. in hysics George Washington U., 1946-59. Served with USNR, 1942-46, 47-48, capt. Res. ret. Mem. Phi Delta Kappa. Home: 908 Allison St Alexandria VA 22302 Office: Office Chief of Naval Operations Washington DC 20370

KENYON, RALPH CLIFFORD, state ofcl.; b. Columbus, Mont. Nov. 14, 1930; s. Vernon P. and Ethel (Weppler) K.; B.Arch., Mont. State Coll., 1953; m. Dalcie Mae Langston, May 1, 1955; children—Jana Sue, Karla Jean. Architect, Drake and Gustafson, Billings, Mont., 1955-63, div. architecture and engring. Dept. Adminstrn., State of Mont., Helena, 1963-65; state controller, Montana, 1965-69; with office of State Planning, Fla., 1969-72, state budget office, 1972—. Served with AUS, 1953-55. Mem. Meth. Youth Fellowship Mont. (pres. 1949-50). Republican. Methodist. Home: 2103 Evergreen Dr Tallahassee FL 32303 Office: Dept Adminstrn Capitol Bldg Tallahassee FL 32303

KENYON, RICHARD LEE, assn. exec.; b. Athens, Ill., Dec. 11, 1917; s. Thomas W. and Elizabeth (Kincaid) K.; A.B., U. Ill., 1938; Ph.D., U. N.C., 1942; m. Carol Ann Elward, July 5, 1951; children—Colleen, Stephanie, Jan, Christopher. DuPont postdoctoral fellow U. Ill., 1942-43; research chemist central research dept. E.I. du Pont de Nemours & Co., Wilmington, Del., 1943-46; asso. editor Chem. and Engring. News, Chgo., 1946-50, editor, 1956-62; asso. editor Indsl. and Engring. Chemistry, Chgo., 1946-50; European editor Chem. and Engring. News, Indsl. Engring. Chemistry, London, Eng., 1950-53; mng. editor Jour. Agrl. and Food Chemistry, Washington, 1953-56; editorial dir. Applied Jours., Am. Chem. Soc., Washington, 1959-62, dir. applied publs., 1962-64, dir. publs. Am. Chem. Soc., 1965-71, dir. pub. affairs and communication, 1971—, dir. planning and information systems, 1967-69. Mem. patent adv. com. U.S. Patent Office, 1968—; mem. sci. information council NSF, 1960-64, chmn., 1964; mem. publs. com. Internat. Union Pure and Applied Chemistry, 1969—. Mem. Am. Chem. Soc., A.A.A.S., Soc. Chem. Industry (Gt. Britain), Chem. Soc. (London). Clubs: Federal City, Cosmos (Washington). Office: 1155 16th St NW Washington DC 20036

KEPNER, WOODY, public relations exec.; b. Millersburg, Pa., June 30, 1920; s. E. Elwood and Charlotte (Dressler) K.; student pub. schs.; m. Palma M. Brown, Feb. 10, 1943; children—Linda Louise (Mrs. Peter G. Henke), Dawn Annette (Mrs. Glenn Kendrick), Tana Lee. Free lance reporter Williamsport Grit, Harrisburg Telegraph, Harrisburg Patriot-News, Harrisburg Sunday Courier, 1935-41; reporter, feature and spl. events writer, photo editor, news editor, news bur. mgr. Miami (Fla.) Publicity Dept., 1945-53, dir., 1953-57; pres., owner Woody Kepner Assos. Inc., Miami, 1957—; dir. Bishopric & Fielden, Inc., advt., Miami. Vice pres. United Fund Dade County, 1963—. Served with USNR, 1942-45. Mem. Pub. Relations Soc. Am., Fla. Pub. Relations Assn., Dade County C. of C. Home: 6901 SW 120th St Miami FL 33156 Office: 3361 SW 3d Av Miami FL 33145 also 919 3d Av New York City NY 10022 also Alexanderlaan 5 Curacao Netherlands Antilles

KEPPEL, DAVID HEARNE, govt. ofcl.; b. Cazenovia, N.Y., Mar. 16, 1909; s. Frederick Dudley and Mary (Hearne) K.; A.B., Syracuse U., 1932; diploma N.Y. Sch. Social Work, Columbia, 1937; m. Ruth Paige, Apr. 23, 1938, children—Judith K. (Mrs. Neal R. Huber), Paige K. (Mrs. Dale E. Bellowich). Dep. commr. Me. Dept. Health and Welfare, 1944-48; dir. welfare city Hartford (Conn.), 1948-64; cons. on vol. agys. Dept. Health, Edn. and Welfare, Washington, 1964-66, program planning specialist Bur. Social Welfare, 1966-68; social work program specialist Med. Services Adminstrn., 1968—; tchr. pub. welfare adminstrn. N.Y. State Pub. Welfare Inst., Cornell U., Ithaca, N.Y., summers 1951-53, Springfield (Mass.) Coll., 1956; mem. Gov's Com. on Unemployment Compensation, 1951. Bd. dirs. Social Adjustment Commn., Hartford. Mem. Am Pub. Welfare Assn. (past dir.), Nat. Assn. Social Workers, Nat. Assn. on Mental Deficiency, Conn. Assn. Local Pub. Welfare Adminstrs. (past pres.). Conglist. Home: 7308 Brookcrest Pl Annandale VA 22003 Office: Health Edn and Welfare South Bldg 330 C St SW Washington DC 20201

KEPPLER, CHARLES BRIEL, physician; b. Richmond, Va., Feb. 13, 1917; s. Philip and Addie (Huffman) K.; B.S., U. Richmond, 1937; M.D., Med. Coll. Va., 1941; m. Myrtis Myrick Elliott, Dec. 1, 1942; children— Charles B., Kristina E., Melinda E. Intern Norfolk (Va.) Gen. Hosp., 1941-42; resident, Norfolk, 1946; practice medicine, specializing in internal medicine, Sewanee, Tenn., 1948-69; mem. staff Emerald Hodgson, Harton Meml., Coffee County hosps.; clin. dir. Multicounty Mental Health Center, Tullahoma, Tenn., 1969—. City councilman, Sewanee, 1965-68. Bd. dirs. Emeral Hodgson Hosp., Learning Disability Center, Sewanee. Served with AUS, 1942-46. Decorated Bronze Star medal with oak leaf cluster. Mem. A.M.A., Tenn., Franklin County med. socs., Phi Beta Pi, Theta Chi. Home: Box 277 Sewanee TN 37375 Office: 1803 N Jackson St Tullahoma TN 37388

KERBY, ANNIE MARGUERITE BEASLEY (MRS. JAMES KENNETH KERBY), nurse, club woman; b. nr. Pontotoc, Miss., Jan. 23, 1927; d. William Cecil and Mary (Lyon) Beasley; student Miss. State Coll. for Women, 1945-47; grad. Bapt. Meml. Hosp. Nursing, Memphis, 1950; student Memphis State U., 1947-48, 58-59, U. Tenn., 1965-66; m. James Kenneth Kerby, Jan. 9, 1954; children—Rebecca Zane, Kenneth Waterman Hewett, Lyon Galloway, Ritchey King. Staff nurse Le Bonheur Hosp., Memphis, 1954-57; nurse Memphis VA Hosp., 1960—. Com. chmn. Maternal Welfare League, 1962-63; vol. 1st aide work A.R.C.; active Memphis Symphony League, 1962—; chmn. spl. features com. Greater Memphis Christian Women's Club, 1968; D.A.R. rep. to Memphis City Beautiful Commn., 1966; organizer, sponsor local chpt. Children Am. Revolution, 1966, sr. pres., 1966-68, state promoter, 1969-70. Mem. D.A.R. (chpt. chmn. hist. markers 1966), Daus. Am. Colonists, Memphis Geneal. Soc., Tenn. League Nursing. So. Dames Am. (sec. 1971—), Internat. Platform Assn., Nat. League Nursing, Tenn. Fedn. Women's Clubs. Club: Luncheon Forum (Memphis). Home: 1849 Central Av Memphis TN 38104 Office: 1030 Jefferson Av Memphis TN 38115

KERCHER, JOHN WESLEY, JR., accountant; b. Columbus, O., Jan. 26, 1915; s. John Wesley and Gudrun C. (Carston) K.; student U. Cin., 1932-34; Antioch Coll., 1934-35; m. Flora Elizabeth Blakeslee, Mar. 26, 1938; children—John Wesley III, William Henry. With Ernst & Ernst, C.P.A.'s, 1942—, partner in charge south central dist., Atlanta, 1957—. C.P.A. in 10 states. Pres. Atlanta Symphony Orch. Mem. Am. Inst. C.P.A.'s, Nat Assn. Accountants, Ga. Soc. C.P.A.'s. Clubs: Capital City, Cheroke Town and Country (Atlanta). Home: 145 Valley Rd NW Atlanta GA 30305 Office: First Nat Bank Bldg Atlanta GA 30303

KERCHER, ROBERT PAUL, ednl. adminstr.; b. Pitts., Aug. 15, 1934; s. George and Laura Fluke (Harvey) K.; A.B., Stetson U., 1956; postgrad. So. Baptist Theol. Sem., 1956-57; B.D., Southeastern Bapt. Theol. Sem., 1960, M.S.T., 1962; Ph.D., Laurence U., 1971; m. Sylvia Williams, July 29, 1960; children—Karis Marie, Kent Williams. Asso. pastor First Bapt. Ch., Hickory, N.C., 1958-60; pastor Fieldstone Presbyn. Ch., Mooresville, N.C., 1962-67; prof. bible Montreat-Anderson Coll., Montreat, N.C., 1967-71, dir. devel., 1971—. Sec.-treas. Planned Properties, Inc., Hickory, N.C., 1967-71. Chmn. Planning Bd., Black Mountain, N.C., 1969-71. Bd. dirs. Catawba Valley council Girl Scouts Am., South Iredell County chpt. A.R.C. Red Cross. Mem. Ministerial Assn. (pres. 1966-67, dir. 1964-67), Am. Acad. Religion, Soc. Biblical Literature, Delta Sigma Phi. Founder systems approach pedagogy. Home: 113 Dogwood Dr Black Mountain NC 28711 Office: PO Box 187 Montreat NC 28757

KERENSKY, VASIL MICHAEL, educator; b. Pontiac, Mich., Dec. 29, 1930; s. Michael Vasil and Traica (Vangeloff) K.; B.S., Central Mich. U., 1953; M.A., U. Mich., 1960; Ed.D., Wayne State U., 1965; m. Elaine Ireland, Dec. 27, 1953; children—Michael William, Richard Alan, John F. High sch. tchr., Grand Blanc, Mich., 1955-56, counselor, 1957-58, dir. guidance, 1959-60; prin. Haslett (Mich.) High Sch., 1961-63; Mott fellow Wayne State U., Flint, Mich., 1964; asst. supt. schs., Waterford, Mich., 1965; prof. edn., also dir. Center for Community Edn., Fla. Atlantic U., Boca Raton, 1966-72, Charles Stewart Mott prof., 1972—. Mem. bd. edn. Holly (Mich.) Pub. Sch., 1957-60. Served with AUS, 1953-55. Nat. Def. Edn. Act fellow, 1960. Mem. Nat. Community Sch. Edn. Assn. (dir. 1968-70, pres. 1970-71), Am. Assn. Sch. Adminstrs., Assn. Supervision and Curriculum Devel., Phi Delta Kappa. Author: (with Ernest O. Melby) Education II: A Social Imperative, 1971. Home: 68 SW 10th Terrace Boca Raton FL 33432

KERLEY, SIDNEY AUSTON, educator; b. Bonham, Tex., Nov. 10, 1915; s. Sidney Houston and Lula (Langston) K.; B.A., Tex. A. and M. U., 1939; M.Ed., N.Tex. State U., 1950; m. Melba Compton, Nov. 24, 1939; children—Michael, Mary Ann (Mrs. David Harrigan), Thomas, Lucinda, Patrick. Coordinator distbv. edn. pub. schs., Sherman, Tex., 1951-52; asso. prof. edn., Tex. A. and M. U., College Station, 1960—, dir. counseling and testing center, 1960—, asso. dean admissions, 1969—. Mem. adv. com. Southwestern region CEEB, Austin, 1968—; pres. bd. Brazos County Youth Counseling Service, 1963-65. Served with AUS, 1942-46. Mem. Am., Tex. personnel and guidance assns., Am. Assn. U. Profs., Phi Delta Kappa, Phi Eta Sigma. Rotarian (bd. dirs.). Author: (with Horace Morse and Paul L. Dressel) General Education for Personal Maturity. Home: 528 Helena St Bryan TX 77801 Office: Acad Bldg Tex A and M U College Station TX 77843

KERN, JOHN WORTH, III, judge; b. Indpls., May 25, 1928; s. John Worth and Bernice (Winn) K.; A.B., Princeton, 1949; LL.B., Harvard, 1952; m. Nancy Alice Park, Aug. 7, 1954; children—John Worth IV, Stephen Guilford. Admitted to D.C. bar, 1954; practiced in Washington, 1959-65; mem. firm Kilpatrick, Ballard & Beasley; asst. U.S. atty. for D.C., 1955-59; asst. to asst. atty. gen. of U.S., 1965-66; asst. to dep. atty. gen. of U.S., 1966-68; asso. judge D.C. Ct. Appeals, 1968—. Home: 5212 Worthington Dr Washington DC 20016 Office: 400 F St NW Washington DC 20001

KERN, JOSEPH HERSCHEL, educator; b. Chillicothe, O., Jan. 31, 1920; s. Herschel Clarence and Agnes Marie (Cruse) K.; B.S. in Pharmacy, Ohio State U., 1949, M.S., 1951, Ph.D. (Am. Found. Pharm. Edn. fellow), 1954; m. Shermania R. Gheen, Feb. 22, 1946; 1 son, Joseph Dana. Teaching asst. pharmacy, Ohio State U., Columbus, 1950-52, instr., 1952-55; asst. prof., U. Fla., Gainesville, 1955-58; prof. pharmacy adminstrn., Northeast La. U., Monroe, 1958—. Chmn. Central dist. Boy Scouts Am., 1971-72. Chmn. bd. dirs., La. Heart Assn., 1969-71. Served with AUS, 1941-46; ETO. Mem. Tchrs. of Pharmacy Adminstn., Am. Assn. Colls. of Pharmacy, (sec.-treas. conf. of tchrs. 1957-63), Am. Pharm. Assn., Nat. Assn. Retail Druggists, Sigma Xi, Rho Chi, Kappa Psi. Roman Catholic (mem. Holy Name Soc.) K.C. Home: 3608 Hanging Moss Lane Monroe LA 71201

KERNS, ROLLAND EDWARD, electric utility exec.; b. Lincoln, Neb., Apr. 13, 1904; s. Charles Edward and Myrta (Hugg) K.; student Bard Coll., Annandale-on-Hudson, N.Y., 1923-26; m. Lillian Theo Looper, Sept. 23, 1926; 1 son, Richard R. With Okla. Gas and Electric Co., 1926—, sec., 1960—, treas., 1966—, financial v.p., 1968—; Assos., 1957—. Sec. Okla. Jr. C. of C., 1937-38. Chmn. investment com. Okla. Gas and Electric Retirement Plan, 1961—; bd. dirs. Okla. Gas and Electric Found., 1966—. Recipient Accounting award Edison Electric Inst., 1935; Brochure award Financial World Analysts, 1964. Mem. Inst. Internal Auditors Oklahoma City (charter), Internat. Accountants Soc. (life), Am. Soc. Corporate Secs., Okla. Soc. Financial Analysts, Oklahoma City, Okla. chambers commerce. Episcopalian (vestryman, treas., lay reader). Clubs: Economic, Exchange, Beacon, Quail Creek Country, Men's Dinner, Sooner Dinner (Oklahoma City). Home: 5817 N Barnes Av Oklahoma City OK 73112 Office: 321 N Harvey Av Oklahoma City OK 73101

KERPER, HAZEL BOWMAN (MRS. W. G. KERPER), lawyer, educator; b. Laramie, Wyo.; d. Elmer E. and Claribel (Colby) Bowman; B.A. with honor, U. Wyo., 1926, J.D. with honor, 1928; postgrad. Stanford Law Sch., 1926-27, Spanish Lang. Sch., San Jose, Costa Rica, 1960-63; certificate in corrections Fla. State U., 1964, M.S. in Criminology, 1965; m. W. G. Kerper, June 17, 1927; children—Minabelle (Mrs. Robert R. Milodragovich), Loujen (Mrs. John S. Bereman), Janeen, Jill (Mrs. Johne M. Lennon). Admitted to Wyo. bar, 1928, Cal. bar, 1942, Tex. bar, 1971; admitted to Fed. Ct. practice, 1932; partner law firm Kerper & Kerper, Cody, Wyo., 1928-40, 43-54; pvt. practice law, Los Angeles, 1940-43; ct. commr. Park County, Wyo., 5th Jud. Dist., 1930-59, asst. atty., 1928-30; mem. pub. relations and publicity staff Children's Orthopedic Hosp. Los Angeles, 1940-43; sec., mgr. Title Ins. and Trust Co., Cody, 1954-59; exec. sec. Avanza Industria, S.A., San Jose, 1959-64, also cons. Kativo, S.A. (Costa Rica, El Salvador, Nicaragua, Panama, Guatemala); asst. prof. sociology and criminal law Sam Houston State U., Huntsville, Tex., 1966-67, asso. prof., 1967-68, prof., 1968—. Recipient Distinguished Prof. award Sam Houston State U., 1967. Mem. P.E.O., Mortar Board, Delta Delta Delta (finance dir., contbr. nat. pub. 1954-59), Phi Kappa Phi, Delta Sigma Rho, Phi Gamma Mu, Delta Tau Kappa. Author: Introduction to Criminal Justice System. Contbr. articles to profl. jours. Home: 2018 Av S Huntsville TX 77340

KERR, BEN JONES, JR., banker; b. Denison, Tex., June 14, 1918; s. Ben Jones and Ethyl (Caldwell) K.; B.A. U. Okla., 1940; M.B.A., Harvard, 1941; m. Marrian Grace Hardie, Sept. 16, 1941; children—Ben Jones III, Janet Lynn (Mrs. Norman U. Smith), Guy Hardie. Joined USN, 1941, served to lt. comdr., ret. 1948; exec. sec. Richard Gill Co., San Antonio, 1950-51; wholesale rep., Nat. Security & Research Corp., N.Y.C., 1951-53; with Merc. Nat. Bank at Dallas, 1953—, asst. trust officer, 1954-55, trust officer, 1955-56, asst. v.p., 1959-66, v.p., exec. trust officer, 1966-70, sr. v.p., exec. trust officer, 1970—; dir. Horn Blueprint Co., Beverly Hills, Inc., King Ranch Oil & Lignite Co. Adviser Southwestern Grad. Sch. Banking So. Meth. U. 1966—; mem. exec. com. Dallas County Heart Assn., 1967—; pres. Dallas Estate Council, 1961-62. Mem. Am. Soc. Corporate Secs. (pres. Dallas regional group 1966-67), Dallas Assn. Security Dealers. Presbyn. Mason (Shriner). Club: Oklahoma University (past pres.) (Dallas). Home: 4444 Larchmont Dallas TX 75205 Office: Mercantile Nat Bank at Dallas PO Box 5415 Dallas TX 75222

KERR, CHARLES MACDONALD, III, inst. exec.; b. New Orleans, July 3, 1912; s. Charles Macdonald, II and Helen M. (Coppee) K.; B.B.A., Tulane U., 1935; postgrad. Seminars Bard Coll., Rhinebeck, N.Y., 1957-58; m. Eleanor Carol Morris, July 8, 1961; children—Charles M. IV, Theresa Helen. Cost accountant Nfld. (Can.) Constructors, Marquise, 1941-42; treas. Cuban Mining Co., El Cristo, Oriente, Cuba, 1943-44; supr. field accounting Pendleton Shipyards, New Orleans, 1944; mem. nat. staff A.R.C., cons. amputee rehab. to Surgeons Gen., U.S. Army, USN, Washington, 1944-47; co-organizer, dir. patient tng. Kessler Inst. Rehab., West Orange, N.J., 1948-50; dir. amputee tng. Hasbrouck Heights (N.J.) Hosp., 1950; office mng. N. Atlantic Constructors, N.Y.C., 1951-52; dir. Nat. Inst. for Amputee Rehb., Montclair, N.J., 1952—; cons. phys. rehab. Ochsner Found. Hosp., New Orleans; cons. phys. edn. dept. Tulane U.; dir. Inst. Devel. Human Performance, 1972—. Tchr. seminars, Phila., N.Y.C., West Orange, Montclair, 1958-63; lectr. Internat. Congress Surgeons, U. Madrid, USPHS, Inst. Gen. Semantics, Lakeville, Conn., N.Y. Soc. Gen. Semantics; pres. Bell-Kerr Realty Co., Bell-Kerr Corp.; dir. Dizzy Dean Corp., Jackson, Miss., master clinician Lifetime Sports Found. Recipient War Dept. commendation for service to injured servicemen World War II, 1945; named Man of Year, Goodwill Industries New Orleans, 1959. Mem. Am. Badminton Assn. Clubs (chmn. nat. rules com., chmn. Nat. Umpires Assn.). Clubs: Tulane (dir. N.Y.C.), Montclair Tennis (pres., dir.). Author: (with Dr. H. H. Kessler) Civilian Amputees in action, 1948; (with Signe Brunnstrom) The Leg Amputee: Pre-Prosthetic Training, 1951; Training of the Lower Extremity Amputee, 1956. Home: Box 4033 New Orleans LA 70118

KERR, GLADYS ELIZABETH MCCAIN (MRS. JAMES DONALD KERR), educator; b. Waxhaw, N.C., July 22,, 1934; d. Robert Maxwell and Isa (Winslow) McCain; B.A., Flora Macdonald Coll., 1956; M.A., George Peabody Coll., 1957; postgrad. NSF Inst. for Math. Tchrs. U. N.C., 1969; m. James Donald Kerr, July 28, 1961; 1 son, James Maxwell. Tchr. math. Arlington (Va.) Pub. Schs., 1957-60; tchr. math., music San Diego Pub. Schs., 1960-61; prof. math. Wingate Coll., N.C., 1961-70, 71—. Cons. S.C. State Math. Dept., 1967; NSF Inst. for Math. Tchrs. in Jr. Colls., U. N.C., Chapel Hill, 1968. Past dist. co-chmn. Union County Heart Fund; pres., Wisackyola Hist. Drama and Festival Assn., 1965-66, dir., 1965-67. Bd. dirs. Union-Anson Counties Community Poverty Com. Mem. Am. Assn. U. Women (treas. 1964-65), Math. Assn. Am., N.C. Acad. Sci., N.C. Tchrs. Math., Delta Kappa Gamma. Democrat. Clubs: Waxhaw Womans (pres. 1965-66, v.p. 1970—). Home: Box 174 Route 3 Waxhaw NC 28173

KERR, HAWLEY COE, lawyer oil co. exec.; b. Tulsa, Nov. 12, 1901; s. Charles William and Annie Elizabeth (Coe) K.; A.B., U. Tulsa, 1922; LL.B., U. Okla., 1925; m. Marguerite Carmen Baca, Dec. 30, 1939; children—Stephen Pendaries, Michael Hawley. Admitted to Okla. bar, 1925, U.S. Supreme Ct., 1949; gen. practice, Tulsa, 1925-37; mem. legal staff Skelly Oil Co., Tulsa, 1937-69, gen. counsel, 1960-66, corp. sec., 1961-66, cons. atty., 1967-69, corp. secretary, 1967—; with firm Ungerman, Grabel, Ungerman & Leiter, 1971—; sec., dir. Skelly Pipe Line Co.; sec.-treas., dir. Skelly Internat. Oil Co.; sec. Skelly Oil Co. of Iran, 1964-70; dir. Hawkeye Chem. Co., Clinton, Ia.; mem. policy com. Chemplex Co., 1966-70. Adv. bd. Internat. Oil & Gas Ednl. Center. Served to lt. col. USAAF, 1942-45. Mem. Am., Okla., Tulsa County bar assns., Ind. Producers Assn., Am. Petroleum Inst., Mid-Continent Oil and Gas Assn., Tulsa C. of C., Sigma Alpha Epsilon. Presbyn. Club: Tulsa. Author treatise. Home: 3153 S Utica St Tulsa OK 74110 Office: Wright Bldg Tulsa OK

KERR, JAMES WILSON, stamp and coin co. exec.; b. Balt., May 21, 1921; s. James W. and Laura Virgia (Wright) K.; B.S. with honors, Davidson Coll., 1942; M.S., N.Y.U., 1948; postgrad. Freiburg U., 1957-60, Brookings Inst., 1970; m. Mary Thomas Montgomery, Feb.

25, 1945; children—April (Mrs. Rodney H. Miller), Catherine (Mrs. Charles M. Wood III) (dec.), Wilson, Andrew. Commd. 2d lt. U.S. Army, 1942, advanced through grades to lt. col., 1964; with inf., World War II, Korea; electronic staff, Ft. Bragg, N.C., 1948-51; weapons research, N.M., 1953-57; adviser French Army, 1957-60; staff electronics, Ft. Monroe, Va., 1960-62; research mgr., div. dir. Civil Def., Pentagon, 1962-64, as civilian, 1964-—; v.p. Latherow & Co., Arlington, Va., 1965-—. Advanced English instr. French Army, 1957-60; cons. Am. Nat. Red Cross Mus., 1968-—, Smithsonian Instn. Dept. Postal History, 1966-—. Vol. fireman N.Y. State, 1946-48, Fairfax County, Va., 1969-—, leader Kit Carson council Boy Scouts Am., 1938-—; chmn. library bd., Orangeburg, N.Y., 1946-48. Decorated Bronze Star medals (4), Purple Heart; recipient Silver Beaver award Boy Scouts Am., 1956. Fellow Explorers Club; mem. Nat. Acad. Scis. (mem. com. on fire research 1970-—), Internat. Assn. Fire Chiefs (chmn. fire research com. 1969-—), Fed. Fire Council, A.A.A.S., S.A.R., Black Forest Mardi Gras (Germany), Nat. Broadcasters Club, Pentagon Officers Athletic Club, Phi Beta Kappa, Gamma Sigma Epsilon, Delta Phi Alpha. Presbyn. (elder 1963-—). Author: Korean-English Phrase Book, 1951; 19th Century Korea Postal Handbook, 1965. Contbr. articles to profl. jours. Home: 6422 Crosswoods Dr Falls Church VA 22044 Office: Sec Def Civil Preparedness Research Pentagon Washington DC 20310

KERR, JOHN HERVEY, JR., Republican state committeeman; b. Lexington, Ky., Oct. 9, 1921; s. John Hervey and Elizabeth (Latham) K.; B.S., U. Ky., 1943; m. Mary LaBach, May 17, 1947; children—John Hervey III, Mary Shepherd, Bettie LaBach. State sec.-treas. Funeral Dirs. Assn. Ky., Inc., 1950-—; partner Kerr Bros. Funeral Home, 1960-—; mem. State Police Merit Bd., Ky., 1950-52; precinct committeeman Fayette County Republican Party, 1952-—; co-commr. Fayette County, 1953-57; co-chmn. Fayette County Rep. Campaign, 1954, 56, 60; asst. state chmn. Ky. Rep. Campaign, 1962, 64, 66, 67, chmn., 1968; city commr., Lexington, 1963-65; del. to Rep. Nat. Conv., 1968; chmn. Ky. Rep. Central Com., 1968-—. Served to 1st lt. AUS, 1943-45; ETO. Decorated Purple Heart; named Outstanding Young Man, Lexington Jaycees, 1953, One of 3 Outstanding Young Men of Ky., Jaycees, 1954. Mem. Am. Legion, Omicron Delta Kappa, Beta Gamma Sigma, Phi Mu Alpha. Mem. Christian Ch. Home: 124 S Ashland Av Lexington KY 40502 Office: 463 E Main St Lexington KY 40507

KERR, JOHN WARD, JR., accountant; b. Fort Monroe, Va., July 30, 1937; s. John Ward and Florence (Bricker) K.; B.B.A., Coll. William and Mary, Norfolk div., 1960; J.D., George Washington U., 1965; m. Carole Anne Alexander, Jan. 18, 1958; children—Katherine Lynne, John Ward III, Elizabeth Carole. Appellate conferee and agt. Internal Revenue Service, Washington, 1960-65; tax dir. Leach, Calkins & Scott, Richmond, 1965-67; tax mgr. Lybrand, Ross Bros. & Montgomery, Richmond, 1967-69; tax mgr. Peat, Marwick, Mitchell & Co., Richmond, 1969-72; tax coordinator J.K. Lasser & Co., Jacksonville, Fla., 1972-—. Instr. taxation Univ. Coll. U. Richmond. Mem. Am. Inst. C.P.A.'s, Va. Soc. C.P.A.'s (tax com. chmn.), Richmond Chpt. C.P.A.'s (tax com. chmn.), Nat. Assn. Accountants, Fed. Govt. Accountants Assn., Alpha Kappa Psi, Pi Kappa Alpha, Phi Alpha Delta. Methodist. Kiwanian. Clubs: Salisbury Country (Midlothian, Va.); Bull and Bear (Richmond, Va.), Va. Mil. Inst. Alumni (Richmond). Home: 8858 Runnymeade Rd Jacksonville FL 32217 Office: Universal Marion Bldg Jacksonville FL 32202

KERR, RALPH WALDO, chemist; b. Mongaup Valley, N.Y., May 19, 1899; s. Marvin Orrin and Minnie (Ballard) K.; A.B., Columbia U., 1921, M.A., 1924, Ph.D., 1924; m. Anne E. Mabbett, Nov. 24, 1949; children—Robert, Barbara, Charlotte. Asst. in chemistry Columbia U., 1922-24, instr. biochemistry, research asso., 1924-29; research chemist Corn Products Co., Argo, Ill., 1929-60, cons., 1960-—. Served with USN, 1918. Mem. Am. Chem. Soc., N.Y. Acad. Scis., A.A.A.S., Fla. Gulf Coast Art Center, Archives Fla. Art, Sigma Xi. Author, editor: Chemistry and Industry of Starch, 1944. Contbr. articles on starch products and chem. derivatives, enzyme chemistry to sci. jours. Patentee starch products, chem. derivatives, prodn. dextrose by enzymatic hydrolysis. Address: 1858 Venetian Point Dr Clearwater FL 33515

KERR, RAYMOND LAWRENCE, ednl. supr.; b. Plainview, Tex., May 18, 1911; s. Lawrence Almon and Dovie (Chumbley) K.; B.S. in Archtl. Engring., Tex. A. and M. Coll., 1935; M.S. in Indsl. Engring., U. Houston, 1954; postgrad. psychology, 1954-65; m. Myrtle Lucile Pine, July 17, 1937; children—Sandra Lucille, Douglas Raymond. Asst. plant engr. Texaco, Inc., 1935-42, asst. mgr., 1946-54, mgr. packaging div., 1954-59; cons. indsl. engring., mgmt., Tex., La., 1959-65; tech. supr. trade, indsl. edn. La. Dept. Edn., Baton Rouge, 1965-68; exec. asst., div. vocational edn. La. Dept. Edn., 1968-—. Chmn. community drive United Fund, Port Arthur, Tex., 1957. Served to lt. col., C.E., AUS, 1942-46. Registered profl. engr., La., Tex. Fellow Royal Soc. Arts (London, Eng.); mem. La. Engring. Soc., Nat. Soc. Profl. Engrs., Am. Inst. Indsl. Engrs., Kappa Phi, Psi Chi. Home: Route 1 Box 82-B Denham Springs LA 70726 Office: La Dept Edn State Capitol Bldg Baton Rouge LA 70804.

KERR, WILLIAM GRAYCEN, lawyer; b. Oklahoma City, Oct. 18, 1937; s. Robert Samuel and Grayce (Breene) K.; B.A., U. Okla., 1959, LL.B., 1962; m. Joffa Gernar, Aug. 4, 1956; children—Joffa, Kavar, Mara. Admitted to Okla. bar, 1962, since practiced in Oklahoma City; v.p. Citizens Finance Co., Oklahoma City, 1963-65; chmn. Citizens Bank Ada (Okla.), 1966-72; dir. Farmers and Mchts. Bank Tulsa; chmn. Bristol, Inc., Downey, Cal., 1970-72, Pub. Leasing Corp., Oklahoma City, 1969-70. Chmn., Okla. Democratic Central Com., 1967-69. trustee, Kerr Found., Nat. Cowboy Hall of Fame. Mem. Phi Delta Theta, Phi Alpha Delta. Home: 2414 Smoking Oak Norman OK 73069 Office: Fidelity Plaza Oklahoma City OK 73102

KERRICK, LOUIS ALLEN, personnel exec.; b. Elizabethtown, Ky., July 11, 1942; s. Merritt Allen and Thelma Pauline (Hunt) K.; B.S., U. Ky., 1964, M.B.A., 1966; m. Margaret Jo Patterson, June 4, 1966; 1 son, Patrick Allen. Personnel mgr. Corning Glass Works, Harrodsburg, Ky., 1966-—. Dir., Shaker Investments, Tempo Investments. Bd. dirs. Mercer County Youth Council, Legend of Daniel Boone Drama. Served with AUS, 1966-67. Named Rotarian of the Year, 1970. Outstanding Young Man of Mercer County, Harrodsburg C. of C., 1970, Jaycee of the Year, 1969. Mer. Harrodsburg Jr. C. of C. (pres. 1971). Baptist (supt. Sunday Sch. dept. 1969-—). Rotarian. Home: 375 College Manor Harrodsburg KY 40330 Office: Corning Glass Works Houghton Dr Harrodsburg KY 40330

KERRY, HENRY EUGENE, lawyer; b. Longview, Tex., Nov. 5, 1932; s. Henry and Mary Louise (Findley) K.; B.B.A., U. Tex., 1954, LL.D., 1957; m. Elizabeth Ladon, July 25, 1953 (div.); children—Linda Louise, Elizabeth Anne; m. 2d. Admitted to Tex. bar, 1957, since practiced in Ft. Worth; mem. firm Hooper & Kerry firms, 1961-—. Chmn. Child Welfare Bd. Tarrant County, 1969-—. Bd. dirs. Ft. Worth Symphony Assn., Ft. Worth Ballet Assn. Served to 1st lt. USAF, 1954-56. Mem. State Bar Tex., Am. (sect. exec. council 1964, exec. council Young Lawyers sect. 1964-65), Ft. Worth-Tarrant County bar assns., Am., Tex. trial lawyers assns., State Jr. Bar Tex. (pres. 1963-64, chmn. 1962-63), Phi Gamma Delta, Phi Alpha Delta. Democrat. Methodist. Home: 4300 Woodwick Ct Fort Worth TX 76109 Office: Ft Worth Club Bldg Fort Worth TX 76102

KERSTING, ALBERT FREDERICK, mgmt. cons.; b. Mobile, Ala., Jan. 2, 1914; s. Albert Frederick and Aileen (Austill) K.; student George Washington U., 1947-49, Tex. Christian U., 1957-60; m. Elizabeth L. George, Nov. 23, 1940; children—Albert Frederick, Elizabeth (Mrs. Milton Drummond Brown), Katherine Austill. Joined USN, 1935, advanced through grades to comdr., 1945, ret., 1957; asst. to dir. prodn. Chance Vought Aircraft Corp., 1957-60; in charge improvement mgmt. LTV Aerospace, Inc., 1960-63; established Kersting & Assos., Dallas, 1959, pres., 1963-—. Active Boy Scouts Am.; mem. S.W. area planning com. YMCA, 1963-69. Ky. Col. Recipient achievement award, sec. Navy, 1945; 1st pl. award, movie contest in work simplification application in industry Indsl. Mgmt. Soc., 1959-62. Mem. Am. Inst. Indsl. Engrs. (adv. bd. aerospace div. 1966, mem. bd. dirs. 1960-65), Soc. for Advancement Mgmt. (Dallas pres. 1961-62, v.p., treas. internat. 1970-71), Indsl. Mgmt. Clubs (nat. exec. council 1963-69), Indsl. Mgmt. Soc., Indsl. Mgmt. Club (Dallas pres. 1960-61, exec. bd. 1959-62), Tex. Mgmt. Cons. Assn. (pres. 1964-65), Tex. Mfrs. Assn., Dallas C. of C., Internat. Work Simplification Inst. (founding mem., exec. v.p. 1970-71, pres. 1971-72, trustee 1967), S.W. Work Simplification Council (founding mem., adv. bd. 1959-67). Episcopalian (licensed lay reader, chmn. laymans work Diocese of Dallas 1963, 70, exec. council). Rotarian. Home: 4447 Alta Vista Lane Dallas TX 75229 Office: 4159 Buena Vista St Dallas TX 75204

KERTZ, HAROLD ALLAN, lawyer; b. Allentown, Pa., Dec. 2, 1906; s. Christian J. and Elizabeth (Rudy) K.; J.D., Georgetown U., 1928; LL.M., Catholic U., 1932; m. Genevieve Hastings, May 1, 1944; 1 son, Robert Allan. Admitted to D.C. bar, 1929; practiced law, Washington, 1928-31; trust officer Nat. Met. Bank, Washington, 1931-40; partner Roberts & McInnis, 1940-54, Mercier, Kertz & Sanders, 1954-57; vice chmn. Pub. Utilities Commn. D.C., 1957-62; prof. of wills and estates, Georgetown U., Washington, 1955-65; dir. Harlowe Typography, Inc., Sho-Tel, Inc., Chesapeake Graphics, Inc., The Chemmet Co., O'Donnell's Sea Grill, Inc., R.E. Darling Co., Basic Boats, Inc., James R. Dunlop, Inc. Mem. ICC Practitioners Assn., FCC Bar, Am., D.C. bar assns., Sigma Nu Phi. Episcopalian. Clubs: Capitol Hill, Columbia Country, University, Nat. Press, Farmington Country, The Counsellors. Legal contbg. editor to Trusts and Estates. Home: 2500 Virginia Av NW Washington DC 20006 Office: 1901 Sunderland Pl NW Washington DC 20036

KERWIN, JOSEPH P., physician, astronaut; b. Oak Park, Ill., Feb. 19, 1932; B.A., Coll. Holy Cross, 1953; M.D., Northwestern U., 1957; m. Shirley Ann Good; 1 dau., Sharon. Intern, D.C. Gen. Hosp., 1957-58; commd. lt. comdr. U.S. Navy, 1958; flight surgeon Marine Air Group 14, Cherry Point, N.C., Fighter Squadron 101, Oceana Naval Air Sta., Virginia Beach, Fla.; staff flight surgeon Air Wing 4, Cecil Field, Fla.; now astronaut Manned Spacecraft Center, Houston. Address: Manned Spacecraft Center Houston TX 77058*

KESNER, DOUGLAS FLOYD, hosp. adminstr.; b. Cleveland, Okla., Aug. 11, 1932; s. Floyd and Jenave H. (Rubert) K.; B.B.A., So. Meth. U., 1960; M.H.A., Trinity U., 1970; m. Miss Cochran, May 23, 1957; children—Denise Kay, Mary Michelle. Adminstr., Parkland Hosp., Dallas, 1960-62, Meth. Hosp., Dallas, 1962-64, Garland (Tex.) Med. Center, 1965-66, Logan (W.Va.) Med. Found., 1967-68, Colonial Convalescent Center, St. Clairsville, O., 1967-68, Nicholas County Hosp. Dist., Lexington, Ky., 1969-—; lectr. Trinity U., Ky. U.; pres. Scott-Willis Hosp., Nursing Home, Clinic Cons.; pres. Crestview Convalescent Centers. Bd. dirs. KNHA, Hunt Med. Found. Served with AUS, 1953-55. Named Health Adminstr. of Year, West Tex., 1965. Fellow Am. Coll. Nursing Home Adminstrs.; mem. Am. Coll. Hosp. Adminstrs., Am., Ky. hosp. assns., Ky. Nursing Home Assn. (pres.), Louisville, Dallas chambers commerce. Club: Optimist (Dallas). Home: 3337 Stanford St Dallas TX 75225 Office: PO Box 1404 Lexington KY 40501

KESSEL, STANLEY PHILLIP, orthodontist; b. Lancaster, O., Dec. 27, 1923; s. Leo and Gerry (Weisman) K.; D.D.S., Ohio State U., 1946, postgrad., 1948-50; m. Anita M. Frankel, May 30, 1963; step-children—Bonni Tischler, Samuel Tischler, Andrew. Practice orthodontics, Cin., 1950-55, Hollywood, Fla., 1956-—. Mem. Citizens Adv. Com. of Hollywood, 1970-—; pres. Hollywood Playhouse, 1967. Served with Dental Corps, USNR, 1946-48. Diplomate Am. Bd. Orthodontics. Mem. Am. Assn. Orthodontists, Fla. Orthodontic Soc., Greater Miami Acad. Orthodontists, Fla., Hollywood dental socs., Hollywood C. of C. (dir. 1970-71), Com. of 100 Hollywood. Jewish Religion. Mason, Rotarian. Contbr. articles to profl. jours. Home: 506 Palm Dr Hallandale FL 33009 Office: 3325 Hollywood Blvd Hollywood FL 33021

KESSLER, EDNA ANNE LEVENTHAL (MRS. MURRAY ARTHUR KESSLER), artist, educator, interior designer; b. Kingston, N.Y., Mar. 13, 1910; d. Max and Dora (Cohen) Leventhal; grad. Parsons Sch. Design, 1929; postgrad. Columbia, N.Y.U., Queens Coll., Instituto San Miguel de Allende (Mexico); m. Murray Arthur Kessler, June 17, 1937; children—Robert Sheldon, Kenneth Charles. Faculty, Parsons Sch. Design, 1928-30; head counselor Camp Co-Ma-Ha, Rock Hill, N.Y., summers 1932-37; pres. Edna Leventhal Millinery Shop, 1935-37, Edna Thal Millinery Shop, N.Y.C., 1937, Edna L. Kessler, Interior Designs, Jamaica, N.Y., 1941-—; art instr. Temple Sholom, Floral Park, N.Y., 1960-—; pvt. instr., Jamaica, 1967-70, Miami, Fla., 1970-—; one-man shows Frederick Thompson Found., Hollis, N.Y., 1962, Little Gallery, N.Y.C., 1964, Manhasset (N.Y.) Art Gallery, 1964, Temple Sholom, Glen Oaks, N.Y., 1965, Hollywood (Fla.) Playhouse, 1972, others; exhibited in group shows at Witte Meml. Mus., San Antonio, Smithsonian Instn., Washington, Parrish Mus., Southampton, N.Y., IBM Gallery, Poughkeepsie, N.Y., many others. Active Cub Scouts. Dir. Jamaica Estates Hebrew Center. Recipient Grand Prix D'Aquarelle, La Biennale Internationale, Vichy, France, 1966; 1st prize Island Art Guild, 1964, L.I. Fair, 1965, Parrish Art Mus., 1965, 67, Art League of Nassau County, 1967, Herrick art Show, 1967; award Met. Miami Art Flower Show, 1969, 70, 71, award Miami Boat Show, 1969, 70, Internat. Boat Show, 1971, award Allied Arts, 1970, 71, Miami Art League, 1971, many others. Mem. Art League L.I. (Gold medal 1961, past dir.), Am. Artist Profl. League, Hudson Valley Art Assn., Island Art Guild, Art League Nassau County (Best in Show award 1962), Malverne Art Assn., Allied Arts N. Miami, Miami Art Center, Miami, Nat., Broward art leagues, Catherine Lorillard Wolfe Art Club. Art work and articles published in fourteen books, U.S., France, Italy. Home: 1170 NE 191st St North Miami Beach FL 33162

KESTENBAUM, LIONEL, lawyer; b. Bklyn., Nov. 10, 1926; A.B., Yale, 1948; LL.B., Columbia, 1951. Admitted to N.Y. bar, 1953, U.S. Supreme Ct. bar, 1955, D.C. bar, 1962; law clk. Dist. Judge So. Dist. N.Y., 1951-52; atty. appellate sect. Civil div. Dept. Justice, 1954-59, asst. chief appellate sect., 1961-65, chief evaluation sect., 1965-68, dir. policy planning Antitrust div., 1968-69; with office gen. counsel AEC, 1959-61; mem. Twentieth Century Fund Task Force Internat. Satellite Communications, 1969-70; now mem. firm Bergson, Borkland, Margolis & Adler, Washington; adj. prof. Georgetown U., 1965-67. Mem. Fed., Am. bar assns. Address: Bergson Borkland Margolis & Adler 21 Dupont Circle Washington DC 20036*

KETCHAM, ORMAN WESTON, judge; b. Bklyn., Oct. 1, 1918; s. Walter Seymour and Arline (Weston) K.; A.B., Princeton, 1940; LL.B., Yale, 1947; m. Anne Phelps Stokes, Dec. 22, 1947; children—Anne Weston, Helen Louisa Phelps, Elizabeth Miner, Susan Stokes. Admitted to D.C. bar, 1948; practiced in Washington, 1948-52; Washington rep. Fund for the Republic, 1953; asst. gen. counsel U.S. Fgn. Operations Agy., 1953-55; trial atty. Antitrust div. U.S. Dept. Justice, Washington, 1955-57; Judge Juvenile Ct. D.C., Washington, 1957-71; asso. judge Superior Ct. D.C., 1971-—. Adj. prof. law Georgetown U. Law Center, 1963-67, U. Va. Law Sch., 1971-—. Mem. council of judges Nat. Council Crime and Delinquency, 1959-—; chmn. Washington Met. Area Council Juvenile Ct. Judges, 1961-64. Served as lt. comdr., USNR, 1941-46. Mem. Am. Bar Assn., Bar Assn. D.C., Nat. Council Juvenile Ct. Judges (pres. 1965-66), Internat. Assn. Youth Magistrates (v.p. 1966-—), Am. Law Inst. Republican. Conglist. Clubs: Cosmos (Washington); Chevy Chase. Author: (with Monrad G. Paulsen) Cases and Materials Relating to Juvenile Courts, 1967. Home: 2 E Melrose St Chevy Chase MD 20015 Office: 410 E St NW Washington DC 20001

KETTLE, JOHN J(OSEPH), bank exec.; b. Dallas, 1895; s. James and Martha (Wallace) K.; student Bryan High Sch., Met. Bus. Sch.; m. Pauline Wood, Mar. 23, 1916; children—Pauline (Mrs. Chas. A. Haynes), Dorothy (dec.). With 1st Nat. Bank, Dallas since 1913, asst. cashier, asst. v.p. and v.p., sr. v.p., 1950-60, vice chmn., 1960-67; vice chmn. bd., dir. Kan. State Bank & Trust Co., Wichita, 1967-—; dir. City Nat. Bank, Plainview, Exchange Savs. and Loan Assn., Dallas. Vice pres., dir. State Fair of Tex.; dir. State Fair Musicals. Mem. Ind. Petroleum Assn., Mid-Continent Oil and Gas Assn., Ind. Producers and Royalty Owners Assn., Am. Inst. Banking, Am., Res. City, Tex. bankers assns. Presbyn. Mason (Shriner, past master). Clubs: Petroleum, Gun, Cipango, Brook Hollow Country, Dallas Country, Dinner Dance (Dallas). Home: 4504 Westway Dallas TX Office: 1401 Elm St Dallas TX

KETTLES, ROBERT CAREW, city ofcl.; b. Ypsilanti, Mich., Jan. 9, 1925; s. Albert Grant and Cora (Stobie) K.; B.A., Mich. State Coll., 1946-52; m. Joanne Attwood, Oct. 25, 1952; children—Brooke Elizabeth, Craig Carew. Mem. Mich. Senate, 1953-54; with Ford Motor Co., Lansing, Mich., 1954-60; pres. Bob Kettles Ford Sales, Caro, 1960-65; v.p. sales Gen. Aviation, Inc., Lansing, 1965-67; adminstr. housing rehab. and neighborhood improvement Orlando, Fla., 1967-—; sales mgr. Stone Island Properties, Enterprise, Fla. Active various community drives. Chmn. finance com. Republican Party, Tuscola County, Fla. Served with AUS, 1943-46, 51-52. Home: 4706 Wayfarer St Orlando FL 32806 Office: PO Box 6 Enterprise FL

KEY, FLOYD MARTIN, county ofcl.; b. Megargel, Tex., Sept. 14, 1926; s. George Andrew and Margaret Estell (Campbell) K.; B.S., Tex. A and M. U., 1948, postgrad., 1967-70; postgrad. Colo. State U., 1969; m. Sarah Beth Mayes, Dec. 30, 1948; children—John Martin, Sally Ann, Spencer Andrew. Farmer, Olney, Tex., 1948-56; asst. county agrl. agent, Brownwood, Tex., 1956-61; county agrl. agent, Meridian, Tex., 1961-65, Comanche, Tex., 1965-—. Trustee Comanche Child Care Center. Served with AUS, 1945-46. Mem. Comanche C. of C. (dir. 1969-70), Epsilon Sigma Phi. Baptist. Lion. Home and Office: Box 705 Comanche TX 76442

KEY, GRIFFIN THEOBALD, III, elec. engr.; b. Eufaula, Ala., Dec. 26, 1924; s. Griffin Theobald and Virginia (Corbitt) K.; B.E.E., Auburn U., 1948; m. Betty Ann Lee, July 28, 1945; children—Deborah Ann (Mrs. Petranka), Judith Corbitt. Mgr. outside constrn. G. T. Key Co., 1948-56, gen. mgr., 1956-65, owner, gen. mgr., 1965-—. Served to 2d lt. USAF, 1943-45. Registered profl. engr. Ala. Mem. Phi Delta Theta. Kiwanian (pres. Capital City club 1971). Home: 1554 Gilmer Av Montgomery AL 36104 Office: 931 N McDonough St Montgomery AL 36104

KEY, JOHN MORRIS, elec. machinery co. exec.; b. Summitville, Ind., Mar. 5, 1922; s. Elmer F. and Margieree (Weaver) K.; student Gen. Motors Inst., 1940-43, U. Wis., 1943-44, U.S. Naval Acad., 1944; m. Alice Fuselier, Sept. 2, 1949; children—Scott, Peggy, Gary. Tool maker Delco Remy, 1940-43; process engr. A.B. Dick Co., 1946-48; pres., mgr. Marine Elec. Repairs, 1948-54; pres., gen. mgr. Owesen & Co., Inc., New Orleans, 1948-69; pres., gen. mgr. Anixter New Orleans, Inc., 1969-—; pres. Anixter Power Systems, Inc., YEK, Inc., H. & K. Equipment Co., Inc. Mem. adv. bd. Salvation Army New Orleans. Served with USNR, 1943-46. Named Man of Year, Salvation Army, 1965. Mason (Shriner). Club: Plimsoll (New Orleans). Home: 5645 Evelyn Ct New Orleans LA 70124 Office: 315 N Notre Dame St New Orleans LA 70130

KEYES, JAY FRASER, hotel exec.; b. N.Y.C., May 22, 1929; s. Warren Jay and Helen Wagner (Sayer) K.; student Orange County Community Coll., 1951; m. Janet Gaynor Dillon, Apr. 20, 1968; children— Benjamin, Seth; stepchildren—Dwight, Susan, Doug. Mgr. Hot Shoppes Inc., Washington, 1951-57; pres. The Key Chain Restaurants, Middletown, N.Y., 1957-60; mgr. Restaurants Assos., N.Y.C., 1960-61; gen. mgr. Hotel Northampton and Wiggins Tavern, Northampton, Mass., 1961-64, The Boar's Head Inn, Charlottesville, Va., 1965-66; asst. to pres. Collonades Hotel, Palm Beach, Fla., 1966-67; gen. mgr. Port-O-Call, Tierra Verde, Fla., 1967-68, Sapphire Bay Resort, St. Thomas, V.I., 1968-69; gen. mgr. Hilton Inn, Williamsburg, Va., 1970-71, v.p. and gen. mgr., 1971; v.p., gen. mgr. Clearwater Point Hilton, Clearwater Beach, Fla., 1971-—. Guest lectr. U. Mass., 1963. Served with USNR, 1948-50. Named Man of the Year, Northampton C. of C., 1963. Mem. Hotel Sales Mgmt. Assn. (founder), C. of C. (dir. 1961-63). Democrat. Episcopalian. Mason. Club: Sertoma (charter mem.) (Clearwater Beach). Address: 715 S Gulfview Blvd Clearwater Beach FL 33515

KEYL, MILTON JACK, educator; b. Decatur, Ill., Mar 5, 1924; s. Norman J. and Anna (Bagenski) K.; B.S., U. Cin., 1947, M.S., 1948, Ph.D., 1957; m. Audrey Fay Shearer, Aug. 21, 1948; children—Mark D., Karen Lynn. Asst. prof. physiology U. Okla. Med. Sch., 1957-60, asso. prof., 1960-66, prof. physiology, research prof. urology, 1966-—. Served with USNR, 1943-46. Mem. Am. Physiol. Soc., Am. Soc. Nephrology, N.Y. Acad. Scis., Internat. Soc. Lymphology, Sigma Xi. Research on kidney. Home: 3605 Sun Valley Oklahoma City OK 73110

KEYWORTH, DONALD ARTHUR, chem. co. exec.; b. Flint, Mich., Apr. 21, 1930; s. Vern and Lillian May (Holcomb) K.; B.S., U. Mich., 1951; M.S., Mich. State U., 1954; Ph.D., Wayne State U., 1958. Head quality controls Lapaco Paint and Varnish Co., Lansing, Mich., 1951-52; research chemist Wyandotte Chems. (Mich.), 1957-61; asso. research dir. Universal Oil Products, Des Plaines, Ill., 1961-67; tech. dir. Scientific and Ednl. Services, Houston, 1967-68; dir. research and devel. Tenneco Hydrocarbon Chemicals div., Pasadena, Tex., 1968-—. Indsl. adv. bd. curriculum devel. Tex. State Tech. Inst., 1971-—. Served with AUS, 1954-56. Mem. Sci. and Ednl. Services (dir. 1967), Am. Inst. Chemists, Am. Chem. Soc. (prof. in charge 1968-69, indsl. cons. to ChemTeC project, 1971), Am. Inst.

Physics, Soc. Applied Spectroscopy, Am. Soc. Testing Materials, Anachems, Sigma Xi, Phi Lambda Upsilon. Author: Chemistry of the Elements, 1971; Chemistry for Technicians, 1969; Flame Emission and Atomic Absorption Spectroscopy, 1968. Contbr. articles to profl. pubs. Home: 5324 Dora St Houston TX 77005 Office: Tenneco Hydrocarbon Chemicals Div P O Box 849 Pasadena TX 77501

KHADHIRI, RIADH KIT, educator; b. Diwaniya, Iraq, June 29, 1932 (came to U.S. 1954); s. Mohammad H. and Lutfia (Khadhiri) K.; B.B.A., U. Miss., 1957, M.S., 1958; D.B.A., Miss. State U., 1970; m. June Morgan, Sept. 5, 1955; children—Diana, Susan. Grad. asst. Miss. State U., State College, 1966-68; asso. prof. Nicholls State U., Thibodaux, La., 1968-71, St. Edward's U., Austin, Tex., 1971—; owner Bus. Research Cons., Thibodaux, 1968-71. Served with Iraqi Army, 1959-60. Named outstanding educator in Am. Nicholls State U., 1971. Mem. Am., So. econ. assns., Acad. Miss. Economists, Arnold Air Soc., Omicron Delta Epsilon, Delta Sigma Pi, Theta Chi. Home: 9302 Heatherwood Austin TX 78704

KHANNA, JASWANT LAL, educator; b. Lehore, Pakistan, July 5, 1925 (came to U.S. 1953, naturalized, 1970); s. Sohan L. and Savitri Devi (Malhotra) K.; B.S., Panjab U., 1943, M.A., 1948; Ph.D. (Fulbright fellow), U. Colo., 1953-56; m. Prabha Bhagat, July 29, 1951; children—Kanwal, Mukti. Lectr. psychology Panjab U., 1956-57, 51-53; sr. psychologist Larned (Kan.) State Hosp., 1957-61; asso. prof. dept. psychiatry U. Tenn. Coll. Medicine, Memphis, 1961—, chief psychologist Perinatal project, 1961—; adj. prof. LeMoyne Owens Coll., 1962—. Cons. Jackson (Tenn.) Mental Health Center, VA Hosp., Memphis. Watumall Found. scholar, 1956. Fellow Am. Orthopsychiat. Assn.; mem. Am., Brit. psychol. assns., Am. Assn. Mental Deficiency, Sigma Xi. Club: Holly Hills Country (Memphis); University of Tennessee Faculty. Home: 474 McElroy Rd Memphis TN 38117

KHOURY, ALBERT JOHN, physician; b. Shreveport, La., Aug. 28, 1920; s. George John and Waddier (Joseph) K.; B.S., Centenary Coll. La., 1941; M.D., U. Nuevo Leon, Monterrey, Mexico, 1948. Intern, Doctor's Hosp., Shreveport, 1947-48, resident, 1948-49; practice gen. medicine, Waskom, Tex.; mem. med. staff, chief cardiology, out-patient dept. U.S. VA Hosp., Shreveport, 1951-54; instr. U. Fla. Infirmary, 1950. mem. Am., Tex. heart assns., Pan-Am. Med. Assn. Home: 2701 Lakeshore Dr Shreveport LA 71109 Office: Khoury Clinic Jefferson Av PO Box 310 Waskom TX 75692

KHOURY, GEORGE HANNA, architect; b. Tripoli, Lebanon, Dec. 11, 1939; s. Hanna G. and Martha (Kallouf) K.; B.S. in Archtl. Engring., U. Miami, 1961, B.S. in Civil Engring., 1964, B.Arch., 1965; m. Elizabeth-Lynn Batho, June 18, 1967; 1 dau., Christine. Engr., Carr Smith & Asso., Miami, Fla., 1964-65; architect Asso. Cons. Engrs., S.A., Beirut, Lebanon, also Washington, 1965-69, head dept. architecture and town planning, 1968; architect Ferendino/Grafton/Pancoast, Miami, 1969—. Cons. advanced hosp. design in assn. with Scandinavian firms. Mem. Order of Lebanese Architects and Engrs., Internat. Union Architects, Royal Inst. Brit. Architects. Home: 427 Santander St Coral Gables FL 33134 Office: 800 Douglas Entrance Miami FL 33134

KIBLER, DAVID BURKE, III, lawyer; b. Lakeland, Fla., Feb. 5, 1924; s. David Burke, Jr. and Bessie (Dew) K.; B.A. cum laude, U. Fla., 1947, J.D., 1949; m. Nell Idalene Bryant, Sept. 26, 1945; children—David Burke IV, Thomas Bryant, Jacquelyn, Nancy Dew. Admitted to Fla. bar, 1949; since practiced in Lakeland; partner firm Holland & Knight and predecessors, 1964—. Dir., v.p. Kibler Agrl. Corp.; dir. Fla. Nat. Bank; Fla. Tile Industries, Inc. (both Lakeland), Chris McGuire, Inc., Ft. Lauderdale, Fla.; sec., dir. Lakeland Fed. Savs. & Loan Assn. Past pres., bd. dirs., exec. com. Lakeland United Fund; mem. Fla. Bd. Regents, 1967—, chmn., 1969—; ex-officio mem. Fla. Council 100. Served to 1st lt. AUS, 1943-46; ETO. Decorated Bronze Star with V, Purple Heart with oak leaf cluster. Mem. Am., 10th Jud. Circuit bar assns., Am. Judicature Soc., Fla. Bar, Am. Legion, Alpha Tau Omega, Phi Delta Phi. Democrat. Presbyn. Rotarian, Elk. Clubs: Lakeland Yacht and Country, Lone Palm Golf (Lakeland); University (Tampa, Fla.). Home: 2113 Fairmont Av Lakeland FL 33802 Office: 92 Lake Wire Dr Lakeland FL 33802

KIDD, AUBREY VIVIAN, banker; b. Richmond, Va., Aug. 1, 1908; s. Robert Henry and Lucy (Warriner) K.; B.S. in Bus. Adminstrn., U. Richmond, 1930; m. Audrey Elizabeth Murray, Sept. 15, 1933; children—Suzanne Murray, Robert Cabell. With The Bank of Va., Richmond, 1927—, part-time bookkeeper, auditor, asst. v.p., cashier, 1927-52, v.p., sec. 1952-66, sr. v.p., 1966—, sec., 1966-71. Lectr., U. Richmond Evening Sch. Bus. Adminstrn., 1936-53; lectr. Sch. Consumer Banking, U. Va., 1953—, trustee, 1960—. Pres. council Boy Scouts Am., 1954-55, mem. exec. bd., 1951-65; chmn. Richmond Local Milk Bd., 1960-62. Trustee Bapt. Ministers' Relief Fund Va., 1959-65. Pres. Consumers Bankers Assn., 1968-69. Mem. Am. Inst. Banking. Home: 7308 Normandy Dr Richmond VA 23229 Office: 800 E Main St Richmond VA 23223

KIDD, BARRON, oil co. exec.; b. Brownwood, Tex., Nov. 12, 1901; s. George W. and Annie (Barron) K.; student Howard Payne Coll., 1918-21; B.A., U. Tex., 1925, B.B.A., 1925; m. Ann Hughes, Apr. 25, 1958; 1 son, Barron Ulmer. With Stark Lumber Co., Orange, Tex., 1925-27; ind. oil operator, Dallas, 1927—; chmn. bd. Cardinal Chem., Inc., Oil Patch Equipment Sales and Rentals Ltd. Mem. Petroleum Club, Phi Gamma Delta. Republican. Presbyn. Clubs: Non Resident Links and River (N.Y.C.); Dallas Country, Brookhollow, Preston Trails Golf (Dallas); Jupiter Island (Hobe Sound, Fla.). Home: 8726 Douglas St Dallas TX 75225 Office: Oak Plaza Bldg 3707 Rawlins St Dallas TX 75219

KIDD, JEROME MCELWEE, city ofcl.; b. East Point, Ga., Mar. 20, 1925; s. Simpson D. and Bessie M. (McElwee) K.; grad. high sch.; m. Melba Jean Acuff, June 3, 1950; children—Kathy Jean (Mrs. Terry A. Loyd), Melanie L., Julie N. Clk. WPB, Washington, 1942-43; with East Point (Ga.) Fire Dept., 1947—, fire chief, 1966—. Bd. dirs. Ga. Christian Children's Home, Valdosta. Served with AUS, 1943-45. Decorated Purple Heart. Mem. Southeastern Assn. Fire Chiefs (pres. 1971-72). Mem. Ch. of Christ. Home: 3125 Carmel Dr East Point GA 30344 Office: 2757 East Point St East Point GA 30344

KIDWELL, JOHN AARON, physician; b. Nocona, Tex., June 5, 1927; s. Paul Dean and Velma Mae (Gentry) K.; B.S., McPherson Coll., 1948; M.D., U. P.R., 1957; m. Delia Cordero, Dec. 24, 1949; children—Doris Wanda, John Paul, James Dean, Debra Ann. Intern Hurley Hosp., Flint, Mich., 1957-58; practice gen. medicine, Weyers Cave, Va., 1958—; mem. med. staff Rockingham Meml. Hosp. Mem. A.M.A., Am. Acad. Gen. Practice, Med. Soc. Va., Rockingham County Med. Soc., Pi Kappa Delta. Mem. Ch. of the Brethren. Club: Ruritan (Weyers Cave, Va.). Home: Box 180 Route 1 Port Republic VA 24471 Office: Box 94 Weyers Cave VA 24486

KIDWELL, ROLLO EUGENE, lawyer; b. Dallas, June 4,, 1908; s. Charles Weems and Lessie Louise (Graber) K.; student So. Methodist U., 1926-28; LL.B., U. Tex., 1933; m. Alice Gertrude Thatcher, July 9, 1945; children—Sue, Molly (Mrs. Foster Jerome Sanders, Jr.). Admitted to Tex. bar, 1933; mem. firm Callaway, Reed, Kidwell & Brooks, Attys., Dallas, 1933-62; v.p., gen. counsel ETMF Freight System, Dallas, 1962—. Mem. Am., Dallas bar assns., State Bar Tex., Motor Carrier Lawyers Assn. Clubs: Tejas (Austin, Tex.); Brookhaven Country (Dallas). Home: 5518 Winston Ct Dallas TX 75220 Office: 2355 Stemmons Freeway Dallas TX 75207

KIEFFER, MARVIN LEWIS, lawyer; b. Weiner, Ark., Mar. 11, 1923; s. Jake and Matilda (Ziegenhorn) K.; B.S. in Pub. Adminstrn., U. Ark., 1950, LL.B., 1951; m. Julia Elizabeth Barker, Aug. 31, 1947. Admitted to Ark. bar, 1951; examining agt. U.S. Bur. Internal Revenue, Little Rock and Jonesboro, Ark., 1951-59; individual practice law, Jonesboro, 1959—. Bd. dirs. Jonesboro YMCA, 1960-70, pres., 1965. Served with AUS, 1943-46. Mem. Craighead County (pres. 1971-72), Ark. (chmn. audit com. 1965-70), Am. bar assns. Baptist. Mason, Kiwanian (lt. gov. Mo.-Ark. div. XVI 1970-71). Club: Jonesboro (pres. 1965). Home: 706 Melton Dr Jonesboro AR 72401 Office: McAdams Trust Bldg Jonesboro AR 72401

KIEK, P. MARTIN, advt. agy. exec. Pres., gen. mgr. Foote, Cone & Belding de Mexico. Address: S A Salamanca 102 10 Piso Mexico City 7 Mexico*

KIEL, GEORGE RALPH, pub. relations exec.; b. Hackensack, N.J., Sept. 24, 1911; s. Frederick William and Olga Madeline (Thoma) K.; B.S., U. Va., 1933; m. Elsie Andrews Lee, May 19, 1945; 1 dau., Carol Anne (Mrs. Thomas O. Otto III). Reporter, Bergen Evening Record, Hackensack, N.J., 1933-37; pub. relations account exec. Arthur L. Green & Assos., N.Y.C., 1937-41; v.p. Hal Leyshon & Assos., Miami, 1941-46; pres. G. Ralph Kiel & Assos., Miami, 1946-50; v.p. Leyshon & Assos., Miami, 1955-60; gen. mgr., dir. publicity Bahamas Devel. Bd., Nassau, 1950-54; v.p. pub. relations Wackenhut Corp., Coral Gables, Fla., 1960—. Bd. dirs. Miami Lighthouse for Blind, 1955-68. Mem. Pub. Relations Soc. Am., Greater Miami Pub. Relations Assn. (pres. 1949-50), U. Va. Alumni Assn., Delta Upsilon. Democrat. Episcopalian. Clubs: Coconut Grove Sailing (Miami); Country (Coral Gables, Fla.); Coconut Grove Civic (v.p. 1960-61) (Miami, Fla.). Contbr. articles to profl. jours. Home: 3911 Battersea Rd Coconut Grove Miami FL 33133 Office: 3280 Ponce de Leon Blvd Coral Gables FL 33134

KIEPPER, ALAN FREDERICK, city ofcl.; b. Syracuse, N.Y., July 3, 1928; s. John Carl and Sarah (McFadden) K.; A.B. cum laude, U. N.H., 1950; M.P.A., Wayne State U., 1960; m. Edith Harper, June 28, 1953; children—Patricia Ellen, Jane Elizabeth, Paul Frederick, Nancy Diana (dec.). Adminstrv. intern City of Richmond, Va., 1953, budget and mgmt. officer, 1953-59; asst. to county mgr. Montgomery County, Rockville, Md., 1959-63; county mgr. Fulton County, Atlanta, 1963-67; asst. city mgr., Richmond, 1967, city mgr., 1967-72; gen. mgr. Met. Atlanta Rapid Transit Authority, 1972—. Bd. dirs Nat. Assn. County Adminstrs., 1965-67, Inst. for Rapid Transit, 1972—; mem. pub. ofcls. adv. council office Econ. Opportunity; mem. Va. Gov.'s Adv. Com. on State-Local Cooperation, 1970-72; chmn. Va. Twin-Trailer Study Commn., 1969, mem. Twentieth Century Fund Task Force on Democratic Devel. of New Towns, 1970. Bd. dirs. Richmond chpt. Nat. Conf. Christians and Jews, 1967-72, Atlanta Assn. Retarded Children, 1964-67; bd. dirs. Richmond area Assn. Retarded Children, 1967-71, pres., 1969. Served to 1st lt. AUS, 1951-53. Mem. Internat. City Mgmt. Assn., Am. Transit Assn., Am. Soc. Pub. Adminstrn. (pres. Va. chpt. 1970), Municipal Finance Officers Assn., Alpha Tau Omega, Tau Kappa Alpha, Phi Kappa Phi, Pi Gamma Mu. Episcopalian. Home: 5614 Queensborough Dr NE Atlanta GA 30328 Office: 100 Peachtree St NW Atlanta GA 30303

KIERAN, WILLIAM A., ins. mgr., economist; b. Decatur, Ill., Aug. 29, 1897; s. William Henry and Mary L. (Maroney) K.; A.B., U. Ill., 1923; m. Adele Hixon, Oct. 16, 1924; children—William Hixon, Robert Edmund. Ins. rep., 1924—; So. mgr. Am. Credit Indemnity Co. of N.Y., 1937-62, credit ins. broker, 1962—. Served Combat Engrs. A.E.F., W.W.I. Mem. V.F.W. Clubs: Downtown, The Club. Home: 712 Rockbridge Rd Birmingham AL 35216 Office: 2151 Highland Av Birmingham AL 35205

KIERN, NAOMI HELEN MOREL (MRS THEODORE WILLIAM KIERN, educator; b. New Orleans, Feb. 28, 1918; d. Felix Charles and Helen (Bartholomew) Morel; student tchr. tng. Margaret C. Hanson Normal Sch., New Orleans, 1934-36; B.A., Tulane U., 1948; M.Ed., La. State U., 1958; m. Theodore William Kiern, Sept. 1, 1954; 1 son, Stephen Theodore. Tchr., Ella Dolhonde Sch., Metairie, La., 1936-38, Metairie High Sch., 1938-51; prin. Bridgedale Elementary Sch., Metairie, 1951-55, 56-66, Phoebe A. Hearst Elementary Sch., Metairie, 1966—. La. rep. Nat. Study Sch. Evaluation, Atlanta, 1971. Mem. La. Tchrs. Assn. (corr. sec. Jefferson Parish unit 1959-61), La. Prins. Assn., Jefferson Parish Pub. Sch. Prins. Assn. (sec. 1965-69), mem. salary com. 1970—), La. Assn. Elementary Sch. Prins. (mem. salary com. 1971—), Am. Assn. U. Women (1st v.p. Metairie-Gretna br. 1965-67, 2d v.p. 1969—), Blue, Blue Violets, Phoebe A. Hearst Elementary Sch. P.T.A. (charter), La. State U. Alumni (charter mem. Jefferson Parish br.), Delta Kappa Gamma (pres. Alpha Delta chpt. 1960-62, parliamentarian 1970—). Episcopalian (a founder, guild chmn., 1964-66). Club: Metairie-Lakeshore Civic. Home: 1408 Bonnabel Blvd Metairie LA 70005 Office: 52[illegible] Wabash St Metairie LA 70001

KIERNAN, OWEN BURNS, ednl. adminstr.; b. Randolph, Mass., Mar. 9, 1914; s. Thomas Francis and Elizabeth (Burns) K.; B.S., Bridgewater (Mass.) State Tchrs. Coll., 1935; M.Ed., Boston U., 1940; Ed.D., Harvard, 1950, L.H.D. (honoris causa), Lesley Coll., 1956; LL.D. (honoris causa), Northeastern U., 1961; Litt.D. (honoris causa), Stonehill Coll., 1965; Ped.D. (honoris causa), Rhode Island Coll., 1966; Sc.D. (honoris causa), Boston U., 1968; m. Esther Harriet Thorley, July 13, 1940; children—Joan Ann, Nancy Elizabeth, John Albert. Prin. Henry T. Wing High Sch., Sandwich, Mass., 1938-44; supt. schs., Wayland and Sudbury, Mass., 1944-51, Milton, 1951-57; commr. edn. State of Mass., 1957-68; exec. sec. Nat. Assn. Secondary Sch. Prins., Washington, 1969—. Past chmn. Mass. Bd. Edn., Mass. Bd. Vocational Edn.; corp. mem. Mass. Inst. Tech.; trustee U. Mass., Lowell Tech. Inst., Mus. Fine Arts, Mus. Sci. Boston, Boston U. Mem. Am. Assn. Sch. Adminstrs., New Eng., Mass. supt. assns., Council Chief State Sch. Officers (pres. 1967), Phi Delta Kappa. Home: 4000 Massachusetts Av NW Washington DC 20016 Office: 1201 16th St NW Washington DC 20036

KIESEWETTER, EVELYN VAUGHT CUNDIFF (MRS. FRANK HOWARD KIESEWETTER), educator; b. Meridian, Miss.; d. William E. and Neatie (Vaught) Cundiff; student Meridian (Miss.) Sch. Music, 1920-27, Cin. Conservatory Music, 1931; A.B., U. Ky., 1938, M.A., 1953, postgrad. 1953—; m. Frank Kiesewetter. Elementary sch. tchr., Lexington, Ky., 1930-57; ednl. cons. Houghton Mifflin Co., Boston, 1957-59; part time mem. faculty U. Ky., Lexington, 1954-60, Morehead State U., 1959; with Zaner-Bloser Co., Columbus, O., summers 1962-69; program dir. Lexington Recreation Dept., 1937. Mem. adv. com. Juvenile Ct., Lexington, 1955-57; mem. Henry Clay Meml. Found., 1955—, Blue Grass Trust for Historic Preservation, 1960—. Bd. dirs. Central Ky. Concert and Lecture Series. Mem. Ky. Edn. Assn., Nat., Buckley Hills Audubon socs., Phi Beta, Kappa Delta Pi. Club: Spindletop Hall. Address: Apt 408 Merrick Place 3516 Milam Lane Lexington KY 40502

KIESEWETTER, FRANK HOWARD, ret. design engr.; b. Covington, Ky.; s. Frank John and Lynda (Pursifull) K.; student U. Cin.; B.S. in Engring., U. Ky.; m. Evelyn Vaught Cundiff. Ret. sr. design engr. Emery Industries, Cin. Past pres. Green Twp. Sch. Bd.; past v.p. Oak Hill Bd. Edn., active Boy Scouts Am.; mem. dist. com. Henry Clay Meml. Found. Served to maj. USAF, World War II. Registered profl. engr., Ohio. Mem. Am. Assn. Cost Engring., Am. Soc. Heating, Refrigerating and Air Conditioning Engrs., Cin. Engring. Soc., U. Ky. Alumni Assn., Blue Grass Trust Hist. Preservation, Nat. Buckley Hills Audubon socs., Demolay Legion of Honor, Cin. Opera Guild. Presbyn. Mason. Club: Spindletop Hall Country. Home: Apt 408 Merrick Pl 3516 Milam Lane Lexington KY 40502

KIEVMAN, MICHAEL S., broadcasting co. exec.; b. Naugatuck, Conn., Apr. 9, 1923; s. Samuel Joseph and Anna (Savage) K.; m. Christine Elizabeth Lyles, June 24, 1948; children—Christopher, Carson, Michele, Corin. Performer Columbia Pictures, Hollywood, Cal., 1946-50; program and production mgr. KOPO-TV, Tucson, 1950-57; sales mgr. ZIV-TV, Los Angeles, 1957-63, Warner Bros.-TV, N.Y.C., 1963-64; gen. sales mgr. sta. WLWD, Dayton, O., 1964-65; v.p. programming Avco Broadcasting, Cin., 1965-68; v.p. programming Cox Broadcasting, Atlanta, 1968—. Guest lectr. U. Ga., Athens, 1968—. Mem. Ohio State Fair Com., 1965-68; mem. steering com. A.R.C., 1963-65. Served with AUS, 1942-46. Decorated Purple Heart, Silver Star. Named Broadcaster of Year, Tucson Broadcasters, 1956. Mem. Nat. Assn. TV Execs. (mem. all industry music com. 1970—), Broadcast Pioneers, Country-Western Assn., Broadcast Exec. Forum. Clubs: Indian Hills Country (Atlanta); Cincinnati Athletic, Summit Hills Country (Cin.). Home: 282 Tara Trail Atlanta GA 30327 Office: 1601 W Peachtree St NW Atlanta GA 30309

KIGER, ROBERT GARY, physician; b. Nashville, Feb. 4, 1934; s. William Odell and Ruby (Munn) K.; B.S., U. S.C., 1954; M.D., Vanderbilt U., 1958; m. Shirley Coker, Sept. 3, 1955; children—Robert Christopher, Mark Ryan. Intern, Vanderbilt Univ. Hosp., Nashville, 1958-59; resident medicine and cardiology Med. Coll. Ga., 1959-63; practice medicine, specializing in cardiology, Columbia, S.C., 1963-66, Nashville, 1967-71; co-dir. cardiac lab. Med. Center NASA, George C. Marshall Spaceflight Center, Huntsville, Ala., 1966-67; acting dir. cardiopulmonary lab. Bapt. Hosp., Nashville, 1968-69; dir. cardiovascular services Providence Hosp., Columbia, S.C., 1972—. Diplomate Am. Bd. Internal Medicine, Am. Bd. Cardiovasular Disease. Fellow A.C.P.; asso. fellow Am. Coll. Cardiology; mem. Middle Tenn. Heart Assn. (dir.). Author: Surgical Forum, 1959. Home: 53 Northlake Rd Columbia SC 29204 Office: Providence Hosp Columbia SC 29204

KILGORE, SAMUEL GORDON, civil engr.; b. Fort Mede, Fla., Oct. 4, 1914; s. John Lewis and Edna Rose (Wood) K.; Chem. E., Ga. Sch. Tech., 1935; m. Joetta Lovelace, Oct. 11, 1952; children—Gordon, Andrew, John Lewis II, William Stewart. Photographer, Atlanta, Miami, Pitts., 1936-42; realtor, West Palm Beach and Tallahassee, Fla., 1946-48; abstractor, right of way agt., civil engr. Fla. Rd. Dept., Tallahassee, 1948—; owner, operator Kilgore's Sales &Service. Served with USAAF, 1943-45. Registered profl. engr., Fla. Home: 1110 Browning Dr Tallahassee FL 32301 Office: Haydon Burns Bldg Tallahassee FL 32303

KILGORE, WILLIAM JACKSON, educator; b. Dallas, Apr. 30, 1917; s. Rather Bowlin and Clara (Cole) K.; A.B., Baylor U., 1938; Th.M., So. Bapt. Theol. Sem., 1941. Th.D. (fellow 1941-43), 1943; Ph.D., U. Tex., 1958; student Columbia, 1949; m. Barbara Schmickle, Dec. 4, 1943; 1 dau., Barbara Sullivan. Interim prof. philosophy and religion Georgetown (Ky.) Coll., 1943; prof, philosophy and Greek, Buenos Aires (Argentina) Internat. Sem., 1944-49; prof. philosophy Baylor U., 1949—, chmn. dept., 1959—; asst. prof. philosophy U. Tex., summer 1958, Grantee Danforth Found., 1957-58, Am. Council Learned Socs., 1961. Mem. Am., Southwestern (council 1961, pres. 1963-64) philos. assns., Am. Assn. U. Profs. (2d v.p.; nat. council 1962-65, 68—; pres. Tex. conf. 1965; chmn. nat. com. on acad. freedom in ch. related instns.), Tex. Philos. Soc., Interam. Soc. Psychology, Alpha Chi. Author: Alejandro Korn's Interpretation of Creative Freedom, 1958; Una evaluacion critica de la philosofia de Alejandro Korn, 1961; One America, Two Cultures, 1965; An Introductory Logic, 1968; also articles in English and Spanish. Home: 305 Guittard Av Waco TX 76706

KILGREN, EVERT WOODROW, petroleum engr.; b. North Manchester, Ind., Nov. 9, 1918; s. Olaf Fritz and Elvira Natalia (Nilsson) K.; B.S. with high honors, Mich. State U., 1940; M.S. with honors, U. Mich., 1941; m. Ellamaye Bogle, Oct. 17, 1942; 1 son, Karl Erik. Research engr. Stanolind Oil & Gas Co., Tulsa, 1941-42; supr. research dept. Magnolia Petroleum Co., Dallas, 1943-46; with Amoco Prodn. Co., Tulsa, 1946—, chief plant engr., 1953—. Mem. Am. Inst. Chem. Engrs., Am. Inst. Mining, Metall. and Petroleum Engrs., Nat. Gas Processing Assn. (pres. elect, dir.), Heat Transfer Research Inst. (dir., chmn. membership com.), Tau Beta Pi, Phi Kappa Phi, Phi Lambda Tau. Home: 2726 E 59th St Tulsa OK 74105 Office: PO Box 591 Tulsa OK 74102

KILLEBREW, JAMES ROBERT, architect, engr.; b. Okmulgee, Okla., Dec. 10, 1918; s. Robert Herman and Edith (Tyler) K.; B.S. in Archtl. Engring., U. Tex., 1948; m. Prebel Lee Thompson, Nov. 14, 1966; children—Debra Lee, Tod Nenian; 1 dau. (by previous marriage), Laura Janice. Sr. partner Killebrew-Rucker and Assos., architects and engrs., Wichita Falls, Tex., 1954—, works include elementary schs., one selected by Tex. Edn. Agv., as one of 25 outstanding since 1950, Bethania Hosp., Parker Sq. State Bank, Texas Hwy. Dept. Bldgs., 1st State Bank, Archer City Hosp., Muenster Meml. Hosp., Gen. Hosp., Plainview, Tex., Vernon (Tex.) Hosp., Vernon Geriatrics Psychiat. Hosp., Wichita Gen. Hosp., Gen. Hosp., Nocona, Tex., addition to Crippled Childrens Hosp., Wichita Falls, Tex., Sci. Bldg., Phys. Edn. Bldg. of Midwestern U., Teenage Drug Addiction Center, Vernon, Tex., hosps. at Eastland, Tex., other pub. bldgs. Asst. instr. Midwestern U. Served from ensign to lt. comdr. USNR, 1940-45, PTO, capt. Res. Archtl. License. Mem. Nat., Tex. (pres. N. Tex. chpt. 1960-61, sec.-treas. 1958-59) socs. profl. engrs., Am. Soc. Archtl. Engrs. (charter mem.), A.I.A. (pres. Wichita Falls chpt. 1966-67), Am. Soc. Heating, Ventilating and Air Conditioning Engrs., C. of C. (chmn. beautification com. 1958-59, bldg. code com. 1955-56, aviation com. 1958-59; dir.), Navy League, U.S. (pres. 1967-68); Tex. Fine Art Soc. (bd. dirs., pres. 1970, chmn. bd. 1972). Mem. Christian Ch. (deacon). Home: 1559 Hanover St Wichita Falls TX 76302 Office: 202 Central Plaza Wichita Falls TX 76302

KILLEBREW, ROSAMOND LOCKETT, radiomicrobiologist; b. Grenada, Miss., Oct. 11, 1913; d. Emmit Savage and Ella Gertrude (Harlan) Lockett; student William Carey Coll., 1931-33; B.E., Delta Bus. U., 1934; B.S., Delta State Coll., 1936; M.S., U. So. Miss., 1959; postgrad. Gulf Coast Research Lab., 1956-59; m. Joseph Killebrew, Oct. 16, 1936; children—Charles J., Linnella S., Mary Regina. Field biologist Miss. Game and Fish Commn., 1936-37; research in ornithology and horticulture with E.A. McIlhenny, Avery Island, La., 1937-40, Am. Mus. Natural History, 1940-45; pvt. bus., food sci., Killebrews, Biloxi, Miss., 1949-55; head sci. dept. Biloxi Municipal

Pub. Sch., 1956-60; asst. prof. biol. sci., Southeastern La. Coll., 1961-62; research sci., instr. of nuclear sci., La. State U., 1962-65; radiomicrobiologist and research, Agrl. Exptl. Sta., 1965—. Recipient NSF-AEC grants, 1957-65. Mem. Miss., La. acads. sci., Am. Nuclear Soc., Am. Assn. U. Profs., A.A.A.S., Ecol. Soc. Am., Animal Behavior Soc., Am. Inst. Biol. Sci., Internat. Oceanographic Soc., Miss. Poetry Soc., Sigma Xi, Gamma Sigma Delta, Alpha Psi Omega, Beta Mu Kappa, Am. Legion Aux. Elks Aux. Designed first flight stamp airmail, 1934. Contbr. profl., sci., poetry jours. Home: 9540 Macedonia St Baton Rouge LA 70810

KILLEN, ROBERT ALLAN, educator; b. Edmonton, Alta., Can., July 28, 1906 (came to U.S. 1937); s. John and Francis (Black) K.; A.B. cum laude, Wheaton Coll., 1938; B.D., Faith Theol. Sem., 1941; Th.M. cum laude, Dallas Theol. Sem., 1945; Th.D., The Free U., Amsterdam, Netherlands, 1956; m. Margaret Huinink, May 24, 1939; children—Richard John, Robert Allan. Ordained to minstry Ref. Presbyn Ch. Evang. Synod, 1941; instr. apologetics Faith Theol. Sem., Phila., 1953-56, prof. theology, 1956-57; prof. theology Covenant Theol. Sem., St. Louis, 1957-61, minister and spl. lectr., 1962-69; v.p. Toronto Bible Coll., 1961-62; asso. prof. Bible and philosophy, Bryan Coll., Dayton, Tenn., 1969-71; prof. contemporary theology, Ref. Theol. Sem., Jackson, Miss., 1971—. Named Outstanding Educator of Am. Bryan Coll., 1971. Mem. Evang. Theol. Soc. Author: The Ontological Theology of Paul Tillish, 1956: Philosophy in a Major Key, 1970: Philosophy and Christian Thought, 1971. Home: 1000 Briarwood Dr Clinton MS 39056

KILLIAN, CARL DAN, state senator; b. Hayesville, N.C., Apr. 10, 1903; s. Paul Bismarck and Maud (Moss) K.; B.S., N.C. State U., 1924; M.A., Columbia, 1927; Ph.D., Ohio State U., 1932; m. Winnie Murphy, Aug. 28, 1940; 1 son, Carl Dan. Mem. faculty Western Carolina U., Cullowhee, N.C., 1935-68, dean sch. psychology and edn., dir. extension div., 1937-38, head dept. edn. and psychology, dir. extension div., 1937-68; chmn. Western N.C. Regional Planning Commn., Asheville, 1969—; exec. dir. State of Franklin Health Council, 1964—; mem. N.C. Senate, 1971—. Mem. Gov.'s Advocacy Commn. Children and Youth, 1971—. Mem. adv. bd. N.C. Assn. for Regional Med. Program. Fellow Royal Soc. Health; mem. Southwestern N.C. Econ. Devel. Commn., 1966—, N.C. Bd. Mental Health, Raleigh, 1965—. Office: Drawer A-J Cullowhee NC 28723

KILLINGSWORTH, ROY WILLIAM, educator; b. Headland, Ala., Apr. 8, 1925; s. Philip Berry and Martha Cora (Granberry) K.; B.S. in Civil Engring., U. Ala., 1948, M.S. in Engring., 1956; m. Johnie Mack Hall, Jan. 21, 1950; children—Daniel William, Sarah Anne. Teaching grad. asst. U. Ala., 1948-49; gen. contractor, Dothan, 1948; field engr. Pressure Concrete Co., 1949-50; v.p. 1950-52; asst. to the dean Coll. Engring., U. Ala., 1952-56, asst. prof. engring., asst. dean Coll. Engring., 1956-57, asso. prof., asst. dean, 1957-63, prof., asst. dean, 1963-67, prof., asso. dean, 1967-70, prof., dir. phys. planning and facilities, 1970—; pvt. cons. Mem. dist. commn. Boy Scouts Am., 1972. Bd. advisers Ala. Hist. Commn., 1971. Served with USNR, 1944-46. Fellow Am. Soc. C.E. (v.p. Ala. sect. 1971-72; mem. Nat., Ala. (pres. Tuscaloosa chpt. 1964, 1st v.p. 1971-72) socs. profl. engrs., Am. Soc. Engring. Edn., A.A.A.S., Greater Tuscaloosa C. of C. (traffic and parking com. 1971), Theta Tau, Tau Beta Pi, Chi Epsilon, Omicron Delta Kappa, Theta Chi. Clubs: University, Indian Hills Country, Tuscaloosa Exchange (dir. 1970). Home: 731 Capstone Ct Tuscaloosa AL 35401 Office: PO Box 1996 University AL 35486

KILLMER, HUGH DOUGLAS, dentist; b. Duluth, Minn., May 24, 1910; s. Raleigh Edward and Pearl Ida (Heath) K.; D.D.S., Washington U., 1936; postgrad. Northwestern U., 1937, U. Tex., Houston, 1955-65; m. Grace E. Perry, Aug. 16, 1952; children—David, Paul, Jonathon, Carey, Robert, Charles, Gwenda, Bill. Individual practice dentistry, St. Louis, 1936-41, 47-49; staff dentist VA Hosp., Alexandria, La., 1944-49; staff dentist VA Hosp., Houston, 1949-57, chief dental service, 1957-66; dental field supr. VA Central Office, Washington, 1966-71; chief dental service VA Hosp., Waco, Tex., 1971—. Adj. prof. Tex. State Tech. Inst. James Connally Campus, Waco. Bd. dirs. D.C. Bapt. Conf. Served with AUS, 1941-47. Decorated Legion of Merit. Fellow Am. Coll. Dentists; mem. Am. Prosthodontic Soc., Am. Assn. Hosp. Dentists, Am. Eguilibration Soc., Internat. Assn. Dental Research, Am. Dental Assn. Baptist (chmn. finance com. 1970-71). Club: Optimist (v.p. 1960-61) (Houston). Home: Qts 21-B V A Hospital Waco TX 76703 Office: VA Hospital Memorial Dr Waco TX 76703

KILPATRICK, CARROLL, newspaper writer; b. Montgomery, Ala., Sept. 2, 1913; s. Andrew Carroll and Mary (Anderson) K.; A.B., Ala. U., 1935; Nieman fellow Harvard, 1939-40; m. Frances Talbot Williams, Mar. 6, 1941; children—Andrew Carroll, Frank Williams. Editorial writer Birmingham News, 1935-37, European assignment, 1937; asso. editor Montgomery Advertiser, 1937-39; nat. affairs writer Newsweek, 1940; Washington corr. Birmingham News and Age-Herald, Raleigh (N.C.) News and Observer, Yorkshire (Eng.) Post, 1940-43. Washington corr. Chgo. Sun, 1943-46; Washington corr. San Francisco Chronicle 1946-51; asst. chief State Dept. press sect., 1951-52; staff writer Washington Post, 1952—. Co-author: The Kennedy Circle, 1961. Editor: Roosevelt and Daniels, A Friendship in Politics, 1952. Contbr. to mags. Mem. White House Corrs. Assn. (pres. 1968-69), Phi Delta Theta, Omicron Delta Kappa. Clubs: Cosmos, Overseas Writers (pres. 1967), Federal City (Washington). Home: 4238 43d St Washington DC 20016 Address: The Washington Post Washington DC 20005

KILPATRICK, CHARLES OTIS, newspaper editor; b. Fairview, Okla., June 16, 1922; s. John E. and Myrtle (Arant) K.; B.A., Stephen F. Austin State Coll., 1942; m. Margie Ada Partin, June 3, 1944; children—Kent Fairles, Millicent Kye, Mark Kevin. With daily newspapers, Nacogdoches, Texas, and also corr. for papers in Houston and Dallas, 1940-42; with Daily Sentinel, Nacogdoches, 1946-48, Courier-Times, Tyler, Tex., 1948-49; regional editor Tyler Morning Telegraph, 1949, mng. editor, 1949-50; mem. staff Evening News, San Antonio, 1950-51; Sunday editor San Antonio Express, 1951-54, asst. mng. editor, 1954-55, mng. editor, 1955-65, now exec. editor; asst. exec. editor, San Antonio Express and San Antonio News, 1957-58, exec. editor, v.p., pub., 1971—. Pulitzer prize journalism juror, 1963, 64, 69, 71. Served with 14th Inf. Bn., USMCR; lt. col. Res., mem. Res. Policy Bd. Mem. Tex. Asso. Pres. Mng. Editors Assn. (past pres. continuing study com.), C. of C. (dir). Episcopalian (board vestry, bishop's com. pub. relations Diocese W. Tex.). Home: 2019 E Lawndale St San Antonio TX 78209 Office: Expenses Pub Co Av E at 3d St San Antonio TX 78205

KILPATRICK, JAMES JACKSON, JR., newspaperman; b. Oklahoma City, Nov. 1, 1920; s. James Jackson and Alma Mia (Hawley) K.; B.J., U. Mo., 1941; m. Marie Louise Pietri, Sept. 21, 1942; children—Michael Sean, Christopher Hawley, Kevin Pietri. Reporter, Richmond (Va.) News Leader, 1941-49, chief editorial writer, 1949-51, editor 1951-67; writer nat. syndicated column; asso. Nat. Rev., 1964—; guest commentator CBS television news, 1971—. Vice chmn. Va. Com. on Constl. Govt., 1962-68; chmn. Va. Magna Carta Com., 1965. Pres. Beadle Bumble Fund, 1954—. Recipient medal of honor for distinguished service in journalism U. Mo., 1953; ann. award for editorial writing Sigma Delta Chi, 1954. Mem. Nat. Conf. Editorial Writers (chmn. 1955-56), Va. Ornithology Soc., Black-Eyed Pea Soc. Am. (No. 1 Pea, pro-tem. 1965—). Club: Rappahannock Hunt. Episcopalian. Whig. Author: The Sovereign States, 1957; The Smut Peddlers, 1960; The Southern Case for School Segregation, 1962. Editor: We the States, 1964. Co-editor: The Lasting South, 1957. Home: White Walnut Hill Woodville VA 22749 Office: The Evening Star 225 Virginia Av SE Washington DC

KILPATRICK, JAMES LOWE, oilwell drilling contractor; b. Haynesville, La., Feb. 8, 1931; s. Dayton Barnett and Illa (Lowe) K.; B.S., La. Poly. Inst., 1953; m. Carolyn Earlene Hargrove, Dec. 27, 1953; children—Barney, Kim, Mark, Pam. Petroleum engr. Monsanto Chem. Co., El Dorado, Ark., 1955-57; petroleum engr. Murphy Corp., El Dorado, 1957-60; petroleum engr., asst. to v.p., gen. mgr. drilling, sr. v.p. Ocean Drilling & Exploration Co., New Orleans, 1960—; dir. Rimrock (U.K.), Rimrock Drilling, Canam Offshore, Odeco Nehon, Odeco (U.K.). Served with USNR, 1953-55. Mem. Am. Inst. Mining, Metall. and Petroleum Engrs., Am. Assn. Oilwell Drilling Contractors (dir.). Home: 2423 Hudson Pl New Orleans LA 70114 Office: 1600 Canal St New Orleans LA 70112

KILPATRICK, JOHN EDGAR, educator; b. Monroe, La., Jan. 3, 1920; s. John Edgar and Myrtle (Ayrant) K.; B.A., Stephen F. Austin Coll., Tex., 1940; M.A., Kan. U., 1942; Ph.D., U. Cal. at Berkeley, 1945; m. Ida C. Williams, June 12, 1960; children—Jan Patricia, Terry Annette, Wendy Lee. Staff, Am. Petroleum Inst. Research project 44 at Nat. Bur. of Standard, 1944-47; prof. chemistry Rice U., 1947—; cons. AEC, 1949—. Mem. Phi Beta Kappa, Sigma Xi. Republican. Home: 5010 Wigton Houston TX 77035

KIM, PO SUNG (PHILIP), publisher; b. Seoul, Korea, July 15, 1929; s. Mu Yop and Tae (Sun) K.; student Yonsei U., Seoul, 1950, Northwestern U., 1956; m. Chul Hyun Sim, Apr. 7, 1951; children—Kathy, Peter. Came to U.S., 1961. Seoul corr. Reuters, Ltd., London, 1950-61; dir. Korean Information Office, Washington, 1961-69; writer weekly column Washington Tidbits Korean Republic, 1962-69; editor-pub. Korea Week, Washington, 1969-70; pub. A-K News Service, Washington, 1970—. Bd. dirs. YMCA Internat. Boys Camp. Mem. Nat. Press Club, Korean Stamp Soc., Tuesday Luncheon Soc., Pub. Relations Soc. Am. Clubs: Advertisement, International (Washington). Home: 3720 Columbia Pike Arlington VA 22204 Office: Nat Press Bldg 14th and F Sts NW Washington DC 20004

KIMBALL, DANIEL P., judge; b. Springfield, La., Oct. 10, 1915; s. Louis R. and Harriet Elizabeth (Sibley) K.; B.A., La. State U., 1938, LL.B., 1947; m. Katherine C. Kleinpeter, Apr. 12, 1941; children—Carolyn Kay (Mrs. Sidney J. Babin), Marilyn Sue, Madelyn Ann. Admitted to La. bar, 1947; practiced in West Baton Rouge, La., 1947-61; city atty. Brusly, La., 1953-61, Rosedale, La., 1960-61; Port Allen, 1953-61, Grosse Tete, La., 1952-61, judge 18th Jud. Dist. Ct., Port Allen, La., 1961—. Dir. Bank of West Baton Rouge, Port Allen. Dist. advancement chmn., vice chmn. dist. exec. com. Boy Scouts Am., 1952-54; sec. Bd. Commrs., Atchafalaya Basin Levee Dist., 1940-42, 46-48; v.p., program chmn. Blue Ridge Inst. for So. Juvenile Ct. Judges, 1966-67, pres., 1967-68; mem. Jud. Council La., 1967—; adv. com. for preparation new juvenile code La., 1970—. Dir. Baton Rouge Port Devel. Assn., 1951-55, Donaldonville Mental Health Center, 1965—, West Baton Rouge Retarded Persons Assn., 1966—. Served with AUS, 1942-45. Mem. La. Bar Assn.(mem. ho. dels. 1955-56), La. Council Juvenile Ct. Judges (sec. 1964-65, v.p. 1965-66, pres. 1966-67), Am. Legion (post comdr., dist. judge adv., vice comdr., dept. judge adv.). Lion (past sec. Port Allen). Office: Port Allen LA 70767

KIMBALL, THOMAS LLOYD, conservationist; b. Los Angeles, Feb. 21, 1918; s. David Patton and Nellie (Nash) K.; student Phoenix Jr. Coll., 1937; B.S., Brigham Young U., 1939; m. Arvella Allen, Sept. 25, 1940; children—Patricia (Mrs. John N. Clark), Pamela (Mrs. Merrill R. Hunt), Kay (Mrs. Stephen Lafleur), Thomas S., Andrea, Allen Kent. With Ariz. Game and Fish Commn., 1939-52, dir., 1947-52; dir. Colo. Game and Fish Commn., 1952-60; exec. v.p. Nat. Wildlife Fedn., Washington, 1960—; sec. Interior's Adv. Bd. Wildlife Mgmt., 1962-68, 71—; chmn. Natural Resources Council Am., 1962-64; cons. Wildlife planning study Cal. Dept. Game and Fish; biologist cons. wildlife affairs Legislative Interim Com. on Wildlife Ore. Mem. Fed. Power Commn. Bd. advisers Crusade for a Cleaner Environment, 1971—; trustee Ding Darling Found.; mem. Pres.'s Air Quality Adv. Bd., 1970—; mem. adv. bd. Dept. Health, Edn. and Welfare Water Quality Criteria Study, Keep Am. Beautiful. Served with USAAF, World War II. Recipient Certificate of Merit Nash Motor Co., 1953, Outstanding Service award Game and Fish Commn. Colo., 1960, Conservation Service award U.S. Dept. Interior, 1964, Distinguished Citizen award U. Ariz., 1964. Mem. Western (pres.), Midwest (pres.) assns. game and fish commrs., Wildlife Soc., C. of C. of U.S. (environmental pollution panel 1971-72), Am. Forestry Assn. Club: Boone and Crockett. Home: 825 Mackall Av McLean VA 22101 Office: 1412 16th St NW Washington DC 20036

KIMBALL, VERA F., editor, writer; b. Seward, Alaska, Feb. 8, 1903; d. Irving L. and Della (Carpenter) Kimball; A.B., Columbia, 1929; m. William T. Castles, Jr., Dec. 2, 1942. On clerical staff Legislature of Ty. of Alaska, 1923; with Alaska R.R., Anchorage, 1923-24, N.A. Newspaper Alliance, Met. Mus. Art, Gen. Foods Corp., Todd-Robertson & Todd (all N.Y. City), part time 1924-29; asst. to sec. Am. Inst. Chemists, 1929-35; editor The Chemist, N.Y.C., 1935-68, asso. editor, 1968—. Mem. N.Y. Acad. Scis., Am. Inst. Chemists (hon. life), A.A.A.S., Cook Inlet Hist. Soc., Alaska (charter mem.), Chester County (S.C.) Hist. Soc. Club: Barnard College (N.Y. City). Author: Firearms and Their Use (with W. T. Castles), 1942; Your Future in Chemistry (with M. R. Bhagwat), 1943. Contbr. World Scope Ency., The Ency. of Chemistry, year books, profl. and popular mags. Office: Route 2 Chester SC 29706

KIMBEL, WILLIAM ANTHONY, govt. cons., corp. exec.; b. N.Y.C., Jan. 5, 1888; s. Anthony and Eleanor (Haubner) K.; B.S., Columbia, 1909; m. L. Maud Windeler, Jan. 17, 1920; children—Joyce (Mrs. Kimbel Gunnels), Richard Anthony. Asst. mil. attache U.S., Embassy, London, 1916; pres. A. Kimbel & Son, archtl. and decorative contractors and mfrs., N.Y.C., 1922-41; asst. to dir. OSS. 1941-45; owner, pub. Myrtle Beach (S.C.) News, 1946-48; adminstrv. dir. Anglo-Am. Council on Productivity, 1948-50; pres. Midcoast Investment, Myrtle Beach, 1950-51, also dir. pub. relations Hi-Q div. Aerovox Corp., Quality Courts United. U.S. rep. Econ. Commn. for Europe, 1954, 55; adviser delegation UNESCO, 1954; cons. Dept. of State, 1953—. Pres. Am. Inst. Decorators, 1938-40, Coastal Ednl. Found. of S.C., 1965; mem. S.C. Adv. Commn. on Edn., 1965—. Served with U.S. Army, World War I, A.E.F. Recipient Medal of Merit, Columbia. Mem. Pilgrims Soc. Am., Am. Camellia Soc., U.S. Seniors Golf Assn., S.C. Hist. Soc., Winyah Indigo Soc. Clubs: Metropolitan, Chevy Chase (Washington) University, Racquet and Tennis. Ardsley Curling (founder, past pres.), Ardsley (N.Y.); Dunes Golf and Beach (founder, dir.) (Myrtle Beach). Home: Wachesaw Plantation Murrells Inlet SC 29576 Office: Box 1526 Myrtle Beach SC 29577

KIMBERLIN, SAM OWEN, JR., assn. exec.; b. Wichita Falls, Tex., Feb. 4, 1928; s. Sam Owen and Ruth (Crowell) K.; B.B.A., U. Tex., 1951, LL.B., 1953; postgrad. Rutgers U., 1972; m. Alison Gray, Dec. 20, 1955; children—Samuel Scott, David Winston. First asst. dist. atty. Travis County, Tex., 1953-54; asst. atty. gen. Tex., 1955-56; gen. counsel Tex. Dept. Banking, 1956-62; exec. dir. Assn. State Chartered Banks in Tex., 1962-64; exec. v.p. Tex. Bankers Assn., 1964—. Pres., Conf. So. Bankers Assn. Execs., 1967-68; mem. Banking Laws Com., Tex. Bar Assn. Bd. dirs. Southwestern Grad. Sch. Banking, Dallas; Sch. of Banking of the South, Baton Rouge. Served with USMCR, 1946-48. Mem. Tex. Bar Assn., Am., Tex. socs. assn. execs., Phi Alpha Delta. Contbr. articles banking jours. Home: 3503 Scenic Hills Dr Austin TX 78703 Office: Vaughn Bldg Austin TX 78701

KIMBERLING, CARROLL FRANKLIN, JR., supermarket exec.; b. Oklahoma City, Aug. 31, 1947; s. Carroll Franklin and June Marie (Joyce) K.; B.B.A., Tex. Christian U., 1969; m. Nancy Farrell Felton, Jan. 2, 1970. Corporate v.p. Kimberlings Supermarkets, Oklahoma City, 1965—. Bd. dirs. Oklahoma City March of Dimes. Mem. Nat. Assn. Retail Grocers U.S., Okla. Retail Grocers Assn (dir.), Oklahoma City C. of C., Oklahoma City All Sports Assn. (dir. 1970—), Oklahoma City Advt. Club, Delta Tau Delta. Republican. Methodist. Club: Young Men's Dinner. Home: 12513 Springwood St Oklahoma City OK 73120 Office: 4545 Windsor Mall Oklahoma City OK 73127

KIMBERLY, GEORGE DOUGLAS, physician; b. Hot Springs, N.C., Nov. 26, 1932; s. David and Willeene Garrison (Glenn) K.; A.A., Mars Hill Coll., 1952; B.S., Wake Forest Coll., 1954; M.D., Bowman Gray Sch. Medicine, 1958; m. Sybil Hope Davis, Sept. 7, 1957; children—Joanna Bess, George Douglas, John Davis. Intern N.C. Bapt. Hosp., Winston-Salem, 1958-60; gen. practice medicine, Bakersville, N.C., 1960-68; partner practice medicine, Mocksville, N.C., 1969—; mem. staff Davie County Hosp., Mocksville, trustee, 1970—. Mem. Am. Cancer Soc. Davie County, 1971-72; mem. Gov.'s Adv. Council Comprehensive Health Planning, 1971—. Mem. Davie-Rowan County Med. Soc., Med. Soc. N.C., A.M.A., Am., N.C. acads. family practice. Home: 715 Magnolia Av Mocksville NC 27028 Office: 717 Hospital St Mocksville NC 27028

KIMBREL, MONROE, banker; b. Miller County, Ga., Aug. 4, 1916; s. Charlie C. and Effie (Folds) K.; B.S., U. Ga., 1936; grad. Stonier Grad. Sch. Banking, Rutgers U., 1949; m. Nita Matlock, Apr. 17, 1941; children—Jenny Wood (Mrs. James Bunn III), Charles Daniel. With Farm Credit Adminstrn., Columbia, S.C., 1936-46; with First Nat. Bank. Thomson, Ga., 1946-65, chmn. bd., 1961-65; chmn. Bank Ft. Valley, Ga., 1963-65; dir. Fed. Res. Bank Atlanta, 1960-65, sr. v.p., 1965, 1st. v.p., 1965-68, pres., 1968—. Mem. Am. (pres. 1962-63), Ga. (pres. 1956-57) bankers assns., U. Ga. Alumni Assn. (pres. 1970-71, 72-73). Rotarian (past dist. gov.). Home: 620 Peachtree St Atlanta GA 30308 Office: Fed Res Bank of Atlanta 104 Marietta St NW Atlanta GA 30303

KIMBROUGH, HARRIS MCDONALD, JR., dentist; b. Amarillo, Tex., Apr. 24, 1932; s. Harris McDonald and Jewel Evelyn (Scales) K.; student Yale, 1950-52, Tex. U., 1952-53; D.D.S., Baylor U., 1957; postgrad. Amarillo Coll., 1971, West Tex. State U., 1971; m. Patsy Ann Hall, May 30, 1964; children—Katrina, Robin, Ned, Risa, Mike, Cinamon. Individual practice dentistry, Amarillo, 1960—, Pampa, Tex., 1962-67; instr. dental assts. course Amarillo Coll., 1969, cons. Alcoholic Recovery Center, 1969—. Dental coordinator Civil Def., 1963-65. Pres., trustee Ceta Glen Conf. on Alcoholism; bd. dirs. Amarillo Mentally Retarded Center, Alcoholic Recovery Center. Served to lt. Dental Corps, USN, 1956-60. Fellow Am. Acad. Pedodontics; mem. Am., Tex. dental assns., Panhandle Dist. Dental Soc. (editor), Am. Acad. Gen. Practice, Am. Soc. Dentistry for Children, Omicron Kappa Upsilon. Club: Amarillo County. Home: 7 Tascociata Circle Amarillo TX 79106 Office: 2312 Georgia St Amarillo TX 79109

KIMBROUGH, JAMES MARION, educator; b. Wales, Tenn., Jan. 27, 1926; s. Ernest Newton and Florence (Bunch) K.; B.A., George Peabody Coll. Tchrs., 1949, M.A., 1950, M.A. in Library Sci., 1961. Tchr. Giles County (Tenn.) Pub. Schs., 1951-61; librarian, Cumberland Coll., Williamsburg, Ky., 1961-64; asst. prof. La. State U., New Orleans, 1964-68; tchr., librarian Martin Coll., Pulaski, Tenn., 1968-70; asst. prof., asst. to dir. Sch. Library Sci., George Peabody Coll. for Tchrs., Nashville, 1970—. Served with USNR, 1944-46. Mem. Am., Southeastern, Tenn. library assns., Pi Gamma Mu, Kappa Delta Phi, Beta Phi Mu. Home: Route 5 Lawrenceburg TN 38464 Office: Sch. Library Sci George Peabody Coll for Tchrs Nashville TN 37203

KIMBROUGH, RALPH BRADLEY, educator; b. Rhea Springs, Tenn., Mar. 12, 1922; s. Robert Bradley and Elizabeth (Crosby) K.; B.S., U. Tenn., 1948, M.S., 1949, Ed.D., 1953; m. Gladys King, Dec. 21, 1946; 1 son, Ralph Bradley. Tchr., Knoxville (Tenn.) High Sch., 1948-49; prin. Nichols Sch., Lenoir City, Tenn., 1950-51; mem. staff So. States Coop Program in Ednl. Adminstrn., 1953-54; prof. U. Tenn., 1954-58; prof. U. Fla., 1958-65, chmn. dept. ednl. adminstrn. and supervision, 1966—. Served with AUS, 1943-45; ETO. Mem. Am. Edn. Research Assn., Am. Assn. U. Profs., N.E.A., Am. Assn. Sch. Adminstrs., Fla. Edn. Assn., Phi Delta Kappa. Author: (with others) Community Leadership for Public Education, 1955; Political Power and Educational Decision-Making, 1964; (with others) Philosophic Theory and Practice in Educational Administration, 1966; Administering Elementary Schools: Concepts and Practices, 1968. Contbr. articles profl. jours. Home: 917 NW 40th Dr Gainesville FL 32601

KIMBROUGH, WILLIAM HORACE, state ofcl.; b. Springville, Ala., Aug. 8, 1913; s. James R. and Bertie (Newman) K.; B.S., U. Ala., 1934, M.A., 1940; LL.D., Jacksonville State U., 1972; m. Thelma Fagan, June 8, 1938; children—Gay Nell, William Edwin. Tchr., Piedmont (Ala.) High Sch., 1934-37, Sylacauga (Ala.) High Sch., 1937-42; supt. Piedmont City Schs., 1942-67; dir. div. adminstrn. and finance State Dept. Edn., 1967—. Sec., Piedmont Community Chest. Mem. Ala. High Sch. Athletic Assn. (pres. 1949-51), Ala. Edn. Assn. (pres. 1959-60), Ala. Assn. Sch. Adminstrs. (pres. 1963-65). Methodist (dir. choir 1943-67). Lion (pres. 1944-46). Home: 2508 Oxford Dr Montgomery AL 36111 Office: State Office Bldg Montgomery AL 36104

KIMERER, NEIL BANARD, SR., psychiatrist, educator; b. Wauseon, O., Jan. 13, 1918; s. William and Ruby (Upp) K.; B.S., U. Toledo, 1941; M.D., U. Chgo., 1944; postgrad. (fellow) Menninger Sch., 1947-50; m. Ellen Jane Scott, May 23, 1943; children—Susan Leigh, Neil Banard, Brian Scott, Sandra Lynn. Intern, Emanuel Hosp., Portland, Ore., 1944; resident psychiatry Winter VA Hosp., Topeka, 1947-50; asst. physician Central State Hosp., Norman, Okla., 1950, cons., 1955—; chief out-patient psychiat. clinic U. Okla. Sch. Medicine, Oklahoma City, 1951-53, instr. dept. psychiatry, 1951-52, asso. prof., 1952-53, asst. prof. dept. psychiatry, neurology and behavioral scis., 1955-61, asso. prof., 1961-69, clin. prof., 1969—; practice medicine specializing in psychiatry, Oklahoma City, 1953—; med. dir. Oklahoma City Mental Health Clinic, 1953-68; cons., spl. lectr. dept. psychology U. Okla., Norman, 1951-58. Mem.

Comprehensive Health Survey Com., Oklahoma City, 1961-—; mem. exec. com. Okla. Family Life Assn., 1958-60; bd. dirs. Oklahoma City Jr. Symphony Soc., 1959. Served as pfc, ASTP, 1943-44; to capt. M.C., AUS, 1945-47, Diplomate Am. Bd. Psychiatry. Fellow Am. Psychiat. Assn.; mem. Am., Okla. State med. assns., Oklahoma County Med. Soc., Oklahoma City Clin. Soc., Okla. Psychiat. Soc., Okla. (pres. 1956, 60-62), Mid-Continent psychiat. socs., A.A.A.S., Okla. Health and Welfare Assn., Alpha Kappa Kappa (pres. Nu chpt. 1943). Rotarian. Author: To Get and Begot, 1971. Contbr. article in field to profl. jour. Home: 2800 NW 25th St Oklahoma City OK 73107 Office: 2600 NW Hwy Oklahoma City OK 73112

KIMMONS, JOSEPH LANIER, dentist; b. Savannah, Tenn., June 25, 1931; s. Joseph Bynum and Willie Mae (Perry) K.; student Tenn. Tech. U., 1949-55; D.D.S., U. Tenn., 1959; m. Elizabeth Marie Cantrell, Aug. 10, 1955; children—Michael Joe, Bynum Lanier. Individual practice dentistry, Ripley, Tenn., 1959-—. County Republican chmn., 1970-—. Pres. Lauderdale County Jr. C. of C., 1964, Lauderdale County chpt. Am. Cancer Soc. Served with USNR, 1950-54. Mem. Am., Tenn., 7th Dist. dental assns., U. Tenn. Alumni Assn. (pres. Lauderdale County), Gideons. Moose, Lion. Home: Lackey Lane Ripley TN 38063 Office: Arcade Bldg Ripley TN 38063

KIMPLE, WILLIAM CARLISLE, packaging co. exec.; b. Dallas, Dec. 13, 1928; s. Louis C. and Gladys (Halsell) K.; student N. Tex. U., 1945-47; B.S., So. Meth. U., 1954; m. Patsy C. Brazil, Feb. 16, 1952; children— Cheryl, Lisa, Robin. With Dixico, Dallas, 1954-—, successively salesman, sales mgr., 1954-61, promotion and advt., 1958-61, sec., 1958-—, dir., 1958-—, v.p., regional mgr., 1965-69, sr. v.p. indsl. relations, 1969-—; dir. Am. Savings & Loan Assn. Served with AUS, 1951-53. Home: 1344 Bar Harbor Dallas TX 75232 Office: 1415 S Vernon St Dallas TX 75224

KINANE, LARRY STARR, banker; b. Austin, Tex., Sept. 18, 1941; s. Ferd J. and Margarett A. (Starr) K.; student St. Edwards U., 1960; B.B.A., Southwest Tex. State U., 1963; m. Felicie A. Drost, May 26, 1962; children—Stephen M., Melissa A. Tchr. math. and history Bloomington (Tex.) Ind. Sch. Dist., 1963-64; tchr., supr. spl. edn. Devereaux Sch., Victoria, Tex., 1964-65; trainee, collection mgr. for accounts Southwestern Investment Co., Victoria, 1965-66; br. loan mgr. Assos. Finance Co., Victoria, Houston, 1966-68; v.p. in charge installment loans, bad debt collections, loan collection dept., new accounts dept., 1968-70; pres., chief exec. officer Bank of Baytown (Tex.), 1971; v.p. comml. loans 1st Bank of Houston, 1971-—. Mem. Houston Jr. C. of C. Lion (pres.), K.C., Rotarian. Home: 8810 Sandstone St Houston TX 77036 Office: PO Box 36708 Houston TX 77036

KINARD, BILLY RUSSELL, SR., football coach; b. Jackson, Miss., Dec. 16, 1933; s. Major Henry and Pearl Marther (Wooley) K.; B.S., U. Miss., 1956; m. Iris Kay Horton; children—Billy Russell, Kathy. Profl. football player, 1956-60; then asst. coach high sch., mem. coaching staff Auburn (Ala.) U., 1961-63, U. Fla., Gainesville, 1964-66, U. Ark., Fayetteville, 1970; head football coach U. Miss., University, 1971-—. Mem. Am. Football Coaches Assn. Home: PO Box 95 University MS 38677

KINARD, DRAYTON TUCKER, educator; b. Dillon, S.C., Feb. 11, 1912; s. Drayton Tucker and Janie (Dew) K.; B.S., Clemson U., 1933; M.S., Va. Poly. Inst., 1941; Ph.D., Mich. State U., 1954; m. Mary Eleanor Turner, Aug. 5, 1938; 1 dau., Mary Nancy. Agrl. engr. Soil Conservation Service, Spartanburg, S.C., 1934-36, Resettlement Adminstrn., Montgomery, Ala., 1936-37; engr. Daniel T. Duncan Engring. Co., Greenwood, S.C., 1937-40, R.H. Bouligny, Inc., Charlotte, N.C., 1940, 41; grad. asst. Va. Poly. Inst., Blacksburg, 1940-41; research asso. U. Ga., Athens, 1941-42, asso. prof., 1946-52, 53-55, prof. agrl. engring., 1955-56; grad. asst. Mich. State U., East Lansing, 1952-53; prof., head dept. agrl. engring. U. Ky., Lexington, 1956-58; prof. agrl. engring. U. Fla., Gainesville, 1958-—, chmn. dept., 1958-68. U.S. AID cons. to Jamaica Minstry Agr. and Lands, 1965. Served from 2d lt. to capt., AUS, 1942-46. Named Ky. Col. Fellow A.A.A.S.; mem. Am. Soc. Agrl. Engrs., Am. Soc. Engring. Edn., Am. Soc. Heating, Refrigeration and Air Conditioning Engrs., Sigma Xi, Phi Kappa Phi, Gamma Sigma Delta, Sigma Pi Sigma, Tau Beta Pi. Methodist. Rotarian. Home: 1841 NW 23d Terrace Gainesville FL 32601

KINARD, FRANK EFIRD, state ofcl.; b. Newberry, S.C., Jan. 15, 1924; s. James C. and Katherine (Efird) K.; B.S., Newberry Coll., 1946, A.B., 1947; M.S., U. N.C., 1950, Ph.D. in Physics, 1953; m. Mary Angelyn McNease, June 25, 1952; children—Sally Garner, Anne Dreher, James McNease (dec.). Instr., U. N.C., 1948-52; physicist E.I. DuPont de Nemours and Co., Aiken, S.C., 1953-63, dir. univ. relations office Aiken, 1963-67; exec. dir. S.C. Commn. Higher Edn., Columbia, 1967; asst. commr., 1968-—. Mem. Oak Ridge Engring. Edn. Adv. Com. Oak Ridge 1965-67. Served with USAAF, 1943-46. Mem. Am. Nuclear Soc. (edn. com. 1964-66), Am. Phys. Soc., A.A.A.S., S.C. Acad. Sci., Sigma Xi. Episcopalian. Home: 801 Albion Rd Columbia SC 29205 Office: 1429 Senate St Columbia SC 29201

KINARD, H(ARGETT) Y(INGLING), cons.; b. York, Pa., May 29, 1912; s. Henry B. and Edith R. (Yingling) K.; student Drexel Inst., Phila., 1928-29; grad. Rider Coll., Trenton, N.J., 1933; m. Pearl E. Greenhill, Aug. 20, 1932; children—Joan S. (Mrs. Edward J. Mercado), Lois (Mrs. Hugh T. Bower), Gail E. (Mrs. Joseph R. Eastburn). Asso. Lybrand, Ross Bros. & Montgomery, Phila., 1933-51; with Electric Storage Battery Co., Phila., 1951-55, comptroller, 1952-55; v.p., treas. Maule Industries, Inc., 1955-58, v.p. finance 1958-59; financial cons. to various firms, 1959-60; exec. v.p., comptroller 1st Union Nat. Bank N.C., Charlotte, N.C., 1960-68; sr. v.p., comptroller 1st Union Nat. Bancorp., Inc., 1968-71, cons. financial activities. C.P.A., Pa. Mem. Am., Pa. insts. C.P.A.'s, N.C. assn. C.P.A.'s, Financial Execs. Inst., Am. Philat. Soc. Presbyn. Kiwanian. Clubs: Carmel Country; Goodfellows, Charlotte Executives. Home: 5825 Lansing Dr Lansdowne Charlotte NC 28211

KINARD, JOHN R., museum exec.; b. Washington, Nov. 13, 1936; s. Robert Francis and Jessie (Covington) K.; B.A., Livingstone Coll., 1960; B.D., Hood Theol. Sem., 1963; m. Marjorie Anne Williams, Nov. 14, 1964; 1 dau., Sarah Alice. East African rep. Operations Crossroads Africa, 1963-64; community organizer S.E. Neighborhood House, 1964-65; project analyst Office Econ. Opportunity, 1965-66; dir. Anacostia Neighborhood Mus., Smithsonian Instn., Washington, 1966-—. Mem. adv. council D.C. Consortium of Univs.; mem. adv. council D.C. chpt. A.R.C.; mem. adv. com. Nat. Parks for the Future project Conservation Found. council Am. Assn. Museums; bd. dirs. Opportunities Utlzn. Center, Washington, Washington Performing Arts Soc., Anacosya Econ. Devel. Corp.; bd. govs. Corcoran Art Gallery, Northeast Museums Conf. Home: 2155 13th St SE Washington DC 20020

KINCAID, GARVICE DELMAR, banker, ins. co. exec.; b. Tallega, Ky., Aug. 9, 1912; s. Douglas and Minnie (Johnson) K.; student Eastern State Tchrs. Coll., 1930-33; A.B., U. Ky., 1934, LL.B., 1937; Litt.D., Ky. Wesleyan Coll., 1961; LL.D., Eastern Ky. State Coll., 1965; m. Nelle Wilson, Oct. 4, 1940; children—Jane and Joan (twins). Admitted to Ky. bar, 1937, since practiced in Lexington; chmn., pres., dir. Central Bank & Trust Co., Lexington, 1945-—, Bank of Danville (Ky.), Corbin Deposit Bank (Ky.), Bank of Williamsburg (Ky.), Blvd. Nat. Bank, Miami, Fla., Dania Bank (Fla.), 1st Nat. Bank, Carlisle, Ky., 1st Nat. Bank, Nicholasville, Ky., 1st Nat. Bank & Trust Co., Georgetown, Ky., Marathon Bank (Fla.), Powell County Bank, Stanton, Ky., Peoples Bank & Trust Co., Berea, Ky., Peoples Comml. Bank, Winchester, Traders Nat. Bank, Mt. Sterling, Citizens Nat. Bank &Trust Co., Somerset, Ky., 1961-—; pres. Ky. Finance Co., Lexington, Ky. Central Life Ins. Co. Lexington, Central Realty Co., Inc., Cardinal Corp., Lexington Ins. Agy., Inc.; owner radio stas. WHOO, WVLK, WINN, WFFG, also WKYT-TV. Mem. Lexington Airport Bd. Founder, chmn. bd. dirs. Boys' Club, Lexington; bd. dirs. Jr. Achievement of Lexington, YMCA; trustee Ky. Ind. Coll. Found., Ky. Wesleyan Coll. Mem. Newspaper Boy Hall Fame, 1965. Co-recipient Horatio Alger Award, 1960; named Ky. Col., 1953, Kentuckian of Year, Ky. Press Assn. Mem. Christian Ch. Mason, Elk. Clubs: Country (Lexington); Jockey (Miami, Fla.). Home: 1800 Richmond Rd Lexington KY 40502 Office: Central Bank Bldg Lexington KY 40507

KINCAID, GEORGE HAROLD, educator; b. Salisbury, N.C., Mar. 6, 1933; s. Herman Calvin and Mildred Roselie (Belt) K.; B.A., U. Fla., 1958, M.R.C., 1959, Ed.D., 1965; m. Margaret Evelyn Barge, Jan. 25, 1959; children—Kevin A., Kerry B., Karl S., Keith C. Counselor, State Dept. Edn., Vocational Rehab., Bartow, Fla., 1959-61; counselor U. Fla., Gainesville, 1961-63, interim instr., 1963-64; asso. prof. Mars Hill, N.C./Asheville-Biltmore Coll., 1964-67; asso. prof. U. South Fla., Tampa, 1967-—. Field coordinator Fla. Protocol Materials Project. Vice pres. Bd. Control Rehab. Ranch, Lakeland, Fla., 1962-63. Served with USN, 1951-55. Mem. Philosophy Edn. Soc., N.E.A., Am. Ednl. Studies Assn., Kappa Delta Pi, Phi Delta Kappa, Delta Upsilon. Contbr. chpt. to The Student in Society. Home: 417 Bannockburn Av Temple Terrace FL 33617 Office: Coll Edn U South Florida Tampa FL 33620

KINDER, JACK DARROW, dentist; b. Andrews, S.C, Dec. 7, 1931; s. Lucian Percy and Sallie Elizabeth (Fitzgerald) K.; student Newberry (S.C.) Coll., 1957-59; D.D.S., Emory U., 1963, M.S.D., 1970; m. Sylvia Talu Oxner, June 4, 1952; children—Stephen Darrow, Lucian Scott. Gen. practice dentistry, Hartsville, S.C., 1963-68; spl. practice orthodontics, Sumter, S.C., 1970-—. Pres. Darlington County Assn. Retarded Children, 1966-68. Mem. Am., S.C. dental assns., Am. Assn. Orthodontists, So. Soc. Orthodontists, Pee Dee Dental Soc. Mason, Kiwanian. Home: 528 Benton Ct Sumter SC 29150 Office: 541 Oxford St Sumter SC 29150

KINDLE, ODIS B. MARTIN, librarian; b. Paris, Tex., Feb. 13, 1926; s. Jesse E. and Laura May (Paschal) K.; B.M.Ed., E. Tex. State Coll., 1949, M.Ed., 1951, B.S. in L.S., 1954; student U. Tex., 1958; student U. Ky., summer 1957, 60-62, M.S. in L.S., 1963; m. Jo Ann Milner, May 30, 1950 (dec. Nov. 1962); 1 son, Paschal Harris; m 2d, Evelyn Miriam Trochesset, Aug. 1969. Tchr. Athens (Tex.) Jr.-Sr. High Sch., 1949-54; librarian Greenville (Tex.) High Sch., 1954-56, librarian Navarro Jr. Coll., Coriscana, Tex., 1956-—, now also dir. library services; faculty Grad. Sch. Library Sci., Our Lady of the Lake Coll., San Antonio, summer 1967-—. Mem. com. adult Christian edn. Episcopal Diocese Dallas. Served with AUS, 1944-46. Mem. Tex. Jr. Coll. Tchrs. Assn. (chmn. library div. 1958-59), Am., Tex. (chmn. dist. 6 1963, mem. publicity com. 1963-64) library assns., Am. Assn. U. Profs. Home: 1215 Elmwood Circle Corsicana TX 75110

KINDRICK, MILLER BENNETT, sch. exec.; b. Mason, Tex., May 24, 1908; s. Samuel Bennett and Iva Lou (Miller) K.; student Tex. A. and M. U., 1929-30, Mary Hardin-Baylor Coll., 1955-58, Baylor U., 1963-70; B.S. in Sociology, Sam Houston State U., 1970; m. Eleanor Highsmith, Mar. 26, 1933; children—Freddy Bennett, Roy Dee. Self-employed grocery and market bus., Junction, Tex., 1930-43; bus. mgr. Gatesville (Tex.) State Sch. for Boys, 1943-44, asst. supt., 1944-62, gen. supt., 1963-—; supt. Mountain View Sch. for Boys, Gatesville, 1962-63. Bd. dirs. A.R.C. Recipient 25 Year Service award Gatesville State Sch. for Boys, 1968. Mem. Nat. Assn. Tng. Schs. and Juvenile Agys., Nat. Conf. Supts. Tng. Schs. and Reformatories, Tex. Parole and Probation Corrections Assn., Tex. Juvenile Officers Assn., Tex. Tchrs. Assn., So. Assn. Tng. Schs. (pres. 1966), Western Conf. Tng. Schs. (pres. 1967). Baptist (deacon). Lion (dir. 1960-62). Address: Box 417 Gatesville TX 76528

KING, ARNOLD KIMSEY, educator; b. Hendersonville, N.C., Dec. 3, 1901; s. William Fanning Pinckney and Julia (Anderson) K.; A.B., U. N.C., 1925; A.M., U. Chgo., 1927, Ph.D., U. 1951; m. Edna Coates, Aug. 31, 1929; children—Arnold Kimsey, William Dennis, Mary Ann. Instr. edn. U. N.C., 1925-26, asst. prof, teaching history, 1927-39, asso. prof. edn., 1939-43, prof. edn., 1943-—, adviser Gen. Coll., 1942-45, asso. dean Grad. Sch., 1945-68, dir. summer session, 1958-64; v.p. inst. research Consol. U. N.C., 1964-—; chmn. ednl. adv. com. NASA Ednl. Programs Br. 1963-—. Local coordinator U. N.C. participation in Coop. Study Teacher Edn. of Commn. on Tchr. Edn., 1939-43; chmn. region 6 Woodrow Wilson fellowship program Assn. Am. Univs., 1952-55. Trustee, N.C. Wesleyan Coll., Meth. Home for Children, Raleigh. Gen. Edn. Bd. fellow U. Chgo., 1933-34; Henry Milton Wolf fellow history, 1935-36. Mem. N.E.A., Assn. for Instl. Research, Phi Beta Kappa, Phi Delta Kappa, Lambda Chi Alpha, Democrat. Methodist (del. to gen. conf. Dallas 1968, St. Louis 1970). Kiwanian. Editor: Secondary Education in the South (with W. Carson Ryan and J. Minor Gwynn), 1946; Research in Progress, vols. 27-35 in U. N.C. Record Series, 1949-57; Planning for the Future, 1958; Long Range Planning, 1969. Home: 512 Dogwood Drive Chapel Hill NC 27514

KING, BOYD FRANKLIN, economist; b. Knoxville, Tenn., Mar. 6, 1937; s. Boyd Edwin and Amy Leeta (Brewer) K.; B.S., U. Tenn., 1959; postgrad. Vanderbilt U., 1961-64; m. Robbie June Whaley, Jan. 28, 1967. Asst. bank examiner Fed. Deposit Ins. Corp., St. Louis, 1959-61; instr. econs. Georgetown U., 1964-69; economist Fed. Res. Bank, Atlanta, 1969-—. Mem. Am., So. econ. assns. Baptist. Home: 1283 Oakdale Rd NE Atlanta GA 30307 Office: Fed Res Bank of Atlanta Fed Res Sta Atlanta GA 30303

KING, BRUCE, state ofcl. Rancher, livestock feeder, Stanley, N.M.; mem. N.M. Ho. of Reps., 1959-68, speaker, 1963-68; gov. of N.M., 1968-70, 71-—. County commr., N.M., 1955-58; legislative mem. N.M. Bd. of Finance, 1961-62; pres. N.M. Constl. Conv.; chmn. N.M. Democratic party, 1966-67; chmn. N.M. Hwy. Users Conf., 1968-69. Bd. dirs. N.M. Farm and Livestock Bur. Served with AUS, World War II. Mem. Nat. Conf. Legislative Leaders, Western Council State Govt., N.M. Cattle Growers Assn., N.M. Soil and Water Conservation (v.p.), No. N.M. Fair Assn. (chmn.), N.M. Wildlife and Conservation Assn., N.M. Amigos, Am. Legion, V.F.W. Elk. Address: Stanley NM 87056

KING, C(HARLES) HAROLD, educator; b. DeWitt, N.Y., Jan. 15, 1899; s. Charles Henry and Jane (Buckman) K.; B.A., Cornell U., 1920, Ph.D., 1935; M.A., N.Y. U., 1930; postgrad. summers Columbia, 1922-23, U. Minn., 1927-28, U. Wis., 1927, Harvard, summers 1937, 57; m. Helen Louise Garlinghouse, May 8, 1947. Instr., asso. prof. Colgate U., 1929-45; asso. prof. history U. Miami, Coral Gables, Fla., 1945-48, prof., 1948-71, emeritus prof., 1971-—. Instr. aerology and nav. USNR, 1943-45; spl. rep. in fund raising A.R.C., 1944-45. Mem. Iron Arrow, Tau Kappa Alpha, Phi Kappa Phi, Phi Eta Sigma, Phi Alpha Theta, Delta Theta Mu, Omicron Delta Kappa. Author: History of Civilization, vol. 1, 1956, rev., 1964; History of Civilization, 1969. Contbr. articles to profl. jours. Home: 7420 SW 53d Pl South Miami FL 33143 Office: Ferre Bldg U Miami Coral Gables FL 33126

KING, CHARLES JAMES, lawyer; b. Atlanta, Feb. 3, 1925; s. Lewis Reed and Mary (Green) K.; J.D., U. Miami, 1955; m. Lydia V. Schuster, May 27, 1950; children—Janet H. (Mrs. Glenn Hargrave), Annette L., James R., Elaine H. Trust officer Broward Nat. Bank, Ft. Lauderdale, Fla., 1955-57; admitted to Fla. bar, 1955; practiced in Ft. Lauderdale, 1957-—; mem. Fla. Ho. of Reps., 1967-70; municipal judge, 1966-67. Mem. Fla., Broward County bar assns., Am. Arbitration Assn., Delta Theta Phi. Home: 621 NW 66th Av Plantation FL 33313 Office: 2425 E Commercial Blvd Fort Lauderdale FL 33308

KING, CHARLES OSSIE, air conditioning contractor; b. nr. Franklin, Ind., Nov. 17, 1919; s. Ossie Lloyd and Lily Mae (Ervin) K.; grad. high sch.; m. Ruth Isabel LePage, July 12, 1944; children—Charles E., Carolyn R., Michael J. Mech. supt. Gen. Am. Transp. Corp., Orlando, Fla., 1946-51; salesman Boys Roofing & S/M Works, Inc., West Palm Beach, Fla., 1951-58; pres. Air Conditioning Designers, Inc., West Palm Beach, 1958-—. Served with USN, 1937-45. Mem. Am. Soc. Heating, Refrigerating and Air Conditioning Engrs. (bd. govs. Gold Coast chpt.), Palm Beach County Roofing and Sheet Metal Contractors Assn. (past pres.), Palm Beach Country Air Conditioning Contractors Assn. (past pres.), Nat. Assn. Sheet Metal and Air Conditioning Contractors (nat. councilor), Refrigeration Service Engrs. Soc., Fla. Roofing, Sheet Metal and Air Conditioning Contractors Assn. (pres.). Rotarian (past pres.). Contbr. articles to jours. Home: 7015 Carissa Circle West Palm Beach FL 33406 Office: 1601 N Military Trail West Palm Beach FL 33406

KING, CHARLES WILLIAM, geophysicist; b. Hannibal, Mo., Sept. 10, 1936; s. William M. and Cleo (Woollen) K.; B.S., Mass. Inst. Tech., 1958; m. Mary Jo Murphy, July 5, 1962; children—Jennifer, Theresa, Christopher. Geophysicist, Mobil Oil Co., 1958-63; geophysicist Union Oil Co. of Cal., Houston, 1963-66, dist. geophysicist, New Orleans, 1966-67, regional geophysicist, Houston, 1968-—. Served with USAF, 1959-60. Mem. Soc. Exploration Geophysicists, Houston Geophys. Soc. Home: 5318 Dumfries St Houston TX 77035 Office: 900 Executive Plaza W Houston TX 77027

KING, CORETTA SCOTT (MRS. MARTIN LUTHER KING, JR.), lectr., writer, civic worker; b. Marion, Ala., Apr. 27, 1927; d. Obidiah and Bernice (McMurray) Scott; A.B., Antioch Coll., 1951; Mus.B., New Eng. Conservatory Music, 1954; L.H.D., Boston U., 1969; m. Martin Luther King, Jr., June 18, 1953 (dec. Apr. 1968); children—Yolanda Denise, Martin Luther III, Dexter Scott, Bernice Albertine. Concert debut, Springfield, O., 1948, numerous concerts throughout U.S.; concerts India, 1959; performances Freedom Concert; voice instr. Morris Brown Coll., Atlanta, 1962; lectr., writer. Del. White House Conf. Children and Youth, 1960; sponsor Sane Nuclear Policy, Com. on Responsibility, Mobilization To End War in Viet Nam, 1966, 67, Margaret Sanger Meml. Found.; pres. Martin Luther King, Jr. Meml. Center; active YWCA. Bds. dirs. So. Christian Leadership Conf., Martin Luther King, Jr. Found. Gt. Britain; trustee Robert F. Kennedy Meml. Recipient Outstanding Citizenship award Montgomery (Ala.) Improvement Assn., 1959, Merit award St. Louis Argus, 1960, Distinguished Achievement award Nat. Orgn. Colored Women's Clubs, 1962, Louise Waterman Wise award Am. Jewish Congress Women's Aux., 1963, Myrtle Wreath award Cleve. Hadassah, 1965, Wateler Peace prize, 1968, numerous others; named Woman of Year, Utility Club N.Y.C., 1962, Woman of Year, Nat. Assn. Radio and TV Announcers, 1968. Mem. Nat. Council Negro Women (Ann. Brotherhood award, 1957), Women Strike for Peace (del. disarmanent conf. Geneva, Switzerland 1962, citation for work in peace and freedom 1963), Women's Orgn. Internat. League for Peace and Freedom, United Church Women (bd. mgrs.), Alpha Kappa Alpha (hon.). Baptist (mem. choir, guild adviser). Club: Links (Human Dignity and Human Rights award Norfolk chpt. 1964). Author: My Life With Martin Luther King, Jr., 1969. Home: 234 Sunset Av NW Atlanta GA 30314

KING, DAN MADISON, librarian; b. Muncie, Ind., Nov. 7, 1914; s. Arthur Daniel and Grace Hamilton (Campbell) K.; A.B., Hanover Coll., 1938; B.S. in L.S., Syracuse U., 1940; postgrad. McGill U., Ball State U., N.Y. U. Asst., Muncie (Ind.) Pub. Library, 1938-39; asst. reference dept. N.Y. Pub. Library, 1940; dist. supr. WPA Library Service Project, Indpls., 1940-42; asst. librarian in charge art sch. library Cooper Union, N.Y.C., 1942-43, librarian in charge, 1943-46; chief reference dept. Grand Rapids (Mich.) Pub. Library, 1946-48; asst. reference dept. N.Y. Pub. Library, 1948-49; librarian Minn. Hist. Soc., St. Paul, 1949-54; head librarian Ky. Wesleyan Coll., Owensboro, 1954-—, asso. prof. library sci., 1954-—. Library cons. Tex. Gas Transmission Gas Corp., Owensboro, Ky., 1960-61; mem. spl. coms. for coll. visitations So. Assn. Colls. and Schs., Atlanta, 1963-—. Mem. Am., Spl. (chmn. nat. museum div. 1953-54), Southeastern, Ky. (pres. 1964-65) library assns., Phi Delta Theta. Presbyn. Club: Filson (Louisville). Contbr. articles to profl. jours. Home: 2313 S York St Owensboro KY 42301 Office: 3000 Frederica St Owensboro KY 42301

KING, E. WILLIAM, pres., treas. Mason & Dixon Lines, Inc. Address: Eastman Rd Kingsport TN 37664*

KING, EDWARD DUNCAN, real estate co. exec.; b. Ga., Feb. 12, 1896; s. Alfred Fawcett and Leila (Sweat) K.; grad. Savannah High Sch.; m. Ruth Holmer, July 12, 1922; 1 son, Carl Duncan. Clk., Nat. Bank of Savannah, 1916-17, Furse & Lawton, cotton brokers, Savannah, 1917; asst. cashier Exchange Bank Savannah, 1919-22; with A.F. King & Son, realtors, Savannah, 1922-—, pres., 1941-—. Pres., Tax Payers Assn. Chatham County, Savannah, 1959-—; treas. Pure Water Council, Savannah, 1962-—; mem. Bd. Policy Liberty Lobby, Washington, Nat. Com. Against Fluoridation, Washington. Bd. dirs. Savannah Vol. Guards. Served with CAC, U.S. Army, 1917-19; AEF in France. Mem. Savannah Real Estate Bd., Ga. Assn. Real Estate Bds., Nat. Assn. Mut. Ins. Agts., Am. Legion, Vets. World War I U.S.A., Sons Confederate Vets., Cinema Ednl. Guild, Hist. Savannah Found., Conservatives. Baptist. Home: 321 E 52d St Savannah GA 31405 Office: 112 Congress St W Savannah GA 31401

KING, FRANK HENRY, mgmt. cons.; b. Washington, Aug. 31, 1918; s. Charles Henry and Julia (Fiorini) K.; B.S., Va. Poly. Inst., 1951; M.S., Okla. State U., 1958; M.B.A., Cal. Western U., 1964; m. Dorothy Elizabeth Earles, June 20, 1951; children—Vicki Faye, Donna Gale, Frank Gregory, Rodney Steven, David Patton, Robin Annice, Raymond Michael. Sr. staff devel. engr. USAF contract mgmt. div., Los Angeles, 1964-65; sr. staff reliability engr. U.S. Army Materiel Command, Gravelly Point, Va., 1965-66; tech. dir. value engring. Hdqrs. USAF Systems Command, Andrews AFB, Md., 1966-70; mgmt. cons., 1970-—; lectr. in field. Served with AUS, 1943-46, USAF, 1953-62. Registered profl. engr., Okla. Mem. Soc.

Am. Value Engrs. dir., Am. Ordnance Assn., Omicron Delta Kappa, Sigma Tau, Pi Tau Sigma. Address: 4725 Pebble Bay Circle Vero Beach FL 32960

KING, FREDERICK ALEXANDER, educator; b. Paterson, N.J., Oct. 3, 1925; s. James Aloysius and Louise (Gallant) K.; student U. San Carlos (Guatemala), 1947-48, Hope Coll., 1946-47, 49-50; A.B., Stanford, 1953; A.M., Johns Hopkins, 1955, Ph.D., 1956; m. Tiia Reet Karell, Aug. 9, 1968. Instr. psychiatry Coll. Medicine Ohio State U., Columbus, 1956-57, asst. prof., 1957-59; mem. faculty Coll. Medicine U. Fla., Gainesville, 1959—, dir. Neurobiol. Scis. Center, 1965—, prof., chmn. dept. anatomical scis., 1969-70, chmn. dept. neurosci., 1970—; mem. psychobiology adv. panel, biol. and med. scis. div. NSF, 1963-67; cons. NIH, 1963—; mem. research sci. devel. rev. com. Nat. Inst. Mental Health, 1969—. Served with USNR, 1943-46, 51. John Carrol Fulton scholar, 1953-55; NIH research fellow, 1955-56; NIH spl. fellow U. Pisa (Italy), 1961-62, Mem. Internat. Neuropsychology Soc. (sec. treas.). Contbr. profl. jours. Home: 3666 NW 13th Pl Gainesville FL 32601 Office: Dept Neuroscience Coll Medicine U Fla Gainesville FL 32601

KING, GERALD LAMAR, investment co. exec.; b. Anniston, Ala., Apr. 12, 1922; s. Thomas Cobb and Sadie (Cox) K.; B.A., U. Ala., 1943, postgrad. in law, 1941-43; m. Martha Morrow Patton, July 29, 1943; children—Gerald Lamar, Thomas Patton, Martha Cox. With T.C. King Pipe & Foundry Co., Anniston, Ala., 1946-61, v.p., 1946-61, sec., 1946-61; partner T.C. King Co., Anniston, Ala., 1945-61; plant mgr. Anniston Soil Pipe div. U.S. Pipe & Fory Co., 1961—; v.p., pres. King Factors, Inc., Anniston, 1961—; dir. Anniston Nat. Bank. Commr. Anniston Airport Bd., 1955—. Trustee Stringfellow Meml. Hosp., Anniston. Served to capt. AUS, 1943-46; PTO. Mem. Nat. Planning Council, Alpha Tau Omega. Club: Anniston Country. Home: 8 Sunset Dr Anniston AL 36201 Office: Front St Anniston AL 36201

KING, GLYNN NATIONS (MRS. HERBERT ANTHONY KING, SR.), textile and laundry co. exec.; b. Resaca, Ga., Apr. 16, 1923; d. Pryor and Mary (Nance) Nations; student W. Ga. Coll., 1941; A.B., U. Ga., 1943; m. Herbert Anthony King, July 3, 1943; children—Herbert Anthony, Martha Maria. Employee, Navy Pre-Flight Sch., Athens, Ga., 1943-44, English tchr. Calhoun (Ga.) High Sch., 1953-56; sec.-treas. Buford Textile, Inc., Calhoun, 1956-62; sec.-treas., in charge nat. sales King Textiles, Inc., also King Laundries, Inc., Calhoun, 1963—. Treas. Gordon County unit Am. Cancer Soc., Calhoun, 1965-72; active Community Chest. Mem. Phi Beta Kappa, Phi Kappa Phi. Baptist (tchr. young people's dept. 1960—). Home: 303 Trammell St Calhoun GA 30701 Office: 129 McConnell Rd Calhoun GA 30701

KING, HERBERT ANTHONY, textile exec.; b. David City, Neb., May 19, 1918; s. Herman Otto and May (Wilson) K.; student pub. schs.; m. Glynn Nations, July 3, 1943; children—Herbert Anthony, Martha Maria. Pres., King Textiles, Inc., Calhoun, Ga., 1963—, King Laundries, Inc., 1963—. Served with USNR, 1941-45. Mem. Am. Legion. Baptist. Rotarian. Home: 303 Trammell St Calhoun GA 30701 Office: McConnell Rd Calhoun GA 30701

KING, HUGER SINKLER, corp. exec.; b. Darlington, S.C., June 15, 1907; s. S. Coker and Mary Simons (Sinkler) K.; student The Citadel, 1923-25; LL.B., U. S.C., 1928; m. Mary Lynn Carlson, May 21, 1932; children—Huger S., L. Richardson, Laurinda C., Michael Lowndes. Admitted to N.C. bar, 1928, practiced in Greensboro, 1928-58, sr. partner King, Adams, Kleemeier & Hagan, 1955-58. Pres. Richardson Corp.; chmn. Piedmont Financial Co. Inc. of N.Y.; dir., chmn. exec. com. Reinsurance Corp. of N.Y.; dir., vice chmn. exec. com. Piedmont Ins. Co.; chmn. exec. com. Piedmont So. Life Ins. Co.; pres. Piedmont Mgmt. Co., Inc.; dir. Richardson-Merrell, Inc., Piedmont Adv. Corp., N.C. Nat. Bank. Trustee, v.p. Richardson Foundation. Past pres. Greensboro Community Chest; chmn. Empty Stocking Fund. Mayor, Greensboro, 1940-42. Vice pres. Richardson Found.; trustee Davidson Coll. Served as lt. comdr. USNR, 1942-45. Mem. Am. Bar Assn., Am. Law Inst., Greensboro C. of C. (past pres.). Presbyn. (elder). Clubs: University (N.Y.C.); Merchants and Manufacturers, Greensboro Country (past pres.) (Greensboro). Home: 701 Sunset Dr Greensboro NC Office: Piedmont Bldg Greensboro NC

KING, IRA JOE, dentist; b. Belgreen, Ala., May 7, 1905; s. William Robert and Mollie Jo (Hester) K.; student Auburn U., 1924, Birmingham So. Coll., 1929-30, Howard Coll., 1931; D.D.S., U. Louisville, 1937; m. Evelyn Lydia Smith, Nov. 2, 1937; children—Jo Ann (Mrs. Ronald Ray Simmons), Mollie (Mrs. Lewis McCoy Martin). Co. dentist West Blocton Coal Mines (Ala.), part time, 1937-41, McWane Cast Iron Pipe Co., Birmingham, part time 1939-56; individual practice dentistry, Birmingham, 1937—; mem. staff Children's Hosp., Birmingham, 1938-39. Vice pres., finance chmn. West End Little League, Birmingham, 1962-66. Mem. Jefferson County Sportsman's Assn. (v.p. 1960-61). Mason (Shriner). Home: 1549 Bay Av Birmingham AL 35211 Office: 1925 29th Av S Homewood AL 35209

KING, IVAN DEWITT, JR., engr., land surveyor; b. Enoree, S.C., Dec. 9, 1925; s. Ivan DeWitt and Clara (Montjoy) K.; B.S., Clemson U., 1949; m. Peggy Anne Eskew, July 6, 1946; children—Richard Kenneth, Bryan Theodore. Tng. program Va. Hwy. Dept. 1949-50, mem. research dept., 1950-51; partner Aldridge, Moon and King, cons. engring., Columbus, Ga., 1951-62; owner King Engring. Service, Winter Haven, Fla., 1962—. Served with USNR, 1942-46. Family named All-American Family from Ga., 1960. Mem. Winter Haven C. of C., Am. Legion, Ga. Soc. Profl. Engrs. (past pres. Columbus chpt.), Fla. Engring. Soc. (past pres. Ridge chpt.), Am. Soc. C.E., Ridge Chpt. Profl. Land Surveyors, Tau Beta Pi, Phi Kappa Phi. Baptist (deacon). Address: 558 E Lake Elbert Dr NE Winter Haven FL 33880

KING, J. T., football coach; B.S., U. Tex., 1938. Mem. faculty Tex. Tech. Coll., Lubbock, 1958—, head football coach, 1961—. Office: Athletic Dept Tex Tech Coll Lubbock TX 79409*

KING, JAMES ALLEN, dentist; b. Dallas, Mar. 4, 1936; s. William Marion and Lillie Belle (Garrett) K.; B.A., North Tex. State Coll., 1958; D.D.S., Baylor U., 1962; m. Sally Ann Latlippe, Dec. 26, 1959; children—James Allen, John Andrew, Peter Daniel, Timothy Vincent. Individual practice dentistry, Irving, Tex., 1964—. Gen. dentist Dental Pub. Health, City of Dallas, 1968—; active YMCA. Served with AUS, 1962-64. Mem. Am., Tex. dental assns., Dallas County Dental Soc., Irving Dental Study Club (sec.-treas. 1971-72). Democrat. Methodist (mem. ofcl. bd. 1971-72). Rotarian. Home: 1944 Valley Oaks St Irving TX 75061 Office: 812 O'Connor St Irving TX 75061

KING, JAMES LAWRENCE, dist. judge; b. Miami, Fla., Dec. 20, 1927; s. James Lawrence and Viola (Clodfelter) K.; B.A. in Edn., U. Fla., 1949, LL.B., 1953; m. Mary F. Kapa, June 1, 1961; children—Lawrence Daniel, Kathryn Ann, Karen Ann, Mary Virginia. Admitted to Fla. bar, 1953; asso. firm Sibley & Davis, Miami, 1953, 55-57, partner Sibley, Giblin, King & Levenson, 1957-64; judge 11th Jud. Circuit, Dade County, Miami, 1964-70; U.S. dist. judge, 1970—; asso. justice Supreme Ct. Fla., 1965; asso. judge 3d Dist. Ct. Appeal, 1965-66. Dir. Miami Nat. Bank, Mount Clements Industries, Inc. Mem. state exec. council U. Fla., 1956-59; mem. Bd. Control Fla. Governing State Univs. and Colls., 1964. Served to 1st lt. USAF, 1953-55. Recipient Service award Presidents State Univs., 1965. Mem. Fla. Bar (pres. jr. bar sect. 1963-64, bd. govs. 1958-63, award of merit young lawyers sect. 1967), Am., Fla., Dade County, Miami Beach bar assns., Univ. Fla. Hall of Fame, Fla. Blue Key, Pi Kappa Tau, Phi Delta Phi. Democrat. Methodist. Kiwanian. Club: University. Home: 11950 SW 67th Ct Miami FL 33138 Office: US Court House 300 NE 1st Av Miami FL

KING, JOE HALE, JR, city ofcl.; b. Birmingham, Ala., Jan. 5, 1925; s. Joseph Hale and Ethel (Key) K.; student U. Ala., 1947-49; m. Annie Belle McDonald, Sept. 15, 1946; children—Joseph H. III, Ethel Marie, Michael Wesley. With Liberty Nat. Life Ins. Co., Birmingham, 1949-68; mayor city Fairfield, Ala., 1968—. Chmn., USS Ala. Battleship Commn., 1963-64; vice chmn. Steel Dist. Officers, Boy Scouts Am., 1968-69, mem.-at-large, 1970—; recipient Century Club award, 1968; mem. Glen Oaks Elementary Sch. P.T.A., 1966—. Served with USMCR, 1943-46; PTO. Recipient several awards Liberty Nat. Life Ins. Co., certificate of Appreciation Birmingham lodge Fraternal Order Police, 1968, George Washington Honor medal award for 1969 Govtl. Unit Activities (as mayor city Fairfield) Freedoms Found. at Valley Forge. Mem. Fraternal Order Police (asso.), Jefferson County Mayor's Assn. (v.p.), V.F.W., Am. Legion, League of Municipalities. Baptist. Mason (Shriner), Elk. Home: 1041 Glen Oaks Dr Fairfield AL 35064 Office: City Hall Fairfield AL 35064

KING, JOHN Q. TAYLOR, coll. pres.; b. Memphis, Sept. 25, 1921; s. John Q. Taylor and Alice (Woodson) King; B.A., Fisk U., 1941; grad. Landig Coll. Mortuary Sci., 1942; B.S., Huston-Tillotson Coll., 1947; M.S., DePaul U., 1950; Ph.D., U. Tex. 1957; m. Marcet Hines, June 28, 1942; children—John Q. Taylor, Clinton Allen, Marjon Alicia, Stuart Hines. Mortician, King-Tears Mortuary, Austin, Tex., 1946—; with Huston-Tillotson Coll., 1947—, prof. math., 1952-65, dean, 1960-65, pres., 1965—, vis. sci. Tex. Acad. Sci., 1960-67; mem. coop. writing com. Pitman Pub. Corp., 1956, 58, 60, 62. Mem. exec. com. Austin Council Human Relations, 1955-67; div. officer Boy Scouts Am., 1956-60; peace edn. com. Am. Friends Service Com., 1959-66; mem. Austin com. USO, 1960—. Mem. gen. bd. edn. United Meth. Ch., 1960-72; exec. com. South Central Jurisdictional Bd. Christian Social Concerns, 1964-72; del. Meth. Gen. and Jurisdictional Confs., 1956, 60, 64, 66, 67, 68, 70, 72. Bd. dirs. Wesley Found., U. Tex., 1953-71, Texas So. U., 1960-71. Tex. Conf. Chs., 1963—, Child and Family Service, 1964-70, Tex. Mental Health Assn., 1966-70, Austin chpt. Nat. Conf. Christians and Jews, Tex. Meth. Student Movement, 1964-70, Community Council of Austin and Travis County, Austin Community Nursery Sch., 1968-70, Travis County unit Am. Cancer Soc., 1966-70, United Fund of Austin and Travis County, 1966-70; trustee Fisk U. Served to capt. AUS, 1942-46; col. Res. Mem. Am. Statis. Assn., Nat. Inst. Sci., Austin C. of C. (v.p., dir.), Sigma Pi Phi, Delta Pi Epsilon, Alpha Phi Alpha, Phi Delta Kappa, Alpha Kappa Mu. Methodist. Mason (33 deg.), Kiwanian. Author: (with wife) The Story of Twenty-Three Famous Negro Americans, 1967. Contbr. numerous articles religious and profl. jours. Home: 2400 Givens Av Austin TX 78722

KING, JOHN R., exec. v.p., gen. mgr. Mason & Dixon Lines, Inc. Address: Eastman Rd Kingsport TN 37664*

KING, LLOYD ELIJAH, JR., physician; b. Mayfield, Ky., Sept. 10, 1939; s. Lloyd Elijah and Mary Frances (Lowe) K.; B.A., Vanderbilt U., 1961; M.D., U. Tenn., 1967, Ph.D., 1970; m. Wanda Gail Waller, Dec. 28, 1968. Postdoctoral fellow U. Tenn., 1968-69; intern, City of Memphis hosps., 1969-70, resident in internal medicine, 1970-71; resident in dermatology U. Tenn. Grad. Sch. Med. Sci., Memphis, 1971-72, instr. anatomy dept., 1971-72; postdoctoral fellow dermatology VA Hosp., Memphis, 1972—. Served with USNR, 1961-63. Mem. Sigma Xi, Phi Chi, Sigma Alpha Epsilon. Democrat. Episcopalian. Home: 1667 Hapano Germantown TN 38138 Office: VA Hosp 1070 Jefferson Av Memphis TN 38103

KING, MARIAN, author; b. Washington; d. Joseph and Jeannette (Michel) King; student Miss Maderia's Sch., Greenway, Va.; studied abroad. Author since 1928; ABC Game Book, 1928; The Mirror of Youth, 1928; ABC Game Cards, 1930; Kees (Jr. Lit. Guild selection), 1930; The Story of Athletics, 1931; The Dutch Mother Goose, 1931; Amnon. A Lad of Palestine, 1932; Skeeta, 1933; The Golden Cat Head, 1933; Kees and Kleintje (Jr. Lit. Guild Selection), 1934; A Boy of Poland, 1934; Sean and Sheela, 1937; It Happened in England, 1939; Piccolino, 1939; Elizabeth: The Tudor Princess, 1940; Young King David, 1948; The Coat of Many Colors, 1951; Young Mary Stuart; Queen of Scots, 1954; Portraits of Children in the National Gallery of Art, 1955; Portfolio for National Gallery Art (Life of Christ), 1950, (Portraits of Children in the National Gallery of Art), 1953; A Gallery of Children, pub. 1955, revised and enlarged edition, published 1967; Portrait of Jesus (King James version and Douav version, separate vols.), 1956; A Gallery of Mothers and Their Children, 1958; What Would You Do; Mary Baker Eddy, Child of Promise, 1968; The Star of Bethlehem, 1968. Children's Book editor The National Observer. Selected Bible Text (King James Version) for Paintings Depicting the Life of Christ for the Nat. Gallery of Art Folder No. 2. Contbr. to books of several sch. book pubs.; also various periodicals. Served with Brit. Supply Missions, Washington, 1940-45. Mem. Authors Guild, English Speaking Union, Nat. Council Women, Childrens Book Guild, Authors Book Guild Am. Club: Longwood Cricket (Chestnut Hill, Mass.). Researcher TV film U.S. One. Home: 4501 Connecticut Av Washington DC 20008

KING, PETER, chemist; b. Boston, Dec. 12, 1910; s. Peter and Isabella (Rodgers) K.; student U. Notre Dame, 1930-31; A.B., U. Cal. at Los Angeles, 1936; Ph.D., Catholic U. Am., 1942; m. Elizabeth Louise Toole, Apr. 25, 1942; children—Peter, Pamela M., Stephan J., Elizabeth A., John R., Victoria L. Chemist, asso. dir. research for materials Naval Research Lab., Washington, 1939-64; sci. dir. Office Naval Research br. office, London, Eng., 1964-66, dep. chief, chief scientist, Washington, 1966—. Recipient Navy Distinguished Civilian Service award, 1960. Mem. Am. Chem. Soc., Washington Acad. Scis., Phlos. Soc., A.A. A.S., Contbr. articles profl. jours. Patentee in field. Home: 1120 Cameron Rd Alexandria VA 22308 Office: Ballston Tower 1 800 N Qunicy St Arlington VA 22217

KING, RALPH BUXTON, JR., dentist; b. Greenwood, Miss., Apr. 24, 1933; s. Ralph Buxton and Eunice Francis (Jones) K.; student La. Poly. Inst., 1951-52, La. State U., 1952-53; D.D.S., U. Tenn., 1956; m. Mary Lee Banner, Nov. 24, 1956; children—Anne Jones, Mary Winston. Dentist Va. Health Dept., 1956-57; individual practice dentistry, Monroe, La., 1959—. Served with AUS, 1957-59, 61-62. Fellow Am. Coll. Dentists; mem. Am., La. dental assns., Am. Assn. Endodontists, So. Endodontic Study Group, Fifth Dist. Dental Soc. (pres. 1959), Kappa Alpha, Psi Omega. Presbyn. (elder, deacon 1961—). Club: Bayou DeSiard Country (dir. 1971—) (Monroe). Home: 2202 Island Dr Monroe LA 71201 Office: 1101 Royal Av Monroe LA 71201

KING, RAY AIKEN, educator; b. Atlanta, Oct. 11, 1933; s. Robert Esrle and Elsie Lurene (Aiken) K.; A.B., Erskine Coll., 1955; B.D., Erskine Theol. Sem., 1958; postgrad. U. Edinburgh (Scotland), 1959-61; Th.M., Austin Presbyn. Theol. Sem., 1971; m. Brenda Kay Taylor, Dec. 21, 1963; children—Ray Aiken Wayne Starr, Kay Allison. Ordained to ministry Asso. Ref. Presbyn. Ch., 1958; pastor Hickory Grove (S.C.) Asso. Ref. Presbyn. Ch., 1958-59; prof. elect ch. history Erskine Theol. Sem., Due West, S.C., 1959-62, prof., 1962—. Mem. bd. fgn. missions Asso. Ref. Presbyn. Ch., 1963-67, chmn., 1965-66, mem. synod com. on ecumenical relations, 1968-71; sustaining mem. Hist. Found. Presbyn. and Ref. Chs., 1965—. Active Boy Scouts Am., 1958-59, 62—. Mem. Presbyn. Hist. Soc. Mason. Author: A History of the Associate Reformed Presbyterian Church, 1966. Mailing address: Erskine Theological Seminary Due West SC 29639 Home: PO Box 177 Due West SC 29639

KING, ROBERT, football coach Furman U. Address: Athletic Dept Furman U Greenville SC 29613*

KING, ROBERT THOMAS, editor; b. Hillside, N.J., Oct. 29, 1930; s. Philip Arthur and Lucy (Davis) K.; ed. Emmanuel Coll. at Cambridge, Eng., 1948-50; B.A., Birmingham (Eng.) U., 1954; postgrad. Shakespeare Inst., Stratford-Upon-Avon, Eng., 1954-55. Trainee Oxford U. Press., N.Y.C., 1957-59; chief copy editor N.Y. U. Press, N.Y.C., 1959-61, editor 1961-63, mng. editor, 1963-66; dir. U. S.C. Press, Columbia, 1966—. Mem. scholarly activities com., publ. subcom. S.C. Tricentennial Commn. Home: 1520 Senate St Columbia SC 29201 Office: University Press Columbia SC 29208

KING, ROLLIN WHITE, airline co. exec.; b. Cleve., Apr. 10, 1931; s. Warren Griffin and Elizabeth (White) K.; student Choate Sch., 1946-48; student Cornell U., Ithaca, N.Y., 1950-54; Ba., Western Res. U., 1955; M.B.A., Harvard, 1962; m. Marcia Gygli, May 10, 1956; children—Rollin White, Edward Prescott. Mem. mgmt. staff NSA, Washington, 1955-60; v.p. King, Pitman Co., investment counsel, San Antonio, 1962-63; pres. Southwest Airlines, Inc., San Antonio, 1963-68; exec. v.p. operation, dir. Southwest Airlines Co., Dallas, 1967—. Cons. air transp. Dept. Communication Royal Thai Govt., Bangkok, 1969. Served with AUS; 1956-58. Mem. Navy League (past pres., co-founder), San Antonio Livestock Exposition (bd. dirs.), Clubs: Harvard Club N.Y.C.; Harvard of Dallas, Oak Hills Country, The Argyle, The St. Anthony (San Antonio). Address: 626 Evans Av San Antonio TX 78209

KING, RUFUS, lawyer; b. Seattle, Mar. 25, 1917; s. Rufus Gunn and Marian (Towle) K.; A.B., Princeton, 1938; post. Stanford, 1940-41; LL.B., Yale, 1943; m. Janice L. Chase, June 15, 1941 (div. June 1951); children—Rufus, Agnes S.; m. 2d, Laura Kinser Barone (dec. Oct. 1965). Instr. Princeton, 1938-39; admitted to N.Y. bar, 1944, D.C. bar, 1948, Md. bar, 1953; partner Rice and King, Washington, 1953-63; pvt. practice in Washington, 1965—; counsel Senate Crime Com., 1951, also other congl. coms.; cons. Pres.'s Commn. Law Enforcement and Adminstrn. Justice, 1966-67. Chmn. joint com, narcotic drugs Am. Bar Assn. and A.M.A., 1956—; chmn. disaster protection com. Washington Bd. Trade, 1956-58; chmn. D.C. Com. on Pub. Schs., 1956-57; pres. Montgomery County Community Psychiat. Clin., 1963-65. Mem. Am. (chmn. criminal law sect. 1957-60, sec. 1954-57, mem. ho. dels. 1960—, spl. com. minimum standards adminstrn. justice 1965—), N.Y., Md. bar assns., Bar Assn. D.C., Am. Law Inst., Scribes (pres. 1968—). Clubs: Princeton (N.Y.), Nassau, Colonial (Princeton); Metropolitan, Lawyers (Washington); American (Miami, Fla.). Author: Gambling and Organized Crime, 1969; The Drug Hang-Up, 1972. Contbr. articles profl. jours. Home: 3524 Williamsburg Lane NW Washington DC 20008 Office: Woodward Bldg Washington DC 20005

KING, STEVEN CLARENCE, govt. ofcl.; b. Plainfield, N.H., Dec. 12, 1921; s. Clarence W. and Flora Belle (Rogers) K.; B.S., U. N.H., 1947; M.S., Cornell U., 1951, Ph.D., 1953; m. Dorothy C. Fentress, Feb. 14, 1967; children—(by previous marriage) Gordon S., Nancy E. Foreman Ken-La Farms, Claremont, N.H., 1947-48; geneticist Fuzzydele Farms, Elverson, Pa., 1948-49; asst. prof. Cornell U., 1953-55, asso. prof. 1955-56; animal geneticist U.S. Dept. Agr., Lafayette, Ind., 1956-59; geneticist Mt. Hope Farm, Batavia, N.Y., 1959-60; br. chief poultry U.S. Dept. Agr., 1960-63, asst. dir. animal husbandry div., 1963-64, staff scientist, 1964-66, asst. dir. animal husbandry div., 1966-68, asst. dir. research devel. and evaluation staff, 1968-70, dep. adminstr. Agrl. Research Service, 1970—. Served to capt. USAAF, 1943-46. Decorated Air medal with oak leaf cluster. Fellow A.A.A.S.; mem. Poultry Sci. Soc., World's Poultry Sci. Soc., Am. Inst. Biol. Sci. Contbr. articles to profl. jours. Home: 12601 Meadowood Dr Silver Spring MD 20904 Office: Nat Agrl Research Center Beltsville MD 20705

KING, STONEWALL CORPUT, JR., educator; b. Calhoun, Ga., Apr. 30, 1931; s. Stonewall Corput and DeAlva (Talley) K.; certificate W.Ga. Coll., 1951; B.S., U. Ga., 1953; B.S. in Pharmacy, Mercer Sch. Pharmacy, 1958; M.S., U. Md., 1960; Pharm.D., U. Mich., 1968; m. Jeanette Hunter, June 16, 1962; children—Stonewall Corput III, Hunter D. Pharmacy resident Johns Hopkins Hosp., Balt., 1958-60; chief pharmacist Leigh Meml. Hosp., Norfolk, Va., 1960-61; chief pharmacist Hamilton Meml. Hosp., Dalton, Ga., 1961-62; asso. prof. U. Ga. Sch. Pharmacy, Athens, 1962-72, asso. prof. Inst. Community and Area Devel., 1968-72; asso. prof., head dept. clin. pharmacy Sch. Pharmacy, Mercer U., 1972—; dir. pharm. edn. Ga. Bapt. Hosp., Atlanta, 1972—; lectr. pharmacology Hall Sch. Nursing, Gainesville, Ga., summers 1965-66, 68. Served with AUS, 1953-55. Recipient Gordon Watson Meml. award W. Ga. Coll., 1951, Lehn & Fink Gold Metal award Mercer Sch. Pharmacy, 1958. Mem. Am., Southeastern (past pres.), Ga. (past pres.) socs. hosp. pharmacists, Am. Pharm. Assn. Rho Chi. Home: 5278 Rosser Rd Stone Mountain GA 30083

KING, VORIS, wholesale grocery co. exec.; b. Lake Charles, La., Jan. 20, 1917; s. Alvin Olin and Willie Lee (Voris) K.; student U. South, 1934-36; m. Frances Thompson, Dec. 19, 1935; children— Charles Stirling, Virginia Lee (Mrs. Sanford Ayres), William Voris, Alvin Bardine. Sec. King Corp., Lake Charles 1958-68; v.p. Little Lake Misere Corp., Lake Charles, 1958—; pres., gen. mgr. Kelly, Weber & Co., Inc., Lake Charles, 1961—; pres. Lake Charles Grain & Grocer Co., Inc., 1961—; dir. Am. Bank Commerce. Chmn. 7th dist. La. U.S.O., 1953—, nat. dir., 1969—; pres. Calcasieu-Cameron chpt. A.R.C., 1957, Calcasieu Area Safety Council, 1960, Lake Charles Marina Bd., 1964; pres. Orange Grove-Graceland Cemetery Assn., 1968—; mem. adv. bd. Salvation Army, 1964-70, adv. bd. laymen Lake Charles Seamen's Center, Inc., 1964—, adv. council area 3 Civil Def., 1953—, Lake Charles Sr. Civilian Adv. Council, 1953—. Bd. dirs. S.S.S., S.W. dist. Fat Stock Show and Rodeo, Inc., Lake Charles Civic Symphony, Calcasieu Area council Boy Scouts Am., La. Heart Assn., Calcasieu Parish Heart Fund Assn., McNeese State Coll. Found. Served with USNR, 1943-45. Recipient Outstanding Citizen award Lake Charles Salvation Army, 1964. Mem. U.S. (v.p. 1962—), La. wholesale grocers assns., Lake Charles Assn. Commerce (civic award 1960, pres. 1964), Better Bus. Bur. (pres. 1958), La. Tourist Assn., Blue Key. Methodist (chmn. bd. trustees). Mason (32 deg., Shriner), Odd Fellow, Rotarian, Elk. Clubs: Lake Charles Golf and Country; Pioneer, Contraband Citizens' Band (pres.), Coastal (dir.).

Home: PO Box 28 Lake Charles LA 70601 Office: Box 1120 Lake Charles LA 70601

KING, WILLIAM BALFOUR, dentist; b. Thomasville, Ga., Nov. 4, 1931; s. John Thomas and Mary (Balfour) K.; student Emory U. at Valdosta, 1951; D.D.S., Emery U., 1956; m. Anne Gatlin, July 29, 1956; children—William Michael, Marianne Rebecca. Individual practice dentistry, Thomasville, Ga., 1958—. Mem. Thomasville Sch. Bd., 1969—. Served with Dental Corps AUS, 1956-58. Mem. Southwestern Dist. Dental Assn. (sec.-treas. 1960-64), Thomasville C. of C. (dir. 1965-70), Ga. Dental Assn. Elk, Rotarian (dir. 1964-65, 71-72, pres. 1963-64). Home: 2720 Old Monticello Rd Thomasville GA 31792 Office: 416 Gordon Av Thomasville GA 31792

KING, WILLIAM HAMPTON, accountant, state ofcl.; b. Heidelberg, Miss., Oct. 1, 1909; s. William E. and Sarah E. (Covington) K.; student Hinds Jr. Coll., 1925-28; B.A., U. Miss., 1930; postgrad. YMCA Grad. Sch., Nashville, 1930-33; m. Eldridge Douglas Banks, July 6, 1934; children—Carolyn Douglas (Mrs. E.J. Andrew), Sarah Kathryn (Mrs. Joe Miklas). Social worker Tenn. Transient Bur. and Resettlement Adminstrn., Nashville, Crossville, 1934-38; cannery mgr. Homesteads Co-op Assn., Crossville, 1938-39; instr. social studies Clarke Jr. Coll., Newton, Miss., 1940; transp. supr. U.S. War Dept., Flora, Miss., 1941-44; accountant Woods Bldg. Supply Co., Jackson, Miss., 1945-47, Scott Bldg. Supply & Allied Corps., Cleveland, Miss., 1947-53; staff auditor Miss. Dept. Audit, Jackson, 1953-55, asst. dir., 1956-61, dir., 1962-63; auditor pub. accounts State of Miss., Jackson, 1964—. C.P.A., Miss. Mem. Am. Inst. C.P.A.'s, Miss. Soc. C.P.A.'s (pres. Jackson chpt. 1959), Nat. Assn. State Auditors, Controllers and Treasurers (treas. 1969, v.p. 1970-72), Municipal Finance Officers Assn., Little Theatre of Jackson, Jackson Music Assn., Jackson Symphony League. Democrat. Methodist (ofcl. bd.). Mason. Clubs: Knife and Fork (dir. 1969-72), Optimist (pres. 1969-70, lt. gov. 1970-71) (Jackson, Miss.). Home: 404 Colonial Circle Jackson MS 39211 Office: PO Box 1060 Capitol Bldg Jackson MS 39205

KING, WILLIAM HENRY, dentist; b. Port Arthur, Tex., June 5, 1929; s. Harry Fielding and Helen Bates (Emerson) K.; student U. Tenn., 1948-50, D.D.S., 1957; student U. Pitts., 1950-51; m. Joan Haralson, June 14, 1960; children—Donald Stewart, William Ronald. Individual practice dentistry, Jackson, Miss., 1958-60; staff dentist VA, Richmond, Va., 1961-63, Waco, Tex., 1963-65, Sepulveda, Cal., 1966-67, Biloxi, Miss., 1967—. Served with USN, 1946-48, 51-53; ETO. Mem. Am. Dental Assn., Am. Legion, Internat. Assn. Dental Research. Home: 29 47th St Gulfport MS 39501 Office: Dental Services VA Center Biloxi MS 39531

KING, WILLIAM RILEY, banker; b. Pineville, La., Dec. 15, 1934; s. William R. and Gertrude (Dillon) K.; student La. State U., 1953-54; B.B.A., La. Coll., 1960; m. Lynn Louise Bagley, Mar. 28, 1959; children—Robert, Donald. Mgmt. trainee Rapides Bank, Alexandria, La., 1958-60; asst. credit mgr. Sears Roebuck & Co., Dallas, 1960-63; asst. credit mgr. Titche-Goettinger, Dallas, 1963-65; v.p., exec. officer retail credit div. Preston State Bank of Dallas, 1965—. Instr., Dallas Inst. Retailing, 1963—, adult div. Dallas Jr. Coll., 1964—. Dir. Nat. Credit Card Sch. for Bankers. Served with USMCR, 1953-57. Fellow Soc. Certified Consumer Credit Execs.; mem. Internat. Consumer Credit Assn. (dir. 1967-71), Charge Account Bankers Assn. (dir. 1971-72), Consumer Credit Assn. Dallas (pres. 1970), Tex. Consumer Credit Assn. (v.p. 1970), Dallas, S.W. football ofcls. assns. Kiwanian. Office: PO Box 12000 Dallas TX 75225 Home: 11320 Buchanan St Dallas TX 75228

KING, WILLIS, govt. ofcl.; b. Fayette County, O., May 24, 1908; s. Harry J. and Alma F. (Dobbins) K.; B.Sc. in Edn., Wilmington Coll., 1929; M.A., Haverford Coll., 1930; Ph.D., U. Cin., 1939; D.Sc., N.C. State U., 1968; m. Frances Hall, June 8, 1935; children— Stephen H., Susan F. (Mrs. Jerry C. Tash), Christopher W. Wildlife technician Great Smoky Mountains Nat. Park, Gatlinburg, Tenn., 1934-40; chief fishery biologist N.C. Wildlife Resources Commn., Raleigh, 1940-49; with Tenn. Game and Fish Commn., Nashville, 1949-51; with U.S. Fish and Wildlife Service, 1951-57, asst. regional dir., Atlanta, 1955-57; chief div. fishery services Bur. Sport Fisheries and Wildlife, U.S. Dept. Interior, Washington, 1957-71, asst. dir., 1971—. Served to lt. USNR, 1944-45. Mem. Am. Fisheries Soc., Am. Inst. Biol. Scis., Sigma Xi. Contbr. articles to publs. Home: 5336 Wapakoneta Rd Washington DC 20016 Office: Bur Sport Fisheries and Wildlife Washington DC 20240

KING, WILLIS ALONZO, JR., dentist; b. Sussex, N.J., Aug. 19, 1941; s. Willis Alonzo and Louise (Collins) K.; student Clemson U., 1958-61; D.D.S., Emory U., 1965, M.S.D., 1969; m. Emily Florilla Willis, Aug. 25, 1961; children—Angela Renee, Michael Willis. Individual practice dentistry, Greenville, S.C., 1969—. Cons. child care groups, 1969—. Served to capt. Dental Corps, AUS, 1965-67. Recipient award Am. Soc. Dentistry for Children, 1965. Mem. Am. Soc. Preventive Dentistry, Am. Soc. Dentistry for Children, Am. Acad. Pedodontics, Am., S.C. dental assns., Southeastern Soc. Pedodontics, Greenville County (sec.-treas. 1970), Piedmont Dist. dental socs., Omicron Kappa Upsilon. Presbyn. Rotarian. Home: 5 Donington Dr Greenville SC 29607 Office: 25 Sweetbriar Rd Greenville SC 29607

KINGMAN, EDWARD ROCKWELL, constrn. co. exec.; b. Somerville, Mass., Jan. 2, 1917; s. Stanley Russell and Grace (Rockwell) K.; A.S.A. with honors, Bentley Coll. Accounting and Finance, 1936; B.B.A. with high honors, Northeastern U., 1951, M.B.A. with high honors, 1955; M.A. with honors, George Washington U., 1955; m. Margaret Hooker, Aug. 9, 1946; children—Edward R., Nancy Margaret. Dir., pres. Security Small Bus. Investment Co., Arlington, Va., 1963-69; exec. v.p., dir. Anderson-Stokes Inc., Rehoboth Beach, Del., 1971—. dir. Washington & Lee Savs. & Loan Assn., Arlington, Fidelity Nat. Bank, Arlington; prin. Kingman Assos. Financial Cons. and Real Estate Brokers, Arlington, 1965—; guest lectr. Navy Financial Mgmt. Program George Washington U., 1955-62. Chmn., Arlington Bd. Edn., 1967; dir., treas. Nat. Assn. Partners of Alliance, 1967-69; v.p., treas. The Nature Conservancy, Washington, 1968-71. Trustee Civil Service Retirement Fund, Arlington. Served to capt. USN, 1941-63; ret., 1963. Mem. Govs. Trade Commn. Brazil, Am. Inst. Banking (Va. legislative adv. com. 1965-66), Va. Edn. Assn., Nat. Sch. Bds. Assn., Nat. Assn. Mil. Comptrollers (nat. v.p. 1962-63). Home: 4851 35th Rd N Arlington VA 22207 Office: 48 Rehoboth Av Rehoboth Beach DE 19971

KINGMAN, HARRY ELLIS, JR., veterinarian, assn. exec.; b. Ft. Collins, Colo., Sept 4, 1911; s. Harry Ellis and Edna E. (Garbutt) K.; D.V.M., Colo. State U., 1933; m. Helen P. Allen, Aug. 3, 1936; 1 dau., Kay Allene. With Dept. Agr., 1934-39; chief vet. Wilson & Co., Inc., 1939-53; dir. profl. relations Am. Vet. Med. Assn., 1953-58, treas., 1952-58, exec. sec., 1958-66; exec. dir. Nat. Soc. Medical Research, 1966—; pres. Livestock Conservation, Inc., 1960-62; mem. livestock adv. com. Dept. Agr., 1955-62; mem. nat. food and drug council Food and Drug Adminstrn., 1964-67. Mem. Phi Delta Theta. Club: University (Chgo.). Home: 6171 Leesburg Pike Falls Church VA 22047 Office: 1330 Massachusetts Av Washington DC 20005

KINGSBURY, GILBERT WILLIAM, SR., broadcasting exec.; b. Covington, Ky., Apr. 27, 1909; s. William P. and Naoma (Runge) K.; A.B. in Econs., U. Ky., 1933; m. Sylvia Irene Phillips, Nov. 21, 1936; 1 son, Gilbert William. Reporter, asst. city editor Ky. Post, 1933-39; asst. dean U. Cin., 1939-41; adminstrv. asst. Senators G. Withers, Earle Clements, 1949-51; news editor Crosley Broadcasting Corp., 1941-45, Washington corr., 1945-49; dir., v.p., 1951—; v.p. Star-Fed. Bldg. & Loan; asst. v.p. U. Ky., Lexington; exec. v.p. Ohio Valley Improvement Assn. Cons. Ky. Turnpike Authority; dep. hwy. commnr. Ky. Past pres. Covington YMCA. Mem. Ky. Ho. Reps., 1958-60. Bd. dirs. Greater Cin. chpt. A.R.C., Dan Beard council Boy Scouts Am., Blue Ridge Assembly; adv. bd. St. Elizabeth Hosp., Covington, Ky.; bd. trustees, mem. exec. com. U. Ky. Recipient Award of Merit, Am. Pub. Relations Assn., 1953-55. Mem. Radio Corrs. Assn., Christopher Gist Hist. Soc. (past pres.), U.S. Savs. and Loan League, Ky. Council Chs. (exec. com.). Democrat. Mem. Ch. of Christ. Clubs: Nat. Press; Optimist, Ft. Mitchell Country. Home: 210 Edgewood Rd Fort Mitchell KY Office: 4017 Carew Tower Cincinnati OH

KINGSLEY, DANIEL T., govt. ofcl.; b. Portland, Ore., Oct. 1, 1932; s. George A. and Jane P. (Powers) K.; grad. Phillips Acad., Andover, Mass., 1950; A.B. in History cum laude, Princeton, 1954; m. Eleanor Bate, Jan. 26, 1955; children—Daniel T., Clay P., Blake M., Christopher W., Elizabeth L., Reed B. Asst. timber mgr. Kingsley Lumber Co., Portland, 1956-57, v.p., sales mgr., 1957-62, pres., gen. mgr., 1962-68; advancement Pres. Nixon, 1968-69; commr. property mgmt. and disposal service Gen. Services Adminstrn., Washington, 1969-71; spl. asst. to Pres., chief personnel office Exec. Office of Pres., Washington, 1971—. Trustee, St. Helen's Hall, Bishop Dagwell Hall, Portland, 1956-58, also mem. exec. com., chmn. pub. relations and devel. com.; trustee Parry Center for Emotionally Disturbed Children, Portland, 1956-68, also 1st v.p., chmn. investment mgmt. com., mem. budget com. Served with AUS, 1954-56. Republican. Episcopalian. Clubs: Multnomah Athletic (trustee 1967-68), Racquet (Portland); Bethesda (Md.) Country. Home: 8000 Herb Farm Dr Bethesda MD 20034 Office: The White House Washington DC 20500

KINGTON, OSWALD MCMINUS, banker; b. Mortons Gap, Ky., Dec. 23, 1891; s. William Ward and Emma Louisa (Lovan) K.; student So. Ky. Coll., 1907-10; m. Lila Jane Jones, Nov. 6, 1912; children—William H., Betty J. (Mrs. Floyd Robert Gilfoil), Oswald McMinus. Sec.-treas. Kinglon Coal Co., Mortons Gap, 1907-20. Judge Hopkins County, 1946. Mem. Woodmen of World. Baptist (chmn. deacons). Club: Madisonville Country. Home: Stone Lane Madisonville KY 42431 Office: 1 S Main St Madisonville KY 42431

KINNAIRD, JOHN MORROW, lawyer; b. Lancaster, Ky., Apr. 11, 1921; s. John Gill and Margaret (Morrow) K.; LL.B., U. Ky., 1948; m. Sarah Anne Denny, Aug. 9, 1942; children—Ann Margaret, Patsy McKee, Jula Jordan. Admitted to Ky. bar, 1948; pvt. practice firm Denny & Kinnaird, Nicholasville, Ky., 1948-55; asst. atty gen., Ky., 1948-49; gen. counsel Ky. State Police, 1949-50; asst. commr. Dept. Motor Transp., Ky., 1950-51, commr. motor transp., 1951-55; asst. to v.p. Consol. Freightways, Inc., Arlington, Va., 1956-58, v.p., 1958-61; admitted to D.C. bar, 1961; practiced law, D.C., 1961—; counsel Galland, Kharasch, Calkins &Lippman, Washington, 1961-65; partner firm Rea, Cross, Knebel & Kinnaird, Washington, 1965-67; exec. sec. Com. Transp. Practices of Nat. Motor Freight Traffic Assn., 1962-67; spl. counsel Am. Trucking Assn., Inc., 1967-69, asst. chief counsel pub. affairs, 1969—, v.p. govt. relations div., 1971—. Served as officer USAAF, World War II. Decorated D.F.C. with oak leaf cluster, Air Medal Mem. Am., Ky. bar assns., Motor Carrier Lawyers Assn., ICC Practitioners Assn., Am. Soc. Traffic and Transp., Phi Delta Phi, Sigma AlphaEpsilon. Presbyn. (elder). Mason. Clubs: Nat. Lawyers, Belle Haven Country. Home: 7108 Park Terrace Dr Alexandria VA 22307 Office: 1616 P St NW Washington DC 20036

KINNAN, ROBERT MACK, banker; b. Marshalltown, Ia., Aug. 18, 1907; s. Edward and Carrie (McConnell) Landt; B.A., U. Ia., 1930, postgrad., 1932-34; m. Betty Ann Carrier, Sept. 8, 1939; children—Mary Gretchen, Robert Mack. Coach, Muscatine, Ia., 1930-39; athletic dir. Washington U., St. Louis, 1939-43; partner in wholesale-retail bus., Austin, Tex., 1945-52; with Capital Nat. Bank, Austin, 1952—; sr. v.p. City Nat. Bank, Austin, 1970—. Chmn. A.R.C., 1946-47; chmn. bd. dirs. Goodwill Industries, Inc., 1968-69. Mem. City Planning Commn., Austin, 1969—. Served with USNR, 1943-45. Mem. Tex. Bankers Assn., Kappa Sigma. Episcopalian (vestryman). Clubs: Admirals, Headliners, Tarry House, Austin (Austin). Home: 2602 Hillview Rd Austin TX 78703 Office: 9th and Congress Austin TX 78701

KINNAN, ROY FRANK, sales exec.; b. Tulsa, Nov. 9, 1915; s. Ralph P. and Dessie J. (Wilson) K.; student U. Tex., 1935-37; m. Mary Emma Paternostro, Mar. 8, 1938; children—Ann Carol (Mrs. John R. Helton), Pamela Kay. Engr., salesman Oil Well Supply Co., Dallas, 1938-41; sales engr. Gates Rubber Co,, Tulsa, 1941-55, sales mgr., Okla. and Ark., 1956-61, southwest sales mgr., Dallas, 1962—. Named Outstanding Nat. Dist. Mgr., 1966. Mem. Dallas C. of C. Methodist. Mason (32 deg.), Toastmaster (award 1963). Royal Oaks Country. Home: 4718 Forest Bend Rd Dallas TX 75234 Office: 1030 Dragon St Dallas TX 75207

KINNEBREW, JACKSON ALLENDER, pub. accountant; b. Pauls Valley, Okla., Aug. 14, 1915; s. Jackson Alvin and Dorella (Allender) K.; A.B., U. Okla., 1935; m. Mary Lucille Metcalfe, Feb. 27, 1940; children—Jackson Metcalfe, James Alvin, Mary Louise. Vice pres. Kinnebrew Motor Co., Oklahoma City, 1935-41, Denison Motor Co., 1946-51; farmer, Pauls Valley, 1951-64; pub. accountant Jack Kinnebrew, 1961—. Served with AUS, 1941-46. Mem. Am. Inst. C.P.A.'s, Okla. Soc. C.P.A.'s, C. of C. (dir., treas. 1963—), Phi Beta Kappa, Beta Theta Pi. Presbyn. Mason (32 deg., Shriner), Elk. Home: 200 Rennie Rd Pauls Valley OK 73075 Office: 1st Nat Bank Bldg Pauls Valley OK 73075

KINNEY, ABBOTT FORD, radio broadcasting exec.; b. Los Angeles, Nov. 11, 1909; s. Gilbert Earl and Mabel (Ford) K.; student Ark. Coll., 1923, 26, 27; m. Dorothy Lucille Jeffers, Sept. 19, 1943; children— Colleen, Joyce, Rosemary. Editor Dermott News, 1934-39; partner Delta Drug Co., 1940-49; pres., gen. mgr. S.E. Ark. Broadcasters, Inc., Dermott and McGhee, 1951—; corr. Comml. Appeal, Memphis, Ark. Gazette, Little Rock, 1935-53; research early aeronautics Inst. Aero. Scis., 1941, castor bean prodn., 1941-42; mem. bd. McGhee-Dermott Indsl. Devel. Corp. Mem. Ark. Geol. and Conservation Commn., 1959-63, Ark. State Planning Commn. 1963—; mem. Miss. River Parkway Commn.; exec. bd. DeSoto Area Council Boy Scouts Am.; past pres. Hosp. Adv. Bd.; mem. Chicot Fair Assn. Bd., Park Commn.; chmn. Chicot County Library Bd. Recipient Silver Beaver award Boy Scouts Am. Mem. Nat. Assn. Radio and TV Broadcasters, Ark. Broadcasters Assn. Ark. (charter mem. Ark. Econ. Council), S.E. Ark. (charter) chambers of commerce, Ark. Hist. Assn. (charter), Am. Numismatic Assn., A.I.M., Chicot County Hist. Soc. (charter). Rotarian (past pres., sec.). Adv. editorial bd. Internat. Broadcasters Soc. Home: Dermott AR 61738 Office: Dermott AR 61738 also McGhee AR 71654

KINNEY, ANNIE LAURIE MAYER (MRS. WILLIAM LIGHT KINNEY), publishing co. exec.; b. Newberry, S.C., Aug. 15, 1902; d. Jacob Luther and Sue Ida (Bouknight) Mayer; grad. Lander Coll., Greenwood, S.C., 1923; m. William Light Kinney, June 18, 1931; 1son, William Light. Bus. mgr. Marlboro County Herald, Bennettsville, S.C., 1931-51, Marlboro Herald-Advocate (merger Marlboro County Herald and Pee Dee Advocate 1951), 1951—; bus. mgr. McColl (S.C.) Messenger, 1952—; v.p., co-owner, sec. Marlboro Pub. Co., Inc., Bennettsville. Tchr. schs. N.C., S.C., 1923-31; owner, mgr. Marlboro Stationery and Gift Shop, Bennettsville, 1935—; columnist local paper, 1931—. Bd. dirs. Marlboro County Tb Assn., A.R.C. Named S.C. Newspaperwoman of Year S.C. Press Assn., 1958, Theta Sigma Phi, 1963; Alumna of Year Lander Coll., 1959. Mem. S.C. Press Assn. (pres, woman's div. 1949-50, 63-64), Bennettsville Garden Club Council (past pres.), Meth. Missionary Soc. (past pres.), D.A.R., Marlborough Hist. Soc. Methodist (Sunday sch. tchr.). Clubs: Read-A-Book Literary (Bennettsville) (past pres.); Pilot (charter pres.). Home: 508 E Main St Bennettsville SC 29512 Office: 201 McCall St Bennettsville SC 29512

KINNEY, BURTON CHESTER, motor carrier exec.; b. Worcester, Mass., Sept. 15, 1917; s. Alfred R. and Edith (Creamer) K.; student Biltmore Jr. Coll., 1937; LaSalle Extension U., 1944; m. Mary Elizabeth Jennings, Sept. 3, 1948; children—Caroline (Mrs. William Michael McConochie), Betty (Mrs. George Bruce Brogdon), Anita Jeanne (Mrs. Dan Thornton). With Ga. Hwy. Express, Inc., Atlanta, 1943-58, successively rate clk., chief rate clk., overcharge claim agt., asst. traffic mgr., 1948-53, gen. traffic mgr., 1953-58; gen. traffic mgr. Terminal Transport Co., Inc., Atlanta, 1958, v.p. traffic, 1958—. Mem. Central and So. Motor Freight Tariff Assn. (dir. 1965-71), Transp. Club Atlanta (pres. 1955), Nat. Classification Com., I.C.C. Practitioners Assn. (chpt. chmn. 1956), Traffic Clubs Internat. (dir. 1957-66, regional v.p. 1966-70), Am. Soc. Traffic and Transp. (certified), Fla. Trucking Assn., So. Shipper and Motor Carrier Council (pres. 1969-70), Nat. Assn. Shipper-Motor Carrier Confs. (treas. 1971), Delta Nu Alpha (chpt. pres. 1955, regional nat. v.p. 1957-61). Club: Lakeshore Country (Jonesboro, Ga.). Home: 406 Homestead Rd Rex GA 30273 Office: 248 Chester Av SE Atlanta GA 30316

KINNEY, ROBERT LEROY, real estate exec.; b. Everett, Wash., Apr. 21, 1938; s. Audrey Ralph and Vera (Davis) K.; student Purdue U., 1956-57; B.B.A. with honors, U. Hawaii, 1960; m. Carol Elizabeth Webster, Aug. 5, 1961; children—Daniel Bryan, Andre Renard. Asst. to pres. Mt. Vernon Sand & Gravel Co. (Wash.), 1960-61; asst. to v.p. commr. and indsl. real estate div. Del E. Webb Corp., Phoenix, 1962-64; v.p. Lomas & Nettleton Financial Corp., Dallas, 1965-69; pres. subsidiary cos. Lomas & Nettleton Properties, Inc., 9900 Meml. Inc., Imperial Interiors, Inc., Dallas, 1967-68, pres, subsidiary Vistamar, Inc., San Juan, P.R., 1968; pres., dir., chief exec. Caribbean Equities Corp., St. Croix, V.I., 1969—. Mem. Photog. Soc. Am., Am. Mus. Natural History, Nat. Audubon Soc., U. Hawaii Found., Phi Kappa Phi. Home: Estate La Grande Princess Christiansted St Croix VI 00820 Office: PO Box 871 Christiansted St Croix VI 00820

KINNEY, WILLIAM ALOYSIUS, mag. editor; b. Newark, Mar. 25, 1907; s. John Francis and Frances (Young) K.; A.B. magna cum laude, Holy Cross Coll., 1928; m. Roseanna McQuesten, Dec. 18, 1943. News corr. United Press Assn., N.Y.C. Bur., 1929-30; staff reporter Newark Star Eagle, 1930-31; asst. night news editor Newark Bur. Asso. Press, 1931-32, night news editor, 1932-33, day news editor, 1933-34, state news editor, 1934-37, spl. assignment N.Y.C. Bur., 1937-40, asst, news editor (night), Washington, 1940-41, night news editor, 1941-42, 46; mem. bd. internat. editors World Report, 1946-47; dir. news service Nat. Geographic Soc., 1948-51, editorial staff Nat. Geographic Mag., 1951-54; self-employed as lit., research, pub. relations cons., 1954-57; publs. cons. Office of Sec. of USAF, 1957, editorial cons. and publ. specialist, 1957-58, contbg. editor, 1958, space sciences editor, The Airman Mag., Washington, 1958—. Served with M.I., USAAF, 1942-46. Fellow Brit. Interplanetary Soc.; mem. Am. Inst. Aeros. and Astronautics, Am. Geophys. Union, A.A.A.S., Md. Hist. Soc., Nat. Geographic Soc. Roman Catholic. Club: Cosmos (Washington). Author: Medical Science and Space Travel, 1959; also short stories in mags. Co-editor, contbr.; Dateline: Washington, 1949; contbr. to Rocket and Missile Technology, 1964. Home: 1818 35th St NW Washington DC 20007 Office: Bolling AFB Washington DC 20332

KINNON, BOBBY RAY, banker; b. Kountze, Tex., Aug. 29, 1939; s. Ray and Dorothy Lee (Thompson) K.; prestandard certificate, Am. Inst. Banking, 1968; m. Kathryn Jeannette Broussard, Aug. 1, 1968; children— Dena, Donna, Deanna, Danita, Dana. Carpenter, Kountze, Tex., 1958-60; then engaged in communications Tex. Dept. Pub. Safety, Beaumont; with Peoples State Bank, Kountze, Tex., 1960-64; with Citizens State Bank, Woodville, Tex., 1965—, cashier, security officer, 1969—. Active various coms. Western Weekend and Dogwood Festival, Woodville, 1966—; scoutmaster Boy Scouts Am., Woodville, 1967—; recipient Scouters award, 1970. Named Boss of Year Tyler County Am. Bus. Women Assn., 1970. Mem. Tyler County C. of C. Democrat. Methodist. Kiwanian (pres. 1968). Home: Livingston Hwy Woodville TX 75979 Office: 102 W Bluff Woodville TX 75979

KINSEY, ROY EDWARD, lawyer; b. Armington, Ill., Sept. 26, 1917; s. Roy Walter and Mabel (Medbery) K.; student St. Petersburg Jr. Coll., 1935-37; B.S., John B. Stetson U., 1939, LL.B., 1941; m. Margaret Elizabeth Cate, July 18, 1942; 1 son, Roy Edward. Admitted to Fla. bar, 1941; practiced in Daytona Beach, Fla., 1946—; mem. firm Kinsey, Vincent & Pyle, 1946—; asst. city atty. Daytona Beach, 1953-54. Served with USNR, 1942-46, to lt. comdr., 1950-52. Mem. Fla. Bar (bd. govs. 1950-51, 53-63), Volusia County Bar Assn. (pres. 1963), C. of C. (bd. govs. 1964-66), Sigma Nu (treas. 1939-41), Phi Alpha Delta. Presbyn. Clubs: Kiwanis (pres. 1958), Halifas River Yacht (dir. 1960-64, sec. 1971), Ocean Dunes (pres. 1958); Oceanside Country. Home: 2900 N Halifax Av Daytona Beach FL 32018 Office: 42 S Peninsula Dr Daytona Beach FL 32018

KINTZLEY, RUSS, newspaper editor; married, 2 children. Asso. editor editorials The Times-Picayune, New Orleans. Mem. Am. Soc. Newspaper Editors, Phi Gamma Delta. Club: Plimsoll. Home: 1239 Eleonore St New Orleans LA 70115 Office: 3800 Howard Av New Orleans LA 70140

KINZBACH, ROBERT BENTON, mech. engring. cons.; b. Houston, Mar. 8, 1908; s. Frank and Anna (McGuire) K.; student U. Tex,, 1926-31; m. Mary Chandler Lyman, Aug. 25, 1931; children—Mary Ellen (Mrs. Richard O. Wilson), Harriett Ann (Mrs. J. DeWitt Morrow, Jr.). Vice pres. Kinzbach Tool Co., Inc., 1931-60; pres. Kinzbach Engring. Co., Houston, 1961 69. gen. mgr., 1967-70; engring. cons., Houston, 1970—. Mem. Am. Soc. M.E. (sect. chmn.), Am. Soc. Tool and Mfg. Engrs., Am. Soc. Metals, Am. Ordnance Assn., Am, Petroleum Inst., Nomads, Houston Engring. and Sci. Soc. (past pres.), Sigma Phi Epsilon, Tau Beta Pi. Presbyn. (elder). Mason, Kiwanian. Patentee in field. Home: 6203 Valley Forge Dr Houston TX 77027 Office: PO Box 36289 Houston TX 77036

KINZEY, BERTRAM YORK, JR., educator; b. Holden, Mass., Sept. 25, 1921; s. Bertram York and Gertrude Frances (Sampson) K.; B.S., Va. Polytech. Inst., 1942, M.S in Archtl. Engring., 1943; m. Ellen Virginia Smith, Nov. 24, 1944; children—Bertram York III, Douglas Webster. Asst. naval architect Norfolk Navy Yard, Portsmouth, Va., 1943-45; archtl. draftsman, jr. structural engr. Baskervill & Son, Richmond, Va., 1945-48; mem. faculty dept. architecture Va. Poly. Inst., Blacksburg, 1948-59, asst. prof., 1948-52, asso. prof., 1952-59; asso. prof. U. Fla., Gainesville, 1959-65, prof., 1965—. Part-time practice architecture, 1948—; cons. in archtl. acoustics. Mem. com. on architecture and acoustics Am. Guild Organists, 1953-60; mem. commn. on architecture Nat. Council Chs., 1953-60. Research Corp. grantee, 1949. Mem. A.I.A. (corporate mem., sec. Fla. North chpt. 1969-71, dir. 1971—), Acoustical Soc. Am., Sigma Xi, Phi Kappa Phi, Tau Sigma Delta. Methodist (adminstrv. bd.). Author: (with H. M. Sharp) Environmental Technologies in Architecture, 1963, also articles. Mailing Address: U Fla Dept Architecture Gainesville FL 32601 Home: 212 S W 42d St Gainesville FL 32601 Office: U Fla Dept Architecture Gainesville FL 32601

KIPLINGER, AUSTIN HUNTINGTON, editor, pub.; b. Washington, Sept. 19, 1918; s. Willard Monroe and Irene (Austin) K.; A.B., Cornell U., 1939; postgrad. Harvard, 1939-40; m. Mary Louise Cobb, Dec. 11, 1944; children—Todd Lawrence, Knight Austin. Reporter Kiplinger Washington Letter, 1939, San Francisco Chronicle, 1940-41; exec. editor Kiplinger mag., Changing Times, 1945-48; columnist Chgo. Jour. of Commerce, 1949-50; news commentator ABC, Chgo., 1951-55, NBC, Chgo., 1955-56; exec. v.p. the Kiplinger Washington Editors, 1956-59, pres., 1959—; editor Kiplinger Washington Letter, 1961—; pub. Changing Times Mag., 1959—. Pres. Juvenile Protective Assn. Chgo., 1955-56; chmn. mayor's adv. com. on youth welfare Chgo., 1956; vice chmn. Nat. Capital Health and Welfare Council, 1960-67; chmn. Montgomery County Community Action Com., 1967-69. Trustee Cornell U., 1960—, Landon Sch., 1960-63, Fed. City Council, Greater Washington Ednl. TV Assn., Nat. Pub. Affairs Center for TV, Washington Journalism Center. Served as naval aviator aboard carriers PTO, 1942-45. Mem. Assn. Radio and TV News Analysts, Phi Beta Kappa, Delta Upsilon, Sigma Delta Chi. Unitarian. Clubs: Metropolitan, Nat. Press, Overseas Writers(Washington); Commonwealth (Chgo.); Cornell (N.Y.); Potomac Hunt; Chevy Chase. Author: (with W. M. Kiplinger) Boom and Inflation Ahead, 1958. Home: Montevideo Poolesville MD 20837 Office: 1729 H St Washington DC 20006

KIPP, DEAN CARL, educator, physician; b. Manhattan, Kan., Apr. 27, 1918; s. Carl Louis and Ethel (McKean) K.; student St. Benedict's Coll., 1935-37; B.S., Kan. State U., 1939; M.D., Kan. U., 1943; m. Mary Elizabeth Davis, May 28, 1943; children—Karen Dean (Mrs. Donald R. McCann, Jr.), Jan Kendree (Mrs. Larry McElwain); Crane Davis. Intern Ohio State U. Hosp., 1943-44, resident surgery, 1947-49; resident pathology Barnes Hosp., St. Louis, 1946-47; clin. asso. prof. surgery Southwestern br. U. Tex. Med. Sch., Dallas, 1962—; chief dept. plastic surgery Baylor U. Med. Center, 1965—. Served with M.C., USNR, World War II; PTO. Diplomate Am. Bd. Plastic Surgery. Fellow A.C.S.; mem. Am., Tex., Dallas med. assns., Am. Soc. Plastic Surgeons, Internat. Fedn. Plastic Surgeons, Tex. Surg. Soc., Tex. Soc. Plastic Surgeons. Home: 3717 Villanova St Dallas TX 95225

KIRBO, CHARLES, Democratic nat. committeeman. Chmn. Ga. Dem. com.; mem. Dem. nat. com. Address: 2401 Bank of Ga Bldg Atlanta GA 30303*

KIRBY, BRIAN GABRIEL, hotel exec.; b. Budapest, Hungary, Aug. 1, 1936 (came to U.S. 1962); s. Ronald G. and Agnes Caroline (Balog) K.; grad. liberal arts Kent Coll., Canterbury, Eng., 1954; degree with honors hotel mgmt. Ecole Hoteliere, Lausanne, Switzerland, 1956-59; m. Virginia Joyce Nixon, Feb. 10, 1962; children—Brian Alan, Patria Christine, Andrea Agnes. Food and beverage mgr. Pontchartrain Hotel, New Orleans, 1962-64; resident mgr. Gran Hotel Bolivar, Lima, Peru, 1964-66; gen. mgr. Pick Nationwide Inn, Columbus, O., 1966-68; asst. gen. mgr. Pick Congress Hotel, Chgo., 1969, v.p., gen. mgr. Exec. House, Washington, 1969—. Mem. Washington Conv. Bur., 1969—, Washington Bd. of Trade, 1969—. Served with Brit. Army, 1954-56. Recipient English Lit. award Kent Coll., 1954; Prix des anciennes eleves Swiss Hotel Mgmt. Sch., 1959; decorated Officer Confrerie de la Chaine des Rotisseurs. Mem. Confrerie de la Chaine des Rotisseurs (vice archiviste Washington chpt. 1969—, bailli Washington chpt. 1972—), Washington Hotel Assn. (dir. 1970—), Hotel Sales Mgmt. Assn., Mem. Ch. of Eng. Lion, Optimist. Club: Skal. Home: 1515 Rhode Island Av NW Washington DC 20005 Office: Executive House Washington DC 20005

KIRBY, GEORGE FRANCIS, mfg. co. exec.; b. Cheneyville, La., Dec. 7, 1916; s. George Francis and Vesta (Mason) K.; B.A., La. Coll., Pineville, 1936; M.S., La. State U., 1938, Ph.D., 1940; m. Nannette Dutsch, Dec. 12, 1941; children—Michael Edward, John Mason. With Ethyl Corp., 1940-69, v.p. research and devel., 1955-62, exec. v.p., 1963-64, pres., 1964-69, also dir.; dir. Tex. Eastern Transmission Corp., 1969—, exec. v.p., 1970-71, pres., 1971—; dir. La. Nat. Bank, Baton Rouge. Bd. dirs. La. State U. Found., Am. Petroleum Inst., Am. Gas Assn.; trustee Gulf Research Inst. Mem. Am. Chem. Soc., Am. Inst. Chem. Engrs., A.A.A.S. Home: 2016 Main St Houston TX 77002 Office: 921 Main St at McKinney St Houston TX 77001 also 320 Park Av New York City NY 10017

KIRBY, HENRY VANCE, physician; b. Harrison, Ark., Apr. 3, 1908; s. Leander Bender and Virgie May (Vance) K.; B.S., U. Ark., 1931; M.D., Washington U., St. Louis, 1933; m. Elva C. Hudson, June 21, 1936; children—Henry Hudson, Carol Anne (Mrs. Ross Lander Fordyce), Helen Vance (Mrs. W. Peyton Daniel, Jr.). Rotating intern DePaul Hosp., St. Louis, 1933-34; gen. practice medicine, Harrison, Ark., 1934—; mem. staff Boone County Hosp., Harrison, 1st chief of staff, 1950; dir. Hudson Packing Co., Harrison, 1946-49. Local examiner Selective Service System, 1940-42; mem. Boone County adv. com. to N.W. Ark. Econ. Devel. Dist., 1969—; active Boy Scouts Am. Mem. bd. Harrison Sch. Dist., 1947-58, pres., 1952-53; 56-58; coroner, Boone County, Ark., 1963—. Served to capt. M.C., AUS, 1942-45. Decorated Bronze Star medal. Mem. Am. Legion, A.M.A., Ark. Acad. Gen. Practice (state dir. 1957-58), Ark. (pres. Ninth Councilor Dist Med. Soc. 1971-72), Boone County (pres. 1940-41) med. socs., N.W. Ark. Wildlife Assn. (dir. 1972—), Lambda Chi Alpha, Phi Beta Pi. Democrat. Presbyn. (elder 1959-62, 71-72). Rotarian. Clubs: Bridge, Supper (Harrison). Home: 1001 W Nicholson St Harrison AR 72601 Office: Boone County Med Center 651 N Spring St Harrison AR 72601

KIRBY, LAVERNE HOWE, architect, engr.; b. Sherman, Tex., Aug. 19, 1912; s. Robert E. and Mabel (Howe) K.; B.S., Tex. Tech, Coll., 1945; m. Lellessee Marcella Hays, Nov. 25, 1936; children—Laverne, Nancy. Partner, Haynes, Strange & Kirby, 1946-47, Haynes & Kirby, 1947-65; gen. practice Laverne H. Kirby, architect and engr., 1965—. Mem. A.I.A., Nat. Soc. Profl. Engrs., Am. Soc. Heating, Refrigeration and Airconditioning Engrs. Presbyn. Clubs: Lions, Lubbock. Home: 2301 29th St Lubbock TX 79401 Office: 1902 Dixie Dr Lubbock TX 79401

KIRCHER, WILLIAM L., labor union exec.; b. Athens, O., Mar. 2, 1915; s. Charles P. and Josephine (McCoy) K.; A.B. in Journalism, Ohio U., 1936; m. Hilda B. Espel, Jan. 20, 1940; children—Thomas J., Mary Jo (Mrs. D. J. Huck). Internat. rep. UAW-CIO, 1942-51, dir. wage stblzn. office, Washington, 1951-53, asst. to v.p., Detroit, 1952-55; asst. dir. orgn. AFL-CIO, 1955-56, asst. regional dir., Ohio and W.Va., 1956-64, asst. nat. orgn. dir., 1964-65, dir., 1965—. Home: 3444 Chiswick Ct Silver Spring MD Office: 815 16th St NW Washington DC

KIRCHHEIMER, WALDEMAR F(RANZ), physician, microbiologist; b. Schneidemuhl, Germany, Jan. 11, 1913; M.D., U. Giessen (Germany), 1947; Ph.D., U. Wash., 1949; m. 1945. Research physician King County Tb Hosp., Seattle, 1942-46; Tb research asso. U. Wash., 1946-47, instr. microbiology, 1948-49; asst. prof. bacteriology Northwestern U. Med. Sch., 1949-53, asso. prof., 1953-56; dep. safety dir., med. bacteriologist, Ft. Detrick, Md., 1956-61; mem. research staff U.S. Inst. Allergy and Infectious Diseases, 1961-62; chief microbiology sect. USPHS Hosp., Carville, La., 1962-64, chief lab. br., 1965—. Sr. surgeon USPHS. Mem. Am. Soc. Microbiology. Research leprosy treatment, immunology. Address: USPHS Hosp Carville LA 70721

KIRCHNER, KING POUDER, oil field drilling co. exec.; b. Kansas City, Mo., Nov. 18, 1927; s. Kenneth Kenton and Thelma (Pouder) K.; B.S., Okla. State U., 1950; B.S. in Petroleum Engring., Okla. U., 1954;; m. Diane Estes, Mar. 18, 1955; children—Kenton, Kyle. Engr., Lufkin Foundry Co., (Tex.), 1950-51; engr., v.p. Unit Drilling Co., Bristow, Okla., 1954-63, pres., 1963—; v.p. Shoreline Oil &Gas Co., Tulsa, 1956—. Served with AUS, 1952-54. Mem. Independent Petroleum Assn. Am. (dir. 1956-70), Young Pres. Orgn., Okla. Independent Petroleum Assn., Petroleum Club of Tulsa (dir., chmn. finance com. 1970-72). Home: 3423 E 56th Pl Tulsa OK 74135 Office: Petroleum Club Bldg Tulsa OK 74119

KIREILIS, RAY WALTER, educator; b. Kenosha, Wis., Mar. 27, 1917; s. Peter and Antoinette (Kasile) K.; B.S., U. Ill., 1941, M.S., 1944; E.Ed., Ind. U., 1950; m. Catherine Camilla, Sept. 9, 1939; children— Ramon, Terry, Robin, Kelly. Instr. physiology dept. U. Ill., 1945-46; instr. phys. edn., swimming coach U. Ore., Eugene, 1946-48; prof. health, phys. edn. and recreation for men. Tex. Technol. Coll., Lubbock, 1950—. Vice pres. South Plains Heart Assn., Lubbock, 1955-56; bd. dirs. pres. Lubbock County Tb Assn., 1952-54; com. chmn. Lubbock County unit A.R.C., 1953-54; W. front dir. Cheppewa Trail Camp, Rapid City, Mich., 1940. Served with AUS, 1945-46. Fellow Am. Coll. Sports Medicine, A.A.H.P.E.R.; mem. Am. Assn. U. Profs., Am. Camping Assn., N.E.A., Tex. Assn. Health Phys. Edn. and Recreation (div. v.p. 1956-57), W. Tex. Pool Operators Assn. (pres. 1955. Amateur Athletic Union (chmn. phys. fitness com. 1959-60). Author: (with T. K. Cureton) Endurance of Young Men, 1945. Home: 4706 28th St Lubbock TX 79410

KIRILL, PETER, metals co. exec.; b. Manhattan, N.Y.C., June 29, 1912; s. Kirill Victor and Tatiana (Prudnick) Bobrowsky; B.C.S., N.Y.U., 1935; m. Beverly Langhorne, June 2, 1944; children— Peter, Langhorne, William D. Dist. sales mgr. Liberty Mut. Ins. Co., N.Y.C., 1946-48; regional mgr. Stewart Warner Corp., Chgo., 1948-57; pres. Alemite Co. Fla., Inc., Jacksonville, 1957—; dir. Fla. Dealer and Growers Bank, Jacksonville. Bd. dirs. Boys Home, YMCA. Served with USNR, 1942-45. Decorated Silver Star medal; recipient citation sec. Navy, 1962-70. Mem. Navy League (nat. v.p.), Gator Bowl Assn. (v.p. 1969—), Jacksonville C. of C. (gov. 1969-70), Phi Gamma Delta. Rotarian. Clubs: University, River, Timuquana, Fla. Yacht, Reveliers (Jacksonville). Home: 2532 Holly Point Rd Orange Park FL Office: 5281 Edgewood Ct Jacksonville FL 32205

KIRILLA, GEORGE MAJER, mgmt. cons.; b. Carthage, Mo., June 14, 1910; s. George and Julianna deCaudroi (Majer) K.; student Rochester U., 1930-31, Northwestern U., 1943-45; B.S., Pacific States U., 1947, LL.D., 1968; postgrad. Harvard, 1957, U. San Francisco, 1962; m. Charmaline Opal Kaufmann, June 23, 1940; children—Charmla Georgine (Mrs. Hermann Novak, Jr.), Dollyna Dee (Mrs. McNair Worrell Perry). Exec., Douglas Aircraft Co., Santa Monica, Cal. and Park Ridge, Ill., 1937-45, Moore Corp., 1945-46, Climax Industries, 1946-47, Cannon Electric Devel. Co., 1948-50; asso., dir. bus. planning pub. relations Booz, Allen & Hamilton, internat. mgmt. consultants, 1950-52; internat. mgmt. cons., adviser U.S. Navy Dept., 1952-54, U.S. Small Bus. Adminstrn., 1954-56, 58-65, U.S. Dept. State/Govt. of Republic of China and Taiwan Provincial Govt., 1956-58, U.S. Dept. Def., 1965—. Cons., adviser U.S. Legislators and House Select Com. on Small Bus., 1966—, U.S. Small Bus. Adminstrn. Council for Small Bus., 1971—; chmn. United Cursade, 1960, 61; adviser World Bus. and Internat. Trade Techniques, U. San Francisco, 1962; co-adminstr. Julianna Kirilla Estate, 1968. Trustee Frank Kirilla Trust. Recipient Presdl. Distinguished Civilian Service medal, 1942; also other citations and awards of merit. Mem. World Affairs Council, Am. Assn. for UN, Dept. Def. Small Bus. and Econ. Utilzn. Council, Nat. Rifle Assn., Psi Sigma Iota (life). Clubs: Peninsula Golf and Country; Grand Hotel Recreation. Author: Incentive System, 1944; Small Business--Its Importance to the American Way of Life, 1969. Address: 2401 Calvert St NW Washington DC 20008

KIRK, CLAUDE R., JR., former gov. Fla.; b. San Bernardino, Cal., Jan. 7, 1926; s. Claude R. and Sarah (McLure) K.; student Emory U., B.S., Duke, 1945; law degree U. Ala., 1949; m. Sarah Stokes; children—Sarah Stokes, Katherine Gilmer, Franklin, William; m. 2d, Erika Mattfeld, Feb. 18, 1967; 1 dau., Claudia Mattfeld. Ins. and bldg. supplies salesman, Birmingham, Ala., 1949; partner Am. Heritage Life Ins. Co., Jacksonville, Fla., 1954, Hayden, Stone, Inc., investment bankers, 1960; founder Kirk Investment Co., Jacksonville, 1964; gov. State of Fla., 1967-70. Candidate for U.S. senator from Fla., 1964. Served with USMCR, 1943-46, 50-52. Decorated Air medal. Episcopalian (lay reader). Office: Kirk Investment Co Jacksonville FL

KIRK, JAMES CURTIS, oil co. exec.; b. Hubbard, Tex., May 10, 1921; s. James Floyd and Edna Pearl (Windham) K.; B.S., Baylor U., 1944; Ph.D., Ohio State U., 1949; m. Esta Mae Thomas, Aug. 11, 1944; children—James Lee, Carol Lyn, Steven Thomas, Gilbert Paul. Analytical chemist Pan Am. Refining Corp., Texas City, Tex., 1944-46; with Continental Oil Co., Ponca City, Okla., 1949-57, 60—, research chemist, supervising research chemist, 1949-57, gen. mgr. research and devel., 1967—; mgr. research Petroleum Chems., Inc., Lake Charles, La., 1957-60. Vice chmn. Okla. Air Pollution Adv. Council, 1967-71; mem. Sch. Bd. for Kay County Vo-Tech. Sch., 1971—. Mem. Am. Chem. Soc. (past sect. chmn.), Soap and Detergent Assn. (past com. chmn.). Republican. Mem. Christian Ch. Kiwanian. Address: Drawer 1267 Ponca City OK 74601

KIRK, VIRGINIA, clin. psychologist; b. Kirksville, Mo., Dec. 22, 1895; d. Sherman and Harriet Rose (White) Kirk; A.B., Drake U., 1917; B. Nursing, Yale, 1927, M.S., 1930; Ph.D., U. Chgo., 1949. Research asst. Yale Psycho-Clinic, 1930-31; dir. nursing Emma Pendleton Bradley Home, Riverside, R.I., 1931-35; research asso. Williamson County Child Guidance Study, Franklin, Tenn., 1935-42; instr. clin. psychology sch. medicine Vanderbilt U., 1943-47, asst. prof., 1947-53, asso. prof., 1953-60, asso. clin. prof., 1960-61, emerita, 1961—; pvt. practice cons. clin. psychologist, 1961—; cons. clin psychologist Family and Children's Service, 1953—; lectr. U. Tenn. Sch. Social Work, 1951-60. Recipient Distinguished Service award Drake U., Drake U. Nat. Alumni Assn., 1965. Fellow Am. Psychol. Assn., Inc.; mem. A.A.A.S., Tenn. Acad. Sci., Southeastern, Midwestern, Tenn. psychol. assns., Am. Assn. Mental Deficiency, Am. Speech and Hearing Assn., Orton Soc. Author articles in field. Home: 666 Timber Lane Regency Park Nashville TN 37215 Office: Med Arts Bldg Nashville TN 37212

KIRK, WELDON, judge; b. Gorman, Tex., June 12, 1925; s. Robert Lee and Ninnie (David) K.; LL.B., U. Tex., 1950; m. Mary Kelley, Aug. 17, 1947. Admitted to Tex. bar, 1949; pvt. practice law, Sweetwater, Tex., 1950-54; Nolan County (Tex.) atty., 1955-61; dist. atty. 32d Jud. Dist., Tex., 1961-70; dist. judge 32d Jud. Dist., Tex., 1971—. Served as 2d lt. USAAF, 1943-46. Named Sweetwater's Outstanding Young Man, 1952. Mem. Nolan County Bar Assn., State Bar Tex. Methodist (steward). Home: 1207 E 14th St Sweetwater TX 79556 Office: Nolan County Ct House Sweetwater TX 79556

KIRK, WILBER WOLFE, marine corrosion lab. exec.; b. Brownsville, Pa., Sept. 21, 1932; s. Wilber Kenneth and Alice (Wolfe) K.; B.S., Otterbein Coll., 1954; M.S. (U.S. Navy Ednl. fellow 1957-59), Ohio State U., 1959; m. Dolores Ruth Tomer, Nov. 13, 1954; children—Kenneth Andrew, Karen Sue, Kelly Lynn, Kevin Thomas. Engr., Bettis Atomic Power Lab., Pitts., 1958-62; engr., Internat. Nickel Co., Inc., Wrightsville Beach, N.C., 1962-67, supr., 1967-68, mgr. Francis L. Laque Corrosion Lab., 1968—. Mem. marine tech. adv. com. Cape Fear Tech. Inst., 1970-72. Served with AUS, 1954-56. Mem. Am. Soc. Metals (chpt. chmn. 1971-72), Nat. Assn. Corrosion Engrs., Am. Soc. Testing and Materials, C. of C. (mem. marine resources com. 1968-71), Sigma Xi. Methodist (trustee 1971-72). Rotarian. Clubs: Port Propeller (edn. chmn. 1971), Cape Fear Country, Executives (Wilmington, N.C.). Home: 5105 Clear Run Dr Wilmington NC 28401 Office: P O Box 656 Wrightsville Beach NC 28480

KIRK, WILLIAM SMITH, dentist; b. Salisbury, N.C., Apr. 22, 1928; s. Frank Walter and Suzanne Sovereign (Smith) K.; student U. N.C., 1944-45, postgrad. 1957-58; D.D.S., Northwestern U., 1949; m. Lois Jean Smith, Feb. 5, 1951; children—William Smith, Margaret Suzanne, Timothy Davis. Individual practice dentistry, Salisbury, 1952-57; practice orthodontics, Salisbury, 1958—. Bd. dirs. North Hills Christian Sch. Served with USAF, 1949-52; ETO. Mem. Am. Dental Assn., Am. Assn. Orthodontists, So. Soc. Orthodontists, N.C. Orthodontic Soc., N.C. Dental Soc., Flying Dentists Assn., World Radio Missionary Fellowship, Inc. (spl. rep. 1964), Second Dist. Dental Soc. N.C. (pres. 1969). Presbyn. (elder 1954). Rotarian. Home: 10 Mulberry Circle Salisbury NC 28144 Office: 1819 Brenner St Salisbury NC 28144

KIRKBY, ARTHUR M(ARTIN), librarian; b. Didsbury, Alta., Can., Sept. 22, 1911; s. Edgar Martin and Anna (Blow) K.; A.B., U. B.C., 1944; B.S., Columbia, 1946; m. Carolyn Elizabeth Pullman, July 24, 1950; children—Arthur Martin, Kevin Reid. Came to U.S., 1945, naturalized, 1952. Asst. Calgary Pub. Library, Alta., 1932-40; adminstrv. asst., dir. central adult services Enoch Pratt Fee Library, Balt., 1946-49, adminstrv. asst., asst. dir., 1949-52; librarian Norfolk (Va.) Pub. Library, 1952—. Mem. Va. Gov.'s Adv. Council on Libraries. Mem. Am. (council 1957-60), Southeastern, Va. (pres. 1967) library assns., Norfolk Hist. Soc. (bd.). Clubs: Rotary, Torch (pres. 1959-60) (Norfolk). Home: 1519 Morris Av Norfolk VA 23517 Office: 301 City Hall Av Norfolk VA 23510

KIRKENDOLL, CHESTER ARTHUR, JR., coll. pres.; b. Searcy, Ark., June 3, 1914; s. Chester Arthur and Mattie (Wyatt) K.; A.B., Lane Coll., 1938; A.M., Northwestern U., 1941; Litt.D., Tex. Coll., 1957; m. Alice Elizabeth Singleton, June 3, 1940; children—Chester, Loretta Jean, Kapel. Dir. leadership edn., also asso. editor ch. sch. publs. Gen. Bd. Christian Edn. Colored M.E. Ch., 1940-50; pres. Lane Coll., 1950—. Bd. dirs. United Negro Coll. Fund; mem. commn. on higher edn. Nat. Council Chs. of Christ in Am. Mem. N.A.A.C.P., Alpha Phi Alpha. Author: Improving the Educational Program of the Local Church, 1949. Home: 566 Lane Av Jackson TN

KIRKHAM, ED SHELTON, city ofcl.; b. Lamar County, Tex., Jan. 4, 1928; s. John F. and Lela Mae (Wood) K.; ed. jr. coll.; m. Oleta Norris, July 3, 1948; children—Daryl Shelton, Joe Mack, Cheryl Beth. With San Angelo (Tex.) Fire Service, 1949-68, chief dept., 1963-68; chief Austin (Tex.) Fire Dept., 1968—. Trustee Austin Boys' Club. Mem. Internat., Tex. fire chiefs' assns., Nat. Fire Protection Assn. Home: 4602 Kiowa Pass Austin TX 78745 Office: 401 E 5th St Austin TX 78701

KIRKLAND, CLARENCE NATHANIEL, JR., city ofcl.; b. Jackson County, Fla., Oct. 31, 1922; s. Clarence Nathaniel and Bernice Eleese (Messer) K.; student U. Fla., 1940-41, Marshall U., 1943, Fla. Police Tng. Course, 1948, U.S. Fgn. Service Inst. in Japanese lang., 1959, U. Md., 1961, U. Ga., 1967, 68; various courses, 1968-70; Baccalaureat in Criminal Justice, Rollins Coll., 1971; m. Mary Extipes, Jan. 5, 1947; children—Tracy Elizabeth, Susan Clarissa, Douglas Raymond. Commd. 2d lt. U.S. Army Air Force, 1943, advanced through grades to maj. U.S. Air Force, 1961; investigator, comdr. spl. investigative units OSI, USAF, 1948-65, assignments involved directing investigations all types criminal and personnel security investigations, violations security regulations and detection Communist and other subversive elements; ret., 1965; chief police, Sumter, S.C., 1965-68; chief police, Titusville, Fla., 1968—. Chmn. North Brevard Eagle Scout Rev. Bd., 1969-70; mem. Brevard County Mental Health Assn., 1970; mem. Gov.'s Council on Criminal Justice, 1971; mem. Salvation Army Adv. Bd., 1971. Mem. Fla. Police Chiefs Assn., Brevard County Police Assn., Internat. Narcotics Enforcement Officers Assn. Methodist (mem. social concerns com. 1971). Rotarian. Home: 3621 Royal Oak Dr Titusville FL 32780 Office: Office Dept Law Enforcement Titusville FL 32780

KIRKLAND, EDGAR LEROY, govt. ofcl.; b. Ft. Davis, Ala., May 2, 1913; s. James Jackson and Mamie (Johnson) K.; grad. high sch.; m. Flora Margaret Law, Aug. 23, 1941. Engr. asst. Macon County (Ala.) Hwy. Dept., 1938-40; equipment insp. U.S. Army Corps Engrs., Mobile, Ala., 1940-43; vet. coordinator, charge vet. tng. program Macon County Bd. Edn., 1947-54; postmaster, Ft. Davis, 1954—. Served with USAAF, 1943-47. Mem. Nat. Assn. Postmasters U.S. Mason. Address: Fort Davis AL 36031

KIRKLAND, EDWIN CAPERS, educator; b. Charleston, S.C., Sept. 14, 1902; s. William Clark and Lalla (Stokes) K.; A.B., Wofford Coll., 1922; M.A., Vanderbilt U., 1924; Ph.D., Northwestern U., 1934; m. Mary L. Neal, Sept. 14, 1930. Various teaching positions, 1922-31; instr. U. Tenn., 1931-37, asst. prof., 1937-41, asso. prof., 1941-46; asso. prof. English, U. Fla., Gainesville, 1946-51, prof., 1951—. Am. consul, cultural officer Am. Consul Gen., Bombay, India, 1954-56. Fulbright Research grantee, Calcutta, India, 1962-63; Am. Philos. Soc., Research grantee Brit. Mus., summer 1963, 66. Mem. Modern Lang. Assn., Am., Asian (exec. bd. 1963—), Indian folklore socs., S. Atlantic Modern Lang. Societe Internationale d'Ethnologie et de Folklore, Southeastern Folklore Soc. (pres. 1939), Phi Beta Kappa.

Editor So. Folklore Quar., 1969—. Home: 629 SW 27th Ct Gainesville FL 32601

KIRKLAND, JAMES STANFORD, city ofcl.; b. Vaucluse, S.C., Oct. 17, 1916; s. Haston Wyman and Annie Kate (Edmunds) K.; B.S., The Citadel; m. Mary Elizabeth Mahoney, Aug. 6, 1942; children—Lynda C., James Standord, David J., Robert G. Office mgr. R. H. H. Blackwell Co., jacksonville, Fla., 1937-38; office mgr. Gulf Oil Corp., Beaufort, S.C., 1938-39; accountant Blue Channel Corp., Port Royal, S.C., 1939-41; treas., City of Beaufort, S.C., 1963—. Served from 1st lt. to maj. AUS, 1941-45. Lion. Home: 1906 Pigeon Point Rd Beaufort SC 29902 Office: Drawer 191 City Hall Beaufort SC 29902

KIRKLAND, JOHN CYRIL, textile co. exec.; b. Ridge Springs, S.C., Sept. 26, 1918; s. Fletcher Lecroy and Minerva (Cullum) K.; B.S., U.S.C., 1940; m. Virginia Sims, July 10, 1943; children—Patricia (Mrs. Larry Brent Lewis), John Cyril, Janet (Mrs. Joe Kenneth Dillard), Earle Fletcher. Accountant, S.C. Hwy. Dept., Columbia, 1940-42; pub. accountant Elliott Davis & Co., accountants, auditors, Greenville, S.C., 1942-49; v.p., sec., dir. Arkwright Mills, Spartanburg, S.C., 1949—. C.P.A., S.C. Baptist (deacon). Home: 136 Marlin Dr Spartanburg SC 29302 Office: South Liberty St Spartanburg SC 29301

KIRKLAND, JOHN DAVID, oil co. exec.; b. McAllen, Tex., June 6, 1933; s. O.D. and Daisy (Donohoe) K.; B.A., Yale, 1955, LL.B., 1958; m. Ann Wales, June 15, 1957; children—David, Solace, Robert. Admitted to Tex. bar, 1958; atty. Baker, Botts, Shepherd & Coates, Houston, 1958-67; v.p. in charge finance Pennzoil Co., Houston, 1967—; dir. Mesa Petroleum Co. Mem. Am., Tex. bar assns. Home: 3620 Inverness Houston TX 77019 Office: Southwest Tower Houston TX 77002

KIRKLAND, JOHN WARE, JR., milling co. exec.; b. Sheffield, Ala., May 5, 1917; s. John W. and Vera (Hurd) K.; B.A., Florence State U., 1939; postgrad. Northwestern U., 1961; m. Frances Elizabeth Renfroe, Jan. 24, 1942; children—Minda Jane (Mrs. Fredric Marshall Martin), Suzanne, John W. III, Sara Beth, Mark D., Harry H., Nancy Lee, Kay Ellen. Field supr. Goodyear Tire & Rubber Co., Birmingham, Ala., 1939-49; dist. mgr. Am. home products Am. Home Foods, Birmingham, Memphis, Columbia, S.C., 1949-53; owner, mgr. Ralston-Purina Co. Agy., Fayette, Ala., 1953-58; gen. sales mgr., dir. Gregs Cookie Co., Birmingham, 1958-64; dir. purchasing Cosby-Hodges Milling Co., Birmingham, 1964—. Served with USAAF, 1942-46; ETO. Decorated Bronze Star medal. Recipient Man of Year award Ralston-Purina Co., 1956. Mem. Nat., Ala. assns. purchasing mgrs., Am., Ala. (dir.) feed mfrs. assns., Ala. Cattleman's Assn. Republican. Christian Scientist (chmn. bd. trustees). Mason (Shriner), Kiwanian. Clubs: Music (dir.), Zamora Golf and Country (Birmingham). Home: 3741 Mountain Park Dr Birmingham AL 35213 Office: 1904 16th St N Birmingham AL 35201

KIRKLAND, WALLACE TALMAGE, real estate appraiser, cons.; b. Guntersville, Ala., July 15, 1931; s. Grover and Ona (McClendon) K.; B.S., Auburn U., 1953; postgrad, U. Fla., 1955-56; m. Martha Alma Cotter, June 2, 1962; children—Lorraine Phyllis, Dawn Ellen, Pres., Kirkland Builders, Guntersville, Ala., 1958-59; asso. regional appraiser Gen. Services Adminstrn., Atlanta, 1959-65; pres. Kirkland & Co., Atlanta, 1965—. Served with USAF, 1953-55. Mem. Am. Inst. Real Estate Appraisers, Soc. Real Estate Appraisers, Pi Kappa Phi, Delta Sigma Pi. Home: 1656 Merton Rd NE Atlanta GA 30306 Office: 15 Peachtree St NE Atlanta GA 30303

KIRKNESS, WALTER, fish and game adminstr.; b. Seattle, Aug. 9, 1920; s. Andrew J. and Hetty (Herman) K.; B.S., U. Wash., 1943; m. Marjorie C. Fall, Oct. 9, 1948; children—Walter Mark, Susan Lee. Biologist, Internat. Salmon Commn., New Westminster, B.C., Can., 1941; fisheries research biologist Wash. Dept. Fisheries, Seattle, 1943-50; fisheries research biologist Alaska Dept. Fish and Game, 1950-53, sr. biologist watershed mgmt., 1954-57, dir. div. comml. fish, 1957-61, commr., Juneau, 1961-67; fishery biologist U.S. Bur. Comml. Fisheries, Washington, 1967—. Served with USMCR, 1943-46. Author: King Salmon and the Ocean Troll Fishery of Southwestern Alaska, 1956. Home: 6212 Beachway Dr Falls Church VA 22041 Office: Interior Bldg Washington DC 20242

KIRKPATRICK, EDITH KILLGORE (MRS CLAUDE KIRKPATRICK), club worker, educator; b. Lisbon, La., Nov. 14, 1918; d. Thomas Morton and Bessie (Melton) Killgore; B.A. summa cum laude, La. Coll., 1938; Mus.M., La. State U., 1965; student Juillard Sch. Music, 1938; m. Claude Kirkpatrick, Aug. 21, 1938; children—Claude Kent, (dec.), Thomas Killgore, Edith Kay, Charles Kris. Tchr. voice, Sulphur, Lake Charles, Jennings, La., 1940-60; instr. voice and music McNeese State Coll., Lake Charles, La., 1956-58; vis. asst. prof. La. State U., 1967-68; choir dir. 1st Bapt. Ch., Sulphur, Jennings, 1938-55, Baton Rouge 1967-68. Vice pres. Burgess Lumber Co., Jennings, 1955-66. Capt. drive A.R.C., 1958, Boy Scouts Am., 1952-56, United Giver 1964; womens' state chmn. La. Coll. Bldg. Fund Crusade, 1967; Bd. dirs. Baton Rouge Symphony, 1969—, pres. aux., 1968-69. Recipient La. Coll. Distinguished Alumni award, 1961. Mem. Nat. Fedn. Music Clubs, (state pres. 1966-69), Nat Fedn. Womens Clubs, La. Bapt. Womans Union (state pres. 1960-63), Nat. Assn. Tchrs. Singing, Nat. Music Tchrs. Assn., Nat. Music Educators Assn., Mortar Bd. Alpha Chi, Beta Pi Theta, Sigma Alpha Iota, Phi Kappa Phi, Pi Kappa Lambda, P.E.O., Baton Rouge Opera Guild (pres. 1970-72). Democrat. Baptist (1st woman mem. La. exec. bd. (1970-73). Co-author: Star Ideals, 1963; also articles in profl. jours. Address: 128 S Lakeshore Dr Baton Rouge LA 70808

KIRKPATRICK, KENNETH LOUIE, constrn. co. exec.; b. Bonham, Tex., Mar. 1, 1920; s. U. and Josephine (Thomas) K.; grad. high sch.; m. Dorothy Estelle Gunn, Sept. 17, 1949; children—Gary Phillips (stepson), Kenneth Louie, Jackie Lynn. With F.W. Woolworth, 1939; mgr. M.E. Moses Co., 1941-47; with Clark Loyd 5 and 10 cent Store, 1948-50; pres. Kirk's Variety Store, Inc., Killeen, Tex., 1951-59; pres. Beauty Homes, Inc., Killeen, 1969—, Jackie Lynn, Inc., Killeen, 1964—, Cove Lanes, Inc., Copperas Cove, Tex., 1952—; owner Kirk's Real Estate, Killeen, 1960—. Pres., Ft. Hood Bd. Realtors, 1969—; dir. Killeen Community Cowhouse Motor Hotel. Mem. Hardin Baylor Citizens Adv. Com., 1970—. Bd. dirs. Killeen Indsl. Found., A.R.C. Served with AUS, 1942. Kirk's Hall, Killeen Girl Scouts Friendship House, named in his honor, 1962. Mem. Homebuilders Assn. (pres. 1971—), Tex. Assn. Realtors (state dir. 1969—), Killeen C. of C. (dir. 1969—), Assn. U.S. Army (dir. 1971—, 1st v.p. 1972-73). Home: 3210 Lake Ann St Killeen TX 76541 Office: 1006 N 38th St Killeen TX 76541

KIRKPATRICK, WILLIAM KIRNEY, physician; b. Beaumont, Tex., Sept. 22, 1929; s. Jewel Bryant and Vera Gladys (Alexander) K.; B.S., S.W. Tex. U., 1952; M.D., U. Tex. at Galveston, 1957; m. Eugenia Maxine Sanders, June 23, 1954; children—Stephen Sanders, Ross Alexander, Sara Katherine. Intern St. Joseph's Hosp., Ft. Worth, 1958; gen. practice, San Antonio, 1962—; mem. staff Santa Rosa, Baptist Meml., St. Benedicts's and Grace Lutheran hosps. Served with M.C., USAF, 1958-61. Biology teaching fellow S.W. Tex. U., 1952; USAF fellow U. Tex. 1956-57. Mem. Am., Tex. acads. family physicians, A.M.A. (Recognition award 1970), Internat. Med. Assembly S.W., Tex., Bexar County med. socs., Alpha Kappa Kappa. Democrat. Episcopalian. Lion. Contbr. articles to profl. jours. Home: 318 Glad Dr San Antonio TX 78223 Office: 2915 S Presa St San Antonio TX 78210

KIRKPATRICK, WILLIAM WALLACE, educator; b. New Rochelle, N.Y., Apr. 8, 1914; s. Frank F. and Mary (Treacy) K.; A.B. magna cum laude, Harvard, 1934; postgrad. Queens Coll., Oxford, 1934-35; LL.B. cum laude, Harvard, 1938. Admitted to N.Y. bar, 1938, U.S. Supreme Ct., 1941, D.C. bar, 1946; spl. asst. to atty. gen. anti-trust div. U.S. Dept. Justice, 1938-42, 46-50, 2d asst., 1954-57, first asst., acting asst. atty. gen., 1958-61; gen. counsel Berlin Element of Office of U.S. High Commr. for Germany, 1950-54; faculty George Washington U., Washington, 1961—, prof. law, 1961—, asso. dean of Nat. Law Center, 1963—. Served from ensign to lt. USNR, 1942-46. Mem. Harvard Law Sch. Assn. Clubs: Army-Navy Country, National Lawyers, Harvard (Washington). Contbr. articles to law jours. Home: 5235 Nebraska Av NW Washington DC 20015

KIRKWOOD, GERALDINE (JERRY), architect; b. Tulsa, Feb. 15, 1928; d. James Wiley and Bula D. (Sparks) Kirkwood; Asso. Sci., Amarillo Coll., 1948; B.Arch., Tex. Tech. Coll., 1954. Draftsman, Hayes and Kirby, Architects-Engrs., Lubbock, Tex., 1954-56, Atcheson, Atkinson and Cartwright, Architects-Engrs., Lubbock, 1956-57; draftsman Tex. Tech. U., Lubbock, 1957-59, architect, 1959—, campus planning com. co-ordinator, 1966—. Mem. A.I.A., Tex. Soc. Architects. Home: Box 610 Route 1 Lubbock TX 79401 Office: Box 4508 Tex Tech U Lubbock TX 79409

KIRSCHKE, WILLIAM, condr., musical dir.; b. Tex.; ed. Tex. Christian U., Ind. U.; pupil Walter Ducloux U. So. Cal.; postgrad. Univ. Conservatorium, Australia; pupil Henri Touzeau Melbourne (Australia) Philharmonic. Formerly condr. Roswell (N.M.) Symphony Orch.; now music dir., condr. El Paso (Tex.) Symphony; numerous guest condr. appearances; participating condr. Am. Symphony League East Coast Inst. Condrs. Recipient Kenan Found. award Young Artist Musicians. Address: 6457 Dawn St El Paso TX 79912*

KIRSCHNER, EDWIN J, business exec.; b. N.Y.C., Dec. 26, 1919; s. M. Betty (Kenner) K.; student U. Florence (Italy), 1945-46, Coll. of William and Mary, Va. Poly. Tech., 1942; B.S., Am. U., 1950, M.A., 1951, postgrad., 1951-54; m. Eleanor Maxwell, Aug. 15, 1956; children—John Erik, Richard Scott, Caroline Lee, Jacqueline Jean. Transp. and aviation officer AID, U.S. Dept. of State, 1957-63; mil. planner USAF, 1952-56; mgr. transp. systems and aerospace mgmt., applied sci. and tech. divs. Litton Systems, Inc., Bethesda, Md., 1967-68; transp. adviser Peat, Marwick, Livingston & Co., Washington, 1968-69; pres. E.J. Kirschner & Assos., 1969—; pvt. transp. cons. to govt. and industry, Washington, 1963-67, 68—; cons. Dept. Transp., 1970—. Mem. faculty Am. U., 1963-64; adj. prof. Niagara U., 1969-70. Nominating com. mem. Aerospace Hall of Fame, 1964—. Mem. transp. adv. bd. to Montgomery County (Md.) Council, 1968—. Served to capt. AUS, 1943-47; now col. Res. Mem. Am. Inst. Aeros. and Astronautics, Am. Airship Assn. (chmn. bd. trustees 1958—), Nat. Def. Transp. Assn. (chmn. edn. com.). Author: The Zeppelin in the Atomic Age, 1957; Civil Aviation, 1958. Contbr. to encys., also articles transp. and aerospace to publs. Home: 5300 Westbard Av Washington DC 20016

KIRSHMAN, HARRY, supt. schs. Supt. Jackson (Miss.) schs. Address: 517 Lexington Av Jackson MS 39209*

KISE, MEARL ALTON, chem. co. exec.; b. Allentown, Pa., Feb. 14, 1908; s. John H. and Emma C. (Wertman) K.; B.S., Lehigh U., 1930; Ph.D., Yale, 1933; m. Julia Bacsics, Sept. 20, 1930; children—John A., Peter E. Instr. chemistry Yale, 1930-32; sr. Textile Found. fellow Yale, 1933-35; research chemist, project leader nitrogen sect., solvay process div. Allied Chem. & Dye Corp., 1935-47, asst. to chief of research, Hopewell, Va., 1948-49; dir. research and devel. Va. Chems. Inc., Portsmouth, Va., 1949-71, v.p. research and devel., 1972—; v.p. VirChem of Can., Ltd., Cornwall, Ont. and Pointe Claire, Que., 1970—. Chmn. Portsmouth Sch. Bd., 1960-72. Pres. Portsmouth Humane Soc., 1970—; treas., trustee Old Dominion U. Research Found., Norfolk, Va.; chmn. bd. trustees Hampton Rds. Ednl. TV Assn., 1968-69. Fellow A.A.A.S.; mem. Am. Chem. Soc. (past chmn. Hampton Rds. sect.), T.A.P.P.I., Am. Soc. Heating, Refrigerating and Air-Conditioning Engrs., Am. Assn. Textile Chemists and Colorists, N.Y., Va. (editor chemistry sect. 1958-63, sec. 1958-59, chmn. 1959-60) acads. sci., Soc. Plastics Engrs., Phi Beta Kappa, Sigma Xi. Lutheran. Contbr. articles to profl. jours. Patentee in field. Home: 112 Monitor Rd Portsmouth VA 23707 Office: 3340 W Norfolk Rd Portsmouth VA 23703

KISSINGER, HENRY ALFRED, govt. ofcl; b. Fuerth, Germany, May 27, 1923; s. Louis and Paula (Stern) K.; A.B. summa cum laude, Harvard, 1950, M.A., 1952, Ph.D., 1954;; m. Ann Fleischer, Feb. 6, 1949 (div. 1964); children—Elizabeth, David. Came to U.S. in 1938, naturalized, 1943. Exec. dir. Harvard internat. 1951-69, lectr. dept. govt., 1957-59, dir. def. studies program, 1958-69, asso. prof. govt., 1959-62, prof., 1962-71, faculty Center Internat. Affairs, Harvard; asst. to the Pres. for nat. security affairs, 1969—; dir. nuclear fgn. policy Council Fgn. Relations, 1955-56; dir. spl. studies project Rockefeller Bros. Fund, Inc., 1956-58. Cons. operations research office, 1950, cons. to dir. Strategy Bd., 1952, cons. Operations Coordinating Bd., 1955-56, cons. weapons systems evaluation group, 1956-60; cons. NSC, 1961-62, U.S. Arms Control and Disarmament Agy., 1961-67; cons. Dept. of State, 1965-69. Served with AUS, 1943-46. Recipient citation Woodrow Wilson prize for best book in fields of govt., politics, internat. affairs, 1958. Mem. Am. Polit. Sci. Assn. Council Fgn. Relations, Am. Acad. Arts and Scis., Phi Beta Kappa. Clubs: Cosmos, Federal City (Washington); St. Botolph (Boston); Century (N.Y.C.). Author: Nuclear Weapons and Foreign Policy, 1957; A World Restored; Castlereagh, Metternich and the Restoration of Peace 1821-22, 1957; The Necessity for Choice: The Prospects of American Foreign Policy, 1961; The Troubled Partnership; A Reappraisal of the Atlantic, Alliance, 1965. Editor: Problems of National Stretegy; Confluence, An Internat. Forum, 1951-58. Contbr. articles to profl. jours. Office: White House Washington DC 20500

KISSLING, FRED RALPH, JR., ins. agy. exec.; b. Nashville, Feb. 10, 1930; s. Fred Ralph and Sarah Elizabeth (FitzGerald) K.; B.A., Vanderbilt U., 1952, M.A., 1958; m. Jane Kirkpatrick, Sept. 12, 1959;children—Sarah FitzGerald, Jane Kirkpatrick. Spl. agt. Northwestern Mut. Life Ins. Co., Nashville, 1953-62, gen. agt., Lexington, Ky., 1962—; pres. Employee Benefit Cons., Inc., Lexington, 1961—; dir. Bank of Lexington. Adv. bd. Salvation Army, Lexington, 1971—. C.L.U. Mem. Am. Soc. Chartered Life Underwriters (chpt. pres. 1969-70), Ky. Gen. Agts. and Mgrs. Assn. (pres. 1963-64), Nat. Assn. Life Underwriters (life mem. Million Dollar Round Table), Am. Soc. Pension Actuaries (dir. 1971—), Sigma Chi. Mason (Shriner). Clubs: Cincinnati; Nashville City; Lexington, Lexington Polo. Author: Sell and Grow Rich, 1966. Editor: Questionaire in Pension Planning, 1971, Questionnaire in Estate Planning, 1971. Home: 728 Old Dobbin Circle Lexington KY 40502 Office: 98 Dennis Dr Lexington KY 40503

KISSNER, JACOB, mfg. co. exec.; b. Frankfurt on Main, Germany; s. Josef and Lina (Sann) K.; ed. business coll.; m. Johanna Ditt, Aug. 27, 1931; 1dau., Olivia. Founder, owner Folbot Works, London, 1932-35; founder, 1935, since pres. Folbot Corp., L.I.; developer Folbot paddle and cruising excursions, White Water Sport, 1937; lectr. Mem. Am. Canoe Assn., Jamaica Estates Assn., Pack and Paddle Soc. Roman Catholic. Clubs: Kiwanis (pres.), Touring Kayak. Author: Foldboat Holidays, 1941; contbr. articles, picture stores to profl., sport publs. Holder Nat. White Water championship, 1941—. Office: Stark Indsl Park Charleston SC 29405

KIT, SAUL, biochemist, educator; b. Passaic, N.J., Nov. 25, 1920; s. Isadore and Minnie (Darvick) K.; A.B., U. Cal. at Berkeley, 1948, Ph.D., 1951; m. Dorothy Anken, Sept. 28, 1945; children— Sally, Malon, Gordon. Post-doctoral fellow U. Chgo., 1951-52; research chemist, asst. biochemist U. Tex. M.D. Anderson Hosp. and Tumor Inst., Houston, 1952-57, asso. biochemist, 1957-60, biochemist, chief sect. nucleo protein metabolism, 1961-62; prof. biochemistry, head div. biochem. virology Baylor U. Coll. Medicine, Houston, 1962—. Served with AUS, 1942-46. Mem. Am. Soc. Cell Biology (pres. 1970-71), Am. Assn. Cancer Research, Am. Soc. Biol. Chemists, Am. Chem. Soc., Am. Soc. Microbiology. Mem. editorial bd. Cancer Research, Internat. Jour. Cancer. Contbr. numerous articles to profl. jours. Home: 11935 Wink St Houston TX 77024 Office: 1200 Moursund Av Houston TX 77025

KITCHEL, GEORGE BEHRMAN, oilwell drilling co. exec.; b. Alta Loma, Tex., June 29, 1909; s. James Roderick and Mary Graham (Behrman) K.; B.S. in Mech. Engring., Rice U., 1931; m. Mariann Adkins, June 9, 1934. With McEvoy Co., Houston, 1931-32, Halliburton Oilwell Cementing Co., 1932, Humble Oil & Refining Co., 1932-35, 36-49, Broderick Boiler Co., Muncie, Ind., 1935-36; with Kerr- McGee Corp., Oklahoma City, 1949—, v.p. contracts Houston, 1955—: v.p. Transworld Drilling Co., Transworld Drilling Co. Ltd., Kerr-McGee Ltd. Registered profl. engr., Tex. Mem. Am. Petroleum Inst. (citation of service 1956, certificate of appreciation 1958), Am. Assn. Oilwell Drilling Contractors (dir.), Ind. Petroleum Assn. Am., Baronial Order Magna Charta, Tau Beta Pi, Clubs: Houston, International Petroleum (Houston). Home: 5519 Tupper Lake Houston TX 77027 Office: 3801 Kirby Dr Houston TX 77006

KITCHIN, LEE, broadcasting exec. Pres., WTAR, WTAR-FM, Norfolk, Va. Address: 720 Boush St Norfolk VA 23510*

KITTRELL, THOMAS SKINNER, banker; b. Edenton, N.C., Nov. 28, 1898; s. Josiah Grudup and Penepole Tucker (Skinner) K.; A.B., U. N.C., 1920; postgrad. Harvard, 1921, U. N.C. Law Sch., 1922; m. Catherine Mills, Feb. 11, 1930. Admitted to N.C. bar, 1922; practice law, Henderson, N.C., 1922—; v.p., sr. trust officer Citizens Bank & Trust Co., Henderson, 1946—, also dir.; dir. Henderson Cotton Mills, Harriet Cotton Mills, Henderson, Home Savs. & Loan Assn., Henderson. Mem. N.C. Ho. of Reps., 1925; judge County Ct., 1928-32. Served to col. AUS, 1940-46. Recipient N.C. State Distinguished Service medal, 1962. Mem. Delta Tau Delta, Phi Delta Phi. Democrat. Episcopalian (jr. warden 1950—, vestryman 1948-52). K.P., Kiwanian Clubs: Henderson Country; Hudson Law (Harvard, Cambridge, Mass.). Home: 334 Belle St Henderson NC 27536 Office: PO Box 1027 Henderson NC 27536

KIVETT, CHARLES THOMAS, judge; b. Carthage, N.C., Jan. 1, 1927; s. Charles Anderson and Sally (Russell) K.; A.B., Catawba Coll., 1950; LL.B., U. N.C., 1955; m. Hilda Lee Kern, Aug. 21, 1951; children—Charles Thomas, Teresa Lee. Accounting div. trainee, Blue Bell, Inc., Greensboro, N.C., 1951-52; trust officer, Security Nat. Bank (now N.C. Nat. Bank), Greensboro, 1955-61, asst. v.p. comml. dept., 1962-63; admitted to N.C. bar 1955, practiced in Greensboro, 1963—, solicitor (pros. atty.), City Ct. Greensboro, 1964-65; dist. solicitor, 12th Dist., State N.C., 1967-69; resident judge Superior Ct., 18th Jud. Dist., Greensboro, 1969—. Mem. N.C. Adv. Council, Small Bus. Adminstrn., 1963-64, N.C. Employment Security Commn., 1964. Active various community fund drives. Mem. nat. com. N.C. Young Democrats, 1959-60, spl. asst. to pres. 1963-64, pres. Guilford County, 1956-57; mgr. county campaign for Sen. B. Everett Jordan, 1960; Dem. nominee N.C. Ho. of Reps., 1964; del. to Atlantic Assn. Young Pol Leaders, Oxford, Eng., 1965. Served with USNR, 1944-46; PTO. Named Outstanding Young Dem. N.C., 1965. Mem. Greensboro Bar Assn. Methodist. Mason (Shriner). Home: 1109 Pamlico Dr Greensboro NC 27402 Office: Guilford County Courthouse Greensboro NC 27402

KIZZIA, COOPER, ins. agt.; b. Murfreesboro, Ark., June 8, 1938; s. Hurley Fred and Clarice (Hare) K.; student Texarkana Coll., 1957-58; B.B.A., So. State Coll., 1961; m. Helen Martin, Dec. 18, 1960; children—James Cooper, Julie Lynn. Concrete technician Midway Constrn. Co., Conway, Ark., 1961-62; with contract dept. Ark. La. Gas Co., Little Rock, 1962-63; mgr. Pike County Ins. Agy., Murfreesboro, Ark., 1963—; dir. Pike County Bank. Chmn. Pike County Housing Authority, 1965—; vice-chmn. Pike County Devel. Council, 1966—; mem. Murfreesboro Water and Sewer Commn., 1968—. City recorder, Murfreesboro, 1969—. Bd. dirs. Pike County Fair Assn. Mem. Ark. Assn. Ins. Agts., Murfreesboro C. of C. (dir.). Methodist. Lion. Home: Box 232 Murfreesboro AR 71958 Office: 101 N Washington St Murfreesboro AR 71958

KJELSON, LEE, music educator; b. Stromsburg, Neb., Aug. 27, 1926; s. Albert V. and Marjorie (Hedbloom) K.; B.M.E., U. Neb., 1948, Mus.M., 1951; Ph.D., U. Ia., 1957; m. Betty Lorraine Aasen, July 31, 1949; children—Lee Richard II, John A. (Jay). Music tchr. pub. schs., Neb. and Ia., 1948-54; grad. asst. Exptl. Sch. Univ. High, U. Ia., 1955-57; asst. prof. music Western State Coll., Gunnison, Colo., 1957-60; prof. music Cal. State Coll., Hayward, 1960-67; prof. music, chmn. dept. music edn. U. Miami (Fla.), 1967—; choral condr. and clinician for state and nat. music edn. assns.; vis. prof. colls. and univs. Mem. Music Educators Nat. Conf. Democrat. Mem. United Ch. Christ. Editor, composer, arranger choral music, Co-author: Basic Series, 1969. Home: 631 Tibidabo St Coral Gables FL 33143

KLASS, PHILIP JULIEN, journalist; b. Des Moines, Nov. 8, 1919; s. Raymond N, and Ann (Traxler) K.; B.S., Ia. State U., 1941. Engr., Gen. Electric Co., Schenectady, 1941-52; sr. avionics editor Aviation Week and Space Tech. mag., Washington, 1952—. Mem. I.E.E.E., Am. Inst. Aeros. and Astronautics, A.A.A.S., Nat. Press Club. Author: UFOs-Identified, 1968; Secret Sentries in Space, 1971. Home: 560 N St SW Washington DC 20024 Office: Nat Press Bldg Washington DC 20004

KLASSEN, ELMER THEODORE, govt. ofcl.; b. Hillsboro, Kan., Nov. 6, 1908; student advanced mgmt. course Harvard Bus. Sch., 1952; m. Bessie Crooks, May 19, 1929; 1 dau., Joan Marie; m. 2d, Marie Callahan, June 8, 1963. With Am. Can Co., N.Y.C., 1925-68, gen. mgr. indsl. relations, 1955-58, v.p. indsl. relations, 1958-61, v.p., asst. gen. mgr. Canco div., 1961-62, v.p., gen. mgr. Canco div., 1962-64, exec. v.p. div. operations, 1964, exec. v.p. corporate operations, 1964-65, pres., 1965-68; dep. postmaster gen. P.O. Dept.,

Washington, 1969-71; bd. govs. U.S. Postal Service, 1971—; postmaster gen. U.S., 1972—. Chmn. bd. Inst. for Collective Bargaining and Group Relations, N.Y.C.; trustee Postgrad Inst. Osteo. Medicine and Surgery, N.Y.C. Republican. Methodist. Elk. Clubs: Sky, Economic, Harvard Business School (N.Y.C.); Capitol Hill (Washington). Office: Postmaster Gen US Postal Service Washington DC 20260 Home: Reeds Bridge Rd Conway MA 01341 also 7224 Arrowood Rd Bethesda MD 20034

KLASSEN, ROBERT LEONARD, govt. ofcl.; b. Patterson, Cal., Nov. 10, 1935; s. George Cornelius and Leah Rachel (Leppke) K.; student Tabor Coll., 1953-55; B.A. with highest honors, Fresno State Coll., 1957; M.L.S., U. Cal. at Berkeley, 1959; m. Beverly Isaak, June 29, 1957; children—Gregory Scott, DeeAnn Joy. Jr. and sr. reference librarian Cal. State Library, Sacramento, 1959-60; head librarian Pacific Coll., Fresno, Cal., 1960-62; asst. supr. Cal. State Library, Sacramento, 1962-68; planning/research program officer Library Programs div. U.S. Office Edn., Washington, 1968-71, planning and legislation officer Bur. Libraries and Ednl. Tech., 1971—. Lectr. extension div. U. Cal. at Davis, 1966-68; U.S. Office Edn. rep. to library work and documentation com. Am. Nat. Standards Inst., 1970—; equal employment opportunity counselor U.S. Office Edn., 1970—, mem. adv. council, 1970. Recipient Civil Service Merit award U.S. Office Edn., 1970; named No. Cal. Librarian of the Year, Cal. Nat. Library Week Com., 1967. Mem. A.L.A., Spl. Libraries Assn. (pres. elect D.C. 1971—), Am. Soc. Information Sci., Beta Phi Mu, Phi Kappa Phi, Pi Gamma Mu. Presbyn. Contbr. articles to profl. jours. Home: 2423 N Roosevelt St Arlington VA 22207 Office: 7th and D Sts SW Washington DC 20202

KLAUS, KENNETH BLANCHARD, musician, educator; b. Earlville, Ia., Nov. 11, 1923; s. Kenneth R. and Iris (Blanchard) K.; B.A., U. Ia., 1947, M.A., 1948, M.F.A., 1949, Ph.D., 1950; m. Marian Ida Fyler, June 8, 1947; children—Kenneth Sheldon, Karl Sherman. Prof., La. State U., Baton Rouge, 1950—, Alumni prof., 1966—; asso. condr. Baton Rouge Symphony, 1965—; prin. viola, 1950—. Served with USAAF, 1942-45; ETO. Mem. Am. Soc. Univ. Composers, Am. Musicol. Soc., Internat. Webern Soc., Berg Soc., Schoenberg Soc., Am. Mus. Library Assn., Am. Fedn. Musicians, Am. String Tchrs. Assn. (state pres.), Phi Mu Alpha, Omicron Delta Kappa, Pi Kappa Lambda, Phi Kappa Phi, Delta Phi Alpha. Author: The Romantic Period in Music. Composer over 60 compositions, 1940—. Home: 230 Albert Hart Dr Baton Rouge LA 70808

KLEBER, FRED MICHAEL, JR., ins. co. exec.; b. Dallas, July 27, 1907; s. Fred Michael and Abbie (Green) K.; B.S. in Bus. Adminstrn., Tex. A. and M. U., 1930; m. Dorothy Coats, May 28, 1932; children—William M., Linda G. With Southwestern Life Ins. Co., Dallas, 1931—, sec., 1962—. Fellow Life Office Mgmt. Assn.; mem. Am. Soc. Corporate Secs. Mason. Home: 859 Misty Glen Lane Dallas TX 75232 Office: 1807 Ross Av Dallas TX 75201

KLECHAK, THOMAS LEWIS, dentist; b. Washington, Sept. 19, 1940; s. Thomas and Margaret Bell (Lewis) K.; B.S., Wake Forest U., 1966; D.D.S., U. Md., 1965; M. Sc., U. N.C., 1971; m. Diane Lorraine Donald, Aug. 15, 1964; children—Thomas Lewis, James Donald. Practicing orthodontist, Jacksonville, Fla., 1971—; mem. faculty Fla. Jr. Coll. Active United Fund, Cancer Crusade, Zero Population Growth. Mem. Young Republicans. Served as capt. Dental Corps, USAF, 1965-69. Mem. Am., Fla. dental assns., N.E. Dist., Jacksonville dental socs., Am. Assn. Orthodontists, So. Soc. Orthodontists, Soc. Dentistry for Children, Acad. Dentistry, Omicron Kappa Upsilon. Clubs: Fairways Executive, Rotary, Century (Jacksonville). Home: 3501 Townsend Blvd Jacksonville FL 32211 Office: 819 Townsend Blvd Jacksonville FL 32211

KLECK, DAVID MILBURN, pub. relations exec.; b. Alexandria, La., Sept. 10, 1921; s. William Rheinhardt and Sidney (Milburn) K.; B.A., Tulane U., 1948; m. Dorothy Cynthia Williams, June 10, 1950; children— John Milburn, Nancy Milburn, Susan Lee. Reporter, sub-editor Times-Picayune, New Orleans, 1948-52; v.p. Gulfside, Inc., New Orleans, 1952-55; New Orleans mgr. Godwin Advt. Agy., 1955-62; owner David M. Kleck & Assos., New Orleans, 1962—. Adviser Jr. League New Orleans, 1965-67. Bd. dirs. Family Service Soc., 1953-54, Travelers Aid Soc., 1960-65, Adv. Com. to Juvenile Cts., 1960-62, La. Soc. Mental Health, 1964-66. Served to lt. USNR, 1943-46. Mem. Pub. Relations Soc. Am., Internat. House New Orleans, Kappa Sigma, Navy League (v.p. 1965-67). Democrat. Club: Lawn Tennis. Home: 5353 Marcia Av New Orleans LA 70124 Office: 520 John Hancock Bldg New Orleans LA 70130

KLEEMAN, RICHARD PENTLARGE, assn. exec.; b. N.Y.C., June 24, 1923; s. Arthur S. and Alice (Pentlarge) K.; grad. Choate Sch., 1940; A.B., Harvard, 1946; m. Rosslyn A. Shore, Jan. 1, 1950; children—Nancy, Alice, Katherine, David. Joined Mpls. Star and Tribune, 1946, reporter, copyreader, 1946-51, asst. city editor, 1951-53, asst. news editor, 1953-54, Sunday news editor, 1954-55, named news editor (edn.), 1955; Washington corr. Mpls. Tribune, 1966-72; asst. dir. Washington office Assn. Am. Pubs., Inc., 1972—. Served to 1st lt. AUS, 1942-46. Recipient Nat. Sch. Bell award, 1961. Mem. Am. Newspaper Guild, Planned Parenthood Fedn. Am. (dir. 1958-61), Planned Parenthood Mpls. (past pres.), Phi Beta Kappa, Sigma Delta Chi (past pres. Minn., past regional dir. SDX Found. bd.) Home: 3642 Upton St NW Washington DC 20008 Office: 1826 Jefferson Pl NW Washington DC 20036

KLEILER, FRANK MUNRO, govt. ofcl.; b. Green Bay, Wis., Apr. 17, 1914; s. Frank Andrew and Addie (Munro) K.; A.B., Antioch Coll., Yellow Springs, O., 1938; student Am. U., Washington, 1937-38; m. Frances Pauline Brezon, Apr. 10, 1939; children—David Allen, James Robert. Reporter, Evening Star, Washington, 1935-36, Boston Herald, 1936-37; clk. to bd. mem. Nat. Mediation Bd., 1937-39; asst. to bd. mem. Nat. Labor Relations Bd., 1939-41, field examiner, Cleve., 1941-42, Indpls., 1942-43, Chgo., 1943-44, regional dir., Pitts., 1944-47, exec. sec., Washington, 1947-51, 53-60; disputes dir. WSB, 1951-52, pub. mem. review and appeals com. 1952-53; dep. commr. Bur. Labor-Mgmt. Reports, Dept. Labor, 1960-62, dir. Office Welfare and Pension Plans, 1962-63, dir. Office Labor-Mgmt. and Welfare Pension Reports, 1963-70, dep. asst. sec. for planning and evaluation, 1970—. Mem. Acad. Polit. Sci., Indsl. Relations Research Assn. Home: 9100 Warren St Silver Spring MD 20910 Office: 8701 Georgia Av Washington DC

KLEIN, BARNEY ISADORE, JR., physician; b. Kerrville, Tex., Apr. 6, 1929; s. Barney Isadore and Zelpha Catherine (Green) K.; student Tex. Western U., 1955-56, Stephen F. Austin State Coll., 1956-58; M.D., U. Tex., 1962; m. Patsy Virginia Johnson, Dec. 21, 1954; children—Howard Felix, Julia Catherine, Cynthia Ann. Intern St. Joseph's Hosp., Ft. Worth, 1962-63; gen. practice Littlefield (Tex.) Hosp. and Clinic, 1963—; health officer Lamb County, 1965-66; med. adviser to A.R.C. chpt., 1967—. Served with AUS, 1954-56. Mem. Tex. Acad. Gen. Practice (v.p. South Plains chpt. 1967), Lamb County Med. Soc. (sec.-treas. 1965, v.p. 1966, pres. 1967), Theta Kappa Psi, Alpha Chi. Methodist (chmn. bd. missions 1966-69, chmn. council on ministries 1969-71). Home: 1414 Cherry Blossom Littlefield TX 79339 Office: 401 W 6th St Littlefield TX 79339

KLEIN, ELIAS, scientist; b. Leipzig, Germany, Oct. 26, 1924 (came to U.S., 1934, naturalized 1943); B.S., Tulane U., 1951, M.S., 1952, Ph.D., 1954; m. Beverly J. Aronowitz, May 9, 1948; children—Jerrold, Jon, Meryl. Head investigation U.S. Dept. Agr. lab., New Orleans, 1954-58; with Courtaulds, Inc., Mobile, Ala., 1958-67, dir. research and devel., 1965-67; sci. dir. Gulf South Research Inst., New Orleans, 1967—. Adj. prof. Loyola U., 1970—; cons. VA Hosp., 1970—. Served with AUS, 1943-45. Fellow Am. Inst. Chemists; mem. Am. Chem. Soc., Sci. Research Soc. Am. Contbr. articles to profl. jours. Patentee in field. Home: 4430 St Bernard Av New Orleans LA 70122 Office: PO Box 26500 New Orleans LA 70126

KLEIN, HERBERT GEORGE, govt. ofcl.; b. Los Angeles, Apr. 1, 1918; s. George and Amy (Cordes) K.; A.B., U. So. Cal., 1940; m. Marjorie G. Galbraith, Nov. 1, 1941; children—Joanne L. (Mrs. Robert Mayne), Patricia A. (Mrs. H. Thomas Howell). Reporter, Alhambra (Cal.) Post-Advocate, 1940-42, news editor, 1946-50; spl. corr. Copley Newspapers, 1946-50, Wash. corr., 1950; with San Diego Union, 1950-68, editorial writer, 1950-52, editorial page editor, 1952-56, asso. editor, 1956-57, exec. editor, 1957-58, editor, 1959-68; mgr. communications Nixon for Pres. Campaign, 1968-69; dir. communications Exec. Br., U.S. Govt., 1969—. Mem. Commn. of Californias. Bd. dirs. San Diego chpt. A.R.C. Publicity dir. Eisenhower-Nixon campaign in Cal., 1952; asst. pres. sec. Vice Pres. Nixon Campaign, 1956; press sec. Nixon inaugural 1957, Nixon campaign, 1958; spl. asst., press sec. to Nixon, 1959-61; pres. sec. Nixon Gov. Campaign, 1962; dir. communications Nixon presdl. campaign, 1968. Served with USNR, 1942-46; comdr. Res. Mem. La Jolla (Cal.) Lamplighters, Am. Soc. Newspaper Editors, Am. Legion, Cal. (Am. del. internat. conv., Manila, P.I. 1950), Alhambra (past pres.) jr. chambers commerce, San Diego Conv. and Visitors Bur. (bd. dirs.), San Diego-Yokohama Friendship Soc. (bd. dirs.), Sigma Delta Chi (nat. com. chmn., gen. activities chmn. nat. conv., 1958), Delta Chi. Presbyn. (elder; bd. Nat. Presbyn. Center). Kiwanian (hon.), Rotarian (hon.). Home: 4917 Crescent St Chevy Chase MD 20015 Office: 1600 Pennsylvania Av Washington DC 20500

KLEIN, LOTHAR, composer, educator; b. Hanover, Germany, Jan. 27, 1932; student Hochschule fur Musik, Berlin, Germany; student with Goffredo Petrassi; B.A., M.A., Ph.D., U. Minn, Fulbright examiner Berlin; dir. music, theater dept. U. Minn.; dir. publs. Schmitt, Hall & McCreary, Minn.; music faculty U. Tex., Austin, 1962—. Recipient Golden Reel, Am. Acad. Film Scis.; Harvey Gaul award. Mem. A.S.C.A.P. Important works include: Symetries for Orchestra I, IV; Cantata II for Actress, Percussion & 3 Soloists on Epigrams of Sappho; A Little Book of Hours. Home: 1806 Pearl St Austin TX 78701

KLEIN, LOUIS SAMUEL, certified pub. acct.; b. Chgo., Sept. 13, 1908; s. Joseph and Lena (Groveman) K.; C.P.A., U. N.Y., 1946; m. Syd Bass, June 2, 1934; children—Letty Sandra, Adele Phylis, Walter Jay. Acct., auditor Federated Purchaser, Inc., N.Y.C., 1932-35; comptroller, acct. Ala. Braid & Ribbon Co., C. M. Offray & Son, Gadsden, 1935-37; practicing C.P.A., 1937—; partner Bloomberg, Max, Louis S. Klein & Co., Gadsden; now partner firm Klein, Harwood & Lambert; pres., dir. Comml. & Financial Corp. Auditor Gadsden Concert Assn., 1961-72; mem. Jewish Welfare Bd. Etowah County. Mem. C. of C., N.Y., Ala. (past v.p., chmn. Gadsden-Anniston chpt.) socs. C.P.A.'s, Am. Inst. C.P.A.'s, Am., So. insts. mgmt., Am. Accounting Assn., B'nai B'rith, Coosa Lodge (past pres.). Mem. Beth Israel Temple (past pres.). Club: Civitan Internat. (past pres., lt. gov.). Home: 102 Cleveland Ct Gadsden AL 35901 Office: 752 Chestnut St Gadsden AL 35901

KLEIN, MILTON, govt. ofcl.; b. St. Louis, Jan. 13, 1924; s. Isador and Ilona (Tichler) K.; B.S. in Chem. Engring., Washington U., St. Louis, 1944; M.B.A., Harvard, 1950; m. Frances Motto, Dec. 28, 1947; children—Richard, Barbara, Janet. Chem. engr. Argonne Nat. Lab., Chgo., 1946-48; with AEC, Chgo., 1950-60, asst. mgr., 1958-60; with NASA/AEC, Washington, 1960-71, mgr., dir. Space Nuclear Systems Office, 1967-71; asso. adminstr. for research, devel., demonstrations Fed. Railroad Adminstrn., Washington, 1971—. Mem. staff dirs. group Pres.'s Space Task Group, 1969. Mem. adv. com. sci. and tech. manpower Ill. Selective Service System, 1957-60. Served with USNR, 1944-46. Mem. Am. Inst. Aeros. and Astronautics, A.A.A.S., Am. Nuclear Soc., Sigma Xi, Tau Beta Pi. Club: Torch (Washington, dir.). Home: 6404 Tulsa Lane Bethesda MD 20034 Office: Fed Railroad Adminstrn Washington DC 20591

KLEIN, NORMAN LESTER, chem. engr.; b. Balt., Feb. 27, 1912; s. George W. and Anna (Willerhausen) K.; student Johns Hopkins, 1930-32; B.S. in Chem. Engring., Ga. Inst. Tech., 1937; m. Mary Leonard, Nov. 25, 1937; children—Roy Alan, Mary Lee. Research engr. Rohm & Haas Co., Phila., 1937-38; lubrication engr. Shell Oil Co., Inc., Balt., 1938-42; chief fuel, lubricants sect. Office Chief Ordnance, Dept. Army, Washington, 1946-59, dep. chief research br., 1959-60, sci. adviser to chief, 1960-62, asst. dep. for labs., 1962—; dir. chemistry and materials research Materiel Command, U.S. Army, 1962—. Mem. sub. com. aircraft fuels NACA, Washington, 1955-60; adv. research com. chem. energy systems NASA, Washington, 1961—. Served as lt. col., AUS, 1942-46. Fellow Am. Inst. Chemists; mem. A.A.A.S., Soc. Automotive Engrs. Contbr. numerous articles in field to jours. Home: 9118 Cherrytree Dr Alexandria VA 22309 Office: care Office Dep for Labs US Army Materiel Command Washington DC 20025

KLEIN, ROBERT M., govt. ofcl.; b. McKeesport, Pa., Jan. 12, 1926; s. Milton E. and Hilda (Lichtenstein) K.; student U. Ky., 1943-44; A.B., George Washington U., 1949, M.A., 1955; m. Jan Lloyd Lawson, Mar. 18, 1950; children—Leslie Jan, Malcolm Lawson, Randal Todd. Asst. Japan desk officer U.S. Dept. Commerce, Washington, 1950-54, sr. Philippine desk officer 1954-60, commerce dept. mem. U.S. Investment Survey Mission to Thailand, 1959, chief Japan-Korea sect., Dept. Commerce, 1962-64, dep. dir. Far East div., 1964—; comml. attache, U.S. Embassy, Seoul, Korea, 1960-62. Lectr. Fgn. Service Inst., 1969-72. Mem. U.S. Civil Service Commn. Bd. of Examiners for Economists, 1965-66; head U.S. delegation to ann. meeting trade com. UN Econ. Commn. for Asia and Far East, 1968. Served with AUS, 1944-46, ETO. Recipient Bronze medal for superior service U.S. Dept. Commerce, 1967. Mem. Am. Econ. Assn. Unitarian. Home: 1608 Sherwood Hall Lane Alexandria VA 22306 Office: US Dept Commerce Washington DC 20230

KLEIN, RODGER W., investment co. exec.; b. Abington, Pa., June 9, 1938; s. Ralph S. and Elizabeth (Field) K.; A.B., Pa. State U., 1960; LL.B., U. Va., 1964; m. Barbara Serr, Aug. 26, 1961; children—Thomas L., Allison E. Admitted to Va. bar, 1964, D.C. bar, 1965; atty. adviser to Judge W.M. Drennen, Tax Ct. of U.S., Washington, 1965-67; asso. atty. Arent, Fox, Kintner, Plotkin & Kahn, Washington, 1967-69; pres., dir. Network Mgmt. Corp., Washington, 1969; pres., dir. Washington Investment Network, Inc., 1969—. Vice pres. Lincoln-Westmoreland Housing Corp., Washington. Mem. Va. State Bar Assn., D.C. Bar Assn., Am. Bar Assn. Home: 7704 Huntmaster Lane McLean VA 22101 Office: Suite 1006 1700 K St NW Washington DC 20006

KLEIN, THOMAS MARTIN, economist; b. Detroit, Aug. 9, 1928; s. Maurice and Ruth (Fink) K.; B.A., U. Mich., 1949, M.A., 1951 Ph.D., 1958; m. Judith Veit Simon, June 20, 1958; children—Michael, Margaret, David, Richard, Edward. Asst. prof. econs. Hamilton Coll., 1957-59; economist balance of payments div. Internat. Monetary Fund, 1959-62; economist div. internat. finance, bd. govs. Federal Reserve System, 1962-67; chief commerce industry and banking div. U.S. Civil Adminstrn., Ryukyu Islands, 1967-69; economist Internat. Bank for Reconstrn. and Devel., Washington, 1969—. Served with AUS, 1950-52. Mem. Am. Econ. Assn., Royal Econ. Soc. Home: 4008 Ingersol Dr Silver Spring MD 20902 Office: 1818 H St NW Washington DC 20433

KLEINER, HENRY EDWARD, JR., pub. exec.; b. Ashland, Ky., Jan. 15, 1928; s. Henry Edward and Marguerite (Wilson) K.; student U. Louisville, 1945-47, Columbia Tech., 1949-50; m. Virginia May Rosenbaum, July 3, 1954; children—Kendra Lee, Lisa Kay. Prodn. dir. The Diplomat mag., Washington, 1952-54; asst. pub., Mechanization mag., 1954-62; bus. mgr. Sports Age mag., 1962-64; bus. mgr. A.I.A. Jour. 1964-70; dir. Bus. Publs., Inc., Silver Spring, Md., 1963-70, v.p., 1970—. Served with AUS. Mem. Am. Water Works Assn., Nat. Solid Wastes Mgmt. Assn. Republican. Episcopalian. Lion Home: 242 Hillside Circle SW Vienna VA 22180 Office: PO Box 1067 Silver Spring MD 20910

KLEINERMAN, MORRIS, psychiatrist; b. Spring Valley, N.Y., May 18, 1907; s. David and Rose (Pilinis) K.; B.S., Coll. City N.Y., 1929; M.D., U. St. Andrews, 1933; m. Gertrude Janet Cohen, June 6, 1945; children—Ruth Anne, Martha Joan, Deena Adrian. Intern Manhattan Gen. Hosp., N.Y.C., 1933-34; resident St. Elizabeths Hosp., Washington, 1934-35, staff psychiatrist, 1935-47; medicine specializing in psychiatry, Washington, 1947—; clin. prof. psychiatry George Washington U. Med. Sch., 1965—. Served to maj. AUS, 1942-46. Fellow Am. Psychiat. Assn. (life); mem. A.M.A., Assn. Am. Med. Colls., Washington Psychiat. Soc. (pres. 1963-64), Phi Delta Epsilon. Home: 7207 Rollingwood Dr Chevy Chase MD 20015 Office: 2520 L St NW Washington DC 20037

KLEINMANN, JACK HENRY, assn. exec.; b. Bronx, N.Y., Sept. 1, 1932; s. Max and Helen (Weinstein) K.; B.A., Bklyn. Coll., 1953, M.A., 1955; Ed.D., Columbia, 1960; m. Ellen Kalberman, June 30, 1954 (div.); children—Laurie, Deborah; m. 2d, Joi Hase Winegar, Sept. 16, 1972. Tchr. pub. schs., N.Y.C., 1953-58; adminstrv. asst. to head of dept. ednl. adminstrn. Tchrs. Coll., Columbia, 1958-59; adminstrv. asst. to supt. schs., White Plains, N.Y., 1959-62; salary cons. and specialist in urban problems N.E.A., Washington, 1962-65, asst. dir. research div., 1965-66, dir. spl. services div., 1966-67, exec. sec., asso. exec. sec. Commn. on Profl. Rights and Responsibilities, 1967-68, dir. planning and organizational devel., 1968—. Served with AUS, 1954-56. Mem. Baroque Arts Soc. Washington (sec.). Author: (with others) Principles of Staff Personnel Administration in Public Schools, 1959; Fringe Benefits for Public School Personnel, 1962; Guidelines for Professional Negotiation, 1963, rev., 1965; Employer Cooperation in Group Insurance Coverage of Public School Personnel, 1964-65, 1966; (with T.M. Stinnett and M. Ware) Professional Negotiation in Public Education, 1966; Profiles of Excellence: Recommended Criteria for Evaluating the Quality of a Local School System, 1966. Contbr. articles to profl. jours. Home: 1330 Massachusetts Av Washington DC 20005 Office: 1201 16th St NW Washington DC 20036

KLEMM, WILLIAM ROBERT, educator; b. South Bend, Ind., July 24, 1934; s. Lincoln W. and Helen (DeLong) K.; student U. Tenn., 1952-54; D.V.M., Auburn U., 1958; Ph.D., U. Notre Dame, 1963; m. Doris Mewha Klemm, Aug. 27, 1957; children—Mark Dolan, Laura Margaret. Gen. practice vet. medicine, Perry, Ga., 1958; research fellow U. Notre Dame, 1960-63; asso. prof. Ia. State U., 1963-66; asso. prof. Tex. A and M U., College Station, 1966-70, prof., 1970—. Served to capt. USAF, 1958-60, maj. Res. Mem. Am. Physiol. Soc., Soc. Neuroscience, Sigma Xi, Phi Kappa Phi, Phi Zeta. Author: Animal Electroencephalography, 1969; Science, The Brain and Our Future, 1972. Contbr. articles to profl. jours. Home: Route 3 Box 179 Bryan TX 77801 Office: Dept Biology Tex A and M U College Station TX 77843

KLEPCZYNSKI, WILLIAM JOHN, astronomer; b. Phila., Apr. 16, 1939; s. William and Theresa (Drzalowski) K.; B.A., U. Pa., 1961; M.A., Georgetown U., 1964; Ph.D., Yale U., 1969; m. Gloria Shell, Oct. 14, 1961. Astronomer U.S. Naval Obs., Washington, 1961—. Mem. Am. Astron. Soc., Internat. Astron. Union, A.A.A.S., Inst. Navigation. Home: 2327 King Pl NW Washington DC 20007 Office: US Naval Obs Washington DC 20390

KLEPPER, ROBERT CLARENCE, county ofcl.; b. Luray, Va., July 25, 1928; s. Clarence D. and Jane (Steele) K.; A.B., Carson-Newman Coll., 1951; postgrad. George Washington U., 1964; m. Jo Dolores Peters, Apr. 12, 1946; children—Robert Clarence, Michael Tyree. City mgr. Altavista (Va.), 1956-60; spl. asst. Norfolk (Va.) Redevel. and Housing Authority, 1960-62; asst. city mgr. Chesapeake (Va.), 1962-66; adminstr. Prince George (Va.) County, 1966-72, New Kent (Va.) County, 1972—. Sec.-treas. Appomattox River Water Authority; sec. Appomattox Basin Indsl. Devel. Corp. Served with AUS, 1946-48. Recipient Meritorious Service award A.R.C., 1955. Mem. Internat. City Mgmt. Assn., Nat. Assn. Counties. Baptist. Mason (Shriner). Club: Prince George (Va.) Ruritan. Home: 2604 Forbes Dr Prince George VA 23875 Office: Environmental Protection Agy Washington DC 20460

KLIEWER, LAWRENCE WYCKOFF, radio and TV exec.; b. Boulder, Colo., July 24, 1923; s. Harry and Lora (Moore) K.; B.A. in Bus. Adminstrn., Coll. William and Mary, 1950; m. Erah Elizabeth Hatten, Dec. 28, 1948; children—Lawrence W., Jr., Linda Elizabeth, Lora Leone. Sports and program dir. Peninsula Broadcasting Corp., Hampton, Va., 1948-53, operations mgr. Peninsula Radio Corp. WVEC and Peninsula Broadcasting Corp., WVEC-TV, Hampton, 1953-55, v.p. operations, 1955—, also dir.; v.p., dir. P.B.K., Ltd., Hampton; v.p., dir. Multra Guard, Inc., Multra Guard of Va., Inc. (both Hampton); mem. adv. com. Bel Meade Corp., Richmond, Va., Pres. Peninsula Community Services Planning Council, 1960-61, Vol. Service Bur., 1959-60; chmn. Newport News (Va.) Planning Commn., 1963—, Newport News Zoning Bd., 1963—; mem. Peninsula Regional Planning Commn., 1967—; bd. dirs. Girls Clubs Virginia Peninsula, 1959-69, Peninsula Council Boy Scouts, 1960-64, Va. Community Funds and Councils, 1961-65. Recipient award for sports broadcasting, Va. Asso. Press, 1953, 54, Peninsula Distinguished Service award, 1958. Mem. Nat. (dir. 1969—, legislative com. 1968—), Va. (pres. 1967-69, dir. 1966—) cable television assns., Va. (sect. chmn. 1967—), Middle Atlantic (v.p. 1968—) golf assns., William and Mary Alumni Assn. (chpt. pres. 1958-59), Kappa Sigma. Clubs: Rotary (pres. 1963-64) (Hampton, Va.); Peninsula Sports (pres. 1959-60), James River Country (bd. dirs. 1966—) (Newport News, Va.). Home: 14 Downing Pl Newport News VA 23606 Office: 1930 E Pembroke Av Hampton VA 23369

KLINE, JOSEPH, govt. ofcl.; b. Rochester, N.Y., May 16, 1907; s. Ruben and Bessie (Shapiro) K.; B.S. in Edn., U. Rochester, 1939; m. Miriam Goldman, June 10, 1946. Tchr. pub. schs., P.R., 1937-42; with plant quarantine div. Dept. Agr., 1946—, now agrl. quarantine insp. Served with AUS, 1942-45. Mem. Fed. Plant Quarantine Insps. Assn., Jewish War Vets. U.S.A. (dept. comdr. 1969-70, editor Nat. Dep. 1965—). Mason (Shriner). Club: B'nai Zion Mens (El Paso). Home: 6001 Fiesta Dr El Paso TX 79912 Office: Dept Agr Cordova Bridge Sta El Paso TX 79912

KLINEFELTER, JAMES LOUIS, lawyer; b. Los Angeles, Oct. 8, 1925; s. Theron Albert and Anna Marie (Coffey) K.; B.A., U. Ala., 1949, LL.B., 1951; m. Mary Lynn Sheffield, Aug. 19, 1971; children (by previous marriage)—Patricia Anne, Jeanne Marie, Christopher Wright. Admitted to Ala. bar, 1951; regional claims rep. State Farm Mut. Auto Ins. Co., Anniston, Ala., 1951-54; partner firm Burnham, Klinefelter, Halsey & Love, Anniston, 1954—; dir. So. Plating & Mfg. Co. Mem. Calhoun County, Ala. Democratic exec. com., 1964—. Served to lt. (j.g.) USNR, 1943-46. Mem. Am., Ala. (sec.-treas. practice and procedure sect.), Calhoun County bar assns., Phi Kappa Sigma, Phi Alpha Theta. Clubs: Kiwanis (past pres.), Anniston Country. Home: 713 Oak St Anniston AL 36201 Office: Comml Nat Bank Bldg PO Box 1618 Anniston AL 36202

KLING, ROBERT EDWARD, JR., govt. ofcl.; b. York, Pa., May 29, 1920; s. Robert Edward and Gladys (Kinneman) K.; m. Doris M. Gilroy, June 11, 1943 (dec.); children—Robert Edward, III, Stephen Campbell, Jonathan Bradford; m. 2d, Mary Apostolou, May 29, 1969. Apprentice Govt. Printing Office, Washington, 1938, various positions, 1938-61, asst. supt. platemaking div., 1961-62, spl. asst. to 14th pub. printer U.S., 1962-70, supt. documents, 1970—. Pres. City Council, Hyattsville, Md., 1960-69. Served to lt. col. C.E. USNR, 1941-45, 50-52. Author: The Government Printing Office, 1970. Home: 701 Notley Rd Silver Spring MD 20904 Office: Supt Documents PO Box 1533 Washington DC 20013

KLINGSBERG, LEONARD, publishing co. exec.; b. Phila., June 10, 1922; s. Louis and Elizabeth (Boxenbaum) K.; student Temple U., 1940-42; m. Elaine E. Tankel, Jan. 3, 1943; Sr. founding partner L. Klingsberg & Co., Phila., 1945-66; pres., Books, Inc., Washington, 1966—; v.p. Pubs. Co., Inc., Washington, 1967—; pres. United Pub. Corp., Washington, 1969—, dir., 1969—; dir. Pubs. Co., Inc., Pubs. Broadcasting Corp. Served with USAAF, 1942-44. C.P.A., Pa. Mem. Am., Pa. insts. C.P.A.'s. Mason. Mailing Address: 5530 Wisconsin Av Washington DC 20015 Home: 7021 Whittier Blvd Bethesda MD 20034 Office: 5530 Wisconsin Av Washington DC 20015

KLOCK, BENNY LEROY, astronomer; b. Washington, Oct. 29, 1934; s. LeRoy and Ertie (Crouse) K.; B.A., Cornell U., 1956, M.S., 1960; Ph.D., Georgetown U., 1964; m. Margaret Ann Sherman, June 1, 1957; children—Mark Steven, Lorri Ann, Brian Lee. Dir. Northern Transit Circle div. U.S. Naval Obs., Washington, 1960—. Com. chmn. Boy Scout troop, Rockville, Md. Served to capt. USAAF, 1957-59. Mem. Internat. Astron. Union, Am. Astron. Soc., A.A.A.S., Sigma Xi. Republican. Contbr. articles in field to profl. jours. Home: 13907 Arctic Av Rockville MD 20853 Office: US Naval Obs Washington DC 20390

KLOCK, DAVID JULIAN, govt. ofcl.; b. Schenectady, May 19, 1938; s. Edwin J. and Eleanor (Taft) K.; B.A., Middlebury Coll., 1960; Ph.D., Columbia, 1969. Internat. economist U.S. Treasury, Washington, 1968—. Served with AUS, 1960-62. Fulbright Student grantee, Philippines, 1966-67. Mem. Am. Econ. Assn. Home: 1500 Massachusetts Av NW Washington DC 20005 Office: 15th and Pennsylvania Av NW Washington DC 20220

KLOEPFER, WILLIAM JOHN, JR., public relations exec.; b. Evanston, Ill., June 14, 1923; s. William John and Alma (Koch) K.; B.S., Northwestern U., 1949;; m. Nancy Lee Henninger, Nov. 26, 1958; children—Joan Helen, Elizabeth Koch. Gen. assignment reporter Athens (Tex.) Daily Rev., 1949-50; Capitol Hill reporter Washington Times-Herald, 1950-51; news editor NBC and Liberty Networks, Washington, 1951-52; asst. to dir. pub. relations Republican Nat. Com., Washington, 1952-55; adminstrv. asst. U.S. Rep. Laurence Curtis (Mass.), Washington, 1955-56; chief Office of Information, CAB, Washington, 1956-59; dir. pub. information Pharm. Mfrs. Assn., Washington, 1959-67; v.p. pub. relations Tobacco Inst., Washington, 1967-71, sr. v.p., 1971—. Served with AUS, 1943-46. Mem. Nat. Press Club, Pub. Relations Soc. Am., Nat. Assn. Sci Writers. Club: Bethesda Country (Md.). Home: 7429 Haddington Pl Bethesda MD 20034 Office: 1776 K St NW Washington DC 20006

KLOEPPEL, ROBERT, II, hotel co. exec.; b. Jacksonville, Fla., Mar. 15, 1942; s. Robert and Lucy Lee (Ellis) K.; B.S., Cornell U., 1964; m. Geraldine Patricia Conroy, Aug. 23, 1963; children—Katharine Ann, Laurie Ellis, David Campbell. With Kloeppel Hotels, Inc., Jacksonville, Fla., 1960—, v.p., 1965—, also dir.; sec.-treas. Consurgico Corp., Tallahassee, 1968—, also dir.; dir. Jacksonville Nat. Bank. Mem. adv. council Fla. Jr. Coll., Jacksonville, 1969—. Mem. Fla., (sec.-treas. 1970—), Jacksonville (pres. 1969-70) hotel and motel assns., Sigma Chi. Republican. Episcopalian. Mason (32 deg., Shriner). Clubs: Merinak (Jacksonville). Mailing Address: PO Box 4517 Jacksonville FL 32201 Home: 9116 Bay Cove Lane Jacksonville FL 32217 Office: PO Box 4517 Jacksonville FL 32201

KLOTZ, HERBERT WERNER, corp. exec.; b. Berlin, Germany, Feb. 24, 1917; s. Herbert and Gertrude (Koppel) Klotz; B.A., Zuoz (Switzerland) Coll., 1935; student U. Zurich (Switzerland), 1935-36; m. Patricia Radford Hopkins, Apr. 3, 1954; children—Radford Werner, Leslie Ritchie, James Taylor. Came to U.S., 1937, naturalized, 1944. With Smith, Barney & Co., and predecessor, N.Y.C., 1937-42, W.E. Hutton & Co., N.Y.C., 1946-48; engaged in mgmt. personal investments, 1949-52; with Winslow, Douglas & McEvoy, N.Y.C., 1953-54; pres., treas. Tex. Securities Corp., N.Y.C., 1954-57, Southwest Adv. Services, Inc. N.Y.C., 1954-57; with Alex Brown & Sons, Washington, 1957-60; spl. asst. to sec. commerce, 1961, dep. to sec. commerce, 1961-62, asst. sec. commerce for adminstrn., 1962-65; exec. v.p. Am. Growth Investment Co., 1966-67; dir. Govt. Systems Center, Kurt Salmon Assos., Inc.; mgmt. cons., 1968-69; pres. Quest Research Corp., 1970—. Dir. Nat. Com. Bus. and Profl. Men and Women for Kennedy-Johnson, 1960. Served to 1st lt. AUS, 1942-45; maj. Res. ret. Democrat. Episcopalian. Clubs: Nat. Press, 1925 F Street, Metropolitan, Federal City (Washington); Warrenton (Va.) Hunt, Fauquier. Home: 1404 Langley Pl McLean VA 22101 Office: 6845 Elm St McLean VA 22101

KLUD, LEON WILLIAM, economist, govt. ofcl.; b. Mena, Ark., Sept. 19, 1941; s. Leo Glenn and Hilta Abilene (Cogburn) K.; student U. Ore., 1959-61; B.A. cum laude, Seattle Pacific Coll., 1963; M. Govtl. Adminstrn. with honors (Pub. Finance Grad. fellow 1963-67), U. Pa., 1965, M.A., 1969, postgrad., 1965-70; m. Patricia Ann Nelson, Dec. 31, 1965. Economist, Joint Com. on Internal Revenue Taxation, U.S. Congress, Washington, 1967—. Mem. Am. Econ. Assn., Nat. Tax Assn., Am. Polit. Sci. Assn., Alpha Kappa Sigma, Beta Gamma Sigma. Mem. Open Bible Standard Ch. (trustee 1968-70, 71—, treas. 1971-72). Clubs: Wharton Graduate School, Capitol Hill Tennis (dir. 1971-72) (Washington). Home: 8431 Forrester Blvd Springfield VA 22152 Office: 5210 New Senate Bldg Washington DC 20510

KLUG, MERVIN LOWAIN, cons. hydrologist; b. North Bend, Neb., Nov. 10, 1924; s. Rhinehold P. and Edna (Witthinrich) K.; B.S., U. Neb., 1950; m. Velva Mae Multer, Nov. 24, 1949; 1 dau., Colleen (Mrs. James Hill). Hydraulic engr., ground water br. U.S. Geol. Survey, Lincoln, Neb., 1950-51, Neb., Kan., Colo., Mont., La., 1952-56; cons. ground water hydrologist William F. Guyton & Assos., Austin, Tex., 1956-61; cons., 1962—; asst. dir. ground water div. Tex. Water Commn., Austin, 1961-62. Served with AUS, 1943-46, C.E., AUS, 1951-52. Mem. Nat. Soc. Profl. Engrs., Am. Soc. C.E.s, Am. Geophys. Union, Nat. Water Well Drillers Assn. Lutheran. Home: 5811 Marilyn Dr Austin TX 78731 Office: 1st Fed Savings Bldg Austin TX 78701

KLUTTS, WILLIAM ALONZO, newspaper editor; b. Ripley, Tenn., June 26, 1928; s. Alonzo and Helen (Given) K.; A.B., U. Chgo., 1947, grad. student, 1947-49. With Chgo. bur. Asso. Press, 1945-49; editor, co-publisher The Lauderdale Co. Enterprise, Ripley, Tenn., 1949-65, editor, pub., 1966—, gen. mgr. Enterprise Comml. & Indsl. Supplies, Ripley, 1961—; v.p., dir. Ripley Devel. Corp. Vice chmn. Ripley Housing Authority, 1962-66, chmn., 1966-69, exec. dir., 1970—. Mem. nat. council Boy Scouts Am., 1955—, mem. W. Tenn. council, 1955-67; pres., 1958; pres. Consol. Charities, Inc., 1955—. Trustee Union U., Jackson, Tenn. 1960-65; adv. council Tenn. Civil War Centennial Commn., 1960-65. Served with AUS, 1950-52, capt. Res.; transferred to lt. USNR, 1966, now lt. comdr. Res. Coroner Lauderdale County, 1956—; exec. sec. West Tenn. Mayors Conf., 1961—. Winner 21 U. Tenn. press awards. Mem. Am. (life), W. Tenn. (life; v.p.) hist. socs., Tenn. Press Assn., Tenn. Future Farmers (hon.), C. of C. (pres. 1954). Baptist (deacon, trustee). Clubs: 30 (Memphis); Rotary (pres. 1957). Contbr. hist. articles profl. jours. Home: 157 Lake Dr Ripley TN 38063 Office: 145 E Jackson St Ripley TN 38063

KLUTTZ, JERRY, writer; b. Clinton, Mo., May 27, 1907; s. Lawson Milo and Adella (McKinney) K.; student Central Coll., Fayette, Mo., 1925-26, U. Mo., 1927-28; B.S., George Washington U., 1931; m. Electa Tassin, Mar. 19, 1935 (dec. July 1971); children—Gerald Eugene, John Lawson, James Edward; m. 2d, Virginia Wanvig Thatcher, Aug. 26, 1972. Reporter, Washington Herald, 1931; reporter Washington Daily News, 1932-40; editor Fed. Diary column Washington Post, 1940-70; founder Fed. Employee Newsletter, 1948, editor, 1948-70; conducted radio news programs, 1938-46. Recipient awards Washington Newspaper Guild, 1947, 53, Clapper-Edson award, 1949. Mem. Nat. Press Club, Fed. (pres.), White House corrs. assns., Internat. Platform Assn., Sigma Delta Chi. Sigma Chi. Club: Washington Golf and Country. Home: 3705 Lorcom Lane Arlington VA 22207 Office: 1515 L St NW Washington DC 20005

KNAPE, CLIFFORD STANLEY, psychologist; b. Austin, Tex., Dec. 7, 1916; s. Carl Johann and Edla (Widerstrom) K.; B.A., U. Tex., 1941, M.A., 1941; M.A., Baylor U., 1951; Ph.D., U. Tex., 1958; m. Anne Sabra Ramsey, May 30, 1942; children—Mildred Anne, Sabra Jane, Carl Guinn. Clk-psychometrist Rehab. div. Tex. Dept. Edn., Austin, 1935-37, parttime, 1937-41; psychologist U.S. VA, Waco, Tex., 1945-51, 53—, now chief psychology service; adj. prof. Baylor U., 1953—. Trustee, Waco Ind. Sch. Dist., 1964—, pres., 1969—; bd. mem. Tex. Rehab. Commn., 1969—. Served with USAAF, 1941-45, to maj. USAF, 1951-53. Mem. Am., Tex. psychol. assns., Nat., Tex. (pres. 1962-63) rehab. assns., McLennan Mental Health Assn. (pres. 1962-63), Tex. Assn. for Mental Health (v.p. for program 1964), Tex. Congress Parents and Tchrs. (state mental health chmn. 1962-65), Phi Beta Kappa. Democrat. Presbyn. Home: 1024 N 18-A St Waco TX 76707 Office: VA Hosp Waco TX 76703

KNAPE, GERALD BEARNDT, newspaper editor, pub.; b. Austin, Tex., Mar. 6, 1912; s. Otto and Hulda (Swenson) K.; student U. Tex., 1929-31; corr. student Nixon Clay Coll., 1932; 1 dau., Frances (Mrs. Robert Wimberley). With Tex. Posten, Austin, 1933—, editor, pub., 1961—. Mem. cav. Tex. N.G., 1931-34, 2d lt., 1967—. Decorated Order Conferred Vasa, Sweden; recipient 50th award Tex. Press Assn., 1965; named hon. commodore Tex. Tidelands Guard, 1953. Mem. Am. Legion Drum and Bugle Corps (drum maj. 1962—). Democrat. Methodist. Mason (32 deg., Shriner). Clubs: Austin Advertising (sec. 1935), Austin Optimist, Austin Scandinavian (pres. 1960). Composer: In the Mist and Fog I See a Light, 1959; Just Let Me Forget, 1963; Honky Tonk Gals from Wilbarger Creek, 1963. Home: 607 Theresa St Austin TX 78703 Office: 900 W Koenig Lane Austin TX 78765

KNAPP, DANIEL C., govt. ofcl.; b. Peoria, Ill., June 19, 1915; s. Christian and Nina (Fernsler) K.; B.A., Bradley U., 1937; M.A., U. Ill., 1938; grad. student Ohio State U., 1944-45; grad. Advanced Mgmt. Program, Harvard, 1962; m. Ruth Weinberger, Dec. 18, 1948; children—Theresa L., Karen D. Govt. intern Nat. Inst. Pub. Affairs, Washington, 1938-39; adminstrv. aide Social Security Bd., 1939-42; chief dept. recruitment and placement VA, 1946-51; exec. officer Dept. Army, Washington and Okinawa, 1951-62; joined U.S. Fgn. Service, 1962; dep. chief career devel. staff state dept., 1962-64, chief manpower resources staff, 1964-66; dir. manpower planning program, 1966-68; dir. personnel Consumer Protection and Environmental Health Service, Dept. Health, Edn. and Welfare, 1968-71; chief personnel policy Environmental Protection Agy., 1971—. Served to 1st lt. AUS, 1942-46. Mem. Am. Soc. Pub. Adminstrn., Soc. Personnel Adminstrn., Pub. Personnel Assn., Pi Gamma Mu. Contbr. articles profl. jours. Home: 15421 Carrolton Rd Rockville MD 20853 Office: Pub Health Service Dept Health Edn and Welfare Washington DC 20853

KNAPP, GEORGE HAWARD, communications supr.; b. Charleston, W.Va., July 31, 1920; s. Arthur O. and Leona (Wilson) K.; student pub. schs.; m. Juanita May Board, Mar. 22, 1956; children—Shirley (Mrs. Roy W. Gossett), Barry, David (by previous marriage). Technician Western Electric Co., Charleston, W.Va., 1941-42; engrs. aide Signal Corps Gen. Devel. Labs., Ft. Monmouth, N.J., 1942; transmitter engr. WTMA, Charleston, S.C., 1946-47; electronics specialist CAA, Charleston, 1947-55; supr. communications div. City of St. Petersburg, 1955—. Served with AUS, 1942-46. Mem. I.E.E.E., Internat. Platform Assn., Asso. Pub.-Safety Communications Officers. Home: 3990 20th St N St Petersburg FL 33714 Office: PO Box 2842 St Petersburg FL 33731

KNAPP, JOHN LAURENCE, govt. ofcl.; b. Washington, Sept. 30, 1935; s. Joseph Grant and Carol (West) K.; B.A., U. Colo., 1957; M.A., Duke, 1960; Ph.D., U. Va., 1970; m. Trilbie Lee Ferrell, Oct. 6, 1962; children—Laurence Freston, Paget Ferrell. Budget analyst U.S. Dept. Agr., 1960; asst. economist Fed. Res. Bank, Richmond, 1960-62; economist A. State of Va. Div. Indsl. Devel. and Planning, Richmond, 1962-66, economist B. Div. State Planning and Community Affairs, 1966, chief research sect., 1967-71, dep. dir., 1971—; instr. Univ. Coll. U. Richmond, 1962-64, 68-72. Served with AUS Res., 1959-65. Mem. Am., So. econ. assns., Phi Beta Kappa. Home: 8601 Julian Rd Richmond VA 23229 Office: 109 Governor St Richmond VA 23219

KNEECE, ROBERT EDWARD, lawyer; b. Columbia, S.C., Dec. 20, 1933; s. Otis Salter and Elise (Blackmon) K.; LL.B., U. S.C., 1958; m. Margaret Ann Medders, June 1, 1957; children—Melanie Carol, Robert Edward, Richard Otis, Milinda Kyle, Rexford Patrick, Margaret Ann. Admitted to S.C. bar, 1958; practiced in Columbia, 1958—; mem. firm Kneece, Kneece & Brown; mem. S.C. Gen. Assembly, 1966—. Dir. Raco Investments. Vice chmn. House Judiciary, 1969, Crime Study Com., 1968, Ins. Study Com., 1969. Mem. Am., S.C., Richland County bar assns., Am., S.C. trial lawyers assns., Columbia C. of C. Mason (Shriner). Club: Palmetto Sertoma, Columbia, S.C. Home: 4110 Parkman Dr Columbia SC 29205 Office: 1406 Bull St Columbia SC 29201

KNEEDLER, WILLIAM HARDING, physician; b. Phila., Aug. 13, 1900; s. Henry Martyn and Alice (Harding) K.; A.B., Princeton, 1922; M.D., U. Pa., 1926; postgrad. London Sch. Tropical Medicine and Hygiene, 1929-30; m. Christina Butler Harris, Apr. 30, 1930; children—Alice Harding (Mrs. J.J. Crate), Cornelia Harris (Mrs. I.B. Hudson Jr.), William Howard. Intern, Pa. Hosp., 1927-29; Presbyn. med. missionary, Thailand, 1930-41, 49-51; cons. tropical medicine Jefferson Hosp., Phila., 1942-47; practice internal medicine, Concord, N.C., 1951—; mem. staff Cabarrus Meml. Hosp., Concord, 1951—; asso. in medicine Jefferson Med. Sch., 1942-47. Diplomate Am. Bd. Internal. Medicine. Fellow A.C.P.; mem. A.M.A., Am. Soc. Internal Medicine. Home: 234 Scenic Dr NE Concord NC 28025 Office: 865 N Church St Concord NC 28025

KNEISEL, RICHARD SAMUEL, educator; b. Louisville, May 31, 1919; s. Robert R. and Lena (Tschopp) K.; B.A., U. Louisville, 1941; M.S. in Edn., U. Ind., 1950. postgrad., 1952-56, 65-66; m. Marjorie Walker, Feb. 25, 1943; children—Richard Craig, Kent Walker, Constance Gail. Chief chemist occupational health div. Ky. Dept. Health, Louisville, 1946-48; tchr., guidance counselor Louisville Pub. Schs., 1948-50; sec., then v.p. App, Johnson & Kneisel., Inc., analytical chemists, Louisville, 1946-51; tchr. Louisville Pub. Schs., 1952-57; edn1. adviser U.S. Army Chem. Sch., Ft. McClellan, Ala., 1957-68; spl. asst. edn. adviser U.S. Army Inf. Sch. Ft. Benning, Ga., 1968—. Served to capt. AUS, 1943-46; 50-51; PTO. Decorated Bronze Star medal. Dept. Army fellow Indiana U., 1965-66. Mem. Am. Personnel and Guidance Assn., Nat. Vocational Guidance Assn., Ky. Personnel and Guidance Assn. (pres. 1955), Louisville Edn. Assn. (v.p. 1954), Assn. U.S. Army, Nat. Soc. for Programmers Instrn., Mil. Testing Assn., Am. Soc. Tng. Dirs., Assn. Supervision Curriculum Devel., Phi Delta Kappa, Theta Chi Delta. Contbr. articles to profl. jours. Home: 5908 Canterbury Dr Columbus GA 31904 Office: US Army Inf Sch Fort Benning GA 31905

KNEZ, EUGENE IRVING, anthropologist; b. Clinton, Ind., May 12, 1916; s. Edward and Ida (Bosonetto) Pearson; A.B., U. N.M., 1941; postgrad. Ind. U., 1941, Yale, 1948, U. Wash., 1949; Ph.D., Syracuse U., 1959; m. Jiae Choi, Mar. 15, 1952; children—Pamela, Alan. Chief, Nat. Bur. Culture, Am. Mil. Govt. in Korea, 1945-46; mus. positions with grad. work Yale Peabody Mus., Wash. State Mus., 1948-49; cultural affairs officer, regional pub. affairs officer Am. embassies, Korea and Japan, 1949-53; instr., lectr. Hunter Coll. and Syracuse U., 1954-59; anthropologist, asso. curator Asian anthropology Smithsonian Instn., Washington, 1959—. Served to capt. AUS, World War II, now lt. col. Res. Decorated Bronze Star medal; recipient Smithsonian Instn. Spl. award, 1965, Republic of Korea commendation, 1962, Asia Found. fellow, 1958. Fellow Am. Anthrop. Assn.; mem. Anthrop. Soc. Washington (former treas.), Smithsonian Senate of Scientists (former councilor), Am.-Korea Soc. Washington (chmn.), Japan-Am. Soc. Washington, A.A.A.S. Author: Korean Mutual Aid Groups: Persistence and Change; A South Korean Village:Sam Jong Dong; sr. author: A Selected and Annotated Bibliography of Korean Anthropology, 1968. Home: 2939 Newark St NW Washington DC 20008 Office: Smithsonian Instn Washington DC 20560

KNEZEVICH, VLADIMIR JOHN, cons. engr.; b. Newcomerstown, O., July 20, 1937; s. Joe Vladimir and Ann (Shirila) K.; B. Indsl. Engring., Ga. Inst. Tech., 1960; postgrad. U. Miami, 1963; m. Wilmeth Gail Austin, Dec. 26, 1958 (div. Jan. 1967); children—Kim, John William; m. 2d, Geraldine Ann Palacino, Apr. 24, 1970. Plant engr. Aerodex, Inc., Miami, Fla., 1960-63, chief engr., 1964-68; project field engr. Aerojet Gen., Homestead, Fla., 1963-64; cons. engr. Howard Needles, Tammen & Bergendoff, Miami, 1968—; chmn. bd. Designs Internat., Miami, 1967—. Cons. engring. pvt. practice, Miami, 1968—; pres. Dovla Corp., Miami Shores, 1972—. Registered profl. engr., Fla. Mem. Greater Miami Jr. C. of C., Nat. Soc. Profl. Engrs., Fla. Engring. Soc. Home: 711 NE 93d St Miami Shores FL 33138 Office: PO Box 2098 AMF Miami FL 33159

KNIGHT, ALLEN MARVIN, machinery co. exec.; b. Los Angeles, Oct. 6, 1931; s. Fredick Allen and Louise (Marvin) K.; B.S. in E.E., U. Tex., 1951; m. Edrie Bradley, May 16, 1959; children—Cheryl Dane, Tracy Allen. Staff engr. Western Electric Co., Chgo., 1955-56; field engr. L. E Wooten Cons. Engrs., Raleigh, N.C., 1956-57; v.p. Carolina Communications Engrs., Statesville, N.C., 1957-63; v.p. Garrison Machinery Co., Statesville, N.C., 1963—, also dir.; dir. Electromec, Statesville. Served with USN, 1951-54. Mem. Am. Mgmt. Assn., Numerical Control Soc. Mason, Elk. Patentee in field. Home: 603 Georgia Av Statesville NC 28677 Office: PO Drawer 391 Statesville NC 28677

KNIGHT, BILLY ROWE, supt. schs.; b. Garner, Tex., Dec. 23, 1933; s. Roy Abner and Martha Cordalia (Holder) K.; A.A., Weatherford Coll., 1957; B.S., North Tex. State U., 1958, M.Ed., 1961; Ph.D., East Tex. State U., 1970; m. Shirlene Leach, Jan. 25, 1958; children—William Mathis, Roland Scott, Joseph Blake. Tchr., Weatherford (Tex.) Ind. Sch. Dist., 1958-61; prin. Millsap (Tex.) High Sch., 1961-65; supt. Saltillo Rural High Sch. Dist., 1965-69, Mineola (Tex.) Ind. Sch. Dist., 1970—. Asst. instr. East Tex. State U., Commerce, 1969-70. Bd. dirs. Mineola (Tex.) Youth Found., Edn. Adv. Com., East Tex. Council Govts. Served with AUS, 1954-56. NSF grantee, 1960. Mem. Am., Tex. assns. sch. adminstrs., Tex. State Tchrs. Assn., So. Assn. Colls. and Schs. (dist. dir. 1970-71), East Tex. Sch. Study Council (dir. 1971-72), Phi Delta Kappa. Methodist (edn. chmn. 1971-72). Mason, Rotarian. Home: 251 Sue Lane Mineola TX 75773 Office: PO Box 360 Mineola TX 75773

KNIGHT, CHARLES RICHARD, gas co. exec.; b. Cleve., Feb. 10, 1920; s. Claude M. and Margarite (Weimer) K.; B.A., Miami U., 1941; M.S. (Alfred P. Sloan fellow), U. Denver, 1942; m. Doris Jane Lamp, Sept. 9, 1941; children—Elizabeth Jane, Charles Richard. Asst. dir. Ala. Legislative Reference Service, Montgomery, 1946-50; dir. research Ala. C. of C., Montgomery, 1950-53; market analyst T.C.I. div. U.S. Steel Corp., Birmingham, Ala., 1953-57, mgr. comml. research, 1957-64; asst. to pres. Ala. Gas Corp., Birmingham, 1964-69, v.p., asst. sec., 1969—. Chmn. Ala. Bus. Research Council, 1965-67. Bd. dirs. Operation New Birmingham. Served to lt. comdr. Supply Corps, USNR, 1942-46. Mem. Am. Marketing Assn., U.S. C. of C., Sigma Nu. Methodist. Club: Exchange Mount Brook, Ala. Home: 94 Crestview Dr Mount Brook AL 35213 Office: 1918 First Av N Birmingham AL 35203

KNIGHT, DELOS LAVERN, JR., pub. relations exec.; b. Bogalusa, La., July 3, 1931; s. Delos Lavern and Ruth (Vineyard) K.; B.A., La. State U., 1952; m. Margaret Frances Rucker, Apr. 10, 1955; children—Delos Lavern III, Kevin T., Anne Ruth, Timothy O. Program dir. radio sta. WIKC, Bogalusa, La., 1954-59; pub. relations

1950. Control chemist Cities Service Refining Co., Braintree, Mass., 1928-29; instr. geology Tufts U., Medford, Mass., 1929-38; recorder U.S. Geol. Survey, Boston, 1939-40; research geologist Assos. of Sci., Harvard, Cambridge, Mass., 1940-42; petroleum geologist Continental Oil Co., Corpus Christi, Tex., 1944; topographic engr. U.S. Geol. Survey, Washington, 1944-52, cartographer, 1952-58, 59-63, geologist, 1959, 63-65; staff cartographer U.S. Bd. on Geographic Names, Washington, 1965—. Olmstead teaching fellow Tufts U., 1927-28, trustees scholar, 1938-39; instr., lectr. Ferry Beach Nature Inst., Saco, Me., 1939-42; dean, 1940-41. Chmn. troop com. Boy Scouts of Am., 1940-41, dist. chmn. sr. scouting, 1941-42. Served with AUS, 1942-43. Fellow Am. Geographic Soc., A.A.A.S., Geol. Soc. Am.; mem. Antarctican Soc., Am. Polar Soc., Am. Soc. Photogrammetry, Am. Assn. Stratigraphic Palynologists, Geol. Soc. Washington, Washington Acad. Scis., Am. Legion, Amvets (founding mem.). Universalist. Home: 2006 Columbia Rd NW Washington DC 20009 Office: Geol Survey Washington DC 20242

KNOX, JOHN GILL, JR., newspaper cartoonist; b. Nashville, Aug. 18, 1910; s. John Gill and Sarah (Sperry) K.; grad. high sch.; m. Edith McCulloch Towler, Apr. 7, 1930; children—John Gill III, Joseph Towler, Phoebe Brownell (Mrs. Robert E. Binkley), Britt Alley. Editorial cartoonist Nashville Evening Tennessean, 1933-34, Memphis Comml. Appeal, 1934-45, Nashville Banner, 1946—. Author, illustrator Riverman, 1971. Home: 2528 Blair Blvd Nashville TN 37212 Office: 1100 Broad St Nashville TN 37202

KNOX, WILLIAM T., govt. ofcl.; B.A., Mercer U.; M.A., Va. Poly. Inst. With Esso Research and Engring. Co., 1938-64; with Office Sci. and Tech. Exec. Office Pres., Washington, 1964-66; v.p. McGraw-Hill, Inc., from 1966; now dir. Nat. Tech. Information Service, Dept. Commerce. Chmn. Council Communication Smithsonian Instn. Mem. Information Industry Assn. (founder; pres.). Address: 3565 Hamlet Pl Chevy Chase MD 20015*

KNUDSEN, KNUD JOHANNES, elec. engr.; b. Sonderho, Denmark, Mar. 15, 1899; s. Henrik and Carolina (Johanson) K.; Examin Artium in Math. and Phys. Sci., State Sch. of Randers, 1919; E.E., Internat. Corr. Schs., 1931; m. Else Lange, Aug. 14, 1928. Came to U.S., 1937, naturalized, 1942. Chief engr. Hickok Elec. Instrument Co., 1937-42; chief instrument engr. Halsey Taylor Co., 1942-43; research engr. U.S. Time Corp., Waterbury, Conn., 1943-44; chief electronics engr. Lewis Engring. Co., Naugatuck, Conn., 1944-48, chief engr., 1948-63, dir. engring., 1963-64, hon. dir. engring., 1964-69; cons. profl. engr., Daytona Beach, Fla., 1969—. Mem. Radio Amateur Civil Emergency Service, Civil Def., 1953-58. Served to 2d lt., F.A., Denmark, 1920-24, army A.C., 1926. Recipient Best Paper prize, Initial Paper prize, McCutcheon award, Am. Inst. Elec. Engrs., 1942; Distinguished Achievement award USAF, 1956. Registered profl. engr., Conn., Fla., Ohio. Fellow I.E.E.E. (life); mem. Cleve. Engrs. Soc. (life), Fla. Engring. Soc., Nat. (life), Conn. socs. profl. engrs. Mason (32 deg., Shriner). Patentee in field. Address: 102 Venetian Way Daytona Beach FL 32019

KNUTSON, GERALD LOYD, univ. adminstr.; b. McLean, Tex., June 8, 1929; s. Youel A. and Margaret J. (Malone) K.; A.A., Graceland Jr. Coll., 1949; student West Tex. State U., 1949-50; B.S., Central Mo. State Coll., 1955, M.S. in Edn., 1956; Ph.D., U. Okla., 1968; m. Norma Audette Smoot, June 7, 1953; children—Linda Kaye, Gary Lynn. Pub. sch. tchr., adminstr., 1955-58; agt. Southwestern Life Ins. Co., Tulsa, 1958-67; instr. U. Okla., Norman, 1967-68, dir. research in gerontology, Extension, Tulsa, 1968-69; dir. ednl. services Okla. State U., 1969—. Cons., Okla. White House Conf. on Aging, since 1970—. Bd. advisers Okla. State U. Student Union. Served with USNR, 1950-54. Grantee in gerontology Dept. Health, Edn. and Welfare, 1958-59. Mem. Adult Edn. Assn., Nat. Assn. for Pub. Continuing and Adult Edn., Phi Delta Kappa. Mem. Reorganized Ch. of Jesus Christ of Latter-day Saints. Rotarian. Home: 1102 N Lincoln St Stillwater OK 74074

KNUTSON, LLOYD VERNON, entomologist; b. Ottawa, Ill., July 4, 1934; s. Floyd Vernon and Jennie Joanna (Valesano) K.; A.B., Macalester Coll., 1957; M.S., Cornell U., 1959, Ph.D., 1963; m. Priscilla Ann Jones, June 8, 1957; children—David, Kari. Research asso. dept. entomology Cornell U., Ithaca, N.Y., 1963-68; research entomologist Systematic Entomol. Lab. U.S. Dept. Agr., Washington, 1968—; resident ecologist Office Ecology Smithsonian Inst., 1971-72. Sci. collaborator Inst. Royal Sci. Nat. Belgique, Brussels. Mem. entomol. socs. Am., Copenhagen, Washington, Fla., Soc. Systematic Zool. Democrat. Baptist. Club: Torch (Washington). Contbr. articles in field to sci. jours. Home: 6005 Welborn Dr Washington DC 20016 Office: Systematic Entomol Lab US Dept Agr US Nat Mus Washington DC 20560

KOBAYASHI, KENJI, violinist; b. Tokyo, Japan, Sept. 5, 1933; s. Yonesaku and Reiko (Hasegawa) K.; came to U.S., 1952; student Julliard Sch. Music, 1952-59; m. Hiroko Kobayashi. Soloist Tokyo Philharmonic Orch., 1950, Nat. Orchestra Assn., Carnegie Hall, N.Y.C., 1957, Juilliard Orch. spring tour, 1959, N.C. Symphony, 1960; recitals at Town Hall, N.Y.C., 1961, Darmstadt (Germany) Contemporary Music Festival, 1961; Concertgebouw, Amsterdam, Holland, 1961; soloist Osaka (Japan) Philharmonic, 1964, Japan Philharmonic, 1965, New Orleans Philharmonic, 1966; mem. string faculty Toho U., Tokyo, 1963—; concertmaster Oklahoma City Symphony, 1967—; artist-in-residence Oklahoma City U., 1967—. Recipient award 1 Hr. Music N.Y.C., 1960. Home: 2410 NW 35th St Oklahoma City OK 73112 Office: Civic Center Music Hall Oklahoma City OK 73102

KOBB, ALEX, dentist; b. N.Y.C., May 28, 1938; s. Louis and Gladys (Landsman) Kobrinetz; B.A., Harpur Coll., 1959; D.D.S., Temple U., 1964; m. Marcia Lynn Goldberg, June 9, 1962; children—Amy Jo, Wendy Lee. Leukemia research asst. Downstate Med. Center, Bklyn., 1959-60; practice dentistry, Hollywood, Fla., 1966—; mem. staff Hollywood (Fla.) Meml. Hosp. Mem. Dade County Dental Research Inst., Miami, 1969—. Campaign worker Jewish Welfare Fedn., Hollywood, Fla., 1967-71; v.p. Young Leaders Council, 1961-72. Bd. dirs. Anti-Defamation League. Served with USNR, 1964-66. Recipient Alumni award Temple U. Sch. Dentistry, 1964. Mem. Am. Dental Assn., Acad. Gen. Dentistry, East Coast Dist. Dental Soc., Fla. Dental Assn., Am. Soc. Preventive Dentistry, Greater Hollywood Dental Soc. (treas. 1972-73), Jewish War Vets. Jewish religion. Home: 622 N Rainbow Dr Hollywood FL 33021 Office: 3816 Hollywood Blvd Hollywood FL 33021

KOBOR, ANNE DIRKES, editor. Illustration editor Nat. Geog. Soc., Washington. Address: Nat Geog Soc 17th and M Sts NW Washington DC 20036*

KOCH, JOHN SUMNER, lawyer; b. Chgo., Dec. 10, 1931; s. Summer Leibnitz and Lucille (Baumann) K.; grad. Phillips Acad., Andover, 1949; A.B., Yale, 1953; J.D., Northwestern U., 1959; m. Constance Chadwell, Oct. 1, 1955; children—Anne Elizabeth, John Sumner, Sarah Grace, Peter Chadwell. Editor, Conn. Shore; 1951; reporter City News Bur. Chgo., Chgo. Daily News, 1955-56; admitted to Ill. bar, 1959, D.C. bar, 1960; asso. Covington & Burling, Washington, 1959-68, partner, 1968—. Mem. Am. Bar Assn., Bar Assn. D.C., Am. Judicature Soc., Aurelian Honor Soc., Scroll and Key. Clubs: University (Chgo.); Yale (N.Y.C.); National Lawyers, City Tavern; Fence; Elizabethan. Home: 2952 Macomb St NW Washington DC 20008 Office: 888 16th St NW Washington DC 20006

KOCH, RONNEY RAY, petroleum engr.; b. Cape Girardeau, Mo., Mar. 29, 1933; s. Calvin John and Mamie (Margraf) K.; B.S. in Chemistry, S.E. Mo. State Coll., 1954; B.S. in Petroleum Engring., U. Okla., 1960; m. Patricia Ione Woody, Feb. 11, 1961; children—Sally Lynn, Carolyn Kay. Chemist, Reynolds Metals Co., Richmond, Va., 1957; engr. Cal. Co., Barataria, La., 1960; engr., devel. engr., group leader Halliburton Services, Duncan, Okla., 1960—. Served with AUS, 1955-57. Registered profl. engr., Okla. Mem. Soc. Petroleum Engrs., Am. Inst. Mining, Metall. and Petroleum Engrs., Tau Beta Pi, Pi Epsilon Tau. Republican. Lutheran (elder, v.p. congregation). Patentee in field. Home: Route 1 Box 255 Duncan OK 73533 Office: PO Drawer 1431 Duncan OK 73533

KOCHAKIAN, CHARLES DANIEL, endocrinologist. educator; b. Haverhill, Mass., Nov 18, 1908; s. Daniel S. and Haigoohee (Nalbandian) K.; A.B., Boston U., 1930, M.A., 1931; Ph.D., U. Rochester, 1936; m. Beatrice Irene Armstrong, July 27, 1940; 1 son, Charles Pedlar. Fellow, U. Rochester (N.Y.) Sch. Medicine and Dentistry, 1933-36, instr. Physiology, 1936-40, asso., 1940-44, asst. prof., 1944-47, asso. prof., 1947-51; prof. research biochemistry U. Okla. Sch. Medicine, 1951-57, head biochemistry and endocrinology, 1951-57; asso. dir. Okla. Med. Research Found., Oklahoma City, 1951-53, coordinator research, 1953-55; prof. physiology U. Ala. Med. Center, Birmingham, 1957-61, 65—, prof. biochemistry, 1961—, prof., dir. exptl. endocrinology, 1961—, acting coordinator research, 1960-61. Fellow A.A.A.S.; mem. Am. Soc. Biol. Chemists, Am. Physiol. Soc., Endocrine Soc., Soc. Exptl. Biology and Medicine, Am. Chem. Soc., Sigma Xi (chpt. sec.-treas. 1942-46, chpt. pres. 1964-65). Presbyn. (elder). Home: 3617 Oakdale RD Birmingham AL 35223 Office: 1919 7th Av S Birmingham AL 35233

KOCHER, JOEL OWEN, city ofcl.; b. Galena, Kan., Sept. 21, 1902; s. Daniel Shanor and Cora (Cullifer) K.; grad. high sch.; m. Anna Margaret Rutherford, Feb. 11, 1940; 1 son, John J. Traffic officer, mgr. Brand Dunwoody Milling Co., Joplin, Mo., 1922-29; mgr. grain dept. Gen. Mills, Incs., Wichita Falls, Tex., 1930-34, Houston, 1935, Wichita, Kan., 1936-56, Enid, Okla., 1957-62; exec. sec., treas. Enid Bd. Trade, 1963—. Recipient Meritorious Service award Okla. 4-H Club, 1966. Mem. Nat. grain Trade Council, Okla. Grain and Feed Dealer Assn. (treas., exec. sec. 1971—), Grain and Feed Dealers Nat. Assn., Nat. Indsl. Traffic League. Republican. Presbyn. (elder). Kiwanian. Club: Oakwood Country. Home: 110 S Coolidge St Enid OK 73701 Office: 1st Nat Bank Bldg Enid OK 73701

KOCIAN, CHARLES JOSEPH, statistician; b. Lansford, Penn., Mar. 31, 1921; s. Emerich S. and Mary (Pavlacka) K.; B.S., Lycoming Coll., 1950; postgrad. Am. U., intermittently 1950—; m. Jean M. Costenbader, Nov. 11, 1950. Statistician welfare, retirement fund United Mine Workers Am., Washington, 1950-61, dental pub. health and research Dept. Health, Edn. and Welfare, 1961, Mil. Sea Transp. Service, USN, 1961-63; supervisory statistician Rural Electrification Adminstrn. U.S. Dept. Agr., 1963-65, Office Surgeon Gen., U.S. Army, 1965—. Dir.Capitol Investment Corp., 1959-60. Served with AUS, 1942-45. Mem. Am. Econ. Assn., Am. Statis. Assn., Nat. Assn. Accountants, Fed. Profl. Assn. Methodist. Mason (32 degree); mem. Order Eastern Star. Patentee steering controlled automobile headlights. Home: 2000 F St NW Washington DC 20006 Office: Forrestal Bldg 10th and Independence Av Washington DC 20315

KOEHLER, ROBERT EARL, editor; b. Oconomowoc, Wis., July 6, 1924; s. George John and Ida Mae (Watterson) K.; B.A., U. Wis., 1948. Asst. editor The Feed Bag, Milw., 1948-49; publicity dir. Spencerian Coll., Milw., 1949-52; asso. editor The Confectioner, Milw., 1952-53; editorial asst. Pacific Builder & Engr., Seattle, 1953-54; editor Architecture/West, Seattle, 1954-62; asso. editor, mng. editor A.I.A. Jour., Washington, 1962-65, editor, 1965—. Recipient Outstanding Publ. award for artwork, layout and makeup Western Soc. Bus. Publs., 1959. Mem. A.I.A. (hon.), Wis. Alumni Assn., Sigma Delta Chi. Editor: 50th Anniversary Annual of The Mountaineers, 1956. Contbg. author to Parents Mag. Yearbook, 1966-70. Home: 1748 Corcoran St NW Washington DC 20009 Office: 1735 New York Av Washington DC 20006

KOENIG, HAROLD PAUL, ecologist; b. Mason City, Ia., Apr. 22, 1926; s. Reuben Harold and Dorothea (Paule) K.; student Ohio Wesleyan U., 1944-45; B.S., Ia. State U., 1947; M.S., Ill. Inst. Tech., 1956; M. Georgia Leisure, Aug. 31, 1947. Asso., Booz Allen & Hamilton, Inc., Chgo., Zurich, Switzerland, 1956-64; asst. to pres. Dresser Industries, Inc., Dallas, 1964, pres. Roots Connersville (Ind.) div., 1964-66, v.p. corporate planning, 1966-67; chmn., pres., chief exec. officer, dir., mem. exec. com. Ecol. Sci. Corp., Miami, Fla., 1967—, dir., officer subsidiaries and affiliates, 1967—. Mem. U.S. Congress ad hoc com. on environmental quality, 1968—. Served with USNR, 1944-46, 51-53. Registered profl. engr., Fla., Ia., Ill., Ind., Minn. Mem. Phi Gamma Delta. Elk, Mason. Methodist. Clubs: Lancers (Dallas); Jockey, Surf (both Miami). Office: 20215 NW 2d Av Miami FL 33169

KOENIG, NATHAN, econs. cons.; b. N.Y.C., Mar. 20, 1907; s. Samuel and Lena (Penner) K.; B.S., U. Conn., 1930; m. Rose Edith Rosenblum, Nov. 24, 1929; children—Judith Barbara (Mrs. Alvin P. Wolfman), Susan Ruth (Mrs. Fredric J. Freed), Martha Jean (Mrs. Stuart L. Bindeman). Agrl. pub., writing, 1930-33; pub. information work U.S. Dept. Agr., Washington, 1933-43; agrl. editor U.S. News and World Report, Washington, 1943-45; exec. asst. to U.S. Sec. Agr., Washington, 1945-48, asst. to sec., confidential asst. to asst. sec. Marketing and Fgn. Agr., Washington, 1948-54; spl. asst. to adminstr. Consumer and Marketing Service, U.S. Dept. Agr., Washington, 1954-65; econ. cons., 1965—. Mem. U.S. Food and Agr. Survey Mission, Japan, Korea, 1947; mem. U.S. delegation spl. cereals conf. Internat. Emergency Food Council, Paris, 1947; rep. U.S. Govt. numerous internat. confs. on internat. food standards. Recipient U.S. Dept. Agr. Superior Service award, 1955, Distinguished Alumni award U. Conn., 1965. Mem. Am. Agr. Econ. Assn., Soc. Internat. Devel., Am. Acad. Polit. and Social Sci., Acad. Polit. Sci., N.J. Agrl. Soc., Pi Kappa Delta, Phi Epsilon Pi. Clubs: National Press, International of Washington. Writer numerous articles, reports in field. Home: 4501 Connecticut Av Washington DC 20008

KOESTER, ENGELBERT LEO, r.r. exec.; b. Cin., Apr. 19, 1913; s. Henry Bernard and Amelia Florence (Klaine) K.; B.A., Xavier U., 1934; m. Helen G. Keefe, Dec. 26, 1942; children—Leacarol (Mrs. Dennis Larkin), Thomas L., Stephen K., David K. Newspaper reporter Cin. Times Star, 1935-46; pub. relations dir. Cin. C. of C., 1946-54; pub. relations dir. Crosley div. Avco Mfg., 1954-60; indsl. devel. mgr. State of Ky., Louisville & Nashville R.R. Co., 1968—. Mem. pub. relations com. Hoover Commn. for Govt. Reorgn., 1956-58; vice-chmn. Ky. Indsl. Devel. Council, 1966-67. Mem. R.R. Pub. Relations Assn., Pub. Relations Soc. Am. (v.p. Bluegrass chpt. 1970-71), Xavier U. Alumni Assn. (pres. 1954). Democrat. Roman Catholic. Contbr. articles to profl. jours. Home: 710 Wicklow Rd Louisville KY 40207 Office: 908 W Broadway Louisville KY 40201

KOHLER, CHARLOTTE, editor; b. Richmond, Va., Sept. 16, 1908; d. Edwin Charles and Augusta F. (Bromm) K.; B.A., Vassar Coll., 1929; M.A., U. Va., 1933, Ph.D., 1936; Litt.D., Smith Coll., 1971. Instr. English, Woman's Coll., U. N.C., 1936-41, asst. prof., 1941-42; mng. editor Va. Quar. Rev., 1942-46, editor, 1946—; asso. prof. English, U. Va., 1965-71, prof., 1971—. Mem. Am. Assn. U. Women, Phi Beta Kappa. Home: 1900 Edgewood Lane Charlottesville VA 22903 Office: One W Range Charlottesville VA 22903

KOHLER, DONALD FROEHLICH, banker; b. Louisville, Apr. 27, 1931; s. Herbert R. and Marie F. (Froehlich) K.; A.B., Princeton, 1953; m. Mary Peabody Mobley, June 1, 1957; children—Elizabeth Fontaine, Mary Peabody, Donald Froehlich. Spl. agt. Northwestern Mut. Life Ins. Co., Milw., 1953-54; v.p. Ky. Trust Co., Louisville, 1956—, First Nat. Bank, Louisville, 1956—; pres. First Ky. Co., Louisville, 1956—; also dir.; dir. Levi Tyler Land Co., T &H Corp., Louisville. Bd. dirs. Rehab. Center, Inc., Louisville, U. Louisville Med. Center; trustee St. Francis Sch., Louisville. Served with AUS, 1954-56. Mem. Am. Inst. Banking. Episcopalian. Clubs: Pendennis, Harmony Landing Country, Owl Creek Country. Home: 146 Westwind Rd Louisville KY 40207 Office: 216 S 5th St Louisville KY 40207

KOHLHOFF, RALPH, govt. ofcl. Dir. div. cultural affairs Fla. Fine Arts Council, Tallahassee. Address: Fine Arts Council Fla The Capitol Tallahassee FL 32304*

KOHLMEIER, CLARENCE FRED, dentist; b. Mackey, Ind., Jan. 20, 1889; s. Fred Ludwig and Susan Catherine (Luehring) K.; student Lockyear's Bus. Coll., 1907-08; D.D.S., Georgetown U., 1916. Practice dental surgery, Washington, 1917—. Bd. dirs. Central Union Mission. Served from 1st lt. to capt. D.R.C., AEF, 1917-19. Mem. Nat. Dental Assn., D.C. Dental Soc. Republican. United Methodist

KOHLMEIER, LOUIS MARTIN, JR., newspaper reporter; b. St. Louis, Feb. 17, 1926; s. Louis Martin and Anita (Werling) K.; B.J., U. Mo., 1950; m. Barbara Anne Wilson, Nov. 15, 1958; children—Daniel Kimbrell, Ann Werling. Staff writer Wall Street Jour., St. Louis and Chgo., 1952-57, Washington, 1960—; staff writer St. Louis Globe-Democrat, 1958-59. Served with AUS, 1950-52. Recipient Nat. Headliners Club award nat. reporting, 1959, Sigma Delta Chi award Washington corr., 1964, Pulitzer prize nat. reporting, 1964. Author: The Regulators— Watchdog Agencies and the Public Interest, 1969. Home: 5902 Madawaska Rd Washington DC 20016 Office: 1015 14th St NW Washington DC 20005

KOHN, JOHN P., JR., lawyer; b. Montgomery, Ala., Dec. 27, 1902; s. John P. and Clementina R. (Cram) K.; ed. Starkes Univ. Sch., Montgomery; St. Louis U.; Spring Hill Coll.; LL.B., U. of Ala., 1925; m. Margaret Thorington, Mar. 6, 1937; 1 dau., Margaret T. In practice of law 1925—; county atty., 1946-64, 68—; spl. atty. for Ala. gov., 1964-65; asso. justice Spl. Supreme Ct. Ala., 1968. Capt. Ala. N.G. 1936; served with U.S. Armed Forces, 1940-45. Mem. Am., Ala., Montgomery (pres. 1931) bar assns., State Dem. Exec. Com. (to fill term 1935), S.A.R., Phi Delta Theta. Clubs: Beauvoir Country (Montgomery), Young Democrats of Alabama (pres. 1933-39), National Young Democratic of America (legal adviser, 1936), Soc. Pioneers of Montgomery (pres. 1958), Men of Montgomery. Author: The Voters Primer, 1939; The Cradle, An Anatomy of A Town, Fact and Fiction, 1969. Home: 2542 Woodly Rd Montgomery AL 36111 Office: 515 S Perry St Montgomery AL 36104

KOHN, RAYMOND F., govt. ofcl. Exec. sec. U.S. Nat. Commn. for UNESCO, Dept. State, Washington. Address: Nat Commn UNESCO Dept State Washington DC 20520*

KOLAR, RONALD EDWARD, constrn. co. exec.; b. Englewood, N.J., Nov. 2, 1936; s. Edward A. and Sara Jane (Emerick) K.; B.S. in Civil Engring., Northwestern U., 1959; m. Janet Sue Harrell, Aug. 15, 1964; children—Eric Scott, Alan Edward. Project engr. B.B. McCormick & Sons, Contractors, Jacksonville Beach, Fla., 1963-65, contract adminstr., 1965-68, v.p., 1968—. Served to lt., C.E., USNR, 1959-63. Registered profl. engr., Fla., Vt. Mem. Am. Soc. C.E., Soc. Am. Mil. Engrs., Alpha Delta Phi. Presbyn. Home: 326 Pablo Rd Ponte Vedra Beach FL 32082 Office: PO Box 248 Jacksonville Beach FL 32250

KOLB, AVERY EGGER, govt. ofcl., author; b. Hattiesburg, Miss., May 14, 1921; s. Avery Egger and Mattie (Giles) K.; student U. So. Miss., 1939-40, Cite U., Paris, 1945, Northwestern U., 1954, Indsl. Coll. Armed Forces, 1967-68, George Washington U., 1968-69; m. Joan Richards, Sept. 19, 1946; children—Avery E. III, Elaine (Mrs. Clifton J. Achee), Jean, June, Evan Richards, Joyce. Artist-author New Orleans, 1945; agt. Eastern Airlines, New Orleans, 1946-48; plans ofcl. Dept. Army, Washington, 1948-56; moblzn. staff ICC, 1956-59; nat. resources planning officer OCDM, 1959-61; economist Office of Emergency Planning, 1962-69; chief guidance and review div. Office Emergency Preparedness, 1969—; free-lance writer, pub., 1959—. Dir. Musart, allied arts instrn., Fairfax, Va. Served to lt. col. AUS, 1940-45. Decorated Croix de Guerre with palm, 1945. Author: Jigger Whitchet's War, 1959. Contbr. articles in field to profl. jours. Home: 6417 Julian St Springfield VA 22150 Office: Office Emergency Preparedness Washington DC 20504

KOLB, CHARLES RUDOLPH, govt. ofcl.; b. Vicksburg, Miss., Apr. 14, 1920; s. Karl and Theresa (Thiel) K.; B.S. in Geology, La. State U., 1947, M.S. in Geology, 1949, Ph.D. in Geology, 1959; m. Bertha Ragsdale, Oct. 9, 1951; 1 son, Charles H. Geologist, Fredrick Snare Engring. Corp., Santiago, Chile, 1949-50; geologist U.S. Army Engr. Waterways Expt. Sta., Vicksburg, 1950-53, asst. chief geology br., 1953-56, chief geology br., 1956-62, chief geology br. Waterways Expt. Sta., 1965—; research scientist, chief environmental scis. div. Research and Devel. Office, Alaska, 1963-64. Lectr. various univs.; instr. Vicksburg Grad. Center, Miss. State U., 1967—; cons. engring geology, 1956—; cons., expert witness engring. geology and litigation Mississippi River Delta and Flood plain, 1965—. Served with USAAF, 1943-45. Decorated Air medal with four oak leaf clusters, D.F.C. with two oak leaf clusters; recipient superior sustained performance award Dept. Army, 1958, Outstanding Performance award, 1963 award for best paper Jour. Sediment Petrology, 1954, best paper award Gulf Coast Geol. Socs., 1965. Fellow Geol. Soc. Am. (chmn. river engring. panel, mem. publs. com.), A.A.A.S.; mem. Am. Inst. Profl. Geologists, Am. Assn. Petroleum Geologists, Miss. Geol. Soc., Internat. Soc. Sedimentation, C. of C., Sigma Xi. Lion. Club: Engineers (pres.) (Vicksburg). Contbr. numerous articles to profl. jours. Home: 3314 Highland Dr Vicksburg MS 39180 Office: Geology Waterways Expt Sta Vicksburg MS 39180

KOLB, JOHN GEORGE, savs. and loan exec.; b. Washington, Nov. 25, 1904; s. John J. and Marie Salome (Jung) K.; B.S., Wharton Sch. Finance and Commerce, U. Pa., 1927; m. Madaline Victoria Showalter, Oct. 6, 1934; children—John George, Ronald Victor. Treas. Oriental Bldg. Assn., 1938-61, pres., 1961—. Mem. Theta Xi.

Mason. Home: 1909 Upshur St NW Washington DC 20011 Office: 600 F St NW Washington DC 20004

KOLB, KENNETH CARLTON, advt. agy. exec.; b. New Orleans, Feb. 20, 1940; s. Guy Carlton and Hazel (Hardin) K.; A.B., Dartmouth, 1961; m. Carolyn Louise Goldsby, Oct. 17, 1964. Account exec. Bauerlein Advt. Agy., New Orleans, 1962-63; merchandising dir. promotion dept. sta. WWL-TV, New Orleans, 1963-65; owner, Kenneth Kolb & Co., New Orleans, 1965—. Bd. dirs. Campfire Girls, New Orleans, 1966-68. Served with USCGR, 1961-62. Democrat. Episcopalian. Club: Mem. Press of New Orleans. Home: 2001 Marengo St New Orleans LA 70115 Office: 126 Carondelet St New Orleans LA 70130

KOLB, WADE STACKHOUSE, city mgr.; b. Sumter, S.C., Dec. 3, 1914; s. James Mack and Ruth (Cubbage) K.; student Draughon's Bus. Sch.; B.S., U. S.C., 1949; m. Rebeca Hoke Bartlett, Dec. 26, 1946; children—Wade Stackhouse, Mack, Robert, Stewart. Warehouse mgr. Union Brokerage Co., Sumter, S.C., prior to army service; city treas., Sumter, 1949-52, city mgr., 1952—. Mem. Am. Legion, V.F.W. Elk, Kiwanian (dir. 1955). Home: Pinewood Rd Sumter SC 29150

KOLE, JOHN WILLIAM, journalist; b. Zeeland, Mich., Jan. 27, 1934; s. John Henry and Una (Messer) K.; B.A., Mich. State U., 1955; M.S., Northwestern U., 1956; Nieman fellow, Harvard, 1962-63; m. Betty Lou Zuege, Sept. 15, 1956; children—Linda Sue, Leslie Ann, James David, Sara Louise, Susan Margaret. Reporter, Milw. Jour., 1956-64, reporter, Washington Bur., 1964-70, chief Washington Bur., 1970—. Recipient awards Am. Polit. Sci. Assn., 1961, Milw. Press Club, 1960-63. Mem. White House Corrs. Assn., Sigma Delta Chi. Clubs: Gridiron, Nat. Press (Washington). Home: 2542 N 23d Rd Arlington VA 22207 Office: Nat Press Bldg Washington DC 20004

KOLENDA, KONSTANTIN, educator; b. Kamien, Poland, May 17, 1923 (came to U.S. 1946, naturalized 1951); B.A., Rice U., 1950; Ph.D., Cornell U., 1953; m. Pauline Moller, June 9, 1962; children—Helena, Christopher. Asst. prof. philosophy Rice U., Houston, 1953-58, asso. prof., 1958-65, prof., 1965—, chmn. dept., 1967—. Fulbright lectr. U. Heidelberg, 1959-60. Mem. Am., Southwestern (pres. 1965) philos. assns., Phi Beta Kappa. Author: The Freedom of Reason, 1964; In Defense of Practical Reason, 1969. Contbr. articles to profl. jours. Home: 2515 Glenhaven St Houston TX 77025

KOLLER, HERBERT R., assn. exec.; b. Cleve., 1921; B.S. in Chemistry, Western Res. U., 1942; J.D., Am. U., 1952; m. Shirley Leavitt; children— Donald, Laura, Mrs. Willard C. Van Horne. Chemist, Indsl. Rayon Co.; research worker information systems U.S. Patent Office; dir. client services EBS Mgmt. Consultants, Washington; prin. information scientist Leasco Systems and Research Corp., Bethesda, Md.; now exec. dir. Am. Soc. for Information Sci., Washington; tchr., lectr. information sci. and tech. Mem. Assn. for Computing Machinery, Am. Chem. Soc., Am. Fedn. Information Processing Socs., Nat. Acad. Scis.-Nat. Research Council, Internat. Fedn. for Documentation. Editor several profl. jours. Office: 1140 Connecticut Av NW Washington DC 20036

KOLLMANN, EDWARD CHARLES, coll. adminstr.; b. N.Y.C., Feb 11, 1915; s. Charles Ferdinand and Emma (Shaefer) K.; B.S. cum laude, Bowdoin Coll., 1941; M.A., Harvard, 1947, Ph.D., 1950; m. Doris Eveline Brand, May 6, 1944; children—Geoffrey, Elise, Deborah, Keith. Asso. prof. philosophy Willamette Coll., Salem, Ore., 1948-52; asst. prof., asso. prof. philosophy Hampton Inst., Va., 1952-58, prof., 1958-67, dir. arts and scis., 1958-67, dir. summer session, 1964—, dean of admissions, 1967-69, acting dean faculty, 1969-70, dean faculty, 1970—. Bd. dirs. Va. Council on Human Relations, 1962-68. Mem. Am. Philos. Assn., Metaphysics Soc., Assn. Asian Studies, Am. Assn. U. Profs. Home: 2 Johnson Ct Hampton Inst Hampton VA 23368

KOMAREK, EDWIN VACLAV, research-agrl.; b. Chgo., June 4, 1909; s. Fredrick Albert and Stella (Hlavka) K.; student U. Chgo., 1927-31; D.Sc., Fla. State U., 1971; m. Elizabeth Hester Barker, July 19, 1935; children—Edwin, Elizabeth B. Mammalogist, Chgo. Acad. Sci., 1928-34; asst. dir. Co-op. Quail Study Assn., 1934-43; agrl. dir. Greenwood Plantation, supt., mgr. Greenwood Seed Co., Thomasville, Ga., 1945—; exec. sec. Tall Timbers Research Sta., Tallahassee, 1958—; hon. research asso. in zoology Smithsonian Instn., 1965—. Mem gov. bd. Agrl. Research Inst., 1965-69. Dir. Tall Timbers Research, Inc. Chmn. Ann. Fire Ecology Conf., Ann. Conf. Ecol. Control Animals by Habitat Mgmt. Mem. Chgo. Acad. Scis., Am. Soc. Mammalogists. Contbr. articles to profl. jours. Home: Birdsong Plantation Thomasville GA 31792 Office: Greenwood Seed Co Thomasville also Tall Timbers Research Sta Tallahassee FL 32301

KOMINSKI, JOHN JOSEPH, staff Library of Congress; b. Springfield, Mass., Oct. 8, 1937; s. Joseph Henry and Jenny Marie (Jarosz) K.; B.A. in Journalism, U. Mass., 1959; LL.B., Georgetown U., 1962, J.D., 1967; m. Frances Janet Saladigo, Sept. 29, 1962; children— Mark, Eric, Therese, Kathryn, Maria. Admitted to Md. bar, 1965; legal specialist Am.-Brit. law Library of Congress, Washington, 1962-67, asst. gen. counsel, 1967-69, gen. counsel, 1970—. Served with AUS, 1963-65. Mem. Am., Md., Fed. (v.p. Capitol Hill chpt. 1969-71, pres. 1971—), Internat. Inst. Space Law. Home: 8611 Portsmouth Dr Laurel MD 20810 Office: Library of Congress 10 1st St SE Washington DC 20540

KONDO, YOJI, astronomer; b. Hitachi, Japan, May 26, 1933; s. Tsuneo and Hama (Yamada) K.; B.A., Tokyo U. Fgn. Studies 1958; M.S., U. Pa., 1963, Ph.D., 1965; m. Ursula Tuetermann, Sept. 10, 1965; children—Beatrice, Cynthia. Came to U.S., 1960; naturalized, 1968. Asst. prof. U. Pa., Phila., summer 1965; Nat. Acad. Scis.-NRC research asso. NASA Goddard Space Flight Center, Greenbelt, Md., 1965-68; staff astronomer NASA Manned Spacecraft Center, Houston, 1968-69, chief astrophysics sect., 1969—; adj. grad. faculty U. Houston, 1968—; adj. asso. prof. U. Okla., 1971-72, adj. prof., 1972—. Fellow A.A.A.S.; mem. Internat. Astron. Union, Am. Aston. Soc. Contbr. articles to profl. jours. Home: 18307 Hereford Lane Houston TX 77058 Office: NASA Manned Spacecraft Center Houston TX 77058

KONDRACKE, MORTON, newspaperman; b. Chgo.; m. Millicent Martinez. Gen. assignment reporter Chgo. Sun-Times, 1963, chief Springfield (Ill.) Bur., from 1964, mem. Washington Bur., 1968—. Recipient newswriting award A.P., 1965, newswriting award Ill. A.P., 1967. Home: 3812 Van Ness St NW Washington DC 20016 Office: Nat Press Bldg Washington DC 20004*

KONIKOFF, BENJAMIN SAMUEL, dentist; b. Chgo., July 16, 1912; s. Samuel and Manya Konikoff; D.D.S., Loyola U., 1945; M.S., La. State U., 1959; student So. State U., 1934-35; m. Gloria V. Stanley, Feb. 3, 1945; children—Benjamin S., Susan Lynn, Charles Edward, Constance, Robert. Practice dentistry, Baton Rouge, 1948—; mem. staff Our Lady of Lake Hosp., Baton Rouge Gen. Hosp.; dental cons. to industry; asso. prof. dept. food sci. and tech. La. State U. Served as lt. Dental Corps, USNR, 1945-47. Fellow Royal Soc. Health (Gt. Britain); mem. La. Dental Soc., Am., La. 6th Dist. dental assns., East Baton Rouge Parish Dental Soc. (pres. 1965-66), Internat. Assn. Dental Research, A.A.A.S., Inst. Food Tech., Pierre Fauchard Acad., Sigma Xi, Delta Sigma Delta, Theta Beta, Gamma Sigma Delta. Democrat. Roman Catholic. Research: milk as a vehicle for fluorides to prevent dental cavities in children. Home: 4457 Broussard St Baton Rouge LA 70808 Office: 4731 North Blvd Baton Rouge LA 70806

KONKEL, RONALD MARION, economist; b. Winona, Minn., Feb. 16, 1939; s. Hubert John and Dorothy Margaret (Ries) K.; A.B., Wichita State U., 1961; M.A., Tulane U., 1968; m. Dorothy M. Terry, June 21, 1958; children—Karen, Christopher, Julie. Tchr., S.E. High Sch., Wichita, Kan., 1961-62; cost analyst NASA Manned Spacecraft Center, Houston, 1964-66; economist NASA Hdqrs., Washington, 1966-72; budget examiner Office Mgmt. and Budget, Washington, 1972—. Mem. Am. Econ. Assn. Home: 709 Smallwood Rd Rockville MD 20850 Office: New Exec Office Bldg Washington DC 20503

KONKLE, WARD WHITNEY, editor, educator; b. Altoona, Pa., Oct. 29, 1908; s. Edson Charles and Mary Catherine (Adams) K.; student Carnegie Inst. Tech., 1927; B.A., U. Pitts., 1930; m. Dorothy Jane Callender, July 18, 1931; children—Patricia L. (Mrs. John Wade), Ronald W., Alan R. Instr. English and radio speech Wooster (O.) High Sch., 1945-52; editor Ohio Agr. Experiment Sta., Wooster, 1952-57; supr. editor Agr. Research Service, USDA, Washington, 1957-58; head tech. pub. sect., supr. tech. writing tech. program ARS, 1958-62; asst. chief publs. br., 1962-63, editor Agrl. Sci. Rev., 1963—, also asst. chief div. information Office Mgmt. Services, 1963—, instr. spl. lectr. Grad. Sch., 1960—. Recipient awards for outstanding performance in teaching tech. writing USDA, 1962, 67. Mem. Am. Assn. Agrl. Coll. Editors, Am. Med. Writers Assn., Am. Radio Relay League. Lutheran. Author: Technical Writing, 1967. Home: 617 Greenbrier Dr Silver Spring MD 20910 Office: US Dept Agr OMS-DI Washington DC 20250

KOOMEN, JACOB, state ofcl. N.C. health dir. Office: Bd Health Cooper Meml Health Bldg Raleigh NC 27602

KOON, ALTON LEON, ednl. adminstr.; b. Irmo, S.C., Sept. 6, 1910; s. Jacob Irby and Lula (Eleazer) K.; A.B., Wofford Coll., 1932; M.A., U. S.C., 1939; m. Marion Doris Faulkenberry, Dec. 5, 1942; children—Alton Leon, Marion Doris, Catherine Lynn, Irby Lee, Nancy Elizabeth. Prin. Folk Elem. Sch., Irmo, 1933-35; prin., coach high sch., Wampee, S.C., 1935-37; prin., coach Floyds Sch., Nichols, S.C., 1937-40, supt., 1940-42; supt. schs., Aynor, S.C., 1946-63; adminstrv. supt. Aynor-Conway (S.C.) Schs., 1963—. Mem. Aynor Health Commn., 1958—; mem. Horry County Bd. Edn., 1948-50. Served to capt. AUS, 1942-46. Mem. Am. Assn. Sch. Adminstrs., Nat., S.C. edn. assns., 40 and 8, Am. Legion (mem. nat. com. law and order 1968-71), Woodmen of the World, Pee Dee Alumni Assn. Wofford Coll. (pres. 1958-60). Methodist (asso. dist. lay leader 1965-70). Lion. Home: P O Box 247 Aynor SC 29511 Office: P O Box 26 Conway SC 29526

KOON, CLYDE HURLSTON, supt. schs.; b. Sheridan, Ark., Feb. 10, 1911; s. Jacob Eddie and Lula (Johnson) K.; B.S., Coll. Ozarks, 1935; M.S., U. Ark., 1947; m. Thelm Beatrice McDougal, July 11, 1937; children—Norman Carrol, Lou L. (Mrs. James Ferguson), Eddie Mac. Sci. tchr., coach Malvern Sch. Dist., 1935-41; sci. tchr., coach, prin. Hughes (Ark.) Sch. Dist., 1941-44; supt. schs. McCrory (Ark.) Sch. Dist., 1944-54, Harrisburg (Ark.) Sch. Dist., 1954-62, Sheridan (Ark.) Sch. Dist., 1962—. Recipient Outstanding Alumni award Coll. Ozarks, 1953. Chmn. Grant County Econ. Opportunity Council, 1966-72; chmn. Grant County Health Adv. Com., 1969-71. Democrat. Baptist (deacon 1942—). Rotarian. Club: Country (Sheridan). Home: Rural Route 2 Box 521 Sheridan AR 72150 Office: 400 N Rock St Sheridan AR 72150

KOON, WARREN HENRY, newspaper editor; b. Spartanburg, S.C., Dec. 6, 1923; s. Henry Smith and Una B. (Finger) K.; B.A., Wofford, Coll., 1948; m. Laura Frances Hudgens, Feb. 14, 1947; 1 son, Kerry Warren; m. 2d, Martha Hamilton Carson, May 30, 1970; stepchildren—Kim, Kevin, Kelly. Pub. relations dir. Wofford Coll., 1948; reporter Spartanburg Herald, 1948; reporter Louisville Times, 1948-51; telegraph editor Asheville (N.C.) Times, 1952-55; exec. sports editor Charleston (S.C.) Post and News-Courier, 1955-65; columnist Charleston Post, 1965-68; mng. editor Rock Hill (S.C.) Evening Herald, 1968-69; mng. editor Tuscaloosa (Ala.) News, 1969-70; editor-pub. Natchez (Miss.) Democrat, 1970—. Served with USMCR, 1942-46. Recipient A.P. S.C. State Writing awards, 1955, 56, 60, 61, 66, 68, U.S. Osteo. Assn. Nat. award for writing, 1968. Mem. So. Conf. Sportswriters (pres.), S.C. Assn. Sportswriters (pres.), Nat. Assn. Writers/Broadcasters (writer of year 1963-64). Author: View From Up Here, 1964. Home: 800 N Union St Natchez MS 39120 Office: 501 N Canal St Natchez MS 39120

KOONCE, MACK RAYFORD, financial service co. exec.; b. Ripley, Tenn., Sept. 18, 1934; s. Robert Malcolm and Alma (McCoy) K.; B.S., U. Ark., 1957; m. Nell Ann Mays, Aug. 29, 1959; 1 dau., Karen Kay. Asst. chief chemist Dierk's Paper Co., Pine Bluff, Ark.,1957-59; salesman Aetna Life Ins. Co., 1959-68; pres. Financial Services, Inc., Pine Bluff, 1968—; v.p., dir. Gen. Life Ins. Co.; Cons., Employee Benefits Cons., Inc. State chmn. March of Dimes, 1967-68. Bd. dirs. United Fund, Heart Found. Recipient Distinguished Service award as outstanding pres. Ark. Jr. C. of C., 1963. Mem. Nat. Assn. Life Underwriters, U.S. (v.p., dir.), Ark. (pres.), Pine Bluff (pres.) jr. chambers commerce, Pi Kappa Alpha. Baptist. Club: Rosswood Country (dir.) Pine Bluff, Ark. Home: 9 Archers Green St Pine Bluff AR 71601 Office: 5th Ave Bldg 115 E 5th Av Pine Bluff AR 71601

KOONTS, ROBERT HENRY, lawyer, ins. co. exec.; b. Greensboro, N.C., May 8, 1927; s. Henry Valentine and Margaret (Andrew) K.; B.S. in Commerce, U. N.C., 1949, LL.B., 1952; grad. exec. program, 1967; m. Edna Mildred Matthes, Mar. 8, 1952; children—Linda Suzanne, Barbara Jane. Admitted to N.C. bar, 1952; gen. practice, High Point, N.C., 1952-57; now v.p., asso. gen. counsel Jefferson Standard Life Ins. Co., Greensboro, N.C.; asso. gen. counsel Jefferson Pilot Corp., Greensboro; sec., dir. Jefferson Standard Broadcasting Co., Charlotte, N.C., Jefferson Standard Broadcasting Co. Va., Richmond; sec. J-P Investments, Inc., Greensboro, Jefferson-Pilot Publs., Inc., Greensboro; sec., dir., gen. counsel Jefferson-Carolina Corp., Greensboro. Served with USNR, 1945-46. Mem. Assn. Life Ins. Counsel, Am., N.C., Greensboro bar assns. Phi Delta Theta, Phi Delta Phi. Presbyn. Club: Greensboro Country. Home: 3600 Starmount Dr Greensboro NC 27403 Office: Jefferson Standard Life Ins Co Greensboro NC 27400

KOONTZ, ELIZABETH DUNCAN, educator, govt. ofcl.; b. Salisbury, N.C., June 3, 1919; d. Samuel Edward and Lena (Jordan) Duncan; A.B., Livingstone Coll., 1938; M.A., Atlanta U., 1941; postgrad. Columbia, Ind. U., N.C. Coll.; L.H.D., Livingstone Coll., Coppin State Coll., Women's Med. Coll. (Pa.), Hobart and William Smith Colls., Keuka Coll.; Litt.D., Atlanta U., Windham Coll.; Ed.D., Howard U.; LL.D., Am. U., Ball State U., Duke; H.H.D., Hofstra U., Eastern Mich. U.; D.Sc. in Edn., Northeastern U., Cedar Crest Coll.; Pd.D., Pacific U., Bryant Coll.; m. Harry Lee Koontz, Nov. 26, 1947. Tchr. Harnett County Tng. Sch., Dunn, N.C., 1938-40, Aggrey Meml. Sch., Landis, N.C., 1940-41, Fourteenth St. Sch., Winston-Salem, N.C., 1941-45, Price High Sch., Salisbury, N.C., 1945-49, Monroe Sch., 1949-65; tchr. spl. edn. Price Jr.-Sr. High Sch., 1965-68; dir. women's bur. Dept. Labor, Washington, 1969—. U.S. del. UN Commn. on Status of Women, 1969; cons. com. status women Nat. Council Adminstrv. Women in Edn. Mem. Rowan County Negro Civic League, Salisbury, 1946—; mem. Youth Commn. of Rowan County, 1955-57; mem. N.C. Gov.'s Commn. Status of Women, 1962; mem. Pres.'s Adv. Council on Edn. Disadvantaged Children, 1965-68. Recipient Distinguished Alumni medallion Livingstone Coll.; Distinguished Tchr. award Civitan Club, Salisbury; Distinguished Citizenship award N.C. Western dist. Civitan Club Internat.; Certificate of Merit, Cheyney State Coll.; Distinguished Service award Federally Employed Women. Mem. N.C., Salisbury tchrs. assns., Nat. Assn. Retarded Children, N.C. Assn. Classroom Tchrs. (pres. 1958-62), N.E.A. (v.p. 1967-68, pres. 1968-69, pres. dept. classroom tchrs. 1965-66), Phi Beta Kappa (hon.), Zeta Phi Beta (hon.). Club: Altrusa (Washington). Home: 1830 16th St Washington DC 20009 Office: Women's Bureau Dept of Labor Washington DC 20210

KOPALD, S.L., JR., food and chem. co. exec.; b. Memphis, Sept. 4, 1921; s. S.L. and Ethel (Goodman) K.; B.S., Washington and Lee U., 1943; Indsl. Adminstr., Harvard Grad. Sch. Bus. Adminstrn., 1943; m. Amelia Daves, Aug. 5, 1946; children—Nancy, Stephen L., Jack D., David R. With Humko Products, Memphis, 1946—, successively purchasing mgr., asst. to pres., 1948-50, v.p., 1950-54, exec. v.p., 1954—; dir. Union Planters Nat. Bank, Bus. Music Corp., Memphis. Chmn. campaign Memphis Community Chest, 1957; mem. Memphis and Shelby County (Tenn.) Planning Commn., 1958-60. Vice chmn. Shelby County Rep. com.; chmn. Tenn. Rep. com. 1971—. Bd. govs., chmn. Hebrew Union Coll.-Jewish Inst. Religion, Cin. Served with AUS, 1943-46; ETO. Mem. Fatty Acid Producers Council (chmn. steering com. 1968—), Omicron Delta Kappa. Republican. Jewish religion. Home: 4880 Lake Dr Memphis TN 38117 Office: 5050 Poplar St Memphis TN 38117

KOPKIND, ANDREW DAVID, journalist; b. New Haven, Aug. 24, 1935; s. Bernard Philip and Esther (Aaronson) K.; A.B., Cornell U., 1957; M.Sc. in Econs., London (Eng.) Sch. Econs., 1961. Reporter, Washington Post, 1958-59; corr. Time mag., 1961-65; asso. editor New Republic, 1965-67, contbg. editor, 1967-69; pres. The New Weekly Project, Inc.; founder, editor Hard Times, 1968-70; editor Ramparts, 1970—; organizer Unicorn News; Washington corr. New statesman, London, 1965-69, Le Nouvel Observateur, Paris, France, 1967-69. Author: The Mixed Curse, 1969. Editor: Decade of Crisis, 1972. Home: 1065 31st St NW Washington DC 20007 Office: PO Box 3097 Washington DC 20010

KOPLIN, ALLEN NORMAN, physician; b. Hartford, Conn., May 15, 1919; s. Samuel and Belle (Black) K.; B.A., N.Y.U., 1939; M.D., Middlesex U., 1943; M.P.H., U. Minn., 1947; m. Pauline Ipsen, July 1, 1946; children—Michael Dean, Kathie Lynn. Intern Knickerbocker Hosp., N.Y.C., 1943-44; with fgn. quarantine div. USPHS, Miami, Fla., 1944, war food adminstrn., Yakima, Wash., 1944-46; chief field demonstration unit Nat. Cancer Inst., 1947-48; area med. adminstr. United Mine Workers of Am. Welfare and Retirement Fund. Birmingham, Ala., 1948-71, area med. adminstr., Knoxville, Tenn., 1963-71, dep. exec. med. officer, Washington, 1971—; lectr. U. Tenn. Sch. Pub. Health Edn., 1969, 70. Chmn. profl. adv. com. Helen McNabb Mental Health Center, Knoxville, 1969; health adv. bd. E. Tenn. Regional Med. Program and Comprehensive Health Planning, 1969. Diplomate Am. Bd. Preventive Medicine. Fellow Am. Coll. Preventive Medicine, Am. Pub. Health Assn. (chmn. com. equal health opportunity 1970). Home: 1509 Gordon Cove Dr Annapolis MD 21403 Office: 907 15th St NW Washington DC 20005

KOPP, EDGAR WILLIAM, univ. dean, educator; b. Louisville, Jan. 28, 1926; s. Edgar W. and Eve (Higbee) K.; B.S., Ga. Tech., 1945, B.S.E. 1947, M.S.E., 1948; m. Carolyn Chesser, June 13, 1948; 1 son, Edgar, Ill. Tech. staff Ford Motor Co., 1948-55; asst. dean engring., prof. U. Fla., 1955-63, asst. dean faculty, prof., 1963-64; dean, prof. engring. U. So. Fla., Tampa, 1964—. Vice pres., mem. bd. dirs. UNIVINC, Inc., 1967-71; bd. dirs. Seminole Bank of Tampa. Mem. council Boy Scouts Am., Tampa, Fla., 1969-71; mem. Com. of 100, Tampa, 1965-70; mem. exec. com. Tampa Arts Council, 1967-70; mem. bd. dirs. Safety Council Tampa, 1967—. Chmn. bd. dirs. Berkely Preparatory Sch., Tampa, Fla., 1968-70; trustee USF Found., 1964-67, 71—. Served to lt. comdr. USNR. Registered profl. engr., Fla. Tau Beta Pi, Omicron Delta Kappa. Rotarian, Mason (Shriner). Home: 811 Grove Park Ave Tampa FL 33609

KOPPERUD, ALVIN HANLEY, ret. lawyer, dentist, real estate developer; b. Grafton, N.D., Jan. 26, 1909; s. Alfred Anderson and Betsey (Sando) K.; student U. Sask. (Can.), 1925-27; B.S.D., Northwestern U., 1931, D.D.S., 1931; LL.B., U. Va., 1938; m. Hallie Eugenia Rudolph, June 13, 1935; 1 son, William Rudolph. Individual practice dentistry, Paducah, Ky. and Lovingston, Va., 1931-39, Murray, Ky., 1947-65, ret., 1965; admitted to Ky. bar, 1939; practice law, Murray, 1939-43; pres. Homeland Developers Inc., Murray, 1965—; pres. Gateway Devel. Corp., Murray, 1964—; chmn. bd. Westlands Trading Corp., Murray, 1972—. Calloway County Atty., 1942-46; dir. Clarks River Watershed Dist., 1965-69. Bd. dirs. Buckhorn (Ky.) Children's Center; pres. Ky. Pub. Library Trustees Assn. Served with Judge Adv. Gen.'s Dept., AUS, 1943-47. Mem. Murray C. of C. (dir.), Psi Omega. Presbyn. (clk. session 1948-61, commr. to gen. assembly 1963). Lion (past pres.). Home: 800 Main St Murray KY 42071 Office: 711 Main St Murray KY 42071

KOPRA, LENNART LAURI, educator; b. Virginia, Minn., Jan. 12, 1924; s. Antti and Ester (Saksinen) K.; B.A., Wittenberg U., 1951; M.A., Northwestern U., 1952, Ph.D., 1954; m. Martha Adelaide Witthoft, June 4, 1951; children—Andrew Charles, Daniel Allan, Timothy Lennart, Lauri Ester. Asst. prof. speech U. Tex. at Austin, 1954-58, asso. prof., 1958-62, dir. speech and hearing clinic, 1961—, prof. speech, 1962-65, prof. speech and edn., 1965—; clin. prof. pediatrics U. Tex. Med. Br. at Galveston, 1967—; cons. in field. Served to lt. USAAF, 1943-46. Fellow Am. Speech and Hearing Assn.; mem. Tex. Speech and Hearing Assn. (pres. 1959), Acoustical Soc. Am., Internat. Soc. Audiology, Speech Communication Assn. Contbr. articles profl. jours. Home: Route 3 Box 137 Leander TX 78641

KORCHIN, LEO, educator; b. Bklyn., July 1, 1914; s. Harry and Rebecca (Halbreich) K.; B.S., Cornell U., 1936; D.D.S., N.Y. U. Sch. Dentistry, 1941; M.S. in Oral Surgery, Georgetown U. Grad. Sch., 1954; m. Esther Goldstein, June 15, 1941; children— Gregory Frank, Paul Maury. Intern Greenpoint Hosp., Bklyn., 1941; individual practice dentistry, Bklyn., 1946-48; officer Dental Corp U.S. Army, advanced through ranks to col., 1942-46, 48-67; prof. oral surgery U. P.R. Sch. Dentistry, San Juan, 1967—; asso. attending oral surgeon Univ. and Oncologic hosps., P.R. Cons. oral surgery USPHS, San Juan, P.R., 1969-70. Decorated Bronze Star medal; recipient Novice award Internat. Assn. Dental Research, 1954. Diplomate N.Y. Bd. Oral Surgery, Am. Bd. Oral Surgery. Fellow Am. Coll. Dentists; mem. Colegio de Cirujanos Dentistas, Am. Dental Assn., Am. Soc. Oral Surgeons, P.R. Soc. Oral Surgeons, Am. Acad. Oral Pathology, Internat. Assn. Oral Surgeons, Am. Assn. Dental Schs. Home: 267

Calle San Jorge Santurce PR 00912 Office: U PR Sch Dentistry San Juan PR 00936Methodist.

KORDA, MARION AMELIA, musician, librarian; b. Portland, Me., June 14, 1922; s. Joseph and Anna (Miller) K.; B.A., U. Me., 1943; M.S. in L.S., Columbia, 1953. Music therapist Camp Edwards, Mass., 1945; Y-teen program dir. YWCA, New Bedford, 1946-47; mem. Louisville Orch. as violinist and violist, 1947—; music librarian, asso. prof. bibliography (music research) U. Louisville Sch. Music, 1947—. Mem. Music (bd. dirs., mem.-at-large), Ky library assns., Am. Assn. U. Profs., Sigma Alpha Iota. Club: Louisville Library. Home: 3111 Talisman Rd Louisville KY 40220

KORDYS, JOSEPH RALPH, JR., architect; b. Newark, Apr. 1, 1933; s. Joseph Ralph and Helen Sophie (Dombrowski) K.; student Ga. Inst. Tech., 1950-55; m. June Atkinson, Aug. 8, 1953; children—J. Scott, Jodi Lynn, Kristi June. With Robert & Co., 1956-62, Gregson & Assos., Atlanta, 1962-64, Wise, Simpson, Aiken & Assos., Atlanta, 1964-68; project architect Bothwell, Jenkins Slay & Assos., Decatur, Ga., 1968-71; asso. architect Cavender Assos., East Point, Ga., 1971—. Mem. A.I.A., Constrn. Specifications Inst. Baptist (deacon). Home: 2876 Battle Forrest Dr Decatur GA 30034 Office: 1677 Dorsey Av East Point GA 30344

KORGEN, REINHARD LUNDE, scientist; b. Newfolden, Minn., Dec. 31, 1906; s. Hans Iverson and Anna Maria (Lunde) K.; A.B., Carleton Coll., 1930; M.A., Harvard, 1931, Ph.D., 1945; m. Dorothy Merriman, Dec. 24, 1942; children—Kristi, Anders. Prof. math. Bowdoin Coll., 1931-65; exec. dir. Northeastern Research Found., Inc., 1959-62; program dir. Coll. Tchr. Programs NSF, Washington, 1963—. Lectr. operations research Tech. U. Denmark, 1958. Fellow A.A.A.S.; mem. Am. Math. Soc., Phi Beta Kappa. Conglist. Clubs: Harvard, Abracadhbra (Washington). Home: 4402 Elm St Chevy Chase MD 20015 Office: Edn Directorate NSF Washington DC 20550

KORNEGAY, HOBERT, dentist; b. Meridian, Miss., Aug. 28, 1923; s. Hobert and Mary Louise (Gaines) K.; B.S., Morehouse Coll., 1945; D.D.S., Meharry Med. Coll., 1948; postgrad. Med. Field Service Sch., 1953, Walter Reed Inst. Dental Research, 1968-71; m. Ernestine Price, June 10, 1948; children—Carmen Kateena, Patricia Louise, James Price, Donna Michele. Individual practice dentistry, Meridian, 1948-53, 1955—; mem. staffs Riley's Hosp., Meridian, Matty Hersee Hosp., Meridian. Cons. preventive dentistry Miss. Head Start, U. P.R. Dental Sch., 1970-71; cons. Miss V.I. Program, 1970-71, USPHS, 1971-72; clinician Jackson Comprehensive Health Clinic, Utica, Miss., 1970-72; dental surgeon Volt Tech. Corp., Atlanta, 1971-72, Westinghouse Learning Corp., Washington and Silver Spring, Md., 1971-72. Mem. Govs. com. Health Needs Children Miss., 1971-72; mem. task force Miss. Council Child Devel., 1971; chmn. Chetaw Area Council Boy Scouts Am., 1955-65; chmn. Lauderdale Econ. Opportunity Program, 1971-72; dir. Meridian Redevel. Authority Urban Renewal, 1971-72. Bd. dirs. St. Francis Homes, 1971—. Served as capt. AUS, 1953-55. Mem. Acad. Gen. Dentistry, Nat., Am. dental assns., N.A.A.C.P. (life), Meridian C. of C., Omega Psi Phi. Republican. Baptist (trustee 1950-72, treas., 1970-72). Mason (Shriner), Elk, Toastmaster (pres. 1969-72). Contbr. articles to newspaper. Home: 1420 39th Av Meridian MS 39301 Office: 2416 5th St Meridian MS 39301

KOROLOGOS, TOM CHRIS, govt. ofcl.; b. Salt Lake City, Apr. 6, 1933; s. Chris T. and Irene (Kolendrianos) K.; B.A., U. Utah, 1955; M.S. (Grantland Rice Meml. fellow 1957; Pulitzer traveling fellow 1958), 1958; m. Carolyn Joy Goff; children—Ann, Philip Chris, Paula. Reporter Salt Lake Tribune, 1950-60, N.Y. Herald Tribune, 1958; account exec. David W. Evans & Assos., Salt Lake City, 1960-62; pres. sec. to Senator Wallace Bennett of Utah, Washington, 1962-65, administrv. asst., 1965-71; spl. asst. to Pres. Nixon, 1971-72, dep. asst., 1972—. Served with USAF, 1956-57. Mem. Ahepa. Greek Orthodox. Home: 8222 Smithfield Av Springfield VA 22150 Office: White House Washington DC 22150*

KORU, SADI SABIT, architect; b. Istanbul, Turkey, Jan. 1, 1910 (came to U.S. 1939, naturalized 1961); s. Osman Sabit and Nuriye (Suleyman) Koruturk; Civil Engr., Istanbul Teknik, 1930; B.S. with honors, U. Fla., 1944, M. Arch., 1956; m. Mary Hiley, May 26, 1941; children—Franklin D., Ronald. Civil engr., Turkey, 1930-39; individual practice architecture, Gainesville, Fla., 1944—; prof. architecture Coll. Architecture, U. Fla., Gainesville, 1947—. Counselor Boy Scouts Am., 1950; mem. Miconopy Arts Center. Served to 1st lt. Turkish Army, 1933-35. Recipient First Prize award Fine Arts Soc. Gainesville, 1967. Mem. Fine Arts Soc., Archtl. League, A.I.A. (pres. North Fla. chpt. 1968-69), Fla. Craftsmen. Works include numerous residences, Gainesville. Home: 1130 SW 9th Rd Gainesville FL 32601 Office: Coll Architecture U Fla Gainesville FL 32601

KOSANOVICH, MICHAEL, physician; b. Gary, Ind., June 21, 1934; s. Nicholas and Sara (Todorovich) K.; A.B., Ind. U., 1956, M.D., 1959; m. Pauline Anne Nielsen, Mar. 4, 1960; children—Michael, Wendy Lynn. Intern, Cook County Hosp., Chgo., 1960; pub. health officer City of Milw., 1961; resident in pathology Ind. U. Med. Center Indpls., 1961-65; practice medicine specializing in pathology, Ft. Benning, Ga., 1965-67; pathologist Baroness Erlanger Hosp., Chattanooga, 1967—, dir. cytogenetics lab., 1965—. Precinct chmn. Republican party, Chattanooga, 1968—. Served with AUS, 1965-67. Mem. Coll. Am. Pathologists, Am. Soc. Clin. Pathology, Internat. Acad. Pathologists, Am. Soc. Microbiology. Episcopalian. Home: 64 Carriage Hill Dr Signal Mountain TN 37377 Office: Baroness Erlanger Hosp Chattanooga TN 37403

KOSBAB, FREDERIC PAUL GUSTAV, physician; b. Berlin, Germany, Mar. 29, 1922; s. Paul A. Waldemar and Elisabeth (Schulze) K.; student U. Berlin, 1940, 44-45, U. Innsbruck, 1941-42, U. Wuerzburg. 1942-43, U. Strasbourg, 1943-44; M.D., Friedrich-Wilhelms U., 1945; postgrad. Neb. Psychiat. Inst., U. Neb., 1958-59, U. Wash. Hosps. 1960-61; m. Marianne Elsbeth Bodmann, May 2, 1951. Came to U.S., 1956, naturalized, 1961. Intern., Swedish Covenent Hosp., Chgo, 1956-57; resident No. State Hosp., Sedro-Woolley, Wash., 1961-62; practice medicine, Kaiserslautern, W. Germany, 1951-55; resident and staff positions various hosps., 1957-62; sr. staff psychiatrist, unit med. dir. Ore. State Hosp., 1962-63; clin. instr. psychiatry U. Ore. Med. Sch., 1962-64; asst. prof. psychiatry Med. Coll. Va., Health Scis. div. Va. Commonwealth U., Richmond, 1964-66, asso. prof., 1966-69, prof. psychiatry, acting chmn., 1969-70, prof., asso. chmn., 1970—, chmn. com. postgrad. tng. dept. psychiatry, 1967-70; pvt. practice psychiatry, Richmond, part-time 1964—. Cons. psychotherapy, residency tng. program Eastern State Hosp., Williamsburg, 1968— Diplomate psy. Am. Bd. Psychiatry and Neurology, in internal medicine W. German Med. Assn. Fellow Am. Psychiat. Assn., Royal Soc. Medicine (London); mem. Am. Med. Writers Assn., Neuropsychiat. Soc. Va., Richmond Acad. Medicine. Author: Neurologie fuer Studierende, 1948. Contbr. articles to publs. Home: 6 Ralston Rd Richmond VA 23229 Office: Med Coll Va Health Scis Div Va Commonwealth U 1200 E Broad St Richmond VA 23219

KOSCHEL, ELMO STERLING, telephone co. exec.; b. New Orleans, July 14, 1918; s. George August and Louisa (Worner) K.; student Loyola U. of South, 1936-40; m. Mildred Campbell, Mar. 4, 1942; children— Clayton, George, Gretchen. With So. Bell Tel. & Tel. Co., New Orleans, 1936—, office mgr., Lake Charles, La., 1946-51, unit mgr., New Orleans, 1951-53, long distance promotion supr., 1953-54, state tng. supr., 1954, sales promotion mgr., Atlanta, 1955-56, comml. practices and tng. supr., Atlanta, 1956-57, Gentilly dist. mgr., New Orleans, 1957-58, La. sales mgr., 1958-59, gen. sales mgr., 1959-64, gen. directory mgr., 1964-67, indsl. devel. mgr., 1967—; pres. Business Research & Surveys, Inc.; chmn. bd. Caltronics, Inc. Mem. U.S. Civil Def. Council, So. Indsl. Devel. Council. Spl. lectr. salesmanship Sales Marketing Execs. Internat., Loyola U., La. State U., New Orleans, 1961-63. Pres., Argonne Property Owners 1952-54; chmn. United Fund Speakers Bur., 1963-65; pres. Vista Park Property Owners Assn., 1965-66. Bd. dirs. YMCA, New Orleans, Nat. Found., New Orleans, La. chpt. Arthritis Found. Served with F.A., AUS, 1941-46. Decorated Bronze Star; named Boss of Year, Nat. Secs. Assn., 1960. Mem. Sales Marketing Execs. (dir.), Bd. Trade, Bur. Govt. Research, New Orleans C. of C. (hon. life mem.), La. Travel Promotion Assn. (pres. 1970-71), Syracuse U. Grad. Sch. Sales Mgmt. and Marketing Alumni Assn. (trustee, v.p.), Blue Key. Clubs: Vista Shores (pres. 1967-68), Import-Export Managers. Author: Hats of a Salesman; Suggestions for Waiter, Waitress and Bellman. Home: 5935 Pratt Dr New Orleans LA 70122 Office: 1215 Prytania St New Orleans LA 70140

KOSCHNY, WILLIAM SIMON, chem. engr.; b. Newport, R.I., Aug. 21, 1921; s. William and Theresa Marie (Czforeck) K.; B.S., Northeastern U., 1949; M.S., McKinley-Roosevelt, Inc., 1952; M.E.A., George Washington U., 1958; postgrad. Am. U., 1958-66; m. Bertha Margaret Clarkin, Jan. 1953 (div. Apr. 1958); children—Theresa Mary and Laura Louise (twins); m. 2d, Mae Margarette McVay Leader, June 20, 1962. Asst. to gen. supt. Lewiston Gas Light Co. (Me.), 1949-50; cadet chem. engr. Lynn Gas & Electric Co. (Mass.), 1950-51; ordnance engr. Bur. Ordnance, USN, Newport, 1951-53, Washington, 1953-54, mech. engr., Bur. Aeros., 1954-56, aero. research engr., 1956-58; mil. intelligence specialist, chief staff intelligence U.S. Army, Washington, 1958-62; supervisory gen. engr. U.S. P.O. Dept., 1962-69, head planning and systems analysis research div., bur. research and engring., Washington, 1962-66, chief design assurance and value engring. div., bur. research and engring., Bethesda, Md., 1966-67, personal staff asst. to asst. dir. engring., Washington, temporary detail as tech. adviser to U.S. Postal Service Inst., Bethesda, Md., 1967-69; tech. adviser/gen. engr. tech. proposal evaluation staff, Bur. Research and Engring., Washington, 1969-71, gen. engr. systems div. Bulk Mail Processing U.S. Postal Service, Washington, 1971—. Served with Air Corps, AUS, 1943. Registered profl. engr., D.C., R.I. Mem. Am. Chem. Soc., Am. Inst. Indsl. Engrs. (rec. sec. 1964-65), Fed. Profl. Assn. Washington (sr.), Soc. Am. Value Engrs., R.I. Honor Soc., Pi Sigma Alpha. Contbr. articles to various publs. Home: 5704 Robinwood Lane Falls Church VA 22041 Office: Bulk Mail Processing US Postal Service Washington DC 20260

KOSKI, AUGUSTUS ALFRED, govt. ofcl.; b. Fairport Harbor, O., June 7, 1908; s. John Kusti and Hilma (Nieminen) K.; B.A. cum laude, Kenyon Coll., 1930; M.A., U. of South, 1934, Columbia, 1949; m. Mildred Mathilda Saari, June 10, 1953. Tchr. lang. St. Andrews (Tenn.) Sch., 1930-31, asst. headmaster, 1931-39, headmaster, 1939-42; civilian information officer Berlin Documents Center, 1946-47; fgn. lang. instr. Randolph-Macon Acad., 1948-50; acad. adviser for comdt. Army Lang. Sch., Presidio of Monterey, Cal., 1951-52, acad. dean, 1952-57; sci. linguist U.S. Dept. State, Washington, 1957-62, publs. chief, 1965— Fgn. lang. research specialist U.S. Office Edn., 1962-65, now ednl. cons.; participant modern lang. and linguistic confs. Served with AUS, 1942-46, 51-52. Mem. Linguistic Soc. Am. Episcopalian. Author: (with Ilona Mihalyfy) FSI Basic Course in Hungarian, 1962, Hungarian Graded Reader, 1968; (with Aili Rytkonen Bell) Finnish Graded Reader, 1968. Contbr. articles to profl. jours. Home: 3411 Annandale Rd Falls Church VA 22042 Office: Fgn Service Inst Dept State SA-3 Washington DC 20520

KOSTENBAUDER, H.B., assn. exec. Pres. Acad. Pharm. Scis., Lexington, Ky. Address: 2121 Nicholasville Rd Lexington KY 40503*

KOSTER, RICHARD M., educator, author; b. Bklyn., Mar. 1, 1934; s. Harry and Lily (Silverstein) K.; B.A., Yale, 1955; M.A., N.Y. U., 1962; m. Otilia Tejeira, July 18, 1959; children—Ricardo, Lily. Mem. faculty Nat. U. Panama, 1960-61; prof. Canal Zone br. Fla. State U., 1964—. Democratic nat. committeeman, C.Z., 1966—; del. Dem. Nat. Convs., 1964, 68, 72. Served with AUS, 1956-59. Author: The Prince, 1972. Home: Calle 47 no 9 Panama Republic of Panama Office: Fla State U Box 930 Albrook Canal Zone

KOSUB, ELMER M., athletic dir. St. Mary's U., Houston. Address: Athletic Dept St Mary's U Houston TX 78228*

KOSZTARAB, MICHAEL, entomologist; b. Bucharest, Romania, July 7, 1927; s. Michael and Berta (Albert) K.; grad. Hungarian U. Agr. Scis., Budapest, 1951; Ph.D., Ohio State U., 1962; m. Matilda Pinter, Oct. 21, 1953; 1 dau., Eva. Extension asst. Hungarian State Bur. Plant Protection Budapest, 1947-50; asst. prof. Hungarian U. Agrl. Scis., 1951-56; cons. entomologist Insect Control and Research, Inc., Balt., 1957-58, asst. dir. research, 1959-60; asso. prof. dept. entomology Va. Poly. Inst., Blacksburg, Va., 1962-68, prof., 1968—. Recipient W. E. Wine Faculty achievement award, Va. Poly. Inst., 1967. Mem Entomol. Soc. Am., Soc. Systematic Zoology, Va. Acad. Scis. Contbr. articles to profl. jours. Home: 614 Woodland Dr Blacksburg VA 24060

KOTT, JOSEPH, architect; b. June 12, 1924; s. John and Michalena (Lyznicki) K.; B.S., U. Kan., 1949; m. Jane Marie Sweeney, June 25, 1945; children—Joy Elva (Mrs. Ralph Emery), Jann Marie John, Joellyn, Jennifer. Chief draftsman Edward M. Fuller, Architect, North Kansas City, Mo., 1949-51; asso. mem. Perkins & Will, Architects, Chgo., 1951-59; exec. v.p. Swenson & Kott, Architects, Nashville, 1959-65; prin. Joe Kott & Assos., 1968—. Served with USNR, 1943-46. Mem. A.I.A., Constrn. Specifications Inst. (chpt. v.p. 1968). Home: 5620 S Hillview Dr Route 2 Brentwood TN Office: 1600 Hayes St Nashville TN 37203

KOTWAL, KEKI RUSI, dentist; b. Bombay, India, Jan. 5, 1939 (came to U.S. 1961, naturalized, 1966); s. Rusl T. and Arnavaz R. (Shroff); B.D.S., U. Bombay, 1960; M.S. in Prosthodontics, U. Ala., 1963, D.M.D., 1965; m. Marie Catherine Cox Graham, Aug. 31, 1962; children—Nevil Eric, Rusty Warren. Individual practice dentistry, Bombay, 1960-61; clin. asst. prosthodontic dept. Sir C.E.M. Dental Sch., 1960-61; commd. capt. U.S. Army, 1965, advanced through grades to maj., 1968; prosthodontist Hosp. Dental Clinic, Ft. Jackson, S.C., 1965-66; comdg. officer Mobile Prosthodontic Team, Korea, 1966-67, prosthodontist Pentagon Dispensary Dental Clinic, Washington, 1967-70; chief prosthodontics William Beaumont Gen. Hosp., El Paso, 1970—. Cons. prosthodontics Whitesands Missile Range Dental Clinic, 1971—, Pub. Health Clinic, Gallup, N.M., 1971—. Social worker Municipalty Social Center, Bombay, intermittently 1958-59. Diplomate Am. Bd. Prosthodontics. Fellow Am. Coll. Prosthodontics; mem. Am. Dental Assn., William Beaumont Gen. Hosp. Prosthodontic Study Club. Home: 579 Hase St El Paso TX 79906 Office: William Beaumont Gen Hosp Box 1235 El Paso TX 79920

KOTZ, NATHAN KALLISON, (NICK), journalist; b. San Antonio, Tex., Sept. 16, 1932; s. Jacob and Tybe (Kallison) K.; grad. St. Albans Sch., 1951; A.B. magna cum laude with high honors in Internat. Relations, Dartmouth, 1955; student London (Eng.) Sch. Econs., 1955-56; m. Mary Lynn Booth, Aug. 7, 1960; 1 son, Jack Mitchell. Reporter Des Moines Register, 1958-64, Washington corr., 1964-70, also for other Cowles Publs. newspapers; nat. corr. Washington Post, 1970—. Bd. dirs. Ia. Bds. Internat. Edn., 1962-64, Suburban Md. Fair Housing, 1966—. Served to 1st lt. USMCR, 1956-58. Recipient Pulitzer prize for nat. reporting, 1968; Raymond Clapper Meml. award, 1966-68; Distinguished Service award Sigma Delta Chi, 1966; Robert F. Kennedy Journalism award, 1968. Mem. Phi Beta Kappa. Club: Nat. Press (Washington). Author: Let Them Eat Promises: The Politics of Hunger in America, 1969. Home: 5508 Montgomery St Chevy Chase MD 20015 Office: National Press Bldg Washington DC 20004

KOURI, RICHARD E., microbiologist; b. Akron, O., May 22, 1943; B.S. in Microbiology, Ohio State U., 1965; M.S. in Radiation Virology, U. Tenn., 1968; Ph.D. in Radiation Biology, U. Tenn., 1970. Teaching asst. U. Tenn., 1966-67, mem. staff Inst. Radiation Biology, 1966-70; trainee Oak Ridge Nat. Lab., 1967-70; postdoctoral fellow dept. mammalian genetics Roche Inst. Molecular Biology, Nutley, N.J., 1970-71; asso. investigator with Council Tobacco Research Microbiol. Assos., Inc., Bethesda, Md., 1971—, also asso. investigator with Nat. Cancer Inst. Mem. Am. Soc. Microbiology, A.A.A.S., Radiation Research Soc., Phi Sigma (pres. chpt. 1969-70). Contbr. articles to profl. jours. Address: Microbiological Assos Inc 4733 Bethesda Av Bethesda MD 20014

KOUW, WILLY ALEXANDER, psychologist, educator; b. Leiden, Netherlands, Dec. 20, 1932; student U. Leiden, 1956-58; B.A., McMaster U. (Can.), 1961; Ph.D., U. Tex., 1965; m. Petronella C. Schnelle, Sept. 9, 1957; children—Brigitte S., Ingrid L., Astrid L. Edith R. Social sci. research asso. U. Tex., 1964-65 fellow clin. child psychology med. br., Galveston, 1965-66, asst. prof. psychology, 1966-67, clin. asst. prof. dept. psychiatry U. Tex. Med. Sch. at San Antonio, 1967—; pvt. Practice psychology, 1967—. Field psychologist U.S. Dept. Health, Edn. and Welfare, summer 1963; field assessment officer Peace Corps, 1965-66; cons. San Antonio State Hosp., Tex. Dept. Mental Health and Mental Retardation; mem. profl. adv. com. Bexar County, bd. trustees for mental health and mental retardation, 1968—; pres. San Antonio Research Found., 1969—. Served with Royal Dutch Army, 1952-54. Mem. Am., Tex. psychol. assns., Bexar County Clin. Psychology Assn. (pres.), Tex. Assn. Children with Learning Disabilities, N.Y. Acad. Scis. Address: 6601 Blanco Rd San Antonio TX 78216

KOVACHEVICH, ELIZABETH ANNE, lawyer; b. Canton, Ill., Dec. 14, 1936; d. Dan and Emilie (Kuchan) Kovachevich; A.A., St. Petersburg Jr. Coll., 1956; B.B.A., U. Miami, 1958; J.D., Stetson U., 1961. Admitted to Fla. bar, 1961, U.S. Supreme Ct., 1968, also fed. cts.; research, adminstrv. aide Pinellas County legislative delegation Fla. Legislature, 1961; asso. DeVito & Speer, 1961-62; house counsel in credit dept. Rieck & Fleece Bldrs. Supplies, Inc., 1962; gen. practice, St. Petersburg, Fla., 1962—; dir., v.p. Staff of Life Bakers, Inc.; dir. Sheraton Inn St. Petersburg. Active Children's Hosp. Guild, St. Petersburg; legal adviser, hon. mem., mem. bd. dirs. Young Women's Residence, Inc., 1968-69; legal adviser, mem. Council for Continuing Edn. Women of Pinellas County, 1968-69, vice chmn., 1969-70; legal adviser, women's residence com., life mem., adv. bd., mem. house com. YMCA; mem. Fla. Gov.'s Commn. Status Women, 1968-71; area chmn. Pinellas County United Fund, 1969. Recipient Cantebury award for scholarship. St. Petersburg Panhellenic Appreciation award, 1964; St. Petersburg Bus. and Profl. Women's award, 1967, Stetson U. Distinguished Alumni award, 1970, Pres.'s award for Community Service Am. Legion Aux., 1970. Mem. Am., Fla., St. Petersburg (past chmn. legislative com., sec. 1969-70) bar assns., Am., Pinellas County trial lawyers assns., West Coast Trial Council, St. Petersburg Panhellenic Assn. (mem. governing bd., dir.), St. Petersburg Legal Secs. Assn. (hon.), Golden Notes St. Petersburg Symphony (charter), Beta Gamma Sigma, Phi Kappa Phi, Phi Delta Delta, Delta Delta Delta. Roman Catholic. Clubs: Seminole Lake Country, Outrigger. Home: 2459 Woodlawn Circle East St Petersburg FL 33704 Office: 3110 First Av N St Petersburg FL 33713

KOVAR, JOHN A., agronomist; b. Ennis, Tex., Nov. 30, 1932; s. John W. and Albina (Novak) K.; B.S., Tex. Tech. U., 1956; M.S., Tex. A and M U., 1963; Ph.D., Ia. State U., 1967; m. Erlece Paree Green, Oct. 28, 1955; children—John Dirk, Tera Lea. Soil scientist U.S. Dept. Agrl., Soil Conservation Service, Lubbock, Tex., 1956, Palestine, Tex., 1959-60; radar aircraft controller USAF, Houston and Germany, 1956-59; research asst. Tex. A and M U., 1960-62; research asso. Ia. State U., 1963-67; agriculturist TVA, Dallas, 1967—. Served to capt. USAF, 1956-59. Named Lone Star Farmer, Future Farmers Am., 1951; Welder Wildlife Found. Fellowship, 1961, 62. Mem.Am. Soc. Agronomy, Soil Sci. Soc. Am., Internat. Soil Sci. Soc., Gamma Sigma Delta. Presbyn. Club: Dallas Agrl. Home: 7607 Rolling Acres Dr Dallas TX 75240 Office: 8428 Kate St Dallas TX 75225

KOWAL, EDWARD, govt. adviser; b. Detroit, July 15, 1920; s. Stephen and Valentine (Kozlowski) K.; B.A., Western Mich. U., 1942; M.Ed., Wayne State U., 1948; m. Claudia Marsh, Nov. 23, 1946; children—Lawrence, Camille. Equal employment opportunity adviser, planner, vocational adviser, USAF Eastern Test Range, Patrick AFB, Fla., 1942-63; pres. Spaceways-Brevard Transit Co., Cape Kennedy, Fla., 1956-69, Rockledge Cab Inc., Cocoa, Fla., 1960-69; planner Eastern Test Range, 1969-70; vocational counselor State Fla., 1968-69. Tchr., Kalamazoo, 1938-40. Violinist Brevard Symphony Orch., Cocoa, 1956—, bd. dirs. 1957—, pres., bd. dirs., 1969-70. Served with USAAF, 1943-46. Home: 15 N Hardee Circle Rockledge FL 32955 Office: PO Box 1105 Cocoa FL 32923

KOWALSKE, RICHARD MACKEY, banker; b. Melbourne, Fla., Jan. 18, 1925; s. Fred Detrick and Eva (Mackey) K.; B.S. in Bus. Adminstrn., U. Fla., 1949, M.B.A., 1950; m. Margaret Elizabeth Maybury, June 23, 1957; children—Richard John, Darren Andrew. Asst. v.p. First Nat. Bank Miami, 1950-59; v.p. William E. Pollock & Co., Miami, 1959-64; sr. v.p. First Nat. Bank, Ft. Lauderdale, Fla., 1965—; v.p., treas. Consol. Bankshares Fla., Ft. Lauderdale, 1970—. Treas. Opera Guild Ft. Lauderdale, 1970 . Bd. dirs., chmn Downtown Devel. Authority; bd. dirs. Broward County Traffic Council, Ft. Lauderdale Mus. Arts; bd. dirs., exec. v.p. Boys Club Broward County. Served with C.E., AUS, 1943-46. Mem. Exec. Assn. Ft. Lauderdale (dir. 1969-71), Phi Gamma Delta, Phi Etta Sigma. Club: Coral Ridge Country (Ft. Lauderdale). Home: 2748 NE 34th St Ft Lauderdale FL 33306 Office: PO Box 8009 Ft Lauderdale FL 33310

KOWERT, ARTHUR HERMAN, newspaper editor; b. Staunton, Ill., July 4, 1911; s. H.G.T. and Mathilde (Schuricht)K.; B.B.A., U. Tex., 1934; m. Elise Weber, Nov. 11, 1937; children—Bruce A., Nancy L. With Fredericksburg Pub. Co. (Tex.), 1935-—, sec.-treas., 1941-—; pres. Johnson City (Tex) Record-Courier, Inc., 1967-—; pres. Hill County Community Press Inc., Fredericksburg, Tex., 1969-—. Mem. Bd. Edn., Fredericksburg, Ind., Sch. Dist., 1951-63. Mem. Tex. (pres. 1953-54), S. Tex. (pres. 1944-45) press assns., Fredericksburg C of C. Lutheran. Lion. Home: 107 E Schubert St Fredericksburg TX 78624 Office: 108 E Main St Fredericksburg TX 78624

KOZELETZ, JOHN F., govt. ofcl.; b. N.Y.C., July 11, 1922; s. Joseph E. and Anna (Klimkowich) K.; A.B., U. Md., 1960; A.M., George Washington U., 1964, postgrad., 1964; m. Laura Evelyn Powell, Feb. 28, 1953. With civilian div. USAF, various locations, Far East, 1946-—, supr. employee devel. specialist 313th air div., Okinawa, 1955-61; employee devel. specialist, directorate civilian personnel, Hdqrs. USAF, Washington, 1961-—; staff instr., mgmt. inst. dir. Hdqrs. USAF Personnel Devel. Center, Maxwell AFB, Ala., 1963-65. Served with A.C., AUS, 1943-46. Mem. Am. Polit. Sci. Assn., Soc. Personnel Adminstrn., Am. Soc. Tng. and Devel. (recipient tng. program award 1962), Soc. Gen. Systems Research, Pi Sigma Alpha. Home: 3309 Spring Lane Falls Church VA 22041 Office: Hdqrs USAF AF/DPCWT Forrestal Bldg Washington DC 20314

KRAENZEL, CARL FREDERICK, educator; b.Hebron, N.D., Nov. 1, 1906; s. Reinhold and Hulda (Weber) K.; student Elmhurst (Ill.) Coll., 1926-29; B.A. U. N.D., 1930; M.A., U. Minn., 1932; postgrad. Harvard 1932-33; Ph.D., U. Wis., 1935; m. Margaret Powell, June 6, 1930; children—Sarah Janet (Mrs. Clinton Nagode), Frederick John, Theodore Carl, James Albert. Research asst. WPA, Wis., Minn., 1934-35; asst. prof. rural sociology Mont. State U., 1935-38, asso. prof., 1938-49, prof. 1949-68; H.Y. Benedict prof. sociology U. Tex. at El Paso, 1968-—. Technician, dir. Near East Found., Tehran, Iran, 1954-56, 59-61; cons. Office Econ. Opportunity Volt Tech. Corp., Kansas City, Mo., 1967-70; mem. health com. Gt. Plains Agrl. Adv. Council, 1955-—. Social Sci. Research Council fellow Harvard 1952-53. Mem. Rural Sociol. Soc., Gt. Plains Inst. (chmn. adv. com. 1957-—). Rocky Mountain Social Sci. Assn., Western States Water and Power Consumers Conf. (dir. 1967-—), Phi Kappa Phi. Author: Great Plains in Transition, 1955. Contbr. articles profl. jours. Home: 1515 Circle Dr El Paso TX 79902

KRAFT, JOSEPH, journalist; b. S. Orange, N.J., Sept. 4, 1924; s. David Harry and Sophie (Surasky) K.; A.B., Columbia, 1947; student Princeton, 1948-49, Inst. Advanced Study, 1950-51; m. Polly Winton, Jan 6, 1960. Editorial writer Washington Post, 1951-52; staff writer N.Y. Times, 1953-57; Washington corr. Harper's mag., 1962-65; syndicated columnist Washington Post, Chgo. Daily News, others, 1963-—. Served with AUS, 1943-46. Mem. Council Fgn. Relations, Phi Beta Kappa. Club: Century (N.Y.C.). Author: The Struggle for Algeria, 1961; The Grand Design, 1962; Profiles in Power, 1966. Contbr. to popular mags. Home: 3021 N St NW Washington DC 20007

KRAFT, LELAND MILO, JR., soil engr.; b. Gloversville, N.Y., Feb. 27, 1942; s. Leland Milo and Doris E. (Snyder) K.; B.C.E., Ohio State U., 1965, M.S., 1965, Ph.D., 1968; m. Rita Anne Lawyer, Sept. 2, 1967; children—Lisa Anne, Michelle Leigh. With Ohio State U., 1964-68, research asso. civil engring. dept., 1967-68; soil engr. Columbus (O.) Testing Lab., 1968-69; asst. prof. civil engring. Auburn U., 1969-—. Cons., Scott Constrn. Co., Opelika, Ala., 1971-—, City of Auburn, 1971-—, Harman, White and Assos., Inc., Opelika, 1970-—. Am. Soc. C.E. (chmn. soil mechanics found. div. tech. activities com. Ala. sect 1970-—), Am. Soc. Testing and Materials, Hwy. Research Bd., Sigma Xi, Chi Epsilon, Tau Beta Pi. Contbr. articles to tech. jours. Office: Civil Engring Dept Auburn U Auburn AL 36830 Home: 218 Redwood Ct Auburn AL 36830

KRAKEL, DEAN, mus. adminstr.; b. Ault, Colo., July 3, 1923; s. Elden A. and Gretta (Cross) K.; B.A., Colo. State Coll., 1950; M.A., U. Denver, 1951; postgrad. U. Colo. Extension Center, 1959; m. Iris Moneta Lesh, June 27, 1947; children—Ira Dean, Susan E. (dec.), Jennie Lynn, Jack Remington. Exhibits preparator Colo. Hist. Soc., Denver, 1951-52; cataloguer, 1951; archivist, asst. prof. in library U. Wyo., 1952-56; Curator, dept. dir., dir. USAF Acad. Mus., Col., 1956-61; dir. Thomas Gilcrease Inst. Am. History and Art. Tulsa, 1961-64; mng. dir. Nat. Cowboy Hall Fame and Western Heritage Center, Oklahoma City, 1964-—, trustee, asst. sec. exec. com., 1969-—. Served with AC, USNR, 1943-46. Mem. Am. Assn. Museums, Western Historians, Cowboy Artists of Am. (hon. mem.), Oklahoma City C. of C., Okla. Zool. Soc. (dir.), Okla. Westerners. Author: South Platte Country, History North Colorado, 1954; The Saga of Tom Horn, 1954; James Boren, Study in Discipline, 1968; Tom Ryan, Painter in Four Sixes Country. Home: 2500 E 122d St Oklahoma City OK 73111 Office: 1700 NE 63d St Oklahoma City OK 73111

KRALOVANEC, PAUL ANDREW, athletic corp. exec.; b. Port Chester, N.Y., Nov. 28, 1938; s. Paul and Anna (Zalman) K.; B.A., Valparaiso U., 1961; m. Dareen Sue Babuska, July 13, 1963; children—Karen, Paul, David. Salesman Campbell Soup Co., Scarsdale, N.Y., 1960-61; office services mgr. Nationwide Ins. Co., White Plains, N.Y., 1962-65; gen. mgr. Causeway Inn South, Tampa, Fla., 1965-71; bus. mgr. HMS Sports Corp., Tampa, 1971-—, dir., 1971-—. Vice pres. Sokol Retirement Home, Inc., Tampa, 1965-71. Mem. Tampa Hotel Assn. (pres. 1968), Fla., Tampa (pres. 1969) restaurant assns., Fla. Motor Hotel Assn. (dir. 1968-71). Lutheran (v.p. 1966-—, dir. Luth. Laymen's League, 1970-—). Clubs: Town and Country Sertoma (dir. 1969-72) Tampa Quarterback (Tampa). Home: 6809 Wilshire Ct Tampa FL 33615 Office: Courtney Campbell Causeway Tampa FL 33607

KRAMER, CLYDE YOUNG, statis. cons.; b. Lebanon, Pa., Feb. 2, 1925; s. Milton George and Bertha (Young) K.; B.S., Va. Poly. Inst., 1951, M.S., 1953, Ph.D., 1957; m. Glenna Lovene Akers, Mar. 17, 1944; 1 son, Bruce Carlton. Prof. statistics, Va. Poly. Inst., 1951-—; vis. prof. Purdue U.; spl. cons. USPHS, 1957-—, USN, 1957-—, N.E.A., 1959; statis. cons. Dow Chem. Co., 1959; cons. Tampax, Inc., Ft. Dietrick, Md., Inst. Textile Tech. Served from pvt. to cpl., AUS. 1943-47. Decorated Purple Heart, Bronze Star medal with oak leaf cluster, Presdl. Citation. Mem. Inst. Math. Statistics, Bimetrics Soc., Am. Statis. Assn., Va. Acad. Sci., Internat. Inst. Statistics, Phi Mu Epsilon, Phi Kappa Phi, Sigma Chi, Phi Sigma. Home: 123 Ellet Dr Box 255 Christiansburg VA 24073 Office: Va Poly Inst Blacksburg VA 24060

KRAMER, EARL JOHN JOSEPH, JR., govt. ofcl.; b. N.Y.C. Mar. 24, 1928; s. Earl Jerome Joseph and Josephine (Szabo) K.; B.C.E., Coll. City N.Y., 1950; m. Jeanette Doris Thompson, Jan. 15, 1955; children—Kathryn Suzann, Paul Anthony. Civil engr. Bur. Reclamation, Fresno, 1950-51; chief civil works sect. U.S. C.E., Mobile (Ala.) Dist. Office, 1951-60; chief civil sect. Ballistic Missile Constrn. Office, Torrance, Cal., 1960-62; chief structural sect., chief Project Mgmt. Office, NASA Marshall Space Flight Center, Huntsville, Ala., 1962-69, dep. chief site support, dir. Safeguard System Command, Huntsville, 1969-—; spl. lectr. engring. Spring Hill Coll. Pres. Whiteburg P.T.A. Mem. Am. Soc. C.E. (pres. Huntsville br. 1963, dir. Ala. sect. 1964-65), Chi Epsilon, Home: 120 Noble Dr Huntsville AL 35802 Office: Safeguard System Command PO Box 1500 Huntsville AL 35807

KRAMER, HOWARD D., govt. ofcl.; b. Dayton, O., Sept. 20, 1907; B.A., Miami U., Oxford, O., 1938, M.A., 1939; Ph.D. in History, State U. Ia., 1942; m. Elizabeth Kramer; children—Mary, John. Acting chief USIS, Philippines, 1945-46; asst. prof. Western Res. U. (now Case Western Res. U.), 1947-54; tech. information officer, social sci. analyst Air Research and Devel. Command, 1954-57; chmn. project, prof. research Am. U., 1957-60; with NSF, Washington, 1960-—, asso. program dir. fellowships program, 1960-65, program dir., head fellowships sect., 1965-66, now div. dir. Grad. Edn. Sci. Fulbright prof. Am. history, India, 1952-54. Home: 5604 Vernon Pl Bethesda MD 20034 Office: NSF 1800 G St NW Washington DC 20550*

KRAMER, JOHN KENNETH, mfg. co. exec.; b. Toledo, O., Jan. 19, 1931; s. Norman J. and Loretta (Lehmkuhle) K.; B.S. in M.E., U. Toledo, 1954; m Violet Marie St. Laurent, May 30, 1959; children—John E., David N., Jennifer M. Sr. indsl. engr. Rubbermaid Inc., Wooster, O., 1961-63, chief indsl. engr., 1963-65, corporate chief indsl. engr., 1965-67; dir. mfg. Rubbermaid Comml. Products, Inc., Winchester, Va., 1967-70; v.p. mfg., 1970-—. Exec. bd. Shenandoah Council Boy Scouts Am., 1971-—. Bd. dirs. United Fund, 1968-72, treas., 1969. Mem. Soc. Plastics Engrs., A.M. Inst. Indsl. Engrs. (dir. 1965-66), Shendadoah Valley Mfrs. Assn. (bd. dirs. 1972-—), Winchester C. of C. Rotarian. Home: Route 6 Box 325 Winchester VA 22601 Office: 3124 Valley Av Winchester VA 22601

KRAMISH, ARVIN MORRIS, govt. ofcl.; b. Denver, July 1, 1924; s. Max and Anne (Kaufman) K.; B.A., U. Denver, 1947, M.A., 1949; J.D., George Washington U., 1956, Ph.D., Am. U., 1970; m. Shirley Kastein, July 1, 1950; children—Marci Jane, Gary Robert. Admitted to Md. bar, 1956; trainee Dept. of State, Washington, 1949-50, U.S. resident officer, Germany, 1950-52, intelligence officer, 1952-55; fgn. affairs officer Office of Civil Affairs, Dept. of Army, Washington, 1955-61; assigned to Nat. War Coll., 1961-62; staff asst. to dir. arms control Office Sec. Def., 1963-65; sr. pvt. investment officer Overseas Pvt. Investment Corp., State Dept., 1965-—. Served with AUS, 1943-46; lt. col. Res. Home: 8214 Larry Pl Chevy Chase MD 20015 Office: OPIC Washington DC 20527

KRANZ, MARTIN EMILE, lawyer; b. New Orleans, Mar. 3, 1900; s. John Martin and Carolyn (Von Behren) K.; B.A., Loyola U., New Orleans, 1920, J.D., 1921, LL.M., 1922; m. Ysabelita Hamilton, Apr. 15, 1926; children—Fritzi (Mrs. Jack L. Martin), Mitzi. Admitted to La. bar, 1921; since practiced law specializing in civil law in New Orleans. Sec., legal adviser bd. assessors La. Assessors Assn., 1938-—, La. Assessors Retirement fund, 1950-—; lectr. ad valorem taxation. Atty., Salvation Army, 1948-—, pres. adv. bd. 1955; exec. bd., New Orleans area Boy Scouts Am., 1947-—, atty., 1961-—. Fellow Internat. Acad. Law and Sci.; mem. Am., La., New Orleans bar assns., Friends Pub. Schs. La. (pres. 1936). Mason (33 deg.). Contbr. articles ad valorem taxation to profl. jours. Home: 1407 Poland Av New Orleans LA 70117 Office: Maison Blanche Bldg New Orleans LA 70112

KRAUSE, FLOYD CARL, rubber co. exec.; b. Akron, O., Feb. 15, 1909; s. Albert Peter and Tillie (Wehnes) K.; B.S. in Mech. Engring., Akron U., 1932; m. Thelma Yvonne Rife, Mar. 29, 1930; children—Ronald, Carol, Gerald. With Armstrong Rubber Co., 1939-41, 45-—, prodn. mgr., West Haven, Conn., 1949-58, asst. factory mgr., Natchez, Miss., 1958-64, factory mgr., 1964-68, gen. mgr., 1968-—. Dist. chmn. Andrew Jackson council Boy Scouts Am., 1967-68; co-chmn. United Givers Fund Dr., 1969-70. Bd. dirs. YMCA, Miss. Safety Council. Served to lt. col. AUS, 1941-46. Decorated Silver Star, Purple Heart. Mem. So. Rubber Group (dir. 1969-—), Natchez-Adams County C. of C. (dir. 1964-—). Republican. Presbyn. Mason (Shriner), Kiwanian. Home: 108 Melrose Av Natchez MS 39120 Office: PO Box 808 Natchez MS 39120

KRAUSE, LAWRENCE BERLE, economist; b. Detroit, Dec. 8, 1929; s. Paul Henry and Lena Blair (Blair) K.; B.A., U. Mich., 1951, M.A., 1952; Ph.D. (Alumni fellow 1952-54); Harvard, 1958; m. Sallye Joan Kirstein, Dec. 20, 1953; children—Leonard Blair, Jason Andrew. Asst. prof. Yale, New Haven, 1958-63; sr. fellow Brookings Inst., Washington, 1963-67, 69-—; sr. staff Council Econ. Advisers, Washington, 1967-69. Lectr. internat. econs. Johns Hopkins U., 1968-—; bd. editors Internat. Orgn., 1969-—; mem. editorial adv. bd. Orbis, 1968-—. Mem. research council Fgn. Policy Research Inst., 1971-—. Served to 1st lt. USMCR, 1954-56. Recipient Osterweil Prize U. Mich., 1951, Sims Prize, 1950. Mem. Am. Econ. Assn. Phi Beta Kappa, Phi Kappa Phi, Phi Eta Sigma. Author: Federal Tax Treatment of Foreign Income, 1964; European Economic Integration and the United States, 1968; Sequel to Bretton Woods, 1971. Home: 3361 Stephenson Pl NW Washington DC 20015 Office: 1775 Massachusetts Av NW Washington DC 20036

KRAUSE, ORVILLE ELLIS, agrl. economist; b. Storm Lake, Ia., Apr. 21, 1914; s. Ellis Llewellyn and Jennie (Waterman) K.; B.A., Marietta Coll., 1938; M.S., U. Wis., 1950, Ph.D., 1957; m. Angela Barney, Dec. 22, 1951. With Wis. Dept. Agr., Madison, 1948-49; statistician U.S. Dept. Agr., Madison, Wis., 1949-62, agrl. economist, Washington 1962-—. Mem. Am. Agr. Econ. Assn., Am. Econ. Assn., Soc. Mayflower Descs., S.A.R. Presbyn. (elder 1955-61). Mason. Home: 630 A St. NE Washington DC 20002 Office: U.S. Dept. Agr ERS-NRED Washington DC 20250

KRAVIS, GEORGE ROBERTS, II, broadcasting exec.; b. Tulsa, Sept. 11, 1938; s. Raymond Field and Bessie (Roberts) K.; grad. U. Okla., 1960. Mem. prodn. dept. stas. KOKH FM/TV, KETA/TV, Oklahoma City, 1959-60, sta. KOED/TV, Tulsa, 1959-60; founder, owner radio sta. KRAV, Tulsa, 1962; owner radio sta. KFMJ, Tulsa, 1966-—; mem. ABC/FM Radio Bd., 1968. Mem. Arts Council of Tulsa, Tulsa Arts Commn., vice chmn. Tulsa Civic Ballet Bd. Bd. dirs. Philbrook Art Center, Cystic Fibrosis, Multiple Sclerosis, Tulsa Philharmonic. Mem. Okla. Broadcasters Assn., Nat. Assn. FM Broadcasters (dir. 1972-73), Nat. Assn. Broadcasters (mem. FM Radio com. 1964). Clubs: Tulsa, Tulsa Press, Tulsa Country; Summit. Address: KRAV/KFMJ PO Box 746 Tulsa OK 74101

KREBS, ROCKNE, sculptor; b. Kansas City, Mo., Dec. 24, 1938; s. Arthur Sandford and Lorine (Fisher) K.; B.F.A., U. Kansas, 1961; m. Denise De Agostino, Apr. 16, 1966; 1 dau., Heather. Exhibited in group shows at Ann. Show of Contemporary Am. Sculpture, 1966, 68, Whitney Mus., N.Y.C., Hemisfair, San Antonio, 1968, Corcoran Gallery, Washington, 1969, 69th Am. Exhbn., Art Inst. Chgo., 1970, Balt. Mus., Balt., 1970, Albright-Knox Gallery, Buffalo, 1971, Walker Art Center, Mpls., 1971, Los Angeles County Mus., 1971, New Orleans Mus., 1971. Vis. artist, Drexel Inst., Phila., 1968, Yale, New Haven, 1970, Corcoran Sch. Art, Washington, 1970-71. Served to lt. USNR, 1962-65. Washington Gallery Modern Art grantee, 1968, Cassandra Found. grantee, 1969, Nat. Endowment for the Arts fellow, 1970. Patentee in light-reflection apparatus, Home: 1861 1/2 Mintwood Pl NW Washington DC 20009 Studio 1737 Johnson Av NW Washington DC 20010

KREGLOW, ALAN FRANK, physician; b. Newcastle, Pa., Mar. 22, 1908; s. Adam Frank and Louise (Miller) K.; student George Washington U., 1926-29; B.S., W. Va., U., 1932; M.D., Med. Coll. Va., 1934; m. Amanda Ellen Chittum, Sept. 27, 1941; children—Alan Frank, Amanda Byington. Intern, Sibley Meml. Hosp., Washington, 1934-35; resident, 1935-36; pvt. practice medicine specializing in internal medicine, Washington, 1936-—; sr. attending physician Doctors Hosp., Washington, 1964-—; also hon. mem. bd. dirs. Recipient Selective Service medal, 1946, Asso. fellow Am. Coll. Cardiology; mem. Am. Soc. Internal Medicine, Am. Soc. for Clin. Pharmacology and Therapeutics (past sec.), A.M.A., Med. Soc. D.C., Am. Heart Assn., Soc. Friendly Sons St. Patrick, Sigma Alpha Epsilon, Omicron Delta Kappa. Republican. Episcopalian. Clubs: Chevy Chase (Md.); University (Washington). Home: 4900 Indian Lane NW Washington DC 20016 Office: 1835 Eye St NW Washington DC 20006

KREIGER, JOHN R., broadcasting exec. Pres., KVET and KASE, Austin, Tex. Address: 705 N Lamar St Austin TX 78701

KREIPKE, MERRILL VINCENT, govt. ofcl.; b. Evansville, Ind., Feb. 14, 1916; s. Charles Edwin and Ida (Hufnagel) K.; student Evansville Coll., 1931-33; B.S. in Civil Engring., Purdue U. 1936; postgrad. George Washington U., 1960-62;; m. Dorothy Louise Neu, July 17, 1937; children—Karen Jean, Jane Ann. Engr., Office of City Engr., Evansville, 1936-39; engr. soil mechanics and materials Army Engrs. Dist., Louisville, 1939-51, chief, found. and materials br., Louisville, 1951, engr. research and devel. Office Chief Engrs., U.S. Army, Washington, 1956-61, engr. Office Chief Research and Devel., Washington, 1961-—, chief terrestrial scis. br. Environmental Scis. div. Office Chief of Research and Devel. Dept. of Army, Washington, 1971-72, chief geophysical scis., 1972-—. Individual practice cons. engr. soils and founds., 1951-56. Permanent sec. Quadripartite Standing Working Group on Ground Mobility (Armies of U.S., U.K., Can., Australia), 1957-—; project officer U.S., NATO Long Term Sci. Study Land Based Mobility, 1966-—; exec. mem. subgroup T (ground mobility) Tech. Coop. Program, U.S. Nat. Leader, 1967-—; project leader U.S., NATO Long Term Sci. Study Complementary Mobility, 1968-—; acting chief Geophys. Scis. Br., Office Chief Research and Devel., Washington, 1969-70, acting chief Terrestrial Scis. Br., 1970-—. Mem. camp site devel. com. N.Va. council Girl Scouts U.S.A., 1957-60. Served from ensign to lt. (j.g.) USNR. 1944-46. Recipient Meritorious Civilian Service medal Dept. Army, 1966. Registered profl. engr., Ky., Ind. Va. Fellow Am. Soc. C.E.; mem. Soc. Am. Mil. Engrs., Internat. Soc. Terrain-Vehicle Systems (charter). Presbyn. (deacon, elder). Home: 3060 Hazelton St Falls Church VA 22044 Office: 3045 Columbia Pike Arlington VA 22204

KREISELMAIER, KURT WALTER, educator; b. Fargo, N.D., Aug. 9, 1934; s. Walter Fredrick and Agnes Lillian (Tenneson) K.; B.S. in Chem. Tech., N.D. State U., 1956; Ph.D. in Inorganic Nuclear Chemistry, Mass. Inst. Tech., 1961; M.B.A., So. Meth. U., 1970; m. Cynthia Ann Jackson, July 21, 1962; children—Brian, Paul Kent. Sect. head Tex. Instruments, Inc., Dallas, 1961-68; v.p. research and devel. Graham Magnetics, Inc. (Tex.), 1968-70; asst. prof. mgmt. and mgmt. sci. Midwestern U., Wichita Falls, Tex., 1970-—; cons., dir. Zentron, Inc., Dallas, 1971-—. Mem. Acad. Mgmt., Sigma Xi, Sigma Iota Epsilon, Beta Gamma Sigma, Phi Kappa Phi, Phi Lambda Upsilon. Lion (v.p. Wichita Falls 1972). Contbg. author: Pigment Handbook. Patentee in field. Developed permanent magnetic computer tape. Home: 1905 10th St Wichita Falls TX 76301 Office: 3400 Taft Blvd Wichita Falls TX 65397

KREITZER, WILLIAM HENRY, oil co. exec.; b. Knightstown, Ind., Sept. 27, 1923; s. Lawrence Edward and Elsie (Jordan) K.; student Ind. U., 1941-42; B.S., Purdue U., 1948; m. Mary Louise Hole, Oct. 26, 1946; children—Crystal Louise, Lawrence William, Karen Lee; m. 2d, Jean Alma Morris, Nov. 8, 1959. Various engring. and supervisory positions, Mobil Oil Corp., St. Louis, Indpls., N.Y.C., 1948-60, operating mgr. S.W. div., 1960-63, wholesale plant mgr., 1963-64, market devel. mgr., 1964, marketing planning mgr., 1964-65, v.p. gas liquids, Houston, 1965-—; pres., chmn. bd. Petrolanc Gas Co., Inc., Natchitoches, La. Served as 2d lt. USAAF, 1943-45. Decorated Purple Heart, Air medal with 2 oak leaf clusters; named Distinguished Engring. Alumnus Purdue U., 1970. Mem. Mo. Soc. Profl. Engrs., Am. Mgmt. Assn., Am. Petroleum Inst., Sigma Alpha Epsilon. Republican. Methodist. Home: 14427 Twisted Oak Lane Houston TX 77024 Office: Houston Natural Gas Bldg 1200 Travis St Houston TX 77002

KRELL, BENNIE WILLIAM, electronic co. exec.; b. Columbia, S.C., Aug. 21, 1904; s. Luther Arthur and Bessie (Brickle) K.; student U.S.C., 1924-26; m. Julia Crosland, July 15, 1928; 1 dau., Jacquelyn (Mrs. Williams). Owner, operation Dixie Radio Supply Co., Columbia, 1929-46; pres., gen. mgr. Dixie Radio Supply Co., Inc., Columbia, 1946-—. Mason (Shriner), Elk. Home: Route 1 Eastover SC 29044 Office: 1900 Barnwell St Columbia SC 29202

KREMER, LOWELL JEROME, wholesale trade exec.; b. Pitts., Feb. 22, 1931; s. Jerome Boris and Betty (Friedman) K.; B.A. in Econs., U. Mich., 1952; m. Lois Ann Steinberg, Dec. 21, 1952; children—Lyn R., Lori Lee, Jeffrey B. Sales mgr. Magnolia Liquor Co., Inc., New Orleans, 1956-59; gen. mgr. United Beverage Co., Oklahoma City, 1959-65; v.p., gen. mgr. Duval Spirits, Inc., Jacksonville, Fla., 1965-—. Served with USNR, 1953-56. Mem. Sales and marketing Execs., Sigma Alpha Mu. Office: PO Box 4670 Jacksonville FL 32201

KRENKEL, PETER ASHTON, educator; b. San Francisco, Jan. 3, 1930; s. Harry N. and Daisy (Ashton) K.; A.A., City Coll. San Francisco, 1951; B.S., U. Cal. at Berkeley, 1956, M.S., 1958, Ph.D., 1960; M. Norma Kay Williams, June 28, 1953. Instr. civil engring. U. Cal. Berkeley, 1958-60; prof. civil engring. Vanderbilt U., Nashville, 1960-65, chmn., prof. dept. environmental and water resources engring., 1965-—; pres. Asso. Water & Air Resources Engrs., Inc., cons. engrs., Nashville, 1967-—. Cons. WHO, Dept. Interior, Pub. Health Service, NSF, U.S. C.E., The Mead Corp., duPont, Farmers Chem. Inc.; mem. State of Tenn. Environmental Health Council, 1967-—. Tb and Respiratory Disease Assn. Air Conservation Commn., 1966-—. Served with C.E., AUS, 1953-55. Recipient research award for san. engring. Am. Soc. C.E., 1963. Mem. Water Pollution Control Fedn., Air pollution Control Assn., Am. Water Works, Assn., Am. Inst. Chem. Engrs., Am. Soc. C.E., Sigma Xi, Tau Beta Pi. Chi Epsilon. Author: (with others) Stream Analysis and Thermal Pollution, 1968; (with F.L. Parker) Engineering and Economic Aspects of Thermal Pollution, 1969; (with F.L. Parker) Biological Aspects of Thermal Pollution, 1969. Home: 1304 Hildreth Dr Nashville TN 37215

KRENTZMAN, BEN, U.S. dist judge; b. Milton, Fla., Mar. 21, 1914; s. Isaac B. and Juanita (Rogers) K.; B.S., LL.B., U. Fla., 1938; m. Wilma McMullen, Nov. 30, 1946; children—John Arthur, Mary Louise, Elizabeth Rogers. Admitted to Fla. bar, 1938; practiced in Clearwater, Fla., 1938-41; 46-67; U.S. judge Tampa Div., Middle Dist.

Fla., 1967—. Served to lt. col. AUS, 1941-46. Decorated Bronze Star. Home: 1541 Walnut St Clearwater FL 33515 Office: PO Box 3209 Tampa FL 33601

KREPS, CLIFTON H., educator; m. Juanita M. Kreps; 3 children. Wachovia prof. banking U. N.C. at Chapel Hill. Address: U North Carolina Sch Bus Chapel Hill NC 27514*

KREPS, JUANITA M. (MRS. CLIFTON H. KREPS), educator, stock exchange exec.; m. Clifton H. Kreps.; 3 children. James B. Duke prof. econs. Women's Coll. Duke U., also asst. univ. provost; dir. N.Y. Stock Exchange. Author books including Sex in the Marketplace: American Women at Work. Address: Office Dean Women's Coll Duke U Durham NC 27708*

KREUTZ, OSCAR R., savs. and loan exec.; b. Sioux City, Ia., April 27, 1898; s. John and Jennie (Peterson) K.; student pub. schs.; m. Marion Frances Benton, June 23, 1926; children—Mary Ann (Mrs. Judson Dodson), Barbara Jane (Mrs. Michael Barrett). Organizer, First Fed. Savs. and Loan Assn., Sioux City, Ia., 1923, mng. officer, 1923-33; sec. Ia. Savs. and Loan League, 1925-33; v.p. Fed. Home Loan Bank of Chgo., 1934; chmn. review com. Fed. Home Loan Bank Bd., 1934-41; gen. mgr. Fed. Savs. and Loan Ins. Corp., 1941-44; exec. mgr. Nat. League Insured Savs. Assn., 1944-53; exec. cons., 1953-54; exec. v.p. First Fed. Savs. and Loan Assn., St. Petersburg, Fla., 1953-54, pres., chmn. bd., 1954-68, chmn. bd., 1968—; dir. Milton Roy Co., Investors Mortgage Ins. Co. Boston, CATV, past mem. task force Fed. Home Loan Bank Bd. cons. to govt. Argentine, AID, 1963. Mem., past pres. Com. of 100; past pres., past gen. campaign chmn. United Fund; past pres. Suncoasters of St. Petersburg, St. Petersburg Progress, Inc.; pres. St. Petersburg Improvement Found., mem. Fla. Council 100; hon. dir. Sci. Center, St. Petersburg Symphony Soc.; adv. bd. Abilities, Inc.; trustee Eckerd Coll.; past trustee Mus. Fine Arts of St. Petersburg. Served in USNR, World War I. Mem. St. Petersburg C. of C., Nat. League Insured Savs. Assn. (pres. 1960), Internat. Union Bldg. Socs. and Savs. Assns. (v.p., mem. council, exec. com.), Fla. Savs. and Loan League (pres. 1961), Navy League U.S., Newcomen Soc. N. Am., Am. Legion. Presbyn. Mason (32 deg.). Clubs: Yacht, Quarterback, Rotary, Lakewood Country, Commerce. Contbr. articles profl. publs. Home: 2028 Brightwaters Blvd Snell Isle St Petersburg FL 33704 Office: First Fed Bldg St Petersburg FL 33731

KREZDORN, ALFRED HERMAN, educator; Ph.D., Tex. A. and M. U. Prof., chmn. dept. fruit crops Inst. Food and Agrl. Scis., U. Fla., Gainesville. Office: U Fla Gainesville FL 32601*

KRIEGEL, HENRY, city treas., Houston. Address: 900 Brazos St Houston TX 77002*

KRIEGMAN, GEORGE, psychoanalyst, psychiatrist; b. Chgo., Sept. 14, 1917; s. Peter Isaac and Bertha (Share) K.; A.B., U. Ill., 1939, M.S., 1942, M.D., 1943; m. Lois Harriet Smason, Jan. 31, 1941; children—Lesley, Diane, Mitchell, Bruce. Candidate, Washington Sch. Psychiatry, 1944-51, Washington Psychoanalytic Inst., 1944-50; intern St. Elizabeths Hosp., Washington, 1943-44, resident, 1944-45; practice medicine, specializing in psychiatry, Richmond, Va., 1947—; asst. prof. Med. Coll. Va., 1950-58; lectr. psychiatry Richmond Profl. Inst., 1951-58, U. Va., 1958-62; instr. Washington Psychoanalytic Inst., 1958-61; asst. clin. prof. psychiatry Med. Coll. Va., 1959-64, asso. clin. prof., 1964-68, clin. prof. psychiatry, 1968—; cons. Family and Childrens Service Soc., 1947—, Va. State Dept. Pub. Welfare, Child Care Bur., 1947-52, VA Hosp., Roanoke, Va., 1652-57; profl. adv. bd. Va. Mental Health and Mental Retardation, 1971—. Served to capt. AUS, 1945-47. Fellow Am. Psychiatry Assn., Am. Acad. Psychoanalysts; mem. Am. Psychoanalyst Assn., Neuropsychiat. Soc. Va., Richmond Acad. Medicine, Acad. Religion and Mental Health. Clubs: Torch, Bull and Bear. Home: 26 Malvern Av Richmond VA 23221

KRISE, EDWARD FISHER, army officer; b. Detroit, June 28, 1924; s. W. Gomer and Dorothy (Fisher) K.; A.B., Brown U., 1949; M.A., U. Chgo., 1950; Ph.D., 1958; m. Elizabeth Ann Bradt, Aug. 5, 1948; children—Patricia Lynn, Thomas Warren. Commd. 1st lt. U.S. Army, 1951, advanced through grades to col., 1968; instr. sociology N.C. State Coll., Ft. Bragg, 1958-61; chief personnel services div. Hq. USCONARC, Ft. Monroe, Va., 1968-69; chief directives and policy Office Surgeon Gen. Washington, 1969-71; dir. Dept. Def. Race Relations Inst., Patrick AFB, Fla., 1971—. Mem. N.M. Conf. Social Welfare, 1954-56. Vice pres. U.S. Power Squadrons, Annapolis, Md., 1967. Decorated Silver Star, Legion of Merit, Bronze Star, Purple Heart. Mem. Nat. Assn. Social Workers, Acad. Certified Social Workers, Council on Social Work Edn., Sigma Nu. Presbyn. Lion. Clubs: Annapolis Yacht, Eau Gallie Yacht; Old Point Comfort Yacht (Ft. Monroe). Home: 206 N A1A Patrick AFB FL 32925 Office: Def Race Relations Inst Patrick AFB FL 32925

KRIVOY, HAROLD LLOYD, govt. ofcl.; b. Newark, N.J., Nov. 26, 1922; s. Samuel and Rose (Hirsch) K.; B.S.in Applied Geophysics, U. Utah, 1950; postgrad. U. Hawaii, 1956-58; m. Glade Anne Smith, Dec. 20, 1949; children—Stephen, Alison, Paul. Geophysicist Gulf Oil, Mobil Oil Exploration Surveys Inc., Tex., Pa., Colo., Uruguay, 1950-56; geophysicist U.S. Coast and Geodetic Survey, Hawaii, 1956-59; geophysicist U.S. Geol. Survey, Hawaii, 1959-64, Denver, 1964-66, Flagstaff, Ariz., 1966-68, Corpus Christi, Tex., 1968—. Served with AUS, 1943-46. Mem. Am. Geophys. Union, Seismol. Soc. Am., Coastal Bend Geophys. Soc. Hawaiian Acad. Sci. Contbr. articles profl. jours. Home: 418 Poenisch Dr Corpus Christi TX 78412 Office: US Geol Survey Marine Geology Box 6732 Corpus Christi TX 78411

KRIVOY, WILLIAM AARON, pharmacologist; b. Newark, Jan. 2, 1928; s. Samuel and Rose (Hirschenhorn) K.; B.S., Georgetown U., 1948; M.S., George Washington U., 1949, Ph.D., 1953. Pharmacologist, Chem. Corps Med. Labs., Army Chem. Center, Md., 1950-54; postdoctoral research fellow U. Pa., 1954-55, dept. pharmacology U. Edinburgh (Scotland), 1955-57; instr. dept. pharmacology Tulane U., 1957-59; asst. prof. dept. pharmacology, Baylor U., 1959-63, asso. prof., 1963-68; with Nat. Inst. Mental Health, Addiction Research Center, Lexington, Ky., 1968—, now pharmacologist. Mem. Am. Soc. Pharmacology and Exptl. Therapeutics, Brit. Pharm. Soc., Soc. Exptl. Biology and Medicine N.Y. Acad. Scis., Am. Coll. Neuropsychopharmacology, Biophys. Soc., Tex. Acad. Sci., Western Pharmacology Soc., Sigma Xi. Contbr. numerous articles to profl. jours. Home: 1565 Alexandria Dr Lexington KY 40504 Office: Nat Inst Mental Health Addiction Research Center Lexington KY 40507

KROCK, ARTHUR, newspaperman; b. Glasgow, Ky., Nov. 16, 1887; s. Joseph and Caroline (Morris) K.; A.A., Lewis Inst., Chgo.; A.M., Princeton, 1908; Litt.D., U. Louisville, U. Ky., 1956, Centre Coll. Ky.; m. Marguerite Polleys, Apr. 22, 1911 (dec. 1938); 1 son, Thomas Polleys; m. 2d, Martha Granger Blair, 1939. Reporter, Louisville, 1907; Washington corr. The Courier Jour. and Louisville Times, 1910-15, editorial mgr., 1915-19, editor-in-chief, 1919-23; asst. to pres. N.Y. World 1923-27; chief Washington corr. N.Y. Times, 1932-53, Washington commentator, 1953-66. Mem. Pulitzer Prize Bd., Sch. of Journalism, Columbia, 1940-53. Contbr. syndicated articles from Peace Conf., Paris, France, 1918-19; one of 3 Am. mems. Inter-Allied Press Com. of Fourteen which induced open sessions Peace Conf.; asst. to chmn., Democratic Nat. Com., 1920. Decorated comdr. Legion d'Honneur (France); Officer's Cross Polonia Restituta; Knights' Cross, Order of St. Olav (Norway). Recipient Pulitzer Prize for Washington Corrs., Pulitzer Prize for Washington Corrs., 1935, 38, nat. corr. 1950 (declined); John Peter Zerga award, U. Ariz. Sch. Journalism, 1967, Presdl. Medal of Freedom, 1970, Freedom Found., 1971. Fellow Sigma Delta Chi. Democrat. Clubs: Metropolitan, Gridiron, 1925 F Street, Princeton (Washington); Nassau (Princeton, N.J.). Author: The Editorials of Henry Watterson, 1923; In the Nation, 1966; Memoirs, 1968; The Consent of the Governed, 1971; Myself When Young, 1973. Home: 2029 Connecticut Av NW Washington DC20006 Office: 1920 L St Washington DC 20036

KROL, JOSEPH, engr., educator; b. Warsaw, Poland, Jan. 14, 1911; s. Kazimierz and Feliksa (Tokarzewski) K.; M.S., Warsaw (Poland) Inst. Tech., 1937; Ph.D. U. London (Eng.), 1947; m. Evelyn Swingland, Apr. 15, 1952. Came, to U.S., 1956, naturalized, 1962. Tech. officer with directorate ammunition prodn. Brit. Ministry of Supply, London, Eng., 1941-45; research scientist U. London, 1946-47; cons. engr., Montreal, Que., Can., 1948-51; asso. prof. mech. engring. U. Manitoba (Can.), 1951-56; prof. indsl. engring. Ga. Inst. Tech., 1956—. Recipient George Stephenson prize, 1951. Registered profl. engr., Ga. Fellow Instn. Mech. Engrs.; mem. Am. Inst. Indsl. Engrs., Engring. Inst. Can., Corp. Profl. Engrs. Que., Am. Econ. Assn., Am. Soc. Mech. Engrs., Instrument Soc., Am., A.A.A.S., Am. Statis. Assn., Econometric Soc., Inst., Mgmt. Scis., Sigma Xi. Author articles on engring. and mgmt. subjects. Home: 210 North Av NW Atlanta GA 30313

KROLL, MILTON P., lawyer; b. Paterson, N.J., 1914; A.B., U. W. Va., 1934; LL.B., Harvard, 1937. Admitted to N.J. bar, 1938, D.C. bar, 1949; atty. SEC, 1940-48, asst. gen. counsel, 1948-52, asso. gen counsel, 1952-53; now mem. firm Freedman, Levy, Kroll & Simonds, Washington; lectr. law George Washington U., 1952-59. Mem. Bar Assn. D.C., Am. Law Inst., Fed., Am. bar assns., Phi Beta Kappa. Address: Freedman Levy Kroll & Simonds 1730 K St NW Washington DC 20006*

KRONCKE, NOEL, hosp. adminstr. Adminstr. Children's Hosp. D.C., Washington. Address: 2125 13th St NW Washington DC 20009*

KRONICK, DAVID ABRAHAM, librarian; b. Connelsville, Pa., Oct. 5, 1917; s. Barnet L. and Rose L. (Miller) K.; B.A., Western Res. U., 1940, B.S. in L.S., 1941; Ph.D., U. Chgo., 1956; m. Marilyn Abramson, Oct. 25, 1959; children—Steven Leonard, Beryl Leah. Librarian, Western Res. U. Sch. Medicine, Cleve., 1946-49, U. Mich. Med. Sch., Ann Arbor, 1955-59; dir. Cleve. Med. Library, 1959-64; chief reference div. Nat. Library Medicine, Washington, 1964-65; dir. med. communications, librarian U. Tex. Med. Sch., San Antonio, 1965—. Pres. Friends San Antonio Pub. Library, 1967-68, Tex. Council Health Scis. Libraries, 1969. Served to capt. M.C., AUS, 1941-46. Council Library Resources fellow, 1971. Mem. Med. Library Assn., Am. Assn. History Medicine, Am. Soc. Information Sci. Mem. B'nai B'rith. Contbr. articles to profl. jours. Home: 1223 Mr Riga Dr San Antonio TX 78229 Office: U Tex Med Sch 7703 Floyd Curl Dr San Antonio TX 78229

KROP, STEPHEN, pharmacologist; b. N.Y.C., Sept. 24, 1911; s. James D. and Mary (Badeker) K.; B.S., George Washington U., 1939; M.S., Georgetown U., 1940; Ph.D., Cornell U., 1942; m. Mary Lulick, July 28, 1934; children—Elaine Stephanie (Mrs. Max W. Wallenburg), Marianne Elizabeth, Paul Nicholas, Thomas Monroe. Faculty Cornell U. Med. Coll., 1939-44, Yale Med. Sch., 1944-46; dir. pharmacological research U.S. Army Chem. Corps Med. Research Labs., 1946-48; exptl. pharmacologist Squibb Inst., New Brunswick, N.Y., 1948-49; dir. pharmacological research Warner Inst., N.Y.C., 1949-51; research asst., dir. Chem. Biol. Coordination Center NRC, 1951-52, mil. chem. research coordinator, 1952-57; dir. pharmacological research Ethlcon, Somerville, N.J., 1957-63; chief drug pharmacology br. Bur. Drugs U.S. FDA, Washington, 1963—. Lectr. Georgetown U. 1963—. Pres. Ethicon Research Found., 1958-63. Fellow N.Y. Acad. Scis., A.A.A.S.; mem. Am. Soc. Pharmacology and Exptl. Therapy, Am. Physiol. Soc., Exptl. Biology and Medicine, Am. Indsl. Hygiene Assn., Soc. Toxicology, Harvey Soc., Sigma Xi Contbr. articles to profl. jours. Home: 7908 Birnam Wood Dr McLean VA 22101 Office: 200 C St SW Washington DC 20204

KRUEGER, JACK BURKE, editor; b. San Antonio, Sept. 26, 1908; s. August and Elizabeth (Hayden) K.; student San Antonio Jr. Coll., U. Tex., 1929; m. Lucille Ann Leibe, Nov. 11, 1937; 1 dau., Kathryn Ann. Reporter San Antonio Light, 1929-36; editor A.P., Dallas, San Francisco, 1936-44; city editor Dallas News, 1945-55, asst. mng. editor, 1955-57, mng. editor, 1957-68, exec. editor, 1968—; dir. A. H. Belo Corp. Mem. Pulitzer Prize jury. Mem. Am. Press Inst. (adv. bd.), A.P. Mng. Editors Assn., Am. Soc. Newspapers Editors, Sigma Delta Chi. Home: 5922 Joyce Way Dallas TX 75222 Office: Communications Center Dallas TX 75222

KRUGER, GUSTAV OTTO, JR., oral surgeon, educator; b. N.Y.C., Sept. 28, 1916; s. Gustav Otto and Anna Charlotte (Mellquist) K.; B.S., George Washington U., 1938, A.M., 1939; D.D.S., Georgetown U., 1939; m. Helyn E. Hollingsworth, Apr. 12, 1947; children—Deborah Ann, Tristram Coffin, Abigail Hollingsworth. Intern Johns Hopkins Hosp., 1939-40; fellow Mayo Found., 1940-42, 45-48; mem. faculty Georgetown U. Sch. Dentistry and Grad. Sch., 1948—, prof. oral surgery, chmn. dept., 1948—, asso. dean, 1966—; chief dental dept. Georgetown U. Hosp., Washington, 1948—; cons. VA hosps., Martinsburg, W.Va., Washington, U.S. Naval Hosp., Bethesda, D.C. Gen. Hosp., Washington; cons. President's physician, 1960-64; cons. Walter Reed Army Med. Center. Mem. med. adv. com. D.C. Dept. Pub. Welfare, 1957-70; chmn. clin. cancer tng. com. NIH, 1969-71. Served to capt., Dental Corps, AUS, 1942-45; CBI, PTO. Named Man of Yr., Georgetown U. Alumni Assn., 1961. Diplomate Am. Bd. Oral Surgery (pres. 1964). Fellow Am., (Washington chmn.), Internat (Washington chmn.) colls. dentists; mem. Am. Dental Assn. (chmn. oral surg. sect. 1961), D.C. Dental Soc. (pres. 1960), Am. (program chmn. 1961), Middle Atlantic (pres. 1952) socs. oral surgeons, Am. Acad. Oral Pathology, Am. Acad. Oral Roentgenology, Internat. Assn. Dental Research, Xi Psi Phi, Sigma Gamma Epsilon, Omicron Kappa Upsilon. Kiwanian. Author: Textbook of Oral Surgery, 1959. Home: 6806 Bradgrove Circle Bethesda MD 20014 Office: 3900 Reservoir Rd Washington DC 20007

KRUGHOFF, ROBERT M., govt. ofcl. Dir. Office Research and Devel. Planning, Dept. Health, Edn. and Welfare, Washington. Address: Dept Health Edn and Welfare 330 Independence Blvd SW Washington DC 20201*

KRUMBEIN, NATHANIEL, furniture co. exec.; b. Alliance, O., June 5, 1914; s. Leo and Esther (Simowitz) K.; B.S., U. Ga., 1937; Ph.G., U. S.C., 1938; m. Amy Meyers, Feb. 15, 1944; children—Charles H., Joyce T., Michael M., Lee B. Asst. mgr. Converse Pharmacy, Spartansburg, S.C., 1938, Armstrong Pharmacy, Greenville, S.C., 1938-39; mgr. Lane Drug Store, Anniston, Ala., 1939-40; pres. Kay Drug Co., Charlotte, N.C., 1946-49; salesman, Heilig-Meyers Furniture Co., Richmond, Va., 1950-51, credit mgr., 1952, store mgr., 1952-58, dist. supr., 1958-66, dir. operations, 1966-68, v.p., 1968-71, mem. exec. com., 1965—, also dir. vice pres., bd. dirs. Jewish Community Center, 1958-60; chmn. exec. com., chmn. regional adv. bd. Va.-N.C. Anti-Defamation League, 1963-71. Bd. dirs. Richmond Jewish Community Council, Nat. Joint Distbn. Com. Served to maj. AUS, 1940-46. Mem. U. Ga. Alumni Assn. (v.p. bd. mgrs. 1963-69; Distinguished Service award 1970), Alpha Epsilon Pi (nat. pres. 1971). Mason. Club: Lakeside Country (Richmond). Home: 17 Oak Lane Richmond VA 23221 Office: 3228 W Cary St Richmond VA 23221

KRUMNOW, WILLIAM EARL, dentist; b. Otto, Tex., Apr. 5, 1929; s. Robert Lee and Anne (Sonntag) K.; student Baylor U., 1946-48; D.D.S., U. Tex. Sch. Dentistry, 1952; m. Georgia Dee Dralle, June 11, 1950; children—Michael, Lana, Dina, Jacob. Individual practice dentistry, Waco, Tex., 1952-53, Taft, Tex., 1955—. City councilman, Taft, 1961-72, mayor, 1972—. Served with AUS, 1953-55. Mem. Am., Tex. dental assns., Nueces Valley Dist. Dental Soc., V.F.W., Psi Omega. Roman Catholic. Rotarian (pres. 1964-65). Home: 727 Field St Taft TX 78390 Office: 231 McIntyre St Taft TX 78390

KRUSE, PAUL ROBERT, librarian, educator; b. What Cheer, Ia., Feb. 26, 1912; s. Carl Fred and Phoebe (Mumby) K.; A.B., John Fletcher Coll., 1933; B.S. in L.S., U. Ill., 1940; Ph.D., U. Chgo., 1958; m. Esther Moe, June 3, 1939; 1 son, Robert Leroy. Librarian, John Fletcher Coll., Oskaloosa, Ia., 1932-33; librarian Bolles Sch., Jacksonville, Fla., 1934-38; reference librarian Jacksonville Pub. Library, 1938-42; reference asst. in charge reference collections Library of Congress, Washington, 1942-45; established library for UN Conf., San Francisco, 1945; instr. library sch. Cath. U., Washington 1943-48; bibliographer Ency. Brit., 1946-47; editor A. N. Marquis Co., 1949; vis. asst. prof. library sch. U. So. Cal., 1950, George Peabody Coll., 1950-51; reorganized library for Rollins Coll., Winter Park, Fla., 1951-52; vis. asso. prof. library sch. U. Ill., 1952-53; asso. prof. library sch. U. Denver, 1954-55; librarian Golden Gate Coll., San Francisco, 1955-65; asso. prof. sch. Library and Information Scis. North Tex. State U., Denton, 1965—. Fulbright lectr., library adviser U. Teheran, 1962-64, U. Ceylon, 1964-65. Library cons. U.S. AID, Universidad Santa Maria la Antigua, Panama, 1968. Active Community and profl. theatre groups. Mem. Am., Tex. library assns., Spl. Libraries Assn. (conf. chmn. 1961). Republican. Methodist. Mason (32 deg., Shriner). Author: The Story of the Encyclopedia Britannica, 1763-1943. Editor Index for Lend Lease Weapon for Victory, 1944; bibliographies for Ten Eventful Years, 1947. Contbr. articles to profl. jours. Home: 1301 Kendolph St Denton TX 76201

KRZYZANIAK, MARIAN, educator; b. Starczanowo, Poland, Feb. 4, 1911; s. Walenty and Stanislawa (Baran) K.; M. Econ. and Polit. Sci., Poznan U., Poland 1932; M.A. Alta U., 1954 Ph.D., Mass. Inst. Tech., 1959; m. Hilda L.R. Baldwin, May 15, 1958; children—Andrzej, Valentine Christopher Baldwin. Came to U.S., 1956, naturalized 1964. Ins. Clk., Poland, 1933-36; civil servant, Poland, 1936-39; dir., asst. mgr., accountant Centrefield Service Co., 1954-56; research asso., lectr., asst. prof., asso. prof. Rice U., Houston, 1958-67, prof. econs. 1967-69, Henry Fox, Sr. Prof. econs., 1969—. Served as 2d lt. Polish Army, 1939-45. Mem. Am. Econ. Assn., Royal Econ. Soc., Polish Arts and Scientists in Am., Econometric Soc., Internat. Platform Assn. Author: (with Richard A. Musgrave) The Shifting of the Corporation Income Tax, 1963. Author, editor: Effects of Corporation Income Tax 1966. Contbr. articles to profl. jours. Editorial bd. Pub. Finance Quarterly. Home: 4103 Durness Way Houston TX 77025 Office: Rice U Houston TX 77001

KUBE, HAROLD DEMING, business cons.; b. Buffalo, Wyo., June 16, 1910; s. Carl C. and Inez (Mather) K.; B.S., U. Neb., 1932; M.B.A., Harvard, 1934; m. Shirley Smith, Aug. 25, 1934; children—Robert Ford, Thomas Smith. Statistician, Internal Revenue Dept., Washington, 1934-35; financial analyst Farm Credit Adminstrn., Washington, 1935-36; indsl. economist Dept. Commerce, 1936-41, economist, 1946-48 economist WPB, 1941-43; dir. planning and research div. Smaller War Plants Corp., 1943-44; with Cambridge Group Study, 1948-50; head econs. and statis. dept. Nat. Found. for Infantile Paralysis, 1950-51; cons. materials policy commn. Pres. of U.S., 1951-52; bus. mgr., treas., asst. sec. Jansky and Bailey div. Atlantic Research Corp., Alexandria, Va., 1952-63; prof. engring. adminstrn. George Washington U., 1963-64; mgnt. cons., asso. Resources Devel. Assos., Washington, 1964—. Dir. Washington Indsl. Investments, Fauquier Savs. & Loan Assn. Mem. Fauquier County Econ. Devel. Com., 1962-68, Fauquier County Planning Commn., 1968—. Served with USNR, 1944-46. Mem. Am. Econ. Assn., I.E.E.E., Beta Gamma Sigma, Beta Theta Pi. Episcopalian. Co-author: Industry Action to Combat Pollution, 1966. Home: RFD 1 Broad Run VA 22014

KUCHMAK, MYRON, chemist; b. Jaworiv, Ukraine, Mar. 26, 1915; s. Paul and Catherine (Fedun) K.; M.S., Lwiv Poly. Inst., 1939; Ph.D. Mich. State U., 1961; m Luba Golenko, Nov. 1, 1943; 1 son, George. Came to U.S., 1950, naturalized, 1961. Instr. Lwiv Poly. Inst., Ukraine, 1939-41; research asst. Lwiv Chamber of Agr., 1941-44; lab., technician Mich. State U., E. Lansing, 1956-58, research asst. 1958-61, NIH fellow, 1961-63; supervisory research chemist Center for Disease Control, Atlanta, 1963-70, chief Lipid standardization lab., 1970—. Recipient Superior Service award Dept. Health, Edn. and Welfare 1965. Mem. Am. Chem. Soc., Am. Oil Chem. Soc., Am. Plant Physiol. Soc. A.A.A.S., in field to profl. jours. Home: 3288 Raymond Dr Doraville GA 30340 Office: 1600 Clifton Rd Atlanta GA 30333

KUEHNER, HERMAN OSCAR, govt. ofcl.; b. San Antonio, Sept. 3, 1932; s. Herman and Concha (Mejia) K.; B.B.A, St. Mary's U., San Antonio, 1954, J.D., 1971; m. Rose Alice Hunt, June 1, 1958; 1 son, Richard Oscar. Auditor U.S. Army Audit Agy., Ft. Sam Houston, San Antonio, 1960-61, contract negotiator Kelly AFB (Tex.), 1961-65, contract auditor Def. Contract Audit Agy., San Antonio, 1965-66, contract adminstr. Def. Supply Agy., San Antonio, 1966—. Served with AUS, 1955-57. Mem. Tex. Soc. C.P.A.'S, Order Sons Hermann, Delta Theta Phi. Roman Catholic. Lion. Home: 4826 Shadydale Dr San Antonio TX 78228 Office: 7071B San Pedro St San Antonio TX 78228

KUEKES, EDWARD GRAYSON, psychologist; b. Berea, O., Aug. 12,, 1924; s. Edward Daniel and Clara (Gray) K.; B.A., Baldwin Wallace Coll., 1949; Ph.D., U. Tex., 1955; student Case-Western Reserve U., 1947-48; m. Roberta Jean Edmonds, June 3, 1950; children—Sherrill Jane, Edward David. Psychology trainee VA Hosp., Temple, Tex., 1951-52, Waco, Tex., 1952-54, VA Mental Hygiene Clinic, San Antonio, 1954-55; staff psychologist San Antonio Mental Hygiene Clinic, 1955-68; chief psychology service VA Hosp., Oklahoma City, 1968—; asso. prof. med. psychology U. Okla., 1968—, asso. dir. Internship Tng., 1968—. Cons. State Alcohol Program, 1955-67, Alpha House, San Antonio, 1967-68. Panel moderator Tex. Employment Commn., 1968. Served with AUS, 1943-46. Decorated Purple Heart. Mem. Am., Okla. psychol. assns.,

Lambda Chi Alpha. Home: Route 13 Box 110AA 6300 Commodore Lane Oklahoma City OK 73132 Office: 921 NE 13th St Oklahoma City OK 73104

KUFFREY, CLYDE EUGENE, dentist; b. Atlanta, July 17, 1929; s. Charles George and Mary Helen (Andrews) K.; student Coll. Arts and Scis. Emory U., 1948-50; D.D.S., Emory U., 1954; m. Valiere Jane Smith, Aug. 30, 1969; children—Lisa Carol, Robert Alton. Individual practice gen. dentistry, Atlanta, 1958—. Pres. Kuffrey Devel. Corp., Atlanta, 1969-70. Served with USNR, 1954-58. Mem. Am., Ga., No. Dist. dental assns., Fifth Dist. Dental Soc., Xi Psi Phi. Republican. Baptist. Mason (Shriner). Home: 4805 Cherrywood Lane Atlanta GA 30342 Office: 702 Medical Arts Bldg Atlanta GA 30308

KUGEL, KENNETH, fgn. service officer; b. Sheboygen, Wis., May 5, 1921; s. Herman Kenneth and Rebecca (von Kaas) K.; B.A., Reed Coll, 1947; M.A., U. Mich., 1948; grad. study George Washington U., 1949; m. Sarajane Moore, Aug. 12, 1944 (div.); children—Kenneth Kaas, Melanie, Candace, Thomas Hans, Carol; m. 2d, Joanne Sheedy Baker, Dec. 30, 1972. Research asst. Republican Nat. Com., 1948; with Library Congress, Bur. Fed. Supply, 1948-49, various assignments natural resources Bur. Budget, 1949-62; dir. Office Thai Regional Affairs, AID, 1962, asst. dir for program mission to Thailand 1962-64; dep. dir. U.S. AID Mission to Panama, 1964-66, asso. asst. adminstr. Vietnam bur., Washington, 1966-67; dir. operational coordination staff U.S. Budget Bureau, Washington, D.C., 1968-70; chief field coordination Office of Mgmt. and Budget, Washington, 1970—. Served to maj. USMCR, 1941-46. Unitarian (trustee). Home: 1600 S Joyce St Arlington VA 22202 Office: Exec Office of Pres Office Mgmt and Budget Washington DC 20503

KUH, FREDERICK ROBERT, newspaperman; b. Chgo., Oct. 29, 1895; s. Dr. Edwin J. and Jennie C. (Cahn) K.; Ph.B., U. Chgo., 1917; m. Renata Boern, Sept. 23, 1929; children—Renata, Dianne. Fomerly reporter Chgo. Herald and Chgo. Eve. Post; Central European corr. London Daily Herald, 1919-23; corr. United Press Assns. in London, Moscow, Berlin and on spl. missions to Manchuria and European countries 1924-42; London corr. Chgo. Sun-Times (formerly Chgo. Sun), 1942-51, Washington corr., 1951—. Club: Cosmos (Washington). Home: 6007 Neilwood Dr Rockville MD 20852 Office: Chicago Sun-Times Nat Press Bldg Washington DC

KUHL, JOSEPH HOWARD, welfare agy. exec.; b. Towner, N.D., Apr. 26, 1908; s. John N. and Marie (Scheuring) K.; student Ia. State U., 1927-28; B.S., U.S. Naval Acad., 1932; postgrad. Naval War Coll., 1947-48; m. Lena Vanette Quina, Dec. 21, 1935; children—Leanne (Mrs. Anthony A. Less), Joseph Howard, Geraldine Ann. Commd. ensign USN, 1932, advanced through grades to capt., 1951; comdr. aircraft carrier, U.S.S. Intrepid, 1958-59; ret., 1962; registered rep. White & Co., Memphis, mem. N.Y. Stock Exchange, 1962-65; exec. dir. Sheltered Occupational Shop, Inc., Memphis, 1965—. Bd. dirs. Memphis Assn. Retarded Children, 1966-67. Decorated Bronze Star medals (2), Order So. Cross (Brazil). Mem. Memphis C. of C., Navy League U.S. Club: Engineers. Home: 3130 Wade St Memphis TN 38128 Office: 616 Minor St Memphis TN 38111

KUHLMAN, CLARENCE EUGENE, educator; b. Austin, Tex., July 14, 1907; s. Henry Lewis and Kate (Cunningham) K.; student U.S. Naval Acad., 1925-28; B.A., U. Tex., 1933, M.A., 1933; Ph.D., U. N.C., 1941; m. Ruth Geist Moss, June 9, 1960. Asso. prof. North Tex. State Coll., Denton, 1935-39; instr. U. N.C., Chapel Hill, 1936-38; supr. WPA Research, Raleigh, N.C., 1939-41; asso. prof. U. Miss., Oxford, 1946-48; prof. U. Tenn., Knoxville, 1948-59; asso. prof. bus. adminstrn. The Citadel, Charleston, S.C., 1959-72. Sr. econ. analyst U.S. Dept. of State, Buenos Aires, Argentina, 1945-46. Bd. dirs. Charleston Opera Co., 1968-69, 72, Footlight Players, 1972—. Served with U.S. Navy, 1925-28; with U.S. Army, 1928-29; served to comdr. USNR, 1941-45. Mem. Am. Arbitration Assn. So. Econ. Assn., Res. Officers Assn., Ret. Officers Assn. (pres. Charleston 1965), Delta Nu Alpha. Home: 954 Tall Pine Rd Mount Pleasant SC 29464

KUHLTHAU, ALDEN ROBERT, educator; b. New Brunswick, N.J., Apr. 29, 1921; s. Harold V., and Emma (Ellison) K.; B.S., Wake Forest U., 1942; M.S., U. Va., 1944, Ph.D., 1948; m. Gay Harris, Sept. 15, 1943; children—Robert Peyton, Richard Harold, Linda Gay. Asst. prof. physics U. N.H., 1948-51; asst. dir. Research Labs. for Engring. Sci., U. Va., Charlottesville, 1951-54, dir., 1954-67, prof. aerospace engring., 1958—, asso. dean Sch. Engring. and Applied Sci., 1961-67, asso. provost for research, 1967-71; pres. Univs. Space Research Assn., 1969—. Mem. Am. Phys. Soc., Am. Assn. Physics Tchrs., Am. Soc. for Engring. Edn., Am. Inst. Aeros. and Astronautics. Home: 1817 Meadowbrook Heights Rd Charlottesville VA 22901 Office: Thornton Hall U Va Charlottesville VA 22903 also Universities Space Research Assn PO Box 5127 Charlottesville VA 22903

KUHN, CHARLES HENRY, civil engr., city ofcl.; b. Cin., Feb. 25, 1902; s. Josiah N. and Clara (Mudersbach) K.; C.E., U. Cin., 1925; m. Florence Mildred Johnson, Aug. 19, 1925; children—C. Richard, Marilyn Ellen (Mrs. Wm. E. Harvey). Civil engr. Pa. R.R. M. of W., 1925; asst. city engr., Ft. Thomas, Ky., 1926-29, city engr., 1930-67, city cons., 1968—. Chmn. Hwy. Commn., 1956—. Vice pres. Campbell County Promotion Council, 1962—; bd. Campbell County YMCA. Named Ky. Outstanding Community Leader, 1952. Mem. Internat. City Mgrs. Assn., Am. Soc. Planning Ofcls., Ky. Soc. Profl. Engrs. Methodist. Mason Home: 32 Crown Point Fort Thomas KY 41075 Office: 130 N Fort Thomas KY 41075

KUHN, HAROLD BARNES, educator; b. Belleville, Kan., Aug. 21, 1911; s. John William and Ida Alice (Morey) K.; diploma Malone Coll., 1934; A.B. magna cum laude, John Fletcher Coll., 1939; S.T.B., Harvard, 1942, S.T.M., 1943, Ph.D. (Hopkins fellow), 1944, postgrad., 1965-67, 70; postgrad. study U. Munich (Germany), 1951-52; D.D., Houghton Coll., 1970; m. Anne Naomi Wicker, June 11, 1934. Ordained to ministry Soc. of Friends, 1935; pastor Rescue (Va.) Friends Ch., 1934-36, Dartmouth (Mass.) Friends Ch., 1939-41, Waldo Congl. Ch., Brockton, Mass., 1941-44; lectr. theology Emmanuel Bible Coll., Birkenhead, Eng., 1936-37; asst., dept. history Harvard, 1942-44; research fellow in philosophy U. Ky., 1944-45; prof. philosophy religion Asbury Theol. Sem., Wilmore, Ky., 1944—, chmn. div. theology, philosophy religion, 1959—; interim minister West Medway (Mass.) Congl. Ch., 1966-67; research scholar univs. Mainz, Erlangen, London, Free U. Berlin, 1960; lectr. World Congress Evangelism, Berlin, 1966: vis. prof. philosophy of religion Eastern Nazarene Coll., 1965-67. Observer, World Council Chs., Amsterdam, Netherlands, 1948; fellow Goethe Inst., Munich, Germany, summer 1967; lectr., retreat leader Ft. Campbell, Ky., U.S. Army, 1968; retreatmaster U.S. Army Europe, summers 1957, 60, 65, 68, 69-72; del. World Conf. Methodism, Oslo, Norway, 1961, Evangelischer Kirchentag, Munich, Germany, 1961, Dortmund, Germany, 1963; chaplains supply, missioner AUS, USAF, Europe, 1953-65; dir., lectr. Flying Seminar to Bible Lands, 1954; ednl. cons. USAF, Europe, 1951-52; prof. Union Theol. Sem., Yeotmal, India, 1957; lectr. U.S. Army War Coll., 1962, Inst. Social Change, Norman, Okla., 1965, 190th Anniversary U.S. Chaplains Corps, Berlin, 1965; protestant del. Notre Dame Conf. on Vatican II, 1966; lectr. Nat. Conf. Adult Christian Edn., Notre Dame, 1972. First aid instr. A.R.C., 1942; active refugee relief and rehab., Germany, 1945—. Trustee Malone Coll., Canton, O.; bd. dirs. Christian Freedom Found. Named Alumnus of Year, Malone Coll., 1968. Mem. Soc. Bibl. Lit., Am. Assn. U. Profs., Evang. Theol. Soc., Acad. Polit. Sci., Am. Assn. Christian Social Ethics, Am. Assn. U. Profs., Am. Philos. Assn. Delta Phi Alpha, Theta Phi. Club: Harvard Faculty. Author: Colossians and Philemon (Aldersgate Bibl. series); An Examination of Liberal Theology, 1943. Editor Asbury Seminarian, 1946—; cons. editor Zondervan Pub. Co. 1964—; editorial bd. Christianity Today, 1956—. Contbr. articles to religious jours. Home: 406 Kenyon Av Wilmore KY 40390

KUIPER, JOHN BENNETT, govt. ofcl.; b. Ann Arbor, Mich., June 22, 1928; s. John and Elizabeth (Bennett) K.; A.B., U. Ky., 1950; postgrad. Ill. Inst. Tech., 1950-51; M.A., U. Ia., 1957, Ph.D. 1960; m. Ellen Tredway, June 27, 1953; children—Anne E., Paul B., John R., Mark T. Cinematographer dir. Reela Films, Inc., Miami, Fla., 1953-55; sound camerman NBC-TV, Africa, summer 1955; asso. prof. TV-Radio Film U. Ia., Iowa City, 1963-67; head motion picture sect. Library Congress, Washington 1965—; adj. prof. Am. U., Washington, 1965—; lectr. U. Minn., U. Ca., Gallery Modern Art, Washington etc. Served with Signal Corps AUS, 1951-53. Recipient Amsterdam Student Union Prize, 1960. Mem. Washington Film Council (pres.), Soc. Cinematologists (pres.), University Film Assn. Contbr. profl. jours. Home: 3801 Underwood St Chevy Chase MD 20015 Office: Library Congress Washington DC 20540

KULSKI, JULIAN EUGENE, architect, urban planner, educator; b. Warsaw, Poland, Mar. 3, 1929; s. Julian S. and Eugenia (Solecka) K.; came to U.S., 1948; naturalized, 1950; student Oxford Sch. Architecture, 1947-48; B.Arch., Yale, 1953, postgrad., 1953-54; Ph.D., Warsaw Inst. Tech., 1966; m. Isabel Gagian, Sept. 3, 1959; children—Helena E., Julian S. Cons. city planning. archtl. practice, New Haven, 1954-59, Washington, 1959—. Vis. prof. architecture, city planning U. Notre Dame, 1960-65; prof. urban planning George Washington U., Washington, 1965-67; dir., prof. dept. city and regional planning Howard U., Washington, 1967—; cons. U.S. AID, Turkey, 1962, World Bank, Malawi, Sudan, Thailand, Peru, Pakistan, Yugoslavia, Mexico, Guatemala, 1963—. Mem. A.I.A., A.I.P., Am. Assn. U. Profs., Am. Inst. Planners, Assn. Collegiate Sch. Architect, Nat. Assn. Housing Redevel. ofcls., Am. Soc. Planning Ofcls., Am. Acad. Polit. and Social Sci., Nat. Trust Historic Preservation, Am. Soc. Pub. Adminstrs. Author: Land of Urban Promise, 1966; Environment in Evolution, 1970; Architecture in a Revolutionary Era, 1971; Evolution or Urban Systems in America, 1970. Address: 6030 Woodland Terrace McLean VA 22101

KULYNYCH, PETRO, bldg. materials co. exec.; b. Smithmills, Pa., June 23, 1921; s. Harry and Mary (Pollick) K.; grad. U.S. Merchant Marine Acad., 1943, Kings Bus. Coll., Charlotte, N.C., 1946; m. Roena Mae Bullis, Dec. 11, 1943; children—Brenda Gail, Janice Lynn. With Dept. Interior, then Dept. War, 1939-42; with Lowe's Cos., Inc., North Wilkesboro, N.C., 1946—, exec. v.p., 1961-71, vice chmn. bd., 1971—, mem. also dir., exec. com. Chmn. Lowe's Charitable and Ednl. Found.; v.p., dir. N.C. World Trade Assn., 1965; bd. dirs. N.C. Dept Conservation and Devel., 1965-69; mem. devel. bd. Lenoir Rhyne Coll., Hickory, N.C., trustee Sullins Coll. Served with USNR, 1943-46. Elk, Mason (Shriner). Clubs: Oakwoods Country (Wilkesboro); Grandfather Golf and Country (Linville, N.C.). Home: 450 Shady Lane Wilkesboro NC 28697 Office: PO Box 1111 North Wilkesboro NC 28659

KUNKLER, DAVID LEE, financial cons.; b. Marion, O., July 27, 1930; s. Donald F. and Marion (Dumm) K.; student Va. Poly. Inst., 1947-48; B.A. Lenoir Rhyne Coll. 1955; M.B.A. U. Fla., 1957; m. Catherine C. Long, Nov. 25, 1950; children—David L., Jeff C., Christopher L. With Arthur Andersen & Co., Atlanta, 1957-69, partner, 1966-69, partner Kunkler, Philip & Spacek, Atlanta, 1969-70; Southeastern regional partner Seidman & Seidman C.P.A.'s N.Y.C., 1970—. Mem. council U.S.O., Atlanta, 1969—; bd. dirs. Goodwill Industries, Atlanta. Served with AUS 1948-52. Mem. Am. Inst. C.P.A.'S, Ga. Soc. C.P.A.'S, Carpet and Rug Inst. Methodist. Mason. Kiwanian. Clubs: Cherokee Town and Country (treas. 1969-71), Peachtree Golf, Commerce. Home: 3965 Vermont Rd NE Atlanta GA 30319 Office: 235 Peachtree St Atlanta GA 30303

KUPERBERG, JOEL, state ofcl. Exec. dir. bd. trustees Fla. Internal Improvement Trust Fund, Tallahassee. Address: Internal Improvement Trust Fund 401 S Monroe St Tallahassee FL 32304*

KUPISZEWSKI, STANLEY DANIEL, JR., lawyer; b. Chgo., Nov. 10, 1932; s. Stanley A. and Joanna (Biedzinski) K.; A.B., Western Mich. U., 1957; J.D., Samford U., 1962; m. Phyllis Irene Kostecki, June 27, 1960; children— Stanley Joseph, Stephen John, John Alexander, Joseph Andrew. Admitted to Fla. bar, 1962; practiced in Lake Wales, Fla., 1962-66, Tallahassee, 1970—; pres. S. J. S. Enterprises, Tallahassee, 1962—; sec.-treas. WalesBilt Hotel Corp.; pres. Ampol Co. Lectr. bus. law and legal aspects for higher edn. Fla. State U., 1969—. Asst. atty. gen. Fla., 1966-67; gen. counsel Fla. Dept. Edn., 1967-69; counsel, Fla. State Bd. Edn., 1970; legislative counsel Fla. Sch. Bds. Assn., 1971; counsel, Flagler County Sch. Bd., 1972. Bd. dirs. Pulaski Found., Inc. Served with AUS, 1954-57. Recipient Nat. Recognition for Achievement Ams. of Polish Extraction, 1967. Mem. Nat. Advocates Soc. (v.p. Fla., 1971—), Fla. Sch. Bd. Attys. Assn. (exec. sec. 1969-70), Fla., Tenn. bar assns., C. of C., Phi Alpha Delta. Democrat. Roman Catholic. Elk. Author: (with Fla. Council Juvenile Ct. Judges) Termination of Parental Rights in the State of Florida, 1967. Home: 2204 Woodlawn Dr Tallahassee FL 32303 Office: 207 Office Plaza Tallahassee FL 32301

KUPKE, DONALD WALTER, educator, scientist; b. Omaha, Mar. 16, 1922; s. George J. and Rose (Rottmann) K.; A.B., Valparaiso U., 1947; M.S., Stanford, 1949, Ph.D., 1952; m. Carol L. Fulton, June 25, 1949; children—Karen, Mark, Heidi, Lise, Mical-Jean. Post-doctoral Carlsberg Laboratorium Copenhagen, Denmark, 1952-53, Uppsala U., Sweden, 1953-54; mem. staff Carnegie Inst., Washington, 1955-56; asst. prof. biochemistry, U. Va., 1957-63, asso. prof., 1963-66, acting chmn. dept. biochemistry 1964-66, prof., 1966—. Served to lt. USNR, 1943-46; PTO. Mem. Am. Chem. Soc., Biophys. Soc., Am. Soc. Biol. Chemistry, Am. Soc. Plant Physiol., Sigma Xi. Co-Author: Advances in Protein Chemistry, 1960; Encyclopedia Plant Phusiol V., 1960; Molecular Biology series, 1972; Methods in Enzymology series, 1972. Contbr. articles in field to profl jours. Home: Rt 1 Box 3L Keswick VA 22947

KURALT, WALLACE HAMILTON, ret. public welfare dir.; b. Springfield, Mass., Feb. 1, 1908; s. Leofold Lester and Louise (Hamilton) K.; B.S., U. N.C., 1931, postgrad. Grad. Sch. Social Work, 1938-39; postgrad. Clark U., 1932; LL.D. (hon.), Davidson Coll., 1971; m. Ina Edith Bishop, Dec. 26, 1931; children—Charles Bishop, Wallace Hamilton, Catherine Tillson (Mrs. Gary Harris). Social case worker, supr. Eastern N.C., 1933-38; field cons. N.C. Dept. Pub. Welfare, Raleigh, 1939-41; pub. welfare analyst U.S. Social Security Bd., Atlanta, 1942-44; dir. Mecklenburg County, N.C. Dept. Pub. Welfare, Charlotte, 1945-72; ret., 1972. Bd. dirs. Charlotte Area Fund, Nat. Council on Alcoholism, Intimate Book Shop, Chapel Hill, N.C. Cons. services to U.S. Senate on family planning and population control. Mem. Mayor's Com. Community Devel.; Gov's. Com. on Delinquency and Crime, White House Conf. on Children and Aging. Mem. Phi Beta Kappa. Pioneer in devel. and adminstrn. of pub. programs of social services to prevent dependency and promote responsible parenthood. Home: 6400 Sharon Rd Charlotte NC 28210 Office: 427 W 4th St Charlotte NC 28202

KURLAND, JORDAN E., assn. exec. Asso. gen. sec. Am. Assn. U. Profs., Washington. Address: 1 Du Pont Circle Washington DC 20036*

KURRAS, HERBERT LEWIS, banker; b. Patchogue, N.Y., Dec. 15, 1932; s. Charles A. and Anna E. (Reuther) K.; B.S., Fla. State U., 1954; LL.B., Stetson Coll. Law, 1959; m. Diane Fisher, Aug. 11, 1956; children— Kevin, Sherylyn, Lisa, Heather. Admitted to Fla. bar, 1960; trust officer First Nat. Bank of Hollywood (Fla.), sr. v.p. Community Nat. Bank & Trust Co., Bal Harbour, Fla., 1964—, also dir.; dir. Geiger Properties, Inc., Miami Beach, Fla. Mem. endowment com. U. Miami, 1967—. Mem. Corporate Fiduciaries Assn. S.E. Fla. (v.p. 1970—), Am., Fla. bar assns., Delta Sigma Pi, Delta Theta Phi. Home: 2100 N 51st Av Hollywood FL 33021 Office: 9600 Collins Av BalHarbour FL 33154

KURTH, WALTER RICHARD, assn. exec.; b. Normal, Ill., Jan. 21, 1932; s. Walter H. and Irene (Freitag) K.; B.S., U. Ill., 1954; m. Mary Elisabeth Taylor, Aug. 23, 1958; children—Mary Helen, Sarah Jane, Elisabeth Irene. Publ. dir. Asso. Credit Burs. of Am., Inc., St. Louis, 1954-57, marketing dir., 1957-62, asst. gen. mgr., 1962-66, asst. gen. mgr., treas., Houston, 1966-68, adminstrv. v.p., treas., 1968-69, exec. v.p., treas., 1969—; pres. ACB Services, Inc., 1970—; sec.-treas. Credit Bur. Automation, Inc., Houston, 1966—, Credit Services Internat., 1970—. Bd. mgrs. Thompson Retreat Center, St. Louis, 1963-64. Mem. Houston Dist. Small Bus. Adminstrn., 1971—. Republican precinct chmn., 1969—, chmn. dist. 15 fund drive, 1970—. Mem. Am. Mgmt. Assn., Adminstrv. Mgmt. Soc., Am., Tex., Houston socs. assn. exec., Star and Scroll (pres. 1953), C. of C., Alpha Kappa Lambda. Presbyn. (elder). Mason (32 deg., Shriner). Home: 13422 Butterfly Lane Houston TX 77024 Office: 6767 Southwest Freeway Houston TX 77036

KURYLO, WALTER, govt. ofcl.; b. Chgo., Oct. 17, 1914; s. William and Mary (Skrzat) K.; J.D., Washington Coll. Law (now Am. U.), 1938; student George Washington U., 1938-43, 46-47; B.S., Am. U., 1949, M.A., 1954, Ph.D., 1960; m. Lydia Margaret Carter, Mar. 2, 1946; children—H. Carter, Wally Clark (dau.). Spl. programs coordinator Bur. Pub. Rds., Dept. Commerce. Washington, 1935-59; mem. hearing bds. on Pollution of Interstate Waters of Mo. River by Sioux City (Ia.) and St. Joseph (Mo.), 1959; profl. staff mem. Senate Com. on Commerce, Transp. Study Group, 1959-61; transp. policy planning officer Bur. Pub. Rds., Dept. Commerce, 1961, exec. sec. Organizing Com. for 9th Pan-Am. Hwy. Congress, 1961-63, sec.-gen., 1963, chief studies and application staff Office Right-of-w-ay and Location, 1964-65; transp. program planning officer Office Planning, 1966-68; chief state programs div. Office Pieline Safety, Dept. Transp., 1968—. part-time faculty mem. Sch. Govt. and Pub. Adminstrn., Am. U., 1957-69. Mem. staff Pres.'s Hwy. Safety Conf., 1946-47, Pres. 1950, Interagy. Water Policy Rev. Com., 1951, Subcom. on Benefits and Costs, Fed. Inter-agy. River Basin Com., 1951-53, Presdl. Adv. Com. on Water Resources, Policy, 1954-55, Interagy. Com. on Water Resources, 1954-59; chmn. Fairfax County Citizen's Com. Sch. Bonds, 1965; mem. Fairfax County School Bd., 1967-70; chmn. Fairfax County Citizens for Superior Environment and Edn. Bonds, 1970—. Served from pvt. to s/sgt. USAAF, 1943-46. Recipient silver service medal Dept. of Commerce; merit award Am. Assn. State Hwy. Ofcls.; Distinguished Service award as sec. gen. 9th Pan Am. Hwy. Congress; named Citizen of Yr. Fairfax County, 1965. Mem. Am. U. Honor Soc., Pi Sigma Alpha, Sigma Nu Phi. Episcopalian. Prin. author: Navigational Clearance Requirements for Highway and Railroad Bridges, 1955; also author tech. papers in profl. and trade jours. Directed nationwide study of navigational clearances in bridges across navigable waterways, 1952-55. Home: 3250 Peace Valley Lane Falls Church VA 22044 Office: Dept Transp Washington DC 20590

KUSHNER, DAVID ZAKERI, educator; b. Ellenville, N.Y., Dec. 22, 1935; s. Nathan and Rita (Forgatsh) K.; Mus.B., Boston U., 1957; Mus.M., U. Cin., 1958; Ph.D., U. Mich., 1967; m. Rebecca Ann Stefan, Dec. 20, 1964; children—Jonathan Moses, Joshua Sanford, Jeremy Avram, Jason Daniel. Asst. prof. music Miss. State Coll. for Women, Columbus, 1964-66; asso. prof. music Radford Coll. (Va.), 1966-68; prof. music U. Fla., Gainesville, 1969—. Bd. dirs. Pro Arte Musica, Gainesville. Mem. Fla. Music Tchrs. Assn., Am. Liszt Soc., (chmn. bd. dirs. 1967—, v.p. 1967), Music Tchrs. Nat. Assn. (life), Am. Musicol. Soc. (chmn. So. chpt., nat. council 1972—), Ernest Bloch Soc., Pi Kappa Lambda (pres. U. Fla. chpt.), Phi Mu Alpha Sinfonia (faculty advisor U. Fla. chpt., life). Commentator weekly program Music from Florida WRUF-FM, Gainesville. numerous publs. Home: 2215 NW 21st Av Gainesville FL 32601 Office: 305 Music Bldg Univ Fla Gainesville FL 32601

KUSS, HENRY JOHN, JR., trade and finance co. exec.; b. N.Y.C., Nov. 10, 1922; s. Henry John and Olga (Sidle) K.; student Coll. of Holy Cross, 1943-44; B.A., St. John's U., 1942; m. Johanna Meta Derouet, June 28, 1944; children—Linda Joy, Karen Lisa. Dir. supply system planning Bur. Ordnance, Dept. Navy, 1947-50; budget analyst Office Sec. Def., 1950-53; dir. Army/Navy Def. Econ. Planning, Paris Office, 1953-55; asst. to under sec. Navy, 1955-57; dir. fgn. mil. resources planning Office Sec. Def., 1957-59, dir. fgn. mil. assistance planning, 1959-61, dep. asst. sec. def. for internat. security affairs, 1962-69; pres. Am. Trade and Finance Co., Arlington, Va., 1969—. Def. mem. Presdl. Commn. on Study Korean Economy, 1953; U.S. rep. NATCO Econ. Cost Com., 1954-55; def. mem. Spl. Internat. Econ. Requirements and Capilitiates Commn., Italy, Norway, Turkey, Greece, 1954; chmn. com. mil. exports Def. Industry Adv. Council, 1962-69. Served with USNR, 1944-47. Recipient Meritorious Civilian Service medal Sec. Def., 1965. Lutheran. Home: 7318 Chatham St North Springfield VA 22151 Office: 2001 Jefferson Davis Hwy Arlington VA 22202

KUTAIT, KEMAL EUGENE, physician; b. Eureka Springs, Ark., Sept. 5, 1930; s. Camil Mahana and Sophia (Rahal) K.; B.S. in Chemistry, Coll. of Ozarks, Clarksville, Ark., 1950, B.S. in Biology, 1951; M.D., U. Ark., 1958; m. Virginia M. Riling, Oct. 25, 1952; children— Kay, Kemal, Karin. Intern Brook Army Hosp., 1958-59; practice medicine, Ft. Smith, Ark., 1963—; sr. partner Dr.'s Kutait, Lilly, Pillstron & Ingram, 1963—; chief staff St. Edward Mercy Hosp., 1970, med. cons. Johnny Cake Child Study Center; clin. instr. family practice U. Ark. Med. Center. Bd. dirs. Ft. Smith Girls Club, United Fund. Served with AUS, 1958-62. Diplomate Am. Bd. Family Physicians. Fellow Am. Acad. Family Physicians; mem. Ark. Acad. Gen. Practice (pres. elect 1971), A.M.A., Ark. Med. Soc. Episcopalian (vestryman, lay reader). Home: 3724 Free Ferry Rd Fort Smith AR 72901 Office: 1120 Lexington Av Fort Smith AR 72901

KUYKENDALL, DAN H., congressman; b. Cherokee, Tex., July 9, 1924; s. Tom G. and Sarah J. Kuykendall; B.S., Tex. A. and M. U., 1947; m. Jacqueline Meyer, July 6, 1951; children—Dan H. Jr., John Meyer, Kathleen Virginia, Jacqueline Kay. Various managerial positions with Proctor & Gamble, Tex., Ky., 1947-55, mgr. 5 mid-south states, Memphis, 1955; with Equitable Life Assurance Soc. U.S., N.Y., 1965-66; pres. D & D Devel. Corp., Owensboro, Ky.; sec. Minit-Stop Corp., grocery drive-ins, Memphis; mem. 90th-92d congresses from 9th dist. Tenn. Co-chmn. Shelby United Neighbor; v.p. Chickasaw council Boy Scouts Am.; chmn. spl. gifts Cancer Soc. Republican candidate for U.S. Senate, 1964. Bd. dirs. Duration Club Home for Retarded Children. Served to lt. USAAF, 1942-45. Methodist (tchr. Sunday sch., chmn. bd., chmn. fund raising. Home: 7902 Greentree Rd Bethesda MD 20034 Office: Longworth Bldg Washington DC 20515

KUYKENDALL, JOHN M., JR., lawyer; b. Charleston, Miss., Sept. 14, 1915; B.A., U. Miss., 1938, LL.B., 1940. Admitted to Miss. bar, 1940, U.S. Supreme Ct. bar, 1956; spl. agt. FBI, 1940-43; asst. atty. gen. State Miss., 1947-51; atty. Miss. Bldg. Commn., 1951-55; now mem. firm Overstreet & Kuykendall, Jackson, Miss. Served to lt. USNR, 1943-46. Mem. Hinds County, Fed., Am. bar assns. Club: Nat. Lawyers. Address: Overstreet & Kuykendall 829 Deposit Guaranty Bank Bldg Jackson MS 39201*

KUYKENDALL, WILLIAM DEAN, banker; b. Henrietta, N.C., Nov. 9, 1936; s. John and Lorena (Banks) K.; bank mgmt. certificate U. Va., 1968; m. Faye Blankenship, Nov. 16, 1957; children—Debra Faye, Deana Louise. Br. mgr. First Nat. Bank of Danville, Va., 1953-65; asst. v.p. Schoolfield Bank & Trust Co., Danville, 1965—. Treas. William T. Sutherlin Acad., 1969, trustee, chmn. finance com., 1969—. Club: Sertoma (past treas., dir.) (Danville). Home: 169 Millerton Rd Danville VA 24541 Office: Corner Patton and Ridge Sts Danville VA 24541

KUYPERS, JOHN MARINUS, educator, b. Rotterdam, Netherlands, Nov. 15, 1900; s. Hendrik Jacobus and Minke (VanderKam) K.; came to U.S., 1914, naturalized, 1921; student Coll. City N.Y., summer 1924, Columbia, summer 1925; A.B. magna cum laude, Carleton Coll., Northfield, Minn., 1926; m. Helen Amelia Sather, Aug. 26, 1935; children—James Hendrik, David Sather, Joseph Andrew; m. 2d, Donatella Martinelli, 1960. Mem. Mpls. Symphony Orchestra, 1926-32; guest lectr. U. Ia., summer sessions 1930-32, dir. Summer Session Orch., 1931-32; dir. music and choirs Hamline U., St. Paul, 1932-42; dir. and judge of state and district music festivals in the midwest; founder, dir. Pro Musica Sinfonietta of St. Paul, 1940-42; guest condr. Minn. Symphony Orch., 1939-41; guest lectr. Bemidji (Minn.) State Tchrs. Coll. summer 1939, U. Washington summer 1949; guest lectr., dir. Summer Session Chorus. U. Ida., 1940-42; acting asso. prof. Cornell U., Ithaca, N.Y., 1942-43, asso. prof., 1942-46, prof., 1946-47, chmn. dept. of music, 1944-47; dir. Cornell U. Glee clubs, Sage Chapel Choir, Chorus, Orch. and Chamber Music Soc., 1942-47; prof. and dir. Sch. Music, U. Ill., 1947-50, prof. music, 1947-61; vis. prof. Dillard U., New Orleans, 1958-60; vis. prof. Newcomb Coll., Tulane U., 1960-61, prof., 1961—; condr. Concert Choir, New Orleans, 1959—; guest condr. New Orleans Phiharmonic-Symphony Orch., 1961-63. Mus. cons. Coronet Ednl. Films; condr. Youth Orch., Chgo., 1948-49, U. Ill. Symphony Orchestra and Sinfonietta, 1947-50; bd. examiners U. Man., Winnipeg, Can., 1939-45. Mem. Music Tchrs. Nat. Assn., Phi Beta Kappa, Pi Kappa Lambda, Phi Mu Alpha, Sigma Delta Pi. Author: How Music Is Built in Our Wonderful World Ency. Contbr. articles on music to profl. jours. Home: 1933 Audubon St New Orleans LA 70118

KUZMICKI, FELIX DAVIS, city ofcl.; b. Wylam, Ala., June 30, 1912; s. William W. and Felicia A. (Thomas) K.; B.A., U. Ala., 1948; m. Alice Elizabeth Tamplin, Aug. 9, 1941. Pres., mgr. S.E. Engring. Service, Monroeville and Birmingham, Ala., 1948-51; engr.-designer John W. Galbreath, Birmingham, Phila., and Twin Harbors, Minn., 1951-54; cons., appraiser, 1954-56; pub. works adminstr., city engr. Office City Engr., Bessemer, Ala., 1956—. Mem. tech. com. Regional Planning Commn., Birmingham, 1967. Served to maj. USMCR, 1942-45. Mem. Am. Pub. Works Assn., Am. Rd. Builders Assn., Inst. Municipal Engring., 3d Marine Div. Assn. (regional v.p. 1967), Kiwanian. Home: 348 Park Av Birmingham AL 35226 Office: 1800 3d St Bessemer AL

KYGER, MURRAY, comml. banker; b. Mason, Tex., Nov. 24, 1905; s. Melvin C. and Lydia (Murray) K.; B.B.A., U. Tex.; LL.B., South Tex. Sch. of Law, 1932; student Grad. Sch. Banking, Rutgers U., 1940; m. Bernice Spiller, May 3, 1930; children—Martha Kay, Thomas Murray. With Houston Bank & Trust Co., 1928-41, v.p., trust officer, dir., until 1941; pres., dir. First Nat. Bank of Ft. Worth, 1941-65, now chmn. bd., dir. Mem. Sigma Iota Epsilon, Beta Gamma Sigma. Home: 110 N Rivercrest Dr Fort Worth TX Office: PO Box 2260 Fort Worth TX

KYLE, FLEMING CLASON, journalist; b. Columbus, Ga., May 5, 1929; s. George Swift and Elizabeth (Clason) K.; B.A., Rollins Coll., Fla., 1953; postgrad. Stanford, 1953-54. Feature writer Ledger, 1961; reporter Arts Critic Enquirer, 1961-63; asso. editor Ledger-Enquirer Sunday Mag., Columbus, 1964—, write weekly travel column On The Go. Mem. bd. Musemont Fine Arts Camp; mem. bd. visitors Barter Theater, Abingdon, Va.; mem. Gov.'s Mansion Fine Arts Com., Westville Historic Crafts. Trustee Springer Opera House; chmn. bd. dirs. Columbus Mus. Arts and Crafts Historic Coll. Found. Named Young Man of Year, Columbus Jr. C. of C., 1963; recipient Garden Club of Ga. merit award, 1963. Mem. Am. Travel Writers, Nat. Trust for Hist. Preservation, Soc. Archtl. Historians, English Speaking Union, Victorian Soc. Am. (dir.), Irish Georgian Soc. Kappa Alpha, Omicron Delta Kappa. Clubs: The Bachelors, Country of Columbus, Big Eddy. Home: 925 Blandford Av Columbus GA 31906 Office: 17 W 12th St Columbus GA 31902

KYLE, GEORGE THOMAS, educator; b. East St. Louis, Ill., Mar. 31, 1904; s. George Thomas and Dollie (Dorsey) K.; A.B., U. Ill., 1926, A.M., 1930; student U. Pa., 1943-44; Ph.D., N.Y.U., 1948; m. Miriam Lavender Pride, May 7, 1932; 1 son, Gregory Pride. Instr. psychology Prairie View (Tex.) Coll., 1927-29; asst. prof. psychology Johnson C. Smith U., Charlotte, N.C., 1930-43; trainee clin. psychology VA Hosp., Tuskegee, Ala., 1946-49; prof. psychol. N.C. Coll., Durham, 1949-53, 63—, undergrad. dean, 1953-64. Mem. N.C. Adv. Council Tchr. Edn., 1960—, N.C. Adv. Com. Guidelines and Standards Tchr. Edn., 1961—. Bd. dirs. Durham Family Service. Mem. Am., Southeastern, N.C. psychol. assns., So. Assn. Philosophy and Psychology, N.C. Tchrs. Assn., N.C. Mental Health Assn. Home: 1203 Crowell St Durham NC

KYLE, WILLIAM LOCKHART, JR., ins. co. exec.; b. Naysville, Ky., May 12, 1927; s. William Lockhart and Rebecca (Winter) K.; B.S. in Bus. Adminstrn., U. N.C., 1949; m. Jane Carol Tagge, Jan. 20, 1957; children—Celia William Lockhart III, Jane. Pres., Carolina Home Life Ins. Co., Jacksonville, Fla., 1958-65; sr. v.p., treas. Voyager Life Ins. Co., Jacksonville, 1965—; v.p. acquisitions Nat. Life of Fla. Corp., Jacksonville, 1968—; dir. Jacksonville Nat. Bank. Served with USNR, 1945-46. Mem. Financial Analysts Soc. Jacksonville, Jacksonville C. of C. Clubs: Timuquana Country, River, University (Jacksonville). Home: 4637 Wadham Lane Jacksonville FL 32210 Office: PO Box 2918 Jacksonville FL 32203

LA BARRE, WESTON, anthropologist; b. Uniontown, Pa., Dec. 13, 1911; s. Isaac Weston and Artemisia van Meter (Hannah) La B.; A.B. summa cum laude, Princeton, 1933; Ph.D., Yale, 1937; m. Maurine Boie, July 9, 1939; children—John Boie Keasbey, David Quinton Lefebvre, Louise Anne Stephens. Research intern, Menninger Clinic, 1938-39; instr. Rutgers U., 1939-43; with war Relocation Authority, Topaz, Utah, 1943; asst. prof. Duke, Durham, N.C., 1946-48, asso. prof., 1948-58, prof., 1958—, James B. Duke prof., 1970—; tchr. summer schs. N.Y.U., 1942, U. Wis., 1947, Northwestern U., 1949, U. N.C., 1951, U. Minn., 1955; vis. clin. prof. U. N.C. Med. Sch., 1955—. Editor-in-chief Landmarks in Anthropology, 1965—; cons. Com. on Adolescence, Group for Advancement Psychiatry. Sponsor Durham Friends Sch. Served with USNR, 1943-46. Recipient Geza Roheim Meml. award, 1958. Sterling fellow Yale, 1937, Guggenheim fellow, 1946. Fellow Am. Anthrop. Assn., Current Anthropology; mem. Phi Beta Kappa, Sigma Xi. Author: The Peyote Cult. 1938; The Aymara Indians of the Lake Titcaca Plateau, Bolivia, 1948; The Human Animal, 1954; Materia Medica of the Aymara, 1960; They Shall Take Up Serpents: Psychology of the Southern Snakehandling Cult, 1962; (with others) Normal Adolescence: Its Dynamics and Impact, 1968; The Ghost Dance: Origins of Religion, 1970. Home: Mt Sinai Rd Rt 1 Durham NC 27705

LABEACH, SAMUEL ALEXANDER, II, govt. ofcl.; b. Panama City, Panama, Apr. 15, 1924; (came to U.S., 1947, naturalized, 1951); s. Samuel A. and Julia (Johnston) LaB.; B.S., Morgan State Coll., 1951; M.A., Howard U., 1962; M.S.W., Cath. U. Am., 1965; m. Nell Ming, July 2, 1951; 1 son, Samuel Alexander III. With D.C. Dept. Recreation, Washington, 1951—, roving leader, 1959-63, field supr. roving leaders, 1963-65, dir. roving leader program, 1965-67, dir. spl. programs, 1967—; tchr. Banneker Jr. High Sch., 1955-56; guest lectr. Howard U., U. Md., Am. U., 1961-66; asst. prof. group work and leadership in recreation Washington Tech. Inst., 1967—; cons., instr. staff Cedar Knoll, Maple Glen, Jr. Village and Receiving Home, 1968—. Active Boy Scouts Am., 1960—; co-founder LeDroit Park Jr. Civic Assn., 1956; mem. Inter-Agy. Staff Com. for Children and Youth for D.C., 1967—; mem. child and adolescent sub-com. on mental health programs Hillcrest Children's Center, 1968—; mem. Mayor's Com. on Mental Retardation, 1968—; nat. chmn. U.S. Youth Games, Washington, 1969. Trustee United Planning Orgn., 1968—. Mem. Nat. Recreation and Park Assn. (chmn. for recruitment and profl. devel. 1962-64), Nat. Assn. Social Workers (chmn. group work sect. 1967—), D.C. Congress Parents and Tchrs. Assn. (life), Kappa Alpha Psi. Baptist (deacon). Contbr. articles to profl. lit. Home: 1330 Leegate Rd NW Washington DC 20012 Office: 3149 16th St NW Washington DC 20010

LABODA, GERALD, oral surgeon; b. Phila., Aug. 15, 1936; s. Lewis and Rose (Waldman) L.; student Temple U., 1954-56; D.D.S., Temple U., 1960; postgrad. U. Pa., 1960-61; m. Sheila Lois Plasky, Aug. 2, 1956; children—Amy Sue, Michele Beth, Alane Cheryl, Bruce Herbert. Intern oral surgery Jefferson Med Coll. Hosp., Phila., 1961-62, resident, 1962-63; practice dentistry specializing in oral surgery. Fort Myers, Fla., 1965—; mem. staffs Lee Meml. Hosp., Fort Myers, Lehigh Acres (Fla.) Gen. Hosp. Pres. Caloosa Aircraft Leasing, Inc.; pres., dir. Lamanda, Inc., Ft. Myers. Bd. dirs. YMCA. Pres. Fla. Dental Soc. Anesthesiology. Served as capt. Dental Corps, AUS, 1963-65. Diplomate Am. Bd. Oral Surgery, Pan Am. Med. Soc. Fellow Internat. Assn. Oral Surgeons, Internat. Assn. Maxillo Facial Surgeons; mem. Am., Southeastern Fla. socs. oral surgeons, Am. Dental Soc. Anesthesiology, Am. Dental Assn., Fla., S.W. Fla., W. Coast Dist. dental socs. Home: 5089 Northampton Dr Fort Myers FL 33901 Office: 3900 S Broadway Fort Myers FL 33901

LABORDE, ADRAS PAUL, editor; b. Bordelonville, La., Dec. 5, 1912; s. Enos J. and Lillie (Bordelon) L.; student Tyler Comml. Coll., 1929; m. Blanche Bordelon, Sept. 30, 1932; children—Joyce L., Adras P. (dec.), Michael A. Radio operator U.S. Mcht. Marine, 1929-32; bi-lingual newscaster radio sta. WWL, New Orleans, 1932-33; owner wholesale drug firm, Marksville, La., 1933-41; telegraph editor Alexandria (La.) Daily Town Talk 1945-50, editor, 1950—. Served with USAAF, 1941-45. Recipient 1st place ann. editorial contest U.P.I., 1962, 63, 64, 66, 68; Meehan conservation award Scripps-Howard Founds., 1966; decorated Knight of St. Gregory, 1972. Mem. Am. Soc. Newspaper Editors, Rapides Wildlife Assn., Young Men's Bus. Club (past pres.). Author: Roger Wilco, 1944; Ransdell of Louisiana: A National Southerner, 1951. Contbr. articles profl. jours. Home: 2107 Texas Av Alexandria LA 71301 Office: 128 Washington St Alexandria LA 71301

LABORDE, MARY PURCELL (MRS. JOSEPH GASTON LABORDE), club woman, ret. educator; b. Pelican, La., May 19, 1905; d. George Dowell and Ela Lee (Browne) Purcell; Christian culture diploma M.E. Ch. S., 1922; licensed instr., Mansfield (LI.). Female Coll., 1923; postgrad. La. State U., 1924, 45, Centenary, 1925-26; certificate N.Y. Sch. Interior Decorating, 1931; B.A., Nicholls State Coll.; m. Joseph Gaston LaBorde, Apr. 14, 1926; 1 son, Joseph Newton. Tchr. Caldwell Parish, La., 1923-25; tchr. S. Highlands Sch., Shreveport, La., 1925-26; tchr. Lady of Mercy Sch., Baton Rouge, 1958-60, St. Theresa's Sch., Sheveport, 1960-61, Trinity Elementary Sch., Baton Rouge, 1969-70. Recipient awards (2) Nat. Soc. So. Dames Am., 1966. 2d v.p. U.D.C., Henry W. Allen chpt., Baton Rouge, 1960-61, 3d v.p. Martha Ried chpt., 1954-57; bd. dirs. Children of Confederacy, Emma Gayle McFadden chpt., Jacksonville, Fla., 1955-57, dir. John McGrath chpt., Baton Rouge, 1958-60; mem. and del. Katherine Livingston chpt. D.A.R., Jacksonville, 1949-52, del. nat. congress, 1950, 63, treas., Kan Yuk Sa, 1955-57, del. state conf., 1964; organized Jr. Nat. Soc. Sons and Daus. of Pilgrims; active Gray Ladies A.R.C.; mem. Confederate Mus., Richmond, Va., 1971-72; hostess Found. for Hist. La., 1965-71. Mem. Descs. Knights of Garter, Plantagenet Soc., Ams. Royal Descent, Nat. Trust Historic Preservation, Magna Charta Dames (v.p. La. Soc. 1967-69), Nat. Soc. Sons and Daus. of Pilgrims (gov. La. br. 1962-64, nat. rec. sec. 1965-66, del. nat. congress 1963, del. Gen. Ct., state registrar 1968-70), Nat. Soc. So. Dames, Am. (award 1966, charter; La. eye bank chmn. 1964-65, v.p. La. 1964-65, award of merit 1967), U.D.C. (nat. com. preservation hist. sites and records 1967-68, nat. and state geneal. records 1967-69, rec. sec. H.W. Allen chpt. 1966-67, chmn. music 1967-68), W.S.C.S., Tchrs. Assn., La. Parliamentarians, Nat. Assn. Parliamentarians, Huguenot Soc. La. (compiled handbook), Marquis Biog. Library Soc. (adv.), Washington Family Descs., Tex. Geneal. Soc. Methodist (youth dir.). Clubs: Music, Baton Rouge Women's; Baton Rouge Music. Home: 11645 Archery Dr Baton Rouge LA 70815

LACAFF, TED BUNCE, JR., oil co. exec.; b. Emporia, Kan., Mar. 9, 1928; s. Ted B. and Doris (Broussard) L.; A.A., Lamar Tech. Inst., 1947; B.S., U. Tex., 1950; m. Mary Conley Jones, Oct. 7, 1951; children— Sally, Becky, Ted, David, Mary Ann. Geol. scout Gulf Oil Corp., Midland, Tex., 1950-52; petroleum geologist Argo Oil Corp., Midland, 1952-59; gen. supt. Tex. Am. Oil Corp., Midland, 1959-61, gen. mgr., 1961-63, v.p., 1963-68, exec. v.p., 1968-69, pres., chief exec. officer, 1969-70, dir., 1966-70; v.p., dir., Australian Oil Corp., Midland, 1963-68; v.p. Western Oil Shale Corp., Midland, 1965-68, pres. 1968-70, dir., 1965-70; v.p. Tex. Am. Sulphur Co., Midland, 1967-69, pres., 1969-70, dir. 1967-70; pres., dir. Pacific Union Gas Co., Midland, 1963-67; sr. v.p., dir. Internat. Energy Co., 1968-69, pres., chmn. bd., dir., 1969-70; pres., dir. Tex. Am. Oil Mgmt. Co., 1969-70; div. mgr. domestic oil and gas Am. Trading & Production Corp., 1970—. Pres. Young Republicans, 1952; dir. Am. Cancer Soc., 1966-67. Mem. Am. Assn. Petroleum Geologists, West Tex. Geol. Soc., Geol. Soc. Australia, Permian Basin Petroleum Assn., Sigma Nu. Roman Catholic. K.C., Elk. Clubs: Racquet, Midland Country. Home: 2100 Seaboard St Midland TX 79701 Office: 300 W Texas St Midland TX 79701

LACATSKI, ALBERT THOMAS, telephone co. exec.; b. Minersville, Pa., Mar. 10, 1926; s. Thomas M. and Anna (Kushlick) L.; B.S., Ind. Inst. Tech., 1951; m. Margaret Jane Mahoney, July 16, 1949; children—James Thomas, Carol Ann. Engr., So. Bell Tel. & Tel. Co., West Palm Beach, Fla., 1951-59, supervising engr., Delray Beach, Fla., 1959-66, dist. engr., Daytona Beach, Fla., 1966—. Served with USAAF, 1944-49. Registered profl. engr., Fla. Mem. Fla. Engring. Soc., Nat. Soc. Profl. Engrs., I.E.E.E. (past sec., vice chmn.). Home: 330 Emory Dr Daytona Beach FL 32018 Office: 711 Volusia Av Daytona Beach FL 32015

LACAYO, HEBERTO, educator; b. Granada, Nicaragua, Jan. 19, 1904; s. Leopoldo and Matilde (Lacayo-Sacasa) L.; B.S., Inst. Nat. de Oriente, Nicaragua, 1922; M.S., U. So. Cal., 1930; Dr. en Letros, U. Nacional, Nicaragua, 1936; m. Maria Perez, Feb. 20, 1931; children—Beverly, Herbert, Susana, Leopoldo, Matilde. Instr., U. So. Cal., 1927-30, Oceanside (Cal.) High Sch., 1930-31, Syracuse U., 1931-41; asso. prof. Russell Sage Coll., 1941-48; asso. prof. Fla. State U., 1948-64, prof. Spanish, 1964—; prof. Spanish Sch., Middlebury Coll., 1946-49; vis. prof. U. Iberoamericana, Mexico City, Mexico, summer 1954; vis. prof. Instituto Technologico de Estudios Superiores Monterrey (Mex.), summers 1955-60, dir. grad. studies, summers 1960—. Mem. Am. Assn. Tchrs. Spanish and Portuguese, Am. Assn. U. Profs., Sigma Delta Pi. K.C. Home: 1730 W Pensacola St Tallahassee FL 32304

LACK, FREDELL, concert violinist; b. Tulsa, Feb. 19, 1922; d. Abram I. and Sarah (Stillman) L.; grad. Juilliard Grad. Sch. Music, 1943; m. Ralph David Eichhorn, July 10, 1947; children—Ardis, Eric Joel. Made debut as soloist with St. Louis Symphony, 1939; Town Hall debut recital, 1943; numerous recitals subsequently, at Town Hall, Carnegie Hall, Philharmonic Hall, Tully Hall (all N.Y.C.); tours in U.S., Can., Central Am., Hawaii, 1943—; featured soloist coast-to-coast Mut. Network radio program, 1946-47; concertmistress Little Orch. Soc., N.Y.C., 1947-49; founder, 1st violin Lyric Art String Quartet, Houston, 1956; rec. for Allegro, Mus. Appreciations: artist in residence, asso. prof. U. Houston, 1961—, mem. Virtuoso Piano Quartet; ann. concert tour, Europe, 1959—; has appeared with orchs. including Pitts., Portland, Salt lake City, Houston, San Antonio, Albuquerque, Tulsa, Baton Rouge (all U.S.), BBC, Royal Philharmonic (London, Eng.), Rias (Berlin, Germany), Oslo, Stockholm Philharmonics, Concertgebouw (Amsterdam). Vice pres. Houston Humane Soc.; founder Young Audiences Chamber Music concerts, Houston. Recipient MacDowell Club Young Artists' award, 1942, Nat. Fed. Mus. Clubs Young Artists' award, 1943, Bklyn. Acad. Mus. Young Artists' award, 1945; one of 12 laureates of Queen Elizabeth of Belgium Internat. Competition, 1951. Home: 4202 S MacGregor St Houston 21 TX 77004

LACKEY, GEORGE FINLEY, engr. exec.; b. Boaz, Ala., Apr. 11, 1927; s. Jesse James and Mae (Bruce) L.; B.S., Auburn U., 1952; m. Lois Jean Garland, Feb. 5, 1955; children—Heather Jean, George Finley. Engr. in tng. Elliott Co., Jeannette, Pa., 1952-53, application engr., 1953-56, field engr. Div. Carrier Corp., Atlanta, 1956-59; mech. engr. Gen. U.S. Army Missile Command, Redstone Arsenal, Ala., 1959-64, chief Aero-GSE Engring. Br., Nike Hercules Project Office, 1964-69, configuration mgr., 1969-71, configuration mgr. Air Def. Spl. Items Mgmt. Office, 1971-72, configuration mgr., chief Product Assurance and Test div., 1972—. Served with USNR, 1945-46. Mem. Am. Soc. M.E., Am. Legion, V.F.W., Assn. U.S. Army, Nat. Rifle Assn., Sigma Phi Epsilon. Episcopalian. Club: Civitan (hon.). Home: 206 Lackey St Boaz AL 35957 Office: Air Defense Special Items Management Office Redstone Arsenal AL 35809

LACKEY, GUY ANNANDALE, educator; b. Sharon, Tenn., July 23, 1891; s. Benjamin F. and Mary E. (Harwell) L.; A.B., U. Okla., 1918; A.M., U. Chicago, 1924, 4 year grad. work; m. Florence Woodard, Apr. 7, 1917; children—Virginia (Mrs. C. C. Mathews), Woodard; m. 2d Wylma Black, Dec. 24, 1944; 1 son, Guy Annadale, Jr. Teacher and supt. pub. schs., Okla., 1910-21; head dept. edn. Chicora (S.C.) Coll., 1921-24, Huron Coll., S.D., 1924-25; summer instr. Central Coll., Okla., 1920, U. S.C., 1923, with Army A.C. Tech. Tng. Sch., 1942-43; collaborator and fellow U. Chgo. human devel. dept., 1943-44; prof. edn. and psychology Okla. State U., 1925-61, prof. emeritus, lectr. edn. and psychology, 1961—; vis. prof. edn. Southwestern Coll., Winfield, Kan., 1964-65; prof. psychology State U. Geneseo, N.Y., 1965-66; participant numerous work-shops, now cons. Mem. A.A.A.S., N.E.A., Nat. Soc. Study Edn., Pi Gamma Mu. Kappa Delta Pi, Phi Delta Kappa, Phi Kappa Phi, Psi Chi, Phi Beta Kappa Democrat. Unitarian. Author books, bulls., numerous articles. Home: 326 S Stallard Ave Stillwater OK 74074

LACKEY, J.M., gen. mgr. WENN, Birmingham, Ala. Address: 1428 5th Av N Birmingham AL 35201

LACKEY, JAMES GILBERT, JR., lawyer; b. Nashville, Aug. 22, 1915; s. James Gilbert and Merrill Margueritte (Everett) L.; B.A., Vanderbilt U., 1936, LL.B., 1938; m. Mary Ellen Smith, Oct. 29, 1942; children— James Gilbert, Ellen Reid. Admitted to Tenn. bar, 1938; practiced in Nashville, 1938-55; mem. firm Stephenson, Lackey & Holman, Nashville, 1955—. Dir. First Fed. Savs. and Loan Assn., 1955—. Tchr. Nashville YMCA Night Law Sch., 1947—, dean, 1955—. Served with USNR, World War II. Decorated Bronze Star. Mem. Nashville (pres. 1964-65), Tenn. (gov. 1969-72), Am. bar assns., Tenn. Def. Lawyers Assn., Order Coif, Alpha Tau Omega, Phi Delta Phi. Episcopalian. Mason (32 deg., Shriner). Clubs: Hillwood Country (pres. 1969-70), Sertoma (Nashville); Capitol City. Home: 419 W Hillwood St Nashville TN 37205 Office: PO Box 2829 Nashville TN 37219

LACKEY, WILLIAM W., lawyer; b. Nashville, Feb. 21, 1917; B.A., Vanderbilt U., 1938, J.D., 1940. Admitted to Tenn. bar, 1940; asst. dist. atty. Davidson County, 1945-48; mem. firm Lackey & Lackey, Savannah, Tenn.; U.S. magistrate, 1965—. Mem. Am., Hardin County, 22d Jud. Dist. (pres. 1969-70) bar assns., Bar Assn. Tenn. (legal aid and referral service com. 1958-59, chmn. domestic relations com. 1962-63, gov. 1968-71), Phi Delta Phi. Office: Lackey & Lackey Main St Savannah TN 38372*

LACOUR, LOUIS CHARLES, lawyer; b. New Orleans, Dec. 29, 1927; s. Septime V. and Effie M. (Bonnette) LaC.; student La. State U., 1946; B.B.A., Loyola U. of South, 1952, J.D., 1956; m. Gloria Anne Comiskey, May 3, 1952; children—Angelique Marie and Adrienne Anne (twins), Gloria Anne, Louis Charles, Vallery James. Parttime instr. econs. and accounting Loyola U. of South, 1951-52; part-time instr. commerce Xavier U., New Orleans, 1956-57; pvt. practice of law, New Orleans, 1956-62, 70—; asst. dist. atty., Parish of Orleans, 1960-62; U.S. atty. Eastern Dist. La., 1962-70. Sec. New

Orleans city affairs com. La. Legislature; mem. Democratic Exec. Com. Parish Orleans. Served with AUS, 1946-48. Recipient Louis N. Pilie award Loyola U., 1952, Distinguished Eagle Scout award, Boy Scouts Am., 1970. Mem. Fed., La. bar assns., St. Thomas More Cath. Lawyers Assn., Holy Name Soc., Blue Key, Sigma Lambda Epsilon. Roman Catholic. K.C. Office: Am Bank Bldg New Orleans LA 70130

LACY, J(OSEPH) TOLBERTTE, coll. dean; b. Augusta, Ga., July 18, 1915; s. James and Sarah (Tolbert) L.; A.B., Paine Coll., 1937; M.A., Atlanta U., 1955, 6th year specialist certificate, 1964; LL.D., Zion Coll., 1970; m. Ruth Yvonne Jefferson, Sept. 21, 1940; children—LaRonce (Mrs. Johnny Grissom), Reta Jo. Supervising prin. Central High Sch., Sylvania, Ga., 1940-71; dean student affairs Paine Coll., Augusta, 1971—; prof. Sch. Edn., Atlanta U., summer sch. Explorer Post adviser Boy Scouts Am., 1940-71; chmn. exec. council Screven County Citizens Betterment Council, 1966. Mem. local bd Selective Service System, Ga. Recipient Silver Beaver award Boy Scouts Am., 1960. Mem. Nat. Assn. Secondary Sch. Prins., Ga. Tchrs. and Edn. Assn. (dir. 1963-65), Ga. Tchr. Edn. Council, Ga. Assn. Educators (chmn. profl. rights and responsibilities commn.). Baptist. Mason. Club: Schoolmasters. Home: 119 Clark Av Sylvania GA 30467

LACY, STERLING SMITH, JR., petroleum engr.; b. El Dorado, Ark., Dec. 5, 1924; s. Sterling Smith and Ruby Lee (Bailey) L.; student Ore. State Coll., 1944-45; B.S., Tex. A. and M. Coll., 1947; m. Emma Lee Morgan, Nov. 29, 1947; children—MaryEllen, Carolyn. With McAlester Fuel Co., Magnolia Ark., 1947—, dist. engr., 1952-54, chief engr., 1954-66, asst. supt., 1967—. Chmn. Magnolia Municipal Water Commn., 1956—. Mem. steering com. U.S. Regional Synod Ark., Okla., La., Tex. Presbyn. Ch., 1972, chmn. task force legal matters, trustees and founds., 1972. Served with AUS, 1944-46; to 1st lt., C.E., AUS, 1951-52. Named Magnolia Young Man of Year, 1959. Registered profl. engr., Tex. Mem. Mid-Continent Oil and Gas Assn. (com. chmn. La. Ark. div. 1962-64), Am. Petroleum Inst. (chpt. chmn. 1950, Soc. Petroleum Engrs., Am. Inst. Mining Engrs., Am. Water Works Assn. Ark. Audubon Soc. (pres. 1967—). Presbyn. (elder; moderator). Home: 203 Troy St Magnolia AR 71753 Office: PO Box 10 McAlester Bldg Magnolia AR 71753

LACY, WILLIAM LARRY, educator; b. Laurel, Miss., June 3, 1936; s. Arthur Roland and Velma Ruth (Brewer) L.; student Ga. Inst. Tech., 1954-57; B.A., Southwestern at Memphis, 1959; Ph.D., U. Va., 1962; m. Nancy Carol Howell, June 30, 1961; children—William Stephen, John Fulton, Mary Anne. Prof. philosophy Southwestern U. at Memphis (Tenn.), 1962—. Presbyn. (elder). Home: 812 West Dr Memphis TN 38112 Office: 2000 N Parkway Memphis TN 38112

LADNER, HEBER A., state ofcl.; b. Lumoerton, Miss., Oct. 4, 1902; s. Webster L. and Velena (Beall) L.; A.B., Millsaps Coll.; A.M., Duke; m. Daisy Bowles, Dec. 22, 1935; children—Mary Eloise, Heber. Mem. Ho. of Reps., Pearl River Co., Miss., 1936-40; sec. Miss. State Budget Commn., 1940-42; clk. Miss. Ho. of Reps., 1942-48; sec. state, State of Miss., 1948—. Mem. Kappa Sigma. Democrat. Baptist. Lion. Mason. Home: 3982 Nassau St Jackson MS 39216 Office: New Capitol Jackson MS 39201

LAFFER, ARTHUR B., economist Office Mgmt. and Budget, Washington. Office: Office Management and Budget Executive Office Bldg Washington DC 20503*

LA FLEUR, ROBERT ALEX, state ofcl.; b. Washington, La., Jan. 26, 1922; s. Alex Golden and Lima (Brignac) LaF.; B.S., La. State U., 1947, M.S., 1956; m. Cora Lee Babin, Nov. 25, 1950. Biologist Tex. A. and M. Research Found., Bryan, 1948-49; La. Wildlife and Fish Commn., New Orleans, 1950-62; exec. sec. La. Stream Control Commn., Baton Rouge, 1962—. Served with USNR, 1943-46. Named La. Conservationist of Year, 1969. Mem. Water Pollution Control Fedn., Am. Water Works Assn., Am. Inst. Biol. Scis., La. Biologists Assn. (chmn. 1961—, sec.-treas. 1962—), State and Interstate Water Pollution Control Adminstrs. (pres. 1970-71). Home: 1859 Shawn Dr Baton Rouge LA 70806 Office: PO Drawer FC La State U Baton Rouge LA 70803

LAFONTAINE, HARRY, motion picture co. exec.; b. Copenhagen, Denmark, May 23, 1913 (came to U.S. 1951, naturalized 1956); s. Henri and Johanne (Jensen) LaF.; B.M.E., Danish Inst. Tech., 1934; M.E.E., Aarhus Tech. U., 1938; m. Edith M. Harris, Oct. 24, 1960. Roving news reel cameraman, 1934-39; produced War in Finland full length documentary feature, several major releases, 1945-50, including Red Menace, 1950; motion picture instr. U. Houston, 1951-53; pres., chmn. Nationwide Sch. Cinematography, Miami, Fla., 1954—; owner LaFontaine Prodns. Served as capt., 1939-40, group comdr. Danish Underground, 1940-45. Decorated Mannerheim War medal, Suomi Vinter War medal. Clubs: Royal Danish Yacht (Copenhagen); International Adventure (London); Racquet and Yacht (Maimi and France). Home: 7930 East Dr Miami Beach FL 33141 Office: Parkley House PO Box 551 Miami FL 33138

LAGAN, HENRY DUANE, physician; b. Enid, Okla., Nov. 30, 1932; s. James Henry and Thelma Estelle (Lyday) L.; B.S., Phillips U., 1954; M.D., U. Okla., 1964; m. Lota Dee Bouher, May 14, 1955; children—Duana Dee, Lynn Alison, Tim Duane, Lee Andrew. Intern Wesley Med. Center, Wichita, Kan., 1964-65; practice gen. medicine, Okeene, Okla., 1965-70, 71—; dir. student health service Oral Roberts U., Tulsa, 1970-71; asso. preceptor U. Okla. Sch. Medicine, 1965—; team physician Okeene High Sch., 1965—. Bd. dirs. Wesley Found., Okla. State U., Stillwater. Served with USAF, 1954-57. Mem. Am. Coll. Sports Medicine, A.M.A., Okla. State Med. Assn., Am. Acad. Family Practice, Am. Coll. Health Assn. Republican. Methodist (mem. ofcl. bd. 1970—, lay del. 1971-72). Home: PO Box 188 Okeene OK 73763 Office: PO Box 389 Okeene OK 73763

LAGATTUTA, VINCENT LOUIS, JR., dentist, educator; b. New Orleans, Mar. 25, 1931; s. Vincent Louis and Evelyn Marie (Bel) L.; B.S., U. Southwestern La., 1953; D.D.S., Loyola U. of South, 1956; certificate U. Pa., 1960; m. Mary Margaret Ehrensing, June 27, 1955; children— Margaret, Vincent H., Mark, Paul, Anne, Louis. Intern in oral surgery Charity Hosp., New Orleans, 1956-57, sr. resident in oral surgery, 1960-61; instr. oral pathology, Loyola U., 1960-61; pvt. practice oral surgery, Baton Rouge, La., 1961—; asst. clin. prof. oral surgery La. State U., Baton Rouge, 1969—; chief dental staff Our Lady of the Lake Hosp., 1966-67, Baton Rouge Gen. Hosp., 1965-66. Served with USAF, 1957-59. Diplomate Am. Bd. Oral Surgery. Fellow Internat. Assn. Oral Surgeons; mem. Am., Southeastern socs. oral surgeons, Pan Am. Med. Assn., La. Soc. Oral Surgeons, A.A.A.S., Am., La., 6th Dist. dental assns., Pierre Fauchard Acad., Blue Key, Xi Psi Phi. K.C. Club: Serra (Baton Rouge). Home: 1659 S Tamarix St Baton Rouge LA 70808 Office: 3850 Convention St Baton Rouge LA 70806

LAHAYE, JIMMIE DONALD, health clubs exec.; b. Port Arthur, Tex., Oct. 4, 1925; s. J. O. and Ida (Darby) LaH.; B.B.A., Tex. U., 1950; m. Evelyn Lawson, June 15, 1947; children—Edward, Andrew, Lauren. Mgr., Johnson & Johnson, Dallas, 1952-62; regional adminstr. Pepsi Cola, Dallas, 1962-64; pres. First Lady Spa, Inc., Houston, 1964—; dir. Trans-Tex. Drive-ins, J & J Credit Union. Served with USMCR, 1942-46. Mem. Purchasing Agts. Assn. (dir. 1959-62). Club: Cosmopolitan (pres. 1969-70) (Houston). Home: 5722 Braesheather St Houston TX 77035 Office: 7255 Clarewood Dr Houston TX 77036

LAHERTY, MICHEAL ALEXANDER educator, b. Raeford, N.C., Aug. 8, 1931; s. Ernest Glenn and Lottie Elizabeth (Shaw) A.; B.A., Lenoir Rhyne Coll., 1953; M.Ed., Appalachian State U., 1958, East Carolina U., 1962, Mich. State U., 1967, Duke, 1959; postgrad. U. Ga., 1968; m. Iris Buford Grigg, June 17, 1956; children—Douglas, Jeffrey, Jonathan, Beth, Robert. Tchr., prin. Catawba (N.C.) Elementary Sch., 1955-60; prin. Wallace-Rose Hill High Sch., Teachey, N.C., 1960-64, Hoke County High Sch., 1964-67; dir. student teaching Pembroke (N.C.) State U., 1967; supt. Hoke County Schs., Raeford, N.C., 1967—. Mem. budget com. United Fund, 1968-71; chmn. Hoke County Bd. Health, 1971-73. Bd. dirs. Region N Health Planning Council. Served with AUS, 1953-55. Mem. Horace Mann League, N.C. Assn. Edn. (pres. dist. supts. div. 1971-72), Grange. Democrat. Baptist. Kiwanian. Home: 603 N Fulton St Raeford NC 28376 Office: 109 E Edinboro Av Raeford NC 28376

LAHM, JACK FREDERICK, comml. diver; b. Ft. Lee, N.J., June 6, 1923; s. Frederick H. and Daisy Eleanor (Parsons) L.; grad. high sch.; m. Dorothy Marie Wright, Sept. 20, 1947; children—Keith David, Marilyn Marie. Served to chief shipfitter (master diver) USN, 1941-63; instr. USN Deep Sea Diving Sch., Washington, 1950-54, 58-63; diving supt. Sanford Bros. Divers, Morgan City, La., 1963-67; pres. Continental Diving Service, Inc., Morgan City, 1967—. Performed diving tasks at Internat. Trade Fair, Solonika, Greece, 1962, Am. Welding Soc. Conv., Phila., 1963. Mem. Comml. Divers Contractors Assn., Marine Tech. Soc., Internat. Oceanographic Found., Fleet Res. Assn., C. of C., Petroleum Club Morgan City, Krewe of Hephaestus. Club: St. Mary Country (Morgan City). Home: 509 Polaris Rd Morgan City LA 70380 Office: PO Box 2484 Morgan City LA 70380

LAHM, SIEGFRIED S., dept. store exec.; b. Saltzburg, Austria, Aug. 26, 1938 (came to U.S., 1949, naturalized, 1958); s. Karl and Anna (Kern) L.; B.S. in Bus. Adminstrn., Econs., Wittenberg U., Springfield, O., 1961; m. Susan Ellen Voorheis, June 11, 1961; children— Heidi, Eric, Corey. Buyer Wren's Allied Stores, Springfield, 1961-64, mdse. mgr., 1964-69, v.p. merchandising, 1969-71; pres. Levys of Savannah (Ga.), 1971—. Chmn. Downtown Core Bus. sect. United Fund, Springfield, 1970-71; pres. Springfield Downtown Mchts. Assn., 1970-71. Mem. Savannah C. of C., Wittenberg U. Alumni Assn., Phi Gamma Delta (trustee). Home: 105 Dombey Rd Wilmington Island Savannah GA 31404 Office: 210 E Broughton St Savannah GA 31402

LAHOOD, CHARLES GEORGE, JR., librarian; b. Omaha, Aug. 29, 1922; s. Charles George and Madeline Teresa (Raven) LaH.; B.S., Cath. U. Am., 1942, M.A., 1943, M.S. in Library Sci., 1952; m. Susanne Bracken, Aug. 28, 1948; children—Charles John, Daniel Edward, Patricia Anne, William David, Thomas George, Robert, Catherine. Staff, Library Congress, 1947—, head serial record sect., 1952-53, asst. chief photoduplication service, 1953-61, chief serial div., 1961-68, chief photoduplication service, 1968—; adj. lectr. Sch. Library and Information Scis., U. Md. Mem. A.L.A. (chmn copy methods sect. policy and research com. 1962-65; chmn. serial sect.), Am. Documentation Inst. (sec. 1956-60, mem. exec. bd., councillor-at-large 1960-62), Nat. Microfilm Assn. St. Vincent de Paul Soc. Roman Catholic. Author: A Survey of Bibliographies and Checklists of Early American Imprints, 1956. Editor: Pictorial Americana, rev. edit., 1955; A Descriptive Checklist of Selected Manuscripts in the Monasteries of Mt. Athos, 1957. Home: 10102 E Bexhill Dr Kensignton MD 20795 Office: Library of Congress Washington DC 20540

LAHR, RAYMOND MERRILL, newspaperman; b. Kokomo, Ind., June 27, 1914; s. Clifford V. and Leone Fern (Groves) L.; A.B., U. Chgo., 1936; m. Sarah Louise Meyer, Oct. 2, 1941. With United Press (now United Press Internat.), 1937—, beginning as staff Midwestern burs., successively labor reporter, Washington, congl. reporter, chief senate staff, 1947-58, chief polit. corr., 1958—. Club: Nat. Press (Washington). Author: (with J. William Theis) Congress: Power and Purpose on Capitol Hill, 1967. Home: 3321 Laurel Ct Falls Church VA 22042 Office: Nat Press Bldg Washington DC 20005

LAIDLAW, JOY, gen. mgr. El Paso (Tex.) Symphony Orch. Office: Pas Del Norte Hotel S El Paso and W San Antonio Sts El Paso TX 79901*

LAIL, EUGENE FRANKLIN, ednl. adminstr.; b. Shelby, N.C., Feb. 8, 1922; s. Tinsley Peter and Hettie Pearl (Parker) L.; B.A., Furman U., 1949, M.A., 1957; Edn. Specialist, U. Ga., 1962; m. Carolyn Elizabeth Brooks, Mar. 21, 1951; 1 dau., Eugenia Elizabeth. Student dir. Furman U. Bands, 1946-49; band dir. pub. schs., Greer, S.C., 1950-53; dir. music, pub. schs., Williamston, 1953-57, coordinator music Crisp County Schs., Cordele, Ga., 1957-62; prin. elementary sch., Vienna, 1962-65; supervising prin. Harlem Pub. Schs., 1965-68; asst. prof. edn. Ga. Coll., Milledgeville, 1968-70; prin. Putnam County High Sch., Eatonton, Ga., 1970—; musical arranger, condr. Lail Merritt Orch., 1951-57; trombonist Greenville (S.C.) Symphony Orch., 1951-57. Cons., Baldwin County Schs., Ga., 1970-72, Ga. Coll. at Milledgeville, 1970-71; dir. vocational edn. Putnam County Schs., Eatonton, 1971-72. Musical arranger, dir. S.C. Am. Legion Drum and Bugel Corps, 1955-56. Served with AUS, 1942-45. Named Star Tchr., Ga. State C. of C., 1959. Mem. Nat., Ga. edn. assns., Nat. Assn. Secondary Sch. Prins., Am. Assn. U. Profs., Woodmen of the World, Phi Delta Kappa. Mason, Kiwanian. Composer: Brazilica, 1957, Street Scenes for Band, 1962. Author: Functional Factors in Native Musical Ability that Relate to School Achievement, 1957. Home: 113 Westminister Dr Eatonton GA 31024 Office: 314 S Washington Av Eatonton GA 31024

LAIN, WILLIAM GLENN, elec. engr.; b. Haskell, Tex., Dec. 9, 1930; s. Robert Griffin and Donna (Moody) L.; B.E.E., U. Tex., 1961; m. Bettey Bob Moore, Aug. 31, 1955; 1 dau., Kimberly Glynn. Chief elec. engr. Bauer Dredging Co., Port Lavaca, Tex., 1961-66; pres., owner Tex. Analytics Inc., Engring. & Mfg. Co., Houston, 1967—; v.p., dir. LSM Inc., Houston. Mem. Corpus Christi Elec. Adv. Bd., 1969—. Served with USN, 1950-56. Mem. Tex. Soc. Profl. Engrs., I.E.E.E. Home: 303 Willow Vista El Lago TX 77586 Office: 17311 El Camino Real Houston TX 77058

LAIR, HARRY REDMON, lawyer; b. Cynthiana, Ky., Apr. 28, 1910; s. Redmon Eugene and Bessie Clay (Dedman) L.; student Ga. Mil. Acad., 1927-29; B.S., U. Ky., 1933; LL.B., Jefferson Sch. Law, 1936; LL.B., U. Louisville, 1951; m. Margaret Jabine Newsom., Dec. 21, 1940; children—Jennie Scott, Harry Redmon. Admitted to Ky. bar, 1936; master commr. Harrison Circuit Ct., 1937—; gen. counsel Harrison Rural Electric Coop. Corp., 1939—; Cynthiana City atty., 1942-54, 58-66; spl. circuit judge Harrison Circuit Ct., 1951, 53, 55; atty. Farmers Nat. Bank, 1957—. Mem. Am., Ky., Harrison County (past pres.) bar assns., Phi Delta Theta, Omicron Delta, Kappa, Delta Sigma Phi. Presbyn. Home: 550 E Pike Cynthiana KY 41031 Office: 11 E Pike St Cynthiana KY 41031

LAIR, NARD, physician; b. Amarillo, Tex., June 7, 1916; s. Albert H. and May (Lair) Jett; B.S., Tex. Tech. U., 1939, M.S., 1940; M.D., U. Tenn., 1947; m. Clara Lee Hethcoat, Feb. 14, 1948; children—Dana, Marcy, Kevin. Intern Baylor U. Hosp., Dallas, 1947-48; resident in surgery Norfolk Gen. Hosp. (Va.), 1948-49; pvt. practice medicine specializing in surgery and aerospace medicine, Dallas, 1952—; mem. staffs Baylor Med. Center, Dallas, St. Paul Hosp., Dallas, NASA, Houston. Cons. FAA, 1958—, med. div. FBI, 1959—, CIA, 1959—. Served with AUS, 1943-46. Named Hon. Med. Cons. to Queen Eng., 1971. Fellow Am. Acad. Family Practice, Dallas So. Clin. Soc., Royal Soc. Health (London), Am. Acad. Air Controllers; mem. Civil Air Med. Assn., Air Medics Med. Aviation Assn., Mensa, Flying Physicians Assn., Am. Guild Organists, Phi Beta Pi. Home: 10215 Van Dyke St Dallas TX 75218 Office: 10710 Shiloh Rd Dallas TX 75228

LAIRD, ANGUS MCKENZIE, investment exec.; b. Opp, Ala., Oct. 9, 1903; s. John Henry and Ada (Zorn) L.; A.B., U. Fla., 1927, M.A., 1928; postgrad. Syracuse U., 1928-29, U. Chgo., 1930-31; m. Myra Adelia Doyle, June 8, 1938; children—Victoria Mell (Mrs. Henry Ackerman), Nan McKenzie (Mrs. Samuel Hughes). Teaching fellow Syracuse U., 1928-29; prof. history and polit. sci. U. Fla., Gainesville, 1929-30, 37-46, U. Denver, 1931-37; dir. Fla. Merit System, Tallahassee, 1946-60; v.p., dir. Municipal Code Corp., Inc., Old St. Augustine Road Estates, Inc.; pres. Huesack Enterprises, Inc.; editor Wakulla News, 1967—. Recipient citation Fla. Cabinet, 1961. Mem. Fla. Pub. Health Assn. (pres. 1955), Fla. Pub. Personnel Assn. (pres. 1953), Pub. Personnel Assn. U.S. and Can. (hon., exec. council 1958-60), Kappa Sigma (historian). Author: City Manager Government in Florida, 1929; (with Wilson K. Doyle) Government and Administration in Florida, 1955; Centennial History of Kappa Sigma, 1969. Home: 507 Plantation Rd Tallahassee FL 32303

LAIRD, EUNICE WARD (MRS. ROBERT ALEXANDER LAIRD), club woman, civic worker; b. New Orleans, Nov. 17, 1893; d. John Joseph and Catherine (McVey) Ward; B.O., New Orleans Coll. Oratory, 1914; m. Robert Alexander Laird, Jan. 31, 1920; children—Katharine Eunice (Mrs. Alfred Friedrichs Livaudais) and Harriet Helene (Mrs. Richard Massie Martin) (twins). Tchr. pub. schs., New Orleans, 1912-19. Mem. exec. bd. Am. Women's Voluntary Service, New Orleans, 1942-46. La. br., 1944-46, organizer, dir. opportunity shop, 1942-46, chmn. ways and means com., 1942-46; active in establishing cancer detection clinic, New Orleans, 1942-44; capt. spl. donors drive women's div. Community Chest, New Orleans, 1942; dir. sect., bd. dirs. Needlework Guild Am., New Orleans, 1942-58, publicity chmn., 1944-56, civil def. chmn., 1950-56; active Chip of Friendship, New Orleans, 1946-47; adv. chmn. Stage Inc., New Orleans, 1949-50; founding bd. mem. Le Petit Theatre, de Vieux Carre Guild, New Orleans, 1950-52, patio chmn., 1952; bd. dirs. Le Petit Salon, 1949-52, publicity chmn., 1945-52; mem. exec. bd., membership chmn. La. Landmarks Soc., 1951-53; mem. founding bd. Army and Navy Club Aux., New Orleans, 1949, sec., 1949-50, pres., 1950-52, bd. dirs., 1949-53; mem. adv. bd. Spring Fiesta Assn., New Orleans, 1942-51, governing bd., 1951-55; mem. founding com. Summer Pops Concerts, New Orleans, 1942, governing bd., 1949-52, chmn. sponsored nights, 1951-52; bd. dirs. New Orleans Philharmonic Soc., 1948-51; bd. dirs. New Orleans Opera House Assn., founding exec. bd. mem. Women's Guild, 1943—, vice chmn., 1949-50, pres., 1959-60, 67-68; co-founder Loyola U. Salon Music, New Orleans, 1951, pres., 1951-53, hon. life pres., 1960—; founding bd. mem. De Paul Hosp. Guild, New Orleans, 1951, pres., 1952-54, hon. life mem. bd. dirs., 1955—, chmn. therapy fund, 1957—; co-founder, organizer St. Mary's Dominican Coll. Assos., New Orleans, 1954, pres., 1954-56, hon. life pres., 1960—; founder, organizer Vous Souvenez-Vous, New Orleans, 1958, pres., 1958-60, 65-67, named hon. life pres., 1960; nat. patroness Phi Beta; mem. exec. bd. Orleans Club, 1957-58, v.p., 1957-58, hon. mem., 1957—; founding com. Preservation New Orleans Cultural Center; mem. New Orleans C. of C. Aux., 1960-61; chmn. coffee forum Fgn. Relations Assn., 1958-60, 62-64, bd. mem., 1956-58, exec. bd., 1958-60, sec., 1964-65; bd. dirs. Community Concerts Assn., New Orleans, 1960—, decorations chmn., 1960-61; chmn. civic hospitality com. women's aux. New Orleans C. of C., 1963-65; chmn. Opera Orientation Series, 1963—; zone chmn. Crippled Children's Easter Seal Campaign, 1964—; mem. 250th Anniversary Com. Founding of New Orleans; 1968; publicity chmn. Evening in Old Creole New Orleans, 1968. Recipient Key to City of New Orleans for outstanding service, Certificate of Merit, 1959; certificate for World War II work Gov. of La., 1945; Times-Picayune Loving Cup for continuous and cumulative service to New Orleans, 1962. Mem. Internat. Platform Assn. Roman Catholic. Home: 5421 St Charles Av New Orleans LA 70115

LAIRD, LESBIA REESE (MRS. DENNIS ELVIN LAIRD), librarian; b. Winfield, Ala., Oct. 24, 1918; d. John Houston and Callie (Gilpin) Reese; student Tex. Coll. Arts and Industries, 1936-37; B.A., Tex. Womens U., 1941; student N. Tex. State U., summer 1942; m. Dennis Elvin Laird, Nov. 24, 1956. Librarian high sch., Mercedes, Tex., 1941-44, U.S. Naval Air Tng. Sta., Corpus Christi, Tex., 1944-46, U.S. Army, Camp Lee, Va., 1946-47, Germany, 1947-52, USAF, Wolters AFB, Mineral Wells, Tex., 1952-55, Brooks AFB, Tex., 1955—. Mem. Tex., Bexar County, Southwestern library assns., Beta Sigma Phi. Democrat. Home: Route 14 Box 345 San Antonio TX 78221 Office: Base Library Brooks AFB TX 78235

LAIRD, MELVIN R, sec. of defense; b. Sept. 1, 1922; s. Melvin R. and Helen (Connor) L.; B.A., Carleton Coll., 1944; D.H.L. (hon.), Lincoln Coll., 1966, St. Leo Coll., 1969; D.Polit. Sci. (hon.), U. Pacific, 1968; LL.D., Ill. Coll., 1971; m. Barbara Masters, Oct. 15, 1945; children—John, Alison, David. Mem. Wis. Senate, 1946-52, chmn. mil. and vets. affairs com., chmn. legislative council, chmn. tax com., mem. Wis. Ednl. Commn.; mem. 83rd-90th Congresses, 7th Dist. Wis., mem. coms. on appropriations, def., commerce, labor, health, edn., welfare, chmn. Joint Senate-House Com. on Statement Rep. Prins., chmn. Rep. Conf., 89th, 90th Congress; U.S. sec. of def., 1969—. Chmn. platform com. Rep. Conv., 1964. U.S. del. WHO, Geneva, 1959, 63, 65. Recipient 15th Ann. Albert Lasker med. award; Man of Year award Am. Cancer Soc., Nat. Assn. Mental Health; Distinguished Service citation Res. Officers Assn., 1950; Ann. award Am. Good Govt. Soc., 1967; Presdl. citation Am. Pub. Health Assn., 1968; Statesman in Medicine award, 1970, numerous others. Mem. D.A.V., Mil. Order Purple Heart, 40 and 8, Am. Legion, V.F.W. Republican. Author: A House Divided: America's Strategy Gap, 1962. Editor: The Conservative Papers, 1964. Home: PO Box 279 Marshfield WI 54449 Office: Dept Def Washington DC 20305

LAIRD, WILSON MORROW, petroleum assn. exec.; b. Erie, Pa., Mar. 4, 1915; s. Charles William and Elizabeth (Morrow) L.; B.A. cum laude, Muskingum Coll., 1936, D. Sc., 1964; M.A., U. N.C., 1938; Ph.D., U. Cin., 1942; m. Reba Allene Latimer, Aug. 8, 1938; children—Douglas, David, Donald, Dorothy (Mrs. Dennis Kaatz). Geologist Pa. Geol. Survey, summers 1936, 37, 40; prof. geology, head dept. U. N.D., 1940-69; dir. Office Oil and Gas, Dept. Interior, Washington, 1969-71; dir. exploration Am. Petroleum Inst., Washington, 1971—; N.D. state geologist, 1941-69; geologist U.S.

Geol. Survey, summers 1944, 45; cons. in field. Fellow Geol. Soc. Am.; Mem. Am. Assn. Petroleum Geologists (Pres.'s award 1947), N.D. Acad. Sci., Washington Geol. Soc., Assn. Geology Tchrs., Sigma Xi, Sigma Gamma Epsilon. Club: International (Washington). Contbr. articles to profl. jours. Home: 1807 Wainwright Dr Reston VA 22070 Office: Am Petroleum Inst 1801 K St NW Washington DC 20006

LAIT, ROBERT MORRIS, wholesale trade co. exec.; b. El Paso, Sept. 1, 1928; s. Jack and Josephine (Saner) L.; B.S. in Civil Engring., U. Tex. at El Paso, 1951; m. Miriam Feinberg, Jan. 30, 1955; children—Linda Sue, Jan Ellen, Amy Jo, Russell M. Constrn. engr. Robert E. McKee, gen. contractor, El Paso, 1950-55; v.p. El Paso Pipe and Supply Co., El Paso, 1955-71. Mem. exec. bd. Yucca council Boy Scouts Am., 1969—; active Jewish Community Center. Served to 1st lt. AUS, 1951. Mem. A.I.M. (mem. pres.'s council 1970-71), Am. Waterworks Assn., N.M. Mining Assn. Jewish religion. Mason (Shriner). Home: 420 Borealis Lane El Paso TX 79912 Office: Southwest Bank Bldg El Paso TX 79901

LAKE, I. BEVERLY, N.C. Supreme Ct. justice; b. Wake Forest, N.C., Aug. 29, 1906; B.S., Wake Forest Coll., 1925; LL.B., Harvard, 1929; LL.M., Columbia, 1940, S.J.D., 1947; m. Gertrude Bell; 1 son, I. Beverly. Admitted to N.C. bar, 1928; prof. law Wake Forest Coll., 1932-51; asst. atty. gen. of N.C., 1952-55; mem. firm Lake, Boyce and Lake, Raleigh, N.C.; now justice N.C. Supreme Ct., Raleigh. Am., N.C., Wake County bar assns., N.C. State Bar, Phi Alpha Delta. Author: Discrimination by Railroads and Other Public Utilities, 1947; North Carolina Practice Methods, 1952. Home: 403 N Main St Wake Forest NC 27587 Office: Justice Bldg Raleigh NC 27601

LAKE, RICHARD HARRINGTON, internat. trade and pub. affairs cons.; b. Carlisle, Pa., Oct. 15, 1919; s. William Harrington and Diana C. (Strube) L.; grad. Strategic Intelligence Sch., 1951, Command and Gen. Staff Coll., 1954; B.S. in Commerce, Roosevelt U., 1958, M.A. in Econs. and Bus., 1961; grad. Fgn. Service Inst., 1965; m. Blair Moody, July 17, 1954; children—Richard Moody, Mary Anne (dec.), William Moody, Sara Blair. Free lance writer, 1937-38; underwriter's asst. Guardian Life Ins. Co., 1938-40; cons. for exhbn. fgn. films in U.S., 1940; commd. 2d lt. U.S. Army, 1940, to lt. col., 1956; comdr. inf. and mil. police units, 1941-46; chief agt. Criminal Investigations Div., U.S. Occupation Forces, Germany, 1947; chief liaison to USSR forces, Berlin, Germany, 1947-48; pub. relations officer Mil. Gov., High Commr. for Germany, 1948-50; staff officer 2d Army Hdqrs., Ft. Meade, Md., 5th Army Hdqrs., Chgo., 1951-53; sr. adviser to Royal Thai Army, Bangkok, Thailand, 1954-56; dir. Indsl. security, enforcement, criminal Investigations U.S. Army, 1957-61; faculty Roosevelt U. Coll. Bus. Administrn., Chgo., 1958-60; cons. internat. affairs Dept. Commerce, Washington, 1961, alternate for sec. commerce to 1st White House Food for Peace Conf., 1961, exec. sec. Fgn.-Trade Zones Bd. U.S., 1961-69, dir. fgn. trade zones staff Bur. Internat. Bus. Operations, 1961-63, Bur. Internat. Commerce, 1963-69; owner Richard H. Lake Assos., 1970—. Mem. Co. Mil. Historians, Permanent Internat. Assn. Navigation Congresses, Am. Assn. Port Authorities (asso.), Soc. for Internat. Devel., Nat. Assn. Bus. Economists, Res. Officers Assn., Ret. Officers Assn., D.A.V., Ill. Assn. Chiefs of Police, Policia Secreta Nacional of Panama (hon.). Episcopalian. Mason (32 deg.). Contbr. articles govt. and bus. publs. Home: 4416 Duncan Dr Annandale VA 22003 Office: PO Box 385 Annandale VA 22003

LAKE, ROY, govt. ofcl.; b. Jefferson, S.C., May 6, 1924; s. William and Sadie (Crawford) L.; B.S. cum laude in Elec. Engring., Agrl. and Tech. Coll. N.C., 1949; m. Geraldine Battle, Sept. 18, 1949; children—Winona M., Michael R., Stephen W., Anita M., Lisa K. Postal clk. U.S. P.O., Washington, 1949-51; patent examiner U.S. Patent Office, Washington, 1951-63, primary examiner, 1963—. Served with USNR, 1942-46. Mem. Washington Patent Office Soc. Home: 1221 Burton St Silver Spring MD 20910 Office: care US Patent Office Washington DC 20230

LAM, CARLOS FEDERICO, JR., educator; b. Panama City, Panama, July 27, 1942; s. Carl Frederick and Cecilia (Fong de) L.; B.S., Clemson U., 1965, M.S., 1967, Ph.D., 1970; m. Ruth Lee Coaplen, Aug. 28, 1965. Grad. research asst. animal sci. Clemson U., 1965-70, grad. dorm counselor, 1965-70, ground instr. Aero Club, 1968-70; prof. physiology U. Panama, 1968—; consul of Republic of Panama in S.C., 1967-68. Mem. Clemson U. Areo Club (pres. 1966-70), Gamma Sigma Delta. Author articles in field. Home: PO Box 3268 Balboa CZ Office: Facultad de Agronomia Univ Panama Republic of Panama

LAMB, JAMES CHRISTIAN, III, educator; b. Warsaw, Va., Aug. 20, 1924; s. James Christian and Renee (Soulie) L.; B.S. in Civil Engring., Va. Mil. Inst., 1947; S.M., Mass. Inst. Tech., 1948, S.E. 1952, Sc.D., 1953; m. Martha Lee McGinnis, June 8, 1948; children—Madeleine C., James Christian IV, Charles D., Robert S., William B. Instr., Va. Mil. Inst., 1948-50; research asst. Mass. Inst. Tech., 1951-53, research asso., 1953-55; san. engr. Am. Cyanamid Co., Bound Brook, N.J. 1955-59; asso. prof. san. engring. U. N.C., Chapel Hill, 1959-65, prof., 1965—. Adj. prof. Newark Coll, Engring., 1955-59; cons. engr., 1948-55, 59—. Served to 1st Lt., AUS, 1943-46. Gen. Edn. Bd. fellow, 1950-51. Diplomate Environmental Engring. Inter-soc. Bd. Mem. Am. Soc. C.E., Am. Pub. Health Assn., Am. Soc. Engring. Edn., Am. Water Works Assn., Water Pollution Control Fedn., Sigma Xi, Delta Omega, Chi Epsilon. Research in water indsl. wastes, treatment processes, 1951—. Home: 612 Greenwood Rd Chapel Hill NC 27514

LAMB, JAMIE PARKER, JR., engring. educator; b. Boligee, Ala., Sept. 21, 1933; s. Jamie Parker and Cletus (Hixson) L.; B.S., Auburn U., 1954; M.S., U. Ill., 1958, Ph.D., 1961; m. Nancy Catherine Flaherty, June 11, 1955; children—David Parker, Stephen Patrick. Asst. prof. engring. mechanics N.C. State U., Raleigh, 1961-63; asst. prof. mech. engring. U. Tex., Austin, 1963-67, asso. prof. 1967-70, prof., 1970—, chmn. mech. engring. dept., 1970—. Cons. LTV Aerospace Corp., Dallas, Marshall Space Flight Center, Huntsville, Ala., Tracor, Inc., Austin, Rocketdyne, McGregor, Tex., ARO, Inc., Tullahoma, Tenn. Served to 1st lt. USAF, 1955-57. Mem. Am. Soc. M.E., Am. Inst. Aeros. and Astronautics, N.Y. Acad. Sci., Am. Soc. for Engring. Edn., Sigma Xi, Pi Tau Sigma, Tau Beta Pi. Baptist. Contr. articles to profl. jours. Home: 2605 Pinewood Terrace Austin TX 78757

LAMB, LAWRENCE EDWARD, cardiologist; b. Fredonia, Kan., Oct. 13, 1926; s. John Robert and Dell M. (Ross) L.; M.D. (Battenfeld Hall scholar), U. Kan., 1949. Intern, U. Kan. Med. Center, 1950, resident, 1950-51, Am. Heart Assn. fellow cardiology, 1954; instr. medicine, fellow cardiology Emory U., 1953-54; fellow cardiology U. Geneva, Switzerland, 1954-55; dir. cardiology dept. internal medicine, 1957-62; chief aerospace and scis. div. USAF Sch. Aerospace Medicine, Brooks AFB, Tex., 1962-66; prof. medicine Baylor U. Coll. Medicine, Houston, 1966- —. Cons. cardiology Project Mercury, NASA, 1960, cons. dir. life scis., 1965. Recipient Arnold D. Tuttle award Aerospace Med. Assn., 1959, Distinguished Civilian Service medal Dept. Def., 1962, Meritorious Civilian Service award Dept. Air Force, 1955-66. Diplomate Am. Bd. Internal Medicine. Fellow Am. Coll. Cardiology, A.C.P., Am. Coll. Chest Physicians, Aerospace Md. Assn., Am. Coll. Clin. Pharmacology and Chemotheraphy, Am. Heart Assn. (council on epidemiology). Author: Fundamentals of Electrocardiography and Vector-cardiography, 1957; Electrocardiography and Vectorcardiography Instrumentation, Fundamentals, and Clinical Applications, 1965; Your Heart and How To Live With It; also numerous articles, monographs, chpts. in books. Editorial bd. Am. Jour. Cardiology, 1964-67, Am. Jour. Electrocardiography, 1966—, Aerospace Medicine, 1964-69, Postgrad. Medicine, 1966—; syndicated med. columnist Newspaper Enterprise Assn., N.Y., 1970—. Home: 135 Downing Dr San Antonio TX 78209

LAMB, THOMAS EUGENE, air force officer; b. Midland, S.D., Aug. 1, 1924; s. Theodore N. and Hazel (McDonald) M.; B.S. Polit. Sci., Am. Internat. Coll., 1960; M.A. Internat. Affairs, U. Md., 1964; grad. Air Command and Staff Coll., 1958; grad. Air War Coll., 1964; m. Syble Rebecca Avery, July 3, 1944; children—Theodore, Marsha (Mrs. Stewart B. Davis). Commd. 2d lt. Army Air Force 1944, advanced through grades to col., 1965; pilot trainee, combat pilot, South Pacific, Philippines, 1944-45; various assignments in US, Okinawa, Azores, Europe; stationed at Hdqrs.-USAF, Washington, 1958-63, 64-66; nuclear planner U.S. European Command, 1967-69; dir. Air Force Jr. ROTC, Air U., Maxwell AFB, Ala., 1969—. Cons. Inst. War and Peace Studies, Columbia U., N.Y.C., 1966-67, also lectr., researcher arms control; mem. Atlantic Seminar and Peace Seminar. Mem. Pi Sigma Alpha. Mason. Home: 105 Poplar St Maxwell Air Force Base AL 36112 Office: Hdqrs Air Force ROTC Maxwell Air Force Base AL 36112

LAMBDEN, DAN R., petroleum refining co. exec.; b. Houston, Sept. 13, 1936; s. Roy L. and Jennie R. (Callicoatte) L.; B.J., U. Tex. at Austin, 1960. Communications specialist Marathon Oil Co., Denver Research Center, Littleton, Colo., 1962-65; editorial asso. Standard Oil Co. of Cal., San Francisco, 1965-67; pub. relations rep. M.P. R.R. Co., Houston, 1967-69; mgr. pub. relations Texaco, Inc., Houston, 1969—. Served to 1st lt. C.E., AUS, 1960-62. Recipient Distinguished Service award Colo. Petroleum Council, 1964. Mem. Pub. Relations Soc. Am., Houston C. of C. (chmn. Operation Sparkle 1970, vice chmn. civic affairs com. 1971), Phi Sigma Kappa, Alpha Delta Sigma. Home: 2121 Fountain View Houston TX 77027 Office: PO Box 52332 Houston TX 77052

LAMBERT, ARTHUR GORMAN, lawyer; b. Washington, Feb. 10, 1899; s. Wilton J. and Elizabeth (Gorman) L.; grad. The Hill Sch., 1918; A.B., Princeton, 1922; LL.B., Harvard, 1925; m. Mary Lemon Sipple, Sept. 4, 1926; children—William S., Arthur Gorman. Admitted to D.C. bar, 1926; partner firm Lambert & Hart, Washington, 1930; asst. U.S. dist. atty., Washington, 1929-33; partner firm Lambert, Furlow & Sheehan and predecessor firms, Washington and Rockville, Md., 1933—; v.p., dir., mem. exec. com. Madison Nat. Bank, Washington. Chmn. bd. mgrs. Village of Chevy Chase (Md.), 1955-64, atty., 1964—. Atty., trustee Suburban Hosp. Assn., Inc., Bethesda, Md. Served with U.S. Army, World War I. Clubs: Metropolitan (Washington); Chevy Chase; Hillsboro (Pompano Beach, Fla.); Wianno (Cape Cod, Mass.). Home: 17 Grafton St Chevy Chase MD 20015 Office: 1629 K St NW Washington DC 20006

LAMBERT, EALON M., state ofcl.; b. Red Level Ala., Dec. 11, 1919; s. Thomas Madison and Estella (Kilpatrick) L.; student Auburn U., 1936-38, 39-40; m. Mary Louise Herndon, May 27, 1967; children—(by previous marriage) Brenda Joyce (Mrs. Joseph Levert Jordan). Marcia Ann; step-children Teresa, Jannie, Suellen Powers. Mem. Opelika (Ala.) City Commn., 1950-63; mayor. Opelika, Ala., 1952-58; mem. Lee County Democratic Exec. Com., 1958—; chmn. Pardon and Parole Bd., Montgomery, Ala., 1963—. Operator Superior Glass Co., Opelika, 1947-67. Del. 3d Congl. Dist. to Nat. Dem. Conv., 1956. Served with USAAF. World War II. Baptist. Home: 45 W Edgemont Av Montgomery AL 36104 Office: State Adminstrv Bldg Montgomery AL 36104

LAMBERT, EUGENE WASDON, JR., educator; b. Taylor, Tex., Nov. 3, 1930; s. Eugene Wasdon and Blonnie Dell (Crowe) L.; B.S. with high honors in Bus. Adminstrn., U. Ark., 1953; M.B.A., U. Tex., 1957; Ph.D., U. Ala., 1963; m. Louanne Hurley, July 26, 1952; children—Eugene Wasdon, III, Ronald Joseph, Anne Kelley, George Kerry. Asst. cashier, asst. mgr. investment dept. Bank of S.W., Houston, 1957-60; asst. prof. finance U. Ala., 1963; asst. prof. U. Tex., Austin, 1963-66; asso. prof. finance U. Tenn., 1966—, chair holder Tenn. Bankers Assn. Chair of Banking; pres. Skylane, Inc., Memphis, Bridal Enterprises, Inc., Asset Mgmt., Inc.; sec. Acad. Enterprises, Inc.; sec.-treas. Financial and Investment Systems, Inc.; partner Skylane East, Memphis. Served with 3800th Air Base Wing, USAF, 1954-56. Recipient L.G. Balfour award Central S.W. province Sigma Chi, 1953; George Currie Faucette award U. Ark., 1953. Mem. Am., Western econ. assns., Am., So., Southwestern finance assns., Nashville Soc. Financial Analysts, Inst. Chartered Financial Analysts, Sigma Chi. Baptist. Home: 673 Kenesaw Av SW Knoxville TN 37919 Office: Dept Finance Alumni Hall Knoxville TN 37916

LAMBERT, FRANKLYN, city ofcl.; b. College Park, Ga., June 29, 1921; s. Chester L. and Maude (Thomas) L.; student West Ga. Coll., 1938-39, Emory U., 1939, Marsh Bus. Coll., Atlanta, 1939-40; m. Lucile Lollar Moore, Oct. 13, 1962; children—Carol Dianne, Cheryl Delma. With Delta Airlines, Atlanta, 1940-41; with Continental Ins. Co., Atlanta, 1941-43; accountant PHA, 1945-47; exec. dir. Housing Authority of Columbus (Ga.), 1947—. Pres., South Columbus Boys Club, 1961; vice chmn. Ga. area Boys Clubs Am., 1966; bd. dirs. Jr. Achievement Columbus; v.p. Columbus Girls Club, 1967—. Served with U.S. Maritime Service, 1943-45. Mem. (past pres. Chattahoochee Valley chpt.), Nat. Housing Conf., Nat. Assn. Housing and Redevel. Ofcls. (v.p. S.E. regional council 1967, pres. 1967-68, bd. govs. 1967-68), S.A.R., Hon. Order Ky. Cols. Methodist. Home: 3011 Meadowview Dr Columbus GA 31906 Office: 1000 Wynnton Rd Columbus GA 31902

LAMBERT, JAMES WELLS, ret. editor, pub.; b. Natchez, Miss., Nov. 23, 1904; s. James K. and Grace (Wells) L.; B.A., Jefferson Coll., 1925; m. Mary Beane, Nov. 17, 1935; children—James Wells, Gay (Mrs. Ellis Lord), Will B. Reporter, Natchez Democrat, 1925-33, city editor, 1933-40, mng. editor, 1940-48, editor and pub., 1948-70. Bd. dirs. Marion Taylor Fund. Mem. Natchez-Adams County C. of C. (dir.), Miss. Press Assn. (pres. 1968-69), La.-Miss. A.P. Assn. (pres. 1968-69). Rotarian, Elk. Home: 208 S Union St Natchez MS 39120 Office: 503 N Canal St Natchez MS 39120

LAMBERT, JAY WILFRED, educator; b. Ryan, Va., Aug. 23, 1906; s. J.D., Jr. and Maude (LeFevre) L.; A.B., Coll. William and Mary, 1927; student Johns Hopkins, 1927-29, 33-34; m. Anne Louise Nenzel, December 15, 1936; children—Charles Francis, Louise Traylor. Psychologist Balt. Health Dept., 1928-29; instr. Loudoun County Hosp. Tng. Sch. Nurses, Leesburg, Va., 1930-31; mem. faculty Coll. William and Mary, 1931—, prof. psychology, 1959—, dean students, 1946-69, v.p. student affairs, 1970—. Mem. Williamsburg City Planning Commn., 1967—. Chmn. trustees William and Mary Alumni Endowment Fund, 1962—. Served to lt. USNR, 1943-46. Mem. William and Mary Alumni Assn. (bd. dirs. 1949-55), Phi Beta Kappa, Sigma Xi, Kappa Sigma. Democrat. Presbyn. Home: 314 Jamestown Rd Williamsburg VA 23185

LAMBERT, PHILLIP E., judge; b. Shawnee, Okla., Dec. 11, 1932; B.A., U. Okla.; J.D., Oklahoma City U.; m. 4 children. Admitted to Okla. bar, practiced in Tulsa; former legal asst. to U.S. Dist. Judge Fred Daughtery; chief judge City of Oklahoma City, also judge Oklahoma City Municipal Criminal Ct., 1965—. Mem. council judges Nat. Council on Crime and Delinquency; commr., cts. chmn. Okla. Crime Commn.; mem. gov.'s com. Prisoner Pre-Release Center; instr. Oklahoma City Police Dept. Police Acad.; mem. adv. bd. Alcohol Safety Countermeasures Program; mem. police- community relations com. Community Relations Commn.; mem. Oklahoma City Traffic Safety Coordinating Com., Criminal Justice Planning Council, Oklahoma City, Mayor's Youth Adv. Com. Bd. dirs. Oklahoma City Council Alcoholism, Oklahoma County Mental Health Assn., Okla. Halfway House; founder, dir. Young Offenders Ct.-Probation Project, Alcohol Rehab. Ct. Class Project. Mem. Am. (adv. com. traffic ct. program), Okla., County bar assns., N. Am. Judges Assn. (chmn. com. on presiding judges), Am. Judicature Soc., Nat. Council Judges, Nat. Conf. Spl. Ct. Judges, Am. Acad. for Jud. Edn. (charter bd. mem.). Address: 700 Couch Dr Oklahoma City OK 73102

LAMBERT, ROY KENNETH, city mgr.; b. Bloomburg, Tex., Oct. 3, 1939; s. Francis Roy and Dora (Berry) L.; B.S. in Civil Engring., Arlington State U., 1962; m. Mollie Jean McDaniel, Sept. 2, 1960; children— Susan Janelle, Cary Gene and Gary Dean (twins). Civil engr. Forrest & Cotton, Inc., cons. engrs., Dallas, 1962-66; civil engr. City of Grand Prairie, Tex., 1967; city mgr., Plano, Tex., 1968-71. Mem. N.Central Tex. Council of Govts. Water Utility Profl. Devel. Tech. Adv. Com., 1969-71, Urban Devel. Manpower Adv. Com., 1969-71. Served with USMCR, 1962. Registered profl. engr., Tex. Mem. E.Tex., Plano (dir. 1969) chambers commerce, Collins County Mayors Assn. (program chmn. 1970), Tex. City Mgrs. Assn., Am. Pub. Works Assn., Tex. Water Conservation Assn., Municipal Finance Officers Assn., Tex. Soc. Profl. Engrs., Tex. Water Pollution Control Assn., Nat. Municipal League. Presbyn. (deacon). Rotarian. Home: 1713 Westridge Dr Plano TX 75074

LAMBERTH, EDWIN GRADY, dentist; b. Alexander City, Ala., Jan. 27, 1929; s. Manuel Grady and Mary Lewis (McIntosh) L.; D.M.D., U. Ala., 1958; m. Elizabeth Ellis, Sept. 5, 1953; children—Lisa, Grady, Kathryn, Brooks. Gen. practice dentistry, Alexander City, 1958—. Replace missionary in Africa, 1967. Served with AUS 1950-52. Decorated Purple Heart, Korean Service medal with 3 bronze service stars. Mem. Am. Dental Assn., 2d Dist. Dental Soc., Sigma Nu. Baptist (deacon). Club: Alexander City Country (past pres.). Home: 409 N Central Av Alexander City AL 35010 Office: 207 Franklin St Alexander City AL 35010

LAMBERTH, EDWIN L, supt. schs; b. Norfolk, Va. Apr. 1, 1907; s. Edgar Stevens and Lillian (Gardner) L.; A.B., Coll. William and Mary, 1928; M.A., U. Va., 1938; postgrad. Harvard Advanced Adminstrs. Inst., 1957; m. Dorothy Smither, June 29, 1933; children—Edwin L., Donna Leigh (Mrs. Donald Hendrix Nash). Tchr. high sch., Eastville, Va., 1928-30, Williamsburg, Va., 1938-39; tchr. high sch., Norfolk, 1930-38, asst. high sch. prin., 1939-44; instr. William and Mary Coll., Williamsburg, 1938-39; now supt. schs., Norfolk. Bd. dirs., chmn. exec. com. Leigh Meml. Hosp.; bd. dirs. United Communities Fund. Fulbright scholar to Europe, Mem. Va. Assn. Sch. Adminstrs. (pres. 1968-69), Phi Delta Kappa, Phi Kappa Tau. Mason (32 deg.), Lion (past pres. Norfolk). Clubs: Harbor, Norfolk Executives (past pres.). Home: 7325 Ruthven Rd Norfolk VA 23505 Office: 800 E City Hall Av Norfolk VA 23510

LAMBETH, JAMES ERWIN, furniture co. exec.; b. Thomasville, N.C., Feb. 2, 1916; s. James Erwin and Mary Helen (McAulay) L.; A.B., Duke, 1937; postgrad. Harvard U. Bus. Sch., 1937-38; m. Katharine Evermond Covington, Aug. 27, 1938; children—James Erwin III, Richard Covington, Mary Katharine (Mrs. Royce Cullens), William Roderick. Gen. supt. Standard Chair Co., 1938-46, sec.-treas., 1946-56; chmn. bd., treas. Erwin-Lambeth, Inc., Thomasville, N.C., 1946—; pres. Piedmont Asso. Industries, Thomasville, 1963-64, now dir.; dir. Home Bldg. and Loan Assn., N.C. Nat. Bank. Mem. N.C. Gov.'s Commn. on Status of Women, 1964, Nat. Citizens' Adv. Council to Status of Women, 1967; pres. Thomasville United Fund, 1964-65; pres. Uwharrie council Boy Scouts Am., 1967-68, commr., 1970-71. Mayor pro-tem, mem. Thomasville City Council, 1963-67. Bd. dirs. Goodwill Industries, Thomasville, 1971-72; trustee Thomasville Community Found., 1963-64, Coll. Found., Inc., 1971—. Recipient Silver Beaver award Boy Scouts Am., 1961. Mem. Thomasville C. of C. (pres. 1962-63), Thomasville (pres. 1970-71), Davidson County (chmn. bd. 1971-72) hist. socs., Newcomen Soc. N.Am., Phi Delta Theta. Methodist (past steward, chmn. stewardship and finance com. 1964-65). Mason, Rotarian (pres. Thomasville 1960-61, gov. Dist. 769, 1966-67, dir. 1972—). Clubs: High Point Executives (pres. 1962-63, dir. 1964—), North State Game (sec. 1971-72). Home: 201 E Holly Hill Rd Thomasville NC 27360 Office: Erwin-Lambeth Inc Julian Av Extension Thomasville NC 27360

LAMBOU, VICTOR WILLIAM, govt. ofcl.; b. New Orleans, Apr. 28, 1929; s. Victor T. and Regina (Byrnes) L.; B.S., La. State U., 1952, M.S., 1953; m. Lorraine Granier, Jan 31, 1953; children—Denita, Geralyn, Roger, Vickie. Fishery research biologist La. Wildlife and Fisheries Commn., 1953-64; dir. fishery research lab., U. Okla., Norman, 1964-66; Fed. Water Pollution Control Adminstrn., U.S. Dept. Interior, 1966—, chief pesticide program. Washington, 1969—. Mem. Biometric Soc., Am. Fisheries Soc., Am. Soc. Ichthyologists and Herpetologists, Am. Soc. Limnology and Oceanography, Wildlife Soc., Ecol. Soc. Am., Fed. Water Quality Assn., Am. Inst. Biol. Sci., A.A.A.S., Gulf and Caribbean Fisheries Inst. Contbr. articles to profl. publs. Home: 7527 June St Springfield VA 22150 Office: Water Program Environmental Protection Agency Washington DC 20242

LAMELL, ROBERT CHARLES, architect; b. Nagyvarad, Oradea, Hungary, Nov. 21, 1913; s. Joseph and Elisabeth (Kiss) L.; Archtl. Engr. degree, Hindenburg Polytechniku, Oldenburg, West Germany, 1935; Diploma Architecture, U. Budapest, Hungary, 1943; violin studies Conservatory Music, Klegenfurt, Austria, 1946-49; m. Marie-Agnes Pachta-Rayhofen, May 26, 1948; children—Arpad, Guido, Anthony. Came to U.S., 1950. Architect, S.A.R. Malaxa, Bucharest, Rumania, 1938-41, Julius Gottwald, Budapest, Hungary, 1941-44, Royal Engrs., British Troops in Austria, 1945-50, Wm. H. Deitrick & J.C. Knight, Raleigh, N.C., 1950-55; architect, v.p. Charles L. Monnot Jr. & Assos. Inc., Oklahoma City, 1955—. U.S. rep. to USIA Am. Architecture Exhibit, Rumania, 1971. Mem. A.I.A. (corporate), Nat. Archtl. Registration Bd. Roman Catholic. Club: Schlaraffia (Klagenfurt, Austria). Exhibited one man shows Austria, Ashville, N.C., Oklahoma City Art Center. Home: 2640 Wilshire Blvd Oklahoma City OK 73116 Office: 4415 N Western Oklahoma City OK 73118

LAMER, CARL F., asst. supt. Bur. Vocational Edn., Ky. Dept. Edn., Frankfort. Address: Bur of Vocational Edn Ky Dept Edn Frankfort KY 40601*

LAMKIN, WILLIAM PIERCE, religious assn. exec.; b. Ansley, La., Oct. 17, 1919; s. John Mays and Carrie Ellen (Posey) L.; student La. Coll., 1941-43; A.B., U. N.C., 1947; m. Irma Hazel Page, Dec. 30, 1948; children—John Page, Mary Jean, Carol Ellen. Copyreader, asst. city editor, night city editor, city editor Charlotte (N.C.) Observer, 1948-61; sec. information Presbyn. Ch. in the U.S., Atlanta, 1961—. Mem. gen. communications and interpretation com. Nat. Council Chs., 1961—; mem. interpretation com. Cons. on Ch. Union; bd. dirs. Presbyn. Survey, TRAV. Served with USAAF, 1943-45. Decorated D.F.C. with 3oak leaf clusters, Air medal with 4 oak leaf clusters. Mem. Pub. Relations Soc. Am. Democrat. Home: 1485A Druid Valley Dr NE Atlanta GA 30329 Office: 341 Ponce de Leon Av NE Atlanta GA 30308

LAMON, HARRY VINCENT, JR., lawyer; b. Macon, Ga., Sept. 29, 1932; s. Harry Vincent and Helen (Bewley) L.; B.S. cum laude, Davidson Coll., 1954; LL.B. magna cum laude, Emory U., 1958; m. Ada Healey Morris, June 17, 1954; children—Hollis Morris, Helen Kathryn. Admitted to Ga. bar, 1958; D.C. bar, 1965; practiced in Atlanta, 1958—; mem. firm Crenshaw, Hansell, Ware & Brandon, 1958-62, Hansell, Post, Brandon, Dorsey, 1962—. Lectr. law Emory U., 1960—; pres. So. Fed. Tax Inst., Inc., 1967—; dir. Sockwell Enterprises, Inc., Baier Corp., Fulton Bros. Electric Co., Leaselite, Inc. Mem. adv. bd. Salvation Army, 1963—; Atlanta Music Club 1962—; adv. bd. Met. Atlanta Boys Clubs, Inc. Served to 1st lt. AUS, 1954-56. Fellow Am. Coll. Probate Counsel, Atlanta Estate Planning Council, Am. Law Inst.; mem. Am., Ga., Atlanta, Fed. bar assns., Lawyers Club Atlanta, Nat. Emory U. Law Sch. Alumni Assn. (past pres.), Phi Beta Kappa, Omicron Delta Kappa, Phi Delta Phi, Phi Delta Theta (province pres. 1964-68). Episcopalian. Mason (32 deg.), Kiwanian (pres. elect Downtown Atlanta). Clubs: Breakfast, Commerce, Capital City, Cherokee Town and Country Contbr. articles prof. jours. Home: 3375 Valley Rd NW Atlanta GA 30305 Office: 1st Nat Bank Tower Atlanta GA 30303

LAMOTTE, STEWART FICKES, JR., circuit judge; b. Red Lion, Pa., May 28, 1921; s. Stewart Fickes and Lottie (Reichard) LaM.; B.B.A., U., Miami, 1943; J.D., 1948; m. Jane Elizabeth Love. Dec. 25, 1950; children— Stewart Fickes, III, Susan Lucille, Sandra Catherine. Admitted to Fla. bar. 1948; practice law, Ft. Lauderdale, Fla., 1948-63; judge indsl. claims Fla. Indsl. Commn., 1961-63; judge County, Ft. Lauderdale, 1963-68; circuit judge, 1968—. Pres., Am. Cancer Soc., Broward County, 1961-63. Served to 1st Lt. USMCR, 1943-46. Decorated Purple Heart. Mem. Am. Legion, Phi Delta Phi. Methodist. Mason (Shriner), Elk. Clubs: High Hampton Country. Lauderdale Yacht (gov.). Home: 103 Fiesta Way Fort Lauderdale FL 33301 Office: Broward County Ct House Fort Lauderdale FL 33301

LAMPARTER, WILLIAM SMITH, furniture mfr.; b. Metuchen N.J., July 1, 1926; s. William George and Irma Lanyon (Smith) L.; student Bowdoin Coll., 1943-45; A.B., Duke, 1947, A.M., 1948. Furniture buyer R.H. Macy & Co., N.Y.C., 1958-66; furniture and contract merchandiser Asso. Merchandising Corp., N.Y.C., 1966-68; v.p. Century Furniture Co., Hickory, N.C., 1968, dir., 1968—; v.p., gen. sales mgr., 1969—. Chmn. exec. com. Friends of Duke U. Library, 1971—; gifts chmn. class of 1947, Duke U. Loyalty Fund; chmn. cultural arts commn. Western Piedmont Council Govts., 1970—. Trustee Jiranek Sch. Furniture Design, N.Y.C., 1964—, Fort Defiance, Inc. (N.C.), 1971—. Mem. Royal Instn. Cornwall (Eng.), Newcomen Soc., Delta Sigma Phi. Republican. Presbyn. Club: Lake Hickory (N.C.) Country. Home: 831 12th Av NW Hickory NC 28601 Office: 401 11th St NW Hickory NC 28601

LAMPKIN, ANDREW JACKSON, chem. engr.; b. Baldwin, Miss., Sept. 11, 1923; s. Andrew J. and Etna (Harrelson) L.; B.S., Miss State Coll., 1950; m. Betty Anne Dent, July 1, 1948; children—Joanne, Deborah Jane, Andrew Jackson, III. Chem. engr. Miss. State Hwy. Dept., Tupelo, 1950; chem. engr. TVA, New Johnsonville, Tenn., 1951-62, mech. engr., Drakesboro, Ky. 1962-68, power plant results supr. Shawnee Plant, Paducah, Kentucky, 1968—. Alderman for New Johnsonville, 1956-60. Served with Signal Corps, AUS, 1944-46. Registered profl. engr. Tenn., Miss. Mem. Internat. Platform Assn., Paducah Art Guild, Alpha Tau Omega, Alpha Phi Omega. Democrat. Baptist (deacon). Home: 452 Cardinal Lane Paducah KY 42001 Office: PO Box 2000 Paducah KY 42001

LAMPTON, ROBERT B., banker; b. Magnolia, Miss., Oct. 26, 1920; s. R.B. and Gertrude (Thompson) L.; B.S. in Engring., Princeton, 1942; postgrad. Grad. Sch. Banking of South, La. State U., 1956-59; m. Katherine Bryan, Aug. 17, 1950: children—Kathy, Mary, Bob, Bryan, Jim. Instr. math. McCallie Sch., Chattanooga, 1946-49; with First Nat. Bank of Jackson (Miss.), 1949—, pres., 1969—, also dir.; dir. First Capital Corp., United Gas, Inc.; lectr. Sch. of Banking of South, La. State U., 1966—. Campaign chmn. United Givers Fund of Jackson, 1962, v.p., 1963, pres., 1964; mem. lay adv. bd. St. Dominics Jackson Meml. Hosp; mem. exec. bd. Andrew Jackson council Boy Scouts Am., 1965—. Bd. dirs., pres. Pearl River Valley Water Supply Dist.; mem. Jackson Planning Bd. Served to lt. USNR, 1942-46. Mem. Jackson C. of C. (pres.-elect), Newcomen Soc., Phi Beta Kappa. Episcopalian. Kiwanian. Clubs: River Hills, Country of Jackson. Home: 125 Woodland Circle Jackson MS 39216 Office: PO Box 291 Jackson MS 39205

LAMSON, BYRON SAMUEL, clergyman, author; b. Boone, Ia., June 4, 1901; s. Danforth C. and Nora (Cussins) L.; student Los Angeles Pacific Coll., 1919-21, Litt.D., 1962; A.B., Greenville Coll., 1923; M.A., U. So. Cal., 1928; postgrad. U. Rochester, 1928, Northwestern U., 1940-42; D.D., Seattle Pacific Coll., 1948; m. Freda Burritt, Sept. 8, 1925 (dec. Aug. 1964); children—Mary Virginia, Lillian Burritt (Mrs. Bradley Sarvis); m. 2d, Betty E. Kline, July 30, 1965. Ordained to ministry Methodist Ch., 1925; pastor Free Meth. Chs., Cal., 1923-27, Ill., 1940-44; dean Los Angeles Pacific Coll., 1927-30, pres., 1930-39; v.p. Greenville (Ill.) Coll., 1939; gen. missionary sec. Free Meth. Ch., 1944-64, dir. research for ch. growth, 1964-71; editor Free Methodist, Free Methodist Pub. House, Winona Lake, Ind., 1964-71; asso. pastor Free Meth. Ch., St. Petersburg, Fla., 1970—. Chmn. Cooperating Home Bds. for Union Bibl. Sem., Yeotmal, India, 1951-64. Mem. Psi. Chi. Author: To Catch the Tide, 1963; Modern Prayer Miracles, 1935; Holiness Teachings of New Testament Literature, 1935; Lights in the World, 1951; Venture, 1960. Address: 2660 52d St N St Petersburg FL 33710

LAMSON-SCRIBNER, DENIS, securities co. exec.; b. Annapolis, Md., June 10, 1934; s. Frank Hamilton and Mercy Dees (Foster) L.S.; B.Chem. Engring., Rensselaer Poly. Inst., 1956; postgrad. Morris Harvey Coll., 1956-61; postgrad. W.Va. U., 1961-63; m. Julia Augusta Moseley, Mar. 31, 1956; children—Julia A., Frank H. III, William F. Prodn. engr. Union Carbide Corp., Charleston, W.Va., 1956-63, financial analyst, N.Y.C., 1963-65, bus. analyst, 1965-66, mgr. reports and analysis, 1966-68; account exec. Frost, Johnson, Read & Smith, Inc., Charleston, S.C., 1968—; v.p., dir., 1969-71, sec., dir., 1971—. Allied mem. N.Y. Stock Exchange, Inc., 1969—. Served to capt. Chem. Corps., AUS, 1957-64. Mem. Am. Inst. Chem. Engrs., Internat. Assn. Financial Planners, Fouragere Soc., Charleston Swim Assn. (v.p. 1971), Sigma Xi. Republican. Episcopalian (treas., vestryman 1969—). Rotarian. Club: Country of Charleston. Home: 1576 Fairway Dr Charleston SC 29412 Office: 49 Broad St Charleston SC 29402

LAMURE, DAVID SYLVESTER, physician; b. Crystal City, Mo., July 8, 1934; s. Percy Woodrow and Marcie (Musgraves) LaM.; A.B., Westminster Coll., 1956; M.D., St. Louis U., 1960; m. Margaret Ann Cinnater, Nov. 27, 1959; children—Marcia Maria, Margaret Collette, David Sylvester, Jeffery William, Elizabeth Ann, Stephen Joseph. Intern Jackson Meml. Hosp., Miami, Fla., 1960-61; resident pathology St. Lukes Episcopal Hosp., Houston, 1969—; med. officer in charge Indian Hosp. USPHS, Schurz, Nev., 1961-63; gen. practice medicine, Tonopah, Nev., 1963-64, Hawthorne, Nev., 1964—; chief staff Mt. Grant Gen. Hosp., Hawthorne, 1968—; bd. dirs. Regional Med. Program, 1967—. Mem. statewide adv. com. for Gov., 1967—, state health facilities adv. council, 1966—; trustee Mineral County Schs., 1966—; bd. dirs. Nev. Heart Assn., 1965—. Recipient commendation on behalf Washoe Indians Surgeon Gen. USPHS, 1963. Republican County campaign chmn., 1966-68. Mem. Houston, Am. socs. clin. pathology, Coll. Am. Pathology, Lahontan Basin Med. Soc. (pres. 1968-69), Phi Beta Pi. Roman Catholic. Home: 12602 Vindon St Houston TX 77024 Office: St Lukes Episcopal Hosp Houston TX 77015

LANCASTER, BOBBY J., columnist Ark. Democrat, Little Rock. Recipient Nieman award. Address: Ark Democrat Capitol Av and Scott St Little Rock AR 72203*

LANCASTER, CARROLL TOWNES, JR., assn. exec.; b. Waco, Tex., Mar. 14, 1929; s. Carroll T. and Beatrice (Hollaman) L.; student U. Tex., 1948-51, 52-53; m. Catherine Virginia Frommel, May 29, 1954; children—Loren Thomas, Barbara, Beverly, John Tracy. Sales coordinator Union Tank div. Butler Mfg. Co., Houston, 1954-56, sales rep., New Orleans, 1956-57, br. mgr., 1957-60; asst. to exec. v.p. Maloney-Crawford Mfg. Co., Tulsa, 1960-62; marketing cons., sr. asso. Market/Product Facts, Tulsa, 1962-63; market devel. asst. Norriseal Controls div. Dover Corp., Houston, 1963-66; area dir. Arthritis Found., Houston, 1966-69, dir. S.W. div., 1969-70; exec. dir. United Cerebral Palsy Tex. Gulf Coast, 1971—. Christian edn. tchr., 1966-70, supr., 1971, asst. youth football coach, Bellaire, 1967-68, 70-71. Bd. dirs. Council Chs. of Greater Houston, 1966-68, v.p., 1968. Served with USNR, 1946-48, 51-52. Recipient award for securing free blood for indigent Harris County Hosp. Dist., 1968. Mem. Am. Marketing Assn., Delta Sigma Phi. Episcopalian. Home: 4711 Fleetwood St Bellaire TX 77401 Office: 4189 Bellaire Blvd Houston TX 77025

LANCASTER, EDGAR HUNTER, JR., lawyer; b. Brookhaven, Miss., June 13, 1918; s. Edgar Hunter and Willie (Butler) L.; B.S., La. Poly. Inst., 1939; LL.B., La. State U., 1948, J.D., 1968; m. Beverly Marie Vedros, Apr. 1, 1944; children—Michael Eugene, Patricia Ann, Edgar Hunter III. Performance supr. U.S. Dept. Agr., 1939-41; admitted to La. bar, 1948; gen. practice law, Tallulah, La., 1948—. Dir. So. Nat. Bank of Tallulah. Rep. La. State Legislature, 1952-68. Mem. council La. Law Inst., 1964—. Trustee, mem. exec. com. Pub. Affairs Research Council La. Served as sgt. AUS, 1942-45. Mem. Madison Parish C. of C. (dir., past pres.). Clubs: Tallulah Rotary, Tallulah Country. Home: 311 Cleveland St Tallulah LA 71282 Office: 510 E Asnew St Tallulah LA 71282

LANCASTER, HARRY CURRENT, athletic dir.; b. Paris, Ky., Feb. 14, 1911; s. Ulman F. and Mayme (Current) L.; A.B., Georgetown (Ky.) Coll., 1928; M.A., U. Ky., 1943; m. Katherine Louise Wright, July 30, 1935 (dec. Aug. 1968); 1 dau., Sonja (Mrs. Dan Spain, Jr.). Asst. coach football, basketball Georgetown (Ky.) Coll., 1932-33, Paris (Ky.) High Sch., 1933-36; tchr., coach basketball Shelby County (Ky.) Schs., 1936, prin., basketball coach, 1936-42; instr. U. Ky. at Lexington, 1942-44, asst. coach basketball, 1950-66, dir. athletics, 1968—. Adviser, Greek Basketball Fedn., summer 1951. Served with USNR, 1944-46. Mem. Thorobred Club. Am., Kappa Alpha. Presbyn. Rotarian. Home: 699 Springridge Rd Lexington KY 40506

LANCASTER, HOWELL, farmer, state legislator; b. Eugene, Fla., July 31, 1911; student U. Fla.; m. Virginia Deen; children—Linda, Margaret, Howell Eugene. Petroleum prodn. jobber; farmer, cattleman; mem. Fla. Ho. of Reps., 1948—, chmn. agr. and citrus com. Past mayor, Trenton, Fla. Baptist. Rotarian (past pres. Trenton). Address: PO Box 66 Trenton FL 32693*

LANCASTER, JAMES OTTO, JR., supt. schs.; b. Natchez, Miss., Sept. 20, 1925; s. James Otto and Ruth (Gillispe) L.; B.S. in Accounting, Northwestern State Coll., 1949; M.A. in Edn. Adminstrn., George Peabody Coll. for Tchrs., 1954; m. Betty Jane Eggers, June 18, 1949; children—James Bruce, John Preston, Marilyn Christine, Allison Carol. Vocational counselor Northwestern State Coll., 1949-50; tchr. math., coach Ferriday High Sch., 1950-55; prin. LaSalle High Sch., 1955-59; supr. scholarships and placement, supr. alumni relations Northeast La. State Coll., 1959-63; supt. schs. Concordia Parish (La.), 1963-69; supt. Ouachita Parish Sch. Bd., Monroe, 1969—. Served with USNR, 1943-46; now comdr. Res. Mem. La. Ednl. Data Systems Assn. (pres. 1966-68, La. Supts. Assn. (pres. 1969—), Am. Assn. Sch. Adminstrs., Phi Delta Kappa. Presbyn. (elder). Kiwanian (pres. 1958—). Home: 27 W Elmwood St Monroe LA 71201 Office: 100 Bry St Monroe LA 71201

LANCASTER, JOSEPHAS JACKSON, educator; b. Gainesville, Ga., Apr. 16, 1924; s. James Walter and Lena (Braselton) L.; student Piedmont Coll., 1941-42, Syracuse U., 1942, U. Ill., 1943-44; B.S. in agr., U. Ga., 1949, M.S., 1952; Ed.D., Cornell U., Ithaca, N.Y., 1959; m. Sarah Frances Waters, July 17, 1954; children—Lynn, Charles, Martha Jane, Joseph. Mem. faculty U. Ga. Coll. Agr., Athens, 1949—, agrl. economist, 1955-59, prof., head dept. extension edn., 1959—. Mem. sub.-com. on staff tng. and devel. Extension Com. on Orgn. and Policy, 1969—, chmn., 1972. Bd. dirs. S.G. Chandler Meml. Scholarship Fund. Served with AUS, 1942-45; ETO. Mem. Ga. Adult Edn. Council (pres.), Adult Edn. Assn. U.S.A. (conf. chmn. 1970, exec. com. 1970-72), Nat. Geog. Soc., A.A.A.S., Phi Kappa Phi, Gamma Sigma Delta. Baptist. Kiwanian. Author: (with others) The Cooperative Extension Service, 1966. Home: Route 3 Box 239 Gainesville GA 30501 Office: Extension Bldg Lumpkin St U Ga Athens GA 30601

LANCASTER, PURVIS TALMADGE, sch. adminstr.; b. Fayetteville, N.C., Aug. 28, 1924; s. James Robert and Mary Elizabeth (Deaton) L.; A.A., Louisburg Coll., 1945; A.B., High Point Coll., 1947; M.A., East Carolina U., 1951; Ed.D., Duke, 1965; m. Earlene Lois Jewett, July 26, 1952; children—Holly, John Talmadge. Supt. schs. Dept. Def. Schs., Central Germany, 1960-61; supt. schs. Dept. Def. Schs., France, 1962-66; supt. Camp Lejeune (N.C.) Dependent Schs., also faculty mem. East Carolina U., 1966—. Served with USNR, 1942. Recipient Letter of Commendation Comdt. USMC, 1968, Commendation for meritorious service Dept. Navy, USMC, 1971; named Boss of Year, Jacksonville (N.C.) chpt. Am. Bus. Women Assn., 1971. Mem. Am. Assn. Sch. Adminstrs., N.C. Supts. Assn., N.E.A., N.C. Assn. Educators, Nat. Sojourners (hon.). Methodist. Kiwanian. Home: 2723 MOQ Camp Lejeune NC 28542 Office: Office of Supt Bldg 855 Marine Corps Base Camp Lejeune NC 28542

LANCE, THOMAS BERTRAM, banker, state ofcl.; b. Gainesville, Ga., June 3, 1931; s. Thomas Jackson and Annie Rose (Erwin) L.; student Emory U., 1948-50, U. Ga., 1951; Grad. Sch. Banking of South, La. State U., 1956; grad. Grad. Sch. Banking Rutgers U., 1963; m. Lethia Belle David, Sept. 9, 1950; children—Thomas Bertram, David Jackson, Stuart Austin, Claude Beverly. Exec. v.p. Calhoun (Ga.) Nat. Bank, 1958-63, pres., 1963—, dir., 1958—; pres. CNB Investments, Inc., Calhoun, 1958—; state hwy. dir. Ga., Atlanta, 1970—; dir. Astro Dye Works, Inc., Calhoun Chem. & Coating Co. Crown Crafts, Modern Fibers, Shaheen Carpet Mills, Multi-Developers, Inc., Edward LaceyMills, Inc. Chmn. 7th Dist. Savs. Bond Drive; chmn. Ga. Hwy. Authority; mem. Ga. Bd. Pub. Safety; active various community drives. Bd. dirs. Ga. div. Am. Cancer Soc. Bd. trustees Ga. Found. Ind. Colls., Reinhardt Coll., Cherokee, Boy's Estate, Dalton, Ga.; mem. adv. council Ga. State Coll. Mem. A.I.M. (pres. council 1965), Ga. Bankers Assn. (2d v.p.), U. Ga. Alumni Soc. (v.p. 7th dist.), Young Presidents Orgn. Methodist (dist. lay leader). Rotarian. Home: 409 E Line St Calhoun GA 30701 Office: 101 Wall St Calhoun GA 30701 also Capitol Sq Atlanta GA 30334

LAND, ELLIOTT LEE, coll. adminstr.; b. Virginia Beach, Va., Oct. 20, 1926; s. Cecil Peter and Berite Aileen (Lee) L.; student Bob Jones U., 1951-53; B.A., Columbia Bible Coll., 1955; M.Ed., U. Va., 1960, D.Ed., 1969; m. Judith Ann Roberts, May 5, 1962; children—Mark Todd, Eric Garth. Tchr., Linkhorn Park Elementary Sch., 1955-56; asst. prin. Kempsville Elementary Sch., 1956-57; prin. Aragona Elementary Sch., 1957-62, Pembroke Elementary Sch., 1962-64, Hermitage Elementary Sch., 1964-66; asst. dir. student teaching U. Va., Charlottesville, 1966-67, asst. cons. to Va. Pub. Sch. Systems, 1966-67, instr. Sch. Gen. Studies, 1967-69; dir. Head Start Program, Fluvanna (Va.) County Sch. Bd., 1967-69; asst. prof. philosophy of edn. Longwood Coll., Farmville, Va., 1967-69, dir. J.P. Wynne Campus Sch., 1969—. Founder, Virginia Beach Tchrs. Bowling League, 1959-64, Aragona Bowling League for Youth, 1960-62; adviser Honors Program, Longwood Coll., 1968—; coordinator Tchr. Aide Program, Prince Edward County Pub. Schs., 1968-69; co-chmn. Sub Region II, White House Conf. on Youth, 1970. Served with USNR, 1944-46. Mem. Nat., South Atlantic philosophy of edn. socs., Am. Assn. U. Profs., Lab. Sch. Adminstrs. Assn., Am. Assn. Sch. Adminstrs., Kappa Delta Pi. Lion. Home: 1001 6th Av Farmville VA 23901

LAND, EUGENE STUART, investment banker; b. Beaumont, Tex., Nov. 18, 1918; s. Amos W. and Mary Marie (Cooper) L.; B.B.A., U. Tex., 1947; m. Mary Jane Dear, May 2, 1943; children—Eugene Cooper, Betty Jane, Donald Stuart. Pres., Inter-Am. Devel. Corp., Houston, 1955-59; pres. Land & Co., Inc., Houston, 1959-66; corporate devel. asso. Dempsey-Tegeler & Co., Inc., Houston, 1966-69; v.p. corporate devel. dept. Rowles, Winston & Co., Inc. Houston, 1969—. Mem. Houston Bd. Realtors. Home: 1712 Hollister Dr Houston TX 77055 Office: Houston Natural Gas Bldg Houston TX 77002

LAND, FREDERIC HERMAN, mfg. co. exec.; b. Batesville, Miss., July 11, 1908; s. Herman Harris and Margaret (Seaton) L.; B.S.C., U. Miss., 1931; m. Johnnie Christine Murphy, Dec. 22, 1934; children—Betty Ann (Mrs. James Carlisle Scott), Nancy Seaton (Mrs. James J. Baldwin III). Asst. store mgr. A & P Tea Co., Columbus, Miss., 1931-35; dist. mgr. So. Oil. Co., Columbus, 1935-37; field supr. USES, Jackson, Miss., 1937-43; field rep. War Manpower Commn., Atlanta, 1943-46; pres. Marshall & Williams So. Corp., Greenville, S. C., 1946-64; exec. v.p. Marshall & Williams Co., Greenville and Providence, 1964-68, sr. v.p., 1968—; dir. Piedmont Food Processing Co., Greenville. Served with USNR, 1944-46. Mem. Greenville C. of C., Am. Textile Mfrs. Assn. (asso.), Kappa Sigma. Republican. Presbyn. Mason (Shriner). Clubs: Greenville Country, Poinsett (Greenville). Home: 709 Byrd Blvd Greenville SC 29605 Office: 620 S Pleasantburg Dr Greenville SC 29606

LAND, JOHN HENRY, judge; b. Columbus, Ga., June 12, 1918; s. Aaron Brewster and Mattie (Miller) L.; LL.B., U. Ga., 1939; m. Rosalie Wilson, Sept. 12, 1943; children—John Henry, Martha Miller (Mrs. Jens Pihlkjaer Christensen), Jeffrey Brooks, Jere Wilson. Admitted to Ga. bar, 1939, practiced in Columbus, 1939-41, 45-55; solicitor gen. Chattahoochee Circuit Ct., Columbus, 1955-64; judge Superior Ct., Columbus, 1964—. Mem. Ga. Senate, 1949-50. Served with AUS, 1941-45. Mem. Assn. U.S. Army, Gridiron Soc., Am. Legion, V.F.W.; Delta Tau Delta. Democrat. Baptist. Mason. Clubs: Exchange, Columbus Lawyers. Home: Route 1 Box 849 Columbus GA 31904 Office: Muscogee County Courthouse Columbus GA 31904

LAND, MARY ELIZABETH, author; b. Benton, La., Sept., 1908; d. Thomas Taylor and Elizabeth (Langford) Land; student Gulf Park (Miss.) Coll., 1924-25; grad. Cheyney-Trent Sch. Poetry, Cal., 1937; children—Patricia (Mrs. Phineas Stevens), George Thomas Land. Staff writer La. Conservation Rev. div. edn. La. Dept. Conservation, 1940-41; editor weekly syndicated column Outdoors South, 1947-48; staff writer So. Outdoors Mag., 1959-61, West Bank Guide, New Orleans, 1962-63; commentator for own conservation, outdoor program Miss. Soundings, WGCM, Gulfport, Miss. Chmn., New Orleans Spring Fiesta, 1947; chmn. spring fiesta La. Poetry Soc., 1948. Recipient certificate of merit Nash Motors, 1953; 1st pl. award for books, short stories and poetry La. Press Women, 1969. Mem. D.A.R. (past program chmn. Metairie Ridge chpt.), Nat. League Am. Pen Women (Blue Ribbon award So. Region Gulf Coast br. 1948, pres. Miss.), Nat. Fedn. Am. Press Women (1st pl. award 1960, 2d pl. award 1969), Colonial Dames XVII Century (certificate of recognition 1971), Nat. Soc. Arts and Letters (co-founder New Orleans chpt., mem. exec. bd.), Outdoor Writers Assn. Am., La. Outdoor Writers Assn. (past dir.), Internat. Womens Fishing Assn., Fedn. Musicians Jackson. Author: (poetry) Shadows of the Swamp, 1940; Mary Land's Louisiana Cookery (co-winner So. Books of Year in ann. So. Books Competition), 1955; New Orleans Cuisine, 1969; (poetry) Abode, 1972. Home: 1314 Williams Av Natchitoches LA 71457

LAND, SAMUEL BUCHANAN, ins. agt.; b. Baskerville, Va., Dec. 15, 1916; s. Samuel Wesley and Mary Beatrice (Buchanan) L.; B.S., Va. Poly. Inst., 1938, M.S., 1939; m. Eunice Gray Caroon, July 6, 1941; children—Samuel Buchanan, Eunice (Mrs. John F. Carroll, Jr.). County agt. Va. Extension Service, 1939-41; marketing specialist Va. Dept. Agr., 1946-47; mgr. coop. Farm Supply Store, South Hill, Va., 1948-53; owner Land Ins. Agy., South Hill, 1953—; dir. Citizens Bank, Inc. Mem. Mecklenburg County Sch. Bd., 1959—. Served from 1st lt. to capt. AUS, 1941-45. Methodist (supt. Sunday sch. 1964-72). Mason, Lion (pres. 1964-65). Home: Route 1 South Hill VA 23970 Office: Box 488 South Hill VA 23970

LAND, WALTER KELLY, county ofcl.; b. Lodi, Miss., Sept. 30, 1917; s. Walter Benjamin and Willie Belle (Emerson) L.; B.A.,1946, M.A., 1948; m. Rosabelle Jordan, June 20, 1944; 1 son, Guy Paul. High sch. prin., Cumberland, Miss., 1942-44, Ingomar, Miss., 1944-46, Abbeville, Miss., 1946-48, Macon, Miss., 1948-53, Big Black, Miss., 1960-62, also guidance counselor, 1948-62; county welfare agt. Webster County, Miss., 1962—. Sec. Webster County Fair Assn., 1955; pres. Eupora Band Boosters, 1965, 68. Named

Rotarian of the year, 1964. Mem. Miss. Edn. Assn., Am. Personnel and Guidance Assn., N.E.A., Montgomery County Tchrs. Assn. (pres.), Miss. Conf. Social Welfare, Miss. Assn. County Welfare Agts. (pres. 1969). Rotarian (pres. 1969). Home: Box 115 Rt 1 Eupora MS 39744 Office: Drawer B Eupora MS 39744

LANDAU, EDMUND A., JR., lawyer; b. Albany, Ga., July 26, 1915; A.B., U. Ga., 1935, LL.B., 1938. Admitted to Ga. bar, 1938; mem. firm Landau, Davis & Farkas, Albany. Sec.-treas. Albany Democratic Exec. Com., 1948-—. Served with AUS, 1942-46. Mem. Am., Ga., Albany, Albany Jud. Circuit bar assns., Phi Beta Kappa, Phi Kappa Phi, Omicron Delta Kappa. Office: Landau Davis & Farkas Citizens and So Bank Bldg Albany GA 31702*

LANDAUER, JERRY GERD, journalist; b. Stuttgart, Germany, Jan. 16, 1932; s. Adolph and Meta (Marx) L. brought to U.S., 1938, naturalized 1944;; A.B., Columbia, 1953; postgrad. U. Bonn (Germany), 1953-54; m. Susan Lois Ecker, June 23, 1963. Local news reporter Washington Post, 1956-60; Capitol Hill reporter U.P.I., 1960-62; reporter Washington bur. Wall St. Jour., 1962-—. Recipient Raymond Clapper Meml. award, 1964; Sigma Delta Chi Distinguished Serviced award for Washington corr., 1964. Mem. Assn. Alumni Columbia Coll., Tau Epsilon Phi. Club: Nat. Press (Washington). Home: 3 Riggs Ct NW Washington DC 20036 Office: Nat. Press Bldg Washington DC 20005

LANDAUER, LEO L., engr.; b. Dallas, Oct. 5, 1907; s. Leo L. and Mabel Cahn (Levy) L.; C.E., Cornell U., 1927; m. Blonda E. Bostick, Aug. 1953. Engr. various offices, 1927-29; cons. engr. C. L. Kribs, Jr., Dallas, 1929-34, partner Kribs & Landauer, Dallas and Houston, 1934-41, pres. Landauer & Shafer, Dallas, Houston, El Paso and Little Rock, 1945-56, Leo L. Landauer & Assos., Inc., cons. engrs., Dallas, Tex., Little Rock, Ark., Baton Rouge, Washington, 1956-—. Served as comdr. USNR, 1941-45. Registered profl. engr., Tex., Okla., Ark., N.M., La., Miss., D.C., Ariz. Mem. Am. Soc. C.E., Nat., Tex. socs. profl. engrs., Am. Soc. Heating, Ventilating & Air Conditioning Engrs., Am. Soc. Mil. Engrs., U.S., Tex. cons. engrs. council. Clubs: Engineers, Cipango (Dallas). Home: 9345 Sunnybrook Lane Dallas TX 75220 Office: 3811 Rawlins St Dallas TX 75219

LANDERS, JOHN DAVID, telephone co. exec.; b. Quiency, Fla., Apr. 28, 1929; s. James Edward and Robbie Ethel (Mayton) L.; grad. high sch.; m. Margorie Elizabeth Townsend, Oct. 11, 1952; children—John David, Jr., Patricia Ann. With Chesapeake & Potomac Telephone Co., Richmond, Va., 1948-—, mgr., Portsmouth, Va., 1961-66, staff supr. pub. relations, Richmond, Va., 1966-70, dist. comml. mgr., 1970-—. Instr. spl. pub. relations programs Va. Commonwealth U., 1966-68. Bd. dirs. A.R.C., 1961-66, YMCA, 1961-66, Salvation Army, 1961-66, Va. Travel Council, 1968, Va. Council Econ. Edn., 1970-71. Named Young Man of Year, Portsmouth Jr. C. of C., 1965. Mem. Pub. Relations Assn. Am., Portsmouth C. of C. (treas. 1964-65), Old Dominion Pub. Relations Assn. (v.p. 1970), Pub. Relations Assn. Am. Methodist. Mason. Home: 4021 Chaparral Dr Roanoke VA 24018 Office: PO Box 1200 Roanoke VA 24006

LANDERS, ROBERT LELAND, agency exec., condr.; b. Durant, Okla., July 31, 1919; s. Charles G. and Sheila (Bratton) L.; student Southeastern State Coll., 1938-40, U. Md; m. Eunice Hassinger, Sept. 4, 1943; children—Robert L., Carol Elaine, Joan, Cynthia, Mary Lynne. Head music dept. McAlester (Okla.) Pub. Schs., 1947-48; dir. bands U. Md., 1950-54; asst. condr. San Carlo Opera Co., 1942-45; commd. warrant officer USAAF, 1940, advanced through grades to capt., 1955, ret., 1965; condr. 529th Air Force Band, Atlantic City and Buckley Field, Colo., 1942-45, Singing Sgts., ofcl. chorus, 1948-65; asso. condr. USAF Band and Symphony Orch., 1963-65; pres. Robert Landers Agy.; former condr. Capital Hill Symphony Orch., Robert Landers Chorale; adminstrv. dir. Fla. Symphony Orch.; minister of music Eldbrooke Meth. Ch., Washington 1949-67; condr. Tampa Oratorio Soc., dir. music Manhattan Av. Meth. Ch., Tampa, Fla., 1967; now minister music First Congl. Ch., Winter Park, Fla. Bd. mgrs. Tampa Boys Club. Mem. Am. Bandmasters Assn., Phi Beta Mu, Kappa Psi. Club: Civitan. Home: 4222 Stonewall Dr Orlando FL 32806 Office: PO Box 782 Orlando FL 32808

LANDIS, FRED STANLEY, constrn. co. exec.; b. Pitts., Feb. 6, 1920; s. Harry and Rebecca (Freedel) L.; B.S. in Civil Engring., Carnegie Mellon U., 1940; m. Ida Evelyn Baty, Jan. 8, 1944; children—James Charles, Carol Thomas Dunne, John Michael. Insp. constrn. Albright & Friel, Aberdeen, Md., 1940-41; v.p., chief engr. Keller Constrn. Corp., New Orleans, 1945-55; pres. Landis Constrn. Co., Inc., New Orleans, 1955-—. Mem. New Orleans Bd. Standards and Appeals, 1967-—. Pres. Jr. Achievement of New Orleans, 1972-—, bd. dirs., 1964-—. Served to lt. col. C.E., AUS, 1941-45; ETO. Decorated Legion of Merit, Silver Star, Bronze Star, Purple Heart (U.S.); Croix de Guerre (France). Mem. Am. Soc. C.E., Asso. Gen. Contractors Am. (chpt. dir. 1968-—), Am. Arbitration Assn. Home: 1473 Nashville Av New Orleans LA 70115 Office: 7410 Prytania St New Orleans LA 70118

LANDIS, RUTH ELLEN, coll. exec.; b. Melrose, Minn., Jan. 5, 1904; d. Richey E. and Ella (Barrett) Landis; B.S., U. Minn., 1925; M.A., Columbia, 1932, Ed.D., Ph.D., 1949. Former chmn. biology and psychology dept. Sr. High Sch., Mt. Vernon, N.Y.; faculty Columbia, summer 1942-44; dir. Counseling Center, St. Francis Coll., Loretto, Pa., 1967-70; dir. Newman Center, San Angelo (Tex.) State U., 1970-—. Instr. psychology, counselor-psychologist Mt. Vernon (N.Y.) Hosp. Sch. Nursing, 1955-67. Active UNESCO com. UN, 1949-50. Mem. N.E.A. (ho. of dels. 1958-65, pub. relations com. edn. N.Y. 1963-65), Pi Lambda Theta, Kappa Delta Phi. Contbr. articles in field to profl. jours. Home: 2704 W Beauregard San Angelo TX 76901 Office: San Angelo U 2451 Dena Dr San Angelo TX 76901

LANDISS, CARL WILSON, educator; b. Clarksville, Tenn., May 6, 1914; s. Clarence W. and Ollie (Dunaway) L.; B.S., Abilene Christian Coll., 1935; M. Ed., Tex. A and M U., 1947; D. Ed., Pa. State U., 1951; m. Georgia Belle Fleeman, Feb. 8, 1936; children—Carolyn Rhea (Mrs. James Byron Graves), William Coleman. Tchr., Sylvester pub. schs., 1935-36; Kansas City pub. schs., 1936-43; prof. Tex. A and M U., College Station, 1943-67, prof., head dept. health and phys. edn., 1967-—. Referee Bluebonnet Bowl, 1963, 68, Cotton Bowl, 1965, 67, 72; mem. College Station Recreational Council, 1967-—, Planning and Zoning Commn., College Station, 1969-—; councilman, College Station, 1958-64. Bd. dirs. College Station United Chest. Served as lt. USNR, 1944-46. Recipient State Honor award Tex. Assn. for Health, Phys. Edn. and Recreation, 1964. Mem. Tex. Assn. for Health, Phys. Edn. and Recreation (past pres.), A.A.H.P.E.R., Internat. Soc. for Psychology of Sport and Phys. Activity, A.A.A.S., S.W. Football Ofcls. Assn., Phi Kappa Phi, Phi Epsilon Kappa, Phi Delta Kappa. Mem. Ch. of Christ. Mason, Kiwanian. Author: (with C.B. Corbin and L.J. Dowell)Concepts and Experiments in Physical Education, 1968. Contbr. articles profl. jours. Home: 803 Dexter Dr College Station TX 77840

LANDREAU, ANTHONY NORMAN, museum curator; b. Washington, Apr. 2, 1930; s. Norman Bayle and Caroline Hill (Griffin) L.; student Catholic U., 1951-52; B.A., Black Mountain Coll. (N.C.), 1956; m. Anita May Jester, Oct. 15, 1965; children—John Celestin, Christopher Anselm, Geoffrey Olson. Cons. textiles, Bolivia, 1965-66; asso. curator Textile Mus., Washington, 1967-70, acting dir., 1971-—. Trustee, Greater Washington Ednl. Telecommunications Assn., Kindler Found., Washington. Served with USNR, 1948-50. Mem. Washington, N.Y. rug socs., Am. Assn. Museums. Author: (with W.R. Pickering) From the Bosphorus to Samarkand: Flat-Woven Rugs, 1969. Contbr. articles on oriental rugs to profl. jours. Home: 507 Greenbrier Dr Silver Springs MD 20910 Office: Textile Museum 2320 S St NW Washington DC 20008

LANDRENEAU, RODNEY EDMUND, JR., physician; b. Mamou, La., Jan 17, 1929; s. Rodney Edmund and Blanche (Savoy) L.; M.D., La. State U., 1951; m. Colleen Fraser, June 4, 1952; children—Rodney Jerome, Michael Douglas, Denise Margaret, Melany Patricia, Fraser, Edythe Blanche. Intern Charity Hosp., New Orleans, 1951-52, resident, 1952-54, 56-58; practice medicine specializing in surgery, Eunice, La., 1958-—; pres., dir. Eunice Med. Center, Inc., 1960-—; mem. staff Moosa Meml. Hosp. Eunice, 1958-—; vis. staff Opelousas Gen. Hosp., 1958-—; cons., staff Lafayette (La.) Charity Hosp. Dir. Acadiana Bank & Trust Co., Mem. La. State Hosp. Bd. Served M.C. AUS, 1954-56. Diplomate Am. Bd. Surgery. Fellow Internat. Coll. Surgeons, A.C.S., (local chmn. com. trauma), Southeastern Surg. Congress, Pan Pacific Surg. Congress; mem. Am. Bd. Abdominal Surgeons. Am. Geriatrics Soc., St. Edmunds Athletic Assn; St. Landry Parish Med. Soc. (pres. 1969-70). Rotarian (dir. Eunice). Home: 1113 Williams St Eunice LA 70535 Office: Eunice Medical Center Eunice LA 70535

LANDRETH, GEORGE H., v.p. Shikar-Safari Internat. Recipient Roy Weatherby Big Game award. Address: Midland TX 77458*

LANDRIEU, MOON, mayor; b. New Orleans, July 23, 1930; s. Joseph and Loretta L.; B.B.A., Loyola U., 1952, LL.B., 1954; m. Verna Satterlee, Sept. 25, 1954; children—Mary, Mark, Melanie, Michelle, Mitchell, Madeline, Martin, Melinda, Maurice. Atty. firm Landrieu, Calogero & Kronlage, 1957-70, mayor City of New Orleans, 1970-—. Mem. La. Ho. of Reps., 1960-66; councilman, New Orleans, 1966-70. Served with AUS, 1954-57. Democrat. Roman Catholic. Home: 4301 S Prieur St New Orleans LA 70125 Office: 1300 Perdido St New Orleans LA 70112

LANDRITH, GEORGE CLAY, constrn. exec.; b. Los Angeles, Nov. 29, 1915; s. William George and Mary (Wickersham) L.; student pub. schs.; m. Frances Jordan, Oct. 28, 1935; children—Nicholas J., George Clay. Vice pres. Thomas L. Dawson, gen. contracting, Kansas City, Mo., 1934-39; owner, operator Landrith Constrn. Co., Alexandria, Va., 1939-45; owner Belle View Apts., Alexandria, 1947-—; dir. 1st Va. Bankshares Corp., Arlington, Va., 1st Commonwealth Ins. Co., Richmond, Va. Mem. Va. Hwy. Commn., 1962-70; mem. Fairfax County Planning Commn., 1948-60, Bd. Fairfax County Suprs., 1960, Richmond Met. Authority, 1966-70, Va. Met. Areas. Transp. Study Commn.; bd. dirs. Alexandria Community Health Center, 1953-54, Alexandria Boys Club, 1958-62; mem. dist. council Salvation Army, 1958-62; sponsor Alexandria Little League, 1953-—; dir. trustees Fairfax County Hosp., 1957-59. Treas., Fairfax County Democratic Com., 1948-49. Trustee George Mason Coll., Fairfax, Va. Mem. Fairfax County C. of C. (dir. 1953, 71). Clubs: Belle Haven Country (Alexandria, Va.); Commonwealth (Richmond, Va.); Farmington Country (Charlottesville, Va.). Home: 6319 Olmi-Landrith Dr Alexandria VA 22307 Office: 1605 Belle View Blvd Alexandria VA 22307

LANDRUM, CARROL FRAZIER, physician; b. nr. Taylorsville, Miss., Apr. 3, 1926; s. Joseph David and Emma Elizabeth (Meadows) L.; student Perkinston Jr. Coll., 1946-47; B.S., Millsaps Coll., 1948; M.D., Tulane U., 1952; postgrad. in pediatrics Harvard, 1969-70. Intern, Brooke Gen. Hosp., Ft. Sam Houston, Tex., 1952-53; practice medicine, Biloxi, Miss., 1954-58, Smith County, Miss., 1958-59, Edwards, Miss., 1959-—. Served to capt. USAF, 1952-54. Mem. Internat. Platform Assn. Baptist. Mason, Rotarian. Research in causes of malignant diseases. Home: PO Box 198 Edwards MS 39066

LANDRUM, JOHN HINTON, librarian; b. Greenwood, S.C., Nov. 25, 1944; s. Julius Parson and Mary Louise (Hinton) L.; student Clemson U., 1962-64; A.B., Erskine Coll., 1966; M.S. in L.S., U. N.C., 1967. Reference librarian S.C. Library, Columbia, 1967-70, dir. reader services, 1970-—. Served with AUS, 1968. Mem. S.C., Southeastern library assns., A.L.A., South Caroliniana Soc., S.C. Hist. Assn., Beta Phi Mu. Home: 5526 Lakeshore Dr Columbia SC 29206 Office: 1500 Senate St Columbia SC 29201

LANDRUM, PHILIP MITCHELL, congressman; b. Martin, Ga., Sept. 10, 1907; s. Philip Davis and Blanche (Mitchell) L.; A.B., Piedmont Coll., Demorest, Ga., 1939; student Mercer U., La. State U.; LL.B., Atlanta Law Sch., 1941;; m. Laura Brown, July 30, 1933; children—Phillip Mitchell, Susan. High sch. athletic dir., coach, Bowman, Ga., 1932-35, Nelson Ga., 1935-37; supt. pub. schs. Nelson, 1937-41; admitted to Ga. bar 1941; asst. atty. gen. State Ga., 1946-47; exec. sec. Gov. Ga., 1947-48; practice of law, Jasper, 1949-—; mem. 83rd-92d Congresses, 9th Dist. Ga. Served USAAF, 1942-45. Mem. Ga. Bar Assn., Am. Legion, V.F.W. Democrat. Baptist. Mason, Elk. Home: Jasper GA 30143 Office: House Office Bldg Washington DC 20515

LANDRY, FRANCES LEGGIO (MRS. JULES F. LANDRY), lawyer; b. Baton Rouge, Aug. 11, 1908; d. George and Josephine (Loicano) Leggio; B.A., La. State U., 1926, LL.B. (valedictorian), 1934; m. Jules F. Landry, Aug. 9, 1934; 1 dau., Frances Harriet. Admitted to La. bar, 1934, since practiced law with husband as Landry & Landry, Baton Rouge; lectr. La. State U. Law Sch., 1942-43; atty. for parish tax collector, 1940-46; spl. asst. atty. gen. La., 1968-70; sec.-treas. Wooddale Comml. Properties, Inc.; dir., owner Lafayette Gallery. Former Beautification Commn. for City Baton Rouge; pres. E. Baton Rouge Parish Library Bd. Control. Formerly active Girl Scouts, Salvation Army. Mem. Internat., Inter-Am., Am. (La. membership chmn. sect. ins.), La., Baton Rouge bar assns., Am., La. (past vice chmn. trustees sect.) library assns., La. State U. Law Sch. Alumni Assn. (pres. 1968-70), Order of Coif, Pi Sigma Alpha, Phi Delta Delta, Phi Kappa Phi, Mu Sigma Rho. Clubs: Woman's, Inc. (bd. mgrs.); Quota (internat. pres. 1942-44). Home: 2036 Lake Hills Pkwy Baton Rouge LA 70801 Office: 348 Lafayette St Baton Rouge LA 70801

LANDRY, HILTON JOHN, JR., holding co. exec.; b. Miami, Fla., Oct. 19, 1938; s. Hilton John and Madge (Borel) L.; B.S., U. Ga., 1961; m. Sandra Smalley, Feb. 8, 1964; children—Hilton John III, Bonnie Jean, Geoffrey Borel. Vice pres. Landry Realty, Inc., 1962-64; pres. Landry Assos., 1964-65; exec. v.p. Dextra Corp., Miami, Fla., 1966-71; pres., chief exec. officer Basic Food Industries Inc., Miami, 1971-—; dir. Berlin Milling Co., Inc. (Md.), Portion-Pak Foods, Inc., Detroit. Served with AUS, 1961-62. Republican. Roman Catholic. Clubs: University, Coral Oaks Tennis (Miami, Fla.); Riviera Country (Coral Gables, Fla.). Home: 3211 Anderson Rd Coral Gables FL 33134 Office: Drawer Z Little River Miami FL 33138

LANDRY, JACOB S., lawyer; b. New Iberia, La., Jan. 20, 1907; A.B., Tulane U., 1926, J.D., 1927. Admitted to La. bar, 1928. Mem. Am., La. State (v.p. 1936-39; pres. 1969-70), Iberia Parish bar assns., Order of the Coif, Phi Delta Phi. Address: PO Box 850 New Iberia LA 70560*

LANDRY, JULES FRANCIS, lawyer, banker, industrialist; b. St. Francisville, La., Nov. 9, 1906; s. Jules F. and Elizabeth (Desposito) L.; LL.B., La. State U., 1932; m. Frances C. Leggio, Aug. 9, 1934; 1 dau., Frances Harriet. Admitted to La. bar, 1932; with firm Landry & Landry, Baton Rouge, 1932-—; chmn. bd. Capital Bank & Trust Co., Baton Rouge, 1955-—, acting pres., 1962; pres., chmn. bd. Bank of Commerce & Trust Co., St. Francisville, La.; pres. Rue Lafayette Mortgage Corp., 1952-—, Bellingrath Hills, Inc., 1955-68, Goodwood Homesites, Inc., 1958-66, Wooddale Comml. Properties, Inc., 1962. Pres. Baton Rouge Symphony Assn., 1962-65; area chmn. U.S. Savs. Bond Com. Mem. La. State U. Found.; trustee Gulf S. Research Inst. Mem. Internat., Inter-Am., La., Am., Baton Rouge bar assns., La. State U. Law Sch. Alumni Assn. Roman Catholic. Elk, K.C. Clubs: Internat. House, Baton Rouge Country, City (Baton Rouge).Home: 2036 Lake Hills Pkwy Baton Rouge LA 70801 Office: Capital Bank & Trust Co Baton Rouge LA also 348 Lafayette St Baton Rouge LA 70801

LANDRY, TOM, profl. football coach; b. Mission, Tex., Sept. 11, 1924; ed. U. Tex.; m. children—Tom, Kitty, Lisa. With N.Y. Yankees, All-Am. Conf., 1949-50; with N.Y. Giants, Nat. Football League, 1950-60, def. halfback, 1950-53, player-coach, 1954, 55, asst. coach, 1956-60; head coach Dallas Cowboys, Nat. Football League, 1960-—. Served with Armed Forces, World War II. Coach Eastern Conf. champions, 1966, 67. Home: Dallas TX 75221 Office: Dallas Cowboys Dallas TX 75221*

LANDRY, WALTER JOSEPH, engring. co. exec.; b. Jeanerette, La., Mar. 14, 1934; s. Walter E. and Dorothy (Rodriguez) L.; student U. Southwestern La., 1952-55; m. Faye Marie Webre, Sept. 17, 1955; children— Susan, Jennifer, Sandra, Michael, Walter, Christine, Julie, Stephen, Rebecca, Robert. Material foreman Dupont Fabricators, 1955-57; sugar cane harvesting contractor, Jeanerette, 1957-59; with J. & L. Engring. Co., Inc., Jeanerette, 1959-—, v.p. operations, 1969-71, exec. v.p., gen. mgr., 1971-—; dir. Sugarland State Bank, Jeanerette, Annelida Acres, Jeanerette, Maquinaria Azucarera, Mexico; pres. Manufacturera 3-M Mexico, 1972-—. Mem. Jeanerette Civil Service Bd., 1970-—. Mem. Jeanerette C. of C. (dir. 1967-—). Democrat. Roman Catholic. Contbr. articles to sugarcane internat. trade mags. Home: 689 Janice St Jeanerette LA 70544 Office: PO Box 620 Jeanerette LA 70544

LANDSMAN, HENRY, elec. engr.; b. Detroit, Nov. 14, 1914; s. Benjamin and Elsie (Streit) L.; B.S. in Elec. Engring., U. Ill., 1934; m. Leah Jeanette Weisberger, May 24, 1936; 1 son, Bennett Albert. Elec. engring. supr. U.S. Navy Dept., 1941-46; elec. engr. Frank H. McEnney, 1946-49; chief engr. U.S. Hoffman Machinery Corp., 1949-57; elec. engr. Lord Electric Co. Inc., Los Angeles, 1957-70, v.p., mgr., 1970-—, contract adminstr., 1961-—, cons. mgmt. adviser, 1954-—. Registered profl. engr., Pa., Conn., Ohio, Del., Ky. Mem. Am. Soc. M.E., I.E.E.E., Am. Ordnance Assn., Am. Soc. Metals, Nat. Soc. Profl. Engrs., U.S. Army Roster of Ammunition. Contbr. articles to profl. jours. Patentee in mech. field. Home: East Town House Apt 306 4590 Beechnut St Houston TX 77035 Office: 5543 Armour Dr Houston TX 77020

LANDY, BURTON AARON, lawyer; b. Chgo., Aug. 16, 1929; s. Louis J. and Clara (Ernstein) L.; B.S., Northwestern U., 1950; LL.B., U. Miami, 1952; student Nat. U. Mexico, 1948; scholar U. Havana, 1951; fellow Inter-Am. Acad. Comparative Law, Havana, Cuba, 1955-56; m. Eleonora M. Simmel, Aug. 4, 1957; children—Michael Simmel, Alisa Anne. Admitted to Florida bar, 1952; gen. practice law in Latin Am. field, Miami, 1955-—; partner law firm Ammerman & Landy, 1957-63, Paul & Landy, 1964-67, Paul, Landy and Beiley, 1967-69, Paul, Landy, Beiley & Bartel, 1969-—; law offices Burton A. Landy, 1963-64; lectr. Latin Am. bus. law U. Miami, 1972-—, also Internat. Law Confs. Mem. Nat. Conf. on Fgn. Aspects of U.S. Nat. Security, Washington, 1958; mem. organizing com. Miami regional conf. Com. for Internat. Econ. Growth, 1958; mem. U.S. Dept. Commerce Regional Export Expansion Council, 1969-—. Dir. Inter-Am. Bar Legal Found. Served with USAF Judge Adv. Gen. Dept., 1952-54, in Korea, 1953-54; maj. USAF Res. Hon. mem. Bar of Republic of South Korea, 1954. Mem. Inter-Am. (asst. sec.-gen. 1957-59, treas. 11th conf. 1959, co-chmn. jr. bar sect. 1963-65, mem. organizing com. I-VI aviation law confs.; mem. council 1969-—), Am. (chmn. com. arrangements internat. and comparative law sect. 1964-65), Spanish-Am., Fla. (vice chmn. adminstrv. law com. 1965, vice chmn. internat. and comparative law com. 1967-68, chmn. aero. law com. 1968-69), Dade County (chairman fgn. laws and langs. com. 1964-65) bar assns., Am. Fgn. Law Assn. (pres. Miami 1958), Miami Jr. C. of C., Phi Alpha Delta. Contbr. articles to legal jours. Home: 6255 Old Cutler Rd Miami FL 33131 Office: Pan Am Bank Bldg Miami FL 33131

LANE, ARTHUR LEE, JR., city ofcl.; b. Esmont, Va., June 12, 1929; s. Arthur Lee and Carrie (Butler) L.; B.S., Va. Poly. Inst., 1958; diploma U. Chgo., 1962, U. Ga., 1969; m. Frances Marie Combs, Nov. 22, 1956; children—Richard Scott, Donna Marie. Asst. city engr., Charlottesville, Va., 1951-56; asst. city mgr., Waynesboro, Va., 1960-65; city mgr., Dublin, Ga., 1965-66, Hopewell, Va., 1966-—. Bd. dirs. YMCA, 1964-—; chmn. Heart Fund dr., 1964; chmn. Hopewell Community Action Com., 1969. Served with AUS, 1948-50; lt. col. Gov.'s Staff, State of Ga., 1965-66. Certified land surveyor, Va., Ga. Mem. Internat. City Mgrs. Assn., Nat. Municipal League, Va. Soc. Profl. Engrs., Va. C. of C. Methodist. Mason (Shriner, 32 deg.). Home: 3311 Walnut St Hopewell VA 23860 Office: Municipal Bldg Hopewell VA 23860

LANE, DAVID CAMPBELL, neurosurgeon; b. Medford, Mass., June 17, 1927; s. Thomas Edward and Jean Matilda (Campbell) L.; B.S., U. Tenn., 1948; M.D., 1951; m. Benita Johnson, June 8, 1958; children—Benjamin J., Brett M., Helen L., David Campbell. Intern, U. Wis. Hosps., 1951-52; resident in neurol. surgery U. Wis., 1952-56; practice medicine, specializing in neurosurgery and neurology, Ft. Lauderdale, Fla., 1956-—. Pres. Lane-Gelety-Woolsey-Centrone Neurosurg. Assos., Ft. Lauderdale, 1962-—; dir. R. K. Cooper Ins. Co., Causeway Med. Corp. Mem. Fla. Senate, 1966-—, minority whip, 1970-—; chmn. Broward County Legislative Delegation, 1971-73; mem. Pres.' Nat. Adv. Health Council, 1970-—. Bd. dirs. Easter Seal Soc., Ft. Lauderdale Mus. Arts, Ft. Lauderdale U., Nat. Rehab. Assn. Served to lt. comdr. USNR, 1944-62. Recipient Allen Morris' award for most outstanding senator, 1970; named Fla. Jaycee's Outstanding Young Man, 1962; Physician of Yr., Broward County Med. Assn., 1971-72. Diplomate Am. Bd. Neurol. Surgery. Fellow A.C.S., Internat. Coll. Surgeons; mem. Ft. Lauderdale Surg. Soc., Am., Fla., Broward County med. assns., Am. Assn. Neurol. Surgeons, Harvey Cushing Soc., Congress Neurol. Surgeons, So. Surg. Soc., So. Neurosurg. Soc., Sigma Chi, Omicron Delta Kappa, Phi Chi. Republican. Episcopalian. Club: Lauderdale Yacht (dir. 1968-72). Home: 1233 N Rio Vista Blvd Fort Lauderdale FL 33301 Office: 300 SE 17th St Fort Lauderdale FL 33316

rep. Crown Zellerbach Corp., Bogalusa, and Baton Rouge, 1959-61, pub. relations mgr., 1961-64, mgr. corp. communications, 1964-71, mgr. pub. affairs, 1972—. Served to 1st lt. AUS, 1952-54. Recipient Distinguished Service award Bogalusa Jr. C. of C., 1956. Mem. Pub. Relations Soc. Am. (pres. Baton Rouge 1970), So. Forest Inst. (chmn. pub. relations com. 1968-70), Sigma Delta Chi. Methodist. Rotarian. Club: Camelot (Baton Rouge). Home: 881 Sinclair Dr Baton Rouge LA 70815 Office: PO Box 3375 Baton Rouge LA 70821

KNIGHT, EDWARD HENRY, psychoanalyst; b. New Orleans, June 14, 1922; s. Edward Henry and Mamie (Lawrence) K.; B.S., La. State U., 1943, M.D., 1945; New Orleans Psychoanalytic Inst., 1960; m. Mary Knox, Aug. 14, 1951; children—Victoria, Alan Henry, Cynthia, Carolyn, Jennifer, Jeremy. Intern Aultman Gen. Hosp., Canton, O., 1945; resident, fellow Menninger Sch. Psychiatry, Topeka, 1948-51; clin. prof. psychiatry La. State U. Sch. Medicine, New Orleans, 1951—; tng. analyst New Orleans Psychoanalytic Inst., 1965—; chief div. psychiatry Truro Infirmary, New Orleans, 1966-67. Mem. assembly's com. on the minister and his work Prsbyn. Ch., Atlanta, 1959—. Mem. Orleans Parish Sch. Bd., 1971—. Served to capt. AUS, 1946-48. Recipient Mental Health award La. Mental Health Assn., 1964. Diplomate in psychiatry Am. Bd. Neurology and Psychiatry. Fellow Am. Psychiat. Assn.; mem. La. Psychiat. Assn. (pres. 1961-62). Home: 7325 Hampson St New Orleans LA 70118 Office: 1303 Antonine St New Orleans LA 70115

KNIGHT, EUGENE STEPHEN, pub. relations dir.; b. Wilmington, N.C., Sept. 21, 1913; s. Eugene Bridgers and Jessie Maude (Frink) K.; B.B.A., N.C. State U., 1935; m. Margaret Hodges Smith, June 14, 1941; children—Eugene Stephen, James Smith. Extension radio specialist N.C. State U., Raleigh, 1935-43; ednl. dir. Central Carolina Farmers, Inc., Durham, N.C., 1946-47; editor Patriot-Farmer Greensboro, N.C. News-Rec., 1947-50; dir. pub. relations and advt. FCX, Inc., Raleigh, N.C., 1950—. Served with AUS, 1943-46. Democrat. Episcopalian (vestryman 1962-65, sec. 1964-65). Home: 2761 Toxey Dr Raleigh NC 27609 Office: PO Box 2419 Raleigh NC 27602

KNIGHT, JAMES L., newspaper exec.; b. Akron, O., 1909. Chmn., chief exec. Knight Newspapers, Inc.; pres. Knight Pub. Co., Charlotte, N.C.; pub. Charlotte Observer, Charlotte News; chmn. bd. Miami (Fla.) Herald Pub. Co. dir. keynoter Pub. Co., Gables Pub. Co., Asso. Press, So. Prodn. Program, Inc., Boca Raton News; pres., dir. Tallahassee Democrat. Mem. Am. (dir.), So. (pres. 1957, chmn. bd. 1958) newspaper pubs. assns. Clubs: Portage Country (Akron, O.); Bath, LaGorce, Indian Creek, Surf (Miami, Fla.); Detroit; Chicago; Key Largo Angelers, Hatteras Marlin, Nat. Press; Lyford Cay (New Providence, Bahamas). Home: The Surf House 8995 Collins Av Surfside FL 33154 Office: care Miami Herald 1 Herald Plaza Miami FL 33101

KNIGHT, JAMES ROLAND, judge; b. Quitman, Ga., Apr. 5, 1911; s. William Roland and Gussie (Jarvis) K.; student South Ga. State Coll., 1931; m. Mary F. Kimble Knight, Dec. 2, 1934; children—Betty Frances (Mrs. John Horton), James R. Profl. baseball player, 1931-34; cafe bus., 1934-39; engr. C.E., 1939-50; investigator U.S. Dept. Labor, 1950-53; sales rep. Ford Motor Co., 1953-64; judge Ct. Ordinary, Brooks County, Ga., 1965—. Chmn., Quitman City Commn., 1959. Mem. Brooks County Live Stock Assn., Brooks County Farm Bur. Baptist. Lion. Home: 203 E Lake Dr Quitman GA 31643 Office: Brooks County Ct House Quitman GA 31643

KNIGHT, JOHN PHILIP, assn. exec.; b. Dayton, O., Apr. 4, 1928; s. Ralph C. and Helen (Drury) K.; B.S., Ohio State U., 1950; M.S., George Williams Coll., 1952; m. Ann Williams, Nov. 22, 1954; children—Karen Elizabeth, John Patrick, Paul Timothy. Asst. youth dir. Wauwatosa br. YMCA Met. Milw., 1954-55, program dir., 1955-58, exec. dir. West Suburban br., 1958-66; asso. met. exec. dir. operations YMCA Greater Oklahoma City, 1966—; career devel. tng. cons. S.W. Area Council of YMCA's. Mem. Mayors Youth Commn., Wauwatosa, 1955-58; mem. Mayors Action for Youth Opportunity Council, 1966—. Bd. dirs. Oklahoma City and County Community Action Program, treas., 1971-72. Served with CIC, AUS, 1952-54. Mem. Assn. Profl. Dirs. YMCAs of U.S., Oklahoma City C. of C. Rotarian, Kwanian. Home: 2808 Orlando Rd Oklahoma City OK 73120 Office: PO Box 1374 Oklahoma City OK 73101

KNIGHT, JOHN SHIVELY, newspaper publisher; b. Bluefield, W.Va., Oct. 26, 1894; s. Charles Landon and Clara Irene (Scheifly) K.; student Tome Sch., Md., 1911-14, Cornell U., 1914-17, LL.D., U. Akron, 1945, Northwestern U., 1947, Kent State U., 1958, Ohio State U., 1961, U. Mich., 1969, Oberlin Coll., 1969, Colby Coll., 1969; medal for achievement in journalism, Syracuse U., 1946; m. Katharine McLain, Nov. 21, 1921 (dec. 1929); children—John Shively (killed in Germany, Mar. 29, 1945), Charles Landon, Frank McLain; m. 2d, Beryl Zoller Comstock, Jan. 24, 1932; 1 dau., Mrs. Kenneth Hewitt. Newspaper reporter and exec., 1920-25; mng. editor Akron (O.) Beacon Journal, 1925-33, editor 1933—; editorial dir. Springfield (O.) Sun. 1925-27, Massillon (O.) Independent, 1927-33, pres., 1933-37; chmn. bd., pub. Miami (Fla.) Herald, 1937-61, now editorial chmn.; pres. Beacon Journal Pub. Co., Knight Newspapers, Inc., to 1966, now editorial chmn.; purchased and discontinued Miami (Fla.) Tribune, 1937; purchased Detroit Free Press, 1940, pres. and editor, 1940-67, now editorial chmn.; owner, editor and pub. Chgo. Daily News, 1944-59, v.p. Charlotte (N.C.) News, 1959—, also Talahassee Democrat. Chief liaison officer between U.S. and Brit. censorship, London, Eng., 1943-44. Trustee Cornell U., U. Miami, Nat. Jewish Hosp.; bd. dirs. N.Y. World's Fair. Served in Motor Transport Corps, 113th Inf., in AAC, AEF, 1917-19. Awarded Frank M. Hawks Meml. Trophy, 1947; Citation of Merit from Poor Richard Club, 1946; honor award, distinguished service journalism, U. Mo., 1949; recipient Brotherhood of Children award, 1946, La Prensa award, 1954, Am.'s Found. award, 1959, John Peter Zenger award, 1967, Pulitzer prize for distinguished editorial writing, 1968. Carr Van Anda award Ohio U., 1970; others; cited outstanding Chicagoan in Inter-Am. relations by U.S.-Uruguay alliance, 1952. Established Knight Meml. Fund commemorating his father; La Prensa Scholarship furthering Inter-Am. understanding. Mem. Am. Soc. Newspaper Editors (past pres.), V.F.W., Am. Legion, A.P. (past dir., chmn. finance com., mem. exec. com.), 40 and 8, Phi Sigma Kappa, Sigma Delta Chi. Episcopalian. Clubs: Portage Country (Akron); Tin Whistles (Pinehurst, N.C.); Bath, Indian Creek (Miami); Union (Cleve.); Detroit, Detroit Athletic, Detroit Economic, Grosse Pointe Country (Detroit); Burning Tree Golf (Washington); Racquet, Chicago, Tavern, Casino, Commercial, Saddle and Cycle (Chgo.); Old Elm (Ft. Sheridan, Ill.); Glenview (Golf, Ill.). Home: 255 N Portage Path Akron OH 44303 Office: 44 E Exchange St Akron OH 44309 also Miami Herald 1 Herald Plaza Miami FL 33101 also Free Press Detroit MI 48226

KNIGHT, OLIVER HOLMES, educator; b. Brownwood, Tex., June 16, 1919; s. Oliver Holmes and Helen Kathleen (Egg) K.; B.A., U. Okla., 1953, M.A., 1954; Ph.D., U. Wis., 1959; m. Wilma Wolff, 1969; 5 children. With Longview (Tex.) News-Jour., 1938. United Press, Washington, 1938-41, Ft. Worth Star-Telegram, 1946-51; copy editor Wis. Stat Jour., Madison, 1954; copy editor Indpls. News, 1960, asst. prof. journalism Ind. U., 1958-61; mem. faculty U. Wis., Madison, 1961-67, prof. journalism, 1966-67; prof. history U. Tex., El Paso, 1967—. Served with AUS, 1943-46. Recipient Frank Luther Mott award Kappa Tau Alpha, 1967. Mem. Am. Hist. Assn., Western Hist. Assn., Orgn. Am. Historians. Mason. Author: Following the Indian Wars, 1960; I Protest, 1966; Ft. Worth: Outpost on the Trinity, 1953; also articles. Home: 5125 Camino de la Vista El Paso TX 79932

KNIGHT, RICHARD BENNETT, educator, cons. engr.; b. Cin., Oct. 11, 1914; s. Harry C. and Helen (Van Horn) K.; B.S., U. Md., 1935; M.S., U. Ill., 1939; m. Sara Kelso Wooten, May 27, 1944; children—Barbara Ann, Richard Bennett. Grad. research asst., Am. Soc. Heating and Ventilating Engrs. fellow in mech. engring. U. Ill., Urbana, 1937-39; air conditioning engr. Md. Refrigeration Co., Balt., 1940, York-Shipley; Inc., York, Pa., 1946; mech. engr. Army Chem. Center, War Dept., Md., 1940-42; vibrations engr. Glenn L. Martin Co., Middle River, Md., 1942-45; asso. prof. heating and ventilating U. Ky., Lexington, 1946-52; LL. Vaughan prof. charge heating and air conditioning curriculum N.C. State U., Raleigh, 1952—. Fulbright vis. lectr. Alexandria (Egypt) U., 1951; UNESCO lectr., Lebanon, Syria, Iraq, 1951; heating and air conditioning cons. to architects and engrs., 1952—; heat transfer and air conditioning cons. Convair, Ft. Worth, Martin Co., Balt., 1953-57; research participant Oak Ridge Inst. Nuclear Studies, 1958-59; heat transfer cons. Oak Ridge Nat. Lab., 1958—; chief scientist P.R. Nuclear Center, Mayaquez, 1961-62, heat transfer cons., 1962; AEC lectr. in univs. and atomic energy labs., Brazil, Argentina, Bolivia, Peru, Columbia, 1962; mem. N.C. Bd. Refrigeration Examiners, 1968—, chmn. bd., 1969—. Registered profl. engr., N.C., Ky. Mem. Am. Soc. for Engring. Edn., Am. Soc. Heating, Refrigeration, Air Conditioning Engrs., Pi Tau Sigma. Presbyn. Lion. Club: Stag, Raleigh Engineers. Home: 3005 Eton Rd Raleigh NC 27608

KNIGHT, RICHARD FINLEY, lawyer; b. Bogalusa, La., Feb. 14, 1933; s. Delos Lavern and Ruth (Vinyard) K.; B.S., La. State U., 1955, LL.B., 1958; m. Sally Ann Powell, July 19, 1958; children—Kathryn Marie, Richard Andrew, Susan Margaret. Jud. adminstr. Supreme Ct. La., 1958-60; partner firm Talley, Anthony, Hughes & Knight, Bogalusa, 1960—. Pres., Bogalusa Area Community Concerts, Inc., 1965; nat. council rep. Boy Scouts Am., 1965-68, v.p. Istrouma Area council, 1969-71, pres., 1971—. Chmn. indigent defender bd. 22nd Jud. Dist. Bd. dirs. Washington Parish chpt. A.R.C.; vice chmn. adv. com. Bogalusa Community Chest. Recipient Silver Beaver, Boy Scouts Am., 1967. Mem. La. State Law Inst., Am., La. bar assns., Am. Judicature Soc., Inst. Jud. Adminstrn., La. State U. Alumni Assn. (chpt. pres.), Omicron Delta Kappa, Phi Delta Phi, Sigma Chi, Beta Gamma Sigma. Methodist (chmn. council ministeries). Rotarian. Home: 1404 Charwood Dr Bogalusa LA 70427 Office: 322 Columbia St Bogalusa LA 70427

KNIGHT, WILLIAM DANIEL, lawyer, farmer; b. Ray City, Ga., Mar. 2, 1934; s. E.M. and Gladys (Daniel) K.; B.S., Valdosta State Coll., 1955; J.D., U. Ga.,1958; m. Jane Stallings, Aug. 6, 1960; children—Edna Elizabeth, William Daniel. Admitted to Ga. bar, 1958, since practiced in Nashville; farmer, Nashville, 1965—. Pres. Berrien County Civic Club, 1966-67; pres. New Lois Community Club, 1968—; mem. City Council, Ray City, 1959-60; Mem. Ga. Ho. of Reps., 1961-66. Bd. dirs. Berrien County Indsl. Bldg. Authority. Served with Ga. N.G., 1958-61. Mem. Am., Ga., Alapaha (pres.) bar assns., Order Gridiron Soc., Phi Delta Phi, Kappa Alpha. Democrat. Baptist (trustee). Home: RFD 2 Nashville GA 31639 Office: PO Box 647 Nashville GA 31639

KNIGHT, WILLYS RAYMOND, educator; b. Whitewater, Wis., May 26, 1917; s. Harry Ray and Esther (Cowan) K.; student Ripon Coll., 1934-37; B.A., U. Wis., 1938, M.A., 1939; student U. Ill., 1941-42; Ph.D., U. Md., 1949; m. Florence E. Hoge, Aug. 5, 1943; children—George, Alice, Bruce. Instr., Miss. State U., 1939-40; teaching asst. U. Ill., 1940-41; civilian pub. service Selective Service, 1941-45; asst. prof. Mich. State U., East Lansing, 1946-51; prof. Ga. State Coll., Atlanta, 1951—. Exec. dir. Ga. Compensation Commn.; pres. Asso. U. Bureaus Bus. Econ. Research. Mem. Am., So. econ. assns., Am. Assn. U. Profs. Author: (with others) Structure of American Industry, 1961; Professional Education for Business, 1965. Home: 6860 Heathfield Dr NW Atlanta GA 30328 Office: 33 Gilmer St SE Atlanta GA 30303

KNIGHT, WOODSON, r.r. exec.; b. Sharpsburg, Ky., Mar. 18, 1913; s. William Rufus and Mary (Cracraft) K.; A.B., U. Ky., 1934; m. Winston Byron, Sept. 28, 1935; children—Robin Woodson, William Robert. With newspapers and A.P., 1935-43; editor Atlantic Richfield Co., Phila., 1945-65; pub. relations dir. Louisville & Nashville R.R., 1965—. Co-chmn. A.R.C., Louisville area chpt., 1970—. Served with USNR, 1943-45. Mem. R.R. Pub. Relations Assn., Pub. Relations Soc. Am., Am. Assn. Indsl. Editors (pres. 1959-60), Delaware Valley Assn. Editors (pres. 1954-55). Rotarian. Home: 3305 Springcrest Dr Louisville KY 40222 Office: 908 W Broadway Louisville KY 40201

KNIPPERS, OTTIS JEWELL, judge; b. Florien, La., Oct. 30, 1913; s. Christopher Columbus and Dona (Lockwood) K.; student Vaughan Sch. Music, 1929-32, U. Minn.; m. Opal Inez Moody, Jan. 28, 1938; children—Jan Carolyn, Ottis Jewell, Nancy Gayle. Profl. singer, 1929-38; operated retail stores, 1938-67; judge Lawrence County Ct., 1966—. Dir. Tenn. River and Tributaries Assn., 1960-64, Duck River Devel. Assn., 1960-64, Tenn. Elk River Devel. Agy., 1963—. Mem. So. Regional Edn. Bd., 1959-61, Mid S. Regional Health Program, 1969—, Tenn. Assn. Advancement Child Care, 1969—, S. Central Tenn. Med. Services Council, 1969—, Tenn. Intergovtl. Com., 1966—, State Tenn. Adv. Council Mental Retardation, 1968—, State Tenn. Adv. Com. Services to Children and Their Families, 1969—; chmn. Lawrence County Gen. Hosp., 1966—; vice chmn. Columbia Area Mental Health Center, 1969—. Mem. Tenn. Ho. of Reps., 1941-44, 49-51, Tenn. Senate, 1956-60. Served from pvt. to sgt. AUS, 1944-46, ETO. Mem. Am. Legion, V.F.W., C. of C., Tenn. Council Juvenile Ct. Judges (sec.-treas. 1968—). Democrat. Methodist (asso. dist. lay leader). Club: Lions (Lawrenceburg). Author, composer, poet. Office: Court House Lawrenceburg TN 38464

KNODEL, DON RICHARD, basketball coach; b. Hamilton, O., Sept. 5, 1931; s. Robert and Teresa (Zeer) K.; B.S. in Edn., Miami (O.) U., 1953; M.A. in Edn., Xavier U., 1960; m. Janet Lois Kindel, June 8, 1957; children—Mark Gregory, Jennifer Dawn, Kristin. Basketball coach Talawanda High Sch., Oxford, O., 1956-58, Harding High Sch., Marion, O., 1958-61; asst. basketball coach Vanderbilt U., Nashville, 1961-66; head basketball coach Rice U., Houston, 1966—. Mem. Nat. Assn. Basketball Coaches, Sigma Chi. Club: Rice Faculty (social chmn.). Home: 1819 Milford St Houston TX 77006

KNODELL, PRESTON GILBERT, JR., educator; b. Austin, Tex., Sept. 23, 1935; s. Preston Gustave and Inez (Whitaker) K.; B.S. in Physics, B.A. in Philosophy, St. Mary's U. of Tex., 1960; M.A. in Philosophy, Catholic U. Am., 1966, Ph.D., 1969; m. Margaret Mary Pollock, Sept. 1, 1962; children—Preston Gilbert III, Peggy Marie. Instr. philosophy Incarnate Word Coll., San Antonio, 1961-62; St. Mary of the Plains Coll., Dodge City, Kan., 1964-65; asst. prof. philosophy U. Tex., San Antonio, 1968—, chmn. dept. philosophy, 1970—. Mem. Am. Catholic Philos. Assn., Nat. Spellol. Soc. Home: 115 Kinder Dr San Antonio TX 78212 Office: 2700 Cincinnati Av San Antonio TX 78228

KNOOP, WERNER CALDWELL, city ofcl., business exec.; b. Hancock County, Ia., Mar. 30, 1902; s. Charles Werner and Jessie (Olmstead) K.; B.S. in Civil Engring., Ia. State Coll., 1924; m. Faith Yingling, Sept. 4, 1926; 1 dau., Athalia May (Mrs. Karl Robert Kullander). Engr. Truscon Steel Co., Youngstown, O., Chgo., Omaha, 1924-29; owner Capitol Steel Co., Little Rock, 1929-40; cons. engr., 1940-46; exec. v.p. Baldwin Co., contractors, Little Rock, 1946-64, pres., 1964—; pres. Eureka Brick & Tile Co., Clarksville, 1949—; v.p. Clarkeville Machine Works, Inc. Dir. Nat. Safety Council. Pres. sch. bd., Little Rock, 1947, mayor, 1957-62; chmn. Little Rock Parking Authority, 1966—; mem. Gov.'s Traffic Safety Adv. Commn. Dir. Johnson-Knoop Found.; mem. internat. com. YMCA World Service; past pres. Little Rock AFB Community Relations Council. Registered profl. engr. Fellow Am. Soc. C.E. (past dir. Mid-South sect.); mem. Nat. Soc. Profl. Engrs., Asso. Contractors Am. (mem. nat. safety com., pres. Ark. chpt.), Little Rock C. of C. (pres. 1970). Presbyn. (elder). Clubs: Rotary, Little Rock, Country of Little Rock. Home: 6 Ozark Point Little Rock AR 72205 Office: 322 Gaines St Little Rock AR 72201

KNOPKE, RAY C., state senator; b. Chgo., Dec. 13, 1913; ed. St. Petersburg Jr. Coll., Ohio State U.; m. Virginia Lacey; children—Susan, Keenan, Ray. Pres. Garden of Memories, Inc.; mem. Fla. Senate, 1966—. Formerly mayor, Temple Terrace, Fla., also councilman; mem. Fla. Ho. of Reps., 1964-66. Served with USAAF. Mem. Fla. C. of C., Com. 100, Am. Legion, V.F.W. Presbyn. (deacon). Mason (Shriner), Elk, Lion. Address: 4207 E Lake Av Tampa FL 33610*

KNOPS, DUANE WILLIAM, advt. exec.; b. South St. Paul, Minn., Mar. 5, 1927; s. Peter and Geneva Lilian (Harrington) K.; student U. Minn., 1946-47, Mills Coll., St. Paul, 1948, Sch. Asso. Arts, 1948-49, Minn. Sch. Bus., 1949-50; m. Margaret Connie Rowell, Nov. 11, 1950; children—Dirk C., Debora L. Account exec. tng. program Campbell-Mithun, Inc., Mpls., 1950-57, account exec., Chgo., 1957-61; account exec. Compton Advt., Inc., Chgo., 1961-67, v.p., mgr., Dallas, 1968-70; account exec. Tracy-Locke, Inc., Dallas, 1970—. Served with USMCR, 1944-46. Mem. Advt. Club Dallas, Advt. League. Republican. Conglist. Home: 4030 Mendenhall Dr Dallas TX 75234 Office: PO Box 50129 1407 Main St Dallas TX 75250

KNOTHE, ADOLF HEINRICH, space scientist, govt. ofcl.; b. Traisa, Germany, Sept. 17, 1921; s. Max Louis and Elisabeth Magdalene (Weingaertner) K.; M.S. in Applied Math., Darmstadt (Germany) Tech. U., 1947, Ph.D., 1952; m. Johanna Krauter, Oct. 18, 1947 (div. 1963); children—Hannelore, Ralph Peter; m. 2d, Hilda Marian Arnold, Nov. 14, 1964. Came to U.S., 1953, naturalized, 1958. Mathematician, Peenemuende (Germany) Rocket Center, 1943-45; asst. prof. Inst. Practical Math., Darmstadt Tech. U., 1947-51; mathematician Farbwerke Hoechst, Germany, 1951-52; chief guidance theory sect. U.S. Army Ordnance Guided Missile Devel. Div., 1953-58; asst. to dir. systems analysis and reliability lab. Army Ballistic Missile Agy., 1958-59, sci. asst. to dir. missile firing lab. 1959-60; chief tech. staff Launch Operations Center, NASA, 1960-64; sr. scientist Kennedy Space Center, 1964—; adj. prof. math. Fla. Inst. Tech., Melbourne, 1965—. Mem. Am. Inst. Aeros. and Astronautics. Home: 102 N Indian Circle Cocoa FL 32922 Office: Kennedy Space Center FL 32899

KNOTT, ROBERT REAVES, radio co. exec.; b. Rotan, Tex., June 21, 1933; s. Proctor B. and Lula Maud (Holderness) K.; B.S., So. Meth. U., 1956. Asst. writer Girard Life Ins. Co., Dallas, 1956-58; asst. advt. and pub. relations mgr., 1959-62, advt. and pub. relations mgr., 1962-64; account exec., pub. relations Kontrak Corp., 1964-67, Workman Advt. Agy., 1967-68; pub. relations mgr. Collins Radio Co., 1968—. Mem. Pub. Relations Soc. Am., Sigma Delta Chi. Home: 4040 Travis St Dallas TX 75204 Office: Collins Radio Co Dallas TX 75207

KNOTTS, BURTON RAY, elec. engr.; b. Pocahontas, Ark., Oct. 24, 1930; s. Burton Dee and Lily (Sago) K.; B.S., U. Ark., 1957; m. Mary Catherine DeClerk, June 9, 1955; children—David Ray, Anna Catherine, Joan Marie. Elec. engr. C.E., U.S. Army, Little Rock dist., 1957—. Mem. U.S. Com. on Large Dams. Served with USAF, 1949-52. Recipient Commendation award for elec. designs U.S. Army, 1966. Registered profl. engr., Ark. Mem. I.E.E.E., Nat. Soc. Profl. Engrs. Toastmaster. Home: 7316 Dahlia Dr Little Rock AR 72209 Office: 700 W Capitol St Little Rock AR 72203

KNOWLES, DOYLE BLEWER, hydrologist; b. Tulia, Tex., July 6, 1924; s. James Hamilton and Sydney (Blewer) K.; B.S., Tex. Technol. Coll., 1944; m. Joe Ann Watkins, Dec. 17, 1955; children—Bobbie Louise, Teresa Ann, William Doyle, Cheryl Lynne, Patricia Elaine. Hydraulic engr. Tex. Bd. Water Engrs., Austin, Tex., 1946-47, U.S. Geol. Survey, various locations, 1947-61; chief water resources div., Geol. Survey Ala., University, 1961-69, sr. hydrologist, publs. officer, 1969—; partner P. E. La-Moreaux Assos., cons. groundwater hydraulogists, Tuscaloosa, Ala., 1961-71, treas., dir., 1971—. Served with USNR, 1944-45. Registered profl. engr., Tex., Ala. Mem. Am. Soc. C.E., Am. Geophys. Union, Am. Water Works Assn., Nat. Water Well Assn., Am. Chem. Soc., Am. Acad. Sci. Contbr. articles to sci. jours. Home: 28 Brookhaven Dr Tuscaloosa AL 35401 Office: PO Drawer O Walter Bryan Jones Hall University AL 35486

KNOWLES, REX HANNA, educator; b. Kansas City, Mo., Jan. 10, 1918; s. Roy Otis and Sarah L. (Canedy) K.; B.A., Wesleyan U., 1940; B.D., Yale, 1943; M.A., U. Neb., 1951, Ph.D., 1958; D.D., Hastings Coll., 1955; m. Jessie Mould, Aug. 24, 1943; children—Nancy, Anne, Rex, Trudy, Mark. Asso. pastor United Ch., New Haven, 1944-46; pastor Cochran Meml. Ch., Oneida, N.Y., 1946-49; univ. pastor U. Neb., Lincoln, 1949-59; dean of Chapel, Centre Coll., Danville, Ky., 1960-66, prof. psychology, 1966—; dir. counseling services, chmn. psychology, 1969—. Pres. Toliver P.T.A., 1963, 64, 65; dist. bd. P.T.A., 1969; pres. bd. YMCA, 1967; v.p. Ky. UN Assn., 1966—; regional chmn. White Conf. Children and Youth, 1969. Named Outstanding Nebraskan for youth work at U. Neb., 1953. Mem. Ky. Psychol. Assn., Nat. Assn. U. Pastors (v.p.) Phi Beta Kappa, Psi Chi, Alpha Chi Rho, Delta Sigma Rho, Omicron Delta Kappa. Presbyn. Rotarian. Contbr. articles to profl. jours. Home: 235 N Maple Danville KY 40422

KNOWLTON, CHARLES W., lawyer; b. Columbia, S.C., 1923; A.B., U. S.C., 1943; LL.B., Harvard, 1949. Admitted to S.C. bar, 1949; now mem. firm, Boyd, Bruton, Knowlton, Tate & Finlay, Columbia. Mem. Am. Coll. Probate Counsel, Am. Judicature Soc., Richland County (pres. 1968-69), S.C. (chmn. exec. com. 1969), Am. bar assns., Phi Beta Kappa, Omicron Delta Kappa. Address: Boyd Bruton Knowlton Tate & Finlay 1250 SCN Center Columbia SC 29201*

KNOX, ARTHUR STEWART, geologist; b. Charlestown, Mass., Jan. 10, 1903; s. Joseph H. and Ada (Stewart) K.; B.S., Tufts U., 1928, M.Ed., 1939; M.A., Harvard, 1931; m. Harriet B. Towne Oct. 21,

LANE, DONALD EDWARD, judge; b. Chevy Chase, Md., June 10, 1909; s. John Albert and Virginia Louise (Payson) L.; B.S., Yale, 1931; ed. George Washington U. Law Sch.; m. Virginia Plugge, Sept. 1, 1938; children—Diana Randall (Mrs. Louis A. Ebersold), Adair Payson. Admitted to D.C. bar, 1935; pvt. practice law, Washington, 1935-41, 45-54; commr. U.S. Ct. Claims, 1954-69; judge U.S. Ct. Custom and Patent Appeals, 1969—. Patent adviser Manhattan Project, 1943. Served to comdr, USNR, 1941-45. Mem. Am. Bar Assn., Am. Patent Law Assn. (past sec., bd. mgrs.), Bar Assn. D.C., Am. Judicature Soc., Washington Patent Lawyers Club (past pres.). Clubs: Columbia Country (Chevy Chase, Md.); University, Cosmos (Washington). Home: 5040 Loughboro Rd NW Washington DC 20016 Office: US Ct Custom and Patent Appeals Washington DC 20439

LANE, EDWARD WOOD, JR., banker; b. Jacksonville, Fla., Apr. 4, 1911; s. Edward Wood and Anna Virginia (Taliaferro) L.; A.B., Princeton, 1933; LL.B., Harvard, 1936; m. Helen Spratt Murchison, Oct. 16, 1948; children—Edward Wood III, Helen Palmer, Anna Taliaferro, Charles Murchison. Admitted to Fla. bar, 1936; partner firm McCarthy, Lane & Adams, and predecessors, Jacksonville, 1941-60; pres., dir. Atlantic Nat. Bank, Jacksonville, 1961—; pres. Atlantic Bancorp; chmn. First Atlantic Nat. of Daytona Beach, Westside Atlantic of Daytona Beach; dir. Fla. Pub. Co. Trustee Cummer Museum Found.; bd. dirs. Jacksonville Community Chest-United Fund. Served to lt. comdr. USNR, World War II. Mem. Jacksonville Area C. of C. (com. 100), Phi Beta Kappa. Clubs: Florida Yacht, Timuquana Country, River, University (Jacksonville); Ponte Vedra (Fla.). Home: 3790 Ortega Blvd Jacksonville FL 32210 Office: Atlantic Nat Bank West Bay Station Jacksonville FL 32203

LANE, HELEN S. MURCHISON (MRS. EDWARD W. LANE, JR.), civic worker; b. Boston, June 1, 1924; d. Charles H. and Helen (Spratt) Murchison; A.B., Sweet Briar Coll., 1946; m. Edward W. Lane, Jr., Oct. 16, 1948; children—Edward W. III, Helen Palmer, Anna Taliaferro, Charles Murchison. Mem. Jacksonville Cultural and Historic Preservation Commn., 1971—. Bd. dirs. Jr. League Jacksonville, Fla., 1954-60, pres., 1959-60; chmn. Symphony Ball, Jacksonville, 1960; restorer 1893 Victorian home; mem. fine arts com. Jacksonville C. of C. Regional dir. exec. com. Alumni Council Sweet Briar Coll., 1968-70; trustee Bartram Sch. Club: Jacksonville Garden (life). Pub.: The Best of Lucifer, 1969; The Queen Victoria Cooks, 1971. Home: 3790 Ortega Blvd Jacksonville FL 32210

LANE, SISTER M. CLAUDE, archivist-librarian; b. Dobbin, Tex., Feb. 7, 1915; d. Michael W. and Mary Lou (Pace) Lane; student U. Tex., 1934-47, U. Houston, 1936-39; B.A., Our Lady of Lake Coll., 1953; M.L.S., U. Tex., 1961. Tchr., choral dir. elementary and high schs. Dominican Sisters Houston, 1934-60; tchr.-librarian elementary and high schs., Tex., Cal., 1953-64; prin. St. Marys Elementary Sch., Orange, Tex., 1958-60; archivist Cath. Archives of Tex., Austin, 1960-61, summers 1961-64, full time 1964-67, 71—, in absentia, 1967-71; tchr. high schs., Tex., Cal., 1961-64; librarian St. Pius X High Sch., Houston, 1967-71. Library cons. Office of Edn., Diocese of Austin, 1964-69, 71—. Shelter mgr. Austin-Travis County Dept. Civil Def., 1965-67. Mem. Am., Cath., Tex. (sec.-treas. Archives Round Table 1967-68, chmn. 1970-71) library assns., Am. Sch. Librarians Assn., Am., Tex., Austin hist. assns., Soc. Am. Archivists, Am. Assn. State and Local History, Harris County Hist Assn., Tex. Hist. Found. and Survey Commn., Soc. Southwest Archivists. Author: Catholic Archives of Texas: History and Preliminary Inventory, 1961. Contbr. profl. jours. Home: Newman Hall Austin TX 78705 Office: 16th and N Congress Sts PO Box 13327 Capitol Sta Austin TX 78711

LANE, MARGARET BEYNON TAYLOR (MRS. HORACE C. LANE), librarian; b. St. Louis, Feb. 6, 1919; d. Archer and Alice (Jones) Taylor; B.A., La. State U., 1939, LL.B., 1942; B.A. in L.S., Columbia, 1941; m. Horace C. Lane, Jan. 6, 1945; children—Margaret Elizabeth, Thomas Archer. Reference and circulation asst. Columbia Law Library, N.Y.C., 1942-44; law librarian, asst. prof. U. Conn. Sch. Law, Hartford, 1944-46; law librarian La. State U. Law Sch. Baton Rouge, 1946-49; recorder documents Sec. of State's Office, Baton Rouge, 1949—. Treas. Delta Iota House Bd. of Kappa Kappa Gamma Frat., 1965-68. Mem. Am., La. library assns., La., Baton Rouge bar assns., Phi Delta Delta, Kappa Kappa Gamma. Club: Baton Rouge Library. Home: 7545 Richards Dr Baton Rouge LA 70809 Office: State Capitol Baton Rouge LA 70804

LANE, MARION POTTER, JR., clergyman; b. Waco, Tex., June 20, 1921; s. Marion Potter and Hattie (Richter) L.; student Peabody Coll., 1939-41; A.B., Wittenberg U., 1943, B.D., 1945; postgrad. Cornell U., 1945-46; M.A., Vanderbilt U., 1959; postgrad. Luth. Theol. So. Sem., 1969; m. Mable Sue Stirewalt, June 23, 1946; 1 son, William Marion. Ordained to ministry Luth. Ch., 1945; missionary Andhra Evang. Luth. Ch., United Luth. Ch. Am., India, 1946-52; mission developer, pastor in Hampton, Va., 1953-56; pastor in Parrottsville, Tenn., 1956-62, St. Paul's Luth. Ch., Shenandoah, Va., 1962—. Sec. central dist. Va. synod Luth. Ch. Am., 1965-72, dean Blue Ridge area, 1972—, chmn. com. on publs., 1967—, valley regional coordinator on ministry. 1971—. Mem. men's com. Japan Internat. Christian U. Found.; bd. dirs. Page County Mental Health Assn.; adv. bd. Massanutten Mental Health Center (pres. 1967-69). Mem. Va., Page County (pres. 1965-66) councils chs., Page County Ministerial Assn. (pres. 1963-65, treas. 1965-66), Luth. Soc. Worship, Music and Arts, Page County Heritage Assn., Page County Farm Bur. Club: Ruritan. Contbr. to devotional quar., also weekly newspaper column. Address: RFD 1 Box 130 Shenandoah VA 22849

LANE, MILLS B., JR., banker; b. Savannah, Ga., 1912; m. Anne Waring; children— Mills B. IV, Anita. Entered banking bus. with Citizens & So. Nat. Bank of Savannah, now vice-chmn., chief exec. officer, Atlanta; dir. Bibb Mfg. Co., Coca Cola Bottling Co. Miami, Ga. Power Co., Winn Dixie Stores. Mem. Young Pres. Orgn. (dir.). Home: 2 W Muscogee Av NW Atlanta GA 30305 Office: Citizens & So Nat Bank 35 Broad St PO Box 4899 Atlant GA 30301

LANE, MONTAGUE, educator, physician; b. N.Y.C., Aug. 28, 1929; s. George and Ida (Korn) L.; B.A., N.Y. U., 1947; M.B., Chgo. Med. Sch., 1952, M.D., 1953; M.S., Georgetown U., 1957; m. Carol Higelman, June 30, 1957; children—Laura Diane, Adam Reuben. Clin. asso. Nat. Cancer Inst., NIH, 1954-56, sr. investigator Clin. Pharmacology and Exptl. Therapeutics Service, attending physician gen. med. br. Nat. Cancer Inst., 1957-60; asso. in medicine George Washington U. Med. Sch., 1957-60; asst. prof.-asso. prof. depts. pharmacology and medicine Baylor U. Coll. Medicine, Houston, 1960-67; prof. depts. pharm. and medicine Baylor Coll. of Medicine, 1967—, head div. clin. oncology dept. pharmacology, 1969—. Mem. study sect. Nat. Cancer Inst., 1966-69; chmn. new agts. com. S.W. Cancer Chemotherapy study group, A.C.P., Am. Inst. for Nutrition, Am. Soc. for Clin. Oncology (program chmn. 1970), Am. Soc. for Pharmacology and Exptl. Therapeutics (exec. bd. clin. div. 1969—), Am. Soc. Clin. Pharmacology and Therapeutics (pres. 1971-72), Am. Soc. for Hematology, Am. Assn. for Cancer Research, Harris County Med. Soc. Editorial adv. bd. Cancer Research, 1970—. Home: 2330 Underwood Houston TX 77025 Office: 1200 Moursund Houston TX 77025

LANE, RICHARD NEWTON, mfg. co. exec.; b. Eagle Pass, Tex., Feb. 6, 1919; s. William Bartlett and Virginia (Gardner) L.; B.A., U. Tex., 1940, M.A., 1941; m. Estelle Speed, Apr. 5, 1942; children—William B., Martha, Richard Newton, Laura. Research asso. Underwater Sound Lab., Harvard, Cambridge, Mass., 1941-42; project engr. sonar sect. RCA, Camden, N.J., 1942-46; project physicist Def. Research Lab., U. Tex., Austin, 1946-48, asst. dir. in charge acoustics div. Def. Research Lab., 1950-57, vis. prof. architecture and planning, 1959-64; mgr. airborne magnetic surveys sect. Edgar Tobin Aerial Surveys, San Antonio, 1948-49; pres., chmn. bd. TRACOR, Inc., Austin, 1955-70, chmn. bd., 1970—; chmn. bd. Tracor Computing Corp., 1970—. Cons. in acoustics, 1950—. Fellow Acoustical Soc. Am. (mem. exec. council 1956-58); mem. I.E.E.E. (sr.), Phi Beta Kappa, Sigma Xi, Beta Gamma Sigma. Club: Austin Yacht. Contbr. articles on archtl. acoustics and solions to tech. jours. Home: 2210 San Gabriel Austin TX 78705 Office: 6500 Tracor Lane Austin TX 78721

LANE, THOMAS ALPHONSUS, journalist, author; b. Revere, Mass., Nov. 19, 1906; s. Thomas Andrew and Julia (Fitzpatrick) L.; B.S., U.S. Mil. Acad., 1928; B.S. in C.E., Mass. Inst. Tech., 1932; grad. Nat. War Coll., 1953; m. Jean Margaret Gee, June 3, 1933; children—Jean, Michael Stuart, Julia Ann (Mrs. Donald Rasmussen), Thomas C. Commd. 2d lt. U.S. Army, 1928, advanced through grades to maj. gen., 1957; exec. officer to Air Engr., Hdqrs., USAAF, 1942; exec. officer, operations officer Engr. sect. Gen. Hdqrs., S.W. Pacific area, 1943-45; joint operations Rev. Bd., 1946; dist. engr. Little Rock, Ark., 1948-50; dist. engr. Okinawa, 1950-52; engr. commr. D.C., 1954-57; comdg. gen. Ft. Leonard Wood, Mo., 1957-60; pres. Mississippi River Commn., 1960-62; ret., 1962; syndicated columnist, author, lectr., 1962—. Instr. civil engring. and mil. history U.S. Mil. Acad., 1935-39; engring. instr. and chief logistics div. Air Command and Staff Sch., 1946-48; exec. dir. Inst. for Human Progress, 1962-63. Pres. Ams. for Constitutional Action, 1965-69. Decorated D.S.M. with oak leaf cluster. Fellow Am. Soc. C.E.; mem. Wash. Soc. Engrs. (hon.). Clubs: Army-Navy (Washington); Army Navy Country (Arlington, Va.); National Press (Washington). Author: The Leadership of President Kennedy, 1964; The War for the World, 1968; Cry Peace: The Kennedy Years, 1969; American on Trial: The War for Vietnam, 1971. Home: 6157 Kellogg Dr McLean VA 22101

LANE, WALTER WISHART, JR., physician; b. Kansas City, Mo., Apr. 4, 1934; s. Walter Wishart and Geraldine (Faley) L.; student The Citadel, 1952-54; B.S., U. Tampa, 1961; M.D., U. Fla., 1965; m. Nancie June Hoopingarner, Nov. 24, 1956; children—Pamela Ann, Sharon Jane, Melissa Ellen, Stacie Lee. Intern, Lloyd Noland Hosp., Birmingham, Ala., 1965-66; pvt. practice medicine, Temple Terrace, Fla., 1966—. Mem. nat. adv. council Council on Econ. Opportunity. Served with USNR, 1955-59. Recipient A.M.A. Gold medal, 1966; named one of Am.'s 10 Outstanding Young Men, U.S. Jr. C. of C., 1966; Alumnus of Year, U. Tampa Alumni Assn. Mem. A.M.A., Am., Fla. (mem. pub. relations com. 1967-68) acads. gen. practice. Columnist, Patient Care mag. Editorial bd. Parent Care, Mgmt. Concepts. Home: 612 Downs Temple Terrace FL 33617 Office: 5202 Busch Blvd Tampa FL 33617

LANE, WILLIAM GUERRANT, educator; b. Reidsville, N.C., June 15, 1919; s. Henry Pritchett and Eva (Smith) L.; A.B. magna cum laude, Furman U., 1939; M.A., Harvard, 1947, Ph.D., 1953; m. Kate Hodge, Sept. 5, 1953; 1 son, Richard Guerrant. Instr. English, Tufts U., Medford, Mass., 1947-50; instr. Duke, 1952-56; asso. prof. S.W. Mo. State Coll., Springfield, 1956-60; asso. prof. U. Colo., 1960-63, prof., 1963-69, chmn. dept., 1964-67; prof., head dept. U. N.C., Greensboro, 1969—. Served to lt. comdr. USNR, 1941-45; PTO. Dexter Traveling scholar Harvard, 1952. Mem. Modern Lang. Assn. Am., South Atlantic Modern Lang. Assn., Keats-Shelley Assn. Am., Research Soc. for Victorian Periodicals, Am. Assn. U. Profs. Democrat. Author: Richard Harris Barham, 1967; Poetry: An Introduction, 1968. Gen. editor: English Language Notes, 1963-68. Home: 3700 Madison Av Greensboro NC 27403

LANEY, JAMES THOMAS, educator, clergyman; b. Wilson, Ark., Dec. 24, 1927; s. Thomas Mann and Mary (Hughey) L.; B.A., Yale, 1950, B.D., 1954; Ph.D., 1966; m. Berta Joan Radford, Dec. 20, 1949; children—Joan, James T., Arthur Radford, Mary, Susan. Chaplain, Choate Sch., Wallingford, Conn., 1953-55; asst. instr. Yale Div. Sch., 1954-55; pastor St. Paul Meth. Ch., Cin., 1955-58; sec. student Christian Movement, prof. Yonsei U., Seoul, Korea, 1959-64; asst. prof. Christian ethics Vanderbilt U. Div. Sch., Nashville, 1966-69; dean Candler Sch. Theology, Emory U., Atlanta, 1969—. Chmn. resources planning commn. Am. Assn. Theol. Schs., 1970—. Pres. Nashville Community Relations Council, 1969. Bd. dirs. Fund for Theol. Edn. Served with AUS, 1946-48. Mem. Am. Soc. Christian Ethics, Soc. for Sci. Study of Religion. Author: (with J.M. Gustafson) On Being Responsible, 1968. Home: 2080 Renault Lane Atlanta GA 30345

LANG, ADELE LEIMAN (MRS. HAROLD LANG), educator; b. N.Y.C.; d. Aaron and Yetta (Katz) Leiman; B.A., N.Y. State Coll. for Tchrs., 1933; M.A., George Washington U., 1960; postgrad. U. Va., 1966, 69-70, Coll. of William and Mary, 1967; m. Harold Lang, Mar. 22, 1936; 1 son, Jeffrey Martin. Tchr. English, Arlington County Sch. System, 1960-64, counselor, 1964—; counselor Gunston Jr. High Sch., Arlington, Va., 1965—. Personnel specialist Fed. Govt. Project for Facilitating Integration under Title I, Arlington, 1966-68. Precinct judge Civic Assn. East Falls, Church, 1953-58; bd. dirs. Arlington County Sch. Fund for Tchrs., 1964-70; mem. Arlington County Secondary Tchrs. Curriculum Council, 1968-70. Mem. N.E.A., Va., Arlington (dir. 1966-68) edn. assns., Am., No. Va. personnel and guidance assns., Am. Sch. Counselors Assn., Delta Kappa Gamma (pres. Alpha Omicron chpt. 1970-72). Democrat. Home: 2718 N Pollard St Arlington VA 22207 Office: 2700 S Lang St Arlington VA 22206

LANG, JAMES RUSSELL, JR., dentist; b. Waco, Tex., Aug. 20, 1939; s. James Russell and Helen (Reutzel) L.; B.S. in Biology, Centenary Coll. La., 1961; D.D.S., Loyola U., New Orleans, 1965; M.S.D. (USPHS fellow), Baylor U., 1969; m. Sara Ann Hitchcock, June 23, 1962; children—Rebecca Ann, Ainsley Helen. Chief resident pedodontics Childrens Med. Center, Dallas, 1968-69; practice dentistry, specializing in pedodontics, Shreveport, La., 1969—. Served to capt. Dental Corps, USAF, 1965-67. Mem. Am. Dental Assn., Am. Soc. Dentistry for Children, Am. Acad. Pedodontics, Kappa Sigma, Omicron Kappa Upsilon. Democrat. Methodist. Home: 4511 Tibbs St Shreveport LA 71105 Office: 5803 Youree Dr Shreveport LA 71105

LANG, JOHN ALBERT, JR., govt. ofcl., educator; b. Carthage, N.C., Nov.15, 1910; s. John Albert and Laura (Kelly) L.; B.A., U. N.C., 1930, M.A., 1931; grad. student Mercer U., 1931-32; m. Catherine Gibson, Nov. 20, 1947; children—John Albert III, Richard Gibson, Laura Catherine, Martha Elizabeth. Head English dept. Ga. Mil. Acad., 1931-33; pres. Nat. Student Govt. Fedn., N.Y.C., 1933-35; asst. to dir., edn. program Civilian Conservation Corps, 1935-38; adminstr. for N.C., NYA, 1938-42; staff asst. Better Health Assn., N.C., 1946-47; adminstrv. asst. to Congressman C.B. Deane, 1947-56; staff specialist govt. operations com. Ho. of Reps., 1956-57; adminstrv. asst. to Congressman R. E. Jones, 1957-61; dep. for Res. and ROTC affairs Office Sec. Air Force, 1961-64; acting spl. asst. to sec. air force for manpower, personnel and res. forces, 1965-66; adminstrv. asst. to sec. air force, 1964-71; professorial lectr. George Washington U., 1969-71; v.p. for external affairs East Carolina U., Greenville, N.C., 1971-72; sec. N.C. Dept. Mil. and Vets. Affairs, 1972—; lectr. profl. civic and ednl. groups, 1933—. Vice chmn. N.C. Democratic Conv., 1946. Bd. dirs. Washington Community Chest. Served from pvt. to maj. USAAF, 1942-46; ETO, PTO; maj. gen. USAF Res. Decorated Legion of Merit, Meritorious Service medal, Air Force Commendation medal, Army Commendation medal; recipient Algernon Sullivan award, 1931; Mangum Oratorial award U. N.C., 1931; citation NYA, 1938-42; scroll appreciation N.C. State Bd. Health, 1946; service citation Congl. Secretaries Club, 1956; Exceptional Civilian Service award Dept. Air Force, 1964, 66; citation N.C. Bur., 1944, Air Force Assn., 1964, 71, Am. Legion, 1962; certificate of recognition Md. Jr. C. of C., 1961; Distinguished Service citation Res. Officers Assn., 1963. Mem. Am. Acad. Polit. and Social Sci., Acad. Mgmt., Am. Soc. Pub. Adminstrn., Res. Officers Assn., Am. Legion, V.F.W., U. N.C. Alumni Assn., Nat. Vocational Guidance Assn., Air Force Assn., Phi Beta Kappa. Elk. Author articles, bulls., studies, surveys, reports in field. Home: 114 King George Rd Greenville NC 27834

LANG, LAWRENCE COPLEY, judge; b. Laredo, Tex., Nov. 14, 1919; s. Arthur Wilton and Katherine (Devine) L.; B.J., U. Tex., 1948, M.J., 1949; LL.B., St. Mary's U., San Antonio, 1956; m. Jeannette Lusk Brickell, Aug. 28, 1949. Tchr., Tex. Southmost Coll., San Antonio Ind. Sch. Dist., 1952-56; admitted to Tex. Bar, 1956; city prosecutor, San Antonio, 1956-58; judge, San Antonio, 1959—. Served as warrant officer, AUS, 1942-46; ETO. Recipient award Nat. Council on Alcoholism, 1967. Mem. Sigma Delta Chi, Delta Theta Phi. Elk. Home: 9910 Titan Dr San Antonio TX 78217 Office: 302 S Laredo St San Antonio TX 78204

LANGDALE, NOAH NOEL, JR., univ. pres.; b. Valdosta, Ga., Mar. 29, 1920; s. Noah N. and Jessie Katherine (Catledge) L.; A.B., U. Ala., 1941, LL.D., 1959; LL.B. Harvard, 1948, M.B.A., 1950; m. Alice Elizabeth Cabaniss, Jan. 8, 1944; 1 son, Michael. Assistant football coach U. Ala., 1942; admitted to Ga. bar, 1951; practiced in Valdosta, Ga., 1951-57; instr. Valdosta (Ga.) State Coll., 1954-55, asst. prof., 1955-57, chmn. bus. adminstrn. and econs. dept., 1955-57; pres. Ga. State U., Atlanta, 1957—. Dir. Guardian Life Ins. Co. Am., N.Y.C., Colonial Stores, Inc. Past chmn. Citizens Adv. com. for Urban Renewal, Atlanta; Ga. chmn. Nat. Football Found., Football Hall Fame. Served as lt. USNR, 1942-46; PTO. Named Georgian of the year, 1961-62; recipient Silver Anniversary All-American award Sports Illus.; Outstanding Civilian Service medal, Myrtle Wreath award Hadassah, 1970. Mem. Am., Ga. bar assns., Ga. Assn. Colls., (pres. 1962-63), S.A.R., Ga. Ednl. Assn., Atlanta C. of C., Phi Beta Kappa, Omicron Delta Kappa, Alpha Kappa Psi, Delta Chi, Phi Kappa Phi. Methodist. Clubs: Rotary, Capital City, Gridiron, Athletic, Touchdown (Atlanta). Home: 3807 Tuxedo Rd NW Atlanta GA 30305

LANGDON, JACK MUNCY, judge; b. Stamford, Tex., Dec. 15, 1910; s. George Muncy and Blanche (Oates) L.; B.S., Tex. Christian U., 1935; LL.B., U. Tex., 1941; m. Dora Lee Byars, Mar. 27, 1937; children—Jane (dec.), John Edmund. Admitted to Tex. bar, 1938; mem. Tex. Ho. of Reps., 1936-40; spl. agt. F.B.I., St. Paul, San Francisco Dallas, Washington, 1940-45; practiced in Fort Worth, 1945-50; judge 17th dist. ct., Fort Worth, 1951-63; presiding judge 8th adminstrv. jud. dist., 1957-63; asso. justice Ct. Civil Appeals, 2d Supreme Jud. Dist. of Tex., 1963—. Chmn. jud. sect. Tex. State Bar, 1968. Del. Nat. Dem. Conv. Phila., 1948. Trustee Tex. Christian U. Mem. Am., Tex., Fort Worth-Tarrant County bar assns. Baptist. Clubs: Kiwanis (dist. gov. 1961), Exchange. Home: 1227 Washington Terrace Fort Worth TX 76107 Office: Civil Cts Bldg Fort Worth TX 76102

LANGDON, JAMES LLOYD, food co. exec.; b. Smithfield, N.C., Oct. 6, 1918; s. James Uriah and Ruth (Dunn) L.; B.S., N.C. State U., 1940; postgrad. Asheville (N.C.) Law Sch., 1948, Northwestern U., 1953, Yale, 1955, Syracuse U., 1965; m. Madelyn Earl Pope, July 10, 1943; children—Madelyn Carol (Mrs. Ben Whitely Baker), Sheila Jeanne (Mrs. Clayton Pierce). Agrl. devel. agt. Carolina Power & Light Co., 1946-49; gen. mgr. Farmer Supply Co., 1949-50; exec. v.p. N.C. Dairy Products Assn., Raleigh, 1950-59; dir. marketing dairy div. Pet, Inc., Johnson City, Tenn., 1959-69, v.p. marketing, 1969, v.p. operations, 1969, exec. v.p., gen. mgr., 1969-70, pres., 1970—; dir. First Peoples Bank. Bd. dirs. So. States Indsl. Council, Milk Industry Found., Nat. Dairy Council, N.C. Dairy Found. Served to lt. col. USAAF, 1941-45. Mem. Pub. Relations Soc. Am., Tenn. Dairy Products Assn. (dir.), Internat. Assn. Ice Cream Mfrs. (dir.), Am. Legion. Mem. Christian Ch. Club: Johnson City Country. Home: Route 4 Knoll Vue Farm Johnson City TN 37601 Office: PO Box O CRS Johnson City TN 37601

LANGDON, ROBERT G., biochemist, educator; b. Dallas, Jan. 18, 1923; s. Clarence I. and Anne (Jones) L.; student So. Meth. U., 1939-42; B.S., U. Chgo., 1944, M.D., 1945, Ph.D. in Biochemistry, 1953; m. Ellen Adams Sandlas, June 16, 1945; children—Cecilia Marie (Mrs. Ben Gadd), Diana Lee, Camelia Sue, Robert Godwin. Mem. faculty Johns Hopkins Sch. Medicine, 1953-67, prof. physiol. chemistry, 1961-67; chmn. dept. biochemistry U. Fla. Sch. Medicine, Gainesville, 1967-69; prof. biochemistry U. Va. Sch. Medicine, Charlottesville, 1969—; cons. NIH, 1961-64, NSF, 1965—. Served to capt., M.C., AUS, 1946-48. Recipient Lederle Med. Faculty award. Mem. A.A.A.S., Am. Chem. Soc., Am. Soc. Biol. Chemists, Sigma Xi, Kappa Alpha. Contbr. to profl. jours. Home: Route 3 Box 193 Charlottesville VA 22901

LANGE, GLEN EVERETT, educator; b. Ft. Madison, Ia., Jan. 22, 1923; s. Clarence Edwin and Mary (Duff) L.; B.C.S, Drake U., 1950, M.A., Hardin-Simmons U., 1960; Ph.D., U. Mo., 1969; m. Thalen Redfern Ogg, Oct. 12, 1947; children—John Redfern, Andrew Charles, Megan Ruth. With Bill Curphy Co., Des Moines, 1950-55; chief accountant Zelrich Co., Dallas, 1955-58; instr. Hardin-Simmons U., Abilene, Tex., 1958-60, U. Mo., Columbia, 1960-62; asso. prof. accounting Western Ky. U., Bowling Green, 1962—, dept. head, 1964—. Commr., City of Bowling Green, 1969—. Served with USAAF, 1943-46. Mem. Delta Sigma Pi. Episcopalian. Home: 2744 Cheyenne Dr Bowling Green KY 42101

LANGE, JEAN RUTHVEN WILSHIRE, writer; b. Eastbourne, Sussex, Eng., Jan. 28, 1902; d. Ruthven Matcham and Millicent Ida (Thomson) Wilshire; student Northfield Pvt. Coll., Watford, Eng., 1919-20; m. Hans Albrecht F. Lange, Apr. 4, 1931 (dec. Aug. 1965); children—Anneliese Johanna, Jack H.; 1 stepdau., Ingeborg Edith. Appeared in Brit. theatre prodns. Rose Marie, 1925-27, The Barretts of Wimpole Street, 1932, Payment Deferred, 1931; appeared in Spanish theatres, Madrid, Barcelona, Valencia, 1924; appeared with Dame May Whitty's Repertory Co., London, 1928-29; news corr. Radio Free Europe, Frankfurt am Main, Germany, 1952-55; dir. pub. relations Montclair (N.J.) Art Mus., 1956-61; writer, producer KLRN-TV, ednl. TV, San Antonio/Austin, 1962—. Mem. U.S. Com. for Refugees, 1960—, Assn. for UN, 1958-61. Recipient citation for services to refugee cause U.S. Com. for Refugees, 1961. Mem. Am. Women in Radio and Television, Internat. Platform Assn., Theta Sigma Phi, Rho Tau Sigma. Contbg. editor San Antonio Mag., 1967-68. Contbr. articles to mags. Home: 8035 Fredericksburg Rd No. 15 San Antonio TX 78229

LANGENFELD, JAMES MICHAEL, dentist; b. Centralia, Ill., June 6, 1942; s. James Richard and Mary Alice (Hill) L.; B.A., Wabash Coll., Crawfordsville, Ind., 1964; D.D.S., Ind. U., 1968; m. Cynthia Ann Glass, Mar. 30, 1962; children—Andrew Michael, Angela Jane. Dental intern U.S. Army Hosp., Ft. Jackson, Columbia, S.C., 1968-69; chief prosthetics periodontal and treatment planning sects. Hunter Army Airfield, Savannah, Ga., 1969-70; stationed in Vietnam, 1970-71; individual practice dentistry, Tifton, Ga., 1971—. Mem. Am., Ga. dental assns., Am. Soc. Dentistry for Children, Southwestern Dist. Dental Soc., Kappa Sigma, Psi Omega, Omicron Kappa Upsilon. Presbyn. Elk. Club: Spring Hills Country (Tifton). Home: 2002 N Central Av Tifton GA 31794 Office: 434 Virginia Av Tifton GA 31794

LANGER, MARSHALL JAY, lawyer, banker; b. N.Y.C., May 30, 1928; s. Samuel and Edna (Klein) L.; B.S. in Econs., U. Pa., 1948; J.D. summa cum laude, U. Miami, 1951; m. Sally Blass, Apr. 3, 1955 (div. 1967); children—Andrew H., Jeffrey S.; m. 2d, Barbara Slatko, Feb. 15, 1970. Admitted to Fla. bar, 1951, since practiced in Miami; mem. firm Bittel Langer & Blass, 1965—; lectr., acting dir. Inter-Am. law program U. Miami Sch. Law, 1955-56, adj. prof., 1965—; exchange prof. law U. Havana, Cuba, 1956; also lectr. tax insts.; pres., mng. dir. Grand Cayman Bank Ltd. (B.W.I.); dir. Internat. Bank, Sterling Bank & Trust Co., Fla. Title Co., N.Am. Investment Fund, N.Am. Bank Stock Fund. Chmn. programs on doing bus. in Caribbean, Practising Law Inst., 1972. Mem. The Fla. Bar (chmn. tax sect. com. on fgn. income 1964-68), Am., Inter-Am. (asst. sec. gen. 1956-61), Dade County bar assns., Am. Fgn. Law Assn. (cht. pres. 1955), Greater Miami Tax Inst. (pres. 1967), Iron Arrow, Zeta Beta Tau (nat. historian, 1959-60), Omicron Delta Kappa, Phi Kappa Phi. Contbr. articles in field. Home: 7330 SW 113th St Miami FL 33156 Office: City Nat Bank Bldg Miami FL 33130 also PO Box 712 Grand Cayman British West Indies

LANGFORD, BOBBY RAY, fire chief; b. Weatherford, Tex., Oct. 6, 1929; s. William L. and Pauliyn (Carter) L.; student Pharmacy Sch., 1948, Tex. A. and M. U., 1956, 60, Civil Def. Sch., Battle Creek, Mich., 1965; m. Dayle Farmer, Mar. 25, 1951; children—David, Larry. With Grand Prairie (Tex.) Fire Dept., 1950—, fire chief, 1961—. Asst. dir. Civil Def., 1965—. Served with AUS, 1947-50. Mem. Dallas County Fire Chiefs Assn. (pres. 1968). Rotarian. Home: 1717 Acosta St Grand Prairie TX 75050 Office: 321 W Main St Grand Prairie TX 75050

LANGFORD, GERALD TALMADGE, exploration co. exec.; b. Kilgore, Tex., Jan. 13, 1935; s. DeWitt and Lillian (Easterling) L.; student Southwestern U., 1952; B.S., U. Tex., Austin, 1957; m. Ora Kay Hess, June 11, 1954; children—Cheryl Kay, Randall Dewitt, Robin Leigh, David Larkin, Matthew, Mary Camille. Gold surveyor, Alaska, 1952; uranium surveyor, Wyo., 1953-55; pres. Tex-L Corp., 1957-67; pres. Cal-L Corp., Santa Barbara, Cal., 1959-68; chief geologist, dir. Sabre Petroleum Corp., 1968-70, pres., chief geologist, 1970—; pres. Am. Energy Corp. Mem. Am. Assn. Petroleum Geologists, Kappa Alpha. Home: Dallas TX Office: 551 Wright Bros Dr PO Box 3122 Addison TX 75001

LANGFORD, JOHN R., sec. Fla. Bd. Vet. Medicine. Address: 932 Mason Av Daytona Beach FL 32017*

LANGFORD, JOHN SHOLAR, JR., judge; b. Atlanta, July 4, 1931; s. John Sholar and Virginia (Flynt) L.; B.S., Auburn U., 1953; LL.B., Emory U., 1958; m. Margaret Hodgson Ellis, June 9, 1956; children—John Sholar III, Martha Ellen, David Ellis. Law clk. to mem. U.S. Ho. of Reps. from Ga., Washington, 1956; admitted to Ga. bar, 1957; mem. firm Bryan, Carter, Ansley & Smith, Atlanta, 1957-66; judge Civil Ct. Fulton County, Atlanta, 1966-68, Juvenile Ct., 1968—. Bd. Dirs. Children's Center Met. Atlanta. Served as 1st lt. USAF, 1954-55. Mem. Am., Ga., Atlanta bar assns., Lawyers Club Atlanta, Am. Judicature Soc., Southeastern Conf. Football Ofcls. Assn. Episcopalian (vestryman 1962-68, jr. warden 1968). Club: Touchdown (Atlanta, pres. 1965). Home: 2765 Northside Dr NW Atlanta GA 30305 Office: 445 Capitol Av SW Atlanta GA 30312

LANGFORD, THOMAS ANDERSON, JR., educator; b. Winston-Salem, N.C., Feb. 22, 1929; s. Thomas Anderson and Louie Mae (Hughes) L.; A.B., Davidson Coll., 1951; B.D., Duke, 1954, Ph.D. (Gurney Harris Kearns fellow, Dempster fellow), 1958; m. Ann Marie Daniel, Dec. 27, 1951; children— Thomas A., James Howard, Timothy Daniel, Stephen Hughes. Mem. faculty, Duke, 1956—, prof. theology, 1966—, chmn. dept. religion, 1965-71, dean Div. Sch., 1971—; vis. prof. U. N.C., Chapel Hill, summer 1962; ordained to ministry Methodist Ch., 1954. Recipient E. Harris Harbison award for distinguished teaching Danforth Found., 1965-66; named to Hall of Fame, Central (Garringer) High Sch., Charlotte, N.C., 1965; named Outstanding Tchr. of Undergrads., Duke, 1965; Am. Council Learned Socs. Study fellow, 1965-66; Soc. for Religion in Higher Edn. Postdoctoral fellow, 1969. Editor: (with George L. Abernathy) Philosophy of Religion, 1962, History of Philosophy, 1965; (with William H. Poteat) Intellect and Hope, Essays in the Thought of Michael Polaany, 1968; Author: In Search of Foundations: English Theology 1900-1920, 1969; (with G. L. Abernathy) Introduction to Western Philosophy: Pre-Socratics to Mill, 1970; also articles. Home: 2002 Dartmouth Dr Durham NC 27705

LANGLAND, CHARLES ALBERT, systems analyst; b. Manchester, Ia., Mar. 28, 1929; s. Thore and Mary Delight (Robison) L.; B.S. in Math., U. S.D., 1951; m. Betty Lou Good, July 2, 1951; children—Ruth Ann, Marc C., Thomas J. Geophysicist, head geophysics-data processing Gen. Geophys. Co., Rocky Mountain and Gulf Coast area, 1951-63; systems engr. IBM Corp., Houston, 1963-67; co-founder, v.p., dir. Asso. Computer Services, Inc., Houston, 1967—. Recipient award for helping install 1st system 360 in world for IBM Mem. Soc. Exploration Geophysicists. Mem. Christian Ch. (mem. bd. 1966-68, mem. bd. 1970—, chmn. deacons 1971—). Home: 10026 Briar Dr Houston TX 77042 Office: 5433 Westheimer Houston TX 77027

LANGLEY, EDWIN, dist. judge; b. Prague, Okla., Oct. 28, 1908; s. Dallas and Katherine (Hobbs) L.; B.S. Harvard, 1932; LL.B., Tulsa Law Sch., 1940; m. Jessie Evans Cosgrove, Nov. 27, 1936; children—Caroline, James Cosgrove. Admitted to Okla. bar, 1940; practiced in Muskogee, 1940-61; U.S. atty. Eastern Dist. Okla., 1961-65; U.S. dist. judge, 1965, chief judge Eastern U.S. Dist. Ct. of Okla, 1965—. Chmn. Okla Indsl. Commn., 1953-54. Mem. Okla. Ho. of Reps., 1949-52. Served to col. AUS, 1942-46. Mem. Okla., Muskogee County bar assns. Club: Muskogee Country. Home: 1011 S Terrace Muskogee OK 74401 Office: Fed Bldg Muskogee OK 74401

LANGLINAIS, JOSEPH WILLIS, clergyman, univ. dean; b. San Antonio, Tex., Aug. 12, 1922; B.S., U. Dayton, 1943; B.A., U. Fribourg, 1952, M.A., 1953, S.T.D., 1954. Ordained priest Roman Catholic Ch.; dir. admissions Chaminade Coll. Prep. Sch., St. Louis, 1957-59; dir. religious formation Marynook Marianist Novitiate, Galesville, Wis., 1959-63; asso. prof. theology St. Mary's U., San Antonio, 1963—, dean Sch. Arts and Scis., 1964—. Mem. Catholic Theol. Soc. Am., Coll. Theol. Soc., Am. Mariology Soc., Religious Edn. Assn., Am. Assn. U. Profs., Am. Archaeol. Soc., Soc. for Sci. Study Religion. Contbr. article to New Catholic Ency. Office: School Arts and Sciences St Mary's University 2700 Cincinnati Av San Antonio TX 78228*

LANGNER, WILLIAM RANKIN, ednl. adminstr.; b. Morrisville, N.Y., Dec. 23, 1931; s. Herbert William and Helen (Rankin) L.; student Coll. William and Mary, 1949-53; B.A., U. Va., 1957. Tchr. Blue Ridge Sch., St. George, Va., 1958-59; chmn. bd., pres., treas., dir. Langner Learning Center, Richmond, Va., 1964—; pres. Langner Found. Mem. Gov's. Study Commn. Vocational Rehab., 1966-68; vice chmn. Va. Adv. Com. on Workshops and Facilities, 1966-68; mem. Va. Bd. Vocational Rehab., 1971—; pres. Richmond Area Rehab. Center, 1971—. Bd. dirs., v.p. Richmond chpt. Easter Seal Soc. Va., 1966-71; pres. Richmond council Internat. Reading Assn., 1968-69, dir., 1971—; mem., former sec.-treas. Central Va. Soc. for Children with Learning Disabilities; chmn. bd. Cordet Found., 1965-71. Recipient Distinguished Service award West End Jaycees, Richmond, Va., 1967. Mem. Paralyzed Vets. Am. (hon.), Jefferson Soc., Alpha Kappa Psi, Kappa Delta Pi. Republican. Episcopalian. Moose. Author: (with William S. Blackwell) Reading Comprehension in Social Studies, 1968; (with Eric A. Foretich) Reading Comprehension in the Natural Sciences, 1968. Address: 102 N Adams St Richmond VA 23220

LANGSTON, FRANK, columnist Dallas Times-Herald. Address: 1101 Pacific St Dallas TX 75202*

LANGSTON, JAMES TAYLOR, JR., metal products co. exec.; b. Houston, Apr. 18, 1923; s. James Taylor and Hazel Diamond (Parker) L.; student Tex. A. and M. U., 1942-43; m. Edith Wanda Barnes, Apr. 6, 1945; children—Leonard, Lynda (Mrs. Wallace Frix), Benjamin, Clay. Vice pres. Tayloe Glass Co., 1947-65, also Tayloe Aluminum Co., 1958-65; vice pres. William Bond, Inc., Memphis, 1969—; dir. W.W. Bond, Inc.; pres. Bond. Mfg. Co., Alumiglas Fronts, Inc. (Tenn., La. and Fla.), 1965-69. Dir. Tenn. N.G. Civil Air Patrol. Served as 1st lt. USAAF, 1943-47. Methodist. Designer, mfr. window wall system of extruded aluminum. Home: 4153 Kriter Lane Memphis TN 38117 Office: 324 E Brooks Rd Memphis TN 38117

LANGSTON, JOANN HANKINS (MRS. DONALD BOBBY LANGSTON), educator; b. Burkburnett, Tex., Jan. 23, 1930; d. John Felix and Mary (Hepner) Hankins; student Madison Coll., 1947-48; B.S., N. Tex. State Coll., 1951; M.Ed., Tex. Wesleyan Coll., 1955; m. Donald Bobby Langston, Jan. 24, 1952; children—Donald Bobby, John David. Tchr. various schs., Tex., 1951-55; faculty Tex. Wesleyan Coll., Fort Worth, 1955—, asst. prof. journalism, 1960—, dir. student publs., 1955—. Reporter, Courier, 1966—. Mem. Nat. Council Coll. Publs. Advisers, Am. Assn. U. Women, Tex. Wesleyan Coll. Alumni Assn. (dir. 1968—), Tex. Intercollegiate Press Advisers Assn. (sec. 1970-71), Pi Delta Epsilon (hon.), Theta Sigma Phi (chpt. v.p. 1959-60, del. nat. conv. 1960), Delta Kappa Gamma. Clubs: Junior Woman's (2d v.p. lit. sect. 1964-65), Woman's, Tex. Wesleyan College Faculty Women's (pres. 1963), Woman's Shakespeare (rec. sec. 1969-70, chmn. press com. 1970-71, mem.-at-large 1971-72, 1st v.p. 1972-73). Contbr. articles profl. publs. Editor: Jr. Jour., 1964-65. Home: 4813 Hollowbrook Rd Fort Worth TX 76103

LANHAM, BEN TILLMAN, JR., univ. adminstr.; b. Edgefield, S.C., Apr. 5, 1917; s. Ben Tillman and Mary (Shaw) L.; B.S., Clemson U., 1937; M.S., U. Tenn., 1938; postgrad. Ia. State U., 1938-39; Ph.D., Mich. State U., 1960; m. Bernice Arnold, June 29, 1941; children—Ben Tillman III, Betty Anne. Research asst. U. Tenn., 1937-38, Mich. State U., 1954-55, Ia. State U., 1938-39; asst. prof. Auburn (Ala.) U., 1939-46, asso. prof., 1946-48, prof., 1948-56, prof., head dept. agrl. econs., 1956-64, asso. dir. Agr. Expt. Sta., asst. dean Sch. Agr., 1964-66, v.p. research, 1966-72, v.p. adminstrn., 1972—. Pres. Research Found., chmn. Research Council, chmn. research grant-in-aid com. Auburn U.; chmn. Ala. Water Resources Research Inst. Council; mem. adv. com. Ala. Program Devel. Office. Served from 2d lt. to maj. Inf., AUS, 1942-46. Mem. A.A.A.S., Am. Farm Econ. Assn., Am., So. econ. assns., Am. Marketing Assn., Am. Acad. Polit. and Social Sci., Am. Sociol. Soc., Assn. So. Agrl. Workers, Internat. Conf. Agrl. Economists, Ala. Acad. Sci., Ala. Edn. Assn., Nat. Council U. Research Adminstrs., Council for Research Policy and Adminstrn. Land-Grant Coll. Assn., Sigma Xi, Gamma Alpha Mu, Gamma Sigma Delta, Omicron Delta Epsilon, Phi Delta Kappa, Omicron Delta Kappa. Baptist. Kiwanian. Contbr. articles profl. jours. Home: 536 S Gay St Auburn AL 36830

LANIER, BILL ED, mfg. co. exec.; b. Ada, Okla., Sept. 5, 1937; s. William Franklin and Jewel Ozella (Martin) L.; B.B.A., U. Okla., 1961; m. Janet Gaye McLin, Jan. 30, 1965; children—Jamie Jan, Christin Gaye, Roderick William. Supr. accounting office Southwestern Bell Telephone Co., Topeka, Kan., 1963; financial analyst Continental Pipeline Co., Ponca City, Okla., 1964-67; dir. personnel, plant mgr., mgr. scheduling systems Sequoyah Industries, Oklahoma City, 1967—. Bd. dirs. Oklahoma City council Boy Scouts Am., 1969-70. Served with AUS, 1961-63. Mem. Soc. Advancement Mgmt., Davis C. of C. (pres., 1969-70), U.S. Armor Officers Assn. (chmn. 1962-63), Beta Gamma Sigma. Methodist. Elk. Home: 10405 Major Av Oklahoma City OK 73120 Office: 4545 N Lincoln Blvd Oklahoma City OK 73105

LANIER, DAVID WILLIAM, lawyer, mayor; b. Newbern, Tenn., Nov. 16, 1934; s. James Parker and Robbye (Sullivan) L.; student Memphis State U., 1952-55; LL.B., U. Tenn., 1958; m. Mary Joan Mills, Dec. 2, 1962; children—Leigh Anne, Robbye Claire. Admitted to Tenn. bar, 1959; since practiced in Dyersburg; mem. firms—David W. Lanier 1959—; mayor, Dyersburg, 1966—. Mem. adv. council Peoples Protective Life Ins. Co., Jackson, Tenn., 1965—. Nat. exec. committeeman Parade Am., 1967, Cerebral Palsy Telethon, 1967, 70. Alderman, Dyersburg, 1966-65; Dyer County campaign mgr. Buford Ellington for Gov., 1966; state chmn. Mayor's for Hooker for Gov. com., 1970; v.p. Tenn. Young Democrats, 1962-67, 8th dist. committeeman, 1966-68. Served with Air N.G. Col.-Aide de Camp, Gov. Buford Ellington's Staff. Bd. dirs. Vocational Rehab. Tng. Center. Mem. Bar Assn. Tenn., Dyer County Bar Assn. (pres. 1971-72), Tenn. Law Enforcement Officers Assn., Fraternal Order Police, Memphis State U. Alumni Assn. (mem. adv. council 1966-68, nat. dir., 1967-71, mem. legislative relations com. 1967-68), Tenn. Municipal League (dir. 1968-71, pres. 1971-72), Downtown Mchts. Assn. (dir.), Jr. C. of C., C. of C. (dir.), Rotary, Phi Delta Phi, Kappa Sigma. Mem. Ch. of Christ. Mason (Shriner), Moose. Club: Dyersburg Boosters (dir.). Home: 2117 Starlight Dr Dyersburg TN 38024 Office: First Citizens Nat Bank Bldg Dyersburg TN 38024

LANIER, ERNEST WILSON, physician; b. Elton, La., Oct. 4, 1918; s. Morgan Martin and Lillian (Clements) L.; A.A., Lamar Coll., 1948; M.D., Southwestern Med. Coll., 1953; student U. Tex., 1948-49; m. Maxine Bailey, Nov. 10, 1939; children—Jacquelyn Ruth, Norman Preston, Michael Roland. Tchr. math. Civilian Conservation Corps, 1937-39; shipping, receiving clk. Sears Roebuck & Co., Port Arthur, Tex., 1939; dock man helper terminal dept. Tex. Co., Port Arthur, 1939-43, bulk oil dept., summers 1946-52; intern VA Hosp., Houston, 1953-54; mem. staff St. Mary's Hosp., mem. staff Park Place Hosp., Port Arthur, v.p. 1970-71. Dir. Rainbow Devel. Corp., Port Arthur, 1960—. Dir Mid-Jefferson County unit Am. Cancer Soc., 1960-61; mem. adv. bd. Jefferson County Chpt. Med. Assts. Assn. Served with USAAF, 1943-46. Mem. Am. Acad. Gen. Practice, Jefferson County Med. Soc. Am., Tex. med. assns., Am. Heart Assn., C. of C., Nat. Rifle Assn., Phi Beta Pi, Phi Theta Kappa. Democrat. Baptist. Rotarian (past pres.). Clubs: Snorkle Skin Divers (med. examiner 1959—), Sabine Neches Sportsman.Home: 65358 Jefferson Blvd Groves TX 77619 Office: 5700 39th St Groves TX 77619

LANIER, JAMES GIBSON, freight co. exec.; b. Birmingham, Ala., Jan. 7, 1920; s. Russel D'Lyon and Martha Henrietta (Gibson) L.; student Coll. Engring., U. Ala., 1936-40; m. Mildred Jeanett Pipes, Jan. 9, 1943; children—James Gibson Jr., Randolph Houston. Engr., Jones &Donan, Madisonville, Ky., cons. engrs., 1946-48; chief engr. Norton Coal Corp., Nortonville, Ky., 1948-52; with Malone Freight Lines, Inc., Birmingham, 1952—, v.p., 1963—, dir., 1963—. Served to lt. comdr. USNR, 1940-46. Decorated Silver Star. Mem. Alpha Tau Omega. Clubs: Birmingham Country, Birmingham Sailing, Relay House (Birmingham). Home: 2832 Hastings Rd Mountain Brook AL 35223 Office: 200 S 35th St Birmingham AL 35202

LANIER, JAMES OLANDA, lawyer; b. Newbern, Tenn., Sept. 8, 1931; s. James Parker and Robbye (Sullivan) L.; student U. Tenn., 1949, U. Tenn. Jr. Coll., 1950-51; B.S., Memphis State Coll., 1955, J.D., Memphis State U., 1969; m. Carolyn Holland, June 1, 1950; children— James Elton, Donna Kay, Robbye Ann (dec.), Amy Claire. Indsl. engr. Milan (Tenn.) Arsenal, 1953-54; social worker Dept. Pub. Welfare, Memphis, 1955-57, sr. social worker, appeals examiner, 1957-58; dir. Surplus Commodities, Dyer County, Tenn., 1958; pres., gen. mgr. Main Sporting Goods, Inc., Dyersburg, Tenn., 1959-62; tech. engr. Milan Ordnance Plant (Tenn.), 1961-63; special investigator Tenn. Dept. Pub. Welfare, Nashville, 1963-67; ins. adjuster U.S. Fidelity & Guaranty Co., 1967-69; pvt. practice law, Dyersburg, Tenn., 1969—; county atty. Dyer County, 1972—. Mem. Tenn. Ho. of Reps., 1959-62, 71-72. Pres. Dyer County chpt. Muscular Dystrophy Assns. Am., 1958-60. Mem. Jr. C. of C. (past treas.) (hon.) Tenn. Law Enforcement Officers Assn., Am., Dyersburg-Dyer County (sec.-treas.) bar assns., Bar Assn. Tenn., Am., Tenn. trial lawyers assns., Am. Judicature Soc., Dyer County C. of C., Sigma Delta Kappa (pres. 1967-68). Democrat (W. Tenn. pres. Young Democrats of Tenn. 1957-63). Mem. Ch. of Christ. Moose (jr. gov. 1959-60, gov. 1960-62, chmn. com. civic affairs, recipient fellowship degree and gov.'s award of merit 1963). Clubs: Dyersburg Kiwanis, Dyersburg Country. Home: 617 Sunset Blvd Dyersburg TN 38024 Office: 105 N Main St Dyersburg TN 38024

LANIER, JOSEPH L(AMAR), textile mfr.; b. Jackson, Ga., Feb. 12, 1906; s. George H. and Marie (Lamar) L.; student Washington and Lee U., 1923-27; m. Lura Fowlkes, Feb. 17, 1931; children—Joseph Lamar, Lura Fowlkes, Anne Rutledge. Chmn. bd., chief exec. officer West Point-Peppell, Inc.; chmn. bd. Wellington Sears Co.; dir. Cabin Crafts, Inc., First Nat. Bank of Atlanta, Atlanta & West Point R.R. Co., Western Ry. of Ala., Rivington Carpets, Ltd. (Brit.). Trustee Inst. Textile Tech., Washington and Lee U., Nat. Safety Council, LaGrange Coll. Mem. Bus. Council, Am. Textile Mfrs. Inst. (dir.). Home: West Point GA 31833 Office: Box 71 West Point GA 31833

LANIER, WILLIAM DONALD, engr., municipal ofcl.; b. Albany, Ga., Sept. 25, 1929; s. Jefferson Bradwell and Angeline (Davis) L.; student North Ga. Coll., 1946-48; B.S.C.E., Ga. Inst. Tech., 1951; m. Sylvia Sue Smith, June 15, 1957; children—Lewis Tod, David Charles, Sue Angeline. Chmn. to party chief Marbury Engring. Co., Albany, 1947-51, party chief, 1954-56; project engr. Wright Contracting Co., Columbus, Ga., 1956-57; asst. city engr., dir. pub. works Albany, Ga., 1957—. Served as 2d lt. AUS, 1951-53. Home: 1318 Gail Av Albany GA 31705 Office: 401 11th Av Albany GA 31705

LANMON, JAMES MONROE, educator; b. Lexington, Tex., Jan. 12, 1917; s. Thomas William and Etta Rosella (Magee) L.; B.A., U. Tex., 1945, M.A., 1947, Ph.D., 1954; m. Virginia May Mehaffey, Sept. 3, 1948; children—Jonathan Thomas, Maynona Louise, James Monroe, Benjamin Herbert. Pastor, Spicewood, Schwertner and McDade Bapt. chs., 1942-47; past asso. prof. edn. Howard Coll., Birmingham, Ala.; teaching fellow ednl. psychology U. Tex., Austin, 1948-52; prof. psychology Miss. Coll., Clinton, 1952-62; asst. prof. psychology E. Tex. State U., Commerce, 1962-64, asso. prof., 1964-67, prof., 1967—, acting head dept., 1967-72, head dept., 1972—. Mem. Am., Miss. (pres. 1960-61), Southwestern, Tex. psychol. assns., N.E.A., Tex. Tchrs. Assn., Phi Delta Kappa. Home: 1620 Bonham St Commerce TX 75428

LANSDELL, SARAH WILKERSON, art critic; b. Sandersville, Ga., Sept. 5, 1920; d. Julian Lyle and Imogene (Swint) Wilkerson; student Armstrong Coll., Savannah, Ga., 1938-40; A.B. in Journalism, U. Ga., 1942; grad. student Tulane U., 1948-49, U. Ga., 1949-50; m. Joseph Truett Lansdell, Apr. 5, 1944 (dec. 1950); 1 dau., Lyle. Reporter, arts critic Savannah Morning News, 1942-44; asso. editor weekly Sandersville (Ga.) Progress, 1946-48; woman's editor, arts critic Macon (Ga.) News, 1950-53; mem. staff Louisville Courier-Jour., 1953—, art editor, critic, 1962—. Mem. Com. to Rescue Italian Art, 1966-67. Mem. Theta Sigma Pi, Sigma Delta Chi. Democrat. Unitarian-Universalist. Office: 525 W Broadway Louisville KY 40202

LANSFORD, DOYLE KEITH, physician; b. Custer City, Okla., Jan. 26, 1931; s. William Harrison and Dorothy Missouri (Baker) L.; B.S., Baylor U., 1951; M.D., Tulane U., 1955; m. Tommie Elizabeth Berry, Feb. 11, 1956; children—James Randal, David Michael, Laura Jean, Elizabeth Ann. Intern, Charity Hosp., New Orleans, 1955-56; practice medicine specializing in family practice, Arlington, Tex., 1959—; mem. staff Arlington Meml. Hosp., Arlington Community Hosp. Served with M.C. USAF, 1956-58. Diplomate Am. Bd. Family Practice. Mem. Am. Acad. Family Practice, A.M.A. Home: 2805 Black Oak Lane Arlington TX 76012 Office: 2306 E Park Row Arlington TX 76010

LANTRIP, ROBERT RYE, city clk.; b. Amory, Miss., Aug. 30, 1924; s. Olen and Ellen (Rye) L.; student E.Miss. Jr. Coll., 1949-50; B.S., Miss. State U., 1953; m. Joyce Marie Keeton, July 2, 1955; children—James Michael, Melinda Ruth, Kimberly Joyce. Accountant, Crown Chem. & Mfg. Co., West Point, Miss., 1953-55; accountant Maddox Motor Co., Aberdeen, Miss., 1955-56; accountant Jones Motor Co., Amory, 1956-68; with Monroe County Welfare Dept., Aberdeen, 1969; city clk., tax collector, adminstr. City of Amory, 1969—. Served with inf AUS, 1943-45; ETO. Decorated Purple Heart. Mem. City Clks. Assn. Miss., Am. Legion, V.F.W. Club: Civitan (treas.). Home: 400 7th Av N Amory MS 38821 Office: PO Box 6 Amory MS 38821

LANTZ, JOHN EDWARD, clergyman; b. Edgerton, O., June 7, 1911; s. John M. and Elizabeth (Conrad) L.; A.B., DePauw U., 1934; B.D., Yale, 1938; M.A., Mich. U., 1942; Litt.D., Evang. Bible Coll.

and Sem., 1969; m. Ruth Esther Cox, Aug. 26, 1937; children—Thomas Edward, John Harvey, Alma Esther. Ordained to ministry Meth. Ch., 1939; teaching fellow U. Mich., 1940-42; instr. McCormick Theol. Sem., 1943-45; editorial staff Meth. Ch., 1945-51; pastor Meth. Ch. South Bend, Ind., 1951-55; exec. dir. so. office Nat. Council Chs., Atlanta, 1955-65; vis. instr. Interdenom. Theol. Conter, Atlanta, 1959-65, asst. prof. speech and communication, 1965-67, asso. prof. communications and ecumenics, 1967—; lectr. speech Vanderbilt U. Sch. Religion, 1946-50; instr. speech U. Tenn. Extension Div., Nashville, 1948-50; vis. instr. Gammon Theological Seminary, 1957-59. Bd. trustees and visitors DePauw U., 1954-57; trustee Protestant Radio and TV Center, Atlanta, 1955-63; mem. men's com. Japan Internat. Christian U. Mem. Ga. Writers Assn., Dixie Council Authors and Journalists, Internat. Platform Assn., UN Assn. Am., World Council Christian Edn. (N.Am. regional com.; voting del. to gen. assembly, Lima, Peru, 1971), Speech Assn. Am., Atlanta Writer's Club. Kiwanian. Club: Druid Hills Golf. Author: Speaking in the Church, 1954; Church Councils in the South, 1957; Reading the Bible Aloud, 1959; (with Ruth Cox Lantz) Bible Characters in Action, 1955, Plays for Happier Homes, 1957; also numerous articles in field. Editor: Best Religious Stories, 1948; Stories of Christian Living, 1950; Stories to Grow By, 1953. Home: 1040 Springdale Rd NE Atlanta GA 30306 Office: 671 Beckwith St SW Atlanta GA 30314

LANTZ, ROBERT BRYAN, clergyman; b. Mansfield, O., Jan. 11, 1936; s. William Bryan and Dorothy (Weatherbie) L.; A.B., Wittenberg U., 1958; graduate Hamma Div. Sch., 1961; m. Katherine I. Isenhour, Aug. 10, 1958. Ordained to ministry Luth. Ch., 1961; chaplain Ohio State Tb Hosp., Columbus, 1959, Univ. Hosp., 1960-61, Trinity Luth. Ch., Akron, O., 1961-63, chaplain Med. Coll. Va., 1963-66; dir. chaplain's dept. Balt. City Hosps., 1965-66; chmn. dept. pastoral care U. Tenn. Med. Units, 1966-69; dir. field edn. and pastoral counseling St. Paul's Coll., Washington, 1969—; asst. prof. pastoral counselling Memphis Theol. Sem., dir. Inst. Medicine and Religion, Memphis. Chaplain Supr. Council for Clin. Tng., Inc., N.Y.C., Lutheran Council U.S.A., N.Y.C. Fellow Am. Assn. Pastoral Counselors; mem. Assn. for Clin Pastoral Edn., Alpha Tau Omega. Kiwanian. Club: Annapolis Yacht (Md.). Home: 1055 Norman Dr Annapolis MD 21403 Office: 3015 4th St NE Washington DC 20017

LANTZ, RUTH COX (MRS. JOHN EDWARD LANTZ), educator; b. Gainesville, Fla., Jan. 11, 1914; d. Harvey Warren and Daisy (Frisbie) Cox; A.B., Emory U., 1934; postgrad. Yale, 1935-36, Pratt Inst., 1936; M.A., U. Mich., 1942; m. John Edward Lantz, Aug. 26, 1937; children—Thomas Edward, John Harvey, Alma Esther. Tchr. Druid Hills Sch., 1934-35; instr. speech Vanderbilt U., 1946-52; speech tchr. St. Mary's Acad., 1952; instr. religious edn. Interdenominational Theol. Center, Atlanta, 1960-69; speaker, dramatic reader various chs., women's groups. Chmn. publicity United Ch. Women of Ga., 1955-56, chmn. individual membership, 1957, chmn. pub. relations, 1961-63; dist. camping chmn. Camp Fire Girls, Atlanta council, 1956-58, pres., 1958-60, program chmn., 1961-64, regional exec. com., 1961—, sec., 1962-66, mem. nat. com. 1966-68; bd. dirs. YWCA, Atlanta, 1963-69; Nashville pres. Fellowship of Reconciliation, 1950-51, mem. nat. council, 1950-55; pres. County Sunday sch. Conv., Monroe, Mich., 1938-39. Mem. women's planning com. Internat. Christian U. Japan. Mem. Am. Assn. U. Women (chmn. creative writing group Atlanta br. 1969—), Religious Edn. Assn. Clubs: Georgia Writers, Atlanta Writers, Atlanta Artists, Am. Bus. Women's Assn. Author: (with J. Edward Lantz) Bible Characters in Action, 1955; Plays for Happier Homes, 1957; also numerous poems, articles, plays in field of art and religion. Editor: The Shepherdess, 1950-58. Illustrator: Speaking in the Church, 1954. Home: 1040 Springdale Rd Atlanta GA 30306

LAPIDUS, MORRIS, architect, interior designer; b. Odessa, Russia, Nov. 25, 1902; s. Leon and Eva (Sherman) L.; came to U.S., 1903, naturalized, 1914; B. Architecture, Columbia, 1927; m. Beatrice Perlman, Feb. 22, 1929; children—Richard L., Alan H. With Warren & Wetmore, N.Y.C., 1926-28, Arthur Weiser, N.Y.C., 1928-30; assn. architect Ross-Frankel, Inc. (now Morris Lapidus Associates), N.Y.C., 1930-42, prin., 1942—; pioneered use of modern in mdsg. field; areas of work include hotels, shopping centers, office bldgs., religious instns.; architect-designer Fontainebleau Hotel, 1954, Eden Roc Hotel, 1955, Americana Hotel, 1956 (all Miami Beach, Fla.), Sheraton Motor Inn, N.Y.C., Cadman Plaza, Bklyn., S.W. Urban Redevel., Washington, Americana Hotel, N.Y.C., Cadman Plaza Devel., N.Y.C., Bedford-Stuyvesant Municipal Swimming Pool, N.Y.C., Paradise Island Hotel, Nassau, Mt. Sinai Continuing Care Pavilion; lectr. store hotel design. Mem. Miami Beach Devel. Commn. Named Citizen of Year in Miami Beach, 1961. Mem. A.I.A., Am. Inst. Decorators, Archtl. League, Nat. Inst. Archtl. Edn., Municipal Art Soc., N.Y., Guild for Religious Architecture, Miami/Beach C. of C. Kiwanian, Elk. Author: Architecture—A Profession and A Business. Home: 3 Island Av Miami Beach FL 33139 Office: 641 Lexington New York City NY 10022

LAPIN, HOWARD SIDNEY, transport planner; b. Los Angeles, Oct. 13, 1922; s. Morris and Sarah (Goldberg) L.; B.S. with honors, Yale, 1947; M.Eng., U. Cal., 1950; Ph.D., Cath. U., 1969. Airport and harbor planner San Francisco Bay area, 1949-52; city planner, research transport planning U. Cal., 1948-49, 52-54; met. planning transport research U. Pa., Phila., 1954-60; on leave as transport planner City Phila., 1955-58; pvt. transp. cons., 1960-65, also transport planning officer Latin Am. bur. AID, 1965-66; chief tech. assistance div. internat. affairs U.S. Dept. Transp., Washington, 1967-72; dir. transp. and urban studies Robert R. Nathan Assos., Washington, 1972—. Mem. Mass. gov.'s adv. com. transp., 1963. Chmn. Cambridge chpt. Am. Assn. UN, 1962-63; bd. dirs. Internat. House Assn., Berkeley, Cal., 1953-54. Served as 1st lt. USAAF, 1942-45. Decorated D.F.C., Air medal with four oak leaf clusters, Purple Heart. NASA predoctoral fellow, 1964. Mem. Am. Inst. Planners, Inst. Traffic Engrs., Transp. Research Forum, Am. Econs. Assn., Regional Sci. Assn., Sigma Xi, Tau Beta Pi. Author: Structuring the Journey to Work, 1964. Contbr. articles profl. jours. Home: 300 M St SW Washington DC 20024 Office: Robert R Nathan Assos 1200 18th St NW Washington DC 20036

LAPO, CECIL ELWYN, musician; b. Flint, Mich., Mar. 12, 1910; s. Clyde E. and Adeline (Draper) L.; student Westminster Choir Coll., Princeton, N.J., 1941; Mus.D., Mt. Union Coll., Alliance, O., 1964; m. Beatrice M. Brodie, Aug. 16, 1931; children—Richard Deane, Carol Anne (Mrs. Roger M. Kunkel). Minister music 1st Presbyn. Ch., Hornell, N.Y., 1934-39, Newtown, Pa., 1939-41, 1st Meth. Ch., Cuyahoga Falls, O., 1941-49, Wichita Falls, Tex., 1949-53, St. Lukes Meth. Ch., Oklahoma City, 1953-61; dir. ministry music United Meth. Ch., Nashville, 1961-70; asso. exec. dir. Choristers Guild, Dallas, 1970-72, exec. dir., 1972—. Bd. dirs. Choristers Guild, Dallas; trustee Westminster Choir Coll. Mem. A.S.C.A.P., Hymn Soc. Am., Woodcarvers Assn. Home: 9805 Audelia Rd Dallas TX 75238 Office: 440 Northlake Center PO Box 38188 Dallas TX 75238

LAPORTE, ANTHONY, hotel co. exec.; b. Elizabethton, Tenn., Jan. 8, 1924; s. Joseph and Minnie Lee (Combs) LaP.; student Milligan Coll., 1942, Wittenberg Coll., 1944; m. Martha Jane Greer, Mar. 25, 1951; children—Anthony, Charlie Greer. Livestock farm, near Cordele, Ga., 1953-62; owner grocery, Cordele, 1954-61; innkeeper, franchise holder Holiday Inns, Inc., Cordele and Calhoun, Ga. and Cartersville, Ga., 1962—; pres. LaPorte, Inc., 1963—; dir. Internat. Assn. Holiday Inns. Mem. Ga. Gov.'s Staff, 1970—; active Little League Assn.; fund chmn. Chehaw council Boy Scouts Am., 1966—. Bd. dirs. Crisp County Planning Commn., Crisp County Airport Authority. Served with USAAF, 1943-45; with USAF, 1949-53; Korea. Named one of Top Ten. Innkeepers, Holiday Inns, Inc., 1967, 68, 70, 71. Mem. Am., Ga. hotel-motel assns., V.F.W., Am. Legion. Baptist (deacon 1970—). Rotarian. Clubs: Pine Hills Country (dir. 1970—) (Cordele); Crisp County Athletic. Home: 24 Av Extension E Cordele GA 31015 Office: PO Box 916 Cordele GA 31015

LAPRADE, JOHN LOVELACE, ret. educator; b. Republican Grove, Va., May 26, 1906; s. John Christian and Lula (Carr) LaP.; B.S., U. Va., 1933; M.S., Va. Poly. Inst., 1937; m. Lucy Finchem, Jan. 10, 1933 (dec. Feb. 1969) children—John C., Patricia A. (Mrs. David McGarvey), Jesse C.; m. 2d, Sue Cox, Nov. 12, 1969. High sch. tchr., Va., 1928-36; agronomist in charge Cigar Wrapper Expt. Sta., Ga. Coastal Plain Expt. Sta., Attapulgus, 1937-48; mem. research faculty tobacco disease research sta. Va. Poly. Inst., Chatham, 1949-70, asso. prof. plant pathology. 1952-70; breeder flue cured tobacco varieties. Mem. Am. Soc. Agronomy, Va. Acad. Sci., Tobacco Workers Conf., A.A.A.S., Sigma Xi. Baptist. Mason. Address: 819 Lowry Lane Tampa FL 33604

LAPRADE, WILLIAM THOMAS, educator; b. Franklin County, Va., Dec. 27, 1883; s. George Washington and Mary Elizabeth (Muse) L.; A.B., Washington (D.C.) Christian Coll., 1906; Ph.D., Johns Hopkins, 1909; m. Nancy Hamilton Calfee, June 11, 1913; 1 dau., Nancy Elizabeth (Mrs. J.D.T. Hamilton). Prof. history Trinity Coll. (now Duke U.), Durham, N.C., 1909-53, prof. emeritus, 1953—; prof. history U. Ill., summers 1916, 30; lectr. history and politics, tng. sch. for secs., YMCA, held at Blue Ridge, N.C., 1918-19; prof. history U. Pa., summer 1925; prof. history U. Mich., summer 1929. Mem. Am. Hist. Assn., Royal Hist. Soc., Am. Polit. Science Assn., Am. Assn. U. Profs. (mem. exec. com. of council 1934-37; chmn. com. on academic freedom and tenure, 1937-48; pres. 1942-43), N.C. State Lit. and Hist. Assn. (pres. 1937), Phi Beta Kappa. Mem. exec. bd. N.C. Dept. Archives and History, 1944—. Mem. Christian (Disciples) Ch. Author: England and the French Revolution, 1909; British History for American Students, 1926; Public Opinion and Politics in Eighteenth Century England, 1936; also articles in Am. Hist. Rev., English Hist. Rev., Am. Polit. Sci. Rev., and series 18 articles on The Teaching of History and Civics, in N.C. Education, 1921-23. Editor Parliamentary Papers of John Robinson (for Royal Hist. Soc.), 1922. Editor the South Atlantic Quar., 1944—. Home: 1108 Monmouth Av Durham NC 27701

LAPSLEY, G. MCIVER, state ofcl., lawyer; b. Ashland, Va., Sept. 28, 1911; s. Robert A. and Vermelle (McCutchen) L.; A.B., Washington and Lee U., 1931; LL.B., U. Richmond, 1949; m. Virginia G. Stonestreet, Dec. 19, 1942; children—Robert Armstrong, Alexander Fraser, Guy McIver. Admitted to Va. bar, 1949; mem. staff Va. Adv. Legislative Council, 1935-50, recording sec., 1950-65; dir. Div. Statutory Research and Drafting, Richmond, Va., 1965—. Mem. Phi Beta Kappa, Sigma Delta Chi. Home: 1207 W Laburnum Av Richmond VA 23227 Office: State Capitol Richmond VA 23219

LARABEE, LOTTIE B(ERTHA), coll. cons., lectr.; b. Sprague, Neb.; d. Arthur Henry and Anna (Bartels) Larabee; Mus.B., U. Sch. Music, Lincoln, Neb.; Mus.M., Am. Conservatory Music; M.A., Ph.D., N.Y. U., 1955. Prin. elementary sch., Beatrice, Neb.; music instr. Albion State Normal Sch.; music instr., dir. extension So. State Coll.; music instr., acting head music dept. Lock Haven State Coll.; dir. own sch. Chgo.; research coll. and univ. adminstrn. and coll. cons., 1953-67, 69—; lectr., 1969—; asst. to pres., acad. asst. to pres., prof. higher edn., v.p. acad. affairs Ft. Lauderdale (Fla.) U., 1967-69. Recipient 1st Distinguished Service award Am. Assn. Ind. Coll. and U. Presidents, 1968. Mem. Am. Assn. Higher Edn., Drs. U.S., A.A.A.S., New Eng. Historic Geneal. Soc., Kappa Delta Pi, Sigma Alpha Iota (past nat. editor). Author: Administrators Who Subvert Learning, Their Residence and Education, 1957; A Parent's Guide to Colleges and Universities, 1963. Home: 1201 SE 2d St Fort Lauderdale FL 33301

LARA-BRAUD, JORGE, church strategist; b. Mexicali, Baja California, Mexico, Apr. 3, 1931; s. Luis and Maria (Braud-Wilson) Lara-Castro; B.A., Austin Coll., 1954, D.D., 1967; B.D., Austin Presbyn. Sem., 1959; doctoral student Princeton Theol. Sem., 1959-62; m. Ruth Marroquin-Pascal, June 6, 1953 (div. 1970); 1 son, Jorge Luis; m. 2d, Carolyn J. Weathersbee, 1970. Came to U.S., 1964. Dean, Presbyterian Sem., Mexico City, 1962-64; prof. missions Austin Presbyn. Sem., Austin, Tex., 1964-66; dir. Hispanic-Am. Inst., Austin, Tex., 1966—. Tex. adv. com. U.S. Commn. on Civil Rights, 1968—. Chmn. bd. dirs. Sanatorio La Luz, Morelia, Michoacan, Mexico, 1968-70; nat. bd. dirs. Joint Action in Community Service, 1968-70; Planned Parenthood-World Population. Mem. Latin Am. Studies Assn., Assn. Seminaries No. Region Latin-Am. (chmn. 1964-65). Home: 4305 Duval Austin TX 78751 Office: 100 E 27th St Austin TX 78705

LARAMORE, DON N., federal judge; b. Hamlet, Ind., Dec. 22, 1906; s. Louis Nelson and Pearl (Stephenson) L.; m. Charlotte M. Schminke, Dec. 29, 1938; 1 dau., Prudence Ann. Admitted to Ind. bar, 1931; judge protempore Starke Circuit Ct. of Ind., 1942-44, judge, 1944-54; judge U.S. Ct. of Claims, Washington, 1954—. Home: 5017 Searsdale Rd Washington DC 20016 Office: US Ct of Claims 17th St and Pennsylvania Av NW Washington DC

LARDNER, GEORGE EDMUND, JR., newspaper reporter; b. Bklyn., Aug. 10, 1934; s. George Edmund and Rosetta (Russo) L.; A.B. in Journalism summa cum laude, Marquette U., 1956, M.A., 1962; m. Rosemary Schalk, July 6, 1957; children—Helen, Edmund, Richard, Charles, Kristin. Copyboy Milw. Sentinel, 1956-57; reporter Worcester (Mass.) Telegram, 1957-59, Miami (Fla.) Herald, 1959-63; with Washington Post, 1963—, reporter, 1963-64, columnist, originator Potomac Watch column, 1964-66, reporter nat. staff, 1966—. Recipient Byline award Marquette U., 1967. Mem. Am. Newspaper Guild, Congl. Press Gallery, Sigma Delta Chi, Alpha Sigma Nu. Roman Catholic. Contbr. free lance articles to nat., local mags. Home: 5604 32d St NW Washington DC 20015 Office: Washington Post 1150 15th St NW Washington DC 20015

LAREW, HIRAM GORDON, educator; b. Independence, W.Va., June 5, 1922; s. H. Gordon and Lula Margaret (Larew) L.; B.S. in Civil Engring., W.Va. U., 1944; M.S., Purdue U., 1951, Ph.D., 1960; m. Mary Jo Thompson, Nov. 22, 1946; children—Jane Jo, Hiram Gordon III, Elizabeth T. Asst. engr. N.Y. Central System, 1946; instr. civil engring. Purdue U., Lafayette, Inc., 1947-56; prof. civil engring. U. Va., Charlottesville, 1956—. Cons. on found. problems to numerous engring., archtl. and contracting firms. Chmn., Charlottesville Bd. Bldg. Appeals, 1964-71. Precinct coordinator Republican party, Charlottesville, 1971—. Bd. dirs. Alcohol-Narcotics Edn. Council of Va. Served with USNR, 1944-46. Mem. Am. Soc. for Engring. Edn., Hwy. Research Bd., Am. Soc. C.E. (pres. Blue Ridge br. 1969-70, sec. Va. sect. 1970—), Va. Acad. Sci. (pres. engring. div. 1967), Am. Road Builders Assn. (bd. dirs. edn. div. 1967-70); Sigma Xi, Tau Beta Pi. Clubs: Boars Head, Community Hunt (Charlottesville). Contbr. articles to tech. jours. Home: 2500 Hillwood Pl Charlottesville VA 22901

LAREY, BETHEL BRYAN, U.S. atty.; b. Texarkana, Ark., Nov. 15, 1933; s. Bert Bethel and Mayno (Britt) L.; B.S. in Engring., Henderson State Coll., 1957; J.D., Vanderbilt U., 1959; m. Emma Lee Tomlinson, Aug. 22, 1954; children—Keith, David. Admitted to Ark. bar; law clk. Ark. Supreme Ct., 1959-60; practiced law, 1963-66; commr. of revenue State of Ark., 1967-69; U.S. atty. Western Dist. of Ark., 1969—. Chmn., Ark. Reciprocity Commn., 1967-69; ex officio sec. Ark. Racing Commn., 1967-69. Mem. Ark. Republican Com., 1966-69. Served with USAF, 1960-63. Methodist (ofcl. bd. 1966). Lion (dir. Texarkana 1965-66). Home: 2323 Jefferson St Texarkana AR 75501 Office: Justice Dept 6th and Rogers Sts Fort Smith AR 72901

LARGE, OSCAR LEON, wholesale trade exec.; b. Rising Star, Tex., Nov. 10, 1923; s. Dewey C. and Jewel B. (Hamilton) L.; student Tex. Tech. Coll., Lubbock, 1941-42, U. Cal. at Berkeley, 1944-45; m. Elizabeth L. Marboe, Feb. 9, 1946; children—Russell D., Linda L. Traffic mgr. A.B. Frank Co., San Antonio, 1946-56, housewares buyer, 1957, toy buyer, 1958; v.p. purchasing Lachman Rose Co., wholesale toy distbr., San Antonio, 1958—. Served with USMCR, 1942-46. Mem. Herman Sons of Tex., Traffic Club San Antonio Home: 4506 Waikiki St San Antonio TX 78218 Office: 3200 E Houston St San Antonio TX 78206

LARGESS, GEORGE JOSEPH, educator; b. Malden, Mass., Oct. 20, 1917; s. James Edmund and Ellen (Hyland) L.; B.S., U.S. Naval Acad., 1939; postgrad. U.S. Naval Postgrad. Sch., 1945, Am. U., 1965—; m. Zoe McCombs, Feb. 2, 1942; children—George Joseph, Robert P., Dennis N., Mary Jude, William M. Commd. ensign USN, 1939, advanced through grades to comdr., 1949; comdr. U.S.S. Altair, 1952-53, U.S.S. Keppler, 1957-58; ret., 1961; project engr. Booz-Allen Applied Research, Inc., 1961-68; instr. math. St. Cecilia's Acad., Washington, 1968-69, D.C. pub. schs., 1968, Bullis sch., Silver Spring, Md., 1969-70, Anne Arundel (Md.) pub. schs., 1970—. Mem. adv. group on electronic warfare U.S. Dept. Def., 1959-61. Pres., Crestwood Citizens Assn., 1960-61, del. D.C. Fedn., 1961-62; pres. Holy Name Soc., 1962-64, del. Archdiocesan Union, 1961-68; pres. Cath. Youth Orgn., 1958-61; leader Capital council Boy Scouts Am., 1953-56; sec. Archdiocesan Union Holy Name Socs., 1968-71; mem. St. Matthew's Cathedral Council, 1968—, Calvert Sch. bd., 1968-70. Recipient Holy Name Soc. Appreciation award, 1964. Mem. Nat. Council Cath. Men, I.E.E.E., Am. Soc. Naval Engrs., A.A.A.S., Armed Forces Communication-Electronics Assn., Washington Operations Research Council, Internat. Platform Assn., N.E.A., Nat. Council Tchrs. Math., Am. Security Council, Phi Delta Kappa. Club: Serra of Washington (trustee). Home: 1908 Quincy St NW Washington DC 20011 Office: Anne Arundel County Schools 112 Green St Annapolis MD 21401

LARIMORE, LEON, clergyman; b. Horse Cave, Ky., July 22, 1911; s. William C. and Myrtie D. (Isenberg) L.; grad. Campbellsville Coll., 1946, D.D., 1962; student Georgetown Coll., 1946; A.B., Western Ky. U., 1949; B.D., So. Bapt. Theol. Sem., 1952; m. Blanche Lile, July 13, 1929; 1 dau., Majorie Bell (Mrs. Levy Ray Broady). Ordained to ministry, Baptist Ch., 1937; pastor Bapt. Chs., Hart, Edmonson, Metcalfe, Green and Monroe Counties, Ky., 1937-57, 3d Av. Bapt. Ch., Louisville, 1957—. Dir. South Central Rural Telephone Coop. Mem. Econ. Security Welfare Commn., 1951-57; chmn. Hart County unit Am. Cancer Soc., 1952-56. Trustee Campbellsville Coll., 1953-70. Mem. Liberty Assn. So. Bapts. (moderator 1942-49, 52-57), Ky. Bapt. Conv. (v.p. 1965), Long Run Assn. So. Bapts. (moderator 1971-72; pres. exec. bd. 1971-72). Mason. Home: 1041 Eastern Pkwy Louisville KY 40217 Office: 1726 S 3d St Louisville KY 40208

LARKIN, ROBERT NELSON, heavy truck mfg. co. exec.; b. Buffalo, Dec. 27, 1931; s. James Crate and Florence W. (Daniels) L.; student Hackley Sch., Tarrytown, N.Y., 1949-50; student Williams Coll., 1952; postgrad. U. Wash., 1969; m. Mary Lou Evans, Apr. 25, 1958; children—Robert Nelson, James S., John T., Mary Kathleen. Pres., Constrn. Transport Ltd., Honolulu, 1958-60; gen. mgr. Consol. Freightways, Inc., Honolulu, 1960-63; mng. dir. Peterbilt Australia Pty. Ltd., Sydney, 1963-65; prodn. mgr. Peterbilt Motors Co., Newark, Cal., 1965-71, plant mgr., Nashville, 1971—. Pres. Atherton (Cal.) Little League, 1969-71; active Boy Scouts Am. Mem. Soc. Automotive Engrs., Delta Upsilon. Clubs: Hillwood Country, City (Nashville); Commonwealth (San Francisco); Pacific (Honolulu). Home: 700 Darden Pl Nashville TN 37205 Office: 430 Myatt Dr Madison TN 37115

LARKINS, JOHN DAVIS, JR., judge; b. Morristown, Tenn., June 8, 1909; s. John D. and Emma (Cooper) L.; B.A., Wake Forest U., 1929, law student, 1930; LL.D., Belin U., 1957; m. Pauline Murrill, Mar. 15, 1930; children—Emma Sue (Mrs. D.H. Loftin), Polly (Mrs. J.H. Bearden). Admitted to N.C. bar, 1930, gen. practice in Trenton, 1930-61; U.S. dist. judge Eastern Dist. N.C., 1961—. Sec. Larkins Stores, Inc.; dir. Life Ins. Co. N.C. Nat. bd. dirs., vice chmn. Am. Cancer Soc. Del.-at-large Democratic Nat. Conv., 1940, 44, 48, 56, 60; sec. N.C. Dem. Exec. Com., 1952-54, chmn., 1954-58; mem. Dem. Nat. Com., 1958-60; mem. N.C. Senate 7th dist., 1936-44, 48-54, pres. pro tem, 1941-42. Chmn. gov.'s adv. budget commn., 1951-53; gov.'s liaison officer and legislative counsel, 1955. Trustee U. N.C., Bapt. Hosp. Served as pvt. AUS, 1945. Recipient distinguished service award Am. Cancer Soc.; Outstanding Alumni Service award Wake Forest U. Sch. Law, 1968. Mem. Am. Legion, 40 and 8, Woodmen of World, Am., N.C. bar assns., N.C. Bar, Inc., Phi Alpha Delta. Baptist (chmn. bd. deacons 1930—). Mason (Shriner), Elk, Moose. Home: Trenton NC 28585 Office: US Post Office and Federal Bldg Trenton NC 28585

LARKS, JACK, engr., educator; b. Chgo., Nov. 16, 1926; s. Israel David and Frieda (Morganstern) L.; student U. Ill., 1947-49; B.S., Mass. Inst. Tech., 1952, M.S., 1953; m. Norma Colwell, Dec. 24, 1957; children—Terri Lynn, Kevin Jon. Research engr. Mass. Inst. Tech., 1953-54; design test engr. Douglas Aircraft, Tulsa, 1955-57, missile operations engr., Cape Canaveral, Fla., 1957-59; facilities engr. Space Tech. Labs., Cape Canaveral, 1959-64; advanced design engr. TRW, Cape Canaveral, 1964-66, dist. rep., Houston, 1966-67, Apollo design engr., 1967-68; marketing rep. Lockheed, Houston, 1968-69, mission planning engr. earth resources, 1969-71; prof. civil tech. U. Houston, 1971—. Instr. surveying Mass. Inst. Tech., 1951-52, U. Mass., 1952-53; instr. math. U. Okla., 1955-56, Brevard Engring. Coll., 1964-65, Coll. Mainland, 1968-69. Bd. dirs. United Fund, Brevard, Fla., 1964-66. Served with AUS, 1945-47. Decorated Purple Heart, Belgian Croix deGuerre. Registered profl. engr., Okla., Fla., Tex. Mem. Research Engrs. Soc. Am., Am. Soc. C.E., Am. Inst. Aeros. and Astronautics, Missiles, Space and Range Pioneers, Sigma Xi, Phi Delta Kappa. Mason, Kiwanian (pres. 1968-69). Home: 1701 Oleander Dr Dickinson TX 77539 Office: U Houston Coll of Technology Houston TX 77058

LARRABEE, CHARLES XAVIER, sci. research exec.; b. Seattle, June 23, 1922; s. Charles Francis and Mary Adele (Brownlie) L.; student Dartmouth, 1940-42; m. Margaret Dwelle, Oct. 8, 1943; children—Giles, Sarah, Meg, Charles, Alexander, Lucy, Jean. Asst. to editor San Francisco Chronicle, 1946-53; adminstrv. asst. to dir. Stanford Research Inst., Menlo Park, Cal., 1953-56; asso. gen. mgr., acting fiction editor Crowell-Collier Pub. Co., N.Y.C., 1956-57; asst. to v.p. United Fruit Co., Boston, 1957-62; mgr. information services Spindletop Research, Lexington, Ky., 1962-64; pub. relations mgr. Research Triangle Inst., Research Triangle Park, N.C., 1964-—. Vice pres. United Fund, 1971. Bd. dirs. Better Bus. Bur. Served with USMCR, 1942-45. Recipient Excellence award Raleigh Pub. Relations Soc., 1968. Mem. Pub. Relations Soc. Am. (dir. N.C. chpt.), Durham C. of C. (task force chmn. 1968-70). Kiwanian. Club: Croasdaile Country (Durham, N.C.). Home: 1114 Woodburn Rd Durham NC 27705 Office: Box 12194 Research Triangle Park NC 27709

LARRICK, ROBERT VERNON, psychiatrist; b. Capon Bridge, W.Va., Feb. 27, 1914; s. James Walter and Myrtle (Powell) L.; A.B., Shepherd Coll., 1941; M.S., W.Va. U., 1943; M.D., Med. Coll. Va., 1946; postgrad. Vanderbilt U., 1953-56; m. Frances Covington; children—Donna, Pamela, Robert Vernon. Sch. tchr., 1934-41; rotating intern Chesapeake and Ohio Hosp., Huntington, W.Va., 1946-48, resident internal medicine, 1947-48; practice of medicine, Winchester, Va., 1950-53; resident psychiatry Vanderbilt U., Nashville, 1953-56; med. dir. Central State Hosp., Nashville, 1959; psychiatrist Hillcrest San., 1958-60; dir. Plateau Mental Health Center, Cookeville, Tenn., 1960-70. Served to maj. AUS, 1948-50. Diplomate Am. Bd. Psychiatry. Mem. Am. Psychiat. Assn., So., Tenn., Middle Tenn., Putnam County med. assns., Phi Chi. Methodist. Home: 855 Loweland Rd Cookeville TN 38501

LARSEN, BRUCE WESTERLY, elec. engr.; b. Everett, Mass., Oct. 25, 1939; s. Nels and Beatrice (Zuercher) L.; B.S., U. Md., 1961; m. Patricia Engstrom, Oct. 5, 1963; children—Sharon Patricia, Wayne Bruce. Analog applications engr. Pratt & Whitney Aircraft, West Palm Beach, Fla., 1961-64; recovery engr. manned spacecraft NASA, Houston, 1964-67, unmanned spacecraft project officer Kennedy Spacecenter (Fla.), 1967-70, Skylab expts. mgr. Apollo-Skylab program office, 1970-—. Registered profl. engr., Fla. Mem. Soc. Am. Mil. Engrs., I.E.E.E., U.S. Naval Inst. Methodist. Home: 514 Bianca Ct Altamonte Springs FL 32701 Office: NASA Kennedy Spacecenter FL 32899

LARSEN, GEORGE EDWARD, librarian; b. N.Y.C., Mar. 26, 1912; s. George and Edythe (Keys) L.; A.B., Williams Coll., 1933; diploma Command and Gen. Staff Coll., 1951, Army War Coll., 1957; M.S., Fla. State U., 1968; m. Hope Harrin, Nov. 11, 1949; children—Margo, Linda, Jeanne, George Edward. Sales mgr. T.M. James & Co., N.Y.C., 1933-43; served from pvt. to col. U.S. Army, 1943-67; faculty Command and Gen. Staff Coll., 1951-54, Army War Coll., 1957-60; ret., 1967; dir. libraries Rollins Coll., Winter Park, Fla., 1968-—. Decorated Legion of Merit. Mem. Am., Fla. library assns., Assn. Am. U. Profs., Delta Phi, Beta Phi Mu. Home: 660 Arjay Way Winter Park FL 32789

LARSEN, RONALD DWIGHT, hosp. adminstr.; b. Sibley, Ia., May 3, 1926; s. Victor D. and Della (Nelson) L.; B.A., Sioux Falls Coll., 1949; M. Hosp. Adminstrn., U. Minn., 1954; m. Deloris Joyce Wik, June 26, 1948; children—Lon M. Scott R., Todd D. Adminstrv. asst. Meth. State Hosp., Mitchell, S.D., 1949-51; adminstr. Rosebud Community Hosp., Winner, S.D., 1951-52; resident Charles Miller Hosp., St. Paul, 1953-54; asst. adminstr. M. D. Anderson Hosp., Houston, 1954-57; adminstr. Pasadena (Tex.) Gen. Hosp., 1957-63, Med. Arts Hosp. of Houston, Inc., 1964-70; exec. dir. Univ. Hosp., Lubbock, Tex., 1970-72, also v.p., sec. bd. trustees; exec. dir. Cook Meml. Hosp., Levelland, Tex., 1970-72; adminstr. Sam Houston Meml. Hosp., Houston, 1972-—. Mem. adminstrv. adv. com. Hosp. Corp. Am., regional adviser 8 hosps., Tex., La., 1972-—; past pres. Houston Area Hosp. Council. Bd. dirs. Pasadena Gen. Hosp., Southmore Hosp., Rockgien Gen. Hosp., Med. Arts Hosp., Williamsburg Nursing Home, 1960-64. Mem. Am. Hosp. Assn., Am. Coll. Hosp. Adminstrs., South Plains Hosp. Assn., Tex. Hosp. Assn. (com. of 100). Rotarian. Home: 14539 Bramblewood St Houston TX 77024 Office: Sam Houston Meml Hosp 1624 Pech St Houston TX 77055

LARSH, HOWARD WILLIAM, educator; b. E. St. Louis, Ill., May 20, 1914; s. John Edgar and Margaret (Kays) L.; B.A., McKendree Coll., 1936; student mycology Washington U., St. Louis, 1936-37; M.S., U. Ill. at Urbana, 1938, Ph.D., 1941; postgrad. med. mycology Duke, also U. N.C., summer 1946; m. Georgia Lee Thomson, Sept. 4, 1938; 1 son, Jonathan Thomson. Mem. faculty U. Okla., 1941-—, prof. med. mycology, 1948-—, research prof., 1961-—, chmn. dept. boatny and microbiology, 1966-—; cons. in field, 1950-—; asso. dir. labs. Mo. Chest Hosp., 1955; research reviewer immunology and infectious diseases com. VA Hosp., Oklahoma City, 1972. Mem. A.A.A.S., Bot. Soc. Am., Soc. Am. Bacteriologists, Am. Pub. Health Assn., Am. Soc. Tropical Medicine and Hygiene, Soc. Exptl. Biology and Medicine, Internat. Soc. Human and Animal Mycology, Reticuloendothelial Soc., Am. Acad. Microbiology, Okla. Acad. Scis., Sigma Xi, Phi Sigma, Lambda Tau. Author articles in field. Home: 611 Broad Lane Norman OK 73069

LARSON, ARTHUR, educator, writer, lectr.; b. Sioux Falls, S.D., July 4, 1910; s. Lewis and Anna Bertha (Huseboe) L.; A.B., Augustana Coll., 1931, LL.D., (hon.), 1953; postgrad. U. S.D. Law Sch., 1931-32; B.A., Jurisprudence, Oxford (Eng.) U. (Rhodes scholar, 1932-35), M.A.- Jurisp., 1938; B.C.L. and D.C.L., 1957; fellow Pembroke Coll., Oxford (hon.); LL.D., Thiel Coll., Valparaiso U., U. S.D., Lenoir Rhyne Coll., Utah State U.; L.H.D., Coe Coll.; m. Florence Faye Newcomb, July 30, 1935; children—Lex, Anna (Mrs. John H. Shenefield). Admitted to Wis. bar, 1935, practiced in Milw. with Quarles, Spence & Quarles, 1935-39; asst. prof. law, U. Tenn. Law Sch., 1939-41; div. counsel, indstl. materials div., O.P.A., Wash., 1941-44; acting price exec., lumber br., 1944; chief, Scandanavian br., Fgn. Econ. Adminstrn., 1944-45; asso. prof. law, Cornell Law Sch., 1945-48, prof. law, 1948-53; dean U. Pitts. Sch. of Law, 1953-54; under sec. of labor, 1954-56; dir. USIA, 1956-57; spl. asst. to Pres., 1957-58, spl. cons., 1958-61; cons. State Dept., 1962-70, Dept. Health, Edn. and Welfare, 1963-65, 70-71, Pres. of U.S. on internat. affairs, 1964-70, Pres.'s Council Econ. Advisers, 1968. Dir. Rule of Law Research Center, prof. law, Duke U., 1958-—; Knapp prof. U. Wis. Law Sch., 1968-69; vis. distinguished prof. Catholic U. Law Sch., 1970-71. Recipient Fulbright Advanced Research Award, 1952, Gerard Henderson Meml. prize, Harvard Law Sch., 1957; World Peace award, Am. Freedom Assn., 1960. Mem. Am. Law Inst., Am. Bar Assn., Brit. Inst. Internat. and Comparative Law, Am. Soc. Internat. Law, Oxford Union Soc. (treas. 1934, librarian 1935), Phi Delta Phi, Order of Coif, Phi Beta Kappa. Lutheran. Club: Cosmos (Washington, D.C.). Author: Cases on Corporations (with R. S. Stevens), 1955; Towards World Prosperity (with M. Ezekiel et al.), 1947; The Law of Workmen's Compensation, 4 vols., 1952; Know Your Social Security, 1959; A Republican Looks at His Party, 1956; What We Are For, 1959; Design for Research in International Rule of Law, 1960; When Nations Disagree, 1961; A Warless World, 1964; Eisenhower, The President Nobody Knew, 1968. Co-author: Economic Security of Americans, 1953; Arms Control, Disarmament and National Security, 1961; Preventing World War III: Some Proposals, 1962; (with J.B. Whitton) Propaganda, 1964; (with Don R. Larson) Vietnam and Beyond, 1965; (with L.T. Lee) Population and Law, 1971. Editor, contbr. Sovereignty Within the Law, 1965. Composer works for organ, string quartet, voice, etc. Home: 1 Learned Pl Durham NC 27707

LARSON, BEN JOHN, accountant, state ofcl.; b. Tulsa, July 11, 1927; s. Ben K. and Pearl (Monks) L.; student Ft. Smith Jr. Coll., 1953-54, Tulsa U., 1954-56; m. Evelyna A. A. Liotta, Dec. 15, 1948; children—Ben T., Michael J., Stephen J., Philip A., David P., Marianne. Various civilian, mil. accounting and financial positions, 1946-61; sr. auditor Mercing & Thomas, 1961-66; audit mgr. Nat. Investors Cos., 1966-68; sr. examiner ins. dept. Ark., Little Rock, 1968-71, chief examiner Ark. securities div., 1971-72; sr. ins. examiner Okla. Ins. Dept., Oklahoma City, 1972-—. Mem. Central Ark. Estate Council, 1969-—. Served with AUS, 1943-46, 47-53. Decorated B.S.M. with oak leaf cluster, C.I.B. with star. Croix de Guerre Mem. Am. Inst. C.P.A.'s, Ark. Soc. C.P.A.'s, Accounting Research Assn. Roman Catholic. K.C. Home: 6417 N Nicklas Oklahoma City OK 73132 Office: Will Rogers Memorial Bldg Oklahoma City OK 73105

LARSON, BILL ALLEN, oil field supply co. exec.; b. Bartlesville, Okla., July 14, 1920; s. Albert D. and Blanche (Stover) L.; B.A., Okla. U., 1942, J.D., 1948; m. Laura L. Pratt, Aug. 5, 1950; 1 dau., Kristen K. Admitted to Okla. bar, 1948; practice in Oklahoma City, 1948-51; asst. to v.p. Consol. Gas Utilities Corp., Oklahoma City, 1953-58; v.p., gen. counsel A.D. Larson Supply Co. Oklahoma City, 1958-64, exec. v.p., 1964-68, pres., 1968-—, also dir.; pres. Larsco, Inc., 1968-—. Mem. boys rehab. com. Okla. County Juvenile Judges. Served to maj. AUS, 1942-46, 51-53; operations officer IX Corps Arty., Korea; lt. col. Judge Advocate, 95th Division (Res.), also hon. marshall. Decorated Air medal with 3 oak leaf clusters; hon. county atty.; hon. justice, practice ct., Okla. U. Coll. Law; hon. mayor Oklahoma City; 95th Div. Outstanding Oklahoman award. Mem. Am., Okla., Oklahoma County bar assns., Am. Petroleum Inst., Res. Officers Assn., Okla. Hist. Soc., Oklahoma City C. of C., Phi Kappa Psi, Phi Alpha Delta. Democrat. Unitarian. Clubs: Petroleum, Oklahoma City Golf and Country (Oklahoma City). Home: 6904 N Grand Blvd Oklahoma City OK 73116

LARSON, CLARENCE E(DWARD), govt. ofcl.; b. Cloquet, Minn., Sept. 20, 1909; s. Louis and Caroline (Ullman) L.; B.S., U. Minn., 1932; Ph.D., U. Cal., 1936; 1 son by previous marriage, Robert Edward; m. 2d, Jane R. Warren, Apr. 20, 1957; children—Ernest Lawrence, Lance Stafford. Nat. Tb Assn. fellow Mt. Zion Research Lab., 1936-37, research asso., 1936-37; prof. chemistry Coll. of Pacific, 1937-40, chmn. chemistry dept., 1940-42; civilian OSRD, 1942; chief analytical sect. radiation lab. U. Cal., 1942-43; asst. supt. Tenn. Eastman Corp., Oak Ridge, 1943-46; dir. research and devel. electromagnetic plant Carbide & Carbon Chem. Corp., 1946-48, plant supt., 1948-50; became dir. Oak Ridge Nat. Lab., 1950, now mem. adv. com. for chemistry; v.p. research Nat. Carbon Co. div. Union Carbide and Carbon Corp., 1955-59; asso. mgr. research Union Carbide Corp., 1959-61; v.p. Union Carbide Nuclear Co., and gen. mgr. Oak Ridge operations, 1961-65, pres. Union Carbide nuclear div., 1965-69; commr. U.S. AEC, Washington, 1969-—; dir. Oak Ridge Inst. Nuclear Studies, Ofcl. del. U.S. delegation Internat. Conf. Peaceful Uses Atomic Energy, Geneva, Switzerland, 1955. Fellow Am. Nuclear Soc.; mem. Am. Chem. Soc., A.A.A.S., Soc. Exptl. Biology and Med., Sci. Research Soc. Am., Inc. (charter), Sigma Xi, Phi Lambda Epsilon, Tau Beta Pi. Rotarian (pres. 1953). Clubs: Bethesda Country, U. (Md.); Cosmos, Capitol Hill (Washington). Contbr. to sci. periodicals. Home: 6514 Bradley Blvd Bethesda MD 20034 Office: US AEC Washington DC 20545

LARSON, JORDAN LOUIS, credit co. exec.; b. Roland, Ia., Jan. 4, 1900; s. Louis and Julia (Johnson) L.; B.A., U. Ia., 1922, M.A., 1931; M.A., Ed.D., Columbia, 1951; m. Mildred Thorson, June 24, 1925; children—Jordan, Jeanne (Mrs. Paul W. Griewe), Marilyn (Mrs. Robert Mau), Leland. Tchr., supt. schs., Littleport, Ia., 1922-24, Garnavillo, Ia., 1924-26, Dunkerton, Ia., 1926-31, Grundy Center, Ia., 1931-36, Ames, Ia. 1936-40, Dubuque, Ia., 1940-46, Mt. Vernon, N.Y., 1946-65; exec. sec. Sch. Facilities Council of Architecture, Edn. and Industry, Prospect Heights, Ill., 1965-—; now pres., chief exec. officer Tower Credit Corp., Tampa, Fla.; vis. prof. Ia. State Coll., summers 1938-40; lectr. N.Y. U., 1947. Chmn. com. on religion and pub. edn. Nat. Council Chs., 1953-61; pres. Asso. Pub. Sch. Systems, 1949-50; mem. U.S. aviation industry adv. panel Air Coordinating Com., 1952-59; v.p. Nat. Aviation Council, 1952-53, pres. 1953-54; adviser to nat. comdr. Civil Air Patrol, 1951-—. Served with U.S. Army, 1918; to lt. col. AUS, 1942-45; ret. col. USAF. Recipient Frank G. Brewer Civil Air Patrol Aerospace award, 1960. Mem. Am. Assn. Sch. Adminstrs. (pres. 1954-55), Ia. Legion Schoolmasters (pres. 1939-40), Ia. Supts. (pres. 1940-41), N.Y. Legion Schoolmasters (pres. 1950-53), European Flying Classroom, Nat. Sch. Facilities Council (pres. 1958-65), Westchester County Chief Sch. Officers (pres. 1957-58), Am. Legion, Alpha Sigma Phi, Phi Delta Kappa. Mason. Club: N.Y. Schoolmasters (pres. 1963), Rotary (pres. 1953-54). Contbr. articles to ednl. mags. Office: 915 Ashley St Suite 306 Tampa FL 33602

LARSON, LEWIS JENNINGS, coll. dean; b. Lincoln, Neb., Sept. 29, 1911; s. Lewis J. and Anna Katherine (Nelson) L.; B.S., Madison Coll., 1938; M.A., George Peabody Coll. for Tchrs., 1947, Ed.S., 1963, Ed.D., 1964; m. Mary Ninaj, Aug. 19, 1934; children—Karl Milan, Elizabeth Ann. Ordained to ministry Seventh-day Adventist Ch., 1956; ednl. and editorial service in India, 1939-61; Ford teaching fellow George Peabody Coll., 1961-62; dean acad. affairs Oakwood Coll., Huntsville, Ala., 1964-69; dean acad. affairs Southwestern Union Coll., Keene, Tex., 1969-—, mem. exec. bd., 1969-—. Mem. ednl. council Gen. Conf. Seventh-day Adventist Ch., India, Burma, Ceylon and Pakistan, 1945-61, N.Am. Ednl. Adv. Council, 1970-—; dep. dir. Ala. Center for Higher Edn., 1968-69. Mem. Am. Sch. Adminstrs., Am. Assn. for Higher Edn., Phi Delta Kappa. Author: Report of First Institute of Scientific Studieo-Bombay, 1956; Story Time, vols. I-10, 1952-57. Editor: Selected Messages, 1961; Health and Longevity, 1957. Editor monthly mags. Herald of Health, 1951-59, Our Times, 1958-59. Address: Southwestern Union Coll Keene TX 76059

LARSON, NETTABELL GIRARD, lawyer; b. Riverton, Wyo.; d. George and Arranetta (Bell) Girard; student Ida. State U., 1957-58; B.S., U. Wyo., 1959, LL.B., 1961; m. Dean M. Larson, Dec.30, 1971. Admitted to Wyo. bar, 1961, U.S. Supreme Ct. bar, 1969; practiced in Riverton, 1963-69; atty.-adviser on gen. counsel's staff Dept. Housing and Urban Devel., assigned Office Interstate Land Sales Registration, Washington, D.C., 1969-70, sect. chief interstate land sales Office Gen. Counsel, 1970-—. Tchr. bus. law Central Wyo. Coll.; guest lectr. at high schs.; condr. seminar on law for layman Riverton br. Am. Assn. U. Women, 1965. Narrator, Progressive Womens Ann. Style Show, 1964, chmn., 1965; narrator style show Country club, 1968; chmn. fund drive Wind River chpt. A.R.C., 1965; chmn. Citizens Com. for Better Hosp. Improvement, 1965; chmn. sub-com. on polit., legal rights and responsibilities Gov.'s Commn. on Status Women, 1965-69, rep. Nat. Conf. Govs. Commn., Washington, 1966; local chmn. Law Day, 1966, 67; mem. state bd. Wyo. Girl Scouts U.S.A.; state vol. adviser Nat. Found., March of Dimes. Pres., Republican Womens Club, 1964-66; precinct committeewoman, 1964-66; mem. exec. bd. County Central Com., 1964-66; Mem. Am., Wyo., Fremont County, D.C., Fed. bar assns., Women's Bar Assn. for D.C., Internat. Fedn. Women Lawyers, Am. Judicature soc., Comml. Law League, Am. Trial Lawyers Assn., Nat. Assn. Women Lawyers (del. Wyo., nat. sec. 1969-70, v.p. 1970-71, pres. 1972-—), Am. Assn. U. Women (br. pres.), Wyoming Federation of Womens Clubs (state editor, pres. elect 1968-69), Kappa Delta. Clubs: Wind River Toastmistress, Riverton chautauqua (pres. 1965-67). Editor: Wyoming Clubwoman, 1966-—; bd. editors Wyo. Law Jour., 1959-61. Writer Obiter Dictum column Women Lawyers Jour. Home: 224 W Sunset St PO Box 473 Riverton WY 82501 Office: Dept of Housing and Urban Development 451 7th St SW Washington DC 20411

LARUE, MARIE T., newspaper editor. Society editor Times-Picayune, New Orleans. Office: 3800 Howard Av New Orleans LA 70140*

LASATER, ROBERT EDWARD, structural engr.; b. Erwin, N.C., Feb. 11, 1930; s. Eugene Herndon and Josephine (Stuart) L.; student Campbell Coll., 1948-50; B.C.E., N.C. State U., 1958; m. Julia Elizabeth Henderson, June 17, 1952; children—Elizabeth, Margaret, Helen, Robert Julia. Designer, draftsman Watson Engrs., Greensboro, N.C., 1958, Holloway-Reeves, Raleigh, N.C., 1959-63, M.J. Andrews, Greensboro, 1964-65; cons. structural engr., Raleigh, 1966-—. Served with USNR, 1950-54. Registered profl. engr., N.C., Ohio. Mem. Am. Soc. C.E., Nat. Soc. Profl. Engrs., Profl. Engrs. N.C., Constrn. Specification Inst. Democrat. Presbyn. (deacon 1971-—). Clubs: North Hills (dir. 1967-—), Optimist (Raleigh); MacGregor Downs Country (Cary, N.C.). Home: 5310 Inglewood Lane Raleigh NC 27609 Office: 1918 Hillsborough St Raleigh NC 17607

LASBURY, LEAH (MRS. CLYDE P. LASBURY), realtor, artist; b. Boca Grand, Fla., Apr. 11, 1915; d. James E. and Nellie (Allen) Bartlett; B.A., Rollins Coll., 1936; B.S., Simmons Coll., 1937; m. Clyde P. Lasbury, Sept. 16, 1939; children—Cherick Pitchford, Dana Lynne, Leah Jean. Exec. trainee G. Fox & Co., Hartford, Conn., 1937-39; real estate broker, Englewood, Fla., 1951-—; sec.-treas. Lee Lasbury, Inc., realtors; dir. J. E. Bartlett & Sons, Inc., Englewood; charter mem. adv. bd. Englewood Bank. One-man shows Englewood Bank, 1960, Community Gallery, Venice, Fla., 1960, Corridor Gallery, Asheville, N.C., 1961, Italian Villa, Venice, 1963, Am. Bank, Sarasota, Fla., 1966; exhibited group shows, 1955-—, including Nat. Assn. Women Artists, N.Y.C., 1959, N.Y.C. Pen and Brush Club, 1959, Ringling Mus., Sarasota, 1961, South Coast Galleries, Corridor Gallery, 1961, Tampa Fair, 1960-61, Lowe Gallery, Miami, 1963, 68, Fla. Artist Group shows, 1964-70, 1st Rollins Coll. Alumni Show., 1966, 67, 68, New Coll. Artists Group, Sarasota Fla., 1966, numerous others; represented in pvt. collections. Organizer Englewood Teen Club, 1952; pres. P.T.A., Broad Brook, Conn., 1945; mem. Englewood Zoning Commn., 1956-57; mem. adv. bd. Sarasota County Library, 1966-—; v.p. Ringling Mus. Mems. Guild, 1960-62; organizer 1st road commn., Englewood, 1956, 1st water commn., 1956; organizer Englewood Library, 1962, bd. dirs., 1962-—; mem. Sarasota County Community Goals Council, 1965-—; dir. Asolo Theatre Festival Assn., 1963-—. Mem. Venice Area Art League (dir.), Englewood Realtors Bd. (organizer, charter pres., dir.), Englewood (past pres.), Sarasota County (publicity com. 1963) chambers commerce, Englewood Women Taxpayers League (organizer, charter pres.), Sarasota Art Assn., Fla. Artist Group (pres. 1972), Internat. Platform Assn., Nat. Assn. Women Artists, D.A.R. (charter Myakka chpt. Venice), Pi Gamma Mu., Phi Mu, Alpha Omega. Republican. Methodist. Clubs: Venice Yacht (charter mem.). Home: 115 Lee Circle Englewood FL 33533 Office: 312 Indiana Av Englewood FL 33533

LASHER, HUMES TRUITT, judge; b. Kittanning, Pa., Oct. 20, 1912; s. John H. and Margaret (Truitt) L.; B.B.A., U. Miami, 1947, LL.B., 1950; m. Evelyn Mae Weitzel, Dec. 21, 1934; children—Humes Truitt, Barry Humes. Admitted to Fla. bar, 1950; practiced in Pitts., 1950-61; partner firm Lasher & Hartwig, Ft. Lauderdale, Fla., 1962-70; judge Ct. of Record, Ft. Lauderdale, 1967-—, Circuit Ct., Fla., 1972-—. Served with USNR, 1942-47. Mem. Internat. Yachtsmen Assn., Under Seas Edn., Better Yachting Council, Broward Artificial Reef, Phi Kappa Alpha, Delta Theta Phi. Republican. Mason, Elk, Rotarian. Home: 1008 Avocado Isle Fort Lauderdale FL 33315 Office: Broward County Ct House Fort Lauderdale FL 33315

LASHMIT, LUTHER SNOW, architect; b. Winston-Salem, N.C., Apr. 22, 1899; s. James Luther and Mary Janette (Snow) L.; student U. N.C., 1917; A.B. in Architecture, Carnegie-Mellon U., 1921, M.A. in Architecture, 1922; postgrad. (scholar), Fontainebleau Ecole des Beaux, 1925-31; m. Mary Lucille Leigh, Jan. 12, 1932. With Northup & O'Brien Architect, Winston-Salem, 1927-49, partner, 1950-52; partner Lashmit Borwn and Pollock Architects-Engrs., Winston-Salem, 1953-68, cons., 1968-—; fed. war housing planner, Atlanta, 1942-45. Instr., Ga. Inst. Tech., 1922-23; asst. prof. Carnegie-Mellon U., 1923-27, asso., 1931-38; cons. Davidson Coll. restoration, 1958. Mem. City Historic Dists. Commn., 1945-65, chmn., 1966-—; chmn. City Codes and Ordinances Com., 1954-63; pres. N.C. Design Found., 1963-64; pres. Episcopal Home for Aging of Diocese of N.C., 1968-69, bd. dirs., 1967-—. Recipient Scholastic medal A.I.A., 1921, Meritorious Service award N.C. chpt., 1958. Mem. A.I.A. (N.C. chpt. pres. 1948). Episcopalian (sr. warden 1963-64, Bishop's award 1969). Club: Twin City (Winston-Salem). Home: 2523 Woodbine Rd Winston-Salem NC 27104 Office: 865 W 4 1/2 St Winston-Salem NC 27101

LASLETT, BASIL GEORGE FREDERICK, architect; b. Hartford, Conn., Jan. 17, 1903; s. Harry Arthur and Ada Maryanne (Henderson) L.; B.Arch., Yale, 1928; m. Persis Louise Lenox, Feb. 22, 1936; children—William L., Basil George Frederick, Lorraine P. Draftsman, Gander, Gander & Gander, Architects, Albany, N.Y., 1928-37; architect Basil G.F. Laslett, Fayetteville, N.C., 1937-63; partner Basil G. F. Laslett and William L. Laslett, Architects-Planners, Fayetteville, 1963-—. Mem. A.I.A., Phi Kappa Epsilon. Democrat. Presbyn. Kiwanian (pres. 1960). Club: Highland Country (Fayetteville). Important works include City Hall, Fayetteville, 1940, Adminstrn. Bldg., Fayetteville City Schs., 1960, Fed. Bldg., U.S. P.O. and Courthouse, 1965, Sci. Bldg., Fayetteville State U., 1967, Cape Fear High Sch., Cumberland County, N.C., 1968, Salvation Army, Fayetteville, 1968, Acad. Bldg., Fayetteville State U., 1972, Health and Social Services Bldg., Cumberland County, 1972. Home: 314 W Park Dr Fayetteville NC 28305 Office: 2090 Fairway Dr Fayetteville NC 28305

LASLETT, WILLIAM LENOX, architect; b. Albany, N.Y., Oct. 5, 1937; s. Basil George Frederick and Persis Louise (Lenox) L.; B.A., Colgate U., 1959; B.Arch., Yale, 1963; m. Elizabeth Southworth Corning, Mar. 9, 1963; children—William Lenox Bradford, Alison Corning. With Basil G. F. Laslett and William L. Laslett, Architects-Planners, Fayetteville, N.C., 1963-—, partner, 1969-—.

Mem. downtown urban planning group, Fayetteville, 1970—. Mem. A.I.A. (sec. N.C. chpt. 1970—, bd. dirs. 1968—, mem. nat. human resources council 1972). Democrat. Presbyn. Clubs: Southern Pines (N.C.) Country. Important works include Science Bldg., Fayetteville State U., 1968, Salvation Army Hdqrs., 1969, Cape Fear High Sch., Cumberland County, N.C., 1970, Acad. Bldg., Fayetteville State U., 1972, Health and Social Services Bldg., Cumberland County, 1972. Home: Weymouth Rd Southern Pines NC 28387 Office: 209 Fairway Dr Fayetteville NC 28305

LASLEY, JAMES BERNARD, textile co. exec.; b. nr. Riedsville, N.C., Oct. 10, 1918; s. Joseph B. and Sallie L. (Strader) L.; B.S. in Mech. Engring., N.C. State U., 1939; exec. program U. N.C., 1961; m. Myrtle Edna Bailey, Sept. 20, 1941; children—Jansen B., John H., Justina. Supt. bldgs. and grounds Meredith Coll., Raleigh, N.C., 1939-41; asst. plant engr. N.C. Shipbldg. Co., Wilmington, N.C., 1941-46; profl. mech. engr., 1946-47; with Springs Mills, Inc., 1947—, plant engr., 1948-60, asst. to v.p. finishing, 1960-62, dir. finishing, 1962-64, v.p. finishing, 1964-66, v.p. corporate devel., 1966-67, exec. v.p. operations, 1968-69, exec. v.p. research, engring. and corporate devel., 1969—, also dir. Trustee Textile Research Inst. Registered profl. engr., N.C. Mem. Am. Soc. M.E. (past chmn. Piedmont sect.), Phi Kappa Phi, Theta Tau, Pi Tau Sigma. Methodist. Patentee Open-width wet processing apparatus, mercerizing frame washing system, pillow tubing opening and detwister. Home: Route 4 Box 334 Lancaster SC 29720 Office: Springs Mills Inc Fort Mill SC 29715

LASLIE, JOHN LEWIS COBBS, banker; b. Montgomery, Ala., May 27, 1917; s. Carney Graham and Isabelle Woodfin (Cobbs) L.; student Phillips Exeter Acad., 1933-35; B.A. magna cum laude, Princeton, 1939; m. Martha Elaine Alexander; 1 dau., Adele Easton. Owner, Cook's Confections, 1950-60; chief adminstrv. officer Continental Barges, Inc., Gentilly Properties, Inc., Financial Securities, Inc., New Orleans, 1957—; v.p., treas., dir. Delta Capital Corp., 1961—; pres., chief adminstr. Aladdin Oil Co., Aladdin Prodn. Co., 1963—; pres. First Nat. Bank, Slidell, La., 1967—; dir. Ceres Devel. Co., So. Cemeteries, Inc., Roane Flying Service, Inc., So. Metal Products, Consmar Corp., Continental Shelf Marine. Chmn. adv. council investment div. Small Bus. Adminstrn., Washington. Chmn. St. Tammany Parish Disaster Fund, 1969, St. Tammany Parish United Fund, 1970. Bd. dirs. Family Service Soc., 1950-54, Gaudet Home, 1953-57. Recipient Nat. Venture Capital award, 1966. Mem. Nat. Assn. Small Bus. Investment Cos. Democrat. Episcopalian. Rotarian. Home: 219 Country Club Blvd Slidell LA 70458 Office: PO Drawer 708 Slidell LA 70458

LASSETER, DILLARD BROWN, lawyer; b. Vienna, Ga., July 23, 1894; s. Edward S. and Lou Anna (Brown) L.; B.A., Emory Coll., Oxford, Ga., 1913; M.A., N.Y. U., 1914; postgrad. Columbia, 1914-15; m. Helen Smith, Nov. 8, 1920. Entered Am. Fgn. Service, Peking, China, 1915, vice consul, Tientsin, 1920, consul, Antung, Manchuria, 1921-23, Hankow, China, 1923-24; in cotton bus. Greenville, S.C., N.Y.C., Chgo., 1925-30; state dir. Ga. NRA, 1934-35, N.Y.A., 1935-40, dep. adminstr., Washington, D.C., 1940-42; counsel House Civil Service Investigating Com., 1943; regional dir. War Manpower Commn., Ga., 1943-46; became adminstr. Farm Security Adminstrn. and Farmers Home Adminstrn., 1946; lawyer and legislative cons., 1954—. Served as officer, B.E.F., France, 1917-18. Mem., Mil. Order World Wars (so. comdr. 1945), Am. Legion, 40 and 8, S.R., Pi Kappa Phi. Clubs: Atlanta Athletic; Chevy Chase (Md.). Home: 4600 Connecticut Av NW Washington DC 20008 Office: 1616 P St NW Washington DC 20036

LASSETTER, CLARENCE RAY, clergyman; b. Harperville, Miss., May 13, 1926; s. Benjamin Poole and Lola Louise (Lyle) L.; student Miss. Coll., 1944; B.A., also B.S., U. Tex., 1947; B.D., So. Bapt. Theol. Sem., 1950, Th.D., 1954; m. Jean Elizabeth Rasco, Jan. 31, 1951; children—Elizabeth Lee, Leslie Ann, Scott Austin, Steven Lyle. Ordained to ministry Bapt. Ch., 1948; pastor Raymond Ch., Webster, Ky., 1948-51, Glen Allen (Va.) Ch., 1953-55, Ft. Mitchell (Ky.) Ch., 1955-64; exec. sec. No. Ky. Assn. Prot. Chs., Covington, 1964-67; program coordinator Comprehensive Care Center, Covington, 1967—; lectr. maths. and philosophy No. Community Coll. of U. Ky., 1966-70; lectr. philosophy No. Ky. State Coll., 1971—. Pres. No. Ky. Bapt. Pastors Conf., 1960, Ky. Alumni Assn. So. Bapt. Theol. Sem., 1960. Pres. No. Ky. Mental Health Assn., 1961-62; sec., dir. Western Recorder, 1960-66; trustee Greater Cin. Council Alcoholism; dir. No. Ky. Health Council, 1962-67. Served with USNR, 1944-46; chaplain Res. Ky. Col. Mem. Ky. Philos. Soc., No. Ky. Assn. Protestant Chs. (pres. 1960-61), No. Ky. Bapt. Assn. (sec.), Phi Beta Kappa. Democrat. Home: 2003 Pieck Dr Covington KY 41011 Office: 207 Garrard St Covington KY 41011

LASSETTER, JAMES GREEN, realtor; b. Villa Rica, Ga., Sept. 13, 1916; s. John G. W. and Addie (Green) L.; student West Ga. Jr. Coll., 1935-36; B.S., U. Ga., 1940; m. Maggie Samples, Apr. 7, 1939; children— Margaret Anne (Mrs. Charles W. Rushing), Mary Lynn (Mrs. Earl Maxwell), James W. Asst. supr. Farm Security Adminstrn., Carrollton, Ga., 1940; soil conservationist Soil Conservation Service, U.S. Dept. Agr., Marianna, Fla., 1941-43, Chipley, Fla., 1943-52, DeFuniak Springs, Fla., 1952-54; real estate broker James G. Lassetter, DeFuniak Springs, 1954-56, Tallahassee, 1956-58; pres. Tallahassee Realty Co., 1958—; pres. Lassetters of Fla., 1959—. Mem. Tallahassee Bd. Realtors (pres. 1964), Fla. Assn. Realtors (dist. v.p. 1962, 65), Fla. Real Estate Exchangers, Nat., Fla. assns. farm and land brokers, Nat. Inst. Real Estate Brokers, Nat. Assn. Real Estate Bds., Internat. Traders Club, Phi Kappa Phi. Baptist. Elk. Home: 1101 Kenilworth PO Box 1333 Tallahassee FL 32302 Office: 1215 Thomasville Rd PO Box 1333 Tallahassee FL 32302

LASSETTER, MAGGIE SAMPLES (MRS. JAMES GREEN LASSETTER), realtor; b. Villa Rica, Ga.; d. Moses Monroe and Ethel (Boyd) Samples; student W. Ga. Coll., 1938-39; m. James Green Lassetter, Apr. 7, 1939; children—Margaret Annette (Mrs. Charles W. Rushing), Mary Lynn (Mrs. Earl Maxwell), James William. Pvt. practice real estate broker, DeFuniak Springs, Fla., 1954-55; partner Tallahassee Realty Co., 1958—, v.p., 1963. Mem. Tallahassee Sister City Commn., Popayan, Colombia, Fla. Adult Edn. Adv. Bd. Mem. Nat. Inst. Real Estate Brokers (regional v.p. 1971), Nat. (gov. 1967), Fla. (dir. dist. 8, 1972; Fla. pres. women's council 1965, dir. Region 10, 1968, pres. Tallahassee 1971, mem. edn. com.; Woman of Year 1965) assns. realtors, Tallahassee Bd. Realtors (pres. 1970, membership com.; Realtor of Year 1970), Am. Bus. Women's Assn. (Woman of Year 1964, pres. Tallahassee 1966), Capitol (pres. 1968), Dist. II (dir.) bus. and profl. women's clubs, Platform Speakers Am., Urban League, Heritage Found., Fla. Traders, Internat. Traders. Baptist. Mem. Order Eastern Star. Clubs: Toastmistress, woman's (chmn. Am. homes dept.) (Tallahassee). Home: 1101 Kenilworth Rd Tallahassee FL 32303 Office: 1215 Thomasville Rd PO Box 1333 Tallahassee FL 32302

LASSWELL, SHIRLEY ANN BASSO SLESINGER (MRS. FRED D. LASSWELL, JR.), lit. promoting co. exec.; b. Detroit, 1924; d. Michael and Clara (Leasia) Basso; grad. high sch.; m. Stephen Slesinger, Oct. 1949 (dec. 1953); 1 dau., Patricia Ann Slesinger; m. 2d, Fred D. Lasswell, Jr., June 1964. Appeared with Olsen & Johnson Show, 1941-49; pres. Stephen Slesinger, Inc., N.Y.C., Tampa, Fla., 1953—; pres. Red Ryder Enterprises, Inc., Hawley Publs., Inc., Tele-Comics, Inc.; owner U.S. and Canadian rights Winnie-the-Pooh Mdse., 1929—; owner comic strips Red Ryder, Little Beaver, King of the Royal Mounted, Ozark Ike; asso. Zane Grey, Inc. in motion picture field, promotion sales comic books based on famous Western stories. Mem. Tampa Aux. Power Squadron, Krewe of Venus. Home: 5108 Longfellow Av Tampa FL 33609 Office: 1111 N Westshore Blvd Tampa FL 33607

LASTRA, JESUS LEOVLGILDO, dentist; b. La Salud, Havana, Cuba, Jan. 5, 1928 (came to U.S., 1961, naturalized, 1968); s. Patricio and Antonia (Martinez) L.; B.S., Inst. of Havana, 1947; D.D.S., Havana U., 1952; D.M.D., U. Ala., 1966; m. Silvia M. Lopez, Aug. 6, 1950; children—Idalia, Teresa. Practice dentistry, Havana, 1952-61; instr. crown and bridge U. Havana, 1952-59, prof., 1959-61, prof. Summer Sch., 1956; instr., research asso. U. Ala., 1966-68; practice dentistry, Miami, Fla., 1968—. Mem. Am., Mexican, Cuban (past v.p., sec. sci. com.), Havana dental assns., Internat. Assn. for Dental Research, Delta Sigma Delta. Lion. Contbr. articles to profl. jours. Home: 2100 SW 21st Terrace Miami FL 33145 Office: 2150 SW 21st Av Miami FL 33145

LASTRA-GONZALEZ, CARLOS JUAN, ednl. adminstr.; b. Ponce, P.R., Aug. 4, 1919; s. Francisco Lastra Carrasquillo and Margarita Gonzalez; B.A. magna cum laude, U. P.R., 1954; M.A., Harvard, 1956, Ph.D., 1961; m. Idalia de Leon; children—Amir, Sarai, Juan C., Daniel, David. Office mgr. Hosp. Supply Co. San Juan, 1938-43; accountant with Julio Rodriguez, San Juan, 1947-48; head accountant Procter and Gamble, San Juan, 1948-49; instr. U. P.R., 1956-57, asso. prof. social scis., dir. indsl. project Social Sci. Research Center, 1957-61; sec. of commerce of P.R., 1961-64, sec. of state, 1965-67; chancellor Inter Am. U of P.R., Area I, 1967-68; dir. Sch. Pub. Adminstr., U. P.R., 1968—. Trustee Presbyn. Hosp., Evangelical Sem. P.R. Recipient Gold medal econs. U. P.R., 1954, scholarship award, 1954; fellowship award John Hay Whitney Found., 1955. Mem. Am. Statis. Assn., Am. Econ. Assn., P.R. Econs. and Statis. Assn., Nat. Assn. Accountants, Gideons Internat. Author: The Impact of Minimum Wages on a Labor Oriented Industry, 1964. Writer weekly financial news column El Mundo, San Juan. Home: 1785 Santa Eulalia Cupey Ext Sagrado Corazon Rio Piedras Office: First Fed Savs Bldg Santurce PR 00910

LASWELL, THOMAS CARROLL, JR., realtor; b. Owensboro, Ky., Sept. 27, 1920; s. Thomas Carroll and Lottie (Omer) L.; A.B., Centre Coll. Ky., 1943; m. Martha Hardin Bosley, Sept. 20, 1943; children—Martha Carroll, Janet Bosley. Realtor, real estate appraiser J.R. Laswell & Sons, Owensboro, 1946—, Laswell Ins. Agcy., Owensboro, 1948—; chmn. bd. Citizens Security Life Ins. Co. Instr. real estate courses Brecia Coll., 1969—. Mayor protem, Owensboro, 1954-57. Bd. dirs. Ky. Soc. Crippled Children, Jr. Achievement, Owensboro. Served to lt. (j.g.) USNR, 1943-45; ETO, PTO. Named Realtor of Year Owensboro Bd. Realtors, 1966. Mem. Am. Right of Way Assn., Ky. Assn. Realtors (dir. 1968, pres. 1971), Ky. Assn. Farm Mgrs. and Rural Appraisers, Ownesboro-Daviess County C. of C. (v.p. 1966), Centre Coll. Alumni Assn. (nat. pres. 1969-70). Mem. Christian Ch. (chmn. congregation 1960-61). Rotarian (gov. dist. 371, 1959-60). Clubs: Owensboro (Ky.) Country; Campbell, Investigators. Home: 2110 S Cedar St Owensboro KY 42301 Office: 2309 Frederica St Owensboro KY 42301

LASZLO, JOHN, physician; b. Cologne, Germany, May 28, 1931; s. Daniel and Edith (Vincze) L.; A.B., Columbia, 1951; M.D., Harvard, 1955; m. Nancy Warner, Mar. 19, 1962; children—Rebecca, Jennifer, Daniel Walter. Came to U.S., 1937, naturalized, 1944. Intern, U. Chgo. Med. Center, 1956; sr. asst. surgeon Nat. Cancer Inst., 1957-58; asso. prof. medicine Duke Med. Center, 1960-71, prof., 1971-72; chief med. service Durham VA Hosp., 1968—. Mem. A.C.P., Am. Soc. Hematology, Am. Assn. Cancer Research, Nat. Cancer Inst. (pharmacology study sect. 1970—). Home: Box 266 Route 1 Durham NC 27705 Office: VA Hosp Fulton Rd Durham NC 27705

LATCHAM, FREDERICK CHARLES, JR., publisher; b. Denver, Aug. 17, 1917; s. Frederick Charles and Louise (Newman) L.; B.A., U. Colo., 1942; m. Joyce Elaine Atkins, Oct. 3, 1953; children—Frederick Charles III, George Geoffery. Line forman Colo. Builders Supply Co., Denver, 1942-43; survey party chief Ford, Bacon & Davis, 1947-49; project engr. Brown & Roote, Miss., Ala., Ga. 1949-53; mng. editor Beeville Pub. Co., Inc. (Tex.), 1953-58, pub., 1958—. Bee County drive chmn. United Fund; mem. United Community Services, Corpus Christi, 1971. Pres. bd. trustees Bee County Coll., 1965—. Served with USAF, 1943-47. Mem. South Tex. (pres. 1966-67), Tex. (dir. 1965-69) press assns., South Tex. (dir. 1967—), Beeville and Bee County (pres.-elect) chambers commerce, Navy League (Beeville council pres. 1960-61, 71—), Chi Psi. Methodist. Rotarian (pres. 1959-60). Home: 210 E Hutchinson St Beeville TX 78102 Office: 109-11 N Washington St Beeville TX 78102

LATHAM, ALICE FRANCES PATTERSON (MRS. WILLIAM JOSEPH LATHAM), pub. health nurse; b. Macon, Ga., Dec. 18, 1916; d. Frank Waters and Ruby (Dews) Patterson; R.N., Charity Hosp. Sch. Nursing, New Orleans, 1937; student George Peabody Coll. Tchrs., 1938-39; B.S. in Pub. Health Nursing, U. N.C., 1954; M.P.H., Johns Hopkins U., 1966; m. William Joseph Latham, July 21, 1940; children—Jo Alice (Mrs. Samuel Earl Wood), Marynette, Lauruby Cathleen. Staff pub. health nurse assigned spl. venereal disease study USPHS, Darien Ga., 1939-40; county pub. health nurse Bacon County, Alma, 1940-41; USPHS spl. venereal disease project, Glynn County, Brunswick, 1943-47; county pub. health nurse Glyn County, 1949-51, Ware County, Waycross, 1951-52; pub. health nurse supr. Wayne-Long-Brantley-Liberty Counties, Jesup, 1954-56; dir. pub. health nursing Wayne-Long-Appling Bacon-Pierce Counties, Jesup 1956—, now dist. nursing dir. S.E. health dist., exec. dir. dist. 2 and 4 and Ware County Home Health Agys. Bd. dirs. Wayne County Mental Health Assn., 1959, 60, 61, Wayne County Tb Assn., 1958-62; a non-alcoholic organizer Jesup group Alcoholics Anonymous, 1962-63; adv. council Ware Meml. Hosp, Sch. Practical Nursing, Waycross, Ga., 1958. Recipient recognition Gen. Service Bd., Alcoholics Anonymous, Inc. Fellow Am. Pub. Health Assn.; mem. Am., 8th Dist. (pres. 1954-58, dir. 1960-62, 1st v.p. 1962), Ga. (exec. bd. 1954-58) nurses assns., Ga. Pub. Health Assn. (chmn. nursing sect. 1956-57). Contbr. to state nursing manuals. Home: 115 Harper St Jesup GA 31545 Office: Southeast Health District Office 1101 Church St Waycross GA 31501

LATHAM, HERALD ROWE, pub. relations co. exec.; b. Durham, N.C., Dec. 13, 1924; s. Romulus Everett and Lucille (Hocutt) L.; student N.C. State Coll., 1945-46, U. N.C., 1946-47, Coll. of William and Mary, 1948-49; m. Emileigh Maxwell, May 26, 1951; children—Lynn and Diann (twins), Herald Jeffrey. Reporter, Norfolk (Va.) Ledger-Dispatch, 1948-51; reporter Charlotte (N.C.) Observer, 1951-52; reporter Norfolk Virginian-Pilot, 1952-54; pub. relations editor Va. State Ports Authority, 1954-55; city editor Kinston (N.C.) Daily Free Press, 1955-60; mng. editor Florence (S.C.) Morning News, 1960-61; copy desk chief Atlanta Jour., 1961-64; asst. mng. editor Indsl. Devel. Mag., Atlanta, 1964-65; pub. relations dir., editor Cin. Mag., Greater Cin. C. of C., 1965-69; pub. relations, v.p., gen. mgr. Harshe-Rotman & Druck, Inc., Memphis office, 1969—; freelance writer. Sec. Cin. Pub. Observance Assn., 1966-69. Served with USNR, 1942-45; PTO. Mem. Cin. Advertisers Club (v.p., dir.), Memphis Advertisers Club, Pub. Relations Soc. Am. Kiwanian. Editor: Memphis Mag., 1970. Home: 5801 Vassar Dr Memphis TN 38138 Office: 100 N Main Bldg Memphis TN 38103

LATHAM, WILLIAM PETERS, composer, educator; b. Shreveport, Jan. 4, 1917; s. Lawrence L. and Eugenia (Peters) L.; student Asbury Coll., Wilmore, Ky., 1933-35, Cin. Conservatory Music, 1936-38; B.Sc. in Music Edn., U. Cin., 1938; B.Mus., Coll. Music Cin., 1940, M.Mus., 1941; Ph.D., Eastman Sch. Music, 1951; student composition with Eugene Goossens, Howard Hanson, Herbert Elwell; m. Joan Seyler, Apr. 18, 1946; children—Leslie Virginia, William Peters, Carol Jean. Mem. faculty N. Tex. State Tchrs. Coll., 1938-39, Eastern Ill. State Tchrs. Coll., 1946; mem. faculty State Coll. Ia., 1946-65, prof. music, 1959-65; prof. composition N. Tex. State U. Sch. Music, 1965—, dir. grad. studies, 1969—. Served to 2d lt. AUS, 1942-46. Scholar in composition Cin. Coll. Music, 1939-41; recipient 1st prize, grad. div. Phi Mu Alpha, 1952. Mem. A.S.C.A.P. (annual awards 1962—), Music Educators Nat. Conf., Phi Mu Alpha, Pi Kappa Lambda. Composer: (for orch.) The Lady of Shalott, 1941, Waltz From a Modern Trilogy, 1941, Fantasy Concerto for Flute and String Orchestra, 1941, Fantasy for Violin and Orchestra, 1946, Suite for Trumpet and String Orchestra, 1951, Sinfonietta, 1953, Concerto for Two Saxophones and Orchestra, 1960, American Youth Performs, 1969; (chamber music) Five Atonal Studies for Clarinet, 1941, Sonata for Oboe and Piano, 1947, Sonatina for Piano, 1949, Sonata for Violin and Piano, 1949, Scatter the Petals, for tenor, harp, viola, alto flute, 1968, Sysiphus, for alto saxophone and piano, 1971; (choral music) Gloria, 1959, A Prophecy of Peace, 1951, Credo, 1959, Glory be to God on High, 1966, Music for Seven Poems, 1958, Blind with Rainbows, 1962; (band music) Proud Heritage, 1955, Brighton Beach, 1954, Court Festival, 1957, Three Chorale Preludes, 1956, Passacaglia and Fugue, 1959, Silver Anniversary, 1961, Escapades, 1965, Dionysian Festival, 1966, Dodecaphonic Set, 1966, Prayers in Space, 1971; (choral music) Te Deum, 1963. Home: Box 13883 NT Sta Denton TX 76203

LATHROP, GEORGE TERRELL, urban planner, educator; b. Asheville, N.C., Aug. 17, 1935; s. Albert Henry and Virginia (Terrell) L.; B.S., N.C. State U., 1957; M. in City Planning, Yale, 1962, certificate Bur. Hwy. Traffic, 1962; postgrad. U. N.C., 1966-69; m. Ann Anthony, Aug. 24, 1957; children—Anthony Terrell, William Park. Urban planner, dir. research Upstate N.Y. Transp. Studies, Albany, 1962-66; lectr. dept. city and regional planning U. N.C., Chapel Hill, 1966—, dir. met. simulation lab., 1968—. Cons. urban and transp. planning agys., 1963—. Served to 1st lt. USAF, 1958-60. Mem. Am. Soc. C.E., Inst. Traffic Engrs., Am. Inst. Planners, Regional Sci. Assn., Tau Beta Pi, Chi Epsilon, Phi Kappa Phi, Sigma Chi. Home: 606 Greenwood Rd Chapel Hill NC 27514

LATIMER, EDWIN PHINNEY, credit co. exec.; b. Honea Path, S.C., Aug. 20, 1909; s. James Clayton and Corrie V. (Phinney) L.; A.B., The Citadel, 1931; m. Katharine Wharton, Sept. 28, 1934; 1 dau., Kay. Instr., Bailey Mil. Acad., 1931-34; with Comml. Credit Co., Columbia, S.C., 1934-37; with Am. Credit Corp. and predecessor cos., Charlotte, N.C., 1937—, pres., 1947-65, chmn. bd., chief exec. officer, 1965—, dir., 1945—, mem. exec. com., 1965—; dir., mem. exec. com. Wachovia Corp., Winston-Salem, N.C. Mem. adv. bd. Salvation Army, Charlotte; bd. dirs. N.C. Citizens Assn., Family and Children's Service, Citadel Devel. Found.; vice chmn. Met. Financial Planning Council, Charlotte. Served to maj. AUS, 1941-46. Mem. Charlotte C. of C. (pres. 1969). Methodist. Clubs: Charlotte Country, Charlotte City, Quail Hollow Country (Charlotte). Home: 1927 Cassamia Pl Charlotte NC 28211 Office: PO Box 2665 Charlotte NC 28201

LATIMER, GEORGE HUBERT, textile co. exec.; b. Honea Path, S.C., Apr. 15, 1911; s. James Clayton and Corrie Virginia (Phinney) L.; A.B., Wofford Coll., 1931; postgrad. U. S.C., 1961; m. Myrtle Thompson, Dec. 31, 1937; children—Ann, Margaret. Asst. mgr. prodn. scheduling LaFrance Industries (S.C.), 1931-33; supt. packing and shipping So. Bleachery and Print Works, Inc., Taylors, S.C., 1933-48; supt. packing and shipping Grace Finishing Plant, Springs Mills, Inc., Lancaster, S.C., 1948-54, divisional supt., 1954-66, asst. plant mgr., 1966-67, plant mgr., 1967-68, gen. mgr., 1968-70, dir. consumer mfg., 1970—. Served with USNR, 1942-46. Mem. Lancaster C. of C. (mem. indsl. council com. 1966—). Episcopalian. Home: 101 Hawthorne Rd Lancaster SC 29720 Office: Grace Finishing Plant Grace Av Lancaster SC 29720

LATTA, HUGH LUSK, designer; b. Corinth, Miss., May 5, 1938; s. Hugh Basil and Ruth (Lusk) L.; B.Design, U. Fla., 1961; M.F.A., Cranbrook Acad. Art, 1963. Instr., Young Peoples Art Center, Cranbrook, Bloomfield Hills, Mich., 1961-62; pres. Design Continuum Inc., Atlanta, 1971—. Asso. prof. Auburn U. Coll. Architecture, 1967—. Chmn. bd. Ga. Interior Designers Found. Mem. Young Men's Round Table, High Mus. Art, Atlanta, 1972—. Named Outstanding Young Man of Atlanta, 1970. Mem. Am. Inst. Designers (nat. gov., chmn. bd. Ga. chpt.), Am. Inst. Interior Designers (nat. edn. chmn. 1971—), Illuminating Engrs. Soc., U. Fla. Alumni Assn., Sigma Chi. Republican. Episcopalian. Contbr. articles to profl. jours. Home: 1857 Walthall Dr NW Atlanta GA 30318 Office: 34 11th St NE Atlanta GA 30309

LATTIER, JOSEPH MALCOLM, JR., dentist; b. Shreveport, La., Sept. 15, 1938; s. Joseph Malcolm and Ozelle (Hadwin) L.; B.A., La. State U., 1961; D.D.S., Loyola U., New Orleans, 1965; m. Mary Martha Martin, Aug. 15, 1964; 1 son, Joseph Martin. Pvt. practice gen. dentistry, Shreveport, 1967—; vis. staff Confederate Meml. Hosp., Willis-Knighton Hosp. Mem. vis. staff Young Men for Good Govt., 1970. Served to capt. USAF, 1965-67. Mem. Am., La. dental assns., La. 4th Dist. Dental Soc. (sci. program chmn., treas. 1972) Acad. Gen. Dentistry, Am. Soc. Dentistry for Children, Shreveport C. of C., Am. Legion, Blue Key, Delta Sigma Delta, Kappa Sigma. Club: Mid-City Optimist (v.p. 1969). Home: 310 Americana St Shreveport LA 71105 Office: 5803 Youree Dr Shreveport LA 71105

LATTING, PATIENCE SEWELL (MRS. TRIMBLE B. LATTING), mayor Oklahoma City, civic worker; b. Texhoma, Okla., Aug. 27, 1918; d. Frank Asa and Leila (Yates) Sewell; A.B. magna cum laude, U. Okla., 1938; M.A., Columbia, 1939; m. Trimble B. Latting, Aug. 23, 1941; children—Francelia, Nancy Sewell (Mrs. Bradley R. Schiller), James Trimble, Cynthia Longley. Asst. to research librarian Chase Nat. Bank, N.Y.C., 1938-39; dir. 1st Nat. Bank, Clinton, Okla.; mayor City of Oklahoma City, 1971—. Mem. Oklahoma City Council. Legislation chmn. Okla. Congress Parents and Tchrs., 1960-67, mem. bd. mgrs., 1959—, mem. exec. com., 1963-67; mem. exec. com., Oklahoma City Council P.T.A.'s, 1960-62; pres. Edgemore P.T.A., Oklahoma City, 1963-64; mem. Okla. Gov.'s Reapportionment Com., 1960, Gov.'s Adv. Com. on Edn., 1964, Mayor's Com. on Internat. Affairs, Oklahoma City, 1962-63, Oklahoma City Citizen's Emergency Finance Com., 1965; mem. bd. Okla. Inst. Justice, 1965—; mem. Okla. Commn. Tchr. Edn. and Profl. Standards, 1965-67; appointed officer of ct. to aid in reapportionment Okla. legislature, 1964; mem. council Oklahoma City, 1967—. Named Woman of Yr. in Civic Work, Oklahoma City chpt. Theta Sigma Phi, 1961, Outstanding Woman award, 1968; named Outstanding Woman of Okla., Soroptimist, 1969; named hon. col. State of Okla., 1960. Mem. Am. Assn. U. Women (state mass media chmn. 1962-63), League Women Voters (mem. Oklahoma City bd. 1958-59), Oklahoma City Tennis Assn. (mem. bd. 1965—), Mortar Bd., Huguenot Soc. Founders of Manakin in the Colony Va., Phi Beta Kappa (v.p. Oklahoma City alumni 1965—), Alpha Lambda Delta, Sigma Alpha Iota, Chi Delta Phi, Pi Mu Epsilon, Pi Beta Phi (pres. Oklahoma City alumni 1947-48). Clubs: 20th Century (sec. 1961-62), Oklahoma City Golf and Country. Instrumental in securing passage of state law permitting local sch. bds. to prohibit high sch. fraternities and sororities, 1953; author of amicus curiae brief field on behalf of Okla. Congress Parents and Tchrs. dealing with reapportionment of state legislature, 1962. Home: 3600 Harvey Pkwy Oklahoma City OK 73118*

LAU, NORMAN EUGENE, ednl. adminstr.; b. Harvey, Ill., July 8, 1930; s. Lawrence J. and Mary Louise (Parent) L.; B.S., Colo. State U., 1953, M.S., 1955; Ph.D., Rutgers U., 1958; m. Eleanor C. Tardy, June 6, 1970; children—1 son, Scott Norman. Entomologist, N.J. Dept. Agr., Trenton, 1958-61; tech. cons. Ratner Pest Control, Atlantic City, 1961-63; product devel. rep. Hooker Chem. Corp., Niagara Falls, N.Y., 1963-65; extension coordinator chems., drugs and pesticides Va. Poly. Inst. and State U., Blacksburg, Va., 1965—. Vice-pres. Niagara County (N.Y.) Mental Health Assn., 1964. Mem. Entomol. Soc. Am., Nat., Va. adult edn. assns., Sigma Xi, Epsilon Sigma Xi. Club: Torch (dir. 1971-72) (Blacksburg). Home: 916 McBryde Lane Blacksburg VA 24060 Office: Va Poly Inst and State U Blacksburg VA 24061

LAU, ROBERT EDMUND, physician; b. York, Pa., Aug. 15, 1917; s. Robert Edmund and Lottie Jane (Trostle) L.; A.B., Gettysburg Coll., 1938; M.D., Jefferson Med. Coll., 1942; m. Ruth Eleanor Haley, May 4, 1954. Intern York Hosp., 1942-43; resident in anesthesiology Oliver Gen. Hosp., Augusta, Ga., 1948-49; commd. capt. M.C., U.S. Air Force; anesthesiologist, flight surgeon, various USAF Hosps., 1950-60; dep. hosp. comdr., 1961-67; dep. dir. for med. staffing and edn. Office of Surgeon Gen., Randolph AFB, Tex., 1968—. Decorated Bronze Star. Diplomate Am. Bd. Anesthesiology. Mem. A.M.A., Am. Soc. Anesthesiologists, Aerospace Med. Assn. Home: 7 Outer Octagon Randolph AFB TX 78148 Office: AF Mil Personnel Center Randolph AFB TX 78148

LAUDERDALE, ROBERT AMIS, JR., educator; b. Harriman, Tenn., July 27, 1922; s. Robert Amis and Ruth (Cashion) L.; B.S., U. Tenn., 1944, M.S., 1948; Ph.D., Mass. Inst. Tech., 1958; m. Maywin Sharp, Aug. 21, 1948; 1 son, David William. Asst. chem. engr. TVA, Knoxville, Tenn., 1944-45; asso. health physicist Oak Ridge Nat. Labs., 1948-52; asst. prof. Mass. Inst. Tech., Cambridge, 1957-58; prof. civil engring. U. Ky., Lexington, 1958—, dir. Water Resources Inst., 1964—. Served with AUS, 1945-47. Mem. Am. Chem. Soc., Water Pollution Control Fedn., Sigma Xi. Home: 3380 Keithshire Way Lexington KY 40503

LAUGHLIN, BOB, athletic dir. Morehead (Ky.) State U. Address: Athletic Dept Morehead State U Morehead KY 40351*

LAUINGER, P(HILLIP) C(HARLES), publisher; b. Oil City, Pa., Aug. 8, 1900; s. Frank T. and Helen (Boyle) L.; A.B., Georgetown U., 1922, LL.D., 1958; Sc.D., St. Bonaventure U., 1957; m. Frances Flaherty, Jan. 19, 1933; children—Philip, Helen, Mary, Frank, Frances, Anthony, Joseph. Staff rep. Oil and Gas Jour., Tulsa, 1922-31, pres., 1931—; dir. Continental Oil Co., Nat. Bank of Tulsa, Home Fed. Savs. & Loan Assn., Derrick Pub. Co., Oil City, Petroleum Pub. Co., Tulsa. Decorated Knight of Malta; knight grand cross Order Holy Sepulchre. Mem. Tex. Mid-Continent Oil and Gas Assn., Natural Gas Assn., Am. Petroleum Inst. Clubs: Tulsa, Southern Hills Country. Author in field. Home: 1357 E 27th Pl Tulsa OK 74114 Office: 211 S Cheyenne Tulsa OK 74103

LAURENT, LAWRENCE BELL, journalist; b. Monroe, La., Mar. 9, 1925; s. Lewis Emeal and Ethel (Dawkins) L.; student U. Va., 1946-49; pvt. study with Dr. W.Y. Elliott, 1954, 55, 56, Dr. Franklin Dunham, 1957-58; m. Margaret F. Goodwillie, Nov. 1, 1949; children—Richard Sandford, Arthur Halliday, Margaret Funsten, Elizabeth McLean. With Bluefield (W.Va.) Daily Telegraph, 1949-50, Charlottesville (Va.) Daily Progress, 1950-51, Washington Post, 1951—. Adj. prof. communications Am. U., Washington, 1963—; chmn. editorial bd. TV Quar., 1963—; guest prof. Syracuse U., 1965; vis. prof. U. Detroit, 1967. Served with USNR, 1943-45. Recipient Front Page award Am. Newspaper Guild, 1964. Mem. Nat. Acad. Television Arts and Scis., White House Corrs. Assn., Am. Assn. U. Profs., Sigma Delta Chi, Pi Delta Epsilon. Episcopalian (vestryman). Club: Nat. Press. Contbr. to books, mags. Editor, author (with Newton N. Minow) Equal Time, 1964. Home: 215 Jefferson St Alexandria VA 22314 Office: 1515 L St NW Washington DC 20005

LAURIE, WILFRID RHODES, ret. lawyer; b. Chatham, Ont., Can., Oct. 5, 1898; s. George E. and Annie (Rhodes) L.; J.D., U. Mich., 1922; m. Margaret Baird Thomas, Mar. 31, 1934. Admitted to Mich. bar, 1922; practiced in Detroit, 1922-25; house atty. Grinnell Bros. and Grinnell Realty Co., 1926-36, v.p., sec., 1933-36; Mich. mgr. charge property mgmt. HOLC, 1937-39; chief legal office Detroit ordnance dist. U.S. Army, 1943-63; now ret. Served with U.S. Army, World War 1. Recipient Meritorious Civilian Service award War Dept., 1945; Exceptional Civilian Service and Ofcl. Commendation for exceptional performance duty, Sec. of Army, 1963. Mem. Fed. Bar Assn. (v.p. Detroit 1959), Land Contract Dealers Assn. Detroit (pres. 1935), First Protestant Soc. Detroit (trustee). Presbyn. Club: Exchange (pres. Detroit 1936). Home: Everglades House 2000 S Ocean Dr Fort Lauderdale FL 33316

LAUTENSCHLAGER, EDWARD WALTER, coll. dean; b. Amsterdam, N.Y., Mar. 1, 1927; s. Edward A. and Carolyn (Haas) L.; B.S., Franklin and Marshall Coll., 1950; M.S., U. Va., 1956, Ph.D., 1963; m. Audrey Mae Warner, June 16, 1948; children—Edward Warner, Carolee Anne, Karen Sue, Garrett Brian, Laurence David. Instr. biology U. Va., 1959-63, asst. prof., 1963-65, registrar, 1959-65; dir. data processing U. Va., 1964-65; prof. biology, dean coll., Roanoke Coll., 1965—. Chmn. Salem Redevelopment and Housing Authority. Trustee Marion Coll., Va. Served with USNR, 1944-46, 51-53, comdr. Res. Mem. Va. Assn. Coll. Registrars and Admissions Officers (past pres.), So. Assn. Coll. Registrars and Admissions Officers (past pres.), Am. Soc. Parasitologists, Am. Soc. Tropical Medicine and Hygiene, Salem-Roanoke County C. of C. (past pres.), Sigma Xi, Omicron Delta Kappa, Phi Sigma Kappa. Research in animal parasitology. Home: 530 E Main St Salem VA 24153

LAVENDER, ROBERT E., justice Okla. Supreme Ct.; b. Muskogee, Okla., July 19, 1926; s. Harold J. and Vergene (Martin) L.; student U. Tulsa, 1946-49, LL.B., 1953; m. Maxine Knight, Dec. 22, 1945; children—Linda, Robert K., Debra, William. Dept. clk. Ct. of Tulsa County, 1946-48, Ct. of Common Pleas, 1949-51; asst. bookkeeper Cain's Coffee Co., 1948-49; claim adjuster Mass. Bond & Ins. Co., Tulsa, 1951-53, U.S. Fidelity & Guarantee, 1953-54; admitted to Okla. bar, 1954; asso. with Joe Francis, Tulsa, 1955-58; practiced in Tulsa, 1958-61; partner firm Bassmann, Gordon, Mayberry & Lavender, Claremore, 1961-65; asst. atty. City of Tulsa, 1954-55; justice Okla. Supreme Ct., 1965—. Served with USNR, 1944-46; PTO. Mem. Am., Okla., Rogers County bar assns., Am. Judicature Soc., Phi Alpha Delta. Republican. Methodist (dir.). Mason, Lion. Home: 2910 Kerry Lane Oklahoma City OK 73120 Office: State Supreme Ct State Capitol Bldg Oklahoma City OK 73120

LAVERDIERE, ERNEST RENE, govt. ofcl.; b. Woonsocket, R.I., Feb. 26, 1918; s. Charles Joseph and Rose (Pariseau) L.; B.Accounting, Hill Coll., 1938; postgrad. Providence Coll., 1938-40, Harvard, 1944, Johns Hopkins, 1946-48; grad. Indsl. Coll. Armed Forces, 1967, Command and Gen. Staff Coll., 1965; m.Marjorie Frances Ellwood, June 8, 1943; children—Ernest Rene, Nancy Lee, Carol Ann. Instr., Hill Coll., Woonsocket, 1938-39, Pequod Bus. Sch., Meriden, Conn., 1940-41; accountant Haskins & Sells, Balt., 1946-47; chief accounting sect. Balt. regional office VA, 1947-52; chief financial policy br. Chem. Corps Material Command, Balt., 1952-55; dep. dir. accounting, finance Air Research and Devel. Command, Andrews AFB, Washington, 1955-60, dir., dep dir. accounting and finance Air Force Systems Command, Washington, 1961—; dep. nat. disbursing officer U.S. Mil. Government, Korea, 1945-46; operator Mgmt. Services Co., Ellicott City, Md., 1959—. Served from pvt. to capt., AUS, 1941-46; col. Res. Mem. Res. Officers Assn., Am. Soc. Mil. Comptrollers (past pres. Balt. chpt.), Fed. Govt. Accountants Assn., V.F.W. Club: Toastmasters (Washington). Home: 3642 Ligon Rd Ellicott City MD 21043 Office: Air Force Systems Command Andrews AFB Washington DC 20331

LAVERTY, JOHN J., adminstr. Univ. Hosp., Lexington, Ky. Office: 800 Rose St Lexington KY 40506*

LAVEY, FREDERICK ADOLPH, lawyer, pub. co. exec.; b. Manchester, Conn., Sept. 15, 1916; s. Frederick Henry and Hilma (Anderson) L.; B.S., Harvard, 1938, postgrad. in bus. adminstrn., 1938-39; postgrad. U. Va. Law Sch. 1940-42, LL.B., 1946; m. Evelyn Heatwole, Jan. 16, 1943; 1 son, Frederick Painter. Admitted to Conn. bar, 1946, D.C. bar, 1947; asso. firm Hewes & Awalt, Hartford, Conn., 1946-47, Awalt Clark & Sparks, Washington, 1947-51; with Pub. Utilities Reports, Inc., 1951—, exec. v.p., 1956-61, pres., 1961—, gen. mgr., 1959—, dir., 1968—; exec. sec. Utilities Publ. Com., 1961—; pres. 2d Class Mail Publs., Inc., 1966-70; pub. mgmt. com. Am. Bus. Press, Inc., 1965-68, dir., 1968-70. Mem. Postmaster Gen.'s Tech. Adv. Com., 1965-68, 70—; chmn. local troop com. Boy Scouts Am.; pres., chmn. bd. dirs. Shenandoah Retreat Civic Assn., 1958-62, 69-70. Served to lt., USNR, 1942-46. Mem. Am. Bar Assn., Bar Assn. D.C., Raven Soc., Delta Theta Phi. Lutheran. Clubs: Harvard Business School, Harvard University of Va., Nat. Lawyers, International Retreat Golf and Country. Home: 4204 Thornapple St Chevy Chase MD 20015 Office: 1828 L St NW Washington DC 20036

LAVINGIA, KISHOR PARMANAND, civil engr.; b. Ahmedabad, India, July 29, 1943; s. Parmanand Popatlal Lavingia and Padmavati Lalchand Shah; came to U.S., 1966; B.C.E., Gujarat U., Ahmedabad, 1964; M.C.E., U. Ky., 1967. Structural engr. Vakil, Mehta, Parikh, Sheth, cons. engrs., Ahmedabad, 1964-66; engr. Watkins & Assos., Inc., Lexington, 1967-70; vis. prof. Sch. Architecture, Ahmedabad, 1970-72. Registered profl. engr., Ky. Home and office: 4b 1037 Cross Keys Rd Lexington KY 40504

LAW, BRUCE, lawyer, mayor, judge; b. Memphis, Dec. 21, 1925; s. Stanley and Mary (Sheperd) L.; B.S., Memphis State U., 1950, LL.B., 1952; postgrad. U. Tenn., 1952; m. Rebekah Jane Bell, July 1, 1955; 1 dau., Lisa Jane. Admitted to Tenn. bar, 1952; practiced in Memphis, 1952—; city judge, mayor, Germantown, Tenn., 1958—. Instr. U. Memphis, 1961-62. City councilman, Germantown, 1958-60. Served with AUS, 1944-46. Decorated Bronze Star medal, Purple Heart. Mem. Tenn., Memphis, Shelby County bar assns., Delta Theta Phi, Lambda Chi Alpha. Democrat. Methodist. Home: 6922 Great Oakes Rd Germantown TN 38038 Office: Sterick Bldg Memphis TN 38103

LAW, JOHN RANDOLPH, orthodontist; b. Morgantown, W.Va., Dec. 16, 1927; s. Harry Randolph and Gail (Davis) L.; A.B., W.Va. U., 1949, M.S. in Zoology, 1951; D.D.S., Georgetown U., 1955; M.S.D. (USPHS, NIH fellow), U. Wash., 1960; m. Margaret T. Hoffman, July 16, 1948; children—John, Carolyn, Christopher, Andrew. Instr. microbiol. technique lab. W.Va. U., 1949-51, instr. ornithology lab. course, 1949-51; asst. curator W.Va. U. Zool. Mus., 1949-51; asso. prof. orthodontics Georgetown U. Sch. Dentistry, 1960-62, asst. clin. prof. orthodontics, 1962-64, guest lectr. dept. anatomy Med. Sch., 1966-68; guest lectr. orthodontics Montgomery Jr. Coll., 1968; asst. prof. orthodontics Howard U. Dental Sch. Grad. Orthodontic Program, 1969; practice orthodontics, Washington, 1962—; partner Drs. Heim & Law, Potomac Real Estate Assos.; cons. Washington Hosp. Center of D.C., Childrens Hosp. of D.C. Mem. Alumni Bd. Georgetown U. Served to lt. USN, 1955-58. Mem. D.C. Dental Soc., Middle Atlantic, Balt. Washington socs. orthodontists, Eastern Strang Tweed, Greater Washington (past pres.) orthodontic study clubs, Am. Soc. Dentistry for Children, A.A.A.S., Am. Soc. Preventive Dentistry, Georgetown U. Dental Sch. Alumni Assn., Phi Kappa Psi, Psi Omega. Kiwanian (past pres.). Club: Potomac Swimming and Tennis (Potomac, Md.). Home: 7543 Sebago Rd Bethesda MD 20034 Office: 4633 41st St NW Washington DC 20016

LAW, WILLIAM HOLDEN, JR., state ofcl.; b. Colonie, N.Y., Feb. 23, 1930; s. William H. and Dorothy (Lant) L.; B.A., U. Me., 1953; M.G.A., U. Pa., 1959; m. Shirley F. Findley, Mar. 31, 1972; children—Richard D., William H. III, Robin Elizabeth. City mgr., Guttenberg, Ia., 1959-61; staff asso. J.K. Jacobs & Co., 1961-62; town mgr. Franklin Twp., N.J., 1962-64; bus. adminstr. Town of Irvington (N.J.), 1964-65; city mgr. City of Pensacola (Fla.), 1965-71; staff dir. Fla. Ho. of Reps., Tallahassee, 1971—; pres. Municipal Cons. Service; trustee Financial Fla. Investors. Bd. dirs. Jr. Achievement; bd. dirs. United Fund, 1966-71, exec. com., 1970-71. Dir. Escambia County Water Devel. Authority, 1969-72; mem. adv. com. to com. rds. and hwys. Legislative Council, 1968-69; mem. space allocation subcom. Fla. Utilities Coordinating Com., 1967-70; mem. resources and adv. com. to com. on transp. Fla. Ho. of Reps, 1969. Served with USNR, 1949-53. Mem. Indsl. Mgmt. Assn., Internat. City Mgmt. Assn., Fla. Mgrs. Assn. (dir.), Fla. League Municipalities, Am. Soc. Pub. Adminstrn., Am. Acad. Polit. Sci., Pensacola C. of C. (dir.). Home: 731 Pensacola Beach Blvd Pensacola Beach FL 32561 Office: Room 303 Capital Bldg Tallahassee FL 32304

LAWDER, LEWIS WAGGNER, assn. adminstr.; b. Balt., Sept. 3, 1919; s. Lewis Waggner and Helen (Heinekamp) L.; student U. Md., 1937-39, Dale Carnegie Sch. Human Relations, 1940, Elmer Wheeler Sales Tng. Sch., St. Louis, 1947, Inst. Orgn. Mgmt. U.S. C. of C. at U. N.C., 1955-56, 57; m. Elizabeth Joan Giles, June 10, 1949; 1 son, Kirk. Gen. mgr. Colonial Fuel Co., Washington, 1946-55; asst. exec. v.p. Met. Washington Bd. Trade, 1955-61; dir. field service div. Nat. Assn. Home Builders, Washington, 1961-68; exec. v.p. Home Builders & Contractors Assn. Palm Beach County (Fla.), 1969—. Bd. dirs. Boys' Club Washington, 1947-57; chmn. Nat. Cherry Blossom Festival Parade, Washington, 1954, 55. Served with AC, AUS, 1942-46; PTO. Decorated Bronze Star. Mem. Fla. Home Builders Assn. (chmn. Fla. exec. officers council 1971), Nat. Assn. Home Builders Exec. Officers Council. Kiwanian (dir. N.E. Washington 1949-51). Home: 7421 W Lake Dr West Palm Beach FL 33406 Office: 2921 Australian Av West Palm Beach FL 33407

LAWLAH, JOHN WESLEY, radiologist, educator; b. Bessemer, Alabama, Aug. 12, 1904; s. John Wesley and Mattie Mae (Lindsey) L.; grad. Morehouse Acad., Atlanta, 1922; B.Sc., Morehouse Coll., 1925, D.Sc., 1941; M.S., U. Wis., 1929; M.D., Rush Med. Coll., 1932; m. Leora Frances McCarrell, Feb. 9, 1933; children—Evelyn Frances, John Wesley, 111. Intern Provident Hosp., Chgo., 1931-32, radiologist, 1935-36, med. dir. and supt., 1936-41; fellow in radiology Billings Hosp., U. Chgo., 1932-35; dean Howard U. Med. Sch., also prof. radiology, 1941-46, clin. prof. radiology, 1946—; cons. radiology Mt. Alto VA Hosp., 1957—; supt. Freedmen's Hosp., Washington, 1942-44, now radiologist. Sec.-Treas. Nat. Conf. Hosp. Adminstrs., 1936-41; mem. panel med. experts selected to draw up preliminary regulations and procedures for med. sect. WHO, 1946; mem. Freedmen's Hosp. Study Commn., 1955—. Mem. pub. health adv. council D.C. Bd. Commrs. Diplomate Am. Bd. Radiology. Fellow Am. Coll. Radiology, Internat. Coll. Surgeons; mem. Radiol. Soc. N.A., Am. Coll. Hosp. Adminstrs., A.M.A., A.A.A.S., Am. Roentgen Ray Soc., Washington Acad. Medicine, Sigma Xi, Alpha Omega Alpha, Sigma Sigma, Alpha Phi Alpha, Sigma Pi Phi. Clubs: Forty (Chgo); Brookland Liberary and Hunting (Washington). Contbr. articles to sci. jours. Home: 32 Bryant St NW Washington 1 DC 20001 Office: 2208 Georgia Av NW Washington DC 20001

LAWLER, EDWARD J., lawyer; b. Chgo., Sept. 15, 1908; s. Edward James and Sarah (Gahan) L.; Ph.B., U. Chgo., 1926-30; LL.B., Harvard, 1933; m. Elizabeth Falls Dunscomb, Dec. 16, 1939. Admitted to Ill. bar, 1933, Tenn. bar, 1941; atty., auditor income tax sect. Office Collector Internal Revenue, Chgo., 1933-34; spl. atty. Bur. Internal Revenue, 1935-36, practicing lawyer, 1937-38, atty. SEC, 1939-40; practiced in Memphis, 1941—. Dir. Ellis Bagwell Drug Co., Chickasaw Bldg. Co. Served as lt. comdr. USNR, 1942-45. Decorated Bronze Star medal. Fellow Am. Bar Found.; mem. Am., Tenn., Memphis Shelby County bar assns., Phi Beta Kappa. Home: 644 S Belvedere Blvd Memphis TN 38104 Office: 1st Nat Bank Bldg Memphis TN 38103

LAWLER, HERMAN ROGER, investor; b. Ben Wheeler, Tex., Mar. 18, 1929; s. William Robert and Frances (Hammock) L.; student U. Tex. at Arlington, 1948-49, So. Methodist U., summers 1949, 50; A.A., San Mateo State Coll., 1953; postgrad. San Jose State Coll., 1954; m. Bertha Faye Thomas, Dec. 21, 1951 (div. Nov. 1969); children—Stephen, Donna, Janette, Bradford, Patricia, Cary; 1 dau. (by previous marriage), Linda Carol; m. Shirley Ann Stevens, June 27, 1970. Tech., engr. Varian Assos., Palo Alto, Cal., 1954-59; pres. Lawler-Williams, Inc., Sunnyvale, Cal., 1959-61, Lawler Properties, Dallas, 1961—; founder Royal Nat. Bank, Dallas. Served with USN, 1946-47, USMCR, 1951-52. Mem. Nat. Assn. Home Builders. Baptist. Mason. Home: 2800 Preston Tower Dallas TX 75225 Office: 1120 Empire Central Pl Dallas TX 75247

LAWLER, ROBERT CLAIR, real estate developer; b. Richmond, Ind., May 9, 1902; s. William F. and Mary M. (McManus) L.; student pub. schs.; m. Elizabeth (Francis), Apr. 28, 1931; children—Mary Louise, Betty Ann, Nancy C. Owner Lawler's, Inc., Richmond, New Castle and Muncie, Ind,. 1932-52; real estate developer, builder shopping centers and apts., Clearwater, Fla., 1952—; dir. Pinellas Central Bank & Trust Co., Bank of Indian Rocks (Largo, Fla.); pres. Lawlers, Inc. Elk, Kiwanian. Home and office: 817 Osceola Rd Belleair Clearwater FL 33516

LAWRENCE, ALEXANDER A., U.S. dist. judge, Savannah, Ga. Address: US Courthouse Savannah GA 31401*

LAWRENCE, CHARLES D., mus. specialist, curator paintings U.S. Navy Art Center, Washington. Address: Combat Art Gallery Bldg 67 Washington Navy Yard Washington DC 20390*

LAWRENCE, DAVID, editor and Washington corr.; b. Phila., Dec. 25, 1888; s. Harris and Dora Lawrence; B.A., Princeton U., 1910; m. Ellanor Campbell Hayes, July 17, 1918 (dec. June 1969); children—David, Mark, Nancy (dec.), Etienne. Joined Washington staff A.P., 1910; Washington corr. N.Y. Evening Post, 1916-19, writing first Washington dispatch to be syndicated nationally by wire; pres. Consol. Press Assn., Washington, 1919-33; founder, pres. U.S. Daily, Washington, 1926-33; pres., editor U.S. News, 1933-48; founder, pres. World Report, 1946-48; editor U.S. News & World Report, Washington, 1948—, pres., 1948-59, chmn. bd., 1959—. Writer of dispatch on nat. and world affairs syndicated to approximately 200 daily newspapers in U.S. Fellow Sigma Delta Chi. Clubs: Nat. Press, Metropolitan, Cosmos, Princeton (Washington). Author: True Story of Woodrow Wilson, 1924; The Other Side of Government, 1929; Beyond the New Deal, 1934; Stumbling Into Socialism, 1935; Nine Honest Men, 1936; Who Were the Eleven Million, 1937; Diary of a Washington Correspondent, 1942; The Editorials of David Lawrence, 1971; also various mag. articles. Office: 2300 N St NW Washington DC 20037

LAWRENCE, DUARD JONES, telephone co. exec.; b. Covington, Ky., July 24, 1923; s. Duard H. and Leona (Jones) L.; student Ohio Mechanics Inst. Applied Sci., 1942; B.S. in Personnel Adminstrn., U. Cin., 1953; m. Loraine Emily Stickling, Apr. 30, 1945; children—Keith C., Denise M., David H. Sales mgr. Cin. & Suburban Bell Telephone Co., 1945-58, marketing sales mgr., 1960-68, gen. labor relations mgr., 1969—; marketing rep. A.T. & T., N.Y.C., 1958-60. Served with USNR, 1942-46. Mem. Am. Marketing Assn. (mem. bd. control 1960-63), Cin. Exec. Assn. (dir. 1965-68), Campbell County (Ky.) C. of C., Indsl. Relations Research Assn. Republican. Mem. United Ch. of Christ. Home: 33 Riverview St Fort Thomas KY 41075 Office: 225 E 4th St Cincinnati OH 45202

LAWRENCE, FRED PARKER, citriculturist; b. Lebanon, Tenn., Mar. 13, 1911; s. Euless Smith and Daisy (Parker L.; B.S., U. Fla., 1934, M.A., 1953; m. Ann Kathryn Williams, Dec. 23, 1934; children—Fred Parker II, Stephen Lawson. With Farmers Home Adminstrn., 1933-42, asst. state dir., 1940-42; citriculturist U. Fla., Agrl. Extension Service, U.S. Dept. Agr., Gainesville, 1947—. U.S. Dept. Agr. citrus breeding and variety dir. Whitmore Found., 1958-60. Active Fla. 4-H Found., U. Fla. Senate. Served to comdr. USNR, 1942-46. Recipient Distinguished Service award Fla. Bankers, 1965. Camp McQuarrie Distinguished Service award Fla. Citrus Growers Assn., 1964. Mem. Am. Soc. Hort. Sci., Soil and Crop Sci. Soc. Am., Tropical Region, Southeastern hort. socs., Fla. State Hort. Soc., Fla. Entomol. Soc., Soil and Crop Soc. Fla., Phi Kappa Phi, Gamma Sigma Delta. Kiwanian. Club: Gainesville (Fla.) Golf and Country. Contbr. articles to profl. jours. Home: 2805 SW 1st Av Gainesville FL 32601

LAWRENCE, HARDING LUTHER, airlines exec.; b. Perkins, Okla., July 15, 1920; s. Moncey Luther and Helen Beatrice (Langley) L.; student Kilgore Coll., 1938-39; B.B.A., U. Tex., 1942; LL.B., South Tex. Coll. Law, 1949; LL.D., U. Portland, 1968; m. Jimmie G. Bland, Jan. 2, 1942; children—James B., Deborah M., State R.; m. 2d, Mary

G. Wells, Nov. 25, 1967; adopted children—Pamela, Katy. Gen. sales mgr., then v.p. sales, dir. Pioneer Air Lines, 1947-55; v.p. sales Continental Air Lines, Inc. 1955-57. v.p.-exec. adminstrn., 1957-58, exec. v.p., dir., 1958-65; pres., chief exec. officer Braniff Airways, Inc., 1965-68; chmn. bd., pres. Braniff Internat., Dallas, 1968-70, chmn. bd., chief exec. officer, 1970-—. Mem. Air Transp. Assn. (dir.), Conquistadores del Cielo. Office: Braniff Airways Inc Braniff Airways Bldg Exchange Park Dallas TX 75235

LAWRENCE, HOMER ALBERT, JR., ednl. adminstr.; b. Texarkana, Tex., June 13, 1930; s. Homer Albert and Earnistene Dawn (Nichols) L.; B.S., East Tex. State U., 1951, M.Ed., 1956; D.Ed., U. Tenn., 1966; postgrad. U. S.C., 1969, U. Ga., 1971; m. Mary Ellen Woodruff, Oct. 6, 1951; children—Marianne, James Albert, Julianna. Instr. engring. U. Tex., Arlington, 1957-60; asst. prof. Memphis State U., 1960-64; research asst. Sch. Planning Lab., U. Tenn., 1964-65; supr. sch. plant div. Tenn. Dept. Edn., Nashville, 1965-67; dir. continuing edn. Jackson (Tenn.) State Community Coll., 1967-70; dir. vocational and adult edn. Jackson City Sch. System, 1970-—; ednl. and sch. planning cons. Committeeman West Tenn. area council Boy Scouts Am., 1971. Bd. dirs. YMCA, 1968-70; mem. tech. adv. com. Tenn. Commn. on Aging. Served with Finance Corps, AUS, 1951-53. Named Civitan of Year, 1969. Mem. Adult Edn. Assn. Am., N.E.A., Tenn. Adult Edn. Assn. (pres.), Am. Assn. Sch. Adminstrs., Vocational Indsl. Clubs Am., Am. Indsl. Arts Assn., Acacia, Pi Omega Pi. Methodist. Mason (Shriner). Club: Civitan (v.p., dir.) (Jackson). Author: Standard Repair Manual, 1956; A Study of Tennessee School Property Accounting, 1966; Dynamic Maturity, 1969. Editor: Tenn. Adult Edn. Assn. Newsletter, 1969-71. Home: 1508 N Royal St Jackson TN 38301 Office: 207 Allen St Jackson TN 38301

LAWRENCE, HOWARD S., food packing co. exec.; b. N.Y.C., June 19, 1923; s. Jack and Irene Lillian (Greenman) L.; B.S., N.Y. U., 1946; m. Lila Frances Bilgore, Aug. 26, 1947; children—David Alan, Debra Sue. With David Bilgore & Co., Inc., Clearwater, Fla., 1950-—, v.p., 1965-—, sec., 1966-—. Instr., Dale Carnegie, 1956-58. Pres., Clearwater Festival, 1966-67; mem. adv. bd. Mease Hosp., 1969-70; mem. Sheriffs Adv. Bd., 1971; mem. County Personal Bd., 1969-70; mem. Mchts. Bd., 1971-—; pres. Big Bros., 1972-73. Mem. exec. bd. Pinellas County Democratic Com., 1970-73. Bd. dirs. Drug Abuse Hosp., Clearwater. Served with USAF, 1942-45; PTO. Recipient Outstanding Pres. award Sertoma Club, 1958; City of Clearwater medal outstanding community service, 1967. Mem. Fla. Gift Shippers Assn. (dir. Fla. chpt. 1968-—, pres. elect 1972-—), Fraternal Order Police (v.p.), Clearwater C. of C. (dir.). Clubs: Sertoma (pres. 1958-59). Jewish religion (pres. temple 1958, bd. dirs. 1959-—). Home: 749 Snug Island Clearwater FL 33515 Office: 702 Franklin St Clearwater FL 33517

LAWRENCE, JAMES LEE, govt. ofcl.; b. Lufkin, Tex., Oct. 12, 1920; s. John Samuel and Arlie Adell (Clark) L.; student Stephen F. Austin State Coll., Mass. Inst. Tech., 1943-44; B.S. in Civil Engring., Tex. A. and M. U., 1949; postgrad. Southwestern Bapt. Theol. Sem., 1952-55; M.S., U. Tex., 1970; m. Dorothy Dell King, Jan. 24, 1942; children—Dorothy Ann, Susan Elizabeth. Civil engr. Tex. Hwy. Dept., Lufkin, 1945-47, Beaumont, 1949-52, Ft. Worth, 1952-60, El Paso, 1960-—; dir. West Tex. State Employees Credit Union. Ordained to ministry Bapt. Ch., 1953; minister Sulphur Springs ch., 1953, Fairview ch., 1954 (both Angelina County, Tex.). Dep. dist. commr. Boy Scouts Am. Served with USAAF, 1942-45. Mem. U.S. Inf. Assn., Am. Right of Way Assn. (past pres. chpt. 35, nat. dir.), North Tex. Soc. Telephone Engrs., Tex. Pub. Employees Assn., Nat., Tex. socs. profl. engrs., El Paso Sportsmen's Assn. Mason (32 deg.), Rotarian. Clubs: Dabblers Investment (pres.), El Paso Kennel, Horizon Country, Del Norte Country. Home: 3025 Cork Dr El Paso TX 79925 Office: 212 N Clark St El Paso TX 79905

LAWRENCE, JAMES MICHAEL, bldg. co. exec.; b. Montgomery, Ala., Aug. 22, 1941; s. James Preston and Evelyn (Freeman) L.; B.S., U. Ala., 1963; M.S. in Civil Engring., 1965; m. Mollie J. Thompson, Sept. 6, 1963; children—Kelly Michele, Reita Leigh, James Michael II. Research asso. U. Ala., Tuscaloosa, 1963-65; asso. Hudson Wright and Assocs., Dothan, Ala., 1965-68; v.p., gen. mgr., Tom Bigbee Light Weight Aggregate Co., Livingston, Ala., 1968; v.p. Koger Properties, Inc., Jacksonville, Fla., 1969-—. Named Jaycee of Year, Dothan Jaycees, 1967. Registered profl. engr., Ala., Fla., Ga., N.C. Mem. Coll. Engring. and Student Engring. Assn. (sec.-treas. 1963-64), Am. Soc. C. E., Nat. Soc. Profl. Engrs., Fla. Engring. Soc., Sigma Xi, Chi Epsilon, Theta Tau, Pi Mu Epsilon, Kappa Alpha. Republican. Methodist. Home: 8833 Coventry Ct Jacksonville FL 32217 Office: PO Box 4520 Jacksonville FL 32201

LAWRENCE, JOHN, corp. exec.; b. Rutland, Vt., Feb. 12, 1911; s. Edwin Winship and Florence (Roby) L.; grad. Phillips Acad., Exeter, N.H., 1928; B.S., Mass. Inst. Tech., 1932; m. Janet Beal, May 28, 1938; children—Carol (Mrs. John Hoffman), Gale, Johanne (Mrs. Ronald La Grange), John Rodney, Ann. Factory mgr. Jones & Lamson Machine Co., 1934-44; gen. factory mgr. SKF Industries, Inc., Phila., 1944-49, tech. v.p. charge mfg., engring. and research, 1950-51; v.p. mfg. Joy Mfg. Co., Pitts., 1951-54, exec. v.p., 1954-55, pres., 1956-57; v.p. Dresser Industries, Inc., Dallas, 1957, exec. v.p., dir., 1957-62, chmn. bd., 1962-70, 72-—, pres., 1965-68, 69-—, also chief exec. officer. Home: 5527 Meaders Lane Dallas TX 75229 Office: Republic Nat Bank Bldg Dallas TX 75221

LAWRENCE, JOHN LEWIS, civil engr.; b. Hinton, W.Va., Oct. 20, 1916; s. Letcher Warren and Ocie Virginia (Pack) L.; B.A. in Indsl. and Civil Engring., Va. Poly. Inst., 1948; m. Gladys M. Peyton, July 26, 1941. Supr. powder plant mfg. E.I. duPont de Nemours & Co., Charleston, Ind., 1940-45; engr. Merritt-Chapman & Scott Marine Constrn., N.Y.C., 1948-52; asst. Brown & Root Marine Operators, Houston, 1952-64; v.p. Ingram Contractors, Harvey, La., 1964-65; pres. Lawrence-Allison & Assos. Corp., cons. engrs., Houston, 1965-—; tchr. applied mechanics night sch., Wilmington, Del., 1948-49. Served with USNR, 1945-46. Mem. Va. Tech. Student Aid Assn., Va. Poly. Inst. Alumni Assn. Presbyn. Mason, Lion. Club: Pine Forrest Country (Houston). Home: 1434 Carolcrest St Houston TX 77024 Office: 3200 Marquart St PO Box 22627 Houston TX 77027

LAWRENCE, JOHN MARSHALL, lawyer; b. Oklahoma City, Nov. 6, 1895; s. John Thomas and Jane (Sawyers) L.; grad. high sch., Oklahoma City; m. Ernestine Grace Bucklin, Nov. 1, 1919; children—Mary Violet (Mrs. William Lee Stubbs), John Marshall Lawrence (killed in action), Donna Jane (Mrs. Rex D. Duhon). Admitted to Okla. bar, 1927, since practiced in Oklahoma City; asst. city atty., Oklahoma City, 1942-46. Served with USN, 1917-18. K.P. (supreme tribune 1954-—), Knight of Khorassan (imperial prince 1953-55). Home: 2609 NW 55th Pl Oklahoma City OK 73112 Office: Leonhardt Bldg Oklahoma City OK 73102

LAWRENCE, PETER, ballet co. ofcl. Formerly dir. devel. Saratoga Performing Arts Center; exec. dir. Fairfax County Cultural Assn.; adminstr. Garden States Arts Center; gen. mgr. Dick Button's Ice-Travaganza; producer Peter Pan, Let's Make an Opera, Shinbone Alley, Shakespeare's Ages of Man; stage mgr. 6 Broadway shows, 3 U.S.O. shows; stage mgr., producer Ballet Theater, Columbia Artists Mgmt., also other groups; with advt. dept., photographer N.Y. Times, also for subsidiary Wide World Photos; film critic Topeka State Jour.; gen. mgr. Atlanta Ballet, 1972-—. Cons., Theater Planning Assos., N.Y.C. Office: 3211 Cains Hill Pl Atlanta GA 30305*

LAWRENCE, RAY VANCE, chemist; b. Ala. July 6, 1910; s. William Monroe and Frances (Ray) L.; B.S., U. Ala., 1931; M.S., U. Tenn., 1933; m. Barbara Frances New, June 22, 1935; children—Robert Craig, Richard Vance. Instr. Marion (Ala.) Mil. Inst., 1932-33; chemist TVA, Muscle Shoals, Ala., 1933-38, Naval Stores Sta., Olustee, Fla., 1938-41, Naval Stores research div., Washington, 1941-43; head rosin research sect., 1950-57, chief Naval Stores Lab., 1958-—. Lectr. terpene chemistry U. Fla., 1953, 58. Mem. Am. Chem. Soc. (chmn. Fla. sect. 1965, Fla. award 1970), A.A.A.S., Am. Soc. Testing Materials, T.A.P.P.I. Patentee in field. Home: 621 W De Soto St Lake City FL 32055 Office: Box 1 Olustee FL 32072

LAWRENCE, STEPHEN SAMUEL, govt. ofcl.; b. Nashville, Tenn., Jan. 6, 1922; s. Stephen James and Margaret (Morel) L.; A.B., Vanderbilt U., 1949, postgrad., 1968; postgrad. Middle Tenn. State U., 1967; m. Martha Vaden West, Aug. 23, 1942; children—Catherine Ashley, Stephen Alfred. With sales dept. Graybar Electric Co., Nashville, 1950-63; dir. Hermitage (Tenn.), home of Andrew Jackson, 1963-67, pres. Heritage Found. Franklin and Williamson County, 1969-—; exec. sec. Tenn. Hist. Commn., Nashville, 1967-69, exec. dir., 1969-—. Chmn. Franklin Historic Tour Commn., 1965-67, Williamson County Civil War Centennial Commn., 1961-65. Served with USNR, 1942-45. Mem. Williamson County Hist. Soc. (pres. 1967-68), Assn. for Preservation Tenn. Antiquities (chpt. dir. 1965-67), Sigma Nu. Home: Route 1 College Grove TN 37046 Office: 7th Av N Nashville TN 37219

LAWRENCE, TELETE ZORAYDA (MRS. ERNEST LAWRENCE), speech and voice pathologist, educator; b. Worcester, Mass., Aug. 5, 1910; d. James Newton and Cora Valeria (Hester) Lester; A.B. cum laude, U. Cal. at Berkeley, 1932; M.A., Tex. Christian U., 1963; pvt. study voice with Edgar Schofield, N.Y.C., 1936-41, drama with Enrica Clay Dillon, N.Y.C., 1937-40; m. Ernest Lawrence, Oct. 9, 1939; children—James Lester, Valerie Alma. Mem. Am. Lyric Opera Co., 1939-—; instr. speech Sch. Fine Arts, Tex. Christian U., Ft. Worth, 1959-66, asst. prof., 1966-71, asso. prof., 1971-—, univ. speech pathologist specializing in voice disorders Speech and Hearing Clinic, 1959-—; pvt. practice speech and voice therapy, 1960-—. Participant, contbr. to internat. congresses, 1965-—. Bd. mem. Sunshine Haven, home for retarded children, 1957-59; gen. chmn. Ft. Worth and Tarrant County, Nat. Retarded Children's Week, 1954; mem. family and child welfare div. Community Council of Ft. Worth and Tarrant County, 1955-57; mem. health and hosp. div., 1959-60; mem. women's com. Ft. Worth chpt. Nat. Conf. Christians and Jews, Inc., 1956-59; exec. v.p. Fine Arts Found. Guild of Tex. Christian U., 1955-56, exec. sec., 1956-58, financial sec., 1958-59. Tex. Christian U. faculty research grant, 1961, on leave to Gt. Britain, Western Europe, Hungary, 1968. Mem. Nat. Council Chs. (bd. dirs. joint com. missionary edn. Pacific Coast area, 1952-55), United Ch. Women of Ft. Worth (chmn. Christian world missions dept. 1955-57, pres., 1957-59), Ft. Worth Area Council Chs. (v.p. 1955-57, exec. com. 1957-59, bd. dirs. 1959-60), U. Cal. Alumni Assn., Am., Tex. speech and hearing assns., Ft. Worth Council for Retarded Children, Speech Communication Assn. Am. (sec. speech and hearing disorders interest group 1962, 63), American Dialect Soc., Am. Assn. U. Profs., Internat. Assn. Logopedics and Phoniatrics, Internat. Soc. Phonetic Scis., Tex. Speech Assn., Phi Beta Kappa, Delta Zeta, Psi Chi, Sigma Alpha Eta. Republican. Mem. Christian Ch. Clubs: Women's; Women of Rotary. Contbr. articles to profl. publs. Home: 3860 South Hills Circle Fort Worth TX 76109

LAWRENCE, WILLIAM HOWARD, radio-TV news reporter; b. Lincoln, Neb., Jan. 19, 1916; s. Edward H. and Daisy (Minner) L.; student U. Neb., 1933; L.H. D., Grinnell Coll., 1967; m. Elizabeth Currie, 1937 (div. 1946); children—William E., Ann; m. 2d, Constance Marcy McGregor, 1951 (div. 1958); m. 3d, Jacqueline Eidal, 1971. Reporter, Lincoln Star, 1932-35, A.P., Lincoln and Omaha, 1935-36, United Press, Chgo., Detroit, Washington, 1936-41; chief corr. N.Y. Times, Moscow, 1943-45, war corr., Pacific, 1945, staff UN Bur., 1946, chief Balkan corr., 1947-48. nat. corr., 1948-61; nat. polit. editor and White House corr. ABC, 1961-68, nat. affairs editor, 1968-—. Recipient George Foster Peabody broadcasting award, 1964. Mem. Sigma Delta Chi. Clubs: International, Nat. Press (pres. 1959-60) (Washington); Burning Tree (Bethesda, Md). Home: 3001 Veazey Terrace NW Washington DC 20008 Office: 1124 Connecticut Av NW Washington DC 20036

LAWRENCE, WILLIAM ROBERT, clergyman; b. Gatesville, Tex., Oct. 12, 1906; s. William Henry and Denia (Millsap) L.; student Baylor U., 1932, S.W. Baptist Sem., 1933-35; m. Inez G. Glaze, Aug. 4, 1930; children—William Robert, Jerry Joe, Janice (Mrs. Cyrus Virl Ruth). Ordained to ministry Baptist Ch., 1928; pastor in Lefors, Tex., 1935-41, Dumas, 1942, McLean, 1947, Delhart, Tex., 1947-49, Clarendon, Tex., 1959-—. Head Bible dept. Clarendon Jr. Coll., 1959-—. Mem. exec. bd. Bapt. Gen. Conv. Tex., pres. Dist 10; chmn. Human Devel. Adv. Bd., Clarendon, 1968-—. Trustee Wayland Bapt. Coll., Highland Bapt. Hosp; pres. Panfork Bapt. Encampment, 1963-—. Dep. wing chaplain Tex. Civil Air Patrol; chaplain Fire Dept., Am. Legion, V.F.W. (all Dalhart). Mem. Child Welfare Bd., Juvenile Delinquency Bd., Dalhart. Served as chaplain USAAF, World War 11, also 1952-53, lt. col. Res. Named citizen of year, Dalhart, 1951. Rotarian (pres. Dalhart 1956), Lion (pres. Clarendon 1964.). Office: Box 936 Clarendon TX 97226

LAWSON, ABRAM VENABLE, univ. adminstr.; b. South Boston, Va., Jan. 9, 1922; s. Abram Venable and Vivien Strudwick (Moseley) L.; B.A., U. Ala., 1946; M.L.S., Emory U., 1950; D.L.S., Columbia, 1969; m. Julia Lee Clark, 1949 (div.); children—Janet Lee, Venable, Mary Vivian. Auditor, Socony-Mobil Oil Co., Denver, 1947-48; teller First Nat. Bank, Altavista, Va., 1948-49; asst. reference dept. Atlanta Pub. Library, 1951, head reference dept., 1954-56, coordinator pub. services, 1956-60; library asst. Harvard Coll. Library, 1951-54; asst. prof. Fla. State U. Library Sch., 1960-65; dir. div. librarianship Emory U., Atlanta, 1965-—. Served with USAAF, 1942-46. Recipient George Virgil Fuller award Columbia, 1964. Mem. A.L.A., Spl. Libraries Assn., Assn. Am. Library Schs., Am. Assn. U. Profs., Am. Soc. for Information Sci. Home: 771 Houston Mill Rd NE Atlanta GA 30329

LAWSON, CHARLES DAVID, mining co. exec.; b. Erwin, Tenn., July 14, 1923; s. Robert Wesley and Lettie (Brown) L.; student Nat. Bus. Coll., Roanoke, Va., 1941-42; m. Miriam Genevieve Ross, June 20, 1953; children—Charles David, Ginny Diane. With traffic dept. Clinchfield R.R., Erwin, Tenn., 1942-45; v.p., sales mgr. Newdale Mica Co. (N.C.), 1945-55; pres. Lawson-Boone Mica Co., Spruce Pine, N.C., 1955-—; sec.-treas. Lawson-United Feldspar & Mineral Co., Spruce Pine, 1956-—; pres. W & L Motor Lines, Inc., Hickory, N.C., 1961-—; dir. Erwin Nat. Bank. Past trustee Spruce Pine Community Hosp. Served with AUS, 1943. Methodist. Moose. Address: Box 309 Spruce Pine NC 28777

LAWSON, MAURICE ANTOINE, real estate exec.; b. Carbon Hill, Ala., May 20, 1918; s. Ellie Fields and Minnie (Buchanan) L.; student Massey Bus. Coll., 1940; m. Ella Earlene Earnest, Sept. 6, 1941; children— Juanita Maurice (Mrs. Jerry Bruce Case) and Martha Antoinette (Mrs. Larry Hugh Graves) (twins), Thomas Henry. Purchasing agt. McCullough Industries, Birmingham, Ala., 1946-49; proprietor Lawson Realty Co., Birmingham, 1950-65; pres. Nat. Mortgage Exchange, Birmingham, 1966-—, Commerce Square, Inc., Birmingham, 1967-—; real estate broker Johnson-Rase & Hays Co., Birmingham, 1967-—, v.p., 1971-—. Mem. Birmingham Real Estate Bd., So. Indsl. Devel. Council. Mem. Jefferson County Water Commn., 1971-—. Served with USAAF 1941-45. Baptist. Mason (Shriner). Clubs: The Club, Roebuck Exchange (pres. 1955), Jade Lake (dir. 1969-—). Home: 636 Elm St Birmingham AL 35206 Office: 1020 S 22d St Birmingham AL 35205

LAWSON, MELVIN ALFRED, ret. banker; b. St. Louis, Nov. 8, 1909; s. Alfred August and Emelia S. (Johansson) L.; grad. Am. Inst. Banking, 1945, Stonier Grad. Sch. Banking, Rutgers U., 1952; m. Eugenia M. Flynn, Jan. 15, 1942. With Worthen Bank & Trust Co., Little Rock, 1928-71, v.p., 1955-71, cons., 1971-—. Chmn. Citizens Traffic Safety Commn., 1966-67. Sec.-treas. Little Rock U. Found., 1947-67; treas. Ada Thompson Meml. Home Endowment Fund, 1956-68, pres., 1968-—; chmn. adv. bd. Salvation Army, 1954. Bd. dirs. United Fund, 1952-55. Mem. Young Businessmens Assn. (pres. 1945), Ark. Bankers Assn. (pres. jr. bankers sect. 1947), Little Rock Sales and Marketing Execs. Assn. (pres. 1955), Little Rock C. of C. (dir. 1955-58). Republican. Methodist. Clubs: Pleasant Valley Country, Little Rock Yacht, Capital (Little Rock). Home: 5540 Grandview Rd Little Rock AR 72207 Office: Worthen Bank & Trust Co Capital Av and Louisiana St Little Rock AR 72201

LAWSON, MYRTLE HAWKINS (MRS. REED LAWTON), civic worker; b. Phenix City, Ala., Mar. 29, 1908; d. Thomas Jefferson and Carrie (Brown) Hawkins; student pub. schs.; m. A. John Bartram, June 8, 1935 (dec. June 1960); m. 2d, Reed Lawton, Aug. 23, 1966. Office sec. J.D. Thomason Realty Co., Columbus, Ga., 1928; compiler rates for fire ins. Ga. Inspection Rating Bur., 1929-31; sec. Dudley Products Co., 1932, White Realty Co., Phenix City, 1933-35; editorial-clk-typist to dir. instrn. and tng. lit. U.S. Army Inf. Sch., Ft. Benning, Ga., 1942-—. Chmn. Family Services, A.R.C., 1963-—; fallout shelter mgr. Civil Def., 1963-—. Mem. East Ala. Genealogy Soc. (chmn. publicity com. 1963-65), Assn. U.S. Army, U.D.C. (pres. Phenix City chpt. 1962-66; chmn. Memorian Program and Year Book), Women of Presbyn. Ch. (v.p. 1960-62, sec. 1958-60, treas. 1972-—, chmn. spiritual growth 1959, chmn. ch. extension 1962-—), Parapsychology Group, Am. Organist Guild. Presbyn. (chmn. music com. 1972-—). Club: Organ. Home: PO Box 333 1112 28th St Phenix City AL 36867 Office: PO Box 1625 Fort Benning GA 31905

LAWSON, THOMAS SEAY, justice Ala. Supreme Ct.; b. Greensboro, Ala., May 3, 1906; s. Lewis Joshua and Amy (Seay) L.; A.B., Davidson Coll., 1926; LL.B., U. Ala., 1929; m. Rose Darrington Gunter, Nov. 30, 1932; (dec.) children—Thomas Seay, Jule Gunter (Mrs. Clifford A. Lanier, Jr.); m. 2d, Kathleen McLean Crampton, Jan. 3, 1970. Admitted to Ala. bar; mem. firm Lawson & Sledge, Greensboro, 1929-31; asst. atty. gen. State of Ala., 1931-39, atty. gen., 1939-42; asso. justice Supreme Ct. of Ala., Montgomery, 1942-—. Trustee, U. Ala. Served to lt. USNR, 1943-45. Mem. Newcomen Soc. N.Am., Sigma Alpha Epsilon, Phi Delta Phi, Omicron Delta Kappa. Home: 3200 Boxwood Dr Montgomery AL 36111 Office: Judicial Bldg Montgomery AL 36104

LAWSON, WILLIAM E., JR., city ofcl.; b. Newport News, Va., Mar. 19, 1923; s. William E. and Ann (Moore) L.; B.S. in Civil Engring., Va. Mil. Inst.; grad. extension course Technique Municipal Adminstrn; m. Ann Weston, Jan. 24, 1948; children—William E. III, Deborah Ann. City engr., Waynesboro, Va., 1947-48; town mgr., South Boston, Va., 1948-51; city mgr., Buena Vista, Va., 1952-54, Delray Beach, Fla., 1954-60, St. Augustine, Fla., 1960-62; dir. pub. works, Newport News, 1962-65, city mgr., 1965-—. Dir. Bank of Hampton Roads, Newport News. Sec., treas. Peninsula Ports Authority. Bd. dirs. Salvation Army. Served with C.I.C., AUS. Home: 51 James Landing Rd Newport News VA 23606 Office: 2400 Washington Av Newport News VA 23607

LAWTON, EDGAR HERBERT, JR., vegetable oil co. exec.; b. Hartsville, S.C., July 12, 1929; s. Edgar H. and Louis (Amis) L.; B.A., Princeton, 1951; M.B.A., Harvard, 1953; m. Drusilla Nan Davidson, June 29, 1957; children—Drusilla Nan, Edgar H. III, John D., Louise Amis. Asst. treas. Hartsville Oil Mill, 1956-62, pres., treas., 1962-—, also dir.; pres., treas. Palmetto Oil Co., Hartsville, 1963-—, also dir.; dir. Sonoco Products Co., Coker's Pedigreed Seed Co., Trust Co. S.C. Trustee Byerly Hosp. Served to lt. (j.g.) USNR, 1953-56. Mem. Nat. Cottonseed Products Assn. (dir. 1963-—). Nat Cotton Council (dir. 1963-64). Baptist. Rotarian. Home: Erwin Rd Hartsville SC 29550 Office: 1501 5th St Hartsville SC 29550

LAWTON, G. CABELL, corp. exec.; b. Richmond, Va., Jan. 4, 1893; s. W. P., Jr. and Sallie Syme (Waddill) L.; ed. high sch.; m. Ruth A. Wells, Oct. 6, 1914; children—G. Cabell, Jr., Floy Leigh, John Courthope. Office mgr. Duplex Envelope Co., 1911-16; treas. Eagle Paper Co., 1916-21, Cushnoc Paper Co., 1917-21, Kennebec Paper Co., 1918-21, Moore and Thompson Paper Co., 1918-21, Hercules Paper Bag Mills, 1919-21, Am. Trust Co., 1928-33; office mgr. Hunton, Williams, Gay Powell & Gibson, 1932-64; pres., dir. Brown Oil Co.; treas., dir. Va.-Ga. Realty Corp., 1935-58; sec., dir. Charles C Haskell and Co., Inc., 1938-58. Clubs: Down Town. Home: 300 W Franklin St Richmond VA 23227 Office: 700 E Main St Richmond VA 23219

LAWTON, RICHARD STANLEY, banker; b. Detroit, Aug. 11, 1931; s. Kenneth E. and Gertrude (Van Keulen) L.; B.A. in Bus. Adminstrn., George Washington U., 1956; student Am. Savs. and Loan Inst., 1957.,; m. Dana Marian Hoop, February 18, 1961; 1 dau. Amy 1957Chief accounting and loan servicing sect. Equitable Life Ins. Co., Washington, 1956-58; asst. treas., mgr. W.W. McCollum, Inc., Arlington, Va., 1958-60; exec. v.p., mgr., dir. Va. Savs. & Loan Assn., Springfield and Fairfax, Va., 1960-64; 1st v.p. Eastern Mortgage Corp., Washington, 1964-65; exec. v.p. Washington-Lee Savs. & Loan Assn., Alexandria, Va., 1965-66, pres., 1966-—, also dir.; dir. Data Systems Corp., Home Builders Assn. Suburban Va., Wilkenton Assos., Inc. Served with AUS, 1951-52. Mem. Va. Savs. and Loan League, Kappa Sigma. Club: Washington Golf and Country. Home: 4501 N 35th Rd Arlington VA 22207

LAWTON, THOMAS, art gallery exec.; b. Somerset, Mass., Feb. 5, 1931; student R.I. Sch. Design, 1949-50; B.S. in Design, Durfee Tech. Inst., 1953; postgrad. Chinese Lang. Tng. Center, Stanford U., Taipei, Taiwan, 1963-64; Ph.D. in Fine Arts (Ford Found. fellow, Univ. scholar), Harvard, 1970. Designer, Cheney Bros., Manchester, Conn., 1953-55; asst. prof. Ia. State U., Ames, 1955-57; asso. curator Chinese art Freer Gallery Art, Washington, 1967-70, curator Chinese art, 1970-71, asst. dir., 1971-—. Adviser, Nat. Palace Mus., Taiwan, 1965-67; hon. lectr. Chinese art U. Mich.; instr. Chinese art Smithsonian Assos., 1970, George Washington U., 1970-71; lectr. to art museums, clubs, univs. Fulbright fellow, 1963-66; John D.

Rockefeller III Fund grantee, 1966-67. Author: (with Li Chu-tsing) The New Chinese Landscape: Six Contemporary Chinese Artists, 1966; (with John A. Pope) The Freer Gallery of Art, Part I, China, 1971, (with Harold P. Stern), Part II, Japan, 1971; Eugene and Agnes E. Meyer Memorial Exhibition, 1971. Translator (from Chinese) Chinese Cultural Art Treasures: National Palace Museum Illustrated Handbook, 1967; A Garland of Chinese Painting, 1967. Contbr. articles to profl. publs. Office: Freer Gallery Art 12th and Jefferson Dr SW Washington DC 20560*

LAWTON, THOMAS OREGON, JR., lawyer; b. Barton, S.C., Nov. 10, 1924; s. Thomas Oregon and Alexania (Easterling) L.; student Wofford Coll., 1941-43; A.B., Duke, 1947, J.D., 1950; m. Bess White Macaulay, July 10, 1952; children—Thomas Oregon, III, Margaret Macaulay, Angus Macaulay. Admitted to S.C. bar, 1950; practiced in Georgetown, S.C., 1950-51, Allendale, S.C., 1951—; mem. firm McNair and Lawton, 1951-65, Lawton and Myrick, 1965—; city atty., Allendale, S.C., 1951—; county atty., Allendale County, S.C., 1951—; county Allendale Recreation Assn., 1958-59, Hampton-Allendale County Community Concert Assn., 1961-65; vice chmn. Allendale County Devel. Bd., 1956-70, chmn., 1970—; vice chmn. Savannah River Basin Devel. Commn., 1966—; chmn. S.C. Tricentennial Commn., 1966-71; curator, v.p. S.C. Hist. Soc. Chmn., Allendale County Democratic Com., 1968—. Served with AUS, 1943-45. Decorated Bronze Star, Purple Heart. Mem. Am., S.C. bar assns., U. S.C. Soc. (dir.), Am. Trial Lawyers Assn., Huguenot Soc. for S.C., Soc. of Cincinnati, Sons Colonial Wars, Sigma Alpha Epsilon, Phi Delta Phi. Democrat. Episcopalian (sr. warden 1968-70). Clubs: Fairdale Country (past pres.); Plantation (Hilton Head Island). Home: Hampton Grove Allendale SC 29810 Office: Memorial Av Allendale SC 29810

LAY, CHESTER FREDERIC, educator, mgmt. cons., accountant, publisher; b. Pope County Ill., Feb. 8, 1895; s. Joseph Lay and Rilda (Chester) L.; B.Ed., Ill. State U., 1917; M.A., U. Chgo., 1923, Ph.D., 1931; m. Harriet Lewis, Sept. 29, 1917; children—Lewis Chester, Coy Lafayette, Lois Jo Harriet Lackore. Instr. grad. sch. social service, also grad. sch. commerce and adminstrn. U. Chgo., 1919-22, prof., 1929-31; head dept. commerce Robert Coll., Istanbul, Turkey, 1922-23; asst. prof. econs. U. Ariz., 1923-24; head div. accounting and mgmt. Ore. State U., 1924-25; prof. mgmt. and accounting U. Tex., 1925-44; pres. So. Ill. U., 1944-48; prof. chmn., dir. grad. studies, mgmt. dept. So. Methodist U., Dallas, 1948-59; sr. prof. mgmt., accounting, grad. studies bus. adminstrn. Trinity U., San Antonio, 1959-63; prof. econs. and bus. adminstrn. Fla. So. Coll., 1963-66, chmn., 1965-66. Vice pres., dir. OBGYN Letters, Inc.; bus. editor Collected Letters Internat. Soc. Obstetricians and Gynecologists. Mem. adv. council Ill. Dept. Pub. Health; mem. Govs. Com. on Edn.; mem. Crab Orchard Lake Com., 1946-48; commr. Fla.-Polk Hist. Commn. C.P.A. Tex., Fla. Served with USN, 1918. C.P.A., Fla. Fellow Acad. Mgmt.; mem. Fla. Acad. Sci., Am., So. (chmn. mgmt. div.) econ. assns., Am. Accounting Assn., Am. Assn. U. Profs., Soc. Advancement Mgmt., S.W., So. mgmt. assns. Nat. Assn. Accountants, Financial Execs. Inst., Newcomen Soc. Eng., Southwestern Social Sci. Assn. (gen. program chmn.), Tex. Soc. C.P.A.'s. Am., Fla. insts. C.P.A.'s. Tenn., N.C., Fla., Ky., S.C., Tex., Mo., Conn., New Eng., Va. hist. socs., Am-Assn. State and Local History, Beta Alpha Psi, Alpha Kappa Psi, Kappa Phi Kappa, Tau Kappa Epsilon. Beta Gamma Sigma, Sigma Delta Pi, Sigma Iota Epsilon (co-founder, pres.). Baptist. Rotarian. Joint author: An Executive Operations Technique, Cost Accounting, Budgeting and Control, 1955; American College Dictionary, 1964, 69; Random House Unabridged Dictionary, 1966; author: Historical Florida Rotary Lakeland, 1968. Contbr. articles to profl. jours. Address: 2809 Berkeley Av Lakeland FL 33803

LAY, COY LAFAYETTE, psysician, surgeon; b. Carbondale, Ill., Feb. 19, 1923; s. Chester Frederick and Harriet (Lewis) L.; student U. Tex., 1939-42; M.D., U. Tex., 1946; M.S. in Obstetrics and Gynecology, U. Minn., 1952; m. Madeline Randolph, Dec. 19, 1943; children—Lois Gretchen, Coy Lafayette, Joel Randolph, John Chester. Clin. asso. prof. U. Wash. Med. Sch., 1947-49; fellow obstetrics and gynecology Mayo Clinic, Rochester, Minn., 1949-51, gynecol. surgery, 1951-52; partner Watson Clinic, Lakeland, Fla., 1952—; chief gynecol. surgery Morrell Meml. Hosp., Lakeland, 1955, 57, chief obstetrics, 1957; cons. gynecology Polk County Hosp., Bartow, Fla., 1956—, So. Bapt. Hosp., Plant City, Fla., 1955—; chmn. dept. obstetrics-gynecology Lakeland Gen. Hosp., 1961, chief gynecology, 1967; clin. asso. U. Miami Sch. Medicine. Owner citrus groves; pres. Sky View Groves & Ranch, 1967, Ob-Gyn Letters, Inc., 1962-63; owner, developer Lake Hollingsworth Hts. subdiv.; pres. Cleveland Hts. Properties, Inc.; dir. Fla. Midlands Real Estate Corp. Pres. Polk County unit Am. Cancer Soc., 1961-62. Served as lt. (j.g.), Med. Res., USN, 1943-49. Diplomate Am. Bd Obstetrics and Gynecology. Fellow A.C.S.; mem. Am., So. (chmn. gynecology sec.), Fla. med. assns., Am. Coll. Obstet. and Gynecol., Fla. Obstetrics and Gynecology Soc., Mayo Clinic Alumni Assn., Am. Fertility Soc. (dir.), So. Gynecol. and Obstet. Soc., South Atlantic Assn. Obstetricians and Gynecologists, Am. Cytology Soc., Chi Phi, Alpha Kappa Kappa, Alpha Epsilon Delta. Rotarian. Editor: Internat. Corr. Soc. Obstetricians and Gynecologists, 1960-70. Home: 419 Lake Hollingsworth Dr Lakeland FL 33803 Office: Watson Clinic Lakeland FL 33802

LAY, EMILY M. (MRS. JAMES SELDEN, JR.), psychiat. social worker, educator; b. Shelby, N.C., Feb. 3, 1913; d. Hugh Graham and Margaret (LeGrand) Miller; B.A., Meredith Coll., 1934; M.S.S., Smith Coll. Sch. Social Work, 1936; m. James Selden Lay, Jr., Feb. 27, 1937; children— Carolyn Miller (Mrs. W. J. Dowd), Patricia L. (Mrs. E.C. Dorsey), Emily (Mrs. P.I. O'Connell). Case worker Guilford County Welfare, Greensboro, N.C., 1934-35; psychiat. social worker Children's Meml. Clinic, Richmond, Va., 1936-37, Bklyn. Bur. Charities, 1937-39, Fairfax County Child Guidance Clinic, Falls Church, Va., 1960-64; supr. family counseling Catholic Family and Children's Services of No. Va., 1964-69; asst. prof., dir. admissions Nat. Catholic Sch. Social Service, Catholic U., Washington, 1969—. Field instr. Va. Commonwealth U. Sch. Social Work, 1961-68; vol. social worker A.R.C., Arlington, Va., 1942-45. Mem. Juvenile Detention Commn. No. Va., 1961-62; mem. bd. dirs. Fairfax Child Guidance Clinic, Falls Church, 1950-60, sec. 1950-52, v.p. 1952-54, pres., 1954-56; mem. regional bd. Health Welfare Council, 1957-59. Active Camp Fire Girls, 1953-60. pres. Fairfax dist., 1953-54, Potomac area, Washington 1956-57; cons. mental health Potomac area Camp Fire Girls, 1961-67. Mem. Nat. Assn. Social Workers, Acad. Certified Social Workers, Council Social Work Edn., Smith, Meredith (pres. Washington chpt. 1950-54) coll. alumnae. Roman Catholic. Home: 202 Forest Dr Falls Church VA 22046 Office: Nat Catholic Sch Social Service Catholic U Washington DC 20017

LAY, JOE LAFAYETTE, food packing co. exec.; b. Knoxville, Tenn., Jan. 17, 1925; s. Ira Vivian and Ava Edna (Parrott) L.; B.S. in Bus. Adminstrn., U. Tenn., 1948, m. Sarah Randolph Lowry, Oct. 15, 1948; children—Sally, Joe Lafayette, Tillman L. With Lay Packing Co., Knoxville, 1948—, sales mgr., 1958-69, v.p. sales, 1969-70, exec. v.p., 1970—. Bd. dirs. Better Bus. Bur. Served with AUS, 1943-45. Mem. Knoxville C. of C., Knoxville Tourist Bur., Am. Meat Inst., Nat. Ind. Meat Packers Assn., Tenn. Ind. Meat Packers Assn. (dir. 1961—), Sigma Nu, Phi Kappa Phi, Omicron Delta Kappa. Rotarian. Home: 4003 Avon Park Circle Knoxville TN 37918 Office: 400 E Jackson Av Knoxville TN 37915Mailing address: 400 E Jackson Av Knoxville TN 37915

LAZZARI, PIETRO, painter, sculptor; b. Rome, Italy, May 15, 1898; s. Pietro and Maria (Giacomelli) L.; Master Artist, Ornamental Sch. of Rome, 1920; m. Evelyn Cohen, Dec. 1, 1934; 1 dau., Nina. Came to U.S., 1929, naturalized, 1936. Free-lance painter, sculptor; executed murals, fine arts sect. U.S. Treasury Dept., 1936-42; faculty Am. U., Washington, 1943-48; head art dept. Dumbarton Coll., Washington, 1948-50; instr. Corcoran Gallery Sch. Art, Washington, 1966-69; executed sculptured busts of Eleanor Roosevelt, Norman Thomas, Adlai Stevenson, Alexander Kerensky, Pope Paul VI; bronze monuments to Edward Miner Gallaudent, Walter Reuther; exhibited Mus. Modern Art, Whitney Mus. Am. Art, Met. Mus., Acad. Design, Venetian Biennial, Art Inst. Chgo., Musee National d'Art Moderne, Paris, Corcoran Gallery, Pa. Acad. Fine Arts, Parsons Gallery, N.Y.C.; represented permanent collections Am. U., Art Inst. Chgo., Corcoran Gallery, Howard U., Smithsonian Instn., Balt. Mus., Mus. Honolulu, Truman Library, Independence, Mo., San Francisco Mus., Hyde Park, Franklin Delano Roosevelt Library, Whitney Mus., Okla. Art Center, Library of Congress, Nat. Collection Fine Arts, Washington. Fulbright research fellow ancient art media, 1950; recipient prizes Ornamental Sch. Rome, Balt. Mus., Corcoran Gallery, Washington Water Color Soc. Developer of polychrome concrete. Home: 3609 Albemarle St Washington DC 20008

LEA, TOM, painter, writer; b. El Paso, Tex., July 11, 1907; s. Tom and Zola (Utt) L.; student Art Inst. Chgo., 1924-26; D.Litt., Baylor U., 1967; L.H.D., So. Methodist U., 1970; m. Sarah Catherine Dighton, July 14, 1938; 1 son, James Dighton. Mural painter, comml. artist, art tchr., Chgo., 1926-33; student in Italy, 1930, N.M., 1933-35; staff Lab. Anthropology, Santa Fe, 1933-35; muralist, easel painter, book illustrator, El Paso, 1936—, writer, 1947—; war corr. Life mag., 1941-46; executed murals pub. bldgs., El Paso, Washington, Dallas, Odessa, Tex., Pleasant Hill, Mo.; easel works represented Dallas Mus. Fine Arts, Life mag. World War II art, collection in Pentagon, also El Paso Mus. Art, pvt. collections. Recipient Distinguished Pub. Service medal for services as war corr. U.S. Navy, 1971. Author and illustrator: Peleliu Landing, 1945; The Brave Bulls, 1949; The Wonderful Country, 1952; The King Ranch, 2 vols., 1957; The Primal Yoke, 1960; The Hands of Cantu, 1964; A Picture Gallery, 1968. Address: 2401 Savannah St El Paso TX 79930

LEA, WALKER ALFRED, JR., physician; b. Port Arthur, Tex., July 31, 1924; s. Walker Alfred and Alice (Townsend) L.; A.A., Lamar Jr. Coll., Beaumont, Tex., 1947; B.S., Baylor U., 1949, M.D., 1954; m. Beverly Barbara Hayes, Dec. 27, 1947; children—Alfred Scott, Walker Alfred III, Jean Kristen. Intern Methodist Hosp., Tex. Med. Center, Houston, 1954-55; resident U. Mich. Hosp., Ann Arbor, 1955-58; clin. instr. U. Mich. Med. Sch., Ann Arbor, 1957-58; chmn. dept. dermatology Scott and White Clinic, Temple, Tex., 1958-69; practice medicine, specializing in dermatology, Waco, Tex., 1970—; cons. in dermatology G., C & S. F. Ry. Hosp., 1958-69, VA Hosp., Temple, 1962-69, vis. dermatologist Ft. Hood Army Hosp., 1960-69; attending dermatologist Cora Anderson Negro Hosp.; lectr. U. Tex. Postgrad. Sch. Medicine, Temple div., 1960-63, U. Tex. Grad. Sch. Biomed. Scis., Houston, 1964-67. Trustee Scott and White Meml. Hosp., 1964-69 treas. 1964-67, 69, exec. com., 1964-69, sec., 1968; bd. dirs., Scott and White Employees Credit Union, 1964-66; vice chmn exec. Chisholm Trail dist. Boy Scouts Am., 1963-64; bd. dirs. Temple United Fund, 1963, 65, 67-69, v.p., 1968; dir. Bell County Bd. Health, 1967-68, Scott, Sherwood and Brindley Edn, and Research Found.; bd. dirs Cultural Activities Center, Inc., 1961-67, pres. bd. dirs., 1962-63. Served with AUS, 1943-45; ETO. Recipient Outstanding Citizen award Temple Jr. C. of C., 1963, Taub Internat. award for research in psoriasis, 1959. Diplomate Am. Bd. Dermatology. Fellow Am. Acad. Dermatology, Am. Soc. Geriatrics; mem. A.M.A., Tex. Med. Assn. (pres. 12th dist. soc. 1965), Bell County Med. Soc. (pres. 1967), Soc. Investigative Dermatology, Tex. Dermatol. Assn., N.Y. Acad. Scis., Tex. Hist. Assn., C. of C., Baylor U. Med., U. Mich. alumni assns., Baylor U. Ex-Student Assn., Magna Charta Barons, Sigma Xi, Alpha Omega Alpha, Phi Sigma, Phi Sigma, Phi Theta Kappa, Phi Beta Pi. Presbyn. (deacon). Mason (32 deg., K.T.), Rotarian (dir. temple 1961-64, 66-67, pres. 1962-63, trustee student scholarship found. 1964-69). Clubs: Bell County Baylor (pres. 1965, past dir.); Rigdwood Country; Hedonia. Contbr. articles to med. jours. Home: 5309 Lake Jackson St Waco TX 76710 Office: 1310 Austin Av Waco TX 76701

LEACH, DAN PAYTON, architect; b. Brooks, Ga., Oct. 30, 1931; s. Dan Payton and Viola (Smith) L.; B.S., Erskine Coll., 1953; B.Arch., Clemson U., 1962; postgrad. U. Tex., 1955-56; m. Mary Ann Kay, Jan. 8, 1951; children—Dan Payton, Donna Victoria. Architect firm James M. Hunt, Elberton, Ga., 1962-65, J. Harold Mack & Asso., Greenville, S.C., 1965—. Mem. Bd. Zoning, Elberton, 1962-65. Served with AUS, 1953-55. Mem. A.I.A. (pub. relations officer S.C. chpt.), Greenville Council Architects (pres.), Nat. Guard Assn. Republican. Baptist. Elk, Lion. Home: Route No. 7 Box 247 Greer SC 29651 Office: 408 N Church St Greenville SC 29601

LEACH, DOUGLAS EDWARD, educator; b. Providence, May 27, 1920; s. Arthur Edward and Saidee Waterman (Raybold) L.; A.B., Brown U., 1942; M.A., Harvard, 1947, Ph.D., 1952; m. Brenda Mason, June 24, 1950; children—Carol Brenda, Bradford Raybold. Instr. to asst. prof. history Bates Coll., 1950-56; asst. prof. to asso. prof. Vanderbilt U., Nashville, 1956-64, prof. history, 1964—. Fulbright lectr. U. Liverpool, 1959-60, U. Auckland, New Zealand, 1967. Served with USNR, 1942-46. Mem. Orgn. Am. Historians, Am. Assn. U. Profs., Am., So. hist. assns., Mass. Hist. Soc., Colonial Soc. Mass., Phi Beta Kappa. Mem. Christian Ch. Author: Flintlock and Tomahawk: New England in King Philip's War, 1958; A Rhode Islander Reports on King Philip's War: The Second William Harris Letter of August, 1676, 1963; The Northern Colonial Frontier, 1607-1763, 1966. Home: 1805 Graybar Lane Nashville TN 37215

LEACH, LESLIE H., educator; b. nr. Russell Springs, Ky., Feb. 16, 1927; s. Leslie H. and Lula (Gosser) L.; B.S., Eastern Ky. U., 1950; M.A., Western Ky. U., 1961; m. Esther Johnson, Jan. 10, 1948; children—Michael, Tamara. Tchr., Barren County Schs., Glasgow, Ky., 1950-60, prin., 1960-61, asst. supt., 1961-63, supt., 1963-67; dir. Traffic Safety Inst., Eastern Ky. U., Richmond, 1967—. Mem. Gov.'s Traffic Safety Coordinating Com., 1968-71. Served with USNR, 1944-46; PTO. Mem. Eastern Ky. U., Western Ky. U. alumni assns., N.E.A., Ky. Edn. Assn., Am., Ky. assns. sch. adminstrs., Ky. Driver and Traffic Safety Assn., Am. Driver and Traffic Safety Edn. Assn., Nat. Safety Council, Nat. Hwy. Research Bd., Phi Delta Kappa. Democrat. Baptist. Mason, Lion, Woodman of World. Home: Deacon Hills Richmond KY 40475

LEACH, MAURICE DERBY, JR., librarian, educator; b. Lexington, Ky., June 23, 1923; s. Maurice Derby and Sallie Eleanor (Woods) L.; A.B., U. Ky., 1945; B.L.S., U. Chgo., 1946; m. Virginia Stuart Baskett, Mar. 16, 1953; 1 dau., Sarah Stuart. Bibliographer, Dept. State, 1947-50; fgn. service officer Dept. State (USIS), vice consul, attache, Cairo and Alexandria, U.A.R., Beirut, Lebanon, 1950-59; chmn. dept. library sci. U. Ky., 1959-66; regional program officer Ford Found., Beirut, 1967-68; librarian, prof. Washington and Lee U., Lexington, Va., 1968—; mem. library adv. bd. Va. Council Higher Edn. Lit. adviser Nat. Library, Egypt, Lebanon and acad. libraries in Middle East. Pres. Lexington br. English Speaking Union. Served with AUS, 1948-49. Episcopalian (vestryman). Rotarian. Club: Tri-Brook Country (Lexington, Va.). Contbr. articles to profl. jours. Home: 1 Courtland Center Lexington VA 24450

LEACH, WARREN BRUCE, JR., lawyer; b. Houston, July 29, 1926; s. Warren Bruce and Sadie (Warren) L.; LL.B., U. Tex., 1951; m. Mary Wilson, June 20, 1952; children—Betty, Barbara, Warren Bruce III, Brenda. Admitted to Tex. bar, 1951; practiced in Houston, 1953—; asst. county atty. Harris County, 1954-56; atty. Marathon Oil Co., Houston, 1956-67, div. atty., 1967—. Pres., Neighborhood Civic Club, 1958-59; P.T.A., 1960-61. Served with USMCR, 1944-46, 51-53. Mem. Am., Tex., Houston bar assns., Tex. Mfrs. Assn., Tex. Mid-Continent, N.M. oil and gas assns. Methodist. Rotarian (pres. chpt. 1965-66). Home: 810 Flint River St Houston TX 77024 Office: PO Box 3128 Houston TX 77001

LEAK, ROBERT E., state ofcl.; b. Charlotte, N.C., Sept. 15, 1934; s. James Pickett and Cornelia (Edwards) L.; B.S., Duke, 1956; M.S., U. Tenn., 1957; m. Martha Councill, Aug. 25, 1956; children— Robert E., James Councill. With Pan. Am. Petroleum Co., Lafayette, La., 1957-59, Allied Securities Corp., Raleigh, N.C., 1961-62, Cameron Brown Mortgage Co., Raleigh, also Charlotte, 1962-64; with N.C. Dept. Conservation and Devel., Raleigh, 1959-61, 64—, adminstr. div. commerce and industry, 1964-71, dir. Office Indsl., Tourist and Community Resources, 1971—; mem. N.C. adv. council Small Bus. Adminstrn. Sec.-treas. N.C. Land Use Congress. Bd. dirs. Raleigh YMCA. Episcopalian (pres. men, lay reader). Mem. Am. Indsl. Devel. Council (certified indsl. developer), Nat. Assn. State Devel. Agys. (v.p.), So. Indsl. Devel. Council, N.C. Indsl. Devel. Assn., So. Assn. State Devel. Agys. (pres., mem. indsl. devel. task force Coastal Plains Commn.). Home: 4900 Rampart St Raleigh NC 27609 Office: Administration Bldg Raleigh NC 27611

LEAKE, GERALD, artist; b. London, Eng., Nov. 26, 1885; s. John William and Jane (Owens) L.; naturalized Am. citizen. Artist, 1905—; exhibited Royal Acad., Royal Soc. Brit. Artists, Walker Art Gallery, Liverpool (Eng.), Nat. Acad., Allied Artists Am., Boston Mus., Chgo. Art Inst., Pa. Acad., Corcoran Gallery, Washington, Albright Gallery, Buffalo, and others. Recipient members 000 prize, Salamagundi Club, 1923, Shaw 000 prize, 1925, Plimpton prize, 1925, small picture exhbn. prizes, 1926, 27; Gold Medal, Allied Artists of Am., 1926; Clark prize figure painting, Nat. Acad., 1934, Gold Medal, 1937; Grumbacher award of merit, 1953; 1st prize, Key West Art and Hist. Soc., 1952, 53. Dir. Island City Art Sch., Key West Art and Hist. Soc. (hon. life.). Mem. N.A.D., Royal Soc. Arts (Eng.). Soc. Illustrators, Nat. Arts Club. Club: Salmagundi. Home: Marathon FL

LEAKE, WOODROW WILSON, govt. ofcl.; b. Rossville, Ga., Dec. 18, 1916; s. James W. and Bertha (Martin) L.; B.S.A., Berry Coll., 1937; postgrad. U. Tenn., 1937, U. Ga., 1938; m. 2d, Lana Mirzayants, Jan. 4, 1957; children—Donald James, Thomas Frank; children of previous marriage—Woodrow Wilson II, Frances Diane. Mgr., owner Leake's Dairy Farm, Chattanooga, 1937-41; supr. FHA, Cartersville, Rossville, Rome, Ga., 1941-47; agr. adviser Army Dept., Chonju, Korea, 1948-49; econ. adviser ECA, Seoul, Korea, 1949-50; agr. adviser, regional dir. ICA, Isfahan, Kerman, Meshed, Iran, 1951-56, chief agr. adviser, Dacca, East Pakistan, 1956-61, chief agrl. adviser, rural devel. officer AID, Blantyre, Nyasaland, 1961-64; chief extension adviser, dep. food and agr. officer AID, Lagos, Nigeria, 1964-66, agrl. specialist instnl. devel. div., Washington, 1966-70, agrl. officer Office North African Affairs, 1970—. Mem. Soc. Internat. Devel. Lion (pres. Dacca 1959-61). Home: 10303 Dickens Av Bethesda MD 20014 Office: AID Dept State Washington DC 20521

LEARD, JOHN EARNSHAW, newspaperman; b. Boston, Aug. 15, 1916; s. John S. H. and Isabelle (Earnshaw) L.; A.B., Bates Coll., 1938; M.S. in Journalism, Columbia, 1939; m. Hazel Elsie Turner, Sept. 28, 1940; children—Linda Earnshaw (Mrs. Raymond Parkin Jr.), Judith Alden (Mrs. Richard Nicholas). Mem. staff Lewiston (Me.) Sun-Jour., 1937; Pulitzer traveling scholar, S.A., 1939-40; editorial asst. Richmond (Va.) News Leader, 1939, reporter, copy editor, asst. city editor, 1941-43, asst. city editor, 1947-51, city editor, 1951-63; mng. editor Richmond Times-Dispatch, 1963-68; exec. editor Richmond Times-Dispatch and Richmond News Leader, 1969—; v.p. Richmond Newspapers, Inc., 1969—; asst. editor Atlantic Monthly mag., Boston, 1940-41; telegraph editor New Haven Register, 1946-47. Trustee, Bates Coll., Lewiston, 1958-63. Served with AUS, 1943-46. Mem. Am. Soc. Newspaper Editors, A.P. Mng. Editors Assn. (bd. 1967-70), Sigma Delta Chi. Episcopalian (former vestryman). Clubs: Westwood (pres. Richmond 1958-60); Hermitage Country. Home: 6207 Monument Av Richmond VA 23226 Office: 333 E Grace St Richmond VA 23219

LEARY, JOSEPH RIVE, JR., osteo. physician; b. Tampa, Fla., July 21, 1908; s. Joseph Robert and Sara (Jones) L.; D.O., Kirksville Coll. Osteopathy, 1930; m. Mary Alice Coppinger, Jan. 1, 1934; children—Alice Patricia Ann (Mrs. C.B. Miller), Joseph Rive III, Elizabeth Roberta (Mrs. William E. Pinder). Technician x-ray dept. Jackson Meml. Hosp., Miami, Fla., 1930-35, Dade County Hosp., Kendell, Fla., 1936-37; x-ray diagnostic practice, Ferguson-McCormick Clinic, Miami, 1937-41; practice medicine, specializing in X-ray diagnosis, Miami, Coral Gables, Fla., 1941—; chief dept. radiology Osteo. Gen. Hosp., North Miami Beach, Fla., 1962—; radiologist N.W. Hosp., Miami. Active Boy Scouts Am., Fla. Civil Def. Mem. Am. Osteo. Assn., Divisional X-ray Soc., Pan-Am. Cancer Cytology Soc., Fla. Soc. Applied Osteopathy, Fla., Dade County (hon. life mem., past pres.) osteo.-med. assns., Sigma Sigma Phi. Baptist (deacon). Club: Atlas. Home: 2332 SW Fifth St Miami FL 33129 Office: Osteopathic Gen Hosp 1750 NE 167th St North Miami Beach FL 33161

LEARY, THOMAS SAMUEL, univ. pres.; b. Rochester, N.Y., May 8, 1915; s. Samuel Walter and Alta C. (Kemp) L.; B.S., Rensselaer Poly. Inst., 1938, M.S., 1939; Ph.D., Ia. State U., 1942; m. Geraldine Kempnich, Nov. 14, 1942; children—Patricia (Mrs. Curtis Padgett), Kathleen (Mrs. J.P. Briggs). Tech. aide to supt. Holston Ordnance Works, 1942-44; responsible engr. Strombert Carlson Co., 1944-46; chief devel. chemist Am. Cyanamid Co., Bound Brook, N.J., 1946-55; mgr. process lab. Cities Service Research & Devel. Co., Lake Charles, La., 1955-61; prof., pres. McNeese State U., Lake Charles, 1961—; cons. engr. Ernest Levingston & Assos., Lake Charles. Bd. dirs. Boy Scouts Am., McNeese Found. Mem. Am. Inst. Chem. Engrs. (nat. program chmn. 1963-64), Nat. Soc. Profl. Engrs., Am. Soc. Engring. Edn., La. Engring. Soc., Sigma Xi, Phi Kappa Phi, Phi Lambda Upsilon, Tau Kappa Epsilon. Clubs: Pioneer of Calcasieu Parish, Bucaneer. Contbr. articles profl. jours. Home: 4130 Ryan St Lake Charles LA 70601

LEASE, GOLDEN RICHARD, constrn. co. exec.; b. Plainville, Ill., June 10, 1908; s. Henry Woodrow and Lucinda (Cook) L.; student U. Chgo., 1930-33, So. Meth. U., 1957-59; m. Zella Mae Long, Sept. 4, 1926; 1 step-son, Bert E. Phillips; children—Marcella June (Mrs. William R. Curry), Richard Wayne. Payroll and cost accountant J.M.

Meltezer Co., N.Y.C., 1931-33; asst. shipping clk. Moorman Mfg. Co., Quincy, Ill., 1934-38; asst. to controller Bechtel-McCone-Parsons, Inc., Birmingham, Ala., 1939-45; mgr., officer, dir. Harman Elec. Constrn. Corp., Dallas, 1946—; sec.-treas., dir. Equipment Rental Corp. Div. mgr. Dallas United Fund, 1957-68. Mem. Cost Accountants Assn. Am., Photog. Assn. Am., So. Meth. U. Alumni Assn. Methodist (mem. ofcl. bd.). Home: 4520 Livingston Av Dallas TX 75205 Office: 4311 Belmont St Dallas TX 75204

LEASENDALE, FRANK OTTO, trucking co. exec.; b. Jersey City, May 15, 1921; s. F. Otto and Lydia (Klix) L.; student Clemson Coll., 1942-43; B.Sc., N.Y.U., 1950, M.B.A., 1955; m. Mildred E. Schlenger, June 12, 1949; children—Nancy, Jeffrey. Chief accountant Gen. Aniline & Film Corp., N.Y.C., 1939-64; mgr. corporate accounting Prentice-Hall, Inc., Englewood Cliffs, N.J., 1964-66; treas. Volkswagen North Central Distbr., Inc., Deerfield, Ill., 1966-69; v.p., treas. Burnham Van Services Inc., Columbus, Ga., 1969—. Instr. budgets and forecasting Coll. City N.Y., 1955-57. Served with AUS, 1942-45. Mem. Nat. Assn. Accountants, Assn. U.S. Army, N.Y. U. Alumni Assn., Am. Trucking Assn., Infantry Museum Assn. Presbyn. (elder). Kiwanian. Club: Green Island Country. Home: 5945 Sherborne Dr Columbus GA 31904

LEATHERS, THOMAS LEE, dentist; b. Central City, Ky., Nov. 30, 1929; s. William Lee and Mae (Ortkiese) L.; B.S., Ill. Wesleyan U., 1953; D.M.D., U. Louisville, 1957; m. Marilyn Alice Marx, Aug. 20, 1955; children—Mark Lee, Thomas Alan. Individual practice dentistry, Crestview, Ky., 1957, Warsaw, Ky., 1957-59, Erlanger, Ky., 1959—. Pres., owner Warsaw Auto Parts, Inc. (Ky.); pres. U. Ky. Dental Sch. Faculty, Lexington, Ky., 1971—. Guest speaker use hypnotism in dental practice. Sec., treas. Boone County Planning Commn., 1967-70. Named Ky. Col. Mem. No. Ky. Dental Study Club (pres. 1966-67), Northeastern Ky. Dental Soc., Am., Ky. dental assns., Am. Inst. Hypnosis. Methodist. Mason. Home: Timberlane Farm Hathaway Rd Union KY 41091 Office: 3818 Dixie Hwy Erlanger KY 41018

LEAVELL, BYRD STUART, physician, educator; b. Washington, Dec. 29, 1910; s. Byrd and Lucie (Browning) L.; B.S., Va. Mil. Inst., 1931; M.D., U. Va., 1935; m. Nancy Butzner, Oct. 7, 1939; children—Anne (Mrs. Herbert Reynolds), Lucie (Mrs. Scott Vogel), Byrd Stuart Jr. Intern, N.Y. Hosp., N.Y.C., 1935-36, asst. resident, 1936-38; practice medicine, specializing in internal medicine, Charlottesville, Va., 1946—; prof. medicine U. Va. Sch. Medicine, 1954—, chmn. dept. internal medicine, 1966-68, asst. dean Sch. Medicine, 1958-61, head div. hematology, 1945-70. Served to maj. M.C., AUS, 1942-46. Decorated Bronze Star medal. Mem. A.M.A., A.C.P., Internat., Am. socs. hematology, A.A.A.S., So. Soc. Clin. Investigation, Am. Clin. and Climatological Assn., Kappa Alpha, Alpha Omega Alpha, Omicron Delta Kappa. Episcopalian. Clubs: Colonnade (pres. 1960), Farmington Country (Charlottesville). Author: The 8th Evac., 1970; (with O. A. Thorup) Fundamentals of Clinical Hematology, 3d edit., 1971. Home: Box 229 Route 2 Charlottesville VA 22901

LEAVELL, CHARLES H., constrn. co. exec. Chmn., pres. C.H. Leavell & Co., El Paso, Tex. Address: 1900 Wyoming St El Paso TX 79987*

LEAVELL, DAVID C(OX), pub. co. exec.; b. New Market, Mo., Aug. 18, 1904; s. Andrew Dean and Nellie Pauline (Cox) L.; student Tex. Christian U., 1923-26; B.J. with honors, U. Mo., 1927; m. Enda Maie Waltrip, May 4, 1934 (dec. Aug. 26, 1957); m. 2d, Pauline Powers Belew, Feb. 14, 1958; 1 son, Jim Belew. Reporter McAllen (Tex.) Monitor, 1919-23; advt. solicitor Ft. Worth Tribune, 1923-24; reporter Ft. Worth Star-Telegram, 1924-26; mem. editorial dept. Marshall (Tex.) News-Messenger, 1927-28; mng. editor, Longview (Tex.) News, 1928-29; mem. editorial dept. Ft. Worth Press, 1929-46; vice pres., gen. mgr. and dir. News Pub. Co. (publs. of Galveston News, Galveston Tribune), 1946-63; v.p., gen. mgr. Galveston County Pub. Co., 1963-66, exec. v.p., 1966—; pub. Tex. City Sun, 1948-63; pres. Southwestn Sch. of Printing, 1955-57. Charter mem. Texas Econ. Commn.; mem. adv. bd. Evening College, Tex. Christian U., 1938-46; pres. Ft. Worth Junior C. of C., 1939; pres. Tex. Christian U. Ex-Students Assn., 1936-38; pres. Galveston C. of C., 1949, 50, exec. com., 1951; bd. dirs. Community Chest. Red Cross; chmn. bd. dirs. Galveston Housing Authority, 1960—; bd. dirs. Greater Galveston Beach Assn.; pres., founder United Fund Galveston, 1953-54, 66-67. Invited by U.S. War Dept. to tour Europe, 1945. Mem. Tex. Daily Newspaper Assn. (treas. 1954-55), Tex. Press Assn. (pres. 1956-57), So. Newspaper Pubs. Assn., Sigma Delta Chi, Delta Sigma Phi. Rotarian (pres. 1953-54). Home: 2901 Beluche Galveston TX 77550 Office: 8522 Teichman Rd Galveston TX 77550

LEAVER, WALTER C., JR., lawyer; b. Nashville, Aug. 11, 1927; B.A., Vanderbilt U., 1949, J.D., 1952. Admitted to Tenn. bar, 1952; mem. firm Barksdale, Whalley, Leaver, Gilbert and Frank, Nashville; asst. city atty. City of Nashville, 1955-63, city atty., 1963. Mem. Am., Nashville bar assns., Bar Assn. Tenn., Am. Judicature Soc., Delta Theta Phi. Office: 7th Floor 3d Nat Bank Bldg Nashville TN 37219*

LEBAILLY, EUGENE BERNARD, air force officer; b. Shoshone, Ida., Jan. 29, 1915; s. Thomas Bernard and Jean Marie (Wilson) LeB.; student Ida. State U., 1933-34; B.S., U. Cal. at Berkeley, 1939; m. Margret Blair, May 3, 1940; children—Stephen B., Jon B. Commd. 2d lt. USAAF, 1940, advanced through grades to lt. gen., 1970; comdr. U.S. Forces Azores, also comdr. 1604th Air Base Wing Lajes Field, Azores, Portugal, 1961-64; dep. dir. info. office Air Force, Washington, 1964-67, dir. info. 1967; comdr. 16th Air Force, Torrejon Air Base, Spain, 1967-70; chmn. Inter-Am. Def. Bd., Washington, 1970—. Mem. exec. bd. Trans-Atlantic council Boy Scouts Am., 1967-70. Decorated D.S.M. with oak leaf cluster, Silver Star. Legion of Merit, D.F.C. with 2 oak leaf clusters, Air medal with 6 oak leaf clusters, Croix de Guerre with silver star (France); Ulchi with silver star (Korea); Cross of Aero Merit (Spain). Mem. Air Force Assn., Cal. Alumni Assn., Order of Daedalian. Home: 68 Westover St Bolling AFB Washington DC 20332 Office: Inter-Am Def Bd 2600 16th St NW Washington DC 20441

LEBER, WALTER PHILIP, army officer; b. St. Louis, Sept. 12, 1918; s. Walter and Bonnie Vera (Blackman) L.; B.S., Mo. Sch. Mines, 1940; M.B.A., George Washington U., 1961; grad. Command and Gen. Staff Coll., 1956, Indsl. Coll. Armed Forces, 1958; m. Bernice Jean Palus, Sept. 9, 1950; children—Randolph Frank, Bonnie Gay, Philip Kevin. Petroleum engr. Stranolind Oil & Gas Co., 1940-41; commd. 2d lt., C.E., U.S. Army, 1941, advanced through grades to lt. gen., 1971; comdr. engring. troops 2d Inf. Div., 1941-42; mem. faculty Engrs. Sch., Ft. Belvoir, Va., 1942; assigned Office Chief Engr. and Advanced Sect. Communications Zone, ETO, 1942-46, Manhattan Engr. Dist., Oak Ridge, 1946-47; chief tech. div. mil. liaison com. AEC, 1947-49; asst. dist. engr., exec. officer Seattle and Walla Walla dist., C.E., 1949-50; comdr. 46th Engr. Battalion, Ft. Sill, Okla., 1950-51; assigned gen. staff logistics Dept. Army, 1951-55; dep. engr. 8th U.S. Army, Korea, also comdr. 2d Engr. Group, Korea, 1956-57; exec. officer to chief engrs. U.S. Army, 1958-61; lt. gov. C.Z., v.p., dir. Panama Canal Co., 1961-63; div. engr. Army Engr. Div., Ohio River, 1963-66; dir. civil works Office Chief Engrs., U.S. Army, Washington, 1966-67; gov. C.Z., pres. Panama Canal Co., 1967-71; system mgr. Safeguard Anti-Ballistic Missile System, Washington, 1971—. Chmn. of gov C.Z. Council Vol. Giving, 1961—. Mgmt. com. Balboa YMCA; exec. bd. C.Z. council Boy Scouts Am.; trustee, exec. com. C.Z. United Fund. Decorated Legion Merit with 2 oak leaf clusters, Bronze Star medal, D.S.M.; Order British Empire; L'Orde de Leopold II (Belgium). Registered profl. engr., D.C. Mem. Soc. Am. Mil. Engrs., Tau Beta Pi, Phi Kappa Phi. Episcopalian. Home: Quarters 53 Fort Belvoir VA 22060 Office: Dept of Army Washington DC 20310

LEBOWITZ, MORTIMER CHARLES, retail co. exec.; b. N.Y.C., Mar. 18, 1912; s. Henry I. and Esther (Roth) L.; A.B., U. Pa., 1932; student N.Y.U. Law Sch., 1933-35; m. Adele Gusack, June 4, 1940; children—John William, Emily, Caroline (Mrs. Richard Simon), Petrina (Mrs. Walter Locke). Buyer, The Mart, Paterson, N.J., 1933-35; founder, pres. Morton's, Washington, 1935—. Bd. dirs. Washington Urban League, 1956—, pres., 1960-61; chmn. Washington Commn. Human Resources, 1962-71; chmn. inner city com. Nat. Capital area council Boy Scouts Am., 1967—, mem. Nat. council, 1970—, mem. interim bicentennial com., 1971—. Trustee Va. Coll.; bd. overseers Coll. V.I.; bd. dirs. Center Met. Studies, 1961-71. Recipient Human Relations award Capitol Press Club, 1961; Merit award D.C. C. of C., 1962; Equal Opportunity Day award, 1963, 67; Silver Beaver award Boy Scouts Am., 1968. Mem. D.C. Bd. Trade, D.C. Retail Bur., Am. Jewish Com., Alpha Phi Omega, Tau Epsilon Phi. Mem. B'nai B'rith. Home: 6319 Georgetown Pike McLean VA 22101 Office: 310 6th St S Arlington VA 22202

LEBOWITZ, RHODA ELEANOR KOVACS (MRS. WALTER BERNARD LEBOWITZ), civic worker; b. Bklyn., Apr. 4, 1934; d. William Gabriel and Shirley (Stone) Kovacs; student U. Miami, 1967, U. Fla., 1968; m. Walter Bernard Lebowitz, Feb. 14, 1954; children—Terry Lynn, Toby Jane. Asso., Joseph Dube Real Estate Co., Miami Beach, Fla., 1964-67; asso. Paul Wimbish Real Estate Co., Miami Beach, 1967—; pres. Travel'n Tours, Inc.; dir. Alarmtec Internat. Corp. Mem. Miami Beach Bd. Realtors. Regional chmn. Miami-Dade County March of Dimes, 1962; pres. Renanah Hadassah, 1966-67. Mem. Miami Beach Democratic Exec. Com., 1959-63; pres. Miami Beach Young Dem. Club, 1960. Bd. dirs. North Beach Elementary P.T.A. Recipient Woman of Year award B'nai B'rith, 1963. Mem. Miami Ballet Soc. (charter, dir. 1970-71, corr. sec. 1971-72), Props, ORT. Jewish religion (dir. Sisterhood 1967-72). Rebecca lodge. Home: 4550 N Bay Rd Miami Beach FL 33140

LEBOWITZ, WALTER BERNARD, lawyer, city ofcl.; b. Newark, May 7, 1930; s. George and Sarah (Kaplan) L.; B.B.A., U. Miami, 1954, LL.B., 1954; m. Rhoda E. Kovacs, Feb. 14, 1954; children—Terry Lynn, Toby Jane. Admitted to Fla. bar, 1954; practiced in Miami Beach, Fla., 1954—; city atty. City of Sweetwater, Fla., 1965-65; municipal judge, Sweetwater, 1965-67; pub. defender City of Miami Beach, 1967—; v.p. Alarmtec Internat. Corp. Gen. council Alarm Cos. of Fla., 1970-72. Democratic committeeman Miami Beach, Dade County Exec. Com., 1956—; atty. Dade County Dem. Com., 1956-58. Served with AUS, 1954-56. Mem. Fla. Municipal Judges Assn. (v.p. 1967-68). Jewish religion (v.p. temple). Moose (past gov.), K.P. Clubs: Bixcayne Democratic (past pres.); South Beach Men's (past pres.). Contbr. articles to various publs. Home: 4550 N Bay Rd Miami Beach FL 33140 Office: 350 Lincoln Rd Miami Beach FL 33139

LEBRECHT, ROGER DONALD DUBLON, radio sta. exec.; b. Kansas City, Mo., Nov. 22, 1937; s. Alphonse and Betty (Roberts) LeB.; student Tex. Western Coll., 1959-61; m. Thelma Jame Mossman, May 4, 1968. Announcer KHMS-FM, El Paso, Tex., 1959-61; gen. mgr. KNDX-FM, Yakima, Wash., 1961-63; gen. mgr. KFRE-FM, Fresno, Cal., 1963-64, WSPA-FM, Spartanburg, S.C., 1964-66; mgr. WBT-FM, Charlotte, N.C., 1966—. Contbg. radio editor Charlotte Ad Club News, 1966-69. Broadcasting adviser Garringer radio dept. Charlotte Pub. Schs., 1970—. Bd. dirs. Fresno Boys Club, 1964-66. Served with AUS, 1956-59. Mem. Nat. Assn. FM Broadcasters (v.p., dir.), Charlotte Advt. Club, English-Speaking Union, British Ry. Modelers of N.Am., Alpha Epsilon Rho, Delta Chi. Home: 9 Stoney Point Lane Charlotte NC 28210 Office: 1 Julian Price Pl Charlotte NC 28208

LECHNER, SISTER JOAN MARIE, coll. pres.; b. Nebraska City, Neb., July 25, 1913, d. John G. and Mary (Tongish) Lechner; A.B., Loras Coll., Dubuque, Ia., 1950; Ph.D., St. Louis U., 1960. Joined Soc. of Ursulines, 1934; instr. English, Latin and commerce St. Joseph's High Sch., Owensboro, Ky., 1936-48, St. Catherine's High Sch., New Haven, Ky., 1948-50; instr. English, Latin and bus., also prin. St. Francis's High Sch., Loretta, Ky., 1950-53; instr. English and bus., also treas. Brescia Coll., Owensboro, 1953-56, pres., 1960—. Recipient St. Louis U. Alumni Merit award, 1968; Liberty Bell Daviess County Bar Assn., 1970; named Citizen of Year, Owensboro Civitan, 1969. Author: Renaissance Concepts of the Commonplaces, 1962. Address: Brescia Coll Owensboro KY 42301

LECUYER, MAURICE ANTOINE, educator; b. Beaune, France, May 25, 1918; Lic. es Let., U. Paris (France), 1943, Dipl., 1944; Ph.D. in French, Yale, 1954. Instr. French, Mt. Allison U., 1946-48, Yale, 1948-52; instr. Romance langs. Queens Coll., 1952-55; asst. prof. U. Ore., 1955-59; asst. prof. French, U. Chgo., 1959-62; asso. prof. French, Rice U., Houston, from 1962, now prof. Mem. Modern Lang. Assn., Am. Assn. Tchrs. French, Soc. Profs. French in Am. Research on linguistics, modern French lit. and criticism. Home: 1710 Wroxton Ct Houston TX 77005*

LEDBETTER, CHARLES ROLAND, lawyer; b. Ft. Smith, Ark., Mar. 25, 1938; s. John H. and Mary Ethel (Reeves) L.; A.B. in Econs. and Physics, Hendrix Coll., 1960; LL.B., U. Ark., 1963, J.D., 1970; m. Doria Jean Fitzgerald, June 27, 1965; 1 dau., Jennifer Lynn. Admitted to Supreme Ct. Ark. bar, 1963; research asst. U.S. Dist. Judge John Miller, Ft. Smith, 1963-65; sr. partner firm Shaw & Ledbetter, Ft. Smith, 1966—; atty. First Nat. Bank, Ft. Smith, Mansfield Bank, Standard Fed. Savs. and Loan Assn. Mem. Hendrix Coll. Alumni Bd. Govs., 1971—. Bd. dirs. Ft. Smith Art Center. Mem. Am. Bar assn. (chmn. Ark. pub. relations sect. 1969—), Phi Alpha Delta. Methodist. Home: 5802 Ellsworth St Fort Smith AR 72901 Office: 212 Mchts Bank Fort Smith AR 72901

LEDBETTER, JACK WALLACE, lawyer, educator; b. El Paso, Tex., Mar. 31, 1930; s. John J. and Leonora (Lackey) L.; B.S., U.S. Naval Acad., 1951; J.D., U. Tex., 1957; m. Iris Geraldine Amick, Sept. 3, 1952; children—John, Robert, Brenda Jean, Glenn. Admitted to Tex. bar, 1957; cons. atty., Austin, Tex., 1958—; prof. bus. law U. Tex., 1958—; gen. counsel State of Tex. Credit Union Dept., 1971—; Austin, gen. counsel Tex. Oil Marketers Assn., 1967—; spl. counsel Tex. Savs. and Loan League, 1961—, Tex. L-P Gas Assn., 1970—; partner firm Baker, Watkins, Ledbetter, Hayden and Ramsey, Austin, 1971—; dir. Stuyvesant Life Ins. Group. Served with USNR, 1947—; now capt. Mem. Am., Tex. bar assns., Naval Res. Lawyers Assn. (orgn. chmn., 1st pres. 1971-72), Phi Delta Phi, Delta Sigma Pi. Author: Mechanics Lien Manual, 1964; Texas Family Law, 3d edit., 1970; co-author Business Law, 2d edit., 1968. Home: 5807 Timber Trail Austin TX 78731

LEDBETTER, ROBERT HARBIN, constrn. co. exec.; b. Rome, Ga., Sept. 24, 1935; s. Allison W. and Rosa (Harbin) L.; grad. Darlington Sch., 1953, Culver Mil. Acad., 1954; B.S., Ga. Inst. Tech., 1958; m. Betty D. Wright, Jan. 19, 1963; children—Robert Harbin, Ernest Wright, David Dandridge. Vice pres., dir. Ledbetter Bros., Inc., Rome, 1960-70, pres., dir., 1970—; v.p., dir. LBI Quarries, Inc., Ledbetter Trucks, Inc.; dir. Echota Realty Co., Rome, Shorter Realty Co.; dir., mem. exec. com. Chesapeake Internat. Corp.; dir. Network Bldg. Systems, Inc., Atlanta Hockey, Inc., Coliseum Promotions, Inc., Atlanta-Fulton County Mgmt. Co., Cloudland Ridge Corp., Atlanta Hawks, Inc. Bd. dirs. Boys Club Rome. Served to lt. (j.g.) USNR, 1958-60. Mem. Nat. Asphalt Pavement Assn., Asso. Gen. Contractors Am., S.A.R., A.I.M. (pres.'s council), Ala. Rome Builders Assn., Ga. Hwy. Contractors Assn. (dir., mem. exec. com., 1st v.p.), Ga. Asphalt Pavement Assn. (dir. 1965—, mem. exec. com., past pres.), Carolina Asphalt Pavement Assn. (dir.), Rome C. of C., Jr. C. of C., Sigma Alpha Epsilon. Presbyn. Clubs: Coosa Country (Rome); Commerce (Atlanta). Home: 1121 Kingston Rd Rome GA 30161 Office: 401 E 1st Av Rome GA 30161

LEDERER, JAMES WEIL, chem. co. exec.; b. Phila., Mar. 6, 1930; s. Harold G. and Ruth (Weil) L.; B.A., U. Pa., 1950; grad. bus. adminstrn. Drexel Inst. Tech., 1951; m. Rosetta Alkus, June 6, 1952 (dec.); children—James Weil, William H., Patricia, Stephanie. Research chemist Publiker Industries, Inc., 1950-52; dist. sales mgr. Richmond Oil, Soap & Chem. Co., Inc., Chattanooga, 1952-61; pres. Lederer Chem. Co., Inc., Greensboro, N.C., 1961-62, now dir.; pres. Cindet-Lederer Chems., Inc., 1962—, also dir.; pres., dir. Cindet Chems., Inc., 1966—, Cindet Investment Co., 1968—; chmn. bd. dirs. Lederfield, Inc., 1969—, Modutron, Inc., 1970—. Bd. dirs. Greensboro Soc. Crippled Children and Adults, 1963—, v.p., 1964-65; bd. dirs. N.C. Soc. Crippled Children and Adults, Guilford chpt. Nat. Found. Served to 1st lt. USAAF, 1955-57. Jewish religion. Home: 4504 Graham Rd Greensboro NC 27410 Office: 2408 Doyle St Greensboro NC 27408

LEDERER, JEROME FOX, govt. ofcl.; b. N.Y.C., Sept. 26, 1902; s. Sigmund and Sophie (Fox) L.; B.S., N.Y.U., 1924, M.E., 1925; m. Sarah Bojarsky, Nov. 1, 1935; children—Nancy (Mrs. John Safarik), Susan. Dir. safety bur. CAB, Washington, 1940-42; tech. dir. Flight Safety Found., N.Y.C., 1947-67, also dir. Cornell-Guggenheim Aviation Safety Center, N.Y.C., 1950-67; dir. Office Manned Space Flight Safety, NASA, Washington, 1967-70, dir. safety, 1970-72; cons. Flight Safety Found., 1972—. Trustee Acad. Aeros., N.Y.C. Recipient Guggenheim medal, Wright Bros. award, Montsanto AWA award, Arthur Williams award, Barbour award, NASA Exceptional Service medal, 1969. Fellow Am. Inst. Aeros. and Astronautics, Royal Aero. Soc.; mem. Nat. Fire Protection Assn., Soc. Air Safety Investigators Nat. Acad. Engring., Am. Soc. M.E., Soc. Automotive Engrs., System Safety Soc. Home: 311 N St SW Washington DC 20024 Office: Flight Safety Found 1800 N Kent Arlington VA 22209

LEDFORD, THERON R., public relations cons., writer; b. Gainesville, Ga., July 30, 1931; s. Theron Clifton and Nell Rose (Robertson) L.; A.B. magna cum laude, Mercer U., 1954; m. Carol Deane Williams, Dec. 23, 1962; 1 dau., Laurie Dianne. With pub. relations dept. Ga. Hwy. Dept., Athens, 1958-70; free-lance writer, pub. relations cons., Gainesville, 1970—. Served with AUS, 1954-56. Mem. Pub. Relations Soc. Am., Alpha Tau Omega. Baptist (Sunday sch. tchr., dir. intermediate tng. union). Contbr. articles to various publs. Home: 790 Park St Gainesville GA 30501 Office: PO Box 744 Gainesville GA 30501*

LEDGARD, RODOLFO, petroleum co. exec.; b. Lima, Peru, Oct. 27, 1920; s. Carlos Enrique and Maria Luisa (Jimenez) L.; student Faculty of Arts and Letters, U. San Marcos, Lima, 1939-42, Faculty of Law, 1942-43, M.A., 1943; m. Isabel Elguera, May 6, 1948; children—Carmen-Maria, Randolph. Journalist, radio scriptwriter, lit. critic, 1940-45; prof. lit. U. San Marcos, 1946-50; dir. radio and motion picture dept. Brit. Information Office in Lima, 1943-45; advt. and sales promotion mgr. Internat. Petroleum Co., Ltd., Peru, 1946-50, pub. relations dept. head for producing and refining, 1950-52, asst. mgr. pub. relations, 1952-60, mgr. pub. relations, 1960-66; pub. relations adviser Esso Inter-Am., Inc., Coral Gables, Fla., 1966-68, sr. adviser pub. affairs, 1968—. Mem. Pub. Relations Soc. Am. Home: 5260 SW 82d Av Miami FL 33155 Office: 396 Alhambra Circle Coral Gables FL 33134

LEDOUX, JACK, race track exec.; b. Orlando, Fla., Oct. 4, 1928; s. Leonard K. and Louise (Downs) L.; B.S. in Journalism, U. Fla., 1950; m. Geraldine C. Collins, Sept. 12, 1949; children—Michele, Lance, Stepehn, Lola. Sportswriter, columnist Orlando Sentinel-Star, 1948-53; pub. relations dir. Sarasota, Daytona Beach (Fla.) Kennel Clubs, 1953-55; gen. mgr., corp. sec. Sanford-Orlando Kennel Club, 1955—; gen. mgr., exec. v.p. Black Hills Kennel Club, Rapid City, S.C., 1964-71; dir. Greyhound Publs., Inc., South Seminole Bank, Tropicana Pools, Inc. Bd. dirs. Black Hills Charity Found. Mem. Fla. Golf Assn. (chmn. adv. com. 1964-65, pres.), Am. Greyhound Track Operators Assn. (publ. and supervisory com. Am. Greyhound Racing Ency., pub. 1963; nat. pres.), World Racing Fedn. (chmn.), World Greyhound Racing Fedn. (pres.), U. Fla. Alumni Assn. (past pres. Sarasota County chpt.), Sigma Delta Chi, Theta Chi. Democrat. Clubs: University, Country, Dubsdread Country (Orlando); Winter Park (Fla.) Racquet. Home: 877 Brock St Winter Park FL 32789 Office: Sanford-Orlando Kennel Club Longwood FL 32750

LEDOUX, JEROME GASTON, clergyman; b. Lake Charles, La., Feb. 26, 1930; s. Peter Louis and Mary Gastonia (Petrie) LeD.; student Divine Word Coll., Epworth, Ia., 1949-51, St. Augustine Maj. Sem., Bay St. Louis, Miss., 1951-57; J.C.D., Pontifical Gregorian U., Rome, Italy, 1961, S.T.L., 1961. Ordained priest Roman Cath. Ch., 1957; tchr. Divine Word Sem., 1961-69; chaplain Xavier U., New Orleans, 1969-71; asso. prof. theology, Xavier U., 1971—; writer syndicated column What's Your Bag. Bd. dirs. Ministries to Blacks in Higher Edn. Mem. Black Cath. Clergy Caucus, Cath. Campus Ministry Assn., Coll. Theology Soc. Home: 1210 Governor Nicholls St New Orleans LA 70116

LEDUC, ALBERT L., educator; b. Vincennes, Ind., June 18, 1911; s. David and Helen (Fish) L.; A.B., Ind. U., 1931, M.A., 1935; Ph.D., U. Wis., 1952; m. Rachel Wineinger, Sept. 1, 1933; children— Albert, Louise (Mrs. Arthur Zierzow). Theodore. Faculty mem. Earlham Coll., 1931-33, Ind. U., 1933-36, Huntingdon Coll., 1936-40, U.S. Mil. Acad., 1942-47; asst. prof. modern langs. Fla. State U., 1947-53, asso. prof., 1953-62; prof. modern langs. Hampden-Sydney (Va.) Coll., 1962—. Vis. prof. S.F. Austin State U., summer 1961, Appalachian State U., summers 1965, 68. Served as col. USAAF, World War II. Mem. South Atlantic Modern Lang. Assn. (officer 1948-49, 59-61), Am. Assn. Tchrs. German, Am. Assn. Tchrs. French (state pres. 1950-53, 65-67, 68-70), Am. Assn. U. Profs., Phi Beta Kappa (pres. Alpha Fla. chpt 1955-56), Pi Delta Phi, Sigma Delta Pi. Methodist. Rotarian (pres. 1967-68). Editor: (with James A. Preu) The Selected Speeches of Robert M. Strozier. Contbr. to French Rev., Am. Travelers Companion, other profl. publs. Home: Hampden-Sydney VA 23943

LEDYARD, WALTER WILLIAM, physician; b. Rockford, Ill., Mar. 6, 1915; s. Walter Riley and Vera (Miller) L.; student Rockford Coll., 1935-36; A.B. summa cum laude, U. Ill., 1942, M.D., 1945; m. Margaret Olga McCarthy, June 22, 1943; 1 dau., Shoon. Intern, U.S. Naval Med. Center, Bethesda, Md., 1945-50; resident U. Va. Hosp., Charlottesville, 1950-53; practice medicine, specializing in neurol. surgery, Columbia, S.C., 1953—; chief staff Columbia Hosp.; mem. staff Bapt., Providence hosps., instr. neurol surgery U. Va. Coll. Medicine, 1951-53; cons. VA Hosp., 1954—. Exhibited one man sculpture show Columbia Mus. Art; exhibited in group shows numerous museums and galleries; represented in permanent collections, including S.C. State Art Collection. Pres. bd. trustees Columbia Mus. Art. Served to lt. (j.g.), M.C., USNR, 1945-50. Diplomate Am. Bd. Neurol. Surgery. Mem. A.M.A., S.C., Columbia med. socs., Harvey Cushing Soc., Am. Assn. Neurol. Surgeons, So. Neurosurg. Soc., So. Med. Assn., S.C. Artists Guild (trustee 1965), Phi Beta Kappa, Alpha Chi Sigma. Alpha Kappa Kappa, Phi Lambda Epsilon. Clubs: Torch (pres. 1956), Kosmos (pres. 1969). Editor: Recorder, 1966-67. Home: 3900 McGregor Dr Columbia SC 29206 Office: 2009 Hampton St Columbia SC 29204

LEE, AFTON MITCHELL, city councilman; b. Eufaula, Ala., June 19, 1898; s. Damon and Aria (West) L.; grad. high sch.; m. Annie Beam, Aug. 15, 1921; children—Afton Mitchell, Arhodia (Mrs. Johnson), Myrtle (Mrs. Edwards), Thelma Lee (Mrs. Newburn), Loretta (Mrs. Jones), Robert Melvin, Reginald Damon. Pres., Damon Lee & Sons Grocery Co., 1909-71; pres. Lee Realty Co., 1925-71; v.p. Citizens Fed. Savs. & Loan Assn., 1957-71; mem. City Council, Homewood, Ala., 1968—. Mem. Zoning Bd., Homewood, 1967-71, Planning Commn., 1968-71, Finance, Pub. Transp. and Utilities Com., 1968-71, City Limits Expansion Com., 1968-71. Home: 1718 27th Av S Homewood AL 35209 Office: 2562 S 18th St Homewood AL 35209

LEE, AMY FREEMAN (MRS. FREEMAN LEE), artist, educator; b. San Antonio, Oct. 3, 1914; d. Joe and Julia (Freeman) Freeman; grad. St. Mary's Hall, 1931; student U. Tex., 1931-34; student Incarnate Word College, 1934-42, Litt.D., 1965; m. Ernest R. Lee, Oct. 17, 1937 (div. Jan. 1941). Art critic San Antonio Express, 1939-41; staff art critic radio sta. KONO, 1947-51; lectr. on art humanities dept. Trinity U., San Antonio, 1954-56, San Antonio Art Inst., 1955-56, Our Lady of Lake Coll., San Antonio, 1969—; one man shows Kilgore Coll., 1969, Incarnate Word Coll., San Antonio, 1969, McLennan Community Coll., Waco, Tex., 1969, U. Tex. Med. Sch., 1970, Woman's Forum, Henderson, Tex., 1970, Beaumont (Tex.) Art Museum, 1970, Tex. Tech U. Museum, Lubbock, 1970, Bee County Coll., 1970, Del Mar Coll., Corpus Christi, Tex., 1971, Southwestern U., Georgetown, Tex., 1971, L. & L. Gallery, Longview, Tex., Pioneer Meml. Library, Fredericksburg, Tex., 1971; exhibited numerous group shows including San Antonio Art League, 1969, Nat. Soc. Painters in Casein, N.Y.C., 1969, 71, Southwest Watercolor Soc. Regional Exhbn., Dallas, 1969, Silvermine Guild, New Canaan, Conn., 1970, Tex. Fine Arts Assn., 1970, Cal. Nat. Watercolor Soc., 1970, 71, L. & L. Gallery, 1970, Jr. League Ann. Collectors Show, San Antonio, 1970, 6th Miniature Paintings Invitation Exhbn., San Antonio, Tex. Fine Arts Assn. Ann. Travelling Exhbn., 1970, 71, Contemporary Artists Group Ann. Travelling Exhbn., 1970, Contemporary Artists Group Ann. Mems. Exhbn., San Antonio, 1970, Day of Fine Arts Exhbn., Crystal City, Tex., 1970, Virginia Museum Travelling Exhbn., 1971, North Star Mall Gallery, San Antonio, 1971, Western Assn. Art Museums, 1971, San Antonio Artists Assn., 1971, Service League of Port Arthur (Tex.) Exhbn., 1971, Painters and Sculptors Soc. N.J., 1971, Del Mar Coll., 1971, Oklahoma City Art Center, 1971, U. Tex. Art Museum, 1971, San Antonio Art League Gallery, 1971, Pioneer Meml. Library, 1971, Ogunquit (Me.) Art Assn., 1971, Ojo Del Sol Gallery, El Paso, 1972; represented in permanent collections Westfall Br. Library, San Antonio, Baylor U. Theater, D.D. Feldman Collection, Dallas, Smith Coll. Mus. Fine Arts, Northampton, Mass., Witte Meml. Mus., San Antonio, Ft. Worth Art Center, Norfolk (Va.) Mus. Arts and Scis., U. Tex. Mus. Fine Arts, Beaumont Art Mus. Recipient numerous prizes including 1st prize 18th Ann. Exhbn., Beaumont Art Mus., 1969; Harwood K. Smith award Southwestern Watercolor Soc., Dallas, 1969; Purchase prize 20th Ann. Tex. Watercolor Soc. Exhbn., 1969; Tex. Fine Arts Assn. citation, 1969; Camellia award Joskes of Tex., 1971; Honorable Mention, 5-State Art Exhbn. 1st Biennial, Gates Gallery and Meml. Library, Port Arthur, Tex.; honored at ann. Woman's Day, Baylor U., Waco, 1967. Bd. dirs. Madonna Neighborhood Centers of San Antonio, San Antonio Blind Assn.; bd. dirs. Friends of San Antonio Pub. Library, pres., 1969; mem. adv. bd. Coll. Fine Arts, U. Tex., 1957-72; bd. dirs. Pub. Information Corp., Austin, Tex., First Repertory Theater, San Antonio, Cultural Art Assn. San Antonio; bd. mgrs. United Colls. San Antonio; mem. consultative bd. Kenwood Community Council, San Antonio; mem. adv. bd. Occupational Edn. and Tech. Dept., Alamo Heights Ind. Sch. Dist. San Antonio. Mem. San Antonio Art League (pres.), Am. Fedn. Arts, Artists Equity Assn., Nat. Soc. Arts and Letters, Tex. Art Educators, Coll. Art Assn. Am., Poetry Soc. Am., Am. Soc. Aesthetics, Assn. Internationale des Critiques d'Art (Paris), Tex. Watercolor Soc. (founder, pres.), Nat. Art Edn. Assn., Internat. Soc. for Edn. Through Art, Nat. Soc. Painters Casein, UN Assn. U.S.A., Tex. Council for Wildlife Protection (dir. 1969), Silvermine Guild Artists, Humane Soc. U.S. (nat. bd. dirs. 1969), Philos. Soc. Tex., Am. Civil Liberties Union, Cal. Nat. Watercolor Soc., Laguna Beach Art Assn. (hon.), Marquis Biog. Library Soc. (adv. mem.), Kappa Pi (hon.), Delta Delta Delta. Author: Hobby Horses, 1940; A Critic's Notebook, 1943, Remember Pearl Harbor, 1945. Works reproduced in Tex. Quar., fall issue 1966, Art & The Creative Teacher, 1971. Contbr. articles to profl. jours. Address: 127 Canterbury Hill San Antonio TX 78209

LEE, BEN STEPHEN, agrl. adminstr.; b. Southampton County, Va., July 20, 1938; s. Vernon and Catherine (Richardson) L.; B.S., Agrl. and Tech. State U., Greensboro, N.C., 1963; m. Dorothy Olivia Gooch, Aug. 17, 1959; children—Regina Marvette, Benita Lavon. Asst. agr. extension agt. Pitt County (N.C.), 1963-64; agr. extension agt. Richmond County (N.C.), 1964-67; vocational agrl. instr. Riverview High Sch., Courtland, Va., 1967-69; agr. extension agt. Greensville County, Va., 1969—. Dir. Harrison Developers, Inc. Mem. Richmond County Recreation Commn., 1966-67. Mem. Nat. Assn. County Agrl. Agts., Am., Va. Soybean assns., Nat. Assn. Extension 4-H Agts., Va. County Agts. Found., Epsilon Sigma Phi, Alpha Phi Alpha. Author articles. Home: Route 2 Box 44 Emporia VA 23847 Office: PO Box 975 Emporia VA 23847

LEE, BRENDA, entertainer; b. Atlanta, Dec. 11, 1944; d. Reuben Lindsey and Grayce (Yarbrough) Tarpley; grad. Hollywood Profl. Sch., 1963; m. Ronald Shacklett, Apr. 24, 1963; children—Julie Leann, Jolie Lenee. Night club appearances at The Flamingo, Las Vegas, 1962, The Deauville, Miami, Fla., 1962, The Sahara, Las Vegas, 1961; TV appearances on shows of Ed Sullivan, Perry Como, Bob Hope, Red Skelton, Danny Thomas, Steve Allen, Tennessee Ernie Ford, Tonight Show, Kraft Music Hall, Hullabaloo; motion picture feature role in Two Little Bears, 1962; command performance for Queen Elizabeth, 1964. Named Worlds' Number One Female Vocalist, New Mus. Express Polls, Eng., 1962, 63, 64, 65; recipient Edison award in Belgium, 1962, Outstanding Vocalist Naras award, 1962, Cashbox and Billboard Best Female Vocalist award, 1962, 63, Aztec award (Mexico), 1971. Home: 5211 Franklin Rd Nashville TN 37220 Office: PO Box 8555 Nashville TN 37211

LEE, BUDGE VAN, indsl. engr.; b. Checotah, Okla., Nov. 30, 1915; s. Budge Van and Whig (Murray) L.; student Southwestern Coll., 1934-35, Hutchinson Jr. Coll., 1935-36, U. Okla., 1937-38, Tex. Christian U., 1945-62; m. Marguerite Louteen Gower, Aug. 16, 1941; children—Carol (Mrs. Jay Loucks), Linda (Mrs. Sidney Neal Shults). With Gen. Dynamics, Ft. Worth, 1942—, chief procurement planning and control, chief material control, 1960-64, procurement research supr., 1964—. Mem. Ft. Worth City Plan Commn., 1954-55, Ft. Worth City Zoning Commn., 1954-55; team capt. United Fund, 1960-72. Recipient Distinguished Service award City of Ft. Worth, 1955. Mem. Am. Inst. Indsl. Engrs., Soc. Am. Value Engrs., Nat. Mgmt. Assn., Aerospace Industries Assn. (small bus. adv. panel 1966—), Ft. Worth C. of C. (life), Delta Tau Delta. Club: Ridglea Country (Ft. Worth). Home: 3476 Wellington Rd Fort Worth TX 76116 Office: Box 748 Fort Worth TX 76101

LEE, CHARLES EDWARD, state ofcl.; b. Asheville, N.C., June 17, 1917; s. Ralph Edwin and Mabel (Robinson) L.; A.B., U. S.C., 1938, A.M., 1939; postgrad. U. Chgo., 1939-41, 46-48; m. Ethel Jane Blizzard, Jan. 20, 1945; children—Christopher Lewes, Janet Castle, Frank Everett Robinson. Editorial asst. Jour. Modern History at U. Chgo., 1939-41; instr. history U. S.C., 1946; asst. prof. history Roosevelt Coll., 1948-50; editor U. S.C. Press, 1952-56, Henry Regnery Co., Chgo., 1956-60; dir. S.C. Dept. Archives and History, Columbia, 1961—. Mem. Nat. Archives Adv. Council, 1968-70, S.C. Parks, Recreation and Tourism Commn., 1967—; v.p. Nat. Conf. State Hist. Preservation Liaison Officers, 1969-72; mem. cons. com. Nat. Survey Historic Sites and Bldgs., Nat. Park Service, 1970—; dep. exec. sec. S.C. Revolutionary Bicentennial Commn., 1971—; mem. adv. panel on research and publs. Heritage '76 com. Am. Revolutionary Bicentennial Commn., 1972—. Vice pres. Hist. Columbia Found., 1964-70. Served as lt. USNR, 1941-45; PTO. Fellow Soc. Am. Archivists (pres. 1971-72); mem. Am. Assn. State and Local History. Clubs: Columbia Forum (sec. 1966-69), Kosmos (v.p. 1971-72). Contbr. articles to profl. jours. Home: 1325 Adger Rd Columbia SC 29205 Office: Box 11188 Columbia SC 29211

LEE, CHARLES EDWIN, civil engr.; b. Baton Rouge, Sept 5, 1920; s. Claude Charles and Ida (Furlow) L.; student Miss. State U., 1938-41; student Miss. State Coll. Extension, 1946, C.Z. Jr. Coll., 1946-47, U. Ill. Extension, 1953, Mass. Inst. Tech., 1960; m. Evelyn Bruce, July 6, 1942. Civilian engr. U.S. Army C.E., 1941-70, with spl. engring. div. Panama C.Z., 1946-48, hydraulic design with Detroit Dist., 1948-50, North Central div., Chgo., 1950-55, New Eng. div., Boston, 1955-60, asst. chief hydraulic design Office Chief Engrs., Washington, 1960-70; asso. D & M Research Co., Glen Burnie, Md., 1970—; also farmer, cons. coastal engr. Cons. engr. in pvt. practice, Halbrook, Mass., 1956-60. Mem. Fed. Adv. Com. Water Data, 1967-70; cons. panel wind and seismic design U.S.-Japan Coop. Program Natural Resources, 1968-70. Mem. planning bd. Town of Halbrook, 1956-60, mem. sch. planning, sch. bldg. coms., 1957-60. Served with USNR, 1942-45. Registered profl. engr., R.I., Mass., Md. Mem. Am. Soc. C.E., Internat. Assn. Hydraulic Research, Coastal Engring. Research Council, Permanent Internat. Assn. Nav. Congresses, Task Com. Small Craft Harbors, Task Com. Groins (chmn.), Washington City Ten Pin Assn. (exec. dir. 1968-70). Research and publs. in field. Address: Ten Pines Farm Rt 1 Box 138 Check VA 24072

LEE, CHARLES HENRY, lawyer, internat. exec.; b. Santiago, Chile, June 28, 1909; s. Charles Henry and Ellen Scott (Wilson) L.; student Columbia, 1927-28; Ph.B. cum laude, Georgetown U., 1931; postgrad. George Washington, Columbia, 1932-33; LL.B., Fordham U., 1937; m. Lulu Vargas-Vila, Aug. 20, 1938; children— Patricia Ellen (Mrs. Lars Schonander), Charles Henry III (dec.), Elisabeth (Mrs. John D. Sevier). Asst. to arbitrator Guatemala-Honduras Boundary Arbitration Tribunal, Washington, 1931-33; admitted to N.Y. bar, 1938, D.C. bar, 1946; practiced in N.Y.C., 1937-41; atty. Coordinator Inter-Am. Affairs, Washington, 1941; atty. Tex. County, N.Y.C., 1941-46; spl. asst. to asst. sec. state Inter-Am. Affairs Dept. State, Washington, 1946-47; mng. dir. E.R. Squibb & Sons Argentina, Buenos Aires, 1947-49, asst. v.p., asst. to pres., dir. Brazilian subsidiary, 1949-56; mng. dir. internat. practice McKinsey & Co., mgmt. cons., N.Y.C., 1956-58; mng. partner Lee, Altieri, Sisto & Assos., mgmt. cons., Mexico City, 1958-61; partner firm Rado & Lee N.Y.C., 1958-61; dir. Econ. Mission of U.S. to Chile, Santiago, 1961-64; v.p. gen. mgr. Hooker Mexicana, 1964—; dir. Compania Minera Sotavento, Minera de Sotavento S.A., de C.V. Mem. Council Fgn. Relations N.Y., 1951—; hon. mem. faculty Catholic U. Chile; chmn. Inter-Am. Council Grad. Sch. Fordham U. With Inter-Am. Def. Bd., Wash., 1942; mil. attache Div. G-2 War Dept., Washington, 1942-43; asst. mil. attache Am. embassy, Argentina, 1943-45. Decorated comdr. Order al Merito (Chile). Mem. Am. C. of C. of Mexico (bus. adv. council, pres.) Mexican-Am. Cultural Inst. (dir.), Mexican Acad. History and Geography, Am. Mgmt. Assn., Am. Bar Assn. (past sec., chmn. Latin Am. law com.), Assn. Bar City N.Y., Am. Chambers Commerce Latin Am. (regional v.p.), Pan Am. Soc. U.S. Roman Catholic. Clubs: Military (Santiago); University (Washington); University (N.Y.C.); University, Campestre Churubusco (Mexico City). Internat. relations editor: Handbook of Latin Am. Studies, 1941. Home: Platon 445 Mexico City Mexico Office: Rio Marne No 17 Mexico City Mexico

LEE, CUTHBERT, artist; b. Boston, June 26, 1891; A.B., Harvard, student Academie Julian, Paris, France. Exhibited in group shows at Studio Guild, Mint Mus. Art, 1946, Jesup Library Art Gallery, Bar Harbor, Me., 1947, Asheville (N.C.) Art Mus., 1952; represented in permanent collections Busch-Reisinger Mus., Harvard, Columbia U., Columbia Club, U. N.C., Ga. Inst. Tech., N.D. Capitol Bldg., Gov.'s Mansion, N.C., De le Brook Manor, Md., Worthington Corp., N.Y.C., Episcopal Cathedrals, Boston and Atlanta, Fed. Ct. Appeals, Am. Hosp. Assn., Chgo. Clubs: Harvard, Pen and Plate, Biltmore Forest Country. Address: 327 Charlotte St Asheville NC 28801*

LEE, DANIEL WARNELL, retail services co. exec.; b. Alma, Ga., June 23, 1919; s. Daniel Marson and Ida (Hyers) L.; B.S. in Agr., U. Ga., 1941; m. Sallie Elizabeth Davis, Dec. 13, 1942; children—Daniel W., James D., Elizabeth C. Soil scientist U.S. Dept. Agr., Walhalla, S.C., 1941-42; tng. specialist VA, Valdosta, Ga., 1946-50, Swainsboro, Ga., 1952-53; with EBSCO Industries, Inc., Birmingham, Ala., 1953—, v.p., regional mgr., 1958—; sec. treas. Lee Land & Timber Co. Inc. Served to capt. AUS, 1942-46, 50-52; ETO. Decorated Congl. Medal of Honor, Purple Heart. Mem. V.F.W. Lion. Home: 1123 Melissa Dr San Antonio TX 78213 Office: 8410 Speedway San Antonio TX 78230

LEE, FREEMAN GORDON, govt. ofcl.; b. Washington, Dec. 31, 1929; s. Freeman Gaylord and Odessa (Wardlaw) L., degree U. Md., 1955; high speed aerodynamics degree U. Cal. at Los Angeles, 1957; m. Mildred Marie Potter, July 19, 1952; children—Lucile Jean, Melodie Susan, Celeste Ann, Montgomery Delta. Controls engr. Vanguard project Glenn L. Martin Co., Balt., 1955-56; flight test analysis engr. Lockheed-MSD, Van Nuys, Cal., 1956-57; analysis engr. aero-space systems Marquardt Aircraft Co., Van Nuys, 1957-58; sr. systems analysis engr. Pershing project The Martin Co., Orlando, Fla., 1958-59; tech. staff, asst. to chief engr. aerospace systems Melpar, Inc., Falls Church, Va., 1959-60; sr. physicist ASW research Aerojet-Gen. Corp., Frederick, Md., 1960-61; sr. systems analysis engr. aero-space projects Naval Air Engring. Center, Phila., 1962-64; electronics project engr., tech. expert land combat systems U.S. Army Missile Command, Redstone Arsenal, Ala., 1964—. Committeeman, Explorer Post 280, Boy Scouts Am., Absecond, N.J., 1962-64, roundtable commr. Tennessee Valley council Arrowhead Dist., 1970—. Served with 88th Blue Devil Div., 1945-49, Italy; with 1092d Combat Engrs., 1951-52, Korea. Recipient Navy commendation for personal contbns. to space effort, 1963; Meritorious award and Medal of Merit, Boy Scouts Am., 1972; Patriotic Civilian Service award Dept. Army, 1971; Humanitarian award Dept. Health, Edn. and Welfare, 1972. Fellow Brit. Interplanetary Soc. (br. chmn. D.C. 1959-61); mem. Am. Rocket Soc. (sect. v.p. 1958), Soc. Am. Mil. Engrs. (nat. award of merit 1966, v.p. 1967-68, 1st dir. 1969-70), Assn. U.S. Army, Am. Astronautical Soc., Am. Legion, Sons Confederate Vets., Order Stars and Bars (vice comdr.-in-chief 1963-64). Conducted controls analysis on all vanguard rockets and post flight analyses of Vikings; designed fuel flow and shock positioning system for BOMARC Missile; system analysis and reentry studies of Pershing Missile; developed airborne radiation analyzer, air def. command and control system, automatic multi-system test equipment for land combat missile systems and support equipment; certified fallout shelter analyst, radiol. officer. Home: 1207 Dodd Dr SW Decatur AL 35601 Office: US Army Missile Command Redstone Arsenal AL 35809

LEE, GEORGE TERRELL, ednl. adminstr.; b. Sylvania, Ga., Nov. 24, 1935; s. George Heath and Nancy Lola (Williams) L.; B.S., Ga. So. Coll., 1959, M.Ed., 1970; m. Aiko Ueda, May 20, 1958; children—James Robert, John David. Football coach, tchr. Kyoto (Japan) U., 1966-69; prin. elementary sch., Hinesville, Ga., 1970-71; now athletic dir. Moultrie Sch. Dist., Charleston, S.C., also prin. Mount Pleasant (S.C.) Acad., 1971—. Served with AUS, 1956-59, USNR, 1962-66. Mem. V.F.W. Methodist. Lion. Club: Isle of Palms Exchange. Home: 117 E Church St Sylvania GA 30467 Office: 605 Center St Mount Pleasant SC 29467

LEE, H. REX, govt. ofcl.; b. Rigby, Ida., Apr. 8, 1910; s. Hyrum and Eliza (Farnsworth) L.; B.S. in Agrl. Econs., U. Ida., 1936, LL.D., 1964; m. Lillian Carlson, May 29, 1937; children—Sherry, Dixie, Linda, Duane Rex, Mark Carlson Economist, U.S. Resettlement Adminstrn., Moscow, Ida., 1936-37; field agt. U. Ida. Extension service, 1937-1938; economist, Bur. Agr. Econs., Berkeley, Cal., 1938-42; field supr., later chief, relocation div., War Relocation Authority, Washington, 1942-46; asst. dir. Office Territories, Dept. Interior, 1946-50; asso. commr., then dep. commr. Bur. Indian Affairs, 1950-61, gov. Am. Samoa, 1961-67; asst. adminstr. AID, Dept. State, Washington, 1967-68; commr. FCC, 1968—. Recipient Pres.'s award for distinguished service, 1966; Distinguished Service award Dept. Interior, 1966. Address: FCC Washington DC 20554

LEE (NELLE) HARPER, author; b. Monroeville, Ala., Apr. 28; d. Amasa Coleman and Frances (Finch) Lee; student Huntingdon Coll., 1944-45, U. Ala., 1945-49. Author: To Kill a Mockingbird, 1960 (Pulitzer prize for fiction 1961). Republican. Methodist. Home: Monroeville AL Office: care Maurice Crain Inc 18 E 41st St New York City NY 10017

LEE, HOWARD NATHANIEL, advt. agy. exec., city ofcl.; b. Lithonia, Ga., July 28, 1934; s. Howard and Lou Temple (Barnes) L.; B.A., Ft. Valley State Coll., 1959; M.S.W., U. N.C., 1966; LL.D., Shaw U., 1971; m. Lillian Wesley, Nov. 24, 1962; children—Angela Denise, Noel Owens, Karin. Probation officer Juvenile Ct., Savannah, Ga., 1961-64; dir. youth services Edn. Improvement Program, Duke, 1966-68; employee relations dir. Duke, 1968-69, dir. human devel., 1969—; mayor City of Chapel Hill (N.C.), 1969—; pres. Graphic Impact Corp., Chapel Hill, 1969—. Second vice chmn. N.C. Democratic Com., 1969-72. Bd. dirs. Day Care and Child Devel. Council Am., So. Regional Council. Served with AUS, 1959-61. Recipient Atlanta N.A.A.C.P. award, 1969, Nat. Urban League-Equal Opportunity Day award, Achievement award Phi Beta Sigma. Mem. Nat. Assn. Social Workers (dir.), Chapel Hill C. of C. (dir.), U.S. Conf. of Mayors. Baptist (deacon). Home: 504 Tinkerbell Rd Chapel Hill NC 27514 Office: City Hall 100 Rosemary St Chapel Hill NC 27514

LEE, J.D., lawyer; b. Tellico Plains, Tenn., May 3, 1929; student Stetson U.; B.S., East Tenn. State U., 1951; J.D., U. Tenn., 1954. Admitted to Tenn. bar, 1954; mem. firm Lee, McGee, Garrett & Chandler, Knoxville, Tenn.; counsel Lester, Hildebrand, Nolan, Lane, Underhill, Mondelli & Thompson, Nashville; clk., master Chancery Ct., 1954-59. Lectr., Profl. Trial Lawyers Inst., 1969. Sec., Tenn. Conservation Commn., 1963-66. Del., Tenn. Constl. Conv., 1953, Democratic Nat. Conv., 1964. Bd. dirs. South Eastern Trial Lawyers Inst., U. Tenn. Coll. Law, 1965—. Mem. Am., Monroe County (pres. 1965) bar assns., Bar Assn. Tenn., Am. (gov. 1964-66, 68—, vice chmn. tort sect. 1966, 68, chmn. basic trial advocacy com. 1969-70, 2d v.p. 1970-71), Tenn. (gov. 1966—) trial lawyers assns., Am. Judicature Soc., Internat. Soc. Barristers, Selden Soc., Phi Delta Phi (province pres. 1957-59). Contbr. articles to legal jours. Office: 205 Clinch Av Knoxville TN 37902 also 200 Sheets Bldg Madisonville TN*

LEE, JAMES RODNEY, lawyer; b. Colorado City, Tex., Jan. 28, 1930; s. James Ralph and Mary (Biggerstaff) L.; B.S., Tex. Christian U., 1951; LL.B., Baylor U., 1956; m. Sara Ann Norman, June 9, 1957; children—Rebecca Ann, Ralph Norman, James Curtis. Admitted to Tex. bar, 1956, since practiced in Waco; partner firm Naman, Howell, Smith & Chase; dir. Word Music, Inc., John M. Hawes Co. Lectr. Baylor U. Law Sch. Pres. U.S.O. council, Waco, 1962-63; pres. Action planning council, Waco, 1969-70; bd. dirs. McLennan County gov.'s com. for aging, 1968; mem. Bd. Adjustment Waco, 1964-68; mem. Heart of Tex. council Boy Scouts Am. Bd. dirs., trustee Greater Waco United Fund. Served to 1st lt. AUS, 1951-54. Mem. Am., Tex., Waco-McLennan County (dir.), Waco Jr. (past pres.) bar assns., Waco C. of C., Phi Delta Phi. Democrat. Disciple of Christ. Comments editor Baylor Law Rev., 1955-56. Home: 5307 Chaparral Dr Waco TX 76710 Office: First Nat Bldg Waco TX 76701

LEE, JAMES STEWART, govt. ofcl.; b. Washington, Sept. 18, 1919; s. Frederic Edward and Edna (Stewart) L.; B.A., U. Ill., 1940; postgrad. (scholar) Clark U., 1940-41, (fellow) U. Wash., 1941; grad. Indsl. Coll. Armed Forces, 1963; m. Madelaine June Fald, Sept. 5, 1943; children—Barbara Susan, Bruce Stewart, Melissa Madelaine. Faculty, U. Wash., Seattle, 1941; geog. and cartographic specialist M.I. Service, War Dept., N.Y.C., 1941-44, with Office Chief Staff, Washington, 1944; with OSS, 1945, Dept. Army, 1946-50; with Dept. Air Force, Washington, 1950-62, air intelligence specialist, 1955-62; supervisory intelligence research specialist, div. chief Def. Intelligence Agy., Dept. Def., Washington, 1963—. Mem. arrangements com. 17th Congress Internat. Geog. Union, Washington, 1952; mem. U.S. delegation Internat. Prodn. Conf., London, Eng., 1955; lectr., seminar leader Dept. Def. Schs., colls., overseas units, 1947—; hon. mem. faculty U.S. Army Intelligence Sch., Ft. Holabird, Md., 1966—. Lt. col. USAF Res. Recipient Civilian Service award War Dept., 1942,

Air Force, 1962. Fellow Am. Geog. Soc.; mem. Am. Assn. Geographers (program mgmt. staff 64th meeting 1968), Am. Ordnance Assn., Am. Soc. Profl. Geographers, Theta Chi. Conglist. Clubs: Officers (Ft. McNair, Washington, Arlington Hall, Va.). Research, developer terrain maps in World War II. Home: 6813 Felix St McLean VA 22101 Office: Def Intelligence Agy Pentagon Washington DC 20301

LEE, JOHN F., JR., city ofcl.; b. El Dorado, Kan., Apr. 7, 1919; s. John F. and Helen (Condell) L.; B.S., U. Mo., 1941; postgrad. U. Kan., 1957-59; m. Lucille Marie Scherlen, Oct. 31, 1964; children— Nancy, Ann, Priscilla, Carol, Cindy, Pamela. City mgr., Victoria, Tex., 1959—. Vice pres. Tex. City Mgrs. Assn., 1973—; bd. dirs. Tex. Municipal League, 1972—. Served with USAAF, 1941-43, 43-45. Mem. C. of C. (1st v.p. 1969). Rotarian. Home: 811 W Stayton St Victoria TX 77901 Office: City Hall Victoria TX 77901

LEE, JOHN HOLMES, constrn. engr.; b. Marion, Ala., Apr. 20, 1919; s. John Holmes and Charlotte (Parks) L.; A.A., Marion Inst., 1939; B.C.E., Ala. Poly. Inst., 1942; m. Sara Frances Yeager, Aug. 10, 1946; children—Eva Frances, John Holmes III, Sara Louise. Jr. engr. Ky. Dam, 1942-43; elec. engr. Navy Dept., Washington, 1943; constrn. engr. locks and dams U.S. Army C.E., Ala., Ga., 1946-65, asst. resident engr., Millers Ferry Lock and Dam, Camden, Ala., 1965—. Mem. Marion City Bd. Edn. Served with USAAF, 1943-46. Registered profl. engr., Ala. Mem. Chi Epsilon. Baptist (deacon). Home: 503 East St Marion AL 36756 Office: PO Box 418 Camden AL 36726

LEE, JOHN LAWRENCE, ret. army officer, lawyer; b. Albertson, N.C., Aug. 12, 1894; s. Ezekiel and Rosa (Davis) L.; diploma Inf. Sch., Ft. Benning, Ga., 1933, Command and Gen. Staff Sch., Ft. Leavenworth, Kan., 1937; LL.B., Duke, 1949, LL.M., Woodrow Wilson Coll. Law, 1951; m. Mary Harlan, Sept. 17, 1932; 1 dau., Linda Joan (Mrs. James Robert Beacham). Served from pvt. to col. Inf., U.S. Army, 1913-46, ret. phys. disability, 1946; admitted to Ga. bar, 1951, practiced in Atlanta and Dunwoody, Ga.; justice 524th Dist. G.M., DeKalb County, Ga., 1957-65. Mem. Justices and Constables Assn. De Kalb County (pres.), Disabled Officers Assn. (nat. exec. committeeman So. Area 1948-58, 60-68, sr. nat. vice comdr. 1958-60, 68—), Ga., Stone Mountain bar assns., Ret. Officers Assn., David Crockett and Martha Stroud Lee Desc. Assn. of Old Duplin County (patriarch-pres. 1960—), Sigma Delta Kappa (scholarship award). Mason (50th yr. award). Club: Old War Horse Lawyers (Atlanta). Home: Rt 1 Box 445 Westbrook Rd Suwanee GA 30174 Office: Suwanee GA 30174

LEE, JOHN RUSKIN, lawyer; b. Olney, Tex., Feb. 16, 1925; s. Harry M. and Lura (Tucker) L.; LL.B., U. Tex., 1950; m. Jannie Lou Dyer, Apr. 29, 1960; children—John Edward, Mary Lucille. Admitted to Tex. bar, 1949; county atty., Winkler County, Tex., 1951-54; dist. atty. 109th Jud. Dist. Tex., 1954-57; city atty. City of Kermit (Tex.), 1960—. Mem. Tex. Ho. of Reps., 1957-58. Served with USNR, 1942-46. Home: 530 N Av D Kermit TX 79745 Office: 204 N Poplar St Kermit TX 79745

LEE, LEWIS SWIFT, lawyer; b. Dallas, Nov. 19, 1933; s. Lenoir Valentine and Margaret (Clendon) L.; student Washington and Lee U., 1954-55; A.B., U. of South, 1955; M.A., Emory U., 1956, LL.B., 1960; m. Frances Ann Childress, Mar. 16, 1956; children—Frances Ann, Lewis Swift, George Childress, Lenoir Valentine II. Admitted to Fla. bar, 1960, since practiced in Jacksonville; partner firm Ulmer, Murchison, Ashby and Ball; sec., dir. Can. Dry Bottling Co. of Fla., Inc. Instr. math. Washington and Lee U., 1955; instr. polit. sci. Ga. State Coll., 1955-56; instr. social studies Ga. Inst. Tech., 1956. Pres., Mental Health Clinic Duval County, 1967; pres. Community Planning Council, Jacksonville, 1969-70, dir. Bd. dirs., sec., counselor Childrens Home Soc. Fla., pres. N.E. div., 1972; former trustee Bartram Sch.; trustee Bolles Sch., U. South, Jacksonville Episcopal High Sch. Found., Willing Hands, Inc., Greater Jacksonville Econ. Opportunity, Inc., Jr. Achievement. Served to 1st lt. AUS, 1956-58. Mem. Maritime Law Assn., Am., Fla., Jacksonville bar assns., Phi Beta Kappa, Phi Delta Theta. Republican. Episcopalian. Clubs: Fla. Yacht, Timuquana Country, River, Ponte Vedra. Home: 3733 Ortega Blvd Jacksonville FL 32210 Office: PO Box 479 Fla Nat Bank Bldg Jacksonville FL 32201

LEE, MARY ANN, journalist; b. Memphis, July 30, 1939; d. Robert Martin and Mattye Veva (Nash) Lee; B.A., Southwestern at Memphis, 1958. Copywriter, John Cleghorn Agy., 1958; continuity dir. WMC-TV, 1959-64; TV columnist Memphis Press-Scimitar, 1964-67, TV-radio editor, 1967—; Memphis corr. Variety, 1968—. Charter mem. Critics Consensus, 1966—. Mem. West Tenn. Council Human Relations; publicity chmn. Chi Omega May Day Festival, 1963. Mem. Democratic Roundtable, 1964; reporter Shelby County Dem. Newspaper, 1965. Mem. UN Assn. (dir. Memphis), Memphis Media Club, Am. Newspaper Guild, Am. Civil Liberties Union (dir. West Tenn. chpt.), League Women Voters (v.p. Memphis 1963). Episcopalian. Home: 3771 Waynoka Av Memphis TN 38111 Office: 495 Union Av Memphis TN 38101

LEE, MARY VIRGINIA, artist; b. Clinton, Okla., Nov. 19, 1924; d. Thomas Joseph and Opal Corbin (Sights) Lee; student (scholar) Bernice Cross-Julia Eckels Studio, 1936-40, (scholar) Am. U., Phillips Meml. Gallery, 1943-45, Corcoran Gallery, 1940-41; grad. Nat. Cathedral Sch., Washington, 1943; student U. N.M., 1947; m. Angelo Marelli, June 29, 1959; children—Luciana, Thomas Giuseppe. Artist in residence Camp Galilee, Lake Tahoe, Nev., 1953, 56, Scuolo Beato Angelico, Milan, Italy, 1958-59; one-man shows Frances Webb Galleries, Los Angeles, Am. Assn. U. Women, Okla. Art Center, Nev. State Art Gallery, N.M. State Art Gallery, Santa Fe, Okla. Southwestern State Coll.; group shows include Mulvane Art Center Washburn U., Topeka, Ann. Confs. Ch. Archtl. Guild Am., Seattle and Dallas, Elmira Coll., N.Y., also Santa Fe, Washington, others; permanent exhibits include Stations of Cross, St. Christopher's Ch., Boulder City, Nev., San Juan Mission Hosp., Farmington, N.M.; represented in pvt. collection Duncan Phillips, Washington, others; stained glass St. Joseph's Ch., Springer, N.M., now working on liturgical commns. in U.S., Europe; artist-designer, v.p. Marelli-Lee, Inc., designers, producers, importers liturgical art. Phillips Meml. Gallery fellow, 1945-46. Mem. Nat. Assn. Women Artists, D.A.R., Kappa Pi. Address: MarelliLee Inc PO Box 132 Clinton OK 73601 also Viale Caterina da Forli 58 Milan Italy 20146 also 626 Canyon Rd Santa Fe NM 87501

LEE, MOLLIE HUSTON, ret. librarian; b. Columbus, O., Jan. 18, 1907; d. Rolla Solmon and Corrina (Smith) Huston; A.B., Howard U., 1929; B.L.S., Columbia, 1934; m. James S. Lee, July 23, 1935; 1 son, James S. Librarian, Shaw U., Raleigh, N.C., 1930-35; tchr. library sci. Atlanta U., summer 1938, N.C. Coll., summer 1939, Shaw U., summer 1941; supr. N.C. Negro Pub. Libraries, 1946-53; supr. Raleigh Pub. Sch. Libraries, 1942-47; head librarian Richard B. Harrison Pub. Library, Raleigh, 1935-72. Supr. Delta Nat. Library Project in Franklin County, also instrumental in establishing Delta Pub. Library, Louisburg, N.C., 1949; mem. Community Council, 1951-53; mem. Mayor's Com. for UN, 1967—; Mid-Atlantic teen-age regional dir. Jack and Jill of Am., Inc., 1956-58; mem. N.C. Gov.'s Coordinating Com. on Aging, N.C. del. White House Conf. Aging, 1961; del. Nat. Conf. U.S. Nat. Commn. for UNESCO, 1961; cons. on library service to disadvantaged A.L.A., 1972; mem. N.C. Gov.'s White House Conf. on Aging, 1971. Trustee, N.C. State Library, 1972—. Named Raleigh Woman of Year for outstanding service to adult edn., 1954; recipient citation N.C. Negro Library Assn. for pioneering in library field and inspiring and encouraging Negro librarians, 1954; citation for outstanding work with mothers of young people Raleigh chpt. Jack and Jill Am., Inc., 1972, citation for outstanding service in library field City of Raleigh, Wake County Commrs., Wake County Library Trustees, 1972. Mem. A.L.A. (past mem. council), N.C. Negro Library Assn. (founder, past pres.), Assn. N.C. High Sch. Library Clubs, N.C., Southeastern Library assns., Adult Edn. Assn., N.C. Fedn. Negro Women's Clubs, Delta Sigma Theta. Episcopalian. Contbr. N.C. Libraries, 1948; also profl. jours. Home: 130 Nelson St Durham NC 27707 Office: 1307 New Bern Av Raleigh NC 27610

LEE, NEAL EDWARD, civil engr.; b. Corpus Christi, Tex., Aug. 6, 1926; s. John T. and Ethyl (Sears) L.; B.S. in C.E., Tex. A. and M. U., 1950; m. Mona Lasemen, Jan. 17, 1922; children—Gregory D., Tammy T. Timekeeper, P.O.B. Montgomery, Wichita Falls, Tex., 1950-51; layout engr. R.F. Ball, San Antonio, 1951; engr. McKinzie Constrn. Co., San Antonio and Beeville, Tex., 1951-56; engr.-estimator Heldenfels Bros., Corpus Christi, 1956—. Served with AUS, 1944-46. Registered profl. engr. Mem. Tex. Soc. Profl. Engrs. (treas. Nueces chpt. 1968-70), Am. Assn. Cost Engrs. Moose. Club: Aggie (Corpus Christi). Home: 302 Cape Hatteras Corpus Christi TX 78412 Office: PO Box 4957 Corpus Christi TX 78408

LEE, RALPH MARION, educator; b. Goldsboro, N.C., Nov. 12, 1898; s. Robert Edward and Emma Daisy (Swinson) L.; A.B., Wake Forest U., 1922; M.A., U. N.C., 1928; postgrad. Mich. State U., 1956; m. Rowena Pittard, July 9, 1924; children—Jane Elizabeth (Mrs. Charles A. Froneberger), Margaret Ann (Mrs. Frank Yandell, Jr.), Martha Lorena (Mrs. Don A. Kraft). Tchr. sci., coach Boiling Springs (N.C.) Acad., 1922-23; prin. Yancey Collegiate Inst., Burnsville, N.C., 1923-26; tchr. history, econs., prin. high sch. div. Mars Hill (N.C.) Coll., 1926-29, acting dean, asst. dean charge of men, 1929-42, acad. dean, chmn. exec. com. of faculty, 1942-69, dean emeritus, 1969, part-time tchr. bus. adminstrn. dept., 1969-71; ret., 1971. Alderman, Town of Mars Hill, N.C., 1935, mayor, 1936-55, justice of peace, 1954-55; mem. Madison County Bd. Edn., 1970—. Served with AUS, 1918; capt. Res. ret. Recipient Citizen of the Year award Mars Hill Civitan Club, 1963-64, Gov.'s award, 1969, Civitan area award, 1970; Distinguished Service citation Wake Forest Coll., 1962; Outstanding Ednl. Service award Anderson Coll., 1961. Mem. Am., So. econ. assns., Jr. Coll. Assn. N.C. (past pres.), N.C. Coll. Conf. (past pres.), N.C. Assn. Acad. Deans (past pres.), So. Assn. Jr. Colls. (pres. 1952-53), So. Jr. Coll. Athletic Assn. (pres. 1932-35), N.C. Coll. Conf. (mem. various coms.), Phi Gamma Mu. Club: Civitan (dist. gov. 1972-73). Home: 160 Bailey St Mars Hill NC 28754

LEE, RAYMOND ALTON, bus. machines co. exec.; b. St. Paul, Aug. 29, 1916; s. Phillip E. and Hildur M. (Belisle-Nordstrom) L.; student Lancaster Bus. Coll., 1938, Yale, 1939; grad U. Minn., 1950, Macalester Coll., 1951; m. Katherine R. Ferschweiler, Sept. 18, 1943; 1 son, Christopher Ray. Editor publs. Peavey Co., 1951-53; dir. publs. Agr. Markets Pub. Co., 1953-54; co. editorial writer Dairy Nat. Assn., St. Paul, 1954-55; pub. relations officer Greater St. Paul Community Chest, 1950; editor, pub. relations mgr. IBM Corp., Austin, Tex., 1956—; tchr. pub. speaking; editor Nat. Assn. Systems; asst. Journalism Inst., Macalester Coll. Chmn. admissions com. Austin United Fund, 1969-70, trustee, 1967—; chmn. publicity com. Vol. Bur., 1968-70; coordinator Jr. Achievement, 1969—. Bd. dirs. Am. Cancer Soc., Austin Arts Council; sec. St. Vincent de Paul. Served with USAAF, World War II and Korea. Decorated D.F.C., Air medal with 6 oak leaf clusters, Silver Star, Purple Heart; recipient Art for Industry awards, 1968, 69. Mem. Pub. Relations Soc. Am., St. Theresa-St. Vincent de Paul Soc., Sigma Delta Chi. Clubs: Rochester (Minn.) Country; Balcones Country (Austin, Tex.). Contbr. articles profl. jours., gen. mags. Home: 4213 Woodway Dr Austin TX 78731 Office: 1325 F M Rd Austin TX 78759

LEE, ROBERT E., govt. ofcl.; b. Chgo., Mar. 31, 1912; s. Patrick and Delia (Ryan) L.; grad. DePaul U., 1935; LL.D. (hon.), St. John's U.; m. Wilma Rector, 1936; children—Patricia, Robert E., Michael B. Agt. fiscal asst. to J. Edgar Hoover F.B.I., 1939-47; dir. surveys and investigations house appropriations com., U.S. Congress, 1947-53; commr. FCC, 1953—, now also vice chmn. FCC mem. Radio Tech. Commn. Aeros.; FCC rep. to Interagy. Group on Internat. Aviation; vice chmn. World Adminstrv. Radio Conf. for Space Telecommunications, 1973 Plenipotentiary Conf., also chmn. interconnection adv. coms. Mem. I.E.E.E. Clubs: Congressional Country, Bolling AFB Officers, Republican (Washington). Home: 3147 Westover Dr SE Washington DC 20020 Office: 1919 M St NW Washington DC 20036

LEE, ROBERT EDWARD, JR., judge; b. Miley, S.C., May 20, 1922; s. Robert Edward and Edna (Chalker) L.; student U. Fla., 1939-40; LL.D., John B. Stetson U., 1949; m. Shirley Hudson, July 8, 1967; children— Virginia M., Mary Edna. Admitted to Fla. bar, 1949, since practiced in Deland; judge Volusia County Juvenile Ct., 1964—. Mem. Fla. Gov.'s Adv. Commn. to Div. Youth Services, 1965—. Bd. dirs. YMCA, 1966-69. Served with S.C., AUS, 1942-45; PTO. Mem. Am., Fla. bar assns., Am. Judicature Soc., Nat., Fla. assns. juvenile ct. judges, Am. Legion, Phi Alpha Delta. K.C. Club: Deland Toastmasters (pres. 1964-65). Home: 2100 N Thorpe Av Orange City FL 32763 Office: 109 W Rich Av Deland FL 32720

LEE, ROBERT WRIGHT, pub., editor; b. Ridley Park, Pa., Mar. 17, 1916; s. Earl and Edna (Durand) H.; student pub. schs.; m. Helen Elizabeth Garrott, Sept. 7, 1940; 1 dau., Sandra. Reporter, then city editor, editorial writer, mng. editor San Francisco News, 1933-59; mng. editor San Francisco News-Call Bull., 1959-62; pub., editor El Paso (Tex.) Herald-Post, 1963—; v.p. Newspaper Printing Corp., El Paso, Herald-Post Pub. Co. Active Boy Scouts Am. Bd. dirs. El Paso Goodwill, YMCA; bd. dirs. El Paso Guidance Center, pres., 1966; bd. dirs. Nat. Conf. Christians and Jews, pres., 1966. Served to 2d lt. USAAF, 1943-45. Decorated Air medal with three clusters. Mem. Sigma Delta Chi. Home: 6321 Snowheights El Paso TX 79912 Office: 401 Mills Av El Paso TX 79999

LEE, SHEW KUHN, optometrist; b. Balt., Apr. 24, 1923; s. Mong Har and Gum Tuey (Wong) L.; Dr. Optometry, Ill. Coll. Optometry, 1949; postgrad. Catholic U. Am., 1957, Md. U., 1959; m. Florence Gin Toy, Oct. 29, 1949; children—Wayson Perry, Davin Jeffrey. Pvt. practice optometry, Washington, 1949—. Lectr. D.C. Traffic Safety Sch.; v.p. D.C. Bd. Optometry, 1959-65; mem. Eye Bank Council; bd. dirs. Eye Bank and Research Found., Washington Hosp. Center. Served with AUS, 1942-45. Decorated Purple Heart, Bronze Star medal with oak leaf cluster. Mem. Am. Optometric Assn., Am. Legion (post comdr. D.C. 1960), D.C. Optometric Soc. (sec. 1956-57), Lees Assn. (trustee), Chinese Consol. Benevolent Assn., Beta Sigma Kappa. Lion (charter pres. Chi-Am 1960, zone chmn. 1961, dep. dist. gov. 1963, hon. mem. Capitol Hill). Research, publs. in field. Home: 2939 McKinley St NW Washington DC 20015 Office: 813 7th St NW Washington DC 20001

LEE, THOMAS EDISON, judge; b. Winter Park, Fla., Jan. 29, 1915; s. Andrew Jackson and Leila Jane (Moss) L.; B.B.A., U. Miami, 1946; J.D., Stetson U., 1949; m. F. Margaret Tough, Dec. 8, 1951; 1 son, Thomas Gregory. Admitted to Fla. bar, 1949; practiced in Miami, Fla., 1949-64; spl. asst. atty. gen., Miami, 1957-58, 61-64; judge Met. Ct. Dade County, Fla., Miami, 1961-71, Circuit Ct., 11th Jud. Circuit in and for Dade County, 1971—. Adviser-dir. Peoples Liberty Nat. Bank of Hialeah, Peoples Liberty Nat. Bank of Miami Shores. Spl. examiner Fla. Real Estate Commn., 1961-64. Past chmn. adv. bd. Fla. Fedn. Blind; mem. local bd. SSS. Served with AUS, 1942-43. Recipient Good Govt. award North Miami (Fla.) Jaycees, 1972; Cooper-Taylor award Greater Miami Jaycees, 1970. Fellow Internat. Acad. Law and Sci.; mem. Am. (mem. com. excise and miscellaneous taxes, sect. taxation), Dade County (dir. 1958-61, 2d v.p. 1963) bar assns., Fla. Bar, Fla. Acad. Trial Lawyers, N.Am. Judges Assn., Am. Judicature Soc., Miami Shores C. of C. (dir.), Internat. Platform Assn., Am. Legion, 40 and 8, Fraternal Order Police (asso.), Marching and Chowder Soc. Miami Shores, Pi Kappa Alpha. Democrat. Presbyn. (chmn. bd. deacons 1970-71). Mason (32 deg., Shriner). Clubs: Sertoma (charter mem., chmn. bd. 1956-57) (Miami); Miami Shores Mens (1st v.p. 1969), Miami Shores Country, Flamingo Dinner (dir. 1959-60, 65-68, pres. 1968-69); Lawyers (Dade County). Home: 11490 W Biscayne Canal Rd Miami FL 33161 Office: Room 500 Dade County Courthouse 73 W Flagler St Miami FL 33130

LEE, VERREN WILSON, agrl. economist; b. Pensacola, Fla., Aug. 24, 1939; s. Verren Delvin and Loney (Walker) L.; A.A., Clarke Meml. Coll., 1962; B.S., Auburn U., 1964; M.S., U. Ariz., 1967; m.; Dorothy Louesa Gaston, June 27, 1965; children—Lance Wilson, Charlotte Louesa. Beaming operator The Chemstrand Corp., Pensacola, Fla., 1958-60; tchr. vocational agr. Lowndes County Bd. Edn., Hayneville, Ala., 1964; asst. county agt. Coop. Extension Service, Moulton, Ala., 1965; grad. research asst. U. Ariz., 1965-67; poultry marketing specialist Auburn (Ala.) U., 1967—. Baptist. Lion. Home: 618 Seminole St Auburn AL 36830 Office: 9-B Extension Cottage Auburn U Auburn AL 36830

LEE, VOYD FRANK, educator; b. Neuville, Tex., Mar. 26, 1911; d. Ernest Christian and Doltie Willie (Willard) Frank; A.A., Lamar State Coll. Tech., 1928; student Mary Hardin-Baylor Coll., 1928-29, Sam Houston State Tchrs. Coll., summers 1929, 32-34; B.S. in Edn., U. Houston, 1953; m. Benjamin Franklin Lee, Mar. 27, 1934; 1 son, Ben Frank. Tchr. Port Bolivar Rural Sch., Tex., 1929, prin., 1930-32, prin. elementary sch., 1935-36; tchr. High Island High Sch., Tex., 1932-35; owner, dir. Kiddie Kollege Nursery Sch., Beaumont, Tex., 1949-52; tchr. Pennsylvania Elementary Sch., Beaumont Ind. Sch. Dist., 1952-53, tchr. French Elementary Sch., 1953—. Mem. adv. com. div. instructional media, Tex. Edn. Agy., 1961—; mem. Sabine area council Tchrs. of Math. Mem. N.E.A., Tex. Congress Parents and Tchrs., Tex. State Tchrs. Assn., Tex., Beaumont classroom tchrs. assns., Tex. (pres. 1960-61; life; mem. workshop planning bd. 1958-62; adviser 1962-63), Beaumont (pres. 1955-57) assns. childhood edn., Internat. Reading Assn., Lamar Area Reading Council, Internat. Platform Assn., Beaumont Assn. Mental Health, Alpha Delta Kappa. Home: Apt 2740 14th St Beaumont TX 77702

LEE, WARDEN SPERRY, lawyer; b. Houston, Dec. 31, 1921; s. Lenoir Valentine and Margaret (Clendon) L.; B.A., U. of South, 1943; LL.B., Washington and Lee U., 1948; m. Patricia Anne Wood, June 16, 1956; children—Warden Sperry, Carlotta. Admitted to Fla. bar, 1948; asso. firm Adair, Kent, Ashby & McNatt, 1948-55, Adair, Ulmer, Murchison, Kent & Ashby, Jacksonville, Fla., 1955-56, partner, 1956-61; partner firm Ulmer, Murchison, Kent, Asby & Ball, 1961-67, Ulmer, Murchison, Asby & Ball, 1967—. Trustee U. of South 1962—, v.p. for classes Asso. Alumni, 1964-65; bd. dirs. Vis. Nurse Assn., pres., 1971-72. Local govt. appeal agt. SSS. Served from apprentice seaman to lt. (j.g.), USNR, 1943-46; as lt., USNR, 1951-53. Mem. Am., Jacksonville bar assns., Am. Judicature Soc., Fla. Bar, Newcomen Soc., Fla. C. of C., Navy League U.S., Ye Mystic Revellers, Phi Delta Theta. Republican. Episcopalian (vestryman). Clubs: Selva Marina, University, Sewanee (past pres.), Fla. Yacht, Timuquana Country, Friars (Jacksonville). Home: 4323 Forest Park Rd Jacksonville FL 32210 Office: Fla Nat Bank Bldg Jacksonville FL 32202

LEE, WILLIAM IVEY, III, oil and gas co. exec.; b. Asheville, N.C., Oct. 8, 1926; s. William I. and Margaret A. (Thrash) L.; student U. Okla., 1946-49; m. Jane Durand, May 28, 1960. Ind. oil producer, 1955-66; pres. Triton Oil & Gas Corp., Dallas, 1966—, chief exec. officer related cos., 1966—, also dir.; dir., chmn. Triton Oil (Australia) Ltd., Triton Oil (Holdings) Australia Ltd., Triton Oil (New Zealand) Ltd., Triton Philippines Oil & Gas Co., Dallas Investments Ltd. (New Zealand); pres., dir. Triton Middle East Oil Co. (Turkey), Antilles Enterprises, Inc., Whalen Corp., Wilco Properties, Inc.; dir. Antilles Enterprises, N.V. Aviation Properties, Inc., Crusader Oil, N.L. (Australia), Inter-Island Devel. Co. (New Zealand), Lubbock Cotton Oil Co., Petroleum Services, Ltd. (New Zealand), Pursuit Oil N.L. (Australia), Sweetwater Cotton Oil Co. Served with USAAF, 1944-45. Clubs: Brook Hollow Golf, Dallas Petroleum, Preston Trail Golf, Dallas (Dallas); N.Y. Athletic (N.Y.C.). Home: 3131 Maple St Dallas TX 75201 Office: Republic Bank Tower Dallas TX 75201

LEE, WILTON AMBROSE, social worker; b. Ponchatoula, La., July 31, 1931; s. Ambrose and Ima (Pritchard) L.; B.A. in Edn., Southeastern La. Coll., 1958; M.S.W., Tulane U., 1959; m. Marilyn Miller, June 25, 1970; 1 son, Warren Davis. Psychiat. social worker S.E. La. State Hosp., Mandeville, 1959-60; psychiat. social worker Chattanooga Psychiat. Clinic, 1960-63, chief social worker, 1963—. Pvt. practice social work, part-time 1962—; faculty So. Missionary Coll., 197-0—; field work supr. U. Tenn. Sch. Social Work, 1962—; cons. in field. Active Chattanooga Little Theatre, 1960—. Served with USAF, 1951-53. Mem. Acad. Certified Social Workers, Nat. Assn. Social Workers (chpt. treas. 1962-63, pres. 1963-64). Home: 525 Briar Park Lane Hixson TN 37343 Office: 1028 E 3d St Chattanooga TN 37403

LEEBER, PHILIP WARD, hosp. adminstr.; b. Beckley, W.Va., Oct. 15, 1939; s. Anthony Philip and Helen (Ward) L.; B.S., Concord Coll., Athens, W.Va., 1961; M.B.A. in Hosp. Adminstrn., George Washington U., 1964; m. Vivian Diane O'Quinn, June 17, 1965; children—Philip Jason, Shannon Dyan. Adminstrv. asst. Bapt. Meml. Hosp., Jacksonville, Fla., 1964-65; asst. adminstr. Appalachian Regional Hosps., Inc., Lexington, Ky., 1965-66; hosp. cons. Fla. Bd. Health, Bur. Health Facilities and Service, Jacksonville, 1967; asst. adminstr. Methodist Hosp., Jacksonville, 1967-69; adminstr. Clearwater (Fla.) Community Hosp., 1969-71; exec. dir. Parkway Gen. Hosp., North Miami Beach, Fla., 1971—; Eastern rep. Am. Med. Enterprises, Inc., 1971—. Mem. Am. Coll. Hosp. Adminstrs., Am., Fla. hosp. assns. Rotarian. Office: 160 NW 170th St North Miami Beach FL 33169

LEEDS, MORTON HAROLD, govt. ofcl.; b. N.Y.C., May 15, 1921; B. in Social Sci., Coll. City N.Y., 1944; M.A., New Sch. Social Research, 1948, Ph.D., 1950; m. Ingrid Rheinstrom, June 25, 1948; children— Wendy, Karen, Lori. Asst. dir. Sephardic Home for Aged, N.Y.C., 1951-52; exec. dir. Borinstein Home, 1953-62; sec. Ind.

Commn. Aging and Aged, Indpls., 1955-62; dir. elderly housing loans program U.S. Dept. Housing and Urban Devel., Washington, 1962-67, dir. plans, programs and evaluation staff, renewal and housing mgmt., 1967-71, dep. dir. Office Program Devel. and Housing Mgmt., 1971—, spl. asst. for elderly to the asst. sec. for housing mgmt., 1972—. Dir. Indpls. Sr. Citizens Center, 1961-62. Served with AUS, 1943-46; CBI. Mem. Nat. Assn. Social Workers (charter). Author: Jackstones, 1970; The Aged, the Social Worker and the Community, 1961. Editor: (with H. Shore) Geriatric Institutional Management, 1964; Washington Colloquium on Science and Society, 1968; Aging in Indiana, 1959. Home: 6219 Lone Oak Dr Bethesda MD 20034 Office: Dept Housing and Urban Devel 451 7th St SW Washington DC 20410

LEEMAN, HAFFORD RANSOM, savs. and loan exec., educator; b. Morgan County, Ala., Nov. 19, 1907; s. James Ervin and Mary Ella (Ransom) L.; A.B., Athens Coll., 1938; B.S., U. Ala., 1939, M.A., 1942; m. Wilma Sue Sheats, Nov. 1, 1936; 1 dau., Charlotte Dianne (Mrs. John Edward Knight, Jr.). Tchr., prin. Morgan County Schs., 1925-47, supt., 1947-53; tchr., prin. Decatur (Ala.) City Schs., 1953-56, supt., 1956-69; faculty Florence State Coll. Summer Sch., 1960, 61, 62. Pres. First Fed. Savs. & Loan Assn., 1969—; dir. Am. Educators Investment Corp., Am. Educators Ins. Co. Mem. So. Assn. Schs. (state secondary com. 1963-69), Ala. Edn. Assn. (chmn. joint com. retirement 1967-69); mem. legislative com.). Baptist (Sunday sch. tchr., deacon). Home: 2110 Woodmont Dr SE Decatur AL 35601 Office: First Fed Savs & Loan Assn 255 Grant St SE Decatur AL 35601

LEEPER, JOHN PALMER, museum exec.; b. Denison, Tex., Feb. 4, 1921; s. John Palmer and Maryanne (Platter) L.; B.Journalism, So. Methodist U., 1942; M.A. in Art History, Harvard, 1947; m. Blanche Wheeler Magurn, Sept. 18, 1948; 1 dau., Maryanne M. Keeper W.A. Clark Collection, Corcoran Gallery Art, Washington, 1948, asst. dir. gallery, 1949-50; dir. Pasadena (Cal.) Art Inst., 1950-53; dir. Marion Koogler McNay Art Inst., San Antonio, 1954—. Instr. Dexter Sch., Boston, 1947-48; lectr. Pasadena Sch. Fine Arts, 1952-53, U. So. Cal., Los Angeles, 1952, Trinity U., San Antonio, 1957-59. Pres. San Antonio Little Theatre. Trustee San Antonio Art Inst. Served with USAAF, 1942-45. Mem. Am. Assn. Museums, Assn. Art Mus. Dirs., Tex. Soc. Arts and Letters (hon.). Club: Harvard (San Antonio). Address: 6000 N Braunfels San Antonio TX 78209

LEFEBER, EDWARD JAMES, physician; b. Wauwatosa, Wis., June 1, 1911; s. Cornelius George and May (McCord) L.; B.S., U. Wis., 1934, M.D., 1936; m. Ellie Hancock Weisiger, June 4, 1938; children—Edward James, Robert Randolph, John Courtney, Ann Elizabeth, Donald Louis, Nancy Ellen. Intern, resident in medicine Med. Coll. Va. Hosps., Richmond, 1936-40; mem. faculty Med. Br., U. Tex., Galveston, 1940—, clin. asso. prof. medicine, 1951—, dir. Student Health Service, 1943-46; practice medicine, specializing in internal medicine with Internal Medicine Assos., Galveston, 1948—; chief out-patient service Galveston office Houston Regional Office, VA, 1946-48; cons. gastroenterology USPHS Hosp., Galveston; pres. staff St. Mary's Infirmary, Galveston, 1961. Mem. home service com. Galveston chpt. A.R.C., 1958—; mem. Galveston Civic Orch., 1957-60. Bd. dirs. Moody House, 1964-65, 67-71, med. dir. Diplomate Am. Bd. Internal Medicine. Fellow A.C.P.; mem. Galveston County Med. Soc. (pres. 1954, sec.-treas. 1948-53), A.M.A., Tex., So. med. assns., Am. Soc. Internal Medicine, Am. Soc. Gastro-Intestinal Endoscopy, Tex. Acad. Internal Medicine, Tex. Club Internists, Houston Gastroent. Soc., Phi Chi. Episcopalian (vestryman). Mason. Home: 2927 Av P Galveston TX 77550 Office: Sealy Smith Profl Bldg 200 University Blvd Galveston TX 77550

LEFER, ALLAN MARK, research scientist, educator; b. N.Y.C., Feb. 1, 1936 s. Judah and Lillian (Gastwirth) L.; B.A., Adelphi Coll., 1957; M.A., Western Res. U., 1959; Ph.D., U. Ill., 1962; m. Mary Elizabeth Indoe, Aug. 23, 1959; children—Debra Lynn, David Joseph, Barry Lee, Leslie Ann. Instr. physiology Western Res. U. Sch. Medicine, Cleve., 1962-64; asst. prof. U. Va. Sch. Medicine, Charlottesville, 1964-69, asso. prof., 1969-72, prof., 1972—. Vis. prof. Hadassah Med. Sch., Jerusalem, Israel, 1971-72. Mem. Am. Physiol. Soc., Am. Soc. Zoologists, Cardiac Muscle Soc., Soc. Exptl. Biology and Medicine, Am. Heart Assn. (basic sci. council; established investigator 1968—), Va. Acad. Sci., Sigma Xi. Contbr. articles to profl. jours. Home: 101 Powhatan Circle Charlottesville VA 22901

LEFTWICH, RICHARD HENRY, educator; b. Burden, Kan., Feb. 1, 1920; s. Rush F. and Nellie (Bailiff) L.; B.A., Southwestern Coll., 1941; M.A., U. Chgo., 1948, Ph.D., 1950; m. Maxine Ellen Dieterich, Mar. 11, 1945; children—Judith E., Gregory V., Bradley R. Asst. prof., asso. prof. Okla. State U., Stillwater, 1948-55, prof. econs., 1955—, head dept. econs., 1966—, Ford Found. faculty research fellow, 1959-60. Vis. prof. U. Chgo., 1962-63; Dir. Ford Found. Faculty Research Seminar, 1960. Served with USAAF, 1942-45. Decorated Bronze Star medal. Mem. Am., Midwest (1st v.p. 1971-72), So. (pres. 1965) econ. assns., Southwestern Social Sci. Assn., Rocky Mountain Social Sci. Assn. (exec. com. 1968-71, pres. 1972-73). Author: The Price System and Resource Allocation, 1955, 4th edit., 1970; An Introduction to Economic Thinking, 1969. Home: 818 W Knapp Av Stillwater OK 74074

LE GARDEUR, GEORGE VERGNES, JR., cons. engr.; b. Shreveport, La., Aug. 4, 1926; s. George Vergnes and Claire (Parkhouse) LeG.; B.S., U. Ala., 1950; postgrad. Tulane U., 1944-45, 58-59; m. Norma Powell, Aug. 24, 1951 (div. Jan. 1970); children—Michael, Susan, Shelley, Deborah; m. 2d, Barbara J. Jett, May 16, 1970. Field constrn. supt. R. P. Farnsworth & Co., Inc., New Orleans, 1950-51; engr. Sverdrup & Parcell, cons. engrs., 1951-53; project engr. H. K. Ferguson & Co., Inc., engrs. and contractors, Cleve., 1953-55; jr. partner, cons. engr. Ewin, Campbell and Gottlieb, cons. engrs., New Orleans, 1955-59; cons. engr. G.V. Le Gardeur, Jr., 1959-66; v.p. H.B. Fowler & Co., Inc., Harvey La., 1966-70, exec. v.p., 1970—. Vice pres. Protestant Home for Aged, 1967. Served with AUS, 1943-44. Registered profl. engr. La., Miss., Ala., Tex., Tenn., Ark. Mem. Cons. Engrs. Council La. (sec.-treas. 1962, pres. 1964), Am. Concrete Inst., Prestressed Concrete Inst., Am. Inst. Steel Constrn., Nat. Soc. Profl. Engrs., La. Engring. Soc., Cons. Engrs. Council, Am. Soc. Testing and Materials, Am. Soc. C.E., St. Pat's Engring. Soc., Theta Tau, Mu Epsilon, Beta Theta Pi, Tau Beta Pi, Chi Epsilon, Omicon Delta Kappa. Methodist. Home: 3845 S Pin Oak Dr New Orleans LA 70114

LEGERE, LAURENCE JOSEPH, research polit. scientist; b. Fitchburg, Mass., Jan. 2, 1919; s. Laurence J. and Aurore (Bean) L.; B.S., U.S. Mil. Acad., 1940; M. Pub. Adminstrn. (Littauer fellow), Harvard, 1948, M.A. (Littauer fellow), 1949, Ph.D., 1951; m. Gail Gordon Paulsen, July 2, 1945. Commd. 2d lt. U.S. Army, 1940, advanced through grades to col., 1966; asst. prof. internat. relations U.S. Mil. Acad., 1945-47; def. asst. to spl. asst. to Pres. Eisenhower, 1956-57; asst. to mil. rep. to Pres. Kennedy, 1961-62, sr. staff mem. NSC, 1962-63, ret., 1966; mem. Center for Internat. Studies Mass. Inst. Tech., 1966-67; research analyst, also dep. div. dir. Inst. Def. Analyses, Arlington, Va., 1968—. Mem. arms control seminar Harvard-Mass. Inst. Tech., 1966-67; mem. nat. policy panel on Europe UN, 1967-69. Decorated Silver Star, Legion Merit, Bronze Star medal, Purple Heart. Mem. Am. Polit. Sci. Assn., Internat. Studies Assn., Am. Mil. Inst. Roman Catholic. Clubs: Army-Navy, Harvard (Washington). Author: The President and the Management of National Security, 1969. Home: 1111 Army-Navy Dr Arlington VA 22202 Office: 400 Army-Navy Dr Arlington VA 22202

LEGERTON, CLARENCE WILLIAM, JR., physician; b. Charleston, S.C., July 8, 1922; s. Clarence William and Winnie Davis (McMaster) L.; student Davidson Coll., 1939-43; M.D., Med. Coll. S.C., 1946; m. Mitzi Foster Herrin, May 31, 1958; children—Clarence William III, Mary Pringle, Gregg McMaster. Intern University Hosp., Balt., 1946-47, med. resident, 1947-48; instr. medicine Duke U. Sch. Medicine, 1950-53; practice medicine specializing in gastroenterology, Conway, S.C., 1953-56, Charleston, S.C., 1956-66; prof. medicine Med. U. S.C., Charleston, 1966—; dir. Citizens and So. Nat. Bank, Charleston, S.C. Vice-chmn. Commrs. Pub. Works, Charleston, 1959—; pres. Charleston Symphony Orchestra Assn., 1967-68; chmn. bd. dirs. Legerton & Co., Inc. Mem. City Council, Charleston, S.C., 1959—, mayor pro-tem, 1960; pres. Charleston County Democratic Convention, 1960. Trustee Montreat-Anderson Coll., vice-chmn., 1962—; trustee Queens Coll. Served to capt. AUS, 1948-50. Fellow A.C.P.; mem. S.C. Soc., Alpha Omega Alpha, Sigma Phi Epsilon, Alpha Kappa Kappa. Presbyn. (pres. corp. 1965—). Club: Carolina Yacht (Charleston). Home: 32 Council St Charleston SC 29401 Office: Medical University Hospital Charleston SC 29401

LEGETTE, CHARLES ERNEST, banker; b. Statesville, N.C., July 21, 1925; s. Charles Henry and Jane (Mills) L.; B.S., U. Ky., 1950; postgrad. U. Va. Grad. Sch. Consumers Banking, 1957, Am. Inst. Banking, 1955, Stonier Grad. Sch. Banking, 1969-71; m. Caroline Lee, Mar. 15, 1929; children—Charles, Caroline Teague, Jane. With South Orlando Nat. Bank (name changed to South Orlando First Nat. Bank 1967), exec. v.p., dir. 1960-63, pres., 1963—. Vice pres. Jr. Achievement, 1965. Bd. dirs. Central Fla. Mus., Orlando, Orlando Pub. Library. Served with USNR, 1943-46. Mem. Orange County Sportsmans Assn. (sec. treas. 1962), Orlando C. of C. (dir. 1967—), Fla. Bankers Assn. (competitive practices com. 1959—), Boone Athletic Boosters Assn. (sec. 1966—), Delta Chi. Episcopalian (vestryman). Kiwanian (pres. 1962). Clubs: Executive, Country Club (Orlando). Home: 813 E Kaley Av Orlando FL 32806 Office: 444 E Michigan Av Box 8157 Orlando FL 32806

LEGIDO, JUSTO, banker; b. Camaguey, Cuba, Dec. 24, 1926; s. Justo and Piedad (Mendiola) L.; B.B.A., U. Havana, 1949; m. Silvia Cueto, Dec. 8, 1957; children—Justo, Jorge, Josiana. Came to U.S., 1961. With Trust Co. Cuba, Camaguey, 1950-56, Banco Continental Cubano, Havana, 1956-61; br. mgr. Peoples Nat. Bank, Miami, 1962-66, auditor, cashier Miami Nat. Bank, 1966-69; sr. v.p., auditor, cashier Bank Miami (Fla.), 1969—. Home: 8860 SW 43d Terrace Miami FL 33165 Office: 110 E Flager St Miami FL 33101

LEGLER, DONALD WAYNE, educator; b. Mpls., Oct. 2, 1931; s. Ernest William and Almira Clarissa (Elness) L.; B.S., U. Minn., 1954, D.D.S., 1956; Ph.D., U. Ala., 1966; m. Janice Carol Cleworth, Dec. 28, 1957; children—Lori Kay, Lee Richard, Catherine Carol. Pvt. practice dentistry, Estes Park, Colo., 1958-62; asst. prof. dentistry U. Ala., 1966-71, prof., chmn. dept. oral biology, asst. dean, 1971—. Served with USAF, 1956-58. Fellowship Swedish Med. Research Council fellow, 1967-68. Mem. Am. Dental Assn., Am. Soc. Microbiology, A.A.A.S., Am. Assn Dental Schs., Sigma Xi. Methodist. Home: 3024 Warrington Rd Birmingham AL 35223 Office: 1919 7th Av S Birmingham AL 35233

LEGNER, STANLEY GAYLE, physician; b. Paw Paw, Ill., Feb. 28, 1920; s. Ernest and Hazel (Girton) L.; A.B., Drake U., 1943; M.D., St. Louis U., 1947; m. Beulah Clem Grah, Oct. 13, 1946; children—David Michael, Robert Eugene. Intern, St. Mary's Hosp., East St. Louis, Ill., 1947-48; resident Woman's Hosp., Chattanooga, 1948-50; practice medicine specializing in family practice, Perryville, Mo., 1950-68, Rossville, Ga., 1968—; mem. staff Hutcheson Meml. Hosp., Ft. Oglethorpe, Ga. Pres., Perry County Pub. Schs., 1962-67. Served with AUS, 1952-54. Mem. A.M.A., Med. Assn. Ga. Presbyn. (elder 1952—), Elk, Lion. Home: 7816 Stongehenge Dr Chattanooga TN 37421 Office: 214 Andrews St Rossville GA 30741

LEGORRETA, LUIS G., banker; b. Zamora, Mex., Jan. 30, 1898; s. Juan de Dios Legorreta and Guadalupe Garcia de Legorreta; student Instituto Cientifico de Mexico City, 1911; m. Gudalupe Vilchis, Dec. 2, 1926; children—Xavier, Isabel, Ricardo, Fernando. Joined Banco Nacional de Mexico S.A., Mexico City, 1913, mem. fgn. dept., 1916, various depts., 1917-22; sec., 1922-26, v.p., 1926-33, pres., 1934-52, vice-chmn., dir. dels., 1952-58, chmn. bd., dir. dels., 1958-70, hon. chmn., 1970—; dir. Banco de Mexico, Cia Fundidora de Fierro y Acero de Monterrey, Celaneses Mexicana, Fabricas de Papel San Rafael, Industria Electrica de Mexico, and other indsl. and financial cos. Chmn. bd. trustees Fundacion Mier y Pesado, pvt. charity orgn. Clubs: Bankers, University of Mexico, Campestre de la Ciudad de Mexico, Jockey Mexicano, Jr. (Mexico City). Home: Montanas Calizas 490 Mexico City Mexico Office: Isabel Catolica 44 Mexico City Mexico

LEGRAND, DUARD, newspaper editor. Editor Post-Herald, Birmingham, Ala. Home: 3325 Hermitage Rd Birmingham AL 35223 Office: 2200 4th Av Birmingham AL 35202*

LEGRAND, HOMER EUGENE, textile mfg. co. exec.; b. Shelby, N.C., Feb. 8, 1922; s. Richard Torrance and Lillian Branham (Fain) LeG.; B.S., N.C. State U., 1946; m. Emma Josephine Beam, Sept. 19, 1943; children—Homer Eugene, Bryan Fain, Anne (Mrs. Calvin J. Augustin), Elisabeth Josephine. Prodn. mgr. Shelby Mills, Inc., 1946-59; plant mgr. Fiber Industries, Inc., 1959—; pres. P & M Warehouse Co., Inc., 1961—; partner Shelby Properties, Ltd., 1963—; dir. First Citizens Bank & Trust Co. Mem. N.C. Gov.'s Council on Occupational Health, 1970-72; council commr. Piedmont council Boy Scouts Am., 1969-71. Bd. dirs. Boys Club, Shelby Life Saving and Rescue Unit, United Fund, Shelter Home of Cleveland Country; bd. advisers Salvation Army, Gardner Webb Coll; trustee Cleve. Meml. Hosp., Cleve. Tech. Inst. Served to capt. AUS, 1943-46. Named Man of the Year, Lions Club, Shelby, 1970. Mem. Shelby C. of C. (v.p. 1971-72). Democrat. Presbyn. Elk, Kiwanian (pres. 1953). Clubs: North Lake Country, Cleveland Country (bd. dirs. 1969-72) (Shelby); Charlotte City, Charlotte Athletic (Charlotte, N.C.). Home: 1000 W Blanton St Shelby NC 28150 Office: Box 1697 Shelby NC 28150

LEGUM, STANLEY HOWARD, dentist; b. Norfolk, Va., Oct. 19, 1939; s. Albert and Janice (Harris) L.; B.A., U. Va., 1961; D.D.S., Med. Coll. Va., 1965; m. Gayle Sue Jacobson, Aug. 4, 1963; children Keith Jon, Robin Denise, Paige Allison, Lisa Joy. Individual practice dentistry, Norfolk, Va., 1965-66, Virginia Beach, Va. 1968—. Served to capt. Dental Corps, USAAF, 1966-68. Mem. Am., Va. dental assns., Tidewater, Virginia Beach dental socs., Norfolk Dental Study Club, Virginia Beach Dental Forum, Alpha Omega. Jewish religion (dir. temple 1969—). Home: 533 Gleneagle Dr Virginia Beach VA 23452 Office: 3712 S Plaza Trail Virginia Beach VA 23452

LEHMAN, DAVID JOHN, JR., physician; b. Newark, Oct. 20, 1915; s. David J. and May (Stern) L.; M.D., U. Va., 1939; m. Henrietta Tichenor, Feb. 27, 1943 (div. July 1961); children—Bonnie (Mrs. Bonnie Maierhoffer), David J. III (dec.), Wendi Ann; m. 2d, Mary Ann Pennington, Oct. 19, 1969. Intern, Newark City Hosp., 1939-41; resident medicine Mount Sinai Hosp., N.Y.C., 1946; practice medicine, specializing in internal medicine and cardiology, Newark, 1947-54, Hollywood, Fla., 1954—; sr. attending in medicine Meml. Hosp., Hollywood, Fla., chief medicine, 1963-64, sec., med. staff, 1964; adj. prof. depts. psychology and sociology Fort Lauderdale U., 1971—; founder, mem. EKG panel Meml. Hosp., 1965—; dir. Dangerous Drugs div. Office of Atty. Gen. of Fla., 1968-69; chmn. Broward Country (Fla.) Council on Aging, 1966-67; organized Teenage and Parental Alert, drug edn. program, 1967; founder, pres. Dangerous Substances Guidance Center, Inc., Broward County, 1969-72; The Starting Place Edn. and Guidance Counseling Center, 1969-72; mem. med. adv. staff the Seed, Rehab. Drug Center for Youthful Drug Offenders, Broward County, 1971—. Served with AUS, 1941-46. Recipient Distinguished Service award Kiwanis Club, Fort Lauderdale, Fla., 1967, Meritorious Citizenship award Fla. Assn. Grand Juries, 1969, citizen of the year award Hollywood Elks, 1970. Diplomate Am. Bd. Internal Medicine. Mem. A.C.P., Broward County Med. Assn. (chmn. drug abuse com. 1967—, v.p. 1964), Fla. Med. Assn. (ad hoc drug abuse com. 1970), Hollywood Men's Golf Assn. (pres. 1965), Am. Legion, Fraternal Order of Police. Elk. Home: 3206 Calle Largo Hollywood FL 33021 Office: 2740 Hollywood Blvd Hollywood FL 33020

LEHMAN, HARVEY EUGENE, zoologist, educator; b. Yuhsien, China, Apr. 19, 1919; s. Algie E. and Mabel (Burke) L.; B.A., Maryville Coll., 1941; M.A., U. N.C., 1944; Ph.D., Stanford U., 1948; m. Lillian Margot Youngs, July 26, 1958. Asst. prof. zoology U. N.C., Chapel Hill, 1948-51, asso. prof., 1951-56, prof., 1956—, chmn. zoology, 1962-67. Dir. NSF tng. program in exptl. embryology Bermuda Biol. Sta., 1960—. Mem. Adminstrv. Bd. Grad. Sch., U. N.C., 1962-67. Mem. A.A.A.S., Am. Inst. Biol. Sci., Am. Soc. Zoology, Am. Soc. Zoologists (sec. div. developmental biology 1969—), Soc. Cell Biology, Soc. Developmental Biology, Am. Soc. Microscopists. Author: General Zoology, 1967, Laboratory Methods for Embryology, 1965. Contbr. articles to profl. jours. Home: Arboretum Dr Chapel Hill NC 27514

LEHMAN, JAMES LUTHER, univ. exec.; b. Kansas City, Mo., June 24, 1929; s. Luther James and Sherrill L. (Arnold) L.; student Oklahoma City U., 1946-47; B.B.A., U. Tex., Austin, 1955; postgrad. Tex. Christian U., 1960; m. Henrietta Rohrer, June 6, 1954; children—Linda Diane, Jamie Denise, Sheryl Esther. Asst. advt. agt. Gulf, Colo. & Santa Fe Ry., Galveston, Tex., 1954-56; asst. dir. pub. relations Tex. Christian U., Ft. Worth, 1956-67, dir. pub. relations, 1967—. Chmn. service to mil. families com. Tarrant County chpt. A.R.C., 1971—. Served with AUS, 1951-53. Mem. Am. Coll. Pub. Relations Assn. (S.W. dist. dir. 1961-62, nat. trustee 1967-70), Advt. Club Ft. Worth (pres. 1966-67), Religious Pub. Relations Council (pres. Ft. Worth chpt. 1963-64), Pub. Relations Soc. Am., Ft. Worth C. of C. (chmn. pub. relations com. 1967-68), Alpha Phi Omega. Home: 3528 Walton St Fort Worth TX 76133 Office: Box 30776 Tex Christian U Fort Worth TX 76129

LEHMANN, GLENN ALBERT, govt. ofcl.; b. Cleve., Sept. 10, 1924; s. Carl G. and Helen (Prindle) L.; B.A., Ohio Wesleyan U., 1948; M.A., Harvard, 1950, Ph.D., 1953; m. Eva Lofstad, Mar. 18, 1955; children— Eric, Christine, Thomas, Kurt. Teaching fellow Harvard, 1950-52; economist U.S. Mission to Norway, 1953-54; U.S. del. to OEEC and NATO, Paris, France, 1955-59; chief economist Bur. for Africa-Europe, AID, Dept. State, 1959-62; econ. adviser AID Mission to Tunisia, 1963-67, acting dep. dir., 1967-68; research asso. Center for Internat. Affairs, Harvard, 1965; sr. econ. adviser AID Mission to Indonesia, 1968; asso. asst. adminstr. for program policy AID, Dept. State, Washington, 1968-71, mem. Sr. Seminar in Fgn. Policy, 1971-72. Served with USAAF, 1943-46. Mem. Soc. Internat. Devel., Am. Econ. Assn., Phi Beta Kappa, Omicron Delta Kappa. Home: 3874 N Tazewell St Arlington VA 22207 Office: AID Dept State Washington DC 20523

LEHMANN, L.C., fire chief, Tampa, Fla. Address: Office of the Fire Chief Tampa FL 33601*

LEHNERT, PETER KARL, wholesale co. exec.; b. Rumburku, Czechoslovakia, May 13, 1938 (came to U.S., 1962); s. Franz and Erna (Hentschel) L.; ed. Gymnasium, Cologne, West Germany; m. Heidrun Lingen, May 26, 1969; children—Natasha, Norman. Mgr. br. Pan Am. Trade Devel. Corp., N.Y.C., 1962-65; founder, pres. Lensteel, Inc., Houston, 1966-68, v.p. mcht. and structural steel dept., 1969—. Mem. Tex. Assn. Steel Importers (v.p.). Home: 510 W Forrest St Houston TX 77024 Office: 1520 Texas Av Houston TX 77002

LEHRER, OTTO FREDERICK, architect; b. Krnoy, Czechoslovakia, June 24, 1907; s. David and Clara (Pohl) L.; student Tech. U. Hannover (Germany), 1925-27; architect/diplom-ingenieur Tech. U. Berlin, Charlottenburg, 1931, postgrad., 1931-33; m. Hilda Fleischer, Feb. 1, 1942; 1 son, Thomas Henry. Came to U.S., 1951, naturalized, 1955. Pvt. practice architecture, Berlin, 1929-33, Portugal, Spain, Port Angola and Port Mocambique, 1933-51, N.Y.C., 1951-55, Miami Beach and Miami, Fla., 1955-59, St. Paul, Minn., 1959-67, Fort Lauderdale, Fla., 1967—. Mem. architects assns. in Berlin, Lisbon, Madrid, N.Y., Fla., Minn. Home: 900 N E 18th Av Fort Lauderdale FL 33304 Office: 808 E Las Olas Blvd Fort Lauderdale FL 33301

LEHRMAN, IRVING, clergyman, b. Poland, June 15, 1912; s. Abraham and Minnie (Dinowitiz) L.; came to U.S., 1921; B.S., City Coll. N.Y., 1936; Rabbi, M.H.L., Jewish Inst. Rabbis, 1942; D.H.L., Jewish Theol. Sem. Am., 1958, D.D., 1968; m. Bella Goldfarb, 1935; children—David, Rosalind. Rabbi, 1942; rabbi Temple Emanu-El, Miami Beach, Fla., 1943-51, life rabbi, 1951—. Former vis. prof. homiletics Jewish Theol. Sem. Am., mem. rabbinical cabinet and bd. rabbinical visitors; hon. chaplain Jewish War Vets.; pres. Synagogue Council Am., 1971—; pres. South Fla. regional Rabbinical Assembly, 1960—, mem. exec. com., 1950—; v.p. Zionist Orgn. Am., Greater Miami Jewish Fedn.; chmn. dialogue com. Nat. Council Christians and Jews. Active numerous civic orgns.; mem. President's Commn. on Obscenity and Pornography; mem. exec. bd. South Fla. council Boy Scouts Am.; mem. Mayor's Adv. Commn. on Juvenile Delinquency. Bd. dirs. United Fund of Dade County, Citizens Housing Found., Bur. Jewish Edn. Greater Miami; bd. dirs., mem. nat. council United Hebrew Immigrant Aid Service. Mem. Am. Technion Soc. (dir.). Home: 2925 Flamingo Dr Miami Beach FL 33140 Office: 1701 Washington Av Miami Beach FL 33139*

LEIBY, GEORGE MARTIN, physician; b. Reading, Pa., Apr. 30, 1902; s. George Francis and Mary Elizabeth (Moyer) L.; B.S., U. N.C., 1929; M.D., Vanderbilt U., 1931; M.P.H., Harvard, 1935; D.P.H., Johns Hopkins, 1938; m. Sara Louise Wilkins, Sept. 6, 1930; children—George Martin, Sara Louise (Mrs. C. Burtt Potter, Jr.). Intern Roper Hosp., Charleston, S.C., 1931; resident Vanderbilt U. Hosp., 1932; fellow Ochsner Clinic, New Orleans, 1943; county, city and state health officer, N.C., Washington and La., 1934-43; hosp. adminstr. VA, 1946-58; asso. prof. preventive medicine Johns Hopkins, 1947; clin. prof. medicine U. Cal. at Los Angeles, 1947-54; chief pub. health adviser AID mission to Brazil, Rio de Janeiro, 1962-64; dir. Stanley County Health Dept., Albemarle, N.C., 1966—; clin. asso. prof. family medicine U. N.C., 1972—. Cons. UN-WHO, Southeast Asia, 1949, UN-WHO, Africa, 1958. Mem. Van Nuys (Cal.) council Boy Scouts Am., 1948-51. Served with A.C., U.S. Army, 1919-22; with M.C., AUS, 1944-46, USAF, 1951-53, 59-62. Diplomate Nat. Bd. Med. Examiners, Am. Bd. Internal Medicine, Am. Bd. Preventive Medicine. Fellow. A.C.P., Am. Coll. Preventive Medicine, Am. Pub. Health Assn.; mem. N.Y. Acad. Medicine, N.Y. Acad. Scis. Baptist (trustee 1955-56). Club: Cosmos (Washington). Home: 907 Honeysuckle Lane Albermarle NC 28001

LEIGH, AURELIA ILEAN, ednl. adminstr.; b. Norfolk, Va., July 28, 1908; d. Benjamin Armstead and Bessie (Ludy) Leigh; B.S., Mary Washington Coll., 1931; Ed.M., U. Va., 1953. High sch. tchr., South Norfolk, Va., 1931-38, asst. prin., 1938-51, acting supt. schs., 1948-49, prin., 1951-59, dir. instrn., 1959-62; elementary supr. Chesapeake (Va.) Pub. Schs., 1962—. Clk., South Norfolk Sch. Bd., 1938-63; tchr. Coll. William and Mary and U. Va. Extension, 1965—. Mem. Va. Edn. Assn. (dist. pres. 1954-56), N.E.A., Regional Suprs. Assn. (sec. 1961-63, v.p. 1966-67), Chesapeake Friends of Music, C. of C. (charter mem. women's div., named Outstanding Woman of Chesapeake 1972), Delta Kappa Gamma (state chmn. publs. and publicity 1971-73), Kappa Delta Pi. Presbyn. (deacon, sec. bd. 1969-70, elder, supt. Sunday sch. 1971—). Club: Pilot (charter). Home: 240 Robert St Chesapeake VA 23320 Office: PO Box 15204 Chesapeake VA 23320

LEIGH, JAMES TILLMAN, investment and devel. cons.; b. Haines City, Fla., Oct. 21, 1925; s. Samuel Garcia and Ethel (King) L.; student Loyola U., New Orleans, 1946, U. Tampa, 1947-48, U. Pitts. Grad. Sch., 1961, Brookings Inst. Advanced Studies 1962; m. Angela Maria Nistal, May 15, 1948; children—Charles Michael, James Joseph, Phillip Martine, Rita Denise, Ramona Diane. Project mgr. Paul Smith Constrn. Co., Tampa, Fla., 1949-51, v.p., 1963-67, also dir.; v.p. Patrick Gardens, Inc., Patrick AFB, Fla., 1951-54, Nat. Engring. & Devel. Corp., Washington, 1954-57; sr. coordinator Urban Renewal Adminstrn., HHFA, Washington, 1958-60, regional dir., Phila., 1960-63; pres., dir. Tampa Plaza, Inc., Waverly Arms, Inc., Tampa; v.p., dir. Golden Eagle, Inc., Durant Bros. Mech. Contractors, Inc., Tom McVey & Assos., Inc., Ray Knox, Inc., Tampa; owner Palm Beach Court, Tampa. Chmn., Mayor's Adv. Com., Tampa, 1963—. Served with F.A., AUS, 1943-46. Decorated Bronze Star. Mem. Tampa C. of C., Tau Omega. Kiwanian (pres., dir. Cocoa Beach, Fla.). Author: Management Handbook for Multifamily Rental Projects, 1956. Home: 2617 Bayshore Blvd Tampa FL 33609 Office: The Leigh Bldg Suite 10 4326 El Prado Blvd Tampa FL 33609

LEIGH, TED F., physician; b. Oxford, Ala., 1911; M.D., Emory U., 1938. Rotating intern Flower Fifth Avenue Hosp., N.Y.C., 1938-40; resident Columbia-Presbyn. Med. Center, N.Y.C., 1946-48; dir. dept. radiology Emory U. Hosp., Atlanta; attending radiologist Grady Meml. Hosp., Atlanta, VA Hosp., Atlanta; prof. radiology Emory U. Sch. Medicine. Served from 1st lt. to maj., M.C., AUS, 1941-46. Diplomate Am. Bd. Radiology. Mem. Am. Coll. Radiology, A.M.A., Radiol. Soc. N.Am., Am. Roentgen Ray Soc. (sec.). Office: Emory University Clinic Atlanta GA 30322*

LEIGH, THOMAS WATKINS, lawyer; b. Winnsboro, La., Apr. 8, 1903; s. Benjamin Watkins and Olive (Buckingham) L.; LL.B., La. St. U., 1924; m. Louise Grisham, July 7, 1942. Admitted to La. bar, 1924; pvt. practice, 1924-29; mem. firm Theus, Grisham, Davis & Leigh, Monroe, La., 1929—. Dir. 1st Nat. Bank of West Monroe. Mem. Gov.'s Spl. Commn. to Study Needs of Higher Edn. in La., 1954—; mem. Gov.'s Spl: Tidelands Adv. Com.; mem. exec. com. Pub. Affairs Research Council La., Council for Better La.; chmn. La. Mineral Bd., 1966—. Bd. suprs. La. State U., 1940-60, chmn., 1948-50. Served as lt. comdr. USNR, 1942-45. Mem. Am. (ho. of dels.), La. (pres. 1954-55, gov.) bar assns., Am. Coll. Probate Attys., Am. Coll. Trial Lawyers, Am., La. (council, v.p.) law insts., Order of Coif, Gamma Eta Gamma, Theta Xi. Episcopalian (vestryman). Clubs: Army and Navy (Washington); Boston, Pickwick (New Orleans). Home: 1401 S Grand St Monroe LA 71201 Office: 400 S Grand St Monroe LA 71201

LEITER, BEULAH G. (MRS. ROBERT PAUL LEITER), lawyer; b. Chgo.; d. Jehiel D. and Rose (Rossman) Liebling; J.D., John Marshall U., 1945, LL.M., 1946; spl. student U. Chgo., U. Ga., Emory U.; m. Robert Paul Leiter, May 9, 1936; children—Darryl J., Paula S. Admitted to Ga. bar, 1945, since practiced in Atlanta; mem. firm Leiter & Leiter, 1946—; dep. sheriff, 1958—. Mem. of Iota Tau Tau, 1951—, So. chancellor, 1955-57, internat. supreme chancellor, 1955-59, mem. supreme council, 1955-63, supreme asso. dean, 1959-61, internat. supreme dean, 1961-63. Mem. Nat. Women's Com. Brandeis U., 1961—. Mem. Internat. Fedn. Women Lawyers (legal edn. com. 1958, penal law, outer space law, UN coms. 1959-60), Nat. Assn. Women Lawyers, Am. Judicature Soc., Com. Women in Pub. Service, Ga. Assn. Women Lawyers (past v.p., rec. sec.), Ga. Bar Assn., Fulton County Lawyers Assn. (charter, trustee 1952, rec. sec. 1956—), Nat. Assn. Claimant Attys., Am. Bus. Women's Assn., P.T.A., Internat. Platform Assn., Am. Trial Lawyers Assn., Nat. Geog. Soc., Phi Kappa Delta. Clubs: Equity (publicity com. 1959-60, 63—), Old War Horse Lawyers, Nat. Travel. Home: 1219 Poplar Grove Dr NE Atlanta GA 30306 Office: 1616 Fulton Nat Bank Bldg 55 Marietta St NW Atlanta GA 30303

LEITH, CARLTON JAMES, geologist, educator; b. Madison, Wis., Sept. 24, 1919; s. Benjamin Donald and Edna (Elkinton) L.; B.A., U. Wis., 1940, M.A., 1941; Ph.D., U. Cal. at Berkeley, 1947; m. Marian Pollensky, June 8, 1941; children—Carol (Mrs. James W. Lee), Ronnie Sue. Asst. prof. geology Ind. U., Bloomington, 1947-49; geologist U.S. Corps Engrs., San Francisco, 1949-51; geologist, geophysicist Standard Oil Co. Cal., 1951-60; project engr. Holmes & Naever, Inc., Los Angeles, 1960-61; prof. geo-sciences N.C. State U., Raleigh, 1961—, head dept. geo-scis., 1967—. Cons. in field. Served with USNR, 1943-46. Mem. A.A.A.S., Am. Assn. Petroleum Geologists, Am. Geophys. Union, Am. Inst. Profl. Geologists, Assn. Engring. Geologists, Geol. Soc. Am., Nat. Assn. Geology Tchrs., N.C. Acad. Sci., Soc. Econ. Paleontologists and Mineralogists. Home: Route 8 Box 202 Raleigh NC 27612

LEITNER, PAUL REVERE, lawyer; b. Winnsboro, S.C., Nov. 11, 1928; s. W. Walker and Irene (Lewis) L.; A.B., Duke, 1950; LL.B., McKenzie Coll., 1954; children—David, Douglas, Gregory, Reid, Cheryl. Admitted to Tenn. bar, 1954; practiced in Chattanooga, 1954; asso. firm Bishop, Thomas, Leitner, Mann & Milburn, and predecessors, 1952-57; partner, 1957—. Treas., dir., Nat. Motor Club of Tenn., Inc., 1956—. Bd. dirs. Family Service Agy., 1957-63; mem. Chattanooga-Hamilton County Community Action Bd.; mem. Juvenile Ct. Commn., Hamilton County, 1955-61, chmn., 1958-59; chmn. Citizens Com. for Better Sch.; mem. Met. Govt. Charter Commn. Bd. dirs. U. Chattanooga Meth. Student Center, Camp Ocoee, YMCA. Recipient Young Man of Year award, Chattanooga area, 1957. Mem. Jr. C. of C. (pres. 1956-57), Am., Chattanooga, Tenn. bar assns., Am. Judicature Soc., Fedn. Ins. Counsel. Methodist (chmn. ofcl. bd., lay leader, dist. bd. lay activities). Address: 330 Pioneer Bldg Chattanooga TN 37402

LEITZSEY, BARNEY BURR, ednl. adminstr.; b. Newberry, S.C., Aug. 2, 1903; s. Barney Burr and Hanna (Brown) L.; A.B., Newberry Coll., 1925; M.A., U. S.C., 1942; postgrad. Winthrop U., Furman U., Newberry Coll.; m. Marie Sease, June 9, 1926. Prin., Stoney Hill High Sch., Prosperity, S.C., 1926-28, Hartford Elementary Sch., Newberry, S.C., 1942-46, Harllee Sch., Florence, S.C., 1948-50, Florence Jr. High Sch., 1929-37; supt. schs., Saleme, S.C., 1928-29, Trenton, S.C., 1950-67; prin., asst. supt., supt. Florence County Schs., 1958-67; asst. supt. Florence Pub. Sch. Dist. 1, 1958-67, bus. mgr., 1958-67, supr. high sch., 1958-67, supr. vocational tng., 1958-67, supr. adult high sch. tng.

LEMAISTRE, CHARLES AUBREY, univ. chancellor, physician; b. Lockhart, Ala., Feb. 10, 1924; s. John Wesley and Edith (McLeod) LeM.; B.A., U. Ala., 1944; M.D., Cornell U., 1947; m. Joyce Trapp, June 3, 1952; children—Charles F., William Sidney, Joyce Anne, Jean Helen. Intern, then resident medicine N.Y. Hosp., 1947-49; research fellow infectious diseases Cornell U. Med. Coll., 1949-51, mem. faculty, 1951-54, asst. prof. medicine, 1953-54; mem. faculty Emory U. Sch. Medicine, 1954-59, prof. preventive medicine, chmn. dept., 1957-59; prof. medicine U. Tex. Southwestern Med. Sch., 1959-66, asso. dean, 1965-66; vice chancellor health affairs U. Tex., Austin, 1966-68, exec. vice chancellor, 1968-69, dep. chancellor, 1969-70; chancellor U. Tex. System, 1971—; cons. epidemiology Communicable Disease Center, USPHS, 1953—; cons. medicine VA, 1954-59, area med cons. Atlanta area, 1958-59; vis. staff physician Grady Meml. Hosp., Atlanta, 1954-59, Emory U. Hosp., 1954-59, Parkland Meml. Hosp., Dallas, 1959-66; med. dir. Woodlawn Hosp., Dallas, 1959-65. Mem. Surgeon Gen. Adv. Com. Smoking and Health, 1963-64; mem. A.M.A.-Edn. Research Found. com. research tobacco and health, 1964-66; chmn. Gov. Tex. Com. Tb Eradication, 1963-64; cons. internal medicine Baylor U. Med. Center, Dallas, 1962—, St. Paul Hosp., Dallas, 1966—; cons. div. hosp. and med. facilities USPHS, 1966—; mem. N.Y.C. Task Force on Tb, 1967; cons. Bur. Health and Manpower, Dept. Health, Edn. and Welfare, 1967—; mem. Tex. Legislature Dept. Health, Edn. and Welfare, 1967—; mem. Tex. Legislature Com. on Organ Transplantation, 1968—, Commn. Non-Traditional Study, 1971—; mem. com. fed. health programs Assn. Am. Med. Colls., 1967—; mem. President's Commn. White House Fellows. Chmn. steering com. Presbyn. Physicians for Fgn. Missions, 1960-62; mem. Ministers Cons. Clinic, Dallas, 1960-62. Bd. dirs. Ga. Tb Assn., 1955-59. Mem. Am. (v.p. 1964-65), So. (pres. 1963-64) thoracic socs., Nat. Tb Assn., Am., Tex., Ga. med. assns., Central Soc. Clin. Research, Dallas County Med. Soc., Dallas Clin. Soc., Alpha Omega Alpha. Presbyn. (deacon). Contbg. author: A Textbook of Medicine, 10th and 11th edits., 1963; Pharmacology in Medicine, 1958. Translating author: The Tubercle Bacillus, 1955. Editorial bd. Am. Rev. Respiratory Diseases, 1955-58. Contbr. articles to med. jours. Home: 1909 Hill Oaks Ct Austin TX 78703 Office: University of Texas System PO Drawer 7969 Austin TX 78712

LEMING, JOE BILLY, mech. engr.; b. Normandy, Tenn., May 30, 1924; s. Charles Winfred and Pearlean (Troxler) L.; B.S., Vanderbilt U., 1949; m. Lelia Barnes, May 17, 1952; 1 son, Charles William. Field engr. Factory Ins. Assn., Chgo., 1949-63; sr. mech. engr. Tenn. Eastman Co., Kingsport, 1963—. Pres., bd. dirs. Kingsport Safety Council. Served with USNR, 1943-46. Registered profl. engr., Tenn. Mem. Nat. Fire Protection Assn., Soc. Fire Protection Engrs., Am. Soc. Safety Engrs. Elk, Moose, Eagle. Home: 800 Meadow Lane Kingsport TN 37663 Office: Tenn Eastman Co B-18 Kingsport TN 37662

LEMMON, MARK, architect; b. Gainesville, Tex., Nov. 10, 1889; s. William Leonard and Cosette (Lipscomb) L.; B.A., U. Tex., 1912; B.S., Mass. Inst. Tech., 1916; m. Maybelle Reynolds, Nov. 14, 1922; children—Dr. Mark Leonard, George Reynolds. Individual practice architecture, Dallas, 1923—; cons. architect U. of Tex. in Austin and brs. Galveston and Dallas; dir. Nat. City Bank of Dallas. Mem. adv. com. Greater Dallas Planning Council; past mem. council, Highland Park. Served as 1st lt., C.E., U.S. Army, World War I; chmn. contract renegotiations bd. Southwestern div. C.E., AUS, 1943-44. Mem. Newcomen Soc. N.Am.; Tex. Philos. Soc., Dallas Hist. Soc., Am. Legion, Sigma Chi. Presbyn. Clubs: City of Dallas, Dallas Country, Friars. Designs executed include Highland Park Presbyn. Ch., 22-story Corrigan Tower, Perkins Sch. Theology for So. Meth. U., U. Tex. Southwestern Med. Sch., Southland Center (cons.), Sheraton Dallas Hotel (cons.); one of two architects Fed. Courthouse and Office Bldg., Dallas; sole architect St. Luke's Meth. Ch., Houston, also pub. schs., Marshall, Longview, Terrell, Grand Prairie, Port Arthur, Sherman and Dallas, Tex. Home: 3211 Mockingbird Lane Dallas TX 75201 Office: Southland Center Dallas TX 75201

LEMMON, MAYBELLE REYNOLDS (MRS. MARK LEMMON), civic worker; b. Longview, Tex.; d. George Thompson and MayBelle (Bruner) Reynolds; grad. Sullins Coll., 1921; postgrad. U. Tex. at Austin, 1921-22; m. Mark Lemmon, Nov. 14, 1922; children—Mark Leonard, George Reynolds. Exhibited group shows at Dallas Mus. Fine Arts, 1962, 63, 64, Jr. League Art Show, 1963. Mem. bd. Jr. League, Dallas, 1938-43; mem. woman's bd. Dallas Civic Opera, 1960-64; mem. bd. Presbyn. Home and Sch., Itasca, Tex., 1944-52; mem. joint adv. bd. So. Meth. U., 1957-63, YMCA, Dallas, 1940-63; women's com. Met. Opera Co., Dallas, 1962. Mem. First Families Va., Nat. Soc. Colonial Dames Am., Dallas Symphony League, Dallas Art Assn., Kappa Kappa Gamma. Clubs: Garden of Am.; Junior League Garden (founder), Dallas Shakespeare (pres. 1963-64), Dallas Garden (bd. mem. 1952-57, v.p. of Founders Garden Club Dallas), Dallas Woman's (pres. 1951-53). Presbyn. (a founder, active Women of Ch.). Home: 3211 Mockingbird Lane Dallas TX 75205

LEMMON, SARAH MCCULLOH, educator; b. Davidsonville, Md., Oct. 24, 1914; d. William Presstman and Ann (Williams) Lemmon; B.S., Madison Coll., 1934; M.A., Columbia, 1936; Ph.D., U. N.C., 1952. Tchr. Annapolis (Md.) High Sch., 1936-40, Oldfields Sch., Balt., 1940-43, LaGrange (Ga.) Coll., 1943-47; asst. prof. Meredith Coll., 1947-56, asso. prof., 1956-63, prof., 1963—, chmn. dept. history and polit. sci., 1962—; vis. prof. N.C. State U., summers 1968-71, spring 1969. Bd. dirs. Wake County Hist. Soc. Gen. Edn. Bd. fellow, 1949-50. Mem. So. Hist. Assn., Orgn. Am. Historians, Hist. Soc. N.C. (pres. 1968), N.C. Soc. Colonial Dames Am., N.C. State Lit. and Hist. Assn. (exec. bd. 1972—), Kappa Delta Pi, Delta Kappa Gamma (local pres. 1972—, internat. scholarship com.). Democrat.Episcopalian (mem. vestry, lay reader). Author: North Carolina's Role in World War II, 1964; North Carolina's Role in the First World War, 1966; Parson Pettigrew of the Old Church, 1970; North Carolina and the War of 1812, 1971. Editor: Builders of the Old North State, 1968; The Pettigrew Papers, Vol. I, 1971. Mem. editorial bd. N.C. Hist. Rev., 1960-72. Home: 917 Brookwood Dr Raleigh NC 27607

LEMMONS, PERRY O., accountant; b. Gaffney, S.C., Nov. 7, 1931; s. Gothard O. and Macie (Wilson) L.; student U. S.C., 1950-52; LL.B., Woodrow Wilson Coll., 1968; m. Betty Clifton, Mar. 16, 1958; children— Kenneth Perry, Laura Lynn. Various accounting positions, Ga., 1945-58; partner Perry O. Lemmons, C.P.A.s, Atlanta, 1963—; admitted to Ga. bar, 1968, since practiced in Atlanta; dir., treas. North Piedmont Sales Co. (S.C.), 1950—; pres., dir. Creative Mgmt., Inc., Atlanta, 1968—, Southland Indsl. Park, Inc., Atlanta, 1969—; sec.-treas., dir. Cleveland Comml. Park, Inc., Atlanta, 1969—. Mem. Evangelism Internat. and Haggai Evangelistic Assn., Atlanta. Treas., chmn. budget com., chmn. govtl. finance com. City of Atlanta Charter Revision Commn., 1971. C.P.A., Ga. Mem. Am., Ga., Atlanta bar assns., Am. Inst. C.P.A.'s, Ga. Soc. C.P.A.'s, Am. Assn. Attys. and C.P.A.'s, Atlanta C. of C. Home: 1938 Lebanon Dr NE Atlanta GA 30324 Office: Fulton Fed Bldg Atlanta GA 30303

LEMMONS, STANLEY LEON, civil engr.; b. Rochester, Tex., Aug. 12, 1925; s. Benjamin and Blanche (Ulshen) L.; B.S. in Civil Engring., Tex. Agrl. and Mech. U., 1949; m. Hazel Bernice Pollard, Sept. 3, 1964; children—Robert, Douglas, Samuel, Paul. Liaison engr. J.E. Greiner Co., Balt., 1950-56; office engr. Turnpike Engrs., Inc., Arlington, Tex., 1956-57; pvt. practice engring., 1957-61; with Tex. Water Rights Commn., Austin, 1961—, dir. water rights div., 1965—. Served with USNR, 1943-46. Registered profl. engr., Tex., Ohio. Jewish religion. Home: 2916 Dover Pl Austin TX 78731 Office: PO Box 13207 Capitol Sta Austin TX 78711

LEMON, DONALD CAMPBELL, artist; b. LaGrange, Ill., Jan. 18, 1913; s. Wendell Morse and Helen Rose (Campbell) L.; student Knox Coll., 1932-33; B.S., Northwestern U., 1934, D.D.S., 1937; m. Barbara Hall, Sept. 24, 1938; children—John Campbell, Nancy (Mrs. Thomas William Walsh). Practice dentistry, LaGrange, 1937-67; exhibited in one man shows at Art Gallery of St. Petersburg (Fla.) 1970, Longboat Key Art Center, Fla., 1971; exhibited in group shows at Winter Park (Fla.& y Art Festival, 1971, Fine Arts Promenade, Oak Brook, Ill.; represented in permanent collections at Merrill Chase Galleries, Chgo. Served with USNR, 1943-45; PTO. Mem. Brown County (Ind.) Art Gallery, Longboat Key (Fla.) Art Center, Sarasota (Fla.) Art Assn., Manatee Art League, Bradenton, Fla. Address: PO Box 352 610 Broadway Longboat Key FL 33548

LEMSER, BERNARD AUGUST, banker; b. St. Joseph, Mo., June 11, 1911; s. August Carl and Edith Marguerite (Dieter) L.; student pub. schs., St. Joseph; m. Mildred Lavon Wadlow, Sept. 18, 1932; children— Lawrence Scott, Daniel Carl. Store mgr. Wohl Shoe Co., St. Louis, 1929-35; mdse. mgr. Sears, Roebuck & Co., Birmingham, Ala., 1935-47; mdse. mgr. Montgomery Ward & Co., 1947-48; gen. mdse. mgr. Aldens, Chgo., 1949-65; v.p. State 1st Nat. Bank, Texarkana, Ark., 1966—; pres. Lake Texarkana Water Supply Corp., Texarkana Manpower & Devel. Corp. Sec.-treas. N.E. Tex. Econ. Devel. Dist.; v.p. Red River Valley Assn. Mem. N.E. Tex. Water Assn., Texarkana C. of C. (past pres., chmn. com. of 15). Lion. Home: 720 W 27th St Texarkana TX 75501 Office: State Line Plaza Texarkana AR 75501

LENCHNER, VICTOR, dentist; b. Bklyn., Feb. 7, 1925; s. Herman and Molly Hildreth (Gerber) L.; D.D.S., N.Y.U., 1948; M.S. in Psychology, U. Miami, 1969; m. Rose Shermer, July 18, 1948; children— Douglas Roy, Julie Claire. Gen. practice dentistry, Bklyn., 1948-50, practice specializing in pedodontics, Miami Beach, Fla., 1953—. Served to capt. Dental Corps, AUS, 1951-53. Recipient Alumni Gold medal N.Y.U., 1948. Diplomate Am. Bd. Pedodontics. Fellow Am. Coll. Dentists, Am. Acad. Pedodontics, mem. Am. (past pres.), Fla. (past pres.) socs. dentistry for children, Miami Beach Dental Soc. (past pres.), Fla. (past pres.), Southeastern (treas.) socs. pedodontists, Psi Chi. Author: What You Should Know About Your Child's Teeth, 1971. Home: 1315 Daytonia Rd Miami Beach FL 33141 Office: 1185 71st St Miami Beach FL 33141

LENFESTEY, FREDRICK THOMAS, jr. coll. pres.; b. Tampa, Fla., Dec. 31, 1920; s. Harold Blondel and Iva (Albaugh) L.; B.S., U. Tampa, 1947; M.S., U. Fla., 1949, Ed.D., 1956; m. Dorothy Louise James, Sept. 3, 1949; children—Harold James, Robert Edward, Eva. Engr. engring. sci. dept. Hookers Point Shipyard, Tampa, 1943; counselor vocational rehab., Tampa, 1946-48; asso. prof. Ga. So. Coll., 1952-55; dean, v.p. Pensacola Jr. Coll., 1955-64, pres. Polk Jr. Coll., Winter Haven, Fla., 1964—. Mem. Gov. of Fla. Childrens Commn., 1957-63; pres. So. Assn, Jr. Colls. Bd. dirs. YMCA, Winter Haven Hosp., 1971-73. Served with AUS, 1943-46, 1950-52. Mem. Profl. Assos. Pensacola, Inc., (v.p. 1962-64), Phi Delta Kappa. Presbyn. Rotarian (pres. 1970). Home: 1300 Lake Mirror Dr NE Winter Haven FL 33880

LENHART, HARRY ALLEN, JR., journalist; b. Pitts., Oct. 11, 1938; s. Harry Allen and Gladys (Pola) L.; A.B., Columbia Coll., 1960; M.A., Fletcher sch. Law and Diplomacy, 1962; postgrad. (Russell Sage Found. Journalism fellow) U. Wis., 1965-66; m. Priscilla Ann Fisher, Sept. 5, 1959; children—Hope Allen, Erik Matthew, Edward Eliot, Christopher Winslow, Benjamin Garrett. Reporter, Providence Jour., 1961-62, Plain Dealer, Cleve., 1962-67; press sec. to U.S. Senator William Proxmire, Washington, 1967-70; reporter, Sr. editor Nat. Jour., Washington, 1970—; editor Photo Journal, Vermilion, O., 1962-63. Media advance man Hubert H. Humphrey Presdl. Campaign, 1968. Congl. fellow Am. Polit. Sci. Assn., 1966-67. Home: 304 Ayrhill Av Vienna VA 22180 Office: 1730 M St NW Washington DC 20036

LENNON, ALTON ASA, congressman; b. Wilmington, N.C., Aug. 17, 1906; s. Rosser Yates and Minnie (High) L.; grad. Wake Forest Coll., 1929; m. Karine Welch, Oct. 12, 1933; children—Edna Lee (Mrs. Lewis R. Frost III), Alton Yates. Admitted to N.C. bar, 1929; mem. N.C. Senate, 1947, 51; U.S. Senator from N.C., 1953-54; mem. 85th to 92d congresses from 7th Dist. N.C., mem. armed services com., mcht. marine and fisheries com., chmn. oceanography subcom. Home: 306 Colonial Dr Wilmington NC 28401 Office: Rayburn House Office Bldg Washington DC 20515

LENNOX, EDWARD NEWMAN, public affairs exec.; b. New Orleans, July 27, 1925; s. Joseph Andrew and May Alice (Newman) L.; B.B.A., Tulane U., 1949; m. Joan Marie Landry, Sept. 3, 1949; children—Katherine Sarah, Anne Victoria, Mary Elizabeth, Laura Joan. Marketing service clk. Shell Oil Co., New Orleans, 1949; with W.M. Chambers Truck Line, Inc., 1950-60, exec. v.p., 1953-60; v.p. Radcliff Materials, Inc., New Orleans, 1961—, So. Industries Corp., New Orleans, 1971—; dir. Mut. Homestead Assn. Mem. La. Bd. Hwys., 1965-67; chmn. New Orleans Aviation Bd., 1965-66; bd. mem. Travelers Aid Soc., 1967; pres. Met. New Orleans Safety Council, 1969-70, Bd. Levee Commrs. of Orleans Levee Dist., 1969-72; bd. dirs. Constrn. Industry Legislative Council, 1969—, Miss. Valley Assn., 1969—; mem. Ala. Gov.'s Adv. Council on Econs., 1971-72, Council on Econs., 1971—, La. Gov.'s Adv. Com. on River Area Transp. and Planning Study, 1971—; chmn. fund campaign Congregation Sisters of Immaculate Conception, New Orleans, 1964—. Bd. dirs. Methodist Hosp., New Orleans, Lower Mississippi River Devel. Assn., 1971—. Served to capt. AUS, 1943-46. Recipient Industry Service award Asso. Gen. Contractors Am., 1967; New Orleans Jr. C. of C. award, 1960; certificate of merit. City New

Orleans, 1964, 67. Mem. La. Tank Truck Carriers (pres. 1953-54), La. Motor Transport Assn. (pres. 1963-64), Am. (v.p. 1962-63), Ala. (v.p. 1956-59) trucking assns., So. Concrete Masonry Assn. (pres. 1963-68), Greater New Orleans Ready Mixed Concrete Assn. (pres. 1966-68), La. Shell Producers Assn. (pres. 1966-68), C. of C. New Orleans Area (dir. 1968-69, v.p. bus. climate 1969—), Lakeshore Property Owners Assn., Internat. House, Tulane Alumni Assn. Clubs: Metairie Country, Traffic (New Orleans). Home: 862 Topaz St New Orleans LA 70124 Office: 1010 Common St Suite 1710 New Orleans LA 70112

LENOIR, WILLIAM BENJAMIN, astronaut; b. Miami, Fla., Mar. 14, 1939; s. Samuel S. and Iona (Yann) L.; S.B., Mass. Inst. Tech., 1962, Ph.D., 1965; m. Elizabeth May Frost, July 4, 1964; children—William Benjamin, Samantha Ellen. Elec. engr. Gen. Radio Co., 1964; instr., then asst. prof. elec. engring. Mass. Inst. Tech., 1964—; scientist-astronaut NASA, 1967—; cons. on meteorol. satellites, 1965—. Recipient C.E. Tucker teaching excellence award Mass. Inst. Tech., 1964. Mem. Am. Geophys. Union, A.A.A.S., Am. Astron. Soc., Am. Inst. Physics, Sigma Xi, Eta Kappa Nu, Sigma Alpha Epsilon. Roman Catholic. Research articles on electromagnetic wave propagation, remote sounding planetary atmospheres, meteorol. satellites; investigator sci. satellite experiments, balloon experiments. Address: NASA-MSC Code CB Houston TX 77058

LENSEN, GEORGE ALEXANDER, historian; b. Berlin, Germany, Nov. 5, 1923; s. Alexander G. and Charlotte A. (Baruchson) L.; came to U.S., 1939, naturalized, 1943; A.B., Columbia, 1947; M.A., Columbia, 1948, Ph.D., 1951; m. Bobbie T'ing-yi Chen, June 1, 1948 (div. Nov. 1968); children—Karen Meng-mei, Kristin Chung-mei; m. 2d, Rumiya Yakhyayevna Shabayeva, Aug. 17, 1969. Instr. Fla. State U., Tallahassee, 1949-51, asst. prof., 1951-55, asso. prof., 1955-59, prof. history, 1959—. Served with AUS, 1943-46; CBI; PTO. Fulbright research scholar Hokkaido U., 1953-54. Social Sci. Research Council grantee, 1957; Am. Philos. Soc. grantee, 1958, 61; Inter-Univ. Com. on Travel Grants, postdoctoral researcher at Leningrad U., 1961; Am. Council Learned socs. grantee, 1961; sr. fellow Nat. Endowment for Humanities for research in Japan, 1967-68. Mem. Assn. Asian Studies, Am. Assn. Advancement Slavic Studies, Am. Soc. Russian Naval History, Phi Alpha Theta. Author: Report from Hokkaido: The Remains of Russian Culture in Northern Japan, 1954; Russia's Japan Expedition of 1852 to 1855, 1955; (with John L. Snell) The Meaning of Yalta, 1956; The Russian Push Toward Japan; Russo-Japanese Relations 1697-1875, 1959; The World Beyond Europe, 1960, 2d edit., 1966; Russia's Eastward Expansion, 1964; Revelations of a Russian Diplomat: The Memoirs of D. I. Abrikossow, 1964; Korea and Manchuria between Russia and Japan: The Observations of Sir Ernest Satow, 1966; The d'Anethen Dispatches from Japan, 1894-1910, 1967; The Russo-Chinese War, 1967; The Soviet Union: An Introduction, 1967; Trading under Sail off Japan 1860-1899: The Recollections of Captain John Baxter Will, 1968; Japanese Diplomatic and Consular Officials in Russia: A Handbook, 1968; Russian Diplomatic and Consular Officials in East Asia: A Handbook, 1968; Faces of Japan: A Photographic Study, 1968; Japanese Recognition of the U.S.S.R.: Soviet Japanese Relations 1921-1930, 1970; April in Russia: A Photographic Study, 1970; War and Revolution: Excerpts from the Letters and Diaries of the Countess Olga Poutlatine, 1971; The Strange Neutrality, Soviet-Japenese Relations During The Second World War, 1941-45, 1972. Home: 1102 Betton Rd Tallahassee FL 32303

LENTZ, JOHN JACOB, ednl. adminstr.; b. Salisbury, N.C., Aug. 20, 1912; s. Jerry R. and Mary (Monroe) L.; B.S., Appalachian State Tchrs. Coll., 1933, M.A., U. N.C., 1949, advanced 6th year program, 1962; grad. Nashville Auto Diesel Sch., 1936; m. Vera M. Broughton, Sept. 7, 1935; children—William Jeremiah, Mary Ella. Tchr., pub. schs., Watauga County, 1933, Pamlico County, 1934-36, 38-42, Hyde County, 1936-38; supt. schs., Sanford, N.C., 1949-66; asst. supt. Greensboro City Schs., 1967—. Served to lt. USNR, 1942-45, ETO. Mem. N.E.A., Horace Mann League, N.C. Edn. Assn., Am. Assn. Sch. Adminstrs., Dept. Rural Edn., Phi Delta Kappa. Rotarian. Home: 2100 Gracewood Dr Greensboro NC 27408 Office: 712 N Eugene St Greensboro NC 27402

LENZI, ALFREDO, Italian diplomat; b. Florence, Italy, Aug. 9, 1903; s. Giuseppe and Olga (Luti) L.; D. Econ., Polit. and Social Scis., U. Florence, 1925; student Sorbonne, Paris; m. Elvira Baratelli, Oct. 14, 1939; children—Guido, Gabriella, Giovanna. Joined Italian Fgn. Ministry; successively comml. attache or econ. counsellor embassies at Bucharest, Lisbon, Addis Ababa, Teheran, Tokyo, Karache, Athens and Cairo; consul gen. from Italy in New Orleans, 1967—. Decorated grand officer Nile; comdr. Order Italy, Order Rumania, Portugal, Persia, Japan, Greece. Home: 1718 Palmer Av New Orleans LA 70118 Office: 231 Carondelet St New Orleans LA 70130

LENZO, JOSEPH FRANCIS, JR., assn. exec., editor; b. Rochester, N.Y., Mar. 21, 1930; s. Joseph Francis and Aida Dora (Finch) Lenzo; Mus.B., U. Tex., 1952, Mus.M., 1953; m. LaVerne Lenzo, 1967; children—Linette, Joseph Francis III. Coordinator vocal music Austin County Bellville, Tex., 1952; tchr. choral music Galena Park (Tex.) Pub. Schs., 1953-63; exec. sec. Tex. Music Educators Assn. and editor Southwestern Musician, Tex. Music Educator, 1963—. Life mem. Tex. Ex-Students Assn., Music Educators Nat. Conf., Tex. Music Educators Assn., Phi Mu Alpha Sinfonia; mem. Tex. (sec.-treas. 1958-59, exec. sec. 1960-63), Am. choral dirs. assn., Tex. Orch. Dirs. Assn. (exec. sec. 1962-63, hon. life mem.), Tex. Bandmasters Assn. Home: 14303 Waterville Way Houston TX 77015 Office: Tex Music Educators Assn Inc PO Box 9908 Houston TX 77015

LEONARD, JERRIS, govt. ofcl.; b. Chgo., Jan. 17, 1931; s. Jerris G. and Marie (Reville) L.; B.S., Marquette U., 1952, J.D., 1955; m. Mariellen C. Mathie, Aug. 22, 1953; children—Mary Alice, Jerris G., John E., Kathleen Ann, Francis X., Daniel J. Admitted to Wis. bar, 1955; practiced in Milw., 1955-69; mem. firm Michael, Best & Friedrich, 1964-69; asst. atty. gen. civil rights div. Dept. Justice, Washington, 1969-71, adminstr. Law Enforcement Assistance Adminstrn., 1971—. Mem. Wis. Assembly from Milwaukee County, 1957-61; mem. Wis. Senate, 1961-69, senate majority leader, 1967-69; pres. Wis. State Agys. Bldg. Corp., 1963-69; chmn. Wis. Legislative Council, 1967-69; Republican candidate for U.S. Senate, 1968. Name One of 5 Outstanding Young Men, Wis. Jaycees, 1965. Mem. Alpha Sigma Nu. Home: 5109 Manning Pl NW Washington DC 20016 Office: Law Enforcement Assistance Adminstrn Dept Justice Washington DC 20530

LEONARD, ROBERT BRUCE, physician; b. Cleburne, Tex., July 11, 1910; s. Andy and Mary (Martin) L.; B.S., E.Tex. State U., 1947; M.D., Baylor U., 1947; m. Fredleen Power, Feb. 5, 1941; children Betty Jo (Mrs. G.R. Singleton), Bonnie (Mrs. W.J. Hyson), Robert F., Theodore W. Intern, Methodist Hosp., Houston, 1947-48; gen. practice medicine, Houston, 1948-63; staff psychiatrist Terrell (Tex.) State Hosp., 1964—. Tchr. adult bible class First Meth. Ch., Terrell, lesson broadcast over KTER each Sunday, 1968—. Mem. A.M.A., Tex. Med. Assn., Kaufman County Med. Soc., Theta Kappa Psi. Home: 202 Melody Lane Terrell TX 75160 Office: Terrell State Hosp Terrell TX 75160

LEONARD, STEWART WALLACE, physician; b. Louisville, Nov. 15, 1905; s. William Kirkland and Lena (Stewart) L.; A.B., Harvard, 1927; M.D. U. Louisville, 1931; m. Beatrice Thomasia Goodmonson, Apr. 14, 1944; children—Cathryn Gail, Linda Lee, Deborah Stewart. Jr. rotating intern Louisville Gen. Hosp., 1931-32, sr. intern pathology, 1932-33, internal medicine, 1933-34, surgery, 1934-35, asst. resident pathology, 1935, surgery, 1936-37; gen. practice medicine, Louisville, 1937-42, 46—. Served from capt. to maj. M.C., AUS, 1942-46; PTO. Mem. Am., Ky., So. med. assns., Am. Geriatrics Soc., Jefferson County Med. Soc., Louisville C. of C. (charter), Ky. Hist. Soc. (life), English Speaking Union. Independent. Methodist. Clubs: Filson, Eexcutives (Louisville). Home: 1801 Windsor Pl Louisville KY 40204 Office: 1983 Douglas Blvd Louisville KY 40205

LEONARD, WARREN GRANT, food co. exec.; b. N.Y.C., May 29, 1918; s. J. Henry and Frances (Grant) L.; B.S. in Indsl. Engring., Lehigh U., 1940; children—Nancy L. (Mrs. T. H. Hamilton III), Carol S. (Mrs. Nicholas R. Parks), W. Grant. Agy. mgr. N.Y. Life Ins. Co., N.Y.C., 1947-51; dir. engring. operations Am. Machine & Foundry Co., N.Y.C., 1951-56; European area dir. Gen. Foods Corp., White Plains, N.Y., 1956-65; v.p. Latin Am. group W.R. Grace & Co., N.Y.C., 1965-69; v.p. splty. foods group Riviana Foods Inc., Houston, 1969—. Served to lt. col. USAF, 1940-47. Decorated Bronze Star. Registered profl. engr., N.H. Clubs: Badminton and Racquet, Royal Canadian (Toronto); Royal Danish (Copenhagen); English Harbour, Mill Reef (Antigua, W.I.); Indian Harbour (Greenwich, Conn.). Home: 10811 Bridlewood Houston TX 77024 Office: 2727 Allen Pkwy Houston TX 77001

LEONARD, WILLIAM, realtor; b. Bryn Athyn, Pa., July 2, 1927; s. Morel and Louise (Davis) L.; student Acad. New Ch., 1946-47; B.Agrl. Engring., Ohio State U., 1951; m. Dorothy Price, Sept. 6, 1952; children—Rebekah (Mrs. Randall Osteen), Cynthia, Kathleen, Tobiah, Wendelin, Timothy. Self-employed as surveyor, Brevard, N.C., 1955-65; realtor, asso. Robert W. Melton Co., Brevard, 1965—. Mem. N.C., Ho. of Reps., 1963; charter mem. Brevard Planning Commn., 1961—; mem. exec. com. Transylvania County Republican Com., 1961—. Served with USNR, 1945-46. Mem. Brevard Bd. Realtors (pres. 1968-71). Swedenborgian religion. Home: 3 Woodland Terrace Brevard NC 28712 Office: 300 N Broad St Brevard NC 28712

LEONARD, WILLIAM TURNER, architect; b. Statesville, N.C., Mar. 19, 1921; s. Joseph Paul and Sudie (Turner) L.; student Mitchell Coll., 1938-39, N.C. State Coll., 1940-42; m. Martha Nell Morrison, May 26, 1951; 1 dau., Paula Kathryn. Final inspection Fairchild Aircraft, 1943-44; flight inspection USMC Cherry Point, 1944-46; sec., treas. Design Asso., Inc., Pendleton, Leonard & Krider, Architect, Statesville, N.C., 1946—. Treas., dir. Statesville Arts Scis. Mus., 1965-67; dir. Tri-States Art Council, 1961-62. Mem. A.I.A., Catawba Valley Council Architects, N.C. Assn. Professions, N.C. Hist. Soc., Mitchell Coll. Alumni Assn., Piedmont Investment Club (treas., pres. 1970-72). Democrat. Baptist. Kiwanian. Club: Statesville City. Home: 390 Oaxwood Dr Statesville NC 28677 Office: PO Box 468 W Broad Statesville NC 28677

LEONARD, WINSTON WHITE, advt. agy. exec.; s.; Elijah Matthew and Elizabeth (Preston) L.; student Mars Hill (N.C.) Coll., 1954-56, Mercer U., Macon, Ga., 1956-58, Walter F. George Sch. Law, 1958-60; m. Karen Laine Wiegand. children—Winston Keith, Mitchell White. Editor, H.L. Peace Publs., New Orleans, 1963-66; pres., chmn. bd., chief exec. officer Crayon, Leonard & Assos., Inc., New Orleans, 1966—. Active Boy Scouts Am., La. chpt. Arthritis Found. Bd. dirs. La. Travel Promotion Assn., Cultural Attractions Fund of New Orleans, Inc., 1970-71. Mem. New Orleans C. of C., Friends of the Cabildo, Internat. House. Republican. Office: 330 Exchange Pl New Orleans LA 70130

LEON-PORTILLA, MIGUEL, author Broken Spears: The Aztec Account of the Conquest of Mexico, 1962; Aztec Thought and Culture: A Study of the Ancient Nahuatl Mind, 1963; Pre-Columbian Literatures of Mexico, 1969. Address: care University of Okla Press 1005 Asp Av Norman OK 70369*

LEON-SOTOMAYOR, LUIS ANGEL, physician; b. Ponce, P.R., Aug. 2, 1931; s. Jose Luis Leon-Parra and Olga Sotomayor-Falcon; B.S. cum laude, U. P.R., 1954, Med. Tech. summa cum laude, 1954, M.D. with highest honors, 1958; m. Rosita Fonfria, June 17, 1955; children—Olga Vanessa, Rose Valerie, Louis Angel, Wanda Linette, Sharon, David. Extern surgery with highest honors Columbia Presbyn. Hosp., N.Y.C., 1957; intern with highest honors Charity Hosp. of La., New Orleans, 1958-59, resident internal medicine Tulane div., 1959-62; fellow in medicine, cardiology Johns Hopkins U., Balt., 1962-63; instr. medicine Tulane U., dir. Alcoholic Research div. Charity Hosp., New Orleans, 1961-62; instr. Med. Coll. Ga., Augusta, 1963-65, U. Tex. Med. Br., Galveston, 1965—; practice medicine, specializing in internal medicine and cardiology, Galveston, 1965—; chmn. dept. medicine Galveston County Hosp., Texas City, 1965-68; mem. staffs John Sealy Hosp., Galveston, St. Mary's Hosp., Galveston, Galveston County Meml. Hosp., Danforth Hosp., Texas City, Clear Lake and Space Center Meml. Hosp., Webster, Tex.; sec. Drs. Clinic, Galveston, 1970—; lectr. in field. Mem. Galveston Bd. Health, 1966-70. Served to capt. M.C., AUS, 1963-65. Recipient grant Tex. Heart Assn., 1969, Bay Area Heart Assn. Diplomate Am. Bd. Internal Medicine, Nat. Bd. Med. Examiners. Fellow A.C.P., Am. Coll. Cardiology, Am. Coll. Chest Physicians, Royal Soc. Health; mem. Sigma Xi, Alpha Omega Alpha. Clubs: Galveston Artillery, Galveston Country, Galveston Boat. Author: Myxedema Coma, 1964; Cirrhosis of Liver and Hepatoma, 1966; Epidemic Diencephalomyelytis, 1969. Contbr. articles to profl. jours. Developer cardiac pacemaker catheter with atrial pressure recorder; co-developer heated ultrasound nebulization machine. Home: 4402 Caduceous St Galveston TX 77550 Office: Drs Clinic 1501 Broadway Galveston TX 77550

LEOPARD, THOMAS FRANK, metals service center exec., computer software exec.; b. Irondale, Ala., Oct. 25, 1928; s. Noah F. and Effie (Clements) L.; certificate in accounting, U. Ala., 1950; m. Ann M. Brothers, May 18, 1957; children—Melanie Ann, Monica Ava. Staff, sr. accountant Ernst & Ernst, Birmingham, Ala., 1950-55; with Haskins & Sells, Birmingham, 1955; asst. to pres. O'Neal Steel, Inc., Birmingham, 1955-59, controller, 1959—; pres. Computer Wares, Inc., Birmingham, 1969—. Served with AUS, 1952-54. Mem. Nat. Assn. Accountants (past dir.), Ala. Soc. Ins. Mgmt. (dir. 1967-69), Am. Accounting Assn., Am. Inst. C.P.A.'s, Financial Execs. Inst., Beta Alpha Psi. Home: 4411 Briarglen Circle Birmingham AL 35243 Office: PO Box 2623 Birmingham Al 35202 also PO Box 31205 Birmingham AL 35222

LEOPOLD, LOUIS, aerospace electronics engr.; b. Boston, Mar. 8, 1918; s. Nathan and Mary (Meyers) L.; B.S., U. Mich., 1941, Ill. Inst. Tech., 1958; postgrad. U. Chgo., 1949-51; m. Wilma Erika Miron, Dec. 27, 1947; children—Robert Louis, Laurence Scott. Electronics devel. engr. Magnecord, Inc., Chgo., 1952-53; sr. electronics project engr., group leader Motorola, Inc., 1953-59; electronics aero. research engr. communications system Project Mercury, NASA, Langley Field, Va., 1950-60, head antennas and microwave systems Project Apollo, Manned Spacecraft Center, Houston, 1961-67; NASA rep. for Project Mercury, McDonnell Aircraft Corp., St. Louis, 1960-61; mgr. NASA office, Apollo High Gain and LEM Steerable High Gain Antennas, Dalmo Victor Co., Belmont, Cal., 1968-69; expt. mgr. NASA Apollo Lunar Orbital Missions, S-band Transponder and Bistatic Radar Expts., 1969—. Cons., A.M.A., Chgo., 1957-59, Motorola, Inc., Thompson Ramo Wooldridge, Inc., 1956-59. Served to capt. USAAF, 1942-46. Recipient NASA Achievement awards, 1963-72. Mem. I.E.E.E. (chmn. aerospace group 1964-65), A.A.A.S., Ill. Acad. Sci., U. Mich. Union, St. Louis Engrs. Club, U. Mich. Alumni Assn. (dir. Houston 1967-68). Home: 7751 El Rancho St Houston TX 77017 Office: NASA Manned Spacecraft Center Houston TX 77058

LEPAGE, WILFRED ALEXANDER, real estate broker; b. Leominster, Mass., June 23, 1902; s. Joseph Alexander and Sarah Katherine (Jewett) LeP.; ed. pub. schs., spl. classes; m. Dorothy Reed Stuart, Aug. 3, 1941; adopted children—Dorothy (Mrs. Martin R. McHugh), Eva (Mrs. Richard Wells) 1 son, Francis J. Supr. erection, draftsman, estimator C.G. Sargents Sons, 1926-41; maintenance engr. Gen. Elec. Co., 1941-44; with Norman E. Day, elec. contractor, 1944-48; owner, builder, operator LePage's Cottage Court, 1948-58; realtor, broker, salesman C.H. Scholfield Realty, Inc., Longboat Key, Fla., 1955—; dir. St. Armands Palmer Bank, Sarasota, Fla., 1961-70. Active A.R.C.; vol. fireman; pres. Longboat Key Civic League, 1960-62; mem. Sarasota Sports Com. First mayor Town of Longboat Key, 1955-57; mem. Longboat Key Bd. Commrs., 1960-62. Served with USN, 1920-23. Mem. Longboat League (dir.). Mason (Shriner), Elk. Club: Stoney Brook Fish and Game (life). Home: 3535 W Forest Lakes Dr Sarasota FL 33580 Office: CH Scholfield Realty Inc Longboat Key FL 33548

LEPHIEW, LOIS CLAYTON DERAINE (MRS. GLYNN LEPHIEW), naturalist, lectr.; b. Ft. Worth; d. Henry Clay and Sadie May (Pope) DeRaine; student (Life scholar) Brantley and Draughon Bus. Coll., 1929-32; m. Glynn LePhiew, Jan. 16, 1932; children—Dorothy June (Mrs. Anderson Hollis), Ann Yvonne (Mrs. Clinton B. McCutcheon), Lois Glynnene (Mrs. Preston R. Ivens III). Real estate broker, 1953-57; lectr., condr. workshops flower arranging to various orgns., Ft. Worth, 1939—; tchr. flower arranging, craft work; judge various flower shows. Guild bd. mem. Ft. Worth Children's Mus., 1960—, chmn. natural sci. and natural history dept., 1966-68; active various community drives. Mem. Ft. Worth Garden Clubs Council (an organizer, historian 1940-72), Ft. Worth Council Nationally Accredited Flower Show Judges (master judge 1962, pres. 1966-67) (pres. 1966-67), Nat. League Am. Pen Women (state 1st v.p. 1968-70), Am. Rose Soc. (charter, pres. 1967-68), Audubon Soc. Clubs: Southside Garden (past pres.), Blue Bonnet (pres. 1972-73), Ft. Worth Woman's (exec. bd.); Woman's (pres. garden dept. 1969-71); Ft. Worth Garden (birds chmn. on exec. bd. 1967-71). Contbr. articles on wild birds to various publs. Home: 2605 Cockrell Av Fort Worth TX 76109

LEPLEY, EDWIN LEE, agrl. adminstr.; b. Louisville, May 19, 1942; s. Ralph Reginal and Bess T. (Woodfin) L.; B.S., Sam Houston State U., 1967; m. Yvonne A. Grothe, June 14, 1963; children—Reginal Carl, Toby Lee. Gen. agt. Eastland and Jack County, Tex. Farm Bur., 1963-65; rural services adviser Tex. Power & Light Co., Palestine, 1966-68; county agrl. agt. Tex. Agrl. Extension Service, 1968—. Bd. dirs. San Jacinto County Fair Assn., 1966—; v.p. Palestine Jaycees, 1968; mem. San Jacinto County Land Bd., 1968-71; pres. San Jacinto County Water Corp., 1972-73. Mem. Tex. County Agts. Assn., Coldspring C. of C. (v.p. 1971), Coldspring Young Farmers. Methodist. Address: Box 67 Coldspring TX 77331

LERNER, ARNOLD STANLEY, radio broadcaster; b. Phila., Feb. 17, 1930; s. Joseph C. and Rose (Friedman) L.; B.S. in Econs., U. Pa., 1951. Asst. to pres. Lerner Bros. and Lerner Coat & Suit Co., Phila., 1951-54; asst. buyer Macy's Dept. Store, N.Y.C., 1955; salesman Sta. WCMS Norfolk, Va., 1956; partner Sta. KOMA, Oklahoma City, 1956-58, KITO, San Bernardino, Cal., 1959; pres. Sta. WADK, Newport, R.I., 1960—, WLLH/WSSH, Lowell/Lawrence, Mass., 1963—. Mem. R.I. Gov.'s Com. to Hire Handicapped, 1962; vice chmn. Newport County Heart Fund drive, 1963; exec. com. Boy Scouts Am., Lowell, 1967; chmn. bus. div. Merrimack Valley (Mass.) March of Dimes, 1969; dir. United Fund, Lowell, 1969, exec. com., 1970; adv. com. St. Joseph's Hosp., Lowell, 1970-72. Bd. dirs., chmn. budget com. Merrimack Valley United Fund, 1971-72. Mem. Nat. Assn. Broadcasters, Mass. Broadcasters Assn. (pres. 1969-70), Newport County C. of C. (dir. 1962-63), Greater Lowell C. of C. (dir. 1969-70, exec. com. 1971-72). Kiwanian; mem. B'nai B'rith (v.p. Newport 1962). Clubs: Newport Yacht, Vesper Country. Home: 9100 W Bay Harbor Dr Bay Harbor Island FL 33154 Office: 4 Broadway Lowell MA 01853

LERNER, SAMUEL HAROLD, physician; b. N.Y.C., June 6, 1917; s. Isadore and Rebecca (Goldstein) L.; A.B., Columbia, 1939; M.D., U. Cin., 1943; m. Mary Elizabeth Sullivan, Feb. 24, 1943; children—Margaret Judith (Mrs. James Krueger), Jo Ann (Mrs. Jon Steen), Deborah Ellen (Mrs. Jack Sweeney), Robert Tod, Caroline Elizabeth. Intern Cin. Gen. Hosp., 1943-44; sr. clin. instr., Western Res. U., 1957-67, asst. clin. prof., 1967-68; asso. clin. prof. Emory U., 1969—. Served to capt. USMCR, 1943-46. Commonwealth fellow Western Res. U., 1946-47, Rockefeller fellow, 1947-48, Diplomate Am. Bd. Psychiatry. Fellow Am. Psychiat. Assn., Am. Orthopsychiat. Assn.; mem. Am. Psychoanalytic Assn., Center Advanced Psychoanalytic Studies (Princeton), Cleve. Psychoanalytic Soc., Phila. Assn. Psychoanalysis. Contbr. articles to profl. jours. Home: 2236 B Peachford Rd Atlanta GA 30341 Office: 3400 Peachtree Rd Atlanta GA 30326

LEROY, L. DAVID, journalist; b. Tignall, Ga., Jan. 2, 1920; s. Lansing Burrows and Glennie (David) LeR.; A.B., U. Ga., 1941; m. Mary Margaret Pridgeon, Sept. 2, 1945; children—David Charles, Gregory Alan. Mem. nat. staff V.F.W., Washington, 1947-48; copyscript writer Gardner Advt. Co., Washington, 1948-49; mng. editor Air Force Times, 1950-53; with U.S. News & World Report, 1953-70, news editor, 1953-64, mem. Capitol Hill staff, 1964-70; dir. publs. Republican Congl. Com., 1970—. Active local Boy Scouts Am. Served with AUS, 1941-46. Decorated Purple Heart Mem. Nat. Rifle Assn., Sigma Delta Chi. Presbyn. (elder). Clubs: Capitol Hill, Nat. Press (past financial sec., treas., gov., chmn. bd. govs., v.p. 1966, pres. 1967); Fairfax Rod and Gun. Editor: Nat. Press Club Record, 1960. Contbr. articles to mil. mags. Home: 4404 N 36th St Arlington VA 22207 Office: Congressional Hotel Washington DC 20003

LESESNE, EDWARD HUGUENIN, govt. ofcl.; b. Charleston, S.C., Oct. 4, 1920; s. Daniel Somers and Emma Rose (Huguenin) L.; B.S. in Civil Engring., Clemson Coll., 1941; m. Sarah Frances Brodie, Apr. 12, 1942; children—Edward Huguenin, Sarah M. (Mrs. John M. Craddock), Elizabeth H., Robert. With TVA, 1941—. asst. dir. water control planning, 1968—. Mem. U.S. Nat. Com. of Internat. Hydrological Decade, 1964-70. Served to capt. AUS, 1942-46. Registered profl. engr., N.C. Fellow Am. Soc. C.E.; mem. U.S. Com. on Large Dams, Sigma Xi, Tau Beta Pi, Chi Epsilon. Prebyn. (elder). Home: 5817 Marilyn Dr Knoxville TN 39914 Office: Evans Bldg Union Av Knoxville TN 37902

LESHER, ARTHUR CARNEY, JR., judge; b. Ambler, Pa., Mar. 8, 1916; s. Arthur C. and Kathryn Marie (Shannon) L.; student Malvern Prep Sch., 1934; A.B., U. Ala., 1938; LL.B., St. Mary's U., San Antonio, 1942; m. Marie R. Palmisano, Sept. 2, 1960. Admitted to Tex. bar, 1942, U.S. Supreme Ct. bar, 1946; asso. firm Eskridge, Croce & Chiles, San Antonio, 1942-45; partner firm Blades, Chiles, Moore & Kennerly, Houston, 1945-48, Chiles, Lawler & Lesher, 1948; pvt. practice 1948; partner firm Kennerly & Leshner, 1956-62; judge Probate Ct., 1962, Ct. Domestic Relations, Houston, 1963-67, 157th Jud. Dist. Ct., 1967—. Bd. dirs. Homes of St. Mark, Variety Boys Club; trustee St. Mary's U. Sch. Law, San Antonio, 1959-61. Mem. Am. Houston, (dir., 1st v.p.) bar assns., State Bar Tex., Delta Theta Phi. Rotarian. Club: Houson. Home: 10130 Shady River Rd Houston TX 77042 Office: Civil Courts Bldg Houston TX 77002

LESHER, EUGENE ALBERT, household chem. co. exec.; b. Sunman, Ind., Sept. 3, 1914; s. Walter E. and Bertha (Miller) L.; student U. Cin., 1932-34; m. Ella M. Brinegar, May 16, 1936; children—Charles E., Thomas A., Katherine J. Clk., A.S. Boyle Co., Cin., 1930-36, salesman, 1936-40; with Boyle Midway div. Am. Home Products Corp., 1944—, v.p. nat. sales, N.Y.C., 1957-66, v.p. So. region, Atlanta, 1967—. Mem. Atlanta Sales and Marketing Execs. (v.p., dir.). Methodist. Clubs: Canadian (N.Y.C.); Cherokee Town and Country (Atlanta). Home: 3540 Old Chamblee Tucker Rd Atlanta GA 30340 Office: 4111 Pleasant Dale Rd Atlanta GA 30340

LESKIN, LOUIS WORON, psychiatrist; b. Chernigov, Russia, Mar. 10, 1913; s. Isidore and Clara (Woronov) L.; came to U.S., 1913, naturalized, 1941; B.S., Coll. City N.Y., 1933; M.D., U. Md., 1937; m. Carolyn Hopkins, May 4, 1941; children—Carol Louise (Mrs. Charles Allen), Abigail (Mrs. Stuart W. Royle), Michael C., Jane H., Edyth Eugenia. Intern, Beth David Hosp., N.Y.C., 1937-38; resident VA Hosp., Waco, Tex., 1946-48; practice medicine specializing in psychiatry Murfreesboro, Tenn., 1940-41, Waco, Tex., 1941-42, 46—; camp physician Civilian Conservation Corps, S.C., Ga., 1939-40; staff physician VA Hosps., Augusta, Ga., 1940, Murfreesboro, 1940-41, Waco, 1941-42; staff psychiatrist VA Hosp., Waco, 1946—. Served with AUS, 1942-45; PTO. Recipient 30 Year Service award VA, 1969. Fellow Am. Psychiat. Assn.; mem. A.M.A., Acad. Religion and Mental Health (pres. Waco Tex. br. 1968-69). Res. Officer Assn. Episcopalian. Home: 2706 Glendale St Waco TX 76710 Office: VA Hosp Memorial Dr Waco TX 76703

LESLEY, GEORGE BRADFORD, geodetic technician; b. Hillsboro, Tex., Jan. 18, 1927; s. George Bradford and Dovie (Bledsoe) L.; diploma Internat. Corr. Schs., 1961; m. Joyce Arcella Jackson, June 20, 1969; 1 dau., Marlies. With Nat. Oceanic and Atmospheric Adminstrn., 1948—, field geodetic surveyor, 1948-65; field supr., spl. electro-optical distance measuring equipment, Corbin, Va., 1965—. Instr. high precision geodetic surveying with Laser instruments to univs., local, state and fed. employees. Served with AUS, 1945-46. Recipient meritorious service award U.S. Dept. Commerce, 1961, Colbert medal Soc. Am. Mil. Engrs., 1968. Mason. Designed and developed precise laser distance measuring instrument, 1966. Home: 1004 Jefferson Davis Blvd Fredericksburg VA 22401 Office: ESSA Coast and Geodetic Survey Fredericksburg Geomagnetic Center Corbin VA 22446

LESLEY, THEODORE LIVINGSTON, estate agt., county ofcl.; b. Tampa, Fla.; s. Theodore and Carrie May (Yancey) L.; student U. Tampa, 1932-36; postgrad. U. Aberdeen, 1959. Mgr., Hartsfield Co., Inc., 1942-46, Gen. Acceptance Corp., 1946-48; estate agt., property mgr., 1948— (all Tampa). Commr. Hillsborough County Hist. Commn. of Records, 1949—, vice chmn., 1955-62, county historian, 1966—; mem. Oaklawn Restoration Com., and asso. mem. Tampa City Park Bd., 1957-58; mem. Fla.'s Gettysburgh Battlefield Monument Adv. Com., 1963, Tampa Barrio Latino Commn., 1970—. Named Knight of Justice, Sovereign Order St. John of Jerusalem, Knight of Malta. Mem. Fla. Hist. Soc. (dir. 1950), Fla. Geneal. Soc. (pres. 1967-68), Territorial Soc. Fla. (pres. 1939), Order Stars and Bars, S.C.V., Soc. of Cincinnati, Braemar Royal Highland Soc. (hon.). Democrat. Episcopalian (past vestryman. jr. warden). Clubs: Sword and Shield, Royal Tennis. Author: The Lesley Family in South Carolina, 1945; The Townsend Memoirs, 1960. Editor: Fla. Geneal. Jour., 1968—. Contbr. numerous hist. and biog. monographs to numerous So. hist. quars. and newspapers. Home: 719 S Delaware Av Tampa FL 33606 Office: County Ct House Tampa FL 33602

LESLIE, HELEN KRAUSS, mech. contracting exec.; b. Newark, Apr. 7, 1921; d. Otto Edmund and Hattie (Windmuller) Krauss; B.S., Ala. Poly. Inst. (now Auburn U.), 1943; m. Wendell Wands Leslie, Aug. 4, 1964. With Krauss Air Conditioning, Inc., 1943-68, successively stenographer, bookkeeper, air conditioning and refrigeration design and layout, draftsman, office mgr., 1943-53, sec., treas., dir., 1953-68; sec., treas., dir. K & W Supply House, Inc., 1943-70, exec. v.p., 1968—; sec., treas., dir. Krauss Roofing Co., Inc., 1953—, Conair Distbrs., Inc., 1956-59; sec.-treas. Stone & Clay Products Corp. Mem. Fla. Citizens Adv. Com. on Hwy. Safety, 1958-62; mem. adv. council St. Petersburg Civil Def. 1958-62; chmn. Gov.'s Commn. on Status Women, 1967-68; mem. exec. com. Goals for St. Petersburg Study Com., co-chmn. pub. safety subcom., mem. Pinellas County Adv. Com. for Vocational and Tech. Adult Edn., Fla. Textbook Evaluation Com., 1964-65. Nat. chmn. Know Your Am. Week of Nat. Fedn. Bus. and Profl. Women's Clubs, 1957, nat. chmn. health and safety, 1958-60, co-chmn. hemispheric friendship com., 1958-60, now mem., treas. nat. fedn., 1960-61, chmn. world affairs, 1961-62, 3d v.p., 1962-63, 2d v.p. 1963-64, chmn. conf. Ams., 1964, chmn. internat. congress, 1965, 1st v.p., 1964-65, pres., 1965-66, mem. membership com., 1971-73; mem. Fla. Com. on Status of Women, Fla. Small Bus. Adv. Council; mem. dist. adv. council Small Bus. Adminstrn., 1970-72, mem. nat. adv. council, 1972—; mem. Women's Nat. Safety Congress. Bd. dirs. Police Athletic League, pres. 1969-70; bd. dirs. St. Petersburg Mayor's Traffic Safety Com.; mem. Nat. Def. Adv. Com. Women in Service, 1969-71, chmn., 1971. Trustee Bus. and Profl. Women's Found., 1969-72. Recipient citation for outstanding service to St. Petersburg, certificate of merit Republic of China. Mem. St. Petersburg C. of C. (chmn. solicitation evaluation com. 1970-71). Republican. Presbyn. Home: Box 13221 St Petersburg FL 33733 Office: 1000 30th St S St Petersburg FL 33712

LESLIE, HENRY ARTHUR, banker; b. Troy, Ala., Oct. 15, 1921; s. James B. and Alice (Minchener) L.; B.S., U. Ala., 1942, J.D., 1948; J.S.D., Yale, 1959; grad. Sch. Banking, Rutgers U., 1964; m. Anita Doyle, Apr. 5, 1943; children—Anita Lucinda (Mrs. David Miller), Henry Arthur. Admitted to Ala. bar, 1948; asst. prof. bus. law U. Ala., 1948-50, 52-54, prof. law, asst. dean Sch. Law, 1954-59; v.p., trust officer Birmingham Trust Nat. Bank (Ala.), 1959-64; sr. v.p., trust officer Union Bank & Trust Co., Montgomery, Ala., 1964—. State chmn. Radio Free Europe Fund. Pres., Childrens Center of Montgomery; mem. Water Improvement Commn. of Ala., Ala. Armory Commn. Chmn. bd. dirs. Ala. Bankers Found.; trustee St. John's Endowment Fund. Served to capt. AUS, 1942-46; now lt. col. Res. Decorated Bronze Star medal. Mem. Fed., Am., Ala. Montgomery bar assns., Am. (state chmn. trust legislative council), Ala. (trust div. pres. 1963-65) bankers assns., Farrah Order Jurisprudence (pres.), Newcomen Soc. N.Am., Delta Sigma Pi, Phi Delta Phi, Omicron Delta Kappa, Pi Kappa Phi. Episcopalian (vestryman). Kiwanian. Clubs: Maxwell Officers; Montgomery Country. Contbr. articles to profl. jours. Home: 3332 Boxwood Dr Montgomery AL 36111 Office: Union Bank & Trust Co Montgomery AL 36104

LESLIE, JOHN CONRAD, publisher; b. Temple, Tex., Sept. 23, 1900; s. John and Pauline (Ross) L.; student So. Meth. U., 1918-20; m. Ollie May Clay, Nov. 1, 1950; children—Carol Jean, John Hamill. With newspapers, Dallas, Galveston, Tex., 1920-23; Asso. Press, Dallas, Austin, Tex., Chgo., 1923-25; ins. editor Chgo. Jours. Commerce, 1925-34; founder Ins. Record, Dallas, 1934, editor, pub., 1934—. Mem. Amalgamated Soc. Trained Seals (founder), Order Blue Goose, Sigma Delta Chi (chpt. treas. 1964-65, dir. 1965-67). Recipient Outstanding Achievement award for Distinguished Service, Tex. Assn. Life Underwriters, 1965; Pub. Service Award for Journalism, Nat. Assn. Independent Insurers, 1970. Methodist. Mason (K.T., Shriner). Home: 9410 Crestedge Dr Dallas TX 75238 Office: 2508 N Haskell Av Dallas TX 75204

LESLIE, JOHN DOUGLASS, research co. exec.; b. Dallas, Sept. 25, 1924; s. John LeGrande and Addie (Caplen) L.; B.S., U. Tex., 1948; m. Celeta Gail Bradford, Feb. 28, 1947; children—John Douglass, Celeta Eve, Jennifer. Test engr. Gen. Electric Co., Schenectady, 1948-50, supr. employee placement, 1950-54, mgr. manpower devel. and communications, 1954-59, mgr. profl. personnel and communications, 1959-63; mgr. personnel research applications Spindletop Research, Inc., Lexington, Ky., 1963-64, mgr. manpower utilization, 1964-66, mgr. econ. devel. div., 1966-68, v.p., 1967—; dir., sec. bd. Appalachian Leadership and Community Outreach. Mem. State Research Steering Com. for Vocational Edn., 1964-68; pres. Central Ky. Regional Mental Health-Mental Retardation Bd., 1971; mem. bd. ednl. cons. Alice Lloyd Coll., 1968-71; mem. pres. adv. council Nat. Grad. U., 1971—; sec. Nat. Area Devel. Inst. Council, 1970; troop com. chmn. Mohawk Valley council Boy Scouts Am., 1958-63. Served with USNR, 1943-45. Mem. Am. Soc. Planning Ofcls. Methodist (trustee 1966-68). Club: Spindletop Hall (Lexington, Ky.). Home: 787 Chinoe Rd Lexington KY 40502 Office: PO Box 481 Lexington KY 40501

LESSENCO, GILBERT BARRY, lawyer; b. Balt., June 19, 1929; s. Jacob David and Sarah (Bank) L.; B.S., Johns Hopkins, 1950; LL.B., Harvard, 1953; m. Elaine Beitler, Sept. 3, 1952; children—Susan Donna, Amy Gail, Robert Howard. Admitted to D.C. bar, 1953; since practiced in Washington; mem. firm Wilner and Bergson, 1953-55; partner Wilner, Scheiner & Greeley, 1955—. Mem. Democratic Central Com., Montgomery County, Md., 1970—. Bd. dirs. Thanks to Scandinavia, Inc. Found; trustee Meridian House Found. Served to lt. USAF, 1953-55. Mem. D.C. Jr. Bar (mem. exec. council 1962-64, named Outstanding Young Lawyer of Year 1965), Phi Sigma Delta. Home: 7928 Robison Rd Bethesda MD 20034 Office: 2021 L St NW Washington DC 20036

LESTER, BARNETT BENJAMIN, editor, govt. ofcl.; b. Toronto, Ont., Can., Aug. 7, 1912; s. Louis and Lena (Rubenstein) L.; came to U.S., 1917; student Cleveland Coll., Western Res. U., 1933; B.A., Oberlin Coll., 1934; scholarships Oberlin Coll., 1930-34, 1934-35, Nat. Inst. Pub. Affairs, Washington, 1935-36, Syracuse U. Acad. Internat. Law, The Hague, 1936, fellow Fletcher Sch. Law and Diplomacy, 1935-36; student Fgn. Service Inst., Dept. of State, 1952, 56; m. Rita Constance Hatcher, May 31, 1943 (dec. Nov. 1960); m. 2d, Claudette Yvonne Gionet, Apr. 19, 1970. Editorial staff Cleve. Plain Dealer, 1928-30; corr. various newspapers, 1930-38; staff reporter and feature writer Cleve. News, 1931-32; with Cleve. bur. Asso. Press, 1933; feature writer Boston Sunday Post, 1935-38; asso. editor The Writer Mag., 1936-38; mng. editor, later editor Exclusive Features Syndicate, Boston, 1936-38; with U.S. Dept. Justice, 1938-41; assigned to Office of Atty. Gen., Washington, 1938-40, editorial and informational asst., 1940-41, information officer, 1941; with Office of Coordinator of Inter-Am. Affairs, 1941-45, asst. dir. feature div., 1941-45, 1943-45; with U.S. Dept. of State, Washington, as asst. dir. feature div., Interim Internat. Information Service (OIAA), 1945; pub. relations exec. Al Paul Lefton Co., Inc., Phila., 1945-46; information specialist, chief motion picture unit, acting chief audio-visual sect. Office of Health Information, USPHS, Office Surgeon Gen., Washington, 1947-48; information specialist Office Publs. and Reports, FSA, 1948-49; chief editorial and prodn. sect., Nat. Heart Inst., 1949-52; pub. information chief, 1950, information specialist, sci. reports br. NIH, 1949-52; rev. officer Dept. State, 1952-61, supervisory publs. editor, 1961-63; editor-writer, 1963—; U.S. Fgn. Service Res. officer, 1965—. Career counselor Oberlin Coll., 1940—. Rep. Office Surg. Gen., USPHS, on interdepartmental com. med. tng. aids, 1947-48; invited participant U.S. Commr. Edn. Conf. Audio-Visual Aids to Edn., 1948; mem. information staff Pres.'s Midcentury White House Conf. on Children and Youth, 1950; mem. spl. survey audio-visual teaching and tng. aids Nat. Heart Inst., USPHS and Assn. Am. Med. Colls., 1951. Recipient Meritorious Honor Group award Dept. State, 1967. Hon. mem. Internat. Rho Pi Phi; fellow Am. Geog. Soc.; mem. Oberlin Coll. Alumni Assn., Alumni Assn. Fletcher Sch. Law and Diplomacy, Tufts U. Alumni Assn., Diplomatic and Consular Officers Ret., Am. Polit. Sci. Assn., Am. Fgn. Service Assn., Acad. Polit. Sci., Am. Acad. Polit. and Social Sci., Fed. Editors Assn. Clubs: Oberlin, Nat. Press, Am. Foreign Service, Internat. (Washington). Author: (with others) The Writer's Handbook, 1936. Writer of articles in mags. and profl. jours., radio and motion picture scripts, and biographies. Home: 2507 N Lincoln St Arlington VA 22207 Office: US Dept State Washington DC 20520

LESTER, GARNER MCCONNICO, utility exec.; b. Jackson, Miss., June 17, 1897; s. John Wallace and Willie (Hoover) L.; B.S., Millsaps Coll., 1919; m. Elizabeth Wilkins, Mar. 10, 1926; children—Elizabeth McConnico (Mrs. Charles H. Foster, Jr.), Garner Wallace. Auditor, treas. Hiawatha Mfg. Co., Jackson, 1919-30; sec., mgr. Miss. Ginning and Mfg. Co., Jackson, 1930-37; owner, mgr. G.M. Lester & Co., cotton products, Jackson, 1937—; v.p. Hinds County Water Co., Jackson 1927-33, pres. 1933—; dir. Deposit Guaranty Bank & Trust Co., Jackson. Bd. dirs. Nat. Tax Equality Assn., 1943-48, pres., 1948-63, chmn. bd., 1963—; organizer 1st pres. Nat. Cotton Council Am., 1941-57. Pres. Jackson YMCA, 1928; exec. com. Andrew Jackson council Boy Scouts Am., 1957—. Served with U.S. Army, World War I. Recipient Silver Beaver award Boy Scouts Am., 1969. Mem. Am. Water Works Assn., Water Pollution Control Fedn. (dir.), Jackson C. of C. (dir.), Am. Legion, Pi Kappa Alpha, Omicron Delta Kappa. Methodist (supt. Sunday sch.). Clubs: Rotary (past pres.), Capital City (Jackson). Home: 2115 Terry Rd Jackson MS 39204 Office: PO Box 369 Jackson MS 39205

LESTER, HAROLD DEWITT, dentist; b. Parksville, Ky., Aug. 18, 1933; s. Marvin DeWitt and Anna Margaret (May) L.; B.A., U. Louisville, 1956, D.M.D., 1963; certificate in pedodontics, Eastman Dental Center, 1965; m. Martha Anne Breland, Dec. 28, 1956; children—Harold DeWitt, Elizabeth Anne. Practice dentistry, specializing in pedodontics, Louisville, 1965—; teaching staff dept. pedodontics U. Louisville Sch. Dentistry, 1971—; mem. staff Louisville Meml. Hosp., Louisville Childrens Hosp. Served to lt. (j.g.) USNR, 1956-59. Mem. Am., Ky. dental assns., Louisville Dental Soc. (past sec.-treas.), Am. Soc. Dentistry for Children, Ky. Soc. Dentistry for Children (past pres.), Am. Acad. Pedodontics, Southeastern Soc. Pedodontics, Ky. Med. Assn., Jefferson County Med. Soc., Psi Omega, Phi Delta. Baptist. Home: 119 Blankenbaker Lane Louisville KY 40207 Office: Semonin Bldg 4812 Hwy 42 Louisville KY 40222

LESTER, HORACE B(AXTER), cons. engr., state legislator; b. Quitman County, Miss., Sept. 5, 1919; s. Simon Edward and Willie (Reid) L.; corr. course in engring.; m. Dora Essie Sanford, May 12, 1942; children—Horace B., Thomas Sanford. With Miss. Hwy. Dept., 1936-40; with U.S., Engrs., 1940-41; with E. I. du Pont de Nemours & Co., 1941-42; engr. City of Jackson, Miss., 1946-47; with EBASCO Services, 1947-49, W. & S. Constrn. Co., 1949-53; cons. engr. as Lester Engrs., Jackson, Miss., 1953—; mem. Miss. Ho. of Reps. Mem. W. Central Miss. Waterway Commn. Served as capt. AUS, 1942-46; col. Res. Mem. Res. Officers Assn. U.S., Am. Soc. C.E., Nat., Miss. socs. profl. engrs., Miss. Water Pollution Control Fedn., Am. Soc. Planning Ofcls., Cons. Engrs. Council U.S., and Miss., Am. Soc. State Legislators, Scabbard and Blade. Rotarian. Home: 1350 Eastover Dr Jackson MS 39211 Office: 555 Yazoo St Jackson MS 39201

LESTER, HUBERT ELISHA, govt. ofcl.; b. Jacksonville, Ala., Jan. 5, 1908; s. Forney Macon and Laura (Dale) L.; student pub. schs.; m. Anne Laurene Harris, Aug., 1929; children—Martha Anne (Mrs. Roy Thomas Ford, Jr.), Cherie (Mrs. Arthur Morris Lockridge), Kirby Lynn (Mrs. William Latham Snowden). Organizer, partner Calhoun Butane & Propane Co., Anniston, Ala., 1947-49; asst. cashier 1st Nat. Bank, Jacksonville, 1930-44; examiner, auditor U.S. Govt. Rent Stblzn. Program, Anniston, 1952, dir. Anniston and Calhoun County, Ala., 1953; partner, v.p., treas. Bethea Furniture Co., Jacksonville, 1954-55; tax assessor Calhoun County, Anniston, 1956—. Dir. Ala. Factoring and Finance Corp. Mayor, Jacksonville, 1941-44; mem. Jacksonville Sch. Bd., 1955—; mem. Ala. Democratic Exec. Com., 1950-58. Treas., Calhoun County chpt. Nat. Found. for Polio, Birth Defects and Arthritis, 1958—; scholarship adv. com. Anniston Meml. Hosp. Served with USNR, 1944-46. Mem. Tax Assessors and Collectors Assn. Ala. (v.p. 1962-63, pres. 1964-65), chmn. legislative com. 1966—), Internat. Assn. Assessing officers, Anniston, Jacksonville chambers commerce, Am. Legion, V.F.W., 40 and 8, Kiwanian. Home: 401 4th St Jacksonville AL 36265 Office: Calhoun County Ct House Anniston AL 36201

LESTER, JAMES ADAMS, editor, clergyman; b. Edison, Ga., Dec. 18, 1928; s. Paul Edwin and Myrtice (Peters) L.; grad. Norman Jr. Coll., Norman Park, Ga., 1946; B.A., Mercer U., Macon, Ga., 1949; B.D., New Orleans Bapt. Theol. Sem., 1953, Th.M., 1955; children—James Earl, Edwin Oliver. Ordained to ministry Bapt. Ch., 1949; tchr. pub. schs., Mitchell County, Ga., 1947, Brooks County, Ga., 1950; dir. News Bur., Mercer U., 1949; mem. staff Times Picayune, New Orleans, 1951-57, copy desk, state news editor, 1955-57; dir. promotion and pub. relations, asso. to exec. sec.-treas. Ga. Bapt. Conv., Atlanta, 1957-68; editor Baptist and Reflector news jour. Tenn. Bapt. Conv., Brentwood, 1968—; pastor Bapt. Chs., La., Miss., Ga. Mem. Pub. Relations Soc. Am., So. Bapt. Press Assn., Bapt. Pub. Relations Assn. Author: A History of the Christian Index, 1822-1953, 1955; A History of the Georgia Baptist Convention, 1822-72, 1972. Contbr. articles to profl. jours. Home: Shenandoah Dr Brentwood TN 37027 Office: Tenn Bapt Conv Franklin Rd Brentwood TN 37027

LESTER, WILLIAM DALE, architect, engring. co. exec.; b. Mayfield, Ky., Oct. 29, 1922; m. Paul and Lottie Pearl (Hawes) L.; student Allegheny Coll., 1943-44; Murray State U., 1946-47; B.S. in Civil Engring., U. Ky., 1949; m. Carolyn Ray, Mar. 16, 1948; children—Dale, Paul. Supr. constrn. Ky. Dept. Hwys., Paducah, 1949-51; area constrn. engr. F.H. McGraw & Co., Paducah, 1951-53; structural and archtl. constrn. supr. Giffels & Vallet, Portsmouth, O., 1953-55; structural designer Rust Engrs., Birmingham, Ala., 1955-56; dept. head hwy. and civil sects. Watson & Co., Tampa, Fla., 1957-65, v.p., prodn. mgr., 1965-69, exec. v.p., 1965—. Cub scout master Boy Scouts Am., 1959; maj. United Fund, 1961. Served with USAF, 1943-45. Mem. Nat. Soc. Profl. Engrs., Fla. Engring. Soc., Am. Soc. C.E. Baptist. Kiwanian (past dir.), Rotarian. Club: Palma Ceia Golf and Country. Home: 3208 Morrison St Tampa FL 33609 Office: 3013 Horatio St Tampa FL 33609

LESUEUR, LAWRENCE EDWARD, news commentator; b. New York, N.Y., June 10, 1909; s. Wallace Robin and Rose Vivian L.; B.S., Univ. Coll., N.Y. U., 1932; m. Dorothy M. Hawkins; children—Lorna, Sarah Amanda. Reporter United Press. Assn., N.Y.C., 1934-39; fgn. corr. CBS, 1939—; fgn. corr. London Paris, and Moscow, 1939-45; news commentator, N.Y.C., 1945-63; polit. commentator Voice of Am., Washington, 1963-64; congl. corr., 1964-66; White House corr., 1966—. Trustee Overseas Corrs. Meml. Fund. Recipient War Office Citation. French Medal of Honor, Legion of Honor. (France); recipient Peabody awards, 1948, 49, English Speaking Union award, 1959. Clubs: Century, National Press, Federal City, Overseas Press. Author: 12 Months That Changed the World, 1943; contbg. author, As We Saw Russia, 1948. Contbr. to mags. Address: US Information Agy 330 Independence Av Washington DC 20547

LE TENDRE, ANDRE, govt. ofcl.; b. Chippewa Falls, Wis., Feb. 26, 1937; s. Allie P. and Mayme (Brown) Le T.; student Wis. State U. at Eau Claire, 1955-58; m. Mary Jean Burich, Sept. 27, 1958; children—Jeanne Marie, Jacqueline Ann, Robert Paul, Jon Pierre. Mgr. radio sta. WXCO, Wausau, Wis., 1964-67; asso. dir. Menzel-Williams & Assos., Stevens Point, Wis., 1967-69; pres. U.S. Jaycees, Tulsa, 1969-70; spl. cons. Dept. Commerce with White House, Washington, 1970-72; asso. nat. dir. citizens coms. Com. for Re-Election of Pres., Washington, 1972. Chmn. Mayors Com. 110, Chippewa Falls, 1959-60; mem. adv. com. Wis. Gov.'s Com. Traffic Safety, 1967-68; mem. Citizens Com. Transp. Quality, Dept. Transp., 1968-69, Pres.'s Commn. 25th Anniversary UN, 1970. Named Wis. Citizen of Year, 1970; recipient Wis. Gov.'s award, 1969, Wis. Legislature citation, 1967. Mem. Wis., U.S. Jaycees. Home: 307 East St NE Vienna VA 22180 Office: 1701 Pennsylvania Washington DC 20006

LETSON, JOHN WALTER, supt. schs.; b. Jasper, Ala., Oct. 22, 1911; s. Jesse Walter and Eugenia (Benton) L.; B.S., Auburn U., 1932; M.A., Columbia, 1942, Ed.D., 1949; LL.D., Emory U., 1969; m. Sara Agnes Wilkes, Aug. 8, 1936; children—Judy, Jimmy, Peggy, Alan, Debbie. Tchr. pub. high schs., Siluria, Coffeeville, Ala., 1932-36; prin. Coffeeville (Ala.) High Sch., 1936-41; prin. Tuskegee (Ala.) High Sch., 1942-44; supt. pub. schs., Bessemer, Ala., 1949-57, Chattanooga, 1957-60, Atlanta, 1960—; area dir. Nat. Youth Adminstrn., Montgomery, Ala., 1941-42; asst. dir. div. adminstrn. and finance Ala. State Dept. Edn., 1946-49. Vis. prof. U. Fla., summers Gainesville, 1954, 56, Florence (Ala.) State Coll., 1957. Mem. Ga. Sci. and Tech. Commn., 1964-70; co-chmn. Phi Delta Kappa Commn. Human Rights, 1964-67. Mem. Nat. Adv. Com. Vocational Edn., Nat. Council on Humanities, 1966-67, Cleve. Conf.; trustee Joint Council Econ. Edn.; mem. Nat. Instrl. TV Adv. Bd. Bd. trustees United Appeal; bd. dirs. Atlanta Met. area Boy Scouts, Teaching Film Custodians, Nat. Found. March of Dimes, Jr. Achievement Atlanta Young Men's Christian Assn., Cerebral Palsy Center Atlanta, Atlanta Boys Club, Am. Cancer Soc. Served as lt., USNR, 1944-46; PTO.

Decorated Liberation medal (P.I.); recipient Distinguished Library Service award Am. Assn. Sch. Librarians, 1972. Mem. Am. Assn. Sch. Adminstrs. (chmn. fed. relations com.; v.p. 1968—), So. Assn. Colls. and Schs. (jr. coll. com. 1953-59, rep. spl. study com. 1959-60, trustee 1963—), Newcomen Soc. N. Am., Horace Mann League, Sales and Marketing Execs. Club. Methodist (ofcl. bd.). Rotarian (pres. City Bessemer 1951, mem. program com. Atlanta, 1961-66, 69, pres. Schoolmaster's 1966). Clubs: Commerce, Capital City. Home: 92 Laurel Dr NE Atlanta GA 30342 Office: 224 Central Av SW Atlanta GA 30303

LETTEER, KATHERINE CALLA VARNADO (MRS. CLARENCE RALPH LETTEER), civic worker; b. Lewiston, La., Oct. 23, 1897; d. Connor Commodore and Rosa May (Lewis) Varnado; student Fla. Parisher Normal Inst. for Tchrs., 1917-19, summers Tulane U., 1925, 27, 28, Draughn's Bus. Coll., 1929-30, La. State U., 1935; m. B.B. Fortinberry, 1920; m. 2d, Percy Leahmon McGehee, 1948 (dec. July 1959); m. 3d, Clarence Ralph Letteer, Oct. 4, 1960. Tchr. elementary sch., Tylertown, Miss., 1920-21; tchr., prin. Bogalusa (La.) City Schs., 1921-28; dir. pub. relations Dept. Agr., Jackson, Miss. summers 1926, 29; asst. prin. Draughn's Bus. Coll., Bogalusa, 1930; pvt., substitute tchr. city schs., 1931-35; journalist two daily papers, Baton Rouge, 1940-48; mem. staff U.S.O., 1942-46; chmn. Gettysburg Meml. Commn., 1966-71. Mem. D.A.R., 1942—, chpt. regent 1964-67, 71—, state chmn. La., 1965—. Mem. La. Soc. Poets in La. (pres. 1969-71), U.D.C. (nat. librarian 1955-59, br. pres.), La. Poetry Soc. Democrat. Baptist. Clubs: Kentwood Garden, Kentwood Music, Literary and Civic Workshop (Baton Rouge); Chicago Woman's Ideal (life). Home: 807 9th St Kentwood LA 70444

LETTS, THOMAS CLINTON, ret. educator; b. El Campo, Tex., Mar. 15, 1911; s. Henry Frank and Clara (Spencer) L.; student U. Houston, 1935-36, 47-48; B.S., Sam Houston State U., 1937; M.S., Tex. A. and M. Coll., 1945, postgrad. 1948-52; m. Margaret Evelyn McDaniel, Oct. 27, 1934; 1 dau., Margaret Sue (Mrs. Rufus Denman Hopper, Jr.). Tchr., prin., supt. pub. schs., Tex., 1929-42; clk. War Dept., 1942; work unit conservationist U.S. Dept. Agr., 1943-46; asso. prof. Sam Houston State U., 1946-58; agriculturist FOA, Tel Aviv, Israel, 1953-54; educationist ICA, Taipei, Taiwan, 1955-57, elementary edn. adviser, Asuncion, Paraguay, 1958-60; tchr. ednl. adviser USOM, Tegucigalpa, Honduras, 1960; elementary edn. adviser, AID, Recife, Brazil, 1963-65; area devel. officer USOM, Dinh Turong Province, Viet Nam, 1965-66, agrl. edn. officer, AID, Saigon, Viet Nam, 1966-71. Pres., Asuncion Coop. Commissary, 1959-60. Exec. com. Wharton County Inter-Scholastic League, 1935-37. Mem. Tex. Tchrs. Assn., S.W. Social Sci. Assn., Walker County C. of C. (dir. 1946-49), Kappa Delta Pi. Clubs: Huntsville Rotary (past pres.); Vocational Agriculture (past pres.). Home: Rt 3 Box 88 Huntsville TX 77340

LEUBA, HARALD RICHARD, govt. ofcl.; b. Berkeley, Cal., Mar. 24, 1936; s. Harald S.C. and Dora (Pooley) L.; B.S., N.M. State U., 1958; M.S., George Washington U., 1963; M.A., Johns Hopkins, 1964, Ph.D. (NSF fellow), 1965; postgrad. U. Wash., 1958-60; m. Nancy Rowena Kingsbury, May 15, 1966; 1 son, Timothy Alan. Asso. engr. Boeing Airplane Co., Seattle, 1958-60; mathematician ARINC Research Corp., Annapolis, Md., 1961-67; asso. prof. Johns Hopkins, Balt., 1963-67; operations research analyst Office Asst. Sec. of Def., Washington, 1967—. Chmn. symposium Quantification of Human Performance, Albuquerque, 1964. Mem. Electronic Industries Assn. (chmn. com. human factors), Human Factors Soc. (asst. editor bull. 1964-66), Soc. Study Social Issues, Sigma Xi. Contbr. numerous articles to profl. jours. Home: 9555 Persimmon Tree Rd Potomac MD 20854 Office: Office Asst Sec of Def Pentagon Washington DC 20301

LE VAN, DANIEL HAYDEN, business exec.; b. Savannah, Ga., Mar. 29, 1924; s. Daniel Hayden and Ruth (Harner) LeV.; grad. Middlesex Sch., 1943; B.A., Harvard, 1950; student Babson Inst., 1950-51. With underwriter's dept. Zurich Ins. Co., N.Y.C., 1951-52; liquified petroleum sales and engring. Gas, Inc., Lowell, Mass., 1952-54; customer relations Lowell Gas Co., 1954-56, in charge LP gas sales and promotion, 1956-58; self-employed agriculturist; dir. Lowell Gas Co., Buzzards Bay Gas Co., Gas, Inc., Lowell Factors, Mass. Assos., Lowell Appliances, Gas Rentals, Inc., Overseas Properties Ltd., N.Y.C. Pres., dir. Fla. br. Internat. Nutria Marketing Assn., 1964-66. Served with AUS, 1943-46. Club: Harvard (N.Y.C.). Home: Box 158 DeLeon Springs FL 32028 also 81 E Merrimack St Lowell MA 01852

LEVENS, JOHNNY BLACKWELL, JR., physician; b. Gulfport, Miss., Dec. 11, 1932; s. John Blackwell and Blanche (Woodcock) L.; B.S., U. Miss., Oxford, 1954-59, M.D., 1961; m. Gayle Larkin, June 26, 1971; children from previous marriage—Sandra, Tracy, John, Mark, Barbara, Sabrina. Intern, Miss. Bapt. Hosp., Jackson, 1961-62; resident Miss. State Hosp., Whitfield; county health dir. Hancock and Pearl River counties, 1962-63; practice medicine, Bay St. Louis, Miss., 1963—; chief staff Hancock Gen. Hosp., Bay St. Louis, 1963-65, 70—, sec. med. staff, 1963-66, chief internal medicine, 1965—. Pres. Waveland Clinic, Inc., 1971; county health officer cons. Hancock County, 1969-71. Pres. Hancock County chpt. Am. Cancer Soc., 1965-68; pres. Hancock County Heart Assn., 1963-70; chmn. K-O Polio campaign, 1964; pres. Hancock County Port and Harbor Commn. Sustaining mem. Nat. Republican Party; chmn. Hancock County Republican Com., 1968-72. Trustee Hancock Gen. Hosp. Med. Staff Pediatric Fund. Served with Inf. AUS, 1951-54. Fellow Am. Coll. Angiology, Am. Clin. Council Cardiology; mem. A.M.A., So. Med. Assn., New Orleans Grad. Med. Assembly, Coast County Med. Soc., Am., Miss. thoracic socs., Am. Acad. Family Practice, Profl. Practice Assn., Am. Legion, V.F.W. Mason. Home: 118 Whispering Pines Waveland MS 39576 Office: 641 Dunbar Av Bay St Louis MS 39520

LEVENTHAL, HAROLD, judge; b. N.Y.C., Jan. 5, 1915; s. Jules Joseph and Sadie (Wolcher) L; A.B., Columbia (Green prize), 1934, LL.B. (Toppan and Ordronaux prizes), 1936; m. Kathryn Kumler, Sept. 18, 1948; children—Philip Henry J., Anne K. Admitted to N.Y. bar, 1936, D.C. bar, 1946; law sec. to Justice Harlan F. Stone, Supreme Ct. U.S., 1936-37, to Justice Stanley Reed, 1938; staff Office Solicitor Gen., 1938-39; chief litigation Bituminous Coal Div., U.S. Dept. Interior, 1939-40; asst. gen. counsel OPA, 1940-43; staff Justice Jackson, Nuerenberg Trials, 1945-46; exec. officer, task force on ind. regulatory commns. Hoover Commn., 1948; chief counsel OPS, 1951-52; mem. law firm Ginsburg & Leventhal and successor firms, 1946-65; gen. counsel Dem. Nat. Com., 1952-65; judge U.S. Ct. Appeals, D.C. Circuit, 1965—; vis. lectr. Yale Law Sch., 1957-62. Served to lt. comdr., USCG Res., 1943-46. Mem. Fed. (past mem. nat. council), Am. bar assns., Bar Assn. D.C., Phi Beta Kappa. Clubs: Nat. Press, Army-Navy. Author articles in legal jours. Contbr. to history OPA. Home: 2406 44th St Washington DC 20007 Office: US Ct Appeals Washington DC 20001

LEVER, CHAUNCEY WALDO, banker; b. Enoree, S.C., Oct. 11, 1925; s. Madison Waldo and Marietta (Boldridge) L.; student The Citadel, Charleston, S.C., 1943-44; B.S., Wofford Coll., Spartanburg, S.C., 1948; grad. Southeastern Inst. Comml. Orgn. Execs., U. N. C., Indsl. Relations Mgmt. Course in Ind. Relations, Williamsburg, Va., 1954; m. Sara Cauthen, Jan. 15, 1949; children—Rachel, Chauncey, Charles. Gen. mgr. C. of C., Jesup and Wayne County, Ga., editor monthly publ., 1948-50; exec. dir. U.S. 25 Hwy. Assn., Inc., 1949-51; gen. mgr. C. of C., Greenwood and Greenwood County, 1950-54; editor monthly publ. Greenwood Progress; dir. indsl. and pub. relations Erwin Mills, Inc., 1954-55; dir. pub. relations Abney Mills and Erwin Mills (plants in S.C., N.C., Miss.), 1955-57; v.p. charge comml. and indsl. devel. S.C. Nat. Bank, 1957-62, v.p. Nat. Div., Corr. Bank Div., 1961-62; div. dir. S.C. State Devel. Bd., 1963-64; v.p., dir. charge nat. div. Fla. Nat. Group Banks, 1965-71; pres., chief exec. officer, dir. Fla. Nat. Banks Fla., Inc., 1971—; pres., chief exec. officer, also mem. exec. com., trust com., pensions bd. Fla. First Nat. Bank Jacksonville, 1972—, dir., 1967—; dir. Fla. Nat. Bank at Lake Shore. Treas. Crippled Children Soc. S.C., Inc., 1960-64; bd. dirs. Carolinas United Community Services, 1957-60; sec. adv. com. Gov.'s Conf. Bus. Edn. Industry and Agr., 1959-64; co-chmn. corp. div. United Fund Greater Jacksonville, 1966-67, vice chmn. area campaign, 1967-68. Bd. dirs. Wesley Manor, Inc.; v.p., dir. Meth. Hosp., Jacksonville, Fla.; bd. visitors Columbia Coll., 1963—; dir. So. Indsl. Devel. Council, 1963-64. Author of The Greenwood Plan for piercing iron curtain, promoting world freedom, peace, 1950, named nat. exec. dir. by Gen. Lucius Clay (nat. chmn. Crusade for Freedom); dir., mem. 1952. Man of South sponsoring com.; asso. chmn. S.C. Crusade for Freedom, 1953-54; mem. Industry Coordinating Com. Fla.; dir Goodwill Industries N. Fla., Inc.; council Jacksonville U. Served with USNR, 1944-46. Recipient man of the year award from Greenwood and Greenwood County Jr. C. of C., 1950, award and distinguished service placque, Feb. 1951; winner award as author Greenwood Nat. Freedoms Found., 1951, 52. Mem. Am. Cotton Mfrs. Inst. (pub. relations com. 1957-58), Am. Indsl. Devel. Council, Pub. Relations Soc. Am., So. (former pres.) Assn. Sci. and Industry, Am. Inst. Banking, Fla. Indsl. Devel. Council, Fla. Bankers Assn. (chmn. indsl. com.), Am. Pub. Relations Assn. (nat. bd. govs.; chmn. Operation Southland 1956-64), Ga. (v.p. 1950, editor monthly publ.), Am. (top nat. award, nat. publs. appraisal 1953; chmn. admissions com. for S.C. 1954), S.C. (sec., editor monthly publs.), So. assns. chamber of commerce execs., Fla. Jacksonville Area (chmn prospect com.), chambers commerce, Am. Public Relations Assn. (nat. awards com.), Travelers Protective Assn. Am. (S.C. div. relations chmn. 1951-54), S.E. Ga. Community Concert Assn. (sec. 1949), Nat. Foreman's Inst. (adv. council), Am. Mgmt. Assn., Columbia Sales Execs. Club. So. States Indsl. Council (dir. 1968—), Jackson Conv. and Visitors Bur. (dir.), Nat. Indsl. Conf. Bd., Wofford Coll. Alumni Assn. (area pres. 1950-51; class agt. 1948-60, pres. Centurion Club 1958-59), Newcomen Soc. N.Am., Am. Legion, Com. 100 (exec. council), Kappa Sigma, Pi Gamma Mu, Blue Key. Methodist (sec. Cokesbury conf. com. 1953-60; chmn. bd. 1957, ch. lay leader; mem. ofcl. bd. 1960—). Clubs: San Jose Country; River (Jacksonville); Rotary, University. Home: 2703 Boquette Av Jacksonville FL 32217 Office: Fla Nat Bank Bldg Jacksonville FL 32201

LEVI, G. KENNETH, publisher; b. Berryville, Va., Feb. 22, 1910; s. George H. and Martha Louise (Williams) L.; student Va. Inst. Tech., 1927-30; m. Evelyn Shiles Dean, Sept. 16, 1929; children— Kenneth Dean, Evelyn Page (Mrs. Henry T. Goode Jr.), Wesley Christopher. Engr. Shenandoah Nat. Park, 1930-31; editor The Clarke Courier, Berryville, 1931-52, owner, pub., 1952—; owner, pub. The Blue Ridge Press, Berryville, 1952—, Spur of Va., 1969—; pres. Spur, Inc. Mem. Clarke County Sch. Bd., 1944—; bd. control Dowell J. Howard Vocational Sch., Winchester, Va. Mem. Berryville C. of C. Democrat. Episcopalian. Clubs: Nat. Press, Touchdown (Washington); Millwood Country (Boyce, Va.); Harpers Ferry (W. Va.) Cooking; Hokie; Virginia Tech (Blacksburg, Va.). Address: Berryville VA 22611

LEVI, WENDELL MITCHELL, lawyer, naturalist; b. Sumter, S.C., Sept. 28, 1891; s. Mitchell and Estella (D'Ancona) L.; A.B., Coll. Charleston, 1912, Litt.D., 1968; Ph.B., U. Chgo., 1915, J.D. cum laude, 1915; m. Bertha Cecil London, June 20, 1921; children—Estella D'Ancona (Mrs. Robert P. Kirchheimer), Patricia London (Mrs. Henry D. Barnett), Wendell Mitchell. Admitted to S.C. bar, 1915; pres. Palmetto Pigeon Plant, 1923-56, chmn. bd., 1956—; pres. Wen-le Corp., Levi Pub. Co., Inc. Vice pres. Sumter County Community Chest, 1954 (gen. chmn. drive 1952-53), United Appeal Bd., 1955; dir. Carolinas United Community Services, 1957—. Commd. 1st lt. inf., Ft. Oglethorpe O.T.C., 1917; spl. duty in charge pigeon sect. Signal Corps, U.S. Army, 1917-18; capt., comdg. Co. L, 323d Inf., 81st Div.; with A.E.F., participated in action, Vosges and Meuse-Argonne, 1918-19. Recipient Cross of Mil. Service U.D.C., 1920. Merit badge counselor Boy Scouts Am., 1934—, mem. council exec. bd. Pee Dee area. Founder bird egg collection Charleston (S.C.) Mus., 1910. Named First Man of Year, Internat. Fedn. Am. Homing Pigeons, 1968; recipient testimonial Los Angeles Pigeon Club, 1971. Mem. Am., S.C., Sumter County (pres. 1970-71) bar assns., Nat. Pigeon Assn. (pres. 1931-33 recipient First Hall of Fame award 1958, also Nat. Pigeon Assn. Service award 1967), Am. Pigeon Club, Am. Carneau Assn. (pres. 1942) V.F.W. (comdr. Sumter County post 1946, dept. S.C. 1948-49, chmn. nat. membership com. 1949-50), Am. Poultry Hist. Soc. (life mem.), S.C. Camellia Soc. (pres. 1954), Am. Legion; hon. life mem. Alumni Assn. Coll. Charleston. Mason (32 deg., Shriner). Kiwanian (Legion of Honor 1972), Elk. Author: The Pigeon, 1941, rev. 1957 -63, 69; Making Pigeons Pay, 1946, rev. 1955, 58, 68; The Visible Pigeon, An Introduction to the World of Birds, 1963; Ency. of Pigeon Breeds, 1965. Editor question and answer dept. Am. Pigeon Jour., 1927—. Home: 417 W Calhoun St Sumter SC 29150 Office: 207 N Washington St PO Drawer 730 Sumter SC 29150

LEVIN, ALBERT ALVIN, mfrs. rep.; b. New Orleans, Sept. 21, 1915; s. Louis and Esther (Yuspeh) L.; B.B.A., Tulane U., 1935; m. Amy Ruth Markby, June 1, 1941; children—David Charles, Louis Aron, Libby Sharon. Mgr. elec. dept. Interstate Electric Co., New Orleans, 1936-46; v.p., sales mgr. United Distbrs., Inc., 1946-51; pres. Al Levin & Assos., Inc., 1951—; pres. World Realty, Inc., 1959—; dir. Universal Furniture. Mem. Elec. Assn. New Orleans, New Orleans Geol. Soc., Square Circle, Kappa Nu. Home: 926 Topaz St New Orleans LA 70124 Office: 1201 S Front St New Orleans LA 70150

LEVIN, ALLEN JAY, lawyer; b. Bridgeport, Conn., May 27, 1932; s. Simon H. and Adele M. (Rossinoff) L.; B.A., N.Y.U., 1954; J.D., U. Miami, 1957; student Boston U., 1954-55; m. Judith Ann Rubinstein, Aug. 18, 1957; children—Jennifer Suzanne, Miriam Adele, David N., Michael A. Admitted to Fla. bar, 1957, Conn. bar, 1958; practiced in Conn., 1958-60, Port Charlotte, Fla., 1960—; judge Small Claims Ct., Charlotte County, Fla., 1963—; atty. bd. commrs. Port Charlotte-Charlotte Harbor Fire Control Dist., 1965—. Instr. Port Charlotte U., 1960-63; legal adviser Port Charlotte Civic Assn., 1960-63; 67—; legal counsel Nat. Police Officers Assn., Am., 1963-67. Bd. dirs. Charlotte County United Fund, 1969—, Charlotte County Family YMCA, 1971-72. Mem. Am., Charlotte County bar assns., Fla. Magistrates and Small Claims Ct. Judges Assn. (v.p. 1970-71, treas. 1971-72), Am. Judicature Soc., Comml. Law League Am., Fla. Bar, Internat. Platform Assn., Bar and Gavel, Alpha Epsilon Pi, Tau Epsilon Rho. Elk, Kiwanian (2d v.p. Port Charlotte 1968). Jewish religion (v.p. Port Charlotte Jewish Community Group 1965-66, dir. 1961-64, 70—, pres. 1967-69. Home: 568 NE Anne Av Port Charlotte FL 33950 Office: 852 S Tamiami Dr Port Charlotte FL 33950

LEVIN, BERNARD MARTIN, govt. ofcl.; b. Oceanside, N.Y., Jan. 17, 1930; s. Abraham and Mabel (Harris) L.; B.A., Colgate U., 1951; M.A., U. N.C., 1954, Ph.D., 1956; m. Shirley Urback, Jan. 19, 1964; children— Suzanne Wendy, Jennifer Hope, Daniel Edward. Research psychologist Am. Inst. Research Washington, 1956-58; operations research analyst Nat. Bur. Standards, 1958—, assigned corporate planning staff Am. Airlines in Pres.'s Govt.-Industry Interchange Program, 1970-71. sci. and tech. fellow Commerce Dept., 1966-67. Mem. Operations Research Soc. Am., Am. Statis. Assn., Inst. Mgmt. Sci., Transp. Research Forum, Psychometric Soc. Home: 6809 Breezewood Terrace Rockville MD 20852 Office: Div 400 Nat Bur Standards Washington DC 20234

LEVIN, DAVID HAROLD, lawyer; b. Pensacola, Fla., Nov. 19, 1928; s. Abe Irvin and Rose (Lefkowitz) L.; A.B., Duke, 1949; J.D., U. Fla., 1952; m. Mona Joyce Lindy, Feb. 16, 1958; 1 dau., Lisa Ann. Admitted to Fla. bar, 1952, since practiced in Pensacola; asst. county solicitor, 1952; asso. Robinson, Roark & Hopkins, 1954-55; partner Levin, Askew, Warfield, Graff & Mabie, 1955—. Pres., dir. Gator Boosters, Inc. Crusade chmn. Pensacola chpt. Am. Cancer Soc., 1964-65, pres., 1966-67; bd. dirs. Pensacola chpt. Am. Heart Assn., 1966-69; chmn. Pensacola United Jewish Appeal, 1967-68; chmn. Fla. Pollution Control Bd., 1971—. Bd. dirs. U. Fla. Found., Inc. Served to capt. USAF, 1952-54. Fellow Fla. Trial Lawyers Assn.; mem. Am., Fla. bar assns., Am. Judicature Soc., Am. Trial Lawyers Assn., Am. Legion, Pensacola U. Fla. Alumni Assn. (pres. 1960), Fla. Council 100. Mason (32 deg., Shriner). Home: 3632 Menendez St Pensacola FL 32503 Office: 250 Profl Bldg Pensacola FL 32501

LEVIN, FREDERIC GERSON, lawyer; b. Pensacola, Fla., Mar. 29, 1937; s. Abe I. and Rose (Lefkowitz) L.; B.S., B.A., U. Fla., 1958, J.D., 1961; m. Marilyn Kapner, June 14, 1959; children—Marci, Deborah, Martin, Kimberly. Admitted to Fla. bar, 1961; practice law, Pensacola, Fla., 1961—; mem. firm Levin, Askew, Warfield, Graff and Mabie, 1961—. Mem. Fla. Trial Lawyers, Am., Fla. bar assns., Ala. Trial Lawyer's Assn., Acad. Fla. Trial Lawyers, Order of Coif, Phi Alpha Delta, Pi Lambda Phi. Home: 3600 Menendez St Pensacola FL 32503 Office: Professional Bldg Pensacola FL 32501

LEVIN, LOUIS, govt. ofcl.; b. Milw., May 9, 1908; s. Jacob and Rebecca (Offengenden) L.; A.B., Kalamazoo Coll., 1929; Ph.D., St. Louis U., 1934; m. Esther Hurwitz, Oct. 25, 1934; children—Miriam (Mrs. Gerald Leventhal), David. Grad. asst. St. Louis U. Sch. Medicine, 1929-34; research asso. anatomy Coll. Phys. and Surg., Columbia U., 1934-45; asst. dir. hematology Michael Reese Hosp., Research Inst., 1945-46; asst. prof. anatomy Coll. Physicians, Columbia, 1946-48; head, sci. div. Office Naval Research, N.Y., 1948-51, head biochemistry br., Washington, 1951-52; program dir. regulatory biology NSF, 1952-58, metabolic biology, 1957-59, dep. dir. div. biol. and med. scis., 1957-60, head Office of Instl. Programs, 1960; dean sci. asso. dean faculties Brandeis U., 1960-64; head Office of Program Devel. and Analysis, NSF, 1964-66, asso. dir. instl. relations, 1966-68, exec. asso. dir., 1968-70, acting dir., 1970, asst. dir. Instl. programs, 1970-72; University prof., also spl. cons. Tex. Tech. U., 1972—. Mem. adv.com. on instl. grants Am. Cancer Soc., 1961-64, 65-67, chmn., 1966-67; mem. adv. com. grad. edn. U.S. Office Edn., 1967-72. Trustee Carver Research Found. Fellow A.A.A.S.; mem. Am. Soc. Biol. Chemistry, Am. Inst. Biol. Scis., Soc. for Exptl. Biology and Medicine, Harvey Soc., Endocrine Soc. Contbr. to profl. jours. Home: 4404 11th St Lubbock TX 79416 Office: Box 4389 Tex Tech U Lubbock TX 79409

LEVIN, RUBEN, editor; b. Warsaw, Poland, Aug. 2, 1902; s. Benjamin D. and Ida (Gochilk) L.; brought to U.S., 1904, naturalized 1917; B.A., U. Wis., 1930; m. Bertha G. Greenberg, June 7, 1931; children—Hilda (Mrs. Alvin Tanenholtz), David A., Jonathan H. Reporter, copyreader on various dailies, 1924-38; with Labor Newspaper, 1938—, editor, mgr., 1953—. Recipient award for distinguished service to journalism U. Wis., 1965. Mem. Am. Newspaper Guild. Democrat. Jewish religion. Contbr. articles to profl. jours. Home: 2712 Blaine Dr Chevy Chase MD 20015 Office: 400 1st St NW Washington DC 20001

LEVIN, SIDNEY HERBERT, broadcasting exec.; b. Balt., May 5, 1935; s. Jack and Ida (Kasoff) L.; B.A., Am. U., 1957; m. Sally Rubin, Feb. 2, 1957; children—Amy, Ira. Announcer, WITH-FM, Balt., 1952-53, program dir., 1953-55; sales mgr. WGMS, Washington, 1955-57; asst. mgr. WKAT, Miami, Fla., 1957-62, exec. v.p., gen. mgr., 1962—; founding dir. Third Century Corp. Guest lectr. U. Miami, 1966. Exec. v.p. Dade County Citizens Safety Council; adviser Dade County Bd. Pub. Instrn. Mem. bd. Tropical council Girl Scouts U.S.A., Anti-Defamation League. Mem. Miami Assn. Food Trades (past pres., dir.), Greater Miami Radio Broadcasters Assn. (founder, past pres.), Radio Advt. Bur., Greater Miami C. of C. (chmn. tourism action com.), Alpha Epsilon Rho. Jewish religion. Club: Miami Touchdown (pres.). Home: 21310 NE 24th Ct Miami FL 33160 Office: 1759 Bay Rd Miami Beach FL 33139

LEVINE, ABRAHAM SETH, govt. ofcl.; b. N.Y.C., July 13, 1920; s. Louis and Fannie (Levine) L.; student Bklyn. Coll., 1937-39; B.A., U. Ia., 1941; M.A., U. Minn., 1947, Ph.D., 1950; m. Rose Marie Gordon, Dec. 17, 1967; children—Victor Bruce, Felicia. Teaching asst., instr. U. Minn., 1946-50; Social Sci. Research Council postdoctoral fellow U. Ill., 1951-52; with U.S. Govt., 1952—, chief social and econ. research br. Dept. Health, Edn. and Welfare, Washington, 1967—. Served with USAAF, 1942-45. Recipient Superior Accomplishment award Fed. Govt., 1965. Fellow Am. Psychol. Assn., A.A.A.S., Social Sci. Research Council; mem. English Speaking Union (sec.-treas. 1954-56), Phi Beta Kappa. Contbr. articles to profl. jours. Home: 1255 N Hampshire Av NW Washington DC 20036 Office: Dept Health Edn and Welfare Washington DC 20201

LEVINE, E(MMANUEL) LESTER, educator; b. Amasa, Mich., May 13, 1933; s. Henry S. and Sophie (Manhoff) L.; B.A. (Knapp & Brandenburg fellow), U. Wis., 1955, M.A., 1956; postgrad. U. Chgo., 1957-59. Research asst. Bur. Govt., U. Wis., 1954-55; instr. Occidental Coll., Los Angeles, 1959-62; lectr. U. Cal., Davis, 1963-64; dir. Cal. Legislature, Assembly Legislative Reference Service, Sacramento, 1962-66; cons. Cal. Joint Legislative Retirement Com., Sacramento, 1966; program planning analyst U.S. Office Edn., Washington, 1966-67; research dir. President's Council on Youth Opportunity, Washington, 1967-68; asso. prof. govt. Fla. State U., Tallahassee, 1968—, asso. dir. Polit. Research Inst., 1968-69, acting dir., 1969-70, asso. dir. Inst. Social Research, 1970—. Mem. adv. com. Wis. Div. for Children and Youth, 1949-52; mem. Mid Century White House Conf. on Children and Youth, 1950; mem. exec. com. Wis. Gov.'s Com. on Children and Youth, 1951-55. Pres. N.E. Los Angeles chpt. Am. Civil Liberties Union, 1961-62; bd. dirs. Madison Neighborhood Centers. Served with Transp. Corps, AUS, 1955-57. Mem. Am. Polit. Sci. Assn., Am. Soc. Pub. Adminstrn. (past chpt. dir., exec. com. univ. govtl. research conf. 1970—), Phi Beta Kappa, Phi Kappa Phi, Phi Eta Sigma. Co-editor: Cooperation and Conflict: Readings in American Federalism, 1969. Book review editor Publius The Jour. of Federalism, 1972—. Home: 2020 Continental Av Tallahassee FL 32304

LEVINE, HAROLD, mfg. co. exec.; b. Newark, Apr. 30, 1931; s. Rubin and Gussie (Lifshitz) L.; B.S., Purdue U., 1954; J.D., George Washington U., 1958; m. Harriet Shapiro, Aug. 17, 1952; children—Linda Ellen, Brenda Sue, Jill Anne, Louise Abby. Admitted to Va. bar, 1958, D.C. bar, 1958, Mass. bar, 1960; marine engr., naval architect Navy Dept., Washington, 1954-55; patent examiner U.S. Patent Office, Washington, 1955-58, with Tex. Instruments Inc., Dallas, 1959-—, mgr. corp. patents, 1966-—, asst. sec., 1968-—, asst. v.p., gen. patent counsel, 1972-—. Mem. Am., Dallas, Fort Worth patent law assns., Assn. Corp. Patent Counsel (sec.-treas. 1971-73), Electronic Industries Assn. (chmn. patents com. 1970-72), Am. Bar Assn. (chmn. com. 407 taxation, patent and trademarks sect. 1971-72), Order of Coif, Alpha Epsilon Pi, Phi Alpha Delta. Kiwanian. Home: 7530 Stonecrest St Dallas TX 75240 Office: 13500 N Central Expressway Dallas TX 75222

LEVINE, JEROME EDWARD, physician; b. Pitts., Mar. 23, 1923; s. Harry Robert and Marian (Finesilver) LeV.; student U. Pitts., 1940-42, 44; M.D., Hahnemann Med. Sch., 1949; postgrad. opthalmology U. Pa., 1951-52; m. Marilyn Toby Hiedovitz, Apr. 14, 1957; children— Loren Robert, Beau Jay. Intern, St. Francis Hosp., Pitts., 1949-50; resident opthalmologist Jefferson Med. Sch. and Hosp., Phila., 1952-54; opthamologist Leech Farm VA Hosp., 1955-59; chief eye dept. Stanocola Clinic, Baton Rouge, 1959-64; pvt. practice medicine specializing in ophthalmology, Baton Rouge, 1964-—. Cons. La. State U. Infirmary, Villa Feliciana Geriatric Hosp., Women's Hosp., Dixon Meml. Hosp., Lane Meml. Hosp.; mem. staff Baton Rouge Gen. Hosp., Our Lady of Lake Hosp.; coding cons. div. blind La. State Dept. Pub. Works; instr. spl. edn. U. Southeastern La., 1971. Served with M.C., AUS, 1942-44. Fellow Am. Geriatric Soc.; mem. La. Eye, Ear Nose and Throat Soc., New Orleans Acad. Ophthalmology, Inst. Glaucoma Research, A.M.A., So., Internat., Indsl., So. med. assns., La., East Baton Rouge Parish med. socs., Pi Lambda Phi, Phi Delta Epsilon. Home: 5876 Glenwood Dr Baton Rouge LA 70806 Office: 4560 North Blvd Baton Rouge La 70806

LEVINE, LEWIS, structural engr.; b. Glasgow, Scotland, Oct. 30, 1899 (came to U.S. 1905, naturalized 1931); s. Elias and Mary (Rosoffsky) L.; C.E., Bklyn. Poly. Inst., 1936, M.C.E., 1940; m. Pearl Margolett Heirshberg, Feb. 29, 1932. Civil engr., Brazil, West Indies, Greece, Turkey, South Burma, 1942-48; fgn. service officer, adv. Ministry of Pub. Works, Greece, 1948-50; structural engr. Tippets, Abbet, McCarthy, Stratton, Greece, 1950-57; chief structural engr. David Volker & Assos., Washington, 1957-—. Served with Royal Brit. Army, 1917-20. Fellow Am. Soc. C.E., Soc. Am. Military Engrs. Home: 4221 16th St N W Washington DC 20011 Office: 5104 MacArthur Blvd N W Washington DC 20016

LEVINE, MAX, dept. store exec.; b. Boston, Aug. 27, 1901; s. Charles and Bessie (Goldstein) L.; A.B., Harvard, 1923, M.B.A., 1925; m. Marcella Lawrence, July 29, 1937; 1 son, John C. Gen. mdse. mgr. A. Polsky Co., Akron, O., 1930-34; div. mdse. mgr. F. & R. Lazarus & Co., Columbus, O., 1934-45; pres., gen. mgr. Foley's, Houston, 1946-64, chmn. bd., 1964-66; v.p., dir. Federated Dept. Stores, Inc., Cin., 1958-65; dir. Houston br. Fed. Res. Bank of Dallas, 1960-63; dir. Fed. Res. Bank of Dallas, 1964-67, 67-—, dep. chmn. bd., 1967-68, 69; dir. Scoa Industries, Inc., Columbus, 1971-—. Bd. dirs., v.p. Houston Symphony Orch.; pres. Houston Mchts. Assn., 1947-48. Jewish religion. Home: 2132 Troon Rd Houston TX 77019 Office: 735 Main Bldg Houston TX 77002

LEVINE, ROBERT ERWIN, editor, writer, economist; b. N.Y.C., Sept. 22, 1930; s. Arnold K. and Beatrice (Euer) L.; student Northwestern U., 1952; B.S., Wharton Sch., U. Pa., 1952; m. Patience Edge Appel, Feb. 21, 1952; children—Andrew Steven, Gregory Roberts, Elizabeth Rengier, Timothy Edge. Jr. accountant Klein, Hinds & Finke, C.P.A.'s, N.Y.C., 1952-53; asst. to pres. Ednalite Optical Co., Peekskill, N.Y., 1953-54; asst. bus. mgr. Billboard Pub. Co., 1954-56; advt. mgr. Rodale Press, Inc., Emmaus, Pa., 1956-59; asst. promotion mgr. House Beautiful mag., 1959-61; copywriter Newsweek mag., 1961-67; market researcher U.S. News and World Report, 1967-68; information and publs. dir. The Urban Land Inst., Washington, 1968-70; asst. editor Bur. Nat. Affairs, Inc., 1971-72; information dir. Opticians Assn. Am., 1972-—. Scoutmaster, com. chmn. Washington Irving council Boy Scouts Am., 1956-66; baseball and basketball coach Little League, 1961-66; bd. dirs. Woodlands High Sch. Scholarship Fund, 1965, Bethesda Fire Dept., 1969-—; bd. dirs., officer Battery Park Citizens Recreation Assn., 1967-—; del. Montgomery County Civic Fedn., 1969. Recipient Writer's award Newsweek, 1967; coach award Greenburgh Recreation Commn., 1965. Mem. Soc. Tech. Writers and Pubs., Pub. Relations Soc. Am., Tau Delta Phi. Jewish religion (bd. dir. congregation 1957-58). Clubs: Nat. Press (Washington); Palisades (Potomac, Md.); Battery Park (Bethesda, Md.). Editor: Calvert Party Ency., 1959; Nine Cities-The Anatomy of Downtown Renewal (Leo Adde), 1969. Founding editor Newsweek Communicator, 1961, Land Use Digest, 1968; exec. editor Urban Land, 1968-—. Home: 5217 Goddard Rd Bethesda MD 20014 Office: 1250 Connecticut Av NW Washington DC 20036

LEVINE, SAM, concrete mfr.; b. Savannah, Ga., Aug. 13, 1919; s. Jacob Herman and Ida (Hershman) L.; student N.Y.U., 1938-39; m. Marilyn Budovsky Grossman, Dec. 24, 1955; children—Jack Jeffrey, Randie Sue, Michael Edward, Nanci Gale, Robert James, and Judith Lynn Levine. Partner, Mursam Block Co., 1946-47, Samson Block Co., 1947-—; pres. Samson Concrete Industries, Inc., 1955-—, Samson Block Co., Inc. of Miami 1957-—; sec., treas. Samson Block Co., Inc. of Homestead, 1957-—; treas., chmn. bd. Builders Finance & Mortgage Co., 1958-—; v.p. Coral Aggregate Corp., 1961-—. Served as lt. (j.g.) U.S. Maritime Service, 1943-45. Mem. Fla. Home Builders Assn., S. Fla. Masonry Assn., C. of C., Zionist Orgn. Am. (pres. Miami Gables dist. 1957-59). Mason (Shriner), Kiwanian; mem. B'nai B'rith. Home: 13575 SW 68th Ct Miami FL 33156 Office: 2665 S Bayshore Dr Way Miami FL 33133

LEVITAN, SAR A., economist, educator; b. Lithuania, Sept. 14, 1914; s. Osher N. and Yocheved (Rapoport) L.; came to U.S., 1931, naturalized, 1935; B.S.S., Coll. City N.Y., 1939; M.A., Columbia, 1939, Ph.D., 1949; m. Brita Ann Buchard, Oct. 16, 1946. Asso. prof. econs. State U. N.Y., 1946-51; pub. mem. review and appeals Wage Stblzn. Bd., 1951-53; specialist labor and econ. devel. Legislative Reference Service, 1954-60; asso. dir. Presdl. R.R. Commn., 1961; research prof. econs. George Washington U., 1962-63, dir. Center for Manpower Policy Studies, research prof. econs., 1967-—; sr. economist W.E. Upjohn Inst., 1964-67; cons. Senate Com. Labor and Pub. Welfare, Gen. Accounting Office, Bur. of Budget, Dept. Health Edn. Welfare, Dept. of Labor. Mem. Nat. Manpower Policy Task Force, 1967-—, vice chmn., 1969-—. Served as capt., AUS, 1942-46. Recipient awards Ford Found., 1962, 67. Mem. Am. Econ. Assn., Indsl. and Labor Relations Research Assn., Nat. Assn. Bus. Economist. Author: Federal Aid to Depressed Areas, 1964; Federal Training and Work Programs in the Sixties, 1969; The Great Society's Poor Law: A New Approach to Poverty, 1969; Programs in Aid of the Poor for the 1970's, 1970; Blue-Collar Workers, 1970; Big Brother's Indian Programs-With Reservations, 1970; Human Resources and Labor Markets, 1972; Work and Welfare Go Together, 1972. Office: 1819 4 St NW Washington DC 20006

LEVITAS, ELLIOTT HARRIS, lawyer; b. Atlanta, Dec. 26, 1930; s. Louis J. and Ida (Goldstein) L.; A.B., Emory U., 1952, LL.B., 1956; B.A. (Rhodes scholar), Oxford U., 1954, M.A., 1958; student U. Mich., 1954-55; m. Barbara Hillman, June 8, 1955; children—Karen, Susan, Kevin. Admitted to Ga. bar, 1958; practiced in Atlanta, 1958-—; mem. firm Arnall, Golden, Gregory, 1958-—; mem. Ga. Ho. of Reps., 1965-—, chmn. com. community affairs and planning. Lectr. Emory U., 1959-60, 68-70. Mem. bd. dirs. Atlanta Jewish Community Center, Atlanta Jewish Welfare Fedn. Served to lt. USAF, 1956-58. Mem. Am., Ga., Atlanta bar assns. Democrat. Home: 829 Castle Falls Dr NE Atlanta GA 30329 Office: Fulton Fed Bldg Atlanta GA 30303

LEVITCH, HERMAN HARRY, jeweler; b. Memphis, Dec. 24, 1916; s. Samuel and Lena (Feingold) L.; LL.B. cum laude, So. Law U., 1941; LL.B., Memphis State U., 1967; grad. Gemological Inst. Am., 1965; m. Frances Wagner, May 31, 1936; 1 son, Ronald Wagner. Jeweler, diamond specialist, jewelry designer, Memphis, 1936-—. Gen. chmn. United Jewish Appeal Southwest Mo. and No. Ark., 1948-50; del. conf. Am.'s problems, Washington, 1967-69, regional conf. U.S. fgn. policy, Louisville, 1969; mem. Memphis Commn. on Drug Abuse, Memphis Community Relations Council. Mem. Shelby County exec. bd. Memphis area March of Dimes, 1966-—; truste Leo N. Levi Nat. Arthritic Hosp., Hot Springs Nat. Park, Ark. Served with USAAF, World War II. Recipient B award Diamonds Internat., 1969. Mem. Memphis area C. of C. (welcoming com. 1965-—), Jewelry Industry Council, Retail Jewelers Am., Moose former trustee), Mason (32 deg., Shriner); mem. B'nai B'rith (v.p. dir. grand Lodge #7 1970-—, Vol. of Year 1966-67, del. leadership conf. Israel 1970). Home: 4972 Peg Lane Memphis TN 38117 Office: 147 Union Av Memphis TN 38103

LEVITT, JOANN NOREEN GORTON, physician; b. Plymouth, Mich.; d. Forrest Warren and Frances (Ford) Gorton; R.N., Edward W. Sparrow Sch. Nursing, 1949; B.S., Mich. State U., 1952; M.D., U. Mich., 1956; m. Robert J. Levitt, Apr. 17, 1947; children—Robert W., Patricia A., William D., Richard H. Intern, Sparrow Hosp., Lansing, Mich., 1956-57; contract physician gen. practice Ireland Army Hosp., 1957-59; individual practice gen. medicine, Ft. Leavenworth, Kan., 1962-63; resident anesthesiology Charity Hosp., New Orleans, 1963-65; individual practice anesthesiology Nat. Orthopedic Hosp., Arlington, Va., Circle Terrace, Jefferson hosps., Alexandria, Va., 1965-—. Med. missionary, Formosa, 1969; cons. in field. Mem. Alexandria Med. Soc., Am., Va. socs. anesthesiology, Alpha Epsilon Iota. Home: 7429 Brad St Falls Church VA 22042 Office: 8301 Arlington Blvd Fairfax VA 22030

LEVITT, PHILLIP RUSSELL, periodontist; b. Cheyenne, Wyo., July 29, 1926; s. Max P. and Alice (Weinstein) L.; B.A., U. Colo., 1950; postgrad. U. Wyo., 1950-51; D.D.S., Northwestern U., 1954; certificate in Periodontics, U. Ala., 1960; m. Helene Sylvia Rosenthal, Feb. 27, 1955; children—Gail Mandi, Ronald Alan, Jeffrey Miles. Pvt. practice gen. dentistry, Denver, 1955-58, specializing in periodontics, Tuscaloosa, Ala., 1961-63, Birmingham, Ala., 1963-—; staff periodontist Ala. State Hosps., 1960-63; clin. instr. dentistry U. Ala., 1966-—. Served with AUS, 1944-46. Mem. Am., Ala. dental assns., Birmingham Dist. Dental Soc., Am. Acad. Periodontology, Ala. Soc. Periodontists, Southern Acad. Periodontology, Phi Sigma Delta, Alpha Omega, Zeta Beta Tau. Jewish religion. Mem. B'nai B'rith. Home: 912 Beech Lane Birmingham AL 35213 Office: 1000 S 19th St Birmingham AL 35205

LEVITT, RONALD L., pub. relations cons.; b. Rochester, N.Y., Mar. 23, 1931; s. Maurice and Pearl (Altman) L.; A.B., U. Miami, 1956; m. Geraldine Rita Wortsman, June 20, 1954; children—Lynn Barbara, Howard Jay. Staff corr. UP, 1956-59; news dir., accounts supr. Mandell/Newman, 1959-60; pres. Ronald Levitt Assos. Inc., pub. relations cons., Coral Gables, Fla., 1961-—. Lectr. pub. relations colls. throughout U.S.; guest lectr. on pub. relations and politics. Served with USN, 1950-54. Recipient Dept. Def. award, 1953; service awards Pub. Relations Soc. Am., 1966, 67, 68, 69. Mem. Pub. Relations Soc. Am. (pres. Fla. 1966; chmn. Southeastern chpt. 1968-70), Internat. Platform Assn., Assn. Indsl. Editors, Am. Assn. Polit. Cons., Fla. Pub. Relations Assn. Clubs: Miami Press, U. Miami Alumni, Palm Bay. Contbr. articles mags. Home: 7170 SW 119th St Miami FL 33156 Office: 141 Sevilla Av Coral Gables FL 33134

LEVITZ, JOEL JACOB, behavioral scientist; b. Phila., Jan. 4, 1935; s. Milton and Sophia (Kurtz) L.; B.S., City Coll. N.Y., 1958; M.A., Sacramento State Coll., 1964; postgrad. City Coll. N.Y., 1959-60, Columbia, 1960-61, U. Denver, 1961-62, Temple U., 1965-—; 1 son, Michael S. Tchr. emotionally disturbed children Hawthorne (N.Y.) Cedar Knolls, 1958-60; tng. supr., tech. rep. Am. Machine & Foundry, Stamford, Conn., 1960-62; engring. psychologist Aerojet Gen. Corp., Sacramento, 1962-64, Philco Ford, Willow Grove, Pa., 1964-66; program mgr. ednl. systems Burroughs Corp., Ardmore, Pa., 1966-70; dir. spl. support services Fed. City Coll., Washington, 1970-—. Cons., No. Natural Gas Co., Environmental Developers Inc. Mem. Human Factors Soc. (exec. council at large 1966-67). Am. Psychol. Assn. (asso.), Psi Chi, Phi Delta Kappa, Phi Theta Tau (hon.). Home: 103 G St SW Box B806 Washington DC 20024

LEVY, JEROME SICKLES, physician; b. Morganfield, Ky., Sept. 27, 1902; s. Phil and Hattie (Sickles) L.; B.S., Washington U., St. Louis, 1923; M.D., 1925; m. Marion Lee, June 15, 1946; children—Carol Lee, Jere-Jane. Intern Jewish Hosp., St. Louis, 1926-27; asst. in surgery Washington U. Sch. Medicine, 1925-26; resident MaPac Hosp., St. Louis, 1927-29; practice medicine, specializing in internal medicine and gastroenterology Little Rock, 1929-—; mem. staff St. Vincent Infirmary, U. Ark., Ark. Baptist Med. Center, Mo. Pacific Hosp.; clin. prof. medicine U. Ark. Sch. Medicine, 1945-—. Vice pres. S.W. regional bd. Am. Jewish Com. 1960-—, also mem. nat. administrv. bd.; mem. administrv. bd. Leo N. Levi Meml. Hosp., Hot Springs, Ark., 1955-—; chmn. Central Ark. Council for Comprehensive Health Planning, 1968-70; adv. bd. Ark. Regional Med. Program. Served with AUS, 1942-46. Diplomate in gastroenterology Am. Bd. Internal Medicine. Fellow A.C.P. (Ark. gov. 1963-71), Am. Coll. Gastroenterology; mem. A.M.A., Pan-Am., Ark. (1st v.p. 1967-68, chmn. com. on medicine and religion 1968-70), So., Pulaski County (pres. 1957) med. assns., Am. Gastroenterol. Assn., Digestive Disease Found. (founding mem.), Zeta Beta Tau. Jewish religion. Mem. B'nai B'rith. Contbr. articles to profl. jours. Home: 3 E Palisades Dr Little Rock AR 72207 Office: 500 S University Av Little Rock AR 72205

LEVY, LARRY, newspaperman; b. Chgo., Nov. 24, 1931; s. Edward Albert and Ruth (Oppenheim) L.; student Colo. Coll., 1950-51; student U. Miami, 1956-57; m. Carole Marie Wolf, Sept. 1, 1962; children— Carrie Ruth, David Jeffrey, Karen Michelle. Reporter, Miami (Fla.) Herald, 1956-57, Southtown Economist, Chgo., 1958-59, Tucson (Ariz.) Citizen, 1959, Daily Oklahoman, Oklahoma City, 1959-62, San Bernardino (Cal.) Sun-Telegram, 1962-63; aviation, mil. writer Daily Oklahoman, Oklahoma City, 1963-67, Oklahoma City Times, 1963-67; aviation writer Tulsa Tribune, 1967-—; free lance magazine writer. Mem. adv. bd. Monte Cussino Sch., Tulsa. Served with USAF, 1951-55. Mem. Oklahoma City Press Club (dir. 1961-66), Aviation Space Writers Assn., Air Force Assn., Sigma Delta Chi, Kappa Alpha Mu. Club: Oklahoma City Gridiron. Home: 7823 S College Pl Tulsa OK 74136 Office: PO Box 1770 Tulsa OK 74102

LEVY, LOUIS, II, cardiologist; b. New Orleans, Nov. 24, 1919; s. Herman and Hannah (Klein) L; B.S., La. State U., 1940, M.D., 1943; m. Dorothy Cobb, Sept. 28, 1945; children—Louis Herman, Larry, Lynda, Leslie, Lizabeth. Intern, resident Charity Hosp., New Orleans, 1943-46, dir. Heart Sta., 1947-—; practice medicine specializing in internal medicine, New Orleans, 1946-—; mem. staff Touro, Hotel Dieu, Mercy, Flint Goodridge, Charity hosps.; instr. medicine La. State U., 1946-51, prof., 1961-—. Diplomate Am. Bd. Internal Medicine and Cardiology. Fellow A.C.P., Am. Coll. Cardiology, Am. Coll. Chest Physicians; mem. A.M.A., So. Med. Assn., New Orleans Acad. Internal Medicine. Home: 5642 Marcia Av New Orleans LA 70124 Office: 3600 Prytania 81 Schick Ct New Orleans LA 70115

LEVY, S. SANFORD, judge, b. 1902; J.D. cum laude, Loyola U. Admitted to La. bar, 1922; judge civil dist. ct., New Orleans; justice ad hoc Supreme Ct., 1970. Office: 421 Loyola Av New Orleans LA 70112

LEVY, WILLIAM EARL, city ofcl.; b. Tallahassee, Fla., Nov. 16, 1910; s. Frederick O'Neal and Bessie (Atkinson) L.; grad. Inst. for Tng. in Municipal Adminstrn.; m. Gladys Hassell Williams, Dec. 28, 1931; children—William Earl Jr., Frederick Cartwright. With City of Tallahassee Fire Dept., 1927-—, chief of dept., 1940-—. Chmn. ednl. com. State Fire Chiefs. Served with AUS, 1944-45. Mem. Fla. Fire Chiefs Assn. (pres. 1968, chaplain), Internat. Fire Service Tng. Assn., Fla. State Firemen's Assn., (pres. Internat. Assn. Fire Chiefs (past pres. Southeastern div.). Baptist (deacon). Kiwanian, Elk, Odd Fellow. Home: 543 E 8th Av Tallahassee FL 32303 Office: 327 N Adams St Tallahassee FL 32301

LEWEY, MERLE CREIGHTON, ret. army officer, govt. ofcl.; b. Coffeen, Ill., Apr. 30, 1921; s. Merle Walter and Flos (Roberts) L.; A.B., James Millikin U., 1948; A.M., U. So. Cal., 1959. Announcer, WSOY, Decatur, Ill., 1941-42; instr. James Millikin U., 1947-48; Announcer WCRA, Effington, Ill., 1950-51; commd. 2d lt. U.S. Army, 1942, advanced through grades to lt. col. 1962; chief audio-visual br. Office Chief Information, Dept. Army, Washington, 1964-66; ret., 1966; audio-visual support officer Office Asst. Chief Staff Communications-Electronics, Dept. Army, 1967-—. Decorated Bronze Star, Legion of Merit. Mem. Soc. Motion Picture and Television Engrs., Acad. TV Arts and Scis., Tau Kappa Epsilon, Alpha Phi Omega, Alpha Epsilon Rho. Home: Cavalier Club 6200 Wilson Blvd Falls Church VA 22044 Office: Office Asst Chief Staff for Communications- Electronics Dept Army Washington DC 20315

LEWIN, GEORGE FOREST, ins. co. exec.; b. Plainfield, N.H., Oct. 25, 1916; s. George Forest and Maude (Walsh) L.; A.B., Middlebury Coll., 1940; J.D., Georgetown U., 1951; m. Barbara DeFord, May 26, 1943. Claims adjuster Liberty Mut. Ins. Co., 1940-41; exec. trainee Provident Mut. Life Ins. Co., 1941-43; asst. Washington rep. Anthracite Coal Industry, 1943-45; asst. traffic mgr. Aircraft Industries Assn., 1945-47; with Govt. Employee Ins. Co., Washington, 1947-—, sr. v.p., 1970-—; sec. Govt. Employees Corp., Govt. Employees Financial Corp.; sec. Criterion Ins. Co., 1964-70. Mem. Washington Bd. Trade. Mem. nat. capitol div. adv. bd. Salvation Army; bd. govs. Nat. Assn. Ind. Insurers. Mem. Am., Va. bar assns., Am. Soc. Corporate Secs., U.S. C. of C., Newcomen Soc., Phi Alpha Delta, Kappa Delta Rho. Republican. Methodist. Home: 5225 Connecticut Av NW Washington DC 20015 Office: 5260 Western Av NW Washington DC 20015

LEWINS, LEON, govt. ofcl.; b. Warsaw, Poland, Jan. 3, 1911; s. Elja H. and Sarah L. (Rosen) Lewinski; came to U.S., 1936; B.S., Coll. City N.Y., 1943; M.A., Am. U., 1951; m. Gertrude R. Weissman, June 15, 1941. Econ. analyst OPA, Washington, 1944-45; economist War Assets Adminstrn., Washington, 1945-47; econ. specialist State Dept., Washington, 1949-61; chief East European Sect., sr. internat. economist Commerce Dept., Washington, 1961-—. Vice pres. Workmen's Circle Home for Aged, Media, Pa., 1963-64. Mem. Am. Econ. Assn., Am. Assn. Advancement Slavic Studies, Assn. Study Soviet Type Economies, Workmen's Circle, Washington Ethical Soc. Author: The Agrarian Problem and Land Reforms in Poland Between the Two World Wars, 1951. Contbr. articles to profl. jours. Home: 4400 East-West Hwy Bethesda MD 20014 Office: Commerce Dept 14th and Constitution Av NW Washington DC 20230

LEWIS, BERNARD LEROY, engring. exec.; b. Storm Lake, Ia., Dec. 19, 1923; s. Leo LeRoy and Francis (Cutchall) L.; B.S. in Physics, Tulane U., 1947, M.S., 1948; m. Dorothy Louise Simoneaux, Feb. 16, 1946; children—David, Michael, Patrick, Timothy. Physicist, Naval Research Lab., Washington, 1948-49; electronic scientist 1949-53, sect. head, 1953-57; radar cons. Systems, Inc., Orlando, Fla., 1957-60; prin. engr. Radiation, Inc., Orlando, 1960-61, Membourne, Fla., 1963-69; chief engr. Airtronics Inc., Washington 1961-63; partner, chief engr. MacDowell Assos., subsidiary Real Eight Corp., 1969-—. Served to lt. USNR 1943-57. Recipient Outstanding Efficiency awards Naval Research Lab., 1956-57; Patent awards Navy Research Lab., Radiation, Inc. Mem. I.E.E.E., Sci. Research Soc. Am., Am. Phys. Soc. Roman Catholic. Contbr. articles to profl. jours. Patentee in field. Home: 1239 Seminole Dr Satellite Beach FL 32935 Office: 900 Pine Tree Dr Indian Harbour Beach FL 32935

LEWIS, C. DOUGLAS, JR., acting chief curator Nat. Gallery Art, Washington. Office: National Gallery Art Constitution Av at 6th St Washington DC 20565*

LEWIS, CEYLON SMITH, JR., physician; b. Muskogee, Okla., July 19, 1920; s. Ceylon Smith and Glenn (Ellis) L.; A.B., Washington U., St. Louis, 1942, M.D., 1945; m. Marguerite Dearmont, Dec. 20, 1943; children—Sarah Lee, Ceylon Smith, III, Carol D. Intern, Salt Lake Gen. Hosp., 1945-46; resident in internal medicine Salt Lake VA Hosp., Salt Lake County Hosp., 1948-51; practice internal medicine and cardiology, Tulsa, 1951-—; asst. clin. prof. medicine U. Okla. Sch. Medicine, 1971-—; cons. internal medicine USPHS Indian Hosp. Trustee Coll. Ozarks, 1964-—; bd. dirs. Am. Heart Assn., 1971-—. Served to capt. M.C., AUS, 1946-48. Diplomate Am. Bd. Internal Medicine. Fellow A.C.P.; mem. Tulsa County Med. Soc. (pres. 1971), Okla. Soc. Internal Medicine (pres. 1971-72). Presbyn. (chmn. med. com. Commn. Ecumenical Missions and Relations). Contbr. articles to profl. jours. Home: 3747 S Wheeling Tulsa OK 74105 Office: 2021 S Lewis Tulsa OK 74104

LEWIS, CHARLES CALBERT, banker; b. Lake Providence, La., Sept. 28, 1908; s. Charles Calbert and Sallie Goslee (Hughes) L.; B.A., La. Coll., 1928; m. Bertha Evelyn Rigsby, Sept. 3, 1936; 1 son, Charles Clinton. Tchr. high sch. and athletic coach, Marion, La., 1928-30, Delhi, La., 1930-36; chief accountant La. Irrigation & Mill Co., Crowley, 1936-—, sec.-treas., 1950-—, also dir.; dir. First Nat. Bank Crowley, 1948-—, v.p., 1952-—; dir. First Nat. Farms, Inc., 1959-—, sec.-treas., 1959-—. Active local Boy Scouts Am., 1936-—. Vice chmn. Crowley Municipal Fire and Police Civil Service Bd.; mem. Municipal Cemetery Bd. Trustee Acadia Baptist Acad. Democrat. Baptist (pres. bd. dirs., treas.). Mason, Rotarian (past pres. Crowley).

Home: 403 E 4th St Crowley LA 70526 Office: First Nat Bank Crowley LA 70526

LEWIS, CHARLES HERBERT, JR., lumber co. exec.; b. Randolph, La., Mar. 23, 1916; s. Charles H. and Mittie Mae (Killgore) L.; B.S., La. State U., 1939; spl. courses Harvard, 1948, U. Houston, 1960-62; m. Annie Lee Cannon, June 26, 1944; children—Charles H. III, Annie Lee, Mary Etta. Forester, Crosby Lumber Co. (Miss.), 1939-41, chief forester, 1945-52; chief forester, wood procurement supt. Crosby Chem., Inc., DeRidder, La., 1952-59; exec. dir. La. Forestry Assn., 1959-65, also gen. mgr., pub. Forest and People mag.; pres., gen. mgr. L.H. Lewis Timber Co., Zachary, La., 1965—; regional forestry mgr. Crossett div. Ga. Pacific Corp., 1971—; comml. pilot. Trustee La. Forestry Found., 1969—, pres., 1969-71. Served as maj. USAAF, 1944-45. Decorated air medal with oak leaf cluster; recipient Distinguished Service award Soc. Am. Foresters, 1966. Mem. La. Forestry Assn. (dir.), Soc. Am. Foresters (nat. council 1963-67, chmn. S.W. La. 1961-62), Nat. Council Forestry Assn. Execs. Rotarian (pres. local clubs 1954, 64). Presbyn. Clubs: Fennwood Hills Country (dir.) Zachary, La.; Delta Yacht (pres.) (Lake St. John, La.). Address: 5744 Fennwood Dr Zachary LA 70791

LEWIS, CHESTER ALFRED, city ofcl.; b. N.Y.C., Nov. 25, 1914; s. Joseph Alfred and Rachel Valentine (Sherry) L.; B.C.E., N.Y.U., 1942; M.S., George Washington U., 1957; m. Jeanne Rose Sorg, Feb. 3, 1940; children—Linda M., Sherry N. Chief of survey party Madigan-Hyland, cons. engrs., N.Y.C., 1935-42; commd. ensign CEC, USN, 1942, advanced through grades to comdr., 1954; ret., 1964; dir. pub. works City of Norfolk, Va., 1969—; dir. Sorg Printing Co., Inc., N.Y.C. Registered profl. engr., Va., N.Y., Hawaii. Mem. U.S. Naval Inst., Am. Pub. Works Assn., Engrs. Club Hampton Rds. (dir.), Mil. Order World Wars, Ret. Officers Assn., Kappa Sigma. Roman Catholic. K.C. Club: Sewalls Point Golf (Norfolk). Home: 7604 Nancy Dr Norfolk VA 23518 Office: City Hall Norfolk VA 23510

LEWIS, DANIEL CURTIS, JR., paper co. exec.; b. Suffolk, Va., Aug. 26, 1918; s. Daniel Curtis and Frances (Rawls) L.; A.B. cum laude, Washington and Lee U., 1942; M.B.A. with distinction, Harvard, 1948, D.C.S., 1954; m. Elizabeth Shirley Baer, June 5, 1948; children—Lawrence S., Clifford R., Robert D. Jr. staff accountant Lybrand Ross Bros. & Montgomery, Boston, 1948-49; asst. prof. commerce Washington and Lee U., 1949-52; research asso. bus. adminstrn. Harvard Grad. Sch. Bus. Adminstrn., 1952-54; asst. to pres. Lynchburg Foundry Co. (Va.), 1954-56, controller, 1956-60, sec., asst. treas., 1960-63; asst. sec. Woodward Iron Co. Birmingham, Lynchburg, 1961-63; asst. to pres. The Chesapeake Corp. Va., West Point, 1963-66, v.p. adminstrn., 1966—, also dir.; sec. Greenlife Products Co., 1969—, also dir.; pres. Chesapeake Bay Plywood Corp., 1967—, also dir.; dir. York River Oyster Research Corp., Cands Lumber Co. Chmn. West Point Sch. Bd., 1965—; mem. Va. Commn. on Higher Edn., 1964-65, Va. Commn. on State and Local Revenues, Expenditures and Related Matters, 1962-63; chmn. Lynchburg Citizens Sch. Study Commn., 1960-61; treas. Va. Found. for Ind. Colls., 1957-63; mem. Va. State Bd. for Community Colls., 1966—, vice chmn., 1970-71, chmn., 1971—. Pres., bd. dirs. Ednl. Found. for Community Colls. Va., 1968—; mem. West Point Bi-racial Com., 1968—. Bd. dirs. United Fund Lynchburg, 1959-61, v.p., 1960-61; bd. dirs. Lynchburg Guidance Center, 1956-59, pres., 1958-59; bd. dirs. Lynchburg chpt. A.R.C., 1956-59, West Point Improvement Assn., 1964-67; trustee Va. Episcopal Sch., 1960-66, Va. Found. Ind. Colls., 1966—, Williamsburg Community Hosp., 1967-70. Served with USNR, 1942-46. Mem. Financial Execs. Inst., Newcomen Soc. N.Am., So. Forest Inst. (pres. 1971). Episcopalian (vestryman). Clubs: Harvard of Va., West Point Country (dir.), Downtown, York River Yacht Haven. Home: Tanager Ct West Point VA 23181 Office: The Chesapeake Corp Va West Point VA 23181

LEWIS, DELANO EUGENE, govt. ofcl.; b. Arkansas City, Kan., Nov. 12, 1938; s. Raymond E. and Enna (Wordlow) L.; B.A., U. Kan., 1960; LL.B., Washburn U., 1963; m. Gayle C. Jones, June 11, 1960; children— Delano Eugene, Geoffrey Paul, Brian Patrick, Phillip David. Gen. atty. Dept. Justice, 1963-65; dep. chief analysis and advice Equal Employment Opportunity Commn., 1965-66; country dir. for Uganda, Peace Corps, 1967-69; legislative asst. to Senator Edward Brooke, Washington, 1970-71; adminstrv. asst. to Walter E. Fauntroy, D.C. del. to Ho. of Reps., 1971—. Mem. Alpha Phi Alpha. Address: 4232 Ingomar St NW Washington DC 20015*

LEWIS, DONALD ELWIN, civil engr.; b. Taylor, Ark., Mar. 5, 1937; s. Herschel A. and Louise (Cheatham) L.; student So. State Coll., 1955-57; B.S.E.E., U. Ark., 1959, B.S. in Civil Engr., 1967, M.S.C.E., 1967; m. Helen Lavelle Goatcher, Oct. 24, 1964; children—Donald Evan, James Todd, Laurie Elizabeth. Elec. engr. Corps of Engrs., Little Rock, 1959-65, civil engr., 1967-70; civil engr. FAA, Memphis, 1970—. Asso. mem. Am. Soc. C.E.; mem. Am. Soc. Profl. Engrs., Internat. Soc. Soils Sechanics and Found. Engrs., Tau Beta Pi, Eta Kappa Nu. Democrat. Baptist (deacon). Home: 3350 Foxgate Memphis TN 38118 Office: 3400 Democrat Rd Memphis TN 38118

LEWIS, E. CROSBY, lawyer; b. Fairfield County, S.C., Mar. 4, 1934; s. Ernest Vann and Nell (Brooks) L.; student U. S.C., 1952-55, LL.B., 1958; m. Cleo B. Dickerson; children—Lisa LaVelle, Allyson Lee, E. Crosby. Admitted to S.C. bar, 1958, since practiced in Columbia. Dir. Riverland Devel. Corp., First Palmetto State Bank & Trust. Vice chmn. S.C. Bd. Edn., 1965-69. Mem. S.C. Ho. of Reps. from Richland County, 1961-64, chmn. mil., pub. and municipal affairs com.; chmn. S.C. Democratic Party, 1967-69; v.p. Nat. Assn. Dem. State Chmn., 1969—. Bd. visitors The Citadel; bd. dirs. S.C. Med. Coll. Hosp. Served with USAF. Named Eagle Scout. Mem. Am., S.C., Richland County bar assns., Columbia C. of C. Methodist. Mason (Shriner). Club: Forest Lake. Home: RFD Winnsboro SC 29180 Office: 1717 Gervais St Columbia SC 29201

LEWIS, EARL MILTON, educator, agrl. engr.; b. Wheaton, Ill., Feb. 4, 1915; s. Roy D. and Carie (Tousley) L.; B.S. in Agrl. Engring., Tex. A. and M. U., 1942; M.S., Okla. State U., 1964; m. Lillian Eugene Payne, June 6, 1942; 1 son, Earl Tousley. With Southwestern Pub. Service Co., Amarillo, Tex., 1946-56, mgr. agrl. devel., 1952-56; exec. mgr. Okla. Farm Electric Council, also extension agrl. engr. Okla. State U., 1956—, asst. prof. agrl. engring., 1966—, traveling lectr., 1970—. Pres. Optimist Club, Plainview, Tex., 1949, Toastmasters Club, Stillwater, 1965. Served to capt. AUS, 1942-46. Mem. Am. Soc. Agrl. Engrs., Illuminating Engring. Soc. Methodist, Mason. Author numerous papers, bulls., fact sheets in field. Home: 1002 Preston Dr Stillwater OK 74074

LEWIS, EDWARD, educator; b. St. Louis, Feb. 10, 1930; s. William and Priscilla (Chambers) L.; B.A., Washington U., St. Louis, 1952, M.A., 1953, Ph.D., 1957; m. Anne Livingston, Oct. 18, 1954; children—William Edward, Patricia Jane, Sophie Eleanor. Asst. prof. U. Kan. at Topeka, 1953-54; asso. prof. modern langs. U. N.C. at Durham, 1954-60, prof., 1960—, chmn. dept. modern langs., 1962-68. Mem. Modern Lang. Assn., Am. Assn. U. Profs., Phi Beta Kappa, Alpha Tau Omega. Contbr. articles to profl. jours. Home: 7908 Gala Ct Raleigh NC 27609

LEWIS, ELLIOT LEON, research co. exec.; b. Boston, Jan. 25, 1925; s. Maurice A. and Dorothy I. (Novogrod) L.; B.S., Boston U., 1948; M.A. (Melville Jacoby fellow), Stanford, 1949; m. Beatriz Giner D'Exremera, Dec. 23, 1963; children—Susan Beth, Gregory Winston. Asst. to pres. Electronics Capital Corp., San Diego, 1960-63; v.p. Garat & Polenitza, investment brokers, Los Angeles, 1963-65; asst. to pres. Electro-optical Systems, Pasadena, Cal., 1965-67; v.p. Econs. Research Assos., Los Angeles, 1963-67; pres., chmn. Leisure Systems Inc., Fort Lauderdale, Fla., 1967—. Served with USCGR, 1942-46; PTO. Recipient Indsl. Film Producers award 1957. Editor, Research for Industry, Stanford Research Inst., 1954-56. Contbr. numerous tech. papers on tourism and recreation to profl. jours. Home: 1021 Hillsboro Mile Hillsboro Beach FL 33062 Office: 2821 E Commercial Blvd Fort Lauderdale FL 33308

LEWIS, GEORGE, banker; b. Tallahassee, Fla., Nov. 4, 1913; s. George Edward and Sarah (Davis) L.; B.S., U. Fla., 1935; grad. Grad. Sch. Banking of Rutgers U., 1939; m. Clifton VanBrunt, Sept. 4, 1940; children—George Edward II, William VanBrunt, Clifton Byrd, Benjamin Bridges. With Lewis State Bank, Tallahassee, 1935—, pres., 1955-67, chmn. bd., 1967—, also dir. Chmn. Fla. adv. com. to U.S. Commn. Civil Rights, 1962-64; treas. Fla. Council Human Relations; mem. so. regional council Am. Civil Liberties Union, Center Study of Dem. Instns., Common Cause, Nation Assos., Bus. Execs. Move for Vietnam Peace and New Nat. Priorities, World Assn. World Federalists. Trustee Fla. Bankers Ednl. Found., 1959-65; bd. dirs. Tallahassee Urban League. Recipient Frontiers Human Relations award, 1963. Mem. Fla. Bankers Assn., World Federalists U.S.A., Inst. Am. Democracy, Fellowship of Reconciliation, UN assn. of U.S., Urban Coalition. Democrat. Episcopalian. Owner Frank Lloyd Wright Fla. House. Home: 3117 Okeeheepkee Rd Tallahassee FL 32303 Office: PO Box 750 Tallahassee FL 32302

LEWIS, GEORGE MCKOY, banker; b. Valley Mills, Tex., Aug. 3, 1902; s. Samuel Knight and Mary Rebecca (Barrett) L.; B.S., A. and M. Coll. Tex., 1924; M.B.A., Harvard, 1927; grad. study U. Chgo., 1929-30; m. Mary Gregory Bunting, Feb. 10, 1940. Mem. staff, div. crop and livestock estimates Dept. Agr., 1924-25; in charge livestock and meat studies Bur. Bus. Research, U. Tex., 1927-29; Inst. Meat Packing fellow U. Chgo., 1929-30; dir. dept. marketing Am. Meat Inst., Chgo., 1939-57, v.p., 1950-63; vice chmn. bd. Jefferson State Bank, San Antonio, 1963—. Vice pres. Am. Meat Inst. Found., 1957-63. Clubs: Quadrangle, Union League, University of Chicago, South Shore Country (Chgo.). Home: 715 Wiltshire Av San Antonio TX 78209 Office: Jefferson State Bank San Antonio TX 78201

LEWIS, GEORGE RUSSEL, librarian; b. Webster County, Miss., July 15, 1929; s. John Terry and Martha (Shaffer) L.; grad. Clarke Meml. Coll., Newton, Miss., 1950; B.A. with honors, Miss. Coll., 1952; M.S. in L.S., La. State U., 1956; student Baylor U., 1957; m. Bobbie Jean McClain, Nov. 26, 1952; children—Karen Denise, Michael Keith. Tchr. English, Forest City (Miss.) Schs., 1952-54; grad. asst. La. State U. Library, 1954-56; asst. pub. service librarian, then cataloger Baylor U. Library, 1956-58; head circulation dept. Auburn U. Library, 1958-62; head librarian Ky. So. Coll., Louisville, 1962-63; dir. libraries Miss. State U., 1963—. Mem. Miss. Library Commn. Mem. Am. (Miss. membership chmn.), Miss., Southeastern library assns., Assn. Coll. and Research Libraries, Phi Kappa Phi, Phi Delta Kappa. Baptist (Sunday sch. tchr.). Lion. Home: PO Box 723 State College MS 39762

LEWIS, GERALD A., lawyer, state legislator; b. Ala.; ed. Harvard, Harvard Law Sch. Practiced in Miami, Fla.; mem. Fla. Ho. of Reps., 1967—. Exec. v.p. Young Democrats Club Dade County. Mem. Fla. N.G. Office: 602 Concord Bldg 66 W Flagler St Miami FL 33130*

LEWIS, GILBERT LASEINE, drug co. exec.; b. Millen, Ga., Oct. 6, 1923; s. Robert Lee and Fannie (Ethridge) L.; student Ga. So. Coll., 1946-47; B.S. in Pharmacy, U. Ga., 1950; m. Betty Ann Camp, Mar. 4, 1929; children—Michael, Elizabeth. Pharmacist Crystal Pharmacy, Moultrie, Ga., 1950-51, Williford Drug Co., Camilla, Ga., 1951-54; pharmacist Pelham Drug Co. (Ga.), 1954-61, now pres.; owner, pres. Lewis Drug Co., Pelham, 1961—; pres. Meigs Pharmacy (Ga.), 1968—; dir. Farmers Bank Pelham. Mem. Pelham City Adv. Com., 1968—; pres. Pelham Devel. Corp., 1965—; chmn. Pelham Recreation Bd. 1966—. Mem. Sch. Bd., Pelham, 1968—; mem. exec. com. Pelham City Democratic party, 1964—. Bd. dirs. Ravenwood Acad., Meigs, Chickasaw Devel. Corp. Served with USAAF, 1942-46. Mem. Pelham C. of C. (dir.), Ga. Pharm. Assn. Methodist (steward). Rotarian. Home: 3 N Legion Dr Pelham GA 31779 Office: 450 W Railroad St Pelham GA 31779

LEWIS, GUY V., basketball coach U. Houston. Office: U Houston Houston TX 77004*

LEWIS, HENRY LEANDER, III, physician; b. Street, Miss., Nov. 26, 1937; s. Henry Leander and Carrie (Carter) L.; A.A., S.W. Miss. Jr. Coll., 1957; B.S., Millsaps Coll., 1959; M.D., U. Miss., 1963; m. Marion Kay Coney, Mar. 22, 1958; children—Jeffrey Carter, Jennifer Kirke, Eric Street, Henry Hunter, Erin McDavitt. Intern Wilford Hall USAF Hosp., San Antonio, 1963-64; practice gen. medicine, Magnolia, Miss., 1967—; mem. staff Beacham Meml. Hosp., Magnolia. Served to capt. USAF, 1963-67. Mem. A.M.A., Miss. Med. Assn., Am. Acad. Family Practice, Miss. Acad. Gen. Practice. Home: 425 W Pine St Magnolia MS 39652 Office: 111 Magnolia St Magnolia MS 39652

LEWIS, HOMER IRVIN, air force officer; b. Asheville, N.C., Feb. 1, 1919; s. Homer Irvin and Edith (Little) L.; grad. Culver Mil. Acad., 1938; student U.S. Naval Acad., 1938-39, U. Tex., 1939-41; m. Dorothy Jane Lehrer, Dec. 14, 1940; children—Peter William, Stephen Wayne, William Lehrer. Commd. 2d lt. Res. Infantry, U.S. Army, 1940; advanced through grades to maj. gen. U.S. Air Force; called to active duty Hdqrs. Gulf Coast Flying Tng. Command AAC, Randolph Air Base, Tex., 1941; numerous assignments including 81st Materiel Squadron, 75th Air Base Group, Foster Field, Tex., 1941-42; glider tng. program, comdt. students 23d Army Air Forces Glider Tng. Detachment, Spencer, Ia., 1942, Hamilton, Tex., 1942-43; comdr. 93d Army Air Forces Coll. Tng. Detachment, Spearfish, S.D., 1943-44; then comdt. cadets twin-engined advanced flying sch. Douglas Army Air Field, Douglas, Ariz; chief U.S. Air Force Res., Hdqrs. U.S. Air Force, Washington, 1971—; comdr. Hdqrs. Air Force Res., Robins AFB, Ga., 1972—; prin. adviser on Res. matters to Chief of Staff U.S. Air Force. Decorated Legion of Merit, Air medal. Mem. Res. Officers Assn. U.S. (past nat pres.). Home: 1744 Olive St Eagle Pass TX 78852 Office: Hdqrs US Air Force Washington DC 20330

LEWIS, HOWARD JOHN, information officer; b. Easton, Pa., Dec. 16, 1919; s. Aaron and Eleanor (Jacobson) L.; A.B., Lehigh U., 1940; M.S., Columbia, 1942; m. JoAnn Sukel, June 8, 1958; children—Deborah, Stephen. Reporter, Bethlehem (Pa.) Globe-Times, 1940-41; publicity dir. Am. Civil Liberties Union, 1942; editor Herald-Tribune edit. This Week Mag., N.Y.C., 1946-49; editor Argosy Mag., N.Y.C., 1949-54; free lance writer, 1954-57; dir. Office Information, Nat. Acad. Scis., Washington, 1957—. Editorial cons., author Ency. Brit. Yearbook Sci. and Future, 1967—; editor newsletter Sci. and Pub. Policy Studies Group, 1969—; pres. Council for Sci. on TV, 1970—. Mem. adv. com. Physics Today, 1968—, Prometheus, 1972—. Served with AUS, 1942-46. Decorated Bronze Star medal. Mem. Nat. Assn. Sci. Writers (exec. com. 1972—), Internat. Sci. Writers Assn. (v.p. 1971—). Author: Complete Book of Bowling, 1955; Complete Book of Pet Care, 1956; Complete Book on Horses, 1957, also numerous articles. Home: 7310 Broxburn Ct Bethesda MD 20034 Office: 2101 Constitution Av Washington DC 20418

LEWIS, HOWARTH LISTER, JR., architect; b. N.Y.C., June 13, 1934; s. Howarth Lister and Edith (Brakmann) L.; B.Arch., U. Fla., 1957; m. Dianna Jean Moore, June 8, 1957. Draftsman, designer Byron Simonson, 1957-58; chief draftsman, designer Howard Chilton, 1958-61; prin. firm Peacock & Lewis Architects, Palm Beach, Fla., 1961—. Pres. Akron, Inc., Palm Beach, 1963—. Chmn. Constrn. Industry Licensing Bd., Palm Beach County, 1969—; chmn. Elec. Bd., Fire Code Revision Com., chmn. Design Rev. Study Com., 1968—, (all of City West Palm Beach). Bd. dirs. St. Andrews Residence, West Palm Beach, Fla. Recipient Anthony Pulara Meml. award for outstanding mem. Fla. chpt. A.I.A., 1971. Mem. A.I.A. (past pres., Fla. chpt. 1968-69), Constrn. Specifications Inst., Alpha Tau Omega. Episcopalian (sr. warden). Kiwanian. Home: 211 Dyer Rd West Palm Beach FL 33405 Office: 400 Royal Paln Way Palm Beach FL 33480

LEWIS, JAMES EDWARD, JR., social worker; b. Little Rock, S.C., Nov. 17, 1918; s. James E. and Hattie (Manning) L.; B.S., Tuskegee Inst., 1941; M.S.W., Cath. U., 1953; certificate youth relations Am. U., 1963; m. Willia P. Johnson, Aug. 28, 1944; 1 dau., Denise D. Recreational specialist agrl. extension dept. Tuskegee Inst., 1937-39, instr., 1940-41; dir. health and phys. edn. Morrison Tng. Sch., 1941-42; exec. dir., Southwest Community House Assn., 1946-48, group worker, 1948-49, exec. dir., 1948-65; adminstr. D.C. Dept. Pub. Welfare Youth Shelter House, 1965—. Coordinator ch. community program for Foundry-Met. Community Council, 1967-69; mem.-at-large bd. Neighbors, Inc., 1960-68; mem. Sheardan Park Civic Assn.; mem.-at-large Police Boys Clubs, 1950; instn. rep. Boy Scouts Am., 1960. Served with AUS, 1942-46. Mem. Nat. Assn. Social Workers, Am. Correctional Assn. Baptist (trustee, deacon). Home: 1354 Tewkesbury Pl NW Washington DC 20012 Office: 1225 Harvard St NW Washington DC 20009

LEWIS, JAMES GRAHAM, govt. ofcl.; b. Sharon, Ga., Oct. 12, 1912; s. William Hill and Louise (Kendrick) L.; student Ga. Sch. Tech., 1929-33; B.S., U. Ga., 1938; m. Virginia Carolina Perry, Oct. 16, 1941; 1son, James Graham. Photogrammetric engr. U.S. Geol. Survey, 1941-58, chief br. research and design, 1958-66, tech. dir. topographic div. McLean Research Center, McLean, Va., 1966—. Mem. Am. Soc. Photogrammetry (bd. dirs. 1966-69), Chi Psi. Methodist. Patentee in field. Home: 3019 Castle Rd Falls Church VA 22044 Office: 1340 Old/Chain Bridge Rd McLean VA 22101

LEWIS, JAMES WOODROW, state supreme ct. justice; b. Darlington County, S.C., Mar. 8, 1912; s. W. J. and Mary Aletha (Bryant) L.; A.B., U. S.C., 1932; m. Alice Lee, Dec. 26, 1936; 1 dau., Barbara (Mrs. Olin D. Haynes). Admitted to S.C. bar 1935; mem. S.C. Hwy. Commn., 1936-40; mem. S.C. Ho. of Reps. from Darlington County, 1935-36, 43-45; judge 4th Jud Circuit S.C., 1945-61; asso. justice Supreme Ct. S.C., 1961—. Address: Darlington SC 29532

LEWIS, JASON RUSSELL, dentist; b. Lewiston, Me., Sept. 16, 1915; s. Nathan H. and Dora C. (Finklestein) L.; B.S., Bates Coll., 1937; D.D.S., U. Md., 1942; m. children—Steven N., Karen (Mrs. Joseph Moates). Intern City Hosp., Worcester, Mass., 1942-43; pedodontist Meml. Hosp., Worcester, 1942-43, Friendly Clinic, 1942-43; dental clinician State of Va., and City of Richmond, 1946-47; practice dentistry specializing in pedodontics, Richmond, 1947—. Instr. asso. Med. Coll. Va., 1948-60, spl. lectr., 1965—. Dental rep. United Givers Fund; mem. Richmond Bd. Health, 1956-62; mem. Va. gov.'s adv. com., 1965—; chmn. legislative com. Council Dental Health, 1954; chmn. fluoridation com. City of Richmond, 1952. Trustee, Richmond Forward. Served with AUS; now maj. Res. ret. Fellow Internat. Coll. Dentists, Va. Dental Assn. (sec.-treas. 1967—); mem. Am. Dental Assn., Richmond Dental Soc. (pres. 1955-56), Southeastern Soc. Pedodontics (pres. 1972), Am. Acad. Pedodontics, Va. Assn. Professions (pres. 1967-68), Am., Va. (pres. 1953) socs. dentistry for children, Omicron Kappa Upsilon, Alpha Omega (pres. Richmond chpt.). Rotarian. Club: Harvard (Richmond). Home: 407 E North Hamilton St Richmond VA 23221 Office: 3605 Grove Av Richmond VA 23221

LEWIS, JOHN FULTON, radio-tv writer, producer; b. Balt., May 28, 1922; s. John A. and Elizabeth (Foreman) L.; student St. John's Coll., Annapolis, 1939-41; children—Christopher, Nancy (by previous marriages), Susan, Scott, Stephen. Polit. reporter A.P., Md., editor, mgr., pub. weekly newspapers, 1941-51; polit. analyst WCBM, Balt., 1951-55; radio-tv information dir. Washington office Am. Farm Bur. Fedn., 1952-57; radiotv news dir. Hearst Stas., Balt., 1957-59; radio-tv adviser/aide Sec. Agr. U.S., 1960-61; Washington producer pub. affairs radio-tv programs Nat. Assn. Ednl. Broadcasters, NBC, others, 1961—; producer-editor Am. Security Council, Washington 1964-69; coordinating editor Com. Internal Security, U.S. Ho. of Reps., 1969—. Mem. Nat. Wildlife Assn., Am. Forestry Assn., China Stamp Soc., Author: (with others) Twenty Years of Tyranny-Communist China 1949-1969. Home: 20 9th St NE Washington DC 20003 Office: House Internal Security Com Cannon House Office Bldg Washington DC 20549

LEWIS, JOHN MARLIN, assn. exec.; b. Furnas County, Neb., Jan. 24, 1932; s. Guy F. and Jessie (Story) L.; B.A., Hastings (Neb.) Coll., 1954; m. Wanda Kay Haussler, Nov. 14, 1954; children—Douglas Scott, James Marlin. Exec. v.p. Shenandoah (Ia.) C. of C., 1956-58, Boone (Ia.) C. of C., 1958-61; asst. to gov. Ia., 1961-63; mem. faculty Ia. State U., 1963-64; dist. mgr. U.S. C. of C., 1964-66; exec. v.p. Ky. C. of C., Louisville, 1966—. Mem. Ky. adv. bd. Small Bus. Adminstrn.; mem. Ky. Partners of the Alliance. Trustee Ky. Ednl. TV Found. Mem. Am. C. of C. Execs., So., Ky. assns. C. of C. execs. Elk, Rotarian. Home: 706 Dorsey Way Anchorage KY 40223 706 Dorsey Way Anchorage KY 40223 Office: 300 W York St Louisville KY 40203

LEWIS, JOHN MILTON, cable TV co. exec.; b. nr. Slocomb, Ala., Mar. 29, 1931; s. Phil Truman and Vermell Beatrice (Avery) L.; grad. high sch.; m. Mary Lee Robledo, June 9, 1951; children—Janet Lee, Lee Michael. With Gulf Power Co., Panama City, Fla., 1949-56; self employed vehicle service co., Panama City, 1956-58; v.p., dir., Burnup & Sims, Inc., West Palm Beach, Fla., 1958-70; mgr. Cable Antenna TV div. Wometco Enterprises, Inc., Miami, Fla., 1970—; pres. Middlesex Cablevision, East Brunswick, N.J., 1971—; pres. Allstate Cablevision, Plainfield, N.J., 1971—, Plainfield Cablevision, 1971— ; also v.p. Wometco Communications, Inc., Miami. Cons. in field. Democrat. Mason. Home: 8385 SW 143d St Miami FL 33158 Office: 316 N Miami Av Miami FL 33128

LEWIS, JOHN ROBERT, assn. exec.; b. Troy, Ala., Feb. 21, 1940; s. Eddie and Willie Mae Lewis; B.A., Am. Bapt. Theol. Sem., 1961; B.A. in Philosophy, Fisk U., 1967; m. Lillian Miles, Dec. 21, 1968.

Chmn., Student Nonviolent Coordinating Con., 1963-66; asso. dir. Field Found., 1966-67; dir. Community Orgn. Project, 1967-70; dir. Voter Edn. Project, Atlanta, 1970—. An organizer Nashville student sit-in movement, 1960; a Freedom Rider, 1961; aleader March on Washington, 1963, March from Selma to Montgomery (Ala.), 1965. Appointee to White House Conf. To Fulfill These Rights, 1966; worker Robert F. Kennedy for Pres. Campaign, 1968. Bd. dirs. So. Christian Leadership Conf., Scholarship Edn. and Def. Fund for Racial Equality; trustee Robert F. Kennedy Meml. Found. Home: 1520 Pinehurst Dr SW Atlanta GA 30311 Office: 52 Fairlie St NW Atlanta GA 30303

LEWIS, JOHN TILLERY, III, ednl. adminstr.; b. Hattiesburg, Miss., Oct. 3, 1930; s. John T. and Jewel (Parkman) L.; B.A., Millsaps Coll., Jackson, Miss., 1953; M.A., U. Miss., 1958, Ph.D., 1963; m. Helen Fay Head, June 10, 1955; children—John Charles, Janis Kay. Clk.-typist USP - FO, Jackson, Miss., 1948-51; adminstrv. asst. Miss. N.G., 1951-57; asst. to adj. Gen. of Miss., 1957-60; instr. Stephen F. Austin State Coll., Nacogdoches, Tex., 1960-61, asst. prof., 1961-64, head dept. psychology, 1964-67, v.p. acad. affairs, 1967—. Active Boy Scouts Am. Served with AUS, 1961-62. Mem. Am., Southwestern psychol. assns. Kiwanian (pres.). Contbr. articles to profl. jours. Home: 620 Bostwick St Nacogdoches TX 75961

LEWIS, J(OSEPH) HEBER, mayor; b. Burnside, Ky., Oct. 17, 1893; s. Robert Owens and Alice Frances (Hardwick) L.; student Berea Coll., 1913, Lindsay Wilson Coll., 1914-15; m. Ruth Upton, December 27, 1916; children—Robert Thomas, Helen Frances (Mrs. Caldwell). Operator Newtonian Hotel, Somerset, Ky., 1915-16; farmer, 1917-19; became petroleum jobber, 1928; pres. J. Heberer Lewis Oil Co., Inc., 1950—, Southeastern Tank Lines, 1951—, J. Heber Lewis Service Sta. Co., Burnside, 1957—; dir Pulaski Service Center, Somerset; dir. Citizens Nat. Bank of Somerset. Mayor City of Burnside, 1948—; mem. Ky. Commn. on Tourist Promotion, 1957-62. Bd. dirs. Ky. Petroleum Council, Ky. Jobbers Council, Masonic Widows and Orphans Home; bd. Lindsey Wilson Coll. Recipient Distinguished Alumnus award Lindsey Wilson Coll., 1956. Mem. A.I.M. (charter mem. pres.'s council), Am. Petroleum Inst., Burnside C. of C. (pres. 1948), Ky. C. of C. (dir. 1965-68), Ky. Petroleum Marketers Assn. (pres. 1949). Methodist (chmn. bd. stewards). Mason (33 deg., grand master Ky. 1951-52; past grand prior York Cross of Honor Ky.). Address: Box 307 Burnside KY 42519

LEWIS, JOSEPH HENRY, systems analyst; b. Springfield, Me., May 4, 1916; s. Harry Abner and A. Louise (Ardron) L.; B.S. in Elec. Engring., U. Me., 1938, M.S. in Econs. and Bus. Adminstrn., 1939; m. Jessie Elizabeth Clinton, June 15, 1945; 1 son, Harry Clinton. Student engr. Consol. Edison Co., N.Y.C., 1939-41; elec. engr., operations research analyst Naval Ordnance Lab., 1941-42; tech. observer U.S. Naval Attache's office, London, Eng., 1942-45; operations research analyst Bur. Ordnance, Navy Dept., 1945-46; gen. mgr. Elec. Machinery Export Co., 1946-47; pres. J.H. Lewis &Co., 1948-49; with Office Sec. Def., 1949-68, project leader Weapons Systems Evaluation Group, 1950-68, project leader Inst. Def. Analysis, Washington, 1956-68, asst. div. dir., 1963-66; developed and directed Weapon Systems Evaluation Group/Inst. Def. Analysis Joint Chiefs Staff Command and Control Group, 1961-68; dir. urban goverance research Urban Inst., Washington, 1968—; dir. evaluation Police Found., 1971—. Recipient Meritorious Civilian Service award Navy Dept., 1945. Fellow A.A.A.S.; mem. Operations Research Soc. Am., Operational Research Soc. Ltd., Tau Beta Pi, Phi Kappa Phi. Contbr. to Operational Research and the Social Sciences, 1966; contbr. articles to profl. jours. Home: 3433 Porter St NW Washington DC 20016 Office: 2100 M St NW Washington DC 20037 also 1015 18th St NW Washington DC 20036

LEWIS, KATHRYN ROSEMARY (MRS. DOUGLAS R. KOTH), physician; b. Battle Creek, Mich., Aug. 8, 1927; d. Theodore and Martha (Rose) Lewis; student Marygrove Coll., 1944-45, John Carroll U., summer 1945, 46, 47; B.A. in Biol. Sci., Ohio State U., 1948; M.D., Marquette U., 1952; m. Douglas R. Koth, Nov. 27, 1952; children—Theodore Lewis, Robert Douglas, Kristin Louise. Intern, Georgetown U. Hosp., Washington, 1952-53, resident, 1953-56; resident, Mt. Alto VA Hosp., Washington, 1953-55; chief resident Georgetown U. Hosp., 1956; spl. fellow in neuropathology Armed Forces Inst. Pathology, Washington, 1956-57; attending physician in neuropathology, Mt. Alto VA Hosp., 1958-60; cons., neuropathologist D.C. Gen. Hosp., Washington, 1958-60; clin. neurologist, Retarded Children's Clinic Georgetown U. Med Center, Washington, 1958-60; research investigator, Armed Forces Inst. Pathology, Walter Reed Army Med. Center, Washington, 1958-60; dir., asst. prof. neuropathology, Georgetown U. Med. Center, 1958—, instr. neurology, 1960—; practice medicine specializing in neurology, Arlington, Va., 1961—; mem. staffs Georgetown U., Arlington, Fairfax, No. Va. Drs., Alexandria (Va.) hosps. Research program coordinator NIH, Nat. Inst. Neurol. Diseases and Blindness and Div. Gen. Med. Services, Washington, 1960-61; research dir. Nat. Children's Rehab. Center, Leesburg, Va., 1965. Mem. A.M.A., Am. Acad. Neurology, Arlington County Med. Soc., Med. Soc. Va., Marquette U. Alumni Assn., Alpha Gamma Delta, Gamma Pi Epsilon, Alpha Epsilon Iota. Contbr. articles to med. jours. Home: 4000 Ridgeview Rd Arlington VA 22203 Office: 3801 N Fairfax Dr Arlington VA 22203

LEWIS, LAWRENCE GLENDON, advt. co. exec.; b. nr. Tuscaloosa, Ala., June 5, 1918; s. Monroe Jordan, Anna (Gardner) L.; student pub. schs.; m. Carrie Mae Hayes, Nov. 7, 1940; children—Robert Jordan, Harriet Anna. Agt., Life & Casualty Ins. Co. Tenn., Nashville, 1939-42, staff mgr. Mobile, 1942-48, tng. supr., 1948, dist. mgr., Jackson, Miss., 1948-56; v.p. Standard Life Ins. Co. of S., Jackson, 1956-65; sales and marketing dir. Mut. Savs. Life Ins. Co., Decatur, Ala., 1965-68; spl. accounts exec., v.p. ins. div. Francis & Lusky Co., Inc., Nashville, 1968—. Served with AUS, 1943-46. Decorated Purple Heart. Mem. Miss. Assn. Life Underwriters (past pres.). Baptist. Mason (32 deg., Shriner); mem. Order of Eastern Star (1st worthy patron). Home: 127 Twin Bay Dr Hendersonville TN 37075 Office: 1450 Elm Hill Rd Nashville TN 37210

LEWIS, LEE H(ONLY), constrn. co. exec.; b. Raymond, Wash., Aug. 25, 1917; s. Burt H. and Myrtle B. (Belles) L.; student U. Wash., 1936-40; B.S., Rutgers U., 1947; m. Marcia Eugenia Wagner, Aug. 20, 1960; children—Tricia (Mrs. Norman Hallonquist, Jr.), Laurie (Mrs. Richard Crossman), Barry, Lawrence. Constrn. engr., div. controller Vitro Corp. Am., N.Y.C., 1947-61; v.p. Century Geophysical Corp., Tulsa, 1961-64, now dis.; owner Rochester Photo Supply, Tulsa, 1965-68; v.p., dir. McMichael Concrete Co., Tulsa, 1968—. Served to lt. USNR, 1942-46. C.P.A., Okla. Mem. Am. Inst. C.P.A.'s, Psi Upsilon, Beta Gamma Sigma. Lutheran. Kiwanian. Home: 5301 E 37th St Tulsa OK 74135 Office: McMichael Concrete Co 431 W 23d St Tulsa OK 74107

LEWIS, MALCOLM RAY, newspaper exec.; b. Newton, Miss., Nov. 11, 1940; s. John Sharp and Lawis Gertrude (Gibbs) L.; student E. Central Jr. Coll., Decatur, Miss., 1959; m. Sandra Kaye Adams, Aug. 29, 1942; children—Lewana, Jena, Christopher. With Meridan (Miss.) Star, 1960—, retail advt. mgr., 1971—. Vice pres. Meridian Gideon Camp, 1970-71. Mem. Meridian C. of C. Baptist (dir. Sunday sch. 1970-71, deacon 1969—). Club: Civitan (past pres. Meridian, past lt. gov.). Home: Route 2 Chandle Rd Meridian MS 39301 Office: 815 22d Av Meridian MS 39301

LEWIS, MARGUERITE GARBER (MRS. WILLIAM LEROY LEWIS), civic worker; b. nr. Bellville, O., July 23, 1911; d. Horatio Seymour and Sylvia (Swank) Garber; B.A., Coll. of Wooster, 1933; M.A., U. Mich., 1936; postgrad. Northwestern U., 1937; m. William Leroy Lewis, June 16, 1937; children—Sylvia Jane, Thomas Leroy, David Garber, Catherine Carol, Linda Evelyn. Tchr., 1933-39. Troop leader Girl Scouts U.S.A., 1960-61, chmn. Am. Field Service, 1962-63; bd. mgrs. N.Y. State Congress Parents and Tchrs., 1962-65; mem. Larchmont-Mamaroneck Motion Picture Council, 1944—, pres., 1957-59; mem. Fedn. Motion Picture Councils, 1960-67, nat. conf. chmn., 1961, nat. pres., 1965-67; radio and TV chmn. Ft. Worth City Council P.T.A.'s, 1967—; moderator weekly TV program Parents in Action, KTVT, 1967—; co-ordinator community services courses, div. spl. courses Tex. Christian U., 1969—. Recipient Distinguished Alumni award Coll. Wooster, 1971. Mem. Am. Assn. U. Women, Delta Sigma Rho, Pi Kappa Delta. Clubs: Wooster, Womans. Presbyn. Editor: Newsreel, 1965-67. Home: 3640 Encanto Dr Fort Worth TX 76109

LEWIS, MARK B., govt. ofcl.; b. N.Y.C., Mar. 26, 1923; s. Philip and Rose (Persoff) Swirsky; B.A., Yale, 1947; m. Lillian Darragh Howard, June 9, 1951; children—Adam, Deborah, Matthew. News dir. radio sta. WWOD, Lynchburg, Va., 1947-49; writer, broadcaster Voice of Am., 1949, corr., Beirut, Lebanon, 1953-54, regional chief, Cairo, Egypt, 1954; information officer USIA, Bombay, India, 1954-55, White House corr., 1955-57, pub. affairs officer Rhodesias and Nvasaland, 1957-61, Ghana, 1962-64, asst. dir. for Africa, 1964-68; mem. Sr. Seminar on Fng. Policy, State Dept., 1968-69; chmn. Television Task Force, USIA, 1969-71; staff dir. Adv. Com. on Arts, 1971—. Served with USAAF, 1943-45; MTO. Mem. Zeta Psi. Home: 515 22d St Washington DC 20520 Office: USIA 1750 Pennsylvania Av NW Washington DC

LEWIS, MARY GENEVIEVE, librarian; b. Vincennes, Ind., Aug. 28, 1911; d. Claudius Ervin and Isa (Hollister) Lewis; B.A., Northwestern U., 1933, M.A., 1935; B.S., Columbia, 1938. Reference asst., reference librarian Oak Park (Ill.) Pub. Library, 1935-37, 38-43, head reference dept., 1938-43, 45-50; instr. English, head dept. Warren Wilson Coll., Swannanoa, N.C., 1950-61; reference librarian Stetson U., DeLand, Fla., 1961—. Chmn. W. Volusia chpt. A.R.C. Served to capt. WAC, 1943-45; ETO. Mem. Am., Fla. library assns. Democrat. Presbyn. Home: 135 W Minnesota Av DeLand FL 32720

LEWIS, MILTON HENRY, JR., utilities co. exec.; b. Pineville, Ky., July 22, 1923; s. Milton Henry and Mary Elizabeth (Broughton) L.; B.S. in Elec. Engring., U. Ky., 1944; m. Marietta Helton, Nov. 18, 1949; children—Milton Henry III, Marietta Lewis, Floyd Allen. Engr., Nat. Adv. Com. for Aeronautics, Langley Field, Va., 1944-47; with Ky. Utilities Co., Pineville, 1947—, mgr. mountain div., 1968—. Gen. chmn. Ky. Mountain Laurel Festival Assn., 1949, bd. dirs., 1968—. Chmn. Pineville Planning Commn., 1968—. Trustee Pineville Pub. Library; trustee, treas. Bell County Pub. Library Dist. Registered profl. engr., Ky. Mem. C. of C. 1971—. Republican. Baptist. Mason, Rotarian. Home: 208 Virginia Av Pineville KY 40977 Office: 120 Kentucky Av Pineville KY 40977

LEWIS, OREN RITTER, U.S. judge; b. Seymour, Ind., Oct. 7, 1902; s. John M. and Emma Anna (Crabb) L.; student Hanover (Ind.) Coll., 1920-23; LL.B., Nat. U., 1939; m. Grace Marguerite Wells, Aug. 12, 1925; children—Oren Ritter, Robert Wells. Admitted to Va. bar, 1939; practice in Arlington, 1939-60; U.S. dist. judge Eastern Dist. Va., 1960—. Mem. Am., Va. Arlington County (pres. 1951) bar assns., Va. State Bar, Phi Delta Theta, Sigma Nu Phi. Kiwanian (lt. gov. 1952). Clubs: Nat. Lawyers, Washington Golf and Country. Home: 3409 N Albemarle St Arlington VA 22207 Office: US Dist Ct Alexandria VA 22314

LEWIS, OSCAR SAMPLE, advt. exec.; b. Adel, Ga., Feb. 23, 1912; s. Falton Kemp and Mary Ellen (Sample) L.; student U. Fla., 1931, Ga. State Coll., 1952, Atlanta Law Sch., 1953; m. Irma Carol Hind, June 3, 1939; children—Linda Carol, Oscar S. Bookkeeper, Fla. Times Union, 1932-36; salesmgr. S.E. div. photo records div. Remington Rand, Inc., 1936-50; sec.-treas. Liller, Neal, Battle &Lindsey, Inc., 1950—. Active United Appeal. Bd. dirs. Annewakee Found. Served with AUS, 1942-43. Mem. Am. Marketing Assn., Atlanta Advt. Club. Mason (Shriner). Home: 2311 Waterton Ct Dunwoody GA 30338 Office: Life of Georgia Tower Atlanta GA 30308

LEWIS, PAUL KERMITH, JR., educator; b. Monticello, Ark., Jan. 24, 1931; s. Paul Kermith and May (Sullivant) L.; B.S. Okla. State U., 1953; M.S., U. Wis., 1955; Ph.D., 1958; m. Jessiemae Keyser, June 18, 1955; children—David, Juanita, Jeannette. Research asst. U. Wis., Madison, 1953-57, asst. prof. dept. animal sci. U. Ark., Fayetteville, 1957-62, asso. prof., 1962-68, prof., 1968—. Mem. Am. Soc. Animal Sci., Am. Meat Sci. Assn., Inst. Food Technologists, Ark. Acad. Sci., Am. Briquette and Agglomerate Assn. Home: Route 6 Fayetteville AR 72701

LEWIS, RICHARD HAYES, lawyer; b. Hopkinsville, Ky., Dec. 3, 1937; s. Fred T. and Nola (Hayes) L.; B.S., Murray State U., 1960; LL.B., U. Ky., 1965; m. Martha Jane Cunningham, June 24, 1961; children—Laura Elizabeth, Cynthia Jane, Katherine Hayes. Asst. city planner Ky. Dept. Commerce, Owenton, 1963; legal aide Ky. Dept. Labor, Frankfort, 1964; admitted to Ky. bar, 1965; practiced in Benton, 1965—; mem. firm Lovett and Lewis, 1965—. City atty., Benton, 1968-70; exec. dir. Benton Municipal Housing Commn., 1966-68; mem. Ky. Ho. of Reps., 1970—. Trustee, Marshall County Law Library; bd. dirs. Marshall County March of Dimes, Purchase Area Devel. Dist., Purchase Area Crime Council. pres. Epsilon Tau Sigma Chi House Corp., Inc., 1967—. Served to capt. AUS, 1960-62. Named outstanding freshman rep. Ky. Ho. of Reps., 1970. Mem. Am., Ky., Marshall County (pres. 1967) bar assns., C. of C. (dir. 1967-69, sec.-treas. 1968-69), Phi Alpha Delta. Democrat. Baptist. Club: Lions (pres. 1968-69). Home: Merrywood Dr Benton KY 42025 Office: 1114 Main St Benton KY 42025

LEWIS, ROBERT CLYDE, accountant; b. Marbury, Ala., Oct. 16, 1932; s. Joseph Clanton and Mary (Cook) L.; student Auburn U., 1955-57; B.S., U. Ala., 1958; m. Dorothy J. Goolsby, Nov. 25, 1954; children— Donald E., S. Yvonne, Ronald C., Richard K., Alan G., Deborah J. Accountant, Frank E. Donilon, Jr., C.P.A., Tuscumbia, Ala., 1958-69; partner Donilon & Lewis, C.P.A.'s, Tuscumbia, 1969—. Pres. Howell Graves Sch. P.T.A., 1963-64. Served with USAF, 1951-55. C.P.A., Ala. Mem. Am. Inst. C.P.A.'s (membership promotion com.), Ala. Soc. C.P.A.'s (mem. council 1970-71; membership com.). Methodist (treas. 1965-69, chmn. finance com. 1970—). Club: Civitan (sec. 1971-72, pres. 1972-73). Home: PO Box 405 Tuscumbia AL 35674 Office: PO Box 405 Tuscumbia AL 35674

LEWIS, SINCLAIR OSCAR, educator; b. Lamont, Miss., Feb. 12, 1930; s. Penny Oscar and Anna Lee (Johnson) L.; B.S., Tougaloo Coll., 1952; M.S. (Nat. Def. Edn. Act fellow), Purdue U., 1963; Ed.D., U. Ky., 1968; m. Eula P. Matthews, Aug. 3, 1968; children—Michael Dennis, Cheryl Lynn. Tchr., counselor Greenville (Miss.) Pub. Sch. System, 1952-65; asso. prof. psychology Ala. State U., 1965-71; prof. psychology, chmn. dept. guidance/counseling and pupil personnel services Jackson (Miss.) State Coll., 1971—. Dir. EPDA Counseling-Guidance Inst., 1969-70, EPDA Fellowship Project, 1970-71. Mem. community council N.A.A.C.P., Montgomery, Ala., 1970-71. Served with AUS, 1946-49. Teaching fellow U. Ky., 1966. Mem. Assn. for Humanistic Psychology, Am. Personnel and Guidance Assn., Am. Assn. U. Profs., Omega Psi Phi, Phi Delta Kappa. Mason. Home: 1081 Pecan Blvd Jackson MS 39209

LEWIS, STANLEY JOSEPH, record co. exec.; b. Shreveport, La., July 5, 1927; s. Frank L. and Lucille (Scalia) L.; grad. high sch.; m. Pauline Marie Taglivore, July 1, 1947; children—Leonard, Susan Marie. Owner, Stans Record Service, Shreveport, 1948—; pres. Su-Ma Pub. Co., Inc. (BMI), Jewel Record Co., Stan's Record Shop, Stan's Record Service of Fla., Inc., Stan's Record Service of Mo., Inc., Stan's Record Service of Okla., Inc., Stan's Record Service of Tenn., Inc., Shreve Advt. Corp., Lenny Pub. Co., Stans Record Service of La., Stans Record Service of Ark., Stans Record Service of Miss., Stans Record Service of Tex., Stans Record Rack Service, Paula Record Co., Ronn Record Co. K.C. Club: Progressive Men's (v.p.). Composer songs. Home: 219 Symphony Lane Shreveport LA 71105 Office: 728 Texas St Shreveport LA 71101

LEWIS, S(UNIE) MADGE, librarian; b. Abilene, Tex.; d. Wiley Everett and Flora (Andrews) Lewis; student Hardin-Simmons U., 1928-30, U. Okla., 1930-31, Tulane U., 1934-35; B.S., Central State Coll., Okla., 1933; M. Christian Tng., New Orleans Theol. Sem., 1942; B.D., Golden Gate Bapt. Theol. Sem., 1949; Th.M., 1950, Th.D., 1951; postgrad. San Francisco State Coll., 1953-55; A.M. in L.S., U. Mich., 1956. Children's librarian Carnegie Pub. Library, Guthrie, Okla., 1934; tchr. Kelton (Tex.) Ind. Sch., 1936-39; asso. missionary Haywood Bapt. Assn., Waynesville, N.C., 1942-45, Brushy Mountain Bapt. Assn., Wilkesboro, 1945-48; acting librarian Golden Gate Bapt. Theol. Sem. Berkeley, Cal., 1951-52, librarian, 1952-56, supr. readers and tech. services, 1956-57; asst. regional librarian Eastern Plains Regional Library, Clovis, N.M., 1958; regional librarian N.E. Regional Library, Cimarron, N.M., 1958-60; acting field librarian N.M. State Library Commn., Santa Fe, 1960; asst. librarian, instr. library sci. Mary Mardin-Baylor Coll., Belton, Tex., 1960-61, librarian, asso. prof. library sci., 1961—. Mem. N.E.A., A.L.A., Southwestern, Tex. library assns., Western Theol. Assn. (pres. 1956), Tex. Council Library Edn. (sec. 1963-65), Tex. Edn. Assn., Bell Fine Arts Assn., Kappa Pi. Home: Box 767 Belton TX 76513

LEWIS, T.E., business exec.; b. Oklahoma City, 1918; grad. Oklahoma City U., 1951, LL.B., 1955. Sec., v.p. TG & Y Stores, Inc., Oklahoma City, also dir. Home: 1209 NW 63d St Oklahoma City OK 73116 Office: PO Box 25967 Oklahoma City OK 73118*

LEWIS, WALTER WOODWARD, state ofcl.; b. Winnsboro, S.C., May 10, 1909; s. Thomas Walter and Mary Ellen (Street) L.; B.S. in Commerce, U. S.C., 1931; postgrad. LaSalle Extension U., 1936-37; m. Florrie Jane Bethea, June 19, 1935; children—Jane Bethea (Mrs. John McNair Turner), Thomas Woodward, Ellen Street (Mrs. Richard P. Fletcher). Clk., Circuit Ct., also register Mesne Conveyances for Fairfield County, Winnsboro, 1933-64; state tax commr. S.C., Columbia, 1964-67; commr. S.C. Alcoholic Beverage Control Commn., 1967—, chmn., 1969-70; judge probate, Fairfield County, 1939; owner, operator Adgerlan Plantation, nr. Winnsboro, 1943—; pres. Mid-County Water Co., 1969—. Treas., exec. sec. Fairfield County chpt. A.R.C., 1937-40; Mem. Nat. Found. for Infantile Paralysis, 1938—, chmn., 1950-53, 64-65. Del., Nat. Democratic Conv., Phila., 1936; sec.-treas. Fairfield County Dem. Exec. Com., 1954-56, chmn., 1956-67. Mem. Nat. Tax Assn. (del. 58th ann. conf. on taxation 1965), Nat., Southeastern (mem. policy com. 1965-67) assn. tax adminstrs., S.C., State Employees' Assn., Nat. Conf. Liquor Adminstrs., Am. Bible Soc. (life), S.C. Assn. Clks. and Registers (hon.), S.C. Assn. Clks. and Registars Mesne Conveyances (pres. 1958-59), Caroliniana Soc. U. S.C., Mt. Zion Soc. Winnsboro (sr. warden 1960—), Fairfield County Hist. Soc. (pres. 1966-67), Am., S.C. rose socs., Delta Sigma Pi. Methodist. Mason, Rotarian. Club: Winnsboro Cotillion. Home: RFD 2 Adgerlan Winnsboro SC 29180 Office: 1710 Gervais St Columbia SC 29202

LEWIS, WILLIAM HUBERT, author, govt. ofcl.; b. N.Y.C., June 4, 1928; s. John S. and Lillian (Rome) L.; student U. Ariz., 1947-48; B.A., George Washington U., 1951, M.A., 1953; postgrad. Johns Hopkins, 1953-54; Ph.D., Am. U., 1960; m. Kathleen Moran, Aug. 20, 1949. With dept. African affairs U.S. Dept. State, 1952-65; vis. prof. Middle Eastern and African studies U. Mich., 1965-66; div. dir. U.S. Dept. State, 1966-67; mem. policy planning staff Office Sec. of Def., Washington, 1967-70; dir. planning and analysis staff, bur. polit.-mil. affairs Dept. State, Washington, 1971—; asso. prof. Middle Eastern and African studies Georgetown and Am. Univs., 1960-69. Served as lt. AUS, 1950-52. Fellow African, Middle Eastern studies assns.; mem. Am. Polit. Sci. Assn. Author: New Forces in Africa, 1962; Modern Middle East, 1963; Emerging Africa, 1964; French-speaking Africa, 1966; Islam in Africa, 1969. Contbr. articles profl. jours. Home: 200 N Nash St Arlington VA 22209 Office: US Dept of State Washington DC

LEWIS, WILLIAM SEXTON, physician; b. Strong, Ark., Mar. 6, 1931; s. William Colvin and Mary Catherine (Hammonds) L.; student La. Poly. Inst., 1949-52; B.S., U. Ark., 1956, M.D., 1956; m. Mary Lynda McCuistion, June 26, 1954; children—John Taylor, Sarah Margaret. Intern, U. Ark. Med. Center, 1956-57, resident, 1957-60; fellow cardiology U. Ark., 1960-61; practice medicine, specializing in cardiology, Little Rock, 1961—; co-founder Little Rock Diagnostic Clinic, 1961—; mem. staffs Bapt. Med. Center, Little Rock, St. Vincent's Infirmary, Little Rock, Meml. Hosp., North Little Rock; co-dir., coronary care tng. of nurses Regional Med. Program, 1970—; co-dir. coronary care unit Bapt. Med. Center, Little Rock, 1970—, dir. cardiac lab., 1966—, chief medicine, 1972-73; asst. clin. prof. medicine U. Ark., 1964—; cons. VA Hosp., 1970—; dir. Profl. Underwriters Life Ins. Served with AUS, 1961-62. Mem. Am. (bd. dirs. 1971—, mem. heart Com. So. region 1967-71), Ark. (pres. 1968-71, mem. exec. com. 1970-71) heart assns., Alpha Omega Alpha. Home: 58 River Ridge Rd Little Rock AR 72205 Office: 900 N University St Little Rock AR 72207

LEY, HERBERT LEONARD, JR., food and drug cons.; b. Columbus, O., Sept. 7, 1923; s. Herbert Leonard and Laura (Spencer) L.; M.D., Harvard, 1946, M.P.H., 1951; m. Doris M. Schoenherr, 1965. Commd. 1st lt., M.C., U.S. Army, 1947, advanced through grades to lt. col., 1955; resigned, 1958, now col. Res.; prof. microbiology George Washington Sch. Medicine, 1958-61; civil service with U.S. Army Research Office, 1961-63; asso. prof. epidemiology and microbiology Harvard Sch. Pub. Health, 1963-68; dir. Bur. Medicine, FDA, 1966-68, commr. FDA, 1968-69; cons. to food and drug industry, 1969—. Decorated Bronze Star. Fellow Am. Coll. Preventive Medicine; mem. Am. Acad. Microbiology. Author sci. articles, contbr. med. texts. Home: 9209 Friars Rd Bethesda MD 20034

LHOTKA, JOHN FRANCIS, JR., educator, physician; b. Butte, Mont., May 13, 1921; s. John Francis and Mary (Backowske) L.; B.A., U. Mont. 1942; M.S. in anatomy, Northwestern U., 1948, M.B., 1949, M.D., 1951, Ph.D., 1953; m. Lois Katherine Clysdale, Sept. 21, 1951. Asst. in anatomy Northwestern U., 1947-50, Stain Commn. fellow summer 1953; asst. prof. anatomy U. Okla. Med. Sch., 1951-55, asso. prof. anatomy, 1955-69, prof. anatomical scis., 1969—. Active in numis. field, especially medieval coinage of Western Europe. Served to 1st lt. CWS, USAAF, 1942-46; PTO. Recipient 4 Health medals, Medal of Merit, Farran Zerbe award, also initial Newell award Am. Numis. Assn. Fellow Am., Royal, Swiss numis. socs., Asociacion Numismatica Espanola, Am. Geriatric Soc., Internat. Acad. Pathology, Royal Soc. Health; patron Am. Numis. Soc., 1962; mem. Am. Assn. Anatomists, Histochem. Soc., Am. Inst. Biol. Scis., Am. Soc. Zoology, Biol. Stain Commn., Soc. for Exptl. Biology and Medicine, Am. Chem. Soc., Archeol. Inst. Am., E. African Wildlife Soc., Nat. Audobon Soc., Wilderness Soc., Nat. Wildlife Fedn., N.Y. Acad. Scis., Co. Mi. Historians, Brit. Museum Soc., Orders and Medals Soc. Am., Midwest Orders and Medals Soc., Order St. Lazarus Jerusalem, Soc. for Promotion of Roman Studies, Sigma Xi, Phi Sigma. Club: Petroleum (Oklahoma City). Author monographs: Introduction to East Roman Coinage, 1957; Medieval Bacteates, 1958; Medieval French Feudal Coinage, 1966; (with P.K. Anderson) Survey of Medieval Iberian Coinages, 1963; also articles. Office: 801 NE 13TH St Oklahoma City OK 73104

LIBBEY, EDWIN BISSELL, educator; b. Bedford, O., Dec. 1, 1908; s. Vernon W. and Nina (Bissell) L.; A.B., Rollins Coll., 1933; A.M., John B. Stetson U., 1939; postgrad. U. Chgo., 1940-41, Okla. A. and M. Coll., 1952-53; m. Dolores Rohde, June 7, 1941; 1 son, Michael R. Tchr., Kissimmee (Fla.) High Sch., 1941-42; tchr. English, Culver (Ind.) Mil. Acad., 1942-46; tchr. humanities Stephens Coll., Columbia, Mo., 1946-49; prof. English and humanities Panhandle State Coll., Goodwell, Okla., 1949—, now chmn. dept. humanities and English. Pres., Goodwell Community Fund, 1964. Mem. Am. Assn. U. Profs. (past pres. Panhandle State Coll. chpt., sec. 1971-72; del. nat. conv. 1968), Nat. Council Tchrs. English, Internat. Reading Assn. (sec. High Plains council 1967-68), Okla. Edn. Assn. (Tchr. of Year citation 1970), Phi Delta Kappa. Methodist. Mason, Lion. Home: PO Box 52 Goodwell OK 73939

LIBEAU, CLAYTON PAYNE, govt. economist; b. Manassas, Va., Oct. 23, 1918; s. Donation and Fannie Byrd (Payne) L.; B.S., U. Md., 1941; M.S., U. Wis., 1949, Ph.D., 1952; m. Jean Reid, Dec. 1, 1945; 1 son, John Reid. Research asst. U. Wis., 1949; agrl. econs. researcher U. Ida., Moscow, 1950-52; asso. agrl. economist U. Neb., Lincoln, 1952-54; agrl. marketing specialist N.C. State U., Raleigh, 1954-59; prof. agrl. econs. U. Wis., 1959-61, N.C. State U., 1961-63; supervisory economist, program analyst U.S. Dept. Agr., Washington, 1963—. Tchr. U. Gadja Mada, Jogjakarkta, Indonisia, 1959-61; program analyst U.S. Forest Service, 1967—. Served with USNR, 1942-43, USMCR, 1943-45. Decorated D.F.C., Air medal with 2 gold stars; recipient indsl. fellowship U. Wis., 1947-49. Mem. Am. Econs. Assn., Am. Agrl. Econs. Assn., Am. Soc. Pub. Adminstrs., Assn. Pub. Program Analysts, Nat. Econs. Club, Alpha Gamma Rho. Clubs: U.S. Dept. Agrl. Toastmasters (treas. 1967-68), Taylor Hibbard (pres. 1971) (Washington). Home: 8312 Still Spring Court Bethesda MD 20034 Office: Room 4229 Forest Service 14th St and Independence SW Washington DC 20250

LICH, ROBERT, JR., educator, physician; b. Sutton, Neb., Feb. 8, 1909; s. Robert and Amalia (Scheidt) L.; A.B., U. Cal. at Berkeley, 1931; M.D., L.I. Coll. Medicine, 1936; M.S. in Pathology, U. Louisville, 1941; m. Edna Troutman, Sept. 24, 1941; children—Robert III, Jonathan Owsley, Nancy Claire; m. 2d, Vivian Martyne Roe, Apr. 1968. Intern John N. Norton Infirmary, Louisville, 1936-37; preceptor Dr. Owsley Grant, 1937-39; resident Louisville Gen. Hosp., 1939-41; pvt. practice, Louisville, 1946—; mem. active staff Louisville Gen., John N. Norton Meml. Infirmary hosps.; courtesy staff Ky. Bapt. St. Anthony, St. Joseph's Infirmary hosps.; cons. staff Children's Hosp.; cons. Meth. Evang., Jewish, VA hosps.; prof. urology, head dept. U. Louisville Sch. Medicine, 1948—. Served with USPHS, USCG, 1941-46. Diplomate Am. Bd. Urology. Mem. A.M.A., A.C.S., Am. Urology Assn., Ky. Surg. Soc., Central Surg. Assn., Am. Assn. Genito-Urinary Surgeons, Internat. Urol. Soc., Clin. Soc. Genito-Urinary Surgeons. Home: Eyry 9402 US Hwy 42 Prospect KY 40059 Office: Med Towers Bldg Louisville KY 40202

LICKLIDER, KAREN LEE, psychiat. counselor; b. Zanesville, O., May 16, 1935; d. LeRoy F. and Theresa (Sheppard) Licklider; B.A., U. Akron, 1957, M.A., 1961. Jr. exec. trainee A. Polsky Co., Akron, O., 1957-58; office mgr. U. Akron, 1958-61; counselor U. Colo., Boulder, 1961-64; dean women N.W. Mo. State Coll., Maryville, 1964-69; counselor State Dept. Vocational Rehab., Mental Health Unit, Orlando, Fla., 1969-71, Orange Meml. Hosp. Mental Health Center, Orlando, 1971—. Named Outstanding Faculty Woman N.W. Mo. State Coll., 1969. Mem. Am. Personnel and Guidance Assn., Am. Coll. Personnel Assn., Am. Assn. U. Women, Nat. (Mo. membership chmn. 1967-69), Mo. assns. women deans and counselors, Nat. Rehab. Assn., Nat. Assn. Social Workers, Nat. Rehab. Counselors' Assn., Embers. Club: Friendship (dir. 1969—). Home: 3610 Dagon St Orlando FL 32806 Office: Orange Meml Hosp Orlando FL 32802

LIDDELL, FRANK AUSTIN, JR., lawyer; b. Houston, Aug. 25, 1928; s. Frank Austin and Virginia (Roby) L.; B.S., Va. Mil. Inst., 1949; M.A., U. Tex., 1952; LL.B., U. Houston, 1958; m. Lise M. Putnam, Dec. 2, 1961; children—Lise A., Frank A. III, Robert Bruce. Research chemist Monsanto Co., Texas City, Tex., 1952-53; admitted to Tex. bar, 1958; practiced in Houston, 1958—; mem. firm Liddell Sapp, Zivley & Brown, 1964—. Dir. S.W. Chem. & Plastics Co., UGC Industries, South Tex. Bank, Houston. Served to 1st lt. USAF, 1953-55. Mem. Am. Bar Assn., Am. Judicature Soc., Am. Soc. for Oceanography, Am. Chem. Soc., A.A.A.S., Tex. Bar Assn., Kappa Sigma. Democrat. Methodist. Clubs: Houston, Houston Country. Home: 6050 Crab Orchard St Houston TX 77027 Office: Gulf Bldg Houston TX 77002

LIDDELL, JAMES LARRY, athletic pub. relations exec.; b. Shreveport, La., June 8, 1942; s. William Walker and Vina Belle (Patman) L.; B.A., Delta State Coll., 1964. Sports information dir. Delta State Coll., Cleveland, Miss., 1960-64; sports editor Clarksdale (Miss.) Press Register, 1964-68; asst. athletic publicity dir. U. Miss., 1968-71; asst. dir. pub. relations New Orleans Saints, 1971-72, dir. pub. relations, 1972—. Served with AUS, 1966. Mem. Nat. Sportscasters and Sportswriters Assn., Miss. Big Eight Conf. Writers Assn., Coll. Sports Information Dirs. Am., Am. Basketball Writers Assn., Coll. Baseball Writers Assn. Am., Profl. Football Writers Assn. Am., Am. Football Writers Assn. Baptist. Lion. Home: 6525 Park Manor Dr Metairie LA 70003

LIDDLE, JOHN ALLEN, banker; b. St. Louis, Nov. 23, 1927; s. Frank M. and Margaret H. (Noble) L.; student U. Tex., 1945-46, Butler U., 1948-49; B.S., Ind. U., 1950; m. Leonardine Smith, July 7, 1951; children—Peggy, John Lee, Suzi, Joan. Accountant Sprole's &Woodard, Fort Worth, 1951-55; with Citizens Nat. Bank, Abilene, Tex., 1955—, sr. v.p., trust officer, 1969—, also dir. Instr. finance and econs. Hardin Simmons U., 1956-58; instr. McMurry Coll., 1970-72. Pres. Abilene Estate Planning Council, 1962. Served with AUS, 1946-48. C.P.A., Tex. Mem. Abilene Soc. C.P.A.'s (pres. 1962). Home: 3126 S Willis St Abilene TX 79605 Office: Box 1251 Abilene TX 79604

LIEBERMAN, JETHRO K., lawyer; b. Washington, Oct. 23, 1943; B.A. cum laude, Yale, 1964; J.D. cum laude, Harvard, 1967. Admitted to N.Y. State bar, 1967, D.C. bar, 1968; since practiced in Washington. Served with USNR, 1968-71. Mem. Pi Sigma Alpha. Author: Court in Session, 1966; Understanding Our Constitution, 1967; Are Americans Extinct, 1968; The Tyranny of the Experts, 1970; Thinking Man in America, 1972. Address: 20 9th St SE Washington DC 20003*

LIEBMAN, SEYMOUR BERTRAM, historian, author, ret. lawyer; b. N.Y.C., Mar. 12, 1907; s. Henry and Fabbie (Abend) L.; LL.B., St. Lawrence U., 1929; M.A. magna cum laude, U. of Americas, 1963; m. Malvina Weiss, June 25, 1950; 1 son, Charles Seymour. Admitted to N.Y. bar, 1929, Fla. bar, 1950; pvt. practice law, N.Y.C., 1929-49, Miami Beach, 1950-60. Tchr., U. of Americas, 1962-66, Fla. Atlantic U., 1968, Miami Dade Jr. Coll., intermittently 1967-71; vis. lectr. at several Am. Univs., also in Eng., Mexico, and Israel; adj. research scholar Inst. Inter-Am. Affairs, U. Miami, 1971. Mem. nat. exec. com. Am. Profs. Peace in the Middle East, 1970—; mem. bar com. on communist tactics and objectives, 1956-70; mem. Com. on Inter-Am. Affairs, 1966-70; exec. com. Greater Miami Jewish Fedn., 1955-59. Bd. dirs. Miami Beach Taxpayers Assn., v.p., 1955-59. Recipient grants or fellowships Meml. Found. for Jewish Culture, 1967, Nat. Found Jewish Culture, 1971, Am. Philos. Soc., 1968, Henry E. Huntington Library, 1966. Mem. Am. Hist. Assn., Haklyut Soc. England, Jewish Hist. Soc. England, Am. Acad. Polit. and Social Sci., Miami Beach Bar Assn. (bd. dirs. 1957-59). Author: Guide to Jewish References in the Mexican Colonial Era, 1964; The Enlightened, 1967; The Jews in New Spain, 1970; The Inquisitors and Jews in the New World, 1972, The Great Auto de Fe of 1649, 1973. Contbr. articles to profl. pubs. Reviewer for Choices, 1969, Hispanic American Historical Review, 1971, Judaism, 1971, Jewish Social Studies, 1972, Jewish Floridian, 1967. Editor: Report Mid East, 1969. Address: 1408 S Bayshore Dr Miami FL 33131

LIEBMANN, SEYMOUR W., constrn. co. exec.; b. N.Y.C., Nov 1, 1928; s. Isidor W. and Etta (Waltzer) L.; B.S. in Mech. Engring., Clarkson Coll. Tech., 1948; grad. Indsl. Coll. Armed Forces, 1963, Command and Gen. Staff Coll., 1966, Army War Coll., 1971; m. Hinda Adam, Sept. 20, 1959; children—Peter Adam, David W. Area engr. constrn. div. E.I. DuPont de Nemours, & Co., Inc., 1952-54; constrn. planner Lummus Co., 1954-56; prin. mech. engr. Perini Corp., 1956-62; v.p. Boston Based Contractors, 1962-66; v.p. A.R. Abrams, Inc., Atlanta, 1967—. Mem. U.S.O. Council, Atlanta. Served to 1st lt. C.E., AUS, 1948-52; col. Res. Registered profl. engr., N.Y., Mass., Ga. Mem. Soc. First U.S. Inf., Res. Officers Assn. U.S. Nat., Ga. socs. profl. engrs., Soc. Am. Mil. Engrs., Engrs. Club Boston. Mason (32 deg., Shriner), Elk. Club: Civitan (Atlanta). Author: Military Engineer Field Notes, 1953‡

LIEDTKE, J. HUGH, natural resources co. exec.; b. Tulsa, 1922; grad. Amherst Coll., 1942, Harvard, 1943, U. Tex., 1947. Chmn., chief exec. officer Pennzoil United Co., Inc., Houston; dir. Penn Grade Assn., Capital Nat. Bank Houston. Mem. Emergency Adv. Com. for Natural Gas, Nat. Commn. on Materials Policy. Mem. Am. Petroleum Inst. (dir.), Nat. Petroleum Council, Tex. Mid-Continent Oil & Gas Assn. (dir.), Nat. Petroleum Refiners Assn. (dir.), Ind. Petroleum Assn. Am. (dir.) Address: Southwest Tower Houston TX 77002

LIESKE, H., clergyman, supt. schs. Supt. schs. So. dist. Luth. Ch., New Orleans. Address: 1425 N Broad St New Orleans LA 70122*

LIETZSEY, BARNEY BURR, ednl. adminstr.; b. Newberry, S.C., Aug. 2, 1903; s. Barney Burr and Hanna (Brown) L.; A.B., Newberry Coll., 1925; M.A., U. S.C., 1942; postgrad. Winthrop U., Furman U., Newberry Coll.; m. Marie Sease, June 9, 1926. Prin., Stoney Hill High Sch., Prosperity, S.C., 1925-26, Hartford Elementary Sch., Newberry, S.C., 1926-28, Harllee Sch., Florence, S.C., 1948-50, Florence Jr. High Sch., 1929-37; supt. schs., Saleme, S.C., 1928-29, Trenton, S.C., 1950-67; prin., asst. supt., supt. Florence County Schs., 1958-67; asst. supt. Florence Pub. Sch. Dist. 1, 1958-67; bus. mgr., 1958-67, supr. high sch., 1958-67, supr. vocational tng., 1958-67, supr. adult high sch. tng., 1958-67, supr. basic adult tng., 1958-61, supr. maintenance new sch. constrn., 1958-67; dir. Marion Mullins Vocational Center, Marion, S.C., 1967-72. Mem. Marion Bd. Health, 1941-67, chmn. bd., 1951-67; chmn. Marion City Easter Seals, 1971-72, chmn. Marion County, 1970-71. Bd. dirs. Tb. Assn., 1938—, pres., 1961-64; bd. dirs. Cancer Soc. Assn., 1961-67. Recipient honor award Florence County Edn. Assn.; recognition award Florence Sch. Dist. 1 Vocational Tchrs., 1967; hon. state farmers del. So. States Conf., 1957, 62, 67. Mem. Nat., S.C., Marion County edn. assns.; past mem. Nat. S.C. assns. secondary sch. prins.; S.C. Adminstrn. Assn., Nat., S.C. adult assns., S.C. Bus. Mgrs. Assn., Nat., S.C. vocational assns. Presbyn. (deacon 1939-52, elder 1952-72). Home: PO Box 695 Marion SC 29571 Office: PO Box 410 Marion SC 29571

LIFQUIST, ROSALIND CARIBELLE, ret. food economist, govt. ofcl.; b. Henning, Minn., June 5, 1903; d. John D. and Frances Myrtle (Wilcox) Lifquist; B.S. with high distinction (Caleb Dorr Scholar 1935), U. Minn., 1935, M.S., 1937; m. Milton H. Simon, May 25, 1927 (dec.). Tchr. home econs. pub. schs., Algoma, Gillette, and Shawano, Wis., 1921-26; dietetics intern U. Minn. Hosp., 1926, U. Wash., 1941; dietitian City Hosp., Lock Haven, Pa., 1926-33; instr. foods U. Minn., St. Paul, 1935-37; asst. prof. foods and nutrition Ia. State Coll., Ames, 1937-41; food economist Bur. Human Nutrition and Home Econs., U.S. Dept. Agr., Washington, 1946-55; consumer econs. specialist Agrl. Marketing Service, also Econ. Research Service, 1955-72. Served from lt. (j.g.) to lt. comdr. WAVES, 1942-46. Recipient certificate of merit U.S. Dept. Agr., 1961. Mem. Am. Home Econs. Assn. (nat. chmn. public relations com. 1958-61), Omicron Nu, Pi Lambda Theta, Phi Upsilon Omicron. Author several govt. publs. on food and food prices, also numerous articles. Home: 1727 Massachusetts Av NW Washington DC 20036

LIGGETT, ALEXANDER COVENTRY, mfg. co. exec.; b. Litchfield, Conn., June 12, 1908; s. Richard Hampden and Lura Moss (Ambler) L.; student, U. Va., 1927-29, 31-34; student, U. Grenoble, France, 1929-30; m. Priscilla W. Watson, Dec. 9, 1936; children—Alexander Winslow, Priscilla Winfield. Admitted to D.C. bar, 1934; practicing atty. Ct. of Claims tax div. Dept. of Justice, 1934-36; Washington rep. Berry & Stevens, 1937-39; pres. Celcure Wood Preserving Co., Jacksonville, Fla., 1949—, also dir.; v.p. Cook Lumber Co., Tampa, 1948—; v.p., dir. Ridge Lumber Co., Lakeland, Fla.; dir. First Nat. Bank Tampa, First Financial Corp. Fla. Pres., dir. Wilson House, Nat. Inst. Historic Preservation. Served as lt. comdr. USNR, World War II; ETO. Mem. S.A.R., Soc. Colonial Wars, Litchfield Hist. Soc. (pres.), Newcomen Soc. N. Am., St. Andrews Soc. Washington, English Speaking Union (dir.), Kappa Alpha. Episcopalian. Clubs: Metropolitan (Washington); Chevy Chase (Md.); University (Tampa, Fla.); Sanctum Country (Litchfield, Conn.); Knickerbocker (N.Y.C.). Home: Litchfield CT 06443 also 2339 Massachusetts Av NW Washington DC 20008 Office: care First Nat Bank Tampa FL 33602

LIGHTBOURNE, JAMES HORN, JR., clergyman; b. Dover, Del., Dec. 26, 1921; s. James Horn and Margaret (Benson) L.; B.A., Elon Coll., 1942, D.D., 1951; M.A., Brown U., 1947, B.D., Hartford Theol. Sem., 1950; m. Carolyn Anderson, Aug. 17, 1946; children—James Horn III, Ernest Anderson, Leslie Hope. Ordained to the ministry United Ch. Christ, 1950; pastor United Ch. of Christ, Holland, Va., 1950-57; supt. Southeast Conv. Conglist. Christian Chs., Atlanta, 1957-65; conf. minister So. Conf. United Ch. of Christ, Burlington, N.C., 1966—. Chmn. Alamanace County Human Relations Council, 1970—. Bd. dirs. Elon Coll., Elon Home for Children, United Ch. Retirement Home, Uplands Center, Frandklinton Center, United Ch. of Christ Stewardship Council. Served with USAAF, 1942-45. Mem. Ga. Council Chs. (pres. 1962-64), N.C. Council Chs. (pres. 1970—). Home: 2903 Amherst Av Burlington NC 27215 Office: PO Box 2410 Burlington NC 27215

LIGHTNER, ARDYCE LEAH STEVENS, educator; b. Leigh, Neb., July 21, 1932; d. John Wesley and Anna (Lueschen) Stevens; B.A., Wayne State Coll., 1952; M.A., Colo. State Coll. at Greeley, 1954, Ed.D., 1966; postgrad. U. S.D., 1958-59, Morehead (Ky.) State U., 1968-69; m. Jerry Preston Lightner, Sept. 13, 1953 (div. May, 1967); children—Jon Tracy, Jean Marie. Instr. Lyons (Neb.) High Sch., 1952-53; grad. asst. Colo. State Coll. at Greeley, 1953-54; instr. math. jr. high sch., Great Falls, Mont., 1962-64; asso. prof. Coll. Great Falls, 1964-67; asso. prof. Morehead State U., 1967-69; asso. prof. Radford (Va.) Coll., 1969—, chmn. dept. bus., 1969-71, mem. grad. council, 1969-70, chmn. undergrad. secondary edn. self-study, 1969-70. Area leader Am. Cancer Soc. drive, Great Falls, 63; co-sponsor Campfire Girls, Great Falls, 1966-67. Mem. Nat., So., Va. bus. edn. assns., Am. Assn. U. Profs., Am., Va. vocational assns., A.A.A.S. Republican. Methodist (tchr.). Contbr. articles profl. jours. Home: 30 Grandview Dr Radford VA 24141

LIGON, JAMES TEDDIE, educator; b. Easley, S.C., Feb. 20, 1936; s. Henry Grace and Gracia Viola (Carson) L.; B.S., Clemson U., 1957; M.S., Ia. State U., 1959, Ph.D. (NSF fellow), 1961; m. Martha Nelle Craig, June 11, 1958; children—Melissa Grace, James Mark, Polly Claire. Asst. prof. agrl. engring. U. Ky., Lexington, 1961-66; asso. prof. agrl. engring. dept. Clemson U., (S.C.), 1966-71, prof., 1971—. Mem. Am. Soc. Agrl. Engrs., Am. Soc. Engring. Edn., Am. Geophys. Union, Sigma Xi, Phi Kappa Phi, Tau Beta Pi, Gamma Sigma Delta. Baptist. Contbr. articles to profl. jours. Home: PO Box 272 Pendleton SC 29670 Office: Agrl Engring Clemson U Clemson SC 29631

LIGON, KATIE WILLIMAS (MRS. WOODIE C. LIGON), educator; b. Tallassee, Ala.; d. Robert Roland and Katie (Roper) Williams; B.S., Ala. A. and M. Coll., 1947; M.A., N.Y.U., 1953; m. Woodie C. Ligon, July 3, 1937. Tchr. Dallas County Tng. Sch., Selma, Ala., 1931-34, Lane Grammar Sch., Birmingham, Ala., 1935-36, Council Elementary Sch., 1936-52; chmn. guidance, adviser to girls Western High Sch., 1952-64; dean women Ala. A. and M. U., 1964-69, dean students, 1969—, v.p. for student affairs, 1970—. Adv. bd. N. Ala. chpt. Multiple Sclerosis Soc., Harris Home for Children, Madison County Assn. Mental Health. Mem. Nat. Assn. Women Deans and Counselors, Am. Personnel and Guidance Assn., Nat. Assn. Student Personnel Adminstrs., Ala. Tchrs. Assn., Alpha Kappa Delta, Alpha Kappa Alpha (regional pub. relations rep.). Methodist. Home: 56 18th Av S Birmingham AL 35205 Office: Ala A and M Univ PO Box 327 Normal AL 35762

LIGON, RONALD SANDERS, travel agy. exec.; b. Lebanon, Tenn., Jan. 6, 1937; s. H. Raymond and Lucille (Sanders) L.; student Vanderbilt U., 1956-58; m. Mary Francis Schmitt, Aug. 2, 1958; children— Ronald Sanders, John Jefferson, Mathew Courtney. Pres., Union Acceptance Corp., Nashville, 1957-62, Security Realty & Mortgage Corp., Nashville, 1958-62; pres. Christus Gardens, Gatlinburg, Tenn., 1959—; dir. Security Ins. Corp., Nashville, Harpeth Enterprises, Inc., Franklin, Tenn., Handy Hardware Co., Inc., Franklin, Woodlawn Constrn. Corp., Inc., Nashville, Volunteer Realty Corp., Ft. Lauderdale, Fla., Harpeth Nat. Bank, Franklin. Chmn. bd. dirs. Harpeth Acad., Franklin; bd. dirs. Monroe-Harding Children's Home, Nashville, Heritage Found., Tenn. Regional Med. Program. Mem. So. Highland Attractions Assn. (past pres.), Blue Ridge Pkwy. Assn. (past pres.), Discover Am. Travel Orgn. (chmn. U.S. Travel Barometer 1970—), Gatlinburg (past pres.), Williamson County (chmn. heritage com. 1971) chambers commerce, Kappa Sigma. Republican. Presbyn. (deacon). Kiwanian, Elk. Clubs: Carnton (Franklin), Elks, Keeneland, Franklin Men's Breakfast (past pres.), Middle Tenn. Pony (dir. 1971—). Home: Riverside Farm Route 2 Franklin TN 37064 Office: 204 3d Av Box 332 Franklin TN 37064

LIKAN, GUSTAV, artist, educator; b. Yugoslavia, 1912; student Munich (Germany) Art Acad., also in Paris, France, Rome, Italy and Amsterdam, Holland. Came to U.S., 1957. One-man exhbns. and group exhbns. in Zagreb and Split, Yugoslavia, also in Paris, Berlin, Germany, Vienna, Austria, other European capitols until 1948; one man exhbn. Kuenstlerhaus, Salzburg, Austria, 1948; exhibited group shows Galeries Georges Petit, Paris, 1932, Nat. Gallery, Oslo, Norway, 1938, Nat. Gallery, Stockholm, Sweden, 1938, Nat. Gallery, Goeteberg, Denmark, 1938, Nat. Mus., Vienna, Austria, 1941, Narodni Mus., Bratislava, 1942, U. Chgo., 1958, Merrill Chase Galleries, Chgo., 1965, 66; lived in Argentina, 1949-57; commd. for portraits and murals; prof., head dept. fine arts Chgo. Acad. Fine Art, 1960-67; instr. Laguna Gloria Mus. Art Sch., Austin, Tex., 1969—. Address: 3203 Shoal Creek Blvd Austin TX 78705*

LIKES, DAVID HENRY, educator, ret. air force officer; b. N.Y.C., Aug. 4, 1914; s. Sylvan Henry and Mamie (Leopold) L.; B.A., Johns Hopkins, 1936; postgrad. Harvard, 1938-39; M.A. (U. fellow), Georgetown U., 1948; Ph.D., 1949; m. Grace Ann McWilliams, Feb. 28, 1948 (dec. Dec. 1971); children—David McWilliams, Lawrence Andrew; m. 2d, Adeline Stuckey, July 15, 1972. Commd. 2d lt. USAF, 1941, advanced through grades to col., 1956; mem. U.S. Mil. North African Mission, Cairo, 1942, Hdqrs. USAF Middle East, 9th Air Force, Desert Air Task Force, 1942-43, Overlord Planning Staff, London, Eng., 1943-44, 1st Allied Airborne Army, 1944-45, Potsdam Conf., 1945; War Plans Div. HQ USAF, 1948-51, standing group NATO, 1951-52, U.S. mission to NATO, Paris, 1953-56, War Plans Div., 1956-58; dep. dir. Nat. Security Council Affairs, Office Sec. Def., 1958-59; faculty Nat. War Coll., 1959-61; mem. aero-space studies inst. Maxwell AFB, 1961-63; ret., 1963; asso. prof., chmn. dept. internat. studies Southwestern Coll. at Memphis, 1963—; research asso. Inst. Internat. Studies of U. S.C. Bd. dirs. Internat. Group Memphis. Decorated Legion of Merit, Bronze Star medal with oak leaf cluster. Ford Found. fellow Duke, 1967-68. Mem. Am. Polit. Sci. Assn., Middle East Studies Assn., Internat. Studies Assn., Inst. Naval Procs., Am. Acad. Polit. Sci., Air Force Assn., Ret. Officers Assn., English Speaking Union, Omicron Delta Kappa, Pi Sigma Alpha. Author: Guerilla Warfare, World War II, 1963. Editor: Organization of the Defense Department, 1963. Home: 2905 Fargo Rd Memphis TN 38128 Office: 2000 North Pkwy Memphis TN 38112

LILES, WOODIE ANDREW, judge; b. Andalusia, Ala., Mar. 19, 1922; s. Andrew Jackson and Era (Rogers) L.; A.B., U. Fla., 1950, J.D., 1953; m. Helen A. Pasquarelli, June 23, 1946; children—Cheryl Marie (Mrs. Hooker), Andrew Jay. Admitted to Fla. bar, 1953; practiced law Orlando, Fla., 1953, Plant City, Fla., 1953-65, Tampa, Fla., 1958-65; city atty., Zephyrhills, Fla., 1955; asst. atty. Hillsborough County (Fla.), 1956-58; mem. Fla. legislature, 1958-65; judge 2d Dist. Ct. of Appeal, Lakeland, Fla., 1965-—, chief judge, 1966-68. Instr. bus. law U. South Fla., Tampa. Chmn. interim com. on mental health retardation Fla. Legislature, 1963-65; mem. cts. task force Gov. Council on Criminal Justice, 1971-—; pres. Tampa area Mental Health Bd., 1971-—, Mental Health Assn. Hillsborough County, 1970-71. Pres. Fla. Young Dems., 1955-57. Bd. dirs. WEDU-TV, Tampa, 1968-—. Served with AUS, 1943-47. Decorated Purple Heart. Named to Hall of Fame, U. Fla.; recipient Good Govt. award Plant City Jaycees. Mem. Am. Judicature Soc., Am., Fla., Hillsborough County, Polk County bar assns., Greater East Hillsborough County C. of C. (past pres.), Blue Key, Am. Legion, Phi Delta Phi, Kappa Alpha. Methodist (tchr. Sunday sch.). Elk, Kiwanian. Home: 706 N Evers St Plant City FL 33566 Office: PO Box 327 Lakeland FL 33802

LILIENFIELD, LAWRENCE SPENCER, med. educator; b. Bkyn., May 5, 1927; s. Henry J. and Lee (Markman) L.; B.S., Villanova Coll., 1945; M.D., Georgetown U., 1949, M.S., 1954, Ph.D., 1956; m. Eleanor Marion Russ, Oct. 22, 1950; children—Jan, Adele, Lisa. Intern, Georgetown U. Hosp., Washington, 1949-50, asst. resident internal medicine, 1950-52-53; instr. dept. medicine Georgetown U., Sch. Medicine, 1955-58, asst. prof., 1958-61, asso. prof. depts. medicine and physiology and biophysics, 1961-64; asst. chief cardiovascular research lab. Georgetown U. Hosp., 1956-63, chmn. dept. physiology and biophysics, 1963-—, prof., 1964-—; vis. prof. Faculty Medicine, U. Saigon, 1965, Tel Aviv U., 1968. Cons., USPHS, 1964-—; mem. NRC-Nat. Acad. Sci., 1965-67. Asso., Com. on Internat. Exchange Persons, 1970-—. Served with USNR, 1944-46, USAF, 1950-52. Fellow A.C.P., A.A.A.S.; mem. A.M.A., Am. Heart Assn., Biophys. Soc., Am. Physiology Soc., Soc. Exptl. Biology and Medicine, Am. Soc. Clin. Investigation, Sigma Xi. Contbr. articles to profl. jours. Home: 6304 Maiden Lane Bethesda MD 20034 Office: 3900 Reservoir Rd NW Washington DC 20007

LILJENQUIST, L(ORENZO) BLAINE, assn. exec.; b. Salt Lake City, Apr. 5, 1912; s. Ezra L. and Mary M. (Wilcox) L.; B.S., U. Ida., 1938; J.D., George Washington U., 1959; m. Sophia Jean Liljenquist, June 1, 1938 (dec. Oct. 1963); children—John Eric, Blaine Lee, David F., Charles Steven, Thomas Richard, Kathryn P., Mark D.; m. 2d, Patricia L. Charters, July 31, 1964. Farmer, agrl. agt. U.S. Dept. Interior, United Pueblos Indian Agy., Albuquerque, 1938-40; agrl. economist Bur, Agrl. Econs., U.S. Dept, Agr., Amarillo, Tex., 1941, with personnel div., 1942-44; Washington rep. Western States Meat Packers Assn., Inc., Washington, 1946-58, v.p., 1958-61, pres., gen. mgr., 1961-70; chmn. Am. Taxpayers and Consumers Assn., Inc., 1970-—. Served to lt. USNR, 1944-46; PTO. Mem. Nat. Assn. Execs. Club, Am., Washington socs. assn. execs., Alpha Zeta. Rotarian. Clubs: 150, Capitol Hill. Mem. Ch. of Jesus Christ of Latter-day Saints (bishop 1951-—). Home: 1234 Meyer Ct McLean VA 22101 Office: 7777 Leesburg Pike Suite 308 Falls Church VA 22043

LILLARD, BILL J., supt. schs. City sch. supt., Oklahoma City. Office: Oklahoma City Bd Edn Oklahoma City OK 73101*

LILLARD, EUGENE PATTERSON, librarian; b. Bowie, Tex., Oct. 6, 1906; s. Orestes Eugene and Julia (Patterson) L.; B.A., Rice U., 1927; M.Ed., So. Meth. U., 1952; M.L.S., Tex. U., 1964. Tchr. Milby High Sch., Houston, 1928-30, Kaufman (Tex.) High Sch., 1930-31; Forney (Tex.) High Sch., 1934-36; mem. faculty Tex. Mil. Coll., Terrell, 1931-34, Edinburg Jr. Coll., 1934-52; prof. Pan Am. Coll., 1952-63; librarian U. Tex., Austin, 1964-—. Served with USAF, 1942-45. Home: 7802 Mullen St Austin TX 78757 Office: Academic Center U Tex Library Austin TX 78712

LILLARD, ROY GLENN, educator; b. Benton, Tenn., June 23, 1912; s. Abraham and Nora (Kimbrough) L.; A.B., Carson-Newman Coll., 1934; M.A., U. Tenn., 1936, postgrad., 1963-64. Asst. librarian Carson-Newman Coll., Jefferson City, Tenn., 1932-34, mem. adv. bd., 1948-—, dir. Off-Campus Sch., 1950-51; grad. asst. U. Tenn., Knoxville, 1935-36; tchr. pub. schs., Knoxville, 1936-43; adminstrv. officer TVA, Benton, Tenn., 1943-67; substitute tchr. Polk County High Sch., Benton, Tenn., 1950-60; instr. Am. history U. Tenn., Knoxville, 1954-55; instr. western civilization Tenn. Wesleyan Coll., Athens, 1961-62; instr. Lee Coll., Cleveland, Tenn., 1965-—; head social sci., bus. and edn. div. Cleveland State Coll., 1967-—. Mem. Am., Tenn., E. Tenn. (pres. 1966-69), So. Bapt., Tenn. Bapt. (chpt. pres. 1968-—), Polk County (past pres.) hist. assns., Orgn. Am. Historians, Am. Assn. for State and Local History, John Sevier Meml. Assn. (pres. 1969-—), Ft. Loudoun Assn., Tenn. Antiquities, Nina Diggers Philol. Assn., Ramsey House Assn. Phi Kappa Phi, Pi Omega Pi, Pi Sigma Alpha. Editor: Studies on Polk County History. Contbr. articles, book revs. to profl. jours. Home: Benton TX 37307 Office: Cleveland State Coll Cleveland TN 37311

LILLEY, HAROLD R., food co. exec.; b. Lumberton, N.C., 1912. Pres., chief operating officer Frito-Lay, Inc. Mason. Home: 5228 Tanbark Rd Dallas TX 75229 Office: Frito-Lay Tower Dallas TX 75235*

LILLIE, WILLIAM HENRY, JR., architect, ret. air force officer; b. Conneaut, O., July 16, 1917; s. William Henry and Kathryn (Green) L.; B.S., Miami U., Oxford, O., 1937-41; m. Janis Crall, July 23, 1942. Commd. 2d lt. U.S. Army Air Force, 1942, advanced through grades to col. U.S. Air Force, 1969; chief architect br. hdqrs., Washington, 1954-58; chief design, Spain, 1958-60; dir. constrn. 3d Air Force, U.K., 1960; chief family housing programs, Washington, 1969-70; base civil engr., Vietnam, 1970; chief civil engr. J-4 Office Joint Chiefs Staff, Washington, 1971; ret., 1971; Washington rep. Neuhaus & Taylor, architects, Houston. Architect F & Y Bldgs., Columbus, O., 1947-50. Decorated Air medal, Army Commendation medal, Air Force Commendation medal with 2 oak leaf clusters, Bronze Star, Legion Merit; recipient Harvey Hiestand design award Miami U., 1940. Mem. Soc. Mil. Engrs. (pres. chpt. 1969), A.I.A. (corporate), Delta Upsilon. Republican. Conglist. Home: 6717 Bulkley Rd Newington VA 22122 Office: Orgn Joint Chiefs of Staff J-4 The Pentagon Washington DC 22030

LILLIEFORS, HUBERT W., educator; b. Reading, Pa., June 14, 1928; s. Manfred and Mabel (Rickenbacher) L.; B.A., George Washington U., 1952. Ph.D., 1964; M.A., Mich. State U., 1953; m. Louise Kiernan, Nov. 14, 1953; children—James Dawson, William Hubert; m. 2d, Jeannette Andre, Aug. 12, 1972. Mathematician Harry Diamond Labs., Washington, 1953-54; sr. scientist Lockheed Missiles & Space Corp., Palo Alto, Cal., 1955-56; operations analyst Operations Evaluation Group, Arlington, Va., 1956-57; mathematician Applied Physics Labs., Silver Spring, Md., 1957-64; asso prof. statistics George Washington U., Washington, 1964-68, prof. statistics, 1968-—. Served with AUS, 1946-47. Mem. Am. Statis. Assn., Inst. Math. Statistics, Operations Research Soc. Home: 13914 Marianna Dr Rockville MD 20853 Office: Statistics Dept George Washington U Washington DC 20006

LILLIOTT, RICHARD WILLOUGHBY, JR., educator; b. Lyons, Ga., Aug. 17, 1912; s. Richard Willoughby and Cornelia (Long) L.; B.A., Rice Inst., 1935; M.A., Colo. U., 1938; m. Martha Bartels, Dec. 28, 1935; children—Richard Willoughby III, Lu Ann. Tchr. pub. schs., Houston, 1935-44; part-time instr. U. Houston, 1941-44, instr., 1944-45, asst. prof., 1945-47, asso. prof., chmn. dept. architecture, 1947-51, prof., chmn. dept., 1951-55, prof., dir. sch. architecture, 1955-59, prof., dean Coll. Architecture, 1959-67, prof., 1967-—. Mem. edn. com. Houston Mus. Fine Arts. Mem. C. of C. (community improvement com.), Assn. Collegiate Schs. Architecture, Phi Kappa Phi, Phi Eta Sigma. Episcopalian. Home: 6 S Wynden Dr Houston TX 77027

LILLY, EDWARD GUERRANT, JR., utility exec.; b. Lexington, Ky., Oct. 29, 1925; s. Edward Guerrant and Elisabeth (Frazer) L.; student U. Va., 1944; B.S., Davidson Coll., 1948; M.B.A., U. Pa., 1949; m. Nancy Cobb, Nov. 25, 1961; children—Penelope Read, Edward Guerrant III, Collier Cobb, Steven Clay. With Citizens & So. Nat. Bank Charleston, S.C., 1949-50; with Wachovia Bank & Trust Co., Durham, N.C., 1952-71, sr. v.p., 1960-71; sr. v.p. finance Carolina Power & Light Co., Raleigh, N.C., 1971-—, also dir. Wachovia Bank and Trust Co. N.A., Raleigh, Gen. Telephone Co. S.E. Served to ensign USNR, 1944-46, lt. 1950-52. Mem. Durham C. of C. (pres. 1968-69, dir. 1964-69). Home: 3728 Lassiter Mill Rd Raleigh NC 27609 Office: PO Box 1551 Raleigh NC 27602

LILLY, JOHN CUNNINGHAM, neurophysiologist, biophysicist; b. St. Paul, Jan. 6, 1915; s. Richard Coyle and Rachel (Cunningham) L.; B.Sc., Cal. Inst. Tech., 1938; student Dartmouth Med. Sch., 1938-40; M.D., U. Pa., 1942; m. Elisabeth Christine Bjerg, June 12, 1959; children—John Cunningham, Charles R., Pamela C., Cynthia R. O. Mem. faculty U. Pa., 1942-56, fellow in biophysicsits E. R. Johnson Found. of Med. Physics, 1942-46, asso., 1946-49, asst. prof. biophysics, 1949-52, asso. prof. med. physics, 1952-56, asso. prof. exptl. neurology dept. neurology and Grad. Sch. Medicine, 1952-56; chief cortical integration sect. Lab. of Neurophys., Nat. Inst. Mental Health, 1953-58; established Communication Research Inst., St. Thomas, V.I., 1959, Miami, Fla., 1960, chmn. bd. trustees, 1959-60, dir. inst., 1960-—; Hixon lectr. Cal. Inst. Tech., 1952; Mayo Found. lectr., 1952; Colloquim lectr. Harvard U., 1954; John Kershman Meml. lectr., 1961; lectr. to laity N.Y. Acad. Medicine, 1962; research prof. in medicine U. Miami Med. Sch., 1960; also lectr. numerous univs., learned socs. Condr. was research for com. on med. research OSRD-USAF, 1942-46 (effective service award 1945); fellowship bd. Nat. Inst. Mental Health, 1954-57; sci. adv. com. for grad. schs. NIH, 1954; bioscis. adv. panel Office Sci. Research, USAF Research and Devel. Command, 1958-61, sci. adv. bd., 1958-63. Recipient John Clark Research prize, 1943. Fellow A.A.A.S., N.Y. Acad. Scis.; mem. Am. Physiol. Soc. (steering com. on neurophysiology 1953-56). Am. Electroencephalographic Soc., I.E.E.E., Biophys. Soc. (charter), Acoustical Soc. Am., Internat. Brain Research Orgn., Aerospace Med. Assn., Washington Acad. Scis., Internat. Fedn. Med. Electronics, Am. Soc. Mammalogists. Assn. Research in Nervous and Mental Diseases, Optical Soc. Am., Soc. Exptl. Biology and Medicine, Sigma Xi, Alpha Mu, Pi Omega. Author: The Mind of the Dolphin, 1961; Man and Dolphin, 1962; Center of the Cyclone, 1971; also sci. papers pub. in jours. Co-author: The Dolphin in History, 1963. Also editor Psychosomatic Medicine, 1957. Address: 3670 Hibiscus St Miami FL 33133

LIMING, WILLIAM SINGLETON, coll. adminstr.; b. Toms River, N.J., Aug. 23, 1910; s. William Lewis and Esther (Singleton) L.; B.A., Bucknell U., 1933; m. Ruth Elizabeth Rohr, June 26, 1936; children—Ruth Gail (Mrs. David E. Ackroyd), Robert Geoffrey. Editor, Ocean County Sun, Toms River, N.J., 1934-36; editorial staff L.I. Daily Press, Jamaica, N.Y., 1936-42; mgr. sales promotion and publicity Met. Life Ins. Co., N.Y.C., 1945-64; v.p. for devel. Erskine Coll., Due West, S.C., 1964-70, instr. journalism, 1966-70; dir. deferred giving devel. dept. Furman U., Greenville, S.C., 1970-—. Mem. Abbeville County Rep. Exec. Com. Trustee Bucknell U., 1964-69. Served to lt. (j.g.) USNR, 1942-45. Recipient Distinguished Service award Bucknell U., 1960. Mem. Am. Coll. Pub. Relations Assn., Am. Assn. Indsl. Editors (pres. 1956-57), Profl. Indsl. Communications Assn. (pres. 1957-59), Bucknell U. Gen. Alumni Assn. (pres. 1962-63), Abeville County Devel. Bd., Tau Kappa Epsilon, Pi Delta Epsilon, Sigma Tau Delta. Associate Reform Presbyn. Rotarian. Club: Poinsett (Greenville, S.C.). Home: PO Box 379 Due West SC 29639 Office: Furman U Greenville SC 29613

LINAM, RONALD HAMPTON, profl. investor; b. Waco, Tex., Nov. 17, 1935; s. Raymond H. and Evelyn (Brooks) L.; B.B.A., Baylor U., 1958; B.S., So. Meth. U., 1961; m.2Georgia Heath, July 1, 1971; children—(by previous marriage) Daniel Kyle, Michael Ray. Dir. investments Transport Ins. Group, Dallas, 1961-70; cons. portfolio mgr., 1970-—; pres. Am. Commonwealth Devel. Corp., dir. Intermed Corp., cons. indsl. engr., 1958-—. Trustee Dallas Bapt. Coll. Mem. Am. Inst. Indsl. Engrs., Dallas Assn. Investment Analysts, Financial Analysts Fedn. Am. Home: Linam Ranch Route 1 Box 13A Krum TX 76249 Office: Adolphus Tower Dallas TX 75202

LINCOLN, GEORGE ARTHUR, army officer, educator, govt. ofcl.; b. Harbor Beach, Mich., July 20, 1907; s. Burr B. and Esther (Hoare) L.; student U. Wichita, 1924-25; B.S., U.S. Mil. Acad., 1929; B.A., M.A., Oxford U., 1932; LL.D. (honorary), U. Pitts., 1968; D. Engring. (hon.), Drexel U., 1972; m. Frederica Bellamy, August 19, 1936; children—Frederica Esther, Daniel Bellamy, Joyce LeFevre, Lorna Harriet. Commd. 2d lt., C.E., U.S. Army, 1929, advanced through grades to brig. gen., 1945, ret., 1969; instr. U.S. Mil. Acad. 1937-41; duty ETO, 1942-43; with Gen. Staff, War Dept., 1943-47; prof. social sci. U.S. Mil. Acad., 1947-69, head dept., 1954-69; dir. Office Emergency Preparedness, Wash., 1969-—; mem. Nat. Security Council, Cost of Living Council; chmn. Oil Policy Com. Mil. adviser to sec. of state, Paris Peace Conf., 1946; dep. to undersec. army, 1948-49; spl. asst. to sec. def., 1951-53; mem. U.S. delegation NATO, 1951-52; staff Pres. Committee to Study Military Assistance Program, 1958; spl. adviser, adminstr. AID, 1964-65. Decorated D.S.M. with oak leaf cluster, Legion of Merit with oak leaf cluster (U.S.); hon. comdr. Order Brit. Empire. Mem. Council Fgn. Relations, Soc. Am. Mil. Engrs., Assn. Am. Rhodes Scholars. Clubs: Army-Navy (Washington); Denver Country. Co-author: Background For Our War, 1942; Economics of National Security, 1954; International Politics, 1954; Dynamics of International Politics, 1962, rev. 1967. Author: Strategy of Minerals, International Realities, 1948. Home: 2828 Albemarle St Washington DC 20008

LIND, DON LESLIE, astronaut; b. Midvale, Utah, May 18, 1930; s. Leslie A. and Elizabeth C. (Whitmore) L.; B.S., U. Utah, 1953; Ph.D., U. Cal. at Berkeley, 1964; m. Kathleen Maughan, Apr. 1, 1955; children—Carol, David, Dawna, Douglas, Kimberly, Lisa. Commd. USN, 1954, advanced through grade to comdr., 1969; naval aviator, 1954-57; space physicist devel. plasma expts. Fields and Plasma br. Goddard Space Flight Center, Greenbelt, Md., 1964-66; astronaut NASA Manned Spacecraft Center, Houston, 1966-—. Mem. Am. Geophys. Union. Office: Code (CB) NASA Manned Spacecraft Center Houston TX 77058

LINDEMANN, LILLIAN CHAMBERS (MRS. BOHN CARL LINDEMANN), physician; b. N.Y.C., Nov. 14, 1922; d. Robert A. and Jean Boalt (Wheeler) Chambers; B.A., Sarah Lawrence Coll., 1944; M.D., Columbia, 1949; m. Bohn Carl Lindemann, Dec. 17, 1948; children—Robert C., A. Louise Laurence, Jean W., Lillian M., Charles S.W. Intern, U. Cal. Hosp., San Francisco, 1949-51; resident Med. Coll. Va., Richmond, 1953-54, 61-64, 64-66; chief maternal and child health Health Dept., City of Richmond, 1955-58; practice medicine, specializing in pediatrics, Richmond, 1958-61, in psychiatry, 1966-—; mem. staff Med. Coll. Va., Richmond Meml. Hosp., Grace Hosp.; instr. dept. pediatrics Med. Coll. Va., 1955-59, clin. instr., 1959-60, clin. asso., 1960, instr. dept. psychiatry, 1964-65, asso., 1965-66, asst. clin. prof., 1967-—. Diplomate Am. Bd. Pediatrics. Clubs: Willow Oaks Country; Deep Run Hunt (Manakin, Va.). Contbr. articles in field to profl. jours. Home: 4708 Cary St Rd Richmond VA 23226 Office: 2223 Monument Av Richmond VA 23220

LINDEMANN, MARCIA ANN RICE (MRS. CHARLES J. LINDEMANN), advt. exec.; b. Huntington, W.Va., Jan. 15, 1931; d. Lloyd Emerson and Beatrice (Odell) Rice; B.A. in English, U. N.C., 1951, M.A. in Comparative Linguistics, 1953; m. Charles J. Lindemann, Feb. 14, 1953; children—Kirstine, Anna Margrethe, Carla. Instr. English, Old Dominion U., 1953-58; copy dir. Atlantic Nat. Adv. Agy., Norfolk, Va., 1961; v.p., co-owner Matthews Advt. Agy. Inc., Norfolk, 1962-71; pres. Hampton Rds. Advt. Inc., 1971-—. Mem. bd., dir. pub. relations Tidewater Arts Council, 1961-—, founder Norfolk Arts Festival, 1961; mem. Norfolk Commn. Community Programming, 1969-—. Mem. Am. Assn. U. Women (dir.), Linguistic Soc. Am., Norfolk C. of C. (dir. women's div. 1967-—) Pub. Relations Soc. Am. Home: 5201 Studeley Av Norfolk VA 23508 Office: 610 W 25th St Norfolk VA 23517

LINDEMANN, OSCAR CURTIS, banker; b. Bartlett, Tex., July 19, 1922; s. Edwin E. and Tecla (Schawe) L.; B.B.A., U. Tex., 1947, M.B.A., 1948; m. Martha Menn, Mar. 19, 1944; children—Richard, Marianne, Carol Beth. Instr. banking and finance U. Tex., 1948-51; with Tex. Bank & Trust Co., Dallas, 1951-—, pres., 1965-—, chmn.; chief exec. officer, 1971-—, also dir., mem. exec. com.; dir. Redman Industries, Dallas, First Bank & Trust Co., Richardson, Tex. Mem. Circle Ten Boy Scout Found.; vice chmn. spl. gifts div. Dallas Baptist Coll. Devel. Fund; mem. Dallas Crime Commn.; sec. investment com. Am. Lutheran Ch., Mpls., 1960-—; mem. Central Bus. Dist. Assn.; pres. Dallas County Campaign Screening Com., 1969-70. Bd. dirs., treas. Dallas County chpt. A.R.C.; bd. dirs. Dallas County United Fund, Dallas Citizens Council, Dallas Assembly, Dallas Summer Musicals, Dallas Zool. Soc., Greater Dallas Council Chs.; trustee Southwestern Med. Found.; bd. devel. Presbyn. Hosp.; pres. Dallas Clearing House Assn., 1969; mem. adv. council U. Tex. Coll. Bus. Adminstrn. Found. Mem. Am., Tex. (v.p. adminstrv. council) bankers assns., Robert Morris Assos., U. Tex. Ex-students Assn. (exec. council), Dallas Zool. Soc. (dir.). Club: Salesmanship. Home: 7407 Malabar Lane Dallas TX 75230 Office: Texas Bank & Trust Co Dallas TX 75250

LINDENBAUM, SOL, govt. ofcl.; b. Lawrenceville, Ill., June 7, 1915; s. Louis and Hilda (Zelmanovitz) L.; A.B., U. Kan., 1936; LL.B., Harvard, 1939; m. Dorothy Wolk, Sept. 11, 1943; children—Joan Frances (Mrs. Michael M. Stern), David Sage. Admitted to Kan. bar, 1939; practiced in El Dorado, Kan., 1940-42; atty. Dept. Justice, Washington, 1946-—, exec. asst. to atty. gen., 1967-—. Mem. Adminstrv. Conf. U.S. Served with AUS, 1942-45. Mem. Phi Beta Kappa. Home: 9921 Pinehurst Av Fairfax VA 22030 Office: Dept Justice 10th and Pennsylvania Av Washington DC 20530

LINDER, CLARENCE H., assn. exec. Pres., Nat. Acad. Engring., Washington. Address: 2101 Constitution Av NW Washington DC 20418*

LINDER, ROBERT EUGENE, agrl. agt.; b. Samson, Ala., May 3, 1926; s. Irvin Vuron and Eula Mae (Owens) L.; B.S. in Agr., Auburn U., 1952, M. in Agr., 1967; m. Barbara Ann Northcutt, Dec. 20, 1953; children— Elaine, Annette, Victoria Jean. Pension counsellor Ala. Dept. of Pensions and Security, Geneva, 1954-60; extension farm agt. Coop. Extension Service, Auburn U., Andalusia, 1960-—. Treas., Andalusia (Ala.) Civitan Club, 1971-72. Served with AUS, 1952-53. Clubs: Andalusia Toastmaster (pres. 1971-72, v.p. 1970-71, sgt. at arms 1969-70). Home: 510 Chapman Andalusia AL 36420 Office: PO Box 519 Andalusia AL 36420

LINDLEY, CLYDE JOE, govt. ofcl.; b. Granite City, Ill., May 7, 1915; s. Clyde Clifford and Lillie Mary (Brady) L.; A.B., U. Mo., 1937; M.A., U. Ia., 1938; postgrad. U. Minn., 1938-41; m. Marie Williams, Dec. 23, 1940; children—Richard Williams, Suzanna (Mrs. Richard D. Summersgill). With VA, Washington, 1946-—, asso. dir. planning, dept. medicine and surgery, 1962-66, exec. sec., spl. med. adv. group, 1967-70, exec. sec., mental health and behavioral scis., 1971-—; sec.-treas. Am. Bd. Counseling Services, Washington, 1960-63, pres., 1963-66; asso. prof. psychology George Washington U., Washington, 1964-66. Served to maj. AUS, 1941-46. Mem. Am. Psychol. Assn., Am. Personnel and Guidance Assn., Nat. Vocational Guidance Assn. Editor: VA Cooperative Chemotheraphy Studies in Psychiatry, vols. 1-6, 1957-61. Home: 1608 Sanford Rd Silver Spring MD 20902 Office: 810 Vermont Av NW Washington DC 20420

LINDLEY, JOHN ELLIS, physician; b. Macon, Miss., Apr. 23, 1926; s. Ancil Levinson and Brancie Ann (Stuart) L.; student Miss. State U., 1943-44, student U. Miss., 1950; B.S., Harvard, 1952; M.D., Baylor U., 1953; m. Helen Marie Puffenbarger, Aug. 21, 1954; children— Mary Lisa, John Ellis II, Mark Andrew. Intern Jefferson Davis Hosp., Houston, 1952-53, resident, 1953-56; practice medicine, specializing in obstetrics, gynecology, Houston, 1956-57; staff obstetrician and gynecologist Jeff Anderson Meml., St. Joseph, Riley hosps., Meridian, Miss.; asst. instr. obstetrics, gynecology Baylor U., 1953-57, instr., 1956-57; asst. prof. obstetrics, gynecology U. Miss., 1957-58. Mem. exec. staff Gov. of Miss., 1960-72; mayor of Marion, Miss. Bd. dirs. Am. Cancer Soc., Lauderdale County, Miss., 1960-63; pres., bd. dirs. Jefferson Davis Acad. Served with USNR, 1944-46. Diplomate Am. Bd. Obstetrics and Gynecology. Fellow A.C.S., Am. Coll. Obstetrics and Gynecology, Central Assn. Obstetricians and Gynecologists; mem. Miss. Obstet. and Gynecol. Soc. (pres.-elect 1965), Am., Miss., So. med. assns., S.W. Postgrad., East Miss. (pres. 1963), Lauderdale County (pres. 1963) med. socs., Miss. Cattlemen's Assn., Sigma Chi. Democrat. Baptist. Contbr. articles to profl. jours.; inventor of Lindley Newborn Resuscitator. Home: Marion MS 39342 Office: 1410 20th Av Meridian MS 39301

LINDLY, JAMES CALVIN, banker; b. Abilene, Tex., Apr. 23, 1923; s. George Calvin and Mary Ellen (Hicks) L.; grad. Southwestern Grad. Sch. Banking, 1963; m. Aileen Faye Riley, July 19, 1945; children— James Riley, Lisa Jan. With First Nat. Bank, Tahoka, Tex., 1941-50; with Levelland State Bank (Tex.), 1956-—, cashier, 1960-—. Chmn. bd. Levelland Pub. Housing Authority. Served with USAAF, 1943-45. Mem. Levelland C. of C. (dir. 1971), Bank Adminstrn. Inst.

(chpt. dir. 1970—). Mem. Ch. of Christ. Kiwanian. Home: 121 Linda Lane Levelland TX 79336 Office: 824 Austin St Levelland TX 79336

LINDOW, LESTER WILLIAM, telecasters orgn. exec.; b. Milw., Apr. 11, 1913; B.A. in Journalism, U. Wis., 1934; m. Andree de Verdor, Dec. 7, 1946; 1 dau., Suzanne Helene. Asso. editor Advt. Almanac, Hearst Newspapers, N.Y.C., 1934-35; comml. dept. sta. WCAE, Pitts., 1935-36, nat. sales mgr., 1936-38, comml. mgr., asst. to the gen. mgr., 1938-40; sec., gen. mgr. WFBM, Inc., Indpls., 1940-42; gen. mgr. stas. WRNY and WRNY-FM, Rochester, N.Y., 1946-47; sec., gen. mgr. Trebit Corp. operators sta. WFDF, Flint, 1947-60, sec., dir., 1948-60, v.p., 1954-60; sec.-treas. Landsmore Corp., 1952-57, v.p., 1954-57; mem. exec. com. NBC Radio Affiliates, 1955-57, chmn. exec. com., 1956-57; exec. dir. Assn. Maximum Service Telecasters, Inc., 1957—, also dir. asst. sec.-treas.; v.p., dir. Grelin Broadcasting Inc., sta. WWRI, West Warwick, R.I., 1957-69, Radio Buffalo, Inc., sta. WWOL and WWOL-FM, Buffalo, 1959-62. Treas., dir. A.R.C., 1953-56, nat. fund vice chmn. for Mich., 1956-57. Served from 1st lt. to lt. col. AUS, 1942-46; apptd. to Gen. Staff Corps, War Dept., 1946-47; col. Res. ret. Mem. Mich. Assn. Broadcasters, Mich. Asso. Press Broadcasters' Assn. (dir.), Res. Officers Assn., Nat. Assn. Radio and TV Broadcasters (dir. AM radio com.), Radio Advt. Bur. (Mich. chmn.), Asso. Press Radio Programming Com. N.Y.C., Assn. Profl. Broadcasting Edn. (dir.) Asso. Press Radio and Television Assn. (v.p., dir.), TV Allocations Study Orgn. (alternate dir.). Union U. Wis. Alumni Assn., Broadcasters Club of Washington (pres. 1964-65, gov. 1959-61, chmn. bd. 1965-66), Internat. Radio and TV Soc., Radio-TV Pioneers Alpha Chi Rho, Sigma Delta Chi, Scabbard and Blade, Iron Cross, White Spades. Elk. Clubs: Flint Golf, Rotary (pres.) (Flint); Radio Executives (N.Y.C.); Nat. Press, Congressional Country, Internat. (Washington). Home: 4000 Massachusetts Av NW Washington DC 20016 Office: 1735 DeSales St NW Washington DC 20036

LINDQUIST, CLARENCE BERNHART, ednl. adminstr.; b. Superior, Wis., Dec. 21, 1913; s. Gust and Hannah (Berentson) L.; B.E., Wis. State U., 1937; M.Philosophy, U. Wis., 1939, Ph.D., 1941; m. Helen Jane Conroy, Dec. 29, 1941; children—Clarence Conroy, Thomas Ward, James Raymond, Robert Michael, Mary Lenore. Instr., U.S. Naval Acad., Annapolis, Md., 1941-42, asst. prof., 1945-46; faculty U. Minn., Duluth, adminstrv. asst. to provost, 1949-51, prof., head math. and engring., 1951-57; program and research adminstr. U.S. Office Edn., Washington, 1957—. Cons. Conf. Bd. Math. Scis. Served to lt. comdr. USNR, 1942-45. Mem. A.A.A.S., N.E.A., Am. Math. Soc., Nat. Council Tchrs. Math., Math. Assn. Am., Res. Officer Assn., Sigma Xi. Lutheran. Author: Mathematics in Colleges and Universities, 1965; Recent Trends in Soviet Scientific and Technical Education, 1964; Soviet Education Programs, 1960; Aspects of Undergraduate Training in the Mathematical Sciences, 1967; NDEA Fellowships for College Teaching, 1971. Home: 6008 Utah Av NW Washington DC 20015 Office: 400 Maryland Av SW Washington DC 20202

LINDQUIST, STUART WILLIAM, hotel chain exec.; b. Worcester, Mass., Dec. 3, 1930; s. Stuart Gustaf and Ida (Rajala) L.; B.S. in Food Mgmt., U. Mass., 1958; m. Audrey Humphriss, June 15, 1957; children— Keith, Brett, Heidi. With Sheraton Corp. Hotels, various locations, 1958—, resident mgr., Mpls., 1964-65, gen. mgr., St. Petersburg, Fla., 1966—. Mem. St. Petersburg Symphony Soc., 1967—, St. Petersburg Community Alliance, 1968—. Served with AUS, 1951-53. Mem. St. Petersburg Hotel and Motel Assn. (pres. 1969), St. Petersburg C. of C. (gov.), Sales Marketing Assn. Presbyn. Mason (Shriner). Home: 6800 34th St S St Petersburg FL 33733

LINDSAY, BRYAN EUGENE, educator; b. Bklyn., Sept. 19, 1931; s. Eugene Fenton and Evelyn (Moors) L.; B.A., Troy State Coll., 1956; M.A., George Peabody Sch. Tchrs., 1962, Ph.D., 1966; m. Mary Ray Moore, children—Eric Evan, Christy, Alyson, Tracey, Jason Moore. Choral, stage band dir. Choctawatchee High Sch., Shalimar, Fla., 1956-61; chmn. dept. humanities, dir. music Okaloosa-Walton Jr. Coll., Valparaiso, Fla., 1965-69; chmn. gen. studies humanities program, prof. humanities Eastern Ky. U., Richmond, 1969—. Mem. Specialist workshop for gifted and talented, Gifted Program Devel. Sect., Ill., Dept. Edn., 1970—. Served with USAF, 1951-54. N.D.E.A. fellow fine arts and humanities, 1961-64, NDEA Inst. fellow in counseling, guidance, 1960; recipient Composer's award A.S.C.A.P., 1964. Mem. A.S.C.A.P., Nat. Acad. Rec. Arts and Scis., Nat. Assn. Jazz Educators, Nat. Assn. Humanities Edn., Am. Film Inst., Ky. Music Educators Assn., Internat. Platform Assn., Ky. Poetry Soc., Music Educators Nat. Conf. Author more than 50 published poems; composer more than 50 compositions. Home: 500 Sherwood Circle Spartanburg SC 29302 Office: Box 381 Converse Coll Spartanburg SC 19301

LINDSAY, CHARLES SIDNEY, architect; b. Tucker, Ga., July 13, 1919; s. Paul Leonard and Gussie (Chewning) L.; B.S., Ga. Inst. Tech., 1942, B.S. in Architecture, 1942; m. Glenna Stubley, Dec. 14, 1946; children—Glenn, Leonard, Carolyn, Richard, Charles. Jr. architect TVA, Knoxville, 1942, 46; partner firm Lindsay & Maples, Knoxville, 1947—, pres., 1970-71. Dir. Cloverleaf Corp. Adviser Tenn. Arts Commn., 1969—; mem. Maryville (Tenn.) Bd. of Appeals, 1960—. Served to capt. USMCR, 1942-46. Decorated Bronze Star. Mem. A.I.A. (pres. East Tenn. chpt. 1963), Tenn. Soc. Architects (pres. 1964). Democrat. Methodist. Club: Green Meadow Country (pres. 1965) (Alcoa, Tenn.). Home: 1318 Young Av Maryville TN 37801 Office: 1301 Hannah St Knoxville TN 37901

LINDSAY, JOHN CALVIN, concrete products co. exec.; b. Oklahoma City, June 20, 1924; s. Murray Dual and Freda Christine (Nau) L.; student Okla. State U., 1943—; m. Syble Charline Piatt, Mar. 24, 1943; children—Carla (Mrs. Robt. Michael Barber), Calvin Glen, Cindy (Mrs. Griffin West Graham). Draftsman Harter Concrete Products, Inc., 1946-47, chief draftsman, 1947-65, prodn. mgr. 1965-69, div. mgr. 1969—; v.p. Heritage Concrete Products, Inc., Oklahoma City, 1971—. Served with USAAF, 1943-46. Decorated Air medal, D.F.C. Home: 1718 Oxford Way Oklahoma City OK 73120 Office: 1628 W Main Oklahoma City OK 73106

LINDSAY, JOSEPH LLOYD, III, dentist; b. Tulsa, Aug. 25, 1940; s. Joseph Lloyd, Jr. and Gennevive (Hollabaugh) L.; student U. Tenn., 1958-60, 61-64, D.D.S., 1964; student Millsaps Coll., Jackson, Miss., summers 1959-60; m. Sandra Faye Brown, June 12, 1963; children—Jeffery Scott, Christie Delane, Jennifer Lynn, Abby Kathleen. Individual practice dentistry, Slidell, La., 1967—; mem. staff Slidell Meml. Hosp. Adult adviser Com. United for Prevention of Illegal Drugs, 1970—; scoutmaster East Carolina council Boy Scouts Am., 1964-67, cubmaster, 1967-70; Ward 9 mem. St. Tammany Parish Sch. Bd., 1971—. Republican mem. Municipal Exec. Com., 1970-71, now mem. parish Exec. Rep. Com.; campaign mgr. Citizens for Nixon, Slidell, 1968; adult adviser Teenage Republicans, Slidell, 1969—. Served to lt. comdr. Dental Corps, USNR. Recipient Order of Arrow, 1957, Eagle Scout award Boy Scouts Am., 1955, Scouters Leadership and Tng. award, 1966, Green Band award, 1967; named Outstanding Young Man of Year, Jr. C. of C., 1969. Mem. Am., La. dental assns., Acad. Gen. Dentistry, Royal Soc. Health, Xi Psi Phi. Mem. Christian Ch. (deacon). Kiwanian (Kiwanian of Year 1971), Elk. Club: Slidell Country. Home: 152 Pinewood Dr Slidell LA 70458 Office: 401 Pontchastrain Dr Slidell LA 70458

LINDSELL, HAROLD, clergyman, educator, editor; b. N.Y.C., Dec. 22, 1913; s. Leonard Anthony and Ella Briggs (Harris) L.; B.S., Wheaton Coll., 1938; M.A., U. Cal., 1939, Ph.D., N.Y.U., 1942; D.D., Fuller Theol. Sem., 1964; m. Marion Joanne Bolinder, June 12, 1943; children—Judith Ann (Mrs. William C. Wood), Joanne Marjorie (Mrs. David Buffam), Nancy Jean (Mrs. Daniel Sharp), John Harold. Prof. hist., missions, registrar Columbia Bible Coll., 1942-44; ordained to ministry Baptist Ch., 1944; prof. missions, asso. prof. church history No. Bapt. Theol. Seminary, 1944-47; prof. Fuller Theol. Sem., 1947-51, registrar, 1947-50, dean, 1950-51, dean faculty, prof. missions, 1951-61, v.p., prof. missions, 1961-64; asso. editor Christianity Today, 1964-67, editor, 1968—; prof. of Bible, Wheaton Coll., 1967-68. Trustee Wheaton (Ill.) Coll., Westmont Coll.; chmn. bd. Gordon-Conwell Theol. Sem. Mem. Tournament of Roses, Nat. Assn. Biblical Instrs., Am. Hist. Assn., Am. Soc. Ch. History, Greater Washington Assn. Evangelicals (pres. 1966-67), Am. Acad. Polit. and Social Scis., Pi Gamma Mu, Pi Kappa Delta, Alpha Gamma Omega. Republican. Club: University (Wheaton, Ill.). Author: Abundantly Above, 1944; The Thing Appointed, 1949; A Christian Philosophy of Missions, 1949; Park Street Prophet, 1951; (with C. J. Woodbridge) Handbook of Christian Truth, 1953; Missionary Principles and Practice, 1955; The Morning Altar, 1956; Daily Bible Readings from the Revised Standard Version, 1957; Christianity and the Cults, 1963; Harper Study Bible (rev. standard version), 1964; When You Pray, 1969. Author articles. Editor: The Church's Worldwide Mission, 1966. Home: 1600 S Eads Arlington VA 22202 Office: Washington Bldg Washington DC 20005

LINDSEY, D. RUTH, corrective therapist, educator; b. Kingfisher, Okla., Oct. 26, 1926; d. Lewis H. and Kenyon (King) Lindsey; B.S., Okla. State U., 1948; M.S., U. Wis., 1954; P.E.D., Ind. U., 1965. Faculty health phys. edn. and recreation Okla. State U., 1948-50, 56—, Monticello Coll., Godfrey, Ill., 1951-54, DePauw U., 1954-56. Counselor, Camp Waldemar, Hunt, Tex., 1948-56; cons. Payne County Child Welfare Dept. and County Health Dept.; fencing cons. Olympic Devel. Com., 2d Nat. Inst. Girls and Women's Sports, 1965; Okla. liaison Nat. Task Force on Perceptual Motor Devel., 1969-70; dir. Workshop on Phys. Edn. for Mentally Retarded, 1967; mem. Gov.'s Phys. Fitness Council, 1966, 69. Bd. dirs. Payne County Sheltered Workshop. Recipient award Danforth Found., 1944. Mem. Amateur Fencers League Am., Nat. Fencing Coaches Assn. Am., Am. (nat. membership chmn.), Okla. (past v.p.) assns. health, phys. edn. and recreation, So., Nat. assns. phys. edn. for coll. Women, Okla. Bd. Women's Ofcls. (past chmn.), Am. Corrective Therapy Assn. Republican. Baptist. Author: (with Jones, Whitley) Body Mechanics, 1968; (with Corbin, Dowell, others) Concepts in Physical Education, 1970. Contbr. articles to profl. jours., mags. Home: 824 Ranch Dr Stillwater OK 74074 Office: Okla State U Stillwater OK 74074

LINDSEY, H. EDWARD, JR., oil well service co. exec.; b. Atlanta, Dec. 17, 1926; s. Hiram Edward D. and Carolyn (Spraggins) L.; B.S., Ga. Inst. Tech., 1948; m. Vangie Theis, Aug. 14, 1954; children—Kristin, Stephen C. Sales engr. Kobe, Inc., Huntington Park, Cal., 1948-50, Internat. Harvester Co., Chgo., 1950-52; pres., owner MWL Tool & Supply Co., Midland, Tex., 1952—; pres. Diamond Oil Well Drilling Co., Midland, 1961—, Helco Fishing Tools, Inc., 1969—, Bond-Coat, Inc., 1969—. Served with USNR, 1943-46. Mem. Soc. Petroleum Engrs., Am. Petroleum Inst. Baptist. Mason (Shriner), Rotarian. Clubs: Midland Petroleum, Midland Country. Home: 1611 Gulf St Midland TX 79701 Office: PO Drawer 631 Midland TX 79701

LINDSEY, HAROLD ARVIS, supt. schs.; b. Gentre, Ala., Apr. 26, 1917; s. William E. and Annie (Holmes) L.; B.S., Berry Coll., 1942; M.Ed., U. Ga., 1950, Ednl. Specialist, 1962; m. Myrtle Vay Davis, Dec. 17, 1947; children—Susan Ann, Elisa Kay. Prin., Rocky Ford (Ga.) Sch., 1943-44, Armuchee (Ga.) Sch., 1946-63; supt. Floyd County Schs., Rome, Ga., 1963—. Served with AUS, 1944-46. Mem. Ga., Floyd County, Nat. edn. assns., Ga. Sch. Supts. Assn., Nat. Library Assn., Nat. Health Assn. Baptist. Mason. Club: Ruritan. Home: Route 1 Armuchee GA 30105 Office: Courthouse Annex Rome GA 30161

LINDSEY, JAMES LESLIE, mining engr.; b. Hopkinsville, Ky., May 16, 1910; s. James Leslie and Mamie (Stone) L.; student pub. schs., Hopkinsville; m. Imogene Dunning, Nov. 18, 1934; children—Arkie Hank, James Philip. Mine supt. Nashville & W.Ky. Coal Cos., 1950-57; gen. supt. Chem. Coke Co., Dawson Springs, Ky., 1957-60; supt. Rialto Coal Co., Inc., Madisonville, Ky., 1963-69, receiver, 1970. Mem. Nortonville City Council, 1963-69; mem. Hopkins County Joint Planning Commn., 1967—. Mem. Ky. Mining Inst., Nat., Ky. (past treas.) socs. profl. engrs., Am. Congress on Surveying and Mapping. Mem. Disciples of Christ Ch. Mason (Shriner). Home: Route 1 Nortonville KY 42442

LINDSEY, REED STERLING, ednl. adminstr.; b. nr. Madisonville, Tex., Oct. 19, 1911; s. James Richard and Zue Ella (McDonald) L.; B.S., Sam Houston State U., 1933; M.A., George Peabody Coll., 1935; m. Frances Ann Smith, Aug. 28, 1938; children—Reed Sterling, John Dewitte, Patsy Ann. Instr. Sam Houston U., Huntsville, Tex., 1933-45, accountant, 1945-50, dean of adminstrn., registrar, 1950—. Dir. Huntsville Nat. Bank, 1960—. Chmn. Huntsville dist. Boy Scouts Am., 1941-44. Trustee Josey Scout Found., 1930—. Mem. Huntsville C. of C. (dir. 1942-45), Assn. Am. Registrars and Adminstrv. Officers, Assn. Tex. Registrars and Adminstrv. Officers, So. Assn. Registrars and Adminstrv. Officers, Kappa Delta Pi. Democrat. Methodist (bd. stewards 1955-60). Kiwanian (pres. 1944). Home: 1604 15th St Huntsville TX 77340

LINDSEY, THOMAS FRANCIS, dentist; b. Frederick, Md., Oct. 6, 1937; s. William Francis and Elizabeth Mae (Cramer) L.; B.A., George Washington U., 1959, M.A., 1964; D.D.S., Georgetown U., 1969; m. Eleanor Jane Hendricks, May 6, 1961; children—Sherrill, Melinda, Von Dubell, Hendricks. Tchr. pub. schs., Arlington County, Va., 1959-65; dir. instrn. Reading Dynamics of D.C., Inc., 1965-69; individual practice dentistry, Arlington, Va., 1969—; instr. No. Va. Community Coll. Dental Aux. Program, 1970—; instr. Georgetown U. Dental Sch., 1971—; pres. Ernest, Inc., 1969—; v.p. Lindsey Farms, Inc., 1965—. Adv. council No. Va. Community Coll. for Dental programs, 1971-72; adviser North Va. Dental Assts. Assn.; mem. Met. Dental Health Council, North VA. Dental Soc. Speakers Bur., 1970-72. Mem. Am., Va. dental assns., No. Va., Arlington County (co-chmn. dental health edn. com. 1970-72) dental socs., Phi Kappa Delta, Delta Tau Delta. Home: 7011 Ellen Av Falls Church VA 22042 Office: 5730 Washington Blvd Arlington VA 22205

LINDVEIT, EARL WAYNE, govt. ofcl.; b. Elmont, N.Y., June 6, 1926; s. Alfred and Julie (Jacobsen) L.; A.B., Bethany Coll., 1950; M.A., Am. U., 1954, Ph.D., 1958; m. Shella Rogers Brown, May 31, 1958; children—Kristin Hill, Eric Brown. Profl. staff U.S. Senate Space Com., Washington, 1959-61; regional mgr. def. systems div. Gen. Motors Corp., Washington, 1961-62; exec. sec. Com. on Sponsored Research, Am. Council on Edn., Washington, 1962-65; sr. scientist Battelle Meml. Inst., Washington, 1965-68; sr. research adminstr. U.S. Dept. Housing and Urban Devel., Washington, 1968—. Cons., Brookings Inst., Inst. for Def. Analyses, Pres.'s Com on Scientists and Engrs. Pres., Westmoreland Citizens Assn., 1970-72; mem. adv. council Aerospace Edn. Found, 1964-66; adv. bd. Washington Colloquium on Sci. and Soc., 1963-66. Served with USAAF, 1944-46. Fellow A.A.A.S.; mem. Acad. Polit. and Social Sci., Am. Polit. Sci. Assn., Am. Soc. for Pub. Adminstrn. Episcopalian. Author: Scientists in Government, 1960. Home: 2 Carvel Circle Washington DC 20016 Office: 451 7th St SW Washington DC 20410

LINEBACK, CHARLES LEON, ret. city ofcl.; b. Cin., Oct. 5, 1908; s. Charles Lineback and Jessie (Pearson) L.; student U. Tenn., 1929-31; m. Ethel Fay Madron, Feb. 18, 1928; children—Charles Leon, Robert Edwin. Dir. pub. safety City of Kingsport, Tenn., 1932-41; spl. agt. FBI, Savannah, Ga., 1942; city mgr., Nevada, Mo., 1946-47, Gainesville, Ga., 1947-49, Statesville, N.C., 1949-55, Salisbury, N.C., 1955-71. Pres. N.C. Civil Def. Assn., 1961—. Bd. dirs. N.C. Local Govtl. Pension System, 1960—. Served with USAAF, 1927-28. Mem. N.C. City Mgrs. Assn. (past pres.), East Tenn. Peace Officers Assn. (organizer, past pres.), N.C. League Municipalities (pres. 1963), Internat. City Mgmt. Assn. (life). Democrat. Methodist. Mason, Rotarian (past pres. Statesville, pres. Salisbury 1964; hon.). Home: 2009 Yost Av Salisbury NC 28144

LINEBARGER, LEON WELSEY, oil co. exec.; b. Cape Girardeau, Mo., Mar. 15, 1923; s. Emery S. and Mable (Sauer) L.; student S.E. Mo. State Coll., 1940-42; B.S. in Commerce and Finance, St. Louis U., 1948; m. Wilma P. Braschler, Jan. 4, 1942; children—Derek Kent, Brian Craig. Auditor, S. D. Liedesdorf & Co., C.P.A.'s, 1948-49; accountant, office mgr. Shell Oil Co., 1949-56; asst. mgr. finance Intercol, Cartagena, Colombia, subsidiary Standard Oil Co. N.J., 1956-58; controller Commonwealth Oil Refining Co., Inc., Ponce, P.R., 1958—. Pres. adv. bd. Ponce Salvation Army, 1965—, Caribbean Sch., Ponce, 1962. Served with USAAF, 1943-46. Named Boss of Year, Ponce chpt. Nat. Secretaries Assn., 1964. Mem. Financial Execs. Inst. Lion. Clubs: Ponce Country (pres. 1965-67), Exchange (Ponce). Home: Calle H 525 La Rambla Ponce PR 00731 Office: PO Box 1406 Ponce PR 00731

LINFORD, VELMA, educator, govt. ofcl.; b. Afton, Wyo., May 30, 1907; d. John A. and Elizabeth (Rowland) Linford; A.B., U. Wyo., 1930, M.A., 1935; postgrad. Denver U., 1939, U. Cal. at Berkeley, summers 1940-41. Tchr. Star Valley High Sch., Afton, Wyo., 1930-33, Laramie High Sch., 1935-45, 46-54; instr. U. Wyo., 1945-46; state supt. pub. instrn. Wyo., 1955-63; ednl. cons. U.S. Dept. Agr., 1964-65; spl. asst. to asso. dir. VISTA; ACTION, Washington, 1965—, acting dir. confs., 1966—. Dir. lay edn. Wyo. div. Am. Cancer Soc., 1946-63; ednl. cons. Dept. Def. Mem. Wyo. Youth Council, 1955—, Provisional Council Adult Edn., 1955—, Gov.'s Com. on Mental Health, 1955—, Gov.'s Com. on Problems of Aged, 1956—. Recipient bronze award for distinguished service Am. Cancer Soc., Wyo. div., 1955, Distinguished Service award to Wyo. edn., 1962. Mem. Nat. (dir. 1949-61, mem. exec. com., 1953-57, pres. dept. rural edn. 1958-59), Wyo. (exec. com. 1949—) edn. assns., Nat. Thespians (dir. 1947-55), ANTA, Wyo. Hist. Soc., Presswomen Wyo. (v.p. 1952), Wyo. Assn. U. Women, Westerners, Delta Kappa Gamma, Theta Alpha Phi. Club: Women's. Author: Wyoming Frontier State, 1947. Home: 3114 Wisconsin St Washington DC 20016 Office: 19th and M Sts Washington DC 20506

LING, JAMES J, electronics co. exec.; b. Hugo, Okla.; s. Henry William and Mary (Jones) L.; ed. St. John's Coll. Prep. Sch., Shreveport, La.) Pres. Ling Electric Co.; pres., chmn. bd., dir. Ling-Temco Electronics, Dallas; chmn. bd., chief exec. officer Ling-Altec Electronics, Dallas, Ling-Temco-Vought, Inc., Dallas; dir. 1st Nat. Bank, Dallas, Dallas Cowboys Football Club. Bd. dirs. Dallas Community Chest, Dallas Symphony Orch., S.W. Center for Advanced Studies; trustee, tech. adv. com. So. Meth. U. Found. for Sci. and Engring.; vice chmn., dir. Dallas Civic Opera Assn.; bd. dirs., mem. chpt. plan com. United Fund Dallas County; dir., mem. council Cotton Bowl Council; trustee St. Mark's Sch. Tex.; mem. adv. council Engring. Found., U. Tex. Served with USNR, World War II; PTO. Mem. Hudson Inst. Home: 10300 Gaywood Rd Dallas TX 75229 Office: PO Box 5003 Dallas TX 75222

LING, JAMES THOMAS, mfg. co. exec.; b. Dallas, May 21, 1944; s. James Joseph and Dorothy (Hill) L.; student So. Meth. U., 1962-63, N. Tex. State U., 1964, N.Y. Inst. Finance, 1965; m. Patricia Francis Looney, Sept. 3, 1971; 1 son, James Joseph. Vice pres. Ling & Co., Inc. (name now LCI, Inc.), Dallas, 1964-70, sec., 1966—, also dir.; adminstrv. asst. to sec. Omega-Alpha, Inc., Dallas, 1971—. Mem. Nat. Guard Assn. Tex. Club: Brook Hollow Golf. Office: PO Box 50046 Dallas TX 75250

LING, SUILIN, mgmt. cons.; b. Shanghai, China, Oct. 13, 1930; s. Chunchen and Maisan (Dunn) L.; came to U.S., 1949, naturalized, 1963; B.S., U. Mich., 1952; Ph.D., Columbia, 1961; m. Avril Marjorie Kathleen Button, Apr. 4, 1964; children—Christopher Charles, Charmian Avril. Mech. engr. Ebasco Services, Inc., 1953-54; with research div. Foster Wheeler Corp., 1954-64; mgmt. cons. The Emerson Cons., Inc., 1964-65; sr. economist Communications Satellite Corp., 1965-67; asst. dir. econ. and mgmt. planning Northrop-Page Communications Engrs., Inc., 1967-69, chief economist, 1969-70; dir., chief economist Teleconsult Inc., Washington, 1970—; lectr. econs. Bernard M. Baruch Sch. Bus. and Pub. Adminstrn., City Coll. N.Y. Mem. Am. Mgmt. Assn., Am. Econ. Assn., Am. Soc. M.E., Am. Acad. Polit. and Social Sci. Author: Economies of Scale in the Steam-Electric Power Generating Industry, 1964. Home: 2401 Calvert St NW Washington DC 20008 Office: 2814 Pennsylvania Av NW Washington DC 20007

LINGAFELT, CHARLES RICHARD, telephone co. exec.; b. Gretna, Va., Sept. 19, 1934; s. Charles Edwin and Essie Jeanette (Walker) L.; student Danville Tech. Inst., 1954; m. Glenna Tillotson, Aug. 14, 1955; children—Steven, Phillip. With Piedmont Broadcasting Corp., 1953-56, Central Va. Broadcasting Corp., 1956-64; plant supt. Peoples Mut. Telephone Co., Gretna, Va., 1964—. Mem. Gretna Vol. Fire Dept. 1959—, 2d lt., 1965—. Baptist (deacon, supt. Sunday sch.) Home: PO Box 38 Gretna VA 24557 Office: PO Box 367 Gretna VA 24557

LINK, ACREE SHREVE, dentist; b. Danville, Va., Mar. 20, 1925; s. Oscar Nathaniel and Lillie May (Shreve) L.; student Va. Poly. Inst., 1946-47; B.S., U. Richmond, 1950; D.D.S., Med. Coll. Va., 1954; m. Barbara DeHardit, Dec. 20, 1952; children—Teresa Joan, Acree Shreve, Michael Joseph. Individual practice dentistry, Newport News, Va., 1954—; mem. staff Riverside Hosp. Bd. dirs. Peninsula United Fund, 1956-59, bd. advs. Mary Immaculate Hosp., 1958-60. Served with AUS, 1943-46. Mem. Am., Va., Peninsula dental assns., Acad. Gen. Dentistry, Omicron Kappa Upsilon, Beta Beta Beta, Phi Kappa Sigma, Psi Omega. Roman Catholic. Club: James River Country. Home: 1201 Mallicotte Lane Newport News VA 23606 Office: 9296 Warwick Blvd Newport News VA 23607

LINK, GEORGE FRANK, petroleum co. exec.; b. Laredo, Tex., Nov. 12, 1913; s. Valentine and Elsie (Distelzweig) L.; grad. high sch.; m. Virginia Rives, Sept. 15, 1936; children—George, Michael, Elizabeth, James, Catherine. Store mgr. Montgomery Ward & Co., 1935-39; export, dist. mgr. Anchor Petroleum Co., 1939-50; pres. Link Petroleum Co., Laredo, 1953-68, Lifco, Inc., 1954-62, Chem. Splty. Co., 1958-62, Equipment Maintenance Co., 1958-62, Porter Oil, Liquid Petroleum Gas Co., McAllen, Tex., 1963-70; asst. v.p. Costal States Gas Producing Co., 1968—; dir. Pan-Tex Hotel Corp. Mem. small bus. adv. council Small Bus. Adminstrn., 1966-67. Mem. Tex. Butane Dealers Assn. (dir. 1954). Home: Star Route Box 34 Laredo TX 78040 Office: 1405 Guadalupe St Laredo TX 78040

LINK, JOSEPH FRANCIS, dentist; b. Dubuque, Ia., Jan. 9, 1917; s. Nicholas John and Martha (McCullough) L.; student Loras Coll., 1934-35; D.D.S., Coll. Dentistry, State U. Ia., 1939; postgrad. Old Dominion U., 1970-71; m. June Roslyn Murray; 6 children. Individual practice dentistry, Dubuque, 1939-41; commd. lt. (j.g.) U.S. Navy, 1941, advancing through grades to capt., 1955; chief dental service, dental officer U.S.S. Repose, 1947-48; chief dental service Naval Hosp., Camp Lejeune, N.C., 1960-62; chief dental service, cons. instr. dental residency tng. program oral surgery Naval Hosp., Great Lakes, Ill., 1962-67; exec. officer Naval Dental Clinic, Norfolk, Va., from 1967; now instr. dental hygiene old Dominion U.; Norfolk; lectr. in field. Diplomate Am. Bd. Oral Surgery (recipient Meritorious Service medal 1971). Fellow Am. Coll. Dentists; mem. Am. Dental Assn., Am. Soc. Oral Surgeons, Am. Dental Soc. Anesthesiology, Inc., Am. Coll. Dentists, Pierre Fauchard Acad., Internat. Assn. Oral Surgeons. K.C. Club: Ryan (pres. 1971—) (Tidewater, Va.). Contbr. articles to profl. jours. Home: 1003 Hanover Av Norfolk VA 23508 Office: Old Dominion U Norfolk VA 23508

LINK, S. GORDDEN, educator, author; b. Chgo., Apr. 9, 1907; s. Joseph S. and Florence (Tannenholtz) L.; B.S., N.Y.U., 1929, A.M., 1930; M.Ed., Harvard, 1932; Ph.D., George Peabody Coll. for Tchrs., 1938; postgrad. Yale, 1931, Columbia U., 1935, George Washington U., 1956, Washington Sch. of Psychiatry, 1958; m. Dr. Mae Mills, Jan 11, 1936. Prof., Limestone Coll., 1930-34; vis. prof. Northeastern U., 1932-33; lectr. George Peabody Coll. for Tchrs., 1934-38; asst. pastor McKendree Meth. Ch., Nashville, 1937-38; prof., chaplain Oglethorpe U., 1938-39; vis. prof. St. Lawrence U., 1939-40; dir. tng., personnel Microstat Corp., 1941-42; dir. writing workshop, McCoy Coll., Johns Hopkins U., 1947-51; cons. office Chief of Staff, U.S. Army, 1948-49; dir. Washington Counseling Center, 1949-61; chmn. div. humanities Anne Arundel Community Coll., Severna Park, Md., 1962-64, prof. English, poet in residence, 1962-66; dir. liberal arts Southeastern U., Washington, 1966-71; professorial lectr. grad. div. Loyola Coll., Balt., 1962-64. Exec. dir. Orgn. Advancement Coll. Teaching, 1964—; pres. Center for Advanced Studies, Amos R. Koontz Meml. Found., Dellbrook campus, Riverton, Va.; writer in residence Shenandoah Coll. and Conservatory Music, 1971—; dir. Dellbrook-Shenandoah Coll. Writers' Conf., 1969—. Trustee Amos R. Koontz Meml. Found. Chmn. Univ. Press Fund. Served from 2d lt. to lt. col. M.I. AUS, 1942-47; lt. col. Res. ret. Decorated Army Commendation medal with Oak Leaf Cluster, Bronze Star (U.S.), Army-Navy Air Force medal, first class (China), Spl. Breast Order Yun Hui with Rosette, Breast Order Pau Tang with Rosette (China). Fellow Am. Assn. Social Psychiatry (Merrill Moore award 1960); mem. Latin Am. Inst. Washington (past pres.), Poetry Soc. Am. (Lola Ridge award, 1948, James Joyce award 1971), Poetry Soc. Va., Baker St. Irregulars, Mil. Order World Wars, Res. Officers Assn. (past v.p. for army, past chaplain D.C. dept.). Republican. Methodist. Author: One Small Unwilling Captain: A Study of the Japanese Mind, 1937, The German Prisoner of War, 1944, The Engineers in the Pacific, 1947; Pocket Guide to Germany, 1951, Three Poems for Now, 1953. Contbr. to poetry anthologies. Home: Dellbrook Riverton VA 22651 Office: Center for Advanced Studies Dellbrook Campus Riverton VA 22651 also 1010 Vermont Av NW Washington DC 20005

LINNENBERG, CLEM CHARLES, JR., economist; b. Houston, May 20, 1912; s. Clem Charles and Maggie (White) L.; student So. Meth. U., 1930; B.A., M.A., U. Tex., 1933; Ph.D., Yale, 1941; postgrad. Am. U., 1954; m. Marianne Sakmann, Aug. 15, 1942. Economist, Dept. Labor, 1934-35, Social Security Bd., 1936, antitrust div. Dept. Justice, 1938-39, Bur. Budget, 1939-51; program planning officer Office Sec. Commerce, 1951-53; chief econ. analysis sect. Office Internat. Trade, Dept. Commerce, 1953; transp. economist Gen. Services Adminstrn., 1953-54, Dept. Agr., 1954-59; chief div. statistics and studies Office Vocational Rehab., Dept. Health, Edn. and Welfare, 1959-62; economist USPHS, 1962-69; ind. cons. in econs. and statistics, 1969—. Lectr. in transp. Georgetown U., 1956-57. Mem. Am. Pub. Health Assn., Phi Beta Kappa, Pi Sigma Alpha, Sigma Delta Pi. Democrat. Methodist. Author: Twixt Chaos and Conformism, 1950; The Agricultural Exemptions in Interstate Trucking: Mend Them or End Them, 1960; Economics in Program Planning for Health, 1966; Organizing and Staffing for the Program Planning Function, 1967; other monographs. Home and office: 3812 Benton St NW Washington DC 20007

LINOWITZ, SOL MYRON, lawyer; b. Trenton, N.J., Dec. 7, 1913; s. Joseph and Rose (Oglenskye) L.; A.B., Hamilton Coll., 1935; J.D., Cornell U., 1938; LL.D., Allegheny Coll., Amhurst U., Bucknell U., Colgate U., Ithaca Coll., Oberlin U., St. John Fisher Coll., St. Lawrence U., Washington U., St. Louis, Marietta Coll., Notre Dame U., Roosevelt U., U. Mich.; L.H.D., Am. U., Yeshiva U.; m. Evelyn Zimmerman, Sept. 3, 1939; children—Anne, June, Jan, Ronni. Admitted to N.Y. State bar, 1938; asst. gen. counsel OPA, Washington, 1942-44; partner firm Sutherland, Linowitz & Williams, 1946-58, Harris, Beach, Keating, Wilcox & Linowitz, Rochester, N.Y., 1958-66; chmn. Nat. Urban Coalition, 1970—. Chmn. bd., chmn. exec. com., gen. counsel Xerox Corp., 1958-66; chmn. bd., chief exec. officer Xerox Internat., 1966; dir. Time Inc., Dreyfus-Marine Midland Corp., sr. partner Coudert Bros., 1969—; ambassador to OAS, 1966-69. Trustee, Hamilton Coll., Am. Jewish Com., Cornell U., Am. Assembly, Council of Ams., Salk Inst., Inst. Internat. Edn.; bd. govs. A.R.C.; dir., co-founder Internat. Exec. Service Corps; chmn. State Dept. Adv. Com. on Internat. Orgns., 1963-66; chmn. Nat. Council Fgn. Policy Assn. Served to lt. USNR, 1944-46. Mem. Am. (pres. N.Y. State), Rochester (pres. 1952) assns. for UN, Rochester C. of C. (pres. 1958), Am., N.Y., Rochester (v.p. 1949-50) bar assns., Am. Assn. UN (dir.), Nat. Planning Assn. (trustee), Council on Fgn. Relations, Phi Beta Kappa, Phi Kappa Phi, Order of Coif. Author articles to profl. jours. Home: 2325 Wyoming Av NW Washington DC 20008 Office: 1 Farragut Sq S Washington DC 20006

LINSKIE, GEORGE ANTHONY, constrn. co. exec.; b. Dallas, Nov. 20, 1915; s. John Joseph and Zoda (Dorsa) L.; M.E., Tex. A. and M. U., 1938; m. Helen Dorothy Lee, Apr. 9, 1939. Mech. engr. Rollins & Forrest Cons. Engrs., Dallas, 1939; mech. engr. U.S. Corps Engrs., Denison, Tex., 1940-42, head mech. engring. dept., 1942-45; v.p. Farwell Co., Inc., Dallas, 1946-50; founder, pres. George Linskie Co., Inc., Dallas, 1950—; dir. Grand Ave. Bank and Trust, Dallas, Gibraltar Life Ins. Co. Chmn. budget, finance com. Children's Med. Center, Dallas, 1968-71, 1st v.p., 1968-71, pres., 1971-72; chmn. task force gen. aviation subcom. Dallas Aviation Com., 1968—. Bd. dirs. State Fair Tex. Mem. Am. Soc. Heating, Refrigerating and Air-Conditioning Engrs., Inc. (nat. bd. dirs. 1962-64; Nat. Distinguished Pub. Service award 1970), Mech. Contractors Assn. Tex. (pres. Tex. 1958), Dallas A&M Club (past pres.), Salesmanship Club Dallas, Engrs. Club Dallas. Club: Dallas Country. Home: 5346 Edmondson Dallas TX 75209 Office: Linwood Bldg 2608 Inwood Rd Dallas TX 75235

LIPMAN, IRA ACKERMAN, security service co. exec.; b. Little Rock, Nov. 15, 1940; s. Mark and Belle (Ackerman) L.; grad. Ohio Wesleyan U., 1960; LL.D., John Marshall U., 1970; m. Barbara Ellen Couch, July 5, 1970; 1 son, Gustave K. Salesman and exec. Mark Lipman Service, Inc., Memphis, 1960-63; pres. Guardsmark, Inc., Memphis, 1963—, chief exec. officer, 1966—, also chmn. bd. Mem. Nat. Alliance Businessmen (Metro chmn. Memphis 1970-71), Internat. Assn. Chiefs Police, Am. Soc. Indsl. Security. Republican. Mem. B'nai B'rith. Club: Ridgeway Country (Memphis). Home: 807 Shady Grove Rd Memphis TN 38138 Office: 540 Madison Av New York City NY 10017 also 22 S 2d St Memphis TN 38103

LIPMAN, JAY STUART, oral surgeon; b. N.Y.C., Feb. 1, 1937; s. Frank and Estelle (Triesteman) L.; student U. Va., 1954-57; D.D.S., Med. Coll. Va., 1961; postgrad. N.Y.U., 1964-65; m. Meryl A. Roberts, Sept. 1970. Intern oral surgery Met. Hosp., N.Y.C., 1963-64; resident Harlem Hosp., N.Y.C., 1965-66; practice oral surgery, Jamaica, N.Y., 1966-70, Hampton, Va., 1970—; cons. VA Hosp., Hampton, Dixie Hosp., Hampton, Riverside Hosp., Newport News, Va. Served with Dental Corps, USNR, 1961-63. Diplomate Am. Bd. Oral Surgery. Fellow Am., Internat. socs. oral surgeons; mem. Va. Soc. Oral Surgeons, Am. Dental Assn., Am. Dental Soc. Anesthesiology. Contbr. articles to profl. jours. Home: 4000 W Mercury Blvd Hampton VA 23366

LIPPERT, KARL MORGAN, hosp. adminstr.; b. Cameroun, W. Africa, Sept. 9, 1906; s. Alfred B. and Isabella (Morgan) L.; brought to U.S., 1908; A.B., U. Cin., 1928, M.B., 1932, M.D., 1933; m. Mary Jane Thier, Aug. 17, 1935. Intern Gen. Hosp., U. Cin., 1932-33; resident, pathology Vanderbilt U., Nashville, 1933-34, also instr., asst. resident pathology Vanderbilt Hosp.; resident surgery Med. Coll. Va., Richmond, 1934-38, also instr. surgery; med. dir., surgeon Chatham County Hosp., Siler City, N.C., 1938-40; pvt. practice surgery, Lancaster, S.C., 1940-42; mem. staff, chief surgeon Columbia (S.C.) VA Hosp., 1946-59, dir., 1965—; area chief surgeon Columbus (O.) VA Hosp.; dep. area med. dir. VA, 1965. Served to lt. col., M.C., AUS, 1942-46. Decorated Bronze Star. Recipient plaques V.F.W., 1966, Disabled Am. Vets., 1968. Diplomate Am. Bd. Surgery, Am. Bd. Thoracic Surgery, Fellow Am., Internat. colls. surgeons, American Coll. Hosp. Adminstrs., S.C. Surg. Soc. S.C. Hosp. Assn. Surgery Trauma; mem. S.C., Columbia (exec. com., program chmn.) med. socs., A.M.A., Am. Coll. Hosp. Adminstrs., S.C. Surg. Soc. S.C. Hosp. Assn. Rotarian. Address: Quarters 11 VA Hosp Columbia SC 29201

LIPSCOMB, EDWARD LOWNDES, pub. relations exec.; b. Hollandale, Miss., Sept. 27, 1906; s. Rev. Thomas Heber and Lutie (Scott) L.; A.B., U. Miss., 1927; m. Cornelia Loper, June 21, 1929; children—Cornelia Blanche, Martha Ethel, Lynda Lowndes. Asst. to prof. English, U. Miss., 1925-27; reporter, newscaster Gulf Coast Guide, Gulfport, Miss., 1927-31, mng. editor, 1931-36; dir. Miss. Advt. Commn., Jackson, 1936-39; dir. pub. relations and sales promotion Nat. Cotton Council, 1939-69; cons., 1969—; advt. cons. Cotton Producers Inst., 1962-69, advt. con. Cotton Council Internat., 1960—; chmn. pub. relations com. of Eisenhower People-to-People Program, 1956-57. Mem. com. orgn. Internat. Pub. Relations Assn., 1953, pres., 1958-59; v.p. Agrl. Relations Council, 1953, pres., 1955; mem. adv. bd. Pub. Relation News, 1953-55; Advt. Fedn. Am. Award, 195?, information adv. com. U.S. Dept. Agr., 1953-54. Trustee Found. Pub. Relations Research and Edn., 1954-59. Recipient Pub. Relations News Ann. Achievement award, 1950, Freedoms Found. Honor medal for pub. addresses, 1950- 52, 53, 60. Mem. Pub. Relations Soc. Am. (pres. 1952; Distinguished Service award, 1958; nat. accreditation bd., 1965-67), Textile Bag Mfrs. Assn. (advt. adv. com. 1944-56, Gulf Coast, Miss. (past sec.) press assns., Barons Magna Charta, Ams. Royal Descent, Huguenot Soc., S.A.R. (pres. Memphis chpt. 1962; pres. Tenn. State, 1963), Beta Theta Pi. Kiwanian (past dist. sec.). Author: Grassroots Public Relations for Agriculture, 1950; Personal Practice of Freedom, 1952; Public Relations or Peasantry, 1960. Contbr. newspaper, mags. articles. Speaker before nat. agrl., profl. groups. Home: 94 N Goodlett Memphis TN 38117 Office: Box 12285 Memphis TN 38112

LIPSCOMB, PEGGY ELAINE, pharmacist, real estate broker; b. Quitman, Tex., July 27, 1924; d. Linsey L. and Essie (Douglass) Lipscomb; student Tex. Women's U., 1941-43; B.B.A., So. Meth. U., 1945; M.Ed., E. Tex. State U., 1951; postgrad. U. Colo., 1953-54; B.S. in Pharmacy, U. Tex., 1959. Tchr., Dallas (Tex.) High Schs., 1951-55; pharmacist Skillern's Drug Stores, Dallas, 1959-63; pharmacist, mgr. Lipscomb's Pharmacy, Quitman, 1963—. Real estate broker Fletcher Realty, Dallas, part-time, 1964—. Del. Tex. Dem. Conv., 1972. Mem. Am., Tex. pharm. assns., Nat. Assn. Retail Druggists, Tex. Real Estate Assn., Millinger Import-Export Assn., Dallas Profl. Women's Club, Internat. Traders, Beta Sigma Phi, Kappa Epsilon (state v.p.). Roman Catholic. Clubs: Holiday Wings, Century 3000, Dallas Gun. Home: 446 Woodland Circle Clear Lakes Village Box 578 Quitman TX 75783 Office: Lipscomb's Pharmacy 101 Lipscomb St Quitman TX 75783

LIPSCOMB, THOMAS ABNER, dentist; b. Mineola, Tex., July 1, 1895; s. Charles Day and Sara Annie (Harris) L.; student North Tex. State U., 1917-18; D.D.S., Baylor U., 1922; m. Bera Oliver Billings, Dec. 2, 1950; 1 son, Thomas Abner. Pharmacist, Dallas, 1918-22; tchr. Baylor Dental Coll., Dallas, 1922-25; dentist, Southwest Med. Clinic, Dallas, 1924-32; individual practice denistry, Dallas, 1932—. Co-founder Mid-Winter Dental Clinic, Dallas, 1929, mgr., 1938, 39, 40; cons. bd. trustees Baylor Dental Coll., 1949-55. Fellow Am. Coll. Dentistry; mem. Dallas County Dental Soc. (pres., 1942-43; named Dentist of Year 1970-71), Federation Dentaire Internationale, Tex. Dental Soc., Am. Dental Assn., Omicron Kappa Upsilon. Baptist. Mason. Home: 6615 Northport Dr Dallas TX 75230 Office: 3707 Gaston St Dallas TX 75246

LIPSEY, JOSEPH, JR., dept. store exec.; b. Selma, Ala., Sept. 12, 1934; s. Joseph and Anna (Bendersky) L.; B.A., La. State U., 1955, LL.B., 1957; student U. Colo., 1952; m. Betty Wellan, June 6, 1960; children—Debora Louise, Joseph III, Elizabeth Ann, Tami Leigh. Admitted to La. bar, 1957, Republic of Korea bar, 1958; practiced in Baton Rouge, 1960-64; gen. mdse. mgr., mng. dir. Wellan's Dept. Store, Alexandria, La., 1965—, v.p., 1965—; v.p., dir. Steinberg Sporting Center, Baton Rouge, 1967—; partner Gulf Purchasing Co. Lectr. mil. law and cts. martial La. State U., 1961-64; legal cons. U.S. Ambassador, Tokyo, Japan, 1958-59. State chmn. Nat. Library Week, 1967-70; mem. Goals for La., Tulane U. So. Assembly, 1969, Columbia U. Am. Assembly, 1971. Bd. dirs. Alexandria Country Day Sch., Rapides Parish Symphony Orch., Attakapas council Boy Scouts Am., Rapides United Givers Fund; bd. dirs. Grand Isle Tarpon Rodeo Internat., 1965—, v.p., 1965—; chmn. COFLEX 1971. Served with USAF, 1957-60. Mem. Baton Rouge Shippers Assn. (pres. 1963), Internat. Bar Assn. Ryukyu Islands, La. State U. Alumni Assn. (chpt. pres. 1968), Alexandria-Pineville C. of C. (pres. 1971), Assn. U.S. Army (chpt. pres. 1968), La., Parish bar assns., Omicron Delta Kappa, Zeta Beta Tau, Phi Delta Phi. Democrat. Jewish religion. Rotarian (dir. Alexandria). Home: 904 Pierson St Alexandria LA 71301 Office: 1200 3d St Alexandria LA 71301

LIPTON, JOSEPH MEYER, savs. and loan exec.; b. Latrobe, Pa., Sept. 9, 1900; s. Isadore and Ida L.; B.S. in Econs., U. Pa., 1922; m. Anne Abrash, Sept. 24, 1933; children—Ronald A., Harriet I. Real estate bus., Miami, Fla., 1925-27; founder, pres. J. M. Lipton Ins. Agy., Inc., Miami, 1927—; co-founder Dade Fed. Savs. & Loan Assn., Miami, 1933, pres., 1935-69, chmn. bd., 1969—. Chmn. fund raising Dade County chpt. A.R.C., 1941; chmn. campaign Greater Miami Combined Jewish Appeal. Bd. govs., pres. Greater Miami Jewish Fedn. Served with U.S. Army, World War I. C.L.U. Mem. U.S. (past dir. Southeastern group; Fla. dir.), Fla. (past pres.) savs. and loan leagues. Jewish religion (pres. temple). Mason (Shriner), Kiwanian. Home: 651 W 47th St Miami FL 33140 Office: 101 E Flagler St Miami FL 33131

LIPTON, ROBERT ISRAEL, lawyer; b. N.Y.C., Dec. 11, 1920; s. Simon and Sadie (Berger) L.; B.S. in Commerce, U. N.C., 1942, J.D. with honors, 1946; m. Cecille Rosenblum, Sept. 9, 1947; children—Howard Alan, Lawrence Jay, Stuart Samuel. Admitted to N.C. bar, 1946; editor-in-chief N.C. Law Review, U. N.C., 1945-46; vis. prof. law U. N.C., 1959; practicing atty., Durham, N.C., 1946—, mem. firm Bryant, Lipton, Bryant & Battle, 1955—; dir numerous comml. corps. Pres., N.C. B'nal B'rith Assn., 1960-61; chmn. State N.C. United Jewish Appeal, 1952-54; del. Internat. Econ. Conf., Jerusalem, Israel, 1953. Bd. dirs. Durham United Fund, 1952-54, Silver Leukemia Found., Leo N. Levy Hosp., Duncan-Fletcher Found., Allied Arts, Inc., B'nai B'rith Found. U.S. Served as pfc., USMC, 1942-43. Mem. Am., N.C., Durham County, Orange County bar assns., Internat. Acad. Law and Sci., Am. Judicature Soc. Beta Gamma Sigma, Order of Coif. Jewish religion (pres. congregation 1962-64. Mem. B'nai B'rith (pres. dist. grand lodge 1964-65). Clubs: Nat. Lawyers (Washington); Durham City, Willowhaven Country (Durham); Chapel Hill (N.C.) Country. Author article law jour. Home: 302 Country Club Dr Durham NC 27705 Office: First Union Bldg Durham NC 27701

LIRETTE, WILLIAM LUM, physician; b. Houston, June 7, 1933; s. Vaughn Andrew and Beulah (Lum) L.; B.A., U. Tex., 1953, M.D., 1957; m. Nan Marlene Eaves, Oct. 8, 1955; children—Kenneth, Stephen, Tracie, Stuart, Janelle, David. Intern Pierce County Hosp., Tacoma, Wash., 1957-58; practice gen. medicine, Killeen, Tex., 1960-61, Temple, Tex., 1961—; mem. staff Scott and White Hosp., King's Daus. Hosp., Santa Fe Meml. Hosp. Chmn. comprehensive health planning com. Central Tex. Council Govts., 1971—. Mem. Bell County Council Alcoholism, 1962—, bd. dirs., 1962-69. Served with USAF, 1958-60. Mem. Tex. Acad. Gen. Practice (dir.), Bell County Med. Soc. (past pres.) Alpha Kappa Kappa. Home: 3505 Buffalo Trail Temple TX 76501 Office: 21 Heritage Pl Temple TX 76501

LISAGOR, PETER I(RVIN), newspaperman; b. Keystone, W.Va., Aug. 5, 1915; s. Paris and Fanny (Simpkins) L.; student Northwestern U., 1933; A.B., U. Mich., 1939; Nieman fellow, Harvard, 1948-49; m. Myra K. Murphy, Feb. 14, 1942; children—P. Scott, Diane M. Sports reporter Chgo. Daily News, 1939-41; gen. news reporter United Press, 1941-42; news editor Paris Post, 1945; gen. news reporter Chgo. Daily News, 1945—, UN corr., 1949, political corr., Washington, 1950-59, chief Washington bur., 1959—. Served with U.S. Army, 1942-45; mng. editor Stars & Stripes, London edit., 1944-45; editor Stars & Stripes mag., Paris, 1945. Recipient Page One award Newspaper Guild, 1948, 49. Clubs: Nat. Press, Overseas Writers (pres. 1960-61) (Washington); Gridiron. Co-author: Overtime in Heaven, 1964. Home: 1528 N Ivanhoe St Arlington VA 22205 Office: Nat Press Bldg Washington DC 20004

LISBY, CARROLL EDWARD, editor; m. Mary O'Mary, children—Gregory, Nina, Jeffrey. Mng. editor Columbus (Ga.) Ledger, Sunday Ledger-Enquirer. Home: 2608 Juniper Av Columbus GA 31907 Office: 17 W 12th St Columbus GA 31902

LISLE, BRIAN ORCHARD, cartographer, historian; b. N.Y.C., July 28, 1915; s. Thomas Orchard and Enid Mary (Lawson) L.; student Petroleum Tech., Sir John Cass Tech. Inst., Eng., 1934-37, N.Y. U., 1940, Ohio U. Extension, 1941-42, Berlitz Sch. Langs., 1947-48, Tex. Christian U., 1961-66, Arlington State Coll., 1963-67, B.S., Ohio Christian Coll., 1968, M.S., 1969; B.A., U. Tex. at Arlington, 1971, M.A., 1972; m. Joan Felise Savage, Mar. 21, 1955; 1 dau., Elizabeth Minka. Editorial asst. World Petroleum, N.Y.C., 1934, London, Eng., 1934-35, asst. editor, N.Y.C., 1937-39; asst. editor Petroleum Times, London, 1935-37; cons. petroleum technologist, publicist, N.Y.C., 1939-41; pub. relations officer, asst. to personnel mgr. Ashland Oil & Refining Co., (Ky.), 1941-42; econ. analyst oil sect. econ. br. Office Mil. Govt. for Germany, U.S. War Dept., Berlin, 1945-46; joint editor-pub. Oil Forum, N.Y.C., 1946-50, Ft. Worth, 1950-57; editor-pub. Internat. Oilman, 1957-61; free-lance petroleum cons., cartographer, Ft. Worth, 1960—; substitute lectr. geography dept. Tex. Christian U., 1962-65; co-ordinator reports and graphics urban planning sect. Tex. Hwy. Dept., Dist. 2, Ft. Worth, 1969—. Republican candidate Tex. Ho. of Reps., Tarrant County, 1954. Served from pvt. to 1st lt., USAAF, 1942-45; ETO. Fellow Nat. Geog. Soc.; mem. A.A.A.S., Assn. Am. Geographers, Am. Geog. Soc., Geog. Assn. (Eng.), Assn. Petroleum Writers, Ft. Worth English Speaking Union (sec.-treas. 1961-63), Southwestern Social Sci. Assn., Tarrant County Humane Soc. (dir. 1951-54), Ft. Worth Urban League (dir. 1952-61, certificate of recognition 1954), Phi Alpha Theta (1st prize, E.C. Barksdale lectr. in Am. history 1971). Author: Tanker Technique, 1700-1936, 1936; (pamphlet) Static Defense of Strategic Oil Installations, 1942; Handbook of Conversion Factors, Formulas, Etc., 1956; Why Drake, 1960. Home: 2617 Sarah Jane Lane Fort Worth TX 76119 Office: Office Transp and Planning Tex Hwy Dept Dist 2 2501 Southwest Loop Fort Worth TX 76115

LISTON, ROBERT TODD LAPSLEY, ednl. adminstr., clergyman; b. Oxford, Ala., Dec. 10, 1898; s. Robert Todd and Isabel Pratt (Lapsley) L.; student McCallie Sch.; A.B., Davidson Coll., 1920; LL.D., 1955; B.D., Union Theol. Sem., Richmond Va., 1924; Th.M. (Charles D. Larus fellow), Union Sem., 1925; postgrad. U. Marburg, 1927; Ph.D., U. Edinburgh, 1930; m. Maria Preston Holman, June 25, 1929 (dec. 1957); children—Robert Holman, Jonathan Miller; m. 2d, Jane Leighton Richards, Aug. 7, 1959. Asst. prof. Hebrew, Union Theol. Sem., 1927-28; pastor Richlands, Va., 1928-37; asso. prof. Bible, Southwestern Coll., Memphis, 1937-40; pres. Davis and Elkins Coll., 1940-43; pres. King Coll., 1943-68; asst. to pres. Milligan Coll., 1970—; vis. prof. Columbia Theol. Sem., 1968-70, Smythe lectr., 1952. Democrat. Presbyn. Author: The Neglected Educational Heritage of Southern Presbyterians, 1956. Address: Milligan College Milligan College TN 37682

LISTON, WILLIAM HARRY, lawyer; b. Natchez, Miss., Mar. 13, 1931; s. William and Hester (Jordan) L.; student Miss. State U., 1950-51, U. Md. Extension (Europe), 1951-52; LL.B., U. Miss., 1958; children—William, III, Lori Layne. Admitted to Miss. bar, 1958; investigator Miss. Dept. Ins., Jackson, 1958; practiced in Winona,

Miss., 1958-—; former mem. firm Liston & Sumner; mem. firm Liston & Upshaw. Served with USAF, 1951-54. Mem. Am., Miss. State, Montgomery County bar assns., Am. Trial Lawyers Assn., Pi Kappa Alpha, Phi Alpha Delta. Methodist. Home: 813 Michelle Dr Winona MS 38967 Office: 128 N Quitman St Winona MS 38967

LITTLE, ALBERT KEIL, lawyer; b. Pitts., May 13, 1885 s. John G. and Sarah (Keil) L.; B.S., Pa. State Coll., 1907; LL.B., U. Pitts., 1910; m. Gladys Ralston, Oct. 17, 1912 (dec. 1927); 1 dau., Sarah (Mrs. A. H. Watson, Jr.); m. 2d, Opal Browder, Dec. 14, 1928; 1 son, William B. Admitted to Pa. bar, 1910; gen. practice law, Pitts., 1910-12; Des Moines, 1913-17; office atty. Hicks Loan & Investment Co., Oklahoma City, 1917-20; gen. counsel Gum Bros. Co., farm and city real estate loans, Oklahoma City, 1920-32; gen. practice law, Oklahoma City, 1932-—; partner firm Little and Hoyt, 1946-72; spl. lectr. bus. adminstrn. U. Okla., 1946-58. Mem. bd. rev. Okla. Employment Security Commn., 1947-53. Mem. Oklahoma City Bd. Realtors, Am., Okla., Oklahoma County bar assns., Oklahoma City Soc. Title Attys., Beta Theta Pi, Phi Kappa Phi. Lutheran. Contbr. articles to legal publs. Home: 1134 NW 37th St Oklahoma City OK 73118 Office: Cravens Bldg Oklahoma City OK 73102

LITTLE, DELMAS CARROLL, instrumentation engr.; b. Bradford, O., Mar. 16, 1907; s. Kenneth and Cora (McCune) L.; B.A., U. Louisville, 1950; m. Gladys Caldwell, Feb. 3, 1955. Chief instrumentation U.S. Army Med. Research Lab., Ft. Knox, Ky., 1945-55; instr. physics U. Louisville, 1953-54; project mgr. Missile Range, N.M., 1955-60; chief instrumentation Army Ballistics Missile Agy., White Sands Missile Range Firing Operations Br., 1960-61; field rep. R & D Directorate, Army Missile Command, Redstone Arsenal, Ala., 1961-63, chief engring. sect. flight operations br., 1963-68. Mem. Instrument Soc. Am. (tech. v.p. 1954, 1st v.p. 1955), Am. Phys. Soc., A.A.A.S., Royal Order of Scotland. Republican. Presbyn. Mason (33 deg.). Home: 4421 Brookhaven Av Louisville KY 40220

LITTLE, ELBERT LUTHER, JR., botanist, dendrologist; b. Ft. Smith, Ark., Oct. 15, 1907; s. Elbert Luther and Josephine (Conner) L.; B.A., U. Okla., 1927, B.S., 1932; M.S., U. Chgo., 1929, Ph.D., 1929; postgrad. U. Mich., 1927, Utah State U., 1928; m. Ruby Rema Rice, Aug. 14, 1943; children—Gordon Rice, Melvin Weaver, Alice Conner (Mrs. Ronald E. Mannan). Asst. prof. biology Southwestern State Coll., Weatherford, Okla., 1930-33; botanist Okla. Forest Service, 1930; from asst. to asso. forest ecologist Forest Service, U.S. Dept. Agr., Tucson, 1934-42, dendrologist, Washington, 1942-67, chief dendrologist, 1967-—; botanist, Ecuador and Costa Rica, 1943, Fgn. Econ. Adminstrn., Colombia, 1943-45, U. Md., Guyana, 1955; prof. dendrology U. Los Andes, Merida, Venezuela, 1953-54, 60; cons., prof. dendrology Interam. Inst. Scis., UN Mission, Turrialba, Costa Rica, 1964-65, 67; cons. UN Mission, Quito, Ecuador, 1965, Nicaragua, 1971; vis. prof. biology Va. Poly. Inst., 1966-67. Collaborator U.S. Nat. Mus., 1965-—. Fellow A.A.A.S., Washington, Okla. acads. scis.; mem. Internat. Commn. Nomenclature Cultivated Plants, Am. Inst. Biol. Scis. (bd. govs. 1956-60), Soc. Am. Foresters, Bot. Soc. Am., Internat., Am. socs. plant taxonomists, Ecol. Soc. Am., Assn. for Tropical Biology, Soc. for Econ. Botany, Phi Beta Kappa, Sigma Xi, Beta Beta Beta, Phi Sigma. Author: Important Forest Trees of the United States, 1949; Southwestern Trees, 1950; Check List of the Native and Naturalized Trees of the United States, 1953; (with Frank H. Wadsworth) Common Trees of Puerto Rico and the Virgin Islands, 1964; Atlas of U.S. Trees, 1971; (with Leslie A. Viereck) Alaska Trees and Shrubs, 1972. Contbr. articles, maps profl. pubs., book revs., articles in encys. Home: 924 20th St S Arlington VA 22202 Office: US Forest Service Washington DC 20250

LITTLE, JAMES SINGLETON, tax exec.; b. Eatonton, Ga., May 27, 1906; s. William Clarence and Laura (Nance) L.; B.S., Mercer U., 1928; m. Helen Elizabeth Salter, Nov. 18, 1937; children—Helen Elizabeth, James Singleton, David Clarence. Accountant E.F. Taylor, C.P.A., Augusta, Ga., 1928-30; accountant gen. office Texaco, Inc., Houston, 1930-33, traveling auditor, 1933-40; spl. accountant Horton Motor Lines, Inc., Charlotte, N.C., 1940-42; chief accountant So. div. Asso. Transport, Inc., Charlotte, 1942-43; asst. to pres., dir. taxes The Mason Dixon Lines, Inc. affiliated corps., Kingsport, Tenn., 1943-—, chmn. trustees Retirement Trusts; dir., sec. The Crown Enterprises, Inc., The Royal Corp. Bd. dirs., sec. The King Found. Mem. Tenn. Soc. C.P.A.'s. Methodist. Home: 1200 Midland Dr Kingsport TN 37664 Office: Eastman Rd Kingsport TN 37660

LITTLE, JAMES WILLIAM, coll. adminstr.; b. Tryon, N.C., Apr. 26, 1918; s. William Frank and Dale (Pritchett) L.; A.B., U. N.C., 1939, M.S., 1949, Ph.D., 1963; m. Sylvia Clare Ingraham, Feb. 6, 1958; children—Margaret, Catherine, Ann Marie. Personnel asst. Ford Instrument Co., Long Island City, N.Y., 1941-43; vocational counselor Univ. Testing Service, U. N.C., Chapel Hill, 1945-49, asso. dir., 1949-63, dir. Guidance and Testing Center, 1964-—, lectr. Sch. of Edn., 1964-—. Served with USAAF, 1943-45. Mem. Nat. Vocational Guidance Assn., Am. Psychol. Assn., Phi Beta Kappa, Phi Delta Kappa. Episcopalian. Home: PO Box 675 Chapel Hill NC 27514 Office: Peabody Hall Chapel Hill NC 27514

LITTLE, LAMAR EUGENE, dentist; b. Winnsboro, La., June 22, 1913; s. Eugene Samuel and Carrie Mae (Butler) L.; B.A., La. Coll., 1935; D.D.S., St. Louis U., 1939; postgrad. N.Y. U., 1943-44, U. Miss., 1959; m. Darlyn McCarty, Jan. 22, 1950; children—Stephen Eugene, Charles McHenry, John Thomas. Individual practice dentistry, Winnsboro, La., 1939-—. Served to lt. comdr. USNR, 1941-45. Mem. Am., La., Fifth Dist. dental assns. Home: P O Box 509 Crowville Rd Winnsboro LA 71295 Office: 610 Prairie St Winnsboro LA 71295

LITTLE, MARGARET C., govt. ofcl. Exec. sec. to sec. Dept. Housing and Urban Devel., Washington. Address: 700 7th St SW Washington DC 20024*

LITTLE, MARY ALICE ENGLAND (MRS. JOE PERRY LITTLE), librarian; b. Sparta, Tenn., June 22, 1916; d. Dallas Carmichael and Althea (Alcorn) England; B.S., Tenn. Tech. U., 1938; M.A. in English, George Peabody Coll., 1946, M.A. in L.S., 1957; m. Joe Perry Little, Dec. 16, 1938; children—Joe Perry, Mary Elizabeth. Tchr., White County High Sch., Sparta, 1938-39, 44-45, Dover (Tenn.) High Sch., 1940-44, Murfreesboro (Tenn.) Central Sch., 1945-51, Sparta Elementary Sch., 1952-56; regional dir. Caney Fork Regional Library, Sparta, 1957-—. Mem. Am. Assn. U. Women (br. pres. 1967-69, chmn. edn. Tenn. div. 1971-—), N.E.A., Nat. (life), Tenn. (life, state dir. 1959-—) congresses parents and tchrs., Gen. Alumni Assn. Tenn. Tech. U. (pres. 1965-67, dir. 1963-68), Pi Gamma Mu, Delta Kappa Gamma (pres. 1968-70). Democrat. Mem. Ch. of Christ. Contbr. articles to profl. jours. Home: Route 4 208 S Spring St Sparta TN 38583 Office: 209 Rhea St Sparta TN 38583

LITTLE, ROBERT NARVAEZ, educator; b. Houston, Mar. 11, 1913; s. Robert Narvaez and Lillian Forrest (Kinney) L.; student U. Tex., 1929-32; B.A., Rice U., 1935, M.A., 1942, Ph.D., 1943; m. Betty Jo Browning, June 1, 1942; children—Scott Robert, Emily Browning. Asst. seismologist Shell Oil Co., 1936-40; asst. prof. U. Ore., 1943-44; research scientist U. Tex., 1944-46, asst. prof. physics, 1946-48, asso. prof., 1948-55, prof. physics and edn., 1955-—; chief nuclear physics Gen. Dynamics Co., Fort Worth, 1953-55. Cons. Los Alamos Sci. Lab., Sandia Corp., Gen. Dynamics Co., Fort Worth, Kaman Nuclear, Tex. Nuclear Corp., Institute Pedagogico de Caracas, Universidad del Valle, Guatemala; dir. physics edn. assistance project NSF, U.S. AID, Consejo Superior Universitario Centroamericano Program, 1965-70. Mem. Am. Assn. Physics Tchrs. (pres. 1970), Am. Phys. Soc., Groupe Internationel de Recherches sur l'Enseignement de la Physique, Sociedad Centro Americano de Fisica, Tex. Acad. Sci. Home: 3928 Balcones Dr Austin TX 78731

LITTLE, ROBERT WARREN, dentist; b. Blacksburg, S.C., Mar. 19, 1920; s. Adolphus Lamar and Mildred Pratt (Waterson) L.; B.S., La. State U., 1942; D.D.S., U. Tex., 1950; m. Theda Inez Childress, July 11, 1942; children—Robert Warren, Steven Louis, Martha Ann. Individual practice dentistry, Waco, Tex., 1954-—. Served with USAAF, 1942-45, with Dental Corps, AUS, 1949-54. Decorated Air medal with two oak leaf clusters. Mem. Acad. Internat. Dentistry, Acad. Gen. Dentistry, Tex. Dental Assn. (mem. ho. of dels. 1969-72), Central Tex. Dist. Dental Soc. (pres. 1962-63), U. Tex. Dental Br. Alumni Assn. (dir. 1968-71), Omicron Kappa Upsilon. Rotarian. Home: 5112 Lake Jackson St Waco TX 76710 Office: 5001 Lakewood Dr Waco TX 76710

LITTLE, SCOTT WELLS, surgeon; b. Winnipeg, Man., Can., Oct. 18, 1926; s. William Scott and Eva (Lapointe) L.; B.Sc., U. Man., 1952, M.Sc., 1954; M.D.:C.M., McGill U., 1958; m. Muriel Sarah Gibbons, May 31, 1958; children—Clare Scott, Bryan William, Robyn Elizabeth. Came to U.S., 1959, naturalized, 1965. Intern, St. Boniface (Man.) Gen. Hosp. 1958-59; resident Gill Meml. Hosp., Roanoke, Va., 1959-62; founder, pres. Little Ear, Nose and Throat Clinic, 1971-—; cons. Salem VA Hosp., Roanoke Valley Speech and Hearing Clinic. Served with Royal Canadian Navy, 1944-45, Winipeg Grenadiers, 1949-54, RCAF 1954-58. Fellow A.C.S., Internat. Coll. Surgeons, Royal Soc. for Preservation Health; mem. A.M.A., So. Med. Assn., Roanoke Acad. Medicine, Med. Soc. Va., Va. Soc. Opthalmology and Otolaryngology. Club: Roanoke Cosmpolitan (pres. 1971). Contbr. articles to profl. jours. Home: 3661 Dogwood Lane SW Roanoke VA 24015 Office: 2036 Colonial Av SW Roanoke VA 24015

LITTLE, THOMAS CHARLES, supt. schs.; b. Moore's Creek, Ky., Jan. 19, 1915; s. Thomas H. and Delila (Dyche) L.; B.A., Eastern Ky. U., 1937; M.A., U. Ky., 1942; Ph.D., George Peabody Coll. Tchrs., 1948; m. Hazel Calico, Oct. 21, 1933. Tchr. Paint Lick Elementary Sch., Garrard County, Ky., 1933-36, Lebanon (Ky.) High Sch., 1937-39; prin. Lebanon Elementary Sch., 1939-40; supt. schs. Columbia, Ky., 1940-44; chmn. edn. div. Ga. So. Coll., Statesboro, 1948-54; asst. supt. bus. affairs Richmond (Va.) Pub. Schs., 1954-69, asso. supt., 1969-72, supt. schs., 1972-—. Ednl. cons. various pub. schs. Mem. adv. council Salvation Army Hosp., 1961-72. Served with USNR, 1944-46. Mem. Am. Assn. Sch. Adminstrs., Nat. Inst. Govtl. Purchasing, Va. Edn. Assn., Assn. Sch. Bus. Ofcls., Council Ednl. Facility Planners, Kappa Delta Phi, Phi Delta Kappa. Rotarian (pres. 1966-67). Club: Commonwealth (Richmond). Contbr. articles to profl. jours. Home: 5306 Riverside Dr Richmond VA 23225 Office: Richmond Pub Schs 301 N 9th St Richmond VA 23219

LITTLE, WALDEN PASKEL, ins. co. exec.; b. nr. Groesbeck, Tex., Mar. 14, 1920; s. Wilmer Preston and Georgia (Cates) L.; A.A., Westminister Coll., 1940; m. Billye Jean Bostick, June 9, 1965; children— Gregory, Regina. With Combined Underwriters Life Ins. Co., Tyler, Tex., 1949-—, pres., 1956-—. City commr. Tyler, 1966-—, mayor, 1968-—. Bd. dirs. YMCA. Mem. Tyler Sales Execs. Club. Mem. Christian Ch. Mason (Shriner), Office: 307 N Glenwood St Tyler TX 75701

LITTLE, WILLIAM BYRD, C. of C. exec.; b. Ripley, Miss., June 30, 1930; s. Byrd Brownlee and Mary (Marsh) L.; B.B.A., U. Miss., 1951; m. Patricia Carruth, Aug. 31, 1951; children—Karen, Cynthia, William Clay. Account exec. Dixie Advt., Jackson, Miss., 1950-51; dir. indsl. council, dir. pub. relations, dir. indsl. dept., Memphis C. of C., 1952-55; mgr. indsl. dept. Greensboro (N.C.) C. of C., 1955-56, exec. v.p., 1957-—. Instr. Nat. Inst. C. of C. Execs. Trustee, Guilford Coll. Recipient Program of Work award C. of C. U.S., 1960. Mem. Am. C. of C. Execs. Assn. (dir., sec.-treas. 1971-72), N.C. Assn. C. of C. Execs. (pres. 1961), Delta Sigma Pi, Pi Kappa Alpha. Methodist. Home: 4217 Tallwood Dr Greensboro NC 27407 Office: 217 N Greene St PO Box 3246 Greensboro NC 27402

LITTLE, WILLIAM D., JR, newspaper exec.; b. Ada., Okla., May 22, 1921; s. William Dee and Willie (Faust) L.; grad. McCallie Sch., 1938; A.B., East Central State Coll., Ada, Okla., 1942; m. Mary Louise Osborne, Sept. 13, 1942; children—Helen Jane, Linda Brooks, William D. III. With News Publ. and Printing Co., Ada, 1942-—, advt. solicitor, asst. to pub., 1946, v.p., bus. mgr., 1947-66, pres., 1966-—; pub. Ada Evening News, 1966-—; dir. Home Fed. Savs. & Loan Assn., Ada, Ada Indsl. Devel. Corp., Okla. Gas & Electric Co. Mem. exec. bd. Valley View Hosp., Ada, chmn., 1963-—; mem. Okla. Econ. Adv. Council, 1963-66, Gov.'s Capital Expenditures Adv. Council, 1967; pres. E. Central Okla. Bldg. Authority, 1965-—; mem. Okla. Health Council, 1968-72; v.p. Okla. Health Scis. Found. Bd. dirs. Scis. and Natural Resources Found. Okla.; mem. Okla. Heritage Found. Mem. Am., So. (dir.) newspaper pubs. assns., Okla. A.P. Mng. Editors Assn. (pres. 1958), Ada. (pres. 1954), Okla. (dir. 1971-—) chambers commerce, East Central Coll. Alumni Assn. (pres. 1949), Newcomen Soc. N. Am. Presbyn. (elder). Home: 422 Highland Av Ada OK 74820 Office: 116 N Broadway Ada OK 74820

LITTLE, WILLIAM FREDERICK, educator; b. Hickory, N.C., Nov. 11, 1929; s. William H. and Mary (Sheely) L.; B.S., Lenoir Rhyne Coll., 1950; M.A., U. N.C., 1952, Ph.D. (Morehead scholar), 1954; m. Edna Dell Hoyle, July 19, 1958; 1 dau., Teresa Dell. Postdoctoral research Univ. Coll., London, 1954-55; instr. Reed Coll., 1955-56; instr. U. N.C., Chapel Hill, 1956-57, asst. prof., 1957-61, asso. prof., 1961-65, prof., chmn., 1965-—; chmn. exec. com. bd. govs., cons. Research Triangle Inst. Mem. Gov's Sci. Adv. Com., 1962-64. Bd. dirs. N.C. Bd. Sci. and Tech.; trustee Lenoir Rhyne Coll. Mem. Am. Chem. Soc. (past chmn. N.C. sect.), A.A.A.S., Sigma Xi. Democrat. Lutheran. Contbr. articles profl. jours. Home: 201 Markham Dr Chapel Hill NC 27514

LITTLEFORD, ROBERT ANTHONY, govt. ofcl.; b. Washington, July 16, 1910; s. William A. and Mary (Carr) L.; B.S., U. Md., 1933, M.S., 1934, Ph.D., 1938; m. Genevieve Everett, Apr. 30, 1938; children—Angela, Elaine, Michael, Eugene, John, Joyce, Thomas, Kathleen. Asso. zoologist Chesapeake Biol. Lab., Solomons, Md., 1937-39; instr. biology Marquette U., 1939-42; instr., asst. prof., asso. prof. zoology U. Md., 1942-54, dir. Seafood Process Lab., 1954-58; dir. biology div. Wards Nat. Sci. Establishment, Rochester, N.Y., 1958-61; grant adminstr. USPHS, Washington, 1961-67; tng. grants adminstr. Fed. Water Pollution Control Adminstrn., Dept. Interior, Washington, 1967-68; chief program evaluation sect. research grants Nat. Center Air Pollution, USPHS, 1968-69, acting dir. Office Research and Tng. Grants, FDA, 1969-71, asso. dir. extramural br. staff ACS, 1971-—. Fellow A.A.A.S., Am. Pub. Health Assn.; mem. Am. Fisheries Soc., Am. Water Works Assn., Water Pollution Control Fedn., Biol. Soc. Washington. Contbr. articles to profl. jours. Home: 4806 Indian Lane College Park MD 20740 Office: 633 Indiana Av Washington DC 20042

LITTLEJOHN, BROADUS RICHARD, supermarket exec.; b. Cedar Springs, S.C., Sept. 24, 1894; s. Wallace W. and Nealie (Willard) L.; student pub. schs., Spartanburg County, S.C.; LL.D. (hon.), Converse Coll., 1966; m. Evelyn Hicks, Oct. 6, 1920; 1 son, Broadus Richard. Formerly with Spartanburg Herald Jour., pres. Community Cash Stores, Spartanburg, S.C., 1921-—; dir. First Nat. Bank S.C., Spartan Broadcasting, Liberty Mut. Ins. Co. Mem. Bd. commrs. Cedar Springs Inst. for Deaf and Blind Sch. for S.C., 1950-70. Councilman, City of Spartanburg. Trustee, vice-chmn. bd. Converse Coll.; trustee Furman U., Spartanburg County Found., Spartanburg Jr. Coll; bd. dirs. Spartanburg County Library. Served with AEF, World War I. Recipient Alernon Sydney Sullivan Medallion Wofford Coll., 1965. Mem. Am. Legion. Baptist (deacon). Kiwanian (Man of Year 1957). Home: 20 Woodburn Rd Spartanburg SC 29301 Office: PO Box 5688 Spartanburg SC 29302

LITTLEJOHN, CAMERON BRUCE, justice S.C. Supreme Ct.; b. Pacolet, S.C., July 22, 1913; s. Cameron and Lady Sara (Warmouth) L.; A.B., Wofford Coll., 1935, LL.D., 1968; LL.B., U.S.C., 1936; m. Inell Smith, Feb. 7, 1942. Mem. S.C. Ho. of Reps., 1937-43, speaker, 47-49; judge 7th Circuit Ct., 1949-67; asso. justice S.C. Supreme Ct., 1967-—. Del. Nat. Conf. State Trial Judges, 1964, 65, 66; del. Nat. Appellate Judges Conf., 1967; mem. Spartanburg adv. bd. registrants Selective Service Act, 1960. Sec. Orgn. Young Dem. Clubs S.C., 1935-36, chmn. Spartenburg County, 1936-37. Served to 1st lt. AUS, 1943-46; PTO. Mem. Wofford Coll. Alumni Assn. (dir. 1966-—), Am. Legion, Blue Key. Baptist (trustee 1962-67). Home: 450 Connecticut Av Spartanburg SC 29302 Office: Supreme Ct SC PO Box 1924 Spartanburg SC 29301

LITTLEJOHN, JAMES DEWITT, assn. exec.; b. El Paso, Tex., June 21, 1931; s. James Franklin and Mary Kathleen (Badgett) L.; B.A., Tex. Christian U., 1954; m. Sunny Gail Wright, May 25, 1968; children (by previous marriage)—Kathleen Marie, Linda Louise. Tchr. pub. schs., San Angelo, Odessa, Tex., 1954-60; pres., Marlo Products Co., Odessa, 1960-61; asst. mgr. Greater Florence (S.C.) C. of C., 1961-63; sports editor, bur. chief Florence Morning News, Savannah (Ga.) Morning News, 1963-69; exec. dir. Hilton Head (S.C.) C. of C., 1969-—; also now chmn. bd., pres. Sunlit Enterprises Ltd. Mem. Am. C. of C. Assn., S.C. Chamber Execs. Assn., U.S., S.C. State chambers commerce. Rotarian. Clubs: Chatham (Savannah, Ga.); Port Royal Golf, Sea Pines Plantation, Palmetto Dunes Golf and Country (Hilton Head). Editor Islander Mag., 1969-—. Home: 7 S Port Royal Dr Hilton Head Island SC 29928 Office: PO Box 1068 Hilton Head Island SC 29928

LITTLEJOHN, TALMADGE DEAN, lawyer; b. Blue Springs, Miss., Oct. 18, 1935; s. Ivy Lee and Annie (Speck) L.; B.A., Miss. Coll., 1957; LL.B., U. Miss., 1960; m. Julia Gray Littlejohn, Sept. 2, 1961; children—Lisa Michele, Christy Madonna. Admitted to Miss. bar., 1960; gen. practice law, New Albany, Miss., 1961-—; mem. Miss. Ho. of Reps., 1960-64; mem. senate, 1964-68, dist. atty. 3d Circuit Ct., 1968-—. Mem. Miss. Planning Council on Mental Retardation, 1964-—; mem. Union County 4-H Adv. Council. Bd. dirs. Regional Rehab. Center, Union County Assn. for Retarded Children. Named outstanding Young Man of Year, New Albany Jr. C. of C., 1963. Mem. Miss., Union County bar assns., Miss. Resource Devel. Com., Miss. Forestry Assn. (dir. 1971), Pi Kappa Delta. Baptist. Club: Civitan (pres. New Albany 1968-69, lt. gov. Miss. dist. 1970-71). Home: 303 Pinecrest Dr New Albany MS 38652 Office: 202 Court Av New Albany MS 38652

LITTLEJOHN, WILLIAM DONALD, physician; b. Oklahoma City, Dec. 30, 1934; s. Arthur Lee and Lucille (Crowe) L.; B.S., Tex. Wesleyan Coll., 1967; M.D., Southwestern Med. Sch., 1967; m. Rosa Louise DuMain, June 13, 1964; children—Linda Joy, Donna Sue, Vicki Lynn, Cynthia Ann. Intern John Peter Smith Hosp., 1967, resident, 1969; practice gen. medicine, Fort Worth, 1969-—; mem. staff St. Joseph Hosp., Ft. Worth Children's Hosp., Harris Hosp., All Saints Episcopal Hosp., Ft. Worth; team physician Fort Worth Braves football team, 1970-—, Fort Worth Wings hockey team, 1970-—. Served with USAF, 1954-61. Mem. A.M.A., Tarrant County Med. Assn., Am. Assn. Gen. Practitioners, Nat. Rifle Assn., Am. Motorcycle Assn., Theta Kappa Psi, Alpha Chi. Home: Rte 1 Box 206 Weatherford TX 76086 Office: 2501 Ridgmar Plaza Fort Worth TX 76116

LITTLETON, ISAAC THOMAS, III, librarian; b. Hartsville, Tenn., Jan. 28, 1921; s. Isaac Thomas and Bessie (Lowe) L.; A.B., U. N.C., 1943, M.A., U. Tenn., 1950; M.S. in L.S., U. Ill., 1951, Ph.D., 1968; m. Dorothy Young, Aug. 12, 1949; children—Sally Lowe, Thomas Young, Elizabeth. Tng. officer VA, 1946-47, head circulation dept., 1951-53; asst. to librarian U. N.C. Library, 1953-58; with D.H. Hill Library, N.C. State U., Raleigh, 1959-—, dir., 1967-—; instr. Peabody Library Sch., summer 1958; cons. in field, 1959-—. Served to lt. (j.g.) USNR, 1943-46. Mem. Am., N.C., Southeastern (treas. 1959-60) library assns., Spl. Libraries Assn., Assn. Southeastern Research Libraries, Beta Phi Mu. Author: Guide to Special Collections in the University of North Carolina Library, 1956; Bibliographic Organization and Use of the Literature of Agricultural Economics, 1967. Editor: North Carolina Union List of Scientific Serials, 1965-67. Home: 4813 Brookhaven Dr Raleigh NC 27609

LITTLETON, J.G., chief of police, Tampa, Fla. Address: Office of the Police Chief Tampa FL 32301*

LITTON, ROBERT BENTON, dentist; b. Shelby, N.C., June 29, 1930; s. Farley Benton and Luta (Smith) L.; student U. N.C., 1948-50; D.D.S., U. Md., 1954; m. Margaret Easom, Aug. 7, 1954; children—Lu, Robert Benton, Margaret S. Oral surgeon intern U. Hosp., Balt., 1954; individual practice dentistry, Shelby, N.C., 1957-—; mem. staff Cleve. Meml. Hosp., Shelby. Served with Dental Corps, AUS, 1955-57. Named Shelby's Man of Year, 1960. Mem. 1st Dist. N.C. Dental Soc. (pres. 1970-71), Western N.C. Swim Assn. (pres. 1971-72). Kiwanian (pres. 1961; dir. 1957-62). Club: Bulldog (pres. 1971-72). Home: 1220 Timberland St Shelby NC 28150 Office: 423 W Marion St Shelby NC 28150

LITVAK, ALLEN LEE, orthodontist; b. Cleve., Mar. 2, 1936; s. David and Bella Litvak; D.D.S. (USPHS fellow), Ohio State U., 1960; M.S., Northwestern U., 1965; m. Ann Florence Gup, Sept. 5, 1959; children—Julia, Michael, Kramer, Allen, Jr. Orthodontist, Pensacola, Fla., 1965-—. Bd. dirs. Pensacola Symphony. Served with USAF, 1960-63. Mem. Alpha Epsilon Pi, Alpha Omega. Republican. Jewish religion (dir. temple 1970). Rotarian (dir. 1969-—). Home: 1241 Durnford Pl Pensacola FL 32502 Office: 220 Plaza Bldg Pensacola FL 32505

LIVAUDAIS, JACQUES ANDRE, banker; b. New Orleans, Dec. 29, 1915; s. Numa and Marie Louise (Friedrichs) L.; night student Loyola U., New Orleans, 1940; student Sch. Banking of South, La. State U., 1950-52; m. Eleanor Lay Riess, Apr. 17, 1941; children—Jacques Andre, Frank Riess, Marie Elizabeth. With Internal Revenue Service, 1940-42; with Bank of New Orleans and

Trust Co., and predecessor, 1945—, exec. v.p., 1961—, also dir. Served as officer USCGR, 1942-45. C.P.A., La. Mem. Am. Inst. C.P.A.'s, La. Soc. C.P.A.'s, Financial Execs. Inst. Clubs: Southern Yacht, Pickwick (New Orleans). Home: 1202 Octavia St New Orleans LA 70115 Office: PO Box 52499 New Orleans LA 70150

LIVER, JOHN WILLIS, civil engr.; b. Paris, Ky., Jan. 8, 1940; s. Willis Rash and Sarah Louise (Stipp) L.; C.E., U. Cin., 1968; m. Barbara Jo Dye, Feb. 24, 1962; children—Lisa Joy, Cynthia Anne. Rodman, Ky. Hwy. Dept., 1958-59; chief designer O.G. Loomis & Son, Covington, Ky., 1959-69; v.p. Loomis Engring. Co., Covington, 1970—. Chmn. water commrs. Boone County Water Dist., 1971—; chmn. Hebron Lutheran Cemetery. Mem. Am. Water Works Assn., No. Ky. Soc. Profl. Engrs. (dir.). Rotarian. Home: 150 Constance Rd Hebron KY 41048 Office: 542 Greenup St Covington KY 41011

LIVERANCE, SARA VANDIVER (MRS. ROBERT E. LIVERANCE), journalist; b. Anderson, S.C., Feb. 21, 1914; d. Thomas Melvin and Mary M. (Brown) Vandiver; grad. high sch.; m. Robert E. Liverance, Oct. 25, 1944. Writer shopping column, reporter Anderson Independent-Daily Mail, 1933-44; promotion, publicity Radio Sta. WAGA, Atlanta, 1944-45; reporter Kannapolis (N.C.) Independent, 1946; local news editor Radio Sta. WABZ, Albemarle, N.C., 1947-48; local news editor, womens editor Radio Sta. WFGN, Gaffney, S.C., 1948-49; chief Anderson Bur., Greenville (S.C.) News, 1949—. Sec. S.C. Conf. on Status Women, 1956; pres. S.C. Council for Common Good, 1960-62; mem. S.C. Gov.'s Commn. on Status Women, 1965-71, com. chmn., 1965-71; staff mem. Synodical Tng. Sch. Presbyn. Ch., 1965-67, sec. Women of Ch. Piedmont Presbytery, 1966-67; rec. sec. Anderson County Hist. Soc., 1967—, bd. govs., 1966—; mem. S.C. Tri-Centennial Com., 1968-71. Bd. trustees State Colls., 1969-73. Recipient Distinguished Service award S.C. Council for Common Good, 1963, Hon. Miss Anderson award Anderson Jr. C. of C., 1967; named Career Woman of Year Anderson Bus. and Profl. Womens Club, 1967. Mem. Anderson Bus. and Profl. Womens Club (past pres., state chmn., conv. del.). Clubs: Altrusa (past pres. Anderson), Anderson County Woman's (2d v.p. 1971-72). Address: PO Box 479 Anderson SC 29621

LIVINGOOD, WILLIAM COOK, physician; b. Graysville, Pa., Feb. 3, 1915; s. John Madison and Frances (Cook) L.; B.S., Waynesburg Coll., 1936; M.D., U. Md., 1940; postgrad. U. Pa., 1949-50; m. Lucille Bernadine Donegan, Aug. 21, 1939; children—Frances (Mrs. James J. Castello), William Cook, Carol (Mrs. R. Stinson Swyers), John M., Charles P., Joan L. Intern Mercy Hosp., Balt., 1940-41; commd. lt. jg. U.S. Navy, 1942, advanced through grades to capt., 1955; ret., 1962; chief of otolaryngology service U.S. Naval Hosp., Phila., 1955-62, head Nat. Naval Aural Rehab. Center, 1955-62, naval flight surgeon Marine Air Wings Pacific, World War II, sr. med. officer U.S.S. Wright, 1947-49; otolaryngologist Guthrie Clinic and Robert Packer Hosp., Sayre, Pa., 1962-70; VA Hosp., Fayetteville, N.C., 1970—; clin. asso. prof. surgery Hahnemann Med. Sch., 1956-70; vis. prof. speech pathology and audiology Ithaca Coll., N.Y., 1966-70. Diplomate Am. Bd. Otolaryngology. Fellow A.C.S., Am. Otologicarhinol. and Laryngol. Soc., A.M.A.; mem. Soc. Mil. Otolaryngologists (nat. pres. 1956-57), Am. Council of Otolaryngology, Deafness Research Found. Club: Centurian. Office: VA Hosp Fayetteville NC 28301

LIVINGSTON, DAVID WARREN, composer; b. Corbin, Ky., Jan. 10, 1925; s. Carl Daniel and Lucy (Darnell) L.; B.S., Western Ky. U., 1951; M.A., U. Ky., 1952; Ph.D., Ohio State U., 1971; m. Joyce E. West, Oct. 5, 1951; children—Pamela, David Timothy. Band dir. Western Ky. U., 1965—; supr. music in Frankfort, Ky., 1953-63. Dir. Civic Symphonette, Frankfort, Ky., 1956-58; dir., arranger Drum and Bugle Corps, 1957-58; tour with band Gemini 15, Europe, 1968. Active Boy Scouts Am. Served with USAAF, 1943-46. Mem. Phi Mu Alpha. Kiwanian. Composer: Theme and Variations, 1952; Adagio for Four Trombones, 1954; How Firm a Foundation, 1956; Saxville, 1962; Prelude and Fugue for Winds, 1963; Pastorale for Winds, 1966. Home: 2325 Bellevue Dr Bowling Green KY 42101

LIVINGSTON, DEAN BENNETTE, newspaper pub., editor; b. North, S.C., Jan. 9, 1933; s. Alex Hamilton and Madge (Rogers) L.; A.B., U. S.C., 1955; m. Grace Dukes, Dec. 22, 1955; children—Donna Grace, Dean. Sports editor Orangeburg (S.C.) Times and Democrat, 1953-55, farm editor, 1955-56, mng. editor, 1959-61, pub., 1961—, editor, 1964—. Served as 1st lt., navagator USAF, 1956-59. Mem. Greater Orangeburg C. of C. (pres. 1967-68), S.C. A.P. Assn. (pres.), S.C. Press Assn. (pres. 1969), Sigma Chi. Mason, Rotarian. Home: 1167 Middleton NE Orangeburg SC 29115 Office: 211 Broughton SE Orangeburg SC 29115

LIVINGSTON, LAWRENCE GORDON, physician; b. Mountain Grive, Mo., Nov. 25, 1905; s. James Harry and Mabel (Beazley) L.; M.D., Washington U. (St. Louis) 1930; m. Gwennie M. Bonham, May 12, 1932 (div. Feb. 1940); adopted children-Janice Mae, Richard Lewis; m. 2d, Alice Jane Pritchett Fletcher, Aug. 19, 1960; children—Phillip Douglas, Harold Arlyn. Intern Okla. State U. Hosp., Oklahoma City, 1930-31, St. Louis Maternity Hosp., 1931-32; practice gen. medicine, surgery, Cordell, Okla., 1933—; mem. staff Cordell Meml. Hosp., also equipment cons.; asso. perceptor Okla. State U. Med. Sch., 1957-58. Dir. Cordell Indsl. Corp., 1960—. Served to lt. col. M.C., AUS, 1940-45; PTO. Mem. A.M.A., Okla. Med. Soc. (councilor 1945-52), Phi Beta Pi, Kappa Sigma. Methodist. Kiwanian. Home: 1414 N Church St Cordell OK 73632 Office: 202 S Market St Cordell OK 73632

LIVINGSTON, R.E., sec. United Brotherhood Carpenters and Joiners of Am., Washington. Address: 101 Constitution Av NW Washington DC 20001*

LLAMAS, PELAYO FLORENTINO, Philippine diplomat; b. Pagsanjan, Laguna, Philippines, June 20, 1916; s. Vicente F. and Feliza (Vidal) L.; LL.B., U. Philippines, 1940; grad. U.S. Fgn. Service Inst., 1946; m. Estuko Ohata, Sept. 7, 1957; children—Elizabeth, Mary Anne, Pelayo Antonio, Carmelita Feliza. Pvt. sec. to 2d dep. commr. immigration, 1941; sec. Philippine delegation UN Gen. Assembly, London, Eng., 1946; mem. Philippine delegation Far Eastern Commn., Wash., 1946-47, 48-49; vice consul, Los Angeles, 1947-48, acting consul, 1948; mem. Philippine mission to UN; vice consul, Shanghai, 1949; acting prin. officer, Shanghai, also charge d'affairs, Nanking, 1949-50, 2d sec., consul, Paris, France, 1951-54; charge d'affairs, London, 1954-55; consul. Hong Kong, also Macao, 1955-56; Kobe, Japan, 1956-60; 1st sec., consul gen., Seoul, Korea, also alternate rep. UN Commns. Unification and Rehab. Korea, 1960-62; prin. officer consulate gen., New Orleans, 1962-66; chief of mission with rank A.E. and P., 1966—; dean Consular Corps, New Orleans, 1967—. Del. ann. conv. Am. Soc. Polit. and Social Sci., Phila., 1948, Internat. Sugar Council Meeting, also Internat. Wheat Council Meeting, 1954; mem. exec. bd. Counsular Corps. New Orleans, 1963—. Bd. dirs. Internat. Trade Mart, New Orleans, 1969-70; Philippine ambassador designate to Rep. of China, Taiwan, 1970. Served as 2d lt. Philippine Army Res., 1941; to capt. AUS, 1941-45. Mem. Am. Acad. Polit. and Social Sci., Philippine Soc. Internat. Law.Home: 7311 Jade St New Orleans LA 70124 Office: Internat Trade Mart New Orleans LA 70130

LLANES, CARLOS GILBERTO, physician; b. Havana Cuba, Mar. 31, 1919; s. Carlos G. and Mirtha (Fernandez) L.; B.S. and B.A., Instituto de la Habana, 1938; M.D., Sch. Medicine U. Havana, 1945; m. Martha Maria Borg, Sept. 18, 1948; children—Carlos Gilberto III, Patricia Ann, Mirtha Maria, Diana Lynn. Came to U.S., 1945, naturalized, 1950. Rotating intern St. Joseph's Hosp., Yonkers, N.Y., 1945-46; resident chest diseases Lakeland Chest Diseases Hosp., Blackwood, N.J., 1946-50; resident radiology Roosevelt Hosp., N.Y.C., 1950-53; spl. course radioactive isotopes Oak Ridge Inst. Nuclear Studies, Tenn., 1953; asso. radiologist Doctors' Hosp., Coral Gables, Fla., 1953-55; chief radiologist Murphy Army Hosp., Waltham, Mass., 1955-56; asso. radiologist Gorgas Hosp., Panama Canal Zone, 1956-57; radiologist, chief cobalt div. Mercy Hosp., Miami, Fla., 1957-59; pvt. practice radiology, Coral Gables, 1959-67, Miami, 1964—; dir. dept. radiology Palm Springs Gen. Hosp., Hialeah, Fla., 1965-67; chief dept. radiology Pan Am. Hosp., Miami, also bd. dirs. Served from capt. to maj., AUS, 1955-57. Diplomate Am. Bd. Radiology. Mem. Am., Fla., Dade County med. assns., Radiol. Soc. N.Am., Greater Miami Radiol. Soc., Fla. Radiol. Soc., Am. Coll. Radiology, Heart Assn. Greater Miami. Lutheran (past pres. congregation). Rotarian. Home: 11225 SW 58th Ct Miami FL 33156 Office: 434 SW 12th Av Miami FL 33130

LLERA SANTOS, FELIX JOSE, dentist; b. Cidra, P.R., July 23, 1939; s. Felix Llera and Carmen Belen (Santos) Barrios; B.S. cum laude, U. P.R., 1960, D.M.D., 1964. NIH fellow in anatomy, 1964-65; gen. practice dentistry, Cidra, 1965—; faculty dept. anatomy U. P.R. Sch. Medicine, Rio Piedras, 1965—, asst. prof., 1970—. Mem. Coll. Dental Surgeons, Dental Grads. Soc. P.R. Sch. Dentistry. Alpha Beta Chi, Delta Sigma Delta (grand master of P.R. 1964). Mem. Popular Democratic Party. Roman Catholic. Rotarian (dir. Cidra 1967—). Research on enervation of teeth. Home: 7 Munoz Barrios St Cidra PR 00639 Office: 21 Gautier Benitez St Cidra PR 00639

LLEWELLYN, CHARLES ELROY, JR., physician, educator; b. Richmond, Va., Jan. 16, 1922; s. Charles Elroy and Pearl Ann (Shield) L.; B.S., Hampden-Sydney Coll., 1943; M.D., Med. Coll. Va., 1946; M.S. (Psychiat.), U. Colo. Postgrad. Med. Sch., 1953; m. Sara Grace Eldridge, Sept. 25, 1948; children—Charles Elroy III, George Eldridge (dec. July 1970), Richard Shield. Intern, Bellevue, N.Y., 1947-48; resident in psychiatry Colo. Psychopathic Hosp., Denver, 1950-53; asso. in psychiatry, asst. chief adult psychiat. outpatient clinic, dept. psychiatry Duke Med. Center, 1955-56, asst. prof. psychiatry, 1956-63, asso. prof. psychiatry, 1963—, head psychiat. outpatient div., 1956—, dir. student mental health service, 1959-69, dir. Duke study group Inter-Univ. Forum for Educators in Community Psychiatry, 1967-71; psychiat. cons., med. services div. Medicaid Program, 1971—; mem. vis. faculty, seminars Lab. Community Psychiatry, Harvard Med. Sch., 1964-67; practice gen. psychiatry, part time 1955—. Sr. psychiat. cons. N.C. Dept. Social Services, 1955—; cons. Family Counseling Service Durham, 1966—, bd. dirs., 1971—; mem. N.C. Mental Health Council, chmn., 1965-69. Cubmaster, Occoneechee council Boy Scouts Am., 1960-66 (named Cubmaster of Year Shawnee dist. 1962). Served to capt. M.C., AUS, 1953-55. Diplomate Am. Bd. Psychiatry and Neurology. Fellow Am., So. psychiat. assns., Am. Orthopsychiat. Assn., Pan Am. Med. Assn.; mem. A.M.A., Am. Group Psychotherapy Assn., Southeastern Group Psychotherapy Soc. (pres. 1965-66), Am. Acad. Religion and Mental Health, N.C. Neuropsychiat. Assn. (pres. 1971-72), N.C., Durham (chmn. med. adv. com. 1957-61) mental health assns. Methodist (pres. Sunday sch. 1957-58; mem. ofcl. bd. 1957-68; chmn. commn. social concerns 1963-68; trustee 1958-59). Office: Duke Univ Medical Center Durham NC 27706 Home: 3550 Hamstead Ct Durham NC 27707

LLOYD, KENNETH BRAWNER, cons.; b. Sinclairville, N.Y., May 25, 1916; s. Lee C. and Charlotte (Brawner) L.; B.A. in Journalism, U. Miami (Fla.), 1938; postgrad. Syracuse U., 1964; m. Myrtle R. Yanchisin, Oct. 23, 1946. Indsl. reporter McGraw Hill Internat., Mexico City, Mexico, 1946; owner, operator advt. agy., Buffalo, 1947-50; project dir. tech. publs. Bell Aircraft Corp., Buffalo, 1950-54; mgr. catalog dept. Kellogg switchbd. div. Internat. Telephone and Telegraph, Chgo., 1955-57; cons. marketing, pub. relations, Buffalo, 1958-60; information services specialist, Gen. Electrics, Syracuse, N.Y., 1961-63; mgr. advt., exhibits Will Sci., Inc., Rochester, N.Y., 1965-67; advt. specialist tech. publs. Bell Aerosystems, Buffalo, 1967-70; condr. marketing seminars for foreign students Syracuse U., 1964. Collector art, 1950-70, exhibitor, lectr. chs., schs., clubs throughout western N.Y. 1958-70; now cons. advt., art and humanities. Mem. Nat. Indsl. Advertisers Assn. Democrat. Episcopalian. Clubs: Aero (Buffalo), Toastmasters (Syracuse). Contbr. articles to profl. jours. Home: 1285 Santa Rosa Dr Clearwater FL 33516

LLOYD, WILLIAM NELSON, lawyer; b. Lewisburg, Tenn., July 24, 1920; s. William Houston and Rhoda (Hastings) L.; student Cumberland U., 1939-40, U. of South, 1941, U.Tenn., 1946; LL.B., Vanderbilt U., 1948, J.D., 1969; m. LaDelle Estes, Sept. 15, 1949; children—William Hastings, Robert Estes. Admitted to Tenn. bar, 1948, since practiced in Lewisburg. Dir. First Nat. Bank of Lewisburg, Oakwood Halls, WSML, Inc. Judge, Ct. of Gen. Sessions, 1950-58; mem. Constl. Conv. Tenn., 1965; del. Democratic Nat. Conv., 1964. Bd. dirs. Medicenter of Lewisburg. Served with USNR, 1942-46. Decorated Silver Star medal, D.F.C. with two oak leaf clusters. Recipient Long Rifle citation Boy Scouts Am., 1960. Mem. Am. Bar Assn., Am., Tenn. (bd. govs.) trial lawyers assns., Am. Judicature Soc. Presbyn. (elder). Home: 343 Forrest St Lewisburg TN 37901 Office: 220 W Church St Lewisburg TN 37901

LOAR, CHARLES R., adminstr. Baptist Med. Princeton Hosp., Birmingham, Ala. Office: 701 Princeton Av Birmingham AL 35211*

LOCKE, ALFRED HAMILTON, elec. engr.; b. McCurtain, Okla., Feb. 9, 1922; s. Blackshear Hamilton and Ethel (Maloney) L.; B.S., U. Okla., 1950; m. Patsy Ruth Kraft, June 5, 1943; children—Linda Kathleen (Mrs. Richard Massey), Jean Louise, Allen Patrick. With Okla. Gas and Electric Co., Oklahoma City, 1950—, now supr. sub-stas. Served to 1st lt. USAAF, 1942-45. Decorated D.F.C., Air medal with 2 oak leaf clusters. Mem. I.E.E.E. (sr., chmn. power group Central Okla. sect.), Am. Soc. Testing and Materials, Oklahoma City Engrs. Club, Nat., Okla. socs. profl. engrs. Baptist (deacon). Kiwanian (dir. 1965-70, pres. 1970-71). Contbr. articles to tech. jours. Home: 5913 NW 58th St Oklahoma City OK 73122 Office: 321 N Harvey St Oklahoma City OK 73102

LOCKE, JOHN FILLMORE, stock market service co. exec.; b. Bklyn., May 10, 1908; s. John Calvin and Adelaide (Fillmore) L.; degrees commerce, chemistry U. Cin., 1936, postgrad. engring.; m. Elsie Jane Nash, Aug. 8, 1942; children—Laura Carolyn, Joy Adelaide, John Noble, Harmon Fillmore. Formerly leader orch., band.; dept. head Avco, Cin., 1942-47; owner, pres. Cyclatron Trading Service, Covington, Ky., 1942—. Mem. child evangelism fellowship YMCA, Cin., 1954-56. Mem. No. Ky. Protestant Assn., Alpha Sigma Phi. Baptist (mem. finance com.). Mason (32 deg.). Author: Cyclotron Stock Market Forecasting, 1946; What is Commodity Trading1956. Contbr. articles to profl. jours. Home and office: 1081 Montague Rd Park Hills Covington KY 41011

LOCKE, LOUIS GLENN, educator; b. Woodstock, Va., May 3, 1912; s. Thomas Glenn and Turah (Funk) L.; A.B., Bridgewater Coll., 1933; A.M., George Washington U., 1934; A.M. (Dexter travelling fellow, 1937, Univ. fellow, 1937-38), Harvard, 1937, Ph.D., 1938; Ford fellow, Harvard and Yale, 1953-54; m. Jeanette Wolfe, Sept. 3, 1940; children—Sarah Anne, Elizabeth Louise. Acting prof. English, U. N.B., Can., 1938-39; asst. prof. English, Mary Washington Coll. of U. Va., 1939-43; head English dept. 20th AAF Coll. Tng. Detachment, 1943-45; asso. prof. English Southwestern U., Memphis, 1945-47; prof. English, Mary Baldwin Coll., 1947-56; chmn. dept. English, dir. div. humanities Madison Coll., Harrisonburg, Va., 1956-69, dean Sch. Humanities, 1969-72, James Madison prof. English, 1972—; vis. prof. Pa. State U., summer 1948, U. N.M., summer 1950. Mem. Modern Lang. Assn. Am., Nat. Council Tchrs. English (chmn. of judges for Va.), English Inst., Coll. English Assn., Omicron Delta Kappa Author: (with William Gibson and George Arms) Toward Liberal Education, 5th edit., 1967; Introduction to Literature, 5th edit., 1967; Readings for Liberal Education, 5th edit., 1967; (with J.P. Kirby and M.E. Porter) Literature Of Western Civilization, 2 vols., 1952; (with George Arms) Symposium, 1954; Tillotson: A Study In Seventeenth-Century Literature, 1954; (with Harris Wilson) The University Handbook, 2d edit., 1966; University Readings, 1961; (with George Arms, W.M. Gibson, George Petty, Jr.) TLE6: Options for the 1970's, 1972. Co-editor, co-founder The Explicator, 1942—. Address: 474 Ott St Harrisonburg VA 22801

LOCKE, WENDELL VERNON, architect; b. Douglas, Kan., Aug. 19, 1924; s. Noel Corbet and Francis (McNutt) L.; student Tex. A. and M. U.; B.A., Okla. State U., 1950, B.Arch., 1953; m. Thyra June Shattuck, Nov. 27, 1947; children—Diane Adele, Jeanne Sharon, Anita Sue, Betty Karen. Draftsman, designer firm Coston, Frankfurt, Short, Oklahoma City, 1953-55; architect firm Caudill, Rowlett, Scott, Oklahoma City, 1955-62; partner, pres. Locke Wright Foster, Inc., Oklahoma City, 1962—. Mem. 1971 Sch. of Month jury. Served with AUS to maj., C.E., AUS, World War II, Korea. Recipient several profl. awards, citations. Mem. A.I.A. (mem. nat. com. architecture for edn.), Council Edn. Facility Planners, Sch. Facilities Council, Soc. Coll. and Univ. Planning. Works include Performing Arts Center, Okla. State U., Stillwater, 1970. Home: Rte 2 Box 122A Oklahoma City OK 73114 Office: 5700 N Portland St Oklahoma City OK 73112

LOCKE, WILLIAM, physician; b. Morden, Man., Can., Mar. 16, 1916; s. Corbet and Ruby Louise (Brown) L.; M.D., U. Man., 1938; M.S. in Medicine, U. Minn., 1947; m. Katherine Elizabeth Acer, Sept. 29, 1945. Fellow in medicine Mayo Clinic, 1938-40, 46-47; research fellow Harvard, 1948-50; mem. staff Ochsner Clinic, New Orleans, 1950—, now head sect. endocrinology and metabolism; faculty dept. medicine Tulane U., 1951—, clin. prof. medicine, 1969—; sr. active staff Ochsner Found. Hosp., New Orleans, 1955—, pres. staff, 1954-55; sr. vis. physician Charity Hosp., New Orleans. Served to lt. comdr. Royal Canadian Navy, 1940-46. Fellow A.C.P.; mem. Endocrine Soc., Am. Diabetes Assn., Sigma Xi. Club: Roundtable (New Orleans). Editor: (with A.V. Schally) The Hypothalamus and Pituitary in Health and Disease, 1972. Contbr. articles profl. jours. Home: 4815 Dryades St New Orleans LA 70115 Office: 1514 Jefferson Hwy New Orleans LA 70115

LOCKETT, AUBREY LEE, cotton co. exec.; b. Wilbarger County, Tex., July 31, 1901; s. Frank S. and Ida (Lowe) L.; student Bowie Comml. Coll., 1918, Tyler Comml. Coll., 1919; m. Jewell Nowlin, May 28, 1924; 1 dau., Linda Lee (Mrs. Wayne R. Underwood). Owner, mgr. Aubrey L. Lockett Gins, Vernon, Tex., 1920—; pres., gen. mgr. Lockett Seed Co., Vernon, 1947-68, chmn. bd., 1968—; mng. partner Lockett Farms, Vernon, 1934—; pres. Waggoner Nat. Bank, Vernon, 1943-50, chmn. bd., 1950-60, hon. chmn. bd., 1960—. Treas. Nat. Cotton Council Am., 1955-62, v.p., 1962-63, pres., 1964, chmn. bd., 1965; treas. Oscar Johnston Cotton Found., 1955-69, chmn. bd., 1968-70; treas. Found. Cotton Research and Edn., 1955-69, chmn. bd. dirs., 1968-70; mem. cotton and cottonseed research and marketing adv. com. Dept. Agr., 1951-62; sec. Santa Rosa Roundup and Livestock Assn., 1946-69. Named Tex. Cotton Ginner of Year, 1959, Nat. Cotton Ginner of Year, 1959. Mem. Nat. (bd. dirs.), Tex (hon. adviser, pres. 1936-38) cotton ginners assns., Tex. Planting Seed Breeders Assn., So. Seedsmen's Assn., Nat. Council Comml. Plant Breeders (charter), Okla. Cotton Ginners Assn. (asso.), Vernon, W. Tex., U.S. chambers commerce. Baptist. Rotarian, Mason (Shriner). Home: 2222 Powell St Vernon TX 76384 Office: PO Box 1579 Vernon TX 76384

LOCKHART, THOMAS ASHE, lawyer; b. Charlotte, N.C., Apr. 5, 1928; s. James Alexander and Sara Laurens (Maffitt) L., Jr.; B.A., U. N.C., 1949, LL.B., 1951; m. Ann Marsh Wilkison, July 12, 1957; children—Thomas Ashe, James Wilkinson, John Laurens, Ann Marsh. Admitted to N.C. bar, 1951, since practiced in Charlotte. Trustee St. Peter's Hosp. Found., Charlotte, Episcopal Radio-TV Found., Inc., Atlanta. Served with AUS, 1952-54. Decorated Bronze Star medal. Mem. Assn. Life Ins. Counsel, Jud. Conf. 4th Circuit. Home: 801 Ardsley Rd Charlotte NC 28207 Office: NC Nat Bank Bldg Charlotte NC 28202

LOCKWOOD, MRS. CHARLES HOWARD (DOROTHY PYLE LOCKWOOD), newspaper pub.; b. Conway, Ark., Nov. 10; d. Lucas Hilliard and Augusta E. (Manes) Pyle; B.A., Central Coll., 1918; postgrad. piano N.Y.C. Sch. Music, 1919-24; m. James Aloysius McGrath, Oct. 1924 (dec. May 1928); m. 2d, Randall B. Terry, Sept. 17, 1931 (dec. May 1955); 1 son, Randall B. Head piano dept. Ark. State Tchrs. Coll., 1920-24; v.p. Burlington (N.C.) Times News, 1955—, High Point (N.C.) Enterprise, 1955—, The Times, Thomasville, N.C., 1958—. Bd. dirs. So. Furniture Expn., 1961. Active Heart Assn., United Fund. Bd. dirs. YMCA, Mem. N.C. Soc. Preservation Antiquities, Presbyn. Clubs: Emerywood Country; Blowing Rock (N.C.) Country. Home: 811 Willowbar Terrace High Point NC 27262 also 1015 Riverview Dr Atchison KS 66002 Office: 210 Church Av High Point NC 27261

LOCKWOOD, MARCIA LOUISE MOSTELLER (MRS. MARION CARL LOCKWOOD), business exec.; b. Cartersville, Ga.; d. Max William and Clarice (Newton) Mosteller; student Ga. State U., 1952; m. Marion Carl Lockwood, Aug. 18, 1951; 1 dau., Kathryn Louise. Sec., retail field office Sears, Roebuck & Co., Atlanta, 1943-46; sec., Archtl. Mfg. Co. Am., Atlanta, 1946-48, bus. adminstr., 1948—. Mem. Phi Chi Theta (pres. Upsilon chpt. 1951-52), Delta Lambda Sigma (treas.). Club: Northside Pilot (pres. 1969-70) (Atlanta). Home: 916 Northcliffe Dr NW Atlanta GA 30318 Office: 1 Permalume Pl NW Atlanta GA 30325

LODOVICHETTI, ARTHUR VICTOR, newsreel sound technician; b. North Bergen, N.J., Mar. 27, 1909; s. Duilio and Anita (Brolli) L.; student Royal Textile U., Italy, 1924-28; radio and elec. engring. student, N.Y.U., Columbia, 1928-30; m. Helen L. Howard, Jan. 13, 1941; 1 dau., Barbara Jean (Mrs. Carl E. Harris). Industry radio technician, 1928-34; design and sales motion picture equipment; free-lance motion picture tech. film prodns. East Coast, 1934-40; chief engr. Condor Films, Caracas, Venezuela, 1940-42; chief prodn. mixer U.S. Naval Photographic Center, 1945-52; newsreel photographer Fox-Movietone News, 1952-63; newsreel sound technician ABC, 1963—. Served with USNR, 1942-45. Mem. White House News

Photographers Assn. (v.p. 1960, pres. 1961), Nat. Geog. Soc., U.S. Capitol Radio-TV Corr. Gallery, Asociacion Mexicana Fotografos de Prensa. Home: RFD Box 4026 Crescent Rd Upper Marlboro MD 20870 Office: ABC Connecticut Av and L St NW Washington DC 20036

LOEB, BEN FOHL, JR., lawyer, educator; b. Nashville, May 15, 1932; s. Ben Fohl and Frances (Paysinger) L.; B.A., Vanderbilt U., 1955, J.D., 1960; m. Anne Nelson, Sept. 23, 1961; children—Charles N., William N. Admitted to Tenn. bar, 1960, U.S. Supreme Ct. bar, 1966; asso. firm Crownover, Branstetter & Folk, Nashville, 1960-64; asso. prof. pub. law and govt., asst. dir. U. N.C. Inst. Govt., Chapel Hill, 1964—. Served to 1st lt. AUS, 1955-57. Mem. Am. Bar Assn., U. N.C. Faculty Club, Am. Assn. U. Profs., Phi Beta Kappa, Phi Delta Phi, Pi Kappa Alpha (chpt. pres. 1955). Democrat. Baptist. Author: Drivers' License Law, 1965; Regulation of Intoxicating Liquors, 1966; Motor Vehicle Law, 1967; Traffic Law and Highway Safety, 1970. Asso. editor Vanderbilt Law Rev., 1960. Home: 812 Emory Dr Chapel Hill NC 27514

LOEBELSON, ROBERT MORRIS, editor, pub.; b. N.Y.C., Feb. 13, 1923; s. Ira and Gertrude (Gordon) L.; student U. Mich., 1943-44; B.A. in Journalism, Ohio State U., 1947; m. Jean Amdur, Jan. 30, 1942; 1 son, Richard Kenneth. Newspaper reporter Ohio State Jour., Cleve. Plain Dealer, Springfield News and Sun, Dayton Herald (all Ohio), 1941-48; editor Tech. Data Digest Mag., Dayton, O., 1948-51; mil. editor Am. Aviation mag., Washington, 1951-56, Space/Aeronautics mag., Washington, 1958-61; mem. pub. relations staff Aerospace Industries Assn., Washington, 1956-58; freelance writer Washington, 1961-66; editor Vertical World Mag., Washington, 1966-70, pres. Vertical World, Inc., 1968-70; pres. Aerospace Communications, Washington, 1970—; dir. Aerosystems Tech. Corp., Franklin, N.J. Served with M.I. AUS, 1943-46. Recipient 1st prize Trans-World Airlines writing competition, 1958. Mem. Aviation Space Writers Assn. (pres. 1960-61), Nat. Press Club. Home: 10001 Sinnott Dr Bethesda MD 20034 Office: National Press Bldg Washington DC 20004

LOEFFLER, DAVID HAROLD, lawyer; b. Bristow, Okla., Oct. 20, 1920; s. Louis and Luva (Sheffel) L.; B.S., Okla. U.; J.D., Harvard; m. Bernice Harpman, June 26, 1949; children—David Harold, Pauli D. Admitted to Okla. bar, 1948; partner Loeffler & Allen and predecessor firms, Bristow, 1948—, Sapulpa, Okla., 1954—, Tulsa, 1971—, sr. partner, 1951—; officer, dir. numerous corps. Chmn., Montfort Jones and Allie Brown Jones Found., 1962—; chmn. Bristow Airport Authority, 1966—. Served to capt. AUS, 1942-45. Mem. Bristow C. of C. (v.p.), Am., Okla. bar assns., Internat. Soc. Barristers. Home: 248 W 6th St Bristow OK 74010 Office: 216 W 6th St Bristow OK 74010

LOEFFLER, FRED PEMBROKE, editor; b. Rochester, N.Y., Dec. 16, 1923; s. Fred Harold and Mildred (Pembroke) L.; grad. Peddie Sch., 1942; A.B., Washington and Lee U., 1948. Mem. staff Roanoke (Va.) Times, 1948—, state editor, 1953-66, gen. copy editor, 1966—. Served to ensign USNR, 1943-46. Home: 2755 Brandon Av SW Roanoke VA 24015 Office: Times World Bldg Roanoke VA 24005

LOEVINGER, LEE, lawyer, investment banking exec.; b. St. Paul, Apr. 24, 1913; s. Gustavus and Millie (Strouse) L.; B.A. summa cum laude, U. Minn., 1933, J.D., 1936; m. Ruth E. Howe, Mar. 4, 1950; children—Barbara Lee, Eric Howe, Peter Howe. Admitted to Minn. bar, 1936, Mo. bar, 1937, D.C. bar, 1966, U.S. Supreme Ct. bar, 1941; asso. law firm Watson, Ess, Groner, Barnett & Whittaker, Kansas City, Mo., 1936-37; trial atty., regional atty. NLRB, 1937-41; atty. antitrust div. U.S. Dept. Justice, 1941-46, asst. atty. gen. charge antitrust div., 1961-63; partner law firm Larson, Loevinger, Lindquist, Freeman & Fraser, Mpls., 1946-60; asso. justice Minn. Supreme Ct., 1960-61; commr. FCC, 1963-68; partner law firm Hogan & Hartson, Washington, 1968—. Gen. counsel Craig-Hallum, Inc., investment banking, Mpls., 1950-60, v.p., dir., 1968—; v.p., dir. Craig-Hallum Corp., Mpls., 1968—; gen. counsel Gen. Securities, Inc., 1951-60; lectr. hosp. and nursing law U. Minn. Med. Sch., 1953-60; vis. prof. jurisprudence, Law Sch., 1961; gen. counsel Minn. Nurses Assn., 1950-60; spl. counsel to subcom. on small bus. U.S. Senate, 1951-52; U.S. del. to com. experts on restrictive bus. practices OECD, 1961-64, vice chmn. com., 1963-64; U.S. del., vice chmn. extraordinary adminstrv. radio conf. Internat. Telecommunications Union, Geneva, 1964, 66. Served to lt. comdr. USNR, 1942-45. Recipient Outstanding Achievement award U. Minn. Regents, 1968. Mem. Am. (mem. law and tech. com. 1969—), D.C., Fed., Minn., Hennepin County bar assns., Am. Judicature Soc., A.A.A.S., Broadcast Pioneers, Phi Beta Kappa, Sigma Xi, Phi Delta Gamma, Delta Sigma Rho, Sigma Delta Chi, Tau Kappa Alpha, Alpha Epsilon Rho. Author: The Law of Free Enterprise, 1949; Jurimetrics, 1949; An Introduction to Legal Logic, 1952. Editor, contbr. Basic Data on Atomic Development Problems in Minnesota, 1958; editorial adviser Jurimetrics Jour.; adv. bd. Antitrust Bull., Performing Arts Rev. Contbr. articles to profl. jours. Home: 5669 Bent Branch Rd Washington DC 20016 Office: 815 Connecticut Av Washington DC 20006

LOEWENSTEIN, JOSEPH MEYER, physician; b. Houston, May 15, 1910; s. Edward Benjamin and Lena (Kapner) L.; B.A., Rice U., 1931; M.D., U. Tex., 1935; postgrad. N.Y. U., 1954, U. London (Eng.), 1965; m. Ethel Lois Fallis, June 6, 1933; children—Joseph Edward, Robert Fallis. Intern John Sealy Hosp., Galveston, Tex., 1935-36; practice gen. medicine, Lovelady, Tex., 1936-38, Port Arthur, Tex., 1938—; partner Parkside Clinic, Port Arthur, 1938—; chief staff St. Mary's Hosp., Port Arthur, 1953; mem. staff Park Place Hosp., Port Arthur. Pres. Port Arthur Little Theater, 1955-59; med. adviser Draft Bd. No. 75, Jefferson County, Tex., 1967—, Schlesinger Convalescent Home, 1967—. Bd. dirs. Gates Meml. Art Mus., Port Arthur, 1958-59. Mem. A.M.A., Tex. Med. Assn., Am. Assn. Gen. Practitioners, Royal Soc. Medicine (London; affiliate mem.), Phi Beta Kappa, Alpha Omega Alpha. Rotarian. Club: Port Arthur Town. Home: 3045 Eugenia Dr Groves TX 77619 Office: 3048 Procter St Port Arthur TX 77640

LOFBERG, ROBERT TOR, govt. ofcl.; b. Gasport, N.Y., Sept. 16, 1922; s. Fritjof Samual and Josephine Ann (Kaufmann) L.; B.A., U. So. Cal., 1959; M.S., Highlands U., 1956; Ph.D., U. N.M., 1958; m. Christine Curry White, Mar. 16, 1955; 1 son, Fredrick Tor. Research scientist Lockheed Aircraft Corp., 1958-59; staff scientist United Tech., 1959-62; chief analytical chemistry sect., div. biochemistry Walter Reed Army Inst. Research, Washington, 1962—. Served with AUS, 1943. Recipient Outstanding Performance awards Dept. Army, 1965, 66, 71. Mem. Am. Chem. Soc., Sigma Xi, Nu Sigma Alpha. Baptist. Contbr. articles to profl. jours. Patentee in field. Home: 11110 Dewey Rd Kensington MD 20795 Office: Walter Reed Army Inst Research Washington DC 20012

LOFROOS, WILLIAM NORMAN, civil engr.; b. Warren, O., June 19, 1931; s. William Eric and Margaret (White) L.; B.E. in Civil Engring., Vanderbilt U., 1954; M.S., U. Fla., 1959; m. Avis Hurst, Aug. 8, 1959; children—Margaret Elizabeth, William Eric. Instr., U. Fla., 1957-59; with Fla. Dept. Transp., Tallahassee, 1959—, now chief bur. planning. Served with USMC, 1954-57, lt. col. Res. Mem. Am. Soc. C.E. (past br. pres.), Fla. Engring. Soc. (past br. pres., past sect. chmn.), Am., Southeastern assns. state hwy. ofcls., Marine Corps Res. Officers Assn. Mason. Home: 1904 Doomar St Tallahassee FL 32303 Office: Fla Dept Transportation Tallahassee FL 32301

LOFTEN, WILLIAM TRAVIS, educator. Asso. prof. edn., chmn. dept. vocational, tech. and adult edn. U. Fla. Home: 210 SE 6th St Gainesville FL 32601 Office: U Fla Gainesville FL 32601

LOFTIS, JAMES STEWART, physician; b. Royse City, Tex., Dec. 3, 1931; s. Laborn Dudley and Mary Nell (Dowell) L.; student So. Methodist U., 1949-52; M.D., Southwestern Med. U., 1956; m. Carrie Jane Whaley, Aug. 27, 1955; children—Amy, Audrey. Intern, Meth. Hosp., Dallas, 1956-57; practice medicine, specializing in family practice, Odessa, Tex., 1959—; mem. staff Med. Center Hosp. Served to capt. USAF, 1957-59. Mem. Andrews-Ector County Med. Soc. (pres. 1970). Home: 3209 Blossom Lane Odessa TX 79760 Office: 1165 E 42d St Odessa TX 79760

LOFTUS, MARTIN L., librarian; b. Sand Creek, Wis., June 9, 1911; s. Samuel and Signe (Carlson) L.; B.S. in L.S., U. Wash., 1932, A.B., 1933; m. Isabel Orr, May 15, 1948. Jr. librarian U. Wash., Seattle, 1933-37; reference asst. N.Y. Pub. Library, N.Y.C., 1937-46; tech. librarian VA, N.Y., 1946; librarian IMF and Internat. Bank for Reconstrn. and Devel., Washington, 1946—. Treas., U.S. Book Exchange, 1964-65. Trustee Pub. Affairs Information Service, 1964—. Served with AUS, 1942-45. Mem. A.L.A., Spl. Libraries Assn. (treas. 1951-52), Am. Documentation Inst., Phi Beta Kappa. Club: Cosmos (Washington). Home: 10407 Montrose Av Bethesda MD 20014 Office: 19 & H Sts NW Washington DC 20431

LOGAN, ALBERT BOYD, lawyer; b. Colorado Springs, Colo., Jan. 27, 1909; s. Glen Hayes and Margaret (McGee) L.; A.B., U. Colo., 1930, J.D., 1932; m. Martha Elizabeth Hutchison, Sept. 28, 1934; children— Marla Lee (Mrs. Al Hollingsworth), Glenda Sue (Mrs. Stephen Harrison). Admitted to Colo. bar, 1932; pvt. practice law, Colorado Springs, 1932-56; with Office Solicitor, U.S. Dept. Interior, Denver, 1956-66; counsel Indian Claims Commn., Washington, 1966-70, Office Gen. Counsel VA, 1970—; lectr. jud. problems. Exec. dir. N.Am. Judges Assn., 1960-67; sec., trustee Jud. Research Found., Washington, 1960-68; cons. Am. Judicature Soc., Nat. Council Alcoholism, U. Colo. Sch. Alcohol Studies, Colo. Commn. Alcoholism, Inst. Law and Psychiatry, Mil.-Jud. Conf. Hwy Safety, Nat. Council Indian Opportunity, Nat. Acad. Metabology. Trustee Harmony Found., Inc. Served with USMCR, 1944-45. Recipient Beyond Call of Duty award Nat. Assn. Municipal Judges, 1961. Mem. Fed., Am., Colo. bar assns., Am. Legion, Am. Judicature Soc., Nat. Inst. Jud. Dynamics (dir.), U.S. Jr. C. of C. (nat. dir), N.Am. Judges Assn. (hon. life mem., Amicus Curiae award 1964), Phi Alpha Delta, Sigma Delta Chi, Alpha Tau Omega. Clubs: El Paso, Exchange (pres. Colorado Springs); National Lawyers. Author: Struggle For Equal Justice, 1968; Justice in Jeopardy, 1972; With Liberty and Justice for All, 1972. Editor: Municipal Ct. Rev., 1960-67, Municipal Ct. Briefs, 1960-67. Contbr. to legal periodicals. Home: 2727 29th St NW Washington DC 20008 Office: National Institute of Judicial Dynamics 2607 Connecticut Av NW Washington DC 20008

LOGAN, LOUIS JAMES, editor; b. Temple, Tex., July 21, 1902; s. James Beauregard and Frances (Schiller) L.; B. Journalism, U. Tex., 1925; m. Iris Allen, Apr. 6, 1929; children—Louis James (dec.), Robert Allen, John Charles, Elizabeth Ann. Advt. mgr. Cameron (Tex.) Enterprise, 1923-24; reporter Austin (Tex.) Am., 1924; staff rep. The Oil Weekly, Houston, 1927-31, staff economist, 1932-34, asso. editor, 1934-46; asso. editor World Oil, Houston, 1947-68; corporate sec., dir. petroleum industry library Gulf Pub. Co., Houston, 1955-68; information coordinator Marathon Le Tourneau Offshore Co., Houston, 1969—. Mem. Sigma Delta Chi. Baptist. Contbr. articles to profl. jours. Home: 1405 Crocker St Houston TX 77019 Office: River Oaks Bank Bldg 2001 Kirby Dr Houston TX 77019

LOGAN, MARGOT BENNETT, museum trustee; b. Atlanta, Aug. 1, 1926; d. W. Hooper and Margaret Logan (Pratt) Bennett; B.A., Newcomb Coll. of Tulane U., 1947; m. Dr. Samuel Logan, Dec. 22, 1947; children—Samuel, Melanie Mynor, George King, Margaret Pratt. Volunteer coordinator Grady Hosp., Atlanta, 1947-48, La. Dept. Pub. Welfare, New Orleans, 1950-52. Bd. trustees Isaac Delgado Mus. Art, New Orleans, 1960—, sec., 1961—; bd. trustees New Orleans Ednl. TV, 1959—, So. Eye Bank, 1959—, Russel Holman Center for Retardates, New Orleans, 1960—, New Orleans Inst. Mental Hygiene, 1960—; mem. bd. womens com. New Orleans Symphony, 1960-62; exec. com. Greater New Orleans Cultural Attractions Fund, 1960—; sec. Jefferson Parrish Med. Auxiliary, 1960-61; now sec. Repertory Theatre of New Orleans, also dir.; bd. dirs. Asso. Councils Arts, Louis S. McGehee Sch.; pres. The Green Door, Inc. (gift shop), Gretna. Mem. Jr. League New Orleans (pres. 1959-60), Pi Beta Phi. Address: 48 Colony Rd Timberlane Estates Gretna LA 70053

LOGAN, THEODORE EDWARD, dental educator; b. Falmouth, Ky., May 16, 1922; s. Archie L. and Chloe Hattie (Bishop) L.; B.S., U. Ky., 1945; D.M.D., U. Louisville, 1949; postgrad. in prosthodontics Ohio State U., 1950; m. Vivian Leach Wiggins, Mar. 4, 1944; children—Theodore Edward, Leslie Ann (Mrs. Peter Compise), Timothy Wilson. Pre-supr. trainee Joseph E. Seagrams, 1945-46; prof., chmn. dept. prosthodontics U. Louisville Sch. Dentistry, 1950—, dir. continuing edn., 1962—, dir. admissions, 1969—; asst. dean, 1971—; practice dentistry specializing in prosthodontics, Louisville, 1961—; cons. Ireland Army Hosp., Ft. Knox, Ky. Mem. Ky. Gov.'s Adv. Council on Med. Assistance. Active Little League, Babe Ruth League. Served to 2d lt. AUS, 1942-44. Fellow Am. Coll. Dentists (pres. Ky. sect. 1970—, ho. of dels. 1963—); mem. Ky. Dental Assn. (pres. 1970-71), Delta Sigma Delta, Phi Delta, Omicron Delta Kappa, Omicron Kappa Upsilon. Mem. Christian Ch. Mason (32 deg.). Club: Philological (Louisville). Contbr. articles to dental jours. Home: 3506 Forest Brook Dr Louisville KY 40207

LOGAN, WILLIAM THOMAS, dentist; b. Dublin, Tex., Dec. 10, 1925; s. James Marvin and Eula (Kiker) L.; B.A., Hardin-Simmons U., 1948; D.D.S., U. Tex., 1952; m. Margaret Elaine Dobbins, May 31, 1947; children—Richard Alan, Diana Lynn. Practice dentistry, Borger, Tex., 1952—. Served with USNR, 1944-46; PTO. Fellow Acad. Gen. Dentistry; mem. Am., Tex. dental assns., Borger (pres. 1959), Panhandle Dist. (pres. 1966-67) dental socs., Am. Acad. Gold Foil Operators, Am. Inst. Oral Biology, Tex. Acad. Gen. Dentistry, Palo Duro (pres. 1960), Clyde Schuyler dental study groups, Tex. Jr. C. of C. (dir. 1954), Psi Omega. Methodist. Mason (Shriner, 32 deg.), Elk, Lion. Clubs: North Plains Knife and Fork (dir. 1962-64). Home: 1400 Bluebonnet Lane Borger TX 79007 Office: 706 S McGee St Borger TX 79007

LOGSDON, GUY WILLIAM, librarian; b. Ada, Okla., May 31, 1934; s. Guy and Mattie Theresa (Marsalas) L.; B.A. in Edn., East Central State Coll., 1957; M.L.S., U. Okla., 1964, postgrad., 1969-70; postgrad. Ind. U., 1968; m. Phyllis Evelyn Landers, Dec. 28, 1953; children—Tamara Lei, Cindy Lou, Susan Elizabeth, Nathalie Marsalas. Photographer Guy Logsdon Studio, Ada, 1954-56; tchr. Norwalk-La Mirada (Cal.) Sch. Dist., 1956-67, Burbank (Okla.) Sch. Dist., 1957-58, Payson (Ariz.) Sch. Dist., 1960-63; salesman Gt. So. Life Ins., Ardmore, Okla., 1958-60; reference librarian Okla. State U., Stillwater, 1964-67; dir. libraries U. Tulsa, 1967—. Mem. Am., Okla., Southwestern library assns., Am., Tex., Cal. folklore socs., Indian Terr. Posse Westerners, Sons of Confederacy, Okla., Western, Rodeo hist. socs., Phi Delta Kappa. Democrat. Methodist. Mason. Editor: Great River and Small (Welborn Hope). Contbr. articles to profl. jours. and encys. Home: 4645 S Columbia St Tulsa OK 74105 Office: U Tulsa 600 S College St Tulsa OK 74104

LOGUE, MICHAEL WOOTEN, mfg. co. exec.; b. Dothan, Ala., July 15, 1933; s. Wilbur Benson and Maym Bell (Wooten) L.; grad. Darlington Sch. cum laude, 1952; B.B.A., Emory U., 1956; student Auburn U., 1953; m. Sara Eleanor Forester, June 13, 1956; children—Amanda Link, Monica Lynn, Wilbur Benson II, Michael Wooten. Sec. Solomon Bros. (name changed to Solomon Fabrics, Inc., 1971), Atlanta and branches, 1962-70, pres., chief exec. officer, 1970—. Served with USAF, 1957-60; Japan. Mem. Sigma Alpha Epsilon. Presbyn. Home: 7090 Riverside Dr NW Atlanta GA 30328 Office: 880 Great Southwest Pky Atlanta GA 30336

LOGUE, THOMAS OTTO, JR., hosp. adminstr.; b. Vicksburg, Miss., Oct. 18, 1932; student Vicksburg Sch. Med. Tech., 1951-53, Withworth Coll., 1969-71, U. Ala., 1971-72; m. Joyce Wilson; children—Tonia, Thomas Edward, Linda. Adminstr., Hancock Gen. Hosp., Bay St. Louis, Miss., 1959-66, Tallahatchie Gen. Hosp., Charleston, Miss., 1966-68, Southwest Miss. Gen. Hosp., McComb, 1968—. Mem. Miss. Manpower Bd., 1970-72; pres. Health Adv. Bd., 1970—; mem. adv. com. Southwest Miss. Jr. Coll., 1970—. Bd. dirs. United Givers Fund. Served to maj. AUS, 1966. Named Outstanding Young Man of Yr., Miss. Jr. C. of C., 1961. Mem. Miss. Hosp. Assn. (bd. govs. 1970—), Am. Coll. Hosp. Adminstrs. (sec.-treas. 71), Am. Legion (comdr. 1971—), Tallahatchie County C. of C. (pres. 1967-68), Bay St. Louis and Mendenhall Jaycees (pres.). Republican. Rotarian (past pres), Mason. Contbr. articles to profl. jours. Home: 1510 Vermont St McComb MS 39648 Office: PO Box 68 McComb MS 39648

LOHR, DERMOT, physician; b. Lexington, N.C., Sept. 1, 1910; s. Andrew Curtis and Fallie (Curry) L.; B.S., U. N.C., 1932; M.D., Jefferson Med. Coll., Phila., 1934; m. Blanche Grimes, Aug. 18, 1935; children—Loyd D., Jacob A., Sarah Jo. Intern, T.C.I. Hosp., Birmingham, Ala., 1934-35; practice medicine, Lexington, 1937-42, 46-57; health dir. Davidson County Health Dept., Lexington, 1959—. Coroner, Davidson County, 1946-50. Served with USN, 1935-37, USNR, 1942-45. Decorated Purple Heart. Mem. Davidson County Med. Soc. (past pres.). Kiwanian (pres. 1950). Home: 20 Vance Circle Lexington NC 27292 Office: N Main St Lexington NC 27292

LOKEY, CLARENCE WALTERS, clergyman; b. Farmersville, Tex., Aug. 21, 1895; s. Thomas Franklin and Luella (Haskin) L.; A.B., Rice U., 1917; M.S., Tex. A. and M. Coll., 1930; Ph.D., 1947; D.D., Southwestern U., 1947; m. Mary Augustine Kerr, Aug. 31, 1918 (dec. 1962); children—Mary Augustine (Mrs. Warren D. Barton), Althea Anne (Mrs. Arthur B. Kelly), Clarence Walters; m. 2d, Zada Olive Maxwell Hamilton, 1967. Traffic supt. Southwestern Bell Telephone Co., Beaumont, Tex. Dist., 1919, supt. toll traffic. Houston, 1920; ordained to ministry Methodist Ch., 1920; pastor in Beaumont, Tex., 1920-21, Doucette, Tex., 1922-24, Edgewood, Tex., 1925-26, Gilmer, Tex., 1930-32, Nacogdoches, Tex., 1932-38; extension sec. Tex. Conf., Gen. Bd. Missions, M.E. Ch. South, 1926-30; presiding elder Marlin dist. Tex. Conf., 1938-40, dist. supt. Bryan dist., 1940-44; exec. sec. home mission bd. Meth. Ch., N.Y.C., 1944-48, sec. Spanish speaking work Meth. Ch., N.Y.C., Phila., also San Antonio, 1948-66. Mem. com. Spanish-Am. work Nat. Council Chs., 1948-66, Nat., Tex. migrant labor coms., 1950-62, treas. Council on Spanish Am. Work, 1963-66; pres. Interdenominational Council Spanish Am. Work, 1959-61. Served to lt. U.S. Army, 1918-19; AEF IN France. Recipient Citation for Distinguished Service, Coll. Bishops, Pastors and Laymen, 1966. Mem. Tex. Acad. Sci., Theta Phi (hon.). Mason, Rotarian. Co-author: Spanish Doorways. Originator, developer Lord's Acre, program of edn. and service for rural and mission chs. and adapted to more gen. application. Home: 7923 Donore Pl San Antonio TX 78229 Office: 53 Bandera Rd San Antonio TX 78228

LOMAN, M(ARY) LAVERNE GLASS (MRS. COY EMIAL LOMAN), educator; b. Stratford, Okla., June 10, 1928; d. Thomas DeWitte and Mary (Goodwin) Glass; student Oklahoma City U., 1944-45; B.S., U. Okla., 1956, M.A., 1957, Ph.D., 1961; m. Coy Emial Loman, Dec. 23, 1944; 1 dau., Sandra Leigh. Grad asst. math. U. Okla., Norman, 1956-57, instr., 1957-61; asst. prof. math. Central State U., Edmond, Okla., 1961-62, asso. prof., 1962-66, prof., 1966—. NSF fellow, 1965-67; named Central State U. Tchr. of Year, 1968. Mem. Math. Assn. Am., Nat., Okla. (dir. 1971—) councils tchrs. math., Okla. Edn. Assn. (pres. local unit 1967-68), Delta Kappa Gamma (pres. Alpha Mu chpt. 1963-65). Home: 2201 Tall Oaks Trail Route 1 Edmond OK 73034

LOMASNEY, THOMAS LAWRENCE, physician; b. Central Falls, R.I., May 29, 1920; s. Thomas Cornelius and Mary (Parks) L.; A.B., Brown U., 1941; M.D., Boston U., 1944; m. Kate Stewart Rutherford, Dec. 17, 1955; children—Robert Rutherford, William Stewart, Sara Wright. Intern Mass. Meml. Hosps., Boston, 1944-45; resident Boston City Hosp., 1946, VA Deans' Com. Hosp., Rutland Heights, Mass., 1947-49, Providence, R.I., 1950-52, Dartmouth Med. Group. Hanover, N.H., 1950; practice medicine specializing in thoracic and cardiac surgery, Knoxville, Tenn., 1952—, Middlesboro, Ky., 1952—; attending thoracic surgeon St. Mary's Hosp., Knoxville, 1952—, Ft. Sanders Presbyn. Hosp., Knoxville, 1952—; attending thoracic surgeon U. Tenn. Meml. Research Center and Hosp., Knoxville, 1961—, instr. thoracic surgery, 1961—; cons. thoracic surgeon Meml. Hosp., Middlesboro, 1956—. Served from lt. (j.g.) to lt. M.C., USNR, 1945-46, 53-54. Diplomate Am. Bd. Surgery, Am. Bd. Thoracic Surgery. Mem. A.M.A., Am. Thoracic Soc., So. Thoracic Surg. Assn., Pan Am. Med. Assn. (diplomate mem., sect. on thoracic surgery), Knoxville Surg. Soc., Soc. Thoracic Surgeons. Contbr. articles to med. jours. Home: 6613 Sherwood Dr Knoxville TN 37919 Office: 2209 White Av Knoxville TN 37916

LOMBARD, ALAIN, condr. Miami Philharmonic. Address: Box 3078 Coral Gables FL 33134*

LOMBARD, EDWARD EMMANUEL, govt. ofcl.; b. Youngstown, O., Jan. 26, 1934; s. Edward Leo and Rita (Vimmerstedt) L.; B.A., Youngstown U., 1959; M.I.A., Yale, 1961; M.S., Stanford, 1968; m. Shirley Elaine Neff, May 11, 1965; children—Edward A. III, Jennifer E. Sr. planning analyst Brunswick Corp., Chgo., 1961-64; lectr. bus. and industry U. Balt., 1964-67; spl. asst. to postmaster gen. P.O. Dept., Washington, 1964-65; dir. data mgmt. Small Bus. Adminstrn., Washington, 1965-69; asst. dir. adminstrn. and program analysis Econ. Devel. Adminstrn., Washington, 1969—; gen. partner, pres. Lland Assos. Spl. cons. U.S. Ho. of Reps., 1969. Served with AUS, 1957. Nat. Inst. Pub. Affairs fellow, 1967-68; recipient award for outstanding performance Small Bus. Adminstrn., 1966, Econ. Devel. Adminstrn., 1971, 72. Mem. Inst. Mgmt. Scis., Operations Research Soc. Am., Assn. Pub. Program Analysts. Roman Catholic. Home:

3166 Juniper Lane Falls Church VA 22044 Office: Dept of Commerce 14th and Constitution Av NW Washington DC 20230

LOMBARDI, LOUIS FELIX, economist; b. Elizabeth, N.J., Aug. 19, 1935; s. Felix Edward and Charlotte Jordan (Morris) L.; B.S. cum laude, Mount St. Mary's Coll., Emmitsburg, Md., 1958; M.A., Fordham U., 1963; LL.B., LaSalle Extension U., 1970; m. Adrienne Jeanette Wire, Dec. 27, 1958; children—Kathleen Ann, Louis Felix II. Asst. trust officer, estate planning Peoples Trust City Bank, Reading, Pa., 1962-65; financial cons., Reading, Pa., 1965; project adminstr. AMF Corp., York, Pa., 1965-66; prin. economist Va. Div. Water Resources, Richmond, 1966—. Mem. adj. faculty VA. Commonwealth U., Richmond, 1969—. Served with AUS, 1958-60. Mem. Am. Econ. Assn. Democrat. Author: Regional Analysis and Forecasting for Regional Areas, 1971. Contbr. articles to publs. Home: 9007 Mapleton Rd Richmond VA 23229 Office: Davenport Bldg 11 S 10th St Richmond VA 23219

LOMBARDI, MAX HABIB, radiation biologist; b. Huanuco, Peru, S. Am., Apr. 25, 1932; s. Maximo David and Maria Eva (Lombardi) L.; B.V.M., U. San Marcos, Lima, Peru, 1958; D.V.M., 1958; M.S., Cornell U., 1961; m. Jeanette Sylvia Dunbar, May 31, 1961; children—Katherine Jeanne, Maria Louisa. Came to U.S., 1963. Instr. exptl. physiology U. San Marcos, Lima, Peru, 1956-59; auxiliar prof. physiology, biochemistry and nutrition, 1960-62, asso. prof. biochemistry, nutrition, radiobiology, 1962-63; scientist Oak Ridge Asso. Univs., 1964-68, sr. scientist, 1966—, coordinator medical radioisotope courses and internat. programs, 1964—. Mem. A.A.A.S., Am. Nuclear Soc. Author: (with L. K. Akers) Radioisotopos en Investigacion Basica, 1967, Radiosotopos en Diagnostico Medico, 1967. Home: Route 17 Guinn Rd Knoxville TN 37921 Office: PO Box 117 Oak Ridge TN 37830

LONDON, GEORGE, opera and concert singer; b. Montreal, Que., Can., May 30, 1920; s. Louis Samuel and Bertha (Broad) Burnstein (father Am. citizen); student Los Angeles City Coll., 1937-39; m. Nora Sheldon, Aug. 30, 1955; children—Marina, Mark. With Am. Music Theater, Los Angeles and Pasadena, Cal., 1940; profl. opera debut as Dr. Grenvil in La Traviata, Hollywood Bowl, 1941; singer Los Angeles and San Francisco civic light opera assns., 1942-44; San Francisco Opera debut in Rigoletto, 1943; baritone soloist, world premiere Hindemith's composition When Lilacs Last in the Dooryard Bloomed, 1946; Vienna State Opera debut in Aida, 1949; singer Glyndebourne Opera, 1950, Bayreuth Festival, 1951-53, 56, 57, 59, 61-64, Salzburg Festival, 1952; Met. Opera debut, Aida, 1951, La Scala debut, 1952; San Francisco, 1959; sang title role Boris Gudunov, Moscow, 1960; title role Am. premiere The Last Savage, 1963-64; artistic adminstr. John F. Kennedy Center for Performing Arts, Washington, 1968—. Apptd. Austrian Kammersaenger (court singer) by pres. of Austria, 1955. Bd. dirs. N.Y.C. Center. Mem. Am. Guild Mus. Artists (pres.). Contbr. articles on music Am. Publs. Recorded title role of Boris Godunov with Bolshoi Ensemble. Home: Les Muses Vufflens-le-Chateau Switzerland also 3125 Chain Bridge Rd NW Washington DC 20016 Office: 726 Jackson Pl NW Washington DC 20566

LONDREY, JAMES LESLIE, life ins. co. exec.; b. Syracuse, N.Y., June 2, 1926; s. Lynn L. and Bertha (Bassler) L.; A.B., Yale, 1950; grad. Basic Advanced Mgmt. Course, U. Va., 1959; m. Jane Gregg, May 24, 1955; children—Gregg L., James F., William G. Underwriter, Marine Office Am., N.Y.C., 1950-53; with Life Ins. Co. Va., Richmond, 1953—, asst. treas. bond div., 1960-64, corp. treas., 1964—, now 2d v.p.; dir. First Va. Mgmt. and Research Corp., Bradford Sch. Corp., Pitts. Chmn. budget com. Richmond United Givers Fund, 1966—, bd. govs., 1964—. Served with USNR, 1944-46. Chartered financial analyst, 1965. Mem. Richmond Soc. Financial Analysts (past pres.). Presbyn. (elder). Clubs: Yale, Downtown (Richmond); Country of Va. Office: 914 Capitol St Richmond VA 23219

LONG, ALFRED B., oil co. exec.; b. Galveston, Tex., Aug. 4, 1909; s. Jessie A. and Ada (Beckwith) L.; student S. Park Jr. Coll., 1928-29, Lamar State Coll. Tech., 1947-56, U. Tex., 1941; m. Sylvia V. Thomas, Oct. 29, 1932; 1 dau., Kathleen Sylvia (Mrs. E.A. Pearson, II). With Sun Oil Co., Beaumont, Tex., 1931—, driller geophys. dept., surveyor engring. dept., engr. operating dept., engr. prodn. lab., 1931-59, regional supr., 1960-69, now ret.; ind. oil cons., Beaumont, Tex., 1969—. Mem. Jefferson County Program Planning Com., 1964. Mem. Soc. Petroleum Engrs., Am. Assn. Petroleum Geologists. I.E.E.E., Houston, Beaumont geol. socs., Gulf Coast Engring. and Sci. Soc. (treas. 1962-65), Am. Petroleum Inst., Houston Petroleum Inst., U.S. Power Squadron. Inventor various oil well devices. Home: 8510 Calder Rd Beaumont TX 77706 Office: PO Box 3265 Beaumont TX 77704

LONG, ARTHUR IRVING, innkeeper; b. Seneca Falls, N.Y., May 8, 1917; s. Arthur I. and Ada Mary (Babcock) L.; student Albany (N.Y.) Bus. Coll., 1938, Cornell U., summer 1952; m. Ruth Arlene Lockwood, May 1, 1940. With Hillsboro Club, Pompano Beach, Fla., 1939-41, E.I. Dupont de Nemours Co., Wilmington, Del., 1941-43; with Royal Park Inn, Vero Beach, Fla., 1946-47; mgr. Holly Inn, Pinehurst, N.C., 1947-71; mgr. The Beach House Motor Inn, Myrtle Beach, S.C., 1971—. Served with USAAF, 1943-46. Mem. So. (v.p. 1967; dir. 1968), N.C. (v.p. 1969-71) innkeepers, Sandhill Area C. of C. Clubs: Pinehurst Country; Tega Cay (Ft. Mill, S.C.). Address: The Beach House Motor Inn 6800 N Ocean Blvd Myrtle Beach SC 29577

LONG, BLANCHE REVERE, Democratic nat. committeewoman; b. Covington, La., Dec. 17, 1904; d. Robert H. and Beulah (Talley) Revere; student Tulane U., 1926-27; m. Earl K. Long, Aug. 17, 1932. Democratic nat. committeewoman for La., 1956-60, 64—. Mem. La. Tax Commn. Mem. bd. La. Assn. Mental Health, Baton Rouge YWCA, Baton Rouge Little Theatre; v.p. bd. La. Arts and Sci. Center, Baton Rouge; chmn. bd. La. Council Music and Performing Arts. Methodist. Address: 7449 Boyce Dr Jefferson Pl Baton Rouge LA 70809

LONG, CHARLES RICHARD, educator; b. Ft. Smith, Ark., Aug. 27, 1940; s. Carl Henry and Margaret Mae (Lane) L.; A.A., Ft. Smith Jr. Coll., 1959; B.A. (Univ. scholar), So. Meth. U., 1961; Ph.D. (Ford scholar), Vanderbilt U., 1965; m. Laura Ellen Garner, Aug. 26, 1963; children—Margaret, Ruth, Richard. Research asst. Nat. Bur. Econ. Research, N.Y.C., 1964; economist Fed. Res. Bank, Atlanta, 1965-68, cons., 1969; asst. prof. econs. Ga. State U., Atlanta, 1968-71, asso. prof., 1971—; cons. Ga. Dept. Health, 1969. Vice chmn. Met. Atlanta Coordinating Com., 1970-71. Trustee Interfaith, Inc., 1968-69. Mem. Am., So. econ. assns., Am. Assn. U. Profs., Regional Sci. Assn. Presbyn. (elder). Club: Peachtree Chess (past pres.) (Atlanta). Home: 1437 Holly Lane NE Atlanta GA 30329 Office: Dept Econs Ga State U Atlanta GA 30303

LONG, E. RAY, city ofcl.; b. Prague, Okla., Oct. 2, 1917; s. L.H. and Susan E. (Clark) L.; B.S., U. Okla., 1940; postgrad. Okla. City U., 1947-50; m. Dorothy Gayle Holmes, Nov. 1, 1940; children— Linda Gayle (Mrs. Ronald E. Fleming), Carolyn J. (Mrs. John Milam), Susan E., John Bradford. With city govt. Oklahoma City, 1946—, city clk., 1967—. Sec., Oklahoma City Airport Trust, Oklahoma City Municipal Improvement Authority, Police, Fire and Employee Pension Systems, 1967—. Served to lt. col. Signal Corps, AUS, 1941-46. Mem. Internal Inst. Municipal Clks., Res. Officers Assn., Am. Legion, Okla. Municipal League, Am. Radio Relay League. Democrat. Methodist. Home: 3207 NW 47th St Oklahoma City OK 73112 Office: Municipal Bldg Oklahoma City OK 73102

LONG, FRED WAYNE, agrl. engr.; b. nr. Bruce, Miss., Aug. 23, 1927; s. Dwight Wayne and Donie Bell (Brasher) L.; B.S., Miss. State U., 1958; m. Scottie Roberta Bray, Dec. 26, 1950; children—Karen Jean, Gregory Wayne. Agrl. engr. Soil and Water Conservation Research div. Agrl. Research Service, Dept. Agr., Oxford, Miss., 1958-60, hydraulic engr., 1960-62, asst. to chief Cornbelt br., St. Paul, 1962-63, hydraulic engr. Soil Conservation Service, Starkville, Miss., 1963—; guest lectr. civil engring. dept. Miss. State U., Starkville, 1968-69. Served with USNR, 1945-47; with USAF, 1950-54. Mem. Am. Soc. Agrl. Engrs. (past chmn. Miss. sect.). Baptist (deacon). Mason (K.T.). Home: Route 3 Box 310 Starkville MS 39759 Office: 208 S Jackson St PO Box 99 Starkville MS 39759

LONG, GEORGE J., lawyer. U.S. dist. atty. Western Ky. dist., Louisville. Address: Office Dist Atty Louisville KY 40202*

LONG, GEORGE ROBERT, assn. exec.; b. Roachdale, Ind., Feb. 23, 1917; s. George Batman and Stella (Sutherlin) L.; A.B., Wabash Coll., 1939; M.A., Ind. U., 1949; postgrad. U. Va., 1949-53; m. Mary Henley Spencer, Dec. 7, 1968. Instr. govt. Ind. U., Bloomington, 1949-53; research fellow Bur. Pub. Adminstrn., U. Va., Charlottesville, 1949-53; planning adminstr. Henrico County, Richmond, Va., 1953-54; field rep. Va. Div. Planning and Econ. Devel., Abingdon, 1954-57; acting commr. Div. Planning and Econ. Devel., 1957-58; exec. dir. Wilson (N.C.) Indsl. Council, 1958-60; mng. partner Robinson, Long & McDonald, Cons., Charlottesville, 1960-62; field cons. League of Va. Counties, Charlottesville, 1962-64; exec. dir. Va. Assn. Counties, Charlottesville, 1964—. Mem. Gov.'s Com. on State and Local Cooperation, 1969—; lectr. on Va. county govt. U. Va., Fed. Exec. Inst., Christopher Newport Coll., George Mason Coll., U. No. Colo. Mem. Met. Areas Study Commn. Va., 1966-68, Mental Health Study Commn., 1964-66, Commn. to Study Rights of Pub. Employees, 1972. Served with AUS, 1941-45. Mem. Nat. Conf. Execs. State Assns. of Counties (pres. 1969-70), Nat. Assn. Counties (dir. 1969-70), Lambda Chi Alpha. Democrat. Presbyn. (elder). Mason. Home: 2310 Tarleton Dr Charlottesville VA 22901 Office: County Office Bldg Charlottesville VA 22901

LONG, HAROLD GLENN, physician; b. Akron, O., July 12, 1933; s. Luke Glenn and Minnie (Caltrider) L.; B.S., North Ga. Coll., 1954; M.D., Med. Coll. Ga., 1958; m. Mary Joel Williams, July 12, 1959; children—Mary Ellyn, Joel Glenn. Intern Athens Gen. Hosp. (Ga.), 1959-60; practice gen. medicine Dahlonega, Ga., 1960—; mem. staff Hall County Hosp., Gainesville, Ga. Active Boy Scouts Am., Ga. Heart Assn. Bd. dirs. Blue Cross and Blue Shield, Columbus, Ga., Named Young Man Year, Dahlonega Jr. C. of C., 1964. Mem. 9th Dist. Med. Soc. Democrat. Methodist. Lion, Elk. Club: Skitts Mountain Golf (Cleveland, Ga.). Home: 2151 Mountain View Dr Dahlonega GA 30533 Office: Memorial Dr Dahlonega GA 30533

LONG, HERMAN HODGE, coll. pres.; b. Birmingham, Ala., May 2, 1912; s. Osie and Ella (Hodge) L.; A.B., Talladega (Ala.) Coll., 1935; A.M., Hartford Sch. Religious Edn., 1936; Ph.D. in Psychology, U. Mich., 1949; m. Henrietta Louise Shivery, May 3, 1938; 1 dau., Ellen. Instr. Miles Coll., 1937-39, dir. summer sch., 1940; field rep. race relations dept. Am. Missionary Assn., Congl. Christian Ch., 1943, field dir., 1944-47, asso. dir., 1947, dir., 1948-64; pres. Talladega Coll., 1964—. Bd. dirs. Carnegie Found. for Advancement Teaching, So. Fellowships, So. Regional Council. Rosenwald fellow and Gen. Edn. Board fellow, 1939-43. Mem. A.A.A.S., Soc. Applied Anthropology, Am. So. social socs., Am., So., Tenn. psychol. assns., Nat. Assn. Intergroup Relations Ofcls. (pres. 1954-55), Inst. on Man and Sci. (mem. bd.). Author: (with C. S. Johnson) People Versus Property. Address: Talladega Coll Talladega AL 35160

LONG, LONNIE LEE, JR., architect; b. Laurens, S.C., Mar. 19, 1940; s. Lonnie Lee and Venice Oleta (Wheeler) L.; B.Arch., Clemson U., 1965; m. Paula Irene Craine, June 24, 1961; children—Venice Helene, Edith Craine, Lonnie Lee III. Draftsman, Lyles, Bissett, Carlisle and Wolff, architects and engrs., Columbia, S.C., 1965-66; architect Lucas and Stubbs Assos., Ltd., Charleston, S.C., 1967-71, Lucas Stubbs and Long Assos., Ltd., architects and engrs., Charleston, 1971—. Mem. A.I.A., Constrn. Specification Inst., Soc. Am. Mil. Engrs., Air Force Assn. Home: 528 Wampler Dr Charleston SC 29412 Office: 255 E Bay St Charleston SC 29401

LONG, PAUL JUNIOR, scientist, artist; b. Tellico Plains, Tenn., May 27, 1927; s. Charles Ody and Maggie Lane (Rogers) L.; B.S., Tenn. Tech. U., 1950; M.S., U. Tenn., 1970; m. Willa Mae Williams, Nov. 16, 1952; children—David Paul, Susan Gayle, Gregory Lessel. Asst. to erector Combustion Engring., Newnan, Ga., 1950; foreman radiographic lab. Union Carbide Corp., Oak Ridge, Tenn., 1951-53, supr. spl. pilot plant operations, 1953-55, supr. ultra-sonic and spl. nondestructive testing group, 1955-63, physicist in charge metall. services lab., 1963-69, head engring. test systems dept., 1969—. Exhibited in group shows at Dulin Art Gallery, Knoxville, Tenn. Committeeman, Boy Scouts Am., Oak Ridge, 1969—; vocational edn. chmn. Jefferson Jr. High Sch. P.T.A., Oak Ridge, 1971—. Served with USAAF, 1945-46. Registered profl. engr., Tenn. Mem. Soc. Nondestructive Testing (charter mem. Oak Ridge, chpt. dir.), S.A.R. Baptist. Author: Our Hill Country Heritage, Vol. I, Williams and Related Families, 1970; Our Hill Country Heritage, Vol. II, Longs and Related Families, 1972. Contbr. articles to profl. jours. Home: 106 Evans Lane Oak Ridge TN 37830 Office: Union Carbide Y 12 Plant Oak Ridge TN 37830

LONG, ROBERT CLARK, physician; b. Louisville, Apr. 8, 1916; s. William Hamilton and Ella (Zinsmeister) L.; A.B., Tulane U., 1936; M.D., U. Louisville, 1940; m. Helen Snyder, Nov. 25, 1937; children— Bill, Jim, Tom, Carolyn, Mary Catherine. Pvt. practice medicine specializing obstetrics and gynecology, Louisville, 1947—; mem. staff Norton Meml. Infirmary, chief obstetrics and gynecology, 1963-64, now chief of staff, 1968—. Chmn. Salk Polio campaign, Louisville, 1957; bd. dirs. Ky. div. Am. Cancer Soc., 1956—; med. adviser mayor Louisville and judge Jefferson County, 1961—. Cons. to Pres. on nat. health manpower; cons. to AID. Bd. mgrs. Louisville YMCA, 1964—. Served to maj. USAAF, 1942-46; CBI. Decorated Bronze Star. Recipient March of Dimes award, 1958, Am. Cancer Soc. award, 1957. Diplomate Am. Bd. Obstetrics and Gynecology. Mem. Am. (bd. dirs., bd. trustees), World (bd. dirs. U.S. com.), Ky. (trustee) med. assns., Am. Coll. Obstetricians and Gynecologists, Central Assn. Obstetricians and Gynecologists, Jefferson County Med. Soc. (chmn. speakers bur. 1961—, arbitration com. 1955-58, pub. relations com. 1957-59, sec. 1952). Home: 5308 Indian Crest Louisville KY 40207 Office: 4122 Shelbyville Rd Louisville KY 40207

LONG, RUSSELL B(ILLIU), U.S. senator; b. Shreveport, La., Nov. 3, 1918; s. Huey Pierce and Rose (McConnell) L.; A.B., La. State U., 1941, LL.B., 1942; m. Carolyn Bason, Dec. 23, 1969; children—(by previous marriage) Katherine (Mrs. Mosely), Pamela Rust (Mrs. McCardell). Admitted to La. bar, 1942; practiced law, Baton Rouge, 1946-47; exec. counsel to gov. La., May-June, 1948; elected to U.S. Senate from La., for unexpired term ending 1950, reelected 1950—, chmn. finance com. Served to of Com., alternate chmn. Joint Com. on Internal Revenue. Served to lt. USNR, 1942-45; MTO, NATO. Mem. Order of Coif, Delta Kappa Epsilon, Pi Delta Phi, Tau Kappa Alpha, Omicron Delta Kappa. Democrat (del. nat. conv. 1952). Elk. Home: Baton Rouge LA Office: Senate Office Bldg Washington DC 20510

LONG, SPEEDY O., congressman; b. Tullos, La., June 16, 1928; s. Felix Franklin and Verda (Pendarivs) L.; B.A., Northwestern State Coll., Natchitoches, La., 1951; J.D., La. State U., 1959; m. Florence Theriot, Sept. 1, 1955; children—Felix Paul, David Theriot. Admitted to La. bar, 1959, since practiced in Jena; mem. La. Senate from 31st Dist., 1956-64; mem. 89th-92nd Congresses from 8th La. Dist. Served with USN, 1946-48, USNR, 1951-52. Mem. Am., La. bar assns., 28th Jud. Bar Assn. La. (pres. 1964), Am. Legion. Baptist. Mason (32 deg., Shriner). Home: PO Drawer L Jena LA 71342 Office: House Office Bldg Washington DC 20515

LONG, STUART MORRISON, editor; b. Portales, N.M., Nov. 15, 1913; s. Jeb Stuart and Elizabeth (Menefee) L.; B.J., U. Tex., 1943; m. Emma Pauline Jackson, July 27, 1936; children—Jeb Jackson, Jefferson Paine. Reporter Austin Am.-Statesman and Internat. News Service, Austin, Tex., 1935-37; pub. Kermit (Tex.) Sun, 1937-40; news editor Austin (Tex.) Statesman, 1940-42; news editor KVET, Austin, 1946-50; editor Long News Service, Austin, Tex., 1946—. Mem. Pres.'s Water Pollution Control Adv. Bd., 1968-71; mem. Tex. Sch. Land Bd., 1970—. Mem. State Democratic Exec. Com., 1948-52. Served with USMCR, 1942-45. Mem. Sigma Delta Chi (chpt. pres. 1967-68, state pres. 1968-70). Mem. Christian Ch. Home: 813 Park Blvd Austin TX 78751 Office: State Capitol Pressroom Austin TX 78711

LONG, WILLIAM BOWMAN, physician; b. Eddy, Tex., June 19, 1921; s. Roderick John and Ester Margueriete (Bowman) L.; D.D.S., Baylor U., 1945, M.D., 1951; m. Mary Cole Farrow, June 3, 1944; children— William F., Daryl E., Robert J., Linda S. Intern Jefferson Davis Hosp., Houston, 1951-52; practice medicine specializing in family practice, Belton, Tex., 1952-68; mem. staffs Sewell-Long Hosp., Belton, Tex.; physician Mary Hardin Baylor Coll., 1969—; cons. Crestview Manor, 1970—. Trustee, Belton Ind. Sch. Dist., v.p. 1966-72. Served with AUS, 1943-44, USNR, 1945-47. Mem. Am. Acad. Gen. Practice, Am., Tex., Bell County med. assns., Belton C. of C. (pres. 1958, Belton Athletic Assn. (pres. 1955-56). Lion (pres. 1959-60). Home: 415 Downing St Belton TX 76513 Office: 205 N Pearl St Belton TX 76513

LONG, WILLIAM DAVID, food co. exec.; b. Crisfield, Md., Sept. 20, 1929; s. Thomas Berry and Etta (Luettinger) L.; student Va. Poly. Inst., 1947-50; m. Barbara Russell, July 15, 1959; children—Lisa Bea, William David, Thomas Beauregard. Pres. Long Farms, Inc., Apopka, Fla., 1961—, Long & Scott Farms, Inc., Apopka, 1964—, Apopka Properties, Inc., 1967—; pres. Apopka Devel. Co., 1970—; sec. Lust & Long Precooler Inc., Apopka, 1960—, Lust & Long Carrot Co., Apopka, 1969—; dir. State Bank Apopka. Vice pres. Orange County Farm Bur., 1967—; v.p., dir. Zellwood Drainage and Water Control Dist., 1962—; mem. Orange County Air and Water Pollution Control, 1970—; mem. Gov.'s Migratory Labor Com., 1967—. Named Outstanding Young Farmer Orange County, Orlando Jr. C. of C., 1964, 65, Outstanding Young Farmer Fla. Jr. C. of C., 1965, 1964, 65, one of four outstanding young farmers in U.S., Nat. Jr. C. of C. and Nat. L. P. Gas Assn., 1966, Ford Found. award in vegetable crop mgmt., 1968; recipient Spl. Resolution 2782 for being selected one of four outstanding young farmers in U.S., Fla. Ho. of Reps., 1965. Mem. Fla. Fruit and Vegetable Growers Assn. (past bd. dirs.), C. of C. (agr. com.). Presbyn. Mason (32 deg., Shriner, Jester), Elk. Club: Zellwood (Fla.) Country (pres.). Home: 2860 E Green Acre Rd Apopka FL 32703 Office: PO Drawer 729 Apopka FL 32703

LONG, WILLIAM EVERETT, JR., utility exec.; b. Oklahoma City, Sept. 3, 1919; s. William Everett and Hazel (Stafford) L.; m. Frances Jeanne Baum, Aug. 7, 1942; children—Susan Jeanne, Nancy Lee. Sales rep. Pan. Am. Airways, Houston, 1946-48; with Houston Natural Gas Corp., 1949—, v.p., asst. gen. mgr. distbn. div., 1968-70, v.p., gen. mgr. distbn. div., 1970—. Chmn. Met. div. United Fund, Houston, 1971—. Served with USAAC, 1941-45, USAF, 1951-52. Mem. Am. Soc. Tng. Dirs. (past pres.), Am. Gas Assn. (recipient Indsl.-Comml. Achievement award 1968), So. Gas Assn., Houston C. of C., Phi Kappa Psi. Mem. Disciples of Christ Ch. Mason, Kiwanian. Clubs: Houston, Lakeside Country. Home: 5010 Westbriar Lane Houston TX 77027 Office: PO Box 1188 Houston TX 77001

LONG, WILLIE CLEVELAND, city ofcl.; b. Jesup, Ga., Oct. 15, 1922; s. Willie C. and Nellie (Smith) L.; grad. Abraham Baldwin Jr. Coll., 1947; B.S., U. Ga., 1949, M.Edn., 1951; m. Ann Richardson, Apr. 3, 1949; children—Bob, Joe. Tchr. VA, Screven, Ga., 1949-50; tchr. Nahunta (Ga.) High Sch., 1951-60; partner Rambler Car. Agy., 1963-66; adminstr. Wayne County, Jesup, Ga., 1966-69, city mgr., 1969—. Mem. Ga. State Senate, 1961-62; justice of peace, 1949-52. Served with AUS, 1943-46. Baptist (deacon). Lion (pres. 1955-56, 69-70). Home: 104 Pierce St Jesup GA 31545 Office: City Hall Cherry and Macon Sts Jesup GA 31545

LONGENECKER, HERBERT EUGENE, univ. adminstr., biochemist; b. Lititz, Pa., May 6, 1912; s. Abraham S. and Mary Ellen (Herr) L.; B.S., Pa. State U. 1933, M.S., 1934, Ph.D., 1936; D.Sc., Duquesne U., 1951; LL.D., Loyola U., 1963; Litt. D., U. Miami, 1972; m. Marjorie Jane Segar, June 18, 1936; children—Herbert Eugene, Marjorie Segar (Mrs. James H. White III), Geoffrey Herr, Stanton Lee. NRC fellow. Univ. of Liverpool, Eng., Cologne, Germany and Queen's, Kingston, Can., 1936-38; sr. research fellow, lectr. in chemistry. U. Pitts., 1938-41, asst. research prof. chemistry, 1941-42, prof. chemistry dir. Buhl Found. Research Project, 1942-44, dean of research in natural scis., 1944-45, dean Grad. Sch. 1946-55; v.p. in charge Med. Center, U. Ill., 1955-60; pres. Tulane U., 1960—. Dir., CPC Internat., Equitable Life Assurance Soc. U.S. Mem. food and nutrition bd. NRC, 1943-53, chmn. com. on chem. warfare, Research and Devel. Bd., 1949-53; mem. research council Chem. Corps Adv. Bd., 1949-63; adv. panel biol. and chem. warfare Office, Asst. Sec. Def. for research and devel., 1953-61; mem. adv. panel R.O.T.C. affairs Office Sec. Def., 1961—, chmn., 1969—; mem. Surg. Gen.'s Cons. Group on Nursing, 1961-63; mem. Nat. Commn. Nursing, 1967-71; mem. commn. fed. relations Am. Council Edn., 1962-65, chmn., 1963-65, nat. selection com. Fulbright Student awards, 1953-55, chmn. West Europe sect., 1954-55. Pres. Pitts Housing Assn., 1948-51. Bd. govs. Inst. of Medicine of Chgo., 1957-60; trustee Council So. Univs., 1960—, pres., 1964; trustees Nat. Commn. on Accrediting, 1961-68, pres., 1964; trustee Nutrition Found., 1961—, chmn. bd., 1965—; trustee Inst. for Def. Analyses, 1960—, Am. Univs. Field Staff, 1960—, S.W. Research Inst., 1960-69, Grad. Research Center of S.W., 1961-72; bd. dirs. Council Financial Aid Edn., 1964-71; environmental health scis. adv. com. NIH, 1970-72; chmn. acad. adv. bd. U.S. Naval Acad., 1966-72; bd. dirs. Internat. Trade Mart, New Orleans, 1961—, United Fund, 1961, YMCA, 1962—, Cultural Attractions Fund, 1961, Information Council of Americas, 1962-64, Bush Found., 1970—, Sloan Found., 1971—,

United Student Aid Funds, 1972—, Nat. Merit Scholarship Corp., 1969—, Nat. Med. Fellowships, Inc., 1965—. Awarded Army and Navy Certificate for service during World War II. Fellow Am. Pub. Health Assn., A.A.A.S., Am. Inst. Chemists; mem. Am. Chem. Soc. (chmn. Pittsburg Sect., 1946-47) Am, Soc, Biol, Chemists, Biochem. Soc. (London); Am. Oil Chemists Soc. (v.p., 1946-47), Am. Inst. Nutrition, Nat. League Nursing, Assn. Am. Univs. (sec.-treas. 1969—), New Orleans C. of C. (dir.), Sigma Xi (exec. com.), Phi Delta Kappa, Sigma Pi. Clubs: Chemists: University (Chgo., N.Y.C.); Round Table, Pickwick, Boston, International House (dir.) (New Orleans). Home: 2 Audubon Pl New Orleans LA 70118

LONGHURST, PHILIP, JR., health adminstr. b. Idaho Falls, Ida., Sept. 14, 1931; s. Philip Alberto and Anna M. (Bolander) L.; B.A., Ida. State Coll., 1956; postgrad. Stanford, 1967-68; M.S. in Health Adminstrn., U. Colo., 1970; m. Joy E. Pullium, May 15, 1952; children—Suzanne Elizabeth, Philip James. Personnel technician Colo. State Civil Service Commn., Denver, 1957-59; personnel dir. Colo. State Hosp., Pueblo, 1959-61; personnel dir. Ft. Logan Mental Health Center, Denver, 1961-69, asst. to dir., 1969-70; exec. dir. Jarett, Rader & Longhurst, Raleigh, N.C., 1970—; asso. Mediscope, Inc., Los Angeles, 1966-67. Democratic precinct committeeman, Denver, 1962. Served with AUS, 1951-53. Recipient Forest Found. award Assn. Mental Health Adminstrns., 1970. Fellow Nat. Inst. Pub. Affairs; mem. Am. Soc. for Pub. Adminstrn., Am. Coll. Hosp. Adminstrs., Am. Soc. Personnel Adminstrn., Assn. Mental Health Adminstrs., Pub. Personnel Assn., Am. Pub. Health Assn. Home: Route 7 Box 364 Raleigh NC 27609 Office: PO Box 27311 Raleigh NC 27611

LONGLEY, JAMES BAIRD, scientist, educator; b. Balt., June 27, 1920; s. William Harding and Hazel (Baird) L.; B.S., Haverford Coll., 1941; Ph.D., Cambridge U., 1950; m. Helen Post Kent, Nov. 5, 1944; children—Gillian, Stephen, Andrew, William. Scientist, NIH, USPHS, Bethesda, Md., 1950-60; asso. prof. Georgetown U. Med. Sch., Washington, 1960-62; prof., chmn. dept. anatomy U. Louisville Sch. Medicine, 1962—. Pres., trustee Biol. Stain Commn. Served with AUS, 1944-46; ETO. Sr. research fellow USPHS, 1960-62. Mem. Histochem. Soc., Am. Assn. Anatomists, So. Soc. Anatomists (pres. 1966-67). Home: 1765 Casselberry Rd Louisville KY 40205 Office: Univ of Louisville Health Sciences Center Louisville KY 40201

LONGSTREET, HARRIET HAMNER, lawyer; b. Greenwood, Miss., July 7, 1912; d. William M. and Sara (Sale) Hamner; student Converse Coll., 1930-32; B.A., U. Mo., 1934; LL.B., Vanderbilt U., 1945;; m. Gilbert W. Longstreet, June 5, 1954. Admitted to Tenn. bar, 1945, U.S. Supreme Ct. bar, 1954; atty. Office Chief Counsel, Internal Revenue Service, 1945—. Mem. Fed., Am. (tax sect.) bar assns., Nat. Lawyers Club, Delta Delta Delta. Episcopalian. Home: 2500 Q St NW Washington DC 20007 Office: Internal Revenue Service Washington DC 20224

LONGSTREET, JAMES RUBERT, educator; b. Daytona Beach, Fla., Apr. 25, 1925; s. Rubert James and Lotto (Reuther) L.; B.S., Antioch Coll., 1949; M.B.A., Northwestern U., 1950, Ph.D., 1956; m. Wilda Graul, June 20, 1948; children—Tacy Jeanne, James Russell, Diane Alicia. Asst. prof. finance U. Cal. at Berkeley, 1953-61; research asso. Wharton Sch. Finance and Commerce, 1961-67; chmn. finance dept. U. So. Fla., 1967—; vis. asso. prof. Northwestern U., summers 1955, 56, 60; dir. Biotronics Inc., Berkeley, 1961-67; producer TV series Investing in Stock Market, 1966; cons. in field. Dir. Family Financial Clinic, Berkeley, 1955-58. Mem. Am. Finance Assn., Am., So., Midwest econ. assns., Nat. Assn. Bus. Economists, Financial Analysts Fedn., Phila. Econs. Soc., Alpha Kappa Psi, Beta Gamma Sigma. Author: Cases in Financial Management, 1964; Investment Banking and the New Issues Market, 1967. Home: 608 Vanderbaker Rd Tampa FL 33620

LOOMANS, KEITH A., ednl. adminstr.; b. Portage, Wis., Aug. 21, 1931; B.S., Concordia Tchrs. Coll. (Ill.), 1954, M.A., 1967. Prin. elementary sch. Trinity Luth. Sch., Brownsville, Tex., 1954-57, Immanuel Luth. Sch., Temple, Tex., 1957-61, Mercedes, Tex., 1961-69; asst. dir. parish service, dir. Luth. schs. Tex. dist. Luth. Ch.-Mo. Synod, 1969—. Mem. Luth. Edn. Assn., N.E.A., Tex. State Tchrs. Assn., Tex. Assn. Ednl. Tech., Phi Delta Kappa. Address: 8100 US Hwy 290 E Austin TX 78724*

LOOMIS, FREDERICK KENT, ret. naval officer, museum treas.; b. Parkersburg, W.Va., May 22, 1904; B.S., U.S. Naval Acad., 1925; M.S. in Diesel Engring., Pa. State U., 1932; m. Katherine A. Widenmann. Commd. ensign U.S. Navy, 1925, advanced through grades to rear adm., 1955; resident insp. naval material Hooven-Owen-Rentschler Co., Hamilton, O., 1935-37; served in U.S.S. Seal, 1937-39; div. engr. staff Comdr. Submarine Div. 15, Submarine Force, U.S. Fleet, Atlantic, 1939; comdr. U.S.S. Skipjack, 1939-41; assigned to staff Comdr. Submarines, 7th Fleet, comdr. Allied Naval Forces, Western Australia, 1941-43, maintenance officer, 1943-45; comdg. officer U.S.S. Napa, 1945-46; comdg. officer Adminstrv. Command and Asst. Comdr., U.S. Naval Tng. Center, Great Lakes, Ill., 1946-48; instr. Indsl. Coll. Armed Forces, 1948-49, chief prodn. br., 1948-49; naval attache, naval attache for air, Tangier, Morocco, 1950-53; dir. Naval Intelligence Sch., 1953-55; ret., 1955. Treas., Truxtun-Decatur Naval Museum. Decorated Legion of Merit with combat V. Mem. Explorers Club. Clubs: Army-Navy, National Press (Washington). Home: 3055 Foxhall Rd Washington DC 20016*

LOOMIS, PHILIP ALBERT, JR., govt. ofcl.; b. Colorado Springs, Colo., June 11, 1915; s. Philip Albert and Sara C. (Jackson) L.; A.B. with highest honors, Princeton, 1938; LL.B. cum laude, Yale, 1941; m. Maryanna H. Oliver, May 28, 1949 (dec. Sept. 1968); children—Sara M., Philip, Margaret. Admitted to Cal. bar, 1941, U.S. Supreme Ct. bar, 1955; rent atty. OPA, 1942-44; asso. counsel Northrup Aircraft, Inc., 1944-46; gen. practice law with O'Melveny & Myers, Los Angeles, 1946-54; dir., asst. sec. Cal. Yacht Anchorage, Inc., 1949-55; lectr. continuing edn. of bar program, State Bar Cal., 1933; spl. cons. revision rules and regulations SEC, 1954-55, asso. dir. div. trading and exchanges, 1955, dir. div., 1955-63, gen. counsel, 1963-70, commr., 1971—. Lectr. in law, U. Va. Law Sch., 1961—. Trustee Webb Sch. of Cal., 1954-59. Recipient Career Service award Nat. Civil Service League, 1964. Mem. Am., Los Angeles bar assns., Am. Judicature Soc., Am. Law Inst., Order of Coif, Phi Beta Kappa. Republican. Episcopalian. Clubs: Capital Hill (Washington); Westerners (Los Angeles); Chevy Chase (Md.). Home: 7108 Beechwood Dr Chevy Chase MD 20015 Office: Securities and Exchange Commn 500 N Capitol St Washington DC 20549

LOONEY, GERALD FRANCIS, financial exec.; b. Westwood, N.J., Sept. 4, 1934; s. James B. and Florence G. (Sims) L.; B.S., Fla. State U., 1960; m. Valerie Tanner, Mar. 29, 1958; children—Michael, Joseph, Kathleen. Accountant, Lybrand, Ross Bros. & Montgomery, Detroit, 1960-64; partner Stockwell, Eaton & Peed, Ft. Lauderdale, Fla., 1964-67; v.p. finance Aloe Creme Labs., Inc., Ft. Lauderdale, 1967—; dir. L.E.R. Distbg., Inc. Mem. Nat. Assn. Accountants, Am. Inst. C.P.A.'s, Am. Inst. Corporate Controllers. Home: 5260 NE 19th Av Ft Lauderdale FL 33308 Office: 4190 NE 5TH Av Ft Lauderdale FL 33308

LOONEY, JUNE PAIGE MURPHY, coll. dean; b. Ivor, Va., June 9, 1919; d. Henry Patrick and Louisa (Crumpler) Murphy; A.B., Elon Coll., 1942; M.A., E. Carolina U., 1961; postgrad. Atlantic Christian Coll., 1956, N.C. State U., 1959; m. John Joseph Williams Looney, Jr., May 30, 1942 (div. Oct. 1969); children—Carolyn Page, Charlotte Anne. Tchr., Norfolk (Va.) County Schs., 1943-45; guidance counselor Rocky Mount (N.C.) City Schs., 1957-60; dir. guidance services Nash County Schs. Nashville, N.C., 1960-62; dir. guidance services Rocky Mount (N.C.) City Schs., 1962-68; asso. dean students Elon Coll. (N.C.), 1968—. Active Girl Scouts U.S.A.; v.p. Mental Health Assn., 1964-68, chmn. mental illness com., 1963-68; city program chmn. Sub-Deb Bd. Advisors, 1962-64, finance chmn., 1965-67; v.p. Rocky Mount Council Parents and Tchrs., 1952-54, pres., 1954-56; active Rocky Mount Arts Center, 1957-68; mem. N.C. Gov's. Council on Mental Retardation, 1965-69. Mem. N.E.A., Am., N.C. personnel and guidance assns., Assn. for Counselor Edn. and Supervision, Am. Sch. Counselor Assn., Nat. Vocational Guidance Assn., Am., N.C. assns. women deans and counselors, Am. Assn. U. Women, N.C. Edn. Assn., N.C. Council Parents and Tchrs., Delta Kappa Gamma, Pi Gamma Mu. Democrat. Episcopalian. Home: 204 N Holt St Elon College NC 27244 Office: Box 2231 Elon Coll Elon College NC 27244

LOONEY, SEBERT TYLER, safety engr.; b. New Castle, Va., Nov. 6, 1927; s. Roscoe F. and Murphy O. (Looney) L.; m. Christine R. Rose, Nov. 21, 1927; children—Carolyn, Watson, Lynn. With Western Electric, Winston-Salem, N.C., 1950-53, Hake Mfg. Co., Roanoke, Va., 1953-57; prodn. mgr. John Martin & Assos., Balt., 1957-63; indsl. engr. Am. Mut. Ins. Co., Richmond, Va., 1953-71; owner Safety Consultants, Richmond, 1971—. Served with USAAF, 1945-48. Mem. Am. Soc. Safety Engrs. (nat. dir. 1968-69), Va. Safety Assn. Mason. Club: Engineers (Richmond). Home: 10541 Duryea Dr Richmond VA 23235 Office: 7825 Midlothian Turnpike Richmond VA 23235

LOONEY, THOMAS CLIFTON, dentist; b. Columbus, Miss., Jan. 14, 1928; s. William Monroe and Mary Etta (Smith) L.; student Livingston U., 1946-48, U. Ala., 1948; D.M.D., U. Ala., 1953; m. Lona Kaye Stegall, July 31, 1968; children—Clifton Lynn, Terry Ann, David Todd. Gen. practice dentistry, Livingston, Ala., 1953—. Master Boy Scouts Am., 1963—, explorer adviser, 1964, mem. exec. bd. Black Warrior council, 1964. Recipient Silver Beaver award Boy Scouts Am., 1953. Mem. Am., Ala. dental assns., Internat. Acad. Orthodontics, Xi Psi. Methodist. Lion (pres. 1958). Address: Box Q Livingston AL 35470

LOOPER, CHARLES EUGENE, banker; b. Greenville, S.C., Dec. 19, 1920; s. James Columbus and Stella (Burdine) L.; B.A., Furman U., 1941; M.A., La. State U., 1942; Ph.D., Georgetown U., 1948; grad. student London Sch. Econs., 1953-54; m. Erma Riggins, May 19, 1944; children—Ann Stewart, Ruth Burdine. Prof. polit. sci., chmn. dept. Furman U., 1948-57; part-time adminstrv. asst. to city mgr., Greenville, 1952-53, 55; with Wachovia Bank & Trust Co., Winston-Salem, N.C., 1957-71, sr. v.p., 1963-71; now with Southeast Banking Corp., Miami. Mem. nat. personnel commn. Nat. Assn. Bank Auditors and Comptrollers, 1960-63. Chmn. Piedmont Indsl. Relations Conf., 1962; charter bd. dirs., exec. com. Winston-Salem Better Bus. Bur., 1960-62; mem. requirements commn., Winston-Salem, 1965-71. Precinct chmn., county del. S.C. Democratic Conv., 1950-57. Chmn. Wake Forest Coll. Inst., 1961-63; adv. bd. Furman U., 1962—; mem. bd. regents Stonier Grad. Sch. Banking, Rutgers U., 1965—; adv. com Ednl. Found. Commerce and Industry N.C., 1966—, Ch. and Industry Inst., Winston-Salem, 1966—; bd. dirs. Goodwill Rehab. Center, Winston-Salem, 1959-64, v.p., 1961-64; bd. dirs., chmn. personnel com. Arts and Crafts Assn., Winston-Salem, 1960-62. Served to lt. USNR, 1942-45. Mem. Am. Bankers Assn., Winston-Salem C. of C. (chmn. edn. com. 1962, chmn. econ. understanding com. 1964). Kiwanian. Clubs: Torch, Forsyth Country (Winston-Salem). Author: (with Emmet Asseff) State Control of Local Government in Louisiana, 1951. Home: 7335 SW 141th Terrace Miami FL 33158 Office: Southeast Banking Corp Miami FL 33151

LOOSBROCK, JOHN FRANCIS, editor; b. Omaha, Nov. 9, 1918; s. John F. and Madonna (McGowan) L.; Ph.B., Marquette U., 1939; m. Margaret Reynolds, July 25, 1942; children—Mary Virginia (Mrs. John G. Miers), John Francis III, Madonna Beatrice. Reporter, Oskaloosa (Ia.) Daily Herald, 1939-40, Milw. Jour., 1945; asso. editor Inf. Jour., Washington, 1945-48; Washington editor Popular Sci. Monthly, 1948-51; mng. editor Air Force Mag., Washington, 1951-58, editor 1958—; editor Aerospace Internat., Washington, 1965-71. Vis. prof. U. Colo. at Boulder, 1965; cons. adminstr. FAA, Washington, 1961-65. Mem. White House Task Force Nat. Aviation Goals, 1961. Served to capt. AUS, 1940-45. Decorated Silver Star, Bronze Star with oak leaf cluster; recipient FAA Distinguished Pub. Service award, 1961. Mem. Air Force Assn., Aerospace Edn. Found., Am. Inst. Aero. and Astronautics, Am. Astronautic Soc., Am. Academy Polit. Sci. Editor: (with Richard Skinner) The Wild Blue, 1961; Space Weapon, 1958; coordinating editor A History of the U.S. Air Force, 1958. Home: 3123 Brooklawn Terrace Chevy Chase MD 20015 Office: 1750 Pennsylvania Av NW Washington DC 20006

LOPEZ, JOAQUIN, aero. engr.; b. Cienfuegos, Cuba, Feb. 9, 1923 (came to U.S., 1967, naturalized 1972); s. Victorino and Amanda (Garcia) L.; B.S., Tri State Coll. Engring., Angola, Ind., 1946; m. Siria Jimenez, Feb. 14, 1948; children—Joaquin, Oscar, Carlos. Asst. to chief engr. Pub. Works Dept., Cienfuegos Dist., Cuba, 1946-49; pres., owner Tractores Centro S.A., Cienfuegos, 1949-63; supt. machinery Agosa S.A., civil engrs., Santander, Spain, 1965-67; aero. engr. Allstate Diesel Inc., Miami, Fla., 1967-69, Growers Ford Tractor Co., Miami, 1969—. Drafting instr. Miami Sr. High Sch., Adult Edn. Training, 1970—. Mem. Am. Soc. Agrl. Engrs., 1952. Roman Catholic. Tech. translator Internat. div. Allis Chalmers Mfg. Co., 1969—. Home: 9210 S W 57th Terrace Miami FL 33143 Office: 3825 N W 32d Av Miami FL 33142

LOPEZ, JUAN D., aux. bishop San Juan, P.R. Address: P O Box 1967 San Juan PR 00903*

LOPEZ REYES, JAIME, consul gen. Colombia, Houston. Address: 914 Main St Houston TX 77002*

LORD, COLUMBUS ELLIS, architect; b. Abbot, Me., Apr. 30, 1897; s. Alvah Brown and Addie Winifred (Colson) L.; student U. Me., 1914-16; B.S. in Arch., Mass. Inst. Tech., 1924; m. Vera Dale Bolan, Feb. 18, 1928; children—Nancy Claire (Mrs. Philip Edwin Graves), Charles Ellis Bolan (dec.). Architect, various firms, Boston, 1924-31; civil engr. City Boston, 1931-34; architect, procurement div. Treasury Dept., Washington, 1934-37; with firm Clarence Wunder, Phila, 1937-38; Quartermaster, U.S. Army, Washington, 1938-41; engr. Corps Engrs. U.S. Army, Washington, 1941-47; chief engr. air facilities Def. Dept., Washington, 1947-67; cons. architect, engr., Arlington, Va., 1967—. Mem. pack council Cub Scouts, Washington, 1953-55; mem. P.T.A., Arlington, Va., 1955-63. Served with Signal Corps, U.S. Army, 1917-19. Registered profl. engr., Va., D.C., Mass., Vt. Registered architect, Va. Mem. A.I.A., Am. Soc. C.E., Nat. Soc. Profl. Engrs., Hwy. Research Bd. of Nat. Acad. Scis., Nat. Aero. Assn., Va. Acad. Sci., Aircraft Owners and Pilots Assn., So. Am. Mil. Engrs. Mason; mem. Order Eastern Star. Clubs: Aero, Mass. Institute Technology (Washington). Home and Office: 2000 N Adams St No. 329 Arlington VA 22201

LORD, EVELYN MARLIN (MRS. SAMUEL SMITH LORD), lawyer, county ofcl.; b. Melrose, Mass., Dec. 8, 1926; d. John Joseph and Janette (Nourse) Marlin; B.A., Boston U., 1948; M.A., U. Del., 1956; J.D., U. Louisville; m. Samuel Smith Lord, Jr., Feb. 28, 1948; children—Steven Arthur, Jonathan Peter, Nathaniel Edward, Victoria Marlin, William Kenneth. Exec. dir. Jefferson County Community Improvement Dist.; adminstrv. asst. to county judge Jefferson County. Mem. Gov.'s Commn. on Status Women. Bd. dirs. Christina Community Center, Wilmington, Del., 1958-60; pres. state League Women Voters, 1961-62; Del. chmn. Radio Free Europe, 1965; adv. bd. Del. Epilepsy Assn., 1964-65; bd. dirs. Neighborhood Garden Assn., Wilmington, 1965, Prisoners' Aid Soc., Del., 1965-66, Del.-Tutorial, Inc., 1965-66, Colonial Inn (mental health), Louisville; bd. dirs. Kentuckiana council Girl Scouts U.S.A., Louisville, 1966-71, pres., 1968-70; mem. women's res. Boy Scouts Am. Mem. Del. Senate, 1962-64; candidate for mayor, Wilmington, 1964. Mem. Am. Acad. Polit. and Social Scientists, Jefferson County Women Lawyer's Assn. (1970-71), Nat. Assn. Women Legislators, Nat. Fedn. Republican Women, Wilmington Panhellenic, Mental Health Assn., Kappa Beta Pi (dean Rho chpt.). Home: 6212 Glen Hill Rd Louisville KY 40222

LORD, FONCHEN USHER (MRS. WILLIAM WALCOTT LORD), artist; b. St. Louis; d. Roland Green and Florence (Richardson) Usher; A.B., Radcliffe Coll., 1933; M.A., Washington U., St. Louis, 1935; m. William Walcott Lord, June 12, 1935; children—Fonya (Mrs. James DeLong), William Pepperell, Carter Usher, Elizabeth Usher. Exhibited invitational one-man shows Stetson U., Deland, Fla., 1969, W.Va. Wesleyan Coll., 1970, Avanti Galleries, N.Y.C., 1970, Miami Mus. Modern Art, 1970, Broward Community Coll., Ft. Lauderdale, 1971; exhibited in group shows at Columbia Mus. Art, Columbus Mus. Arts and Crafts, Birmingham Mus. Art, Atlanta High Mus., Norton Gallery, Dulin Gallery Art, Ringling Mus. Art, Butler Inst. Am. Art, Jacksonville Art Mus., many others; represented in permanent collections Miami Mus. Modern Art, W.Va. Wesleyan Coll., Lowe Mus., New Coll., Sarasota, Fla. Pres., Palm Island Corp., Bartow, Fla., 1954-64, Braden River Ranchettes, Bartow, 1964-71; asst. treas. Paris Tanning Co., South Paris, Me., 1944-48. Recipient Merit award Fla. State Fair, 1964; Clearwater Art Seminar award, 1961, 63; 1st prize Sunshine Art Festival, 1962; 1st prize Polk County Ann., 1963, 67, awards, 1965, 66, 70; Chautauqua Nat. award, 1968; awards Festival of States Ann., 1963, 65, 66, 68. Fellow Royal Soc. Arts (London); mem. Fla. Artists Group, Nat. Assn. Am. Pen Women, Zeta Tau Alpha. Episcopalian. Home: 4305 Oak Glen Rd Lakeland FL 33803

LORD, JOHN WESLEY, bishop; b. Paterson, N.J., Aug. 23, 1902; s. John James and Catherine (Carmichael) L.; grad., Montclair (N.J.) State Normal Sch., 1922; A.B., Dickinson Coll., 1927; B.D., Drew Theol. Sem., Ph.D., 1930; U. Edinburgh, Scotland, 1930-31; grad. work, Rutgers U., 1931-34; D.D., Dickinson Coll., 1943, LL.D., 1949; S.T.D., Boston U., 1949; H.H.D., Western Md. Coll., 1963; D.D., Morgan State Coll., 1966; m. Margaret Farrington Ratcliffe, April 29, 1931; 1 dau., Jean Phillips (Mrs. Arnold C. Cooper). Tchr., prin. in N.J. schs., 1922-24; asst. pastor Emory Methodist Ch., Jersey City, 1927-30; pastor (during constrn. with vol. labor) Union (N.J.) Community Ch., 1931-34, 1st Meth. Ch., Westfield, N.J., 1938-48; resident bishop. Boston Area, Meth. Ch., 1948-60, Washington Area, Meth. Ch., 1960—. Del. to Gen. Conf., Meth. Ch., 1944-48, also mem. commn. ecumenical affairs, pres. gen. bd. pensions; pres. council bishops United Meth. Ch., 1970-71. Mem. gen. bd. Nat. Council Chs; pres. Mass. Council Chs., 1953-55; pres. Meth Corp., Washington. Trustee Sibley Meml. Hosp., Washington, Am. U., Western Md. Coll.; chmn. bd. govs. Wesley Theol. Sem.; bd. dirs. Bishops Coll for Peace and The Self-Devel. of Peoples. Mem. Phi Kappa Sigma, Tau Kappa Alpha. Republican. Mason (33 deg.). Home: 2020 Plymouth St NW Washington DC 20012 Office: 100 Maryland Av NE Div World Peace Washington DC 20002

LORD, MARION E. MANNS, educator; b. Ft. Huachuca, Ariz., Dec. 17, 1914; d. George Wiley and Annie (Pellett) Manns; student R.I. State Coll., 1932; B.S., Northwestern U., 1936; postgrad. Breadloaf Coll., summer 1936; M.Ed., Harvard, 1962; M.A., Ph.D. (E. B. Fred fellow), U. Wis., 1968; m. William Shepard Lord, Apr. 29, 1938 (div. May 1965); children—Caroline B. (Mrs. Martin L. Gross), Marion F. (Mrs. Fred W. Steadman), Jane B. (mrs. Jared Chapin). N.H. State rep. Gen. Ct., Concord, N.H., 1957-62; dean of women, dir. guidance New Eng. Coll., Henniker, N.H., 1962-64; edn. program specialist, asst. to dir. div. coll. support Bur. Higher Edn., Office of Edn., Washington, 1968-71, dir. women's project Nat. Center Ednl. Statistics, 1971—. Vice pres., dir. N.H. Council for Better Schs., 1957-64; county co-chmn. Nat. Found. Infantile Paralysis-March of Dimes, Laconia, N.H., 1958; dir. N.H. Council on World Affairs, 1957-63, Laconia Hosp. Mem. Am. Psychol. Assn., Am. Polit. Sci. Assn., D.C. Sociol. Soc. (mem. com. on status of women), Nat. Council Adminstrv. Women in Edn., Federally Employed Women, Order Women Legislators, N.H. State Soc. in Washington, Am. Personnel and Guidance Assn., Nat. Assn. Women Deans and Counselors, League Women Voters, Am. Assn. U. Women, Bus. and Profl. Womens Club. Republican. Home: 800 4th St SW Washington DC 20024 Office: 400 Maryland Av SW Washington DC 20202

LORENZ, JOHN GEORGE, librarian; b. N.Y.C., Sept. 28, 1915; s. John W. and Theresa T. (Wurtz) L.; B.S. (Library fellow), Coll. City N.Y., 1939; B.S. in L.S., Columbia, 1940; M.S. in Pub. Adminstrn., Mich. State U., 1952; m. Josephine R. Trumbull, Oct. 1, 1944; children—Laurence T., Janice R. Reference asst. Queens Borough (N.Y.) Pub. Library, 1940-44; head bus. and tech. div. Schenectady Pub. Library, 1941-44; head reference div. Grand Rapids (Mich.) Pub. Library, 1944-46; asst. librarian Mich. State Library, 1946-56; with U.S. Office Edn., 1957-65, dir. div. library services and ednl. facilities, 1964-65; dep. librarian Library of Congress, 1965—, Liaison mem. com. sci. and tech. information Exec. Office of Pres., 1966—. Recipient Superior Service award Dept. Health, Edn. and Welfare. Mem. Am. (council 1960-64, 69—, exec. bd. 1971—, chmn. panel UNESCO 1965-70), D.C. library assns., Assn. State Libraries (exec. bd. 1962-71), Internat. Fedn. Library Assns. (pres. com. library statistics and standards 1964—), Nat. Book Com. (exec. bd. 1968—), Nat. Library Steering Com. (chmn. 1969). Club: Kenwood Golf and Country (Bethesda). Contbr. numerous articles in field, chpts. in books. Home: 5629 Newington Rd Bethesda MD 20016 Office: Library of Congress Washington DC 20540

LORENZEN, KENNETH ELBERT, dentist; b. Burlington, Ia., Apr. 16, 1923; s. Harry A. and Lilly (Love) L.; student Tex. Tech. U., 1946-47; D.D.S., Creighton U., 1952; m. Jo Anne Wolaver, Nov. 29, 1944; children—Sandra (Mrs. Richard Barrett), Kenneth R., Malcolm C. Gen. practice dentistry, Arcadia, Neb., 1952-54, Lubbock, Tex., 1954—; occasional clinician. Served with USNR, 1942-46. Mem. Am., Tex., South Plains (past pres.) dental socs., Phi Eta Sigma. Republican. Methodist. Home: 5412 28th St Lubbock TX 79407 Office: 1608 Aven St Lubbock TX 79401

LORIA, FRANK LEO, surgeon; b. Vacherie, La., Jan. 19, 1898; s. Paul and Phyllis (Cipolla) L.; B.S., Tulane U., 1921, M.D., 1923; m. Pauline Quaglino, Feb. 12, 1924 (dec. Oct. 1966); children— Paul Leonard, Philip Ronald; m. 2d, Octavie Livaudais, July 27, 1968. Gen. surg. practice, 1925—; surg. preceptorships Prof. Rudolph Matas, 1925-27, Prof. Maurice Gelpi, 1928-31; asst. in surgery, sch. medicine Tulane U., 1925-27, instr. in surgery, 1927-50, in charge lab. operative surgery, 1932-38, in charge lab. of surg. anatomy, 1938-41, lectr. in anatomy phys. diagnosis and minor surgery, sch. phys. edn., 1932-52, prof. hygiene Coll. Arts and Scis., 1958-61; chmn. surg. sects. Charity Hosp. La., 1942-44, later sr. vis. surgeon; chmn. surg. sect. Hotel Dieu Hosp., 1956-57, chief of staff, 1959, now sr. attending surgeon; vis. surgeon Sara Mayo, Flint-Goodridge hosps. (all New Orleans). Past pres. Virgilian Soc, New Orleans, New Orleans chpt. Dante Alighieri Soc.; past dir. New Orleans chpt. A.R.C., Travelers' Aid Soc., New Orleans Opera House Assn. Served as pvt. U.S. Army, World War I. Decorated silver medal Italian Govt., 1937; named adm. Gt. Navy of State of Neb. Diplomate Am. Bd. Abdominal Surgery. Fellow A.C.S., S.E. Surg. Congress, Am. Soc. Abdominal Surgeons; mem. Am., So. med. assns., La., Orleans Parish med. socs., New Orleans Acad. Sci. (life), Mediaeval Acad. Am., Shakespeare Soc. New Orleans, La. Hist. Soc. (pres.), Internat. Boswell Inst., Tulane Alumni Assn. (life), Stars and Bars Soc., Alpha Omega Alpha, Alpha Tau Omega. Mason (Shriner). Clubs: Round Table, Metairie Country. Author: Monti's Antonio Scarpa—(a translation), 1957; Historical Aspects of Abdominal Injuries, 1968; also sci. med. and surg. papers. Ex-asso. editor New Orleans Med. and Surg. Jour. Home: 223 Audubon Blvd New Orleans LA 70118 Office: Maison Blanche Bldg 921 Canal St New Orleans LA 70112

LORTON, WILLIAM DAVID, JR., city ofcl.; b. Radford, Va., Feb. 9, 1915; s. William David and Nelia Snow (Howell) L.; student Safety and Security Sch., Anniston, Ala., 1943, Va. Central Police Tng. Sch., 1947; diploma in fingerprinting and photography Chgo. Inst. Applied Sci., 1952; grad. FBI Acad., 1954; m. Pauline Elizabeth Rotenberry, Oct. 7, 1950; 1 dau., Lois (Mrs. Raymond Crockett Horton). With police dept. City of Radford (Va.), 1946-50, police sgt., 1952-57, chief police, 1957—; investigator Hercules Powder Plant, 1950-52. Chmn. Hwy. Safety Com., City Radford, Va., 1969—. Served with AUX. Mil. Police, AUS, 1943-46. Named Boss of Year Jr. C. of C., 1961. Mem. Nat. FBI Acad. Assos. Commonwealth Va. (pres. 1967-68), Va. Assn. Chief Police (mem. exec. com. 1970-71). Mem. Christian Ch. Mason (Shriner), Kiwanian. Home: 611 Calhoun St Radford VA 24141 Office: Radford Police Dept 1st and Wadsworth St Radford VA 24141

LORY, HILLIS, fgn. service officer; b. Sutherland, Ia., Nov. 13, 1900; s. Rev. James A. and Cora J. Lory; A.B., Morningside Coll., Sioux City, Ia., LL.D., 1945; A.M., Columbia; m. Sarah Miriam Drury, June 18, 1924; children—Priscilla (Mrs. Jonathan Bickings Kulp), Nancy. Faculty Hokkaido Imperial U., Japan, 1925-29; travel and residence in Orient, 1927, 29, 34, 37; Roberts fellow public law Columbia, 1929-31; acting head dept. polit. sci., Denison U., Granville, O., 1931-33; invited mem. Carnegie Endowment Inst. of Internat. Law, U. Mich., summer 1933; mem. faculty in polit. sci., Stanford U., 1933-34; lectr. Far Eastern politics, also Carnegie Endowment for Internat. Peace; Honnald Found. lectr. Knox Coll., 1934; Porter Found. lectr. Beloit Coll., 1935; mem. faculty Far Eastern Area and Language Sch., Stanford, 1943-44; officer Japanese Affairs div. Dept. State, 1944—; spl. asst., fgn. affairs officer, 1953-58; fgn. officer charge U.S.-USSR Indsl. and Tech. Exhanges, 1958—. Chmn. Fairfax County Bd. Edn., 1956—. Author: Japan's Military Masters (with foreword by the Honorable Joseph C. Grew, former ambassador to Japan and under-sec. of State, 1943). Contbr. on Far Eastern politics to various jours. Home: Fair Hills Old Ox Rd Fairfax Station VA Office: Dept of State Washington DC 20520

LOTT, H(ENRY) ALVIN, constrn. co. exec.; b. Pearl River, La., Sept. 8, 1908; s. John Alexander and Minnie (Till) L.; student Internat. Corr. Schs.; m. Edna Joiner, Feb. 12, 1931; children—Harold Alvin, Edna Inez (Mrs. Harold T. Dokupil). With R.P. Farnsworth Co., New Orleans, 1927-49, supt., 1935-41, gen. supt., 1941-49; v.p. constrn. Farnsworth & Chamber Co., Inc., Houston, 1949-57; organizer H.A. Lott, Inc., Gen. Contractors, Houston, 1957, chmn. bd. Bd. dirs. Meml. Bapt. Hosp. System, Houston. Recipient Merit award U.S. Dept. Housing and Urban Devel., 1966. Clubs: Houston, Lakeside Country. Joint contractor of domed stadium, Houston, 1963. Home: 3502 Amherst St Houston TX 77005 Office: 6315 Gulfton Houston TX 77036

LOTT, REUBEN, furniture co., securities, real estate exec.; b. Ararat, Ala., Jan. 8, 1897; s. George Franklin and Carrie (Craft) L.; student North Manchester (Ind.) Coll., 1917-18; m. Blondie Clara Powell, Apr. 20, 1927. Partner, Foster & Lott Retail Furniture Co., Laurel, Miss., 1919; owner, mgr. Lott Furniture Co., Laurel, 1923; pres. Laurel Furniture Co., Inc., 1946—; former pres. Lott Furniture Co. Meridian, Inc. (Miss.), Lott Furniture Co. Brookhaven, Inc. (Miss.), Lott Furniture Co. Jackson, Inc. (Miss.), Lott Furniture Co. Forest, Inc. (Miss.), Lott Furniture Co. McComb, Inc. (Miss.); dir. 1st Nat. Bank, Laurel. Chmn., Laurel Housing Authority; mem. Miss. Econ. Council. Chmn. bd. trustees Clarke Coll. Served with U.S. Army, 1919. Mem. Nat., Miss. retail furniture assns., Miss. Mchts. Assn., U.S., Miss., Laurel (dir.) chambers commerce, Am. Legion. Baptist (deacon). Mason. Home: 1005 15th St Laurel MS 39440 Office: 318-22 Front St Laurel MS 39440

LOTT, YANCY DAVIS, railroad exec.; b. Jackson, Miss., Aug. 28, 1906; s. Y. D. and Annette (Heintz) L.; A.B., Spring Hill Coll., 1927; LL.B., Georgetown U., 1932; m. Sarah C. Hunter, Nov. 20, 1935; children—Sally, Yancy Davis, Annette, Thomas, Lillis, Catherine. Spl. agt. FBI, 1932-34; admitted to D.C. bar, 1931, Miss. bar, 1934, Ala. bar, 1935; atty. G. M. & N. R.R., 1934-40; gen. atty. G. M. & O. R.R., 1940-50, gen. solicitor, 1950-55, v.p., comptroller, 1956—; dir. Gulf Transport Co., G. M. & O. Land Co., New Orleans Gt. No. Ry. Co., Mchts. Nat. Bank Mobile. Bd. dirs. Providence Hosp., America's Jr. Miss Pageant. Mem. Spring Hill Coll., Georgetown U. (gov.) alumni assns., Soc. Former Spl. Agts. FBI, Am., Ala., Miss., Mobile bar assns., Assn. Am. R.R.'s (past chmn. accounting div.). Clubs: Touchdown, Internat. Trade, Athelstan, Mobile Country (Mobile); University (Chgo.). Home: 11 E Wimbledon Dr Mobile AL 36608 Office: 104 St Francis St Mobile AL 36602

LOTTERHOS, WILLIAM EAST, physician; b. Crystal Springs, Miss., Nov. 22, 1914; s. Julius L. and Bessie (East) L.; student Millsaps Coll., 1932, Miss. State U., 1934; B.S., U. Miss., 1938; postgrad., 1937-38; M.D., U. Tenn., 1940; m. Elizabeth Teat, Oct. 19, 1943; children—William East, George, Elizabeth, Richard, John Howard. Intern, Miss. Baptist Hosp., Jackson, 1940-41; resident Methodist Hosp., Memphis, Tenn.,1946-47; practice medicine, specializing in family medicine, Jackson, Miss., 1947—; prof., also chmn. dept. family practice Med. Coll. Ga., Augusta, 1972—; mem. staffs St. Dominic's, Bapt., Doctor's, Hinds Gen., Univ. hosps. (all Jackson). Pres., Jackson Council on Alcoholism, 1959; mem. Nurse's Examining Bd., Miss., 1959-66; mem. bd. License for Phys. Therapy, 1966—; mem. Gov.'s Council Comprehensive Health Planning, 1968—; chmn. Com. Area Wide Health Planning, Gov.'s Com. on Rehab., 1968—; bd. dirs. Central Miss. Home Health Agy. Served to lt. col. M.C., AUS, 1941-46. Decorated Bronze Star, Purple Heart, Legion of Merit; Italian Mil. Cross of Valor. Diplomate Am. Bd. Family Practice. Fellow Am. Geriatric Soc.; mem. Am. Acad. Gen. Practice (pres. 1970-71, chmn. bd. dirs. 1968-70), Central Med. Soc. (pres. 1958-59), Miss. Med. Assn. (speaker Ho. of Dels. 1968-73), A.M.A., (chmn. sect. gen. practice 1965—, mem. council sci. assembly). Home: 920 Millege Rd Augusta GA 30904 Office: Med Coll Ga Adminstrn Bldg Augusta Ga 30902

LOUGHERY, RICHARD MILLER, hosp. adminstr.; b. Edinburg, Ind., Aug. 7, 1920; s. Roger S. and Margaret (Miller) L.; B.A., Ind. U., 1941; m. Miriam B. McGuire, Aug. 31, 1943; children—Suzanne, Cynthia, Richard, Michelle. Adminstrv. asst. Meth. Hosp., Indpls., 1946-53; asst. adminstr. Garfield Meml. Hosp., Washington, 1953-55, adminstr., 1955-58; dep. adminstr. Washington Hosp. Center, 1956-59, adminstr., 1959—; preceptor grad. program hosp. adminstrn. George Washington U.; mem. Hosp. Research and Devel. Inst.; cons. surgeon gen. USAF, 1959-68. Mem. Washington Bd. Trade. Chmn. hosp. adv. com. Health Facilities Planning Council, 1965-72; mem. Langley Forest (Va.) Citizens Assn., 1956—. Bd. dirs. D.C. Tb Assn., 1959-71; exec. com. Hosp. Council Nat. Capital Area, 1958-70, 72; 1st v.p. adv. group Regional Med. Program D.C., 1968-70. Served to capt. USMCR, 1942-46. Fellow Am. Coll. Hosp. Adminstrs. (chmn. book award com. 1965, chmn. com. publs. and information 1968-70, Council of Regents 1969-71, gov. 1971—, ho. of dels. 1972—), Am. (council on adminstrn. 1964-66, vice chmn. council on legislation 1972, ho. of dels. 1960-62, 72—, Md.-D.C. Del. (pres. 1961, sec. 1965, trustee 1956-70), Fairfax County, D.C. (pres. 1956-57) hosp. assns. Contbr. articles profl. jours. Home: 6901 Benjamin St McLean VA 22101 Office: 110 Irving St NW Washington DC 20010

LOUPE, SYLVAIN ROBERT, ret. fgn. service officer; b. White Hall, La., Apr. 29, 1907; s. Joseph Auxiliaro and Arcise (Dupuy) L.; B.A., La. State U., 1930, M.A. 1932; postgrad. U. Paris, 1951; m. Willie Mae Dietsch, Nov. 24, 1932; children—Judith Arbeth (Mrs. James Dunton), Sylvain MacRobert, Roberta Mae (Mrs. David Bankston), Donna Noelle. Prin. Central Espana (Cuba) Grammar Sch., 1930-31; tchr. Demonstration High Sch., La State U., 1931-32, asst. prof. mil. sci. and tactics 1941-42; prin. Doyle (La.) High Sch., 1932-33; dist ednl. adviser U.S. Dept. Interior, Atlanta, 1934-41; with U.S. Dept. of State, 1941-67, courier, S. Am. asst. communications officer, Cairo, Egypt, communications officer, Shanghai, China, regional supr. and attache Am. embassy, Paris, chief diplomatic pouch and courier br., Washington, chief gen. services div. and attache Am. embassy, Bonn, Germany, 1941-55, fgn. service officer class 3, 1st sec. embassy, consul, Bonn, 1956-60, counselor embassy, Rio de Janeiro, 1960-66; spl. rep. for excess personal property Am. embassy, Paris, 1966-67; fgn. service officer class 2 and full col.; now hon. cons. fgn. service State Dept. Adviser. Council for Devel. of French in La., 1969—. Bd. dirs. Am. Sch. of Rio, Our Lady of Mercy Sch. of Rio. Served as 1st lt. U.S. Army, 1933-34; to capt. to lt. col., AUS, 1941-42. Recipient citation and commendation Dept. Def., Meritorious Service medal Dept. State. Mem. Res. Officer Assn. (chmn. com. ret. officers 1969—, exec. v.p. La. dept. 1972-73), N.E.A., Nat. Medn. Fed. Employees (pres. Alexandria chpt. 1938-39), La. Tchrs. Assn., Fed. Postal Employees Assn., Atlantic Council U.S., Am. Soc. Pub. Adminstrn. (sr.), Internat. Platform Assn., U.S. Diplomatic Courier Assn. (charter), Nat. Adult Edn. Assn., Rio de Janeiro C. of C. (membership, program com.), Am. Security Council. K.C. (3 deg.). Clubs: American, Flamengo, Naval (Rio de Janeiro); Yacht (Brasilia); Nat. Travel (N.Y.C.); Wayfarer; Les Enchantes Dance (treas. 1971) (Gonzales, La.); Cabaret (London, Eng.); Nat. Travel. Home: White Hall Route 1 Box 308 Springfield LA 70462

LOURIE, ABRAHAM M., retail co. exec.; b. St. George, S.C., July 17, 1926; s. Louis and Ann Gertrude (Friedman) L.; student U. Ga., 1946-47; m. Nancy Jean Elfenbaum, Mar. 7, 1954; children—Allison Beth, Louis Steven, Joan Ellen, Adam Neal. With Lourie's Inc., Columbia, S.C., 1950—, v.p. 1954—. Pres. Loubro Co., Inc., Columbia, S.C., 1959—, Lourie's Dutch Sq., Columbia, 1970, Columbia Jewish Community Center, 1966-67. Team capt. United Fund, 1957-58. Bd. dirs. House of Peace Synagogue, 1957-59, Carolina Assn. Clothiers and Furnishers, 1965-67. Mem. Greater Columbia C. of C. Downtown Bus. Assn. (pres. 1970), Greater Columbia C. of C. (dir. sports com. 1969-70), Phi Epsilon Pi. Mason; mem. B'nai B'rith. Club: Country (Columbia). Home: 6210 Eastshore Rd Columbia SC 29206 Office: 1601 Main St Columbia SC 29201

LOURIE, ISADORE EDWARD, lawyer, state legislator; b. St. George, S.C., Aug. 4, 1932; s. Louis and Ann (Friedman) L.; LL.B., U. S.C., 1956; m. Susan Reiner, Nov. 29, 1959; children—Lance, Joel, Neal. Admitted to S.C. bar, 1956, since practiced in Columbia; partner Lourie and Draine, 1966—; mem. S.C. Ho. of Reps., 1965—, chmn. County House delegation, 1966-72. Dir., First Palmetto State Bank & Trust Co. Pres. S.C. Young Democrats, 1957-58; del. Nat. Dem. Conv., 1972. Pres. Happy Time Center for Mentally Retarded Children. Named Columbia's Young Man of Year, 1960. Mem. Am., S.C., Richland County bar assns., Am. Trial Lawyers Assn., Columbia Jr. C. of C. (past pres.). Jewish religion. Mason; mem. B'nai B'rith. Club: Civitan (Columbia). Home: 6308 West Shore Rd Columbia SC 29206 Office: 1224 Pickens St Columbia SC 29201

LOVE, BENTON FOOSHEE, banker; b. Vernon, Tex., Nov. 19, 1924; s. Benton Fooshee and Nell (Scott) L.; student (Debate scholar) Trinity U., 1941; B.B.A., U. Tex., 1947; postgrad. Southwestern Grad. Sch. Banking, So. Methodist U., 1968; m. Margaret Janelle McKean, Sept. 20, 1947; children—Jeffrey Benton, Janelle Margaret, Julie McKean. Founding pres. Gift-Raps, Inc., Houston, 1948-65; pres. River Oaks Bank & Trust Co., Houston, 1965-67; sr. v.p. Tex. Nat. Bank Commerce, Houston, 1967-68, exec. v.p., head comml. banking dept., 1968-69; pres. Tex. Commerce Bank, Houston, 1969—, also dir.; pres. Tex. Commerce Bancshares, Inc.; dir. Morrison-Knudsen Co., Inc., Proler Steel Corp. Active United Fund, 1969—, co-chmn. agy. operations com., 1969-70; mem. adv. bd. Salvation Army, 1967—, Meml. Hosp., Houston, 1969—; chmn. indsl. div. Pin Oak Charity Horse Show, 1966-69; mem. exec. com., sec. treas., bd. dirs. Nat. Space Hall Fame, 1969—; chmn. finance com. Holly Hall, Houston, 1969-70, bd. dirs., 1967-69; pres. Houston Grand Opera Assn., 1970—; treas. Houston Com. on Fgn. Relations, 1970—; chmn. finance com., treas., bd. dirs. Houston YMCA, 1969—; mem. adv. council Coll. Bus. Adminstrn. Found., U. Tex. at Austin, 1968—. Bd. dirs. Brazos Presbyn. Homes, 1968-69, Nat. Conf. Christians and Jews, Better Bus. Bur. Served to capt. USAAF, 1943-45; ETO. Decorated D.F.C. Mem. Houston C. of C. (chmn. cultural affairs com.), U. Tex. Ex-Students' Assn. (pres. 1968, exec. com. 1969—), Res. City Bankers Assn., Young Presidents Orgn. (chmn. S.E. Tex. 1966-67), Rice U. Assos. Presbyn. (past deacon). Clubs: Ramada, Houston, River Oaks, Plaza (dir.) (Houston). Home: 808 E Friar Tuck Houston TX 77024 Office: PO Box 2558 Houston TX 77001

LOVE, CHARLES ROBERT, constrn. co. exec.; b. Toppenish, Wash., May 31, 1919; s. C. Minter and Elizabeth (Soden) L.; student Central Wash. State Coll., 1938-42; hon. grad. U.S. Mcht. Marine Acad., 1944; B.A., U. Wash., 1946; m. Barbara Ann Boston, May 4, 1963 (div.); children—Timothy John, Deborah Dianne, Malissa Woods. Spl. agt. FBI, Atlanta, Pitts., San Francisco, 1945-48; dir. safety Stanford, 1958-60, lectr. Health edn., 1958-60, lectr. Sch. Nursing, 1958-67; v.p., dir. Corrigan Communications, Inc., Palo Alto, Cal., 1960-62; v.p. Edex Corp., Palo Alto, 1962-65; pres. C. Robert Love Assos., Los Altos, Cal., 1965-70; pres. Structural Systems Internat., Inc., Washington, 1970—; mem. adv. bd. Inst. Aerospace Safety and Mgmt., U. So. Cal., 1964—; sr. systems cons. Litton Industries; sr. systems cons., coordinating sec. Helene Fuld Health Found.; cons. Ore. System Higher Edn.; dir. edn. and tng. Tuskegee Inst. Housing Found. Cons. N.C. Baptist Hosp.'s Sister City Program, Bucaramango, Colombia. Served to lt. (j.g.) USNR, 1942-45; PTO. Recipient Scholarship award U.S. Mcht. Marine Acad., 1944. Mem. Soc. Former Agts. FBI, San Francisco Press Club, Nat. Assn. Ednl. Broadcasters, Nat. Assn. Pub. Sch. Adult Educators, N.E.A. Club: Sequoia Yacht (Redwood City, Cal.). Contbg. editor: Law and Order Mag., 1959-61. Creator cartoon Kelly at the Desk. Office: 1100 17th St NW Washington DC

LOVE, FRANK CRINER, oil co. exec.; b. Purcell, Okla., Apr. 29, 1908; s. Frank Criner and Louamma (Edwards) L.; LL.B., U. Okla., 1930; m. Margaret Eugenia Vessels, Dec. 29, 1931. Admitted to Okla. bar, 1931, practiced in Oklahoma City until 1934; with legal dept. Shell Oil Co., Tulsa, 1935-36; with firm Emby, Johnson, Crowe & Tolbert, Oklahoma City, 1937-48; with Kerr-McGee Corp., Oklahoma City, 1948—, exec. v.p., 1956-67, pres., 1967—, also dir., mem. exec. com.; dir. Fidelity Nat. Bank and Trust Co., Kermac Nuclear Fuels Corp., Bd. dirs. U. Okla. Research Inst. Named knight of St. Gregory, 1949. Mem. Order of Coif. Clubs: Oklahoma City Golf and Country (dir.), Petroleum (dir.) (Oklahoma City). Home: 3243 Northwest 19th St Oklahoma City OK 73102 Office: Kerr-McGee Bldg 2d and Robinson Sts Oklahoma City OK 73102

LOVE, FRANKLIN SADLER, trade assn. exec.; b. Rock Hill, S.C., Nov. 9, 1915; s. Franklin Sadler and Edna (Hull) L.; A.B., Presbyn. Coll., Clinton, S.C., 1937; m. Jessie Huggins, Apr. 10, 1943; children—Judith (Mrs. J. L. Freeman), Beverly (Mrs. Z.V. Cockerham), Franklin Sadler III, Glenn. Sec., Cotton Mfrs. Assn. of S.C., Clinton, 1937-42, Am. Cotton Mfrs. Assn., Charlotte, N.C., 1946-49; sec.-treas. Am. Textile Mfrs. Inst., 1949—. Adviser, Internat. Cotton Adv. Com., 1958. Mem. Charlotte adv. bd. Salvation Army; bd. dirs. Council on Alcoholism; bd. visitors Davidson Coll. Served to capt. Ordnance Dept., AUS, 1942-46. Mem. Charlotte C. of C., Def. Supply Assn., Am. Trade Assn. Exec., Phi Psi. Presbyn. Rotarian (del. 1961, pres. 1961-62). Clubs: City, Executives (sec.-treas. 1960-61), Goodfellows (Charlotte).Home: 1601 Providence Rd Charlotte NC 28207 Office: Johnston Bldg 212 S Tryon St Charlotte NC 28202

LOVE, JAMES C., III, hwy. constrn. co. exec.; b. Ruston, La., Sept. 25, 1938; s. James C. and Helen (James) L.; B.S. in Civil Enging. and Gen. Bus., La. Tech. U., 1962; m. Patricia Chapman, Jan. 29, 1960; children—James C., Helen Elizabeth, Daniel, Patricia. With T.L. James & Co., Inc., Ruston, 1962—, project mgr. hwy. constrn., 1964-67, cost engr. in charge data processing, cost accounting, field clerical personnel, 1967—, also dir. Bd. dirs. Lincoln Parish Sch., Ruston, La., Peach Festival Assn., Ruston; bd. dirs. La. Tech. U. Wesley Found Bd., pres., 1971; bd. dirs. Greater Tech. Found., pres., 1968. Mem. La. Tech. U. Alumni Assn., Kappa Sigma. Methodist (adminstrv. bd.). Home: Route 1 Box 530 Ruston LA 71270 Office: PO Box O Ruston LA 71270

LOVE, JEFF RAY, garment mfg. exec.; b. Jones Prairie, Tex., Dec. 10, 1902; s. Philip H. and Clara (Bozeman) L.; student Howard Payne Coll., 1919-20; m. Benita Harthcock, Jan. 24, 1931; children—Grace (Mrs. James Narramore), Betty (Mrs. George Shepherd), Jeff Ray. With Cheeves Bros. Dry Goods, Cameron, Tex., 1920; mgr. Duke & Ayres Variety Store, Bryan, Tex., 1926-35; designer Lovknit Mfg. Co., Greenville, Tex., 1936-47; pres. J.R. Love Co., Celeste, Tex., 1948—. Baptist. Mason. Home: 1 Meadow Lane Greenville TX 75401 Office: 218 Sanger St Celeste TX 75423

LOVE, MIRON ANDERSON, dist. judge; b. Houston, Oct. 25, 1920; s. Robert William and Josephine (Moody) L.; student So. Meth. U., 1946-48; LL.B., S. Tex. Law Sch., 1951; m. Marjorie Ruth Skiles, Dec. 21, 1948; children—Mark Lowry, Ross William. Admitted to Tex., bar, 1951; asst. dist. atty., 1952-54; city judge Houston, 1955-58; state dist. judge, Houston, 1958—. Bd. dirs., pres. Tex. Bill of Rights Found., 1960—; bd. dirs. Travelers Aid, March of Dimes. Served to 1st lt. USAAF, 1943-46. Mem. Am. (mem. adv. com. standards for criminal justice 1969—), Tex., Houston bar assns., Delta Theta Phi. Home: 3526 Garrott St Houston TX 77002 Office: Court House 301 San Jacinto St Houston TX 77002

LOVE, PHILIP HAMPTON, editor, writer, lectr.; b. Balt., Dec. 19, 1905; s. Philip H. and Madeline (MacDonald) L.; student Calvert Hall Coll., 1921-25; m. Ann Purcell, Dec. 29, 1928; 1 dau., Ann (Mrs. Edward A. Greene). Freelance cartoonist-writer, Balt., 1922-29; cartoonist-columnist Cartoons Mag., Balt. 1925-27; re-write man-feature writer Balt. Post, 1929-31; reporter, Washington Star, 1931-35, asst. city editor, 1935-38, asst. Sunday editor, 1938-45, feature editor, 1945-71, Sunday mag. editor, 1947-63; lectr. journalism George Washington U., 1942-52. Weekly columnist Love on Life, Bell-McClure Syndicate and N.Am. Newspaper Alliance, 1963-71, McNaught Syndicate, 1971—; editor Greater Buffalo Press, 1971—; guest lectr. colls. and univs. Mem. Chevy Chase Citizens Assn., Hawthorn Citizens Assn., Dares Beach Assn., St. Mary's County Hist. Soc., St. Mary's Art Assn. Bd. govs. Arts Club Washington, 1947-54. Mem. Nat. Press Club, Am. Assn. Sunday and Feature Editors, White House Corrs. Assn. Author: Andrew W. Mellon: The Man and His Work, 1929; Phil Love Talks of Comics, 1964; also articles in mags., newspapers. Home: 3015 Beech St NW Washington DC 20015 also Star Route Box 71C1 Leonardtown MD 20650 Office: 3015 Beech St NW Washington DC 20015

LOVE, RICHARD HARVEY, lawyer; b. Washington, Aug. 31, 1915; s. Leo Young and Grace Marie (Jett) L.; A.B., U. Md., 1936, LL.B., 1938; m. Betty Zane Schofield, Nov. 14, 1942 (dec. Sept. 1967); children— Richard, Robert, Edward, William, Elizabeth. Admitted to Md., D.C. bars. 1939; legal research asst. to Hon. W. Calvin Chesnut, U.S. dist. judge, Md., 1938-40; pvt. practice law, 1940-41, 46—; counsel Bd. Zoning Appeals, Prince Georges County, Md., 1953-55. Served from pvt. to maj. AUS, 1941-46; ETO; col. Judge Adv. Gen. Corps, Res. Decorated Legion Merit, Am. Def., Am. Service, European, African, Middle East, World War II Victory, Armed Forces Res. medal. Mem. Am., Md. bar assns., Bar Assn. D.C., Judge Advs. Assn. (exec. sec.), Mil. Order Fgn. Wars (judge adv. gen. Nat. commandery), Assn. U.S. Army, Mil. Law Inst., Phi Kappa Phi, Order of Coif. Republican. Roman Catholic. Editor: Judge Adv. Jour. Home: 6905 Carleton Terrace College Park MD 20740 Office: 1010 Vermont Av Washington DC 20005

LOVE, ROBERT MITCHELL, assn. exec.; b. Chgo., Aug. 7, 1928; s. Quill Horace and Jemma (Mitchell) L.; student Monterey Peninsula Jr. Coll., 1960-61; grad. Inst. for Orgn. Mgmt., U. Houston, 1968, Advanced Mgmt. Studies, Tex. Christian U., 1971; m. Shari Lee Cook, Dec. 12, 1964; children—Mark, Gregory, Wendi. Customer service agt. Am. Airlines, Memphis, 1951-55, customer service mgr., Washington, 1955-59, mgr. mil. traffic office, San Francisco, 1959-63;

mgr. customer service and operations Mohawk Airlines, N.Y.C., 1963-65; mgr. conv. and visitors bur. Little Rock C. of C., 1965-67; exec. v.p., also gen. mgr. Jonesboro (Ark.) C. of C., 1967-71; dir. indsl. services Knoxville (Tenn.) C. of C., 1971-72; exec. dir. Melton Hill Regional Indsl. Devel. Assn., 1972—. Served with AUS, USAF, 1946-51. Decorated Bronze Star medal, Purle Heart. Mem. Am. Soc. Assn. Execs., Am. Soc. C. of C. Execs.. Ark. C. of C. Mgrs. Assn. Methodist. Mason. Home: 7508 Berkshire Blvd Powell TN 37849 Office: 705 Gray St Knoxville TN 37902

LOVE, ROBERT WORRELL, city ofcl.; b. Madisonville, Tenn., Sept. 5, 1916; s. Robert John and Lillian Dee (Worrell) L.; student Vanderbilt U., 1933-34; B.S., U.S. Mil. Acad., 1938; M.B.A., Harvard, 1948; m. Cornelia Gambill, Sept. 16, 1939; children—Candace (Mrs. E.C. Dimitri), Robert, Wheless, Anne, Jenelle. Commd. 2d lt. U.S., Army, 1938, advanced through grades to col.; div. engr. Mo. River Div., Omaha, 1966-68; ret., 1968; urban renewal project mgr. Nashville Housing Authority, 1968—. Decorated D.S.M., Silver Star, Bronze Star, Legion of Merit (U.S.); Croix de Guerre (France). Fellow Am. Soc. C.E.; mem. Soc. Am. Mil. Engrs., Nat. Assn. Housing, and Redevel. Ofcls., Assn. U.S. Army. Presbyn (elder 1970—). Club: Exchange (Nashville). Home: 4505 Price Circle Rd Nashville TN 37205 Office: 309 Fifth Av N Nashville TN 37219

LOVE, TERRENCE LESTER, planner, architect, educator; b. Covington, Va., Feb. 6, 1937; s. James Harold and Patsy (King) L.; B.Arch., Va. Poly. Inst., 1961; M.B.A. in Real Estate and Urban Affairs, Ga. State U., 1969, Ph.D. in Land Econs., 1970; m. Valerie Gay LeCraw, Nov. 20, 1965; 1 son, Terrence Lester. Architect Aeck Assos., Inc., Atlanta, 1965-67; urban planner Adley Assos., Inc., Atlanta, 1967-70; asso. prof. Ga. State U., Atlanta, 1970—. Cons. in real estate feasibility, urban design and econ devel. Bd. dirs. Atlanta Arts Festival, 1970—; chmn. Atlanta Inter-Profl. Learning Team, 1970—. Served with AUS, 1961-62. Mem. A.I.A. (life), Am. Inst. Planners (life), Am. Real Estate and Urban Econ. Assn. (life, editor newsletter), Beta Gamma Sigma, Delta Sigma Pi. Home: 506 Manor Ridge Dr NW Atlanta GA 30305 Office: 33 Gilmer St SE Atlanta GA 30303

LOVE, WARREN LEE, banker; b. Washington, Apr. 2, 1919; s. Luther Lee and Elsa (Watson) L.; B.C.S. in Accounting, Benjamin Franklin U., 1940; M.C.S., Southeastern U., 1942; m. Mary Dolores McCarthy, Oct. 6, 1945; children—Sharon, Brian, Sheila, Maureen, Michael, Kevin. Spl agt. FBI, Washington, 1942-70; v.p. marketing First Nat. Bank Washington, 1970—. Chmn. troop, counselor Nat. Capital Area council Boy Scouts Am., 1960-66; pres. Donaldson Run Recreation Assn., Arlington, Va., 1965; treas., bd. dirs. Bellvue Forest Citizens Assn., Arlington, 1965, 70. Served with USNR, 1938. Recipient Certificate Appreciation, Boy Scouts Am., 1964, Optimists Internat., 1963. Mem. D.C. Bankers Assn. Methodist. Optimist. Home: 3607 N Peary St Arlington VA 22207 Office: 1701 Pennsylvania Av NW Washington DC 20006

LOVE, WILLIAM SYDNEY, JR., chemist; b. Galveston, Tex., Sept. 27, 1929; s. William Sydney and Inez Fischer (Bell) L.; student Southwestern U., 1946-48; B.S., U. Tex., 1957; m. Martha Evelyn Bickley, Aug. 10, 1951; children—Lloyd Stokes, Evelyn Elizabeth. Chemist Neches Butane Products Co., Port Neches, Tex., 1957-63; lab. supr. Southwest Chem. and Plastics Co., Seabrook, Tex., 1963—. Pres. Oyster Bay Assn., LaPorte, Tex., 1968—, sec. LaPorte Planning and Zoning Commn. 1969—. Served to 1st lt. AUS, 1951-53. Mem. Am. Chem. Soc. Republican. Methodist (bd. stewards 1958-61, 64-67). Lion (pres. 1966-67, dep. dist. gov. 1970-71). Club: Clear Lake Sailing. Home: 9 Bay Harbor Dr LaPorte TX 77571 Office: PO Drawer 478 Seabrook TX 77586

LOVELACE, BARNES FLOURNOY, lawyer; b. Brewton, Ala., June 23, 1910; s. Edwin Marshal and Frances Flournoy (McKinzie) L.; LL.B., U. Ala., 1932; m. Barbara Blount, Nov. 5, 1948; children—Sharon, Yancey Edwin, Barnes Flournoy, Barbara, Wynton Houston. Admitted to Ala. bar, 1932; since practiced in Brewton, Ala. Pres. Peoples Ins. Agy., Brewton, 1955—; v.p. S. Ala. Land Co., 1940—; dir. Bank of Brewton; pres. Lovelace Lumber Co., Brewton, Ala., 1932—. Public defender Escambia County (Ala.), 1970—; mem. City of Brewton Council, 1936-40; mem. Ala. Legislature, 1938-42, 46-50. Served to lt. USNR, 1942-46. Democrat. Episcopalian. Rotarian. Home: 1407 Poplar Av Brewton AL 36426 Office: Court House Annex Brewton AL 36426

LOVELACE, JOHN HENRY, lawyer; b. Waco, Tex., Oct. 26, 1926; s. Carl and Lucile (Hill) L.; B.A., U. Okla., 1948; J.D., U. Tex., 1951; m. Sarah Elizabeth Sadler, Oct. 20, 1951; children—John Henry, Sarah Elizabeth. Admitted to Tex. bar, 1951; with firm Sheehy, Cureton, Westbrook, Lovelace & Nielsen and predecessors, Waco, 1951—, partner, 1957—. Dir. Nat. City Bank Waco. Lectr. Baylor U. Sch. Law, 1965-68. Gen. chmn. Grass Roots Orgn. Waco, 1964; mem. exec. com. Citizens Adv. Com., 1970—. Served with AUS, 1944-46. Mem. State Bar Tex., Am. Bar Assn., Kappa Alpha Order (nat. bd. dirs. 1963-69, certificate of honor 1970), Phi Alpha Delta. Home: 3420 Oakridge Lane Waco TX 76708 Office: American-Amicable Bldg Waco TX 76701

LOVELL, JAMES A., astronaut; b. Cleve., Mar. 25, 1928; s. James A. and Blanche Lovell; student U. Wis., 1946-58; B.S., U.S. Naval Acad., 1952; grad. Aviation Safety Sch., U. So. Cal., 1961; hon. D., Ill. Wesleyan U.; D.Sc. (hon.), Rockhurst Coll., 1970; m. Marilyn Gerlach; children—Barbara Lynn, James Arthur, Susan Kay, Jeffrey C. Commd. 2d lt. U.S. Navy, advanced through grades to capt., 1965; test pilot Navy Air Test Center, Patuxent River, Md., 1958-61; then flight instr., safety officer Fighter Squadron 101, Naval Air Sta., Oceana, Va.; astronaut with Manned Spacecraft Center, NASA, 1962—; made 14 day orbital Gemini 7 flight, Dec. 1965, including rendezvous with Gemini 6, Gemini 12 Mission, 1966; command module pilot Apollo VIII, 1968; backup spacecraft comdr. Apollo XI; spacecraft comdr. Apollo XIII, 1970. Spl. cons. President's Council on Phys. Fitness and Sports, 1967—. Recipient Distinguished Service award NASA, 1965, Harmon Internat. Trophy, 1966, 67, Flight Achievement award Am. Astronautical Soc., 1966, 68, DeLaval Medal, 1967, Gold Space Medal, 1967, Gen. Thomas D. White Space trophy USAF, 1968, Robert J. Collier trophy, 1968, Henry G. Bennett Distinguished Service award, 1969, Robert H. Goddard Meml. trophy, 1969, H.H. Arnold trophy, 1969, Golden Plate award Am. Acad. Achievement, 1969, Gold Medal N.Y.C., 1969, Medal for valor City of Houston, 1969, Hubbard Medal Nat. Geographic Soc., 1969, Spl. Trustees award Nat. Acad. TV Arts and Scis., 1969, award Inst. Nav., 1969, Distinguished Alumni Service award U. Wis., 1970, Haley Astronautics award Am. Inst. Aeros. and Astronautics 1970, Presdl. medal for Freedom, 1970, Exceptional Service medal (two) NASA; decorated D.F.C. (two), Distinguished Service medal (Navy). Club: Toastmasters. Address: Manned Spacecraft Center NASA 2101 NASA Rd Houston TX 77058

LOVELL, JOE W., utilities ofcl.; b. Wartrace, Tenn., Oct. 2, 1912; s. Hall and Mattie (Jernigan) L.; student pub. schs., Murfreesboro; m. Flora Mae Qualls, Aug. 4, 1935. House electrician Tenn. Coll., 1926-29; bookkeeper, plumber, steamfitter Standard Plumbing & Heating Co., 1930-32; meter reader, cashier Murfreesboro (Tenn.) Water Dept., 1932-38, supt. Water Dept., 1938-56, Water and Sewer Dept., 1956—. Chmn., Tenn. Water and Wastewater Certification Bd., 1971—, Com. for Tng. Water and Wastewater Plant Operators in Tenn., 1968-72. Bd. dirs. Tenn. Municipal League, 1964-65. Recipient Samuel A. Greeley Service award, 1962; George Warren, Fuller award, 1967. Mem. Am. Water Works Assn. (life mem.; chmn. Ky.-Tenn. sect. 1957-58), Am. Pub. Works Assn. (pres. Tenn. 1964-65), Water Pollution Control Fedn. Presbyn. (elder, treas. 1944-51). Mason. Office: PO Box 700 Murfreesboro TN 37130

LOVELL, JOHN, JR., educator; b. Asheville, N.C., July 25, 1907; s. John and Zula (Pope) L.; A.B., Northwestern U., 1926, M.A., 1927; Ph.D., (Rockefeller Found. fellow), U. Cal. at Berkeley, 1938; m. Nancy Merritt, Sept. 6, 1940 (div. Mar. 1951); 1 dau., Taunya Marita; m. 2d, Marian Giles Mouzon, July 31, 1954 (dec. Oct. 13, 1966). Instr. English, W. Va. State Coll., 1927-29; asst. prof. English, Howard U., Washington, 1930-46, asso. prof., 1946-58, prof., 1958—, asso. dean Coll. Liberal Arts, 1964-68, acting head dept. English, 1968-69, chmn. dept., 1972—; vis. prof. in Ia., Cal., Am. Friends Service Com., 1948; vis. prof. U. Pacific, summers 1950, 56; lectr., cons. seminars for exec. devel. U.S. Dept. Agr. Fulbright lectr., Japan, 1960-61. Served to 1st lt. AUS, 1943-46. Mem. Modern Lang. Assn. Am., Am. Lit. Sect., Am. Studies Assn., Am. Soc. for Theatre Research, Am. Ednl. Theatre Assn., Assn. for Asian Studies, Folklore Soc. Greater Washington, Internat. Theatre Inst., ANTA, Authors League Am., Nat. Council Tchrs. English, Washington Urban League, N.A.A.C.P. (sec. 1939-42), Kappa Alpha Psi. Democrat. Author: Digests of Great American Plays, 1961; Black Song: The Forge and the Flame, 1972. Contbr. articles to profl. jours. Research, lectr. native drama and folklore. Home: 201 I St SW Washington DC 20024

LOVEMAN, ADOLPH BERNARD, physician; b. Birmingham, Ala., 1903; M.D., U. Mich., 1929, M.S. in Dermatology and Syphillis, 1933. Intern, Univ. Hosp., Ann Arbor, Mich., 1929-30, resident dermatology and syphillis, 1930-31, jr. instr. dermatology and syphillis, 1931-32, sr. instr., 1932-33; mem. active staff Jewish Hosp., Louisville Gen. Hosp., Norton Meml. Infirmary; clin. prof., chmn. dermatol. service U. Louisville. Diplomate Am. Bd. Dermatology. Mem. Am. Acad. Dermatology, A.M.A., So. Med. Assn. Office: 332 W Broadway Louisville KY also Medical Towers S Louisville KY 40202*

LOVERING, LEALAND LLOYD, lawyer; b. Revere, Mass., Oct. 21, 1926; s. Ernest E. and Gladys (Libbey) L.; student U. N.H., 1945-46; J.D., U. Fla., 1959; m. Dorothy D. Smith, Oct. 12, 1957; 1 stepson, Frederick Dailey Smith. Admitted to Fla. bar, 1959; mem. firm Smith & Lovering, 1960-63, Owen, Wagner & Nugent, 1963-64; partner firm Cone, Wagner, Nugent, Johnson, McKeown & Dell, Rockledge, Fla., 1964—. Pres. Okaloosa County chpt. Am. Cancer Soc., 1961-62, Okaloosa County Shrine Club, 1962. Bd. dirs. Brevard County Mental Health Assn. Served with AUS, 1944-45. Mem. Am., Palm Beach County, Brevard County (chmn. legal aid 1966, exec. com. 1967—) bar assns., The Fla. Bar (bd. govs. 1968—), Acad. Fla. Trial Lawyers (dir. 1970—), Am. Trial Lawyers Assn., Soc. Hosp. Attys., Am. Judicature Soc., U. Fla. Alumni Club (pres. 1962). Home: 510 Old Settlement Rd Merritt Island FL 32952 Office: 1259 S Florida Av Rockledge FL 32955

LOVING, JOE HILTON, JR., municipal judge; b. Dallas, Dec. 12, 1935; s. Joe Hilton and Lola Julia (Anders) L.; B.A., So. Meth. U., 1958, LL.B., 1960; postgrad. Southwestern Bapt. Theol. Sem., 1969—; m. Mary Leone Carpenter, June 8, 1963; children—Donna Michelle, Sheryl Diane, Kimberly Dawn. Admitted to Tex. bar, 1960, practiced in Grand Prairie, 1961; asst. city atty., Dallas, 1961-68; judge municipal ct., Dallas, 1968—. Ordained to ministry Bapt. Ch., 1969. Mem. Tex., Dallas bar assns., N.Am. Judges Assn., Delta Theta Phi. Home: 623 Oceanview Dr Dallas TX 75232 Office: Police and Courts Bldg Main and Harwood Sts Dallas TX 75201

LOVVORN, MARTIN CRAFT, banker; b. Dallas, Apr. 15, 1928; s. Ben H. and Floyd (Craft) L.; B.B.A., So. Meth. U., 1948; m. Mary Carolyn Goodman, Nov. 18, 1950; children—Janet, Mark, Linda, Laurie. Chmn. bd. Lewisville (Tex.) Nat. Bank, 1963-65, Tex. Nat. Bank, Dallas, 1965—; pres. 1st Nat. Bank, Richardson, Tex., 1964—, Dynamerica Corp., Dallas, Tex., 1969—. Bd. dirs. Bapt. Found. of Tex.; trustee annuity bd. So. Bapt. Conv. Served to lt. (j.g.) USNR. 1951-52. Home: 3820 W Bay Circle Dallas TX 75214 Office: 808 S Central Expressway Richardson TX 75080

LOW, GEORGE MICHAEL, govt. ofcl.; b. Vienna, Austria, June 10, 1926; s. Arthur and Gertrude (Burger) L.; B.Aero. Engring., Rensselaer Polytech. Inst., 1948, M.S. in Aero. Engring., 1950, honorary D.Eng., 1969; D.Sc., U. Fla., 1969; m. Mary R. McNamara, Sept. 3, 1949; children—Mark S., Diane E., G. David, John M., Nancy A. With NASA, and predecessor, 1949—, dep. asso. adminstr. manned space flight, 1963-64, dep. dir. Manned Spacecraft Center, Houston, 1964-67, mgr. Apollo spacecraft program, 1967-69, dep. adminstr. NASA, 1969—, chmn. select com. original studies leading to Manned Lunar Landing Program. Trustee Rensselaer Poly. Inst. Recipient outstanding Leadership medal NASA, 1962, Distinguished Service medals (2), 1969; Arthur S. Flemming award U.S. Jr. C. of C., 1963; Space Flight award Am. Astronautical Soc., 1968; Paul T. Johns trophy Arnold Air Soc., 1969; Louis W. Hill Space transp. award Am. Inst. Aeronautics and Astronautics, 1970; Nat. Space Club Astronautics Engr. Award, 1970. Fellow Am. Astronautical Soc., Am. Inst. Aeros. and Astronautics; mem. Nat. Acad. Engring., Aerospace Med. Assn. (hon.), Nat. Aero. Assn. (dir). Research fields aerodynamic heating, boundary layer theory and transition, internal flow in supersonic and hypersonic aircraft. Club: Cosmos (Washington, DC). Office: Deputy Adminstr NASA Washington DC 20546

LOW, JAMES PATTERSON, orgn. exec.; b. Hartford, Conn., July 25, 1927; s. Marshall and Margaret (Fleming) L.; B.A., U. Md. 1953; M.B.A., Fla. Atlantic U., 1972; m. Patricia Marion Siegman, Nov. 20, 1956; children—Lisa Patricia, Lori Patterson. Mgr., Pulaski County (Va.) Indsl. Devel. Corp. and C. of C., 1953-55; asst. mgr. assn. service dept. C. of C. U.S., Washington, 1956-58, mgr., 1958-66; exec. v.p. Am. Soc. Assn. Execs., 1966—. Instr., Insts. for Ogn. Mgmt., Yale, Mich. State U., Syracuse U., Stanford, 1958—. Pres., River Oaks and Langley Forest Citizens Assn., McLean, Va., 1964. Chmn. finance com. Fairfax County (Va.) For Congressman Broyhill, 1964-65; mem. Fairfax County steering com. Republican party, 1963—. Served with USMCR, 1945-46; to capt. AUS, 1951-54. Decorated Bronze Star. Mem. Washington Trade Assn. Execs., Am. Soc. Assn. Execs., Nat. Assn. Execs. Club (dir.), Sigma Nu. Club: Congressional Country. Author: Basic Operating Policies of Trade and Professional Associations, 1960; Association Legislative Handbook, 1962; Association Executive Contracts, 1965. Home: 8463 Brook Rd McLean VA 22101 Office: 1101 16th St NW Washington DC 20036

LOW, JOHN T(HOMAS) C(UYAMA), bank exec.; b. N.Y.C., Nov. 20, 1918; s. James Joseph and Charlotte (Manning) L.; A.B., Colgate U., 1939; J.D., Columbia, 1942; m. Virginia Ball Kull, Aug. 2, 1941; 1 dau., Virginia Nichols. Admitted to N.Y. bar, 1942, practiced N.Y.C., with Davis, Polk, Wardwell, Sunderland & Kiendl, 1942-45, Dewey, Ballantine, Bushby, Palmer & Wood, 1947-57; vice president, sr. trust officer Lincoln National Bank and Trust Company, Syracuse, N.Y., 1957-68; exec. v.p. Citizens Fidelity Bank & Trust Co., 1968—; confidential law asst. Gov. Thomas E. Dewey, 1945-47; lectr. law Pace Coll., N.Y.C., 1947-52. Admitted to Ky. bar, 1968. Mem. Am., Ky. bar assns., Am. Bankers Assn. Author articles on taxation. Home: 2310 Merrick Rd Louisville KY 40207 Office: PO Box 1140 Louisville KY 40201

LOWBEER, LEO, physician; b. Vienna, Austria, May 30, 1901; s. Alfred and Pauline (Sobotka) L.; M.D., U. Vienna, 1927; m. Gertrude Neuhut, Sept. 28, 1940; 1 dau., Carol Ann. Came to U.S., 1938, naturalized, 1944. Intern dept. pathology Vienna Municipal Hosp., 1927-28, rotating intern 1928-29, 1st asst. to Prof. Jakob Erdheim dept. pathology, 1929-32, resident dept. metabolic and nutritional diseases, 1932-33, sr. resident dept. geriatric medicine, 1933-37; pathologist Hillcrest Meml. Hosp., Tulsa, 1939-45; chief pathologist, dir. dept. pathology Hillcrest Med. Center, Tulsa, 1945-67, emeritus, 1967—; chief cons. pathologist Hillcrest Med. Center and Okla. Bd. Medicolegal Investigations, 1967—; distinguished lectr. dept. pathology U. Okla. Sch. Medicine, Oklahoma City, 1947—; cons. pathologist FAA; cons. U.S. Dept. Justice; dir. Hillcrest Poison Center, Tulsa, 1961—. Recipient citation for meritorious service North Tulsa Community Service, 1954; certificate appreciation, 1969, Service to Mankind award, 1971 (both Tulsa Sertoma Club). Diplomate Am. Bd. Pathology. Fellow Am. Assn. Pathologists and Bacteriologists, Coll. Am. Pathologists, Am. Soc. Clin. Pathologists, Internat. Acad. Pathology; mem. Am. (life), So., Okla. med. assns., Tulsa County Med. Soc. (life mem., alternate del.), Am. Acad. Forensic Scis., A.A.A.S., Soc. Exptl. Biology and Medicine, Nat. Assn. Med. Examiners, Am. Assn. Poison Control Centers, Am. Acad. Clin. Toxicology, Okla. Assn. Pathologists (pres. 1950), Tulsa Philharmonic Assn. Democrat. Methodist. Clubs: Tulsa Ski, Concertime, Tulsa Tennis. Contbr. articles to med. jours. Home: 2547 S College St Tulsa OK 74114 Office: Hillcrest Medical Center 1120 S Utica St Tulsa OK 74104

LOWDEN, FRANCIS VIELE, JR., lawyer; b. Elizabeth, N.J., Aug. 27, 1915; s. Francis V. and Mabel (Horning) L.; grad. Pingry Sch., 1933; A.B., Dartmouth, 1937; LL.B., U. Va., 1942; m. Barbara Clarke, June 24, 1939; children—Francis V. III, Katherine C., Frederick C. Admitted to Va. bar, 1941, since practiced in Richmond; mem. firm Hunton, Williams, Gay & Gibson. Mem. Commn. to Study Rights of Pub. Employees in Va., 1972-73. Served to lt. USNR, 1943-46. Mem. Am., Va. (chmn. labor law com. 1971—), Richmond bar assns., Order of Coif, Raven Soc., Sigma Nu Phi, Beta Theta Pi. Home: 110 College Rd Richmond VA 23229 Office: 700 E Main St Richmond VA 23212

LOWE, A(LVIN) J(ENKINS), educator; b. Lawrence, Mass., Sept. 26, 1931; s. George Alfred and Helen (West) L.; B.A., Miss. So. Coll., 1958, M.A., 1959; Ed.D., U. Va., 1967; m. Elizabeth Munson; children— Katherine, Frederick, Ralph, Owen. Clinician reading clinic Miss. So. Coll., 1957-58, instr. Sch. Edn. and Psychology, 1958-59; instr. reading U. Va., 1959-62; dir. reading center Loyola U., New Orleans, 1962-66, asst. prof. edn., 1962-66; asst prof. reading edn. U. South Fla., Tampa, 1966-69, asso. prof., 1969—. Reading tchr. George Hurst Elementary Sch., 1956-57, St. Anne's Sch., 1960-62, Holy Name Sch., 1962-66; reading cons. various schs., ednl. programs, govt. agys.; announcer, engr. various TV and radio stas. Served with AUS.; Korea. Mem. Am. Psychol Assn., Am. Ednl. Research Assn., Internat. (mem. evaluation com. 1968-71), Coll. reading assns., Nat. Reading Conf. (conf. mgr. 1963—, dir. 1969—), Hillsborough County Reading Council, Nat. Soc. Study Edn., Soc. Profs. Edn., Nat. Council Tchrs. English, Am. Acad. Polit. and Social Sci., Nat. Council Measurement Edn., Am. Assn. U. Profs., Phi Delta Kappa (chpt. pres. 1970-71), Kappa Delta Pi. Club: Civitan. Contbr. numerous articles to profl. jours. Home: 8417 Boxwood Dr Tampa FL 33615

LOWE, HARRY, museum curator; b. Opelika, Ala., Apr. 9, 1922; s. Harry Foster and Lois (Fletcher) L.; B.F.A., Auburn U., 1943, M.F.A., 1949; student Cranbrook Acad., 1951, 53. Prof. art, dir. Art Gallery, Auburn U., 1957-59; dir. Tenn. Fine Arts Center, Nashville, 1959-64; curator exhbn. and design Nat. Collection Fine Arts, Smithsonian Instn., 1964-72, asst. dir. operations, 1972—. First pres. Tenn. Assn. Museums, 1960. Served with F.A., AUS, World War II; ETO. Home: 1517 30th St Washington DC 20007 Office: Nat Collection Fine Arts Smithsonian Instn Washington DC 20560

LOWE, HUGH WASHINGTON, accountant, tax cons.; b. Temple, Okla., Apr. 24, 1909; s. Joe and Viola Ann (Johnson) L.; B.S., Southeastern State Coll., Durant, Okla., 1934; M.S., Okla. State U., 1939; diploma in personnel and guidance Colo. State Coll., 1948, postgrad. summers 1948-52; m. Jacqueline Wilkins, July 27, 1938; children—Jackie Ann (Mrs. Billy Carl Gunn), David H. Prin. elementary jr., sr. high schs., 1934-42; plans and tng. supr., sr. instr. Air Force Tech. Sch., 1942-44; dir. guidance, appraiser for VA, Southeastern State Coll., 1946-49; dir. guidance, Temple (Okla.) Sch., 1949-51, Dept. of Air Force, Wichita Falls, Tex., 1951-54; accountant, tax cons., Temple, 1954—; chief exec. officer Lowe's Accounting & Tax Service; v.p., dir. Okla. Independent Ins. Contractors Agy., Inc., Oklahoma City; mem. adv. bd. Gt. Mo. Life Ins. Co., Springfield. Served with USNR, 1944-46. Recipient Am. Community Leader award News Pub. Co., Raleigh, N.C., 1968. Mem. Am. Personnel and Guidance Assn., Nat. Vocational Guidance Assn., Okla (dist. mem. exec. personnel and guidance div.), S.W. Okla. (guidance chmn.) edn. assns., Kappa Delta Pi. Lion (pres. Temple club 1958-59). Author: Teachers Handbook, 1942; (with Dr. John W. Morris and others) Let's Orient Ourselves, 1948. Contbr. to profl. publs. Home: 719 N Commercial Av Temple OK 73568 Office: 127 N Commercial Av Temple OK 73568

LOWE, THOMAS ELTON, physician; b. Nacogdoches, Tex., Oct. 3, 1906; s. Thomas Edmund and Ellie (Eilliot) L.; student Rice U., 1928; M.D., Tulane U., 1933; m. Evelyn Althea Reisig, Nov. 9, 1935; children—Thomas Elton, Robert James, Ronald C. Intern So. Bapt. Hosp., New Orleans, 1933-34; practice gen. medicine, Houston; mem. staff St. Joseph Hosp., Houston, Meml. Baptist. Hosp., Houston, Hermann Hosp., Houston, Methodist Hosp., Houston. Served to maj. M.C., AUS, 1942-46. Mem. A.M.A., Tex., Am. assns. gen. practice, Tex., Harris County med. socs., Theta Kappa Psi. Home: 12330 Perthshire St Houston TX 77024 Office: 715 Telephone Rd Houston TX 77023

LOWE, MRS. THOMAS JACKSON (ROSE WALKER MAYNE), assn. exec.; b. Athens, Ga.; d. George Stovall and Rosa Montgomery (Walker) Mayne; A.B. in Edn. (U.D.C. scholar), M.S. (U. fellow), U. Ga.; Nat. Soc. Crippled Children and Adults, Inc. and Alpha Chi Omega scholar U. Mich. and Mich. State Normal Coll.; m. Thomas Jackson Lowe; 1 dau., Harriet Rose. Cerebral palsy coordinator S.C. Soc. Crippled Children and Adults, 1949-50, exec. dir., 1951—; adviser, cons. health related tax-supported agys.; vis. lectr. state univs., colls. Sponsored legislation to provide edn. to handicapped children in Ga., S.C. Mem. Gov.'s, Mayor's coms. on handicapped. Named Columbia Career Woman of Year, 1965, S.C. Career Woman of Yr. 1966; recipient State S.C. Rehab. award of yr., 1969. Mem. Internat. Council Exceptional Children (past dist. pres.; former S.C. pres.), Am. Assn. Easter Seal Execs., Nat., S.C. rehab. assns., Daus.

Colonial Wars, Colonial Dames 17th Century, Nat. Soc. Magna Charta Dames, S.C. Psychol. Assn., S.C. Acad. Sci., S.C. Conf. Social Work, Jamestowne Soc., Soc. Descs. Knights of Garter, Daus. 1812, Dau. Am. Colonists, D.A.R., U.D.C., Plantagenet Soc., Psi Chi, Xi Phi Xi. Methodist. Home: 4017 MacGregor Dr Columbia SC 29206 Office: 3020 Farrow Rd Columbia SC 29203

LOWE, WEBB, restaurant chain exec.; b. Lambertsville, Mich., July 18, 1931; s. Webster and Pearl (Peters) L.; student U. Toledo, 1950-51, Northeastern U., 1966-67, So. Methodist U., 1970; m. Katherine Wagenhauser, Aug. 21, 1954; children—Webster, Kevin, Kelly, Lisa. Exec. v.p. McDonald's Corp., Chgo., 1968-69; pres., chief exec. officer Bonanza Internat., Inc., Dallas, 1969—. Post adviser Circle Ten council Explorer Scouts Am., 1969—. Mem. Young Pres.'s Orgn. Home: 7237 Joyce Way Dallas TX 75231 Office: 6116 N Central Expressway Dallas TX 75206

LOWELL, JOHN FREDERICK, clothing retail chain exec.; b. London, Eng., Oct. 27, 1938; s. Hans and Jessie (Schoen) von Fraunhofer; student Clark's Coll. (London), 1952-56, Columbia U., 1957-59, N.Y. U., 1959-61; m. Judith Ann Weitzner, Aug. 30, 1962; children—David John, Brian Phillip, Jennifer Brooke. Came to U.S., 1956, naturalized, 1964. Buyer gifts dept. Abercrombie & Fitch Co., N.Y.C., 1962-65, men's clothing and sportswear dept. R.A.M. div. Genesco, N.Y.C., 1965-68, Julius Garfinckel, Washington, 1968-69; pres., chief exec. officer Farnsworth-Reed Ltd., Washington, 1969—. Instr. clothing and dress Southeastern U., Washington, 1968—. Home: 5375 Duke St Alexandria VA 22304 Office: 1341 F St NW Washington DC 20004

LOWENS, IRVING, musicologist, music critic; b. N.Y.C., Aug. 19, 1916; s. Harry and Hedwig (Abramovich) L.; B.S., Columbia, 1939; M.A., U. Md., 1957, postgrad., 1957—; m. Margery Louise Morgan, Feb. 1, 1969. Contbg. music critic Washington Eve. Star, 1953-60, chief music critic, 1961—; reference librarian for sound recs. music div. Library of Congress, Washington, 1959-61, asst. head reference sect. music div., 1961-66. Research cons. Moravian Music Found., 1956—; mem. adv. bd. Inter-Am. Inst. for Mus. Research, Tulane U., 1961—, Hist. Inst. Am. Music, 1965—; bd. dirs. Am. Music Center, 1966-72; chmn. bd. dirs. Am. Mus. Digest, 1967-70; trustee Robert Owen Lehman Found., 1964-66. Recipient Moramus award for distinguished service to Am. music, 1960; Am. Council Learned Socs. travel grantee, Germany, 1962, research grantee, 1965-66; Martha Baird Rockefeller Fund travel grantee, Austria, 1964, Romania, 1967; U.S. State Dept. travel grantee, Venezuela, 1968, Greece and Cyprus, 1970; Nat. Endowment for Arts research grantee, 1969. Fellow Am. Antiquarian Soc.; mem. Am. (mem. council 1956-59, 61-64, 68-71, exec. bd. 1964-65), Internat. musicological socs., Am. Studies Assn., Am. Folklore Soc., Internat. Assn. Music Libraries, Bibliog. Soc. Am., Internat. Folk Music Council, Soc. Ethnomusicology, Music Library Assn. (exec. bd. 1962-64, pres. 1965-66), Music Critics Assn. (pres. 1971—), Hymn Soc. Am., Manuscript Soc. Club: Cosmos (Washington). Author: Music and Musicians in Early America, 1964; other books and monographs. Contbr. numerous articles on history, bibliography and lit. early Am. music to profl. jours. Office: Evening Star 225 Virginia Av SE Washington DC 20003

LOWENSTEIN, CHARLES DOUGLAS, ednl. services co. exec.; b. Bayonne, N.J., Apr. 22, 1942; s. Irving Eric and Barbara (Goldenberg) L.; B.S. in Commerce and Econs., U. Vt., 1963; m. Leslie Ann Diamond, Sept. 5, 1965; children—Lee Jay, Andrea Michelle. Supt. Lowenstein Metals Inc., Newark, 1964-67; registered prin. Penn Securities Co., East Orange, N.J., 1967-68; asst. dir. Nelson Sch. Securities, Mountainside, N.J., 1968-69; v.p. sales Ga. Internat. Securities Co., Atlanta, 1969-70; pres. Investment Tng. Inst., Inc., Atlanta, 1969—; tng. cons. Wiesenberger Services, Inc., N.Y.C., 1971—. Mem. task force to design new industry tng. standards Nat. Assn. Securities Dealers, 1971. Served with AUS, 1963. Mem. Internat. Assn. Financial Planners, Jr. C. of C., Nat. R.R. Hist. Soc., Tau Epsilon Phi. Jewish religion. Home: 1830 Cameo Ct Tucker GA 30084 Office: PO Box 29151 Atlanta GA 30329

LOWENSTEIN, GEORGE WOLFGANG, UN cons.; b. Germany, Apr. 18, 1890; s. Julius Max and Augusta Victoria (Klettschoff) L.; student Royal William Coll., Germany, 1909, Frederik Williams U., Germany, 1919, London (Eng.) Sch. Tropical Hygiene and Medicine, 1939; m. Johanna Sabath, Nov. 27, 1923; children—Peter F. Lansing and Ruth Edith (Mrs. Roger G. Gallagher) (twins). Intern Berlin III U. Clinic, 1919; resident Berlin Charity Hosp., 1920; dir. pub. health Berlin Neubabelsberg, 1920-22; dir. pub. health and welfare, Berlin, Germany, 1923-33; pvt. practice medicine in Berlin, 1933-38, Chgo., 1940-46, Chebeague and Dark Harbor, Me., 1947-58; permanent cons. for Internat. Abolitionists Fedn. at ECOSOC, UN, 1947—; med. cons. German Consulate (Atlanta) for Fla. Social Econs. Research; pres. Aripeka Corp. for Devel., 1958-66; med. cons. Pasco County Civil Def., 1958-66; lectr. Morton Plaut Hosp., Clearwater, also Clearwater campus St. Petersburg Jr. Coll. Vice pres. Allied Art Council West Pasco, 1960-66. Bd. dirs. Aripeka Meml. Library, Richey Symphony Assn., West Pasco County Hosp. Assn., 1959-66. Co-founder German Hygiene Mus., Dresden; county chmn. first aid A.R.C., 1958-66, vol. program cons. nat. A.R.C., 1958-66; vol. worker A.R.C., 52 years. Civilian Def., Chebeague and Dark Harbor, Me., 1946-57. Served with German Army, 1914-18. Decorated Cross Merit I Class, Germany, 1965; recipient Commendation awards Pres. U.S., 1945, 70; 50 Year Gold Service Pin, A.M.A. and A.R.C., 1970; Service to Mankind award Sertoma, 1972, others. Fellow A.A.A.S., Am. Coll. Sport Medicine (emeritus), Am. Pub. Health Assn. (life); mem. A.M.A., Am. Assn. Mil. Surgeons, Acad. Gen. Practice (charter mem., life mem.) sec. 1948-52), Steuben Soc. Club: City (Chgo. chmn. hygiene sect. 1946-46). Rotarian, Mason (Shriner, Comdr., 32 deg.). Home: 1007 Woodside Dr Clearwater FL 33516

LOWERY, GEORGE HINES, JR., zoologist, educator; b. Monroe, La., Oct. 2, 1913; s. George Hines and Pearl (Connaughton) L.; B.S., La. State U., 1934, M.S., 1936; Ph.D., U. Kan., 1949; m. Jean Tiebout, Mar. 12, 1937; children—Jeanette (Mrs. Edward Moore), Carol Lynn. Mem. faculty La. State U., 1936—, dir. Mus. Natural Sci., 1936—, prof. zoology, 1950—, Boyd prof., 1955—. Mem. Am. Ornithologists Union (pres. 1959-62; Brewster medal 1955), Am. Soc. Mammalogists, Soc. Study Evolution, Soc. Systematic Zoologists, A.A.A.S., Sigma Xi, Phi Kappa Phi. Author: Louisiana Birds, rev. edit., 1960; also numerous articles. Home: 6255 Chandler Dr Baton Rouge LA

LOWERY, JAMES HARLTON, city ofcl.; b. Remlig, Tex., July 10, 1923; s. James Frank and Lillian (Mitchell) L.; grad. Port Arthur Bus. Coll., 1944. Clk. Lumus Constrn. Co., N.Y.C., 1944; parts mgr. Hempel Motors Co., Orange, Tex., 1953-54; auditor Tex. Employment Commn., Houston, 1955-56; with City of Port Arthur (Tex.), 1957—, dir. finance, 1964—. Mem. C. of C., Municipal Finance Officers Assn. Baptist (deacon chmn. finance com. 1967—). Home: 2749 31st St Port Arthur TX 77640 Office: 400 4th St Port Arthur TX 77640

LOWERY, LEE LEON, JR., civil engr.; b. Corpus Christi, Tex., Dec. 26, 1938; s. Lee Leon and Blanch (Dietrich) L.; B.S., Tex. A. and M. U., 1960, M.S., 1962, Ph.D., 1966; m. Evelyn Frances Lindsey, Sept. 4, 1960; children—Kelli Lane, Christianne. Asso. research engr. Tex. Transp. Inst., Bryan, 1960—; asso. prof. depts. civil engring., aerospace engring., archtl. engring. Tex. A. and M. U., 1960—; research engr. Albritton Engring. Corp., 1963-66; sr. partner Pile Dynamics, Inc., 1968—; pres. Anderson-Lowery & Assos. Profl. engring. cons. Esso Prodn. Research, Brown & Root, Kaiser Steel Co., Chgo. Bridge & Iron Works. Mem. Am. Soc. C.E., Nat., Tex. socs. profl. engrs., Am. Soc. Engring. Edn., Sigma Xi, Tau Beta Pi, Phi Kappa Phi, Chi Epsilon. Kiwanian. Contbr. articles to profl. jours. Patentee in field. Home: 2404 Wayside St Bryan TX 77801 Office: 4015 Texas Av Bryan TX 77801

LOWERY, RAYMOND, newspaper editor; b. Patterson Springs, N.C., Jan. 13, 1918; s. William and Ida (McBrayer) L.; student Oak Ridge Mil. Inst., 1935-36; A.B., U. N.C., 1936-39; m. Jeanne DeKam, Mar. 13, 1948; children—David, Danny. Mng. editor Los Angeles Comml. News, 1948; telegraph editor Shelby (N.C.) Daily Star, 1948-50; entertainment editor The News and Observer, Raleigh, N.C., 1952-60, Sunday editor, 1960-69, copy editor, feature writer, 1969—. Dir. N.C. State Ballet, Raleigh Concert Music Assn., N.C. Music Assn. Served with USAAF, 1942-46. Home: 4306 Lambeth Dr Raleigh NC 27609 Office: News and Observer 215 McDowell St Raleigh NC 27602

LOWITZ, DONALD SYLVAN, govt. ofcl.; b. Chgo., Apr. 16; s. Leo H. and Hattie (Levow) L.; B.Legal Sci., Northwestern U., 1950, LL.B., 1952; m. Shana Labovitz, Aug. 10, 1952; children—Amy, Theodore, Joshua. Admitted to Ill. bar, 1952; practiced in Chgo., 1952-54; asst. U.S. atty. charge civil tax matters No. Dist. Ill., Chgo., 1954-59; mem. firm Lowitz, Vihon, Lowitz & Stone, Chgo., 1959-69; asst. dir., gen. counsel Office Econ. Opportunity, Washington, 1969—. Mem. Am. Jewish Com. Congl. campaign mgr. 13th Dist. Ill., Republican Com., 1968; active Rep. Presdl. campaign, 1968. Bd. dirs. Bresler Found., Chgo. Mem. Am., Ill., Chgo., Fed. bar assns., Order of Coif. Jewish religion (past dir. and treas. congregation). Mem. B'nai B'rith. Home: 6109 Durbin Rd Bethesda MD 20034 Office: 1200 19th St NW Washington DC 20506

LOWREY, AMOS CLARK, JR., city ofcl.; b. Little Rock, July 12, 1916; s. Amos Clark and Nettie May (Dean) L.; student U. Md., European extension, Frankfurt, German, 1952-53; corr. Internat. Accountants Soc., 1963; m. Hazel Marie Sweat, Sept. 4, 1938; 1 dau., Sandra Gail (Mrs. Julian Reed Hodges, Jr.). Bookkeeper, Eli Witt Cigar Co., Tampa, Fla., 1937-42; mem. internat. dept. Marine Bank & Trust Co., Tampa, 1963-66; finance dir. City of Pinellas Park (Fla.), 1966-69, City of Clearwater (Fla.), 1969—. Served to maj. USAF, 1942-63. Decorated Air medal with 5 oak leaf clusters (U.S.); Croix de Guerre avec palme (France). Mem. Municipal Finance Officers Assn., Municipal Treasurers Assn., Ret. Officers Assn., Nat. Assn. Uniformed Services. Club: Officers (MacDill AFB, Fla.). Home: 4415 Vasconia St Tampa FL 33609 Office: PO Box 4748 Clearwater FL 33515

LOWREY, RUSSELL HARMON, dentist; b. Montgomery, Ala., Mar. 21, 1942; s. Allen Benjamin and Lillian Anna (Russell) L.; student Huntingdon Coll., 1959-61; B.S., U. Ala. at Tuscaloosa, 1963, D.M.D. cum laude, 1967, certificate orthodontics, 1971; m. Sheryl Delane McCain, May 25, 1968. Practice orthodontics, Huntsville, Ala., 1971—. Served to capt. USAF, 1967-69. Mem. Am. Dental Assn., Am. Assn. Orthodontists, So. Soc. Orthodontists, Psi Omega, Lambda Chi Alpha. Baptist Home: 11314 Crestfield Dr Huntsville AL 35803 Office: 2323 Whitesburg Dr Huntsville AL 35801

LOWREY, THOMAS JEFFERSON, physician; b. Slick, Okla., July 4, 1927; s. Estel Jack and Bertha Vineta (Conner) L.; student Okla. U., 1944-45, Northeastern State Coll. (Okla.), 1945-46; B.S., So. Methodist U., 1950; M.D., U. Tex., 1954. Intern Univ. Hosps., Oklahoma City, 1954-55, resident, 1955-56; resident internal medicine VA Hosp., Oklahoma City, 1956-57; practice gen. medicine, Yukon, Okla., 1957—; mem. staff Parkview Hosp., El Reno, Okla., chief staff, 1966-68, Deaconess, Baptist hosps., both Oklahoma City. Served with AUS, 1946-48. Diplomate Am. Bd. Family Practice. Mem. A.M.A., Am. Acad. Family Practice, Okla., Canadian County med. assns., Alumni Assn. U. Tex. Med. Br., Alpha Omega Alpha, Theta Kappa Psi. Lion. Mem. Christian Ch. (elder). Home: 716 Kingston Dr Yukon OK 73099 Office: 331 Main St Yukon OK 73099

LOWRY, RODNEY L., physician. Acting adminstr. D.C. Gen. Hosp., Washington. Office: 19th and Massachusetts Av SE Washington DC 20003*

LOWRY, ROY FRANK, supt. county schs.; b. Pasqualank, N.C., Dec. 21, 1907; s. William and Daisy E. (White) L.; A.B., U. N.C., 1930, M.A. in Sch. Adminstrn., 1936; m. Mary Katherine Goodson, 1932; children—Katherine (Mrs. D.R. Donovan), Roy Frank. Tchr., coach Union Grove High Sch., Iredell County (N.C.), 1930-31, prin., 1931-33; prin. Cameron High Sch., Moore County (N.C.), 1933-42, Thomasville (N.C.) High Sch., 1942-44, Wakelon High Sch., Zebolon, N.C., 1944-47; supt. Washington (N.C.) County Schs., 1947-61, Northampton (N.C.) County Schs., Jackson, 1961—. Past pres. Albemarle Sch. Masters Club, Wake County Sch. Masters Club. Mem. N.C. Assn. Educators (past pres. Moore and Wake counties; past pres. supts. N.E. dist.; past chmn. N.C. elementary edn. com.). Rotarian, Lion. Home: Box 503 Jackson NC 27845 Office: Box 158 Jackson NC 27845

LOWRY, ROYE LLEWELLYN, govt. ofcl.; b. Norwood, O., Oct. 2, 1917; s. Roye Valentine and Blanche (Hartman) L.; B.A., George Washington U., 1941, M.A., 1947; postgrad. Cornell U., summer 1953, Harvard, 1953-54, Middlebury Coll., summer 1954, Grenoble U., 1945; m. Betty Lu Steere, Apr. 13, 1946; children—Nicholas, Elizabeth. Budget examiner U.S. Bur. of Budget, Washington, 1941-43, 46-47; fgn. Service officer Am. consulate, Liverpool, Eng., 1947-50, Am. embassy, Warsaw, Poland, 1951-53, USIA, 1954, Am. embassy, Moscow, USSR, 1955-57, Dept. of State, 1957; exec. sec. Fed. Statistics Users Conf., Washington, 1957-66; analytical statistician Bur. of the Budget, Washington, 1966-69; clearance officer Office of Mgmt. and Budget, Washington, 1969—. Mem. Arlington (Va.) County Bd., 1962-65, chmn., 1964; pres. Met. Washington Council of Govts., 1964, chmn. exec. bd., 1965; sec.-treas. No. Va. Transp. Commn., 1965-66. Mem. bd. of control George Mason Coll., 1965-69. Served with AUS, 1943-46. Mem. Am. Statis. Assn., Am. Econ. Assn., A.A.A.S., Phi Beta Kappa. Home: 668 S Jefferson St Arlington VA 22204 Office: Office of Management and Budget Washington DC 20503

LOWRY, WALLACE EDWIN, coll. adminstr.; b. Holliday, Tex., Sept. 3, 1903; s. Jasper A. and Flora A. (Blakemore) L.; B.A. in Math. and Spanish, Southwestern U., 1923, B.S. in Chemistry and Physics, 1928; M.A. in Adminstrn. and English, U. Tex., 1935, D. Ed., 1951; m. Julia M. Wallace, June 4, 1932; children—Wallace Edwin, Burt Lewis. Prin., Huntsville (Tex.) High Sch., 1929-35; supt. schs., Orange, Tex., 1936-39; dir. pub. services Sam Houston State Coll., 1940-42, dean of college, 1951-65, v.p. acad. affairs, 1965—; asst. commr. edn., State of Tex., 1945-50. Mem. com. armed forces edn. Dept. Def., 1949-52; mem. nat. commn. for vocational edn. U.S. Dept. Health, Edn. and Welfare, 1969—. Bd. visitors U.S. Marine Corps Inst., 1959-62. Served to maj. USAAF, World War II. Decorated Bronze Star; recipient Silver Beaver award. Mem. Scabbard and Blade, Order of the Arrow, Pi Kappa Alpha (nat. pres. 1968—), Phi Delta Kappa, Kappa Kappa Psi, Alpha Kappa Delta, Alpha Phi Omega. Methodist. Rotarian. Author: Evaluative Study of Veterans Education Contiguous to Texas, 1947. Editor: Texas State Plan for Vocational Education, 1947; Bull. of So. Conf. Tchr. Edn., 1961-66. Home: 2020 Av O Huntsville TX 77340

LOYACANO, STEPHEN, 1st v.p. New Orleans Jazz Museum. Address: 7320 Zimple St New Orleans LA*

LOYD, LOYE CARROLL, glass co. exec.; b. Yantis, Tex., May 19, 1926; s. Edward M. and Ava (Gilbreath) L.; student So. Meth. U., 1949-50; m. Barbara Ray, Feb. 16, 1952; children—Stanley Alan, Terry Ray. Mgr., Mid-West Glass Co., Midland, Tex., 1955-62; owner Glasco Glass Co., Midland, 1962—; pres. Temple Glass & Mirror Co., Inc. (Tex.), 1969—, Bell Glass & Mirror Co., Killeen, Tex., 1970—, El Paso Glass & Mirror Co., Inc. (Tex.), 1970—; sec.-treas. Barber Glass & Mirror Co., Inc., Big Spring, Tex., 1968—; dir. Tex. Glass Distbrs., Inc., Ft. Worth, Odessa Glass &Mirror Co., Inc. (Tex.). Served with USNR, 1943-46. Mem. Assembly of God Ch. Rotarian (sec. 1965-66). Home: 2503 Dartmouth St Midland TX 79701 Office: 24 Industrial Loop Midland TX 79701

LU, JIMMY KIEN-TEH, physician; b. Shanghai, China, May 26, 1937; s. Yun Chun and Shu Yun (Peh) Lu (came to U.S. 1958, naturalized 1970); student Centenary Coll. La., 1959-61, East Tex. Baptist Coll., 1958-59; M.D., Tulane U., 1965; m. Sandra Lee Anderson, Sept. 17, 1966; children—Monica, Jimmy K., Jason. Intern Methodist Gen. Hosp., Dallas, 1965-66, resident surgery, 1966-67; practice gen. medicine, Dallas, 1967—; mem. staff Meth. Hosp. Mem. A.M.A., Tex., Dallas County med. soc. Home: 5807 Fox Hill Lane Dallas TX 75232 Office: 214 Westcliff Profl Bldg Hampton Rd at Ledbetter St Dallas TX 75224

LUBBE, CATHERINE CASE (MRS. JOHN A. LUBBE), author; b. Villa Park Ill., Sept. 24, 1898; d. John Joseph and Frances A. (Darmstadt) Case; student No. Ill. State Normal Coll., 1917; grad. Columbia Conservatory, 1923; L.H.D., l'Universitie Libre (Asie), 1970; m. John Andrew Lubbe, 1929; children—John Andrew, Kaye Don. Tchr. pub., pvt. schs., Ill., 1916-25; author poems pub. in numerous mags., newspapers, anthologies, including Poets Am., Book of Year, Poetry Soc. Tex., Child Welfare, Dallas Morning News, Colo. Springs Gazette and Telegraph, Kaleidograph, Elmhurst Press, South and West, others; dramatic reader poetry on various radio, television programs, 1922-57. Active A.R.C. Recipient World Fair Gold Medal Poetry Day award, 1940; Nyogen Senzaki Meml. Haiku award, 1966; UN day Leadership award (P.I.), 1967; gold medal award United Poets Laureate Internat., 1968 Leadership in Poetry award Internat. Acad. Leadership, Philippines, 1970. Mem. Poetry Soc. Tex. (hon. life mem., corr. sec. 1952-56, dir. 1957—, librarian, poetry critic, mem. poetry day com. editorial com.; Old South award 1971, Edsel Ford Meml. award 1971), Nat. Fedn. State Poetry Socs. (2d v.p. 1972—), La. Poetry Soc., St. Edward's Altar Soc., Eugene Field Soc. (hon.), United Poets Laureate Internat. Roman Catholic. Clubs: Lakewood Garden, Competriots. Home: 419 Clermont Av Dallas TX 75223

LUBELL, SAMUEL, writer; b. Poland, Nov. 3, 1911; s. Louis and Mollie (Reitkop) L. came to U.S., 1913; student Coll. City N.Y. eves. 1927-31; B.S., Sch. Journalism, Columbia, 1933; m. Helen Sopot, Mar. 22, 1941; children—Bernard, Walter. Travel in Europe on Pulitzer traveling scholarship Columbia, 1934; reporter and rewrite man L.I. Daily Press, 1935-36; reporter, Army and Navy editor, writer column Federal Diary, Washington Post, 1936-37; copy desk, labor editor Richmond (Va.) Times-Dispatch, 1937; reporter, rewrite man Washington Herald, 1937-38; free lance writer for nat. mags. including Sat. Eve. Post., 1938-41; writer Office Facts and Figures, later OWI, 1941; gen. sec. Rubber Survey Com. (Baruch Com.), 1942; asst. to James F. Byrnes, dir. Office Econ. Stblzn., 1942; asst. to Bernard M. Baruch, adv. unit on war and post-war adjustment policies Office War Moblzn. War corr. Sat. Eve. Post; European corr. Providence Jour. 1946; dir. Opinion Reporting Workshop, Sch. Journalism, Columbia U., N.Y.C., 1958-68. Woodrow Wilson Found. award Am. Polit. Sci. Assn., 1952; Guggenheim fellow, 1951, 54. Ind. Democrat. Mem. Nat. Press Club. Author: The Future of American Politics, 1952; Revolution in World Trade, 1954; Revolt of the Moderates, 1956, White & Black, 1964; The Hidden Crisis in American Politics, 1970. Commentator, CBS and NBC, TV and Radio, 1952-60; polit. analyst, commentator RKO Gen. TV & Radio, 1964, Voter Speak Reports, 1952-68. Author syndicated column The People Speak. Home: 3200 New Mexico Av NW Washington DC 20016

LUBIN, SAMUEL, govt. ofcl.; b. Washington, Sept. 16, 1914; s. Israel H. and Annie (Cohen) L.; B.S., Wilson Tchrs. Coll., 1936; M.S.W., Nat. Cath. Sch. Social Work, 1947; m. Frances C. Reichman, Nov. 5, 1945; children—Michael Evan, Amy Ilene. Dir. UNRRA operations, U.S. Zone Germany, 1945-47; adminstr. Jewish Social Service Agys., 1949-63; regional dir. Am. Jewish Com., 1956-58; regional dir. Council Jewish Fedns. for S.E. States, 1958-63; manpower adminstrn. rep., regional youth and program cons. S.E. region U.S. Dept. Labor, Atlanta, 1963—. Served with AUS, 1942-45. Mem. Acad. Certified Social Workers. Home: 1602 Adelia Pl NE Atlanta GA 30329 Office: 1371 Peachtree St NE Atlanta GA 30306

LUBKE, GEORGE WILLIAM, JR., mortgage banker; b. Yonkers, N.Y., Dec. 10, 1919; s. George William and Valeska (Kostka) L.; student N.Y.U., Columbia, N.Y. Tech. Inst., Newark U., 1938-42, Stetson U., 1946-47, Northwestern U., 1953-56; LL.D., Fla. Research Inst., 1970; m. Alice Myra Painter, Jan. 26, 1944; children—Robin Alice, George William III. Salesman, Mut. Benefit Life Ins. Co., Daytona Beach, Fla., 1946-49; founder George W. Lubke, Inc., Daytona Beach, 1949, pres., 1949—; pres. Amcount Systems, Inc., Miami. Chmn., Tax Study Com., Volusia County, 1954; commr. on aging, State of Fla., 1962-67, chmn. exec. com., 1963-68. Vice pres. Young Democratic Clubs Fla., 1953-55. Chmn. bd. Daytona Beach Housing Authority, 1958-69. Served with N.Y. State N.G., 1941-42; with AUS, 1942-46. Named Man of Year, Daytona Beach Jr. C. of C., 1949. Mem. Am., Fla. mortgage bankers assns., Nat. Housing Conf. (dir., v.p.), Nat., Fla. (pres.) assns. housing and redevel. ofcls., D.A.V. (past treas. Fla.). Home: 311 Shady Pl Daytona Beach FL 32014 Office: 250 Midway Daytona Beach FL 32020

LUCAS, ALFRED SPEAR, JR., banker; b. Birmingham, Ala., Jan. 10, 1921; s. A. S. and Angela (McCaffrey) L.; student St. Bernard Jr. Coll., Cullman, Ala., 1938-40; B.S., Auburn U., 1942; m. Winifred Strohmeyer, Oct. 22, 1949; children—Thomas William, Alfred John, Mary Angela, Winifred Loretta, Michael Joseph, William Patrick, Cecelia Anne. With Birmingham Trust Nat. Bank, 1942—, v.p. in charge nat. accounts, 1957-67, v.p. bus. devel., 1967—. Mem. Downtown Improvement Assn., 1968—, Com. of 100, 1968—, Downtonw Action Com., 1968—, exec. bd. Birmingham area council, Boy Scouts Am., 1968—; adv. mem. Jefferson County Community Chest; 1968—; v.p., nat. dir. Leukemia Soc., Am. Inc., 1968—. Bd. dirs. Vol. Bur., Girls' Club. Served with AUS, 1942-46.

Bestowed Knight of St. Gregory by Pope Pius XII, 1961. Life mem. C. of C.; mem. Bank Marketing Assn. (past dir.), Pub. Relations Assn. Ala., Ala. Bankers Assn. (chmn. pub. relations com., 1965-66), Delta Sigma Pi. Kiwanian. Home: 106 Azalea Rd Birmingham AL 35213 Office: 112 N 20th St Birmingham AL 35202

LUCAS, EARL STANCIL, mayor; b. Mound Bayou, Miss., Jan. 1, 1938; s. William Hymon and Lillie Bell (Rushing) L; B.S., Dillard U., 1957; postgrad. Depauw U., 1953-57, Beloit (Wis.) U.; m. Marilee Lewis, Sept. 13, 1959; children—Eric, Vicki, Carla, Tina, Mark. Dir. pub. edn., Mound Bayou, 1965—, dir. adult edn., 1965—; mayor, Mound Bayou, 1969—. Trustee Mound Bayou Community Hosp., Fund for Edn. and Community Devel., Am. Civil Liberties Union, Nat. Council Chs. Elk. Home: PO Box 476 Mound Bayou MS 38762 Office: Drawer H Mound Bayou MS 38762

LUCAS, GEORGE JOSEPH, physician; b. Bridgeport, Conn., Oct. 25, 1929; s. George Michael and Louise (Dziack) L.; B.S., Georgetown U., 1951, M.D., 1955; m. Margaret E. Droyd, June 25, 1955; children— George M., Rosemary A., Brian J. Intern, D.C. Gen. Hosp., Washington, 1955-56; resident Mt. Alto VA Hosp., Washington, 1956-57, U. Wis., Madison, 1959-61; asst. chief neurology D.C. Gen. Hosp., Washington, 1964-65; practice medicine, specializing in neurology, Washington, 1964-69; chief neurol. service VA Hosp., Little Rock, 1969—; mem. staff St. Elizabeth Hosp.; clin. asst. prof. neurology Georgetown U., 1966-69; asst. prof. neurology U. Ark. Med. Center, 1969—. Chmn., Potomac Valley chpt. Myas Thenia Gravis Found., Washington, 1968-69. Served with USAF, 1957-64. Diplomate Am. Bd. Neurology and Psychiatry. Fellow A.C.P., Am. Acad. Neurology; mem. A.M.A., Pulaski County, Med. Soc., Ark. State Med. Soc., A.A.A.S., Am. EEG Soc. (asso.). Home: 5320 Edgewood Rd Little Rock AR 72207 Office: 300 E Roosevelt Rd Little Rock AR 72206

LUCAS, J. LYNN, lawyer; b. Luray, Va., Dec. 27, 1898; s. Edwin L. and Minnie C. (Strickler) L.; A.B., Roanoke Coll., 1925; law, U. Va., 1928; m. Vivian D. Shenk, July 21, 1931. Admitted to Va. bar, 1928, since practiced in Luray. Past chmn. Democratic Com. of Page County, Va. Mem. Am., Va. (v.p. 1937, mem. council 1972—), Page County (pres. 1957-60), Luray bar assns., Columbia Hist. Soc., S.A.R. (past pres. Shenandoah Valley chpt.), Internat. Assn. Ins. Counsel, Va. Trial Lawyers Assn., Am. Judicature Soc., Sigma Chi, Phi Alpha Delta. Lutheran. Mason (Scottish Rite, York Rite, Shriner), Lion (past pres. Luray). Home: 165 S Court St Luray VA 22835 Office: Lucas Bldg 15 S Court St Luray VA

LUCAS, JACK, ednl. adminstr.; b. nr. Montrose, Ga., Mar. 21, 1931; s. William Robert and Mattie Mae (Herndon) L.; B.S., Ga. So. Coll., 1957, M.A., 1960; life prin. certificate, Mercer U., 1961; m. Florrie Odesa Daniel, June 20, 1965; 1 dau., Mattie Virginia. Prin. Limestone Elementary Sch., Cochran, Ga., 1953-63; prin. Bleckley County Elementary Sch., Cochran, 1963—. Chmn. reception Ga. Elementary Prin. Conf., 1965. Chmn. Bleckley County Heart Fund, 1970-71. Recipient alumni certificate Nat. 4-H, 1964, farmer's friend award First Ga. Farm Bur., 1965, vol. honor certificate Am. Cancer Soc., 1965. Mem. Nat., Ga., Bleckley County (pres. 1962-63) edn. assns., Nat., Ga. (dist. pres. 1965) elementary prins. assns. Home: Route 1 Montrose GA 31065 Office: Route 3 Cochran GA 31014

LUCAS, JAMES ARTHUR, JR., lumber co. exec.; b. Grand Prairie, Tex., July 5, 1917; s. James Arthur and Mattie Lou (Eden) L.; B.S., Tex. Tech U., 1947; m. Prudence Howard, Mar. 10, 1945; children—Nancy, Prudence. Engr., Lone Star Gas Co., Fort Worth, 1947-52; with Hurst Lumber Co., (Tex.) 1952—, pres., 1968—; dir. First Nat. Bank of Hurst. Tchr. math. Tex. Christian U., Fort Worth, 1959-60. Mem. Met. Regional Hwy. Com., Fort Worth Region, 1966—. Served to maj. AUS, 1944-47. Mem. Euless C. of C. (pres. 1960-61). Lion (pres. 1959-60). Home: 1213 Greenbriar Lane Arlington TX 67013 Office: 104 E Hurst Blvd Hurst TX 76053

LUCAS, JIM GRIFFING, reporter; b. Checotah, Okla., June 22, 1914; s. Jim Bob, Jr. and Effie Lincoln (Griffing) L.; student U. Mo., 1932-33. Reporter, feature writer Muskogee (Okla.) Daily Phoenix and Times-Democrat, 1934-38; news broadcaster, sta. KBIX, Muskogee, 1936-38; reporter, feature writer Tulsa Tribune, 1938-42; Marine combat corr. battles Guadalcanal, New Georgia, Russell Islands, Tarawa, Saipan, Tinian, Iwo Jima, 1942-45; corr. Scripps-Howard Newspaper Alliance, Washington, 1945. Served as 1st lt. USMC, World War II. Decorated Bronze Star. Recipient Nat. Headliners award best combat reporting, 1943; George Polk Meml. award, 2 Ernie Pyle awards, Omar Bradley Gold Medal; Pulitzer Prize; Korean Nat. Medal; Marine Corps Res. Officers Assn. award; 1st annual Fourth Estate award Am. Legion, 1958; First Annual Mark Watson award, 1968. Mem. Amvets (charter mem.), White House Corrs. Assn., Assn. U.S. Army, Nat. Headliners, Air Force Assn., Sigma Delta Chi. Methodist. Clubs: Nat. Press (Washington); Overseas Press. Author: Combat Correspondent, 1944; Battle for Tarawa (with Capt. Earl J. Wilson, Sgts. Samuel Shaffer, Cyril Peter Zurlinden), 1944; Dateline-Vietnam, 1966. Home: 6036 Richmond Hwy Alexandria VA 22303 Office: 1013 13th St Washington DC

LUCAS, MELVIN ALLEN, ednl. adminstr.; b. LaGrange, Ga., Oct. 19, 1932; s. Harper and Bessie (Railey) L.; B.S., Troy State Coll., 1953; M.A., George Peabody Coll. for Tchrs., 1956, Ed.D., 1963; m. Lamona Hall, Mar. 22, 1953; children—Dawn Yvonne, Deborah Susan. Asst. football coach Lanett High Sch., 1953; park supr. Recreation Dept., Nashville, 1955-56; supr. elementary phys. edn. Arlington County (Va.), 1956-57; football coach Forest Park (Ga.) High Sch., 1957-59; baseball coach, asst. football coach Troy (Ala.) State Coll., 1960-64; baseball coach U. S. Ala., Mobile, 1964-68, athletic dir., 1964—. Mem. youth com. Group Aid for Retarded Children, Inc., Mobile, 1967—; pres. Ala. Deep Sea Fishing Rodeo, 1969; chmn. Mobile County March Dimes, 1972; Ala. games chmn. Spl. Olympics, 1972; mem. Gov.'s Commn. on Phys. Fitness, 1972—, Mobile Mayor's Commn. on Recreation, 1972—. Served with AUS, 1953-55. Recipient Algernon Sidney Sullivan award George Peabody Coll., 1959. Named Baseball Coach of Year Ala. Collegiate Conf., 1961. Fellow A.A.H.P.E.R.; mem. Ala. Assn. Health, Phys. Edn. and Recreation (sect. chmn. 1961-62), Mobile Track and Field Assn. (pres. 1964-65), Mobile Jr. C. of C. (v.p. 1966-67), Kappa Delta Pi, Phi Delta Kappa. Baptist. Club: Mobile Touchdown. Home: 815 Nassau Dr Mobile AL 36608

LUCAS, OPAL (ELIZABETH) (MRS. GEORGE L. LUCAS), bakery co. exec., editor; b. Stuttgart, Ark., Dec. 9, 1910; d. Ernest William and Ida (Williford) McCollum; student U. Ark. Extension Center, 1960-63; m. George Luther Lucas, Dec. 1, 1934; 1 son, John Allen. Sec., Commonwealth Bldg. & Loan Assn., Little Rock, 1929-32, Fed. Res. Bank., Little Rock, 1933-34, Little Rock Tech. High Sch., 1954-55, sec.-supt. schs. Little Rock, 1955; exec. sec., editor Meyer's Bakeries, Inc., Little Rock, 1955—. Vol., A.R.C., 1950-55; den mother Cub Scouts, 1951-54; active P.T.A.; bd. dirs. Better Bus. Bur. Inc., Ark. Mem. Am. Bus. Women's Assn. (nat. pres. 1968-69, 1st v.p. 1967-68, v.p. S. Central dist. 1966-67). Cath Daus. Am. (lectr. Our Lady Perpetual Help Ct. 1967-70), state chmn. civic involvement 1971-73), Am. Mgmt. Assn., Nat. Secs. Assn. Roman Catholic. Author, editor: The Baker Boy (co. mag.). Club: Altrusa (chmn. community services). Home: 617 N Spruce St Little Rock AR 72205 Office: 1301 W 7th St Little Rock AR 72201

LUCAS, ROSEMARY DEAN, broadcasting exec.; b. Los Angeles; d. Roy and Juarita (Damer) Dean; grad. Ind. U., 1953; m. children—Kim, Jim. Hostess, producer Mid-Day, also weather girl WAPI-TV, Birmingham, Ala., 1962—. Mem. Birmingham Press Club. Office: WAPI-TV Box 1310 Birmingham AL 35201

LUCCA, WILLIAM JOSEPH, JR., assn. exec.; b. N.Y.C., Jan. 21, 1929; s. William Joseph and Mary (Berschefsky) L.; student The Citadel, 1948-49; B.S., Georgetown U., 1953, LL.B., 1956; grad. student Mich. State U. Sch. Organizational Mgmt., 1960-61; m. Janice Elizabeth Pyles, Aug. 17, 1960; children—Robert William, Elizabeth Anne. Adminstrv. asst. U.S. reps. Antoni N. Sadiak, Washington, 1958-59, Harold C. Ostertag, 1959-60; asst. mgr. assn. service dept. C. of C. of U.S., Washington, 1960-62; exec. dir. Commd. Officers Assn. of USPHS, Washington, 1962—. Exec. sec. ad hoc com. study by-laws Ret. Officers Assn., 1964; chmn. Washington Legislative Group, 1963. Recipient Award of Merit exec. com. Commd. Officers Assn., 1963. Mem. Am. Pub. Health Assn., Am. Soc. Assn. Execs., Washington Trade Assn. Execs. Clubs: Nat. Assn. Executives, Bull Elephants. Home: 9705 Manteo Ct Oxon Hill MD 20022 Office: 1750 Pennsylvania Av NW Washington DC 20006

LUCIUS, CARLETON SIMMONS, banker; b. Belleview, Fla., Jan. 15, 1926; s. John Harley and Ollie Gertrude (Harsey) L.; B.S. in Bus. Adminstrn., U. Fla., 1946; grad. Sch. Banking of the South, La. State U., 1958; m. Jean Nixon Pinder, Mar. 5, 1971; children by previous marriage—Stephen Michael, Cheryl Diane (Mrs. William G. Wallace). With Sears Roebuck & Co., Ocala and Gainesville, Fla., 1950, Met. Life Ins. Co., Panama City, Fla., 1950-51, Lovell Bros., Ocala, 1951, Fed. Deposit Ins. Corp., Atlanta, 1951-60; pres., dir. Lake Region Bank of Commerce, Winter Haven, Fla., 1960-65; pres., dir. So. Bank of West Palm Beach, Fla., 1965—; dir. Fla. So. Bank, Palm Springs. Bd. dirs. Emergency Natural Resources Palm Beach County, Fla., United Fund Palm Beach County, Chris Halfway House. Served with AUS, 1944-46. Decorated Purple Heart. Mem. Sales and Marketing Execs. Internat. (treas. 1969-71), Am. Legion. Mason. Methodist (adminstrv. com. 1966—). Club: Exchange (pres. 1971-72). Home: 1822 Caribbean Rd West Palm Beach FL 33406 Office: 7320 S Dixie Hwy West Palm Beach FL 33405

LUCKAM, THOMAS GRANT, dentist; b. Newport News, Va., Jan. 7, 1935; s. Grant Hiram and Mary (Thompson) L.; student Randolph Macon Coll., 1953-56; B.S., D.D.S., Med. Coll. Va., 1960; m. Elizabeth Madison Hargrave, Sept. 12, 1959; children—Thomas G., Mary Elizabeth, Sarah Madison. Pvt. practice dentistry, Gloucester Point, Va., 1962—; asso. State Health Dept., 1969—. Den leader Boy Scouts Am., Gloucester Point, 1971—. Served as lt. comdr. USNR. Mem. Am., Va. dental assns., Peninsula Dental Soc., Acad. Gen. Dentistry, Am. Analgesia Soc., C. of C., Omicron Delta Kappa. Episcopalian. Lion. Clubs: York River Yacht (commodore 1968-69) (Gloucester Point); Ware River Yacht (dir. 1971—) (Gloucester, Va.). Address: Box 112 Gloucester Point VA 23062

LUCKETT, PAUL HERBERT, III, fiber and textile co. exec.; b. El Paso, Tex., Feb. 6, 1935; s. Paul Herbert and Maxine Revelle (Mooney) L.; B.S. in Chem. Engring., Mass. Inst. Tech., 1956; grad. Advanced Mgmt. Tng. Program, U. Tex., 1970; m. Caroline Curtis Foisie, Oct. 6, 1956; children—Elizabeth Winkler, Christopher Lloyd. Process engr. El Paso Products Co., Odessa, Tex., 1956-59, sales rep., 1960-65, marketing exec., 1966-69, asst. v.p., 1969-70; exec. v.p. operations Beaunit Corp., 1970-72, exec. v.p., gen. mgr. Fibers div., Research Triangle Park, N.C., 1972—. Bd. dirs. Odessa-Midland Symphony Assn., 1967-70, Odessa Jazz Assn., 1966-70. Served with AUS, 1957. Mem. Man-Made Fiber Assn., Am. Textile Mfrs. Inst., Tau Beta Pi, Delta Kappa Epsilon. Republican. Roman Catholic. Home: 821 Faulkner Pl Raleigh NC 27609 Office: PO Box 12234 Research Triangle Park NC 27709

LUCKEY, CARL FREEMAN, physician; b. Jackson, Tenn., July 16, 1914; s. David William and Mabel Dent (Freeman) L.; B.A., Union U., 1936; M.D., Vanderbilt U., 1941; m. Althea Ann Colvin, Dec. 31, 1938; children—Carl Freeman, George DeLansone. Intern, John Gaston Hosp., Memphis, 1941-42; resident Vanderbilt U. and VA Hosp., Nashville, 1947-50; practice medicine, Franklin, Tenn., 1945-47, Florence, Ala., 1950—; mem. staffs Coffee and Colonial Manor hosps., Florence, Colbert County, Shoals hosps., Sheffield. Bd. dirs. Colonial Manor Hosp., Florence, 1970—. Served to maj. M.C., AUS, 1941-45. Fellow A.C.P.; mem. A.M.A., Ala., So. med. assns., Sigma Xi, Phi Beta Pi, Alpha Tau Omega. Episcopalian. Club: Turtle Point Yacht and Country. Home: 2101 Arlington Blvd Florence AL 35630 Office: 419 N Court St Florence AL 35630

LUCKEY, GEORGE PAUL, ret. bus. exec.; b. Ontario, Cal., Apr. 4, 1891; s. George W. A. and Bertha (Musson) L.; A.B., U. Neb., 1910, M.A., 1912, D.Engring. (hon.), 1952; postgrad. U. Goettingen, Germany, 1912-14; m. Olive Lehmer, July 12, 1922; children—George William, Helen L. Staff, Mt. Wilson Solar Obs., Pasadena, Cal., 1915; Charles E. Brush fellow Nela Research Lab., Cleve., 1916; physicist Westinghouse Research Lab., East Pittsburgh, Pa., 1917-1919-20; physicist, instrument and equipment sect. McCook Field, Dayton, O., 1920-26, asst. chief equipment sect., 1926-27; with Hamilton Watch Co., Lancaster, Pa., 1927-54, head tachometer div., 1927-30, dir. research, asst. gen. supt., 1930-33, factory mgr., 1933-40, v.p. charge mfg., 1940-52, pres., chmn. bd., 1952-54, dir., 1947-54, ret., 1954; dir. Nuclear Research Chems., Orlando, Fla., 1960-67. Mem. adv. bd. Phila. Ordnance Dist., 1950-54. Served with AC, U.S. Army, 1918. Recipient certificate of Appreciation, Joint Chiefs of Staff, 1951. Mem. A.A.A.S., Am. Ordnance Assn., Horological Inst. Am. (hon.), Am. Phys. Soc., Winter Park C. of C., Sigma Xi. Clubs: Orlando Country; University (Winter Park, Fla.). Patentee in field. Home: 461 Virginia Dr Winter Park FL 32789

LUCKIE, CHARLES ADAMS, circuit judge; b. Montgomery, Ala., Nov. 27, 1906; s. Arche Carter and Orlene (Goodwyn) L.; LL.B., Stetson U., 1931; m. Suzanne Knox, Nov. 27, 1963. Admitted to Fla. bar, 1931; practiced law, Jacksonville, Fla., 1931-50; partner Rogers, Towers & Bailey, 1931-50; mem. Fla. Ho. of Reps., 1941, 47, 49; circuit judge, Jacksonville, 1950—. Served to col. AUS, 1941-46. Decorated Legion of Merit, Bronze Star, Army Commendation medal. Mem. Fla. Bar, Jacksonville Bar Assn. Democrat. Presbyn. (elder). Home: Ortega Blvd Apts Jacksonville FL 32210 Office: County Courthouse Jacksonville FL 32202

LUDDEN, FOREST EDWIN, state ofcl.; b. Lewiston, Me., July 10, 1932; s. William Robinson and Dorothy (Barry) L.; B.S., So. Ill. U., 1959, M.S., 1960; M.P.H., U. Mich., 1962; Ed. D., U. Ala., 1970; m. Theresa Marie Shotts, Nov. 27, 1954; children—Sandra Ann, William Roger, James Alan. Dir. Bur. Primary Prevention, Ala. Dept. Pub. Health, Montgomery, 1962-69, dir. div. narcotics and dangerous drugs, 1969—; asst. to state health officer, 1968—, state registrar, 1971—. Treas., Montgomery Council Indsl. Editors, 1965—; field supr. Nat. Health Council, 1959; pres. Jackson County (Ill.) Health Council, 1960. Served with USNR, 1951-55. Fellow Soc. Pub. Health Educators; mem. Am., Ala. pub. health assns., N.E.A., Ala. Heart Assn., Phi Delta Kappa. Lion. Club: Bonnie Crest Country. Home: 1012 High Point Rd Montgomery AL 36109 Office: State Office Bldg Montgomery AL 36104

LUDDEN, JOHN FRANKLIN, economist, govt. ofcl.; b. Michigan City, Ind., May 6, 1930; s. Charles Franklin and Marie Bernadette (Kelley) L.; B.S., U. Wis., 1952, M.S., 1955; postgrad. U. Mich., 1955-58; m. Edna Adriana Abadie-Abarca, Dec. 13, 1964; children—Charles Robert, Anne Marie, John Michael, James Edward. Storekeeper, U.S. Army Corps Engrs., 1947-48; wage and hour investigator U.S. Dept Labor, Washington, 1960, mgmt. intern, 1960-61, economist, tng. instr., 1961-63, labor economist, 1963; industry economist Internal Revenue Service, Treasury Dept., Washington, 1963—. Served with AUS, 1952-54. Recipient Spl. Service award Treasury Dept., 1967, 69. Mem. Am. Econ. Assn. Home: 8503 Fairburn Dr Springfield VA 22152 Office: Audit Div US Internal Revenue Service Washington DC 20224

LUDWIG, WILLIAM MICHAEL, physician; b. N.Y.C., July 6, 1937; s. Saul and Blanche (Ober) L.; B.A., U. Pa., 1957; M.D., N.Y.U., 1961; m. Carolee Ann Frum, June 20, 1964; children—Adam Nathan, Alexandra. Intern, U. Pitts., 1961-62, resident medicine, 1964-66; NIH postdoctoral fellow in gastroenterology, 1967; practice medicine, Miami Beach, Fla., 1968—; clin. instr. medicine U. Miami. Served with USPHS, 1962-64. Fellow A.C.P.; mem. Phi Beta Kappa. Home: 7441 Wayne Av Miami Beach FL 33141 Office: 1680 Meridian Av Miami Beach FL 33139

LUEBKE, NEIL ROBERT, educator; b. Pierce, Neb., Sept. 15, 1936; s. Robert Carl and Cinderetta Amelia (Guthmann) L.; B.A. in English, Midland Coll., 1958; M.A. in Philosophy, Johns Hopkins U., 1962, Ph.D. in Philosophy, 1968; m. Phyllis Jean Madsen, June 15, 1957; children—Anne Elizabeth, Karen Marie. Asst. prof. philosophy Okla. State U., Stillwater, 1961-71, asso. prof. philosophy, 1971—. Dir. Esso Ednl. Found. Critical Thinking Project, 1971—. Woodrow Wilson Nat. fellow, 1958-59. Mem. Am. Philos. Assn., Am. Assn. U. Profs. (pres. local chpt. 1971-72), Southwestern Philos. Soc., Mountain-Plains Philosophy Conf. (mem. exec. com. 1970-71, chmn. 1971-72), Blue Key, Pi Kappa Delta. Lutheran (con. v.p. 1971—). Author: Paul Tillich's Philosophy and Theology of History, 1968; also articles. Home: 616 Harned Pl Stillwater OK 74074 Office: Hanner Hall Oklahoma State U Stillwater OK 74074

LUECKE, FRANK MARTIN GEORGE, JR., journalist; b. Mountain Grove, Mo., July 17, 1931; s. Frank Martin George and Mabel Clare (Bedingfield) L.; B.J., U. Mo., 1953; m. Janet Emma Wright, Oct. 29, 1953; children—Leslie Ruth, Martin Wright. News editor, adman Purcell (Okla.) Register, 1955-56; pub. Grand Prairie (Tex.) Banner, 1956-57; co-owner, editor, pub. Cameron (Tex.) Herald, 1957—. Pres., Cameron Pub. Library Bd.,1966-67. Bd. dirs. Central Tex. Symphony Assn., 1965-67, pres., 1968-69; bd. dirs. Cultural Activities Center, Temple, Tex., Cameron Indsl. Found., St. Edward Hosp. Devel. Fund. Served to 1st lt. AUS, 1953-55. Recipient 1st prize editorials Okla. Press Assn., 1955, hon. mention editorials, 1956; Golden Pencil award 1970; Golden Dozen editorialist award Internat. Conf. Weekly Newspaper Editors, 1970. Mem. Cameron C. of C. (dir. bd.), Cameron Jr. C. of C. (dir. 1958-59), Nat. Newspaper Assn. (com. chmn. 1969-72), Tex. Press Assn. (prizes 1958, 62, sec., treas. 1968-69), Dallas Press Club. Rotarian (pres. 1966-67). Club: Cameron Country. Contbr. articles to mags. Home: 806 E 7th St Cameron TX 76520 Office: 108 E 1st St Cameron TX 76520

LUEDECKE, WILLIAM HENRY, engring. co. exec.; b. Pittsburg, Tex., Apr. 5, 1918; s. Henry Herman and Lula May (Abernathy) L.; B.S., U. Tex., 1940; m. Mary Anne Copeland, June 3, 1939; children—William Henry III, John Copeland. Mech. engr. Columbian Gasoline Corp., Monroe, La., 1940-41; supr. ship bldg., mech. entr. USN, Orange, Tex., 1941-42; gen. supr. factory mgrs. N. Am. Aviation Co., Dallas, 1942-44; air conditoning engr. Westinghouse Elec. Corp., Dallas, 1944-46; mech. engr., charge Chrysler Airtemp. div. Chrysler Corp., Los Angeles, 1946-50; owner Luedecke Engring. Co., Austin, Tex., 1950—, also Luedecke Investment Co.; dir. City Nat. Bank, Austin, Mut. Savs. Instn., Austin, Electro-Mechanics Co., Inc., Austin. Bd. Dirs. Travis County Heart Fund. Austin YMCA. Named Man of Yr., Tex. Barbed Wire Collectors Assn. Registered profl. engr., Tex. Mem. Am. Soc. Heating, Refrigerating, Air Conditioning Engrs. (dir., pres. Austin chpt.), Tex., Nat. socs. profl. engrs., C. of C., Econ. Devel. Council, Better Bus. Bur., Nat. Fedn. Ind. Bus. (dist. chmn.). Methodist. Rotarian. Club: Westwood Country (dir.). Home: 3403 Foothills Pkwy Austin TX Office: 1007 W 34th St Austin TX

LUEHRSEN, HANNES, architect, city planner; b. Bargteheide, Holstein, Germany, Mar. 13, 1907; s. Alfred and Mathilde (Hirsch) L.; B.Arch., Tech. U. Berlin-Charlottenburg, 1930-33; M.Arch. and Planning, Tech. U. Aachen, 1934; m. Ruth Schumacher, Sept. 4, 1948; children—Regine, Thomas. Came to U.S., 1945, naturalized, 1955. With Office Prof. Egon Eiermann, Berlin, 1935-36; with Office Fritz Ebhardt, Berlin, 1936-37; with Office Prof. Otto Firle, Berlin, 1937-38; pvt. practice architecture, Berlin, 1938-41; planner, designer Rocket Research and Devel. Center, Peenemuende, Baugruppe Schlempp, Berlin-Karlshagen, Germany, 1941-43; chief architect, planner German Rocket Center, Electro Mechanische Werke, Peenemuende, Germany, 1943-45; chief planner, architect with Dr. von Braun team of rocket scientists and technicians Dept. of the Army, Research and Devel. Div., Fort Bliss, Tex., 1945-50; chief planning office Dept. of the Army, Ordnance Missile Labs., Huntsville, Ala., 1950-54, chief master planning office, Redstone Arsenal, Ala., 1954-60; chief master planning office, planning cons., archtl. adv. NASA, Marshall Space Flight Center, Huntsville, 1960-69; individual practice city planning, Heidelberg, Germany, 1969—. Mem. A.I.A. Prin. works include comprehensive master plan Marshall Space Flight Center, Huntsville, 1960-65, comprehensive master plan Michoud Operations, La., 1964, basic studies for master plan Miss. Test Operations, Miss., 1962, master land use plan Pearlington Beach, Miss., Lacombe, La., 1965, master plan U. Ala. Research Inst., Huntsville, 1963, master plan for future devel. Historic City of Heidelberg, 1968. Home: 1101 Edgewood AV S E Huntsville AL 35801 Office: 69 Heidelberg Hirschgasse 19 Germany

LUGN, A(LVIN) L(EONARD), geologist; b. Mediapolis, Ia., Nov. 22, 1895; s. Victor Richard and Ellen Aurora (Bergsten) L.; A.B., Augustana Coll., 1916; postgrad. Columbia, 1916-17; M.S., State U. Ia., 1925, Ph.D., 1927; m. Rubie Bloomberg, June 29, 1921 (dec. 1955); children—Alvin Leonard, Richard Victor; m. 2d, Katharine Fritz Aderholdt, June 5, 1957. Instr. sci., Upsala Coll., East Orange, N.J., 1916-17; prof. chemistry and physics Lenoir-Rhyne Coll., Hickory, N.C., 1919-23; grad. asst. geology State U. Ia., 1923-26; prof. geology and biology Midland Coll., Fremont, Neb., 1926-27; instr. geology U. Neb., 1927-28, asst. prof. 1928-34, asso. prof. 1934-38, prof., 1938-62, prof. emeritus, 1962—, dir. summer field courses geology, 1947-62; geologist Ia. Geol. Survey, 1924-26, Neb. Geol. Survey, 1929-62; cons. Miss Geol. Survey, 1953; prof. geography and earth scis., chmn. dept. Lenoir-Ryne Coll., Hickory, N.C., 1962—; cons. geol. and research; expert in ground water litigation, water supply econ. geology; research asso. Stanford U., 1957. Served with

U.S. Navy, 1917-19, World War I, chemist Naval engring., expt. sta., Annapolis, Md.; served as lt. comdr., USN 1942-46; in naval communications and at Navy Hydrographic Office; now lt. condr. ret. Res. Recipient Distinguished Achievement award Augustana Coll., Rock Island, Ill., 1964. Fellow Geol. Soc. Am.; mem. Soc. Econ. Geologists, Am. Assn. Petroleum Geologists, Soc. Econ. Mineralogists Paleontologists, Population Assn. Am., Am. Geog. Soc., N.C. Acad. Sci., Neb. Acad. Sci. (past pres.), Sigma Xi. Lutheran. Republican. Author: Geology of Lucas County, Iowa; Sedimentation in the Mississippi River; Geology and Ground Water Resources of South-Central Nebraska; Deep Wells of Nebraska; Pleistocene Geology of Nebraska; Laboratory Exercises in Physical, Structural and Historical Geology; Laboratory Exercises on Minerals and Rocks; Workbook in General Geology; Origin of Loess; compiler, writer of classified Naval Air Navigation publs., World War II; also numerous articles on geol. subjects. Home: 510 7th Av NE Hickory NC 28601

LUGO-RODRIQUEZ, JORGE E., educator; b. Lajas, P.R., Oct. 21, 1929; s. Jorge Lugo and Dolores Rodriquez; B.A., Poly Inst. at San German (P.R.), 1948; Med. Technologist, U. P.R., 1951, M.D., 1955; m. Vidalina Lugo, July 15, 1957; children—Edwin I., Diana. Intern Fajardo (P.R.) Dist. Hosp., 1955-56; resident VA Hosp., 1959-61, San Juan City Hosp., 1956-57; fellow cardiology U. Wis., 1961-63; mem. staff med. dept. cardiology Sch. Medicine, U. P.R., Rio Piedras, 1963—, asso. prof. medicine, 1971—, dir. cardiac labs. univ. hosps. and P.R. Med. Center, 1963—. Cons. cardiology San Juan City Hosp., 1966, USPHS, V.I., 1967. Pres. P.T.A., High Sch. of U. P.R., 1971-72. Served with AUS, 1957-59. Diplomate Am. Bd. Internal Medicine. Asso. fellow Am. Coll. Cardiology; fellow Am. Fedn. Clin. Research; mem. P.R. Med. Assn., Am., P.R. (dir. 1969) heart assns. Home: 435 San Lino Rio Piedras PR 00926

LUHRS, CARO ELISE, physician; b. Dover, N.J., Jan. 21, 1935; d. Albert Weigand and Ethel Adelaide (Voss) L.; A.B., Swarthmore Coll., 1956; M.D., Harvard, 1960. Intern medicine and pediatrics U. N.C. at Chapel Hill, 1960-61, resident mdeicine, 1961-62; fellow hematology Georgetown U. Med. Sch., Washington, 1962-64, instr. medicine, 1964-67, dir. hematology labs. and blood bank, 1966-68, asst. prof. medicine, 1967-69, clin. asst. prof. medicine, 1969—; med. adviser Sec. Agr., Washington, 1969—. Bd. dirs. U. S. Dept. Agr. Grad. Sch., 1971—. Recipient Superior Service award U.S. Dept. Agr., 1971. White House fellow, 1968-69. Diplomate Am. Bd. Internal Medicine. Fellow Royal Soc. Health, A.C.P.; mem. Am. Soc. Hematology, Internat. Soc. Hematology, A.M.A. (council on food and nutrition 1970—, council on rural health 1971—), Med. Women's Internat. Assn., Am. Med. Women's Assn., D.C. Med. Soc., Am. Pub. Health Assn., Internat. Assn. Agrl. Medicine. Club: Zonta. Home: 2939 Van Ness St NW Washington DC 20008 Office: Office of the Secretary US Dept Agriculture Washington DC 20250

LUIGS, CHARLES RUSSELL, mfg. exec.; b. Evansville, Ind., Apr. 4, 1933; s. Charles Anthony and Agnes (Russell) L.; student St. Edwards U., 1951-52; B.S., U. Tex., 1957; m. Mary M. McClaine, Sept. 7, 1957; children—Charles Edwin, James Russell, Carol Lynn, Susan Nadine, Michael Allan. Vice pres. sales U.S. Industries De Venezuela, Anaco, Venezuela, 1958-63, v.p. engring. petroleum equipment div. U.S. Industries, Inc., Longview, Tex., 1963-66, v.p. marketing petroleum-chem. equipment group, Houston, 1966-67, v.p. corporate devel. So. U.S.A. group, Dallas 1967-68, chmn. furnishings group, Dallas, 1968-69, exec. chmn. Northeast group, also corporate v.p. 1969-70, exec. group chmn. So. U.S.A. group, 1970-71, exec. v.p., dir. corp., 1971—. Mem. Nat. Soc. Profl. Engrs., Am. Inst. Mining Metall. and Petroleum Engrs. Home: 4475 Royal Lane Dallas TX 75229

LUIKART, MARGARET LUCILLE CLARK (MRS. FORDYCE WHITNEY LUIKART), educator; b. Euclid, O., Aug. 19, 1909; d. James Benjamin and Lucie (Snyder) Clark; B.A., Ohio Wesleyan U., 1931; postgrad. Case Sch. Applied Sci., 1932-33, Western Res. U., 1928; m. Fordyce Whitney Luikart, Sept. 7, 1935; children— Clark Whitney, James Louis, John Ford. Tchr., 1931-35; asst. buyer sportswear C.E. Chappell & Sons, Syracuse, N.Y., 1935-37; substitute tchr., 1937-42; founder Mother's Club of YWCA Nursery Sch., Kifissia, Greece, 1949-50; tutor Remedial Edn. Center (name changed to Kingsbury Center, 1969), Washington, 1956-67, coordinator of tutoring, 1967-68, acting dir., 1968-69, asst. to dir., 1969—, trustee, 1968—. Mem. Daus. of Mayflower, Washington Panhellenic Assn. (pres. 1958-59), Delta Gamma (Washington chpt. Alumnae pres. 1955-57, nat. chmn. constn. and by-laws 1957-61). Methodist (Sunday sch. tchr. 1950-64). Club: Ohio Wesleyan Monnett (Washington chpt. pres. 1941). Home: 3257 Beech St NW Washington DC 20015 Office: 2138 Bancroft Pl Washington DC 20008

LUIS CANO, SERGIO, govt. ofcl. Sub-minister industry and commerce Mexico. Office: Irving SA de CVCiudad Del Risco 151 Mexico City Mexico*

LUKE, JAMES LINDSAY, physician; b. Cleve., Aug. 29, 1932; s. James Lindsay and Parthenia (Burke) L.; student Yale, 1950-52; B.S., cum laude, Columbia, 1956; M.D., Case Western Res. U., 1960; m. Marcia Gene Alley, Oct. 5, 1957; children—Lindsay Jean, Sarah Chisolm, Alexandra Blair. Intern, Yale Med. Center, New Haven, 1960-61; resident, then chief resident in pathology Univ. Hosps. of Cleve., 1961-63; staff researcher Lab. Exptl. Pathology, Nat. Inst. Arthritis and Metabolic Diseases, NIH, Bethesda, Md., 1963-65; asso. med. examiner Office Chief Med. Examiner, N.Y.C., 1965-67; state med. examiner, Okla., Oklahoma City, 1967-71; chief med. examiner, D.C., 1971—; prof. forensic pathology U. Okla. Med. Center, 1967-71; prof. pathology George Washington U., 1971—, Georgetown U., 1971—, Howard U., 1971—. Served with USPHS, 1963-65. Recipient Distinguished Faculty award U. Okla. Med. Center, 1969. Fellow Am. Acad. Forensic Scis. (pres. 1966); mem. Am. Assn. Pathologists and Bacteriologists, Nat. Assn. Med. Examiners (exec. com. 1970—). Contbr. articles to profl. jours. Home: 5240 Loughboro Rd NW Washington DC 20016 Office: 1901 E St SE Washington DC 20003

LUKSTA, ROBERT, basketball coach Loyola U., New Orleans. Address: Athletic Dept Loyola U New Orleans LA 70118*

LUMB, ROBERT MONTY, dentist; b. Vancouver, B.C., Can., July 9, 1928; s. Robert John and Anna Margaret (Burgess) L.; student Staunton Mil. Acad., 1947, U. Houston, 1954-56, Emory U. Sch. Dentistry, 1956-60; m. Shirlee Anne Young, Sept. 12, 1958; children—Julie Anne, Linda Lee, Robert Scott. Individual practice dentistry, Miami, Fla., 1960-65, Homestead, Fla., 1965—. Mem. staff Dade County Research Clinic, Miami, 1961-63. Served with AUS, 1951-53. Mem. Am. Dental Assn., Fla., East Coast, South Dade dental socs., C. of C. (essay chmn. 1966-67). Baptist. Mason (Shriner). Clubs: Civitan (dir. 1969) Toastmaster (Homestead). Home: 28550 SW 172d Av Homestead FL 33030 Office: 1555 N Krome Av Homestead FL 33030

LUMLEY, JOHN MORRIS, educator; b. Vineland, N.J., Feb. 10, 1906; s. John and Flossie (Zaner) L.; B.A., Muhlenberg Coll., 1928; M.Ed., Pa. State U., 1945; D.Ed., Waynesburg Coll., 1955; m. Kathryn Wentzel; 1 son, Joe Ernie. Tchr.-prin. Eagles Mere (Pa.) Sch., 1928-30; prin. Dushore (Pa.) High Sch., 1930-32; supervising prin. Dushore Borough schs., 1932-38; supt. schs., Sullivan County, Pa., 1938-52; dep. supt. pub. instrn. Pa., 1952-55; supt. city schs., Wilkes Barre, Pa., 1955-57; exec. asst., dir. div. fed. relations N.E.A., Washington, 1957-67, asst. exec. sec. for legislation and fed. relations, 1967-71, also mem. nat. legislative commn., now nat. legislative cons., 1971—. Pres. Pa. Edn. Assn., 1951. Chmn. Sullivan County Tb Soc., 1940-51, Sullivan County Tb and Heart Assn., 1950-51, Sullivan County council Boy Scouts Am., 1950. Trustee Mansfield (Pa.) Tchrs. Coll.; bd. dirs. Multiple Sclerosis Soc. Washington, 1949-53. Recipient Alumni Achievement award Muhlenberg Coll., 1955. Mem. N.E.A., Am. Assn. Sch. Adminstrs., Phi Delta Kappa. Lutheran. Mason. Home: 3315 Morrison St NW Washington DC 20015 Office: 1201 16th St NW Washington DC 20036

LUMPKIN, ALVA M., lawyer; b. Columbia, S.C., Nov. 25, 1921; A.B., U. S.C., 1943, LL.B., 1947. Admitted to S.C. bar, 1947; since practiced in Columbia; mem. firm Lumpkin and Lafaye; spl. atty. S.C. Legislative Research Council, 1950-51; spl. asst. U.S. atty., trial atty. OPS, 1951-52. Vice chancellor Episcopal Diocese of Upper S.C., 1956-65. Fellow Am. Coll. Probate Counsel; mem. Am., S.C. bar assns., Am. Counsel Assn., Am. Judicature Soc., Assn. Bar City N.Y. Office: 907 Barringer Bldg Columbia SC 29201*

LUMPKIN, JOSEPH ARNOLD, hosp. ofcl.; b. Rome, Ga., Aug. 17, 1918; s. Charles Henry and Willie N. (James) L.; student Carroll Lynn Bus. Coll., 1945-47; m. Frances Irene Chasteen, May 24, 1940; 1 son, Joseph Darrell. Office mgr. Floyd Hosp., Rome, Ga., 1947-48, adminstr. asst., 1948-50, asso. dir., 1950-57; adminstr. Douglas-Coffee County Hosp., Douglas, Ga., 1957-67, Blount Meml. Hosp., Oneonta, Ala., 1967—. Mem. Community Service Council. Bd. dirs. A.R.C., United Givers Drive. Served with USNR, 1943-45; ETO. Decorated Bronze Star. Mem. Am. Assn. Hosp. Accountants (dir. Ga. Chpt.), Ga. (treas. 1964), S.E. Ga. (pres. 1960-61) hosp. assns., Ala. Assn. Hosp. Execs. Mason (Shriner), Elk, Rotarian (v.p. club). Home: 907 Magnolia St Oneonta AL 35121 Office: Blount Meml Hosp Oneonta AL 35121

LUNCEFORD, BILL EUGENE, educator; b. Lanett, Ala., Apr. 30, 1929; s. Mabry O'Neal and Annie (Cooksey) L.; A.B., Howard Coll., 1952; B.D., So. Bapt. Theol. Sem., 1954, M.Th., 1955; M.A., Middle Tenn. State U., 1959; D.Ed., Auburn U., 1961; m. Malena Roark, July 3, 1953; children—Beth Ann, William Mark, Jane Laurie. Ordained to ministry Bapt. Ch., 1950; student pastor Bapt. chs., Ala., Ky., Tenn., 1950-59; grad. fellow Auburn U., Ala., 1959-61; prof. edn. and psychology, asst. to dean students Samford U., Birmingham, Ala., 1961-63, dir. student personnel services, 1963-65, interim registrar, dir. admissions, 1965-67, prof. edn. and psychology, dir. testing, 1965-70; asst. regional dir. Southeastern regional office Am. Coll. Testing Program, 1970—. Treas., bd. dirs. Jefferson County Assn. for Mental Health, 1966—; bd. dirs. Ala. State Mental Health Assn. NSF fellow Beloit Coll., 1967. Mem. Am., Ala. personnel and guidance assns., Ala. Psychol. Assn., Omicron Delta Kappa, Kappa Phi Kappa, Phi Delta Kappa. Home: 3301 Henderson Mill Rd Chamblee GA 30341

LUNDBERG, GUSTAVE HAROLD, educator; b. Fremont, Neb., Sept. 5, 1901; s. Gustave Emil and Clara (Lindquist) L.; B.S., Midland Coll., 1924; M.A., Colo. State Coll., 1937, Vanderbilt U., 1942; Ph.D., George Peabody Coll., 1951; m. Hazel Alice Glenny, Oct. 30, 1939. Faculty, Dana Coll., 1924-28; tchr. Consol. High Sch., Crowley, Colo., 1929-37, Allen Acad., Bryan, Tex., 1938-40; instr. Vanderbilt U., Nashville, 1942-45, asst. prof., 1945-53, asso. prof., 1953-56, prof. applied math., 1956-67, prof. emeritus, 1968—; prof. math. Austin Peay State U., 1967-72; faculty participant Boeing Airplane Co., summers 1955-56; research participant Oak Ridge Nat. Lab., summer 1957; faculty George Peabody Coll., summers 1961-62. Mem. Am. Math. Assn., Am. Math. Soc., Engring. Assn. Nashville, Am. Soc. Engring. Edn., Tenn. Acad. Sci. (pres. 1969), Sigma Xi, Phi Delta Kappa. Editor: Jour. Tenn. Acad. Sci., 1963-66. Contbr. articles to profl. jours. Home: 2001 21st Av S Nashville TN 37212

LUNDBLADE, HOBERT PHILIP, dentist; b. Sandstone, Minn., Oct. 12, 1929; s. Joseph M. and Hilda C. (Nordgren) L.; B.S., U. Minn., 1952, D.D.S., 1954, M.S. in Dentistry, 1955; m. Evelyn Eleanore Parvey, Sept. 12, 1953; children—Deborah Diane, Gregory Scott. Practice dentistry, St. Paul, 1954-55; teaching asst., clin. instr. U. Minn., Mpls., 1954-55; practice endodontics, San Antonio, 1958—; instr. dental assisting San Antonio Coll., 1961-68. Sec., dir. Beverage Consultants Am., Inc. Alderman, mayor City of Castle Hills, Tex. Served to capt. Dental Corps, AUS, 1955-58. Fellow Am. Coll. Dentists; mem. Am., Tex. dental assns., San Antonio Dist. Dental Soc. (bd. dirs. 1967—, pres.-elect), Am. Assn. Endodontists, U.S. Power Squadron, Omicron Kappa Upsilon, Psi Omega. Research with isotopes on root canal sealers. Home: 228 Herweck Dr San Antonio TX 78213 Office: 1019 Shook Av San Antonio TX 78212

LUNDE, ANDERS STEEN, statistician, govt. ofcl.; b. Bridgeport, Conn., Dec. 10, 1914; s. Anders and Cecelia (Steen) L.; A.B., St. Lawrence U., 1938; M.A., Columbia, 1947, Ph.D., 1955; m. Eleanor Sheldon, Sept. 9, 1939; children—Erik Sheldon, Peter Steen, Anthony Gulliver, Anne Louisa. Faculty, Rutgers U., New Brunswick, N.J., 1948-51, St. Lawrence U., Canton, N.Y., 1951-55; prof., dir. research Gallaudet Coll., Washington, 1955-58; chief natality statistics br. Nat. Vital Statistics div. USPHS, Washington, 1962-64, dep. dir. div. vital statistics Nat. Center for Health Statistics, 1964-67, dir. Office State Services, 1967—; adj. prof. dept. biostatistics U. N.C., 1968—. Served to maj. Chaplain Corps, AUS, 1943-46. Fellow Am. Sociol. Assn., A.A.A.S., Am. Pub. Health Assn.; mem. Population Assn. Am. (sec.-treas. 1965-68, dir. 1968-71), Am. Statis Assn. Author: (with S.K. Bigman) Occupational Conditions Among the Deaf, 1959; other publs. Home: 1120 Sourwood Dr Chapel Hill NC 27514 Office: PO Box 12214 Research Triangle Park NC 27709

LUNDE, DAVID ARLAND, coll. adminstr.; b. Pittsfield, Mass., Oct. 12, 1938; s. Harold Theodore and Bernice (Bradway) L.; student Ill. Inst. Tech., 1956-57; B.Arch., U. Pa., 1961; m. Carol Lee Buckley, Dec. 22, 1962; 1 dau., Laura Lee. Apprentice, Aeck Assos., Atlanta, 1964-67, architect, 1967-68; campus architect U. Ga., Athens, 1968—. Served with USNR, 1961-64. Mem. A.I.A., Soc. Coll. and Univ. Planners, Delta Tau Delta. Presbyn. (deacon, supt. Sunday sch.). Toastmaster (pres.). Archtl. works include Walton House, Northrope House, both 1969, Jefferson (Ga.) City Hall, 1972, Lunde House, 1972. Home: 245 Bishop Dr Athens GA 30601 Office: Old Coll Bldg U Ga Athens GA 30601

LUNDERMAN, CHARLES JOHNSON, JR., lawyer; b. Paducah, Ky., Dec. 26, 1922; s. Charles Johnson and Loretta Corine (Bacon) L.; student Ky. State Coll., 1940-43; LL.B., Lincoln U., 1949; m. Belma Delores Pleasant, July 16, 1950; Admitted to Ky. bar, 1949; since practiced in Louisville. Instr. bus. law Foust-Obannon Sch., 1951-52; judge Quar. Ct., 1965-66; mem. Air Pollution Hearing Bd., 1968—. Vice pres. Jefferson County Republican Exec. Com., 1964—. Bd. dirs., mem. legal redress com. Louisville br. N.A.A.C.P. Served with USAAF, 1943-46. Mem. Nat. (dir. 1967—), Louisville bar assns., Nat. Assn. Claimants Counsel Am., Nat. Inst. Municipal Law Officers, Urban League. Club: Epicurean (Louisville). Office: 319 W Jefferson St Louisville KY 40203 Home: 4021 Grand St Louisville KY 40203

LUNDGREN, LAWRENCE EDWARD STANLEY, physician; b. St. Alban's, Vt., Sept. 27, 1920; s. Eric Vanner and Gladys (Judson) L.; B.S., Tufts U., 1941; M.D., Magistri-Chirurgiae, McGill U., 1945; m. Mary Frances Knowles, June 24, 1960; children—Christian Stewart, Jay Andrew. Intern Montreal (Que., Can.) Gen. Hosp., 1944-45; resident Margaret Hague Maternity Hosp., Jersey City, 1947-52; cons. Miss., Tex. State Bd. Health, 1952-53; practice medicine, specializing in obstetrics and gynecology, Jackson, Miss., 1953-57, Houston, 1957—; chief of service, obstetrics and gynecology Meml. Bapt. Hosp.; mem. staff St. Lukes Episcopal, Meth., St. Joseph's hosps.; clin. instr. U. Miss., 1955-57. U. Tex., 1957-59, Baylor Sch. Medicine, 1957—. Founding mem. Houston Mus. Med. Sci., Houston Grand Opera Guild. Bd. dirs. Civic Music Assn., 1958-61. Served as capt. USAF, 1945-47. Fellow Am. Coll. Obstetrics and Gynecology (1st prize award for sci. exhibit 1971); mem. Am., Tex. (recipient sci. award, 1958) med. assns., Harris County Med. Soc. (mem. exec bd., chmn. adjudication and med. testimony bd.), Postgrad. Assembly of Tex., Osler Soc., Am. Soc. Abdominal Surgeons, SACRES Soc., S.A.R. Baptist. Contbr. articles in field to profl. jours. Home: 32 S Wynden Dr Houston TX 77027 Office: Meml Profl Bldg Houston TX 77002

LUNGER, IRVIN EUGENE, univ. pres., clergyman; b. Williamsport, Pa., June 28, 1912; s. George Lee and Mabel Clara (Griggs) L.; A.B. magna cum laude, Bethany Coll., 1934; B.D., U. Chgo., 1935, A.M., 1936, Ph.D., 1938; student U. Munich, Germany, 1936-37; Litt.D., Bethany Coll; 1959; L.H.D., U. Ala., 1965; m. Eleanor Jeanne Zink, Feb. 10, 1939 (dec. Aug. 1955); children—Susan Ann (Mrs. Lee C. Brown), Kathryn Elizabeth (Mrs. Bob Willis); m. 2d, Kay Walsh Ritchey, June 19, 1957; foster son, Owsley Ritchey. Ordained to ministry Disciples of Christ Ch., 1932; minister Christian Ch., Morristown, O., 1930-34, University Ch. Disciples of Christ, Chgo., 1939-55; prof. religion, dean Morrison Chapel, Transylvania U., Lexington, Ky., 1955-56, acad. dean, 1956-57, pres., 1958—. Dir. United Fund, 1959-65, pres. bd. dir., 1962-64; pres. dir. Bd. Higher Edn., Disciples of Christ, 1963-64; pres. bd. dirs. Henry Clay Found., Lexington, 1968—; chmn. exec. com. Ky. Ind. Coll. Found., 1967-68; Ky. chmn. Rhodes Scholarship Selection Com., 1960-67; mem. Ky. Gov.'s Commn. Higher Edn., 1964-69; mem. Lexington-Fayette Found., 1960—. Chmn. bd. dirs. Living Arts and Sci. Center, Inc., 1968-69. Bd. dirs. Ednl. Adv. and Reference Corp., N.Y.C., 1965-70; chmn. bd. dirs. Lexington Pub. Library, 1966-70. Named Ky. col., 1959. Mem. Council Ind. Ky. Colls. and Univs. (pres. 1966, 68), Conf. Ch.-Related Colls. of South (pres. 1970), Omicron Delta Kappa, Tau Kappa Alpha, Beta Theta Pi. Democrat. Kiwanian. Clubs: Informal (Lexington); Idle Hour Country, Filson. Contbr.; Faith of the Free, 1940. Home: 469 N Broadway Lexington KY 40508

LUNN, EDWARD WALLACE, SR., boiler supply co. exec.; b. Chgo., Aug. 9, 1912; s. George B. and Margaret (McDermott) L.; grad. high sch.; m. Gladys Elizabeth Hunter, Sept. 25, 1934; children—Beverly (Mrs. Warren F. Young), Gloria (Mrs. Charles G. Allison), Wallace Edward. Asst. to Gerald B. Howard, Engr. So. Engring. & Appraisal Co., 1929-34; chief engr., supt. Nashville Linen Service, 1934-42; founder, pres. Boiler Supply Co., Inc., Nashville, 1942—. Juror, Freedoms Found., 1968; mem. adv. bd. Belmont Coll., Harrison Chilitowee Acad., Tenn. Assn. Retarded Children and Adults. Sec., Davidson County Democratic Com., 1954-58; col. on staff Tenn. Govs. Ellington, Clement. Bd. dirs. Nashville Union Mission. Maj., Tenn. State Guard, 1941-47. Recipient numerous bus. awards. Mem. Am. Soc. M.E., Am. Soc. Heating, Air-Conditioning and Refrigerating Engrs., Am. Ordinance Assn., Nashville Engring. Assn., Nat. Assn. Profl. Engrs., Middle Tenn. Indsl. Dist. Assn., C. of C., Indsl. Devel. Team Tenn. Baptist (deacon). Mason (32 deg. Shriner), Elk. Clubs: Nashville Boosters (pres. 1959), Civitan Internat. (pres. 1968-69). Home: 2903 Tyne Blvd Nashville TN 37215 Office: 490 Craighead St Nashville TN 37204

LUNNON, BETTY SHEEHAN (MRS. JAMES LUNNON), librarian; b. Montgomery, Ala., May 29, 1908; d. Merrill Ashurst and Martha (Guice) Sheehan; student U. Ala., 1928, 30, 32-34; A.B., George Washington U., 1938; M.A., Appalachian State Tchrs. Coll., 1959; m. David White, Nov. 27, 1927 (div. 1936); m. 2d, James Lunnon, May 13, 1939 (dec. Nov. 1954); 1 dau., Penelope Anne (Mrs. Darrell F. Fleeger). Tchr., librarian Hayneville (Ala.) Pub. Sch., 1927-29, Seale (Ala.) Pub. Sch., 1929-31, Dadeville (Ala.) Pub. Sch., 1931-32; case worker Ala. Dept. Pub. Welfare, Fed. Emergency Relief Adminstrn., 1933-35; statis. cataloger U.S. Govt., 1937-38; librarian Miami Edison Sr. High Sch., 1938-42, Fairlawn Elementary Sch., 1952-54; supr. Dade County Sch. Libraries, Miami, 1954-68; supr. libraries Dept. Edn., Pago Pago, American Samoa, 1968—; asst. prof. U. Miami, summer 1960, evening sch., 1961, 63-66; prof. summer workshop Drexel Inst., 1965; library com. cons. Field Enterprises Ednl. Corp. Gray Lady, A.R.C., 1949-52; dir. Fla. Hearing and Speech Center, 1962-63. Mem. Am. Assn. U. Women (br. v.p. 1950-51), D.A.R., Nat., Fla. edn. assns., Am. (nat. chmn. sch. library suprs. 1966-67), Fla. (pres. 1961-62) library assns., Dade County Sch. Library Assn. (pres. 1953), Am. (dir. southeastern states 1962-64, chmn. suprs. sect. 1966-67, dir. 1962-64), Fla. (pres. 1956) assns. sch. librarians, Kappa Delta Pi, Delta Kappa Gamma. Club: Quota (lt. gov. 27th dist.). Author: Jacarezinho Vadico, 1946; Two Shoes, 1951. Contbr. articles profl. jours. Home: 1002 Granada Blvd Coral Gables FL 33134 Office: Library American Samoa Pago Pago American Samoa 96920

LUPARDUS, JOHN WILLIAM, constrn. co. exec.; b. Sapulpa, Okla., Apr. 19, 1920; s. Otto Orban and May (Hughes) L.; student Okla. State U., 1946; m. Sally Thomas Harris, Aug. 29, 1947; children—John William, Joseph Thomas, Jeffrey Orban, Jan, James Lewis. Sales rep. Nat. Tank Co., Hobbs, N.M., 1947-50, mgr. city sales, Midland, Tex., 1950-52; with BL&B Constrn. Inc., Midland, 1952—, partner, 1952-55, pres., 1955—; co-owner Equipment Rental Co., Midland, Tank Rentals Co., Midland, 1965—. Served with USAAF, 1942-45. Decorated D.F.C., Air medal with one oak leaf cluster. Mem. Hobbs Jr. C. of C., Lambda Chi Alpha. Club: Ranchland Hill Country (Midland). Home: 2601 W Dengar St Midland TX 79701 Office: 4000 W Indsl St Midland TX 79701

LUPER, HAROLD LEE, educator; b. O'porto, Portugal, Dec. 21, 1924; s. Albert Ward and Fannie (Hawkins) L.; A.B., Western Mich. Coll., 1949; M.A., Ohio State U., 1950, Ph.D., 1954; m. Mary West Leatherwood, Jan. 24, 1944; children—John Stephen, Robert Louis, Sally Ann. Asst. prof. speech Central Mich. Coll., Mt. Pleasant, 1950-51; instr. speech Ohio State U., Columbus, 1951-54; asst. prof., asso. prof. speech correction U., Ga., Athens, 1954-63; prof., head dept. audiology and speech pathology U. Tenn., Knoxville, 1963—, dir. Hearing and Speech Center, 1966—. Fellow Am. Speech and Hearing Assn. (v.p. adminstrn. 1971—); mem. Tenn. (pres. 1966), Ga. (pres. 1962) speech and hearing assns. Contbr. articles to profl.

jours. Author: (with Robert L. Mulder) Stuttering: Therapy for Children, 1964. Editor: (asso.) Exceptional Child, 1964-68; Jour. Speech and Hearing Disorders, 1966-71; dsh Abstracts, 1962-66. Home: 7705 Sabre Dr Knoxville TN 37919

LUPINE, ELMER ALAN ROY, civil engr.; b. Pasadena, Cal, Nov. 19, 1908; s. Joseph Edward and Philipa Anne (Caracaus) L.; B.S., U. Ala., 1931; C.E., Roosevelt Grad. Coll., Chgo., 1944; postgrad. Columbia U., 1936-38; m. Mary Mac Smith, Aug. 2, 1955. Civil engr. Ala. State Hwy Dept., Tuscaloosa, 1931-32, Carl B. Call, Architect, N.Y.C., 1933-34, Office of the Borough Engr., N.Y.C., 1934-39, mem. staff of Dept. Engr., San Juan, P.R., 1939-40; civil engr. design div. Dept. of Navy, Atlantic Div. Naval Facilities Engring. Command, 1940-60, fecilities mgmt., 1961-69, facilities planning, 1969—. Registered profl. engr., Va. Fellow Am. Soc. C.E. (mem. various coms.). Club: Norfolk Boat. Home: 212 86th St Virginia Beach VA 23451 Office: Atlantic Division Naval Facilities Engineering Command Norfolk VA 23511

LUPO, ROBERT MAXCY, JR., indsl. engr.; b. Hendersonville, N.C., Nov. 17, 1928; s. Robert Maxcy and Dessie (Dixon) L.; B. Indsl. Engring., Ga. Inst. Tech., 1949; m. Carolyn Simpson, Sept. 5, 1954 (div. May 1969); children—Douglas Robert, Carol Lynne; m. 2d, Gretchen Minnich, Jan. 30, 1970; step-children—John L. Kaufmann, Paul M. Kaufmann, Elizabeth K. Kaufmann. Engr., So. Bell Tel. & Tel. Co., Augusta, Ga., 1949-63; tech. study mgmt. advanced engring. and planning br. NASA, Kennedy Space Center, Fla., 1963—. Served with USNR, 1952-54. Mem. Ga., Ala. socs. profl. engrs., Am. Inst. Indsl. Engrs., Air Force Communication Electronics Assn., Sigma Chi. Republican. Methodist. Club: Cape Kennedy Ga. Tech. Home: PO Box 731 Titusville FL 32780 Office: Kennedy Space Center FL 32899

LUSK, CLU FLU, physician; b. Eros, La., June 26, 1921; s. Frank E. and Helen (Remington) L.; B.S., La. Tech. U., 1942; M.D., Tulane U., 1950; m. Betty Morse, Jan. 1, 1944 (div. June 1945); 1 son, Frederick; m. 2d, Shirley C. Dieterich, June 17, 1950; children—Alan, Jane, John, Claire. Intern Shreveport (La.) Confederate Memorial Hosp., 1950-51, resident H.P. Long Hosp., Pineville, La., 1951-52; practice medicine, specializing in family practice, Weimar, Tex., 1952-53, Gainesville, Tex., 1953—; chief staff Gainesville Mem. Hosp., also bd. dirs. Served with USCGR, 1942-45; ETO, PTO. Diplomate Am. Bd. Family Practice. Mem. Kappa Sigma, Phi Chi, Omicron Delta Kappa, Alpha Omega Alpha. Home: Woodbine Rd Gainesville TX 76240 Office: 314 N Grand St Gainesville TX 76240

LUSSKY, WARREN ALFRED, librarian; b. Chgo., Apr. 16, 1919; s. Arthur W. and Alma (Proegler) L.; B.A., U. Colo., 1946; M.A., U. Denver, 1948; student U. Ill., 1941-42;; m. Mildred Joann Island, June 12, 1948. Asst. librarian Pacific Luth. Coll., Parkland Wash., 1948-49; librarian Hopkins Transp. Library, Stanford, 1950, Rocky Mountain Coll., Billings, Mont., 1950-55; head librarian Neb. Wesleyan U., Lincoln, 1955-56; dir. library, asso. prof. Tex. Luth. Coll., Sequin, 1956—. Mem. accrediting team Tex. Edn. Agy., U. Corpus Christi, Tex., 1961. Mem. Am., Tex. (dist. vice chmn. 1965, chmn. 1966), Pacific N.W. (personnel adminstrn. com. 1951-53), S.W. library assns. Prin. contbr. to design new Tex. Luth. Coll. Library; research and publs. on design and functions coll. library bldgs. Home: 357 Irvington Dr San Antonio TX 78209 Office: Texas Luth College Library Seguin TX 78155

LUSTER, GEORGE LOWELL, educator; b. Middleburg, Ky., Oct. 24, 1921; s. George Cochran and Deedy (Martin) L.; student Berea Coll., 1940-42; B.S. in Agr., U. Ky., 1947; M.S., Ohio State U., 1952, Ph.D., 1954; m. Hazel Marie Wall, May 28, 1944. Pub. high sch. tchr., Ky., 1947-51; research asst. Ohio State U., Columbus, 1953-54; faculty U. Ky. Coll. Edn., Lexington, 1954-69, asso. prof., 1958-69, prof., 1969, dir. instructional materials lab. for vocational edn., 1966-69; dir. (pres.) S.E. Community Coll. of U. Ky., Cumberland, 1969-72; asst. dir. for acad. affairs Elizabethtown Community Coll. of U. Ky., 1972—; Am. dir. Ahwaz (Iran) Agr. Coll., 1962-64. Cons. Ohio State U., 1965, Md. Dept. Edn., 1967. Dir., Alcor Inc. Mem. exec. bd. Blue Grass council Boy Scouts Am., 1971; mem. Upper Cumberland Council on Alcoholism and Drug Abuse, 1972, Regional Adv. Com. for Vocational Edn., 1971-72; mem. community adv. council Harlan (Ky.) Appalachian Regional Hosp., 1970-72. Served with Signal Corps, USAAF, AUS, 1943-45; ETO, PTO. Recipient Centennial award, dept. agrl. edn. Ohio State U., 1970. Mem. N.E.A., Am. Assn. Tchr. Educators in Agr. (treas. 1968, 69), Am. Vocational Assn., Harlan (Ky.) Mining Inst. (hon.), Alpha Zeta, Phi Delta Kappa (chpt. pres. 1961-62), Gamma Sigma Delta. Baptist (deacon 1959-62, 65-68, 70-72, trustee 1966-69, past mem. finance, nominating coms.). Mason, Rotarian. Contbr. articles to profl. jours. Home: 593 Charlemagne Blvd Route 3 Elizabethtown KY 42701

LUSTIG, STANLEY HOWARD, accountant; b. Bklyn., July 11, 1927; s. Emil and Ethel (Isaacson) L.; B.B.A., Coll. City N.Y., 1948, postgrad., 1949-52; LL.B., Bklyn. Law Sch., 1955; postgrad. N.Y. U. Law Sch., 1956-57; m. Joan Gottscho, Dec. 25, 1954; children—Eric, Margo, Robin. Accountant, Louis J. Hollander Co., C.P.A.'s, N.Y.C., 1948-51, Bernhard H. Frank, C.P.A., N.Y.C., 1951, Finkelstein & Goldstein, C.P.A.'s, N.Y.C., 1951-54, 54-55; asst. in adminstrn. Robert H. Feldman, N.Y.C., 1954; tax dept. Anchin, Block, Anchin, C.P.A.'s, N.Y.C., 1955-57; comptroller Cole of Palm Beach, Inc. (Fla.), 1957-58; accountant Harry Silett, C.P.A., Palm Beach, 1958-63; pub. accountant Harry Silett Co., Palm Beach, 1963-65; pvt. practice pub. accounting, Palm Beach, 1965-66; pub. accountant Ganz, Brenner & Lustig, Palm Beach, 1966-68, Ganz, Brenner, Lustig, Oken & Anderson and predecessor firm, Palm Beach and North Palm Beach, 1968—; mem. adv. bd. First Nat. Bank, Riviera Beach. Served with USNR, 1945-46. C.P.A., N.Y., Fla. Mem. Am., Fla. (chpt. pres.), N.Y. insts. C.P.A.'s, East Coast Estate Planning Council. Jewish religion. Home: 418 Oyster Rd North Palm Beach FL 33408 Office: 636 US Hwy 1 North Palm Beach FL 33408

LUSZKI, MARGARET BARRON (MRS. WALTER A. LUSZKI), psychologist; b. Washington, Mar. 24, 1907; d. Charles Henry and Helena (Johnson) Butler; A.B., U. Mich., 1928; M.A., U. Md., 1930; postgrad. Cath. U. Am. Sch. Social Work, 1939-40, Wash. Sch. Psychiatry, 1945-47, Mass. Inst. Tech., 1947-48; Ph.D., U. Mich., 1951; m. Walter A. Luszki, Mar. 15, 1950. Employee counselor Social Security Bd. and FSA, 1939-43; chief employee relations sec. U.S. Dept. Health, Edn. and Welfare, 1943-50; lectr. U.S. Dept. Agr. Grad. Sch., 1945-47; lectr. Am. U., 1951; project coordinator work confs. in Mental Health Research, Nat. Tng. Labs., 1951-57; cons. in student personal adjustment Paine Coll., Augusta, Ga., 1957-58; psychologist VA Hosp., Augusta, 1958-59; psychol. cons. Crippled Children's div. Ga. Dept. Health, 1958-59; study dir. Research Center for Group Dynamics, Inst. for Social Research, U. Mich., 1960-61; clin. psychologist and vocational counselor VA Hosp., Ann Arbor, Mich., 1961-66; research asso. Center for Research on Utilization of Sci. Knowledge, Inst. for Social Research, U. Mich., 1961-66; clin. psychologist VA Hosp., Charleston, S.C., 1966-72 clin. asso. in psychiatry (psychology) dept. psychiatry S.C. Med. U., 1968—; cons. psychologist, 1962—. Fellow Am. Psychol. Assn., Soc. for Psychol. Study Social Issues, Am. Sociol. Assn.; mem. Nat. Rehab. Assn. Unitarian. Author: Interdisciplinary Team Research: Methods and Problems, 1958; (with Fox and Schmuck) Diagnosing Classroom Learning Environments, 1966. Contbr. articles to profl. jours. Home: Box 361 Folly Beach SC 29439 Office: 165 Maple St Charleston SC 29403

LUTHER, ELBERT FARMER, JR., civil engr.; b. Burns, Tenn., May 27, 1923; s. Elbert Farmer and Helen (Ligon) L.; B.S., Tenn. Tech., 1949; m. Florine Bell Owen, June 16, 1951; children—Robert S., Randy Owen. Civil engr. Ill. Div. Waterways, Springfield, 1949-52; cost reduction engr. E.I. Du Pont de Nemours & Co., Inc., Aiken, S.C., 1952-53; civil engr. Tenn. Dept. Hwys., Nashville, 1954-55, field engr., 1956—, sr. road design engr., 1969—; field engr. Ford Glass Plant, Nashville, 1955-56; pres. Line & Grade Inc., contractors, Brentwood, Tenn., 1970—. Asst. scout master Boy Scouts of Am., 1958-69. Served with AUS, 1943-46. Registered profl. engr., Tenn. Mem. Christian Ch. (Sunday Sch. coordinator). Club: Melrose Civitan (sec. 1971-72). Home: 5005 Trousdale Dr Nashville TN 37220

LUTKEN, DONALD CURRY, utility exec.; b. Jackson, Miss., Mar. 26, 1924; s. Peter Koch and Erma (Curry) L.; student Miss. State U.; B.S., U.S. Naval Acad., 1946; m. Melissa McNeill Turner, June 11, 1946; children—Melissa (Mrs. Hugo Newcomb, Jr.), Isabel (Mrs. W.L. Eggart), Donald, Lucie, Edwin Poteat. With Miss. Power and Light Co., 1949—, engr., Jackson, 1949, plant supt. Natchez Steam Elec. Sta., 1950-53, Delta Steam Elec. Sta., Cleveland, 1953-57, supt. prodn., Jackson, 1957-63, asst. chief engr., 1963-65, chief engr., 1965-67, v.p., chief engr., 1967-68, v.p. operations, 1968-69, exec. v.p., dir., 1969-70, pres., dir., 1970—, chief exec. officer, 1971—; dir. Magna Corp., Jackson, 1st Fed. Savs. & Loan Assn. Mem. exec. bd. Andrew Jackson council Boy Scouts Am., also mem. exec. com. Region V.; Miss. chmn. U.S. Savs. Bond div. Treasury Dept. Bd. dirs. United Givers Fund, YMCA; trustee St. Andrews Episcopal Day Sch., Southeastern Electric Exchange. Served with USNR, 1946-49. Mem. Am. Soc. M.E., U.S. Naval Inst., Am. Soc. Naval Engrs., Miss. Soc. Profl. Engrs., Nat. Assn. Electric Cos., Jackson C. of C., I.E.E.E. Presbyn. Rotarian. Clubs: Capital City Petroleum, Jackson Country; Engineers (New Orleans). Home: 1618 Pine Ridge Pl Jackson MS 39211 Office: PO Box 1640 Jackson MS 39205

LUTON, FRANK HARPER, psychiatrist; b. Decaturville, Tenn., Oct. 18, 1898; s. William Oliver and Corilla (Harper) L.; M.D., Vanderbilt U., 1927; m. Milbrey Young, June 8, 1927; children—Deborah (Mrs. Thomas Randolph Cate), Melissa (Mrs. William H. Bradford). Intern, Phipps Psychiat. Clinic, Johns Hopkins Hosp., Balt., 1927, resident, 1929-31; clin. clk. Queen's Sq. Hosp., London, 1931, Judge Baker Found., Boston, 1932, Boston City Hosp., 1933; practice psychiatry, Nashville, 1931—; cons. VA Hosp., Thayer, State Hosp., Nashville, 1947-60, clin. dir., 1960-69; vis. psychiatrist Mental Health Clinic Vanderbilt U. Hosp., Nashville, 1947-60; commr. Tenn. Dept. Mental Health, Nashville, 1969-71, dir. tng. and research, 1971—; Instr. psychiatry Johns Hopkins, 1930-31; asst. prof. Vanderbilt U., 1931-37, asso. prof., 1937-42, prof. psychiatry, 1942-64, prof. emeritus, 1964—. Mem. A.M.A. So. Med. Assn., Am. Assn. Mental Deficiency, Am. Psychiat. Assn., Am. Coll. Psychiatrists, Assn. for Research Nervous and Mental Disorders, Nat. Assn. Mental Health. Home: 5401 Stanford Dr Nashville TN 37215 Office: Central State Psychiatric Hospital 1501 Murfreesboro Rd Nashville TN 37217

LUTON, SHELTON, judge; b., 1906; LL.B., Vanderbilt U. Admitted to Tenn. bar, 1930; judge, Davidson County (Tenn). Office: County Ct House Nashville TN 37201*

LUTTRELL, CURTIS C., state ofcl. Commr. labor La. Office: PO Box 44094 Baton Rouge LA 70804*

LUTTRELL, JOHN MORTER, lawyer; b. Norman, Okla., June 16, 1916; s. John Edmund and Mary Elizabeth (Morter) L.; B.A., U. Okla., 1938; postgrad. (Rhodes Scholar), Oxford U., 1938-39; LL.B., U. Okla., 1941; m. Josephine Nell Watters, Aug. 23, 1941; children—John S., Susan N. Admitted to Okla. bar, 1941; gen. practice, Norman, 1941—; city atty., Norman, 1954-63; dir. First Nat. Bank & Trust Co. Bd. visitors U. Okla., 1969-72. Served with USNR, 1943-46, 51-53. Fellow Am. Coll. Trial Lawyers, Am. Bar Found.; mem. Okla. Bar Assn. (v.p. 1972), C. of C., Phi Beta Kappa, Beta Theta Pi. Democrat. Episcopalian. Home: 1125 S Ponca Av Norman OK 73069 Office: 104 E Eufaula St Norman OK 73069

LUTTRELL, LESTER LEE, dentist; b. Columbus, Ga., June 22, 1933; s. Lester Lee and Alice Eloile (Brinson) L.; B.S., North Ga. Coll., 1954; D.D.S., Emory U., 1958, certificate in orthodontics, 1966; m. Jo Beth Rice, July 11, 1959; children—Dena Jan, David Reed, Linda Dayle. Intern Brooke Gen. Hosp., San Antonio, 1958-59, rotating intern, 1964-66; practice dentistry, specializing in orthodontics, Griffin, Ga., 1966—; mem. staff Griffin Spalding County Hosp. Served to maj. Dental Corps, AUS, 1958-64. Mem. Ga. Soc. Orthodontists, So. Soc. Orthodontists, Am. Assn. Orthodontists, Am. Dental Assn., Ga. Conservancy, Orthodontic Edn. and Research Found., Delta Sigma Delta. Baptist. Clubs: Exchange (pres. 1971-72) (Griffin, Ga.); Sierra. Home: 1005 Springer Dr Griffin GA 30227 Office: 218 Addevale St Griffin GA 30223

LUTZ, GERALD WHISNANT, dentist; b. Shelby, N.C., Aug. 30, 1934; s. John Reid and Madge Marie (Whisnant) L.; student Gardner-Webb Jr. Coll., 1952-53; B.S. in Geol. Engring., N.C. State U., 1956; grad. Med. Coll. Va. Sch. Dentistry, 1965; m. Frances Ann Fowler, Apr. 25, 1959; children—Janet Lynn, Kimberly Ann. Engring. geologist Nello Teer Constrn. Co., Durham, N.C., 1956-57; gen. practice dentistry, Fallston, N.C., 1965—. Served from ensign to lt. (j.g.) USNR, 1957-61. Mem. Am. Dental Assn., N.C. Dental Soc., Am. Forestry Assn., Isothermal Dental Soc. (pres. 1969), Am. Inst. Mining Engrs., Am. Soc. Dentistry for Children, Omicron Kappa Upsilon, Sigma Zeta, Delta Sigma Delta. Methodist. Club: Rutherford Country (Rutherfordton; N.C.). Address: Box 138 Fallston NC 28042

LUTZ, KEITH WILLIAM, state ofcl.; b. Shannon, Ill., Feb. 22, 1922; s. Otis and Ada Marie (Boyd) L.; B.S., U. Okla., 1948; grad. Central Flight Instr. Sch.; m. Suzannelle Hall, June 10, 1952; 1 son, Kenneth W. Formerly flight instr., faculty pilot U. Okla., corporate pilot, pilot Air Transport Command United Airlines; dir. Okla. Aeros. Commn., 1963—. Served with USAF. Recipient Certificate of Merit Aviation Distbrs. and Mfrs. Assn., 1971. Mem. Am. Assn. Airport Execs., Aircraft Owners and Pilots Assn., Nat. Pilots Assn., Nat. Assn. State Aviation Ofcls., Quiet Birdmen, Phi Delta Theta. Kiwanian. Home: 6809 Ann Arbor Terrace Oklahoma City OK 73132 Office: 424 United Founders Tower Oklahoma City OK 73112

LUTZ, THERESA PENCE (MRS. C. RALPH LUTZ), ednl. adminstr.; b. nr. Greensboro, N.C.; d. Claude S. Stroud and Lelia (Powell) Pence; B.A., Mary Washington Coll., 1947; M.Ed., U.Va., 1956, postgrad., 1956-57; postgrad. George Washington U., summer 1961, 61-62, Am. U., 1963, Coll. William and Mary, 1964-71; m. C. Ralph Lutz, May 30, 1931; children— Patricia (Mrs. Edward L. Plummer, Jr.), Phillip (dec.). Tchr., New Market (Va.) Elementary Sch., 1944-46, New Market High Sch., 1946-47, Wilson Meml. High Sch., Fishesville, Va., 1947-57; tchr., counselor Mt. Vernon High Sch., Alexandria, Va., 1957-58; dir. guidance Lee High Sch., Springfield, Va., 1958-67; counselor, instr. grad. edn. No. Va. Center, U. Va., also instr., counselor West Springfield High Sch. Trustee, Marion Coll. Mem. N.E.A. (life), Va. (chmn. tchr. and profl. standards com. 1966—), Fairfax edn. assns., Am., Va., No. Va. personnel and guidance Assns., Adult Edn. Assn. Am., Internat. Platform Assn., Nat. Vocational Guidance Assn., Va., Guidance Assn., Delta Kappa Gamma (chpt. pres. 1972—). Lutheran (counselor Luther League 1961-63). Author: (with Lillian W. Eisenberg) Central Evangelical Lutheran Church and Christ Evangelical Lutheran Church, 1953. Home: 5803 Accomac St Springfield VA 22150 Office: 6100 Rolling Rd Springfield VA 22152

LUTZ, WILLIAM FLETCHER, govt. ofcl.; b. Red Lion, Pa., July 8, 1922; s. William Fletcher and Aurelia Gardner (Lichtenberger) L.; B.S. in Econs., Franklin and Marshall Coll., 1947; postgrad. George Washington U., 1948-49; m. June Miller, May 11, 1945 (dec. Aug. 1951); 1 dau., Sharon Jane; m. 2d, Alta Louise Casper, May 2, 1953. Supervisory accountant, regional mgr. U.S. Gen. Accounting Office, Mpls.-St. Paul, 1947-58; with U.S. CAB, 1958—, chief field audits div., 1958-61, dept. dir. Bur. Econs., Washington, 1961-72, dir. Bur. Accounts and Statistics, 1972—. Instr. accounting U.S. Dept. Agr. Grad. Sch. Bd. dirs., exec. com., pres., comptroller Central Atlantic Conf. United Ch. Christ; past dir., treas. United Ch. Christ Home, Inc., Silver Spring, Md. Served to 1st lt. Q.M.C., AUS, 1943-46. Recipient Superior Accomplishment award CAB, 1960, 66; Distinguished Service award Fed. Govt. Accountants Assn., 1961, Robert W. King meml. award, 1970. C.P.A., N.C. Mem. Fed. Govt. Accountants Assn. (pres. 1966-67), Am. Inst. C.P.A.'s, Am. Accounting Assn., Pi Gamma Mu. Mem. United Ch. Christ (moderator, trustee, treas., auditor). Clubs: Nat. Aviation, Aero, Internat. (Washington). Home: 6459 Oakwood Dr Falls Church VA 22041 Office: Universal Bldg 1825 Connecticut Av NW Washington DC 20428

LUVISI, LEE, concert pianist, educator; b. Louisville, Dec. 12, 1937; student Curtis Inst. Music, 1952-57; m. Nina Hussey, June 20, 1959; 1 son, Brian. Mem. faculty Curtis Inst. Music, 1957-62; artist in residence U. Louisville Sch. Music. Home: 1703 Trevillian Way Louisville KY 40205

LYBRAND, RAYMOND DONOVAN, bank exec.; b. Columbia, S.C., Sept. 9, 1922; s. Fritz Otis and Elizabeth A. (Murphy) L.; student U. S.C., 1947-48, Am. Inst. Banking, 1954-64, Carolinas Sch. Banking U. N.C., 1962-65; m. Doris Louise Eastman, June 2, 1945; children—Ted D., Donna Dee. With Citizens and So. Nat. Bank, Columbia, 1941-51; store auditor Edens Food Stores, Columbia, 1951-52; teller First Nat. Bank S.C., Spartansburg, 1952-53, head teller, 1953-55, asst. cashier, 1955-61, cashier operations, 1961-66; with First State Nat. Bank, Jackson, S.C., 1966—, v.p., cashier in charge operations, 1966—. Served with USNR, 1942-45, 50-51; Korea. Mem. Bank Adminstrn. Inst. (dir. 1957-58). Methodist (chmn. finance commn., 1959-62, bd. trustees, 1963-65, vice chmn. bd., 1964-65, financial sec., 1967-69). Clubs: Silverton Agricultural (Jackson); Civitan (pres. 1961-62, dir., 1957-63, lt. gov., 1964) (Union, S.C.). Home: Lions Club Rd Jackson SC 29831 Office: First State Nat Bank PO Box 128 Jackson SC 29831

LYKES, RICHARD WAYNE, govt. ofcl.; b. Trenton, N.J., Aug. 19, 1919; s. Ira Timothy and Mary E. (Smith) L.; B.A., Wooster Coll., 1941; M.A., U. Pa., 1948; Ph.D. Am. U., 1960; m. Irene Ida Wargo, Mar. 13, 1943; children—Barbara Joan (Mrs. Armstrong), Liliane Mary. Tchr., social studies River Edge (N.J.) High Sch., 1941-42; instr. dept. history Temple U., Phila., 1947-48; prof. history U. Va. Extension Div., Petersburg, Arlington, 1949-55, 59—; historian Nat. Park Service, Petersburg, Va., 1948-51; historian mil., tech. history Q.M. Tech. Tng. Comand, Ft. Lee, Va., 1952-56; educationist U.S. Office Edn., Washington, 1956-60, sr. specialist internat. edn., 1960—; lectr. history, edn. to various orgns. Pres., dir. Fed. Employees Credit Union of Fort Lee, 1954-55. Speaker, bur. Civil Def., Petersburg-Hopewell, Va., 1952—; chmn. bur. United Givers Fund Speakers, Petersburg, 1956. Served with AUS, 1942-46; Res. Recipient Achievement certificate Q.M. Tng. Command, Ft. Lee, Va., 1956. Mem. Am. Hist. Assn., Am. Studies Assn., Eastern Nat. Park and Monument Assn., Mil. Govt. Assn., Ret. Officers Assn., Phi Alpha Theta. Presbyn. (trustee; v.p. Mens Orgn., 1961). Mason. Club: Wooster (Ohio) Letterman. Contbr. articles to various jours., numerous hist. pamphlets. Home: 3304 Parkside Terrace Fairfax VA 22030 Office: care US Office Edn Dept Health Edn and Welfare Washington DC 20202

LYLE, GUY REDVERS, librarian; b. Lloydminster, Sask., Can., Oct. 31, 1907; s. John Percival and Mary (Lynch) L.; B.A., U. Alta., 1927, LL.D., 1964; B.S., Columbia U. Sch. of Library Service, 1929, M.S., 1932; grad. study U. Ill., 1942-43; m. Margaret White, Nov. 27, 1930; children—John D., Jennifer Ann, Christopher, Margaret Ellen. Came to U.S., 1927, naturalized, 1935. Librarian and instr. library science Antioch Coll., O., 1929-35; asso. U. Ill. Library Sch., 1935-36; librarian Woman's Coll. of U. N.C., 1936-44; dir. libraries La. State U., 1944-54, Emory (Ga.) U., 1954—. Author: Classified List of Periodicals for the Coll. Library, 1934, rev. (with Virginia Trumper), 1948; Coll. Library Publicity, 1935; Adminstrn. of Coll. Library, 1944; Bibliography of Christopher Morley, 1952. Co-author: (with K. Guinagh) I Am Happy to Present, 1953, 2d edit., 1968; The President, the Professor, and the College Library, 1963; The Librarian Speaking, 1970. Contbr. to library jours. Home: 2229 Tanglewood Rd Decatur GA 30033 Office: Emory U Emory GA

LYLE, JOHN EMMETT, lawyer; b. nr. Boyd, Tex., Sept. 4, 1910; s. John Emmett and Ethel (Goodwin) L.; student Jr. Coll. Wichita Falls, 1928-29, U. Tex., 1929-32, Houston Law Sch., 1932-33; m. Gertrue Swanner, Mar. 21, 1937. Admitted to Tex. bar, 1934, practiced in Corpus Christi, 1934-61; mem. Lyle & Burney, 1934-55, Head & Lyle, 1955-61; practice law, Houston, 1961—. Dir., Lincoln Liberty Life Ins. Co., Houston. Mem. Tex. Ho. of Reps., 1941-44; mem. 79th to 83d congresses from 14th Tex. Dist., 1945-55. Served with AUS, 1942-44. Mem. Christian Ch. Clubs: River Oaks Country, Corpus Christi Country, Carriage, Warwick. Home: 3435 Westheimer 1011 Houston TX 77037 Office: Lincoln Liberty Life Bldg Houston TX 77002

LYLE, ROYSTER, JR., library curator; b. Danville, Va., Dec. 10, 1933; s. Royster and Frances (Sale) L.; B.A., Hampden-Sydney Coll., 1956; student U. Va. Sch. Arch., 1968-70; m. Katherine Paul Letcher, Mar. 16, 1963; 1 son, Royster Cochran. Mng. editor Spearhead Newspaper, Frankfurt, Germany, 1956-58; broker Francis I. duPont, N.Y.C. and Danville, Va., 1959-62; sec. George C. Marshall Research Found., Lexington, Va., 1962—, curator, asst. to dir. Marshall Library, 1964—. Bd. dirs. Historic Lexington Found., New Market Battlefield Meml., Va. Citizens Planning Assn., Conservation Council of Va., Assn. for Preservation of Va. Antiquities, Rockbridge Hist. Soc. Mem. Pub. Relations Soc. Am., Soc. Archtl. Historians, Am. Assn. Museums, Chi Phi, Omicron Delta Kappa. Home: 110 McDowell St Lexington VA 24450 Office: George C Marshall Research Library VMI Parade Lexington VA 24450

LYLE, TERRY ALAN, dentist; b. Temple, Ga., Oct. 10, 1939; s. Cecil Morgan and Lorene (Carroll) L.; B.S. in Chemistry, Ga. State U., 1963; D.D.S., U. Tenn., 1967; m. Annette Marcelle Barnette, Oct. 5, 1959; children—Marcus Lonnie, Jonathan Lee, Michael Terry. Individual practice dentistry, Forest Park, Ga., 1967—. Cons., dentist Christian City Orphans Home, College Park, Ga., 1970-71. Recipient Deans award U. Tenn., 1967. Mem. Clayton County C. of C., Am., Ga. dental assns., No. Dist. Dental Soc., South Fulton Dental Study Group, Omicron Ki Upsilon. Kiwanian (chmn. com. 1968-70). Home: 5686 Skyland Dr Forest Park GA 30050 Office: 1124 Main St Forest Park GA 30050

LYLES, GEORGE ROBERT, research co. exec.; b. Flint, Mich., Oct. 27, 1931; s. Robert H. and Ruth J. (Newland) L.; B.S., Ark. State U., 1951; M.S., La. State U., 1958; m. Ann C. Forrester, Aug. 12, 1951; children—Larenda, Roberta, George R. Chief chemist Jonesboro City Water & Light Dept., (Ark.); with Kem Tech Labs., Inc., Baton Rouge, 1955—, chemist, 1958-59, gen. mgr., 1959-65, pres., 1965—. Cons. air and water pollution, gen. chem. and trace techniques Humble Oil and Refining Co., Ethyl Corp., Gen. Chem. div. Allied Chem. Corp., Kaiser Aluminum & Chem. Corp., Am. Cyanamid Co., Monsanto Chem. Co., Texaco, Inc., others. Served to lt. USMCR, 1953-55. Mem. Am. Chem. Soc. Contbr. articles to profl. jours. Home: 944 W Lakeview St Baton Rouge LA 70810 Office: 16550 Highland Rd Baton Rouge LA 70810

LYLES, ROYCE, city ofcl. Dir. dept. finances City of Jacksonville. Home: 7104 Merrill St Jacksonville FL 32207 Office: City Hall Jacksonville FL 32202*

LYLES, WILLIAM GORDON, architect; b. Whitmire, S.C., Oct. 23, 1913; s. John Thomas and Maggie (Livingston) L.; B.Arch., Clemson Coll., 1934; m. Louise Stork, Jan. 15, 1937; children—William Gordon, Robert Thomas. Apprentice several archtl. offices, 1934-38; architect Stork and Lyles, Columbia, S.C., 1938-41, 45-47; pres., chmn. bd. Lyles, Bissett, Carlisle & Wolff, Columbia, 1947—; chmn. bd. Asso. Investments, Inc., 1952—; dir. Bankers Trust, (Columbia), Bank Commerce, Prosperity, S.C. and Chapin, S.C. Chmn. Columbia and Richland Country's Indsl. Devel. Commn., 1958-61; co-chmn. Columbia Community Relations Council, 1963-70, chmn., 1970—; co-chmn. ad hoc com. on design and constrn. evaluation study for Gen. Services Adminstrn., Washington, 1963-64, mem. pub. adv. panel on archtl. services, 1965-67; mem. Gov.'s Adv. Com., 1964-70; mem. Mayor's Adv. Coms., 1958-70; mem. Richland County Historic Commn., 1962—. Mem. adv. bd. Commn. on Higher Edn., 1965-68; trustee United Community Services, 1968—; co-chmn. Columbia Guidance Center, 1965-70. Served to col. C.E. AUS, 1941-45. Decorated Legion of Merit; recipient 27 awards and citations for excellence in design. Fellow Nat. Am. Inst. Architects (mem. govt. affairs com. 1964-70, chmn. 1970; mem. interprofl. com. architects and engrs. concerning fed. procurement A-E services 1966—, vice chmn. 1969—; chmn. interregional com. on fees and practices 1970—; mem. Columbia Council Architects 1956—); mem. A.I.A. (S.C. chpt.; chmn. com. to publish regulations and booklets governing practice architecture S.C. 1952, 61, 69-70), Columbia C. of C. (dir. 1958-62, 70—), U.S. C. of C. (constrn. and civic devel. com. 1961-63), Newcomen Soc. N.Am. Lutheran (mem. ch. council 1954-57, 60-64, 66-70; chmn. pastor's selection com. 1963). Clubs: Cosmos (Washington); City (Raleigh); Forest Lake Country; Spring Valley Country; Palmetto (Columbia). Archtl. works include: Langley Bath Clearwater Sch.; Russell House U. S.C., also Undergrad. Library; Elmwood Cemetery Meml. Tower; libraries at S.C. State Coll. and Wofford Coll.; Orangeburg-Calhoun TEC, U. S.C. Coliseum, U.S.C. Humanities Center, numerous others. Home: 5625 Lakeshore Dr Columbia SC 29206 Office: 1800 Gervais St Columbia SC 29202

LYNCH, ALMA MARTHA HIRSCH (MRS. WILLIAM WRIGHT LYNCH), civic worker; b. Wheeling, W.Va.; d. Conrad and Alma (Hanszen) Hirsch; B.A., U. Tex.; grad. Sullins Coll.; m. William Wright Lynch, Oct. 18, 1930; children—William Wright, Harry Hanszen. Dir., Ins. Bldg. Corp. Chmn. exec. com. Dallas Council World Affairs, 1963-66, chmn. W. Dallas Scholarship Com., 1962-66; dir. Soc. Animal Protection, 1964-66, W. Dallas Community Centers, 1962-66; mem. exec. com. fine arts bd. So. Meth. U., 1964-66; trustee Lynch Found., Ednl. Opportunities, Dallas; mem.-at-large, mem. steering com. Nat. Com. Children and Youth; chmn. women's bd. Dallas Civic Opera, 1967-68; mem. bd. devel. Bishop Coll. Bd. dirs. Tex. Women's Council Dallas County, 1967-69, Planned Parenthood, Dallas, Dallas Theater Center, Dallas Symphony Orch., Dallas Civic Ballet, Douglas MacArthur Acad. Freedom, Brownwood, Tex. Recipient Zonta Service award, 1967. Mem. Chi Omega, Sigma Alpha Iota. Episcopalian. Club: Brook Hollow Golf. Home: 3941 Glenwick Lane Dallas TX 75205

LYNCH, HOWARD WAYNE, banker; b. Hamilton, Tex., Mar. 2, 1902; s. William Warner and Martha Isabella (Miller) L.; B.A., Centre Coll., Danville, Ky., 1925; M.A., U. Ky., 1933; m. Dolly Gretna Hanna, Nov. 2, 1925; children—William Hanna, Howard Wayne, Dan Winsett. Prin., tchr., coach Franklin (Ky.) High Sch., 1925-30; tchr., asst. football coach Amarillo (Tex.) High Sch., 1930-37, head football coach 1937-50, asst. prin., 1950-58; prin. Tascosa High Sch., Amarillo, 1958-67; asst. v.p. Tascoasa Nat. Bank, Amarillo, 1967-68, v.p., 1968—. Mem. Panhandle Sports Hall of Fame, 1964. Mem. Tex. High Sch. Coaches Assn. (Hall of Honor, 1963), Tex. Tchrs. Assn., N.E.A., Tex. Assn. Secondary Sch. Prins., Nat. Assn. Secondary Sch. Prins., Phi Kappa Tau, Omicron Delta Kappa, Phi Delta Kappa. Methodist. Rotarian. Home: 1000 Western St Amarillo TX 79106 Office: 3601 W 15th St Amarillo TX 79106

LYNCH, JOHN FRANCIS, newsman; b. La Moure, N.D., Sept. 17, 1917; s. William David and Ana (Cruden) L.; B.S., N.D. State U., 1940; m. Barbara Ruth Washburn, Feb. 2, 1951; children—Amanda Ruth, William Dana. Printer's devil LaMoure Chronicles, 1934-35; reporter Fargo (N.D.) Forum and WDAY, Inc., 1940-43; reporter-editor Midwest burs. U.P., 1943-51; TV newswriter-producer NBC, 1951-58; dir. pub. affairs CBS, 1959-60; with ABC News, 1960—, Washington bur. chief, 1965—. Home: 2920 Upton St Washington DC 20008 Office: 1124 Connecticut Av NW Washington DC 20036

LYNCH, JOSEPH P., newspaper advt. exec.; b. Grand Rapids, Mich., May 27, 1919; s. Joseph Patrick and Ellen Joan (Lynch) L.; ed. Northwestern U., Harvard Grad. Sch. Bus.; m. Patsy Elizabeth Ashbolt, Apr. 29, 1944; children—Joseph P. III, Michael L., David, Pamela E., Anthony J. Mdse. mgr. asst. to advt. mgr., promotion mgr. Grand Rapids Press, 1946-54; promotion mgr. Washington Post, 1954-61, classified advt. mgr., 1961-67, advt. mgr., 1967-69, v.p. advt., 1969—. Mem. plans bd. Bur. Advt.; dir. Advt. Council. Active Boy Scouts Am. Bd. dirs. Cath. Youth Orgn., Met. Boys Club. Served to 1st lt. AUS, 1941-43. Mem. Internat. Newspaper Promotion Assn. (past pres.), Assn. Newspaper Classified Advt. Mgrs. (past v.p.), Internat. Newspaper Advt. Execs. (dir.). Clubs: University (Washington); Burning Tree. Home: 5215 Portsmouth Washington DC 20016 also Trappe MD Office: 1515 L St Washington DC 20005

LYNCH, KENNETH CLYDE, physician; b. New Tazewell, Tenn., Oct. 13, 1926; s. Brownlow M. and Pearl (Sowder) L.; student Lincoln Meml. U., 1946-47; M.D., U. Tenn., 1961; m. Bobbie Lee Ryder, Sept. 24, 1948; children—Elizabeth Jean, Donald Wayne. Intern, Holston Valley Community Hosp., Kingsport, Tenn., 1961-62, co-dir. diabetic clinic, 1962—, dir. med. staff out-patient clinic, chmn. dept. gen. practice, mem. med. staff exec. com., 1967—, pres. med. staff, 1971; operator Blomingdale Med. Clinic, Kingsport, 1962—. Served with AUS, World War II. Fellow Royal Soc. Health; mem. Am., Tenn. med. assns., Sullivan-Johnson County Med. Soc. (pres. 1972), Am. Acad. Gen. Practice, Am. Diabetic Assn. Republican. Kiwanian. Home: 1417 Linville St Kingsport TN 37664 Office: 2901 Bloomingdale Pike Kingsport TN 37660

LYNCH, KENNETH MERRILL, coll. ofcl.; b. Hamilton, Tex., Nov. 27, 1887; s. William W. and Martha (Miller) L.; M.D., U. Tex., 1910; LL.D., U. S.C., 1930, Coll. of Charleston, 1945; D.Sc. (hon.), Clemson Coll., 1954; m. Lyall Wannamaker, Nov. 9, 1941; children—Merrill (Mrs. C.S.F. Smith), William; children by previous marriage—Kenneth Merrill, Martha (Mrs. William W. Humphreys). Resident pathologist Phila. Gen. Hosp., 1910-11; instr. pathology U. Pa., 1911-13; asst. pathologist Phila. Gen. Hosp., also U. Hosp., Phila., 1911-13; prof. pathology Med. Coll. S.C., 1913-21, 26-60, prof. emeritus, 1960—, vice dean, 1935-43, dean, 1944-49, pres. and dean faculty, 1949-60, chancellor, 1960—. Mem. council Nat. Inst. Neurol. Diseases and Blindness, 1957-61; mem. sci. adv. bd. Council For Tobacco Research, USA, 1954—, chmn. 1958; mem. S.C. Bd. Health, 1935-45, chmn. 1940-44; chmn. of S.C. Cancer Commn. 1939-44; mem. Summerville (S.C.) Bd. Health, 1966—. Served as capt. M.C., U.S. Army, 1918. Recipient gold medal for sci. exhibit, A.M.A., 1921, research medal, So. Med. Assn., 1921, distinguished service award, 1957; Distinguished Service awards Am. Cancer Soc., 1958, U. Tex., 1967, Med. Coll. S.C., 1968. Fellow A.C.P. (gov. 1925-27, 36-37); mem. A.A.A.S., Am. (v.p. 1935-36), So. (councillor 1935-42) med. assns., Am. Soc. Tropical Medicine (pres. 1930), Am. Soc. Clin. Pathology (pres. 1930), Am. Soc. Cancer Control (dir. 1939-43), Am. Assn. Pathologists, Am. Soc. Cancer Research, Phi Beta Kappa, Alpha Omega Alpha, Alpha Mu Pi Omega, Omicron Delta Kappa. Democrat. Episcopalian. Club: University (N.Y.C.). Author: Protozoan Parasitism of the Alimentary Tract., 1930; Green's Manual of Pathology, 1934; Medical Schooling in South Carolina, 1970; also articles. Former mem. editorial bds. several profl. jours. Home: PO Box 811 Summerville SC 29483 Office: 80 Barre St Charleston SC 29401

LYNCH, MINNIE-LOU CHITTICK (MRS. WELDON JEROME LYNCH), lectr., civic leader, library cons.; b. Cutler, Inc., Feb. 28, 1916; d. Loren Maconn and Mae (Callane) Chittick; student Maryville Coll., 1934-36; m. Weldon Jerome Lynch, Mar. 24, 1940; children—Jenny Callane (Mrs. Robert L. Royer), Bridget Dorn (Mrs. Matt V. Hargrove IV). Book reviewer for audiences, 1938—; Book Theater presentations, 1950—; lectr., Can., U.S. Organizer, Allen Parish (La.) Com. Library Devel., 1950, chmn., 1950-57; pres. Allen Parish Library Bd. Control, 1957-65, v.p., 1968—; mem. com. library standards State Dept. Edn., 1965-67; chmn. La. Library Devel. Com., 1964-68, mem. library survey sub-com., 1967-69; cons. Coastal Bend Planning Commn., Corpus Christi, Tex., 1969; cons. inservice tng. La. Central Dist. Libraries, 1968-69; coordinator spl. programs La. State Library, 1968-70; dir. S.W. Libraries Motivation Study Project, 1971-72; chmn. com. to advise Students to Dallas project, 1970-72; mem. exec. com. La. Adv. Council on Libraries, 1971—; mem. U.S. com. for Am. Library in Paris, 1970—. Recipient citation La. Soil and Water Conservation Commn., 1971. Mem. A.L.A. (Trustee citation 1964, adv. com. to pub. relations office 1964-68, membership com. exec. bd. 1966-68), La. Council Performing Arts, Am. Library Trustee Assn. (nat. pres. 1961-63), Southwestern, La. (Modisette award 1963, sect. chmn. 1960) library assns., Nat. Book Com. (nat. bd.), Internat. Platform Assn., Psi Iota Xi, Pi Kappa Delta. Clubs: Matinee Music, Oakdale Garden (organizer). Author monograph: Guidelines for Holding a Governor's Conference on Libraries, 1963, rev., 1968; contbg. author: The Library Trustee, 1968. Home: 404 E 6th Av Oakdale LA 71463

LYNCH, ROBERT RAMSAY, JR., univ. ofcl.; b. Mansfield, O., Jan. 30, 1935; s. Robert R. and Muriel (Parker) L.; B.S. in Journalism, U. Fla., 1956; m. Joan Halberstadt, Dec. 26, 1957; 1 dau., Donna. Sports writer Fort Lauderdale (Fla.) News, 1958-62, sports editor, 1962-64, news and feature editor U. Fla., 1964-65, dir. information services, 1965—. Fla. advt. rep. Golf World Mag., 1961-64. Served with AUS, 1956-58. Recipient Pompano Beach Jr. C. of C. award 1962. Mem. Am. Coll. Pub. Relations Assn. (trustee 1971—, sec. 1971-73, dist. dir. 1970-71), Fla. Pub. Relations Assn. (v.p. 1969-71, chpt. pres. 1969), U. Fla. Alumni Assn. (pres. Alachua County 1968, dist. v.p. 1970-72), Delta Chi, Sigma Delta Chi. Kiwanian. Home: 111 NW 26th St Gainesville FL 32601 Office: Bldg H U Fla Gainesville FL 32601

LYNCH, THOMAS FRANCIS, supt. schs.; b. N.Y.C., May 2, 1912; s. Patrick J. and Annie (Prior) L.; A.B., Cath. U. Am., 1932; M.A., Fla. State U., Tallahassee, 1954; postgrad. Columbia, Fordham U., N.Y. U., Fla. State U., U. Miami; m. Lucy T. Thornton, Aug. 18, 1945; 1 dau., Kathleen (Mrs. Jack A. Norris, Jr.). Instr. math. Prep Sch., 1932-36; salesman, estimator Burns Bros., N.Y.C., 1936-41; instr. Am. Hardware Corp., New Britain, Conn., 1941-42; asst. chief adminstrv. div. VA, Pitts., 1946-49; instr., supr., prin. Dade County Pub. Schs., 1949-71, ret. 1971; supt. schs. Archdiocese Miami (Fla.), 1971—. Unit chmn. United Fund, 1971, 72; mem. Red Cross Planning Com., 1971, 72; mem. Fla. Youth Primary Com., 1972; mem. accreditation com. Fla. Cath. Conf. Served with AUS, 1942-46, 50; PTO. Mem. Fla. Edn. Assn., Internat. Reading Assn., Am. Assn. Sch. Adminstrs., Nat. Council Tchrs. Math., Central Assn. Math. and Sci. Tchrs., Nat. Assn. Secondary Sch. Prins., So. Assn. Colls. and Schs. (vis. com. accreditation), Cath. War Vets., Nat. Cath. Edn. Assn. K.C. (4 deg.). Editor: Post High School Tech. and Bus. Program, 1957. Home: 315 NE 111th St Miami FL 33161 Office: 6180 NE 4th Ct Miami FL 33137

LYND, JAMES PAUL, social worker; b. Ironton, O., Jan. 16, 1928; s. Ben H. and Frances (Schmitt) L.; student Rio Grande Coll., 1948-49, Cedarville Coll., 1949-51, Miami U. (Ohio), 1952; B.I.S., U. Mid-Fla., 1971; m. Lucille Randolph, July 20, 1956. Supr., Cal. Youth Authority, Norwalk, 1954-55; field counselor Ohio Juvenile Placement Bur., Dayton, 1955-59; supt. Butler County Juvenile Center, Hamilton, O., 1959-63, Orange County Juvenile-Parental Homes, Orlando, Fla., 1963—. Bd. dirs. Edgewood Boys Ranch, Gil-Lyn Guest Home, Drug Abuse Treatment Center. Served with USNR, 1945-46. Mem. Fla. (chpt. pres. 1965-66), Nat. councils on crime and delinquency, Nat. Juvenile Detention Assn. (sec.-treas. 1971-72), D.A.V. Lutheran. Mason (32 deg., Shriner). Club: Sertoma (dir. 1966-68). Address: 1718 E Michigan Av Orlando FL 32809

LYNE, JAMES COLEMAN, lawyer; b. Logan County, Ky., Aug. 7, 1908; s. Coleman Sanford III and Myrtle (Thomerson) L.; A.A., Bethel Coll., 1928; J.D., U. Ky., 1932; m. Lucy L. Linton, Nov. 10, 1936; children—June Carolyne, James Coleman; m. 2d, Lucille Nunn Forcum, June 17, 1961. Admitted to Ky. bar, 1933, since practiced in Russellville; mem. firm Felts & Lyne, 1935-37; atty. City of Russellville, 1943-48, Logan County, Russellville, 1948-57; atty. 7th jud. dist. Commonwealth of Ky., Russellville, 1962—; pres., dir. 1st Fed. Savs. & Loan Assn., Russellville, 1934—. Trustee Logan-Todd Bookmobile Commn.; chmn. bd. trustees Logan County Hosp. Mem. Am., Ky., Logan County bar assns., Tenn. Valley Golf Assn. (pres. 1959, 65), Phi Alpha Delta, Sigma Alpha Epsilon, Phi Mu Alpha. Democrat. Baptist. Kiwanian (pres Russellville 1963). Home: Daleview Circle Cloverland Russellville KY 42276 Office: First Federal Bldg Russellville KY 42276

LYNE, LEWIS FREDERICK, III, banker; b. Jersey City, Feb. 4, 1921; s. Lewis Frederick, Jr. and Roberta (Dillon) L.; B.A., Vanderbilt U., 1943; m. Caroline Reid, June 28, 1946; children—Rosalie, Roberta, Ann. Salesman, Equitable Securities Corp., Nashville, Dallas, 1945-50; S.W. regional mgr. municipal bond dept. Merrill, Lynch, Pierce, Fenner & Smith, Inc., Dallas, 1950-52; v.p., exec. v.p., mgr. municipal bond dept., Mercantile Nat. Bank, Dallas, 1952—; dir. So. Equitable Life Ins. Co., Little Rock. Mem. Dallas Assembly, 1964—. Served to lt. (j.g.) USNR, World War II. Mem. Vanderbilt U. Alumni Assn. (dir.), Sigma Chi. Episcopalian. Home: 4595 Rheims Pl Dallas TX 75205 Office: PO Box 5415 Dallas TX 75222

LYNHAM, JOHN MARMADUKE, lawyer, banker; b. Washington, Feb. 19, 1908; s. Edgar Hardwicke and Mera Elsie (Marmaduke) L.; B.S. in Govt., Am. U., 1935; J.D., George Washington U., 1931, LL.M., 1932; m. Adele Randolph Pugh, May 22, 1947; children—Adele Cameron (Mrs. Robert B. Shanks), John Marmaduke, Mary Hardwicke, Gale Randolph. Admitted to D.C. bar, 1931; Md. bar, 1953; mem. firm of Drury, Lynham & Powell (formerly Minor, Gatley & Drury), Washington, 1930-69; v.p., trust officer Nat. Savs. & Trust Co., Washington 1969-72. Bd. mgrs. Chevy Chase Village, 1963—, vice chmn., 1969—. Trustee Nat. U., 1947-54; trustee Landon Sch., 1966—, chmn. bd., 1967—; dir. Gunston Hall Sch., 1941-46; trustee Nat. Ballet Soc., 1969-72. Served from lt. (j.g.) to comdr., USNR, 1941-45. Fellow Am. Bar Found.; mem. Am. Bar Assn., Bar Assn. D.C., Am. Judicature Soc., Acad. Polit. Sci., Lawyers Club, The Barristers (pres. 1960), Inst. Jud. Adminstrn. Clubs: Chevy Chase (gov. 1949-55, 59-65, pres. 1954-55); Metropolitan (gov. 1968—, chmn. exec. com. 1971—), Nat. Lawyers (Washington). Author: The Chevy Chase Club—A History, 1958. Home: 14 Oxford St Chevy Chase Vilage MD 20015 Office: 719 15th St NW Washington DC 20005

LYNN, JOSEPH THOMAS, educator, physicist; b. Bell Buckle, Tenn., May 30, 1911; s. Joseph T. and Flora (Lynch) L.; A.B., Vanderbilt U., 1934; postgrad. U. Va., 1937-38; M.S., Ohio State U., 1940; m. Aileen Ingram, June 15, 1933; 1 dau., Elizabeth Lynn (Mrs. Rueben Y. Leonard). Instr. physics dept. N.C. State U., 1942-45, asst. prof., 1945-56, asso. prof., 1956-65, prof., grad. adminstr., 1965—, acting head, 1962-63, 64-65. Mem. Am. Assn. Physics Tchrs., A.A.A.S., Phi Beta Kappa (pres. Wake County assn. 1961-62). Home: 400 Lake Boone Trail Raleigh NC 27608

LYNN, MELVYN STUART, mathematician; b. London, Eng., July 7, 1937; s. Richard and Julie (Shavick) L.; B.A., Oxford U., 1958, M.A., 1964; M.A., U. Cal. at Los Angeles, 1960, Ph.D., 1962; m. Barbara Berkson, Aug. 26, 1960; children—Monica Georgette, Anthea Suzanne, Matthew David. Open exhibitioner Merton Coll., Eng., 1955-58; research asst. numerical analysis research, U. Cal. at Los Angeles, 1959-62; research fellow Nat. Phys. Lab., Teddington, Eng., 1962-63, sr. sci. officer, 1963-64; staff mem. IBM, Los Angeles Sci. Center, 1964-65, mgr. math. dept. Houston Sci. Center, 1965-66, mgr. research dept., 1966-67, mgr. center, 1967-71; prof. math. scis., dir. Inst. for Computer Services and Affiliations, Rice U., Houston, 1971—. Mem. Assn. for Computing Machinery (editor in chief Communications of the ACM, chmn. editorial com.), Soc. Indsl. and Applied Math. Contbr. articles to profl. jours. Home: 931 Magdalene St Houston TX 77024 Office: Rice Univ Houston TX 77001

LYNN, ROBERT DEWESE, headmaster; b. Brighton, Tenn., Oct. 20, 1913; s. Lucius Ross and Edith Lenora (DeWese) L.; A.B., Presbyn. Coll., 1934; M.S. in Social Work, Coll. William and Mary, 1935; M.A., Memphis State U., 1961, Ed.D., 1968; m. Evelyn McDowell, June 28, 1941; children—Sara Frances, Robert DeWese, Elizabeth Jane. Athletic dir. Dublin (Ga.) High Sch., 1935-43; instr. econs. Presbyn. Coll., Clinton, S.C., 1943-45; field sec. Pi Kappa Alpha frat., Atlanta, 1945-46, exec. sec., Memphis, 1946-59; headmaster The Hutchison Sch., Memphis, 1959—. Adminstr. Nat. Chpt. House Loan Fund; exec. v.p. Pi Kappa Alpha Meml. Found., 1948-59, chmn. scholarship com., 1960—. Mem. Coll. Frat. Secs. Assn. (pres.), Coll. Frat. Editors Assn. (pres.), Memphis Assn. Ind. Schs. (pres.), Nat. Assn. Prins. Schs. for Girls, Nat. Interfrat. Conf. (exec. com. 1962—, pres. 1970—), So. (exec. com. 1963—, pres. 1965-66), Mid-South (pres. 1969-70, exec. com. 1965—) assns. ind. schs., Am. Assn. Sch. Adminstrs., Newcomen Soc. N.Am., Blue Key. Presbyn. (elder; lectr. Men's Bible Class). Clubs: Kiwanis, Rivermont (dir.), University, Executive. Editor Shield and Diamond mag., 1949—. Home: 1738 Ridgeway Rd Memphis TN 38138 Office: 1740 Ridgeway Rd Memphis TN 38138

LYNN, ROSS MCCAIN, headmaster; b. Jacksonville, Fla., Apr. 1, 1911; s. Lucius Ross and Edith (DeWese) L.; A.B., Presbyn. Coll., 1931, LL.D., 1952; M.A., U. N.C., 1948; m. Halcyon Roach, July 20, 1960; stepsons—Richard Charlton Moore, Jr., Thurston Roach Moore. Tchr., coach Dublin (Ga.) High Sch., 1931-32; tchr., coach Darlington Sch., Rome, Ga., 1932-41, tchr., dean, 1946-51; headmaster Presbyn. Day Sch., Memphis, 1951-55, Memphis U. Sch., 1955—. Trustee William R. Moore Sch.; bd. dirs. Ednl. Records Bur.; sec. bd. Memphis U. Sch. Served from 2d lt. to lt. col. USAAF, 1942-46. Decorated Bronze Star. Mem. Memphis, So., Mid-South assns. ind. schs., Tenn. Edn. Assn., N.E.A., Nat. Assn. Secondary Sch. Prins., Nat. Assn. Ind. Schs. (dir.), Country Day Sch. Headmasters Assn., Mil. Order World Wars, Am. Legion, Blue Key, Pi Kappa Alpha. Presbyn. (elder). Clubs: University, Memphis Country (Memphis). Home: 1288 Ridgeway Rd Memphis TN 38138 Office: 6191 Park Rd Memphis TN 38138

LYNN, SHERWOOD CHANG, physician; b. Anju, Korea, Oct. 4, 1904 (came to U.S. 1921, naturalized 1954); s. Dong Shang and En Sang (Park) C.; B.A., U. Dubuque (Ia.), 1930; M.D., Emory U., 1935; m. Martha Owen Hood, Aug. 25, 1931 (dec. Aug. 1970); children—Jennie (Mrs. John Watts Jamison), Mary (Mrs. Laurence George Jenewein), Sherwood Chang, Leigh (Mrs. Jimmie Edward McClendon). Intern Quincy (Mass.) City Hosp., 1936; resident Norfolk County Hosp., South Braintree, Mass., 1937-38; practice medicine, specializing in family practice, Savannah, Ga., 1939-55, Houston, 1957—. Hon. pres. Korean-Am. Friendship Assn. Houston, 1961-70, pres., 1970—; pres. Korean Sunday Sch., South Main Baptist Ch., Houston, 1969—. Mem. Tex. Med. Assn. Presbyn. Mem. Slavonic Benevolent Order State Tex. (supreme lodge). Home: 4502 University Oaks Blvd Houston TX 77004 Office: 5515 Griggs Rd Houston TX 77021

LYNN, WILLIAM JOSEPH, basketball coach; b. Cullman, Ala., Aug. 24, 1924; s. Luther A. and Florence (Mann) L.; grad. St. Bernard Jr. Coll., 1948; B.S., Auburn U., 1950; m. Martha Rudisal Hawthrone, Dec. 22, 1951; children—Martha Ann, William Joseph, Katherine,

Jenifer, David. Freshman basketball coach Auburn (Ala.) U., 1950-56, asst. coach, 1956-62, head coach, 1962—; partner Furniture Mart, Auburn. Served with USNR, 1944-46. Mem. Sigma Pi. Methodist (steward). Elk. Home: 553 Cary Dr Auburn AL 36830

LYNNE, SEYBOURN HARRIS, judge; b. Decatur, Ala., July 25, 1907; s. Seybourn Arthur and Annie Leigh (Harris) L.; B.S., Ala. Poly. Inst., 1927; LL.B., U. Ala., 1930; m. Katherine Donaldson Brandau, June 16, 1937; 1 dau., Katherine Roberta. Admitted to Ala. bar, 1930; practiced Decatur, 1930-34; judge Morgan (Ala.) County Ct., 1934-41; judge 8th Jud. Circuit of Ala., 1941-42; judge U.S. Dist. Ct., No. Dist. Ala., 1946—, chief judge, 1953—; dist. judge rep. Jud. Conf. U.S., 5th circuit, 1958-60. Served as lt. col., Judge Advocate Gen. Dept., AUS, 1942-46. Decorated Bronze Star. Mem. Ala. State Bar, Am. Bar Assn., Blue Key, Scabbard and Blade, Pi Kappa Alpha, Phi Kappa Phi, Phi Delta Phi, Omicron Delta Kappa. Democrat. Baptist. Kiwanian (dist. gov. 1938). Club: Birmingham Country. Home: 3323 Briarcliff Rd Birmingham AL 35223 Office: Federal Bldg Birmingham AL 35203

LYNSKEY, WILLIAM WALLACE, corp. exec.; b. Huntsville, Ala., Jan. 20, 1927; s. Randall William and Katherine (Drake) L.; student U. Chattanooga, 1946-47, Ga. Inst. Tech., 1948-49; m. Ruby Thompson, Mar. 14, 1956; children—Mark Edward, William David, Theresa Anne, Christopher Paul, Timothy Joseph. Teller, The Hamilton Nat. Bank, Chattanooga, 1950; salesman Vance Iron & Steel Co., 1951; purchasing agt. Chattanooga Boiler & Tank Co., 1952-67; pres. Threadco, Inc., 1962—, Tenn. Machine Works, 1967—. Served with USNR, 1945-46. Mem. Nat. Rifle Assn., Pi Kappa Alpha. Roman Catholic. Clubs: Chattanooga Yacht, Loret Yacht (dir.) (Chattanooga). Home: Bayshore Dr Harrison TN 37341 Office: Latta St PO Box 8035 Chattanooga TN 37411

LYON, HENRY LOUIS, JR., clergyman; b. Tuscaloosa, Ala., Aug. 1, 1907; s. Henry L. and Dorothy (Lucius) L.; A.B., Samford U., 1930, D.D. (hon.), 1948; Th.M., So. Bapt. Theol. Sem., 1932; LL.D., U. Ala., 1964; m. Louise Jackson, Dec. 23, 1929; 1 son, Henry Louis III. Ordained to ministry Bapt. Ch., 1929; pastor Powderly Bapt. Ch., Birmingham, Ala., 1932-38, 66th St. Bapt. Ch., Birmingham, 1938-43, Highland Av. Bapt. Ch., Montgomery, Ala., 1946—. Pres., Ala. Bapt. Conv., 1955-56; mem. home bd. missions So. Bapt. Conv., 1950-56, mem. relief and annuity bd., 1963-69. Mem. Ala. Textbook Com., 1966—. Bd. dirs. Montgomery Bapt. Hosp. Served to capt. USAAF, 1943-46. Recipient Cross of Mil. Service U.D.C., 1959. Mem. S.C.V., S.A.R., Kappa Phi Kappa. Mason (32 deg., K.T., Shriner). Club: Exchange (pres. 1954). Home: 2606 Oxford Dr Montgomery AL 36111 Office: 1931 Highland Av Montgomery AL 36111

LYON, ROWLAND, art curator, artist; b. Washington, July 16, 1904; s. Gideon Allen and Florence (Russell) L.; grad. Pa. Acad. Art, 1925, Corcoran Sch. Art, 1926, Cape Cod Sch. Art, 1939; A.B., George Washington U., 1929, M.A., 1932; m. Mary Frances Fort, July 14, 1938. Instr. art George Washington U., 1936-38; artist Evening Star, Washington, 1938-42; color specialist map div. Dept. State, Washington, 1942-49; cataloger, draftsman map div. CIA, Washington, 1949-50; cartographer, environmental protection sect. Q.M. Gen., U.S. Army, Washington, 1950-51; curator art Smithsonian Instn., Washington, 1951—. Exhibited group shows Corcoran Art Gallery, Washington, Arthur U. Newton Galleries, N.Y.C., Arnot Art Gallery, Elmira, N.Y., Washington Art Club, Nat. Collection Fine Arts, Washington, Madrid, Bilbao, Barcelona, Seville, Valencia, Spain, Genoa, Italy, Athens, Greece; collections Arts Club, Washington, also pvt. collections. Recipient prizes Soc. Ind. Artists, 1933, Fedn. Women's Clubs, 1934, W. & J. Sloane Purchase prize, 1935, Landscape Club Washington, 1937, 45, 47, Harper's Ferry Art Show, 1955, others. Mem. Washington Water Color Assn. (past pres.), Soc. Washington Artists (prizes 1935, 42, 43, 44), Washington Printmakers, Artists Guild Washington, Washington Arts Club, Landscape Club Washington, Sigma Nu. Club: Pyramid (Washington). Home: 3835 S St Washington DC 20007 Office: Smithsonian Instn Washington DC 20560

LYONS, LOUISE BOOTH (MRS. DWIGHT K. LYONS), educator; b. Johnson City, Tenn., Mar. 17, 1932; d. Alvin Robert and Pearl (Deakins) Booth; B.S., E. Tenn. State U., 1952; M.A., 1955; specialist in edn. degree, U. Ky., 1966, postgrad., 1967—; m. Dwight K. Lyons, Aug. 15, 1959. Tchr. elementary schs. Washington County, Tenn., 1952-54, Kingsport, Tenn., 1954-57, Brevard County, Fla., 1957-58; elementary supervising tchr. demonstration sch. Appalachian State Tchr. Coll., Boone, N.C., 1958-59; elementary tchr., librarian Jefferson County, Ky., 1959-61; coordinator instructional media, asst. prof. library sci. Eastern Ky. U., Richmond, 1961-69; instructional media specialist, asst. prof. edn. U. Louisville, 1969—. Pres., Richmond Bus. and Profl. Women's Club, 1963-64; chmn. Am. home dept. Richmond Woman's Club, 1963-64; mem. Woman's Club Central Ky., Lexington, 1965-69; sec. Saturday Matinee Musical Richmond, 1965-67. Mem. Ky. Audio-Visual Assn. (treas.), Ky. Edn. Assn., N.E.A., Ky. Library Assn., A.L.A., Ky. Assn. Sch. Librarians, Nat. Assn. Ednl. Broadcasters, Am. Assn. Sch. Librarians, Assn. Ednl. Communications and Tech., Assn. Higher Edn., Speed Art Museum, Ky. Col., Pi Tau Chi, Kappa Delta Pi. Mem. Order Eastern Star. Baptist. Home: The 800 800 S 4th St Louisville KY 40203

LYONS, PHILLIP MITCHELL, ins. exec., real estate broker; b. Gueydan, La., Nov. 22, 1941; s. Joseph Bosman and Elder (Richard) L.; student McNeese State Coll., 1959-62, Alvin Jr. Coll., 1964; m. Wynona Faye Meyers, Apr. 28, 1962; children—Phillip M., Wilton J. Adminstrv. trainee Am. Nat. Ins. Co., Galveston, Tex., 1965, asst. mgr., acting mgr. policy issue dept., 1966-67, mgr., 1967—, systems analyst, 1971-72, div. mgr., policyholders service div., 1972—; partner Lyons Real Estate, Sulphur, La., 1966—. Solicitor, United Fund, 1966-69. Mem. Jr. C. of C. (dir. 1972, state dir. 1972-73). Elk. Club: Neuman. Home: 1602 Bayou Shore Galveston TX 77550 also 1012 S Stanford St Sulphur LA 70663 Office: 1 Moody Plaza Galveston TX 77550 also 1339 Cypress St Sulphur LA

LYONS, THOMAS WILLIAM, clergyman; b. Washington, Sept. 26, 1923; s. Thomas William and Nora (Bagley) L.; student St. Charles Coll., 1937-43; A.B., St. Mary's Sem., Balt., 1945, S.T.B., 1946, postgrad. 1946-48. Ordained priest Roman Catholic Ch., 1948; served at St. John the Evangelist Ch., Silver Spring, Md., 1948-49, St. Matthew's Cathedral, Washington, 1949-53; dir. Mackin High Sch., Washington, 1953-57; asst. dir. edn. archdiocese Washington, 1954-64, dir., 1964—; pastor St. Francis de Sales Ch., Washington, 1963-66, St. Thomas Apostle Ch., Washington, 1966—. Chmn. Archdiocesan Commn. on Sacred Music, 1966-71. Mem. Nat. Cath. Ednl. Assn. (v.p. 1965-69), Assn. Cath. Sch. Supts. (chmn. 1968-70). Home: 2665 Woodley Rd NW Washington 20008 Office: 1200 17th St NW Washington 20036

LYSTAD, ROBERT ARTHUR, educator; b. Milw., Aug. 10, 1920; s. Arthur Frederick and Lulu (Lunde) L.; B.A., U. Wis., 1941; B.D., Drew Theol. Sem., 1944; Ph.D., Northwestern U., 1951; m. Mary Agnes Hanemann, June 21, 1953; children—Lisa Douglass, Anne Hanemann, Mary Lunde, Robert Douglass, James Hanemann. Ordained to ministry Meth. Ch., 1945; minister Meth. Chs., Columbus, O., 1944-47. also Millersport, O.; prof. anthropology Tulane U., New Orleans, 1951-61; prof. African studies, Sch. Advanced Internat. Studies, Johns Hopkins U., Washington, 1961—. Author: The Ashanti: A Proud People, 1958; The African World: A Survey of Social Research, 1965. Home: 4900 Scarsdale Rd Washington DC 20016 Office: 1740 Massachusetts Av NW Washington DC 20036

LYTLE, ROY COBB, lawyer; b. Pitts., Oct. 18, 1902; s. Louis Edward and Emma Elizabeth (Cobb) L.; A.B., Cornell U., 1924; J.D., Harvard, 1927; m. Virginia Baugh, Oct. 12, 1927; children—Camilla (Mrs. Alex P. Aven), Margaret (Mrs. John A. Griner III); m. 2d, Joanne Harper, May 16, 1966. Admitted to Okla. bar, 1927, since practiced in Oklahoma City; mem. firm Lytle, Soule & Emery, 1927—; counsel Better Bus. Bur., 1930—; prof. emeritus Okla. U. Sch. Medicine. Chmn. bd. Va. Blue Ridge Ry., Lynchburg; dir. City Nat. Bank & Trust Co., Oklahoma City, Swanson's Tire Co., Governair Corp. Past pres. Greater Oklahoma City United Appeal; mem. adv. com. St. Anthony Hosp. Mem. A.M.A. (affiliate), Okla. Med. Hall of Fame, Okla. Bar Assn., Am. Law Inst., Am. Judicature Soc., Phi Beta Kappa, Phi Kappa Phi, Alpha Tau Omega. Republican. Episcopalian. Mason(32 degree). Clubs: Oklahoma City Country, Beacon. Home: 6806 NW Grand Blvd Oklahoma City OK 73116 Office: 2210 First Nat Center Oklahoma City OK 73102

MAAS, ROY WALTER, engring. co. exec.; b. Utica, Mich., Nov. 12, 1931; s. Walter C. and Eleanor (Pruchs) M.; B.C.E., Valparaiso U., 1955; postgrad. U. Louisville, 1971—; m. Barbara Jean Strombeck, June 4, 1955; children—David, Caron, Roger. Field engr. J. S. Watkins Cons. Engrs., Valparaiso, Ind., 1955-56, design engr., Lansing, Mich., 1958, Charleston, W.Va., 1958-62, Ind. Dept. Hwys., Indpls., 1962-63; v.p. Watkins & Assos. Inc., Cons. Engrs., Louisville, 1963—, dir., 1968—. Served to lt. USNR, 1956-57. Registered profl. engr., Ill., Ind., Ky., W.Va., Va. Mem. Am. Soc. C.E.'s, Nat. Soc. Profl. Engrs., Am. Road Bldrs. Assn., Am. R.R. Engrs. Assn., Am. Water Works Assn., Ky. C. of C. Lutheran (pres. ch. council 1970-71). Home: 9813 Longwood Circle Anchorage KY 40223 Office: PO Box 1284 Louisville KY 40201

MABRY, NELLOISE JOHNSON, educator; b. Valdosta, Ga., Sept. 8, 1921; d. Hansford Duncan and Maudelle (Williams) Johnson; student Bethel Woman's Coll., 1938-39, Wesleyan Conservatory, 1941; A.B., Mercer U., 1943, M.Ed., 1949; m. William Herbert Mabry, Mar. 5, 1942 (div. Nov. 1947); 1 son, William Herbert. Tchr., Cynthia H. Weir Elementary Sch., Macon, Ga., 1950—. Mem. Nat., Ga., Bibb edn. assns., Ga. Assn. for Childhood Edn. (pres. 1964-66), Delta Kappa Gamma (chpt. scrapbook chmn. 1966-68), Am. Assn. U. Women, Alpha Delta Pi, Alpha Psi Omega. Democrat. Baptist. Home: 1575 Adams St Macon GA 31204

MACAGY, DOUGLAS GUERNSEY, arts adminstr.; b. Winnipeg, Man., Can., July 8, 1913; s. Douglas Drillio and Elisabeth (Guernsey) MacA.; student U. Toronto, 1933-35, Barnes Found., Merion, Pa., 1936-39; U. Pa., 1938-39; A.B., Western Res. U., 1940; m. Jermayne Smart, Mar. 24, 1941 (div. Dec. 1954); m. 2d, Elizabeth Tillett, Feb. 19, 1955; children—Ian Douglas, Caitlin Elisabeth. Came to U.S., 1936. Asst. ednl. dept. Cleve. Museum Art, 1939, asst. painting dept., 1940-41; curator San Francisco Museum Art, 1941-43; chief Japan sect. Propaganda div. FarEast Bur. Office War Information, 1943-45; dir. Cal. Sch. Fine Arts, 1945-50; v.p. Orbit Films, Seattle, 1950-51; exec. sec. N.Y. Museums Commn. UNESCO, 1951-52; spl. cons. to dir. Museum Modern Art, N.Y.C., 1953-56; dir. research Wildenstein & Co. Inc., N.Y.C., 1956-59; dir. Dallas Museum Contemporary Arts, 1959-63; cons., 1963-68; dep. chmn. Nat. Endowment Arts, Nat. Council Arts, Washington, 1968—, acting chmn., 1969; dir. exhbns. Joseph H. Hirshhorn Mus., Washington, 1971—. Mem. Am. Soc. Aesthetics (trustee 1946-48), Coll. Art Assn., Am. Assn. Museums. Club: Players (N.Y.C.). Author: The Museum Looks in on TV, 1956; (with Elizabeth MacAgy) Going for a Walk with a Line, 1959; Art that Broke the Looking Glass, 1961. Contbr. articles to art jours. Home: 3309 35th St NW Washington DC 20016 Office: 1000 Jefferson Dr SW Washington DC 20560

MACALUSO, CHARLES ANTHONY, environmental products co. exec.; b. Paterson, N.J., Sept. 1, 1928; s. Vincent J. and Virginia (Pasqualletti) M.; M.E., Stevens Inst. Tech., 1950, M.S., 1958; m. Arlene DeYoung, Jan. 26, 1952; children—Steven C., Nancy L., Marc D. Chief engr. Worthington Corp., capital goods machinery products, Harrison, N.J., 1950-63; mgr. advanced product planning, Buffalo, N.Y., 1963-68; v.p. corporate devel. Ecological Sci. Corp., environmental products and services, Miami, Fla., 1969—; dir. Western Supply Co., Tulsa, Pritchard-ECO, Inc., Tulsa, Adache Assos., Inc., Cleve., Dyna Tech., Inc., Sioux City, Ia. Dir., sec. Episcopal Charities of Western N.Y., 1966-68. Served with Ordnance Corps, AUS, 1951-53. Registered profl. engr., N.J., Fla. Mem. Am. Soc. M.E. (bd. chmn. Turbomachinery Inst. 1970—), Tau Beta Pi. Episcopalian (lay reader 1960-68). Patentee in field. Home: 7450 N W 7th Court Plantation FL 33313 Office: 20215 NW 2d Av Miami FL 33169

MACARTHUR, ALLEN GRANT, banker; b. Detroit, Aug. 2, 1939; s. Alexander Grant and Corrinne Ann (Mellon) MacA.; student Provincial Inst. Mining, 1955-57; A.A., St. Petersburg Jr. Coll., 1962; B.S. in Bus. Adminstrn., Fla. State U., 1965; m. Mary Paula Karlavage, Nov. 29, 1969; children—Allen Joseph, Ann Marie, John Allen. Nat. bank examiner Tallahassee, Fla., 1965-68; exec. v.p. Southeast Nat. Bank, Dunedin, Fla., 1968, pres., 1968—; Plasti-Craft Corp., Dunedin, Fla. Bd. dirs. Anclote Psychiat. Centre, Tarpon Springs, Fla. Mem. Dunedin C. of C. (dir. 1971—), Delta Sigma Pi. Presbyn. Home: 2307 Jones Ct Dunedin FL 33528 Office: 2494 Bayshore Blvd Dunedin FL 33528

MACARTHUR, DIANA TAYLOR, public affairs cons.; b. Santa Fe, July 7, 1933; d. Antonio J. and Elizabeth (Steele) Taylor; B.A., Vassar Coll., 1955; student U. Geneva, 1953-54; children by previous marriage —Elizabeth, Alexander; m. 2d, Donald Malcolm MacArthur, Mar. 31, 1962. Cons. economist Checchi & Co., Washington, 1957-61; v.p., dir. Washington office Thomas J. Deegan Co., 1961-62; dep. chief West Africa, Peace Corps, 1963, regional program officer North Africa, Near East, South Asia, 1964, dir. div. pvt. and internat. orgns., 1965-66; coordinator Nat. Youth Conf. on Natural Beauty and Conservation, 1966-68; self-employed cons. pub. affairs to corps., assns., Washington, 1968—. Mem. citizens adv. bd. Pres.'s Council on Youth Opportunity, 1968-69; adviser Youth Orgns. United, 1968—. Bd. dirs. African Student Aid Fund of Phelps Stokes Fund, 1971—; trustee Menninger Found., 1972—. Mem. Phi Beta Kappa. Home: 5313 Albemarle St NW Washington DC 20016

MACARTHUR, DONALD MALCOLM, water pollution control exec.; b. Detroit, Jan. 7, 1931; s. Donald J. and Margaret (MacAuley) MacA.; B.Sc. with honors, St. Andrews (Scotland) U., 1954; Ph.D., Edinburgh (Scotland) U., 1957; m. Diana Taylor, Mar. 31, 1962; children—Elizabeth, Alexander. Mem. faculty U. Conn., 1957-58; mgr. research center Melpar Inc., subsidiary Westinghouse Air Brake Co., 1958-66; dep. dir. research and tech. Office Sec. Def., 1966-70; pres. Enviro Control, Inc., Washington, 1970—; cons. water pollution Dept. Interior. Fellow Am. Inst. Chemists; mem. Am. Chem. Soc., A.A.A.S., Am. Water Works Assn., N.Y. Acad. Scis. Author tech. articles. Home: 5313 Albemarle St Washington DC 20016

MACARTHUR, HARRY, theatrical editor Washington Star. Address: 225 Virginia Av SE Washington DC 20003*

MACAULAY, ANGUS HAMILTON, lawyer; b. Spartanburg, S.C., Apr. 1, 1928; s. Angus H. and Margaret (White) M.; A.B., The Citadel, 1950; LL.B., Yale, 1955; m. Amanda C. Tevepaugh, May 12, 1962; children—Angus H., Alexander M., Katherine. Admitted to S.C. bar, 1955, Va. bar, 1956, since practiced in Richmond, Va.; mem. firm Mays, Valentine, Davenport & Moore, 1961—. Dir. Colonial Life & Accident Ins. Co., Columbia, S.C. Mem. Richmond Air Pollution Control Bd., 1965—; pres. Richmond Community Action Program, 1969-70. Mem. Richmond 3d Dist. and State Central Democratic Coms. Trustee Richmond Forward, 1965-70; bd. dirs. United Givers Fund, Marymont Found. Served with AUS, 1946-47, to 1st lt., 1951-53. Mem. Am. (exec. council jr. bar conf. 1960-62), Va. (chmn. young lawyers sect. 1959-60, chmn. joint com. pub. information 1966-68), Richmond bar assns. Presbyn. Club: Downtown (Richmond). Home: 502 Henri Rd Richmond VA 23226 Office: Ross Bldg Richmond VA 23219

MACAULAY, NEILL WEBSTER, JR., educator; b. Columbia, S.C., Apr. 10, 1935; s. Neill Webster and Eliza Singleton (Barron) M.; A.B., Citadel, 1956; M.A., U. S.C., 1962; Ph.D., U. Tex., 1965; m. Nancy Jane Copenhaver, Aug. 15, 1958; children—Charles Stuart, Robert Bruce, James Douglas. Planter, exporter Finca Nancy Plantation, San Cristobal, Cuba, 1959-60; asst. prof. history U. Fla. at Gainesville, 1964-69, asso. prof., 1969—. Guest lectr. U.S. Mil. Acad., 1970, Armed Forces Staff Coll., Norfolk, Va., 1970, Nat. War Coll., Washington, 1972. Bd. mgrs. U. Fla. Press, 1968—. Served with inf. AUS, 1956-58, to 1st lt. Cuban Rebel Army, 1958-59. Ford Found. Postdoctoral fellow, 1964-66, Nat Endowment for Humanities fellow, 1972-73. Mem. Phi Beta Kappa. Republican. Author: The Sandino Affair, 1967; A Rebel in Cuba, 1970. Home: RFD 1 Box 212 Micanopy FL 32667 Office: History Dept U Fla Gainesville FL 32601

MACBRIDE, DEXTER DUPONT, assn. exec.; b. Elizabeth, N.J., Aug. 18, 1917; s. Charles Munnerlyn and Flora T. (Jerome) MacB.; student William & Mary Coll., 1936-37; LL.B., Cumberland U., 1938; m. Grace Anderson, Dec. 23, 1963; 1 son, Charles Dexter. Admitted to Va. bar, 1939; practiced in Norfolk, 1939-41; sr. right of way agt. City of Los Angeles, 1946-47; supervising right of way agt. State of Cal., Sacramento, 1948-63, asst. chief right of way agt., 1963-70; exec. v.p. Am. Soc. Appraisers, Washington, 1970—. Mem. Pub. Relation Round Table Sacramento, Am. Right of Way Assn. (nat. sec.; exec. com., sr. mem.), Am. Arbitration Assn. (nat. panel arbitrators), Am. Soc. Pub. Adminstrs., Audubon Soc., Am. Soc. Assn. Execs., Am. Soc. Appraisers. Club: Commonwealth. Author: Power and Process. Editor: Valuation Quar. Home: 1668 Chimney House Rd Reston VA 22070 Office: Dulles Internat Airport PO Box 17265 Washington DC 20036

MACCALLUM, THOMAS ADRIAN, journalist; b. Plainfield, N.J., Oct. 14, 1939; s. Thomas E. and Mildred (Bergen) MacC.; student Wilmington Coll., 1957-59. Reporter, Star-News Newspapers, Inc., Wilmington, N.C., 1960-61, city editor, 1965-69; editor Hanover Sun, weekly, Wilmington, 1969-71, Cheraw (S.C.) Chronicle, 1971—. Served with AUS, 1962-65. Unitarian. Mailing Address: 114 Front St Cheraw SC 29520 Home: 38 Janice Circle Cheraw SC 29520 Office: Cheraw Chronicle Cheraw SC 29520

MACCART, VIRGINIA RAHM (MRS. RAYMOND D. MACCART), club woman; b. Pitts., May 18, 1887; d. Edward and Maude (MacDonald) Rahm; student pvt. schs.; m. Raymond D. MacCart, Oct. 1, 1919. Mem. Permanent Com. Prevention Juvenile Delinquency N.Y., 1955—; hon. life regent D.A.R., 1950—; nat. rec. sec. gen. Nat. Soc. New Eng. Women, 1942-45; hon. pres. gen. Nat. Soc. Daus. Union 1861-1865, 1951-54; hon. 1st v.p. gen. Colonial Dames of 17th Century, 1953; pres. Nat. Soc. Congress of States Soc., Inc., N.Y., 1949-62. Recipient medal for war work Nat. Soc. New Eng. Women, 1945; Mary Mildred Sullivan award Lincoln Meml. U., 1953. Mem. Daus. Am. Colonists, Colonial Dames Vt. Soc., Pa. Huguenot Soc., Pa., N.Y. hist. socs., Gen. Fedn. Women's Clubs, Washington Philatelic Soc., English-Speaking Union, Nat. Soc. Patriotic Women (nat. chaplain), Daus. Pa. in N.Y., N.Y. Bible Soc., Salvation Army Aux. (stamp chmn.), Nat. Am. philatelic socs., Bur. Specialist Stamp Assn., First Day Cover Soc. Republican. Lutheran. Clubs: Political Study, Woman's Washington City, Washington, Capitol Hill (Washington); Past Regents (N.Y.); Navy Wives; Stamp Collector's (Boston); Wilson (N.Y.) Yacht. Home: 4301 Massachusetts Av NW Washington DC 20016 also 201 N Riverside Dr Pompano Beach FL 33062

MACCLENAHAN, GEORGES ALBERT, French diplomat; b. Paris, France, Aug. 12, 1914; s. Georges and Camille Lentz (de Villaine) MacC.; grad. Ecole Nationale de la France, d'Outremer; m. Monique Durand, Sept. 5, 1951; children—Georges E., Florence Villemot, Patrick A. Adminstr. for French Overseas Tys., Oubangui-Chari, 1946-49, Ivory Coast, 1957-60; consul in Kenya, 1951-56, Lagos, Nigeria, 1960; col. Suez Expdn., 1956; 1960; counsellor French embassy, Rio de Janeiro, 1961-66; consul gen., Houston, 1967—. Served with French Army, 1939-45. Decorated Officer Legion of Honor, French War Cross with bars, Colonial medal. Home: 5695 Longmont St Houston TX 77007 also 1 Rue de Villersexal Paris VII France Office: Esperson Bldg Houston TX 77002

MACCONNELL, JAMES HAMILTON, clergyman; b. Athens, Pa., Dec. 19, 1912; s. James H. and Frances (Baker) MacC.; B.A., U. of South, 1936; B.D., St. Luke's Sem., Sewanee, Tenn., 1939; A.C.P., Coll. of Preceptors, London, 1958; M.Ed., Loyola U., New Orleans, 1967; m. Elizabeth Lay Eastwood, Nov. 25, 1940; children—Mary Frances (Mrs. William J. Ferry), James Hamilton, Sean Michael. Ordained to ministry Protestant Episcopal Ch. as deacon, 1939, priest, 1940; with Owego Asso. Missions, N.Y., 1939-42; rector St. James', Leesburg, Fla., 1942-45, St. Paul's, Key West, Fla., 1945-50; vicar St. Philip's, Matthewtown, Inagua, Bahamas, 1953-59; prin. W. India Chems. Sch., Inagua, 1956-59; headmaster St. Michael's Sch., Savannah, Ga., 1960-63; rector St. Michael's, Chickasaw, Ala., 1963-65; prin. All Saints Sch., St. Thomas, V.I., 1965-67; diocesan missionary in charge St. Ursula's, St. John's Island, V.I., 1967-69; canon All Saints Cathedral, St. Thomas, 1969—; vicar St. Andrew's Ch., St. Thomas, 1971—. Instnl. chaplain St. Thomas; ecumenical chmn. Diocese V.I.; exec. com. Inter-Faith Commn., St. Thomas. Mem. dist. bd. Fla. Welfare Bd., 1946-50, chmn., 1947-49. Mem. Nat. Assn. Secondary Sch. Prins., Alpha Psi Omega, Kappa Delta Pi. Address: PO Box 777 St Thomas VI 00801

MACDONALD, GWENDOLINE, nurse educator; b. Brockville, Ont., Can.; d. Stanley Abott and Mary (Nute) MacDonald; came to U.S., 1923, naturalized, 1941; diploma Monmouth Meml. Hosp. Sch. Nursing, 1943; B.S., Syracuse U., 1950; M.A., Columbia U. Tchrs. Coll., 1958; Ed.D., 1964. Staff nurse, head nurse, White Plains and Syracuse, N.Y., 1946-50; dep. chief nurse, then chief nurse A.R.C.

Blood Program, Washington, also Balt., 1950-53; pub. health nurse, supr. Pub. Health Dept., Norfolk, Va., 1953-55; instr. Vassar Sch. Nursing, Poughkeepsie, N.Y., 1955-57; asst. dir. dept. diploma and asso. degree programs Nat. League for Nursing, N.Y.C., 1958-61, project dir. dept. baccalaureate and higher degree programs, 1961-64; prof., dir. Sch. Nursing, Mich. State U., East Lansing, 1964-70; dean Sch. Nursing, U. Miami, Coral Gables, Fla., 1970—. Ednl. cons. to collegiate schs. nursing; condr. survey nursing schs. and hosps. Sisters of Mercy, Detroit Province, 1964; mem. com. on health professions to asst. sec. for health and sci. affairs Dept. Health, Edn. and Welfare, 1970—; mem. nat. citizens com. WHO, 1958—; fund raiser Mental Health Assn., 1961-64; mem. profl. adv. com. various health and welfare orgns. Bd. dirs. Dade County Vis. Nurse Assn. Mem. Am., Mich., Fla. nurses assns., Adult Edn. Assn., Am. Pub. Health Assn., Assn. for Higher Edn., Nat. League for Nursing (pres. 1969-71), Alumni Assn. Syracuse U., Am. Ednl. Research Assn., Columbia U. Tchrs Coll. Nursing Edn. Alumni Assn. (pres. 1972—), Pi Lambda Theta, Kappa Delta Pi. Club: Zonta. Author: The Development of Standards and Accreditation in Collegiate Nursing Education, 1965. Contbr. articles and reports to profl. lit. Office: School of Nursing U Miami Box 875 Biscayne Annex Miami FL 33152

MACDONALD, L(ELAND) LLOYD, lawyer; b. Marfa, Tex., July 19, 1931; s. John E. and Myrtle (Barnett) MacD.; B.B.A., Baylor U., 1952, LL.B., 1957; m. Juanice Koen, Nov. 22, 1958; children—David Allen, Kathryn Ann. Tchr. pub. sch., San Antonio, 1954-55; admitted to Tex. bar, 1957; title analyst Shell Oil Co., Midland, Tex., 1957-60; practiced law, Midland, 1960—; mem. firm L.L. MacDonald, 1960-64, Kerr, Fitz-Gerald & Kerr, 1964—. Mem. youth council YMCA, 1963-64; chmn. adv. bd. Salvation Army, 1969-72. Served to 1st lt. 1952-54 Mem. Midland County Bar Assn. (v.p. 1964), State Bar Tex., Baylor Law Alumni Assn. (dir. 1967-69). Baptist. Mason, Rotarian (dir. 1969-71, v.p. 1972). Home: 1515 Community Lane Midland TX 79701 Office: Midland Tower Midland TX 79701

MACDONALD, THOMAS COOK, JR., lawyer; b. Atlanta, Oct. 11, 1929; s. Thomas Cook and Mary (Morgan) MacD.; B.S., U. Fla., 1951, LL.B., 1953; m. Gay Anne Everiss, June 30, 1956; children—Margaret Anne, Thomas William. Admitted to Fla. bar, 1953; practiced in Tampa, 1953—; mem. firm Shackleford, Farrior, Stallings & Evans, 1953—. Legislative counsel Gov. of Fla., 1963. Mem. Fla. Student Scholarship and Loan Commn., 1963-67, Hillsborough County Pub. Edn. Study Commn., 1965. Bd. dirs. Univ. Community Hosp., Children's Home of Tampa. Served to 1st lt. Judge Adv. Gen. Corp., USAF, 1953-55. Mem. Am. Law Inst., Am. Bar Assn. (com. on ethics and profl. responsibility 1972—), Fla. Bar (mem. com. on profl. ethics 1964-72, chmn. 1966-70, Fla. W. Coast Sports Assn. (sec. 1965—), U. Fla. Athletic Assn. (dir.), Gasparilla Krewe, U. Fla. Alumni Assn. (pres. elect 1972), Phi Kappa Phi, Phi Delta Phi, Fla. Blue Key, Kappa Alpha. Episcopalian. Home: 1904 Holly Lane Tampa FL 33609 Office: PO Box 3324 Tampa FL 33601

MACDONALD, WARREN HARDING, govt. ofcl.; b. Prince William County, Va., Mar. 31, 1921; s. George H. and Esther (Stiles) MacD.; student George Washington U., 1939-41, postgrad. 1970-71; B.S. in Social Sci. with distinction, Am. U., 1955, postgrad. 1955-56; m. Martina H. Connors, Jan. 10, 1944. Accredited rep. Vet.'s Claims and Appeals, Am. Legion, Washington, 1945-51, supr. appeals sect. Nat. Rehab. div., 1951-55, research analyst, 1955-59, dep. dir. Nat. Rehab. Com., 1959-61, dir. research and fgn. relations, 1961-69; spl. asst. to adminstr. vets. VA, 1969—. Served with USAAF, 1943-45. Decorated Air medal. Mem. Am. Legion. Republican. Author numerous research reports for Am. Legion. Home: 4619 Edgefield Rd Bethesda MD 20014 Office: 810 Vermont Av NW Washington DC 20240

MACDOUGALL, WILLIAM RODERICK, lawyer, govt. ofcl.; b. Nevada City, Cal., May 14, 1914; s. William Stewart and Ethel (Hutchinson) MacD.; student Sacramento Jr. Coll., 1930-32, U. Cal. at Berkeley, 1933-34; LL.B., McGeorge Coll. Law, 1941; m. Carol Bernie Keane, May 1, 1937; children—Marcia Keane, James Stewart. Various positions State of Cal., 1932-42; admitted to Cal. bar, 1941; gen. counsel, mgr. County Supr. Assn. Cal., 1946-70; exec. dir. Adv. Commn. on Intergovtl. Relations, Washington, 1970—. Mem. Cal. Major Hwy. Devel. Com., 1952-61, Fed. Pub. Assistance Adv. Council, 1959-61, Cal. Gov.'s Commn., on Met. Area Problems, 1959-61, Cal. Constl. Revision Commn., 1964-70, Cal. Council on Criminal Justice, 1968-70. Exec. dir. Cal. County Govt. Edn. Found., 1966-70. Served from ensign to lt., USNR, 1943-45; in U.S.S. Whitehurst. Mem. Nat. Assn. County and Pros. Attys. (founder), Nat. Assn. Counties (sec.-treas. Western regional dist. 1954-61, chmn. home rule com. 1962-70, sec. pub. welfare com. 1961-70, chmn. conf. state assn. execs. 1956-58), Nat. Municipal League, Am., Fed. bar assns., Chi Psi. Clubs: Nat. Lawyers; Commonwealth of Cal. Home: 9905 Hillridge Dr Kensington MD 20795 Office: Advisory Commn Intergovtl Relations 726 Jackson Pl NW Washington DC 20575

MACE, ALMON TURLEY, economist, educator; b. Orleans, Ind., Mar. 30, 1911; s. Almon Gallatin and Una (Turley) M.; B.S., Purdue U., 1934, M.S., 1936; postgrad. U. Cal. at Berkeley, 1936; Ph.D., George Washington U., 1956; m. Lucyle Harrod, Feb. 5, 1934; children— William Harrod, Mary Lee. With Farm Security Adminstrn. and Farmers Home Adminstrn., U.S. Dept. Agr., Washington, 1938-55, asst. dir. budget and statistics div., 1950-55, program analyst Commodity Stblzn. Service, 1955-61, dir. rural areas devel. program, asst. to sec. agr., 1961-66; prof. econs., head dept. econs. and bus. adminstrn. Madison Coll., Harrisonburg, Va., 1967—; dir. Rochdale Coop. Chmn., Council of Chs. Inner City Program, Washington, 1957; pres. Dominion Hills Civic Assn., Arlington County Council P.T.A.'s. Recipient certificate of merit Dept. Agr., 1960. Mem. Am., So. econs. assns., Am., Internat. agrl. econs. assns., Ceres, Alpha Zeta, Phi Delta Theta. Presbyn. (elder). Mason (Shriner). Home: 216 Governor's Lane Harrisonburg VA 22801

MACEKURA, JOSEPH, ednl. adminstr.; b. Ridgewood, Pa., Sept. 9, 1921; s. Matthew and Tekla (Linko) M.; B.A., George Washington U., 1949, M.A., 1951; student Am. U., 1960—, U. Mass., 1968; m. Evelyn Wladika, June 18, 1949; 1 son, Mark. Tchr., Arlington (Va.) Pub. Schs., 1950-54, counselor, 1955-56, dir. guidance, 1957-60, asst. prin., 1961-66, asso. prin., 1967-69, prin. Jefferson Jr. High Sch., 1969—. Mem. Claremont Civic Fedn., 1955—. Served with AUS, 1942-46. Mem. Nat., Va. edn. assns., Nat., Va. assns. secondary sch. prins., Phi Delta Kappa. Contbr. Monthly Labor Review, 1955-56, Am. Sings, 1947; Sewanee Review, 1963; Mademoiselle mag., 1964; McCalls mag., 1964-65; A Good Day's Work, 1969; Today's Education, 1970. Home: 4935 S 25th St Arlington VA 22206 Office: 816 S Walter Reed Dr Arlington VA 22204

MACESICH, GEORGE, economist, educator, author; b. Cleve., May 27, 1927; s. Walter Vaso and Milka (Tepavac) M.; A.A., George Washington U., 1951, B.A., 1953, M.A., 1954; Ph.D., U. Chgo., 1958; m. Susana Sonia Svorkovich, Feb. 16, 1955; children—Maja Susana Radmila, Milka Milena Milica, George Milan Peter. Research asso. U. Chgo., 1956-58; research economist U.S. C. of C., Washington, 1958-59; dir. Fla. Council on Econ. Devel., Tallahassee, 1961-63; asst. prof. econs. Fla. State U., Tallahassee, 1959-61, asso. prof., 1961-63, prof. econs., 1963—, also dir. Center Slavic and East European studies, 1965—, mng. editor Slavic Papers, 1967—. Econ. cons. U.S. Dept. Commerce. 1961—. Served with USN, 1944-53. Mem. Am., So. (editorial bd. jour. 1961-65) econ. assns., Am. Statis. Assn., Am. Econ. History Assn. Mem. Serbian Orthodox Ch. Author: Commercial Banking and Regional Development, 1965; Yugoslavia; Theory and Practice of Development Planning, 1964. Contbr. numerous articles and revs. to U.S. and fgn. profl. jours. Home: 2401 Delgado Dr Tallahassee FL 32304

MACFARLAND, ALFRED T., judge; b.Lebanon, Tenn., Apr. 23, 1917; B.A., U. Ala., 1940; J.D., Cumberland U., 1941. Admitted to Tenn. bar, 1942, U.S. Ct. Customs and Patent Appeals bar, 1948, U.S. Dist. Ct. bar, 1948, U.S. Tax Ct. bar, 1948, U.S. Ct. Appeals bar, 1949, U.S. Supreme Ct. bar, 1950, U.S. Ct. Mil. Appeals bar, 1953. Prof. law, Cumberland U., 1947-48; gen. counsel, R.R. and Pub. Utilities Commn., 1951-55; now with MacFarland, Reed & Kinnard, Lebanon. Mem. Tenn. Ho. of Reps., 1945-47, Tenn. Senate, 1951-53; commnr. Revenue Dept. Tenn., 1959-61. Mem. Am., Tenn., Lebanon bar assns.; Barristers Club, Blue Key. Office: 107 W Market St Lebanon TN 37087*

MACFARLANE, HARPER, lawyer; b. Chatham, Ont., Can., Jan. 26, 1901; s. Alexander and Helen (Swearingen) M.; L.B., U. Tex., 1924; m. Inez Canaday, Nov. 10, 1927. Asso. Templeton Brooks, Napier & Brown, San Antonio, 1924-35, mem. firm Brooks, Napier, Brown & Matthews 1935-42, Brewer, Mathews, Nowlin & Macfarlane, 1942-56, Matthews, Nowlin, Macfarlane & Barrett, 1956—. Served to lt. col. AUS, 1942-45. Mem. Am., San Antonio bar assns., State Bar Tex., Nat. Assn. R.R. Trial Counsel, Am. Legion, Mil. Order World Wars, Sigma Nu. Clubs: San Antonio Country, San Antonio Petroleum, Kiwanis. Home: 1016 Wiltshire Av San Antonio TX 78209 Office: Alamo Nat Bldg San Antonio TX 78205

MACGREGOR, ALICIA AMORY DUPONT (MRS. GEORGE PURNELL MACGREGOR), bus. exec.; b. Wilmington, Del., Aug. 1, 1903; d. Alfred Irenee and Alicia (Bradford) duPont; pvt. edn.; m. Harold Sanford Glendening, June 27, 1922 (div.); 1 son, Alan Sanford; m. 2d, Frank Leslie Fraser, Oct. 11, 1947 (dec. 1962); m. 3d, George Purnell MacGregor, Mar. 29, 1965. Pres., Fla. Paper Converters, 1962-68; dir. Am. Nat. Bank, 1962-69. Pres. women's aux. St. Anthony Hops., 1954-55; founder Queen of Hearts Ball, fund-raising event for Sun Coast Heart Assn., 1959. Recipient certificates of appreciation Am. Heart Assn., 1956, 57, 63, Silver medal, 1958, 59, Gold medal, 1960, 61; citation Nat. Assn. for Mental Health, 1962. Home: 360 Coffee Pot Riviera St Petersburg FL 33704

MACGREGOR, CLARK, polit. ofcl.; b. Mpls., July 12, 1922; s. William Edwin and Edith (Clark) MacG.; grad. cum laude, Dartmouth, 1946; J.D., U. Minn., 1948; m. Barbara Porter Spicer, June 16, 1948; children—Susan Clark (Mrs. Joseph S. Wheelwright), Laurie Miller, Eleanor Martin. Admitted to Minn. bar, 1948, practiced in Mpls. until 1961; partner firm King & MacGregor, 1952-61; mem. 87th-91st congresses from 3d Dist. Minn., mem. jud. com.; counsel to Pres. for congl. relations, 1971-72; campaign dir. Com. for Re-election of the Pres., 1972—. Active local A.R.C., Community Chest. Served to 2d lt. AUS, 1942-45; CBI. Named One of Mpls. 100 Newsmakers of Tomorrow, Time mag., 1953. Mem. Am., Minn., Hennepin County, bar assns. Presbyn. Home: 2834 Foxhall Rd NW Washington DC 20007 Office: 1701 Pennsylvania Av NW Washington DC 20006

MACGREGOR, GEORGE LESCHER, utilities exec.; b. Little Rock, Oct. 29, 1901; s. Arthur William and Irene (Lescher) MacG.; B.S., U. Tex., 1923; LL.D., Southwestern U.; m. Jean Edge, Dec. 7, 1929; children—Gregor Carmichael, George Lescher. Joined Dallas Power & Light Co., 1929, mgr., pres., 1940-53, chmn. bd., 1944-53, dir. until 1968; v.p., dir. Tex. Utilities Co., Dallas, 1945-53, pres., 1953-57, chmn. bd., 1967-72; chmn. Tech. Services, Inc., until 1967. Bd. dirs. State Fair Tex.; pres., trustee Southwestern Med. Found.; trustee, past pres. Tex. Research Found.; trustee Hoblitzele Found., Childrens Med. Center; past pres. Community Chest, Citizens Council. Recipient Distinguished Engring. Grad. award U. Tex., Dallas County Hosp. award, 1969. Registered profl. engr. Mem. Edison Electric Inst. (past dir.), Philos. Soc. Tex., Newcomen Soc. Eng., Sons Republic Tex., Phi Gamma Delta, Episcopalian, Mason, Kiwanian. Clubs: Electric, Country, Brook Hollow Golf, City (Dallas); Recess (N.Y.C.). Home: 6322 Westchester Dr Dallas TX 75205 Office: 1506 Commerce St Dallas TX 75201

MACGREGOR, GEORGE LESCHER, JR., banker; b. Dallas, Sept. 15, 1936; s. George Lescher and Jean (Edge) MacG.; B.B.A., U. Tex., 1958; m. Nancy Clement, Feb. 16, 1963; children—George Lescher III, Michael F. Asst. cashier 1st Nat. Bank, Dallas, 1960-64, asst. v.p., 1964-68; v.p. Nat. Bank Commerce, Dallas, 1968-70, sr. v.p. charge nat. accounts, 1970—. Served with AUS, 1959-60; mem. Res. Mem. Am. Inst. Banking, Phi Gamma Delta. Episcopalian. Clubs: Dallas Country, Idlewild, Terpscichorian (Dallas). Home: 7614 Southwestern Blvd Dallas TX 75225 Office: 1525 Elm St Dallas TX 75201

MACHADO, LUIS, diplomat; b. Guanabacoa, Cuba, Sept. 25,, 1899; s. Luis and Maria L.(Ortega) M.; student Candler Coll., Havana, Cuba, 1916; A.B., Inst. Havana, 1917; degree civil law, U. Havana, 1920, degree pub. law, 1922; m. Genoveva Silva y Murray, Feb. 7, 1925; children—Irene (Mrs. Adrian Macia, Jr.), Elena (Mrs. Andreas F. Lowenfeld), Natalia (Mrs. Agustin Maruri). Admitted to Bar of Cuba; practiced in Havana; mem. law firm Nunez Mesa y Machado; exec. dir. Internat. Bank for Reconstruction and Devel., 1946-48, gov. for Cuba, 1949; pres. Econ. Commn. for Latin Am., 1949; Ambassador of Cuba to U.S.A., 1950-52, exec. dir. Internat. Bank of Reconstruction and Devel., Internat. Finance Corp., Internat. Devel. Assn., representing Mexico, Peru, Nicaragua, Venezuela, Haiti, Costa Rica, Guatemala, El Salvador, Honduras and Panama. Mem. Cuban delegation to Peace Conf., Versailles, 1919; del. of Cuba to Financial and Monetary Conf., Bretton Woods, 1944, to Internat.-Am. Conf. on Problems of War and Peace, Chapultepec, Mexico, 1945, to Third Internat. Conf. on Radio Communications, Rio de Janeiro, 1945, to Conf. on Trade and Employment, Havana, 1948, to Japanese Peace Conf., San Francisco, 1951. Decorated: Comdr. of the Order of Merit, Chile, 1938; Order of El Sol del Peru, 1945; Great Cross, Carlos Manuel de Cespedes, Cuba, 1950; Great Cross of Quetzal of Guatemala, 1962; Order of Balboa (Republic of Panama), 1963. Pres. of the Good Neighbor Found., 1936. Mem. Nat. Mfrs. Assn. Cuba (pres., 1941-45), Nat. Tourist Commn. (pres., 1937-39), Geog. Soc. Cuba, Cuban Inst. Internat. Law, Bar Assn. Havana (mem. governing bd., 1936), Y.M.C.A. (pres., 1924). Clubs: Country of Havana, Miramar Yacht, Havana Yacht, Vedado Tennis, Union, Rotary (pres., 1929), Rotary Internat. (dir., 1931-34), Havana Biltmore Yacht and Country, International Nautical, The American, The British, Ateneo (Havana); The Lawyers, Metropolitan (N.Y.C.); Burning Tree, Metropolitan (Washington). Author: The Platt Amendment, 1922; International Legislation of the Air, 1923; Necessity for the Adoption of a Policy on Foreign Trade, 1929; Cuba, the Cork Island, Essay on Cuban Economy, 1936; Cuban Fiscal Index, 1944. Home: 6832 Tulip Hill Terrace Washington DC 20016 Office: 1818 H St Washington DC 20433

MACIEL-AGUILAR, SERGIO ROMAN, educator, physician; b. Guadalajara, Mex., Oct. 18, 1933; s. Ramon Maciel-Marin and Maria Aguilar de Maciel; M.D., U. Guadalajara, 1957; m. Virginia Medina-Elizondo, Nov. 6, 1965; children—Cecilia, Sergio, Virginia. Resident in anesthesiology Sud-Pacifico Hosp., Guadalajaro, Mex., 1958-59, State U. Ia. Hosps., Iowa City, 1961-63; intern Good Samaritan Hosp., Phoenix, 1959-60; asst. prof. anesthesiology Escuela de Medicine, U. Guadalajara, 1966—. Mem. Am. Soc. Anesthesiologists (affiliate), Associacion de Anestesiologos de Jalisco Soc. (sec. 1958-59), Football Club Asociacion Civil. Home: 2702 Bogota Frac Providencia Guadalajara Jal Mexico Office: U Guadalajara Gualdalajara Mexico

MACINNES, W. C., utility co. exec.; b. N.S., Can., Feb. 19, 1902; M.E.E., Mass. Inst. Tech., 1927; m. Martha L. Sorensen; 1 son, William P. Formerly elec. engr. Savannah Electric & Power Co. (Ga.), then asst. to pres. Sierra Pacific Power Co., Reno; with Stone & Webster Service Corp., N.Y.C., 1935-37, v.p., 1941-54; pres. West Coast Power Co., Portland, Ore., 1937-41; pres. Tampa Electric Co. (Fla.), 1954-69, chmn., chief exec. officer, 1969—, also dir.; v.p., dir. Gulfcoast Transit Co., Mid South Towing Co.; dir. Exchange Nat. Bank Tampa, Citizens Gas Fuel Co., Green Mountain Power Corp., Nat. Gas & Oil Corp., Tampa So. R.R. Co., South Atlantic Life Ins. Co. Pres. Southeastern Electric Exchange, 1960, now dir. Chmn. industry and policy planning com. Fla. Council of 100, 1961-62; pres. Fla. West Coast Ednl. Television, Inc., 1960, now dir.; pres. Citizens Safety Council Hillsborough County, 1960, now dir.; dir. Fla. State Fair and Gasparilla Assn., Fla. Financial Forum; pres. Tampa Horse Show Assn.; regional v.p. Tenn. Walking Horse Assn. Trustee U. Tampa; bd. dirs., Boys Clubs Tampa, MacDonald Tng. Center Found. Named Outstanding Citizen of Year, Tampa Civitan Club, 1960; recipient Mgmt. Achievement award Soc. Advancement Mgmt., 1960. Mem. Fla. (dir.), Greater Tampa (pres. 1957-58) chambers commerce, Ye Mystic Krewe of Gasparilla. Presbyn. (deacon), Mason (Shriner), Rotarian (dir. Tampa). Clubs: University (dir.) (Tampa); Palma Ceia Golf. Home: 98 Martinique St Tampa FL 33606 Office: 111 N Dale Mabry St Tampa FL 33606

MACINTYRE, A(LFONSO) EVERETTE, lawyer, govt. ofcl.; b. nr. Burlington, N.C., Feb. 3, 1901; s. William Seymour and Ella Mary (Clark) MacI.; A.B., U. N.C., 1926; LL.B., George Washington U., 1929; m. Reita Jane Lyons, Aug. 20, 1930; 1 son, Miles Everette. Admitted to N.C. bar, Va. bar, D.C. bar; practiced in Washington, 1929—; mem. legal staff FTC, Washington 1930-55, chief antimonopoly trial staff, 1945-50, asst. dir. antimonopoly bur., 1950-55, chief div. investigation and litigation, 1950-54, adviser on antimonopoly, 1954-55, mem. FTC, 1961—. staff dir., gen. counsel select com. on small bus. U.S. Ho. Reps., Washington, 1955-57, gen. counsel, 1957-61. Mem. Am., Fed. bar assns., Am. Judicature Soc., Acad. Polit. Sci. Home: 1564 Colonial Terrace Arlington VA 22209 Office: FTC Washington DC 10025

MACIULA, L. ANDREW, mech. engr.; b. Bartlesville, Okla., Nov. 1, 1915; s. Andrew Joseph and Carrie (Wujceak) M.; B.S., Okla. State U., 1934; m. Reba Norris, July 14, 1939; children—Edward A., Kenneth M., Robert C., Roger Eric, Thomas J. Plant engr. Watervliet (N.Y.) Arsenal, 1939-46; asst. to mgr. engring. dept. Phillips Petroleum Co., Bartlesville, Okla., 1946-52, asst. plant mgr., Rocket Fuels Div., 1952-58; mgr. adminstrn. Phillips-Astrodyne-N.Am. Aviation, McGregor, Tex., 1958-60; cons. L.A. Maciula & Assos., 1960-68; exec. v.p., gen. mgr. Slurry Seal, Inc., Waco, Tex., 1961-65; gen. mgr., dir. Prodn. CommandAire Corp., Waco, 1965-67; exec. dir. Nat. Slurry Seal Assn., 1965-67; dir. mech. engring. labs., hydroclome engring. Okla. State U., Stillwater, 1968—. Bd. dirs., trustee Waco United Fund, 1956-60; Camping, activities chmn. Heart O' Tex. council Boy Scouts Am., 1957-61; mem. bd. Providence Hosp., Waco, 1965-68. Registered profl. engr., N.Y., Okla., Tex. Mem. Nat. Soc. Profl. Engrs., Am. Rocket Soc. K.C. (past grand knight, dist. dep. 1964-68, state committeeman 1956-64). Home: 729 Lakeshore Dr Stillwater OK 74074 Office: Okla State U Stillwater OK 74074

MACIVER, PEGGE FARMER (MRS. DONALD GORDON MACIVER), monodramatist, educator; b. Colon, C.Z.; d. Alfred Gibson and Minnie (Cuckler) Farmer; B.A., Ohio U., 1935; B.L.L., Cin. Conservatory Music, 1938; M.A., George Washington U., 1964; m. Donald Gordon MacIver, June 7, 1957; 1 stepson, Neil. Monodramatist, lectr., writer touring U.S., Can. writing, performing own plays for one woman theatre presentations, 1938-59; speech therapist D.C. Pub. Schs., 1959-67, tchr. in-service tng. programs, program coordinator Ednl. Resources Center, 1967-70, asst. dir. Developmental Center for Spl. Edn., 1970—; tchr. in-service tng. programs D.C. Tchrs. Coll. TV moderator, panelist Its Your World and World Headliner programs; mem. speakers burs., Dayton (O.) Council World Affairs, League Women Voters, 1950-57. Mem. Nat. League Am. Pen Women, Am., D.C. speech and hearing assns., N.E.A., D.C. Edn. Assn., Internat. Platform Assn., Phi Beta Kappa, Pi Beta Phi, Alpha Delta Kappa, Delta Kappa Gamma. Contbr. articles to profl. publs. Home: 8500 New Hampshire Av Silver Spring MD 20903 Office: DC Pub Schs Washington DC 20007

MACK, LEO MOSES, JR., oral surgeon; b. Jacksonville, Fla., Mar. 7, 1938; s. Leo Moses and Irene Ada (Schulhofer) M.; student U. Miami, 1956-59; D.D.S., Emory U. Sch. Dentistry, 1963, M.S.D. in Dentistry, 1966; m. Ingeborg Gietz, June 21, 1964; children—Stephanie, Kirsten, Nils. Intern, Washington U. Sch. Dentistry, St. Louis, 1963-64; resident in oral surgery VA Hosp., Atlanta, 1964-66; pvt. practice oral surgery, Atlanta, 1968—; mem. staff Northside Hosp., Atlanta, Atlanta Hosp., Doctors Meml. Hosp., Atlanta; oral surgeon Ben Massell Dental Clinic, Atlanta, 1968—; clin. instr. oral surgery Emory U. Sch. Dentistry, 1969—. Served with USAF, 1966-68. Diplomate Am. Bd. Oral Surgery. Decorated Air Force Commendation medal. Mem. Am. Dental Assn., Am., Ga. socs. oral surgeons, No. Dist., Fifth Dist., dental socs., Met. Atlanta Oral Surgery Study Group, Alpha Omega. Home: 370 Hunters Ridge Atlanta GA 30060 Office: 6075 Roswell Rd NE Atlanta GA 30328

MACK, WILBUR OLLIO, educator; b. Seward, Okla., Aug. 11, 1919; s. Colister L. and Addie Lee (Lowe) M.; B.S., Langston (Okla.) U., 1947; M.S., Okla. State U., 1954; m. Julia Mae Hobbs, May 19, 1945 (dec. Mar. 1968); children—Ronald Wilbur, Waymond Ollio, Larry Wayne, Wilma Denise; m. 2d, Martha Margaret Mayo, Aug. 11, 1970. Tchr., Prairie View (Tex.) Coll., 1953-57, So. U., Baton Rouge, 1957-62; asst. prof. engring. Fla. A. and M. U., Tallahassee, 1962—. Served as 1st lt., AUS, 1941-45. Registered profl. engr., Tex., La. Mem. Am. Soc. Agrl. Engrs., Nat. Safety Council, Kappa Alpha Psi. Democrat. Baptist. Mason (32 deg.). Home: 710 Stafford St Tallahassee FL 32304

MACKAY, JAMES LESTER, psychologist; b. St. Louis, Sept. 23, 1891; s. James T. and Clara L. (Messmer) MacK.; B.S., U. Mo., 1920, M.A., 1924; Ph.D., N.Y.U., 1944; student U. Tex., summer 1956, Mills Coll., summer 1946; m. Mabel G. Crouch, Jan. 28, 1920; children— William Robert, Edward James. Sch. adminstrn., Philippine Islands, 1914-16; prin. Elias Michael sch. for Crippled Children, St. Louis, 1925-30, Carondelet Sch., 1930-37; Exptl. edn., St. Louis, 1920-46; chief VA Guidance Center, U. Ariz. at Tucson, 1946-48; dir. guidance South San Antonio (Tex.) Schs., 1949-59;

practice of psychology, San Antonio, 1948—. Pres., Mental Health Assn. Bexar County, 1959; del. White House Conf. on Aging, 1971. Served with inf. 1918. Mem. Acad. Religion and Mental Health, World Fedn. Mental Health, Am. Personnel & Guidance Assn., Nat. Vocation Guidance Assn., Am. Psychology Assn., Nat. Soc. Study, Edn., Phi Delta Kappa. Episcopalian. Home: 3737 Fredericksburg Rd San Antonio TX 78201

MACKENZIE, JOHN A., U.S. dist. judge, Norfolk. Office: U S Courthouse Norfolk VA 23510*

MACKENZIE, ROLAND REDUS, realtor; b. Washington, Mar. 13, 1907; s. Albert Redus and Mary J. (Hummer) MacK.; grad. Brown U., 1929; m. Louise Parker Fownes, May 11, 1940; children—Clark Fownes, Margot Fownes. Rep. U.S. Walker Cup Golf Team, 1926, 28-30; with Dupont Laundry, Washington, 1930-32; golf profl. Colorado Springs Country Club (Colo.), Congl. Country Club, Washington, 1933-37; pres., dir. Shamrock Properties, Inc., Balt., 1938—, pres. Shamrock Realty Co., Greentree Realty Co., Towson, Md.; pres., dir. S.E. Airmotive, Charlotte, N.C., 1958—. Pres., dir. Big Pebble Assn., Pinehurst, N.C. Presbyn. Club: Foxfire Golf and Country (chmn. bd.) (Pinehurst, N.C.); Gulf Stream Golf (Del Ray Beach); Elkridge-Greenspring (Balt.). Home: McCaskill Rd Pinehurst NC 28374 also Shamrock Farm Cockeysville MD Office: MacKenzie Bldg Southern Pines NC

MACKENZIE, WALTER BRANDT, pipe line co. exec.; b. Rockville Centre, N.Y., Mar. 14, 1921; s. Walter Jackson and Marie (Brandt) M.; B.S., Sch. Commerce, N.Y. U., 1950, M.B.A., Grad. Sch. Bus. Adminstrn., 1955; m. Edith Stewart Hooker, Feb. 7, 1943; children—Nancy (Mrs. Gary A. Perryman), Susan, David Walter, Janet. Various accounting, financial positions Standard Oil Co. (N.J.), N.Y.C., 1940-59; adminstrn. asst. to sec.-treas. Plantation Pipe Line Co., Atlanta, 1960, sec., 1960-63, sec.-treas., 1963-64, dir., 1963—, v.p. adminstrn., 1964, pres., 1964—. Bd. trustees Luth. Theol. So. Sem., Columbia, S.C., 1968—, Ga. Found. Ind. Colls., 1971—; mem. bd. advisers La. Found. Pvt. Colls., 1971—. Served with USCG, 1942-45. Mem. Am. Petroleum Inst. (chmn. com. 1967-68), Am. Mgmt. Assn., Pres's Assn., Assn. Oil Pipe Lines (co. rep. 1964—). Lutheran. Office: 3390 Peachtree Rd NE Atlanta GA 30326 5310 Northland Dr NE Atlanta GA 30342

MACKEY, BENJAMIN FRANK, judge; b. Atlanta, Dec. 1, 1904; s. James M. and Dora (Gaddy) M.; student pub. schs., Little Rock, Ark.; m. Maxie Walker, Feb. 12, 1928; children—Mary Frances (Mrs. Robert E. Phillips), B. Frank, Maxilee (Mrs. John J. Williams). Policeman, Little Rock, Ark., 1937-58; agt. 1st Pyramid Life Ins. Co., Little Rock, Ark., 1958-62; sheriff Pulaski County, Little Rock, Ark., 1963-68, county judge 1969—. Mem. Little Rock Sch. Bd., 1959-62. Mem. central bd., YMCA, 1963-65; mem. chmn. bd. Pulaski County March of Dimes, 1969—. Mem. Ark. Sheriffs Assn. (pres. 1968), Ark. Law Enforcement Assn. (1st v.p. 1962-69), Nat. Sheriffs Assn. (dir. 1967-68). Methodist. Mason (33 deg.). Home: 1700 Pinewood Dr Little Rock AR 72204 Office: Pulaski County Courthouse Little Rock AR 72204

MACKEY, LYLA THRASHER (MRS. ALEXANDER B. MACKEY), librarian; b. Highway, Ky.; d. John D. and Myrtie (Smith) Thrasher; A.B., Central State Coll., Edmond, Okla., 1934; M.A., George Peabody Coll., 1937, B.S. in L.S., 1943; m. Alexander B. Mackey, Feb. 15, 1935. Tchr. pub. schs., Clinton County, Ky., 1929-32; asso. prof. Trevecca Coll., Nashville, 1935-43, Librarian, 1944—, spl. counselor young women, 1950-64. Mem. N.E.A., Am. (Tenn. recruitment network), Southeastern, Tenn., Nashville library assns., Am. Assn. U. Women, Ladies' Hermitage Assn. Mem. Ch. of Nazarene. Home: 700 Harding Pl Nashville TN 37211 Office: 333 Murfreesboro Rd Nashville TN 37210

MACKEY, M(AURICE) CECIL, JR., univ. pres.; b. Montgomery, Ala., Jan. 23, 1929; s. M. Cecil and Annie Laurie (Kimrey) M.; B.A., U. Ala., 1949, M.A., 1953, LL.B., 1958; Ph.D., U. Ill., 1955; postgrad. Harvard, 1958-59; m. Clare Siewert, Aug. 29, 1953; children—Carol, John, Ann. Asst. prof. econs. U. Ill., 1955-56; asso. prof. econs. USAF Acad., 1956-57; admitted to Ala. bar, 1958; asst. prof. law U. Ala., 1958-62; with FAA, 1963-65, U.S. Dept. Commerce, 1965-67; asst. sec. U.S. Dept. Transp., 1967-69; exec. v.p., prof. law Fla. State U., Tallahassee, 1969-71; pres. U. South Fla., Tampa, 1971—. Asst. counsel sub-com. on antitrust and monopoly U.S. Senate, 1958-62. Recipient Arthur S. Flemming award Washington Jaycees, 1967. Mem. Artus, Chi Alpha Phi. Home: 10410 Butia Pl Tampa FL 33618

MACKEY, OSCAR POWELL, III, state ofcl.; b. Memphis, Aug. 13, 1938; s. Oscar P. and Lucy C. (Wallace) M.; B.B.A., U. Miss., 1960, LL.B., 1963, J.D., 1968. Admitted to Miss. bar, 1963; practiced in Coffeeville, 1963-65, Water Valley, 1965-70; mem. firm Oscar P. Mackey III, 1965-70; asst. atty. gen. State Miss., 1970—. Mem. Miss. Ho. of Reps., 1967-72. Mem. Am., Yalobusha County bar assns., Miss. State Bar, Order of DeMolay, Water Valley Jr. C. of C. (pres. 1965), Delta Kappa Epsilon, Alpha Phi Omega. Presbyn. Home: 5155 Wayneland Dr Apt B-8 Jackson MS 39211 Office: State Office Bldg Room 800 Jackson MS 39205

MACKEY, PAUL RETTIG, ednl. adminstr.; b. Galion, O., Apr. 22, 1912; s. Charles Alvan and Minnie (Rettig) M.; B.A., Emory and Henry Coll., 1935; M.A., Ohio State U., 1940; postgrad. George Washington U., 1950-51; m. Kathryn Campbell Scott, Oct. 26, 1935. Coach, tchr., Johnson City, Tenn., 1935-36, Norton, Va., 1936-39, Galion, O., 1940-41, Bristol, Tenn., 1941-43; tchr.-coach, Alexandria, Va., 1943-48, tchr. guidance, 1948-56, asst. supt. constrn.-planning, 1956-69; dir. bldgs. and constrn. Loudoun County Schs., Leesburg, Va., 1969—. Mason, Lion, Kiwanian. Home: Rural Route 1 Box 1R Purceilville VA 22132 Office: 30 W North St Leesburg VA 22075

MACKEY, WILLIAM STURGES, JR., med. co. exec.; b. St. Louis, May 27, 1921; s. William S. and Dorothy Frances (Allison) M.; B.A., Rice U., 1943; M.B.A., U. Tex., 1950; m. Margaret Wescot Powell, Dec. 10, 1943; children—Dorothy (Thomas Robben), John, James. Asso. prof. accounting Rice U., Houston, 1946-62; partner Simons & Mackey, Houston, 1946-62; v.p., treas. Mandrel Industries, Houston, 1962-66; v.p. finance Tex. Internat. Airlines, Houston, 1966-69; chmn., pres. Medenco, Inc., Houston, 1969—. Served to 1st lt. USAAF, 1946. C.P.A., Tex. Mem. Am. Inst. C.P.A.'s, Tex. Soc. C.P.A.'s, Beta Gamma Sigma. Clubs: Lakeside Country, University, Plaza. Episcopalian. Home: 11335 Holidan St Houston TX 77024 Office: 3 Greenway Plaza E Houston TX 77046

MACKIN, CATHERINE PATRICIA, journalist; b. Balt., Aug. 28, 1939; d. Francis Michael and Catherine (Gillooly) Mackin; B.A. cum laude, U. Md., 1960; postgrad. (Nieman fellow) Harvard, 1967-68. Gen. assignment reporter, asst. to pub. Free State News, College Park, Md., 1958-60; gen. assignment reporter, city desk rewriter Balt. News Am., 1960-63; with Washington bur. Hearst Newspapers, 1963-69, White House corr., 1965-67, urban affairs corr., 1968-69; news corr. NBC, Washington, 1969—. Mem. White House Corr. Assn., Alpha Omicron Pi. Club: Women's Nat. Press (Washington). Home: 2320 20th St NW Washington DC Office: NBC 4001 Nebraska Av NW Washington DC 20016

MACKIN, JOHN GILMAN, JR., constrn. co. exec.; b. Ada, Okla., July 17, 1930; s. John Gilman and Dorothy Doris (Hatchett) M.; B.S. in Civil Engring., Tex. A. and M. U., 1955; m. Mary Louise Bunch, May 29, 1949; children—Jana (Mrs. Gary Cathy), Ina Carol, Renata Diane, John Gilman. Offshore constrn. engr. Cal. Co., 1955-56; project engr. Brown & Root, Inc., Houston, 1957-61, mgr. marine industries group, 1962-67; v.p. Divcon, Inc., also pres. Descon Engrs., Houston, 1968; v.p., gen. mgr. Fluor Ocean Services, Inc., Houston, 1969—. Vice pres. Maplewood North-South Community Improvement Assn., 1962-66, pres., 1966, dir., 1962-65. County and Tex. del. Democratic Conv., 1958, 59, 68. Served with AUS, 1950-51. Registered profl. engr., Tex., La. Mem. Am. Soc. C.E., Am. Soc. Oceanography-Marine Tech. Soc., Houston C. of C. (mem. sci. com. 1967—), Nat. Oceanography Assn. (dir. 1970—). Patentee offshore structural system for offshore regions with ice flow, guidance structure for deepwater pipeline constrn. Office: PO Box 36878 Houston TX 77036 Home: 13710 Apple Tree St Houston TX 77024

MACKINNON, GEORGE E., U.S. judge; b. St. Paul, Apr. 22, 1906; s. James Alexander Wiley and Cora Blanche (Asselstine) MacK.; student U. Colo., 1923-24; LL.B., U. Minn., 1929; m. Elizabeth Valentine Davis, Aug. 20, 1938; children—Catharine Alice Wilson, James Davis, Leonard Davis. Admitted to Minn. bar, 1929, U.S. Supreme Ct. bar; asst. gen. counsel Investors Syndicate, Mpls., 1929-42; engaged pvt. practice law, 1949-53, 58-61; elected mem. Minn. Ho. of Reps. from 29th dist., 1934, 36, 38, 40; mem. 80th Congress 1947-49, 3d Minn. Dist.; U.S. dist. atty. for Minn., 1953-58; spl. asst. to U.S. atty. gen., 1960; gen. counsel, v.p. Investors Mut. Funds, Mpls., 1961-69; judge U.S. Ct. Appeals for D.C. Circuit, 1969—. Republican nominee for gov. of Minn., 1958. Served to comdr. U.S. Navy Air Force, 1942-46; Cited for meritorious service by comdr. Air Force U.S. Atlantic Fleet. Mem. Am., Minn., Hennepin County bar assns., Delta Tau Delta, Phi Delta Phi. Republican. Episcopalian. Clubs: Minneapolis, Wayzata County. Author: Minn. State Reorganization Act, 1939; State Civil Service Law, 1939; Old Age Assistance Act, 1936. Home: 11333 Willowbrook Dr Potomac MD 20854 Office: US Court House Washington DC 20001

MACKINTOSH, DAVID MCNABB, JR., architect; b. McClellanville, S.C., Apr. 25, 1916; s. David McNabb and Mamie (Peacock) M.; student Clemson U., 1936-39; m. Ida H. Watson, June 26, 1940; children—David McNabb III, Ida Gayle. Prin. D. M. Mackintosh Assos., 1948-63; asso. archtl. engr. J. N. Pease Assos. Archtl. Engr., Charlotte, N.C., 1963—. Served with Armed Forces, 1942-45. Decorated Bronze Star. Registered architect, N.C., S.C., Ga. Mem. A.I.A. (sec., treas. South Atlantic dist., 1959-62, chmn. com. 1961-62). Prin. works include Kilgo Meth. Ch., Charlotte, N.C., Porsey's Furniture Co., Charlotte, Allied Security Ins. Co., Fleet Ballistics Mil. Facility, Troops Complex. Home: 2516 Belvedere Av Charlotte NC 28205 Office: 2925 Independence Blvd Charlotte NC 28205

MACKLE, FRANK ELLIOTT, JR., real estate developer; b. Atlanta, July 23, 1916; s. Francis Elliott and Theresa (Roche) M.; B.C.E., Vanderbilt U., 1938; m. Virginia Steward, Sept. 3, 1940; children—Frank Elliott III, Nancy Radcliffe. Vice pres. Mackle Co., Miami, Fla., 1948—; pres., dir. Gen. Devel. Corp., 1958-61, chmn. bd., 1961; pres., dir. Deltona Corp., Miami 1963—; Marco Island Devel. Corp., Miami 1964—. Mem. Fed. Housing Adminstrn. Bd., 1961-62; mem. lay adv. com. Barry Coll., 1972—. Mem. lay adv. bd. Mercy Hosp., Miami, 1962—; mem. lay bd. trustees U. Notre Dame (Ind.), 1964—; trustee United Fund of Dade County; bd. dirs. Catholic Welfare Bur. Miami. Served as lt. USNR, 1943-46. Mem. Horseman's Benevolent and Protective Assn. (state pres. 1964-65, nat. pres. 1964-69), Home: 1410 W 25th St Sunset Island 2 Miami Beach FL 33140 Office: 3250 SW 3d Av Miami FL 33129

MACKNIGHT, HARRY DAVID, city ofcl.; b. Bellevue, Ky., Apr. 3, 1917; s. James Edwin and Hermina Henrietta (Lakamp) MacK.; student Cin. YMCA Sch., 1936-37; certificate in bus. adminstrn. U. Cin., 1954; m. Priscilla Bates Hanscom, Feb. 9, 1957; 1 stepdau., Suzanne (Mrs. Gerald F. Sparks); children—David, Richard, Helen. Cashier sch. office Cin. YMCA, 1937; board marker I.F. Westheimer Co., Cin., 1938; asst. bookkeeper Hock's Buick Co., 1939-41; machine operator Wright Aero. Corp., Cin., 1941-42; clk. Johnston Co., 1947; mem. payroll dept. Western Electric Co., 1948-50; with Baldwin Piano Co., Cin., 1951-52; city treas., tax collector City of Ft. Thomas, Ky., 1953—; treas. Ft. Thomas Municipal Properties Corp., 1966—; sec., treas. Policemen's and Firemen's Pension Fund, Ft. Thomas, 1953—. Served to staff sgt. AUS, 1942-46. Mem. Municipal Finance Officers Assn. U.S. and Can., Ky. Municipal Officers Assn. (exec. bd. 1969-70, 71, v.p. 1972—). Mem. United Ch. of Christ (deacon 1953-56, 69-70; treas. men's club). Club: Fort Thomas Veterans Social and Athletic (past treas.). Home: 62 Miller Lane Ft Thomas KY 41075 Office: City Bldg 130 N Ft Thomas Av Ft Thomas KY 41075

MACLAURY, D(ONALD) W(AYNE), research worker, educator; b. Waterbury, Conn., Feb. 28, 1905; s. Wayne and Ruth (Case) MacL; certificate in elec. engring. Pratt Inst., 1925; B.S., Cornell U., 1937; M.S. (fellow 1938-40), Ia. State Coll., 1940, Ph.D., 1955; m. Meita Hiteman, Aug. 10, 1946; 1 son, Keith. Instr. Ia. State Coll., 1937-38; asst. poultry husbandry, U. Ky., 1940-50, asso., 1950-54, poultry husbandman, 1954-59, prof. poultry sci., 1959-66, prof. animal scis., 1966—. Fellow A.A.A.S.; mem. Poultry Sci. Assn., Genetics Soc. Am., Am. Statis. Assn., Biometric Soc., Ky. Acad. Sci. Am. Inst Biol. Scis., World Poultry Sci. Assn., Sigma Xi, Gamma Sigma Delta. Contbr. articles to profl. jours. Home: 106 Brigadoon Pkwy Lexington KY 40503

MACLAY, DOUGLAS WELLER, mfg. co. exec.; b. Houston, Nov. 29, 1927; s. Edgar Gleim and Erin (Weller) M.; A.B., Rice U., 1950; B.B.A., U. Colo., 1950; M.B.A., Harvard, 1952; m. Sue Lykes, July 7, 1954; children—Leslie, Martha, Douglas Weller, Mallory, Susan. Salesman Republic Steel, Dallas, 1952-54; chmn. bd. Maclay Hurst, Houston, 1955-65; chmn. Burgess Industries, Dallas, 1965—; dir. Armstrong Assos., Dallas, 1968—. Mem. Dallas Citizens Council, Dallas Assembly. Trustee Dallas Art Mus., Dallas Womens Day Center; trustee Hockaday Sch., chmn. ann. fund drive, 1970-71. Served with USCGR, 1945-46. Presbyn. (deacon). Home: 5105 Shadywood Lane Dallas TX 75209 Office: 8101 Carpenter Freeway Dallas TX 75209

MACLAY, W(ILLIAM) DAYTON, govt. ofcl.; b. Auburn, Neb., June 22, 1905; s. Fred D. and Gertrude (Smelser) M.; B.Sc., U. Neb., 1928, Ph.D., 1931; m. Alberta Elizabeth Grandy, Dec. 28, 1927; children—Janet Noreen (Mrs. Kenneth E. Stockard), William Dayton, Ronald Douglas. Asst. prof. chemistry Minicipal U. of Omaha, 1932-36; research chemist NIH, 1936-40; with U.S. Dept. Agr., 1940—, dir. No. Regional Research Lab., Peoria, Ill., 1954-59, asst. adminstr. Agrl. Research Service, Washington, 1959-65, dir. research program devel. and evaluation staff, 1965—. Mem. Am. Chem. Soc., Inst. Food Technologists, Sigma Xi, Phi Lambda Upsilon. Club: Cosmos (Washington). Author articles. Patentee in field. Home: 3565 S Leisure World Blvd Silver Spring MD 20906 Office: US Dept of Agriculture Washington DC 20250

MACLEAN, HECTOR, banker, lawyer; b. Balt., Sept. 15, 1920; s. Angus W. and Margaret (French) McL.; B.S., Davidson Coll., 1941; LL.B., U. N.C., 1948; m. Lyl Francis Warwick, Dec. 18, 1944; 1 dau., Lyl Billings. Admitted to N.C. bar, 1948; pvt. practice, 1948—; pres. So. Nat. Bank of Lumberton, 1955—, So. Nat. Bank of N.C.; director, pres. Lumberton Implement Co., Va. and Carolina So. R.R.; dir. Kay & Co. Mem. N.C. Senate. Mayor of Lumberton 1949-53. Dir. N.C. Tb Assn., Med. Found. of N.C.; trustee St. Andrews Presby. Coll. Served from lt. to capt., AUS, 1942-46. Decorated Bronze Star medal. Mem. Robeson County Hist. Soc. (pres. 1955), C. of C., Am., N.C. bar assns., Omicron Delta Kappa, Phi Delta Phi. Home: 2101 Elm St Lumberton NC 28358 Office: 550 N Chestnut St Lumberton NC 28358

MACLEAN, PAUL D(ONALD), neurophysiologist; b. Phelps, N.Y., May 1, 1913; B.A., Yale, 1935, M.D., 1940; postgrad. U. Edinburgh, 1935-36; m. 1942; five children. Intern, Johns Hopkins Hosp., 1940-41; asst. resident medicine New Haven (Conn.) Hosp., 1941-42; asst. pathologist Yale Med. Sch., 1942; clin. instr. medicine, Washington Med. Sch., 1946-47; resident fellow psychiatry USPHS, Harvard Med. Sch., also Mass. Gen. Hosp., 1947-49; asst. prof. physiology, Yale Med. Sch., 1949-51, asst. prof. psychiatry, 1951-53, asso. prof., 1953-56, physiologist, 1956; chief Limbic Integration and Behavior Sect., NIH 1957—Dir., Electroencephalogical Lab., New Haven Hosp., 1951-52; attending physician Grace-New Haven Hosp., 1953-56. Trustee Prof. Percival Bailey Ednl. Project. Served to maj., M.C., AUS, 1942-46. Recipient Distinguished Res. award Assn. Residents Nervous and Mental Disease, 1964. NSF sr. resident fellow, Switzerland, 1956-57. Mem. Electroencephalogical Soc., Neurol. Assn., Assn. Hist. Med., Am. Physiol. Soc. Office: Lab of Neurophysiology Nat Inst Mental Health Bethesda MD 20014*

MACLEAY, DONALD, lawyer; b. Tacoma, Dec. 27, 1908; s. Lachian and Mabel (Nye) M.; student Hill Mil. Aca., Portland, Ore., 1922-24, Phillips Acad., Andover, Mass., 1924-25; LL.B., U. Colo., 1931; m. Elizabeth Hall Fesser, Jan. 27, 1934; children—Donald, Linda (Mrs. J. L. Dewell), Murdo Lachlan. Admitted to Colo., Ill., D.C. bars, 1931-33; com. prevention and punishment of crime Chgo. Assn. Commerce, 1931-32; gen. practice law, 1933—; now mem. firm Macleay, Lynch, Berhard & Gregg. Served to lt. USNR, 1943-45. Mem. Am., Maritime Administrv. bar assns., Bar Assn. D.C., Am. Judicature Soc., Assn. Interstate Commerce Practitioners Maritime Law Assn. U.S., Phi Delta Phi, Chi Psi. Episcopalian. Clubs: University, Propeller (Washington); Belle Haven Country (Alexandria, Va.); Pickwick, Internat. House (New Orleans); Fairfax Hunt (Fairfax County, Va.); Jefferson Island, Nat. Lawyers (Washington). Home: 1800 Edgehill Dr Belle Haven Alexandria VA 22307 Office: 1625 K St Washington DC 20006

MACLEISH, RODERICK, fgn. corr., author; b. Bryn Mawr, Pa., Jan. 15, 1926; s. Norman Hillard and Lenore (McCall) MacL.; student St. George's Sch., Newport, R.I., Art. Inst. Chgo., U. Chgo.; m. Diana Sumner Chapin, May 20, 1950 (div. 1968); children—Eric, Cynthia Sumner; m. 2d, Doris Ethel Inch, Apr. 20, 1970. Staff United Press, N.Y.C., 1946-47; staff ABC, 1947-49, script editor ABC-TV, 1949-50; news dir. Sta. WLAW, Boston, 1950-55; news commentator sta. WBZ, 1955-57; chief Washington bur. Westinghouse Broadcasting Co., 1957-59, chief European corr., London, Eng., 1959-66, radio-TV commentator, Washington, 1966-68, sr. commentator, 1968—. Named One of 10 Outstanding Young Men of Greater Boston, Jr. C. of C., 1956. Mem. Assn. Am. Corrs. London (pres. 1965). Independent. Episcopalian. Clubs: Federal City (Washington); Reform (London). Author: A Time of Fear, 1958; The Sun Stood Still, 1967; The Guilty Bystander, 1971; A City on the River, 1972; also author TV plays. Contbr. articles to mags., also polit. columns to Christian Sci. Monitor. Home: 4215 38th St NW Washington DC 20016 Office: Westinghouse Broadcasting Co Inc 1625 K St NW Washington DC 20006

MACLELLAN, ROBERT LLEWELLYN, ins. exec.; b. Chattanooga, Nov. 1, 1906; s. Robert J. and Cora (Llewellyn) M.; A.B., Dartmouth, 1928; LL.D., Maryville College, 1968; m. Kathrina Howze, Sept. 2, 1939; children—Anne Llewellyn, Robert Howze. Agy. sec. Provident Life & Accident Ins. Co., Chattanooga, 1930-32, agy. v.p., 1932-35, v.p., 1935-51, pres., 1952-69, chmn., chief exec. officer, 1969-71, also dir., mem. exec. com.; dir. Am. Nat. Bank & Trust Co., Forest Hills Cemetery Assn. Mem. exec. com. Am. Life Conv., 1966-68. Vice pres. McCallie Sch., Chattanooga, 1937-71, also trustee. Chmn. Community Chest dr., 1946. Trustee U. Chattanooga; bd. dirs. Bd. Annuities, Presbyn. Ch. U.S.; bd. dirs., exec. com. Greater Chattanooga Devel, Com.; bd. dirs. So. States Indsl. Council; chmn. Chattanooga Downtown Devel. Com.; bd. dirs. Life Ins. Med. Research Fund, Huebner Found., Chattanooga YMCA; bd. dirs. v.p., exec. com. United Fund of Chattanooga, pres., 1969,70; pres. Maclellan Found.; mem. devel. council U. Tenn. Com.; bd. visitors Berry Coll. Mem. Inst. Life Ins. (dir. 1962-64, chmn. 1965), Life Ins. Assn. Am. (dir. 1961-64), Newcomen Soc., Alpha Sigma Phi. Presbyn. (elder). Clubs: Lookout Mountain Golf, Chattanooga Golf and Country, Lookout Mountain Fairyland, Mountain City (Chattanooga); University (N.Y.C.). Died Dec. 15, 1971. Home: Lookout Mountain TN 37350 Office: Fountain Sq Chattanooga TN 37402

MACLEOD, JOHN, basketball coach U. Okla. at Norman. Office: Athletic Dept U Okla Norman OK 73069*

MACLEOD, NORMAN RICHARD CLAUDE, social work exec.; b. Ft. Sheridan, Ill., Oct. 3, 1903; s. Norman and Elizabeth (Keene) M.; student San Antonio Jr. Coll., 1920-22; B.S., U. Tex., 1924; m. Irma Roberta Hicks, Feb. 8, 1925; children—Mildred (Mrs. J.W. Turner, Jr.), Grace (Mrs. J.L. Nelms), Norman Richard. Worker, YMCA, San Antonio, Tex., 1924-28, dir. youth program, 1928-33; city-wide youth dir. YMCA, Houston, 1933-41, asso. gen. sec., 1941-44; gen. sec. YMCA, Wichita Falls, Tex., 1944-51; met. exec. dir. Greater Oklahoma City YMCA, 1951—; mem. exec. com. internat. div. YMCA of U.S. Mem. Morse Found. Com., 1960—; participant White House Conf. on Youth, 1950, 60. Bd. dirs. Community Action Program of Office Econ. Opportunity, Nat. YMCA; bd. regents U. Tex. Sch. Social Work, 1944-51, U. Okla. Sch. Social Work, 1955—. Mem. Nat. Council YMCA's, Gen. Secs. U.S. and Can. (pres. 1962-67), Oklahoma City C. of C. (dir.). Rotarian (pres.). Presbyn. (elder). Home: 2109 NW 61st St Oklahoma City OK 73112 Office: PO Box 1374 Oklahoma City OK 73101

MACMILLAN, CHARLES JAMES BARR, educator; b. Auburn, N.Y., Apr. 30, 1935; s. John Walker and Margaret Ethel (Barr) M.; B.A., Cornell U., 1957, Ph.D., 1965; M.A., Colgate U., 1959; m. Joan Tyler Reinberg, June 15, 1958; children—Ann Tyler, Tyler Lash. Acting asst. prof. U. Cal. at Los Angeles, 1962-64; asst. prof., asso. prof., dir. Gen. Edn. Program for Tchrs., Temple U., 1964-70; asso. prof., head dept. foundational studies in edn. Fla. State U., Tallahassee, 1970—. Mem. Philosophy Edn. Soc. (mem. exec. com.), Seal and Serpent Soc., Sherwoods of Cornell, Phi Kappa Phi, Phi Delta Kappa. Bd. editors Studies in Philosophy and Education, 1970. Editor: (with B. Paul Komisar) Psychological Concepts in Education, 1966; (with Thomas W. Nelson) Concepts of Teaching, 1968. Home: 2316 Armistead Rd Tallahassee FL 32303

MACNABB, ALEXANDER STUART, govt. ofcl.; b. Bay Shore, L.I., N.Y., Aug. 24, 1929; s. Francis Patrick Glennon and Helen Theresa (Monahan) MacN.; A.B., Colgate U., 1956; J.D., Washington and Lee U., 1959; postgrad. N.Y. U. Law Sch., 1960-61; m. Kathleen Marie Noonan, June 29, 1963; children—Helen Marie, Margaret Ann, Mary Alice, Ian Christopher, Joshua Finlay. Pres., Alexander MacNabb Assos., Advt., Bay Shore, 1960-67; pres. Town Almanac Pub. Co., Bay Shore, 1960-67; mem. Pres.'s Com. on Manpower, U.S. Office Econ. Opportunity, 1966-67, spl. asst. to dir. Community Action Program, 1967-69; Office Econ. Opportunity rep. to presidentially established Nat. Program for Vol. Action, Washington, 1969-70; dir. Office Operating Services, U.S. Dept. Interior, Bur. Indian Affairs, Washington, 1970-71, dir. Office Engring., 1971—; v.p. Newmark, Posner && Mitchell, N.Y.C., 1961; dir. Munston Electronic Mfg. Corp., Islip, N.Y., 1962. Chmn., Boy Scouts Am. fund drive, L.I., 1960, Arlington, Va., 1968-69, mem. exec. bd. Nat. Capital Area Council; asso. adviser Explorer Post, Arlington, commr. Boy Scout Roundtable, Arlington, mem. Scout World Jamboree Com. 1971, mem.-at-large nat. council; chmn. Girl Scouts U.S.A. fund drive, 1968; chmn. Washington and Lee Law Sch. fund drive, 1967-69. Bd. dirs. Nat. Capital Area Big Bros. Served with USNR, 1952-54. Mem. Am. Polit. Sci. Assn., Am. Sociol. Assn., Am. Acad. Polit. and Social Scis., Nat. Congress Am. Indians (Micmac Tribe), Am. Indian Movement, Nat. Indian Youth Council, Canoe Criusers Assn., Blue Ridge Voyaguers, Nat. Speleological Soc., Phi Alpha Delta, Pi Sigma Alpha. Roman Catholic. Clubs: Potomac Speleological (Arlington); Potomac Appalachian Trail (Washington). Home: 129 N Oakland St Arlington VA 22203 Office: Bureau Indian Affairs 1951 Constitution Av NW Washington DC 20242

MACNAMARA, DAVID CLAUDE, city ofcl.; b. Phila., Sept. 21, 1924; s. Gerald C. and Elizabeth C. (Ramspacher) MacN.; B.S. in Bus. Adminstrn. St. Joseph's Coll., Phila., 1949; m. Mary P. Schott, Sept. 10, 1949; children—Mary Lynn (Mrs. Robert A. Heekin), Margaret, Stephen, Sharon, Leslie, Lee Ann, Claudia. High sch. athletic dir., Lansdale, Pa., 1949-55; agy. mgr., dir. tng. State Farm Ins. Cos., Jacksonville, Fla., 1955-62; exec. dir. Greater Jacksonville Safety Council, 1962-68; sec. City Council, Jacksonville, 1968—; lectr. Jacksonville U., 1960—. Dir. Title Ins. Co. of South. Pres. Mental Health Assn. Duval County, 1968-70; founder Suicide Prevention Center, Jacksonville, 1969. Trustee Jones Coll., Jacksonville. Served with USMCR, 1942-46. K.C. (4 deg.), Rotarian. Home: 711 Seabrook Pkwy Jacksonville FL 32211 Office: City Hall Jacksonville FL 32202

MACNAUGHTON, JAMES ROBERT, accountant; b. Fredericton, N.B., Can., Apr. 11, 1918; s. Herbert R. and Jennie (Gamble) MacN.; came to U.S., 1923, naturalized, 1942; B.B.A., U. Minn., 1941; m. Emilie Borgwald, Jan. 19, 1944; children—Carol, James, Ann. With Ernst & Ernst, C.P.A.'s, 1941—, partner, Des Moines, 1956-70, partner in charge Mid-Atlantic dist., Washington, 1970—. Pres. elect Wis. Soc. C.P.A.'s, 1952. Pres. Jr. Achievement Des Moines, 1963-64; regional bd. mem. Midwest Jr. Achievement, 1964—; pres. Music Under Stars, Des Moines, 1964—. Bd. dirs. Ia. Taxpayers Assn., 1965—, CIRAS, Salvation Army, Boys Home of Ia. Served to lt. (j.g.) USCGR, 1942-45. C.P.A., Ia., 6 other states. Mem. Am. Inst. C.P.A.'s, Ia. Soc. C.P.A.'s (pres. 1957-58), Des Moines C. of C. (dir.), Beta Gamma Sigma (hon.), Beta Alpha Psi (hon.). Episcopalian. Mason (Shriner, Jester), Rotarian. Clubs: Golf and Country (pres. 1960), Des Moines Wakenda (Des Moines); International, Congressional Golf and Country, Touchdown, Terrapin (Washington). Home: 9605 Weathered Oak Ct Bethesda MD 20034 Office: 1225 Connecticut Av NW Washington DC 20036

MACNAUGHTON, WILLIAM ALEXANDER, lawyer; b. Winchester, Ky., Jan. 18, 1922; s. Archibald John and Anne (Epperson) MacN.; B.B.A., U. Tex., 1943, LL.B., 1948; m. Anne Cherlene O'Hair, Aug. 23, 1943; children—Anne Lynn, Virginia Sue, William Alexander, James Robert, Charles Thomas. Admitted to Tex. bar, 1948; since practiced in Houston, 1948—; mem. firms MacNaughton & Levevidge, 1948-50, Townes & Townes, 1950-54; pvt. practice law, 1958-66; gen. atty. Ginther, Warren &Ginther, 1955-58; city judge Bellaire, Tex., 1951-56; partner MacNaughton, Brady & Marlatt, Houston, 1966-68, MacNaughton & McWhorter, 1968—. Pres., So. Assos., Inc., 1967—; gen. partner MacNaughton & Assos., Ltd., 1963—. Mem. Houston Bar Assn. (v.p. 1958). Home: 2148 Inwood St Houston TX 77019 Office: 614 Southwest Tower Houston TX 77002

MACNEES, VALERIE CATHERINE KOOPS (MRS. JAMES BARRY MACNEES), journalist; b. LaCrosse, Wis., Sept. 11, 1912; d. Edward Charles and Minnie (Morley) Koops; B.A., Wis. State U., 1933; postgrad. U. Wis., 1936-37; m. James Barry MacNees, June 5, 1940; children—Valerie Ann (Mrs. James R. Youmans), James Michael. Tchr. pub. schs., Wis., 1933-40; clk. U.S. Census Bur., Washington, 1940-42; classification clk. WPB, Washington, 1942-43; editor Fgn. Broadcast Intelligence, Washington, 1944-45; mem. editorial staff N.C.W.C. News Service, Washington, 1946-51; womens editor Catholic Standard, Washington, 1951-63, feature editor, 1963—. Weekly columnist Prince Georges Post, Hyattsville, Md., 1969—. Author: Catholic Churches in Montgomery County, 1966. Home: 2007 Brighton Rd Washington DC 20018 Office: 1711 N St Washington DC 20006

MAC NERNEY, JOHN SHERIDAN, educator; b. N.Y.C., Jan. 10, 1923; s. John Sheridan and Lillian (Egelhofer) MacN.; student Trinity Coll., 1939-41; B.A. with highest honors, U. Tex., 1948, Ph.D., 1951; m. Kathleen Mary O'Connor, Dec. 8, 1945. Vibration analyst, United Aircraft Corp., E. Hartford, Conn., 1941-43; instr. pure math. U. Tex. 1948-51; instr. math. Northwestern U., 1951-52; asst. prof. math., U. N.C., 1952-56, asso. prof. 1956-62, prof., 1962-67; prof. math. U. Houston, 1967—. Served as cpl. USAAF, 1943-46. Mem. A.A.A.S., Am. Math. Soc., Elisha Mitchell Sci. Soc., Math. Assn. Am., N.C. Acad. Sci., Circolo Matematico di Palermo, Phi Beta Kappa, Sigma Xi (pres. N.C. chpt. 1966-67). Home: 2016 Main St Houston TX 77002

MACON, EDWARD MALCOLM, physician; b. Washington, Jan. 24, 1928; s. Edward Bailey and Anne Isobel (Carpenter) M.; B.S., George Washington U., 1951, M.D., 1955; m. D. Anne Ferguson; children—Michael Gilbert, Patricia Jane, Elizabeth Anne. Intern McLaren Gen. Hosp., Flint, Mich., 1955-56; resident internal medicine Washington (D.C.) Gen. Hosp., 1956-57; gen. practice medicine, Vienna, Va., 1957-69; physician emergency room Prince Georges Hosp., Cheverly, Md., 1969—. Served with AUS, 1946-47. Mem. A.M.A., Am. Coll. Emergency Physicians, Med. and Chirurgical Faculty State Md. Home: 9831 Vale Rd Vienna VA 22180 Office: Prince Georges Hospital Cheverly MD 20785

MACON, GEORGE WILSON, JR., tobacco mfg. co. exec.; b. Henderson, N.C., Aug. 21, 1909; s. George W. and Pattie Boddie (Alston) M.; m. Sarah Elizabeth Bass, July 23, 1937; children—Emily Jane (Mrs. James Hamilton Baird), George Wilson III, Anne Alston (Mrs. Harry Hobbs Goodwin). Pres. Universal Leaf Tobacco Co., Inc. of China, 1946-50; with Philip Morris, Inc., Richmond, Va., 1950—, v.p., 1959—; dir. Philip Morris Overseas, Va. Trust Co., Richmond. Home: 215 Ampthill Rd Richmond VA Office: Philip Morris Inc Box 1895 Richmond VA

MACON, SETH CRAVEN, ins. co. exec.; b. Climax, N.C., Mar. 22, 1919; s. Oren T. and Kate (Craven) M.; A.B., Guilford Coll., 1940; grad. Am. Coll. Life Underwriters, 1949; attended So. Meth. U. Inst. Ins. Marketing, 1947, U. N.C. Exec. Program, 1958; m. Hazel Lee Monsees, June 27, 1942; children—Carol Susan, Randall Seth. With Jefferson Standard Life Ins. Co., 1940—, supt. agys., 1946, sales dir., Greensboro, N.C., 1956-58, asst. agy. mgr., 1958-62, 2d v.p., asso. agy. mgr., 1962-64, v.p., asso. agy. mgr., 1964-67, v.p., agy. mgr., 1967-70, sr. v.p. agy., 1970—, also dir. Trustee Guilford Coll. Served with USA-AF, 1942-46. Baptist (deacon, mem. finance com.). Clubs: Greensboro Rotary, Starmount Forest Country, Piedmont Sales Execs. Home: 3803 Madison Av Greensboro NC 27403 Office: P O Box 21008 Greensboro NC 27420

MACPEAK, THOMAS JOHN, lawyer; b. N.Y.C., July 6, 1933; s. Samuel Daniel and Gertrude (Carroll) M.; B.S. in Chemistry, LeMoyne Coll., 1955; LL.B., Georgetown U., 1958; m. Carol Ann Conboy, July 3, 1965; children—Anne-Marie, Mark Daniel. Admitted to D.C. bar, 1959; practice law, Washington, 1959—; with Sughrue, Rothwell, Mion, Zinn and Macpeak and predecessor firm, 1960—, partner, 1961—. Served with AUS, 1959. Mem. Am., D.C. bar assns., Am. PatentLaw Assn., Inter-Am. Bar Assn., Internat. Assn. Protection Indsl. Property, Lawyers Club. Club: International (Washington). Home: 4706 Jamestown Rd Bethesda MD 20016 Office: 1776 K St NW Washington DC 20006

MACPHERSON, JANET TAYLOR WOLFENDEN (MRS. HERBERT GRENFELL MACPHERSON), civic worker; b. Phila.; d. Edward Musker and Annette (Robertson) Wolfenden; B.S., M.A., U. Pa.; m. Herbert Grenfell MacPherson, June 5, 1937; children—Janet Lynne, Robert Duncan. Pres., Franklin Sch. P.T.A., 1954-56; chpt. dir. Am. Assn. U. Women, 1957-59; pres. League Women Voters, Oak Ridge, 1961-63, Tenn., 1967-69; pres. Oak Ridge Civic Music Assn. Women Guild, 1963-64; pres. Friends Oak Ridge Pub. Library, 1966-67; mem. Nat. Com. for Support Pub. Schs., 1967-70; mem. Comm. 100 Found. for Better Govt. for Tenn., 1967—; mem. salary structure study com. Bd. Edn. Oak Ridge, 1969-71; bd. dirs. Awareness House of Oak Ridge, Inc., 1970—; mem. Tenn. com. for 1970 White House Conf. on Children and Youth, 1969-70; mem. state planning com. Air Quality Project for Tenn., 1970-71. Editor: This Is Oak Ridge, Tenn., 1961. Home: 102 Orchard Circle Oak Ridge TN 37830

MACY, ARTHUR WARREN, lawyer; b. Phila., July 1, 1919; s. Arthur Warren and Marietta (Nyland) M.; student U. Colo., 1939-41, 45-48; J.D., La. State U., 1952; m. Frances Walts, Sept. 7, 1948; children— Patricia Ann, Susan Lyn, Mary Jane, Barbara Warren. Research asst. history dept. U. Colo., 1947-48; tchr. San Carlos (Ariz.) Apache Reservations, 1948-49; research asst. legal biography La. State U., 1949-50; admitted to La. bar, 1952; practiced in Hammond, La., 1952—; mem. firm Reid & Reid, 1952-54, Reid & Macy, 1955-68, Macy, Kemp and Newton, 1969-71, Macy & Kemp, 1971—; law clk. 1st Circuit Ct. of Appeal, State of La., 1962—. Served with USNR, 1941-45. Mem. Am., La., 21st Jud. Dist. La. (pres. 1965-67), bar assns., Order of Coif, Phi Kappa Phi, Phi Delta Phi, Pi Gamma Mu, Phi Kappa Psi. Democrat. Episcopalian. Mason (K.T.), Rotarian, Lion, Kiwanian. Asso. editor: La. Law Rev., 1951-52. Home: Route 4 Box 171M Hammond LA 70401 Office: 220 W Thomas St Hammond LA 70401

MACY, JOSEPH, educator; b. Bklyn., Mar. 29, 1927; s. John and Anna Maria (Maurer) M.; A.A., Palm Beach Jr. Coll., 1962; B.A., Fla. Atlantic U., 1966, M.Ed., 1967; postgrad. FBI Nat. Acad., 1961; m. Shirley Walden, Oct. 15, 1949; children—Michael Joseph, John Francis, Kathryn Ann, Ralph William. With Palm Beach Police Dept., 1950-51; patrolman to asst. chief West Palm Beach Police Dept., 1951-68; prof. law enforcement Palm Beach (Fla.) Jr. Coll., adj. prof. law enforcement Fla. Atlantic U., 1969—. Founder traffic violators sch. Palm Beach County, 1968. Mem. adv. com. State Dept. Edn. on Higher Edn. for Police Officers, 1966—; mem. Gov.'s Police Standards Council, 1967—. Bd. dirs. Palm Beach County Mental Health Assn., 1963—, Comprehensive Community Mental Health Center, 1966—, Gulfstream council Boy Scouts Am., 1951—. Served with USNR, 1944-48. Recipient J. Edgar Hoover medal for excellence, 1961. Mem. Fla. Peace Officers Assn., Am. Assn. Jr. Colls., Internat. Assn. Chiefs of Police, Palm Beach County Firemans Guild, Phi Theta Kappa. Democrat. Roman Catholic. K.C. Home: 224 Belmonte Rd West Palm Beach FL 33405 Office: 4200 S Congress Av Lakeworth FL 33460

MADAMBA, JORGE JUDY, dentist; b. Central Tinunga Isabelia, Negros Occidental, P.I., Jan. 26, 1936 (parent Am. citizen); s. Jorge Arzaga and Iva (Harrison) M.; B.S., Okla. State U., 1960; D.D.S., U. Mo., 1967; m. Drucilla Pemberton, Oct. 25, 1969; 1 son, Ryan Koby. Instr., U. Mo. Dental Sch., Kansas City, 1967; pvt. practice dentistry, Tulsa, 1967—. Mem. Dental Health Edn. Com., Tulsa, 1971—, Vocational Edn. Com., Tulsa, 1971—, adv. com. Tulsa Pub. Health Dept., 1971—. Mem. Am. Dental Assn., Okla., Tulsa County dental socs., Am. Soc. Preventive Dentistry, Acad. Gen. Dentistry, Am. Soc. Clini. Hypnosis, Endodontics Study Club (pres. 1970), Okla. State U. Alumni Assn. (chpt. pres. 1972), Sigma Chi. Kiwanian. Home: 2931 E 77th St Tulsa OK 74136 Office: 4142 S Harvard St Tulsa OK 74135

MADDEN, JAMES HOWARD, mech. engr.; b. Muskogee, Okla., Apr. 16, 1930; s. Joseph H. and Buena Vista (Harris) M.; B.S., Okla. State U., 1957; postgrad. Okla. U., 1965-67; m. Archie Robertson, Apr. 11, 1953; children—Joseph H., Buena Faye, Jimmy Don, Carol Ann, Mable Ann, Suzanne Lynn. With Internat. Petroleum Co., Coral Gables, Fla., 1957-58, Thiokol Chem. Co., Marshall, Tex., 1959-61; with Civil Service Commn., Abilene, Tex., 1961, Mobile, Ala., 1963-65, mech. engr. Tinker AFB, Okla., 1965—. Rancher raising Charolais and Herefords, McLoud, Okla., 1967—. Served with AUS, 1950-52. Decorated Bronze Star medal; recipient Recognition for service certificate U.S. C.E., 1961. Mem. Okla., Mil. engrs. socs. Home: Route 2 Box 75 McLoud OK 74851 Office: Tinker AFB Oklahoma City OK 73145

MADDEN, MARTHA ANN, coll. dean; b. Shreveport, La., Apr. 5, 1937; d. James H. and Velma (Fletcher) Madden; B.S., So. Methodist U., 1959; M.A., 1963. Tchr math. Dallas Ind. Sch. Dist., 1959-62; guidance counselor Thomas Rusk Jr. High Sch., Dallas, 1962-65; dir. Florence Moore Hall, dean student staff Stanford, 1965-67; dean of women N.E. La. U., Monroe, 1967—. Dean students World Campus Afloat, spring 1970; N.E. La. U. adviser, mem. exec. bd. World Campus Afloat Assn., 1971—, mem. exec. council 1971-73, asst. counselor, summer 1972. Hon. mem. adv. bd. vol. workers VA Hosp., Palo Alto, Cal., 1967; mem. San Francisco Symphony Found., 1965-67; rep. Monroe Panhellenic Council, 1969—. Bd. dirs. Methodist Wesley Found., N.E. La. U., bd. govs. Ouachita Parish chpt. A.R.C., 1971. Mem. La. Tchrs. Assn., La. Assn. Deans of Women (v.p. 1969), Am., La. personnel and guidance assns., Nat. Assn. Women Deans and Counselors (La. membership chmn.), La. Vocational Guidance Assn. (membership chmn. 1972), So. Coll. Personnel Guidance Assn., Nat. Vocational Guidance Assn., Am. Assn. U. Women, Internat. Platform Assn., Zeta Tau Alpha, Alpha Lambda Delta, Pi Lambda Theta. Clubs: Altrusa; Toastmistress. Home: 1604 Shannon St Monroe LA 71201

MADDEN, ROBERT BOWMAN, airline co. exec.; b. Sharon, Pa., Aug. 28, 1912; s. Edward Aloysius and Nannie Aletta (Bowman) M.; B.S., U.S. Naval Acad., 1933; M.S., Mass. Inst. Tech., 1938; postgrad. Harvard, 1947; m. Mary Norman Hopkins, June 18, 1935; children—Nancy Helen (Mrs. Linwood Banks Simmons), Robert Hopkins. Commd. ensign USN, 1933, advanced through grades to capt., 1953; adminstrv. asst. to chief Bur. Ships, 1953-54; head marine engring. dept. U.S. Naval Acad., 1954-57; dir. ship design Bur. Ships, 1957-59; comdr. Charleston Naval Shipyard, 1959-60; v.p. engring. Am. Pres. Lines, San Francisco, 1961-63; mgr. marine engring. Pan Am. World Airways, Inc., Patrick AFB, Kennedy Space Center, Fla., 1963-65, mgr. facilities engring., 1964-70; project mgr. engring. support services project NASA, 1970—. Mem. bd. control U.S. Naval Inst., 1954-59. Registered profl. engr., D.C. Mem. Am. Soc. Naval Engrs. (asst. sec.-treas. 1950-59), Soc. Naval Architects and Marine Engrs., Soc. Am. Mil. Engrs. (pres. Canaveral post 1971-72), Sigma Xi. Republican. Methodist. Asst. editor Jour Am. Soc. Naval Engrs., 1950-59. Home: 102 W Bay Dr Cocoa Beach FL 32931 Office: Pan Am World Airways Inc Kennedy Space Center FL 32899

MADDEN, TOM J., clergyman; b. Enid, Okla., Apr. 14, 1919; s. Thomas J. and Ama (Sigmon) M.; A.B., Okla. Bapt. U., 1943; postgrad. Baylor U., 1943-44; Th.M., Southwestern Bapt. Theol. Sem., 1948; m. Edna Earle Parker, June 27, 1946; children—Thomas J. III, Jane Elizabeth. Ordained to ministry Bapt. Ch., 1941; prof. Bible, Arlington State U., Tex., 1947-48; pastor Calvary Bapt. Ch., Mexia, Tex., 1948-51, Greenbrier (Tenn.) Bapt. Ch., 1951-54, 1st Bapt. Ch., Tullahoma, Tenn., 1954—. Pres., Tenn. Bapt. Conv., 1968—, Tenn. Bapt. Found., 1963—, Tullahoma Ministerial Alliance, 1957-58; exec. com. So. Baptist Conv., 1966—. Trustee Bapt. Hosp., Nashville. Rotarian. Home: 124 Oak Park Tullahoma TN 37388 Office: Grundy at Washington Tullahoma TN 37388

MADDEN, WALES HENDRIX, JR., lawyer, univ. regent; b. Amarillo, Tex., Sept. 1, 1927; s. Wales Hendrix and Kathryn (Nash) M.; B.A., U. Tex., 1950, LL.B., 1952; m. Alma Faye Cowden, Nov. 8, 1952; children—Wales Hendrix III, Straughn. Admitted to Tex. bar, 1952, practiced in Amarillo. Dir. First Nat. Bank of Amarillo, Wainco Oil Co.; chmn. exec. com. Mesa Petroleum Co. Mem. bd. regents Amarillo Coll., 1958-59; bd. regents U. Tex., 1959-65, also mem. univ. devel. bd.; mem. Tex. Coll. and Univ. System Coordinating Bd. 1964—; mem. Amarillo Area Found., Amarillo Airport Bd., Cal Farley's Boys Ranch. Trustee Trinity U., San Antonio. Served with USNR. Named Outstanding Young Man of Amarillo, 1957. Mem. Am., Amarillo (pres. 1956) bar assns., Amarillo C. of C. (pres. 1968), State Bar Tex., State Jr. Bar Tex. (pres. 1956), Friar Soc., Phi Alpha Delta, Phi Delta Theta, Phi Eta Sigma, Pi Sigma Alpha. Presbyn. (elder). Home: 2701 Teckla St Amarillo TX 79106 Office: 700 W 9th St Amarillo TX 79101

MADDLONE, JOSEPH S., corp. exec.; b. Bklyn.,, 1912; C.B. Rutgers U. Grad. Sch. Banking, 1948. Vice pres., asst. sec. Gulf Am. Corp.; sec., dir. Andrew Hotel Corp., Cape Coral Constrn. Co., Cape Coral Mortgate Co., Cape Coral Realty, Inc., Collgerry Realty, Inc., Pine Corp., Am. Ins. Agy., Inc., Caves Devel. Corp., Gulf Am. Galleries, Inc., Guild Life Ins. Co. Am., Gulf Communicators, Inc., Hobby House Am., Inc., Hobbyland U.S.A., Inc., Homeowners Title Co., Lee Investment Co., Pkwy. Mortgage Co., Brand Names, Inc., Congress New Orleans East, Inc., Fed. Ins. Agy., Inc., Golden Gate Inn, Inc., Golden Gate Realty, Inc., Gulf Am. Sales Corp., Modern Air Transp., Inc., Remuda Ranch Clubs, Inc., Fort Myers Constrn. Co., Gulf Am. Land Corp. Ariz., Gulf Guaranty Land & Title Co., N.M. Am. Land Corp., Surety Acceptance Co., Tropical Attractions, Inc., Utah Am. Land Corp., Amco Budget Corp.; v.p., sec., dir. Gulf Key Enterprises, Inc., Country Club Inn, Inc., Pin-World, Inc., River Ranch Acres Clubs, Inc., Tropical Paradise, Inc.; v.p., asst. sec. Rosen Investment Corp.; asst. sec. Golden Gate Estates, Inc.; sec., treas., dir. Oriental Displays, Inc., Gulf Am. Land Corp. (1966)., Mem. Am. Mus. Natural History, UN Assn. U.S.A., Smithsonian Assos. Clubs: Golden Gate Golf and Country (sec., dir); Jockey (Miami); Racquet. Home: 2501 Cordova St Coral Gables FL 33134 Office: 7880 Biscayne Blvd Miami FL 33138

MADDOX, CARL, dir. athletics La. State U. at Baton Rouge. Address: Dept Athletics La State U Baton Rouge LA 70803*

MADDOX, DAN WAITE, credit corp. exec.; b. Easonville, Ala., June 9, 1909; s. William Notley and Minnie (Waite) M.; student Ga. Sch. Tech., 1925-29; m. Margaret Huffman, June 21, 1969; children—Judith E. (Mrs. Frank Isbel Nebhut), Ellen King (Mrs. Norman Christianson), James Notley. With Universal C.I.T. Corp., N.Y.C., 1930-41; founder, chief exec. officer Assos. Capital Corp., Nashville, Tenn., 1943—; dir. Assos. Corp. North Am., South Bend, Ind., mem. exec. com., 1964—; dir. Capital Life Ins. Co., Denver, Colo., Shoney's Big Boy Enterprises, Nashville, Commerce Union Bank, Nashville; chmn. bd. Cumberland Life Ins. Co., Nashville. Mem. Economic Devel. Com., State of Tenn., 1971—. Tenn. Agrl. and Indsl. Commn., 1972—. Trustee, African Wildlife Leadership Found., Washington; trustee Childrens Museum, Nashville, v.p., 1971—; trustee Maddox Found. Recipient Weatherby award Shikar Safari Internat., 1967. Mem. East African Profl. Hunters Assn., Shikar Safari International (pres. 1965). Clubs: Mill Reef (Antigua, West Indies); Explorers (N.Y.C.). Home: 1228 Chickering Rd Nashville TN 37215 Office: 601 Broadway Nashville TN 37203

MADDOX, EDWARD ALDRIDGE, JR., physician; b. Atlantic City, Feb. 23, 1921; s. Edward Aldridge and Jennie Elizabeth (Jackson) M.; B.A., Lincoln U., 1943; M.D., Meharry Med. Coll., 1946; m. Gloria Bernice Demby, Jan. 1, 1947; children—Edward Aldridge III, Allen Rodrick. Intern, Hubbard Hosp., Nashville, 1946-47; gen. practice medicine, Selma, Ala., 1947—; med. dir. Civil Rights, Selma-Montgomery, 1963, Head Start Perry County, Ala., 1965—, Selma Head Start, 1971, Green County (Ala.) Office Econ. Opportunity, 1971—; grand med. dir. Order Eastern Star, 1948-53; pub. health physician, 1962-63. Dist. commr. Boy Scouts Am., 1963-65. Bd. dirs. Selma YMCA. Served with M.C., AUS, 1943-46; to maj. M.C., USAF, 1953-55; officer Res. Mem. Nat. (del. 1966), Ala. (past pres.) med. assns., Alpha Phi Alpha, Beta Kappa Chi. Elk. Club: Chesterfield (Selma). Home: 1511 Mabry St Selma AL 36701 Office: 811 1st Av Selma AL 36701

MADDOX, GEORGE LAMAR, JR., educator; b. McComb, Miss., July 2, 1925; s. George Lamar and Dimple Mae (McEwen) M.; B.A., Millsaps Coll., 1949; M.A., S.T.B., Boston U., 1952; Ph.D., Mich. State U., 1956; m. Frances Evelyn Godbold, June 9, 1946; children—Patricia Alise, George David. Asst. prof. to prof. Millsaps Coll., 1952-60; asso. prof., prof. Duke, Durham, N.C., 1960—. chief div. med. sociology Med. Center, 1967—, also dir. Center for Study of Aging and Human Devel. Spl. USPHS postdoctoral research fellow U. London, 1968-69; cons. NIH, 1958—. Served with inf. AUS, 1942-45. Kent fellow Danforth Found., 1954-56, Russell Sage fellow, 1960-62. Mem. Am. Sociol. Assn., A.A.A.S., Gerontol. Soc. Democrat. Methodist. Author: Drinking Among Teenagers, 1964; The Domesticated Drug, 1970; The Future of Aging and the Aged, 1971; Human Behavior, 1971. Home: 2750 McDowell St Durham NC 27705

MADDOX, JAMES GRAY, economist; b. Rison, Ark., Feb. 4, 1907; s. Ernest Ray and Eve (Gray) M.; B.S.A., U. Ark., 1927; M.S., U. Wis., 1930; M.P.A., Harvard, 1948, Ph.D., 1950; m. Alice Batten, June 15, 1934; children—Susanna (Mrs. Stephen A. Tripp), Jeannie (Mrs. Walter P. Sy), Mclinda (Mrs. Albert S. Boyer), Swanee (Mrs. John H. Austin). Economist, FCA, 1933-36, A.A.A., 1936-37, Resettlement Adminstrn., 1937-39; div. dir. Farm Security Adminstrn., 1939-43; asst. to chief Bur. Agrl. Econs., Dept. Agr., 1943-47; asst. dir. Am. Internat. Assn., 1949-52; v.p. Internat. Devel. Services, N.Y.C., 1953; mem. staff Am. U. Field Staff, 1953-58; prof. agrl. econs. N.C. State Coll., Raleigh, 1958-—, asst. dir. Agrl. Policy Inst., 1960-67, dir., 1967-70; dir. research study Econ. Devel. and Manpower Requirements in South, 20th Century Fund, 1962-66. Mem. Am. Econ. Assn., Am. Farm Econ. Assn. Author: Technical Assistance by Religious Agencies in Latin America, 1956; The Advancing South: Manpower Prospects and Problems, 1967. Home: Route 6 Box 266 Raleigh NC 27609

MADDOX, LESTER GARFIELD, former gov. Ga.; b. Atlanta, Sept. 30, 1915; ed. Atlanta pub. schs.; student accounting and engring.; m. Virginia Cox; children—Linda (Mrs. Don Densmore), Lester Garfield, Virginia Louise, Larry. Formerly supr. Atlanta indsl. plant; entered retail bus. and opened Pickrick Restaurant; formerly engaged in real estate sales, devel., grocery field; established Pickrick Furniture; later gov. of Ga., now lt. gov. Mem. U.S., Ga. chambers commerce, Atlanta Better Bus. Bur., Nat. Retail Furniture Assn., Travelers Protective Assn., Ga. Sheriffs Assn. (hon.), Peace Officers Assn. Ga. (hon.), Justices of Peace and Constables Assn. Ga. (hon.), Westgate Mchts. Assn. (pres.). Baptist. Mason (Shriner). Moose; mem. Jr. Order United Am. Mechanics. Club: Buckhead Fifty. Address: 205 The Prado Atlanta GA 30309

MADDOX, ROBERT LEE,, SR., chem. co. exec.; b. Atlanta, Apr. 25, 1909; s. Clarence Earl and Carrie Lee (Bennett) M.; student elec. engring. Internat. Corr. Schs., 1934; m. Virginia Manley Causey, Apr. 12, 1931; children—Robert Lee, Michael, Louis, David P. and Donald P. (twins). With Ga. Power Co., 1932-39; supr. elec. div. U.S. Naval Shipyards, Portsmouth, Va., 1941-44; partner Portsmouth Appliance and Service, 1945-47; appraiser elec. engring. Bales & Womach, Atalanta, 1950-51; salesman Guardian Chem. Co., Atlanta, 1952-60; sr. v.p., dist. sales mgr. Momar, Inc., 1960-—; partner Holiday Inn Franchise, Bainbridge, Ga.; pres. Clear View Nursing Care, Thomaston, Ga. Mem. Clarkston (Ga.) City Council, 1940-41. Mem. Gideons Internat. (v.p. Ga. 1966, treas. Ga. 1963, zone trustee 1971). Baptist (deacon). Mason (32 deg., Shriner). Home: 507 Hill St Thomaston GA 30286 Office: 1830 Ellsworth Industrial Dr NW Atlanta GA 30318

MADDOX, WILLIAM BAILEY, fire chief; b. Anderson, S.C., July 19, 1908; s. William Lee and Frances Elizabeth (Vandiver) M.; student Clemson U., 1925-27; m. Annie Laura Breazeale, Nov. 9, 1935 (dec.); children—Frankie Lee (Mrs. Robert Lee Squires), James M. With engring. dept. S.C. State Hwy. Dept., late 1920's; with Anderson (S.C.) Fire Dept., 1931-—, chief, 1950-—. Pres., bd. dirs. Booster Club Local High Sch., 1954-55; bd. dirs. United Fund, 1958-60. Mem. Internat. Assn. Fire Chiefs, S.C. Firemens Assn. (pres.), S.C. State Fire Chiefs (pres.), Anderson Meml. Hosp. Assn., Clemson U. IPTAY. Mason. Home: 605 E Orr St Anderson SC 29621 Office: 401 S Main St Anderson SC 29621

MADDOX, WILLIS HENRY, mayor; b. Graford, Tex., Dec. 4, 1913; s. Finis Willis and Eva (Holland) Maddox; student North Tex. State U., 1931-33, U. Tex., 1934-36; LL.B., Cumberland U., 1938; m. Eugenia Freeman, May 28, 1938; children—Ann (Mrs. Don H. Stenhouse), Robert Willis. With Maddox Devel. Co., petroleum, Pittsburg, Tex., 1938-40; partner, sec.-treas. Auto Parts and Service Co., Lebanon, Tenn., 1941-54; owner Maddox Real Estate, Lebanon, 1954-—; mem. Lebanon City Council, 1948-57, mem. finance com., 1958-59, mayor, 1970-—. Pres., Tenn. Parents Council for Handicapped, 1950-53; v.p. Tenn. Assn. on Mental Retarded, 1969-70, pres., 1970-71; mem. Tenn. Gov.'s Adv. Bd. Mental Retardation, 1968-71; pres. Wilson County Vocational Center, 1968-—. Mem. Tenn. Senate, 1955-56. Bd. dirs. McFarland Hosp. Mem. Tenn. Municipal League (dir.), Mid-Cumberland Council Govts. (dir.), Lambda Chi Alpha. Mason (Shriner), Rotarian. Home: 103 Oak Hill Circle Lebanon TN 37087 Office: City Hall 119 S College St Lebanon TN 37087

MADEWELL, CARL EDWARD, economist; b. Spencer, Tenn., May 11, 1935; s. Erastis E. and Annie Lee (McCoy) M.; B.S., Tenn. Tech. U., 1957; M.S., U. Tenn., 1960; M.A., U. Wis., 1968, postgrad., 1966-68; m. Dorothy Jean Holingsworth, Aug. 15, 1958; children—Alan Edward, Jared Lee. Farmer, Spencer, Tenn., 1951-53; rubber mfg. inspector Ohio Rubber Co., Willoughby, 1954-57; r.r. signal mechanic N.Y. Central R.R., Willoughby, O., 1956-57; marketing specialist U.S. Dept. Agr., Balt., 1960-62; agrl. economist TVA, Muscle Shoals, Ala., 1962-—. Served with AUS, 1958. Recipient Scholarship award Tenn. Farmers Coop., 1953-54. Mem. Am. Econs. Assn., Am. Marketing Assn., Am., So. agrl. econs. assns., Catfish Farmers Am. Assn., Alpha Tau Alpha. Baptist. Club: Exchange (Florence, Ala.). Home: 2316 Bower Dr Florence AL 35630 Office: TVA Nat Fertilizer Devel Center Muscle Shoals AL 35660

MADIGAN, JOHN ALPHONSUS, JR., lawyer; b. Monesson, Pa., Apr. 15, 1919; s. John Alphonsus and Edna L. (Scales) M.; B.S., U. Miami, 1940; J.D., George Washington U., 1948; postgrad. U. Fla., 1940-42; m. Mary Louise Green, Sept. 29, 1946; children—John Raymond, Terrell Courtney. Mem. staff U.S. War Dept., Washington, 1942-43, 46-48, U.S. Dept. Air Force, 1948-50; admitted to Fla. bar, 1948, D.C. Bar, 1948; practiced in Tallahassee, 1950-—; asst. atty. gen., Fla., 1950-53; mem. firm Madigan, Parker, Gatlin, Truett & Swedmark and predecessor firms, Tallahassee, 1958-—, sr. partner, 1970-—; pres. Seminole Ventures, Inc., Tallahassee, 1970-—; dir. Univ. Bus. Asso., Univ. Comml. Asso., Tallahassee; vice chmn. Fla. capital office First Fed. Savs. & Loan Assn. of St. Petersburg; chmn. Parkway Nat. Bank, Tallahassee. Pres. United Fund, Tallahassee, 1965. Bd. dirs. Extended Care of Tallahassee, 1971-—; trustee, vice chmn. Tallahassee Community Coll. Served to comdr. USNR, 1943-46. Mem. Am., Fla., Tallahassee bar assns., 2d Jud. Bar Assn. (pres. 1964), Phi Delta Phi, Pi Kappa Alpha. Kiwanian. Clubs: Capital City Country (pres. 1970), Killearn Golf and Country, Tiger Bay (Tallahassee). Home: 1410 Alban Av Tallahassee FL 32301 Office: PO O Box 669 Tallahassee FL 32302

MADISON, BLAINE MARK, ret. juvenile correction ofcl.; b. Olin, N.C., Feb. 13, 1906; s. Charles Martin and Molly (White) M.; A.B., High Point Coll., 1929; M.A., Duke, 1933, M.Ed., 1939; m. Helen Williams, May 15, 1935. Prin. N.C. Pub. Sch., 1929-42; head. Meth. Orphanage Schs., Raleigh, N.C., 1942-52; asst. dir. Prisons for State N.C., 1952-55; commr. Juvenile Correction for N.C., 1955-71. Mem. profl. council Nat. Council on Crime and Delinquency; del. planning commn. Nat. Inst. Crime and Delinquency. Mem. Parks and Recreation Bd. of City Raleigh, 1954-—; mem. Raleigh Community Ambassador Project, 1955-—, pres., 1960-—. Chmn. N.C. Gov's. Com. Juvenile Delinquency and Youth Crime, 1962-—; spl. cons. to President's Com. on Juvenile Delinquency and Youth Crime. Trustee High Point Coll. Mem. Am. Prison Assn., N.E.A., Am. Assn. Sch. Adminstrs., N.C. Conf. Social Service, Nat. Assn, Tng. Schs. and Juvenile Agencies (pres. 1965-67), Kappa Delta Pi. Home: 1809 McDonald Lane Raleigh NC 27608

MADISON, ELIHU, economist, financial cons.; b. Yoakum, Tex., Oct. 5, 1905; s. George Hiram and Mattie (Smythe) M.; B.B.A., U. Tex., 1927; M.B.A., N.Y.U., 1936, Ph.D., 1952; m. Virginia J. Duncan, Jan. 4, 1946; 1 dau., Dolly Madison. With Texaco, Inc., N.Y.C., 1929-70, mgr. econs. dept., 1949-62, gen. mgr. finance and econs., 1962-70; financial cons., 1970-—. Home and Office: 104 Capri Austin TX 78746

MAECHLING, CHARLES, JR., lawyer, govt. ofcl.; b. N.Y.C., Apr. 18, 1920; s. Charles and Eugenie H. Maechling; B.A., Yale, 1941; LL.B., U. Va., 1949; m. Janet Leighton, Sept. 2, 1944; children—Philip Leighton, Eugenie Elisabeth. Admitted to N.Y. State bar, 1949, D.C. bar, 1957; asso. firm Sullivan & Cromwell, N.Y.C., 1949-51; atty. Office Sec. Air Force, 1951-52; mgr., counsel govt. relations dept. Electronics Industries Assn., Washington, 1953-56; partner firm Shaw, Pittman, Potts & Maechling, 1956-61; dir. for internal def. Dept. State, Washington, 1961-63, spl. asst. to undersec. for polit. affairs, 1963-65, spl. asst. to ambassador-at-large, 1965-66; dep. gen. counsel, spl. asst. to dir. NSF, Washington, 1966-—; gen. counsel Fairways Corp., 1959-61. Served to lt. comdr. USNR, 1941-46. Editor-in-chief Va. Law Rev., 1948-49. Contbr. articles to profl. jours. Home: 3403 Lowell St NW Washington DC 20016

MAEGLI, HALLO, graphoanalyst, airway service agt.; b. Hamburg, Germany, Jan. 25, 1924; d. Juan and Gertrud M. (de Maegli) Maegli; pvt. tutoring Germany and Guatemala, Central Am., 1936-42; m. George Nesbit Urice, Sept. 18, 1947 (div. June 1953); 1 dau., J. Melanie. Came to U.S. 1945, naturalized 1953. Passenger service agt., ticket agt. Delta Airlines, Miami, Fla., 1945-49; passenger service agt. internat. documentation agt., ticket dept. Braniff Airways, Miami, 1952-72. Tchr. course in graphoanalysis and interpretation of fgn. langs. for various airlines, 1952-—; chmn. Internat. Congress Graphoanalysts, Chgo., 1963, asst. co-ordinator, 1964-72. Mem. Internat. Graphoanalysis Soc., Fla. Graphoanalyst (chmn. study group), Internat. Platform Assn., Am. Horse Show Assn., Opera Guild Miami (asso.). Democrat. Presbyn. Died Apr. 3, 1972. Home: 850 Nightingale Miami Springs FL 33166 Office: care Braniff Internat Airways Miami FL 33159

MAEHL, WILLIAM HENRY, JR., educator; b. Chicago Heights, Ill., June 13, 1930; s. William Henry and Marvel Lillian (Carlson) M.; B.A., U. Minn., 1950, M.A., 1951; postgrad. (Fulbright fellow), King's Coll., U. Durham (Eng.), 1955-56; Ph.D., U. Chgo., 1957; m. Audrey Mae Ellsworth, Aug. 25, 1962; 1 dau., Christine Amanda. Asst. prof. Montclair (N.J. State Coll., 1957-58; asst. prof. Washington Coll., Chestertown, Md., 1958-59; asst. prof. U. Okla., Norman, 1959-64, asso. prof., 1964-70, prof. English history, 1970-—; vis. prof. U. Neb., summer, 1965. Served with AUS, 1953-55. Leverhulme Research fellow, 1961-62; grantee Am. Philos. Soc., 1961-62, 67-68, 71. Fellow Royal Hist. Soc.; mem. Am. Hist. Assn., Conf. on Brit. Studies, Soc. for Study Labour History, Southwestern Social Sci. Assn., Econ. History Soc., Am. Assn. U. Profs. Author: The Reform Bill of 1832, 1967; also articles. Home: 2601 Meadowbrook Dr Norman OK 73069 Office: Room 406 455 W Lindsey St Norman OK 73069

MAFFETT, THELMA ELIZABETH, educator, artist; b. Peoria, Ill.; d. Robert Henry and Vada (Whitaker) Maffett; B.A., diploma art, Belhaven Coll., 1931; postgrad. U. Ky., summer 1939, U. Wis., summer 1940, U. Alaska, summer 1958; M.A., George Peabody Coll., 1950. Sec., Continental Life Ins. Co., also Fidelity Mut. Life Ins. Co., Jackson, Miss., 1931-38; comml. tchr. Delta State Coll., Cleveland, Miss., 1938; art tchr. city schs., Jackson, 1939-45; art instr. Bethel Woman's Coll., Hopkinsville, Ky., 1945-47; asso. prof. art Belhaven Coll., Jackson, 1947-—. Part-time instr. art edn. Millsaps Coll., Jackson, 1957-65, Univs. Center, Jackson, 1956-—. Crafts counselor Camp DeSoto, Mentone, Ala., 1960, Camp Montreat (N.C.), summer 1945. Active various mus. assns., Miss. Arts Festival. Mem. Nat. Art Edn. Assn., Miss. Art Assn., Jackson Photog. Soc. (pres. 1964, Jerry Darbes award 1964), Jackson Internat. Salon (treas. 1956-—), Alpha Delta Kappa (state historian, chpt. pres.). Presbyn. Club: Belhaven Faculty (pres. 1954, 62). Home: 115 Highland Circle Jackson MS 39211

MAGDA, LOUIS STEPHEN, educator; b. Besenyotelek, Hungary, Aug. 18, 1919; s. Lajos Marton and Katalin Erzsebet (Szabo) M.; B.S., Jozsef Nador U., 1944, B.B.Ed., 1945, Ph.D., 1949; m. Maria Adel Vucsics, Dec. 24, 1951; 1 son, Louis Andre IV. Came to U.S., 1956, naturalized, 1961. Tchr. High Sch. Budapest, Hungary, 1944-45; stockbroker Magda Bankhouse, 1944-46; tchr. Police Acad., 1945-46, Jozsef Nador U., 1946-54; asst. prof. Buffe Vall, 1954-56; indsl. worker Grabler Mfg. Co., 1957-59, Huron Rd. Hosp., Cleve., 1959-67; tchr. Ashtabula (O.) High Sch., 1964-65, Wooster (O.) High Sch., 1965; prof. econs. Morehead (Ky.) State U., 1966-—. Served with Hungarian Army, 1939-41. Mem. Am. Econ. Assn. Home: Route 4 Morehead KY 40351

MAGEE, DENNIS ELTON, physician; b. Picayune, Miss., Aug. 18, 1931; s. Cooper Ray and Wilder (Patten) E.; B.S., U. So. Miss., 1955; M.D., U. Miss., 1958; m. Jamis Calhoun, July 4, 1952; children—Don, Mary Kathryn, Denise. Intern, Miss. Bapt. Hosp., Jackson, 1958-59; gen. practice medicine, Pearl, Miss., 1960-61, Picayune, Miss., 1962-—; mem. staff Crosby Meml. Hosp., chief staff, 1962-63. County health officer Miss. Bd. Health, Picayune, 1960-62. Mem. Pearl River County Med. Soc., Miss. Med. Assn., A.M.A. Club: Civitan International (past pres.). Home: 529 River Rd Picayune MS 39466 Office: 220 E Canal St Picayune MS 39466

MAGEE, JOHN MELVIN, clergyman; b. Mize, Miss. Sept. 24, 1915; s. John Grenaid and Emma Catherine (Carr) M.; B.A., Maryville Coll., 1941; B.D., Columbia Theol. Sem., 1944, postgrad., 1948-50, M.Div., 1971; m. Margaret Christine Sisk, May 20, 1943; children—Connie Louise, Mary Rebecca, Nancy Christine. Ordained to ministry Presbyn. Ch., 1944; pastor, Nettleton, Saltillo, Plantersville, Tupelo, Bucy Garden chs. (all Miss.), 1944-48, Decatur, Ga., 1948-51, Union City, Tenn., 1951-55, Norris Memphis Ch., Memphis, 1955-62; asst. minister Covenant Ch., Memphis, 1962; pastor 1st Presbyn. Ch., Hammond, La., 1962-65, Concord (Tenn.) Presbyn. Ch., 1965-69; stated supply Chota Presbyn. Ch., Concord, 1965-69; pastor 1st Presbyn. Ch., Union City, Tenn., 1969-—. Past moderator Memphis Presbytery, Knoxville Presbytery; chmn. com. evangelism, mem. interch. relations com. Synod Tenn.; chmn. interch. relations com. Memphis Presbytery; chmn. com. TV, radio and vis. synod of Appalachia; chmn. wom's. work Presby. of Knoxville; mem. com. on Christianity and health New Orleans Presbytery. Chmn. advancement com. Chickasaw council S.W. Dist., Boy Scouts Am. Served with USMC, 1933-37; lt. col., dep. wing chaplain Tenn. Wing, Civil Air Patrol, 1969, wing chaplain, 1971-—. Mem. Memphis, Union City (past pres.), Tangepahoa Parish (v.p.), Obion County (treas. 1970) ministerial assns., Knoxville Presbyn. Ministers Assn. (sec.-treas. 1967). Mason (K.T., illustrious grand chaplain) Kiwanian. Home: 609 E Main St PO Box 898 Union City TN 38261

MAGEE, NELSON MOORE, constrn. exec.; b. nr. Wakefield, Va., Oct. 10, 1930; s. E. Daniel and Elva (Laine) M.; B.S., Va. Poly. Inst., 1952; m. Edna Yolanda Perez, Jan. 30, 1953; children—Gregory Nelson, Shane Bradford, Karen Yolanda. Partner, Magee & Son, Gen. Contractors, Wakefield, 1954-55; estimator, engr. Reid & Hope Constrn. Co., Suffolk, Va., 1955-57; field estimator E.I. DuPont de Nemours & Co., Inc., Waynesboro, Va. and Old Hickory, Tenn., 1957-58; estimator, engr. Harbert Constrn. Corp., Birmingham, Ala., 1958-60; v.p., gen. mgr. Constructors of Fla., Inc., Orlando, 1960-62; v.p., chief engr., dir. Ledbetter-Johnson Co. and Ledbetter Bros., Inc., Rome, Ga., 1962-—. Cubmaster, Boy Scouts Am., 1962-68; chmn. Berry Acad. Parents Orgn. Served to 1st lt. AUS, 1952-54. Mem. Asso. Gen. Contractors, Nat. Asphalt Paving Assn., Am. Rd. Builders, Am. Legion. Elk. Club: Optimist. Home: 341 Mt Alto Rd Rome GA 30161 Office: 401 E 1st Av Rome GA 30161

MAGER, GERALD, judge; b. Bklyn., June 1, 1934; s. Morris David and Adele (Lapter) M.; B.A., U. Miami, 1956, J.D., 1959; postgrad. George Washington U., 1959; m. Naomi Himmelstein, Aug. 24, 1956; children—Mark Adam, Scott Alan, Russ Evan, Seth Lee. Admitted to Fla. bar, 1959; asst. atty gen. State of Fla., Tallahassee, 1959-67, gen. counsel to gov., 1967-70; judge 4th Dist. Ct. Appeals Fla., West Palm Beach, 1970-—. Chmn. Inter-agy. Com. on Mental Retardation Planning, 1964-66; mem. Adv. Council on Mental Retardation, 1965-66, chmn., 1966-67; mem. Fla. Oil Compact Com., 1967-70, Fla. Law Enforcement Planning Council, 1968-70, Fla. Jud. Council, 1970-—. Recipient Outstanding Legislative Service award Fla. Psychology Assn., 1961; spl. recognition for legislative service Fla. Jud. Council, 1963; State Govtl. Affairs award Fla. Jaycees, 1965; certificate of appreciation Radio Free Europe, 1963-66; named Jaycee of Month, Tallahassee Jaycees, 1965. Mem. Am. (appellate judges sect.), Broward County, Palm Beach County, Orange County, Brevard County bar assns., Fla. Bar (com. on jud. selection, tenure and compensation), Am. Judicature Soc., Fla. Govt. Bar, Tau Delta Phi (founder), Tau Epsilon Rho, Omicron Delta Kappa (hon.). Jewish religion. Kiwanian, Elk, Woodmen of World, Toastmaster. Home: 3105 Palm Aire Dr Pompano Beach FL 33060 Office: 1525 Palm Beach Lakes Blvd West Palm Beach FL 33402

MAGGARD, JAMES ELMER, engr.; b. Cumberland, Ky., Dec. 25, 1933; s. James Elmer and Hazel (White) M.; B.C.E., U. Ky., 1956, student, 1951-56; student U. Cin., 1962-64; m. Lois Ann Grove, Aug. 19, 1961; 1 son, James Joseph. Constrn. engr. Balt. & Ohio R.R. Co., Cin., 1959-62; design engr. Larson, McKinney & Miller, Cin., 1962-64; engr. Watkins & Assos., Consulting Engrs., Lexington, Ky., 1964-72, asst. v.p., dir. 1972-—. Mem. Ky. Planner-in-Charge Review Bd., 1971-—. Served to capt. USAF, 1956-59. Registered land surveyor, Ky.; certified planner-in-charge, Ky. Mem. Nat., Ky. socs. profl. engrs., Cons. Engrs. Council, Am. Legion, Jaycees. Home: 673 Bayswater Way Lexington KY 40503 Office: 446 E High St Lexington KY 40508

MAGIDSON, ADOLPH, lawyer; b., 1907; ed. N.Y. U., Coll. City N.Y.; J.D. St. Johns U. Admitted to bar, 1931; now general counsel Bur. of Nat. Affairs. Office: Bur of Nat Affairs 1231 Twenty-fifth St NW Washington DC 20037*

MAGILL, HENRY FRASER, army officer; b. Badin, N.C., May 3, 1928; s. Ora Basel and Sally (Jenkins) M.; B.S. in Engring., Clemson A. and M. Coll., 1951; M.S. in Engring., U. Ala., 1960; advanced arty. officer course, 1952, electronic fire control, 1955, guided missile course, 1957, advanced ordnance officer course, 1961; student Army Command and Gen. Staff Coll., Army War Coll.; m. Janice Francis Kirby, June 27, 1964; 1 dau. Engr., Owens-Corning Fiberglas Corp., N.Y.C., 1952; commd. maj. AUS, 1963, advanced through grades to lt. col.; arty. officer, Korea, 1953, comdr. officer ordnance co., 1954; aide-de-camp Maj. Gen. J.B. Medaris, Army Ballistic Missile Agy. and mil. asst. to Dr. Wernher von Braun, 1956-58; chief plans br. Antimissile and Space Def. Projects. Office, Redstone Arsenal, Ala., 1960-62; project officer Atomic Task Force High Altitude Atomic Tests, Down Range Antimissile Measurement Program, Atlantic Missile Range, 1963; project officer phys. scis. div. Army Research Office, Arlington, Va., 1963-67; battalion comdr. 3d Armored div., Germany, 1968; ordnance officer U.S. Forces, Berlin, German, 1969; sta. office sec. def. advanced research projects agy., Vietnam, 1970-72; chief plans and programs Kwajalein Missile Range, Marshall Islands Trust Ty. Pacific Islands, 1972; chief requirements div. Safeguard System Command, 1973-—. Mem. Community Concert Series, Huntsville, Ala., 1956. Mem. Am. Inst. Indsl. Engrs., Soc. Profl. Engrs., Am. Inst. Aeros. and Astronautics, Am. Ordnance Assn. Methodist. Club: Army-Navy Country. Contbr. articles to profl. jours. Home: 7744 Mallard Rd Huntsville AL 35802 Office: Hq Safeguard System Command Huntsville AL 35809

MAGILL, RICHARD VINCENT, JR., librarian; b. Greenville, S.C, Mar. 13, 1941; s. Richard Vincent and Kathryn Audrey (McKnight) M.; B.S., Clemson U., 1962; postgrad. Mich. State U., 1962-63; M.S., Fla. State U., 1968; m. Frances Carolyn Burgess, Mar. 8, 1969; 1 son, Richard, Travis. Guide, U.S. Capitol Guide Force, 1963; circulation asst. Greenville County (S.C.) Library, 1966-69, head of spl. collections, 1969-71, head gen. reference, 1971-—. Served with AUS, 1963-65. Mem. Southgate Christian Ch. (bd. deacons 1970-—). Home: 107 Burgess Av Greenville SC 29609 Office: 300 Cottege St Greenville SC 29601

MAGILL, VERNON ROY, mech. engr.; b. McCook, Neb., June 18, 1933; s. Van H. and Leila (Hoffman) M.; B.S. in Mech. Engring., U. Neb., 1956; M.S. in Indsl. Engring., U. Okla., 1965; m. Connie Jean Lindly, Aug. 15, 1954; children—Michael A., Scott L., Lee A. Jr. engr. Boeing Co., Wichita, Kan., 1956; asso. engr. Chance Vought Aircraft Co., Dallas, 1958-60; project engr. USAF, Tinker AFB, Okla., 1960-66, sr. engr., 1966-70, supr. prodn. mgmt., 1970-—. Served to 1st lt. C.E., AUS, 1956-58. Registered profl. engr., Okla. Mem. Tinker Mgmt. Club, Sigma Xi, Delta Sigma Phi. Episcopalian. Author: Simplified Method for Preliminary Design of Thermal Anti-Icing Systems, 1960; Emergency Escape From High Performance Aircraft, 1965; Awakening of Middle Management to Value Engineering, 1967. Home: 7308 NW 19th St Bethany OK 73008 Office: OCAMA Tinker Air Force Base OK 73145

MAGINNISS, HOWARD PICHON, JR., aircraft co. exec.; b. Phila., Feb. 25, 1912; s. Howard Pichon and Mary Leona (Meyers) M.; student U. Kan., 1931-32; m. Muriel A. Starbecker, Feb. 1, 1964; children—Vicki Mae, Lee Kirk. Reporter, editor Tulsa Tribune, 1933-42; plant pub. relations mgr. Douglas Aircraft Co., Tulsa, 1942-46, pub. relations exec., 1951-60; Washington mgr. Douglas Aircraft, also McDonnell Douglas Corp., 1960-—; dir. advt. and pub. relations Nat. Bank of Tulsa, 1946-51. Mem. Pub. Relations Soc. Am., Aero Club of Washington, Nat. Aviation Club, Nat. Space Club. Clubs: Nat. Press, Washington Golf and Country; Chesapeake Country (Lusby, Md.). Home: 3987 N River St Arlington VA 22207 Office: 1150 17th St NW Washington DC 20036

MAGNANT, KENNETH KARL, mech. engr.; b. Rhinelander, Wis., Aug. 2, 1937; s. Earl Hamilton and Elsie (Segerlund) M.; B.M.E., U. Fla., 1960; student U. Ala., 1968-—; m. Catherine Anne Slater, Dec. 22, 1962; children—Lance Kenneth, Mark Raymond. Mech. engr.

Brookley AFB, Mobile, Ala., 1960; mech. engr., aerospace technologist NASA, Huntsville, Ala., 1961-64; mech. engr. U.S. Army Missile Command, Redstone Arsenal, Ala., 1964—; partner L &M Cons., Huntsville, 1967—. Registered profl. engr., Ala. Patentee air bourne missile launcher. Home: 3616 Crestmore Av Huntsville AL 35805 Office: US Army Missile Comd Redstone Arsenal AL 35809

MAGNES, WILLIAM DAVID, advt. agy. exec.; b. N.Y.C., May 22, 1916; s. Isaac David and Stella (Haberman) M.; student Yale, 1934-36, Columbia, 1936-38; m. Mary Rutherford Bull, Oct. 17, 1946. With Gussow, Kahn & Co., N.Y.C., 1946-48, Doherty, Clifford & Shenfield, N.Y.C., 1948-50; pub. relations dir. Columbia Artists Mgmt., N.Y.C., 1952-56; creative dir. Larrabee Assos., Washington, 1956-60; creative dir., exec. v.p. Robert Gamble, Jr., Inc., Washington, 1960-65; pres. William Magnes Advt., Inc., Washington, 1965—. Instr. advt. copy Am. U., Washington, 1959-60; pub. relations cons. to various orgns. Pres. Georgetown Workshop Theatre, Inc., 3020 Tilden St N.W., Inc. Served to capt. AUS, 1942-46, 50-52. Mem. Met. Washington Bd. of Trade, Am. Advt. Fedn., English-Speaking Union. Author short stories, novelettes. Home: 3020 Tilden St NW Washington DC 20008 Office: 1775 K St NW Washington DC 20006

MAGRUDER, HELEN ELAINE HAKALA (MRS. EUGENE ROSS MAGRUDER), govt. ofcl.; b. Republic, Mich., Dec. 31, 1918; d. Jacob and Mary Louise (Lahenpera) Hakala; student Badger-Green Bay Bus. Coll., 1937-38, U. Dayton, 1956-59, U. Md., 1960-62; m. Harold Eugene Canada, May 14, 1948 (dec. Dec. 31, 1951); m. 2d, Eugene Ross Magruder, July 15, 1955; stepchildren—Lee Ann (Mrs. Richard Lee Naragon), Lawrence Ross, Kevin Michael. Claims adjuster Internal Revenue Service, Milw., 1943-49; adminstrv. asst. to sr. officer Displaced Persons Commn., Camp Grohn, Germany, 1949-50; chief custodial services br. Dept. Army, Nurnberg, Germany, 1950-51, chief real estate br., 1951; sec. psychol. warfare Hdqrs. U.S. Army, Washington, 1951-55; position classification specialist Air Force Logistics Command, USAF, Wright-Patterson AFB, Dayton, O., 1955-59; sec. counterintelligence div. Office Spl. Investigations USAF, Misawa Air Base, Japan, 1959-60, chief classification and wage adminstrn. br. 39th Air Div., 1960-62; position classification specialist aerospace med. div. USAF, Brooks AFB, San Antonio, 1962-64, chief classification and wage adminstrn. br., 1964-65; personnel mgmt. specialist Hdqrs. USAF, Washington, 1965-67, program devel. officer, 1967-71; chief operations br. div. personnel Office Mgmt. Services, Dept. Agr., Washington, 1971—. Grad. instr. advanced flower arranging Ikenobo Sch. Japanese Flower Arrangements, Tokyo, Japan, 1962. Sr. troop leader Girl Scouts U.S.A., 1947-48. Wis. state rep. Army Emergency Relief Soc., 1948-49, mem. Gray Ladies A.R.C., 1952-54. Recipient Scholastic Achievement medallion U. Md., 1961. Superior Performance awards U.S. Air Force, Misawa, 1960, 62, Brooks AFB, 1965, Achievement awards Hdqrs. U.S. Air Force, Washington, 1966, 68. Mem. Soc. Personnel Adminstrn. (program coordinator Dayton chpt. 1957-59), Classification and Compensation Soc. (charter). Mem. Order Eastern Star. Clubs: Faculty Women's, George Washington U. Home: 2801 New Mexico Av NW Washington DC 20007 Office: Dept of Agriculture 14th and Independence Avs Washington DC 20250

MAGRUDER, JOHN HOLMES, III, mus. ofcl.; b. Rochester, N.Y., July 1, 1919; s. John Holmes, Jr. and Esther (Hosmer) M.; B.S., U.S. Naval Acad., 1941; m. Georgene Lee, Oct. 16, 1954 (dec. June 1964); children—John Holmes IV, Lee Malcolm. Vice pres. Fgn. Adv. Ser. Corps, N.Y.C., 1946-50; v.p. Magruder, Inc., Washington, 1952-63, dir., 1952-69; dir. Nat. Armed Forces Mus. Adv. Bd., Smithsonian Instn., Washington, 1963—. Vice pres. Fgn. Adv. Ser. Corps, N.Y.C., 1946-50; dir. Marine Corps Museums, 1952-69; ex-officio mem. Marine Corps Uniform Bd., 1954-69; mem. Marine Corps Historic Sites Bd., 1966-69; mus. planning cons., 1960—. Mem. Prince William County (Va.) Hist. Commn., 1969—; cons. Fauquier County (Va.) Hist. Assn., 1969—; grand marshal Bicentennial Commemoration of James Smithson, 1965; founder Marine Corps Mus., Quantico, Va., 1960, Marine Corps Meml. Mus., Phila., 1965; organizer art exhbn. The History of the U.S. Navy as Seen through Eyes of Contemporary Artist, Palais de Chaillot, Paris, France, 1963. Trustee Naval Hist. Found. Served from 2d lt. to col. USMC, 1942-46, 52-69; PTO. Decorated Legion of Merit, Bronze Star with V (U.S.); knight Order of Orange-Nassau (Netherlands). Fellow Co. Mil. Historians (bd. govs. 1954—, editor-in-chief 1957-60, v.p. 1969—), Am. Mil Inst., Clan Gregor Soc. Episcopalian. Club: Army and Navy (Washington). Contbr. numerous articles to popular mags., profl. jours. Home: 1814 24th St NW Washington DC 20008 Office: Smithsonian Institution Washington DC 20560

MAGRUDER, WILLIAM A., govt. cons. Formerly dir. comml. engring. Lockheed California Co., Subsidiary Lockheed Aircraft Corp.; chief U.S. supersonic transport program, 1970-71; research staff for high-technology products for export Office of Pres., Washington, 1971—. Office: Exec Offices The White House Washington DC 20500*

MAGUIRE, JACK RUSSELL, univ. ofcl.; b. Denison, Tex., Apr. 10, 1920; s. Jeff Edward and Elizabeth (Russell) M.; student N. Tex. State Coll., 1940-41; B. Journalism, U. Tex. at Austin, 1944; m. Patsy Jean Horton, Aug. 11, 1946; children—Jack Russell, Kevin Maguire. Reporter AP, Austin, 1943-44; pub. relations rep. M.-K.-T. R.R., St. Louis. 1945-50, T.P. & P. Ry., Dallas, 1950-51; dir. pub. relations Tex. Ins. Adv. Assn., Austin, 1950-56; exec. dir. U. Tex. Ex-Students' Assn., 1956—; pvt. practice as pub. relations cons., Austin 1950—. Dir. Univ. State Bank, Austin; trustee Ednl. Projects for Edn., Inc., Washington. Mem. Am. Ry. Mag. Editors Assn., Pub. Relations Soc. Am., Am. Alumni Council (dir,) Sigma Delta Chi. Presbyn. Clubs: Rotary, Westwood Country, Headliner; Forty Acres. Editor: A President's Country. Columnist: Talk of Texas. Contbr. articles profl. jours. Home: 1306 Belmont Pkwy Austin TX 78703 Office: Box 7278 Univ Station Austin TX 78712

MAGUIRE, PAT HORTON (MRS. JACK RUSSELL MAGUIRE), editor; b. Houston, Apr. 23, 1926; d. Pat Arthur and Hilda (West) Horton; B.A., U. Tex., 1946; m. Jack Russell Maguire, Aug. 11, 1946; children—Jack, Kevin. Free lance writer, researcher St. Louis, Dallas, Austin, 1946-56; dir. pub. relations Austin Presbyn. Theol. Sem., 1956-61; acting mng. editor U. Tex. Alumni Mag., ALCALDE, 1961, mng. editor, 1961—, dir. alumni publs., 1964—; dir. communications Ex-Students' Assn. U. Tex., 1971—. Mem. Internat. Assn. Bus. Communicators, Theta Sigma Phi, Alpha Phi. Clubs: Westwood Country, The Headliners, The Forty Acres (Austin). Home: 1306 Belmont Pkwy Austin TX 78703 Office: 2110 San Jacinto St Austin TX 78712

MAHAFFEY, JAMES PERRY, sch. ofcl; b. Greenville, S.C., Sept. 29, 1935; s. Earl P. and Flora V. (Painter) M.; B.A., Furman U., 1957; M.A. George Peabody Coll. Tchrs., 1958; postgrad. U. Tenn., summer 1965, U. Chgo., summer 1967; U. S.C., 1969, U. Md., 1969; m. Nora D. Padgett, Dec. 22, 1961. Reading coordinator, tchr. Hillcrest High Sch., Simpsonville, S.C., 1958-62; supr. reading, English, Sch. Dist. Greenville County, Greenville, 1962-65; supr. reading S.C. Dept. Edn., Columbia, 1965-69; dir. instrn. Anderson (S.C.) Pub. Schs., 1969—. Lectr. edn. Converse Coll., Spartanburg, S.C., 1962-65, Appalachian State U., summers, 1970, 71; cons. to sch. dists. Tex., N.C., Va., Ala., Fla. Assn. for Supervision and Curriculum Devel. (pres. 1968-69), N.E.A., Internat. Reading Assn., Greenville County Edn. Assn. (pres. 1963-64), Assn. State English and Reading Specialists, S.C. Internat. Reading Assn. of Edn. (chmn. 1966—), Nat. Soc. Study Edn. Jr. C. of C., Kappa Phi Kappa, Kappa Delta Pi. Home: 1201 Hanover Rd Anderson SC 29621 Office: Box 439 Anderson SC 29621

MAHAN, JOHN WILLIAM, govt. ofcl.; b. Missoula, Mont., June 24, 1923; s. John William and Iola (Morgan) M.; student Carroll Coll., Helena, Mont., 1945-46; LL.B., U. Mont., 1949; m. Shirley Touhy, Aug. 4, 1943; children—Kim (Mrs. John R. Dunham), Shelley, Bartley, John William III. Admitted to Mont. bar, 1949; pvt. practice, 1949-52, 56-66; spl. asst. atty. gen. Mont., 1952-56; chmn. Subversive Activities Control Bd., 1966—. Trial lawyer Hugh O'Brien Youth Found., 1968—; dir., co-chmn. Nat. Pollution Control Found., 1968—. Nat. chmn. Vets. for Kennedy and Johnson, 1959-60, Vets. for Johnson and Humphrey, 1963-64. Served to maj. USNR and USMCR, World War II; PTO. Mem. Am., Mont. bar assns., V.F.W. (nat. comdr. 1958-59), Am. Legion, Disabled Am. Vets, Navy League, Sigma Alpha Epsilon. Episcopalian. Mason (32 deg., Shriner). Home: 4746 N Dittmar Rd Arlington VA 22207 Office: 811 Vermont Av NW Washington DC 20445

MAHAN, JOSEPH BUFORD, museum dir.; b. Rydal, Ga., June 11, 1921; s. Joseph Buford and Lola Virginia (Garrison) M.; A.B. in Journalism, U. Ga., 1946, M.A., 1950; Ph.D., U. N.C., 1970; m. Katherine Hines, Aug. 25, 1956. Dir. pub. relations Reinhardt Coll., Waleska, Ga., 1946-49; asst. prof. history U. Ga., 1952-59; curator Columbus (Ga.) Mus. Arts and Crafts, 1959-65; cons. Ga. Office Econ. Opportunity, 1965-66; dir. edn. and research Columbus Mus. Arts and Crafts, 1966-71; dir. Westville Historic Handicrafts, Lumpkin, Ga., 1972—; cons., lectr. in field. Bd. dirs. Columbus Hist. Found. Served with AUS, 1942-45. Decorated Purple Heart. Mem. Ga. Hist. Soc., Sigma Delta Chi. Democrat. Baptist. Home: 2339 Burton St Columbus GA 31904 Office: PO Box 848 Lumpkin GA 31815

MAHAN, STANLEY MICHAEL, JR., dentist; b. Montevallo, Ala., June 29, 1934; s. Stanley Michael and Mary Ethyl (Wood) M.; B.S., Auburn U., 1956; M.A., Ala. Coll., 1961; D.M.D., U. Ala., 1966; m. Linda Chambers, Sept. 1, 1962; children—Susan Margaret, Stann Melinda. With H.H. Tchakarian & Sons, organ builders, part-time, 1952-56; dir. faculty-student services Ala. Coll., 1957-61; sales rep. Upjohn Drug Co., 1961-62; bass player Birmingham Symphony Orch., 1965-66; practice dentistry, Montevallo, 1966—; mem. faculty U. Ala. Sch. Dentistry, 1966-69. Chmn. Montevallo Community Chest, 1970. Dep. sheriff Shelby County, Ala., 1961-72; sec.-treas. Montevallo Fire Dept., 1958-61, asst. chief, 1970-71, chief, 1971—; Shelby County finance chmn. Albert P. Brewer campaign for gov., 1970. Bd. dirs. Musemont Fine Arts Camp, Birmingham Area council Boy Scouts Am. Recipient Vulcan award Boy Scouts Am., 1970. Mem. Ala. Fire Chiefs Assn., Montevallo C. of C., Ala. Conservancy, North-South Skirmish Assn., Phi Mu Alpha, Beta Beta Beta, Delta Sigma Delta (dep. 1966-72), Delta Tau Delta. Democrat. Methodist (mem. adminstrv. bd.). Mason, Lion (1st v.p. Montevallo 1961), Rotarian (dirs. Montevallo 1968, 71). Home: Montebrier Brierfield AL 35035 Office: 266 Salem Rd Montevallo AL 35115

MAHANEY, R. DAN, govt. ofcl.; b. Dubois, Pa., Dec. 23, 1918; s. Daniel Thomas and Nora (Hepburn) M.; m. Lois C. Campbell, June 28, 1952; children—Michael, Patricia. Chief operations and safety CAA, Washington Nat. Airport, 1945-57; chief operations and safety FAA, Bur. Nat. Capital Airports, Washington, 1957-65, mgr. Dulles Internat. Airport, 1965-72, mgr. Nat. Capital Airports, 1972—. Served with USAAF, 1940-45. Mem. Am. Soc. Safety Engrs., Am. Assn. Airport Execs., Nat. Aviation Club, Washington Aero. Club. Home: 3466 Roberts Lane Arlington VA 22207 Office: Hangar 9 Washington Nat Airport Washington DC 20001

MAHER, ALVIN MICHAEL, research co. exec.; b. Houston, Aug. 9, 1929; s. Alvin Michael and Lucile Germaine (Guillaume) M.; B.S., Tulane, 1957; postgrad. U. Md., 1957, George Washington U., 1958; m. Marianne Sprinkle, Nov. 21, 1952 (div. July 1968); children—Christopher, Katherine, Robert; m. 2d, Renate Erika Betterman, July 5, 1968; children—Wayne, Debra, Karina. Supr. applied reliability engring. Melpar, Inc., Arlington, Va., 1957-60; dir. quality assurance div. Keltec Industries, Inc., Alexandria, Va., 1960-64; v.p. operations Gen. Testing Labs., Springfield, Va., 1964—; pres., dir. Inland Testing Labs., Inc., Morton Grove, Ill., 1969—; v.p., treas., dir. M-S Marine Corp., Annapolis, Md., 1970—; tech. expert on shock and vibration U.S. Internat. Electrotech. Commn., 1967—; dir. constrn. Injun II Earth Satellite, 1961. Served with USAF, 1951-55. Mem. Am. Council Ind. Labs., Am. Ordnance Assn., Inst. Environmental Scis. (sr. pres. 1966-67, nat. bd. dirs. 1967-68), Pi Kappa Alpha. Patentee in field. Home: 8301 Weller Av McLean VA 22101 Office: 6840 Industrial Rd Springfield VA 22151

MAHFOUZ, HAPPY, dir. athletics, basketball coach Little Rock U. Address: Dept Athletics Little Rock AR 72204*

MAHLA, CURTIS HARRY, civil engr.; b. San Antonio, Mar. 6, 1925; s. W.A. and Lottie (Walsh) M.; A.A. in Aero. Engring., Spartan Sch. Aeros., 1948; B.S. in Civil Engring., U. Tex., 1952; m. Lucille F. Furnatter, Dec. 20, 1958; children—Philip, Susan, Sharon. Research engr. Southwest Research Inst., San Antonio, 1954-55; engr. Tex. Power & Light Co., Dallas, 1955-56, Unit Structures, Magnolia, Ark., 1956-57; bridge design engr. Ark. Hwy. Dept., Little Rock, 1957-64; civil engr. Dept. Air Force, Little Rock AFB, 1964—. Served with USNR, 1944-46, AUS, 1952-53. Registered profl. engr., Tex., Ark. Mem. Am. Soc. C.E., Chi Epsilon, Tau Beta Pi. Home: Route 1 Box 212 Cabot AR 72023 Office: Base Civil Engrs Little Rock AFB AR 72076

MAHON, ELDON BROOKS, govt. ofcl.; b. Loraine, Tex., Apr. 9, 1918; s. John Bryan and Nola May (Muns) M.; B.A., McMurry Coll., 1939; LL.B., U. Tex., 1942; m. Nova Lee Groom, June 1, 1941; children—Jana, Martha, Brad. Admitted to Tex. bar, 1942; law clk. Tex. Supreme Ct., 1945-46; county atty. Mitchell County, Tex., 1947; dist. atty. 32d Jud. Dist. Tex., 1948-60; dist. judge, 1960-63; v.p. Tex. Electic Ser. Co., Ft. Worth, 1963-64; practice law, Abilene, Tex., 1964-68; U.S. atty. No. Dist. of Tex., Justice Dept., Ft. Worth, 1968—. Pres. W. Tex. council Girl Scouts U.S.A., 1966-68. Trustee McMurry Coll., Abilene. Served with USAAF, 1942-45. Named one of 5 Outstanding Tex. Prosecutors, Tex. Law Enforcement Found., 1957. Mem. Am., Fed., Ft. Worth-Tarrant County bar assns., Am. Judicature Soc., State Bar Tex. Methodist (del. gen. conf. 1964, jurisdictional conf. 1963). Home: 4167 Sarita Fort Worth TX 76109 Office: 206 US Court House Fort Worth TX 76102

MAHON, GEORGE HERMAN, congressman; b. Mahon, La., Sept. 22, 1900; s. John Kirkpatrick and Lola Willis (Brown) M.; A.B., Simmons U., 1924; LL.B., U. Tex., 1925; postgrad. U. Minn., summer 1925; LL.D. (hon.), Waynesburg Coll., 1951, Wayland Coll., 1960, Tex. Technol. Coll., 1962, Hardin Simmons U., 1964, Pepperdine Coll., 1965; m. Helen Stevenson, Dec. 21, 1923; 1 dau., Daphne. Began practice at Colorado City, Tex., 1925; elected county atty. Mitchell County, Tex., 1926; apptd. dist. atty. 32d Jud. Dist. Tex., 1927, elected without opposition, 1928, 30, 32; mem. 74th to 92d Congresses, 19th Tex. Dist., chmn. house appropriations com., 1964—, chmn. house subcom. def. appropriations, 1949-52, 55—, author ann. def. appropriation bills, chmn. joint senate-house com. on reduction of fed. expenditures. Democrat. Methodist. Mason (33 deg.). Home: Lubbock TX 79408 Office: House Office Bldg Washington DC 20515

MAHON, JOHN KEITH, educator; b. Ottumwa, Ia., Feb. 8, 1912; s. John Keith and Ellen (Stoltz) M.; B.A., Swarthmore Coll., 1934; Ph.D., U. Cal. at Los Angeles, 1950; m. Enid Pasek, Feb. 28, 1948; 1 son, John Keith III. Sec., treas. Samuel Mahon Co. wholesale, grocery bus., Ottumwa, 1934-42; instr. Colo. A. and M. Coll. (now Colo. State U.), 1950; instr. U.S. history, U. Cal. at Los Angeles, 1950-51; asst. prof., U. Fla., 1954-60, asso. prof., 1960-66, acting chmn. dept. history, 1965, prof., chmn. dept. history, 1966—. Mem. Fla. Antiquities Commn., Air Force Hist. Found. Trustee Am. Mil. Inst.; bd. dirs. Duke Fla. Indian History Project. Served to capt., field artillery, AUS, 1942-46; civilian mil. historian Office of Chief of Mil. History, U.S. Army, 1951-54, acting chief orgnl. history and honors br., 1953-54. Research grantee U. Fla., 1963, Am. Philos. Soc., 1963, 67; recipient Blue Key Distinguished Faculty award U. Fla., 1965. Mem. Am. Mil. Inst. (bd. trustees 1951-54, bd. editors 1951-56, editorial panel 1958—), U.S. Nav. Inst., Am. (speaker symposia 1952, 65, panel chmn. conv. 1959), So. hist. assns., Orgn. Am. Historians (conv. panel chmn. 1968), Fla. Hist. Soc. (bd. editors 1965—), Am. Assn. U. Profs., Phi Alpha Theta. Club: University (Washington). Author: History of the Second Seminole War, 1968; The War of 1812, 1972; U.S. Army manuals, USAF manuals, monographs mil. history. Editor: Reminiscences of the Second Seminole War (John Bemrose), 1966. Contbr. articles profl. jours., papers profl. assns. Home: 4129 SW 2d Av Gainesville FL 32601

MAHONEY, VERNON LLOYD MIKE, city planner; b. Asheville, N.C., Feb 14, 1925; s. Vernon Litsinger and Esther (Newberg) M.; student U. Ariz., 1942-43; B.S., U. N.M., 1945; postgrad. U. Tex., 1947, U. Okla., 1949, 50-51 children—Lloyd S., Molly F., D. Kirkman, Ellen N. Instr. civil engring. U. Ariz., 1947-48; planning asst. Tucson-Pima County, Ariz., 1948; asst. planning dir., 1951-53; asst. planning engr. City of El Paso, Tex., 1948-50; research asst. U. Okla., 1950-51; planning dir. Austin, Tex., 1953-58, City and County of Yuma, Ariz., 1958-62; asst. planning dir., City of Phoenix, 1962-64; planning dir. Ft. Worth, 1964-69; pres. Mike Mahoney & Assos., Inc., urban planning cons., Ft. Worth, 1969—. Pres., Austin Council Chs., 1958, Yuma council Camp Fire Girls, 1961, chmn. long range planning com. Maricopa council, 1963, mem. bd. Tarrant County council, 1965, pres., 1966, 67. Dir. Ft. Worth-Tarrant County Community Council, 1968-70, Fort Worth Chamber Devel. Corp., 1968-70. Served with USNR, 1943-46. Mem. Am. Inst. Planners, Am. Soc. C.E., Am. Soc. Planning Ofcls., Theta Chi. Office: 1612 Summit Av Fort Worth TX 76102

MAI, LUDWIG HUBERT, educator; b. Mannheim, Germany, Mar. 27, 1898; s. Hubert C. and Anna Maria (Specht) M.; Diploma, U. Manneheim, 1920; Diploma Com. Ed, Goethe U., 1921, Dr. Rer. Pol., 1924; came to U.S., 1950; m. Ilse Behrend, Feb. 12, 1927; children—Veronica (Mrs. J.R. Reynolds), Klaus L., Ursula (Mrs. Gordon White). Prof. econs. St. Mary's U., San Antonio, 1950—, dean grad. sch., 1959-68, Univ. prof., 1968—, dir. Inst. Internat. and Pub. Affiars, 1968—; cons. Southwest Research Inst., San Antonio, 1956-66. Mem. Am., So., econ. assns., Assn. for Social Econs. (v.p. 1970), Royal Econ. Soc., S.W. Social Sci. Assn., Assn. Evolutionary Econs., Omicron Delta Epsilon, Pi Gamma Mu. Home: 343 Shadwell Dr San Antonio TX 78228

MAIKEN, PETER TRUEBLOOD, editor; b. Washington Island, Wis., Sept. 9, 1934; s. John Andrew and Grace (Trueblood) M.; B.A. in History, Beloit Coll., 1955; M.A. in History, Northwestern U., 1966; m. Gail Bradley, Dec. 19, 1959; children—Eric Bradley, Terrence Trueblood, Steven Chancellor. Reporter, Freeport (Ill.) Jour.-Standard, 1961; staff writer Rockford (Ill.) Register-Republic, 1962; editor Chgo. Tribune Mag., 1963-68, mng. editor, 1969-70; editor Washington mag. of The Sunday Star, 1970—. Served to lt. USNR, 1956-60. Mem. Sigma Alpha Epsilon. Presbyn. Home: 2290 Dunster Lane Rockville MD 20854 Office: 225 Virginia Av SE Washington DC 20003

MAILEN, TYSON HARVEY, oil co. exec.; b. Cottonwood Falls, Kan., Jan. 26, 1911; s. Francis Charles and Jennie Bird (Harvey) M.; B.A., Kan. U., 1939; M.S., Okla. State U., 1941; m. Caroline Watson, Nov. 15, 1963; children—Tarry Watson, Tyson Harvey. Research fellow Okla. State U., 1939-41; with Phillips Petroleum Co., Bartlesville, Okla., 1941—, mgr. agrl. chems. Chem. Dept., 1963—. Asst. commr. Cherokee Area council Boy Scouts Am., 1954-57. Served to 1st lt., AUS, 1941-45. Mem. Entomological Soc. Am., Sons of God Evangelistic Assn. (dir. 1971—), Sigma Phi Epsilon. Presbyn. (ordained deacon). Mason (32 deg., Shriner), K.T., Elk. Club: Frank Phillips Mens. Patentee in field. Home: 101 N Seneca St Bartlesville OK 74003 Office: 15C4 Phillips Bldg Bartlesville OK 74004

MAINOUS, ARCH GLASS, JR., banker; b. Lexington, Ky., Oct. 29, 1933; s. Arch G. and Juanita (Cornett) M.; B.S., U. Ky., 1955, postgrad., 1958-60; m. Rosalie Redding, June 16, 1956; children—Rosalie O'Dell, Arch Glass III. Teller Lincoln Bank & Trust Co., Louisville, 1955-56; bank examiner Fed. Deposit Ins. Corp., 1956-58; with Citizens Union Nat. Bank & Trust Co., Lexington, Ky., 1958—, asst. cashier, 1961-62, asst. v.p., 1962-63, v.p., dir., 1963-71, mem. discount com., 1967—, pres., 1971—. Mem. Ky. Indsl. Devel. Finance Authority, 1970—; mem. regional adv. com. Comptroller Currency, 1972—. Div. chmn. United Community Fund, 1961, 62, 64; treas. Fayette County Heart Fund, 1963-69; treas. Blue Grass council Boy Scouts Am., 1965-66, vice chmn. fund com., 1972; pres. Lexington Clearing House, 1967-68. Chmn. bd. Fayette County Recreation and Parks Bd., 1968-71; mem. Lexington-Fayette County Met. Recreation and Parks Bd., 1968-69; treas., mem. exec. com. Fayette County Republican Com., 1969—. Trustee, mem. exec. com. Good Samaritan Hosp.; trustee Ky. Bankers Assn. Sch. Banking, 1971—; bd. dirs. Cardinal Hill Children's Hosp., 1971—. Named Outstanding Young Man Fayette County Jr. C. of C., 1968. Mem. Robert Morris Assos. (pres. Ohio Valley chpt. 1972-73), Sigma Chi. Mason (Shriner). Club: Spindletop Hall (dir. 1967—). Home: 1684 Donelwal Dr Route 6 Lexington KY 40505 Office: Citizens Union Nat Bank and Trust Co Lexington KY 40507

MAJESTY, MELVIN SIDNEY, psychologist, air force officer; b. New Orleans, June 6, 1928; s. Sidney Joseph and Marcella (Kieffer) M.; B.A., La. State U., 1949; M.S., Western Res. U., 1951, Ph.D., 1967; m. Bettye Newanda Gordon, Dec. 18, 1955; 1 dau., Diana Sue. Research asso. personnel Research Inst., Cleve., 1950-51; commd. 2d. lt. U.S. Air Force, 1951, advanced through grades to lt. col.; dep. chief personnel testing Hdqrs. SAC, 1951-52; coordinator research devel. Human Resources Research Center, Lowry AFB, Colo., 1952-58; human factors test engr. Hdqrs. Air Force Ballistic Systems Div., Norton AFB, Cal., 1958-64; behavioral scientist Air Force Inst. Tech., 1964-67; research psychologist Aerospace Med. Research Lab.,

1967-68; asst. chief tng. research div. Air Force Human Resources Lab., Wright-Patterson AFB, O., 1968-69, chief profl. edn. div., Brooks AFB, Tex., 1969—. Served with AUS, 1946-47. Decorated Air Force Longevity award, Air Force Commendation medal. Mem. Am. Psychol. Assn., Soc. Air Force Psychologists, Am. Ednl. Research Assn., Psi Chi. Patentee listening center. Home: 11002 Whispering Wind St San Antonio TX 78230 Office: PO Box 35446 Brooks AFB TX 78235

MAJOR, ALEXANDER DAVID, physician; b. Madison, Wis., Nov. 18, 1916; s. David Maggard and Leta Elliot (Allen) M.; A.S., U. Tex. at Arlington, 1935; M.D., Baylor U., 1939; m. Mabel Kathryn Chandler, Dec. 9, 1941; children—Kay (Mrs. Tom Telle), Carol (Mrs. Tom Grow), Mike, Chan, Sandy, Brent, Kris. Intern City County Hosp., Ft. Worth, 1939-40; resident, 1940-43; practice medicine, specializing in surgery, Nocona, Tex., 1946—; mem. staff Major Clinic Hosp., Bowie Meml. Hosp.; med. dir. Consol. Aircraft Co., Fort Worth, 1943-44; owner, dir. Major Clinic Hosp., 1946-71. Pres., Nocona Bd., 1949-60. Served to lt. col. M.C., AUS, 1943-46: PTO. Recipient Man of Year award from Nocona C. of C., 1950. Decorated Bronze Star. Mem. Tri-County Med. Soc. (past pres.), Tex. Med. Assn., A.M.A., Am. Assn. Gen. Practice. Home: Route 3 Nocona TX 76255 Office: Box 239 Nocona TX 76255

MAJOR, SAMUEL JAMES, bldg., constrn. co. exec.; b. Lebanon, Pa., July 11, 1918; s. Ralph M. and Sallie Wengert (Kreider) M.; B.S., U.S. Naval Acad., 1939; M.B.A., Harvard, 1947; m. Mary Elizabeth Jonitz, June 14, 1941; children—Samuel J., Elizabeth. Commd. ensign U.S. Navy, 1939, advanced through grades to capt., 1957; with So. Materials Co., Inc., Norfolk, Va., 1966—, treas., 1967—. Republican. Episcopalian (vestryman 1969). Rotarian. Clubs: Army Navy Country (bd. govs. 1952-55), (Arlington, Va.); Elizabeth Manor Country (bd. dirs. 1965-67) (Portsmouth, Va.); Virginia, Harbor (Norfolk); Cedar Point (Crittenden, Va.). Home: 4701 River Shore Rd Portsmouth VA 23703 Office: PO Box 420 Norfolk VA 23501

MAJORS, RIAS HILTON, govt. ofcl.; b. Montgomery, Ala., Mar. 8, 1924; s. Rias Benjamin and Roby (Parker) M.; B.S., Auburn U., 1948, M.S., 1950; Ph.D., U. Ga., 1965; m. Hazel Lois Mims, Dec. 1, 1943; children—Gary Lee, Ronald Parker, Chief animal husbandry sub-unit Communicable Disease Center, USPHS, Atlanta, 1950, chief animal husbandry unit, virus and rickettsia sect., 1950-59, acting chief sci. services sect., lab. br., 1959-60, chief, 1960—. Served to 1st USAAF, 1943-46. Mem. Am. Assn. for Lab. Animal Sci., Sci. Research Soc. Am., USPHS Commd. Officers Assn., Alpha Zeta, Gamma Sigma Delta. Home: 1963 Briarlyn Ct NE Atlanta GA 30345 Office: 1600 Clifton Rd NE Atlanta GA 30333

MAKOVER, SYLVAN AARON, clothing co. exec.; b. Baltimore, Jan. 28, 1914; s. Thomas and Mollie Eva (Land) M.; LL.B., Atlanta Law Sch., 1933; m. Frances Katz, Sept. 26, 1940; children—Marilyn (Mrs. Mitchell Shapiro), Bette. With Shirley of Atlanta, Inc., mfr. ladies and childrens sportswear, Atlanta, Ga., 1928—, pres., 1964—. Vice pres. Jewish Nat. Fund of Atlanta, 1970—, Southeast Region of United Synagogues of Am., 1970—. Vice pres., bd. dirs. Atlanta Jewish Community Center; bd. dirs. Jewish Home of Atlanta. Mem. Jewish religion (pres. congregation 1968-69, bd. dirs. 1958—). Mem. B'nai B'rith. Clubs: Standard, Progressive. Home: 3020 Nancy Creek Rd NW Atlanta GA 30327 Office: 4200 Shirley Dr SW Satlanta GA 30336

MALAC, BARRY FORREST, forestry research exec.; b. Vienna, Austria, Dec. 12, 1923; s. Gustav Josef and Antonie (Kostlanova) M.; came to U.S., 1949, naturalized, 1952; student U. Prague, 1946-48; M. Forestry, Duke U., 1952; m. Marian Martha Bartak, Apr. 16, 1949; children—Roy David, Deborah Ruth, Timothy Alan. Crew Kirby Lumber Co., Silsbee, Tex., 1950; research asst. Duke U. Sch. Forest, Durham, N.C., 1953; project leader Union Camp Corp., Savannah, Ga., 1953-65, mgr. woodlands research dept., 1965—. Methodist (dist. lay leader 1969—). Home: 710 Windsor Rd Savannah GA 31406 Office: Box 570 Savannah GA 31402

MALARKEY, MARTIN FRANCIS, JR., radio and cable TV exec.; b. Pottsville, Pa., May 1, 1918; s. Martin Francis and Gertrude (Cress) M.; B.S. in Law and Accounting, LaSalle Coll., Phila.; m. Catherine Clare McCarthy, May 30, 1935; 1 dau., Clare Ann (Mrs. John E. Hampford); m. 2d, Elizabeth Koehn Onesto, May 29, 1961. Vice pres. Malarkey's, Inc., Pottsville, 1939-42, pres., 1946-50; pres., dir. Trans Video Corps., Washington, 1950-59, Onesto Hotel Corp., 1960-71, radio sta. WRTA, Altoona, Pa., 1956—; owner Eastern Shore Microwave Relay Co., Washington, 1961—; pres. Malarkey, Taylor and Assos., Inc., Washington, 1959—; treas., dir. radio sta. WMBT, Shenandoah, Pa., Served with USNR, World War II. Mem. Nat. Cable TV Assn. (founder, 1st pres.). Clubs: Nat. Broadcasters (pres. 1966-68); Georgetown, Internat.; City Tavern Assn. (Washington); Pottsville. Pioneer in devel. cable TV. Home: 1534 28th St NW Washington DC 20007

MALBON, WENDELL ENDICOTT, educator; b. Norfolk, Va., July 18, 1918; s. Joseph Clyde and Letha (Barnes) M.; B.Ch.E., U. Va., 1941, M.A., 1952, Ph.D., 1955; m. Alice Bell Cochran, June 27, 1942; 1 dau., Alice Belle (Mrs. Belle M. Evjen). Gen. contractor, 1946-49; faculty U. Va., Charlottesville, 1955-69, asso. prof. math., 1959-69, chmn. applied math. div., 1957-64; prof. math. Old Dominion U., Norfolk, Va., 1969—. Cons. math., edn. NASA, 1955-67. Served to maj. AUS, 1941-46. Mem. Am. Math. Soc., Math. Assn. Am., Sigma Xi, Tau Beta Pi, Omicron Delta Kappa, Kappa Alpha, Theta Tau. Democrat. Episcopalian. Rotarian. Home: 1104 E Bay Shore Dr Virginia Beach VA 23451

MALCOM, JOHN PAUL, lumber co. exec.; b. Okolona, Ark., Dec. 3, 1918; s. John Franklin and Nellie C. (Hare) M.; grad. high sch.; m. Frances Jane Hardin, June 9, 1945; children—Mary Karol (Mrs. Edwin Dale), Paula Jane, (Mrs. John L. Griffin). With Gurdon (Ark.) Lumber Co., 1939—, sales mgr., 1958—. Mem. Gurdon City Council, 1962-66; mem. Gurdon Sch. Bd., 1964—. Served with USAAF, 1942-45. Baptist. Mason, Rotarian. Club: Hoo Hoo Lumbermens. Home: 903 E Main St Gurdon AR 71743 Office: Gurdon Lumber Co Hwy 67 Gurdon AR 71743

MALDONADO, SIERRA E.D., psychiatrist; b. Ponce, P.R., 1909; M.D., Columbia, 1936; postgrad. neurology, psychiatry, U. Pa., 1952-53. Intern, San Juan Mil. Hosp., P.R., 1937-38; resident chest diseases, Seton Hosp., N.Y.C., 1936-37; psychiat. resident Friends Hosp., Phila., 1953-54; psychiat. fellow, Pa. Hosp., Phila., 1954-56; exec. dir. P.R. Inst. Psychiatry, Bayamon, 1956—. Lectr., P.R. Med. Fellow A.C.P., A.C.S.; mem. A.M.A., Am. Psychiat. Assn., Am. Psychosomatic Soc. Office: PR Inst of Psychiatry Inc Box 127 Bayamon PR*

MALEK, FRED VINCENT, govt. ofcl.; b. Oak Park, Ill., Dec. 22, 1936; s. Fred W. and Martha (Smickles) M.; B.S., U.S. Mil. Acad., 1959; M.B.A., Harvard, 1964; m. Marlene A. McArthur, Aug. 5, 1961; children— Fred W., Michelle A. Asso. McKinsey & Co., Inc., Los Angeles, 1964-67; chmn. Triangle Corp., Columbia, S.C., 1967-69, now dir.; dep. under sec. Dept. Health, Edn. and Welfare, 1969-71; dep. asst. to Pres. for nat. security affairs, 1971—. Adj. prof. U. S.C., 1968-69. Mem. Cal. Republican Central Com., 1967-68. Bd. dirs. Teach Found. Served to 1st lt. AUS, 1959-62. Clubs: Harvard of Southern Cal. (dir., 1st v.p. 1965-67), University (com. chmn. 1966-68) (Los Angeles). Contbr. articles to mgmt. jours. Home: 6709 Lupine Lane McLean VA 22101 Office: Executive Office of President White House Washington DC 20500

MALIK, ANAND KUMAR, educator; b. Main Channu, India, Apr. 10, 1924; came to U.S., 1954; s. Arjan Das and Kartar (Kaur) M.; F.Sc., Panjab U., India, 1942, B.A., 1944, M.A., 1946; P.G.C.E., U. London (Eng.), 1952, D.Ed., 1954; Ed.D., Columbia, 1955; m. Vik Chandler, Sept. 20, 1958; children—Arun Kumar, Ashwin Kumar, Avinash Chankumar. 1954. Lectr. Govt. Coll., Rohtak, India, 1949-52; vis. prof. edn. U. Ida., 1957-60; head div. Asiatic studies U. Bahia, Salvador, Brazil, 1960-63; head Sch. Edn. of Panjab U., 1963-64; asst. prof. U. Sask. (Can.), 1964-67; prof. philosophy of edn. U. Tenn., 1967—; cons. Sch. Planning Lab., Knoxville, Tenn., 1960, Fla. Sch. Desegregation Center, Coral Gables, 1971. Mem. Brit. Mus. Soc. Recipient research award Can. Council Humanities and Social Scis., 1965-67, postgrad. research award U. Tenn., 1970; named Top Tchr. of Year U. Tenn., 1971, lectr. of year Phi Kappa Phi, 1972. Fellow Philosophy of Edn. Soc.; mem. Delta Tau Kappa, Phi Delta Kappa. Author: From the Five Continents, 1956; Current Themes in Philosophy of Education, 1967; Social Foundations of Canadian Education, 1969; Comparative Theories of Knowledge, 1971. Editor of Internat. Edn. Home: 7709 Sussex Circle Knoxville TN 37919

MALKEMUS, JOHN DAVID, chem. co. exec.; b. Louisville, Sept. 6, 1913; s. David S. and Catherine (Carr) M.; B.S., DePaul U., Chgo., 1934, M.S., 1936; Ph.D., Northwestern U., 1939, postgrad., 1939-40; m. Deidre DeVries, June 11, 1939; children—Deirdre (Mrs. Gary Norton), David W., Douglas S., Dean, Diana. Chemist, Colgate-Palmolive-Peet Co., Jersey City, 1940-46; dir. products application div. Jefferson Chem. Co., Austin, Tex., 1946-59; asst. gen. mgr., tech. dir. specialty chems. div. Reichhold Chems., Inc., Austin, 1959—. Mem. Am. Chem. Soc., Soc. Plastics Engrs. Contbr. articles profl. jours. Patentee in field. Home: 4603 Crestway Dr Austin TX 78731 Office: PO Box 9405 Austin TX 78766

MALLALIEU, FRANK ARTHUR, architect; b. Springfield, Mass., Apr. 14, 1937; s. Herbert and Charlotte Alden (Howe) M.; B.S. (Edward W. Edwards scholar) in Arch., U. Cin., 1963; postgrad. George Washington U., 1964-66; m. Judith Ann Conover, June 15, 1963; children—Todd Stephen, Lori Elizabeth. Asst. sect. chief Office Constrn. and Preliminary Planning Service, VA, Washington, 1963-69; sr. asso. William Phillips Brown & Assos., Alexandria, Va., 1969-71; project mgr. Enviro-Med, Ind. med., ednl. facility planners, LaJolla, Cal., Washington, 1971—. Archtl., constrn. mgmt. cons. Gerald A. Schwab, Alexandria, Va. Mem. Arlington (Va.) Community Action Com., 1966—, Civic Assn. Hollin Hills (Va.), 1967—. Served with USNR, 1954-62. Recipient 3d award Illuminating Engring. Soc., 1961; named Outstanding Young Architect in Washington D.C. area D.C. Council Engring. and Archtl. Socs. and Washington Acad. Scis., 1966. Mem. A.I.A., Acacia, Delta Phi Delta. Club: Hollin Meadows Swim and Tennis (Alexandria). Prin. archtl. works include Gar-Field Sr. High Sch., Prince William County, Va., 1970; Stafford Sr. High Sch., Stafford County, Va., 1971. Home: 2115 Mason Hill Dr Alexandria VA 22306 Office: Enviro-Med Inc 1120 Connecticut Av NW Washington DC 20036

MALLAN, JOHN POWERS, polit. scientist; b. Cambridge, Mass., Dec. 20, 1922; s. Thomas Francis and Anna (Powers) M.; B.S., U. N.H., 1942; M.A., U. Chgo., 1948; Ph.D., Harvard, 1964; m. Lucy Margaret Bunzl, Aug. 7, 1965; 1 son, Thomas Walter: stepchildren—Elizabeth Augustine, Margaret Augustine. Instr., Boston U., 1948-50; asst. prof. Simmons Coll., 1950-51; teaching fellow Harvard, 1952-55; instr., asst. prof. Smith Coll., 1955-57, 60-65; dir. Mass. Audit of State Needs, 1957-60; trustee Mass. Bd. Community Colls., 1960-65; mem. sr. staff Am. Assn. Jr. Colls., 1965-68, 69—; mem. sr. research staff Urban Inst., Washington, 1968-69. Mem. Northampton (Mass.) Sch. Com., 1962-63; sec. Mass. Higher Ednl. Facilities Commn., 1964-65. Served with AUS, 1944-46. Mem. Am. Polit. Sci. Assn. Home: 3235 38th St NW Washington DC 20016 Office: 1 Dupont Circle NW Washington DC 20036

MALLARD, RAYMOND B., judge; b., 1908; grad. Wake-Forrest U. Admitted to N.C. bar, 1931; presently asso. judge, Ct. Appeals, Raleigh, N.C. Home: 523 Wade Av Raleigh NC 27605 Office: 1 W Morgan St Raleigh NC 27601*

MALLE, ALBERT LEON, educator; b. Pittsburg, Kan., Sept. 30, 1914; s. Albert Edward and Maude Florence (Guthrie) M.; D.V.M., Kan. State U., 1939; m. Thela Fern Chesnut, June 28, 1936; children—Diane Lee (Mrs. Martin Jon Beeman), Kathy Jo (Mrs. Thomas John Dearinger). Pvt. practice vet. medicine, Pierson, Ia., 1939-51; mem. faculty Okla. State U., Stillwater, 1951—, prof. pathology, 1968—, dir. extension Coll. Vet. Medicine, 1968—. City councilman, Pierson, Ia., 1940-47; mayor, Pierson, 1949-51. Mem. Am., Okla. vet. med. assns., Am. Assn. Avian Pathologists, Phi Zata. Methodist. Mason. Home: 1819 W 5th St Stillwater OK 74074 Office: Okla State U Coll Vet Medicine Stillwater OK 74074

MALLEN, SAUL TWOM, textile mfg. exec.; b. Boston, Dec. 18, 1914; s. Joseph and Ida (Seltzer) M.; LL.B., Northeastern U., 1937; m. Muriel S. Goldberg, June 10, 1939; children—Ted A., Steven L., Peter J, Admitted to Mass. bar, 1938; with Sport-Wear Hosiery Mills, Inc. (co. name changed to Sport Wear Mills, Inc., 1968), Phila., 1938—, exec. mgr., Etowah, Tenn., exec. v.p., sec. treas., dir., chmn. 1942—; Officer, chmn. bd. dirs. Windsor Hosiery Mills, Inc., Etowah; co-founder, exec. v.p., treas., chmn., Internat. Yarn Corp., San Juan, P.R., 1963, Cleveland, Tenn., 1967—; co-founder, dir., chmn. Knitco, Inc., N.Y.C., 1966—. Pioneer drive to establish first blood bank in McMinn County, Tenn.; mem. Jewish Community Center; active Ochs Meml. Temple, Chattanooga, 1941—, dir. 1965-67; patron Bright Sch., Chattanooga, 1946—; charter mem., dir. Cleveland Regional Speech and Hearing Center (Tenn.), 1971—. Bd. dirs., McCallie Sch., 1953-61, patron, 1953—. Mem. Nat Assn. Am. Hosiery Mfrs., Am. Sci. Yarn Mfrs. Mason (32 deg., Shriner), Elk; mem. B'nai B'rith. Club: Valleybrook Golf and Country. Home: 3408 Harcourt Dr Chattanooga TN 37411 Office: Sport Wear Mills Inc Etowah TN 37331

MALLERY, WILLIAM HENRY, III, city ofcl.; b. McComb, Miss., Dec. 15, 1935; s. William Henry and Tot (McManus) M.; B.Pub. Adminstrn., U. Miss., 1958; postgrad. So. Meth. U.; m. Cecil Nolan, July 12, 1958; children—David, Mark, Kathy, William Henry 1V, John Paul. Asst. to city mgr., Farmers Branch, Tex., 1958-59; mgr. C. of C., Farmers Branch, 1959; self-employed as pub. relations, counsellor, Pub. Relations Council, 1960; dir. pub. relations, asst. sales mgr. Magnolia Mobile Homes Sales Corp., 1961; purchasing agt., Vicksburg, Miss., 1962; program officer Program of Advances for Pub. Works Planning, U.S. Dept. Housing and Urban Devel., 1963-66; city mgr., Punta Gorda, Fla., Belle Glade, Fla., 1966—. Named Jaycee of the Month Vicksburg Jr. C. of C., 1963. Mem. Internat., Fla., Palm Beach County (sec.-treas.) city mgrs. assns. Unitarian. Home: 225 NW Av C Belle Glade FL 33430 Office: 33 W Av A Belle Glade Fl 33430

MALLETTE, JOHN MICHAEL, biologist, educator; b. Houston, Aug. 6, 1932; s. Jules L. and Lydia (Myers) M.; B.S. Xavier U., 1954; M.S., Tex. So. U., 1958; Ph.D. (Nat. Found fellow), Pa. State U., 1962; m. Pazetta Berryman, Aug. 19, 1959; children—John M., Adelaide Veronica, Pazetta Ann. Research technician Dental Br. U. Tex., Houston, 1957-58; instr. Tex. So. U., 1958-59; prof. biology, chmn. grad. research program Tenn. Arts and Industry State U., Nashville, 1962-71; dir. allied health Meharry Med. Coll., Tenn. State U., Nashville, 1971—. Dir. NSF Undergrad. Research Participation Program, 1964—; cons. So. Assn. Colls. and Schs., NIH, United Negro Coll. Fund, Middle Tenn. Tchrs. Assn. Cubmaster, Boy Scouts Am., 1966—. Bd. dirs. Catholic Charities of Tenn., People United for Restoration of Environment. Decorated Knight of St. Gregory the Great. Served with AUS, 1954-56. Home: 4011 W Hamilton St Nashville TN 37218

MALLIN, JAY, journalist; b. N.Y.C., Dec. 10, 1927; s. Albert Milton and Cecilia (Jaffe) M.; A.B., Fla. So. Coll., 1949; m. Caroll Sue Driftmeyer, Jan. 31, 1959; children—Jay, Linda Anne. News editor Havana (Cuba) Herald, 1951-53; stringer corr. Time and Life, 1956—. Research scientist Center for Advanced Internat. Studies, Miami, 1967-69; cons. The Wackenhut Corp., Coral Gables, 1970-71. Author: Fortress Cuba, 1965; Caribbean Crisis, 1965; Terror in Viet Nam, 1966; Guevara on Revolution, 1969; Strategy for Conquest, 1970; Terror and Urban Guerrillas, 1972. Contbr. gen., acad., mil. jours. Home: 406 Savona Av Coral Gables FL 33146

MALLORY, ARENIA CORNELIA, coll. pres., assn. exec.; b. Jacksonville, Ill., Dec. 28, 1905; d. Edward James and Mazy (Brooks) Mallory; student Whipple Acad. Music, 1918-22; B.S., Simmons Coll., 1927; M.A., U. Ill., 1950; LL.D., Bethune-Cookman, 1951; M.A. (hon.), Jackson Coll., 1936; m. A. C. Clemmons, June 4, 1927; 1 dau., Andrea Mazy. Pres. Saints Jr. Coll., Lexington, Miss., 1927—. Del., Internat. Council Women, 1954, Montreal, 1957, Rome, 1962, vice convener edn., Commn., Istanbul, Turkey, 1961; pres. Friends Liberian Youth; manpower devel. specialist Dept. Labor, 1963. Mem. Holmes County Bd. Edn., 1968—. Dir. Lillian Brooks Coffey Rest Home, Detroit, 1948—. Recipient woman yr. award Utility Club, N.Y.C., 1956; award as one of twelve outstanding women Am., Nat. Council Negro Women, 1946; outstanding woman in govt. award Delta Sigma Theta; Sojourner Truth award Negro Women, 1964. Fellow So. Regional Conf., Assn. Higher Edn.; mem. Nat. Council Negro Women (v.p. 1953-57), Nat. Council Women U.S. (3d v.p. 1956—, del. internat. council 1959), Nat. Soc. Prevention Juvenile Delinquency (N.Y.C. v.p. 1956—), Am. (life), Miss. (state chmn. human relations council, Merit award 1970) tchrs. assns., Internat. Platform Assn., N.E.A., Acad. Polit. Sci., Women's Orgn. Higher Edn., Adminstrn. of Rural Edn., Negro Bus. and Profl. Women's Clubs, Women in Community Service (nat. dir.), Phi Delta Kappa. Address: Saints Jr Coll Lexington MS 39095

MALLORY, JAMES GUY, JR., dentist; b. Cairo, Ill., Jan. 8, 1914; s. James Guy and Birdie Elizabeth (Clutts) M.; student Tulane U., 1932-33, St. Louis U., 1933-34; D.D.S., Loyola South U., 1939; m. Grace Lenore Chapman, Sept. 7, 1940; children—Nancy (Mrs. John Christian Archer), Jamie (Mrs. Watson Van Benthuysen), Janet, Susan. Pvt. practice dentistry, New Orleans, 1939—; mem. staff Mercy Hosp. Active Young Men's Bus. Club. Served with Dental Corps, USNR, 1941-46. Fellow Internat. Coll. Dentistry; mem. Am., La., New Orleans dental assns., Mil. Order World Wars, Psi Omega, Phi Kappa Sigma. Democrat. Baptist. Mason. Home: 8001 Sycamore St New Orleans LA 70118 Office: Maison Blanche Bldg New Orleans LA 70112

MALLORY, TOMMY GLENN, city ofcl.; b. Lindale, Tex., Mar. 12, 1934; s. Wylie Franklin (dec.) and Esta Lee (Bowers) M.; A.A., Tyler Jr. Coll., 1961; B.S., East Tex. State U., 1966; m. Patricia Allison, Oct. 15, 1955; children—Traci, Trent, Terrell. Asst. water supt. City of Tyler, Tex., 1955-68, dir. utilities, 1968—. Dir. Tyler City Employees Credit Union. Served with AUS, 1954-55. Mem. Tex. Water Utilities Assn. (v.p. 1971-72; named Man of Month 1966), Am. Waterworks Assn., Water Pollution Control Fedn. Mason. Home: 407 Knoxville St Tyler TX 75701 Office: PO Box 2039 Tyler TX 75701

MALLOU, FERNANDO, physician; b. Cadiz, Spain, Mar. 15, 1929; s. Anthony V. and Magdalen (Labrador) M.; B.A., B.S., Ofcl. U. Zaragossa, 1947; M.D., Ofcl. U. Spain Sch. Medicine, 1953, M. Med. Sci., U. Madrid, 1956; m. Rebecca Vento, Jan. 3, 1963; children—Edward, Magdalen, Lewis. Came to U.S., 1956, naturalized, 1966. Intern, Kans. Gen. Hosp., Wichita, 1956; resident surgery U. Tex., Galveston, 1957-58, resident anesthesiology, 1958-60; anesthesiology fellow Anderson Hosp., Houston, 1961; charge of anesthesia dept., pulmonary research and therapy Tex. Tb. Hosp., Harlingen, 1962-64; anesthesiologist Knapp Meml. Hosp., Weslaco, Tex., 1964-66, Irving Hosp., Meth. Hosp., Dallas, 1966—; cons. in anesthesiology; bd. dirs. Vanderbilt Resources Corp., Dallas. Mem. Am., Tex. med. assns., Am. Geriatric Soc., Am., Tex., Dallas County anesthesiology socs., Dallas County Med. Soc., Am. Oceanographic and Forestry Assn., Am. Assn. Fgn. Med. Grads. Office: Dr. Fernando Mallou Exchange Bank Tower Dallas TX 75235

MALLOY, IRMA THOMAS (MRS. JAMES E. MALLOY), counselor; b. Stockton, Ala., Aug. 30, 1936; d. Tom and Alberta (Askew) Thomas; B.A., Tenn. State U., 1957, M.S., 1967; postgrad. Temple U., 1965; m. James E. Malloy, July 15, 1958; children—Darryl Lynn, Christopher Thomas. Social caseworker Ala. Indsl. Sch., Mt. Meigs, 1957-58, Womens Christian Alliance, Phila., 1960-63; counselor Daniel Boone Pub. Sch., Phila., 1964-65; dean of women Dillard U., New Orleans, 1966-68; counselor Tex. So. U., Houston, 1969-71, dir. Counseling Center, 1971—, also bd. dirs. Model Cities Cuney Homes tutoring program. Dir. Lady Bronze Cosmetic Salon, Houston. Troop leader Girl Scouts U.S.A., 1959-60; asst. dir. Harris Home for Children, Huntsville, Ala. 1965-66; chmn. curriculum and guidance com. James H. Law Elementary Sch. P.T.A. Mem. Am. Personnel and Guidance Assn., Nat. Vocational Guidance Assn., Am. Sch. Counselor Assn., Coll. Student Personnel Assn., N.A.A.C.P., Tenn. State U. Alumni Assn. Delta Sigma Theta (chmn. mental health com.). Home: 4019 Redwin Circle Houston TX 77047

MALMI, A. CARL, govt. ofcl.; b. Duluth, Minn., Oct. 20, 1917. Andrew and Mary (Ojaniemi) M.; student Duluth Bus. U., 1936; B.C.S., Columbus U., 1949, M.F.A., 1950; m. Bobbie Grace Simmons, Oct. 18, 1942; children—Carol L., Robert A. File clk. Social Security Agy., Balt., 1941; payroll clk. State Dept., Washington, 1941-46, group supr., 1946-47, orgn. and methods examiner 1947-51; area budget officer USIA, Nr. East, South Asia, Africa, 1951-56, 60-62; adminstrv. officer Voice of Am., 1962-65; exec. officer, 1965—; budget planning and procedures officer, Washington, 1956-58; budget and finance Officer Am. Nat. Exhbn. in Moscow, Dept. of Commerce, 1958-59, adminstrv. officer in Washington, U.S. Sci. Exhibit, Century 21 Exposition, 1959-60. Pres. Fernwood Citizens Assn., 1961-62. Served with AUS, 1942-45, ETO. Democrat. Methodist. Home: 9705 Holmhurst Rd Bethesda MD 20034 Office: 1776 Pennsylvania Av Washington DC 20006*

MALONE, DUMAS, historian; b. Coldwater, Miss., Jan. 10, 1892; s. John W. and Lillian (Kemp) M.; A.B., Emory Coll., 1910; B.D., Yale, 1916, A.M., 1921, Ph.D., 1923; LL.D., Northwestern U., 1935; Litt.D., Emory U. and U. Rochester, 1936. Dartmouth Coll., 1937; L.H.D., U. Chattanooga, 1962; m. Elisabeth Gifford, Oct. 17, 1925; children—Gifford Dumas, Pamela. Instr. history, Yale U., 1919-23; asso. prof. history U. Va., 1923-26; prof. 1926-29; vis. prof. Am. History, Yale, 2d term, 1926-27; sr. Sterling fellow (traveling), Yale, 1927; an editor Dictionary Am. Biography, 1929-31, editor in chief, 1931-36; dir. Harvard U. Press, 1936-43; prof. history, Columbia, 1945-59; Thomas Jefferson Found. prof, history U. Va., 1959-62, biographer-in- residence, 1962—. Bd. dirs. Thomas Jefferson Meml. Found.; mem. adv. cons. on publ. Papers of Jefferson and Madison. Pvt., later 2d lt., USMC, 1917-18. Mem. Am. Hist. Assn. (exec. council, 1934-38), Am. Antiquarian Soc., Am. Acad. Arts and Scis., Mass. Hist. Soc., So. Hist. Assn. (pres. 1967-68), Va. Hist. Soc. (hon.), Phi Beta Kappa. Recipient John Addison Porter prize, Yale, 1923; Guggenheim fellowship, 1951-52, 58-59; Thomas Jefferson award U. Va., 1964; Wilbur Lucius Cross medal Yale, 1972. Clubs: Century, Virginians (N.Y.C.); Cosmos (Washington). Democrat. Author: The Public Life of Thomas Cooper, 1926; Saints in Action, 1939; Edwin A. Alderman; A Biography, 1940; Jefferson the Virginian (vol. I of projected 6 vol. work entitled Jefferson and His Time), 1948; Volume II; Jefferson and the Rights of Man, 1951; Vol. III: Jefferson and the Ordeal of Liberty, 1962, Vol. IV: Jefferson the President, First Term, 1970; The Story of the Declaration of Independence, 1954; Thomas Jefferson as Political Leader, 1963; (with Basil Rauch) Empire for Liberty, 2 vols., 1960, 6 vol. edit., 1962. Joint-author with others, The Interpretation of History (1943). Editor: Correspondence between Thomas Jefferson and P. S. du Pont de Nemours, 1930. Contbr. mags. Editor with Allen Johnson of Dictionary of Am. Biography, vols. IV to VII, 1930-31, as editor in chief, vols VIII to XX, 1932-36; editor Hist. Book club 1948—. Cons. Nat. Assn. Ednl. Broadcasters on The Jeffersonian Heritage, 1952. Mng. editor Polit. Sci. Quar., 1953-58. Home: 2000 Lewis Mountain Rd Charlottesville VA 22903 Office: Alderman Library U Va Charlottesville VA 22901

MALONE, JEWELL WORKMAN (MRS. BEN F. MALONE), ednl. adminstr.; b. Wichita Falls, Tex.; d. John E. and Caroline (Harty) Workman; B.S., North Tex. U., 1941; M.Ed., West Tex. U., 1951, postgrad., 1951-72; postgrad. N.M. State U., U. Colo., San Jose State U., George Peabody State Coll., Cal. State U.; m. Ben F. Malone, June 23, 1942; 1 dau., Patsy Caroline. Tchr. elementary schs., New Liberty, Clay County, Tex. 1939-42, Argyle, Denton County, Tex., 1942-43, Letot, Dallas County, Tex., 1943-44, Deep Elm, N.C., 1944, Grand Prairie, Tex., 1945, Mountain Creek, Dallas County, 1945-46, Portales, N.M., 1946-49, Hereford, Tex., 1949-51, Bunavista Elmentary Sch., Borger, Tex., 1951-52; elementary tchr., prin. Huber Elementary Sch., Borger, 1952-58; supr. primary grades Borger Pub. Schs., 1958-69, co-ordinator elementary curriculum, 1969—. Summer dir., tchr. Headstart Program, Borger, 1966. Pres. city council P.T.A., Borger, 1965-67. Mem. N.E.A., Tex. Tchrs. Assn., Borger Edn. Assn., Tex., Nat. assns. supervision and curriculum devel., Tex. Elementary Prins. and Suprs., Tex. Congress Parents and Tchrs. (pres. dist. 19), Panhandle Sch. Leaders Assn., Delta Kappa Gamma. Club: North Plains Knife and Fork (Borger). Home: 410 Santa Fe St Borger TX 79007 Office: Adminstrv Center 9th and Weatherly Sts Borger TX 79007

MALONE, JOHN WARRICK, dentist; b. St. Louis, Jan. 11, 1921; s. John Warrick and Rosabelle (Houts) M.; A.A., Harris Tchrs. Jr Coll., 1943; D.D.S., St. Louis U., 1946; certificate orthodontics N.Y.U., 1970; m. Elizabeth Cahall Scott, Feb. 18, 1950; children—Marilyn Cahall, Charles Warrick, John Scott, Robin Elizabeth. Dentist, U.S. Vets Adminstrn. Hosp., Washington, 1950-57; practice of dentistry, Falls Church, Va., 1957—; instr. prosthetics and operative dentistry, Georgetown U. Dental Coll., Washington, 1954-57; chief dentist U.S. Army Res. Hosp., Rockville, Md., 1967—. Leader Civic Assn., East Falls Church, Va., 1964-65. Served as dental surgeon, USCGR, 1947-49; served as col., AUS, 1961-62. Richard Ross fellow, 1952-53; named Elk of the Year, 1967. Mem. Am., N. Va., Fairfax County dental socs., Pedodonic Found., Project Concern. Presbyn. (elder 1968-70). Home: 1821 Briar Ridge Court McLean VA 22101 Office: 313 Park Av Falls Church VA 22046

MALONE, LEE HARRISON BROWN, art mus. dir.; artist; b. Las Cruces, N.M., May 28, 1913; s. Lee Quayle and Doris Jennison (Brown) M.; A.B., Yale Art Sch., 1939; m. Joan Gilroy Reilly, Sept. 29, 1945; children— Michael, Caroline, John S., Monica, Thomas, Mary Christina. Artist, 1934—; art historian; lectr.; exhibited Clearwater, Fla., 1935, 36, 37; curator Clearwater Art Mus., 1936-37; instr. history art Notre Dame Coll. of S.I., 1939-40; aide to co-ordinator inter-Am. affairs Dept. State, 1940-41; dir. Columbus (O.) Gallery Fine Arts and Columbus Art Sch., 1946-53, Mus. Fine Arts Houston, 1953-59; exec. dir. nat. devel. com. Pierpont Mogran Library, N.Y.C.; dir. Mus. Fine Arts, St. Petersburg, Fla., 1968—. Served as lt. comdr. USNR, 1943-46. Mem. Assn. Art Mus. Dirs., Am. Assn. Museums, Am. Fedn. Arts, Coll. Art Assn., Inter-Mus. Lab. Roman Catholic. Author: Sacred Art, 1953; Chagall and deChirico, 1955; also exhibit catalogs and mag. articles. Home: 1222 Brightwaters Blvd NE St Petersburg FL 33704 Office: 255 Beach Dr N St Petersburg FL 33701

MALONE, MIKE, program dir. WUNI, Mobile, Ala. Address: 1257 Springhill Av Mobile AL 36604*

MALONE, RUTH M. MOORE (MRS. CHARLES EDMUND MALONE), author; b. Clarendon, Ark.; d. John Burton and Bessie (Branch) Moore; grad. Ward Belmont Coll., Tenn.; student U. Ark.; m. Charles Edmund Malone; children—Margaret Branch (Mrs. Hubert de Marcy), Mary Bess (Mrs. Dick Lankford). Free lance writer Am. Home, Good Housekeeping, Parents, Sunday mags., Memphis Comml. Appeal, Shreveport (La.) Times, Ark. Democrat, Ark. Gazette, 1944-65; weekly syndicated feature Palmer Media Group, S. Ark. newspapers, 1959-65; asso. editor State mag., 1961-62; food editor Holiday Inn mag., 1962—. Mem. Tenn. Fedn. Womens Clubs, Ark. Fedn. Womens Clubs (dist. pres. 1960-62), Nat. League Am. Pen Women (br. pres. 1966-68), Ark. Press Women, Nat. Fedn. Press Women, Pi Beta Phi (alumni pres. 1964-65). Author-editor: Where to Eat in the Ozarks—How its Cooked, 1961, 62-64; Swiss Holiday Recipes, 1966; editor Holiday Inn International Cook and Travel Book, 1962—. Author: Dogpatch Cook Book for Dogpatch USA, 1970. Home: 1 River Ridge Rd Little Rock AR 72207 Office: PO Box 18216 3756 Lamar Av Holiday City Memphis TN 38118

MALONE, WILLIAM WARREN, JR., lawyer; b. Athens, Ala., Feb. 12, 1916; s. William Warren and Daisy (Warten) M.; student Birmingham-So. Coll., 1933-34; A.B., U. Ala., 1937, LL.B., 1939; m. Mitzi Browning Chambers, Nov. 18, 1946; children—Miriam Lane, William Warren III, Patrick B. Admitted to Ala. bar, 1939; since practiced in Athens. Dir. East Lauderdale Banking Co. Past pres. N.Ala. Tb. Assn., Athesn Jr. C. of C. Presdl. elector Ala., 1960. Served with USAAF, 1942-45. Mem. Am. Legion (past post comdr.). Home: 400 S Beaty St Athens AL 35611 Office: PO Box 711 Athens AL 35611

MALONEY, CHARLES G., bishop; b. Sept. 9, 1912. Ordained priest Roman Cath. Ch., 1937; titular bishop of Capsa and aux. to archbishop of Louisville, 1954—. Address: 212 E College St Louisville KY 40203

MALONEY, CLEMENT GARLAND, corp. and govt. cons.; b. Hot Springs, Ark., July 4, 1917; s. James C. and Dorothy (Clement) M.; student Northwestern U., 1937-40. 1 son, Thomas C. Vice pres. Kollsman Instrument Corp., N.Y.C., 1961-64; cons. to sec. def., Washington, 1964-66; internat. marketing cons. Philco Corp. div. Ford Motor Co., 1966-67; cons. internat. sales and export financing Office Sec. Def., 1967-69; spl. asst. to the pres. Control Data Corp., 1969—. Served as col. USAAF, World War II; now col. USAF Res. Recipient Exceptional Civilian award U.S. Air Force. Mem. Washington Bd. Trade, Internat. Platform Assn., Inst. Aeros. and Astronautics, Internat. Assn. Cybernetics, Mil. Comptrollers, Nat. Security Indsl. Assn., Air Force Assn. U.S. Mil. Order of Carabao, Am. Ordnance Assn., Am. Mgmt. Assn., Clubs: Fort Myers Officers; Bolling AFB Officers; Nat. Aviation, Army Navy (Washington). Home: Crystal Plaza Apt 405 S 2111 Jefferson Davis Hwy Arlington VA 22202

MALONEY, JOHN ALEXANDER, hosp. adminstr.; b. Knoxville, Tenn., Mar. 1, 1927; s. Harry Lotspeich and Gertrude (Blaetz) M.; student U. Tenn., 1947-50; certificate in hosp. adminstrn. Ga. State Coll., 1958; m. Doris Ann Akes, Oct. 21, 1964; children—John Patrick, Chris topher Michael; stepchildren-Thomas Kent Gaskins, Shelley Gaskins, William Glenn Gaskins, Jr. Adminstr., Lawrence County Gen. Hosp., Lawrenceburg, Tenn., 1958-60, Morristown-Hamblen (Tenn.) Hosp., 1960-64, Central State Psychiat. Hosp., Nashville, 1964-67, Eastern State Psychiat. Hosp., Knoxville, 1967-71, R. J. Taylor Meml. Hosp., Hawkinsville, Ga., 1972—. Served with USNR, 1944-46; to 2d lt. AUS, 1952-53. Mem. Am. Coll. Hosp. Adminstrs., Tenn. Hosp. Assn., Knoxville Hosp. Council (pres. elect), Pi Epsilon Rho. Episcopalian. Kiwanian. Rotarian. Address: RJ Taylor Meml Hosp Hawkinsville GA 31036

MALONEY, JOSEPH FARGIS, educator; b. N.Y.C., June 24, 1926; s. Thomas E. and Marie Celeste (Fargis) M.; A.B., Fordham U., 1950, M.A., 1951, Ph.D., 1955; m. Margaret Gough, Mar. 29, 1948; children—Joseph, Margaret. Mem. faculty Fordham U., 1950-60; exec. dir. Mass Transp. Commn., Commonwealth of Mass., 1961-64; sr. cons. pub. adminstrn. U. Ife Inst. Adminstrn., Ibadan, Nigeria, 1964-66; prof. polit. sci., dir. Urban Studies Center, U. Louisville, 1966—, dir. Inst. Community Devel. Asst. gov. State of Mass., 1960. Trustee Bellarmine-Ursuline Coll. Served with AUS, 1945-46. Mem. Am. Acad. Polit. Sci., Am. Acad. Polit. and Social Sci., Am. Polit. Sci. Assn., Nat. Assn. Housing and Redevel., Am. Soc. Planning Ofcls., Am. Soc. Pub. Adminstrn., Nigerian Inst. Mgmt., Royal Inst. Pub. Adminstrn. (U.K.). Contbr. articles to profl. jours. Home: 1910 S 3d St Apt 5 Louisville KY 40208

MALONEY, MARTIN FRANCIS, govt. ofcl.; b. Littleton, Colo., Jan. 4, 1910; s. James Edward and Margaret Gertrude (Flynn) M.; B.S. in C.E., U. Colo., 1930; m. Eloise Lucille Griffin, Oct. 1, 1938; children—Patricia (Mrs. Donald T. Wolpert), John Edward, Martin David, Mary Jo. Draftsman, Am. Bridge Co., Gary, Ind., 1931-32; supt. Lallier Constrn. Co., Denver, 1932-35; structural engr. Colo. Hwy. Dept., Denver, 1935-39; with U.S. Bur. Pub. Rds., 1946—, regional bridge engr., Denver, 1954-59, chief interstate hwy. div., Washington, 1959-62, asst. to adminstr., 1962-69, dir. office engring., 1969-71, asso. adminstrn. engring. and operations Fed. Hwy. Adminstrn., 1971—. Served to capt. USNR, 1939-46 Recipient Meritorious Service Silver medal award Dept. Commerce, 1962. Fellow Am. Soc. C.E.; mem. Sigma Tau, Chi Epsilon, Alpha Tau Omega. Home: 2517 Crest St Alexandria VA 22302 Office: 400 7th St SW Washington DC 20590

MALONEY, ROBERT SIDNEY, savs. and loan exec.; b. New Orleans, Dec. 10, 1937; s. Paul H. and Evelyn (Hardie) M.; student pub. schs., New Orleans; m. Bonny Booth Babin, May 31, 1958; children—Bobbie Jean, Robert S., Kurt Brian, Julie Ann, Craig Stewart. Office boy Maloney Trucking & Storage Co., New Orleans, 1957; estimator Gallagher Transfer & Storage Co., New Orleans, 1958-59, sec.-treas., 1959-62, pres., 1966—; v.p. Citizens Homestead, New Orleans, 1960-66; pres. Maloney Truck Leasing Corp., 1967—, Citizens Homestead Assn., 1967—, Maloney Trucking & Storage, Inc., 1967—, Malone Carloading, Inc., 1967—, all New Orleans. Adv. dir. Nat. Am. Bank, New Orleans, 1966—, Better Bus. Bur., 1966—. Home: 5828 Sylvia Dr New Orleans LA 70124 Office: 945 Magazine St New Orleans LA 70130

MALOOF, LOUIS NASSIR, architect; b. Copperhill, Tenn., Feb. 27, 1935; s. Nassir Ackle and Adline (Ferris) M.; B.S., Ga. Inst. Tech., 1957, B.Arch., 1962; m. Sue Ann Thomason, June 7, 1958; 1 son, Noel. With Heery & Heery, Inc., Atlanta, 1960—, exec. v.p., 1967—. Served to lt. (j.g.) USNR, 1957-59. Mem. A.I.A., Pi Kappa Alpha. Roman Catholic. Kiwanian. Home: Route 3 Box 396 Buford GA 30518 Office: 880 W Peachtree St Atlanta GA 30309

MALOOLY, DONALD ALBERT, physician; b. El Paso, Tex., May 9, 1930; s. Elias A. and Mamie (Coury) M.; student Rice U., 1947-49; B.A., Tex. Western Coll., 1950; M.D., U. So. Cal., 1954; m. Mary Hill, July 9, 1955; children—Donald Ellis, Mary Elizabeth, Mark Hill. Intern, William Beaumont Army Hosp., Ft. Bliss, Tex., 1954-55; resident Scott and White Clinic, Temple, Tex., 1957-59, Long Beach (Cal.) VA Hosp., 1959-60; fellow Mayo Clinic, Rochester, Minn., 1960-61; practice medicine, specializing in cardiology, El Paso, 1962—; mem. staff Providence Meml., St. Joseph's, Sun Towers hosps., Hotel Dieu. Served to capt. M.C., AUS, 1954-57. Diplomate Am. Bd. Internal Medicine, also cardiovascular bd. Fellow Am. Coll. Chest Physicians, Am. Coll. Cardiology, Royal Soc. Promotion Health; mem. A.M.A., Am. Heart Assn. (fellow council on clin. cardiology, mem. council high blood pressure research, arteriosclosis, basic sci.), Tex. Acad. Internal Medicine, Tex. Med. Assn., Alpha Omega Alpha, Phi Rho Sigma, Phi Kappa Phi, Tau Kappa Epsilon. Episcopalian. Contbr. articles to profl. jours. Home: 6249 Westwind Dr El Paso TX 79912 Office: 1100 N Stanton St El Paso TX 79902

MALOY, RICHARD JOSEPH, newspaper editor; b. New Castle, Pa., June 7, 1924; s. Frank Joseph and Helen (Flynn) M.; A.B., U. Mich., 1949; m. Berneice A. Kinahan, Apr. 7, 1951; children—Michael, Timothy. Reporter, Balt. Sun, 1949-50, Detroit Free-Press, 1950-51; telegraph editor Lorain (O.) Jour., 1951-52; mem. staff Washington Post, 1952-67, city editor, 1964-65, London editor, 1965-66; chief Washington bur. Thomson Newspapers, 1970—. Served with inf. AUS, World War II; ETO. Decorated Bronze Star. Mem. White House Corr. Assn., Assn. Am. Corr. London. Sigma Delta Chi. Club: Nat. Press (Washington). Home: 8313 Meadowlark Lane Bethesda MD 20015 Office: 1135 Nat. Press Bldg Washington DC

MALOY, THEODORE HASKELL, pub. relations exec.; b. nr. Delhi, Okla., Aug. 26, 1907; s. Pumphrey Angelo and Nettie Josephine (McGowen) M.; A.B., U. Okla., 1929; m. Dorothy Inez Fluck, June 2, 1929; 1 dau., Amy Lynn (Mrs. Richard R. Lindsly). Editor Elk City (Okla.) Daily News, 1929-32; staff corr., bur. mgr., S.W. div. news editor UP, 1932-44; br. mgr. Braun & Co., Dallas, 1944-57; Dallas region pub. relations mgr. Safeway Stores, 1957-62; sr. partner VanCromkhite & Maloy, Inc., Dallas, 1962—; v.p. Suburban Newspapers, Inc., Ft. Worth. Named one of five Friends of Tex. Press award, Tex. Press Assn., 1956. Mem. Pub. Relations Soc. Am., Sigma Delta Chi. Ind. Democrat. Presbyn. Clubs: Dallas Press, Dallas Rotary. Home: 3710 Granada St Dallas TX 75205 Office: Suite 600 2949 Stemmons Freeway Dallas TX 75247

MALOY, WILLIAM LEWIS, state ofcl., educator; b. Des Moines, Oct. 15, 1927; s. William Lewis and Helen (Chaves) M.; B.S., U. Neb., 1949, M.S., 1954; Ed.D., Fla. State U., 1958; m. Sarah Anne Brown, Aug. 26, 1953; children—William L., Brian, Robert, Bruce. Asst. prin. Escambia High Sch., Pensacola, Fla., 1958-59; cons. Inst. Systems, Fla. Dept. Edn., Tallahassee, 1959-63; resident prof., dir. off-campus program Fla. State U., Tallahassee, 1963-64, dir. univ. placement, 1964-65, asst. dean, asso. prof. edn. adminstrn. Coll. Edn., 1965-69; spl. asst. for ednl. affairs to gov. of Fla., Tallahassee, 1969, now exec. sec. Gov.'s Citizens Com. on Edn. Cons. Philco-Ford Corp., Ft. Washington, Pa., 1967—; program cons. Office Naval Research, Washington, 1961—; chmn. research and studies com. Fla. Council on Elementary Edn., Tallahassee, 1962—; chief naval tng., Pensacola, Fla., 1971—. Local chmn. U.S.O., 1967—. Bd. dirs. S.E. Scholarship and Research Found.; adv. bd. So. Assn. Rural Edn. Improvement Project. Served to capt. USNR, 1944-46, 50-52, 61-62. Mem. Navy League U.S. (pres. chpt.), Phi Delta Kappa, Kappa Delta Pi. Democrat. Episcopalian. Rotarian. Office: Governor's Office The Capital Tallahassee FL 32304

MALPASS, LESLIE FREDERICK, educator; b. Hartford, Conn., May 16, 1922; s. Frederick and Lilly (Elmslie) M.; B.A., Syracuse U., 1947, M.A., 1949, Ph.D., 1952; m. Winona Helen Cassin, May 17, 1946; children—Susan H. (Mrs. John F. Poulton), Peter Gordon, Jennifer Joy, Michael Andrew. Psychologist, Child Guidance Center, Syracuse, N.Y., 1948-52; asst. prof., asso. prof. So. Ill. U., Carbondale, 1952-60; vis. prof. U. Fla., Gainesville, 1959-60; prof. U. S. Fla., Tampa, 1960-65; dean arts and sci. Va. Poly. Inst., Blacksburg, 1965-68, v.p., 1968—. Dir 1st Nat. Exchange Bank of Va., Blacksburg; cons. U.S. Office of Edn., NSF, Peace Corps. Bd. dirs. Showalter Hosp., Blacksburg, Va. Served with AUS, 1945-46. Fellow Am. Psychol. Assn.; mem. A.A.A.S., Am. Assn. U. Profs. Author: Human Behavior, 1965; Social Behavior, 1967; Handbook Mental Deficiency, 1962; Automated Teaching, 1967; Psychological Research in Mental Deficiency, 1968; also numerous articles in profl. jours. Home: 1416 Highland Circle Blacksburg VA 24060

MALTZMAN, SYLVIA, writer; b. Spring Lake, N.J.; d. Israel and Libbie (Samet) Maltzman; B.A., Woodbury, Coll., Los Angeles, 1949, U. Americas, Mexico, 1950. Staff writer Post Press, El Centro, Cal., 1950-53, 56-59, New-Jour., Daytona Beach, Fla., 1953-55, Daily Report, Ontario, Cal., 1955-56, Sun-Tattler, Hollywood, Fla., 1959-60, Ft. Lauderdale (Fla.) News, 1960—. Served with USMCR, 1943-46. Mem. Theta Sigma Phi. Home: 520 SW 27th Rd Miami FL 33129 Office: 320 S E 1st Av Ft Lauderdale FL 33316

MAMALAKIS, MARIE J., educator, news corr.; b. Shreveport, La., Sept. 15, 1913; d. John and Demetria (Passadakis) Mamalakis; A.B., Southwestern La. Inst., 1933; B.S. in L.S., La. State U., 1940; postgrad. U. Chgo., 1948. Tchr. St. Landry Parish Schs., 1934-40; librarian and tchr. St. Landry Parish Opelousas High Sch., 1938-41; circulation librarian U. Southwestern La., Lafayette, 1941-65, dir. publs., prof. 1965—; mng. editor Lafayette Progress, 1951-54, editor, 1954-62. Free-lance feature story writer local papers. Field work disaster relief A.R.C., 1940. Mem. Nat. Fedn. Press Women, A.L.A., La. Library Assn., La. Tchrs. Assn., La. Press Women's Assn. (treas. 1957-58), Pi Gamma Mu, Beta Phi Mu, Phi Kappa Phi, Sigma Sigma Sigma, Phi Alpha Theta, Omicron Delta Epsion. Mem. Order Eastern Star. Contbr. articles to profl. jours. Home: 1018 Auburn Av Lavayette LA 70501

MAN, EUGENE HERBERT, univ. adminstr.; b. Scranton, Pa., Dec. 14, 1923; s. E. Lester and Celia (Cohen) M.; A.B., Oberlin Coll., 1948; Ph.D. (Office Naval Research fellow, E.I. duPont fellow), Duke, 1952; m. Gladys Greenberg, Mar. 7, 1945; children—Elizabeth Sue (Mrs. Carl B. Eichenberger), Barbara Ruth, Linda Jeanne, Bruce Jonathan. Research chemist E.I. duPont de Nemours & Co., Inc., Wilmington, Del., 1952-60, supr. tech. sect., Chattanooga, 1960-61, sr. supr., 1961-62; coordinator research U. Miami, Coral Gables, Fla., 1962-66, dean research coordination, 1966—. Vis. investigator Scripps Instn. Oceanography, 1971-72. Bd. dirs. Health Planning Council, Dade County, Fla.; mem. Mental Health Consortium, Dade County, pres., 1970-71; dir., chmn. Gulf Univs. Research Consortium, 1969-71; trustee, v.p. Community Mental Health Services, Dade County; trustee United Fund Dade County, 1967-69. Served to 1st lt. AUS, 1943-46. Recipient Harry N. Holmes award in chemistry, Oberlin Coll., 1948. Fellow Am. Inst. Chemists; mem. Am. Chem. Soc., A.A.A.S., Nat. Council Univ. Research Adminstrs. (exec. com. 1967—), Sigma Xi, Phi Beta Kappa, Phi Lambda Upsilon. Contbr. articles profl. jours. Patentee in field. Home: PO Box 8542 U Miami Coral Gables FL 33124 Office: Ferre Bldg U Miami Coral Gables FL 33124

MANAHAN, HELEN MARIE, educator; b. Piqua, O., Nov. 14, 1906; d. George W. and Mary Caroline (Dunker) Manahan; B.S. in Edn., Ohio State U., 1929, M.S. in Physiology, 1930; M.S., Columbia, N.Y. Sch. Social work, 1947; postgrad. U. Mich., 1939-41, Smith Coll., 1954, Tulane Sch. Social Work, 1957-58. Instr. health, phys. edn. Ia. State Tchrs. Coll., Cedar Falls, 1930-32; caseworker Montgomery County, Hamilton County Welfare Depts., O., 1933-37; psychiat. social worker Newberry (Mich.) State Hosp., 1939-40, Pontiac (Mich.) State Hosp., 1940-42, St. Elizabeth's Hosp., Washington, 1942-45; psychiat. caseworker cons., N.Y. chpt. A.R.C., 1946-48; asst. prof. Tulane Sch. Social Work, New Orleans, 1949-59; asst. prof. dept. social work Fla. State U. Sch. Social Welfare, Tallahassee, 1959-69; free-lance writer. Mem. Senate, Tulane U., 1954-56, Fla. State U., 1963-65; participant Pilot Demonstration Workshop for Nurses, Tallahassee, 1963, 6th Ann. Fla. Nursing Home Short Course, Gainesville, Fla., 1964; del., Internat. Congress on Mental Health, London, Eng., 1948; condr. seminars Little Rock, 1959, Jacksonville, Fla., 1960, St. Petersburg, Fla., 1960, Montgomery, Ala., 1963, Tampa, Fla., 1964, Clearwater, Fla., 1966. Mem. LeMoyne Art Found. Mem. Nat. Assn. Ret. Tchrs., Am. Assn. U. Profs. Home: 1922 Sunset Lane Tallahassee FL 32303

MANASCO, CARTER, lawyer, public relations exec.; b. Townley, Ala., Jan. 3, 1902; s. John Claude and Dora Letitia (Beaty) M.; student Howard Coll., Birmingham, Ala., 1920-22; LL.B., U. Ala., 1927; m. Mae Emma Guyton, Aug. 1, 1942 (dec. June 1963); 2 sons. Admitted to Ala. bar, 1927; legislative counsel Nat. Coal Assn., 1949—; mem. Ala. Ho. of Reps. 1930-34; mem. 77th-80th congresses from 7th Ala. Dist. Mem. Commn. on Orgn. Exec. Br. of Govt. (Hoover Commn.). Democrat. Mem. Ala. Bar Assn. Mason, Lion. Home: 5932 Chesterbrook Rd McLean VA 22101

MANCEAUX, WILSON JOHN, physician; b. Kaplan, La., Jan. 6, 1935; s. Elias and Nessie (Hebert) M.; B.S., Southwestern U., 1956; M.D., La. State U., 1960; m. Priscilla Pate, Oct. 11, 1969; children—Wilson John, Derrell, Michael, Cheryl. Intern, Confed.

Meml. Hosp., Shreveport, La., 1960-61; pvt. practice medicine, Kaplan, La., 1964—; mem. staff Abram Kaplan Meml. Hosp. Served with AUS, 1962-64. Lion (pres. 1967-68). Home: Route 2 Box 396-H Kaplan LA 70548 Office: 801 N Cushing St Kaplan LA 70548

MANDEL, BENJAMIN J., govt. ofcl.; b. Russian-Poland, Sept. 1, 1912; s. Joseph and Nechama (McKay) M.; came to U.S., 1923, naturalized, 1926;; B.S., Coll. City N.Y., 1934; M.A., George Washington U., 1938; Licentiate Economie, Sch. Econ. and Bus. Adminstrn., Gothenborg, Sweden, 1967; postgrad. Am. U., 1941-66; m. Silvia Rosenthal, Apr. 22, 1937; children—Sondra Edith (Mrs. Bernard Snyder), Myra Louise (Mrs. Richard Grand). Chief statistics div. Social Security Adminstn., Balt., 1944-60; prof. statistics U. Balt., 1946—, chmn. dept., 1948-70; dir. Office Statis. Programs and Standards, U.S. Post Office Dept., Washington, 1962-70; Prof. statistics U.S. Dept. Agr. Grad. Sch., Washington, 1963—; vis. prof. statistics U.S. Civil Service Commn., Washington, N.Y.C., Chgo., San Francisco, 1965—. Recipient Merit Citation, Seward Park High Sch., N.Y.C., 1966; Director's citation Social Security Adminstrn., 1959; Superior Accomplishment award U.S. Post Office Dept., 1967, 70, Meritorious Service award, 1968. Mem. Am. Statis. Assn., Am. Soc. Quality Control, NSF. Author: Statistics for Management, 1972; The Regression Control Chart--A Valuable Tool of Management, 1969. Contbr. numerous articles to profl. jours. Home: 6101 16th St NW Washington DC 20011 Office: US Post Office Dept Washington DC 20260

MANDEL, BERNARD, educator; b. Phila., Mar, 31, 1911; s. Morris and Anna (Borish) M.; B.A., U. Pa., 1933, M.A., 1934, Harrison scholar, 1935, Harrison fellow, 1936; m. Ruth Sigmond, Oct. 17, 1937; 1 son, Robert Sigmond. Research asst. Nat. Research Project, Phila., 1936-39; inspr. U.S. Wage & Hour Div., Phila., 1939-42; economist U.S. Dept. Labor, Washington, 1942-49; statistician U.S. Dept, Navy, Washington, 1949-61, operations research analyst, 1961-67; instr. econs. No. Va. Community Coll., 1966-67, instr. developmental math., 1967-72, asst. prof., 1972—. Served with AUS, 1943-46. Mem. Am. Econ. Assn. Home: 9736 Ranger Rd Fairfax VA 22030 Office: Northern Virginia Community College Central Campus Annandale VA 22003

MANDELL, GERALD LEE, educator; b. N.Y.C., Aug. 20, 1936; s. Herman H. and Sylvia L. (Keller) M.; B.A., Cornell U., Ithaca, N.Y., 1958, M.D., 1962; m. Judith H. Rensin, Dec. 20, 1960; children—James, Pamela, Scott. Instr. Cornell U. Med. Coll., N.Y.C., 1968-69; asst. prof. medicine U. Va., Charlottesville, 1969—, asso. prof. internal medicine, 1972—, head div. infectious diseases, 1969—. Served with Indian Health Service, USPHS, 1963-65. Mem. So. Soc. Clin. Investigation, Infectious Disease Soc. Am., Soc. for Exptl. Biology and Medicine, Phi Beta Kappa, Alpha Omega Alpha. Contbr. articles to profl. jours. Home: 106 Powhatan Circle Charlottesville VA 22901 Office: Box 251 Univ Va Sch Medicine Charlottesville VA 22901

MANDERSON, JAMES FRANK, state ofcl; b. Brookwood, Ala., Jan. 30, 1909; s. Custis Lee and Mattie (Lindsey) M.; grad. U. Ala., 1934; m. Gussie Standeffer, July 4, 1935; children—Francis Elizabeth (Mrs. Ernest Everett Hale), Diane. Operator laundry, dry cleaning bus., Tuscaloosa, Ala., 1934-42; mfr.s rep. Endicott Johnson Shoe Corp., Endicott, N.Y., 1946-56, Craddock Terry Shoe Corp., Lynchburg, Va., 1956-63; state dir. Civil Def., 1963—. Pres. North Port (Ala.), P.T.A., 1960-61. Served with USNR, 1942-45. Ky Col., Ark. Traveler. Mason, Lion (pres. 1957-58). Home: 2001 22d Av North Port AL 35476 Office: Administrn Bldg Montgomery AL 36104

MANDRELL, WILLIAM F(RANCIS), former realtor; b. London, Eng., Apr. 5, 1888; s. Frank H. and Catherine (Brockbank) M.; student pub. schs.; m. Maude Lloyd, Feb. 19, 1911 (dec. Dec. 1970); 1 son, Edward (dec.); m. 2d, Regina Moreno Kirchoff, Oct. 20, 1971. Realtor, 1926-66. Pres. Mobile Rescue Mission, 1953-55; trustee Lexington (Ky.) Theol. Sem.; pres. State Bd. Christian Ch. Ala. Mem. Mobile Real Estate Assn. (pres. 1955), C. of C. Mem. Christian Ch. (past mem. finance com. of internat. conv.). Mason (32 deg.). Home: PO Drawer AM Fairhope AL 35632

MANG, CONRAD DELL, educator; b. Lockhart, Tex., Mar. 29, 1920; s. Frank Adam and Dollie (Martin) M.; B.S., M.Ed., U. Houston, 1947, M.L. in Religion, 1950; Ed.D., U. Tex., 1957; m. Nelle Oliver, Aug. 7, 1943; children—Diane Lynette, Suzanne Kay. Elementary tchr. Houston Ind. Sch. Dist., 1947-50; prin. elementary sch. Lamar (Tex.) Consol. Sch. Dist., 1950-52; tchr. Austin (Tex.) Ind. Sch. Dist., 1952-54, prin. 1954-57; prof. edn. Lamar State Coll. Tech., Beaumont, 1957-67, head dept. edn., 1969—, exec. dir. Region V Edn. Service Center, 1967-69. Vis. prof. Nat. Def. Edn. Act Insts., 1965-67; cons. numerous schs. in Tex. Bd. dirs. Rothwell Bible Chair, Camp Fire Girls Am. (chmn.), Beaumont Remedial Clinic, Beaumont Tchrs. Credit Union; chmn. Beaumont City Parks Commn., 1971—. Served with USCGR, 1942-45. Mem. Tex. Assn. Coll. Tchrs., Houston Council Edn. (pres. 1950), Beaumont C. of C. (bd. dirs.), Phi Kappa Phi, Phi Delta Kappa, Kappa Delta Pi. Rotarian. Author brochure: Curriculum Practices in Southeast Texas, 1964. Contbr. articles to profl. jours. Home: 3110 Redwood Dr Beaumont TX 77703

MANGAN, ROBERT MARTIN, lawyer; b. Binghamton, N.Y., Aug. 23, 1916; s. Martin John and Olive (Perrault) M.; A.B., U. Wis. 1939; student U. Minn., 1940-41, U. N.C., 1941; LL.B., Georgetown U., 1949; m. Dorothy Dobson, Aug. 16, 1941; children—Kathleen (Mrs. Robert F. Poi), R. Lawrence, Peter, Norma (Mrs. Bob Weakley), Michele. Research asst. Minn. Municipal Reference Bur., 1940-41; teaching fellow U. N.C., 1941; various civilian adminstrv., personnel and legal positions, War Dept. and Dept. Army, 1942-61; spl. asst. to asst. sec. interior for pub. land mgmt. Dept. Interior, 1961-63, dep. asst. sec. interior for pub. land mgmt., 1963-65; dep. under sec. Dept. Interior, 1965-69; asst. to commr. Fed. Power Commn., 1969-72; pvt. law practice, Washington, 1972—; sec. V.I. Corp., 1962-64. Mem. Fairfax County Council Human Relations. Mem. D.C. Bar, Fed. Bar Assn., Smithsonian Assos. Unitarian (trustee 1958-60). Author articles. Asso. editor Personnel Adminstrn., 1942-45. Home: 2449 Fardale St Vienna VA 22180 Office: 1625 I St NW Washington DC 20006

MANGE, EDWARD CARL, corp. exec.; b. N.Y.C., Jan. 12, 1941; s. Ralph A. and Edith (Gogel) M.; student Del Mar Coll., 1958-59, Tex. A. and M. Coll., 1959-60; m. Heleen Simon, Nov. 9, 1962; children—Jody Lynn, Andrew Martin. Pres., gen. mgr. Metals Inc. div. Western Metal Co., 1961-71, Metals Inc., Metals Inc. Overseas Export Corp., 1971—. Mem. acquisition com. United Fund Corpus Christi. Bd. dirs. Jewish Community Council Corpus Christi. Mem. Nat. Assn. Secondary Material Industries. Jewish religion (tchr. temple Sunday sch.). Mem. B'nai B'rith (treas.). Patentee wire stripper. Home: 338 Palmetto St Corpus Christi TX 78412 Office: 3000 Agnes St Corpus Christi TX 78403

MANGRUM, FRANKLIN MAYER, educator; b. Mayfield, Ky., June 1, 1925; s. Louis Varon and Harriet Elizabeth (Mayer) M.; A.B., Washington U., St. Louis, 1949; Ph.D., U. Chgo., 1957; m. Jessie Graves, Aug. 25, 1945. Tchr. philosophy, chmn. humanities div. Shimer Coll., Mt. Carroll, Ill., 1956-59; mem. faculty Morehead (Ky.) State U., 1959—, prof. philosophy, 1962—, head dept., 1966—. Tchr. Rockford (Ill.) Coll., summers, 1958, 59. Faculty mem. bd. regents Morehead State U., 1968-71. Served with AUS, 1944-46. Decorated Bronze Star. Recipient Distinguished Faculty award Morehead State U. Alumni Assn., 1969. Mem. Ky. Philos. Assn. (pres. 1966-67), Am. Philos. Assn., Metaphysical Soc. Am., N.E.A., Ky. Edn. Assn., Ky. Col., Blue Key, Delta Tau Delta. Baptist. Home: 416 Allen Av Morehead KY 40351

MANGRUM, JOHN EDWARD, ins. co. exec.; b. Dallas, Sept. 12, 1913; s. Oscar Austin and Elizabeth (Hume) M.; student U. Tex., 1930-32; m. Saravee Megarity, Oct. 23, 1932; children—Doris Kathleen (Mrs. Robert A. Vallerga), John Charles. With Southland Life Ins. Co., Dallas, 1933—, now sr. v.p., treas., dir.; dir. Hillcrest State Bank, Med. Computer Systems Inc., Computer Control Systems Inc. (all Dallas). Chmn. investment adv. com. Tex. Tchr. Retirement System. Mem. Financial Execs. Inst. (pres. Dallas chpt.). Clubs: Dallas Country, Las Colinas Country, Dallas Athletic. Home: Manco Ranch Route 2 Lewisville TX 75067 Office: PO Box 2220 Dallas TX 75222

MANGU, JOHN, JR., truck lines co. exec.; b. Akron, O., Nov. 4, 1925; s. John and Elizabeth (Stoica) M.; B.C.E., U. Akron, 1950; m. Donna Jean Smith, Sept. 24, 1951; children—Pamela Beth, Jean Marie, Linda Ann. Field engr. Clemmer Constrn. Co., Akron, 1950-55, MileHi Constrn. Co., Akron, 1955-56; dir. properties Roadway Express, Inc., Akron, 1956-69; dir. properties and real estate Ryder Truck Lines Inc., Jacksonville, Fla., 1970—; chmn. bd. Terminal Properties Exchange. Served with AUS, 1944-46. Registered profl. engr., 28 states; registered land surveyor La., Ky., S.C. Fellow Am. Soc. C.E., Nat. Soc. Profl. Engrs. Home: 3857 Musket Trail Jacksonville FL 32211 Office: PO Box 2408 2050 Kings Rd Jacksonville FL 32211

MANGUM, EDWARD, educator; b. Greenville, Tex., Dec. 11, 1913; s. Edward Pinkney and Clare (Perkins) M.; B.A., E. Tex. State U., 1936; M.A., Cath. U. Am., 1947. Dir., Mt. Vernon Players, Washington, 1937-47; asst. prof. drama George Washington U., Washington, 1947-50; founder, mgr. dir. Arena Stage, Washington, 1950-52; dir. Honolulu Community Theatre, 1952-54; cons. Am. Nat. Theatre and Acad., N.Y.C., 1954-58, Asia Soc., N.Y.C., 1958; theatre specialist State Dept., Ankara, Turkey, 1958-59; dir. State Theatres, Frankfurt/Main, Bamberg, Germany, 1959-61; asst. prof. English, Southwestern U., Georgetown, Tex., 1962-65; prof. drama St. Edwards U., Austin, 1965—, chmn. dept. fine and performing arts, 1970—. Mem. Actors Equity, Internat. Platform Assn., Am. Assn. U. Profs. Home: 2904 Gem Circle Austin TX 78704

MANGUM, FRANK I., JR., dentist; b. Greeneville, Tenn., Mar. 5, 1931; s. Frank Issac and Junita (Emmerson) M.; B.S., Tenn. State U., 1956; D.D.S., U. Tenn., 1958; m. Frances Ann Holloway, June 24, 1961; children—Cynthia Ann, Scott Holloway. Dir. Dental Health, Lake County, Leesburg, Fla., 1959-60; practice dentistry, Orlando, Fla., 1960-62, Leesburg, 1962—; mem. staff Leesburg Gen. Hosp. Served with USAF, 1950-53. Mem. Lake County (pres. 1967-69), Orange County, Central Dist. dental socs., Am., Fla. (ho. of dels.) dental assns., Acad. Gen. Dentistry, Acad. Operative Dentistry (charter), U. Fla., U. Tenn., Tenn. State U., Tusculum Coll. alumni assns., So. Acad. Clin. Nutrition, Acad. Dental Information, Fla. Dental Study Group. Republican. Presbyn. (deacon). Kiwanian, Elk. Club: Silver Lake Country. Home: 6161 S Silver Lake Dr Leesburg FL 32748 Office: 1376 North Blvd West Leesburg FL 32748

MANGUM, GROVER CLEVELAND, ednl. adminstr.; b. Pageland, S.C., July 5, 1918; s. Grover Cleveland and Lillie (Gathings) M.; A.A., Wingate Jr. Coll., 1937; A.B., Wofford Coll., 1939; M.A., U. S.C., 1947, M.Ed., 1948; postgrad. U. Me., 1959; m. Alice Bryant, May 17, 1942; 1 son, Anthony Bryant. Prin., McCall High Sch., 1940-42; supt. Ruby (S.C.) Schs., 1943-49, Ridgeland Schs., Jasper County, 1950-56, Darlington (S.C.) Schs., 1956-58; supt. edn. Darlington County (S.C.), Darlington, 1969—. Mem. exec. com. S.C. Crippled Children's Soc., 1966—. Sec.-treas. bd. trustees Wingate (N.C.) Jr. Coll., 1945-48. Served with USMCR, 1942-43. Mem. N.E.A., Am. Assn. Sch. Adminstrs., S.C., Darlington County (pres. 1959-60) edn. assns., Jr. C. of C. (hon.). Mason, Kiwanian, Lion. Club: Civitan (hon.). Home: Min-Lou Circle Darlington SC 29532 Office: Courthouse Darlington SC 29532

MANGUS, SAMUEL JAMES, army med. officer; b. Dundalk, Md., July 13, 1929; s. Samuel Jason and Nellie Pauline (Mordica) M.; B.S. in Chemistry, Washington Coll., 1952; M.D., U. Md., 1956; grad. student Baylor U., 1968-69; m. Ruth Drucilla Bertram, July 3, 1954; children—Bonnie D., Paula A., Sherrie V., Ruth D. Enlisted in M.C., U.S. Army, 1946, advanced through grades to col., 1971; intern Valley Forge Army Hosp., 1956-57; resident internal medicine Ft. Howard VA Hosp., 1957-59, Madigan Army Gen. Hosp., 1960-61; assigned Sch. Aviation Medicine, Brookes AFB, 1964; chief dept. medicine Ft. Meade, Md., 1961-64, Deep Sea Diving Sch., U.S. Navy, 1966; chief profl. services Ft. Eustis Hosp., 1964-67, 69-70; comdr. med. dept. Ft. Monroe, Va., 1970—. Decorated Bronze Star, Air medal, Commendation medal. Mem. A.C.P., Am. Hosp. Assn., Tidewater Hosp. Assn., Am. Coll. Hosp. Adminstrs., Army Aviation Assn. Am., Mil. Surgeons, Assn. U.S. Army, Nat. Sojourners, Heros of '76. Mason. Clubs: Army and Navy (Washington); Ft. Monroe Yacht. Home: 307 Grafton District Rd Yorktown VA 23490 Office: MEDDAC US Army Health Clinic Fort Monroe VA 23351

MANIGAULT, PETER, newspaper pub.; b. Charleston, S.C., Jan. 13, 1927; s. Edward and Mary (Hamilton) M.; A.B., Princeton, 1950; m. Landine Sanford Legendre, Aug. 8, 1959; children—Gabrielle, Pierre. With Eve. Post Pub. Co., also The News and Courier Co., Charleston, 1950—, pres. pub. 1960—, v.p. Buenos Aires Herald, 1969—, Aiken (S.C.) Standard, 1969—, Cambridge (Md.) Banner, 1972—. Trustee Nat. Trust Historic Preservation, 1963, vice chmn., 1966—. Served with USNR, 1945-46, 52-53; capt. Res. Decorated Legion of Merit with combat V; Order Mil. Merit (Republic Korea). Mem. Inter-Am. Press Assn. (dir.), Nat. Audubon Soc. (dir.). Home: 71 Anson St Charleston SC 29401 Office: 134 Columbus St Charleston SC 29402

MANISCALCO, TINA CANINO (MRS. PETER MANISCALCO), bus. exec.; b. Houston, May 23, 1915; d. Anthony and Vincent Mary (Fasullo) Canino; student pub. schs.; m. Peter Maniscalco, June 20, 1935; children—Margaret (Mrs. Sam Desterfano), Joseph S., John A., Tracy C. Legal sec. Stewart, Burgess & Morris, Houston, 1947-48; bookkeeper, underwriter, secretarial work Universal Security Life Ins. Co., Houston, 1948-66, pres., chmn. bd., 1966-69, exec. v.p., 1969—; pres., chmn. bd. Universal Security Co., Inc., Houston, 1966-69, pres., 1969—. Mem. Tex., Houston legal res. ofcls. assn., Charity Guild Catholic Women (treas. 1968-69), St. Joseph Hosp. Aux. Roman Catholic. Clubs: Summit, Ladies of Unico, St. Thomas Alumni Mothers, Alpha Gamma Delta Alumni Mothers. Home: 6224 San Felipe Rd Houston TX 77027 Office: 1625 Main St Houston TX 77002

MANLEY, RICHARD SHANNON, lawyer, state legislator; b. Birmingham, Ala., June 23, 1932; s. Richard Sabine and Alice (Hughes) M.; B.S., U. Ala., 1953, LL.B., 1958; m. Lillian Grace Cardwell, Aug. 23, 1953; children—Richard Shannon, Alyce Hughes. Admitted to Ala. bar, 1958, U.S. Dist. Ct. So. Dist. Ala., U.S. 5th Circuit Ct. of Appeals, U.S. Supreme Ct., U.S. Ct. Mil. Appeals; practiced in Demopolis, 1958—; mem. Ala. Ho. of Reps., 1967—. Dir. New Southland Nat. Ins. Co.; v.p. Demopolis Cable TV Co., Inc.; sec. Demopolis Constrn. Co., Inc. Pres. Bd. Edn., Demopolis, 1969—, Demopolis Jr. C. of C., 1961-62; v.p. Ala. Jr. C. of C., 1960-61; dir. U.S. Jr. C. of C., 1962-63. Bd. dirs. Marengo County Hist. Soc., Marengo County Mental Health Assn.; bd. advisers Ala. Hist. Commn., Gen. Holland M. Smith Meml. Served with USMCR, 1953-56. Mem. Am., Ala., 17th Judicial Circuit (past pres.) bar assns., Am. Trial Lawyers Assn., Comml. Law League Am., Am. Judicature Soc., Demopolis C. of C. (dir., past pres.), Marine Corps Res. Officers Assn., U. Ala. Nat. Alumni Assn. (v.p. 1967-68), Farrah Law Soc., Phi Delta Phi, Delta Chi. Methodist (trustee). Rotarian. Clubs: Demopolis Country (past pres., dir.), Demopolis Athletic, U. Ala. Alumni (pres. Marengo County 1965-66); Indian Hills Country (Tuscaloosa, Ala.); The Club (Birmingham, Ala.). Home: 1501 Country Club Dr SW Demopolis AL 36732 Office: 105 S Walnut Av Demopolis AL 36732

MANLEY, WILLIAM TANNER, govt. ofcl.; b. nr. Owingsville, Ky., Aug. 18, 1929; s. Nathan and Flora (Whaley) M.; B.S., U. Ky., 1951, M.S., 1955; Ph.D., U. Fla., 1958; m. Vertna Jane Alexander, Oct. 29, 1951; 1son, William Conway. Asst. prof. U. Fla., 1958-63, asso. prof., 1963-65; economist U.S. Dept. Agr., Gainesville, Fla., 1960-65, dep. dir., marketing econs. div., Washington, 1966-68, dir., 1968—. Served to 1st lt. USAF, 1951-53. Recipient Certificates of Merit, U.S. Dept. Agr., 1963, 69. Mem. Am. Agrl. Econs. Assn., Gamma Sigma Delta, Omicron Delta Epsilon. Home: 6928 Girard St McLean VA 22101 Office: 14th and Independence Sts Washington DC 20205

MANN, BARNETT DONALD, supt. schs.; b. Valley Mills, Tex., May 12, 1932; s. Mitchell and Vada (Barnett) M.; B.S., North Tex. State U., 1953, M. Edn., 1962, postgrad., 1969—; m. Patsy Rae Jones, July 18, 1953; children—Michael, Stephen, Paige. Tchr., Belton Ind. Sch. Dist., 1953-54, Killeen, Tex., 1954-56; high sch. prin., Groesbeck Ind. Sch. Dist., 1958-61, Nocona Ind. Sch. Dist., 1961-64; supt. schs. Gold-Burg Ind. Sch. Dist., 1964-67, New Deal (Tex.) Ind. Sch. Dist., 1967-69, Graham (Tex.) Ind. Sch. Dist., 1969—. Active Boy Scouts Am.; bd. dirs. Little League Assn., New Deal, Tex., 1968-71; adult adviser Leo Lions Club, Graham, Tex., 1970-71. Mem. Tex., Graham tchrs. assns., Am., Tex., Region 9 assns. sch. adminstrs., Tex. Farm Bur., Graham C. of C. (dir. 1970-72). Mason, Elk, Lion. Home: 1401 Hillcrest St Graham TX 76046 Office: 1000 Kentucky St Graham TX 76046

MANN, CECIL WILLIAM, psychologist; b. Sydney, Australia, Oct. 13, 1895; s. John Wills and Martha (Harvey) M.; B.A., U. Sydney, 1927, M.A., 1929; Ed.D., Stanford, 1937; m. Helene Powner, Oct. 16, 1937; 1 dau., Jennifer O. Lectr., Tchrs. Coll., Sydney, 1928-38; asso. prof. psychology Claremont Coll., Cal., 1938-39; asso. prof. psychology U. Denver, 1939-42; dir. guidance bur. La. State U., 1942-45; prof. psychology Tulane, 1945-62, prof. emeritus, 1962—, head dept., 1946-51; prof. psychology Western Carolina U., Cullowhee, N.C., 1961-67, prof. emeritus, 1967—. Chmn. Commn. of Enquiry, Fiji Islands, 1934. Carnegie Research fellow, Fiji Islands, 1935; psychol. cons. VA, 1947-51; dir. research project Office Naval Research. Pres. La. Psychologists, Inc., 1960-61. Fellow Am. Psychol. Assn., A.A.A.S., Sigma Xi. Club: Town and College (pres. 1965-66). Author: Education in Fiji, 1935. Contbr. numerous articles and reports of research in exptl. psychology to govt. publs. and sci. jours. Home: Route 3 Box 203 Sylva NC 28779

MANN, CHARLES SCOTT, dentist; b. Lufkin, Tex., Apr. 17, 1926; s. David L. and Blanche Catherine (Scott) M.; student Stephen F. Austin U., 1942-44; D.D.S., U. Tex., 1947; postgrad. U. Tenn., 1959, U. Ala., 1959; m. Leah Catherine Mann, Sept. 1949; children—Charles Scott, Barbara Kay. Individual practice dentistry, Lufkin, Tex., Amarillo, Houston, now Austin, Tex.; dentist Gary Job Corps, San Marcos, Tex. Served to lt. col. Dental Corps, AUS, World War II, Korea; lt. col. Res., moblzn. designee 5th Army Dental Surgeon. Mem. Army Dental Surgeon. Mem. Am., Tex. dental assns., Austin Dental Soc., Assn. Mil. Surgeons, Res. Officers Assn., Xi Psi Surgeons, Res. Officers Assn., Xi Psi Phi. Methodist. Kiwanian. Home: 4204 North Hills Dr PO Box 9709 Austin TX 78766 Office: 103 W 5th St Austin TX 78701

MANN, DANIEL SIGLE, supt. schs.; b. Horatio, Ark., July 14, 1926; s. George Daniel and Irene (Bush) M.; B.A., Northeastern State Coll., 1951; M.Ed., West Tex. State U., 1959; postgrad. Okla. State U., 1951-65; m. Kathryn Overby, Dec. 26, 1946; children—Larry Daniel, Zereta Irene. Prin. high sch., Hitchita, Okla., 1950-53; supt. schs., Plemons, Tex., 1954-60, Big Cabin, Okla., 1960-65, Coweta, Okla., 1965-70, Waukomis, Okla., 1970—. Mem. Okla. Edn. Assn. (county pres. 1971-72), Okla. Bus. Adminstrn., Okla. State Adminstrn., Nat. Assn. Sch. Adminstrs. Baptist. Home: Box 70 Waukomis OK 73773 Office: Box 70 Waukomis OK 73773

MANN, DAVID PERRY, JR., furniture co. exec.; b. Woodville, Tex., Apr. 18, 1927; s. David Perry and Hattie Lucille (Barclay) M.; student U. Tex., 1945; B.B.S., So. Meth. U., 1952; m. Alpha Jane Bazzoon, July 25, 1964; 1 son, Lee Perry. Owner, Mann Furniture Co., Woodville, Tex., 1964—; v.p., dir. Citizens State Bank, Woodville. Served with USNR, 1945-47. Mem. Retail Furniture Assn. Tex. (dir.). Methodist. Kiwanian. Home: PO Box 626 Woodville TX 75979 Office: 206 W Bluff St Woodville TX 75979

MANN, FLOYD HULON, state ofcl.; b. Daviston, Ala., Aug. 20, 1920; s. Walter Curtis and Bessie (Purcell) M.; student FBI Nat. Acad., 1947, 49, 51-52, Armory Sch., Denver, 1941; m. Grace Dodd, Nov. 25, 1944; children—Paul, Lane, Deana, Kay, Patsy. Chief of police Opelika, Ala., 1950-59; asst. to v.p. personnel services West Point-Pepperell, Inc. (Ga.), 1963-68; dir. Ala. Dept. Pub. Safety, Montgomery, 1959-63, 68—; dir. First Fed. Savs. & Loan Assn., West Point, 1968—, Ala. Liquified Petroleum Gas Co., 1968—. Mem. Aeros. Commn., 1959—, Peace Officers Annuity and Retirement Bd., 1969—. Served with USAAF, 1942-45. Decorated D.F.C. with oak leaf cluster, 4 Air medals. Mem. Peace Officers Assn., FBI Acad. Assos. Democrat. Baptist. Mason (Shriner), K.P. Home: 117 S Anton Dr Montgomery AL 36105 Office: 500 Dexter Av Montgomery AL 36102

MANN, FORBES, aerospace co. exec.; b. Rochester, N.Y., Sept. 25, 1918; s. Abram Joseph and Helen (Forbes) M.; student Phillips Acad., Andover, Mass., 1933-34, Peekskill Mil. Acad., 1934-36, grad. Brown U., 1940; m. Elizabeth Reese Jones, June 7, 1942; children—Robin Gvoyal, Richard Forbes. Design engr. Brewster Aeros. Corp., Long Island City, N.Y., 1940-41; with Ling-Temco-Vought, Inc., Bridgeport, Conn., Dallas, 1941—, chief preliminary design, 1947-52, chief mil. sales, 1952-55, program control mgr., 1955-57, dir. long range planning 1957-59, v.p., Washington, 1959-69; pres. Vought Aeronautics div. LTV Aerospace Corp., Dallas, 1969-70, pres. LTV Aerospace Corp., 1970-72; sr. v.p. LTV Corp., Dallas, 1972—. Cubmaster, scoutmaster D.C. council Boy Scouts Am., 1959-63. Bd.

dirs. Jr. Achievement Dallas. Mem. Air Force Assn., Navy League, Assn. U.S. Army, Aero. Club Washington, Phi Gamma Delta. Clubs: Burning Tree (Washington); Preston Trail Golf, Northwood (both Dallas). Home: 5106 Shadywood Lane Dallas TX 75209 Office: PO Box 5003 Dallas TX 75222

MANN, FRANK EUGENE, lawyer, city ofcl.; b. Mart, Tex., Jan. 15, 1909; s. Cary and Pearl (Alden) M.; m. Janice Jones, Aug. 28, 1948; children—Frank Eugene, Donna (Mrs. Addison Thornhill), Sharon (Mrs. Neal Kinholt), Patricia. Admitted to Tex. bar, 1932, since practiced in Houston; fire commr., dir. fire def. Houston and Harris County, 1939-42; mem. Houston City Council, 1959—. Mem. Tex. Ho. of Reps., 1937-38, 57-58. Served from pvt. to capt. AUS, 1942-45. Mem. Tex., Harris County, Houston bar assns., Am. Legion, V.F.W., Sons of Herman, Harris County Mounted Sheriff's Posse (life mem., past pres.). Eagle (past pres.), Nat. Rifle Assn. (life), Bayou Rifles. Lion. Home: 5430 W 43d St Houston TX 77018 Office: Chronicle Bldg Houston TX 77002

MANN, HELENE DAVIS P(OWNER) (MRS. CECIL W. MANN), psychologist; b. Greensburg, Ind., June 30, 1899; d. Charles Tracy and Olive (Davis) Powner; student U. Ariz., 1917-19; A.B., U. Cal. at Berkeley, 1922; M.A., U. So. Cal., 1927; postgrad. U. So. Cal., The Sorbonne, Paris, U. Madrid, 1927; pvt. study, France, U.S.A.; m. Cecil William Mann, Oct. 16, 1937; 1 step-dau., Jennifer O. Psychologist, tchr. gifted children Pasadena (Cal.) city schs., 1925-29; chief psychologist Los Angeles County Juvenile Hall Clinic, 1929-39; spl. lectr. U. Denver, 1939-41; psychologist Bur. Testing and Guidance, also Specialized Tng. and Reassignment Unit, U.S. Army, La. State U., 1943-45; dir. Tulane U. Reading Improvement Program, 1953-57; pvt. practice psychology, New Orleans, 1957-61, Sylva, N.C., 1962—; clin. psychologist Bur. of Indian Affairs, Dept. of Interior, Cherokee, N.C., 1961-69. Mem. Am., Southeastern, N.C. psychol. assns., Am. Assn. U. Women, League Women Voters (br. v.p.), Pi Beta Phi. Contbr. articles to sci. jours.; also children's stories. Home: Route 3 Box 203 Sylva NC 28779

MANN, HORACE DEWEY, chemist; b. Flowery Branch, Ga., Nov. 4, 1907; s. Horace Darwin and Shasta Viola (Edwards) M.; student Maryville Coll., 1926-30, George Washington U., 1934-36; m. Clara Mae Barron, Feb. 28, 1948; 1 dau., Franes Diane. Sci. Aide Dept. Agr., Washington, 1934-41, analytical chemist, Beltsville, Md., 1941-53, research chemist, Kerrville, Tex., 1953—. Mem. Am. Chem. Soc., Entomol. Soc. Am. Contbr. articles to profl. jours. Home: 601 Mockingbird Lane Kerrville TX 78028 Office: PO Box 232 Kerrville TX 78028

MANN, JAMES ROBERT, congressman; b. Greenville, S.C., Apr. 27, 1920; s. Alfred Cleo and Nina (Griffin) M.; B.A., The Citadel, 1941; LL.B. magna cum laude, U. S.C., 1947; m. Virginia Thomason Brunson, Jan. 15, 1945; children—James Robert, David Brunson, William Walker, Virginia Brunson. Admitted to S.C. bar, 1947; practice in Greenville, 1947—; partner firm Mann, Foster, Richardson & Fisher, 1969—; del. S.C. Ho. of Reps. from Greenville County, 1949-52; solicitor 13th Jud. Circuit, 1953-63; mem. 91st and 92nd Congresses from 4th Dist. S.C. Dir. Palmetto State Life Ins. Co. Sec., Greenville County Planning Commn., 1963-67; chmn. Greenville County Heart Assn., 1952; mem. bd. devel. New Orleans Bapt. Theol. Sem. Bd. dirs. Family Service Agy., 1952; trustee Greenville Hosp. System, 1965-68; bd. visitors Presbyn. Coll. Served to lt. col. AUS, 1941-46. Mem. Am., S.C., Greenville County bar assns., Am. Judicature Soc., Greater Greenville C. of C. (pres. 1965), V.F.W. (dep. comdr. 1951-52), Am. Legion, Phi Beta Kappa, Omicron Delta Kappa. Democrat. Baptist. Mason (Shriner), Kiwanian, Elk; mem. Woodmen of the World. Home: 118 W Mountain View Av Greenville SC 29609 Office: Longworth House Office Bldg Washington DC 20515

MANN, JANEAN LEE, exec. asst.; b. Riverdale, Md., Sept. 14, 1943; d. Francis Lee and Jean (Hughes) Mann; B.A. in Journalism, U. S.C., 1966. With Americana Corp., 1962-63; staff writer Birmingham (Ala.) Post-Herald, 1966-69; press sec. U.S. Rep. John H. Buchanan, Jr. (Republican-Ala.), 1969-71, exec. asst., 1971—. Recipient pub. service award U.S. Treasury Dept.; newswriting award A.P. Mem. House Republican Communications Assn. Theta Sigma Phi. Republican. Club: Greater Birmingham. Home: 5713 MacArthur Blvd NW Washington DC 20016 Office: Longworth House Office Bldg Washington DC 20515

MANN, LAWRENCE CASEY, II, archtl. designer, educator; b. Atlanta, Sept. 12, 1942; s. Lawrence Casey and Charline Almarie (Beard) M.; student (NSF fellow) Morris Brown Coll., 1959; B.Arch., Howard U., 1967, M. City Planning, 1972; postgrad. N.Y. U., 1972—; m. Miriam Ann Hewitt, June 18, 1966; 1 son, Lawrence Casey III. Planning aide Daniel, Mann, Johnson, Mendenhall, 1963, William H. Metcalf, Jr. and Assos., Washington, 1964; designer Bucher-Meyers and Assos., Washington, 1964-65; mem. prodn. staff Fry and Welch, Architects, Washington, 1965-66; designer, mem. prodn. staff Sheridan, Behm and Assos., Washington, 1966-67; cons. Howard U., Washington, 1967; office mgr. Charles Irving Bryant and Assos., Washington, 1967; urban designer, planner Planners Collaborative, Inc., Washington, 1967-68; pres. bd. dirs., staff cons. 2MJQ Environmental Research Devel. Corp., Washington, 1967—; asst. dir. Urban Design Center, Urban Am., Inc., Washington, 1968-69; acting dept. chmn., asst. prof. dept. community planning and devel. Fed. City Coll., 1970-71. Community Planning Edn. grantee Model Cities Program, Washington, 1969—; aid to minority planning student Dept. Housing and Urban Devel., 1969—. Mem. Met. Washington Planning and Housing Assn., Nat. Assn. Profl. Bureaucrats, Nat. Tech. Assn., Council Black Archtl. Schs. (a founder), Inst. Community Planning and Devel. Mason. Home: 430 Delafield Pl NW Washington DC 20011

MANN, LOWELL KIMSEY, mfg. exec.; b. LaGrange, Ga., June 28, 1917; s. Otis A. and Georgia B. (Mundy) M.; advanced mgmt. student Harvard, 1962; m. Helen Margaret Dukes, Feb. 11, 1944; 1 dau., Margaret Ellen. Foreman, Callaway Mills, LaGrange, 1935-39, indsl. engr., 1939-42; indsl. engr. Blue Bell, Inc., Greensboro, N.C., 1946-52, chief engr., 1952-61, v.p. engring., 1961-62, v.p. mfg., 1962-68, dir., 1963—, exec. v.p., 1968—; dir. Shadow Line, Inc., Morgantown, 1968—. Active Nat. Multiple Sclerosis Soc. Bd. dirs. Learning Inst. N.C. Served to capt. AUS, 1942-46. Mem. Piedmont Asso. Industries, Civitan Internat. Democrat. Baptist. Home: 5503 Currituck Pl Sedgefield Greensboro NC 27407 Office: 335 N Church St Greensboro NC 27401

MANN, MONTY, advt., pub. relations, motion picture and audiovisual co. exec.; b. Oklahoma City, Aug. 12, 1906; s. John Thomas and Rebecca (Mantoux) M.; grad. high sch.; m. Martha Ross Putman, Feb. 4, 1933; children—Monty, Thomas William. Vice pres., gen. mgr. Tracy-Locke Co., Dallas, 1927-49, v.p., br. mgr. Glenn Advt., Dallas, 1949-51; v.p., account exec. Lowe Runkle Co., Oklahoma City, Okla., 1951-63; pres. Monty Mann Sports, Oklahoma City, 1963-66; exec. v.p. Creative Communicators, Oklahoma City, 1964-70, dir. 1966-70, exec. producer motion picture prodns. div., 1964-70; exec. v.p. Monty Mann Prodns., Oklahoma City and Peoria, Ill., 1970-71; owner, exec. producer Monty Mann Communications, Oklahoma City, 1971—. Active Boy Scouts Am. Served with USMC, 1944. Mem. Am. (past chmn. S.W. council), Southwestern (past pres.; dir. 1967—) assns. advt. agys., Soc. Motion Picture and TV Engrs., Nat. (tng. counselor 1960—), Okla. (past pres.) rifle assns., Oklahoma City C. of C. Rotarian. Clubs: Oklahoma City Press, Oklahoma City Gun, Western Wildcats Rifle. Home: 3024 NW 41st St Apt 59 Oklahoma City OK 73112 Office: Monty Mann Communications 2809 NW Expressway Oklahoma City OK 73112

MANN, RICHARD DEAN, iron works exec.; b. Valley Mills, Tex., Nov. 3, 1926; s. Eddie and Winnie Belle (Elder) M.; B.S., W. Tex. State U., 1950; m. Penny Anderson, Nov. 25, 1947; children—Deannie (Mrs. Tommy Hill), Donald Edward. Draftsman, Amarillo Iron Works Co. (Tex.), 1947-55, chief sales engr., 1955-69, gen. mgr., 1969—. Served with AUS, 1945-47. Mem. Am. Inst. Steel Constrn. Baptist. Club: Optimist of Amarillo (sec., treas.). Home: 524 W Hastings St Amarillo TX 79108 Office: Box 1507 Amarillo TX 79105

MANN, ROBERT TRASK, appellate judge; b. Tarpon Springs, Florida, June 5, 1924; s. William Edgar and Eunice (Trask) M.; B.S., in Bus. Administrn., U. Fla., 1946, LL.B., 1951; M.A. in Govt., George Washington U., 1948; LL.M., Harvard, 1953; LL.M., Yale, 1968; m. Elizabeth Brown, Dec. 27, 1947; children—Robert Trask, Margaret Elizabeth. Instr. bus. organization and control U. Md., 1947-48; admitted to Fla. bar, 1951, Mass. bar, 1952; asst. prof. law Northeastern U., 1951-53; practice law, Tampa, Fla., 1953-68; mem. firms Graham & Mann, 1956-58, Whitaker, Mann & Stagg, 1959-63; Campbell, Mann & Hampton, 1964-66; now judge Dist. Ct. of Appeal, Lakeland, Fla. Fla. Ho. of Reps., 1956-68. Served with AUS, 1943-45. Named Young Man of Year, Tampa, Jr. C. of C., 1958; recipient outstanding rep. award, St. Petersburg Times, 1967. Mem. Am. Law Inst. Methodist (mem. gen. conf., 1960, 64, 68, 72, World Council 1965, Southeastern jurisdictional council 1960-68). Home: Lake Weeks Seffner FL 33584 Office: District Court Appeal Lakeland FL 33802

MANNERS, GEORGE EMANUEL, educator; b. N.Y.C., Nov. 26, 1910; s. John Emanuel and Demetra (Kremida) M.; B.S. in Commerce, Ga. State U., 1935; M.B.A. in Econs., U. Ga., 1946; Ph.D. in History, Emory U., 1959; m. Claire Gibson, Oct. 14, 1939; children—George Emanuel, Susan Demetra. Bookkeeper, accountant in Ga., 1927-37; engaged in practice pub. accounting, 1937—; high sch. tchr., Atlanta, 1937-39, 41-42, 46-47; test technician merit system Ga. Labor Dept., 1939-41; mem. faculty Ga. State U., and predecessor, 1947—, dean Sch. Bus. Adminstrn., 1950-69, asst. v.p., 1969-70, asso. v.p., 1970-71, Regents prof., 1971—. Mem. Met. Planning Commn., Atlanta, 1949-59, Atlanta Regional Export Expansion Council. Served to maj. AUS, 1942-46. Mem. Am. Assn. Collegiate Schs. Bus. (past mem. exec. com.), So. Econ. Assn., So. Hist. Assn., Atlanta C. of C., Hellenic Study Group, Delta Sigma Pi, Beta Gamma Sigma, Omicron Delta Kappa, Alpha Tau Omega. Methodist (Sunday sch. tchr.). Kiwanian. Author: History of Life Insurance Company in Georgia, 1891-1955, 1959; also articles. Home: 338 Nelson Ferry Rd Decatur GA 30030 Office: 33 Gilmer St SE Atlanta GA 30303

MANNHEIMER, WALTER HERBERT, physician; b. Mainz, Germany, June 24, 1911; s. Eugene and Hedwig (Weiss) M.; B.S., U. Freiburg, 1931, M.D., U. Basel, 1934; m. Ilse Holz, Jan. 20, 1937; children—Irene (Mrs. Gabriel Mirkin), Hedy (Mrs. Richard B. Dunn). Came to U.S., 1936, naturalized, 1942. Intern, Wichita Gen. Hosp., Wichita Falls, 1936-37; resident Charity Hosp., New Orleans, La., 1949-50; practice medicine, specializing in anesthesiology, Seguin, Tex., 1937-49; chief anesthesia sect. VA Hosp., Houston, 1955—; asso. prof. anesthesia Baylor Coll. Medicine, 1955—. Served with M.C., AUS, 1944-46. Author: Histopathologic Effects of Local Anesthetic Drugs, 1961. Contbr. articles to profl. pubs. Home: 5114 Jackwood St Houston TX 77035 Office: VA Hospital Houston TX 77031

MANNING, ALLEN BRYANT, physician; b. Mills County, Tex., Nov. 21, 1936; s. Marvin H. and Artiste Cozette (Bryant) M.; student McMurry Coll., 1955-57, Hardin-Simmons U., 1956-58, Abilene Christian Coll., 1958; M.D., U. Tex., Galveston, 1962; m. Vivian Gay Holmes, Aug. 23, 1958; children—Debra Gay, Jeffrey Holmes. Rotating intern John Peter Smith Hosp., Ft. Worth, 1962-63, resident, 1963-64, vice chmn. dept. gen. practice, 1970—; gen. practice medicine, Arlington, Tex., 1964—; pres. med. staff Arlington Community Hosp., 1969-70; sec. med. staff Arlington Meml. Hosp., 1972-73; aviation med. examiner FAA, 1966—. Bd. dirs. Arlington Boys Club, 1967-70. Recipient NSF research grant U. Tex. Med. Br., 1959-61, Mead Johnson award gen. practice residency, 1963-64, Physicians Recognition award A.M.A., 1969. NSF fellow, 1969-71. Diplomate Am. Bd. Family Practice. Mem. A.M.A., Tex. Med. Assn., Tarrant County Med. Soc., Am., Tex., Tarrant County acads. gen. practice, Am. Assn. Physicians and Surgeons, Am. Coll. Emergency Physicians, N.Central Tex. Council Med. Staffs Pvt. Hosps., Phi Chi, Mu Delta. Home: 1008 Live Oak Lane Arlington TX 76013 Office: 1300 S Fielder Rd Arlington TX 76013

MANNING, ALMA SQUIRES (MRS. T. WESLEY MANNING), nursing adminstr.; b. New Middleton, Tenn., Sept. 9, 1912; d. James T. and Florence (Hays) Squires; diploma St. Thomas Sch. Nursing, Nashville, 1941; certificate Middle Tenn. Tchrs. Coll., Murfreesboro, 1931; B.S. in Nursing Edn., Cath. U. Am. 1955; m. T. Wesley Manning, Aug. 26, 1947. Substitute tchr. Smith County Schs., Carthage, Tenn., 1931-38; instr. nursing St. Thomas Sch. Nursing, Nashville, 1941-44, St. Mary's Sch. Nursing, Knoxville, Tenn., 1944-48; dir. nursing Nashville Met. Gen. Hosp., 1948—. Mem. bd. examiners Tenn. Com. on Nursing Edn. and Nursing Practice, 1945-50; mem. Tenn. Bd. Nursing, 1952-54; Named one of 5 outstanding execs. of year Davidson County, Bus. and Profl. Women's Club, 1963. Methodist. Club: Zonta (charter). Home: 2514 Joya Dr Nashville TN 37214 Office: Nashville Met Gen Hosp Nashville TN 37210

MANNING, ARTHUR BREWSTER, newspaper editor; b. Atlanta, Mar. 31, 1913; s. James Arthur and Rose (Word) M.; m. Mildred J. Dalton, July 11, 1945; children—March Word, James Brewster, William Dalton. Editorial positions Atlanta Constn., 1932-55; press-radio dir. Ga. War Finance Com., 1944-46; copy chief Robert Scott Advt. Agy., Atlanta, 1943-50; with Jacksonville (Fla.) Times-Union, 1955—, mng. editor, 1959—. Mem. Alpha Kappa Psi. Rotarian. Club: University. Home: 414 Oglethorpe Rd Jacksonville FL 32216 Office: PO Box 1949 Jacksonville FL 32201

MANNING, BILLY RANDOLPH, ednl. adminstr.; b. Roanoke, Va., Apr. 27, 1934; s. Daris William and Irma (Hundley) M.; B.S., Va. Poly. Inst., 1955; m. Shirley Ann Scott, Sept. 10, 1955; 1 son, Michael Scott. Designer Newport News (Va.) Shipbldg. and Dry Dock Co., 1957-61; structural engr., Fort Lee, Va., 1961-63, Office Civil Def., Olney, Md., 1963-65; civil engr. C.E. U.S. Army, Olney, 1965-68; dir. profl. adv. center Auburn U., Birmingham, 1968—. Mem. Birmingham Area Manpower Planning Council, 1972—. Served to lt. AUS, 1955-57. Registered Profl. Engr., Ala., W.Va., Mem. Profl. Soc. Nuclear Def., Nat. Soc. Profl. Engrs. (course dir., instr. 1969—). Lutheran (dir. mission edn. 1969-72). Clubs: Shades Valley Optimist, Green Valley Country. Home: 1616 Colesbury Circle Birmingham AL 35226 Office: City Hall Annex Birmingham AL 35203

MANNING, FRANCIS SCOTT, educator; b. Barbados, W.I., Sept. 16, 1933; s. Francis Fyles and Eileen (Robinson) M.; B.Eng. with honors, McGill U., Montreal, Que., Can., 1955; M.S.Engring., Princeton, 1957, M.A., 1957, Ph.D., 1959; m. Nancy Elizabeth Free, Apr. 16, 1960; children—Francis Charles, Helen Eileen. Came to U.S., 1955, naturalized, 1964. Instr. dept. chem. engring. Carnegie-Mellon U., Pitts., 1959, asst. prof., 1959-64, asso. prof., 1964-68; prof., head dept. chem. engring. U. Tulsa., 1968—. Barbados scholar, 1951. Registered profl. engr., Tex., Okla., Pa. Mem. Am. Inst. Che. Engrs., Am. Soc. Engring. Edn. (vice chmn. Allegheny (Pa.) sect. 1965, chmn. 1966), Am. Inst. Metall. Engrs. (R.W. Hunt Silver medal 1969), Sigma Xi, Tau Beta Pi. Author: (with L.N. Canjar) Thermodynamic Properties and Reduced Correlations for Gases, 1967. Contbr. articles to profl. jours. Home: 5227 S 68th East Pl Tulsa OK 74145 Office: U Tulsa Tulsa OK 74110

MANNING, FRANK WILLIAM, electronic engr.; b. Chariton, Ia., July 26, 1917; s. Frank Eli and Margaret (Fowler) M.; B.E. in Elec. Engring., Ia. State Coll., 1938; m. Margaret Elizabeth Rollins, Mar. 2, 1946; children—Margaret Elaine, William Frank, Susan Amy, Jane Elizabeth. With Central States Power & Light Corp., West Union, Ia., 1938-41; engr. Interstate Power Co., Dubuque, 1941; mem. aircraft radio lab. staff U.S. War Dept., Dayton, O., 1942-47; with Oak Ridge Nat. Lab., 1947—, supervising engr. electronics sect., 1949—. Engring. cons. Democritus Nuclear Center, Greece, 1963-64; v.p. Hilltop Corp., Norris, Tenn., 1960—. Commr., Norris Water Commn., 1952-54; mem. Norris Municipal Pub. Works Com., 1954-66, chmn. 1956-65. Councilman, City of Norris, 1969-70, vice mayor, 1971-72. Mem. Anderson County Republican exec. Com., 1960—. Registered profl. engr., Ohio Tenn. Mem. I.E.E.E., A.A.A.S., Am. Nuclear Soc. Rep. Episcopalian (warden ch. 1959-64, 65-66). Mason. Patentee in field. Home: 14 Hilltop Pl Norris TN 37828 Office: PO Box X Oak Ridge TN 37830

MANNING, GLENN FRANKLIN, lawyer; b. Huntsville, Ala., July 10, 1922; s. Frank C. and Lucile (Davis) M.; student Auburn U., 1940-41; student U. Ala., 1941-43, LL.B., 1948; student Georgetown U., 1943-44; LL.M., George Washington U., 1949; m. Mary Elizabeth Kirkpatrick, Oct. 16, 1954; children—Frank R., Mary K., Alice E., Sam D. Admitted to Ala. bar, 1948; atty. FTC, 1948-49; practice law, Huntsville, Ala., 1949-50; state dist. atty. 23d Jud. Circuit of Ala., 1951-58; practice law, Huntsville, 1958—; partner firm Martinson, Manning, and Martinson, Huntsville, 1963—. Instr. polit. sci. U. Ala., 1952-55. Mem. Madison County (Ala.) Democratic Exec. Com., 1958-64, Madison County Republican Exec. Com., 1965-70; del. Ala. Rep. Conv., 1968, 70; mem. Ala. State Rep. Com., 1969-70. Bd. dirs. U. Ala. Law Sch. Found. Mem. Am., Ala. (bd. commnrs.), Huntsville-Madison County (pres. 1969-70) bar assns., Farrah Order Jurisprudence, Ala. Trial Lawyers Assn., Am. Trial Lawyers Assn. Episcopalian. Home: 2603 Ridgeview Circle SE Huntsville AL 35803 Office: 217-221 Uptown Bldg Huntsville AL 35804

MANNING, ISAAC STANFORD, dentist; b. Valdosta, Ga., Apr. 19, 1920; s. Ollie and Mamie (Serman) M.; student Fla. Meml. Coll., 1940-42, Fisk U., 1945-47; D.D.S., Meharry Med. Coll., 1951; m. Johnnie Ruth Chestnut, Jan. 26, 1962; 1 son, Isaac Stanford. Pvt. practice dentistry, Orlando, Fla., 1953—. Vice pres., dir. Washington Shore Fed. Savs. & Loan Assn.; dir. Dr. P. Phillips Nursing Home. Vice chmn. Orlando Uban Renewal Com., 1963-65; mem. Adv. Com. on Housing Rehab., Orlando, 1965—; mem. Orange and Seminole Counties Adv. Com. on Recreation, 1967—. Served with AUS, 1942-45, Dental Corps, AUS, 1951-53. Mem. Nat. (state v.p. 1966-69), Am. dental assns., Fla. Med. and Dental Assn. (pres. 1966-67), Fla. Meml. Coll. (pres. Orange County), Meharry Med. Coll. alumni assns., Alpha Phi Alpha. Democrat. Baptist (trustee). Mason, Elk. Home: 806 Lake Mann Dr Orlando FL 32805 Office: 708 W Jackson St Orlando FL 32805

MANNING, RAYMOND BRENDAN, mus. ofcl.; b. Bklyn., Oct. 11, 1934; s. Franklin B. and Elizabeth (Smith) M.; student U. Fla., 1952-53; B.S., U. Miami, 1956, M.S., 1959, Ph.D., 1963; m. Lilly D. King, Aug. 1, 1957; children—Marian, Barbara Ann, Elaine. Research instr. Inst. Marine Scis., U. Miami, 1959-63; asso. curator div. marine invertebrates Nat. Mus. Natural History, Smithsonian Instn., 1963-64, curator div. crustacea, 1965-67, chmn. dept. invertebrate zoology, 1967—. Mem. Biol. Soc. Washington, A.A.A.S., Am. Inst. Biol. Scis. Home: 2401 Jackson Pkwy Vienna VA 22180 Office: Dept Invertebrate Zoology Mus Natural History Smithsonian Instn Washington DC 20500

MANNING, ROBERT LISBON, TV cinematographer; b. Nashville, May 18, 1933; s. Robert Lisbon and Katherine (Kallock) M.; student Vanderbilt U., 1952-54. With WSM-TV, Nashville, 1950-54, 56—, news cinematographer, reporter, 1956-60, chief cinematographer, 1960—. Bd. dirs. Cath. Communication Commn. Tenn. Served with Signal Corps, AUS, 1954-56. Mem. Radio-TV News Dirs. Assn., Nat. Press Photographers Assn., Soc. Motion Picture and TV Engrs., Mid-Tenn. News Photographers Assn., Sigma Delta Chi (chpt. dir.). Roman Catholic. Home: 6668 S Upton Ct Nashville TN 37209 Office: 5700 Knob Rd PO Box 100 Nashville TN 37202

MANNING, WALTER SCOTT, educator; b. nr. Yoakum, Tex.; B.B.A., Tex. Coll. Arts and Industries, 1932; M.B.A., U. Tex., 1940; m. Eleanor Mary Jones, Aug. 27, 1937; children—Sharon Frances, Walter Scott, Robert Kenneth. Asst. to bus. mgr. Tex. Coll. Arts and Industries, Kingsville, 1932; tchr., Sinton (Tex.) High Sch., 1933-37, Robstown (Tex.) High Sch., 1937-41; prof. Tex. A. and M. Coll., College Station, 1941—. Cons. C.P.A. Mem. athletic council Tex. A & M U. C.P.A., Tex. Mem. Am. Assn. U. Profs., Am. Accounting Assn., Am. Inst. C.P.A.'s Tex. Soc. C.P.A.'s, College Station C. of C. (past pres.), Tex. Assn. U. Instrs. in Accounting (pres. 1963-64), Knights York Cross of Honor, Alpha Chi. Democrat. Presbyn. (elder). Mason (32 deg., Shriner, K.T.), Kiwanian. Home: 405 Walton Dr E College Station TX 77840

MANNING, WILLIAM RAYMOND, supt. schs.; b. Vancouver, B.C., Can., May 17, 1920; s. William and Mary (Gysels) M.; came to U.S., 1922, derivative citizen; B.A., San Jose (Cal.) State Coll., 1941; M.A., U. Pacific, 1949; Ed.D., Stanford, 1956. Tchr., Galt, Cal., 1946-49; prin., Lodi, Cal., 1949-50; supt. schs., Orangevale, Cal., 1950-58, Petaluma, Cal., 1958-64, Lansing, Mich., 1964-67, Washington, 1967—. Vis. prof. U. Hawaii, Sacramento State Coll., San Francisco State Coll., No. Mich. U., Mich. State U. Served with USAAF, 1942-46. Contbr. articles to profl. jours. Home: 3900 Watson Pl NW Washington DC 20016 Office: 415 12th St NW Washington DC 20004

MANOR, HAROLD CARL, coll. pres.; b. Ft. Wayne, Ind., Sept. 20, 1913; s. Carl E. and Mabel (Timmis) M.; B. Music Edn., Ind. U., 1936, M.A., 1938, Ed.D., 1947; postgrad. U. Fla., 1954-56; D. Humane Letters, Fla. Atlantic U., 1972; m. Dorothy Beatrice McCormick, June 6, 1937; 1 dau., Marcia Lee. Supr. music, Rockville, Ind., 1936-38, Winchester, Ind., 1938-44; instr., critic Ind. U., 1944-47;

chmn. fine arts dept. Ark. State Coll., 1947-53; instr. St. Petersburg Jr. Coll., 1953-55, dean evening div., 1955-57; asst. pres. Palm Beach Jr. Coll., Lake Worth, Fla., 1957-58, pres., 1958—. Mem. Assn. for Higher Edn. Am., So. Assn. Colls. and Schs. (mem. commn. on colls.), Phi Delta Kappa, Phi Mu Alpha. Presbyn. Mason, Rotarian. Home: 3570 S Ocean Blvd Palm Beach FL 33480 Office: 4200 Congress Av Lake Worth FL 33460

MANOS, GEORGE, pianist, conductor; b. Greensboro, N.C., Mar. 10, 1930; s. Spyros and Marina (Skalas) M.; diploma Peabody Conservatory Music, 1952; student Julliard Sch. Music, 1947. Dir. ProArte Chamber Orch., Washington, 1946-48, Peabody Opera Chorus, Balt., 1948-51, Nat. Assn. Am. Composers and Condrs. Chamber Orch., 1957-59, Nat. Oratorio Soc., Washington, 1957-67, D.C. Bach Festivals, 1960-67; founder, music dir., condr. Killarney Bach Festival, Republic of Ireland, 1971—; mem. tour Columbia Mgmt., 1957-58, European Athens Artist Bur., 1967-69; solo appearances; condr. Nat. Ballet, 1964-65; faculty Madeira Sch., 1964-67, Am. U., 1967, Cath. U., 1967-71; exec. dir. Wilmington (Del.) Sch. Music, 1971—. Served with USMCR, 1948-52. Recipient ecclesiastic order Archbishop Australia for cultural contbn., 1957, commendation Royal House Greece, 1955. Clubs: Friday Morning Music Arts (Washington). Home: 6905 Millwood Rd Bethesda MD 20034 Office: Wilmington Sch Music 4101 Washington St Wilmington DE 19802

MANSFIELD, JIM HOLLAND, optical mfg. co. exec.; b. Bandera, Tex., Oct. 8, 1936; s. James Roy and Beverly Jenny (Boles) M.; B.S. in Indsl. Engring., Okla. State U., 1959; postgrad. So. Ill. U., 1959-60; m. Sue Jane Kallenberger, Aug. 25, 1956; children—Sherry Lynn, Melanie Sue. Sr. mgmt. cons. Lifson, Wilson, Ferguson & Winick, Dallas, 1961-68; dir. operations Internat. Optical Co., Dallas, 1968-69; v.p. mfg. Home Metal Products Co., Plano, Tex., 1969-72; v.p., gen. mgr. Internat. Optical, Dallas, 1972—. Cons. county hosps. Bd. dirs. Collin County United Fund, 1971-72. Registered profl. engr., Tex. Mem. Am. Inst. Indsl. Engrs. (sr. mem.), Sigma Phi Epsilon (treas. 1954). Republican. Methodist. Home: 7039 Town Bluff Dallas TX 75240 Office: 750 Central Expressway Plano TX 75074

MANSFIELD, LAWRENCE FREDERICK, economist, educator; b. St. Petersburg, Fla., Sept. 19, 1922; s. Ernest Joshua and Annie (Bradshaw) M.; B.A., Washington and Lee U., 1947, B.S., 1947; M.A., U. Fla., 1949; Ph.D., U. N.C., 1960; m. Frances Cornelia Walker, Apr. 4, 1962; step- children—Alan, Sean. Asst. prof. U. Tenn., Knoxville, 1953-57, Fla. State U., Tallahassee, 1957-59, Hollins Coll., Roanoke, Va., 1959-61; economist Fed. Reserve Bank, Atlanta, 1961-65, 67-68; econ. adviser AID, Guinea and Nigeria, 1965-67; prof. econs. U. Miami, Coral Gables, Fla., 1968—. Served to lt.(j.g.) USNR, 1943-46. Mem. Am., So. econ. assns., So. Finance Assn., Royal African Soc., So. Finance Assn. (exec. com. 1969-70), Phi Kappa Phi. Home: 8175 SW 185th St Miami FL 33157 Office: Econs Dept U Miami Coral Gables FL 33124

MANSHIP, CHARLES P(HELPS), JR., publisher; b. Baton Rouge, Aug. 13, 1908; s. Charles Phelps and Leora (Douthit) M.; M.B.A., Harvard, 1932; B.Jour., U. Mo., 1930;; m. Paula Garvey, Aug. 27, 1938. Reporter State-Times and Morning Adv., Baton Rouge, 1926-27, gen. mgr., 1938-42, pub., 1946—; advt. salesman Times-Picayune, 1932-34; sec., treas. Baton Rouge Broadcasting Co. 1946—, La. TV Corp., Mobile Video Tapes, Co.; pres. Capital City Press; dir. Internat. Trade Mart, Gulf States Utilities Co., La. Nat. Bank, Capital Bldg. & Loan Co. Mem. So. Newspaper Pubs. Assn. (pres. 1959, Kappa Alpha. Rotarian. Clubs: Internat. House, Boston (New Orleans); Country, City (Baton Rouge). Home: 2250 Kleinert Av Baton Rouge LA Office: 525 Lafayette St Baton Rouge LA

MANSHIP, DOUGLAS, radio, TV, newspaper exec.; b. Baton Rouge, Nov. 3, 1918; s. Charles P. and Leora (Douthit) M.; student La. State U., 1936-41, U. Heidelberg, 1937, U. Colo., 1938-39; m. Jane French, Jan. 31, 1942; children—Douglas Lewis, Richard French, David Charles, Dina. Reporter State Times and Morning Advocate, 1945-47; with Baton Rouge Broadcasting Co., 1947—, pres. 1948—; pres., gen. mgr. La. TV Broadcasting Corp. 1953—; sec.-treas. Capital City Press, 1951-70, pub., 1970—; dir. City Nat. Bank, La. Fire Ins. Co., TV Stas. Inc. Dir. civil def., La., 1951-52; campaign chmn. Community Chest, 1950, bd. dirs., 1950-52, pres. 1951. Served with USAAF, World War II. Mem. Baton Rouge (pres. 1963), La. (v.p.) chambers of commerce, Assn. for Profl. Broadcasting Edn., Council for A Better La., Assn. La. Chambers Commerce, Kappa Alpha. Episcopalian. Rotarian. Home: 5470 Claycut Rd Baton Rouge LA 70806 Office: 1650 Highland Rd Baton Rouge LA 70802

MANSKE, WALLIS HENRY, lawyer; b. Oldenburg, Tex., Jan. 30, 1922; s. Herbert G. and Eleanora (Ahlhorn) M.; student Tex. Luth. Coll., 1940-42; LL.B., U. Louisville, 1949; m. Ethel Mae Price, May 19, 1946; 1 dau., Patricia Ann. Admitted to Ky. bar, 1950; practiced in Louisville, 1950—. Served with USAAF, 1942-45. Decorated Bronze Star medal. Mem. Am., Ky., Louisville bar assns., World Peace Through Law, Nat., Ky. assns. trial attys., Ky. Hist. Soc. Mason. Home: 3318 Autumn Way Louisville KY 40218 Office: Marion E Taylor Bldg Louisville KY 40202

MANSKE, WALTER EARL, banker; b. Waco, Tex., Sept. 2, 1928; s. Walter Louis and Lillie Emily (Witte) M.; A.A., Tex. Lutheran Coll., 1947; B.B.A., Baylor U., 1950; m. Phyllis Mae Reichle, Mar. 26, 1955; children—Sharon, Diane. New bus. supr. Tex. Power & Light Co., Waco, 1955-59; mgr. farmers br. Carrollton, 1959-69; v.p., loan officer Central Bank & Trust Co., Farmers Branch, Tex., 1969—. Pres. Dallas area adv. council Dallas area Chambers Commerce, 1971. Served with USAF, 1950-54. Recipient Outstanding Citizen award Farmers Branch Community Red Cross, 1966. Chmn. United Fund, 1964-65, Cancer Soc., 1968-69. Mem. Greater N.W. (pres. 1970), Farmers Branch (pres. 1962) chambers commerce. Rotarian, Mason. Club: Brookhaven Country. Home: 3128 Rolling Knoll St Dallas TX 75234 Office: 12875 Josey Lane Dallas TX 75234

MANSON, PETER C., b. 1918; grad. U. Fla., 1951. Mem. faculty Sch. Law U. Va., Charlottesville. Office: School Law Univ Va Charlottesville VA 22901

MANSON-HING, LINCOLN ROY, educator; b. Guyana, May 20, 1926; s. Rupert and Agatha (Too-Chung) M.; D.M.D., Tufts U., 1948; M.S., U. Ala., 1961; m. Joyce Louise Chin, Aug. 21, 1959; children—Collin J., Jennifer L., Jeffrey P. Pvt. practice dentistry, Kingston, Jamaica, 1948-56; asst. prof. dentistry U. Ala., Birmingham, 1956-59, asso. prof. dentistry, chmn. dept. dental radiology, 1959-72, prof. dentistry, 1968—. Fulbright-Hays lectr. to Egypt, 1964-65; cons. VA Hosp., Birmingham, Ala., Am. Dental Assn., Am. Nat. Standards Inst. Mem. Am. Acad. Dental Radiology (pres. 1967), Internat. Assn. Dental Research, Am. Dental Assn., Am. Acad. Dental Radiology, Sigma Xi, Omicron Kappa Upsilon. Author: (with A.H. Wuehrmann) Dental Radiology, 1969. Contbr. articles to profl. jours. Home: 205 Mecca Av Birmingham AL 35209 Office: 1919 7th Av S Birmingham AL 35233

MANTHEY, J.H., JR., publishing co. exec.; b. Lexington, Mo., June 13, 1906; s. John H. and Lydia (Ahrens) M.; student Central Wesleyan Coll., Warrenton, Mo., 1926-28; student bus. courses U. Tex., Nat. Bus. Inst., Chgo.; m. Phyllis M. Schowengerdt, Dec. 24, 1933; 1 son, John Bradford. Editor, mgr. Lexington Advertiser Daily News, 1929-32; pub. Cleveland (Tex.) Adv., 1932-68; pres. Trinity Pub. Co., Liberty, Tex., pubs. Liberty Vindicator, Dayton News, Liberty County News, Hull-Daisetta Progressive Outlook, Liberty County Press, Anahuac Progress, Winnie-Stoval Chronicle, 1939-67; pub. San Jacinto Times, East Tex. Progress, East-Tex. Shopper, until 1968; owner, mgr. Cleveland Printers & Stationers; v.p. Farmers State Bank; operator farm and real estate holdings. Mem. state adv. council dept. journalism Tex. A. and M. U., 1958—. Mem., ofcl. Trinity River Assn., Lower Trinity Valley Assn.; charter mem., officer Cleveland Vol. Fire Dept.; mem. Tex. Gov.'s Planning Com., Traffic Safety Com.; Liberty County rep. San Jacinto River Authority; hon. mem. Tex. Atty. Gen.'s Staff; hon. dir. Tex. Safety Council; mem. Tex. Industrialization Com. Sec., city mgr. City of Cleveland, 1935-54; sec. Liberty County Democratic Exec. Com., 1942-54; past officer Liberty County Young Dem. Club, Tex. Young Dem. Club. Recipient numerous awards in field newspaper pub., community service, polit. activities. Mem. Tex. (dir., editorial bd., officer 1932—), Tex. Gulf (charter pres. 1939, editor mag.), South Tex., North and East Tex. press assns., Tex. Editorial Assn. (officer), East Tex. (dir., asst. editor mag.), Cleveland (chmn. organizing com., past sec., mgr., pres., Bus. Man of Year 1951) chambers commerce, Sigma Delta Chi (hon.). Methodist (lay mem., steward, mem. choir, Sunday sch. tchr., pastor's asst.). Mason, Rotarian (charter Cleveland, past pres., dist. officer), Lion (charter Cleveland, past pres.). Club: Liberty Country. Home: 506 Plum Grove Rd Cleveland TX 77327 Office: 104-106 Houston St PO Box 368 Cleveland TX 77327

MANTLE, PETER JOHN, aerospace co. exec.; b. South Harrow, Eng., Apr. 29, 1935; s. George Henry and Winifred (Coyne) M.; student Southampton U., 1952-53; D.C. Ae., Coll. Aeronautics, 1958; M.S., magna cum laude, Laval U., 1960; Ae. E., Cal. Inst. Tech., 1964; m. Lisa Popoff, June 26, 1965; children—Tracy Lynn, Christopher James. Aerodynamicist Saunders-Roe, Engring., Isle of Wight, Eng., 1953-56; research engr. Canadian Armament Research & Devel. Establishment, Quebec, 1958-60; chief engr. Vehicle Research Corp., Pasadena, Cal., 1960-64; engr. Gen. Dynamics, Groton, Conn., 1965-67; tech. dir. Bell Aerospace Co., New Orleans, 1967-68, engring. mgr., 1969-70, program mgr., 1970—. Teaching asst. Cal. Inst. Tech., 1960-62; cons to NASA Aeroballistics, 1961-63. Mem. Am. Inst. Aero. and Astronautics (mem. tech. com. 1970), Am. Soc. Mech. Engrs., Royal Aero. Soc., U.S. Naval Inst., Sigma Xi. Patentee in field. Home: 4621 Senac Dr Metairie LA 70003 Office: PO Box 29307 New Orleans LA 70129

MANUCCIA, HERBERT, cons. engr., educator; b. N.Y.C., Sept. 15, 1905; s. Louis and Constance (Speciale) M.; City Coll. N.Y., Cooper Union, George Washington U.; m. Marie Serena, Jan. 27, 1928; 1 son, Herbert Louis. With Herbert Manuccia, P.E. and Assos., cons. engrs., Washington; prof., staff Sch. Engring. and Architecture Cath. U. Am. Prin. works include design multi story bldgs., subways, Ind. Subway System, N.Y.C.; bridges, ships, Maritime Commn.; stress analysis N.Y. World's Fair; mil. structures, including Pentagon Bldg., Arlington, Va.; engr. cons. foreign mil. installations; overseas engring. cons. mil. installations. Vice chmn. Alexandria City Bd. Zoning Appeals. Past rep. D.C. council Archtl. and Engring. Socs., former officer and past chmn. various coms. in these socs. Former chmn. No. Va. com. Boy Scouts Am. Registered profl. engr., Va., D.C., Md., N.C. Certified by Nat. Council State Bds. Engring. Exams. Recipient Outstanding Engr. award D.C. Soc. Profl. Engrs., 1955, Va. Soc. Profl. Engrs., 57. Mem. Am. Assn. U. Profs., Am. Soc. Engring. Edn., A.A.A.S., Soc. Am. Mil. Engrs., Municipal Engrs. Soc. City N.Y., Nat. (past nat. dir.; past nat. sec. cons. engineers, nat. gov.), Va. (past dir.), No. Va. (past pres.), D.C. (past pres., now state chmn.) socs. profl. engrs., Holy Name Soc. Roman Catholic. Home: 716 Pryor St Alexandria VA 22304 Office: Shirlington Trust Bldg 2740 S Randolph St Arlington VA 22206

MANUEL, MAURICE, JR., dentist; b. Mamou, La., Dec. 24, 1930; s. Maurice and Armida (Young) M.; B.S., U. Southwestern La., 1951; postgrad. U. Ill., summers 1951, 52; D.D.S., Loyola U., 1955; m. Lois Lorene Henderson, Aug. 23, 1955; children—Maurice III, Charles Cary. Instr. crown and bridge dentistry Loyola U. Sch. Dentistry, New Orleans, 1955; practice dentistry, Lafayette, La., 1959—. Served to maj. Dental Corps, USAF, 1955-59. Mem. Am., La., Lafayette dental assns. Roman Catholic. K.C. Rotarian (pres. 1969). Home: 1003 Greenbriar Rd Lafayette LA 70501 Office: Bldg E 1144 Collidge St Lafayette LA 70501

MANUEL, SADAY J., city ofcl.; b. Basile, La., Mar. 28, 1922; s. Valentin and Valentine M.; student Jefferson Davis Vocational-Tech. Sch., 1951-52; m. Ellen Ardoin, Nov. 26, 1946; children—Brenda Joy, Sidney Joel, James Steven. Owner store, Jennings, La., 1939-52, G. B. Zigler Shipyard, Jennings, 1952-56; city clk. City of Jennings, sec.-treas. Jennings Vol. Fire Dept., 1956—; asst. fire chief. Mem. Democratic Exec. Com., 1957—. Served with AUS, 1942-45. Mem. Am. Legion, V.F.W. Roman Catholic. K.C., Lion. Home: 523 W Division St Jennings LA 70546 Office: City Hall Jennings LA 70546

MANUPELLI, FRANK, indsl. exec.; b. San Antonio, Feb. 24, 1924; s. Daniel and Ora (Hogan) M.; student Hampden-Sydney Coll., 1943-44, U.N.C., 1944, U. Tex., 1946-47; LL.B., St. Marys U., 1950; m. Lauretta Buschell, Jan. 19, 1952; children—Stephen Daniel, Jeffrey Scott, Laura. Spl. agt. FBI, Washington, N.Y.C., N.J., 1950-53; dir. personnel City of San Antonio, 1953-56; dir. indsl. relations, asst. gen. mgr. Bus. Aircraft Corp., San Antonio, 1956-64; exec. v.p. Hemisfair '68, San Antonio, 1964-68, Ellison Industries, San Antonio, 1968—. Chmn., Fire and Police Civil Service Commn., San Antonio, 1963—. Served with USNR, 1943-46. Mem. Tex. Mfrs. Assn. (dir. 1961-62), Soc. Former Spl. Agts. FBI, St. Marys U. Alumni Assn. (dir. 1968—). Home: 8100 Countryside Dr San Antonio TX 78209 Office: 103 Springdale Dr San Antonio TX 78227

MANVEL, ALLEN DAILEY, statistician; b. Spokane, Wash., June 29, 1912; s. Arthur M. and Agnes (Johnson) Dailey; A.B., Occidental Coll., 1934; postgrad. U. Chgo., 1935-36, Harvard, 1939-40; m. Helen L. DeWerthern, Oct. 9, 1937; children—Sarah (Mrs. Warren K. Porter, Jr.), Bennett. Statistician, Cal. Med.-Econ. Survey, Beverly Hills, 1934-35; asst. supr., research and statistics Ill. Dept. Finance, Springfield, 1936-39, acting state budget supr., 1942-43; analyst U.S. Bur. Budget, Washington, 1943-46; chief Govts. Div., U.S. Bur. of Census, Washington, 1946-60, 62-67; asso. dir. Nat. Commn. on Urban Problems, Washington, 1967-68; asst. dir. Adv. Commn. on Intergovtl. Relations, Washington, 1968-70; cons. statistics, govt. finance, 1970—. Mem. Tax Inst. Mem. Phi Beta Kappa. Club: Cosmos (Washington). Contbr. articles in field to profl. jours. Home: 6221 Western Av NW Washington DC 20015

MAPLES, JOHN, JR., banker; b. Omaha, Ga., Dec. 21, 1913; s. John and Mary (Portis) M.; student Auburn U., 1932-35, Rutgers U., 1945-47; m. Susie Hayes, Apr. 24, 1937; 1 dau., Mary Sue (Mrs. J. Donald Thornburgh). Sr. v.p. Birmingham Trust Nat. Bank (Ala.), 1935-64; exec. v.p., dir. Union Bank & Trust Co., Montgomery, Ala., 1964—. Treas., Ala. Heart Assn., 1958-65, chmn. bd., 1966—; Ala. treas. Radio Free Europe, 1964-68, state chmn., 1968; mem. budget com. Am. Heart Assn., 1967-68; bd. dirs. United Appeal, Montgomery, Downtown Unlimited. Mem. Theta Chi. Baptist. Club: Montgomery Country, Kiwanis (bd. dirs.). Home: 3107 Pinehurst Dr Montgomery AL 36111 Office: 60 Commerce St Montgomery AL 36103

MAPLES, JOHN CLIFTON, civil engr.; b. Cromwell, Ky., Oct. 18, 1921; s. Orson C. and Pearl (Renfrow) M.; B.S. in Civil Engring., U. Ala., 1951; postgad. Okla. State U., 1969—; m. Florence Utley, Apr. 6, 1946; children—Stephen J., Patricia. Civil engr. design TVA, Knoxville, 1951-53, constrn. engr. Johnsonville Steam Plant, 1956-58; constrn. engr. U.S. C.E., Wilmington Dist., N.C., 1953-56, constrn. engr., designer, Tulsa Dist., 1958-60, project engr. Keystone Dam, Tulsa Dist., 1960-62, constrn. mgmt. engr., Tulsa Dist., 1962-66, resident engr. Ark. Navagation Project, Locks Dam 18, Tulsa Dist., 1966-71, chief navigation br., Tulsa dist., 1971—. Cubmaster, Boy Scouts Am., 1955-56, scoutmaster, 1959-61, explorer leader, 1961-62. Served with AUS, 1942-45; ETO. Registered profl. engr., Okla. Mem. Am. Soc. C.E., Chi Epsilon. Baptist (supt. Sunday Sch. 1967—). Home: 14660 E 11th Pl Tulsa OK 74108 Office: Box 30 Inola OK 74036

MAPP, ALF JOHNSON, JR., author, historian; b. Portsmouth, Va., Feb. 17, 1925; s. Alf Johnson and Lorraine (Carney) M.; A.A., Coll. William and Mary, 1945, A.B., 1961; m. Hartley Lockhart, Mar. 28, 1953; 1 son, Aif Johnson III; m. 2d, Ramona Hartley Hamby, Aug. 1, 1971. Editorial writer Portsmouth Star, 1945-46, asso. editor, 1946-48, editorial chief, 1948-54; news editor, editorial writer Virginian-Pilot, Norfolk, 1954-58; free lance writer, 1958—; lectr. Old Dominion Coll., 1961—, also asst. prof. English, history, journalism and creative writing; profl. lectr., 1948—. Mem. Portsmouth-Norfolk County Savs. Bond Com., 1948-51; Va. Com. Library Devel., 1949-50; editorial com. Commemoration of 350th Anniversary of Rep. Govt. in Am., 1966-69; publs. com. War of Independence Commn., 1967—, Jamestown Found., 1967—; chmn. Am. independence bicentennial coms. Norfolk and Portsmouth hist. socs.; Portsmouth chmn. Am. Revolution Bicentennial Commn. Dir. Portsmouth Pub. Library, 1948-58, v.p., 1954-56; bd. dirs. Portsmouth Area Community Chest, 1948-52. Del. Va. State Democratic Conv., 1946. Named Portsmouth Young Man Yr., 1951; recipient Freedoms Found. Honor medal, 1951; English award Old Dominion Coll., 1961, Troubadour Outstanding Tchr. award, 1969; Outstanding Educator award, Chgo., 1972. Mem. Va., Portsmouth, Norfolk (dir. 1965—), No. Neck hist. socs., Am. Hist. Assn., S.A.R., Am. Assn. U. Profs., Authors Guild, Va. Library Assn. (legislative com. 1950-51), Assn. Preservation Va. Antiquities, Internat. Platform Assn., Va. Writers Club, Modern Lang. Assn. Am., Phi Theta Kappa, Delta Phi Omega. Author: The Virginia Experiment, 1957; Frock Coats and Epaulets, 1963; America Creates Her Own Literature, 1965; Just One Man, 1968. Editorial rev. bd. Hist. Socs. Eastern Va. Contbr. articles to nat., pop. mags., met. newspapers, scholastic jours.; author film scripts. Home: 225 Grayson St Portsmouth VA 23707 Office: Old Dominion U Norfolk VA 23508

MAPP, ERWIN EDGAR, JR., librarian; b. LaGrange, Ga., Sept. 13, 1923; s. Erwin Edgar and Elizabeth (Williams) M.; student U. Ga., 1946-47; B.A., La. State U., 1950, B.S. in Library Sci., 1951; postgrad. Columbia U., 1954; m. Elizabeth Virginia Beavers, Sept. 12, 1953; 1 dau., Rhonda Denise. Student library asst. Engring., Math., Physics Library, La. State U., 1947-51; asst. bus. and industry div. Atlanta Pub. Library, 1951-52, Eastern Parkway br. Bklyn. Pub. Library, 1953-54; dir. Lanier Lake Regional Library, Lawrenceville, Ga., 1954-62; chief librarian State U. N.Y., Agrl. and Tech. Coll., Alfred, 1962-65; tech. librarian West Point Pepperell Corp. research div., Shamut, Ala., 1965-66; dir. Jackson (Miss.) Municipal Library, 1966—. Exec. dir. Miss. Nat. Library Week, 1969-70; campaign dir. Gwinnett County March of Dimes, (Ga.), 1960. Served with USNR, 1943-46. Recipient certificate of recognition steering com. Nat. Library Week, 1970. Mem. Am., Southeastern, Ga. (treas. 1961-62), Miss. (chmn. spl. libraries sect. 1971) library assns., Spl. Libraries Assn. (chpt. pres. 1970-71), Am. Soc. Information Sci. Home: 5145 Shirlwood Dr Jackson MS 39211 Office: 301 N State St Jackson MS 39201

MAPP, LOUIS EDGAR, concrete pipe co. exec.; b. Hattiesburg, Miss., June 30, 1937; s. William Claud and Mary Elizabeth (Faulkner) M.; student U. Miss., 1955-56, U. So. Miss., 1957-58, La. State U., 1958-59; m. Melinda McWilliams, Aug. 18, 1959; children—Louis E., Claude M., Leslie Lynn. With Faulkner Concrete Pipe Co., Hattiesburg, Miss., 1958—; v.p., 1960-72, pres., 1972—, also dir., v.p., dir. Carter Bldg., Inc.; dir. First Miss. Nat. Bank. Chmn. Forrest County Savs. Bond Drive, 1970. Mem. City Planning Commn., Hattiesburg, 1969—. Bd. dirs. Forrest County Indsl. Bd., Pine Burr Area council Boy Scouts Am., Southeastern Miss. Air Ambulance Dist., Hattiesburg Boys Brotherhood, Hattiesburg YMCA, Sch. Engring. U. Miss., U. So. Miss. Found. Served with AUS, 1957. Mem. Am. Concrete Pipe Assn. (region bd. dirs. 1969—), Hattiesburg C. of C. (pres. 1971, bd. dirs. 1969—). Presbyn. (deacon 1970—). Kiwanian (bd. dirs. 1970—), Elk. Club: Hattiesburg Country (pres. 1971—) bd. dirs. 1969—). Home: 104 Hillendale Dr Hattiesburg MS 39401 Office: PO Box 992 Hattiesburg MS 39401

MAPULA, ROBERT MICHAEL, dentist; b. El Paso, Tex., Feb. 13, 1935; s. Jesus Ralph and Amelia (Ybarra) M.; B.A., Tex. Western Coll., 1957; D.D.S., U. Tex., 1963; m. Olga Marcella Arreola, Dec. 30, 1961; children— Melissa Monique, Robert Michael II, Jaime David. Med. technician Southwest Gen. Hosp., El Paso, Tex., 1955-60, Tex. Childrens Hosp., Houston, 1960-63; pvt. practice dentistry, El Paso, 1963—. Cons. Father Rahm Clinic, El Paso, 1970; cons., staff mem. Thomason Gen. Hosp., El Paso, 1963; mem. staff Providence Meml., Sun Towers hosps. Chmn. fund raising com. Mayors Coll. Opportunity Fund, 1970; pres. 20-30 Internat., El Paso, 1966-67. Mem. Acad. Gen. Dentistry (pres. 1969), Am., Tex., El Paso dental socs., Rocky Mountain Analgesia Soc. Democrat. Roman Catholic. Home: 228 Fremont Lane El Paso TX 79912 Office: 3630 Pershing Dr El Paso TX 79903

MARABLE, EUGENE RUSSELL, JR., lawyer; b. Prince George County, Va., Feb. 7, 1921; s. Eugene Russell and Laura Enola (Simmons) M.; A.B., Washington and Lee U., 1946, LL.B., 1948; m. Martha Mitchell Kinsey, May 22, 1952; children—Benjamin Thomas Kinsey, Martha Mitchell. Admitted to Va. bar, 1955; with trust dept. Wachovia Bank & Trust Co., Winston-Salem, N.C., 1948-49; investigator Dun & Bradstreet, Richmond, Va., 1949-52; underwriter Atlantic Life Ins. Co., Petersburg, 1952-55; practice of law, Petersburg, 1955—; mem. firms Spotswood & Marable, 1955-59, Bohannan, Kinsey & Marable, 1959-62, Bohannan & Marable, 1962-64, Marable &Jones, 1964—; city atty. City of Petersburg, 1964—. Asso. judge Municipal Ct., Petersburg, 1955-59, judge, 1959-64; asso. judge Juvenile and Domestic Relation Ct., Petersburg, 1955-59. Bd. dirs. A.R.C., Petersburg, 1956-60; Travelers Aid Soc., Petersburg, 1956-58, YMCA; mem. adv. bd. Petersburg Welfare Dept., 1955-63; sec.-treas., Bollingbrook Day Sch., Prince George County, 1958—, also trustee. Served with U.S. Army, 1943-46. Mem. Va. State Bar, Am., Va. State, Petersburg (pres. 1970) bar assns., Am.

Trial Lawyers Assn., Am. Judicature Soc., Petersburg C. of C., Phi Kappa Sigma, Phi Alpha Delta, Omicron Delta Kappa. Episcopalian. Clubs: Country (Petersburg); PTG Country (dir.). Home: 1523 Westover Av Petersburg VA 23803 Office: Marable and Jones PO Box 107 Petersburg VA 23803

MARAVICH, PRESS, basketball coach; B.A., B.S., Davis and Elkins Coll.; M.S., W.Va. U. Formerly basketball coach N.C. State U., Raleigh; now basketball coach La, State U. Address: Athletic Dept La State U Baton Rouge LA 70803

MARBURY, CARL HARRIS, educator; b. Leeds, Ala., Mar. 24, 1935; s. Will and Mary E. (Davis) M.; B.S., Ala. A and M U., 1957; B.D., Oberlin Coll., 1962; M.A., 1962; Ph.D., Harvard, 1968; postgrad. San Jose Coll., 1958, Ecumenical Inst. U. Geneva (Switzerland), 1961, Wayne State U., 1959. Teaching fellow O.T. Oberlin (O.) Coll., 1960-62, philosophy religion, 1960-61, instr. Koine Greek, 1961-62; instr. classical Greek Concord Acad., 1964-66; teaching fellow Harvard, 1966-67; prof. philosophy Ala. A and M U., Normal, 1968-—, Dean Sch. Library Media, 1969-—, travelling asst. to prof. O.T. langs. and lit. to Middle East, summer 1961, instr. Summer Sch., 1967. Cons. East-West Center, U. Hawaii. Mem. Ala. Council on Human Relations, 1971-—; mem. regional adv. group Ala. Regional Med. Program, 1971-—; asst. dir. pub. relations Internat. Assn. Educators for World Peace, 1970-—; bd. dirs. Ala. League for Advancement Edn., 1971-—; vice chmn. A and M's Instnl. Self Study, 1970-—; cons to Huntsville VISTA program, 1970-—; mem. U. Ala. at Birmingham Sch. Medicine com. on identifying and recruiting Blacks for study medicine, 1971-—. Bd. dirs. Harris Home for Children; exec. dir. Assn. Ednl. and Profl. Opportunities Found. Monroe fellow, 1962-66; Presbyn. Grad. fellow, 1966-68. Mem. Ala. Acad. Sci., Student Govt. Assn. (adviser), Kappa Alpha Psi. Home: 9633 Meridian St Huntsville AL 35811 Office: Alabama A and M Univ Normal AL 35762

MARBURY, RITCHEY MCGUIRE, III, civil engr.; b. Albany, Ga., May 18, 1938; s. Ritchey McGuire and Kathryn (Van Houten) M.; B.C.E., Ga. Inst. Tech., 1960, M.C.P., 1966; m. Fonda Gayle Starnes, June 16, 1962; children—Mary Kathryn, Ritchey McGuire IV. Planning intern Wichita-Sedgwick County Met. Planning Dept., 1961; partner Marbury Engring. Co., Albany, 1965-—; now pres. Marbury, Ritter, Scott; Turner, Inc., cons. engrs. Instr. algebra Albany Area Tech. and Vocational Sch., 1966. Served with C.E., AUS, 1963-65. Mem. Am. Soc. C.E. (pres.), Ga. Soc. Registered Profl. Land Surveyors (sec.-treas., dir.), Surveying and Mapping Soc. Ga. (v.p.), Cons. Engrs. Councils Ga., U.S., Am. Congress Surveying and Mapping, Phi Gamma Delta, Phi Kappa Phi. Mem. Ch. of Jesus Christ of Latter-day Saints (pres. br.). Rotarian. Home: 1824 Green Valley Lane Albany GA 31705 Office: 2330 Whispering Pines Rd Albany GA 31705

MARBURY, WILLIAM ARDIS, JR., banker, ins. exec.; b. Ruston, La., July 22, 1917; s. William Ardis and Leola R. (Ridgdill) M.; B.A., La. Poly. Inst. 1936; m. Virginia Lomax, Sept. 5, 1943; children—Rebekah, Caroline. Organized William A. Marbury & Co., Ruston, 1944; pres. Am. Home Plan Corp., Marbury Investment Corp., Bankers Life of La., Marbury Bldg. Corp., So. States Gen. Agy.; pres., dir. Home Nat. Bank (La.), Ruston State Bank & Trust Co. (La.); dir. La. Bank & Trust Co., Shreveport. Chmn. Am. Cancer Soc. Pres. (first) Greater Tech Club, Inc.; mem. Alumni bd. La. Poly. Inst.; former mem. Lincoln Parish Sch. Bd. Mem. Young Pres.' Orgn., Homer (dir., exec. com.), Ruston (past pres., dir.) chambers commerce, Beta Gamma Sigma, Kappa Sigma. Episcopalian. Home: N Trenton St Ruston LA 71270 Office: 605 N Vienna St Ruston LA 71270

MARCANO, HIPOLITO, Puerto Rican Senator; b. Humacao, P.R., Aug. 13, 1913; s. Miguel and Josefa (Ortiz) M.; A.B., Inter-Am. U. P.R., 1937, LL.D. (hon.), 1963; LL.B., U. P.R., 1940; div.; children—David, Hipolito. Legal counsel Dept. of Labor, P.R., 1942-43; mem. Puerto Rican Senate, 1956-—, majority leader, 1969-—; gen. counsel Puerto Rican Fedn. Labor, AFL-CIO, 1943-—; dean Inter-Am. U. P.R. Sch. Law, 1960-—. Sec., dir. Labor Bank of P.R., 1962-—. Mem. central com. Popular Dem. Party, 1956-60, 64-—. Mem. Am., Inter-Am., Fed. bar assns., Internat. Acad. Law and Sci., Am. Acad. Social Sci., Puerto Rican Acad. Polit. Sci., Inter-Am. U. Alumni Assn., Cigarmakers Internat. Union, Internat. Soc. Devel. Mem. Ch. of Christ. Mason (Shriner), Elk; mem. Order Eastern Star. Home: 804 Ponce de Leon Av Santurce PR 00907 Office: Capitolio Box 1648 San Juan PR 00903

MARCHANT, TRELAWNEY ESTON, lawyer; b. Columbia, S.C., Dec. 9, 1921; s. Trelawney Eston and Lila (Cave) M.; B.S., U. S.C., 1942, LL.B., 1947; m. Caroline Melton Bristow, Nov. 10, 1951; children—Trelawney Eston III, Walter Bristow, Caroline Melton, Nancy Lila. Admitted to S.C. bar, 1947; practiced in Columbia, 1948-—; mem. firm Marchant, Bristow & Bates, 1952-—; judge Municipal Ct., Columbia, 1956-61. Dir., 1st Palmetto Bank & Trust Co. Chmn., Richland County chpt. Nat. Found., 1954-55. Chmn., Richland County Democratic Com., 1963-68. Bd. dirs., v.p. U. S.C. Ednl. Found.; trustee U. S.C., 1965-70, chmn. bd. trustees, 1970-—. Served to capt. USMCR, 1942-46, now col. S.C. Nat. Guard. Mem. Am., S.C., Richland County (pres. 1970-71) bar assns., Am. Judicature Soc., Acad. Polit. Sci., U. S.C. Alumni Assn. (past pres.), Am. Legion, Mil. Order of World Wars (past pres.), Omicron Delta Kappa, Sigma Nu. Episcopalian. Kiwanian (dir.). Clubs: Forest Lake Country; Cotillion, Columbia Ball, Torch. Home: 5046 Courtney Rd Columbia SC 29201 Office: 1306 Main St Columbia SC 20201

MARCHBANKS, CLAUDE VANCE, JR., textile mill products exec.; b. Gastonia, N.C, Sept. 12, 1923; s. Claude V. and Ethel May (Wilbanks) M.; student Central Wesleyan Coll., 1956-57, grad. exec. program U. N.C., 1969; m. Carolene Elizabeth Lewis, Mar. 26, 1944; children—Marshall Vance, Sherry Lynn. With Deering Milliken, Inc., 1945-—, mng. dir. Europe, 1966-67, asst. gen. mgr., 1968, gen. mgr., 1969-—; dir. Mgmt. Development, Inc. Dist. commr. Boy Scouts Am., 1969-71, mem. exec. council, 1971; pres. S.C. dist. Wesleyan Men 1969-—; vice chmn. bd. trustees Central Wesleyan Coll., Clemson U. Republican. Mem. Wesleyan Ch. (mem. bd. adminstrn. 1968-72). Lion. Home: 242 Grove Dr Box 531 Clemson SC 29631 Office: Box 449 Laurens SC 29360

MARCHBANKS, JERRY LEE, bus. exec.; b. San Antonio, Oct. 26, 1935; s. James Lee and Neva R. (Dixon) M.; B.S., Tex. A. and M. U., 1959; M.B.A., St. Marys U., 1965; m. Janice E. Lancaster, Sept. 2, 1961; children—Deborah Lynne, Michael Lee, Stephen Lance. Chief indsl. engr. Kelly AFB, Tex., San Antonio, 1960-64; mgr. Ernst & Ernst, San Antonio, 1964-68; v.p., dir. Computer & Bus. Mgmt., Inc., San Antonio, 1968-70; v.p., fir. CBM Edn. Centers, San Antonio and Baton Rouge, 1968-—. Served with USAF, 1959-60. Mem. Am. Inst. Indsl. Engrs. (chpt. pres. 1964-65), Tex. Soc. Profl. Engrs., Data Processing Mgmt. Assn. Contbr. articles to profl. jours. Home: 129 Meadowbrook Dr San Antonio TX 78232 Office: 501 Urban Loop San Antonio TX 78207

MARCOM, ORVAL WELDON, coll. adminstr.; b. Royse City, Tex., Jan. 2, 1908; s. George Ralph and Hattie (Jones) M.; student So. Meth. U., 1926-27; B.A., Tex. Tech. Coll., 1936, M.A., 1949, Ed.D., 1961; m. Laura Lucille Latimer, Mar. 15, 1929; children—Patsy (Mrs. William B. Methvin), George W., Marilyn (Mrs. Robert F. Wham). Tchr., prin. pub. schs., Tex., 1928-47; supt. schs., Levelland, Tex., 1947-61; academic dean San Jacinto Coll., Pasadena, Tex., 1961-67, academic v.p., 1967-—. Mem. Tex. State Tchrs. Assn. (dist. past pres.), C. of C., Phi Delta Kappa. Mason, Rotarian. Home: 2611 Shenandoah St Pasadena TX 77502

MARCOTT, PAUL, pub. relations exec.; b. Buffalo, Mar. 8, 1915; s. Samuel C. and Elsa (Newman) M.; student U. Buffalo, 1933; m. Lorena M. Smith, Aug. 30, 1941. Indsl. editor Am. Optical Co., 1946-47; prodn. mgr., account exec. Warman & Co., 1947-48; copy chief Lansheft, Inc., 1947-48; indsl. editor Western Electric Co., 1948-50 (all Buffalo), asst. dir. pub. relations Bell Helicopter Co., Buffalo, 1950-56, advt. mgr., Fort Worth, 1956-—. Vice pres. bd. Community Hosp. Planning Bd., 1965-67. Served with USAAF, 1942-46. Mem. Am. Helicopter Soc., Am. Marketing Assn., Assn. U.S. Army, Dallas Ad League, Ft. Worth Ad Club, Hurst-Euless C. of C. (pres. 1967, dir. 1965-67), Sigma Delta Chi (past dir.). Republican. Mason (Shriner). Patentee in field. Home: 4625 Mackey Dr Fort Worth TX 76118 Office: PO Box 482 Fort Worth TX 76101

MARCUS, IRWIN M., psychoanalyst, educator; b. Chgo., Mar. 18, 1919; s. Max U. and Belle (Rothbaum) M.; B.S., U. Ill., 1939, M.D., 1943; postgrad. Columbia, 1946-49; m. Dorothy Mann, June 29, 1948; children—Randall, Sherry, Melinda. Asso. psychoanalyst dept. psychiatry Columbia, 1949-51; asso. prof. Tulane U., 1951-56, clin. prof., 1956-—, also spl. lectr. sch. Social Work and Tchr. Edn. Center; clin. prof. La. State U. Med. Center, New Orleans, 1956-—; pres. New Orleans Psychoanalytic Inst., 1967-71, now dir. Child Psychoanalysis Div.; chmn. dept. psychiatry Touro Hosp., 1972-—, Charity Hosp. sr. cons. Children's Bur., Dept. Public Welfare, Orleans, Jefferson and St. Bernard parishes. Served to capt. AUS, World War II. Fellow Bd. Profl. Standards, Am. Psychoanalytic Assn., Am. Group Psychotherapy Assn. (past dir.), Am. Orthopsychiat. Assn., Am. Psychiat. Assn., Am. Acad. Child Psychiatry (chmn. program com. 1971-—); mem. Internat. Assn. Child Psychiatry, Assn. Child Psychoanalysis (councillor), Sigma Xi. Author: Costume Play Therapy, 1966: Learning Problems, 1967. Co-editor: Family Book Child Care, 1957. Editor Currents in Psychoanalysis, 1972. Contbr. articles to profl. jours. Home: 4231 Vendome Pl New Orleans LA 70125 Office: 3619 Prytania St New Orleans LA 70115

MARCUS, JACK LOWELL, auto rental exec.; b. Lassy, Roumania, July 23, 1917; s. Morris Lowell and Ruth Ethel (Leibovici) M.; came to U.S., 1931; B.S., Purdue U., 1939; m. Mildred Louise Given, Feb. 27, 1946; children—Ruth Ellen (Mrs. Robert B. Jacobson), Susan (Mrs. Stewart Forbes), David G., Ronald L. Elec. engr. Am. Elec. Co., Indpls., 1939-41; v.p. Given Bros., El Paso, Tex., 1946-69; pres. Dollar a Day Rent a Car, El Paso, 1969-—. Vice pres. bd. El Paso Girls Club; pres. bd. El Paso Children's Day Care; bd. dirs. Booth Home of Salvation Army. Served to capt., AUS, 1941-46: ETO. Mason (32 deg.), Kiwanian (lt. gov. internat. 1967, pres. local club). Home: 711 Blanchard St El Paso TX 79902 Office: 1515 Airways St El Paso TX 79925

MARCUS, STANLEY RAYMOND, govt. research dir.; b. Providence, Feb. 29, 1916; s. Lyon A. and Mabel (Phillips) M.; B.S., U. R.I., 1938; M.S. in Engring. Adminstrn., George Washington U., 1958; postgrad. Mass. Inst. Tech., Pa. State U.; m. Beatrice Perry, Sept. 26, 1942; 1 son, Malcolm Jeffrey. Mech. engr. U.S. Naval Torpedo Sta., Newport, R.I., 1940-45; asst. chief engr. div. war research Columbia U., Newport, 1945-56; ind. practice, Providence, 1946-51; project engr. Bur. Ordnance, Washington, 1951-56, coordinator underwater Office Naval Research, 1956-59, coordinator anti-submarine warfare weapons Dep. Chief Naval Operations, 1959-60, asst. tech. dir. systems planning, 1960-63, dir. research div. Bur. Naval Weapons, Washington, 1963-66, exec. dir., chief scientist research and tech. directorate Naval Ordnance Systems Command, Washington, 1966-—. Registered profl. engr., R.I. Mem. Acoustical Soc. Am., Am. Inst. Physics, Operations Research Soc. Am., Wash. Operations Research Council, Nat. Soc. Profl. Engrs., A.A.A.S., Am. Soc. of Cybernetics, Am. Ordnance Assn., Philos. Soc. Washington, Alpha Epsilon Pi. Mem. editorial bd. Navy Tech. Forum. Home: 2111 Jeff Davis Hwy Arlington VA 22202 Office: Naval Ordnance Systems Command Dept Navy Washington DC 20360

MARDAN, OMAR, newspaperman; b. Richmond, Va., June 21, 1924; s. Omar and Willoughby (Hull) M.; B.A., U. Richmond, 1945; m. Jacqueline Mae Lewis, 1969. With Richmond Times-Dispatch, 1945-—, news editor, 1960-69, asst. mng. editor, 1969-—. Mem. Sigma Phi Epsilon, Omicron Delta Kappa, Sigma Delta Chi (chpt. pres. 1965). Clubs: Willow Oaks Country. Home: 607 W 25th St Richmond VA 23225 Office: 333 E Grace St Richmond VA 23219

MARDEN, LUIS, journalist; b. Chelsea, Mass., Jan. 25, 1913; s. Louis and Celia (Pote) M.; ed. pub. schs., Quincy, Mass.; m. Ethel Cox, Oct. 5, 1939. Free-lance writer and photographer, 1932-34; mem. staff Nat. Geog. mag., 1934-—, mem. fgn. editorial staff, 1940-66, chief fgn. staff, 1966-—; spl. research underwater photography, deep sea diving journalism; producer documentary films. Mem. Confrerie des Chevaliers du Tastevin. Clubs: Oxford and Cambridge University (London, Eng.); Anglers (N.Y.C.); National Press, Cosmos (Washington); Royal Suva Yacht (Fiji Islands). Author: Color Photography with the Miniature Camera, 1934; also articles. Home: Fontinalis 600 Chain Bridge Rd McLean VA 22101 Office: Nat Geog Soc 17th and M Sts NW Washington DC 20036

MARDER, ESTELLE ROTHENBERG, mus. ofcl.; b. Bklyn.; d. Max and Ida (Milman) Rothenberg; student Alpha Bus. Sch., State U. N.Y., 1926-28; m. David Marder, July 3, 1932 (dec. Sept. 1965); 1 dau., Rita Muriel (Mrs. Alan Barton). Med. sec. Dr. Herman Besser, N.Y.C., 1928-29; exec. sec., advt. mgr. Thrift Service and Thrista Holding Co., Bklyn., 1929-33; exec. sec. Winsoney Furnishers, Inc., N.Y.C., 1933-34; exec. sec., curator edn., Asheville (N.C.) Art Mus., 1966-—. N.C. rep. Nat. Zionist Emergency Council, 1942-48; chmn. Citizens Food Conservation Com., 1947-48. Mem. Nat. Council Jewish Women (v.p. 1948-49), Hadassah (pres. Asheville chpt. 1942-45), Sigma Beta Sigma. Jewish religion(pres. temple sisterhood 1946-48). Home: 16 Maplewood Rd Asheville NC 28804 Office: 152 Pearson Dr Asheville NC 28801

MARECEK, PETER STEPHEN, supt. schs.; b. Rowena, Tex., Feb. 9, 1909; s. Joseph and Anna (Bohacek) M.; B.A., Howard Payne Coll., 1932; M.A., Tex. Arts and Industry U., 1957; postgrad. U. Tex., summers 1937, 38, 40, 48-50, 52, 54; m. Alice Fern Jackson, Sept. 4, 1934; children—Patricia Ann (Mrs. LeRoy Andrews) Carolynn Sue (Mrs. Carl Vernon Helgren). Prin., coach Brookesmith (Tex.) Rural High Sch. Dist., 1930-31, Mirando City (Tex.) Ind. Sch. Dist., 1931-34, Runge (Tex.) Ind. Sch. Dist., 1934-36; Pawnee (Tex.) Ind. Sch. Dist., 1936-38; supt. Pawnee Ind. Sch. Dist., 1938-—. Trustee, Bee County Jr. Coll. Mem. Tex. Tchrs Assn., Tex. assns. sch. adminstrs., N.E.A., Tex. Assn. Sch. Bds. Presbyn. Lion (1st pres. 1950, 69-70, treas. 1962-66, 67-68). Home: PO Box 567 Pawnee TX 78145 Office: PO Box 568 Pawnee TX 78145

MARGULIES, HAROLD, govt. ofcl.; b.Sioux Falls, S.D., Feb. 13, 1918; s. Samuel Saul and Nellie (Graceman) M.; A.B., U. Minn., 1938, M.S. (fellow), 1948; B.S., U. S.D., 1940; M.D., U. Tenn., 1942; m. Marjory Gutfreund, Apr. 12, 1952; children—Marc, Amy. Pvt. practice medicine, Des Moines, 1949-61, also mem. staff Ia. Meth. Hosp.; prof. medicine, chief of party Ind. U. Adv. Group, AID Contract, Postgrad. Med. Center, Karschi, Pakistan, 1961-64; adviser on med. edn. WHO, Alexandria, UAR, 1965-66; asso. dir. div. internat. med. edn. Assn. Am. Med. Colls., also dir. Assn./AID Contract Project, 1965-67; asso. dir. A.M.A. div. socio-econ. activities, Washington, 1967-68, sec. Council on Health Manpower, 1968-69; dep. asst. adminstr. for program planning and eval. Health Sers. and Mental Health Adminstrn., U.S. Dept. Health, Edn. and Welfare Rockville, Md., 1969-71, acting dir. Regional Med. Programs Service, USPHS, 1969-71, dir. Regional Med. Programs Service, 1971-—. Cons. in internal medicine VA., 1949-61, White House Office of Sci. and Tech., 1966-67, Nat. Adv. Commn. on Health Manpower, 1966-67. Diplomate Am. Bd. Internal Medicine. Fellow A.C.P., Am. Pub. Health Assn., mem. A.M.A., Assn. Am. Med. Colls., Mayo Alumni Assn., Sigma Xi. Author: Foreign Medical Graduates in the United States, 1969; also articles. Home: 5408 Albemarle St Washington DC 20016 Office: 5600 Fishers Lane Rockville MD 20852

MARIE, SISTER JOAN, coll. pres.; b. Nebraska City, Neb., July 25, 1913; d. John G. and Mary (Tongish) Lechner; A.B., Loras Coll., Dubuque, Ia., 1950; Ph.D., St. Louis U., 1960 Joined Soc. of Ursulines, 1934; instr. English, Latin and commerce St. Joseph's High Sch., Owensboro, Ky., 1936-48, St. Catherine's High Sch., New Haven, 1948-50; instr. English, Latin and bus., also prin. St. Francis' High Sch., Loretta, 1950-53; instr. English and bus., also treas. Brescia Coll., Owensboro, 1953-56, pres., 1960-—. Recipient merit award St. Louis U. Alumni, 1968; Citizen of Yr. award, 1969; Liberty Bell award Daviess County Bar Assn., 1969. Address: Brescia Coll Owensboro KY 42301

MARINACCIO, ANTHONY, educator; b. Bridgeport, Conn., Aug. 26, 1912; s. Paul and Louisa (DeLibero) M.; B.E., Conn. State Coll., 1937; M.A., Ohio State U., 1939; Ph.D., Yale, 1949; LL.D., Parsons Coll., 1961; m. Elsie Kleps, Sept, 5, 1936 (dec. Sept. 1964); children—Warren, Karen (Mrs. John Beacon), Dianna (Mrs. Joseph Carlisi), Nancy (Mrs. David Wilber), Linda, Lee; m. 2d, M. Maxine Reynolds, Oct. 15, 1965. Tchr. Jr. High Sch., Hartford, Conn., 1935-41; elementary sch. prin., 1941-46; prof. edn., prin. campus sch. Tchrs Coll., State U. N.Y. at Oswego, 1946-49; asst. supt. charge instrn. and supervision pub. schs., Peoria, Ill., 1949-53; supt. schs., Mexico, Mo., 1953-55, Kankakee, Ill., 1955-59, Davenport, Ia., 1959-64; dean Parsons Coll., 1964-65; pres. The Hiram Scott Coll., Scottsbluff, Neb., 1964-69; prof. grad. edn. George Washington U., Washington, 1969-—; professorial lecturer edn. George Washington U., summers, 1952-69; prof. edn. Bradley U., part time, 1949-53, supervision of instrn. research extension courses, 1956-58; vis. prof. secondary edn. Ohio State U., summers, 1953-54. Speaker various civic and ednl. groups. Active various local civic, religious and ednl. groups; organized South End Council, Hartford, Conn., 1944-46, Peoria Citizens' Council for Pub. Schs., 1951-52, in service tchr. edn. program, Peoria, 1949-53; pres. Kankakee Community Chest (Ill.), 1957-58. Mem. Davenport (Ia.) Planning Commn., 1960-63. Bd. dirs. Peoria Council Boy Scouts Am., 1951-53, A.R.C., Peoria, 1951-53; trustee Hiram Scott Coll., 1964-69. Mem. Sheldon Forum, Phi Delta Kappa, Epsilon Pi Tau, Phi Sigma Phi, Psi Phi. Mason (Shriner). Author: Exploring the Graphic Arts, 1959. Contbr. articles to profl. pubs. Home: 13919 Turnmore Rd Silverspring MD 20906 Office: The George Washington University Washington DC 20006

MARINO, AMERIGO, conductor, Birmingham (Ala.) Symphony Orch. Home: 134 Stratford Circle Birmingham AL 35209 Office: 710 N 20th St Birmingham AL 35203*

MARINO, ANGELO FRANCES, epidemiologist; b. North Adams, Mass., Feb. 5, 1912; s. Gregory John and Helen (Downs) M.; grad. pub. schs.; m. Mary Elizabeth Harrell, Feb. 9, 1944; children—Ramon, Helen (Mrs. Robert Stamps), Ronald, Gregory. With Norfolk (Va.) Health Dept., 1938-—, epidemiologist, 1940-—. Guest lectr. Old Dominion U. Served with USNR, 1929-33, 42-45. Mem. Am. Venereal Disease Assn. (exec. sec. 1970, treas. 1972-—), Tidewater Rose Soc. (treas. 1970-71). Roman Catholic. Home: 615 Maury Av Norfolk VA 23517 Office: 401 Colby Av Norfolk VA 23507

MARINO, CHARLES BENJAMIN, oil co. exec.; b. Bryan, Tex., Nov. 12, 1928; s. Ben and Mary (Viviani) M.; B.S. in Geology, U. Houston, 1950; m. Valeta Purrington, Sept., 1961; children—Charles L.R., Dena Maria. Geologist Highland Oil Co., Houston, 1950, 54, Brit. Am. Oil Co., Houston, 1954-58; ind. oil operator Charles B. Marino Co., Houston, 1958-—; dir. Sweeney Citizen State Bank (Tex.), 1969-—; dir. Snap-Pac Corp., Houston, 1966-—, pres. 1967-—; dir. Italian-Am. Oil Co., Houston, 1964-—, pres., 1964-—; dir. Power Oil Co. Served with USMCR, 1946-47, 50-53. Home: 4055 Falkirk St Houston TX 77025 Office: 3703 Yoakum St Houston TX 77006

MARINO, SALVADOR ANTHONY, elec. engr.; b. Birmingham, Ala., Dec. 28, 1927; s. Joseph Salvador and Mary (Raia) M.; student Birmingham So. Coll., 1946-48; B.E.E., Auburn U., 1951; m. Josephine Musso, Sept. 17, 1951; children—Joseph, Anthony, Salvador. Design engr. Ala. Power Co., Birmingham, Ala., 1951-55, system planning engr., 1955-65, sr. system planning engr., 1965-—. Active Boy Scouts Am., 1961-70; pres. St. Joseph Sch. P.T.A., 1960-61. Served with USNR, 1945-46. Registered profl. engr., Ala. Mem. I.E.E.E., Tau Beta Pi, Eta Kappa Nu, Phi Kappa Phi. Roman Catholic (pres. St. Joseph Holy Name Soc., 1960-61, chmn. finance com. 1969-70, pres. Parish council 1970-—). Home: 1437 27th St Birmingham AL 35218 Office: 600 N 18th St Birmingham AL 35202

MARINO, SAMUEL JOSEPH, librarian, educator; b. New Britain, Conn., Nov. 29, 1916; s. Mariano and Josephine (Pandolfo) M.; A.B., La. State U., 1940, B.S., 1948, M.A. in French, 1949; A.M. in L.S., U. Mich., 1952, Ph.D., 1962; m. Dorothy Quinney, Feb. 7, 1949; children— Mary Leila, Joseph, Michael. Acting dir. libraries U. Miss., 1952-53; dir. libraries, chmn. dept. library sci. Ind. State Tchrs. Coll., 1954-58; head librarian McNeese State College, Lake Charles, La., 1958-67; prof. library sci. Tex. Woman's U., Denton, 1967-—. Dir., chmn. library sect. La. Coll. Conf. Dir., Pirateland Devel. Co., Inc. Bd. dirs. Terre Haute (Ind.) Civic Symphony. Served to capt. AUS, 1942-46. Mem. Am., Tex. (publs. com.), La. (chmn. coll. and univ. sect., 2d v.p. 1965-66) library assns., Phi Mu Alpha Sinfonia, Beta Phi Mu, Phi Sigma Iota. Club: Civitan. Author: French Travellers in the United States, 1765-1932, 1961. Editor: La. Library Assn. Bull. Contbr. articles to profl. jours. Home: 3205 Darby Lane Denton TX 76201

MARION, JOHN BAPTIST, III, architect; b. West Palm Beach, Fla., Aug. 21, 1928; s. John Baptist II and Alice Esther (Dickeson) M.; A.A., Palm Beach Jr. Coll., 1950; B. Arch., U. Fla., 1953; m. Earline Rippy, Apr. 17, 1954; children—Deborah Marie, John Baptist IV, Kurt Gregory. Chief draftsman Myrl Hanes Architect, Gainseville, Fla., 1953-56, asso. Myrl Hanes Assos.-Architects, 1956-58; owner John Marion Architect & Assos. (and predecessor), Palm Beach, Fla., 1959-67; mng. partner Marion, Baber, Paluga, Kaisrlik & Snell Architects-Engrs., Palm Beach, 1967—; asso. prof. archtl. design U. Fla. at Gainesville, 1956-57. Mem. West Palm Beach Bldg. Bd. Appeals, 1960-67, West Palm Beach Civic Auditorium Com., 1963, West Palm Beach Bldg. Code Revisions Com., 1969—; mem. West Palm Beach Zoning Bd. Appeals, 1967—, chmn., 1969-70. Bd. dirs. Brown Br. YMCA; adv. bd. Salvation Army. Served with N.G., 1947-56. Mem. A.I.A. (past officer Palm Beach chpt.; honors and awards com, bd. dirs. Fla. Assn. 1967-69, commn. pub. affairs 1969-70, budget com. 1970-71), Gargoyle Soc., Phi Kappa Phi, Alpha Tau Omega (pres. alumni 1964). Mason (Shriner), Kiwanian. Club: Tuscawilla (West Palm Beach). Prin. works include Fire Sta., 1963, 4th Dist. Ct. Appeals, 1970 (West Palm Beach); Palm Beach Internat. Airport Terminal Complex, 1966, Palm Beach Gardens High Sch., 1967; Boca Raton (Fla.) Jr. High Sch. 1969; Avis S.E. Regional Hdqrs. and Service Center, Miami, Fla., 1971. Home: 725 Dobbins St West Palm Beach FL 33405 Office: 234 Royal Palm Way Palm Beach FL 33480

MARIS, JACK LEONARD, ednl. adminstr.; b. Franklin, Tex., Aug. 4, 1921; s. Edgar Lee and Elna P. (Jackson) M.; M.Ed., Sam Houston U., Huntsville, Tex., 1956, B.S., 1949.; m. Evelyn Janelle Petty, June 27, 1947; children—Mike, Marsha. Asst. county supt. schs., Franklin, Tex., 1949-56; bus. mgr. Hearne (Tex.) Pub. Schs., 1956-62, Gorsicana (Tex.) Pub. Schs., 1962-68, Bratosport Coll., Lake Jackson, 1968—. Served with AUS, 1942-45. mem. Mason, Lion. Home: 112 Rose Trail Lake Jackson TX 77566 Office: 500 College Dr Lake Jackson TX 77566

MARK, CHARLES CHRISTOPHER, publisher; b. Milw., Oct. 12, 1927; s. Aloysius and Gertrude (Wolf) M.; M.S.W., U. Wis., 1954; m. Alice Claire Resnick, June 13, 1954; children—Christopher Joshua, Hilary Beth. Exec. dir. Winston-Salem Arts Council (N.C.), 1958-61; founder, exec. dir. St. Louis Arts and Edn. Council, 1961-64; spl. cons. to cultural adviser White House, Washington, 1964-65; dir. State and Community Operations Nat. Found. on Arts and Humanities, Washington, 1965-67; dir. planning analysis Nat. Endowment for the Arts, Washington, 1967-69; pres. Performing Arts Council, Los Angeles Music Center, 1969; founder, pub. The Arts Reporting Service, Washington, 1970—; sr. lectr. U. Cal. at Los Angeles, 1969-70; del., cons. UNESCO. Served with USAAF, 1946-47. Author: Run Away Home, 1960; A Study of Cultural Policy in the U.S.A., 1969. Contbr. articles profl. jours. Home: 9214 Three Oaks Dr Silver Spring MD 20901

MARK, SIDNEY CARL, broadcasting exec.; b. N.Y., Feb. 27, 1914; s. Henry and Sarah (Berkowitz) M.; B.A., Coll. City N.Y., 1934; m. Patricia Greenfield, Jan. 18, 1946; children—Priscilla, Jonathan Greenfield, Mary Alice, Sarah Edna, Henry Greenfield. Announcer, producer radio sta. WHN, N.Y., 1935; spl. events prodn. mgr., radio sta. WHK-WCLE, Cleve., 1937-43; radio-TV dir. Al Paul Lefton Co., 1943-48; pres., gen. mgr., radio sta. WTTM, Trenton, N.J., 1948-53; pres. Swern & Co. (Lit Brothers), Trenton, 1954-62; chmn., pres. Mark/way, Inc. (radio sta. KAKC AM-FM, Tulsa, WAKC, Bloomington-Normal, Ill., KFUN, Las Vegas, N.M.); dir. Bankers Bond & Mortgage Co. Am. Instr. radio-TV announcing and prodn. Western Res. U., Cleve., also Coll. City N.Y., 1937-53. Chmn. Trenton Planning Bd., 1955-59; v.p. Trenton Philharmonic Soc., 1953-63; v.p. Del. Valley United Fund, 1954-56; bd. dirs. Greater Phila.-S. Jersey Council, 1949-53; trustee Greater Trenton Council, 1956-62; bd. dirs. Tulsa chpt. A.R.C., Tulsa Recreation Center for Physically Ltd.; bd. dirs., v.p. Tulsa Civic Ballet; v.p. Jr. Achievement of Tulsa, Inc.; pres. Concertime, Inc. of Tulsa; bd. dirs. Tulsa Philharmonic Soc., Inc.; chmn. Tulsa Central YMCA; finance chmn. Boy Scouts; treas. adv. council Salvation Army, Tulsa; mem. Jewish Community Council, Tulsa. Pres. N.J. Broadcasters Assn., 1951-52. Mem. Mensa (chmn. Tulsa). Clubs: Petroleum, Tulsa Tennis. Home: 6766 S Columbia Av Tulsa OK 74136 Office: KAKC Bldg 51st and S Peoria Box 970 Tulsa OK 74101

MARKER, HOWARD WILLIAM, physician; b. Dallas, Nov. 16, 1932; s. Al B. and Menah (Rubinsky) M.; A.A., Tyler Jr. Coll., 1951; B.A., U. Tex., 1953, M.D., 1958; m. Fay Bussel, Aug. 16, 1956; children— Michael Barry, Jeffrey Harold, Edward Andrew, Cynthia Elaine. Intern, Memphis (Tenn.) Hosps., 1958-59, resident in internal medicine, 1961-65; pvt. practice specializing in internal medicine, Memphis, 1966—; mem. staff Bapt. Meml., St. Joseph, Meth., William Bowld hosps.; clin. asst. prof. internal medicine U. Tenn. Med. Units, Memphis, 1966—. Chmn. med. and sci. com. West Tenn. chpt. Arthritis Found., 1969—. Served with USAF, 1959-61. NIH fellow, 1963-65. Diplomate Am. Bd. Internal Medicine. Fellow Am. Coll. Physicians; mem. A.M.A., Tenn. Med. Soc., Am. Rheumatology Assn. Mem. B'nai B'rith (v.p. 1970—, treas. 1970-71). Home: 90 Grovedale St Memphis TN 38117 Office: 210 Jackson St Memphis TN 38105

MARKERT, WILLIAM NORMAN, fabricated metal products mfg. co. exec.; b. Louisville, May 14, 1923; s. William Reese and Anna (Gruner) M.; B.M.E., U. Ky., 1949; m. Marie LaVerne Bauer, June 27, 1949; children— Janice Kaye, Suzanne Marie. Design engr. Schmutz Mfg. Co., Louisville, 1949-52; sr. engr. Tube Turns div. Chemetron, Louisville, 1952-66; chief mfg. engr. Grinnell Corp., Princeton, Ky., 1966—. Chmn. bd. dirs. Caldwell County Airport, 1971—. Served with AUS, 1943-46. Registered Profl. Engr., Ky. Mem. Soc. Mech. Engrs., Order Ky. Cols. Home: 33 Dogwood Lane Princeton KY 42445 Office: ITT Grinnell Corp Welding Products Div PO Box 647 Princeton KY 42445

MARKEY, GENE, author; b. Jackson, Mich., Dec. 11, 1895; s. Eugene Lawrence and Alice (White) M.; B.S., Dartmouth, 1918; student Art Inst. Chgo., 1919-20; L.H.D., Rollins Coll., 1957; m. Joan Bennett, 1932 (div. 1937); 1 dau., Melinda; m. 2d, Hedy Lamarr, 1939 (div. 1940); m. 3d, Myrna Loy (div. 1950); m. 4th, Lucille Parker Wright, 1952. Served as 1st lt., 19th Inf., AUS, 1917-19; with USNR 1930-55; on active duty, 1941-46; promoted comdr., 1945; ret. rear adm., 1955. Spl. asst. Sec. of Navy, 1944, 1946. Decorated Legion of Merit, Bronze Star, Navy Commendation Medal; star of solidarity (Italy); Legion of Honor (France). Mem. Delta Kappa Epsilon. Roman Catholic. Clubs: Buck's, White's (London); Jockey, Knickerbocker, Brook (N.Y.C.); Travellers (Paris, France); Author: Literary Lights, 1923; Men About Town, 1924; (with Charles Collins) The Dark Island, 1928; The Pumpkin Coach, 1928; Stepping High, 1929; The Road to Rouen, 1930; His Majesty's Pyjamas, 1934; The Great Companions, 1949; Kingdom of the Spur, 1953; Kentucky Pride, 1956; That Far Paradise, 1960; Women, Women, Everywhere, 1964; (plays) Right You Are, 1925; (with Samuel Hoffenstein) The Eskimo, 1926. Contbr. short stories to mags. Home: Calumet Farm Lexington KY 40501

MARKHAM, JEROME DAVID, physician; b. Rockville Centre, N.Y., Jan. 27, 1917; s. Benjamin Abravanel and Sophia (Newmark) M.; B.A., Columbia Coll., 1937; M.D., Med. Coll. Va., 1941; m. Sara Farber, June 4, 1941; children—Shelley, Richard Bryan, Barbara Frances. Intern, Queens Gen. Hosp., Jamaica, N.Y., 1941-42; resident Mt. Sinai Hosp. of N.Y., 1946, VA Hosp. Richmond, Va., 1947-48; pvt. practice medicine, specializing in internal medicine and cardiology, Richmond, 1948—; mem. staffs Med. Coll. Va. Hosp., St. Mary's Hosp., Richmond Meml. Hosp.; asst. prof. applied physiology, Med. Coll. Va., 1950-53, asso. prof., 1953-57, clin. asso. in medicine, 1955—, vol. part-time faculty, 1950—; bd. dirs. Richmond Area Heart Assn., 1953—, Easter Seal Soc., 1967, Beth Sholom Home for the Aged, 1965. Served with AUS, 1942-46. Diplomate Am. Bd. Internal Medicine. Fellow A.C.P.; mem. Richmond Acad. Medicine, Richmond Soc. Internal Medicine, Med. Soc. Va. (conv. del. 1970, 72), So. Med. Assn., Am. Heart Assn. Club: Columbia Univ of Va. (pres. 1950-55, dir. 1970-71). Contbr. articles to profl. publs. Home: 7101 Glen Pkwy Richmond VA 23229 Office: 5700 Old Richmond Av Richmond VA 23226

MARKHAM, JOHN STEWART, hosp. adminstr.; b. Richmond, Va., May 4, 1933; s. Curtis Owen and Lucy Mildred (Hall) M.; student U. Va., 1952-53; B.S., U. Richmond, 1958; M.H.A., Med. Coll. Va., 1967.; m. Betty Ann Johns, Feb. 13, 1954; children—Mary Lucy, Catherine Ann, Ernest Owen. Pub. accountant, Va., 1958-65; asst. adminstr. Meml. Mission Hosp., Asheville, N.C., 1967-68; adminstr. Culpeper (Va.) Meml. Hosp., 1968-72, Nat. Orthopaedic and Rehab. Hosp., Arlington, Va., 1972—. Lectr.; prof. in residence Lynchburg (Va.) Tng. Sch. and Hosp., spring 1972. Mem. com. on income Va. White House Conf. on Aging, 1971. Bd. dirs. Culpeper chpt. Va. Heart Assn., Am. Cancer Soc. Served with AUS, 1953-55. C.P.A., Va. Fellow Va. Soc. C.P.A.'s; mem. Am., Va. (dir.) hosp. assns., Am. Coll. Hosp. Adminstrs. Author: Cost Accounting in Health Care Management, 1971. Home: 5223 Spalding Ct Burke VA 22015 Office: 2455 Army Navy Dr Arlington VA 22206

MARKHAM, MEELER, religious assn. exec.; b. Fort Worth, Mar. 8, 1914; s. Henry Nathan and Mattie Viola Jane (Sanders) M.; student Howard Payne Coll., 1934-35, U. Tex., 1936, Tex. Christian U., 1943, Southwestern Bapt. Theol. Sem., 1943-45, summer 1947; m. Myrtie Lesselle Manlove, June 18, 1937; 1 son, Edwin Meeler. With Soil Conservation Service, U.S. Dept. Agr., Kenedy, Tex., 1937-40; insp. Q.M.C., 1941, chief insp., 1942-43; ordained to ministry Bapt. Ch.,; asst. pastor, choir dir. First Bapt. Ch., Beeville, Tex., 1945; pastor First Bapt. Ch., Carrizo Springs, 1945-51; pastor First Bapt. Ch., Mercedes, 1951-55; supt. missions Lower Rio Grande Bapt. Assn., Tex., 1955-60; missions sec. Kan. Conv. So. Bapts., Wichita, 1960-65; sec. Mission Property Services, Home Mission Bd., So. Bapt. Conv., Atlanta, 1966-70, asst. dir. div. associational services, pubs., 1971—. Trustee Valley Bapt. Acad., Harlingen, Tex., 1953—, sec., 1954—; bd, dirs. Alto Frio Bapt. Encampment, Tex., 1953-57, pres., 1954-57. Mem. Winter Garden Bapt. Assn. (moderator 1947-48), Bapt. Gen. Conv. Tex. (exec. bd. 1950-51), So. Tex. Pastor's Conf. (pres. 1960). Mason, Rotarian (pres.). Author: This Confident Faith, 1968; contbg. author: Every Day: Five Minutes with God, 1969. Contbr. articles, writer column profl. pubs. Home: 678 E Paces Ferry Rd NE Atlanta GA 30305 Office: 1350 Spring St NW Atlanta GA 30309

MARKHAM, RAY WALTER, accountant; b. Lake City, Fla., Nov. 5, 1933; s. William Walter and Donnie (Hancock) M.; B.S., Jacksonville U., 1962; m. Dorothy Cason, June 22, 1952; children—Garry, Cheryl Ann, Karen, Ray Walter. Rate clk. Tamiami Freightways, Inc., Jacksonville, Fla., 1954-56; postal clk. U.S. Post Office, Jacksonville, 1956-62; staff accountant Smoak, Davis, & Nixon, C.P.A.'s, Jacksonville, 1962-66, partner, 1966—. Mem. budget com. United Fund, Jacksonville, 1967—. Trustee Bapt. Bible Inst., Graceville, Fla. Served with AUS, 1952-54. Mem. Am. Fla. (sec. 1969) insts. C.P.A.'s, Hosp. Financial Mgmt. Assn., Nat. Assn. Accountants, Alpha Kappa Psi. Baptist (deacon). Mason (32 deg.). Club: Toastmasters (pres. 1967). Home: 1406 Belleshore Circle Jacksonville FL 32218 Office: Fla Title Bldg Jacksonville FL 32202

MARKLE, DONALD M., judge; b. Palestine, Tex., July 9, 1911; s. Frank Barrows and Carrie (McDonald) M.; A.B., LL.B., U. Tex., 1937. Admitted to Tex. bar, 1937; formerly asso. with Wayman & Kleinecke; mem. firm McDonald & Markle, 1946-50; judge Tenth Dist. Ct., Tex., 1950—. Mem. Ho. of Reps., Tex., 1941-48. Mem. Beta Theta Pi. Episcopalian. Home: 2903 Dominique Dr Galveston TX 77550 Office: County Courthouse Galveston TX 77550

MARKMAN, SHERMAN, jewelry mfg. co. exec.; b. Denver, Aug. 21, 1920; s. Abe and Julia (Rosen) M.; student So. Methodist U., 1962-64; m. Sande Kartus, July 24, 1942; children—Stephen Michael, Joan Susan, Lori Ann. Vice pres. Lester's, Inc., Oklahoma City, 1940-59; exec. v.p. Besco Enterprises, 1960-61; sr. v.p. Zale Corp., Dallas, 1962-69; pres. Designcraft Jewel Industries, N.Y.C., 1969—, chief exec. officer, 1969—. Mem. Dallas Council World Affairs, 1962—. Served with USMCR, 1942-45; PTO. Mem. Jewelry Mfrs. Assn. N.Y., Nat. Assn. Christians and Jews. Clubs: Press, Columbian (Dallas). Home: 7207 Joyce Way Dallas TX 75225 Office: 380 2d Av New York City NY 10010

MARKS, EDWARD ARCHIBALD, JR., lawyer; b. Newark, June 25, 1909; s. Edward A. and Mary C. (Blodgett) M.; B.S., U. Va., 1931, LL.B., 1933; m. Irene Dwight Patterson, June 21, 1932; children—Irene (Mrs. Rowland Anthony Rupp, Jr.), Edward Archibald III. Admitted to Va. bar, 1932; practiced in Richmond, 1933—; mem. firms King & Marks, 1936-42, Sands, Marks & Sands, 1945-61, Sands, Anderson, Marks & Clarke, 1961—; commr. in chancery Chancery Ct. of Richmond, Circuit Ct. of Henrico County, Va. Dir. Hankins & Johann, Inc., Central Va. Shippers Assn., J.M. Fry Co., Inc., Nat. Cab Co., Inc. (all Richmond), Hoofprint Hill Stables, Inc., Goochland, Va. Bd. dirs. Richmond Natural History Soc. Recipient Order of Merit, Boy Scouts Am., 1946. Fellow Am. Coll. Trial Lawyers; mem. Va. State Bar, Am., Richmond City bar assns., Internat. Assn. Ins. Counsel, Def. Research Inst., U.S. Power Squadron, Va. Soc. Ornithology, Nat. Trust for Historic Preservation, Wilderness Soc., Order of Coif, Nat. Wildlife Fedn., Nat. Audubon Soc., Phi Beta Kappa, Phi Alpha Delta. Episcopalian (trustee). Home: 7200 W Franklin St Richmond VA 23226 Office: Fidelity Bankers Life Bldg 9th and Main Sts Richmond VA 23219

MARKS, HENRY SEYMOUR, historian, educator; b. Greensboro, N.C., May 26, 1933; B.B.A. in Mgmt. U. Miami (Fla.), 1955, M.A. in History (Food Fair Found. fellow), 1956; postgrad. U. Ala. 1960-61, 62-64; m. Marsha Kass. Faculty, U. Miami (Fla.), 1955-56, Jacksonville (Ala.) State Coll., 1958-60, U. Ala., 1960-61, Florence (Ala.) State Coll. 1961-62, U. Ala., Huntsville, 1964-68, Ala. A. & M. Coll. 1968-69. Lectr. ednl. subjects; judge social sci. fairs, Ala. Mem. Am., Ala. So., Fla. hist. assns., Hist. Assn. S. Fla., Hakluyt Soc., Am. Soc. Pub. Adminstrn., Phi Alpha Theta. Jewish religion (pres. temple). Author: The Failure of the United States to Maintain the Independence of Korea and the Effect of the Failure upon Americans in Korea. Contbr. book reviews and abstracts to Huntsville (Ala.) Times and numerous publs. in field. Address: 102 Clinton Av W Huntsville AL 35801

MARKS, HERBERT EDWARD, lawyer; b. Dayton, O., Nov. 3, 1935; s. I.M. and Sarah (Schiff) M.; A.B., U. Mich., 1957; LL.B., Yale, 1960; postgrad. George Washington U., 1966-69; m. Marcia Frager, June 5, 1966; 1dau., Jennifer Lynn. Admitted to Ohio bar, 1960, D.C. bar, 1964; law clk. to chief judge U.S. Ct. Claims, Washington, 1964-65; practiced in Washington, 1965—; partner firm Wilkinson, Cragun & Barker, 1969—. Lectr. bus. law Am. U. Extension, 1962-63. Asso. gen. counsel Presdl. Inaugural Com., 1969. Sec., gen. counsel Am. Historic and Cultural Soc., Inc. Served to capt. USAF, 1961-64. Mem. Bar Assn. D.C., Am., Fed. bar assns., Fed. Communications Bar Assn., Phi Beta Kappa, Pi Sigma Alpha. Republican. Jewish religion. Clubs: Lawyers, Army and Navy. Home: 5317 Cardinal Ct Spring Hill Bethesda MD 20016 Office: 1616 H St NW Washington DC 20006

MARKS, JAMES JOHN, restaurateur, developer; b. Chgo., Aug. 23, 1911; s. Nicholas John and Stella (Gourety) M.; B.S., U. Mich., 1936; m. Christine Constance Tampary, Nov. 11, 1939; children—Lianna Sandra, James John. Forestry technician U.S. Forestry Service, Ava, Mo., 1934; forest supr. Mich. Conservation Dept., Lansing, 1934-35; cons. forester, Ann Arbor, Mich., 1936-37; owner Martine's Restaurant, Pensacola, Fla., 1942—, Martine's Ice Cream Co., Pensacola, 1942—; pres. Esquire House, Warrington, Fla., 1934—, Martine's, Pensacola, 1947—, Marwood Motors, Pensacola, 1955—, Ky. Fried Chicken, Biloxi and Gulfport, Miss., 1964—, Ky. Fried Chicken, Mobile, Ala., 1964—, New Orleans, 1967—, Col. Sander's Ky. Fried Chicken Corp.; sec.-treas. Circle Sanitation, Pensacola, 1959—. Mem. adv. bd. Fla. Hotel and Restaurant Commn., 1961-62; mem. bd. Fla. Hospitality Edn. Program, 1962-63; chmn., pres. Fla. Tourism Council, 1962-63; mem. Fla. Council of 100, 1963—, mem. exec. com. Served to comdr. USNR, 1937-45. Mem. Am. Restaurants Hall of Fame, 1961. Mem. Nat., Fla. (pres. 1961-62) restaurant assns., Sales Execs. Club. Mem. Hellenic Orthodox Ch. Rotarian (past local pres.). Clubs: Toastmasters; Mobile Country, Pensacola Country. Home: 4002 Marlane Dr Pensacola FL 32506 Office: 4101 Mobile Hwy Pensacola FL 32506

MARKS, LEONARD HAROLD, lawyer; b. Pitts., Mar. 5, 1916; s. Samuel and Ida (Lewine) M.; B.A., U. Pitts., 1935, LL.B., 1938, L.D., 1965; m. Dorothy Ames, June 3, 1948; children—Stephen Ames, Robert Evan. Admitted to Pa. bar, 1938, D.C. bar, 1946; asst. prof. law U. Pitts. Law Sch., 1938-42; prof. law Nat. U., 1943-55; asst. to gen. counsel FCC, 1942-46; partner firm Cohn & Marks, Washington, 1946-65; 69—; head USIA, 1965-68; dir. Communications Satellite Corp., 1963-65; chmn. bd. Rollins Communications Inc., 1969—. State Dept. lectr. administrv. and constl. law, India, 1958, Pakistan, Afghanistan, Iran, Turkey, 1961; Am. del. Internat. Broadcasting Conf., Mexico City, 1948, N.Am. Regional Broadcasting Conf., Montreal, 1949; mem. U.S. delegation Internat. Telecommunications Conf., Geneva, Switzerland, 1959, 63, Summit Conf., Honolulu and Manila, 1966, Latin Am. Presidents Conf., Punta del Este, Uruguay, 1967; chmn. U.S. delegation, ambassador, chmn. Internat. Conf. on Communication Satellites, Washington, 1969. Mem. Am. (mem. ho. of dels. 1962-64), Fed. Communications (pres. 1959-60), Allegheny County, Inter-Am., Internat. bar assns., Bar Assn. D.C., Order of Coif, Phi Beta Kappa, Omicron Delta Kappa, Sigma Delta Chi. Clubs: Cosmos, Federal City, Internat., Broadcasters (pres. 1957-59) (Washington). Home: 2833 McGill Terrace NW Washington DC 20008 Office: 1920 L St NW Washington DC 20547

MARKS, MEYER BENJAMIN, pediatric allergist; b. Chgo., Feb. 16, 1907; s. Simon and Rose (Block) M.; B.S., U. Ill., 1929, M.D., 1933, M.S., 1934; m. Golda A. Nathan, Sept. 27, 1932; children—Linda, Stephen. Intern, Cook County Hosp., 1934-35, resident 1935-36; pvt. practice pediatrics, 1937-57; cons. pediatric allergist Mt. Sinai Hosp., Miami Beach; dir. pediatric allergy clinic Jackson Meml. Hosp.; pediatric allergy and gen. allergy, 1957—; chief med. officer Asthmatic Children's Found. Residential Treatment Center, North Miami Beach; cons. pediatric allergist Variety Children's Hosp., Miami; clin. prof. pediatrics U. Miami Sch. Medicine. Hon. pres. med. div., Southeastern div. Am. Friends Hebrew U. Pres. Asso. Convalescent Homes and Hosp. for Asthmatic Children, 1971. Diplomate in pediatric allergy Am. Bd. Pediatrics. Fellow Am. Acad. Pediatrics, Am. Coll. Allergists, Am. Acad. Allergy; mem. A.M.A., Dade County Med. Assn., Fla., Miami (pres. 1954-55) pediatric socs., Fla. Med. Assn., Fla. Allergy Soc. (pres. 1970), Sigma Xi. Jewish religion. Contbr. articles to med. books and jours. Home: 105 E San Marino Dr Miami Beach FL 33139 Office: 333 Arthur Godfrey Rd Miami Beach FL 33140

MARKS, MORTON, JR., interior designers co. exec.; b. Richmond, Va., July 31, 1926; s. Morton and Hannah (Dombrower) M.; student N.C. State U., 1943-44, Va. Poly. Inst., 1944, Biarritz-Am. U., France, 1945; B.A., U. Richmond, 1949; m. Helen Lucille Wallerstein, June 30, 1949; children—Linda H., Robert M., Kathryn A., Morton Marks III. Asst. dir. pub. relations Am. Fidelty and Casualty Co., and affiliate Markel Service, Inc., Richmond, Va., 1948-51; exec. v.p.-treas. Morton Marks & Sons, Inc., contract furnishings and interior designers, 1951—. Pres. Kanawha Recreation Assn., 1971—, Tuckahoe Elementary P.T.A., 1964, Harry F. Byrd Middle Sch. P.T.A., 1971. Bd. dirs. Credit Bur. of Richmond, Inc., Rainbow Found. Served with AUS, 1944-46. Decorated, D.S.M., Bronze Star medal, Purple Heart. Recipient Key Man award Richmond Jr. C. of C., 1956. Mem. Am. Inst. Interior Designers, Inst. Bus. Designers (internat. treas. 1972—), Retail Mchts. Assn. Greater Richmond (v.p. 1972—), Va. Retail Mchts. Assn. Va. Mus. Fine Arts, Va. Congress of Parents and Tchrs. (hon. life mem.), Rainbow Div. Vets. (nat. exec. com. 1952-53), Cross of Mil. Service, United Daus. of Confederacy, Omicron Delta Kappa, Pi Delta Epsilon. Mem. Jewish religion. (bd. mgrs. temple 1965-69). Mason. Clubs: Bull and Bear, Kanawha, Richmond First. Contbr. articles to profl. pubs. Home: 411 Westham Pkwy Richmond VA 23229 Office: Main at 13th St Richmond VA 23211

MARKS, PAUL H., lawyer; b. Key West, Fla., Feb. 8, 1908; s. Herman and Pauline (Rosenthal) M.; J.D., U. Fla., 1930; m. Martha Gilchrist Frame, 1949; children—Patricia, Paul, Stephen. Admitted to Fla. bar, 1930, since practiced law in Miami; counsel to M. A. Smith, state bank liquidator, 1933-38, HOLC, Miami, 1934-36; gen. counsel Overseas Bridge Commn., 1937-39; counsel Gulf Life Ins. Co., 1934—; chmn. bd. Flagler Fed. Savs. & Loan Assn., Miami. Pres. Miami Downtown Business Council, 1959-62; dir. Crime Commn.; chmn. Orange Bowl Stadium Com., 1961—. Served to lt. comdr. USNR, 1942-45. Recipient City of Miami Outstanding Citizen award, 1964; citations from City of Miami, Orange Bowl Com., USN, Pi Lambda Phi, U. Fla. Alumni, State of Fla., Miami-Dade C. of C., Fla. Savs. and Loan League. Charter mem. Orange Bowl Com. and Adv. Council. Mem. Fla. Savs. and Loan League (pres. 1964-65), Dade County Bar Assn. (past dir.), U. Fla. Alumni (past pres. Miami), Fla. Blue Key, Miami-Dade C. of C. (past dir., mem. adv. council). Home: 6464 Caballero Blvd Coral Gables FL 33146 Office: 101 NE 1st Av Miami FL 33132

MARKS, WILLIAM BURNELL, ednl. adminstr.; b. Warsaw, Va., Apr. 4, 1903; s. Henry Thomas and Elizabeth (France) M.; A.B., Coll. Williams and Mary, 1925; Ed.M., Duke U., 1932; M.A., U. Mich., 1936; postgrad. Ohio State U., 1947, U. Tenn., 1948, U. Wis., 1950,

George Washington U., 1955, U. Md., 1957; m. Fanny Elizabeth Young, Dec. 26, 1928; children—William Burnell, Kenneth Livingston. Asst. prin. Herndon High Sch., Fairfax, Va., 1925-26; tchr.-coach Washington-Lee High Sch., Arlington, Va., 1926-28; prin. Fincastle (Va.) High Sch., 1928-30; vice-prin., coach Sandy Spring High Sch., Montgomery, Md., 1930-34; counselor Bethesda-Chevy Chase (Md.) Sr. High Sch., 1934-35; prin. Takoma Park Jr. High Sch., Silver Spring, Md., 1935-46; supr. Montgomery County (Md.) Schs., 1946-52; counselor Montgomery Blair Sr. High Sch., Silver Spring, 1952-61; prin. Lively (Va.) pub. schs., 1961—. Asso. Smithsonian Instn. Washington. Mem. Lancaster, Va. edn. assns., Va. PTA, Kappa Phi Kappa, Phi Delta Kappa. Methodist (chmn. pastor parish relations com. 1965—). Mason (32 deg., Shriner), Lion. Mem. Order Eastern Star. Club: Ruritan (past dist. gov. 1967-68, dist. dir. 1969-72). Home: Rt 2 Box 280 Lancaster VA 22503 Office: PO Box 17 Lively VA 22507

MARKWELL, NOEL GENE, psychologist; b. Covington, Ky., May 24, 1933; s. Quentin Roosevelt and Lelia (Workman) M.; A.B., Lafayette Coll., 1955; M.S., Purdue U., 1958, Ph.D., 1959; postgrad. U. Stockholm, 1959-60, U. London, 1962. Psychology intern Ohio State U. Med. Center, 1960-61; psychologist Warley Hosp., Brentwood, Essex, Eng., 1961-62, D.C. Dept. Pub. Health, 1962-66; psychologist Georgetown U., Washington, 1966-71, asst. clin. prof. psychology Med. Sch., 1966—; pvt. practice psychotherapy, 1972—; cons. psychologist Group Health Assn., 1970—, Inst. Psychiatry and Fgn. Affairs, 1971—. Diplomate Am. Bd. Profl. Psychology. Mem. Am. Psychol. Assn., Am. Polit. Sci. Assn., A.A.A.S., Sigma Xi. Home: 5038 MacArthur Blvd NW Washington DC 20016

MARLAND, EMILY JANE STAHLEM (MRS. JACKSON THORNE MARLAND), educator, author; b. Valley City, N.D., Feb. 14, 1926; d. Arthur David and Evelyn (McInnes) Stahlem; student N.D. State U., 1943-45; B.A. (Cal. P.T.A. scholar), U. Cal. at Los Angeles, 1947; M.A., Columbia, 1948; m. Jackson Thorne Marland, June 30, 1949 (dec. July 1960); children—Albert MacInnes, Jackson Thorne, Tchr., Mary E. Bennett Sch. for Deaf, Los Angeles, 1948-49; pvt. tutor deaf and aphasic children, Washington, 1950-60; faculty Hearing and Speech Center, Gallaudet Coll., Kendall Green, Washington, 1962-67, asst. prof., 1968—. Appeared in various TV shows; hearing testor pre-sch. children Washington Hearing Soc., 1949-50. Mem. Alexander Graham Bell Assn. for Deaf, Am. Assn. U. Profs., Conv. Am. Instrs. of Deaf, Council Exceptional Children, Hearing and Speech Assn. D.C., Washington Assembly, Internat. Platform Assn., Kappa Kappa Gamma. Republican. Episcopalian. Club: Garden (Westmoreland Hills). Author: Idioms - How to Teach Them to the Deaf, 1969; A Handbook for Teachers, 1969; A Workbook for Students, 1969. Home: 5404 Albemarle St Washington DC 20016

MARLIN, CLIFTON BOYD, educator; b. Dorsey, Miss., Oct. 24, 1920; s. Gordon and Minnie (Farris) M.; B.S., Miss. State U., 1943; M.F., Duke, 1949; m. Dorothy Ree Moore, Mar. 20, 1945; 1 son, Roger B. With Forestry Dept., Miss. State U., 1949-50; with Miss. Forestry Commn., Jackson, 1951-61, dir. forest mgmt., 1953-56, state forester, 1956-61; asst. prof. La. State U., Baton Rouge, 1961—. Mem. exec. com. Smokey Bear program Nat. Coop. Forest Fire Prevention, 1957-60; chmn. So. Group State Foresters, 1960. Served from cpl. to capt. AUS, World War II; ETO. Decorated Purple Heart. Mem. La., Miss. (past dir.) forestry assns., Am. Assn. U. Profs., Soc. Am. Foresters, Scabbard and Blade, Sigma Xi, Gamma Sigma Delta, Sigma Pi, Beta Beta Beta, Alpha Zeta. Baptist. Contbr. articles to profl. jours. Home: 5822 Clematis Dr Baton Rouge LA 70808

MARLIN, ERVIN R., assn. ofcl.; b., 1909; ed. Trinity Coll., Dublin. Personnel officer Farm Credit Adminstrn., Washington, 1935-36, Social Security Bd., 1936-39; asst. dir. personnel FSA, 1939-42; spl. asst. to U.S. ministr., Dublin, to U.S. ambassador, London, 1942-44; adminstrv. analyst Bur. Budget, Washington, 1944-45; external relations officer, dir. Tech. Assistance Bur., Internat. Civil Aviation Orgn., Montreal, 1945-62; sr. dir. UN High Commr. for Refugees, Geneva, Switzerland, 1962-65; dir. Office Internat. Orgn. Recruitment, Dept. State, Washington, 1965-71; dir. internat. relations Am. Assn. Retired Persons, Washington, 1971—. Office: Dept State Washington DC 20520

MARLOW, H(OBSON) MCKINLEY, lawyer; b. Cookeville, Tenn., Sept. 20, 1931; s. H.M. and Birtha (Bryant) M.; B.S., Tenn. Tech. U., 1954; LL.B., Vanderbilt U., 1957; m. Dorothy Fay Teal, June 18, 1960; children—Darryl McKinley, Stephen Teal, Eric Martin. Admitted to Tenn. bar, 1957; gen. practice, Nashville, 1957—; pres. Image, Inc., Motivation Mgmt. Inc., Image Pub. Co., Ashwood Music Co.; treas. Music Industries Corp. Mem. Am. (copyright com.), Nashville bar assns., Am. Trial Lawyers Assn., Bar Assn. Tenn. Mason (Shriner). Author: ABC's of Copyright Law for Songwriters, 1960. Home: Lynn Dr Nashville TN 37211 Office: Parkway Towers Nashville TN 37219

MARLOW, W(ILLIAM) H(ENRY), mathematician, educator; b. Waterloo, Ia., Nov. 26, 1924; s. Clifford William and Ella Louise (Murphy) M.; B.S., St. Ambrose Coll., Davenport, Ia., 1947; M.S., U. Ia., 1948, Ph.D., 1951; m. Delphine Elizabeth Meisch, Aug. 9, 1948; children—William J., David T., Michael L., Mary D., Anne T. Research asso. logistics research project George Washington U., 1951-56, prin. investigator, 1956-69, dir. Inst. for Mgmt. Sci. and Engring., 1969—, prof. applied sci., 1969-71, prof., chmn. operations research, 1971—. Asso. research mathematician U. Cal. at Los Angeles, 1954-55. Served to lt. (j.g.) USNR, 1943-46. Mem. Math. Soc., Math Assn., Navy Inst., Washington Operations Research Council, Operations Research Soc. Am., Inst. Mgmt. Scis., Soc. for Indsl. and Applied Math., Am. Soc. for Engring. Edn., Sigma Xi. Asso. editor Navy Research Logistics Quart., 1956—. Home: 4038 27th Rd N Arlington VA 22207 Office: George Washington U Washington DC 20006

MARLOWE, JAMES MILTON, physician; b. Jacksonville, Fla., Aug. 15, 1930; s. Thomas Lee and Ola (Cannte) M.; B.S., Fla. So. Coll., 1955; M.D., U. Miami, 1959; m. Selma Paterson, Nov. 1, 1952; children—Robert Charles, Ronald Jack, Richard James, Russell George. Intern, U.S. Naval Hosp., Portsmouth, Va., 1959-60; pvt. practice medicine, specializing in family practice, New Port Richey, Fla., 1963—; sr. mem. Richey Med. Center, New Port Richey, 1970—; chief staff West Pasco Hosp., New Port Richey, 1968-69; sec., treas. New Port Richey Community Hosp., 1970—, dir. edn., 1970-72; v.p., dir. Richey Manor, Inc., 1964-72; mem. staffs Tarpon Springs (Fla.) Gen. Hosp., Morton Plant Hosp., Clearwater, Fla. Instr. sex edn. and drug edn. Pasco County Sch. System, 1968-72; team physician dept. athletics Gulf High Sch., New Port Richey, Fla., 1963-72. Mem. exec. bd. Pinellas Area council Boy Scouts Am., 1968-72, council rep. to Nat. and Regional councils, scoutmaster, 1964-72. Mem. pres.'s council Fla. So. Coll., Lakeland, 1969-72. Served with USNR, 1950-53, 1959-63. Diplomate Am. Bd. Family Practice. Mem. Pasco-Hernandos-Citrus County Med. Soc. (pres. 1972), Fla. Med. Assn., A.M.A., Am. Acad. Family Physicians, Am. Diabetes Assn. Democrat. Methodist (trustee 1968-71, del. ann. conf. 1963-71). Home: 917 River Rd N New Port Richey FL 33552 Office: PO Box 1058 New Port Richey FL 33552

MARMION, CHARLES GRESHAM, bishop; b. Houston, Aug. 19, 1905; s. Charles Gresham and Katherine Angie (Rankin) M.; B.B.A., U. Tex., 1930; B.D., P.E. Theol. Sem. in Va., 1933, D.D. (hon.), 1954; D.D. (hon.), U. of South, Swanee, Tenn., 1954; m. Doris Anita Dissen, July 1, 1937; children—Beverley Anne, Sara Katherine, Dana Elizabeth. Bank clk., Houston, 1921-26; rector Christ Episcopal Ch., Eagle Lake, also St. John's Ch., Columbus, Tex., 1933-37; asst. rector St. Alban's Ch., Washington, 1937-40; rector St. George's Ch., Port Arthur, Tex., 1940-45, Ch. of Incarnation, Dallas, 1945-54; bishop Diocese of Ky., P.E. Ch., 1954—; pres. Province of Sewanee, Episcopal Ch., 1969-71. Mem. nat. council P.E. Ch., 1948-54, dep. to gen. conv., 1943, 52. Chmn. Port Arthur chpt. A.R.C., 1942-45. Mem. Beta Alpha Psi, Theta Xi. Mason, Rotarian. Mem. Legion of Honor, Order of DeMolay. Club: Pendennis (Louisville). Home: 147 W Wind Rd Louisville KY 40207 Office: 421 S 2d St Louisville KY 40202

MARMION, WILLIAM HENRY, bishop; b. Houston, Oct. 8, 1907; s. Charles Gresham and Katherine (Rankin) M.; A.B., Rice Inst., 1929; B.D., Va. Theol. Sem., 1932, D.D. 1954; m. Mabel Dougherty Nall, Dec. 28, 1935; children—William Henry, Roger Mills Nall. Ordained deacon Episcopal Ch., 1932, priest, 1933; priest in charge St. James, Taylor, Tex., and Grace Ch., Georgetown, 1932-35; asso. rector St. Mark's Ch., San Antonio, 1935-38; rector St. Mary's-on-Highland, Birmingham, Ala., 1938-50; St. Andrew's Ch., Wilmington, Del., 1950-54; consecrated bishop Episcopal Diocese of Southwestern Va., Roanoke, 1954—. Former dir. diocesan camps for young people in Tex. and Ala., headed diocesan youth work several years; dep. to Gen. Conv. Episcopal Ch., 1943, 46, alternate dep., 1949, 52; del. to Provincial Synod; mem. exec. council Episcopal Ch., 1963—. Chmn. Ala. Com. on Interracial Cooperation, 4 yrs. Trustee Va. Theol. Sem. Rotarian. Home: 2730 Avenham Av SW Roanoke VA Office: 1000 1st St SW Roanoke VA

MARQUES, RENE, author; b. Puerto Rico, 1919. Author plays: El Hombre y Sus Suenos, 1948; Palm Sunday, 1949; El Sol y Los MacDonald, 1950; La Carreta, 1952; Juan Bobo y la Dama de Occidente, 1956; La Muerte No Entrara en Palacio, 1957; Los Soles Truncos, 1958; Un Nino Azul Para Esa Sombra, 1959; La Casa Sin Reloj, 1961; Carnaval Afuera, Carnaval Adentro, 1962; short stories: Cuentos Puertorriquenos de Hoy, 1959; Otra Dia Nuerstro, 1955; En Una Ciudad Llamada San Juan, 1960; books: La Vispera del Hombre, 1958; Oxcart, 1969. Address: care Charles Scribner's Sons 597 Fifth Av New York City NY 10017*

MARQUEZ-DIAZ, NESTOR, educator, lawyer; b. Caquas, P.R., Mar. 7, 1936; s. Mario and Angela (Diaz) M.-D.; B.S., U. P.R., 1955; M.A., Ind. U., 1956; Ph.D., U. Madrid, 1958; LL.B., Tulane U., 1961. Admitted to La. bar, 1961; economist P.R. Treasury Dept., 1954-55; economist P.R. Econ. Devel. Adminstrn., 1956-59; lectr. Loyola U., New Orleans, 1959-61, co-dir. Inter-Am. Labor Mgmt. Center, 1961; partner firm Pilie, Nelson & Limes, New Orleans, 1961-62; prof. bus. adminstrn. Nicholls State Coll., Thibodaux, 1961-70; prof. bus. adminstrn. Tex. A & I U., Laredo, 1970—; pvt. practice law, New Orleans, 1962—; sr. partner Marquez-Diaz & Parker, 1967—; legal and econ. cons.; asst. atty. gen. State of La. Vice pres. Inter-Am. Pub. Corp., New Orleans, 1961-62, Interam. Shipbldg. Corp., La. Rose, La., 1961-63; sec.-treas. All-state Marine & Investment Services, Inc., New Orleans; pres. Marquez-Diaz & Parker Arms Co. Lectr. L. P.R., 1958; tech. adviser to rector U. of Central Am., Managua, Nicaragua, 1961—; indsl. promotion and econ. devel. cons. AID, San Jose, Costa Rica, 1963; econs. cons., New Orleans, 1961—. Spl. agt. La. State Police; dep. sheriff Lafourche Parish. Pres. New Orleans West Civic Assn. Vice pres. Spanish Am. Union of La., 1963. Chmn. Seven Eighty Niners Dem. Orgn., 1963; pres. Citizens for Democratic Action. Bd. dirs. U. Coahuila, Torreon, Mexico. Recipient Juarez award Govt. of Mex.; Order of Quetzal medal Govt. of Guatemala. Mem. Am., La., Inter-Am. bar assns., Am. Econ. Assn., Nat. Planning Assn., Acad. Polit. Sci., Phi Alpha Delta, Phi Delta Gamma. Roman Catholic. Clubs: Pass Christian Yacht; International House, New Orleans Press, Import-Export, Young Mens Business; Bayou Country. Author: An Analysis of the Banking System of Costa Rica, 1962; The Furniture Industry of Puerto Rico; Notes and Comments on the Ministry of Industry of Costa Rica; Foreign Capital and Its Role in Economic Development. Home: 2311 Victoria Villa Angela Apts Laredo TX 78040 Office: PO Box 537 Laredo TX 78040

MARREN, JANET, artist. Address: 21 Chiapa de Corzo San Cristobel las Casas Chiapas Mexico*

MARRIOTT, ALICE SHEETS (MRS. JOHN WILLARD MARRIOTT), restaurant chain exec., Rep. nat. committeewoman; b. Salt Lake City, Oct. 19, 1907; d. Edwin Spencer and Alice (Taylor) Sheets; A.B., U. Utah, 1927; m. John Willard Marriott, June 9, 1927; children—John Willard, Richard Edwin. Partner Hot Shoppes, Inc. (name changed to Marriott Corp. 1967), Restaurant chain, Washington, 1927—; v.p., dir., 1929—. Mem. Republican Nat. Com., 1959—, vice chmn., 1965; mem. Rep. Coordinating Com., 1965; exec. com. D.C. Rep. Com.; treas. Rep. Nat. Conv., 1964, 68, 72; vice chmn. inaugural com., 1969; chmn. distinguished ladies reception for the inaugural, 1969. Mem. Nat. Adv. Commn. Children and Youth; chmn. Pres.'s Adv. Com. on Arts of John F. Kennedy Center for Performing Arts, 1970—, trustee, 1972—. Bd. dirs. Washington Ballet Guild, Goodwill Guild, Washington Home Rule Com., Arthritis and Rheumatism Found. of Met. Washington. Mem. League Republican Women D.C. (v.p. 1957-61), Nat. Symphony Orch. Assn., Am. Newspaper Womens Club, Chi Omega, Phi Kappa Phi. Mem. Ch. of Jesus Christ of Latter-day Saints. Clubs: Capitol Speakers (membership chmn.), Washington, Capitol Hill, Women's Nat. Republican, F Street, Welcome to Washington Internat. (treas.). Home: 4500 Garfield St Washington DC 20007 Office: 5161 River Rd Washington DC 20016

MARRIOTT, J(OHN) WILLARD, JR., restaurant-hotel chain exec.; b. Washington, Mar. 25, 1932; s. John Willard and Alice (Sheets) M.; B.S. in Banking and Finance, U. Utah, 1954; m. Donna Garff, June 29, 1955; children—Deborah, Stephen Garff, John Willard III. Pres. Marriott Motor Hotels, 1957-65; v.p. Hot Shoppes Inc., 1959-64, exec. v.p., 1964; pres. Marriott-Hot Shoppes, Inc. (now Marriott Corp.), 1964—, also dir.; adv. bd. brs. Riggs Nat. Bank, Washington. Bd. dirs. Met. Washington Bd. Trade, Downtown Progress, Washington, Washington Nat. Symphony; apptd. by Pres. Nixon to Adv. Council for Minority Enterprise; mem. Pres.'s Nat. Tourism Resources Review Commn. Served to lt. USNR, 1954-56. Mem. Am. Hotel and Motel Assn., Nat. Restaurant Assn., Sigma Chi. Clubs: Burning Tree, Columbia Country (Bethesda, Md.). Home: 5214 Parkway Dr Chevy Chase MD 20015 Office: 5161 River Rd Washington DC 20016

MARSDEN, ELIZABETH HARLOW, educator; b. Nashville, Mar. 17, 1923; d. Frank Ernest and Harriet Ellsworth (Rees) Harlow; Mus.B., U. Miami, 1944; M.A., Columbia, 1945; m. Edward Derwood Marsden, Dec. 23, 1946 (div. Jan. 1971); children—Elizabeth Rhys, Margaret Lee, Catherine Harlow, Harriet Ann. Tchr., Southeastern La. Coll., 1945-47; asst. prof. music U. Miami, 1947-52; supr. music Penn Hills Sch., Pitts., 1954-59; tchr. piano, voice, Pitts., 1959-61; judge Music Educators Nat. Conf., Miami, 1953, Tampa, Fla., 1953; tchr. Dade County (Fla.) Schs., 1964, Brevard County (Fla.) Schs., 1966-72; minister of music Coral Way Presbyn. Ch., Miami, 1964-66, First Presbyn. Ch., Titusville, 1966-72; music cons. Marietta (Ga.) City Schs., 1972—. Lectr. U. South Fla., 1967-72, Rollins Coll., 1971, U. Ga., 1972—. Mem. Am. Assn. U. Profs., Am. Assn. U. Women, Am. Guild Organists, Music Educators Nat. Conf., N.E.A., Classroom Tchrs. Assn., Fla. Elementary Tchrs. Assn., Brevard Edn. Assn., Brevard Music Edn. Assn. (v.p.), Delta Kappa Gamma, Chi Omega, Sigma Alpha Iota. Presbyn. (v.p. women's guild). Clubs: College, Tuesday Music, Mt. Lebanon Women's (Pitts.); Coral Gables Garden, Flamingo Dinner. Home: Box 584 Marietta GA 30060 Office: 145 Dodd St Box 6066 Marietta GA 30060

MARSH, BURTON WALLACE, transp. and traffic engr., assn. exec.; b. Worcester, Mass., Jan. 9, 1898; s. Luman Wallace and Florence Duncan (Wells) M.; B.S. in Civil Engring., Worcester Poly. Inst., 1920, D.Eng. (hon.), 1961; postgrad. Yale, 1920-21; m. Mary Elizabeth Allison, Oct. 8, 1927; children—Jean Allison (Mrs. John K. Adams), Mary Elizabeth, (Mrs. Harold R. McCartor), Alan Burton. Work on housing projects, city planning, zoning, traffic planning various cities, including Worcester, Norfolk, Va., Dayton, O., 1921-24; city traffic engr., Pitts., 1924-30, Phila., 1930-33; dir. traffic engring. and safety dept. Am. Automobile Assn., Washington, 1933-64, exec. dir. Found. for Traffic Safety, 1964-66, Inst. Traffic Engrs., Washington, 1967-70; cons. engr. traffic and safety, 1970—. Lectr., instr. dean in traffic courses and schs. including Traffic Engring. and Traffic Officer Tng. Schs. at Yale, Harvard, Northwestern U., Pa. State U., U. Md.; pioneer municipal traffic engr. Mem. transp. systems planning group. Hwy. Research Bd., mem., past chmn. Hwy. Research Bd. NRC; mem., past chmn. Nat. Com. Uniform Traffic Laws and Ordinances, Nat. Adv. Com. on Uniform Traffic Control Devices. Bd. mgmt. Central br. YMCA, Washington; former trustee Worcester Poly Inst., 1953-67; mem. bd. Theodore M. Matson Meml. Fund, Inc. Recipient Paul Gray Hoffman award, 1959; Theodore M. Matson Meml. Award 1960, Arthur Williams Meml. award, 1970. Mem. Inst. traffic Engrs. (past pres.), Am. Soc. C.E., Sigma Xi, Tau Beta Pi. Presbyn. Club: Cosmos (Washington). Address: 3126 Rittenhouse St NW Washington DC 20015

MARSH, CHARLES FRANKLIN, educator; b. Antigo, Wis., Aug. 18, 1903; s. Charles Osborne and Mae (Barnett) M.; A.B., Lawrence Coll., 1925; M.A., U. Ill., 1926, Ph.D., 1928; LL.D., Furman U., 1968; m. Chloro Nancy Thurman, Sept. 8, 1928; children—John Charles, Nancy (Mrs. Richard Scribner Stowe). Instr. econs. and bus. Am. U., Washington, 1928-30; asso. prof. Coll. William and Mary, Williamsburg, Va., 1930-33, prof., 1933-50, chancellor, prof. econs. and bus., 1950-58, chmn. dept. bus. adminstrn., 1941-54, dean of faculty, 1952-58, lectr. bus. adminstrn., 1968—. Asst. dept. adminstr. NRA, Washington, 1935-36; prin. economist Fed. Bd. Investigation and Research, Washington, 1940-42; coordinator adv. council Va. Economy, Richmond, 1949-50; pres. Wofford Coll., Spartanburg, S.C., 1958-68. Chmn. commn. on colls. So. Assn. Colls. and Schs., 1964. Pres. bd. Williamsburg Community Living, Inc., 1969-71; mem. exec. com., bd. edn. Va. conf. United Meth. Ch., 1948-56, lay del. S.C. Conf. to ann., jurisdictional and gen. conf., 1960-68 lay leader Peninsula dist., 1969, cons. coll. coordinating council Western N.C. conf., 1968—, mem. Commn. on Ecumenical Affairs, 1971—, chmn. local council on ministries, 1971-72. Dir. war bd. City of Williamsburg, 1943-45, chmn. postwar planning commn., 1945-46, mem. city planning commn., 1946-48, mem. city council, 1948-52; chmn. adv. commn. on long-range planning City of Spartanburg (S.C.), 1963-68; pres., dir. Council for Spartanburg County, 1961-68. Recipient Outstanding Civilian Service medal Dept. Army, 1965, Citizen of Yr. award Spartanburg (S.C.) Kiwanis Club, 1967, Distinguished Service award Greenville (S.C.) Lions Club, 1968; residence hall named in his honor Wofford Coll., 1969. Mem. Am. Econ. Assn., Va. Social Sci. Assn. (pres. 1942), S.C. Assn. Colls. (pres. 1965), S.C. Assn. Pvt. Colls. (chmn. 1964-66), Williamsburg C. of C. (pres. 1945), Phi Beta Kappa, Omicron Delta Kappa, Alpha Phi Omega, Phi Kappa Tau. Rotarian. Club: Middle Plantation (Williamsburg, Va.). Author: The Hampton Roads Communities in World War II, 1951; Opportunities for Improvement of the Virginia State Tax Structure, 1945; United Methodist Colleges in Western North Carolina: A Study in Relationships, 1969. Home: 705 Powell St Williamsburg VA 23185

MARSH, JOHN O., JR., lawyer, former congressman; b. Winchester, Va., Aug. 7, 1926; s. John Otho and Nell Virginia (Wayland) M.; LL.B., Washington and Lee U., 1951; m. Glenn Ann Patterson, July 22, 1950; children—John O. III, Rebecca Patterson, Scot Wayland. Admitted to Va. bar, 1952, D.C. bar, 1970; practiced in Strasburg, Va.; mem. Shenandoah County Sch. Bd., 1959-60; judge, Strasburg, 1954-62; town atty., New Market, Va., 1954-62; mem. 88th to 91st Congress, 7th Dist. Va., mem. appropriations com. 89th to 91st Congresses; now engaged in practice law, Washington. Mem. Am. Revolution Bicentennial Commn.; adv. com. Papers of George Washington. Served with AUS, 1944-47; lt. col. Va. N.G. Named Outstanding Young Man of Year, Va. Jr. C. of C., 1959. Mem. Am. Bar Assn., Va. State Bar, Am. Legion (Distinguished Service medal Dept. Va. 1962), Va. Jr. C. of C. (life), V.F.W., Assn. U.S. Army, N.G. Assn. U.S., Va. N.G. Assn., Phi Kappa Psi, Phi Delta Phi, Omicron Delta Kappa. Presbyn. Mason. Home: Strasburg VA 22657 3425 N Albemarle St Arlington VA 22207 Office: 1701 Pennsylvania Av NW Suite 1120 Washington DC 20008

MARSH, WARREN ELDON, banker; b. DuBois, Neb., Mar. 9, 1925; s. Daniel Booker and Katherine Molly (Hartman) M.; ed. USN spl. courses, Southwestern Grad. Sch. Banking; m. Alpha Mae Holt, Jan. 28, 1956; children—Stephanie Yvonne, Ronald Eugene, Angelia Dean. Sr. v.p. 1st Pasadena State Bank (Tex.), 1945—. Served with USNR, 1943-45. Mem. Am. Inst. Banking, Pasadena C. of C. Mem. Reorganized Ch. Jesus Christ of Latter-day Saints. Mason, Elk. Club: Pasadena Optimist (past pres.). Home: 1804 Glencrest St Pasadena TX 77502 Office: 1001 Southmore St Pasadena TX 77502

MARSH, WOODROW LEE, JR., supt. schs.; b. Pinson, Ala., July 5, 1924; s. Woodrow Lee and Pearl (Loggins) M.; B.A., Miss. Coll., 1947; M.A., U. Miss., 1949, Ed.D., 1968; postgrad. Nat. Acad. Sch. Adminstrs., 1969, Tchrs. Coll. Columbia U., 1971; m. Adelia Bell Rogers, Apr. 29, 1944; children—Carol (Mrs. Charles Felix Humphrey), James Rogers, Barbara Elaine. Tchr., coach Canton (Miss.) High Sch., 1947-49; prin. Yazoo City High Sch., 1949-53, Greenwood High Sch., 1953-57; asst. supt. Greenwood pub. schs., 1957-61; supt. schs., Moss Point, 1961-66; dir. consultative services for schs. U. Miss., 1966-67; supt. schs. Bolivar Sch. Dist. IV, Cleveland, Miss., 1967—. Vis. prof. Miss. State U., summer 1958, Delta State Coll., summer 1968, 70. Mem. Legislative Recess Ednl. Study Com., chmn. Policies and Procs. Com. 1970—. Served with AUS, 1943-46. Decorated Bronze Star medal. Mem. Am. (bicentennial commn. 1971—), Miss. assns. sch. adminstrs., Nat., Miss., Bolivar County edn. assns., Miss. Assn. Sch. Supts. (pres. 1965-66), Miss. High Sch. Activities Assn. (state councilman 1969—), Cleveland C. of C. (bd. dirs. 1967—), Bolivar County Farm Bur. Mason, Rotarian (pres. 1964-65). Home: 512 Hillcrest Circle Cleveland MS 38732 Office: 305 Merritt Dr Cleveland MS 38732

MARSHALL, C(HARLES) HERBERT, physician; b. Washington, June 26, 1898; s. Charles H. and Pauline L. (Jennings) M.; Sc.B., Howard U., 1921, M.D., 1924; m. Esther Ophelia Tibbs, July 21, 1939; 1 son, Charles Herbert 3d. Intern Freedman's Hosp., Washington, 1924-25; pvt. practice medicine, Washington, 1925—; asst. instr. dept. medicine Howard U., Washington, 1928-32. Mem. Jr. Police and Citizens' Corps; mem. exec. bd. Nat. Capital area Boy Scouts Am.; mem. bd. Whipper Maternity Home; vice chmn. Commr.'s Youth Council, D.C., Citizens Joint Com. on Nat. Rep. D.C.; mem. Mayors Com. for Employment of Handicapped. Bd. dirs. Citizens Assn. of Georgetown, Citizens' Crime Commn. Met. Washington, So. Conf. Ednl. Fund, Met. Police Boys Club. Served with SATC, 1918. Recipient SSS Medal. Mem. Rock Creek Citizens Assn. (pres. 1935—), D.C. Fedn. Civic Assns. (pres. 1952-54), Nat. Med. Assn. (chmn. bd. trustees 1944-47, pres. 1949-50), N.A.A.C.P. (D.C. pres. 1941-43). Baptist. Club: Pigskin (v.p.). Home: 2710 P St NW Washington DC 20007

MARSHALL, CLIFTON JAMES, architect; b. Owensboro, Ky., Aug. 17, 1919; s. Elmer and Audrey (Farmer) M.; B.S., U. Ill., 1949; student Wash. U., St. Louis, 1941-42; m. Valerie K. Zarvis, June 3, 1946 (dec. Jan. 1956); 1 dau., Geraldine Ann; m. 2d, Margaret Jagoe Smith, May 23, 1959. Partner Roberts & Marshall, Asso. Architects, Owensboro, Ky., 1950-54; project mgr. O'Connor & Kilham, Architects, N.Y.C., 1954-56; asst. prof. U. Kan., Lawrence, 1956-57; ind. practice architecture Owensboro, Ky., 1957-66; asso. univ. architect U. Ky., Lexington, 1966-69, univ. architect, dir. design and constrn. div., 1969—; asso. prof. Clemson (S.C.) U., 1964-66. Organizer, dir. Lincoln Fed. Savs. & Loan Assn., Owensboro. Mem. coordinating com. Lexington Transp. Planning Study; mem. design rev. bd. Urban Renewal Commn., City of Lexington. Served with C.E., AUS, 1942-45. Mem. A.I.A., Ky. Soc. Architects, Assn. U. Architects, Soc. Coll. and U. Planning, Am. Assn. Hosp. Planning, Scarab. Baptist. Mason, Rotarian. Home: 814 Glendover Circle Lexington KY 40502

MARSHALL, DANIEL PARR, JR., lawyer; b. Lexington, Ky., Nov. 25, 1922; s. Daniel Parr and Jennie Pettit (Simmons) M.; student U. Ky., 1940-43; A.B., U. Louisville, 1948, LL.B., 1950; m. Lillian Bertram, May 13, 1944; children—Daniel Parr III, Anne O., William F. III. Admitted to Ky. bar, 1950; practiced in Louisville, 1950-63, 70—; mem. firm Duncan, Humphrey, Peabody & Oldham, 1950-53, Johnson & Marshall, 1953-55; individual practice, 1955-62; judge Juvenile Ct., Jefferson County, Ky., 1962-63; judge First Chancery div. Jefferson Circuit Ct., Louisville, 1964-69; partner Marshall & Gailor, Louisville, 1970—; lectr. English, U. Louisville, 1958-61, lectr. bus. law, 1961-63, 70—. Mem. Health and Welfare Council, 1964—; mem. Juvenile Ct. Adv. Bd., 1964-69, chmn., 1967-69; bd. dirs. Family and Children's Agy. Trustee Louisville Law Alumni Found. U. Louisville, 1962-64. Served to 2d lt. Inf., AUS, 1943-46. Mem. Sierra Club, Wilderness Soc., Am., Ky., Louisville (past pres., com. chmn.) bar assns., Am. Trial Lawyers Assn., Kappa Alpha, Omicron Delta Kappa, Phi Alpha Delta, Alpha Chi Sigma. Republican. Unitarian. Home: 410 Belgravia Ct Louisville KY 40208 Office: Republic Bldg Louisville KY 40202

MARSHALL, ERSTON LELAND, ret. ins. exec.; b. Gaylord, Mich., Apr. 6, 1886; s. Anthony D. and Emma J. (Felter) M.; A.B., U. Mich., 1908. J.D., 1912; m. Mabel C. Wilson, Dec. 31, 1913; children—Arleen I. (Mrs. Charles Jorgeson), Jean L. (Mrs. Benjamin Z. Maltz). Actuary LaFayette Life Ins. Co., 1912-17; cons. actuary, Indpls., 1917-20, Des Moines, 1920-29; v.p. LaFayette Life Ins. Co., 1929-49, pres. 1949-52, pres. emeritus, 1952—, dir., cons. Fellow Soc. Actuaries; mem. Internat. Congress Actuaries (permanent com.), Internat. Platform Assn., Am. Inst. Actuaries (gov. 1924-27, 33-48), Order of Coif. Methodist (ofcl. bd.). Mason (32 deg., Shriner), Rotarian. Author: Net Premiums and Reserves For Ages Below Fifteen, 1928. Contbr. articles to ins. jours. Home: Apt 19J Peachtree Towers 300 W Peachtree St Atlanta GA 30308

MARSHALL, JAMES STANLEY, univ. pres.; b. Cheswick, Pa., Jan. 27, 1923; s. Walter and Mildred (Crawford) M.; student Pa. State Tchrs. Coll. at Slippery Rock, 1940-43, U. Chgo., 1943-44; B.S., Pa. State Tchrs. Coll., Slippery Rock, 1947; M.S., Syracuse U., 1950, Ph.D., 1956; m. Ruth Cratty, June 10, 1944 (div. Apr. 1966); children—David Stanley, Sue Ellen, John Dodds; m. 2d. Shirley Slade, Sept. 10, 1966; children—Kimberly, James Andrew. Tchr. sci. Mynderse Acad., Seneca Falls, N.Y., 1947-52; asst. prof. sci. State U. N.Y. Coll. Edn., Cortland, 1953-55, asso. prof., 1956, prof., 1957-58; instr. Syracuse U., 1955-56; prof. sci. edn., head dept. Fla. State U., Tallahassee, 1958, asso. dean Sch. Edn., 1965-67, dean Coll. Edn., 1967-69, acting pres., 1969, pres., 1969—; cons. Turkish Ministry Edn.; dir. Turkish Nat. Sci. High Sch. Project, 1963-67; ednl. cons. state, local sch. dists. Vice pres., bd. dirs. So. Scholarship and Research Found.; bd. dirs. Southeastern Ednl. Corp. Fellow A.A.A.S. (mem. commn. sci. edn. 1962-67); mem. Am. Inst. Physics, Nat., Fla. sci. tchrs. assns., N.E.A., Fla. Edn. Assn., Am. Assn. Physics Tchrs., Nat. Assn. Research Sci. Teaching, Fla. Acad. Scis., Sigma Xi, Phi Delta Kappa. Contbg. author: Curriculum Planning for the Gifted, 1960; New Curricula, 1963. Editor: Jour. Research in Sci. Teaching, 1963-67. Co-author: Current Trends in Science Education. Contbr. articles to sci., ednl. jours. Home: 1030 W Tennessee St Tallahassee FL 32304 Office: President's Office 200 Westcott Fla State U Tallahassee FL 32306

MARSHALL, JEROME BENJAMIN, JR., dentist; b. Wilkes-Barre, Pa., Sept. 27, 1929; s. Jerome Benjamin and Anna Montford (Stoneham) M.; student Wyo. Sem., 1943-47; B.A., Princeton U., 1951; D.D.S., U. Pa., 1955, postgrad. 1965-66; m. Nancy Elisabeth Brader, Dec. 27, 1955; children—Elisabeth Stoneham, Jerome Benjamin III, Sarah Atherton. Chief oral surgery Wilkes-Barre (Pa.) Gen. Hosp., 1959-61; commd. 2d lt. Dental Corps, USAF, 1961, advanced through grades to lt. col., 1970, resigned, 1970; pvt. practice dentistry specializing in oral surgery, Alexandria, Va., 1970—; instr. in oral surgery U. Pa. Sch. Dentistry, 1957-58, Med. Sch., 1966-67; dir. The Shank Land Co. Chmn. The Alexandria Lyceum Restoration Campaign, 1971; chmn. Greater Washington Area 125th anniversary dr. Wyo. Sem., 1971. Bd. dirs. The Hist. Alexandria Found. Mem. Am., Alexandria dental assns., Va., Alexandria (dir.) dental socs., Delta Sigma Delta, Omicron Kappa Upsilon. Episcopalian. Mason. Clubs: Belle Haven Country (Alexandria, Va.); Irem Temple Country (Dallas, Pa.); Westmoreland (Wilkes-Barre, Pa.). Home: 213 Prince St Alexandria VA 22314 Office: 1451 Belle Haven Rd Alexandria VA 22307

MARSHALL, JOHN DAVID, librarian; b. McKenzie, Tenn., Sept. 7, 1928; s. Maxwell Cole and Emma (Walpole) M.; B.A summa cum laude, Bethel Coll., McKenzie, Tenn., 1950; M.A., Fla. State U., 1951, postgrad., 1951-52. Grad. asst. Office of Dean of Sch. of Library Sci., Fla. State U., 1951-52; reference librarian Clemson (S.C.) U. Library, 1952-55; head reference dept. Auburn (Ala.) U. Library, 1955-57; head acquisitions div. U. Ga. Library, Athens, 1957-67; univ. librarian Middle Tenn. State U., Murfreesboro, 1967—. Cons. Library Sci. Inst., Tenn. Tech. U., 1971-72. Mem. Am., Southeastern (chmn. coll. and univ. section, 1972-74), Tenn. (chmn. intellectual freedom com. 1969-70) library assns., Am. Library History Round Table (sec. 1969—), Assn. Coll. and Research Libraries (pub. com. 1957-62), Bibliog. Soc. Am, English Speaking Union, Tenn. Hist. Soc., Tenn. Edn. Assn., Phi Kappa Phi, Beta Phi Mu. Author: Books in Your Life, 1959; A Fable of Tomorrow's Library, 1965; Louis Shores: A Bibliography, 1964. Editor: Of, By, and For Librarians, 1960; An American Library History Reader, 1961; In Pursuit of Library History, 1962; Mark Hopkins' Log and Other Essays of Louis Shores, 1965; Approaches to Library History, 1966; Library in the University, 1967; (with Louis Shores and Wayne Shirley) Books, Libraries, Librarians, 1955. Book rev. editor Jour. of Library History, 1966—; gen. editor Shoe String Press contbrns. to Library Literature series, 1963—; contbg. editor So. Observer, 1953-66. Editorial bd. Alabama Librarian, 1956-57. Book reviewer Library Jour., 1953-64. Home: 802 E Main St Apt 34 Murfreesboro TN 37130

MARSHALL, MARA BLUMBERG (MRS. SYLVAN MITCHELL MARSHALL), artist; b. Nice, France, July 21, 1926 (parents Am. citizens); d. Joseph and Leah (Kristeller) Blumberg; grad. Scudder-Culver Jr. Coll., 1945, N.Y. Sch. Interior Decoration, 1946; Student Art Students' League, N.Y.C., 1945-46; m. Sylvan Mitchell Marshall, Feb. 11, 1951; children—Douglas Wayne, Bradley Ross. One-man show First Fed. Gallery, Chgo., 1971, Nat. League Pen Women, Washington, 1972; exhibited group shows Cosmos Club, Washington, Am. Art League Exhibit, Washington, Exhibit for Kennedy Center for Performing Arts, Washington, Julius Garfinckel & Co., Am. Art League Gallery, Washington, Washington Gallery Art, Nat. League Am. Pen Women, 1970, 72, Pres. Park Exhibit, Washington; represented in permanent collections. Mem. bd. Salvation Army Aux., 1954-56; mem. Pan Am. Liaison Com. of Women's Orgns., 1954—; mem. White House Spanish-Portuguese Study Group, 1953—, mem. bd., corr. sec., 1956-57. Mem. Nat. League Am. Pen Women (Ann. award Biennial Contest in Art, D.C. br. 1967, 69, Ann. award, 1st prize oils nat. biennial contest 1969, exec. bd. D.C. br. 1968-70, corr. sec., 1968-70, pres. D.C. br. 1970-72, 1st prize accryllics 1971), Artists Equity Assn. Am. Art League. Club: International. Home: 2929 Ellicott St NW Washington DC 20008

MARSHALL, SAMUEL FREDERIC, union ofcl.; b. Salem, O., May 10, 1930; s. Norris Clayton and Ursula (Aleisch) M.; student Kent State U., 1949-50; m. Glenda May Spencer, Aug. 23, 1952; children—Walter Lon, Marie Lynette, Spencer Lee, Josef Lowell. Reporter, Canton (O.) Repository, 1946-49; mem. staff Cleve. Plain Dealer, 1952-64, labor writer, 1963-64; editor Communications Workers Am. News, Washington, 1965-68; dir. publs. and pub. relations Am. Fedn. State, County and Municipal Employees. AFL-CIO, Washington, 1968—. Cons. to govt., 1966—. Recipient George Polk Meml. award, 1964, Cleve. Press Club award, 1960, 65, Internat. Labor Press Assn. Nieman Fellows awards, 1966, 67. Mem. Am. Newspaper Guild. (treas. local 1, Cleve. 1963-64), Kent State U. Alumni Assn., Sigma Delta Chi (sec., v.p. Buckeye chpt. 1962-64). Democrat. Clubs: Nat. Press (Washington). Office: 1155 15th St Washington DC 20005

MARSHALL, SAMUEL HAYES, city ofcl.; b. McLoud, Okla., Dec. 7, 1907; s. Henry H. and Caroline (Holder) M.; B.S., U. Fla., 1933; m. Charlotte Josephine Rempe, Dec. 8, 1934; 1 son, James Rempe. Accountant, Joseph E. Phillips, C.P.A., 1935-39; city auditor-clk. City of Ft. Lauderdale, Fla., 1939-54, dir. finance, 1954—. Served with Finance Dept., AUS, 1943-45. Mem. Nat. Assn. Accountants, Municipal Finance Officers Assn. U.S. and Can., Bankers Club N.Y.C. Republican. Presbyn. Mason, Elk. Home: 1405 NE 4th Pl Fort Lauderdale FL 33301 Office: 100 N Andrews Av Fort Lauderdale FL 33302

MARSHALL, SYLVAN MITCHELL, lawyer, TV producer; b. N.Y.C., May 14, 1917; s. Louis H. and Kitty Markowitz; B.A., Coll. City N.Y., 1938; LL.B., Harvard, 1941; m. Mara Byron, Feb. 11, 1951; children—Douglas Wayne, Bradley Ross. Admitted to N.Y. bar, 1946, Washington bar, 1953; mem. firm Garey & Garey, N.Y.C., 1946-51; spl. asst. to chief counsel OPS, Washington, 1951-53; partner Granik & Marshall, Washington, 1953-58; asst. producer Youth Wants To Know and Am. Forum, NBC-TV and radio, 1953-58; spl. dep. atty. gen., N.Y., 1946-50; pvt. practice Washington, 1958—; sr. partner law firm Marshall & Soll, Washington; partner Soll, Connelly & Marshall, N.Y.C.; Washington counsel Community Fed. Savs. & Loan Assn., St. Louis, First Fed. Savs. & Loan Assn., Chgo., First Fed. Savs. & Loan of Miami, First Fed. Savs. & Loan Assn., Jacksonville, Fla., Standard Fed. Savs. & Loan Assn., Cin., St. Petersburg Fed. Savs. & Loan of Wis., Milw., First Fed. Savs. & Loan, St. Petersburg, Fla., First Fed. Savs. &Loan Assn., Madison, Wis. Hon. dep. police commr. N.Y.C., 1950-53. Served from 2d lt. to lt. col., AUS, 1941-46. Decorated knight comdr. Order of the Falcon (Iceland); Knight comdr. Order of Vasco Nunez de Balboa (Republic of Panama); comdr. Order of Lion (Finland); Order of Taj (Iran); Order of So. Cross (Brazil); Order of Ruben Dario (Nicaragua). Mem. Acad. Television Arts and Scis. Clubs: International, Cosmos (Washington). Home: 2929 Ellicott St NW Washington DC 20008 Office: 1825 K St NW Washington DC 20006 also 130 Park Av New York City NY 10017

MARSHALL, THORD MASON, sch. supt.; b. Dayton, Pa., July 27, 1909; s. Mason Forbes and Viola (Borland) M.; B.S., Pa. State Coll., 1932; M.Ed., U. Pitts., 1939; Ph.D., Fla. State U., 1955; m. Mildred Cline, July 20, 1937; children—James, Sue Ann. Head coach, asst. prin. Cowanshannock Twp., 1937-39; athletic dir., coach, tchr. Mt. Lebanon, Pitts., 1939-46; high sch. prin., Hollywood, Fla., 1946-50, Tallahassee, 1951-55; asst. supt. schs., Broward County, Ft. Lauderdale, 1955-63; supt. Savannah-Chatham County pub. schs., Savannah, Ga., 1963—. Active Boy Scouts Am. Served from lt. (j.g.) to lt. comdr., USNR, 1943-45. Decorated D.F.C., 3Air Medals; recipient Broward County Outstanding Citizen award Ft. Lauderdale Bus. Men's Club, 1962. Mem. Am. Legion, Phi Delta Kappa, Kappa Delta Pi. Rotarian (pres. Ft. Lauderdale 1962-63). Author: Educational Opportunities in White Public Secondary Schools of Leon County, Florida, 1955. Home: 603 E 57th St Savannah GA 31405

MARSHALL, THURGOOD, asso. justice U.S. Supreme Ct.; b. Balt., July 2, 1908; s. William & Norma A. (Williams) M.; A.B., Lincoln U., 1930, LL.D., 1947; LL.B., Howard U., 1933, LL.D., 1954; LL.D., Va. State Coll., 1948, Morgan State Coll., 1952, Grinnell Coll., 1954, Syracuse U., 1956, N.Y. Sch. Social Research, 1956, U. Liberia, 1960, Brandeis U., 1960, U. Mass., 1962, Jewish Theol. Sem., 1962, Wayne U., 1963, Princeton U., 1963, U. Mich., 1964; m. Vivian Burey, Sept. 4, 1929 (dec. Feb. 1955); m. 2d, Cecilia A. Suyat, Dec. 17, 1955; children—Thurgood, John. Admitted to Md. bar 1933, individual practice, Balt., 1933-37; asst. spl. counsel N.A.A.C.P., 1936-38, spl. counsel, 1938-50, dir., counsel legal def. and ednl. fund, 1940-61; U.S. circuit judge for 2d jud. circuit, 1961-65; solicitor gen. of U.S., Dept. Justice, Washington, 1965-67; asso. justice Supreme Ct. U.S., Washington, 1967—. Civil rights cases argued include: Tex. Primary Case, 1944; Restrictive Covenant Cases, 1948; U. Tex. and Okla. Cases, 1950; sch. segregation cases, 1952-53; visited Japan and Korea to make investigation of ct. martial cases involving Negro soldiers, 1951. Mem. N.Y. State Commn. World's Fair. Cons. Constl. Conf. on Kenya, London, 1960; rep. White House Conf. Youth and Children. Bd. dirs. John F. Kennedy Meml. Library; mem. coll. electors Hall of Fame N.Y. U. Recipient Spingarn medal, 1946; Living History award Research Inst. Mem. Am., Nat. bar assns., Assn. Bar City N.Y., N.Y. County Lawyers Assn., Alpha Phi Alpha. Episcopalian. Mason (33 deg.). Home: 6233 Lakeview Dr Falls Church VA 22041 Office: Supreme Court US Washington DC 20543

MARSHALL, VIRGIL HARRISON, dentist; b. Newport News, Va., May 7, 1922; s. Albert Holman and Vera Adel (Hall) M.; student Va. Poly. Inst., 1942-43 45-46; D.D.S., Med. Coll. Va., 1950; m. Evelyn Ruth Gardner, June 16, 1947; children—Virgil Harrison, Marilyn Gardner, David Randolph. Intern in oral surgery Med. Coll. Va. Hosp., 1950-51; practice of gen. dentistry, Charlottesville, Va., 1951—; pres. Beaver Dam Land Corp., Charlottesville, 1964, V.H.M. Corp., 1962; v.p. M & O Corp. 1967, Terrace Devel. Corp., 1965; dir. Farmington, Inc., 1971—; Va. Nat. Bank, Farmington Property Owners, Inc. Bd. dirs. United Givers Fund, 1961-66, vice chmn. campaign, 1965, chmn. campaign, 1966. Served to 1st lt., USAAF, 1943-45. Fellow Va. Dental Assn.; mem. Am. Dental Assn. (mem. at large exec. council 1968-70), Va. Artificial Kidney Assn. (pres. 1967—), Atwood Wash Soc., Omicrom Kappa Upsilon, Psi Omega. Episcopalian (vestryman 1968-71). Mason (Shriner), Rotarian. Contbr. to ency. Home: 3 Oak Circle Farmington Charlottesville VA 22901 Office: 306 E Jefferson Charlottesville VA 22901

MARSHALL, WALLACE, physician, surgeon; b. Appleton, Wis., July 19, 1904; s. Victor F. and Fanny (Levy) M.; B.A., U. Wis., 1930; B.M., Northwestern U., 1932, M.D., 1933; m. Louise Marjorie Clayton, Aug. 14, 1953; 1 dau., Victoria Louise. Intern, Wesley Hosp,, Wichita, Kan., 1932, Los Angeles County Gen. Hosp., 1932-33; pvt. practice medicine, Two Rivers, Wis., 1949-59, Watertown, Wis., 1959-61, Florida, Ala., 1961-62, Heflin, Ala., 1962, Anniston, Ala.; instr. physiol. chemistry, medicine U. Ala., 1936-37; asso. prof. physiol. chemistry Spring Hill Coll., 1947; lectr. sci. research St. Norbert Coll., 1953; fellow psychiatry La. State U.-Charity Hosp. of La., New Orleans, 1966-67; med. cons. to pharm. firms; prof. psychology Auburn U., Montgomery, 1971—; staff psychiatrist Bapt. Hosp., Montgomery, Jackson Hosp., Montgomery. Recipient certificate of award Med. Econs., 1967. Fellow A.A.A.S., Am. Med. Writers Assn. (life), Miss. Valley Med. Soc. (life dir., Wis. v.p. 1959-61), Royal Soc. Health, Acad. Psychosomatic Medicine; mem. Indian Assn. Dermatologists and Venereologists (life), Nat. Writers Club, A.M.A., Am. Fedn. Clin. Research, Wis, (sec., program chmn. 5th councillor dist., 1956-57), Montgomery County med. socs., Med. Assn. State Ala., So. Med. Assn., Am. Acad. Gen. Practice (past chpt. pres.). Mason (32 deg., Shriner). Author: Noise of Great Waters (1st prize Am. Physicians Literary Guild), 1947; Essentials of Medical Research, 1953; numerous med., surg. articles. Asso. editor: Med. Times, 1943-63; cons. editor gen. practice of Med. Digest, 1957—; abstract editor Psychol. Reviews, 1938-40; book review editor Mississippi Valley Med. Jour., Clin. Medicine, 1959-61; hon. cons. editor Med. Digest, Bombay, India, 1960—. Discovered and produced microcirculatory constrictor from crude liver, Kutapressin, 1950; co-discoverer Marshall-White syndrome, 1965; originator theory of psychoallergy. Address: 2326 Winchester Rd Montgomery AL 36111

MARSHBURN, JOSEPH HANCOCK, educator; b. Josselyn, Ga., Jan. 11, 1890; s. M. Thomas and Alice Verina (Hendricks) M.; A.B., U. Ga., 1911, A.M., 1912; A.M., Harvard, 1919; Yale fellowship, 1923; Ph.D., Cornell, 1927; m. Mary Amoss, Jan. 17, 1919; 1 son, Joseph Hancock. Instr. English, U. Ga., 1912-14; head dept. English, Ga. Mil. Coll., 1914-16, v.p., 1916-17, pres., 1917-20; prof. English, U. Okla., 1920—, ret. chmn. dept. Reader, Folger Shakespeare Library, 1936, Brit. Mus., 1948-49; David Ross Boyd prof. English lit., 1949. Mem. Royal Soc. Lit., Modern Lang. Assn., Am. Assn. U. Profs., Sigma Chi, Phi Beta Kappa. Democrat. Episcopalian. Mason (K.T., Shriner), Lion. Author: Murder and Witchcraft in England, 1550-1640, 1972. Home: 652 Reed Av Norman OK 73069

MARTELL, HELEN MARIE, civic worker; b. Boston, Mar. 12, 1906; d. Charles Joseph and Helen (Contee) Martell; LL. B., George Washington U., 1939, A.B., 1940. With Potomac Electric Power Co., 1933-71, asst. sec., 1950-71, asst. treas., 1961-68, treas., 1968-71. Former area co-chairman United Givers Fund; mem. membership and budget com. Health and Welfare Council, Nat. Capital Area, Washington. Mem. Colonial Dames of Am. (chmn. com. 1971—), Descs. of Lords of Md. Manors, Order of Coif, Panhellenic (Washington pres. 1937-38), Phi Delta Delta, Delta Zeta. Republican. Roman Catholic. Clubs: Zonta (Washington pres. 1969-70). Washington. Contbr. articles to profl. mag. Student editor: George Washington Law Rev., 1938-39. Home: 9622 Alta Vista Terrace Bethesda MD 20014

MARTH-SNADER, ELLA CAROLYN MARTH (MRS. DANIEL W. SNADER), educator; b. Alton, Ill.; d. Louis George and Elizabeth (Krauskopf) Marth; A.B., Harris Tchrs. Coll., 1930; M.S., St. Louis U., 1935, Ph.D., 1944; m. Daniel W. Snader, July 28, 1956. Tchr. pub. schs., St. Louis, 1930-44; asst. prof. math. Harris Tchrs. Coll., 1945-47, dean of women, asso. prof., 1947-52; prof., chmn. div. math. and bus. edn. D.C. Tchrs. Coll., 1952-56, prof., 1960—; asso. prof. div. math. Chgo. Tchrs. Coll., 1956-59; specialist elementary math. U.S. Office of Edn., Washington, 1959. Cons. elementary math. Mem. St. Louis Assn. for Human Relations, 1950. Mem. Am. Math. Soc., Nat. Council Tchrs. Math., Central Assn. Sci. and Math. Tchrs. (dir. 1949, 51-53), N.E.A., Am. Personnel and Guidance Assn., Sigma Xi, Pi Mu Epsilon, Delta Kappa Gamma. Unitarian. Contbr. articles to profl. jours. Home: 3701 Connecticut Av NW Washington DC 20008 Office: 1100 Harvard St NW Washington DC 20009

MARTIN, ABE OTHEL HERSHEL, univ. athletic dir.; b. Jackson, Tex., Oct. 18, 1908; s. Tim and Molly (Swan) M.; B.Ed., M.A., Tex. Christian U.; m. Sally Ann Martin, Aug. 17, 1932; 1 son, Don D. Coach high sch., El Paso, Tex., 1932-36, Lubkin, Tex., 1936-43; with Standard Oil Co. Tex., 1943-44; coach Paschal High Sch., Ft. Worth, 1944-45; football coach, athletic dir. Tex. Christian U., 1945-69, athletic dir., 1969—. Mem. Am. Football Coaches Assn. (pres. 1965). Home: 3700 Wedghill Way Fort Worth TX 76133

MARTIN, ALBERT BOYNTON, coll. pres.; b. Wanza, Brit. E. Africa, Nov. 27, 1912; s. Albert Ephraim and Catherine Marie (Cilliers) M.; A.B., S.W. Tex. State Coll., 1934; Ed.M., U. Tex., 1941, Ed.D., 1949; m. Pauline Buchwald, Feb. 15, 1936. Tchr., coach Santa Rosa High Sch., 1934-35; prin. Tabasco High Sch., La Joya, Tex., 1935-39, supt. schs., 1939-41; dep. state supt. Tex. Dept. Edn., 1941-42, dir. equalization, 1945-47, dir. curriculum, 1948-49; dir. extension, dir. summer session, and prof. edn. U. Miss., 1949-51; v.p. Fla. State U., 1951-59; pres. Amarillo (Tex.) Coll., 1960—. Chmn. State Commn. on Edn., Tex., 1946-47; mem. State Com. on Certification Regional Edn., 1957-58; chmn. State Fulbright Com., 1957-59; exec. dir. Tex. Gov.'s Com. on Edn. Beyond the High Sch., 1963; mem. Potter and Randall County (Tex.) Citizen's Com.; bd. dirs. YMCA, Amarillo, United Fund, Amarillo. Served as lt. comdr. with USNR, 1942-45. Mem. Tex. Jr. Coll. Assns., Am. Assn. Jr. Colls. (mem. commn. instruction), Fla. Edn. Assn., Fla. Assn. Coll. and Univs. (pres. 1958-59), Assn. Tex. Colls. and Univs. (chmn. commn. on classification and membership 1969-70), Amarillo C. of C. (dir.), Am. Legion, Phi Delta Kappa, Phi Delta Theta, Omicron Delta Kappa, Gold Key. Methodist. Mason. Rotarian (pres. Amarillo 1966).

Club: Amarillo Knife and Fork (pres. 1965). Author bulls. on curriculums. and sch. and coll. adminstrn. Home: 2617 Curtis Dr Amarillo TX 79109

MARTIN, ALBERT ERSKINE, JR., fiber producer exec.; b. Rome, Ga., Jan. 22, 1919; s. Albert Erskine and Pauline (Taylor) M.; B.S., Tulane U., 1945, M.S., 1946; postgrad. Brown U., 1947-50; m. Rosemay Yvonne Carrere, Aug. 22, 1958; 1 son, Albert Erskine III. Sr. physicist U.S. Dept. Agr., So. Regional Research Lab., New Orleans, 1950-57; head textile physics sect. textile research and devel. Courtauld, Inc., Mobile, Ala., 1957-62; mgr. tech. services Firestone Synthetic Fibers Co., Hopewell, Va., 1962—, now mgr. applications research. Spl. lectr. physics Spring Hill Coll., Mobile, 1957-59; instr. physics Tulane U., 1945-47, 52-57, Brown U., 1947-50; mem. research adv. council Auburn U. Textile Sch., 1959-61. Committeeman, merit badge counsellor Boy Scouts Am., Richmond, Va., 1962—. Bd. dirs. Old Dominion chpt. Nat. Cystic Fibrosis Research Found. Mem. Fiber Soc., Am. Soc. for Testing Materials, Am. Assn. Textile Technologists, Am. Radio Relay League. Patentee in field. Home: 4221 Stratford Rd Richmond VA 23225 Office: PO Box 450 Hopewell VA 23860

MARTIN, ALLEN JACKSON, JR., hosp. adminstr.; b. Ruffin, N.C., Sept. 12, 1931; s. Allen Jackson and Pearl (Kennedy) M.; A.B., Elon Coll., 1958; m. Mary Anne Ward, June 18, 1954; children—Allen Jackson, Jeffrey Ward, Mary Celeste. Asst. adminstr. Meml. Hosp., Danville, Va., 1959; adminstr. Washington County Hosp., Plymouth, N.C., 1959-66, Lower Florence County Hosp., Lake City, S.C., 1966-69; cons. for planning Edgefield (S.C.) County Hosp., 1969-71, adminstr., 1971—. Bd. dirs. Albemarle Area Devel. Corp., 1964-66. Mem. N.C. (dist. pres. 1965-66), S.C. hosp. assns., Plymouth and Washington County C. of C. (pres. 1965). Presbyn. (deacon, elder, lay minister). Rotarian. Home: Bausket St Edgefield SC 29824 Office: Edgefield County Hosp Edgefield SC 29824

MARTIN, BENNY WORTH, dentist; b. High Point, N.C., May 9, 1931; s. Jesse Worth and Murphy Irene (Joyce) M.; B.S., High Point Coll., 1954; D.D.S., U. N.C., 1958; M.S.D., U. Minn., 1964; m. Shirley Goodale Purinton, July 25, 1959; children—Jesse Worth, George Kinner, Dennis Vernon, Gordon Hunter, Amy Purinton. Clin. Instr. Sch. Dentistry, U. N.C. Dept. Oral Surgery, 1958-59, cons., part time instr., 1970—; intern oral surgery Mayo Clinic, Rochester, Minn., 1961-62, resident oral surgery, 1962-64; practice dentistry specializing in oral surgery, Raleigh, N.C., 1954—. Oral surgery cons. N.C. Dept. Correction, Raleigh, 1964—, Wayne County Meml., Johnston County Meml., Wilson Meml. hosps.; mem. staff Wake County Meml. Hosp., Rex Hosp., Raleigh. Chmn. dental div. N.C. Cancer Soc., 1967, 68; mem. exec. com., bds. dirs. N.C. div. Am. Cancer Soc., 1967, 68. Served to capt. Dental Corp, USAF, 1959-61. Diplomate Am. Bd. Oral Surgery. Mem. Am., N.C. dental assns., Am. N.C. socs. oral surgeons, Am., N.C. socs. dental anesthesia, Sigma Phi Epsilon, Psi Omega. Methodist. Home: 5424 Thayer Dr Raleigh NC 27609 Office: Building E Glenwood Professional Village Raleigh NC 27608

MARTIN, BROOKS, architect; b. Colorado, Tex., Sept. 23, 1913; s. A.D. and Ury (Brooks) M.; B.Arch., Tex. A. and M. Coll., 1940; B.Arch., Harvard, 1952, M.Arch., 1953; m. Orabel Foster, May 16, 1941. Pvt. practice, Bryan, Tex., 1948-51, San Antonio, 1959—, Mexico, 1962—; asst. architect Tex. A. and M. Coll. system, 1945-48; cons. architect Fehr & Granger, Austin, Tex., 1950; designer-architect Carl Kock, Boston, 1952; asso. architect Hugh Stubbins, Jr., Boston, 1952-54; architect Samuel Glaser Assos., Boston, 1955; sr. research architect Southwest Research Inst., San Antonio, 1956-58; vis. critic design Harvard, 1953, Boston Archtl. Center, 1955; group exhbn. San Antonio Press Club, 1962; prin. works include St. Mary's U. Law Sch., 1959, Cambridge Oval Apts., Alamo Heights, 1959, Canyon Creek Country Club, 1959, St. Cecelia's, also St. Margaret Mary parish schs. and rectory, 1959, McDavitt Lester Ins. Bldg., 1958, residences for John Fonveilles, 1959, Elbert DeCourseys, 1959, W. S. Lights, 1960, Navarro Houses restoration, 1962-64, Aransas Pass subdiv., 1962, Cambridge Oval Duplex, 1964, McCullough Med. Center, 1962, Dougherty Tea House, also Dougherty Office Bldg., 1964, town houses Cambridge Oval, 1964, Chandler Bldg. remodeling, 1964; resident architect W.S. Light Devel. Co., 1959—; archtl. adviser, pres. Jackson Todd Memorial Found. Cancer Research; interior design project Dempsey-Tegler, 1960, N. Star Mall and McCrelless Shopping Center, 1960; coordinating architect St. Mary's U., 1964; resident architect Fomento Economico Monterrey, S.A., Mexico, 1959; prin. works in Mexico City include Cine Tacubaya, 1963, apt. house project, 1963. Recipient Guptill certificate Tex. A. and M. Coll., 1941; winner U.S. Plywood Co. regional competition, 1940, Fenestra Co. regional competition, 1940. Sec. Savannah Corp., San Antonio, Argyle Investment Co., San Antonio. Bd. dirs. Jackson Todd Cancer Research Found., 1960—, La Prensa, 1959-61. Served with AUS, World War II. Decorated Purple Heart. Mem. A.I.A. (2d prize nat. journalism award 1959), Tex. Soc. Architects (award merit 1963), San Antonio Conservation Soc. (hon.), San Antonio C. of C. (chmn. projects com.), Alpha Rho Chi (medal 1952). Democrat. Episcopalian. Kiwanian. Home: 122 Downing St San Antonio TX 78209 Office: L-28 Kallison Tower San Antonio TX 78212 also Hamburgo Mexico City 6 Mexico

MARTIN, CHARLES ALVIN, JR., frozen food industry exec.; b. Nashville, Sept. 5, 1923; s. Charles Alvin and Maude (Cameron) M.; grad. pub. schs.; m. Mary Virginia Tate, Oct. 22, 1946; children—Charles Douglas, Harriett Julia (Mrs. James P. Bennett), Deborah Tate. Vice pres., gen. mgr. Polar Refrigerated Services, Inc., Nashville, 1946-66, asst. to pres., 1966-72, pres., 1972—, also dir.; v.p. Frozen Foods Inc., Nashville, 1952-57; pres. Frozen Food Distbrs., Inc., St. Petersburg, Fla., 1959-69; v.p. Winter Garden Freezer Co., Inc., Bells, Tenn., 1969-71; gen. mgr., dir. Agrl. Services Assn., Bells., 1971—; comml. warehouse service officer Dept. Def., Chgo., 1950-51. Served with 1st Inf. Div., AUS, 1942-46. Decorated with two Bronze Star medals. Mem. Nat. Assn. Refrigerated Warehouses (mem. exec. com. 1960-63), Am., So. (dir. 1959-62) frozen food assns. Club: Exchange (Nashville). Home: 5821 Beauregard Dr Nashville TN 37215 Office: Polar Refrigerated Services Inc PO Box 1174 Nashville TN 37202

MARTIN, CHARLES EDWARD, educator; b. Mantee, Miss., Sept. 3, 1930; s. James Aaron and Armenda (Vaughn) M.; B.A., Miss. Coll., 1951; M.A., Tulane U., 1958, Ph.D., 1965; m. Anne Armstrong, Aug. 7, 1953; children—Carol Anne, James Charles, Ellen Elaine. Asst. prof., asso. prof., prof. Spanish, Miss. Coll., Clinton, 1957—, head dept. fgn. langs., 1966—, v.p. for acad. affairs, 1969—. Danforth asso. Served with AUS, 1951-54. Mem. Am. Assn. Honors Councils, Am. Assn. Tchrs. Spanish and Porguguese, Am. Council Tchrs. Fgn. Langs., South Central, Miss. (v.p.) modern lang. assns., Am. Assn. U. Profs. (past chpt. pres., sec. state conf.), Omicron Delta Kappa, Phi Sigma Iota, Phi Delta Kappa. Baptist (deacon). Home: 107 Billy Byrd Dr Clinton MS 39056

MARTIN, CHARLES KNOX, JR., coll. chancellor; b. Doniphan, Mo., Dec. 13, 1909; s. Charles Knox and Alva (Withers) M.; A.B., S.W. Mo. State Coll., 1932; M.A., U. Mo., 1935; Ph.D., Yale, 1939; m. Marguerite Peebles, Dec. 29, 1941; children—Charles Knox, Ann Withers. Tchr. Dixon (Mo.) High Sch., 1931-32, prin., 1932-34; supt. schs., Dixon, 1934-36; teaching asst. dept. edn. Yale, 1936-39; prof. edn. and psychology Mary Washington Coll. of U. Va., and 1939-52; pres. Radford (Va.) Coll., 1952-72, chancellor, 1972—. Dir. 1st and Mchts. Nat. Bank. Mem. brotherhood commn. So. Bapt. Conv. City councilman, Fredericksburg, 1948-52. Trustee Bluefield (Va.) Coll., Radford Community Hosp. Served as comdr., USNR, 1942—. Mem. Va. Edn. Assn., Am. Assn. Sch. Adminstrs., Am. Legion (past post comdr.), Omicron Delta Kappa, Phi Delta Kappa, Phi Kappa Phi. Kiwanian (past pres.). Home: 105 Dogwood Lane Radford VA 24141

MARTIN, MRS. CHESTER E., club woman; b. College Park, Ga., June 29, 1902; d. James Franklin and Etta (Doyal) Lambert; student U. Ga., 1919, Draughon's Bus. Coll., 1920; m. Chester Earle Martin, Nov. 4, 1922; 1 dau., Elsie Lambert (Mrs. John Wen Lundeen Jr.). Hon. consul for Guatemala to Atlanta, 1955-65. Pres., Hapeville Woman's Club, 1926, woman's council First Christian Ch., Atlanta, 1927, United Ch. Women Atlanta 1950-51, United Ch. Women Ga., 1952-53, Ga. Fedn. Women's Clubs, 1952-54, life dir.; southeastern council Gen. Fedn. Women's Clubs, 1954-56, gardens chmn., 1954-58, chmn. dept. fine arts, 1960-62, treas., 1964-66, pres. Past State Presidents Club, 1962-64; chmn. UN Day Observance, Atlanta, 1951, mem. bd. Atlanta UN, 1967—; bd. mem. Atlanta Goodwill Industries, 1948-58, Atlanta Girls' Club, 1955-57, United Ch. Women Atlanta, 1946-70; pres. Atlanta Music Club guild, 1972—; bd. mem. Atlanta Council Girl Scouts, 1948-57, mem. Juliett Low Regional Commn., 1954-66; mem. adv. bd. Fulton County Juvenile Ct., 1954-65; pres. bd. dirs. Savannah St. Mission Inc., 1958-65, finance chmn., 1965—; pres. Ga. Roadside Council, 1966; pres. Peachtree unit Parliamentary Law, 1969-71; parliamentarian women's com. Atlanta Symphony Guild, 1966-68; chmn. Japanese Internat. Christian U. Ga. Recipient Woman of Year in Civic Service award, Atlanta, 1950, master certificate for flower show judging Nat. Council State Garden Clubs, 1961. Life mem. Disciples of Christ Hist. Soc. Mem. Christian Ch. (pres. Altar guild). Club: Pan American (pres. Atlanta 1960-62). Author: Reverend James Franklin Lambert, 1965. Home: 300 Blackland Rd NW Atlanta GA 30342

MARTIN, CORA ARLETA, personnel specialist; b. Dean, Tenn., Sept. 30, 1923; d. Thomas Crawford and Florice (Gardner) Martin; certificate Bowling Green Bus. U., 1943. Clk. typist War Dept., Tullahoma, Tenn., 1943-46; payroll clk. VA and U.S. Dept. Agr., Atlanta, 1946-51; personnel rep. U.S. Army Corps of Engrs., Tullahoma, Tenn., 1951-60; placement and employee mgmt. relations specialist Army Rocket and Guided Missile Agy. and U.S. Army Missile Support Agy., 1960-69; personnel staffing specialist, fed. women's program coordinator U.S. Army Missile Command, 1969—. Chmn. Bedford County Heart Unit, 1964-67, vice chmn., 1967—. Mem. Soc. for Personnel Adminstrn., Shelbyville Bus. and Profl. Women's Club, Tenn. Fedn. Bus. and Profl. Women's Clubs, Inc. (pres. 1963, parliamentarian 1965-66, 71-72), Bedford County African Violet Soc., Federally Employed Women (chpt. pres. 1971-72). Home: 502 Riverview Dr Shelbyville TN 37160 Office: Civilian Personnel Office Redstone Arsenal AL 35809

MARTIN, CRAWFORD COLLINS, state ofcl.; b. Hillsboro, Tex., Mar. 13, 1916; s. William Marvin and Daisy (Beavers) M.; student U. Tex. Law Sch., 1936-38; LL.B., Cumberland U., 1939; m. Margaret Ann Mash, May 14, 1941; children—Sherry (Mrs. Tom Hill), James, Nancy. Admitted to Tex. bar, 1939; practiced in Hillsboro, 1939-63; mem. firm Martin & Martin, Hillsboro, 1946-63; sec. state State of Tex., Austin, 1963-67; atty. gen. of Tex., 1967—. Chmn. bd. Hillsboro State Bank, 1958—. Mayor, Hillsboro, 1946-47; mem. Tex. Senate, 1948-63. Served with USCGR, 1942-45. Mem. Am. Bar Assn., State Bar Tex. Democrat. Mason, K.P., Lion. Home: 5314 Western Hills Dr Austin TX 78731 Office: Supreme Ct Bldg Austin TX 78711

MARTIN, DAN ALTON, banker; b. Temple, Tex., Oct. 27, 1937; s. Alton C. and Lois (Garner) M.; B.S., Abilene Christian Coll., 1960, M.S., 1968; m. Meta Jan Caskey, June 26, 1961; 1 dau., Jan Catherine. Asst. trust officer, asst. cashier Frost Nat. Bank, San Antonio, 1961-67; v.p., cashier Lamesa Nat. Bank (Tex.), 1967—. Auditor, United Fund, Lamesa, 1969-70; treas. Dawson County unit Am. Cancer Soc., 1968, chmn., 1971; chmn. Dawson County chpt. Nat. Multiple Sclerosis Soc., 1968—, bd. dirs. Permian Basin chpt., 1971—. Bd. dirs. Dawson County Community Action Council, 1970-71, Boys Club. Mem. C. of C. (legislative com. 1970—). Optimist (pres. 1971-72). Mem. Ch. of Christ (Sunday sch. tchr.). Home: 805 N 17th St Lamesa TX 79331 Office: 112 N Houston St Lamesa TX 79331

MARTIN, DONALD THOMAS, ry. exec.; b. Richmond, Va., Dec. 6, 1913; s. Clarence Vincent and Pearl (Thirston) M.; B.S. in Bus. Adminstrn., Va. Poly Inst., 1934; m. Louise Whitehurst, June 12, 1937; children—Donald Thomas, Robert Eugene, Charles David. Terminal mgr., Brooks Transp. Co., Washington, 1935-41; mgr. Ft. Terminal VA, Richmond, Va., 1946-48; gen. mgr. Cabell Eanes Advt. Agy., Richmond, 1947, v.p., 1954-56; pvt. practice pub. relations cons., Richmond, 1955-58; dir. pub. relations, advt., A.C.L. R.R., Jacksonville, Fla., 1958-60, asst. v.p., 1961-67; asst. v.p. pub. relations and advt. Seaboard Coast Line R.R. Co., Jacksonville, 1967—; dir. Fla. Pub. Co. Jacksonville. Active various community drives; past pres. Duval county unit Am. Cancer Soc.; mem. univ. council Jacksonville U. Bd. dirs. Children's Home Soc., North Fla. council Boy Scouts Am., United Community Services, U.S.O., St. John's Country Day Sch.; chmn. bd. trustees Fla. Jr. Coll. at Jacksonville. Served to lt. col. AUS, 1941-46. Mem. Assn. Am. R.R.'s, R.R. Pub. Relations Assn., Fla., N.C., S.C. pub. relations assns., Pub. Relations Soc. Am., Assn. R.R. Advt. Mgrs. Roman Catholic. Rotarian. Club: Timuquana Country. Home: 4620 Avon Lane Jacksonville FL 32210 Office: 500 Water St Jacksonville FL 32202

MARTIN, DWIGHT WESLEY, broadcasting co. exec.; b. Kalamazoo, June 16, 1910; s. Arba and Virgie (Frantz) M.; A.B., Ohio Wesleyan U., 1931; LL.B., U. Cin., 1934; m. Jeannette B. Nichols, Sept. 7, 1936; children— Sally N., Jeannette F., Dwight Wesley (dec.). Admitted to Ohio bar, 1934; with trust dept. Central Trust Co., Cin., 1934-35; asso. Dinsmore, Shohl, Sawyer & Dinsmore, 1935-45, partner, 1945-46; v.p. Crosley Broadcasting Corp., 1946-52; v.p., dir. Gen. Teleradio, Inc. 1952-55, RKO Teleradio, 1955-56; exec. v.p. Lion Television Corp., 1956-59; chmn. bd. Modern Broadcasting Co. of Baton Rouge, Inc., 1956-64; v.p., treas., dir. Royal St. Corp., 1962—; pres., dir. Royal St. Investment Corp., New Orleans, Interchange Realty Co., Inc., 1963—; dir. Mission Hills Ranch, Inc., Royal St. Devel. Co., Inc., Broadcast Music, Inc., New Orleans Armature Works, Inc., New Orleans Electric Supply, The Urban Corp., Greater Park City Co. Bd. dirs. Cin. United Fund, 1950-52, Met. Crime Commn. Served as lt. comdr. USNR, 1943-45. Mem. Nat. Assn. Broadcasters (dir. 1958-62), Order of Coif, Phi Beta Kappa, Omicron Delta Kappa. Home: 415 Park Rd Metairie LA 70005 Office: 520 Royal St New Orleans LA 70130

MARTIN, EDMUND CLYDE, state ofcl.; b. Gainesville, Ga., Mar. 8, 1923; s. Webster W. and Winnie (Wood) M.; B.S., U. Ga., 1943, M. Edn., 1951, SU-6, 1953, Ed.D., 1964; m. Leila Carolyn Langford, July 28, 1946; children—Barbara Joan (Mrs. Loren H. Hill), Edmund Clyde. Tchr., Hall County Bd. Edn., Gainesville, Ga., 1946-49; prin., Maysville High Sch., 1949-51, Ila High Sch., 1951-54, Hart County High Sch., Hartwell, 1954-59, Cartersville High Sch., 1959-61; supt. schs., Cartersville City Schs., 1961-65; exec. dir. Ga. Ednl. Improvement Council, Atlanta, 1965—. Mem. Ga. Edn. Coordinating Com., 1966—, Lunch Room Council, 1969—, Ga. Regional Med. Program Regional Adv. Group, 1970—, Treas. Health Careers Council, Inc., 1968-70. Bd. dirs. Ga. State League for Nursing, 1969—. Served with AUS, 1943-46. Mem. N.E.A., Ga. Assn. Educators, Am. Assn. Sch. Adminstrs, Phi Delta Kappa, Kappa Delta Pi. Democrat. Baptist (ordained deacon, chmn. bd. deacons, 1950-60, supt. Sunday sch. 1963-64, Bapt. tng. union dir. 1964-65). Author: College Enrollment of Georgia's 1968 High School Graduates, 1969; Directory of Educational Opportunities in Georgia, 1968-69, rev. edit., 1970-71; (with David J. Tucker) Georgia Scholarship Guide, 1969-70, (with David J. Tucker) Investment and Implementation, 1966, (with Charles E. Hopkins) New Directions for Education in Georgia, 1966. Home: 2289 Shasta Way NE Atlanta GA 30345 Office: 7 Hunter St Bldg Atlanta GA 30334

MARTIN, EDWARD, physician; b. Atlanta, Nov. 24, 1910; s. John and Rosemarie (Claxton) M.; B.S., Cornell U., 1931; M.D., Chgo. Med. Sch., 1933; m. Alice Cartwright, Sept. 25, 1935; children—Edward, Benjamin, Hamilton. Intern, Presbyn.-St. Lukes Hosp., Chgo., 1933-34, resident, 1934-35; pvt. practice medicine, Decatur, Ga., 1935—. Cons., Decatur Bd. Pub. Health, 1956—. Served as capt. M.C., AUS, 1944-46. Diplomate Am. Bd. Family Practice. Fellow A.C.P.; mem. Ga., Decatur med. socs., A.M.A., Sigma Chi, Alpha Omega Alpha. Address: 3978 Phylis Pl Decatur GA 30032

MARTIN, EDWIN DAVIE, educator; b. Midlothian, Tex., Dec. 2, 1902; s. Raleigh and Annie Laura (Davie) M.; A.B., Abilene Christian Coll., 1923; M.S., Tex. A. and M. Coll., 1927; Ed.D., Colo. State Coll., 1941; m. Jewel McDonald, Aug. 12, 1923; 1 dau., Jean (Mrs. R. L. Sanders). Tchr. English, Mineral Wells, Tex., 1923-25; elementary prin., 1925-26; supt. A. and M. Consol., College Station, Tex., 1926-28; asst. prin. Hamilton Jr. High, Reagan Sr. High schs., Houston, 1928-36; prin. Hamilton Jr. High Sch., 1936-42; dir. research Houston Pub. Schs., 1946-55, asst. supt., 1955-61, dep. in charge of secondary edn., 1961-66; prof. edn. Houston Bapt. Coll., 1966—. Chmn. Census Tract div. Research Com., 1950—. Served to maj. AUS, 1942-46; lt. col., USAF Res. Recipient Honor Key award Kappa Delta Pi, 1963. Mem. Tex. Assn. Secondary Sch. Prins. (pres. 1938), N.E.A., Am. Ednl. Research Assn., Tex. Tchrs. Assn., Am. Statis. Assn., Am. Assn. U. Profs., S.A.R., (chpt. pres. 1970-71), Kappa Delta Pi (alumni counselor nat. exec. council 1968-71). Phi Delta Kappa. Mem. Ch. Christ (elder). Research in field. Home: 2341 Quenby St Houston TX 77005

MARTIN, EDWIN WILSON, JR., govt. ofcl.; b. Oceanside, N.Y., Sept. 3, 1931; s. Edwin W. and Jean (Carbone) M.; A.B., Muhlenberg Coll., 1953; M.A., U. Ala., 1955; Ph.D., U. Pitts., 1961; m. Margaret Anne Smith, Sept. 5, 1953; children—Scott Andrew, Bruce Leslie. Instr., U. Ala., 1955-57; clin. supr. U. Pitts., 1957-60; asst. prof., asso. prof. speech, co-dir. Speech and Hearing Clinic, U. Ala., 1960-67; dep. asso. commr. Bur. of Edn. for Handicapped, U.S. Office of Edn., Washington, 1967-69, asso. commr., 1969—. Dir. subcom. on handicapped U.S. Ho. of Reps., 1966-67. Fellow Am. Speech and Hearing Assn. (asso. editor 1961-62, cons. editor 1965-69); mem. Am. Psychol. Assn., Council for Exceptional Children. Home: 7013 Churchill Rd McLean VA 22101 Office: Bur Edn Handicapped US Office of Edn Washington DC 20202

MARTIN, FARRIS JAMES, JR., librarian; b. Greenville, Ala., Dec. 21, 1933; s. Farris James and Myrtiss Katherine (Germany) M.; B.S., U. Ala., 1956; M.A., Fla. State U., 1958; m. Emma Jean Worley, Aug. 27, 1959; 1son, Farris James III. Chemist, Ala. Hwy. dept., Montgomery, 1956-58; librarian sci., tech. social sci. depts. Enoch Pratt Free Library, Balt., 1959-60; head sci., indsl. dept. Dallas Pub. Library, 1960-61; dir. Montgomery Pub. Library, 1961—; library planning cons. Mem. Am., Ala. (past div. pres.) library assns., Phi Beta Kappa, Beta Phi Mu, Phi Kappa Sigma (past pres.). Author: Nonfiction Space Travel Literature, 1960. Home: 3560 N Georgetown Dr Montgomery AL 36109 Office: 445 S Lawrence St Montgomery AL 36104

MARTIN, FRANCIS LINTON, lawyer; b. Chattanooga, Jan. 6, 1891; s. Francis and Lydia (Linton) M.; Ph.B., Yale, 1912; LL.B., Columbia, 1915; m. Emily T. Kelley, Aug. 17, 1933; 1 dau., Caroline T. (Mrs. Erwin Brady Bartusch). Admitted to Tenn. bar, 1916, since practiced Chattanooga; mem. firm Miller, Martin, Hitching, Tipton, Lenihan & Waterhouse, 1923—. Served as 1st lt., 17th F.A., 2d Div., U.S. Army, 1917-19; AEF in France. Decorated Silver Star (U.S.); Fourragere of Croix de Guerre (France). Mem. Am. Bar Assn., Assn. Life Ins. Counsel. Clubs: Mountain City, Chattanooga Half Century. Home: 1914 Poplar Av Memphis TN 38104 Office: Volunteer Bldg Chattanooga TN 37402

MARTIN, GEORGE DAN, lawyer, state sen.; b. Jackson, Miss., Nov. 29, 1936; s. George Drew and Maggie Lee (O'Quinn) M.; student Ind. U., 1955-56; LL.B., Jackson Sch. Law, 1961; m. Marianna McLain, Dec. 27, 1959; children—Dana Virginia, Garron Patrick. With First Nat. Bank, Jackson, Miss., 1958-59, U.S. P.O., Jackson, 1959-60; admitted to Miss. bar, 1961; practiced in Brandon, 1961—; mem. firm Martin & Martin, 1966—. Partner Farm Bur. Ins. Cos., Rankin County, 1960-67; mem. Miss. Senate, 1968—. Served with USAF, 1955-58. Recipient Distinguished Service award Brandon Jaycees, 1962. Mem. Am., Miss., Rankin County bar assns., Miss. Jr. C. of C. (state pres. 1966-67), Rankin County C. of C., Sigma Delta Kappa. Baptist (chmn. bd. deacons 1969-70). Home: Bentonwood Dr Brandon MS 39042 Office: Box 9 Corner Hwy 18 and 80 Brandon MS 39042

MARTIN, HAROLD C., ednl. adminstr. Mem. Ala. Bd. Edn., Montgomery. Office: State Bd Education Education Bldg Montgomery AL 36104*

MARTIN, HAROLD EUGENE, newspaper pub.; b. Cullman, Ala., Oct. 4, 1923; s. Rufus John and Emma (Meadows) M.; B.A. with honors, Howard Coll., 1954; M.A., Syracuse U., 1956; m. Jean Elizabeth Wilson, Nov. 25, 1945; children—Brian, Anita. Asst. bus. mgr. Syracuse (N.Y.) Herald Jour., 1957-58; asst. prodn. mgr. St. Louis Globe Dem., 1958-60; asst. gen. mgr. Birmingham (Ala.) News, 1960-63; editor, pub. Montgomery (Ala.) Advertiser-Jour., 1963—; tchr. Howard Coll., 1961; v.p. Service Engraving Co., Advertiser Co.; pres. So. Publs., Inc., Baxter County Newspapers, Inc., Mountain Home, Ala., Ashley County Newspapers, Inc., Crosset, Ark., Cookeville Newspapers, Inc. (Tenn.). Adv. bd. Sch. Journalism Syracuse U. Mem. Mayor's Com. on Community Affairs. Bd. dirs. A.R.C. Served with USMCR, 1942-45. Recipient Citation mass communications Howard Coll., 1965, Green Eye Shade citation Sigma Delta Chi, 1969, Community Service award Ala. Asso. Press Assn., 1969, Pulitzer prize for local reporting, 1970; named Alumnus of Yr., Samford U., 1970. Mem. Downtown Unlimited. Baptist (bd. dirs. Ala. Bapt. publ., adv. com. Ala. Bapt. Home Mission Bd.).

Kiwanian. Home: 3620 McCurdy St Montgomery AL 36111 Office: 107 S Lawrence St Montgomery AL 36102

MARTIN, HAROLD HARBER, mag. writer, columnist; b. Commerce, Ga., Sept. 17, 1910; s. Gabriel Pierce and Mary Edna Augusta (Harber) M.; A.B. in Journalism, U. Ga., 1933; m. Boyce Lokey, Apr. 23, 1935; children—Marian Hamilton (Mrs. E. Thorpe Mealing), Harold Harber, John P., Nancy Boyce (Mrs. David E. Sparks). Sports writer Atlanta Georgian and Sunday Am., 1932-34; feature writer Atlanta Constn., 1934-39, columnist, 1939-43, 46-66; contbr. Harper's, Collier's, Liberty, Sat. Eve. Post, 1944-45, 50; asso. editor Sat. Eve. Post, 1951-53, contbg. editor, 1958-63, editor at large, 1964-69. Served to 1st lt. USMCR, 1943-45. Decorated Bronze Star. Mem. Sigma Delta Chi (Distinguished Service award and Bronze medal 1958). Club: Nat. Press (Washington). Episcopalian. Author: (with Gen. M. B. Ridgway) Soldier, 1956; (humor) Father's Day Comes Once a Year and Then it Always Rains, 1960; The Incredible Starlifter, 1972. Address: 2895 Normandy Dr NW Atlanta GA 30305

MARTIN, H(AROLD) LINDY, ednl. adminstr.; b. Christie, Va., May 29, 1931; s. R.M. and Beauty Martin; A.B., Pembroke State U., 1952; postgrad. Southeastern Sem., 1952-53; M.Ed., Auburn U., 1955; m. Anna Sue Ellard, June 11, 1955; children—John Lind, Sue Effin, Lumary Elizabeth, Leigh Frances, David Douglas. Ordained to ministry Bapt. Ch., 1952; grad. counselor Auburn U., 1954-55, head counselor, 1955-57; dir. student affairs Samford U., Birmingham, Ala., 1957-63, dir. aux. services, 1963-70, dean div. student services, 1970—. Chmn. bd. Nat. Entertainment Assos., Inc., Atlanta. Chaplain, Birmingham YWCA, 1963-68; mem. com. Operation Native Sons and Daus., 1968-69. Recipient Distinguished Service award Savannah (Ga.) State Coll., 1966; Outstanding Alumnus award Pembroke (N.C.) State U., 1968. Mem. So. Coll. Personnel Assn., So. Univs. Student Govt. Assn. (exec. dir. 1960-67, dir. div. creative and performing arts 1967-69), Birmingham C. of C. (edn. com. 1968-69), Pi Kappa Alpha, Phi Delta Kappa, Omicron Delta Kappa, Alpha Phi Omega. Author: A Handbook of Student Government, 1963; Student Representation in College and University Affairs, 1964. Home: 2749 Cherokee Rd Brimingham AL 35216

MARTIN, HENRY FAIN, bank exec.; b. Island Grove, Fla., May 9, 1903; s. Henry Coalson and Mittie Ann (Tompkins) M.; student Jacksonville Bus. Coll., 1920-21; m. Mae Stewart, June 10, 1928. Sec. to pres. Cumberland & Liberty Mills Co., Jacksonville, Fla., 1922-24; chief clk. to supt. sales Fla. dist. Tex. Co., 1924-26; pub. accountant, Jacksonville, 1926-28; clk. Atlantic Coast Line R.R. Co., Jacksonville, Fla., 1928-30, chief clk. to gen. agt., 1930-35, traveling freight agt., 1935-39, comml. agt., Perry, Fla., 1939-41, Orlando, Fla., 1941-48, supt. mine service, Mulberry, Fla., 1948-49, supt. Port Tampa Terminals, Port Tampa, Fla., 1949-60, mgr. Port Tampa Docks, 1960-67, dir. port traffic, 1967-68, ret., 1968; pres., Comml. Bank Tampa, Fla., 1960-66, chmn. bd., 1960—. Pres. Tampa Bay chpt. Nat. Def. Transp. Assn., 1960-61. Mem. Port Tampa C. of C. (pres. 1958-59). Baptist (trustee 1964—). Mason. Home: 3310 McKay Av Tampa FL 33609 Office: Comml Marine Bank 1770 N 50th St Box 5066Y Tampa FL 33605

MARTIN, IRA JAY, III, educator; b. Pawtucket, R.I., Sept. 2, 1911; s. Ira Jay and Vivian (Kinne) M.; Ph.B., Brown U., 1933; B.D., Andover Newton Theol. Sem., 1936; Th.D., Boston U., 1942; m. Ethel Virginia Augenstein, June 3, 1936; 1 dau., Rita Elaine Gay. Ordained to ministry Bapt. Ch., 1937; pastor Calvinistic Bapt. Ch., Woolwich, Me., 1934-35, Littleton Bapt. Ch., Littleton Common, Mass., 1936-41, First Bapt. Ch., Athol, Mass., 1941-44; instr. Bible; Berea (Ky.) Coll., 1944-50, asst. prof., 1950-59, asso. prof., 1959-66, Henry Mixter Penniman prof., 1966—. Dir. student work Bapt. Chs. Mass., 1936-44; dir. Wesley Found., 1948-62. Mem. Nat. Assn. Bibl. Instructors, Am. Acad. Religion (1st pres. 1964), Nat. Soc. Bibl. Lit. (sect. pres. 1961), Am. Inst. Archaeology, Am. Schs. Oriental Research, Am. Assn. U. Profs. Author: Faith of Jesus, 1956; Faith of Paul, 1965; Glossolalia in the Apostolic Church, 1960; Glossolalia: A Bibliography, 1970. Contbr. articles to profl. pubs. Home: 118 Van Winkle Dr Berea KY 40403

MARTIN, JACK, columnist; b. Buford, Ga., June 13, 1905; s. Vines and Azzie Lee (Barrett) M.; grad. high sch. Edna Mae Holcomb, July 31, 1937; 1 dau., Vanita Dolores (Mrs. Edwin Eugene Arnold). Salesman, Whittemore Shoe Polish Co., 1932-38, Tetley Tea Co., 1938-50, Taylor Bros., Inc., 1950-53, Goody's Mfg. Co., 1953-59; columnist Banner Herald, newspaper, Athens, Ga., 1963—. Portrayer Santa Claus in personal appearances, ann. radio shows, Athens Area, 1930's-65; program dir. Empty Stocking Fund, Athens, 1932-33; hon. historian Ga., 1971—. Recipient citation of appreciation Mayor of Athens, 1962; awarded 2d Ecumenical medal Pope Paul VI; awarded cruise aboard polaris nuclear submarine, 1967; named hon. historian of Athens, Ga., also historian Clarke Country; hon. citizen Okla., Fla. Mem. United Comml. Travelers (grand counselor Ga.-Fla. 1947-48), Nat. Showmens Assn., Circus Fans Assn., Circus Hist. Soc., Internat. Platform Assn. Democrat. Presbyn. (past chmn. bd. deacon). Elk, Moose. Address: 190 Best Dr Athens GA 30601

MARTIN, JACK T., basketball coach, educator; b. Desdemona, Tex., Aug. 15, 1922; s. Ernest William and Elizabeth (Meyers) M.; student Tarleton State Coll., 1939-41, Creighton U., 1943; B.S., Hardin-Simmons U., 1948, M.S., 1949; m. Shirley Gene Stephens, June 27, 1947; 1 dau., Sharon Lee. Prof., basketball coach Hardin-Simmons U., 1948-51, Lamar U., Beaumont, Tex., 1951—. Squadron comdr. Tex. Air N.G. Bd. dirs. Little League, Beaumont, 1960. Served with USAAF, 1942-45; PTO; now col. Res. Named coach of yr. Southland Conf., 1969, 70. Mem. Tex. N.G. Assn. (dir.), Nat. Basketball Assn. U.S.A. Lion. Home: 630 Zavalla Dr Beaumont TX 77705

MARTIN, JAMES D., mem. Republican Nat. Com., oil co. exec.; b. Tarrant, Ala., Sept. 1, 1918; s. Dick and Mary (Graham) M.; ed. bus. coll., law sch.; m. Patricia Huddleston, Dec. 27, 1959; children—James Douglas, Annette Graham, Richard Huddleston. Began career with Am. Oil Co., 1937; began Martin Oil Co., 1946, now pres.; mem. 89th Congress from Ala. Past pres., chmn. bd. Ala. Asso. Industries. Candidate for U.S. Senate, 1962; now mem. Republican Nat. Com. Served to maj. AUS, 1941-46; ETO. Kiwanian (past pres. Gadsden, Ala.). Home: 407 Country Club Dr Gadsden AL 35901

MARTIN, JAMES GLESGOW, JR., govt. ofcl.; b. Hendersonville, Tenn., May 8, 1918; s. James Glesgow and Edith (Coolidge) M.; student Falls Bus. Coll., Nashville, 1937-38, Internat. Accounting Soc., Chgo., 1949-52; m. Marjorie Collins, Nov. 9, 1942; children—James Glesgow III, John S. Formerly with Gen. Shoe Corp., Gallatin, Tenn.; revenue officer Internal Revenue Service, Chattanooga, 1945-51, div. chief spl. tax fraud squad, Nashville, 1951-52, acting chief Delinquent Accounts and Returns br., Nashville, 1952-54, chief, 1954-59, chief collection div., 1959-62, asst. to dist. dir., 1962-63, asst. dist. dir., Jackson, Miss., 1963-64, dist. dir., 1964-71, asst. regional commr. accounts, collection and prepayor service, southwest region, Atlanta, 1971—. Chmn. finance and fund raising com. Hiawatha dist. Boy Scouts Am., 1967-68, mem. Andrew Jackson council, 1966-68; chmn. Combined Fed. Campaign, Fed. agys., 1969. Pres. bd. dirs. Interagy. Bd. U.S. Civil Service Com. for Miss.; trustee United Givers Fund. Served to capt. AUS, 1941-45. Decorated Bronze Star with bronze oak leaf cluster, Purple Heart, Silver Star; recipient Superior and Outstanding Performance awards Internal Revenue Service. Mem. Jackson Fed. Execs. Assn. (pres.). Presbyn. Kiwanian (pres. 1969). Club: Colonial Country (Jackson). Home: 3819 N Stratford Rd NE Atlanta GA 30342 Office: Federal Office Bldg Peachtree Baker St Atlanta GA 30301

MARTIN, JAMES ROBERT, JR., U.S. dist. judge; b. Greenville, S.C., Nov. 30, 1909; s. James Robert and Lyda (Rankin) M.; LL.B., Washington and Lee U., 1931; m. Lydia Prichard, Dec. 19, 1929; children—Belle Mead (Mrs. Robert V. Heckel), Lydia (Mrs. Ben M. Sawyer, Jr.), Bobbie Jane (Mrs. Charles W. Traylor). Admitted to S.C. bar, 1931; practice in Greenville, 1931-44; judge 13th Jud. Circuit S.C., 1944-61; U.S. dist. judge Eastern and Western Dists. S.C., 1961-67; chief district judge U.S. Dist. S.C., 1967—. Mem. S.C. Ho. of Reps. from Greenville County, 1943-44. Mem. Am., S.C., Greenville County bar assns. Presbyn. Home: 401 Crescent Av Greenville SC 29605 Office: Federal Bldg and US Courthouse Greenville SC 29603

MARTIN, JOHN BEISEL, JR., dentist; b. Freeland, Pa., Oct. 25, 1927; s. John Beisel and L. (Virgil) M.; student Va. Poly. Inst., 1945-46, Ursinus Coll., 1947-49; D.D.S. U. Pa., 1953; m. Sandra Arline Anderson, Dec. 26, 1965. Instr., U. Pa., 1953-55; dentist Saucer Dental Clinic, Phila., 1953-55, Boston-Miami (Fla.) Clinic, 1955—; pvt. practice dentistry, Phila., 1953-55, Coconut Grove, Fla., 1955—. Minister of dissent Soverign Nation of New Atlantis, apptd. by Pres. Leicester Hemingway, 1965—; bd. dirs. Charity Dental Clinic, Coconut Grove Cares, 1970—; supt. Dade County Youth Fair, 1970—; pres. Miami Indoor Aircraft Assn., 1964—; asso. Salvation Army Charity Clinic, 1964—, Smithsonian Instn., 1968—. Served with AUS, 1945-47. Mem. Psi Omega. Republican. Mem. Christian Ch. Club: Miami Sports Car (pres. 1958-60). Editor Pa. Dental Jour., 1951-53. Address: 3225 Darwin St Coconut Grove FL 33133

MARTIN, JOHN BENNETT, JR., agronomist; b. West, Miss., Sept. 19, 1926; s. John Bennett and Lena (Weaver) M.; student Miss. Delta Jr. Coll., 1946-48; B.S., Miss. State U., 1951, M.S., 1954; postgrad. Ohio State U., 1957-59; Ph.D., Va. Poly. Inst., 1961; m. Sue Pounders, June 8, 1957; children—Richard John, Charles David. Field rep. Olin Mathieson Chem. Corp., Jackson, Miss., 1955; asst. agronomist Auburn (Ala.) U., 1956-57; asso. prof. agronomy and chemistry La. State U., Alexandria, 1961-66; agronomist TVA, Muscle Shoals, Ala., 1966—. Served with USNR, 1944-46, AUS, 1951-53. Mem. Am. Soc. Agronomy, Sigma Xi. Home: Route 7 Russellville AL 35653 Office: TVA Muscle Shoals AL 35660

MARTIN, JULIAN ALGERNON, law enforcement coordinator; b. Gibsland, La., May 22, 1908; s. Louis Frederick and Rosa (Cammack) M.; B.S., La. State U., 1931, M.S., 1933, J.D., 1936; m. Catherine Elizabeth May, Aug. 29, 1936; children—Julian Clark, Charles Russell, John Ashton. Technician, La. State Livestock Sanitary Bd., Baton Rouge, 1933-36; spl. agt. F.B.I., Ky., W.Va., Washington, 1936-45, sr. resident agt., Baton Rouge, 1945-60; coordinator La. State U. Law Enforcement Tng. Program, Baton Rouge, 1960-71, head dept. law enforcement, 1971—. Cons. law enforcement and training. Chmn. La. Commn. Standards and Edn., 1966-69; co-chmn. La. Commn. on Law Enforcement, 1967-69. Mem. Soc. Former Spl. Agts. F.B.I. (chpt. chmn. 1968-69). Baptist (deacon). Mason. Clubs: Kiwanis, High-Twelve. Home: 1331 Pickett St Baton Rouge LA 70808 Office: Pleasant Hall La State U Baton Rouge LA 70803

MARTIN, LEONARD WATSON, lawyer, state legislator; b. Nashville, Tenn., Aug. 9, 1935; s. Henry Watson and Winnie Dell (Thompson) Martin; B.S., U. Tenn., 1960, J.D., 1962; m. Margaret Helen Holcomb, July 6, 1956; children—Lee Watson, Sean Conrad, Kitty Suzanne. Admitted to Tenn. bar, 1962; mem. firms Gillenwater & Martin, Knoxville, Tenn., 1962-64, Stuart & Martin, Dickson, Tenn., 1965—; mem. Tenn. Ho. of Reps., 1968—, house majority leader, 1971—; sec., dir. West Hills Devel. Corp., Dickson, 1969; pres. Ventures, Inc., Dickson; dir. Farmers & Mchts. Bank, White Bluff, Tenn. Chmn. Heart Fund Campaign, 1966. Served with USMCR, 1953-57. Mem. Am., Tenn., Dickson County (pres. 1967), Dickson bar assns., Am., Tenn. trial lawyers assns., Am. Judicature Soc., Marine Corps Res. Officers Assn., Dickson County C. of C. (pres. 1970—), U. Tenn. Alumni Assn. (pres. Dickson County 1966). Mason, Rotarian (pres. 1968-69). Clubs: Country, Peckerwood (Dickson). Home: Rock Church Rd Dickson TN 37055 Office: 223 N Main St Dickson TN 37055

MARTIN, LEROY ALBERT, univ. chancellor; b. Morristown, Tenn., Jan. 15, 1901; s. Burton McMahan and Julia (Haggard) M.; student Tenn. Wesleyan Coll., 1921. LL.D., 1959; A.B., U. Chattanooga, 1924, D.D., 1946; S.T.B., Boston U., 1928; A.M., Drew U., 1931; m. Ruth Duckwall, Aug. 10, 1927; children—Julia Carolyn (Mrs. Clifford A. Betts Jr.), Elizabeth Blackburn (Mrs. Archibald Calder Willingham III). Tchr., Baylor School, Chattanooga, 1924-25; ordained to ministry Methodist Ch., 1927; minister, Bristol, Tenn., 1928-30, Paterson, N.J., 1932-36, Hackettstown, N.J., 1936-37, Madison, N.J., 1937-45; supt. Western Dist., Meth. Conf., Newark, 1945-50; lectr., practical theol. Drew Theol. Sem., 1948-49; pres. Tenn. Wesleyan Coll., Athens, 1950-59; pres. U. Chattanooga, 1959-66, chancellor, 1966—, prof. classics, 1968—. Mem. exec. com. Chattanooga-Hamilton County chpt. A.R.C. Bd. dirs. Community Found. of Greater Chattanooga. Elected Athens Man of Year, 1955; recipient Outstanding Civilian Service medal Dept. Army. Mem. Chattanooga C. of C., Newcomen Soc., Blue Key, Pi Gamma Mu, Alpha Soc. (U. Chattanooga), Sigma Chi. Clubs: Monday (past pres. N.Y.C.); Rotary (pres. 1968-69), Fairyland, Mountain City. Author: A History of Tennessee Wesleyan College, 1857-1957. Home: 619 W Brow Rd Lookout Mountain TN

MARTIN, LOIS ESTELLE, educator; b. Berry, Ala., Jan. 1, 1914; d. John W. and Eliza (Moore) Baker; B.S., North Tex. State U., 1940, Ed.D., 1964; M.S., U. Ill., 1942; m. H. Gebhard Martin, Aug. 26, 1933 (dec. Jan. 1952); children—Jois Elizabeth (Mrs. James A. Ross), Kenneth Gebhard. Tchr. elementary sch., Cleburne, Tex., 1934-39, Forsan, Tex., 1939-40, Sweetwater, Tex., 1941-42; elementary and secondary tchr., counselor, Wichita Fallas, Tex., 1952-64; prof. edn. Hardin-Simmons U., Aiblene, Tex., 1964-67, dir. guidance edn., 1965—, head dept. spl. edn. and guidance, 1970—. Cons. jr. coll. Pres. Woman's Missionary Soc., 1950-51; dist. chmn. Guidance Assn., 1959-60; pres. P.T.A., 1937-38; coordinator Guidance Services, 1963-64; sponsor Tex. Student Edn. Assn., 1964—. Recipient Distinguished Alumni award North Tex. State U., 1964. Mem. Am. Assn. U. Women, U. Women's Club (pres. 1966-67), City Tchrs. Assn. (pres. 1962-63), Women's Study Club (pres. 1956-57), Tex. Soc. Coll. Tchrs. Edn., N.E.A., Tex. Tchrs. Assn., Tex. Personnel and Guidance Assn., Delta Kappa Gamma (pres. 1965-66). Baptist (Sunday sch. tchr. 1942-46, tng. union dir. 1942-51, Sunday sch. supt. 1947-62). Mem. Order Eastern Star (past worthy matron). Contbr. to mags., newspapers. Home: 641 Westwood Dr Abilene TX 79603

MARTIN, MACEO CONRAD, banker; b. Pittsylvania County, Va., June 18, 1897; s. Romey Orlando and Hattie Rosina (Inge) M.; student Pittsylvania Indsl. Inst., 1912-14, Va. Union U., 1915-17; m. Elaine Henderson, Nov. 26, 1920 (dec. 1931); children—Hattie Irene, Maceo Conrad, Edwina Mae; m. 2d, Georgia Hortense Person, Dec. 11, 1943; 1 dau., Paula K. Cashier Danville Savings Bank & Trust Co. (Va.), 1919-46; exec. v.p., cashier, 1942-51, pres. successor co., First State Bank 1952—, also chmn. bd. dirs.; pres. Washington-Douglas Drug Co., 1952—. pres., Va. Council on Human Relations, 1967—. Trustee Va. Union U., 1958—. Mem. Nat. Bankers Assn. (sec. 1929-52), pres. 1952—). Democrat. Baptist. Mason (33 deg., Shriner). Home: 1145 Piney Forest Rd Danville VA Office: 201 N Union St Danville VA

MARTIN, MARTIN HOWARD, grocery co. exec.; b. Lubbock, Tex., July 2, 1916; s. Ronald Hilton and Mary Emily (Gilmore) M.; student Tex. Tech. U., 1940-41, Dunwoody Inst., Mpls., 1936-37; m. Billie A. Macha, Sept. 18, 1933; children—Sandra Kathleen (Mrs. Chester A. Gutzman), Carol Ann (Mrs. Richard W. Smith). Br. mgr. Red Star Yeast & Products Co., Dallas 1942-43, supervising br. mgr., Oklahoma City, 1943-44; bakery mgr. H.E. Butt Grocery Co., Corpus Christi, Tex., 1944-54, dir. bakery operations, 1954-67, dir. mfg., 1968, v.p. mfg., 1968—. Mem. Tex. Bakers Assn. (pres. 1965-66), Am. Soc. Bakery Engrs. Mason (K.T.). Home: 5006 Wooldridge Rd Corpus Christi TX 78413 Office: PO Box 9216 Corpus Christi TX 78408

MARTIN, MELVIN LEWIS, mech. engr.; b. Elgin, Neb., Mar. 26, 1923; s. Ernest C. and Goldie M. (Norton) M.; student U. Denver, 1941-42, Rockhurst Coll., 1943; B.S., U. Colo., 1948; postgrad. Am. U., 1966-68; m. Bettie Leigh Richardson, Jan. 24, 1943; children—Lawrence R., Donald K., Douglas C. Engr., Goodyear Tire & Rubber Co., Akron, O., 1948-49, Texas Co., Denver, 1949-51; engr. C.E., U.S. Army, Omaha, 1951-56, Los Angeles, 1956-62, supervisory engr. Office Chief Engrs., Washington, 1962—. Cons. welding, pipelines, pressure vessels. Com. chmn. Boy Scouts Am., Whittier, Cal., 1958-60, Alexandria, Va., 1963, scoutmaster, 1967—; v.p. dir. membership Rose Hill Farms Community Center, 1967-71. Served with USAAF, 1943-46. Recipient Performance award Engrs. Joint Council, 1969. Registered profl. engr., Colo., Tex., D.C. Mem. Am. Soc. M.E., Am. Welding Soc., Am. Vacuum Soc. Presbyn. Mason. Home: 6211 Redwood Lane Alexandria VA 22310 Office: Forrestal Bldg Washington DC 20314

MARTIN, NORENE DANN (MRS. JOSEPH W. MARTIN), assn. exec.; b. Fulton, N.Y., Mar. 22, 1917; d. Lee F. and Grace (Brown) Dann; grad. Black Mountain Coll., 1939; M.A., Columbia, 1940; student inst. for orgn. mgmt. Yale, 1958; grad. Inst. for Advanced Mgmt., Syracuse U., 1964; m. Joseph W. Martin, June 5, 1939; children—David Clark, Sara Walford, Martha Brown. Editorial asst. Macmillan Pub. Co., N.Y.C., 1942-46; editor Nat. Parking Assn., Washington, 1952—, asst. to the dir., 1958-65, exec. dir., 1965-68, exec. v.p., 1968—. Mem. parking com. Hwy. Research Bd., traffic safety com. Met. Washington Bd. Trade; dir. United Cerebral Palsy of Washington, 1964—, pres., 1969—. Mem. Am. Soc. Assn. Execs., Am. Hist. Assn., Washington Trade Assn., Washington Guitar Soc., Am. Assn. Univ. Women. Episcopalian. Editor: All Saints' Bull., monthly religious publ. 1958-64. Home: 3705 McKinley St NW Washington DC 20015 Office: 1101 17th St NW Washington DC 20036

MARTIN, OKIE RAYMOND, architect; b. Memphis, Jan. 13, 1924; s. Okie Raymond and Willie Martha (Peterson) M.; student Southwestern Coll., 1946, Tulane U., 1950; M.S. in Architecture, Va. Poly. Inst., 1953; m. Hazel Mae Brown, Jan. 29, 1949; children—Vann Raymond, Catherine Lynne, Dorothy Leith. Owner, Raymond Martin, Architect, Memphis, 1955-57; partner Martin & Adams, Architects, Memphis, 1957-61; pres., treas. Martin & Adams Architects, Inc., Memphis, 1961-62; pres., treas. Raymond Martin & Assos. Architects, Inc., Memphis, 1962—; v.p. Century Bldg. Corp., 1962—. Gen. chmn. Shelby and Crittenden counties Muscular Dystrophy Assn. Am., 1963, pres. Mid-South chpt., 1970—, nat. v.p., 1970—; col., aide de camp on staff Gov. Winfield Dunn, 1971—. Served to 1st lt. AUS, 1942-46, 50-52. Mem. A.I.A. (Silver medal award 1952, chpt. pres. 1962), Guild for Religious ArchitectureTenn. Soc. Architects (past v.p., dir.), Memphis C. of C., Tau Sigma Delta, Sigma Nu. Baptist (chmn. deacons). Clubs: Executives; Park Woodland Civic (past pres.). Important works include Century Bldg., Memphis, 1959, First Assembly of God Ch., Memphis, 1962, Liberty Nat. Bank-Suburban Bldg., Louisville, 1962, Memphis State U. Sch. Edn. and Campus Sch., 1963, Univ. Center, 1967, Wooddale High Sch., Memphis, 1967, Activities Bldg. for Walnut St. Bapt. Ch., Louisville, 1970, Memphis State U. Engring Sci. Bldg., 1970, Engring. Tech. Bldg., 1971. Home: 180 S Goodlett St Memphis TN 38117 Office: 3294 Poplar Av Memphis TN 38111

MARTIN, PATRICK GLENN, fire chief; b. Childress, Tex., Apr. 3, 1930; s. John Middleton and Ila May (Waller) M.; grad. high sch.; m. Jacqueline Pearl Hargett, Nov. 29, 1969; children—Patrick Glenn, Jr., Alana, Barbara, Brenda, Cheri. Fireman, Arlington, Tex., 1952-56, Capt., 1956-58, tng. officer, 1958-62, asst. chief, 1962-65, fire chief, 1965—. Asst. field supr. fire fighting course Tex. A. and M. U., 1970-71. Mem. adv. com. fire protection Tarrant County Jr. Coll., 1968-71. Served with AUS, 1947-50; Korea. Recipient Civil Def. Award Merit Ft. Worth, Tarrant County Civil Def. Office, 1957. Mem. N. Tex. Firemans Assn. (pres. 1970-72), Tex. Fire Chiefs, Southwestern Fire Chiefs, Internat. Fire Chiefs. Baptist. Home: 2611 Monterrey St Arlington TX 76015 Office: 403 W Main St Arlington TX 76010

MARTIN, PAUL ELLIOTT, ret. bishop; b. Blossom, Tex., Dec. 31, 1897; s. Charles E. and Willie (Black) M.; A.B., So. Methodist U., 1919, LL.D., 1945; D.D., Southwestern U., 1938, Hendrix Coll., 1945; D.S.T., Oklahoma City U., 1968; m. Mildred Helen Fryar, June 29, 1920. Prin., Blossom (Tex.) High Sch., 1919, supt. pub. sch., 1920-22; ordained to ministry Methodist Ch., 1922, ordained deacon, 1924, elder, 1926 (North Tex. Conf.); pastor, Cedar Hill, 1922-24, Maple Av. Ch., Dallas, 1924-27, Henrietta, 1927-29, Iowa Park, 1929-30, Kavanaugh-Greenville, 1930-35; dist. supt. Wichita Falls Dist., 1935-38; pastor First Ch., Wichita Falls, 1938-44; bishop Meth. Ch. (elected at South Central Jurisdictional Conf.), 1944-68; assigned to Ark.-La. area, Little Rock, La. and North Ark. Confs., 1944-60, Houston Area, Tex. and Rio Grande Confs., 1960-68. Del. to Gen. Conf. of M.E. Ch., South, 1938, to Uniting Conf. of Meth. Ch., 1939, to Gen. Conf., Meth. Ch., 1940, 44; pres. council world service and finance, pres. council bishops Meth. Ch., 1961-62; chmn. U.S. sect. World Meth. Council; spl. lectr., counselor ch. adminstrn. Perkins Sch. Theology, So. Methodist U., 1968—. Trustee So. Meth. U., Southwestern U., Lon Morris Coll., Am. U., Tex. Meth. Children's Home, Lydia Patterson Inst., Sacritt Coll. Western Meth. Assembly and Meth. Hosp. Served as lt. inf. U.S. Army, World War I. Mem. Nat. Council Chs. of Christ Am., Sigma Alpha Epsilon, Tau Kappa Alpha, Theta Phi. Mason (33 deg.). Home: 6211 W Northwest Hwy Dallas TX 75225

MARTIN, PAUL LOGAN, mag. editor; b. Ft. Worth, Dec. 23, 1912; s. Rev. Logan and Julia (Pritchard) M.; A.B., Texas Christian U., 1933; student Harvard, 1935-36; m. Kathleene Gibbs, June 17, 1950; 1 dau., Susan P. Reporter, Oklahoma City Times, 1933-35; rewrite man Boston Herald, 1935-36, Boston Am., 1937; mng. editor Quincy (Mass.) Eve. News, 1936-37; polit. and legal corr. A.P., state capitol, Harrisburg, Pa., 1937-40; radio news editor Press Assn., Inc., A.P., N.Y.C., 1940-42; reporter Los Angeles Examiner, 1946; polit. and legal corr. Gannett Newspapers, Washington, 1947-50, chief bur., 1950-66; gen. editor nat. staff U.S. News & World Report, 1965—. Served to maj. USAAF, 1942-46; maj. Air Force Res. Recipient Raymond Clapper award, 1950. Mem. White House Corrs. Assn., Overseas Writers, Senate and House Press Galleries, Sigma Delta Chi. Clubs: Washington Golf and Country. Nat. Press, Gridiron, Metropolitan, 1925 F Street. Home: 3615 N Glebe Rd Arlington VA 22207 Office: 2300 N St NW Washington DC 20037

MARTIN, RACHEL SANGSTER, librarian; b. Mt. Olive, N.C., Aug. 18, 1918; d. Leon Forrest and Bertha (Reaves) Martin; B.A., Brenau Coll., 1939; B.S. in L.S., U. N.C., 1949; M.A., State U. Ia., 1955. Tchr. pub. schs., N.C., 1939-49; asst. reference librarian Auburn (Ala.) U., 1949-51; librarian Mary Baldwin Coll., Staunton, Va., 1951-56; head humanities div. library Fla. State U., Tallahassee, 1956-57; reference and serials librarian Furman U., Greenville, S.C., 1957—. Mem. Am. (reference and subscription books rev. Com. 1968—, Southeastern (chmn. nominating com. reference services div. 1960, vice chmn., chmn. reference services div. 1964-66), S.C. (sec. 1959, chmn. membership com. 1960-61) library assns., Am. Assn. U. Profs. (pres. Furman U. chpt. 1962-63), Delta Kappa Gamma, Beta Phi Mu, Zeta Tau Alpha. Baptist. Club: Altrusa (rec. sec. Greenville, 1959-61, archivist 1961-63, pres. 1966-68, parliamentarian 1970-71). Compiler index to articles Furman Studies 1959. Home: 219 Courtney Circle Greenville SC 29609 Office: Furman U Library Greenville SC 29613

MARTIN, ROBERT B., broadcasting exec. Vice pres., sta. mgr. WGBS, Miami, Fla. Office: 710 Brickell Av Miami FL 33131*

MARTIN, ROBERT RICHARD, coll. pres.; b. McKinney, Ky., Dec. 27, 1910; s. Henry Franklin and Annie Frances (Peek) M.; A.B., Eastern Ky. State Coll., 1934; M.A., U. Ky., 1940; Ed.D., Columbia U. Tchrs. Coll., 1951; m. Anne French Hoge, May 31, 1952. Tchr., prin. pub. schs., Mason and Lee counties, Ky., 1935-48; with Ky. Dept. Edn., 1948-60, successively auditor, dir. finance, head bur. adminstrn. and finance, 1948-55, supt. pub. instrn., 1956-59, commr. of finance, 1959-60; pres. Eastern Ky. U., 1960—. Assisted devel. found. program for financing of edn. in Ky.; mem. So. Regional Edn. Bd. Bd. dirs. Civil War Roundtable. Served as tech. sgt. USAAF, 1942-46, meterologist. Recipient Outstanding Alumnus award Eastern Ky. State Coll., 1956, Outstanding Kentuckian award Ky. Press Assn., 1964, Meritorious Service award Alumni Council Ky., 1970, Outstanding Civilian Service Medal Dept. of Army, 1971; grantee Danforth Found., 1971. Mem. N.E.A., Am. Assn. Sch. Adminstrs., Ky. Edn. Assn., Ky Council on Pub. Higher Edn., Council Chief State Sch. Officers, Am. Assn. State Colls. Univs. (pres. 1971-72), Phi Delta Kappa, Kappa Delta Pi. Democrat. Presbyn. (deacon). Mason, Rotarian. Home: 507 Lancaster St Richmond KY 40475

MARTIN, ROY BUTLER, JR., mayor; b. Norfolk, Va., May 13, 1921; s. Roy Butler and Anne (Holman) M.; student Norfolk div. William and Mary Coll., 1939-40; B.S. in Commerce, U. Va., 1943; m. Louise F. Eggleston, 1948; children—Roy Butler III, Ann Beverly. Pres. Foote Bros. and Co., food brokers; mayor Norfolk; dir. First Nat. Bank Norfolk. Mem. adv. bd. Nat. League of Cities; mem. com. on community devel., v.p. U.S. Conf. Mayors; past pres. Va. Municipal League. Bd. dirs. Norfolk Boys Club, Old Dominion Coll. Ednl. Found.; nat. adv. bd. MacArthur Meml. Found.; trustee Tidewater Va. Devel. Council. Mem. Norfolk Food Brokers Assn. (past pres.), Am. Legion (past comdr. post). Episcopalian. Clubs: Harbor, Princess Anne Country, Norfolk Yacht and Country. Home: 1519 Commonwealth Av Norfolk VA 23505 Office: City Hall Norfolk VA 23510

MARTIN, RUBY LEE GRANT (MRS. HENRY MARTIN), lawyer; b. Lake Village, Ark., Feb. 18, 1933; d. Ben F. and Jessie Grant; B.A., Fisk U., 1956; LL.B. cum laude, Howard U., 1959; m. Henry Martin, Oct. 21, 1961; 1 son, Tony. Admitted to Ohio bar, 1959; investigator civil rights div. Cleve. Community Relations Bd., 1959-60; staff atty. U.S. Commn. Civil Rights, 1960-65; asst. to civil rights program U.S. Dept. Health, Edn., Welfare, Washington, 1965-67, dir. office civil rights, 1967—. Bd. govs. Capitol Hill Day Sch. Named among Outstanding Women Am., 1967; named Outstanding Negro Woman of Year women's aux. Nat. Dental Assn., 1968; recipient Distinguished Service award Dept. Health, Edn., Welfare, 1968. Mem. Ohio Bar, Alpha Kappa Alpha. Episcopalian. Author publs. sch. desegregation for Commn. Civil Rights. Contbr. articles to law jours. Home: 3624 Southern Av SE Washington DC 20020

MARTIN, THEODORE KRINN, coll. ofcl.; b. Blue Mountain, Miss., Jan. 2, 1915; s. Thomas Theodore and Ivy (Manning) M.; A.B., Georgetown (Ky.) Coll., 1935; M.A., La. State U., 1941; Ph.D., George Peabody Coll., 1949; m. Lorene Garrison, Sept. 6, 1947; children—Glenn Krinn, Mary Ann, Janet Kay. Tchr., Consol. Sch., Dumas, Miss., 1935-36; prin. Mississippi Heights Acad., 1936-39; tchr. Murphy High Sch., Mobile, Ala., 1940-41; registrar Miss. State U., State College, 1949-53, registrar, adminstrv. asst. to pres., 1953-56, dean Sch. Edn., 1956-61, adminstrv. asst. to pres., 1959-61, exec. asst. to pres., 1961-66, v.p., 1966—, dir. Summer Sch., 1956—. Served as capt. AUS, 1941-46. Mem. Miss. Edn. Assn., Kappa Alpha, Phi Kappa Phi, Omicron Delta Kappa, Kappa Delta Pi, Phi Delta Kappa. Presbyn. Mason: Home: Sheely Hills State Coll MS

MARTIN, THOMAS JOHN, educator; b. Braddock, Pa., Aug. 12, 1935; s. Thomas John and Hazel (House) M.; B.S., Slippery Rock State Tchrs. Coll., 1958; M.Ed., U. Pitts., 1960; Ed.D., Fla. State U., 1964; m. Marilyn Jane Carson, Dec. 29, 1959; children—James Thomas, Kirk Stanley, Tamara Lynn. Grad. asst. Fla. State U., 1961-64; asst. prof. East Carolina Coll., Greenville, 1964-66; asso. prof. health and phys. edn. Va. Poly. Inst. and State U., Blacksburg, Va., 1966-71; asso. prof. health and phys. edn., chmn. dept., dir. athletics Roanoke Coll., Salem, Va., 1971—. Vis. prof. Slippery Rock State Coll., summers 1966, 67. Chmn. youth com. Blacksburg Community Fedn., 1966-71, v.p., 1970-71; chmn. Blacksburg Recreation Adv. Bd., 1970-71; pres. Blacksburg United Fund, 1971. Recipient Blacksburg Outstanding Young Man award, 1970. Mem. Va. Acad. Sci., Phi Epsilon Kappa (chpt. pres. 1962-63), Phi Delta Kappa, Sigma Delta Phi, Lambda Chi Alpha. Republican. Presbyn. Mason (32 deg.). Home: 3648 Barn Swallow Circle Roanoke VA 24018 Office: Roanoke College Salem VA 24153

MARTIN, VERNON NORTHFLEET, educator; b. Benham, Ky., Mar. 25, 1930; s. Oscar F. and Nancy Ellen (Burkhart) M.; B.A., U. Ky., 1955, M.A., 1958, Ph.D., 1968; m. Jessie Mae Worley, Oct. 15, 1950; children— Rebecca, Mark, John. Head polit. sci. dept. Cumberland Coll., Williamsburg, Ky., 1956-63; head. govt. dept. Western Ky. U., Bowling Green, 1963—. Served with USNR, 1948-49, 52-53. Home: 2031 Honeysuckle St Bowling Green KY 42101

MARTIN, WADE OMER, JR., state ofcl.; b. Arnaudville, La., Apr. 18, 1911; s. Wade O. and Alice (Mills) M.; B.A., Southwestern La. Inst., 1932, LL.B., La. State U., 1935; m. Juliette Bonnette, Oct. 25, 1938; children—Merle Mary, Marcelle, Wade O., III, David, Wallace, Gregory. Admitted to La. bar, 1935; asst. atty. gen., Baton Rouge, 1935-40; practice of law, Baton Rouge, 1940-44; sec. of state of La., 1944—. Mem. Am., La., East Baton Rouge Parish bar assns., Nat. Assn. Secs. of State (past. pres.; exec. com.), Nat. Assn. Ins. Commrs. (past pres.), Gamma Eta Gamma, Kappa Sigma. K.C. Home: 210 LSU Av Baton Rouge LA 70808 Office: State Capitol Baton Rouge LA 70804

MARTIN, WILLIAM CURTIS, educator; b. San Antonio, Dec. 31, 1937; s. Lowell Curtis and Joe Bailey (Brite) M.; B.A., Abilene Christian Coll., 1958, M.A., 1960; S.T.B., Harvard, 1963, Ph.D., 1969; m. Patricia Dale Summerlin, Dec. 31, 1957; children—Rex William, Jeffrey Summerlin, Elisabeth Dale. Instr. religion Dana Hall Sch., Welesley, Mass., 1965-68, chaplain, 1967-68; asst. prof. sociology Rice U., Houston, 1968—. Instr. Police Acad., Houston, 1970—. Pres., Fellowship for Racial and Econ. Equality, 1970-72. Bd. dirs. Houston Council on Human Relations, 1970—. Danforth Found. asso., 1970—. Recipient Nicolas Salgo Outstanding Tchr. award Rice U., 1971. Mem. Am. Sociol. Assn., Am. Soc. of Christian Ethics, Soc. for Sci. Study Religions. Democrat. Author: These Were God's People, 1966, Christians in Conflict, 1972. Contbr. articles to profl. jours. Home: 2148 Addison St Houston TX 77025

MARTIN, WILLIAM FREDERICK, oil co. exec.; b. Blackwell, Okla., Mar. 31, 1917; s. Fred and Emma (Buchholz) M.; B.S., U. Okla., 1938; m. Betty Jean Randall, Mar. 24, 1941; children—Sharol Ann, William Scott. With Phillips Petroleum Co., Bartlesville, Okla., 1939—, gen. clk. treasury dept., clk. charge war bond sect., clk. charge banks, notes, reconcilements and fgn. funds, asst. finance mgr. treasury dept., 1939-50, asst. sec., asst. treas., 1950-59, sec., asst. treas., 1959-60, treas., 1960-62, sec.-treas., 1962-65, sr. v.p., 1965-68, exec. v.p., 1968-71, pres., 1971—, also dir.; dir. Nat. Bank of Tulsa, 1st Nat. Bank, Bartlesville. Bd. dirs. YMCA. Served to 1st lt. USAAF, 1942-44. Mem. Bartlesville C. of C. (dir.), Ind. Natural Gas Assn. Am., Am. Petroleum Inst. (dir.), Am. Legion, Phi Delta Theta, Beta Gamma Sigma. Mason (Shriner, Jester). Home: 615 E 16th Pl Bartlesville OK 74003 Office: Phillips Bldg Bartlesville OK 74004

MARTIN, WILLIAM MCCHESNEY, JR., broker; b. St. Louis, Dec. 17, 1906; s. William McChesney and Rebecca (Woods) M.; B.A., Yale, 1928; student Benton Coll. Law, St. Louis, 1931; grad. student Columbia (part time), 1931-37; LL.D., Temple U., Amherst Coll., Tulane U., Marietta Coll., Washington U., Trinity Coll., U. Pa., Yale U., Bowdoin Coll., Washington and Lee U., Hamilton Coll., Harvard, Tufts U., Princeton, Columbia, N.Y.U., Rutgers U., Middlebury Coll., Bishop's U., Williams Coll., New Sch. Social Research, U. Del., U. Mich.; m. Cynthia Davis, April 3, 1942; children—Cynthia, Diana, William III. In bank examination dept. Fed. Res. Bank, St. Louis, 1928-29; head statis. dept. A. G. Edwards & Sons, St. Louis, 1929-31, partner, 1931-38; mem. N.Y. Stock Exchange, 1931-38, gov., 1935-38, chmn. com. on constitution, 1937-38, sec. of Conway Com. to reorganize the Exchange, 1937-38, chmn. bd., pres. protem, 1938, pres., 1938-41; pub., editor Econ. Forum, 1932-34. Asst. to exec. Munitions Assignments Bd., Washington, asst. exec. Pres.'s Soviet Protocol Com.; apptd. mem. bd. dirs. Export-Import Bank, 1945, chmn. bd., 1946-48; asst. sec. of Treasury, 1949; U.S. exec. dir. Internat. Bank Reconstrn. and Devel., 1949-52; chmn. bd. govs. Fed. Res. Bd., 1951-70. Chmn. bd. trustees Berry Schs.; trustee Yale U., New Haven, Johns Hopkins U., Balt., Fgn. Service Ednl. Found. Served to col., AUS, 1941-45. Presbyn. Clubs: West Side Tennis, Yale, Metropolitan, Alibi, Chevy Chase (Washington). Home: 2861 Woodland Dr NW Washington DC 20008 Office: 800 17th St NW Washington DC 20006

MARTIN, WILLIAM ROGERS, educator; b. Raleigh, N.C., May 30, 1926; s. Alfred A. and Elizabeth (Rogers) M.; B.S., Hampton Inst., 1951; M.A., Columbia, 1957; m. Ann Reaves, June 16, 1955; children— Claudette Elizabeth, William R. Tchr., Oakland High Sch., Haines City, Fla., 1952-57; chmn. indsl. arts dept. Dillard High Sch., Ft. Lauderdale, Fla., 1957-61; asst. prin., 1963-71; prin. Parkway Middle Sch., Fort Lauderdale, 1971—. Adminstr. Dillard Adult Center, 1959-62, Broward County Adult Center, Ft. Lauderdale, 1963; dean Wingate Jr. High Sch., Ft. Lauderdale, 1961-63. Served with AUS, 1944-45. Mem. Nat. Soc. for Study Edn., Nat., Fla., Ft. Lauderdale edn. assns., N.A.A.C.P., Omega Psi Phi. Baptist. Home: 320 NW 19th Av Fort Lauderdale FL 33311

MARTINDELL, DAVID JACKSON, publisher; b. Orange, N.J., July 3, 1928; s. Jackson and Edna (Conboy) M.; B.B.A., Upsala Coll., 1951. Engaged in pub. relations, 1951-60, in advt., 1960-62; founder, 1963, pres., dir. Yachting Club Am.; originator, compiler Who's Who in Am. History, 1962—, Who's Who in Yachting, 1966—, Am. Yacht Register, 1965—. Served with AUS, 1952-54; Korea. Clubs: Yachting of Am., Everglades Yacht and Tennis (Ft. Lauderdale); Racquet (Miami, Fla.). Home: 2425 Barcelona Dr Fort Lauderdale FL 33301 Office: Sunrise Professional Bldg Fort Lauderdale FL 33304

MARTINEZ, ANGEL VIERA, speaker P.R. Ho. of Reps. Office: Ho of Reps Capitolio San Juan PR 00903*

MARTINEZ, ANITA (MRS. ALFRED MARTINEZ), city ofcl.; b. Dallas, Dec. 8, 1925; d. Joe Franco and Anita Trevinio (Mongaras) Nanes; student Dallas Coll. So. Meth. U., 1945; m. Alfred Martinez, Jan. 27, 1946; children—Alfred Joseph, Steve Dan, Patricia Ann, Rene Orlando. Mem. Dallas City Council, 1969—. Mem. Dallas Community Action Head Start Program, 1969—; fund solicitor West Dallas Youth Center, 1965—; mem. criminal justice com. N. Tex. Central Council Govts.; mem. text book adv. com. Dallas Ind. Sch. Dist.; mem. designs of city com. Goals for Dallas; active fund raising Children's Med. Center; founder Mexican-Am. Block Partnership Program; mem. gen. council Dallas Young Adult Inst.; mem. Jesuit Parents Club, Children's Sch. Safety Com.; active Mobility Adjustment Retrained Workers, So. Meth. U.; initiated Weekly Council Report column in El Sol newspaper. Bd. dirs. Met. YWCA, Nat. Center for Vol. Action. Recipient Worthy Woman award Citizens Nat. Bank, 1968; named One of Ten Outstanding Women News Shapers, Dallas Times Herald, 1968, 69, 70. Mem. ladies aux. Dallas Restaurant Assn. (promoter Tasting Bee for charity), Women's Council Dallas County, St. Monica Spanish Lit. Guild, Tex. Municipal League. Home: 3866 Beutel Ct Dallas TX 75229 Office: City Hall Dallas TX 75201

MARTINEZ, ELVIN L., state legislator; b. Tampa, Fla., 1935; ed.U. Tampa; B.A., LL.B., Stetson U.; m. 4 children. Admitted to Fla. bar; mem. Fla. Ho. of Reps., 1967—. Del., Democratic Nat. Conv., 1968. Mem. Nat., Fla. bar assns. Optimist (pres. West Tampa club). Address: 2305 W Buffalo Av Tampa FL 33603*

MARTINEZ, OLIMPIO R(AMON), constrn. mgmt. cons.; b. Santurce, P.R., July 26, 1926; s. Oscar O. and Soledad (Munoz) M.; B.S. in Civil Engring., Va. Poly. Inst., 1946; m. Isabel Llado, Dec. 18, 1948; children— Amalia I., Elisa S., Lucia M. Jr. structural engr. P.R. Water Resources Authority, San Juan, 1946-47, asst. structural engr., 1947-48, asst. constrn. engr., 1948-59, structural design engr., 1952-54; constrn. engr. Oscar Martinez, Inc., San Juan, 1950-51; structural design engr. Robert L. Brown & Assos. Co., Roanoke, Va., 1951-52; asst. project engr. Raymond Internat., Inc., San Juan, 1954-56, project engr., 1956-58, asst. dist. mgr., 1958-63; project mgr. Frederick Snare Corp., San Juan, 1963-64, Interstate Gen. Contractors, Inc., San Juan, 1964-66, Glenwal Constrn. Corp., San Juan, 1966-67; prin. partner Martinez & Torres Constrn. Mgmt. Cons., Santurce, P.R., 1967—. Mem. P.R. Inst. Architects, Engrs. and Surveyors, Am. Soc. C.E., Soc. Am. Mil. Engrs., Nat., Va. socs. profl. engrs., Constrn. Specification Inst. Home: 9-B 4 St Parkside Guaynabo PR 00920 Office: El Monte Mall Hato Rey PR 00918

MARTINEZ, RADAMES REMIGIO, physician; b. Matanzas, Cuba, Oct. 1, 1922; s. Tomas L. and Ana (Alvarado) M.; B.S., Havana High Sch., 1942; M.D., Havana U., 1949; m. Lilia Villate, July 24, 1942; children—Lilia, Lupe, Radames Remigio, Robert, Raymond, Reynold, Linda. Came to U.S., 1962, naturalized, 1967. Intern, Havana U. Hosp., 1947-49, intern orthopedics, 1949-51, resident, 1951-53; instr. orthopedic chair Havana U., 1953-56, asst. prof., 1960; resident physician VA Hosp., Coral Gables, Fla., 1962; chief orthopedic service Tucson VA Hosp., 1962-64; staff orthopedic surgeon Med. Center Hosp., Odessa, Tex., 1964—. Fellow Internat. Coll. Surgeons, A.C.S. Roman Catholic. Home: 3106 Bonham St Odessa TX 79760 Office: 520 W 5th St Odessa TX 79760

MARTINEZ, ROBERT, assn. exec.; b. Tampa, Fla., Dec. 25, 1934; s. Serafin M. and Ida (Carreno) M.; B.S., U. Tampa, 1957; M.A., U. Ill., 1964; m. Mary Jane Marino, Dec. 19, 1954; children—Sharon Marie, Robert Alan. Tchr. social studies Hillsborough County (Fla.) Bd. Pub. Instrn., Tampa, 1957-62, 63-66, dept. head, 1957-62; exec. dir. Hillsborough Classroom Tchrs. Assn. Inc., Tampa, 1966—; sec.-treas. CTA River Apts., Inc. Instr. econs. U. Tampa, summer 1965; mgmt. cons. labor and indsl. relations, 1964-67. Sec., Hillsborough Polit. Action Com. for Edn., 1966—; lobbyist for edn. Fla., 1967—. Mem. Model Cities Adv. Com. on Edn. Mgmt. trustee Employee Welfare Trust Fund, Tampa, 1965—. Mem. N.E.A. (task force commn. on urban edn. 1968), Fla. Edn. Assn., Hillsborough Classroom Tchrs. Assn., U. Ill., U. Tampa alumni assns., Urban Com. Exec. Secs., Greater Tampa C. of C., Fla. Council on Urban Edn. Assns. (sec.-treas.). Democrat. Club: Tampa Bay Boulevard School Dad's. Contbr. articles to publs. Home: 4647 San Jose St Tampa FL 33609 Office: 4505 N Rome Av Tampa FL 33603

MARTINEZ, RODOLFO, educator; b. Corpus Christi, Tex., Oct. 17, 1927; s. Martin and Manuela (Cortez) M.; B.S., U. Utah, 1954, Ph.D., 1968; M.A., U. Tex., 1955; m. Mary Tanguma Torres, Nov. 27, 1952; 1 son, Daryl. Acting chmn., instr. div. social sci. Navarro Jr. Coll., Corsicana, Tex., 1955-59; chmn., instr. div. social sci. Casper (Wyo.) Coll., 1959-61; teaching asst. Wash. State U., Pullman, 1961-63; teaching asso. U. Utah, Salt Lake City, 1963-65; instr. Brigham Young U., Provo, 1965-67, asst. prof., 1967-68; asso. prof. polit. sci. Eastern Ky. U., Richmond, 1968-70; dir. academic devel. Gov.'s State U., Park Forest, Ill., 1970-71; dir. Northeast Area Manpower Inst. Devel. Staff, R.I. Dept. Edn., Cranston, 1971—. Fulbright lectr. Universidad Nacional de Cuyo, Mendoza, Argentina, 1969-70. Mem. Orem (Utah) Planning Commn., 1968. Served with AUS, 1945-46, 50-52. Mem. Am., So. polit. sci. assns. Democrat. Home: 2233 Nogales St Corpus Christi TX 78416 Office: 1150 Narragansett Bvld Cranston RI 02905

MARTINEZ DEL CAMPO, JUAN, JR., b. Mexico City, Mexico, Aug. 31, 1927; student Central U. Madrid; Licentiate in Law, U. Mexico. Admitted to bar, Mexico, 1951; sec. Consultive Commn., Tariffs Dept., Ministry of Communications, 1954-59; prof. comml. and adminstrv. law, U. Mexico, 1956-57, U. Nuevo Leon, 1962-63; pres., dir., mem. exec. commn. Mexican Electric Chamber, 1967-68. Bd. dirs., Nat. Advt. Council, 1969-71. Mem. Mexican Electric and Electronics Assn., Indsl. Chamber Mexico (exec. com.), Asociacion Nacional de Fabricantes de Aparatos Domesticos (pres., 1971—), Barra Mexicana-Colegio de Abogados. Office: 102 Salamanca 302 Despacho Mexico City 7 Mexico*

MARTINEZ-TEJEDA, JUAN J., mfg. co. exec.; b. Hda. Hornos, Coah., Mexico, June 7, 1908; s. Claudio J. and Luz Maria (Tejeda) M.; M.E., Cornell U., 1927; m. Maria Teresa Orvananos, May 12, 1936; children— Claudio, Maria Teresa. With Mexican Light & Power Co., Ldt., 1927-60; pres., gen. mgr. Autoelectrica, S.A. de C.V., Toluca and Mexico City, 1961-68, Simpson S.A. de C.V., 1964—, Automagneto, S.A. de C.V., 1966-68; pres. Durit, S.A. de C.V., Toluca and Mexico City, 1968—; dir. Immobiliaria Edison, S.A., 1968—, Immobiliaria Geografos, S.A., 1961—, Immobiliaria Circunvalacion, S.A., 1961—, Union de Sequros, S.A., Mexico City, Mexico, 1966—. Mem. bd. Nat. Chamber Electricity, 1946-47; mem. bd., exec. com. Confedn. Chambers of Industry, 1959-60. Trustee Cornell U., 1961-66; chmn., trustee Centro Educacional Ing. Juan Martinez Tejeda, A.C., Toluca, 1966—. Recipient Cornell medal, 1966. Mem. Phi Kappa Theta. Clubs: Cornell (Mexico and N.Y.C.); University (Mex.). Home: Paseo de la Reforma 2125 Mexico City 10 Mexico Office: Taine 134-A Mexico City 5 Mexico also PO Box 260 Toluca Mexico

MARTZ, GLENN EVERETT, author, lectr.; b. Livonia, Mo., Sept. 1, 1900; s. Seth Thomas and Lydia Dea (Speak) M.; student Kirksville (Mo.) State Tchrs. Coll., 1924, No. State Tchrs. Coll., S.D., 1926-27; m. Beverly Margaret Smith, June 4, 1936 (dec.); children—Dale Ellsworth, Glenn Eldon, Sally Ann (Mrs. Edward Southgate), Mary Lou (Mrs. Malcolm Minor); m. 2d, Anne Louise Monen, June 2, 1972. Editor Am.-News, Aberdeen, S.D., 1930-36, A.P., Bismarck, N.D., 1945-46, U.P.I., Washington, 1947-53, Banner, Nashville, 1965-69; staff writer Look Mag., Des Moines, 1940; pub. Washington News Beat, 1954-63; editorial writer Pensacola (Fla.) New-Jour. Field mgr. Office Def. Transp., Minn., N.D., 1943-45; dir. pub. relations Marine Resources div. Ala. Dept. Conservation, 1971-72. Republican. Roman Catholic. Home: 534 Jackson St Summerdale AL 36580

MARTZELL, JOHN ROBERT, lawyer; b. Shreveport, La., Feb. 9, 1937; s. Victor Jean and Catherine (Caverlee) M.; B.S. cum laude, U. Notre Dame, 1958, J.D., 1961; student Loyola U., New Orleans, 1962; m. Veronica Elizabeth Porteous, Aug. 18, 1962; children—Justin Caverlee, Christiane Selton, Andrew Hilman, Benjamin Porteous. Admitted to La. bar, 1962; with firm Covington & Burling, Washington, 1960; law clerk J. Skelly Wright, judge, U.S. Dist. Ct., New Orleans, 1961-62, Frank B. Ellis, 1962-63; practiced in New Orleans, 1963—; mem. firm Ungar and Dulitz, 1963-66; partner firm Ungar, Dulitz and Martzell, 1966-71; partner Martzell & Montero, 1971—. Spl. counsel Civil Rights, Bogalousa, La., 1965-66; spl. counsel gov. State of La., 1967—; exec. dir. La. Com. on Human Relations, Rights and Responsibilities, 1966-67; vis. lectr. St. Mary's Coll., Notre Dame, Ind., 1959-61. Chmn., Archidiocesian Confraternity of Christian Doctrine, New Orleans Catholic Archdiocese, 1967. Mem. La. Trial Lawyers Assn. (sec.-treas.

1968-69, v.p. 1971-72), Am., New Orleans (dir. 1968—) trial lawyers assns. Home: 515 Hillary St New Orleans LA 70118 Office: 1012 Richards Bldg New Orleans LA 70112

MARVIN, JOHN GEORGE, clergyman, ch. orgn. exec.; b. Summit, N.J., May 8, 1912; s. George and Caroline (Whitman) M.; B.S., Davidson Coll., 1933; Th.B., Princeton, 1936; D.D., Coll. Emporia, 1964; LL.D., Tarkio Coll., 1964; m. Elizabeth Anne Wheater, June 30, 1944; children—Caroline Wheater, Elizabeth Anne, Martha Jane, Frances Alice. Ordained to ministry Presbyn. Ch., 1936; pastor, Windsor, N.Y., 1936-37, Montrose, Pa., 1937-44, Lewistown, Pa., 1944-52, Denton, Tex., 1952-61; presbytery exec. Greater Kansas City, Mo., 1961-65; pastor 1st Presbyn. Ch., Bartlesville, Okla., 1965-69; sr. minister Chevy Chase Presbyn. Ch., Washington, 1969—. Mem. exec. com. Pa. Council Chs., 1949-52, Tex. Council Chs., 1953-61; mem. exec. com., long range chmn. Greater Kansas City Council Chs., 1962-65; chmn. campus Christian Life Tex. Synod, 1958-61; chmn. nat. mission Pa. Synod, 1949-52; sec. nomination com. Gen. Assembly U.P. Ch., 1955-58, chmn. com. on baptized children, 1969-70, mem. com. of nine on synod boundaries, 1970-72; bd. dirs. Midwest Christian Counseling Center, 1963-69, Presbyn. Homes of Okla., Inc., 1966-69; mem. jud. commn. Synod of Okla.-Ark., 1966-69; mem. strategy com. Bd. Nat. Missions, 1968-70. Bd. dirs., mem. exec. and acad. coms. Tarkio Coll., 1961-67; bd. dirs. Westminster Found., Pa. State U., 1945-52, N. Tex. State U., 1952-61; chmn. constnl. procedures Washington City Presbytery, 1969-72. Mem. Beta Theta Pi. Republican. Rotarian. Contbr. articles to religious publs. Home: 11912 Gregerscroft Rd Potomac MD 20854 Office: One Chevy Chase Circle Washington DC 20015

MARVIN, MURRAY JOSEPH, life ins. co. exec.; b. Green County, O., June 15, 1913; s. Murray Joseph and Iona (Gee) M.; B.S., W.Va. State Coll., 1936; M.B.A., U. Chgo., 1960; m. Delores Kathleen Jackson, Dec. 31, 1946. Partner with wife Marvin & Marvin, pub. relations and advt. agy., Chgo., 1947-52; exec. dir. Nat. Ins. Assn., Chgo., 1950-61; dir. planning N.C. Mut. Life. Ins. Co., Durham, 1961-71, v.p. planning and communication, 1971—; instr. Grad. Sch. Bus. N.C. Central U., Durham, part time, 1962-66. Mem. 3 man cons. team reviewing activities local anti-poverty agy. Operation Breakthrough, 1965-66; mem. Pres. Nixon's Urban Renewal Task Force, 1969; mem. budget com. United Fund, 1966-71. Bd. dirs. Children's Mus. Served with USNR, 1944-46. Recipient Crosthwait award Chgo. Ins. Assn., 1961, 40th Anniversary award Nat. Ins. Assn., 1961. Mem. Am. Mgmt. Assn., Am. Inst. Mgmt., Pub. Relations Soc. Am., Life Advertisers Assn., Kappa Alpha Psi. Republican. Episcopalian. Home: 909 Dupree St Durham NC 27701 Office: Mutual Plaza Durham NC 27701

MARVIN, OSCAR MCDOWELL, hosp. adminstr.; b. Statesville, N.C., Apr. 12, 1924; s. Oscar McDowell and Gladys (Early) M.; A.B., U. N.C., 1948; M.B.A., U. Chgo., 1953; M.S., U. Louisville, 1970; m. Jane Everitt Krauss, June 16, 1951; children—Frederick McDowell, Elizabeth Anne, Robert Doyle. Foreman, Hanes Dye & Finishing Co., Winston-Salem, N.C., 1948-51; hosp. adminstrv. resident N.C. Baptist Hosp., Winston-Salem, 1952-53; asst. adminstr. City Meml. Hosp., Winston-Salem, 1953-55, N.C. Med. Care Commn., Raleigh, 1955-57; hosp. adminstr., missionary Bd. World Missions Presbyn. Ch. U.S., Yodogawa Christian Hosp., Osaka, Japan, 1957-60; asst. adminstr. City Memphis Hosp., 1960-62, adminstr., 1962-68; lectr. dept. preventive medicine U. Tenn., 1963-68, asso. prof. Coll. Pharmacy, 1965-68; exec. dir. Louisville Med. Center, Inc., 1968—. Sr. cons. Internat. Hosp. Cons. Service, 1970—. Treas. Memphis Hosp. Council, 1963, v.p., pres., 1965. Sec. Memphis Inst. Medicine and Religion, 1966-68; mem. Mayor's Com. to Employ Handicapped, Memphis, 1963; chmn. hosp. div. Shelby United Neighbors, Memphis, 1965. Bd. dirs. Med. Benevolence Found. Served with AUS, 1942-45. Mem. Am. Coll. Hosp. Adminstrs., Am. Assn. Hosp. Accountants (organizer N.C. chpt. 1954, pres. 1955-56), Tenn. Hosp. Assn. (chmn. Council Adminstrv. Practice), Assn. Coop. Hosp. Laundries (sec.-treas. 1970-71), Sigma Nu. Presbyn. (deacon, elder). Rotarian. Contbr. articles profl. jours. Home: 2442 Parkdale Av Louisville KY 40220 Office: 334 E Broadway St Louisville KY 40202

MARZETTI, LAWRENCE ARTHUR, govt. ofcl.; b. Mt. Vernon, O., Apr. 17, 1917; s. Joseph and Pia (DiPiero) M.; A.B. in Edn., Morehead State Coll., 1939; postgrad. George Washington U., 1940-41, 47-48; M.A. in Pub. Adminstrn., Am. U., 1952; m. Josephine Palazzo, July 26, 1942; children—Loretta Ann, Lawrence Anthony, Joseph Vincent, Philip John, Alfred Paul. With U.S. Bur. of Census, Washington, 1940—, tech. adviser subcom. census and statistics Post Office and Civil Service Com. Ho. of Reps., 1970—, with Internat. Statis. Programs 1956-70, chief cons. br., 1956-61, asst. dir. overseas cons. and research office, 1961-66, chief, 1966-70. Pres., Silver Hill Boys' Club Devel. Corp., Hillcrest Heights, Md., 1968—. Served to capt. USMCR, 1943-46. Recipient Meritorious Honor award U.S. Dept. Commerce, 1952, named Italian-Am. Man of Year Sons of Italy, 1972. Mem. Am. Statis. Assn., Soc. Internat. Devel., NSF Register Sci. and Tech. Personnel. Roman Catholic (chmn. parish council edn. com.). Home: 5932 25th Av SE Washington DC 20031 Office: Bur Census Washington DC 20233

MASCIOCCHI, PIUS JAMES, bldg., constrn. exec.; b. Dudley, Pa., Nov. 25, 1913; s. Joseph and Paulina (Mosca) M.; B.S. in C.E., Drexel U., 1937. With E.I. duPont de Nemours & Co., Wilmington, Del., 1936—, cost contract supr. engring. dept., Wilmington, 1941-47, project closing supr., 1947-51, engring. office supt. Savannah River Plant, AEC, Augusta, Ga., 1951—. Chmn. United Fund, 1968. Fellow Am. Soc. C.E. (mem. local qualifications com. 1954—, br. pres. 1954, state dir. 1957, 69); mem. S.C. Soc. Engrs. (dir. 1966). Roman Catholic (pres. Holy Name Soc. 1960). K.C. (4 deg.). Home: 2426 Kings Way Augusta GA 30904 Office: E I DuPont de Nemours & Co PO Box 117 Augusta GA 30903

MASDEN, HOWARD SEEFELD, social work exec.; b. Milw., Feb. 15, 1909; s. Charles Pitman and Louise (Seefeld) M.; student Lawrence Coll., 1929-30; B.A., U. Ia., 1953; M.S. in Social Work, U. Tex., 1955; children—(by previous marriage) Sally Louise (Mrs. Horace Houston), Nancy Lee (Mrs. J.O. Duncan, Jr.); m. 2d, Annie Laurie Davis, Dec. 22, 1950. With Tex. Dept. Pub. Welfare, 1950-63, asst. dir. child welfare, 1958-63; dir. child care, edn. and tng. Tex. Youth Council, Austin, 1964-72, dir. ednl. program adminstrn., 1972—. Active United Fund, 1958; Sponsor S.W. Tex. Ednl. TV Council, 1969. Bd. dirs. Tex. Social Welfare Assn., 1960-64, treas., 1963-64. Recipient Gov.'s citation for service to mentally retarded, 1966. Mem. Nat. Assn. Social Workers, Acad. Certified Social Workers, Nat. Assn. Tng. Schs. and Juvenile Agys., A.A.A.S., Phi Alpha Delta. Methodist. Home: 2005 Mimosa Dr Austin TX 78745 Office: 201 E 14th St Austin TX 78701

MASHBURN, MARIAN GRIFFIN, realtor, civic worker; b. Tallapoosa, Ga., June 13, 1919; d. Charter W. and Emma (MacDonald) Griffin; U. Ala., 1942; m. John Blaine Mashburn, Oct. 24, 1942; 1 dau., Marsha Anita. Sales rep. W.C. and A.N. Miller Devel. Co., Washington, 1955-60; asso. realtor Belle Harris Realtor, Jacksonville, Fla., 1961-64, Stockton, Whatley, Davin & Co., 1964-69; realtor, 1970—. Publicity dir. Girl Scouts Am. Wilmington, N.C., 1953; bus. mgr. Jr. League Children's Theatre, Wilmington, 1954; docent Smithsonian Inst. Washington, 1955; mem. advt. staff Antique Show, Washington, 1959; mem. Jr. League Am., 1949. Recipient White House Youth Conf. award, 1959. Mem. Jacksonville Bd. Realtors. Home: 4613 Waverly Lane Jacksonville FL 32210 Office: 218 W Adams St Jacksonville FL 32202

MASHMAN, JOSEPH, aircraft co. exec.; b. Chgo., Apr. 17, 1916; s. Smauel and Rebecca (Lechman) M.; student Armour Inst. Tech., 1933-37; postgrad. U. Buffalo, 1943-45; m. Barbara Bridges, Apr. 3, 1965; children (by previous marriage)—Joanne Susan, Barbara Jean (Mrs. Michael M. Reese), Steve Edgar, Sally Elizabeth (Mrs. Richard Pfeffer). Sr. exptl. test pilot Bell Aircraft Corp., Niagra Falls, N.Y., 1943-45; chief exptl. test pilot Bell Helicopter Corp., Niagra Falls, 1945-51, dir. market devel., Fort Worth, 1951-60, asst. v.p. marketing projects, 1960-68, v.p. spl. projects, 1968—. Rep. U.S. Vertical Lift Industry on FAA Com., 1958-63; cons. on helicopters to White House, Washington, 1964-69; mem. research engring adv. com. Nat. Security Indsl. Assn., 1970—. Decorated Gold Medal Award for Valor (Peru); Presidential Cavaliere dell'Ordinae (Italy); recipient Golden Plate award Am. Acad. Achievement, 1965. Fellow Am. Helicopter Soc. (hon.), Australian Helicopter Soc. (hon.), Helicopter Soc. India (hon.), Am. Inst. Aeronautics and Astronautics (asso.), Royal Aero. Soc. Great Britain (asso.); mem. Am. Helicopter Soc. (pres. 1970-71, chmn. bd. 1971-72), Am. Acad. Achievement (bd. govs. 1965—), Assn. U.S. Army, Army Aviation Assn. Am., Quiet Birdmen, Internat. Order Characters, Soc. Exptl. Test Pilots, Helicopter Assn. Am., Twirly Birds Soc. (founding mem). Home: 3310 Fairmount St Dallas TX 75201 Office: PO Box 482 Fort Worth TX 76101

MASIKO, PETER, JR., coll. pres.; b. Vera Cruz, Pa., Mar. 18, 1914; s. Peter, Sr., and Sophia (Baker) M.; B.A. with highest honors, Lehigh U., 1936; M.A. (fellow), U. Ill., 1937, Ph.D., 1939; m. Anna E. Fetterolf, July 9, 1932; children—Elaine Irene (Mrs. James Salapotas), Peter, III. Instr. U. Ill., 1936-39; with Wright Jr. Coll., Chgo., 1939-62, successively instr., chmn. social sci. dept., asst. dean, became dean, 1950; exec. dean Chgo. City Jr. Coll., 1956-62; pres. Miami-Dade Jr. Coll., Miami, Fla., 1962—; economist Bd. Investigation and Research, Washington, summer 1942. Mem. U.S. Dept. Def. adv. com. on edn.; mem. edn. div. Dade County Community Relation Bd. Mem. exec. bd. S. Fla. council Boy Scouts Am.; bd. dirs. Dade County Med. Research and Health Services Found., United Fund, United Health Found., Health Planning Council, Council Internat. Vistors; mem. Dade County Oceanographic Sci. Park Adv. Com. Mem. steering com. mental health tng. and research So. Regional Edn. Bd. Mem. Am. Econ. Asso., Assn. Higher Edn., Am. Assn. Sch. Adminstrs. (mem. com. on funds.), Am. Assn. Jr. Colls. (mem. jr.-sr. coll. com., mem. constl. revision com.; dir., mem. adv. com. new instrs.), N.E.A., N. Central Assn. (commr. commn. on colls., univs. 1956-60), Am. Council on Edn. (mem. commn. on fed. relations), Fla. Jr. Coll. Pres.'s Council, Greater Miami C. of C., Phi Beta Kappa, Phi Kappa Phi. Lutheran. Kiwanian. Author: Introduction to Social Sci. (with Atteberry, Auble and Hunt), rev. edit., 1951. Home: 10270 SW 102d Terrace Miami FL 33156 Office: 11011 SW 104th St Miami FL 33156

MASINTER, RALPH, lawyer; b. Marietta, O.; s. Elias Michael and Rachel Leah (Shereshefsky) M.; LL.B., Washington and Lee U., 1926; LL.M., N.Y. U., 1929; m. Miriam Beilin, Apr. 16, 1939; 1 dau., Enid Renee. Admitted to W.Va. bar, 1927, N.Y. bar, 1933, Va. bar, 1956; gen. practice Roanoke, Va., 1956—; spl. asst. to atty. gen. N.Y., 1933, Va., 1956-64; U.S. trial commr. N.Y., Pa., N.J., Del., Md., D.C., 1943-44; asso. editor Am. Trial Lawyers Jour., 1962—. Lectr. advanced legal tng. Past pres. Midway Jewish Community Center, Forest Hills, N.Y. Past mem. Democratic County Com., N.Y. County; past pres. Mid-Manhatton Dem. Club; past mem. speakers bur. Dem. Nat. Com.; alt. del. Dem. Nat. Conv., 1960; mem. exec. cof. Dem. City Com. Bd. dirs. Va. Assn. for Mental Health. Mem. Va., Roanoke, N.Y. State bar assns., Am., Va. trial lawyers assns., Va. State Bar, Comml. Law League Am., Ground Hog Club Am. (v.p. Roanoke), Jewish Nat. Council, C. of C., Delta Sigma Rho, Phi Epsilon Pi. Jewish religion (past chmn. bd. synagogue; past pres. Men's Club). Mason (32 deg. Shriner); mem. B'nai B'rith (past v.p., exec. mem. Tristate Anti-Defamation League). Contbr. articles to profl. jours. Home: 1867 Blenheim Rd SW Roanoke VA 24015 Office: State and City Bldg Roanoke VA 24011

MASON, ALVIN HUGHLETT, cons. scientist and engr.; b. Harborton, Va., Feb. 3, 1905; s. Alvin T. and Elizabeth (Hughlett) M.; B.S. with honor in Civil Engring., U. S.C., 1929; M.S., U. Pa., 1931, Ph.D., 1953; m. Mary R. Crow, Sept. 3, 1937. Physicist Nat. Bur. Standards, Washington, 1937-39; stress analyst, torsional vibration analyst U.S. Navy and U.S. Maritime Commn., 1939-48; physicist Office of Chief of Staff, U.S. Army, 1953-63. Registered profl. engr., Washington. Fellow A.A.A.S.; mem. Am. Geophys. Union, Va. Acad. Sci., Philos. Soc. Washington, Washington Soc. Engrs. Democrat. Methodist. Author: The Journal of Charles Mason and Jeremiah Dixon, 1969. Contbr. articles to profl. jours. Home: 2407 N Kenmore St Arlington VA 22207

MASON, BARRY JEAN, banker; b. Big Spring, Tex., June 3, 1930; s. Vernon E. and Irene (Owen) M.; student Tex. Arts and Industries Coll., 1947-50; B.S., U. Tex., 1957; B. Fgn. Trade, Am. Inst. for Fgn. Trade, 1958; postgrad. U. Hawaii, 1968; m. Alexana Petroff, Aug. 31, 1958; children—Scott Alexander, Lydia Claire. Trainee, First Nat. City Bank of N.Y., N.Y.C., 1958-59, trainee, Hong Kong, 1959-60, asst. accountant, Tokyo, 1960-63, asst. mgr., Tokyo, 1963-66, mgr., Hong Kong, 1966-67, resident v.p., Hong Kong, 1967-68, resident v.p., Tokyo, 1968-69, v.p., 1969; v.p. Republic Nat. Bank of Dallas, 1969-70, sr. v.p., 1970—. Mem. corporate adv. bd. Internat. Sch., Hong Kong, 1967-68; trustee Am. Sch. in Japan, 1969. Served with AUS, 1948-49, USNR, 1952-53, USMCR, 1953-55. Mem. Bankers Assn. for Fgn. Trade, Am. Bankers Assn., Am. C. of C. in Japan (chmn. budget com. 1966). Rotarian. Home: 7730 Yamini Dr Dallas TX 75230 Office: Pacific at Ervay Dallas TX 75201

MASON, BRIAN HAROLD, geologist; b. New Zealand, Apr. 18, 1917; s. George Harold and Catherine (Fairweather) M.; M.Sc., U. New Zealand, 1938; Ph.D., U. Stockholm, 1943. Came to U.S., 1947, naturalized, 1953. Lectr. geology Canterbury Coll., New Zealand, 1944-47; prof. mineralogy Ind. U., 1947-53; chmn. dept. mineralogy Am. Mus. Natural History, N.Y.C., 1953-65; research curator U.S. Nat. Mus., Washington, 1965—. Sec. Internat. Commn. Meteorites, 1960-68. Fellow Mineral. Soc. Am., Geol. So. Am.; mem. Geochem. Soc., Royal Soc. New Zealand, Swedish Geol. Soc. Author: Principles of Geochemistry, 3d edit., 1967; Meteorites, 1962; The Literature of Geology, 1953; (with L.G. Berry) Mineralogy, 1959; (with W.G. Melson) The Lunar Rocks, 1970. Office: US Nat Museum Washington DC 20560

MASON, CHARLES C., supt. schs.; b. Jonesburg, Mo., Nov. 23, 1904; s. James L. and Susie (Opie) M.; A.B., Central Wesleyan Coll., 1926; M.S., Washington U., 1928; Ed.D., Colo. State Coll., 1941; postgrad. U. Colo., 1927, U. Mo., 1929; D.Sc. (hon.), U. Tulsa, 1959; m. Myrtle J. Smith, Mar. 23, 1932; children—James David, Sue Ann. Tchr., prin., supt. schs., Jonesburg, Mo., 1924-27; tchr., prin. pub. schs., Tulsa, 1928-35, asst. supt. schs., 1935-44, supt. 1944—. Dir. Tulsa Fed. Savs. & Loan Assn. Lectr. U. Okla., U. Tulsa, Central Wesleyan Coll., Colo. State Coll. Edn.; mem. Joint Council Econ. Edn.; mem. Bd. Edn. Okla. Dept. Pub. Instrn.; cons. Okla. Council for Handicapped Children, Inc. Asso. trustee Okla. Frontiers Sci.; trustee Hillcrest Med. Center, Am. Hist, and Art Mus., Gilcrease Mus.; bd. dirs. Community Chest, YMCA; mem. adv. bd. Am. Citizenship Tng. Center, Okla. Christian Coll.; chmn. Tulsa Edn. Meml. Trust Found. Recipient award Mr. Supt. of Okla., 1956; Am. educator's award Freedom Found., 1960. Mem. C. of C. (mem. bd.), N.E.A., Am. Assn. Sch. Adminstrs. (dir., mem. exec. com., legislative steering com.), Okla. Assn. Sch. Adminstrs., Nat. P.T.A. (life), Okla. P.T.A. (life), S.A.R., Okla. Edn. Assn., Phi Delta Kappa, Sigma Phi Epsilon. Mem. Christian Ch. Rotarian. Co-author textbooks on spelling. Home: 1123 S Evanston Tulsa OK 74104 Office: 3027 S New Haven Tulsa OK 74114

MASON, CHARLES NATHAN, ret. govt. ofcl.; b. Billings, Mont., Mar. 9, 1909; s. Joseph E. and Anna E. (Ganser) M.; B.A., Mont. State U., 1930, M.A., 1934; postgrad. U. Wis. Extension, 1940, advanced mgmt. program Harvard, 1959; m. Mabel Rebecca Smith, Dec. 24, 1929;children—Charles Nathan, Gary F., Kent W., Mark S. Laborer, Gt. Western Sugar Co., Billings, 1924-25; bookkeeper Midland Nat. Bank, Billings, 1926; clk. to asst. registrar Mont. State U., Missoula, 1927-35, instr., 1934-35; various adminstrv. positions U.S. Dept. Agr., Missoula, Milw., Indpls., 1935-42, chief div. accounting Office Budget and Finance, Dept. Agr., Washington, 1942-46; budget officer CCC, Washington, 1946-50; systems accountant Gen. Accounting Office, Washington, 1951-52; budget officer CIA, Washington, 1952-62, asst. dir. finance, 1962-69; ret. Instr. Dept. Agr. Grad. Sch., 1943-55, 65-69; professorial lectr. accounting George Washington U., 1953, 54. Pres. Chevy Chase Citizens Assn., 1970-72. Recipient CIA Merit medal, 1959. Mem. Am. Accounting Assn., Fed. Govt. Accountants Assn., Nature Conservancy (treas. 1960-69, bd. 1969-70), Wilderness Soc., Am. Ornithologists Union, Wilson Ornithol. Soc., Wis. Soc. for Ornithology, Nat. Audubon Soc., Audubon Soc. of Central Atlantic States (treas. 1961-63), Fed. Union, Md. Ornithol. Soc. (v.p. Montgomery County 1964-67), Alpha Kappa Psi (silver service award, 1951; dist. dir. 1957-68). Episcopalian. Home: 6432 31st St NW Washington DC 20015

MASON, C(HARLES) RUSSELL, conservation exec.; b. Doylestown, Pa., Oct. 28, 1895; s. William and Mary Adelaide (Dubs) M.; B.S., Pa. State U., 1917; M.S.A., Purdue U., 1920; m. Elizabeth Park Stewart, Dec. 1, 1917 (dec.); 1 son, Richard Stewart; m. 2d, Jessie M. Horne, Sept. 6, 1926 (dec.). Instr., asst., asso. prof. hort. and extension Purdue U., 1917-20, Pa. State Coll., 1920-23, 24-26; farmer, 1923-24; wholesale seed mgr. for S.E., v.p. F.C. Stokes &Co., 1926-34; with W. Atlee Burpee Co., 1935-39; exec. dir. Mass. Audubon Soc., 1939-57, exec. dir. Fla. Audubon Soc., 1957-72, dir. Pan Am. and Tours div., 1971-72. Chmn. Fla. Conservation Council, 1957—; pres. Flying Carpet Tours, 1972—. Mem. N.E. Wildflower Soc. (dir.), Am. Ornithologists Union, Cornell Lab. of Ornithology, Phi Kappa Phi, Sigma Nu. Author: Picture Primer of Bird Attraction, 1954; Field Guide to the Birds of the Guianas. Contbr. articles to profl. jours. Home: S Clyde Av Kissimmee FL 32741 Office: 700 W Vine St Kissimmee FL 32741

MASON, CLINTON KENNETH, investment co. exec.; b. Boston, May 22, 1931; s. Clinton Kenneth and Irene Mary (Perham) M.; A.B., Dartmouth, 1953; M.B.A., N.Y. U., 1957; m. Elaine Durham, Aug. 3, 1962; children—Lauren Irene, Clinton Kenneth III, Scott Thomas. Buyer, Western Electric Corp., 1953-60; account exec. F.I. Du Pont, Oklahoma City, 1960-68; v.p. Parker Bishop & Welsh, Oklahoma City, 1969-70; v.p. instl. sales Parker Welsh & Hadden, 1970-71; officer Lenz-Newton, Oklahoma City, 1971—; v.p., sec., treas., dir. Gamma Financial Assn., Oklahoma City. Officer, United Fund, Oklahoma City, 1967-68. Bd. dirs. Oklahoma City Jr. Symphony, 1967-68. Mem. Opera Guild, Oklahoma City C. of C. Republican. Methodist. Clubs: Sportsmans, Dartmouth (Oklahoma City). Financial columnist Pulse mag., 1971—. Home: 3828 N W 69th Terrace Oklahoma City OK 73116 Office: Suite 302 City Nat Bank Tower Oklahoma City OK 73102

MASON, DONALD GREY, banker; b. Ferrum, Va., Oct. 11, 1927; s. Able Grey and Roxie (Buckner) M.; B.S., Coll. William and Mary, 1957; m. Mary Clay Nichols, Dec. 23, 1956; children—Donald Grey, Nancy Elizabeth, Ellen Kay. Asst. v.p. Va. Nat. Bank, Norfolk, 1957-69; v.p. First Va. Bankshares, Springfield, 1969—. Served with AUS, 1950-52. Home: 3825 King Arthur Rd Annandale VA 22003 Office: 6400 Arlington Blvd Falls Church VA 22042

MASON, FRANKLIN GASQUE, dentist; b. Mullins, S.C., Nov. 20, 1924; s. Edison I. and Mary (Gasque) M.; B.S., Clemson U., 1949; D.D.S., Emory U., 1953; m. Lucy Farrow Reames, June 18, 1947; children—Mary Lydia, Lucy Anne, Deborah Lynn, Francis Elizabeth. Practice dentistry, Mullins, S.C., 1953—. Adv. com. Florence Darlington Tech. Sch., 1969-72; vis. lectr. Sch. Dental Medicine, Med. U. S.C., 1970-71. Pres., Mullins United Fund, 1965; chmn. Mullins Recreation Bd., 1960-61. Trustee Baptist Coll. at Charleston (S.C.); bd. dirs. S.C. Eye Bank. Served with C.E., AUS, 1943-46. Named Mullins Young Man of Year, 1959. Mem. Am., S.C. (pres. 1965) dental assns., Pee Dee Dental Soc. (pres. 1959), S.C. Soc. Dentistry for Children, S.C. Lions Sight Conservation Assn. (v.p. 1970). Baptist (deacon, supt. Sunday sch. 1960-64, mem. bldg. com. 1960-70, chmn. finance com. 1969-70). Lion (dist. gov. 1967-68). Club: Pinewood Country. Home: S Main St Mullins Sc 29574 Office: 160 E Wine St Mullins SC 29574

MASON, GILBERT RUTLEDGE, physician; b. Jackson, Miss., Oct 7, 1928; s. Willie Atwood and Adlean (Jackson) M.; B.S., Tenn. State U., 1949; M.D., Howard U., 1954; m. Natalie Lorraine Hamlar, July 29, 1950; 1 son, Gilbert Rutledge. Intern Homer G. Phillips Hosp., St. Louis, 1954-55; gen. practice medicine, Biloxi, Miss., 1955—. Med. dir. Harrison County Head Start, 1969—; mem. tissue and drug coms. Howard Meml. Hosp., Biloxi, 1967—, chief family practice sect., 1971—. Vice chmn. bd. Greater Gulf Coast Land Devel. Corp., 1970—; dir. Miss. Indsl. Spl. Services, Inc. Pres. N.A.A.C.P., Biloxi, 1960—; chmn. USO, 1959-60, 70—; chmn. Community Action Program, 1966-69; mem. City Planning Commn., 1969—; mem. state adv. com. U.S. Civil Rights Commn., 1965—; mem. Gov.'s Emergency Council, 1969-71; vice chmn. state adv. com. to Cabinet Com. on Pub. Edn., 1970—; mem. state adv. com. Div. Comprehensive Health Planning, 1969—; scoutmaster Boy Scouts Am., 1959—; pres. Biloxi Civil League, 1960-69. Mem. Harrison County Democratic Exec. Com., 1968—. Recipient Silver Beaver award Boy Scouts Am., 1963; Outstanding Alumnus citation Semi-centennial Celebration Tenn. State U., 1962; named Citizen of Year, 1959, 64; Outstanding Citizen, 1970. Fellow N.Y. Research Found. Diplomate Am. Bd. Family Practice. Fellow Am. Acad. Family Practitioners; mem. A.M.A., Nat. Med. Assn., Alpha Phi Alpha. Baptist. Elk, Mason (32 deg.). Home: 119 Alicia Dr Biloxi MS 39531 Office: 433 E Division St Biloxi MS 39530

MASON, JAMES MIDDLETON, investment co. exec.; b. Augusta, Ga., Mar. 19, 1908; s. James Middleton and Daisy Claire (Bacon) M.; student Augusta Coll., 1926; m. Emma Louise Lester, Sept. 29, 1934; 1 son, Benjamin Lester. With Johnson, Lane, Space, Smith & Co.,

Augusta, 1933—, salesman, 1944-61, v.p., 1961—, also dir. Asso. mem. N.Y. Stock Exchange. Served with AUS, 1943-44. Episcopalian. Elk. Clubs: Augusta Country, Pinnacle. Home: 1211 Milledge Rd Augusta GA 30904 Office: 721 Broad St Augusta GA 30904

MASON, JOHN CLARKE, lawyer, former govt. ofcl.; b. Charlotte, N.C., May 2, 1912; s. Edwin Lowell and Mamie (Badgett) M.; student Furman U., 1930-31; A.A., George Washington U., 1936, J.D., 1940; m. Germaine Jeanne Bernard, Aug. 27, 1939; children—John Clarke, Germaine J., Kathleen M., Janice M., Claire Anne (dec.), Michael J. Admitted to D.C. bar, 1940, U.S. Supreme Ct. bar, 1953, other U.S. cts.; clk. Fed. Power Commn., Washington, 1934-41, atty., 1941-53, asst. gen. counsel, 1953-56, dep. gen. counsel, 1956-60, gen. counsel, 1960-61, dep. gen. counsel, 1961-67; asso. Morgan, Lewis & Bockius, Washington 1967—; rep. Fed. Power Commn. on Adminstrv. Conf. U.S., 1961-62. Mem. Pub. Utilities Commn., Fairfax County, Va., 1951-52; adv. council U.S. Land Law Rev. Commn. Active Boy Scouts Am., Poplar Heights Citizens Assn., Poplar Heights Recreation Assn. Served from lt. (j.g.) to lt., USNR, 1944-46, PTO. Mem. Fed. (council), Am. bar assns. Home: 1029 Poplar Dr Falls Church VA 22046 Office: 1140 Connecticut Av NW Washington DC 20036

MASON, MARTIN ALEXANDER, cons. engr.; b. Washington, Apr. 23, 1907; s. Alexander Kemp and Elizabeth (Arenz) M.; B.S. in Engring., George Washington U., 1931; postgrad. (John R. Freeman scholar in hydraulics) Johns Hopkins, 1936-37; Ingenieur-Docteur, U. Grenoble (France), 1938; m. Winnifred Maupin Meade, Nov. 5, 1932; children—Ann Winnifred, Martin Everard. Hydraulic engr. Nat. Bur. Standards, 1925-40; chief engr. Beach Erosion Bd., 1940-51; dean engring. George Washington U., 1951-67; pres. Capitol Inst. Tech., 1967-71, also trustee. Cons. engr. Mem. Am. Soc. Washington, C.E., Am. Soc. M.E., Washington Soc. Engrs. (Outstanding Engr. award 1966), Washington Acad. Scis. (Outstanding Engr. Award 1947), Am. Soc. Engring. Edn., Am. Geophys. Union, Nat. Soc. Profl. Engrs., Sigma Xi, Sigma Tau, Tau Beta Pi. Club: Cosmos (Washington). Home: 3621 Raymond St Chevy Chase MD 20015

MASON, MORTON F., physician. Editor: Jour. Forensic Scis. Office: Parkland Memorial Hosp 5201 Harry Hines Blvd Dallas TX 75235*

MASON, PHILIP MINOR, ednl. adminstr.; b. Marion, Ala., Dec. 1, 1910; s. William Henry and Elise (Minor) M.; A.A., Marion Inst., 1929; B.A., U. Ala., 1931, M.A., 1932, LL.D., 1972; m. Emma Alison, Aug. 23, 1935;children—Alison (Mrs. William Paul McNutt), Philip Minor, Samuel Alison. Tchr. high sch. Monroe County, Ala., 1932-35; prin. jr. high sch., Choctaw County, Ala., 1935-38; prin. elementary sch., Baldwin County, 1938-53; asst. dir. Mobile Center, U. Ala., 1953, dir. Huntsville Center, 1953-64, dir. devel. and external affairs, Huntsville, 1964—. Chmn., Madison County Sesquicentennial Com., 1969; coordinator N. Ala. Regional Sci. Fair, 1964-69. Bd. dirs. United Givers Fund, Huntsville Achievement Sch., Madison County Assn. Mental Health, Huntsville Arts Council, pres. 1965-66, Met. Y.M.C.A., pres. 1967-69. Recipient Outstanding Kiwanian award, Huntsville, 1966, commendation Pres. U.S., 1970. Mem. Ala. Edn. Assn. (dist. pres. 1946), Elementary Prins. Assn. Ala. (pres. 1940), Huntsville C. of C. (bd. dirs. 1965-69), Lambda Chi Alpha, Phi Delta Kappa. Democrat. Episcopalian. Kiwanian (dist. lt. gov. 1971). Home: 1807 Big Cove Rd Huntsville AL 35801 Office: PO Box 1247 Huntsville AL 35807

MASON, RICHARD ALLEN, banker; b. Little Rock, July 15, 1934; s. Thomas Allen and Pauline (Thompson) M.; B.S. in Commerce, Tex. Christian U., 1957; m. Janford Smith, Aug. 30, 1956; children—Tracy, Leslie, Hilary. With data processing div. IBM, 1958-66; with Ft. Worth Nat. Bank, 1966—, sr. v.p. marketing div., 1969—. Mem. faculty Tex. Christian U., 1968—, bd. dirs. Ft. Worth C. of C. Devel. Corp., 1969-71. Chmn. bus. div. United Fund Campaign Cabinet, 1968; group dir. Tex. Christian U. Research Found., 1969-70. Served to 1st lt., Transp. Corps, AUS, 1956. Mem. Am. Bankers Assn., Bank Pub. Relations and Marketing Assn., Sales and Marketing Execs., Tex. Christian U. Alumni Assn. (dir. 1969-70), Tex. Christian U. M.J. Neeley Sch. Bus. Alumni Assn. (pres. 1969-70), Kappa Sigma. Republican. Baptist. Home: 2309 Medford Ct E Fort Worth TX 76109 Office: 800 Main St Fort Worth TX 76102

MASON, ROBERT, editor; b. Charlotte, N.C., Sept. 1, 1912; s. Walter L. and Irene (Peterson) M.; A.B., U. N.C., 1933; m. Frances Fulton, Feb. 11, 1939; 1 dau., Frances Fulton II (now Mrs. Robert Baldwin, Jr.). City editor Sanford (N.C.) Herald, 1933-35, editor, 1952-57; reporter Raleigh (N.C.) News & Observer, 1935-37; city editor Durham (N.C.) Herald, 1937-41; Sunday editor Norfolk (Va.) Virginian-Pilot, 1941-43, 46-52, asso. editor, 1957-59, mng. editor, 1959-62, editor, 1962—. Chmn. Norfolk Civil War Centennial Commn.; mem. Pres.'s Nat. Citizens Com. for Community Relations. Trustee, Chrysler Mus., Norfolk. Served to lt. USNR, 1943-46. Mem. Am. Soc. Newspaper Editors, N.C. Hist. Soc., N.C. Editorial Writers Conf. (chmn. 1955-56), Va. Press Assn., Norfolk Assembly, Navy League, Newcomen Soc., Alpha Tau Omega. Democrat. Episcopalian. Clubs: Princess Anne Country, Harbor, Virginia; Federal City, Nat. Press (Washington). Home: 1412 Trouville Av Norfolk VA 23505 Office: 150 W Brambleton Av Norfolk VA 23510

MASON, THOMAS BOYD, lawyer; b. Lynchburg, Va., Jan. 12, 1919; s. Leonard Tyree and Beulah Elizabeth (Coffey) M.; student Hampden-Sydney Coll., 1936-38; LL.B., U. Va., 1941; m. Emily Ann Wilkins, Jan. 22, 1949; children—Martha Wyatt, Ann Corinne Courtney. Admitted to Va. bar, 1940; practice in Arlington, 1941-42, Lynchburg, 1946-56; mem. trust dept. Peoples Nat. Bank & Trust Co., Lynchburg, 1956-61; U.S. atty. Western dist Va., 1961-69; gen. atty. N.&W. Ry., 1969—. Served with USNR, 1942-46. Mem. Va. State Bar, Am., Va., Roanoke bar assns., Pi Kappa Alpha, Phi Alpha Delta. Home: 2608 Richelieu Av SW Roanoke VA 24014 Office: 8 N Jefferson St Roanoke VA 24011

MASON, (MARY) THOMASINE GRAYSON (MRS. E. FLEMING MASON), lawyer, state ofcl.; b. Summerton, S.C., Nov. 7, 1918; d. James Fulton and Anne (Gentry) Grayson; A.B., U. S.C. 1938, LL.B., 1942; m. Edgar Fleming Mason, June 30, 1939. Recruiter, personnel worker U.S. Civil Service Commn., Ga., also S.C., World War II; admitted to S.C. bar, 1941, since practiced in Manning; asso. Grayson-Elliott, Inc., 1952-63, sec. bd. dirs., 1947—; trial atty. civil div. U.S. Dept. Justice, Washington, 1968-72; hearing examiner Bur. Hearings and Appeals, Social Security Adminstrn., Dept. Health, Edn. and Welfare, 1972—; mem. S.C. Senate, 1966-68. Dist. vice chmn. A.R.C., 1955-56; chmn. TB seals dr., 1965-67. Del. nat. conv., Democratic party, 1960. Bd. dirs. Palmetto Girls State; trustee Clarendon Meml. Hosp. Mem. Clarendon Co. Farm Bur., Clarendon Co. C. of C. D.A.R., Am. Legion Aux. (v.p. S.C. dept.), S.C. Bar Assn. (v.p. 3d jud. circuit 1965-67), Am. Trial Lawyers Assn., Am. Bar Assn., Alpha Delta Pi. Clubs: Booster; Garden (Summerton); Business and Professional Women's, Executive (Sumter, S.C.). Home: Apt 106 Chateau de Ville Apts 3600 Chateau Dr Columbia SC Office: 221 Middleburg Plaza Columbia SC

MASON, TIM ROBERT, educator; b. Hereford, Tex., Apr. 26, 1930; s. Homer Basil and Naomi Estelie (Aldridge) M.; B.S., Abilene Christian Coll., 1953; M.S., Texas Tech. U., 1955; Ph.D., Tex. A. and M. U., 1963; m. Bettie Louise Justice, Mar. 31, 1953; children—Jacque Lynn, Judy Ann, Jeff Alan. Asst. prof. Abilene Christian Coll., 1956-64; dir. tech. services Profl. Feeds, Kansas City, Mo., 1964-66; prof. Tarleton State Coll., Stephenville, Tex., 1966—; pres. Stephenville Research Inst., 1968—. Pres. bd. dirs. Sherwood Foster Home for Children. William Elwood Soil Conservation fellow, 1954. Mem. Am. Soc. Animal Sci., Plains Nutrition Council. Mem. Ch. of Christ (elder). Club: Optimist (Stephenville). Home: Route 3 Box 42-A Stephenville TX 76401

MASSELL, SAM, mayor of Atlanta; b. Atlanta, Aug. 26, 1927; s. Sam and Florence (Rubin) M.; student Emory U., 1944-45, U. Ga., 1947-48; LL.B., Atlanta Law Sch., 1949; B.C.S., Ga. State U., 1951, postgrad. certificate in selling, 1952, postgrad. diploma in real estate, 1953; m. Doris M. Middlebrooks, Oct. 25, 1952; children—Cynthia Diane, Steven Alan, Melanie Denise. Chief publs. Nat. Assn. Women's and Children's Apparel Salesmen, Inc., 1949-51; with Allan-Grayson Realty Co., 1951-69, v.p., 1955-69; v.p. Mallin Developers, Inc., 1956-65; vice mayor, pres. Atlanta Bd. Alderman, 1962-69; mayor City of Atlanta, 1970—. Instr. in real estate Smith-Hughes Atlanta Vocational Sch., 1956. Councilman, City of Mountain Park (Ga.), 1950-52; sec., Atlanta City Exec. Com., 1953-61. Served with USAAF, 1946-47. Democrat. Jewish religion. Clubs: Standard, Commerce. Home: 2750 Wyngate NW Atlanta GA 30305 Office: 206 City Hall 68 Mitchell St SW Atlanta GA 30303

MASSENGALE, R. GLENN, clergyman, educator; b. Stewart, Ala., June 4, 1915; s. Warren Grover and Mattie (Spencer) M.; A.B., Birmingham-So. Coll., 1935; B.D., Yale, 1939, Ph.D., 1950; m. Lessie Elizabeth Clements, Aug. 16, 1938; 1 dau., Ellona Lois. Jr. sec. YMCA, Ansonia, Conn., 1936-39; dir. religious and social life Emory U., Atlanta, 1939-41; dir. Wesley Found., Yale, 1941-43; ordained to ministry Methodist Ch., 1941; pastor Meth. Ch., Decatur, Miss., 1943; chaplain U. S.C., Columbia, 1946-49; prof. religious edn. Scarritt Coll., Nashville, 1949-51; prof. religion and philosophy, dean of men Huntingdon Coll., Montgomery, Ala., 1951-57, prof. religion and philosophy, dir. library, 1957—. Served as chaplain USNR, 1944-46; comdr. USNR. Mem. A.L.A., Am. Acad. Religion, Sigma Alpha Epsilon, Omicron Delta Kappa. Rotarian. Contbr. to ch. publs. Home: 1346 Wedgewood Dr Montgomery AL 36111

MASSENGILL, RAYMOND MCCELLAN, JR., educator, researcher; b. Bristol, Va., Dec. 8, 1937; s. Raymond McCellan and Mary Louise (Myers) M.; B.S., U. Tenn., 1959, M.S., 1959; Ed.D., U. Va., 1968; m. Harriet Hargreave, Dec. 20, 1958; children—Kimberly, Deborah, Raymond McCellan III, Andrew. Dir. med. speech pathology Duke U. Med. Center, Durham, N.C., 1964—, asso. prof. dept. surgery, 1971—, chmn. campus Christian Life com., 1970—. Dept. Health, Edn. and Welfare trainee, 1963; Nat. Elks Found. scholar, 1963, Vocational Rehab. Assn. scholar, 1963, research grantee Nat. Insts., 1966. Fellow Am. Speech and Hearing Assn.; mem. Am. Cleft Palate Assn., So. Speech Communication Assn. (chmn. speech pathology sect. 1971). Author: Hypernasality: Considerations in Causes and Treatment Procedures, 1971. Contbr. articles to sci. publs. Editorial cons. Am. Jour. Speech and Hearing Disorders, 1971—. Home: 2734 Spencer St Durham NC 27775

MASSEY, CECIL EARL, city mgr.; b. Stamford, Tex., Sept. 16, 1921; s. Hugh Thomas and Ella May (Grisby) M.; student Washington and Lee U., 1945; B.B.A., Baylor U., 1949, M.A. 1950; postgrad. West Tex. State Coll., 1951; m. Mary Ann Burton, Dec. 30, 1949; children—Cleve, Neal, Mark, Linda. Mgr., Canyon (Tex.) C. of C., 1950-51, Deaf Smith County C. of C., Hereford, Tex., 1951-53; mgr. City of Hereford (Tex.), 1953-56, City of Haltom City (Tex.), 1956-57, City of Weatherford (Tex.), 1957-62, City of Weslaco (Tex.), 1962—. Active Boy Scouts Am.; bd. commrs. Waco Methodist Children's Home; past pres. Hereford Lions Club: past zone chmn., Lions Internat., dist. gov., 1960-61, now internat. counselor, pres. gov.'s council Tex. Lions Clubs, 1960-61, past officer Canyon and Haltom City Lions Clubs. Served with AUS, 1942-45. Named Man of Year, Weslaco, 1967. Rockefeller Found. Fellow, N.Y.C., Nat. Theatre Conf. fellow, N.Y.C. Mem. Baylor Ex-Lettermen's Assn. (chmn. bd. dirs. 1953-57), State Hwy. 60 Assn. (sec. 1952), Internat., Tex. city mgrs. assns., S.W. Conf. Football Ofcls. Methodist (mem. ofcl. bd., asso. dist. lay leader). Mason. Home: 904 Border Weslaco TX 78596 Office: City Hall Bldg Weslaco TX 78596

MASSEY, DONALD WAYNE, ednl. adminstr.; b. Durham, N.C., Mar. 7, 1938; s. Gordon Davis and Lucille Alma (Gregory) M.; student U. Hawaii, 1959, U. Ky., 1965; m. Violet Sue McIlvain, Nov. 2, 1958; children— Kimberly Shan, Leon Dale, Donn Krichele. Head microfilm sect. Ky. Hist. Soc., Frankfort, 1961; dir. microfilm center U. Ky., Lexington, 1962-67; dir. photographic services and graphics U. Va., Charlottesville, 1967—. Instr., U. Va. Sch. Continuing Edn., 1971-72. Served with USMCR, 1957-60. Mem. Am., Va. library assns., Soc. Reprodn. Engrs., Nat., Va. (pres. 1971), Ky. (Outstanding award 1967, pres. 1964-67) microfilm assns. Contbg. editor Va. Librarian, 1970-71, Micro-News Va. Microfilm Assn., 1970-71. Contbr. articles to profl. pubs. Home: Route 2 Box 82F Scottsville VA 24590 Office: U Va Library Charlottesville VA 22903

MASSEY, DYAR EDWIN, JR., univ. adminstr.; b. Greenville, S.C., Dec. 1, 1916; s. Dyar Edwin and Lydia (Nix) M.; A.B. in Journalism, U. Ga., 1937, M.A., 1938; m. Nancy Caldwell, Oct. 10, 1943; children—James Edwin, David Dyar, Barbara Ann. Instr. social sci. U. Ga., Athens, 1938-39, dir. pub. relations, alumni sec., also asst. prof. journalism, 1939-41, dir. pub. relations, 1951-54; dir. Community Chest of Greater Greenville, 1941-45; editor, pub. Wrightsville (Ga.) Headlight, 1946-51; dir. devel. Furman U., Greenville, 1954-59; dir. devel. Emory U., Atlanta, 1959-71, asst. v.p. devel., 1972—. Bd. mem., agy. relations div. Met. Atlanta Community Services, 1960-63; dir. U. Ga. Sesquicentennial Celebration, 1950-51; mem. financial devel. council Urban Coalition. Bd. dirs. Goodwill Industries of Atlanta, 1962—. Mem. Am. Coll. Pub. Relations Assn. (pres. 1967-68), Pub. Relations Soc. Am. (pres. Ga. chpt. 1972), Ga. Soc. Fund Raisers (pres. 1968), Ga. Jr. C. of C. (v.p. 1949-50), Phi Beta Kappa, Phi Kappa Phi, Omicron Delta Kappa, Sigma Delta Chi. Kiwanian (pres. Greenville 1958). Baptist. Home: 1691 Mason Mill Rd NE Atlanta GA 30329

MASSEY, EDWIN DWIGHT, hosp. adminstr.; b. Leslie, Ark., Feb. 11, 1926; s. Daniel B. and Louisa Belle (Stephenson) M.; student McNeese State Coll., 1968, La. State U., 1969-70, U. Ala., 1970-71; m. Bonnie Lucile Williams, Aug. 7, 1946; children—Linda (Mrs. William Riley Milner II), Larry D., Paul D., Michael Edwin. Computer, Petty Geophys. Engring. Co., San Antonio, 1947-53; party chief Liberty Exploration Co., Houston, 1953-59; bus. mgr. Beauregard Meml. Bapt. Hosp., DeRidder, La., 1959-60, adminstr., 1960—. Named col. Staff La. Gov., 1969—. Mem. Am. Acad. Med. Adminstrs., La. Hosp. Assn., La. Nursing Home Assn., DeRidder C. of C. Baptist. Kiwanian. Club: DeRidder Duck. Home: 105 Henderson St DeRidder LA 70634 Office: 502 S Pine St DeRidder LA 70634

MASSEY, GILMORE HAROLD, educator, univ. ofcl.; b. Monroeville, Ala., Jan. 5, 1921; s. Gilmore and Myrtle (Hudson) M.; B.S., Auburn U., 1944; postgrad. So. Bapt. Theol. Sem., 1944-45; M.A., George Peabody Coll., 1946; Ed.D., Tex. Tech. Coll., 1956; m. Elizabeth Martin, Apr. 4, 1945; children—Martha Elizabeth, Ruth Lynn. Dir., Bapt. Union, U. Miami (Fla.), 1946-50; dean students Wayland Coll., Plainview, Tex., 1950-53, Belmont Coll., Nashville, 1953-57; dir. counseling, asst. dean U. So. Miss., 1957-60; dir. counseling, adminstr. Office Registrar, Fla. State U., Tallahassee, 1960-64; dean admissions and records Tenn. Tech. U., Cookeville, 1964-69, also prof. edn.; dir. Madisonville Community Coll. of U. Ky., 1969—. Ednl. cons., conf. speaker and cons. Mem. Am. Psychol. Assn., Am. Personnel and Guidance Assn., Nat. Vocational Guidance Assn. Baptist (chmn. bd. deacons 1963-64). Rotarian. Contbr. to youth publs. Home: Grampian Hills Madisonville KY 42431

MASSEY, HOWARD CECIL, entomologist; b. Sylvarena, Miss., Mar. 19, 1912; s. Howard Clinton and Jenny Theodora (Lowe) M.; student Miss. State Coll., 1931-32; m. Gladys Sedwich, Sept. 17, 1937. With U.S. Dept. Agr., various locations, 1932—, plant pest insp., Harlingen, Tex., 1936-57, work unit supr., Seguin, Tex., 1957—. Served with AUS, 1943-46. Recipient Merit certificate sustained outstanding performance U.S. Dept. Agr., 1966. Mem. Entomol. Soc. Am. Democrat. Presbyn. Mason (K.T., 32 deg.). Club: Rod and Gun (v.p.). Home: 708 E Weinert St Seguin TX 78155 Office: PO Box 48 Seguin TX 78155

MASSEY, JACK TAYLOR, life ins. co. exec.; b. Frederick, Okla., May 7, 1927; s. James A. and Viola (Taylor) M.; B.B.A., U. Okla., 1951, LL.B., 1957; m. Sue Neal, Nov. 10, 1951; children—Sarena L., Cynthia S., J. Taylor, Neal E. Admitted to Okla. bar, 1957; agt. Mass. Mut. Life Ins. Co., Oklahoma City, 1951-62; self employed ind. ins. agt., ins. cons., Oklahoma City, 1962-64; with United Founders Life Ins. Co., Oklahoma City, 1964—, exec. v.p. 1966—, also dir., mem. exec. com.; exec. v.p. United Founders Life Ins. Co. of Ill., Arlington Heights, 1968—, also dir.; dir. Reis Corp., Oklahoma City, Gen. Life of Tenn. Ins. Co., Columbia, United Founders Life Ins. Co. of Tex., Dallas. Served with USNR, 1945-46. C.L.U. Mem. Am. Soc. C.L.U.'S, Okla.-Oklahoma County Bar Assn., Lawyers Tax Group, Beta Theta Pi, Phi Alpha Delta. Methodist (adminstrv. bd.). Lion. Club: Quail Creek Golf and Country, Beacon, Oklahoma City Boat. Home: 2308 NW 58th St Oklahoma City OK 73112 Office: 5900 Mosteller Dr Oklahoma City OK 73112

MASSEY, JAMES CARLTON, archtl. historian; b. San Gabriel, Cal., Apr. 8, 1932; s. Carlton Justice and Marion (Steltz) M.; B.Arch., U. Pa., 1955; m. Anne E. McLaughlin, Nov. 12, 1955. Architect, Nat. Park Service, Dept. Interior, Phila., 1955-66, chief Historic Am. Bldgs. Survey, 1966-72; dir. dept. historic properties Nat. Trust for Historic Preservation, Washington, 1972—. Bd. dirs. Historic Delaware County, 1964-66, Radnor Hist. Soc., 1963-67. Served with AUS, 1956-57. Ford Found. grantee, 1966. Mem. Soc. Archtl. Historians (editor Newsletter, 1962—, dir.), Athenaeum of Phila., Soc. Am. Archivists, Arts Club Washington. Unitarian. Home: 614 S Lee St Alexandria VA 22314 Office: 740 Jackson Pl NW Washington DC 20006

MASSEY, LUTHER M., dentist; b. Wakefield, N.C., July 4, 1895; s. Daniel D. and Eldora Frances (Hood) M.; student Wake Forest Coll., 1913-16; D.D.S., Med. Coll. Va., 1918; grad. implant dentistry Inst. Grad. Dentists, N.Y.C., 1969; m. Vivian Dawson, June 24, 1927; 1dau., Carolyn Vivian. Practicing dentist, Zebulon, N.C., 1919—; farmer; dir. N.C. Farm Bur. Service Co.; mem. exec. com., dir. N.C. Farm Bur. Mut. Ins. Co. Mem. N.C. Bd. Edn., 1939-44; chmn. Wake County Bd. Elections, 1939-41. Chmn. bd. trustees Meredith Coll., 1952-68, trustee, 1968—; bd. dirs. Wake County Opportunities, Inc., State N.C. Tchrs. and State Employees Retirement System; trustee agrl. found. State Coll., N.C., chmn. research fund; trustee dental found. U.N.C. Served with Dental Co. No. 1, World War I; 1st lt. Dental Res., until 1936. Mem. Am., 4th Dist. (pres.) dental assns., D.C. Dental Soc., N.C. (pres. local county unit, dir.), Four County (past pres.) heart assns., Internat. Soc. Implant Dentistry, N.C. Farm Bur. Fedn. (exec. com.), Am. Legion. Baptist (chmn. finance com.). Mason (32 deg.), Rotarian (pres.). Club: Carolina Country. Home: Zebulon NC 27597

MASSEY, ROBERT LEE, dentist; b. Detroit, Tex., Dec. 24, 1902; s. Robert Price and Frances Elizabeth (Coleman) M.; D.D.S., Baylor U., 1927; m. Agnes High, Apr. 19, 1930; children—Roberta (Mrs. Jack B. Ramsey), Elizabeth (Mrs. Mac Kehoe), Carole (Mrs. E.E. Dean). Gen. practice dentristry, Tulia, Tex., 1928—. Recipient Order Good Fellow, 1955. Mem. Am. (life), Tex. (life) dental assns., Panhandle Dental Soc., Xi Psi Phi. Baptist. Home: 507 N Donley St Tulia TX 79088 Office: First Nat Bank Bldg Tulia TX 79088

MAST, STEWART DALE, airport exec.; b. Kalamazoo, Mich., May 10, 1924; s. Virgil S. and Sarah L. (Rippey) M.; student U. Mich., 1942, Argubright Coll. Bus. Adminstrn., 1946, Spartan Sch. Aeros., 1947; m. Mary F. Smith, Aug. 1, 1945; children—Peter S., Frances A. Mgr. city airport, Battle Creek, Mich., 1948-60; airport dir., County of Milw., 1960-66; mgr. airports Hillsborough County Aviation Authority, Tampa, Fla., 1966—. Mem. bd. review Milw. council Boy Scouts Am., 1964-65. Served to 2d lt. USAAF, 1943-45. Mem. Am. Assn. Airport Execs. (dir. 1965-67). Mason. Home: 5114 Homer Av Tampa FL 33609 Office: PO Box 22287 Tampa FL 33622

MASTEN, JOHN TALBOT, educator; b. Newark, Mar. 13, 1914; s. Glenn Arnold and Janet (Turner) M.; student Springfield (Ill.) Jr. Coll., 1932-34; B.S., U. Ill., 1936, M.S., 1937; Ph.D., U. N.C., 1942; m. Elizabeth Ida Bluemke, Aug. 17, 1938; children—Patricia Sue (Mrs. Charles Judd Barnes), John Talbot. Regional price economist Bur. Labor Statistics, Chgo., 1945-47; chmn. dept. econs. Kalamazoo Coll., 1947-48; asso. prof. U. Ky., Lexington, 1948-57, prof. econs., 1957-67, dir. grad. studies in econs., 1963-66, chmn. dept., 1964-66; Ga. Bankers Assn. prof. banking U. Ga., Athens, 1967—. Cons. Ky. Bankers Assn., 1964—; ednl. dir. Ga. Banking Sch., Athens, 1968—; faculty Banking Sch. of South, Baton Rouge, 1964-69. Mem. Fayette County Recreation Bd., Lexington, 1957-62. Mem. Am., So. econ. assns., Am. Finance Assn., Beta Gamma Sigma. Author: (with W. Warren Haynes) Programmed Text in Money and Banking, 1969. Contbr. articles to profl. jours. Home: 130 Devereux Dr Athens GA 30601

MASTERS, GEORGE MALLARY, educator; b. Savannah, Ga., June 19, 1936; s. George Mallary and Edna Lee (Brabham) M.; student King Coll., 1954-56; B.S., magna cum laude, Columbia, 1960; M.A., Johns Hopkins, 1962, Ph.D., with distinction, 1964. Asst. prof. French, U. Mo., Columbia, 1964-66; asst. prof. Romance langs. State U. N.Y. Binghamton, 1966-69, asso. prof., 1969-70; asso. prof. Romance langs. U. N.C., Chapel Hill, 1970—. Recipient research grants U. Mo., 1965-66, State U. N.Y., 1967-70, U. N.C., 1970-73; Nat. Def. Edn. Act fellow, 1960-63, Hon. Woodrow Wilson fellow, 1960-61, Woodrow Wilson Dissertation fellow, 1963-64, Am. Council Learned Socs. fellow, 1968, Nat. Endowment for Humanities fellow, 1968. Mem. N.C. Hist. and Lit. Assn., Ga. Hist. Soc., Am. Assn. Tchrs. French, Modern Lang. Assn., Renaissance Soc. Am., Medieval Acad. Am., Herb Soc. Am., Phi Beta Kappa, Phi Sigma Iota. Author:

Rabelaisian Dialectic and the Platonic-Hermetic Tradition, 1969. Contbr. articles to profl. jours. Mem. adv. bd. Romance Notes, 1970—; mem. editorial bd. Studies in Philology, 1972—. Home: Box 907 201 W Trollinger Av Elon College NC 27244 Office: Dey Hall U NC Chapel Hill NC 27514

MASTERS, WILLIAM PEYTON, credit agy. exec.; b. Atlanta, Mar. 17, 1916; s. James Marvin and Cecelia (Hale) M.; grad. U. S.C., 1937; m. Virginia Watson, Dec. 20, 1941; children—Ansley (Mrs. Robt. T. Lyles), Sally (Mrs. David C. Wakefield), Virginia W., Lila S. Co-founder Carolina Fleets, Inc., 1952 (merged into Am. Discount 1961, then merged with Home Finance to form Am. Credit Corp. 1965), pres., 1952-70; exec. v.p. Am. Credit Corp., Charlotte, N.C., 1970—. Served to capt. USAF, 1941-46. Club: Anderson (S.C.) Country (bd. govs.). Home: Marryot Av Charlotte NC Office: 201 S Tryon St Charlotte NC 28101

MASTERSON, FRANCIS T., exec. dir. U.S. Fgn. Claims Settlement Com. Office: Foreign Claims Settlement Com 1111 20th St NW Washington DC 20230*

MASTERSON, WILLIAM HENRY, univ. pres.; b. Houston, Mar. 16, 1914; s. Leigh C. and Aileen (Sharp) M.; B.A., Rice U., 1935; M.A., U. Pa., 1946, Ph.D.,1950; m. Orvetta T. Weston, Aug. 18, 1945; children— David Glen (dec.), Amanda Roane, Aileen Talbott. Instr. history Baylor Sch., Chattanooga, 1935-41, 47-48; asst. instr. history U. Pa., 1945-47; faculty Rice U., Houston, 1948-66, prof. history, 1955-66, asst. to pres., 1951-55, master Hanszen Coll., 1957-66, dean humanities, 1959-66, pres., 1969—; pres. U. Chattanooga, 1966-69. Vis. prof. U. Wis., 1957. Trustee St. Stephens Sch., Austin, Tex. Served to capt. AUS, 1941-45. Mem. Am. Mississippi Valley, So., Tex. Gulf Coast (pres. 1957-60, v.p. 1960—) hist. assns., Houston Philos. Soc., C. of C. (met. council) Newcomen Soc. Phi Beta Kappa. Episcopalian. Rotarian. Author: William Blount, 1950. Editor: John Gray Blount Papers; Jour. So. History, 1959-61. Office: Rice University Houston TX

MASTRAN, DAVID VINCENT, systems analyst; b. El Paso, Tex., Dec. 14, 1942; s. Joseph Lee and Mary (Black) M.; B.S., U.S. Mil. Acad., 1965; M.S., Stanford, 1966; postgrad. George Washington; U., 1969-72; m. Shelley Ellen Smith, June 12, 1965; children—David Bruce, Susannah Mary. Commd. 2d lt. U.S. Air Force, 1965, advanced through grades to capt. 1971; reliability analyst Directorate of Spl. Weapons, San Antonio, 1966-67; operations research analyst Hdqrs. 7th Air Force Operations Analysis Office, Tan Son Nhut Air Base, Viet Nam, 1967-68, Hdqrs. Air Force Operations Analysis Office, Washington, 1968-71; ret., 1972; operations research analyst Office Asst. Sec. Def. (Systems Analysis), 1972—. Decorated Bronze Star, Air Force Commendation medal. Mem. Operations Research Soc. Am., Washington Operations Research Council, Inst. Mgmt. Sci., Assn. Pub. Programs Analysis, West Point Alumni Assn. Home: 933 Mackall Av McLean VA 22101 Office: Office of Assistant Secretary of Defense (Systems Analysis) The Pentagon Washington DC 20330

MASTRO, NICK, state ofcl.; b. Jacksonville, Fla., Jan. 9, 1924; s. L.K. and Mary (Gionis) Mastrogianakis; B.C.E., U. Fla., 1946; M.P.H. in Engring., U. Mich., 1952; m. Eva Yeatropoulos, Oct. 4, 1953; children—Mary Christine, Elain Sophia. Jr. engr. Smith & Gillespie, cons. engrs., Jacksonville, 1946-47; with Fla. Bd. Health, Jacksonville, 1947—, regional san. engr., 1949-67, dir. div. indsl. waste, 1967-68, asst. chief bur. san. engring., 1968—. Registered profl. engr., Fla. Fellow Water Pollution Control Fedn.; mem. Fla. Pub. Health Assn., Nat. Soc. Profl. Engrs., Air Pollution Control Assn., Fla. Water Pollution Control Operators Assn., Fla. Engring. Soc., Sigma Tau, Sigma Phi Epsilon. Mem. Greek Orthdox Ch. (trustee, v.p.). Clubs: University Park Country, University Park Civic (dir. 1965-68) (Jacksonville). Home: 5413 Coppedge Av Jacksonville FL 32211 Office: Fla Div Health 1217 Pearl St Jacksonville FL 32201

MASY, JACK, display specialist USIA since early 1950's—, designer U.S. exhibit Montreal World's Fair, Osaka World's Fair; presently supr. Am. Revolution Bicentennial Commn. Office: Am Revolution Bicentennial Commn 736 Jackson Pl NW Washington DC 20076*

MATA, EDUARDO, conductor; b. Mexico City, Mexico, 1942; student Nat. Conservatory Music; student of Carlos Chavez, 1960-65; advanced conducting work with Igor Kipnis, Max Rudolph, Erich Leinsdorf, 1964; m. Carmen. Resident conductor Tanglewood, 1964; guest conductor featuring Mexican music with orchestras Mexico, Brazil, Chile, Peru, Poland, Yugoslavia, Luxembourg, France, U.S.; presently music dir., conductor Orch. Nat. U. Mexico. Named Conductor of the Year, Nat. Assn. Critics Mexico, 1967. Address: Orquesta Universidad Nacional Autonoma Ciudad Universitaria Mexico City Mexico*

MATARESE, JOHN, real estate exec.; b. Bronx, N.Y., Mar. 5, 1917; s. Giovanni and Civita (DePaola) Matarese; student extension courses N.Y. Coll., Cornell U., 1948-52; m. Norma Jean Wilson, Nov. 16, 1960; 1 son, Monte Dean. With Matarese Food Store, N.Y.C., 1933-37; produce mgr. First Nat. Food Stores, White Plains, N.Y., 1937-40, 46-57, Grand Union Food Stores, New Canaan, Conn., 1957-58; real estate salesman Punta Gorda Isles, Inc. (Fla.), 1959-62, gen. sales mgr., 1962-68, v.p., gen. sales mgr., 1968—; adv. bd. Port Charlotte Bank (Fla.). Bd. dirs. St. Joseph Hosp., Port Charlotte. Served with AUS, 1941-46. Clubs: Punta Gorda Isles Yacht; Brunt Store Golf (Punta Gorda). Home: 2111 Palm Tree Dr Punta Gorda FL 33950 Office: 1625 W Marion Av Punta Gorda FL 33950

MATEER, RICHARD SHELBY, educator; b. Fredericktown, Mo., Sept. 2, 1923; s. Thomas Joseph and Helen Veronica (Donihee) M.; B.S. in Metall. Engring., Mo. Sch. Mines, 1944; M.S., Carnegie Inst. Tech., 1947; Ph.D., U. Pitts., 1950; m. Myrtle Ann Rider, Jan. 11, 1952; children—Margaret, Susan, Thomas. Fellow Mellon Inst. Indsl. Research, 1950-52; research engr. Kaiser Aluminium Co., 1952-54; asst. prof., then asso. prof. U. Pitts., 1954-58; prof. metall. engring., head dept. U. Ky., 1958—; acad. visitor Imperial Coll., London, Eng., 1965; research stellite div. Union Carbide Corp., 1967; cons. in field. Research grantee dental amalgam Dept. Health, Edn. and Welfare, 1964—. Mem. Am. Inst. M.E., Am. Soc. Metals, Sigma Xi. Home: 247 Shady Lane Lexington KY 40503

MATEKER, EMIL JOSEPH, JR., geophysicist; b. St. Louis, Apr. 25, 1931; s. Emil J. and Lillian A. (Broz) M.; B.S., St. Louis U., 1956, M.S., 1959, Ph.D., 1964; m. Lolita A. Winter, Nov. 25, 1954; children—Mark Steven, Anne Marie, John David. Geophysicist, Stanolind Oil & Gas Co., Midland, Tex., 1956, Standard Oil Co. of Cal., Salt Lake City, 1957, 58-60; instr. geophysics St. Louis U., 1960-63; asst. prof. geophysics Washington U., St. Louis, 1963-66, asso. prof., 1966-69; mgr. geophys. research Western Geophys. Co., Houston, 1969-70, v.p. research and devel., 1970—. Cons. U.S. Army C.E., St. Louis Met. Sewer Dist., Fred Weber Constrn. Co., Traylor Bros. Constrn. Co., Pam Am. Petroleum Co., others. Served to 2d lt., inf. AUS, 1952-54. Mem. Soc. Exploration Geophysicists, Seismol. Soc. Am., Am. Geophys. Union, European Assn. Exploration Geophysicists, A.A.A.S., Sigma Xi. Author: A Treatise on Modern Exploration Seismology, 1965, also others. Asst. editor Geophysics, 1968-69. Home: 419 Hickory Post Houston TX 77024 Office: PO Box 2469 Houston TX 77001

MATHENY, CHARLES WOODBURN, JR., engr., city ofcl.; b. Sarasota, Fla., Aug. 7, 1914; s. Charles Woodburn and Virginia (Yates) M.; B.S. in Civil Engring., U. Fla., 1936; grad. Army Command and Gen. Staff Coll., 1944; m. Jeanne Felkel, July 12, 1942; children— Virginia Ann, Nancy Carolina, Charles Woodburn III. Civil engr. Fla. East Coast Ry., 1939-41; commd. 2d lt. U.S. Army Res., 1936, 1st lt. U.S. Army, 1941, advanced through grades to col., 1955; gen. staff Dept. Army, 1948-51; arty. bn. comdr., Germany, 1945-46; aviation officer 25th Inf. Div., Korea, 1952; dep. comdt., dir. combat devel. Army Aviation Sch., 1954; dep. dir., research dir., dept. tactics Arty. Sch., 1955-57; aviation officer 7th U.S. Army, 1957-58; Munich sub area comdr. So. Area Command, Europe, 1959, dep. chief staff for information, 1960; Mich. sector comdr. VI Army Corps, 1961-62; ret., 1962; asst. supt. Dept. Pub. Works and Engring., City of Tampa (Fla.), 1963—. Active Boy Scouts Am., various community and ch. activities. Decorated Bronze Star with oak leaf cluster, Air Medal with three oak leaf clusters. Registered profl. engr., Ga. Mem. Assn. U.S. Army, Army Aviation Assn., Am. Helicopter Soc., S.A.R., Alpha Tau Omega. Episcopalian. Initiator tactical use of helicopters in Army, 1949. Home: 4802 Beachway Dr Tampa FL 33609 Office: 404 Jackson St Tampa FL 33602

MATHENY, HERSCHEL ALBERT, indsl. engr.; b. Guntersville, Ala., July 28, 1930; s. Ernest Bradford and Martha (Alexander) M.; student Snead Jr. Coll., 1954-55; B.S., U. Ala., 1957; m. Lynne Shirley Wietfeld, Sept. 27, 1969; 1 son, Ernest Alexander. Engr. Reynolds Metals Co., Sheffield, Ala., 1957-60; dir. program mgmt. Teledyne Brown Engineering, Huntsville, Ala., 1960—. Served with AUS, 1951-53. Mem. Nat. Mgmt. Assn., Tau Beta Pi, Alpha Pi Mu. Democrat. Methodist. Home: Signal Point Rd Guntersville AL 35976 Office: 300 Sparkman Dr Huntsville AL 35807

MATHENY, ROBERT DUANE, clergyman; b. Long Beach, Cal., Nov. 17, 1924; s. Harry and Ethel (Brothers) M.; B.A., Tex. Christian U., 1945, B.D., 1949; postgrad. U. Chgo., 1960, Pacific Sch. Religion, Berkeley, Cal., 1966, Furman U., 1969, 71; m. Norma Elizabeth Cheverton, June 22, 1949; children—Sarah (Mrs. Dennis Carlson, Jr.), Paul. Ordained to ministry Disciples of Christ Ch., 1950; minister, Conroe, Tex., 1948-50, Houston, 1950-51, Center, Tex., 1951-53. Jacksonville, Tex., 1953-63, First Christian Ch., Richardson, Tex., 1963-68, Atlanta, 1968-70, Winter Park (Fla.) Christian Ch., 1970—. Trustee Tex. Christian Chs., 1959-62, pres. dist. 14, 1957-59, bd. mem. Fla. Christian Chs. Disciples of Christ, 1971—; corr. The Christian, 1949—; trustee Christmount Christian Assembly, Black Mountain, N.C., 1968—; mem. Council Christian Unity, Disciples of Christ Hist. Soc.; Disciples of Christ rep. Fla. Council of Chs., 1971—; music and drama critic. Pres. Jacksonville Civic Music Assn., 1958-63; committeeman Boy Scouts Am.; pres. Richardson Ministerial Alliance, 1966. Bd. dirs. Central Fla. Heart Assn., 1970—. Recipient Distinction of Merit award U.S. Com. for UN, 1957, Tb Christmas Seal Drive award, 1959. Mem. Brite Div. Sch. Alumni Assn. (v.p.), Tex. Christian U. Ex-Students Assn., Tex. Council Chs. (pres. 1964-65), Winter Park Ministerial Assn. (pres. 1971—), Central Fla. Civic Music Assn., Alpha Psi Omega. Democrat. Mason, Rotarian. Home: 1217 Denton Rd Winter Park FL 32789 Office: 760 N Lakemount Av Winter Park FL 32789

MATHENY, TOM HARRELL, lawyer; b. Houston, June 30, 1933; s. Whitman and Lorene (Harrell) M.; B.A., Southeastern La. U., 1954; J.D., Tulane U., 1957. Admitted to La. bar, 1957; partner firm Pittman & Matheny, Hammond, La., 1957—; trust counsel 1st Guaranty Bank; v.p. Edwards & Assos., So. Brick Supply, Inc. Faculty, Southeastern La. U., 5 years, Holy Cross Coll., New Orleans, 3 years; mem. com. on conciliation and mediation of disputes World Peace through Law Center. Chmn. advancement com. Boy Scouts Am., Hammond, 1960-64, mem. dist. council, 1957-66, mem. exec. bd. Istrouma council, 1966—; pres. Tangipahoa Parish Mental Health Assn.; sec. Chep Morrison Scholarship Found.; mem. men's com. Japan Internat. Christian U. Found.; mem. com. on community action and crime prevention La. Commn. on Law Enforcement and Adminstrn. Criminal Justice. Bd. dirs. La. Moral and Civic Found., Tangipahoa Parish A.R.C., 1957-67, Hammond United Givers Fund, 1957-68, La. Council Chs., Southeastern Devel. Found., La. Mental Health Assn., Wesley Found., La. State U., 1965-68, 70—; trustee Centenary Coll., 1964-70; hon. trustee John F. Kennedy Coll. Recipient Man of Year award, Hammond, 1961, 64, also La. Jr. C. of C., 1964. Fellow Harry S. Truman Library Inst. (hon.); mem. Am. (com. on probate and trust), La. (past gen. chmn. com. on legal aid), 21st Jud. Dist. (past sec.-treas., v.p. 1967-68, 71—) bar assns., Comml. Law League Am. (past mem. com. on ethics), La. Alumni Council (past pres.), Acad. Religion and Mental Health, La. Assn. Claimant's Compensation Attys., Southeastern La. U. (dir., pres. 1961-62, dir. spl. fund 1959-62, past dir. Tangipahoa chpt.), Tulane Sch. Law alumni assns., Am. Trial Lawyers Assn., Am. Judicature Soc., Law-Sci. Inst., World Peace Through Law Acad., Acad. Polit. Sci., Am. Acad. Polit. and Social Sci., Internat. Acad. Law and Sci., Common Cause, Internat. Platform Assn., UN Assn., La. Hist. Assn., Friends of Cabildo, Acad. Religion and Mental Health, Gideons Internat., Nat. Assn. Conf. Lay Leaders (pres.), Assn. Conf. Lay Leaders South Central Jurisdiction (pres.), Hammond Assn. Commerce (dir. 1960-65), Phi Delta Phi, Phi Alpha Delta. Democrat. Methodist (steward, adminstrv. bd., dist. lay leader 1960-64, past co-chmn. conf. bd. lay activities, lay minister, lay leader La. area conf., numerous other ch. activities). Mason, DeMolay (Legion of Honor), Kiwanian (v.p., dir.). Home: Pleasant Ridge Hammond LA 70401 Office: Guaranty Bank Bldg Hammond LA 70401

MATHESON, PAUL TAYLOR, fire chief; b. Asheville, N.C., June 15, 1910; s. Dallas G. and Nora (Towe) M.; A.B., U. Miami, 1936; m. Alice M. Hill, Apr. 28, 1940; 1 dau., Joy E. With Fire Dept., Coral Gables, Fla., 1936—, lt. charge tng., 1945-55, fire chief, 1955—. Vice pres. bd. dirs. Coral Gables Municipal Credit Union; trustee Coral Gables Fireman's Relief and Pension Fund. Served with AUS, 1941-42. Recipient Cooper Taylor Meml. award Jr. C. of C., 1960. Mem. Internat., Southeastern assns. fire chiefs, Fla., Dade County (past pres.) fire chiefs assns., Nat. Fire Protection Assn., Iron Arrow U. Miami. Elk. Club: U. Miami Gridders. Home: 5765 SW 46th Terrace Miami FL 33155 Office: 2325 Salzedo St Coral Gables FL 33134

MATHEWS, FORREST DAVID, univ. pres.; b. Grove Hill, Ala., Dec. 6, 1935; s. Forrest Lee and Doris (Pearson) M.; A.B., U. Ala., 1958, M.A., 1959, LL.D., 1969; Ph.D., Columbia, 1965; m. Mary Chapman, Jan. 24, 1960;children—Lee Ann, Lucy McLeod. With U. Ala., University, 1960—, pres., 1969—, also faculty history dept. Dir. Birmingham br. Fed. Res. Bank, Atlanta. Mem. Nat. Programming Council for Pub. Television, 1970—; mem. adv. com. intern program Am. Council on Edn., 1970—; mem. Council on Coll.-Level Exams., Coll. Entrance Exam. Bd., 1971—; bd. advisers Outstanding Young Men Am., 1971—; state chmn. March of Dimes, 1971—; bd. dirs. So. Regional Edn. Bd., 1970—; trustee Judson Coll., 1968—, Charles F. Kettering Found. Served with inf., AUS, 1959. Named One of 10 Outstanding Young Men, U.S. Jr. C. of C. Mem. Nat. Assn. State Univs. and Land-Grant Colls. (chmn. com. on ednl. opportunities for minority groups 1970—), Phi Beta Kappa, Omicron Delta Kappa. Home: PO Box B University AL 35486

MATHEWS, GEORGE A., adminstr. Bapt. Meml. Hosp., Jacksonville, Fla. Office: Bapt Meml Hosp 800 Prudential Dr Jacksonville FL 32207*

MATHEWS, HARLAN, state ofcl.; b. Walker County, Ala., Jan. 17, 1927; B.A., Jacksonville State Coll., 1949; M.A., Vanderbilt U.; m. Betty Cox, 1947; children—Stanley, Richard, Lester. Admitted to Tenn. bar, 1962; with Tenn. State Planning Commn., 1950-54; mem. Tenn. Budget Staff, 1955-59, dep. commr. finance and adminstrn., 1959-61, commr. finance and adminstrn., 1961—. Served with USNR, 1944-46. Mem. Nat., Tenn. municipal finance officers assns., Nat. Assn. State Auditors, Comptrollers and Treasurers. Democrat. Baptist. Address: Dept Finance and Adminstrn State Capitol Nashville TN 37219*

MATHEWS, JOHN ELIE, JR., state senator; b. Jacksonville, Fla., June 20, 1920; A.B., Emory U., 1942; LL.B., Harvard, 1948; m. Gwendolyn Howard; children—Josiah Game, Kimball Irene, Barbara Alice, John Elie III. Admitted to Fla. bar; dep. commr. Fla. Indsl. Commn., 1950-51; mem. Fla. Ho. of Reps., 1956-62; mem. Fla. Senate, 1962—, pres., 1969—. Served to lt. comdr. USNR, World War II. Decorated Bronze Star. Mem. Jacksonville C. of C., Phi Beta Kappa, Sigma Chi (Balfour award). Democrat. Methodist. Mason (Shriner, 32 deg.). Address: State Capitol Tallahassee FL 32304*

MATHEWS, THOMAS RICHARD, assn. exec.; b. Salt Lake City, Aug. 1, 1921; s. Wesley Chase and Edith Blanche (Alm) M.; B.A., U. Utah, 1942; m. Bonnie Johnson, Dec. 27, 1942; children—Thomas Richard, Colin Dee, Anne. Sunday editor Salt Lake City Tribune, 1946-51; reporter San Francisco Chronicle, 1951-60; dir. information Peace Corps, Washington, 1961-62; dep. asst. sec. for congl. relations U.S. Dept. State, Washington, 1963-64, also White House cons., 1963; dir. pub. relations Lincoln Center for Performing Arts, N.Y.C., 1965-68; v.p. communications Urban Coalition, Washington, 1969; spl. asst. to John W. Gardner, chmn. Common Cause, Washington, 1970—. Washington press sec. Robert Kennedy for Pres. campaign, 1968. Served as 1st lt. 10th Mountain Div., AUS, 1943-45. Decorated Air medal with 4 oak leaf clusters. Recipient Christopher award for outstanding journalism, 1960. Democrat. Clubs: Brooklyn Heights Casino (Bklyn.), St. Albans Tennis (Washington). Home: 2311 Connecticut Av NW Washington DC 20008 Office: Common Cause 2100 M St NW Washington DC 20037

MATHEY, F(ABYAN) COURTENAY, newspaper exec.; b. N.Y.C., July 14, 1932; s. C. Fabyan and Edith (Barber) M.; student Princeton, 1950-53; B.S., U. Ark., 1957, M.B.A., 1960; m. Emily Gail O'Rear, July 12, 1958; children—Fabyan Courtenay II, C. Robinson. Cons., Peat, Marwick, Mitchell & Co., Dallas, 1960-64; accountant E.L. Gaunt &Co., Little Rock, 1964-65; partner Rothwell & Mathey, C.P.A.'s, Dallas, 1965-69, Travis, Ramsey & Mathey, C.P.A.'s, Dallas, 1969-70; controller Dallas Times Herald, 1970—; treas., dir. Systems Devel., Inc. Pres., George B. Dealey Elementary Sch. Dad's Club, 1969—. Served with AUS, 1953-55. C.P.A., Tex., Ark. Mem. Am. Inst. C.P.A.'s, Tex. Soc. C.P.A.'s. Clubs: Princeton (v.p.), Exchange of North Park (pres.) (Dallas). Home: 6429 Orchid Lane Dallas TX 75230 Office: Herald Sq Dallas TX 75202

MATHIS, EVAN THOMAS, JR., mining co. exec.; b. Americus, Ga., Dec. 23, 1925; s. Evan Thomas and Lois (McMath) M.; student Ga. Southwestern Jr. Coll., 1942-43; B.S., U.S. Naval Acad., 1946; m. Nell McGehee, June 24, 1950; children—Lane, Nell, Carol, Commd. ensign U.S. Navy, 1946, advanced through grades to lt., 1950; shipboard officer in U.S.S. Stormes, 1946-48, U.S.S. Patrol Craft Escort 903, 1948; naval aviator, Atlantic and Caribbean, 1948-54; with Marble Products Co., Atlanta, 1954—, sales mgr., 1954-58, treas., 1958-59, v.p., 1959-62, dir., 1959—, pres., 1962—; exec. v.p., dir. Fla. Terrazzo Supplies, Inc., Miami, Fla., 1960-65, pres., 1965—; exec. v.p., dir. Bilbrough Marble Co., Austin, Tex., 1964—; treas. Imperial Chems., Inc., West Palm Beach, 1960-65, pres., 1965—; co-owner Peachtree Park Office Bldg., Atlanta, 1963—; v.p., dir. Citizens Bank of Americus; adv. dir. Citizens & So. Nat. Bank, Atlanta; dir. Conseehee Carpets, Inc., Ellijay, Ga.; partner MSM Farms, Whitestone, Ga. Mem. Atlanta Freight Bur. (dir.), Young Pres.'s Orgn. Methodist (steward). Kiwanian. Clubs: Capital City, Gyro, Piedmont Driving. Home: 547 Spring Valley Rd NW Atlanta GA 30318 Office: 67 Peachtree Park Dr Atlanta GA 30309

MATHIS, LOYD BURL, cons. elec. engr.; b. Beaver, Okla., Jan. 11, 1908; s. Lee B. and Anna (Cooke) M.; B.S. in Elec. Engring., Okla. State U., 1930; postgrad. Panhandle A. and M. Coll., 1931, Alexander Hamilton Bus. Sch., 1947; m. Thelma R. Reeves, July 27, 1930; 1 dau., Carol J. (Mrs. Albert J. Bird). Tchr. math. and sci. Beaver High Sch., 1931-35; technician, engr. Ariz. Edison Co., Phoenix, 1937-43; instr. radio U.S. Naval Tng. Sch., Stillwater, Okla., 1943-45; engr. C.H. Guernsey & Co., Oklahoma City, 1945—, v.p., 1962—. Registered profl. engr., Okla., Colo., Utah, Wyo., Neb., Ark., La., N.M., Ore. Mem. I.E.E.E., Eta Kappa Nu. Home: 4714 Harvey Pkwy Oklahoma City OK 73118 Office: PO Box 53247 Oklahoma City OK 73105

MATHIS, ROBIN HOOD, broadcasting exec.; b. Houlka, Miss., Nov. 29, 1929; s. Henry Lacy and Annie Nina (Cole) M.; B.S. in Agronomy, Miss. State U., 1952; postgrad. Elkins Radio Sch., 1958; m. Shirley Lorraine Carroll, June 29, 1958; children—Melanie Carol, Leslie, Sharon. Announcer WHOS, Decatur, Ala., 1955; partner, mgr. WCPC-AM/FM, Houston, Miss., 1955-67, pres., gen. mgr., 1967—; partner WSJC-AM-FM, Magee, Miss., 1957—, WXTN, Lexington, Miss., 1958—, WSAO, Senatobia, Miss. Dir. Chickasaw Devel. Found. Served from 2d lt. to 1st lt., USAF, 1952-54. Recipient Silver Beaver award Boy Scouts Am. Mem. U.P.I., Nat. Assn. Broadcasters, Daytimers (nat. dir.), Miss. (state dir.) broadcasters assns. Miss. Econ. Council (dir. 1967-69), U.S. Jr., Miss. Jr. (pres. 1962-63) chambers commerce. Baptist. Club: Exchange (pres. Houston 1967-68). Home: Route 2 Box 29 Houston MS 38851 Route 2 Box 29 Houston MS 38851 Office: PO Box 569 Houston MS 38851

MATLOCK, KENNETH JEROME, bldg. materials co. exec.; b. Oak Park, Ill., May 30, 1928; s. Harvey and Lillian (Sivertsen) Samuelson; student James Millikin U., 1946-48; B.S. in Accountancy, U. Ill., 1950; postgrad. Northwestern U. Inst. Mgmt., summer 1963; m. Dorothy Belowski, Nov. 3, 1956; children—Geoffrey, Barbara, Gail, Paul. Sr. audit mgr. Price Waterhouse & Co., Chgo., 1950-64; with Celotex Corp., Chgo., 1964-65, v.p. financial operations, Tampa, Fla., 1965-70; asst. to v.p. Jim Walter Corp., Tampa, 1966-70, controller, 1970—; v.p. Jim Walter Research Corp., St. Petersburg, Fla., 1967—; controller, dir. Walter Land Co., Tampa, 1970—. Adviser, Jr. Achievement, Chgo., 1958-60; active Heart Fund, United Fund, Chgo., 1956-58. Served with USNR, 1945-46. C.P.A., Ill., Fla. Mem. Am. Inst. C.P.S.s, Ill., Fla. socs. C.P.A.s. Home: 1401 87th Av N St Petersburg FL 33702 Office: 1500 N Dale Mabry Hwy Tampa FL 33607

MATLOCK, ROBERT JOE, dentist; b. Dumas, Ark., July 20, 1940; s. Robert Gray and Josephine (Edington) M.; B.A., U. Ark., 1962; D.D.S., U. Tenn., 1965; m. Darlene Burnett, July 19, 1969; 1 dau.,

Jennifer Gray. Dentist, Wayne County Health Dept., Greenville, Mo., 1965; pvt. practice dentistry, Rogers, Ark., 1969—; mem. staff Rogers Meml. Hosp. Served to maj. Dental Corps, AUS, 1965-69. Mem. Am., Ark., Northwest Ark. dental assns., Ozark Dental Study Club, Am. Soc. Dentistry for Children, Rogers C. of C., Delta Sigma Delta. Methodist. Elk. Home: 904 S 14th Pl Rogers AR 72756 Office: 321 N Second St Rogers AR 72756

MATOUSEK, O(TTO) RALPH, lawyer; b. Chgo., May 29, 1923; s. Otto J. and Helen (Filip) M.; B.A., Stetson U., 1944; postgrad. Harvard, 1944-45; J.D., Northwestern U., 1949; m. Lillian Elizabeth Graw, Dec. 28, 1946; children—Robert, Charles, Martha Lynne. Admitted to Ill. bar, 1949, Fla. bar, 1949, U.S. Supreme Ct. bar, 1961; practiced in Chgo., 1949, Homestead, Fla., 1949—; spl. asst. atty. gen., Homestead, 1952-64; city atty., Homestead, 1953-61; dir., gen. counsel First Nat. Bank, Fla. Title Co.; pres., chmn. Homestead Radio Sta. WIII; founding dir. Fla. Title Co., Miami, First Nat. Bank of Princeton-Naranja. Served to lt. comdr. USNR, 1943-46. Named Boss of Yr., Homestead Secs. Assn., 1959. Mem. Fla. Bar, Am., Ill., Homestead (pres. 1968-70) bar assns., Am. Legion, V.F.W., Sigma Nu, Delta Theta Phi, Phi Alpha Theta, Pi Gamma Mu. Democrat. Presbyn. Elk (exalted ruler 1953, state v.p. 1958, dist. dep. 1959), Rotarian (pres. 1963), Moose (gov. Homestead 1971). Home: 4 NW 22d St Homestead FL 33030 Office: 234 N Krome Av Homestead FL 33030

MATSAERT, HERMAN JOZEF, Belgian diplomat; b. Bulskamp, Belgium, June 28, 1927; s. Leo Karel and Martha (van Themsche) M.; Dr. Juris, U. Louvain (Belgium), 1951, M.A. in Polit. and Diplomatic Scis., 1952; m. Christine Jenny t'Joen, May 29, 1963; children—Kristina, Frank, Patricia, Ann. Fgn. policy columnist, newspaper Het Laatste Nieuws, Brussels, 1954-57; with Belgian civil service, Magistrature, 1957-61; with Belgian fgn. service, 1961—, with Ministry Fgn. Affairs, Brussels, 1961-63, 1st sec. Belgian embassy Dar-es-Salaam, Tanzania, 1963-64, consul, consul gen. Bukavu, Democratic Republic Congo, 1964-66, consul gen. Houston, 1967—. Served as lt. arty. Belgian Army res., 1952-54. Decorated Order of Crown (Belgium). Home: 27 Willow End Dr Houston TX 77024 Office: Consulate Gen Belgium River Oaks Bank & Trust Tower 2001 Kirby Dr Houston TX 77019

MATSON, JESSIE BALDWIN, ret. govt. ofcl.; b. Omaha, July 18, 1904; d. William Arthur and Elizabeth M. (Bratt) Baldwin; student Grinnell Coll., 1922-25; A.B., U. Neb., 1926; postgrad. U. Utah, 1945-47; children—John Hanthorn (dec.), Joanne Sandra. Writer Omaha Daily Jour. Stockman. 1926-30; syndicate writer Corn Belt Farm Dailies, 1930-34; state dir. women's div. Ia. Emergency Relief Adminstrn., 1934-35; Ia. dir. women's and profl. projects WPA, 1935-40; with Archives Security, Air Force, 1942; faculty mem. U. Utah, 1945-46; tchr. Guam, Mariannas Islands, 1946-47; coordinator women's activities St. Paul Civil Def., 1950-70; now ret.; tchr. So. Cross Sch., Miami, Fla., 1971-72. Former comdr. Ramsey County Cancer Soc.; founder St. Paul Council Human Relations, 1948; former chmn. Nat. Thanksgiving Day Assn.; past v.p. pub. affairs Soroptimist Fedn. Ams.; life mem. past pres. St. Paul Club. State chmn. Luther W. Youngdahl campaign for gov., 1949-50. Recipient certificate of merit Gov. of Minn., 1961, 70; numerous others. Mem. V.F.W. Aux., Am. Legion Aux., Bus. and Profl. Women, Ret. Govt. Profl. Employees Assn., Inter-Club Council (founder 1944, pres. 1948-49, bd. mem.), League Women Voters, P.E.O., Theta Sigma Phi, Alpha Phi, Gamma Alpha Chi. Christian Scientist. Clubs: University, Women's City, Toastmistress (founder 1st St. Paul club). Home: 234 SE Beeney Rd Port Charlotte FL 33950

MATSON, ROGER ALLEN, govt. economist; b. Minot, N.D., July 29, 1938; s. Walfred Gustav and Zella Katherine (Martinson) M.; B.A., Concordia Coll., 1960; Ph.D., U. Colo., 1965; M. Regional Planning, U. N.C., 1970; m. Sandra Frances Winn, Sept. 2, 1967; 1 son, Todd Allen. Instr. U. Montana at Missoula, 1963-64; chief econ. research staff TVA, Knoxville, 1965-70; part-time lectr. U. Tenn., Knoxville, 1969-70; regional economist Dept. Commerce, Washington, 1970—. Woodrow Wilson fellow, 1960, USPHS fellow, 1964. Mem. Am. Econ. Assn., Regional Sci. Assn. Lutheran. Home: 3132 Cedar Grove Dr Fairfax VA 22030 Office: 2400 M St NW Washington DC 20203

MATSON, THOMAS EDWARDS, geologist; b. Washington, May 30, 1917; s. George Charlton and Beulan (Edwards) M.; B.S., U. Okla., 1939; m. Virginia R. Matych, Aug. 19, 1943; children—Susan, Kathryn, Thomas E., Josephine. Div. geologist S.W. Producing Pure Oil Co., 1944-51; partner Manhart, Millison & Beebe, 1951-55; chief geologist, v.p. exploration Home-Stake Prodn. Co., Tulsa, 1955-59, cons., 1959-66; pres. Matson Royalty Co., Gemini Oil Co.; mgr. Okla. div. N.Am. Royalties, Inc., 1971—. Served with USAF, 1942-44. Mem. Am. Assn. Petroleum Geologists, Tulsa, Oklahoma City, Kan. geol. socs. Home: 231 E 20th St Tulsa OK 74119 Office: Philtower Bldg Tulsa OK 74103

MATTESON, LEWIS WHITFORD, JR., data processing co. exec.; b. Houston, Nov. 24, 1924; s. Lewis Whitford and Lillian (Hall) M.; B.S. in Elec. Engring., Rice U., 1949; m. Betty Irene Dykes, Dec. 16, 1954; children— Sherry, Whit, Debbie, Ricky. Partner, Matteson S.W. Co., Houston, 1950-62, v.p., 1962-67; chmn. bd., 1967-71; owner, chmn. bd., pres. Matteson Transformers Inc., Houston, 1957-70; owner, mgr. Matteson Devel. Co., Houston, 1970—; v.p., sec., treas., dir. Plaza Lincoln-Mercury, Inc., Houston, 1971—. Served with Signal Corps, AUS, 1943-46. Mem. I.E.E.E., Phi Theta Kappa. Episcopalian. Club: Racquet (Houston). Home: 211 Paul Revere Dr Houston TX 77024 also Casa del Rio Hunt TX 78024 Office: 9426 Old Katy Rd Houston TX 77055

MATTHEWS, ALAN BRUCE, communications co. exec.; b. Clarksburg, W.Va., Dec. 11, 1923; s. Ezra Wilson and Hilma (Nelson) M.; B.S., Ohio U., 1945; m. Marjorie Phillips, 1944 (div. 1962); children—Bruce, Thomas, David, Jennifer, Michelle, Bradford, Christopher; m. 2d, Marjorie L. Nelson, 1963. With Arthur Andersen & Co., 1945-65, gen. partner, 1956, partner in charge Denver office, 1956-65; financial v.p. Communications satellite Corp., Washington, 1965-70, also dir.; pres. Bliss & Laughlin Industries, Inc., Chgo., 1970-71; chmn., pres. Nat. Cable Communications Corp., Washington, 1971—; dir. University Nat. Bank, Am. Security Corp. Pres., Jr. Achievement Met. Denver, 1960-62, chmn. bd., 1962-64, chmn. bd. Western region, 1964-66, nat. exec. com., 1962—; pres. Graland Country Day Sch., 1960-61, treas., 1964-65, trustee, 1959-65; treas. Denver Symphony Soc., 1964-65, trustee, 1958-65; chmn. Red Rocks Music Festival, 1960-61. Trustee Nat. Symphony Orch., Avery Coonley Sch.; bd. dirs. Chgo. Crime Commn., 1970-72. Served with AUS, 1942-43, Mem. Am. Inst. C.P.A.'s, Nat. Assn. Accountants (dir. 1963-64)., Newcomen Soc. Home: 3019 Dumbarton Av NW Washington DC 20007 Office: Astrol Bldg L'Enfant Plaza Washington DC 20024

MATTHEWS, BURNITA SHELTON, judge; b. Burnell, Miss., Dec. 28, 1894; d. Burnell and Lora Drew (Barlow) Shelton; LL.B., Nat. U. Law Sch., 1919, LL.M., 1920, LL.D., 1950; LL.D., Am. U., 1966; m. Percy Ashley Matthews, Apr. 28, 1917. Admitted to D.C., Miss., U.S. Supreme Ct. bars; practiced in Washington from 1920; active in securing equal right for women; former mem. faculty Washington Coll. Law; judge U.S. Dist. Ct. for D.C., 1949—. Past mem. Com. Experts on Women's Work of ILO; former mem. research com. Inter-Am. Commn. of Women; former mem. nat. council Nat. Woman's Party. First v.p. nat. bd. woman's Med. Coll. Pa.; mem. nat. devel. com. Am. U. Recipient Distinguished Service award Bar Assn. of D.C., 1968. Mem. Am. Bar Assn., Nat. Assn. Women Lawyers (ex-pres.). Drafted many laws sponsored by Nat. Women's Party. Home: 4500 Connecticut Av NW Washington DC Office: US Court House Washington DC

MATTHEWS, CARL LEWIS, supt. schs.; b. Smiths Grove, Ky., Mar. 17, 1924; s. Jerman Walter and Lula D. (Rountreee) M.; A.B., Westery Ky. State U., 1951, M.A., 1954; m. Dorothy Coop, Sept. 9, 1950; children— Monie, Sheila, David, Mark. Social studies tchr., Hopkinsville, Ky., 1951-52, Park City, 1952-54; asst. prin. high sch., Hilliard, Fla., 1954-56, Munfordville, Ky., 1956-60; supt. schs., West Point, Ky., 1960—. Active Boy Scouts Am., Girl Scouts Am., local Heart Fund. Chmn. Recreation Commn., West Point, 1961-72; chmn. Zoning Appeals Bd., West Point, 1969-72. Served with USAAF, 1942-46. Mem. Nat., Ky. edn. assns., Am., Ky. assns. sch. adminstrs., Internat. Platform Soc., Ky. Hist. Assn. Republican. Mem. Ch. of Christ. Home: 1502 Geoghegan St West Point KY 40177 Office: PO Box 367 West Point KY 40177

MATTHEWS, DALLAS BENJAMIN, ret. sch. adminstr.; b. Eva, La., May 17, 1907; s. Calvin and Molly (Hall) M.; B.S., So. U., Baton Rouge, 1933; M.A., Mich. State U., 1942; m. Helen Long, Dec. 24, 1937. Tchr., Benton, La., 1933-35; dir. vocational edn. Grambling (La.) Coll., 1935-37; supr. Negro vocational edn. in La., So. U., 1937-47; supt. La. Tng. Inst., Baton Rouge, 1947-71; ret., 1971; dep. sheriff East Felicina Parish (La.). Bd. dirs. Blundon Home, Baton Rouge; bd. dirs., v.p. So. Tchrs. and Parent Fed. Credit Union, Baton Rouge. Mem. Nat. Assn. Tng. Schs. and Juvenile Agys. (dir.), La. Edn. Assn., Nat. Conf. Supts. Correctional Instns. for Men, Girls and Women, So. U. Alumni Fedn. (life), Phi Beta Sigma (chpt. treas.). Mason (32 deg.). Home: PO Box 47 Ethel LA 70730

MATTHEWS, DANIEL GEORGE, editor; b. Lawrenceville, Va., Dec. 18, 1932; s. George Daniel and Evelyn (Goodrich) M.; student George Washington U., 1956-64; m. Annette P. Delaney, Jan. 13, 1959. Analyst, VA, Washington, 1953-54; library asst. cataloging U.S. Dept. State, Washington, 1954-63, intelligence and research specialist, 1964-66; editor-in-chief African Bibliographic Center, Washington, 1963—, exec. dir., 1966—. Editorial cons. Greenwood Press, N.Y.C., 1967—; pres. Washington Task Force on African Affairs, 1969—; mem. exec. com. coordinating council Internat. Ednl. Exchange, 1969—; lectr., cons. to acad. instns. on Africana collections and U.S. fgn. policy toward Africa. Served with AUS, 1950-53. Mem. African Studies Assn. (asso.), African Heritage Studies Assn. (chmn. liaison com.), A.L.A. Author: Soviet View of Africa, 1957, A Current Bibliography on Ethiopian Affairs, 1967, 72. Editor-in-chief A Current Bibliography on African Affairs 1963—; editor African affairs for General Reader, 1967, Current Themes in African Hist. Studies, 1970. Mem. editorial bd. African Books in Print, Ife, Nigeria. Home: 1816 New Hampshire Av NW Washington DC 20009 Office: 1346 Connecticut Av NW Washington DC 20036

MATTHEWS, DORIS BOOZER (MRS. CHARLES L. MATTHEWS), educator; b. Lexington, S.C., Aug. 18, 1932; d. Otto Raymond and Ruth (Sox) Boozer; B.S., Newberry Coll., 1952; M.Ed., U.S.C., 1955, 6-Yr. Certificate, 1971, Ph.D., 1972; m. Charles L. Matthews, Aug. 20, 1952; children—Shirley Ruth, Carles Ray, Sylvia Ann. Tchr., Brennen Sch., Columbia; S.C., 1952-64; supr. counseling S.C. State Employment Service, Columbia, 1964-66; counseling supr. and basic edn. specialist S.C. Com. for Tech. Edn., Columbia, 1966-68; instr. elementary edn. U. S.C., Columbia, 1968-72; asst. prof. S.C. State Coll., Orangeburg, 1972—. Chmn. Columbians Youth Com., 1968-72, chmn. Cayce Neighborhood Center, 1967-70. Mem. S.C. Edn. Assn., S.C. Assn. Supervision and Curriculum Devel., Assn. Student Teaching, Employment Counselors Assn., Am. Vocational Guidance Assn., Am., S.C. personnel and guidance assns., S.C. Dept. Audio-Visual Instrn., Am. Vocational Assn. Lutheran. Clubs: Cayce Womens (pres. 1965-67), Fashion Rose Garden (pres. 1962-64). Home: 101 Deliesseline Rd Cayce SC 29033 Office: SC State Coll Orangeburg SC 29115

MATTHEWS, EDGAR MORTON, supermarket chain exec.; b. Atlanta, Mar. 7, 1922; s. Paul Bell and Leta (Puckett) M.; student U. Neb., 1943-44; B.A. in Journalism, U. Ga., 1949; m. Anne Estelle Wetmore, Apr. 7, 1951; children—Charles Wetmore, Paul Edward. With U.S. Engr. Dept., 1941-43; asst. dir. advt. Piggly Wiggly Corp., Jacksonville, Fla., 1949-51, dir. advt., 1951—, asst. v.p., 1970—; gen. conv. chmn. Nat. Piggly Wiggly Operators Assn., 1962—. Bd. dirs. East Duval County (Fla.) Arthropod Control Dist., 1961-68, chmn., 1964-67; mem. Neptune Beach Adv. Planning Bd., 1964-69, pres., 1968. Served with AUS, 1943-46. Mem. Advt. Club of Jacksonville (dir., 1958-63, pres., 1962; award, 1961). Home: 1306 Kings Rd Neptune Beach FL 32250 Office: Piggly Wiggly Corp PO Box 149 Jacksonville FL 32201

MATTHEWS, ERNEST CRAWFORD, III, lawyer; b. Nashville, Nov. 29, 1927; s. Ernest Crawford and Ozella (Young) M.; B.A., Vanderbilt U., 1949, J.D., 1952; m. Jo Ann Hammack, Dec. 23, 1950; children—Ernest Crawford IV, David M., Craig M., Charles C. Admitted to Tenn. bar, 1952, since practiced in Nashville; mem. firm Tyne, Sugg & West, 1952-56, Murray & Matthews, 1956-68, Matthews, Proctor & Gray, 1968—. Lectr. law U. Tenn., Nashville, 1953, 54, 56-57. Mem. Nashville Estate Planning Council. Served with AUS, 1946-48. Fellow Am. Coll. Probate Counsel; mem. Am., Tenn. (gov. 1954-55, 58-59, chmn. real estate, probate and trust law sect. 1967-68), Nashville (sec., treas. 1961, dir. 1969-72) bar assns., Jr. Bar Conf. (pres. 1958-59), Order of Coif, Phi Beta Kappa, Phi Delta Phi, Sigma Chi. Baptist. Mason (33 deg.). Club: Hillwood Country. Home: 305 Clarendon Av Nashville TN 37205 Office: Stahlman Bldg Nashville TN 37201

MATTHEWS, JAMES HARVEY, physician; b. Liberty, Mo., June 11, 1916; s. Ollie G. and Antoinette Thompson (Craig) M.; B.S., Okla. Baptist U., 1937; M.D., Vanderbilt U., 1941; m. Doris Marie Parish, June 11, 1939; children—Annette (Mrs. Ray M. Woodlief), Rebecca (Mrs. Michael H. Barnes), Jeanne (Mrs. Ward B. Masden, Jr.). Physician VA Hosps., Asheville, N.C. and Nashville, 1946-60; chief, pulmonary disease research, VA Central Office, Washington, 1960-68, asst. dir. research service, 1968—. Served with M.C., AUS, 1942-46. Fellow A.C.P., Am. Coll. Chest Physicians; mem. Am. Thoracic Soc., A.M.A., Alpha Omega Alpha. Editor: Transactions, VA Armed Forces Pulmonary Disease Conferences, 1960-68. Home: 3037 Hazelton St Falls Church VA 22044 Office: VA Central Office Washington DC 20420

MATTHEWS, JAMES SEALE, dentist; b. Ocala, Fla., Jan. 13, 1928; s. John Roy and Elizabeth Ann (Seale) M.; B.S., U. Fla., 1951, M.S., 1952; D.D.S., Emory U., 1957; m. Billie Ann Hahn, July 10, 1950; children—Deborah Ann (Mrs. E. Wayne Smith), Susan Elizabeth. Research asst. U. Fla. at Gainesville, 1952-53; gen. practice dentistry, Gainesville, 1957-69, Hawthorne, Fla., 1968—. Mem. Am. Dental Assn., Fla., Alachua County (sec. 1959-60, pres. 1960-61) dental socs., Hawthorne C. of C. (pres. 1972—, bd. dirs.), Psi Omega, Beta Theta Pi (sec. bd. trustee student aid fund U. Fla. 1968-69, pres. bd. trustees 1969—). Democrat. Methodist (chmn. adminstrv. bd. 1969—). Home: PO Drawer 518 Hawthorne FL 32640 Office: Doctors Med Bldg Hawthorne FL 32640

MATTHEWS, JAY ARLON, JR., publisher, editor; b. St. Louis, Apr. 13, 1918; s. Jay Arlon and Mary (Long) M.; student San Jose State Coll., 1939-41, U. Tex., 1946-47; m. May Clark McLemore, Jan. 16, 1944; children—Jay Arlon III, Emily Cochrane, Sally McLemore. Asst. dir. personnel Adj. Gen.'s Dept. Tex., 1947-53, dept. adj., 1957-65, mil. support plans officer, 1965-69, chief emergency operations, 1965-71; pub. Presidial Press, Mil. History Press. Past dir. Civil Def., Austin; mem. adv. bd. Confed. Research Center, Hill Jr. Coll. Served with AGC, Tex. N.G., 1946—, col., 1965—. Mem. Austin (state v.p. 1951-52) U.S. (chmn. nat. security com. 1952-53) jr. chambers commerce, Tex. Safety Assn. (dir. traffic safety), N.G. Assn. U.S. (chmn. publicity 81st Gen. Conf.), Instituto Internationale de Historia Militar (hon. life), Co. Mil. Historians, Assn. U.S. Army. Episcopalian. Club: Exchange. Editor: Mil. History of Tex. and S.W. Quar. Home: 1807 Stamford Lane Austin TX 78703 Office: 6529 South Interregional US 35 Austin TX 78744 and PO Box 5248 Austin TX 78703

MATTHEWS, M.D., utility exec.; student Ark. State U.; B.A., U. Ark. Asst. constrn. Tex. Gas Transmission Corp., 1948-56; v.p., sec., treas. Fish Service Corp., 1956-58; with Internat. Pipeline Constrn. SA Panama, 1958-62; pres. Fish Internat. Argentina, 1962; v.p. Valley Gas Prodn., Inc., 1963; with Houston Natural Gas Corp., 1964—, sr. v.p., treas., 1969—. Served with AUS, World War II. Address: Houston Nat Gas Bldg Houston TX 77002*

MATTHEWS, MARTIN, accountant, educator; b. nr. Timmonsville, S.C., June 30, 1915; s. Martin L. and Elizabeth (Sansbury) M.; B.S., U. S.C., 1938, M.Accountancy, 1971; grad. LaSalle Extension U., 1944. Accountant, U.S. Govt., 1938-39, Standard Oil Co. of N.J., 1939-42; pub. accountant, 1946-54; gen. practice C.P.A., 1954-60; partner Matthews & Yates, C.P.A.'s, Columbia, S.C., 1960-64, owner, mgr., 1964-72, partner, 1972—; asso. prof. accounting S.C. State Coll., 1967—. Treas., Columbia Covenant Council of Lutheran Chs., Mo. Synod. Served with AUS, 1942-46. Mem. S.C. Assn. C.P.A.'s, Am. Inst. C.P.A.'s, Nat. Assn. Accountants, Am. Assn. Univ. Profs., S.C. C. of C. Lutheran (past pres.). Mason, Elk. Clubs: Optimist (past dist. lt. gov., S.C. dist. gov. 1970-71), Columbia Breakfast Optimist (past pres.). Home: 2931 Forest Dr Columbia SC 29204 Office: 2230 Devine St Columbia SC 29205

MATTHEWS, RAY SORY, agrl. cons.; b. Springfield, Tenn., Nov. 16, 1927; s. John Hallums and May Jo (Darden) M.; student U. Tenn., Chattanooga, 1945-46; B.S., U. Tenn. Tech., 1950; M.A., George Peabody Coll., 1951; m. Marjorie Ann Ewell, Mar. 12, 1950; children— Debra JoAnn, Janice Marie. Instr. biology Ga. Bd. Edn., 1950-52; with U.S. Dept. Agr., 1952-55; sr. biologist Va.-Carolina/Chem. Co., Richmond, Va., 1955-57; research and devel. rep. for Southwestern and Southeastern states Am. Cyanamid Co., Princeton, N.J., 1957—; agr. cons. to industry and growers in prodn. foods and fibers. Served with Paratroopers, 1946-48. Mem. Entomol. Soc. Am. (chmn. recruitment 1962), Miss. Entomol. Soc. (dir. 1963), Ark. Plant Food Inst., La. Entomol. Soc., Federated Pecan Growers Assn., Nat. Aerial Applicators Assn., Tex. Agrl. Chems., S.E. and Southwestern Pecan Growers Assn. Presbyn. (bd. deacons 1964—). Home: 3810 Norman PO Box 5021 Alexandria LA 71301 Office: Am Cyanamid Co PO Box 400 Princeton NJ 08540

MATTHEWS, RICHARD ABNER, banker; b. Duncan, Miss., Apr. 15, 1924; s. Richard and Viola (Massey) M.; student U. Ala. Extension, 1946-47, Grad. Sch. Banking, La. State U., 1966-68; m. Louise Dean Brannon, Jan. 22, 1930; children—Susan Kirk, Elizabeth Lucille. Asst. br. mgr. Mchts. Nat. Bank, Mobile, Ala., 1941-57; v.p. Bank for Savs. & Trusts, Birmingham, Ala., 1957-63; v.p. Birmingham Trust Nat. Bank, 1963—. Served with AUS, 1943-46; to 1st lt., 1950-52; Korea, now lt. col. Res. Mem. Asso. Industries Ala., Am. Inst. Banking, Bank Adminstrn. Inst. (past chpt. pres.), Birmingham C. of C. Republican. Presbyn. (deacon). Home: 3828 Williamsburg Circle Birmingham AL 35243 Office: 112 N 20th St Birmingham AL 35290

MATTHEWS, RITA SUE, assn. exec.; b. Durant, Okla., Dec. 18, 1925; d. Edward Sam and Lois (Sharpless) Matthews; A.A., No. Okla. Jr. Coll., 1946; B.A. in Journalism, U. Okla., 1949. News editor Sentinel (Okla.) Leader, 1949-50, Tonkawa (Okla.) News, 1950-51; women's editor radio sta. KWHW, Altus, Okla., 1951-54; health information sec. Tulsa County Pub. Health and Heart Assn., 1954-56; field rep. Okla. Heart Assn., 1956-64, exec. dir., 1965—. Mem. Gov.'s Com. on Rehab., 1966-67, Gov's Council on Regional Med. Program, 1966—; mem. nat. com. on rehab. Am. Heart Assn., 1968-70. Mem. Okla. Pub. Health Assn. (v.p. 1969-70), Okla. Health and Welfare Assn., Okla. Assn. Voluntary Health Agys. (pres. 1970-72), Theta Sigma Phi. Republican. Presbyn. Home: 800 NE 15th St Oklahoma City OK 73104 Office: 825 NE 13th St Oklahoma City OK 73104

MATTHEWS, THOMAS A., lawyer; b. Chgo., Aug. 3, 1901; s. Thomas Henry and Lorena (Stewart) M.; A.B., Northwestern U., 1922, J.D., 1925; m. Elsie S. Spears, June 27, 1925; children—Thomas Alexander, Byron Stewart. Admitted to Ill. bar, 1925; practiced in Chgo., 1926-71; specialist on municipal law; editor Edward Thompson Law Pub. Co.; counsel for Ill. Municipal League, 1927-65. Presbyn. Author complete code of ordnances for about 150 cities and villages in Ill. Author: Municipal Ordinances, 2 vols.; pamphlets: Handbook for Municipal Officials; How To Levy Taxes; Municipal Licensing Powers; Forms for Special Assessment Proceedings. Contbr. to Ill. Municipal Rev. Editor: Current Municipal Problems Mag. Home and Office: 926 Sandstone Dr Bartlesville OK 74003

MATTHEWS, THOMAS LEROY, JR., aluminum co. exec.; b. Phila., Nov. 5, 1918; s. Thomas LeRoy and Elsie (Von Zingraf) M.; B.A., U. Va., 1941, M.A., 1950; mgmt. certificate U. Richmond, 1954; B.S. (hon.), Ga. Inst. Tech., 1958; m. Nellie Louise Early, June 7, 1941; 1 dau., Carol Loraine. Research asso. Dept. Air Force, 1948-50; head psychology VA Center Va., Charlottesville, 1948-50; with Reynolds Metals Co., 1950—, personnel mgr., mgr. personnel research, Richmond, Va., 1957-61, div. personnel mgr. cable and can divs., 1961-67, dir. manpower planning and devel., 1967—. Mem. adj. faculty Va. Commonwealth U.; mem. vis. faculty U.S. Army Logistics Mgmt. Center; vis. lectr. U. Va., U. Minn. Served to capt. AUS, 1942-46. Mem. Am., Southeastern psychol. assns., Am. Mgmt. Assn., Va. Acad. Sci., A.A.A.S., Am. Soc. Personnel Adminstrn., Sigma Xi, Sigma Nu, Theta Kappa Psi. Contbr. articles to profl. jours. Home: Beechwood Box 216 Route 1 Doswell VA 23047 Office: 6601 W Broad St Richmond VA 23218

MATTHEWS, TOM, asst. to dir. Common Cause, Washington. Home: 2311 Connecticut Av NW Washington DC 20008 Office: Common Cause 2100 M St NW Washington DC 20037*

MATTHEWS, WILLIAM BUSH, lawyer; b. Memphis, Feb. 12, 1931; s. Joseph Warren and Jewel (Bush) M.; B.A., U. Tenn., 1952; LL.B., Vanderbilt U., 1956; m. Florence Carroll, Jan. 22, 1955; children—William Bush, Maurine Carroll, Warren Carroll. Admitted to Ala. bar, 1956; practice law, Ozarks, Ala., 1956—; asst. dist. atty. Dale County, 1959—. Dir. Bank of Ozark. Mem. Ala. Bar Commn., 1966—. Chmn., Dale County March of Dimes, 1957-58, Dale County Red Cross, 1959-60. Served with AUS, 1953-55. Mem. Delta Sigma Phi, Phi Delta Phi. Rotarian (pres. 1966-67); Ozark Quarterback. Methodist. Home: Squirrel Dr Ozark AL 36360 Office: PO Box 1145 Ozark AL 36360

MATTHIAS, WILLARD C., govt. ofcl.; b. Fennimore, Wis., Mar. 6, 1914; s. Nathaniel and Ernestine Caroline (Braun) M.; B.A. magna cum laude, U. Ia., 1936; M.A., U. Minn., 1938; M.A. (Littauer fellow 1938-39), Harvard, 1944; m. Sally L. Seashore, June 26, 1937; children—Jane Iris, Theodore Willard. Staff mem. Brookings Instn., Washington, 1939-40; instr. then asst. prof. govt. Miami U., Oxford, O., 1940-43; intelligence officer CIA, 1947-58, 59-64, 66—; U.S. rep. Brit. Joint Intelligence Com., London, 1953-55; fellow Center Internat. Affairs, Harvard 1958-59; 1st sec. Am. embassy, Rome, Italy, 1964-66; mem. bd. nat. estimates CIA, 1961-64, 66—. Served with AUS, 1943-46. Mem. Phi Beta Kappa. Episcopalian. Home: 408 Clover Way Alexandria VA 22314

MATTINGLY, JAMES WILLIAM, JR., apparel mfg. co. exec.; b. Lexington, Ky., Nov. 9, 1920; s. James William and Geneva (White) M.; A.B., U. Ky., 1949; m. Kitty Richardson, Oct. 6, 1950; children—John Basil, Laura Lee, Todd Davenport. With Cowden Mfg. Co., Lexington, Ky., 1951—, salesman, 1954-61, account exec., 1961-67, v.p. merchandising, 1968—, also dir. Served with USMCR, 1942-45. Episcopalian (vestryman). Clubs: Lexington Country, Lansdowne (Lexington). Home: 3415 Brookhaven Dr Lexington KY 40502 Office: 300 New Circle Rd NW PO Box 2500 Lexington KY 40501

MATTINGLY, THOMAS K., astronaut; b. Chgo., Mar. 17, 1936; s. Thomas K. Mattingly; B. Aero. Engring., Auburn U., 1958. Commd. officer U.S. Navy, 1958, now lt.; astronaut NASA Manned Spacecraft Center, Houston; pilot command module Apollo XVI, 1972. Address: NASA Manned Spacecraft Center Houston TX 77001*

MATTISON, CHARLES RAY, city ofcl.; b. Belton, S.C., July 13, 1929; s. Clyde Calhoun and Carrie Lucinda (Fant) M.; grad. Cecil's Inst. Accountancy, Greenville, S.C., 1949; m. Betty Lucille Vaughn, Aug. 20, 1954; 1 dau., Connie Faye. Shipping clk. Textron, Inc., Belton, 1949-51; city clk., treas. Town of Belton, 1951-52; teller, internal control accountant S.C. Nat. Bank, Belton, 1952-57; mgr. Greer & Campbell Ins. Agy., Belton, 1957-59; accountant J. Marion Campbell & Co., Anderson, S.C., 1960-61; city clk., treas. City of Belton, 1962—. Sec., Belton Jr. C. of C., 1956-57, treas., 1957-58. Recipient Outstanding Civic Leaders of Am. award, 1967. Mem. Internat. Inst. Municipal Clks., Anderson County Municipal Assn. (asst. sec., treas.). Baptist. Home: 437 Forest Lane Belton SC 29627 Office: PO Box 520 201 O'Neal St Belton SC 29627

MATTOX, JOSEPH HERBERT, JR., univ. pub. relations exec.; b. Chillicothe, O., Sept. 5, 1914; s. Joseph Herbert and Mary Olive (Blaney) M.; student La. State U., 1934-37, 49-51; m. Mary Bertha Willis, Dec. 20, 1940; 1 dau., Ilse. Writer, editor Baton Rouge State-Times and Morning Adv., 1936-37; pub. relations counsel La. Welfare Dept., also La. Hosp. Bd., 1937-40; editor Monroe (La.) Morning World, 1940-41, Memphis Comml. Appeal, 1941-42; dir. pub. relations La. State U. System, Baton Rouge, 1948—. Pub. relations cons. Chillicothe Sesquicentennial Commn., 1946-47. Served from pvt. to lt. col., inf. AUS, 1942-46; ETO. Decorated Bronze Star. Mem. Am. Coll. Pub. Relations Assn. (dist. pres. 1952), Pub. Relations Soc. Am. (pres. Baton Rouge chpt. 1961-63). Democrat. Episcopalian. Author: The Future of Educational Public Relations, 1951. Editor: Welfare, 1937-40. Contbr. articles profl. jours. Home: 2425 June St Baton Rouge LA 70808 Office: Louisiana State University, Baton Rouge LA 70803

MAUCK, HENRY PAGE, JR., educator, physician; b. Richmond, Va., Feb. 3, 1926; s. Henry Page and Harriet Hutcheson (Morrison) M.; student Wash. and Lee U., 1942-43; B.A., U. Va., 1948, M.D., 1952; m. Janet Garrett Horsley, May 14, 1955; children—Henry Page III, John Waller. Asst. prof. medicine, pediatrics Med. Coll. Va., Richmond, 1961-66, asso. prof., 1966-72, prof., 1972—; cons. McGuires VA Hosp., Richmond, Langley Field Air Force Hosp., Hampton, Va. Served with AUS, 1944-46. Am. Heart Assn. fellow, 1956-57. Diplomate Am. Bd. Internal Medicine. Fellow A.C.P., Am. Coll. Cardiology; mem. So. Soc. Clin. Investigation, So. Soc. for Clin. Research, Am. Fedn. Clin. Research. Contbr.: Pathophysiology, Autonomic Control of Cardiovascular System, 1971. Home: 113 Oxford Circle West Richmond VA 23221

MAUGHAN, DON, dir. Water Resources Council, Washington. Office: Water Resources Council 2120 L St Washington DC 20037*

MAULDIN, E. EUGENIA, librarian; b. Baldwyn, Miss., Nov. 4, 1916; d. Thomas Andrew and Reba (Welsh) Mauldin; B.A., Millsaps Coll., 1938; M.Ed., U. Miss., 1950; M.L.S., U. Ill., 1956. Tchr., Carmichael (Miss.) High Sch., 1938-39, Ashland (Miss.) Grade Sch., 1939-41, Glen Allan (Miss.) Grade Sch., 1941-42, Guntown (Miss.) Grade Sch., 1942-43, New Albany (Miss.) Grade Sch., 1946-47; librarian Baldwyn High Sch., 1947-51; teaching asst. U. Ill. Grad. Sch. Library Sci., 1955-56; librarian Corinth (Miss.) High Sch., 1956-57; asst. prof. dept. library service Coll. Edn., U. Tenn., Knoxville, 1957-69, asso. prof., Grad. Sch. Library and Information Sci., 1971—; instr. library service Miss. State U., summer 1966. Mem. com. on tchr. edn. So. Regional Edn. Bd., 1964-67. Acting editor Tenn. Librarian, 1958-59. Mem. E. Tenn. Edn. Assn. (chmn. audiovisual sect. 1960-61), Tenn. Library Assn. (A.L.A. councilor 1965-69), Am. Assn. Sch. Librarians, Southeastern (chmn. librarianship as a career com. 1968-70), Miss. library assns., N.E.A., Am. Assn. U. Profs., Alpha Beta Alpha, Pi Lambda Theta (v.p. local chpt. 1967-69), Delta Kappa Gamma. Home: 1631 Laurel St Knoxville TN 37916

MAURER, ALAN OWEN, economist; b. N.Y.C., May 5, 1939; s. Morris and Anne (Knauer) M.; B.A., Coll. City N.Y., 1961; postgrad. U. Cal. at Berkeley, 1961-62; M.A., Am. U., 1966; m. Elayna Niesen, May 18, 1969. Economist, U.S. Commerce Dept., Washington, 1962-65; financial economist Fed. Home Loan Bank Bd., Washington, 1965-66; regional economist Bur. Internat. Commerce, Washington, 1966—. Mem. faculty Montgomery Coll. Evening Sch., Takoma Park, Md. Mem. Am. Econ. Assn., Am. Statis. Assn., Nat. Honor Soc. Econs. (v.p. 1961). Author pamphlets Basic Data on German Economy, 1967, Basic Data on Italian Economy, 1967. Contbr. articles to profl. jours. Research in econ. devel., consumer durables. Home: 2517 Buck Lodge Terrace Adelphi MD 20783 Office: Bur Internat Commerce US Commerce Dept 14th St and Constitution Av NW Washington DC 21230

MAUTZ, ROBERT BARBEAU, univ. chancellor; b. Marion, O., Jan. 22, 1915; s. Albert Edward and Bessie (Barbeau) M.; B.A., Miami U., 1937, L.H.D., 1969; J.D., Yale, 1940, postgrad., 1949-50; postgrad. U. Mexico, 1950, 53; L.H.D., U. Fla., 1968, U. Miami, 1970; LL.D., Jacksonville U., 1968, Miami U., 1970; D.Sc., Fla. Inst. Tech., 1971; m. Esther Guthery, Feb. 22, 1947. Admitted to N.Y. State bar, 1941; practiced in N.Y.C., 1940-41; asso. firm Root, Clark, Buckner & Ballantine, N.Y.C., 1940-41; atty. Pan Am. Airways, Brit. West Africa, 1941-42; exec. officer legal div. Office Mil. Govt., Berlin, Germany, 1945-48, dep. legal dir., Hesse, 1948-49; prof. law, asst. dean Coll. Law, U. Fla., 1950-58, dean acad. affairs, 1958-63, v.p. acad. affairs, 1963-68; chancellor Fla. State U. System, Tallahassee, 1968—. Commr. from Fla. to Edn. Commn. of States, 1968—. Bd. dirs. LeMoyne Art Found., Tallahassee, 1969—, Micanopy (Fla.) Art Found., 1965-68. Mem. Am. Bar Assn., Am. Jurisprudence Assn., Assn. Exec. Officers State Wide Bds. Higher Edn. (dir.), So. Regional Edn. Council (dir.), Fla. Council of 100, Ohio Soc. of N.Y., Order of Coif, Blue Key, Phi Beta Kappa, Phi Alpha Delta, Beta Theta Pi, Omicron Delta Kappa. Rotarian. Contbr. articles to profl. jours. Home: 819 E Park Av Tallahassee FL 32301 Office: 107 W Gaines St Tallahassee FL 32304

MAVRIS, NICHOLAS BENNIE, pipe line co. exec.; b. Oklahoma City, Nov. 23, 1923; s. George and Ada Virginia (Diles) M.; B.S. in Mech. Engring., Okla. State U., 1948, M.S., 1949; m. Elizabeth Ann Shaver, July 3, 1943; children—Virginia Ann (Mrs. Earl Eugene Humes), George Samuel, Kathryn Ann, Nicola Ann. Instr., Okla. State U., 1948-49; engr. Interstate Oil Pipeline Co., 1949-51; asst. regional mgr. Rocky Mountain region Continental Oil Co., 1963-67, mgr. transp., 1967-68; with Continental Pipe Line Co., 1951-63, 68—, pres., chief exec. officer, Ponca City, Okla., 1969—, also dir.; dir., pres. Yellowstone Pipe Line Co., 1969—, Cherokee Pipe Line Co., Glacier Pipe Line Co., 1969—; dir. Butte Pipe Line Co., Arbuckle Pipe Line Co., Platte Pipe Line Co., West Shore Pipe Line Co., Explorer Pipeline Co., Seadock, Inc. Served with AUS, 1943-46. Mem. Rocky Mountain Oil and Gas Assn. (dir.), Am. Petroleum Inst. (div. transp. central com. 1968—), Assn. Oil Pipe Lines. Clubs: Pupe Liners (dir.) (Tulsa); Ponca City Country. Home: 2208 Meadowbrook St Ponca City OK 74601 Office: PO Drawer 1267 Ponca City OK 74601

MAX, PETER, economist; b. Utica, N.Y., Mar. 19, 1933; s. Theodore Louis and Marian (Smith) M.; B.A., Williams Coll., 1955; postgrad. Cornell U., 1955-59; m. Susanne Widtman, Aug. 10, 1953; children—Eric, Gregg, Peter. With Cornell U., 1955-59, Carnegie Inst. Tech., 1959-60; sr. cons. Boni Watkins Jason & Co., N.Y., 1960-61, Nat. Econ. Research Assos., N.Y.C., 1961-63; chief bus. econs. Battelle Meml. Inst., Columbus, O., 1963-65; sr. cons. NERA, Inc., Washington, 1965-69; v.p. Nat. Econ. Research Assos., 1970—. Mem. Am. Econ. Assn., Am. Statis. Assn., Nat. Assn. Bus. Econ., Phi Beta Kappa, Phi Gamma Delta, Phi Kappa Phi. Clubs: International, Williams (Washington); Nat. Economists (pres. 1970, chmn. bd. govts. 1971). Address: 1211 Connecticut Av NW Washington DC 20036

MAXEY, JACK U., YMCA exec.; b. Oilton, Okla., Aug. 23, 1925; s. Jack and Ann (Miller) M.; student Salt City Bus. Coll., 1946-48, Hutchinson (Kan.) Jr. Coll., 1948-49, Bethany Coll., Lindsborg, Kan., 1949-51, George Williams Coll., Chgo., 1951-52; m. Melba Aleen Sims, Aug. 19, 1944; children—Ronald, Rommie Lee, Lynda, Danny, Randy. Phys. dir. YMCA, Chgo., 1951-53; phys. dir., program dir. YMCA, Streator, Ill., 1953-56; men's phys. dir. YMCA, Topeka, 1956-60; exec. dir. YMCA, Perryton, Tex., 1960-63, Greenville, Tex., 1963-69, Enid, Okla., 1969—. Served with A.C., USNR, 1942-46. Recipient Distinguished Service awards Perryton Lions Club, 1962, Perryton YMCA, 1960, Greenville YMCA, 1969 Mem. Assn. of Dirs., Sigma Delta Alpha. Methodist. Rotarian. Home: 119 S Watson St Enid OK 73701 Office: 415 W Cherokee St Enid OK 73701

MAXFIELD, DONALD VINCENT, food service co. exec.; b. Centralia, Ill., Apr. 19, 1914; s. Hurem Allen and Blanche (Copple) M.; B.S. in Accounting, U. Ill., 1936; m. Elizabeth A. Hartz, May 19, 1945; children— James Allen, Susan Mary. Sr. accountant Grey, Hunter, Stenn, C.P.A.'s, Marion, Ill., 1936-39; asst. to controller Ill. Agrl. Assn., Chgo., 1939-41; asst. controller Clinton Foods (Ia.), 1945-50; systems analyst Hotpoint, Inc., Chgo., 1950-51; controller Peter Fox Brewing Co., Chgo., 1951-53; asst. auditor No. Trust Co., Chgo., 1953-57; asst. v.p., asst. controller Continental Casualty Co., Chgo., 1957-58, controller, 1958-62, v.p., 1960-62; v.p., treas. Canteen Corp., Chgo., 1962-64, financial v.p., 1964-68, adminstrv. v.p., 1968, also dir. subsidiaries; financial v.p. Ky. Fried Chicken Corp., Nashville, 1968-70; pres., chief exec. officer, chmn. bd. Satellite 3 In 1 Corp., 1970-71; financial v.p., treas. Equity Nat. Industries, Atlanta, 1971—; dir. Mdse. Nat. Bank Chgo. Served to maj. AUS, 1941-45. Decorated Purple Heart. Mem. Financial Execs. Inst., Am. Mgmt. Assn., Nat. Rifle Assn. Home: 8925 Huntcliff Lake Ct Atlanta GA 30338 Office: 2700 Nat Bank of Ga Bldg 34 Peachtree St NW Atlanta GA 30303

MAXFIELD, JACK GEORGE STREETER, physician, radiologist; b. Waco, Tex., Apr. 28, 1913; A.B., Baylor U., 1936, M.D., 1940; postgrad. U. Cal. Med. Sch. Extension, San Francisco, 1947, Oak Ridge Inst. Nuclear Medicine, 1949, 52; m. Louis Gribble; 2 daus. Intern So. Pacific Hosp., San Francisco, 1940-41; resident Maxfield Clinic Hosp., 1947-49, now adminstr.; resident Tex. Radiation and Tumor Inst., 1949-51; staff St. Paul Hosp., Dallas, Parkland Hosp., Dallas, Morton Inst. Molecular Medicine, Dallas; former staff Cottage Hosp., Santa Barbara, Cal. Served to lt. col. M.C., AUS, 1941-46. Decorated Legion of Merit, Bronze Star. Mem. A.M.A., S.W. Soc. Nuclear Medicine (past pres.), Dallas County Med. Soc., Am. Coll. Radiology, Rocky Mountain, Tex. radiol. socs., Radiol. Soc. N.Am., Am. Radium Soc., Dallas County Clin. Soc., Brit. Inst. Radiology, Internat. Coll. Surgeons, Pvt. Clinics and Hosps. Tex. (past pres.). Home: Triple 7 Ranch Carrollton TX 75006 Office: 2711 Oak Lawn Dallas TX 75219

MAXWELL, (OTIS) ALLEN, editor, publisher; b. Waco, Tex., Nov. 24, 1915; s. Otis Allen and Myra (Vesey) M.; B.A., So. Methodist U., 1937, B.S. in Commerce, 1937; M.A., 1940; m. Emma Vee Dunlap, Aug. 31, 1940; children—Otis Allen III, Mary Susanna, Rebecca Agnes. Asst. book editor Dallas Morning News, 1937-42, 48-58, book editor, 1958—; asst. dir. So. Methodist U. Press, 1939-42, dir., 1946—; mng. editor Southwest Rev., 1939-42, editor, 1946-63. Editor: The Present Danger: Four Essays on American Freedom, 1953, (with Mody C. Boatright and Wilson M. Hudson) Folk Travelers: Ballads, Tales, and Talk, 1953, Texas Folk and Folklore, 1954, Mesquite and Willow, 1957, Madstones and Twisters, 1958, And Horns on the Toads, 1959; Singers and Storytellers, 1961, The Golden Log, 1962, A Good Tale and a Bonnie Tune, 1964; (with Lon Tinkle) The Cowboy Reader, 1959; (with Hudson) The Sunny Slopes of Long Ago, 1966. Vice pres. Assn. Am. Univ. Presses, 1955. Mem. adv. fine arts com. Dallas C. of C., chmn. 1948-50. Mem. exec. com. Jno. E. Owens Meml. Found., 1954—, chmn., 1955-57. Served from ensign to lt. comdr., Supply Corps, USNR, 1942-46. Mem. Tex. Inst. Letters (v.p. 1953-57, 61-62, councilor 1957-61), Tex. Folklore Soc. (treas. 1951-57, asso. editor 1953-67), Phi Beta Kappa, Kappa Sigma. Democrat. Methodist. Home: 6610 Northwood Rd Dallas TX 75225 Office: So Methodist U Dallas TX 75222 also Dallas Morning News Dallas TX 75222

MAXWELL, AMY BRYAN, ret. variety chain store exec.; b. Cairo, Ga., June 17, 1912; s. Harry Albert and Bessie (Bryant) M.; grad. high sch.; m. Katherine Wilkes, Sept. 30, 1935; children—Albert Bryan, Sandra Katherine (Mrs. Ronald Dean Bohlender). Trainee, McCrory Stores Corp., Inc., Tallahassee, 1929, asst. mgr., 1930; store mgr. Christos Stores, Inc., Panama City, Fla., 1931-38; founder, chmn. bd., pres. Dixieland Stores, Inc., Fernandina Beach, 1939-68; founder, chmn. bd., exec. v.p. Dixieland 5-10-25 &. 00 Stores, Inc., Fernandina Beach, 1945-68; exec. v.p., dir., Super Dollar Stores, Inc., Fernandina Beach, 1965-72. Mem. Nashville (Ga.) Sch. Bd., 1946; chmn. bd. Berrien Housing Authority, 1949-54; pres., chmn. bd. Berrien Organized Aid, 1945; bd. dirs. Okefenokee council Boy Scouts Am., 1951-52; commr. Fernandina Beach Housing Authority, 1961-64. Mem. A.I.M. (fellow pres.'s council). Methodist (past chmn. bd. stewards, trustee). Mason (Shriner). Clubs: Ponte Vedra (Fla.); Deerwood, University (charter) (Jacksonville, Fla.); Kiwanis (dir. Fernandina Beach 1954-68, pres. 1969), chmn. internat. conv. attendance div. 4, 1969). Home: S Fletcher Av PO Box 748 Fernandina Beach FL 32034

MAXWELL, DAVID OGDEN, govt. ofcl.; b. Phila., May 16, 1930; s. David Farrow and Emily Ogden (Nelson) M.; B.A., Yale, 1952; LL.B., Harvard, 1955; m. John Clark Paddock, Dec. 14, 1968. Admitted to Pa. and D.C. bar, 1955; with firm Obermayer, Rebmann, Maxwell & Hippel, Phila., 1959-67, partner, 1963-67; ins. commr., Pa., 1967-69, sec. adminstrn. and budget sec., 1969-70; gen. counsel Dept. Housing and Urban Devel., Washington, 1970—; mem. med. assistance adv. council Dept. Health, Edn. and Welfare, 1969-70. Exec. vice chmn. Pa. Citizens for Shafer, 1966; dir. Nixon-Agnew campaign, Pa., 1968; trustee Republican Citizens Com. U.S., 1963-65. Served with USNR, 1955-59. Mem. Am., Pa., Fed., D.C. bar assns., Am. Bar Found., Am. Judicature Soc. Episcopalian. Home: 4404 29th St NW Washington DC 20008 Office: 451 7th St SW Washington DC 20410

MAXWELL, GROVER CLEVELAND, ret. retail exec.; b. Resaca, N.C., Nov. 6, 1887; s. Gilbert Motier and Mary Jeannette (Grady) M.; student pub. schs.; m. Corrie Ann Meares, Sept. 22, 1926; children—Gorver Cleveland, George Motier, William Thomas. Former pres. Maxwell Bros., Inc., Augusta, Ga., ret., 1968; chmn. bd. emeritus Ga. R.R. Bank & Trust Co. Bd. visitors Presbyn. Coll. Served with Q.M.C., 1918. Mem. Augusta C. of C., Augusta Retail Assn., Ga. Bankers Assn. Mason. Clubs: Augusta Country, Augusta National, Pinnacle. Author: Maxwell Brothers Furniture Business, 1968. Home: 2353 McDowell St Augusta GA 30904 Office: Ga R R Bank Bldg Augusta GA 30902

MAXWELL, HENRY FAVILLE, educator, clergyman; b. Esidumbini, Natal, South Africa, Mar. 18, 1908; s. Charles Henry and Katherine L. (Sullivan) M.; B.A., Carleton Coll., 1929; B.D., Chgo. Theol. Sem., U. Chgo., 1932; diploma in theology Mansfield Coll., Oxford, Eng., 1934; B.Litt., St. Catherine's Coll., Oxford, 1935 Oxford U., 1935; m. Mary Elizabeth Ketron, Sept. 30 1934; 1 son, Henry Ketron. Ordained to ministry United Ch. of Christ, 1934; pastor 1st Congl. Ch., Ashland, Wis., 1934-37, Ladysmith, Wis., 1937-40, Flossmoor (Ill.) Community, Ch., 1940-44; commd. lt. (j.g.) U.S. Navy, 1944, advanced through grades to lt. comdr., 1954; staff chaplain Philippine Sea Frontier, 1945-46, 1st Marine Div., Tientsin, China, 1946-47, in U.S.S. Lake Champlain, 1957-59, U.S.S. F.D. Roosevelt, 1953-54; ret., 1965; asso. prof. sociology Limestone Coll., Gaffney, S.C., 1965-70; prof. sociology Dakota Wesleyan U., Mitchell, S.D., 1970-71; dir. pastoral services Med. Univ. of S.C., Charleston, 1971—. Chaplain to students, interim prof. sociology, econs. Northland Coll., Ashland, Wis., 1934-47. Mem. Ill. Conf. United Ch. of Christ, Oxford Soc., Corinthian Lit. Soc. Kiwanian. Home: 1474 Burning Tree Rd Charleston SC 29412

MAXWELL, JAMES LIVINGSTON, cons.; b. Tulsa, May 12, 1926; s. William Raymond and Mary Pauline (O'Donnell) M.; B.A., Okla. State U., 1950. Mayor, Tulsa, 1958-66; cons. U.S. Dept. Commerce; pvt. cons. on urban affairs. Bd. mem. Tulsa Library Adv. Com.; pres. Tulsa Real Estate Investment Trust. Served with AUS, 1944-46. Mem. Tulsa County Hist. Soc. (chmn.), Am. Legion, V.F.W., C. of C., Sigma Chi. Home: 4124 E 46th Pl Tulsa OK 74135

MAXWELL, MARY DALE BRETT (MRS. CHARLES LEROY MAXWELL), educator, clubwoman; b. Cordell, Okla., July 5, 1910; d. Rutherford and Gertrude (Whitaker) Brett; B.F.A., U. Okla., 1938; m. Charles Leroy Maxwell, Mar. 9, 1944; children—Marilyn Dale, William Brett. Tchr. pub. sch. and music, Verden, Okla., 1931-36, Alva Pub. Schs., 1938, Ardmore Pub. Schs., 1939-43; screener Bechtel McCone Fgn. Employment Corp., Los Angeles, 1943-44; corr. U.S. Treasury, Chgo., 1944; job adviser USES, Chgo., 1944-45. Active A.R.C., United dr., Boy Scouts Am., Girl Scouts U.S.A., March of Dimes. Pres. Alva Research Club, 1955-56. Mem. D.A.R. (regent Cherokee Outlet chpt. 1960-62, del. Continental Congress, Washington 1961—), P.E.O. (pres. local chpt. 1956-58, treas. Okla. State chpt. 1968-69, corr. sec. 1969-70, rec. sec. 1970-71, organizer 1971-72), Alva Women's Golf Assn. (pres. 1968), Alpha Phi. Baptist. Home: 502 Lake Dr Alva OK 73717

MAXWELL, MILDRED L LAYMAN (MRS. GEORGE ROBERT MAXWELL), educator; b. Bristow, Okla., Sept. 18; d. Harry Elmer and Myrtle A. (Knight) Layman; student Wichita U., 1937-38; B.S., Okla. State U., 1941; M.E., U. Ark., 1967; m. George Robert Maxwell, Dec. 30, 1939; children—Robert Richard, Jon Michael. Tchr. pub. schs., Searcy, Ark., 1960-62. Searcy Sr. High Sch., 1962-65; guidance counselor Searcy Jr. High Sch., 1965—. Mem. exec. bd., sec.-treas. Sheltered Workshop. Mem. Am. Assn. U. Women, Am., Ark. personnel and guidance assns., Ark. Sch. Counselors Assn., Searcy Edn. Assn. (exec. bd.), Zeta Tau Alpha, Omicron Nu, Beta Sigma Phi (pres. 1968-70), P.E.O. (pres. 1970-72). Baptist. Home: 110 Ridge Pl Searcy AR 72143

MAXWELL, VIRGINIA OMO, govt. ofcl.; b. Vandergrift, Pa.; d. Charles H. and Lennie (Pheasant) Omo; B.A., Am. U., 1939; m. Leonard W. Maxwell, Sept. 22, 1946 (div.); 1 son, Charles Christopher. Dir. women's programs, traffic mgr. radio sta. WGAY, Silver Spring, Md., 1953-58; personnel officer Dept. Air Force, Washington, 1942-49, information specialist, 1958-61; registrar, adminstrv. officer Nat. Bur. Standards Grad. Sch., Washington, 1961—. Sec. Nat. Bur. Standards Ednl. Com., 1961—; v.p. Page Hill Citizens Assn., Bethesda, Md., 1953-54. Bd. dirs. Nat. Bur. Standards Welfare Assn., 1960-61; pres. bd. dirs. Once Upon a Time, radio plays for children, 1948-61. Mem. Md. (chmn. radio-TV 1949-51), Montgomery County (radio chmn. 1948-49) fedns. women's clubs, Beta Beta Beta, Phi Mu. Episcopalian. Club: Woman's (publicity chmn. 1952-53) (Bethesda). Office: Nat Bureau of Standards Washington DC 20234

MAXWELL, WILLIAM JAMES, dentist; b. Florence, S.C., Feb. 27, 1935; s. William James and Hannah (Harrell) M.; B.S., The Citadel, 1957; D.D.S., Med. Coll. Va., 1961; m. Mary Nell Wilson, Dec. 27, 1957; 1 son, William James, Jr. Dir. dental assisting program

Florence-Darlington Tech. Edn. Center, 1967-69; pvt. practice gen. dentistry, Florence, 1963—. Bd. dirs. Am. Cancer Soc., 1969; mem. Pee Dee Comprehensive Health Planning Council, 1968—. Served to capt., Dental Corps, AUS, 1961-63. Mem. Am., S.C. dental assns., Pee Dee Dental Soc. (pres. 1969—), Pee Dee Dental Study Club (sec. 1968—), Psi Omega. Baptist. Kiwanian (dir. 1966-69). Home: 1019 Park Av Florence SC 29501 Office: 614 W Palmetto St Florence SC 29501

MAY, ALAN MUTNICK, restaurant chain exec.; b. N.Y.C., Apr. 23, 1935; s. Jack and Madeline (Mutnick) M.; S.B., Mass. Inst. Tech., 1957; M.B.A., N.Y. U., 1959; m. Marcia Wolfson, June 6, 1963; 1 dau., Alexandra Nicole. Asst. treas. Bankers Trust Co., N.Y.C., 1957-60, asst. v.p., 1960-65; v.p. finance Elcor Chem. Corp., Midland, Tex., 1965-69; exec. v.p., dir. Steak and Ale Restaurants of Am., Inc., Dallas, 1970—. Mem. Financial Execs. Inst. Home: 3601 Turtle Creek Blvd Dallas TX 75219 Office: 3505 Turtle Creek Blvd Dallas TX 75219

MAY, ALETHA BARRETT (MRS. DONALD W. MAY), advt. exec.; b. Trenton, Tex., July 11, 1911; d. James Absalom and Lois (Adams) Barrett; student Tex. Women's U., 1928-29; B.S., E. Tex. State Coll., 1940; m. Donald Wright May, Sept. 3, 1944; 1 dau., Janis Susan. Tchr. pub. schs., Tex., 1930-31; county home demonstration agt. Brooks County, Tex., 1941-44; editor, staff home economist Producer-Consumer, Amarillo, Tex., 1944-48; v.p. Don May Advt., Inc., Dallas 1958—. Home: 6149 Brandels Lane Dallas TX 75214 Office: PO Box 9736 Lakewood Station Dallas TX 75214

MAY, CLARENCE EDWARD, educator, bank dir.; b. Weyers Cave, Va., Apr. 12, 1903; s. William Henry and Eliza (Rankin) M.; B.A., Bridgewater Coll., 1924; M.A., U. Va., 1931; postgrad. Columbia U., 1936-38; U. Manchester (Eng.), 1949; U. London, 1961; m. Frances Zoll, Feb. 2, 1928; 1 son, Clarence Edward. Tchr. various pub. schs. W.Va., Hawaii, Va., C.Z., 1924-44; prin. Culpeper (Va.) High Sch., 1945-46; head English dept. Bridgewater (Va.) Coll., 1946-68; lectr. English lit. Madison Coll., Harrisonburg, Va., 1969-70; dir. Valley Nat. Bank, Harrisonburg, Va., 1967—. Councilman Town of Bridgewater, 1956-58, mayor, 1958-68. Committeeman, Rockingham County Democratic Com.; Va. Dem. Com., del. 1959, 63, Dem. Nat. Conv., 1964; county gubernatorial campaign mgr., 1965; Chmn. Bridgewater 100th Anniversary Celebration Com., 1967. Mem. Phi Delta Epsilon, Lambda. Mason, Rotarian. Author: One Hundred Years of Masonry in the Town of Bridgewater, 1965; (with Russell L. Stultz) A History of the Shenandoah Valley Electric Cooperatives, 1968. Editor, Philomathean, 1967-68. Home: 421 E College St Bridgewater VA 22812

MAY, DONALD CURTIS, JR., govt. ofcl.; b. Ann Arbor, Mich., May 31, 1917; s. Donald Curtis and Alice Inglis (Smith) M.; B.A., U. Mich., 1938; M.A., Princeton, 1940, Ph.D., 1941; m. Helen E. Byrn, Feb. 21, 1942. Math. analyst Navy Bur. Ordnance, Washington, 1941-59; systems analysis officer Bur. Naval Weapons, Washington, 1959-63; asst. for analysis Surface Missile Systems Project, U.S. Navy Dept., Washington, 1963—. Mem. Washington Acad. Sci., Operations Research Soc. Am. Author: (with R. S. Burington) Handbook of Probability and Statistics, 1953. Home: 5931 Oakdale Rd McLean VA 22101 Office: PMO-403 Ordnance Systems Command Navy Dept Washington DC 20360

MAY, DONALD WRIGHT, advt. agy. exec.; b. Leonard, Tex., June 18, 1911; s. Robert C. and Mary Agnes (Wright) M.; m. Aletha Barrett, Sept. 3, 1944; children—Janis Susan, Robert Arthur. Editor, Memphis Democrat, Bay City Tribune, 1933-38; asso. prof. journalism Tex. A. and M. Coll., 1938-43; became dir. pub. relations and edn. Consumers Coops. Asso., 1943; dir. sales Farmers Coop. Exchange, Raleigh, N.C., 1952-54; asso. McCarty Co., advt. counselors, Dallas, 1954-58; pres. Don May Advt., Inc., Dallas, 1958—. Mem. Am. Assn. U. Profs., Tex., Panhandle press assns. A.I.M. (pres.'s council). Republican. Home: 6149 Brandeis Lane Dallas TX 75214 Office: PO Box 9736 Lakewood Sta Dallas TX 75214

MAY, EDWARD DEAN, ednl. adminstr.; b. Lansing, N.C., Sept. 8, 1940; s. Robert Todd and Ethel (Graham) M.; B.S., Appalachian State U., 1962; M.S., Radford Coll., 1967; m. Brenda Sue Johnson, May 11, 1963. Tchr., Jefferson (N.C.) Elementary Sch., 1962-63; park ranger Blue Ridge Parkway, summers, 1963-65; tchr. Oakland Elementary Sch., Galax, Va., 1963-65, prin., 1965—. Mem. Carroll County, Va., Nat., N.C. edn. assns., Jaycees. Clubs: Ruritan, Lions, Collegiate Civic. Home: Rt 4 Taylorwood Galax VA 24333

MAY, FRANCIS BARNS, educator; b. Cascilla, Miss., Dec. 24, 1915; s. James Marshall and Hallye (Rice) M.; B.B.A. with highest honors, U. Tex., 1941, M.B.A., 1943, Ph.D., 1957; m. Janice Evelyn Christensen, June 9, 1956. Instr. bus. statistics U. Tex., Austin, 1941-43, asst. prof., 1947-58, asso. prof., 1958-61, prof. 1961—, chmn. dept. gen. bus., 1964-68, research scientist Bur. Bus. Research, 1954-57, statistician, 1958-64, cons. statistician, 1964—. Vis. prof. statistics U. Minn., Mpls., 1960; dir. San Antonio br. Dallas Fed. Res. Bank, 1966-71, chmn. bd., 1968, 70. Served from pvt. to capt., USAAF, 1943-46. Mem. Am. Statis. Assn. (council, pres. Austin chpt. 1964-66), Southwestern Social Sci. Assn. (chmn. bus. research sect. 1956-57, editor 1958, pres. 1968-69), Econometric Soc., Operation Research Soc., Inst. Mgmt. Scis., Phi Kappa Phi, Phi Eta Sigma, Beta Gamma Sigma, Sigma Iota Epsilon, Beta Alpha Psi. Club: Social Science (pres. Austin 1965-66). Author: Introduction to Games of Strategy, 1970. Asso. editor Tex. Bus. Rev., 1963-64. Contbr. numerous articles to profl. jours. Home: 6504 Auburnhill Austin TX 78723

MAY, JOHN LAWRENCE, bishop; b. Evanston, Ill., Mar. 31, 1922; s. Peter Michael and Catherine (Allare) M.; M.A., St. Mary of Lake Sem., Mundelein, Ill., 1945, S.T.L., 1947. Ordained priest Roman Catholic Ch., 1947; asst. pastor St. Gregory Ch., Chgo., 1947-56; chaplain Mercy Hosp., Chgo., 1956-59; v.p., gen. sec. Catholic Ch. Extension Soc. U.S., 1959-67, pres., 1967—; techr. St. Gregory High Sch., Chgo., 1949-56, Loyola U., Chgo., 1948-49; lectr. Cana Conf. Chgo., 1949-65; defender of bond, met. tribunal Archdiocese of Chgo., 1949-58, prosynodal judge, 1958-69; aux. bishop of Chgo., 1967-69; bishop Diocese of Mobile (Ala.)., 1969—; Office: Office of Bishop Diocese of Mobile Mobile AL 33601

MAY, JOSEPH LESERMAN, hosiery co. exec.; b. Nashville, May 27, 1929; s. Daniel and Dorothy (Fishel) M.; B.A., Yale, 1951; LL.B., N.Y.U., 1958; grad. Harvard Program Mgmt. Devel., 1969; m. Natalie McCuaig, Apr. 12, 1957; children—Benjamin Tallman, Andrew Leserman, Joshua McIntosh, Maria Catherine. Salesman, May Hosiery Mills, N.Y.C., 1955-58, pres. Nuweave Socks div., Nashville, 1958-64; exec. v.p. May Hosiery Mills div. Wayne Gossard Corp., Nashville, 1965—; admitted to Tenn. bar, 1959. Pres., Nashville Jewish Community Center, 1969-71. Served with AUS, 1951-54. Mem. Tenn. Bar Assn. Rotarian (pres. Nashville 1971-72). Club: Old Oak (Nashville). Home: 2305 Hampton Av Nashville TN 37215 Office: 425 Chestnut St Nashville TN 37202

MAY, KEN EVERETT, motel exec.; b. Little Rock, July 27, 1941; s. Lawrence A. and Carra Jewel (Halsey) M.; student N.M. Highlands U., 1960-61, N.M. State U., 1962-64; m. Sylvia Raye, Apr. 27, 1963. Mgr., Ramada Inn, Tucumcari, N.M., 1964-66; mgr. Ramada Inn, Carlsbad, N.M., 1967-69; mgr. Holiday Inn, Lubbock and Amarillo, Tex., 1969—; v.p. Beaus & Belles Pants West, Inc. Bd. advisers Hotel-Restaurant Sch., Amarillo Coll. Mem. N.M. Hotel-Motel Assn. (dir. 1965), Panhandle Motel Assn. (pres. Amarillo), Amarillo Jr. C. of C. (v.p.). Address: 1911 I-40 at Ross Amarillo TX 79105

MAY, MORTIMER, hosiery mfr.; b. Laconia, N.H., Dec. 20, 1892; s. Jacob and Rebecca (Weingarten) M.; B.S., Columbia, 1914; m. Gertrude Bloch, Dec. 26, 1917; children—Reba (Mrs. Robert Blum), Leon. Sec., May Corp., Nashville, 1914, pres., 1946-58, chmn., 1958—. Bd. govs. Devel. Corp for Israel; mem. nat. council Am. Friends of Hebrew U.; past pres. Zionist Orgn. Am.; mem. bd. United Israel Appeal, Jewish Nat. Fund, Am. Com. for Weizman Inst.; mem. exec. com. Union Am. Hebrew Congregations. Mem. World Zionist Orgn. (gen. council), Am. Jewish Congress (bd.), World Jewish Congress (bd.), United Tenn. League (bd.). Club: Barnard Astronomical. Home: 5024 Alton Rd Miami Beach FL 33140 Office: 425 Chestnut St Nashville TN 37203

MAYBORN, FRANK WILLIS, newspaper editor and publisher; b. Akron, O., Dec. 7, 1903; s. Ward C. and Nellie C. (Welton) M.; B.A., U. Colo., 1927. With Dallas News, 1926, Stone & Webster Corp., Ft. Worth, 1927-29; bus. mgr. Temple (Tex.) Telegram, 1929-45, editor, pres., pub., 1945—; founder, pres., 1936-70, operator radio sta. KTEM, Temple; founder, pres., 1953—, operator KCEN-TV, Temple; owner Sherman (Tex.) Democrat, 1945—; pres., part owner, operator Killeen (Tex.) Herald, 1952—, Taylor (Tex.) Press, 1959—; founder, operator radio sta. WMAK, Nashville, 1947-54; pres., dir. Bell Pub. Co., Temple, 1945—, Bell Broadcasting Co., Temple, 1936-70, Sherman Democrat Co., 1945—, Killeen (Tex.) Herald Pub. Co., 1952—, Taylor (Tex.) Pub. Co., 1959—, Channel 6, Inc., 1962—, County Developers, Inc., 1967—, FWM Properties, 1965—; dir. 1st Nat. Bank, Temple. Dir. Temple Indsl. Found., pres., 1963; mem. Tex. Hist. Found., 1967-68, Tex. Hist. Survey Com., 1966-69; mem. adv. council U. Tex. Journalism Found., 1964-66, Tex. A. and M. U. Dept. Journalism, 1958-59; mem. adv. and devel. bds. Tex. Indsl. Commn.; mem. Ft. Hood Civilian Adv. Com., Baylor U. Broadcast Council; mem. adv. bd. Scott and White Hosp. Found., Temple. Mem. Tex. Democratic Com., 1948. Bd. dirs. Temple Boys Choir, 1969, Waco Symphony Assn., 1968-69; trustee Peabody Coll., 1970—, Central Tex. Med. Found., 1970—; chmn. bd. trustees Kinsolving Youth Center, 1971—. Served from pvt. to maj., AUS, 1942-45; ETO. Decorated Bronze Star Medal; recipient Outstanding Citizens award, Temple, 1948, Tex. award for outstanding service V.F.W., 1955, award for contbn. to soil and water conservation Soil Conservation Service, 1959; Citizenship award Jr. C. of C., 1951, Man of Year award, 1971, 4-H award for outstanding service to 4-H Clubs, 1971. Mem. Am. Soc. Newspaper Editors (past dir.), Tex. Daily Press League (dir. Tex. Sunday comic sect.), Temple C. of C. (dir., past pres.), Retail Mchts. Assn. Temple, Tex. Daily Newspaper Assn. (past pres.; award 1946), Am. (fed. laws com.), So. (pres. 1962, chmn. bd. 1963) newspaper pubs. assns., Tex. Council Higher Edn., Assn. U.S. Army (life, certificate of achievement 1969), Phi Kappa Psi, Sigma Delta Chi. Presbyn. (elder). Mason, Rotarian (hon.). Clubs: Nat. Press (Washington); Advertising (past pres.) (Ft. Worth); Dallas Athletic, Lancers (Dallas); Headliners (Austin); Temple Country. Office: 17 S 3d St Temple TX 76501

MAYBORN, WYTHEL LOUWEEN KILLEN (MRS. FRANK W. MAYBORN), pub. co. exec.; b. Union, Ore.; d. William Lane and Ida (Creasey) Killen; student Strayers Bus. Coll., 1938-39; m. Frank W. Mayborn, Apr. 20, 1947. With fed. law sect. Library of Congress, 1939-41; sec. Senator Alben W. Barkley, 1941-47; v.p., Bell Pub. Co., Temple, Tex., 1947—, Channel 6, Inc., Temple, 1954—, FWM properties, Inc., Temple, 1960—, Frank W. Mayborn Found., Temple, 1962—; dir. Red River Valley Pub. Co., Sherman, Tex.; dir., asst. sec. Community Enterprises, Inc., Temple. Mem. Bell Profit Sharing Com., Red River Valley Profit Sharing Com., 1959—; mem. Temple Arno Art League, 1948—. Del.-at-large Democratic Conv., Atlantic City, 1963. Bd. dirs. Sr. Citizens Activities, Bell County Mental Health and Mental Retardation; trustee Harvest House, Temple; mem. woman's bd. Dallas Civic Opera Co. Mem. City Fedn. Women's Clubs (pres. 1970-71). Presbyn. Home: 603 W Shell Av Temple TX 76501 Office: 17 S 3d St Temple TX 76501

MAYER, CLAUDIUS FRANCIS, govt. med. officer; b. Eger, Hungary, July 6, 1899 (came to U.S. 1931, naturalized 1936); s. George and Julianna (Berze) M.; A.B., Cistercian Gymnasium, Eger, 1917; M.D., Royal Hungarian Peter Pazmany U., 1925, Columbia, 1931; m. Jeanette Eva Bodnar, Aug. 7, 1927. Attending physician Urol. Clinic, Budapest, 1926-28; clin. pathologist Hungarian Social Security Inst., 1928-31; med. dir. Lindsay Labs., Inc., Bklyn., 1931-32; sci. editor Index-Catalogue of Surgeon Gens. Library, U.S. War Dept., Washington, 1932-54; med. officer Civilian Employees' Health Service, U.S. Dept. Def., Washington, 1955—. Served to lt. col. AUS, 1948-54. Fellow A.A.A.S.; mem. Washington Soc. Pathologists, Assn. Mil. Surgeons U.S., Chevy Chase Citizens' Assn., N.Y. Acad. Scis. Author: History of Medicine, 1927; Monastic Medicine, 1930; Albertus Magnus, 1928; Ramazzini de Morbis Artificum, 1928; Biobibliography of 16th Century Medical Authors, 1941; Epidemic Hemorrhagic Fever, 1951; Genesis of Genetics, 1953; History of Genetics, 1961. Editorial bd. Acta geneticae medicae, Rome, 1953—; columnist Mil. Medicine, 1953-63. Home: 5513 39th St NW Washington DC 20015 Office: Pentagon Washington DC 20025

MAYER, PHIL, hotel exec.; b. Naponoch, N.Y., Nov. 15, 1918; s. Julius and Helen (Pineles) M.; B.A., Cornell U., 1940; m. Harriet Minushkin, June 10, 1945; children—Hal Norris, Jack Burton. Owner, operator Queen Mountain Country Club, Ferndale, N.Y., 1940-56; mgr. Lombardy Hotel, 1956-58, Singapore Motel, 1958-64, Barcelona Hotel, 1964-67; partner, exec. dir. Desert Inn, 1967— (all Miami Beach, Fla.); dir. Senogas Corp., Miami, Fla. Served with USAAF, 1941-45. Decorated Bronze Star, Air Medal with 3 oak leaf clusters. Mem. Miami Beach Motel Assn. (dir. 1971—). Home: 300 Diplomat Pkwy Hallandale FL 33009 Office: Desert Inn 17201 Collins Av Miami Beach FL 33154

MAYER, RAYMOND CHARLES, trade assn. exec.; b. Bklyn., Aug. 12, 1921; s. Raymond C. and Sybil (Peacock) M.; B.A., Colgate U., 1947; m. Grace E. Fleming, Feb. 20, 1949; children—Raymond C., Nancy Ruth, Hollis E., Sybil F., Margo G. From student trainee to exec. staff dir. Raymond C. Mayer & Assos., Inc., N.Y.C., White Plains, N.Y., 1954-60, v.p., 1960-62, exec. v.p., 1962, pres., 1962-69; pub. relations counsel, sci. engr. various trade assns., 1954-69; exec. dir. Elec. Council Fla., Tampa, editor Elec Fla., 1970—, also dir. Active Cub Scouts Am., Boy Scouts Am., United Fund, A.R.C. Served to lt. AUS, 1942-55. Mem. A.A.A.S., Pub. Relations Soc. Am. (sec., dir.), Colgate U. Council on U. Relations, Sigma Nu. Republican. Conglist. Club: Colgate University (N.Y.C., dir.); Sertoma. Contbr. articles to trade and news mags. Home: 2704 Fountain Blvd Tampa FL 33609 Office: 5445 Mariner St Tampa FL 33609

MAYES, FAY MCWHORTER (MRS. CHARLES R. MAYES), clubwoman; b. Roopville, Ga., Aug. 2, 1916; d. Lorenza B. and Agnes (Ward) McWhorter; B.B.A., U. Miami (Fla.), 1970; R.N., Middle Ga. Hosp., 1937; m. Charles Robert Mayes, Jan. 2, 1942 (dec. Oct. 1967); children—William McWhorter, Robert Holder. Pres., Fla. Fedn. Garden Clubs, Inc., 1959-61; pres. Fla. chpt. 99's, 1944; editor Fla. Gardener, 1955-57; asso. editor Nat. Gardener, 1955-57; pres. Fla. Assn. Parliamentarians, 1961-63; life mem., past pres. Fla. Atlantic Music Guild, Inc.; life mem. Norty Broward Soc. Symphony, Inc.; bd. govs. Nature Conservancy, Washington, 1960-63, past pres. Fla. chpt.; mem. bd. Fla. Fedn. Garden Clubs; life mem. Nat. Council State Garden Clubs. Author: Program Patterns, 1958; The New Program Patterns, 1961; Public Relations and Pubicity Pointers. Home: 1100 S Ocean Blvd Pompano Beach FL 33062

MAYES, HAROLD, ret. steel co. exec.; b. Graham, Tex., July 13, 1905; s. Charles Homer and Louisa (Shoemaker) M.; B.S., Tex. A. and M. Coll., 1927; m. Audra Loraine Millican, Nov. 22, 1932; children—Elizabeth (Mrs. W. R. Merritt II), Harold. Draftsman, Austin Brothers Steel Co., Dallas, 1927-34, plant supt., 1934-53; partner Oliver-Mayes Steel Co., Dallas, 1953-54; works mgr. Mosher Steel Co. of Louisiana, Inc., Shreveport, 1954-70; v.p. Tri-State Metal Bldgs., Inc., Shreveport, 1970-72. Served to maj. AUS, 1942-45. Mem. Am. Welding Soc., La. Mfrs. Assn. (state pres. 1965-66). Baptist. Lion (pres.). Home: 102 Lynn Av Shreveport LA 71105

MAYES, JAMES JEFFRIES, dentist; b. Danville, Ala., Nov. 10, 1922; s. Alversa Donald and Amanda (Sims) M.; B.A., Fisk U., 1950; D.D.S., Meharry Med. Coll., 1954; m. Vivienne Lucile Malone, Sept. 1, 1952. Gen. practice dentistry, Waco, Tex., 1954—. Trustee, McLennan Community Coll., Greater Waco United Fund. Served with AUS, 1941-45; PTO. Decorated Bronze Star medal. Mem. Am., Nat., Tex., Gulf State dental assns., Omicron Kappa Upsilon. Democrat. Baptist. Kiwanian. Home: Route 7 Box 336 Waco TX 76705 Office: 1227 Chestnut Av Waco TX 76704

MAYES, MARTIN, govt. ofcl.; b. Richmond, Mo., July 3, 1905; s. Jewell and Edith (Martin) M.; A.B., William Jewell Coll., 1928; B.J., U. Mo., 1929; postgrad. U. Vienna (Austria), 1931; Ph.D., U. Heidelberg (Germany), 1934; m. Victoria von Tiesenhausen, Mar. 16, 1934 (div.); children—Renate Elizabeth, Monika Annette (Mrs. Kenneth A. Kiley); m. 2d, Jane Cannon, Dec. 29, 1959. Editor, pub. Missourian, Richmond, 1934-44, Missourian Press, 1938-44; served with U.S. Strategic Bombing Survey in Europe, 1945; chief of sect. U.S. Mil. Govt., State of Hesse, Germany, 1946; dep. chief edn. and religious affairs br., Bavaria, Germany, 1947-48; ednl. adviser Commr. for Bavaria, U.S. Dept. State, 1949-50, chief edn. br., Munich, Germany, 1951-52; cons. Multikrete Corp., Wilmington, Del., 1952-53; also dir.; legislative aide to Senator Hennings, Washington, 1953-54; cons. U.S. Senate Com., Washington, 1955-56; with U.S. Office Edn., Washington, 1957—, successively chief sch. laws sect., liaison officer, acting dir. Office Information, spl. asst. Bur. Higher Edn., 1970—. Cons. to Learning Resources Inst., N.Y.C., Chgo. Dir. Workshop Criminal Behavior, Adams State Coll., Alamosa, Colo., 1956. Bd. dirs. Found. for Advancement Edn., Bavaria, 1948-52, Fgn. Study Commn., Munich 1., 1949-51, dir. Am. Assn. Sch. Adminstrs.-N.E.A. Internat. Field Study Projects in Germany, 1964-66, 68-72; sec. Adv. Com. Nat. Orgns., 1957-61; bd. dirs. Nat. Interagy. Council on Smoking and Health, 1964—. Fellow Am. Sociol. Assn.; mem. Am. Hist. Assn., A.A.A.S., Assn. Higher Edn., N.E.A., Mo. Soc. (pres. Washington 1963-64), Am. Assn. Sch. Adminstrs., Profl. Edn. Assn. in U.S. Office Edn. (pres. 1969-72). Club: Nat. Press (Washington). Author govt. publs., also articles in profl. jours. Editorial dir. Schule and Gegenwart, 1950-51. Patentee piston ring and piston. Home: 2000 S Eads St Arlington VA 22202 Office: US Office Edn Washington DC 20202

MAYES, RICHARD LEON, candy co. exec.; b. Earlsboro, Okla., Oct. 29, 1928; s. Sterling L. and Alberta Beatrice (Follmar) M.; B.B.A., U. Okla., 1952; postgrad. N.Y.U., 1958-59, Central State U., 1971-72; m. Jo Ann McKibben, July 14, 1951; children—Cynthia Ann, Deborah Sue, Beverly Gayle, Julie Kay. Asst. mgr. Oklahoma City Safety Council, 1952-55; with pub. relations dept. Assn. Casualty and Surety Cos., 1955-57; account supr. Batten, Barton, Durstine & Osborn, N.Y.C., 1957-62, account group supr., Boston, 1962-64; v.p. sales and marketing, dir. Bunte Candies Inc., Oklahoma City, 1964—; partner Sheridan Assos. Instr. Oklahoma City U., 1954, mem. tennis adv. com., 1970—. Served with AUS, 1946-48. Mem. Oklahoma City All Sports Assn. (dir.). Unitarian (trustee). Club: Quail Creek Golf and Country. Home: 2713 NW 59th St Oklahoma City OK 73112 Office: 129 E California St Oklahoma City OK 73104

MAYES, SAMUEL HUBERT, JR., lawyer; b. Little Rock, Sept. 6, 1931; s. S. Hubert and Charlotte (McIntosh) M.; J.D., U. Ark., 1954; m. Mary J. Schallhorn, Aug. 30, 1933 (div. 1966); children—Jean, Charlotte, Melissa; m. 2d., L. Susan Harrell, Dec. 30, 1971. Admitted to Ark. bar, 1954; atty. Ark. Revenue Dept., 1954; dep. pros. atty. 6th Jud. Dist., Little Rock, 1957-58; spl. asst. atty. gen. State of Ark., 1963; partner firm Fulk, Lovett &Mayes, Little Rock, 1960—. Asst. sec. Ark. Senate, 1953. Served with USAF, 1955-57. Mem. Delta Theta Phi, Omicron Delta Kappa, Sigma Chi. Democrat. Methodist. Home: 2021 Beechwood St Little Rock AR 72207 Office: 807 W 3d St Little Rock AR 72201

MAYEUX, DONALD ARCILE, wholesale grocer; b. Mamou, La., Mar. 26, 1920; s. Aurelis and Aza (Vidrine) M.; B.S., La. State U., 1939, M.S., 1941; m. Gladys Guillory, July 13, 1940; children—Donald Lynn, Margaret (Mrs. Robert Kinler), Andre, Philip. Mgr., co-owner Mamou Wholesale Grocery Co., 1946—; dir. Gulfco Investment Group, Inc. Pres. Evangeline Parish unit Am. Cancer Soc., 1960—, pres. La. div., 1968-69, state crusade chmn., 1970-71; mem. Evangeline Parish Dept. Pub. Welfare, 1961—. Served to maj. AUS, 1942-46. Named man of year in Mamou, 1958. Mem. La. Wholesale Grocers Assn. (pres. 1960-61). K.C. (4 deg.), Rotarian (pres. 1954-55). Home and office: Box 130 Mamou LA 70554

MAYFIELD, HENRY DAVIS, JR., architect, educator; b. San Antonio, Jan. 18, 1913; s. Henry Davis and Emma (Slavitchek) M.; B.S. in Archtl. Design, Tex. A. and M. U., 1935, M.Ed., 1971; m. Virginia Estelle Schell, Feb. 17, 1939 (dec. Mar. 1968); children—Jenny Lee (Mrs. George Edward Walker), Henry Davis III, William Jack Roy; m. 2d, Ethel Inez Maracle Byford, 1971. Individual practice architecture, Bryan, Tex., 1939-41, 46-56; system architect Tex. A. and M. Coll., 1956-61; univ. architect Duke, 1961-66; cons. univ. architect, Waco, Tex., 1966-69; mem. office facilities planning U. Okla., 1969—; prof. Tex. State Tech. Inst., Waco, 1969—. Served to col., arty. AUS, 1941-46. Mem. A.I.A., Tex. Soc. Architects, Constrn. Specifications Inst., Assn. Univ. Architects, Chatham County Hist. Soc. Rotarian. Clubs: Briarcrest Country (Bryan); Lake Waco Country. Home: 215 Robins Loop Waco TX 76705 Office: Tex State Tech Inst Waco TX 76705

MAYFIELD, MARIETTA JUNE, wholesale co. exec.; b. Dallas, Oct. 15, 1932; d. Willie David and Hattie Irene (Redd) Pilgrim; grad. Burroughs Accounting Sch., 1953; exec. secretarial course Draughns Bus. Coll., 1967; m. Jerry Charles Mayfield, May 4, 1951; children—

Joy Lynne, Julie Anne. With credit card dept. Texaco, Inc., 1950-57, asst. supt., 1956-57; stenographer Tidewater Asso. Oil Co., San Francisco., 1953-54; gen. accountant Dresser Electronics, 1959-61; controller Hall-Mark Electronics Corp., Dallas, 1962-70, corporate sec., 1969—; corporate sec. T Bar M, Inc., 1971—, also dir.; dir. Elmer Wheeler Internat., Inc.; co-owner Mayfield Furniture Co., Mesquite, Tex., 1965-71. Republican. Baptist. Club: T Bar M Racquet (Dallas). Home: 1709 Iroquois St Garland TX 75040

MAYLAN, ARTHUR GEOFFREY, civil engr.; b. Mansfield, Eng., Apr. 5, 1930; s. Arthur Leslie and Katie Roma (Perrin) M.; nat. certificate bldg. Barnsley Tech. Coll. (Eng.), 1952; m. Irene Edwards, July 15, 1967. Came to U.S., 1957, naturalized, 1963. Civil engr., Salisbury, So. Rhodesia, 1952-57, Louis Berger & Assos., East Orange, N.J., 1957-58, Boswell Engring Co., Ridgefield Park, N.J., 1958-60, Fla. Dept. Transp., Tallahassee, 1960—. Treas., Tallahassee Little Theater, 1965-67. Registered profl. engr., Fla. Mem. Am. Soc. C.E. Episcopalian. Mason. Club: Killearn Golf and Country (Tallahassee). Home: 3604 Donegal Dr Tallahassee FL 32303 Office: Haydon Burns Bldg Tallahassee FL 32304

MAYLE, FRANCIS CARL, JR., physician; b. Newark, June 5, 1928; s. Francis C. and Pauline (Finkbeiner) M.; B.S., Georgetown U., 1949, M.D., 1953, M.S. in Neurophysiology, 1959; m. Barbara Mollach, May 30, 1953; children—Marjorie, Francis Carl III, Katherine, Paul. Intern U.S. Naval hosp., St. Albans, N.Y., 1953-54; resident Georgetown U. Hosp., Washington, 1956-59, Mt. Alto VA Hosp., Washington, 1956-59, D.C. Gen. Hosp., 1957; practice medicine specializing in neurology, Bethesda, Md., Washington, 1959—; mem. staffs Providence, Georgetown U. Children's, Sibley hosps., Washington Hosp. Center (all Washington), Suburban Hosp., Bethesda; Holy Cross Hosp., Silver Spring, Md.; asst. clin. prof. neurology Georgetown U. Sch. Medicine, 1959—. Chmn. regional adv. com. Met. Washington Regional Med. Programs, 1969—. Served with USNR, 1953-56. Diplomate Am. Bd. Neurology. Fellow A.C.P., Am. Geriatric Soc.; mem. A.M.A., Am. Epilepsy Assn., So. Med. Assn., Montgomery County (sec. 1967-68), D.C. med. socs., St. Luke's Soc., Georgetown Clin. Soc., Washington Med. and Surg. Soc., Am. Acad. Neurology (press and pub. relations chmn. 1969—), Georgetown U. Alumni Assn. (senate). K.C. Home: 4903 Scarsdale Rd Washington DC 20016 Office: 8218 Wisconsin Av Bethesda MD 20014

MAYNARD, A(MOS) LEE, pub. relations exec., editor; b. Kenova, Va., July 26, 1936; s. Amos Maynard and Minnie (LeMaster) M.; B.S. in Tech. Journalism, W.Va. U., 1961; postgrad. Marshall U., 1965-68; m. Helen Brooks, July 10, 1959; children—Darel Lee, Toran Brooks. Asst. pub. relations officer W.Va. Dept. Natural Resources, Charleston, 1962-65; dir. pub. relations W.Va. C. of C., Charleston, 1965-66; adminstrv. exec. sec. W.Va. Commn. on Manpower, Tech. and Tng., Charleston, 1966-68; nat. dir. operations Outward Bound, Inc., Reston, Va., 1968—. Home: 11420 Links Dr Reston VA 22070 Office: Isaac Newton Sq Reston VA 22070

MAYNARD, JOHN GARY, JR., dentist; b. Bennettsville, S.C., Apr. 14, 1936; s. John Gary and Grace Evelyn (Lee) M.; A.B. in Econs., Davidson Coll., 1958; D.D.S., Med. Coll. Va., 1958-62; certificate of periodontics U. Ky., 1967; m. Sara Jean Mason, Aug. 2, 1958; children—Sara Grason, Catherine Mason, John Gary. Intern, Walter Reed Hosp., 1962-63; practice periodontics, Richmond, Va., 1967—; part-time faculty dept. periodontics U. Ky., 1966-67, U. Pa., 1969-70; asst. clin. prof. periodontics Med. Coll. Va., Richmond, 1970—. Served to capt. Dental Corps, AUS, 1962-65. Decorated Army Commendation medal. Mem. Am., Va. dental assns., Richmond Dental Soc. (treas. 1971-72), Am., Va. (organizer, pres. 1968-70) socs. periodontists, Am. Acad. Periodontology, So. Acad. Periodontology (mem. membership com. 1969-71). Presbyn. (deacon 1969—). Rotarian. Club: Westwood Racquet (Richmond). Home: 29 Twin Lake Lane Richmond VA 23229 Office: 4909 Grove Av Richmond VA 23226

MAYNARD, W. NEIL, banker; b. Winthrop, Ark., Jan. 22, 1942; s. J. D. and Eurby (Abney) M.; B.S., U. Ark., 1963; postgrad. Ark. Law Sch., 1963-65, La. State U. Sch. Banking, 1968-70; m. Marianne Crank, June 15, 1963; children—Eric Neil, Jason Hunter. Trainee, Worthen Bank & Trust Co., Little Rock, 1963-66; asst. cashier First Nat. Bank, Stuttgart, Ark., 1967, cashier, 1968, exec. v.p., 1969, pres., 1970—, also dir. Pres., Stuttgart Indsl. Devel. Corp., 1970; chmn. Boy Scout Fund drive, 1969, Ark. County chpt. Crippled Childrens Assn., 1969-71. Bd. dirs. Grand Prairie Home Builders Assn. Named Outstanding Young Man, 1971. Mem. Am. Inst. Bankers (chmn. Grand Prairie), Life Underwriters Assn., Ark. Bankers Assn. (vice chmn.), Ark. Polled Hereford Assn., Stuttgart C. of C. (pres.), Acacia. Lion. Home: 1511 S Forter St Stuttgart AR 72160 Office: PO Drawer 908 Stuttgart AR 72160

MAYNE, ALVIN, mgmt. and econ. cons. co. exec.; b. Chgo., May 14, 1914; s. Oscar A. and Sahra (Greenberg) M.; B.A., U. Chgo., 1936; M.B.A., U. Chgo., 1940; m. Jeannette Ladin, June 20, 1937; 1 dau., Evelyn. With NRA, Washington, 1934-36; adviser to Q.M. Gen., 1942-45; economist Moody's Investor Service, 1945-48; faculty Wharton Sch., U. Pa., Phila., 1948-51, 53-54; dep. asst. adminstr. Nat. Prodn. Authority, Washington, 1951-53; adviser Exec. Office of Pres., Washington, 1953-54; econ. adviser Govt. P.R., 1954-61; adviser U.S. coordinator Alliance for Progress, 1962-64; pres. Clapp & Mayne, Inc. of P.R., Santurce, 1965—. Mem. Soc. Internat. Devel. (chpt. pres. 1970—), Am. Econ. Assn., Econometric Soc., Am. Statis. Assn., Sigma Xi. Contbr. articles to various publs. Home: 61 Kings Ct San Juan PR 00911 Office: 1606 Ponce de Leon Av Santurce PR 00909

MAYNICK, CAPUS MILLER, cons.; b. Rockingham County, N.C., Dec. 23, 1889; s. Joshua James N. and Anna (Moore) W.; student U. N.C., 1907-09; m. Elizabeth McBee, June 19, 1915. Reporter, Greensboro Daily Record, 1911-13, Charlotte Observer, 1913-14; editor Greensboro Daily Record, 1915-17, pub., 1920-22; editor High Point (N.C.) Enterprise; acting adminstr. Point 4 Program, 1950; A.E. and P. to Nicaragua, 1950-51; ambassador to Columbia, 1951-53; adj. gen. N.C., 1957-61; exec. v.p. Richardson Found., N.Y.C., 1961-63; adviser to N.C. Gov. on Negro citizenship equality, 1963-65. Dir. for N.C., Nat. Reemployment Service, 1933-34; chmn. N.C. Hwy. and Pub. Works Commn., 1934-37, chmn. state planning bd., 1937; founder, dir. Health Edn. Inst., to 1949; mem. nat. adv. council U.S. Dept. Agr., 1965-69. Mem. N.C. Ho. of Reps., 1931, N.C. Senate, 1933; chmn. N.C. Democratic Party, 1948. Served with inf., U.S. Army, 1918. Presbyn. Author: North Carolina Roads and Their Builders, 1953. Co-author: North Carolina and the Negro, 1964. Home: 1713 Beaucrest Av High Point NC 27260

MAYO, CHRISTIAN JOYCE WILKES (MRS. GARNETTE F. MAYO), librarian; b. Lyons, Ga., Sept. 11, 1916; d. Robert Quitman and Ruby (Wilkes); B.S., Ga. State Coll. Women, 1946; student Fla. State U., 1953-54; m. Garnette E. Mayo, June 26, 1938. Tchr. Sidney Lanier Sch., Brunswick, Ga., 1943-45, Toombs Central Sch., Lyons, 1945-48, Lyons (Ga.) High Sch., 1948-50; sch. librarian Okaloosa County Sch., Eglin AFB, Fla., 1950-55; tech. librarian Eglin AFB, 1955-58, base librarian, from 1958; now supervisory librarian U.S. Army Mil. Police Sch., Ft. Gordon, Ga. Trustee Fort Walton Beach (Fla.) Pub. Library, 1953-65. Mem. Am., Southeastern, Ga. library assns., Central Savannah River Area Assn. Presbyn. Home: 4115 Windsor Spring Rd Hephzibah GA 30815 Office: US Army Military Police School Library Ft Gordon GA 30905

MAYO, HIRAM JOHNSON, supt. schs.; b. Mesic, N.C., July 11, 1924; s. Wiley S. and Alice (Lupton) M.; A.B., East Carolina U., 1944, M.A., 1948; postgrad. Columbia; m. Leah Ross, May 4, 1945; children—Hiram Johnson, Rita Leah. Asso. prof. edn. State Tchrs. Coll., Livingston, Ala., 1950-52; supt. schs., Edenton, N.C., 1960-67, Craven County Schs., New Bern, N.C., 1967—. Mem. Craven County Health Bd., 1967-72. Served with USNR, 1944-45. Mem. Am. Assn. Sch. Adminstrs., N.C. Edn. Assn. (past pres. Dist. 14). Methodist. Mason (32 deg.), Rotarian (sec.). Home and office: PO Box 969 New Bern NC 28560

MAYO, JOHN CALDWELL CALHOUN, financier, industrialist; b. Paintsville, Ky., Dec. 18, 1900; s. John C.C. and Alice (Meek) M.; student Amherst Coll., 1919-20; m. Mary Nancy McClure, June 17, 1938; children—Thomas Jefferson, John C.C. III, Andrew Jackson, Nancy McClure, Alice Margaret. Pres., dir. Mayo Oil Service Co., 1921—, Mayo Equipment Co., 1923—, Mayo Arcade Co., 1925—, Midland and Atlantic Bridge Corp., 1926—, Mayo Co., 1930—; chmn. bd. 2d Nat. Bank, Ashland, Ky., 1948—, S.P. Hager & Son, Co., Ashland, 1947—; pres. Olive Hill Refractories Co., Ashland, 1941—, Collins-Mayo Collieries Co., Ashland, 1940—; v.p. Ky. River Coal Corp., Lexington, 1945—; chmn. bd. Watterson City, Inc., Louisville, 1960—; pres., dir. many other corps. Mem. Ky. Unemployment Compensation Commn., 1937-43, 48-60. Mem. Phi Delta Theta. Democrat. Episcopalian. Home: 1508 Lexington Av Ashland KY 41101 Office: Mayo Arcade Bldg Ashland KY 41101

MAYO, ROBERT BOWERS, museum dir.; b. Phoenixville, Pa., Apr. 26, 1933; s. Newton Tabb and Mary (Dabney) M.; B.F.A., Richmond Profl. Inst., 1959; m. Margaret Gwynn Thomas, Dec. 1, 1956; children—Pamela Elizabeth, Mary Beth, Margaret Bingham. Curator interpretation and exhibits Jamestown (Va.) Festival Park, 1959-61; curator exhibits N.C. Dept. Archives and History, Raleigh, N.C., 1961-66; dir. Valentine Mus., Richmond, Va., 1966—; cons. mus. planning, mus. exhibits design and fabrication. Trustee Historic Richmond Found. Served with USNR, 1951-55. Mem. Am. Assn. Museums, Va. History Fedn., Va. Postal History (v.p. 1971—), United Methodist Historic Soc., Assn. for Preservation Va. Antiquities, Am. Assn. Museums, Assn. State and Local History, Am. Philatelic Soc. Clubs: Isaak Walton League, Ducks Unlimited. Home: 1401 Winslow Rd Richmond VA 23235 Office: 1015 E Clay St Richmond VA 23219

MAYO, WALLACE C., dentist; b. Century, Fla., Feb. 10, 1914; s. James Lawrence and Lula Mae (Tompkins) M.; student U. Fla., 1932-33; D.D.S., Emory U., 1937; m. Jean Kingsbery, Jan. 11, 1941; children— Donna Jean, Susan, Clair, Howard. Intern Ft. Oglethorpe, Ga., 1938; pvt. practice dentistry, Pensacola, Fla., 1939-41, specializing in periodontics, 1945—. Chmn. adv. council Emory U. Sch. Dentistry; mem. adv. com. U. Fla. Sch. Dentistry, Pensacola Jr. Coll. Sch. Dental Hygiene; mem. dental adv. com. Dept. Def. Served with Dental Corps, AUS, 1941-45; ETO; NATOUSA. Fellow Internat. Coll. Dentists, Am. Coll. Dentists; mem. Fla. Soc. Peridontology, Am. Dental Assn. (ho. of dels.), Fla. (past pres., chmn. council on dental edn.), N.W. Fla. Dist. (past pres.), Pensacola (past pres.) dental socs., Am., So. (past pres.) acads. peridontology, Acad. Internat. Dentistry, Fedn. Dentaire Internationale, Res. Officers Assn. (past pres. Fla. dist.), Pensacola C. of C., USCG Aux. (insp. examiner). Baptist. Clubs: Exchange (past pres.), Yacht, Scenic Hills Country. Home: 2920 E Blackshear St Pensacola FL 32503 Office: 901 N 12th Av Pensacola FL 32501

MAYO, WILLIAM TAYLOR, state ofcl.; b. Summerfield, Fla., Dec. 10, 1917; s. Nathan and Nora (Newsome) M.; student U. Fla., 1934-36; m. Elizabeth Blalock, Aug. 6, 1939; children—William T., Elizabeth Jean, Nathan M., Joe Bryan. Co-owner automobile agy., Tallahassee, 1946-62; mem. Fla. Rd. Bd., 1961-64, also adminstr. Interstate Hwy. System; mem. Fla. Pub. Service Commn., Tallahassee, 1964—, chmn., 1966-70. City commr., Tallahassee, 1950-62, mayor, 1953-54. Recipient award for exceptional achievements in pub. service Kiwanis, 1964. Methodist. Elk. Club: Exchange (Tallahassee). Home: 1548 Lee Av Tallahassee FL 32303 Office: 700 S Adams St Tallahassee FL 32304

MAYORAL-BIGAS, JORGE WALTER, physician; b. Adjuntas, P.R., Sept. 5, 1927; s. Angel Maria and Felicia (Bigas) Mayoral; B.S. magna cum laude, U. P.R., 1947; M.D., Boston U., 1951; m. Nilda Maldonado, June 16, 1962; children—Georyanna, Jorge Walter, Michael, Nilmarie. Intern, resident internal medicine San Juan City Hosp., 1951-53; resident internal medicine San Juan VA Hosp., 1953-54; resident gastroenterology Kennedy VA Hosp., Memphis, 1956-58; practice medicine, specializing in gastroenterology, Ponce, P.R., 1958—; head dept. medicine Damas Hosp., Ponce. Served with USAF, 1954-56. Mem. A.C.P., P.R. Med. Assn., P.R. Soc. Gastroenterology. Author: Dubib-Johnson Disease, 1967. Home: Santa Maria A-51 Ponce PR 00731 Office: 33 Concordia Ponce PR 00731

MAYS, AVERY, constrn. co. exec.; b. Morgan County, Ala., Mar. 11, 1911; s. Walter Ernest and Millie Ann (Blankenship) M.; ed. pub. schs., Tex.; m. Eva Blanche Ponder, Mar. 27, 1932; children— Evelyn Joyce (Mrs. Tom C. McClellan), Gerald Avery. Retail lumberman, 1929-42; residential builder and land developer, 1943-55; gen. contractor, 1955—; treas., dir. Red Bird Indsl. Devel., Inc., Dallas, 1963—; dir. Lone Star Gas Co., Great Am. Res. Ins. Co., Oak Cliff Bank and Trust Co., State Fair of Texas. Mem. Dallas Ind. Sch. Dist., 1947-53; chmn. Dallas County A.R.C., 1965-66; pres. Greater Dallas Planning Council, 1966-67; bd. dirs. Dallas Citizens Council, pres., 1968; pres. Dallas United Fund; bd. dirs. Dallas County Boys Home; past pres. bd. Meth. Hosp., Dallas. Recipient Constrn. Industry Brotherhood citation Nat. Conf. Christians and Jews, 1962; named Oak Cliff Man of Year, 1962. Mem. Dallas Home Builders Assn. (pres. 1949; Hugh Prather Distinguished Service trophy 1960), Nat. Assn. Home Builders (dir. 1949-52), Dallas C. of C. (pres. 1961-62), Dallas Real Estate Bd. (Easterwood trophy 1960), Asso. Gen. Contractors (pres. Dallas 1967). Mason (32 deg., Shriner), Kiwanian (past pres. Oak Cliff). Home: 950 Kessler Pkwy Dallas TX 75208 Office: 625 Frito Lay Bldg PO Box 35612 Dallas TX 75235

MAYS, GERALD AVERY, constrn. co. exec.; b. Dallas, Nov. 24, 1939; s. Avery and Eva Blanche (Ponder) M.; B.S. in Civil Engring., So. Meth. U., 1962; postgrad., 1962-63; m. Shirley Ann Pike, Dec. 31, 1970 children—(by previous marriage) Gerald Avery, Sandra Jo, Sherrie Lynne. Player Kansas City Chiefs Football Club, 1961-70; v.p. Avery Mays Constrn. Co., Dallas, 1963-71, pres., 1971—; partner George Mays Assn. Ins. Agency, Dallas, 1963—; structural engr. Howard, Needles, Tammen & Bergendoff, Kansas City, 1964-66, Boyd, Brown & Stude, Kansas City, 1966-67. Trustee Baker U. Named Sportsman of the Year, Am. Football League, 1965; named to Kansas City Chiefs Hall of Fame, 1972. Registered profl. engr., Mo., Kan. Mem. Sigma Tau, Chi Epsilon, Blue Key. Home: 4468 Twinpost Rd Dallas TX 75234 Office: Box 35612 Dallas TX 75235

MAYS, MAX CARROLL, dentist; b. Beaumont, Tex., Dec. 2, 1935; s. Ed Kellie and Edith Joan (Miller) M.; B.S., So. Methodist U., 1958; D.D.S., U. Tex., 1963; m. Laura Lee Alvis, June 4, 1960; children—Roy Kellie, Matthew Carroll, Amanda. Gen. practice dentsitry, Silsbee, Tex., 1965-67, Lake Jackson, Tex., 1967—. Mem. City Charter Rev. Commn., 1971. Served to lt. Dental Corps, USNR, 1963-65. Mem. Am., Tex. dental assns., 9th Dist. Dental Soc., Brazoria County Dental Study Club (pres.), Brazosport C. of C., Alpha Tau Omega, Xi Psi Phi, Omicron Kappa Upsilon. Republican. Methodist. Kiwanian. Home: 316 Forest Dr Lake Jackson TX 77566 Office: 82 Flag Lake Rd Lake Jackson TX 77566

MAYS, RICHARD DUDLEY, lawyer; b. Dallas Dec. 28, 1939; s. Carl Cecil and Bonnie Jean (Troutt) M.; B.B.A., U. Tex., 1963, LL.B., 1965; m. Patricia Ridgway, Dec. 23, 1960; children—Allison Lynn, Erik Reagan. Admitted to Tex. bar, 1965; partner firm Mays & Mays, Dallas, 1965-67; asst. dist. atty. Dallas County, Dallas, 1967—. Precinct chmn. Dallas Democratic Com., 1966-68. Served with USCGR, 1959-60. Mem. Am., Dallas, Dallas Jr. bar assns., State Bar Tex., Delta Tau Delta. Club: Dallas Athletic. Home: 3804 Villanova St Dallas TX 75225 Office: Dallas County Courthouse Dallas TX 75202

MAYS, WILLIAM ARLIE, investor, developer; b. Gilbert, Ark., Feb. 23, 1901; s. James Franklin and Dora Bell (Box) M.; ed. pub. schs.; m. Eva Agnes Campbell, Sept. 19, 1920; children—Taylor F., Troy M. Pres. Mays Investment Co., Amarillo, Tex., 1951—; pres. Agridustrial Financing, 1954-56, sec.-treas., 1966-70; pres. Eighth Av. Corp., Amarillo, 1956—; founder W.A. Mays and Agnes Mays Trust No. 2, 1963—, co-developer Wolflin Square Subdiv., Amarillo, 1962; dir. Southwestern Investment Co., Amarillo. Founder, trustee Mays Found; chmn. bd. trustees Wayland Bapt. Coll., Plainview, 1950-60. Recipient Merit Award citation Wayland Bapt. Coll., 1959; Citizenship award Civitan Club, 1964; citation for distinguished service Bapt. Found. Tex., 1969. Baptist (deacon 1946—). Home: 1503 Lamar St Amarillo TX 79102 Office: 914 Tyler St Amarillo TX 79101

MAYSHARK, CYRUS, coll. adminstr.; b. Atlantic City, Aug. 3, 1926; s. Casimer and Jessie Rose (Whitney) M.; B.A., Williams Coll., 1949; M.Ed., Boston U., 1952; Ph.D. in Health and Safety, Ind. U., 1954; M.S. in Hygiene, Harvard, 1962; m. Barbara Anne Fisher, Sept. 12, 1947; children—Gail (Mrs. Scott Allen), Pamela (Mrs. Odis Chambers), Lee, Linda, Laura. Phys. dir. YMCA, Boston, 1949-52; state rep. Me., N.H., Vt. Nat. Found. Infantile Paralysis, Inc., Portland, Me., 1954-57; asst. prof. health edn. Ore. State U., Corvallis, 1957-60, asso. prof. health edn., 1960-65; prof., chmn. health edn. U. Tenn., Knoxville, 1965-68, asso. dean Coll. Edn., 1968-72; dean Sch. Edn. U. Tex., El Paso, 1972—. Pres., Mayshark, Newman & Assos., Inc. cons. comprehensive health edn. programs, Knoxville, 1969—; mem. Mid-Eastern Tenn. area adv. group, Regional Med. Program, 1969—; mem. adv. bd. tng. and tech. program AEC, Union Carbide and asso. univs., Oak Ridge, 1968—. Served with 11th airborne div. AUS, 1944-46; PTO. USPHS fellow, 1961-62; Mace bearer, Phi Kappa Phi lectr. U. Tenn., 1969-70. Fellow Soc. Pub. Health Edn.; mem. A.A.A.S., Am. Assn. U. Profs., Am. Pub. Health Assn., Am. Assn. Health, Phys. Edn. and Recreation, Am. Assn. Higher Edn., Am. Sch. Health Assn., N.E.A., Phi Delta Kappa. Author: (with R.H. Kirk and R.P. Hornsby) Personal Health in Ecologic Perspective, 1972; (with R.A. Foster) Health Education in Secondary Schools, 3d edit., 1972; (with D.D. Shaw) The Administration of School Health Programs, 1967; (with R.A. Foster) Methods in Health Education, 1968. Contbr. to profl. jours. Home: 753 Sunset Dr El Paso TX 79912

MAYTAG, LEWIS B., airline exec.; b. Rochester, Minn., 1926; ed. Colo. Coll. Founder Maytag Aircraft Corp., Colorado Springs, Colo., 1948, Maytag-Waynick Corp., Colorado Springs, 1952; pres. Frontier Airlines, Denver, 1959-62; chmn. bd., pres. Nat. Airlines, Inc., Miami, Fla.; dir. Maytag Co.; mem. adv. bd. dirs. First Nat. Bank Miami. Mem. Nat. C. of C. (dir. 1968-70, chmn. membership com.), Air Transport Assn. (dir.). Office: Box 2055 Airport Mail Facility Miami FL 33159

MAZA, LUIS, set designer; b. Cuba; student painting Karl Zerbe, Fla. State U. Tech. dir., designer Tallahassee Little Theater, Pocket Theatre, 1961-67; resident designer Spelman Coll., 1967-70; owner Luis Maza Studios, Atlanta, 1970—; set designer Alliance Theatre Co., Atlanta, 1971—. Home: 848 Durant Pl Atlanta GA 30308 Studio: 535 Courtland NE Atlanta GA 30308*

MAZAN, WALTER LAWRENCE, govt. ofcl.; b. Center Rutland, Vt., June 5, 1921; s. Lawrence Walter and Henrietta (Mazur) M.; student Norwich U., 1941; B.S. in Commerce, U. Vt., 1949; LL.D., So. Colo. State Coll., 1971; m. Lee Duffy, July 14, 1956; children—Walter Lawrence II, Lorilee, Michelle, Michael. With investigations dept. Gen. Adjustment Bur., N.Y.C., 1949-52; dir. civil def. for Vt., also asst. to gov., 1951-57; with Office Emergency Preparedness, Exec. Office Pres., 1957-69, dir. Office Liaison, 1969; asst. sec. of transp. for pub. affairs, 1969-70; dir. intergovtl. affairs White House Conf. on Children and Youth, 1970-71, exec. dir., 1971—. Lectr. in field, 1963—. Vice pres. Nat. Conf. State Socs., 1967; pres. Office Emergency Preparedness Credit Union, 1965-66. Served with USAAF, 1942-46. Recipient Outstanding Performance award Office Emergency Preparedness, Sustained Superior Performance award, 1967; Merit certificate Nat. Jr. Achievers, 1970; Recognition award U. Tenn., 1969; Appreciation certificate U. Fla., 1970. Mem. Nat. Geog. Soc., Arlington County Civic Assn., Vt. State Soc., Nat. Platform Assn. Roman Catholic. Author reports. Home: 4856 N 35th Rd Arlington VA 22207 Office: Exec Office Bldg 17th and Pennsylvania Av NW Washington DC 20304

MAZO, EARL, writer; b. Warsaw, Poland, July 7, 1919; s. Samuel George and Sonia (Portugal) M.; grad. Clemson Coll., 1940; m. Rita Vane, 1941; children—Judith Frances, Mark Elliot. Staff Charleston (S.C.) News and Courier, also Greenville News, 1939-41; editor, editorial page Camden (N.J.) Courier Post, 1945-50; staff N.Y. Herald Tribune, 1950-64, nat. polit. corr.; with N.Y. Times, N.Y.C., 1964-65, Reader's Digest, 1965—; polit. commentator WTOP-TV, CBS, Washington, 1969—. Served to lt. AUS, World War II; combat corr. European Star and Stripes. Decorated Air medals, Bronze Star medal, Presidential citations. Mem. Acad. Polit. Sci., Sigma Delta Chi. Clubs: Overseas Press (N.Y.C.); Nat. Press (Washington). Author: Richard Nixon, A Political and Personal Portrait, 1959; The Mindreaders, 1964. Home: 5915 Nebraska Av NW Washington DC 20015

MAZUR, PETER, biologist; b. N.Y.C., Mar. 3,, 1928; s. Paul M. and Adolphia (Kaske) M.; grad. Lawrenceville Sch. (N.J.), 1945; A.B. magna cum laude, Harvard, 1949, Ph.D., 1953; m. Drusilla Stevens, May 25, 1953; 1 son, Timothy. NSF postdoctoral fellow Princeton, 1957-59; staff biologist biology div. Oak Ridge Nat. Lab., 1959—, group leader cell physiology, 1966.—. Mem. Am. Inst. Biol. Sci. adv. com. to environmental biology br. NASA. Trustee Coll. of Oak Ridge, Webb Sch., Knoxville, Tenn. Served ast 1st lt. USAF, 1953-57. Fellow A.A.A.S.; mem. Soc. Gen. Physiologists, Am. Soc. Microbiology, Bot. Soc. Am., Biophys. Soc., Soc. Cryobiology (pres.-elect 1971, gov., founding mem.), Phi Beta Kappa, Sigma Xi. Club: Cosmos (Washington). Mem. editorial bds. Cryobiology Biodynamica. Contbr.

articles to profl. jours. Home: 125 Westlook Circle Oak Ridge TN 37830 Office: Biology Div Oak Ridge Nat Lab PO Box Y Oak Ridge TN 37830

MAZZE, EDWARD M., educator; b. N.Y.C., Feb. 14, 1941; B.B.A., Coll. City N.Y., 1961, M.B.A., 1962; Ph.D., Pa. State U., 1966; m. 1 child. Lectr. bus. adminstrn. Baruch Coll., City U.N.Y., 1961-62; doctoral research asst. Pa. State U., 1963-66, instr. marketing and internat. bus., 1965-66; asso. prof. marketing U. Detroit, 1966-68; asso. prof. marketing W. Va. U., 1968-70, dir. spl. programs in bus. adminstrn., 1968-70; prof. marketing Va. Poly. Inst. and State U., 1970—, coordinator marketing program, 1970—, dir. bus. extension Coll. Bus., 1971-72; vis. asso. prof. bus. adminstrn. U. Pitts. Grad. Sch. Bus., 1970; cons. world trade, manpower devel. Greater Detroit Bd. Commerce and Regional Export Expansion Council Mich., 1966-68; cons. coop. bus. devel. program Office Equal Opportunity, 1969-70. Mem. N.Y.C. Employees Com. Brotherhood Week, 1963. Mem. Acad. Mgmt., Am. Inst. Decision Scis., Am. Marketing Assn., Assn. Edn. Internat. Bus., Soc. Advancement Mgmt. (pres. Detroit chpt. 1967-68), Beta Gamma Sigma, Chi Sigma Nu, Mu Gamma Tau, Pi Sigma Epsilon. Author: (with Milton Alexander) Sales Management: Theory and Practice (prize European Assn. Sales Cons.), 1965; International Marketing Administration, 1967; The Management of Retail Enterprises: Decision Exercises, 1971; contbg. author: The Academic Community Looks at Library Management, 1972. Editor: (with Huxley Madeheim and Charles S. Stein) Readings in Organization and Management, 1963, International Business: Articles and Essays, 1963; (with Alexander) Case Histories in Sales Management, 1965; (with William J. Schultz) Marketing in Action: Readings, 1963, 68; Introduction to Marketing: Readings in the Discipline, 1970. Gen. editor Basic Management Series, 1964-69. Mem. editorial staff Marketing Abstracts Sect. Jour. Marketing, 1971-75. Contbg. columnist Mgmt., 1971-72, Apparel Mfr., 1971-72. Contbr. book revs., articles to profl. jours. Address: 902 Elliott Dr Blacksburg VA 24060

MCADAMS, BASIL ALVIN, cons. engr.; b. Flasher, N.D., Nov. 30, 1916; s. Homer Green and Lydia (Gettman) McA.; B.S., Ia. State U., 1938; m. Velma L. Leeper, Jan. 24, 1941; 1 dau., Ann E. (Mrs. John William Thompson, Jr.). Field and office engr. Howard R. Green Co., Cedar Rapids, Ia., 1938-44, G.D. Hall & Assos., Yakima, Wash., 1946-51; san. engr. Duval County Health Dept., Jacksonville, Fla., 1951-53; project mgr. Rader & Assos., Miami, Fla., 1953-61; owner B.A. McAdams, cons. engr., Miami, 1961; partner Greenleaf Engrs., Miami, 1961-63, Greenleaf-Telesca, Miami, 1964-69; v.p., treas. Greenleaf Enterprises, Inc., Miami, 1963—; owner B.A. McAdams, engrs., Miami, 1969—. Served to ensign USNR, 1944-46. Diplomate Am. Acad. Environmental Engrs. Mem. Nat. Soc. Profl. Engrs., Air Pollution Control Assn., Am. Soc. M.E. Mason (Shriner). Patentee in field. Home: 1691 Nethia Dr Miami FL 33133 Office: 18800 NW 2d Av Miami FL 33169

MCADAMS, HERBERT HALL, banker; b. Jonesboro, Ark., June 6, 1915; s. H.H. and Stella (Patrick) McA.; B.S., Northwestern U., 1937; postgrad. Harvard, 1937-38, Loyola U., Chgo., 1938-39; LL.B., U. Ark., 1940; m. Ruth Noyes, Apr. 3, 1938; children—Judith (Mrs. Walter A. DeRoeck), Sandra (Mrs. Robert C. Connor), Hall, Penny. Admitted to Ark. bar, 1940, since practiced in Jonesboro; pres., chmn. bd. Citizens Bank, Jonesboro, 1959—; chmn. Home Fed. Savs. & Loan Assn.; dir. Ark. La. Gas Co. Sec. drainage dist. No. 25, Craighead County, Ark., 1946-60; Ark. chmn. Citizens Com. on Edn., 1950; mem. Uniform State Laws Commn., 1961-66; chmn. Ark. Indsl. Devel. Commn., 1967—; mem. Ark. Adv. Council For Elementary and Secondary Edn., 1964-65. Pres. bd. dirs. Jonesboro Spl. Sch. Dist., 1957; pres. Peoples Property Assn.; bd. dirs. Student Loan Found., Ins. and Bank Stock Fund, Inc., Ark. Mental Health Assn., mem. adv. bd. St. Bernard's Hosp. Served with USNR, World War II. Mem. Am., Ark. bar assns., Am., Ark. (chmn. state legislative com.) bankers assns., U. Ark. Alumni Assn. (dir.), Jonesboro (chmn. aviation com.), Ark. (bd. dirs. 1961-63, 65—) chambers commerce. Presbyn. (elder). Clubs: Rotary (Jonesboro); Little Rock Country, Little Rock, Top of the Rock (Little Rock); Summit, Top of the 100, Tennessee (Memphis). Home: 1420 Elmwood Pl Jonesboro AR Office: Citizens Bank Bldg Jonesboro AR 72401

MCADAMS, JOHN M., internat. ofcl.; b. Vega Baja, P.R., July 15, 1916; s. Walter Q. and Barbara (Martinez) McA.; A.B., U. P.R., 1937; A.M., Fordham U., 1938, Ph.D., 1952; grad. student Inf. Sch., Ft. Benning, Ga., Command and Gen. Staff Coll., Ft. Leavenworth, Kan.; m. Elizabeth L. Simmons, Apr. 14, 1948; children—Elizabeth B., John M., Walter L., Mary E., Michael P. Instr., U. P.R., 1939-42; acting mil. attache Am. embassy, Paraguay, 1942-44; instr., editor Command and Gen. Staff Coll., Ft. Leavenworth, 1945-47; chief tech. information office Dept. Army, Pentagon, 1947-49; dir. publs. office, gen. secretariat OAS, Washington, 1949—. Lectr. personnel mgmt. for execs. Army Tng. Center, Washington, 1962—, Washington Internat. Center, 1966—. Pres., Bethesda (Md.) Fire Bd., 1967—. Served from lt. to maj. AUS, 1940-49. Decorated Orden Nacional del Merito (Paraguay). Mem. Am. Polit. Sci. Assn. Roman Catholic. K.C. Home: 5606 Forest Pl Bethesda MD 20014 Office: 19th and Constitution Av NW Washington DC 20006

MCADAMS, WILBOURN BAKER, accountant; b. Houston, Nov. 23, 1937; s. Wilbourn A. and Laura (Baker) McA.; B.S. in Physics, U. Tex., 1960, M.B.A., 1962; m. Penelope Elizabeth Pojman, Sept. 2, 1961; children— Natalie Ann, Mark Baker. Mem. audit staff Arthur Andersen & Co., Houston, 1963-64, adminstrv. services div., 1964-68, mgr., 1968—. Mem. Am., Tex. socs. C.P.A.'s. Presbyn. Home: 207 Lakemere St Houston TX 77024 Office: 910 Travis St Houston TX 77002

MCAFEE, JAMES ALVIE, sports writer; b. Wichita Falls, Tex., Apr. 3, 1941; s. Hubert A. and Margie (Tarver) McA.; student Midwestern U. 1959-60, Odessa Jr. Coll., 1961-62; m. Betty Ann Phillips, July 16, 1960; children—Lorri Lizabeth, Jamie Denise, Tamara. Sports writer Wichita Falls Record News, 1959-60, Odessa (Tex.) Am., 1960-63; sports writer Abilene (Tex.) Reporter-News, 1963-64, sports editor, 1964-71, news editor, 1971; golf writer Tulsa Tribune, 1971—. Home: 11437 E 37th Pl Tulsa OK 74145 Office: 318 S Boulder St Tulsa OK 74102

MCAFEE, KENNETH EMBERRY, lawyer; b. Spadra, Ark., Aug. 27, 1903; s. Thomas W. and Corah M.B. (Dowell) McA.; B.S., LL.B., U. Okla., 1934; m. Maxine Maples, Apr. 21, 1930; 1 dau., Jacquelyn (Mrs. Gary Wayne Williams). Admitted to Okla. bar, 1934; mem. firm McAfee, Taft, Cates, Mark, Bond & Rucks, Oklahoma City, 1934—. Bd. dirs. U. Okla. Found. Served to lt. comdr. USNR, 1942-45. Fellow, U. Okla. Mem. Am. Bar Assn., Am. Inst. C.P.A.'s, Inc., Okla. Heritage Assn. (dir.), Order of Coif, Beta Gamma Sigma. Lion. Clubs: Sirloin, Economics (Oklahoma City); Mens Dinner. Home: 1120 Glenwood Oklahoma City OK 73116 Office: 100 Park Av Bldg Oklahoma City OK 73102

MCALEXANDER, KENNETH LOCKE, dentist; b. Paris, Tex., Oct. 28, 1927; s. Jesse Locke and Cora Lee (Williams) McA.; B.S., Baylor U., 1950, D.D.S., 1955; m. Dorothy Gwendolyn Walker, May 27, 1950; children—Stephen Locke, Carol Lee. Practice dentistry, Dallas, 1955; chief dental staff Garland Hosp., 1959-60, 65-68; mem. faculty Butler U. Coll. Dentistry, 1955-64; cons. Conn. Gen. Life Ins. Co., 1960—. Served with USMCR, 1943-44, 50. Decorated Purple Heart. Mem. Am., Tex., Dallas County dental assns., Am. Acad. Gen. Practice, Internat. Acad. Orthodontics (pres. Dallas chpt.). Optimist (pres. White Rock 1959, dist. gov. 1960). Club: Dallas Gun. Home: Route 1 Box 179 Mesquite TX 75149 Office: 2345 Gusthomasson St Dallas TX 75228

MCALINDON, HAROLD ROBERT, hosp. co. exec.; b. Munger, Mich., May 30, 1940; s. John Joseph and Barbara Margaret (Henika) McA.; J.D., Blackstone Sch. Law, 1965; M.S. in Psychology, Ohio Christian Coll., 1967, Ph.D. in Mgmt., 1969; m. Cheryl Ann Streb, July 8, 1967. Chief accountant St. Mary's Hosp., Saginaw, Mich., 1965-67; asst. supt. Saginaw County Hosp., Saginaw, 1967-68; controller Mercy Hosp., Jackson, Mich., 1968-69; adminstr. Our Lady of the Way Hosp., Martin, Ky., 1969-71; dir. human resources Hosp. Corp. Am., Nashville, 1971—. Cons. human resources and organizational devel., 1968—. Sec., Floyd County (Ky.) Cath. Parish, 1969-71; mem. Health Careers in Ky. Com., 1970; mem. Found. for Christian Living, 1969—. Served with AUS, 1963-65. Named Hon. Ky. col., 1970; cited by Dept. Econ. Security for Tng. Disadvantaged People, 1970. Fellow Am. Acad. Med. Adminstrs. (regional v.p. 1970—); mem. Ky. Hosp. Assn. (personnel and health edn. steering com. 1969—), Am. Soc. for Tng. and Devel., Am. Mgt. Assn., Internat. Platform Assn., Hosp. Financial Mgmt. Assn., A.A.A.S., Council for Christian Service, Am. Soc. for Hosp. Edn. and Tng., Alpha Psi Omega (nat. bd. dirs.). Club: Executive. Contbr. articles to profl. jours. Home: 1025 Perry Warner Blvd Nashville TN 37205 Office: 242 25th Av Nashville TN 37203

MCALISTER, DURWOOD, newspaper editor; b. Bolivar, Tenn., June 16, 1927; s. Turner D. and Mary (Brown) McA.; B.A., Howard Coll., 1949; m. Dorris Fay Curenton, June 15, 1950; children—David Bruce, Jane Kimberly, Donald Kent. Reporter, Birmingham (Ala.) Age-Herald, 1948-50; reporter, news editor Anniston (Ala.) Star, 1950-54; with Atlanta Jour., 1954—, news editor, 1957-63, asst. mng. editor, 1967-68, mng. editor, 1968—; Sunday editor Atlanta Jour.-Constn., 1963-67. Served with USNR, 1945-46. Mem. A.P. Mng. Editors Assn. (nat. dir.), Sigma Delta Chi. Home: 2491 Glenrock Dr Decatur GA 30032 Office: PO Box 4689 Atlanta GA 30302

MCALLISTER, HORACE ALEXANDER, JR., city mgr.; b. Waynesville, N.C., Apr. 4, 1921; s. Horace Alexander and Anne Ruby (Alexander) McA.; B.S., C.E., Carnegie Inst. Tech., 1950; postgrad. Columbia, 1950-51, Manhattan Coll., 1961; m. Rachel Eleanor Nelms, July 18, 1942; 1 dau., Katherine Helen. Cons. engr. bridges and soil mechanics, N.Y.C., 1950-58; town engr., pub. works dir., Meadville, Pa., 1959-65, 67-69, city adminstr., 1966-67; city mgr., Newton, N.C., 1969—. Served with USNR, 1944-46. Fellow Am. Soc. C.E., Internat. City Mgmt. Assn. Presbyn. (elder). Kiwanian. Home: 1402 N Frye Av Newton NC 28658 Office: City Hall Newton NC 28658

MCALLISTER, KENNETH, tobacco exec.; b. Coraopolis, Pa., May 25, 1916; s. Arthur Walker and Ethalinda May (Correll) McA.; B.S. in Mech. Engring., Rutgers U., 1939; m. Betty Proudfoot, Sept. 21, 1940; children—Keith, Craig. Sales promotion mgr. radio sta. WGY, Schenectady, 1940-41; advt. exec. Columbia Records, 1941-43, 46-50; v.p., sec. plans bd. Sullivan, Stauffer, Colwell & Bayles, Inc., 1953-55; sr. v.p., dir. Benton & Bowles, Inc., N.Y.C., 1950-53, 55-61; v.p. advt. Thomas J. Lipton, Inc., 1961-63, exec. v.p., 1963-67, dir. 1961-67; pres., dir. Good Humor Corp., 1965-67; pres. M & M/Mars Candy div. Mars, Inc., 1967-68; pres. cigarette and tobacco div. Liggett & Myers, Inc., 1969—, also dir., mem. exec com., exec. v.p. parent co. Served with USNR, 1943-46. Mem. Phi Beta Kappa, Tau Beta Pi. Clubs: Winge'd Foot (Mamaroneck, N.Y.), Stanwich (Greenwich); Plantation, Harbour Town, Hilton Head Golf (Hilton Head, S.C.). Home: Catbird Lane Hilton Head Island SC 29928

MCALLISTER, WALTER WILLIAMS, savs. and loan exec.; b. San Antonio, Mar. 26, 1889; s. Frank Williams and Lena (Stumberg) McA.; E.E., U. Tex., 1910; m. Lenora Alexander, Mar. 26, 1913 (dec. May 1969); children—Elizabeth (Mrs. O. J. Solcher, Jr.), Walter Williams, Gerald N.; m. 2d, Cleo T. Sterne, Dec. 14, 1970. Chmn. bd. San Antonio Savs. Assn., 1921—, South States Oil Co., San Antonio, 1961—; dir. Mortgage Guaranty Ins. Corp., Milw.; mayor City of San Antonio, 1961-71. Chmn., Fed. Home Loan Bank Bd., Washington, 1953-56. Pres. Navarro Improvement Co., San Antonio, 1931—; pres. Tex. Municipal League, 1965; mem. San Antonio River Beautification Commn., 1933, Tex. Finance Commn., 1952-53; hon. co-chmn. Hemis Fair; commr. Urban Renewal Agy. Bd. dirs. Research and Planning Council, Edni. TV, Channel 9, Austin; chmn. bd. dirs. Witte Mus., 1952-53; trustee Internat. Union Bldg. Socs. and Savs. and Loan Assn.; pres. bd. trustees San Antonio Union Jr. Coll., 1945-60. Recipient Golden Deeds award San Antonio Exchange Club, 1956; Outstanding Citizen award San Antonio Council of Presidents, 1964. Mem. U.S. (mem. legislative com., past pres.), Southwestern (past pres.), Tex. (past pres.) savs. and loan leagues, San Antonio C. of C. (past pres.). Mason (33 deg., Shriner), Kiwanian (past pres. San Antonio). Clubs: Argyle; San Antonio Country. Home: 103 Bushnell Pl San Antonio TX 78212 Office: PO Box 1810 San Antonio TX 78296

MCAMIS, ROBERT JAMES, physician; b. Fort Worth, Aug. 5, 1930; s. Robert Wesley and Yvonne (Kerr) McA.; student U. Tex., 1949-50, Baylor U., 1951; M.D., Southwestern branch U. Tex., 1955; m. Christine Mullins, Apr. 30, 1959; children—Sharon, Ronald Lee, Robert James. Intern, DuPage County Meml. Hosp., Elmhurst, Ill., 1955-56; practice medicine specializing in gen. practice, Channelview, Tex., 1956—; mem. staff, bd. govs. Tidelands Gen. Hosp., Channelview. Dir. Channelview Bank, Hosp. Affiliates, Inc. Mem. Am., Tex. med. assns., Harris County Med. Soc., Am. Acad. Gen. Practitioners. Home: 908 Westmont St Houston TX 77015 Office: 15101 E Freeway Channelview TX 77530

MCANALLY, CHARLES VAUGHAN, educator; b. Weatherford, Tex., May 6, 1928; s. Thomas Owen and Clota M. (Vaughan) McA.; A.A., N. Tex. Agrl. Coll., 1947; B.S., Tex. Tech., 1950, M.Ed., 1959; m. Nell Ruth Bloodworth, Dec. 27, 1957; children—Shane, Laurie, Kent. Tchr., Aledo (Tex.) Ind. Sch. Dist., 1954, supt., 1962—; prin. Aledo Elementary Sch., football coach Aledo High Sch., 1955-62. Trustee Weatherford Coll. Served with AUS, 1951-53. Mem. Am., Tex. assns. sch. adminstrs. Address: PO Box D Aledo TX 76008

MCANULTY, MARY CATHERINE CRAMER (MRS. CHARLES GILBERT MCANULTY) ret. educator; b. Braddock, Pa., June 26, 1908; d. Albert R. and Sara (Kelly) Cramer; A.B., Fla. So. Coll., 1929, M.A., Columbia, 1937; postgrad. Fla. State U., 1946-50; m. Charles Gilbert McAnulty, Dec. 25, 1937. Elementary tchr. Lake Ann Sch., Lake Garfield, Fla., 1930-31, elementary prin., 1932-34; prin. South Winter Haven Elementary Sch., Winter Haven Fla., 1935-55; adminstrv. asst. to supervising prin. Winter Haven Area Schs., 1956-60; prin. Fred Garner Elementary Sch., Winter Haven, 1961-67, Lake Alfred Elementary Sch., 1968-69, ret. First v.p., chmn. vols. Winter Haven chpt. A.R.C., 1969-70. Recipient achievement award Fla. chpt. Delta Kappa Gamma, 1965. Mem. Assn. Supervision and Curriculum Devel., Internat. Reading Assn. (chpt. chmn. 1967), Am. Childhood Edn. Assn., N.E.A., Fla. Edn. Assn. (dist. dir. dept. elementary prins. 1965-67), Polk County Elementary Prins. Assn. (sec.), League Women Voters (local dir. 1962), Am. Assn. U. Women (local br. chmn. status women com. 1963), D.A.R. (chpt. auditor 1963-64, treas. 1967-68, regent 1970-72, chmn. Jr. Am. Citizens 1972—), Internat. Platform Assn., Fla. So. Coll. Alumni Assn. (v.p. 1965-66), P.E.O. (treas. 1969—), Pi Gamma Mu, Delta Kappa Gamma (Fla. pres. 1962-63, mem. internat. research com., 1968-70). Methodist (chmn. commn. edn. 1959-60, mem. ofcl. bd. 1966-69, mem. ch. nominating com. 1966-69, mem. worship commn, supt. study program 1969-70, organist). Clubs: Pilot (charter; dir. 1952-53, 56-57, pres. 1954-55, 61-62), Poinsettia Garden (sec.), Winter Haven Women's (chmn. edn. com. 1967-68), Winter Haven Music; Lake Region Home Extension. Home: 999 Piedmont Dr SE Winter Haven FL 33880

MCARTHUR, CHARLES MORTIMER, dairy products mfr.; b. Miami, Fla., Mar. 10, 1937; s. Bivian Burrage and Frances Marie (Heffernan) McA.; B.S., U. Fla., 1959; m. Nadean Ann Orr, June 12, 1959; 1 dau., La Nae. Pres., Charles McArthur Dairies, Inc., Okeechobee, Fla., 1959—, chmn. bd., 1964—; chmn. bd. Americable, Inc., 1969—; dir. 1st Nat. Bank of Miami, Worth Av. Nat. Bank, Palm Beach, Fla., Okeechobee County Bank, Charter Co., Jacksonville, Fla., Nat. Life of Fla. Corp. Bd. dirs. West Palm Beach Goodwill Industries; chmn. bd. trustees Eckerd Coll., St. Petersburg, Fla., 1971—, Charles McArthur Found., 1968—. Mem. Com. of 100 of Miami Beach; White House fellow, spl. asst. to Postmaster Gen., 1969-70. Mem. Young Pres.'s Orgn. (v.p., dir.). Republican. Episcopalian (lay reader, vestryman). Clubs: Surf, Miami (Miami); Everglades (Palm Beach); Metropolitan (N.Y.C.). Home: 309 Stafford Pl Okeechobee FL 33472 Office: PO Box 1205 Okeechobee FL 33472

MCASHAN, S.M., JR., business exec., 1904; A.B., Princeton, 1927; m. Chmn. bd., chief exec. officer, chmn. exec. com. Anderson, Clayton & Co., 1966—; dir. Houston & Shell Oil Co. Address: Tennessee Bldg Houston TX 77002*

MCAULEY, JAMES ARTHUR, petroleum co. exec.; b. Pampa, Tex., Aug. 18, 1930; s. James Arthur and Lillie (Robertson) McA.; B.S. in Petroleum Engring., Tex. Technol. U., 1953; m. Joanne Elaine Guest, Sept. 1, 1952; 1son, James Kelly. Engr., Sun Oil Co., 1953-56, Nortex Oil & Gas Corp., 1956-60, Ryan Consol. Petroleum Corp., 1958-60 (all Dallas); partner, petroleum engr. Gandy-McAuley, Dallas, 1960-68; pres. Oilfield Prodn. Services, Inc., 1964—, also dir., v.p. parent co. Served with AUS, 1953-55. Mem. Am. Inst. Mining and Metall. Engrs., Ind. Petroleum Assn. Am., Soc. Petroleum Engrs., Am. Petroleum Inst., Tex. Mid-Continent Oil and Gas Assn., Tex. Tech. Ex-Students Assn. (pres. 1960). Mem. Christian Ch. (elder). Clubs: Red Raider (pres., dir. Dallas 1969-70), Dallas Athletic. Contbr. articles to profl. jours. Home: 11524 E Ricks Circle Dallas TX 75230 Office: 1610 Fidelity Union Tower Dallas TX 75201

MCAVOY, BLANCHE, educator; b. Mitchell, Ind., Sept. 11, 1885; d. George and Mary (McIntire) McAvoy; B.A., U. Cin., 1909; M.A., Ohio State U., 1912; postgrad. Columbia, 1916; Ph.D., U. Chgo., 1930. Tchr., Kennedy Heights (O.) Pub. Sch., 1909-11; teaching fellow Ohio State U., 1911-14; tchr. Watterman (Ill.) Hall, 1914-15, Mt. Healthy (O.) High Sch., 1915-18, Wyoming (O.) High Sch., 1918-21; asst. prof. Ball Tchrs. Coll., 1921-25; substitute tchr. Western Coll. for Women, 1925; instr. Ill. State Normal U., 1926-31, asst. prof., 1931-45, asso. prof., 1945-51, prof., 1951-54, prof. emeritus, 1954—. Fellow A.A.A.S.; mem. Am. Bot. Soc., Ecol. Soc. Am., Acad. Sci. Ind. and Ill., Sigma Xi, Sigma Delta Epsilon, Gamma Theta Upsilon (nat. sec.-treas.). Author: Biology A Study Guide, 1939. Home: 3701 N Cincinnati Av Tulsa OK 74106

MCBEE, GEORGE GILBERT, agrl. adminstr.; b. Eastland, Tex., Aug. 15, 1929; s. Floyd Pierce and Stella (Reese) McB.; A.A., Ranger Jr. Coll., 1948; B.S., Tex. A. and M. U., 1951, M.S., 1956, Ph.D., 1965; m. Ida Jane Maspero, June 25, 1954; children—Cynthia Kay, Nancy Gail. Asst. county agt. Tex. Agr. Extension Service, San Antonio, 1953-54, research asso. Tex. A. and M.U., College Station, 1954-56, agronomist Tex. Agr. Expt. Sta., 1956-60, state extension specialist, 1960-62, research asso., 1962-65, resident dir. Tex. Agr. Expt. Sta., Lubbock, 1969—, asso. prof., 1965-69. Dir., Water, Inc. Cons. on turf and agrl. chemistry. Com. chmn. dist. level Boy Scouts Am., 1969. Served with AUS, 1951-53; maj. Res. Mem. Am. Soc. Agronomy, Am. Soc. Plant Physiology, Am. Soybean Assn. (dir.), Weed Sci. Soc. Am., West Tex. Water Inst. (dir.), Sigma Xi, Phi Theta Kappa, Phi Kappa Phi, Alpha Zeta. Contbr. articles to profl. jours. Home: 6223 Louisville Dr Lubbock TX 79413 Office: Tex A&M U Research and Extension Center Route 3 Lubbock TX 79401

MCBRAYER, ROBERT VAUGHAN, ins. exec.; b. Draketown, Ga., June 19, 1911; s. William A. and Dona (Vaughan) McB.; grad. high sch.; m. Beatrice Hatchett, Dec. 24, 1937; children—Robert Vaughan, Lynda Clay, William David. With Interstate Life & Accident Ins. Co., Atlanta, 1931, dist. mgr., 1945-55, asst. div. mgr., Chattanooga, 1955-58, asst. agy. mgr., 1958-64, v.p., mgr. agys., 1964-66, adminstrv. agy. v.p., 1966—, recipient co.'s leading dist. mgr. award, 1950. Mem. Chattanooga C. of C., Chattanooga Estate Planning Council. Democrat. Baptist. Mason. Home: 4424 Lilac Lane Chattanooga TN 37411 Office: 540 McCallie Av Chattanooga TN 37411

MCBRIDE, JEROLD ROBERT, clergyman; b. Rocky Ford, Colo., Sept. 20, 1932; s. Harold Henry and Verna (Todd) McB.; student La. Coll., 1950, Wayland Coll., 1951; B.S., Hardin-Simmons U., 1953; B.D., Southwestern Bapt. Theol. Sem., 1956, Th.D., 1960; m. Elizabeth Jane Basore, June 25, 1954; children—Cheryl Renee, Charlotte Ann, Murray Todd. Ordained to ministry Baptist Ch., 1951; pastor Calvary Bapt. Ch., Breckenridge, Tex., 1951-56, Tabernacle Bapt. Ch., Gainesville, Tex., 1956-59, Southside Bapt. Ch., Palestine, Tex., 1959-61, 1st Bapt. Ch., Chickasha, Okla., 1961-64, Ponca City, Okla., 1964-69, San Angelo, Tex., 1971—; exec. sec. dept. evangelism Bapt. Gen. Conv. Okla., Oklahoma City, 1969-70, also bd. dirs. Asst. in Greek, Hardin-Simmons U., 1952-53; teaching fellow Southwestern Bapt. Theol. Sem., Ft. Worth, 1957-58; guest prof. Okla. Coll. Liberal Arts, 1961-62; chaplain Okla. Senate, 1963. Trustee Southwestern Bapt. Theol. Sem. Contbr. numerous articles to profl. jours. Home: 2802 Vista del Arroyo San Angelo TX 76901 Office: 37 E Harris Av San Angelo TX 76901

MCBRIER, C. ROBERT, retail co. exec.; b. Newburgh, N.Y., Feb. 29, 1916; s. Charles E. and Bertha (McNeil) McB.; B.S. in Accounting, Syracuse U., 1938; m. Margaret E. Tenhet, Mar. 1, 1941; children—Quay (Mrs. M. Luther Peters), Jane (Mrs. Daniel McLean), Charles Robert, Carlyle E. Sec., treas., controller Burdines, Inc., Miami, Fla., 1949-52; dir. research Frederick Atkins Inc., N.Y.C., 1952-53; sr. v.p. finance, treas. Woodward &Lothrop, Washington, 1953—, also dir.; dir. Am. Nat. Bank, Washington. Bd. dirs. Nat. Capital Area council Boy Scouts Am. C.P.A., Va. Mem. Theta Chi, Phi Kappa Phi, Beta Alpha Psi. Presbyn. (elder). Rotarian. Club: Congressional Country (Bethesda). Home: 6630 Hillmead Rd

Bethesda MD 20034 Office: Woodward and Lothrop 11th and F Sts NW Washington DC 20014

MCBRYDE, MYRON HOMER, banker; b. Sanford, N.C., July 27, 1923; s. Forrest Glenn and Anne (Stone) McB.; B.A., Rollins Coll., 1950; J.D., U. Miss., 1964; m. Ann Elizabeth Garner, Aug. 4, 1950; children— Bruce Garner, Lory Joan. Spl. agt. FBI, 1951-61; admitted to Miss. bar, 1964, U.S. Supreme Ct. bar, 1968; atty., Columbus, Miss., 1964-67; dir. N.C. Bur. Investigation, 1967-69; security officer Wachovia Bank & Trust Co., Winston-Salem, N.C., 1969—. Faculty criminology Miss. State Coll. for Women, 1964. Bd. dirs. Youth Service Bur., Winston-Salem. Served with AUS, 1943-46. Mem. Am. Bar Assn., Bank Adminstrn. Inst. (chmn. security commn. 1970—, dir. 1970—), N.C. Bankers Assn. (chmn. protective com. 1970—), Kappa Alpha, Phi Alpha Delta. Home: Route 3 Beaver Brook Rd Clemmons NC 27012 Office: Box 3099 Winston Salem NC 27102

MCCABE, DESOTO BEN, JR., civil engr.; b. Kansas City, Mo., Nov. 15, 1919; s. DeSoto Ben and Nedetta (McPherson) McC.; B.C.E. cum laude U. Mo., 1943; m. Katheryn Elizabeth Welch, Sept. 9, 1939; children—Edward Glen, Kathleen (Mrs. Alan Ray Lamarche)), Colleen. Engr.-in-charge Fed. Pub. Housing Authority, Sioux City, Ia., 1946; city mgr. Clarinda, Ia., 1947-49, Park Ridge, Ill., 1950-52; chief engr. McCabe Assos., Engrs., Chgo., 1953-65; project mgr. World Bank Water and Sewer Project, East Pakistan, 1966-68; chief san. engr. Barnhouse-McCabe Engrs., Columbus, O., 1969-70; chief san. engr. Rader & Assos., Miami, Fla., 1970-71; chief engr. McCabe Assos. Ltd., Miami, 1971—. Served with USNR; P.T.O. Registered profl. engr., Fla., W.Va., Tenn., Ky., Mo., Ill., Ga., Ariz., Ind., Ia., Ohio. Mem. Inst. Engrs. of Pakistan, Am. Soc. C.E., Am. Water Works Assn., Am. Pub. Works Assn., Am. Water Resources Assn., Water Pollution Control Fedn., Am. Soc. Pub. Adminstrn., Am. Soc. Planning Ofcls., Internat. City Mgrs. Assn. Home and office: 12390 SW 8th St Miami FL 33144

MCCABE, GERARD BENEDICT, univ. library adminstr.; b. N.Y.C., Jan. 22, 1930; s. Patrick Joseph and Margaret Irene (McDonald) McC.; B.A. in English, Manhattan Coll., 1952; A.M. in L.S., U. Mich., 1954; M.A. in English, Mich. State U., 1959; m. Jacquelyn L. Maloney, Aug. 3, 1963; children—Theresa Marie, Rebecca Mary. Library service scholar U. Mich., 1952-53, library service fellow, 1953-54; asst. acquisitions dept. U. Neb. Library, Lincoln, 1954-56; chief bibliog. acquisitions dept. Mich. State U. Library, East Lansing, 1956-58, librarian Inst. for Community Devel. and Service, Mich. State U., 1958-59; acquisitions librarian U. S. Fla., Tampa, 1959-66, asst. dir. planning and devel., 1967-70; asso. dir. U. Ark. Library, Fayetteville, 1966-67; dir. univ. libraries Va. Commonwealth U., Richmond, 1970—. Mem. A.L.A., Va., Southeastern library assns., Bibliog. Soc. Am. Home: 1519 Village Grove Rd Richmond VA 23233 Office: 901 Park Av Richmond VA 23220

MCCABE, RICHARD EDMUND, clergyman, social worker; b. Milw., Sept. 15, 1929; s. John and Margaret M. (Burke) McC.; B.S., Regis Coll., 1951; M.S.W., Worden Sch., 1962; postgrad. U. Detroit, 1951, Marquette U., 1953-54. Founder, dir. Catholic Charities, Diocese of Austin, Tex., 1962—. Disaster cons. Nat. Conf. Catholic Charities, St. Vincent de Paul Socs. Pres., Austin Council Chs., 1969-70, Austin Council on Alcoholism, 1969-70; chmn. bd. Austin Rehab. Center, Inc.; founder, dir. Big Brothers of Austin; dir. Austin Parents League, Tex. Bd. for Emotionally Disturbed Children; sec. Med.-Dental Referral Service, Inc., Tex. Conf. Catholic Charities, Internat. Coops., Inc., founder Caritas of Austin, Caritas of Waco. Served with AUS, 1951-53. Mem. Nat. Assn. Social Workers, Acad. Certified Social Workers, Austin Social Welfare Assn., Am. Orthopsychiat. Assn. Home: 2630 Exposition Blvd Austin TX 78703 Office: 2600 E 19th St Austin TX 78702

MCCABE, WILLIAM GORDON, JR., textile exec.; b. Petersburg, Va., July 11, 1911; s. W. Gordon and Frances C. (Spicer) McC.; grad. Woodberry Forest Sch., 1930; B.S., U. Va., 1933; m. Lydia Phillips, Apr. 14, 1936; children—Katharine Gordon, Mary Scott. Asso., Am. Cotton Coop. Assn., New Orleans, 1933-36, mgr. Greenville (S.C.) office, 1936-39; partner Donkle & McCabe, Inc., Greenville, 1939-48; dir. raw cotton purchases J.P. Stevens & Co., Greenville, 1948-51, dir. raw cotton and wool policies and procurement, 1951-52, v.p., 1952-70, group v.p., 1970—, also dir. S.C. Nat. Bank. Mem. marketing adv. com. U.S. Dept. Agr.; mem. Cotton Promotion Com. S.C., 1958—. Bd. dirs. Greenville County Found. 1959—; chmn. bd. Greenville Gen. Hosp., 1950-56. Served to lt. (j.g.) USNR, 1943-46; PTO. Mem. N.Y. (nat. adv. com., dir. Wool Assos.), New Orleans (dir.) cotton exchanges, Nat. Cotton Council, S.C. Textile Mfrs. Assn., Am. Textile Mfrs. Inst. Episcopalian. Clubs: Boston (New Orleans); Biltmore Forest Country (Biltmore, N.C.); Poinsett (past pres.), Green Valley Country (dir.), Cotillion (past pres.) (Greenville); Racquet and Tennis, Weavers, Metropolitan (N.Y.C.); Admirals. Home: Kenmure Farms Flat Rock NC 28731 Office: PO Box 1209 JP Stevens & Co Inc Greenville SC 29602

MCCAFFREY, JOSEPH FRANCIS, broadcasting co. journalist; b. Poughkeepsie, N.Y., May 9, 1920; s. Philip Francis and Kathryn (Shally) McC.; student State U. N.Y., 1939; m. Mildred M. Barrington, Oct. 27, 1945; children—Sally Ann (Mrs. Dennis Shumaker), Michael. With Poughkeepsie (N.Y.) Courier, 1939-41; corr. CBS, Washington, 1944-48, MBS, Washington, 1948-54; chief corr., commentator Evening Star Broadcasting Co., Washington, 1954—. Chmn. standing com. Congl. Radio-TV Galleries, 1956, 71. Chmn. No. Va. Easter Seal drive, 1964; chmn. No. Va. Christmas Seal Dr., 1970. Served to 1st lt. AUS, 1941-44. Recipient Ted Yates award Washington Acad. Tv Arts and Scis., 1971, Emmys, 1960, 61, 64, 68. Mem. Radio Tv. Correspondents Assn. (pres. 1955-56, 70-71). A.F.T.R.A. (local v.p. 1957-58). Author: Election Guide, 1954. Home: 1309 Sunnyside Lane McLean VA 22101 Office: 4461 Connecticut Av Washington DC 20008

MCCAGHREN, ALLEN DREW, dentist; b. Dallas, Feb. 4, 1938; s. Henry Clarence and Alma (Hudgins) McC.; B.S., Abilene Christian Coll., 1960; D.M.D., U. Ala., 1961, M.S., 1970; m. Peggy Joyce Roberts, Oct. 29, 1960; children—Scott Allen, Lani Michelle. Pvt. practice pediatric dentistry, Gadsden, Ala., 1970—; faculty U. Ala. Sch. Dentistry; mem. staff Bapt. Meml. Hosp. Spl. chmn. Polio Campaign, Gadsden, 1972. Served to lt. comdr. Dental Corps, USNR, 1964-68. Mem. Am., Ala. dental assns., Am. Soc. Dentistry for Children, Am. Acad. Dentistry for Handicapped, Am. Acad. Pedodontics, Southeastern Soc. Pedodontics, Ala. Pedodontic Soc., Costa Valley Dental Study Club (pres. 1972). Home: Route 2 Box 227 Attalla AL 35954 Office: 1019 Forrest Av Gadsden AL 35901

MCCAHILL, WILLIAM PAUL, govt. ofcl.; b. Marshalltown, Ia., June 29, 1916; s. William J. and Louise (Stradella) McC.; B.S., Marquette U., 1938, M.A., 1940; m. Louise G. McBride, May 26, 1945; children—Mary Geraldine, Robert John, William Thomas. With A.P., Milw., 1940-41, Dept. Labor, Washington, 1946-47; exec. sec. Pres.'s Com. on Employment of Handicapped, Washington, 1947—. Chmn. exec. com. People to People Com. for Handicapped, 1965-72; mem. nat. adv. com. Blinded Vets. Assn., 1966—, Nat. Easter Seal Soc., 1966—. Bd. dirs. D.C. div. Am. Cancer Soc.; bd. mem. Maj. Gen. Melvin J. Maas Meml. Rehab. Found., Washington. Served to maj. USMCR, 1941-46; now col. Res. Ret. Decorated Legion of Merit; recipient awards including Distinguished Service award Dept. Labor, 1964. Mem. Marine Res. Officers Assn. (exec. dir. 1946-53), D.A.V., V.F.W., Amvets, Am. Legion, Catholic War Vets., Nat. Rehab. Assn., Internat. Assn. Personnel Employment Security, Am. Fedn. Govt. Employees, Vocational Rehab. Commn., Internat. Soc. Rehab. Disabled (vice chmn. 1960-63, com. bd. mem.). Clubs: Army-Navy Country, International, Nat. Press. Author: Hit The Beach, 1943; First to Fight, 1947; U.S. Marine Corps Reserve: A History 1916-66, 1966. Home: 2761 N Wakefield St Arlington VA 22207 Office: 14th and Constitution Av NW Washington DC 20210

MCCAIN, MAURICE EDWARD, uniform co. exec.; b. Denver, Feb. 14, 1909; s. Thomas C. and Fannie (Burke) McC.; grad. high sch.; m. Florence Inez Snowden, Dec. 27, 1927. With McCain Tailoring Co., 1927-34; mgr. uniform dept. Yielding Bros., 1934-39; with McCain Uniform Co., Inc., Birmingham, Ala., 1939—, pres., 1954—; v.p., dir. Decatur Transit Truck Lines (Ala.), 1954-61; pres., dir. Banner Uniform Co., Inc., Atlanta, 1962—; v.p., dir. Burke Uniform Co., Houston, 1967—. Served with USAAF, 1943-45. Mem. Nat. Assn. Uniform Mfrs. (dir.), Birmingham C. of C., Birmingham Traffic and Transp. Club, Birmingham Motor Truck Club, Aero Club. Baptist. Mason (Shriner), Elk. Clubs: Civitan, City Salesmen's (pres. 1967-68), Birmingham Area, Vestavia Country, The Club, Downtown. Home: 3756 Locksley Dr Birmingham AL 35223 Office: 2208 3d Av N Birmingham AL 35203

MCCAIN, VIRGIL BOWDEN, JR., coll. pres.; b. Oneonta, Ala., Mar. 9, 1910; s. Virgil Bowden and Jessie (Roberts) McC.; B.A., Birmingham-So. Coll., 1932; exchange fellow Lycee David, Angers, France, 1932-33; M.A., U. Ala., 1934; postgrad. (Austin grad. fellow) Harvard, 1934-35; L.H.D., Athens (Ala.) Coll., 1957; m. Martha Elizabeth Freeman, May 28, 1938; children—Virgil Bowden III, Robert Freeman. Tchr., asst. coach Corinth (Miss.) High Sch., 1935-38; techr. Lanier (Ala.) High Sch., 1938-40; prin. Pine Level Sch., also Pike Rd. High Schs., Montgomery County, Ala., 1940-42; supt., bus. mgr. Methodist Childrens Home, Selma, Ala., 1942-48; dean men, head edn. dept., dir. pub. relations Huntingdon Coll., Montgomery, Ala., 1948-54; pres., bus. mgr. Snead Coll., Boaz, Ala., 1954-59; pres. Athens Coll., 1959-65, Pershing Coll., Beatrice, Neb., 1965-67, Snead State Jr. Coll., Boaz, 1967—. Pres. So. Methodist Childrens Home Workers, 1944, Ala. Conf. Child Caring Instns. and Agys., 1945; mem. conf. bd. lay activities Meth. Ch., 1954-66, commn. promotion and cultivation, 1960-64; del. Gen. Conf. Meth. Ch., 1960, 64. Chmn. bd. dirs. Emanual Brown Tng. Sch., Minter, Ala., 1952-65. Recipient Man of Year award Boaz Civitan Club, 1958, Athens Civitan Club, 1960; Eyes Upon You award Ala. Optometric Assn., 1959. Mem. Ala. Edn. Assn. (pres. div. higher edn. 1953-59), Am. Coll. Pub. Relations Assn. (nat. dir. 1957-59, pres. Southeastern dist. 1953), Assn. Am. Colls., Ala. Assn. Ind. Colls. (pres. 1963-66), Omicron Delta Kappa, Kappa Phi Kappa. Club: Civitan. Home: 308 Mann Av Boaz AL 35957

MCCAIN, WILLIAM DAVID, univ. pres.; b. Bellefontaine, Miss., Mar. 29, 1907; s. Samuel Woodward and Sarah Alda (Shaw) McC.; B.S., Delta State Coll., Cleveland, Miss., 1930; A.M., U. Miss., 1931; Ph.D., Duke U., 1935; Litt.D., Miss. Coll., 1967; m. Minnie Leicester Lenz, Oct. 3, 1931; children—William David, John Woodward (dec.), Patricia. Teaching fellow history U. Miss., 1930-31; head math. dept. East Central Jr. Coll., Decatur, Miss., 1931-32; head social sci. dept. Copiah-Lincoln Jr. Coll., Wesson, Miss., 1932-33; fellow history Duke U., 1933-35; historian Morristown (N.J.) Nat. Hist. Park, 1935; asst. archivist Nat. Archives, Washington, 1935-37; acting asso. prof. history U. Miss., summers 1942-41; lectr. history Millsaps Coll., 1941-42, 46-47; historian Miss. dept. V.F.W., 1946—; historian dept. Miss., Am. Legion, 1946-55; dir., sec. bd. trustees Miss. Dept. of Archives and History, 1938-55; pres. U. So. Miss., Hattiesburg, 1955—. Chmn. Miss. Library Commn., 1941-43, Miss. Hist. Commn., 1948-55; mem. Miss. Geol. Commn., 1938-55. Served as 1st lt. A.A.A., Coast Arty., AUS, 1943-45, 51-53; maj. gen. Res. Mem. Soc. Am. Archivists (founding, council 1939-44, pres. 1951-53), Miss. Hist. Soc., Miss. Library Assn. (pres. 1941-44), Miss. N.G. Assn., Alpha Tau Omega. Democrat. Baptist. Lion. Author: The United States and the Republic of Panama, 1937; The Story of Jackson: A History of the Capitol of Mississippi, 1821-1951, 1953. Editor: Jour. Miss. History, 1939-56. Contbr. to jours. and newspapers. Address: Southern Sta Box 1 Hattiesburg MS 39401

MCCALEB, E. HOWARD, chief justice Supreme Ct. La.; b. New Orleans, Dec. 25, 1897; s. Edwin Howard and Elodie Louise (Barriere) McC.; LL.B., Washington and Lee U., 1919; m. Louise Marion Wright, July 9, 1920; children—Marion (Mrs. John F. Marshall), E. Howard. Admitted to La. bar, 1920; practiced with father, firm McCaleb & McCaleb, New Orleans, 1920-24, 25-36; asst. U.S. atty. Eastern Dist. of La., 1924-25; mem. Ct. of Appeal of La., 1936-47; asso. Justice Supreme Ct. La., 1946-70, chief justice, 1970—. Mem. S.A.R., Order of Coif. Delta Tau Delta, Phi Alpha Delta. Democrat. Episcopalian. Clubs: New Orleans Country, Pickwick. Home: 6333 Perrier St New Orleans LA 70118 Office: Supreme Court Bldg 301 Loyola Av New Orleans LA 70112

MCCALEB, MICHAEL, holding co. exec.; b. Fort Worth, Jan. 12, 1939; s. Maurice and Bonnie (Smith) McC.; student Del Mar Jr. Coll., 1961; B.B.A., Tex. A. and I. U., 1963; m. Mary Ann Hohstadt, July 8, 1961; children—Alison Blair, David Keith. Audit mgr. Arthur Andersen & Co., Pub. Accountants, Houston, 1963-69; financial v.p. Stratford of Tex., Inc., Houston, 1969—. Served with Transp. Corps, AUS, 1959-60. C.P.A., Tex. Mem. Tex., Houston socs. C.P.A.'s. Lion. Home: 12443 Honeywood Trail Houston TX 77077 Office: Tenneco Bldg 1010 Milam Houston TX 77002

MCCALL, ABNER VERNON, univ. pres.; b. Perrin, Tex., June 8, 1915; s. Harry Vernon and Gertrude Elizabeth (Rhoades) McC.; LL.B., Baylor U., 1938, A.B., 1942; LL.M., U. Mich., 1943; m. Frances Laura Bortle, Dec. 25, 1940 (dec. June 1969); children—Anne, Bette Gail, Richard Vernon, Kathleen; m. Mary Wilson Russell, 1970. Admitted to Tex. bar, 1938; mem. firm Gibson, McCall & Dawson, Longview, Tex., 1938-42; instr. law Baylor U., Waco, Tex., 1938-42, prof. law, 1946-48, dean law sch., 1948-59, exec. v.p. univ., 1959-61, pres., 1961—; asso. justice Supreme Ct. Tex., 1956; spl. agt. FBI, 1943-46. Pres. Bapt. Gen. Conv. Tex., 1963-65; mem. Tex. Civil Jud. Council, 1954—, pres., 1955-58; mem. Edn. Commn. of States Pres. Assn. Tex. Colls. and Univs., 1968, Ind. Colls. and Univs. Tex., Inc., 1965-71. Mem. Delta Theta Phi. Baptist. Mason. Home: 3205 Austin St Waco TX 76710

MCCALL, CHARLIE CAMPBELL, lawyer; b. Causeyville, Miss., Mar. 23, 1895; s. Charles Edward and Mary Rebecca (Collins) McC.; ed. bus. coll., prep. sch., Starkes (Ala.), Edgar's (Ala.), Denna's (N.Y.) and Ga. Mil. Acad.; LL.B., Georgetown U., 1921, LL.M., 1922, M.P.L., 1922; LL.M., Nat. U., 1922, M.P.L. 1922, S.J.D., 1936; LL.M. in Dp., Am. U., 1923; student U. Ala., U.S. Mil. Acad. (resigned 1913); grad. Sch. Mil. Govt. U.S. Army, Charlottesville, Va., 1944, AAF Sch. Applied Tactics, (Orlando, Fla.), Sch. Applied Personnel Mgmt., 1945; m. Nellie Curtis Cave, Apr. 16, 1924; 1 dau. (by previous marriage), Dorothy. Admitted to D.C. bar, 1920, Ala. bar, 1920; U.S. Supreme Ct. bar, 1926, Va. bar, 1957; pvt. sec. to Congressman John McDuffie of Ala., 1919-20; capt. judge adv. Judge Adv. Gen.'s Dept. Washington, 1921-23; examiner pub. accounts, Ala., 1924-27; atty. gen. of Ala., 1927-31; spl. asst. atty. gen. of Ala., 1931-32; counsel RFC, Washington, 1932-33; chief counsel pub. bodies sect. legal div. Fed. Emergency Adminstrn. Pub. Works, 1933-34, chief legal adviser N.Y. State office, 1934-35; counsel PWA, 1935-38, asst. gen. counsel, 1938-39, acting gen. counsel, 1939-40, gen. counsel, 1940-41; acting gen. counsel P.R. Reconstrn. Adminstrn., San Juan, 1937; spl. asso. gen. counsel Fed. Works Agy., 1941-42, asst. gen. counsel, 1945-48; practiced in Birmingham, Ala., 1948-49; chief financing atty. div. law Slum Clearance Staff, HHFA, Washington, 1949-58, spl. counsel, office gen. counsel, 1954-57, spl. asst. to gen. counsel, 1957-58; pvt. law practice, 1958—. Served at 1st lt., cav., U.S. Army, 1917-19, capt. 1920-24, maj. cav., U.S.R. and Ala. N.G., 1925-34; lt. col., AC, U.S. Army, 1942-45; lt. col. USAF Res. ret. Mem. Am., Va., Fed., Birmingham bar assns., Bar Assn. D.C., Nat. Assn. Attys. Gen. (pres. 1929), Mil. Order World Wars, Sigma Nu Phi, Chi Psi Omega. Mason (32 deg., Shriner). Home: 8525 Crestview Dr Fairfax VA 22030

MCCALL, DANIEL THOMPSON, JR., justice Supreme Ct. Ala.; b. Butler, Ala., Mar. 12, 1909; s. Daniel Thompson and Caroline (Bush) McC.; B.A., U. Ala., 1931, LL.B., 1933; m. Mary Edna Montgomery, Apr. 3, 1937; children—Mary Winston (Mrs. Rogers Neilson Laseter), Daniel Thompson III, Nancy (Mrs. John Worrell Poynor). Admitted to Ala. bar, 1933; practiced in Mobile, 1933-60; partner firm Johnston, McCall & Johnston, 1943-60; circuit judge 13th Circuit, 1960-69; asso. justice Ala. Supreme Ct., Montgomery, 1969—. Mem. Mobile County Bd. Sch. Commrs. 1950-56, 58-60. Trustee U. Ala., nat. alumni pres., 1963. Served to lt. USNR, World War II. Mem. Am., Ala., Mobile County (past pres.) bar assns., Jr. Bar Assn. Ala. (past pres.), Am. Judicature Soc., Nat. Conf. State Trial Judges, Ala. Assn. Circuit Judges, Inst. Jud. Adminstrn., Ala. Law Inst., Am. Trial Lawyers Assn., Farrah Law Soc., Ala. Hist. Soc., Wildlife and Conservation Assn., Navy League U.S., Am. Legion, 40 and 8, S.A.R., Sons of Confederacy, Sigma Nu, Phi Delta Phi, Omicron Delta Kappa. Democrat. Episcopalian. Clubs: Bienville, Indian Hills Country, Athelstan, Hickory Hill Hunting. Home: 118 Ryan Av Mobile AL 36607 Office: PO Box 218 Montgomery AL 36101

MCCALL, DUKE (KIMBROUGH), clergyman, sem. pres.; b. Meridian, Miss., Sept. 1, 1914; s. John William and Lizette (Kimbrough) McC.; A.B., Furman U., 1935, D.D., 1949; Th.M., So. Bapt. Theol. Sem., 1938, Ph.D., 1942; LL.D., Baylor U., 1945; m. Marguerite Mullinnix, Sept. 1, 1936; children—Duke Kimbrough, Douglas H., John R., Michael W. Ordained to ministry Baptist Ch., 1937; pastor Broadway Ch., Louisville, 1940-43; pres. New Orleans Bapt. Theol. Sem., 1943-46; exec. sec. of exec. com. So. Bapt. Conv., treas. conv., 1946-51; pres. So. Bapt. Theol. Sem., Louisville, 1951—. Mem. exec. com. Bapt. World Alliance. Bd. dirs. Louisville Fund, 1957—. Rotarian. Author: God's Hurry, 1949; co-author Passport to the World, 1951; Broadman Comments, 1958, 59. Editor: What Is the Church, 1958. Office: 2825 Lexington Rd Louisville KY 40206

MCCALL, HARLEY, ins. co. exec.; b. Indian Bayou, La., July 28, 1918; s. Jessie A. and Savanah (Dailey) McC.; grad. Southwestern La. U., 1937; D.D., Am. Bible Sch., McNeese State Coll.; m. Alberta DeHart, Nov. 22, 1940; children—Thomas Harley, Darryl Jessie, Jacqueline Ann, Barry Lane. Policeman, 1940; with Dun & Broadstreet, 1943-44, Radiant Labs. & Ins., 1944-48; steamfitter, 1949-50; exec. positions various ins. cos., 1950-57; founder Harley McCall & Assos., Lake Charles La., 1957—. Sec., La. Ins. Commn., 1964-65. Evangelist People's Methodist Ch. Exec. dir. Democracy in Action, 1959—. Del., La. 7th Dist. Democratic Assn., 1960-63. Served with AUS, 1942-43. Democrat. Home: 2215 Lake St Lake Charles LA 70601

MCCALL, JOHN WILLIAM, JR., physician; b. Meridian, Miss., Oct. 4, 1918; s. John William and Lizette (Kimbrough) McC.; student Southwestern U., 1937-38; A.B., Miss. Coll., 1940; M.D., U. Tenn., 1943; m. Ellen Edens, June 17, 1943; children—Carol (Mrs. E. Greer Richardson), John W. III, David Timmons. Intern, Baptist Meml. Hosp., Memphis, 1944-45, chief surg. resident, 1950; resident So. Baptist Hosp., New Orleans, 1948-49; practice medicine, specializing in surgery, Memphis, 1948—; mem. staffs Baptist, Meth., St. Joseph, City of Memphis hosps. Served with M.C., AUS, 1946-47; ETO. Fellow A.C.S.; mem. Southeastern Surg. Assn., Am., Tenn., So., Memphis, Shelby County med. assns. Republican. Baptist (deacon). Kiwanian. Club: Executive. Home: 2816 Lombardy St Memphis TN 38111 Office: 27 N Cleveland St Memphis TN 38104

MCCALL, LEMUEL ALLSOBROOK, museum trustee; b. Florence, S.C., June 29, 1913; s. Lemuel Allsobrook and Irene (French) McC.; B.A., Presbyn. Coll. (Clinton, S.C.), 1935; m. Carolyn Elizabeth Heriot, Apr. 22, 1949; children—Ann Richards, Elizabeth Allsobrook, Susan Heriot. Asst. state dir. Nat. Youth Adminstr., S.C., 1935-37; pres. Fairfield Dairy, Florence, S.C., 1937-45; owner Fairfield Farms, Florence, 1938-71; pres. Darlington Motor Co., (S.C.), 1946-53; lay Hi-Y dir. Florence (S.C.) YMCA, 1940-70; trustee Florence (S.C.) Museum, 1954—. Pres. Florence County Farm Bur., 1960; mem. S.C. State Mental Health Bd., 1967; mem. Florence County Mental Health Bd., 1964-70. Served with AUS, 1936-37. Accredited flower judge. Mem. Florence Garden Council (pres. 1970-71), S.C. Huguenot Soc., S.C. Hist. Soc., Florence Choral Soc., Florence County Hist. Soc., Pi Kappa Alpha. Democrat. Club: Country of S.C. Home: Cashua Ferry Rd Route 2 Florence SC 29501 also (summer) Litchfield Beach SC Office: Cashua Ferry Rd Route 2 Florence SC 29501

MCCALLIAN, RICHARD JONES, engring. cons.; b. Dayton, O., Jan. 5, 1913; s. Edwin Lewis and Mary (Marsh) M.; B.S., Tri-State Coll., 1934; postgrad. U. Ga., 1963-65; m. Louise Garnett, Aug. 4, 1969. Metallurgist, U.S. Steel Corp., Gary, Ind., 1936-44; engring. cons., Phila., 1945-48; dist. sales mgr. Stulz-Sickles Co., Elizabeth, N.J., 1949-62; indsl. devel. cons., Port Richey, Fla., 1963—; pres., Florestate Park, Inc., Oceanographic Minerals, Inc., Port Richey, 1967—; dir. Chasco Fiesta, Inc., Port Richey. Bd. dirs. Boy Scouts Am., Port Richey. Mem. Fla. Travel Council, Fla. Indsl. Devel. Council, Am. Marketing Assn., Fla. C. of C. Methodist (certified lay speaker 1967—, asso. dist. lay leader 1968—). Author: Potential Economic Benefits of Cross Florida Barge Canal, 1965. Patentee in field. Home: 30 Gulf Breeze N Port Richey FL 33568 Office: 19 N Main St Port Richey FL 33568

MCCALLISTER, CLOVIS EARL, telephone co. ofcl.; b. Seminole, Okla., Aug. 1, 1941; s. Calvin Earl and Freda (Baughn) McC.; B.A., Tex. A. and M. U., 1964; m. Mary Patricia Barlow, Aug. 28, 1963; 1 son, Brian Alan. Reporter, Midland (Tex.) Reporter-Telegram, 1965-66; editor Sweetwater (Tex.) Reporter, 1966-69; farm and ranch editor Abilene (Tex.) Reporter News, 1969-71; pub. information asst. Gen. Telephone Co. of S.W., San Angelo, Tex., 1971—. Mem. Sigma Delta Chi. Home: 233 Nottingham Trail San Angelo TX 76901 Office: Box 1001 San Angelo TX 76901

MCCALLUM, WALTER HAMILTON, farmer; b. nr. Magee, Miss., Nov. 12, 1914; s. William Hugh and Eva Marie (Shivers) McC.; student Copiah Lincoln Jr. Coll., Wesson, Miss., 1934-35; m. Dora Pauline Yelverton, Mar. 14, 1940; children—Walter Hamilton, Paul E., Mary Elizabeth Shivers. Farmer, Magee, 1943—, dir. Miss. Farm Bur. Mut. Ins. Co. Bd. dirs. Simpson County Council on Aging; bd. dirs., mem. exec. com. Magee Coop.; mem. Farm Home Adminstrn. Com., 1956-59. Mem. Simpson County Democratic Exec. Com., 1951-72. Recipient Simpson County Outstanding Farm Family award Mendenhall C. of C., 1961, Outstanding Service award Sampson County Farm Bur., 1966. Mem. Miss. Farm Bur. Fedn. (dir. 1965, conv. del. 1968), Simpson County Farm Bur. (dir. 1951-72, pres. bd., 1953-66), Simpson County Jr. Livestock Assn. (dir. 1958-59). Presbyn. (elder). Mason. Club: Laurel Hill Hunting. Address: Box 176 RFD 2 Magee MS 39111

MCCAMMON, WILLIAM CLINTON, city and county ofcl.; b. nr. Knoxville, Tenn., Jan. 5, 1903; s. William Clinton and Pearl (Dodson) McC.; B.S., U. Tenn., 1926; postgrad. U. Mich., 1927-28; m. Eleanore Jewell Williams, Aug. 19, 1935; 1 dau., Carolyn Eleanore. Landscape designer W.C. McCammon, Knoxville, 1929-33; landscape technician Nat. Park Service, Great Smoky Mountains Nat. Park, Gatlinburg, 1933-40; exec. dir., planning engr. Knox County (Tenn.) Planning Commn., 1940-56; chief operations Met. Planning Commn. of Knoxville and Knox County, 1956-64, exec. dir., 1964—. Registered profl. engr., Tenn., Mem. Am. Soc. Planning Ofcls., Am. Inst. Planners, Knoxville Tech. Soc., Tenn. Soc. Profl. Engrs. (Knoxville sec.-treas. 1951-53), Am., Smokey Mountain orchid socs., S.R., James White's Fort Assn. (dir.). Baptist. Clubs: Men's Garden (pres. 1948), Executive, Deane Hill Country. Home: 6909 Cresthill Dr Knoxville TN 37919 Office: Bldg A City Hall Park Knoxville TN 37902

MCCAMY, ROBERT JULIAN, textile co. exec.; b. Lindale, Ga., July 18, 1911; s. Robert and Bernice (Herring) McC.; grad. Darlington Sch., 1928; B.S. in Textile Engring., Ga. Inst. Tech., 1932; m. Charlotte Powers, June 5, 1936; children—Robert J., Donald Howard, Mary Deane, Charles Powers. Trainee, Pepperell Mfg. Co., Lindale, Ga., 1932-37, 38-39, supt. dyeing, 1939-42, asst. plant supt., 1942-47, plant supt., 1947-55, asst. mgr., 1955-61, v.p., 1961-65, v.p. West Point-Pepperell, Inc., 1965—; tech. sales So. Dyestuff Corp., Charlotte, N.C., 1938-39. Pres., TB Assn., Rome, Ga., 1963—. Trustee Darlington Sch.; bd. dirs. Textile Edn. Found. Mem. C. of C. (dir. 1960), Phi Psi, Tau Beta Pi, Pi Kappa Phi. Methodist (trustee). Mason. Club: Riverside Country. Home: 209 Hamilton Dr West Point GA 31833 Office: West Point-Pepperell Inc West Point GA 31833

MCCANDLESS, BRUCE, II, astronaut; b. Boston, June 8, 1937; s. Bruce and Sue (Bradley) McC.; B.S., U.S. Naval Acad., 1958; M.S. in Elec. Engring., Stanford, 1965; m. Alfreda Bernice Doyle, Aug. 6, 1960; children—Bruce III, Tracy. Commd. ensign U.S. Navy, 1958, advanced through grades to lt. comdr., 1966; naval aviator, 1960, with Fighter Squadron 102, 1960-64; astronaut Manned Spacecraft Center, Houston, 1966—. Mem. I.E.E.E., U.S. Naval Inst., Nat. Geog. Soc. Episcopalian. Home: 314 Whitecap Dr Seabrook TX 77586 Office: Code CB NASA Manned Spacecraft Center Houston TX 77058

MCCANDLESS, CHARLES EMERY, educator; b. Dallas, July 26, 1931; s. Dewey Taylor and Clara (Askins) McC.; B.S., Tex. A. and M. U., 1956, M.Ed., 1958; Ed.D., North Tex. State U., 1966; m. Joyce Elaine Thompson, Apr. 8, 1951; children—Cathy, Sharon, Debra. Head coach Silsbee (Tex.) Jr. High Sch., 1956-58; counselor Silsbee High Sch., 1958-60; part-time instr. health, phys. edn., recreation North Tex. U., Denton, 1960-61; asst. prof. health and phys. edn., intramural athletics dir. Tex. A. and M. U., College Station, 1963-66, chmn. freshman courses dept. edn. and psychology, 1964-66, dir. adj., chmn. counselor edn., 1966-67, asso. prof. edn. and psychology, 1967—, asso. dean liberal arts, 1966—, coordinator univ. self study, 1971—. Pres., College Station Recreation Council, 1968—. Served with USAF, 1951-53. Recipient Student-Faculty Relations award Coll. Liberal Arts, 1969. Mem. College Station C. of C., College Station Progress Assn. (dir. 1969-71), Am. Personnel and Guidance Assn., Am. Coll. Personnel Assn., Assn. Counselor Edn. and Supervision, Tex. Personnel and Guidance Assn., Tex. Psychol. Assn. Assoc. dir. several profl. jours. Home: 212 Redmond Dr College Station TX 77840

MCCANLESS, GEORGE FOLSOM, justice Supreme Ct. Tenn.; b. Morristown, Tenn., June 8, 1904; s. Michael C. and Nannie Louise (Folsom) McC.; A.B., Vanderbilt U., 1926, LL.B., 1928; m. Sarah Gaut Hardcastle, Apr. 9, 1929; children—Sarah, George Folsom. Admitted to Tenn. bar., 1928, practiced in Morristown, 1928-37, 46-54; chancellor 13th Chancery Div. Tenn., 1937-38, commr. finance and taxation Tenn., 1939-46; atty. gen. Tenn., 1954-69; justice Supreme Ct. Tenn., Nashville, 1969—. Mem. Tenn. Hist. Commn., 1961—. Mem. Tenn. Hist. Soc. (pres. 1959-61), Phi Kappa Sigma, Phi Delta Phi. Presbyn. Home: 700 Crescent Rd Nashville TN 37205 Office: Supreme Ct Bldg Nashville TN 37219

MCCANN, KELLY FRANKLIN, battery mfg. co. exec.; b. Oklahoma City, Apr. 3, 1928; s. Ralph Williamson and Thelma Jane (Franklin) McC.; B.B.A., Baylor U., 1949; m. Ethel Hurr, Dec. 23, 1949; children—Kelly Franklin, James Ralph, William Lee. Reporter, Dun & Bradstreet, Inc., 1949-50; with Continental Battery Mfg. Corp., 1950—, pres., 1960—, also dir.; dir. Tex. Nat. Bank, Dynamerica Corp. (all Dallas). Bd. mgmt. Town North YMCA, Dallas, 1967—. Mem. Ind. Battery Mfrs. Am. (past trustee). Baptist (deacon). Rotarian. Club: Preston Trail Golf (dir. Dallas). Home: 6805 Midcrest Dr Dallas TX 75240 Office: 4919 Woodall St Dallas TX 75247

MCCANN, RALPH WILLIAMSON, battery mfg. co. exec.; b. Jacksonville, Fla. Mar. 28, 1897; s. William A. and Joanna (Williamson) McC.; student comml. law U. Tex. Extension, 1922-23; m. Thelma J. Franklin, Nov. 29, 1922; children—Joanna (Mrs. John G. Heard), Kelly F., Ralph Williamson. Comml. reporter R.G. Dun & Co., Jacksonville, Fla., Denver, 1916-19; salesman, dist. and zone mgr. Firestone Tire & Rubber Co., Akron, O., 1920-42; co-founder Continental Battery Mfg. Co., Dallas, 1932—, pres., 1950—; chmn. bd. Continental Battery Co., 1959—, McCann-Continental Bldg. Co., Dallas, 1963—. Mem. Dallas Council Social Agys., 1946-48; adv. council Dallas Community Chest Trust Fund. Mem. Dallas Sch. Dist. Bd., 1950-52. Founder Thelma J. McCann 4-year scholarship Baylor U., 1962. Recipient certificate of distinguished service Dallas Sch. Bd., 1952. Mem. Am. Assn. Battery Mfrs., Dallas C. of C. Baptist (deacon). Clubs: Rotary, Dallas Athletic, Dallas Salesmanship (past v.p., camp bd. chmn.), Glen Lakes Country (past pres.). Donor (with wife) dept. of electrocardiology and electroencephalography to Baylor U. Med. Center, 1967, also Presbyn. Hosp. Devel. Fund, Dallas Bapt. Coll. Home: 7501 Rambler Rd Dallas TX 75231 Office: 4919 Woodall St Dallas TX 75247

MCCANN, RALPH WILLIAMSON, JR., battery co. exec.; b. Dallas, Aug. 1, 1932; s. Ralph Williamson and Thelma Jane (Franklin) McC.; B.B.A., Baylor U., 1954; m. Bobbie Louise Barclay, May 22, 1954; children—Ralph Williamson III, Charles B. Credit reporter Dun & Bradstreet, Inc., Houston, 1954-55; marketing mgr. Continental Battery Co., Dallas, 1957—. Pres., Northwood P.T.A., 1969-70; commr. Little League, 1971. Served to capt. USAF, 1955-57. Baptist. Club: Canyon Creek Country (Richardson, Tex.). Home: 7170 Briar Cove Dallas TX 75240 Office: 4919 Woodall St Dallas TX 75247

MCCANN, SAMUEL MCDONALD, physiologist, educator; b. Houston, Sept. 8, 1925; s. Samuel Glenn and Margaret (Brokaw) McC.; student Rice U., 1942-44; M.D., U. Pa., 1948; m. Barbara Loraine Richardson, 1950; children—Samuel Donald, Margaret, Karen Elizabeth. Intern, Mass. Gen. Hosp., Boston, 1948-49, asst. resident medicine, 1949-50; instr. physiology U. Pa. Sch. Medicine, Phila., 1952-54, asst. prof., 1954-58, asso. prof., 1958-64, prof., 1964-65; prof., chmn. U. Tex. Southwestern Med. Sch., Dallas, 1965—. Mem. endocrinology study sect. NIH, 1967-69. Served to capt. M.C., AUS, 1951-52. Recipient Lindback award for distinguished teaching U. Pa., 1965; Oppenheimer award for research in endocrinology Endocrine Soc., 1966. Mem. Am. Physiol. Soc., Endocrine Soc., Soc. Clin. Investigation, Soc. Exptl. Biology and Medicine, A.A.A.S., N.Y. Acad. Scis. Mem. editorial bd. Endocrinology, 1963-68, Neuroendocrinology, 1965—. Home: 7025 Hillgreen Dr Dallas TX 75214

MCCANTS, CHARLES SPENCER, physician; b. Winnsboro, S.C., Jan. 14, 1890; s. James Glenn and Nancy Thornwell (Wardlaw) McC.; B.S., Davidson Coll., 1912; M.D., Med. Coll. Va., 1918; m. Isabel Gooding, Sept. 4, 1918; children—Eleanor (Mrs. Herbert T. Surrency), Laura (Mrs. Frank J. Dana, Jr.), Isabel (Mrs. E. Wilson Yates, Jr.), Nelle (Mrs. John G. Smith). Intern, Stuart Circle Hosp., Richmond, Va., 1917-18, Florence (S.C.) Infirmary, 1918-19; resident Postgrad N.Y. Hosp., 1921, Meml. Hosp., Richmond, 1923; practice gen. medicine, Winnsboro, S.C., 1919—; mem. staff Fairfield Meml. Hosp., Winnsboro, 1955—, staff Fairfield Meml. Hosp., 1956-58, 69-71, adminstr., 1964-67, trustee, 1956-62. Pres., Mchts. & Planters Bank, 1967, vice chmn., 1968—, also dir., pres., dir. Community Fed. Savs. & Loan Assn., 1934—. Pres., Mt. Zion Soc., 1963-66. Chmn. bd. trustees Sch. Dist., 1920-45; bd. dirs. Fairfield Devel. Bd. Mem. Fairfield C. of C. (bd. dirs., pres. 1960), Fairfield County Med. Soc. (pres. 1969-71), S.C. (councilor 1954-64), Tri-State (pres. 1964 med. assns., A.M.A., Kappa Sigma, Phi Chi. Democrat. Presbyn. (elder). Club: Fairfield Country. Home: 222 Bratton St Winnsboro SC 29180 Office: 113 W Moultrie St Winnsboro SC 29180

MCCARROLL, EARL LUCAS, banker; b. Holly Springs, Miss., May 2, 1915; s. John Ramsay and Marie (McKie) McC.; extension student Northwestern U.; certificate Am. Inst. Banking, 1941; grad. Rutgers U. Grad. Sch. Banking, 1949; m. Helen Shannon, Oct. 15, 1938; children— Earl Lucas, Eileen (Mrs. James J. McDonald), Michael Shannon. With Union Planters Nat. Bank, Memphis, 1933-52, asst. vice pres. charge comml. loans, 1950-52; with First Nat. Bank, Little Rock, 1952-59, exec. v.p., 1955-58, pres., 1958-59; exec. v.p. Union Nat. Bank, Little Rock, 1959-63, pres., 1963-68, also dir. mem. exec. com., chief exec. office; 1967-68; pres. Farmers Bank & Trust Co., Blytheville, Ark., 1968—. Treas. Little Rock Sch. Dist., 1956-64; former sec. bd. trustees Little Rock U., 1963—; pres. Blytheville United Fund; dist. chmn. U.S. Savs. Bond Program. Mem. Am., Ark., (exec. council) bankers assns., Am. Inst. Banking (pres.), Memphis (1946-48), Little Rock C. of C. (pres. 1961). Episcopalian (past vestryman, chmn. finance com.). Rotarian. Club: Blytheville Country (pres.). Home: 710 N 16th St Blytheville AR 72315 Office: PO Box 688 Blytheville AR 72315

MCCARTER, JAMES THOMAS, engring. co. exec.; b. Greenville, S.C., Sept. 24, 1932; s. Thomas Avery and Emily (Street) McC.; B.M.E., Clemson U., 1954; m. Patricia Marie Hood, Feb. 14, 1959; children—Steven Thomas, Bruce Hood, David Christopher. Engr., Western Electric Co., Burlington, N.C., 1954-55, J.E. Sirrine Co., Engrs., Greenville, 1957-58; resident engr. U.S. Army, Charlotte, N.C., 1958-59; project engr. Davis Mech. Contractors, Greenville, 1959-64; v.p. Piedmont Engrs., Architects and Planners, Greenville, 1964—, also dir. Served to 1st lt. AUS, 1955-57. Registered profl. engr., S.C., N.C., Ga., Ala., Tenn., N.J., Me. Mem. Am. Soc. M.E. (vice-chmn. 1962-63, chmn. 1963-64), Am. Soc. Heating, Refrigeration and Air Conditioning Engrs. (chpt. treas. 1964-65, 2d v.p. 1965-66, 1st v.p. 1966-67, pres. 1967-68), Nat. Soc. Profl. Engrs (chpt. pres. 1968-69), Phi Kappa Phi, Tau Beta Pi. Baptist (deacon 1965—). Patentee in field. Home: 228 McSwain Dr Greenville SC 29607 Office: PO Box 1717 Greenville SC 29602

MCCARTHA, WALTER HAYNE, civil engr.; b. Batesburg, S.C., May 13, 1908; s. Walter Jacob and Henryetta (Towill) McC.; B.S. in Civil Engring., The Citadel, 1930, C.E., 1936; postgrad. in econs. George Washington U., 1930-31; in architecture, 34-35; postgrad. U. Mo. at Rolla, 1963, 64, 68, Civil Service Commn., 1966, USPHS, 1969, U. Md., 1962; m. Virginia Jean Ritchhart, June 3, 1957. Valuation engr. aide ICC Washington, 1930-31; archtl. engr. Pub. Bldgs. Service, Washington, 1931-40; engr., chief materials engring. group, 1950-57; chief specifications engr. for constrn. VA, Richmond, Va., 1946-49; archtl. gen. engr. charge specification standards for constrn. Directorate of Civil Engring., Hdqrs. U.S. Air Force, Washington, 1957—. Dir. Joint Bd. on Sci. Edn., Washington, 1955-64, 72—, chmn., 1958-59; mem. tri-service com. for constrn. research Nat. Bur. Standards, 1971—. Served to col. USAAF, 1940-46. Recipient Civil Engring. Meritorious Achievement award Dept. Air Force, 1962. Registered profl. engr. D.C. Mem. Nat., D.C. (pres. 1954-55, dir. 1963-66) socs. profl. engrs., Soc. Am. Mil. Engrs., Washington Soc. Engrs. (dir. 1969-70, v.p. 1972—), D.C. Council Engring. and Archtl. Socs. (chmn. 1956-57), Am. Soc. Testing and Materials. Baptist. Mason (32 deg. Shriner). Clubs: Chantilly Nat. Golf and Country (Centerville, Va.). Contbr. constrn. chpts. to Air Force Manuals, 1960, 61, 64-72. Home: 3804 14th St N Arlington VA 22201 Office: Engring Div Directorate of Civil Engring Hdqrs US Air Force Bolling AFB Washington DC 20332

MCCARTHY, JUSTIN GERALD, editor; b. Chgo., May 15, 1915; s. Justin Gerald and Myra (Hanecy) McC.; student U. Ill., 1932-33, Northwestern U., 1937; Neiman Fellow, Harvard, 1947-48; m. LaVerne Maxine Williams, Nov. 1, 1961; children—Justin Gregory, Kathleen (Mrs. Melvin M. Romine). With Chgo. Daily News, 1935-43, Chgo. Sun, 1943-47; dir. news bur. United Mine Workers Am., 1948-55, editor jour., 1955—. Mem. Nat. Council Alcoholism, Washington Area Council Alcoholism, Arlingtonians for a Better County. Mem. Soc. Nieman Fellows, Am. Newspaper Guild, Am. Pub. Health Assn. Democrat. Unitarian. Club: Nat. Press (Washington). Home: 6016 N 19th St Arlington VA 22205 Office: 1437 K St NW Washington DC 20005

MCCARTNEY, HELEN KEELER (MRS. J. ROBERT MCCARTNEY), ret. dental asst.; b. Greenville, Tex., Apr. 29, 1897; d. Edward Franklyn and Nellie (Abbe) O'Dell; B.C.S., Bowling Green Bus. U., 1924, dental asst. degree Chgo. Sch. Nursing 1928; m. James Robert McCartney, Dec. 31, 1924 (dec. Apr. 1963). Head commerce dept. Winnfield (La.) High Sch., 1922-27; dental asst., office mgr., accountant, Shreveport, La., 1927-63. Recipient nat. wildlife conservation awards. Mem. Nat. Audubon Soc., Am. Forestry Assn., 4th Dist. Dental Aux., Women's Aux. La. Dental Assn., Nat., La. tchrs. assns., Am. Legion Aux., Internat. Platform Assn., Nat. Wayfarers Club, Lady's Club El Karubah Shrine. Democrat. Presbyn. Home: Robin's Hill Thorton Rd Plain Dealing LA 71064

MCCARTNEY, RICHARD THOMAS, pub. relations co exec.; b. Ozark, Ark., Aug. 18, 1927; s. Herbert Earl and Carrie (Adcock) McC.; B.A., John Brown U., 1947, L.H.D., 1967; B.D., Southwestern Theol. Sem., 1956; postgrad. Baylor U., 1967-68; m. Barbara Anne Treadwell, Oct. 1, 1947; children—Judith Anne, Mary Kathleen, Michael David. Mem. staff radio and TV stas., 1947-57; dir. pub. relations Baptist Gen. Conv. of Okla., Oklahoma City, 1957-62, Bapt. Gen. Conv. of Tex., Dallas, 1962-68; exec. v.p. Arthur Davenport Assos., Inc., Oklahoma City, 1968-69, pres., 1969—. Mem. fund campaign team Okla. Bapt. U., 1969-70. Recipient Distinguished Service in Religious Journalism award Lambda Lambda Lambda, 1959. Mem. Pub. Relations Soc. Am. (pres. Oklahoma City chpt., 1969—, chmn. S.W. dist. 1971, vice chmn. honors and awards com. 1972; chmn.'s citation 1971), John Brown U. Alumni Assn. (nat. pres., 1967-69). Democrat. Lion. Home: 7328 Hammond Circle Oklahoma City OK 73132 Office: Arthur Davenport Assos Inc 13 NW 41st St Oklahoma City OK 73118

MCCARTY, GEORGE COURTNEY, athletic dir.; b. Bassetts, Tex., Oct. 18, 1915; s. James Thomas and Lucy (Arnold) M.; B.S., N.M. State U., 1950, M.A., 1951; m. Marietta Young, Apr. 4, 1942; children—Sandra Kay (Mrs. Rucker Ashmore), Thomas Michael. With prodn. dept. Hanlon Buchanon Oil Co., 1946-47; coach McLean High Sch., 1948-49, N.M. State U., 1949-54; coach Tex. Western Coll., 1954-59, dean men, 1959-62; dir. athletics U. Tex. at El Paso, 1962—. Served with USAF, 1940-46. Mem. Lambda Chi Alpha. Democrat. Baptist (mem. bd. deacons). Kiwanian. Club: Touchdown. Home: 2009 N Campbell St El Paso TX 79902 Office: PO Box 180 El Paso TX 79999

MCCARTY, JOHN M., judge; b. Fort Pierce, Fla., Nov. 23, 1915; B.A., U. Fla., 1937, LL.B., 1941, J.D., 1967. Admitted to Fla. bar, 1941, U.S. Dist. Ct. bar, 1942, U.S. Ct. Appeals bar, U.S. Supreme Ct. bar, 1960; municipal judge Fort Pierce, 1947-51; asst. to gov., 1953; judge, 9th Judicial Circuit, 1957-59; Mem. Fla. Constn. Revision Commn., 1965-67. Fla. senator, 1962-67. Trustee, U. Fla. Law Center Assn., 1964—. Served to major, F.A., AUS, 1942-46. Mem. St. Lucie County (pres. 1948), Am. bar assns.; The Fla. Bar (bd. govs. 1963-69, pres. 1971); Am. Judicature Soc. (dir. 1969—), Acad. Fla. Trial Lawyers, Fla. Blue Key, Phi Delta Phi. Address: Box 4412 Fort Pierce FL 33450*

MCCAUL, THOMAS VADEN, JR., lawyer, securities co. exec.; b. Clemson, S.C., Dec. 30, 1911; s. Thomas Vaden and Waldine Byrd (Scearce) McC.; LL.B., U. Fla., 1935; m. Sammy Anne Wills, Apr. 26, 1957. Admitted to Fla. bar, 1935; practiced in Miami, Fla., 1936-54; mem. firm Bouvier, Helliwell & McCaul, Miami, Fla., 1948-50; spl. asst. to atty. gen. of Fla., Tallahassee, 1941-43; prin. Wall St. Corp. Am., Inc. security dealers, Miami, 1963—, v.p., treas., 1965—, also dir. Mem. Nat. Assn. Security Dealers. Pi Kappa Alpha. Democrat. Home: 530 N E 133rd St North Miami FL 33161 Office: Wall St Corp Am Inc 3390 Coral Way Miami FL 33145

MCCAULEY, HAROLD HOMER, mech. engr.; b. Stockton, Kan., Aug. 26, 1923; s. Homer Wilson and Hilda (Moore) McC.; B.S., Kan. State U., 1949; m. Patricia June Canfield, July 22, 1951; children—Carol Linn, Barbara Jean, Avis Dee, Allan Wade. Civilian engr. U.S. Army Corps Engrs., Kansas City Dist., 1949-54; elec.-mech. engr. Servis, Van Dorn & Hazard, cons. engr., Topeka, 1954-59; supr. engr. Corps Engrs., ICBM Launcher Sites, 1959-63; mech. engr. Office Chief of Engrs., Washington, 1963-70, supervisory engr., 1970—. Mem. Am. Nat. Standards Inst. B31.4 sect. com.; adviser Jr. Engr. Tech. Soc. local high sch., 1965-69. Treas., P.T.A., 1965-66, 68-71, pres. Woodlawn Citizens Assn., 1971. Served with USNR, 1945-46. Recipient letters of commendation, certificates of achievement Dept. Army, 1962, 64. Mem. Nat. Soc. Profl. Engrs., Sigma Tau, Pi Tau Sigma. Presbyn. Home: 5017 Rosemont Av Alexandria VA 22309 Office: Forrestal Bldg Washington DC 20315

MCCAULEY, LOYD CECIL, dentist; b. Canton, Tex., Sept. 2, 1913; s. Sidney James and Florence Eva (Prater) McC.; student N. Tex. State Tchrs. Coll., 1930-32; D.D.S., Baylor U., 1936; m. Claudia Alethe Moore, Aug. 30, 1934; children—Phillip Ray, Ronald Cecil, Danny Paul. Pvt. practice dentistry, Alba, Tex., 1938-42, Mt. Pleasant, Tex., 1942—; courtesy staff Titus County Meml. Hosp., Mt. Pleasant. Pres., Mt. Pleasant Ind. Sch. Bd., 1952-56. Mem. Am. Dental Assn., Tex., First Dist. (pres. 1954) dental socs., Pierre Fauchard Acad., Order of Goodfellow. Mem. Ch. of Christ. Home: 303 Chester St Mount Pleasant TX 75455 Office: PO Box 508 Mount Pleasant TX 75455

MCCLAIN, DAVID H., state senator; b. Macon, Ga., June 4, 1933; s. Joseph A. Jr. and Laura (Burkett) McC.; B.A., Duke, 1957; M.A. (Scottish Rite fellow 1958), George Washington U., 1961; LL.B., Stetson Coll. Law, 1961; m. Leslie McNevin, Dec. 20, 1968; 1 dau., Linda N. Partner, MacFarlane, Ferguson, Allison & Kelly, Tampa, Fla., 1961—; legislative liason Fla. Gov.'s office, 1967; mem. Fla. Senate, 1970—. Mem., Fla. Law Review Commn., 1970-71. Vice chmn. Bd. Pub. Relations and Conf. Facilities, Tampa. First v.p. Hillsborough County Young Republican Club, 1967-68, pres., 1969-70; mem. Hillsborough County Rep. Club, legal adv. exec. com., 1969-70. Served with AUS. Mem. Fla., Am., Tampa, Hillsborough County bar assns., Tampa Jr. C. of C., Beta Theta Pi, Delta Theta Phi. Mason (Shriner). Club: Interbay Sertoma (sec. 1970-71). Home: 4611 Fig St Tampa FL 33609 Office: PO Box 1531 Tampa FL 33601*

MCCLAIN, JAMES WRIGHT, dept. stores exec.; b. Chgo., Nov. 4, 1907; s. T.B. and Margaret (Wright) McC.; m. Bernice J. Fisher, Mar. 5, 1935; 1 dau., Carolyn Sue (Mrs. Edward L. Auffert). With Dillard Dept. Stores Inc., Tulsa, formerly v.p. accounting, now corporate v.p., also dir. Mem. Nat. Assn. Accountants, Tulsa C. of C. Methodist. Mason (shriner, 32 deg.). Home: 1755 E 59th St Tulsa OK 74105 Office: PO Box 1950 Tulsa OK 74102

MCCLAIN, RICHARD HERBERT, bus. orgn. exec.; b. Dallas, May 3, 1925; s. Fred H. and Edith (Haman) McC.; B.B.A., So. Methodist U., 1950; m. Eugenia Nolan, Sept. 3, 1953; children—Michael Richard, Kathryn Nolan. Sales and advt. Schaeffer Pen Co., Ft. Madison, Wis., Millers Falls Tool Co. (Mass.), Carnation Milk Co., Los Angeles, 1950-55; trade practice cons. Better Bus. Bur. Dallas, 1955-58; exec. v.p. Better Bus. Bur. Mobile County, Tex., 1958-62; exec. v.p. Better Bus. Bur. Houston, 1962-71, pres., 1971—. Chmn. mgmt. com. Council Better Bus. Burs., 1971—. Mem. Tex. Motor Vehicle Commn., 1971. Served with USMCR, 1943-46. Mem. Soc. Fund Raisers, Am. Soc. Assn. Execs., Houston Advt. Club, Tex. Bill of Rights Found. Presbyn. Home: 314 Fawnlake St Houston TX 77024 Office: Main Bldg Houston TX 77002

MCCLANAHAN, WILLIAM J., cartoonist Dallas Morning News. Address: Communications Center Dallas TX 75222*

MCCLARRIN, WILLIAM OTTO, govt. ofcl.; b. Atlanta, Ga., Apr. 11, 1918; s. Mozell and Geneva (Radden) McC.; B.A., Howard U., 1949; postgrad. Am. U., evenings 1949-55, New Sch. Social Studies, N.Y.C., 1953, U. Notre Dame, 1969; m. Frances Justine Morsell, Feb. 14, 1942; children—Vaughn Otto, Lynn Frances. Reporter, artist Afro-Am., newspaper, Balt., 1936-40, copy editor, artist, 1940-41;

publicity agt. Howard U., Washington, 1941-43, dir. pub. relations, 1947-56, 69-70; sr. artist, designer OPA, 1943; editor Newspic mag., Birmingham, Ala., N.Y.C., 1945-46; asst. editor Consumers Union Pubs., N.Y.C., 1946-47; pub. affairs officer USIA, Indonesia, 1956-58; chief information office, illustrator U.S. Commn. on Civil Rights, 1958-62; pvt. practice pub. relations, U.S., Africa, 1962-66; dir. community relations community action program U.S. Office Econ. Opportunity, Washington, 1966-69, dir. spl. communications programs Office Pub. Affairs, 1970-72, dir. editorial div., 1972—. Pub. relations cons. various businesses, profl. orgns. Pub. relations com. Washington chpt. A.R.C., 1965—; chmn. pub. relations com. Health and Welfare Council Nat. Capital area, 1967-69, UN Assn., Washington, 1971—; mem. citizens adv. com. Washington Zoning Commn., 1966—. Served with USAAF, 1943-45. Lucy E. Moton Travel fellow Howard U., 1941. Mem. Nat., Capital (Ann. awards 1948, 50, Newsman trophy 1960) press clubs, Pub. Relations Soc. Am., Coll. Pub. Relations Assn., Am. Alumni Council (Merit award 1949, 52), Advt. Club Met. Washington, Omega Psi Phi. Episcopalian. Clubs: Gourmets, Consorts (Washington). Editor: Oracle mag., 1970—. Home: 1712 Allison St N W Washington DC 20011 Office: 1200 19th St N W Washington DC 20506

MCCLARTY, BILLYE GEORGE, dentist; b. Quanah, Tex., Jan. 10, 1933; s. George H. and Faye (Hoffmeyer) McC.; D.D.S., Baylor U., 1957; m. Fredna Ann Howard, Nov. 8, 1953; children—Kimice Sue, Mark Howard, Karen Beth, Kelley Ann. Individual practice dentistry, Amarillo, Tex., 1959-68; mem. dental staff VA Hosp., Tuskegee, Ala., 1968-69, Dallas, 1970—; chief dental service VA Center, Reno, 1968-69, VA Hosp., Muskogee, Okla., 1969—. Served with USAF, 1957-59. Mem. Am. Dental Assn., Am. Acad. Gen. Dentistry. Home: 2403 Linda Dr Ennis TX 75119 Office: VA Hosp 4500 Lancaster Rd Dallas TX 75216

MCCLARY, GEORGE OSCAR, ednl. psychologist; b. Rapidan, Va., June 27, 1923; s. Haywood Oscar and Jane Irene (Hopkins) McC.; B.A., U. Richmond, 1949; M.S., Pa. State U., 1954; Ph.D. in Psychology, George Washington U., 1969. Office mgr., personnel supr., shipwright dept. Newport News Shipbldg. & Dry Dock Co. (Va.), 1940-44; publs. analyst VA, Richmond, Va., summer 1946; case record asst. Va. Dept. Corrections, 1947-48; psychiat. aide Western State Hosp., Staunton, Va., summer 1949; counselor Norfolk (Va.) Consultation Service, Va. Bd. Edn., 1949-52; dir. student workshop John Marshall High Sch., Richmond, summers 1957-58; instr. Richmond Profl. Inst., Coll. William and Mary, 1957-59; instr. U. Va. Extension Div., 1959; psychometrist, sch. psychologist, dir. guidance and psychol. services, supr. guidance services Richmond Pub. Schs., 1952-66, dir. pupil personnel services, 1966—. Instr., George Washington U., 1961, U. Va., 1962, 64, 68, 70, U. Richmond, 1966, 71, 72, William and Mary Coll. Extension, 1963; mem. Govs. Com. on Employment of Physically Handicapped, 1961-62; edn. com. Richmond Mental Health Assn., 1961-64, 65-67, bd. dirs., 1967-71; bd. dirs. Meml. Guidance Clinic, Richmond, 1966-69; bd. dirs. Va. Council on Social Welfare 1968-71, mem. exec. com., 1969-71; bd. dirs., 1968-71; bd. dirs. Va. Inst. Pastoral Care, 1970—; mem. Richmond Youth Com., 1963-67; mem. Mental Health Execs. Roundtable, Richmond Area Community Council, 1964-67; bd. dirs. Speech Center, Med. Coll. Va., 1956-60, Big Sister Assn. Richmond, 1956-60, Shakespeare Players, Inc., 1963-65. Served with AUS, 1944-46. Diplomate in sch. psychology Am. Bd. Profl. Psychology. Mem. Am. (exec. council 1963-66), Va. (pres. elect 1960-61, pres. 1961-62), Richmond (treas. 1955-56, v.p. 1958-60, pres. 1960-61) personnel and guidance assns., Am. Sch. Counselor Assn. (pres. elect 1963-64, pres. 1964-65, gov. 1960-66), Nat. Vocational Guidance Assn., Assn. for Measurement and Evaluation in Guidance, N.E.A., Assn. for Counselor Edn. and Supervision, Am., Va., Richmond psychol. assns., Va. Edn. Assn., Nat. Assn. Pupil Personnel Adminstrs. (editor news bull. 1969, 70, pres. 1972—). Presbyn. Club: Va. Boat. Author: Interpreting Guidance Programs to Pupils, 1968. Home: 213 N Plum St Richmond VA 23220

MCCLEARY, WILLIAM ERNEST, librarian, educator; b. Alexandria, La., May 29, 1927; s. Ernest Earl and Laura (Hearte) McC.; B.A., Centenary Coll. La., 1948; M.A. in Journalism, La. State U., 1950, M.S. in L.S., 1958; certificate advanced studies librarianship U. Ill., 1971. Tchr., Caddo Parish Sch. Bd., Shreveport, La., 1950-58; catalog, acquisitions librarian Shreve Meml. Library, 1958-60; librarian Union Producing Co., 1961-67; reference librarian La. State U., 1967-72, documents librarian, 1972—, instr., summer 1972. Served with USMCR, 1945-46, 50-51. Recipient scholarship City of Oslo, Norway, 1953, assistantship La. State U., 1957-58, U. Ill., summer 1970, grantee La. State U., 1971. Mem. Am. Assn. U. Profs., Spl., Southwestern, La. (treas. 1964-65; chmn. subject specialist sect. 1971-72) library assns., North La. Hist. Assn. Episcopalian (vestryman). Club: Caddo Bossier Library (pres. 1964-65, 70-71) (Shreveport). Bull. editor La. Library Assn., 1965-66, La. chpt. Spl. Libraries Assn., 1965-66, 68, 72-73. Home: 6147 Creswell Rd Shreveport LA 71106 Office: 8515 Youree Dr Shreveport LA 71105

MCCLELLAN, JOHN LITTLE, U.S. senator; b. Sheridan, Ark., Feb. 25, 1896; s. Isaac Scott and Belle (Suddleth) McC.; ed. pub. schs.; m. Eula Hicks, Nov. 2, 1913 (dec.); children—Max Eldon, Doris; m. 2d, Lucille Smith, Nov. 8, 1922 (dec.); children—John L., James, Mary Alice; m. 3d, Norma Myers Cheatham, Nov. 10, 1937. Admitted to Ark. bar, 1913, and began practice at Sheridan; pros. atty. 7th Jud. Dist. of Ark. 2 terms, 1927-30; mem. 74th and 75th Congresses from 6th Ark. Dist.; U.S. senator from Ark., 1942—. Served at 1st lt., A.S.S.C., Wrold War I. Recipient Distinguished Pub. Service award, Nat. Tax Found., 1957; George Washington award, Am. Good Govt. Soc., 1959; Hatton W. Sumners award, S.W. Legal Found., 1959. Democrat. Baptist. Home: Camden AR Office: Senate Office Bldg Washington DC 20510 also Union Life Bldg Little Rock AR Federal Office Bldg Little Rock AR

MCCLELLAND, WILLIAM AGNEW, psychologist; b. N.Y.C., Nov. 8, 1918; s. William Cecil and Charlotte (Brooks) McC.; A.B., Brown U., 1941; M.A., U. Minn., 1946, Ph.D., 1948; m. Dorothy Ann Nelson, Sept. 16, 1942; children—Katherine E., Richard B. Instr., dept. psychology U. Minn., Mpls., 1946-48; asst. prof., dept. psychology Brown U., Providence, 1948-51; research psychologist U.S. Air Force, 1951-55; dir. research, dept. dir., asso. dir. Human Resources Research Office, George Washington U., Washington, 1955-69, profl. lectr. dept. psychology, 1966—; exec. v.p. Human Resources Research Orgn., Alexandria, Va., 1969—. Served from pvt. to capt., USAAF, 1942-46. Fellow Am. Psycholol. Assn., A.A.A.S.; mem. Am. Edn. Research Assn., Psychonomic Soc., D.C. Psychol. Assn. Home: 7813 Accotink Pl Alexandria VA 22308 Office: 300 N Washington St Alexandria VA 22314

MCCLENDON, CARLEE THOMAS, ednl. TV network ofcl.; b. Edgefield, S.C., Aug. 15, 1940; s. Ralph Thomas and Sadie (Jackson) M.; B.A. in Journalism, U. S.C., 1965; m. Juliet McCreary Refo, June 10, 1967; 1 dau., Julie R. Tchr. history Langley-Bath-Clearwater High Sch., Aiken County, S.C., 1965-66; asst. historic resources coordinator S.C. Dept. Archives and History, 1966-67; mng. editor Edgefield Adv., 1967-68; coordinator local events S.C. Tricentennial Commn., Columbia, 1968-71; edn. editor SC ETV Network, Columbia, 1971—. Organizer historic homes tours, 1966-71; restoration cons. Edgefield's Magnolia Dale, 1965-68; founder Pottersville Mus., 1970. Mem. Edgefield Jr. C. of C., Am. Assn. State and Local History (merit award for Edgefield County Hist. Soc. 1967, state membership chmn. 1969), Nat. Trust Historic Preservation, S.C., Edgefield (v.p. 1960—) hist. socs., South Caroliniana Soc., Sigma Delta Chi, Sigma Phi Epsilon. Methodist. Author: 1790 and 1800 Federal Census Records of Edgefield District, 1960; Edgefield Marriage Records, 1970. Home: 312 S Woodrow St Columbia SC 29205 Office: Drawer L 2712 Millwood Av Columbia SC 29205

MCCLENDON, CHARLES YOUMANS, football coach; b. Lewisville, Ark., Oct. 17, 1923; s. Leigh Alexander and Susie (Robey) McC.; B.A., U. Ky., 1950, M.A., 1951; m. Dorothy Faye Smart, Dec. 24, 1947; children—Dolores Kaye, Charles Scott. Asst. football coach U. Ky., 1951, Vanderbilt U., 1952; asst. coach La. State U., Baton Rouge, 1953-62, head coach, 1962—. Served with USNR, 1943-46. Office: Athletic Dept La State U Baton Rouge LA 70803

MCCLENDON, JAMES LOWELL, dentist; b. Houston, Jan. 29, 1927; s. Ezra James and Bessie Edith (Day) McC.; student Tex. A. and M. U., 1943-44; B.A., U. Tex., 1950, D.D.S., 1954; m. Anne Cecelia Glavin, Apr. 24, 1957; children—Theresa Ann, James Lowell. Fellow in oral surgery Mayo Clinic, 1954-57; pvt. practice oral surgery, Houston, 1954—; clin. asso. clin. prof. dept. pathology U. Tex. Dental Br., Houston, 1957—. Cons. oral pathology M. D. Anderson Hosp. and Tumor Inst., Houston, 1964-72; chief oral surgery Meml. Baptist Hosp. Systems, 1967-72. Bd. dirs. Harris County and Tex. chpts. Am. Cancer Soc. Served with USNR, 1945-48. Recipient Bronze Exhibit award Am. Acad. Dermatology. Diplomate Am. Bd. Oral Surgery. Fellow Internat. Assn. Oral Surgeons; mem. Am. Soc. Oral Surgeons, Am. Dental Assn., U. Tex. Dental Br. Alumni Assn. (trustee 1959-62), Omicron Kappa Upsilon. Republican. Roman Catholic. Optimist (pres. Houston 1960). Contbr. articles to profl. jours. Home: 11835 Stuckey Lane Houston TX 77024 Office: 1118 Meml Profl Bldg 1019 Lamar St Houston TX 77002

MCCLENNEY, EARL HAMPTON, coll. pres.; b. Marion, Ala., Mar. 4, 1907; s. Henry Clay and Mary (Moore) McC.; student Lincoln Normal Sch., Marion, Ala., 1921-26, Talladega (Ala.) Coll., 1926-28, Agrl. and Tech. Coll., 1928-30, LL.D., 1954; B.S., Cornell U., 1939; M.S., Pa. State Coll., 1942; m. Madeline Jones, Nov. 9, 1939; children— Earl, Clifton; m. 2d, Fannie M. Midder, Aug. 19, 1960; 1 dau., Elizabeth Gail. Tchr. high sch. Thomasville, N.C., 1931-32, prin. high sch., 1932-36; miscellaneous sch. and assn. work, 1936-49; pres. St. Paul's Coll., Lawrenceville, Va., 1949—. Vice pres. N.C. Coll. Conf., 1948-49; bd. dirs. YMCA, Raleigh, N.C.; mem. state adv. com. on schs. and colls.; mem. exec. bd. Va. Council on Human Relations. Bd. dirs. South Side Community Coll., Lawrenceville. Mem. N.E.A., Assn. Coll. and U. Profs., Assn. Episcopal Colls. (pres. 1970—), Va. Tchrs. Assn., Va. Edn. Assn., Alpha Kappa Mu, Alpha Beta, Omega Psi Phi. Episcopalian. Address: St Paul's Coll Lawrenceville VA 23868

MCCLESKY, J. C., supt. schs.; b. Lambert, Miss., Feb. 14, 1923; s. Ellis E. and Jewel (Rose) McC.; B.S., Tex. A. and M. U., 1944; M.E., Midwestern U., 1954; m. Aline Irene Graf, Apr. 9, 1944; children—Betty Jewel, Phyllis Diane, William Ellis. Efficiency engr. N. Am. Aviation Co., Dallas, 1944-45; store mgr. Goodyear Tire & Rubber Co., Grand Prairie, Tex., 1945-46; tchr. Chillicothe (Tex.) Pub. Schs., 1946-49, prin. high sch., 1949-56, supt., 1956-60; supt. Shamrock (Tex.) Pub. Schs., 1960-69, Slaton (Tex.) Pub. Schs., 1969—. Mem. dist. exec. com., also mem. exec. com. Adobe Walls council Boy Scouts Am. Mem. N.E.A. (chmn. Tex. Panhandle 1962-65), Tex. Tchrs. Assn., Am. Assn. Sch. Adminstrs., U. Interscholastic League (mem. regional com. 1962-66), Assn. Former Students Tex. A. and M. U., West Tex., Slaton (pres. 1971) chambers commerce, St. Patrick's Assn. (chmn. 1965). Baptist. Mason (Shriner), Lion (pres. Shamrock 1962-63, dist. sec. 1962-63, 1st v.p. Slaton 1971), Rotarian. Club: Shamrock Boosters. Home: 1435 W Crosby St Slaton TX 79364 Office: 300 S 9th St Slaton TX 79364

MCCLINTOCK, SIMMS, polit. scientist, educator; b. Lake Village, Ark., July 10, 1927; s. William Richey and Lilly (Simms) McC.; B.A., Hendrix Coll., 1951; M.A., Columbia, 1953. Coordinator social studies Crossett (Ark.) High Sch., 1953-65; asso. prof. history and polit. sci. State Coll. Ark., Conway, 1966—. Faculty adviser State Coll. Ark. Young Democrats, 1966—. Faulkner County Hist. Soc. Sec., bd. dirs. Carmichael Found. Served with USNR, 1945-48, 51-52. Recipient Distinguished award Ark. Jr. C. of C., 1962; named Ark. Tchr. of Year, U.S. Office Edn. and Look Mag., 1963. John Hay fellow Columbia, 1965-66. Mem. Classroom Tchrs. Ark. (pres.), N.E.A., Ark. Edn. Assn., Faulkner County Hist. Soc. (pres.), Phi Delta Kappa. Episcopalian. Author: Guide To Teaching Citizenship, 1961; Guide To Teaching Economics, 1965. Home: 120 Baridon St Conway AR 72032

MCCLOUD, DARELL EDISON, educator; B.S., Purdue U., 1945, M.S., 1947, Ph.D., 1949. Asst. and asso. prof. agronomy U. Fla., Gainesville, 1948-57, chmn. dept. agronomy Inst. Food and Agrl. Scis., 1965—; head humid pasture and range investigations Agrl. Research Service, U.S. Dept. Agr., 1957-65. Fellow Am. Soc. Agronomy; mem. Crop Sci. Soc. Am. (pres. 1969), Sigma Xi, Phi Sigma, Phi Kappa Phi. Office: Dept of Agronomy Inst Food and Agrl Sciences University of Fla Gainesville FL 32601

MCCLUNEY, JOE ALFRED, assn. exec.; b. Oxford, Ala., Sept. 9, 1924; s. Olin A. and Myrtle (Hartline) McC.; B.S. in Gen. Bus., U. Ala., 1949; postgrad. U. N.C., 1956-62, Mich. State U., 1963-65; m. Margaret Elizabeth Locke, May 13, 1949; children—Sandra Etoile, Margaret Judson, Joe A. Mgr. Geneva (Ala.) C. of C., 1956-58, Ozark (Ala.) C. of C., 1958-59, Atmore (Ala.) C. of C., 1959-63, mgr., exec. v.p. Jasper (Ala.) area C. of C., 1963—. Chmn. Geneva County (Ala.) March of Dimes, 1957; adviser Jr. Achievement, Opelika, Ala., 1954; active United Fund. Bd. dirs., mem. exec. com. community Service Council. Served with AUS, 1944-46; ETO. Mem. Am., So., Ala. (pres. 1963-64, sec.-treas. 1964—) chambers commerce execs. assns. Methodist (mem. bd., treas.). Rotarian (treas. Altmore, Ala. 1962). Home: Chamber Bldg PO Box 972 Jasper AL 35501 Office: 816 8th Av Jasper AL 35501

MCCLUNG, CLOYD HARRELL, librarian; b. Waco, Tex., Sept. 11, 1916; s. Sampson Reece and Ethel (Reding) McC.; B.A., Baylor U., 1938; M.R.E., Southwestern Theol. Sem., 1941; M.A. in L.S., Fla. State U., 1953; m. Doris Wilson, July 3, 1943; 1 son, Reece Alfred. Ednl. dir. Calvary Bapt. Ch., Fort Worth, 1940-42, Allapattah Bapt. Ch., Miami, 1945-48, 1st Bapt. Ch., Fort Pierce, Fla., 1948-49, Panama City, Fla., 1949-54; Tidwell Bible librarian Baylor U., Waco, 1954-64; librarian Polk Jr. Coll., Winter Haven, Fla. 1964-68, Eckerd Coll., St. Petersburg, 1968—. Librarian, U.S.A. World Fair, summer 1965. Served with USAAF, 1941-46. Mem. Am., Tex., Southwestern, Southeastern Fla. library assns. Baptist. Home: 2667 Granada Circle St Petersburg FL 33712

MCCLUNG, JAMES COWAN, newspaper pub.; b. Kerens, Tex., May 17, 1912; s. Luther Thurman and Carrie J. (Miller) M.; grad. high sch.; m. Evelyn Louise Terry, Nov. 19, 1936; children—James Cowan, Katrina Sue (Mrs. James Thomas Williams). With Dallas Dispatch, 1930-37; with Dallas Times Herald, 1937—, prodn. mgr., 1956—. Mem. Am., So. newspaper pub. assn., Tex. Daily Newspaper Assn. Mason (32 deg., Jester, Shriner). Home: 4128 Drowsy Lane Dallas TX 75233 Office: 1101 Pacific Av Dallas TX 75202

MCCLUNG, LUTHER THERMAN, oil operator, rancher; b. Kerens, Tex., Oct. 30, 1909; s. Luther T. and Carrie J. (Miller) McC.; student pub. schs., Dallas; m. Evelyn Louise Loe, Aug. 6, 1927; children—Lucian Louise (Mrs. Murl R. Richardson), Barbara Ann (Mrs. William R. Wells). Circulation mgr. Courier-Times, Tyler, Tex. and Ft. Worth Press, 1927-40; asst. bus. mgr. Longview (Tex.) News-Jour., 1927-40; gen. contractor Luther T. McClung & McClung Constrn. Co., 1940-48; pres. McClung Oil Corp., 1958—, Cross Plains Grain & Peanut Co., 1965—; asso. Coastal States Gas Producing Co., Midland, 1958—; owner, operator Luther T. McClung 4M Ranch, Kiowa, Okla., 1948—, 4M Ranch, Rising Star, Tex., 1960—. Mem. Am. (dir. 1950-56), Tex. (pres. 1950, dir. 1948-52) Angus assns. Home: 1014 Denton St Midland TX 79701 also Route 5 Box 99 Comanche TX 76442 Office: Continental Bank Bldg Fort Worth TX also Wilco Bldg Midland TX 79701

MCCLUNG, RALPH CLAY, dentist; b. Collinsville, Ala., Apr. 21, 1907; s. James Newton and Virginia Ida (Jones) McC.; student Auburn U., 1925-26, Birmingham So. Coll., summer 1926; D.D.S. cum laude, Emory U., 1930; m. Olive Ann Greagan, Aug. 8, 1950; 1 son, Ralph Clay. Practice dentistry, Birmingham, Ala., 1930—. Pres. Bachelors Cotillion, 1933; king Christmas Carnival, 1940, Linly Heflin Festival, 1933. Served to capt. Dental Corps, AUS, 1943-44; ETO. Fellow Acad. Internat. Dentistry, Am. Dental Assn., Internat. Coll. Dentists (pres. 1972-73), Pierre Fauchard Acad.; mem. Acad. Anesthesiology, Ala. Dental Assn., Birmingham Dist., Chgo. dental socs., Am. Acad. Restorative Dentistry (pres. 1958-59), Am. Assn. Dental insultants (pres. 1971-73), Psi Omega, Omicron Kappa Upsilon. Methodist. Rotarian. Clubs: Birmingham Country, Birmingham Aero (pres. 1943); Ace Flying (pres. 1942); The Club; Hole-in-one; Quarterback. Home: 2918 Overhill Rd Birmingham AL 35223 Office: Profl Arts Bldg Birmingham AL 35205

MCCLUNG, ROY CORNELIUS, coll. pres.; b. Frederick, Okla., Sept. 17, 1917; s. Joseph Leonard and Ethel (Robinson) McC.; B.A., Okla. Bapt. U., 1941; Th.M., So. Bapt. Theol. Sem., 1944, Th.D., 1948; m. Genelle Bucklew, Aug. 5, 1941; children—Michael, Nancy (Mrs. RoGene Chaddick), Mark. Ordained to ministry Bapt. Ch., 1938; pastor in Hiseville, Ky., 1945-47, Louisville, 1947-54, Ada, Okla., 1954-58, Plainview, Tex., 1958-63; pres. Wayland Bapt. Coll., Plainview, 1963—. Chmn. Haynes dist. Council Boy Scouts Am., 1961-64. Lion. Mason. Home: 1307 W 6th St Plainview TX 79072

MCCLURE, CECIL DAVIS, agr. exec.; b. Anderson, S.C., July 4, 1913; s. William John and Dessie Cinderella (Hall) M.; grad. high sch.; m. Norma Malinda Griffin, Feb. 2, 1935; children—Alma Ann (Mrs. Arthur J. Harrell), Eugene Norman Plant mgr. Pure Oil Co., Anderson, S.C., 1935-38, Monroe, N.C., 1938-43; farm mgr. Chamblee Farms, Inc., Belle Glade, Fla., 1943—, mem. bd., 1962—. Supr., Palm Beach Broward Soil and Water Conservation Dist., 1964—, chmn., 1969-70. Bd. dirs. City Belle Glade Housing Authority, Mem. Belle Glade Farm Bur., Fla. Celery Exchange (dir.). Presbyn. (deacon 1952-56, elder 1957-65) Mason. Home: PO Box 115 Belle Glade FL 33430 Office: PO Box 509 Belle Glade FL 33430

MCCLURE, CHARLES KING, distillery exec.; b. St. Louis, July 10, 1910; s. Charles King and Mary (Hicks) McC.; A.B., Westminster Coll., 1931; m. Mary Chenault Van Winkle, Oct. 2, 1939; children—Mary Chenault (Mrs. P. M. Conway, Jr.), Charles King III. Jr. exec. Lord & Taylor, N.Y.C., 1931-33; exec. Stewart Dry Goods Co., Louisville, 1933-40; with Stitzel Weller Distillery, Louisville, 1940—, sec., 1941-47, sec.-treas., 1947-65, chmn. bd., 1965—, also dir.; dir. Commonwealth Life Ins. Co., Louisville. Past pres., chmn. bd. Distilled Spirits Inst., Washington; dir. Bourbon Inst.; dir., past sec. License Beverage Industries, N.Y.C. Bd. overseers U. Louisville; bd. dirs. Louisville Safety Council; trustee Westminster Coll., Fulton, Mo. Mem. Ky. Distillers Assn. (past pres., chmn. bd.), Louisville C. of C. (dir.), Phi Delta Theta. Clubs: Louisville Country, Wynn Stay, Pendennis, Filson (Louisville). Home: 5822 Orion Rd Glenview Heights Louisville KY 40222 Office: PO Station D Louisville KY

MCCLURE, LEE ROPER, constrn. co. exec.; b. Greenville, S.C., Apr. 5, 1927; s. Lee Lafayette and Ivor (Roper) McC.; B.E.E., Ga. Inst. Tech., 1951; m. Mable Keel, Dec. 29, 1950; children—Michael Lee, Lisa Ellen, Teresa Anne. Instr., Ga. Inst. Tech., Atlanta, 1951-52; design and sales engr. F.J. Evans Engring. Co., Atlanta, 1952-57; v.p., sec. Ammons, McClure & Caldwell, Inc., Atlanta, 1957-62; exec. v.p. Kahn So. div. M.B. Kahn Constrn. Co., Columbia, S.C., 1962-68, also dir; v.p., mgr. comml. and indsl. div. Algernon Blair, Inc., Atlanta, 1968—. Served with USNR, 1945-46. Mem. S.C. Indsl. Developers Assn. (pres. 1967), Am. Soc. Heating, Refrigeration and Air Conditioning Engrs., Nat. (state treas. 1966, Engr. of Year S.C. 1966, sec. 1967, nat engrs. week chmn. 1970-71), Ga. (pres. 1971-72) socs. profl. engrs., Ga. Indsl. Devel. Assn., So. Indsl. Devel. Council. Presbyn. Home: 6750 River Springs Lane NW Atlanta GA 30328 Office: PO Box 56205 Atlanta GA 30343

MCCLURE, MILTON DALLAS, lawyer, processing co. ofcl.; b. Chattanooga, May 24, 1926; s. Ardie Elbert and Gena (Mitchell) McC.; A.B., Colgate U., 1948; LL.B., Emory U., 1951, D. Law, 1971; m. Patricia Ellen Lynch, Dec. 22, 1950; children—Robert Lynch, Alan Andrew. Admitted to Tenn. bar, 1952, U.S. Supreme Ct. bar, 1956; asst. commr. revenue State of Tenn., 1951-53; asso. firm Folts, Brammer, Bishop & Thomas, attys., Chattanooga, 1953-56; partner firm McClure, Moore, Anderson & Meyer, 1956-64; v.p. Air Terminal Parking Co., Inc., 1964-66; comptroller, v.p. finance Potato Processing Co., Inc., Atlanta, 1967-72; mem. firm Henderson, Haley & Thurman, Marietta, Ga., 1972—. Gen. counsel Tenn. Law Enforcement Officers Assn., Inc., 1956-63. Bd. dirs., v.p. Cumberland Youth Found., Inc., Chattanooga. Served with USMCR, 1943-46; PTO. Mem. Emory U. (dist. pres.), Colgate U. (v.p. Tenn.) alumni assns., V.F.W., Sigma Nu, Phi Alpha Delta. Elk. Clubs: Civitan, Colgate University of N.Y. Contbr. articles to law enforcement jour. Office: Henderson Haley & Thurman 219 Roswell Rd Marietta GA

MCCLURE, ROBERT EDWIN, JR., accountant; b. Duluth, Ga., Dec. 28, 1921; s. Robert Edwin and Gladys (Rhodes) McC.; student U. Fla., 1941-42; B.B.A., U. Ga., 1951; m. Marian Pauline Duft, Aug. 30, 1958; children— Robert Edwin III. Martin Rhodes, John Duft, Susan Lucinda; 1 stepson William Peter Treblas, Jr. Civil service Wright-Patterson AFB, Dayton, O., 1946-49; auditor Ernst & Ernst, Atlanta, 1951-54; accountant Maule Industries, Miami, Fla., 1954-55, Smethurst & Dessaint, C.P.A.'s, Miami, 1955-56; controller Harold Rabin Co., Inc., Belle Glade Fla., 1957; auditor W.J. Callahan & Co., C.P.A.'s, Miami, 1957-58; mgr., consolidations and reports Ryder System, Inc., Miami, 1959-65; mgr.-partner Smith, Braley & Johnson, C.P.A.'s, Miami, 1965-69, Peat, Marwick, Mitchell & Co., C.P.A.'s, Miami, 1969—. Served with USAAF, 1942-45; ETO. C.P.A., Fla. Mem. Am. Inst. C.P.A.'s, Greater Miami C. of C., Beta Gamma Sigma. Democrat. Methodist. Club: Sertoma (Past treas., dir.). Home: 7520 SW 84th Ct Miami FL 33143 Office: 1000 Brickell Av Miami FL 33131

MCCLURE, WILLIAM JASPER, ednl. adminstr.; b. Fulton, Mo., Jan. 26, 1914; s. William C. and Mary (McCue) McC.; B.A. cum laude, Westminster Coll., 1936, L.H.D., 1958; M.A., Gallaudet Coll., 1937; M.A. in Adminstrn., George Washington U., 1942; m. Mary Lillian Bruce, Oct. 20, 1934; children—Mary Hughes (Mrs. Thomas Kendrick), William, Helen Lee (Mrs. Donald Bush), George. Instr., Gallaudet Coll., 1937-39, asst. prof., 1939-41, asso. prof., 1941-46, prof., 1946-50, dir. tchr. tng., 1946-50; supt. Tenn. Sch. Deaf, Knoxville, 1950-57, Ind. Sch. Deaf, Indpls., 1957-67; pres. Fla. Sch. for Deaf and Blind, St. Augustine, 1967—. Pres. Conf. Execs. Am. Schs. Deaf, 1960-63; mem. adv. com. to U.S. commr. of edn., 1962—; pres. Council on Edn. of Deaf, 1963-65. Mem. Phi Delta Theta, Phi Delta Kappa. Methodist. Rotarian. Editor: Proc. Am. Instrs. Deaf, 1951—. Contbr. articles to profl. jours., chpt. to book. Home: 27 Milton St St Augustine FL 32084 Office: Fla School for Deaf and Blind PO Box 1209 San Marco Av St Augustine FL 32084

MCCLURKIN, JOHN BRAXTON, librarian; b. Neenah, Ala., Jan. 2, 1912; s. John Marvin and Sarah Olivia (Watson) McC.; B.A., U. Ala., 1932, certificate in L.S., 1934, M.A., 1939; M.A., U. Chgo., 1966; m. Margaret Viola Lawson, Feb. 27, 1954; children—Margaret Ann, John Braxton. Tchr., librarian Tupelo (Miss.) Mil. Inst., 1932-34; library asst. reading room Library of Congress, 1935, reference asst. Legislative Reference Service, 1936-43; economist editor U.S. Bur. Labor and Statistics, Washington, 1943-44; economist librarian U.S. Alien Property Custodian, 1944; economist librarian U.S. Fed. Home Loan Bank Adminstrn., 1945; reference librarian civics dept. Chgo. Pub. Library, 1946-47; research librarian Legislative Reference Bur., Honolulu, 1947-50; dir. Supreme Comdr. for Allied Powers Civil Information Edn., Information Center, U.S. Army, Okayama, Japan, 1950-52; bibliographer Air Univ. Library, Maxwell AFB, Ala., 1952-58, tech. asst. to dir., 1958-62, circulation librarian, 1962-65, med. service sch. librarian, 1965; chief librarian Breckinridge Library, USMC Edn. Center, Quantico, Va., 1966—. Chgo. Grad. Library Sch. scholar, 1945. Mem. Ala. Library Assn. (treas. 1962-63), Spl. (Ala. chpt., pres. 1960-61, editor Bull. 1955-56, chmn. mil. librarians div. 1968-69) Southeastern, Va. library assns. Democrat. Methodist. Editor: Union List of Serials in Honolulu Libraries, 1950; Alabama Librarian, 1957-59. Home: 18217 Possum Point Rd Dumfries VA 22026 Office: Breckinridge Library USMC Edn Center Quantico VA 22134

MCCOACH, BLAKE ALEXANDER, JR., newspaper editor; b. Middletown, N.Y., Oct. 17, 1920; s. Blake A. and Kathleen A. (Cute) McC.; student pub. schs.; m. Dorothy M. Marshall, May 16, 1943; children—Gary Alexander Alan Jeffrey. News, announcer Sta. WENY, Elmira, N.Y., 1945-46, WSLB, Ogdensburg, N.Y., 1946-47, WENT, Gloversville, N.Y., 1947-50, WABY, Albany, N.Y., 1950-57; columnist Hearst Times Union, Albany, 1955-57; pub. Dade County Times Union, Miami, Fla., 1960-64; became v.p., editor Hialeah (Fla.) Miami Springs Jour., 1965; pres., pub.-editor Greater Miami Jour., 1965—. Pub. relations Democratic Registration drive State of Fla., 1964. Served with USAAF, 1940-45. Mem. Broadcast Music. Methodist. Lyricist for songs, including Take Care of My Heart, Save the Last Waltz for Me, Lawrence Welk Polka, Forever and Ever and Ever, others. Home: 10271 SW 49th St Miami FL 33165 Office: 45 E 9th Ct Hialeah FL 33010

MCCOLLAM, WILLIAM, JR., utilities exec.; b. New Orleans, Mar. 15, 1925; s. William and Marie (Mason) McC; B.S. in Arts and Scis., La. State U., 1943; B.S. in Engring., U.S. Mil. Acad., 1946; M.S., Mass. Inst. Tech., 1954; m. Hope Flower Joffrion, Apr. 20, 1947; children—Ellen Dale, William Cage, Stephen Mason. Commd. 2d lt. C.E., U.S. Army, 1946, advanced through grades to lt. col., 1958; resigned, 1961; exec. asst. to pres. Ark. Power & Light Co., Little Rock, 1961-64, v.p., 1964-67, sr. v.p., dir., 1967-70; exec. v.p. New Orleans Pub. Service Inc., 1970-71, pres., chief exec. officer, 1971—, also dir.; dir. Middle South Utilities, Inc., Middle South Services, Inc., La. Power & Light Co., System Fuels, Inc., 1971—. Decorated Bronze Star medal. Episcopalian. Clubs: New Orleans Country, Internat. House, Boston, Plimsoll (New Orleans). Home: 1315 Webster St New Orleans LA 70118 Office: 317 Baronne St PO Box 60340 New Orleans LA 70160

MCCOLLOUGH, J.B., aerospace engr.; b. Webb, Okla., Sept. 25, 1930; s. Bill Bryan and Dorothy (Trogdon) McC.; student Central State Coll., Edmond, Okla., 1952-54; B.S. in Aero. Engring., U. Okla., 1956; m. Joyce Renee Pitt, Aug. 1, 1953; children—Val Jay, Lori Gay, Loretta Kay, Angela Fay. Flight test engr., aero-dynamicist Cessna Aircraft Co., Wichita, Kan., 1956-61; aerospace engr., flight test FAA Acad., Oklahoma City, 1961-65, tech. asst. to chief engring. and mfg., 1965-66, chief flight standards resident tng. devel., 1966-68; aerospace engr. Office Tng., FAA Hdqrs., Washington, 1968-71, program mgr. Sonic boom research, 1971—. Served with USMC, 1948-52. Registered profl. engr., Kan., Okla. Mem. Am. Inst. Aeros. and Astronautics, Sigma Gamma Tau. Club: Toastmasters. Home: 4125 Mason Ridge Dr Annandale VA 22003 Office: 800 Independence Av Washington DC 20553

MCCOLLOUGH, SAMUEL WARD, refining co. exec.; b. Chicora, Pa., Aug. 19, 1913; s. Oliver Merle and Hannah Elizabeth (Garing) McC.; student Pa. State U. Extension, 1936-39; m. Mary Elva Powell, Sept. 21, 1939; children—Janice K., Lee Ward, Randy Fred. With Pa. Refining Co., Karns City, 1931-41; foreman White Oil Treating Plant, Karns City, 1942-63; co-owner Mineral Oil Refining Co., Dickinson, Tex., 1942—, v.p., 1963—, dir., 1964—, chmn. profit sharing trust, 1968—. Mem. exec. com. Bay Area council Boy Scouts Am., 1960. Bd. dirs. Mainland United Fund, 1970-72; trustee Dickinson Ind. Sch. Dist., 1954-68, pres., 1964-68. Served with AUS, 1943-46. Mem. Tex. Mfrs. Assn. (chpt. pres. 1964), Dickinson C. of C. (dir. 1968-72, Sr. Man of Year 1963, 70), Order of Arrow. Methodist (chmn. bd. 1954). Mason, Rotarian (pres. 1971). Home: 5121 Oak Ct Dickinson TX 77539 Office: PO Drawer C Dickinson TX 77539

MCCOLLUM, EDWARD NEWTON, physician; b. San Antonio, Oct. 7, 1933; s. William Howard and Verda (Davis) McC.; grad. Ark. State Tchrs. Coll., Conway, 1954; M.D., U. Ark., 1958; m. Winona Christine Miller, Dec. 21, 1954; children—William E., Kim, Michelle, Michael, Kelly. Intern, St. Vincents Infirmary, Little Rock, 1959; gen. practice medicine McCollum Clinic, Decatur, Ark., 1959—; vol. med. expdn. to Guatemala with team from Duke, 1968. Dir. Decatur State Bank, Dunhall Pharms., Inc. Vice pres. Decatur Sch. Bd., 1962—; v.p., sec.-treas., dir. Decatur Devel. Com., 1968—. Mem. exec. bd. Benton County Republican Com., 1965-69. Bd. dirs. Gravette Manor Rest Home, 1964-69, Gravette Med. Center, 1968-70. Mem. Am., Ark. acads. gen. practitioners, Benton County Med. Assn. (past pres.), Ark. Simmental Cattle Assn. (founding dir.), Phi Alpha Zeta, Phi Sigma Pi. Presbyn. (elder). Mason (32 deg.), Elk. Home: School St Decatur AR 72722 Office: Box 127 Decatur AR 72722

MCCOLLUM, LEONARD F(RANKLIN), business exec.; b. Bradford, Tenn., Mar. 20, 1902; s. Samuel Winfield and Mary Isabelle (McDaniel) McC.; A.B., U. Tex., 1925; m. Margaret Wilson, Jan. 30, 1927; children—Olive Glennell, Leonard Franklin. Div. geologist Humble Oil & Refining Co., Amarillo and San Antonio, 1927-34; exploration mgr. Carter Oil Co., Tulsa, 1934-36, dir., 1936-38, v.p., dir., 1938-41, pres. 1941-43; asst. coordinator prodn., Standard Oil Co. (N.J.) and exec. v.p., Creole Petroleum Co., N.Y.C., 1943-44; coordinator, producing activities Standard Oil Co. (N.J.), 1944-47; pres., dir., Continental Oil Co., Ponca City, Okla., Houston, 1947-64, chmn. bd., 1964—, chief exec. officer, 1964-67; chmn. bd. Capital Nat. Bank, Houston; adv. dir. Morgan Guaranty Trust Co. N.Y. Trustee Cal. Inst. Tech., Bus. Council; mem. chancellors council U. Tex. Mem. Am. Petroleum Inst., Mid-Continent Oil and Gas Assn. (dir.), Am. Assn. Petroleum Geologists, Inst. Mining and Metall. Engrs. Clubs: Augusta National; Blind Brook; Bayou; Ramada, River Oaks Country; Houston, Petroleum (Houston). Home: 3435 Westheimer St Houston TX 77027 Office: PO Box 2197 Houston TX 76101

MCCOLLUM, RUBY INEZ MYERS (MRS. RUFUS K. MCCOLLUM), educator, lodge exec.; b. Tamaha, Okla., Nov. 4, 1914; d. Ola T. and Bursha Bell (Culver) Myers; B.S. in Edn., Northeastern State Coll., 1940, M. Teaching, 1955; m. Rufus K. McCollum, Dec. 31, 1937 (dec. Oct. 1966). Tchr. rural schs., Haskell County, Stigler, Okla., 1934-38, Adair County, Stillwell, Okla., 1946-50, Cherokee County, Tahlequah, Okla., 1939-46, 50-66; tchr. Westville (Okla.) Jr. High Sch., 1966-68, Westville High Sch., 1968—. Mem. Nat., Okla. edn. assns., Am. Legion Aux., Cherokee County 4-H Club Leaders (sec. 1964-66), Night Circle Womens Missionary Union (sec., 1965-66, pres., chmn. circle), Northeastern State Coll. Alumni Assn. (life), Kappa Kappa Iota (royal high lady Tahlequah 1953-55, exec. bd. Zeta conclave). Republican. Baptist (asso. supt., sec. beginners dept. Sunday sch., supt. various depts.). Rebekah (noble grand 1959-60, jr. noble grand 1960-61, lodge dep. 1961-63). Home: 215 S College St Tahlequah OK 74464 Office: Westville High Sch Westville OK 74965

MCCONNELL, ALVIN HAYGOOD, lawyer; b. Mobile, Ala., Apr. 23, 1909; s. Robert Haygood and Laura Gertrude (Tippin) McC.; student Auburn U., 1927-28; J.D., U. Ala., 1933; m. Adele Robins Hope, June 16, 1934; 1 dau., Adele Robins (Mrs. Thomas E. Perry III). Admitted to Ala. bar, 1933; since practiced in Mobile; asst. Ala. dist. atty., 1939-42; asst. U.S. dist. atty., 1943-45. Trustee Mobile chpt. Nat. Multiple Sclerosis Soc. Mem. Am., Fed., Ala., Mobile County (pres. 1962) bar assns., Ala. Trial Lawyers Assn., Mobile C. of C. Methodist (trustee). Kiwanian. Home: 23021/2 Dauphin St Mobile AL 36606 Office: Van Antwerp Bldg Mobile AL 36602

MCCONNELL, JOHN EDGAR, med. ins. exec.; b. Forks of Elkhorn, Ky., Aug. 14, 1914; s. Willie Gayle and Effie Ann (Goins) McC.; B.S., Eastern Ky. U., 1938; m. Anna Gene Wells, Nov. 5, 1938. Field scout exec. Boy Scouts Am., 1938-42; with Blue Cross and Blue Shield Ky., 1942—, pres., 1967—. Pres., McConnell Bros. Inc.; dir. Louisville Trust Co., Leisure Industries, Inc. Bd. dirs. Goodwill Industries Louisville, Louisville Automobile Assn. Served to lt. USNR, 1942-45. Recipient Outstanding Alumnus award Eastern Ky. U., 1966. Mem. Louisville C. of C. (pres. 1966), Louisville Sales and Marketing Execs. (pres. 1960), Alumni Assn. Eastern Ky. U. (pres. 1945). Presbyn. Rotarian (pres. Louisville 1967), Mason (Shriner). Home: 3320 Bardstown Rd Louisville KY 40218 Office: 3101 Bardstown Rd Louisville KY 40205

MCCONNELL, JOSEPH HOWARD, lawyer, bus. exec.; b. Chester, S.C., May 13, 1906; s. Joseph Moore and Eliza Howard (Riggs) McC.; A.B., Davidson (N.C.) Coll., 1927; LL.B., U. Va., 1931; m. Elizabeth H. Bernard, Oct. 31, 1936; children—Elizabeth (Mrs. Samuel Eells, Mary (Mrs. David Lowance), Catharine (Mrs. Tory Peterson). Admitted to Fla., N.C., N.Y. bars; practiced in Fla., N.C., 1931-33; atty. NRA, 1933-35; asso. law Cahill, Gordon, Zachry & Reindel, N.Y.C., 1935-41; with RCA, Camden, N.J., v.p. charge finance, exec. v.p., 1941-49; pres. NBC, 1949-52; pres. Colgate-Palmolive-Peet Co. 1953-55; gen. counsel, dir. Reynolds Metals Co., 1955-59, exec. v.p., 1959-63, pres. chief adminstrv. officer, 1963-71, now dir.; dir. Basic, Inc., Brit. Aluminum Co., Ltd., Canadian Reynolds Metals Co.; chmn. bd., dir. Communications Satellite Corp., 1971—. Rector bd. visitors U. Va. Mem. Phi Beta Kappa, Kappa Alpha. Presbyn. Clubs: Links, Blind Brook, Augusta National. Home: Bellona Midlothian VA 23113 Office: Reynolds Metals Bldg Richmond VA 23261 also 950 L'Enfant Plaza SW Washington DC 20054

MCCONNELL, RONALD CLEO, dentist; b. Stafford, Kan., Apr. 29, 1937; s. Cleo Carl and Jenny Lois (Wagner) McC.; Asso. Sci., Arlington State Jr. Coll., 1957; student Tex. Christian U., 1957-58; B.S., Tex. Wesleyan Coll., 1959; D.D.S., Baylor U., 1963, M.S.D., 1965; m. Patricia Anne Schmid, July 2, 1960; children—Ronald Todd, Patrick Sean. Resident in pedodontics Children's Med. Center, Dallas, 1963-65; practice dentistry for children, Richardson, Tex., 1965—. Asso. prof. pedodontics Baylor U. Coll. Dentistry, 1965-70. Active YMCA. Bd. dirs. Richardson Pub. Library, 1967-69. Diplomate Am. Bd. Pedodontics. Mem. Internat. Assn. Orthodontics, Am. Soc. Preventive Dentistry, Am., Tex., Dallas County (dir., dir. continuing edn. programs 1970-71) dental assns., Am. (certificate of merit 1963), Tex. (pres. 1970-71) socs. dentistry for children, Southwestern Soc. Dental Analgesia (pres. 1970-71), Southwestern Soc. Pedodontists, Greater Dallas (pres. 1968-69), Richardson (pres. 1970-71) dental study research groups, Baylor U. Grad. Pedodontic Alumni Assn. (pres. 1967-68), Delta Sigma Delta (dep. supreme grand master Baylor chpt. 1963—). Rotarian. Club: Toastmasters (Richardson); Royal Oaks Country, Lancers (Dallas). Home: 1222 Mohawk Trail Richardson TX 75080 Office: 204 S Cottonwood TX 75080

MCCONVILLE, EDWARD PATRICK, JR., banker; b. Albany, N.Y., Nov. 5, 1932; s. Edward Patrick and Anna Dolores (Leonard) McC.; student U. Notre Dame, 1950-53; J.D., Union U., 1956; m. Lois Ann Bessette, June 30, 1956; 1 son, Stephen Patrick. Admitted to N.Y. bar, 1958, Ind. bar, 1965, U.S. Supreme Ct. bar, 1969, D.C. bar, 1971; asst. house counsel AMF, Inc., N.Y.C., 1958-63; asst. counsel Lincoln Nat. Life Ins. Co., Fort Wayne, Ind., 1963-66; mem. office chief counsel Econ. Devel. Adminstrn., U.S. Dept. Commerce, Washington, 1966-68; sr. v.p. First Nat. Bank, Washington, 1968—. Bd. dirs. Cath. Youth Orgn., D.C., Model Cities Econ. Devel. Corp., D.C. Served with AUS, 1956-58. Home: 4903 Flint Dr Washington DC 20016 Office: 1701 Pennsylvania Av N W Washington DC 20006

MCCOOL, WOODFORD BETHEL, govt. ofcl.; b. McPherson, Kan., May 7, 1915; s. John H. and Nancy M. (Shirley) McC.; B.A., U. So. Cal., 1942; m. Lois Lucille Wells, Aug. 7, 1953; children—John Michael, Sandra Kim. Communications officer U.S. Mission to UN, 1946-51, for sec. 0f state 2d and 3d session UN Gen. Assembly, 1947-48; asst. dir. Exec. Office Sec. Def., 1951-53; asst. sec. of commn. AEC, Washington, 1943-54, sec. of commn., 1954—. Served to lt. USNR, World War II. Recipient Outstanding Service award AEC, 1957. Mem. Am. Soc. Pub. Adminstrn., Am. Polit. Sci. Assn. Democrat. Presbyn. Club: Kenwood Country (Washington). Home: 7501 Democracy Blvd Bethesda MD 20034 Office: Atomic Energy Commn Washington DC 20545

MCCORD, GUYTE PIERCE, JR., judge; b. Tallahassee, Sept. 23, 1914; s. Guyte Pierce and Jean (Patterson) McC.; student Davidson Coll., 1933-34; B.A., J.D., U. Fla., 1940; m. Laura Elizabeth Mack, Dec. 16, 1939; children—Florence Elizabeth, Guyte Pierce III, Edward LeRoy. Admitted to Fla. bar, 1940; practiced in Tallahassee, 1940-60; dep. commr. Fla. Insl. Commn., 1946-47, pros. atty. Leon County, 1947-48, asst. gen. counsel Fla. Pub. Service Commn., 1949-60; judge 2d Jud. Circuit Fla., Tallahassee, 1960—. Pres. Murat House Assn., Inc., 1967-69; bd. dirs. Fla. Heritage Found., 1969-70, mem. exec. com., 1965-69. Served to comdr. USNR, 1942-46, 52-53. Mem. Res. Officers Assn. (v.p. Tallahassee 1961-64), Tallahassee C. of C., Am. Legion, Fla. Conf. Circuit Judges (sec.-treas. 1970, chmn. 1972), Phi Delta Phi, Sigma Alpha Epsilon. Presbyn. (elder 1960—). Kiwanian (dir. 1958-59). Home: 502 S Ride St Tallahassee FL 32303 Office: PO Box 1028 Tallahassee FL 32302

MCCORD, MOLLIE ROYALL, lawyer, clubwoman; b. Atlanta; d. Claude Manley and Mollie (McCormick) McCord; B.A., Southwestern at Memphis; LL.B., Memphis State U., 1954. Owner, mgr. Meter Splty. Co., Memphis, 1941—; admitted to Tenn. bar, 1954; priorities and indsl. analyst WPB, Civilian Prodn. Adminstrn., Memphis, 1942-47; dir. Memphis Legal Aid Office, 1954-55; practiced in Memphis, 1954—. Pres. Memphis Art League, 1958-59, 63-64, Josephine Circle, 1954-55, Memphis Panhellenic Assn., 1946-47, Mid-Day Study Club, 1956-57, Women's Inter-Club Golf Assn., 1970; mem. Royal Club of Cotton Carnival, Soc. Preservation Tenn. Antiquities, Memphis Symphony League, In His Name II Circle, King's Daus. Mem. Tenn., Memphis, Shelby County bar assns., Brooks Art Gallery League, Delta Delta Delta (pres. local alumnae 1940-41, woman of year 1954), Phi Delta Delta. Presbyn. Clubs: Review (pres. 1967-69), Memphis Country (chmn. orgn. women golfers 1967); Chickasaw Garden (sec.). Home: 2909 Central Av Memphis TN 38111

MCCORD, ROBERT SANFORD, editor; b. Camden, Ark., Apr. 4, 1929; s. Mose Sanford and Myrtle (Hutchinson) McC.; B.J., U. Ark., 1951; M.S. in Journalism, Columbia, 1954; m. Muriel Helene Stuck, Dec. 16, 1951; children—Kim Sanford, Jeffrey Sanford, Stacey Elise. Reporter, Sunday mag. editor Ark. Democrat, Little Rock, 1954-57, asso. editor, v.p., dir., 1967—; editor, pub. North Little Rock (Ark.) Times, 1957-67; dir. First Nat. Bank of Little Rock. Trustee Little Rock U., 1965-70. Served with AUS, 1951-53. Mem. Ark. Press Assn. (treas. 1963—), Am. Soc. Newspaper Editors, Fgn. Policy Assn., North Little Rock C. of C., Blue Key, Kappa Sigma, Sigma Delta Chi (regional dir. 1968—). Methodist. Rotarian. Home: 2039 Topf Rd North Little Rock AR 72116 Office: 5th and Scott Sts Little Rock AR 72203

MCCORKINDALE, LAURENCE DANIEL, entomologist; b. Lexington, Mo., Mar. 12, 1909; s. Nicholas Quinn and Mary Annie (Peterson) McC.; A.A., Fullerton (Cal.) Dist. Coll., 1929; B.S., U. Ariz., 1932; m. Frances Adeline Benton, Mar. 24, 1956; 1 son, Kim Eugene. Sr. agrl. insp. Los Angeles County, 1936-59; agrl. commr., Butte County, Cal., 1959-60, Fresno County, Cal., 1960-66; dir. Food Orgn., Ariz. Div. Emergency Services, Phoenix, 1966—; dir., state entomologist Ariz. Commn. Agr. and Horticulture, Phoenix, 1966—. Chmn., Western Plant Bd.; exec. sec. Internat. Pink Bollworm Com.; mem. Nat. Plant Bd.; mem. Ariz. Legislative Fiscal Economist Adv. Com. Pres., San Joaquin Valley Agrl. Commrs. Assn., 1962-64; chmn. Fresno County Dept. Head Council, 1963; dir. student visitations from Nat. Sch. Agr., Mexico City, 1964-66. Recipient Distinguished Service award Kiwanis Internat., 1964; certificate appreciation Danish Creamery Assn., 1965. Mem. Entomol. Soc. Am., Nat. (chmn. plant industry com. 1971—), Western (sec.-treas.) assns. state depts. agr., Cal. Assn. Agrl. Commrs. (hon. life), Sigma Alpha Epsilon (life). Christian Scientist. Club: Commonwealth of Cal. (San Francisco). Home: 3425 E Mountain View Rd Phoenix AZ 85028 Office: 1688 W Adams St Phoenix AX 85007

MCCORKLE, CHARLES HOWARD, supt. schs.; b. Elizabethton, Tenn., Apr. 8, 1909; s. Arthur Emmert and Bessie D. (Williams) McC.; B.S., Milligan Coll., 1931, LL.D. (hon.), 1972; postgrad. E. Tenn. State U., 1932, State U. Ia., 1952, George Peabody Coll., 1938; M.A., Vanderbilt U., 1936; m. Elizabeth L. Connell, June 9, 1936; children—Nancy Williams (Mrs. Olan W. Hay), Elizabeth Louise (Mrs. Michael Ludwig). Elementary tchr. Johnson City (Tenn.) Pub. Schs., 1932-34, elementary prin., 1934-36, asst. prin. jr. high, 1936-41, prin. jr. high, 1941-42, prin. sr. high, 1942-52, supr., 1952-56, supt., 1956—. Mem. exec. com. Assn. Drug Edn., 1969-70; mem. Gov's. Com. for Mentally Retarded, 1967-70. Bd. dirs. Johnson City United Fund, 1950-60; trustee, mem. exec. com. Milligan Coll. Mem. N.E.A. (life), City Supts. Assn. (pres. 1960-62), Tenn. (pres. 1953), E. Tenn. (pres. 1964-65) edn. assns., Tenn. Secondary Sch. Athletic Assn. (legislative council 1958-66), Tenn. Supts. Study Council (chmn. curriculum com. 1963-70), Am., Tenn. (pres. 1964) assns. sch. adminstrs., Kappa Sigma. Mem. Christian Ch. (Bible Sch. supt. 1944-50). Kiwanian. Home: 427 Highland Av Johnson City TN 37601 Office: S Roan St Johnson City TN 37601

MCCORKLE, ELLIS REA, safety engr.; b. Sedalia, Mo.; s. William Earl and Sarah Blanche (Peters) McC.; student Clark U., 1943-44; B.C.E., Finlay Engring. Coll., 1948; student Internat. Corr. Schs., 1951-55; m. Katie Jeanette Brame, Apr. 20, 1946; children—Philip Rea, Cynthia Kay, Mark Ellis, Teresa Lee, Sarah Ann. Safety engr. Central Surety Ins. Corp., Little Rock, 1948-56; ground safety dir. 34th Air Div. Def., Albuquerque, 1956-58; asst. chief protection br. Gen. Services Adminstrn., Chgo., 1958-59; field engr. Johnson & Scott, Memphis, 1959-68; safety cons. indsl. process research and devel. Ellis R. McCorkle & Assos., North Little Rock, Ark., 1968—. Cons., lectr. in field. Served with AUS, 1942-46; ETO. Decorated Bronze Star. Registered profl. engr., Ark., N.M.; certified safety profl. Mem. Am. Soc. Safety Engrs., Nat. Soc. Profl. Engrs., Am. Soc. Heating, Refrigeration and Air Conditioning Engrs. Baptist (deacon). Club: Lakewood Outboard Boat (North Little Rock). Address: 1425 Garland Av North Little Rock AR 72116

MCCORKLE, JAMES LORENZO, JR., educator; b. Jackson, Miss., May 17, 1935; s. James L. and Lois (Wilson) M.; B.A. (Naval R.O.T.C. scholar), Auburn U., 1957; M.A. (Nat. Def. Edn. Act fellow), U. Miss., 1962, Ph.D., 1966. Asst. prof. history Northwestern State Coll., Natchitoches, La., 1966—, chmn. acad., profl. standards com., 1968-69. Served to lt. (j.g.) USNR, 1957-60. Mem. Am., So. hist. assns., Orgn. Am. Historians, Acad. Polit. Sci., Phi Alpha Theta, Phi Kappa Phi. Presbyn. (deacon 1968-72 elder 1972—). Home: Fleur de lis 100 S Williams Av Natchitoches LA 71457

MCCORMACK, AUSTIN FRANCIS, JR., pollution control co. exec.; b. Bklyn., Feb. 9, 1924; s. Austin Francis and Irene (Halligan) McC.; M.E., Stevens Inst., 1945; m. June Doyle, June 25, 1949; children—Austin III, William, Kathryn, Daniel, Thomas, Ann. Dist. engr. Permutit Co., Rochester, N.Y., 1946-49, dist. engr., Dallas, 1961-63; chief engr. Comml. Chem Products, Midland Park, N.J., 1959-61; formed McCormack Equipment Co., Dallas, 1963; pres. McCormack Corp., Dallas, 1967—; chmn. bd., dir. Automation Equipment & Controls Co. Inc., Dallas, 1968—. Neighborhood commr. Boy Scouts Am., 1961-67; co-chmn. Jesuit Sustentation Fund, 1968, 69, 71; pres. Bishop Lynch Athletic Assn., 1970. Served as ensign USNR, 1945-46. Registered profl. engr., Tex., Okla. Mem. Am. Water Works Assn., Water Pollution Control, Fedn., Tex. Soc. Profl. Engrs., Dallas C. of C. (water pollution com. 1969). Roman

Catholic. Club: Dallas Athletic. Patentee in field. Home: 9424 Sherwood Glen Dallas TX 75228 Office: 3505 Turtle Creek Blvd Dallas TX 75219

MCCORMACK, CAROL HARTFORD, financial exec.; b. Redfield, S.D., Jan. 15, 1920; s. Elliott Hartford and Inger Dorthea (Stapp) McC.; B.S., Drake U., 1953; postgrad. La. State U. Sch. Banking, 1957; m. Virginia Dare Rothgeb, June 12, 1946; 1 dau., Patricia Ann. Dist. mgr. Universal C.I.T. Credit Corp., Des Moines, 1946-50; v.p., controller La. Nat. Bank, Baton Rouge, 1953-56; cons. mgr. Ernst & Ernst, St. Louis, 1956-59; exec. v.p., dir. Am. Nat. Bank, Portsmouth, Va., 1959-60; treas. Merc. Mortgage Co., St. Louis, 1960-62; sr. industry analyst IBM, N.Y.C., 1962-67; financial v.p. Waddell & Reed, Inc., Kansas City, Mo., 1967-68; self-employed as financial cons., Kansas City, Mo., 1968-69, Houston, 1969—; founder, owner, operator C.H. McCormack & Assos., Inc., Houston, 1971—. Cons. various banks and domestic corps. Bd. dirs., trustee Low Heywood Sch., Stamford, Conn. Served to capt. AUS, World War II; PTO. Decorated Bronze Star with oak leaf cluster. Clubs: Stamford (Conn.) Yacht, Brookridge Country (Overland Park, Kan.). Author: Bank Investment Portfolio, 1964; Bond Trade Analysis Program, 1964; Optimum Bond Bidding Program, 1966; Accounting for Debt Securities, 1972. Inventor portfolio control system, inter-portfolio trade locater. Home: 811 Patchester Dr Houston TX 77024

MCCORMACK, JAMES, ret. air force officer, industry exec.; b. Chatham, La., Nov. 8 1910; s. James and Mary E. (Garner) McC.; grad. Riverside Mil. Acad., 1928; B.S., U.S. Mil. Acad., 1932; postgrad. Oxford U., 1935, Mass. Inst. Tech., 1937; m. Eleanor Morrow, May 15, 1936; children—Ann Martha (Mrs. James Stanton), James Rudolph. Served in army engrs. and air force in successive grades from 2d lt. to maj. gen., 1932-55; former v.p. Mass. Inst. Tech.; chmn. chief exec. officer Communications Satellite Corp., 1965-70; chmn. bd. Aerospace Corp., 1970—; dir. COMSAT, Bulova Watch Co., Eastern Air Lines. Decorated D.S.M. and other U.S. and fgn. medals. Baptist. Home: 1001 Wilson Blvd Arlington VA 22209 Office: L'Enfant Plaza SW Washington DC 20036

MCCORMACK, JAMES STUCKEY, mgmt. cons.; b. Peru, Ill., Mar. 12, 1931; s. Joseph Hume and Eva (Stuckey) McC.; B.S. in Mech. Engring., 1953; M.S. in Indsl. Engring, Ohio State U., 1956; postgrad. in statistics N.C. State U., 1966-67; m. Elayne Parrish, Dec. 4, 1964; children—James Parrish, Hallie Suzanne. Mech. engr., E.I. du Pont de Nemours & Co., Inc., Wilmington, Del., 1953-54; plant engr. Corning Glass Works, (N.Y.), 1956-58, product engr., 1958-61, dist. sales mgr., 1961-64, plant indsl. engr., 1964-66; mgmt. cons. G.A. Schwenk & Asso., Inc., Charlotte, N.C., 1966—. Faculty, Queen's Coll., Charlotte, 1968-69. Mem. personnel com. Mercy Hosp. Served with USAF, 1954-56. Mem. Am. Hosp. Assn., Nat. Assn. Bus. Economists, Am. Inst. Indsl. Engrs., Nat. Soc. Profl. Engrs. Republican. Baptist. Contbr. articles to tech. jours. Home: 1009 Bearmore Dr Charlotte NC 28211 Office: 2915 Providence Rd Charlotte NC 28211

MCCORMICK, EDWARD MACK, govt. ofcl.; b. Neck City, Mo., June 7, 1920; s. Edward Franklin and Ida (McKay) McC.; B.S., Kan. State Coll. at Pittsburg, 1941, M.S., 1947; Ph.D., Am. U., 1970; m. Cleta Gail Steward, Nov. 7, 1943; children—Susan, Patti. Tech. editor Nat. Radio Inst., Washington, 1946-49; electronic engr. Goodyear Aircraft Corp., Akron, O., 1949-51; with U.S. Naval Ordnance Lab., Corona, Cal., 1951-59, head data assessment div., 1955-59; asso. program dir. NSF, Washington, 1959-64, head data processing center 1964-68; with Office Information Systems, Dept. Agr., Washington, 1968—. Lectr. U. Cal. at Los Angeles, 1955-59; profl. lectr. Am. U., 1960—. Served with USAAF, 1943-46. Mem. Assn. for Computing Machinery. Democrat. Mem. Disciples of Christ Ch. Author: Digital Computer Primer, 1959. Contbr. chpt. to book, articles to profl. jours. Home: 8720 Ewing Dr Bethesda MD 20034 Office: Office Information Systems Dept Agr Washington DC 20250

MCCORMICK, JOHN HOYLE, judge; b. Pensacola, Fla., July 30, 1933; s. Clyde H. and Orrie B. (Frink) McC.; B.S., U. Fla., 1955; J.D., Stetson U., 1958. Admitted to Fla. bar, 1958, U.S. Supreme Ct. bar, 1964; practice law, White Springs, Fla., 1958-60, Jasper, Fla., 1960—; mayor White Springs, 1959-60; county judge Hamilton County, Fla., 1960—; atty. Hamilton County Bank, Jasper, 1966—, v.p., 1968—; also dir.; dir. First Fed. Savs. & Loan Assn., Live Oak, Fla.; local counsel So. Ry. System, 1967—; atty. Hamilton County Devel. Authority, 1966—; approved loan closing atty. First Fed. Savs. & Loan Assn., Live Oak, Fed. Land Bank of Columbia, S.C., VA, Farmers Home Adminstrn., John Hancock Mut. Life Ins. Co.; approved atty. Lawyers Title Ins. Corp., Richmond, Va., Lawyers' Title Guaranty Fund, Orlando, Fla., Title & Trust Co. Fla., Jacksonville, Peninsular Title Ins. Co., Jacksonville. Mem. Hamilton County C. of C. (pres. 1961), Am. Bar Assn., Fla. Bar, Am. Arbitration Assn., Fla. County Judge's Assn., Phi Delta Phi. Methodist. Kiwanian. Mason. Club: Suwanee River Valley Country (dir. Jasper). Address: PO Drawer O Jasper FL 32052

MCCORMICK, RONALD ROBERT, psychologist; b. Chgo., June 19, 1929; s. Robert D. and Gladys (Swain) McC.; B.S., Northwestern U. 1951, M.A., 1952; postgrad. North Tex. State U., 1959-62; m.2Shirlee B. Boggs, Sept. 5, 1952 (div. 1964); children—Brian, Kelly, Melinda; m. 2d, Barbara Anderson, Aug. 30, 1968; 1 son, Daniel. Psychologist, Dallas County Juvenile Ct., Dallas, 1957-61; sr. human factors psychologist System Devel. Corp., Paramus N.J., 1961-62; lead human factors psychologist Ling-Temco-Vought Corp., Dallas, 1962-66; engr.-scientist Tracor., Inc., Austin, Tex., 1966-67; vocational rehab. psychologist Fla. Dept. Edn., Ft. Lauderdale, 1967; research asso. and asst. dir. testing and evaluation Fla. Atlantic U., Boca Raton, 1967—; cons. Western Union Computer Utilities Corp., Ft. Lauderdale, 1968—; pres., founder Internat. Data Interchange, Inc., Boca Raton, Fla., 1969—, Trademark Design Products, Inc., Boca Raton, 1970—. Personnel cons. Broward County Mfrs. Assn., Ft. Lauderdale, 1967-69. Served to capt. USAF, 1952-57. Mem. Am. Psychol. Assn., Am. Ednl. Research Assn., Phi Delta Kappa. Co-author: Broward County Computer-Assisted Wage and Salary Survey; author Mastery-Commitment Education; The McCormick Job Performance Measurement Rate--Scales. Home: 97 NW 12th Av Boca Raton FL 33432 Office: Testing and Evaluation Center Fla Atlantic U Boca Raton FL 33432

MCCORMICK, WILLIE MAE WARD (MRS. WALTER WITTEN MCCORMICK), tech. specialist; b. Centerville, Tex. Oct. 17, 1908; d. William Sylvester and Lucy (Marshall) Ward; B.A., Mary Hardin Baylor Coll., 1929; M.A., Hardin Simmons U., 1931; postgrad. So. Methodist U., Tex. Woman's U.; m. Walter Witten McCormick, May 29, 1929; 1 dau., Elizabeth Ward (Mrs. Billy Joe Wilcox). Tchr. chemistry and algebra Big Spring (Tex.) High Sch., 1941-44, 45-48; analytical chemist Dow Chem. Co., Freeport, 1944-45; calculator Chance Vought (now Ling-Temco-Vought), Dallas, 1951-55, structural engr., 1955-63, sci. programmer, 1963-67, tech. specialist, 1967-69; sr. program analyst Univ. Computing Co., Arlington, Tex., 1970—. Mem. A.A.A.S., Assn. Computing Machinery, Math. Assn. Am., Soc. Indsl. and Applied Math., Fedn. Am. Scientists, Am. Assn. U. Women (treas.); Am. Soc. Information Sci., Trainmen's Aux. (pres. 1940-41). Democrat. Baptist (supt. adult dept. Sunday sch.). Mem. Order Eastern Star (past worthy matron). Home: Route 1 Box 66 Euless TX 76039 Office: Computer Technology Arlington TX 76010

MCCOTTER, BURNEY RICHARD, life ins. co. exec.; b. Grantsboro, N.C., Feb. 9, 1920; s. John Lawrence and Flora (Tingle) M.; A.B., Atlantic Christian Coll., 1941; grad. exec. program U. N.C., 1965; m. Margaret R. Palmer, June 21, 1946; children—Richard, Karen. Tchr. high sch., N.C., 1941-42; agt. Jefferson Standard Life Ins. Co., 1946-47, 48-50; gen. agt. Franklin Life Ins. Co., 1947-48; mgr. Occidental Life Ins. Co., N.C., 1950-52, agy. asst., Raleigh, 1952-55, agy. sec., 1955-60, asst. v.p., 1960-64, v.p., 1964, v.p., sec., 1964-66, v.p. operations, 1966-70, sr. v.p., 1970—. Served to 1st lt. USAAF, 1942-46. Decorated Air medal with two oak leaf clusters. C.L.U. Mem. Am. Soc. Chartered Life Underwriters (chpt. pres. 1961), Atlantic Christian Coll. Alumni Assn. (past pres.), Soc. for Preservation and Encouragement Barber Shop Quartet Singing in Am. Democrat. Presbyn. (deacon 1960-64, elder 1969—). Kiwanian. Club: Carolina Country. Home: 332 Buncombe St Raleigh NC 27609 Office: 1001 Wade Av Raleigh NC 27605

MCCOTTER, MARGARET ROSEMOND PALMER (MRS. BURNEY RICHARD MCCOTTER), librarian; b. Thomasville, N.C., Nov. 7, 1921; d. Jacob Alexander and Etna (Little) Palmer; A.B., Catawba Coll., 1942; B.S., U. N.C., 1944; m. Burney Richard McCotter, June 21, 1946; children—Richard Palmer, Karen Ellen. Librarian So. Pines (N.C.) Sch. System, 1944-47; post librarian Fort Story (Va.), 1950-51; librarian LeRoy Martin Jr. High Sch., Raleigh, N.C., 1959-62, 65—; library cons. N.C. Dept. Pub. Instrn., Raleigh, 1963-65. Mem. N.E.A., United Daus. Confederacy, N.C. Library Assn., N.C. Assn. Educators, Beta Phi Mu, Sigma Pi Alpha. Democrat. Presbyn. Club: Carolina Country (Raleigh). Author: (with others) AV Cataloging and Processing Simplified, 1971. Editor: Reference Materials for School Libraries, 1965. Home: 332 Buncombe St Raleigh NC 27609 Office: 1701 Ridge Rd Raleigh NC 27607

MCCOWAN, R(OBERT) T(AYLOR), oil co. exec.; b. Carlisle, Ky., July 29, 1928; s. William Ray and Susan (Taylor) McC.; B.S., U. Ky., 1951; postgrad. U. Ill., 1964; m. Nyle Eleanor Yates, Dec. 6, 1953; children— David Wayne, Susan Jill. With Ashland Oil, Inc., 1951—, salesman, Cin., 1951-54, div. mgr., Chgo., 1954-59, spl. rep., Ashland, Ky., 1959-64, asst. mgr. refinery sales, 1964-65, exec. asst., 1965-67, v.p., 1967-68, adminstrv. v.p., 1968-70, sr. v.p., 1970-72, exec. v.p., 1972—, also dir. Active Ashland (Ky.) YMCA, 1963—. Mem. Am. Petroleum Inst., Nat. Petroleum Refiners Assn., Ashland (dir.), Ky. chambers commerce, Asphalt Inst. (dir.), U. Ky. Alumni Assn. (pres. Boyd County), Omicron Delta Kappa, Beta Gamma Sigma (dir.'s table), Delta Tau Delta. Mem. Christian Ch. Club: Bellefonte. Home: 2311 Forest Av Ashland KY 41101 Office: 1409 Winchester Av Ashland KY 41101

MCCOWN, JAMES KIMBOL, dentsit; b. Philadelphia, Miss., Sept. 14, 1915; s. James Monroe and Lou Ada (Green) McC.; student Miss. State U., 1935-37, U. Miss., 1937-38; D.D.S., Loyola U. of South, New Orleans, 1943; m. Mary Victoria Lee, Sept. 8, 1940. Practice dentistry, Amory, Miss., 1946—; pres. Glendale, Inc., Amory, 1970—; owner Glendale Shopping Center, Amory, 1970—. Served with Dental Corps, AUS, 1943-46. Mem. Am. Dental Assn., Miss., Northeast Miss. dental socs. Democrat. Baptist. Home: 808 Town and Country Lane Amory MS 38821 Office: 107 N 3d St Amory MS 38821

MCCOWN, THEODORE VEDELL, JR., govt. ofcl.; b. Johnson City, Tenn., Jan. 14, 1932; s. Theodore Vedell and Sarah (Brown) McC.; B.S., E. Tenn. State U., 1953; m. Jane Rector McCown, Jan. 6, 1955; 1 dau., Sarah Jane. Office mgr. Gen. Shale Products Corp., Kingsport, Tenn., 1956-62; adminstrv. asst. to city mgr. City of Kingsport, Tenn., 1962-69, dir. personnel and pub. relations, 1969—, asst. city mgr., 1972—. Chmn. comml. div. United Fund Campaign, 1970, gen. chmn., 1971. Chmn. bd. Appalachian Preaching Mission, 1967, area chmn., 1968—; bd. dirs., area chmn., publicity dir. Nat. Found.-March of Dimes; bd. dirs. A.R.C., Community Aid Agy., Community Chest of Kingsport. Served with AUS, 1954-56. Mem. United Comml. Travelers, Alpha Phi Omega. Presbyn. (deacon, elder). Moose Club: Sertoma (pres. 1963, chmn. bd. 1964). Home: 3833 Telstar Dr Kingsport TN 37664 Office: 225 W Center St Kingsport TN 37660

MCCOY, ARTHUR, broadcasting exec. Pres., WQXI, WQXI-FM, Atlanta. Address: 2970 Peachtree Rd NW Atlanta GA 30305*

MCCOY, FRANCIS TYRONE, educator; b. N.Y.C., Oct. 15, 1922; s. Francis Thomas and Gladys (Parker) McC.; B.A. Fla U., 1944, M.A., 1947, J.D., 1955; postgrad. (fellow) Yale Law Sch., 1963-64. Admitted to Fla. bar 1955; vice consul U.S. Fgn. Service, 1947-52; asst. law librarian U. Fla., Gainesville 1955-56, law librarian, 1956-62, asst. prof. law, 1956-65, asso. prof., 1965-70, prof., 1970—. Served to 2d lt. AUS, 1943-45; lt. col. Res. Mem. Fla. Bar, Phi Beta Kappa, Kappa Alpha. Episcopalian. Home: 28 NW 36th St Gainesville FL 32601

MCCOY, GENE GUY, advt. exec; b. Oskaloosa, Ia., May 11, 1926; s. Guy Gene and Edith (Seaman) McC.; B.B.A., U. Wis., 1951; M.A. in Marketing, State U. Ia., 1952; m. Idella Maria Brown, Aug. 8, 1947; children—Gene Guy III, Vicki V., Randi R., S. Sherman. Advt. mgr. W.M. McAllister Co., Sycamore, Ill., 1952-53; account exec. Gerald T. LeFever & Assos., Little Rock, 1953-55, partner, 1956-57; pres. Ad Craft of Ark., Inc., Little Rock, 1958—. Asst. prof., chmn. dept. advt. U. Ark. at Little Rock. Mem. Ark. Atty. Gen.'s Study Com. for Consumer Protection Legislation; cons Model Cities Program. Served with AUS, 1944-47. Named Ark. Traveler, 1969. Mem. Am. Advt. Fedn. (dir. 10th dist. 1958—, gov. 10th dist. 1969-70, nat. dir. 1969-70, lt. gov. 1968-69), Pub. Relations Soc. Am., Little Rock Advt. Club (pres. 1958-60), A.I.M. (pres. council), Am. Marketing Assn., Alpha Delta Sigma (nat. v.p. 1971-72), Alpha Kappa Psi, Sigma Alpha Epsilon. Author publs. in field. Home: 12000 Rivercrest Dr Little Rock AR 72207 Office: 3d and Cross St Little Rock AR 72203

MCCOY, IDELLA MARIA THERESA BROWN (MRS. GENE GUY MCCOY), bus. exec.; b. Woodriver, Ill., July 21, 1928; d. Mayo Clinton and Loretta (Weisaupt) Brown; student Shurtleff Coll., Ill., 1946-48; m. Gene Guy McCoy, Aug. 8, 1948; children—Gene Guy III, Vicki V., Randall R., S. Sherman. Prodn. mgr. Ad Craft of Ark., Inc., Little Rock, 1958, sec.-treas., 1958-65, exec. v.p., 1965—. Residential chmn. United Fund Pulaski County, 1962-63, pub. relations, 1969. Mem. Am. Advt. Fedn. (dir. S.W. dist.), Little Rock Advt. Club (pres. 1970-71), Gamma Alpha Chi (Spl. Service award 1969). Home: 12000 Rivercrest Dr Little Rock AR 72207 Office: 1122 W 3d St Little Rock AR 72201

MCCOY, JEROME DEAN, physicist, educator; b. Liberty, Mo., Feb. 28, 1931; A.B., William Jewell Coll., 1952; M.A., U. Mo., 1957; Ph. D., Helsinki U., 1964; m. 1954; 2 children. Instr. physics U. Mo., 1957-58; asst. prof. U. Tulsa, 1958—. Cons., N. Am. Aviation, Inc. Mem. A.A.A.S., Assn. Physics Tchrs. Address: 3104 E 48th Pl Tulsa OK 74105*

MCCOY, JOSEPH HENRY, JR., dentist; b. Norfolk, Va., Feb. 15, 1933; s. Joseph Henry and Frances Louise (Rogers) McC.; A.A., Coll. William and Mary, 1953; B.S., Med. Coll. Va., 1956, D.D.S., 1957; m. Shirley Mae Perry, Mar. 31, 1956; children—Yvonne Vicki, Sheryl Anne. Pvt. practice dentistry, Virginia Beach, Va., 1959—. Pres., Haven Heights Civic League, 1965-68. Bd. visitors Old Dominion U.; bd. dirs., vice-chmn. Tidewater Community Coll. Served to capt. Dental Corps, USAF, 1957-59. Mem. Virginia Beach (pres. 1970), Tidewater (exec. committeeman 1970—) dental socs. Mason (Shriner), Lion. Home: 4041 Sherwood Lane Virginia Beach VA 23455 Office: 4920 Virginia Beach Blvd Virginia Beach VA 23462

MCCOY, WILLIAM HENRY, III, coll. pres.; b. Jacksonville, Fla., Feb. 8, 1928; s. William Henry and Thelma (Windham) McC.; B.A. in History, U. Fla., 1949, M.Ed. in Adminstrn., 1966, Specialist's Certificate in Adminstrn., 1967, Ed.D. in Coll. Adminstrn., 1968; m. Diane Christine Grieco, June 9, 1962. Tchr. Fla. pub. schs. Dade County, 1955-56, Duval County, 1957-61; dir. news bur. Jacksonville U., 1961-62, dir. placement, 1962-64, registrar, 1964-66; spl. asst. to pres., asst. prof. edn. U. Fla., Gainesville, 1968-69; pres. Lord Fairfax Community Coll., Middletown, Va., 1969—. Pres. St. Thomas Chapel Trust, Middletown, 1971—. Bd. dirs. Va. Nat. Trust for Hist. Preservation. Served with AUS, 1950-53; Far East. Mem. So. Coll. Placement Assn., Phi Delta Kappa, Phi Kappa Phi, Phi Delta Theta, Blue Key. Rotarian. Home: Route 2 Box 172B Berryville VA 22611 Office: PO Drawer E Middletown VA 22645

MCCRABB, LOUISE BOOTHE (MRS. J.F. MCCRABB), ret. educator; b. Cuero, Tex.; d. Sterling Price and Belle (Jolley) Boothe; B.A., Sul Ross State Coll., 1958, M.A., 1961; M.L.S., Tex. Woman's U., 1962; archivist studies U. Denver, 1969; m. J.F. McCrabb, Apr. 29, 1946 (dec. 1954). Tchr. pub. schs., Cuero, Tex., 1932-37, 54-60; instr. library sci., librarian Sul Ross State Coll., Alpine, Tex., 1962-64, asst. prof. library sci. and history, 1964—. Mem. Tex. Library Assn., Tex. Tchrs. Assn., Tex. Assn. Coll. Tchrs., Am. Assn. U. Profs., Tex., El Paso hist. socs., Phi Alpha Theta, Kappa Delta Pi, Delta Kappa Gamma, Tau Kappa Epsilon. Club: Hawthorne Study (pres. 1956-57) (Cuero). Home: W 368 Shadow Mountain Dr Apt 232 El Paso TX 79912

MCCRACKEN, FRANKLIN ALLEN, banker; b. Covington, Ky., Sept. 6, 1901; s. Clarence C. and Lucy (Swindler) McC.; grad. high sch.; m. Margaret Teegarden, Aug. 30, 1930; children—Joyce (Mrs. Robert B. Patrick), Ruth Ann (Mrs. Gilbert D. Cheatham). With Fifth Third Bank, Cin., 1920-29; pres., trust officer Newport (Ky.) Nat. Bank, 1929—. Mem. No. Ky. C. of C. Mason, Optimist. Club: Highland Country (Ft. Thomas, Ky). Home: 234 S Fort Thomas Av Fort Thomas KY 41075 Office: PO Box 190 Newport KY 41072

MCCRACKEN, JOSEPH GLENN, supt. schs.; b. Fairview, N.C., Oct. 21, 1913; s. Cicero McAfee and Laura Helen (Clayton) McC.; A.B., Wake Forest U., 1938; M.A., U. N.C., 1942; LL.D., Limestone Coll., 1957; m. Katherine Frenger Mason, Dec. 16, 1939; children—Katherine Mason, Jo Ann. Tchr. high sch., Greensboro, N.C., 1938-40; dean of boys Needham Broughton High Sch., Raleigh, 1940-41; prin. Elizabeth City High Sch., 1941-44, supt., Elizabeth City pub. schs., 1944-49; dir. div. ins. N.C. State Bd. Edn., 1949-50; supt. schs., Spartanburg, S.C., 1950—. Edn. cons. sch. dist. reorgn. finance, architecture.; commr. Edn. Commn. of States, Compact for Edn., 1966-68. Mem. Spartanburg Planning Commn., 1965-69. Bd. dirs., mem. planning bd. Spartanburg YMCA; council assos. Wofford Coll.; bd. dirs. S.C. Blue Cross-Blue Shield. Recipient outstanding service certificate Am. Econ. Found., 1962, citizen's distinguished service award Wofford Coll., 1968, outstanding service award Spartanburg Civitan Club 1969. Mem. S.C. Edn. Assn. (pres. 1967-68), S.C. (pres. 1944-45), Am. (bd. dirs. nat. acad. sch. execs. 1968—) assns. sch. adminstrs., Appalachian Regional Ednl. Adv. Com., S.C. Congress Parents and Tchrs., Wake Forest U. Alumni Assn. (pres. 1961-62; spl. merit award 1961-62). Methodist. Rotarian (pres. 1957-58). Author: (with Am. Assn. Sch. Adminstrs. Commn.) State Associatons of School Administrators, 1968. Contbr. articles to profl. pubs. Home: 144 Shoreham Rd Spartanburg SC 29302 Office: Spartanburg City Schools PO Box 970 Spartanburg SC 29301

MCCRACKEN, JOSEPH HILL, III, lawyer; b. Dallas June 12, 1927; s. Joseph Hill and Mary Frances (Hall) McC.; B.S., Okla. A. and M. Coll., 1950; LL.B., So. Methodist U., 1956. Admitted to Tex. bar, 1956; asso. firm Carrington, Gowan, Johnson, Bromberg & Leeds, Dallas, 1956-58; partner firm Hughes, Donosky, McCracken & Hunt, Dallas, 1958- 63, McCulloch, Ray, Trotti & Hemphill, Dallas, 1963-66; practiced in Dallas, 1966—. Mem. com. edn. Southwestern Law Jour., So. Meth. U., 1955-56, now cons, Mem. S.A.R., Sons Republic of Tex., Tex. Bar, Dallas Bar Assn. (sec-treas., dir. 1958), Nat. (dir. 1965-69), Tex. (hon. life dir.) skeet shooting assns. Huguenot Soc., Am. Soc. Arms Collectors, Barristers, Sigma Alpha Epsilon, Delta Theta Phi. Methodist. Clubs: Dallas Gun (dir. 1963—), Terpsichorean, Idlewild. Contbg. biog. author Tex. State Hist. Assns.'s. Handbook of Texas-Supplement, 1969. Home: 4401 Highland Dr Dallas TX 75205 Office: 211 North Ervay Bldg Dallas TX 75201

MCCRANIE, RUDOLPH GERALD, dentist; b. West Palm Beach, Fla., Mar. 28, 1935; s. Rudolph Guyton and Bessie Pauline (Walker) McC.; student Mercer U., 1953-55; D.D.S., Emory U., 1959; m. Norma Sue Frye, Dec. 22, 1956; children—Susan Elizabeth, Virginia Carol, Melissa Leigh, Jerri Elaine. Pvt. practice dentistry, Adel, Ga., 1961—. Mem. adv. staff Gov. Carter, 1971—; rep. city of Adel, Coastal Plains Area Planning and Devel. Commn., Valdosta, Ga., 1970-71; chmn. Citizens Adv. Com., Adel, 1969-71. Adv. staff Rep. Bill Stuckey, 1967-71. Served to lt. Dental Corps, USNR, 1959-61. Mem. Am., Ga. dental assns., Sigma Nu, Psi Omega. Democrat. Baptist. Club: Circlestone Country (dir.). Home: 724 S Forrest St Adel GA 31620 Office: 206 E Memorial Dr Adel GA 31620

MCCRARY, DENNIE LOCKHART, real estate devel. co. exec.; b. Macon, Ga., Mar. 7, 1938; s. Dennie Lockhart and Mary Marguerite (Barksdale) McC.; B.S., U.S. Naval Acad., 1960; M.B.A., Harvard, 1966; m. Frances Roberta Parker, June 24, 1961; children—Jennifer Lane, Thomas Parker, Catherine Barksdale. Asst. to pres. Sea Pines Co. real estate devel., resort operations, Hilton Head Island, S.C., 1966-68, v.p. finance, 1968-70, v.p. finance, gen. mgr., 1970-71, exec. v.p., 1972—; dir. Sea Pines Co., First Carolina Bank, Beaufort, S.C. Trustee Sea Pines Acad. Served to 1st lt. USAF, 1960-64. Decorated Air Force Commendation Medal. Mem. Hilton Head Jr. C. of C., Hilton Head C. of C. (v.p.). Presbyn. (deacon). Rotarian, Toastmaster. Home: 8 Surf Scoter Rd Hilton Head Island SC 29928 Office: Sea Pines Co Hilton Head Island SC 29928

MCCRARY, GEORGE AUTREY, physician; b. Nashville, Ark., Aug. 31, 1939; s. Matthew Marcellus and Addie Mae (Young) McC; student U. Ark., 1957-60, M.D., 1964; m. Mary Ann Frizzell, Aug. 25, 1961; children— George Autrey, Jr., Mary Lynn. Intern, Bapt. Med. Center, Little Rock, 1964-65; physician Johnson Durham Clinic, Jacksonville, Ark., 1967-71, Durham-McCrary, P.A., Jacksonville, 1971—; mem. staffs Rebsamen Meml. Hosp., Jacksonville, Ark. Meml. Hosp., North Little Rock. Mem. Ark. Merit System Council, 1969-71. Served with USNR, 1965-67. Mem.

Jacksonville C. of C. (dir.) Ark., Pulaski County med. socs., A.M.A. Baptist (trustee). Home: 1 Red Fox Lane Jacksonville AR 70276 Office: 2 Crestview Plaza Jacksonville AR 70276

MCCRARY, MARY JANE KING (MRS. CARL MCCRARY), historian; b. Brevard, N.C.; d. Alexander Henry and Hessie (Clayton) King; student Furman U. (formerly Greenville Woman's Coll.), 1915-17; Mus. Arts, Tift Coll., 1918; m. Hugh R. Walker, Oct. 1, 1920 (dec.) children—John S., Jane (Mrs. Jon T. Freeman); m. 2d, Carl McCrary, Jan. 20, 1931; children—Thomas K., Martha (Mrs. Joseph W. McGuire, Jr.). Tchr. pub. sch. music, Brevard Schs., 1923-25; owner, mgr. Walker Ins. Agy., 1929-57; pres. Brevard Bd. of Realtors, 1964-65; mem. Nat. Real Estate Bd. County chmn. blood com. A.R.C.; mem. N.C. Am. Revolution Bicentennial Commn., N.C. Confederate Centennial Commn.; chmn. Transylvania County Hist. Commn., 1960—. Recipient Blue, purple ribbons for paints, ceramic works. Mem. Cherokee Hist. Assn. (mem. exec. bd.), Nat. Soc. Am. Colonists, D.A.R., League Am. Pen Women, N.C., Western N.C. hist. assns. Episcopalian. Home: 228 Maple St Brevard NC 28712 Office: 37 W Jordan St Brevard NC 28712

MCCRAW, GORDON DEW, resort exec.; b. Lynchburg, Va., Oct. 22, 1913; s. Robert Lee and Ella Blanche (Sampson) McC; student Fla. So. Coll., 1947-48, Fla. State U., 1948-49; m. Catherine Lydia Chamberlain, Jan. 10, 1945; 1 dau., Leila Rae (Mrs. James Mack Barron, III). Salesman, Connor Produce Co., Lynchburg, 1937-41; mgr. J.H. Chamberlain Hotels, Ocean Grove, N.J., Lake Alfred, Fla., Asheville, N.C., 1945-50, Ponte Vedra (Fla.) Surf Club, 1950, Timuquana Country Club, Jacksonville, Fla., 1951, Courtney Restaurants, Atlanta, 1952, Morrison's Cafeteria Co., Imperial House Restaurants, Daytona Beach, St. Petersburg Beach, West Palm Beach, Orlando (all Fla.), 1952-55; mgr., supr. Slater System, Inc., Atlanta, Danville, Va., Dayton, O., 1955-57; relief mgr. Howard Johnson Restaurants, Miami, Fla., 1957; mgr. M&M Cafeteria Co., Miami, 1957-58, Nantahala Village, Bryson City, N.C., 1960—; resort mgr. Bryson City Duval Hotel, Tallahassee, 1958-60. Served with USAAF, 1937-41, 41-45. Mem. Am., N.C. hotel and motel assns. Presbyn. Rotarian, Mason. Home: 127 Lipona Rd Tallahassee FL 32304 Office: Nantahala Village Bryson City NC 28713

MCCRAY, WILLIAM EDWARD, educator; b. Memphis, Sept. 20, 1930; s. Charlie C. and Ethel (Davis) McC.; B.S., LeMoyne Coll., 1955, M.A., N.Y.U., 1957, Ph.D., 1963; student Valentina Litvinoff Studio of Dance 1960-63; M.A., Tchrs. Coll., Columbia U., 1970. Instr. speech, drama Miss. Vocational Coll., Itta Bena, 1957-58; instr. English and drama St. Paul's Coll., Lawrenceville, Va., 1958-59; asso. prof. English, dancer, choreographer, asso. dir. Orchesis, modern dance group, Grambling (La.) Coll., 1963—. Served with AUS, 1952-54. Mem. Am. Assn. U. Profs., Speech Communication Assn. Am., Am. Dance Guild, Am. Theatre Assn., Nat. Council Tchrs. English. Home: 1651 Rozelle Cove Memphis TN 38114 Office: PO Box 468 Grambling LA 71245

MCCREA, THEODORE H., clergyman. Ordained to ministry Episcopal Ch.; now suffragen bishop Dallas. Address: 2220 Main St Dallas TX 75201*

MCCREARY, JOSEPH SAMUEL, JR., dentist; b. Buffalo, Tex., Jan. 7, 1934; s. Joseph Samuel and Edna Emma (Jones) McC.; B.S., Baylor U., 1954, D.D.S., 1958; m. Linda Frances Severin, June 21, 1958; children—Melissa Lynn, Joseph Samuel III. Pvt. practice dentistry, Fort Worth, 1960—. Dental dir. Head Start, 1969. Served to capt. Dental Corps, AUS, 1958-60. Mem. Nat. Fedn. Ind. Bus., Am. Soc. Dentistry for Children, Am., Tex. (del. 1968-69, 71-72) dental assns., Fort Worth Dist. Dental Soc. (v.p. 1971-72), Fort Worth C. of C., Psi Omega. Methodist (bd. mem. 1956—). Kiwanian. Club: Ridglea Country (Fort Worth). Home: 3932 Thistle Lane Fort Worth TX 76109 Office: 6013 Wedgwood Dr Fort Worth TX 76109

MCCROCKLIN, GEORGE WILSON, chem. co. exec.; b. Campti, La., Feb. 26, 1919; s. Claude and Georgie (Thompson) McC.; student So. Meth. U., 1936; m. Bonnie Woodfin, June 13, 1936; children—Alicia (Mrs. Frank B. Clayton), Lydia (Mrs. Tom Robinson), Teresa (Mrs. Alan Beall Price). Pres., Tech. Maintenance, Inc., Pasadena, Tex., 1960—; chmn. bd. Emsco, Inc., 1964—; dir. Pasadena Nat. Bank, 1st Nat. Bank, Lake Jackson, Tex. Chmn., United Fund, Pasadena, 1967; chmn. adv. bd. Salvation Army. Trustee San Jacinto Found. Named Small Bus. Man of Year, Small Bus. Adminstrn., 1969. Mem. Small Bus. Adminstrn. Houston (adv. bd.), Pasadena C. of C. (pres.), Rodeo Assn. Houston (life). Mason (Shriner), Rotarian. Club: Pasadena (pres.). Home: 802 Shadow Lane Pasadena TX 77502 Office: 909 W Harris St Pasadena TX 77502

MCCRORY, HARVEY FRED, veterinarian, state ofcl.; b. Kosciosko, Miss., Oct. 6, 1921; s. Harvey Lee and Hettie (Adams) McC.; B.S. in Animal Husbandry, Miss. State U., 1942; postgrad., 1967-68; D.V.M., Tex. A and M U., 1949; m. Nadine Elizabeth Weaver, May 20, 1944; children—Sharon Lee, Katyn Ann, Virginia Ruth, John Charles. Mem. dept. vet. sci. Miss. State U., State College, 1949-71, prof., acting head dept., 1966-69; dir. Vet. Diagnostic Lab., state veterinarian Miss. Bd. Animal Health, Jackson, 1971—. Bd. dirs., pres. Felix Long Meml. Hosp., Starkville, Miss., 1960-71. Served with A.C., AUS, 1943-45. Named Miss. Veterinarian of Year, 1971. Mem. Am., N.E. Miss. (sec. 1960), Miss. (exec. sec. 1961) vet. medicine assns., Oktibbeha County C. of C. (1st v.p. 1969-70, pres. 1970-71), Acacia. Mason (Shriner). Home: 17 Cedar Cove Brandon MS 39042 Office: Veterinary Diagnostic Lab PO Box 4356 Jackson MS 39216

MCCRORY, MARTHA, educator; b. Quincy, Ill.; d. Joseph W. and Florence (Bastert) McCrory; student Northwestern U., 1937-38; B.M., U. Mich., 1941; M.M., Eastman Sch. Music, 1944, also artists diploma; postgrad. U. London, summer 1955, Berkshire Music Center, 1941, Music Acad. of West, 1952. Cellist, All Am. Youth Orch., 1940, U. Mich. Little Symphony, 1940, Rochester Philharmonic, 1942-46; asst. prof. music Drake U., 1946-47, Trinity U., San Antonio, 1947-52; asst. prin. cello San Antonio Symphony, 1947-53, Chattanooga Symphony, 1955-62, mgr., 1958-62; asst. prof. music U. of South, Sewanee, Tenn., 1962-69, asso. prof., 1969—; dir. Sewanee Summer Music Center, 1963—; cellist Chattanooga, Nashville, Knoxville symphonies, Cumberland Trio, 1967—. Mem. adv. panel Tenn. Arts Commn. Mem. Nat. Sch. Orch. Assn. (chpt. chmn, chpt. pres.), Tenn. Fedn. Music Clubs (dir.), Tenn. String Tchrs. Assn. (pres.), Pi Beta Phi, Sigma Alpha Iota, Pi Kappa Lambda. Republican. Conglist. Home: Sewanee TN 37375 Office: U of the South Sewanee TN 37375

MCCUEN, DAVID M., picture editor Nat. Geog. Soc., Washington. Office: Nat Geog Soc 17th and M Sts Washington DC 20036*

MCCULLOCH, ELIZABETH HARDY HUDSON (MRS. EDWARD RUSSELL MCCULLOCH), educator; b. Atlanta, Nov. 14, 1907; d. John LaFayette and Lily (Hardy) Hudson; A.B., Agnes Scott Coll., 1928; M.Ed., Ga. So. Coll., 1966; m. Edward Russell McCulloch, Dec. 26, 1933 (dec. Oct. 1956); children—John Russell, Nancy Ruth (Mrs. Ernest Parks Davis). Tchr. high sch. Fulton County Bd. Edn., Atlanta, 1928-34, 1957-63; counselor Sandy Springs High Sch., Atlanta, 1963—. Mem. Ga. Tchr. Edn. Council, Ga. Personnel and Guidance Assn. (treas. 1970-71), Ga. Assn. Sch. Counselors (dist. pres. 1967-70), Fulton County Tchrs. Assn., Ga. Edn. Assn., Am. Personnel and Guidance Assn. Presbyn. (elder). Home: 754 Crestridge Dr NE Atlanta GA 30306

MCCULLOUGH, ANDREW DOSSETT, investment cons.; b. McAllen, Tex., Nov. 24, 1935; s. Leland Graves and Elizabeth Brown (Dossett) McC.; student U. Wash., 1953-54; B.B.A., U. Tex., 1958; m. Elizabeth Anna Asche, July 14, 1962; children—Anna Bermingham, Andrew Dossett, Jr. Investment banker Underwood, Neuhaus & Co., Inc., Houston, 1958-63, Schneider Bernet & Hickman, Inc., 1963-67; sr. v.p., treas., sec., dir., founder First of Tex., Inc., 1967-70; pvt. practice as pvt. investment and bus. cons., 1970—; dir. Eagle Mgmt. & Trust Co. Trustee Houston Ballet Found., v.p., 1968-70; trustee Tex. Children's Hosp., sec., 1968—; trustee Contemporary Arts Mus., v.p., 1971-72; trustee Chinquapin Sch., vice chmn. bd., 1972—; bd. dirs. Houston chpt. Leukemia Soc. Am. Mem. U.S. Air N.G., 1958-64. Mem. Sigma Alpha Epsilon. Republican. Episcopalian. Clubs: Houston Country, Ramada, Bayou. Home: 4001 Inverness Dr Houston TX 77019 Office: 1212 River Oaks Banks Tower Houston TX 77019

MCCUNE, SHANNON, educator; b. Son Chon, Korea, Apr. 6, 1913; s. George Shannon and Helen Bailey (McAfee) McC.; B.A., Coll. of Wooster, 1935; M.A., Syracuse U., 1937; Ph.D., Clark U., 1939, LL.D., 1960; LL.D., U. Mass., 1962, Eastern Nazarene Coll., 1966; m. Edith Blair, June 30, 1936; children—Antoinette (Mrs. Kieran Kennedy), Shannon (Mrs. Jonathan Wagner), George Blair. Asst. prof. geography Ohio State U., Columbus, 1939-47; econ. analyst, econ. intelligence officer Bd. Econ. Warfare, Fgn. Econ. Adminstrn., Washington, 1942-45; asso. prof., prof. geography Colgate U., Hamilton, N.Y., 1947-55; provost U. Mass., Amherst, 1955-61; dir. dept. edn. UNESCO, Paris, France, 1961-62; civil adminstr. U.S. Civil Adminstrn. Ryukyu Islands, 1962-64; staff asso. pres's. office U. Ill., Urbana, 1964-65; pres. U. Vt., Burlington, 1965-66, research prof., 1966-67; dir. Am. Geog. Soc., N.Y.C., 1967-69; prof., chmn. dept. geography U. Fla., Gainesville, 1969—. mem. Assn. Am. Geographers, Phi Beta Kappa, Sigma Xi. Mason. Author: Korea's Heritage: A Regional and Social Geography, 1956; Korea: Land of Broken Calm, 1966. Home: 1617 NW 7th Pl Gainesville FL 32601

MCCUNE, WILLIAM STANLEY, surgeon; b. Petoskey, Mich., June 4, 1909; s. William George and Helen (Allen) McC.; B.A. summa cum laude, Swarthmore Coll., 1931; M.D. cum laude, Harvard, 1935; m. Doris Douglas, July 8, 1936; children—Carol, Cynthia (Mrs. Philip Allen III), Barbara, Mary. Intern, Mass. Gen. Hosp., 1935-37; resident Peter Bent Brigham Hosp., Boston, 1937-39; house physician Boston Lying-in Hospital, 1939-40; practice medicine specializing in surgery, Mich., 1940-43, Washington, 1946—; research grantee for vascular surgery, 1954-58, pancreatic x-ray visualization, 1960-64, NIH research on duo-denoscopy pancreatic surgery, 1965-68; clin. prof. surgery George Washington U. Sch. Medicine, 1958—; cons. in surgery Walter Reed Hosp. NIH VA Hosp., D.C. Mem. adv. bd. Care-Medico, 1964—; bd. dirs. Medico, Bloedorn Found., Washington. Served to maj., M.C., AUS, 1943-46. Fellow Am. (v.p. 1963), So. (v.p. 1971) surg. assns., Royal Soc. Medicine; mem. Soc. Surg. Alimentary Tract (founder), Med. Soc. D.C. (pres. 1968, chmn. exec. bd. 1972), A.C.S. (chmn. state adv. com, 1969), Southeastern Surg. Congress (council 1965—), Internat. Soc. Surgery, Orgn. State Med. Soc. Presidents (steering com. 1967-68), A.M.A., Soc. Alumni and Friends of Care/Medico (pres. 1966-67), N.Y. Acad. Sci., Washington Acad. Surgery, (pres.-elect 1972), Phi Beta Kappa, Alpha Omega Alpha. Episcopalian (sr. warden). Author: (with B. Blades) Nash's Surg. Physiology, 1953; Cancer of Digestive Tract, 1968. Contbr. articles to profl. jours. Home: 2510 Virginia Av NW Washington DC 20037 Office: 2520 L St NW Washington DC 20037

MCCURDY, PATRICK PIERRE, editor; b. Angers, France, Sept. 14, 1928 (parents Am. citizens); s. Joseph Alexander and Constance Yolande (DeBoiseferon) McC.; B.S. in Chem. Engring., Carnegie Inst. Tech., 1949; m. Eiko Yamada, May 30, 1953; children—Alan J., Wendy C., Alec J., Jeffrey R. Chem. engr. Humble Oil & Refining Co., Baytown, Tex., 1949-50, Callery Chem. Co. (Pa.), 1955-56; sr. chem. engr. research and devel. lab. U.S. Army, Fort Belvoir, Va., 1956-60; with Chem. & Engring. News, Washington, N.Y.C., Frankfurt, Germany, Tokyo, Japan, 1960—, mng. editor, Washington, 1967-69, editor, 1969—. Served to 1st lt. C.E., AUS, 1950-54. Mem. Am. Chem. Soc., Chemists' Club N.Y., Phi Kappa Phi, Tau Beta Pi, Theta Tau. Clubs: Foreign Correspondents (Tokyo); Tokyo American. Home: 8349 Orange Ct Alexandria VA 22309 Office: 1155 16th St NW Washington DC 20036

MCCURDY, RICHARD CLARK, govt. ofcl.; b. Newton, Ia., Jan. 2, 1909; s. Ralph Bruce and Florence (Clark) McC.; A.B., Stanford, 1931, E.M., 1933; m. Harriet Edith Sutton, Sept. 11, 1933; children—Gregor, Richard, Carolyn, Robert. Engring. and prodn. Shell Oil Co., 1933-47; prodn. mgmt. Shell Caribbean Petroleum Co., 1947-50; gen. mgr. Shell Group Cos., Venezuela, 1950-53; pres. Shell Chem. Co., N.Y.C., 1953-65; dir. Shell Oil Co., mem. exec. com., 1959-69, pres., chief exec. officer, 1965-69; asso. adminstr. orgn. and mgmt. NASA, Washington, 1970—. Trustee United Seamans Service, 1954—. Bd. dir. Mfg. Chemists Assn., 1955-65, chmn. bd., 1961-62, chmn. exec. com., 1964-65. Trustee Stanford U., 1965-70, Hood Coll., 1968-70. Mem. Am. Inst. Mining, Metall. and Petroleum Engrs., Am. Phys. Soc., Am. Petroleum Inst., Beta Theta Pi. Clubs: N.Y. Yacht; Noroton (Conn.) Yacht (commodore); Tokeneke (Darien, Conn.); Pacific Union (San Francisco); Links (N.Y.C.). Home: 2500 Virginia Av Watergate East Apts 717-S Washington DC 20037 Office: 400 Maryland Av SW Washington DC 20002

MCCURRY, WALTER KNORBOURNE, criminologist; b. Norfolk, Va., July 13, 1906; s. Ernest Swepson and Anabelle (Saunders) McC.; student LaSalle Coll., 1930-32, U. Mich., 1936, U. Ky., 1959; m. Ruth Jones, July 30, 1925; children—James K., Patricia M. (Mrs. Andrew M. Johnson). (dec.). Sr. adminstrv. officer Bur. Prisons, U.S. Dept. Justice, Lexington, Ky., 1929-59; exec. v.p. McCurry, Henderson, Enright Advt. Agy., Inc., Norfolk, 1959-66; warden Norfolk Prison Farm, 1966—. Served with USNR, World War II. Decorated Purple Heart. Mem. V.F.W. (past nat. chief of staff). Republican. Episcopalian. Mason (32 deg., Shriner). Clubs: Norfolk Cosmopolitan, Norfolk Executive. Home: 632 John Etheridge Rd Chesapeake VA 23322 Office: 701 Sanderson Rd Chesapeake VA 23322

MCCUTCHEN, JOSEPH KELLY, JR., carpet co. exec.; b. Chattanooga, Nov. 14, 1939; s. Joseph Kelly and Christine Mercier (Bandy) McC.; grad. McCallie Sch., 1958; B.S., Ga. Inst. Tech., 1962; m. Elizabeth Mills McDonald, Dec. 19, 1964; children—Joseph Kelly III, Elizabeth Shannon. Asst. to pres. J & C Carpet Co., Inc., Ellijay, Ga., 1962-64, nat. sales mgr., 1964-69; pres., dir. Universal Carpets, Inc., Ellijay, 1969—. Served with AUS, 1963-69. Mem. Carpet and Rug Inst., Sigma Alpha Epsilon. Republican. Methodist (adminstrv. bd.). Lion. Clubs: Cotillion, Quarterback, Piedmont Driving. Home: Blue Ridge Rd Ellijay GA 30540 Office: Indsl Blvd Ellijay GA 30540

MCCUTCHEON, CHESTER MYERS, investment co. exec.; b. Monroeville, Pa., Oct. 30, 1907; s. William Erwin and Margaret Kelso (Myers) McC.; student Westinghouse Tech. Night Sch., East Pittsburgh, Pa., 1926-30, La Salle Extension U., 1933-35, Am. Savs. and Loan Inst., Atlanta, 1947-54; m. Helen Sophia Clawson, Nov. 3, 1944; children—Ronald R., Brian L., Brenda (Mrs. Ernest Mosley), Lynn Ellis, Bruce A., Curtis W. Cost accountant Westinghouse Electric & Mfg. Co., Pitts., 1926-33; tax collector No. Huntingdon Twp., Westmoreland County, Pa., 1934-40; examiner Fed. Home Loan Bank Bd., Washington, 1941-47; comptroller Fulton Fed. Savs. & Loan Assn., Atlanta, 1947—; v.p. Fulton Investment Co., 1958-60, pres., 1960-65; dir. Southeastern Capital Co.; pres. Cherokee Enterprises, Tuxedo, Inc. Chmn. Cobb County Republican Exec. Com., Marietta, Ga., 1964-66; co-chmn. finance com. Callaway for Gov. Campaign, 1966. Mem. thesis rev. bd. Grad. Sch. Savs. and Loan, Ind. U., 1960—. Mem. Nat. Soc. Controllers and Financial Officers (past pres.). Presbyn. (deacon). Contbr. articles to profl. jours. Home: 96 Whitlock Av Marietta GA 30060 Office: Fulton Fed Bldg 11 Pryor St NE Atlanta GA 30303

MCCUTCHEON, NANCY SUSAN, educator; b. Columbia, S.C., July 10, 1937; d. Samuel Durant and Nancy (Milford) McCutcheon; B.A., U. S.C., 1957, M.Ed., 1966, Ph.D., 1969; diploma, tchrs. certificate in piano Sherwood Music Sch., Chgo., 1959. Tchr., Belvedere Elementary Sch., Columbia, 1957-65; grad. teaching asst. Sch. Edn., U. S.C., Columbia, 1965-68, instr., 1968-70, asst. prof., 1970—. Pvt. piano tchr., 1955—; cons. substitute teaching program Williamsburg County, S.C., 1969-70; coordinator Career Opportunities Program, Williamsburg County, 1970—. Mem. N.E.A., S.C. Edn. Assn., S.C. Assn. Student Teaching, Assn. Supervision and Curriculum Devel., Soc. Research Child Devel., Am. Ednl. Research Assn., Columbia Music Tchrs. Assn. (sec. 1964-66), So. Assn. Schs. and Colls. (vis. com.) Nat. Assn. Edn. Young Children, S.C. Fedn. Music Clubs (adjudicator piano festivals 1960—), Nat. Council Tchrs. English, Nat. Soc. Study Edn., So. Assn. Children Under Six, Phi Beta Kappa (sec.-treas. Alpha of S.C. chpt. 1970—), Kappa Delta Epsilon, Alpha Delta Kappa, Delta Kappa Gamma, Beta Sigma Phi (chpt. pres. 1961-62), Baptist. Club: Sherwood Music School Seminar (pres. 1967, 68). Contbr. to profl. publs. Home: 2911 Devine St Columbia SC 29205

MCDANIEL, BENNIE OSBORNE, physician; b. Springville, Miss., Apr. 28, 1896; s. William Brantley and Dora Sedera (Smitherman) McD.; B.S., U. Miss., 1922; M.D., Northwestern Med. Sch., 1925; m. Mildred Luther, Jan. 2, 1929; children—Nan Ellen (Mrs. Kenneth Largent), Bennie Ann (Mrs. James P. Walker). Intern, Bapt. Meml. Hosp., Memphis, 1924-25, house surgeon, 1925-26; practice medicine, Merigold, Miss., 1926-34, Elk City, Okla., 1934-41, Amherst, Tex., 1941-54, Muleshoe, Tex., 1954—; co-owner West Plains Hosp., Clinic and Nursing Home, 1954-68; Bailey County health officer, 1954—. Mem. A.M.A., So., Tex., Lamb, Bailey, Cochran and Hockley County med. assns., Am. Assn. Physicians and Surgeons. Democrat. Baptist. Home: 310 W 9th St Muleshoe TX 79347 Office: 708 S 1st St Muleshoe TX 79347

MCDANIEL, CHARLES POPE, JR., supt. schs.; b. Tucker, Ga., Dec. 28, 1922; s. Charles Pope and Loreno (Britt) McD.; A.B., Mercer U., 1947, M.Ed., 1949; postgrad. Columbia U., 1950-53; Ed. D., U. Ga., 1967; m. Beatrice Schroeder Martin, Apr. 19, 1946; children—Mary Elizabeth, Margaret Anne, Charles William. Instr. Ga. Mil. Coll., Millegeville, 1947-53; supervising prin. Metter Pub. Schs., 1953-56; prin. Druid Hills High Sch., Atlanta, 1956-60; supt. Thomasville (Ga.) City Schs., 1960-69, Clarke County (Ga.) Schs., 1969—. Bd. dirs. Thomasville Youth Center, 1962, Thomasville YMCA; trustee Mercer U. 1965. Served from pvt. to 1st lt., USMCR, 1942-46. Decorated Purple Heart; named Thomasville Man of Yr., 1965. Mem. C. of C., Nat., Ga. edn. assns., Ga. Psychol. Assn., Druid Hills Civic Assn. Am. Assn. Sch. Adminstrs., Ga. Sch. Supts. Assn. (dist. dir.), Am. Legion (past comdr.), Sigma Nu, Kappa Phi Kappa. Democrat. Baptist. Kiwanian (pres. 1956), Rotarian (pres. 1964-65), Lion. Home: 250 Cedar Creek Dr Athens GA 30601 Office: PO Box 1708 Athens GA 30601

MCDANIEL, CHESTER MORLEY, dentist; b. Ewing, Va., Aug. 1, 1915; s. Tipton Leman and Mary Ellen (Morley) McD.; student U. Ky., 1934-36; D.M.D., U. Louisville, 1940; m. Joyce Marie Crim, Jan. 27, 1940; children—Jeneanne (Mrs. Keith Russell Sieck), Phyllis Ellen. Pvt. practice dentistry, Middlesboro, Ky., 1940—. Mem. Ky. Bd. Health, 1968—; fund drive chmn. Middlesboro Community Chest, 1948—, A.R.C., 1950-51; curriculum com. Middlesboro Bd. Edn., 1968-70; chmn. Middlesboro Bd. Zoning Adjustment, 1964-69. Served to capt. Dental Corp, AUS, 1942-45. Decorated Bronze Star. Fellow Am. Coll. Dentists; mem. Am., Ky., Southeastern (pres. 1956, 67-68) dental assns., Middlesboro C. of C. Republican. Methodist (chmn. bd.) Rotarian. Home: 210 Petersboro St Middlesboro KY 40965 Office: 2215 W Cumberland St Middlesboro KY 40965

MCDANIEL, DALE FRANKLIN, lawyer; b. Tulsa, Jan. 23, 1927; s. Lando and Bonnie (Terrill) McD.; B.S. in Bus. Adminstrn., U. Tulsa, 1956, LL.B., 1959; m. Kathryn Hope Foster, May 23, 1948; children—Kathryn Lynn, Brian Dale. Admitted to Okla. bar, 1959; atty. Sanders, McElroy & Whitten, Tulsa, 1960-66; partner Church & McDaniel, Tulsa, 1966-68, Whitten & McDaniel, Tulsa, 1968—; dir. CCC, Inc., Customade Products, Inc., Tulsa. Bd. dirs. Tulsa County Legal Aid Soc. Served with USNR, 1945-46; PTO. Mem. Fedn. Ins. Counsel, Am., Okla., Tulsa County bar assns., Def. Research Inst., Am. Judicature Soc., Am., Okla. trial lawyers assns., Phi Alpha Delta. Home: 3508 E 7th St Tulsa OK 74135 Office: NBT Bldg Tulsa OK 74103

MCDANIEL, EARL RUSSELL, fire chief; b. Lexington, Ky., Dec. 24, 1912; s. Thomas Jefferson and Patsy Ann (Atwood) McD; student Transylvania Coll., 1933-34; m. Margaret Elizabeth Umstead, June 18, 1937; children—Marsha, James (Mrs. Elmer Caton), Charles Auburn, Earl Russell II. With Lexington Fire Dept., 1941—, capt. 1948-49, asst. chief, 1949-50, chief, 1950—. Active Little League Baseball, 1950-64; div. chmn. Community Chest drive, 1949-71; chmn. first aid div. A.R.C., 1950-70; mem. state Armed Forces Adv. Com., 1950-60; mem. Ann. Community Fire Works Program, 1955—; chmn. Easter Seal drive, 1959, Polio drive, 1960, Gov.'s Fire Commn., 1971; arrangements chmn. Billy Graham Crusade, 1971. Bd. dirs. Polio Drive, 1948-65, A.R.C., 1951-69. Recipient U.S. C. of C. Fire Safety award, 1966-68; Man of Year, Optimist Club, 1958-59. Mem. Jr. C. of C. (nat. chmn. fire prevention 1948-49), State Firemens Assn. (pres. 1952), Southeastern Fire Chiefs Assn. (pres. 1954), Internat. Assn. Fire Chiefs. Mason (32 deg., Shriner, master 1960, potentate shrine 1965). Home: 203 Idlehour Dr Lexington KY 40502 Office: 219 E 3d St Lexington KY 40508

MCDANIEL, ERNEST EARL, JR., elec. engr.; b. Chattanooga, Mar. 5, 1934; s. Ernest E. and Edith (Catlett) McD.; Vanderbilt U., 1957; postgrad. U. Tenn., 1961-62; m. Kathryn D. Vaughn, Nov. 22, 1968. Sr. plant engr. Avco Corp., Nashville, 1958-64; pres. McDaniel Engring., Nashville, 1964-66; chief engr. Tech.-Trainer Corp., Chattanooga, 1966—; v.p. engring. Sound-Tronic, Inc., Chattanooga, 1967—. Cons. NASA, Huntsville, Ala., 1962-63. Registered profl. engr., Tenn. Mem. Tenn. Soc. Profl. Engrs. Baptist. Designer sound level meter for measurement vehicle noise, 1968, numerical control system for ednl. use, 1969. Home: 3504 Wauchula St Chattanooga TN 37406 Office: 2001 Elmendorf St Chattanooga TN 37406

MCDANIEL, ESTES CRUDEN, farmer, state legislator; b. Pontotoc, Miss., June 28, 1909; s. Thomas L. and Janie (Inzer) McD.; B.S., U. Okla., 1931; M.A., George Peabody Coll., 1941; m. Grace B. Gary, June 30, 1951. Supervising high sch. prin. Morgan County (Ala). Bd. Edn., 1934-50; farmer nr. Greenwood Miss., 1952—; mem. Miss. Ho. of Reps. from 15th Dist., 1964—. Mem. Nat. Soc. State Legislators (charter mem., del. nat. conv. 1966, 68-70, charter pres. Miss. chpt. 1968-69, nat. gov. 1969-72), Farm Bur., Am. Miss. Angus assns., Rivers and Harbors Assn., Am. Soybean Assn., Miss. Cattlemen's Assn., Greenwood C. of C., Kappa Phi Kappa. Democrat. Presbyn. Mason (Shriner), Elk, Lion, Woodman of World; mem. Order Eastern Star. Home: 301 E Claiborne St Greenwood MS 38930

MCDANIEL, FELIX CARSON, beverage co. exec.; b. Lake Lure, N.C., Sept. 2, 1939; s. Donald Gordon and Jessie C. (Flynn) McD.; asso. Lees McRae Jr. Coll., 1957-59; B.S. in Bus. Adminstrn., Berea Coll., 1961; M.B.A., Ind. U., 1962; m. Janice Mayhall, Aug. 26, 1961; children—Stanley, Brian. Staff accountant, Arthur Young & Co., C.P.A.'s, 1963-65; controller Pepsi-Cola Bottling Co., Inc., Springfield, O., 1965-68; treas. All Am. Beverages, Winston-Salem, N.C., 1968—. Mem. Springfield Golf Commn., 1969—. C.P.A., N.C., Ohio. Mem. Am. Inst. C.P.A.'s, Beta Gamma Sigma, Beta Alpha Psi. Lion (pres. 1970—). Home: 2639 Amesbury Rd Winston Salem NC 27103 Office: 1664 Stadium Dr Winston Salem NC 27107

MCDANIEL, JACK WILLIS, consultant; b. Goodman, Miss., May 2, 1934; s. Major C. and Anise (Pickering) McD.; B.A., Miss. Coll., 1956; certificate in social work La. State U., 1957; M.S.W., Fla. State U., 1960; m. Nancy Worley, June 9, 1956; children—Jack Willis, Nancy Roselyn. Child welfare worker, supr., Miss. Dept. Pub. Welfare, Tupelo, 1956-61, dist. supr., 1961-65; exec. dir. Lift, Inc., Tupelo, 1965-71; owner McDaniel's Book Store & Toy Box, Tupelo, 1968-71; exec. dir. Tech. Assistance Tng. and Edn. Resources, Jackson, Miss., 1971—. Mem. Community Devel. Found., 1965-71. Bd. dirs. Community Concert Assn., Tupelo, 1966-71. Served with AUS, 1963. Mem. Miss. Community Action Agy. Dirs. Assn. (past pres.), Nat. Assn. Social Workers, Miss. Conf. Social Work (adv. com. early childhood edn. 1966—), S.E. Regional Assn. Community Action Agys. (bd.), Pi Gamma Mu. Presbyn. (minister music 1966-71). Kiwanian (dir. Tupelo 1967-69). Research in pre-sch. edn. Home: 751 Windward Rd Jackson MS 39206 Office: Box 5367 Jackson MS 39216

MCDANIEL, RAYMOND, exec. dir. Shreveport (La.) Times. Home: 422 Ontario St Shreveport LA 71106 Office: Shreveport Times 222 Lake St Shreveport LA 71002*

MCDANIEL, THOMAS ZERE, gas co. exec.; b. St. Petersburg, Fla., July 27, 1925; s. Robert H. and Susie J. (Lovelace) McD.; B.S., Auburn U., 1950; postgrad. Rice U., 1963, U. Houston, 1960-64; m. Olga M. Caceres, Sept. 5, 1970; 1 dau., Dorothy B. Home and bldg. designer, salesman Phillips Bros., Inc., Roanoke, Ala., 1950-54; jr. engr. Transcontinental Gas Compressor Sta., Roanoke, 1954-55; constrn. engr. Transco Gas Corp., Linden, N.J., 1955, div. pipeline engr., Baton Rouge, 1956-57, acting dist. pipeline supt., Laurel, Miss., 1958-59, engr. meter sta. design, Houston, 1959-62, sr. engr. in charge Tex., La., Ga. Pa., N.J., N.Y. stas., 1963—. Mem. instructional staff W.Va. U., 1962-71, U. Okla., 1966-68, U. Houston, 1968. Served with inf., AUS, World War II; ETO. Decorated Bronze Star medal, French and Belgian Fourragere. Mem. Instrument Soc. Am. (past edn. dir.), Nat. Soc. Profl. Engrs., Engrs. Council Houston (past councilor), Am. Soc. M.E., U.S. Jr. C. of C. (past v.p. and acting pres.), Dramatic Order Knights of Khorassan. Mason, K.P., Rotarian. Contbr. articles to profl. jours. Home: 2119 DeMilo St Houston TX 77018 Office: PO Box 1396 Transco Gas Corp Houston TX 77001

MCDAVID, CHARLES WILLIAM, steel co. exec., mayor; b. Waxahachie, Tex., Sept. 21, 1914; s. William Allen and Alice (Gibson) McD.; B.S. in Archtl. Engring., Tex. Tech. U., 1938; m. Katrina Louise Brewer, Jan. 30, 1938; children—William Terry, Martha Jane (Mrs. David Earl Barber). With Central Tex. Iron Works, Waco, 1938—, asst. mgr. sales, 1959-66, mgr. prodn. control, 1966—; mayor pro tem City of Waco, 1971, mayor, 1972—. Instr. engring. Tex. Agrl. and M U., 1942-43. Chmn., Waco Tornado Cleanup Task Force, 1953; loaned exec. United Fund Drive, Waco, 1966; chmn. Plumbing Bd. Waco, 1968; mem. Planning Commn. Waco, 1969, Waco City Council, 1969—; sec.-treas. Heart of Tex. Council of Govts. Recipient 20 Year commendation Tex. Tech. Loyalty Fund, 1968; named Central Tex. Engr. of Year, 1970. Registered profl. engr., Tex. Mem. Tex., Nat. socs. profl. engrs., Cen-Tech Exes (past pres.), Central Tex. Geneal. Soc., S.A.R. (Tex. v.p. 1971-72), Tau Beta Pi. Rotarian. Club: Ridgewood Country (Waco). Home: 3115 Cumberland St Waco TX 76707 Office: 2025 Webster St Waco TX 76703

MCDAVID, CONSTANCE LOUISE WEBB (MRS. HOMER GEORGE MCDAVID), county ofcl.; b. Covington, Ky., Aug. 27, 1896; d. Joseph F. and Josephine H. (Herrington) Webb; grad. Houston pub. schs.; m. Homer George McDavid, Apr. 27, 1924; children—Raymond H., Donald G. With treas.'s office, Harris County, Tex., 1935—, county treas., 1948—. Worker, United Fund, Salvation Army. Named Outstanding Treas. in Tex., 1970; recipient civic award River Oaks Bus. and Profl. Women's Club woman of year, 1958, 65. Mem. County Treas.' Assn. Tex., Nat. Assn. County Ofcls., Nat. Assn. County Treasurers and Finance Officers (dir. 1959). Methodist. Home: 1718 Monarch Oaks St Houston TX 77055 Office: 301 San Jacinto St Houston TX 77002

MCDAVID, FREDERICK RHODES, cons. mech. engr.; b. Sanford, N.C., Dec. 26, 1924; s. James Philip and Nora (Foy) McD.; B. Mech. Engring., N.C. State U., 1948; postgrad. Carnegie Inst. Tech., 1949; m. Janet Frances Smiley, Jan. 19, 1950; children—Frederick R., Philip A., Susan K., Nora J., Robert J. Process engr. U.S. Steel Corp., Pitts., 1947-49; design engr. Walter Hook & Assos., Charlotte, N.C. 1950-51, H.K. Ferguson Co., Cleve., 1951-53; partner Kluckhuhn & McDavid, Washington, 1954—. Cons. engr. master plan Haile Selassie I Univ., Ethiopia. Chmn., Fairfax County (Va.) Bd. Plumbing Examiners and Appeals, 1968—. Organizer, troop com. chmn. Nat. Capitol Area council Boy Scouts Am. Served with AUS, 1944-46. Registered profl. engr., D.C., Va., Md., Pa., Ohio, Fla., Conn., N.Y. Mem. Am. Soc. M.E., Cons. Engrs. Council, Am. Legion. Republican. Methodist (dir. 1960-61). Elk. Home: 9321 Convento Terrace Fairfax VA 22030 Office: 2430 Pennsylvania Av Washington DC 20037

MCDERMOTT, ROBERT FRANCIS, business exec., former univ. dean; b. Boston, July 31, 1920; s. Alphonsus F. and Anna C. (Thygeson) McD.; grad. Boston Latin Sch., 1937; student Norwich U., 1937-39; B.S., U.S. Mil. Acad., 1943; M.B.A., Harvard, 1950; LL.D., St. Louis U., 1962; Litt.D., St. Bernard Coll.; m. Alice P. McDermott, Jan. 20, 1943; children—Patricia A. Beynet, Robert Francis, David W., Mary A., Mark S. Commd. 2d lt. U.S. Army, 1943, advanced through grades to brig. gen. U.S. Air Force, 1959; with 9th Air Force, Europe, World War II; personnel staff officer Hdqrs. USAF, 1946-48; asst. prof. social scis. U.S. Mil. Acad., 1950-54; prof. econs., vice dean U.S. Air Force Acad., 1954-56, dean faculty, 1956-68, 1st permanent prof., 1957-68; ret., 1968; exec. v.p. United Services Automobile Assn., San Antonio, 1968-69, pres. 1969—; dir. Straus-Frank Co. Trustee S.W. Research Inst., Social Sci. Found. U. Denver, St. Mary's Hall, Air Force Village Found. Decorated Legion of Merit, D.S.M. (U.S. Army, USAF), Bronze Star, Air medal with clusters. Mem. Order of Daedalians, Fedn. Ins. Counsel, Nat. Assn. Ind. Insurers (dir.), San Antonio C. of C. (dir.), Theta Chi. Clubs: San Antonio Country, Oak Hills Country, Harvard, West Point Soc. Author: Principles of Insurance, 1953; (with others) Economics of National Security, 1953; Principles of Personal Finance, 1954. Home: 823 Eventide Dr San Antonio TX 78209 Office: 4119 Broadway San Antonio TX 78288

MCDILL, EDWIN BRANDAO, librarian; b. New Orleans, June 11, 1936; s. James Delph and Esther Mary (Brandao) McD.; B.S., Spring Hill Coll., 1958; M.S., La. State U., 1960; m. Lucinda Lanning, July 12, 1963; 1 dau., Lucinda Amy. Librarian, Cranwell Sch., Lenox, Mass., 1960-62; reference librarian Holy Cross Coll., Worcester, Mass., 1962-64; reference asst. Greensboro (N.C.) Pub. Library, 1964-67; asst. librarian Guilford Tech. Inst., Jamestown, N.C., 1967—. Active Buten Mus. Wedgewood, Merion, Pa., Dyson Perrins Mus., Worcester, Eng., Friends Salisbury (Eng.) Cathedral. Mem. Am. Vocational Assn., Southeastern, N.C. library assns., Guilford Library Club, Greensboro Preservation Soc., Wedgwood Soc. London. Home: 2301 W Pisgah Church Rd Greensboro NC 27408 Office: Box 309 Jamestown NC 27282

MCDIVITT, JAMES A., astronaut; b. Chgo., June 10, 1929; s. James and Margeret (Maxwell) McD.; student Jackson Jr. Coll., 1948-50; B.S. in Aero. Engring., U. Mich., 1959, D. Astronautic Sci. (hon.), 1965; D.Sc., Seton Hall U., 1969, Miami U. (O.), 1970; m. Patricia Ann Haas; children—Michael A., Ann Lynn, Patrick W., Kathleen M. Joined U.S. Air Force, 1951, advanced through grades to brig. gen., 1972; served in Korean action; student Exptl. Test Pilot Sch., Edwards AFB, 1959-60, Aerospace Research Pilot Course, 1961; then exptl. flight test officer Edwards AFB; astronaut, 1962-69, command pilot Gemini IV spacecraft, 1965, comdr. Apollo IX, 1969; mgr. lunar landing operations, 1969; mgr. Apollo spacecraft program, 1969—. Mem. Soc. Exptl. Test Pilots, Am. Inst. Aeros. and Astronautics, Am. Astronaut. Soc. Office: NASA Manned Spacecraft Center Houston TX 77058

MCDONALD, A. P., engr., author, educator; b. Leesville, La., Dec. 4, 1908; s. Jesse Nelson and Annie (Gibson) McD.; B.S., A. and M. Coll. Tex., 1930, M.S., 1943; m. Verne Satterwhite, Aug. 22, 1931; children—Cynthia Anne (Mrs. Leslie B. Williams, Jr.), Jerry Nelson, Gwendolynn Kay (Mrs. Robert R. Miller). Tech. employee Am. Tel. & Tel., St. Louis, Wichita, Kan., 1930-32; elec. contractor, Leesville, La., 1933-34; engr. Tex. Power & Light Co., Dallas, 1936; instr. Allen Mil. Acad., Bryan, Tex., 1938, A. and M. Coll. Tex., 1938-43; asst. prof. Centenary Coll., Shreveport, 1943-45; engr. charge system studies George C. Hengy & Co., 1945-48; asst. prof. charge extension drawing courses Indpls. dist. Purdue U., 1948-53; asst. prof. Rice U., Houston, 1953-57, asso. prof., 1957, chmn. dept. engring. graphics, 1953-69, mgr. dept. printing and reprodn., 1964—. Served from 2d lt. to 1st lt., AUS, 1934-47. Mem. Am. Soc. Engring. Edn. (advt. mgr. Jour. Engring. Graphics 1957-60, chmn. S.W. sect. 1963-64, treas. div. engring. graphics 1969—), Am. Assn. U. Profs., Clan Donald Soc. Am. (dist. convener Tex. br. 1958-61, dist. toshachdeor 1961—), Bur. Issues Assn., Nat., Tex. (chpt. v.p. 1966-67) socs. profl. engrs., Houston Engring. Edn. Com. Democrat. Methodist. Mason. Author: Differential Equation Supplement, 1957; Technical Graphics, 1957. Home: 2228 Robinhood Rd Houston TX 77005

MCDONALD, EDGAR HASKELL, state ofcl.; b. Cloud Chief, Okla., Sept. 18, 1907; s. James Edgar and Corda McDonald; B.S., Southwestern State Coll. Weatherford, Okla., 1933; M.A., Western State Coll., Gunnison, Colo., 1939; m. Kathryn O'Hara Waggoner, May 13, 1944; children—Stephen, Deborah. Tchr., adminstr. pub. schs., Carter, Walters, Vimson, Verden, Gracemont, Noble (all Okla.); dep. and asst. supt. edn. State of Okla., Oklahoma City. Served with AUS. Mem. Okla. Assn. Sch. Adminstrs., N.E.A. Mason (32 deg.), Lion. Home: 4508 NW 32d St Oklahoma City OK 73122 Office: Room 328 State Capitol Bldg Oklahoma City OK 73105

MCDONALD, ERWIN LAWRENCE, clergyman, editor; b. London, Ark., Oct. 31, 1907; s. Frank Floyd and Rebecca Geneva (Powell) McD.; grad. Ark. Poly. Coll., 1932; A.B., Ouachita Coll., 1943; B.D., So. Baptist Theol. Sem., 1947; Litt. D., Georgetown Coll., 1958; m. Mary Elsie Price, Mar. 1, 1930; children—Avis Jeannine (Mrs. Sam H. Jones, Jr.), Judy Carole (Mrs. J. W. Lucas). Press corr., Russellville, Ark., 1932-37; city editor Daily Courier-Democrat, 1937-41; ordained to ministry Baptist Ch., 1938; editor So. Standard, Arkadelphia, Ark., 1941-43; instr. Ouachita Coll., 1943-44, pastor Washington (Ark.) Bapt. Ch., 1942-44, Sligo Ch.Pendleton, Ky., 1944-47; dir. pub. relations So. Bapt. Theol. Sem., 1944-51, editor The Tie, 1947-51; dir. pub, relations Furman U. and editor Furman U. Mag., 1951-54; exec. sec. edn. Gen. Assn. Bapts. in Ky., 1954-57; editor Ark. Bapt., Little Rock, 1957-72; religion editor Ark. Democrat, Little Rock, 1972—. Chmn., Ark. Literacy Com., 1965; mem. Ark. adv. com. U.S. Commn. on Civil Rights. Dir. Christian Civic Found. Ark., Inc.; bd. dirs. Asso. Ch. Press, 1969-72; asso. dir. Scotland Bapt. Evangelistic Crusade, 1961. Recipient Distinguished Alumnus award Ouachita Coll., 1960, Distinguished Bapt. Minister award So. Bapt. Coll., 1963; hon. Ky. col., 1963; named Alumnus of Yr., So. Bapt. Theol. Sem., 1972. Mem. C. of C., So. Bapt. Press Assn. (pres. 1965), Greater Little Rock Ministerial Assn. (pres. 1965), Inst. Fundamental Communication (rec. sec. 1965). Democrat. Rotarian. Author: The Church Using the Newspaper, 1961; 75 Stories & Illustrations from Everyday Life, 1964; (with Ralph Creger) A Look Down the Lonesome Road, 1964; Across the Editors Desk, 1966; Stories for Speakers and Writers, 1970. Editor: The Church Proclaiming and Witnessing, 1966. Home and Office: 1419 Garland Av North Little Rock AR 72116

MCDONALD, FRANK GOODALL, appellate judge; b. Meridian, Tex., Apr. 9, 1916; s. John Francis and Helen Leonese (Tomlinson) McD.; student Hillsboro Coll., 1933-34; B.A., Baylor U., 1936; LL.B., U. Tex., 1938; m. Artie Louise Vanderford, Dec. 22, 1948; 1 dau., Luann Leonese. Admitted to Tex. bar, 1938; practiced in Hillsboro, 1938-40; judge 66th Jud. Dist. Tex., Hillsboro, 1947-52; chief justice Ct. Civil Appeals, Waco, 1953—. Served from pvt. to col., AUS, 1940-46. Mem. Am., Waco bar assns., State Bar Tex., Am. Legion, V.F.W., Delta Theta Phi. Democrat. Episcopalian. Mason (K.T., Shriner), K.P., Odd Fellow, Lion. Home: 2407 Starr St Waco TX 76710 Office: Courthouse Waco TX

MCDONALD, GERALD A., supt. Cath. Schs., El Paso, Tex. Address: 1300 Lamar St El Paso TX 79903*

MCDONALD, HENRY BURNSIDE, constrn. co. exec.; b. Yatesville, Ga., June 15, 1912; s. John Braxton and Henrietta May (Burnside) McD.; student U. Ga., 1929-32; m. Margaret Lee Wade, Sept. 12, 1943; children— Betty Ann (Mrs. M. John Thomas), Henry Burnside, James Malcolm. Jr. engr. U.S. Dept. Agr., 1932-35; party chief surveys W.S. Lee Engring. Co., 1935-37; design engr. J.E. Greiner Co., 1937-40; gen. supt. Blythe Bros., 1940-42, 51-53; asst. mgr. Koppers Co., 1946-50; v.p. Wright Contracting Co., Columbus, Ga., 1954—. Gov., Md. Safety Council, 1961-64. Served to lt. comdr. USNR, 1942-46. Registered profl. engr., Md. Mem. Am. Soc. M.E., Am. Soc. C.E., Am. Soc. Hsy. Engrs., Moles. Home: 15 Greensland Vista Standing Boy Rd Columbus GA 31904 Office: Box 1580 506 Coolidge Av Columbus GA 31902

MCDONALD, HEYWARD E., lawyer; b. Winnsboro, S.C., Sept. 27, 1925; student Davidson Coll.; B.S., U.S. Naval Acad. 1946; LL.B. magna cum laude, U. S.C., 1958. Admitted to S.C. bar, 1958; now with Rogers, McDonald, McKenzie and Fuller, Columbia, S.C. Chmn. State Supreme Ct. Com. on Character and Fitness of Applicants for the Bar, 1962-66; mem. Nat. Commn. Archtl. Barriers, 1966-70. Pres., Richland County chpt. Nat. Found., 1961-63, Bd. dirs. Easter Seal Soc.; trustee Columbia City Schs., 1968-70. Mem. S.C. Ho. Reps., 1962-66. Named S.C.'s Outstanding Handicapped Citizen, 1963. Mem. Richland County (chmn. Grievance Com. 1964), S.C., Am. bar assns., Wig and Robe, Phi Beta Kappa, Phi Delta Phi. Office: Rogers McDonald McKenzie and Fuller Barringer Bldg 1338 Main StColumbia SC 29201*

MCDONALD, MARY JANE KETCHIN (MRS. HARRY MCCASKILL MCDONALD), educator; b. Winnsboro, S.C., Feb. 9, 1929; d. James Shaw and Statia (Phillips) Ketchin; B.A., Fla. So. Coll., 1950; postgrad. Winthrop Coll., 1953, U. Ariz., 1954; M.Ed., U. S.C., 1967; m. Harry McCaskill McDonald, Mar. 26, 1955. Tchr. elementary schs., Auburndale, Fla., 1950-51, Hartsville, S.C., 1951-53, 54-55, 59-64, Tucson, Ariz., 1953-54, Orangeburg, S.C., 1955-59; jr. high sch. tchr., Hartsville, S.C., 1953-54; elementary sch. counselor, supr. Hartsville (S.C.) City Schs., 1964—. Instr. Coll. Gen. Studies, U. S.C., 1968, 69; cons. S.C. Dept. Edn., 1965-70; mem. visitation and accreditation teams So. Assn. Schs. and Colls., 1966-67. Mem. Gov's Com. for 1970 White House Conf. on Children and Youth, 1970-71; mem. bd. Community Concerts Assn., Hartsville, 1964-66; mem. scholarship com. Klepman Mills, Inc., Society Hill, S.C. Mem. N.E.A., Am. Personnel and Guidance Assn., Darlington County Edn. Assn. (pres. 1963-64), S.C. Edn. Assn., S.C. Personnel and Guidance Assn. (pres. 1970-71), Assn. for Childhood Edn., S.C., Darlington County assns. for retarded children, S.C., Darlington County assns. for mental health, Delta Kappa Gamma. Presbyn. Contbr. articles to profl. jours. Mailing address: PO Box 425 7 Erwin Rd Hartsville SC 29550 Office: Thornwell Elementary Sch Hartsville SC 29550

MCDONALD, OLIN KENNETH, sch. adminstr.; b. Marshville, N.C., Apr. 7, 1919; s. John Norman and Ruth (Dees) McD.; A.B., U. S.C., 1941, M.Ed., 1949; m. Ann McCutchen, July 12, 1942; children—John Michael, Robert Norman. Tchr. pub. sch., Camden, S.C., 1947-55; prin. Willow Dr. Elementary Sch., Sumter, S.C., 1955-60, McLaurin Jr. High Sch., Sumter, 1960—; coordinator instructional media Dist. 17. Instr. extension div. U. S.C., 1949—. Bd. dirs. Art Mus. Served to capt. USAAF, 1941-47; lt. col. Res. Decorated Air medal with three oak leaf clusters, D.F.C, with oak leaf cluster. Mem. Nat. Assn. Secondary Prins., S.C. Edn. Assn., Am. Legion, Blue Key, Pi Kappa Phi. Democrat. Presbyn. (supt. sr. dept. 1964-65). Elk (youth com.). Home: 120 Willow Dr Sumter SC 29150

MCDONALD, OWEN PETER, govt. ofcl.; b. Yankton, S.D., June 5, 1916; s. Peter Joseph and Beatrice (Cogan) McD.; teaching certificate Black Hills Tchrs. Coll., 1936; B.A., Neb. State Coll., 1939; M.A., Am. U., 1954; m. Elinor Dawn Johnson, Sept. 24, 1942; children— Kathleen Ann, John Owen, Lawrence Edward. Tchr., adminstr. Shannon County Pub. Schs., Denby, S.D., 1939-41; personnel classification analyst WPB, 1941-42; mem, planning staff, asst. adminstr, for constrn., supply and real estate VA, Washington, 1946-48; analyst mgmt. div. Hdqrs. USAF, Washington, 1948-51, chief systems and procedures br. mgmt. div., 1951-55; specialist for analysis and rev. properties and installations Office Asst. Sec. Def., Washington, 1955, staff asst., 1955-56, chief mgmt. div., 1957-58, realty officer Dept. Def., 1958-65, chief mgmt. and reporting div. contract support services directorate, 1965-70, contract specialist, 1970—; spl. asst. to adminstr. Gen. Services Adminstrn., Washington, 1956. Served from 2d lt. to capt., AUS, 1942-46; CBI; col. USAF Res, Decorated Bronze Star medal. Mem. Am. Polit. Sci. Assn. Roman Catholic. Home: 9000 Linton Lane Stratford on the Potomac Alexandria VA 22308 Office: Pentagon Washington DC 20330

MCDONALD, ROBERT WADE, mech. engr.; b. Raleigh, N.C., Mar. 17, 1933; s. Norman Capel and Esther (Riggan) McD.; B.S., N.C. State Coll., 1956; m. Catherine Patterson Coley, Jan. 12, 1952; children—Miriam, Beverly. Comml. sales Mpls. Honeywell, Greensboro, N.C., 1956-60; chief engr. Stahl Rider, Inc., Raleigh, 1960-61; div. heating-cooling specialist Carolina Power & Light Co., Southern Pines, N.C., 1961-62, Raleigh, 1962-67, system heating-cooling engr., 1967-72, prin. engr. transmission location, 1972—. Mem. Nat. Soc. Profl. Engrs. N.C., Am. Soc. Heat, Refrigeration and Air Conditioning Engrs., N.C. Soc. Engrs., Sigma Phi Epsilon. Republican. Presbyn. Club: Carolina Country. Home: 1103 Cowper Dr Raleigh NC 27608 Office: PO Box 1551 Raleigh NC 27602

MCDONALD, ROY, newspaper puslisher; b. Graysville, Tenn., Nov. 25, 1901; s. Frank Jones and Nannie (Ketner) McD.; m. Elizabeth Williams, Dec. 8, 1923. Chmn. bd., pub. Chattanooga News-Free Press Co., pub. Chattanooga News-Free Press; chmn. bd. Tenn. Blue Cross-Blue Shield. Home: 405 Scenic Hwy Lookout Mountain TN 37350 Office: 400 E 11th St Chattanooga TN 37402

MCDONALD, WALTER SCOTT, city mgr.; b. Pilot Point, Tex., July 23, 1908; s. George Edwin and Jessie (Scott) McD.; B.S. in Civil Engring., So. Meth. U., 1931; m. Evelyn Foster Moore, June 8, 1934; children—Walter Scott, Steve George, Lynn Elizabeth, (Mrs. Robert Murray). Asst. dist. engr., resident engr. Tex. Hwy. Dept., 1931-42; with City of Dallas, 1942—, city mgr., 1966—. Recipient Distinguished Engr. Alumnus award Inst. Tech., So. Meth. U., 1967; Outstanding Achievements award civil engring. Nat. Engrs. Week, 1967; Louis Brownlow Meml. award Internat. City Mgmt. Assn., 1969. Registered profl. engr., Tex. Mem. Am. Soc. C.E. (Nat. Civil Govt. award 1970), Nat., Tex. socs. profl. engrs., Dallas Tech. Club. Rotarian. Contbr. articles to profl. jours. Home: 6814 Desco Dr Dallas TX 75225 Office: City Hall Dallas TX 75201

MCDONALD, WILLIAM BART, assn. exec.; b. Mountain Park, Okla., Dec. 9, 1908; s. John Christopher and Elsie Greenwood (Urbach) McD.; student U. Okla., 1927; m. Ernestine Lou Hershey, Apr. 18, 1937; children—John Kris, Pamela (Mrs. Michael Lynn Nicholson). Asst. cashier First Nat. Bank, Snyder, Okla., 1927-35; motor license agt. Okla. Tax Commn., Hobart, 1935-38; distbr. Champlin Refining Co., Hobart, Okla., 1938-52; owner, Mac's Sportshop, Hobart, Okla., 1952-67; mgr. Hobart C. of C. (Okla.), 1968—. Mem. Okla. Ho. of Reps., 1941-45; mem. Hobart (Okla.) City Council, 1947-51; treas., Hobart, Okla., 1955—. Recipient Community Service award Hobart C. of C., 1971. Mem. Hobart C. of C. (pres. 1938). Democrat. Methodist. Kiwanian. Home: 505 N

Hitchcock St Hobart OK 73651 Office: 411 S Main St Hobart OK 73651

MCDONELL, WILLIAM ROBERT, chemist; b. New Rockford, N.D., Mar. 8, 1925; s. Arthur Phillip and Eva Pearl (Williamson) McD.; B.S. in Chemistry, U. Mich., 1947, M.S. in Chemistry, 1948; Ph.D., U. Cal., 1951; m. Donnalee M. Lissaman, Mar. 20, 1955; children—James D., Melinda L. Chemist, Argonne Nat. Lab., E.I. duPont de Nemours & Co., 1951-53; engr. Savannah River Lab., Aiken, S.C., 1953-60, supr., 1960-70, sr. research scientist, 1969, research asso., 1970-—. Mem. Am. Chem. Soc., Am. Nuclear Soc., Phi Beta Kappa, Sigma Xi. Home: 1318 Evans Rd Aiken SC 29801 Office: Savannah River Lab Aiken SC 29801

MCDONOUGH, MARTIN PATRICK, librarian; b. Chgo., Jan. 28, 1914; s. Partrick and Delia (Flanagan) McD.; B.A., Villanova U., 1938; B.A. in L.S., Rosary Coll., 1941; postgrad. U. Chgo., 1947-48; m. Barbara June Scarborough, June 30, 1946; children—Martin Patrick, Christine Marie. Librarian, St. Rita High Sch., Chgo., 1939-41; asst. librarian Wright Jr. Coll., Chgo., 1946, 50-51; research librarian Chgo. Dept. Subways and Superhighways, 1946; tech. librarian Q.M. Food and Container Inst., Chgo., 1947-49; dir. Library Sch., East Tex. Coll., Commerce, 1949-50; base and tech. librarian Ellington AFB, Tex., 1952-54; chief librarian Houston Post, 1954-62; chief librarian U.S. Army Arty. and Missile Sch., Ft. Sill, Okla., 1962-64; head processes sect., tech. information dissemination br. NASA Manned Spacecraft Center, Houston, 1964-—. Sec. San Jacinto Assn. for Retarded. Served with USAAF, 1942-45. Mem. Tex. Library Assn., Spl. Libraries Assn. Home: 1103 Wedgewood Circle Pasadena TX 77502 Office: Tech Library NASA Manned Spacecraft Center Houston TX 77058

MCDONOUGH, THOMAS JOSEPH, bishop; b. Phila., Dec. 5, 1911; s. Michael Francis and Margaret Mary (Nolnan) McD.; A.B., St. Charles Sem., Phila., 1935; J.C.D., Catholic U. Am., 1941. Ordained priest Roman Cath. Ch. in Cathedral of Phila, May 26, 1938; asst. pastor, Cathedral and St. Charles parish, Phila., 1938-40; vice-chancellor,chancellor, vicar gen. officialis, diocese of St. Augustine, Fla., 1941-48; pastor of Cathedral, St. Augustine, 1943-45; apptd. domestic prelate, 1945; consecrated bishop, St. Augustine, 1947; bishop of St. Augustine, 1947-57; aux. bishop of Savannah, Ga., 1957-60, archbishop, 1960-67; archbishop of Louisville, 1967-—. Author: Apostolic Administrators, 1941. Home: 40 Cathedral Place Louisville KY 40203 Office: 212 E College St Louisville KY 40203

MCDOUGALL, GEORGE EDWARD, constrn. co. exec.; b. Moose Jaw, Sask., Can., Apr. 7, 1918; s. George C. and Edith (Armstrong) McD.; B.S., U. Alta., 1942; m. Barbara Gillman, Dec. 5, 1942; 1 dau., Barbara Dianne. Came to U.S. 1947, naturalized, 1957. Hwy. bridge engr. Pub. Roads Adminstrn. Edmonton, Alta., also Whitehorse, Can., 1942-44; field engr., expediter, purchase agt., project mgr. Daniel Constrn Co., Greenville, S.C., 1947-48, div. mgr., v.p., gen. mgr. Daniel Internat., 1968-—, also dir.; dir. S.C. Nat. Bank, Greenville, Yorktown Corp., Greenville, Materiales y Equipos de la Construccion, S.A. Registered profl engr., S.C. Mem. S.C. Soc. Profl. Engr., Clan McDougall Soc. Episcopalian. Clubs: Green Valley Country, Greenville Country, Poinsett. Home: Rt 9 Altamont Rd Greenville SC 29609 Office: Daniel Bldg Greenville SC 29602

MCDOW, WILLIAM LEE, physician; b. nr. Lancaster, S.C., Nov. 30, 1926; s. Edward Lee and Helen C. (Williamson) McD.; B.S., The Citadel, 1947; M.D., Med. Coll. S.C., 1951; m. Sue Clements, Mar. 14, 1953; children—Pamela Ann, Lee Martin, Kimberly Jane, William Curry, Benjamin Charles, Carl Edward. Intern, Baroness Erlanger Hosp., Chattanooga, 1951-52; gen. practice medicine, Kershaw, S.C., 1952-—; chief of staff Marion Sims Meml. Hosp., 1957-67. Dir. Kershaw br. 1st Nat. Bank of S.C. Vice chmn. Lancaster County Commn. Higher Edn., 1957-—. Served with USNR, 1945-46. Mem. A.M.A., S.C. Med. Assn., Lancaster County Med. Soc. (past pres.), Kershaw C. of C. (pres. 1968). Presbyn. (elder). Home: 209 Park Dr Kershaw SC 29067 Office: W Marion St Kershaw SC 29067

MCDOWELL, CHARLES RICE, JR., journalist; b. Danville, Ky., June 24, 1926; s. Charles Rice and Catherine (Feland) McD.; B.A., Washington and Lee U., 1948; M.S., Columbia, 1949; m. Ann Lewis Webb, Apr. 26, 1952; children—Jenny, William, Catherine. Columnist, Richmond (Va.) Times-Dispatch, 1949-—, Washington corr., 1965-—, chmn. standing com. corrs., 1970. Served with USNR, 1944-45. Clubs: Gridiron (Washington); Gauley Bridge (W.Va.) Fortnightly. Author: One Thing After Another, 1960; What Did You Have in Mind, 1962; Campaign Fever, 1965. Home: 2005 Stirrup Lane Alexandria VA 22308

MCDOWELL, CLOYD DELBERT, trade assn. exec.; b. Cumberland Falls, Ky., July 14, 1910; s. Joseph B. and Cora (Barnett) McD.; A.B., Morehead State U., 1935; m. Lillian West, June 1, 1931; 1 dau., Peggy Reigh (Mrs. George T. Curlin). Mem. War Manpower Commn., 1941-45; asst. sec. Operators Assn. Williamson Field, 1946-50; asst. sec. Harlan County Coal Operators Assn., Harlan, Ky., 1950-56, sec., 1956-57, pres., 1957-—; pres. Nat. Ind. Coal Operators Assn., 1971-72. Mem. Sec.'s Adv. Com. on Coal Mine Safety Research, 1970-—. Commr., Harlan Water Works, Harlan, 1966-—. Chmn. bd. dirs. Harlan County Airport, 1960-—, Little Shepherd Trail Assn., 1966-—; bd. regents Morehead State U. Recipient Silver Beaver award Boy Scouts Am. Kiwanian (chmn. bus. and pub. affairs com. 1966-—, v.p. club 1972-73). Presbyn. Home: 403 Central St Harlan KY 40831 Office: 1st and Court Sts Harlan KY 40831

MCDOWELL, DAWSON CLAY, educator; b. Chgo., July 19, 1913; s. Dawson and Helen (Kennedy) McD.; B.S., U. Chgo., 1935, M.S., 1942; m. Bonita Kirtley, Nov. 25, 1936; 1 dau., Valerie. Metallurgist, Ryerson Steel Co., Chgo., 1936-41; instr. U. Chgo., 1943-45; prof. U. P.R., Rio Piedras, 1945-—, also dir. Inst. Tropical Meteorology. Mem. Am. Meteorol. Soc. Home: Box 22931 U PR Sta Rio Piedras PR 00931

MCDOWELL, THEODORE NOYES, govt. ofcl.; b. Washington, Oct. 20, 1925; s. Ralph Walker and Ruth (Noyes) McD.; B.A., Duke, 1947; m. Mildred Norton Bowen, May 13, 1945; children—Patricia Bowen, Janet Ruth, Theodora Noyes, Theodore Noyes. Reporter, Washington Star, 1947-50, asst. promotion mgr., 1950-51; editor, pub. South Newsletter, Washington, 1952; account exec. Evening Star Broadcasting Co., 1953-54, program mgr., 1955-61, mgr. news, pub. affairs, 1962-70; dir. pub. affairs U.S. Dept. Transp., Washington, 1970-71, Southeastern regional rep., Atlanta, 1971-—. Mem. exec. com. Children's Hosp., Washington, 1964-70, also bd. govs. Nat. Cathedral Sch., Washington, 1964-70. Served with USNR, 1943-46. Mem. Washington Acad. TV Arts and Scis. (a founder), A.P. Radio and TV Assn. (dir.), Chesapeake A.P. (pres. 1962), Washington Jr. C. of C. (sec. 1950), Pres's. Cup Regatta Assn. (v.p.), Nat. Hon. Mil. Soc. Pershing Rifles, Nat. Press Club, Radio-TV News Dirs. Assn., Broadcast Pioneers, Pi Kappa Phi, Sigma Delta Chi. Home: 4040 E Brookhaven Dr NE Atlanta GA 30319 Office: 1720 Peachtree Rd NW Atlanta GA 30309

MCDOWELL, WILETT EDWIN, pulpwood co. exec; b. Damascus, Ga., Dec. 9, 1914; s. Edd C. and Nancy Lou (Wiley) McD.; student pub. schs; m. Pearl Willis, Jan. 18, 1941; children—Ladon, Dolores Ann, Janis Regina. Farmer, Damascus, 1937-—; owner McDowell's Garage & Service Sta., Damascus, 1951-—; partner Harper Lumber Co., Blakely, Ga., 1954-—; dealer Gt. No. Paper Co., Cedar Springs, Ga., 1963-—; pres., owner W.E. McDowell Pulpwood Co., Inc., Damascus, 1967-—. Mem. Early County Bd. Edn., 1966-—. Mem. Cattlemens Assn., Early County Farm Bur. Baptist. Mason (Shriner). Home: Route 1, Box 163 Damascus GA 21741 Office: Route 1 Damascus GA 31741

MCDOWELL, WILLIAM RALSTON, lawyer; b. Shreveport, La. Jan. 18, 1917; s. Milas R. and Mollie (Ayres) McD.; B.B.A., U. Tex., 1940, LL.B., 1940; m. Fern Bronstad, Sept. 15, 1939; children—Rebecca Gail (Mrs. W. Lionel Carver), Mollye Aleda (Mrs. F. Folson Bell) (dec.). Admitted to Tex. bar, 1940; spl. agt. FBI, Washington, 1940-41; adminstrv. asst to dir., 1941-45; asso. law firm McBride & Johnson, Dallas, 1945-47; asst. dist. atty. Dallas County, 1947-48; atty. gen. atty. T. & P. Ry., Dallas, 1948-58. v.p., gen. counsel, 1959-—; gen. counsel So. Lines, M.P. R.R., Dallas, 1962-—; dir. Abilene & So. Ry., Gt. S.W. R.R., Mchts. Cold Storage, Tex-N.M. Ry. Co. Mem. Am.,Dallas bar assns. State Bar Tex. Am. Judicature Soc., ICC Practioners, Soc. Former Agts. FBI. Lutheran. Home: 5353 Edmondson St Dallas TX 75209 Office: Fidelity Union Tower Dallas TX 75201

MCDUFF, MARJORIE MCLEAN (MRS. JOSEPH REA MCDUFF), pub. co. exec.; b. New Orleans, July 22, 1918; d. Clarence Eugene and Leah (Briede) McLean; grad. high sch.; m. Joseph Rea McDuff, June 8, 1940; children—Rebecca Lynn (Mrs. Anthony T. Kramer), Alan Rea, Nancy Gail (Mrs. Randolph J. Ross). Office asst. Geiger Printing Co., Hattiesburg, Miss., 1936-38; office mgr., asst. treas. Julius Kayser & Co., Hattiesburg, 1938-41; office mgr., asso. editor, sec. Who's Who in Am. Edn., Inc., Hattiesburg, Nashville, 1955-68, asso. editor Presidents and Deans of Am. Colls and Univs., Leaders in Am. Sci., 1955-68; mng. editor CCM Corp. subsidiary Crowell Collier Ednl. Corp., 1968-72; treas., bookkeeper Univ. and Coll. Press of Miss., 1972-—; asso. editor Who's Who in Am. Coll. and Univ. Adminstrn., 1970, Ofcl. Museum Directory, 1970. Sec., Forrest County Safety Council, 1957-58. Mem. Jr. Aux. Hattiesburg. Republican. Episcopalian. Club: Hattiesburg Country. Home: 800 S 17th Av Hattiesburg MS 39401 Office: RC Cook Student Union Bldg U So Mississippi Hattiesburg MS 39401

MCDUFFIE, GLENN LARIN, electric co. exec.; b. Samson, Ala., May 24, 1918; s. James Hosea and Mary (Dannelley) McD.; B.S. in Elec. Engring., U. Ala., 1948; postgrad. U. Pitts., 1948-49, N.Y. U., 1949-50; m. Harriet Beasley Davis, Jan 4, 1951; children—Philip, Mary. Mgr. missile programs Tex Instruments, Inc., Dallas, 1955-57; with Westinghouse Electric Internat. Co., N.Y.C., 1948-55, mgr. thermal electric power plant projects, 1953-55, area rep. def., space products, Houston, 1958-—. Comdt., U.S. Army Res. Sch., Houston, 1964-—. Served with AUS, 1940-46, 50-53. Registered profl. engr., Tex. Mem. Tex. Soc. Profl. Engrs., I.E.E.E., Am. Inst. Aeros. and Astronautics, Am. Soc. Oceanography, Tau Beta Pi. Initiated devel. TV camera used on 1st manned moon landing. Home: 12222 Old Oaks Dr Houston TX 77024 Office: 1275 Space Pk Dr Houston TX 77058

MCEACHERN, WILBUR WASHINGTON, banker; b. Hazelhurst, Ga., Oct. 8, 1904; s. Andrew Oliver and Sarah (Yawn) McE.; B.A., Ga. Normal Coll., 1919; grad. Am. Inst. Banking, 1923; m. Bonnie Loree Ehler, Sept. 8, 1925 (dec.); children—Mary Lou (Mrs. Wallace D. Trevillian), Jo Ann (Mrs. John W. Hyde); m. 2d Jean Gunter Arnau, Aug. 7, 1964. With Atlantic Nat. Bank, Jacksonville, Fla., 1919-24, 1st Nat. Bank and 1st Security Bank, St. Petersburg, Fla., 1924-30; pres. Union Trust Co., St. Petersburg, 1931-44, vice chmn., 1944-46; exec. v.p. The Bank of Va., Richmond, 1946-50; pres. First Nat. Bank, Greenville, S.C., 1950-57; pres. South Carolina Nat. Bank, Greenville, 1957-66, chmn. chief exec. officer, 1966-—; dir. Fed. Reserve Bank of Richmond, Charlotte br. Pres. bd. trustees Greater Greenville Community Chest; chmn. steering com. United Fund of Greenville County, 1955; bd. visitors Clemson Coll., 1963; gov. Greenville unit Shriner's Hosp. for Crippled Children. Mem. Am. (adv. com. on fed. legislation 1961-62, mem. legislative com. 1964, pres. state bank div. 1944, mem. exec. council nat. bank div. 1960-63), Fla. (pres. 1941), S.C. (pres. 1958-59) bankers assns., S.C. C. of C. (dir.). Episcopalian. Mason (K.T., Shriner). Clubs: Poinsett (Greenville); Country Club of Va., Commonwealth (Richmond). Home: 127 Knollwood Lane Greenville SC 29607 Office: 13-15 S Amin St Greenville SC 29601

MCELHINNEY, JOHN, physicist; b. Phila., Mar. 25, 1921; s. Joseph and Mary (Kearney) McE.; B.S., Ursinus Coll., 1942; M.S., U. Ill., 1943, Ph.D., 1947; m. Geraldine E. Walters, Dec. 28, 1942; children— Ruth Elaine, Barbara Jill (Mrs. Chester Garner). Spl. research asso. U. Ill., Urbana, 1947-48; research asso. Los Alamos (N.M.) Sci. Lab., 1948-49; supervisory scientist Nat. Bur. Standards, Washington, 1949-55; br. head Naval Research Lab., Washington, 1955-66, supt. nuclear physics div., 1966-—. Recipient Superior Accomplishment award Nat. Bur. Standards, 1954; Presdl. citation Naval Research Lab., 1964. Fellow Am. Phys. Soc., Wash. Acad. Scis.; mem. Am. Nuclear Soc., A.A.A.S., Philos. Soc. Wash., Research Soc. Am. Home: 11601 Stephen Rd Silver Spring MD 20904 Office: Naval Research Lab Washington DC 20390

MCELRATH, ROBERT LEE, supt. schs.; b. Candler, N.C., July 4, 1928; s. Alonzo and Nova (Peebles) McE.; student Mars Hill Jr. Coll., 1945-49; A.B., Baldwin-Wallace Coll., 1951; M.P.H., U. N.C., 1957; Ed.D., U. Tenn., 1968; m. Betty A. Duck, Dec. 24, 1948; children—Richard S., Robin L. Tchr., Buncome County Schs., Asheville, N.C., 1951-56, prin. elementary sch., 1958-59, prin. sr. high sch., 1956-66; asso. dir. sch. planning lab. U. Tenn., 1966-68; supt. schs., Greeneville, Tenn., 1968-—. Vis. lectr. U. Tenn., summers 1969-70, Tusculum Coll., 1969-—; sch. plant cons. Bd. dirs. Greeneville YMCA. Served with AUS, 1946-48. Mem. Am. Assn. Sch. Adminstrs., N.E.A., Council Ednl. Facility Planners. Lion. Home: 1410 Brentwood Dr Greeneville TN 37743 Office: PO Box 30 Greeneville TN 37743

MCELROY, EDGAR HOOD, JR., mfg. co. exec.; b. Waxahachie, Tex., June 20, 1921; s. Edgar Hood and Myrle (Anderson) McE.; B.S. in Mech. Engring., Tex. Tech. U., 1947; m. Dorothy Clift, Apr. 25, 1948; children— Edgar Hood III, Oliver C. Power engr. Tex. Power & Light Co., Dallas, 1947-55; dir. area devel., 1955-57; v.p., gen. mgr. Tex. div. Capitol Products Corp., Sherman, Tex., 1957-63; dir. indsl. div. Hardwicke-Etter Co., Sherman, 1963-64; pres. Medco, Inc., Sherman, 1961-—, Day Mfg. Co., Sherman, 1964-—, Bodie Corp., Sherman, 1964-—, DMC Bus. Forms, Inc. Sherman, 1968-—; mgr.-partner Grayco Investments, Sherman, 1969-—; dir. Grayson County State Bank, Sherman, Recovery Co., Sherman. Served with USNR, 1945-47. Decorated Air medal. Registered profl. engr., Tex. Mem. Sherman C. of C. (past pres.), Tex. Mfrs. Assn. (past v.p., dir.), Nat. Paperboard Box Assn., Tex. Soc. Profl. Engrs. Rotarian. Home: 610 N McKown St Sherman TX 75090 Office: Box 907 Sherman TX 75090

MCELROY, SAM MARTIN, farm mgr.; b. nr. Morganfield, Ky., Apr. 14, 1921; s. Caswell Bennett and Lola Elizabeth (O'Nan) McE.; B.S., U. Ky., 1943; m. Annie Maria Meacham, May 24, 1947; children— James Bennett, Sam Martin, Susan, Charles Tandy. Farm planner Soil Conservation Service, 1945-47; instr. vets. farm tng. Union County Bd. Edn., 1947-60; profl. farm mgr., W. Ky., So. Ill., 1960-—; dir. Morganfield Nat. Bank. Mem. Gov's. Com. on Agr., 1964-68; sec.-treas. Union County Soil Conservation Dist., 1968-—. Served to capt. AUS, 1943-46; ETO. Decorated Purple Heart with oak leaf cluster, Bronze Star medal with oak leaf cluster. Mem. Ky. Assn. Soil Conservation Dists. (pres. 1966-68), Union County Farm Bur., C. of C., Am. Legion, Pi Kappa Alpha. Democrat. Mason. Presbyn. (deacon 1947-—). Home: Route 3 Box 203 Morganfield KY 42437 Office: Morganfield Nat Bank Bldg Morganfield KY 42437

MCELROY, WILLIAM D(AVID), biochemist, govt. ofcl.; b. Rogers, Tex., Jan. 22, 1917; s. William D. and Ora (Shipley) McE.; B.A., Stanford, 1939; M.A., Reed Coll., 1941; Ph.D., Princeton, 1943; m. Nella Winch, Dec. 23, 1940; children—Mary Elizabeth, Ann Reed, Thomas Shipley, William David. War research, com. med. research OSRD, Princeton, 1942-45; NRC fellow, Stanford, 1945-46; instr. biology dept. Johns Hopkins, 1946, successively asst. and asso. prof., prof. biology, 1951-—, chairman biology department, 1956-—, also dir. McCollum-Pratt Inst.; now dir. NSF, Washington. Mem. Sch. Bd. Balt. Trustee Asso. Univs. Inc., Marine Biol. Lab., Woods Hole, Mass. Recipient Barnett Cohen award in bacteriology. Inst. of Biol. Scis. (pres. 1968), Am. Chem. Soc., Nat. Acad. Sci., Am. Soc. Biol. Chemists (pres.) Soc. Gen. Physiology (pres.), Soc. Naturalists, Soc. Zoologists, Bot. Soc. Am., Am. Acad. Arts and Scis. (Rumford prize), Am. Physiol. Soc., Am. Soc. Bacteriologists, Sigma Xi, Kappa Sigma. Author textbook. Editor: Copper Metabolism (with Bentley Glass), 1950; Phosphorus Metabolism, 2 vols., 1951, 52; Mechanism of Enzyme Action, 1954; Amino Acid Metabolism, 1955; The Chemical Basis of Heredity, 1957; The Chemical Basis of Development, 1959; Light and Life, 1961; Cellular Physiology and Biochemistry, 1961. Home: 220 Ridgewood Rd Baltimore MD 21210 Office: Nat Sci Found 1800 6 St NW Washington DC 20550

MCELVEEN, THOMAS M(ELVIN), ins. adjuster, appraiser, marine surveyor; b. Florence, S.C., July 6, 1902; s. Joseph McSwain and Frances (Hicks) McE.; grad. Spartan Acad., 1921; B.S., Furman U., 1925; m. Alice Senn, June 20, 1929; children—Thomas Melvin, William Lawrence, Allice Palmer. Gen. adjuster Travelers Ins. Co. of Hartford, Conn., Charlotte, N.C., 1926-36, Glens Falls Ins. Group, Columbia, S.C., 1934-39; organized Thomas M. McElveen Co., Miami, Fla., 1939, pres., 1939-—; pres. Thomas M. McElveen, Bolivia, S.A., Thomas M. McElveen Internat. Corp., Miami, Fla. Mem. Fla. Assn. Ind. Ins. Adjusters, (past pres.), S. Fla., S.C. claims men assns., Internat. Chartered Inst. Loss Adjusters (founder, pres. 3 terms), Nat. Assn. Ind. Ins. Adjusters, C. of C. Baptist. Mason (Shriner). Contbr. articles trade mags. Home: 5867 SW 49th St Miami FL 33155 Office: 121 SW 8th St Miami FL 33130

MCELYA, OLIVER RACINE, cons. engr.; b. Clarendon, Tex., Jan. 11, 1907; s. Oliver Racine and Elvira (Punchard) McE.; student Abilene Christian Coll., 1924; B.S., Tex. Tech. Coll., 1934; student So. Meth. U., 1942; m. Eunice Martin, Dec. 28, 1925; children—Hal Martin, Carey Lynn. Civil engr. Santa Fe R.R., Clovis, N.M., 1927-31, Slaton, Tex., 1936-38; resident engr. Tex. Hwy. Dept., Dallas, 1934, 38-45; sales engr., Dallas, 1946-—; cons. engr., 1946-—; resident engr. Tex. Turnpike Authority, 1955-57; sec. treas. Dallas Tex. Computers, Inc., 1961-—, Central Enterprises, 1958-—. Mem. Tex. State Bd. Registration Pub. Surveyors. Pres. White Rock Community Council, Dallas, 1951; mem. Dallas City Plan. Commn., 1951-52. Trustee, mem. phys. properties com. Christian Coll. S.W.—Dallas. Mem. Tex. Surveyors Assn. (pres. 1964), Am. Soc. C.E., Nat., Tex. socs. profl. engrs., Engrs. Club of Dallas, Am. Congress on Surveying and Mapping, Kappa Kappa Psi. Mem. Ch. of Christ (deacon). Home: 9214 Poppy Lane Dallas TX 75218 Office: 3901 San Jacinto St Dallas TX 75204

MCENNIS, LEONARD J., JR., govt. ofcl.; b. Houston, Oct. 10, 1912; s. Leonard J. and Marie Ida (Whips) McE.; B.J., U. Mo., 1934; m. Bernice A. Thoma, June 21, 1941; children—Michael J., Mary Beth, Thomas C. Reporter The Herald-Post, Louisville, 1934-35; publicist, writer, editor Nat. Safety Council, Chgo., 1935-40; dir. publs. The Traffic Inst., Northwestern U., Evanston, Ill., 1940-59; asst. v.p. communications Ins. Inst. for Hwy. Safety, Washington, 1959-70; dep. dir. information FTC, Washington, 1970-—. Served with USNR, 1942-46. Mem. Pub. Relations Soc. Am. Home: 6517 Wilmett Rd Bethesda MD 20034 Office: Fed Trade Commn Washington DC 20580

MCEVER, VIRGLE WASHINGTON, JR., physician; b. Moultrie, Ga., May 11, 1925; s. Virgle Washington and Mary Elizabeth (Johnson) McE.; B.S cum laude, North Ga. Coll., 1948; M.S., U. Ala., 1949; M.D., Med. Coll. Ga., 1953; m. Amelia Elizabeth Calabrese, Aug. 20, 1945; children—Michael Paul, Joseph Anthony, Virgle Washington, III. Intern Brooke Army Med. Center, 1953-54; resident surgery St. Joseph's Infirmary, 1959-63; pres., chmn. bd. Warner Robins (Ga.) Clinic, Inc., 1960-—, med. dir., 1954-65; pres., chmn. bd. Doctors Clinic Profl. Assn., Warner Robins, 1966-—; pvt. practice medicine specializing in surgery, Warner Robins, Ga., 1963-—; chief surgery Houston County Hosp., Warner Robins, 1964-—; dir. med. services Pabst Brewing Co. (Ga.), 1970-—; mem. staffs Houston County, Ga. Peachbelt, Hallmark hosps. Dir., mem. exec. com. Citizens & So. Bank, Warner Robins, 1966-—; dir. Burke Corp., Warner Robins, 1967-—. Mem. Houston County Bd. Health, Perry, Ga., 1957-59, 68-—; mem. Warner Robins City Council, 1957-59; mem. Robins AFB Community Council, 1958-59; pres. Warner Robins Library Bd., 1965-—. Mem. Houston County Republican Com., 1964-—. Served with AUS, 1943-46, 53-54; PTO. Fellow A.C.S., Southeastern Surg. Congress, Pan-Pacific Surg. Assn.; mem. Peach Belt Med. Soc. (pres. 1970-71), Med. Assn. Ga. (del. 1966-—), A.M.A., So. Med. Assn., Phi Chi. Episcopalian (sr. warden 1956-58, 1970-—, del. Diocesan Council 1964-—, mem. exec. bd. Diocese Ga. 1968). Mason (32 deg., Shriner), Elk. Clubs: Lake Country (Houston); Optimist (distinguished pres. 1956-57, chmn. bd. 1958) (Warner Robins). Home: 108 Tanglewood Dr Warner Robins GA 31093 Office: 212 Hospital Dr Warner Robins GA 31093

MCEWIN, JOHN BEN, mech. engr.; b. Paris, Tex., Feb. 22, 1914; s. Fernie Fae and Cora (Weikel) McE.; B.S., Tex. Technol. Coll., 1942 Test engr. Gen. Electric Co., Schenectady, 1942-43; mech. engr. Humble Oil & Refining Co., Baytown, Tex., 1943-46; field engr. Peerless Pump Div., Oklahoma City, 1946-51; project engr. Sandia Corp., Albuquerque, 1951-55; mech., elec. engr. U.S. Army C.E., Perrin AFB, Tex., 1956-57, USAF, 1957-64, Goodfellow AFB, Tex., 1964-—. Cons. engr., 1963-—. Mem. Nat., Tex. socs. profl. engrs., Nat. Rifle Assn. Methodist. Club: San Angelo Gun (treas. 1966). Home: 3354 Cumberland Dr San Angelo TX 76901 Office: Goodfellow AFB San Angelo TX 76901

MCFALL, FREDERICK GLEASON, JR., oral surgeon; b. Tampa, Fla., June 8, 1928; s. Frederick Gleason and Clara (Cox) McF.; student N. Ga. Coll., 1946-48; D.D.S., Emory U., 1953; postgrad. U. Ala., 1956-59; m. Virginia Ray, Mar. 13, 1954; children—Frederick

Gleason III, James William, Stephanie Virginia. Practice dentistry, Atlanta, 1953-54; pvt. practice oral surgery, St. Petersburg, Fla., 1959—; chief oral, maxillo-facial and plastic surgery Bayfront Med. Center, 1970—. Pres. 4200, Inc.; treas. Fidelity Capital, Inc; dir. Liberty Nat. Bank, Magnadine Financial Corp., Bankers Fire & Casualty Corp., Universal Acceptance Corp., N.E. Nat. Bank. Vice chmn. roads and bridges com. Com. of 100, 1969—. Bd. dirs. Nat. Center for Voluntary Action, Washington. Served with USAF, 1954-56. Mem. Am. Dental Assn., Fla., Southeastern socs. oral surgery, Fla., West Coast Dist., Pinellas County dental socs., Am. Dental Soc. of Anesthesiolgy, Xi Psi Phi. Club: Sertoma Internatioal (internat. pres.). Home: 11150 131st St N Seminole FL 33540 Office: 4200 Central Av St Petersburg FL 33711

MCFALL, ROBERT WILLIAM, clin. psychologist; b. Endicott, N.Y., Mar. 9, 1938; s. Robert S. and Ruth (Sutton) McF.; B.S., U. Ky., 1961, M.A., M.A., 1963, Ed.D., 1965; m. Gene Ann Carter, Aug. 12, 1967. Research, teaching asst. U. Ky., 1961-65; dir. psychology Frankfort (Ky.) State Hosp., 1965-67; asst. dir. diagnosis and evaluation service Dept. Mental Health, Frankfort, 1967-68; clin. research psychologist Nat. Inst. Mental Health Clin. Research Center, Lexington, Ky., 1968-71, chief male treatment service, 1971—. Vis. prof. U. Ky., 1968-70; cons. Ky. Dept. Mental Health, 1968—. Mem. Am., Ky. psychol. assns., Am., Ky. seech and hearing assns., A.A.A.S., Central Ky. Mental Health Assn. Home: 3045 Montavesta Rd Lexington KY 40502 Office: Leestown Pike Lexington KY 40507

MCFARLAND, HAROLD RICHARD, food co. exec.; b. Hoopeston, Ill., Aug. 19, 1930; s. Arthur Bryan and Jennie (Wilkey) McF.; B.S. in Agr., U. Ill., 1952; m. Sarah Forney, Dec. 30, 1967. Mgr. purchasing Campbell Soup Co., Camden, N.J., 1957-67; dir. procurement Keebler Co., Elmhurst, Ill., 1967-69; v.p. purchasing and distbn. Ky. Fried Chicken Corp., Louisville, 1969—. Served to 1st lt. USAF, 1952-54. Decorated Korea Sygman Rhee unit citation. Recipient Ky. Fried Chicken Pres.'s award, 1970. Mem. Louisville C. of C., Ky. Restaurant Assn. (dir.), Nat. Broiler Council (dir. 1972—), Delta Upsilon. Presbyn. Home: 4110 Lime Kiln Lane Louisville KY 40222 Office: 1441 Gardiner Lane Louisville KY 40213

MCFARLAND, PAUL HEDRICH, JR., oral surgeon, army officer; b. Hagerstown, Md., Dec. 11, 1925; s. Paul Hedrich and Beulah Lee (McDonald) McF.; B.A., Gettysburg Coll., 1948; D.D.S., U. Md., 1952; B.S. in Dentistry, Baylor U., 1960, M.S. in Dentistry, 1962; m. Mabel Louise Gardner, Aug. 24, 1951; children—Stephen Scott (dec.), Richard Paul, Pamela Lee. Served with AUS, 1944-46; commd. 1st lt., Dental Corps, U.S. Army, 1952, advanced through grades to col., 1971; chief oral surgery Murphy Army Hosp., Waltham, Mass., 1954-55, 130th Sta. Hosp., Heidelberg, Germany, 1956; oral surgeon, Ft. Sam Houston, Tex., 1957-59; resident in oral surgery Brooke Gen. Hosp., Ft. Sam Houston, 1960-62; chief dental service, also chief oral surgery 121st Evacuation Hosp., Ascom, Korea, 1962-63, asst. chief oral surgery Ireland Army Hosp., Ft. Knox, Ky., 1963-65; chief oral surgery, 1965-68, chief hosp. dental service, 1966-68; chief dept. dentistry and oral surgery service 97th Gen. Hosp., also cons. oral surgery Frankfurt (Germany) Med. Service Area, 1968-71; asst. chief profl. br. Office of Asst. Surgeon Gen. for Dental Services, Dept. of Army, Washington, 1971-72, chief profl. br., 1972—. Instr. oral surgery U. Md. Sch. Dentistry, 1952-54; faculty ann. post-grad. course oral surgery Walter Reed Gen. Hosp., Washington, 1967-68, 72, Letterman Gen. Hosp., San Francisco, 1968, 72; cons. oral surgery 8th U.S. Army, also Surgeon Gen. Republic of Korea Army, 1962-63, 1st U.S. Army, 1968; chmn. program com. U.S. Army Europe Ann. Dental Tng. Conf., Garmisch, Germany, 1969, gen. chmn., 1970. Pres. bd. govs. Officers' Open Mess, 121st Evacuation Hosp., Korea, 1962-63, 97th Gen. Hosp., Frankfurt, 1969-70. Decorated Army Commendation medal with oak leaf cluster. Diplomate Am. Bd. Oral Surgery (adv. com. 1967-68). Fellow Am. Coll. Dentists, Internat. Assn. Oral Surgeons; mem. Am., Brit. socs. oral surgeons, Am., Korean (hon.) dental assns., Assn. Mil. Surgeons, Assn. U.S. Army. Methodist (mem. ofcl. ch. bd. 1960-62, chmn. commn. on edn. 1961-62). Contbr. articles to dental jours., chpts. to Current Therapy in Dentistry. Lectr. profl. meetings, hosps., seminars. Home: 1225 Old Stable Rd McLean VA 22101 Office: Profl Br Office Asst Surgeon General (Dental) Office Surgeon General Dept of Army Washington DC 20314

MCFEATERS, MARVIN CLYDE, govt. ofcl.; b. Kingman, Kan., Dec. 21, 1914; s. Ralph Clyde and Mary Jane (Beitler) McF.; B.C.S., Strayer Coll. Accountancy, Washington, 1939; B.A., George Washington U., 1942, M.A., 1948; postgrad. Johns Hopkins, 1959; m. Verna Marjorie Smith, Sept. 5, 1936; children—Marvin Clyde, Carol Elaine (Mrs. David Dunlap). City editor Alva (Okla.) Daily Record, 1933-35; clk. various govt. agys., Washington, 1935-42; economist, editor Bavarian Economist, Office Mil. Govt., Munich, Germany, 1946-47; commodity analyst ECA, Mut. Security Agy., Washington, 1948-55; chief procurement analysis br. ICA, Washington, 1955-56; controller U.S. Operations Mission to Thailand, Bangkok, 1957-59, program officer, Lebanon, 1962; mem. Fgn. Affairs Information Mgmt. Project, 1965: chief commodity import div. AID Mission to Brazil, Rio de Janeiro, 1966—. Prof. accounting Strayer Coll., 1948-50; mem. spl. procurement mission to Bolivia, 1954, Pakistan, 1955, State Dept. Econ. Study Team to Laos, Cambodia, 1956, spl. Econ. Trade Survey to Korea, South Vietnam, Thailand and Pakistan, 1960. Nat. editor Mil. Govt. Jour. and Newsletter, 1948-54. Served with AUS, U.S. Mcht. Marine, 1943-45. Recipient Meritorious award AID Rio de Janeiro, 1966. Mem Am. Econ. Assn., Soc. for Internat. Devel., Pi Gamma Mu. Conglist. Club: Propellor (Beirut). Home: 305 N Virginia Av Falls Church VA 22046 Office: Agency for Internat Development Latin American Bureau Washington DC 20523

MCGAFFIN, WILLIAM, newspaperman; b. David City, Neb., Oct. 2, 1910; s. Hugh M. and Nelle M. (Derby) McG.; A.B., U. Neb., 1932; B.Sc., Columbia, 1935; m. Jean Fuller, July 22, 1949; children—Christopher M., Nicholas P. Reporter, Neb. State Jour., Lincoln (Neb.) Star, Omaha World Herald, 1931-34; telegraph editor Columbus (Neb.) Telegram, 1934; writer, editor A.P., N.Y.C., 1935-37, corr. in London, Paris, French N. Africa, Egypt, Libya, India, China, Russia, 1937-44; corr. Chgo. Daily News in PTO, Japan, China, Manchuria, Czechoslovakia, Russia, London, 1944-53, UN, 1953-56, Washington 1956—; covered fall of France, Battle of Britain, 1940. Battle of Malta, 1942; War Corr. U.S. forces in India, China, 1942-43, battles of Saipan, Guam, Iwo Jima, Okinawa, 1944-45. Hitchcock scholar, 1934-35. Mem. Sigma Nu, Sigma Delta Chi. Episcopalian. Clubs: Nat. Press, Overseas Writers (Washington). Co-author: Anything But the Truth; Scandal in the Pentagon. Contbr. to numerous mags. Home: 6208 Beachway Dr Falls Church VA 22041 Office: Chgo Daily News Nat Press Bldg Washington DC 20005

MCGALLIARD, AC RUBLE, librarian; b. Stanton, Tenn., June 1, 1905; d. Alexander Caldwell and Sallye (Wells) Ruble; A.B., Davis and Elkins Coll., 1927; B.S., U. N.C., 1934; m. Harry Woodrow McGalliard, Apr. 17, 1937; 1 dau., Ac Ann (Mrs. William Davidson Brunson, Jr.). With library U. N.C., 1927-40, sec. dept. history, 1941, sec. librarian, 1942-45; head circulation dept. Battle Creek Pub. Library, 1945-46; librarian, News & Observer Pub. Co., Raleigh, N.C., 1949-54; library, N.C. State U., Raleigh, 1955—. Mem. Beta Phi Mu, Wake County Democratic Women, N.C. Library Assn., Southeastern Library Assn. Presbyn. Author junvenile stories. Home: 408 Glascock St Raleigh NC 27604 Office: Ref Dept D H Hill Library N C State U Raleigh NC 27607

MCGALLIARD, HARRY WOODROW, state ofcl.; b. Connelly Springs, N.C., July 19, 1911; s. William Theodore and Agnes (Presson) McG.; A.B., U. N.C., 1929, J.D., 1935; postgrad. Harvard, 1929-30; m. Ac Ruble, Apr. 17, 1937; 1 dau., Ac Ann (Mrs. W. D. Brunson, Jr,). Admitted to N.C. bar, 1935; asst. dir. N.C. Inst. Govt., 1935-40; mem. N.C. atty. genls. staff, Raleigh, 1940-51, asst. N.C. atty. gen., 1951-63, dep. atty. gen., 1963-70, chief dep. atty. gen., 1970—. Commr. on uniform state laws, 1946-55; mem. N.C. jud. council, 1959-61, 62-66. Served with AUS, 1943-46. Home: 408 Glascock St Raleigh NC 27604 Office: N C Atty Gen Office Raleigh NC 27602

MCGALLIARD, WILLIAM ALVA, pub. co. editor; b. Maxwell, Okla., Aug. 23, 1912; s. Don Dempsey and Julia May (Walker) McG.; student extension courses U. Okla., 1952-53; m. Bessie Brunetta Sweat, Dec. 3, 1932; children—Glorianna (Mrs. George Chapman), Helen Janet (Mrs. J.L. Bullard), Judith Carol (Mrs. B.J. Nelson), Nicholas Alva. County mgr. farm program U.S. Dept. Agr., Carter County, Okla., 1942-51; writer, editor The Daily Ardmoreite, Ardmore, Okla., 1951-56, writer, editor, pub. relations rep., 1963—; pub. relations dir. The Noble Found., Ardmore, 1957-58; free lance writer, photographer, Ardmore, 1958-62; Pres., Ardmore Sheltered Workshop, 1970. Bd. dirs. Ardmore Pub. Library, 1964-67, chmn., 1967. Served with AUS, 1944-45. Named hon. Indian Chief, Chickasaw Tribe, 1966, outstanding citizen, Ardmore C. of C., 1970, recipient citizen recognition award Okla. Library Assn., 1967. Mem. Okla. Writers. Fedn., Am., Okla. library assns. Okla. Council Libraries (chmn. 1968-69), Okla. Dept. Libraries Bd. (vice chmn. 1970-71), Ardmore C. of C. (mem. edn. council, 1965-71, chmn. council 1967-69). Mason (32 deg., Shriner). Author: The Seeker and the Explorer, 1961. Home: 1209 Wolverton St Ardmore OK 73401 Office: 115 W Broadway Ardmore OK 73401

MCGARRAGHY, JOSEPH C., judge; b. Washington, Nov. 6, 1897; s. Andrew and Mary Imogene McGarraghy; LL.B., Georgetown U., 1921; m. Marian Boyd Cameron, Feb. 24, 1939 (dec. June 1970). Asst. corp. counsel, 1924-25; mem. law firm Colladay, McGarraghy, Colladay & Wallace, 1925-40, Wilkes, McGarraghy & Artis, 1940-54; judge U.S. Dist. Ct., Washington, 1954—. Pres. Washington Bd. Trade. Chmn. Greater Nat. Capital Com., 1945-50. Chmn. Republican State Com., D.C., 1949-54; del. Rep. Nat. Conv., 1952; chmn. Eisenhower-Nixon Inaugural Com., 1953. Served with Engr. Corps, U.S. Army, 1917-20. Mem. The Barristers (pres. 1937-38), Am., D.C. (1st v.p. 1941-42) bar assns., Gamma Eta Gamma. Clubs: Metropolitan, Columbia Country (Washington). Address: US Ct House Washington DC 20001

MCGAVOCK, POLLY P(OLITT), realtor; b. Walton, Ky., Feb. 7, 1904; d. Flor S. and Shirlie (Tucker) Politt; student Marshall Coll., 1921-22; A.B., Randolph-Macon Women's Coll., 1925; m. John Fulton McGavock, June 9, 1925 (div.); 1 dau., Shirley (Mrs. Richard Estabrook McConnell), Asso. H. T. Van Nostrand & Co., 1948; realtor, 1948—. Mem. exec, bd, Charlottesville A.R.C., 1943-46, rotating mem. bd,, 1948—; pres, Charlottesville and Albemarle Child Welfare Assn., 1944-46; co-chmn. Community Chest Campaign, 1955; mem. bd. Charlottesville div. Am. Cancer Soc., 1956-57. Head A.R.C. Motor Corp, World War II. Asso. U. Va. Library. Mem. Nat. Assn. Real Estate Appraisers, C. of C., Charlottesville and Albermarle Real Estate Bd. (pres. 1954), Nat., Va. (regional v.p. 1961, bd. dirs. 1965) real estate assn., Va. Assn. Realtors (legislative com. 1972), Internat. Real Estate Fedn., Nat. Inst. Real Estate Brokers (state membership chmn. 1962), Nat. Inst. Farm and Land Brokers, Nat. Assn. Real Estate Bds. (women's council), Internat. Platform Assn., Kappa Delta. Episcopalian. Clubs: Farmington Hunt, Farmington Country (Charlottesville); Boar's Head. Home: 314 Kent Rd Charlottesville VA 22903 Office: 1 Boar's Head Lane Charlottesville VA 22901

MCGAW, JESSIE BREWER, author, educator; b. Clarksville Tenn., Oct. 17, 1913; d. Lewis Vernon and Birdie (Basford) Brewer; B.A., Duke, 1935; M.A., Peabody Coll., 1940; postgrad. Columbia, 1948-50; student (Fulbright scholar) Am. Acad. Rome, 1959; m. Howard Franklin McGaw, Dec. 28, 1939 (div. 1958); children—Miriam Katherine, Vernon Howard; m. 2d, Harold Lorenz Geis, Aug. 29, 1964 (div. 1972). Tchr. Latin, Ward Belmont Sch., Nashville, 1938-40; tchr. Lausanne Sch., Memphis. 1940-42; became tchr. English and Latin, U. Houston, 1952, now asst. prof. Bd. dirs. YWCA, 1957-59, Day Care Assn., 1956-61, Houston Civic Music Assn., 1958-60, Houston Council Human Relations. Mem. S. Central Modern Lang. Assn., Classical League Assn., Vergilian Soc., League Women Voters, Am. Assn. U. Women, Tex. Inst. Letters, U. Houston Women's Assn. (pres. 1967-68), Houston Council Tchrs. Fgn. Lang. (treas. 1967-68), Kappa Kappa Gamma, Delta Kappa Gamma (grantee to Greece, 1972). Democrat. Methodist. Club: University Houston Woman's (pres. 1955). Author: How Medicine Man Cured Paleface Woman, 1956; Painted Pony Runs Away, 1958; Little Elk Hunts Buffalo, 1961; America; History of Houston YWCA. Translator (from Latin to English) Heptaplus. Home: 2405 Dickey Pl Houston TX 77019

MCGAW, JESSIE BREWER, author, educator; b. Clarksville, Tenn., Oct. 17, 1913; d. Lewis Vernon and Birdie (Basford) Brewer; A.B., Duke, 1935; M.A., Peabody Coll., 1940; postgrad. Columbia, 1948-50; student (Fulbright scholar) Am. Acad. Rome, 1959; m. Howard Franklin McGaw, Dec. 28, 1939 (div. 1958); children—Miriam Katherine, Vernon Howard; m. 2d, Harold L. Geis, Aug. 1964 (div. Mar. 1972). Tchr. Latin, Ward Belmont Sch., Nashville, 1938-40; tchr. Lausanne Sch., Memphis, 1940-42; tchr. English and Latin, U. Houston, 1952—. Bd. dirs. YWCA, 1957-59, Day Care Assn., 1956-61, Houston Civic Music Assn., 1958-60, Houston Council Human Relations. Recipient Cokesburg Juvenile award; Theta Sigma Phi lit. award; research grant, 1964. Mem. Tex. Folklore Soc., South Central Modern Lang. Assn., Houston Council. Tchrs. Fgn. Lang. (treas.), League Women Voters, Am. Assn. U. Women, Tex. Inst. Letters, U. Houston Women's Assn. (pres. 1967-68), Kappa Kappa Gamma. Democrat. Methodist. Club: University Houston Woman's (pres. 1954-55). Author: How Medicine Man Cured Paleface Woman, 1956; Painted Pony Runs Away, 1958; Little Elk Hunts Buffalo, 1961; History of Houston YWCA; translator Heptaplus. Home: 2405 Dickey Pl Houston TX 77019

MCGEE, DEAN ANDERSON, petroleum exec.; b. Humbolt, Kan., Mar. 20, 1904; s.. George Gentry and Gertrude Hattie (Sayre) McG.; B.S. in Mining Engring., Kan. U., 1926; LL.D., Oklahoma City U., 1957; D.Sc., Bethany Nazarene Coll., 1967; D. Eng., Colo. Sch. Mines, 1968; m. Dorothea Antoinette Swain, June 28, 1938; children—Marcia Ann (Mrs. Charles P. Bieber), Patricia Dean (Mrs. C. Burke Maino). Geology instr. Kan. U., 1926-27; petroleum geologist Phillips Petroleum Co., Bartlesville, Okla., 1927, chief geologist, 1935-37; v.p. charge prodn., exploration Kerr-McGee Oil Industries, Inc. (name changed to Kerr-McGee Corp. 1965.), Oklahoma City, 1937-42, exec. v.p., 1942-54, pres., 1954-67, chmn. bd., 1963—, also dir.; pres., dir. Kerr-McGee Bldg. Corp., Kerr-McGee Chem. Corp., Tascosa Gas Co.; dir. Kerr-McGee Pipeline Corp., Kermac Contractors, Inc.; chmn. bd., pres. Bison Gas Co.; pres., dir. Kerr-McGee Australia, Ltd.; v.p. Downtown Airpark, Inc.; chmn. bd. Kerr-McGee Iranian Oil Co.; dir. Triangle Refineries, Inc., Gen. Electric Co., Cato Oil & Grease Co., Moss-Am., Inc., Bighole Drillers, Inc., Cloverleaf Serv.-Stas., Inc., Okla. Industries, Inc., Okla. Natural Gas Co., Am. Potash & Chem. Corp., Kerr-McGee of Can., Ltd., Internat. Creosoting & Constrn. Co., Knox Industries Corp., Fidelity Bank N.A., First Nat. Bank & Trust Co. of Muskogee; owner McGee-Keesee Angus Ranch. Adv. com. So. Interstate Nuclear Bd.; trustee Southwest Research Inst., Presbyn. Med. Center, Midwest Research Inst., Kansas City, Mo.; dir., chmn. bd. Oklahoma City U. Found., Inc.; indsl. counselor mem. Okla. U. Research Inst.; pres., dir. Kerr-McGee Found., Inc.; Mc-Gee Found., Inc.; dir., 2d v.p., v.p. Okla. Med. Research Found.; trustee, mem. exec. com. Oklahoma City U., Nat. Cowboy Hall of Fame; chmn. bd. trustees Am. Assn. Petroleum Geologists Found.; trustee Kan. U. Endowment Assn., Cal. Inst. tech., Oklahoma City arts Council, Okla. Zool. Soc., Jr. Achievement of Greater Oklahoma City, Inc., Mid-Continent Regional Ednl. Lab., Oklahoma City Indsl. and Cultural Facilities Trust, Scis. and Natural Resources Found. Okla.; chmn. Gulf dist. com. for selection of scholarships Rhodes Scholarship Trust, 1968-71; v.p., dir. exec. com. Frontiers of Sci. Found. of Okla., Inc.; bd. dirs. (life) Oklahoma City Symphony Soc., Nat. Conf. Christians and Jews; vice chmn. bd. trustees, dir. Okla. Safety Council; pres., dir. Okla. State Fair and Expn.; met. bd. dirs. YMCA; chmn. exec. com. Okla. Health Scis. Found., Inc., mem. corp. Okla. Art Center; incorporator Oklahoma City Community Found., Inc.; bd. dirs. Okla.-Ark. Presbyn. Found., Tex.-Mid-Continent Oil & Gas Assn., Ark. Basin Devel. Assn. Recipient Erasmus Haworth Distinguished Alumni Citation for Distinguished Service, Kan. U., 1951; elected to Okla. Med. Scis. Hall of Fame, 1958, Okla. Hall of Fame, 1958; Nat. Brotherhood citation Nat. Conf. Christians and Jews, 1961; Outstanding Civilian Service award Dept. Army, 1965; Distinguished Service citation U. Okla., 1966; Headliner award, Industrialist of Year, Oklahoma City Press Club, 1968; Outstanding Okla. Oil Man award Okla. Petroleum Council, 1970; Golden Plate award Am. Acad. Achievement, 1969. Fellow A.A.A.S., Okla. Acad. Sci., U. Okla. Acad of Fellows; mem. Oklahoma City C. of C. (dir.), Am. Inst. Mining, Metall. and Petroleum Engrs. (hon.), Okla. Hist. Soc., Oklahoma City Geol. Soc., Am. Inst. Profl. Geologists, Nat. Petroleum Council (dir.), Inst. Internat. Edn. (adv. com.), Am. Assn. Petroleum Geologists, Am. Petroleum Inst. (adv. com. mid-continent dist., div. prodn.), Ind. Petroleum Assn. Am. (dir.), Nat., Okla. socs. profl. engrs., Ind. Natural Gas Assn. Am. (dir.), Urban League Oklahoma City, Newcomen Soc. N. Am. (honoree 1970), Mid-Continent Oil and Gas Assn., Soc. Econ. Paleontologists and Mineralogists, Atomic Indsl. Forum, Navy League U.S., Colo. Sch. Mines Alumni Assn. (hon.), Sachem, Sigma Xi, Tau Beta Pi, Theta Tau, Delta Sigma Pi (hon.), Pi Epsilon Tau (hon.). Democrat. Presbyn. (elder). Mason (32 deg., Shriner, Jester). Clubs: Beacon, Oklahoma City Golf and Country, Mayfair, Men's Dinner, Sirloin, Touchdown (mem. exec. com.), Oklahoma City Petroleum, 25 Years of Petroleum Industry. Contbr. articles profl. jours. Home: 7300 N Country Club Dr Oklahoma City OK 73116 Office: Kerr-McGee Bldg Oklahoma City OK 73102

MCGEE, ELIAS THOMAS, JR., civil engr.; b. Anderson, S.C., Feb. 15, 1931; s. Elias Thomas and Helen (Wiles) McG.; B.S., Clemson Coll., 1952, postgrad., 1954-55; m. Joy Young, Mar. 25, 1953; children—Joy Karen, Lisa Kimberly. Engr., Santee Elec. Coop, Inc., Kingstree, S.C., 1955-56; engr. United Fruit Co., La Lima, Honduras, C.Am., 1956-59; engr. Allied Chem. Corp., Ironton, O., 1959-62; engr. Ohio Div. Water, Columbus, 1962-63; civil engr. C.E., Dept. Army, Huntington, W.Va., 1963—. Cons. engr., land surveyor. Served with USAF, 1952-54. Registered profl. engr., land surveyor, Ky.; certified fallout shelter analyst. Mem. Am. Soc. C.E., Ky. Hist. Soc. Republican. Presbyn. Home: 102 Pike St Louisa KY 41230 Office: 502 8th St Huntington WV 25721

MCGEE, HOWELL WALTON, educator; b. Marshall, Ill., July 10, 1916; s. Seale Walton and Mabel (Howell) McG.; B.A., Northeastern State, 1937; M.A., U. Okla., 1942, Ph.D., 1960; m. Eileen Davison, June 25, 1939; children—Sharon Sue (Mrs. Robert Steele), Rosemary (Mrs. David James Howe), Rebecca Jan. Prin., Chandler High Sch., 1937-42, Hartshorne High Sch., 1942, Idabel, 1942-50, McAlester High Sch., 1950-52; editor U. Okla., Norman, 1952-53, asst. dir. Sch. and Community, 1953-54, dir. evening classes, 1954-60, dir. adult admission and records, 1960—, cons. job corps staff tng., 1965-70; cons. Okla. Employment Services, 1967; cons. Office Edn., Dept. Health, Edn. and Welfare. Sec., Coalition of Adult Edn. Orgns. Served with USNR, 1943-46. Mem. Assn. U. Evening Colls. (exec. sec. 1963—, recipient Leadership Citation 1971), Okla. Edn. Assn. (chpt. pres. 1967-68), Okla. Adult Edn. Assn., Kappa Delta Pi, Delta Psi Omega, Sigma Tau Gamma. Democrat. Mem. Christian Ch. (elder, trustee). K.P. Contbr. articles to profl. jours. Home: 1635 Crestmont Norman OK 73069 Office: 1700 Asp Norman OK 73069

MCGEE, NEALE STRATTON, banker; b. Oklahoma City, Nov. 18, 1924; s. Leonard Kyle and Thelma (Selcer) McG.; student U. Colo., 1943; B.S. magna cum laude, Oklahoma City U., 1948, J.D., 1954; grad. Stonier Grad. Sch. Banking Rutgers, 1968; m. Ruth Rauch, June 22, 1946; children—Melanie Alison, Patrick Neale, Valerie Ann. Sales mgr. Gen. Motors Acceptance Corp., Oklahoma City, also Amarillo, N.Y.C., Denver, 1948-59; area mgr. Ford Motor Credit Co., Dallas and Detroit, 1960-64; asst. v.p. Bank Commonwealth, Detroit, 1965-67; v.p. Republic Nat. Bank Dallas, 1967—, now v.p. and rep.-Mexico, Mexico City. Served to lt. comdr. USNR, 1943-46. Mem. Sales and Marketing Internat., Robert Morris Assos., Am. Inst. Banking, Naval Res. Assn., Navy League, Naval Order U.S. Club: Dallas Athletic and Country. Presbyn. Republican. Clubs: Mexico City Country, University, Bankers (Mexico City); Dallas Athletic, Dallas Athletic Country. Home: 9765 Audelia Rd Dallas TX 75238 also Fuego 990 Jardines del Pedregal Mexico 20 DF Mexico Office: Reforma 509 3er piso Mexico 5 DF Mexico

MCGEE, TOM G., supt. schs.; b. Bison, Okla., May 23, 1904; s. Jess and Mary Chesley (Van Dusen) McG.; B.S., Phillips U., 1952, M.E., 1953; m. Margaret Irene Burns, Aug. 13, 1944 (div. July 1952). Tchr., 1927-46; supt. schs. Kingfisher County, Okla., 1946—; local corr. newspapers, 1932—. Mem. Okla. Edn. Assn. (co-chmn. area planning bd.), Okla. County Supts. Assn., Okla. County Officers Assn. Author. An Incident on the Chisholm Trail, 1938; Tom's Rules of English Grammar, 1969. Author, dir.: Pat Hennessey Massacre Pageant, 1939; Who Killed Pat Hennessey, 1941; Auntie's Money, 1940; Buddy the Boomer, 1939; The Ruby Knot, 1942; Pat Hennessey Story, 1956; Songs Turkey Creek, 1957; Half Past Noon, 1957; Trails Past Oklahoma, 1958; Their Children's Hour of Verse, 1958; The Revised Pat Hennessey Massacre, 1963. Home: 4121/2 S Main St Hennessey OK 73742 Office: Court House Kingfisher OK 73750

MCGEHEE, CARDEN COLEMAN, banker; b. Franklin, Va., Aug. 11, 1924; s. Clopton Vivian and Laura (Coleman) McG.; student Va. Poly. Inst., 1941-43; B.S., U. Va., 1947; grad. Rutgers U. Grad. Sch. Banking, 1955-58, Harvard Bus. Sch. Advanced Mgmt. Program, 1970; m. Carolina Yarnall Casey, Apr. 21, 1951; children—Carden

Coleman, Stephen Yarnall, Margaret Fox Verner. With First & Mchts. Nat. Bank, Richmond, Va., 1948—, asst. trust officer, 1954-56, trust officer, 1956-59, v.p., 1959-62, sr. v.p., 1962-66, exec. v.p., 1966-68, chief adminstrv. officer, 1968—, pres., 1969—, also dir.; dir. 1st and Mchts. Corp., 1st Nat. Bldg. Corp. Bd. visitors Va. Commonwealth U.; bd. govs. St. Christophers's Sch., Retreat Hosp.; bd. govs., pres. United Givers Fund; bd. dirs. Central Richmond Assn. Served with AUS, 1943-46; maj. Va. N.G. Mem. Assn. Res. City Bankers, C. of C., Beta Theta Pi, Delta Sigma Rho, Phi Alpha Delta. Rotarian (pres. Richmond Club 1971—). Clubs; Commonwealth, Country Club of Va., Bull and Bear. Home: 6128 St Andrews Lane Richmond VA 23226 Office: 817 E Main St Richmond VA 23217

MCGEHEE, CORENE E., accountant; b. Corpus Christi, Tex., Feb. 22, 1935; s. Adrian B. and Cora Mae (Minton) McG.; A.A., Delmar Jr. Coll., 1954; B.B.A., U. Tex., 1956, M.B.A., 1967 Jr. accountant Frazer & Torbet, C.P.A.'s, Corpus Christi, 1956-58, semi-sr. accountant, 1958; accountant Coastal States Gas Producing Co., Corpus Christi, 1958-65, sr. accountant, 1963-65; accountant Gifford-Hill & Co., Inc., Dallas, 1967—, asst. to corporate controller, 1969—. C.P.A., Tex. Mem. Beta Alpha Psi. Home: 3929 Inwood St Dallas TX 75209 Office: 2949 Stemmons St Dallas TX 75247

MCGEHEE, REGINALD BEN, food broker; b. Summit, Miss., Oct. 4, 1911; s. Louis Hooker and Stella (Scott) McG.; student Southwest Jr. Coll., Summit, 1930-32; m. Rebecca Felder, Oct. 18, 1933; children—Reginald Ben, Millie. Soda mgr. Liggett Drug Co., Washington, 1934-40; salesman Rumford Chem. Corp. (R.I.), 1940-50; mgr. R. B. McGehee Co., food brokers, Jackson, Miss., 1950-54; sec.-treas., partner McGehee Brokerage Co., Inc., Jackson, 1954—, now pres. Mem. Jackson Food Brokers Assn. (sec.-treas. 1957, pres. 1958), Grocers-Mfrs. Assn. Jackson. Democrat. Baptist. Clubs: Shady Oaks Country, Central Miss. Traffic, Liveoaks Golf. Home: 5358 S Venetian Way Jackson MS 39211 Office: 126 Ricks St Jackson MS 39211

MCGILL, JOHN CHARLES, physician; b. Clover, SC., Aug. 3, 1922; s. Waldo Knox and Elsie (Sullivan) McG.; B.A., Erskine Coll., 1943; M.D., Vanderbilt U., 1946; m. Mabel Lindsay Hamilton, Oct. 6, 1950; children—Frances, Meredith, John, Elizabeth, Hamilton. Intern, Med. Coll. Va., Richmond, 1946-47, Charlotte (N.C.) Meml. Hosp., 1949-50; practice medicine specializing in family practice, Williamston, S.C., 1950-51, Kings Mountain, N.C., 1951—; mem. staff Kings Mountain, Gaston Meml. hosps. Pres., Kings Mountain Savs. & Loan Assn., 1971—. Served with AUS, 1947-49. Mem. A.M.A., So. Med. Assn., N.C. Med. Soc., Am. Bd. Family Practice (charter). Presbyn. (elder). Rotarian. Home: 703 Hillside St Kings Mountain NC 28086 Office: 103 Watterson St Kings Mountain NC 28086

MCGILLICUDDY, LILLIAN GRACE, mem. Republican Nat. Com.; b. Chgo., May 12, 1893; d. Gustave and Louise (Peters) Flumey; degree household arts and home econs. Chgo. Tchrs. Coll., 1912; m. Shelby Martin Boorhem, Apr. 5, 1916; children—Shelby Martin (dec.), William; m. 2d, Frank McGillicuddy, Jan. 22, 1938. Tchr., Chgo. pub. schs., 1912-16; chmn. Hot Spring County (Ark.) Rep. Com., 1952-56; vice chmn. Ark. Rep. Central Com., 1942-64; del. Rep. Nat. Conv., 1940, 44, 48, 52, 64; co-chmn. for Ark., Eisenhower Presdl. Campaigns, 1952, pres. Little Rock Rep. Women's Club, 1964-65, Pulaski County Rep. Women's club, 1958-60; mem. Rep. Nat. Com. for Ark, 1964—. Chmn. Hot Spring County chpt. A.R.C., 1942-48; mem. Ark. Art Center, 1960—. Mem. Nat, Soc. Arts and Letters (pres. Little Rock 1964-66), Nat. League Am. Pen Women. Episcopalian. Mem. Order Eastern Star. Club: Fine Arts (Little Rock). Author column: W.R. Campaigner, 1963-64; contbr. Ark. Outlook, 1965—. Address: 12 Lombardy Lane Little Rock AR 72207

MCGIMSEY, CHARLES ROBERT, III, educator; b. Dallas, June 18, 1925; s. Charles Robert, Jr. and Ellen (Parks) McG.; student Vanderbilt U., 1942-43, U. of South, 1943-44; B.A. in Anthropology, U. N.M., 1949; M.A. (teaching fellow), Harvard, 1954, Ph.D. in Anthropology, 1958; m. Mary Elizabeth Conger, Dec. 20, 1949; children—Charles Robert, Brian Keith, Mark Douglass. Instr., U. Ark. at Fayetteville, 1957, asst. prof., 1958-62, asso. prof., 1962-67, prof. anthropology, 1967—, chmn. dept., 1969-72, asst. curator U. Ark. Mus., 1957-59, dir., 1959—. Dir. Ark. Archeol. Survey, 1967—; chmn. Ark. Mus. Study Commn., 1967-71; mem. Ark. rev. com. Ark. Historic Preservation Program, 1969—; collaborator Nat. Park Service, 1972—. Served to lt. (j.g.) USNR, 1943-47. Fellow Am. Anthrop. Assn.; mem. Am. Assn. Museums, Ark. Archeol. Soc. (editor 1960—), Soc. Am. Archeology (exec. com. 1971—), Southeastern Museums Conf. (council 1962-71, editor 1964-71). Author: (with G.R. Willey) Monagrillo Culture of Panama, 1954; Mariana Mesa, 1958; Indians of Arkansas, 1969; Public Archeology, 1972. Research in archeology, N.M., 1948-51, Panama, 1952, 55-56, 61-62, Ark., 1957—. Home: 435 Hawthorn St Fayetteville AR 72701

MCGIMSEY, RICHARD GIBBS, constrn. exec.; b. Caldwell County, Lenoir, N.C., Mar. 7, 1928; s. Gamewell Charles and Bertha Irene (Deaton) McG.; B.S., Catawba Coll., 1951; m. Rachel Louise Grant, Aug. 14, 1954; 1 son, Richard Gibbs. Dir. purchasing Lowe's Hardware & Bldg. Supply, North Wilkesboro, N.C., 1953-57; partner McGimsey-Sutton Co., North Wilkesboro, 1957-58; sr. v.p., dir. marketing Moore's Super Stores, Roanoke, Va., 1958—; v.p. City Flour & Feed Co., Lenoir, N.C., 1967—; pres. Contractors Builders Services Corp., Roanoke, 1968—. Vice pres., bd. dirs. Big Bros. Roanoke, 1970—. Served with AUS, 1951-53. Mem. Roanoke Valley (dir.) Va. (state dir.) home builders assns. Methodist (chmn. com. 1969—). Clubs: Shenandoah, Country, Hunting Hills Country (Roanoke). Home: 3701 Peakwood Dr SW Roanoke VA 24014 Office: 45 Reserve Av SW Roanoke VA 24016

MCGINNES, FRANKLIN PIERCE, seafood co. exec., automobile dealer; b. Mollusk, Va., Feb. 22, 1927; s. Thomas Dix and Aileen (Poole) McG.; B.S., U. Va., 1947; postgrad. Gen. Motor Inst., Flint, Mich., 1948; m. Nancy Madison Crawford Hubbard, Aug. 14, 1965;1 stepdau., Anne C. Hubbard. Gen. mgr. T.D. McGinnes, Inc., Kilmarnock, Va., 1948-64, pres., 1964—; exec. v.p., mgr. Va. Seafoods, Inc., Irvington, 1964—; pres. MCCO Enterprises, Inc., Kilmarnock, Va. Pet Foods, Inc., Irvington; v.p. Kilmarnock Motor Sales, Inc. Dir. Nat. Fisheries Inst. Served with USNR, 1944-46, 52-53. Mem. No. Neck Automobile Dealers Assn. (past pres.), Va. Canners Assn. (past pres.), Shellfish Inst. N.Am. (pres.), Mid-Atlantic Food Processors Assn. (pres.). Rotarian. Home: Bell Tower Irvington VA 22480 Office: Irvington VA 22480

MCGINNIS, FLOYD HAROLD, instrument engr.; b. Neodesha, Kan., May 14, 1932; s. Earl and Margaret (Lesco) McG.; student Bismarck Jr. Coll., 1957; m. Alice Louise Moore, Jan. 9, 1952; children—Danny, Marlene, Cregg, Linda. Instrument technician Am. Oil Co., Mandan, N.D., 1954-60; instrument engr. Western Petrochem. Co., Chanute, Kan., 1960-64; sales engr. SEISCOR div. Seismograph Service Corp., Tulsa, 1964-69, sales mgr. indsl. instruments, 1969—. Served with USN, 1950-54. Mem. Instrument Soc. Am., Soc. Plastics Engrs. Engrs. Joint Council, Am. Water Works Assn. Home: 901 E Elgin PL Broken Arrow OK 74012 Office: PO Box 1590 Tulsa OK 74102

MCGINNIS, HERMAN GARRARD, constrn. co. exec.; b. Cedartown, Ga., Mar. 16, 1924; s. John Henry and Rosie (Miller) McG.; student U. Ga., 1946-48; m. Virginia Lee Brannon, Aug. 25, 1946; children—Kathy, Herman G., Mary Ann. With Ledbetter Bros., Inc., Rome, Ga., 1942—, sec.-treas., 1960—. Served with AUS, 1943-45. Baptist. Home: 304 Lavendar Dr Rome GA 30161 Office: 401 E 1st Av Rome GA 30161

MCGINNIS, JOHN THOMAS, III, civil engr.; b. Shelbyville, Ky., Oct. 2, 1941; s. John Thomas and Louise (Griffin) McG.; B.C.E., U. Ky., 1965; m. Connie Ann West, Aug. 17, 1963; 1 dau., Mindy Lee. Civil engr. L. E. Gregg & Assos. Inc., Lexington, Ky., 1965-66, 68—; asst. civil engr. Post Engrs., U.S. Army, Ft. Sill, Okla., 1967-68, asst. civil engr. 92d Engr. Bn., Vietnam, 1968. Mem. Am. Soc. C.E. Home: 2409 Reims Rd Lexington KY 40504 Office: PO Box 1325 Lexington KY 40501

MCGINTY, JACK EARL, accountant; b. Akron, O., Nov. 23, 1925; s. Truman and Essie (Saunders) McG.; B.B.A., U. Ga., 1953; m. Jan Douglas, Feb. 18, 1950; children—Melinda, Melissa. Practice pub. accounting, McRae, Ga., 1953—. Pres., McRae-Helena P.T.A., 1955-56; chmn. Heart of Ga. Planning and Devel. Commn., 1967. Served with AUS, 1944-45. Mem. Ga. (v.p. bd. trustees 1963-64), Waycross (pres. 1963-64) socs. C.P.A.'s, McRae-Telfair (pres. 1956-57), Ga. (v.p. 1957-58, treas., 1958-59) junior chambers commerce, Pi Kappa Alpha. Methodist (lay leader 1956-60, S.Ga. conf. bd. lay activity 1960-65, treas. S.Ga. conf. 1972—). Mason, Rotarian (pres. McRae, 1967-68). Telfair C. of C. (pres. 1969-70). Home: 410 W Graham St McRae GA 31055 Office: 205 S 2d St McRae GA 31055

MCGINTY, VEAZEY CORNELIUS, educator; b. Norwood, Ga., Jan. 24, 1911; s. Newton Elliott and Susie (Veazey) McG.; A.B., Mercer U, 1931; M.Ed., U. Ga., 1951; postgrad. Tex. Tech., summer 1932, Fla. U., summer 1948, Western Carolina Coll., 1960; m. Mary Esther Harvey, Aug. 21, 1945. Prin., Morven (Ga.) High Sch., 1931-33, Valdosta (Ga.) High Sch., 1933-34, Porter Mil. Acad., Charleston, S.C., 1934-36, Millersburg (Ky.) Mil. Inst. Jr. Sch. 1936-37; asst. prin. Riverside Acad. Jr. Sch., Gainesville, Ga., 1937-39; athletic dir. Waynesboro (Ga.) High Sch., 1939-46, Newnan (Ga.) High Sch., 1946-49, Athens (Ga.) city schs., 1949-52; supt. Quitman (Ga.) city schs., 1952-65; adminstrv. asst. spl. programs, Thomasville, Ga., 1965-72. Mem. Nat. (life), Ga. edn. assns., So. Assn. Colls. and Secondary Sch. Edn. (mem. elementary com. 1960-63), Internat. platform Assn., Kappa Alpha. Baptist (deacon). Kiwanian (v.p. Quitman Brooks County Ga. 1959-60). Home: 2404 Patterson St Thomasville GA 31792 Office: 2404 Patterson St Thomasville GA 37192

MCGLAMRY, MAX REGINALD, lawyer; b. Wilcox County, Ga., Sept. 12, 1928; s. Edgar Lee and Allie Bea (Faircloth) McG.; B.S., Auburn U., 1948; J.D. cum laude, Mercer U., 1952; m. Jean Louise Hilyer, Dec. 28, 1950; children—Sharon Kay, Michael Lee. Admitted to Ga. bar, 1953; individual law, practice law, Columbus, Ga., 1954-64; partner Swift, Pease, Davidson & Chapman, Attys., Columbus, 1964-70, Swift, Page & Chapman, Columbus, 1971—. Exec. com. Muscogee County Democratic party, 1956-60. Served with USNR, 1948-49. Mem. Am., Ga. bar assns., State Bar Ga., Am. Judicature Soc., Blue Key, Phi Kappa Phi, Phi Alpha Delta, Alpha Epsilon Delta, Pi Kappa Alpha. Democrat Baptist. Clubs: Columbus Lawyers (pres. 1964), Lions (pres. 1967), Green Island Hills Country. Home: 2937 Lynda Lane Columbus GA 31906 Office: 1043 3d Av Columbus GA 31902

MCGOWAN, CARL, judge; b. Hymera, Ind., May 7, 1911; A.B., Dartmouth, 1932; LL.B., Columbia, 1936; m. Josephine V. Perry, Jan. 20, 1945; children—Mary Rebecca, John, Hope. Admitted to N.Y. bar, 1936, Ill. bar, 1940. D.C. bar, 1948; sr. mem. firm Ross, McGowan, Hardies & O'Keefe, Chgo., 1953-63; gen. counsel C.& N.W. Ry., 1957-63; judge U.S. Ct. Appeals for D.C. Circuit, 1963—. Mem. Am., Chgo., Ill. bar assns., Bar Assn. D.C., Am. Law Inst., Phi Beta Kappa. Home: 4717 Quebece Av NW 20016 Washington DC Office: U.S. Court of Appeals Washington DC 20442

MCGOWAN, E(DGAR) L(EON), state ofcl., lawyer; b. Conway, S.C., June 1, 1920; s. Edgar L. and Francis (Mishoe) McG.; student U. Ala., 1938-41; B.S., U. S.C., 1947, M.S., 1950, LL.B., 1957; m. Mildred Parris, Apr. 3, 1941; 1 son, E. Linden. Instr. U. S.C., 1947-51, asst. prof., 1950-58, asso. prof., 1958—; pvt. accounting practice, Columbia, S.C., 1947-57; pvt. practice law, 1957-71; v.p., dir. Investment Life & Trust Co., Mullins, S.C.; commr. labor State of S.C., 1971—. Sec.-treas. S.C. Democratic party; sec. Richland County Dem. party. Mem. Am. Accountants Assn., Am., S.C., Richland County bar assns. Methodist. Mason (Shriner), Lion. Club: Palmetto. Office: 1710 Gervais St Columbia SC 29211

MCGOWEN, MARVIN CARROLL, dentist; b. Baird, Tex., Mar. 27, 1910; s. John Henry and Lella (Thaxton) McG.; D.D.S., Baylor U., 1933; m. Ethelyn Clark, Nov. 1, 1935; 1 dau., Carol Lynn (Mrs. Robert Griffin Mizell). Practice dentistry, Baird, 1933—. Sec.-treas. Callahan Sherriff's Posse, 1960-70. Served to lt. comdr. USNR, 1942-45: PTO. Fellow Am. Coll. Dentists; mem. 17th Dist., Tex. dental socs., Am. Dental Assn., Am. Acad. Gen. Dentistry, Internat. Assn. for Orthodontics, Delta Sigma Delta. Methodist. Lion. Club: Abilene Camera. Home: 951 Cherry St Baird TX 79504 Office: 201 Market St Baird TX 79504

MCGRAIL, THOMAS HUGH, lawyer; b. Albany, N.Y., Sept. 6, 1920; s. Thomas H. and Katherine (Fischer) McG.; A.B., Harvard, 1947, LL.B., 1950; m. Ruth Ann Hutton, June 15, 1957; children—Mary Ann, Katherine, Margaretha, Elizabeth. Admitted to D.C. bar, 1956; trial atty. U.S. Dept. Justice, 1951-55; mem. com. counsel, judiciary com. U.S. Ho. of Reps., 1955-56; asst. U.S. atty., Washington, 1956-59; individual law practice, 1959-61; partner Thompson, McGrail & O'Donnell, Washington, 1962—. Served to capt., inf. AUS, 1941-46. Home: 9730 Shreiner Lane Great Falls VA 22066 Office: Union Trust Bldg Washington DC 20005

MCGRAIN, PRESTON, geologist; b. Corydon, Ind., Dec. 10, 1917; s. Albert M. and Eva (Shuck) McG.; student Antioch Coll., 1935-39; A.B., Ind. U., 1940, M.A., 1942, postgrad., 1946-47; m. Magdalene Schlotthauer, Feb. 16, 1959. Field asst., geologist Ind. Geol. Survey, Bloomington, summers 1940, 46, 47; geologist Ind. Flood Control and Water Resources Commn., Indpls., 1947-50; asst. state geologist Ky. Geol. Survey, U. Ky., Lexington, 1950—. Teaching asst. dept. geology Ind. U., Bloomington, 1940-42. Served to capt. C.E., AUS, 1942-46. Fellow Geol. Soc. Am., Ind. Acad. Sci.; mem. Am. Assn. Petroleum Geologists, Geol. Soc. Ky. (pres. 1955-56), Am. Inst. Mining, Metall. and Petroleum Engrs. Christian Scientist. Contbr. articles to profl. jours. Home: 1221 Providence Rd Lexington KY 40502 Office: Ky Geol Survey U Ky Lexington KY 40506

MCGRATH, HAROLD MORRIS, educator; b. Cortez, Colo., June 1, 1916; s. Michael A. and Bernice (Holt) McG.; B.A., Colo. State Coll., 1956, M.A., 1957, Ed.D., 1964; m. Mildred M. Taylor, Mar. 26, 1950; children— Patricia Ann., Michael Arthur. Prin., Kuner Sch. Dist., Kersey, Colo., 1951; with Ideal Grocery Inc., Greeley, Colo., 1952-56; salesman Miller Supermarkets, Greeley, 1956-58; faculty E. Carolina U., Greenville, 1957—, prof. bus. edn., 1964—. Served with USCGR, 1942-45. Mem. N.E.A., N.C. Edn. Assn., Greeley Numis. Soc. (pres. 1948-51), Pi Omega Pi (hon.), Phi Delta Kappa, Delta Pi Epsilon, Beta Gamma Sigma. Moose. Club: Civitan. Home: 103 Deerwood Dr Greenville NC 27834

MCGRATH, KYRAN MURRAY, assn. exec., lawyer; b. Chgo., Aug. 24, 1934; s. George E. and Annabelle (Colten) G.; B.S. cum laude Georgetown U., 1956, LL.B., 1959; m. Rosemary McVeigh, June 16, 1956; children—Kyran Murray, Jr., Eileen, Thomas, Roseann. Admitted to D.C. bar, 1959; gen. practice, Washington, 1959-61; legislative counsel Senator Paul H. Douglas, Washington, 1961-65; chief Ill. Dept. Bus. and Econ. Devel., Washington, 1965-67; spl. asst. to chmn. Nat. Adv. Commn. on Civil Disorders, Washington, 1967-68; dir. Am. Assn. Museums, Washington, 1968—. Lectr., cons. U.S. Dept. Labor, 1967; mem. U.S. nat. commn. to UNESCO, 1970. Pres., P.T.A., Washington, 1967. Roman Catholic. Club: Happy Hour Investment (pres. 1965-67) (Washington). Office: Am Assn Museums 2233 Wisconsin Av NW Washington DC 20007

MCGRATH, ROGER GREGORY, III, oil co. exec.; b. Greenwood, Miss., Feb. 19, 1930; s. Roger Gregory and Xavier (Brickell) McG.; student St. Bernard Coll., 1947-48, Miss. State U., 1948-49; m. Barbara Peaster, July 14, 1956; children—John Gregory, Barbara Lynn. With Southland Oil Co., Yazoo City, Miss., 1949—, exec. asst. to chmn. of bd., 1965-72, v.p., dir., 1972—. Chmn., Yazoo County United Givers Fund, 1966. Served with AUS, 1951-52. Mem. Am. (bd. dirs.). Miss. (bd. dirs., pres. 1972) trucking assns., Yazoo County C. of C. (pres. 1969). Club: Yazoo Country (pres. 1969). Home: 2254 Wildwood Terrace Yazoo City MS 39194 Office: 112 E Broadway St Yazoo City MS 39194

MCGRAW, EARL CLYDE, utilities exec.; b. Elwood, Neb., Dec. 15, 1903; s. Earl J. and Ella P. (Swan) McG.; B.S., U. Neb., 1927; m. Mildred Louise Skoda, Dec. 17, 1926; children—Thomas Edward, Richard Lee, Stephen Clyde. Successively engr., local supt., asst. dist. supt., dist. supt. Western Pub. Co., 1927-37; gen. supt. Tex.-N.M. Utilities Co., 1937-41; operating div. Stone & Webster Service Corp., N.Y.C., 1941-45, v.p. Boston office, 1945-49, v.p. N.Y.C. office, 1949-50; pres. Montaup Electric Co., v.p. Haverhill Gas Light Co., Fall River Gas Works Co., and Tampa Electric Co., 1945-49; v.p. Transcontinental Gas Pipe Line Corp., Houston, 1950-55, exec. v.p., 1955-57, pres., 1957-67, chmn. bd., 1967—, also dir. Profl. engr., Mass., N.J., Tex., Ala., Ga., Md., Miss., N.Y., N.C., S.C., Va. Mem. Am. Inst. E.E., Am. Inst. M.E., Soc. Gas Lighting, Houston Petroleum Club. Presbyn. Mason. Clubs: Austin (Tex.); River Oaks Country, Houston, Engineers (Houston). Home: 5917 Green Tree Rd Houston TX 77027 Office: 3100 Travis St Houston TX 77006

MCGRAW, JACK ELMER, ednl. fund exec.; b. Barwick, Ga., July 8, 1928; s. Henry Harris and Carrie (Vanlandingham) McG.; B.S., Fla. State U., 1950; m. Lynnette Emily Forrester, June 26, 1949; children— Jacquelyn Carol, Russell Howard, Lynnette Elise. Asst. mgr. bookstore Fla. State U., Tallahassee, 1950-52; administrv. asst. Fla. State U. Alumni Assn., 1952-54, asst. exec. sec., 1957-60; dir. pub. relations Valdosta (Ga.) State Coll., 1954-57; asst. sec. Pickett & Hatcher Ednl. Fund, Inc., Columbus, Ga., 1960-63, sec., 1963—. Bd. dirs. Columbus br. Nat. Conf. Christians and Jews, Columbus chpt. A.R.C. Served with AUS, 1946-47. Mem. Ga. Assn. student Financial Aid Adminstrs. (v.p. 1968-70). Baptist (chmn. bd. deacons). Kiwanian (pres. 1969. dist. lt. gov. 1969-70.) Home: 2646 Edgewood Rd Columbus GA 31906 Office: 1800 Buena Vista Rd Columbus GA 31902

MCGREEVY, MARTIN KENNETH, ins. co. exec.; b. Central Falls, R.I., Jan. 17, 1931; s. John Martin and Elizabeth Mary (Coderre) McG.; A.B., Providence Coll., 1952; M.A., Boston U., 1953; m. Amy Whitfield Jones, Feb. 19, 1955; children—Brian Kenneth, Marion Elizabeth. Tchr. pub. schs., Pawtucket, R.I., 1953; ins. agt. various cos., Atlanta, 1956-60; br. sales mgr. Am. Mut. Fire Ins. Co., 1960-63, multi peril underwriting mgr., Charleston, S.C., 1963-66, underwriting mgr., 1966-67, v.p. underwriting, 1967—; v.p. underwriting Carolina Am. Life Ins. Co., 1969—. Active United Fund, Citadel Ednl. Found. Bd. dirs. Ins. Forum Adv. Bd., U. S.C. Served to 1st. lt. AUS, 1953-55. Mem. Soc. C.P.C.U.'s (chpt. pres. 1970-72, regional adv. bd. 1971-72), S.C. Windstorm and Hail Underwriting Assn. (chmn. bd. dirs. 1971—), Ga. Property Ins. Facility (dir.), Ga. Automobile Ins. Plan (dir.), S.C. Hist. Soc., Phi Alpha Theta. Episcopalian (sr. warden 1969-71, conv. del. 1970). Rotarian (chmn. internat. youth projects com. 1971-72). Club: Charleston Country. Home: 221 Shady Lane Charleston SC 29407 Office: 100 Broad St PO Box 838 Charleston SC 29402

MCGREW, CLINTON JACKSON, JR., physician; b. Marion, O., Dec. 25, 1930; s. Clinton Jackson and Esther Gertrude (Harris) McG.; A.A., George Washington U., 1950, A.B., 1952, M.D., 1955; M.S., U. Rochester, 1957; m. Olga Marion Dunbar, Apr. 29, 1955; children—Jason Lee, Alan Carle, David Mark, Donna Lee, Cathy Ann. With M.C. USN, 1955—, advanced through grades to capt., 1971; resident internal medicine Bethesda Naval Hosp., 1962-65; head disposition sect. Surgeon Gen. Office, 1965-68; med. research adviser Def. Atomic Support Agy., 1960-61; chief medicine Naval Hosp., Orlando, Fla., 1968-70; chief recruit dispensary Naval Tng. Center, Orlando, Fla., 1970—. Bd. dirs. Agape Ministries. Mem. A.M.A., Christian, Fla. State, Orange County med. socs., Tau Kappa Epsilon. Baptist. Club: Sailing (Orlando, Fla.). Home: 2743 Summerfield Rd Winter Park FL 32789 Office: Naval Hosp Glenridge Way Orlando FL 32813

MCGREW, GERALD L., oil co. exec.; b. Gas, Kan., Aug. 17, 1918; s. Ora C. and Frankie L. (Forrester) M.; student Iola Jr. Coll., 1936-38; B.S., U. Kan., 1947; m. Mary Jane Reid, June 22, 1947; children—Stephen R., Christi Sue. With engring dept. Cities Service Gas Co., 1940-41; gen. engring dept. Cities Service Oil Co., 1947-49, Bartlesville, Okla., 1947-49, purchasing dept., 1949-51, rep., Washington, 1951-52, with crude oil supply div., 1952-58, v.p. supply and transp., 1958-66, v.p. pub. and indsl. relations, dir., Tulsa, 1966—. Served to maj. C.E., AUS, 1941-46. Mem. Nat. Alliance Businessmen for Eastern Okla. (chmn. 1969-71), Met. Tulsa C. of C. (dir., v.p. 1969-71), Oklahoma C. of C. Mason. Clubs: Southern Hills Country, Tulsa, Summit (Tulsa); Austin, Wichita Petroleum (Kan.). Home: 2956 E 57th Place Tulsa OK 74105 Office: Cities Service Bldg PO Box 300 Tulsa OK 74102

MCGRORY, MARY, newspaperwoman; b. Boston; d. Edward Patrick and Mary (Jacobs) McGrory; A.B., Emmanuel Coll. Reporter, Boston Herald Traveler, 1942-47; book reviewer Washington Evening Star, 1947-54, feature writer for nat. staff, 1954—. Recipient George Polk Meml. award. Office: Washington Evening Star 225 Virginia Av SE Washington DC 20003

MCGUFFEE, HERBERT BUFORD, JR., marketing and merchandising co. exec.; b. Brookhaven, Miss., Dec. 11, 1925; s. Herbert Buford and Lillie May (Holloway) McG.; B.B.A. in Marketing and Merchandising, U. Miss., 1949; m. Mary George McCarty, Dec. 19, 1969. Operating mgr. Montgomery Ward and Co., 1949-50; 1st floor mgr. R.E. Kennington Co., Inc., Jackson, Miss., 1951-52; Statistician Miss. Ins. Commn., 1953-55; salesman Woolley Bros. Inc., Jackson, 1955-60; pres., gen. mgr. Woolley & McGuffee, Inc., Jackson, 1969; chmn. bd. Herbert B. McGuffee, Inc., Jackson, 1969—. Served with AUS, World War II. Mem. Jackson C. of C. (mem. good govt. and distbrs. com.), Natchez Trace Pkwy. Assn. Miss., Jackson Floor Covering Assn., USCG Aux. (membership tng. and pub. edn. officer). Methodist. Rotarian. Home: 110 S Park Dr Jackson MS 39211 Office: 927 Palmyra St Jackson MS 39203

MCGUFFEY, CARROLL WADE, educator; b. nr. Nora, Ky., May 8, 1922; s. Logan Herschel and Kate Ida (Wade) McG.; B.S., Eastern Ky. State U., 1948; M.A., George Peabody Coll. for Tchrs., 1949; D.Ed., Fla. State U., 1957; m. Dorothy Jane Landers, Sept. 2, 1950; children— Carroll Wade, Janie Sue, Linda Lou, Patrick William, Donald Eugene. Math. tchr. Fitzgerald (Ga.) High Sch., 1949-50; survey cons. Ga. Dept. Edn., 1950-51, coordinator field studies, 1952-53, supr. sch. plant services, 1953-54, chief Office Sch. Plant Service, 1956-58; grad. research asst. Fla. State U., 1954-55; sch. plant adminstr. Fla. State Dept. Edn., 1958-60, asst. dir. sch. plant adminstrn., 1960-64; exec. dir. Asso. Cons. Edn., Inc., Tallahassee, 1964-68; prof. edn., dir. edn1. planning and devel. studies U. Ga., Athens, 1968—. Vis. prof. Fla. State U., 1962-68; pres. Ednl. Cons., Inc., Athens, Ga., 1969—; pres. Interstate Sch. Bldg. Service, 1962; adviser Fla. Sch. Plant Mgmt. Assn., 1960-64. Served to capt. AUS, 1942-46, 51-52. Recipient citation Exec. Office Pres. U.S., 1964; certificate of Merit, Fla. Civil Def. Council, 1964. Mem. Council Ednl. Facility Planners Internat. (Distinguished Service award 1971, pres.-elect 1971-72), Am. Assn. Sch. Adminstrs., Assn. U. Profs., Assn. Sch. Bus. Ofcls., Southeastern Council Ednl. Facility Planners (chmn. 1970-71), Phi Delta Kappa. Contbr. articles to profl. jours. Home: Route 1 Deerfield Rd Bogart GA 30622 Office: Coll Edn U Ga Athens GA 30601

MCGUIRE, FRANK JOSEPH, basketball coach; b. N.Y.C., Nov. 8, 1916; s. Robert J. and Anne (Lynch) McG.; B.S., St. John's U., 1936; M.S. in Phys. Ed., N.Y. U., 1949; L.H.D., Belmont Abbey Coll., 1961; m. Patricia Johnson, Apr. 14, 1941; children—Patricia Jeanne (Mrs. Stephen F. Johnson), Carol Anne, Frank Joseph. Asst. football coach, baseball coach St. Xavier High Sch., N.Y.C,, 1937-47; basketball coach, baseball coach St, John's U., N.Y,C,, 1947-52; head basketball coach U, N.C., Chapel Hill, 1952-61, Phila. Warriors, Nat. Basketball Assn., 1961-62; head basketball coach, asso. athletic dir. U. S.C., 1964—. Lectr. basketball various clinics. Pres. N.C. Cerebral Palsy Found., 1958-59; chmn. N.C. Heart Fund Campaign, 1959-60; state dir. S.C. Multiple Slerosis Drive, 1965. Bd. dirs. Nat. Cerebral Palsy Found.; adv. bd. Fellowship of Christian Athletes. Served to lt. USNR, 1942-46. Named U.S. Basketball Coach of Yr., Met. N.Y.C. Writers, 1952, U.P.I., A.P., U.S. Basketball Coaches Assn., 1957. Roman Catholic. Author: Offensive Basketball, 1958; Defensive Basketball, 1959. Home: 268 Sandhurst Rd Columbia SC 29210

MCGUIRE, HORACE MOHLER, physician; b. Sweetwater, Tenn., Feb. 7, 1918; s. Horace Mohler and Margaret (Gaut) McG.; B.S., Carson-Newman Coll., 1940; M.D., U. Tenn., 1944; m. Elizabeth Leonard Harrison, Oct. 10, 1940; children—Ann (Mrs. Gary A. Grooms), Margie (Mrs. Eugene Hancock), Horace Mohler III. Intern Bapt. Meml. Hosp., Memphis, 1944-45; resident various Army hosps., 1945-47; gen. practice medicine, Madisonville, Tenn., 1947—; mem. staff Sweetwater (Tenn.) Hosp. Dir. Sweetwater Valley Bank, Madisonville. Mem. Madisonville City Council, 1950-53,; mem. Madisonville Planning Commn., 1969—. Served with AUS, 1943-46. Mem. Am., Soc., Tenn., Monroe County med. assns., Acacia (hon.) Clubs: Optimist, Madisonville Golf; Senators (Knoxville, Tenn.). Address: Box 487 Madisonville TN 37354

MCGUIRE, HUBERT EVERETT, elec. equipment co. exec.; b. Littlefield, Tex., Dec. 6, 1927; s. Albert Roger and Maude (Hutton) McG.; B.S. in Elec. Engring., Tex. Technol. U., 1952; m. Marilyn Swanson, Sept. 27, 1948; children—Thomas Michael, Diana (Mrs. Michael T. Wright). Project engr. Melpar, Inc., Fairfax, Va., 1953-58; engring. mgr. Martin Marietta Corp., Orlando, Fla., 1958-66, NASA programs mgr., 1966-67; v.p. Airtronics Internat. Corp., Fort Lauderdale, Fla., 1966; v.p. Ground/data Corp., Fort Lauderdale, 1967-71, pres., 1971—, also dir.; dir. John McGuire Builders, Inc., Fort Lauderdale, scoutmaster, Cub Scouts Am., Fairfax, Va., 1958. Served with USNR, 1946-48. Mem. Armed Forces Communications and Electronics Assn., A.I.M. Patentee in field. Home: 5780 SW 4 Ct Plantation FL 33314 Office: 4014 NE 5 Terr Fort Lauderdale FL 33308

MCGUIRE, JAMES DONALD, police chief; b. Comanche, Mont., July 18, 1909; s. James Barker and Nettie Clay (Wheeler) McG.; grad. high sch.; m. Alma Stambaugh, Oct. 1, 1927; children—James Donald, John Lynn. With Tulsa Police Dept., 1934-54; with Haltom City (Tex.) Police Dept., 1955—, now chief. Holder certificates Tex. Commn. on Law Enforcement, Nat. Com. on Profl. Law Enforcement Standards. Mem. Nat., Tex. chiefs of police assns., Tex. Law Enforcement Assn. (dir.). Elk, Moose, Old Fellow. Home: 3029 Haltom Rd Haltom City TX 76117 Office: 5024 Broadway Haltom City TX 76117

MCGUIRE, MATTHEW F., judge; A.B., Holy Cross Coll., Worcester, Mass., 1921, LL.D., 1941; LL.B., Boston U., 1926; m. Eleanor G. McCarthy, Feb. 1, 1936. Admitted to Mass. bar, 1926, began practice in Boston; spl. asst. to U.S. atty. gen., 1934, 1939, asst. to atty. gen. U.S., 1940-41; chief U.S. dist. judge in D.C., 1961-66, sr. dist. judge, 1966—. Served USN, 1918. Mem. Am. Bar Assn., Am. Legion, Holy Cross Coll. Alumni. Democrat. Roman Catholic. Home: 2701 Connecticut Av NW Washington DC Address: US Court House Washington DC

MCGUIRE, WILLIAM BULGIN, power co. exec., lawyer; b. Franklin, N.C., July 26, 1910; s. William Boyd and Margaret Virginia (Bulgin) McG.; A.B., Davidson Coll., 1930; LL.B., Duke, 1933; m. Grace Mosely Robinson, Oct. 2, 1940; children—Elizabeth Eagles, William Bulgin, John O'Brien, Robert Boyd. Admitted to N.C. bar; mem. legal dept. Duke Power Co., Charlotte, N.C., 1933-56, asst. to pres., 1956-58, pres., 1959—, also dir.; dir. Piedmont & No. R.R., Edison Electric Inst. Mem. N.C. Bar 26th Jud. Dist. Alpha, Order of Coif, Omicron Delta Kappa. Clubs: Charlotte Country, Charlotte City. Home: 2611 Sherwood Av Charlotte NC 28207 Office: Duke Power Co 442 S Church St Charlotte NC 28202

MCGUIRK, WILLIAM EDWARD, JR., banker; b. N.Y.C., Dec. 31, 1917; s. William Edward and Loretta B. (Lanigan) McG.; B.S., U.S. Naval Acad., 1939; postgrad. Harvard, 1939-40; m. Mary Paige, Aug. 2, 1942. Syndicate mgr. Kuhn, Loeb & Co., N.Y.C., 1945-50, 52-54; asst. to commnr. AEC, 1950-52; exec. v.p. Davidson Chem. div. W.R. Grace & Co., 1954-56, pres., 1956-65; chmn. exec. com., dir. Mercantile-Safe Deposit & Trust Co., Balt., 1965—, now chmn. bd.; chmn. bd., dir. of ECL Industries, Ltd., Nassau, Bahamas; dir. A.S. Abell Co., Balt., Atlantic Coast Line Co., Balt., Mt. Vernon Mills, Balt., Canton Co., Balt., Cottman Co., Balt., Murray Mfg. Co., Samuel Kirk & Son, Inc., A.C.L.R.R., Jacksonville, Fla.; chmn. exec. com. Louisville & Nashville R.R., Louisville. Mem. Md. Agrl. Adv. Bd. Trustee, vice chmn. Johns Hopkins Hosp.; bd. visitors Johns Hopkins U. Sch. Medicine. Served as lt. comdr. USNR, 1941-45; comdg. officer U.S.S. Palmer. Clubs: Harvard, Union League, Links (N.Y.C.); Maryland, Elkridge (Balt.). Home: Marylea RD 1 Box 426 Bel Air MD 21014 Office: 13 South St Baltimore MD 21202

MCGURN, BARRETT, fgn. service officer; b. N.Y.C., Aug. 6, 1914; s. William Barrett and Alice (Schneider) McG.; A.B., Fordham U., 1935, Litt.D., 1958; m. Mary Elizabeth Johnson, May 30, 1942 (dec. Feb. 1960); children—William Barrett III, Elizabeth (Mrs. John J. Hehn), Andrew; m. 2d, Janice Ann McLaughlin, June 19, 1962; children—Summers, Martin Barrett, Mark Barrett. With N.Y. Herald Tribune, 1935-66, reporting staff, N.Y.C., 1936-42, 62-66, asst. corr., Rome, 1939, bur. chief Rome 1946-52, 55-62, bur. chief, Paris, 1952-55, acting chief bur., Moscow, 1958, assignments in Morocco, Algeria, Tunisia, Hungary (1958 revolution), Egypt, Greece, Yugoslavia, Poland, Austria, Switzerland, French Equatorial Africa; press attache Am. embassy, Rome, 1966-68; dep. dir. U.S. Govt. Press Center, Vietnam, 1968, dir., 1968-69; counselor for press affairs U.S. embassy, Vietnam, 1969—; dep. spokesman Dept. of State, press liaison between White House, Dept. of Def., Dept. of State, 1969—. Mem. State Dept. Com. to Determine Policy on Computerization of Files of Pub. Policy Statements, 1970; mem. interagy. task force to rescue Americans in danger in Amman, Jordan, 1970; chmn. policy drafting com. of information com. Cabinet Com. on Drug Control. Mem. Am. embassy com. to select Italian fellowship winners for study in U.S., 1950-52. Trustee Corrs. Fund, 1965-68, trustee Overseas Press Club Found.; adv. council, Fordham U.; journalism adv. council Iona Coll. Served to sgt. AUS, 1943-45; corr. Yank, covered assignments Peliliu Invasion in Marianas, Solomon Islands, New Hebrides, New Zealand and Hawaiian Islands. Decorated Purple Heart, Italian Order of Merit; recipient Polk award for outstanding fgn. reporting L.I. U., 1955; named best press corr. abroad Overseas Press Club, 1957; recipient Christopher award for one of ten most inspiring books of yr., 1960; named man of yr., Cath. Inst. Press, 1962; Fordham U. Alumni Man of Yr. in communications, 1963; co-winner ann. Golden Typewriter award N.Y. Newspaper Reporters Assn., 1965, outstanding pub. service award N.Y. chpt. Sigma Delta Chi, 1965; Page One award, 1966; Silurians award, 1966; award N.Y. Newspaper Reporters' Assn. 1966. Mem. Fgn. Press Assn. Italy (pres. 1960-62), SHAPE Corrs. Assn. (treas. Paris 1955). Roman Catholic. Clubs: Overseas Press (pres. 1963-65, life gov.) (N.Y.C.); The Anglo-American Press (Paris); Cercle Sportif (Saigon); Circolo del Ministero degli Affari Esteri (Rome). Author: Decade in Europe, 1959; A Reporter Looks at the Vatican, 1962; A Reporter Looks at American Catholicism, 1967. Contbg. author: The Best from Yank, 1945; Yank, The GI Story of the War, 1946; Highlights from Yank, 1948; Combat, 1950; Overseas Press Club Cook Book, 1962; I Can Tell it Now, 1964; How I Got that Story, 1967; Heroes of Our Times, 1968; also numerous mags. Author initial study N.Y., Herald Tribune series, New York City in Crisis. Early life papers on deposit in U.S. journalism collection Wis. State Hist. Soc. Home: 5229 Duvall Dr Westmoreland Hills Washington DC 20016 Office: Dept of State S/PRS 2109 22d and C Sts Washington DC 20520

MCGURN, JOHN MARTIN, utilities exec.; b. El Paso, Tex., Oct. 25, 1913; s. Martin James and Margaret (McGovern) McG.; student St. Edward's U., Austin, Tex. 1930-32; B.S., N.M. State U., 1934; m. Catherine Pinner, Nov. 12, 1946; children—John Martin, Katrina C., Arthur S., Teresa C., Christopher P., Monica N. With El Paso Electric Co., 1934-41; with Vepco Co., Richmond, Va., 1941—, v.p., 1963-66, sr. v.p., 1966-67, pres., chief exec. officer, dir., 1967-70, vice chmn. bd., 1970-71, chmn. bd., chief exec. officer, 1971—; dir. Bank of Va., Va. Commonwealth Bankshares, Interstate Corp. Mem. Va. Gov.'s Adv. Com. Indsl. Devel. Mem. Va. (dir.), Richmond (v.p.) chambers commerce, Nat. Assn. Electric Cos. (dir.), So. Electric Exchange (v.p.), N.A.M. Pub. Utilities Assn. Virginias (mem. exec. com.). Edison Electric Inst. (mem. adv. com.). Roman Catholic. Kiwanian. Home: 4100 W Franklin St Richmond VA 23221 Office: PO Box 26666 Richmond VA 23261

MCHARD, JAMES DALE, govt. ofcl.; b. Blackwell, Okla., Oct. 28, 1933; s. William Carl and Ruby (Thomas) McH.; B.S., Okla. State U., 1956; M.P.H., U. Mich., 1962; m. Mary Janett Bush, Aug. 20, 1961; children—Dale, Janet Marie. Jr. engr. Alcoa, Point Comfort, Tex., 1956-58; asst. engr. Okla. State Dept. Health, Oklahoma City, 1958-61, engr., 1962-69, dir., div. occupational and radiol. health, 1969—. Served with AUS, 1957. Registered profl. engr., Okla. Mem. Am. Air Pollution Control Assn., Am. Pub. Health Assn., Conf. on Radiol. Health, Am. Conf. Govtl. Indsl. Hygienists, Acad. Environmental Health Scientists. Republican. Methodist. Home: 812 NW 42 St Oklahoma City OK 73118 Office: 3400 N Eastern St Oklahoma City OK 73105

MCHENRY, RICHARD JOSEPH, pub. relations counselor, publisher; b. Parkersburg, W.Va., June 15, 1934; s. Edward E. and Ethel (Wood) McH.; student Ohio State U., 1952-54; B.A., Marshall U., 1958; m. Eleanor B. McRae, Feb. 19, 1961; children—Richard J., Karen M. Reporter, Orlando (Fla.) Sentinel-Star, 1959-65; pub. relations dir. Botts Advt. Inc., Orlando, 1965-66; pres. Dick McHenry Pub. Relations, Orlando, 1966—, also Dick McHenry Publs., Inc.; pub. Fla. Industries Guide, 1971—. Television producer WFTV Apt. Guide, Orlando, 1969. Bd. dirs. Miss Fla. Pageant. Served with USNR, 1954-56. Mem. Fla. Pub. Relations Assn. (chpt. pres. 1969-70), Pub. Relations Soc. Am., Sigma Alpha Epsilon. Presbyn. Rotarian. Home: 910 S Osceola Av Orlando FL 32806 Office: 20 W Lucerne Circle Orlando FL 32801

MCHENRY, SILAS LEE, govt. ofcl., educator, agrl. specialist; b. Spokane, Wash., Aug. 30, 1918; s. Silas Laura and Marian C. (Rodibaugh) McH.; B.S., U. Del., 1939, M.S., 1958; Ed.D., Pa. State U., 1960; m. Myrtle Alice Tull, Feb. 20, 1943; children—Silas Lee, Linda Jane. Tchr. vocational agr. Greenwood High Sch., Del., 1939-40; tng. officer U.S. VA, Newark, 1946-47; agrl. agt. Rutgers U., Bridgeton, N.J., 1947-49; extension poultry specialist U. Del., Newark, 1949-51, 53-58; state specialist in poultry sci. U. Hawaii, Honolulu, 1959-64, asso. prof., 1959-62, grad. faculty, 1962-63, prof., 1963-64, chmn. poultry sci. dept., supr. research, teaching, extension, 1963-64; pub. information specialist div. industry advice, bur. edn. and vol. compliance FDA, U.S. Dept. Health, Edn. and Welfare, Washington, 1964-65, industry information officer div. industry edn., program leader chem. contamination, 1966-68, bur. vol. compliance div. industry services, 1968-70, industry relations br. bur. vet. medicine, 1970—. Chmn. food task group Hawaiian Civil Def., 1962-63; participant numerous seminars and workshops U.S., 1966-68; presented results of nation-wide survey extension teaching methods at World's Poultry Congress, Sydney, Australia, 1962. Scoutmaster Boy Scouts Am. Served to lt. comdr. USNR, 1940-45, 51-53. Mem. Am. Assn. U. Profs., Am. Assn. Agrl. Coll. Editors, World's Poultry Sci Assn., Res. Officers U.S.A., S.A.R., Am. Legion, V.F.W., Fed. Editors Assn., Gamma Sigma Delta. Contbr. numerous articles in field to profl jours. Home: PO Box 9811 Chevy Chase MD 20015 Office: US Food and Drug Adminstrn Washington DC 20204

MCHUGH, RAYMOND JOSEPH, newspaperman; b. Fond du Lac, Wis., Oct. 29, 1924; s. Raymond George and Anita (Bast) McH.; student Marquette U., 1941-42; B.A., U. Wis., 1947; m. Phoebe Rose Suetmeyer, Jan. 3, 1946; children—Michael Lyn, Robin Shawn, Taylor Erin. Sports writer Wis. State-Jour., Madison, 1946-47; sports editor, then mng. editor Kewanee (Ill.) Star Courier, 1948-53; asst. exec. editor San Diego Union, 1953-58; asst. news editor Des Moines Register, 1958-59; news editor San Diego Evening Tribune, 1959-60; news editor Conley News Service, San Diego, 1960-63, chief Washington bur., 1963—; editorial adviser Navy League U.S., 1964—. Served with AUS, 1943-45. Mem. V.F.W., Am. Legion, Sigma Delta Chi. Clubs: Nat. Press, Nat. Aviation, Internat. (Washington); Overseas Press (N.Y.C.). Home: 6817 Old Chesterbrook Rd McLean VA 22101 Office: 1629 K St NW Washington DC 20006

MCILVAIN, ERNEST HADLEY, JR., govt. ofcl.; b. Prescott, Ariz., Oct. 29, 1918; s. Ernest Hadley and Ellen (Throne) McI.; B.S., Colo. State U., 1940; M.S., Utah State U., 1948; m. Mary Jane Covey, Mar. 1, 1941; children—Ruth Ann, Michael J. Range ecologist Agrl. Research Service, U.S. Dept. Agr., Woodward, Okla., 1940-54, research agronomist, supt., 1954—. Research cons. Rockefeller Found., 1958—. Scoutmaster Boy Scouts Am., Woodward, 1946-50, 65—. Served with AUS, 1942-46. Decorated Bronze Star medal. Mem. Am. Soc. Range Mgmt., Woodward C. of C. Mem. Christian Ch. Address: So Great Plains Field Sta Woodward OK 73801

MCILVAIN, JESS HALL, architect; b. Denton, Tex., Mar. 29, 1933; s. Charles Lee and Edith (Hall) McI.; B.Arch., Tex. Tech. U., 1959; m. Joni Wimberley, Aug. 23, 1959; children—James Sean, Sheila Maria. Designer Nesmith & Lane, Architects, El Paso, Tex., 1959, Garland & Hilles, Architects, El Paso, Tex., 1960-63; designer, project mgr. William Metcalf Architect, Washington, 1963, Cooper & Auerbach, Architects, Washington, 1963-65, Bucher-Meyers Architects, Washington, 1966-67 project mgr. Weihe, Black, Kerr, Architects, Washington, 1967-68 designer Callmer & Milstead, Architects, Washington, 1968. Archtl. dir Tile Council of Am., Inc. 1969. Mem. Tex. Tech. U. Century Club. Served with AUS, 1953-55. Recipient Horizon Homes Regional award for residential design, 1962. Mem. A.I.A. (chpt. exec. bd. 1968, chmn. house com. 1969), Tex. Tech. U. Alumni Assn. (pres. Washington chpt. 1971-72), Sigma Chi. Club: Kenwood (Bethesda, Md.). Address: 6012 Woodacres Dr Washington DC 20016

MCINERNEY, ROONEY, justice Okla. Supreme Ct., b. 1930; ed. U. Okla.; LL.B., U. Tulsa. Admitted Admitted to Okla. bar, 1954; asso. justice Okla. Supreme Ct., Oklahoma City. Office: State Capitol Oklahoma City OK 73105

MCINNIS, CURTIS EUGENE, TV broadcasting co. exec.; b. Shreveport, La., Sept. 3, 1942; s. Curtis Columbus and Willie Paulean (Sanders) McI.; grad. high sch.; m. Jo Ann Cato, June 27, 1943; children—Gena Ann, Jeffery Todd. With KTBS TV, Inc., Shreveport, La., 1965—, pub. service dir., promotion mgr., 1968—. Served with USMCR, 1961-65. Recipient citation, D.A.V., 1971. Home: 7204 Suntan St Shreveport LA 71108 Office: 312 E Kings Hwy Shreveport LA 71104

MCINNIS, JAMES DANIEL, physician; b. Darlington, S.C., Apr. 10, 1936; s. James Daniel and Mary Isabel (Roberts) McI.; B.S., The Citadel, 1958; M.D., Med. U. S.C., 1962; m. Betty Ann Harleston, Dec. 29, 1959; children—James Daniel, David Motte, Mark Langley. Intern, Columbia (S.C.) Hosp., 1962-63; gen. practice medicine, Darlington, 1965—; mem. staff Coleman-Aimar Hosp., Darlington. Med. adviser Darlington Rescue Squad, 1966—. Active Boy Scouts Am. Bd. dirs. S.C. Heart Assn., Darlington Housing Commn.; bd. dirs., adviser Allied Health Center, Florence-Darlington Tech. Edn. Center. Served with M.C., AUS, 1963-65. Mem. A.M.A., Am. Acad. Family Practice, S.C., Darlington County med. assns., Darlington County Asso. Clubs, Darlington C. of C. (dir.). Presbyn. (deacon 1967-69, 72—). Kiwanian. Club: Darlington Country (pres. 1971-72). Home: 103 Tennessee Dr Darlington SC 29532 Office: 120-22 Cashua St Darlington SC 29532

MCINNIS, JOHN ROBERT, physician, surgeon; b. Moore County, N.C., July 15, 1908; s. James Dalton and Florence Elizabeth (Blue) McI.; student Davidson Coll., 1927-29, U. Okla., 1931; A.B., U. N.C., 1933; M.D., U. Tenn., 1956; m. Esther Alice Hurley, Dec. 26, 1941; children—John Robert, Charles Hurly, Marilyn Esther, Nancy Catherine. Vice pres., mgr. Caroline Handerchief Co., Inc., West End, N.C., 1935-42; accountant, office mgr. Sandhill Furniture Corp., 1947-51; intern. surgery resident Mercy Hosp., Oklahoma City, 1956-58; pvt. practice medicine and surgery, 1956—; mem. staffs Mercy, Bapt. Meml., Doctors Gen, South Community hosps. (all Oklahoma City). Chmn. sch. bd. West End (N.C.) Pub. Schs., 1959-61. Served from pvt. to capt. AUS, 1942-47; col. M.C. Res. ret. Mem. A.M.A., Am. Acad. Family Practice, Okla., Oklahoma County med. socs., Oklahoma City Clin. Soc., Ret. Officers Assn., Capitol Hill, Oklahoma City chambers commerce. Presbyn. (elder, trustee). Mason (32 deg., Shriner); mem. Order Eastern Star (past patron). Club: Hillcrest Golf and Country (Oklahoma City). Home: 7008 S Country Club Dr Oklahoma City OK 73159 Office: 4515 S Pennsylvania St Oklahoma City OK 73119

MCINTOSH, G. J., supt. schs. City sch. supt., Newport News, Va. Office: Newport News VA 25407*

MCINTOSH, LAWRENCE WHITE, banker; b. Hapeville, Ga., Aug. 3, 1934; s. Eddie and Bobbie I. (White) McI.; B.S., Davidson Coll., 1956; postgrad. Harvard Bus. Sch., 1967; m. Marjorie Faye McDuffie, Oct. 6, 1957; children—Lawrence White, Laura Michele. With Citizens & So. Nat. Bank, Atlanta, Ga., 1956-68, v.p., 1966-68; pres. Store Services, Inc., convenience retailing, 1968; exec. v.p. Jacksonville (Fla.) Nat. Bank, 1968-70, pres., 1970-72; pres., dir. First Nat. Bank, St. Petersburg, Fla., 1972—; exec. v.p., chief operating officer, dir. Charter Bankshares Corp., Jacksonville, 1972—. Pres., dir. Fla. Crown Minority Enterprise, Small Bus. Investment Co., Jacksonville, 1971-72; mem. Jacksonville U. Council, 1970-72; pres. Jacksonville Clearing Assn., 1972. Served to 2d lt. AUS, 1957. Mem. Jacksonville C. of C. (com. of 100, 1969-72; v.p. finance, dir. 1972). Republican. Episcopalian. Clubs: River (Jacksonville); Ponte Vedra (Ponte Vedra Beach, Fla.); Commerce, St. Petersburg Yacht. Home: 2260 Coffee Pot Blvd NE St Petersburg FL 33704 Office: PO Box 1689 St Petersburg FL 33731

MCINTYRE, MARY SHELLEY, musician; b. Good Pine, La.; d. Archibald Ormsby and May (Rawlings) McIntyre; student Ward-Belmont Jr. Coll., 1 year, New Orleans Conservatory; 1 year; grad., also postgrad. Juilliard Inst. Mus. Art, N.Y.C.; student Columbia, 1 summer, pupil Vlado Kolitsch, N.Y.C. Solo violinist concert ensemble The Homestead, Hot Springs, Va., 8 years; solo violinist concert ensemble Lauderdale Beach Hotel, Ft. Lauderdale, Fla., 5 winters; solo violinist concert ensemble Grindstone Inn, Winter Harbor, Me., 3 summers; violinist Houston Symphony, 1943—; violist Brevard (N.C.) Festival 2 seasons. Mem. Am. Fedn. Musicans. Presbyn. Home: 2724 Nottingham Rd Houston TX 77005 Office:

Houston Symphony Soc Jesse H Jones Hall for Performing Arts 615 Louisiana St Houston TX 77001

MCIVER, JULIA WHILDEN, newspaper exec.; b. Charleston, S.C., May 7, 1909; d. William Whilden and Petrona (Royall) McI.; B.A., Winthrop Coll., 1931; M.A., U. S.C., 1952; postgrad. U. Tex., Coll. William and Mary. Elementary tchr. Mt. Pleasant (S.C.) Acad., 1931-41; tchr. art Hyatt Park Elementary Sch., 1941-42; classification specialist WAVES, 1942-45; vocational adviser VA, 1945-51; personnel mgr. News and Courier, also Charleston (S.C.) Evening Post, 1952-—. Mem. Am. Soc. for Personnel Adminstrn., Newspaper Personnel Relations Assn. Republican. Presbyn. (deacon, mem. exec. com. Synod Guidance Program 1965-—). Home: 111 Hibben St Mount Pleasant SC 29464 Office: 134 Columbus St Charleston SC 29402

MCKAMIE, EDGAR MORAN, electric supply co. exec.; b. Moody, Tex., June 14, 1925; s. William Henry and Nancy Ida (Permenter) McK; grad. high sch.; m. Lura Fay Snowden, May 20, 1949; children—William Michael, David Edgar. Trainee Celanese Corp., Kingsville, Tex., 1947; salesman Corpus Christi (Tex.) Hardware, 1948-50; with Dealers Elec. Supply Co., Waco, Tex., 1950-—, sales mgr., 1955-58, store mgr., 1958-61, v.p. sales and purchasing, 1961-—; partner Eimak Industries, Waco, 1971-—. Active United Fund drive, 1959-70; cubmaster Boy Scouts Am., 1959, scoutmaster, 1966-68, explorer adviser, 1968-71, dist. commr., 1961-64, 1968-71, council explorer chmn., 1970-71; v.p. Waco Teenage Baseball, 1969-71; pres. Dist. 15 Christian Mens Fellowship, 1963-65; pres. Northwestern Little League, 1965; pres. elect Christian Mens Fellowship Tex., 1973-74. Del., Democratic County Conv., 1956, 58. Bd. dirs. Lake Air Little League. Served with U.S. Mcht. Marine, 1943-46. Recipient Silver Beaver award Boy Scouts Am., 1966. Mem. Christian Ch. (chmn. bd. 1961-62, 1968, 70). Club: Woodland West Country (Waco). Home: 5409 Edinburgh St Waco TX 76710 Office: 1808 Washington St Waco TX 76703

MCKAY, ANN BALL, sanitary engr.; b. N.Y.C., Sept. 27, 1934; d. George L. and Helen (Ellsworth) Ball; B.S., Allegheny Coll., 1956; M.S., U. Fla., 1958; m. Milton E. McKay, Jr., Jan. 17, 1959 (div. May 1970); children—Tracy Ann, Shari Ellen, Scott E. Research asso., san. engring. research U. Fla. at Gainesville, 1958-59, research asso., dept. obstetrics and gynecology, 1959-62; san. engr. Hutcheon Engrs., Inc., Palm Beach, Fla., 1966-67; cons. chemist, water and indsl. waste problems, Belle Glade, Fla., 1967-71; mgr. labs. Fla. Atlantic U., Boca Raton, 1971-—; tchr. Belle Glade Jr. High Sch., 1967-69. Mem. Palm Beach County Sch. Bd., 1969-—, chmn., 1972-—. Treas., dir. Glades Republican Club, 1968-—. Mem. Sigma Xi (asso.) Home: 4053 Sandra Lane West Palm Beach FL 33406 Office: Dept Chemistry Fla Atlantic U Boca Raton FL

MCKAY, CHARLES FLINT, bus. cons.; b. St. Johnsbury, Vt., Nov. 18, 1930; s. Littleton Kirk and Mabel (Flint) McK.; B.B.A., U. Miami, 1954; m. Margaret Eileen Mund, June 14, 1956; children—Lisa Charlene, Sharon Lee. U.S. fgn. service officer Am. embassy, Quito, Ecuador, 1956-57, Am. consulate, Puerto la Cruz, Venezuela, 1957-59, Am. embassy, Uruguay, 1959-62; pres. chmn. bd. North & Latin Am. Devel. Corp., 1962-—; pres., founder Charles McKay & Assos., Inc., Miami, Fla., 1964-—. Mem. exec. res. U.S. Dept Commerce, 1967; mem. Regional Export Expansion Council, del. to nat. council conf., Washington, 1970, vice chmn. S. Fla. council, 1971, 72. Founding mem., bd. dirs. Nat. Fedn. Export Mgmt. Cos., 1972-—, Internat. Center, Inc., 1972-—, bd. dirs. Bd. Internat. Trade, 1969-—. Served to 1st lt. AUS, 1955-56. Mem. Dominican-Am. C. of C. (pres.) Fla. Colombia Alliance, Miami-Dade County C. of C. (bd. dirs.), C. of C. of Ams. (dir. 1970, 71, chmn. world trade com. 1972), Center for Advanced Internat. Studies (mem. council), Fla. World Trade Assn. (founder, pres. 1968-—). Rotarian. Contbg. author: Guidelines to Operating in Latin America, 1970. Author: AProfile of International Business in Dade County, Florida, 1972; Caribbean Yachting Facilities, 1972. Home: 7550 SW 141 St Miami FL 33158 Office: 299 Alhambra Circle Coral Gables FL 33134

MCKAY, CHESTER EARL, rubber co. exec.; b. Columbus, Ga., Dec. 20, 1917; s. C.E. and Vivian (Bunt) McK.; B.S. in Physics, U. Ga., 1950; grad. Command and Gen. Staff Sch., 1944, Adj. Gen.'s Sch., 1942; m. Alma Pylant, Apr. 16, 1948; children—Michael L., Charles P. Enlisted as pvt. USAAF, 1936, advanced through grades to lt. col, USAF 1952; resigned, 1952; with Sears, Roebuck & Co., Chgo., 1952-66; pres., chmn. bd. Copolymer Rubber & Chem. Corp., Baton Rouge, 1966-—; dir. La. Nat. Bank. Mem. exec. bd. Istrouma Area council Boy Scouts Am., 1966-69. Trustee Pub. Affairs Research Council, Gulf South Research Inst.; bd. dirs. Council Better La. Decorated Croix de Guerre. Mem. Internat. Inst., Synthetic Rubber Producers. (bd. dirs.), Baton Rouge C. of C. (pres.), La. Mfrs. Assn. (bd. dirs.), La. Chem. Assn. (bd. dirs.). Baptist. Home: 5053 Blue Bell Dr Baton Rouge LA 70808 Office: PO Box 2591 Baton Rouge LA 70821

MCKAY, CONNALLY, judge; b. Eddy, Tex., Sept. 22, 1914; s. Daniel Sparks and Lila (Connally) McK.; LL.B., Baylor U., 1937; m. Glee McCrary, Mar. 26, 1938; children—Diane (Mrs. Thomas W. Gilliam), Elaine (Mrs. Walker Harman), Robert Connally. Admitted to Tex. bar, 1937; county atty., Wood County, Tex., 1941-43, 46; dist. atty. Smith, Wood & Upshur Counties, Tex., 1946-49; referee in bankruptcy, 1949-52; dist. judge 114th Jud. Dist., Tyler, Tex., 1953-69; asso. justice Ct. of Civil Appeals, 12th Supreme Jud. Dist. of Tex., Tyler, 1969-—; dir. Citizens First Nat. Bank of Tyler. Mem. Tex. Jud. Qualifications Commn. of Tex., 1965-69. Pres., East Tex. Fair Assn., 1960, Tyler Indsl. Found., 1966-67, East Tex. Hosp. Found. 1970-—; mem. devel. council Baylor U., 1971-—; mem. Human Welfare commn. Baptist Gen. Conv. of Tex., 1971-—. Bd. dirs. Bapt. Found. Tex. Served to lt. USNR, 1943-46. Recipient T.B. Butler award as outstanding citizen, T.B. Butler Pub. Co., 1965. Mem. Tyler C. of C. (pres. 1965-66), Baylor U. Ex-Students' Assn., Am. Bar Assn., State Bar Tex. Baptist (chmn. bd. deacons 1959-60). Mason (Shriner). Home: 3110 Belmead St Tyler TX 75701 Office: 306 County Courthouse Tyler TX 75701

MCKAY, EDWARD S., educator; b. Sept. 10, 1923; B.S., St. Vincent Coll., 1949; M.S., Ohio State U., 1950, Ph.D., 1956; m. Louise McKay. With Ohio Dept. Agr., 1951-56; faculty Ohio U., Athens, 1958-64; now prof., head dept. chemistry, U. Tulsa. Mem. Am. Chem. Soc. (chmn. Tulsa sect.), Okla. Acad. Sci., Sigma Xi. Author: Selected Experiments in Chemistry, 1968. Contbr. articles analytical chemistry to profl. journals. Office: U Tulsa 600 S College St Tulsa OK 74104*

MCKAY, EDWIN DOUGLASS, physician; b. Canton, Miss., Dec. 4, 1921; s. Joseph William and Edna (Douglass) McK.; student Centenary Coll., 1938-41; M.D., La. State U., 1950; m. Lucienne Hollard, Dec. 22, 1946 (dec. Nov. 1968); m. 2d, Alice Beebe Pace, Nov. 25, 1970. Intern McKeesport (Pa.) Hosp., 1950-51; practice gen. medicine, Blanchard, La., 1951-—; founder Blanchard Clinic, 1951-—; practice emergency medicine Baptist Meml. Hosp., San Antonio. Mem. Caddo Parish Bd. Health, 1960-—, pres.; health officer City of Blanchard. Served with AUS, 1942-46; ETO. Mem. Am. Acad. Gen. Practice, So. Med. Assn., La., Shreveport, Tex., Bexar County med. Socs., Lambda Chi Alpha. Democrat. Kiwanian (pres. Blanchard 1957). Home: Route 5 Box 322 Shreveport LA 71007 Office: P O Box 38 Blanchard LA 71009

MCKAY, EGBERT ROBERT, police chief; b. Mecklenburg County, nr. Charlotte, N.C., Nov. 3, 1911; s. Elmer Ranson and Mary Arlena (Benfield) McK.; student Mecklenburg County Police Tng. Sch., 1946-47, 67-68; m. Edith Isenhour, Dec. 17, 1935; 1 son, James Carroll (dec.). Mgr. Vicks Lunch, Concord, N.C., 1931-36; agt. Pilot Life Ins. Co., Concord, 1936-41; Weave room Cannon Mills, Concord, 1942; with Concord (N.C.) Police Dept., 1943-—, police chief, 1969-—. Served with USNR, 1943-45. Mem. Piedmont Law Enforcement Acad. (dir. 1966-—), N.C. Law Enforcement Officers Assn. (dir. 1969-—), N.C. Police Execs. Assn., Internat. Assn. Chiefs Police, Inc. Lutheran (stewardship chmn. 1970-71, mem. council, congl. v.p.). Lion, Mason. Home: 629 Propston St NW Concord NC 28025 Office: 8 Barbrick Av SW Concord NC 28025

MCKAY, GRIFFITH HEAD, cons. engr.; b. Jackson, Miss., Oct. 20, 1907; s. John Peyton and Alice Rose (Strait) McK.; B.S. in Civil Engring., Miss. State U., 1930, Jr. engr. Ark.-La. Gas Co., Shreveport, La., 1930-32, natural gas engr., 1932-42; cons. engr. WPB, Washington, 1942-43; asst. to v.p. Tenn. Gas Transmission Co., Houston, 1943-45, mgr. sales, 1945-47, v.p., 1947-48; v.p., dir. East Tenn. Natural Gas Co., Chattanooga, 1948-49; cons. engr., mgmt., gas, fuels, real estate leasing, rentals, financing, Houston, 1959-—. Tchr. gas engring. Centenary Coll., 1939-41. Registered profl. engr., Tex., Washington. Mem. Nat., Tex. socs. profl. engrs., Houston Engring, and Sci, Soc, Democrat. Club: Houston. Contbr. articles to trade mags. Designer (with R.M. Hutchins) Slide-High Pressure Gas Transmission. Home: 1220 Southmore St Houston TX 77004 Office: 1215 Oakdale St Houston TX 77004

MCKAY, JAMES ALVIN, JR., judge; b. San Antonio, Nov. 22, 1917; s. James Alvin and Margaret (Basala) McK.; LL.B., U. Tex. 1941; m. Ida Lucille Camiade, Dec. 4, 1941; children—Michael, Madelyn, Patrick, Dennis, Marie. Admitted to Tex. bar, 1943, practiced in San Antonio, 1946-62; judge 150th Dist. Ct., Bexar County (Tex.), San Antonio, 1963-—. Participant nat. conf. Justice for the Child, U. Chgo., 1961, Nat. Inst. for Juvenile Ct. Judges, U. Okla., 1963, Nat. Inst. Juvenile Ct. Judges, U. Minn., 1966; mem. Tex. Council on Adminstrn. Justice, 1958-—. Mem. Tex. Ho. of Reps., 1959-60. Pres., Community Welfare Council San Antonio, 1955-56; chmn. San Antonio Planning and Zoning Commn., 1957-58; chmn. Bexar County Juvenile Bd., 1963-69. Recipient citation for outstanding service Pres.'s Com. on Nat. Employ the Physically Handicapped Week, 1951. Served from pvt. to capt. AUS, 1942-46; PTO. Mem. San Antonio Bar Assn. (pres. 1955), State Bar Tex., Harp and Shamrock Soc. Tex. (v.p.), Am. Legion (comdr. 20th Dist. 1952-54, judge adv. Tex. 1948-49), Cath. Lawyers Guild, Roman Catholic (past legislation chmn. Archdiocesan Council Cath. Men.). Home: 807 Patricia Dr San Antonio TX 78216 Office: Bexar County Courthouse San Antonio TX 78204

MCKAY, JOY H. (MRS. SAMUEL J. MCKAY), assn. exec.; b. Warrenville, N.J., June 14, 1914; d. Arthur and Helen (Milius) Hofheimer; grad. Dalton Sch., N.Y.C., 1932; grad. Sarah Lawrence Coll., 1934; m. Joseph J. Siccardi, Sept. 5, 1934 (div. 1952); children—Helene Gay, Carol Ann (Mrs. William Williams Wyman), Arthur J., Marilyn Jill (Mrs. Thomas Iullucci, Jr.); m. 2d, Raymond Roth, Aug. 25, 1955 (dec.); m. 3d, Samuel J. McKay, Dec, 1970. Mem. bd. of edn. Warren Twp., N.J., 1940-47, pres. 1947; chmn. Warren Twp. A.R.C.; v.p. Mental Hygiene Soc. Union County, N.J., 1946-49, pres. 1949-51; bd. mgrs. N.J. Neuropsychiat. Inst., Princeton, N.J., 1951-55, v.p., 1953-54; trustee Woods Schs., Langhorne, Pa., 1955-62, Pres. N.J. Assn. for Mental Health, 1951-56, mem. bd., 1951-64, exec. com. 1951-63, chmn. planning com., 1958-62; chmn. com. orgn., Nat. Assn. Mental Health, 1953-57, dir., 1951-62, mem. exec. com., 1953-62, chmn. planning com. 1959-61, mem. program com., 1961-63, chmn. direct services com., 1961-63; exec. dir. Somerset County Assn. for Mental Health, 1965-67; dir. div. services N.J. Heart Assn., 1967-70; supr. Heart Sunday Broward County (Fla.) Heart Assn., Ft. Lauderdale 1971, assn. fund-raising dir., 1971-—. Trustee Nathan Hofheimer Found., 1945-70. Unitarian. Home: 750 NE 40th St Boca Raton FL 33432

MCKAY, LAFAYETTE CAMP, engring. exec.; b. San Antonio, Jan. 5, 1926; s. Seth Shepard and Bama Lawson (Camp) McK.; B.S. in Mech. Engring., Tex. Technol. U., 1947; m. Mary Otie Lynn, May 29, 1947; children—Lafayette Camp, Nancy Melynn. With Haynes & Kirby, architects-engrs., Lubbock, Tex., 1947-49, Landauer & Guerrero, cons. engrs., Dallas, 1949-50, Atcheson & Atkinson, architects-engrs., Lubbock, 1950-52; self employed Lafayette C. McKay, cons. engr., Lubbock, 1952-68; supr. bldg. systems engring. Benham-Blair & Affiliates, Oklahoma City, 1968-70; sr. project mgr. Herman Blum Cons. Engrs., Dallas, 1971-—. Registered profl. engr., Okla., Tex., N.M., Ariz., Ia., Miss. Mem. Nat., Okla., Tex. socs. profl. engrs., Am. Soc. Heating, Refrigerating and Air Conditioning Engrs. (chpt. pres. 1954-55), Soc. Environmental Engrs. Home: 7168 Lyre Lane Dallas TX 75214 Office: 1015 Elm St at Griffin Dallas TX 75202

MCKAY, SAMUEL LEROY, clergyman; b. nr. Charlotte, N.C., Oct. 15, 1913; s. Elmer Ranson and Arlena (Benfield) McK.; A.B. cum laude, Erskine Coll., 1937; B.D. cum laude, Erskine Theol. Sem., 1939; postgrad. U. Ga., 1941-42, Union Theol. Sem., 1957; m. Martha Elizabeth Caldwell, Apr. 29, 1939; children—Samuel LeRoy, Mary Louise, William Ranson. Ordained to ministry of Presbyn. Ch., 1940; pastor Prosperity Asso. Ref. Ch., Fayetteville, Tenn., 1942-46, Bethel Asso. Ref. Ch., Oak Hill, Ala., 1946-50, 1st Asso. Ref. Ch., Salisbury, N.C., 1950-53, 1st Ch. U.S., Dallas, N.C., 1953-60, First Ch., Kernersville, N.C., 1960-66, Cooleemee (N.C.) Presbyn. Ch., 1966-69, Broadway-Salem Presbyn. Ch., Broadway, N.C., 1969-—. Stated clk. Gen. Synod Asso. Ref. Presbyn. Ch., 1950-53; commr. Gen. Assembly Presbyn. Ch. U.S., 1960, 69; permanent clk. Winston-Salem Presbytery, 1961-69, chmn. leadership edn. com., 1962-66, chmn. Christian edn. com., 1967-68; supr. chaplaincy program Davre County Hosp., 1968-69. Pres. Dallas P.T.A., 1955-56. Bd. mgrs. Kernersville YMCA, 1962-66, chmn. membership com., 1963, treas., 1964, pres., 1965-66; bd. dirs. Winston-Salem-Forsyth County YMCA, 1965-66. Mem. Kernersville Area Ministers Assn. (pres. 1963-64), N.C. Poetry Soc. (dir. 1971-—, chmn. poetry contests 1970-72, pres. 1972-—), Clan MacKay Soc. N.Am. (pres. 1971-—). Lion. Contbr. articles and sermons to periodicals and publs. Home: PO Box 268 Broadway NC 27505 Office: Broadway Presbyn Ch Main at Mcleod Broadway NC 27505

MCKEAN, H(ERBERT) ALAN, govt. ofcl.; b. Sitka, Alaska, May 10, 1920; s. Herbert Allen and Alice (Mann) McK.; B.A., Reed Coll., 1941; postgrad. Am. U., 1947; M.A., Whitman Coll., 1950; m. Alta Deloris Olsen, June 14, 1942; children—Sherry Ann, Robert Alan, Nancy Deloris. Personnel asst. U.S. Dept. Labor, 1941-43, classification specialist, 1946-48; farmer, Baker, Ore., 1948-49; tchr. pub. schs., Richland, Wash., 1950-51; classification specialist, insp., personnel mgmt. specialist U.S. Civil Service Commn., Washington, Seattle, 1951-61; mgmt. analyst Internal Revenue Service, Washington, 1961-62; chief div. employment U.S. Dept. Labor, Washington, 1964-69, dep. dir. personnel, 1969-70; chief spl. projects office U.S. Civil Service Commn., Washington, 1970-—. Served with USAAF, 1943-46. Finalist Arthur S. Flemming award competition, 1960. Mem. United Ch. of Christ. Developed personnel standard for research sci. positions, gen. supervisory standards, digital computer occupations. Home: 1801 Glen Park Dr Silver Spring MD 20902 Office: US Civil Service Commn Washington DC 20210

MCKEAN, RANDOLPH ANDREWS, accountant; b. Bronxville N.Y., Dec. 27, 1941; s. Norman Francis and Jane (Clayberger) McK.; B.S., Auburn U., 1964; m. Judith Levenstein, Nov. 20, 1966; children—Steven Andrew, David Scott. Staff accountant Arthur Andersen & Co., Atlanta, 1964-68, tax mgr., Miami, Fla., 1968-—. Active Jr. Achievement, 1966-67. Served with USMC, 1961-67. Mem. Am., Fla. insts. C.P.A.'s, Ga. Soc. C.P.A.'s, Nat. Assn. Accountants. Home: 10300 SW 98th St Miami FL 33156 Office: 150 SE 2d Av Miami FL 33131

MCKEAN, RICHARD LEON, JR., dentist; b. Mobile, Ala., Oct. 23, 1917; s. Richard Leon and Edith Marie (Sutton) McK.; D.D.S., Emory U., 1951; m. Virginia Singletary, June 6, 1947; 1 son, Richard Leon III. Pvt. practice dentistry, Mobile, 1951-—. Served with USMCR, 1942-45. City tennis champion-twice. Mem. Am., Ala. dental assns., 1st Dist. Dental Soc., Alpha Tau Omega, Zeta Iota Psi. Methodist. Clubs: Touchdown, Mobile Country. Home: 10 Drury Lane Mobile AL 36608 Office: 1729 Springhill Av Mobile AL 36604

MCKEE, HERBERT CHARLES, research adminstr.; b. San Antonio, Feb. 26, 1920; s. James E. and Agnes (Parr) McK.; B.S., Muskingum Coll., 1942; M.S., Ohio State U., 1947, Ph.D., 1949; m. Eileen Lou Sechler, Sept. 25, 1948; children—Bruce, Carolyn. Research asso. Ohio State U. Research Found., 1948-50; chem. engr. Jefferson Chem. Co., Austin, Tex., 1950-53; with Southwest Research Inst., San Antonio and Houston, 1953-—, engr., sect. mgr., asst. dir. dept. chemistry, chem. engr., 1953-—. Chmn., Tex. Air Control Bd. Served to 1st lt. USAAF, 1942-46. Mem. Am. Chem. Soc., Am. Inst. Chem. Engrs., Air Pollution Control Assn., Sci. Research Soc. Am., Am. Indsl. Hygiene Assn., Am. Soc. for Oceanography, Am. Soc. for Testing and Materials. Home: 8010 Neff St Houston TX 77036 Office: 3600 S Yoakum St Houston TX 77006

MCKEE, MELVIN JAY, editor; b. Webb City, Mo., June 22, 1934; s. Daniel H. and LaVeta (Cook) McK.; B.A. cum laude, Tenn. Temple Coll., 1958; M.A., U. Ga., 1959; postgrad. (fellow) Emory U., 1962-64, Ga. State U., 1969. Founder, editor DeKalb Lit. Arts Jour., Clarkston, Ga., 1966-—; founder, editor, publisher This Issue, The Magazine of the New Creative, Atlanta, 1971-—.Mem. faculty Young Harris Coll., 1959-61, U. Tenn., 1961, West Ga. Coll., 1961-62, DeKalb Coll., 1964-—. Served with Air Force USNR, 1952-54. Named Ga. Young Writer of Year So. Festival, U. Ga., 1959. Mem. South Atlantic Modern Lang. Assn., Modern Lang. Assn., Nat. Council Tchrs. English, Internat. Composers Guild, Poetry Soc. Am. Home: 110 E Maple St Decatur GA 30030 Office: 555 Indian Creek Rd Clarkston GA 30021

MCKEE, WALTER TATE, ret. supt. schs.; b. Newton, Ala., May 7, 1909; s. John Thomas and Maude (Cobb) McK.; B.S. in Edn., U, Ala., 1933, M.S. in Edn., 1936; postgrad. Peabody Coll., summers 1937, 38, 40; m. Corrie Elizabeth Davis, Aug. 25, 1936; 1 son, Walter Tate. Tchr. Montgomery (Ala.) Pub. Schs., 1928-31, prin., 1931-43, asst. supt., 1943-54, asso. supt., 1954-58; supt. Montgomery City and County Schs., 1958-72. Mem. steering com. Edn. Commn. of the States, 1966-67. Pres., Montgomery Area council Boy Scouts Am. Bd. dirs. United Appeal, Salvation Army, A.R.C., Family Guidance Center, YWCA (all Montgomery). Mem. Am. Assn. Sch. Adminstrn., Ala. Congress Parents and Tchrs. (past mem. bd. mgrs.), Nat. (past mem. resolutions com.), Ala. (v.p. 1941-42, chmn. fed. relations com. 1955-70, chmn. welfare com. 1944-45, new bldg. com. 1948-50) edn. assns., Phi Delta Kappa. Presbyn. (elder). Lion. Home: 2501 Gladlane Dr Montgomery AL 36111

MCKEE, WILLIAM E., educator; b. Apr. 15, 1924; s. Elmer W. McK.; B.M., Syracuse; M.M., Eastman Sch. Music; Ph.D., N. Tex. State U.; m. Margaret Ruby; children—George, Jonathan, Timothy, Robin. Faculty, U. Tulsa, 1950-—, presently prof., head Sch. Music. Mem. Am. Musicological Assn., Phi Mu Alpha, Lambda Chi Alpha. Composer: Introduction and Dance. Contbr. articles to profl. journals. Office: Sch Music U Tulsa 600 College Av S Tulsa OK 74104*

MCKEITHEN, JOHN JULIAN, past gov. of La., lawyer; b. Grayson, La., May 28, 1918; s. Jesse Japheth and Agnes DeEtte (Eglin) McK.; student High Point Coll., 1936-38, LL.D., 1964; A.B., 1941; LL.B., La. State U., 1942; m. Marjorie Funderburk, June 14, 1942; children—Jay, Fox, Rebecca, Melissa, Pamela, Jenneva Maude. Admitted to La. bar, 1942; practiced in Columbia, La., 1945-64, 72-—, Monroe, La., 1954-64; mem. La. Pub. Service Commn., 1954-64; gov. State of La., Baton Rouge, 1964-72. Chmn. Interstate Oil Compact Commn.; exec. com. Nat. Govs. Conf. Dir. Caldwell Bank & Trust Co., Columbia. Mem. La. Ho. of Reps., 1948-52; Democratic candidate for lt. gov. La., 1952. Served with AUS, 1942-45; PTO. Mem. V.F.W., La. Farm Bur., Delta Council, La., Am. bar assns., Am. Legion. Methodist (lay speaker, mem. ofcl. bd.). Mason, Kiwanian. Home: Hogan Plantation Columbia LA 71418

MCKELLAR, DOUGLAS HOWARD, railroad exec.; b. Louisville, June 17, 1917; s. Robert Lide and Mattie-Sevier (Bonnie) McK.; grad. Hotchkiss Sch., 1935; B.S., Yale, 1939; m. Jessie Barker, May 4, 1943; 1 son, Douglas Howard. Salesman, Campbell Soup Co., Camden, N.J., 1939-41, Ky. Color & Chem. Co., Louisville, 1945-51; with sales, marketing dept. Reynolds Metals Co., Louisville, 1951-58; pres. Louisville Flying Service, Inc., 1958-—; v.p. sales L. & N. R.R. Co., Louisville, 1961-—. Served to lt. col. USAAF, 1941-45; ETO. Decorated D.F.C., Air medal with four clusters. Home: 160 Westwind Rd Louisville KY 40207 Office: 908 W Broadway Louisville KY 40201

MCKELWAY, BENJAMIN MOSBY, newspaperman; b. Fayetteville, N.C., Oct. 2, 1895; s. Alexander Jeffrey and Lavinia Rutherford (Smith) McK.; ed. Va. Poly. Inst. and George Washington U.; m. Margaret J. Prentiss, Sept. 14, 1920; children—Benjamin Mosby, William Prentiss, John MacGregor. Reporter Washington Times, 1916; editorial writer and news editor New Britain (Conn.) Herald, 1919-20; successively reporter, city editor, news editor, mng. editor, asso. editor Washington Star, 1921-46, editor, 1946-63, editorial chmn., 1963-—; v.p. Evening Star Newspaper Co. Pres. A.P., 1958-63; pres. Washington Bd. Trade, 1945-46. Trustee Nat. Geographic Soc., George Washington U., D.C. Public Library; trustee Rockefeller Found., 1958-61; trustee Library of Congress Trust Fund Bd. Served as 2d lt. U.S.A., 1st lt. and a.d.c. to Brig. Gen. L. M. Brett, 1917-18. Mem. Washington Nat. Monument Soc., Am. Soc. Newspaper Editors (pres. 1949-50), Delta Tau Delta. Presbyn. Clubs: Cosmos, Nat. Press, Metropolitan, Chevy Chase, Alibi, Gridiron (pres. 1958). Home: 4920 Palisade Lane NW Washington DC 20016 Office: Evening Star Washington DC

MCKENNA, THOMAS ADAM, JR., analytical chemist; b. Natchez, Miss., Mar. 14, 1922; s. Thomas Adam and Blanche (Korndorffer) McK.; student Copiah-Lincoln Jr. Coll., 1938-39; B.S. in Chemistry, La, State U., 1944; student U. Miss., 1955, Podbielniak Inst., 1956; m.

Peggy Marie McCrosky, June 2, 1949; children—Mary Lucille, Thomas Adam III, Michael Gerard, Patrick Joseph. With Motor Fuels Lab., Dept. Revenue, State La.; with Firestone Tire & Rubber Co., Orange, Tex., 1944-—, successively shift control chemist, spl. problems chemist, spl. problems chemist, lab., mgr. and chief chemist, 1956-—; owner, dir. work Marian Labs., Lake Charles, La., 1955-—, Lectr. Lamar Coll. Tech., 1963. Mem. dist. advancement com. Boy Scouts Am.; pres. St. Mary's Home and Sch. Assn., 1963-64; active Community Concert Assn. Fellow Am. Inst. Chemists; mem. Gulf Coast Spectroscopic Group (chmn.), Am. Soc. Quality Control (area dir. S. Tex. sect. 1959-—; chmn. membership com. Sabine subsect.; sr. mem.), Am. Chem. Soc. (chmn. S.W. La. 1954-—; sec. Tex.-La.-Gulf sect. 1961-62), Am. Soc. Testing Materials (com. chmn.), A.A.A.S., C. of C., Alpha Tau Omega. K.C. Editor: The Newletter, 1949-54. Author numerous articles in profl. jours.; also papers. Home: 2001 W Rio Grande Pl Orange TX 77631 Office: PO Box 1269 Orange TX 77631

MCKENNA, WILLIAM FRANCIS, lawyer; b. Meriden, Conn., May 14, 1910; s. Frank Joseph and Alice (Downes) McK.; Ph.B., Yale, 1930, LL.B., 1932; m. Catherine Agnes Donahue, June 25, 1935; children—William Francis (dec. 1966), Daniel Joseph. Admitted to Conn, bar, 1932; with Buckley, Creedon & Danaher, Hartford, 1932-35; counsel, acting chief pub. loans sect. legal div. RFC, Washington, 1935-42; counsel Def. Supplies Corp., 1942; chief airports br. War Assets Adminstrn., 1945-47; counsel com. banking and currency U.S. Senate, 1947-57, U.S. Joint Com. Def. Prodn., 1950-51; administrv. asst. U.S. Senator William Benton, 1950; asso. Ford Motor Co., Washington Office, 1957-58; house counsel Nat. Assn. Mut. Savs. Banks, N.Y.C., 1958-59; dir- counsel Washington office Nat. Assn. Mut. Savs. Banks, Washington, 1959-63; gen. counsel, v.p. Nat. League Insured Savs. Assns., Washington, 1963-—. Comdg. officer USNR Law Co. 5-11, Washington, 1956-57, 64-65. Pres. Conn. Democrats D.C., 1939-40. Served from lt. (j.g.) to lt,, USNR, 1943-45, capt. USNR ret. Mem. Am. Inter-Am., Fed., Md. bar assns., Bar Assn. D.C., Yale Law Sch. Assn., U.S. Senate Assn. Adminstrv. Assts. and Secs., Assn. Former Senate Aides, Assn. Bar City N.Y., Nat. Lawyers Club, Clubs: Yale, University, Exchequer (past chancellor) (Washington); Yale (N.Y.C.); Men's (Silver Spring, Md.). Editor in chief Nat. League Mgrs. Manual; writer Nat. League legal bulls; lectr. savs. and loan topics. Home: 8004 Park Crest Dr Silver Spring MD 20910 Office: 1200 17th St NW Washington DC 20036

MCKENZIE, BRYAN WALLACE, dentist; b. San Augustine, Tex., Sept. 24, 1930; s. Hallie B. and Bertha (Pate) McK.; B.S., Stephen F. Austin State Coll., 1950; postgrad. U. Houston, 1955-57; D.D.S., U. Tex., 1962; m. Virginia Mae Cain, Oct. 3, 1952; children—Linda Carol, Gregory Bryan. Research chemist Monsanto Chem. Co., Texas City, Tex., 1955-58; gen. practice dentistry, Dickinson, Tex., 1962-—; dir. Pine Dr. Profl. Center. Mem. Dental Health Com. 9th Dist., 1967-—; dental dir. Galveston County Health Clinic, 1962-65. Mem. adv. com. Dickinson High Sch. Vocational Indsl. Clubs Am. and Health Occupations Tng. Programs, 1970-—; active Boy Scouts Am. Served with USNR, 1951-54. Mem. Am., Tex. dental assns., 9th Dist. Dental Soc. (pres. 1971-72), Tex. Soc. Dentistry for Children, Am. Profl. Practice Assn., Am. Soc. Preventive Dentistry, Dickinson C. of C., Optimist Internat. (pres. Dickinson 1967-68, lt. gov. S.E. Tex. dist. 1968-69). Presbyn. (sec. 1967-68, deacon). Home: 5201 Desel Dr Dickinson TX 77539 Office: 2108 1/2 Pine Dr Dickinson TX 77539

MCKENZIE, LAWSON MORELL, physicist, govt. ofcl.; b. Sheridan, Indiana, Nov. 7, 1912; s. Lawson Walter and Bertha Ethel (Sims) McK.; B.S., George Washington U., 1934, M.A., 1937; m. Louise Martha Erk, June 10, 1941; children—Martha Joyce (Mrs. Adam), John Lawson. Textile insp. U.S. Dept. of Agr., 1935; reference librarian Library of Congress, 1935-40; patent examiner U.S. Patent Office, 1940-42; physicist Bur. of Ships, Navy Dept,, 1942-43; tech. aide Nat. Def. Research Com., OSRD, 1943-46; physicist Office Naval Research, 1946-50, head physics br., 1951-52, spl. asst, 1954-55; exec. dir. Naval Research Adv. Com., 1953-59; exec. sec. of Defense Sci. Bd., 1959-62; tech. asst. to v.p. scientific research Ford Motor Co., 1962-63, research planning associate, 1964-68; exec. sec. Interdepartmental Com. Sci. Research and Development, 1953-54; exec. sec., govt. research com. Nat. Acad. Sci. Nat. Research Council, 1954-56; cons. Sec. Def., Dept. of Defense, 1962-63, Office Naval Research, 1963-65, NSF, 1963-67; spl. asst. to pres. Nat. Acad. Scis., 1967-69; sec.-treas. Univs. Space Research Assn., 1969-70; sci. policy analyst Office U.S. Sec. Transp., Washington, 1970-—. Recipient Naval Ordnance Devel. award, 1945, Army-Navy Certificate of Appreciation, 1948. Fellow A.A.A.S., Wash. Acad. Scis.; mem. Am. Phys. Soc., Sci. Research Soc. Am., Internat. Platform Assn., Nat. Conf. Adminstrn. Research (conf. com.), Philos. Soc. Wash. (pres. 1961), U.S. Naval Inst. Sigma Pi Sigma, Delta Tau Delta. Presbyn. Author: (with others) New Weapons for Air Warfare, 1947; The Technical Report, 1954; articles tech. reports, jours. Home: 5311 Westpath Way Fort Sumner MD 20016 Office: US Dept of Transportation Washington DC 20590

MCKENZIE, SAM PHILLIPS, superior court judge; b. Blytheville, Ark., Oct. 30, 1920; s. William Morrell and Rose Elizabeth (Phillips) McK.; J.D. with 1st honors, U. Ga., 1944; m. Margaret Mundy, Nov. 20, 1948; children—Sam Phillips, Judith Ann, Michael Morrell, Margaret Mundy. Admitted to Ga. bar, 1944; mem. firm Carter, Carter & McKenzie, Atlanta, 1944-49, McKenzie, Kaler & Shulman, Atlanta, 1949-56; individual practice in Atlanta, 1956-62; judge Superior Ct., Atlanta Jud. Circuit, 1962-—. Lectr., Atlanta Law Sch., 1944-64; faculty Nat. Coll. State Trial Judges, U. Nev., Reno, 1966-68, bd, dirs., 1970-—. Pres., Atlanta Tb Assn., 1956-58, bd. dirs., 1963-64; pres. Cath. Social Services, 1956-59; Ga. mem. Council for Christian Unity, 1963; pres. bd. dirs. Holy Family Hosp. 1962-64. Named Atlanta Young Man of Year, Jr. C. of C., 1948. Mem. Am. (mem. adv. com. on judges function), Ga., Atlanta bar assns., Nat. Conf. State Trial Judges (exec. com.; chmn. 1971-72), Am. Law Inst., Inst. Jud. Adminstrn. (com. on standards criminal justice), Phi Delta Theta (internat. pres. 1962-64). Clubs: Atlanta Lawyers; Cherokee Town and Country; Atlanta Athletic. Co-author: State Trial Judge's Book, 2d edit., 1969. Home: 3370 E Wood Valley Rd NW Atlanta GA 30327 Office: Fulton County Court House Atlanta GA 30303

MCKIE, EDWARD F., JR., lawyer; b. Albany, N.Y., Oct. 29, 1924; B.E.E., Rensselaer Poly. Inst., 1948; LL.B., Georgetown U., 1952. Admitted to D.C. bar, 1952; now with Birch, Swindler, McKie & Beckett, Washington. Adj. prof. Georgetown Law Sch., 1963-67; chmn. Nat. Counsel Patent Law Assns., 1969-70; sr. adviser U.S. Del. Diplomatic Conf., on Patents, Copyrights, Trademarks, 1970. Mem. Bar Assn. D.C., Am. Bar Assn. (chmn. sect. patent, trademark, copyright law, 1967-68), Am. Patent Law Assn. (treas. 1961-64, mem. bd. mgrs. 1964-67), Phi Delta Phi. Asso. Editor: Georgetown Law Jour., 1951-52. Office: Birch Swindler McKie & Beckett 1000 Connecticut Av Washington DC 20036*

MCKIM, CHARLOTTE B., civic worker; b. Bklyn., Apr. 20, 1899; d. David Peyton and Maude (Logan) Bevans; student Art Student's League, 1920-23, Harvard, summer 1934; m. William Lee McKim, Oct. 15, 1924. Sec. Soc. Four Arts, 1951-56, dir,, 1951-—. Mem. Norton Gallery Art, Mus. Modern Art N.Y.C., English-Speaking Union Palm Beach. Compiler: The Salles Letters 1825-50, 1957. Address: 322 Eden Rd Palm Beach FL 33480

MC KIM, WILLIAM LEE, civic worker; b. Cooperstown, N.Y., Oct. 19, 1894; s. William J. A. and Maud Stewart (Lee) McK.; grad Hill Sch., Pottstown, Pa., 1913; B.A., Yale, 1918; m. Charlotte Frances Bevans, Oct. 15, 1924. Salesman, Blair & Co., Inc., stocks and bonds, 1919-29; art collecting and assembling art exhbns. in Palm Beach, 1939-54. Dir. Soc. Four Arts, Palm Beach, 1941-—, v.p., 1952-—. Served cpl. to sgt. 1st class, CWS, AEF, 1917-19. Mem. Palm Beach Civic Assn., English-Speaking Union (dir.), Soc, Colonial Wars. Episcopalian. Clubs: Knickerbocker (N.Y.C.); Baltusrol Golf (Springfield, N.J.); The Beach, Everglades (Palm Beach, Fla.). Address: 322 Eden Rd Palm Beach FL 33480

MCKINLEY, JIMMIE JOE, librarian; b. Bertram, Tex., July 23, 1934; s. Joseph Crofford and Velma Anne (Barnett) McK.; B.J. cum laude, U. Tex., 1955; M.S., U. Ky., 1964. Asst. librarian Bethel Coll., McKenzie, Tenn., 1961-63, reference librarian, 1966-70, acting head librarian, 1970-71. Mem. Assn. Coll. and Research Libraries, A.L.A., Carroll County (Tenn.) Hist. Soc., Sigma Delta Chi. Presbyn. Home: PO Box 2106 Longview TX 75601

MCKINLEY, WILLIAM EDWARD, lawyer, county ofcl.; b. Mize, Miss., Jan. 3, 1931; s. William W. and Hazel (Stringer) McK.; B.A., Millsaps Coll., 1954; LL.B., Jackson Sch. of Law, 1958; m. Joy White, July 24, 1955; children—William Bruce, Karl Dibrell, Kathleen Marie. Claims mgr. Crawford & Co., Ins., Allstate Ins. Co., Hartford Accident & Indemnity Co., 1954-60; admitted to Miss. Bar, 1958; practiced in Jackson, Miss., 1958-—; mem. Miss. Ho. of Reps., 1964-68; mem. Miss. State Senate, 1968-72; clk. Hinds County Circuit, 1972-—. Vice pres. Childre Enterprises, Inc., Jackson, 1963-—; instr. ins. law Central High Sch., Jackson, 1960-—. Treas., Boys' Club Alumni Assn., Jackson, 1964-65, v.p., 1960-61, pres., 1961-62; mem. alumni bd. Millsaps Coll. Bd. dirs. Hinds County (Miss.) Mental Health Assn. Served with AUS, 1951-52. Mem. Am., Miss., Hinds County, Jr. bar assns., Am. Legion, Kappa Sigma, Sigma Delta Kappa. Methodist. Mason (Shriner), Moose. Club: Civitan (past officer Jackson, Miss.). Home: 2073 Shady Lane Jackson MS 39204 Office: 418 Yazoo St Jackson MS 39201 also Hinds County Court House Jackson MS 39201

MCKINNEY, JOHN ROBERT, research inst. exec.; b. Chattanooga, Dec. 2, 1928; s. Charles Dana and Kathryn (Simmons) McK.; B.S., U. Chattanooga, 1950; postgrad. U. Va., 1955-56; M.H.A., Med. Coll. Va., 1959; m. Marion Teresa Coan, Aug. 29, 1959;children—John Robert, Susan K., Maureen S., Collin C., Catherine C. Asst. dir. U. Va. Hosp., Charlottesville, 1959-60, Hosp. Council Nat. Capital Area, Washington, 1960-62; exec. dir. Health Facilities Planning Council for Met. Washington, 1962-72; pres. Inst. for Health Care Research, Washington, 1972-—. Clin. asst. prof. dept. community medicine Georgetown U. Sch. Medicine, 1969-72; guest lectr. Med. Coll. Va. Sch. Hosp. Adminstrn., 1965-—. Pres. citizens adv. bd. Arlington County (Va.) Mental Health Clinic, 1966-69. Served to lt. USNR, 1951-55. Fellow Am. Coll. Hosp. Adminstrs. mem. Am. Assn. Hosp. Planning. Home: 1214 N Columbus St Arlington VA 22205 Office: 1812 K St NW Washington DC 20006

MCKINNEY, JOSEPH F., corp. exec.; b. Phila., 1931; student St. Joseph's Coll.; M.B.A., Harvard, 1957; married. Mgr. Phila. research dept. Reynolds & Co., 1957-59; dir. research Warner, Jenkins, Mandel & Longstreth, 1959-60; founder, pres. Electro-Sci. Investors Inc., Richardson, Tex., 1960-63; v.p. Brown, Allen & Co., 1963-64; ind. cons., 1964; dir. corporate finance Ling & Co., 1964-65, Goodbody & Co., 1965-66; pres., chief exec. officer Saturn Industries, Inc., also dir.; now pres. Tyler Corp. Home: 7339 Elmridge Dr Dallas TX 75240 Office: 3121 S Indian Center Dallas TX 75201*

MCKINNEY, WARD LYNN, equipment mfg. co. exec.; b. Sherman, Tex., May 15, 1920; s. James Ward and Helen Maud (Lynn) McK.; student Del Mar Coll., 1953-56, Grayson Coll., 1968-69; m. Dorthell Grider, May 19, 1940; children—Lynda (Mrs. Aubrey L. Rangley), Vicki (Mrs. Peter D. Doremus), Robin. Chief pilot Jaques Power Saw Co., Denison, Tex., 1945-48; field salesman Hardwick-Etter Co., Vernon, Tex., 1948-51, Corpus Christi, Tex., 1951-55; dist. mgr. Heco Truck Cranes, Los Angeles, 1955-58, gen. sales mgr., Sherman, 1958-60; v.p., dir. sales Texoma, Inc., Sherman, Tex., 1960-—. Mem. Mil. Affairs Com., 1969. Served with USAAF, 1942-45. Mem. Power and Communications Contractors Assn. (adv. com. 1961-—), Asso. Equipment Distbrs. (spl. affairs com. 1968-70). Mason (32 deg., Shriner). Club: Tanglewood Hills (Sherman). Home: 2613 River Crest Dr Sherman TX 75090 Office: Hwy 75 N Sherman TX 75090

MCKINNEY, WILTON JOHNSON, textile exec.; b. Greer, S.C., Apr. 14, 1921; s. Boyd Brown and Alice (Johnson) McK.; B.S. in Accounting, U. S.C., 1947. Accountant, S.D. Leidesdorf & Co., C.P.A.'s, 1947-50, Ely & Walker Mills, 1950-55; with Burlington Industries, Inc., 1955-—, controller Burlington Cotton Co., Greenville, S.C., 1968-—. Varsity tennis coach Greenville (S.C.) Sr. High Sch., 1948-—. Treas., Greenville Fine Arts Festival; 1966-—; chmn. Selective Service Bd., Greenville, 1963-—. Served to lt. USNR, 1943-46. Mem. Adminstrv. Mgmt. Soc., So. Lawn Tennis Assn. (v.p. 1963-65), S.C. Tennis Assn. (pres. 1963, sec.-treas. 1964-—), Sigma Alpha Epsilon, Omicron Delta Kappa. Presbyn. (deacon). Rotarian (sec. 1964-68). Club: Greenville Country (hon.). Home: 238 Byrd Blvd Greenville SC 29605 Office: PO Box 3846 Greenville SC 29608

MCKINNIS, GEORGE EDEN, JR., lawyer, business exec.; b. Shawnee, Okla., July 23, 1901; s. George E. and Mary (Dickson) McK.; student Okla. Bapt. U., 1919-22; A.B., U. Wis., 1923; LL.B., Harvard, 1927; m. Marion Harris, June 7, 1935; children—George Courtney, Sarah Ann. Admitted to Okla. bar, 1928, since practiced in Shawnee; v.p. Shawnee Realty & Investment Co., 1935-—; v.p. First Fed. Savs. & Loan Assn., 1947-57, pres., 1957-72, chmn. bd., gen. counsel, 1972-—. Atty., Shawnee Bd. Edn., 1954-62; hearing officer SSS, Dept. Justice, 1946-50. Chmn. adv. bd. Salvation Army, 1965; mem. adv. com. 4th Army, 1948-54; vice chmn. Okla. Election Bd., 1950-54; pres. Shawnee Community Concert Assn., 1946-50; dir. Shawnee YMCA, 1948-60; mem. Greater Seminole Area council Camp Fire Girls, 1950-54. Mem. Shawnee Bd. City Commrs., 1946-50, mayor, 1946-48. Trustee Okla. Bapt. U., 1949-52, Shawnee Indsl. Found., 1970-—. Served as lt. comdr. USNR, 1941-45; PTO. Mem. U.S. (com. on Fed. Home Loan Bank system 1969-70), Okla. (v.p. 1964-66, pres. 1967-68) savs. and loan leagues, S.W. Savs. and Loan Conf. (dir. 1964-68), Am., Okla. (ho. dels.), Pottawatomie County (pres. 1962) bar assns., Shawnee C. of C. (dir. 1970-—), Am. Legion, V.F.W., Delta Upsilon, Phi Delta Phi, Pi Kappa Delta, Theta Alpha Phi. Presbyn. (trustee, former elder). Mason (K.T.), Elk (exalted ruler Shawnee 1962), Lion (pres. Shawnee 1938, dist. gov. 1950). Club: Knife and Fork (pres. 1949-50). Home: 1506 N Union St Shawnee OK 74801 Office: 330 N Broadway Shawnee OK 74801

MCKITTRICK, JAMES LIVINGSTON, mfg. exec.; b. Saluda, S.C., Mar. 6, 1914; s. James R. and Carrie (Parks) M.; B.A., Furman U., 1933; postgrad. Benjamin Franklin U., 1939-40; m. Nancy Katherine Buntin, June 9, 1956; 1 dau., Nancy Rebecca. Tchr. schs. and colls., until 1947; mgr. C.E. Luttrell & Co., Greenville, S.C., 1947-52; sec. Franklin Nat. Life Ins. Co., 1953-57; gen. mgr. Acme Cloth Reel Co., 1958-—. Served with USAAF, 1942-43. Democrat. Baptist. Lion. Home: 401 Garrison Rd Simpsonville SC 29681 Office: 214 W McBee Av Greenville SC 29601

MCKNIGHT, COLBERT AUGUSTUS, newspaper editor; b. Shelby, N.C., Aug. 19, 1916; s. John Samuel and Norva (Proctor) McK.; B.S., Davidson Coll., 1938; LL.D., Colby Coll.; m. Margaret Belle Henderson, Mar. 29, 1941 (div. 1968); children—John Peter, Margaret C., David P.; m. 2d, Gail Oliver Ehle, Oct. 30, 1968; 1 dau., Colby Augusta. Reporter Charlotte News, 1939-42, news editor, 1944-48, mng. editor, 1948-49, editor, 1949-54; editor San Juan (P.R.) World Jour., also Asso. Press war corr., 1942-44; exec. dir. So. Edn. Reporting Service, 1954-55; editor Charlotte (N.C.) Observer, 1955-—; v.p., dir. Knight Pub. Co., 1956-—. Pres. N.C. Fund, 1963-65; chmn. bd. So. Edn. Reporting Service, 1963-65. Trustee Charlotte Coll., 1960-65. Mem. Am. Soc. Newspaper Editors (dir. 1965-—, pres. 1971-72), Nat., N.C. confs. editorial writers. Presbyn. Home: 1627 Beverly Dr Charlotte NC 28207 Office: 600 S Tryon St Charlotte NC 28202

MCKNIGHT, FELIX R., pub. co. exec.; b. Dallas, Aug. 2, 1910; s. Luther Knox and Nancy Cate (Bates) McK.; grad. Tex A. and M. Coll., 1932; m. Elizabeth Terrell, Oct. 19, 1934; children—Joan Elizabeth, Anne Terrell. Reporter, San Antonio Light, 1928-32, A.P., 1933-41; staff corr. Dallas Morning News, 1941, asst. mng. editor, 1943-50, mng. editor, 1950-57; v.p., editor Dallas Times Herald, from 1957, now sec., co-pub.; dir. Am. Press Inst., Columbia 1954-—. Pres. Circle Ten region Boy Scouts Am. Named outstanding young man of Tex., C. of C., 1943; recipient Distinguished Nat. Service award for best editorial Sigma Delta Chi, 1944. Mem. Am. Soc. Newspaper Editors (dir. 1952-—), Cotton Bowl Athletic Assn. (pres. 1954-55), A.P. Mng. Editors Assn. (past dir.), Sigma Delta Chi. Methodist. Club: Nat. Press. Home: 6326 Westchester St Dallas TX 75205 Office: 1101 Pacific St Dallas TX 75202

MCKNIGHT, GLEN DEAN, JR., physician; b. Covington, Va., May 17, 1932; s. Glen Dean and Virginia Catherine (Benson) McK.; B.S., A.B., Washington and Lee U., 1956; M.D., U. Va., 1960; m. Shirley Ann Greene, Dec. 6, 1936; children—Roberta, Christopher, Billy, Jeannine, Stephanie, Dean. Intern, Naval Hosp., Pensacola, Fla., 1960-61; resident Sch. Aviation Medicine, Pensacola, 1961-62; practice medicine specializing in family practice, Alexandria, Va., 1965-—; mem. staffs Duke St., Sem. hosps., Alexandria, Fairfax (Va.) Hosp., cons. Pharmacology Assn., Bethesda, Md., 1967-—. Served with AUS, 1952-54, USNR, 1959-65. Mem. Am., Aerospace med. assns., Med. Soc. Va., Alexandria Med. Soc. Met. Washington Sports Medicine Assn. (charter), Phi Kappa Sigma, Alpha Epsilon Delta. Club: Belle Haven Country (dir.). Home: 1209 Burtonwood Court Alexandria VA 22308 Office: 1302 Lafayette Dr Alexandria VA 22308

MCLAIN, EUGENE MILTON, lawyer, state senator; b. Cragford, Ala., Feb. 14, 1931; s. Eugene Milton and Louise (Leftwich) McL.; B.S., Auburn U., 1953; postgrad. Cambridge (Eng.) U., 1953-54; LL.B., U. Ala., 1959; m. Geraldine Phillips, Aug. 23, 1953; children—David Scott, Caroline. Admitted to Ala. bar, 1959, since practiced in Huntsville; partner firm Bell, Richardson, Cleary, McLain & Tucker; mem. Ala. Ho. of Reps., 1966-70; mem. Ala. Senate, 1970-—. Dir. Bank of Huntsville. Served with USAF, 1954-56. Recipient George Washington Honor medal, 1955; named One of Four Outstanding Young Men of Ala., 1960, Huntsville's Young Man of Year, 1961. Mem. Ala. Bar Assn. (past pres. young lawyers sect.). Democrat. Baptist. Rotarian, Elk. Home: 4101 Piedmont Dr SE Huntsville AL 35802 Office: 408 Franklin St SE Huntsville AL 35801

MCLAIN, LEE ROY, drilling co. exec.; b. Normangee, Tex., Mar. 29, 1927; s. Etcil and Evie Irene (Hamilton) McL.; B.B.A., U. Houston, 1949; m. Ima Jean Mathis, June 4, 1949; 1 dau., Cindy. Exec. v.p. Butler Drilling Co., Houston, 1964-—, aslo dir.; dir. Prodn. Maintenance Co., Tex. Gulf Coast Leasing, Inc. Bd. dirs. Com. Sound Am. Edn., pres. council Houston Bapt. Coll. Served with C.E., AUS, 1945-47; ETO. Baptist (deacon 1954-72). Clubs: University, Racquet (Houston). Office: 7440 Cullen Blvd Houston TX 77021

MCLANE, H. ARTHUR, lawyer; b. Valdosta, Ga., Apr. 2, 1939; s. Carson H. and Philena (Tyson) McL.; B.A., Emory U., 1961; J.D., U. Ga., 1963; m. Jane Campbell Bennet, June 17, 1961; children—Mary Campbell, Paul Corbett. Admitted to Ga. bar, 1963; practiced in Valdosta, Ga., 1963-—; county atty. Lowndes County (Ga.), 1965-—; atty. Echols County Bd. Edn., 1966-—. Adv. bd. Valdosta Area Vocational Tech. Sch., 1967-—. Bd. dirs. Valdosta Boys Club, 1966-—, pres., 1971-72; bd. dirs. Valdosta Entertainment Assn., 1968-71. Named Outstanding Young Man, 1972. Mem. State Bar Ga., Valdosta Bar Assn., Am. Judicature Soc., Sigma Alpha Epsilon, Phi Delta Phi, Phi Kappa Phi. Methodist. Elk. Club: Valdosta Country (dir., pres. 1971). Office: 504 N Patterson St Valdosta GA 31601

MCLARRY, LACY, concertmaster; b. Tex.; student of violin with Philip Williams, Dallas; grad. So. Meth. U., also Master's degree. Currently concertmaster Okla. City Symphony Orch., N.H. Music Festival Orch.; mem. string quartet Western Arts Summer Music Festival, Laramie, Wyo.; violin tchr. Kan. State Tchrs. Coll., Emporia. Served with USN. Office: Oklahoma City Symphony Orch Civic Center Music Hall Oklahoma City OK 73102*

MCLARTY, CLEYLON LEE, educator; b. Oxford, Miss., Apr. 10, 1923; s. Walter Eugene and Ada (Livingston) McL.; B.Mus., U. Miss., 1951, M.Ed., 1958, Ed.D., 1963; m. Mildred Hale, Feb. 26, 1948; children—Michael, Patricia, Dianne, Phillip. Tchr., counselor pub. schs., Miss., 1949-59; grad. asst. U. Miss., Oxford, 1959-60; asst. to dean of students, dir. devel. U. Ga., Athens, 1960-61; instr. Miss. State U., Starksville, summer 1962, U. Miss., summer 1964; asso. prof. Delta State Coll., Cleveland, Miss., 1962-66; prof. edn., coordinator rehab. counseling program Ark. State U., Jonesboro, 1966-—. Mem. Am. Ednl. Research Assn., N.E.A., Am. Personnel and Guidance Assn., Assn. for Counselor Edn. and Supervision, Assn. for Measurement and Evaluation in Guidance, Nat. Assn. for Student Tchrs., Ark. Personnel and Guidance Assn., Ark. Sch. Counselors Assn., Assn. for Higher Edn., Phi Delta Kappa, Kappa Delta Pi. Home: 1901 W Oak St Jonesboro AR 72401 Office: Ark State U State University AR 72467

MCLARTY, MARY ADELAIDE, librarian; b. Memphis, Aug. 3, 1925; d. John Robert and Edith (Wiggins) McLarty; A.A., Stephens Coll., 1945; B.A. with honors, U. N.C., 1949, B.S. in L.S., 1953. Tchr., librarian pub. schs., Shaw, Miss., 1949-51; extension librarian Wilson County Pub. Library, Wilson, N.C., 1953-57; librarian Onslow County Pub. Library, Jacksonville, N.C., 1957-67; dir. Davidson County Pub. Library, 1967-70; extension librarian Rowan Pub. Library, Salisbury, N.C., 1970-—; asst. treas. S.M. Fewel & Co., Vance, Miss. Bd. dirs. Jacksonville-Camp Lejeune U.S.O.; charter mem. Salisbury Hist. Found. Recipient community woman award Jacksonville Jr. C. of C., 1964. Mem. A.L.A., N.C., Southeastern library assns., N.C. Hist. and Lit. Soc., Cath. Daus. Am., Onslow Hist. Soc., Jacksonville C. of C. Democrat. Home: 308 Queens Rd PO Box

249 Lexington NC 27292 Office: Rowan Public Library Salisbury NC 28144

MCLAUGHLIN, A.A., business exec., b. 1910; ed. Robert Morris Sch. Bus.; m. With Pennzoil Co., 1927-68, controller, 1964-67, treas., 1967-71; treas., asst. sec. Pennzoil United Inc., Houston. Address: Southwest Tower Houston TX 77002*

MCLAUGHLIN (EDWARD) BRUCE, lawyer; b. Omaha, Apr. 2, 1921; s. Charles F. and Margaret (Bruce) McL.; student Mercersburg Acad., 1935-38; B.S., Georgetown U., 1943; postgrad. George Washington U., 1950-51; LL.B., U. Miami, 1953. Announcer Sta. KTSM, El Paso, Tex., 1943-44; news editor KFRE, Fresno, Cal., 1944; with McKesson-Robbins, San Francisco, 1945-46; radio prodn. Sta. KOSA, Odessa Tex., 1947-49, Sta. KPHO, Phoenix, 1949; TV prodn. Sta. WITV, Miami-Ft. Lauderdale, Fla., 1953-55; admitted to Fla. bar, 1955, since practiced in Miami. Served with Signal Corps, AUS, World War II. Mem. Fla. Bar, Am., Dade County bar assns., Lawyers Club Dade County (dir. 1969-70), Screen Actors Guild (pres. Fla. br. 1965-69, mem. Fla. council 1962-—, mem. nat. bd. dirs. 1968-—), Am. Legion, Gamma Eta Gamma. Democrat. Roman Catholic. Clubs: Coral Gables (Fla.) Country; Jockey (Miami, Fla.); University (Washington). Home: 45 Antilla Av Coral Gables FL 33134 Office: Ainsley Bldg Miami FL 33132

MCLAUGHLIN, CHARLES BORROMEO, clergyman; b. N.Y.C., Sept. 26, 1913; ed. St. Joseph Sem., St. John Sem. Ordained priest, Roman Catholic Ch., 1941; titular bishop Risinium and aux. of Raleigh (N.C.), 1964; bishop St. Petersburg, Fla., 1968-—. Address: 4960 Bogie Av N St Petersburg FL 33710*

MCLAUGHLIN, DAVID, protozoologist, educator; b. Sumter, S.C., Nov. 1, 1934; s. Arthur S. and Iris (Ladson) McL.; B.S., Clark Coll., Atlanta, 1956; M.S., Howard U., 1962, Ph.D., 1965; m. Pauletta Fellows, Sept. 7, 1963. Research asst., USPHS grantee Howard U., Washington, 1957-62, teaching and research supr. NSF Summer Research Participant for High Sch. Tchrs., 1957-58, NSF Summer Research Participant for High Sch. Students, 1958-64, research asso., USPHS grantee, 1962-65, supr. summer undergrad. research participation, 1965-66, prof. zoology, coordinator Ind. Research Lab., 1965-—. Postdoctoral studies Bio-Space Tech. Tng. Program NASA Wallops Sta., 1965, Gemini Summary Conf. NASA Manned Space Craft Center, Houston; participant 3d Internat. Congress on Protozoology, Leningrad, USSR, 1969. Mem. Soc. Protozoologists, Am. Inst. Biol. Sci., A.A.A.S., Am. Micros. Soc., Am. Soc. Zoologists, N.A.A.C.P., Sigma Xi, Beta Kappa, Omega Psi Phi. Baptist. Contbr. articles to profl. jours. Home: 907 Cox Av Hyattsville MD 20783 Office: 415 College St NW Washington DC 20001

MCLAUGHLIN, LEO PLOWDEN, univ. ofcl.; b. N.Y.C., July 30, 1912; s. Leo and Sallie (Rowan) McL.; A.B., Georgetown U., 1938; Ph.Licentiate, Woodstock (Md.) Coll., 1939; A.M., Catholic U. Am., 1940; Th. Licentiate, Weston (Mass.) Coll., 1946; D. es L., U. Paris, France, 1950; LL.D., U. Wyoming, 1970. Instr. Bklyn. Prep. Sch., 1940-42; vis. lectr. Georgetown U., summers 1942-45; ordained priest Roman Cath. Ch., 1945; dir. radio sta. WFUV-FM, 1950-53; chmn. dept. communication arts Fordham U., 1952-53, dean of coll., 1953-59; dean St. Peters Coll., 1959-65, pres., 1965; pres. Fordham U., 1965-69, chancellor, 1969-70; dir. freshman studies Johnson C. Smith U., Charlotte, N.C., 1970-—. Dir. Met. Applied Research Center. Mem. adv. com. U.S. Army Command and General Staff Coll. Mem. Assn. Urban Univs. (v.p. 1968, pres. 1969), Phi Delta Kappa. Address: Johnson C Smith Univ Charlotte NC 28208

MCLAUGHLIN, LLOYD ALPHONSE, JR., physician; b. New Orleans, June 30, 1921; s. Lloyd A. and Manilla (Bourdeaux) M.; B.S., Tulane U., 1949, M.D. 1952; m. Vilma Moncada, July 7, 1956; children—Gayle Elizabeth, Barry Joseph, Brooks Gerard, Maureen Marie, Laura Louise. Intern Mercy Hosp., New Orleans, 1952-53; gen. practice medicine, New Orleans, 1953-54; resident Touro Infirmary, New Orleans, 1954-55; fellow Ochsner Found., New Orleans, 1955-56; practice medicine specializing in pediatrics, 1957-—; mem. staffs Hotel Dieu, Mercy Hosp., Sara Mayo Hosp., Crippled Children's Hosp. (all New Orleans); sr. vis. pediatrician Charity Hosp., New Orleans; asst. clin. prof. pediatrics Tulane U., 1955-—. Pres. Greater New Orleans chpt. Muscular Dystrophy Assn. Am., 1961. Served with USAAF, 1941-45. Mem. A.M.A., La., Orleans Parish med. socs., La. Pediatric Soc., Am. Acad. Pdiatrics. Research in field. Home: 1913 Elizabeth Av Metairie LA 70003 Office: 501 N Jefferson Davis Pkwy New Orleans LA

MCLAUGHLIN, MARTIN MICHAEL, govt. ofcl.; b. Portland, Ore., June 23, 1918; s. Chatham Ewing and Julia (Costello) M.; A.B., U. Portland, 1938; M.A., U. Notre Dame, 1941, Ph.D., 1948; m. Patricia Claire Ollivier, Dec. 28, 1948; children—Martin P., Peter C., Christopher P., Michael J., Stephen A., Mark B. Asst. prof. DePaul U., Chgo., 1948-51; ofcl. of U.S. high commn., Germany, 1952-54; exec. officer Dept. Def., 1954-57; U.S. embassy to NATO, 1957-60; spl. asst. Dept. State, 1960-65; dep. dir. Office Internat. Tng. AID, Washington, 1965-—. Lectr. George Washington U., Catholic U., U. Md. Founder U.S. Nat. Student Assn., 1947. Served with USAAF, 1942-46. Roman Catholic. K.C. Home: 3325 N 20thSt Arlington VA 22207 Office: 1901 Pennsylvania AV Washington DC 20535

MCLAUGHLIN, MAX VICTOR, physician; b. Blue Springs, Ala., Nov. 4, 1928; s. James Daniel and Dovie Alma (Whigham) McL.; B.S., U. Ala., 1952; M.D., Med. Coll. Ala., 1956; m. Sally Girard Schofield, Dec. 23, 1954 (dec. July 1968); 1 son, Max Victor. Intern Mobile (Ala.) Gen. Hosp., 1956-57, resident, 1957-58; practice gen. medicine, Mobile, 1958-—. Mem. Ala. Bd. Corrections, 1963-—, chmn., 1972-—. Bd. dirs. Doctors Hosp., Mobile. Served with AUS, 1946-48. Mem. Med. Assn. State of Ala., Med. Assn. Mobile County, Am. Acad. Family Practice, Phi Gamma Delta, Phi Beta Pi, Omicron Delta Kappa. Episcopalian. Mason, Kiwanian (charter mem. West Mobile). Home: 13 N Springbank Rd Mobile AL 36608 Office: 2218 Fulbrook Center Mobile AL 36605

MCLAUGHLIN, ORVEL VEARL, banker; b. Nowata, Okla., Feb. 14, 1921; s. Gerald Beatrice and Lillian Maysey (Bell) McL.; B.A., Oklahoma City U., 1949, LL.B., 1953; m. Doris Mae Bozarth, Oct. 3, 1947; children— Gerald Stephen, Janet Lee. Page to head bookkeeper Tradesmens Nat. Bank, 1941; auditor, installment loan officer, asst. cashier charge installment loans, comml. loan officer First Nat. Bank, Oklahoma City, 1948-61; pres., chief exec. officer Village Bank, Oklahoma City, 1961-—; chmn. bd., pres. Village Bldg. Corp. Vice pres., bd. mgmt. North Side YMCA; bd. dirs. Oklahoma County Mental Health Assn. Served with USNR, 1942-46. Recipient Distinguished Service award Village Jr. C. of C., 1968, Boss of Year award, 1969. Hon. mayor, The Village, 1967. Mem. Okla. Installment Bankers Assn., Okla., Oklahoma County bar assns., Am. Legion (past post comdr., treas.), Oklahoma City C. of C. Democrat. Baptist. Lion. Club: Toastmasters (past pres.). Home: 3004 Kent Dr Oklahoma City OK 73120 Office: 9520 May Av Oklahoma City OK 73120

MCLAUGHLIN, WILLIAM LOWNDES, physicist; b. Stony Point, Tenn., Mar. 30, 1928; s. John Calvin Brown and Fannie (McCaa) McL.; student Potomac State Coll., 1945-47; B.S., Hampden Sydney Coll., 1949; postgrad. Duke, 1949-50, Tubingen U. (Germany), 1950-51; M.S., George Washington U., 1962; m. Nancy Elizabeth Shepherd, Mar. 27, 1951; children—Peter Shepherd, David Wallace. Physicist, Nat. Bur. Standards, Washington, 1951-54, 54-—. Cons. radiation effects and radiation processing. Served with AUS, 1954-56. Recipient silver medal Dept. Commerce, 1969. Mem. Am. Phys. Soc., Optical Soc. Am., Health Physics Soc., A.A.A.S., Radiation Research Soc., Soc. Photog. Scientists and Engrs. (dir. 1965-67). Presbyn. Home: 3901 Albemarle St NW Washington DC 20016 Office: Center for Radiation Research Nat Bur Standards Washington DC 20234

MCLAWHORN, WALTER RALEIGH, physician; b. Greenville, S.C., May 12, 1920; s. Walter Raleigh and Lula (Carpenter) McL.; B.S., Furman U., 1941; M.D., S.C. Med. U., 1944; postgrad. gross pathology Algemenis Krahenhouse, Vienna, Austria, 1947; m. Dorothy Mae Noblett, June 16, 1943; children—Walter Leigh, Marilyn Elizabeth. Intern, Roper Hosp., Charleston, S.C., 1944-45, resident in surgery Columbia (S.C.) Gen. Hosp., 1945-46; house physician Spartanburg (S.C.) Gen. Hosp., 1948-49; practice medicine specializing in gen. practice, Fountain Inn, S.C., 1954-—, owner, operator McLawhorn Clinic, 1954-—; mem. staff Hillcrest Hosp., Simpsonville, S.C.; sec.-treas. Fountain Labs., Inc., 1954-—. Chmn., Fountain Inn Red Cross drive, 1955. Bd. dirs. Fountain Inn Emergency Relief Agy. Served to capt. U.S. Army, 1942-48. Mem. Am. Acad. Gen. Practice, C. of C. (man of year 1955). Greenville County Alston Wilkes Soc. (pres. 1968-69), Alpha Epsilon Delta, Phi Rho Sigma. Republican. Methodist (chmn. bd. 1954-55). Lion (pres. 1960-61), Mason. Club: Fountain Inn Simpsonville Country. Home: Wilson Bridge Rd Fountain Inn SC 29644 Office: 203 S Weston St Fountain Inn SC 29644

MCLEAN, AUGUSTUS ALEXANDER, JR., physician; b. Lenoir, N.C., Feb. 2, 1920; s. Augustus Alexander and Hallie (Hall) McL.; B.S., Davidson Coll., 1942; M.D., Med. Coll. Va., 1945; m. Margaret Stephenson, Sept. 30, 1944; children—Margaret (Mrs. James Womble), Patricia, Augustus Alexander III, Gay, Benjamin. Intern, U. Va. Hosps., 1945-46; practice family medicine, Lenoir, 1948-50, Murfreesboro, N.C., 1950-—; mem. staff Roanoke Chowan Hosp., Ahoskie, N.C. Farmer, Murfreesboro. Mem. Tri County Airport Authority. Bd. dirs. Pine Forest Rest Home. Served to capt. AUS, 1946-48. Mem. Am., So., N.C. (del. 1961-62), Seaboard (v.p. 1970-71) med. assns., Hertford County (pres. 1956-58), 1st Dist. (sec.-treas. 1955-56) med. socs., Murfreesboro Hist. Assn., Murfreesboro C. of C. Rotarian (pres. 1969-70). Home: 615 Woodridge Dr Murfreesboro NC 27855 Office: 200 S Wynn St Murfreesboro NC 27855

MCLEAN, HUGH K., lawyer; b. Milan, Tenn., Oct. 19, 1918; A.B., Cumberland U., 1940; J.D., Vanderbilt U., 1949. Admitted to Tenn. bar, 1948, U.S. Dist. Ct. bar, Western Dist. Tenn. bar, 1951, U.S. Supreme Ct. bar, 1961, U.S. Ct. Appeals bar, 1966; since practiced Tenn.; city atty., Paris, Tenn., 1959-—. Mem. Paris-Henry County (pres. 1964-68), Tenn., Am. bar assns., Blue Key, Delta Theta Phi. Lion. (pres. Paris 1954). Office: 504 Comml Bank Bldg Paris TN 38242*

MCLEAN, JAMES DOUGLAS, JR., paleontologist, geologist; b. Newport, R.I., Dec. 18, 1919; s. James D. and Emma (Carter) McL.; B.A., Washington and Lee U., 1944; postgrad. Bryn Mawr Coll., 1945; M.S., La. State U., 1947. Acting head dept. geology Va. Mil. Inst., Lexington, 1948-49; dir. McLean Paleontol. Lab., pubs. sci. books, papers, data cards, Alexandria, Va., 1950-—; cons. geologist, Alexandria, 1950-—; cons. electronic data processing in geol. and sci. work. Mem. Am. Assn. Petroleum Geologists, Paleontol. Soc., Paleontol. Research Inst., Soc. Econ. Paleontologists and Mineralogists, Societe Geologique de France, Am. Mus. Natural History, Paleontol. Assn. (Eng.), Soc. Ind. Profl. Earth Scientists, Am. Assn. Profl. Geologists, Am. Arbitration Assn. (bd. expert panelists). Editor: McLean Card Catalogue of American Foraminifera, vols. I-XIV and continuations, 1950-—; Reports from McLean Paleontol. Lab., nos. 1-5 and continuation, 1952-—; McLean Card Catalogue of Ostracoda, vols. I-VIII and continuations, 1956-—; Manual of Micropaleontological Techniques, vols. I-VI and continuation, 1959-—; distbr., pub., H,S. Puri Card Catalogue of Recent Ostracoda, vols. I-VI, and continuations, 1960-—; Strata Data, 1962-—; Manual Micropaleontological Stratigraphy, vols. I, II, and continuation, 1963-—. Author numerous sci. papers and monographs. Research on micropaleontol. subjects and stratigraphy. Home: 1927 Summit Terrace Belle Haven Alexandria VA 22307 Office: PO Box 916 Alexandria VA 22312

MCLEAN, LEON MOORE, supt. schs.; b. Rowland, N.C., Dec. 15, 1928; s. Arless Lester and Maggie Mae (McRimmon) McL.; B.S., Appalachian State U., 1949; M.Ed., U. N.C., 1957, advanced supt. certificate, 1967; m. Janie Rae Britt, June 22, 1951; children—Steven, Donna. Tchr., coach Massey Hill Sch., Fayetteville, N.C., 1949-52, Littlefield Sch., Lumberton, N.C., 1955-57; prin. Garland (N.C.) Sch., 1957-63; supt. sch. system, Fairmont, N.C., 1963-—. Chmn. Robeson County March of Dimes Campaign, 1963. Served with AUS, 1952-55. Mem. N.C. Edn. Assn. (pres. supt.'s div. Southeastern N.C. dist. 1966). Rotarian. Home: 701 Gertrude St Fairmont NC 28340 Office: 106 Trinity St Fairmont NC 28340

MCLEAN, WILLIAM YOUMANS, architect; b. Vidalia, Ga., Aug. 9, 1927; s. John Archibald and Alma (Tod) McL.; student U.S. Naval Acad., 1945-47; B.S., Ga. Inst. Tech., 1947, B.Arch., 1950; m. Larue Jane Wells, June 9, 1951; children—William Youmans, Jonathan Wells, Amanda Jane. Archtl. draftsman, designer Wm. J.J. Chase & Assos., Atlanta, 1951-52, 55-58; architect Harvey & Elliott, Rome, Ga., 1959-60, M.G. Turner, Rome, 1960-61; partner Turner & McLean, Architects, Rome, 1961-62; asso. Hugh Gaston Assos., Albany, Ga., 1962-63; owner William Y. McLean, Architect, Albany, 1963-67, Tifton Ga., 1967-—. City commr., vice mayor Tifton, 1972-—. Served as lt. (j.g.) USNR 1952-55. Mem. A.I.A. (organizer, 1st pres. S.W. Ga. chpt. 1965-66, dir. Ga. council, 1966-67, dir. s. Atlantic regional council 1966). Democrat. Episcopalian (mem. diocesan council 1971-—). Elk, Rotarian. Home: 202 W 26th St Tifton GA 31794 Office: 215 N Central Av Tifton GA 31794

MCLELLAN, JOHN S., lawyer; b. Kingsport, Tenn., Nov. 19, 1921; grad. U. Ky. Admitted to Tenn. bar, 1944, U.S. Appeals Ct. bar, 6th Circuit, 1955, U.S. Appeals Ct. bar, 7th Circuit, 1956, U.S. Appeals Ct. bar, 1st, 5th Circuits, 1957; since practiced Tenn. Chmn., TVA bd. commrs. for Fed. Ct., Eastern Dist. Tenn., 1968-—. Mem. Kingsport, Tenn. (del. 6th Circuit Judicial Conf. 1969-70, chmn. Labor Law Sect. 1970), bar assns., Am. Judicature Soc. Office: 421 E Market St Kingsport TN 37660*

MCLELLAND, ROBERT ALLEN, city ofcl.; b. Houston, Aug. 17, 1931; s. Otis A. and Eunice V. (Merrill) McL.; student U. Ala., 1954-56; B.A., Ga. State Coll., 1960; m. Florence Teresa Moriarty, July 27, 1957; children—Albert, Robert, Jeffery. Supr., Allstate Ins. Co., Atlanta, Ga., 1959-61; dir. personnel and safety activities City of Sarasota, Fla., 1961-68, city auditor, clk., 1968-—. Instr. adult edn. classes Fla. State Bd. Edn., 1969-70. Children's parade chmn. Sarasota County Pageant Assn., 1966-67, grand parade chmn., 1967-68, crew purser, 1968-69, ex-officio purser, 1969-70, bd. dirs., 1969-—. Served with USAF, 1950-54. Recipient citation for community service United Appeal, 1967. Mem. Pub. Personnel Assn., Fla. Assn. Civil Service and Personnel Agys., Am. Soc. Safety Engrs., Ala. Alumni Assn., Internat. City Clks. Assn., Internat. City Mgrs. Assn., Municipal Finance Officers Assn, Delta Chi. Elk. Home: 3185 Bay St Sarasota FL 33580 Office: 1565 1st St Sarasota FL 33578

MCLEMORE, ANDREW JACKSON, III, librarian; b. Memphis, Feb. 6, 1932; s. Andrew Jackson and Willia (Rogers) McL.; A.B., Morehouse Coll., 1954; M.S. in Library Sci., Atlanta U., 1960; grad. Ga. So. Coll., 1970; m. Willie George Scott, July 30, 1964; children—Mignon, Andrew, Victor. Asst. librarian Atlanta U., 1958-62; librarian Miles Coll., Birmingham, Ala., 1962-66, Savannah (Ga.) State Coll., 1966-—. Served with AUS, 1955-57. Recipient fellowship Nat. Urban League, 1969. Mem. Am., Ga., Southeastern library assns., Alpha Phi Alpha. Mason. Editor faculty research bull. Savannah State Coll., 1966-—. Home: 1412 Stillwood Dr Savannah GA 31406 Office: PO Box 20394 Savannah State Coll Savannah GA 31404

MCLEMORE, ETHEL WARD, research geophysicist, mathematician; b. Sylvarena, Miss., Jan. 22, 1908; d. William Robert and Frances Virginia (Douglas) Ward; B.A., Miss. Woman's Coll., 1928; M.A., U. N.C., 1929; postgrad. U. Chgo., 1931, Colo. Sch. Mines, 1941-42, So. Meth. U., 1962-64; m. Robert Henry McLemore, June 30, 1935; 1 dau., Mary Frances. Head math. dept. Miss. Jr. Coll., 1929-30; instr. chemistry, math. Miss. State Coll. for Women, 1930-32; research mathematician Humble Oil & Refining Co., Houston, 1933-36; ind. geophys. research, Tex. and Colo., 1936-42, Ft. Worth, 1946-—; geophysicist United Geophys. Co., Pasadena, Cal., 1942-46; tchr. chemistry, physics Hockaday Sch., Dallas, 1958-59, tchr. math., 1959-60, tchr. chemistry, 1968-69; tchr. chemistry Ursuline Acad., Dallas, 1964-67. Mem. Am. Math. Soc., Math. Assn. Am., Am. Geophys. Union, Seismol. Soc. Am., Soc. Exploration Geophysicists, A.A.A.S., Soc. Indsl. and Applied Math., Tex. Acad. Sci., Sigma Xi. Contbr. articles to profl. jours. Home: 11625 Wander Lane Dallas TX 75230

MCLEMORE, LEE, city ofcl.; b. Hohenwald, Tenn., June 6, 1915; s. Adlai and Minnie (Murray) McL.; student pub. schs.; m. Dorothy Wallace, June 5, 1936 (div. 1960); 1 son, Wayne Lee; m. 2d, Ensley Gardiner, 1969. Display advertiser, 1936-55; active in pub. relations, sales promotion, constrn. and real estate; city councilman, Houston, 1954-—, now mayor pro-tem. Regional co-chmn. United Fund, Community Chest; active P.T.A.; com. chmn. Houston Beautiful Campaign; pres. Civic Council Houston; past pres. Houston Galveston Area Council. Candidate for Tex. State Senate, 1972. Bd. dirs. Harris County Welfare Bd., Houston-Harris County Lighthouse for Blind; County Welfare Bd., Houston-Harris County Lighthouse for Blind; charter mem. Houston Youth Fair and Rodeo, Houston Big Bros. Assn., Community Council. Served with USAAF, 1942-45. Named One of Outstanding Young Texans, 1952; recipient Charles A. Perlitz award Jr. C. of C., 1966. Mem. Houston C. of C. (dir. Houston Outstanding Young Man award 1951), Harris County Mayor and Council Assn., Houston Jaycee Alumni Assn. (past pres.), Houston Tourist Assn. (pres.), Sign Mfrs. Assn. (chmn.), River Oaks Bus. and Profl. Assn. Optimist, Elk, Eagle. Clubs: Houston Advertising, Houston Yacht, Montagu, Variety. Home: 4944 Woodway St Houston TX 77027 Office: 3701 Allen Pkwy Houston TX 77019

MCLEMORE, RICHARD AUBREY, state ofcl.; b. Perry County, Miss., June 6, 1903; s. Hezekiah and Tabitha (Small) McL.; A.B., Miss. Coll., 1923, Litt.D., 1969; A.M., George Peabody Coll., 1926; Ph.D., Vanderbilt U., 1933 (fellow in history, 1930-33); m. Nannie Pitts, 1927; 1 son, Harry Kimbrell. Supt. village schs., Miss., 1923-26; instr. history, and dean, Jones County Jr. Coll., 1926-30, 33-34; prof. history and dean Judson Coll., 1934-38; prof. Miss. So. Coll., 1938-57, dean, 1945-54, 55-57, acting pres., 1955; pres. Miss. Coll., Clinton, 1957-68; dir. Miss. Dept. Archives and History, 1969-—. Mem. Am., So., Miss., So. Bapt. hist. assns. Baptist (deacon). Mason (33 deg., Shriner), Lion (past dist. gov., state historian, internat. counselor). Author: The Natchez County, 1936; Franco-American Diplomatic Relations, 1816-1836, 1940; Mississippi Through 4 Centuries (with wife), 1945, rev., 1949, 60, Outline of Mississippi History, 1941, rev., 1944, 46, 51, 59, 69; (with Blough and Switzer) Fundamentals of Citizenship, 1950, rev., 1957; Our Nation's Story (with Everett Auguspurger), 1954, rev., 1962; (with Boyd C. Shafer and Everett Augspurger) A United States History for High Schools, 1966, rev., 1969, 1865 to the Present: A United States History for High Schools, 1966; A History of Mississippi Baptists, 1970. Contbr. to Encys.; also to hist. jours. Hist. editor: Official Map of Mississippi, 1953. Editor in chief Jour. Miss. History, 1969-—. Home: 224 Kitchings Dr Clinton MS 39056

MCLEMORE, MRS. RICHARD AUBREY, educator, author; b. Harvest, Ala., Sept. 21, 1900; d. James Ervin and Lola (Sanderson) Pitts; A.B., Athens Coll., 1921; M.A., George Peabody Coll. Tchrs., 1927; postgrad. Vanderbilt U., 1930-31; m. Richard Aubrey McLemore, June 2, 1927; 1 son, Harry Kimbrell. Instr. history Northport (Ala.) High Sch., 1921-22, Escambia County High Sch., 1922-24, Monrovia High Sch., 1924-25; head dept. history McComb (Miss.) High Sch., 1925-27; prof. history Jones County Jr. Coll., 1927-30, 33-34; instr. history Perry County High Sch., Ala., 1936-37. Mem. Miss. Hist. Soc., Am. Assn. U. Women (Miss. div. pres. 1950-52), Miss. Geneol. Soc. Democrat. Baptist. Author: (with Richard Aubrey McLemore) Outline of Mississippi History, 1941; Mississippi Through Four Centuries, 1944; The Mississippi Story, 1959, rev. 1969; also articles in field. Address: 224 Kitchings Dr Clinton MS 39056

MCLENDON, BILLYE BURRELL, psychologist; b. Copperas Cove, Tex.; d. Norwood W. and Lena Mae (McGonagill) McLendon; A.A. with 1st Honors, Temple Jr. Coll., 1948; B.A. magna cum laude, U. Tex., 1950, M.A., 1956, Ph.D., 1965. Secretarial positions, 1946-50, 52; classroom tchr. Ind. Sch. Dist., Port Arthur, Austin, Tex., 1950-54; research and teaching asst. dept. psychology U. Tex., 1955-56, asst. psychologist, intern Testing and Counseling Center, 1957-59, teaching asst., lectr. dept. ednl. psychology, 1959-61; psychologist Austin Community Guidance Center, 1956-57; sch. psychologist St. Andrews Episcopal Sch., 1958; clin. psychologist Child Psychiatry Center, Milw. Children's Hosp., also instr. psychology depts. psychiatry and pediatrics Marquette U. Sch. Medicine, Milw., 1964-67; practice counseling and clin. psychology, 1965-—; elementary multi-school counselor and psychologist San Antonio Ind. Sch. Dist., 1969-70; psychologist Harlandale Ind. Sch. Dist., 1970-71. Delta Delta Delta scholar U. Tex., 1949. Mem. Am., Southwestern, Tex. psychol. assns., UN Assn., Nat. Council on Family Relations, Internat. Platform Assn., Am. Mus. Natural History, Nat. Wildlife Fedn., Phi Beta Kappa, Pi Lambda Theta, Psy Chi. Democrat. Methodist. Contbr. articles to profl. jours. Research on origins of the person, creativeness, student-centered teaching, psychotherapy, community mental health. Home: 211 W French Pl San Antonio TX 78212

MCLENDON, GORDON BARTON, broadcasting, film exec.; b. Paris, Tex., June 8, 1921; s. Barton Robert and Jeanette (Eyster) McL.; student Kemper Mil. Sch., 1938; A.B., Yale, 1943;

children—Jan, Bart, Kristen, Anna Gray. Owner radio sta. KNET, Palestine Tex., 1948; pres., owner Liberty Broadcastin System, Dallas, 1948-52; owner KLIF, Dallas, KABL, San Francisco, WNUS, Chicago, WYSL, Buffalo, WWWW, Detroit, KNUS-FM, Dallas, KABL-FM, San Francisco, KOST, Los Angeles, WYSL-FM, Buffalo, KCND-TV, Pambina, N.D., US Sales, X-TRA News; pres. The McLendon Corp., McLendon Pacific Corp., Sunshine Broadcasting Corp., McLendon Radio Pictures, Tex, Triangle, Inc.; partner Tri-State Theatres, Tex. State chmn. March of Dimes, 1958. Democratic candidate for nomination U.S. Senator Tex., 1964; candidate for nomination gov., 1968. Served as Japanese lang. officer, intelligence, USNR, 1943-45. Named outstanding football announcer Sporting News, 1950; one of 10 outstanding young men U.S. Jr. C. of C., 1951, Pulse, Inc. Man of Yr., 1967; recipient Golden Plate award Am. Acad, Achievement, 1966; award Am. Mothers' Com., 1967. Mem. Nat. Assn. F.M. Broadcasters (dir.), Chi Psi. Methodist. Clubs: City, Brook Hollow Golf, Dallas Country (Dallas). Author: The Old Scotchman's Scrapbook; Fun Style in the use of English, Way to a More Colorful Vocabulary. Home: Manor House 1315 Commerce Dallas TX 75201 Office: McLendon Bldg 2008 Jackson St Dallas TX 75201

MCLENDON, R.D., coll. pres.; b. Quitman, Miss., May 23, 1905; s. Rosier Alexander and Mary Ann (McLemore) McL.; B.S., Miss. So. Coll., 1929; M.S., U. Tex., 1938; m. Corinne Hipps, May 1, 1938. Prin. Leaksville (Miss.) High Sch., 1929-31, Waynesboro High Sch., 1931-33, Madison-Ridgeland High Sch., 1933-35; supt. Lumberton (Miss.) High Sch., 1935-40, Woodville High Sch., 1940-42; pres. Pearl River Jr. Coll., Poplarville, Miss., 1942-53, N.W. Miss. Jr. Coll., Senatobia, 1953-—. Named col. gov.'s staff. Mem. Instns. Higher Learning Miss. (trustee), Miss. Jr. Coll. Assn. (pres. 1947-49), Miss. Assn. Colls. (pres. 1953-54), Mason, Rotarian. Address: Senatobia MS 38668

MCLEOD, BO, newspaper editor; b. Ocala, Fla., Aug. 23, 1926; s. Robert M. and Addie (Hill) McL.; grad. pub. high sch.; m. Carolyn Willis, July 22, 1950; children—Mary Janet, Sandra Jo, Carol Ann. With Donalsonville (Ga.) News, 1943-—, editor 1951-—; columnist Atlanta Jour., 1961-—. Served with AUS, World War II. Mem. Donalsonville (Ga.) C. of C. Presbyn. (elder). Lion (pres. 1961-62). Home: PO Box 324 Donalsonville GA 31745 Office: PO Box 338 Donalsonville GA 31745

MCLEOD, DANIEL ROGERS, atty. gen. S.C.; b. Sumter, S.C., Oct. 6, 1913; s. D. Melvin and Bertie (Guyton) McL.; student Wofford Coll., 1931-32; LL.B., U. S.C., 1948; m. Ellen D. LaBorde, May 20, 1941 (dec.); children—Daniel R., Elizabeth Ann; m. 2d, Virginia B. Hart, July 31, 1962; stepchildren—John E. Hart, Robert S. Hart. Admitted to S.C. bar, 1948; asst. atty. gen. S.C., 1950-58, atty. gen., 1958-—. Mem. Am., S.C. bar assns. Methodist (ofcl. bd.). Home: 4511 Langrave Rd Columbia SC 29202 Office: Wade Hampton Office Bldg Columbia SC 29202

MCLEOD, HAROLD MCCALLUM, govt. ofcl.; b. Timmonsville, S.C., Oct. 27, 1907; s. William Rogers and Ellen (Byrd) McL.; A.B., Wofford Coll., 1928; m. Carolyn Keller Bowman, Apr. 27, 1935; children—Harold McCallum, John Bowman. Tchr., prin. pub. schs., 1928-33; with Internal Revenue Service, 1933-—, asst. dist. dir., Columbia, S.C., 1952-60, dist. dir., 1960-—. Trustee Wofford Coll.; bd. dirs., trustee United Community Services Lexington and Richland Counties. Served with AUS, 1942-46; PTO; col. Res. Mem. Mil. Govt. Assn., Res. Officers Assn., Clan MacLeod Soc. U.S., St. Andrews Soc. Middle South, S.A.R., Am. Legion, Fed. Exec. Council (past pres.), Kappa Alpha. Methodist. Lion. Home: 922 Russell St SE Orangeburg SC 29115 Office: Fed Office Bldg 901 Sumter St Columbia SC 29201

MCLEOD, JOHN PURL UTTLEY, physician; b. Fayetteville, N.C., Nov. 5, 1911; s. James Luther Torquil and Geneva Gertrude (Allran) McL.; premed. student So. Missionary Coll.; M.D., Loma Linda U., 1939; m. Wilma Georgia Dickerson, July 30, 1935; children—Geneva Irene (Mrs. Donald Ellis Blood), John Purl Uttley, Wayne Torquil. Intern, Glendale (Cal.) Sanitarium and Hosp., 1938, Highsmith Hosp., Fayetteville, N.C., 1938-39; practice family medicine, Marshville, N.C., 1939-—; dir. McLeod Clinic, 1941-45; pres. Bio-Factor Labs., Marshville, 1936-—; pres. McLeod Airport, Wingate, N.C., 1948-62; acting dir. Anson County Health Dept., 1968-—; coronor Union County, N.C., 1957-58; med. examiner, 1958-60; justice of peace, 1967-69. Comdr., capt. Civil Air Patrol, 1945-48; active A.R.C. Diplomate Nat. Bd. Med. Examiners. Fellow Am. Assn. Gen. Practice; mem. A.M.A., So. Med. Assn., N.C., Tri-State, Union County (past pres.) med. socs., N.Y. Acad. Scis., N.C. Art Soc. (life). Lion (charter mem. Marshville, treas. 1963-—). Contbr. articles to med. jours., newspapers, mags. Author: Ish and Isha, 1967. Home: 301 White St Marshville NC 28103 Office: 103 S Elm St Marshville NC 28103

MCLEOD, WALTON JAMES, JR., lawyer; b. Lynchburg, S.C., Aug. 7, 1906; s. Walton James and Pauline (Mullins) McL.; grad. Porter Mil. Acad., 1923; A.B., Wofford Coll., 1926; LL.B., U. S.C., 1930; m. Rhoda Lane Brown, Feb. 2, 1935; children—Walton James III, Peden B, William Mullins, Thomas Gordon III. Admitted to S.C. bar, 1930; practice of law, Walterboro, 1930-—; mem. firm Jefferies, McLeod, Unger & Fraser, 1956-—; city atty., Walterboro. Mem., vice chmn. S.C. Hwy. Commn., 1946-50. Mem. nat. exec. com. Young Democrats, 1938-42; Dem. chmn. Colleton County, 1950-60; mem. S.C. Dem. Exec. Com., 1960-—. Trustee Walterboro pub. schs,, 1936-46, Wofford Coll., 1954-66, Served to lt. comdr, USNR, 1942-46. Mem. Coll. Trial Lawyers, Am. Legion (comdr. S.C. 1949-50, mem. nat. exec. com. 1951-52), Am. (ho dels. 1950-64, bd. govs. 1964-67, chmn. resolutions com. 1961-62), S.C. (pres.), Colleton County (pres. 1962-—) bar assns., Kappa Alpha, Phi Delta Phi. Methodist. Mason (Shriner). Home: 109 Savage St Walterboro SC 29488 Office: 111 E Washington St Walterboro SC 29488

MCLEOD, YANCEY A., lawyer; b. Bishopville, S.C., Nov. 22, 1909; A.B., U. S.C., 1930, LL.B., 1932. Admitted to S.C. bar, 1932; since practiced in Columbia; partner firm McLeod and Singletary; spl. asst. to U.S. atty., 1951-55. Mem. S.C. Senate from Richland County, 1946-50; chmn. S.C. Dem. Com., 1964-66. Served to maj. USMCR, World War II. Mem. Am., S.C. (sec.-treas. 1939-42, chmn. legislative com. 1960-61, chmn. judicial system rev. com. 1962), Richland County (pres. 1961) bar assns. Office: Barringer Bldg Columbia SC 29201*

MCMAHAN, HOWARD DANE, govt. ofcl.; b. Topeka, July 11, 1930; s. Irl O. and Anna (Wilson) M.; B.A. with highest honors Geneva Coll., 1952; M. in Pub. Adminstrn., U. Kan., 1955; m. Myrtle Shucart, Dec. 8, 1954; children—Deborah Lynn, Brenda Ann, Michael Howard. Budget analyst, Kansas City, Mo., 1956-59; dir. finance, Boulder, Colo., 1959-62; city mgr., Littleton, Colo., 1962-66; dir. finance, Fort Worth, 1966-67, city mgr., 1967-71; regional dir. Region VI, Dept. Health, Edn. and Welfare, Dallas, 1971-—. Treas. YMCA, Fort Worth, 1969; resource mem. Tex. Urban Devel. Commn., 1970-71; vice chmn. Dallas-Ft. Worth Fed. Exec. Bd., 1972; mem. Tex. Adv. Commn. on Intergovtl. Relations, 1971-—; chmn. Southwest Fed. Regional Council, 1972-—. Bd. dirs. Tarrant County United Fund, 1968-71, Community Council, 1968-71. Served with AUS, 1954-56. Mem. Dallas Fed. Bus. Assn. (vice chmn. 1971-72), Internat. City Mgmt. Assn., Am. Soc. Pub. Adminstrn. Home: 5708 Wonder Dr Fort Worth TX 76133 Office: 1114 Commerce Dallas TX 75102

MCMAHON, JAMES ROBERT, educator; b. Tell City, Ind., July 16, 1932; s. Clarence William and Nell Edith (Hess) McM.; B.F.A., Ind. U., 1960; M.F.A., U. Fla., 1962; m. Levelle Sue Rosenberger, Mar. 7, 1959; children—Shawna Marie, Mark James, Shannon Marell, Ian Robert. Instr. dept. architecture U. Fla., 1961-62; prof. Manatee Jr. Coll., Bradenton, Fla., 1962-—, chmn. dept. art and music, 1968-—. Lectr. Am. Internat. Acad., Rome, Italy, 1966-72. Bd. govs. Allied Arts Counsel of Sarasota and Manatee Counties, 1963-70, exec. com., 1969-70, v.p., 1970-71, pres., 1971-72. Served with USAF, 1951-55. Recipient Roger Gould Wolcott award Indpls. Art Assn.; Meritorious Tchr. awards Manatee Jr. Coll., 1966-71. Mem. Am. Assn. U. Profs, Sarasota Art Assn., Assn. Coll. and U. Concert Mgrs., Fla. Assn. Pub. Jr. Colls. Home: 2715 48th St Bradenton FL 33505 Office: 5840 26th St W Bradenton FL 33505

MCMAHON, JOHN MARTIN, physician; b. Buffalo, Dec. 24, 1915; s. Charles A. and Mary (Fox) McM.; B.S., Georgetown U., 1936, M.D., 1940; M.S. in Medicine, U. Minn., 1950; m. Virginia Mary Tracy, Mar. 21, 1942; children—John Martin, Edward, Barbara, Robert, Bruce, Tommy. Intern, Georgetown U. Hosp., Washington, 1940-41; practice medicine specializing in internal medicine, Bessemer, Ala.; asso. Browne-McHardy Clinic, New Orleans, 1950-52; partner Bessemer Clinic, 1952-—; prof. clin. medicine U. Ala., 1952-—, dir. Arthritis Clinic Med. Center; attending cons. VA Hosp., Birmingham; chief of medicine Bapt. Med. Center-Princeton, Birmingham; mem. staff Bessemer Meml. Hosp. Served to capt. AUS, World War II; PTO. Recipient Benemerenti award Pope Paul VI, 1968. Diplomate Am. Bd. Internal Medicine. Fellow A.C.P., Am. Coll. Gastroenterology (past pres., abstract staff Jour. Gastroenterology, 1957-70). Contbr. articles to profl. jours. Home: 106 Waverly Circle Bessemer AL 35020 Office: 800 Clinic Lane Bessemer AL 35020

MCMAHON, RICHARD WARREN, motel corp. exec.; b. Memphis, Aug. 12, 1939; s. Warren Greenway and Ometra (Simpson) McM.; B.S., Memphis State U., 1962; m. Laura LeLievre, Jan. 18, 1964; 1 dau., Valerie Jones. With Holiday Inns, Inc., Memphis, 1962-—, dir. sales for operations, 1963-66, dir. nat. sales, 1966-69, dir. marketing western region, 1969-70, dir. sales and promotion, inns and restaurants, 1970-—. Recipient Distinguished Sales award Memphis Sales Execs. Assn., 1968; named Salesman of Year, Holiday Inns, 1968. Mem. Hotel Sales Mgmt. Assn. Internat. (dir. 1971-72), Discover Am. Travel Orgn., Am. Marketing Assn., Memphis Sales and Marketing Execs. Club, Mid-South Football Ofcls. Assn., Pi Sigma Epsilon, Psi Chi, Omicron Delta Kappa, Chi Beta Phi, Sigma Alpha Epsilon. Unitarian. Home: 5840 Ridgevale Memphis TN 38138 Office: 3796 Lamar Av Memphis TN 38118

MCMAKIN, WILLIAM ISAAC, JR., wholesale trade exec.; b. LaGrange, Ky., June 7, 1912; s. William Isaac and Elizabeth (Emerson) McM.; student Eastern U., 1931, U. Ky., 1932, Transylvania U., 1932-33; m. Kathryn Hardin, Oct. 17, 1940; children—William Isaac III, Ronald Albert. Salesman, Belknap, Inc., No. Ky., 1936-62, buyer wholesale hardware, 1962-72, v.p., 1972-—, also dir.; dir. Bank of Oldham County, LaGrange, Ky. Mem. Christian Ch. (chmn. bd. 1969-70). Mason (32 deg. Shriner, dist. dep. grand master 1956), Rotarian. Home: Route 1 Box 55 LaGrange KY 40031 Office: 111 E Main St Louisville KY 40202

MCMANIS, LOUIS BARBER, electronics mfg. co. exec.; b. Blackwell, Okla., Nov. 30, 1916; s. Robert L. and Roxie (Barber) McM.; B.S., Kan. State Coll., 1938; M.S., Okla. U., 1956; m. Delores Geraldine Christoson, Apr. 6, 1946; children—Robert Louis, Paul E., Bruce Milan. Mktg. mgr. Dresser Electronics, Houston, 1956-60; sr. v.p. Geo Space Corp., Houston 1961-66; pres. Digital Data Systems, Inc., Houston, 1967-—. Served with USAAF, 1941-46. Mem. I.E.E.E., Soc. Exploration Geophysicists, European Assn. Exploration Geophysicists, Geophys. Soc. Houston, Instrument Soc. Am. Home: 10549 Gawain St Houston TX 77024 Office: 7415 Hillcroft Av Houston TX 77036

MCMANUS, EUGENE F., bus. exec., b. 1921; B.S., U. Ill.; m. With Touche, Ross, Bailey & Smart, C.P.A.'s, until 1951; then controller Detroit Creamery Co., Spreckles Sugar Co.; with Nat. Services Industries Inc., Atlanta, 1965-—, treas., 1967-69, v.p. finance, treas., 1969-—. Home: 4400 Paper Mill Rd Marietta GA 30060 Office: 1180 Peachtree Mill Rd Marietta GA 30309*

MCMANUS, LYDIA MARIE TESTA (MRS. WILLIAM JAMES MCMANUS), bank exec.; b. Waterproof, La., Sept. 8, 1923; d. Charles Thomas and Christine (Forte) Testa; grad. Bish Mathis Inst., 1942; m. William James McManus, Feb. 8, 1964; 1 son, Michael Charles. Bookkeeper Massony & Altick Cotton Office, Winnsboro, La., 1942-44; bookkeeper Bank St. Joseph and Trust Co., Waterproof, 1945-47, asst. cashier, 1947-—. Mem. Waterproof City Council, 1958-—; commd. col. staff Gov. La., 1965-—. Sec.-treas., Waterproof Givers Fund, 1961, 62. Roman Catholic. Home: Waterproof LA 71375 Office: Bank of St. Joseph & Trust Co Waterproof LA 71375

MCMASTER, JOHN GREGG, lawyer; b. Florence, S.C., Mar. 16, 1914; B.S., U. S.C., 1936, LL.B., 1938. Admitted to S.C. bar, 1938; since practiced in Columbia; mem. firm Tompkins, McMaster and Thomas. Code commr. State of S.C., 1953-54; vice chmn. S.C. Aeros. Commn., 1952-56, chmn., 1956-57; exec. dir. Assn. S.C. Life Ins. Cos., 1956-—. Mem. ho. reps. S.C. Gen. Assembly, 1945-48. Fellow Am. Coll. Trial Lawyers; mem. Am., S.C., Richland County (dir. 1941, sec. 1945) bar assns., Nat. Assn. R.R. Trial Counsel, S.C. Def. Attys. Assn., Omicron Delta Kappa. Office: Security Fed Bldg Columbia SC 29201*

MCMELLON, JOHN ALTON, mfg. co. exec.; b. Mansfield, La., June 3, 1921; s. Otis and Della (Butler) McM.; grad. high sch.; m. Sandra Robbins, Apr. 14, 1963; children—John Alton, Lisa. Pattern, quality control supr. Mid-Continent Steel Casting Corp., Shreveport, La., 1950-57, works mgr., 1963-66, v.p., works mgr., 1966-70; research, quality control supr. HICA Corp., stainless steel foundry, 1957-60, works mgr., 1960-63; v.p., mfg. mgr. Kast Metals Corp. and HICA Corp., 1970-—. Served with USAAF, 1942-45. Decorated Air medal, Purple Heart. Mem. Shreveport C. of C., Am. Legion. Democrat. Methodist. Club: East Ridge Country. Home: 546 N Marlborough St Shreveport LA 71106 Office: PO Drawer 6611 Shreveport LA 71106

MCMILLAN, ANN ALTA, psychologist; b. Tallahassee, May 16, 1936; d. Robert Alton and Margaret (Smith) McMillan; B.A., Blue Mountain Coll., 1958; M.Ed., U. Miss., 1966, Ed.D., 1967; m. J.R. Null, June 26, 1958 (div. Mar. 1960); children—Robert Alton, David Bruce. Dir. guidance Keystone High Sch., Keystone Heights, Fla., 1963-65; instr. counselor U. Miss. Counseling Center, Oxford, 1965-67; dir. student personnel services Blue Mountain Coll., Miss., 1967-68; sch. psychologist Orange County (Fla.) Sch. System, 1968-69; childrens psychologist Guidance Center, Inc., Daytona Beach, Fla., 1969-—. Cons. psychol. services. Mem. Volusia County Mental Health Assn., Am., Fla. personnel and guidance assns., Nat., Fla. assns. women deans and counselors, Nat. Assn. Sch. Psychologists, Kappa Delta Pi. Home: 1109 Richardson Rd Tallahassee FL 32301 Office: 1220 Willis Av Daytona Beach FL 32014

MCMILLAN, HENRY WILLIAM, adj. gen. Fla.; b. Osyka, Miss., Aug. 12, 1910; s. Henry W. and Essie Belle (Strickland) McM.; grad. Army Inf. Sch., 1940, Command and Gen. Staff Coll., 1941, Air Ground Operations Sch., 1954, Army War Coll., 1964; D.Latin Am. History (hon.), U. Paraguay, 1946; m. Louise Ford, Feb. 7, 1932; children—Karen Louise (Mrs. Thomas E. Houston), Julie Frances. Enlisted Fla, N.G., 1929, advanced through grades to maj. gen., 1961; active duty U.S. Army, 1940-46; 1st chief U.S. Mil. Mission Paraguay, S. Am., 1944-46; div. chief staff 51st Inf, Div,, Fla. N.G., 1946-52, asst. div. comdr., 1952-61, comdg. gen., 1961-62; adj. gen. Fla., 1962-—. With Internal Revenue Service, Dist. Fla., 1937-62, chief collection div., 1954-62. Chmn. adv. com. to gov. Fla. on Cold War Edn., 1962-—. Mem. St. Augustine Quadricentennial Coordinating Com., 1963-—; exec. bd. North Fla. council Boy Scouts Am., 1963-—. St. Augustine chpt. Am. Cancer Soc., 1963-—. Decorated Army Commendation medal, various area and service ribbons, also Fla. decorations; Orden Nacional Del Merito, Order del Defensor de la Republica (Paraguay). Mem. Phi Kappa Tau. Home: 86 Marine St St Augustine FL 32084 Office: Mil Dept State Florida St Augustine FL 32084

MCMILLAN, HUGH DIX, JR., mfrs. rep.; b. Shreveport, La., Sept. 15, 1925; s. Hugh Dix and Edna (Self) McM.; B.S., Tex. A. and M. Coll., 1947; m. Dorothy Jean Sawyer, May 10, 1952; children—Hugh Dix III, Janet Lynn. Design engr. Coastal Equipment Co., Houston, 1947-48; design and sales engr. D & S Sales, Inc., 1948-49; sales engr, J.R. Dowdell & Co., 1949-55; pres. McMillan Equipment Co., 1955-—. Dir. F.E. Giesecke Meml. Fund Austin, Tex. Served with AC, AUS, 1944-45. Mem. Am. Soc. Heating, Refrigerating and Air Conditioning Engrs. (past pres. Houston chpt., nat. dir., regional chmn. Houston Engring. and Sci. Soc., Nat., Tex. socs. profl. engrs. Baptist. Mason (Shriner). Club: Pine Forest Country. Home: 13302 Apple Tree Houston TX 77024 Office: 1336 W Clay Houston TX 77019

MCMILLAN, JAMES BRYAN, judge; b. Goldsboro, N.C., Dec. 19, 1916; s. Robert Hunter and Louise (Outlaw) McM.; grad. Presbyn. Jr. Coll., 1934; A.B., U. N.C., 1937; LL.B., Harvard, 1940; m. Margaret Blair Miles, Feb. 27, 1944; children—James Bryan, Marjorie Miles. Admitted to N.C. bar, 1941; mem. staff N.C. atty.-gen., 1940-42; partner Helms, Mulliss, McMillan & Johnston, Charlotte, 1946-68; U.S. dist. judge Western Dist. N.C., 1968-—; judge pro tem Charlotte City Ct., 1947-51. Mem. N.C. Cts. Commn., 1963-—. Pres. Travelers Aid Soc., 1957-59; bd. visitors Davidson Coll. Served from apprentice seaman to lt. (s.g.), USNR, 1942-46; ETO. Fellow Internat. Acad. Trial Lawyers; mem. Am., 26th Dist. (pres. 1957-58), N.C. (pres. 1960-61) bar assns., United World Federalists, Newcomen Soc., St. Andrews Coll. Alumni Assn. (pres. 1965-66), Omicron Delta Kappa. Democrat. Presbyn. Clubs: Charlotte City, Charlotte Country. Home: 1930 Mecklenburg Av Charlotte NC 28205 Office: US Dist Ct Charlotte NC 28201

MCMILLAN, JOHN ALEXANDER, III, holding co. exec.; b. Charlotte, N.C., May 9, 1932; s. John Alexander and Mildred Elizabeth (Shepherd) McM.; A.B. in History, U. N.C., 1954; M.B.A., U. Va., 1958; m. Caroline Hill Houston, Nov. 21, 1959; children—Elizabeth Houston, John Alexander IV. Vice pres. Carolina Paper Bd. Corp., Charlotte, 1958-60; v.p. John C. Shepherd Lumber Corp., Charlotte, 1960-63; v.p. R.S. Dickson & Co., Charlotte, 1963-68; v.p., treas. Ruddick Corp., Charlotte, 1968-—; dir. Am. & Efird Mills, Charlie's Girls, Inc., Harris-Teeter Supermarkets, Jordan Bus. Forms, Inc., Asso. Auto Parts, Inc., Lowndes Hill Realty Co., Knapdale Properties, Ltd. Served with AUS, 1954-56. Mem. Sigma Alpha Epsilon. Republican. Presbyn. (deacon 1965-—, treas. 1971, elder 1972-—). Mem. Order of Gimghoul. Clubs: Charlotte Country, Charlotte City. Home: 754 Museum Dr Charlotte NC 28207 Office: First Union Jefferson Tower Charlotte NC 28282

MCMILLAN, JOHN JOHNSON, psychologist, assn. exec.; b. Mokanshan, China, Aug. 5, 1922 (parents Am. citizens); s. Henry Hudson and Leila (Memory) McM.; B.A., Wake Forest Coll., 1943; M.A., Duke U., 1948, Ph.D., 1951; m. Valleria Page Rankin, June 17, 1950; children—Ronald T., Stephen H. Clin. Psychologist VA Hosp., Richmond, Va., 1951-55; psychologist research grants and fellowship br. Nat. Inst. Mental Health, Bethesda, Md., 1956-57; exec. sec. behavioral sci. study sect., div. research grants NIH, Bethesda, 1957-58; psychologist Rohrer, Hibler and Replogle, Atlanta, 1958-59; asso. prof. psychiatry Med. Coll. Va., 1960-65; adminstrv. officer Am. Psychol. Assn., Washington, 1965-—. Served with USNR, 1943-46; PTO. Mem. Am., Va. psychol. assns., Phi Beta Kappa, Sigma Xi, Omicron Delta Kappa. So. Baptist. Home: 5105 Kenwood Dr Annandale VA 22003 Office: 1200 17th St NW Washington DC 20036

MCMILLAN, JOHN LANNEQU, congressman; b. Mullins, S.C.; s. M. S. and Mary Alice (Keith) McM.; grad. Mullins High Sch.; student U. N.C.; m. Margaret English, Oct. 31, 1936. Mem. 76th-92d Congresses, 6th S.C. Dist. Mem. Am. Legion. Democrat. Baptist. Mason, Elk. Home: Florence SC 28801

MCMILLAN, L(ATTA) STARR, JR., county ofcl.; b. Fayetteville, N.C., Apr. 28, 1923; s. Latta Starr and Eva (McLean) McM.; student Campbell Coll., 1941-44; m. Jewel Southerland Baker, Apr. 20, 1946 (dec. Nov. 1968); children—Martha Jewel (Mrs. Robert E. Spell), Latta Starr III, JoAnn (Mrs. Phillip Murray). Pharm. buyer Bellamy Drug Co., Wilmington, N.C., 1944-70; county coroner New Hanover County, Wilmington, 1963-—. Dir. Ogden Vol. Fire Dept., 1963-64, Ogden Rescue Squad, 1962-64. Mem. Jr. Order United Am. Mechanics. Democrat. Elk, Moose. Clubs: Optimist. Home: 210 Green Meadows Dr Wilmington NC 28401

MCMILLAN, LOUIS KELLY, JR., operations research analyst; b. Little Rock, Feb 8, 1929; s. Louis Kelly and Josephine (McNally) McM.; B.S., U.S. Naval Acad., 1952, M.S., 1962; m. Helen Moore, Sept. 5, 1959; children—Mary Cameron, Mark Douglas. Dir. operations research group Tracor, Inc., Rockville, Md., 1966-68; sec., dir. comml. systems div. Vertex Corp., Kennsington, Md., 1968-—. Chmn. bd. Chemmark of Washington, Inc., 1968-—; cons. USN, 1969-—. Active Va. Civic Assn., 1966-—. Served from ensign to lt. comdr. USN, 1952-66. Mem. Operations Research Soc. Am., Mil. Operations Research Soc. Lion. Home: 6103 Sherborn Lane Springfield VA 22152 Office: 10400 Connecticut Av Kennsington MD 20795

MCMILLAN, RONALD JAMES, architect, civil engr.; b. Wellington, New Zealand, Feb. 11, 1915; s. James Lawrence and Lucy (Jenner) McM.; student Wellington Coll., Victoria U., Mil. Sch. Instrn.; m. Myrtle Emeline Clark, June 17, 1942; children—Pamela, Heather. Dir. C.M.B. Constrn. Co., 1947-51; pres. Ronald J. McMillan, Inc. cons. engrs., architects, 1952-66 (both New Zealand);

asso. Davis-Yohalem Cons. Engrs., Ft. Lauderdale, Fla., 1969—; dir. Plaza South Assn., Inc. Served to sr. capt. Royal New Zealand Engrs., 1943-46. Decorated Spl. Service (USN). Fellow Inst. New Zealand Architects (asso.), Instn. Structural Engrs. (Eng.), Am. Soc. C.E.; mem. New Zealand Instn. Engrs., Am. Concrete Inst. Clubs: United Officers (Wellington); Manawatu (Palmerston). Principal works include New Zealand Breweries; St. Mary's Cath. Ch., Glaxo Labs., Palmerston. Home: 4230 N Ocean Dr Ft Lauderdale FL 33308 Office: Davis Yohalem Cons Engrs 233 Commercial Blvd Ft Lauderdale FL 33308

MCMILLEN, WHEELER, author; b. nr. Ada, O., Jan. 27, 1893; s. Lewis D. and Ella (Wheeler) McM.; student Ohio No. U., LL.D. (hon.), 1940; D.Litt., Parsons Coll., 1953; m. Edna Doane, May 28, 1915; 1 son, Robert Doane. Reporter Cincinnati Post, 1912; owner Covington Republican, 1914-18; farmer, Hardin County, O., 1918-22; asso. editor The Country Home (formerly Farm and Fireside), 1922-34; editor, 1934-37, editorial dir. 1937-39; editor-in-chief Farm Jour., 1939-55; v.p., dir. Farm Journal., Inc., 1955-63; dir. Bankers Nat. Life Ins. Co. Pres., chmn. Nat. Farm Chemurgic Council, 1937-62; Am. Assn. Agrl. Editors, 1934-38. Mem. nat. exec. bd. Boy Scouts Am., v.p. nat. orgn., 1959-63; mem. adv. com. Pres.'s Council Youth Fitness, 1957-58. Chmn. N.J. Public Health Council, 1947-49. Exec. dir. commn. on Increased Indsl. Use of Agrl. Products, 1956-57. Recipient Silver Buffalo and Antelope awards from Boy Scouts; Hon. Am. Farmer from Future Farmers Am.; citation Nat. 4-H Clubs; Louis Bromfield gold medal Melabar Farm Found., 1965. U.S. del. Internat. Congress Indsl. Chemistry, Milan, 1950. Mem. Phila. Soc. Promoting Agr. (pres. 1960-62), Grange, Kappa Tau Alpha, Alpha Zeta. Republican. Club: Cosmos (Washington). Author: The Farming Fever, 1924; The Young Collector, 1928; Too Many Farmers, 1929; New Riches from the Soil, 1946; Land of Plenty, 1961; Why the United States is Rich, 1963; Possums, Politicians and People, 1964; Bugs or People, 1965; Fifty Useful Americans, 1965; Farmers in the United States, 1966; The Green Frontier, 1968; Weekly on the Wabash, 1969. Editor: Harvest: An Anthology of Farm Writing, 1964. Home: Box 999 Anna Maria FL 33501

MCMILLIN, CLARENCE VADEN, dentist; b. Campobello, S.C., Mar. 26, 1906; s. Landrum Reid and Sallie Janet (Bishop) McM.; B.A., Wofford Coll., 1938; B.S., George Washington U., 1933; D.D.S., U. Md., 1938; m. Ruth Jane Looper, June 18, 1941; 1 son, Clarence Vaden. Pvt. practice dentistry, Inman, S.C., 1938-42, 47—; dir. Mut. Nat. Bank S.C., Landru. Served to maj. Dental Corps, AUS, 1942-47. Mem. Am., S.C. dental assns., Piedmont Dist. Dental Soc. (pres. 1953-54), Assn. Mil. Surgeons, Chi Beta Phi, Psi Omega. Baptist (vice chmn. bd. deacons 1964-65). Rotarian. Home: 8 Wingo St Inman SC 29349 Office: PO Box 53 4 Bishop St Inman SC 29349

MCMILLON, REGNAL LUTHER, ins. co. exec., pub. speaker; b. Guion, Tex., Apr. 23, 1921; s. James Luther and Tennessee Jones (Haynie) McM.; student Tarleton State Coll., 1938; m. Elsie Eugenia Roberts, Dec. 14, 1941; children—Toni Karen, Steven Grant. Internat. speaker for convs., clubs, other orgns.; with Bus. Men's Assurance Co., Abilene, Tex., 1946-71, dist. mgr., 1956-60, br. mgr., Abilene, Tex., 1961-71; gen. agt. Washington Nat. Ins. Co., Lubbock, Tex., 1971—. Dir. Nat. Gen. Agts. and Mgrs. Conf.; trustee Life Underwriters Tng. Council U.S., pres., 1965-66. Served with USAAF, 1942-46. Named Ins. Field Man of Yr. in Life Ins. in U.S., 1962; Internat. Health Ins. Man of Yr., 1965; recipient Harold R. Gordon Meml. award Internat. Assn. Health Underwriters, 1965, Distinguished Service award Vocational Agr. Tchrs. Tex., 1965; John Newton Russell award, 1967. Mem. Nat. (pres, 1961-62), Tex. (pres. 1956-57) assns. life underwriters, Tex. Assn. Health Underwriters (pres. 1954-55), Author numerous articles on selling, human relations. Home: 3508 37th St Lubbock TX 79413 Office: 2321 50th St Lubbock TX 79412

MCMINN, WILLIAM GENE, architect, educator; b. Abilene, Tex., Aug. 27, 1931; s. Ollie and Mabel (Renfro) McM.; B.A., Rice U., 1952, B.S. in Architecture, 1953; M. Architecture, U. Tex., 1954; m. Joan Gentry, Dec. 10, 1955; children—Kevin, Tracey. Asst. prof. Tex. Tech. Coll., Lubbock, 1956-58, asst. campus architect, 1958-59; asso. prof. architecture Clemson (S.C.) U., 1959-63; asst. to dean Sch. Architecture and Arts, Auburn (Ala.) U., 1964-66, head dept. architecture, 1966-69; dir. design Six Assos., Architects, Asheville, N.C., 1969-71; head dept. architecture La. State U., Baton Rouge, 1971—. Mem. Auburn (Ala.) planning commn., 1966-68. Served with C.E., AUS, 1954-56. Mem A.I.A. Home: 742 Druid Circle Baton Rouge LA 70808

MCMULLAN, JOHN EDWIN, newspaper editor; b. Elberton, Ga., June 14, 1921; s. Thomas O. and Ruth (Haley) McM.; student U. Ga., 1938-41; LL.B., U. Miami (Fla.), 1955; m. Betty Mesker, Mar. 20, 1942; children— Pamela Jean, Linda Kathleen. City editor Miami Daily News, 1950-55; news dir. Knight Newspapers, Washington bur., 1963-65; exec. editor Miami Herald, 1966—. Home: 12100 SW 65th Av Miami FL 33156 Office: 1 Herald Plaza Miami FL

MCMULLAN, THEODORE NEWTON, librarian; b. Jackson, Miss., June 25, 1908; s. Marcus Theodore and Lucy (Grace) McM.; B.S. in Elec. Engring., La. State U., 1931, M.S., 1932, B.L.S., 1934; grad. Command and Gen. Staff College; m. Hortense Corynne Shearer, Sept. 5, 1936; children—Janice (Mrs. William Higgenbottom), Theodore Newton, Frederick Marcus. Head circulation dept. La. State U. Library, 1934-41, 45-55, acting dir. libraries, 1955-56, asso. dir., 1956-61, dir. library, 1961—. Chmn. Nat. Library Week for La., 1958; chmn. librarian's sect. La. Coll. Conf., 1962-63. Served from 2d lt. to lt. col., AUS, 1941-45. Mem. Am. Assn. U. Profs. (past v.p.), So. Assn. Colls. and Schs. (evaluation team 1963), Res. Officers Assn. (pres. La. chpt., Baton Rouge chpt.), A.L.A. (resolutions com.; La. rep. to council 1966—), La. Tchrs. Assn., Southeastern, Southwestern (past chmn. coll. and univ. sect.; 2d v.p.), La. (pres. 1958) library assns., Baton Rouge Library Club (pres.), Scabbard and Blade, Sigma Pi (faculty adviser). Methodist. Editor of La. Newspaper (La. Library Assn. and Assn. Southwestern Research Libraries). Kiwanian. Contbr. articles to profl. jours. Editor: Southwestern Newsletter, 1965-66, La. Newspapers ASERL, Statistics of Southern College and University Libraries. Home: 544 Magnolia Woods Dr Baton Rouge LA 70808

MCMULLEN, ALEXIS BRENIER, ret. assn. exec.; b. Forrest, Ill., Feb. 22, 1896; s. George A. and Gertrude (Curyea) McM.; B.A., Valparaiso U., 1915; postgrad. Cal. Poly. Sch. Engring., 1916-17; m. Iris Neville Smith, Mar. 5, 1921; children—Sara Ann (Mrs. Douglas G. Lindsey), Alexandria, Virginia. Chief engr. with architect, Richmond, Va., 1921-23; pres. McMullen Aircraft Corp., Tampa, Fla., 1925-32; state dir. aviation, Fla., 1933-36; chief airports div. CAA, Washington, 1936-41, exec. dir. Air Res. Assn., Washington, 1949-53; exec. v.p. Nat. Assn. State Aviation Ofcls., Washington, 1963-70, ret., 1970, dir., 1948-62; treas. Asso. Investors Syndicate, 1955-57; dir. Avemco Life Ins. Co., Silver Spring, Md. Served to lt. Army Air Service, 1917-20; served from maj. to col. USAAF, 1941-47. Decorated Legion Merit (U.S.); Commandeur de l'Ordre du Ouissam Alaouite Cherifien (Morocco, Africa). Mem. Nat. Aviation Club, Air Force Assn., Aviation Space Writers Assn., OX-5 Club Am. (named to Aviation Hall Fame 1971). Club: Army-Navy Country. Home: 6103 Woodmont Rd Alexandria VA 22307

MCMULLEN, NEIL CAMPBELL, judge; b. Tampa, Fla., Aug. 30, 1913; s. Donald C. and Mary (Ball) McM.; student Emory U., 1931-33; A.B., U. Fla., 1937, J.D., 1937; m. Ruth R. L'Engle, Nov. 29, 1947; children—Neil Campbell, Ruth, Donald Frederick. Admitted to Fla. bar, 1937, practiced in Tampa; asst. city atty. Tampa, 1956-60; judge 13th Jud. Circuit Fla., Tampa, 1960—, now chief judge. Mem. Am., Tampa, Hillsborough County (pres. 1951) bar assns., Fla. Bar (pres. jr. bar sect. 1942, rep. Fla. legislature 1942-50, chmn. rules of civil procedure 1954), Nat. Conf. State Trial Judges, Am. Judicature Soc., Tampa C. of C., Kappa Alpha. Methodist. Elk. Home: 19 Treasure Dr Tampa FL 33609 Office: Courthouse Tampa FL 33602

MCMURRAY, CLAUDE SWANSON, ednl. adminstr.; b. Hiltons, Va., Feb. 19, 1912; s. Ulysses Simpson and Frances (Hart) McM.; B.A., King Coll., 1937; M.A., E. Tenn. State U., 1955; m. Agnes Taylor, July 25, 1938. With Scott County Sch. Bd., Gate City, Va., 1937—, prin. Clinchport Jr. High Sch., 1940-41, Rye Cove High Sch., 1941-65, gen. supr. Scott County Schs., 1965—. Mem. Va., Scott County edn. assns. Democrat. Club: Gate City Civitan (treas. 1960-61, pres. 1968-69). Home: Route 1 Box 165 Gate City VA 24251 Office: PO Box 307 Gate City VA 24251

MCMURRAY, JAMES EDWIN, hotel exec.; b. Hubbard, O., Dec. 7, 1931; s. Homer Dewey and Edith (Mason) McM.; student Youngstown Coll., 1956-58; m. Ellen Wagner, Feb. 10, 1952; 1 dau., Bess Marla. Owner, mgr. Lakeside Lodge, Geneva-on-the-Lake, O., 1956-62; v.p., gen. mgr., dir. Wedgewood South Corp., Hilton Inns of N.C., Winston-Salem, 1959—; treas., dir. Wedgewood Enterprises, Inc. Served with AUS, 1952-54. Mem. N.C. (pres. elect), Winston-Salem (past pres.) innkeepers assns., N.C. Travel Council, Am. Hotel and Motel Assn., Winston-Salem C. of C. (dir.). Home: 1211 Meade Lane Winston-Salem NC 27106 Office: 420 High St Winston-Salem NC 27101

MCMURRY, WILLIAM SCOTT, oral surgeon; b. Poteau, Okla., Apr. 10, 1921; s. Ulysses Scott and Synthia Alice (McDonald) McM.; student Northeastern State Coll., D.D.S., U. Mo., 1950, grad. oral surgeon, 1966; m. Kathryn Elizabeth Robison, Feb. 2, 1946. Pvt. practice dentistry, Okmulgee, Okla., 1950-60; resident oral surgery U. Mo., 1963-66; oral surgeon Bay Pines (Fla.) VA center, 1967—. Clin. instr. oral surgery U. Mo., 1966-67; prof. pathology, embryology, histology St. Petersburg (Fla.) Jr. Coll., 1967—. Served with USAAF, 1941-46. Mem. Am., Okla. (pres. eastern dist. 1957-58) dental assns., Am. Acad. Oral Pathologists, Am., Midwestern, Fla. socs. oral surgeons. Mason. Home: 10319 106th Terrace North Largo FL 33540 Office: PO Box 4005 Bay Pines FL 33504

MCNAB, M(AHON) TERRY, lawyer, corp. exec.; b. Tampa, Fla., Feb. 1, 1927; s. Robert Calvin and Hazel (Kirkconnel) McN.; B.S. in Bus. Adminstrn., U. Fla., 1950; J.D., Stetson U., 1958; m. Marjorie Katherine Huddleston, Apr. 6, 1963. Staff accountant Ernst & Ernst, C.P.A.'s, Tampa, 1950-53; instr. accounting U. Fla., Gainesville, 1953-55; admitted to Fla. bar, 1958; partner firm Mabry, Reaves, Carlton, Fields & Ward, Tampa, 1958-62; practice in Tampa, 1962-66; v.p., gen. counsel, dir. Kenflo Corp., Tampa, 1966-71; exec. v.p., founder EDCO, Inc., Tampa, 1971—. Lectr. law Stetson U., 1958. Served to lt. (j.g.), USNR, 1945-46. C.P.A., Fla. Mem. Am., Fla., Tampa, Hillsborough County bar assns., Am., Fla. insts. certified pub. accountants, Aircraft Owners and Pilots Assn., Tampa C. of C., Phi Delta Phi, Alpha Kappa Psi, Phi Delta Theta. Episcopalian (instr. Sunday Sch. 1964-65, bd. ushers 1965—). Clubs: Merrymakers (pres. Tampa 1958); Tampa Yacht and Country; Ye Mystic Krewe of Gasparilla. Home: 563 Luzon Av Tampa FL 33609 Office: 512 Florida Av Tampa FL 33602

MCNABB, GERALD COLEMAN, JR., advt. exec.; b. Dallas, Dec. 17, 1934; s. Gerald Coleman and Dorothy (Horton) McN.; A.B., Dartmouth, 1956; postgrad. U. Chattanooga, 1958-61; m. Barbara Carole Monarch, May 4, 1956; children—David Ashley, Susan Carole. Tchr. McCallie Sch. for Boys, Chattanooga, 1958-59; mem. dept. pub. relations, advt. Blue Cross-Blue Shield, Chattanooga, 1960-63, Olin Film Div., Pisgah Forest, N.C., 1964-67, v.p., creative dir. Price/McNabb Advt. Agy., Inc., Asheville, 1967—. Instr. advt. Western Carolina U., 1969. Served with USNR, 1956-58. Mem. C. of C., Advt. Fedn. Western N.C. (v.p.). Unitarian-Universalist. Clubs: Rotary, Carolina Mountain (pres. 1971-72). Home: 5 Graystone Rd Asheville NC 28804 Office: 400 Northwestern Bank Bldg Asheville NC 28804

MCNABB, ROBERT EUGENE, state ofcl.; b. Newport, Tenn., June 20, 1932; s. Hugh F. and Lena Mae (Kennedy) McN.; B.A., Carson-Newman Coll., 1955; M.S. in Social Work, U. Tenn., 1960; m. Mary Hu Medlin, Oct. 8 1955; 1 dau., Lora Annette. Staff social worker Central State Psychiat. Hosp., Nashville, 1960-62, VA Hosp., Murfreesboro, Tenn., 1962-64; chief psychiat. social worker Clover Bottom Hosp. and Sch., Nashville, 1964-66; dir. psychiat. social work Tenn. Dept. Mental Health, Nashville, 1966—. Mem. Nat. Assn. Social Workers, Acad. Certified Social Workers, Am. Pub. Health Assn., Conf. Social Workers in State and Territorial Mental Health Programs (chmn. elect), Tenn. Conf. Social Welfare, Am. Assn. on Mental Deficiency. Baptist. Mason. Home: 2709 Western Hills Dr Nashville TN 37214 Office: Cordell Hall Bldg Nashville TN 37219

MCNAIR, GROVER CLEVELAND, JR., constrn. co exec.; b. Winston-Salem, N.C., May 17, 1924; s. Grover Cleveland and Renna (Klinetob) McN.; student Mass. Inst. Tech., 1943-44; B.S. in Archtl. Engring., N.C. State U., 1949; m. Jane Marilyn Casstevens, Dec. 8, 1951; children— Grover Cleveland III, Julia Owen, Mary Lyn. Pres., Grover McNair Constrn. Co., Inc., Winston-Salem, 1954—. Pres., Casstevens Hosp., 1964—; founder Med. Park Hosp., 1969— (both Winston-Salem). Served with AUS, World War II, ETO. Decorated Combat Inf. Badge. Mem. Nat. Assn. Home Builders (nat, dir.), Fedn. Am. Hosps. (dir.), Sigma Phi Epsilon, Mu Beta Psi. Democrat. Presbyn. (deacon). Kiwanian. Club: Old Town (Winston-Salem). Home: 130 Pine Valley Rd Winston-Salem NC 27104 Office: 747 Summit St Winston-Salem NC 27102

MCNAIR, LARRY DELANO, profl. engr.; b. Macon, Ga., June 21, 1934; s. William Oscar and Annie (Buchannan) McN.; B.Ch.E., Ga. Inst. Tech., 1956; student Okla. A. and M. U., 1956, U. Chattanooga, 1959; m. Mary Lee Padgett, Aug. 3, 1953; children—Jennifer Scott, Mary Shannan, Jeffery Webb, Andrew Buchannan. Process engr. Continental Oil Co., Ponca City, Okla., 1956-57; design engr. Combustion Engring. Inc., Chattanooga, Tenn., 1957-61, research engr., Windsor, Conn., 1961-65; sr. engr. So. Services Inc., Birmingham, Ala., 1965—. Mem. Midwest Benthol. Soc., Nat. Soc. Profl. Engrs., Am. Inst. Chem. Engrs., Am. Chem. Soc., A.A.A.S., Air Pollution Control Assn., Nat. Fire Protection Assn., So. Services Leadership Assn. (v.p. 1971). Patentee furnace explosion prevention systems. Home: 804 Vestavia Lake Dr Birmingham AL 35216 Office: PO Box 2625 Birmingham AL 35202

MCNAIR, ROBERT EVANDER, former gov. of S.C., lawyer; b. Cades, S.C., Dec. 14, 1923; s. Daniel Evander and Claudia (Crawford) McN.; A.B., U. S.C., 1947, LL.B., 1948, LL.D., 1967; m. Josephine Robinson, May 30, 1944; children—Robert Evander, Robin Lee, Corinne Calhoun, Claudia Crawford. Admitted to S.C. bar, 1948, practiced in Allendale, 1948-62; mem. S.C. Ho. of Reps., 1951-62, chmn. labor, commerce and industry com., 1953-54, judiciary com., 1955-62; lt. gov. S.C., 1962-65, gov., 1965-71; practiced in Columbia, 1971—; pres. Investors Heritage Life Ins. Co. of South; dir. Airco, Inc., So. Ry. System, Ga.-Pacific Corp., R.L. Bryan Co. Mem. adv. com. Am. Enterprise Inst. Mem. Jud. Council; mem. Legislative Council, 1955-65. Chmn., Nat. Conf. Lt. Gov.'s, 1965-66; chmn. So. Govs.' Conf., 1968-69, chmn. human resources com., 1969-70; chmn. Nat. Democratic Govs.' Conf., 1968-69, mem. exec. com.; mem. exec. com. Nat. Govs.' Conf.; Dem. gov.'s liaison to Dem. Nat. Com., 1971-72. Mem. steering and exec. coms. Nationwide Compact for Edn.; chmn. So. Regional Edn. Bd., 1967-68; chmn. Edn. Commn. of States, 1968-69; states co-chmn. Appalachian Regional Commn., 1970, Coastal Plains Regional Commn., 1967-68; mem. Com. Assessing Progress of Edn., Nat. Com. Support of Public Schs. Served with USNR, 1942-46; PTO. Mem. Am. Legion, Farm. Bur., Blue Key, Kappa Sigma Kappa. Democrat. Baptist (chmn. bd. deacons 1957-59). Mason (Shriner), Lion (dep. dist. gov. 1951). Address: Sunturf Circle Spring Valley Columbia SC 29204

MCNAMARA, DOLORES MABEL LACOUME (MRS. ROBERT J. MCNAMARA), editor; b. Galveston, Tex., Apr. 26, 1913; d. James G. and Lucille (Rizzo) LaCoume; student pub. and parochial schs.; m. Robert J. McNamara, Apr. 27, 1938; 1 dau., Linda Ann (Mrs. Joseph Paul Polivka, Jr.). With Tex. Prudential Ins. Co., Galveston, Tex., 1930-32; clk.-typist Am. Nat. Ins. Co., Galveston, 1932-39, asst. supr., 1940-44; asso. editor Star Bull., Galveston, 1946—. Club: Altrusa (corr. sec. 1966-67) (Galveston, Tex.). Home: 2714 John Dr LaMarque TX 77568 Office: One Moody Plaza Galveston TX 77551

MCNAMARA, JOHN, supt. schs. Ordained priest Roman Catholic Ch.; supt. schs. Diocese of Corpus Christi (Tex.). Address: 620 Lipan St Corpus Christi TX 78401*

MCNAMARA, JOHN JOSEPH, airport mgr.; b. Burkburnett, Tex., Feb. 20, 1916; s. Patrick Joseph and Jane (Taylor) McN.; A.A., Tyler Jr. Coll., 1968; m. Marjorie Katherine Downs, May 18, 1957. Oil lease operator Am. Liberty Oil Co., 1934-42; city airport attendant, Tyler, Tex., 1946-50, airport mgr., 1950—. Served with USAAF, 1942-46; ETO. Mem. Am. Assn. Airport Execs. (past pres. Tex. chpt.), Air Force Assn. Democrat. Roman Catholic. K.C. (4th deg.). Home: RFD 2 Box 364 Tyler TX 75701 Office: PO Box 2039 Tyler TX 75701

MCNAMARA, NEDRA, univ. exec.; b. New Castle, Pa., Mar. 4, 1914; d. John Fleming and Ann (Hartland) McNamara; student U. Miami, Coral Gables, Fla., 1931-34; A.B., Fla. State U., 1935. Reporter, Miami (Fla.) Herald, 1932-35; tchr. English, head journalism dept. Coral Gables High Sch., 1935-42; exec. asst. Pleasantville Constrn. Co., Nassau, B.W.I., 1942-44; adminstrv. asst. Office Personnel Narratives, USAF Intelligence, Orlando, Fla., N.Y.C., 1944-45; exec. asst., editor house organ First Nat. Bank Miami, 1945-49; staff writer U. Miami Pub. Information Office, 1949—, news editor, 1951, asst. dir., 1958-62, acting dir., 1962-64, dir. pub. information, 1964-66, dir. news bur., 1966—; asst. to editor U. Miami Press, 1949-57; free lance contbr. Rendezvous, 1940-41. Mem. Am. Coll. Pub. Relations Assn., Alpha Epsilon Rho, Theta Sigma Phi (v.p. Greater Miami 1959-60), Mortar Board, Kappa Alpha Theta. Office: U Miami Coral Gables FL 33124

MCNATT, CHARLES DANIEL, county ofcl.; b. Parkton, N.C., Mar. 17, 1918; s. J.C.D. and Mary Elizabeth (Hancock) McN.; A.B., E. Carolina U., 1938; M.A., U. N.C., 1955; m. Madeleine Homer Byrum, Aug. 8, 1942; children—Charles Milton, James Daniel. Tchr. history Gray's Creek High Sch., Fayetteville, N.C., 1938-41, Mineral Springs High Sch., Winston-Salem, N.C., 1959-61; tng. officer VA, VARO, Winston-Salem, 1946-59; owner, operator Bookmark, 1961-66; officer Vets. Service, Forsyth County, Winston-Salem, 1966—. Mem. Winston-Salem Draft Bd., 1968-70. Asst. chmn. Democratic party Speas Sch. Precinct, 1964, registrar, 1964-66. An organizer Forsyth County Kidney Found., 1971, pres., 1971-72. Served with AUS, 1941-46. Mem. Am. Legion (vice comdr. Winston-Salem 1969, adj. comdr. 1970—, 2d v.p. 1971-72). Presbyn. (deacon). Club: Old Town Civic (pres. Winston-Salem 1962-63, 70, dir. 1972). Home: 2830 St Claire Rd Winston-Salem NC 27106 Office: 3d St Winston-Salem NC 27101

MCNEAL, ARCHIE LIDDELL, librarian; b. Ruleville, Miss., Sept. 3, 1912; s. Archibald Walter and Amelia (Thompson) McN.; B.S., Memphis State Coll., 1932; B.L.S., George Peabody Coll., 1936; Ph.D., U. Chgo., 1951; m. Billie Irene Cornett, Feb. 11, 1946 (dec. April 1968); m. 2d, Dorothy M. Johnson, June 11, 1969. Reference asst. Cossitt Library, Memphis, 1932-34; librarian Millington (Tenn.) High Sch., 1934-36; East Tenn. State Coll., 1936-43, 46-48; chief readers services div. U. Tenn., 1948-52; dir. libraries U. Miami (Fla.), 1952—; vis. prof. Fla. State U. Library Sch., summers 1954, 55, 57, U. N.C. Sch. of Library Sci., 1959, 61, Columbia U., summer 1964, 67, 69. Mem. Fla. State Library and Hist. Commn., 1966-69, chmn. commn., 1968-69. Cons. libraries, gen. edn., Dept. State, India, 1957; mem. adv. council on library resources U.S. Office Edn., 1966—. Served to first lt., AUS, 1943-46; with Far East Air Forces, 1945; overseas Australia, New Guinea. P.I. and Japan, 1943-46. Mem. A.L.A., (mem. council 1955-65, pres. library adminstrn. div. 1960-61, chmn. intellectual freedom com. 1959-64, exec. bd., 1961-65, 1968-69, 2d v.p. 1968-69), Am. Assn. U. Profs., Assn. Coll. and Research Libraries (pres. 1964-65), Southeastern (pres. 1964-66), Fla. (past pres.), Tenn. (pres. 1940-42) library assns., Phi Kappa Phi. Democrat. Conglist. Home: 1414 Certosa Av Coral Gables FL 33146 Office: U Miami Coral Gables FL 33124

MCNEEL, EDWARD CONNER, lawyer; b. Louisville, Miss., Apr. 7, 1933; s. Clem Taylor and Martha Mae (Williams) McN.; student Baylor U., 1950-52; B.A., La. Coll., 1954; LL.B., Tex. U., 1958; m. Jane Ann New, Aug. 18, 1956; children—Martha Ann, Elizabeth Ann. Admitted to Tex. bar, 1958; practiced in Odessa Tex., 1958—; mem. firms Rogers, Kimarough & Halsell, 1958-59, McNeel & Bock, 1959—; v.p., sr. trust officer First Nat. Bank, 1961—; dir. Exec. Leasing Corp. City judge Odessa, Tex., 1960-61; asst. dist. atty. Ector County, 1961. Del., Democratic State Conv., 1964-70. Chmn., Ector County Child Welfare Bd., 1969-70. Bd. dirs. Cancer Soc., Odessa, 1962—, pres., 1965—; bd. dirs. Wayland Bap. Coll., Plainview, Tex.; chmn. bd. Ector County Med. Center Hosp. Recipient Community Leader of Am. award News Pub. Co., 1969. Mem. Tex., Ector County (dir.) bar assns., Ector County Bapt. Assn. (treas. 1960-62), C. of C. Baptist (deacon 1967-70). Lion, Rotarian. Home: 1510 Ridgecrest St Odessa TX 79760 Office: 700 N Grant St Odessa TX 79760

MCNEELEY, HARRY DRAKE, chem. co. exec.; b. Orlinda, Tenn., Feb. 23, 1914; s. H.W. and Lemma (Drake) McN.; B.S., Carson-Newman Coll., Tenn., 1935; m. Murray Lee Stone, Mar. 6, 1940; children—William S., Susan Brooke. With Tenn. Eastman Co., 1935—, devel. chemist, asst. to div. supt., asst. to gen. supt., adminstrv. asst., 1935-42, 47-50, asst. supt. explosives div., asst. to works mgr. Holston Ordnance Works, 1942-44; asst. to works mgr. Clinton Engr. Works, 1944-47; asst. to pres. Tenn. Eastman Co. div. Eastman Kodak Co., Kingsport, 1950-53, v.p., 1953-59, exec. v.p., 1959-63, pres., 1963-—; dir., mem. exec. com. Eastman Kodak Co., 1967-—, v.p., 1968-—; chmn. Tex. Eastman Co., Eastman Chem. Products, Inc.; pres. Carolina Eastman Co.; v.p., dir. Eastman Chem. Inter-Am. Ltd.; chmn. bd. Holston Def. Corp.; chmn. bd. 1st Nat. Bank of Sullivan County. Pres., Kingsport Community Chest, 1961. Bd. dirs. Holston Valley Community Hosp.; trustee Carson-Newman Coll. Mem. Am. Chem. Soc., Kingsport C. of C. Democrat. Baptist. Clubs: Ridgefields Country (Kingsport); University (N.Y.C.). Home: 4527 Preston Court Kingsport TN 37664 Office: Tenn Eastman Co Kingsport TN 37662

MCNEELY, JESS EDWARD, rubber co. exec.; b. Ardmore, Okla., Apr. 15, 1938; s. Jesse Guy and Winnie Faye (Oaks) McN.; student U. Houston, 1956-60, Fullerton Jr. Coll., 1964-65, Cal. State Coll. at Long Beach, 1965-66; m. Melvaline Anderson, Aug. 31, 1957; children—Lisa, Dana, Sheryl. Asst. plant mgr. Houston Rubber Co., 1957-60; west coast sales mgr. Bettis Rubber Co., Whittier, Cal., 1961-67; pres. Houston Sales Co., 1967-—, owner, 1969-—. Bd. dirs. P.T.A. Westwood Elementary Sch., Houston, 1967-70. Mem. Los Angeles Rubber Group, Nat. Oil Equipment Mfrs. and Dels. Soc., Soc. for Preservation and Encouragement Barbershop Quartet Singing in Am. Methodist. Home: 10303 Knoboak St Houston TX 77043 Office: Box 9174 Houston TX 77011

MCNEIL, MARSHALL, newspaper corr.; b. San Antonio, Mar. 29, 1904; s. Clarence W. and P. Jane (Taylor) McN.; ed. pub. schs.; m. Blanche Venable, May 2, 1925 (dec. Feb. 1962); 1 son, Neil Venable; m. 2d, Jennie June Langer, Sept. 11, 1963. Newspaperman, San Antonio and Beaumont, Tex., to 1926, later Pensacola and Jacksonville, Fla.; city editor Houston Press, 1926-29; mng. editor Jacksonville Jour., 1929-30; corr., mng. editor Scripps-Howard Newspaper Alliance, Washington, 1930-34, corr., 1937-—; editor Knoxville (Tenn.) News-Sentinel, 1934-37. Episcopalian. Club: Gridiron (pres. 1954). Home: 2845 29th Pl NW Washington DC 20008

MCNEIL, NORMAN LAIRD, univ. pres.; b. San Antonio, Oct. 3, 1915; s. Bert and Annie (Fite) McN.; B.A., U. Tex., 1937, M.A., 1944, Ph.D., 1956; m. Kathleen Howard, Feb. 7, 1941; children—Laird Howard, John Robert. Instr. English, U. Tex., 1954-56; prof. English, Tex. A. and I. U., Kingsville, 1956-65; pres. Sul Ross State U., Alpine, Tex., 1965-—; field collector folk materials Library of Congress, 1940-41; Am. specialist lectr. Dept. of State, 1962. Served with USAAF, 1943-44. Recipient E.D. Farmer Internat. fellowship award for collection folklore in Mexico, U. Tex., 1941. Mem. Tex. Folklore Soc. (pres. 1946-49). Episcopalian. Spl. research British folk ballad in Am., folk ballad in Mexico. Home: President's House Sul Ross State Coll Alpine TX 79830

MCNEIL, WALTER HARVE, sales rep.; b. Harlan, Ky., Apr. 21, 1920; s. John Charles and Marie E. (McBrayer) McN.; student Pikeville Coll., 1956-59; grad. Squadron Officer Sch., 1955, Air Command and Staff Coll., 1960; m. Nellie Dean, June 1, 1946; children—Kay Francis (Mrs. Barry Runyon), Paula Jean (Mrs. Freddy Branham). With Sycamore Coal Corp., Patterson, Va., 1937-42; enlisted pvt. USAAF, 1942, commd. 2d lt. U.S. Army, 1943, advanced through grades to capt., 1946; staff communication officer Hdqrs. ETO; trans. to USAF Res., 1946, advanced through grades to lt. col., 1967, ret., 1970; liaison officer Air Force Acad. coordinator W.Va., Ky., So. Ohio, 1961-70; with Foster Thornburg Hardware Corp., Huntington, W.Va., 1946-61; sales rep. Banks-Miller Supply Co., 1961-—. Named Outstanding Liaison Officer Coordinator in South, USAF Acad., 1965. Charter mem. Armed Forces Communications and Electronics Assn.; mem. Air Force Assn., Internat. Platform Assn., U.S. Capitol Hist. Soc., USAF Hist. Found. (life), Met. Opera Guild, Res. Officers Assn., Nat. Mgmt. Assn. Democrat. Baptist (deacon). Mason. Club: Army and Navy (Charleston, W.Va.). Home: 508 5th St Pikeville KY 41501 Office: PO Box 2097 Pikeville KY 41501

MCNEILL, FRED DOUGLAS, JR., educator; b. Durham, N.C., Jan. 15, 1932; s. Fred D. and Lottie (Hill) McN.; B.S., N.C. State Coll., 1953, M.S., 1957, postgrad., 1961, 63; postgrad. Wis. State U., 1962; m. Myrtle Jones, Aug. 18, 1956; children—Sheila Colette, Veta Runette. Sci. tchr., coach Mary Potter High Sch., Oxford, N.C., 1957-63; asst. exec. sec. N.C. Tchrs. Assn., Raleigh, 1963-68; program asso., dir. children center Learning Inst. of N.C., Durham, 1968-70, program asso. for bus. and finance, 1970-—. Cons. Tchr. Edn. and Profl. Standards Commn. N.C., Raleigh, 1963-—, Upward Bound Program, Office Econ. Opportunity, 1966-—; mem. statewide ad hoc com. N.C. Div. Sch. Planning. Mem. Durham (N.C.) Human Relations Council, 1966-—; v.p. Royal Oaks Community Orgn., 1967-—; pres. Royal Oaks Community Council; pack chmn. Cub Scouts; vice chmn. Durham County Bd. Edn. Chmn. bd. dirs. Operation Breakthrough, Durham; bd. dirs. Carolina Friends Sch. Served with M.C., AUS, 1953-56. Mem. Durham Bus. and Profl. Chain, Am. Tchrs. Assn. (trustee), A.A.A.S., Nat. Field Service Assn., N.C. Acad. Sci., Am. Inst. Biol. Sci. Mem. A.M.E. Zion Ch. (bus. adminstr., budget chmn.). Club: Toastmasters (pres.), Home: 1100 Cana St Durham NC 27707 Office: 1006 Lamond Av Durham NC 27701

MCNEILL, KINDEL PARKER, data processing co. exec.; b. Wichita Falls, Tex., July 1, 1931; s. Lester P. and Velma (Parker) McN.; B.A., Tex. Christian U., 1957; m. Linda F. Lang, Feb. 23, 1963; children— Julie Ellen, Suzanne Elizabeth. Exploration geologist Pan Am. Petroleum Corp., Houston, Tyler, Tex., Alaska, 1957-65; marketing dir. McDonnel-Douglas Automation Co., Houston, 1965-68, cons. geology, geophysics; v.p. Geocom, Inc., New Orleans, 1968-70, Houston, 1970-—. Adviser Jr. Achievement, 1965-66. Served with USAF, 1951-53. Mem. Phi Delta Theta. Toastmaster (v.p. 1964-65). Home: 9025 Gaylord Dr Houston TX 77024 Office: 3311 Richmond Av Houston TX 77006

MCNELIS, THOMAS ANTHONY, JR., editor; b. Kingston, N.Y., Feb. 8, 1929; s. Thomas Anthony and Marjorie (O'Reilly) McN.; B.S., Fordham U., 1952; M.S., Columbia, 1953; m. Victoria Zakseski, Aug. 22, 1953; children— Marilyn Judith, Robert Thomas, James William. Sports writer Binghamton (N.Y.) Press, 1953-54, Evening Sun, Balt., 1954-55; communications and pub. relations specialist Bayonne (N.J.) Refinery, Standard Oil Co. (N.J.), 1955-59, Bayway Refinery, Linden, N.J., 1959-61; editor Humble Extra service sta. pub. Humble Oil & Refining Co., Houston, 1961-—. Pres., Green Brook Twp. Republican Club, 1959-60. Chmn., Green Brook Recreation Com., 1960-61; dist. dir. Bronco div. Boys Baseball, 1968-—. Served with AUS, 1946. Mem. Spring Br. Meml. Sports Assn. Roman Catholic. Kiwanian. Lion. Home: 12803 Traviata St Houston TX 77024 Office: PO Box 2180 Houston TX 77001

MCNERNEY, JULES JOHN, physician; b. Dallas, Mar. 27, 1918; s. Dennis and Amie (Wilkerson) McN.; B.S., St. Mary's of Tex., 1937; M.D., La. State U., 1942; m. Arvia Ruby Murphy, Oct. 17, 1941; children— Cheryl, Jules John. Intern, Church Home and Infirmary, 1942, Walter Reed Army Hosp., 1942-43; resident Oliver Gen. Hosp., Augusta, Ga., 1948-50, Med. Coll. Ga., 1950-52; practice medicine specializing in internal medicine and adminstrn., U.S. Army, 1952-68, Hopkinsville, Ky., 1968-—; mem. staff Jennie Stuart Meml. Hosp., Hopkinsville. Area coordinator S.W. Ky., Tenn. Mid-South Regional Med. Program, Hopkinsville, 1968-—; cons. internal medicine 3d U.S. Army Surgeon, 1966-68; asst. clin. prof. medicine Med. Coll. Ga., Augusta, 1950-52, prof. mil. sci. and tactics, 1950-52. Pres., Ft. Campbell (Ky.) Sch. Bd., 1964-68. Decorated Legion of Merit. Fellow A.C.P.; mem. Internat. Platform Assn., A.M.A., Assn. Mil. Surgeons, Pan Am., So., Ky. med. assns., Christian County (sec.-treas. 1972), Muldraugh Hill County (pres. 1955-56) med. socs., Phi Chi. Republican. Home: 306 Deepwood Dr Hopkinsville KY 42240 Office: 310 Richard St Hopkinsville KY 42240

MCNIEL, GEORGE WILLIAM, state ofcl.; b. San Marcos, Tex., Feb. 21, 1931; s. William and Lora Mae (Riley) McN.; B.B.A., Baylor U., 1952; student S.W. Tex. State U., 1948-50; m. Barbara Jo Metz, June 12, 1953; children—Mark William, Earl Wayne, Glen Daniel. Staff auditor Arthur Andersen & Co., Houston, 1955-56; staff auditor firm Mulholland & Conklin, Austin, Tex., 1956-57; treas. Rich Plan of Austin Inc., 1957-60; partner firm Mulholland, McWhirter & McNiel, Austin, 1960-62; staff auditor Tex. Auditor's Dept., 1962-64, supervising asst., 1964-66, 1st asst., 1966-68, state auditor, 1968-—. Served to 1st lt. USAF, 1952-54. Mem. Beta Alpha Psi, Delta Sigma Pi. Baptist (deacon, chmn. bd.). Home: 6507 NE Dr Austin TX 78723 Office: 319 Sam Houston State Office Bldg Austin TX 78711

MCNITT, HAROLD AUSTIN, internat. economist; b. Dec. 6, 1924; s. Harold Anson and Margaret (Austin) McN.; student Western Res. U., 1945; A.B., U. Mich., 1949, M.A., 1953, Ph.D., 1956; postgrad. (Fulbright fellow) U. Copenhagen, 1954-55, (SSRC fellow) U. Uppsala, Sweden, 1957-58; m. Roberta Frank, June 8, 1946. Instr. philosophy U. Mich., 1955-56, Western Res. U., 1956-57, Johns Hopkins, 1958-59; European area specialist Dept. of Commerce, Washington, 1961-—; trade devel. officer U.S. Trade Mission to Sweden, 1963. Served to 2d lt. USAAF, 1943-45. Mem. A.A.A.S., Am. Assn. U. Profs., Am. Philos. Assn., Am. Fgn. Service Assn., Phi Beta Kappa, Phi Kappa Phi. Club: Washington Philosophy. Contbr. articles to profl. jours. Home: 4918 Belt Rd NW Washington DC 20016 Office: US Dept Commerce Washington DC 20230

MCNIVEN, MALCOLM ALBERT, soft drink co. exec.; b. Oceanside, N.Y., Dec. 8, 1929; s. William and Hazel (Summers) McN.; B.A., Denison U., 1951; M.S. Ohio U., 1952; Ph.D., Pa. State U., 1955; m. Elaine Vellacott, June 12, 1954; children—Geoffrey David, Susan Leslie, Jane Elizabeth. Asst. prof. U. Md., College Park, 1956-57; supr. indsl. testing Pa. State U., University Park, 1957-59; research psychologist advt. research sect. E.I. du Pont de Nemours, Wilmington, Del., 1957-59, sect. mgr., 1959-67; mgr. marketing research dept. The Coca Cola Co., Atlanta, 1967-71, v.p., 1968-—, v.p. marketing services Coca-Cola U.S.A., 1971-—. Vis. prof. U. Pa., Phila., 1966-67, Ga. Inst. Tech., Atlanta, 1969-—. Trustee Denison U. Fellow Am. Psychol. Assn.; mem. Inst. Mgmt. Sci., Nat. Indsl. Conf. Bd. (mem. council on marketing research 1967-—), Lambda Chi Alpha. Editor: How Much to Spend for Advertising, 1969-—. Home: 810 Edgewater Trail NW Atlanta GA 30328 Office: 310 North Av NW Atlanta GA 30313

MCNORTON, CLAUDE, educator; b. Repton, Ala., Mar. 25, 1908; s. John Thomas and Emily (Mixon) McN.; A.B., U. Ala., 1935; M.S., La. State U., 1937; M.A. (research fellow 1941), N.Y.U., 1951; grad. U.S. Army Sch. Personnel Services, Washington and Lee U., 1945; m. Elizabeth Moore Kyser, Dec. 9, 1943; 1 dau., Emily Frances (Mrs. Robin Thomas Read). Tchr. social studies Ensley High Sch., Birmingham, Ala., 1946; mem. history and polit. sci. faculty Ala. Poly. Inst., Auburn, 1946-68; mem. polit. sci. faculty Auburn (Ala.) U., 1968-—, adviser to Auburn UN assns., 1949-55, Auburn Conf. Internat. Affairs, 1958-63, 65-69, Auburn Student Internat. Relations Forum, 1971-—, Student Vet. Assn., 1960-—, sponsor Horizons Symposium, 1970. Mem. nat. voter adv. bd. Am. Security Council, 1970-—. Served to capt. USMCR, 1942-46. Decorated Royal Yugoslav Commemorative War Cross, Royal Yugoslav Army; recipient Certificate of Merit, 1967, Distinguished Service Key, 1970 (both Alpha Phi Omega); named Outstanding Alumnus, Delta Chi, 1964. Mem. Ala. Hist. Assn., Ala. Acad. Sci., Acad. Polit. Sci., Internat., Am., So. polit. sci. assns., S.C.V. (state historian 1964-65, chmn. monuments and memls. com. 1966-67), UN Assn. U.S.A., Delta Chi (life mem., alumni trustee; exec. sec. E. Ala. alumni assn., mem. internat. constrn. and by-laws com. 1970-—), Alpha Phi Omega (life mem., chmn. adv. com. 1966-70, chpt. adviser at large 1970-—), Pi Sigma Alpha, Phi Alpha Theta, Omicron Delta Kappa, Lambda Alpha Epsilon. Presbyn. Rotarian (mem. dist. found fellowship com. 1957, chmn. internat. contacts com. Auburn club 1972-73). Home: 448 Hare Av Auburn AL 36830

MCNULTY, JOSEPH PETER, dist. ct. appeals judge; b. N.Y.C., May 11, 1925; s. Peter J. and Charlotte (Morton) McN.; student Slippery Rock State Tchrs. Coll., 1943-44, St. Petersburg Jr. Coll., 1947-48, St. John's U., 1948-50; LL.B., Stetson U., 1952; m. Norma Virginia McInerney, Feb. 3, 1962; children—Maura Rose, Joseph Peter, Stephen Edward, Colleen Marie. Admitted to Fla. bar, 1952; practice law St. Petersburg, 1952-57; atty. Pinellas County Legislative Delegation, 1955; asst. U.S. atty., So. Dist. Fla., 1955-56; judge Civil and Criminal Ct., Pinellas County, 1957-62; circuit judge, Clearwater, Fla., 1963-68; judge Dist. Ct. Appeals, 1968-—. Served to lt. USAAF, 1943-45. Mem. Pi Kappa Alpha, Phi Alpha Delta. K.C., Eagle, Moose, Elk. Club: West Side Exhange (St. Petersburg). Home: 2001 16th Av SW Largo FL 33540 Office: District Court of Appeals Lakeland FL 32202

MCNULTY, MATTHEW FRANCIS, JR., educator, health sci.-service adminstr.; b. Elizabeth, N.J., Nov. 26, 1914; s. Matthew Francis and A. Helen (Dwyer) McN.; B.S., St. Peters Coll., 1938; law student Rutgers U., 1939-41; M. Hosp. Adminstrn., Northwestern U., 1949; M.P.H., U. N.C., 1952; D.S.C., U. Ala., 1969; m. Mary Nell Johnson, May 4, 1946; children—Matthew Francis III, Mary Lauren. Contract writer, mgmt. trainee actuarial div. Prudential Life Ins. Co. of Am., N.J., 1938-41; dir. med. adminstrn. VA, 1946-54; adminstr. U. Ala. Hosp., Birmingham, 1954-63; gen. dir. U. Ala. Hosps. and Clins., 1963-66; prof. hosp. adminstrn. U. Ala. Grad. Sch., 1954-69, vis. prof., 1969-—, dir. grad. program hosp. adminstrn., 1964-66, prof. epidemiology and preventive medicine U. Ala. Sch. Medicine, Birmingham, 1964-69, vis. prof., 1969-—, dean Sch. Health Services Adminstrn. 1966-68; prof. community medicine and internat. health Georgetown U., Washington, v.p. for med. center affairs, 1969-71, exec. v.p. med. center affairs, 1971-—; chmn. bd. trustees Georgetown U. Community Health Plan, Inc.; W.K. Kellogg Found. Vis. prof. Central U. Venezuela, 1967; dir. Council Teaching Hosps., also asso. dir. Assn. Am. Med. Colls., 1966-69; hosp. cons., 1953-—; preceptor hosp. adminstrn. George Washington U., U. Ia., U. Minn. Mem. nat. adv. com. health research projects Ga. Inst. Tech., 1959-65; nat. adv. com. health research projects U. Pitts., 1956-60; adv. com. W.K. Kellogg Found., 1960-65; vis. cons., lectr. Ministry of Health and Social Welfare, Venezuela, 1967-69. Bd. dirs. Blue Cross-Blue Shield of Ala., 1960-61, 65-68, Greater Birmingham United Appeal, 1960-66; trustee Jefferson County Tb Sanatorium, 1958-64; mem. Health Services Research Stude Section, NIH, 1963-67; cons. com. on profl. nurse traineeships USPHS, 1959, 63; mem. White House Conf. on Health, 1965, White House Conf. on Medicare Implementation, 1966, Nat. Conf. on Group Practice, 1967, Nat. Conf. on Costs of Health Care Facilities, 1967, Sec. Labor Conf. on Health Manpower, 1966. Served from pvt. to lt. col. USAAF, 1941-46. Fellow Am. Pub. Health Assn., Am. Coll. Hosp. Adminstrs. (bd. regents and council of regents 1961-67); mem. Am., Ala. (past pres.) hosp. assns., Nat. (bd. dirs. 1971-—), Ala. (past dir.) leagues for nursing, Internat. Hosp. Fedn., Jefferson County Vis. Nursing Assn. (past pres.), Ala. Pub. Health Assn. (past chmn. med. care sect.), Southeastern Hosp. Conf. (past dir.), Birmingham Hosp. Council (past pres.), Assn. Univ. Programs in Hosp. Adminstrn., Greater Birmingham Area C. of C., Soc. Advancement Mgmt., Am. Assn. Med. Colls. (chmn. teaching hosp. council 1964-65), Royal Soc. Health, Orgn. Univ. Health Center Adminstrs., A.A.A.S., Santa Gertrudis Breeders Internat. Author articles in field. Clubs: University (Ala.); Cosmos, City Tavern (Washington); Bethesda (Md.) Country. Home: 10000 Carter Rd Bethesda MD 20034 Office: 3750 Reservoir Rd NW Washington DC 20007

MCNUTT, BILLY JOE, cosmetic mfg. exec.; b. Paris, Tenn., May 29, 1930; s. Thomas L. and Lena (Barton) McN.; student Murray State U., 1948-50; B.S., U. Tenn., 1953, postgrad., 1960, 63, 66; m. Mary Ann Coursey, June 15, 1952; children—Debra Ann, Randall Joe. Pharmacist, Hamlet Drug Co., Paris, 1954-57; chemist Golden Peacock, Inc., Paris, 1957-60, chief chemist, 1960-62, tech. dir., 1962-66, v.p. tech div., 1966; v.p. tech. div. Mitchum Co., Paris, 1966-—. Mem. Toilet Goods Assn., Tenn., 8th Dist. (pres. 1961) pharm. assns., Soc. Cosmetic Chemists, Kappa Psi (treas. 1951), Rho Chi. Baptist. Mason, Lion (past pres.), Elk. Club: Paris Country. Home: Anderson Dr Route 2 Paris TN 38242 Office: 2700 S Wood St Paris TN 38242

MCPHAUL, MARY OLIVE, ednl. adminstr.; A.B., Samford U., Birmingham, Ala.; M.A., U. Ala. Formerly residence counselor Fla. State U., instr. dept. English Sam Ford U.; asst., asso., dean of women U. Southwestern La., now coordinator, adminstr. dept. student personnel. Mem. Am. Assn. U. Women, Hypatia Soc., Phi Kappa Phi, Alpha Lambda Delta, Kappa Delta Pi, Pi Delta Pi, Alpha Delta Pi, Delta Kappa Gamma. Club: University Women's. Office: Univ Southwestern Louisiana Lafayette LA 70501

MCPHEETERS, HAROLD LAWRENCE, physician; b. N.Y.C., Mar. 10, 1923; s. Harry Halstead and Ethel (Brush) McP.; A.B., Lafayette Coll., 1945; M.D., U. Louisville, 1948; m. Phyllis Merrill, Dec. 24, 1951; children— David, Doris, Thomas, Amy. Intern, City Hosp., Springfield, O., 1948-49; resident U. Louisville (Ky.) Hosp., 1949-52; asst. psychiatrist Ellis Hosp., Schenectady, N.Y., 1954-55; asst. commr. Ky. Dept. Mental Health, Louisville, 1955-57, commr., 1957-64; dep. commr. N.Y. Dept. Mental Hygiene, Albany, 1964-65; dir. mental health So. Regional Edn. Bd., Atlanta, 1965-—; instr. Albany Med. Coll., 1954-55; asst. prof. psychiatry U. Louisville, 1955-64; clin. asso. prof. psychiatry Emory U., 1970-—. Bd. dirs. Louisville Child Guidance Clinic, 1957-64, Atlanta Area Community Council, 1970-—. Served with AUS, 1943-46; served to lt. M.C., USNR, 1952-54. Mem. Am., Ky. (pres. 1960), Ga. psychiat. assns., A.M.A., Am. Pub. Health Assn. Contbr. articles in field to profl. jours. Home: 435 Forest Valley Rd NE Atlanta GA 30342 Office: 130 6th St NW Atlanta GA 30313

MCPHERON, ALAN BEAUMONT, judge; b. McAlester, Okla,, July 6, 1914; s. Robert Lee and Jeannette (Kridler) McP.; LL.B., U. Okla., 1937; m. Mary Jane Bass, Apr. 8, 1938; 1 dau., Jill. Admitted to Okla. bar, 1937; practice law, Durant, 1946-65, dist. judge 1965-—; asst. county atty., 1939-43; judge 19th Jud. Dist. Okla. Chmn. War Vets. Commn. of Okla., 1949-51; chmn. Bd. Review, Okla. Employment Security Commn., 1951-59. Served with U.S. Army, 1943-46. Recipient Bronze Star, Croix de Guerre. Home: 2010 W Liveoak Durant OK 74701 Office: Bryan County Court House Durant OK 74701

MCPHERSON, ALICE RUTH, physician, educator; b. Regina, Sask., Can., June 30, 1926; d. Gordon and Viola (Hoover) McP.; B.S., U. Wis., 1948, M.D., 1951. Intern Santa Barbara Cottage Hosp., 1951-52; resident anesthesiology Hartford Hosp., 1953, resident ophthalmology Chgo. Eye, Ear, Nose and Throat Hosp., 1953, U. Wis. Hosp., 1953-55; ophthalmologist Davis & Duehr Eye Clinic, 1955-57, Scott and White Clinic, 1958-60, Houston, 1960-62; fellow retina service Mass. Eye and Ear Infirmary, 1957-58; practice medicine, specializing in ophthalmology, retinal diseases, Houston, 1962-—; mem. staffs Meth. Hosp., Houston, St. Luke's Hosp., Houston, Tex. Children's Hosp., Houston; clin. instr. U. Wis., 1956-58; clin. asso. prof. ophthalmology Baylor Coll. Medicine, Houston, 1960-63, 1969-—, asst. prof. ophthalmology, 1963-69, chief retina service dept. ophthalmology, 1960-—. Lectr. ophthalmology U. Tex., 1958-—; cons. retinal diseases VA Hosp., 1959-—, Ben Taub Hosp., Houston, 1960-—. Diplomate Am. Bd. Ophthalmology, Fellow Am. Acad. Ophthalmology and Otolaryngology, A.C.S.; mem. A.M.A., Tex., Pan.-Am. med. assns., Soc. Cryosurgery, Internat. Coll. Surgeons. Harris County Med. Soc., Houston Ophthal. Soc., Am. Med. Women's Assn., Nat. Med. Found. for Eye Care, Pan-Pacific Surg. Assn., French Ophthal. Soc., Internat. Med. Assembly Southwest Tex., Am. Assn. Ophthalmology, So. Med. Assn., Assn. Research Ophthalmology, Assn. Am. Physicians and Surgeons, Retina Soc., Soc. Eye Surgeons, Jules Gonin Club. Author: New and Controversial Aspects of Retinal Detachment, 1968. Office: 6436 Fannin Med Center Profl Bldg Houston TX 77025

MCPHERSON, DAVID LEE, banker; b. Wellston, Okla., Nov. 11, 1942; s. D. D. and J. D. (Holt) McP.; student Okla. State U., 1960, U. Tulsa, 1961-62; grad. Okla. Sch. Banking, 1968; m. Sandra Lynn Dollins, Sept. 22, 1963; children—Cynthia Kay, Paul Gavin. Salesman, Petty's Shoes and Trippett's Shoes, 1961-62; teller Security Nat. Bank, Sapulpa, Okla., 1962-64, asst. cashier, 1964-67; cashier 1st Nat. Bank, Edmond, Okla., 1967-—, v.p., 1972-—. Bd. dirs., state dir., treas., 1st v.p., pres. Sapulpa Jr. C. of C., 1962-67; treas., bd. dirs. Sapulpa Campfire Girls Assn., 1965-67. Mem. Bank Adminstrn. Inst., Okla. Bankers Assn., Edmond (v.p., treas., dir. 1967-—), Edmond Jr. (pres., dir. 1967-—) chambers commerce. Republican. Home: 1007 Crown Dr Edmond OK 73034 Office: PO Box 309 Edmond OK 73034

MCPHERSON, KARL, ret. govt. ofcl.; b. Cuthbert, Ga., Mar. 5, 1912; s. Duncan A. and Rebecca (Parkerson) McP.; student U. Ga., 1929-32, Ga. State Coll., 1938, Woodrow Wilson Coll. Law, 1938-40, Harvard Bus. Sch., 1962; m. Ola M. Maffett, Apr. 1, 1933; children—Karl M., Carolyn R. (Mrs. Percy W. Baker), Martha A. (Mrs. A.W. Quillian IV), Massee E. Rate clk. Fed. Power Commn., 1935-39; spl. rep. U.S. Civil Service Commn., 1939-42; dir. civilian personnel Warner Robins Air Material Area, Ga., 1942-71, dep. chief personnel and administrn., also chief civilian personnel div. Methodist (steward). Kiwanian. Home: 2480 Kingsley Dr Macon GA 31204

MCQUADE, WILLIAM MICHAEL, editor; b. Ann Arbor, Mich., Nov. 11, 1943; s. Thaddeus B. and Clarissa (Palmer) McQ.; B.Sc., Ohio State U., 1965; postgrad. Nat. Law Center George Washington U., 1969-72; m. Jane Ellen Wales, Sept. 12, 1964; 1 son, Thadd

Michael. Naturalist Ohio Dept. Natural Resources, 1964; foreman R.B. Stout Landscaping Inc., Beth, O., 1969; staff asst. Whiteman Digest Internat. Law Office Legal Advisor U.S. Dept. State, 1970-71; adminstrv. editor Jour. Internat. Law and Econs., George Washington U. Nat. Law Center, Washington, 1970-71, editor in chief, 1971—. Served to capt. AUS, 1966-69. Home: 5811 N 19th St Arlington VA 22205 Office: 714 21st St NW Washington DC 20006

MCQUAIDE, HENRY CHARLES, physician, surgeon; b. Vicksburg, Miss., Dec. 27, 1920; s. Henry C. and Marguerite (McGinty) McQ.; student Tex. A. and M. Coll., 1937-41; M.D., Baylor U., 1944; m. Sara Bess Barber, Dec. 26, 1943; children—Henry C. III, Carol Ann, Mary Kay. Intern, U.S. Navy Hospital, San Diego, 1944-45; resident in surgery Nan Travis Hosp., Jacksonville, Tex., 1946-47, U.S. VA Hosp., Houston, 1950-52; mem. surg. staff Travis Clinic, 1947-49, VA Hosp., Temple, Tex., 1953-55; pvt. practice surgery, Bryan, Tex., 1956—; surg. cons. Tex. A. and M. Coll., 1956—, Allen Mil. Acad., 1956—. Co-owner K-M Ranch, Burleson Milan Counties. Served to lt. (j.g.) M.C. USNR, 1944-46; served to capt. M.C., USAF, 1953-55. Diplomate Am. Bd. Surgery. Fellow A.C.S. Home: 3614 Sweetbriar Bryan TX 77801 Office: 2719 Osler Blvd Bryan TX 77801

MCRAE, ROBERT MALCOLM, JR., U.S. dist. judge; b. Memphis, Dec. 31, 1921; s. Robert Malcolm and Irene (Pontius) McR.; B.A., Vanderbilt U., 1943; LL.B., U. Va., 1948; m. Louise Howry, July 31, 1943; children— Susan Campbell, Robert Malcolm III, Duncan Farquhar, Thomas Alexander Todd. Admitted to Tenn. bar, 1948; practice in Memphis, 1948-64; partner firm Apperson, Crump, Duzane & McRae, 1955-59, Larkey, Dudley, Blanchard & McRae, 1959-64; judge Tenn. Circuit Ct., 1964-66; U.S. dist. judge Western Dist. Tenn., 1966—. Served to lt. USNR, 1943-46. Mem. Beta Theta Pi, Phi Delta Phi, Omicron Delta Kappa. Episcopalian (pres. Episcopal Churchmen of Tenn. 1964-65). Home: 2886 Iroquois Rd Memphis TN 38111 Office: 167 N Main St Memphis TN 38103

MCRAE, VINCENT VERNON, govt. ofcl.; b. Columbia, S.C., Sept. 2, 1918; s. Thomas Tyson and Clireta (Avery) McR.; student U. Chgo., 1944-45; B.S., Miner Tchrs. Coll., 1940; M.S., Cath. U., 1944, Ph.D. in Math., 1955; m. Mae Agnes Smith, June 27, 1941; children—Vincent Vernon, Ronald G.S. Tchr., D.C. Pub. Schs., 1940-42; operations analyst Operations Research Office, Johns Hopkins, Balt., 1952-61; chief strategic div. Operations Research Office, chief air def. div. chmn. armour group and stratspiel group, 1952-61; chief strategic div. Research Analysis Corp., McLean, Va., 1962-64; cons. Office Spl. Asst. to Pres. for Sci. and Tech., Washington, 1962-64; tech. asst. Office Sci. and Tech., The White House, Washington, 1964—. Mem. staff Gathier Commn., 1956, Coolidge Arms Control Com., 1958; mem. U.S. delegation Conf. on Surprise Attack, Geneva, Switzerland, 1957. Sec., Brookland Civic Assn., Washington. Served to 2d lt. U.S. 1944-47. Fellow A.A.A.S.; mem. Am. Math. Soc., Operations Research Soc., N.E.A., N.A.A.C.P., D.C. Fedn. Civic Assn., Sigma Xi, Rho Delta Rho. Home: 1501 Emerson St NW Washington DC 20011 Office: Office Sci and Tech Exec Office Bldg Washington DC 20001

MCRAE, WILLIAM ALLAN, JR., U.S. judge; b. Marianna, Fla., Sept. 25, 1909; s. William Allan and Mary (Parker) McR.; A.B., U. Fla., 1932, J.D., 1933; Rhodes scholar Christ Ch., Oxford U. (Eng.), 1933, B.A. in Jurisprudence, 1935, B.Litt., 1936, M.A. in absentia, 1946; m. Aline Virginia Dearing, Aug. 29, 1942; children—Aline Virginia, William Allan III, Dearing. Admitted to Fla. bar, 1933; practiced with firm Knight, Adair, Cooper & Osborne, Jacksonville, 1936-38, Giles J. Patterson, 1938-40; mem. firm Holland, Bevis, McRae & Smith, Bartow, 1946-61; judge U.S. Dist. Ct., Middle Dist. Fla., 1961—, chief judge, 1971—. Prof. law U. Fla., 1940-41; mem. Fla. constn. adv. com. Sr. cons. AEC, Washington, 1946. Trustee U. Fla., U. Fla. Law Center Assn. Endowment Corp.; chmn. bd. trustees Jacksonville U.; bd. govs. Fed. Jud. Center, 1968-70. Served from lst lt. to col. USAAF, 1942-45. Decorated Legion of Merit. Fellow Am. Coll. Trial Lawyers; mem. Am. (chmn. Fla. com. sect. jud. adminstrn.), Fed. bar assns., Am. Law Inst., Selden Soc., Jud. Council Fla. Bar, Am. Judicature Soc. (past dir.), U. Fla. Alumni Assn. (pres. 1949-50), Order of Coif, Blue Key, Phi Beta Kappa, Phi Kappa Phi, Phi Delta Phi, Omicron Delta Kappa, Alpha Tau Omega (pres. Fla. 1931). Rotarian (pres. Bartow 1947-49). Club: Florida Yacht. Home: Jacksonville FL 32201 Office: US District Court PO Box 4070 Jacksonville FL 32202

MCREE, JOHNSON, JR., accountant; b. Richmond, Va., June 11, 1923; s. Johnson and Elizabeth Goodridge (Sale) McR.; student Hampden-Sydney Coll., 1940-42; B.S. in Commerce, Washington and Lee U., 1948; m. Elizabeth Temple Johnston, Oct. 22, 1949; children—Edith Battaile, Annie Belle Sackett, Elizabeth Goodridge. Staff accountant T. Coleman Andrews & Co., Richmond, Va., 1948-51; sr. staff accountant, auditor City of Richmond, 1951-52; sr. staff accountant firm Baker, Brydon, Rennolds & Whitt, Richmond, 1952-54, office mgr., Manassas, Va., 1954-58, resident partner, office mgr., 1958-61; comptroller, treas., dir. Georator Corp., Manassas, 1961-63; sr. partner firm Brydon, McRee & Smith, Richmond, Manassas, and Chester, Va., 1963—. Treas., dir. Tax Council, Washington, 1967—. Served with AUS, 1943-46, 50-51. C.P.A., Va. Mem. N.A.M. (tax com. 1961—), Am. Inst. C.P.A.'s, Va. Soc. C.P.A.'s, Manassas C. of C. (pres. 1962-63), N.C. Soc. Cincinnati (standing com.), Pi Kappa Alpha. Episcopalian (former vestryman, treas.). Kiwanian (pres. Manassas 1964). Producer Manassas Jazz Festival, Fat Cat Jazz records. Home: 9213 West St Manassas VA 22110 Office: 9125 Center St Manassas VA 22110

MCSOUD, LAWRENCE ANTHONY, lawyer; b. Bristown, Okla., May 11, 1933; s. Charles and Evelyn (Nahan) McS.; B.Ed., Okla. State U., 1955; J.D., U. Tulsa, 1959; m. Kay Ann Davie; 2 children. Tchr. Tulsa Pub. Sch. System, 1956; admitted to Okla. bar, 1959; asst. dist. atty. Creek County, Okla., 1959-62, dist. atty., 1962-64; asst. U.S. atty. No. Dist. Okla., Tulsa, 1964-66, first asst. U.S. atty., 1966-67, U.S. atty., 1967-69; asso. Houston, Kline & Davidson, Tulsa, 1969—; lectr. Tulsa U. Law Sch.; mem. jud. selection com. Tenth Jud. Dist. Bd. dirs. Sapulpa (Okla.) Salvation Army, 1962; post adviser Indian Nations council Boy Scouts Am., 1968. Vice pres. Young Democrats, Creek County, Okla., 1961. Mem. Fed. (1st v.p. Tulsa chpt. 1968—), Okla., Tulsa County (mem. exec. com., 1968—), Creek County (v.p. 1962) bar assns., Sapulpa C. of C., Phi Alpha Delta, Xi Mu. Democrat. Roman Catholic. K.C., Kiwanian, Elk. Clubs: University (Tulsa); Oaks Country. Home: 232 E 28th St Tulsa OK 74114 Office: 630 W 7th St Tulsa OK 74127

MCSWEEN, DONALD MURDOCH, recreation co. exec.; b. Newport, Tenn., May 18, 1915; s. William Daniel and Rowena (Jones) McS.; ed. U. Tenn., 1933-37, Cumberland U., 1939-40; m. Louise Valentine, Aug. 20, 1938. Admitted to Tenn. bar, 1942; practiced in Newport, 1945-62, Nashville, 1959-62; atty. City of Newport, 1946-49; v.p. Diversified Mgmt. Corp. (now Downtowner Corp), Memphis, 1959; pres. Diversified Securities Corp., Memphis, 1959-61, With TVA, VA, War Manpower Commn., 1940-45; Tenn. commr. of employment security, 1953-59; Tenn. commr. of conservation, 1963-67; S.C. dir. state parks and recreation, 1967-71; pres. Travel Retreats Internat., also Holiday Camps Am., Inc., Alcoa, Tenn., 1971—. Served with Signal Corps, AUS, World War II. Named Outstanding Young Man Yr., Tenn. Jr. C. of C., 1947. Mem. Am., Cocke County bar assns., Bar Assn. Tenn., S.E. State Park Dirs. Assn. (pres. 1968-69), Nat. Conf. State Parks (chmn. legislative com. 1968—, bd. dirs. 1969—), Am. Legion (Tenn. comdr. 1947-48), also numerous employment security, conservation, recreation and travel orgns. Presbyn. Mason (32 deg., K.T., Shriner), Elk, Kiwanian. Home: Old Glory Rd Smoky View Estates Rt 2 Maryville TN 37801 Office: 243 Calderwood St Alcoa TN 37701

MCTAGGART, JAMES ARTHUR, govt. ofcl.; b. Enid, Okla., Jan. 21, 1928; s. Guy Earl and Hazel (White) McT.; student Oklahoma City U., 1950-53; D.D.S., Baylor U., 1957; M.P.H., U. Cal. at Berkeley, 1965; m. Sandra Babb Gilley, May 17, 1950; 1 dau., Stacey Lynn. Commd. sr. dental surgeon USPHS, 1965, advanced through grades to capt., 1971; dental intern USPHS Hosp., Seattle, 1957-58; clin. dentist USPHS Outpatient Clinic, San Juan, P.R., 1958-60; dentist, Operation DeepFreeze, Antarctica, 1960-61; regional rep. Bur. Radiol. Health, Dallas, 1964—. Vis. lectr. U. Cal. at Los Angeles, 1963; guest lectr. Baylor U. Coll. Dentistry, 1971. Served with USNR, 1946-49. Fellow Am. Pub. Health Assn.; mem. Delta Omega. Office: 1100 Commerce St Dallas TX 75221

MCTERNAN, JAMES J., JR., communications co. exec.; b., 1921; B.A. in Econs., Yale, 1945; m. mgr. gen. accounting Packard Motor Car Co., 1952-54; financial controller Studebaker-Packard Corp., 1954-57; asst. to v.p. N.Y. Central R.R. Co., 1957-58; asst. v.p. Penn Central Co., 1968-70; v.p. finance and adminstrn. Communications Satellite Corp., Washington, 1970—. Served with USAF, 1952-54. Home: 10028 Garrett St Vienna VA 22180 Office: 955 L'Enfant Plaza SW Washington DC 20024*

MCVICKAR, RONALD, aviation co. exec.; b. N.Y.C., Feb. 17, 1922; s. James and Louise (Hinck) M.; student Stuyvesant Sch., 1940; m. Mary Grafton Filley, Aug. 30, 1944; children—David, Louise, Oliver. Dist. sales mgr. Northwest Orient Airlines, Newark and Chgo., 1945-60, Washington, 1960-63; asst. v.p. N.W. Airlines, Inc., 1963-70, v.p., 1970—. Mem. Met. Washington Bd. Trade, Nat. Def. Transp. Assn. Clubs: Metropolitan, Internat. Aviation; Aero (Washington). Home: Home Port Route 1 456 Honereng Trail Annapolis MD 21401 Office: 1660 L St Washington DC 20036

MCVICKER, EDGAR LEONARD, govt. ofcl.; b. Vici, Okla., Mar. 1, 1914; s. Jesse Allen and Clara (Hendrick) McV.; B.S., Okla. State U., 1941; m. Jessie Lorraine Polk, Oct. 14, 1930; children—J. Robert (dec.), Vicki Lou. Economist, U.S. Dept. Agr. Washita River Devel. Project, Chickasha, Okla., 1949-56; exec. dir. Okla. Cotton Ginners, Crushers and Research Found., Oklahoma City, 1956-58; indsl. devel. specialist Bur. Indian Affairs, Anadarko, Okla., 1958—. Mem. Okla. Indsl. Adv. Com., 1968-72. Pres., Okla. County Muscular Dystrophy Assn., 1958. Mem. Okla. Ho. of Reps., 1936-40. Served with AUS, 1943-44. Mem. Okla. State U. Alumni Assn. (dir.), Am. Legion, Nat. Fedn. Fed. Employees. Mem. Ch. of Christ. Rotarian. Home: 1005 London Dr Anadarko OK 73005 Office: Fed Bldg Anadarko OK 73005

MCWANE, KENNETH GOODWIN, hwy. engr.; b. Lynchburg, Va., Oct. 29, 1900; s. Charles William and Cora Lee (Wilkinson) McW.; student U. Va., 1919-21; m. Ruth Leon Henson, Oct. 30, 1926; 1 dau., Ruth (Mrs. Robert Lee Mason). With Va. Dept. Hwys., 1921-52; engr. traffic and operations Hwy. Research Bd., Nat. Acad. Scis. NRC, Washington, 1952-64. Registered profl. engr., Va. Fellow Am. Soc. C.E.; mem. Inst. Traffic Engrs. (mem. tech. council 1960-64), Va. Assn. Traffic Engrs. Democrat. Methodist (mem. adminstrv. bd.). Elk. Home: 4011 Morrison Dr Lynchburg VA 24503

MCWHIRTER, WELDON HAYS, SR., bank exec.; b. Gainesville, Tex., Oct. 30, 1931; s. Sidney Hays and Olive Roberta (Ballard) McW.; B.S., So. State Coll., 1953; m. Billie Jean Boyd, May 7, 1953; children—Weldon Hays, Pamela Jean. Asst. cashier First Nat. Bank Magnolia, Ark., 1955-62; v.p. First Nat. Bank Warren, Ark., 1962-68, pres., 1968-69; pres., dir. Met. Nat. Bank, Little Rock, 1969—. Mem. Bd. Edn., Warren, 1967-69. Served with AUS, 1953-55. Mem. Warren C. of C. (pres. 1967). Lion (treas. 1964—, v.p. 1965-66, dir. 1966-69). Home: 6104 Senate St Little Rock AR 72209 Office: 5601 S University St Little Rock AR 72209

MCWHORTER, JOHN ALEXANDER, JR., lawyer; b. Greensboro, Ga., July 19, 1925; s. John Alexander and Annie (Sanders) McW.; A.B., Washington and Lee U., 1947, LL.B., 1950; LL.M., George Washington U., 1956. Admitted to Va. bar, 1950, D.C. bar, 1955; atty. Office Chief Engrs., Dept. Army, Washington, 1950-55; practiced in Washington, 1955—; mem. firm King & King, 1955—. Mem. Fed., Am. (chmn. pub. contracts sect. 1972—), D.C., Va. bar assns., Phi Delta Phi, Phi Kappa Sigma. Club: Nat. Lawyers. Home: 2301 E St NW Washington DC 20037 Office: 1320 19th St NW Washington DC 20036

MCWHORTER, WILLIAM HORACE, ednl. adminstr.; b. Montgomery, Ala., Jan. 9, 1928; s. Abbott Milton and Leona Estelle (White) McW.; B.S., Jacksonville State U., 1949; M.A., George Peabody Coll. for Tchrs., 1956; Ed.D., U. Ala., 1969; m. Kathleen Story, Jan. 31, 1954; children—William Timothy, Lillian, Suzanne. Tchr., coach high sch., Oxford, Ala., 1949-51; instr. Jacksonville State U., 1952-53; tchr., coach high sch., Blue Springs, Ala., 1951-52, Wildwood, Fla., 1956-57; prin. high sch., White Springs, Fla., 1957-59; dir. Colegio Internat., Valencia, Venezuela, 1959-66; dean Faulkner State Jr. Coll., 1966-68; pres. Lurleen B. Wallace State Jr. Coll., Andalusia, Ala., 1969—. Cons. research and higher edn. State of Ala., 1968—. Served with AUS, 1953-55. Mem. Am. Assn. Sch. Adminstrs., Andalusa C. of C. (dir.), Phi Delta Kappa, Kappa Delta Pi, Beta Beta Beta. Methodist (adminstrv. bd. 1969—). Rotarian. Home: 1409 Sunset Dr Andalusia AL 36420 Office: PO Drawer 1418 Andalusia AL 36420

MCWILLIAMS, JETTIE MANNING CRISP (MRS. WILEY E. MCWILLIAMS, JR.), educator; b. nr. Mt. Creek, Ala., May 5, 1928; A.B., Berea Coll., 1958; postgrad. Bluffton Coll., 1957, Ohio State U., 1964; M.A. (Haggin fellow), U. Ky., 1963, Ed.D., 1966; m. Robert Alton Crisp, Jr., May 5, 1949 (dec. Mar. 1961); children—Jane Rae, Victoria Anne, Kathryn Dianne, Yvonne Nell; m. 2d, Wiley E. McWilliams, Jr., June 4, 1967. Pub. high sch. English tchr., Wheelwright, Ky., 1950-52, Pandora, O., 1959-61; guidance counselor Bryan St. Jr. High Sch., Lexington, Ky., 1963-64; instr. U. Ky., Lexington, 1965-66; asst. prof. ednl. psychology and guidance, then asso. prof. Tenn. Tech. U., Cookeville, 1966—. Cons. ednl. systems and Project Upper Cumberland, Cookeville, 1967—. Leader, Girl Scouts U.S.A., Beaverdam, O. 1959-61; sec. Cookeville P.T.A., 1960-61, historian, 1961-62, 2d v.p., 1967-68. Bd. dirs. Tenn. Vocational Tng. Center, Cookville, 1967-70. Recipient Outstanding Alumnus award Bluffton Coll., 1971. Mem. Am. Assn. U. Women, Am. Personnel and Guidance Assn., Nat. Vocational Guidance Assn., Am. Coll. Personnel Assn., Am. Assn. U. Profs., Tenn. Assn. Counselor Educators and Suprs., Nat. Tenn. edn. assns., Internat. Platform Assn., Kappa Delta Pi, Beta Sigma Phi. Contbr. articles to profl. jours. Home: 1131 Flatt Circle Cookeville TN 38501

MCWILLIAMS, ROBERT WHEALTON, life ins. co. exec.; b. Portsmouth, N.C., July 8, 1910; s. Charles S. and Annie T. (Toler) McW.; student U. N.C., 1930-31, Eastman Coll., 1932-33; m. Dorothy J. Osborne, May 20, 1950; children—Robert Wheelton, Ann Cullen. With Life Ins. Co. Va., Portsmouth, 1933—, successively agt., staff mgr., Portsmouth, mgr. Staunton, Lynchburg, Newport News, Norfolk and Portsmouth, divisional supr., asst. v.p., 1946-50, 2d v.p., 1955-56, now dist. mgr. Past dir. Lynchburg Staunton, Norfolk Life Underwriters. Pres., Norfolk Found., Inc. Mem. Peninsular Assn. Life Underwriters (past pres.), Portsmouth Assn. Life Underwriters (pres., dir.). Baptist. Mason (Shriner). Clubs: Cosmopolitan (past pres.), Norfolk (Va.) Yacht and Country; Virginia; Cedar Point Country (Crittenden, Va.). Home: 1215 S Fairwater Dr Norfolk VA 23508 Office: 808 Loudoun Av Portsmouth VA 23707

MEACHAM, ELLIS KIRBY, lawyer; b. Chattanooga, Sept. 5, 1913; s. Cowan White Kirby and Jean (Ellis) M.; A.B., U. Chattanooga, 1935; LL.B., Vanderbilt U., 1937, J.D., 1969; m. Jean Bevan Austin, Feb. 12, 1940; children—G.B. Kirby, Jere Ellis. Admitted to Tenn. bar, 1937; gen. practice civil law, Chattanooga, 1937—; atty. City of Chattanooga, 1948—. Served as comdr. USNR, 1941-45. Recipient award for fiction Friends of Am. Writers, 1969. Mem. Am., Tenn., Chattanooga bar assns., Authors Guild, Authors League Am. Episcopalian. Club: Fairyland (Lookout Mountain, Tenn.). Author: The East Indiaman, 1968; On the Company's Service, 1971. Home: 414 S Crest Rd Chattanooga TN 37404 Office: Hamilton Bank Bldg Chattanooga TN 37402

MEAD, EDWIN BUDGE, banker; b. Rockford, Ill., June 7, 1901; s. D. Ray and Jeanette (Wisegarver) M.; grad. Exeter Acad., 1919; B.A., U. Wis., 1923. Vice pres. Mead Constrn. Co., Miami, Fla., 1923-41; v.p., treas. Mead Bros., Miami, 1924-66; pres. Ill. Nat. Bank & Trust Co., Rockford, 1931-35; founder, chmn. bd. First Nat. Bank & Trust Co., Eustis, Fla., 1956—, Bank of Mt. Dora (Fla.), 1965—; dir. Brown Sugar Corp.; treas., dir. radio sta. WLBE: pres. Rockford Safe Deposit Co., 1941-69. Vice pres. Lake County Tb Assn., 1956-64; pres. Waterman Meml. Hosp. Assn., 1961—. Served to lt. col. USAAF, 1942-44. Mem. Theta Delta. Clubs: Mt. Dora Yacht, Honeydew (Mt. Dora); Surf, Bath, Miami Beach, Miami, Biscayne Bay Yacht (Miami); Citrus (Orlando, Fla.); Pine Meadows (Eustis). Home: Far Reach Ranch Deer Island Mount Dora FL 32757 Office: PO Drawer 38 Eustis FL 32726

MEAD, FREDERICK M.M., communications co. exec.; b., 1915; B.S., N.Y. U., 1940; m. Mng. accountant Price Waterhouse & Co., 1940-55; asst. to controller Kearfott Co., Inc., 1955-58; controller Mallinckrodt Chem. Works, 1958-64; comptroller Communications Satellite Corp., 1964—, treas., 1969—. Office: 955 L'Enfant Plaza Washington DC 20024*

MEADE, EDWARD GRANT, educator; b. Phila., Apr. 6, 1914; s. Edward and Elizabeth (Grant) M.; A.B., Dartmouth, 1935; M.A., U. Wis., 1936; M.A.L.D., Fletcher Sch. Law and Diplomacy, 1938; Ph.D., U. Pa., 1948; postgrad. Harvard, 1945, Air War Coll., 1960-61; m. Courtenay Frances Etheridge, Oct. 21, 1949; children—Elise Stokes, Courtenay Etheridge, Sydney Ingram, Elizabeth Grant, Celestia Loyall. Chmn. polit. sci. dept. Haverford Coll., 1946-48; U.S. cultural attache, Bangkok, Thailand, 1955-56, U.S. pub. affairs attache, Thailand, 1956-60, Lagos, Nigeria, 1961-64; coordinator book program USIA, Europe, Africa, Washington, 1964-65; prof., chmn. polit. sci. dept. Old Dominion U., Norfolk, Va., 1965—. Spl. prof. polit. sci. faculty Chulalongkorn U., Bangkok, Thailand, 1956-60. Dir. pub. relations Norfolk (Va.) A.R.C., 1954-55; vice chmn. Fulbright Found., Thailand, 1955-60; bd. dirs. John E. Peurifoy Found., Bangkok, 1956-60, Social Sci. Assn. Thailand, 1957-60, Norfolk Forum, 1969—. Served with USNR, 1941-46, 48-55. Fletcher fellow, 1936-38. Mem. Am. Hist. Assn., Am. Acad. Polit. and Social Sci., Am. Polit. Sci. Assn., Am. Soc. Internat. Law, Am. Assn. U. Profs., Am. Fgn. Service Assn., Cum Laude Soc., Mil. Order Fgn. Wars, Pa. Soc., S.R., Pub. Relations Soc. Am., Delta Kappa Epsilon. Clubs: Norfolk Yacht and Country; Merion Cricket (Haverford, Pa.). Author: American Military Government in Korea, 1951. Contbr. articles to profl. jours. Home: 1000 Cambridge Crescent Norfolk VA 23508

MEADE, EVERARD WILSON, ednl. adminstr.; b. Pohick, Va., Jan. 2, 1914; s. Emmett Augustus and Katie Elizabeth (Wilson) M.; B.A., U. Va., 1935; m. Virginia Valentine Walker, Mar. 28, 1935; 1 dau., Elizabeth Valentine (Mrs. John Winship Howard). Asst. to pres. Am. Tobacco Co., 1945-48; v.p. Young & Rubicam, Inc., 1948-53, Ogilvy Benson & Mather, Inc., 1955-57; spl. asst. to dean U. Va. Grad. Sch. Bus. Adminstrn., Charlottesville, 1956—. Served with USNR, 1942-45; PTO. Mem. Kappa Alpha. Episcopalian. Clubs: Farmington Country, Boar's Head (Charlottesville). Author: The Golden Geese, 1968. Contbr. articles to profl. jours. Home: 1 Blue Ridge Lane Farmington Charlottesville VA 22901

MEADE, GEORGE PETERKIN, ret. sugar refiner; b. Cumberland, Md., Dec. 26, 1883; s. Philip Nelson and Sarah (Rannells) M.; B.S., N.Y.U., 1905, Chem.E., 1921, D.Eng. (hon.), 1955; student U. Mich., 1914; D.Sc., La. State U., 1954, Tulane U., 1970; m. Eleanore Felicia Hussey, Aug. 7, 1912 (dec.). Asst. chemist Nat. Sugar Refinery, Yonkers, N.Y., summers 1901-05, full time, 1905-07; asst. chemist Fajardo (P.R.) Sugar Co., 1908; chemist and asst. supt. Colonial Sugars Co., Gramercy, La., 1909-13; supt. and mgr. Cuban Sugar Refining Co., Cardenas, also dir. Central Control Lab. Cuban-Am. Sugar Co., 1913-23; gen. supt. Colonial Sugars Co., 1923-28, mgr., 1928-56, dir., 1950-59. Mem. sugar com. 8th Internat. Congress Applied Chemistry, N.Y., 1912; chmn. U.S. Nat. Com. on Sugar Analysis, 1953-60; del. Internat. Commn. Uniform Methods of Sugar Analysis, London, 1936, Brussels, 1949, Paris, 1954, v.p. Internat. Commn., 1954-62, hon. v.p. Internat. Commn., Hamburg, 1962, chmn. U.S. Nat. Commn., Washington, 1958. Mem. tech. adv. com. Sugar Research Found.; trustee Pub. Affairs Research Council La.; mem. Bur. Govtl. Research, New Orleans. Pres. St. James Parish (county) Sch. Bd., 1932-56. Recipient Dyer award Sugar Man of Yr., 1961; award Sugar Industry Technologists, 1963. Fellow A.A.A.S., Am. Inst. Chemists, Herpetologists League, N.Y. Acad. Scis.; mem. Am. Chem. Soc. (named man of year carbohydrate div. 1953), La. Engring. Soc., Am. Inst. Chem. Engrs., Internat. Soc. Sugar Cane Technologists (hon.), Am. Soc. Icthyologists and Herpetologists tv.p.), N.Y. Zool. Soc., S.C.V., Phi Beta Kappa, Tau Beta Pi, Alpha Chi Sigma. Democrat. Episcopalian. Clubs: Chemists (N.Y.C.); Round Table Louisiana, (New Orleans). Pres. Bone Char Research Project, Inc. 1948-49. Author: Cane Sugar Handbook 9th edit., 1963; Athletic Records: The Whys and Wherefores, 1966. Contbr. tech. articles to Indsl. and Engring. Chemistry, Internat. Sugar Jour., Sports Illustrated, Sci. Monthly, Ency. Brit., etc.; also articles on Habits of La. Harmless Snakes; Asso. editor Sugar Jour. (New Orleans), monthly column, The Proof Stick. Home: Pontchartrain Hotel New Orleans LA 70140

MEADERS, LOREN BRYCE, oil exec.; b. Richfield, Ill., Oct. 28, 1907; s. Frederick E. and Anna (Bahr) M.; student Kan. U., 1926-27, Okla. U., 1927-28, Advanced Mgmt. Program, Harvard, 1951; m. Georgia Burnett, Dec. 1, 1934 (dec.); children—John B., Thomas F.; m. 2d, Martha P. Hester, Jan. 15, 1970. Worked in oil fields, Borger,

Tex., 1927-28; with Halliburton Co. (formerly Halliburton Oil Well Cementing Co.), 1928, successively driver open-cab cement truck, supr., div. mgr. S.W. Tex. div., mgr. testing and tools dept., regional v.p., v.p. field operations, 1950-53, pres., dir., 1953—, chief exec. officer, 1963—; dir. Otis Engring. Corp., Brown & Root, Inc. Trustee Halliburton Employees Benefit Fund. Mem. Am. Petroleum Inst., Am. Inst. Mining Metall. and Petroleum Engrs., Ind. Petroleum Assn. Am., Mid-Continent Oil and Gas Assn., C. of C. Clubs: Dallas Petroleum, Dallas Country. Home: 3601 Turtle Creek Blvd Dallas TX 75219 Office: 3211 Southland Center Dallas TX 75201

MEADOR, BRUCE BARNES, newspaper exec.; b. Haskell, Tex., Aug. 27, 1910; s. Clay Bruce and Sarah (Alsbrook) M.; B.S., McMurry Coll., 1932; m. Margaret Henson, Jan. 28, 1932; 1 dau., Margie Ann (Mrs. Robert E. Shackelford). C.P.A., Abilene, Tex.; dir., vice chmn. exec. com., sec. Harte Hanks Newspapers, Inc., San Antonio; dir. Times Pub. Co., Wichita Falls, Tex., Surety Life Ins. Co., Salt Lake City. Trustee Bernard Hanks Estate, Abilene, Eva May Hanks Estate, Abilene. Mem. Am. Inst. C.P.A.'s, Tex. Soc. C.P.A.'s. Democrat. Methodist. Home: 123 Brackenridge San Antonio TX 78206 Office: PO Box 269 San Antonio TX 78291

MEADOR, CLIFTON KIRKPATRICK, physician, educator; b. Selma, Ala., Sept. 7, 1931; s. Daniel John and Mabel (Kirkpatrick) M.; B.A., (Walter O. Parmer scholar), Vanderbilt U., 1952, M.D., 1955; m. Helen Allen, June 17, 1955; children—Clifton Kirkpatrick, Aubrey Allen, Ann Graham, Elizabeth Garrett. Intern, Presbyn. Hosp., N.Y.C., 1955-56, asst. resident medicine, 1956-57; asst. resident medicine Vanderbilt U. Hosp., 1959-60; fellow endocrinology Vanderbilt U., 1960-61, instr. dept. medicine Sch. Medicine, 1960-61; practice medicine, specializing in endocrinology, Selma, 1961-62, pvt. practice; asst. prof. medicine Sch. Medicine, U. Ala., 1962-64, asso. prof., 1964-66, prof., 1966—; asst. chief-of-staff U. Ala. Hosp., 1966-68; dean Sch. Medicine, U. Ala., 1968—. Served as capt., M.C., AUS, 1957-59. Recipient Founders medal for scholastic honors Vanderbilt Sch. Medicine, 1955. John and Mary R. Markle scholar, 1963. Fellow A.C.P.; mem. Am. Diabetes Assn., Am. Fedn. for Clin. Research, Endocrine Soc., N.Y. Acad. Sci., Phi Beta Kappa, Sigma Xi, Alpha Omega Alpha. Mem. editorial bd. So. Med. Jour., 1969—. Contbr. articles profl. jours. Home: 3188 Overhill Rd Birmingham AL 35213

MEADOWS, ALGUR HURTLE, oil co. exec.; b. Vidalia, Ga., Apr. 24, 1899; s. John Morgan and Sally (Dailey) M.; grad. Centenary Coll. Law Sch., 1926, LL.D. (hon.), 1969; D.Hum., So. Meth. U., 1965; m. Virginia Garrison Stuart, Dec. 11, 1922 (dec. 1961); 1 son, Robert Al.; m. 2d, Elizabeth Boggs Bartholow, July 12, 1962. Accountant, Standard Oil Co. La., Shreveport; 1921-29; v.p. Gen. Finance Co., 1929-30, Gen. Am. Finance System, Inc., 1930-36; v.p. Gen. Am. Oil Co. Tex., 1936-41, pres., 1941-50, now chmn. bd. and exec. com.; dir. Republic Nat. Bank Dallas. Trustee So. Meth. U.; bd. dirs. St. Mark's Sch., Dallas, Wadley Research Center. Mem. Am. Petroleum Inst., Ind. Petroleum Assn. (bd. dirs.), Dallas Petroleum Club, Dallas Art Assn., Sigma Nu. Democrat. Presbyn. Mason (Shriner). Clubs: Gun, Dallas Country, Brook Hollow Golf, Preston Trails Country (Dallas); Sleepy Hollow Country (N.Y.); Jupiter Hills; Everglades, Seminole, Bath and Tennis (Palm Beach). Home: 6601 Turtle Creek Blvd Dallas TX 75205 also 261 El Bravo Way Palm Beach FL 33480 Office: Meadows Bldg Dallas TX 75206

MEADOWS, CHRISTINE, curator. Curator, Historic House & Museum, Mount Vernon, Va. Office: Mt Vernon Ladies Assn Mount Vernon VA 22121*

MEADOWS, DANIEL THOMAS, dentist; b. Salem, Ala., June 5, 1917; s. Daniel Porter and Gemmie Bruce (Browning) M.; B.S., Auburn U., 1939; D.M.D., U. Ala., 1953; m. Agatha Joan Fischer, Mar. 31, 1944; children— Gemma (Mrs. Thomas W. Stanford, Jr.), Daniel Thomas. Pvt. practice dentistry, Birmingham, Ala., 1953; resident in prosthodontics U. Ala., 1955-57; staff dentist Birmingham VA Hosp., 1954-55, 57-62, chief dental service, 1962-68, 69—. Prof. clin. dentistry U. Ala., Birmingham, 1968—. Served to col. Dental Corps, AUS, 1942-46, 68-69. Decorated Army Commendation medal with oak leaf cluster. Fellow Am. Coll. Dentists; mem. Am. Prosthodontic Soc., Am., Ala. dental assns., Am. Legion, Southeastern Acad. Prosthodontics, Birmingham Dist. Dental Soc. (exec. council 1968-72), Phi Kappa Phi, Gamma Sigma Delta, Kappa Delta Pi, Xi Psi Phi. Editor: Ala. Farmer, 1939. Home: 4309 Corinth Dr Birmingham AL 35213 Office: 700 S 19th St Birmingham AL 35233

MEADOWS, JACK E., ednl. adminstr. Mem. Ark. Bd. Edn. Office: Education Bldg Little Rock AR 72203*

MEADOWS, WILLIAM ANSE, JR., U.S. atty.; b. Goodman, Miss., June 19, 1919; s. William Anse and Willie (Rosemond) M.; B.B.A., LL.B., U. Miami (Fla.), 1949; m. Evelyn Carpenter, Dec. 25, 1941; children—Daniel William, Guy Robert. Admitted to Fla. bar, 1949; tchr. U. Miami, 1951-52; with OPS, 1951-52; asst. state atty., Miami, 1955-57; partner firm Sams, Anderson, Alper, Meadows & Spencer, Miami, 1958-60; circuit judge, Dade County, Fla., 1961-63; U.S. atty. So. Dist. Fla., 1963—. Lay leader Fla. Conf., Meth. Ch., mem. Gen. Bd. Lay Activities. Served with USMCR, 1940-45, 52-54. Fellow Internat. Acad. Trial Lawyers; mem. Am., Dade County, Fla. bar assns., Com. of 100, Phi Delta Phi. Home: 11820 SW 70th Av Miami FL 33101 Office: Post Office Bldg Miami FL 33101

MEAKIN, JOHN LEONARD, lighting products distbr.; b. Washington, Dec. 8, 1918; s. Frances Hardie and Marguerite (DeSale) M.; B.A., U. Md., 1941; m. Betty R. Korbel, Sept. 18, 1941; 1 son, John William. Commd. 2d lt. U.S. Army, 1941, advanced through grades to maj., 1956; assigned to Hdqrs. U.S. European Command, Heidelberg, Germany, 1950-53, Office Dep. Chief Staff Logistics, Dept. Army, 1954-56; resigned, 1956; commd. col. Res., 1967; exec. v.p. Mason Mortgage & Investment Corp., Washington, 1955-61; gen. mgr. Reed A. Thursby & Co., St. Petersburg, Fla., 1961; owner, pres. Howlen Assos., Inc., St. Petersburg, 1961-63; v.p. Hardee's Food Systems, Inc., Rocky Mount, N.C., 1963-68, Unico Corp., Virginia Beach, Va., 1968-70; owner Eterna S of Tidewater, Norfolk, Va., 1970—. Mem. Am. Drive-In Operators' Assn. (pres. 1970), Aircraft Owners and Pilots Assn., Eastern Carolina Airmen's Assn. Republican. Presbyn. Home: 504 Sandy Valley Ct Virginia Beach VA 23452 Office: 4991 Cleveland St Virginia Beach VA 23462

MEALING, ISABEL THORPE, social worker; b. Townsend, Ga., Oct. 4, 1907; d. Elisha McDonald and Maude (Davis) Thorpe; student Ga. State Tchrs. Coll., 1924-26; A.B., Randolph-Macon Woman's Coll., 1928; M.S.W., Tulane U., 1943; postgrad. U. Va., 1929; m. John Pace Mealing, Jr., Aug. 15, 1929 (div. Dec. 1939); children—Elisha Thorpe, Margaret Mae (Mrs. Wayne Frederick Orlowski). Visitor Fulton County Dept. Pub. Welfare, Atlanta, 1937-38; dir. McIntosh County Dept. Pub. Welfare, Darien, Ga., 1938-40; child welfare cons. State of Ga., Atlanta, 1941-44; social worker A.R.C., Lawson Gen. Hosp., Atlanta, 1944-45; asst. field dir. Lawson Gen. Hosp., and Station Hosp., Ft. Benning, Ga., 1945-46; chief social work service VA Regional Office, Ft. Jackson, S.C., 1947-48; pub. welfare officer Dept. Army, Japan, 1949-51; sr. social worker Valley Forge Army Hosp., 1951; chief social work service VA Hosp., Richmond, Va., 1951-52, VA Center, Wadsworth, Kan., 1952-68, Dublin, Ga., 1968—. Mem. Social Planning Council, Leavenworth, Kan., 1952-68, v.p., 1955-56, 67-68, pres., 1956-57; bd. dirs. A.R.C., Leavenworth, Kan., 1960-68; bd. govs. United Fund, Leavenworth, 1967-68; bd. dirs. YWCA, Leavenworth, 1962-68, pres., 1964-65; chmn. welfare com. Mayor's Adv. Com., Leavenworth, 1968; mem. organizational bd. Leavenworth Community Action Program, 1966; adviser Explorer Scouts Am., 1972; bd. dirs. Dublin Mental Health Assn., v.p., 1972—. Mem. Nat. Assn. Social Workers (exec. bd. Mo.-Kan. chpt. 1954-56, pres. central Ga. chpt. 1970-71, del. to assembly 1971), Am. Assn. Med. Social Workers (pres. Mo.-Kan. chpt. 1954-55), Nat., Internat., Ga. (nominating com. 1945) confs. on social welfare, Daus. Am. Colonists, Colonial Dames, Dublin Social Workers Club (pres. 1971-72). Address: VA Center Dublin GA 31021

MEANS, CRAIG RAY, educator; b. Shreveport, La., Aug. 16, 1922; s. Frank Alvin and Marie Evelyn (Washington) M.; student Howard U., 1946-48, D.D.S., 1954; B.S., So. U., 1950; M.S., Ohio State U., 1962. 1 dau., Stephanie Claire. Pvt. practice dentistry, Salisbury, Md., 1955-59, Camden, N.J., 1959-61; asst. prof. removable prosthodontics Howard U., Washington, 1961-66, asso. prof., chem. dept., 1966-70, prof., asso. dean. undergrad. affairs, 1970—; dental intern Freedmen's Hosp., Washington, 1954-55; resident maxillofacial prosthetics Meml. Hosp. for Cancer, N.Y.C., 1963-64. Served with AUS, 1941-45. Louise C. Ball Fund fellow, 1962-64. Fellow Am. Coll. Dentists; mem. Am., Nat. dental assns., Am. Prosthodontic Soc., Am. Assn. Dental Schs., C.O. Boucher Prosthodontic Conf., Omicron Kappa Upsilon. Editor newsletter Howard U. Dental Alumni, 1968—. Contbr. articles to profl. publs. Home: 6101 16th St NW Washington DC 20011

MEANS, ERNEST, govt. ofcl. Sec. ex-officio Legislation Commn. for Promotion of Uniformity in Law, State of Fla. Office: Holland Bldg Tallahassee FL 32304*

MEANS, MARIANNE HANSEN, polit. columnist; b. Sioux City, Ia., June 13, 1934; d. Ernest Maynard and Else Marie Johanne (Andersen) Hansen; B.A., U. Neb., 1956. Copy editor Lincoln (Neb.) Jour., 1955-57; woman's editor No. Va. Sun, Arlington, 1957-59; Washington bur. corr. Hearst Headline Service, 1959-61, White House corr., 1961-65; polit. columnist King Features Syndicate, 1965—. Mem. D.C. Woman's Savs. Bond Com., 1959-62. Recipient Front Page award N.Y. Newspaper Women, 1962. Mem. White House Corrs. Assn., Phi Beta Kappa, Delta Delta Delta, Theta Sigma Phi, Kappa Tau Alpha, Gamma Alpha Phi. Club: Washington Press. Author: The Woman in the White House, 1963. Home: 1521 31st St NW Washington DC 20007 Office: 1701 Pennsylvania Av Washington DC 20006

MEANS, WILLIAM WALTER, judge; b. Sand Springs, Okla., Mar. 29, 1933; s. Paul Willard and Marie (Conkey) M.; student U. Okla., 1951-53, 55-57; J.D., U. Tulsa, 1961; m. Mary Ellen Faulkner, Aug. 6, 1960; children—Karl W., Karen A. Admitted to Okla. bar, 1961; practice law, Tulsa, 1961-62; asst. dist. atty., Tulsa, 1962-66; chief civil asst. dist. atty., Tulsa, 1966-67; judge Ct. Common Pleas, Tulsa, 1967-68; asso. judge, 14th dist., Tulsa, 1969-71, dist. judge, 1971—. Served with AUS, 1953-55. Mem. Am., Okla., Tulsa County bar assns. Presbyn. Kiwanian. Home: 5519 S Marion St Tulsa OK 74135 Office: Tulsa County Court House Tulsa OK 74103

MEANY, DAN, geologist. Trustee, Nat. Conf. Christians and Jews. Address: 1201 Lantana Corpus Christi TX 78407*

MEANY, GEORGE, labor ofcl.; b. N.Y.C., Aug. 16, 1894; s. Michael Joseph and Anne (Cullen) M.; ed. pub. and high sch., N.Y.C.; recipient of numerous honorary degrees; m. Eugenia A. McMahon, Nov. 26, 1919; children—Regina Clare (Mrs. Robert C. Mayer), Eileen (Mrs. Ernest S. Lee), Genevieve (Mrs. John S. Lutz). Began career as apprentice plumber, 1910, journeyman plumber, 1915; business rep. Plumbers Local Union No. 463, N.Y.C., 1922-34; pres. N.Y. State Fedn. of Labor, 1934-39; sec.-treas. AFL, 1940-52, pres. from 1952; pres. new combined orgn. AFL-CIO, 1955—. Mem. Nat. War Labor Bd., 1942—. Del. 12th, 14th Gen. Assembly UN. Democrat. Catholic. Home: 8819 Burdette Rd Bethesda MD 20034 Office: AFL-CIO Washington DC 20006

MEARS, ALLEN LAVERN, JR., county agt.; b. Haynesville, La., Dec. 18, 1925; s. Allen Lavern and Icy (Martin) M.; B.S., La. State U., 1951, M.S., 1962; postgrad. U. Ark., 1955; m. Joyce Cockrell, June 24, 1951; children—James, John. Asst. county agt. Webster Parish, Minden, La., 1951-53, county agt., area livestock agt., 1967—; asst. county agt. Beauregard Parish, De Ridder, La., 1953-66; asso. county agt. Caddo Parish, Shreveport, La., 1966-67. Served with AUS, 1945-46; PTO. Mem. Farm Bur. (dir.), Cattlemens Assn. (dir.), Hog Marketing Assn. (dir.), Cattle and Pasture Demonstration (dir.), Feed and Pig Assn. (dir.), County Agt. Assn., Hon. Coop. Extension Orgn., V.F.W., Am. Legion. Mason. Club: Civitan (Minden). Home: 910 Nella St Minden LA 71055 Office: Box 836 Minden LA 71055

MEARS, J. HOLMES, JR., food co. exec.; b. Milw., Aug. 28, 1922; s. J. Holmes and Rebecca (Glenn) M.; student Tulane U., 1943-46; m. Fern Wingerter, Feb. 22, 1969. Treas., Carver Foods Co., Houston, 1955—; sec. Patio Confections, Inc. Mgr. Carver Found.; trustee Employees Profit-Sharing Trust. Served with USNR, 1945-47. Mem. Quill and Scroll. Democrat. Episcopalian. Office: PO Box 2101 Houston TX 77001

MEBS, RUSSELL WILLIAM, ret. physicist; b. Columbus, O., Feb. 21, 1906; s. George Henry and Myrtle (Clevenger) M.; B.E.E., Ohio State U., 1927, M.Sc., 1932, Ph.D., 1940; m. Elizabeth Haseltine, Mar. 20, 1934. Grad. engring. student Westinghouse Electric Co., East Pittsburgh, Pa., 1927-28; research engr. Stackpole Carbon Co., St. Marys, Pa., 1928-30; research engr. Union Switch & Signal Co., Swissvale, Pa., 1930-31; metallurgist, solid state physicist Nat. Bur. Standards, Washington, 1935-72. Recipient George Kimball Burgess Meml. award, 1960. Fellow Washington Acad. Scis.; mem. Am. Soc. for Metals, Washington Soc. Engrs. Home: 6620 32d St N Arlington VA 22213

MECKLER, GERSHON, profl. engr.; b. Bklyn., Jan. 27, 1927; s. Morris and Irma (Herring) M.; B.S., Pa. State U., 1949; m. Nina Tanenbaum, June 29, 1952; children—Eileen Susan, Marcia Ann, Jeffrey Elliot. Sr. mech. project engr. Voorhees, Walker, Smith & Smith, Architects, N.Y.C., 1951-55; chief mech. engr. Samborn, Steketee and Assos., Engrs. and Architects, Toledo, 1955-57; owner Meckler Engring. Co., Cons. Engrs., Toledo, 1957-62; sr. partner Meckler-Hoertz & Assos., Engrs. and Architects, Toledo, 1962-64; pres. Space Conditioning Corp., Toledo, 1963-64; v.p. Lithonia Lighting, Inc., Conyers, Ga., 1964-68, Environmental Systems Corp., Conyers; pres. Bldg. Dynamics, Inc., Atlanta, 1968—; pres. Bldg. Research Inst., Washington; dir. Rusco Industries, Los Angeles. Cons. H.H. Robertson Co., Inland Steel Co., Westinghouse Electric Corp. Mem. bldg. research adv. bd. NRC-Nat. Acad. Scis. Mem. Mayors Com. on New Devel., Toledo, 1964. Served with USNR, 1945-46. Registered profl. engr., Conn., Ga., Ill., Ind., Mich., Ohio, Pa., W.Va.; holder certificate of qualification Nat. Council Engring. Examiners. Mem. Illuminating Engring. Soc., Am. Soc. Heating, Refrigerating and Air Conditioning Engrs., Bldg. Research Inst., Am. Phys. Soc., Am. Inst. Physics, Nat. Soc. Profl. Engrs., Nat. Acad. Scis. (fed. constrn. council). Jewish religion. Mason (32 deg., Shriner). Patentee thermoelectric luminaire. Home: 2750 Ridge Valley Rd NW Atlanta GA 30327 Office: 2750 Ridge Valley Rd NW Atlanta GA 30327

MECOM, JOHN E., JR., pres. New Orleans Saints Football Team. Office: 944 St Charles St New Orleans LA 70130*

MECOM, JOHN WHITFIELD, ind. oil producer; b. El Paso, Jan. 13, 1911; s. Harvey Mercer and Louise (Elam) M.; student Rice U., 1927, U. Okla., 1928-31; m. Mary Elizabeth Withers, May 14, 1937; children— John Whitfield, Betsy, Lannie. Propr. John W. Mecom, ind. oil producer, Houston, 1938—; owner Cardwell Mfg. Co., Wichita, Kan., 1954—, U.S. Oil of La., Houston and New Orleans, 1954—, Boonton Plastic Co. (N.J.), 1954—, Gran Hotel, Houston, 1962—, Keystone Drug Co., Houston, 1960—; part owner Reed Roller Bit Co., Houston, 1960—; dir. Tex. Commerce Bank N.A., Houston; chmn. bd., chief exec. officer, 1966. Gov. adviser Rice U. Mem. Sigma Alpha Epsilon. Democrat. Episcopalian. Clubs: Houston Country, River Oaks Country, Ramada (Houston); Boston (New Orleans). Home: 2960 Lazy Lane Houston TX 77019 Office: 1500 Gray St Houston TX 77002*

MEDCALF, WINFRED LOUIS, physician; b. Tecumseh, Okla., Oct. 21, 1928; s. Reat Ira and Anna Mae (Edwards) M.; A.A., Pasadena City Coll., 1950; B.S., Okla. State U., 1954; M.D., U. Okla., 1957; postgrad. Southwestern Bapt. Theol. Sem., 1959-60; m. Patricia Sue Hensley, June 18, 1950; children—Paul Ira, Timothy Wayne, Pamela Sue, Valerie Louise, Michael Louis. Intern, Mercy Hosp., Oklahoma City, 1957-58, resident in surgery, 1958-59; practice medicine specializing in gen. practice, Marlow, Okla., 1959-60, 63-64, 67-68, practice limited to arthritis and internal medicine Arthritis Clinic, Ardmore, Okla., 1968—; apptd. first med. missionary to Thailand by So. Bapts., 1959-67, established Bangkla (Thailand) Bapt. Hosp., 1964; mem. staffs Mercy Hosp., Oklahoma City, Talley-Walker Hosp., Marlow, Meml. Hosp., Ardmore, Ardmore Seventh Day Adventist Hosp. Coach, Little League Baseball, 1969-70; pack dir. Cub Scouts, 1968-69. Served with AUS, 1946-48. Mem. Am., Okla. med. assns., Tri-County Med. Soc., Okla. Arthritis Found., Am. Rheumatism Assn. Democrat. Baptist. Home: 421 Monroe St NW Ardmore OK 73401 Office: 207 C St NW Ardmore OK 73401

MEDFORD, BENJAMIN SAVAGE, musician, ret. educator; b. Oxford, N.C., Nov. 4, 1906; s. John Joseph and Mary (Savage) M.; B.A., Radford Coll., 1947; M.S., Va. Poly. Inst., 1953. Tchr., pianist on radio, in concert; prof. music Radford (Va.) Coll., 1936-72. Served with USNR, 1942-46. Mem. Am. Assn. U. Profs., Am. Radio Relay League, Va. Music Tchrs. Assn. Episcopalian. Address: Windsor Hill Radford VA 24141

MEDFORD, FRANK ELDRIDGE, physician; b. Asheville, N.C., July 18, 1935; s. Clarence Columbus and Madell Elizabeth (Hardin) M.; B.S., Wake Forest Coll., 1957; M.D., Bowman Gray Sch. Medicine, 1961; m. Eva Sharon Phillips, Oct. 27, 1962; 1 dau. Cheryl Dawn. Intern, Charleston (W.Va.) Meml. Hosp., 1961-62, resident, 1962-65; fellow W. Va. U. Hosp., Morgantown, 1964-65; med. dir. Tech. Center, Union Carbide Corp., South Charleston, W. Va., 1965-68; practice medicine, specializing in internal medicine, Newport News, Va., 1968—; mem. staff Riverside Hosp., Newport News. Diplomate Am. Bd. Internal Medicine, Nat. Bd. Med. Examiners. Mem. Newport News Med. Soc. Home: 106 Sandpiper St Newport News VA 23602 Office: 316 Main St Newport News VA 23601

MEDLEN, AMMON BROWN, educator; b. Lockhart, Tex., Sept. 12, 1908; s. Robert Milton and Caledonia Frances (Brown) M.; B.A., Baylor U., 1930, M.A., 1932; Ph.D., Tex. A. and M. U., 1952; m. Sue Myrtle Williams, June 6, 1936; children—Robert Byron, Suzanne Isabelle. Instr., Baylor U., 1932-34; tchr. prin. pub. schs., Tex., 1935-40; asst. prof. Ouachita Coll., 1940-43; instr. U. Houston, 1946; instr. dir. Tex. A. and M. Coll., 1946-41; asst. prof., 1951-54, asso. prof., 1954-65; prof., head biology dept. Tarleton State Coll., Stephenville, Tex., 1965—. Served with USNR, 1942-45. Fellow Tex. Acad. Scis.; mem. A.A.A.S., Am. Assn. U. Profs., N.Y. Acad. Scis., Am. Soc. Zoologists, Sigma Xi, Beta Beta Beta. Lion (pres. 1955-56, dep. dist. gov. 1956-57). Home: 881 Rome Av Stephenville TX 76401

MEDLEY, PAUL, JR., librarian; b. San Angelo, Tex., Mar. 9, 1936; s. Paul and Lucille (Cauble) M.; B.A., So. Meth. U., 1958; M.S. in L.S., U. Tex., 1969, postgrad. Law Sch., 1961-62; m. Margaret Sue Robbins, Sept. 30, 1960; children—Mark, Marshall. With Vari-Typer Corp., Austin, Tex., 1962-64; library asst. U. Tex. Library, Austin, 1964-66; pub. services librarian Abilene (Tex.) Pub. Library, 1966-67; dir. Waco-McLennan County Library, Waco, Tex., 1967—. Team capt. local United Fund. Pres., dir. W. Tex. Library Film Circuit. Mem. Am., Tex., Southwestern, Waco (pres.) library assns. Rotarian. Home: 1717 Mountainview Dr Waco TX 76710 Office: 1717 Austin Av Waco TX 76701

MEDLOCK, THOMAS TRAVIS, lawyer, state legislator; b. Joanna, S.C., Aug. 28, 1934; s. Melvin Kelly and Mayme (DuBose) M.; A.B., Wofford Coll., 1956; LL.B., U. S.C., 1959; m. Laura Virginia Orr, Oct. 11, 1969. Admitted to S.C. bar, 1959; asso. atty. Roberts, Jennings, Thomas & Lumpkin, Columbia, 1959-61; asst. atty. gen. for S.C., 1961-62; partner Lumpkin, Kemmerlin & Medlock, Columbia, 1962-67; individual practice law, Columbia, 1967-69; partner Medlock, Rentz & Anders, Columbia, 1969—; mem. S.C. Ho. of Reps., 1964—. Vice pres. S.C. Adv. Com. on Children and Youth, 1967—; mem. S.C. Tri-Centennial Commn., Columbia Youth Commn. Active Boy Scouts Am.; pres., dir., United Cerebral Palsy of Midlands, S.C., 1963—; bd. dirs. Meth. Bethlehem Community Center, Columbia, 1964—, S.C. Coffee House; founder, chmn. Richland Housing Found. Served with AUS, 1957. Mem. Columbia C. of C., Blue Key, Phi Beta Kappa, Kappa Sigma, Pi Gamma Mu. Democrat. Methodist (ofcl. bd.). Club: Civitan (dir. 1966—). Home: 1012 Duke Av Columbia SC 29204 Office: 1340 Pickens St Columbia SC 29201

MEDWEDEFF, FERDINAND MARSHALL, dentist; b. Flint, Mich., Nov. 20, 1926; s. Marshall Herbert and Elsie Ella (Miller) M.; student Mich. State Coll., 1944-45; B.S., U. Mich., 1949; D.D.S., Emory U., 1954; m. Joan Lenore Kampmeier, June 17, 1950; children—Carol, Linda, John. Jr. health officer Tenn. Dept. Pub. Health, 1954-55; pvt. practice dentistry, Nashville, 1955—; asst. clin. prof. Vanderbuilt U. Med. Staff, 1955—; founder, pres. Precision X-Ray Co., 1964. Served with USAAF, 1945. Recipient 1st award in sci. exhibit Am. Dental Assn., 1963. Fellow Am. Acad. Dental Radiology. Contbr. articles to profl. jours. Patentee in field. Home: 4505 Wayland Dr Nashville TN 37215 Office: 21st and Hayes Med Bldg Nashville TN 37203

MEECE, O'LEARY MELROSE, supt. schs.; b. nr. Somerset, Ky., Mar. 20, 1911; s. George Linville and Eva E. (Silvers) M.; A.B., Western Ky. U., 1938; M.A., U. Ky., 1948; m. Marjorie Elaine Sears,

June 23, 1942; 1 dau., Anne Louise (Mrs. Charles Bennett Farris). Elementary tchr. Pulaski County Schs., 1933-35; elementary prin. Somerset (Ky.) Pub. Schs., 1936-39; secondary tchr. Somerset High Sch., 1939-42, 47-50; dir. instrn. Somerset Pub. Schs., 1950-54, supr., 1954—. Bd. mgrs. Ky. P.T.A. Served with USAAF, 1942-47. Decorated Bronze Star medal with 2 oak leaf clusters. Mem. Ky. (dir.), Middle Cumberland Dist. (sec.) edn. assns., Am. Legion, Phi Delta Kappa. Methodist (trustee). Rotarian. Contbr. articles profl. jours. Home: 306 College St Somerset KY 42501 Office: Somerset Schs College St Somerset KY 42501

MEEK, PAUL D., oil and chem. co. exec.; b. McAllen, Tex., 1930; grad. U. Tex. at Austin, 1953. Pres., dir. Cosden Oil && Chem. Co., Big Spring, Tex.; v.p., dir. Cos-Mar, Inc.; v.p., dir. Am. Petrofina, Inc. Mem. Am. Inst. Chem. Engrs., Am. Petroleum Inst., Am. Inst. Chemists. Office: Box 1311 Big Spring TX 79720

MEEKER, CHARLES RUTHERFORD, JR., mgmt. cons.; b. Parkersburg, W.Va., Apr. 30, 1913; s. Charles R. and Estella (Tate) M.; student So. Meth. U., 1932-36; m. Doris Alton Shaw, Feb. 4, 1939; 1 son, Charles Rutherford III. With Interstate Theaters, 1936-44, successively publicity dir. Palace and Majestic Theatres, Dallas, mgr. State Theater, Amarillo, asst. city mgr. Dallas theaters; mgr. dir. State Fair Musicals, Dallas, 1944-59, v.p., 1951-59; gen. mgr. Cary Schneider Investment Corp., 1961-62; cons. to pres. Gt. S.W. Corp. and Six Flags over Tex., 1961-71; chief exec. officer Teen Am. Assos., also producer Miss Teenage Am. Pageant, 1962-71; pres. Miss Teenage Am., Inc., 1968—; gen. partner Charles R. Meeker, Jr. & Assos., 1968—; cons., chmn. bd. Cedar Point, Inc., Sandusky, O., 1968—; cons., pres. Dr. Pepper Co., Dallas; cons., gen. mgr. Seven Seas, Arlington, Tex.; dir. Hillcrest State Bank; cons. Carter Properties, Dallas. Bd. dirs. Dallas Lighthouse for Blind. Mem. Christian Ch. Clubs: Salesmanship, Dallas Country, Conferie Des Chevaliers Du Tastevin, Cipango, Les Amis d'Escoffier. Author articles in field. Home: Park Towers 3310 Fairmount Dallas TX 75201 Office: 1165 Empire Central Place Dallas TX 75247

MEEKER, LEONARD CARPENTER, lawyer, ambassador; b. Montclair, N.J., Apr. 4, 1916; s. Irving Avard and Elizabeth Louise (Carpenter) M.; grad. Deerfield Acad., 1933; A.B., Amherst Coll., 1937; LL.B. Harvard, 1940; m. Christine Rhoda Halliday, Sept. 27, 1947 (dec. Feb. 1958); children—Richard Halliday, Charles Carpenter, Sarah Louise; m. 2d, Beverly Joan Meeker, June 14, 1969; 1 dau., Eliza Ann Hunt. Admitted to D.C. bar, 1940, Cal. bar, 1941; with Office Gen. Counsel, Treasury Dept. Wash., 1940-41, Office Solicitor Gen., Dept. Justice, Washington, 1941-42; with Office Legal Adviser, Dept. State, Washington, 1946-51, asst. legal adviser, 1951-61, dep. legal adviser, 1961-65, legal adviser, 1965-69; ambassador to Rumania, 1969—. Trustee Potomac Sch., 1959-67, chmn., 1960-63. Mem. Am., Fed. bar assns., Am. Soc. Internat. Law, St. Nicholas Soc. City of N.Y. Home: 3000 Chain Bridge Rd NW Washington DC 20016 Office: Am Embassy Bucharest Rumania

MEER, KURT, broadcasting exec. Pres. WMQM, Memphis. Office: 272 S Main St Memphis TN 38103*

MEFFEN, JAMES DOUGLAS, educator; b. N.Y.C., Aug. 7, 1927; s. James Douglas and Edith (Anderson) M.; A.B., Gordon Coll., 1949; S.T.B., Harvard, 1951; M.A., Suffolk U., 1957; Ed.D., Calvin Coolidge U., 1959; H.H.D., Arubaanse Handels Academie, 1970; m. Ruth Freer, 1948; children—James Douglas III, David Mark, Melodee Joy, LaMarre Cherie; m. 2d, Janet Searles, 1960; children—Faith, Martha, Scott, Alison; m. 3d, Jean Mutschler, 1972. Ordained to ministry Christian Ch. (Congl. Christian), 1951; minister Christian chs., West Mansfield, Mass., 1950-51, Hallandale, Fla., 1954-55, Boston, 1955-56; chaplain S. Fla. State Hosp., West Hollywood, 1957-58; prin. Deerborne Sch., Coral Gables, Fla., 1959-63; adminstr. of Coral Gables Acad. and Inst. Reading, 1963—. Cons., United Cerebral Palsy; field cons. Commn. on High Quality Tchr. Edn. of Internat. Reading Assn., 1971. Served from 1st lt. to capt., chaplain USAF, 1951-54. Fellow Am. Orthopsychiat. Assn.; mem. Nat. Assn. for Retarded Children, Assn. for Children with Learning Disabilities, Am. Assn. on Mental Deficiency, Am. Personnel and Guidance Assn., Nat. Vocational Guidance Assn., Assn. for Measurement and Evaluation in Guidance, Am. Sch. Counsellor Assn., Internat. Reading Assn., Am. Pub. Health Assn., Internat. Platform Assn., Am. Coll. Personnel Assn., Nat. Assn. Secondary Sch. Prins., Council for Exceptional Children, Am. Legion, D.A.V. Democrat. Home: 2925 SW 106th Av Miami FL 33165 Office: 7700 Miller Rd Miami FL 33155

MEFFERT, GEORGE HENRY, profl. engr.; b. Arlington, Minn., Apr. 4, 1907; s. Henry Conrad and Johanna (Duehimeier) M.; B.C.E., U. Minn., 1930; m. Alice Denny, Sept. 6, 1945; children—Nancy, Joanne, Marsha. Sales engr. Carrier Air Conditioning Co., various locations, 1930-36; chief engr. Carrier Bock Corp., Dallas, 1936-42, Martin-Johnson Engring. Co., Dallas, 1946-49, Roscoe DeWitt, Architect, Dallas, 1949-69; project engr. Tippetts-Abbett-McCarthy-Stratton, Engrs., Arlington, Tex., 1969-70; project engr. Ratliff-Purdy-McGuire, Cons. Engrs., Dallas, 1971—. Bd. dirs. Central Bus. Dist. Assn., Dallas, 1961. Served to lt. comdr. USNR, 1942-46; PTO. Registered profl. engr., Tex. Mem. Am. Soc. Heating, Refrigerating, and Air Conditioning Engrs. (recipient Distinguished Service award, 1967; past chpt. pres.), Nat., Tex. socs. profl. engrs., Engrs. Club Dallas, Scabbard & Blade, Triangle, Chi Epsilon. Lutheran. Home: 3328 Greenbrier Dr Dallas TX 75225 Office: 4300 Sigma Rd Dallas TX 75234

MEGARGEE, EDWIN INGLEE, psychologist, educator; b. Plainfield, N.J., Feb. 27, 1937; s. S. Edwin and Jean (Inglee) M.; B.A. magna cum laude, Amherst Coll., 1958; Ph.D., U. Cal. at Berkeley, 1964; m. Ann Therese Piemonte, Aug. 1, 1959; children—Elyn Jean, Edwin Inglee, Christopher John, Stephen Andrew. Clin. psychologist Alameda County Probation Dept., San Leandro, Cal., 1961-64; asst. prof. dept. psychology U. Tex., Austin, 1964-67; asso. prof. psychology dept. Fla. State U., Tallahassee, 1967-70, prof., 1970—, also dir. splty. tng. program in psychology of crime and delinquency; cons. psychologist Fed. Correctional Instn., Tallahassee, 1967—. Cons. Nat. Commn. on Causes and Prevention of Violence, 1968-69, U.S. Secret Service, 1968, Nat. Inst. Mental Health, 1968—, Hogg Found. for Mental Health, 1965-67. Fellow Soc. Personality Assessment (finance com.), Am. Sociol. Assn.; mem. Am. Psychol. Assn., Am. Assn. Correctional Psychologists (pres. elect), Phi Beta Kappa, Sigma Xi, Delta Sigma Rho. Club: Killearn Country. Author 2 books. Editor FCI Research Reports, also 2 books; asso. editor Jour. Abnormal Child Psychology; cons. editor Jour. Personality Assessment, Jour. Criminal Law, Criminology and Police Sci. Contbr. articles to profl. jours. Home: 2241 Monaghan Dr Tallahassee FL 32303

MEGLA, GERHARD KARL, elec. engr.; b. Berlin, Germany, Jan. 22, 1918; s. Karl Franz and Margarete (Behrens) B.; B.S., U. Berlin, 1938, M.S., 1940; Ph.D. in Engring., Tech. U., Dresden, Germany, 1955; m. Wiltrud Engelmann, Feb. 19, 1942; 1 dau., Cornelia. Came to U.S., 1960, naturalized, 1965. Design engr. group mgr., head microwave lab., C. Lorenz AG, Berlin, 1939-47; dir. research and devel. Sachenwork, Radeberg, Germany, 1947 55; prof., dir. high frequency tech. Tech. U., Ilmenau, Germany, 1955-59; sr. sci. engr. Martin Co., Orlando, Fla., 1960-61; sr. scientist Hoffman Electronics Co., Santa Barbara, Cal., 1961-63; research mgr. Corning Glass Works, Raleigh, N.C., 1963-66, dir. research lab., 1966—; prof. elec. engring. N.C. State, U. N.C., 1964—. Fellow I.E.E.E.; mem. Optical Soc. Am. Author: Transmission of Information with Ultra High Frequencise, 1954; Microwave Theory and Techniques, 5th edit., 1961; Structure of Information, 1961; articles in Am. and German sci. jours. Home: 3029 Randolph Dr Raleigh NC 27609 Office: 3800 Electronics Dr Raleigh NC 27604

MEGOW, LAWRENCE FREDRICK, steel fabricator; b. Corlis, Wis., Feb. 19, 1910; s. Fritz Louis and Anna Marie (Briesemeister) M.; student U. Wis., 1928-32, Stephen F. Austin U., 1965-67, U. Houston, 1962—; m. Sylvia Winifred Pleva, July 8, 1933; children—Barbara (Mrs. Louis Basile), Carol (Mrs. Odis Echols), Ronald, Donald. Clk. to factory mgr. A.O. Smith Corp., 1928-54; with Hahn & Clay, Houston, 1955—, v.p. charge prodn., 1963—. Tchr., Marquette U., World War II. Bd. dirs. Space Hall of Fame. Commd. adm. Tex Navy, 1971. Recipient certificate for achievement in oceanography State of Tex., 1970. Mem. Am. Welding Soc. (past chmn. Houston sect.), U.S. Naval Inst., Am. Ordnance Assn. (past chmn. S. Tex. sect.), Marine Tech. Soc., Am. Oceanographic Soc., Soc. Tech. Writers and Publs., Houston Engring. and Sci. Soc., Houston C. of C., Am. Rocket Soc. (past chmn.), Rocket Research and Devel. Soc., Deep Submersible Pilots Assn. (hon.), Kappa Tau Alpha, Engrs. Club Houston. Roman Catholic. Editor: Slide Rule, 1967-69. Contbr. articles to profl. jours. Home: 3342 Arbor St Houston TX 77004 Office: 5100 Clinton Dr Houston TX 77020

MEHAFFEY, EUGENE LEE, dir. athletics; b. Bklyn., Nov. 18, 1932; s. Charlie D. and Josephine (Lee) M.; A.A., Tenn. Wesleyan Jr. Coll., 1952; B.S., So. Meth. U., 1954; M.S., Ind. U., 1955, Doctorate in Phys. Edn., 1966; m. Barbara Jane Wilson, June 11, 1967; 1 dau., Melodie Michelle. Asst. basketball coach Bristol (Tenn.) High Sch., 1955-56; coach, tchr. Big Stone Gap (Va.) High Sch., 1958; head basketball coach, athletic dir. Parry McCluer High Sch., Buena Vista, Va., 1958-62; asst. basketball coach U. Va., 1962-67; head basketball coach, athletic dir., chmn. phys. edn. dept. Carson-Newman Coll., Jefferson City, Tenn., 1967—. Served with AUS, 1956-58. Mem. Nat. Assn. Basketball Coaches, A.A.H.P.E.R., Phi Delta Kappa. Office: Box 2021 Carson-Newman Coll Jefferson City TN 37760

MEHAFFY, PAT, circuit judge; b. Little Rock, Oct. 8, 1904; s. Thomas Miller and Annie (Poe) M.; student Hendrix Coll.; LL.B., Ark. Law Sch., 1927; m. Kathryn Kurtz, June 4, 1932; children—Thomas Michael, Kathryn. Admitted to Ark. bar, 1927; asst. atty. gen., 1929-34; chief dep. pros. atty., 1934-38; pros. atty. 6th Jud. Dist. of Ark., 1939-40; practiced in Little Rock; circuit judge U.S. Ct. of Appeals for 8th Circuit, Little Rock, 1963—. Dir., mem. exec. com. First Nat. Bank of Little Rock. Lectr. torts and criminal law Ark. Law Sch., 1947-50; chmn. appeal bd. SSS. Democratic nat. committeeman 1960-63. Mem. Am. Trial Lawyers Assn. Home: Westriver Apts Little Rock AR 72202 Office: Federal Bldg Little Rock AR 72201

MEHALLIS, GEORGE, educator; b. Wheeling, W.Va., Feb. 14, 1923; s. Gus and Eva (Bizakis) M.; B.S., Ohio State U., 1945, M.A., 1948, Ph.D., 1963; m. Rita Jane Gaddy, Apr. 23, 1957; children—Constance West, George. Tchr., Ashtabula (O.) Harbor High Sch., 1945-48, Miami Beach (Fla.) Sr. High Sch., 1948-50; asst. prof. indsl. edn. U. Miami, 1950-56, asso. prof., 1956-60, chmn. dept. indsl. edn., 1961-64; instr. Ohio State U., 1960-61; dir. tech.-vocational studies Miami (Fla.)-Dade Jr. Coll., 1964—. Mem. Fla. State Supts. Adv. Council Indsl. Arts, 1963-68; cons. Am. Assn. Jr. Colls.; mem. com. occupational edn. instns. So. Assn. Colls. and Schs.; mem. editorial adv. bd. Prakken Publs.; cons. Gen. Learning Corp., 1968-70. Chmn., Occupational Program Coordinating Council Dade County, 1971. Served with USNR, 1942-44. Mem. Am. (pres. 1971-72), Fla. tech. edn. assns., Am., Fla. vocational assns., Am. Indsl. Arts Assn., Nat. Aerospace Edn. Council, Greater Miami Aviation Assn., Phi Delta Kappa, Kappa Delta Pi, Epsilon Pi Tau. Contbr. articles to profl. jours. Home: 614 Aledo Av Coral Gables FL 33134 Office: 11380 NW 27th Av Miami FL 33167

MEHEARG, LILLIEN ERL (MRS. GEORGE E. VOLZ), psychologist, educator; b. Parkdale, Ark.; d. Thomas Albert and Lillie (Massey) Mehearg; B.A., Millsaps Coll., 1957; M.A., La. State U., 1958; Ph.D., U. So. Miss., 1963; m. George E. Volz, Jan. 2, 1956 (dec. 1959). Intern psychology N.Y. State Dept. Mental Hygiene, Poughkeepsie, 1959-60; psychologist, dir. Lake Charles (La.) Mental Health Center, 1960-61; psychologist, research dir. Hammond (La.) Mental Health Center, also coordinator Region VII Mental Health Planning Council, also chief psychologist Hammond State Sch. Retarded, 1962-64; asst. prof. U. So. Miss., Hattiesburg, 1964-65, asso. prof., 1965-68, prof., 1968—, dir. Psychol. Clinic, 1964—, dir. psychol. tng., 1966—. Cons. VA, Family Cts., various state agys. Chmn. Miss. Bd. Psychol. Examiners. Mem. Am., Miss., Southeastern, Southwestern psychol. assns., A.A.A.S., Assn. Advancement Behavioral Therapies, Psi Chi, Phi Kappa Phi. Home: 3601 Morningside Dr Hattiesburg MS 39401

MEHRTENS, WILLIAM OSBORNE, judge; b. Savannah, Ga., Jan. 24, 1906; s. Leo W. and Cornelia (Millen) M.; LL.B., U. Fla., 1932; m. Jaime H. Hancock, Nov. 4, 1936; 1 son, William Osborne. Admitted to Fla. bar, 1932; mem. firm Mershon, Sawyer, Johnston, Dunwody, Mehrtens & Cole, 1933-42, partner, 1945-65; now judge U.S. Dist. Ct. Fla. Mem. Fla. Supreme Ct. Permanent Adv. Com. on Appellate Rules, 1958—. Trustee Internat. Oceanographic Found.; bd. dirs. Miami Heart Inst. Served from lt. (j.g.) to lt. comdr., USNR, 1942-45. Fellow Internat. Acad. Trial Lawyers, Am. Coll. Trial Lawyers, Acad. Fla. Trial Lawyers; mem. Fla. Bar (bd. govs. 1955-64, past pres. jr. sect., past dir.), Am., Dade County bar assns., Acad. Fla. Trial Lawyers, Blue Key, Phi Beta Kappa, Sigma Alpha Epsilon, Phi Kappa Phi, Phi Delta Phi. Clubs: Riviera Country (Coral Gables, Fla.); Coral Reef Yacht, Palm Bay (Miami, Fla.); Miami Beach Rod and Reel (Miami Beach); Panama Marilin, Bermuda Anglers. Home: 1441 SW 11th St Miami FL 33135 Office: PO Box 2379 Miami FL 33101

MEIER, FRANK LORENZ, architect; b. Dallas, June 21, 1936; s. Lorenz Godfrey and Io (Briggs) M.; B.Arch., Tex. A. and M. Coll., 1960; m. Barbara Elane Brooks, Aug. 29, 1959; children—Michelle Elane, Andrea Catherine, Melanie Ann. Designer, draftsman Thomas, Jameson & Merrill, Architects, Dallas, 1956-57, Collins, Dryden &Assos., Architects, Dallas, 1958-63; architect Dales Y. Foster &Assos., Dallas, 1963-64; architect, v.p., Dales Y. Foster, Inc., Dallas, 1964—; pres. Research House, Inc., 1966-68; v.p. Otis Internat., Inc., Dallas, 1969-71; chmn. bd. Computer Designs, Inc., 1971—; v.p., sec., treas. Contemporary Properties, Inc. Mem. adv. bd. YWCA, Dallas, 1968—. Mem. A.I.A., Tex. Soc. Architects, Dallas Bldg. Owners and Mgrs. Assn., Soc. Coll. Univ. Planning. Episcopalian (vestryman 1968-72). Home: 7230 Walling Lane Dallas TX 75231 Office: LTV Tower Dallas TX 75201

MEIER, WILBUR LEROY, JR., educator; b. Elgin, Tex., Jan. 3, 1939; s. Wilbur Leroy and Ruby (Hall) M.; B.S., U. Tex., Austin, 1962, M.S., 1964, Ph.D., 1967; m. Judy Lee Longbotham, Aug. 30, 1958; children—Melynn, Marla, Melissa. Planning engr. Tex. Water Devel. Bd., Austin, 1962-66; research engr. U. Tex., Austin, 1966-67; asst. prof. Tex. A. and M. U., College Station, 1967-68, asso. prof., 1968-70, prof. indsl. engring., 1970—; cons. Computer Graphics Internat., Inc., Bryan, Tex., Tex. Water Devel. Bd., Austin, Tex. Gov.'s Office, Austin, Water Resources Engrs., Inc., Walnut Creek, Cal., Environments for Tomorrow, Inc., Washington, Kaiser Engrs., Inc., Oakland, Cal. Named Outstanding Young Engr. of Year, Travis chpt. Tex. Soc. Profl. Engrs., 1966. Mem. Am. Inst. Indsl. Engrs., Operations Research Soc. Am., Inst. Mgmt. Scis., Am. Soc. C.E. (past br. sec.-treas.), Tex. Soc. Profl. Engrs. (past chpt. dir.), Am. Soc. Engring. Edn. (pres. chpt.), Sigma Xi, Tau Beta Pi, Alpha Pi Mu, Chi Epsilon. Contbr. articles profl. jours. Home: 1819 Shadowwood Dr College Station TX 77840

MEIER, WILLIAM LUDWIG, JR., dentist; b. Teague, Tex., Apr. 12, 1924; s. William Ludwig and Irene Emma (Senter) M.; student Tex. Tech. U., 1941-43, 46-47; D.D.S., Northwestern U., 1951; meteorology certificate Cal. Inst. Tech., 1944; m. Juanita Champion, Oct. 18, 1952; children—Clark, Carolyn. Pvt. practice dentistry, Austin, Tex., 1951—. Mem. adv. bd. Central Tex. Dist. Campus Crusade for Christ, 1965—, chmn., 1970. Served with USAAF, 1943-46. Mem. Austin Dist. Dental Soc. (pres. 1967-68). Kiwanian. Home: 405 Almarion St Austin TX 78746 Office: 1307 E 38 1/2 St Austin TX 78722

MEIROSE, LEO HARRY, librarian; b. Cin., Oct. 25, 1922; s. Leo and Clara (Baude) M.; A.B. cum laude, Xavier U., 1945; M.S. in Library Sci., Case Western Res. U., 1950; m. Ruth Ruddell, Jan. 24, 1948; children—Leo Harry, Mary, JoAnn, Martha, John, Judith. Asst. librarian Xavier U., Cin., 1945-51; asst. head films and recordings center Pub. Library Cin. and Hamilton County, Cin., 1951-55, head schools dept., 1955-61, personnel dir., 1961-62, chief branches and extension services, 1963-64; dir. Fort Lauderdale (Fla.) Pub. Library, 1964—. Instr. Xavier U., 1945-64. Mem. community adv. bd. Fort Lauderdale U., 1969—. Mem. A.L.A., Southeastern Fla. (pres. 1971-72) library assns. Home: 6271 NW 16th Pl Fort Lauderdale FL 33313 Office: 1300 E Sunrise Blvd Fort Lauderdale FL 33304

MELCHIOR, ARIEL, JR., publisher, editor Charlotte Amalie Daily News. Address: 5 Wimlskfts Charlotte Amalie Virgin Islands 00801*

MELENDEZ, EFRAIN SANTIAGO, clergyman, govt. ofcl.; b. Comerjo, P.R., Feb. 17, 1930; s. Jose Antonio and Justina (Melendez) Santiago; student Defenders Theol. Sem., 1957-61, Psychol. Inst. P.R., 1967-69; m. Gwendolyn Page, July 18, 1953; children—Jeffery Lee, Brian Mallory, Lorinda Sue, Merikay. Ordained to ministry Methodist Ch., 1961; pastor Wesleyan Meth. Ch. of P.R., 1957-64; pres. Weleyan Conf. P.R., 1962-64; pres. Safway Sales Co., Rio Piedras, P.R., 1959-63; V.P. Halco Sales Co., Rio Piedras, 1960-68; pres. Andamios, Inc., 1965-68; sec. Social Services of P.R., Santurce, 1969—. Coordinator, dir. Billy Graham Evangelistic Assn. in Latin Am., 1964-68. Mem. adv. com. Columbia U.; mem. Samaritan Found.; mem. exec. bd. council Boy Scouts Am. Vice pres., mem. presdl. bd. Progressive Party of P.R., 1967—. Bd. dirs. Ciudad del Retiro, LOGOI. Served with USNR, 1953-57. Recipient various honors. Mem. Nat. Council Family Relations, Nat. Rehab. Assn., Am. Pub. Welfare Assn., Nat. Council Illegitimacy, Acad. Polit. Scis., Am. Legion, Logia Soberana de P.R., P.R. League against Cancer. Internat. Platform Assn. Home: Calle Tulipan 178 Urb San Francisco Rio Piedras PR 00927 Office: Box 11697 Santurce PR 00908

MELICH, EDWARD IDEL, physician; b. N.Y.C., May 17, 1906; s. Morris and Esther (Schwartz) M.; student Columbia, 1926-27; A.B., George Washington U., 1929, M.D., 1932; m. Virginia Miller Param, Oct. 23, 1971; children by previous marriage—Henry A., Arthur E., Karen Marie (Mrs. Marvin Solomon). Intern, Jersey City Med. Center, 1932-34; physician VA, 1936-68, chief sect. gastroenterology VA Center, Bay Pines, Fla., 1946-48; pvt. practice medicine, St. Petersburg, Fla., 1969—; mem. staff Palms Pasadena, St. Petersburg Gen. hosps. Served to capt. M.C., AUS, 1942-46. Fellow A.C.P., Am. Coll. Gastroenterology (past gov. Fla., past chmn. bd. govs., past v.p.); mem. Am. Heart Assn. Contbr. articles to profl. jours. Home: Box 6755 St Petersburg FL 33756 Office: 1609 Pasadena Av S St Petersburg FL 33707

MELICH, MITCHELL, lawyer, govt. ofcl.; b. Bingham Canyon, Utah, Feb. 1, 1912; s. Joseph and Mary (Kalembar) M.; LL.B., U. Utah, 1934; m. Doris M. Snyder, June 3, 1935; children—Tanya (Mrs. Noel L. Silverman), Michael, Nancy (Mrs. Timothy J. Funk), Robert A. Admitted Utah bar, 1934; pvt. practice, Moab, 1934-63; city atty., Moab, 1935-51; atty. Grand County, 1941-42; sec., dir. Utex Exploration Co., Moab, 1953-62; pres., dir. Uranium Reduction Co., Moab, 1954-62; dir. pub. relations Atlas Minerals div. Atlas Corp., 1962-65; dir., treas. New Park Mining Co., 1962-65; dir. Ideal Nat. Ins. Co., Salt Lake bd. First Security Bank of Utah, 1962-69; apptd. solicitor Dept. Interior, Washington, 1969—. Mem. of Colorado River Com. of Utah, 1945-47, Utah Water and Power Bd., 1947. Mem. Utah Senate, 1943-50; mem. Utah Legislative Council, 1949-54; del. Republican Nat. Conv., 1952-60, mem. Nat. Com. for Utah, 1961-64; Republican candidate gov., 1964. Bd. regents U. Utah, 1961-65, also mem. devel. fund com. Mem. Am. Bar Assn., U.S. Supreme Ct., Fed. bar assns. Utah State Bar, Utah Mining Assn. (pres. 1962-63), Kappa Sigma. Republican. Mason (Shriner). Club: Alta, Salt Lake Country (Salt Lake City). Home: 4100 Cathedral Av NW Washington DC 20016 Office: Dept Interior Washington DC 20240

MELIUS, FREDERIC NICHOLAS, JR., freight co. exec.; b. N.Y.C., May 17, 1907; s. Frederic Nicholas and Mae (Wagner) M.; A.B., Colgate U., 1929; LL.B., Columbia, 1932; m. Coralie Harper, Oct. 3, 1935; children—Jane C. (Mrs. H. Clayton Cook). Frederic Nicholas III. Admitted to N.Y. bar, 1932, asst. gen. counsel U.S. Freight Co. and subsidiaries, N.Y.C., 1937-57, v.p., 1957-66, sec., gen. counsel, 1963-66, pres., 1966—, also dir.; chmn. bd. Western Carloading Co., Freeport Cruise Lines Ltd., Bahama Cruise Lines; dir. Great Dane Trailer Co., Tropical Gas Co., Waterman S.S. Co., Fed. Home Loan Bank N.Y.; adv. bd. Bankers Trust Co. Trustee, bd. dirs. United Seaman's Service; bd. dirs. West Side Assn., N.Y.C., 1966—. Mem. Traffic Club N.Y., Nat. Def. Transp. Assn. (nat. v.p.), Transp. Assn. Am., Freight Forwarder Inst., Nat. Freight Traffic Assn., Phi Delta Phi, Beta Theta Pi. Clubs: Nat. Propeller (exec. com.); Le Club International (Ft. Lauderdale); Capital Yacht, Nat. Lawyers (Washington). Home: 3017 NE 57th St Fort Lauderdale FL 33308 Office: 711 3d Av New York City NY 10017

MELLADO, RAMON, govt. ofcl.; m.; children—Elena, Ramon, Ricardo, Manuel. Pub. sch. adminstr., 1931-41; under-sec. edn., Govt. of P.R., 1941-43; prof., dir. dept. pedagogy Coll. Edn., U. P.R., 1943-48, dean of adminstrn., 1948-56, prof. grad. sch. edn., 1957-68; sec. edn. Commonwealth of P.R., 1968—. Mem. Constl. Covn., Commonwealth of P.R., 1952. Mem. Am. Acad. Social and Polit. Sci., P.R. Tchrs. Assn. Author: Designing a Science Curriculum, 1941; Culture and Education in Puerto Rico, 1948; Puerto Rico y Occidente, 1963. Home: Centrum Plaza Condominium Hato Rey PR 00919 Office: Dept Edn Commonwealth of PR Box 759 Hato Rey PR 00919

MELLOWN, WILLIAM EWING, JR., state ofcl.; b. York, Ala., Jan. 17, 1931; s. William Ewing and Mildred (Harris) M.; B.S., Livingston State Coll., 1952; M.A., U. Ala., 1953; postgrad. Columbia, 1956, Syracuse U., 1964; m. Jeanette Steedley, Aug. 31, 1952; 1 son, William E. III. Grad. asst. dept. history U. Ala., 1953-54; tchr. Bibb County Bd. Edn., Centerville, Ala., 1954-55; tchr., asst. prin. Alexandria (Ala.) Sch., 1955-57; prin. Saks High Sch., Anniston, Ala., 1957-64; asst. ednl. TV coordinator State Dept. Edn., Montgomery, Ala., 1964-67; asst. coordinator Title I, Elementary and Secondary Edn. Act, 1965-67, coordinator, 1967-71, coordinator Title III, 1965-71, Title V, 1967-71, Title VII and VIII, fed. projects coordinator, 1971—. Bd. dirs. Prattville (Ala.) YMCA. Mem. Ala. Edn. Assn., Am. Assn. Sch. Adminstrn., N.E.A., Phi Delta Kappa. Kappa Phi Kappa. Club: Civitan (sec.-treas. 1963-64). Home: 116 Heritage Hills Dr Prattville AL 36067 Office: State Office Bldg Montgomery AL 36104

MELTON, CHANCELLOR GARLAND, optometrist; b. Yellville, Ark., Apr. 28, 1899; s. William Thomas and Mary Elizabeth (Sims) M.; O.D., No. Ill. Coll. Optometry, 1923; m. Josephine McGill, Dec. 31, 1924; children— Garland, Betty Jo (Mrs. James H. Bennett). Practice optometry, Fayetteville, Ark., 1923—. Organizer, sr. v.p., mem. bd. Investors Preferred Life Ins. Co., Little Rock, 1959—. Mem. Ark. Bd. Optometric Examiners, 1937-68, pres. bd., 1940-50. Mem. Washington County Bd. Health, 1928-45, Fayetteville City Hosp., 1928-40, Washington County A.R.C., 1928-45, Fayetteville Boys Club, 1941-48, U.S.O., 1942-45, Ark. Savs. Bond, 1941—; organizer Washington County Crippled Children, 1933, 1933-54, pres., mem. bd., 1933-54; mem. bd., 1st v.p. Fayetteville Community Chest, 1933-34; Washington County War Bond chmn., 1941-48. Mem. central com. Washington County Democrats, 1937-40. Mem. optometric bd. trustees So. Coll., 1962-69, chmn. bd., 1965-69; mem. Fayette Sch. Bd., 1935-54, Huntsville Vocational, 1940-55. Named Ark. Optometrist of Year, 1971; Optometrist of Yr., So. Council Optometry, 1971; hon. crew mem. U.S.S. John F. Kennedy, 1970. Fellow Am. Acad. Optometry, Am. Research Council Optometry; mem. Am. (mem. council edn. 1946-62, mem. legal-legislative com. 1934-60), Ark. (pres. 1935-36) optometric assns., Grad. Clinic Found., Am. Optometric Found. (mem. original bd. 1952-54), Fayetteville C. of C., Beta Sigma Kappa. Methodist (bd. stewards 1924—, chmn. 1933-40, chmn. bd. edn. 1946-48, dist. lay leader 1929-32, conf. rep. 1933-40). Lion (pres. 1930-31, dep. dist. gov. 1930-31), Mason (Shriner). Home: 418 Ila St Fayetteville AR 72701 Office: 230 N Block St Fayetteville AR 72701

MELTON, DOUGLAS ALBERT, fire chief; b. Putnam, Ala., June 20, 1909; s. Albert Gallington and Sadie (Woolsey) M.; student courses in fire engring. and fire schs.; spl. tutoring U. Ala.; m. Nora Margerory Griffin, Apr. 19, 1944; children—Douglas Albert II, Penny Jean, Eva Kathryn, Teenie Louise, Vivian Olivia, Lisa Iris. With Mobile Fire Dept., 1935—, chief, 1967—; tchr. short course firemanship U. Ala. Served with USCG, 1926-27. Mason (Shriner). Home: 200 Kenan St Mobile AL 36606 Office: 701 St Francis St Mobile AL 36602

MELTON, FREEMAN H., JR., supt. schs.; b. Wellington, Tex., Jan. 15, 1926; s. Freeman H. and Sudie (Stephens) M.; B.S., West Tex. State Coll., 1950, M.S., 1952; m. Rosemary Phillips, Aug. 14, 1949; children— Stephen Earl, Julie Carol, Margaret Joyce, Paul Freeman. Coach, tchr. pub. schs., Earth, Tex., 1950-51, McLean, Tex., 1951-52; sch. prin., McLean, 1952-54, supt. schs., 1954-60; supt. schs., Panhandle, Tex., 1960—. Mem. Panhandle Bd. City Devel.; chmn. A.R.C., Panhandle. Served with USNR, 1944-46. Recipient service citation A.R.C., 1958. Mem. N.E.A., Am., Tex. assns. sch. adminstrs., Tex. Tchrs. Assn. Mason. Lion (McLean Lion of Year 1960). Home: 1406 Maple St Panhandle TX 79068 Office: Box 68 Panhandle TX 79068

MELTON, HOWELL WEBSTER, circuit ct. judge; b. Atlanta, Dec. 15, 1923; s. Holmes and Alma (Combee) M.; LL.B., U. Fla., 1948; m. Margaret Catherine Wolfe, Mar. 4, 1950; children—Howell Webster, Carol Anne. Admitted to Fla. bar, 1948, since practiced in St. Augustine; with firm Upchurch, Melton & Upchurch, 1948-61; circuit ct. judge 7th Jud. Circuit of Fla., 1961—. Mem., past sec. St. Johns County Blood Bank; mem. St. Johns County Welfare Fedn.; Trustee Flagler Hosp., St. Augustine. Served with AUS, 1943-46. Recipient Distinguished Service award Fla. Jaycees, 1953. Mem. Am., St. Johns County bar assns., Fla. Bar (past chmn. council of bar presidents), Am. Judicature Soc., U. Fla. Alumni Assn., Phi Delta Theta, Phi Delta Phi. Methodist (past chmn. ofcl. bd.). Mason. Club: Ponce de Leon Country (St. Augustine). Home: 41 Carrera St St Augustine FL 32084 Office: County Courthouse St Augustine FL 32084

MELTON, JAMES OTHO, educator, cons. engr.; b. Hastings, Okla., Sept. 25, 1922; s. Hannie Benjamin and Mary (Rankin) M.; B.S., U. Okla., 1948, M.Engring., 1949; postgrad. Okla. State U., 1962—; m. Margaret Jean Shorney, Nov. 7, 1943; children—James Benjamin, Nancy Anne. Faculty, U. Okla., Norman, 1947-63, prof. indsl. mgmt. engring., aerospace and mech. engring., civil engring. U. Okla., 1962-63, acting chmn. Sch. Indsl. Mfg. and Engring., 1961-63; research cons. Geolograph Co., Oklahoma City, 1955-62; chief engr. Jamco, Inc., 1963-72; chief engr. Jamco div. Wagner Electric Co., 1972—; mgmt. cons. Speco, Inc., Oklahoma City, 1962-69; ind. cons. engr., Norman, 1952—. Served with AUS, 1943-46, 50-52. Mem. Am. Soc. M.E., Am. Soc. Engring. Edn., Am. Soc. Testing Materials, Nat., Okla. socs. profl. engrs., Am. Soc. Tool and Mfg. Engrs., Soc. Exptl. Stress Analysis, Soc. Nondestructive Testing, Am. Soc. Testing Materials, Soc. Automotive Engrs., Sigma Xi, Tau Beta Pi, Sigma Tau, Sigma Gamma Tau, Alpha Sigma Phi. Presbyn. Patentee in field of oil field service equipment, automotive front end equipment. Home: 1208 Cruce St Norman OK 73069

MELTON, JAMES P., govt. ofcl. Asst. supt. Bur. Adminstrn. and Finance, Dept. Edn., State of Ky., Frankfort. Office: Dept Edn Frankfort KY 40601*

MELTON, JOSEPH COLLINS, banker; b. LeFlore, Miss., Sept. 8, 1922; s. Jesse Collins and Mai B. (Rogers) M.; B.S. in Accounting and Bus., Bowling Green Bus. U., 1951; m. Katherine Weis, Nov. 3, 1956; children—Terraseta (Mrs. Thomas H. Hodges), K. Camille, Joseph Collins. Vice pres. Holmes County Bank & Trust Co., Vaiden, Miss., 1952—; pres. Indsl. Devel. Corp. Carroll and Montgomery Counties; dir. Crossroads Indsl. Devel. Corp. Dir. devel. com., Town of Vaiden. Bd. dirs. Winona Acad. Served with AUS, 1941-45. Mem. Miss. Econ. Council, Am. Legion, Toppers Frat. Methodist. Lion. Home: Hwy 35 Vaiden MS 39176 Office: Vaiden Bank Vaiden MS 39176

MELTON, OLIVER QUIMBY, JR., newspaper editor, state rep.; b. Americus, Ga., Feb. 12, 1922; s. Oliver Quimby and Mary (Davenport) M.; A.B. in Journalism, U. Ga., 1942; LL.D., John Marshall Law Sch., Atlanta, 1956; LL.B., LaSalle Extension U., 1958, Woodrow Wilson Coll. Law, 1961; m. May Wingfield, June 30, 1943; children—Oliver Quimby III, Mary W., Laura, Leila. Editor, mng. editor Griffin Daily News, 1945—; mem. Ga. Ho. of Reps., 1959—; admitted to Ga. bar, 1961. Mem. bd. regents Univ. System Ga., 1955-60. Served as lt., cav., AUS, World War II. Decorated Purple Heart; recipient George Washington honor medals for editorials (two), Freedoms Found., 1951, 55; citations for editorials on religious understanding Nat. Conf. Christians and Jews, 1947, 48; citation for work with handicapped people Nat. Am. Legion, 1949; H.H. Dean trophy for best editorial in daily Ga. newspaper Ga. Press Assn., 1952; Salvation Army War Cry awards, 1945, 46; citation for fire prevention campaign Nat. Bd. Fire Underwriters, 1947; named Ga. Citizen of Yr., 1955; Most Fearless Editorial award Ga. Press Assn., 1955, 60. Mem. Ga. Press Assn. (bd. mgrs. 1952-56, pres. 1955-56), 4th Dist. Press Assn. (pres. 1953), Kappa Alpha. Methodist (steward). Mason, Elk. Club: Commerce. Author: History of Griffin, 1959. Home: RFD Route C Griffin GA 30223 Office: Griffin Daily News Griffin GA 30223

MELTON, ROBERT ELWIN, educator; b. Preston, Kan., Aug. 19, 1914; s. Daniel W. and Bessie M. (Hayson) M.; B.S., Kan. State Tchrs. Coll., 1939; M.S., Fla. State U., 1962; m. Betty Ann Robinson, Dec. 1, 1945; 1 dau., Janet Denise. Tchr. high sch., Burr Oak, Kan., 1939-41; commd. 2d lt. USAAF, 1941, advanced through grades to lt. col., 1950; lead navigator Middle E., CBI, 1942-44; supr. radar officer tng. Air Tng. Command, 1944-47; staff Air U., 1949-52, Hdqrs. USAFE, 1953-56, Hdqrs. USAF, 1957-59, Hdqrs. TAC, 1960-61; ret., 1961; prof. econs. Manatee Jr. Coll., Bradenton, Fla., 1962—, chmn. dept. bus. adminstrn., 1964—. Decorated Air medal, D.F.C. Mem. Am. Accounting Assn., Am. Assn. U. Profs., Nat. Faculty Assn., Fla. Bus. Edn. Assn., Anna Maria Island Power Squadron, Phi Delta Kappa, Sigma Tau Gamma. Mason. Home: 3911 Plumosa Terrace Bradenton FL 33505

MELTON, ROSSER B., educator; b. Appleby, Tex., Nov. 21, 1910; s. William B and Rosa Belle (Blacksher) M.; B.S., Stephen F. Austin State U., 1934; M.A., U. Tex., 1937, Ph.D., 1940; m. Frances Elizabeth Couch, Dec. 21, 1938; children—Rosser B., Lynn Ayres, William C. Prof. sociology Sam Houston State U., 1940-45; asso. prof. econs. U. Ark., 1945-47; prof. econs. North Tex. State U., 1947—. Mem. Am., S.W. econ. assns., S.W. Social Sci. Assn., A.A.A.S., Assn. Evolutionary Econs., Alpha Chi, Alpha Kappa Delta, Pi Gamma Mu. Contbr. articles to profl. jours. Home: 1605 Kendolph St Denton TX 76201

MELTON, VERA BOLICK, educator, librarian; b. Lenoir, N.C., Jan. 27, 1924; d. Jessie R. and Ethel (Miller) Bolick; B.S., Appalachian State Tchrs. Coll., 1949, M.A., 1953; m. Jerome H., Aug. 11, 1944. Tchr. Winston-Salem (N.C.) schs., 1944-46, Granite Falls, N.C., 1946-51; librarian Hudson (N.C.) High Sch., 1951-53; supr. libraries Caldwell County, Lenoir, 1953-55; head librarian Needham Broughton Sr. High Sch., Raleigh, N.C., 1955-66; library supr. Bd. Edn., Waynesville, N.C., 1966—; dir. ednl. media Haywood County Consol. Schs., 1968-69; coordinator of library services Community Coll., 1969-70, dir. library services, 1970—. Dir. standards, N.C. Libraries, 1959—; N.C. exec. dir. Nat. Library Week, 1970. Pres. Sir Walter Lions Aux. 1956-57; bd. dirs. Easter Seal, Caldwell County. Mem. N.C. Edn. Assn. (chmn. 1957-58), N.E.A., N.C. (chmn. 1958-61, exec. sec. 1966—), Southeastern Am. (chmn. N.C. implementation standards 1960), library assns., Beta Sigma Phi (pres. 1953-54). Democrat. Baptist. Club: Jr. Women's (pres. 1954-55). Author, editor handbooks; mem. revision bd. World Ency., 1964—. Home: 5513 Parkwood Dr Raleigh NC 27609 Office: 100 Harrington St Raleigh NC 27603

MELTZER, MILTON, physician, psychoanalyst; b. Rochester, N.Y., May 11, 1923; s. Louis and Clara (Ratner) M.; B.A. cum laude, Ohio State U., 1943, M.D., 1946; grad. Washington Psychoanalytic Inst., 1960; m. Sallie Rabinoff, Mar. 23, 1946; children—Gail Miriam, Steven Marc. Intern, St. Elizabeth's Hosp., Washington, 1946-47, resident psychiatry, 1947-50; chief med. officer Alcatraz Fed. Penitentiary, 1951-52; gen. practice psychoanalysis and psychiatry Washington, 1952—; psychiatric cons. D.C. Dept. Vocational Rehab., 1953—; tng. and supervising analyst Washington Psychoanalytic Inst., 1965—. Served with USPHS, 1951-53. Fellow Am. Psychiat. Assn., A.A.A.S.; mem. Am. Psychoanalytic Assn. (mem. exec. council 1967—), Washington Psychiatric Soc. (pres. 1967-68), Phi Beta Kappa, Alpha Omega Alpha. Address: 2934 Fessenden St NW Washington DC 20008

MELVILLE, C.E., adminstr. Jefferson Hosp., Pine Bluff, Ark. Address: Jefferson Hosp Pine Bluff AR 71601*

MELVILLE, PHILLIP LAURENT, civil engr.; b. Paris, France, June 11, 1922; s. Edmond and Alice (Grener) M.; came to U.S., 1942, naturalized, 1949; B.A., B.S., U. Montpellier (France), 1940; B.S. in Civil Engring., U. N.M., 1944; M.S., Purdue, 1945; m. Sheila Drury, June 5, 1954; children—Anne Helen, Laura Charlotte. Grad. asst. Purdue U., 1944-45; research engr. Va. Dept. Hwys., 1945-59; hwy. research engr. Va. Hwy. Research Council, 1949-55; asst. chief soil sect. civil engring. br., engring. div. mil. constrn. Office Chief Engrs. U.S. Army, Washington, 1955-62, chief materials sect., 1962-70; tech. asst. airports service FAA, Washington, 1970—. Lectr., U. Va., Charlottsville, 1949-55, instr. No. Va. Center, Arlington, 1955-70; cons. found., materials for bldgs., pavements. Named Outstanding Young Engr. in Govt., U.S. Army, 1956; recipient ofcl. commendation Dept. Army, 1965, 68; Spl. Achievement award FAA, 1971. Registered profl. engr., Va. Fellow Am. Soc. C.E.; mem. Am. Concrete Inst. (tech. com. 1961—), Nat., Va. (chpt. pres. 1967-68, state pres. 1971) socs. profl. engrs., Hwy. Research Bd. (tech. com. 1949—), Am. Soc. Testing Materials (tech. com. 1962-70), Sigma Xi, Sigma Tau, Tau Kappa Alpha. Home: 6116 Edgewood Terrace Alexandria VA 22307 Office: 800 Independence Av SW Washington DC 20591

MELVIN, DOROTHY MAE, parasitologist; b. Fayetteville, N.C., Jan. 27, 1923; d. Willie James and Lillie (Bain) Melvin; A.B., U. N.C., 1942, M.S., 1945; Ph.D., Rice Inst., 1951. Med., X-ray technician Goldsboro (N.C.) Hosp., 1942-43; tng. officer med. parasitology Nat. Communicable Disease Center, USPHS, Atlanta, 1945-49, 51-57, supervisory parasitologist microbiology tng. lab., 1957-62; chief parasitology tng. unit, 1962—; instr. parasitology bacteriology dept. Emory U., 1951-67, asst. prof., 1967—. Diplomate in med. and pub. health parasitology Am. Acad. Microbiology. Mem. Internat. Coll. Tropical Medicine, Am. Inst. Biol. Scis., Am. Soc. Parasitologists, Am. Soc. Tropical Medicine and Hygiene, Research Soc. Am., Wesleyan Service Guild, Sigma Xi. Methodist. Contbr. articles to profl. jours. Home: 2418 Kingscliff Dr NE Atlanta GA 30345 Office: Parasitology Tng Unit Center for Disease Control USPHS Atlanta GA 30333

MELZAC, VINCENT, curator. Chief exec. officer Corcoran Gallery of Arts. Office: 17th and New York Av Washington DC*

MEMOLI, FRANK, architect; b. Bklyn., Feb. 2, 1913; s. Albert and Rosa (DeFeo) M.; student N.Y. U., 1943, U. Cin., 1944-48; m. Inez M. Wikoff, Jan. 1, 1949. With various archtl. firms, Ohio, 1945-63, Lexington, Ky., 1964—; now with Clotfelter & Johnson. Mem. A.I.A., Constrn. Specifications Inst. Mason. Author: Vanity and Value, 1954; The Game of Civilization, 1970. Home: 705 Sunset Dr Lexington KY 40502 Office: 556 N Broadway Lexington KY 40508

MENDELL, DAVID, psychiatrist; b. N.Y.C., May 10, 1909; s. Morris H. and Sarah (Kahn) M.; B.S., Coll. City N.Y., 1929; M.D., U. Vienna, 1934; m. Miriam Wydra, June 27, 1944; children—Jeffrey V., Mark Judson. Intern, Bellevue Hosp., N.Y.C., 1934-35, St. Joseph Infirmary, Houston, 1935-36; pvt. practice medicine, Houston, 1937-42; resident fellow psychiatry Langley Porter Clinic, San Francisco, 1946-47, asst. chief child psychiatry dept., 1947-48; practice medicine, specializing in psychoanalysis, San Francisco, 1948-50, specializing in psychiatry, psychoanalytic group and family, Houston, 1950—; candidate, clin. asso. San Francisco Inst. Psychoanalysis, 1946-50; instr. psychiatry U. Cal. Med. Sch., San Francisco, 1947-48; clin. asso. prof. psychiatry U. Tex. Grad. Sch. Bio-Med. Sci., 1953—, Baylor Coll. Medicine, 1959—; clin. prof. psychiatry U. Tex. Sch. Med. Houston, 1972—; cons., dir. group therapy program Baylor Coll. Medicine, 1963-70; cons. staff VA Mental Hygiene Clinic, San Francisco, 1948-50; cons. USAF Hosp., San Antonio. Served from capt. to lt. col. USAAF, 1942-46. Diplomate Am. Bd. Psychiatry and Neurology. Fellow Am. Group Psychotherapy Assn., Am. Psychiat. Assn.; mem. Am. Acad. Psychotherapists (pres. 1967-68), Group for Advancement Psychiatry (com. on family 1956—, chmn. com. on family 1971—), UN Assn. of U.S.A. (mem. chpt. adv. com.). Asso. editor Family Process. Contbr. articles to profl. jours. Home: 3611 N Braeswood Blvd Houston TX 77025 Office: Medical Towers Houston TX 77025

MENDELL, HENRY ELIAS, physician; b. Key West, Fla., Feb. 27, 1925; s. Julius and Clara (Rothman) M.; M.D., U. Tex., 1947; m. Muriel Friedman, Dec. 6, 1958; children—Jeffrey Neal, Robin Sheryl. Rotating intern St. Louis City Hosp., 1947-48; intern in medicine Barnes Hosp., St. Louis, 1948-49; resident in internal medicine Baylor U. Affiliated Programs, Houston, 1949-51; practice medicine, specializing in internal medicine, Houston, 1954—; asso. internist M. D. Anderson Hosp. and Tumor Inst., Houston, 1954-71; mem. staff Ben Taub, Hermann, Meth., Meml., St. Luke's, St. Joseph, Bellaire Gen. hosps., Houston; clin. asso. prof. internal medicine Baylor Coll. Medicine, Houston, 1964—. Served to capt. M.C., USAF, 1951-53. Diplomate Am. Bd. Internal Medicine. Mem. A.M.A., A.C.P., Tex. Acad. Internal Medicine, Houston Soc. Internal Medicine, Alpha Omega Alpha. Republican. Jewish religion. Home: 5735 Ariel St Houston TX 77035 Office: 4003 Bellaire Blvd Houston TX 77025

MENDELSON, DONALD ALVIN, elec. engr.; b. Washington, July 7, 1925; s. Joseph Aaron and Anne L. (Cash) M.; student Wilson Tchrs. Coll., Washington, 1941-43; B.S. in Elec. Engring., U. Ky., 1950; M.S. in Environmental Engring. Fla. Inst. Tech., 1972. Engr., AVCO Mfg. Co., Cin., 1950-51; project engr. Wright Air Devel. Center, Dayton, O., 1951-54; sr. devel. engr. Goodyear Aircraft Corp., Akron, O., 1954-61; specialist N.Am. Rockwell Corp., Columbus, O. also Cocoa, Fla., 1961-69. Cons. elec. engr., 1950—; staff cons. engr. Dayton State Hosp., 1948-61. Served with AUS, 1943-46. Registered profl. engr., Ky., Ohio, Fla. Mem. I.E.E.E. (sr.). Developer advanced tech. mgmt. systems, mil. electronic systems, marine and environmental measurement systems. Home: 295 Belair Av Merritt Island FL 32952

MENDENHALL, JOHN RYAN, accountant; b. Des Moines, Jan. 17, 1928; s. Merritt Blake and Elizabeth (Ryan) M.; B.Sc., U. Notre Dame, 1950; LL.B., Harvard, 1953; m. Joan Lois Schaefer, June 20, 1953; children— Thomas, James, Jane, Julie, Robert. With tax dept. Arthur Andersen & Co., C.P.A., Cleve., 1953-66, partner, 1963—, dir. taxes, Chgo., 1966—. Served with AUS, 1946-47, C.P.A., Ohio, Mich., Ia., Ill. N.C. Mem. Ohio Soc. C.P.A.'s, Am. Inst. C.P.A.'s, Roman Catholic. Clubs: University, Harvard (N.Y.C.). Contbr. articles to tech. tax jours. Office: 815 Connecticut Av NW Washington DC 20006

MENDENHALL, WILLIAM, III, educator; Ph.D., N.C. State U. Chmn. dept. statistics Coll. Arts and Scis., U. Fla. Office: U Fla Gainesville FL 32601

MENDEZ, ALFRED F., clergyman; b. Chgo., June 3, 1907; ed. U. Notre Dame, Holy Cross Coll. Ordained priest Roman Catholic Ch., 1935; 1st bishop of Arecibo (P.R.), 1960—. Address: Box 606 Arecibo PR 00613*

MENDEZ, CARMINA, broadcasting co. exec.; b. San Juan, P.R.; d. Emiliano and Isabel (Jimenez) Mendez; ed. Sacred Heart Coll., San Juan, Marymount Coll., N.Y.C.; m. E. Schroder, Apr. 4, 1944 (div.); children—Henry, Carmina, Elsie S. (Mrs. Fernando Ruiz), Marianne. Pres., Sta. WHOA, San Juan, 1954—; pres., co-owner Sta. WSTE-TV, Fajardo, P.R. Mem. Citizens Adv. Com. to Mayor San Juan. Recipient Top Mgmt. award as outstanding exec. in communications field S.M.E., Mem. Broadcasters Assn. P.R. (dir.), Federacion Publicitaria de P.R. (founder, sec.). First to introduce English lang. comml. broadcast to P.R. Home: Park Blvd Cond Apt 1013 San Juan PR 00913 Office: 105 Padre Las Casas St Hato Rey San Juan PR 00918*

MENDEZ, FELIX GILBERTO, advt. and pub. relations exec.; b. Lares, P.R., July 31, 1932; s. Edelmiro Mendez and Inocencia Soto M.; B.S., U. P.R., 1954; postgrad. Am. U., Cornell U., Lares Sch. Commerce; m. Antonia Gonzalez, Dec. 21, 1954; children—Felix Antonio, Mercedes, Rosa, Francisco, Marife. Med. rep. Endo Pharm. Co., 1956-59, Armour Pharm. Co., 1959-61; supr. Smith, Miller & Patch, 1961-62; pub. relations dir. Interstate Gen. Contractor, 1962-63; mgr. govt. relations, asst. dir. pub. relations, I.T.T., 1963-69; dir. Econ. Devel. Adminstrn. P.R. Office Information and Pub. Relations 1969-70; pub. relations counsellor Coop. Devel. Adminstrn. and Govt. Housing Bank, 1970—; v.p. Admakers, also pres., co-owner San Juan Pub. Relations, Inc. (P.R.), 1971—. Cons. Served as 2d lt. AUS, 1954-56. Mem. Pub. Relations Soc. P.R. (past pres.), InterAm. Pub. Relations Soc. (dir.), Pub. Relations Soc. Am., Casino de P.R., San Juan Pub. Relations (pres.), Alpha Beta Chi (nat. past pres.). Mem. New Progressive Party (county pres., treas. municipal com.). Roman Catholic. K.C., Lion (sec.). Home: C-29 Rufino Rodriguez Villa Clementina Guaynabo PR 00657 Office: 1120 Ashford Av San Juan PR 00907 also GPO Box 2114 San Juan PR 00936

MENDEZ, JUSTO A., senator P.R.; b. Lares, P.R., Dec. 2, 1917; s. Justo and Cristina (Rodriguez) M.; B.S. in Chem. Engring., 1942; m. Providencia Oliver, Sept. 6, 1943; children—Povines (Mrs. Humberto Torres), Justo, Lumen. Gen. supr. Los Canos Sugar Mill; exec. v.p. Central Fed. Savs. & Loan Assn.; pres. San Martin Mortgage Corp.; vp. bd. P.R. Housing Bank; now mem. P.R. Senate, minority leader. Mem. P.R. exec. council Boy Scouts Am., 1956; mem. Citizens' Com. Arecibo Edn., 1958. Pres. Local planning bd., 1954-59. Served with AUS, 1943-46. Mem. P.R. Coll. Architects, Surveyors and Engrs., P.R. Coll. Chemists, Navy League U.S., P.R. Planning Soc. Home: C-71 Ebano Caparra Heights PR 00920 Office: Senate El Capitolio San Juan PR 00904

MENDEZ, LEOPOLDO, artist; ed. San Carlos Acad. Fine Arts (Mexico); sch. of painting, Chimalistac. Artist for newspapers, 1923-25; asst. stage designer, Mexico City, Mexico; head fine arts sect. Ministry Popular Edn., 1932; tchr. drawing various tech. schs., Mexico City; founder-mem. LEAR; a founder Taller de Grafica

Popular. Del. Warsaw (Poland) Peace Congress, 1948, Peace Congress, Vienna, Austria, 1953. Exhibited in shows at Los Angeles, 1930, numerous shows Europe and U.S.; represented in permanent collections Mexico and U.S. Recipient 1st prize Book Fair, 1944, 1st Mexican Graphic Art prize, 1946. Address: care Mexican Life Sa Boerareli 85 Mexico City Mexico

MENDICINO, JOSEPH FRANK, educator; b. Cleve., Nov. 22, 1930; s. Sam F. and Rose (Gangale) M.; B.S., Case Inst. Tech., 1953; Ph.D., Western Res. U., 1958; m. Martha Vettor, June 9, 1951; children—David, Kathryn, Sylvia, Darryl, Derek, Rosemary. Postdoctoral fellow, Buenos Aires, Argentina, 1958-62; asst. prof. Ohio State U., Columbus, 1962-68; asso. prof. biochemistry U. Ga., Athens, 1968—. Mem. Soc. Biol. Chemists, Am. Chem. Soc. Home: 125 Brookwood St Athens GA 30601

MENDONSA, ARTHUR, city ofcl.; m.; 2children. Formerly asst. prof. U. Ga.; formerly exec. asst. to chmn. DeKalb County Bd. Commrs., Decatur, Ga.; now city mgr., Savannah, Ga. Mem. Am. Soc. Pub. Adminstrn., Mem. Am. Inst. Planners, Internat. City Mgrs. Assn. Author: Simplified Financial Management for Local Government. Home: 302 E 46th St Savannah GA 31405 Office: City Manager's Office City Hall Savannah GA 31401

MENEFEE, J. M., state ofcl. Commr. conservation La. Office: PO Box 44275 Baton Rouge LA 70804*

MENENDEZ-MONROIG, JOSE M., state senator; b. San Juan, P.R., June 22, 1917; s. Albert Seaman Menendez and Agustina Monroig; B.A., U. P.R., 1939, LL.B., 1941; m. Lyda M. Cortada, Aug. 3, 1946; children—Jose Antonio, Michele Marie. Admitted to P.R. bar, 1941; asso. atty. Pub. Service Commn., 1946; adjudicator VA, 1947. Mem. P.R. Senate, 1969—; sec. gen. New Progressive party, Mem. Am. Bar Assn., Colegio de Abogados de P.R. Roman Catholic. Home: 54 Krug St Santurce PR 00911 Office: Box 3183 San Juan PR 00904*

MENGER, JAMES MEREDITH, JR., govt. ofcl.; b. Vicksburg, Miss., Sept. 17, 1923; s. James Meredith and Anne Genevieve (Thornton) M.; student Hinds Jr. Coll., Miss., 1939-40; A.B., Harvard, 1948, LL.B., 1952; m. Margaret Ann Weymuller, June 18, 1949; children—Sarah (Mrs. Bruce Geoffrion), Caroline Anne, James Charles. Admitted to Miss. bar, 1952; asst. counsel Office Legislative Counsel, U.S. Ho. of Reps., Washington, 1952-63; profl. staff mem. Com. Interstate and Fgn. Commerce, U.S. Ho. of Reps., 1963—. Served with USAAF, 1940-45. Decorated D.F.C., Air medal with 2 oak leaf clusters. Mem. Miss. Bar Assn. Home: 7606 Marian Ct Falls Church VA 22042 Office: Rayburn Bldg Washington DC 20515

MENHINICK, HOWARD KENNETH, city and regional planner; b. Lansing, Mich., Jan. 28, 1901; s. George Edward and Anna Sofia (Tornblom) M.; B.S., Mich. State Coll., 1923; M.L.A.C.P., Harvard, 1928; m. Dorothea Mary Fulton, July 13, 1929; children—Edward Fulton, Robert John. Landscape engr. O. C. Simonds, Chgo., 1923-25; visited U.S. cities, compiling materials for Our Cities Today and Tomorrow, by Hubbard and Hubbard, 1928-29; instr. Sch. City Planning, Harvard, 1929-31, asst. prof. 1931-36; asso. cons. Nat. Resources Planning Bd. and to state planning bds. of Mass. and R.I., 1935-37; with TVA, 1937-51, dir. regional studies div., 1941-51; Regents prof. city planning Ga. Inst. Tech. emeritus; instr. Inst. for Tng. in Municipal Adminstrn., Chgo., 1945-48; dir. hdqrs. planning staff UN (on leave from TVA), 1946; pres. Menhinick & Little, Inc., cons. city planners; dir. planning and devel. Keck & Wood, Inc., Atlanta, 1968-71. Chmn. adv. com. Met. Atlanta Rapid Transit Authority. Chmn. Met. Atlanta Transit Study Commn., 1962. Pres. Assn. Collegiate Schs. Planning, 1962. Mem. Am. Inst. Planners (gov. 1954—; Distinguished Service award 1966), Am. Soc. Planning Ofcls. Internat. City Mgrs. Assn. Presbyn. Author: (with H. V. Hubbard) Sect. Airports in the City Plan, in Airports: Their Location, Administration, and Legal Bases, 1930. Editor: Planners Jour., 1935-37; Revision of Local Planning Administration, 1948. Home: 4370 Spalding Dr Dunwoody GA 30338

MENIUS, ESPIE FLYNN, JR., elec. engr.; b. New Bern, N.C., Mar. 5, 1923; s. Espie Flynn and Sudie Grey (Lyerly) M.; B.E.E., N.C. State Coll., 1947; adopted children—James Benfield, Ruben Hughes. With Carolina Power & Light Co., 1947-63, asst. to dist. mgr., Raleigh, Henderson, N.C., Sumter, S.C., 1947-50, elec. engr., Asheville, Southern Pines, Dunn, N.C., 1950-52, dist. engr. Hartsville, S.C., 1952-63; sr. elec. engr. Sonoco Products Co., Hartsville, 1963—. Instr. Florence-Darlington Tech. Ednl. Center. Mem. Hartsville Vol. Fire Dept., 1958—; Eagle Scout, Boy Scouts Am., 1938, scout troop leader New Bern, N.C., 1940-41, Raleigh, N.C., 1941-47, Henderson, N.C., 1948-49, Asheville, N.C., 1950, Southern Pines, N.C., 1951-52, Sumter, S.C., 1949-50, Hartsville, S.C., 1952-64. Served with AUS, 1943-46. Recipient Silver Beaver award Boy Scouts Am., 1959; named Hartsville's Citizen Yr., Rotary, 1960. Registered profl. engr., N.C., S.C., Tenn., Ga. Mem. I.E.E.E., A.A.A.S., Nat. Assn. Engrs., Knight of St. Patrick, Scabbard and Blade, Eta Kappa Nu, Pine Burr, Phi Eta Sigma, Theta Tau. Presbyn. (elder, tchr. men's Bible class). Club: Civitan (past dir.). Author articles in field. Home: 423 Richardson Circle W Hartsville SC 29550 Office: Sonoco Products Co N 2d St Hartsville SC 29550

MENKE, RICHARD JOHN, orthopaedic surgeon; b. Covington, Ky., July 31, 1930; s. Richard Herman and Mary (Kerstein) M.; student Xavier U., 1946-49; M.D., St. Louis U., 1953; m. Mary Ann Rice, June 30, 1956; children—Mary Elizabeth, Richard C., Patricia Ann, Paul G., Jeanne Marie, John Joseph, Thomas Edward. Intern, St. Elizabeth Hosp., Covington, 1953-54; resident gen. surgery Henry Ford Hosp., Detroit, 1954-57, resident orthopaedic surgery, 1957-60; practice medicine, specializing in orthopaedic surgery, Covington, 1960—; chief surgery St. Elizabeth Hosp., 1972; mem. staff Wm. Booth Hosp. Pres., W & M Corp., Covington, 1966—, Menke-Runge Johnson P.S.C. Mem. adv. bds. St. Charles, Madonna Manor nursing homes. Served to capt. M.C., AUS, 1955-57. Mem. A.M.A., Ky., Campbell-Kenton County (pres. elect) med. socs., Ky. Orthopaedic Soc., Am. Acad. Orthopaedic Surgery, C. of C. Democrat. Roman Catholic. Home: 2 Flower Ct Fort Mitchell KY 41014 Office: 823 Scott St Covington KY 41011

MENN, JOE KARL, coll. pres.; b. Yorktown, Tex., Dec. 28, 1933; s. Hubert L. and Martha (Boch) M.; B.A., Tex. Luth. Coll., 1955; B.D., Capital U., 1960; M.A., U. Tex., 1962, Ph.D., 1964; m. Myrtle Vassberg, Sept. 1, 1957; children—Esther, Kristine, Jonathan. Instr. English, Capital U., Columbus, O., 1959-60; instr. history Tex. Luth. Coll., Seguin, 1957-59, 62-63, asst. to pres., 1962-63, dean of coll., 1968-69, pres., 1969—; asst. to asso. prof. history Augustana Coll., Sioux Falls, S.D., 1964-68. Vis. prof., lectr. U. Me., summer 1967. Mem. bd. theol. edn. Am. Luth. Ch.; mem. exec. council Ind. Colls. and Univs. Tex.; sec. exec. com. Tex. Found. Voluntarily Supported Colls. and Univs.; sec. Council Ch. Coll. Presidents Am. Luth. Ch. Bd. dirs. Luth. Ednl. Council N.Am. Mem. Orgn. Am. Historians, Assn. So. Historians. Author: The Large Slaveholders of Louisiana, 1964. Home: 605 Fleming Dr Seguin TX 78155

MENNIS, EDMUND ADDI, banker; b. Allentown, Pa., Aug. 12, 1919; s. William H. and Grace A. (Addi) M.; B.A., Coll. City N.Y., 1941; M.A., Columbia, 1946; Ph.D., N.Y.U., 1961; m. Selma Adinoff, Sept. 25, 1945; children—Ardith Grace, Daniel Liam. Fellow econs. dept. Coll. City N.Y., 1941-42; jr. analyst Eastman Dillon & Co., N.Y.C., 1945-46; sr. research asst. Am. Inst. Econ. Research, Great Barrington, Mass., 1946-50; security analyst Wellington Mgmt. Co., Phila., 1950-61, economist, 1953-60, dir. research, 1958-61, v.p., economist, 1960-66, mem. investment com., 1958-66; sr. v.p., chmn. trust investment com. Republic Nat. Bank of Dallas, 1966—. Mem. econ. adv. bd. U.S. Sec. of Commerce, 1967-68; tech. cons. Bus. Council, 1962-66, 72—. Mem. exec. com. Dallas Symphony Orch., 1968—. Served to 1st lt. AC, AUS, 1942-45, and to capt. USAF, 1951-53. Fellow Nat. Assn. Bus. Economists (council, 1966-69); mem. Conf. Bus. Economists, Inst. Chartered Financial Analysts (trustee 1968—, v.p. 1969-70, pres. 1970-72, trustee research found. 1971—), Financial Analysts Fedn. (dir. 1970-72), N.Y., Dallas socs. security analysts. Clubs: Chaparral, Lakewood Country (Dallas). Asso. editor Financial Analysts Jour., 1960—; editor C.F.A. Digest, 1971—. Home: 3611 Milton Av Dallas TX 75205 Office: Republic Nat Bank of Dallas PO Box 241 Dallas TX 75221

MENSCHER, BARNET GARY, steel co. exec.; b. Laurelton, N.Y., Sept. 5, 1940; s. Samuel and Louise (Zaimont) M.; student Centenary Coll., 1958-59; B.B.A., U. Tex., 1963; m. Diane Elaine Gachman, June 12, 1966; 1 dau., Melissa Denise. Vice pres. marketing Ella Gant Mfg., Shreveport, La., 1964-66; warehouse mgr., dir. material control Gachman Steel Co., Fort Worth, 1966-68, gen. mgr., Houston, 1968-70, sales mgr. Gulf Coast, 1971—. Investment cons. D & L Enterprises, 1966—. Mem. solicitation com. United Fund, 1969-71; mem. Nat. Alliance of Businessmen Jobs Program, 1969—. Served with AUS, 1963-65. Mem. Tex. Assn. Steel Importers, Purchasing Agts. Assn. Houston, Credit Assn. Houston, Am. Mgmt. Assn., Phi Sigma Delta, Alpha Phi Omega. Democrat. Jewish religion. Club: Porsche of America (Houston). Home: 314 Tealwood Dr Houston TX 77024 Office: PO Box 40448 Houston TX 77040

MERA, ANDRES, dentist; b. Bayamo, Cuba, Aug. 19, 1914; s. Andres Ibo and Pauline Victoria (Statzer) M.; Cirujano Dentista, U. Havana, 1939; D.D.S., N.Y.U., 1949; m. Maria Dolores Cintron-de-Mera, Mar. 16, 1957; children—Ana Celina, Andres, Victor, Daniel, Rex, Diana. Came to U.S., 1947, naturalized, 1952. Dental technician, gen. practice dentistry, Havana, Cuba, 1939-47; gen. practice dentistry, N.Y.C., 1947—; head dental group, N.Y.C. Served to capt. U.S. Army, 1953-55. Mem. Am. Dental Assn., 1st Dist. Dental Soc., Am. Dental Soc. Anesthesiologists, Colegio Cirujanos Dentistas de PR. Home: Turquesa 2116 Rio Piedras PR 00927 Office: 162 W 72d St New York City NY 10023

MERCER, RONALD EUGENE, assn. exec.; b. Ipava, Ill., June 17, 1938; s. Clifford Irwin and Ila (Onion) M.; student Humboldt Inst., 1956-57, U. Colo., 1966-68, U. Okla., 1967-69, Tex. Christian U., 1969-71; m. Janet Sue Adcock, Jan. 27, 1957; children—Ronald Eugene, Pamela Sue. Rate clk. Central Transfer Co., Peoria, Ill., 1957-58; freight bill auditor, Burlington Truck Lines, Inc., Galesburg, Ill., 1958-62, asst. traffic mgr., 1962-63, asst. traffic mgr. marketing, 1963-65; chief exec. C. of C., Sidney, Neb., 1965-67, Scottsbluff, Neb., 1967-68, Helena, Ark., 1969-72; Big Spring, Tex., 1972—; dir. econ. devel., Salina, Kan., 1968-69. Exec. dir. Nat. River Acad. U.S.A., Helena, Ark., 1970—. Asst. scoutmaster Ark. Area council Boy Scouts Am., 1969-72; Scoutmaster Buffalo Trail Area council, 1972—; mgr. Little League Baseball, Sidney, Scottsbluff, 1965-68; chmn. Ark. Task Force for Continuing Edn., Inst. for Orgn. Mgmt., Tex. Christian U., 1972—; mem. Tex. Indsl. Devel. Council, Tex. Tourist Council. Bd. dirs. Big Spring United Fund. Mem. Am., So. indsl. devel. councils, Am., Ark. chambers commerce execs., So. Assn. C. of C. Execs., Tex. C. of C. Mgrs. Home: 1718 Yale Big Spring TX 79720 Office: 215 E 3d Big Spring TX 79720

MERCER, THEODORE CHELTON, coll. pres.; b. Spring City, Tenn., Sept. 3, 1920; s. Robert and Minerva Jane (Lewis) M.; A.B., Bob Jones U., 1943, M.A., 1944; postgrad. U. Chgo., 1946; Litt. D., Houghton Coll., 1952; m. Ora Alice Moore, Aug. 24, 1944; children—Theodore Chelton, John Moore, David Mark. Licensed to preach Meth. Ch., 1938; ordained to ministry Bapt. Ch., 1942; mem. faculty in English, Bob Jones U., 1943-53, dean men, 1944-47, registrar, 1947-53, asst. to pres., 1949-53; dir. publicity, also asst. in devel. Muskingum Coll., 1953-56; pres. Bryan Coll., Dayton, Tenn., 1956—. Local historian Rhea County; mem. Council Advancement Small Colls.; bd. dirs. Tenn. div. Am. Cancer Soc., 1962-68; chmn. county United Fund, 1968—. Mem. Am. Assn. Higher Edn., Am. Coll. Pub. Relations Assn., Newcomen Soc. N. Am., Tenn. Hist. Soc. Rotarian (pres. 1972—). Home: Bryan Coll Dayton TN 37321

MERCER, WALTER ALEXANDER, JR., educator; b. Lumberton, Miss., Jan. 20, 1925; s. Walter A. and Flozzella (Grissom) M.; student Jackson State Coll., 1946-48; A.B., Fisk U., 1950; M.S. in Edn., Ind. U., 1952, Ed. D. (Danforth Found. spl. grad. fellow 1959-60), 1961; m. Mary Martin, Dec. 27, 1958; children—James, Apryl. Supervising tchr. student teaching Powell Lab. Sch., Savannah (Ga.) State Coll., 1952-55, Coll. supr. student teaching, 1956-57, dir. audio-visual aids center, 1957-58, dir. student teaching, 1958-62; prof. edn. and student teaching Fla. A. and M. U., Tallahassee, 1962-71. Vice pres. Lee Manor Improvement Assn., 1965-70. Served with AUS, 1943-46. Mem. Assn. Student Teaching (mem. Fla. unit exec. com. 1967—), Fla. Assn. Tchr. Educators (pres. 1972-73), Phi Delta Kappa, Alpha Phi Alpha. Home: 1111 Hastie Rd Tallahassee FL 32304

MERCHANT, G.C., JR., state ofcl.; m., 2 sons. Dir. S.C. Aeros. Commn. Home: 5655 Ravenwood Dr Columbia SC 29206 Office: Aeronautics Commn Box 88 West Columbia SC 29169

MERCHANT, WALTER MAYFIELD, orgn. exec.; b. Haskell, Tex., Feb. 1, 1927; s. Walter Herbert and Gladys Adelia (Mayfield) M.; student Southwestern U., 1944-45, 46-47; B.A., U. Tex., 1949; m. Charles Rhea Blocker, Nov. 26, 1947; 1 dau., Donna Rhea. Incorporator, sec. Am. Coll. Musicians, Austin, Tex., 1947-51; salesman Western Auto Co., Austin, 1951-54; owner Self-Merchant's Service Stas., Austin, 1954-59; owner-operator Self-Merchant's Student House for U. Tex. Boys, 1959-62; sales Prudential Life Ins. Co., Austin, 1961-64; editor, v.p. pub. relations, chmn. account schedule Am. Coll. Musicians, 1962—; incorporator Coll. Aid Agy., Austin, sec.-treas., 1969—, editor Piano Guild Notes, 1964—. Served with USNR, 1944-45. Named to Hall of Fame, Am. Coll. Musicians, 1969. Mem. Tex. Ex's, Kappa Alpha. Methodist (treas. 1950-54, mem. bd. 1950—, pres. Sunday sch. class 1969—). Home: 5801 Marilyn Dr Austin TX 78731 Office: 808 Rio Grande St Austin TX 78767

MERCIECA, CHARLES, educator; b. Malta, Feb. 3, 1933; s. Carmel and Julia (Brincat) M.; came to U.S., 1961, naturalized, 1971; A.B. in English, Loyola Coll., Malta, 1955; A.B. in Philosophy, Instituto Filosofico, Milan, Italy, 1958; M.S. in Sch. Adminstrn., Kan. State U., 1964; B.S. in Social Work, St. Louis U., 1965; Ph.D. in Social Founds., U. Kan., 1966; m. Sherry Jean Watson, May 28, 1970; 1 dau., Juliette Ruth. Instr. elementary teaching Loyola Coll., Malta, 1951-55; instr., supr. St. Aloysius' Coll., Malta, 1958-61; tchr. St. Marys (Kan.) Pub. High Sch., 1962-64; asso. prof. Chgo. State U., 1966; asso. prof. Fresno (Cal.) State Coll., 1967; prof. edn. Ala. A. and M. U., Huntsville, 1967—, dir. Center for Intercultural Studies, 1971—. Fellow Philosophy Edn. Soc.; mem. Internat. Edn. Assn. (pres. Ala. 1970—), Soc. Profs. Edn., Am. Assn. U. Profs., Internat. Council Edn. for Tchrs., Comparative and Internat. Edn. Soc., Internat. Assn. Educators for World Peace (founder 1969), Delta Tau Kappa (U.S. chancellor 1968—). Contbr. articles to profl. jours. Home: 810 W Arbor Dr NW Huntsville AL 35811

MEREDITH, FLORA MARIE, educator; b. Hagerstown, Md., July 30, 1902; d. Harry Lionel and Marie (Maisch) Meredith; A.B., Duke, 1923, postgrad; M.A. (Gen. Edn. Bd. fellow 1938-39), Tchrs. Coll. Columbia, 1939. Tchr. English, Girls High Sch., Hagerstown, Md., 1923-25; head English dept. Ft. Pierce (Fla.) High Sch., 1925-28; counselor Woman's Coll., U. N.C., 1928-35; social dir. East Campus, Duke, summers 1934-43; dean women, asso. prof. psychology Hendrix Coll., 1935-43; personnel dir. Limestone Coll., 1943-45; dean of women Tusculum Coll., 1945-51; prof. psychology, placement dir. East Tenn. State U., Johnson City, 1951—. Mem. Hazen Found. Conf., 1949-50. Bd. dirs. Oakland Park Juvenile Home. Mem. Am. Psychol. Assn., Nat. Instnl. Tchr. Placement Assn., A.A.A.S., So. Coll. Placement Officers Assn., Am. Personnel and Guidance Assn., Tenn. Edn. Assn., Bus. and Profl. Women's Club, Monday Club Aux., Phi Beta Kappa, Zeta Tau Alpha, Delta Kappa Gamma, Chi Delta Phi, Kappa Delta Pi. Home: 1205 Southwest Av Johnson City TN 37601

MEREDITH, OWEN NICHOLS, museum dir.; b. Etowah, Tenn., Mar. 27, 1924; s. Owen Habner and Ora (Nichols) M.; B.A., U. Va., 1946; postgrad. Fla. State U., 1949, U. Mo., 1950, Alliance Francaise (Paris), 1951; M.A., Syracuse U., 1952; Editor, Circuit Rider, sub-features editor Together mag. Meth. Pub. House, Nashville, Chgo., 1953-57; pub. information dir. Nasvhile-Davidson County chpt. A.R.C., 1957-70; dir. Tenn. State Mus., Nashville, 1970—. Sec., Tenn. Exec. Residence Preservation Found. Mem. Inter-Mus. Council of Nashville and Davidson County (pres. 1970—), Tenn. Assn. Museums (arrangements chmn. 1971 state conv.). Home: 413 Chesterfield Av Nashville TN 37212 Office: War Meml Bldg Nashville TN 37219

MERHIGE, ROBERT REYNOLD, JR., U.S. dist. judge; b. N.Y.C., Feb. 15, 1919; s. Robert Reynold and Eleanor (Donovan) M.; LL.B., U. Richmond, 1942; m. Shirley Galleher, Apr. 24, 1957; children—Robert Reynold III, Mark Reynold. Admitted to Va. bar, 1942; practice in Richmond, 1942-67; judge U.S. Dist. Ct., Richmond, 1967—. Lectr. trial tactics U. Va. Law Sch.; appeal agt. Henrico County Draft Bd., 1954-67. Mem. Richmond Citizens Assn.; mem. citizens adv. com. San. Dist. A. Henrico County. Served with USAAF, World War II. Decorated Air medal with 4 clusters; recipient Amara Civic Club award, 1968; Citizen of Yr. award 3d Dist. chpt. Omega Psi Phi, 1971-72; Spl. award in field of justice and human relations Judicial Council, Nat. Bar Assn., 1972. Mem. Am., Va., Richmond (pres. 1963-64) bar assns., Va. State Bar, Va. Trial Lawyers Assn. (chmn. membership com. 1964-65), Va. Trial Lawyers Assn. Home: 5 Kanawha Rd Richmond VA 23226 Office: Post Office Bldg Richmond Va 23219

MERIN, SIDNEY JULIUS, psychologist; b. Altoona, Pa., Jan. 22, 1927; s. Morris and Lillian (Foreman) M.; B.S., Pa. State U., 1950, Ph.D., 1956, M.A., Temple U., 1952; m. Arlene R. Merrow, Dec. 31, 1945; children—Cheryl Ann, Debra Kay, Michele Lee, Jeffrey Michael. Psychol. asst. Psychol. Clinic, Temple U., 1950-51; psychol. intern Elgin (Ill.) State Hosp., 1952; psychologist Child Guidance Clinic St. Petersburg, Fla., 1953-54; psychol. asst., asst. supr. Psychol. Clinic, Pa. State U., 1954-55; clin. psychologist Child Guidance Clinic, St. Petersburg, 1955-56; staff psychologist Byron Harless & Assos., Tampa, Fla., 1956-60; sr. psychologist Samuel G. Hibbs, M.D. & Assos., Tampa, 1960-64; pvt. practice as clin. psychologist, Tampa, 1964—. Cons. to Clearwater Adult Mental Health Clinic, 1961—, Reading Edn. and Devel. Clinic, 1962—, dir. Ednl. Services Clinic; faculty U. South Fla., 1962—; dir. psychology, pres. Clin. Center for Reading and Learning, Inc. Mem. profl. services com. Community Resources Council; co-chmn. Mayor's Com. to Investigate Civil Service Practices, 1969. Bd. dirs. Hillsborough County Assn. Mental Health, Inter Profl. Family Council. Served with AUS, 1945-46; ETO. Diplomate Am. Bd. Examiners Profl. Psychology. Mem. Am., Fla. (pres. 1970-71, chmn. standards and ethics com.), Tampa Bay (pres. 1957, chmn. standards and ethics com.) psychol. assns., Council on Exceptional Children, Council on Family Relations, Hillsborough County Soc. Clin. Psychologists, Internat. Acad. Law and Sci., Fla. Bd. Examiners Psychology, Sigma Alpha Eta, Phi Delta Kappa. Contbr. articles to profl. jours. Research in psychol. factors in identical twins, wives of men on hazardous duty, psychol. and psychiat. influence in ct. decisions regarding child custody. Home: 4509 San Rafael St Tampa FL 33609 Office: 41 Davis Blvd Tampa FL 33606

MERIWETHER, CHARLES MINOR, drug co. exec.; b. Memphis, Feb. 15, 1911; s. Charles Minor and Leslie Allen (Stevens) M.; student U. Tenn., 1932; LL.B., Cumberland U., 1933; m. Beverly Alston, June 7, 1939; children—Leslie Ann (Mrs. James Atkins), Beverly (Mrs. Frank Lockridge, Jr.), Charles Minor. Engaged in ins. law and ins. mgmt., Memphis, 1933-42, in retail and wholesale drug bus., Birmingham, Ala., 1944-58; dir. finance, Ala., 1958-61; bd. dirs. Export-Import Bank Washington, 1961-65; v.p. Dewberry Drug Co., Inc., Birmingham, Ala., 1965—. Pres. Ala. Ednl. Authority, 1958-61, Ala. Hwy. Authority, 1958-61; chmn. investment com. Tchr. Retirement Fund and Employees Retirement Fund, Ala., 1958-61; dir. Ala. Adjustment Bd., 1958-61. Chmn. dirs. Ala. chpt. Nat. Multiple Sclerosis Soc., 1958-59. Served with U.S. Mcht. Marine, 1942-43. Mem. Birmingham City Salesmen's Club, Phi Gamma Delta. Methodist. Odd Fellow. Clubs: Nat. Press (Washington); Birmingham Downtown, Birmingham Relay House. Home: 803 Essex Rd S Birmingham AL 35222 Office: City Fed Bldg Birmingham AL 35203

MERIWETHER, JOHN T., city mgr., Little Rock. Office: City Hall Little Rock AR 72201*

MERIWETHER, RICHARD EARL, hosp. adminstr.; b. Clarksville, Tenn., July 31, 1920; s. William Douglas and Doris (Crosman) M.; B.S., Austin Peay State U., 1943; M.S., Northwestern U., 1959; m. Pauline Keller, Jan. 30, 1949; children—William Walton, Margaret Ann, John Barker. Farmer, nr. Guthrie, Ky., 1946-50; buyer Covington Grain Co., Guthrie, 1950-52; office mgr. Tenn. Roofing Co., Clarksville, 1952-55; asst. adminstr. Western State Hosp., Hopkinsville, Ky., 1955-57, adminstr., 1957-62; dir. hosp. adminstrn. Ky. Dept. Mental Health, Louisville, 1962-65; adminstr. Muhlenberg Community Hosp., Greenville, Ky., 1965-70, Bowling Green (Ky.)-Warren County Hosp., 1971—. Mem. adv. council Ohio Valley Regional Med. Program, 1966-69; dir. Western Ky. Hosp. Services, Inc., 1968-70; mem. bd. Blue Cross Hosp. Plan, 1968-69. Mem. adv. bd. Freed-Hardeman Coll., Henderson, Tenn., 1961-68; bd. dirs. Mid-Western Mental Health Mental Retardation, Madisonville, Ky., 1965-69, vice chmn., 1968. Served with USAF, 1943-46. Recipient William A. Wycoff Meml. award Twin Lakes dist. Ky. Hosp. Assn., 1967. Mem. Greenville C. of C. (sec., treas. 1968-70, pres. 1967-68), S.A.R. (chpt. pres. 1969), Am. Coll. Hosp. Adminstrs., Nat. Assn. Hosp. Purchasing Agts. (regional v.p. 1961), Ky. Hosp. Assn. (trustee

1966-68, pres. 1968-69), Nat. League Nursing, Ky. League Nursing (mem. bd. 1962). Kiwanian (pres. 1969). Contbr. articles to profl. jours. Home: 1412 Scottsville Rd Bowling Green KY 42101 Office: PO Box 56 Bowling Green KY 42101

MERKER, FRANK FERDINAND, hosp. adminstr.; b. Bklyn., July 2, 1909; s. August and Mathilda (Schmidt) M.; student Balt. Poly. Inst., 1924-27; B.S., Johns Hopkins, 1931; M.D., Med. Coll. Va., 1943; postgrad. Menninger Sch. Psychiatry, 1946-49; m. Edith Marjorie Greer, Feb. 6, 1937; 1 dau., Mathilda Sue. With Balt. Gas & Electric Co., 1931; with Glenn L. Martin Aircraft Co., 1933-35; with Civilian Conservation Corps, 1935-40; intern U.S. Marine Hosp., Balt., 1944; resident psychiatry VA Hosp., Topeka, 1946-49, asst. sect. chief, 1949-51, sect. chief, 1952-54, asst. dir. profl. services, 1954-55, dir. profl. services, 1954-58; practice medicine, specializing in psychiatry, Topeka, 1946-58, Salem, Va., 1958-60, Roseburg, Ore., 1960-66; dir. profl. services VA Hosp., Salem, 1958-60; dir. VA Hosp., Roseburg, Ore., 1960-66, VA Hosp., Coatesville, Pa., 1966-69, VA Hosp., Richmond, Va., 1969—; asso. prof. psychiatry Med. Coll. Va., 1969—. Served to capt., M.C., USAAF, 1944-46. Fellow A.A.A.S., Am. Psychiat. Assn.; mem. A.M.A. Conglist. Address: VA Hosp Richmond VA 23219

MERKIN, WILLIAM IRVING, govt. ofcl.; b. N.Y.C., July 19, 1918; s. Samuel and Rae (Mishin) M.; B.A. in Econs., Coll. City N.Y., 1940; postgrad. Harvard Grad. Sch. Bus. Adminstrn., 1945; m. Lucile B. Dannenberg, Sept. 14, 1940; 1 son, William Stuart. With various U.S. Govt. burs., depts., 1940—; dir. Office Adminstrn., Domestic and Internat. Bus., Dept. Commerce, 1960-68, asso. dir. U.S. Bur. Census, Washington, 1968—. Served to 1st lt. USAAF, 1942-45. Decorated D.F.C., Air medal with clusters. Recipient Meritorious Service medal Dept. Commerce, 1951, Exceptional Service medal, 1967. Clubs: International (Washington); Wood Lawn Country (Alexandria, Va.). Home: 2510 Virginia Av NW Washington DC 20037 Office: US Dept Commerce Bur Census Washington DC 20233

MERLO, THOMAS JOHN, public accountant; b. Scranton, Pa., Dec. 3, 1930; s. Vito and Mildred (Gatto) M.; student U. Scranton, 1953-54; B.B.A., U. Miami, 1957; m. Ann Piccioni, May 18, 1957; children—Robin, Thomas, Kim Marie, William, Lisa. Utilities cons. Morgan, Altemus & Barrs, Miami, Fla., 1963-66; dir. fiscal affairs Jackson Meml. Hosp., Miami, 1966-68; dir. internal auditing Dade County, Miami, Fla., 1968-71; sr. partner Thomas J. Merlo, C.P.A., Miami, 1971—; utilities cons.; dir. Nat. Properties, Inc., Miami. Chmn. Dade County Employees United Fund Campaign, 1968-69; bd dir. Dade County United Fund, 1969—. Served with USN, 1949-52. Mem. Am. Inst. C.P.A.'s, Fla. Inst. C.P.A.'s, Internal Auditors Assn. Fla., Nat. Assn. Accountants, Unico Southwest (pres. 1971). Clubs: Serra (treas.), Southwest Lions (treas. 1962). Home: 2010 Alhambra Circle Coral Gables FL 33134 Office: 2138 Biscayne Blvd Miami FL 33137

MEROS, GEORGE NICHOLAS, lawyer; b. Abbeville, S.C., Mar. 21, 1923; s. Nicholas G. and Pearl (Peterson) M.; B.S., U. Fla., 1950, LL.B., 1953; m. Anne Shropshire, Nov. 30, 1946; children—Peter, Dede, George Nicholas, John. Admitted to Fla. bar, 1953, since practiced in St. Petersburg; mem. firm Meros, Hobson & Wilkinson and predecessor firms, 1956—; pres. Jebb, Inc., St. Petersburg; lectr. Stetson Law Sch.; dep. commr. Fla. Indsl. Commn., 1953-58. Bd. dirs. Mound Park Hosp. Served with AUS, 1941-45. Mem. Am., Fla. bar assns., Com. of 100, Alpha Tau Omega, Phi Delta Phi. Clubs: Lakewood Country, St. Petersburg Yacht. Kiwanian. Contbr. articles to profl. jours. Home: 4627 Sunrise Dr S St Petersburg FL 33705 Office: 432 7th St S St Petersburg FL 33701

MERRELL, CURTIS HARLAN, supt. schs.; b. Crawfordsville, Ark., Feb. 18, 1935; s. William and Golda (Banks) M.; B.A., Ouachita Baptist U., 1957; M.S., La. State U., 1960; Ed.D., U. Ark., 1969; m. Virginia Ramona Moody, Aug. 28, 1954; children—Scott Carleton, Stephen Craig, Drew Christopher. Grad. teaching asst. La. State U., 1959-60; coach, athletic dir., asst. prin., math. tchr. Central High Sch., Helena-West Helena, Ark., 1960-67; head resident Pomfret Hall, U. Ark., 1967-69; dir. S.E. Ark. Ednl. Service Center, Monticello, 1969-71; supt. schs., Monticello, 1971—. Chmn. Phillips County Assn. Crippled Children; pres. Drew County Mental Retardation Council, 1972-73. Served with AUS, 1957-59. Named Outstanding Young Educator, Helena-W. Helena, 1966. Mem. Nat., Ark. (chmn. legislative com. dept. classroom tchrs. 1962-64) edn. assns., Am., Ark. assns. sch. adminstrs., Ark., S.E. Ark. sch. study councils, S.E. Ark. Schoolmasters, Drew County C. of C., Phi Delta Kappa. Baptist. Club: Monticello Country. Home: 211 McKnight Dr Monticello AR 71655 Office: 136 W College St Monticello AR 71655

MERRIAM, WILLIAM R(USH), communications co. exec.; b. Washington, Oct. 4, 1912; s. John H. and Rose (Wallach) M.; A.B., Lehigh U., 1933; m. Maria Teresa Ippoliti, Feb. 16, 1946; children—Rosemary, Laura Elizabeth, Asst. to drama editor Washington Times, 1934; pub. relations account exec. John Price Jones Corp., N.Y.C., 1935-40, fund raising campaign dir., 1946-47; membership sec. Fedn. Ry. Progress, 1948-49, dir. pub. relations, 1950-52, v.p., 1953, v.p., sec., treas., 1954-57; spl. asst. pub. relations Assn. Am. Railroads, 1957-60; asst. v.p., dir. Washington relations Internat. Tel. & Tel. Corp., 1961-67, v.p., dir. Washington relations, 1967—. Bd. Washington Tennis Patrons Found., Internat. Rescue Com. Served to capt. Q.M.C., U.S. Army, 1941-46. Decorated commendatore Al Merito della Repubblica Italiana (Italy). Mem. Pub. Relations Soc. Am., Alpha Chi Rho. Episcopalian. Clubs: Nat. Press, 1925 F Street, Metropolitan, Chevy Chase. Home: 1808 45th St NW Washington DC 20007 Office: 1707 L St NW Washington DC 20036

MERRICK, EUNICE PEACOCK (MRS. GEORGE E. MERRICK), civic worker; b. Coconut Grove, Fla.; d. Alfred and Lillian (Frow) Peacock; student pvt. and pub. schs.; m. George Edgar Merrick, Feb. 5, 1916. Treas. George E. Merrick, Inc., real estate, 1934-42, pres., 1942-45. Active in establishing Dade County Schs., Coral Gables, 1922-25. Recipient Book of Golden Deeds, Exchange Club Coral Gables, 1957. Mem. Hist. Soc. So. Fla., Fla. Hist. Soc., Nat. League Am. Pen Women (patroness), Sigma Alpha Iota (patroness). Christian Scientist. Clubs: Coral Gables Woman's (charter mem., dir.), Coral Gables Garden (past pres.). George E. Merrick, the original owner, founder Coral Gables, Fla. Home: 3926 Segovla St Coral Gables FL 33134

MERRICK, HARRY LEONCE, advt. exec.; b. Portsmouth, O., Oct. 12, 1903; s. Harry L. and Georgia (Crawford) M.; ed. pub. schs.; m. Mary Heine, Aug. 9, 1952; children—Harry Leonce, David, Mary, William. With Kal, Ehrlich & Merrick Advt. (co. name changed to Kal & Merrick Advt., Inc.), Washington, 1925—, pres., 1946—; dir. Jefferson Fed. Savs. & Loan Assn., Pepsi Cola Bottling Co. Washington; adv. bd. Riggs Nat. Bank. Pres., Washington Bd. Trade, 1953-54; chmn. Washington Conv. and Visitors Bur., 1956-59. Program chmn. Eisenhower-Nixon inaugurals. Recipient Printers Ink Silver medal award Am. Fedn. Advt.; Silver Beaver, Boy Scouts Am. Kiwanian (past pres. Washington); Mason (Shriner, Jester). Home: 3730 Cardiff Rd Chevy Chase MD 20015 Office: 2141 Wisconsin Av Washington DC 20007

MERRICK, WARD SPRAGUE, JR., petroleum engr.; b. Ardmore, Okla., Jan. 4, 1928; s. Ward Sprague and Jinks (Ikard) M.; student Okla. U., 1945-50; m. Marianne Brown, Mar. 24, 1951; children—Ward Sprague III, Vaida, Frank W., Robert B. Mgr., geologist, engr. Ward S. Merrick, Ardmore, 1950—. Alternate nat. del. Republican Conv., 1964. Chmn., So. Okla. Meml. Found.; v.p. Frontiers of Sci. Fedn. Okla., Merrick Found.; past pres. United Fund drive; chmn. So. Okla. Hosp. Authority. Bd. dirs. Midcontinent Environmental Center Assn. Served to capt. AUS. Mem. Midcontinent Oil and Gas Assn., Independent Petroleum Assn., Hereford Heaven Cattle Assn. (dir.), Ardmore C. of C. (Americanism award 1962). Home: 700 Q St SW Ardmore OK 73401 Office: Box 998 Ardmore OK 73401

MERRIFIELD, LESTER LEVERN, dentist; b. Dill City, Okla., Feb. 1, 1921; s. Conrad Cecil and Ivery Lea (Guthrie) M.; B.S., Okla. State U., 1941; D.D.S., Baylor U., 1946; M.S. in Dentistry, U. Mo., 1950; m. Jan Marlene McVicker, Oct. 4, 1967; children—Terri Ann, Shawn Lea. Practice dentistry, Chickasha, Okla., 1946-48; practice orthodontics, Ponca City, 1951—. Tchr., Tweed Found. for Orthodontic Research, 1953-60, co-dir., 1960-70, dir., 1970—. Served with USAAF, 1943-45, 50-51. Diplomate Am. Bd. Orthodontics. Mem. Nat., Okla., County dental assns., Nat. Orthodontic Assn. Contbr. articles to profl. jours. Home: Route 3 Ponca City OK 74601 Office: 111 Patton St Ponca City OK 74601

MERRILL, FRED L., ednl. adminstr. Mem. Ala. Bd. Edn. Office: Dept Edn State of Alabama Montgomery AL 36104*

MERRILL, HUGH DAVIS, JR., lawyer, state legislator; b. Anniston, Ala., Apr. 2, 1913; s. Hugh Davis and Martha (Chitwood) M.; A.B., U. Ala., 1935, LL.B., 1937; m. Martha Holcombe, Dec. 28, 1951; children—Hugh, David, Paul, Nancy. Partner law firm Merrill, Merrill, Vardaman &Williams. Mem. Ala. Ho. of Reps., 1955—, speaker pro tem, 1967-71. Mem. Ala. Democratic Com., 1951-58; del. Dem. Nat. convs., 1944, 52, 56, 64. Chmn. bd. trustees Jacksonville State U. Served to lt. AUS, 1944-46. Mem. Am. Legion, Sigma Alpha Epsilon. Baptist. Mason, Kiwanian, K.P. Home: 2312 Ridgeview Rd Anniston AL 36201 Office: Legislative Bldg Montgomery AL 36104

MERRILL, PATRICIA KOKEN (MRS. JACK H. MERRILL), civic worker; b. Toronto, Ont., Can., Jan. 12, 1926; d. Frank W. and Violet (Vernon) Koken; B.J., Ohio State U., 1948; m. Jack Hilton Merrill, Aug. 7, 1948; children—Jeffrey Leeson, Lisa Marie. Adviser, Kappa Delta, 1948-59, province pres., 1960-63, nat. press dir., 1963-65, nat. v.p., 1965-67, nat. pres., 1967—, membership chmn. Cleve. chpt. 1962-63, v.p., 1963-64, pres., 1964-65; den mother Cub Scouts Am., 1961-63, area adviser to den mothers, 1962-63; sec. Ohio State U. Alumnae Assn., Toledo, 1958; room mother Avon (O.) Elementary Sch., 1960-61, Crestwood Elementary Sch., Richmond, 1970; room mother Rocky River (O.) Elementary Sch., 1963-64, chmn. ways and means, 1965-66; del. Va. Congress Parents and Tchrs. Conv., 1971; 3d alternate area adviser, for 34 colls., N.C., Va., W. Va., chmn. quota-limitation com. Nat. Panhellenic Conf., 1971—. Del., Chesterfield County Republican Conv., 1971, Va. Rep. Conv. 1971; canvass chmn. Crestwood Precinct Rep. Com., 1971, 72. Conglist (asst. dir. Bible sch. 1957-58, sec. Couple's Club 1958—). Home: 1620 Creekside Rd Richmond VA 23235

MERRILL, PELHAM JONES, judge Supreme Ct. Ala.; b. Heflin, Ala., Dec. 1, 1907; s. Walter Benjamin and Lilla (Jones) M.; A.B., U. Ala., 1926, LL.B., 1934; m. Gladys Morrison, Aug. 21, 1936. Tchr., coach West Blocton (Ala.) High Sch., 1926-31; admitted to Ala. bar, 1934, since practiced in Heflin; asso. justice Supreme Ct. of Ala., 1952—. Mem. Ala. Ho. of Reps., 1936-38, 47-52, speaker pro tem, 1949, 51; mem. Ala. State Democratic Exec. Com., 1938; chmn. Cleburne County Dem. Exec. Com., 1936-42. Served from 2d lt. to maj. USAAF, 1942-46; col. Res. ret. Mem. Am. Legion. Baptist. Mason. Home: 2008 Commodore St Montgomery AL 36106 Office: Judicial Bldg PO Box 218 Montgomery AL 36101

MERRIMAN, JERRY JOHNSON, religious ofcl.; b. Lufkin, Tex., Jan. 10, 1939; s. Gratton Johnson and Audrey Faye (Beasley) M.; B.S., (Baseball scholar), Miss. State U., 1961; M.R.E., Southwestern Bapt. Theol. Sem., 1963; postgrad. Southwestern Bapt. Sem., 1965, European Bapt. Sem., 1967; m. Rhonda Jean Cox, June 27, 1970. Religious youth counselor Christian Life Crusade, 1963-69; dir. Bapt. Student Union, Miss. State U., State College, 1969—. Cons. youth activities com., pulpit supply com. First Bapt. Ch., Starkville, Miss., 1971—; soloist for religious, sch., civic groups, 1963—. Counselor, tribal dir. Camp Rockmont for Boys, Black Mountain, N.C., summers 1961, 66. Mem. Miss. State Alumni Assn. Baptist (deacon 1971—). Kiwanian. Club: M (State College). Author: (with Chester E. Swor) The Teenage Slant, 1963, Youth at Bat, 1968, To Enrich Each Day, 1969. Home: 302 Greensboro St Starkville MS 39759 Office: PO Box 4035 State College MS 39762

MERRITT, A(RTHUR) R(AYMOND), banker; b. Clearfied County, Pa., Dec. 20, 1895; s. Elijah and Mary (Shimp) M.; student Am. Inst. Banking, 1925-30; grad. Sch. Banking of South, La. State U., 1956, grad. Grad. Sect., 1959; m. Leta Smith, May 9, 1917. Cashier Bank of Sherrill, 1923-40, v.p., 1940-42, pres., 1942-53; Ark. bank commr., 1953-55; dir. Simmons 1st Nat. Bank; owner A.R. Merritt Co., plantation mgmt. Mem. exec. bd. area council, mem. nat. council Boy Scouts Am.; bd. dirs. Jefferson Comprehensive Care Center, Ark. Soc. Crippled Children; chmn. bd. trustees Jefferson Hosp. Recipient Silver Beaver award Boy Scouts Am. Mem. S. Ark. Livestock Show Assn. (pres.). Presbyn. Mason (32 deg., past comdr., past potentate, Shriner, Jester, K.T.), Royal Order Scotland, Red Cross of Constantine (past sovereign), Rotarian. Address: Sherrill AR 72152

MERRITT, GILBERT STROUD, lawyer; b. Nashville, Jan. 17, 1936; s. Gilbert Stroud and Angie Fields (Cantrell) M.; B.A., Yale, 1957; LL.B., Vanderbilt U., 1960; LL.M., Harvard, 1962; m. Louise Clark Fort; children—Gilbert Stroud III, Louise Clark, Rufus Elijah Fort. Admitted to Tenn. bar, 1960; pvt. practice with Boult, Hunt, Cummings & Connors, Nashville, 1962-63; city atty. Nashville and Davidson County, Tenn., 1963-66; U.S. atty. gen. Middle Dist. Tenn., Nashville, 1966-69; partner Gullet, Steele, Sanford, Robinson & Merritt, Nashville, 1970—. Sec., treas. So. Properties, Inc., 1960—; instr. Vanderbilt U., 1960-61, asso. prof. law, 1969-70. Del. Tenn. Constl. Conv., 1965. Acting dir. Vanderbilt Urban Devel. Center, 1970-71; trustee Fisk U. Mem. Am., Nashville, Tenn. bar assns. Democrat. Episcopalian. Contbr. articles to profl. jours. Home: 612 Fair St Franklin TN 37064

MERRITT, LINTON JACK, business exec.; b. Dothan, Ala., Sept. 19, 1923; s. Pearl Girard and Rebecca Faye (Miller) M.; ed. pub. schs.; m. Kathleen Faust, Jan. 29, 1971. Oilfield and pipeline equipment operator and bookkeeper, 1946-56; office mgr., asst. gen. mgr. Luke Constrn. Co., Houma, La., 1956-60; self-employed in home bldg., 1960-62; with Houma Welders, Inc., 1962—, adminstr., 1964—. Part-time dep. sheriff, Houma, 1970—. Served with AUS, 1940-45; with U.S. Maritime Service, 1945-46. Mason. Home: 1007 Peach St Houma LA 70360 Office: 1100 Oak St Houma LA 70360

MERRITT, LUCIAN GERALD, instrument mfg. dir.; b. Waco, Tex., Aug. 8, 1936; s. Lucian Henry and Hester Novel (Perdue) M.; B.B.A., Baylor U., 1958, M.S., 1960; postgrad. St. Mary's U., 1960-62; m. Tommie Pierce, Dec. 22, 1956; 1 dau., Lezli Diane. Mgr. div. purchasing, space and information systems div. N.Am. Aviation, Inc., Downey, Cal., 1962-67; dir. material services Tracor, Inc., Austin, Tex., 1967-71, dir. mfg. operations, 1971—; dir. Merritt, Inc. Past pres. Austin Gideon Camp; past bd. dirs. Campus Crusade for Christ. Served from 2d lt. to 1st lt. USAF, 1959-62; capt. Res. Mem. Am. Mgmt. Assn., Nat. Purchasing Mgmt. Assn., Gideons, Order of Artus, Alpha Chi. Mason. Home: 100 Wallis St Austin TX 78746 Office: 6500 Tracor Lane Austin TX 78721

MERRITT, MARION WILLIAM, retail store exec.; b. Belton, S.C., Apr. 20, 1921; s. Marion Shafter and Nell Blyth (Williamson) M.; B.S., The Citadel, 1943; m. Inez Hill Bussey, Dec. 4, 1943; children—Marion William, Kathy (Mrs. Harry Stinson), Inez. With Winn-Dixie Stores, Inc., Greenville, S.C., 1946-55, Jacksonville, Fla., 1955-58, Louisville, 1958-63, div. mgr., v.p., Atlanta, 1969—. Served with AUS, 1942-45. Decorated Bronze Star medal. Home: 3825 Dumbarton Rd NW Atlanta GA 30327 Office: 5400 Fulton Indsl Blvd Atlanta GA 30336

MERRITT, PAUL BURWELL, ins. exec.; b. Chincoteague, Va., Dec. 23, 1924; s. Leslie Uphsur and Aletia (Tarr) M.; student LaSalle U., 1949-53; m. Helen Mae Potts, June 3, 1943; 1 son, Gregory Paul. Comptroller, Naval Air Sta., Fed. Civil Service, 1947-59; owner Paul B. Merritt Co., Chincoteague, 1959—; pres. Pony Penninl Enterprises, Inc., 1962—, also dir.; pres. Misty Meadows Devel., 1970—. Vice-mayor Chincoteague, 1952-54, mem. Accomack County Bd. Suprs., 1963—. Served with USNR, 1943-45; PTO. Mem. V.F.W. (comdr. 1949-52), Chincoteague C. of C. (exec. sec. 1953-57, 63-68). Democrat. Baptist (Sunday sch. supt. 1957-71). Mason, Kiwanian. Home: 111 Maddox Blvd Chincoteague VA 23336 Office: 201 Maddox Blvd Chincoteague VA 23336

MERRITT, ROBERT EDWARD, hosiery mill exec.; b. Mt. Airy, N.C., Mar. 27, 1927; s. Oscar Kochtitzky and Catherine Roth (Hubbard) M.; B.S. in Elec. Engring., N.C. State Coll., 1949; m. Cava Mary Clarkson, Dec. 29, 1951; children—Caroline, Frances, Edward, Mary Louise, Sallie. Engr., Am. Machine & Foundry Co., Raleigh, N.C., 1951-53; asst. mgr. Merritt Machine & Supply Co., Mt. Airy, 1953-55; asst. supt. Renfro Hosiery Mills Co., Mt. Airy, 1955-65, pres., 1965—. Trustee Surry Community Coll. Served with USNR, 1945-46. Recipient Spl. award Nat. Assn. Hosiery Mfrs., 1968; named Jr. C. of C. Young Man of Yr., 1960. Mem. Internat. Fedn. Knitting Technologists, Nat. Assn. Hosiery Mfrs. (dir. 1963-69). Episcopalian. Rotarian. Patentee in field. Home: 832 Country Club Rd Mount Airy NC 27030 Office: PO Box 908 Mount Airy NC 27030

MERRY, FRANCES ROBINSON (MRS. ERNEST BRISCOE MERRY, JR.), civic worker; b. Jacksonville, Fla., May 15, 1914; d. Philip Frank and Lorene (Youngblood) Robinson; student Ward-Belmont Sch., Nashville, 1930-32, Mary Baldwin Coll., 1932-33; m. Ernest Briscoe Merry, Jr., Nov. 1, 1933; children—Frances Robinson (Mrs. George Bryan Simkins), Ernest Briscoe III, Philip Robinson, Anne Somers. Bd. dirs. Girl Scouts U.S.A., Augusta, Ga. area, 1938-40; bd. dirs. Jr. League, 1936-41, 50-53; pres. Episcopal Day Sch. Assn., 1951-52; with Gray Ladies A.R.C., 1942-44; bd. dirs. Augusta Assembly, 1955-56; chmn. meml. petit point furnishing St. Paul's Episcopal Ch., 1957-66, dir. Jr. Dau. King, 1954-55, pres. Women's Aux., 1943-44. pres. Augusta Symphony Orch. Guild, 1961-64; bd. dirs. Augusta Symphony and Historic Augusta, Inc.; trustee Augusta Prep. Sch., 1961—. Clubs: Augusta Country; Town and Country Garden (pres. 1951-52, 66-67). Pinnade. Home: Magnolia Villa Augusta GA 30904

MERSCH, EDWARD BERNARD, surgeon; b. Covington, Ky., Nov. 20, 1908; s. Bernard H. and Mary C. (Kruetzman) M.; B.S., Xavier U., 1931; M.B., U. Cin., 1935, M.D., 1936; m. Margaret W. Rettig, Sept. 11, 1940; 1 dau., Mary Margaret. Surg. resident Louisville Gen. Hosp., 1936-39; asst. surg. clinician Cin. Gen. Hosp., 1940-53; practice medicine specializing in surgery, Covington, 1953—; mem. surg. staff St. Elizabeth Hosp., 1940—, Booth Meml. Hosp., 1940—, St. Luke's Hosp., Ft. Thomas, Ky., 1954—. Fellow A.C.S.; mem. A.M.A., Ky. Med. Assn. (pres. 1957-58), Southeastern Surg. Congress, Cin. Surg. Soc. Lion (past pres. Covington). Club: Art (Cin.). Home: 3261 Turkeyfoot Rd S Fort Mitchell KY 41017 Office: 722 Scott St Covington KY

MERSKY, ROY MARTIN, lawyer, educator; s.; Irving and Rose (Mendelson) M.; B.S., U. Wis., 1948, LL.B., 1952; M.A. in L.S., 1953; m. Deena Hersch, Feb. 3, 1951; children—Alisa Judith, Deborah Ann, Ruth Elizabeth. Admitted Wis. bar, 1952, Tex. bar, 1967; practiced law, Wis., 1952-54; municipal reference librarian, Milw., 1953-54; asst. librarian Yale, 1954-59; dir. Washington State Law Library, 1959-63; exec. sec. Washington Jud. Council, 1959-63; commr. Wash. Supreme Ct. Reports, 1959-63; prof. law, law librarian U. Colo., 1963-65, U. Tex. 1965—; acting dir. Jewish Nat. and U. Library, Hebrew U., Jerusalem, 1972-73. Mem. Am. Bibliog. Center; mem. adv. bd. Congressional Information Service. Bd. dirs. Tex. bd. Am. Civil Liberties Union, Tex. chpt. Am. Civil Liberties Union. Served with AUS, 1944-46. Decorated Bronze Star Medal. Mem. Am., Wis. bar assns., Tex. Library Assn., State Bar Tex., Am. Assn. Law Schs., Am. Assn. Law Libraries, Am. Judicature Soc., Am. Soc. Legal History, A.L.A., Spl. Libraries Assn., N.A.A.C.P., Am. Assn. U. Profs., Tex. Assn. Coll. Tchrs., Mental Health Assn., Urban League. Jewish religion. Author: Louis Dembitz Brandels, 1856-1941; A Bibliography, 1958; Water Law Bibliography 1947-65; Sources Book on U.S. Water and Irrigation Studies, 1966; Law Books for Non-Law Libraries and Laymen, A Bibliography, 1966; Index to Periodical Articles Related to Law, 1970. Editor publs. in field. Contbr. articles legal Jours. Book review editor Law Library Jour., 1965-72, Criminal Law Bull., 1972—; assoc. editor Bankers Law Jour., Real Estate Law Jour. Home: 1419 Gaston Av Austin TX 78703

MERTINS, CHRISTIAN CARL, JR., banker; b. Pensacola, Fla., July 10, 1926; s. Christian Carl and Helen (Bond) M.; B.S., U. Fla., 1950; m. Dorothy Gertrude Nobles, Jan. 4, 1952; children—Clifton Karl, Laura Marie, David Laurence. Mgmt. trainee Newport Industries, Inc., Pensacola, 1950-51; v.p., cashier First Bank & Trust Co., Pensacola, 1953—, also dir.; pres. Barnett Bank Pensacola, 1953—. Dir. Fla. Sch. of Banking. Pres. Jr. Achievement of Pensacola. Bd. dirs. Children's Home Soc. W. Fla., Children's Home Soc. of Fla., Pensacola Port Authority. Served with AUS, 1944-46, 51-53. Mem. Assn. for Bank Audit, Control and Operations, Unit Bankers W. Fla., Pensacola C. of C. (pres.), Scabbard and Blade, Pi Kappa Alpha. Clubs: Exchange, Pensacola Country. Home: 1765 Texar Dr Pensacola FL 32503 Office: 100 W Garden St Pensacola FL 32502

MESADA, LILLIAN C. (MRS. AUGUSTINE M. MESADA), ret. assn. exec.; b. Wakefield, Mass., Oct 24, 1908; d. Walter Huntley and Florence (Karcher) Comee; B.S., Northwestern U., 1942; M.A., Columbia, 1952; m. Augustine M. Mesada, Nov. 19, 1960. Tchr. phys. edn. Colby Jr. Coll., 1931-43; clubmobile worker A.R.C., ETO, 1943-45; tchr. phys. edn. Kimberley Sch., Montclair, N.J., 1946-48;

program exec. Armed Services dept. YMCA, Key West, Fla., 1948-71. Bd. dirs. Old Island Restoration Found., 1971—, sec., membership chmn., 1971; mem. adv. bd. Salvation Army, 1971—. Mem. A.R.C. Clubmobile Assn. (pres. 1952-53), Bus. and Profl. Women's Club (pres. 1966-67), Beta Sigma Phi (named chpt. Girl of Year 1970). Home: 2514 Linda Av Key West FL 33040

MESH, HOWARD ALAN, accountant; b. Chgo., Oct. 3, 1933; s. William B. and Rose (Kanter) M.; B.B.A., U. Miami, 1955; m. Sandra Ann Rosen, June 26, 1955; children—Ronna Fern, Scott Everett. Sr. accountant Pentland, Purvis, Keller & Co., 1955-60; pvt. practice accounting, 1960-61; partner H.N. Miller & Co., 1961-63, Miller, Beer & Co., 1963-68; mgr. Peat, Marwick, Mitchell & Co., Miami, Fla., 1969-70; sr. partner Mesh, Dick & Baum, 1970—. Mem. leaders div. United Jewish Appeal, 1966—. Bd. dirs. United Fund of Dade County; bd. dirs., treas. V.I.P. Sch., Inc. Served with AUS, 1956-58. Mem. Am., Fla. (chmn. com. on mgmt. services 1967-68, chpt. v.p.) insts. C.P.A.'s, Accounting Soc. U. Miami (founder, charter pres.). Jewish religion (bd. dirs., youth commr. congregation). Club: Optimist of Southwest Miami (charter, pres. 1961-62). Home: 1224 SW 89th Av Miami FL 33156 Office: 1000 Brickell Av Miami FL 33131

MESSENGER, JOHN NELSON, accountant; b. Friona, Tex., Mar. 11, 1942; s. George C. and Beulah (Weaks) M.; B.B.A., W. Tex. State U., 1965; m. Anita Faye Wimberley, Aug. 28, 1965; 1 son, John Nelson II. Accountant, Steve Messenger, Friona, 1965-67; partner Messenger &Co., C.P.A.'s, Friona, Hereford, Tex., 1967-70; partner Kernaghan, Harvey & Co., C.P.A.'s, Dallas, also Hereford, 1971-72; partner Baldridge & Co., C.P.A.'s, San Marcos, Tex., 1972—. Mem. accounting adv. council W. Tex. State U. C.P.A., Tex. Mem. Am. Inst. C.P.A.'s, Tex. Soc. C.P.A.'s, Accounting Research Assn., Amarillo Area Estate Planning Council, Alpha Kappa Psi. Baptist. Lion (mem. dist. gov.'s cabinet 1966-67). Home: 2711-B Parker Lane Austin

MESSENGER, STEVE, accountant; b. Friona, Tex., Sept. 24, 1923; s. George C. and Ruth (Kirk) M.; B.B.A., West Tex. State U., 1953; m. Narcia Evelyn Finney, July 18, 1954; children—Michael Brent, Jay Corwin, Troy Wayne. Self-employed accountant, Friona, 1953-66; sr. partner firm Steve Messenger & Co., Hereford, also Friona, 1966-70; partner Kernaghan, Harvey & Co., Dallas, also Friona, Hereford, Amarillo, 1970—. Gen. chmn. United Fund, 1966, city chmn., 1967—; mem. Amarillo Area Estate Planning Council, 1966—. Recipient Golden Rule award United Fund. C.P.A., Tex. Mem. Am. Inst. C.P.A.'s, Tex. (state dir. Panhandle chpt. 1971-72), Amarillo socs. C.P.A.'s, Accounting Research Soc., Tex. Tech. Tax Inst. (v.p. 1969), Friona (dir., sec. 1960-61, v.p. 1961-62, 68-69, pres. 1969-70), West Tex. (mem. legislative, ednl. coms. 1970—) chambers commerce, Tex. Cattle Feeders Assn. Baptist. Mason, Lion (pres. 1969, Hi-Plains Eye Bank dir. 1965-70). Home: 6203 Jameson St Amarillo TX 79106 Office: Am Nat Bank Amarillo TX 79101

MESSER, H(ARRY) DONALD, mgmt. and tech. cons. co. exec.; b. N.Y.C., Apr. 19, 1931; s. Harry Andrew and Sue (Metzger) M.; B.S., N.Y. U., 1952; M.S., Cornell U., 1955; Dr. Engring., Johns Hopkins, 1963; m. Jeanine Louise Aline Sizorn, Mar. 28, 1956; children—Michael Alan, Philip Daniel. Physicist, Hughes Aircraft Co., Los Angeles, 1954-55; sr. engr. Martin Co., Balt., 1957-61; mgr. systems engring. Fairchild-Hiller Corp., Hagerstown, Md., 1961-63; prin. scientist Booz Allen Applied Research, Inc., 1963-64, research dir., 1964-66, v.p., 1966-67; v.p. Booz Allen and Hamilton, Inc., Washington, 1967-70; v.p. Orkand Corp., Silver Spring, Md., 1970-71; pres. Messer Assos., Inc., Silver Spring, 1971—. Served with AUS, 1955-57. Mem. Operations Research Soc. Am., Inst. Mgmt. Cons. (founding), A.A.A.S. Club: University (Washington). Home: 6425 31st Pl NW Washington DC 20015 Office: 1400 Spring St Silver Spring MD 20910

MESSERSMITH, LLOYD LOWELL, ret. educator; b. Francisco, Ind., Jan. 29, 1905; s. Martin Lewis and Amelia (Rogers) M.; B.A., DePauw U., 1928; M.A., Columbia, 1932; Ed.D., Ind. U., 1942; m. Fae Elizabeth Houston, Aug. 22, 1929; children—Martha Ann (Mrs. Lindsay B. Smith), Betty Jean (Mrs. James Cole), Alice Kay (Mrs. James Collins). Tchr. pub. schs., Francisco, Ind., 1922-24, Shortridge High Sch., Indpls., 1928-30; instr. history, basketball coach DePauw U., Greencastle, Ind., 1930-45; prof. phys. edn. So. Meth. U., Dallas, 1945-70. Mem. evaluation team Nat. Council Accreditation Tchr. Edn., 1965-66, Tex. Edn. Agy., 1966-67. Chmn. group work div. Council Social Agys. Dallas, 1949-50; mem. phys. edn. com. S.W. area YMCA, 1950-68; mem. adv. com. Dallas Mus. Health and Sci., 1960-68. Bd. dirs. YMCA, Dallas, 1946-56. Recipient Honor awards Ind. Assn. Health, Phys. Edn. and Recreation, 1950, So. dist., 1956, Tex. Assn. Health, Phys. Edn. and Recreation, 1956, A.A.H.P.E.R., 1961. Fellow A.A.H.P.E.R. (v.p. phys. edn. div. 1962-63, chmn. recognition awards com. 1967-69, dist. pres. 1959-61), Am. Coll. Sports Medicine, Am. Pub. Health Assn., Am. Sch. Health Assn.; mem. Ind. (pres. 1936-37), Tex. (pres. 1955-56) assns. health, phys. edn., recreation, Am. Acad. Phys. Edn., Am. Assn. U. Profs., Lambda Chi. Methodist. Author: (with others) Physical Education Handbook, 1954, 5th rev. edit., 1969. Mem. editorial com. Tex. Assn. Health, Phys. Edn., Recreation Jour., 1968-71. Contbr. articles to profl. jours. Home: 3513 Purdue St Dallas TX 75225

MESSINGER, HENRY M., land surveyor; b. New Orleans, June 2, 1912; s. Frank L. and Anna Dorothy (Zachau) M.; student pub. schs.; m. Lucille Bradley, July 25, 1936; children—Martha Ann, Frank Lee III. Parish surveyor Morehouse Parish; also pres. Morehouse Parish police jury. Mem. La. Engring. Soc., La. Land Surveyors Assn. (pres. 1967), Bastrop-Morehouse C. of C. (dir.), Am. Soc. C.E., Am. Congress Surveying and Mapping. Presbyn. (deacon, elder). Mason. Home: 401 Jackson St Bastrop LA 71220 Office: 331 Jackson St Bastrop LA 71220

MESSMER, H(ERMAN) PAUL, govt. ofcl.; b. Columbus, O., Aug. 7, 1913; s. Herman L. and Doris (Fishinger) M.; B.A., B.S. in Edn., Ohio State U., 1937; m. Clara Kathryn Stuckey, May 14, 1936; children—Barbara Kay (Mrs. John L. Stevens), Lawrence P. Tchr., Fairfield Twp Schs., Huron County, O., 1937-42, supt., 1942-46; supr. counseling and services to handicapped Ohio Employment Service, Columbus, 1946-50, chief counseling, 1950-61, chief community projects Manpower Devel. and Tng., 1961-64; employment adviser, liaison officer President's Com. on Employment Handicapped, Washington, 1964-68, dep. asst. exec. sec., 1968-70, asst. exec. sec., 1970—. Exec. dir. Ohio Worker Tng. Com., 1961-64; exec. sec. Ohio Gov.'s Com. Employment Handicapped, 1954-63. Mem. Nat. Rehab. Assn. (charter treas. Ohio; pres. job placement div. 1970; mem. bd. 1970—), Internat. Assn. Personnel in Employment Security (past pres. Ohio), Nat. Vocational Guidance Assn., Am. Personnel and Guidance Assn., Internat. Platform Assn. Home: 6006 16th St N Arlington VA 22205 Office: President's Com on Employment of Handicapped Washington DC 20210

MESSNER, SAMUEL THEODORE, JR., investment broker; b. Binghamton, N.Y., Oct. 21, 1916; s. Samuel T. and Bessie (Eastwood) M.; B.S., U. Pa., 1939; m. Ruth Eleanor MacNeill, Sept. 20, 1941; children—Richard, Mary Elizabeth. With 30 Minute Laundry and Sixty Minute Clean, 1946-57; asso. mgr. E.I. du Pont de Nemours & Co., Inc., St. Petersburg, Fla., 1957-61; v.p., allied mem. Walston & Co., Inc. (mem. N.Y. Stock Exchange), St. Petersburg, 1962—. Chmn., dir. fund raising div. Heart Fund, 1959-60. Bd. dirs. Girl Scouts U.S.A., St. Petersburg, 1960-63, All Childrens Hosp. Guild. Served to capt. USAAF, 1942-46. Mem. St. Petersburg Stock and Bond Club. Episcopalian. Home: 136 Sunshine Lane St Petersburg FL 33701 Office: 300 West Bldg St Petersburg FL 33733

MESTER, JORGE, condr.; b. Mexico City, Mexico, 1935; came to U.S., 1945; studied with Jean Morel, Leonard Bernstein, Albert Wolff. Condr. concerts Mozart Festival, Lincoln Center, N.Y.C., summers 1966, 67; condr. Nat. Symphony, Mexico City, 1966, Boston Symphony, 1967, Pitts. Symphony, 1968; prin. condr. Aspen (Colo.) Music Festival, 1969, now music dir.; guest condr. Boston, New Orleans, Indpls. orchs., Japan Philharmonic, Trieste Philharmonic, Los Angeles Philharmonic; now music dir. Louisville Philharmonic Soc. Home: 3200 Tucker Station Rd Louisville KY 40299 Office: 321 W Broadway Louisville KY 40202

METCALF, IRBY G., JR., banker; b. Bokchito, Okla., Oct. 23, 1922; s. Irby G. and Lennie (Bracket) M.; student Southwestern Coll., Durant, Okla., 1939; B.A., Dallas Coll., 1946; grad. Stonier Grad. Sch. Banking, Rutgers U., 1953, Inst. Financial Mgmt., Harvard, 1961; m. Jacquita Ann Knight, Aug. 5, 1944. Nat. bank examiner, Dallas, 1948-54; pres. First Nat. Bank, Post, Tex., 1954-65; with Continental Nat. Bank, Ft. Worth, 1965—, exec. v.p., 1966-67, pres., 1967—; v.p., dir Citizens State Bank, Slaton, Tex., 1964—; dir. First Nat. Bank, Grand Prairie, Tex. Mem. exec. bd. Longhorn council Boy Scouts Am.; mem. bd. All Sts. Episcopal Hosp., Tarrant County United Fund, Southwestern Expn. and Fat Stock Show. Served to 1st lt., inf., AUS, World War II. Home: 4312 Bellaire Dr S Fort Worth TX 76109 Office: 714 Houston St Fort Worth TX 76101

METCALF, SHELBY, basketball coach. Head basketball coach Tex. A. and M. Coll. Office: Tex A and M Coll College Station TX 77843*

METCALF, WILLIAM HENRY, JR., architect; b. Memphis, Feb. 9, 1928; s. William Henry and Myrtle (Tittle) M.; B.A., Yale, 1949, B.Arch., 1951, M.Arch. (Magnus T. Hopper fellow), 1952; postgrad. U. Oslo, Norway, summer 1950; m. Barbara Ann Keller, Oct. 8, 1955; children— Ramsay Katherine, Anne Louis. Architect, Washington, 1958-65; partner Metcalf & Assos., Architects and Engrs., Washington, 1966—; vis. critic Carnegie-Mellon U., 1959-60, Catholic U., 1961, Howard U., 1962, Tex. A. and M. U., 1968. Served to capt. USAF, 1953-56. Nuffield fellow Div. Archti. Studies, London, 1957-58, Rehmann fellow A.I.A., 1958. Mem. A.I.A., Am. Hosp. Assn., Internat. Hosp. Fedn., Am. Assn. Hosp. Planning. Presbyn. Clubs: International (Washington), Washington Golf and Country (Arlington, Va.). Important works include: Health Centers, Lagos, Nigeria; U. Lagos Teaching Hosp. and Med.-Dental Sch.; Anne Arundel Gen. Hosp., Annapolis, Md.; Fairfax Hosp., Falls Church, Va.; Montgomery Gen. Hosp., Olney, Md.; Bapt. Meml. Hosp., Jacksonville, Fla.; John Andrew Meml. Hosp., Tuskegee Inst., Ala.; U.S. Embassy, Vientiane, Laos; Nat. Zool. Park; Master Plan and Phase Six, Smithsonian Instn., Washington: Staff Housing U.S. Embassy, Monrovia, Liberia. Home: 4201 Fairfax Rd McLean VA 22101 Office: 1054 31st St NW Washington DC 20007 also 150 E 58th St New York City NY 10022

METCALFE, JOSEPH DAVIS, constrn. co. exec.; b. Pearsall, Tex., Sept. 29, 1916; s. Joseph Davis and Mary (Hudson) M.; B.S., Tex. A. and M. U., 1937; m. Antoinette Barnwell Mazyck, Aug. 11, 1939; children— Joseph Davis, Marilyn (Mrs. Douglas L. Inhofe), John Barnwell. Engr. Ark. Natural Gas Corp., 1937-41, Bucyru-Erie Co., 1946-48; v.p. Tecon Corp., 1948-55; with Standard Industries, Inc., Tulsa, 1955—, pres., dir., 1967—; pres., dir. J.D. Metcalfe, Inc., Tulsa, 1962—. Served to lt. col. C.E., AUS, 1941-46; ETO. Decorated Bronze Star. Registered profl. engr., Okla., Tex. Mem. Assn. Gen. Contractors (br. v.p. 1967), Nat. Crushed Stone Assn. (v.p. S.W. region 1972—), Okla. Asphalt Pavement Assn. (dir. 1972—); Tulsa Indsl. Execs. Council (vice chmn. 1971—), Nat. Soc. Profl. Engrs. Episcopalian (vestryman 1963-66). Home: 2128 E 31st Pl Tulsa OK 74105 Office: Box 15670 Tulsa OK 74115

METKO, GERALD EARL, bus. adminstr.; b. Evanston, Ill., Oct. 23, 1930; s. John Arthur and Blanche (Heinz) M.; student Lake Forest Coll., 1948-50; B.S., No. Ill. U., 1957; postgrad. Stetson U., 1957-58; m. Ann Sumner, June 14, 1952; children—LorAnn, Scott. Asst. pub. relations mgr. Allstate Ins. Co., St. Petersburg, Fla., 1959-64; exec. dir. St. Petersburg Housing Authority, 1964-68; mgr. bus.-govt. relations and community devel. St. Petersburg Area C. of C., 1969—; devel. dir. All Childrens Hosp., 1969-71; v.p. First St. Petersburg Service Corp., 1971—. Mem. Mayor's Adv. Com. for Elimination of Slums and Blight, 1966-69; moderator, participant Gov.'s Conf. on Cities, Tallahassee, Fla., 1968; mem. Mayor's Com. for Relocation of Displaced Persons, 1966-69; mem. St. Petersburg Ann. Christmas Parade Com., 1967-68; chmn. St. Petersburg Motorcade Com. honoring President Kennedy, 1963; mem. Mayor's Green Spot Com., 1968-69. Vice pres. Vis. Nurses Assn.; dir. CACEP, Presbyn. Social Ministries, Villa Maria Housing, Inc., Project Find. Neighborly Center; commr. St. Petersburg Housing Authority. Served with USNR, 1950-54. Recipient Outstanding Service award City of St. Petersburg, 1969, 71, Key to City St. Petersburg, 1968, 71. Mem. Fla. Assn. Housing and Redevel. Ofcls. (past pres.). Club: St. Petersburg Exchange (pres.). Home: 5120 Huntington Circle NE St Petersburg FL 33703 Office: First Federal Savings & Loan Bldg 4th and Central Av St Petersburg FL 33701

METTS, DANIEL LAMAR, JR., librarian; b. Pulaski, Tenn., June 9, 1925; s. Daniel Lamar and Ruth MacMurray (Feagin) M.; A.B., Emory U., 1947, M.A., 1948, M.L.S., 1950; m. Evelyn Bates, Aug. 26, 1949; children— Martha, Catherine, Marguerite. Asst. in acquisitions Fla. State U., Tallahassee, 1950-53, head serial acquisitions, 1954-56; asst. head acquisitions Library U. Minn., St. Paul, 1956-63; librarian Mercer U., Macon, Ga., 1963—. Served with USNR, 1943-46. Mem. Southeastern, Ga. library assns., Am. Soc. Information Sci. Alpha Tau Omega. Home: 3020 Clairmont Av Macon GA 31204 Office: Stetson Memorial Library Mercer U Macon GA 31207

METZER, JAMES FREDRICK, lawyer; b. Tulsa, Mar. 24, 1933; s. James Ambrose and Marian Edith (Harkness) M.; B.B.A., U. Okla., 1956, LL.B., 1957; m. Waltraud Margarete Brand, June 5, 1959; children—Greg Anthony, Marilyn Karin. Admitted to Okla. bar, 1957; mem. firm Ungerman, Grabel, Ungerman & Leiter, Tulsa, 1959-61; staff atty. Halliburton Co., Duncan, Okla., 1961-64; sec., gen. atty. Republic Supply Co., Oklahoma City, 1964—. Served to capt. AUS, 1957-59. Mem. Am., Okla. bar assns., Oklahoma City C. of C., Sigma Alpha Epsilon. Republican. Lutheran. Home: 3813 NW 69th Terrace Oklahoma City OK 73116 Office: 135 Couch Dr Oklahoma City OK 73102

METZGER, SIDNEY M., bishop; b. Fredericksburg, Tex., July 11, 1902; s. Francis and Ida (Dietz) M.; student St. Mary's Sch., Fredericksburg, 1910-15, St. John's Sem., San Antonio, 1915-22; Th.D., North Am. Coll., Rome, Italy, 1925; Dr. Canon Law, Pontifical Inst. of Canon and Civil Law, Rome, 1928; LL.D., St. Edwards U., 1940. Ordained priest St. John Lateran Basilica, Rome, 1926; prof. St. John's Sem., San Antonio, 1928-33, rector, 1933-40; regent St. Mary's U. Law Sch., San Antonio, 1935-40; consecrated aux. bishop of Santa Fe (titular bishop of Birta), 1940; installed as coadjutor of El Paso, with the right of succession, 1942; succeeded to the See of El Paso, 1942. Decorated Knight Comdr. Equestrian Order of Holy Sepulchre of Jerusalem; Grand Cross of King Alfonso X, The Wise (Spain). Doctor Mundunae Sapientiae of Boswell Soc., 1963. Address: 1012 N Mesa Av El Paso TX 79902

MEWHORTER, WILLIAM JOSEPH, banker; b. Mpls., May 17, 1925; s. William Henry and Cathryn Mary (Dwyer) M.; B.B.A., Tex. Coll. Mines, 1948; m. Anne Beys, Feb. 17, 1950; children—William Paul, Anne Lynn. Asst. v.p. State Nat. Bank, El Paso, 1948-62; v.p. First Nat. Bank, Roswell, N.M., 1963-66, First Nat. Bank, Midland, Tex., 1966-72; pres., dir. Western State Bank, Midland, 1972—. Served with USNR, 1942-45. Democrat. Roman Catholic. Home: 1700 Culver Dr Midland TX 79701 Office: 1030 Andrews Hwy Midland TX 79701

MEYER, ALPHONSE HERMAN, JR., surgeon, educator; b. Memphis, Feb. 3, 1919; s. Alphonse Herman and Eulalie (Ashner) M.; student U. Va., 1936-38; S.B., Harvard, 1940, M.D., 1943; m. Janis Floe Hays, Aug. 13, 1949; children—James Hays McIntosh (stepson), Gregory Allison, Andrew Hays. Intern Barnes Hosp., St. Louis, 1944; asst. resident surgery Barnes Hosp., 1946-48, Albany Hosp., 1948-49; asst. in surgery Washington U. Med. Sch., 1946-48, Albany Med. Coll., 1948-49; chief resident surgery Queens Gen. Hosp., 1949-51; mem. faculty U. Tenn. Sch. Medicine, Memphis, 1951—, asst. clin. prof. surgery, 1962—; practice medicine specializing in surgery, Memphis, 1951—; mem. staffs Bapt. Meml., Meth., St. Joseph, LeBonheur Children's, City of Memphis hosps. (all Memphis). Served with M.C., USNR, 1944-46. Diplomate Am. Bd. Surgery, Am. Bd. Abdominal Surgery. Mem. A.C.S., Southeastern Surg. Congress, Am. Soc. Abdominal Surgeons, Am. Coll. Gastroenterology. Contbr. articles to profl. jours. Home: 79 W Galloway Dr Memphis TN 38111 Office: 20 S Dudley St Memphis TN 38103

MEYER, ALVIN FELIX, JR., govt. ofcl.; b. Shreveport, La., Sept. 3, 1920; s. Alvin Felix and Bertha (Weil) M.; B.S., Va. Mil. Inst., 1941; postgrad. George Washington U., 1962; m. Vivian Burford, June 13, 1942;children—Alvin Felix III, Carolyn Burford (Mrs. Ronald Rhode). Commd. 2d lt. USAAF, 1941, advanced through grades to col., 1960; chief biomed. sci. corps, 1965-69, chmn. Dept. Def. Environmental Pollution Control Com., 1965-69; spl. asst., legislative affairs Consumer Protection and Environmental Health Service, U.S. Dept. Health, Edn. and Welfare, Washington, 1969-70; dir. Office Noise Abatement and Control, U.S. Environmental Protection Agy., Washington, 1970—. Chmn. bd. Abe Meyer Corp., Shreveport, La., 1969—; pres. Alvi Corp., Arlington, Va., 1965—. Fellow Am. Soc. C.E., Am. Pub. Health Assn., Aerospace Med. Assn. (asso.); mem. Nat. Soc. Profl. Engrs. Contbr. articles to profl. jours. Home: 1600 Longfellow St McLean VA 22101 Office: Environmental Protection Agency Washington DC 20460

MEYER, BEN FRANKLIN, journalist; b. San Antonio, Aug. 18, 1903; s. Ben Franklin and Emily (Peters) M.; student Baylor U., 1923-26; m. Christine Richardson, Feb. 8, 1927. With San Antonio Light, 1918-19; with San Antonio Express, 1919-21; with Cuero Daily Record, 1921-23; with Waco News-Tribune, 1923-24; gen. mgr. Electra (Tex.) News, 1926; corr. A.P., Atlanta, 1927-38, chief bur., Mexico City, Mexico, 1938-41, exec. rep. for Caribbean, Havana, Cuba, 1941-43, 48-54, chief bur., Santiago, Chile, 1943-45, exec. rep. for N.C. and S.C., 1946, exec. rep., Ill., Ind., 1947, Latin Am. affairs specialist, Washington, 1954-68; chief press div. OAS, 1969-70. Lectr. Georgetown, U., Catholic U. Am., Baylor U., U. Tex. Mem. White House, State Dept. corrs. assns., Sigma Delta Chi. Democrat. Episcopalian. Club: Nat. Press (Washington). Home: 2632 S Grant St Arlington VA 22202

MEYER, CHARLES APPLETON, govt. ofcl.; b. Boston, June 27, 1918; s. George von L. and Frances (Saltonstall) M.; B.A., Harvard, 1939; m. Suzanne Seyburn, June 15, 1940; children—Brooke (Mrs. Harald Franzgen), Nancy S. With Sears, Roebuck & Co., 1939-69, Sears subsidiary, Bogota, Colombia, 1953-55, v.p., 1955-60, v.p., dir. Southwestern terr., Dallas, 1960-66, v.p., dir. Eastern terr., Phila., 1966-69; asst. sec. state for inter-Am. affairs Dept. State, Washington, 1969—. Bd. dirs. Children's Hosp., Phila., Jarvis Christian Coll. Served to capt. AUS, World War II. Clubs: Harvard, Brook (N.Y.C.); Racquet (Chgo.); Shoreacres (Lake Bluff, Ill.); Gulph Mills Golf; Onwentsia (Lake Forest, Ill.); Metropolitan (Washington). Home: 3010 Woodland Dr NW Washington DC 20008 Office: Dept State Washington DC 20520

MEYER, CHARLES EDWARD, constrn. co. exec.; b. New Orleans, Aug. 20, 1938; s. Elbert J. and Ruth (Thomas) M.; B.S. in Mech. Engring., Tulane U., 1960; M.B.A., Loyola U., 1965; m. Myrna Knight, Dec. 29, 1956; children—Richard Charles, Randall James, Ronald Scott. Engr., U.S. Gypsum Co., 1960-62; sr. tool engr. Boeing Co., 1962-65; sec., treas. Hamilton, Meyer & Assos., Inc., Metairie, La., 1964—; pres. La. Housing & Urban Devel. Corp., Metairie, La., 1967—, La. Housing & Urban Devel. Constrn. Co., Metairie, 1968—. Registered profl. engr., La. Mem. Am. Soc. M.E., La. Engring. Soc., Am. Pilots Assn. Home: 6 Shady Oak Lane New Orleans LA 70123 Office: PO Box 763 Metairie LA 70004

MEYER, FLOYD RAYMOND, librarian; b. Oak Park, Ill., Dec. 4, 1915; s. Roman N. and Cecil (Ayers) M.; B.Sc. in Edn., U. Neb., 1938, Ed.D., 1957; M.A. in L.S., U. Denver, 1949; m. Marjorie Marie Carie, June 7, 1938; children—Philip R., Karen M. (Mrs. Danny Eugene Myers). Tchr., prin. jr. high sch. Howells (Neb.) Pub. Schs., 1938-40, Cedar Bluffs (Neb.) High Sch., 1940-41, Stratton (Neb.) High Sch., 1946-47; librarian North Platte (Neb.) Pub. Schs., 1947-48; asst. edn. librarian, instr. dept. secondary edn. U. Neb., 1948-50, asst. librarian social studies div., instr. secondary edn., 1950-53, asst. librarian tech. services div., asst. prof. secondary edn., 1953-56, librarian U. High Sch., asst. prof. secondary edn. in charge library edn., 1956-57; dir. East St. Louis Residence Center Library, So. Ill. U., 1957-58; dir., prof., chmn. dept. library sci. Kan. State Coll., Pittsburg, 1958-66; library dir. Stephen F. Austin State U., Nacogdoches, Tex., 1966-71, documents librarian, 1971-72, serials recs. librarian, 1972—. Chmn. Resident Center Libraries, East St. Louis, Ill., 1957-58. Served from 1st lt. to lt. col. AUS, 1941-46. Mem. Am. Legion, Pi Mu Epsilon, Phi Delta Kappa. Democrat. Roman Catholic. Club: Piney Woods Country (Nacogdoches). Author: Nebraska School Library Handbook, 1952; Look to Your Library, 1953, rev., 1956. Home: 4104 Forest Lane Nacogdoches TX 75961

MEYER, FREDERICK GUSTAV, botanist; b. Olympia, Wash., Dec. 7, 1917; B.Sc., Wash. State U., 1939, M.Sc., 1941; Ph.D., (Univ. scholar), Washington U., St. Louis, 1949. Lab. asst. botany Wash. State U., 1939-51; dendrologist Mo. Bot. Garden, 1951-56; botanist new crops research br. Agrl. Research Service, U.S. Dept. Agr., 1957-63; research botanist in charge herbarium, U.S. Nat. Arboretum, Washington, 1963—. Served with AUS, 1942-46. Mo. Bot. Gardens grantee Univ. Coll., London, 1949-51, NSF fellow, 1955—. Mem. Botanical Soc., Am. Soc. Taxonomy, Hort. Soc., Soc. Study Evolution, Internat. Soc. Plant Taxonomy. Office: US Nat Arboretum Washington DC 20250*

MEYER, HENRY ALBERT, state ofcl.; b. St. Louis, June 15, 1904; s. Albert George and Mary Gertruce (Bruns) M.; B.S., U. Ill., 1930, M.E., 1938; Ed.M., U. Fla., 1963, Ed.S., 1964, Ed.D., 1966; m. Elizabeth M. Shea, Oct. 2, 1931. Commd. ensign USCG, 1930, advanced through grades to capt., 1952; with USCG Dist. 3, 1955-57, Dist. 5, 1957-61; ret., 1961; dir. evening program Edson Jr. Coll., 1966-68; dir. operations research Vocational Rehab., Fla. Dept. Health and Rehab. Services, Tallahassee, 1968—. Mem. Am. Assn. Sch. Adminstrs., Assn. for Supervision and Curriculum Devel., Ret. Officers Assn., Fla. Vocational Assn., Nat., Fla. rehab. assns., Am. Legion, U. Ill. Alumni Assn., Phi Delta Kappa, Kappa Delta Pi, Alpha Kappa Delta. Home: 420 E Park Av Tallahassee FL 32301 Office: 725 S Bronough St Tallahassee FL 32304

MEYER, HENRY EDWIN, educator; b. Jeffersonville, N.Y., July 23, 1890; s. Henry August and Eliza (Weber) M.; Tchrs. diploma, Ithaca Conservatory, 1910, artists diploma, 1914; B.A., Southwestern U., 1934; B.M., Ithaca Conservatory, 1935, B.S., 1935; M.A., S.W. Tex. State Coll., San Marcos, 1942; m. Rodney Leal, Sept. 23, 1914; children—Jean, Gregory, Henry, Rodney. Head music dept. Howard Payne Coll., Brownwood, Tex., 1918-20; dean music Daniel Baker Coll., 1920-24; dean music Southwestern U., Georgetown, Tex., 1926-42; dean sch. fine arts, 1942-61, prof. piano and organ, 1926-61; vis. prof. U. Tex., Sul Ross Coll. Mem. Tex. Music Tchrs. Assn. (pres. 1926-28), Tex. Assn. Music Schs. (pres. 1947-48). Rotarian. Methodist. Republican. Home: 810 E University St Georgetown TX 78626

MEYER, JOSEPH WILLIAM, airline exec.; b. St. Louis, Aug. 24, 1908; s. Fred L. and Elizabeth (Bastian) M.; grad. high. sch.; m. Lorraine Buchmann, Oct. 15, 1936; children—Jerry, Robert, John. Bookkeeper, Smith, Moore & Co., St. Louis, 1927-31, R. E. Funsten Co., St. Louis, 1931-36; with Delta Air Lines, St. Louis, Memphis, Atlanta, 1936—, asst. v.p. customer relations, 1967—. Episcopalian. Home: 3132 Argonne Dr NW Atlanta GA 30305 Office: Atlanta Airport Atlanta GA 30320

MEYER, JULIEN H(ERMAN), surgeon, obstetrician, gynecologist; b. Enfield, N.C., May 7, 1914; s. Joseph and Hennye (Lehman); B.S., U. N.C., 1935; M.D., Med. Coll. Va., 1937; m. Dorothy Rose Kahn, July 14, 1940; children—Julien Herman, Carol Joan. Intern. Greater Balt. Med. Center, 1937-38; resident in obstetrics and gynecology St. Joseph's Hosp., Balt., 1938-40; postgrad, course gynecol. pathology Johns Hopkins Hosp., 1940; practice obstetrics and gynecology, Roanoke, Va., 1940—; attending obstetrician, gynecologist Roanoke Meml. Hosps., 1940—, chief obstetrics and gynecology, 1961-62; cons. gynecology VA Hosp., 1946—; courtesy staff Lewis-Gale Hosp., 1946—; staff Community Hosp. of Roanoke Valley. Fellow A.C.S., Am. Coll. Obstetricians and Gynecologists; mem. A.M.A., Med. Soc. Va., Va. Obstet. and Gynecol. Soc., Roanoke Acad. Medicine, So. Med. Assn., Roanoke Valley Assn. Obstetricians and Gynecologists (pres. 1965-66). Home: 4925 Crossbow Circle SW Roanoke VA 24014 Office: Med Center Bldg 127 McClanahan St SW Roanoke VA 24014

MEYER, LAWRENCE JOSEPH, lawyer; b. Chgo., July 7, 1927; s. Joseph Benjamin and Sarah (Peilet) M.; student Roosevelt Coll., Chgo., 1948-50; LL.B., U. Miami, 1954; m. Roslyn Simon, Mar. 28, 1953; children—Sandra Leigh, Janice Beth, Pamela Sue. Admitted to Fla. bar, 1955; individual practice law, Hollywood, Fla., 1955—; small claims judge Broward County, 1963—. Past chmn. T-Y Park Bd. Broward County. Served with USNR, 1945-48. Mem. Broward (treas., mem. exec. com.), South Broward (past dir.) bar assns. Mason (Shriner). Home: 5000 McKinley St Hollywood FL 33021 Office: 2435 Hollywood Blvd Hollywood FL 33020

MEYER, PHILIP EDWARD, journalist; b. Deshler, Neb., Oct. 27, 1930; s. Elmer Edward and Hilda (Morrison) M.; B.S., Kan. State U., 1952; M.A., U. N.C., 1963; postgrad. Harvard, 1966-67; m. Mary Sue Quail, Aug. 5, 1956; children—Caroline, Katherine, Melissa, Sarah. Asst. state editor Topeka (Kan.) Daily Capital, 1954-56; grad. asst., part-time instr. U. N.C., 1956-58; reporter Miami (Fla.) Herald, 1958-62; Washington corr. Knight Newspapers, 1962-69, 70—; project dir. Russell Sage Found., 1969-70; dir. Negro attitude surveys, Detroit, Miami, 1967-68. Served with USNR, 1952-54. Recipient Pub. Affairs Reporting award Am. Polit. Sci. Assn., 1960. Nieman fellow, 1967. Mem. Am. Polit. Sci. Assn. Episcopalian. Club: Harvard (N.Y.C.). Contbr. articles on social scis. to profl. jours. Home: 11650 Mediterranean Ct Reston VA 22070 Office: Nat Press Bldg Washington DC 20004

MEYER, SYLVAN HUGH, newspaper editor; b. Atlanta, Oct. 7, 1921; s. David Norman and Ray (Levinsohn) M.; A.B. in Journalism, U. N.C., 1943; m. Annemie Heineman, Jan. 19, 1947; children—Erica, David, Jason. Reporter, Daily Times, Gainesville, Ga., 1947-48; mng. editor, 1948-50, editor, v.p., 1950-69; editor Miami (Fla.) News, 1969—. Chmn. Ga. adv. com. U.S. Commn. Civil Rights, 1958-65; mem. nat. com. Am. Civil Liberties Union, 1959—; mem. adv. bd. Pulitzer prize, 1968—. Served to lt. USNR, 1943-46. Nieman fellow, Harvard, 1951; recipient award Sidney Hillman Found., 1961, Dept. of Army Patriotic Civilian Service award, 1961. Mem. Am. Soc. Newspaper Editors (dir. 1965—), Nat. Planning Assn., Greater Miami C. of C. (bd. govs.), Sigma Delta Chi (Distinguished Service award for editorial writing 1957), Tau Epsilon Phi. Clubs: Miami, Standard. Author: (with Walter Spearman) Racial Crisis and the Press, 1960. Home: 248 W Rivo Alto Dr Miami Beach FL 33139 Office: Miami News 1 Herald Plaza Miami FL 33101

MEYER, VAUGHAN BENJAMIN, lumber co. exec.; b. Eagle Pass, Tex., Dec. 13, 1920; s. Otto C. and Genevieve C. (Vaughan) M.; B.S., Rice U., 1941; postgrad. Cal. Inst. Tech., 1941-42; m. Courtenay Langdon Lyon, May 25, 1946 (div. Feb. 1969); children—Catherine (Mrs. Richard Abbott Lange), Beverly. Exec. v.p. Alamo Lumber Co., San Antonio, 1948-61; pres. Eagle Lumber Co., San Antonio, 1956—, Eagle Lumber Co. of Tex., 1961—; dir. George C. Vaughan & Sons, San Antonio, Lumbermen's Investment Co., Lumbermen's Underwriters, Austin, Tex. Councilman, mayor pro tempore City of Terrell Hills, 1965-68. Trustee S.W. Found. for Research and Edn., Vaughan Found., Raymond Dickson Found., St. Marys Hall. Served to lt. comdr. USNR, 1942-46. Mem. S.A.R., Soc. Colonial Wars, Tex. Cavaliers, Sigma Xi. Episcopalian. Clubs: Argyle, San Antonio Country, Pilon. Home: 202 Ruelle San Antonio TX 78209 Office: PO Box 6985 San Antonio TX 78209

MEYER, WILLIS G(EORGE), petroleum geologist; b. Bellwood, Neb., Jan. 21, 1906; s. George David and Ella V. (Carrigan) M.; A.B., U. Neb., 1930; A.M., U. Cin., 1933, Ph.D., 1941; m. June Allison, June 26, 1937; children—Nancy Rebecca, Ann Marie. Geologist, Amerada Petroleum Corp., Tex. and Okla., 1934-38, DeGoyler & MacNaughton, Dallas, 1938-47; partner Meyer & Achtschin, Dallas, 1947-57; owner, mgr. Willis G. Meyer (formerly Willis G. Meyer & Assos.), also cons. in petroleum engring. and geology, 1957—. Fellow Geol. Soc. Am.; mem. Am. Asso. Petroleum Geologists (past v.p.), Am. Geophys. Union, A.A.A.S., Soc. Ind. Profl. Earth Scientists (past pres.), Am., Dallas (past pres.) geol. socs., Sigma Xi, Acacia. Unitarian. Clubs: Engineers, Dallas Country, Petroleum (Dallas). Author geol. papers. Home: 4950 Rheims Pl Dallas TX 75205 Office: Republic Nat Bank Bldg Dallas TX 75201

MEYERCORD, EDWARD BERNARD, door mfg. co. exec.; b. Chgo., June 21, 1912; s. George Rudolph and Agnes (Adams) M.; B.L.S., Northwestern U., 1934; m. Carol Duffield, Nov. 13, 1937; children—Edward Bernard, Jr., Susan (Mrs. Patrick J. Rice), Francis D., Pamela Ann (Mrs. Michael P. Mitchell). Unit mgr. Comml. Credit Co., Chgo., 1935-37; sec. Meyercord Compound Lumber Co., Mobile, Ala., 1937-40, pres., 1940-49; owner Meyercord Sales Co., Mobile, 1949—; pres., treas. Meyercord Door Corp., Mobile, 1957—. Bd. dirs., v.p. Mobile Symphony, 1957-67; bd. dirs. Providence Hosp., Mobile, 1959—, chmn., 1968-69. Club: Country (pres. 1946-47) (Mobile). Home: 8 Springbank St S Mobile AL 36608 Office: Box 7187 Mobile AL 36607

MEYERS, GRANT ULYSSES, foundry co. exec.; b. Moline, Ill., May 1, 1913; s. George C. and Lillian (Rommel) M.; B.S.C., Northwestern U., 1933; M.B.A., U. Chgo., 1955; m. Doris M. Fraser, Jan. 23, 1953; children—Stuart, Joan, Glen, Eric, Marcia. Mgr. accounting dept. Wis. Steel Works div. Internat. Harvester Co., Chgo., 1933-55; v.p., comptroller Radiant Mfg. Corp., Morton Grove, 1955-59; sec.-treas. Security-Columbian Banknote Co., N.Y.C., 1959-60, financial v.p., sec., 1960-65; owner, chmn., pres., chief exec. officer Oil City Iron Works, Inc., Corsicana, Tex., 1965—. Mem. Financial Execs. Inst., Nat. Assn. Accountants (internat. pres. 1969-70), Acacia, Beta Gamma Sigma, Beta Alpha Psi. Mason. Clubs: Metropolitan (N.Y.C.); Cipango, Lancers (Dallas); Corsicana Country; Chicago Yacht; Canyon Creek Country (Richardson, Tex.). Home: 2514 Big Horn Lane PO Box 725 Richardson TX 75080 Office: PO Drawer 1560 Corsicana TX 75110

MEYERS, TEDSON J., lawyer; b. Bayonne, N.J., May 6, 1928; A.B., N.Y. U., 1949, M.A., 1950; J.D., Harvard, 1953. Admitted to D.C. bar, 1953, N.Y. State bar, 1957; since practiced in Washington; govt. regulation counsel ABC, 1958-61; adminstrn. asst. to chmn. FCC, 1961-62; spl. asst. to dir. Peace Corps, 1963-68. Mem. D.C. City Council, 1972—; mem. White House Task Force on Ednl. TV Overseas, 1966-68; pub. mem. Criminal Justice Coordinating Bd., D.C., 1970—. Mem. Bar Assn. D.C. (mem. adminstrv. law sect.), Am., FCC bar assns. Home: 1828 Wyoming Av NW Washington DC 20009 Office: 1200 18th St NW Washington DC 20036*

MICHAEL, CYRIL, judge, musician; b. Charlotte Amalie, St. Thomas, V.I., Jan. 22, 1898; s. Andreas and Wilhelmina (Fusborg) M.; student music extension U. Chgo., 1932; LL.B., La Salle Extension U., 1947; m. Elizabeth T. Davis, Dec. 23, 1940; children—Edna, Dale, Elba, Betsey-Mae. Admitted to V.I. bar, 1945; organizer orch., tchr. comml. class Frederiksted (V.I.) High Sch., 1921-22; sec. to govt. and dist. attys., 1933-37, also acting ct. reporter; clk. U.S. Dist. Ct., dist. ct. commr., ct. interpreter, law clk. to dist. ct. judge, 1937-51; acting judge Police Ct., intermittently, 1937-51, judge Municipal Ct., St. Thomas and St. John, 1957-65; presiding judge Municipal Ct. of V.I., 1965—; U.S. atty. Dist. of V.I., 1951-54, mem. V.I. bar examining Com., 1947-56. Mem. dist. com. P.R. council Boy Scouts Am., 1944—, v.p. V.I. council; chmn. Police Commn., 1947-55. Mem. U.S. Navy Band, 1917-33, acting bandmaster, Guantanamo Bay, 1932. Mem. Am., Nat., V.I. bar assns., Fleet Res. Assn. (pres.) Am. Legion (past comdr.). Roman Catholic. Author articles in local newspapers. Home: Box 297 Charlotte Amalie St Thomas VI

MICHAEL, JAMES HARRY, JR., lawyer, state senator; b. Charlottesville, Va., Oct. 17, 1918; s. James Harry and Reuben (Shelton) M.; B.S., U. Va., 1940, LL.B., 1942; m. Barbara E. Puryear, Dec. 18, 1946; children—Jarrett, Victoria. Admitted to Va. bar, 1942; since practiced in Charlottesville; mem. firm Michael and Musselman, 1946-54, J.H. Michael, Jr., 1954-59, Michael and Dent. 1959—; asso. judge Juvenile and Domestic Relations Ct., Charlottesville, 1954-68; mem. Va. Senate, 1968—. Exec. dir. Inst. Pub. Affairs, U. Va., 1952; mem. governing bd. Council State Govts. Mem. Charlottesville Sch. Bd., 1951-62; bd. govs. St. Anne's Sch. Bd., 1954—; sec. Charlottesville Com. Fgn. Relations, 1950—. Served with USNR, 1942-46, comdr. Res. ret. Wilton Park fellow Wilton Park Conf., Sussex, Eng., 1971. Mem. Am., Va. State (v.p. 1957-58), Charlottesville-Albemarle (pres. 1966) bar assns., C. of C., Am. Judicature Soc., Nat. Consumer Finance Assn., 4th Jud. Conf., Va., Am. trial lawyers assns., Raven Soc., Sigma Nu Phi, Omicron Delta Kappa. Episcopalian (vestryman). Elks. Clubs: Downtown (Richmond, Va.); Farmington Country (Charlottesville, Va.); Redland. Home: 900 Rugby Rd Charlottesville VA 22901 Office: 414 Park St Charlottesville VA 22901

MICHAEL, JOSEPHUS ALBERT, ednl. adminstr.; b. Harrisonburg, Va., July 26, 1934; s. Olin Bain and Alberta (Hunsucker) M.; B.A., Randolph Macon Coll., 1956; M.S., U. Va., 1961; m. Sylvia Jane Johnson, July 3, 1959; 1 dau., Teresa Lynn. Tchr., asst. prin. Nelson County High Sch., Lovingston, Va., 1958-61; prin. Goochland (Va.) High Sch., 1961-62; asst. prin. Henrico High Sch., Richmond, Va., 1962-63; prin. Manchester High Sch., Richmond, 1963-65; asst. prin. Herndon (Va.) High Sch., 1965-67; prin. Herndon Intermediate Sch., 1967—. Served with AUS, 1956-58. Mem. Nat., Va., Fairfax edn. assns., Nat., Va. assns. secondary sch. prins., No. Va. Power Squadron, Nelson County Edn. Assn. (v.p. 1959), Dist. C Prins. Assn. (sec.-treas. 1963-65), Jaycees. Clubs: Ruritan, Commodore White Sands Yacht. Home: 15017 Carlbern Dr Centreville VA 22020 Office: 224 Locust St Herndon VA 22070

MICHAEL, WILLIAM SHAW, lawyer; b. Athens, Ga., Jan. 14, 1936; s. Leroy and Katherine Grace (Shaw) M.; A.B., U. N.C., Chapel Hill, 1957; LL.B., U. Mich., 1962; m. Patricia Ann Dillon, Aug. 31, 1958; children—Helen Katherine, Caroline Fleming, Patricia Dillon. Admitted to N.C. bar, 1963; trust officer, counsel First Union Nat. Bank of N.C., Charlotte, 1962-66; v.p., gen. counsel The Ervin Co., real estate devel., Charlotte, N.C., 1966—. Trustee, Center for Creative Living, Athens, Ga. Served with AUS, 1957-58. Mem. Am., N.C. bar assns., Kappa Sigma, Phi Delta Phi. Democrat. Episcopalian. Home: 618 Museum Dr Charlotte NC 28207 Office: 4037 E Indepence Blvd Charlotte NC 28205

MICHAELIAN, CHARLES THOMAS, accountant; b. Jersey City, Nov. 23, 1927; s. Karekin P. and Katharine (Sprauer) M.; student Drexel Inst. Tech., 1945-46; B.B.A. cum laude, Pace Coll., 1952; m. Joan Morledge, July 20, 1957; children—Thomas J., Richard C., Paul K., Margaret J. Sr. staff accountant Arthur Andersen & Co., N.Y.C., 1952-56; asst. controller Am. Export Lines, Inc., N.Y.C., 1956-62; controller Adam Young, Inc., N.Y.C., 1962-63; divisional accountant C.F. Braun & Co., Murray Hill, N.J., 1964-65; mgr. financial analysis Newport News (Va.) Shipbldg. & Dry Dock Co., 1966—. Instr. Sch. World Trade, N.Y.C., 1960-62. Treas., Hidenwood Presbyn. Kindergarten Bd., Newport News, 1966-69, Richard T. Yates P.T.A., Newport News, 1969-70. Served with ordnance dept. AUS, 1946-49. C.P.A., N.Y. Mem. Am. Inst. C.P.A.'s. Republican. Presbyn. (elder). Kiwanian. Home: 97 Stonewall Pl Newport News VA 23606 Office: 4101 Washington Av Newport News VA 23607

MICHAELIS, FRED JACOB, JR., ins. and finance exec.; b. New Orleans, Nov. 15, 1919; s. Fred Jacob and Louise (Beck) M.; student pub. schs.; m. Ruth Louise Holls, Oct. 14, 1946; 1 son, Jonathan Frederick. Clk., Marshall J. Smith & Co. Ltd., New Orleans, 1937-39; spl. agt. Gottschalk Gen. Ags., New Orleans, 1939-40, Fire Assn. Phila., La. and Miss., 1945-50, R. Kirk Moyer Agy., Shreveport, La., 1950-54; ins. agt. Love Ins. Agy., Shreveport, 1954-57, Allied Services, Shreveport, 1957—; exec. asst. to dir. La., Office of Emergency Planning, 1965-67; econ. planner Coordinating and Devel. Council N.W. La., 1968—. Pres., Muscular Dystrophy Assn., Shreveport, 1960-64. Served to capt. AUS, 1940-45. Decorated Purple Heart with oak leaf cluster. Mem. Nat. Assn. Ins. Agts., Home Builders Assn. Shreveport. Democrat. Lutheran. Clubs: Kiwanis (pres. 1962), Shreveport Progressive Mens (pres. 1964-65), Riverside Swimming (pres. 1967-68). Home: 216 E Southfield Blvd Shreveport LA 71105 Office: 2942 Youree Dr Shreveport LA 71104

MICHAELS, ROBERT PHILLIP, JR., tobacco co. exec.; b. nr. Morrisville, N.C., Jan. 11, 1917; s. Robert Phillip and Caroline (Searcy) M.; student U. N.C., Chapel Hill, 1935-37; m. Margaret Brown Martin, Apr. 27, 1946; children—Robert Phillip III, Margaret Martin, Gail Brown, Richard Gregory. Vice-pres., dir. Venable Tobacco Co., Inc., Durham, N.C., 1949-54; v.p. fgn. sales A.C. Monk & Co., Inc., leaf tobacco, Farmville, 1954—. Mem. Pitt County (N.C.) Devel. Commn., 1962—. Mem. Bethel Twp. (N.C.) Sch. Bd., 1962—. Served with USAAF, 1941-45. Decorated 3 Air Medals, D.F.C. Methodist (ofcl. bd. 1960-64). Home: PO Box 396 Bethel NC 27812 Office: A C Monk & Co Farmville NC 27828

MICHAELS, WILLARD A., broadcasting co. exec.; b. Omaha, May 13, 1917; s. Gus M. and Bessie (Kerstine) M.; B.A., U. San Antonio, 1940; m. Helen Louise Mintel, Nov. 20, 1938; children—Marcella (Mrs. Lawrence Pickell), Lawrence Richard, Betty (Mrs. Robert Westbrook). Asst. sports editor San Antonio Express, 1937-40; sports announcer, sales mgr., gen. mgr. sta. KABC, San Antonio, 1940-53; v.p. sta. WJBK-TV, Detroit, 1955-61; dir. Storer Broadcasting Co., Miami Beach, Fla., 1960—, TV v.p., 1961-66, exec. v.p., 1966-67, pres., 1967—; pres., dir., mem. exec. com. Northeast Airlines. Pres., bd. dirs. Storer Found.; bd. dirs. Miami Heart Inst., Heart Assn. Greater Miami. Methodist. Clubs: Old Baldy (Saratoga, Wyo.); Indian Creek Country, La Gorce Country, Bath (Miami Beach); Pine Valley Golf (Clementon, N.J.); Bloomfield Hills (Mich.) Country. Home: 11 La Gorce Circle Miami Beach FL 33141 Office: 1177 Kane Concourse Miami Beach FL 33154

MICHAELSON, LOUIS HENRY, ind. oil operator; b. Wichita, Kan., Feb. 22, 1919; s. I.T. and Regula (Schenebricker) M.; B.S., Wichita State U., 1941; m. Ruth Foster White, Mar. 30, 1946; children—Eric Lance, Kristin Rae. With Gulf Oil Corp., Wichita, 1936-42; exptl. geologist Skelly Oil Co., Midland, Tex., 1946-48; div. geologist Tex. Gulf Producing Co., 1948-65; v.p. Green & Michaelson Producing Co., Midland, 1965—, Texam Oil Corp., 1965-67. Vice pres. Permian Basin council Girl Scouts U.S.A., 1969. Served with USAAF, 1942-45. Recipient Silver Beaver award Boy Scouts Am., 1969. Mem. Am. Assn. Petroleum Geologists, Geol. Soc. Am., W. Tex. Geol. Soc., Soc. Econ. Paleontologists and Mineralogists. Presbyn. (deacon 1959-62, 65-67, treas. 1961-62, 67). Home: 2008 Douglas St Midland TX 79701 Office: Bldg of Southwest Midland TX 79701

MICHAELSON, NEIL FREDERICH, city ofcl.; b. Detroit, Mar. 22, 1938; s. Arthur John and Doris Marie (Vincent) M.; student Detroit Coll. Bus., 1963-65; B.S., U. Miami, 1971; m. Marion Helen Fargo, Sept. 25, 1966; children—Steve Matthew, Clint Patrick. City clk., treas., purchasing agt. City of Garden City, Mich., 1965-66; interim city mgr., city clk., auditor City of New Smyrna Beach, Fla., 1966-68; asst. city mgr. City of Winter Haven, Fla., 1968-69; asst. city mgr., financial dir. City of South Miami, Fla., 1969—; instr. municipal finance adminstrn. Inter-City Mgmt. Assn. Served with USMC, 1955-58, U.S. Army, 1959-61. Mem. Internat. City Mgmt. Assn., Municipal Finance Officers Assn., Municipal Treasurers Assn., Dade County City Mgrs. Assn., Am. Soc. Pub. Adminstrn., South Miami-Kendall Jr. C. of C. (v.p. 1970). Home: 14120 Kendall Lakes Blvd Miami FL 33143 Office: 6130 Sunset Dr South Miami FL 33143

MICHALSKI, EDWARD MATTHEW, engring. sales corp. exec.; b. Orange, N.J., Sept. 29, 1926; s. Matthew Joseph and Katherine (Zachariziewicz) M.; B.S., U.S. Mcht. Marine Acad., 1947; postgrad. Hays Sch. Combustion, 1953; m. Carol Swafford, Nov. 9, 1949. Third engr. Mcht. Marines, 1948; service engr. Combustion Engring., Inc., N.Y.C., 1949-54, burner engr. engring dept., 1954-55, supr. Fuels Equipment Engring. div., 1955-58, mgr., 1958-62; pres., owner Matthew Engring. Co., Chattanooga, 1962-64; v.p., treas. P-V-F Suppliers, Inc., 1964-65; pres., chmn. bd. dirs. Mike Michalski &Co., Chattanooga, 1965—. Served with USNR, 1945-46. Registered profl. engr., Tenn. Mem. Nat. Tenn. socs. profl. engrs., Chattanooga Engrs. Club, Am. Soc. M.E., Instrument Soc. Am., Am. Inst. Plant Engrs. Methodist. Clubs: Chattanooga Golf and Country, Rivermont Golf and Country. Patentee in field. Home: 1234 Dallas Rd Chattanooga TN 37405 Office: 1203 Hixson Pike Chattanooga TN 37405

MICHELI, GENE SAUL, psychologist; b. Astoria, N.Y., Jan. 15, 1928; s. Gino and Marie (Bartolomei) M.; B.A., N.Y. U., 1949, Ph.D., 1966; M.A., Fordham U., 1952; m. Evelyn Chatterton, Nov. 1, 1958; children—Jacquelyn, Robert. Research psychologist Met. Life Ins. Co., N.Y.C., 1953-59, Naval Tng. Device Center, Orlando, Fla., 1959—. Served to lt. AUS, 1951-53. Mem. Am. Psychol. Assn., A.A.A.S., Human Factors Soc. Research in field. Home: 703 Albertson Pl Orlando FL 32806 Office: Naval Tng Device Center Orlanda FL 32813

MICHELIN, EDWARD EUCLIDE, clergyman; b. Cheboygan, Mich., May 5, 1922; s. Euclide A. and Rose (Marchand) M.; B.S., U. Detroit, 1948, St. Paul Sem., St. Paul, 1950; postgrad. St. John Sem., Little Rock, 1950-54 Ordained priest Roman Cath. Ch., 1954; asst. pastor St. Peter's Co-Cathedral, Jackson, Miss., 1954, St. Alphonsus Ch., Ocean Springs, 1960-62; financial sec. Diocese of Natchez-Jackson, 1962-66; vice chancellor, 1962—; pastor St. John's Ch., Crystal Springs, 1963-66; exec. dir. Cath. Charities, Inc., Jackson, 1962—, exec. v.p., 1966—. Designated domestic prelate, 1965. Bishop's rep. for Cath. hosps., 1957—; exec. dir. Miss. Conf. Cath. Hosps., 1957—, St. Mary's Home and D'Evereaux Hall Child Care Corps., 1968—; pres. Cath. Charities Housing Assn. Biloxi, Cath. Charities Housing Assn. Jackson, Homes for Mississippians, 1968—, also various housing corps. for elderly and low income people; chmn. bd. Am. Health Congress, 1971-72. Served to ensign USNR, 1942-46. Mem. Cath. Hosp. Assn. U.S. (pres. 1970-71, trustee). Home: 2911 Hemingway Circle Jackson MS 39209 Office: 237 E Amite St Jackson MS 39205

MICHELIS, ADOLPH NEWTON, dredging co. ofcl.; b. Port Clinton, O., July 2, 1937; s. Adolph and Elizabeth (Newton) M.; student Armstrong Jr. Coll., 1955-56; A.S., So. Tech. Inst., 1959; m. Sara Glenda Bevill, Apr. 5, 1958; children—Lisa Lynn, Pamela Ann. Civil technician Ga. Hwy. Dept., Moultrie, 1959-60; asst. engr. Savannah && Atlanta Ry. Co., 1960-63, So. Ry. Co., Atlanta, 1963-64; v.p. dredging Parkhill-Goodloe Co., Inc., Jacksonville, Fla.,

1964-—. Served with USMC, 1955-56. Mem. World Dredging Assn. Clubs: Jacksonville Propeller. Home: 7646 Holiday Rd S Jacksonville FL 32216 Office: PO Box 8707 Jacksonville FL 32211

MICHELS, KENNETH M., univ. adminstr.; b. Chgo., Sept. 17, 1922; A.B., Emory U., 1949, M.A., 1950; Ph.D., U. Wis., 1953; m. Esther Eloise Baker, Feb. 1, 1946; children—Kenneth M., Jeanne Ann. Asst. prof. Purdue U., 1953-56, asso. prof., 1956-60, prof., 1960-64, coordinator off-campus grad programs, 1960-62, asst. dean univ. extension adminstrn., 1962-64; prof. psychology, chmn. dept. Fla. Atlantic U., Boca Raton, 1964-67, acting chmn. dept. sociology, 1966-67, dean Coll. Social Sci., 1967-68, dean Coll. Sci., 1968-71, v.p. acad. affairs, 1971-—; research scientist summer faculty program Mil. Operations Research div. Lockheed Aircraft Corp., Marietta, Ga., 1957; summer vis. investigator Roscoe B. Jackson Meml. Labs., 1962; vis. prof. U. Cal. at Berkeley, summer 1964. Cons., Courtney and Co., Phila., 1957-58, Aircraft Armaments, Inc., Cockeysville, Md., 1956-—, VA, 1959-64, System Scis. Affiliates, Columbus, O., 1960-—, Columbus div. North Am. Aviation, 1962-63, behavioral scis. tng. com. Nat. Inst. Gen. Med. Scis., 1964-—, Northrop Corp., 1966-—, USPHS, 1967-—. Served with USAAF, 1941-45; now lt. col. Res. Mem. Am. Psychol. Assn., Midwestern Psychol. Assn., Assn. Study Animal Behavior, Ecological Soc., N.Y. Acad. Scis., Psychonomic Soc., A.A.A.S., Phi Beta Kappa, Sigma Xi. Contbr. articles to profl. jours. Office: Florida Atlantic Univ Boca Raton FL 33432

MICHELSON, AARON IVAN, librarian; b. Cleve., Oct. 3, 1927; s. William and Florence Beatrice (Slesnick) M.; B.S., Case-Western Res. U., 1949, M.S. in L.S., 1950; postgrad. U. Chgo., 1956-59; m. Fairlie A. Brown, Aug. 27, 1955; children—Katherine, Mary, Susanna, Sarah. Reference asst. Detroit Pub. Library, 1950-51; librarian, instr. library sci. N.D. State Coll., 1954-56; reference asst. U. Chgo. Library, 1956-59; dir. Okla. Library-Community Project, 1959-60; asst. prof., asso. prof. U. Okla. Sch. Library Sci., 1960-65; directing editor, head librarian Scott, Foresman & Co., ednl. pubs., Glenview, Ill., 1965-66; library dir. U. South Ala., Mobile, 1966-—. Mem. Library Services and Constrn. Act Adv. Com. Ala., 1971. Served with AUS, 1951-54. Mem. A.L.A., Ala. (chmn. coll., univ. and spl. libraries div.), Southeastern library assns., Adult Edn. Assn. U.S., Urban League. Editor: Oklahoma Library-Community Project Newsletter, 1959-60. Contbr. articles profl. jours. Home: 1107 Fribourg St Mobile AL 36608 Office: Library U South Ala Mobile AL 36688

MICHELSON, EDWARD J., newspaper corr.; b. Northampton, Mass., Apr. 3, 1915; s. Isadore Henry and Fannie (Avrich) M.; B.A., Williams Coll., 1937; m. Dorothea Adair Pohlman, Feb. 3, 1938; children— Kathleen (Mrs. Frederick D. Meloan), Paul, Emily (Mrs. Thomas D. Crews). Reporter St. Louis Post-Dispatch, 1937-38; writer pub. relations div. Westinghouse Electric Co., 1939-40; day editor, internat. shortwave news div. CBS, 1941-44; spl. asst. Office Sec. War, 1946; mem. hist. sect. strategic services unit War Dept., 1946; asso. Robert S. Allen, syndicated columnist, 1946-50; Washington corr. N. Am. Newspaper Alliance, also New Eng. dailies, 1946-—; Washington editor Forbes mag., 1956-63, Printer's Ink mag., 1958-63; mag. editor Ocean Sci. News, 1968-69; Washington editor Sci. and Tech. mag., 1969-—. Exec., Enterprises Publs. Research dir. pub. works subcom. on water Resources U.S. Ho. of Reps., 1951. Served with OSS, AUS, 1944-46. Mem. Aviation/Space Writers Assn., White House Corrs. Assn., Washington Soc. Investment Analysts, Gargoyle Soc. Clubs: Williams (N.Y.C.); Nat. Press (Washington). Contbr. to gen. financial and spl. bus. periodicals. Editor: Our American Government (Wright Patman) 1948. Home: 2153 Florida Av NW Washington DC 20008 Office: Nat Press Bldg Washington DC 20004

MICHELSON, RONALD KEITH, dentist; b. San Francisco, July 10, 1936; s. Charles Dean and Mary (Bettencourt) M.; student Coll. San Mateo, 1954-56, Georgetown U. Coll. Arts and Scis., 1959-61; D.D.S., Georgetown U., 1965; 1 son, David Keith. Intern oral surgery Norfolk (Va.) Gen. Hosp., 1965-66; individual practice dentistry, Virginia Beach, Va., 1967-71; 2d year resident oral surgery Jackson Meml. Hosp., U. Miami, 1971-72, chief resident, 1972-73. Served with AUS, 1956-59. Mem. Virginia Beach Power Squadron, Tidewater, Va., Am. dental assns., Delta Sigma Delta. Episcopalian. Contbr. articles to profl. jours. Home: 2105 Brickell Av Apt 202 Miami FL 33129

MICHERO, W.H., bus. exec.; b. Fort Worth, 1925; grad. Tex. Christian U., 1948. Vice-pres., sec., Tandy Corp., Fort Worth. Home: 1300 Mistletoe Dr Fort Worth TX 76110 Office: 2727 W 7th St Fort Worth TX*

MICHIE, LUCILE EASTHAM (MRS. J. TEVIS MICHIE), psychologist; b. Charlottesville, Va., Jan. 22, 1907; d. Rosser J. and Helen H. (George) Eastham; student Coll. William and Mary, 1924-26; B.S. in Edn., U. Va., 1929, M.Edn., 1960, advanced grad. student, 1963-72; m. J. Tevis Michie, Aug. 6, 1929;children—Robert Kinloch, Martha Tevis. Tchr. pub. schs. Wakefield County, Va., 1929-30, Clark Sch., Charlottesville, Va., 1931-39; sec.-treas., dir. Helen G. Eastham Shop, Inc., 1931-50; tchr. Lane High Sch., Charlottesville, 1931-45, counselor, 1957-60, counselor-psychometrist, 1960-63; sch. psychologist Charlottesville Pub. Schs., 1963-72; cons. Children and Youth Center, Pediatric Dept., U. Va. Hosp., 1972-—; supr. sch. psychology practicum students, 1968-72. Cons. Nat. Guidance Inst., U. Va., Charlottesville, 1960-61; treas. Country Day Sch., 1948-54; vice pres. Va. Assn. Mental Health Parliamentarian. Pres. bd. dirs. Children's Service Center, Charlottesville, 1954-56, bd. dirs., 1954-57; bd. dirs. Charlottesville, Albemarle County community chests. Recipient service award Charlottesville Mental Health Assn., 1959. Mem. Nat., Va., Charlottesville (past pres., dir., parliamentarian) edn. assns., Nat. Vocational Guidance Assn., Va., Piedmont (past pres.), Am. personnel and guidance assns., U. Va. Edn. Alumni Assn., Am. Assn. U. Women, League Women Voters, Bus. and Profl. Women's Club (pres. Charlottesville 1939-41, pres., dir. Va. Fedn. 1944-46; dir. nat. fedn.), Charlottesville Mcht. Assn. (treas. 1946-49), Alumni Assn. Coll. William and Mary, U. Va. Alumni Assn. (life mem.), Am. (asso.), Va. psychol. assns., Va. Assn. Sch. Psychologists (mem. profl. affairs com.). Delta Kappa Gamma, Kappa Delta Pi (life mem., chpt. treas. 1959-69, service award 1969). Republican. Episcopalian. Clubs: Keswick (Va.) Country, Colony (Richmond, Va.). Author articles on mental health and handling children's problems. Home: PO Box 3445 Charlottesville VA 22903 Office: Children and Youth Center the Towers Charlottesville VA 22903

MICHOT, LOUIS J., ednl. adminstr. Mem. La. Bd. Edn. Office: State of La Dept Edn Box 44064 Baton Rouge LA 70804*

MICKLER, JOHN ELLIS, aerospace exec.; b. Klamath Falls, Ore., Oct. 26, 1911; s. Malcolm Peterson and Alice Jane (Ellis) M.; B.M.E., Ga. Inst. Tech., 1932; B.I.E., U. Fla., 1937; postgrad. U. Tenn. Space Inst., 1971; m. Jimmie McClendon, Oct. 3, 1964; children—Brian Ellis, Jan Temko, Karen Yarborough, Lindsay Rae, Nan Henderson, William R. Collins. Pres., M.P. Mickier & Son, Inc., Kissimmee, Fla., 1948-55; supt. Columbia Hardboard Co., Everett, Wash., 1957-58; project engr. Boeing Co., Seattle also Huntsville, Ala., 1958-70; program mgr. Tech. Micronics Control Inc., Madison, Ala., 1971-—. Served to capt. AUS, 1940-45. Mem. Soc. Logistics Engrs. Democrat. Baptist. Home: 10010 Hampshire Dr SE Huntsville AL 35803 Office: Hwy 20 Madison AL 35826

MICKUM, GEORGE BRENT, III, lawyer; b. Washington, Jan. 13, 1928; s. George Brent and Anna (Love) M.; B.S. cum laude, Georgetown U., 1949, LL.B., 1952; m. Lora Ann Mattare, June 27, 1953; children—George Brent, Luke Anthony, Ann Elizabeth, Paul Christopher, Joseph Benedict, Mark Andrew. Admitted to D.C. bar, 1952; clk. Charles Fahy, U.S. Ct. of Appeals, D.C. Circuit, Washington, 1952-53; elk. Stanley F. Reed, Supreme Ct. of U.S., Washington, 1953-54; practiced in Washington, 1954-—; mem. firm Steptoe & Johnson. Served with AUS, 1945-47. Mem. Delta Theta Phi, Pi Gamma Mu. Democrat. Roman Catholic. Home: 44 Grafton St Chevy Chase MD 20015 Office: 1250 Connecticut Av NW Washington DC 20036

MIDDLETON, EDWIN GHEENS, lawyer, Republican nat. committeeman; b. Louisville, June 11, 1920; s. Charles G. and Anita (Gheens) M.; grad. Woodberry Forest Sch., 1938; B.A., U. Va., 1941; LL.B., U. Louisville, 1948; m. Mary Jane Lampton, July 11, 1942; children—Edwin Gheens, Anita G., Huntley L. Admitted to Ky. bar, 1948; partner firm Middleton, Seelbach, Wolford, Willis & Cochran, 1948-—; dir., gen. counsel Am. Life & Accident Ins. Co.; dir. Louisville Title Ins. Co. Chmn. bd. Louisville and Jefferson County Children's Home, 1957-60, trustee, 1953-66; sec. Louisville Park Theatrical Assn., 1956-66; trustee, sec. Louisville Country Day Sch., 1957-67; trustee Louisville Collegiate Sch., 1956-—. Chmn. exec. com. Louisville and Jefferson County, Republican party, 1958-63; finance chmn. Citizens for Eisenhower, 1952; del. Rep. Nat. Conv., 1964; permanent chmn. Ky. Rep. Conv., 1964; mem. Rep. Nat. Com. for Ky. Chmn. bd. trustees U. Louisville. Served from pvt. to maj. USMC, 1941-46. Decorated Bronze Star Medal, Purple Heart. Mem. Am., Ky., Louisville bar assns. Episcopalian. Clubs: Filson, Salmagundi, Louisville Country (pres., dir. 1963-69). Office: 501 S 2d St Louisville KY 40202

MIDDLETON, ELWYN LINTON, lawyer; b. Pamona, Fla., Oct. 16, 1914; s. William Spencer and Lizzie A. (Williams) M.; LL.B., Stetson U., 1939; m. Annie L. Fielding, Dec. 7, 1942; children—Elwyn Linton, Mary Ann, John David, Phillip Fielding. Admitted to Fla. bar, 1939, since practiced in Palm Beach; asso. E. Harris Drew, 1939-42; mem. firm Burns, Middleton, Farrell & Faust (formerly Burns, Middleton, Rogers & Farrell), 1946-—; town atty., Palm Beach, 1953-—. Dir. Bank of Palm Beach & Trust Co., Palm Beach. Trustee Fla. Presbyn. Coll. Served from ensign to lt. USNR, 1942-46. Mem. Am., Palm County (pres. 1951) bar assns., Fla. Bar (gov. 1954-56), Phi Alpha Delta. Democrat. Presbyn. Home: 242 Dunbar Rd Palm Beach FL 33480 Office: 205 Worth Av Palm Beach FL 33480

MIDDLETON, JOHN ALBERT, coll. pres.; b. Foreston, S.C., Jan. 2, 1914; s. Brewington and Lula (Hayes) M.; A.B., Allen U., 1939, LL.D., 1966; B.D., Howard U., 1942; Th.M., Iliff Sch. Theology, 1956; LL.D., Payne Coll., 1966, Bethune-Cookman Coll., 1967, Payne Theol. Sem-Wilberforce U., 1970; m. Merlissie Tyson, Dec. 24, 1943; children—Ann Fay (Mrs. Ronald Reed), Johnsy Althea, Phillip Brewington. Ordained minister A.M.E. Ch., 1938; pastor churches in Va. and Md., 1942-47; prof. Morris Brown Coll. and Turner Theol. Sem., Atlanta, 1947-56; pastor Allen Temple A.M.E. Ch., Atlanta, 1956-65; pres. Morris Brown Coll., Atlanta, 1965-—. Campaign dir. United Negro Coll. Fund; mem. Ga. Council on Human Relation. Mem. Atlanta Bd. Edn., 1969-—. Bd. dirs. Interdenominational Theol. Center, Atlanta, Carrie Steel Pitts Home, Atlanta, Atlanta U. Center Corp., Atlanta council Boy Scouts Am. Mem. Frontiers Internat., Sigma Phi Pi, Alpha Phi. Home: 601 University Pl NW Atlanta GA 30314

MIDDLETON, JOHN TYLOR, educator; b. Chgo., Sept. 15, 1912; s. Walter Guy and Gertrude (Baldwin) M.; B.S., U. Cal. at Berkeley, 1935; Ph.D., U. Mo., 1940; m. June R. White, Aug. 20, 1939 (dec.); children—Peter Cornell, David Burke, Mary Russell, Sara Parke; m. 2d, Diana J. Clarkson June 16, 1961. Asst. in botany U. Mo., 1936-39; faculty U. Cal., 1939-—, as jr. plant pathologist, asst. plant pathologist, asso. plant pathologist, 1939-54, plant pathologist, 1954-67, prof., chmn. dept. plant pathology, Los Angeles, also Riverside, 1957-63, dir. Statewide Air Pollution Research Center, 1962-67; prof. emeritus 1967-—; dir. Nat. Center for Air Pollution Control, 1967-68; commr. Nat. Air Pollution Control Adminstrn., cons. pathologist, 1950-—. Chmn., Cal. Motor Vehicle Pollution Control Bd., 1960-62, vice chmn., 1962-63, mem. bd. 1964-67; spl. cons. USPHS, 1963-67. Office Sci. and Tech., Exec. Offices of Pres.; adviser WHO, 1963. Bd. dirs. Riverside Community Planning Forum. Mem. Air Pollution Control. Assn., Am. Inst. Biol. Scis., Am. Phytopath. Soc., Am. Geog. Soc., Internat. Assn. Plant Taxonomy Mycol. Soc. Am., Torrey Bot. Club, Nederlandse Planteziektenkunidige Vereniging, A.A.A.S., Sigma Xi, Alpha Zeta, Gamma Alpha. Rotarian. Club: Commonwealth (Cal.). Cons. editor: Environmental Research; mem. editorial adv. bd. Western Grocers Assn., Internat. Jour. Air Pollution. Contbr. articles to profl. publs. Home: 2811 Albermarle St NW Washington DC 20008 Office: 801 N Randolph St Arlington VA 22203

MIDDLETON, NORWOOD CRONK, newspaper editor; b. Sumter, S.C., May 26, 1918; s. Walter P. and Mattie (Cronk) M.; A.B., Roanoke Coll., 1939; m. Lucille Hood, June 28, 1941; children—Kenneth Norwood, David Lynn. Reporter Roanoke (Va.) World-News, 1940-46; mng. editor Pulaski (Va.) Southwest Times, 1946-49; with Roanoke (Va.) Times, 1949-—, successively swing deskman, city editor, news editor, 1949-57, mng. editor, 1957-—. Mem. exec. bd. Blue Ridge council Boy Scouts Am., pres. 1966-67. Moderator Montgomery Presbytery, Presbyn. Ch. U.S., 1967. Served from pvt. to capt. USAAF, 1942-45. Mem. Salem C. of C. (past dir.), Va. Press Assn. (pres. 1966-67). Presbyn. (elder). Kiwanian. Home: 1149 Forest Lawn Dr Salem VA 24153 Office: 201 Campbell Av SW Roanoke VA 24010

MIDLEN, JOHN HOLBROOK, lawyer; b. Phila., June 2, 1910; s. Edward B. and Lilian (Lewis) M.; B.S. in Econs., U. Pa., 1931; J.D., Georgetown U., 1938, LL.M., 1954; m. Gertrude H. Robertson, Oct. 12, 1940; children—John H., Margaret R. (Mrs. Manda). Admitted tp D.C. bar, 1935; gen. counsel Delta Sigma Phi, 1940-47, 51-53; practice law in Washington, 1945-—; sr. partner Midlen & Reddy, 1968-—. Mem. FCC Nat. Industry Adv. Com., 1960-—, FCC Industry Adv. Group U.S.-Mexico Standard Broadcast Agreement Negotiations, 1966-70; communications counsel Nat. Religious Broadcasters, 1968-—. Pres., Spring Valley-Wesley Heights Citizens Assn., Washington, 1959-60. Served to lt. col. AUS, 1941-45. Decorated Army Commendation ribbon with oak leaf cluster. Mem. Fed. Communications Bar Assn. (sec., treas., exec. com.), Am. Bar Assn., Bar Assn. D.C. Presbyn. (elder). Home: 4800 Tilden St NW Washington DC 20016 Office: 1990 M St NW Washington DC 20036

MIDLO, MAURY AVRAM, radio, TV exec.; b. New Orleans, Mar. 12, 1935; s. Charles and Natalie Alissa (Strauss) M.; B.A., Tulane U., 1956; m. Florence Ann Abram, July 8, 1956; children—Bennett, Marianne. Editorial research asst. WDSU-TV, New Orleans, 1958-59, promotion asst., 1959-60, promotion coordinator, 1960-64, dir. promotion and merchandising, 1964-—. Instr. Loyola U., New Orleans, part-time, 1969; chmn. NBC-TV Affiliates Promotion Com., 1971-72. Bd. dirs. Am. Civil Liberties Union La., 1966-69, Jewish Community Center, 1968-70, Anti-Defamation League, Friends New Orleans Pub. Library, Orleans Audubon Soc., 1969-72. Served with AUS, 1956-58. Mem. Broadcasters Promotion Assn. (dir. 1967-69,, 71; sec. 1972). Home: 1603 Fern St New Orleans LA 70118 Office: 520 Royal St New Orleans LA 70130

MIERS, HENRY VIRGIL, newspaper editor, critic; b. Texarkana, Tex., Jan. 19, 1925; s. Henry Virgil and Willa Neta (Castleman) M.; B.A., Tex. Technol. Coll., 1947; m. Patricia Nancy Locke, Aug. 7, 1954; children—Peggy Castleman, Roslyn Southwick, Douglas Locke. With Dallas Times Herald, 1947-—, amusements editor, 1953-—; critical writer Christian Sci. Monitor, others, 1956-—. Mem. Margo Jones Nat. Award Com., mem. regional com. ANTA; program com. YMCA; mem. Dallas profl. Arts Alliance. Served with USNR, 1944-46. Mem. Nat. Screen Council, Broadway Theater League (dir.), Alpha Tau Omega. Club: Variety. Home: 3600 Armstrong Av Dallas TX 75205 Office: Dallas Times Herald Herald Sq Dallas TX 75202

MIERS, MILEY L., II, dentist; b. Montgomery, Ala., Feb. 6, 1927; s. Miley L. and Luna (Browder) M.; A.B., Washington U., St. Louis, 1953, D.D.S., 1953; m. Patricia Malloy, Sept. 5, 1959; children—Melanie Anne, Michael Lawrence, Michelle Lynn, Miley L. III. Practice gen. dentistry, St. Louis, 1953-54, Tallahassee, 1954-—; mem. dental staff Tallahassee Meml. Hosp., 1954-—; asst. sec. Fla. Bd. Dental Examiners, 1963-67. Pres., Boys Club Leon County, 1969-—; head dental div. Leon County United Fund, 1958-61. Mem. Fla. Ho. of Reps., 1966-—. Bd. dirs. Tallahassee YMCA. Served with USNR, 1944-46. Recipient George Washington Gold medal award Freedoms Found. at Valley Forge, 1968; voted one of most outstanding mems. Fla. Legislature, 1969, 70. Fellow Am., Internat. coll. dentists; mem. Leon County (pres. 1958-59), N.W. Dist. (pres. 1962-63) dental socs., Am. (mem. Fla. delegation 1964-67), Fla. dental assns., Am., Fla. acads. gen. dentistry, Fla. Acad. Dental Practice Adminstrn., Fla. Prosthodontic Soc., North Fla. Dental Research Com. (pres. 1965), Am. Acad. Dental Practice Adminstrn., Am. Equilibration Soc., Am. Soc. Oral Physiology and Occlusion, Pierre Fauchard Acad., Fedn. Dentaire Internationale, Southeastern Acad. Prosthodontics, Am. Prosthonodontic Soc., Tallahassee C. of C. Methodist (mem. ofcl. bd.). Mason (32 deg., Shriner), Toastmaster (dir., past pres. Tallahassee), Rotarian (dir. Tallahassee). Clubs: Seminole Booster, Tip-Off (Fla. State U.); Century (Washington U. Dental Sch.). Home: 614 Short St Tallassee FL 32303 Office: 1213 Miccosukee Rd Tallahassee FL 32303

MIGDOL, MARVIN JACOB, pub. relations and personnel exec.; b. Rochester, N.Y., Jan. 11, 1937; s. Frank and Dorothy (Krieger) M.; B.A., U Buffalo, 1959; postgrad. U. Miami, 1959-60; M.S., Boston U., 1961; m. Sharon Grace Miron, 1970. Sec. for communications Rensselaer Poly. Inst., Troy, N.Y., 1963-64; pub. relations cons., pres. Migdol Assos., New Orleans, Buffalo, 1964-68; pres. Snelling & Snelling, Dallas, 1968-—. Lectr. inst. Boston U., 1960-61, Pa. State U., 1961-63, State U. N.Y., 1966-68. Active Jewish Welfare Fedn. Bd. dirs. Acad. Hosp. Pub. Relations, Inst. Information and Communication in Israel. Mem. Am. Assn. Indsl. Editors, Am. Coll. Pub. Relations Assn., U. Buffalo Alumni Assn. (pres. 1964-65), N.W. Pa. Internat. Council Indsl. Editors, Pub. Relations Assn. Western N.Y., Alpha Epsilon Pi (regional gov. 1966-67). Author: Public Relations Handbook, 1962; Comics as a Public Relations Tool in Communications, 1970. Contbr. numerous articles to profl. jours. Home: 7853 La Casa Dr Dallas TX 75240 Office: Noel Page Bldg Dallas TX 75206

MIGLIONICO, NINA, lawyer; b. Birmingham, Ala., 1913; A.B. with honors, Howard Coll. (now Sanford U.); LL.B., U. Ala., 1936. Admitted to Ala. bar, since practiced in Birmingham; mem. Birmingham City Council; tax cons. Pres., Ala. Joint Legislative Council; past pres. Ala. Merit System. mem. President's Commn. on Status of Women; mem. adv. com. to commr. Internal Revenue Service. Named Ala. Woman of Achievement, 1954, Birmingham Woman of Year, 1963; recipient Nat. Top Hat award. Mem. Am. (ho. of dels. 1959-61), Birmingham bar assns., Nat. Assn. Woman Lawyers (past pres.), Ala. Fedn. Bus. and Profl. Women's Club (past pres.), Ala. Women Lawyers Assn. (past pres.). Roman Catholic. Club: Zonta (past pres. Birmingham). Author: Voting Habits of Women in Jefferson County, Alabama; Law Pertaining to Family Relations in Alabama. Contbr. articles on status of women and legislative problems in Ala. to profl. publs.

MIGLIORE, PHILIP JOSEPH, physician; b. Pitts., Dec. 18, 1931; s. Salvatore and Clara (Pergola) M.; B.S., U. Pitts., 1954, M.D., 1956; m. Ann Nixon, July 20, 1957; children—Philip Victor, Cynthia Ann, Todd Nixon. Intern West Pa. Hosp., Pitts., 1956-57, resident, 1959-60; resident U. Pitts. Presbyn. Hosp., 1960-61; fellow M.D. Anderson Hosp., 1961-64; practice medicine specializing in pathology, Houston, 1964-70; asst. pathologist Meth. Hosp., 1969-—; asst. prof. pathology Baylor Coll. Medicine, 1969-—; asst. pathologist, asst. prof. pathology M.D. Anderson Hosp. and Tumor Inst., 1964-69. Served to capt. USAF, 1957-59. Diplomate Am. Bd. Pathology. Mem. A.M.A., A.A.A.S., Am. Soc. Clin. Pathologists, N.Y. Acad. Scis., Phi Beta Kappa, Alpha Omega Alpha. Presbyn. (elder). Contbr. articles to med. jours. Home: 3602 Grennoch St Houston TX 77025 Office: Meth Hosp Houston TX 77025

MIHAILOVICH, VASA D., educator; b. Prokuplje, Yugoslavia, Aug. 12, 1926; s. Dragutin and Vidosava (Petkovic) M.; A.B., Wayne State U., 1956, M.A., 1957; Ph.D., U. Cal. at Berkeley, 1966; m. Branka Jancetovic, Dec. 28, 1957; children—Draggan Paul, Zoran Mark. Came to U.S., 1951, naturalized, 1956. Instr. U. N.C., Chapel Hill, 1961-63, asst. prof., 1963-68, asso. prof., 1968-—. Mem. exec. bd. So. Conf. Slavic Studies, 1967-70. Mem. Am. Assn. Tchrs. Slavic and East European Langs. (v.p. 1970), Modern Lang. Assn. Contbr. to anthologies; contbr. articles and reviews on Russian and Yugoslav lit. to profl. jours. Home: 403 Long Leaf Dr Chapel Hill NC 27514

MIKI, ROBERT T., govt. ofcl.; b. Honolulu, Sept. 21, 1930; s. Thomas L. and Alice (Terada) M.; B.B.A., U. Hawaii, 1952; M.A., U. Ill., 1954; Ph.D., U. Minn., 1957. Instr. econs. U. Minn., 1955-57; prof. Williams Coll., 1957-63; with U.S. Dept. Commerce, Washington, 1963-—, research, 1963-65; spl. asst. to dep. asst. sec. econ. devel., 1965-66; dep. dir. Office Econ. Research, 1966-67, sr. economist Office Asst. Sec. Commerce for Econ. Affairs, 1967-—; prof. grad. dept. econs. Georgetown U.; cons. in field. Mem. Am. Econ. Assn., Econometric Soc., So. Regional Sci. Assn. (pres. 1971-72), Omicron Delta Gamma. Contbr. articles in field to profl. jours. Editor, Rev. Regional Studies. Home: 4701 Willard Av Chevy Chase MD 20015 Office: Office Asst Sec Econ Affairs US Dept Commerce Washington DC 20230

MIKULAK, DANIEL, JR., hotel exec.; b. N.Y.C., Aug. 8, 1937; s. Daniel and Mary (Nemec) M.; A.A., Prince George Coll., 1959; B.S., U. Denver, 1961; m. Anna Marie Dixon, July 19, 1958; children—Ruth Ann, Daniel III. Exec. asst. mgr. Rainbow Hotel, Great Falls, Mont., 1962-63; cons. Western Internat. Hotels Co., 1963-64, area controller St. Francis Hotel, San Francisco, 1965-66; exec. asst. mgr. Continental Plaza Hotel, Chgo., 1967; gen. mgr.

Fairmount Roosevelt Hotel, New Orleans, 1967—. Mem. Mayor's Mardi Gras adv. com. City of New Orleans; v.p. Greater New Orleans tourist and conv. com.; chmn. New Orleans Super Bowl Task Force; mem. La. Council Music and Performing Arts, Greater New Orleans Ednl. TV Found. Bd. mgrs. Delgado Coll.; trustee So. La. chpt. Leukemia Soc. Am. Mem. La. (dir.), Greater New Orleans (v.p.) hotel assns., Greater New Orleans C. of C. (dir., mem. com. 50, mem. com. mgmt.), Urban League Greater New Orleans (dir.), Am. Hotel and Motel Assn. (chmn. nat. adv. council career devel. div.), Confrerie de la Chaine des Rotisseurs, Internat. Wine and Food Soc. New Orleans. Home: Fairmount Roosevelt Hotel New Orleans LA 70140

MIKULIN, ROBERT LEONARD, civil engr.; b. Dime Box, Tex., Aug. 27, 1931; s. Leonard and Millie (Marek) M.; A.A , Blinn Coll., 1951; B.S., U. Tex., 1953; m. Eleanor Klopsteck, May 29, 1954. Engr. Tex. Hwy. Dept., Brenham, 1953-54, 56—. Served with AUS, 1954-55. Registered profl. engr., Tex. Mem. Am. Soc. C.E., Nat. Soc. Profl. Engrs. Lutheran (sec. 1967-69). Home: 1403 Chappell Hill St Brenham TX 77833 Office: PO Box 770 Brenham TX 77833

MILAM, CARL MAX, govt. ofcl.; b. Cecil, Ark., July 13, 1930; s. Carl J. and Letha (Staton) M.; A.B., Okla. Bapt. U.,1954; M.A., U. Okla., 1958, Ph.D., 1962; m. Marilyn Jeanne Cline, Feb. 13, 1948; children—Sherryl Marie, Laura Jeanne, Kathleen Ione. Gen. mgr. Bison Press, Shawnee, Okla., 1955-56; asst. prodn. mgr. Phillips & Van Orden, San Francisco, 1956-58; asst. prof. Central State Coll., Edmond, Okla., 1958-61, U. Ky., Lexington, 1961-66; asso. prof., chmn. dept. polit. sci. U. Ark., Fayetteville, 1966—; dir. adminstrn. State of Ark., 1969—. Home: 3800 Sevier St North Little Rock AR 72116 Office: State Capitol Bldg Little Rock AR 72201

MILAM, JOHN THOMAS, physician; s.; Benjamin Burl and Bessie Mable (Crites) M.; B.S., W.Va. U., 1936; postgrad. W.Va. U., 1938-39; grad. Command and Gen. Staff Sch., 1943; M.S., Tulane U. Sch. Medicine, 1946-50; m. Helen Carolyn Graham, May 27, 1946; children—John Benjamin, James Thomas, Lynn Elise. Sci. tchr. Sissonville High Sch., 1936-37, Charleston High Sch., 1938-39; intern Charity Hosp., New Orleans, 1950-51; practice gen. medicine, Cleveland, Miss., 1951—. Pres., Russel Bldgs. Corp., Cleveland, 1964—; sec. Cleveland Clinic Bldg. Corp., 1966—; sec.-treas. Holiday Enterprises, 1970—; v.p. Arcade Shoes, Inc., Cleveland; dir. Exec. Services, Jackson, Miss. Chief of staff East Bolivar County Hosp., Cleveland, 1962, 65. Served from 2d lt. to maj. AUS, 1940-46. Mem. A.M.A., Am. Acad. Gen. Practice, Miss. State Med. Assn., Delta Med. Soc. Methodist. (steward 1968—), Rotarian. Home: 1108 Farmer St Cleveland MS 38732 Office: Cleveland Clinic Hwy 8 E Cleveland MS 38732

MILAM, MARY WELLS, welfare and civic vol.; b. Miami, Fla., Dec. 7, 1922; d. Marcus Alexander and Omega Gardner (Wigginton) Milam; B.S., U. Miami, 1944. Sec., dir. Ramico Inc., Miami; dir. R.M. Co. of Miami, Inc. Dir., past chmn. exec. com., family and child care div., past v.p. Welfare Planning Council of Dade County, Fla.; past vice chmn. Dade County chpt., past mem. nat. council U.S.O.; dir. Travelers Aid Soc. of Miami, 1958, chmn. joint bd. Nat. Survey Service; mem. Nat. Budget and Consultation Com.; bd. dirs., past v.p. Dade County Assn. Child Guidance Clinics; chmn. Family and Child Care Survey Dade County, 1958—; del. White House Conf. Children and Youth, 1960; corporate mem. Nat. Assembly Social Policy and Devel. Trustee N. Miami, 1957, Mus. Sci. and Natural History of Miami; bd. dirs., v.p. Family and Children's Services of Dade County; bd. dirs., mem. exec. council Nat. Council for Homemaker-Home Health Aide Services; pres., bd. dirs. Travelers Aid-Internat. Social Services. Mem. Nat. Travelers Aid Assn. (sec.), Am. Assn. U. Women, Women's Panhellenic Assn. Miami, Miami Civic Music Assn., Miami Opera Guild, Fla. Cooperating Council, Lowe Gallery, Chi Omega, Baptist. Home: 405 SW 11th Av Miami FL 33136

MILAM, ROBERT WILSON, physician; b. Nashville, Nov. 2, 1930; s. Daniel Franklin and Mary Louise (Wilson) M.; student Harvard, 1946-48, U. N.C., 1948-49; M.D., Columbia, 1953; m. Anna Mary Simac, June 9, 1952; children—Anamari Camis, Robert Wilson, Edward Nicholas, Daniel Franklin, Benjamin Rush, Stanley Nemec. Intern, Jefferson Davis Hosp., Houston, 1953-54; resident Baylor Med. Sch. Affiliated Hosps., Houston, 1954-56, Children's Hosp., Boston, 1958-59, Mass. Gen. Hosp., Boston, 1959; mem. staff Scott and White Clinic, Temple, Tex., 1959-61; practice medicine specializing in orthopaedic surgery, McAllen, Tex., 1961—; mem. staff McAllen Gen., Mission Municipal, Edinburg Municipal, Knapp Meth. hosps.; cons. Harlingen (Tex.) State Tb Hosp.; instr. orthopaedic surgery Baylor U., 1954-56, U. Tex., 1959-61. Pres., Easter Seal Soc. for Crippled Children and Adults Tex., 1966-68. Served to capt. M.C., USAF, 1956-58. Diplomate Am. Bd. Orthopaedic Surgeons. Fellow A.C.S.; mem. Am. Acad. Orthopaedic Surgeons, Tex., Western orthopaedic assns. Address: 3200 S 2d St McAllen TX 78501

MILBRODT, PAUL EUGENE, electronic engr.; b. Wilson, Ark., Mar. 21, 1923; s. Paul and Ola (Sanders) M.; student Ark. State Coll., 1946-49; B.S. in Elec. Engring., U. Ark., 1951; M.S., George Washington U., 1969; m. Edna Louise Lindenberg, Aug. 3, 1951; 1 dau., Cathy Louise. Electronic engr. Nat. Union, 1951-54, Melpar Inc., 1954-57; prin. electronic engr. Budd Co., 1963-65; sr. electronic engr. Control Sci. Corp., 1965-67; asst. dir. engring. Airtronics, Inc., Chantilly, Va., 1968—. Digital cons., Va., 1967-69. Served with USAAF, 1941-45. Registered profl. engr. Home: 12001 Central Dr Fairfax VA 22030 Office: 3001 Centerville Rd Chantilly VA 22021 also Box 17186 Dulles Airport Washington DC 20041

MILES, ALGENE STEVENS, JR., banker; b. Louisville, Nov. 30, 1929; s. Algene Stevens and Edna May (Rietze) M.; B.A., Washington and Lee U., 1951; grad. Grad. Sch. Banking Rutgers-State U., 1964; m. Ann Berry Houston, Nov. 6, 1954; children—Frank, Elizabeth. Trainee First Nat. Bank Louisville, 1954-59, asst. cashier, 1959-61, asst. v.p., 1961-64, v.p., 1964-68, sr. v.p., 1968-70, exec. v.p., 1970—. Campaign dir. Planned Parenthood dr., 1968, Easter Seal dr., 1969. Bd. dirs. United Way, 1970, treas., 1970; bd. dirs. Salvation Army Boys Club; bd. dirs. St. Joseph's Infirmary, 1968-70, vice chmn., 1970. Served to 2d lt. AUS, 1951-53. Clubs: Louisville Country (dir. 1969-71); Pendennis (Louisville). Home: 613 Club Lane Louisville KY 40207 Office: PO Box 1019 216 S 5th St Louisville KY 40207

MILES, CATHERINE E. (MRS. JAMES R. MILES), educator; b. Reform, Ala.; d. Leven Handy and Mary (Sibley) Ellis; B.S., U. Ala., 1949, M.S., 1950, Ph.D., 1953; J.D., Emory U., 1963; m. James R. Miles, Mar. 1952; children— Jeannette (Mrs. B. L. Smith), Maxine (Mrs. J.A. Bayly). Indsl. accountant Batson-Cook Co., West Point, Ga., 1937-42; prof., chmn. dept. Ga. State U. at Atlanta, 1952—. Named Atlanta's Woman of Yr. in Edn., 1967. Mem. Nat. Assn. Accountants, Ga. Soc. C.P.A.'s, Am. Accounting Assn. (sec.-treas.), Am. Soc. Women Accountants, State Bar Ga., Am., Atlanta bar assns., Beta Gamma Sigma, Beta Alpha Psi. Author: (with Joe Lane) Business and Personnel Taxes, 1967, rev. edit., 1973. Office: Ga State U Dept Accounting 33 Gilmer St Atlanta GA 30303

MILES, HENRY HARCOURT WATERS, physician; b. Burnside, La., Sept. 18, 1915; s. William Porcher and Harriette (Waters) M.; B.S., Tulane U., 1936, M.D., 1939; m. Margaret Bemis Hart, Nov. 29, 1939; children—Sarah Beirne, Robert Hart. Intern, Touro Infirmary, New Orleans, 1939-40, Johns Hopkins Hosp., 1940-41; resident Med. Coll. Va., 1941-42, Mass. Gen. Hosp., 1946-52, Boston Psychoanalytic Inst., 1947-52; individual practice psychiatry and psychoanalysis, New Orleans, 1952—; tng. and supervising analyst New Orleans Psychoanalytic Inst., 1957—; prof. psychiatry Tulane U., 1966—. Mem. La. Hosp. Planning Adv. Council, 1964—, med. adv. bd. Dept. Pub. Welfare, 1966—. Served with M.C. AUS, 1942-46. Fellow Am. Psychiat. Assn.; mem. A.M.A., Am., Internat. psychoanalytic assns., A.A.A.S., Am. Psychosomatic Soc., Alpha Omega Alpha. Author: (with S. Cobb and H. Shands) Case Histories in Psychosomatic Medicine, 1952. Contbr. articles to profl. jours. Home: 1446 Arabella St New Orleans LA 70115 Office: 1430 Tulane Av New Orleans LA 70112

MILES, HERBERT JACKSON, educator; b. Clarence, Mo., July 7, 1907; s. Joseph Edward and Sarah Ellen (Stanley) M.; A.B., Westminster Coll., Fulton, Mo., 1932; Th.M., Southwestern Baptist Sem., 1935; M.A., Baylor U., 1949; Ph.D., U. Mo., 1953; m. Dorothy Elizabeth Wilson, May 22, 1932; 1 son, Stanley Wilson. Ordained to ministry Bapt. Ch., 1930; pastor in Mabank, Tex., 1932-36, Macon, Mo., 1936-38, West Frankfort, Ill., 1938-43, Springfield, Mo., 1944-47; instr. sociology Baylor U., 1948-49, Okla. Bapt. U., 1949-53; prof. sociology Carson-Newman Coll., Jefferson City, Tenn., 1953—; Russell Bradley Jones faculty lectr., 1966; Lyceom lectr. Morristown Coll., 1967; marriage and family life cons. Pres. Bapt. Pastors Conf., Springfield, 1945-46. Mem. Am. Assn. Marriage and Family Counselors, So. Sociol. Soc., Jefferson City C. of C., Alpha Kappa Delta, Phi Sigma Tau. Republican. Elk. Clubs: Civitan. Author: Sexual Happiness in Marriage, 1967; Sexual Understanding Before Marriage, 1971. Home: 713 Branner Av Jefferson City TN 37760

MILES, JOHN BENJAMIN, lawyer; b. Greensboro, N.C., Oct. 19, 1930; s. John Richard and Lois (Wilson) M.; A.B., Guilford Coll., 1952; LL.B., Wake Forest Coll., 1955; m. Daphne Adele Rees, June 25, 1960; children—Lois Rose, John Benjamin, Jr. Admitted to N.C. bar, 1958, practiced in Greensboro, 1958-61, 68—; judge Municipal-County Ct., Greensboro, 1961-68. Bd. dirs. Greensboro Oratorio Soc. Served with CIC, AUS, 1955-58. Mem. N.C., Greensboro bar assns., Wake Forest U. Lawyers Alumni Assn. (exec. com. 1968-70), Phi Delta Phi. Presbyn. (elder). Home: McLeansville NC 27301 Office: Southeastern Bldg Greensboro NC 27401

MILES, LEROY MITCHEL, banker; b. Maysville, Ky., Nov. 12, 1907; s. Ernest Swift and Mary (Mitchel) M.; B.S., U. Ky., 1928; M.B.A., Harvard, 1930; m. Margaret Garland Haskins, Aug. 23, 1937; children— Jeanne, Richard. With First Nat. Bank & Trust Co. (consol. 1st Security Nat. Bank & Trust Co.), Lexington, Ky., 1930—, successively asst. cashier, v.p., exec. v.p., 1930-58, pres., 1958—; dir. Cin. br. Fed. Res. Bank of Cleve., 1960-62, Gen. Telephone Co. Ky., 1962—. Pres. Lexington chpt. A.R.C., 1938-39, Community Chest, 1947-48. Treas. Ky. Med. Found. Served from capt. to col., inf., AUS, 1941-46. Mem. Lexington C. of C. (v.p. 1949-50), Ky. C. of C. (pres. 1968-70), U. Ky. Alumni Assn. (pres. 1948-49). Home: 421 Bristol Rd Lexington KY 40502 Office: 167 W Main St Lexington KY 40501

MILES, R.A., city ofcl. Police chief, Austin, Tex. Office: 120 W 8th St Austin TX 78764*

MILES, RICHARD VANCE, JR., forester, surveyor, pulp and paper exec.; b. Opelousas, La., May 21, 1911; s. Richard Vance and Mathilde (LaCombe) M.; B.S.F., La. State U., 1932; m. Georgia Evelyn Shute, Aug. 18, 1934; children—Richard Vance III, Donald Cooper. Forester, officer U.S. Forest Service in Ala., Tenn., Ga., N.C., Washington, 1933-42; with Gulf States Paper Corp., Tuscaloosa, Ala., 1942—, as chief forester, 1942-49, mgr. div. forestry, 1949-59, mgr. pub. relations div., 1954-58, v.p. forestry, 1959-61, v.p. natural resources and pub. affairs, 1961-64, v.p. industry relations and pub. affairs, 1964-69, v.p. govtl. relations, 1969—. Mem., past chmn. Ala. Bd. Registered Foresters; past chmn. Keep Ala. Green. Chmn. bd. trustees Ala. Acad. Sci., past v.p.; trustee Ala. Wildlife Res. Found. Recipient Order of Golden Pine Cone award Ga. Forestry Assn., 1959; Hon. Tex. Citizen award, 1960; Gov's award for distinguished forestry practice, 1963; named Ky. Col.; lt. col., aide-de-camp. Ala. Gov.'s staff. Fellow Am. Congress Surveying and Mapping; mem. Soc. Am. Foresters (sr. mem., past. chmn. S.E. sect.). Forest Farmers Assn. (dir.), So. Forest Inst. (past pres., dir.), Ala. Forest Products Assn. (past chmn. legislative com., pres. 1966-67), So. Forest Disease and Insect Research Council (past exec. com.), Alumni Assn. Sch. Forestry La. State U., Am. Forestry Assn. (past dir., hon. v.p.). Ala. Soc. Profl. Land Surveyors, Ala. Forestry Council (past chmn. legislative com.), Nat. Geog. Soc., La. State U. Alumni Fedn. (mem. exec. council 1958-59, life mem.), Greater Tuscaloosa, U.S., Ala. (dir. 1965—) chambers commerce, Tuscaloosa Mfrs. Forum (chmn.), Internat. Platform Assn., Trade Relations Assn., Kappa Sigma (pres. Tuscaloosa alumni chpt.). Episcopalian. Clubs: Lions (pres. 1950-51), Tuscaloosa Country (pres. 1964-65), University (Tuscaloosa); Ponte Vedra (Fla.), Rudder Hill Hunt, Lake Wildwood. Home: 1014 Myrtlewood Dr Tuscaloosa AL 35401 also Milestone Lake Wildwood Cottondale AL Office: Gulf States Paper Corp Tuscalossa AL 35401

MILES, ROBERT IRVING, dentist; b. Glenside, Pa., Aug. 2, 1917; s. William Schooley and Jennie Mae (Keller) M.; student Duke, 1935-36; D.D.S., Med. Coll. Va., 1940; m. Katherine Elizabeth Scherer, Nov. 29, 1941; children—Robert Irving, Elizabeth Scherer, Margaret Carolyn, William Scherer. Pvt. practice dentistry, Richmond 1940-41, 1945—. Tchr. dept. operative dentistry Med. Coll. Va., Richmond, 1940-59. Served to capt. 9th Inf. Div., AUS, 1941-45. Decorated Bronze Star. Mem. Richmond Dental Soc., Va., Am. dental assns., Va. Assn. Professions, McKee Study Club, Delta Sigma Delta. Lutheran. Home: 2215 Wedgewood Av Richmond VA 23228 Office: 3604 Monument Av Richmond VA 23230

MILES, THOMAS PEYTON, lawyer, judge; b. Appling County, Ga., Dec. 20, 1921; s. Thomas Peyton and Elizabeth (Faulkner) M.; LL.B., Mercer U., 1950, A.B., 1951; m. Mary Jacqueline Fernnell, Sept. 2, 1944; children—Mary Cathy, Constance Ann, Elizabeth Paulette, Thomas Peyton Miles III. Admitted to Ga. bar, 1950; practice law, Baxley, 1950—; solicitor City Ct., 1955-58, judge, 1959—; judge Juvenile Ct., Appling County, 1963—. Dir. Appling Devel. Corp. Mayor, Surrency, Ga., 1953-60. Served with USAAF, 1940-45. Decorated Air Medal with 10 oak leaf clusters, Purple Heart. Mem. Brunswick Bar Assn. (pres. 1963-64), V.F.W., Am. Legion, Delta Theta Phi. Mason, Moose, Elk, Kiwanian (past pres. Baxley, past lt. gov. 4th div.). Home: PO Box 412 Baxley GA 31513 Office: PO Box 412 Baxley GA 31513

MILES, WALDO GARLAND, lawyer; b. Wise, Va., June 12, 1911; s. Wade M. and Mollie S. (White) M.; student U. Richmond, 1930-33; A.B., Washington and Lee U., 1934, LL.B., 1938; m. Christine Junchen, Feb. 9, 1944; children—LaRue Carter Hicks, Christine Mollie. Admitted to Va. bar, 1937; asso. firm Carter & Williams, Danville, 1938-41; partner firm Williams, Miles & Williams, Danville, 1941-48, Woodward, Miles & Flannaghan and predecessor firms, Bristol, Va. 1948—. Mem. Va. Mental Health Study Commn., 1963-65, Va. Mental Retardation Planning Council, 1964-70, Va. Adv. Legislative Council Sub-com. Studying Grants-in-aid, 1965, Va. Adv. Council on Econ. Edn., 1965—; pub. mem. Va. Tax Study Commn., 1956-57, 62-63; mem. Bristol Sch. Bd., 1958-63, chmn., 1962; mem. Va. Bd. Edn., 1963-71, chmn., 1970-71; chmn. Gov.'s Regional Conf. on Edn., 1967; vice chmn. Va. Pub. Defender Commn., 1972—. Mem. Va. exec. com. Democratic State Central Com., 1960-68. Pres. Bristol Mental Health Clinic, 1957, Bristol Meml. Hosp., 1958-60, bd. dirs., 1956-65; bd. dirs. Bristol chpt. A.R.C., 1954-60; bd. visitors Va. Poly. Inst., 1966-70, Sullins Coll., trustee Va. Council Health and Med. Care. Served as lt. comdr. USNR, 1942-45; lt. comdr. Res. Fellow Am. Coll. Probate Counsel; mem. Bristol C. of C. (dir. 1952-54, 56-58, 68-72, exec. com. 1960-64). Am., Fed., Va. pres. 1962-63), Bristol (past pres.) bar assns., Am. Judicature Soc., Am. Law Inst., Va. C. of C. (dir.), Washington and Lee U. Law Sch. Alumni Assn. (mem. council 1963-65, pres. 1964-65), Omicron Delta Kappa, Pi Delta Epsilon, Phi Delta Phi, Phi Gamma Delta. Methodist. Clubs: Bristol (Va.) Country; Commonwealth (Richmond, Va.). Home: 17 Long Crescent Dr Bristol VA 24201 Office: 115 Johnson St Bristol VA 24201

MILES, WILLIAM JOHN, textile co. pres.; b. Adams, Mass., Apr. 17, 1929; s. John Andrew and Julia Ann (Mendel) M.; B.S., R.I. Sch. Design, 1951; S.M. in Textile Tech. Mass. Inst. Tech., 1957, S.M. in Indsl. Mgmt., 1958; m. Clara Elizabeth Leigh, Mar. 19, 1954; 1 son, Michael William. Supt. Deering-Milliken, Spartanburg, S.C., 1960-65, dir. mfg., knitted outerwear div., 1965-68; dir. mfg. Texfi/Lively Knits, Fayetteville, N.C., 1968-70, pres., 1970—. Served to lt. (j.g.) USNR, 1951-54: Korea. Mem. V.F.W., Nat. Rifle Assn. Republican. Episcopalian. Mason. Home: 3408 Melba St Fayetteville NC 28301 Office: Hoffer Dr Fayetteville NC 28302

MILGRAM, ABRAHAM SAMUEL, constrn. exec.; b. Tel-Aviv, Palestine, Sept. 25, 1936; s. Jaime and Esther (Reich) M.; came to U.S., 1952; B.S., U. Tex., 1958; postgrad. Central U. Venezuela, 1958-59, Northwestern U., 1958; m. Zelma K. Milgram. Field engr. Atlantic Refining Co., Port Arthur, Tex., 1958; design engr. Orinoco Mining Co., Port Ordaz, Venezuela, 1958-63; gen. mgr. Bella Co., Beaumont, Tex., 1963-66, exec. v.p., 1966—, also dir.; exec. v.p., dir. Hurco, Inc., Beaumont, 1967—; dir. Tex. Bank Beaumont. Dir., sec.-treas. Asso. Maintenance Contractors; trustee Sabine area Carpenters Apprenticeship Tng. Fund; v.p. Sabine area Piping Contractors Assn. Mem. Am. Soc. for Testing Materials, Am. Concrete Inst., Am. Soc. C.E., Nat., Tex. socs. profl. engrs. Home: 680 Heritage Lane Beaumont TX 77706 Office: PO Box 5421 Beaumont TX 77706

MILHOUSE, PAUL WILLIAM, bishop; b. St. Francisville, Ill., Aug. 31, 1910; s. Willis Cleveland and Carrie (Pence) M.; A.B., Ind. Central Coll., 1932; D.D., 1950; B.D., Am. Theol. Sem., 1937, Th.D., 1946; L.H.D., Westmar Coll., 1965; S.T.D., Oklahoma City U., 1969; D.D., So. Meth. U., 1969; m. Mary Frances Noblitt, June 29, 1932; children—Mary (Mrs. R.L. Hauswald), Pauline (Mrs. Arthur Vermillion), Paul David. Ordained to ministry Methodist Ch., 1931; pastor, Birds, Ill., 1928-29, Mt. Vernon, Ill., 1932, Elliott, Ill., 1932-37, Olney, Ill., 1937-41, Decatur, Ill., 1941-51; asso. editor Telescope-Messenger, Harrisburg, Pa., 1951-59; exec. sec. Gen. Council of Adminstrn., Dayton, O., 1959-60; bishop, Kansas City, 1960-68, Oklahoma City, 1968—. Pres., Decatur (Ill.) Council of Chs., 1945-49, Bd. of Arbitration, Decatur, 1946, Bd. of Evangelism, Dayton, 1960-68. Trustee So. Meth. U., Oklahoma City U., United Sem., Meth. Home, Boys Ranch. Mem. Epsilon Sigma Alpha. Author: Enlisting and Developing Church Leaders, 1946; Come Unto Me, 1946; Doorways to Spiritual Living, 1950; Except the Lord Build the House, 1949; Christian Worship in Symbol and Ritual, 1953; Lift Up Your Eyes, 1955; Laymen in the Church, 1957; At Life's Crossroads, 1959; Philip William Otterbein, Pioneer Preacher to German Speaking Americans, 1968. Editor Facing Frontiers, 1960. Contbr. articles to profl. jours. Home: 2213 NW 56th Terrace Oklahoma City OK 73112 Office: Gravens Bldg Oklahoma City OK 73102

MILLAR, HUDSON COLQUHOUN, JR., broadcasting co. exec.; b. Orange, N.J., Dec. 22, 1920; s. Hudson C. and Margaret B. (Baird) M.; B.A. in Bus. Adminstrn., Washington and Lee U., 1943; m. Katherine Gross, Apr. 5, 1966; children—Randolph, Gregory, Jeffrey, 1 step-dau., Connie Sue. With Cullman Broadcasting Co. (Ala.), 1949-67, pres., 1948-66, dir., 1948—, treas., 1968—; pres., dir. Gt. So. Mills, 1956-59; pres., dir. Airmedia, Inc., Ft. Pierce, Fla., 1965—, Indian River Broadcasting Co., Ft. Pierce, 1967—. Instr., St. Bernard Coll., 1962-63, mem. lay bd., 1963-67. Chmn., Ft. Pierce Citizens Adv. Com., 1970-71. Pub. relations dir., Ala. Republican Party, 1966-67. Served with USAAF, 1943-46. Mem. White Friars, Phi Kappa Psi. Kiwanian. Home: 1705 S 8th St Ft Pierce FL 33450 Office: Box 3032 Ft Pierce FL 33450

MILLARD, JAMES ABIA, JR., clergyman, ch. ofcl.; b. Bristol, Tenn., Apr. 8, 1912; s. James Abia and Elsie Minor (McCutchan) M.; B.A., Hampden-Sydney Coll., 1932; B.D., Union Theol. Sem. in Va., 1935, Th.M., 1936, Th.D., 1942; D.D., Ark. Coll., 1951; m. Sunshine Hooper, June 12, 1937; children—Eleanor Hooper (Mrs. Steuart E. Vest), Pamela Anne, Lora O'Cain. Ordained to ministry Presbyn. Ch., 1936; pastorates in Va., La., Ark., 1935-52; prof. ch. polity and adminstrn. Presbyn. Theol. Sem., Austin, Tex., 1952-55, homiletics, 1956-59; clk., treas. Presbyn. Ch. U.S., Atlanta, 1959—. Home: 455 Boone Lane Fairhope AL 36532 Office: 341-E Ponce de Leon St NE Atlanta GA 30308

MILLARD, MARVIN LAYTON, banker; b. Danville, Ark., Sept. 20, 1908; s. John M. and Roxie (Hunt) M.; student Ark Poly. Coll., U. Tulsa; m. Willette Eustice, Feb. 10, 1940; 1 son, William M. With Exchange Nat. Bank, Tulsa, 1927-33; with Nat. Bank Tulsa, 1933—, exec. v.p., 1958-60, pres., 1960—, chmn. bd., chief exec. officer, 1964—, also dir. Chmn. Okla. Turnpike Authority. Trustee U. Tulsa. Served from lt. (j.g.) to lt. USNR, World War II. Mem. Okla. Bankers Assn. (pres.), Kappa Alpha. Mem. Christian Ch. Club: Southern Hills Country (pres.). Home: 3631 S Birmingham St Tulsa OK 74105 Office: PO Box 2300 Tulsa OK

MILLEDGE, MRS. STANLEY (SARAH FRANKLIN MILLEDGE), civic worker; b. Melrose, Mass., July 8, 1906; d. Albert Barnes and Edith (Bradbury) Franklin; B.A., Wellesley Coll., 1927; m. Stanley Milledge, Sept. 1, 1928 (dec. Oct. 1965); children—Allan Francis, Sarah Woodman (Mrs. Harold S. Nelson), Eleanor Franklin (Mrs. Barry Decker). Dir. women's community affairs WCKT-TV, Miami, Fla., 1962—, also dir. community service; dir. Sunbeam TV Corp. Pres. Miami Shores P.T.A., 1938-39; pres. Girl Scouts U.S.A., Dade County, 1948-50, chmn. region 6. 1952-56, nat. dir., 1952—, chmn. nat. nominating com., 1963-66, mem. nat. exec. com., 1958, council pres., 1961-62; pres. Children's Service Bur., 1950-52, Vis. Nurse Assn., 1952-54; chmn. Dade County recreation div. Welfare Planning Council, 1949-51, chmn. health div., 1956—; mem. Children's Com., 1951-56; sec. Community Chest, 1953—; v.p. Council Community Relations, 1954-56, Civil Liberties Assn., 1954-57; sec. Protestant Service Bur., 1955-56 (all Dade County); v.p. James E. Scott Community Assn., 1957—; mem. state bd. Fla. Council Human Relations, 1958-62; sec. Fla. Co-operating Council

Children and Youth; chmn. Fla. Com. for Children and Youth, 1968; bd. St. Petersburg Community Welfare Council, 1958-62; sec. South Pinellas Mental Health chpt., 1959-62; bd. dirs. Girl Scouts Tropical Fla., Dade County Welfare Planning Council, Vis. Nurse Assn., Miami Travellers Aid, United Cerebral Palsy Assn., United Ch. Women Greater Miami; chmn. Miami Wellesley Club Fund; trustee Everglades Sch. Girls, Miami, Fla., 1955-60; bd. dirs. Miami YWCA, pres., 1968-—; sec. Womens Com. of 100, Miami; chmn. Miami Council for Continuing Edn. of Women, 1971-72. Recipient Fla. regional award Nat. Conf. Christians and Jews, 1957; named Woman of Achievement, Dist. 12 Fla. Bus and Profl. Women, 1967. Mem. Am. Assn. UN (chpt. bd. 1958-—, local chpt. treas. 1959-62, vice chmn. Miami 1971-—), Soc. Mayflower Descs., Theta Sigma Phi. Conglist. Clubs: Zonta, Miami Wellesley (pres. 1947-49). Home: 1600 Bayshore Dr Miami FL 33133 Office: Station WCKT Miami FL 33138

MILLER, AGNES CHAMBLESS (MRS. FRED MAHER MILLER), univ. dean; b. Ruston, La., Apr. 8, 1918; d. Marion Christopher and Rhoda (Liner) Chambless; B.S., La. Tech. U., 1938; M.S., La. State U., 1944; Ph.D., Fla. State U., 1964; m. William L. Cofer, Aug. 17, 1949 (div. 1959); children—Rhenda Scott, Claire Frances; m. 2d, Fred Maher Miller, Aug. 7, 1965. Tchr. high sch., Belcher, La., 1938-40; asst. dining hall dir. La. State U., 1941; food service dir. Standard (Oil) Restaurant Co., Baton Rouge; tchr. high sch., Start and Rayville, La., 1942-44; supr. nutrition and lunchroom edn. A.E. Phillips Tchr. Tng. Sch., La. Tech. U., Ruston, 1944-46, instr. food and nutrition, 1946-49, prof. home econs., 1955-59, 61-62, 64-—, dean Coll. Home Econs., 1970-—; parish sch. lunch supr. Natchitoches, La., 1949-50, Lake Charles, La., 1954-55. Mem. Am., La. (pres. elect 1972) home econs. assns., Nat., Gulf Coast sect. assns. inst. food technologists, La. Tchrs. Assn. (chpt. v.p. 1967-68), So. Assn. Agrl. Workers, Coll. and U. Tchrs. Food and Nutrition (sect. pres. 1968-69), Soc. Nutrition Edn., Am. Assn. Adminstrs. Home Econs., La. Acad. Sci., La. Coll. Conf. (sec. home econs. sec. 1971-72). Alpha Tau Delta, Phi Kappa Phi, Delta Zeta. Baptist. Home: 503 S Sparta Ruston LA 71270

MILLER, ALBERT HENDERSON, cons. engr.; b. Newport, Ark., Nov. 30, 1932; s. Albert Jackson and Dovie (Murphy) M.; student Ark. State Tchrs. Coll., 1950-51; B.S. in Agrl. Engring., U. Ark., 1955; M.S. in Agrl. Engring., U. Mo., 1957; m. Lynette Alexander, Dec. 31, 1957; children—Alison Lyn, Albert Alexander. Sales engr. Delta Irrigation Co., Memphis, 1955; grad. asst. U. Mo., 1955-57; field engr. Short & Brownlee Constrn. Co., Inc., Newport, Ark. and Kansas City, Mo., 1957-59; br. mgr. Brownlee & Rogers, Inc., El Dorado, Ark., 1960; v.p. H.D. Kantor & Son, Inc., Clarksdale, Miss., 1961; pres. Miller Engring. Co., Inc., Clarksdale, 1961-63, Miller-Newell Engrs., Ltd., Newport, Ark., 1963-—; partner A.J. Miller & Son Farms, Newport, 1963-—; sec.-treas. Miller-Newell Abstract Co., Inc., Newport, 1967-—. Registered profl. engr., Ark., Miss., Mo., Ala. Mem. Am. Soc. Agrl. Engrs. (chmn. Ark. chpt. 1971), Nat. Soc. Profl. Engrs., Newport Area C. of C. (pres. 1971), Phi Delta Theta (chpt. pres. 1954, pres. alumni club 1967), Gamma Sigma Delta, Kappa Kappa Psi, Gamma Alpha (chpt. pres. 1957). Episcopalian. Rotarian (dir. 1964-68). Home: 1001 Walnut St Newport AR 72112 Office: 308 Walnut St Newport AR 72112

MILLER, ALFORD DONALD, city ofcl.; b. Shamokin, Pa., Sept. 14, 1928; s. Alford Franklin and Edna (Arbogast) M.; student Charlotte Fire Coll., 1958-61, U. N.C., 1969, 71; m. Amanda Damaris Francis, Jan. 15, 1949; children—Nancy Damaris, Karen Diane. Armature winder Electro Motive div. Gen. Motors Corp., Halethorpe, Md., 1948-51; control tower operator Piedmont Airlines, Winston-Salem, N.C., 1955-64; vol. fire chief Pilot Fire Dept., Thomasville, N.C., 1956-64; fire chief Tarboro, N.C., 1964-67; civilian fire chief Pacific Architects and Engrs., Los Angeles, Vietnam, 1967-69; fire chief Shelby, N.C., 1969-—; fire rescue instr. N.C. Field Service. Dir. Davidson County Little League Football, 1962-64; chmn. Edgecombe County March of Dimes, 1966. Served with USAF, 1951-55. Mem. N.C. Firemens Assn., N.C. Fire Chief's Assn. (v.p. 1966-67), Nat. Fire Prevention Assn., Am. Legion. Home: 305 S Poston St Shelby NC 28150 Office: 16 Graham St Shelby NC 28150

MILLER, ANDREW PICKENS, state ofcl.; b. Fairfax, Va., Dec. 21, 1932; s. Francis Pickens and Helen (Hill) M.; A.B. magna cum laude, Princeton, 1954; postgrad. New Coll., Oxford U., 1954-55; LL.B., U. Va., 1960; m. Dorothy Andrews Brown, Aug. 14, 1954; children—Julia Lane, Andrew Pickens, Elise Givhan. Admitted to Va. bar, 1960; asso. Penn, Stuart & Stuart, 1960-62; partner Penn, Stuart & Miller, Abingdon, Va., 1963-69; atty. gen. Commonwealth of Va., Richmond, 1970-—. Vice chmn. So. Conf. Attys. Gen., 1972-—. Pres. Washington County United Fund, Inc., 1963-64; dir. S.W. Tb and Respiratory Disease Assn., 1967-69; pres. Va. Highlands Festival, Inc., 1963-65; chmn. Va. Law Day Observance, 1966. Pres., Young Democratic Clubs of Va., 1966-67; chmn. Washington County Democratic Com., 1967-69; del. Dem. Nat. Conv., 1968; mem. Dem. State Central Com., 1968-71. Bd. dirs., sec.-treas. Barter Found., Inc., 1962-69; trustee King Coll., 1966-—; mem. adv. com. Old Dominion Found. Fellowship Program, 1966-71. Served as 1st lt. AUS, 1955-57. Recipient Distinguished Service award Jaycees, 1963. Mem. Va. (chmn. young lawyers sect. 1967-68, mem. com. constl. revision 1968-69), Am. (mem. ho. dels. 1971-—) bar assns., Raven Soc., Order of Coif, Phi Beta Kappa, Phi Alpha Delta, Omicron Delta Kappa. Democrat. Presbyn. (chmn. bd. deacons 1966-67). Rotarian (pres. Abingdon, Va. 1965-66). Home: 13 Glenbrooke Circle West Richmond VA 23229 Office: Supreme Ct Appeals Bldg 11th and Broad St Richmond VA 23219

MILLER, AUGUSTUS TAYLOR, JR., educator; b. Arlington, Tex., Apr. 14, 1910; s. Augustus Taylor and Maude (Duckett) M.; B.S., Emory U., 1931, M.S., 1933; Ph.D., U. Mich., 1939; M.D., Duke U., 1953; m. Adeline Helen Porombovics, Oct. 17, 1938; 1 son, Robert David. Instr., dept. physiology U. N.C. Sch. Medicine, 1939-41, asst. prof., 1941-44, asso. prof., 1944-50, prof., 1950-—. Cons. on environmental medicine Surgeon Gen., U.S. Army. Mem. Am. Physiol. Soc., Soc. Neurobiology, A.A.A.S. Home: 804 Old Mill Rd Chapel Hill NC 27514

MILLER, BANKS LEROY, JR., pub. relations cons.; b. San Juan, Tex., Jan. 31, 1924; s. Banks Leroy and Zella Ellen (Williams) M.; B.B.A., U. Tex., 1948; M.S., Boston U., 1949; m. Martha Ellen Bonner, July 1, 1950; children—Banks Leroy III, Mark M. Advt. mgr. Tenn. Products & Chem. Corp., Nashville, 1950-53; v.p. Western Republic Life Ins. Co., Austin, Tex., 1954-60; owner Asso. Enterprises, Austin, 1960-69; partner Christian, Miller & Honts, Austin, 1969-—. Vis. prof. U. Tex. Sch. Communications, 1965. Pres., Casis P.T.A., 1965-66. Served with USAAF, 1943-45. Mem. Pub. Relations Soc. Am. (pres. Austin chpt. 1970), Am. Tex. socs. assn. execs., Tex. Pub. Relations Assn., Austin Advt. Club (past pres.), Austin C. of C. (dir.), Phi Kappa Sigma. Presbyn. Rotarian. Clubs: Headliners, Citadel, Westwood Country. Home: 2706 Mt Laurel Lane Austin TX 78703 Office: PO Box 772 Austin TX 78767

MILLER, BARBARA ANN KAUFMAN (MRS. HAROLD I. MILLER), lyric soprano; b. Morgantown, W.Va., Aug. 2, 1932; d. Nathan and Ethel (Ritchin) Kaufman; student U. Mich., 1950-51, Pa. State U., 1951-53; A.B., U. Pitts. 1955; m. Harold I. Miller, Feb. 10, 1963; 1 son, Bruce. Lyric soprano appearing with popular mus. shows, 1958-—, including Call Me Madam, 1953, Blossom Time, 1953, Gentlemen Prefer Blondes, 1953, The Mikado, 1953, Louisiana Purchase, 1953, Naughty Marietta, 1953, Three Wishes for Jamie, 1953, Music In The Air, 1953, Lady In The Dark, 1953, The Great Waltz, 1953. Performer for community and charity orgns., Altonna, Pa., 1954-—, Danville, Ky., 1963-—. Mem. Council Jewish Women (gen. chmn. spl. projects Lexington 1963-—), Sisterhood Adath Israel Temple, Lexington, Ky., Ohio Valley Fedn. Temple Sisterhoods (mem. bd. 1968-—, program chmn.), Little Garden Club of Danville, Am. Assn. U. Women, Women Guild Lexington Philharmonic, Sigma Delta Tau, Hadassah (bd. mem. 1963-64). Home: 470 Boone Trail Danville KY 40422

MILLER, BYRON ALLEN, social worker; b. Campbellsville, Ky., Oct. 16, 1911; s. Isacc Newton and Lula (Allen) M.; B.A., Western State U., 1932; M.A., U. Ky., 1937; M.S.W., La. State U., 1954; m. Mildred Jones, Apr. 11, 1946. Tchr., Taylor County High Sch., Cambellsville, Ky., 1933-40; faculty officer Ky. Mil. Inst., Lyndon, Ky. and Venice, Fla., 1940-42; tng. specialist VA Regional Office, Little Rock, Ark., 1946-52; psychiatric social worker VA Regional Office, New Orleans, 1954-55; mem. outpatient psychiat. team St. Alban's Pvt. Psychiat. Hosp., Radford, Va., 1956-63; coordinator Alcoholism Research Lab., Houston VA Hosp., 1963-71; asst. prof. dept. psychiatry Baylor Coll. Medicine, 1972-—. Served with AUS, 1942-46. Decorated Bronze Star medals (five). Mem. Nat. Assn. Social Workers, Acad. Certified Social Workers, Am. Orthopsychiat. Assn. Contbr. articles to profl. jours. Home: Rt 2 Box 141AA Livingston TX 77351 Office: Houston VA Hosp 2002 Holcombe Blvd Houston TX 77031

MILLER, CHARLES F., oil co. exec.; b. Lake Charles, La., June 12, 1918; s. Edgar and Ruth (Williams) M.; B.S. in Petroleum Engring., Tex. A. and M. Coll., 1940; m. Marijo Brigham, May 22, 1948; children— Charles B., Lucy Lee, Mary E. Petroleum engr. Gulf Oil Co., Fannett, Tex., 1940-41, from petroleum engr. to dist. engr., Tex., So. La., Houston, 1947-53; with Kerr-McGee Corp., Oklahoma City, 1953-—, gen. supt., gen. mgr. prodn., 1953-60, mgr. fgn. drilling and prodn., 1961, gen. mgr. fgn. and domestic prodn., oil and gas operations, 1968-—, v.p. Oil and Gas div., group v.p. oil and gas operations, 1969-— v.p. Kerr-McGee Pipeline Corp., White Shoal Pipeline Corp., Triangle Refineries, Inc. Served to maj. AUS, 1941-46; CBI. Mem. Am. Inst. Mining Engrs., Am. Petroleum Inst., Mid-Continent Oil and Gas Assn. Episcopalian. Home: 3332 Goodger Dr Oklahoma City OK 73112 Office: Kerr-McGee Corp Kerr-McGee Bldg Oklahoma City OK 73102

MILLER, CHARLES HENDERSON, educator; b. Salisbury, N.C., Oct. 26, 1905; s. Charles Henderson and Laura (Kluttz) M.; A.B., Duke, 1928, J.D., 1934; m. Maude McCracken, Apr. 14, 1949; children—Charles Henderson, John Merriman. Fellow Legal Clinic, Duke Law Sch., Durham, N.C., 1931-34, asst., 1934-47; admitted to N.C. bar, 1933, Tenn. bar, 1949; cons. Nat. Probation Assn., N.Y.C., 1945-47; cons., dir. instns. N.C. Dept. Pub. Welfare, Raleigh, 1946-47; dir. legal clinic, prof. law U. Tenn., Knoxville, 1947-—. Bd. dirs. Salvation Army of Knoxville, Family Service Assn. Knoxville; trustee Med. Research Found., Knoxville. Mem. Nat. Council Legal Clinics, Nat. Council Profl. Responsibilities, Am., N.C., Tenn., Knoxville bar assns., Order of Coif, Phi Kappa Phi, Phi Delta Theta. Methodist (mem. adminstrv. bd. 1947-—). Author: (with W.E. Cole) Social Problems: a Sociological Interpretation, 1965; also articles. Home: 4622 Wye Way Lane Knoxville TN 37020

MILLER, CHARLES VALENTINE, physician; b. Omaha, Apr. 23, 1915; s. Lloyd Herman and Jennette L. (Wiegand) M.; B.S., U. Wyo., 1938; M.D., U. Rochester, 1942; m. Ann Clark, Apr. 28, 1945; 1 son, John Allyn. Intern U. Neb. Hosp., 1942-43, fellow U. Rochester Sch. Medicine, 1946-48; resident and instr. U. Tenn. Coll. Medicine, 1948-51; fellow hematology Pratt Diagnostic Clinic, Boston, 1958-59; practice medicine, Chattanooga, 1954-58, Ft. Worth, 1959-61; dir. labs., hematologist Mary Washington Hosp., Fredericksburg, Va., 1961-—. Bd. dirs. Fredericksburg chpt. A.R.C., Fredericksburg bd. Am. Cancer Soc.; med. bd. Va. chpt. Leukemia Soc. Am. Served from 1st lt. to maj., AUS, 1943-46; as maj. USAF, 1951-53; ETO. Diplomate Nat. Bd. Med. Examiners, Am. Bd. Pathology. Fellow Am. Soc. Clin. Pathologists, Internat. Soc. Hematology, Assn. Clin. Scientists, Soc. Nuclear Medicine; mem. A.M.A., Va. Med. Assn., Sigma Chi, Gamma Sigma Epsilon. Presbyn. Kiwanian. Research in field. Home: 1109 Westwood Dr Fredericksburg VA 22401 Office: Med Arts Bldg Fredericksburg VA 22401

MILLER, C(HARLES) WALLACE, agronomist; b. Paonia, Colo., Sept. 13, 1911; s. Frank M. and Mabel (Hall) M.; B.S., Okla. State U., 1934; m. Emabel Offutt, Aug. 12, 1941; 1 son, Charles Wallace. Soil scientist Soil Conservation Service, Gallup, N.M., 1934-40, soil conservationist, Phoenix, 1944-46; soil surveyor U.S. Grazing Service, Albuquerque, 1940-42; agronomist C.E., Tulsa, 1942-44, CAA, Ft. Worth, 1946-52, Mil. Land Mgmt., Hdqrs. Air Tng. Command, USAF, San Antonio, 1952-66; chief land mgmt. sect. Office Chief Engrs., Dept. Army, Washington, 1966-71; profl. agronomy and land mgmt. cons., San Antonio, 1971-—; cons. turf mgmt. Alamo Heights Sch., 1954-—. Mem. Am. Soc. Agronomy (past dir.), Am. Soc. Mil. Engrs., Tex. Turf Grass Assn., Soil Conservation Soc. Am., Phi Kappa Phi, Alpha Zeta, Phi Sigma. Baptist. Contbr. articles to profl. jours. Home and office: 639 Nottingham Dr San Antonio TX 78209

MILLER, CLARENCE ROSS, physician; b. Navasota, Tex., Jan. 17, 1893; s. Ross Joseph and Minnie Lee (Teague) M.; M.D., U. Tex., 1913; m. Bertha George Fouts, Nov. 14, 1918. Intern Scott and White Hosp., Temple, Tex., 1913; mem. staff Austin (Tex.) State Hosp., 1957-—, supt., 1965-67; neurol. physician USPHS, also VA hosps. at Greenville, S.C., Sheridan, Wyo., Northport, L.I., N.Y., Boston, N.Y.C., Chgo., Ft. Lyon, Colo., Lyons, N.J., Coatesville, Pa., Jackson, Miss., Marlin, Tex. Mil. Cons., Tex. Rehab. Commn. service, World War I. Diplomate Am. Bd. Psychiatry and Neurology. Fellow A.M.A., Am. Psychiat. Assn.; mem. Tex. Med. Assn., Travis County Med. Soc. Episcopalian. Rotarian (dist. gov. 1955-56). Clubs: Austin, Headliners (Austin). Home: 1801 Lavaca St Austin TX 78701

MILLER, CLARENCE WILLIAM, hosp. adminstr.; b. Erwin, Tenn., July 5, 1918; s. Hyder Robert and Cecil (Miller) M.; student U.S. Naval Sch. Hosp. Adminstrn., 1952, Mercer U., 1955-56; m. Sharlene Ruth Hansen, May 3, 1969; 1 son Wayne Preston. Commd. officer, USN, 1937; served with Hosp. Corps; ret., 1957; asst. adminstr. Lake Wales (Fla.) Hosp., 1957-59, adminstr., 1959-—. Elk. Club: Lake Wales Country. Home: 1104 Circle Dr Lake Wales FL 33853 Office: 410 11th St Lake Wales FL 33853

MILLER, CLAUDE RUSSELL, JR., army dentist; b. Etowah, Tenn., Nov. 4, 1929; s. Claude Russell and Bleeka (Knox) M.; D.D.S., U. Tenn., 1952; student Command and Gen. Staff Coll., 1966-67; m. Barbara Gail Rutledge, Oct. 8, 1950; children—James Russell, Walter Richard, William Everett, Ann Rutledge. Pvt. practice dentistry, Ashland City, Tenn., 1952; commd. 1st lt. U.S. Army, 1952, advanced through grades to col., 1971; served in Europe, 1953-55, Japan, 1960-63; comdr. 932d Dental Profl. Service, Vietnam, 1971-72; assigned to Ft. Jackson, S.C., 1972-—. Home: 2027 Cheltenham Lane Columbia SC 29206 Office: US Army Dental Service Oliver Dental Clinic Fort Jackson SC 29207

MILLER, DANIEL CARLOS, advt. agy. exec.; b. Birmingham, Ala., Sept. 12, 1916; s. Walter Grover and Mercedes (Goldsmith) M.; B.A., U. Houston, 1934-38; postgrad. Sorbonne, 1937, Harvard, 1938; m. Polly Henry, Dec. 6, 1966; children—Carol (Mrs. Bart Bragg), Dulce (Mrs. John David Bell). With South Am. Gulf Oil Co., Barranquilla, Colombia, 1938-39; welder, foreman Panama Canal, 1940-43; account exec. Bozell & Jacobs, Houston, 1948-49; prin. Miller & Assos., Houston, 1950-—. Served with U.S. Mcht. Marines, 1943-46. Recipient Vern award French Govt., 1938. Presbyn. Rotarian (dir. 1965-69). Address: 357 N Post Oak Lane Houston TX 77024

MILLER, DAVID EDMOND, physician; b. Biscoe, N.C., June 6, 1930; s. James Herbert and Elsie Dale (McGlaughon) M.; A.B., Duke, 1952, M.D., 1956; m. Marjorie Willard Penton, June 4, 1960; children—Marjorie Dale, David Edmond. Intern, Duke Med. Center, Durham, N.C., 1956-57, resident in internal medicine, 1957-58, 59, 60, research fellow cardiovascular disease, 1958-59, 61, asso. internal medicine and cardiology, 1963-—; practice medicine, specializing in internal medicine and cardiology, Durham, 1964-—; attending physician internal medicine div. cardiology Watts Hosp., Durham, 1964-—, also chmn. med. staff patient care com. Served to lt. comdr., USNR, 1961-63. Diplomate Am. Bd. Internal Medicine. Fellow A.C.P.; mem. Am., So. med. assns., Am. Heart Assn. (council clin. cardiology 1963-—), N.C., Durham-Orange County med. socs., Am., N.C. socs. internal medicine, Am. Fedn. Clin. Research. Methodist (mem. chancel choir, adminstrv. bd.; pres. men's group; chmn. pastor-parish relations com.; lay del. N.C. ann. conf.). Contbr. articles profl. jours. Home: 1544 Hermitage Ct Durham NC 27707 Office: 1200 Broad St Durham NC 27705

MILLER, DAVID WADSWORTH, accountant; b. Balt., Dec. 26, 1920; s. Samuel H. and Florence (Wadsworth) M.; B.S., U. Fla., 1943; m. Margarett R. Ragsdale, Jan. 27, 1945; 1 dau., Anne C. Accountant Russell S. Bogue, C.P.A., Tampa, Fla., 1943-45; internal auditor Borden Co., Tampa, 1945-55; prof. Stetson U., Deland, Fla., 1955-65; accountant, Deland, 1955-—. Cost cons. Fla. Concrete and Products Assn., 1958-—. C.P.A., Fla. Mem. Fla., Am. insts. C.P.A.'s. Presbyn. (elder 1961-—). Home: 1236 W New York Av Deland FL 32720 Office: Whitehair Bldg Deland FL 32720

MILLER, DONALD HOPE, headmaster; b. Lexington, Mass., July 3, 1907; s. Hugh and Clara Hazeltine (Fay) M.; grad. Deerfield Acad., 1925; A.B., Princeton, 1929; postgrad Harvard Mass. Inst. Tech. U. Pa.; m. Peter Marsters, May 15, 1930; children—Malcolm Fay, Eileen (Mrs. Kenneth Sloan). With R. H. Macy Co., N.Y.C., 1929-30, Provident Mut. Life Ins. Co., N.Y.C., 1930-31; tchr. Beacon Sch., Wellesley Hills, Mass., 1931-32; tchr. Belmont (Mass.) Hill Sch., 1932-43, head sci. dept., 1936-43; tchr. Phillips Exeter Acad., Exeter, N.H., 1943-47, Shady Side Acad., Pitts., 1947-52; headmaster Newark Acad. 1952-56, Germantown Acad., 1956-66, Gulf Stream Sch., Delray Beach, Fla., 1967-—. Examiner in biology Ednl. Records Bur., 1939-51; Coll. Entrance Exam. Bd., 1946; v.p. Fla. Assn. Acad. Non-Pub. Schs.; dir. Fla. Council Ind. Schs. Active Boy Scouts Am. Trustee St. Andrew's Sch., Boca Raton, Fla., Gulf Stream Sch. Found., Inc.; mem. ednl. adv. bd. Jacksonville Episcopal High Sch. Mem. Headmasters Assn., Country Day Sch. Headmasters Assn. Unitarian. Rotarian. Clubs: Tower (Princeton); Seagate Beach, Delray Beach (Fla.); Princeton (Phila.). Home: 3525 Oleander Way Delray Beach FL 33444 Office: Gulf Stream School 3910 N Ocean Blvd Delray Beach FL 33444

MILLER, DONALD LANE, pub. relations co. exec.; b. Pitts., May 14, 1918; s. Donald Edwin and Arvilla (Lane) M.; A.B., Kenyon Coll., 1940; Russian interpreter certificate U. Colo., 1946; postgrad. U. Pitts., 1947-48; m. Norma Reno, Feb. 2, 1951. Reporter, Pitts. Sun-Telegraph, 1940-42, Washington Post, 1946; pub. relations Westinghouse Electric Corp., Pitts., 1947-51; reporter Billboard and Tide, 1953; pub. relations dir. Nat. Agrl. Chem. Assn., Washington, 1954-58; sec. Donald Larch & Co., Washington, 1958-61; pres. Asso. Pub. Relations Counselors, Washington, 1961-—. Exec. dir. All Am. Conf., Washington, 1962-—. Editor, GOP Nationalities News, Rep. Nat. Com., 1960; pub. relations nationalities div. Rep. Nat. Com., 1964; coordinator life underwriters sect. Citizens for Nixon-Agnew, 1968. Served from ensign to lt. USNR, 1942-46; from lt. to lt. comdr. 1951-53. Mem. S.A.R., Am. Legion, V.F.W., Amvets, Phi Beta Kappa, Delta Tau Delta. Clubs: National Press, Capital Hill (Washington). Author: Strategy for Conquest, 1966. Contbg. editor Washington New Approach, 1971-—. Home: 309 Green St Alexandria VA 22314 Office: 1028 Connecticut Av NW Washington DC 20036

MILLER, DORIS HOPE HUNTINGTON (MRS. RALPH STANLEY MILLER), educator; b. nr. Rensselaer, Ind., Oct. 18, 1922; d. Henry Jay and Lura Mary (Yeoman) Huntington; B.S., Manchester Coll., 1945; M.S. in Edn., Syracuse U., 1947; postgrad. U. Denver, summer 1955, Stanford, summer 1964, Pacific U., summer 1968; m. Ralph Stanley Miller, June 16, 1951. Asso. dir. residence hall Rochester (N.Y.) Inst. Tech., 1947-50, instr. English, 1947-50, 52-54, dir. Student Union, 1952-56; counselor sophomore women, asst. dir. residence hall Ia. State Tchrs. Coll., Cedar Falls, 1950-51; dir. teenage program YWCA, Rochester, 1951-52; tchr., registrar, girls counselor, head social studies dept. St. John's Sch., Santurce, P.R., 1957-63; guidance counselor Antilles High Sch., Ft. Buchanan, San Juan, P.R., 1963-—. Mem. evaluating com. Middle States Assn. Colls. and Secondary Schs., 1963, 69. Membership chmn. P.R. Women's Coll. Club, 1958-59, publicity chmn., 1963, v.p., 1963-64, pres., 1965-67, mem.-at-large, 1967-69, 71-—. Mem. Am. Guidance and Personnel Assn., Nat. Vocational Guidance Assn., Nat. Assn. Social Workers, Am. Assn. U. Women, Natural History Soc. P.R., Caribbean Counselors Assn., P.R. Assn. Nat. Honor Soc. Chpts. (exec. sec. 1968-71), Pi Lambda Theta. Methodist (rec. sec. Women's Guild 1958-59, chmn. worship com. 1970-—). Home: 1509 Calle Las Marias Santurce PR 00911 Office: Antilles High Sch Ft Buchanan San Juan PR 00934

MILLER, EARL LEWIS, adhesive co. exec.; b. Etowah, Tenn., Mar. 4, 1921; s. Enoch Earl and Lockey (Derrick) M.; grad. high sch.; m. Mildred Toomey, June 2, 1940; children—Gary Earl, Timothy Lewis. Brakeman L & N R.R., 1938-47; salesman H.B. Fuller Co., Atlanta, 1947-51, Empire Labs., Atlanta, 1951-52, Polymer So., Springdale, Conn., 1952-61, Holt Mfg., Birmingham, Ala., 1961-62; with Big Bear Adhesive & Chem. Co., Inc., Etowah, 1962-—, pres. train plant personnel, 1968-—. Camping chmn. Unaka dist. Boy Scouts Am., 1968-69, scoutmaster, 1969-70, recipient Order of Arrow; pres. P.T.A., Etowah, 1952. Baptist. Mason (32 deg., Shriner). Club: Senators (Knoxville, Tenn.). Home: 306 Louisiana St Etowah TN 37331 Office: Hwy 30 W Etowah TN 37331

MILLER, EBERHARD HAMMEL, educator; b. Denver, Feb. 11, 1922; s. Eberhard Oscar and Pearl (Hammel) M.; B.S. in Mech. Engring., U. Mo., 1946, B.S. in Elec. Engring., 1947, M.S. in Mech. Engring., 1948; m. Myra Lee Wiegmann, Jan. 20, 1945; children—Joan (Mrs. Kenneth Hillman), Susan J. (Mrs. David G.

Cooper). Engr., head detonator lab. Olin Industries East Alton, Ill., 1948-52; field engr. R.W. Booker & Assos., St. Louis, 1952-54; research engr. Schlumberger Well Surveying Co., Houston, 1954-57; engring. coordinator Clevite Corp., Houston, 1957-58; asst. prof. gen. engring. Tex. Coll. Arts and Industry, Kingsville, 1958-63; asst. prof. sci. U. Corpus Christi, 1963—. Asso. dir. home study course in natural gas distbn. So. Gas. Assn., 1960-63; liaison explosives Civil Def., Houston, 1964-68; cons. heat transfer, accident studies to industry, 1958-63. Mem. adult com., Girl Scouts U.S.A.; 1958-62. Served with Intelligence Corps, AUS, 1942-46. Registered profl engr., Mo., Tex. Mem. I.E.E.E., Am. Soc. M.E. (past chmn.), Nat. Radio Inst. Alumni Assn. Mason. Home: 4129 Bray Dr Corpus Christi TX 78413 Office: PO Box 6010 6500 Ocean Dr Corpus Christi TX 78411

MILLER, ERMA LOUISA EDWARDS (MRS. HOWARD ALBERT MILLER), musician, educator; b. Shannon City, Ia., Dec. 18, 1907; d. George Judson and Rose (Ewing) Edwards; normal certificate Simpson Coll., 1928; student St. Theresa Coll. for Women, 1931-32; B.S., U. Ark., 1945; m. Howard Albert Miller, Dec. 31, 1928; children—George Edwards (dec.), Patricia Lee (Mrs. Anthony Walker), Howard Albert. Organist, 1st Meth. Ch., Villisca, Ia., 1920-26; asst. organist 1st Bapt. Ch., Winona, Minn., 1931-32, Meth. Ch., Ogdon, Utah, 1935; pvt. tchr. music, Winona, Minn., 1930-33, Ogden, Utah, 1934-35, St. Charles, Ark., 1936-41, Marietta, Ga., 1946—; tchr. music appreciation Faith Luth. Sch., Marietta, 1958-65. Organizer, Marietta Community Symphony, 1951; chmn. bd. Marietta Symphony, 1958-67; mgr. Marietta Community Symphony, 1952-69, trustee, 1967—; Marietta rep., mem. bd. Atlanta Symphony, 1948-50; sr. leader Girl Scouts U.S.A., Marietta, 1946-47. Mem. Music Educators Nat. Conf., Marietta Writers Club, Ga. Music Educators Assn. Clubs: Marietta (Ga.) Music (pres. 1952-54); Fish and Wildlife Service Woman's (pres. 1956-57); Forest Service Wives; Atlanta Woman's Aero. (sec. 1954-55). Home: 511 Sybil Lane Marietta GA 30060

MILLER, ESTELLE LEE (MRS. T. E. MILLER), polit. worker, lawyer; b. N.Y.C., Nov. 30, 1929; d. Jacob and Theresa (Smith) Lieberman; A.B., Bklyn. Coll., 1949; LL.B. U. Wis., 1954; student U. Miami, 1952-53; m. Robert M. Ague, Jr., Mar. 28, 1952 (div. Jan. 1966); children—Robert M. III, Lindajean Duff; m. 2d, T. E. Miller. Tchr. pub. schs., N.Y.C. 1949-51; admitted to Wis. bar, 1954; practiced in Janesville, 1955-56; research asst. U. Wis. Law Sch., 1954; trial lawyer FTC, Washington, 1956-58, Fed. Power Commn., 1958; opinion writer CAB, Office of Gen. Counsel, Washington, 1958-61; instr. congl. campaign workers, Va., Tex., Okla., Ga.; spl. cons. Republican Nat. Com., Washington. Mem. Ga. Fedn. Republican Women (pres. 1965-67, dir. 1964—), Nat. Fedn. Rep. Women (dir. 1965—; chmn. nat. ednl. adv. com.), D.C. League Rep. Women, Cobb County Fedn. Rep. Women (founder, pres. 1964). Mem. Am., Fed., Wis. bar assns. Republican. Episcopalian. Clubs: Columbus (Ga.) Country; Capitol Hill (Washington). Contbr. articles to profl. jours. Home: 627 Westmoreland Columbus GA 31904

MILLER, EUGENE LESLIE, engine mfg. exec.; b. Tulsa, Apr. 23, 1919; s. Joseph G. and Flora (Shorten) M.; B.S. in Engring., Okla. A. and M. Coll., 1941; m. Doris Cooley, May 6, 1942; children—Melinda, Matthew, Melissa. With Mid Continent Petroleum Corp., Tulsa, summers 1937-40; project engr. Cooper-Bessemer Corp., Mt. Vernon, O., 1946-54, asst. gen. mgr., 1954-56, gen. mgr., 1956-57, pres., gen mgr. 1957-65, pres., chief exec. officer, 1965—, chmn., 1967—; chmn., chief exec. officer Cooper Industries, Inc., Houston; dir. First-Knox Nat. Bank. Served as lt. col. C.E. AUS, 1942-46. Mem. Blue Key, Pi Tau Sigma, Sigma Tau. Presbyn. Address: 631 Hunters Grove Houston TX 77024

MILLER, FANNIE (MRS. SHERMAN E. MILLER), educator; b. Winchester, Ky., May 30, 1914; d. Sam and Ethel (Schwartzman) Herman; A.B., U. Ky., 1935, M.A., 1937; postgrad. Columbia, summer 1936, U.Ky.; m. Dr. Sherman E. Miller, May 30, 1937; children—Freda Grace (Mrs. Michael H. Lerner), Joseph Herman, Samye Norene (Mrs. Norman Auerback), Faith Sarah. Supervising tchr. English, speech, drama U. Sch., U. Ky., Lexington, 1936-41, substitute tchr., 1944-59, supervising tchr., 1959-62, coordinator student teaching, 1962—, asst. prof. student teaching, 1966—. Cons. English tchrs., English depts., 1960—; mem. editorial adv. bd. Lit. Cavalcade, 1964-67. Pres., 7th dist. P.T.A., 1960-63; mem. state bd. mgrs. Ky. Congress Parents and Tchrs., 1960-63; pres. Lexington City Council, 1957-58, bd. mem., chmn. 7th dist. com. Reading and Library Service, 1966—; mem. Ky. Gov.'s Citizens Com. for Ky. Village, 1964, Gov.'s Commn. Status Women, 1964-66; chmn. area resource com. Midwest Porgram Airborne TV Instrn., 1960-63; founder Lexington Children's Theater, 1964-65; mem. budget com. United Community Fund; trustee, vice chmn. Lexington Pub. Library. Recipient United Jewish Appeal award, 1950; YMCA citation for Outstanding Service to Youth of Lexington and Fayette County, 1952; March of Dimes certificate appreciation, 1954; Delta Zeta Outstanding Woman on Campus award, 1968; Assn. Women Students at U. Ky. as outstanding woman faculty mem., 1970; ann. citation religious leadership Temple Adath Israel, 1972. Mem. Ky. Congress Parents and Tchrs. (life), Nat., Ky., Central Ky. (pres. English sect. 1964-65) edn. assns., Assn. Tchr. Educators, Ky. Speech Assn. (past v.p.), Nat., Ky. (pres. 1967-68) councils tchrs. English, Mortar Bd., Delta Kappa Gamma (hon.), Gamma Beta Phi (adviser), Phi Beta Kappa, Kappa Delta Pi. Jewish religion (past pres. sisterhood; past religious sch. supt.). Home: 311 Holliday Rd Lexington KY 40502

MILLER, FLOYD FREEMAN, physician; b. Skiatook, Okla., Mar. 15, 1930; s. Floyd Edwin and Elsie Hazel (Rader) M.; B.S., U. Okla., 1953; M.D., 1956; m. Mary Adeline Fowler, Aug. 16, 1953; children—Michael Floyd, Steven Fowler. Intern, Univ. Hosp., Ann Arbor, Mich., 1956-57, resident internal medicine, 1957-60, allergy fellow, 1960-61; practice medicine specializing in allergy, Tulsa, 1963—; mem. staff St. John's, St. Francis hosps., Tulsa. Instr. U. Mich. Sch. Medicine, 1960-61. Bd. visitors U. Okla. Sch. Medicine, Oklahoma City, 1970-72. Served with USAF, 1961-63. Fellow A.C.P., Am. Acad. Allergy; mem. Tulsa County Med. Soc. (pres. elect 1972), Tulsa Internists Soc. (pres., 1971), Tulsa C. of C., Okla. Soc. Internal Medicine (sec.-treas. 1970-72), Am. Thoracic Soc., Phi Beta Kappa, Phi Eta Sigma, Alpha Omega Alpha. Club: Southern Hills Country, University. Home: 3736 E 43d Pl Tulsa OK 74135 Office: 3233 E 31st St Tulsa OK 74105

MILLER, FORRESTT ALLEN, coll. dean; b. Pinetop, Ariz., July 15, 1931; s. Joseph L. and Allyne Elizabeth (Kendrick) M.; B.A., Chico State Coll., 1956; M.A., U. Cal. at Berkeley, 1959, Ph.D., 1962; m. Suzanne Joy Schneebeli, June 25, 1955; children—Bradford Edwin, Kristina Suzanne. Instr. history U. Mass. at Amherst, 1961-62; mem. faculty Vanderbilt U., Nashville, 1962—, prof., 1971—, asso. dean Coll. Arts and Scis., 1971—. Cons. Random House, 1962-63, Dept. Health, Edn. and Welfare, 1970-71. Rapporteur Nashville Com. Fgn. Relations, 1967-71. Served with USAF, 1950-55. Mem. So. Conf. Slavic Studies (pres., 1970, exec. com., 1967-70), Am. Hist. Assn., Am. Assn. Advancement Slavic Studies, Am. Acad. Social and Polit. Sci. Author: Dmitrii Miliutin and the Reform Era in Russia, 1968. Home: 6813 Cloudland Dr Nashville TN 37205

MILLER, FRANCIS PICKENS, govt. ofcl.; b. Middlesboro, Ky., June 5, 1895; s. Henry and Flora (McElwee) M.; A.B., Washington and Lee U., 1914; B.A. (Rhodes scholar), Oxford U., 1921, M.A., 1923; student Grad. Inst. Internat. Studies, Geneva, Switzerland, 1927-28; LL.D. (hon.), Centre Coll., 1954; D.Litt. (hon.), Washington and Jefferson Coll., 1959; LL.D. (hon.), Davis and Elkins Coll., 1964; m. Helen Day Hill, Aug. 25, 1927; children—Andrew Pickens, Robert Day. Asso. with YMCA, 1914-26; sec. World's Student Christian Fedn., Geneva, 1927-28, chmn., 1928-38; field sec. Fgn. Policy Assn., 1934-35; with Raymond Leslie Buell organized Nat. Policy Com., 1935 (sec. 1935-38, vice chmn. 1938-42), Pub. Affairs Com., 1936 (exec. sec. 1936-37); sec. So. Policy Com., 1935-40; orgn. dir. Coms. on Fgn. Relations of Council on Fgn. Relations, N.Y., 1938-41. With Henry P. Van Dusen and Herbert Agar organized movement to secure transfer destroyers to Britain in return for bases, 1940; nat. vice chmn. Fight for Freedom Com., 1941; mem. bd. Freedom House, 1958—; chmn. planning bd. Fgn. Information Service of Coordinator of Information, 1942; cons. Dept. State, 1950-52; mem. Nat. Com. for Effective Congress, 1966—, Am. Revolution Bicentennial Commn., 1967-69; mem. bd. visitors Davidson (N.C.) Coll.; chmn. bd. visitors Fla. Presbyn. Coll., St. Petersburg, Fla., 1968-71; past mem. bd. colls. and univs.; moderator of the Presbyn. Synod Va., 1953-54; mem. Central Com. World Council chs., 1954-61; pres. Va. Council Chs., 1957-59; exec. sec. Friends of Presbyn. Union, 1954-55; coordinator Va. Com. on Religious Freedom, 1960; mem. bd. So. Regional Council, 1959—. Mem. Va. Ho. of Dels., 1938-41; candidate for gov. Va., 1949, U.S. Senate, 1952; spl. asst. Ednl. and Cultural Affairs, Dept. State, Washington, 1962-65. Served with AEF, 1917-19; mem. staff OSS, 1942-43; commd. lt. col. AUS, 1943, col. Gen. Staff Corps, 1945; on staff G-2, SHAEF, 1944-45, and O.D.I. Office Mil. Govt., Germany, 1945-46. Decorated Legion of Merit with cluster (U.S.); Order Brit. Empire; Legion of Honor, Croix de Guerre with palms (France); Order Leopold I with palm, Croix de Guerre with Palm (Belgium). Mem. Council Fgn. Relations, Soc. of Cincinnati, Oxford Soc., Phi Beta Kappa, Phi Gamma Delta, Omicron Delta Kappa. Democrat. Presbyn. Clubs: Century, Yale, Cosmos, City Tavern. Author: (with Helen Hill) The Giant of the Western World, 1930; (with H. R. Niebuhr, W. Pauck), The Church Against the World, 1935; The Blessings of Liberty, 1936; Man from the Valley, 1971. Contributed chpts. to: Church and Campus, 1956; Christians are Citizens, 1957; What the Christian Hopes for in Society, 1957; We Dissent, 1962. Address: 2810 P St NW Washington DC 20007

MILLER, FRANK DICKSON, army officer; b. Brush Prairie, Wash., May 27, 1914; s. Frank O. and Lora (Dickson) M.; B.S., U.S. Mil. Acad., 1938; m. Margaret Fay Prickett, Sept. 23, 1939; children—Frank Dickson, Brink P., Maile M. (Mrs. William J. Doyle), Robert M., Jeremy K., Margaret C., Mary V. Commd. 2d lt. U.S. Army, 1938, advanced through grades to maj. gen., 1967; with 77th Inf. div., 1943, asst. chief staff G-3 77th div., 1944, regtl. exec. officer, acting comdr. 307th Inf. Rgmt., 1945; dep. mil. gov., Japan, 1945; with G-3 sect. hdqrs., Pacific Forces, 1946-49; with dept. tactics U.S. Mil. Acad., 1949-53; assigned U.S. Army Caribbean, 1954; asst. chief staff G-4, 1954-56; comdg. officer 20th Inf. Regt., 1956-57; with Office Asst. Chief Staff G-4 Hdqrs. Continental Army Command, Ft. Monroe, Va., 1958-61; with Mil. Assistance Adv. Group, Vietnam, 1961, asst. chief staff J-4, 1962; chief staff MAAG, 1963; exec. officer Office Dept. Chief Staff Logistics Dept. Army, 1963-65; asst. chief staff G-4 8th Army, Korea, 1965-66; dep. chief staff plans and operations U.S. Army Vietnam, 1966-67, asst. dep. comdg. gen., chief staff, 1967; asst. dep. chief staff logistics Dept. Army, 1967-69; ret., 1970. Decorated D.S.M. with oak leaf cluster, Legion of Merit with 2 oak leaf clusters, Bronze Star medal with oak leaf cluster, Air medal, Combat Inf. badge, Korean Order Chung Mu; Vietnamese Nat. Order. Mem. Assn. U.S. Army, Ret. Officers Assn., Army Athletic Assn., West Point Soc., Bestline Dist. Assn. Episcopalian (licensed lay reader). Club: Army-Navy (Washington). Address: 4130 Watkins Trail Annandale VA 22003

MILLER, GENE EDWARD, newspaper reporter; b. Evansville, Ind., Sept. 16, 1928; s. Paul E. and Irene (Hudson) M.; A.B. in Journalism, Ind. U., 1950; Nieman fellow, Harvard, 1967-68; m. Electra Sonia Yphantis, Apr. 13, 1952; children—Janet Irene, Theresa Jean, Thomas Raphael, Roberta Lynn. Reporter, Jour.-Gazette, Ft. Wayne, Ind., 1950-51, Washington bur. Wall St. Jour., 1953-54, Richmond (Va.) News Leader, 1954-57, Miami (Fla.) Herald, 1957—. Served with AUS, 1951-53. Recipient Headliner award, 1966, 69, Heywood Broun award, 1966, Pulitzer prize, 1967. Author: 83 Hours till Dawn. Investigative reporting led to freedom and exoneration of two persons wrongly convicted of murder in separate cases. Home: 8831 SW 20th St Miami FL 33165 Office: 1 Herald Plaza Miami FL 33101

MILLER, GEORGE A., TV exec., state senator; b. Montrose, Colo., Apr. 3, 1927; s. George A. and Verdie (Sallee) M.; student East East State Coll., 1946-48, Okla. State U., 1948-50; m. Mary E. Cox, June 11, 1948; children—George E., John D., Robert W., Mary Ann. Chief engr. KADA Broadcasting, Inc., Ada, Okla., 1950-60; news dir. Eastern Okla. Television, Inc., Ada, 1955—; mem. Okla. State Senate, 1964—, chmn. senate com. edn., 1968—. Served with USNR, 1945-46. Mem. Nazarene Ch. Optimist. Home: 1021 E 6th St Ada OK 74820 Office: 1600 Arlington St Ada OK 74820

MILLER, GEORGE CARPENTER, banker; b. Columbus, O., July 16, 1918; s. Orlando Carpenter and Susan (Siebert) M.; B.Sc. in Bus. Adminstrn., Ohio State U., 1940; m. Mary M. Kritzer, Nov. 4, 1947; children—Shelby, Jack, Martha. With Armstrong Cork Co., 1941-51; with Time Motor Freight Co., Lubbock, Tex., 1953-60, dir. sales and traffic, 1955-60; with Citizens Nat. Bank, Lubbock, 1963—, sr. v.p., trust officer, 1965—, dir., 1966—. Chmn., Lubbock Symphony, 1960, Lubbock Tb Assn., 1958, Lubbock Urban Renewal Commn., 1969, Citizens Traffic Commn., 1968. Trustee Methodist Hosp., Lubbock, chmn., 1970-71. Served to maj. USAAF, 1942-46. Decorated Bronze Star (U.S.); Croix de Guerre (France). Mem. Phi Gamma Delta. Episcopalian. Home: 3213 43d St Lubbock TX 79413 Office: Box 841 Lubbock TX 79408

MILLER, GEORGE EDWARD, judge; b. Akron, O., Aug. 23, 1920; s. George Dewey and Etta May (Hagerman) M.; B.S., U. Houston, 1949, J.D., 1951; m. Edith M. Booker, Apr. 4, 1944; children—Jackie (Mrs. Dale Davenport), Pamela. Admitted to Tex. bar, 1951; practiced in Houston, 1951-54; asst. dist. atty. Harris County, Houston, 1954-58; partner firm Tynes, Turk & Miller, Houston, 1958-61; judge County Criminal Ct. at Law 1, Harris County, 1961-67, 113th civil dist. ct., 1967—. Served to 1st lt. USAAF, 1942-46; ETO. Recipient St. John Garwood award U. Houston Law Sch., 1949, Mem. State Bar Tex., Houston, Am. bar assns. Democrat. Methodist. Mason (Shriner). Home: 4944 Woodway St Houston TX 77027 Office: Civil Courts Bldg Houston TX 77002

MILLER, GEORGE HAROLD, supt. schs.; b. Beteravia, Cal., Feb. 23, 1917; s. James Allen and Effie (Shell) M.; B.S., East Tenn. State U., 1940; M.A., Appalachian State U., 1951; m. Elizabeth Alberta Helton, Oct. 12, 1940; children—Gwen, Penny. Tchr. Gastonia (N.C.) city schs., 1940-42, 1947-48, elementary prin., 1948-61, asst. supt., 1961-68; asst. supt. Gastonia county schs., 1968—. Served to lt. (j.g.) USNR, 1943-46; PTO. Mem. N.C. Edn. Assn., Am. Assn. Sch. Adminstrs., N.E.A., Assn. Childhood Edn. (state pres. 1969—), Phi Delta Kappa. Methodist. Club: Civitan (sec. 1964-66) (Gastonia). Home: 806 St Michaels Lane Gastonia NC 28052 Office: Gastonia County Schs Gastonia NC 28052

MILLER, GEORGE TYLER, former coll. pres.; b. Washington, Va., July 25, 1902; s. John J. and Evelyn M. (Tyler) M.; grad. Randolph-Macon Acad., 1919; B.S., Va. Mil. Inst., 1923; postgrad. U. Va., 1931-48; LL.D., Bridgewater (Va.) Coll. 1955; m. Kathryn G. Waver, May 7, 1929 (dec. 1935); children—G. Tyler, William W.; m. 2d, Elise Reaguer, July 25, 1947 (dec. 1956); 1 dau., Elise; m. 3d, Elizabeth Mauzy, Aug. 18, 1968. Tchr., asst. prin. Washington (Va.) High Sch., 1923-24, prin., 1924-25; real estate bus. Okeechobee and Miami, Fla., 1925-26; gen. ins. and farming, Washington, Va., 1926-28; div. supt. schs., Warren and Rappahannock Counties, Front Royal, Va., 1928-45; supt. city schs. Charlottesville, Va., 1945-46; supt. pub. instrn. State of Va., 1946-49; pres. Madison Coll., Harrisonburg, Va., 1949-71, ret. Dir., 1st Nat. Bank of Harrisonburg. Pres., bd. dirs. Front Royal Recreation Center, 1939-45. Dir. coordinator Civilian Def., Front Royal and Warren County, 1941-45; bd. dirs. Va. Library Bd., 1946-49, Va. Planning Bd.; mem. adv. council Va. Economy (ex-officio); sec., treas. mem. exec. com. Nat. Commn. Accrediting, 1963-67; mem. adv. council instructional TV, So. Regional Edn. Bd. Ex-officio mem. bd. visitors, U. Va., Med. Coll. Va., Coll. William and Mary, Va. Poly. Inst., Va. Mil. Inst., Va. Sch. for Deaf and Blind, 1946-49; vice chmn. bd. trustees Rockingham Meml. Hosp.; (chmn. disaster com. Warren County chpt. A.R.C., 1942-45; mem. Regional Council for So. Edn., 1948-49; mem. bd. control So. Regional Edn., 1948-55. Mem. Am. Assn. State Colls. and Univs. (dir. 1960-62, pres. 1968), Assn. Va. Colls. (pres. 1955-56), Am. Assn. Sch. Adminstrn., Chief State Sch. Officers (nat. council, 1946-49). Va. Acad. Sci., Va. Edn. Assn. (dist. pres., 1944, pres., 1945-46), Nat. Commn. on Accrediting (sec.-treas., exec. com.), Phi Delta Kappa. Episcopalian (vestrymen). Rotarian. Contbr. articles to Va. ednl. publs. Home: 126-B Pleasant Hill Rd Harrisonburg VA 22801

MILLER, GERALD SHELDON, motel exec.; b. Miami, Fla., Sept. 14, 1934; s. Jack and Theresa (Reisman) M.; B.B.A., U. Miami, 1956; m. Barbara Marilyn Robins, Feb. 14, 1960; children—Jack David, Toni Lynn. Mem. adminstrv. staff Nat. Brands, Inc., Miami, 1956-63; purchasing agt. Carillon Hotel, 1963-66; exec. dir. Sans Souci Hotel, 1966-71 (both Miami Beach, Fla.); exec. dir. Howard Johnson's Motor Lodge, Hollywood Beach, Fla., 1971—. Mem. City of Hollywood Advt. Adv. Bd., 1971—. Bd. fellows Mt. Sinai Hosp., Miami Beach. Served with USNR, 1952-56. Mem. South Fla. Hotel and Motel Assn., Hollywood C. of C. (dir. 1970—). Jewish religion. Mason (Shriner). Home: 1211 94th St Bay Harbor Islands FL 33154 Office: Howard Johnson Motor Lodge 2501 N Ocean Dr Hollywood Beach FL 33020

MILLER, GILES EDWIN, lawyer; b. Dallas, Aug. 2, 1920; s. Clarence R. and Esther (Connell) M.; A.A., Terrill Jr. Coll., 1940; B.A., So. Meth. U., 1941; m. Betty Jane Stewart, Oct. 25, 1941 (div.); children—Giles Edwin, Stewart Ransom, Donovan Connell; m. 2d, Narene McGough, Dec. 13, 1960; children—Sonya, Scott, Leonard, Jonathan Edwards Bryan. Admitted to Tex. bar, 1944; exec. v.p. Conro Mfg. Co. and Miller Bros. Fabrics, 1945-50; pres. Tex. Textile Mills, 1950-55; with Miller Cotton and Investment, 1955-58; pub., editor Park Cities News, 1958-62; chmn. bd. Legal Security Life Ins., Co., Dallas, 1959-65; pres., treas. Radio KPCN, Inc., Dallas, 1962-68, Radio KBUY, Inc., Amarillo, 1960-66; now engaged in writing and research; civil asst. dist. atty. Chmn. bd. Goins Found. Mem. Am., Dallas bar assns., State Bar Tex., Soc. Advancement Mgmt., Dallas Mgmt. Assn., Terrill EX-students Assn. (1st v.p.), Navy League. Club: Rock Creek (mem. bd.). Home: 3312 Dartmouth St Highland Park TX 75205 Office: Records Bldg Dallas TX 75202

MILLER, GLENN CURREY, ins. co. exec.; b. Chattanooga, Oct. 13, 1946; s. Willard and Fonza (Swafford) M.; student U. Tenn., 1964-66. With Vol. State Life Ins. Co., Chattanooga, 1967—, advt. asst., 1967-68, mgr. advt. and promotion, 1968-70, dir. advt. and promotion, 1970—. Mem. pub. relations com. United Fund, 1969-70; spl. gifts com. Am. Cancer Soc., 1971; actor Chattanooga Little Theatre, 1967—. Mem. campaign staff U.S. Sen. Albert Gore, 1970. Mem. Chattanooga Advt. Fedn. (pres. 1972-73), Chattanooga Assn. Bus. Communicators (pres. 1969-70), Life Advertisers Assn. Democrat. Episcopalian. Jaycees. Home: 3314 Pinewood Terrace Chattanooga TN 37411 Office: PO Box 1369 Chattanooga TN 37411

MILLER, HARRY A., JR., physician, surgeon; b. Morrisville, Mo., Dec. 29, 1914; s. Harry Arthur and Nella M. (Oliver) M.; B.S., U. Mich., 1938, M.B., 1939, M.D., 1940; m. Gladys Jeannette Bauer, July 6, 1945; children—Ann, Marvin, Thomas. Resident surgeon Wayne County Gen. Hosp., Eloise, Mich., 1940-42; sr. resident, chief resident surgeon, 1946-48; chief surg. staff Mercy Hosp., 1955. Served as lt. comdr. USN, 1942-45; lt. comdr. Res. Decorated Silver Star, Bronze Star. Diplomate Am. Bd. Surgery. Fellow A.C.S., Southwest Surg. Congress. Mason. Home: 1344 Honeydale Rd Brownville TX 78520 Office: 301 E Washington St Brownville TX 78520

MILLER, HARRY EUGENE, basketball coach; b. Morgantown, Ind., Jan. 26, 1927; s. Vernon E. and Jessie E. (Richardson) M.; B.A., Eastern N.M. U., 1951; M.A., Western Colo. State Coll., 1955; m. LaNora E. Graham, Aug. 12, 1951; children—Robert E., Thomas Allen, Gary E. Basketball coach House (N.M.) High Sch., 1951-52; basketball coach, asso. prof., phys. edn. Colo. Western Coll., Gunnison, 1952-58, Fresno State Coll., 1960-65, Eastern N.M. U., Portales, 1965-70; basketball coach North Tex. State U., Denton, 1970—; asst. basketball coach N.M. U., Albuquerque, 1958-60. Dir., Fresno Coaching Sch., 1965. Served with USAAF, 1945-47. Named Coach of Year dist. 7 Nat. Assn. Intercollegiate Athletics, 1967, area 2, 1968. Mem. Nat. Assn. Basketball Coaches. Republican. Rotarian, Elk. Contbr. articles to profl. jours. Home: 2228 Yorkshire Dr Denton TX 76201

MILLER, HELEN HILL, journalist; b. Highland Park, Ill., July 7, 1899; d. Russell Day and Lucia Elliott (Green) Hill; student Ferry Hall, Lake Forest, Ill.; A.B., Bryn Mawr Coll., 1921; Diploma in Econs. and Polit. Sci., Oxford (Eng.) U., 1922; Ph.D., U. Chgo., 1928; certificat Inst. U. Geneva, 1928; m. Francis Pickens Miller, Aug. 25, 1927; children—Andrew Pickens, Robert Day. Tutor Bryn Mawr Summer Sch. for Women Workers in Industry, 1921, 23, 26; research worker on grant from Am. Assn. Adult Edn., 1926-27; European study and travel, 1927-30; free-lance writer, 1930-34; writer on staff U.S. Dept. Agr., 1934-40; with Social Security Bd., 1935; vis. lectr. St. John's Coll., 1939-40; administrative sec. Nat. Policy Com., 1938-41, exec. dir., 1941-47; corr. London Economist, 1940, Am. editorial rep., 1943-50; corr. Washington bur. Newsweek, 1950-52; free lance, 1953—; contbg. editor New Republic, 1958-66; sr. tutor, Am. U., 1965; exec. sec. Edgar Stern Family Fund, 1956-63; contbr. nat. mags. Bd. dirs. Bryn Mawr Coll., 1948-52; bd. visitors Fla. Presbyn. Coll.; cons. U.S. Dept. Labor, 1962-63. Mem. Am. Polit. Sci. Assn. Democrat. Clubs: Cosmopolitan (N.Y.C.); Washington Press (pres. 1955-56), City Tavern Assn. (Washington). Author or co-author several books, 1928—, latest, Greece, 1965; The Case for Liberty, 1965; Sicily and the Western Colonies of Greece, 1965; Bridge to Asia; the Greeks on the Eastern Mediterranean, 1967; The Realms of

Arthur, 1969; Greece Through The Ages, 1972. Address: 2810 P St NW Washington DC 20007 also Tamasee Kitty Hawk NC 27949

MILLER, HENRY BATES, chem. co. exec.; b. Muldrow, Okla., June 5, 1910; s. Ernest Ary and Leila Adine (Bates) M.; student Middle Tenn. State U., 1939-42; certificate in electronics and chem. engring. Vanderbilt U., 1945; m. Bessie Pearl Oliver, Aug. 13, 1938; children—Oliver Bates, Frances C. (Mrs. Ralph Bartholomew), Ernest A., Anne J. (Mrs. David Robinson), Rebecca L. (Mrs. Russel Prince). Devel. chemist Genesco, Nashville, 1941—; with Life & Casualty Ins. Co., 1943-45; Genesco, 1941—; owner H.B. Miller Electronic Organ Service, Nashville, 1950—. Mem. Tenn. N.G., 1933-41. Recipient Silver Star, Gen. award Genesco, 1965. Mem. Am. Guild Organists, Am. Assn. Textile Chemists and Colorists, Nat. Investigations Com. on Aerial Phenomena. Kiwanian. Home: 550 Croley Dr Nashville TN 37209 Office: 6100 Centennial St Nashville TN 37209

MILLER, HERBERT LYNN, coll. adminstr.; b. Newark, Oct. 7, 1923; s. Herbert Arthur and Harriette Dorothy (Niebuhr) M.; B.S., Ga. Inst. Tech., 1948, M.S., 1955; postgrad. (fellow) U. Fla., 1959-60; m. Barbara Joyce McKerrow, Sept. 16, 1956; 1 son, Michael Andrew. Financial analyst Citizens and So. Nat. Bank, Atlanta, 1948-54; instr. corp. finance Ga. Inst. Tech., Atlanta, 1956-62; mem. faculty, Central Fla. Community Coll., Ocala, 1962—, dir. div. bus. and social scis., 1968—. Dir. Marion County Tchrs. Credit Union, 1964—, sec., 1967—. Served with AUS, 1943-46. Mem. Ocala-Marion County C. of C. (chmn. pub. affairs com., 1964-65), Am., So. econs. assns. Democrat. Episcopalian. Rotarian. Contbr. book reviews to Choice mag. Home: 1119 NE 16th Av Ocala FL 32670 Office: PO Box 1388 Ocala FL 32670

MILLER, HILLMAN BOYCE, farmer; b. Eunice, La., Aug. 2, 1910; s. Arteleus and Barbara (Brandt) M.; grad. high sch.; m. Agnes Hornsby, Dec. 19, 1934; children—Darby Donald, Alura Kay (Mrs. Robert Steven Mitchell). Farmer, cattleman, Church Point, La., 1934—; dir. Farmer's State Bank, Church Point. Recipient Banker's Assn. Soil Conservation award, 1970. Mem. Arcadia Parish Cattlemen's Assn. Methodist (sec., treas. 1935—, trustees 1935—, chmn. bd. 1940—). Home: Route 1 Box 417 Church Point LA 70525

MILLER, HOWARD ALBERT, cons. forester, biologist; b. Indianola, Ia., Dec. 22, 1906; s. Edward Luther and Viola (Lower) M.; A.B., Simpson Coll., 1928; M.F., Yale, 1930; m. Erma Edwards, Dec. 31, 1928; children—Patricia (Mrs. Anthony R. Walker), George E. (dec.), Howard Albert. Jr. forester Bur. Biol. Survey, 1930-42, chief wildlife refuges, 1946-57; chief br. wildlife mgmt. U.S. Forest Service, 1957-66; cons. forester and biologist, Marietta, Ga., 1966—. Chmn. forest resources N. Am. Wildlife and Natural Resources Conf., 1964; mem. Gov.'s com. Goals for Ga., 1971. Served to capt. C.E., AUS, 1942-46. Decorated Bronze Star. Recipient award for superior service U.S. Dept. Agr., 1964. Mem. Soc. Am. Foresters (div. chmn. 1955-65), Wildlife Soc. (com. chmn. 1963-65), Ga. Acad. Sci., Am. Inst. Biol. Sci. Author: How to Know The Trees, 1972; Let's Get Acquainted With Mushrooms, 1968; The Fascinating World of Carnivorous Plants, 1970; The Third Forest And Our Environment, 1971. sr. author Fleshy Fungi Eaten by Southern Wildlife, 1969. Address: 511 Sybil Lane SE Marietta GA 30062

MILLER, HUBERT STAUFFER, JR., architect; b. Panama, C.Z., June 7, 1936; s. Hubert S. and Amy (Hilborn) M.; B.Arch., Cath. U. Am., 1959. Designer, draftsman Box & Pratt, 1959-60, Charles Jennings, Architect, 1962-63; designer, draftsman constrn. supt. Jon Carsey, Architect, 1960-62; v.p. planning and architecture Vantage Co., 1963-66; self-employed architect, Dallas, 1966—; owner Noble Property Co., Dallas, Hub Miller Assos., Dallas, Tex. Canadian Constrn. Co., Dallas. Mem. A.I.A. Works include Woodway Sq. project, Houston, 1966, Willow Creek project, Dallas, 1968, Exec. Plaza project, Dallas, 1969. Address: 3612 Noble Av Dallas TX 75204

MILLER, ISRAEL BERNARD, scrap metal co. exec.; b. Huntsville, Ala., June 11, 1926; s. Louis and Elsie (Ratner) M.; B.S. in Indsl. Mgmt., Ga. Inst. Tech., 1948; m. Dolores Evelyn Katz, Feb. 6, 1947; children—Joy (Mrs. Kenneth Jay Greenberg), Solomon Ira, Sara Gayle. Partner, L. Miller & Son, Inc., Huntsville, 1948-58, treas., mgr., 1958-66, pres., 1966—; bus mgr. Technique, Ga. Inst. Tech., 1947. Mem. Huntsville United Jewish Appeal Com., 1948-59, Huntsville United Jewish Fund, 1959—. Nat. Joint Distbn. Com., 1964—. Bd. dirs. region Anti-Defamation League, B'nai B'rith, 1967—. Served with USNR, 1944-46. Mem. Indsl. Mgmt. Soc., Inst. Scrap Iron and Steel, Am. Welding Soc., Nat. Welding Supply Assn., Alpha Epsilon Pi, Pi Delta Epsilon. Jewish religion (past pres. and trustee temple). Mason (Shriner); mem. B'nai B'rith (pres. 1956, 67). Rotarian. Home: 1101 Fraser Av SE Huntsville AL 35801 Office: PO Box 1207 Huntsville AL 35807

MILLER, J. ROBERT, state ofcl.; b. Monroe County, Ky., June 5, 1920; s. Harlan Ross and Ina (Chapman) M.; B.S. in Agr., Western Ky. U., 1948, M.Sc., 1955; m. Naomi Bowman, June 30, 1942; children—John Robert II, Rhoda Beth, Joseph Jesse. Tchr. elementary schs. Monroe County, 1939-42; tchr. vocational agr. Tomkinsville (Ky.) pub. schs., 1948-67; Ky. commr. agr., 1968—. Mem. bd. trustees U. Ky., 1968—. Served with USAAF, 1942-46. Mem. Nat. Farm Orgn., Farm Bur., Artificial Breeding Assn. Home: Route 3 Tomkinsville KY 42167 Office: Capital Annex Bldg Frankfurt KY 40601

MILLER, JACK EVERETT, lawyer; b. Monroe, La., Dec. 10, 1921; s. Herman M. and Syble (Harrison) M.; student Ga. Tech., 1942-43; grad. Gilbert Johnson Law Sch., 1948; m. Vivian Geraldine Bagby, May 13, 1945 (div.); children—Jack E., John A.; m. 2d, Kathryn Woodard Garriss, Dec. 23, 1970. Admitted to Ga. bar, 1948; formerly mem. firm Duffy, Miller, Duffy; now individual practice, Savannah. Served with USAAF, 1943-45, with USAF, 1951-53, lt. col. Res. Judge Adv. Gen. Dept. Mem. Am. Trial Lawyers Assn., Am., Ga., Savannah bar assns., Am. Legion. Elk. Club: American Business (chpt. pres. 1959, dist. gov. 1964-65). Home: 13511 Rockingham Rd Savannah GA 31401 Office: 122 E Oglethorpe Av Savannah GA 31401

MILLER, JAMES GREGORY, pharm. co. exec.; b. B.W.I., Oct. 29, 1927 (came to U.S. 1949, naturalized 1956); s. John Gregory and Sylvia (Brennan) M.; student McGill U., 1944-45; D.V.M., V.S., U. Toronto, 1949, D.V.Sc., 1956; M.S., Cornell U., 1950; postgrad. U. Mich., 1953-56; m. Ruth Jordan, June 16, 1950; children—Ralph Gregory, Virginia Ann, Lynn. Asst. prof. La State U., 1950-53; group leader Arthur D. Little, Inc., 1956-60; prof., head dept. animal diseases, U. Ga. at Tifton; 1960-66; pres. Miller Assn., Tifton, 1966—. Chmn., Com. on Vet. Lab. Accreditation, 1969—. Mem. Am., South Ga. (sec. 1960—), Ga. (dir.), La. vet. med. assns., Nat. Conf. Vet. Lab. Diagnosticians (chmn. 1964—), U.S. Animal Health Assn. Rotarian, Elk. Home: 3100 NE 43d St Fort Lauderdale FL 33308 Office: Box 353 Tifton GA 31794

MILLER, JAMES ROBERT, life ins. exec.; b. Live Oak, Fla., Feb. 10, 1904; s. Marion Paschal and Hattie (Williams) M.; student pub. schs.; m. Laurel Armstrong, May 5, 1930; children—James Robert, Martha June, Donald Kay. Agt., Met. Life Ins. Co., Jacksonville, Fla., 1933-37, asst. mgr., Macon, Ga., 1937-45; free-lance salesman chems., 1945-46, 47-49; partner Modern Heating Co., Macon, 1946-47; gen. agt. Guarantee Mut. Life Ins. Co., Omaha, 1949-55; organizer chmn. Md. Fried Chicken Am., Inc., Cherokee Nat. Life Ins. Co.; organizer, pres. First Macon Corp. Mem. Macon Assn. Life Underwriters (past pres.), Macon Gen. Agts and Mgrs. Assn. (past pres.), U.S., Ga., Macon chambers commerce. Baptist (deacon). Mason (Shriner), Kiwanian. Home: 2959 Crestline Dr Macon GA 31204 Office: 1122 Gray Hwy Macon GA 31201

MILLER, JARRELL ETSON, radiologist, educator; b. San Antonio, Nov. 14, 1913; s. Etson Lee and Mabel (Braddock) M.; B.A., St. Mary's U., 1934; M.D., Baylor U., 1938; m. Virginia Edith Gallagher, June 24, 1939; children—Gwen Janet, Dwight Leigh, Beverly Diane, Pamela Anne. Intern Robert B. Green Meml. Hosp., San Antonio, 1938-39; resident radiology Cleve. City Hosp., 1939-42; radiologist Parkland Hosp., Dallas, 1946-49; Children's Med. Center, Dallas, 1947-65, Baylor U. Med. Center, 1949-66, St. Paul Hosp., 1967—; cons. VA Hosp., Lisbon, Tex., 1946-57; VA Hosp., McKinney, Tex., 1946-57; mem. faculty Southwestern Med. Sch., U. Tex., Dallas, 1947—, clin. prof., radiology, 1956—; lectr. med. br. U. Tex., Galveston. Vice pres. med. activities Dallas Citizens Traffic Commn., 1960-67. Bd. dirs. Dallas County unit Am. Cancer Soc., 1950—, pres., 1956-57, exec. com., Tex. div., 1957—, pres., 1963; bd. dirs. Dallas Tb Assn., 1953-68, pres., 1960-61; bd. dirs. Tex. Tb Assn., 1961-63, Dallas Heart Assn., 1954-60; bd. govs. St. Mary's U., 1958-63. Served with M.C., AUS, 1942-46; ETO. Recipient Alumnus of Year award St. Mary's U., 1961. Diplomate Am. Bd. Radiology (guest examiner 1965, 69-71). Mem. Am. (alternate del. 1962—), Tex. (chmn. council sci. advancement 1959-68, exec. bd. 1959—) med. assns., Dallas County (pres. 1965, chmn. bd. dirs. 1966), Collin County (pres. 1948) med. socs., Am. Coll. Radiology (chmn. bd. chancellors, 1966, pres. 1967), Dallas-Ft. Worth, Tex. (pres. 1953, sec. 1956-58), Rocky Mountain radiol. socs., Radiol. Soc. N.Am., Am. Roentgen Ray Soc., Dallas So. Clin. Soc. (Marchman award 1962), Flying Physicians Assn., Dallas C. of C. (v.p. pub. health com. 1964, mem. legislative com. 1965—), Aircraft Owners and Pilots Assn. Theta Kappa Psi, Alpha Pi Alpha. Contbr. articles to med. jours. Home: 6115 D Averill Way Dallas TX 75225

MILLER, JARVIS ERNEST, research adminstr.; b. Orange Grove, Tex., May 30, 1929; s. Richard C. and Ethel (DuBose) M.; B.S., Tex. A. and M.U., 1950; M.S., Purdue U., 1951, Ph.D., 1954; m. Alma Howell, June 20, 1952; children—Susan, Kathleen, Margaret, Carolyn. Asst. prof., asso. prof. agrl. econs. Tex. A. and M. U., College Station, 1955-61; chief of AID party Santo Domingo, Dom. Rep., 1965-67, asst. dir. Agr. Expt. Sta., 1967-71, asso. dir., 1971—; agr. economist, acting rural devel. officer AID, Buenos Aires, Argentina, 1961-65. Served to lt. USAF, 1953-54. Mem. A.A.A.S., Am. Acad. Arts and Scis., Am. Agr. Econs. Assn., Internat. Assn. Agrl. Economists. Home: 3502 Stillmeadow Dr Bryan TX 77801 Office: Tex Agrl Expt Sta College Station TX 77843

MILLER, JOE ANDREW, textile co. exec.; b. Westminster, S.C., July 2, 1936; s. John and Lois (Crenshaw) M.; student Clemson U., 1954-58; student Grad. Sch. Bus. U. Va., 1969; m. Norma Jean Turner, Dec. 24, 1955; children—Andrea Norma, Robyn Agatha. With Cone Mills Corp., various locations, 1958—, asst. gen. mgr., Cliffside, N.C., 1963-66, gen. mgrs., 1966—. Pres., dir. Cliffside R.R. Co., 1966—; dir. 1st Citizens Bank & Trust Co., Cliffside. Mem. Isothermal Devel. Commn., 1969—. Trustee Royster Meml. Hosp., Boiling Springs, N.C., 1970—. Mem. So. Textile Assn. Methodist. Rotarian. Club: Piedmont (Spartanburg, S.C.). Home: 5 Washington St Cliffside NC 28024 Office: 1 Main St Cliffside NC 28024

MILLER, J(OHN) BROUGH, educator, artist; b. Ithaca, Mich., April 4, 1933; s. Henry Arthur and Mildred (Walter) M.; B.S., Central Mich. U., 1960, postgrad., 1962-64; M.F.A., Cranbrook Acad. Art, 1964; m. Janet Marlene Pabst, June 10, 1959; children—Heidi Lynn, Maija Grotell, Maclan Brough. Tchr., Brandon Schs., Ortonville, Mich., 1959-63; mem. faculty Tex. Woman's U., Denton, 1964—, asso. prof. grad. studio ceramics and welded metal sculpture, 1967—. Mem. faculty, Dallas Mus. Fine Arts Mus. Sch., 1968-69; exhibited group shows Internat. Fold Mus., Santa Fe, 1965, S.W. Craftsman, Dallas, 1968-70, also Dallas Mus. Fine Arts, Contemporary Gallery, Dallas. Served with USN, 1950-54. Research grantee Tex. Coordinating Bd., 1966-69. Mem. Tex.-Designer-Craftsman, Am. Assn. U. Profs. Unitarian-Universalist. Home: Route 1 Fairway Acres Country Club Rd Argyle TX 76226

MILLER, JOHN FRANK, JR., lawyer; b. Hickory, N.C., Oct. 31, 1897; s. John Frank and Cordella (Clay) M.; J.D., Nat. U., 1931; m. Bertha L. Yordy, Jan. 15, 1921; 1 son, John Frank III. Tech. adviser, dep. commr. income tax unit Internal Revenue Service, Treasury Dept., Washington, 1920-51, tech. adviser, dir. tax rulings div. Office Asst. Commr. Tech., 1951-57; admitted to D.C. bar, 1931; practice law specializing in taxes, Washington, 1957—. Served with U.S. Army, World War I, AEF. Decorated Purple Heart. Mem. Am. Bar Assn., Am. Legion. Mason, Elk. Address: 3056 Chestnut St NW Washington DC 20015

MILLER, JOHN HENRY, JR., civil engr.; b. Manila, P.I., Nov. 21, 1939 (parents Am. citizens); s. John Henry and Louise (Rutherford) M.; B.S., Tex. A. and M. Coll., 1963; m. Shelby Fairfax Stone, June 29, 1968; 1 son, John Alan, Jan. 20, 1972. Engring. draftsman Temco Electronics & Missiles Co., Greenville, Tex., 1961-62; engring. asst. Tex. Hwy. Dept., Dallas, 1963-67, asso. design engr., 1967-68, asso. resident engr., Denton, Tex., 1968-69, resident engr., 1969—. Served with AUS, 1962. Registered profl. engr., Tex. Mem. Am. Soc. C.E., Tex. Soc. Profl. Engrs., Tex. Pub. Employees Assn. Presbyn. Home: PO Box 13437 1218 Stanley St Denton TX 76203 Office: PO Box 694 Denton TX 76201

MILLER, JOHN RICHARD JOSEPH, textile products co. exec.; b. Hickory, N.C., Nov. 16, 1933; s. Henry Grady and Anna Barbara (Haase) M.; B.S., N.C. State Coll., 1956; m. Exia Lorraine Boliek, May 20, 1961; 1 dau., Regena Lorraine. Supt. processing, mng. dir. Hickory Dyeing & Winding Co., Hickory, N.C., 1958-59, v.p. charge prodn., 1959—, also dir. Served to 1st lt. AUS, 1956-58. Mem. Hickory Jr. C. of C. (sec. 1963), Tau Kappa Epsilon. Lutheran (tchr. Sunday sch. 1964-71). Designer, supr. constrn. complete plant expansion facility doubling work area and new office location, 1966-67. Home: Route 2 Box 643 G Hickory NC 28601 Office: PO Box 1975 Hickroy NC 28601

MILLER, JOHN ULMAN, clergyman; b. N.Y.C., Dec. 9, 1914; s. Clarence John and Edythe Gladys (Shaffer) M.; B.A. cum laude, Taylor U., 1937; M.A., Butler U., 1942; D.D., Geneva Theol. Coll., 1968; m. Marcella E. Hubner, June 12, 1937; children—John U., Mark C., Mary Kay (Mrs. Charles Bolin), Gretchen (Mrs. Ernest Micka). Ordained to ministry Bapt. Ch., 1937; pastor 1st Bapt. Ch., Bluffton, Ind., 1946-49, Boston, 1949-56, Tabernacle Ch., Utica, N.Y., 1956-63, United Ch. of Christ, Hagerstown, Ind., 1963-66, St. John's Evang. Ch., Louisville, 1967—. Participant, Churchmen Weigh News, WNAC, Boston, 1953-56; Meml. Chapel preacher, instr. religion N.Y. State Masonic Home, Utica, 1957-62; broadcast weekly services WKBV, Richmond, Ind., 1965-66; preacher Fellowship Chapel WHAS, Louisville, 1967—; maintains 24 hour Dial-A-Prayer, Louisville, 1968—. Chmn. campaigns Crippled Children, Tb, U.S.O., 1946-49. Served to capt. USAAF, 1942-45; PTO. Named Community Leader Am., News Pub. Co., 1969; Ky. col. Mem. Ind.-Ky. Conf. United Ch. of Christ, Bach Soc. Louisville. Home: 3404 Kirby Lane Louisville KY 40299 Office: 637 E Market St Louisville KY 40202

MILLER, JOHN WILLIAM, govt. ofcl.; b. Toomsboro, Ga., Mar. 1, 1921; s. John Ennis and Ivaline (Stubbs) M.; A.B., Mercer U., 1942; M.Ed., U. Ga., 1969; m. Edythe Loraine Billue, Jan. 19, 1955; children—Lynn, John Wade. With U.S. Dept. Agr., Fort Valley, Ga., 1947; tchr. Wilkinson County (Ga.) Bd. Edn., Irwinton, 1948-49, supt. schs., 1949-69; project dir. Neighborhood Youth Corps. U.S. Dept Labor, Milledgeville, Ga., 1969—. Pres. Pine Grove Poultry Farm, Inc., Toomsboro, 1966-69, Chmn. Wilkinson County Easter Seal, 1957-65. Bd dirs. Oconee Area Community Action Agy., Milledgeville. Served to capt. AUS, 1942-46. Mem. N.E.A., Ga. Edn. Assn., Ga. Supts. Assn., Nat. Assn. Sch. Adminstrs., Am. Legion, Farm Bur., Woodmen of World. Baptist (trustee). Home: Toomsboro St Irwinton GA 31042 Office: 131 N Jefferson St Milledgeville GA 31061

MILLER, JOSEPH LEWIS, JR., govt. ofcl.; b. Boothbay Harbor, Me., Aug. 21, 1913; s. Joseph Lewis and Addie T. (Perkins) M.; B.S., U. N.H., 1936; student Am. U., 1954-55, Advanced Mgmt. Program, Harvard, 1961; m. Allice Ruth Boyer, June 17, 1939; 1 son, Donald Earl. Exec. trainee Jordan Marsh Co., Boston, 1936-37; food broker J. R. Poole Co., 1937-40; commd. ensign, USN, 1940, advanced through grades to comdr., 1954; invasion Casablanca, 1942, Philippines. 1944; attached cruiser 3d Fleet invasion and surrender Japan. 1944-45; served in Pacific, 1951; exec. officer Large Supply Depot, 1948-51; capt. res.; chief VA br. Bur. of Budget, Washington, 1954-56; dir. mgmt. engring, office FCDA, Battle Creek, Mich., 1956-58; spl. asst. to asst. dir. resources and prodn. OCDM, Washington, 1958-61; asst. chief resources moblzn. br. Office Emergency Planning, Exec. Office of Pres., Washington, 1961-63, officer-in-charge Ghana-Sierra Leone Desk, AID, Dept. State, Washington, 1963-64, asst. dir. mgmt. support Bur. Africa, 1964-67, dir. Office Adminstrv. Services, 1967—. Vice pres. Barcroft Terrace Citizens Assn.; active Boy Scouts Am., Little League Baseball. Recipient Am. Legion Citizenship award, Bklyn., 1928; Eagle Palm, Boy Scouts Am., 1929. Mem. Am. Fgn. Service Assn., Res. Officers Assn. (pres. Battle Creek, Mich.), Am. Soc. Pub. Adminstrn., Potomac River Power Squadron, Harvard U. Alumni Assn., Harvard Advanced Mgmt. Assn., Ret. Officers Assn., Alpha Tau Omega. Clubs: Harvard (Boston and Washington); New Hampshire University Alumni (Washington); Rotary; Annapolis (Md.) Country. Home: 140 E Lake Dr Annapolis MD 21403 Office: US Dept State (AID) Washington DC 20520

MILLER, JOSEPH SIDNEY, wire co. exec.; b. Vancouver, B.C., Can., June 30, 1921; s. Sidney Wilfred and Phyllis Elizabeth (Laidlaw) M.; B.A.Sc. in Mech. Engring., U. B.C., Vancouver, Can., 1950; m. Dorothy Masters Hebb, June 17, 1942; children—Malcolm, Carlyle, Marion, Andrew, Ian. Mgr., Johnson Wire Products, Montreal, Que., Can., 1950-56; gen. mgr. West Coast Wire Works, Vancouver, 1957-58; pres., dir. Atlanta Wire Works, Jonesboro, Ga., 1959—; Johnson Foils, Inc., Springfield, Mass., 1970—, Drytex, Inc., Jonesboro. Served with RCAF, 1942. Mem. Clayton County C. of C. (v.p. 1968-70). Clubs: Capital City, Cherokee Town and Country (Atlanta). Home: 2888 Habersham Rd Atlanta GA 30305 Office: 1117 Battle Creek Rd Jonesboro GA 30236 Mailing Address 1117 Battle Creek Rd Jonesboro GA 30236

MILLER, JOSEPH THOMAS, food chemist; b. Barre Plains, Mass., Oct. 30, 1919; s. Alfred Fredrick and Margaret (Sullivan) M.; B.S., U. Mass., 1941; m. Claire E. Tyler, June 8, 1942; children—Joseph, Michael, Kathleen (Mrs. William Kastner III), Peter, James, Claire. Food chemist Blue Channell Corp., Port Royal, S.C., 1941-44, plant mgr., Belhaven, N.C., 1949-59, v.p. quality control and research and devel., Port Royal, S.C., 1959—. Served to ensign USNR, 1944-46. Mem. Inst. Food Technologists. Roman Catholic. Home: 1003 S Ribaut Rd Beaufort SC 29902 Office: Blue Channel Corp Port Royal SC 29935

MILLER, JUDITH MIRIAM STATMAN (MRS. PAUL P. MILLER), advt. exec.; b. Dallas, June 1, 1938; d. Joseph and Lillian (Tolmich) Statman; student U. Tex., 1955-56; m. Paul P. Miller, Dec. 20, 1970; 1 stepson, Steven Miller. With Bloom Advt., Dallas, 1957-71, head media dept., 1965-71; supr. broadcast Tracy-Locke, Dallas, 1971—. Mem. Assn. Broadcast Execs. Tex. (sec. 1963-64, 65-66, 67-67). Home: 5039 Cedar Springs 210 Dallas TX 75235 Office: 1407 Main St Dallas TX 75250

MILLER, KEITH RICE, dentist; b. Chandler, Okla., Nov. 17, 1920; s. Harry Winter and Helen Merian (Rice) M.; A.B., East Central State Coll., 1943, B.S., 1945; D.D.S., U. Mo., Kansas City, 1950; m. Anna Frances Adair, July 15, 1943; children—Cynthia Calvert, Gail Armstrong, Keith Adair, David Rice, Megan Joann Girault. Bookkeeper, Ada Milling Co. (Okla.), 1938-43; chemist, physicist Okla. Ordnance, 1943-45; grad sch. prin., Latta, Okla., 1945-46; instr. E. Central State Coll., 1945-46; night clk. Schyler Hotel, Kansas City, Mo., 1946-50; practice dentistry, Woodville, Miss., 1950—; chief dental staff Field Meml. Hosp., 1961-62, exec. sec. med. staff, sec. med. staff, 1967—. Water safety chmn. A.R.C.; chmn. Feleciano dist. Boy Scouts Am., 1954-56, vice chmn. Houma dist. 1965-70, vice chmn., dist. commr. Avondale dist., 1969-71, mem. exec. bd. Istrouma Area council; scoutmaster Philmont Scout Ranch for Tng. 1965—, dist. chmn., 1971—. Mem. Am., Miss. dental assns., Sigma Tau. Methodist (vice chmn. bd.). Odd Fellow, Lion. Address: PO Box 517 Woodville MS 39669

MILLER, KENNETH DAYTON, educator; b. N.Y.C., May 3, 1914; s. Dewey Harold and Ray (Wilber) M.; A.A., Marin Jr. Coll., 1935; B.S., U. Ore., 1937, M.S., 1938; Ph.D., U. Mich., 1948; m. Floy Conner Minor, Aug. 7, 1944; children—Kenneth, Dabney, Craig. Tchr., coach Liberty Union High Sch., Brentwood, Cal., 1938-41, State Tchrs. Coll., Lock Haven, Pa., 1946-48; asso. prof. Fla. State U., 1948-53, prof., 1953—, head dept. phys. edn., health and recreation, 1957-70. Served with USNR, 1942-46; PTO. Decorated Air medal. Mem. Am. (pres. So. dist. 1969-70), Fla. (pres. 1963-64) health, phys. edn. and recreation assns., Aircraft Owners and Pilots Assn., Phi Kappa Phi, Sigma Delta Psi, Phi Epsilon Kappa, Phi Delta Kappa, Chi Psi. Republican. Episcopalian. Author: (with others) Physical Education Activities for College Men and Women, 1963; Track and field for Girls, 1964, (with Billie J. Jones), rev. edit., 1972; (with Rita Horky) Modern Basketball for Women, 1970. Contbr. articles to profl. jours. Home: 1504 Argonne Dr Tallahassee FL 32303

MILLER, LOYE WHEAT, JR., journalist; b. Knoxville, Tenn., Mar. 20, 1930; s. Loye Wheat and Sara Vance (Davis) M.; A.B., Dartmouth, 1951; M.S. in Journalism. Columbia, 1952; m. Joan Wethey Stromenger, Dec. 18, 1954; children—Lissa Wethey, Loye Wheat. Mem. staff Charlotte (N.C.) Observer, 1955-59, asst. city editor, 1959; corr. Washington bur. Time mag., 1959-64, 1969-70, chief Midwest news bur. Time-Life mags., 1964-69; corr. Washington

Bur. Knight Newspapers, 1970—. Served to lt. (j.g.) USNR, 1952-55. Home: 5113 Dalecarlia Dr Washington DC 20016 Office: Knight Newspapers Inc Nat Press Bldg Washington DC 20004

MILLER, LUTHER TABOR, JR., bldg., constrn. co. exec.; b. Ft. Worth, Nov. 13, 1914; s. Luther Tabor and Hulda Estelle (Franklin) M.; B.S., (scholar), Tex. Christian U., 1935, M.A., 1937; m. Grace Nichols, Apr. 2, 1952; children—Cliff, Steve, Janis Ann. C.P.A., Fort Worth, 1939; faculty, acting dir. Tex. Christian U. Sch. Bus., 1939-40; partner Patterson, Leatherwood, Miller, Talkington & Ward, Ft. Worth, 1943-47; sec., treas., v.p., controller, dir. McVean & Barlow, Inc., Odessa, Tex., 1952—. Prof., McMurrey Coll., 1948; cons. Casualty Ins., 1960-70. Bd. dirs. Indsl. Found., Odessa, 1960-70, pres., 1968-69. C.P.A., Tex. Recipient Spl. award Odessa C. of C., 1957, Mem. C. of C. (chmn. com. 1960-65), Tex. Soc. C.P.A.'s, Am. Inst. C.P.A.'s, Am. Assn. Ins. Mgrs., Tex. Mfg. Assn. (past ofcl.), Am. Mgmt. Assn. Club: Optimist (Fort Worth). Home: 3103 Eastover Dr Odessa TX 79760 Office: Box 4517 Odessa TX 79760

MILLER, MALCOLM DRENNAN, lawyer; b. Waverly, Ill., May 26, 1909; s. Malcolm Foote and Ethel May (Pease) M.; B.A., Grinnell Coll., 1931; postgrad. U. Ill. Coll. Law, 1932-34; LL.B., Georgetown U., 1935; m. Martha Ann Riggs, Aug. 26, 1937; children—William, Malcolm, Margaret (Mrs. Philip Filiatrault), Winifred (Mrs. Robert Payne). Admitted to D.C. bar, 1935, Va. bar, 1945; atty. ICC, 1936-43; atty., chief counsel, common carrier sect. OPA, 1943-46; practice administrv. law, Washington, 1946-56; trial atty. P.O. Dept., Washington, 1947-50; atty., asst. gen. counsel Gen. Services Adminstrn., Washington, 1956-61, asst. commr., Transp. and Communications Service, 1961-62, dep. commr., 1962-66, dep. gen. counsel, 1966-67, mem. bd. contract appeals, 1967-69. Lectr., Am. U., Washington, 1947-58. Mem. Arlington (Va.) Citizens Com. for Sch. Improvement, 1946-52; chmn. Arlington Com. of 100, 1969-70. Recipient Star Cup award Arlington County Civic Fedn., 1950; Meritorious Service award Gen. Services Adminstrn., 1962. Mem. Fed. Bar Assn., Va. State Bar. Club: National Lawyers (Washington). Home: 1701 N Huntington St Arlington VA 22205

MILLER, MARGARET HARDWICK, educator; b. Tyler, Tex., Feb. 21, 1910; d. Charles Pennington and Agnes (Hughes) Hardwick; B.A., Tex. U., 1930; postgrad. U. Mexico, 1933; m. Dr. Will M. Miller, June 29, 1935; children—Margaret Rose (Mrs. Butler), Thomas A. Tchr. pub. schs., Corsicana, Tex., 1930-35, part-time tchr., 1935-39. Mem. Corsicana Bd. Edn., 1951-58, pres., 1956-58; mem. Tex. State Bd. Edn., 1959—; v.p. Nat. Assn. State Bds. Edn., 1961-64, hon. life mem.; mem. White House Conf. Children and Youth, 1960; mem. nat. bd. dirs, Camp Fire Girls, Inc., 1958-60; mem. state bd. trustees Home for Retired Tchrs., 1959—; del. Nat. Conf. Rural Youth, 1963; mem. Nat. Com. Support Pub. Schs., 1963—; Gov.'s Council Youth Fitness, 1963—; bd. trustees Corsicana Pub. Library, 1969—. Recipient Nat. Award Merit, D.A.R., 1956. Mem. Nat. Sch. Bds. Assn. (life; exec. com. 1958-59), Tex. Assn. Sch. Bds. (pres. 1957; Distinguished Service award 1971), Tex. Congress Parents and Tchrs. (bd. mgrs. 1956-58), Tex. Library Assn., D.A.R. (hon. regent, state treas. 1950-53), Daus. Am. Colonists (state rec. sec. 1955-57), Sons and Daus. Pilgrims (state corr. sec. 1959-61), Magna Charta Dames, Colonial Dames Am., Ams. Royal Descent Order of Crown, Huguenot Soc., Internat. Soc. Genealogy and Heraldry, Delta Kappa Gamma, Beta Sigma Phi, Kappa Delta. Presbyn. Home: 1405 Oak Lawn Dr Corsicana TX 75110 Office: Box 715 Corsicana TX 75110

MILLER, MARVIN ALWIN, librarian; b. Wilkesboro, N.C., Oct. 25, 1903; s. George W. and Jane (Anderson) M.; A.B., U. N.C., 1926; B.S., Columbia, 1929; m. Alice Lee Long, June 1, 1927 (dec. Oct. 1961); children—Marilyn Louise, Brian Stephen; m. 2d, Violet Lanneau Borden, Sept. 10, 1966. Asst., U. N.C. Library, 1923-26; tchr. Leaksville (N.C.) High Sch., 1926-27; part time supr. stacks N.Y.C. Pub. Library, 1928-29, reference asst. information desk, 1929-32; librarian, U. N.H., 1932-40; librarian U. Ark., 1940-47, dir. libraries, 1947-71. Dir. Victory Book Campaign for Ark., 1943; mem. sub-com. Bd. on Resources of Am. Libraries. Mem. Am. (councilor 1945-49, chmn., chmn. membership com. for Ark. 1952, 53), Ark. (pres. 1946-47; chmn. constn. com., 1957-58), Southwestern (treas. 1949-50, v.p. 1951-52, pres. 1953-54; chmn. scholarship com., 1958-64), library assns. Assn. Coll. and Reference Libraries (state rep. 1958-60, exec. com. engring. sch. library sect. 1942-45, chmn. Oberly meml. award com. 1948). Contbr. articles to profl. jours. Home: Route 5 Rogers AR 72756

MILLER, MARY FRANCES (MRS. SHANNON O. MILLER), office mgr.; b. Richards, Tex., June 11, 1919; d. Albert Nolan and Lynn (Wood) Cecil; high sch. grad.; m. Shannon, O. Miller, Jr., Apr. 7, 1944 (dec. 1960); children—Shannon O. III, Martha. Office mgr. Navarra Motors, Key West, Fla., 1945-49. Peebles Motor Co., South Norfolk, Va., 1949-52, Can. Dry Bottling Co., New London, Conn., 1952-55, Crippo Motor Co., 1955-57, Snelling Motor Co., Houston, 1957-60, Pores, Inc., Ft. Pierce, Fla., 1960-68, also sec.; past office mgr. Taylor Buick Corp., Ft. Pierce; sec.-treas. Dave Snelling Lincoln, Mercury, Inc., Houston, from 1968, now office mgr. Leo Jarnagin Pontiac Center, Houston. Presbyn. Home: 8354 Ruthby Houston TX 77017 Office: Leo Jarnagin Pontiac Center Co 2600 Travis StHouston TX 77006

MILLER, MARY RUTH, educator; b. Bartow, Fla., Dec. 22, 1926; d. Willie Boyd and Ruth (Anderson) Miller; A.B. in Edn., Fla. State U., 1948; M.A., George Peabody Coll., 1951; Ph.D., Duke, 1966; postgrad. Columbia, summer 1953, U. So. Cal., summer 1954, Shakespeare Inst., Stratford-on-Avon, Eng., summer 1955, U. Edinburgh (Scotland), summer 1969. Tchr. elementary sch., Palatka, Fla., 1948-49; tchr. high schs., Bell, Fla., 1949-50, Brandon, Fla., 1950-51, Webster, Fla., 1951-53; tchr. English, dir. pub. relations Reinhardt Coll., 1953-59; asst. prof. English, Fla. So. Coll., 1962-67; prof. English and chmn. dept. Tenn. Wesleyan Coll., Athens, 1967—. Recipient Lewis State Tchr.'s Scholarship, Fla. State U., 1945-48; Danforth Tchrs. Summer Scholarship, U. So. Cal., 1954; Cokesbury award in Coll. Teaching, Duke U., 59-60, 61-62, grad. research assistantship, 1960-61. Mem. Nat. Council Tchrs. English, Conf. Coll. Composition and Communication, South Atlantic Modern Lang. Assn., Coll. English Assn., Modern Lang. Assn., S.E. Renaissance Conf., Tenn. Coll. English Assn., Renaissance Soc. Am. Democrat. Methodist. Home: 422 Gettys Lane Athens TN 37303

MILLER, MERLE RUSSELL, educator; b. Louisville, Apr. 21, 1915; s. Hiram and Clara (Perkins) M.; A.B., Western Ky. U., 1937; A.B., Bowling Green Coll. Commerce, 1940; J.D., U. Louisville, 1950; LL.M., Georgetown U., 1966; m. Sara Louise Ray, Nov. 25, 1938; children—Patricia Anne (Mrs. Richard Crisp Downing), Russell Hiram. Tng. officer VA, Louisville, 1946-50; Admitted to Ky., 1950; individual practice law, Somerset, Ky., 1950-51; sr. investigator OPS, Louisville, 1951-52; investigator U.S. Gen. Accounting Office, Louisville, 1952-56; contract personnel officer, investigation specialist AEC, Aiken, S.C., 1959-62, Washington, 1964-66, Atlanta, 1966-70; tchr. Ark. State U., Jonesboro, 1970—. Adj. prof. Augusta Coll., 1958, 62, Ga. State U., 1970. Ednl. chmn. Am. Cancer Soc., Aiken, 1960-62. Served with AUS, 1942-46. Named Ky. col. Mem. Ky., S.C. bar assns., Ky. Hist. Soc. Mason (Shriner), Kiwanian, Lion. Home: 2217 Indian Trails Jonesboro AR 72401

MILLER, META HELENA, educator; b. Balt., Jan. 29, 1897; d. Charles A. A. J. and Mary (Bonnet) Miller; A.B., Goucher Coll., 1917; M.A., Johns Hopkins, 1919, Ph.D., 1922; postgrad. Columbia, Sorbonne; certificat d'etudes pratiques de prononciation Institut de Phonetique, 1931. Instr. French, Wells Coll., 1919-21; with U. N.C., Greensboro, 1922—, successively asst. prof. Romance langs., asso. prof., 1927-37, prof., 1937-66, prof. emeritus, 1966—, acting head dept., 1953-56, head dept., 1956-62. Active Am. aid to France, 1940-45. Mem. Modern Lang. Assn., South Atlantic Modern Lang. Assn., Am. Assn. Tchrs. French, Am. Assn. Tchrs. Spanish, N.C. Edn. Assn., Am. Archaeol. Soc., World Federalists, Alliance Francaise, Luth. Acad. Scholarship, P.E.O., Kappa Kappa Gamma, Alpha Delta Pi, Tau Psi Omega. Democrat. Lutheran. Club: Johns Hopkins. Author: Chateaubriand and English Literature, 1925; (with Chinard, Gilbert, others) Les Natchez, 1932; (with Hooke, Malcolm) French Review Grammar, 1945. Home: 1908 Walker Av Greensboro NC 27403

MILLER, MILTON LEONARD, educator; b. McKeesport, Pa., Feb. 12, 1904; s. Wolf and Sarah (Speer) M.; A.B., Harvard, 1925, M.D. cum laude, 1929; m. Bernice Saul, May 6, 1938; 1 son, Jeffrey. Intern Mass. Gen. Hosp., Boston, 1930-32, tng. in psychiatry and neurology, 1932-35, psycho-analysis trainee, Chgo. Psychoanalytic Inst., 1936-40, mem. staff, 1939-42; practice medicine, specializing in psychiatry and psychoanalysis, 1948-59; pres. So. Cal. Psychoanalytic Inst., 1950-59; prof. psychiatry U. N.C. Med. Sch., Chapel Hill, 1959—, dir. U.N.C.-Duke psychoanalytic tng. program, 1960—; attending psychiatrist N.C. Meml. Hosp. Psychiat. cons. Health, Edn., Welfare Bd., Raleigh, N.C. Served to lt. col. M.C., AAF, 1942-46. Mem. Am. Psychoanalytic Soc. (life), Am. Psychiat. Assn. (life), Am. Psychosomatic Soc., A.A.A.S., A.M.A. Author: Nostalgia, a Psychoanalytic Study of Marcel Proust, 1956. Home: Box 87 Route 6 Chapel Hill NC 27514

MILLER, MINOS D., JR., judge; b. Jennings, La., Sept. 9, 1920; s. Minos D. and Ruth (Ingram) M.; B.S., La. State U., 1947, J.D., 1947; m. Ruth Means Loyd, Dec. 22, 1942; children—Bonner, Minos D. III, J. Valcour. Admitted to La. bar, 1947; mem. firm Adams & Miller, 1947-53; dist. judge 31st Jud. Dist. Ct. La., 1953-69; judge Ct. Appeal 3d circuit, 1969—; spl. assignment judge La. Supreme Ct., 1958, La. Appeals, 1961-62. Active Boy Scouts; chmn. Jefferson Davis Parish Planning Bd., 1963. Vice-pres. Am. Legion Hosp., Jennings. Served to lt. (sr. grade) USNR, 1941-46. Decorated Purple Heart. Mem. Am., La., S.W. La., Jefferson Davis Parish bar assns., La. Dist. Judges Assn. (past pres.), Am. Judicature Soc., V.F.W., Am. Legion, Lambda Chi Alpha, Phi Eta Sigma, Omicron Delta Kappa, Phi Delta Phi. Democrat. Methodist. Home: PO Box 1309 Jennings LA 70546 Office: PO Box 3000 Lake Charles LA 70601

MILLER, MITCH, state ofcl.; b. Mentone, Ala., Oct. 4, 1930; s. Henry Thomas and Ruth (Miller) M.; student U. Ga., 1959, Ohio State U., 1962; m. Minnie Lyn Martin, Feb. 19, 1950; children—Charles Martin, Myron Baynor. With Dept. of Def., USAF, 1948-62, electronics engr., 1948, logistics mgr., 1962, cons. mgmt., marketing electronics products, 1962-69; mem. Ga. Ho. of Reps.; regional marketing mgr. Emerson Electric Co., 1963—. Mem. Am. Legion. Mason (Shriner), Moose. Home: 3859 Mathis St Macon GA 31206 Office: 1000 Executive Ct Warner Robins GA 31093

MILLER, MONTE MACK, banker; b. Winchester, Va., June 12, 1933; s. George Franklin and Reatha (Hubbard) M.; B.A. in Biology, U. Va., 1956, M.B.A., 1963; m. Carolyn Winn Miller, Sept. 12, 1961; children—Virginia Corydon, Elizabeth Carter, Meredith Winn. Asst. to headmaster Christ church (Va.) Sch., 1958-60; staff Virginian-Post, Norfolk, Va., 1960-61; joined Nat. Bank Commerce of Norfolk, 1962, staff methods and systems div., 1962, (merger Va. Nat. Bank 1963) staff marketing div., 1963-64, nat. accounts div., 1964, asst. cashier, 1964, asst. v.p., 1966-67, v.p. loans, 1967-69, v.p. charge card, 1969—. Chmn. Azalea Festival, Norfolk, 1970, Norfolk Community Concerts, 1968—. Commr. Model Cities Commn., Norfolk, 1969—; mem. adv. com. Norfolk City Council, 1969—. Bd. dirs. Ghent Neighborhood League, Va. Student Aid Found. Mem. U. Va. Alumni Assn., Norfolk, Va. Chambers Commerce Tidewater Horse and Pony Assn., Kappa Alpha. Episcopalian (vestryman). Clubs: Norfolk Yacht and Country, Princess Ann Country, Harbor (Norfolk). Home: 535 Fairfax Av Norfolk VA 23507 Office: 3300 E Princess Ann Rd Norfolk VA 23502

MILLER, NATHAN, journalist; b. Balt., May 26, 1927; s. David and Jennie (Miller) M.; B.A., U. Md., 1950, M.A., 1951; m. Jeanette Martick, Feb. 22, 1963. With Balt. Sun., 1954-69, corr. Washington Bur., 1966-69; asso. editor Editorial Research Reports, Washington, 1970-71, Kiplinger Washington Letters, 1971—. Served with USNR, 1945-46. Recipient award for pub. service reporting Am. Polit. Sci. Assn., 1961. Mem. White House, State Dept. corrs. assns. Club: Overseas Press (N.Y.C.). Home: 4916 Western Av Chevy Chase MD 20016 Office: 1729 H St NW Washington DC 20006

MILLER, NATHAN ANDERSON, educator; b. Dandridge, Tenn., May 24, 1914; s. Thomas Norman and Leutitia (Davis) M.; A.B. magna cum laude, Carson-Newman Coll., 1936; M.S., U. Tenn., 1944; m. Alfreda Rowena Reed, July 5, 1949; children—Gwenna, Thomas. Tchr. grammar sch., Jefferson City, Tenn., 1936-38, prin. high sch., 1943-44; tchr. O'Keefe High Sch., Atlanta, 1938-43; dir. tchr. internes Carson-Newman Coll., 1944; dean Little River Sch., Miami, Fla., 1945-55; dean of boys Madison Jr. High Sch., 1955-56; cons. Reader's Digest, Pleasantville, N.Y., 1956-58; tchr. North Miami (Fla.) High Sch., 1958-65; asst. prin. North Dade High Sch., 1965-67, Miami Springs (Fla.) Jr. High Sch., 1967—; owner, dir. Camp Sky-Top, Rosman, N.C., 1950—; cons. Ednl. Testing Service, Princeton, N.J., 1955—; chmn. interviewing com. for Exchange Tchrs., U.S. Office Edn., 1952—. Chmn., Jefferson County A.R.C. Fund, 1943-44; v.p. Little River Youth Center Found.; bd. dirs. Fla. Youth Found. Mem. Nat. Council Tchrs. English (dir., chmn. audio visual aids com. 1942-50, co-editor Speak-Look-Listen 1943), Dade County Classroom Tchrs. Assn. (hon. life; pres. 1948-49), Nat. Soc. for Study Communication (charter mem.), Jefferson County Bapt. Assn. (Sunday sch. supt.), Phi Kappa Phi, Phi Delta Kappa. Rotarian. Editor: Atlanta Teacher, 1941-43; co-founder, editor: Dade County, Fla. Teacher, 1946-48; editorial collaborator Reading Skill Builders, 1957-58. Home: 570 Hunting Lodge Dr Miami Springs FL 33166 Office: 150 Royal Poinciana Blvd Miami Springs FL 33166

MILLER, NORMAN, lawyer; b. Boston, Dec. 6, 1925; s. Harry and Ethel (Feldman) M.; student Northeastern U., 1942-44, U. Glasgow (Scotland), 1945-46, Boston Coll., 1946-47; LL.B., U. Miami, 1952; m. Constance Hope, Nov. 23, 1952; children—Clifford Michael, Debra Caryl, Edward Harris; m. 2d, Patricia Ann Miller; 1 son, Jason William. Admitted to Fla. bar, 1952; asst. to the city atty., Miami, Fla., 1951-52; practice law, Miami, 1952—; judge Town of Medley, 1960-65. Served as cpl. AUS, 1944-46, ETO. Decorated Bronze Star medal. Mem. Nat. Assn. Claimants Compensation Attys. (state v.p. 1959-60, asso. editor bar jour.; past pres. South Fla.), Fed. (Fla. rep. 1956—), Am., Fla., Dade County bar assns., U. Miami Law Alumni Assn., Fla. Municipal Judges Assn. (pres. 1964-65), Acad. Fla. Trial Lawyers, Am. Arbitration Assn., Am. Trial Lawyers Assn. (safety liaison officer), D.A.V., Jewish War Vets. (local comdr.). Mason (32 deg.). Home: 422 Bargello Coral Gables FL 33134 Office: Biscayne Bldg Miami FL 33130

MILLER, PATRICK DWIGHT, clergyman, ch. ofcl.; b. Franklin County, Ga., Jan. 13, 1900; s. John C. C. and Florence (McWhorter) M.; A.B., Davidson Coll., 1922, D.D., 1933; B.D., Union Theol. Sem. Va., 1926, Th.M., 1927; m. Lila Morse Bonner, Mar. 7, 1931; children— Belle Neel (Mrs. George R. McMaster), Mary Bonner (Mrs. Walter A. Brueggemann), Patrick Dwight. Ordained to ministry Presbyn. Ch., 1927; minister Rabun County, Ga., 1927-29 Raleigh, N.C., 1934-41, San Antonio, 1941-49, Atlanta, 1949-55; sec. exec. com. home missions Presbyn. Ch. U.S., 1929-34, exec. sec. bd. ch. extension Presbyn. Ch. U.S., 1955-65, moderator, 1968—; guest prof. homiletics Columbia Theol. Sem., Decatur, Ga., 1965-69, ret. Home: 1327 Fairview Rd NE Atlanta GA 30306

MILLER, PAUL JACKSON, JR., lawyer; b. nr. Phenix City, Ala., Mar. 2, 1924; s. Paul J. and Maori (Jackson) M.; student Auburn U., 1946-47; J.D., U. Ala., 1951; m. Agnes Frances Zagar, Apr. 21, 1946; children— Paul, Scott, Leigh, Claire, Dawn, Gwen. Admitted to Ala. bar, 1951; spl. agt. FBI, 1951-54; practice law, Phenix City, Ala., 1954—; judge Russell County Ct., 1956-59. Chmn., Ala. Milk Control Bd., 1959-62; active Springer Theatre. Served with USMCR, 1942-46. Decorated D.F.C., Air medal with 3 gold stars. Mem. Phenix City Jr. C. of C. Mem. Am., Ala. bar assns., Am. Trial Lawyers. Roman Catholic (pres. ch. council 1969—). Home: 1306 32d St Phenix City AL 36867 Office: Phenix Girard Bank Phenix City AL 36867

MILLER, R.C., ednl. adminstr. Mem. Ky. Bd. Edn. Address: Ky Bd Edn Frankfort KY 40601*

MILLER, RALPH ALEXANDER, aviation co. exec.; b. Washington, May 28, 1935; s. Ralph G. and Marie Therese (Von Degenfeld) M.; B.A., U. Va., 1957; m. Katharin S. Lloyd-Rees, Dec. 16, 1961; children—Ralph George, Mary Lloyd, Robert Alexander, Anthony Otto. Pres., Ram Aviation, Newport News, Va., 1963-69, chmn. bd., 1969-70, pres., 1971—; vice-chmn., dir. First City Bank Newport News. Served to lt. USNR, 1957-62. Mem. Va. Aviation Trades Assn. (pres. 1968-69), Internat. Order Characters. Episcopalian. Rotarian. Club: Metropolitan (Washington). Home: 1042 Algonguin Rd Norfolk VA 23505 Office: Patrick Henry Airport Newport News VA 23602

MILLER, RALPH STANLEY, accountant; b. Dansville, N.Y., June 13, 1918; s. Jay A. and Dora (Saxton) M.; grad. Jamestown (N.Y.) Bus. Coll., 1938; B.S., Syracuse U., 1948; m. Doris Hope Huntington, June 16, 1951. Bookkeeping and gen. office Swift & Co., Jamestown, 1939-41, Syracuse, N.Y., 1941-42; staff accountant Wilson, Shults & Co., C.P.A.'s, Rochester, N.Y., 1948-56; accountant, office mgr. Price Waterhouse & Co., San Juan, P.R., 1956—. Served with AUS, 1942-45; ETO. Mem. Am. Inst. C.P.A.'s, N.Y. State Soc. C.P.A.'s, Instituto de Contadores Publicos Autorizados de P.R., Nat. Assn. Accountants, P.R. Natural History Soc., Beta Alpha Psi. Methodist. Club: Exchange (San Juan). Home: 1509 Calle Las Marias Santurce PR 00911 Office: Chase Manhattan Bank Bldg Hato Rey PR 00927

MILLER, REUBEN GEORGE, educator; b. Phila., Mar. 28, 1930; s. George and Edna (Fuchs) M.; B.A., LaSalle Coll., 1952; diploma, U. Stockholm (Sweden), 1954; MA., U. Mont., 1956; Ph.D, Ohio State U., 1966; m. Sylvia Raigla, June 22, 1955. Asst. instr. Ohio State U., Columbus, 1954-57; acting asst. prof. Oberlin (O.) Coll., 1957-58; asst. prof. U. Mass., Amherst, 1959-67; asso. prof. econs. Smith Coll., Northampton, Mass., 1967-70; Charles A. Dana prof. econs., chmn. econs. dept. Sweet Briar (Va.) Coll., 1970—. Fulbright-Hayes lectr. econs. Coll. of Law, Nat. Taiwan U., Republic of China, 1965-66. Recipient Am.-Scandinavian Found. fellowship, 1952-53, Research Tng. fellowship Social Sci. Research Council, 1958-59. Mem. Am. Econ. Assn., Am. Finance Assn., Royal Econ. Soc. Contbr. articles in field to profl. jours. Office: Dept Econs Sweet Briar Coll Sweet Briar VA 24595

MILLER, ROBERT, city editor Dallas Morning News. Office: Communications Center Dallas TX 75222*

MILLER, ROBERT ALVIN, social worker; b. Oklahoma City, Feb 21, 1937; s. George Henry and Pearl (Laughlin) M.; B.A., Baylor U., 1959; M.S.W., Fla. State U., 1963; m. Vera Lavell Conrad, Oct. 2, 1964; 1 son, Robert Conrad. Child welfare worker Tex. Dept. Pub. Welfare, 1959; caseworker Waco State Home, Tex., 1959-61; dir. social service, tng., psychiat. social worker Fla. Sch. for Boys, Marianna, 1963-67; chief counselor Ct. of Record, juvenile div. Escambia County, Pensacola, Fla., 1967-71; now criminal justice specialist Intergovtl. Program Office, Pensacola. Prof. sociology U. West Fla. at Pensacola, 1968. Treas., Boys Club Escambia County, 1969. Mem. Fla. Counselors Assn. (bd. dirs. 1969-70), Fla. Council Crime and Delinquency (bd. dirs. N.W. Fla. chpt., 1969-70), Acad. Certified Social Workers, Alpha Kappa Delta. Optimist (pres. Pensacola, 1970-71). Home: 2931 Swan Lane Pensacola FL 32504 Office: 803 N Palafox St Pensacola FL 32501

MILLER, ROBERT ATKERSON, state ofcl.; b. Nashville, Nov. 3,, 1931; s. Chester C. and Dorothy (Atkerson) M.; B.A., Vanderbilt U., 1953; m. Shirley Wright, Feb. 20, 1954; children—Lynn Allison, Lisa Ann. With div. geology, Dept. Conservation of Tenn., Nashville, 1956—, chief geologist, 1969; instr. geology U. Tenn., Nashville, 1964—. Recipient Beautiful Am. award Holiday Mag. 1969. Mem. Am. Inst. Profl. Geologists. Geol. Soc. Am., Tenn. Acad. Sci., Audubon Soc., Tenn. Citizens Wilderness Planning, Tenn. Scenic Rivers Assn. (founder 1966. pres. 1966-68, bd. advisers 1968—). Home: 709 Templeton Dr Nashville TN 37205 Office: State Office Bldg Nashville TN 37205

MILLER, ROBERT LAMAR, lawyer; b. Gonzales, Tex., Aug. 29, 1906; s. William Tecumseh and Louise Estelle (Robinson) M.; B.A., Washington and Lee U., 1928; LL.B., U. Tex., 1930; m. Eral Jahn, June 15, 1933. Admitted to Tex. bar, 1930; practiced in Gonzales, 1930—; mem. firm Miller & Miller. Chmn. bd. First Nat. Bank, Gonzales; dir. Gonzales County Savs. & Loan Assn., Holmes Foods, Inc., Nixon, Tex., Nixon Processing Co., Nixon Feed & By-Products. Active Holmes Meml. Hosp., Gonzales, Tex., 1969—, Gonzales Warm Springs Assn., 1960—. Served with USNR, 1942-45. Decorated Bronze Stars (2); recipient Order Bronze Shoe, Found. Crippled Children, 1963. Presbyn. (elder 1952—). Mason. Home: 310 Darst St Gonzales TX 78629 Office: 503-1/2 St Joseph St Gonzales TX 78629

MILLER, ROBERT TREADWELL, physician; b. N.Y.C., Mar. 8, 1920; s. Edward Grover and Hattie (Robson) M.; B.S., Tufts U., 1942, M.D., 1945; m. Mary Catharine Bolster, Nov. 3, 1945; children—Marjorie Bolster, Christopher Robson. Intern Nat. Naval Med. Center, Bethesda, Md., 1945-46; resident Boston City Hosp., 1948, D.C. Gen. Hosp., Washington, 1948-50; med. dir., also bd. dirs. Orange Grove Center, 1958—, United Cerebral Palsy Child Devel. Center, 1960—, Team Evaluation Center, 1962—; med. adv. staff United Cerebral Palsy Tenn., Siskin Found., 1958—. Bd. dirs. Tenn. Camp for Diabetic Children. Served to lt. (j.g.), M.C., USNR,

1945-47, to lt., 1953-54. Recipient citation, 1954. Diplomate Am. Bd. Pediatrics, Nat. Bd. Med. Examiners. Fellow Am. Acad. Pediatrics, Am. Acad. Cerebral Palsy; mem. Tenn. Pediatric Soc., A.M.A. Tenn., County med. socs. Home: 4100 Tacoma Av Chattanooga TN 37405 Office: 4100 Tacoma Av Chattanooga TN 37405

MILLER, ROBERT WILEY, govt. ofcl.; b. Linden, Cal., June 8, 1928; s. Raymond Wiley and Florence (Burke) M.; student Pacific U., 1946-48; A.B., Coll. of Pacific, 1950; postgrad. in journalism U. Tulsa, 1953; M.B.A., Harvard, 1956; D.C.S. (hon.), Drake Coll., 1964; m. Betty Brown, Nov. 15, 1953; children—Janet Ruth, Stephen Wiley. Dir. pub. relations radio sta. WOL, Washington, 1950-51; asst. mgr., dir. pub. relations Automobile Club of Okla., Am. Automobile Assn., 1953-54; exec. v.p. Pub. Relations Research Assos., Inc., World Trade Relations, Inc., Washington, Ottawa, Ont., Can., 1956-61; dir. program pub. relations Columbia U., Sch. Gen. Studies N.Y.C., 1960-65; prof., dir. bus. govt. relations program Sch. Bus. Adminstrn., Am. U., Washington, 1965-70, dir. Center Study of Pvt. Enterprise, 1968-70; dir. Office Domestic Bus. Policy, Dept. Commerce, Washington, 1970-71; exec. dir. White House Conf. Indsl. World Ahead-A Look at The Indsl. World in 1990, 1971-72; spl. asst. to Pres., 1972—. Lectr. Am. U., Washington, 1957-60; cons. to numerous bus., govt. and industry clients; mem. N.Y. Regional Export Expansion Council, 1963-65. Mem. Nat. council Boy Scouts Am., 1960—. Trustee Ft. Lauderdale U. Served with AUS, 1951-53. Mem. Pub. Relations Soc. Am., Pub. Affairs Council (dir. 1967-70), U.S. C. of C. (mem. pub. affairs com. 1968-70). Methodist. Mason. Clubs: Nat. Press, Kenwood Golf and Country, Cosmos (Washington); Harvard of New York. Author: Profitable Community Relations for Small Business, 1960; Corporate Policies and Public Attitudes, 1965; The Creative Interface: The New Relationships between Business and Government, 1968. The Creative Interface II: International Business-Government Relations, 1969; The Creative Interface III: Private Enterprise and the Urban Crisis, 1971; Corporate Ambassadors to Washington, 1970. Contbr. numerous articles to bus. and profl. jours. Home: 5037 Westrath Terrace Washington DC20016

MILLER, ROBERTA LEMONS, librarian; b. Penrod, Ky., Oct. 8, 1941; s. James William and Ina (Dickinson) L.; B.S., Murray State U., 1962; M.S. (King grantee 1962), George Peabody Coll., 1963; m. Charles D. Miller, Apr. 20, 1968. Catalog librarian Vanderbilt U. Med. Library, Nashville, 1963-66; reference librarian U. Ky. Med. Library, Lexington, 1966-67; automation librarian U. Va. Med. Library, Charlottesville, 1967-68; chief tech. processing Henrico County Pub. Library, Richmond, Va., 1968-71, dir., 1971—. Instr. library sci. Va. Commonwealth U., Richmond, 1971. Recipient K. T. Distbr. Scholarship award, 1959. Mem. Am., Va. library assns., Potomac Tech. Processing Librarians (chmn. 1970-72). Home: 8311 Whistler Rd Richmond VA 23227 Office: PO Box 27032 Richmond VA 23261

MILLER, SAUL, editor; b. N.Y.C., Sept. 23, 1918; s. Louis and Kate (Zizmor) M.; B.S., N.Y. U., 1941; m. Beatrice Elbaum, Nov. 10, 1945; children—David, Kate, Judith, Jonathan. Reporter, Gazette &Daily, York, Pa., 1945-48; copy editor Richmond (Va.) Times-Dispatch, 1948-49; news editor Jamestown (N.Y.) Sun, 1949-51; dir. New Newspaper Service, Washington, 1951-55; asso. editor AFL News Reporter, 1955; mng. editor AFL-CIO News, 1955-58; dir. publs. AFL-CIO, Washington, 1958—. Served with AUS, 1942-45. Mem. Am. Newspaper Guild. Nat. Press (Washington). Home: 3410 Highview Ct Silver Spring MD 20902 Office: Dept Publications AFL-CIO 815 16th St Washington DC 20006

MILLER, STERLING KIMSEY, city ofcl.; b. Santa Fe, N.M., Sept. 2, 1933; s. Lester Lynn and Velma (Sterling) M.; B.B.A., Tex. Technol. Coll., 1955; m. Mavis Louise Fluke, Jan. 30, 1954; children—Rebecca, Deborah, Sterling Kimsey, Teresa. Internal auditor City of Lubbock (Tex.), 1958-65, dir. finance, 1965—; resident auditor Greenham Common AFB, Newbury, Eng., 1957-58; staff auditor Nouasser Air Depot, Casablanca, Morocco, 1955-57. Sec.-treas. Lubbock Firemen's Relief and Retirement Fund, 1971—. bd. dirs. Tex. Municipal Retirement System, 1971—. Recipient award Municipal Adv. Council. Mem. Municipal Finance Officers Assn. (1st v.p. Tex. chpt. 1971—). Club: Treasure Island Golf Center (dir. 1963—). Home: 4903 15th St Lubbock TX 79416 Office: PO Box 2000 Lubbock TX 79457

MILLER, TERRY PARKINSON, dentist; b. Wagoner, Okla., May 20, 1933; s. Howard S. and Evie (Parkinson) M.; B.A., Okla. State U., 1955; D.D.S., U. Mo. at Kansas City, 1959; m. Martha Puckett, Aug. 4, 1956; children—Stephen Howard, Amy Elizabeth. Practice dentistry, Stillwater, Okla., 1961—. Chmn. Heart Sunday, Payne County, 1965-67; pres. Payne County Heart Assn., 1965-67. Served with AUS, 1959-61. Mem. Stillwater Dental Soc. (past pres.), Okla. (ho. dels.), Am. dental assns., Acad. Gen. Dentistry (pres. Okla. chpt.), Stillwater C. of C. (dir.), Sigma Nu. Episcopalian (vestryman). Lion (pres.). Club: Century (past pres.) (Stillwater). Home: 22 Fox Ledge Lane RR 4 Stillwater OK 74074 Office: 900 S Walnut St Stillwater OK 74074

MILLER, THOMAS LLOYD, educator; b. Commerce, Tex., Sept. 21, 1913; s. Thomas Lewis and Ottie (Cotton) M.; B.A., East Tex. State U., 1935, M.A., 1945; Ph.D. (teaching fellow 1948-49, 52-53), U. Tex. at Austin, 1956; m. Dorothy Marie LoBello, Dec. 25, 1948; children—Marilyn Marie (Mrs. Don B. Leinhart), Thomas Allen. Tchr. history McCamey (Tex.) High Sch., 1936-42; mem. faculty Tex. A. and M. U., College Station, 1946, instr., 1946-53, asst. prof., 1953-57, asso prof., 1957-68, prof. history, 1968—. Served with AUS, 1942-44. Mem. Am. Assn. U. Profs., Agrl. History Soc., Tex. Hist. Assn., Orgn. Am. Historians, Phi Alha Pheta. Author: Bounty and Donation Land Grants of Texas, 1835-1888, 1967; The Public Lands of Texas, 1519-1970, 1971. Office: Tex A & M U College Station TX 77843

MILLER, WALTON SANSOM, financial mgmt. co. exec.; b. Dallas, Sept. 21, 1932; s. William Henry and Eveline (O'Hara) M.; B.B.A., So. Methodist U., 1954; m. Barbara Ann Russell, May 29, 1954 (div. Sept. 1964); children—Sheralyn, Walton Sansom, James Russell, Shawna Marie; m. 2d, Gladys Vines, Oct. 12, 1968; 1 son, David Arthur. Mng. partner Henry Miller Ins. Agy., Dallas, 1955-70; pres. Walton Miller Cos., 1970— Metro Terra Properties, Inc., 1970—, Financial Planning Assos., 1970—, Protein Industries, Bovine Internat., Inc., 1970—; chmn. bd. U.S. Financial Corp., Dallas, 1970—; dir. Traders Compress Co., Oklahoma City, also others. Lectr., So. Methodist U., 1958—, U. Tex., Austin, 1968—. C.P.C.U. Mem. Nat. Assn. Life Underwriters, Million Dollar Round Table, Dallas, North Dallas chambers commerce, North Dallas Parents League, Blue Key, Phi Delta Theta. Methodist. Clubs: City, Brookhaven Country, Shady Oaks Country, Dallas Press, Dallas Tennis Assn., Mustang, M Assn. Home: 3883 Turtle Creek St Dallas TX 75204 Office: Walton Miller Bldg Dallas TX 75204

MILLER, WAYNE W., ednl. adminstr.; b. Hydro, Okla., Mar. 8, 1920; s. Grover Cleveland and Vada Lucille (Talkington) M.; B.S., Okla. State U., 1942; M.S., U. Ill., 1957; m. Sara Ellynn Pickens, June 11, 1946; children—Michael Wayne, Cynthia Ellynn. Asst. county agt., Muskogee County, Okla., 1945-46; div. project leader, extension service Okla. State U., Stillwater, 1952-58, v.p., 1972—; head div. agr. Okla. State U. Sch. Tech. Tng., Okmulgee, 1946-51, asst. dir., 1958-63, dir., dean, 1963-72, dir., 1972—. Mem. Pres.'s Com. on Employment of Handicapped; mem. Gov.'s Adv. Com. on Rehab. Facilities; mem. Gov.'s Com. on Employment of Handicapped; prin. investigator, project dir. Nat. Conf. on Residential Vocational Edn.; spl. cons. Div. Vocational Edn., U.S. Office of Edn. Served with USMCR, 1942-45; PTO; served to maj. USMCR, 1951-52. Decorated Bronze Star. Mem. Am. Vocational Assn. (life), Nat. Tech. Soc. Am., Okmulgee C. of C. (dir.), Okla. State U. Alumni Assn. (life), Blue Key, Alpha Zeta, Gamma Sigma Delta, Alpha Gamma Rho. Mason (32 deg.), Rotarian. Methodist. Home: Box 1 Okla State Tech Okmulgee OK 74447

MILLER, WESLEY, lawyer; b. Jay, Okla., Mar. 28, 1918; s. William M. and Leah (Boyd) M.; B.A., Northeastern State Coll., 1939; postgrad. U. Okla. Sch. Law, 1939-41; m. Louise Heflebower, Mar. 30, 1963; children—Teresa Lynn, Mark Wesley. Admitted to Okla. bar, 1945; practice law, Tahlequah, Okla., 1945—. Referee, Nat. Mediation Bd., Kansas City, Mo., 1961, Honolulu, 1961, Mpls., 1965, Nat. R.R. Adjustment Bd., Chgo., 1962-71. Pres., Okla. League Young Democrats, 1949-50. Served to capt. AUS, 1941. Recipient 20 Year Selective Service medal, 1969. Mem. Okla. (mem. ho. of dels. 1967—), Cherokee County (pres. 1952-55) bar assns., Tahlequah C. of C., Am. Legion, V.F.W., Phi Beta Epsilon, Phi Delta Phi. Democrat. Methodist. Kiwanian (pres. 1955). Home: 100 Bluff Av Tahlequah OK 74464 Office: 214 S Muskogee St Tahlequah OK 74464

MILLER, WILBERT ELWOOD, social worker; b. Reidsville, N.C., Nov. 26, 1925; s. George James and Irene (Walker) M.; B.S., Howard U., 1951, M.S.W., 1958; postgrad. Catonville Community Coll., 1970; m. Gloria Thompson Hall, July 2, 1959; children—Rene Joseph Hall, Jacqueline Yvonne. Counselor, Lorton (Va.) Reformatory, 1953-54; caseworker Child Welfare Div., Washington, 1954-55, Pub. Assistance Div., 1955-56; counselor Maple Glen Tng. Sch., Laurel, Md., 1957-58; sr. caseworker Boys Village, Cheltenham, Md., 1958-63, supr. casework services, 1963—; field supr. for students Sch. Social Work, Howard U., U.N.C.; field supr. Md. Summer Careers Program. Served with AUS, 1944-46, to 1st lt., 1951-52. Recipient Ten Year award for pub. service to State Md., 1968. Mem. Nat. Assn. Social Work, Acad. Certified Social Workers, Nat. Assn. Tng. Schs. and Juvenile Agys., Md. Classified Employees Assn., Md. Tchrs. Assn., Howard U. Sch. Social Work Alumni Assn., Middle Atlantic States Conf. of Correction. Author: Boys' Village of Maryland Student Handbook, 1969. Home: 611 7th St NE Washington DC 20002 Office: Boys Village of Md Cheltenham MD 20623

MILLER, WILBUR K., judge; b. Owensboro, Ky., Oct. 9, 1892; s. Reuben A. and Margaret (Morehead) M.; student U. Mich.; m. Marie Louise Hager, June 2, 1917. Admitted to Ky. bar, 1916, and practiced in Owensboro; county atty., Daviess County, 1922-30; chmn. Pub. Service Commn. of Ky., 1934-35; judge Spl. Ct. of Appeals of Ky., 1940-41; judge U.S. Ct. of Appeals for D.C., 1945—. Served in F.A., U.S. Army, World War I. Mem. Phi Delta Phi, Phi Kappa Sigma. Home: Westchester 4000 Cathedral Av NW Washington DC 20016 Office: US Ct House Washington DC 20001

MILLER, WILLIAM ANDREW, JR., judge; b. West Newton, Pa., June 21, 1904; s. William Abraham and Maggie May (Knopp) M.; LL.B., South Tex. Sch. Law, 1936; m. Ruby Allen Miller, June 6, 1932; children—Daryl Marie, William Stephen. Admitted to Tex. bar, 1936; judge, Harris County, Tex., 1954—. Mem. Tex. Ho. Reps., 1946-54. Mem. Houston Democratic Exec. Com., 1940-42. Mem. bd. regents South Tex. Coll., 1953—. Served from 2d lt. to capt., AUS, 1942-46, Res. ret. Mem. Houston Fat Stock Show, Am. Legion, Tex. Christian Endeavor Union (trustee), Delta Theta Phi. Mem. Christian Ch. (licensed minister). Mason (K.T., Shriner), Eagle. Clubs: Houston Yacht, Ellington Air Force Base Officers Farm and Ranch. Home: 6504 Auden St Houston TX 77005 Office: County Civil Ct at Law Civil Sts Bldg Houston TX 77002

MILLER, WILLIAM BARRETT, elec. engr.; b. Galveston, Tex., Nov. 22, 1926; s. William Herman and Margaret (Steinbach) M.; B.S., Tex. A. and M. U., 1948; postgrad. U. Houston, 1949, So. Meth. U., 1951-52, Tex. U., 1957; m. Bernice A. Smith, June 25, 1949; children—William Barrett, Margaret Ann. Asst. rate engr. Houston Light & Power Co., 1948-50; electronic design engr. Convair, Ft. Worth, 1950-52; project engr. Bovay Engrs., Houston, 1953-62; individual practice elec. engr., 1962-63; elec. engr. H. Wayne Holland, 1963; project elec. engr. CRS Design, Houston, 1963-64; sr. elec. design engr. Tellepsen Petro Chem. Constructors, Houston, 1964-70; with Universal Energy Systems, 1970—. M C Ever Engring., 1970-71; elec. engr. B & R, Inc., 1971—. Sec. cub scouts Sam Houston Area council Boy Scouts Am., 1961; bus. mgr. sr. div. Little League, 1964. Bd. dirs. Ross Sterling Athletic Dad's Club. Mem. Nat., Tex. socs. profl. engrs., Am. Inst. Elec. Engrs. (past sec.), I.E.E.E., A.A.A.S., Instrument Soc. Am., Inst. Radio Engrs. Clubs: St. Philip Neri Men's; Crestmont Park Civic. Home: 5503 Grace Point Lane Houston TX 77048 Office: 4100 Clinton St PO Box 3 Houston TX 77001

MILLER, WILLIAM DURELL, educator; b. Jacksonville, Fla., Dec. 3, 1916; s. Frank Hoten and Verna (Sharp) M.; B.A., U. Fla., 1939; M.A., Duke, 1942; Ph.D., U. N.C., 1952; m. Rhea Bond, Aug. 27, 1944; children—William D., Francis Lloyd, Christopher Paul, Robert Holt, Carol Maria, Richard Girard, Edmund Bond. Asso. prof. Memphis State Coll., 1948-57; prof. Marquette U., Milw., 1958-68; prof. Am. social and intellectual history Fla. State U., Tallahassee, 1969—. Author: Memphis During the Progressive Era, 1957; Mr. Crump of Memphis, 1964. Home: Lloyd FL 32337 Office: Fla State U Tallahassee FL 32306

MILLER, WILLIAM ERNEST, fed. judge; b. Johnson City, Tenn., Feb. 3, 1908; s. Samuel Ernest and Grace (Barlow) M.; A.B., U. Tenn., 1930, J.D. (hon.), 1968; LL.B., Yale, 1933; m. Carolyn Gies, Dec. 1, 1934; 1 dau., Susan Barlow (Mrs. Charles E. Wright, Jr.). Admitted to Tenn. bar, 1933; mem. firm Cox, Epps, Miller & Weller, Johnson City, 1933-55; chancellor First Chancery Div. Tenn., 1939; U.S. dist. judge Middle Dist. Tenn., 1955-70, judge 6th Circuit Tenn., 1970—; lectr. Vanderbilt Law Sch. Chmn. Washington County chpt. A.R.C., 1938-40; chmn. Tenn. Rhodes Scholarship Com.; mem. Tenn. Adv. Council, Higher Edn. Act, 1965. Presdl. elector, 1940; mem. Constl. Conv. Tenn., 1953. Mem. athletic bd., trustee U. Tenn. Served as maj. USAAF, World War II. Recipient award of merit U. Tenn. Law Sch., 1966. Mem. Internat. Platform Assn., Tenn. Hist. Soc., Am., Fed. (hon.), Tenn., Va. (hon.), Nashville bar assns., Am. Judicature Soc., Am. Counsel Assn., Am. Law Inst., Order of Coif, Am. Legion, Phi Beta Kappa, Phi Alpha Delta, Sigma Alpha Epsilon. Republican. Methodist. Rotarian. Clubs: Johnson City Country, Hurstleigh (Johnson City, Tenn.); Cumberland, Belle Meade Country, Round Table (Nashville); Nat. Lawyers (Washington). Contbr. to law revs. Home: 228 Vaughans Gap Rd Nashville TN 37205 Office: US Courthouse Nashville TN 37203

MILLER, WILLIAM STEVENSON, design engr.; b. West Lafayette, Ind., Dec. 12, 1919; s. William Todd and Leona (Allen) M.; B.S., Purdue U., 1942; m. Rosemary V. Easterwood, May 23, 1941; children—William Stevenson, Sister Rose William. With Huffman Wolfe So. Corp., Atlanta, 1946-59, v.p., mgr., 1957-59; with Clarence Coston Inc., West Palm Beach, Fla., 1961-63; design engr. heating and air conditioning piping with NASA, Kennedy Space Center, Fla., 1963—. Served to maj. AUS, 1942-46. Decorated Bronze Star. Registered profl. engr., Ga. Home: 449 Espanol St Cocoa FL 32922 Office: NASA Design Engring Mech Systems Div 52 Kennedy Space Center FL 32899

MILLETT, RALPH LINWOOD, JR., editor; b. Memphis, Oct. 30, 1919; s. Ralph Linwood and Alice (Campbell) M.; student U. Wyo., 1938-40; B.J., U. Mo., 1942; m. Mary Virginia Smith, Dec. 10, 1944; children—Mary Jo, Alice Virginia, Jan Vasco, Ralph Linwood III. Copy reader, copy desk chief, news editor Knoxville (Tenn.) News-Sentinel, 1947-66, editor, 1967—. Served to lt. USNR, 1942-45. Mem. Am. Soc. Newspaper Editors, Sigma Chi, Sigma Delta Chi, Kappa Tau Alpha. Presbyn. Rotarian. Clubs: Cherokee, Racquet. Home: 4168 Towanda Trail Knoxville TN 37919 Office: 204 Church St Knoxville TN 37901

MILLIGAN, MANCIL WOOD, educator; b. Shiloh, Tenn., Nov. 21, 1934; s. Mancil Abernathy and Ivy (Wood) M.; B.S., U. Tenn., 1956, M.S., 1958, Ph.D., 1963; postgrad. U. Wash., 1958, Stanford, 1964; m. Arlys Joyce Cushman, Sept. 15, 1956; children—Mancil Wood, Jr., Matthew Wayne. Research engr. Boeing Co., Seattle, 1956-57, 58-59; instr. mech. engring. U. Tenn., Knoxville, 1957-58, prof. mech. and aerospace engring., 1959—. Cons. Union Carbide Nuclear Co., Oak Ridge, 1959—. Mem. Am. Soc. Mech. Engrs., Am. Soc. Engring. Edn., Tech. Soc. Knoxville, Am. Inst. Aeros. and Astronautics, Pi Tau Sigma, Tau Beta Pi, Sigma Xi. Home: 3624 Cherrylog Rd Knoxville TN 37921 Office: 442 Dougherty Hall U Tenn Knoxville TN 37916

MILLIGAN, RAY KEITH, computer co. exec.; b. Carmi, Ill., Oct. 17, 1934; s. Ray and Margaret Ethel (Barbre) M.; B.A. in Econs., Fla. State U., 1957; postgrad. in finance Wayne State U., 1958-59, Chrysler Inst. Engring., 1958-59; m. Dian Helene Hoskins, May 24, 1956; children—Miachel Keith, Dian Kimberly, Sean Hoskins, Wade Ferrell, Melissa Davis. Systems analyst Chrysler Corp., 1947-49; asst. to pres. Soroban Engring., Melbourne, Fla., Soroban Engring. Co., 1959-61; nat. sales mgr. electronics research and devel. Geo Space Corp., Melbourne, 1964-65; dir. systems div. D. Brown Assos., Melbourne, 1965-67; mgr. computer tech. Quantum Sci. Corp., N.Y.C., 1967-68; pres., chmn. bd. founder, mfr. computer systems HETRA Computer & Communications, Melbourne, 1968—. Mem. Brevard County Overall Econ. Devel. Program Com., 1970—. Mem. Melbourne C. of C., Soc. for Information Display, Am. Ordnance Orgn., Phi Delta Theta. Episcopalian. Contbr. articles to tech. jours. Home: 915 S Riverside Dr Indialantic FL 32901 Office: 1151 S Eddie Allen Rd Melbourne FL 32901

MILLIKEN, JAMES BUTLER, lawyer, judge; b. Louisville, Aug. 7, 1900; s. Herbert Bryant and Sarah Ann (Neeld) M.; A.B., Centre Coll., 1922; LL.B., Yale, 1926; m. Janet Pugh, June 2, 1938; children—Sara Lee, Cynthia Marshall. Admitted to Ky. bar, 1926, Ohio bar, 1927, since practiced in Newport, Ky. and Cin.; asso. justice Ct. Appeals Ky., 1950, judge, 1950-56, chief justice, 1956-59; judge Ct. of Appeals, 6th Appellate Dist., 1959—, chief justice, 1963-64, 71—, asso. justice, 1965-71. Dir. Ft. Thomas-Bellevue (Ky.) Bank. Mem. Am., Ky. bar assns., Am. Judicature Soc. (dir.), Phi Kappa Tau, Phi Delta Phi. Office: State Capitol Frankfort KY 40601

MILLINGTON, CLAYTON BLAKE, govt. ofcl., educator; b. Elk City, Okla., Dec. 4, 1927; s. Chester B. and Fay (Abernathy) M.; B.S., Okla. State U., 1951, M.S., 1956; Ph.D., Mich. State U., 1964; m. Patsy Darlene Unterkircher, June 28, 1951; children—Philip Allen, Eric Lee. Tchr. high sch., Claremore, Okla., 1953-54; instr. Okla. State U., 1954-56, 56-57, Mich. State U., 1957-60; asst. prof. Okla. State U., Stillwater, 1960-61, asso. prof., 1964-69, prof., 1969—, exec. dir. Okla. Council on Econ. Edn., 1960—, dir. Bus. Extension Service, 1961—, dir. Center for Econ. Edn., 1967—; exec. sec. Okla. Dept. Edn. Curriculum Com. on Econ., 1964—; asso. program dir. NSF, Washington, 1971-72. Chmn. Nat. Council Econ. Edn. Dirs., 1971—. Counselor, bd. dirs. local council Boy Scouts of Am., 1967—; chmn. United Fund, 1965, 1st v.p. 1966, pres. 1967; chmn. Stillwater Sales Tax Dr., 1964. Served to 1st lt. with USAF, 1951-53, lt. col. Res. Mem. Nat. Bus. Edn. Assn., Nat. Council for Social Studies, Okla. Soc. Assn. Execs., Nat. Council for Small Bus. Mgmt. Devel. (v.p. 1965, mem. adv. bd. 1966—), Delta Pi Epsilon (chpt. pres. 1957, 61), Phi Delta Kappa. Methodist. Contbr. articles in field to profl. jours. Home: 1111 S Kings Hwy Stillwater OK 74074

MILLOWAY, JOHN EUGENE, real estate appraiser and cons., shopping center developer; b. High Point, N.C., May 11, 1931; s. John E. and Eugenia (Bennett) M.; B.B.A., U. Miami, Coral Gables, Fla., 1954. Asso., W. L. Harris, real estate appraiser and cons., Miami, Fla., 1951-56; mem. firm Milloway & Coulter, appraisers, consultants, 1956-62; practice as real estate appraiser and cons., 1963—, shopping center developer, 1971—. Alternate del. Nat. Democratic Conv., 1956. Served as 1st lt. USAF Res., 1954-60. Mem. Am. Inst. Real Estate Appraisers, Am. Soc. Appraisers, Soc. Real Estate Appraisers, Am. Right-of-Way Assn., Pi Kappa Alpha. Presbyn. Clubs: Palm Bay, Jockey, University (Miami); LaGorce Country (Miami Beach, Fla.). Home: 1086 NE 91st St Miami FL 33138 Office: Greater Miami Fed Bldg Miami FL 33131

MILLS, ALFRED PRESTON, educator; b. Fallon, Nev., Jan. 8, 1922; s. Percy Edward and Ruth (Candee) M.; B.S. in Chemistry, U. Nev., 1943; Ph.D., Tulane U., 1949; m. Josephine Elizabeth Sullivan, Aug. 6, 1946; children—James Everett, Nancy Louise. Instr. chemistry U. Miami, 1949-51, asst. prof., 1951-56, asso. prof., 1956—, acting asst. dean grad. sch., 1964-65, chmn. div. natural sci. and math., 1960-61, dir. Radioisotopes Lab., 1954-62, pres. U. Miami Credit Union, 1965-68; S.E. regional dir. U. Profs. for Acad. Order, 1971—. Dir. South Fla. Regional Sci. Fair, 1954-58; mem. sci. edn. panel NSF. Bd. dirs. Fla. Found. Future Scientists, 1960-63; dir. Fla. State Sci. Talent Search, 1967. Served to lt. comdr. USNR, 1943-46, 52-53, now capt. Res.; comdg. officer Naval Res. Officers Sch., 1965-68; South Fla. coordinator Naval Acad. Information Program, 1970—. Mem. Am. Chem. Soc. (nat. council, chmn. personnel com., chmn. South Fla. subsect., chmn. phys. chemistry exams. com. 1963—, chmn. Fla. sect. 1971), Am. Phys. Soc., A.A.A.S., Fla. Acad. Sci. (pres. 1962), Fla. Lawn Tennis Assn. (pres. 1964-65, jr. ranking chmn. 1967, jr. tournament chmn. 1968—), Naval Res. Assn. (chpt. pres. 1966-67), Res. Officers' Assn. (chpt. pres. 1959-60), Am. Assn. U. Profs., Phi Kappa Phi (pres. U. Miami chpt. 1965-66). Club: Royal Palm Tennis (pres. 1968; sec. 1971). Author: Laboratory Manual in Physical Chemistry, 1953. Abstractor Chem. Abstracts, 1933—. Editor Fla. Acad. Scis. Newsletter; Fla. regional editor Tennis, USA. Home: 7540 SW 28th St Miami FL 33155 Office: Dept Chemistry U Miami Coral Gables FL 33124

MILLS, CHELSIE JOE, govt. ofcl.; b. Winfield, Ala., July 31, 1926; s. Chelsea Franklin and Frieda Beatrice (Harper) M.; B.S., U. Ala. 1949; postgrad. U. Mich., 1954-55; m. Mary Helen Weeks, Mar. 22,

1947; children—Myra Helen, William Joe. Agt., U.S. Internal Revenue Service, Birmingham, Ala., 1949—, appellate conferee, 1958—. Served with AUS, 1945-46. Mem. Ala. Soc. C.P.A.'s (chpt. treas. 1964-65; chpt. vice chmn. 1966-67), Am. Inst. C.P.A.'s, Alpha Kappa Psi, Beta Alpha Psi. Methodist (steward). Clubs: Toastmasters (pres.), Civitan (v.p. 1952-53). Home: 3225 Oriole Dr Birmingham AL 35226 Office: 2121 Bldg Birmingham AL 35203

MILLS, DON, newspaper editor; b. Lexington, Ky., May 1, 1936; s. Elbert Rhey and Maurine (Plain) M.; A.B., U. Ky., 1958; postgrad. (Rotary fellow) Edinburgh (Scotland) U., 1958-59. Reporter, The Sun-Democrat, Paducah, Ky., 1960-61; press sec. to Gov. Edward T. Breathitt, Frankfort, Ky., 1963-67; editor The Herald, Lexington, 1968—. Pres. Young Democrats Ky., 1969-70. Served to lt. AUS, 1960-62. Named one of the three outstanding men in Ky., Ky. Jr. C. of C., 1965. Home: 2135 Georgian Way Lexington KY 40504 Office: 239 W Short St Lexington KY 40504

MILLS, E. BONNIE, lawyer; b. Carthage, Miss.; d. Clarence V. and Fannie La Nora (Grimes) Mills; student Miss. So. Coll., Hattiesburg, 1939; LL.B., U. Miss., 1950. Admitted to Miss. bar, 1950, practiced, Jackson, 1950-51; legal retainer Sanders Industries, 1950-51; asst. gen. counsel War Claims Commn., 1953-55; asst. gen. counsel Gen. Services Adminstrn., 1955-56, gen. and trial atty., 1956-70. Feature writer for various drives including U.S.O., Cancer Soc., Def. and Bond Savs. Programs, Community Chest weekly radio programs for pub. affairs, bus. and profl. women's club. Served as capt. WAC, Dept. of Def., Washington, 1951-53. Mem. Am. (mem. coms.), Miss., Fed. (pres. D.C. 1968-69, dir. 1956-70), Nat. Fed. (nat. council 1963—, nat. resolutions com.) bar assns., Miss. Soc. Washington (sec.), Miss. Art Assn., Jackson Little Theater, League Women Voters, Jackson Bus. and Profl. Women's Club (past pres.), Miss. Fedn. Bus. and Profl. Women's Clubs (past pres.), Am. Assn. U. Women, Phi Delta Delta. Baptist. Mem. Order Eastern Star. Club: National Lawyers. Asso. editor Miss. Law Jour. Office: 209 N Van Buren St Carthage MS 39051 also 1746 Brecon Dr Jackson MI 39211

MILLS, EARL WAYNE, publisher; b. Valliant, Okla., July 18, 1912; s. James Walter and Annie Newman (Ward) M.; grad. high sch.; m. Ethel Alma Mason, Sept. 9, 1933; 1 son, Larry Earl. Printer, Valliant (Okla.) Tribune, 1928, pub., 1932-39; printer McCurtain Democrat, Idabel, Okla., 1928-32; pub. Boswell (Okla.) News, 1939-63; pub. Broken Bow (Okla.) News, 1964—; dir. First Nat. Bank, Broken Bow. Treas. Sch. Dist. 1, Boswell, 1940-56; jury commr., Choctaw County, Okla., 1949; sec. Choctaw County Election Bd., 1953-61; chmn. McCurtain County Election Bd., 1967—. Democrat. Methodist. Mason, Lion. Home: 304 S Wallace St Broken Bow OK 74728 Office: 108 Broadway Broken Bow OK 74728

MILLS, EDGAR F., YMCA exec.; b. Windsor, Ont., Can., Sept. 3, 1927; s. Harry and Helen (Lowry) M.; brought to U.S., 1938, naturalized, 1948; B.S., Manchester Coll., 1950; m. Mary Esther Brown, Aug. 21, 1949; children—Stewart Jon, Todd Nelson. Youth dir. Down River br. YMCA, Detroit, 1950-54, Northeastern br., 1954-58; exec. dir. Owosso, Mich., 1958-62; exec. dir., Amarillo, Tex., 1962—. Mem. Potter Randall Citizens Com. Served with AUS, 1946-47. Mem. United Good Neighbors of Amarillo. Kiwanian. Home: 1815 Virginia St Amarillo TX 79102 Office: 816 Van Buren St Amarillo TX 79101

MILLS, JOHN HENRY, state ofcl.; b. Florence County, S.C., Jan. 24, 1913; s. W.N. and Victoria (Jones) M.; m. Josie Blackmon, Apr. 21, 1934. With S.C. Hwy. Patrol, 1937-42; mem. S.C. Ho. of Reps., 1943-45, sgt.-at-arms, 1945-66; now comptroller gen., S.C. Served with USCGR, 1942-44. Office: Hampton Office Bldg Columbia SC 29402*

MILLS, JOHN MICHAEL, social worker; b. Ranger, Tex., Oct. 8,, 1937; s. Onos Roland and Marie (Jones) M.; student Arlington State Jr. Coll., 1956-58; B.A., U. Tex., 1961; M.S.W., Tulane U., 1965; m. Suellen Speer Mills, May 30, 1964; children—Scott Allen, Heather. Psychiat. social worker Oaks Unit Brown Sch., Austin, Tex., 1965-69, social work supr., 1968-69; dir. Settlement Club Home, Austin, 1969-71; dir. Abilene (Tex.) Youth Center, dir. Abilene Clin. Mgmt., Inc., 1971—. Field instr. Worden Sch. Social Work, San Antonio, 1967-69. Served with Med. Service Corps, AUS, 1961-63. Mem. Nat. Assn. Social Workers (exec. com. Austin area chpt. 1969-70), Acad. Certified Social Workers, Am. Orthopsychiat. Assn. Baptist (deacon). Home: 2209 Shoreline Dr Abilene TX 79602 Office: 4225 Poplar St Abilene TX 79605

MILLS, JOHN PARDON, JR., state ofcl.; b. Binghamton, N.Y., Jan. 29, 1911; s. John Pardon and Maude (Brooker) M.; B.S. in Civil Engring., Va. Poly. Inst., 1936; m. Lena Reaves, Apr. 15, 1938; children—Gerald, Dennett. With Va. Dept. Hwys., Richmond, 1936—, asst. traffic and planning engr., 1950-52, state traffic and planning engr., 1952-71, state traffic and safety engr., 1971—; mem. No. Va. Transp. Commn., 1965—, Va. Hwy. Research Bd., 1952—. Registered profl. engr., Va. Mem. Inst. Traffic Engrs. Home: 7614 N Pinehill Dr Richmond VA 23228 Office: 1221 E Broad St Richmond VA 23219

MILLS, LEWIS BENSON, basketball coach; b. Roanoke, Va., Feb. 5, 1937; s. Robert Herbert and Daisy M.; B.S., Va. Poly. Inst., 1960; m. Diann Rierson, July 30, 1959; children—Carrie, Scott. Asst. freshman basketball coach Va. Poly. Inst., Blacksburg, 1960; head football coach, head basketball coach, athletic dir. Roanoke Cath. High Sch. (Va.), 1961-62; freshman basketball coach, U. Richmond (Va.), 1962-63, head basketball coach, 1963—. Office: U Richmond Richmond VA 23173

MILLS, MARY LEE, nurse. Nurse cons. Office Community Health Service, Dept. Health, Edn. and Welfare, Washington. Recipient Distinguished Service award Dept. Health, Edn. and Welfare, 1971; Rockefeller Pub. Service award, 1971. Address: 7107 9th St NW Washington DC 20012*

MILLS, MAUBERT R., lawyer; b. Madison County, Ky., Nov. 6, 1925; A.B., U. Ky., 1948, LL.B., 1950. Admitted to Ky. bar, 1950, since practiced in Madisonville. Mem. Gov.'s Criminal Procedure Com., 1958-62; chmn. Gov.'s Task Force on Corrections, 1963; chmn. Gov.'s Task Force on Criminal Justice, 1964-66. Mem. Am., Ky. (gov. 1957-69, pres. 1969-70), Hopkins County bar assns., Commonwealth Attys. Assn. (pres. 1963). Office: Madisonville KY 42431*

MILLS, ROBERT LEE, coll pres.; b. Erlanger, Ky., Nov. 13, 1916; s. John Clifford and Dixie Lee (Morris) M.; A.B. in Math. and Physics, U. Ky., 1938, M.A. in Ednl. Adminstrn., 1941, Ed.D., 1951; m. Mildred Sizer, June 24, 1942; children—Robert Lee, Dixie Louise, Barbara Jean. Tchr., Covington (Ky.) Pub. Schs., 1938-41; head hydraulics br. Air Force Tech. Sch., Lincoln, Neb., 1942-44; mem. supervisory staff electromagnetic plant, Oak Ridge, 1944-48; research asst. U. Ky., 1948-51, dean admissions, registrar, 1954-57; dir. research, head bur. adminstrn. and finance Ky. Dept. Edn., 1951-54; chmn. dept. ednl. adminstrn. U. Tex., 1957-59; pres. Georgetown (Ky.) Coll., 1959—. Exec. sec. Ky. Adv. Commn. Ednl. Policy 1952-54; v.p. Ky. Assn. Colls. and Secondary Schs., 1962-63, mem. exec. com., 1959-64, pres., 1963-64; chmn. exec. com. Ky. Ind. Coll. Found.; mem. Ky. Commn. on Higher Edn., 1967—; mem. Ky. Govt. Council, 1968—; adviser Tex. Assn. Sch. Bds., 1957-59; cons. Pres. Com. White House Conf. Edn., 1955; mem. Ky. Devel. Council, 1961—. Mem. Nat., Ky. edn. assns., Newcomen Soc., So. Assn. Baptist Colls. (pres. 1965-66), Baptist World Alliance (chmn. mens dept. 1965—), Kappa Delta Pi, Phi Delta Kappa, Phi Kappa Tau. Democrat. Baptist. Kiwanian. Contbr. articles to profl. jours. Home: 444 E Main St Georgetown KY

MILLS, WILBUR D(AIGH), congressman; b. Kensett, Ark., May 24, 1909; s. Ardra Pickens and Abbie Lois (Daigh) M.; ed. Hendrix Coll., Harvard Law Sch.; m. Clarine Billingsley, May 27, 1934 children—Martha Sue, Rebecca Ann. Admitted to Ark. bar, 1933, began practice in Searcy. County and probate judge, White County, 1934-38; cashier Bank of Kensett, 1934-35; mem. 76th to 92d Congresses, 2d Ark. Dist., Chmn. House Ways and Means Com. Democrat. Methodist. Mason (33 deg.). Home: Kensett AR 72082 Office: Searcy AR 72143 also Little Rock AR 72203

MILLS, WILLIAM ANDREW, accountant; b. nr. Sandersville, Ga., Apr. 7, 1910; s. Oscar L. and Willie Mae (Griffin) M.; B.S. in Commerce, U. Ga., 1934; m. Ruth H. Waters, Aug. 31, 1940. Staff accountant M.H. Barnes & Co., C.P.A.'s, Savannah, Ga., 1934-43; partner Barnes, Askew, Mills & Co., C.P.A.'s, Savannah, 1947-61, Haskins & Sells, pub. accountants, Savannah, 1961—. Served to capt. AUS, 1943-46, C.P.A., Ga., La., N.C. Mem. Am. Inst. C.P.A.'s, Ga. Soc. C.P.A.'s, Beta Gamma Sigma, Phi Kappa Phi, Beta Alpha Psi. Kiwanian. Home: 802 E 41st St Savannah GA 31402 Office: 1st Fed Bldg Savannah GA 31402

MILLS, WILLIAM HAROLD, gen. contractor; b. Birmingham, Ala., Feb. 19, 1911; s. Charles W. and Mary (Parker) M.; student Woodberry Forest Sch. (Va.), 1928-29, U. Fla., 1929-30; B.S. in Civil Engring., Mass. Inst. Tech., 1934; m. Helen D. Cooper, Nov. 16, 1963; children—William Harold, Susan Ann, Caroline Bridget, Mary Danforth. Partner, Clarson & Mills, St. Petersburg, Fla., 1935-46; pres., chief exec. officer Mills & Jones Constrn. Co., 1946—; dir. St. Louis Nat. Baseball Club, Inc., First Nat. Bank, St. Petersburg, Gen. Telephone Co. Fla., First St. Petersburg Service Corp., Founders Life Assurance Co. Mem. vis. com. dept. civil engring. Mass. Inst. Tech. Mem. Fla. Council 100, St. Petersburg Com. 100, Newcomen Soc., Tampa Horse Show Assn., Greater St. Petersburg C. of C. (past pres.), Suncoasters, Delta Tau Delta. Episcopalian. Clubs: St. Petersburg Yacht, Bath, Dragon, Lakewood Country; Racquet (Miami, Fla.); Pasadena Country. Home: 901 40th Av N St Petersburg FL 33703 Office: PO Box 1257 St Petersburg FL 33731

MILLS, WILLIAM HAROLD, JR., bldg. exec.; b. St. Petersburg, Fla., July 24, 1939; s. William Harold and Caroline (Bonfoey) M.; B.C.E., U. Fla., 1961; m. Sylvia Carol Ludwig, Mar. 2, 1962; children—William Harold III, Robert Michael, Leslie Ann. Vice pres. bus. devel. Mills & Jones Constrn. Co., St. Petersburg, 1964-68; v.p. Wellington Corp., Atlanta, 1968-71; v.p. Mills & Jones Constrn. Co., 1971—. Chmn. blue ribbon zoning com., City St. Petersburg, 1965-68; mem. Tampa Bay Aviation Adv. Com., 1967-68. Bd. dirs. United Fund, Pinellas County, 1966-68. Served to lt. (j.g.) USPHS, 1962-64. Mem. St. Petersburg C. of C., Am. Soc. C.E., Nat. Soc. Profl. Engrs., Mensa, Sigma Alpha Epsilon. Democrat. Episcopalian. Clubs: St. Petersburg Yacht, Dragon (St. Petersburg); Racquet (Miami, Fla.). Home: 220 Maron St NE St Petersburg FL 33704 Office: PO Box 1257 St Petersburg FL 33731

MILLSAPS, FRED RAY, banker; b. Blue Ridge, Ga., Apr. 30, 1929; s. Samuel Hunter and Ora Lee (Bradshaw) M.; A.B., Emory U., 1951; postgrad. U. Wis., 1958, Harvard Bus. Sch. Mgmt. Devel. Program, 1962; m. Audrey Margaret Hopkins, June 22, 1957; children—Judith Gail, Stephen Hunter, Walter Scott. Auditor, Fed. Res. Bank, Atlanta, 1953-58, dept. mgr., 1958-61, asst. cashier, 1962-63, asst. v.p., New Orleans br., 1964-65, v.p., Atlanta, 1965; financial v.p. Fla. Power & Light Co., Miami, 1965-69; pres., dir. First Nat. Bank Ft. Lauderdale (Fla.), Consol. Bankshares of Fla., Inc.; vice chmn., dir. Guaranty 1st Nat. Bank Ft. Lauderdale; vice chmn. Plantation First Nat. Bank (Fla.); dir. Ocean 1st Nat. Bank, Ft. Lauderdale; vice chmn., dir. Security 1st Nat. Bank, Ft. Lauderdale, Indsl. Devel. Corp., Orlando, Fla. Bd. dirs. Sta. WPBT-TV, community TV, Miami; vice chmn.; trustee Fla. So. Coll. Served with CIC, AUS, 1951-53. Mem. Econ. Soc. South Fla. (dir.), Fla. Assn. Registered Bank Holding Cos. (dir.). Methodist. Rotarian. Clubs: Lauderdale Yacht, Coral Ridge Country. Home: 2665 NE 37th Dr Ft Lauderdale FL 33308 Office: 1 Financial Plaza Ft Lauderdale FL 33394

MILLSAPS, LUTHER LEE, telephone co. exec.; b. West Point, Miss., Oct. 14, 1926; s. Hiram and Evie (Ellis) M.; student spl. courses U. Miss., Emory U.; m. Lucile Loreta Curtis, Nov. 8, 1949; 1 dau., Loreta. With S. Central Bell Telephone Co., Tupelo, Miss., 1947—, comml. supr., 1969—. Pres. 4-H Adv. Council, Aberdeen, Miss., 1965, life mem. 4-H Honor Club; pres. Rotary Kidney Found., 1972. Served with AUS, 1945-46.Recipient awards including Aberdeen Rotarian of Year award, 1967. Mem. Miss. Econ. Council. Methodist (conf. and dist. dir. lay speaking, vice chmn. conf. pub. com. 1970—). Mason (33 deg., K.T., Shriner), Rotarian (pres. 1966, chmn. dist. extension com. 1969-70). Clubs: 120, Civitan (pres. 1962). Home: 1623 Patterson St Tupelo MS 38801 Office: 330 Jefferson St Tupelo MS 38801

MILNE, DOUGLAS BISSET, food co. exec.; b. The Dalles, Ore., July 9, 1915; s. John J. and Mary (Thompson) M.; B.S., U. Ore., 1938, B.B.A., 1938; m. Betty Lucille Fagerland, Oct. 4, 1941; children—Douglas John, Mary Susan, Jack Fagerland. Salesman, Closset & Devers Coffee Co., Portland, Ore., 1938-42; owner, pres. Doug Milne Co., Inc., Jacksonville, Fla., 1946—; dir. Five Points Guaranty Bank, Jacksonville. Chmn. bd. dirs. YMCA, Jacksonville Univ. Athletic Assn. Served with inf., AUS, 1942-46. Mem. Phi Delta Theta. Elk, Rotarian. Home: 3632 Pine St Jacksonville FL 32205 Office: 1357 W Beaver St Jacksonville FL 32209

MILNER, CHARLES FREMONT, univ. adminstr.; b. Leesburg, O., Aug. 18, 1909; s. Fremont Beverly and Ella Margaret (Walker) M.; student Earlham Coll., 1926-27; B.A., Guilford Coll., 1933; M.A., U. N.C., 1941; m. Eloyse Sargent Postlethwaite, Aug. 21, 1936 (dec. Apr. 1958); children—Charles Fremont, Beverly, Clyde A. II; m. 2d, Evelyn Ogburn Petway Mowery, June 12, 1959. Tchr. sci. high sch., 1933-36, Central Jr. High Sch., Greensboro, N.C., 1936-37; head bur. visual instrn. U. N.C., Chapel Hill, 1937-42, asso. dir. extension div., 1945-56, acting dir., 1956-59, dir., 1959—. Vis. instr. visual edn. Clemson Coll., summer 1939; cons. audiovisual program U.S. War Dept., Japan, 1948; vis. prof. U. Teheran; U.S. Dept. of State cons. to Ministry of Edn., Iran, 1952-53. Sec. adv. conf. com. off-campus services N.C. Bd. Higher Edn., 1960—; mem. Chapel Hill Sch. Bd., 1955-61; chmn. adv. com. N.C. Recreation Commn., 1957-63. Served with USNR, 1942-45, comdr. Res. Mem. Nat. Univ. Extension Assn. (pres. 1966-67), Guilford Coll. Alumni Assn. (v.p. 1961). Democrat. Mem. Soc. of Friends. Kiwanian (pres. Chapel Hill 1949). Home: 8 Woodhaven Rd Chapel Hill NC 27514

MILTON, DIXIE TYLER, librarian; b. Boston, Aug. 17, 1910; d. John William and Emma Ray (Tyler) Milton; B.S., Tex. State Coll for Women, 1941, B.S. in L.S., 1952. Librarian, Garden City High Sch. Library 1940-41, Waco (Tex.) Army Air Force Library, 1942-46, Waco Pub. Library, 1947-49, Mo. State Library, Jefferson City, Baylor U. Library, Waco, 1950-53; librarian Masonic Grand Lodge Library, Waco, 1953—. Cons. librarian Lee Lockwood Library and Mus., Waco. Mem. A.L.A., Spl. Libraries Assn. Republican. Baptist. Home: 4109 Sherry Lane Waco TX 76711 Office: 715 Columbus St Waco TX 76703

MILTON, LORIMER D., banker; b. Washington, 1899; ed. Brown U., 1920. Pres., Citizens Trust Co., Atlanta; partner Yates & Milton; chmn., treas. Southeastern Fidelity Fire Ins. Co.; pres. Citizens Trust Co. Chmn. bd. trustees Howard U. Home: 529 Waterford Rd NW Atlanta GA 30303 Office: 212 Auburn Av NE Atlanta GA 30303*

MILWIT, SANFORD CHARLES, orgn. exec.; b. Vancouver, Wash., Dec. 1, 1939; s. Herbert H. and Ida (Nusbaum) M.; B.S., U. Md., 1963; postgrad. course, George Washington U., 1968, Washington U., 1972; m. Ada Josephine Gritz, Aug. 11, 1963; children—Daniel, Kyle. Spl. asst. S.M., Vinocour, pub. relations cons., Washington, 1962-63; advt. mgr., asst. to pub. relations dir. Am. Automobile Assn., Washington, 1963-65; dir. pub. relations D.C. div. Am. Cancer Soc., 1965-69, dir. pub. relations and pub. edn., 1969—. Pub. relations chmn. Nat. Diabetic Detection Week Met. D.C. Area, 1964. Mem. Georgetown Village Civic Assn., 1965-67; vol. bowling instr. U. Md. Named Best Athlete of Year, Alpha Epsilon Pi, 1961-62; recipient award of merit Am. Diabetes Assn., 1965; Distinguished Service citation Nat. Assn. and Council Bus. Schs., 1966. Mem. Pub. Relations Soc. Am., D.C. Pub. Health Assn., Advt. Club Met. Washington, Sigma Delta Chi, Tau Mu Epsilon, Alpha Epsilon Pi. Prepared spl. project for Am. Cancer Soc. Home: 1909 Snowdrop Lane Silver Spring MD 20906 Office: 1825 Connecticut Av NW Washington DC 20009

MIMS, LAMBERT CARTER, city ofcl.; b. Uriah, Ala., Apr. 20, 1930; s. Jeff and Carrie (Lambert) M.; grad. high sch.; m. Reecie Philips, Aug. 17, 1946; children—Dale, Danny. Engaged in retail and wholesale food bus., 1949-65; owner, Mims Brokerage Co., Mobile, Ala., 1958-70; pub. works commr., City Mobile, 1965-68, 69—. Mayor, City Mobile, 1968-69, 72—. Chmn. Sts. and Hwys. Com., Ala. League Municipalities, 1966-68, now chmn. Human Resources Com.; mem. Human Resources Com. Nat. League Cities. Trustee Judson Coll., Marion, Ala. Named Mobile's Most Outstanding Young Man, 1965. Mem. Ala. Pub. Works Assn. (pres. 1969-70, 72—). Baptist (deacon; chmn. bd. 1950-65; 1st v.p. Ala. Bapt. State Conv. 1969-70, 70-71; mem. Mobile Camp Gideons, pres. 1962-65; mem. christian businessmen's com. internat. 1965-70; bd. dirs. Mobile rescue mission). Kiwanian. Author: For Christ and Country, 1969.Address: PO Box 1827 Mobile AL 36601

MIMS, NANCY CROCKETT (MRS. MATTHEW HANSFORD MIMS), editor, librarian; b. Stony Point, Tenn., Nov. 6, 1909; d. Stuart Raper and Marie Langley (Ramsey) Crockett; A.B., Agnes Scott Coll., 1931; postgrad. Grensboro Coll. for Women, 1932; m. Charles R. McCarty, Dec. 27, 1933 (dec. Mar. 1936); m. 2d, Matthew Hansford Mims, Feb. 21, 1940; children—Julian Landrum III, Matthew Hansford, Marie Crockett. Tchr. English dept. Waynesville (N.C.) High Sch., 1931-33, Wilkes County (Ga.) pub. schs., 1935-37, Edgefield High Sch., 1937-39, Franklin (N.C.) High Sch., 1939-40; editor Edgefield Advertiser, county weekly, 1942-45, Johnston Herald, 1942-45, Palmetto White Ribbon, W.C.T.U. publ., 1945—; corr., feature writer Augusta (Ga.) Chronicle, Augusta Herald, 1949—, Columbia (S.C.) Record, 1949-59; head librarian Edgefield County Aiken-Barnwell-Edgefield Regional Library, 1958—. Dir. Civic League Courtesy Center, 1967—. S.C. exec. dir. Nat. Library Week, 1967; Edgefield County chmn. Tricenteniary. Chmn. bd. trustees D.A. Tompkins Meml. library, 1943—; Edgefield County chmn. White House Conf. on Children and Youth, 1960. Vice chmn. County Democratic Conv., 1956. Recipient spl. grant Porter Fleming Found., 1964, Community Leader of Am. award, 1968. Mem. Edgefield County Hist. Soc. (sec. 1960—), S.C. Library Assn. (sec. pub. library sect. 1960-61), Caroliniana Soc., Clan Campbell Am., D.A.R. (chpt. regent 1964-66), Daus. Colonial Wars, Daus. Am. Colonists, Nat. Soc. So. Dames Am., U. Archives Inst. Contbr. to Chronicle Sunday Mag., 1953-55. Home: 610 Buncombe St Edgefield SC 29824

MIMS, ROBERT BRADY, investment and ins. co. exec.; b. Jackson, Miss., June 6, 1935; s. Robert P. and Edith (Brady) M.; B.A., Millsaps Coll., 1957; m. Susan Medley, Dec. 27, 1957; children—Melissa M., Robert D. Agt., Mut. Benefit Life Ins. Co., Newark, 1957-60, asst. dir. tng., 1960-62, Miss. mgr., 1962-69; v.p., regional dir. Financial Service Corp., Jackson, Miss., 1969—, also dir. Served with AUS, 1957-58. Mem. Jackson Assn. Life Underwriters (past pres.), Miss. Gen. Agts. and Mgrs. Assn. (past pres.), Jackson C. of C., C.L.U.'s (pres. Miss. chpt. 1971-72), Million Dollar Round Table (life). Home: 4321 N Honeysuckle Lane Jackson MS 39206 Office: 880 Lakeland Dr Jackson MS 39216

MIMS, SAMUEL STEWART, chem. co. exec.; b. Easley, S.C., Apr. 10, 1931; s. Samuel Stewart and Frances Elizabeth (Perry) M.; student Clemson Coll., 1948-50; B.S., La. State U., 1952, Ph.D., 1958; m. Inka Ann Fredotovich, Aug. 25, 1956; children—Tania, Sammy, Inka, Benjamin. Project engr. Thiokol Chem. Corp., Huntsville, Ala., 1954-55; sect. leader research and devel. R. J. Reynolds Tobacco Co., Winston-Salem, N.C., 1958-66; asst. dir. research and devel. El Paso Products Co., Odessa, Tex., 1966—. Served with U.S. Army, 1952-54. Mem. Am. Chem. Soc. Contbr. articles to profl. jours. Patentee in field. Home: 2831 Teakwood St Odessa TX 79760 Office: PO Box 3986 Odessa TX 79760

MIMS, THOMAS JEROME, ins. co. exec.; b. Sumter, S.C., Dec. 12, 1899; s. Lazarus and Sarah Rebecca (White) M.; A.B., Furman U., 1921; m. Valma Gillespie, Dec. 14, 1926; children—Thomas Jerome, George Franklin. Apprentice, Recording & Statis. Corp. of N.Y., Detroit, 1921, N.Y.C., 1921-22, asst. mgr., Phila., 1922-25, mgr., Indpls., 1925-27, Boston, 1927-29; salesman Burroughs Adding Machine Co., Detroit, Boston, 1929-31; ins. spl. agt. State N.J., also Morley Gen. Agy., Camden, N.J., 1931-32; mgr. William R. Timmons Agy., Greenville, S.C., 1933—; v.p., sec., dir. Canal Ins. Co., Greenville, 1942-48, pres., treas., dir., 1948—; v.p. Century-Lincoln Mercury, Inc. Gov. Internat. Ins. Seminar. Bus. mgr. Greenville Little Theater, 1951-53, 64-66, council, 1951-68, v.p., 1956-57, pres., 1957-58; pres. Rotary Charities, Inc., 1964-65; mem. adv. bd. S.C. Safety Council, 1969-70, pres., 1970-71. Bd. dirs. United Fund Greenville; vice-chmn. Found. Modern Liquor Regulations and Control; adv. council Furman U. Named Boss of Yr., Greenville Jr. C. of C., 1964, Greenville Assn. Ins. Women, 1966. Mem. Nat., S.C., Greenville (past pres.) assns. ins. agts., S.C. Motor Transp. Assn. (chmn. ins. com. 1951-63), S.C., U.S. (membership com. 1961-62, 64-68, ins. co. 1959-61, 63-65), Greenville (chmn. community relations com. 1964-68, dir. 1969-72) chambers commerce, Am. Mgmt. Assn., A.I.M. (fellow pres.'s council), Truck and Heavy Equipment Claims Council (charter mem., chmn. membership com.), Assn. S.C. Property and Casualty Ins. Cos. (pres. 1962-63, mem. exec. com. 1963-68), Internat. Platform Assn., Presidents Assn., Am. Acad.

Polit. and Social Sci. Baptist (mem. finance com.) Elk, Rotarian (dir. Greenville 1957-58, pres. 1963-64, v.p. 1964-65). Clubs: Touchdown (charter mem.; pres. 1963-64), Greenville City (pres. 1965, dir. 1964, chmn. bd. dirs., 1966-67), Poinsett, Forum (Greenville): Palmetto (Columbia, S.C.). Home: Knollwood Dr Route 6 Greenville SC 29602 Office: 417 E North St Greenville SC 29602

MINEAR, LEON PIERSON, govt. ofcl.; b. San Antonio, Mar. 20, 1915; s. Joseph H. and Monnie M. (Guin) M.; A.B. cum laude, San Francisco State Coll., 1938, M.A., 1941; Ed.D., Stanford, 1947; m. Dolores F. Goetzee, Aug. 20, 1939; 1 son, Roger Leon. Tchr. pub. jr. and sr. high schs., Oakland, Cal., 1938-42; flight radio officer Pan Am. World Airways, 1942-43, sr. communications rep. South Pacific, 1944, asst. supt. tng., 1944, supt. tng., 1945-46; vice prin. Carmel High Sch., Carmel-by-the-Sea, Cal., 1946-47; asst. to dean Denver Jr. Coll., 1947-49; pres. Stockton (Cal.) Jr. Coll., 1949-52; prin. Benson Poly. Sch., 1952-61; supt. pub. instrn. Ore., Salem, 1961-68; dir. vocational-tech. edn. U.S. Office Edn., Washington, 1968—, research cons., 1962-68. Chmn. Nat. Task Force on Vocational-Tech. Edn., Edn. Commn. of States; dir. study Ore. ednl. improvements Ford Found., 1962-66; chmn. Higher Edn. Coordinating Council, 1963, 65; adviser Ednl. Policies Commn.; sec. gov.'s adv. council Ore. juvenile instns., 1955-61; chmn. Gov.'s Policy Planning Commn. for Human Resources, Ore. Water Resources Bd., Ore. Interagy. Legislative Com. on Migratory Labor, 1961-64, Ore. Outdoor Edn. Comm, Ore. SSS Appeals Bd., 1958-65; chmn. Portland (Ore.) Met. Youth Commn., 1960-61; mem. White House Com. Aging, 1962, Pres.'s Com. Vocational Edn., 1962, Ore. chmn., mem. nat. bd. dirs.; mem. U.S. Armed Forces adv. com., 1959-60; dir. study state schs. of adminstrn. Carnegie Found. Condr., Monteray Regional Symphony, 1946-47, Denver Community Symphony, 1947. Bd. dirs. Save the Children Fedn., Stanford U., 1964—, Ore. Mus. Sci. and Industry, 1961—, Monteray County Symphony Assn., 1946, Denver Businessmen's Symphony Assn., pres., 1947-49. Mem. Portland High Sch. Prins. Assn. (pres. 1956-57), Salem C. of C. (edn. com.), Am. Assn. Sch. Adminstrs., N.E.A., Ore. Edn. Assn., Cal. Tchrs. Assn., Ore. Sch. Activities Assn. (dir.), Council Chief State Sch. Officers, Ore. Hist. Soc., Phi Delta Kappa, Kappa Delta Pi, Sigma Alpha Eta. Co-author ednl. texts. Contbr. articles to ednl. jours. Home: 4241 Alderbrook Av Salem OR 97302 Office: Public Service Bldg Salem OR 97302

MINER, MARYALICE FAIRBANK (MRS. JOHN H. K. MINER), civic leader; b. Ft. Sam Houston, Tex., Apr. 30, 1925; d. Leigh Cole and May (Romig) Fairbank; student Washington Conservatory Music, 1941-42; A.A., Endicott Jr. Coll., 1945; m. John Hanson Kennard Miner, June 5, 1946; children—David Christopher, Steven Kennard, John Hanson Fairbank, Merileigh Fairbank. Vol. coach swimming Pascagoula (Miss.) Recreation Dept., 1955-65; co-founder Aquatic Club of Jackson County, Pascagoula, 1965, sec., 1965—; leader sr. scouts Girl Scouts U.S.A., 1953-56; den mother Cub Scouts Am., 1956-60; mem. Pasagoula Civic Guild, 1953—, v.p., 1966-67; dir. PasPoint Little Theatre, 1955—, sec., 1964-67, dir., drama coach jr. players, 1960; dir. aquatics, St. Andrews-on-Gulf, Ocean Springs, Miss.; ofcl. hostess for Pascagoula, Mardi Gras, 1970; founder, pres. Marmin Enterprises. Recipient Keys to City, Baton Rouge, 1964, New Orleans, 1964; commendatory resolution Pascagoula City Council, 1968. Mem. Am., Nat. Inter-scholastic swimming coaches assns., Internat. Platform Assn., Amateur Athletic Union (chmn. So. women's swimming com. 1964—). Author: Dolly the Dolphin's Do's and Don't's for Swimming. Home: 103 St Andrews Dr St Andrews-on-the-Gulf Ocean Springs MS 39564 Office: 1810 Government St Ocean Springs MS 39564

MINGE, JERRY LEE, lawyer; b. Rome, Ga., Sept. 23, 1934; s. Willie Lee and Mary (Moore) M.; B.B.A., U. Ga., 1959, LL.B., 1959; m. Carol Bland, Mar. 27, 1958; children—Mary Angela, Jennifer Bland, Anne Marquerite. Admitted to Ga. bar, 1958; partner Scoggin & Minge, Attys., Rome, 1959-63, Hamilton, Anderson & Minge, Attys., Rome, 1963—; judge City Ct. of Floyd County, Ga., 1967-69. Mem. Ga. Ho. of Reps., 1965-67. Mem. Am., Ga., Rome (pres.) bar assns., Jr. C. of C. (past pres.), Phi Delta Phi, Sigma Nu. Baptist. Mason, Elk. Clubs: Coosa Country, Nine O'Clock Cotillion, Exchange. Home: 10 Saddle Mountain Rd Rome GA 30161 Office: PO Box 746 237 N 5th Av Rome GA 30161

MINGES, COYTE ROSCOE, dentist; b. Catawba, N.C., Nov. 5, 1912; s. Franklin Alexandria and Mittie Naome (Setzer) M.; student U. N.C., 1930-32; D.D.S., Med. Coll. Va., 1936; m. Jean Lewis, Feb. 5, 1952; children—Clyde, Franklin, Laura. Gen. practice dentistry, Rocky Mount, N.C., 1936—. Dir. First Union Bank, Rocky Mount. Mem. Nash County (N.C.) Bd. Health, 1959—. Served with AUS, 1942-47. Fellow Am. Coll. Dentists; mem. Am., N.C. dental assns., Am. Legion (past post comdr., dist. comdr.), N.C. Res. Officers Assn. (past pres.), Delta Sigma Delta. Democrat. Lutheran. Mason, Elk. Clubs: Civitan (past pres.), Benvenue County (both Rocky Mount). Home: 3305 Hawthorne Rd Rocky Mount NC 27801 Office: PO Box 192 Rocky Mount NC 27801

MINGIONE, ANN DISSINGER (MRS. DONALD LEO MINGIONE), clin. psychologist; b. Berwyn, Ill., Mar. 6, 1936; d. Clarence and Geneva (Hutton) Dissinger; B.A., DePauw U., 1958; M.A., U. N.C., 1961, Ph.D., 1961; m. Donald Leo Mingione, Jan. 16, 1964; 1 son, Daniel Jeffrey. Intern clin. psychology Inst. Living, Hartford, Conn., 1961-62; asst. prof. U. Hartford, 1962; clin. psychologist Guidance Clinic, Portsmouth, Va., 1962-64; practice clin. psychology, Portsmouth, 1964—. Cons. psychologist U.S. Naval Hosp., Portsmouth, 1964-66, Community Psychiat. Clinic, 1964-66. Saint Mary's Infant Home, Norfolk, 1968—, Catholic Family and Children's Service, Norfolk, Child and Family Service Agy., Portsmouth, 1969—. Bd. dirs. Kirk-Cone Rehab. Center, Chesapeake, Va. 1965-67. Served as lt. MSC USNR, 1963-65. Mem. Va., Am. psychol. assns., Soc. for Psychol. Study of Social Issues, Portsmouth Service League, Alpha Phi. Home: 2840 Meadow Wood Dr W Chesapeake VA 23321 Office: The Pass House Crawford at London Sts Portsmouth VA 23704

MINGIONE, DONALD LEO, physician; b. Paterson, N.J., Aug. 10, 1933; s. John R. and Mary (Brown) M.; M.D., Creighton U., 1957; m. Dorothy Ann Dissinger, Jan. 16, 1964; 1 son, Daniel Jeffery. Intern, also resident in medicine Med. Centre, Jersey City, N.J., 1957-59; fellow in psychiatry Inst. of Living, Hartford, Con., 1959-62; staff mem. Maryview Hosp., Portsmouth, pres. gen. med. staff, 1970; Portsmouth (Va.) Gen. Hosp., Norfolk (Va.) Gen., Louise Obici, Suffolk, Va., 1963—; gen. practice psychiatry, Portsmouth, Va., 1964—; clin. asst. psychiatry N.J. Coll. Medicine, 1958-59; asst. prof. U. Hartford, 1960-62; cons. Child and Family Service, Catholic Charities; cons. psychiatry USPHS Hosp., Norfolk, Va.; cons. child psychiatry St. Mary's Infant Hosp., Norfolk, Va.; cons. Suicide Prevention Center. Bd. dirs. Mental Health-Mental Retardation Bd., Portsmouth. Served as lt. comdr. USNR, 1962-64. Mem. Portsmouth Acad. Medicine, Soc. Psychol. Study of Social Issues, Neuropsychiat. Soc. Va., Am. Psychiat. Assn., Phi Rho Sigma. Elk, Kiwanian. Home: 2840 W Meadowwood Dr Chesapeake VA 23322 Office: The Pass House Crawford at London Sts Portsmouth VA 23704

MINICK, NORMAN R., lawyer; b. Shade Gap, Pa., Apr. 3, 1899; student Washington and Lee U., LL.B., Vanderbilt U., 1920. Admitted to Tenn. bar, 1920, since practiced in Nashville; partner firm Trabue, Minick, Sturdivant & Harbison. Mem. Am., Tenn., Nashville bar assns. Office: Life and Casualty Tower Nashville TN 37219*

MINIS, ABRAM, investment counselor; b. Savannah, Ga., Nov. 6, 1903; s. Abram and Mabel (Henry) M.; B.S. in Chemistry, Harvard, 1926, M.B.A., 1928; m. Florence Powell, Nov. 22, 1941 (dec. Dec. 1971); children—Robert P., Marguerite Ann (Mrs. Brian Colt Jerome), Henry H. With statist. dept. First Nat. Bank Boston, 1928-30; chmn. bd. Minis & Co., Inc., Savannah, Ga., 1931—; chmn. bd. Carson Chem. Co., Savannah, 1965—. Trustee, chmn. The Hodge Found., Inc., Savannah, 1962—; trustee Savannah Found., 1955—, Widener Coll., Chester, Pa., 1968—. Mem. Inst. Chartered Financial Analysts, So. Acad. Arts, Letters and Scis. (trustee), N.Y. Soc. Security Analysts. Home: 112 E 45th St Savannah GA 31405 Office: PO Box 8306 Savannah GA 31402

MINK, JOHN ROBERT, educator; b. Peru, Ill., Sept. 8, 1927; s. Monte Franklin and Marcella (White) M.; B.A., Ind. U., 1951, D.D.S. with honors, 1956, M.S. in Pedodontics, 1961; m. Barbara Joanne Merrill, June 21, 1952; children—Sarah, Teresa, Kathleen, Mary, James, Elizabeth. Instr. Ind. U., Indpls., 1957-60, asst. prof., 1960-62; dir. dental Clinic Handicapped Children, James Whitcomb Riley Hosp. for Children, Indpls., 1957-62; mem. faculty U. Ky., Lexington, 1962—, prof. pedodontics, 1966—. Cons. pedodontics USPHS, 1969-72, Am. Dental Assn., 1972—. Vice pres. Vols. Bur. Lexington, Ky., 1971-72. Served with AUS, 1946-47. Diplomate Am. Bd. Pedodontics. Fellow Am. Acad. Pedodontics, Internat. Coll. Dentists; mem. Am. Soc. Dentistry for Children (bd. dirs. 1969-72), Ky. Soc. Dentistry for Children (pres. 1967—), Am. Assn. Dental Schs., Internat. Assn. Dental Research, Delta Upsilon. Office: Coll Dentistry U Ky Lexington KY 40506 Home: 1944 Linstead Pl Lexington KY 40504

MINNET, JAMES FRANCIS, judge; b. Detroit, Dec. 25, 1913; s. Charles Joaquim and Rose (Goike) M.; student Lawrence Inst. Tech., 1935-36; LL.B., Columbus Sch. Law of Cath. U., 1939; LL.M., M.P.L., Southeastern U., 1940; student U. Mich., 1943-44, U. Miami, 1945, U. Colo., 1966; m. Rapheal M. Trapolino, Aug. 26, 1939; children—Linda Anne, James Francis, Rapheal Mary. Admitted to D.C. bar, 1939, Fla. bar, 1948; atty. examiner ICC, Washington, 1940-41, 45-49; materials analyst Gen. Motors Corp., Detroit, 1941-45; practice law, Ft. Lauderdale, Fla., 1949-65; sr. mem. Minnet, Allsworth, Doumar, Schuler & Elliott, 1952-65; judge Circuit Ct. for Broward County, Fla., 1965—. Dept. commr. Fla. Indsl. Commn., Ft. Lauderdale, 1956-61; U.S. commr., Ft. Lauderdale, 1962-65; spl. counsel City of Ft. Lauderdale, 1963-65. Mem. Am., Fed. bar assns., Fla. Bar, Bar Assn. D.C. Democrat. K.C., Elks. Club: Woodlands Country. Home: 5714 Bamboo Circle Fort Lauderdale FL 33313 Office: Broward County Ct House Fort Lauderdale FL 33301

MINNICK, ROBERT C., educator; b. Houston, Feb. 7, 1926; B.A., Johns Hopkins, 1950; A.M., Harvard, 1951, Ph.D. in Applied Math., 1953. Instr. applied math. Harvard, 1953-54, asst. prof., 1954-57; sr. physicist Burroughs Corp., 1957-60; sr. research engr. Stanford Research Inst., 1960-65; prof. elec. engring. Montant State U., from 1966; now prof. elec. engring. and computer sci. Rice U., Houston. Mem. I.E.E.E. Designer digital computer subsystems and systems, cellular logic components. Office: Dept Elec Engring Rice Univ Houston TX 77001*

MINNICK, WILLIAM DAVID, metal co. exec.; b. Boston, Pa., Oct. 30, 1924; s. Harry Atwater and Sarah Jane (Carnahan) M.; B.S., So. Meth. U., 1950; m. N. Jeanne Cole, Aug. 5, 1945; children—Susan Lynn (Mrs. Michael Downie), Barbara Jean. With A.O. Smith Corp., various locations, 1952—, sales mgr., Milw., 1962-68, dir. marketing Houston, 1968—. Served with AUS, 1943-46. Decorated Combat Infantryman Badge. Clubs: Houston Petroleum, Lakeside Country. Home: 1804 Stoney Brook St Houston TX 77042 Office: First City Nat Bank Bldg Houston TX 77002

MINOR, GEORGE RIDGWAY, surgeon, educator; b. Cannel City, Ky., Oct. 18, 1913; s. Hugh and Lillie (Faulkner) M.; B.S., U. Va., 1936, M.D., 1940; M.S., U. Mich., 1948. Intern U. Va. Med. Center, 1942-43; resident surgery, 1943-44, thoracic surgery U. Mich., 1944-45, instr., 1945-46, gen. surgery 1947-48; asst. prof. surgery, U. Ill., Chgo., 1948-49; practice medicine specializing in surgery U. Va. Hosp., Charlottesville, 1949—, 1949-53, asst. dean Sch. Medicine, 1963-71, prof. surgery, 1964—; on leave surg. cons., proj. surgery Project Hope, Tunisia 1972—. Diplomate Am. Bd. Surgery, Am. Bd. Thoracic Surgery. Mem. Albemarle County Med. Soc. (pres. 1967-68), Med. Soc. Va., A.C.S., Am. Thoracic Soc., Soc. Thoracic Surgeons, Am. Assn. Thoracic Surgery, So. Thoracic Surg. Soc., Va. Surg. Soc., Southeastern Surg. Congress, Soc. Internat. de Chirurgie. Home: Monroe Hill Charlottesville VA 22903 Office: Univ Va Hosp Charlottesville VA 22901

MINOR, JAMES ROLAND, elec. products co. exec.; b. Sulligent, Ala., Dec. 31, 1935; s. Noah R. and Louise (Dove) M.; B.A., Athens U., 1958; postgrad. Vanderbilt U. 1959; m. Patricia Ann Mitchell, June 5, 1955; children—Angela Diane, Richard Byron. Dist. scout exec. Boy Scouts Am., Huntsville, Ala., 1960-64; mgr. purchasing Cornelius Co., vending, Scottsboro, 1964-70; purchasing mgr. Fedders Corp., Decatur, 1970-72; asst. purchasing agt. Magic Chef Corp., Cleveland, Tenn., 1972—. Mem. dist. com. Tenn. Valley council Boy Scouts Am., 1960-71; exec. dir. United Givers Fund, Scottsboro, Ala., 1964-71. Mem. North Ala. Purchasing Mgrs. (pres. 1970-71, bd. dirs. 1967-70, dir. nat. affairs 1971-72). Club: Scottsboro Rifle (v.p. 1968-69). Home: 1501 20th St NW Cleveland TN 37311 Office: King Edward Av Cleveland TN 37311

MINOR, W.F., columnist New Orleans Times-Picayune. Office: 3800 Howard Av New Orleans LA 70140*

MINOR, WILLIAM HAROLD, machinery co. exec.; b. Roanoke, Mo., Jan. 19, 1928; s. Julius Harold and Sarah Virginia (Markland) M.; student Central Mo. State Coll., 1945, Brown U., 1945-46; B.S., U. Mo., 1950; m. Joan Garner, Feb. 3, 1950; children—Sandra Lynn, William Markland. Cons., Pate Engring. Co., Tulsa, 1950-56, Sverdrup & Parcel Engring. Co., St. Louis, 1956-58; engr. contracting Standard Industries, Tulsa, 1958-63; engr. Portland Cement Assn., Tulsa, 1963-68; v.p. sales CMI Corp., Oklahoma City, 1968—. Served with USNR, 1945-46. Registered profl. engr., Okla. Mem. Nat., Okla. socs. profl. engrs., Am. Mil. Engrs., Chi Epsilon. Home: 5900 Tiffany Circle Oklahoma City OK 73132 Office: Box 1985 Oklahoma City OK 73101

MINTER, JAMES CARL, banker; b. Thomasville, Ga., Sept. 10, 1906; s. John Arthur and Sarah (Tomlinson) M.; grad. high sch.; m. Miriam G. Garrison, Aug. 6, 1941; children—Sarah M., Timmerman Carl, John Gorham. With Bank of Thomasville, 1926-32; with Citizens Bank, Cairo, Ga., 1932—, pres., 1955—. Dir. S.W. Ga. Planning Commn., 1964-68, Ga. Municipal Assn., 1965-68; chmn. Grady County Hosp. Authority, 1953-63, Mayor pro-tem City of Cairo, 1958-68. Trustee Ga. Bapt. Children's Home, 1958-62; Norman Coll., 1968, Cairo High Sch., 1953—; bd. dirs. Grady County Recreation Commn., 1968—. Recipient U.S. Treasury award, 1941-45. Mem. C. of C. (pres. 1955). Democrat. Baptist (deacon). Kiwanian (pres. 1942), Elk, Mason. Club: Country (Cairo). Home: 540 S Broad St Cairo GA 31728 Office: PO Box 28 Cairo GA 31728

MINTER, RICHARD C., mcht., lawyer; b. Monticello, Ga., Apr. 28, 1922; s. Chester Lane and Bessie (Hardin) M.; LL.B., Mercer U., 1950; m. Elizabeth K. Thompson, Oct. 27, 1963; children—Wanda Faye Thompson (Mrs. Hamilton), Jay Wall Thompson. Admitted to Ga. bar, 1950, practiced law, Eastman, 1951; v.p. Stuckey's Inc., Eastman, 1951-57; sec., treas., dir. Pecan Shoppe of Dinwiddie, Fredericksburg, Va., 1957—. Served with USNR, 1942-46. Mem. Am., Ga. bar assns., Phi Alpha Delta, Kappa Sigma. Methodist. Lion, Mason (32 deg., Shriner). Home: PO Box 387 Eastman GA 31023

MINTZ, MORTON ABNER, newspaper reporter; b. Ann Arbor, Mich., Jan. 26, 1922; s. William and Sarah (Solomon) M.; A.B. in Econs., U. Mich., 1943; m. Anita Inez Franz, Aug. 30, 1946; children—Margaret Ruth, Elizabeth Diane, Roberta Joan, Daniel Robert. Reporter, St. Louis Star-Times, 1946-50; reporter, asst. city editor St. Louis Globe-Democrat, 1951-58; reporter Washington Post, 1958—. Recipient Heywood Broun, Raymond Clapper, George Polk Meml. awards for journalism, 1962. Author: The Therapeutic Nightmare, 1965; Nightmare, 1965; By Prescription Only, 1967; (with Jerry S. Cohen) America, Inc., 1971. Home: 3022 Macomb St NW Washington DC 20008 Office: 1515 L St NW Washington DC 20005

MIRANDA, FAUSTO R., lawyer; b. Mexico City, Mexico, June 7, 1910; ed. Tex. Coll. Mines, French Coll. Mexico; LL.B., U. Mexico, 1936; postgrad. Harvard. Admitted to Mexican bar, 1935, since practiced in Mexico City; mem. firm Miranda Santamarina Steta. Office: Paseo de la Reforma 76 Mexico City Mexico*

MIRES, A(LBERT) HAROLD, accounting firm exec.; b. Kaplan, La., Jan. 15, 1928; s. Ivy and Rose (Bourque) M.; student U. Southwestern La., 1948-50; m. Rosie Mae Pellesier, Nov. 26, 1953. Accountant, office mgr. Vinton Co-Op Drier, Inc. (La.) 1950-57; pvt. practice accounting, Sulphur, La., 1957—; sr. partner Mires & Broussard, C.P.A.'s, Sulphur, 1967—. Lectr. McNeese State Coll., Lake Charles, La., 1967; mem. S.W. La. Estate Planning Council. Exec. bd. Calcasieu area council, Boy Scouts Am., 1969—, dist. chmn., 1972—. Served with USNR, 1946-48. C.P.A., La. Mem. Am. Inst. C.P.A.'s. La. Soc. C.P.A.'s, West Calcasieu Assn. Commerce (dir.). Rotarian (pres.). Office: 126 W Napoleon St PO Drawer W Sulphur LA 70663

MIRO CARDONA, JOSE, Cuban polit. leader; b. Havana, Cuba, 1902; s. Jose Miro Argenter and Luz Cardona de Miro; grad. U. Havana Law Sch.; m. 2 sons. Practiced in Havana, 1938-58, 59-60, specializing in criminal law; prof. penal law U. Havana, to 1960, also dean Law Sch. Organized Cuban exile group to protest dictatorship of Batista, 1958; prime minister Castro govt. of Cuba, 1959; Cuban ambassador to Spain. 1960; pres. Cuban Revolutionary Council, opposition to Cuban premier, 1961-63. Mem. Cuban Coll. Lawyers (pres.), Soc. Friends of Republic, Group Civic Instns. Home: 1034 Michigan Av Miami Beach FL 33139*

MISCHEL, PHILIP BURTON, chem. co. exec.; b. N.Y.C., Sept. 19, 1935; s. Stephen and Dorothy (Schwam) M.; B.S. in Chemistry, Coll. City N.Y., 1957; postgrad. U. Buffalo, 1958-61; m. Ann Marlene Cohen, June 15, 1958; children—Russell, Jeffrey, Andrea. Supr. prodn. plastics div. Allied Chem. Corp., Buffalo, 1957-63; mgr. marketing Petrochems. Co., Inc., Ft. Worth, 1963—. Bd. dirs. Cub Scouts Am., Ft. Worth, 1971-72; leader Civic Music Assn., Ft. Worth, 1971-72. Mem. Am. Assn. Textile Chemists and Colorists, So. Agrl. Chemists Assn., Am. Chem. Soc., Chem. Splty. Mfrs., Fertilizer Roundtable Discussion Group. K.P. Club: Ft. Worth Advertising (instr. sales and marketing execs. marketing seminars courses 1970—). Patentee in field. Office: Petrochems Co Box 2199 Ft Worth TX 76101

MISCHO, OTHMER JOSEPH, labor union exec.; b. Mt. Calvary, Wis., Nov. 20, 1904; s. Frank and Mary (Harter) M.; student U. Wis., 1924-27; B.Ed., Milw. State Tchrs. Coll., 1932; m. Ivy Mae Rymer, Aug. 14, 1932; children—Ivan, Dennis, Jay, Alana. Mem. Amalgamated Transit Union, 1933—, internat. v.p., 1941-46, internat. sec.-treas., 1946—. Home: 4910 River Rd Washington DC 20016 Office: 5025 Wisconsin Av NW Washington DC 20016

MISHELEVICH, DAVID JACOB, computer center exec., physician; b. Pitts., Jan., 1942; s. Benjamin and Sarah (Bachrach) M.; B.S., U. Pitts., 1962; M.D. (Henry Strong Denison scholar), Johns Hopkins, 1966, Ph.D. in Biomed. Engring., 1970; m. Elaine Carol Grumer, Aug. 18, 1963. Post-sophomore research fellow Johns Hopkins Sch. Medicine, 1964-65; intern Balt. City Hosps., 1966-67; sr. asst. surgeon USPHS, 1967-68, surgeon, 1968-69; staff asso. NIH, Bethesda, Md., 1967-69; NIH spl. fellow in biomed. engring. and medicine Johns Hopkins Sch. Medicine, 1969-71; v.p. Nat. Ednl. Cons., Inc., Balt., 1970-71, chief computing and profl. records div., 1970-72, exec. v.p., 1971—, dir. Med. Computing Resources Center, U. Tex. Southwestern Med. Sch. at Dallas, 1972—, asst. prof. computer sci., asst. prof. internal medicine, 1972—. Mem. A.A.A.S., Am. Physiol. Soc., Am. Soc. Information Sci., Assn. for Computing Machinery, I.E.E.E., Internat. Platform Assn., Nat. Microfilm Assn., Phi Beta Kappa, Omicron Delta Kappa. Democrat. Jewish religion. Contbr. articles, abstracts to profl. jours. Home: 12866 Noel Rd Dallas TX 75230 Office: Med Computer Resources Center Univ Tex Southwestern Med Sch 5323 Harry Hines Blvd Dallas TX 75235

MISKIMEN, GEORGE WILLIAM, educator; b. Appleton, Wis., May 21, 1930; s. George Oscar and Gladys Matilda (Burns) M.; B.S., Ohio U., 1953, M.S., 1955; Ph.D., U. Fla. at Gainesville, 1966; m. Carmen Milagros Rivera-Batlle, Apr. 19, 1963; children—Kathryn Ann, Teresa Marie, Elizabeth Joan, Carmen Mildred. Entomologist V.I. Agrl. Program U.S. Dept. Agr., St. Croix, 1958-61; research entomologist, investigations leader entomology research div. U.S. Dept. Agr. Mayaguez, P.R., 1962-66; dir., prof. biology Entomol. Pioneering Research Lab. U. P.R. at Mayaguez, 1966—. Served with AUS, 1947-51. U. Fla. Academic fellow; Hatch Scientific grantee, NSF grantee. Mem. Entomol. Soc. Am., Internat. Orgn. Biol. Control, Soc. Systematic Zoology, Internat. Soc. Sugarcane Technologists, Coleopterist's Soc., Assn. Tropical Biology, Soc. Study Coleoptera, U.S. Coast Guard Aux. (Flotilla comdr. 1968—, div. tng. officer 1970), Sigma Xi, Gamma Sigma Delta, Delta Upsilon (sec. 1954, pledge pres. 1953). Episcopalian. Mason, Rotarian. Clubs: Boqueron Yacht (Boqueron, P.R.); Deportivo del Oeste (Mayaguez, P.R.); Casino de Mayaguez (P.R.). Contbr. articles to scientific jours. Home: Box 1420 Km 4 O Miradero Rd Villa Sonsire Mayaguez PR 00708 Office: Entomol Pioneering Research Lab University PR at Mayaguez Mayaguez PR 00708

MISKOVSKY, GEORGE, lawyer, ex-state senator; b. Oklahoma City, Feb. 13, 1910; s. Frank and Mary (Bourek) M.; LL.B., U. Okla., 1936; m. Nelly Oleta Donahue, Dec. 30, 1932; children—George,

Gary, Grover, Gail Marie. Admitted to Okla. bar, 1936, since practiced in Oklahoma City; sr. mem., head firm Miskovsky, Sullivan, Embry & Miskovsky, Oklahoma City; pub. defender Oklahoma City, 1936; county atty. Oklahoma County, 1943-44; mem. Okla. Ho. of Reps., 1939-42; mem. Okla. Senate, 1950-60. Sec. Economy Square, Inc. and Penn 74 Inc. Shopping Centers. Mem. Am., Okla., Oklahoma County bar assns., Am. Judicature Soc., C. of C., Am., Okla. trial lawyers assns., U. Okla. Law Assn., Order of Coif, Pi Kappa Alpha, Phi Alpha Delta. Democrat. Episcopalian. Mason (Shriner). Clubs: Lions, Oklahoma City Golf and Country, Oklahoma City Press. Sooner Dinner. Home: 1511 Drury Lane Oklahoma City OK 73116 Office: Hightower Bldg Oklahoma City OK 73102

MITCHELHILL, JAMES MOFFAT, govt. ofcl.; b. St. Joseph, Mo., Aug. 11, 1912; s. William and Jeannette (Ambrose) M.; B.S., Northwestern U., 1934, C.E., 1935; m. Maurine Hutchason, Jan. 9, 1937 (div. 1962); children—Janis Maurine (Mrs. Ross W. Johnson), Jeri Ann (Mrs. Charles T. Riney). Engring. dept. C., M., St. P. & P.R.R. Co., Chgo. and Miles City, Mont., 1935-45; asst. mgr. Ponce & Guayama R.R. Co., Aguirre, P.R., 1945-51, v.p., gen. mgr., 1969-70; mgr. Central Cortada, Santa Isabel, P.R., 1951-54; r.r. supt. Braden Copper Co., Rancagua, Chile, 1954-63; staff engr. Coverdale & Colpitts, N.Y.C., 1963-64; asst. to exec. v.p. Central Aguirre Sugar Co., 1964-67; v.p., gen. mgr. Coddea, Inc., Dominican Republic, 1967-68; asst. to gen. mgr. Land Adminstrn. of P.R., La Nueva Central Aguirre, 1970-71, for Centrals Aguirre Lafayette and Mercedita, 1971-—. Registered profl. engr., Mont., licensed civil engr., P.R. Fellow Am. Soc. C.E., Am. Geog. Soc. N.Y.; mem. Am. Ry. Engring. Assn., Colegio de Ingenieros Arquitectos Y Agrimensores de P.R., Asociacion de Technicos Azucareros de P.R. Sigma Xi, Tau Beta Pi. Home: PO Box 137 Aguirre PR 00608 Office: care Snow White Sugar Refinery Mercedita PR 00715

MITCHELL, ARTHUR LLOYD, educator; b. Richlands, Va., May 5, 1926; s. Arthur L. and Mary Lyde (White) M.; student William and Mary Coll., 1943; A.B., Emory and Henry Coll., 1946; M.A., Columbia, 1950. Tchr., Marion (Va.) High Sch., 1946-51, 53-58, Va. High Sch., Bristol, 1951-52, Lane High Sch., Charlottesville, Va., 1952-53; faculty Emory and Henry Coll., Emory, Va., 1958-—, prof. English, 1958-—, dir. admissions, 1965-—, asst. registrar, 1969-70, registrar, 1970-—. Pres. Smyth County (Va.) Young Democratic Club, 1953; treas. Washington County (Va.) Dem. Com., 1969-—. Trustee Washington County Pub. Library. Mem. Va. Assn. Tchrs. of English, Nat. Council Tchrs. of English. Methodist. Lion, Rotarian. Asst. editor Va. English Bull., 1952-53. Home: PO Box 1 Emory VA 24327

MITCHELL, CHARLES GRIFFITH, JR., architect; b. Frankfort, Ky., July 16, 1927; s. Charles Griffith and Mary Ellen (Duke) M.; B.S. in Archtl. Engring., U. Ky., 1951; m. Mary Ann Turner, Mar. 21, 1951 (div. July 1965); children—Mark T., Marie Ellen, Rebecca Ann. Began as a designer for Mallett & Assos., Architects and Engrs., Jackson, Miss., 1951-52, John L. Turner & Assos., Architect, Jackson, 1952-54; pvt. practice architecture, Jackson, 1955-—. Wing comdr. Miss. Wing, Civil Air Patrol, 1958-60. Served with USNR, 1945-46; PTO. Registered profl. architect, engr., Miss. Mem. A.I.A., Nat. Soc. Profl. Engrs., Delta Chi. Methodist. Clubs: Country, Optimist (Jackson). Prin. works include Peeples-Newman Office Bldg., Vicksburg, Miss., 1960; Hattie Casey Sch., Jackson, 1961; Neshoba County Gen. Hosp., Philadelphia, Miss., 1962; Thomas Street Sch., Tupelo, Miss., 1963; Union County Gen. Hosp., New Albany, Miss., 1963; McComb (Miss.) City Hosp., 1965; Itawamba County Hosp., Fulton, Miss., 1966, Vicksburg Convalescent Home, 1966, Walter Sillers State Office Bldg., Jackson, 1967, dormitories Miss. Valley State Coll., 1968, 69, Indsl. Arts Bldg. Miss. Valley State Coll., 1970, and others. Home: 127 Chiswick Circle Jackson MS 39211 Office: 5155 Galaxie Dr Jackson MS 39206

MITCHELL, CLARENCE M., JR., assn. exec.; b. Balt., Mar. 8, 1911; s. Clarence M. and Elsie (Davis) M.; A.B., Lincoln U., Chester County, Pa., 1932, hon. LL.D.; LL.B., U. Md.; postgrad. U. Minn., Atlanta U.; LL.D., Morgan State Coll., Balt.; m. Juanita Elizabeth Jackson, Sept. 7, 1938; children—Clarence M. III, Keiffer J., Michael B., George D. Admitted to Md. bar; newspaper reporter; various govt. posts including dir. field operations. Fair Employment Com., 1943, War Manpower Commn., WPB; labor sec. N.A.A.C.P., 1945-50, dir. Washington bur.,1950-—; legislative chmn. Leadership Conf. Civil Rights. Mem. Pres.'s Com. to Employ Physically Handicapped. Recipient Spingarn medal N.A.A.C.P., 1969. Mem. Am., Fed. bar assns., Am. Judicature Soc. Methodist (chmn. bd. trustees). Office: Congl Bldg 422 1st SE Washington DC 20003

MITCHELL, CLARENCE WILMORE, county agrl. agt.; b. Clay, Ky., June 28, 1916; s. Henry and Mollie (Lively) M.; B.S., Western Ky. Tchrs. Coll., 1940; M.S., U. Ky., 1947; m. Lena Mae Watson, Aug. 7, 1942. Tchr., Dixon, Ky., 1940-42; county agt. Extension Service, U. Ky., Lexington, 1947-—. Served with AUS, 1943-46. Recipient distinguished service award Nat. Assn. County Agrl. Agts., 1964. Mem. Nat. County Agts. Assn., C. of C., Epsilon Sigma Phi. Methodist. Lion. Home: 508 N 3d St Nicholasville KY 40356 Office: Court House Nicholasville KY 40356

MITCHELL, CLYDIE SHERLENE KNOTT (MRS RAY MITCHELL), ednl. adminstr.; b. Natchitoches, La., Dec. 5, 1936; d. Rufus Winfield and Willa (Bruce) Knott; B.A., Northwestern State Coll., 1959, M.A., 1964; m. Ray Mitchell, June 22, 1960; 1dau., Elizabeth Ann. Speech therapist Caddo Sch. System, Shreveport, La., 1960-63, coordinator spl. edn., 1967-69, supr. spl. edn., 1969-—; speech and hearing cons. Northwestern State Coll., 1963-65; dir. Speech Correction Center, Shreveport, 1965-67. Pvt. practice as speech pathologist, 1963-69. Mem. Assn. Children with Learning Disabilities, La. Tchrs. Assn., Caddo Suprs. Assn., Am., La. (pres. 1968), Shreveport (pres. 1965-67) speech and hearing assns., Council Exceptional Children (membership chmn. 1966-68), La. Schs. Suprs. Assn., Nat. Council Adminstrs. Spl. Edn., Kappa Delta Pi, Alha Delta Kappa (membership chmn. 1968-69). Methodist. Mem. Order Eastern Star. Clubs: Zonta (Shreveport pres. 1968, 69, 70), Meadow Lake Golf. Home: 8924 Acacia Lane Shreveport LA 71108 Office: 1969 Midway Shreveport LA 71108

MITCHELL, DOLPHUS BURL, optometrist; b. Birmingham, Ala., Sept. 9, 1922; s. Allen T. and Gertrude (Robinson) M.; student Alcorn A. and M. Coll., 1941-43, Monroe Coll. Optometry, 1946; Dr. Optometry, No. Ill. Coll. Optometry, 1949; LL.D., Union Bapt. Sem., 1952; m. Rebecca Woodfin, Mar. 16, 1960; children—Dawn Bonita, Dolphus Burl II (dec.), Donald Brian, Dora Bertine. Individual practice optometry, Birmingham, Ala., 1949-—, asso. prof. optometry U. Ala., part-time 1970-71. Vol. staff mem. U. Ala. Child Devel. and Learning Disabilities Center, 1969-71. Commr. Boy Scouts Am., Birmingham, 1951-53; v.p. North Smith Civic League, 1971-72. Served with AUS, 1943-46. Recipient Service Award Booker T. Washington Bus. Coll., 1971. Fellow Royal Soc. Health; mem. Ala. Optometric Assn., Nat. Assn. Retarded Children, Am. Pub. Health Assn., Nat. Assn. Children with Learning Disabilities, Am. Acad. Polit. and Social Scis., Internat. Platform Assn., N.A.A.C.P. Baptist (deacon). Mason (32 deg., Shriner). Home: 2130 Leola Circle Birmingham AL 35207 Office: 507 17th St N Birmingham AL 35203

MITCHELL, DONALD POOLE, ednl. adminstr.; b. Newton, Mass., Sept. 4, 1917; s. A. Earle and Edith (Poole) M.; student U. N.H., 1935-37; B.S., Mass. State Coll., 1940; Ed.M., Harvard, 1947, Ed.D., 1953; m. Dorothy Collinge Zipf, June 19, 1948; children—Gay Collinge (Mrs. Kelly), Jill Poole. Tchr., elementary prin. pub. schs., Seekonk, Mass., 1940-42; tchr., asst. prin. pub. schs., Greenwich, Conn., 1946-47; specialist sch. dist. orgn. Sch. Bldg. Commn., Boston, 1949-50; asst. dir. center field studies Harvard Grad. Sch. Edn., 1950-52, asso. dir., 1952-54; dir. div. field studies and research Rutgers U. Sch. Edn., New Brunswick, N.J., 1954-56, asso. prof., 1954-56; dir., treas. Kargman, Mitchell & Sargent, Inc., Boston, 1956-60; exec. sec. New Eng. Sch. Devel. Council, Cambridge, Mass., 1960-65; dir. Washington Internships in Edn., 1965-70; dir. Leadership in Pub. Edn. Study, Acad. Ednl. Devel., Inc., 1970-72; dir. Ed. D. program, Nova U., Ft. Lauderdale, Fla., 1972-—. Asso. edn. Harvard Grad. Sch. Edn., 1960-65, lectr. edn., 1961-62; cons. to various schs., sch. systems, univs. Served from 2d lt. to capt. inf. AUS, 1942-45. Mem. Sigma Alpha Epsilon, Phi Delta Kappa. Democrat. Unitarian-Universalist. Home: 200 Eldorado Pkwy Plantation FL 33314 Office: Nova U Fort Lauderdale FL 33314

MITCHELL, EDGAR DEAN, astronaut; b. Hereford, Tex., Sept. 17, 1930; s. Joseph T. and Ollidean (Arnold) M.; B.S. in Indsl. Mgmt., Carnegie Inst. Tech., 1952; B.S. in Aero. Engring., U.S. Naval Postgrad. Sch., 1961; Sc.D. in Aeros. and Astronautics, Mass. Inst. Tech., 1964; Sc.D., N.M. State U., 1971; D.Eng., Carnegie Mellon U., 1971; m. Louise Elizabeth Randall, Dec. 21, 1951 (div. Jan. 1972); children—Karlyn Louise, Elizabeth Randall. Joined U.S. Navy, 1952, commd. ensign, 1953, advanced through grades to capt., 1966; naval aviator, 1954, with patrol squadron 29, Okinawa, 1955, pilot heavy attack squadron 2, U.S.S. Bon Homme Richard also U.S.S. Ticonderoga, 1957-58, research project pilot air devel. squadron 5, 1958-59, chief project mgmt. div. Navy Field Office Manned Orbiting Lab., Los Angeles, 1964-65, assigned to Aerospace Research Pilot Sch., Edwards AFB, Cal., 1965-66; astronaut Manned Spacecraft Center, Houston, 1966-—, prime crew Apollo XIV Lunar Exploration, 1970. Explorer scout leader West Newton (Mass.) council Boy Scouts Am., 1962-63. Decorated D.A.R. Naval Aviator award, Presdl. Medal Freedom, D.S.M. NASA, D.S.M. USN. Mem. Parapsychol. Assn., Soc. Exptl. Test Pilots, Am. Inst. Aeros. and Astronautics, Sigma Xi, Kappa Sigma.

MITCHELL, EDWARD THOMAS, lumber co. exec.; b. Jakin, Ga., Sept. 9, 1934; s. James Powell and Naomi (Carter) M.; grad. high sch.; m. Annie Lee Durham, Jan. 3, 1954; children—Peggy, Susan, Brenda. Head bookkeeper, note teller First State Nat. Bank, 1951-56; reporter Agrl. Stblzn. and Conservation Service Office, U.S. Dept. Agr., Bainbridge, Ga., 1956-60; salesman, Willis Lumber Co., Bainbridge, 1960-68, v.p., co-owner, 1968-—. Mem. Bd. Edn., Decatur County, 1968-—; city councilman, Brinson, Ga., 1962-—. Mem. Bainbridge Home Builders Assn. (dir. 1965). Methodist (mem. bd. stewards 1960-—). Rotarian. Club: Country (Bainbridge, Ga.). Home: PO Box 637 Brinson GA 31725 Office: PO Box 98 Bainbridge GA 31717

MITCHELL, GERA ALONZA, fire chief; b. Opelika, Ala., Oct. 13, 1915; s. William Osborn and Sallie Lou (Wright) M.; student pub. schs., Opelika; m. Golden Garrett, June 11, 1936; children—William Ellis, Earl Franklin. With City of Opelika Fire Dept., 1928-42, fire chief, 1947-—, fire chief Army Depot, Anniston, Ala., 1942-45; Mem. Internat. Assn. Fire Chiefs (treas., dir.). Presbyn. Office: PO Box 629 Opelika AL 36801

MITCHELL, HARVEY LEE, constrn. co. exec.; b. Houston, Aug. 8, 1921; s. Milton Edgar and Edith May (Wulfert) M.; B.A., Rice U., 1944; m. Emma Jane Shirley, Apr. 8. 1944; 1 son, Wayne Lee. Pub. accountant Alwin Adams & Co., C.P.A.'s, Houston, 1943-44; chief accountant Farnsworth & Chambers Co., constrn., Houston, 1944-56; with Spaw-Glass, Inc. constrn., Houston, 1956-—, v.p., treas., 1968-—, also dir. Scoutmaster, committeeman scouting Cub Scouts Am., Houston, 1946-54, committeeman scouting Boy Scouts Am., 1954-56. Mem. Nat. Assn. Accountants. Rotarian. Club: Inwood Forest Country (Houston). Home: 2704 Helberg St Houston TX 77018 Office: Spaw Glass Inc PO Box 25025 Houston TX 77005

MITCHELL, HUGH GORDON, former UN ofcl.; b. Statesville, N.C., Oct. 5, 1902; s. Richard Page and Amedia (Leinster) M.; B.S., U. N.C., 1924; student of law, 1924-26. Practice of law, 1926-—, asso. gen. counsel, 3d v.p. Alexander R.R. Co.; county atty., Iredell County, 1956-62. Mem. N.C. Senate, 1943, 45; spl. legal adviser on adminstrv. matters for UN, 1946-48. Dir. N.C. State Assn. for Blind; chmn. Zebulon Baird Vance Meml. Commn. N.C.; chmn. War Savs. Staff, Iredell Co., N.C., 1942; govt. appeal agt., Selective Service, Iredell Co. Bd. No. 1, 1940-42; former mem. army adv. com. 3d U.S. Army. Bd. dirs. Patterson Sch. Mem. nat. awards jury Freedoms Found., 1951. Recipient Lions Internat. pres. award, 1956-57. Mem. Am. Coalition Patriotic, Civic and Fraternal Socs. (pres. 1965-72), Patriotic Order Sons Am. (pres. N.C. camp 1928-31, nat. pres. 1935-43, 49-51, nat. dir.-gen. 1951-—, nat. sec. 1951-—), Am. Judicature Soc. Am., N.C. State, N.C., 22d Jud. Dist. (v.p. 1970-71), Iredell County (pres. 1964-65) bar assns., Delta Sigma Phi. Democrat (del. nat. conv. 1936, 40, 44, 56, 60, alternate del. 1948). Presbyn. Lion (internat. counsellor, chmn. internat. relations com. dist. 31-B). Home: 123 Kelly St Statesville NC 28677 Office: Law Bldg Statesville NC 28677

MITCHELL, I. S., III, utility exec.; b. Atlanta, Mar. 2, 1915; s. Frank Rice and Jay (McBride) M.; A.B., U. Ga., 1936, LL.B., 1938; m. Elizabeth Boyd Nance, May 22, 1953; children—Elizabeth Nance, Sanford. Admitted to Ga. bar, 1938; land title atty. Ga. Power Co., Atlanta, 1938-57, asst. to pres., 1957-64, asst. sec., asst. to chmn., 1964-67, v.p., sec., 1967-—. Trustee Fulton- DeKalb County Nat. Found. March of Dimes, Ga. State Y.M.C.A. Served to 1st lt. Intelligence, AUS, 1942-46. Mem. Atlanta, Ga. chambers commerce, Chi Phi, Phi Delta Phi. Rotarian. Clubs: Commerce, Piedmont Driving (Atlanta). Home: 10 Peachtree Battle Av NW Atlanta GA 30305 Office: 270 Peachtree St NW Atlanta GA 30303

MITCHELL, JACK HARRIS, JR., educator, research scientist; b. Auburn, Ala., Sept. 15, 1911; s. Jack Harris and Ethel (Blasingame) M.; B.S., Clemson U., 1933; postgrad. Columbia, 1936-37; Ph.D. in Biochemistry, Purdue, 1941; m. Annie Lee Knox, Oct. 7, 1944; children—Jack H., Scott K., Lee W., Miriam U. Research chemist Am. Meat Inst., Chgo., 1941-42; head biochem. sect. So. Research Inst., Birmingham, Ala., 1947-50; asst. chief stability div. Q.M. Food &Container Inst., Chgo., 1950-55, chief chem. and microbiology div., 1955-57; head food tech. and human nutrition dept. Clemson U., 1957-64, prof. food sci. and biochemistry, 1964-—. Served to capt. AUS, 1942-46. Mem. Inst. Food Technologists (chmn. Dixie sect. 1972-73), A.A.A.S., Am. Inst. Chemists, Assos. U.S. Army Natick (Mass.) Labs. (bd. dirs. 1964-67), Sigma Xi, Gamma Sigma Delta. Methodist. Contbr. articles to profl. publs. Patentee in field. Home: 101 Bradley St Clemson SC 29631

MITCHELL, JAMES DANIEL, physician; b. Union City, Tenn., July 6, 1925; s. James Daniel and Eliza (Lambert) M.; B.A., U. Miss., 1952; med. certificate U. Miss., 1954; M.D., U. Tenn., 1956; m. Mary Hamill, Jan. 29, 1950; children—Susan, Charles Howard. Intern, St. Joseph's Hosp., Memphis, 1956-57; practice medicine specializing in family practice, Lexington, Miss., 1957-60, Jackson, 1960-—; mem. staffs Hinds Gen. Hosp., chief staff, 1968-69, Miss. Bapt. Hosp.; cons. Miss. State Bd. Health; chmn. Central Miss. Health Planning Council, 1968-69; mem. Miss. Medicaid Commn. Served with AUS, 1943-46. Mem. Am. (chmn. M-PAC 1969), Miss. (v.p. 1969-70) med. assns., Central Miss. Med. Soc. (chmn. pub. health and legislative com. 1964-67, mem. grievance com. 1970-—), U. Miss. Alumni Assn. (bd. dirs. 1969-—). Club: Optimist, Touchdown (pres. 1965-—) (Jackson, Miss.). Home: 1050 Beasley Rd Jackson MS 39209 Office: 4613 Clinton Blvd Jackson MS 39209

MITCHELL, JOHN NEWTON, former U.S. atty. gen.; b. Detroit, Sept. 5, 1913; s. Joseph Charles and Margaret Agnes (McMahon) M.; LL.B., Fordham U., 1938; postgrad. St. John's U. Law Sch., 1938-39; m. Martha Beall; 1 dau., Martha; children (by previous marriage)—John Newton III, Jill Elizabeth (Mrs. Edwin C. Reed). Admitted to N.Y. bar, 1938; practiced N.Y.C., 1938-68; partner firm Nixon, Mudge, Rose, Guthrie, Alexander & Mitchell, and predecessor firms, 1938-68; atty. gen. U.S., 1969-72. Campaign mgr. for Richard M. Nixon, 1968, 72. Bd. dirs., trustee action. Served with USNR, 1943-46. Mem. Am. (mem. sect. local govt.), N.Y. State bar assns. Home: Watergate East Washington DC 20037

MITCHELL, JOHN PATRICK, dentist; b. Butte, Mont., Sept. 8, 1904; s. Frank Joseph and Mary Margaret (McVeigh) M.; student Carroll Coll., 1923-25; D.D.S., Creighton U., 1929; postgrad. Baylor U., 1965-66, Creighton U., 1971, Northwestern U. Pvt. practice dentistry, Dallas, 1929-—. Clinic research tchr., cons. numerous dental meetings. Mem. Am., Tex., (recipient Order of Good Fellow), Mont., Chgo., Dallas County dental assns., Omnicron Kappa Upsilon. K.C. Club: Mustang (So. Meth. U.). Research in vertical-horizontal denture magnetic occlusal balance and retention of artificial teeth. Home and office: 3301 Greenville St Dallas TX 75206

MITCHELL, JOSEPH BRADY, mil. historian, author; b. Ft. Leavenworth, Kan., Sept. 25, 1915; s. William A. and Margery (Brady) M.; B.S., U.S. Mil. Acad., 1937; m. Vivienne French Brown, Aug. 20, 1938; children—Sherwood N., J. Bradford. Mem. operations div. War Dept. Gen. Staff, 1945-49; chief historian Am. Battle Monuments Commn., 1950-61, hist. cons., 1969-—; curator Ft. Ward Mus., Alexandria, Va., 1964-—. Trustee Nat. Temple Hill Assn. Served from 2d lt. to lt. col., 5th inf. div., AUS, 1937-45; ETO. Decorated Bronze Star. Recipient Am. Revolutionary Round Table prize for best book in field, 1962. Mem. Soc. of Cin., Civil War Round Table Alexandria and D.C. Episcopalian. Author: Decisive Battles of the Civil War, 1955; Decisive Battles of the American Revolution, 1962; Twenty Decisive Battles of the World, 1964; Discipline and Bayonets, 1967; The Badge of Gallantry, 1968; Military Leaders in the Civil War, 1972. Home: 606 Beverly Dr Alexandria VA 22305 Office: 4301 W Braddock Rd Alexandria VA 22304

MITCHELL, JOSEPHINE GRAY (MRS. T. A. MITCHELL), musician, past owner lumber bus.; b. Bonham, Tex.; d. Moses Vashti and Bertie (Hoy) Gray; B.S., Tex. Women's U., 1926, M.A., 1971; m. T.A. Mitchell, Mar. 21, 1929 (dec. 1964); children—Richard Gray, Thomas Albert. Pianist profl. concerts, Tex., Okla., Colo., 1927-—; tchr. music Port Arthur (Tex.) High Sch., 1928-29; formerly owner, operator T.A. Mitchell Lumber Co., Ft. Worth. Condr. Statewide Tex. Composers Contests, 1952-72; judge piano auditions Nat. Piano Guild, 1964-72; Music of Tex. Composers lecture recitals. Bd. dirs. Ft. Worth Civic Music, Tex. Girls Choir, Ft. Worth Youth Symphony. Recipient citation Nat. Fedn. Music Clubs, 1962, 68, Nat. Fedn. Musicians, 1966, 69; named 1st lady of music Ft. Worth, 1966, Tex. State citation composers, 1956, 71. Mem. Fort Worth League Composers (founder, chmn. 1958-68, pres.), Nat. Fedn. Music Clubs (nat. citation; asst. nat. folk music archivist 1963-66, archivist, chmn. folk music research S. Central region 1966-68, nat. chmn. folk music 1970-72), Tex. Fedn. Music Clubs (pres. 4th dist. 1964-66), Tex. Composers Guild (state chmn. 1952-58, 62-72), Tex. Women's U. Alumnae Assn. (past pres.), Ft. Worth Ballet Assn., Symphony League, Opera Guild, Sigma Alpha Iota (pres. 1961-62; recognition award), Lady Lions. Episcopalian. Clubs: Fort Worth Women's (chmn. Joint Twilight Musicales 1970-72), E. Clyde Whitlock Music, Euterpean Music (pres. 1952-54). Author: Texas Composers and Their Works, 1950-70. Compiler: (with others) Texas Composers Catalogue of Works, 1964, 68. Editor: Tex. Composers Guild Handbook, 1955. Home: 5120 Malinda Lane S Fort Worth TX 76112

MITCHELL, LANSING LEROY, judge; b. Sun, La., Jan. 17, 1914; s. Leroy A. and Eliza Jane (Richardson) M.; B.A., La. State U., 1934, J.D., 1937; postgrad. U. Mich., 1943; m. Virginia Jumonville, Apr. 18, 1938; children—Diane Mitchell (Mrs. Parker), Lansing Leroy. Admitted to La. bar, 1937; practice law, Pontchatoula, La., 1937-38; spl. agt. FBI, Washington, 1938-41; atty. U.S. SEC, Washington, 1941-42; asst. U.S. atty., Eastern Dist. of La., 1946-53; partner firm Deutsch, Kerrigan & Stiles, New Orleans, 1953-66; U.S. dist. judge Eastern Dist. of La., New Orleans, 1966-—. Mem. Municipal Com. on Finance, City of New Orleans, 1955-57, Municipal Auditorium Adv. Com., 1957-61; vice chmn. New Orleans Heart Fund Campaign, 1959-60, Armed Forces Day in New Orleans, 1964, 65; pres. Camp Fire Girls of Greater New Orleans, 1965-68; mem. Small Bus. Adv. Council for State of La. La. state chmn. Lawyers for Kennedy-Johnson, 1960. Served from 1st lt. to lt. col. AUS, 1942-46; ETO; now col. Res. Mem. New Orleans C. of C. (chmn. nat. security com. 1963-66), Inter-Am., Am., La., New Orleans bar assns., Maritime Law Assn. U.S., Judge Advocates Assn., Soc. Former Spl. Agts. FBI, Am. Legion, Mil. Order World Wars, Navy League, Assn. U.S. Army (past pres. La.), S.A.R., Soc. War 1812, Scabbard and Blade, Phi Delta Phi, Pi Kappa Alpha. Mason (Shriner, K.T.). Clubs: Paul Morphy Chess; Press of New Orleans; Bienville; Pendennis; Royal Order St. George; Bienville. Home: 6027 Hurst St New Orleans LA 70118 Office: 400 Royal St New Orleans LA 70130

MITCHELL, LAWRENCE DU-WAYNE, physician; b. Henderson, Ky., Feb. 23, 1925; s. Edward Preston and Martha Alma (Martin) M.; B.B.A., Sam Houston U., 1948; B.A., U. Tex., 1952; M.D., Baylor U., 1956; M.A., Sam Houston U., 1966; m. Ethel Clark, July 3, 1964; children— Michael Warren, Melissa Ann. Intern. Midstate Baptist Hosp., Nashville, Tenn., 1957; practice of gen. medicine, San Jacinto County, Tex., 1957-65; Grimes County, 1965-—; med. staff Tex. Dept. Corrections, Huntsville, 1967-—; mem. staffs Grimes Meml. Hosp., Navasota, Tex., Huntsville Meml. Hosp., Tex. Served with USNR, 1943-46. Decorated with Bronze Star medal. Mem. Am., Tex. med. assns., Tri-Med. Soc., Royal Soc. Health, The Smithsonian Assos., Tex. Farm Bur., Lambda Alpha Epsilon, Phi Chi. Mason. Home: Route 2 Box 250 Huntsville TX 77340 Office: 2 Main St Box 1056 Anderson TX 77340

MITCHELL, MARTHA JOY, librarian; b. Rome, Ga., Mar. 29, 1925; d. John T. and Edith (Terrell) Mitchell; B.A., Tenn. Temple Coll., 1954; B.A., George Peabody Coll. for Tchrs., 1958, M.A. in Library Sci., 1960. Head librarian Tenn. Temple Coll., Chattanooga, 1954-57, 60-64; librarian Dalewood Jr. High Sch., Chattanooga, 1964-66; head librarian Franklin High Sch., Nashville, 1966-—. Named Ky. Col. Mem. N.E.A., Tenn. Edn. Assn., Tenn., Am. library assns., Women's Nat. Book Assn. (pres. 1971-73). Home: 2406 Blair

Blvd Nashville TN 37212 Office: Franklin High Sch Franklin TN 37064

MITCHELL, MARY BELL (MRS. JAMES R. MITCHELL), banker; b. Lynn Haven, Fla., Mar. 20, 1913; d. Robert Benjamin and Lula (Ward) Bell; student pub. schs.; m. James R. Mitchell, June 29, 1935; children—Sarah J. (Mrs. Gerald M. Williams), Mary James (Mrs. Robert Daniel Evans). Trainee clk.-sec. First Nat. Bank, Miami, Fla., 1931-33; sec.-clk. Fla. Nat. Bank & Trust Co., 1933-35; clk. Gulf Oil Corp., 1935-37, Merc. Nat. Bank, Miami Beach, Fla., 1937-39; with City Nat. Bank, Miami, 1939-—, gen. ledger bookkeeper, 1945-48, asst. cashier, asst. operations and personnel, 1948-50, cashier, asst. operations, personnel, 1950-54, v.p., cashier, operations and personnel, 1954-64, sr. v.p., cashier, operations, personnel, and data processing, 1964-—; v.p. City Nat. Bank Corp., 1971-—. Mem. Fla. Bankers Assn. (past chmn. research com., mem. com. on date processing 1965-—), Nat. Assn. Bank Auditors and Comptrollers (past dir.), Nat. Assn. Bank Women. Presbyn. Home: 25081 SW 128 Ct Princeton FL 33171 Office: 25 W Flagler St Miami FL 33130

MITCHELL, MEMORY F. (MRS. T.W. MITCHELL), editor; b. Raleigh, N.C., Jan. 21, 1924; d. James S. and Foy (Johnson) Farmer; A.B., Meredith Coll., 1944; postgrad. Cornell U. Law Sch., 1944-45; J.D., U. N.C., 1946, A.M., 1949; m. B. W. Blackwelder, July 14, 1955 (div. Feb. 1960); m. 2d, Thornton W. Mitchell, Sept. 7, 1963; children—James Thornton and David Wingate (twins). Tchr., Meredith Coll., 1949-50; adminstrv. asst. N.C. Bd. Pub. Welfare, 1950-54; judge Cabarrus County (N.C.) Domestic Relations Ct., 1954-55; supr. N.C. Office Archives and History, 1956-61, dir. div. publs., 1961-—, editor N.C. Hist. Rev., 1962-—. Trustee Olivia Raney Library, 1961-69. Named Woman of Yr., Raleigh, 1961. Mem. N.C. Bar, Orgn. Am. Historians, Hist. Soc. N.C., So., Wake County hist. socs., Am. Assn. U. Women (pres. Raleigh 1961-63), N.C. Lit. and Hist. Assn. Democrat. Baptist. Author: Legal Aspects of Conscription and Exemption in North Carolina, 1861-1865, 1965. Editor: Messages, Addresses and Public Papers of Terry Sanford, Governor of North Carolina, 1961-65, 1966; Messages, Addresses and Public Papers of Daniel Killian Moore, Governor of North Carolina, 1965-69, 1971. Mem. editorial bd. American Archivist, 1972-—. Contbr. articles to various publs. Home: 2431 Medway Dr Raleigh NC 27608 Office: 109 E Jones St Raleigh NC 27611

MITCHELL, O(LIN) JACKSON, architect, educator; b. Little Rock, Sept. 19, 1931; s. Olin and Florence (Jackson) M.; B. Arch., Washington U., St. Louis, 1954; M. Arch., M. City Planning, U. Pa., 1961; m. Carolyn Jean Edrington, Oct. 20, 1962; children—James Jackson, Mark Taylor. With Wittenberg, Delony & Davidson, Little Rock, 1954-56, 61-66, partner in charge design, 1961-66; with Hellmuth, Obata & Kassabaum, St. Louis, 1956-57; with Caudill, Rowlett & Scott, Houston, 1957-58, 66-67, project designer, 1966-67; asso. prof. Rice U. Sch. Architecture, Houston, 1966-67, asso. dir. sch., 1967-69, prof., dir. grad. studies Sch. Architecture, 1969-—. Asst. prof. Sch. Architecture Tex. A. and M. U., College Station, 1957-59; pres. Omniplan Urban Design and Planning, Houston, 1970-—. Bd. dirs. S.W. Center for Urban Research, Houston. Registered architect. Mem. A.I.A. (chpt. corporate mem.), Sigma Alpha Epsilon. Prin. works include So. State Coll. dormitories, Magnolia, Ark., housing projects, Hot Springs, Ark. Home: 2223 Bolsover St Houston TX 77005

MITCHELL, ROBERT HARTWELL, physician; b. Plainview, Tex., Dec. 6, 1911; s. Robert Hartwell and Eudora (Alexander) M.; M.D., U. Tex., 1935; m. Vernon Richardson Mitchell, June 1, 1935; children—Martha Elizabeth, Leah Jane. Intern, U. Ia. hosps., 1935-36; individual practice, Fort Worth, 1946-55, Plainview Tex., 1955-—; dir. diagnostic div. Terrell's Labs., Fort Worth, 1946-55, chmn. dept. medicine John Peter Smith Hosp., All Saints Hosp., Cook Meml. Hosp. Center for Children, 1946-55; med. dir. Fort Worth Heart Assn. and Heart Lab., 1953-55; chmn. dept. medicine, dir. coronary unit, chief staff Central Plains Gen. Hosp., Plainview, 1955-—. Fort Worth Lab. for Surg. Research, Southwestern Med. Sch., 1953-55. Served from 1st lt. to col. M.C., AUS, 1941-46. Diplomate Am. Bd. Internal Medicine. Fellow A.C.P., Am. Coll. Cardiology; mem. Am. Heart Assn. (fellow council clin. cardiology; dir., mem. exec. com., central com., past v.p.), Tex. Heart Assn. (dir. and mem. exec. com. 1961-—, pres. 1964), A.M.A., Tex. Med. Assn., Tex. Rheumatism Assn. (past pres. and dir.), Tex. Acad. Internal Med. (pres. 1960), Inter-Am. Congress Cardiology (dir. 1968-72). Episcopalian. Clubs: Fort Worth, Ridglea Country (Ft. Worth); Plainview (Tex.) Country; Lancers (Dallas); 40 Acres (Austin). Contbr. articles to med. jours. Office: Skaggs Bldg Plainview TX 79072

MITCHELL, ROBERT SYDNEY, clergyman; b. Sumter, S.C., Mar. 29, 1933; s. Talmadge Wadford and Mattie Felicia (Heckel) M.; A.B., Trevecca Nazarene Coll., 1961; M.A., Austin Peay State U., 1964; m. Emmaline Craft, Dec. 19, 1954; children—Robert Sydney, Donald and Ronald (twins), Thomas, Nethla, Melinda. Ordained to ministry Ch. Nazarene, 1962; minister Ch. of Nazarene, Newberry, S.C., 1953-58, Erin, Tenn., 1961-—. Tchr., Houston County Schs., Erin, Tenn., 1961-67, supt., 1967-71. Chmn. Citizens Adv. Com., Erin, 1968-70; exec. sec. Highland Rim CEO, 1967-70. Bd. dirs. Erin Housing Authority, 1968-—. Del., spl. 8th dist. Dem. Conv., 1968. Mem. Am. Assn. Sch. Adminstrs., N.E.A., Tenn. Edn. Assn. Rotarian. Club: Civitan (pres.). Home: Route 3 Box 128 A Erin TN 37061

MITCHELL, ROLAND BURNELL, med. sci. research dir.; b. Denton, Tex., Mar. 24, 1910; s. Robert Marion and Robbie (Hawkins) M.; B.S. North Tex. State U., 1932; M.A., U. Tex., Ph.D., 1939; m. Julianne Still, Sept. 6, 1938; children—Bonnie Ann, Susan. Sci. tchr. Tex. pub. schs., 1928-34; supervising sci. tchr. S.W. Tex. Tchrs. Coll., 1935-37; bacteriologist bur. plant industry U.S. Dept. Agr., 1937-42, Tex. Pub. Health Labs., 1942; asst. dir. bur. labs. Fla. Bd. Health, 1946-48; prof. pub. health bacteriology U. Fla., 1947-48; chief dept. aerobiology Sch. Aviation Medicine, USAF, 1948-51, chief dept. microbiology, 1951-57, acting dir. med. sci. div., 1954-57, dir., 1957-59; chief med. scis. div. Aerospace Med. Center, Brooks AFB, Tex., 1959-61, dir. biosystems research div. aerospace med. div. Sch. Aerospace Medicine, 1962-63, dir. bioscis. and sr. scientist DCS Research and Devel., Aerospace Med. div., 1963-64, chief biol. scis. div. Directorate of Research and Devel., Aerospace Div., 1964-71; chief Bur. Research, Fla. Div. Health, 1971-—. Served from 1st lt. to maj. USAF, 1942-46. Fellow Am. Acad. Microbiology, Am. Pub. Health Assn.; mem. Am. Soc. Microbiology Soc. Am. Bacteriology, Soc. Exptl. Biology and Medicine, Aerospace Med. Assn., Assn. Mil Surgeons, Sigma Xi. Methodist. Home: 7253 Tahiti Rd Jacksonville FL 32216 Office: Bur Research Div Health Dept Health and Rehab Services PO Box 210 Jacksonville FL 32201

MITCHELL, ROY DEVOY, mgmt. engr., govt. ofcl.; b. Hot Springs, Ark., Sept. 11, 1922; s. Watson W. and Marie (Stewart) M.; B.S., Okla. State U., 1948, M.S., 1950; B.Indsl. Mgmt., Auburn U., 1960; m. Jane Caroline Gibson, Feb. 14, 1958; children—Michael, Marilyn, Martha, Stewart, Nancy. Instr., Odessa (Tex.) Coll., 1953-56; prof. engring. graphics Auburn (Ala.) U., 1956-63; field engr. HHFA, Community Facilities Adminstrn., Atlanta, Jackson, Miss., 1963-71; area engr. Met. Devel. Office, Dept. Housing and Urban Devel., 1971-72, chief architecture and engring., 1972-—. Cons., Army Balistic Missile Agy., Huntsville, Ala., 1957-58, Auburn Research Found., NASA, 1963; mem. state tech. action panel Coop. Area Manpower Planning System. Mem. Central Miss. Fed. Personnel Adv. Council. Served USNR, 1943-46. Commended by Sec. of Dept. Housing and Urban Devel. Registered profl. engr., Ala., Miss. Mem. Nat. Soc. Profl. Engrs., Am. Soc. for Engring. Edn., Miss. Soc. Profl. Engrs., Nat. Assn. Govt. Engrs. (charter mem.), Jackson Fed. Execs. Assn., Central Miss. Safety Council, Am. Water Works Assn., Iota Lambda Sigma. Methodist (trustee, mem. bd. 1959-60). Home: 324 Valley Vista Dr Jackson MS 39211 Office: Dept Housing and Urban Development 300 Woodrow Wilson WJackson MS 39213

MITCHELL, WALTER M., county ofcl., textile industry exec.; b. Cordele, Ga., Aug. 22, 1901; s. James Northern and Rosalie Wade (Marshall) M.; A.B., Ga. Mil. Coll., 1919; B.S., Ga. Inst. Tech., 1923; m. Ethel Niall, Oct. 16, 1926; children—Walter M., William N., Wade T. Dir., v.p., Draper Corp., Atlanta; dir., chmn. Pan Am. Investment Co., Fed. Res. Bank of Atlanta; dir. Alpha Mut. Fund, Alpha Investors Fund, Am. Resorts, Inc. Rich's Inc., Bank of Ga. Commr. roads and revenue Fulton County (Ga.), now chmn. commrs. Trustee, pres. Ga. Tech. Found; trustee Atlanta Childs Home, Lewis H. Beck-Ga. Tech. Scolarship Fund; chmn. Ga. Conservancy. Mem. Am. Cotton Mfrs. Assn., Cotton Mfrs. Assn. Ga., Phi Delta Theta. Rotarian (past pres.). Clubs: Capital City, Piedmont Driving, North Fulton Dads' (past pres.), Peachtree Racket (Atlanta); Piedmont (Spartanburg, S.C.). Home: 45 Montclair Dr NE Atlanta GA 30309

MITCHELL, WARREN EUGENE, coll. basketball coach; b. Lynchburg, Va., Apr. 1, 1933; s. Samuel Aubrey and Roxie (Cline) M.; B.A., U. Richmond, 1957; m. Annette LaFoon, Oct. 24, 1959; 1 son, Warren Eugene. Tchr., coach York High Sch., Yorktown, Va., 1959-60; head basketball coach Newport News (Va.) High Sch., 1960-64; asst. basketball coach Davidson (N.C.) Coll., 1964-66; head basketball coach William and Mary Coll., Williamsburg, Va., 1966-—. Served with AUS, 1957-59. Mem. So. Conf. Basketball Assn. (pres. 1972), Sigma Alpha Epsilon. Kiwanian. Contbr. articles to coaches' mags. Home: 522 Prince Georges St Williamsburg VA 23185

MITCHELL, WILEY FRANCIS, JR., lawyer; b. Youngsville, N.C., July 23, 1932; s. Wiley F. and Irene (Edwards) M.; B.A., Wake Forest U., 1952, J.D., 1954; m. Marshale Moody, May 31, 1953; children—Katherine Lee, Frances Dale. Admitted to N.C. bar, 1954, D.C. bar, 1962; practiced in Raleigh, N.C., 1954-61, Washington, 1962-—; asso. Joyner & Howison, attys., Raleigh, 1954-60; partner Joyner, Howison & Mitchell, attys., Raleigh, 1961-62; gen. atty. So. Ry. System, Washington, 1962-69, gen. solicitor, 1969-—. Mem. Va. Revenue Resources and Econ. Study Commn., 1970-—; mem. Va. Commn. on City-County Relations, 1972-—. Vice chmn. Alexandria Republican Com., 1967; mem. city council, Alexandria, Va., 1967-70, vice mayor, 1970-—. Mem. Am., N.C., Va. (hon. life) bar assns., Nat. Assn. R.R. Trial Counsel (v.p. 1968-70, pres. 1971), Bar Assn. D.C., Alpha Sigma Phi, Omicron Delta Kappa, Phi Delta Phi. Baptist (deacon 1966-—). Rotarian. Clubs: Am. Business (chpt. pres. 1961) (Raleigh); Alexandria (Va.) Sportsmen's. Home: 511 Canterbury Lane Alexandria VA 22314 Office: 920 15th St NW Washington DC 20013

MITCHELL, WILLIAM ALEXANDER, govt. ofcl.; b. Clemson, S.C., May 29, 1917; s. Jack Harris and Ethel (Blasingame) M.; B.S., Clemson U., 1938; M.A., U. N.C., 1939; fellow Duke, 1939-41; M.A., Princeton, 1942, Ph.D., 1948; m. Helen Warner Dart, June 5, 1950. Instr., Princeton U., 1941-42, 46-47; asst. prof. U. Va., 1947-49; asso. prof. U. Mass., 1949-52; mem. staff CIA, Washington, 1952-63; mem. staff Office Mgmt. and Budget, Exec. Office of Pres., Washington, 1963-—. Served from 2d lt. to maj. AUS, 1942-46. Home: 6202 Winston Dr Bethesda MD 20034 Office: Exec Office Bldg Washington DC 20503

MITCHELL, WILLIAM AVERY, JR., dentist; b. Greenville, S.C., Apr. 26, 1933Js. William Avery and Eva (Rigdon) M.; B.S., Furman U., 1955; D.D.S., Emory U., 1959, M.S.D., 1967; m. Patricia Ann Scott, June 26, 1965; 1 son, William A. III. Practice orthodontics, Decatur, Ga., 1963-69, Greenville, S.C., 1969-—. Instr., Emory U. Sch. Dentistry, 1965-68. Bd. dirs. United Speech and Hearing Services, 1972-—. Served to capt. Dental Corps, AUS, 1959-61. Mem. Am., S.C. (del. 1972), Ga. dental assns., Greenville County Dental Soc. (sec. 1970, v.p. 1971, pres. 1972), Am. Assn. Orthodontists, So. Soc. Orthodontists, S.C., Ga. orthodontics socs., Furman U. Alumni Assn. (past pres. Atlanta area). Baptist (asso. deacon 1971). Rotarian. Home: 132 Seven Oaks Dr Greenville SC 29605 Office: 13 S Calhoun St Greenville SC 29601

MITCHELL, WILLIAM NED, bus. exec.; b. nr. Winston-Salem, N.C., Feb. 14, 1940; s. Shirley Hill and Dorothy (Nelson) M.; B.S. in Transp., U. Tenn., 1965-—; m. Beryl Helen Roberts, Apr. 26, 1964; children—Cheryl Hill, William Ned. With Hennis Freight Lines, Inc., Winston-Salem, 1966-71, v.p., 1966-71; v.p. M & M Tank Lines, Inc., 1965-71; v.p. Piedmont Motor Sales, 1965-71; mgr. Homestead Industries, Winston-Salem, 1971-—. Mem. Delta Nu Alpha, Mason. Home: 3740 Will Scarlet Rd Winston-Salem NC 27104 Office: 2734 Robinhood Rd Winston-Salem NC 27106

MITCHINER, J(OSEPH) ELTON, lawyer; b. Smithfield, N.C., Apr. 29, 1919; s. Edwin Joseph and Lola (Talton) M.; A.B., Wake Forest Coll., 1940; postgrad. U. N.C. Law Sch., 1940-42; m. Gretchen Parrish, July 18, 1942; children—Carol Leigh, Judy, Joe. Admitted to N.C. bar, 1943, Fla. bar, 1956; asst. clk. Superior Ct. Johnston County (N.C.), 1943-44; pvt. law practice, specializing in taxation and estates, Smithfield, 1944-54; spl. trial atty. regional counsel Internal Revenue Service, 1954-56; pvt. practice law, specializing in taxation, estates, corporate law, Raleigh, N.C., Ft. Lauderdale, Fla., 1956-—; dir., gen. counsel Cook & Pruitt Masonry Contractors, Inc., Miami, Fla., MA-Leek Woodcrafts, Inc. and affiliates, Wingate, N.C., Charles McArthur Dairies and affiliated corps., Okeechobee, Fla. Republican. Baptist. Mason (Shriner). Home: 1200 Kimberley Dr Raleigh NC 27609 Office: Branch Bank and Trust Bldg Raleigh NC 27601 also Bayview Bldg Ft Lauderdale FL 33304

MITKO, FRANCIS CONSTANTINE, govt. ofcl.; b. Salt Lake City, Utah, Mar. 16, 1940; s. Frank and Esther (Papanicholes) M.; B.A. in Psychology, U. Utah, 1964; M.A. in Econs., San Francisco State Coll., 1970; m. Madeline Kikuno Romero, June 8, 1964. Alcohol and tobacco tax specialist Internal Revenue Service, San Francisco, 1965-67; economist mineral forecasts U.S. Bur. Mines, San Francisco, 1967-70, economist platinum specialist, Arlington, Va., 1970-—. Faculty econ. forecasting, microecons., operations research Golden Gate Coll., evenings 1969-70. Served with USMCR, 1958. Mem. Am. Econ. Assn., I.F.P. Investment Club (sec.-treas. 1969-—). Democrat. Unitarian. Publisher: Mineral Industry in California, 1968, others. Home: 1117 N Kenilworth St Arlington VA 22205 Office: 4015 Wilson St Arlington VA 22203

MITLIN, NORMAN, educator, entomologist; b. Bklyn., Feb. 13, 1918; s. Joseph and Fannie Rachel (Goldfein) M.; B.S., N.Y. U., 1945; postgrad. U. Md., 1957-60; m. Luceille Liston, Mar. 14, 1942; 1 son, Laurance R. Research entomologist, U.S. Dept. Agr., State Coll., 1949-—; asso. prof. entomology, Miss. State U., State College, 1969-—. Trustee Starkville Pub. Library, chmn. bd., 1968-—. Served with USAAF, 1942-43. Mem. A.A.A.S., Entomological Soc. Am., Am. Chem. Soc., Soc. Southeastern Biologists, Miss. Acad. Scis., Miss. Entomological Assn., Miss. Library Assn. (chmn. trustees section 1970-71). Home: 513 Poplar Rd Starkville MS 39759 Office: Box 5367 State College MS 39762

MITTENDORF, THEODOR HENRY, paper mfg. cons.; b. Clay Center, Kan., Jan. 14, 1895; s. Theodor Henry and Antonie (Carls) M.; B.S., Okla. State U., 1917; m. Dorothy E. Solger, May 18, 1919; 1 dau., Laone M. (Mrs. D. R. Hoerl) Lectr. extension div. Okla. State U., 1917; lectr., free-lance writer, 1919-20; dept. supt. Armour & Co., Chgo., 1920-22; sec., dir. sales and advt. Mid-States Gummed Paper Co., Chgo., 1922-38; v.p. charge sales Indsl. Tng. Inst., 1938-39, v.p., gen. mgr. Gummed Products Co., Troy, O., 1940-48; v.p. charge sales Hudson Pulp and Paper Corp., N.Y.C., 1948-56, exec. v.p., 1956-58, cons., 1958-—; dir. 5 East 71st St. Corp. Bd. dirs. Muscular Dystrophy Assn. Served from 2d lt. F.A. to 1st lt. AS, U.S. Army, World War I, AEF. Named to Okla. State U. Alumni Hall of Fame, 1961. Mem. Kraft Paper Assn. (dir., mem. exec. com. 1951-58), Gummed Industries Assn. (pres. 1955-56). Paper Bag Inst. (pres. 1955-56). Paper Club N.Y., Am. Legion, Symposiarchs, Kappa Sigma, Alpha Zeta, Pi Kappa Delta. Republican. Methodist. Mason; mem. Order Eastern Star. Clubs: Mt. Dora (Fla.) Golf, Mt. Dora Yacht; Ponte Vedra (Fla.); African Safari of Fla. Home: Route 1 Box 102 Lake Shore Dr Tavares FL 32778 Office: 477 Madison Av New York City NY 10022

MITTON, JOHN HERBERT, civil engr.; b. Washington, July 28, 1911; s. Philip Francis and Mary Lillian (Gibbons) M.; B.S. cum laude, U. Md., 1931, C.E., 1935; LL.B., Catholic U. Am., 1934; m. Josephine Elizabeth Locraft, Nov. 24, 1938; children—John Herbert, Josephine M. (Mrs. Thaddeus E. Kowynia), Joanne E., Jeanne B. (Mrs. John Van der Vossen), Judith E. (Mrs. John Martucci). Traffic engr. D.C. Govt., 1931-69, asst. dir. Dept. Vehicles and Traffic, 1953-59, chief traffic planning and design Dept. Hwys. and Traffic, 1959-69; cons. traffic engr., Washington, 1969-—. Lectr., Cath. U.Am., 1961-70; admitted to D.C. bar, 1934; U.S. Ct. Appeals for D.C., U.S. Supreme Ct.; expert witness before Fed. and State Cts., ICC, Pub. Service Commns., County Councils. Mem. Nat. Com. on Uniform Traffic Laws and Ordinances, Hwy. Research Bd.; tech. cons. to Pres.'s Com. for Traffic Safety, 1955-58; mem. St. Vincent de Paul Soc., 1951-—, past pres. St. Martins Conf.; mem. Presdl. Inaugural Coms., 1949, 53, 57, 61, 65. Recipient award of merit D.C. Govt., 1969. Mem. Washington Soc. Engrs. (past pres.), Inst. Traffic Engrs. (trustee Pension Plan, past sect. pres., com. chmn.), Road Gang and Lamplighters, Tau Beta Pi, Phi Kappa Phi. Contbr. articles to profl. jours. Address: 1736 Holly St NW Washington DC 20012

MITTS, ERNEST, exec. dir. Atlantic States Marine Fisheries, Tallahassee. Address: Box 2784 Tallahassee FL 32304*

MITZE, CLARK H., arts adminstr.; b. Cedar Falls, Ia., Mar. 28, 1918; s. George H. and Alace (Brown) M.; B.A., Ia. State Tchrs. Coll., 1939; M.A., U. Ia., 1946; m. Verla Diekman, May 20, 1942; children—Thomas, Michael Terry, Robert. Tchr. pub. schs., LeMars, Ia., 1947-50, Clayton, Mo., 1950-52; faculty Washington U., St. Louis, 1952-66; dir. Mo. Council on Arts, 1965-68; dir. state and community operations Nat. Endowment for Arts, Washington, 1968-—; music critic St. Louis Globe-Democrat, 1963-68; contbg. critic Washington Post. Served to lt. col. USAAF, World War II. Mem. Phi Mu Alpha, Omicron Delta Kappa. Office: 806 15th St Washington DC 20506

MIXON, ALVIN, farmer, mcht., cattleman; b. Georgiana, Ala., Dec. 19, 1908; s. Samuel Henderson and Lela (Cook) M.; grad. Massey Bus. Sch., Birmingham, Ala., 1930; m. Frances Brassell, May 15, 1936; 1 son, Alvin. Salesman, interior decorator Morgan Bros. Dept. Stores, Birmingham, Georgiana and Evergreen, Ala., 1930; founder, owner S. H. Mixon's Store, Gin & Milling Co., Georgiana, Alvin Mixon Merc., Harper Merc. Co., Belleville; cattleman, Georgiana, 1952-—. Organizer So. Pine Electric Co-op, Brewton, Ala., 1938; pres. So. Electric Co-op, Brewton, 1957-—; dir. Ala. Electric Power Generation Plants and High Voltage Transmission Lines, Andalusia. Mem. Ala. Energy Adv. Council. Asso. dir. SSS, Conecuh County, 1938-42; organizer Conecuh County United Fund. Organizer Conecuh County Hosp., 1954, bd. dirs., 1954-—. Mem. Ala. Forest Products Assn., Am., Ala. Angus assns., Ala., Conecuh County cattlemens assns., Conecuh County Hist. Soc., Conecuh Farm Bur. (dir.), Georgiana, Evergreen chambers commerce, Internat. Platform Assn., Woodmen of World. Methodist (steward, layman). Mason (Shriner), Rotarian, Kiwanian. Club: Quarterback (Georgiana). Address: Route 1 Georgiana AL 36033

MIXSON, CHARLES ANDREW, physician; b. Montgomery, Ala., Nov. 24, 1931; s. Dwight Lyman and Katherine Maude (Killebrew) M.; student Washington and Lee U., 1950-51; B.S., U. Ala., 1954; M.D., Med. Coll. Ala., 1958; m. Marian Louise Suggs, Nov. 5, 1960; children— Melinda, Charles Andrew, Ashley Ann. Intern, Tampa (Fla.) Gen. Hosp., 1958-59; resident Santa Cruz (Cal.) County Hosp., 1959-60; practice gen. medicine, Milton, Fla., 1960-—; mem. staff Santa Rosa County Hosp., Milton. Mem. Am., Fla. med. assns., Assn. Am. Physicians and Surgeons. Home: Route 2 Box 352A Milton FL 32570 Office: 1100 Stewart St Milton FL 32570

MIXSON, THOMAS GOODWIN, banker; b. Levy County, Fla., Oct. 12, 1893; s. Archibald James and Mattie Ella (Mims) M.; grad. Draughon's Bus. Coll., Atlanta, 1910; m. Alma Claire Odell, Aug. 27, 1917; 1 son, James G. With Roess Lumber Co., Ocala, Fla., 1910-12; bookkeeper Ocala Nat. Bank, 1912-15; cashier Greek Am. Bank of Tarpon Springs, Fla., 1915-18; with Exchange Nat. Bank, Tampa, Fla., 1918-45, successively clk., asst. cashier, cashier, v.p., 1940-45, dir., 1935-45; pres., dir. The First Nat. Bank, St. Petersburg, Fla., 1945-56; pres., The City Bank and Trust Co., 1959-71, dir., 1959-—, chmn. bd., 1971-—; chmn. bd., dir., pres. The Suncoast City Bank, 1970-—. Chmn. com. Tampa Taxpayers Assn., 1944-45; campaign chmn. Tampa chpt. A.R.C., 1945-46. Bd. dirs. All Children's Hosp., Inc. Mem. St. Petersburg (com. of 100), Tampa (pres. 1943-44) chambers commerce. Baptist. (deacon 1962-—). Clubs: St. Petersburg Yacht, Lakewood Country (St. Petersburg); Commerce, Innisbrook Golf and Country (Tarpon Springs). Home: 501 Bayview Dr NE St Petersburg FL 33704 Office: 301 4th St N St Petersburg FL 33701 also PO Box 13504 St Petersburg FL 33733

MIZE, GILBERT, supt. schs.; b. Viola, Ark., Nov. 6, 1908; s. William Aaron and Sarah Elizabeth (Johns) M.; B.A., Sul Ross State U., 1932; M.A., Tex. Tech. U., 1939; m. Dannie Brown Stark, May 30, 1936; children—Dennie Jean (Mrs. A. L. Schnell, Jr.), Sara Elizabeth, Charles Lovett, Gilbertine. High sch. tchr., athletic coach, Dunn, Tex., 1932-35; high sch. prin., coach, Fluvanna, Tex., 1935-42; jr. high sch. prin., Perryton, Tex., 1942-48, supt. schs., 1948-—. Pres. United Fund, 1970. Bd. dirs. YMCA. Served with AUS, 1944-46. Mem. C. of C. (dir. 1967-69). Methodist (chmn. bd. 1964-66). Home: 1705 Drake St Perryton TX 79070 Office: 821 SW 17th St Perryton TX 79070

MIZE, JOHN THOMAS, dentist; b. Landrum, S.C.; s. Walter J. and Elizabeth Oxley (Eldridge) M.; A.B., Maryville Coll., 1942; D.D.S., Emory U., 1945; m. Margaret Calhoun Fain, June 11, 1943; children— Elizabeth, Margaret, Jessie, John, Joseph, Walter. Pvt. practice dentistry, Tyron, N.C., 1946—; mem. staff St. Luke's Hosp. Chmn. Democratic Precinct Com., Tyron, 1958-64. Bd. dirs. Tyron Sch., Isothermal Community Coll. Served to lt. comdr. USNR, World War II and Korea. Mem. Am., N.C. dental assns., Isothermal Dental Soc. (pres. 1950), Pierre Fauchard Acad. Conglist. (v.p.). Rotarian. Clubs: Red Fox Country, Tyron Country (bd. dirs.); Gun (Spartanburg, S.C.). Home: 801 Doubleday Rd Tyron NC 28782 Office: 301 Carolina Dr Tryon NC 38782

MIZE, RONDAL CURTIS, mech. engr.; b. Cullman, Ala., Jan. 10, 1938; s. Herbert Jackson and Pearl (Young) M.; B.M.E., Auburn U., 1960; m. Sara Ruth Vandiver, July 30, 1961; children—Belinda Suzanne, Rondal Curtis Jr. With NASA, Huntsville, Ala., 1960—, mech. engr., 1960-61, aerospace engr., 1961-65, supr. aerospace engr. flight systems, 1965-71, aerospace engr. spl. projects, 1971—. Registered Profl. Engr., Ala.; Registered Fallout Shelter Analyst. Mem. Am. Soc. Nondestructive Testing (pres. Ala. chpt. 1970-71), Am. Soc. Mech. Engrs., Nat., Ala. socs. profl. engrs. Baptist (deacon 1960-72, pianist-organist 1960-72). Club: Civitan Internat. Home: 907 Nunnelly Av Cullman AL 35055 Office: NASA MSFC Huntsville AL 35812

MIZELL, WILMER DAVID, congressman; b. Vinegar Bend, Ala., Aug. 13, 1930; s. Walter David and Addie (Turner) M.; grad. Leaksville (Miss.) High Sch.; m. Nancy Ruth McAlpine, Nov. 16, 1952; children—Wilmer David, James Daniel. Major league baseball pitcher with St. Louis Cardinal orgn., Pitts. Pirates, N.Y. Mets, until 1962; engaged in sales and pub. relations Winston-Salem Pepsi-Cola Bottling Co. (N.C.), 1962-68; mem. 91st-92d Congresses 5th Dist. N.C. Commr. Little League Baseball. Mem. N.C. Republican Exec. Com., Forsyth County Young Reps.; chmn. Davidson County (N.C.) Bd. Commrs., 1966-68; mem. adv. council N.C. Fedn. Teen-Age Reps., Nat. Fedn. Teen-Age Republicans. Served with AUS, 1953-54. Named Distinguished Citizen, George Washington U., 1969; Christian Athletic of Year, So. Baptist Sports Assn., 1951. Mem. U.S. Army Athletic Assn. (hon.), Am. Legion (mem. nat. distinguished guests com.), U.S. Naval Acad. Athletic Assn. (hon.). Republican. Home: RFD 5 Winston-Salem NC 27101 Office: 429 Cannon House Office Bldg Washington DC 20515

MIZELLE, MERRIMOND BROWN, govt. ofcl.; b. Jamesville, N.C., Sept. 15, 1924; s. William Mayo and Mary (Brow) M.; B.C.E., N.C. State U., 1946; m. Elsie Virginia James, Aug. 14, 1948; children—Pamela James, William Russell, Michael Brown. Engr. South Eastern Underwriters Assn., Atlanta, 1946-54; spl. agt. Continental Ins. Co., Raleigh, N.C., 1954-67; sales supr. Great Am. Ins. Co., Raleigh, 1971—; asst. fire and casualty actuary N.C. Dept. Ins., Raleigh, 1971—. Registered real estate broker, N.C.; registered profl. engr., N.C.; Chartered Property and Casualty Underwriter. Mem. Chartered Property and Casualty Underwriters Soc. Democrat. Methodist. Patentee drain cleaner. Home: 3437 Churchill Rd Raleigh NC 27607 Office: N C Dept Ins Raleigh NC 27602

MMAHAT, JOHN ANTHONY, lawyer; b. New Orleans, Sept. 5, 1931; s. Joseph and Mary (Bertucci) M.; B.A., Tulane U., 1956, J.D., 1958; m. Arlene Cecile Montgomery, Aug. 12, 1967; children—Arlene Cecile, Amy Montgomery. Admitted to La. bar, 1958, since practiced in Metairie; sr. partner Mmahat, Gagliano & Duffy, 1958—. Chmn. bd. Medallion Realty, Inc., 33 Flavors of South, Inc.; pres. Gulf Fed. Savs. & Loan Assn., Exec. House Bldg., Inc. Vice chmn. New Orleans Aviation Bd., 1964—; mem. Gov.'s Task Force Com. to Draft Goals for La., 1969. Mem. La. Democratic Central Com., 1960-64; judge ad hoc First Parish Ct., Jefferson Parish, 1965. Bd. dirs. Muscular Dystrophy Assn. Am.; mem. men's adv. com. League Women Voters. Served with USAF, 1951-53. Recipient Glendy Burke medal for oratory Tulane U., 1956; Distinguished Service award as outstanding young man of Greater New Orleans Jr. C. of C., 1965. Mem. Am., La. bar assns., La. Landmarks Soc., Friends of Cabildo, Delgado Art Mus., Metairie Bus. Assn. K.C. Club: New Orleans Athletic. Home: 1239 1st St New Orleans LA 70130 Office: 5416 Veterans Meml Blvd Metairie LA 70003

MOAK, FRANKLIN EDWIN, educator; b. Bogue Chitto, Miss., Dec. 22, 1925; s. David Silas and Carrie (Greer) M.; B.B.A., U. Miss., 1949; M.A., Columbia, 1954, Ed.D., 1956; m. Helen Gibson Hutchcraft, June 28, 1950; children—Polly Ann, Franklin Edwin, Amanda Winn, Andrew David, Elizabeth Wadsworth, James Hutchcraft. Clk., I.C.R.R., Jackson, Miss., 1943-45; comml. rep. So. Bell Telephone Co., Atlanta, 1948-50; recreation asst. Tchrs. Coll., Columbia, N.Y.C., 1954, supr. internat. teaching service bur., 1954-55, counselor student orgns., 1955-56, dir. placement, 1956-57, asst. provost, asst. prof., 1957-60; asso. prof. edn., dir. placement and financial aids U. Miss., Oxford, 1960-64, dean div. student personnel, prof. edn., 1964—; Fulbright cons. Universidad Indsl. de Santander, Bucaramga, Colombia, S.A., 1967. Cons., Passaic (N.J.) Bd. Edn., 1958-59, cons. nat. grad. study grants selection bd. Girl Scouts U.S.A., 1959-60; exec. bd. area council Boy Scouts Am., 1967. Trustee St. Anthony Ednl. Found., Inc., N.Y., 1968—; bd. dirs. Hosp. Crippled Adults, Memphis, 1969—; ho. of dels. Nat. Interfrat. Conf., 1968-70, mem. nominating com., 1970. Served from 2d lt. to capt. AUS, 1950-53. Recipient Rotary Found. Group Study award to Switzerland, 1967. Mem. Am. Assn. Sch. Adminstrs., N.E.A., Assn. Higher Edn., Am. Personnel and Guidance Assn., So. Coll. Placement Assn., Assn. Sch., Coll. and Univ. Staffing (exec. com. 1958-60), Am. Coll. Personnel Assn., Miss. Edn. Assn., Oxford-Lafayette C. of C. (dir. 1969—), Kappa Delta Pi, Phi Delta Kappa, Delta Sigma Pi, Delta Psi, Omicron Delta Kappa. Presbyn. (elder). Mason (32 deg., K.T., Shriner), Rotarian (dir. 1962-64, pres. 1965-66, dist. gov. 1968). Clubs: Oxford Country; St. Anthony (N.Y.C.). Contbr. articles ednl. publs. Home: Pinecrest Dr Oxford MS 38655 Office: U Miss University MS 38677

MOAK, SAMUEL KUHN, educator; b. Yonan, Korea, Dec. 15, 1929; s. Young Moon and Ham Am (Park) M.; came to U.S., 1957; B.S., Colo. State U., 1959; M.S., U. Ky., 1962; Ph.D., N.C. State U., 1966; m. Soon Wha, May 10, 1945; 1 dau., Joanne. Instr. econs. N.C. State U., Raleigh, 1965; asst. prof. Campbell Coll., Buies Creek, N.C., 1966; asso. prof. econs. U. Richmond, Va., 1967—. Served to capt. Republic of Korean Army, 1950-56. Mem. Am., Korean econ. socs., Am. Agrl. Econ. Assn., Gamma Sigma Delta, Beta Epsilon. Presbyn. Club: Nat. Economists. Home: 7019 Monument Av Richmond VA 23226

MOBLEY, CARLTON, justice Supreme Ct. Ga.; b. nr. Hillsboro, Ga., Dec. 7, 1906; s. Jesse Aidine and Little Pearl (Jackson) M.; A.B., LL.B. cum laude, Mercer U., 1928; m. Margaret Elrod, Jan. 6, 1934; 1 dau., Margaret Elrod. Admitted to Ga. bar, 1928; mem. U.S. Congress. 6th Dist. Ga., 1932-34; practice law, 1937-41. 46-54; sec. exec. dept. State Ga., 1934-47; asst. atty. gen. Ga., 1941-42; asso. justice Supreme Ct. Ga., 1954—. Served from lt. to lt. comdr. USNR, 1943-46. Mem. Am., Ga., Macon bar assns., Sigma Pi. Delta Theta Phi. Baptist. Mason (Shriner), Elk, Kiwanian. Home: 3163 Habersham Rd NW Atlanta GA 30305 Office: Jud Bldg State Capitol Atlanta GA 30303

MOBLEY, ELGIE RONALD, JR., banker; b. Red Rock, Tex., July 8, 1930; s. Elgie R. and Mary (Wright) M.; B.B.A., U. Tex., 1951; m. Billie Marie Conrad, Nov. 23, 1950; children—Elgie Ronald, Melanie Marie, Kevin Reid, Darren Fendall. Asst. cashier Jefferson State Bank, San Antonio, 1952; asst. examiner Tex. State Banking Dept., Austin, 1952-54; office mgr. South Tex. White Truck Service, Corpus Christi, 1954-56; with Victoria Bank & Trust Co. (Tex.), 1956—, v.p., cashier, 1969-72, sr. v.p., cashier, 1972—. Bd. dirs. Tex. Gulf Coast chpt. The Arthritis Found., Houston. Lutheran. Home: 404 Cannon Rd Victoria TX 77901 Office: PO Box 1698 Victoria TX 77901

MOBLEY, JOHN HOMER, II, lawyer; b. Shreveport, La., Apr. 28, 1930; s. John H. and Beulah (Wilson) M.; A.B., U. Ga., 1951, J.D., 1953; m. Sue Lawton, Aug. 9, 1958; children—John Lawton, Anne Davant. Admitted to Ga. bar, 1952; practiced in Atlanta, 1955; mem. firm Kelley & Mobley, 1956-63, Gambrell & Mobley, 1963—. Served as 1st lt. Judge Adv. Gen. Corps, USAF, 1953-55. Mem. Am., Atlanta bar assns., State Bar Ga., Am. Judicature Soc., Phi Delta Phi, Kappa Alpha Order. Episcopalian. Clubs: Lawyers, Atlanta Athletic, Piedmont Driving, Atlanta Country, Commerce. Home: 4348 Sentinel Post Rd NW Atlanta GA 30327 Office: 1st Nat Bank Bldg Atlanta GA 30303

MOBLEY, WILFORD REAGAN, JR., stock broker; b. Fort Oglethorpe, Ga., June 25, 1923; s. Wilford Reagan and Frankie A. (Mobley) M.; B.B.A., U. Tex., 1948; m. Billie Janice Wilkerson, Feb. 20, 1954; children—Mark Reagan, Jennifer Ann. Sales mgr. Scobey Moving & Storage Co., San Antonio, 1958-62; with R.L. Stewart & Co., Inc., securities, 1962—, chief exec. officer, 1968—. Mem. camp bd. mgmt. YMCA, San Antonio, 1968-69; mem. Tex. Lions Crippled Children Camp Com., 1966-71; chmn. camp capers com. Episcopal Diocese of West Tex., 1965-70; dist. commr. Alamo Area council Boy Scouts Am., 1951-53, asst. scoutmaster, 1967—. Served with USAF, 1942-46, 50-53. Mem. Internat. Assn. Financial Planners, Pi Kappa Alpha. Episcopalian (lay reader 1962—). Lion (sec. 1953—, chaplain 1969-71, bd. dirs. 1954-59). Home: 122 Ridgehaven Pl San Antonio TX 78209 Office: 5140 Broadway San Antonio TX 78209

MOCH, RONALD WILBUR, army officer, veterinarian; b. St. Louis, Dec. 23, 1942; s. Wilbur Fred and Mildred Ede (Koop) M.; B.S., U. Mo., 1964, D.V.M., 1966; M.L.A., Johns Hopkins, 1972; m. Judith Kay Zircher, Aug. 28, 1966; children—Kathy, Kimberly. Practice vet. medicine, St. Louis, 1966-67; commd. capt. U.S. Army, 1967; student Army Vet. Sch., Chgo., 1967; student, faculty devel. course Ft. Sam Houston, Tex., 1967; grad. psychol. warfare course, Ft. Bragg, N.C., 1968; asst. chief spl. projects and food tech., Chgo., 1967, acting chief, 1967-68; asst. chief Combat Service Support, Chgo., 1968, acting chief, 1968; resident vet. pathology Edgewood Arsenal, Md., 1968-72; head vet. medicine dept. NAMRU-3, Cairo, Egypt, 1972—; grad. med. officers career course, Ft. Sam Houston, 1970. Mem. Harford County Interfaith Assn., 1968. Leader, unit guide, faculty Am. Youth Found., 1963—. Decorated Army Commendation medal. Outstanding Agrl. Freshman scholar from Mo. U. to Sr. Camp Conf. for Young Men, Danforth Assn., 1963; Outstanding Young Men of Am., 1972. Mem. Am., Mo. vet. med. assns., Am. Assn. Mil. Surgeons, Am. Assn. Vet. Anatomists, Unicorn. Address: NAMRU-3 FPO New York City NY 09527

MOCK, FRED, municipal judge, b. 1921; B.B.A., U. Okla.; LL.B., U. Tulsa. Municipal judge, Tulsa. Office: City Hall Tulsa OK 73101*

MOCK, JOHN EDWIN, scientist; b. Altoona, Pa., Sept. 29, 1925; s. Daniel Raymond and Sarah (Lorenz) M.; B.S., U.S. Mil. Acad., 1947; B.S., Purdue U., 1950, M.S., 1950, Ph.D., 1960; M.S., Ohio State U., 1953; M.S., George Washington U., 1966, M.B.A., 1968; m. Jeannette Daly, Oct. 25, 1947; children—Donna Jean, Susan Jean. Project scientist Wright Air Devel. Center, O., 1949-54; staff scientist Hdqrs. U.S. Air Force, Germany, 1955-58; scientist Def. Atomic Support Agy., Washington, 1960-64; prof., exec. officer dept. 7ath. U.S. Air Force Acad., 1964-65; scientist Advanced Research Projects Agy., Washington, 1966-68; asso. prof. math. George Washington U., 1960-64, U. Va., 1966-67; dir. Ga. Sci. and Tech. Commn., Atlanta, 1968—, Ga. Inst. for Research in Biotech., 1969—. Cons. Kaman Nuclear, Nuclear Research Assos., Dept. Def., Coastal Plains Regional Commn., Appalachian Regional Commn., mem. Ga. Boundary Commn., 1968—, Ga. Econ. Devel. Policy Council, 1968—; rep. com. on natural resources and environmental mgmt. Nat. Gov's Conf., 1969—; chmn. Nat. Govs.' Council Sci. and Tech., 1970-71; dir. Coastal States Orgn., 1969-70; cons. Office Sec. Def., 1968-71, Nat. Acad. Engring. Com. Cities of Future, 1970—, NSF Intergovtl. Sci. Programs and Project RANN, 1971—, Council State Govts. Com. Sci. and Tech., 1969—. Bd. dirs. So. Interstate Nuclear Bd., Gulf U. Research Corp., State Tech. Services Program. Recipient Mark Mills award Am. Nuclear Soc., 1960. NSF study grantee 1965. Mem. Am. Nuclear Soc., A.A.A.S., Am. Geophys. Union, Operations Research Soc. Am., Am. Physics Soc., N.Y., Ga. acads. scis., Am. Soc. Engring. Edn., Am. Soc. for Oceanography, Marine Tech. Soc., Ga. Inventor's Assn., Sigma Xi. Home: 7220 Dunhill Terrace Atlanta GA 30328 Office: Ga Sci and Tech Commn Box 32745 Atlanta GA 30332

MOCK, PRESLEY JOE, physician; b. Hillsboro, Tex., May 17, 1910; s. Presley Miller and Inda May (Coleman) M.; A.A., Hillsboro Jr. Coll., 1928; B.A., U. Tex., 1931, M.D., 1935; m. Hazel Estell Barger, June 20, 1937; children—Presley Joe, Sue Gale (Mrs. Wesley Wayne Kooken). Rotating intern Jefferson Davis Hosp., Houston, 1935-37; gen. practice medicine and surgery, LaPorte, Tex., 1937—; mem. staffs Pasadena-Bayshore, Southmore hosps., Pasadena, Tex., Baptist Meml. Hosp., Houston. Dir. Medico Investment, Ltd., Pasadena, Medico Investment Co., Inc., Pasadena. Trustee LaPorte Ind. Sch. Dist., 1953-57. Bd. dirs. Pasadena Chamber Music Soc. Recipient Meritorious medal N.G., 1947. Fellow Am. Acad. Family Practice; mem. A.M.A., Tex Med. Assn., Harris County Med. Soc., Houston Acad. Medicine, LaPorte Bayshore C. of C. (dir. 1945-64, v.p. 1956). Mason (32 deg., Shriner), Rotarian (pres. 1942-43). Home: 410 S 1st St LaPorte TX 77571 Office: 815 S Broadway La Porte TX 77571

MOCK, WAYNE L., govt. ofcl.; b. Jeannette, Pa., Apr. 2, 1937; s. Harry L. and Ruth (Larimer) M.; S.B. in Chem. Engring., Mass. Inst. Tech., 1959; M.B.A. with high distinction, U. Mich., 1960, M.A. in Psychology, 1963, Ph.D. in Bus. Adminstrn., 1964; m. Lois S. Felson, June 9, 1963. Asst. prof. U. Mich. Grad. Sch. Bus., 1964-65, Columbia U. Grad. Sch. Bus., 1965-66; program and tng. officer Peace Corps, Peru, 1967-69; dir. research Peace Corps, Washington, 1969, spl. asst. to dep. dir., 1970-71; dir. programs Inter-Am. Social Devel. Inst., 1971—. Cons. to Equal Employment Opportunities Commn., 1966. Mem. Phi Beta Kappa, Beta Gamma Sigma. Home: 5700 26th St N Arlington VA 22207 Office: 806 Connecticut Av Washington DC 20525

MODLIN, DAVID GUY, JR., educator; b. Williamston, N.C., Oct. 23, 1943; s. David Guy and Nettie (Meador) M.; B.S., N.C. State U., 1966, M.S., 1968, Ph.D., 1971; m. Karen Jean Cockerham, June 7, 1969. Trainee Cal. State Hwy. Commn., Los Angeles, summer 1965; asst. structural engr. Singletary-Fowler Inc., Clarkton, N.C., summer 1966; asst. plant engr. Weyerhaeuser, Plymouth, N.C., summer 1967; project engr. N.C. State Hwy. Commn., Raleigh, N.C., 1968-71; asst. prof. civil engring., campus traffic planner La. State U., 1971—. Mem. Am. Soc. C.E., Inst. Traffic Engrs., Transp. Systems Planning Group of Hwy. Research Bd., Am. Soc. Engring. Edn., Am. Road Builders Assn., La. Engring. Soc., Phi Eta Sigma, Tau Beta Pi, Chi Epsilon, Phi Kappa Phi, Phi Kappa Tau. Baptist. Home: 1288 Kimbro Dr Baton Rouge LA 70808 Office: Dept Civil Engring La State U Baton Route LA 70803

MODLIN, GEORGE MATTHEWS, univ. chancellor; b. Elizabeth City, N.C., July 13, 1903; s. John William and Nannie E. (Matthews) M.; A.B., Wake Forest U., 1924; LL.D., 1947; M.A., Princeton 1925, Ph.D., 1932; LL.D., Stetson U., 1962, Hampden-Sidney Coll., 1971, U. Richmond, 1971; m. Virginia Pendleton Brinkley, June 2, 1928. Asst. in econs. Princeton, 1927-28, instr., 1928-32, asst. prof., 1932-38; part-time lectr. econs. Rutgers U., 1936-38; prof. econs., dean Sch. Bus. Adminstrn. U. Richmond (Va.) 1938-46, pres., 1946-71, chancellor, 1971—. Dir., 1st and Mchts. Nat. Bank, Richmond, C. & P. Telephone Co., Va. Pub. panel mem. War Labor Bd., 1943-45. Trustee Keesee Ednl. Fund, Inc. Mem. Richmond C. of C. (pres. 1951), So. U. Conf. (pres. 1955), So. Assn. Baptist Schs. and Colls. (pres. 1952), Assn. Va. Colls. (pres. 1952), Am., So. econ. assns., Assn. Am. Colls. (pres. 1962), Phi Beta Kappa, Kappa Alpha, Omicron Delta Kappa. Clubs: Country of Virginia, Commonwealth. Author: (with F. T. De Vyver) Development of Economic Society, 1936, rev., 1946; (with A. M. McIsaac) Social Control of Industry, 1938. Home: 2Bostwick Lane University of Richmond VA 23173

MODRALL, AUGUSTUS WILLIAM, JR., architect; b. Dallas, Dec. 24, 1930; s. Augustus William and Corinne (Sowell) M.; B.Arch., U. Tex., 1953; m. Janis Marie Dechman, Dec. 4, 1954; children—Gayle Lynn, Gretchen Ellen. Draftsman, architect, Golemon & Rolfe, Houston, 1953-59; architect Cowell & Neuhaus, Houston, 1959-63; with Koetter, Tharp & Cowell, Houston, 1964—, architect, 1964-65, asso. partner, 1965-70, v.p., 1970-72, sr. v.p., 1972—. Mem. A.I.A. (sec. Houston), Tex. Soc. Architects. Presbyn. (elder, deacon). Home: 6126 Reamer St Houston TX 77036 Office: 1535 W Loop South Houston TX 77027

MOEHLMAN, WILLIAM FREDERICK, metals co. exec.; b. Madison, Wis., Aug. 7, 1897; s. William Frederick and Dorothea (Niederer) M.; B.S., U. Wis., 1922; m. Constance Kennedy, Sept. 3, 1969. Dist. engr. Armco Drainage & Metal Products, Middletown, O., 1927-30, municipal and airport engr., 1930-33; sales mgr. Tenn. Metal Culvert Co., Nashville, 1934-45, v.p., mgr., dir., 1945-62, chmn., sec., 1962—; dir. Home Fed. Savs. & Loan Assn., Knoxville, Tenn., 1950—; chmn., sec. Knox Concrete Products Inc., Knoxville, 1962—, Southeastern Inc., Knoxville, 1962—. Served with AUS, 1918-19. Mem. Gt. Smoky Mountain Conservation Assn. (pres.), Nat. Soc. Profl. Engrs., Am. Soc. C.E., Knoxville C. of C. (pres. 1947-50), Am. Heart Assn. (dir. 1959-62), Tau Beta Pi. Mason. Home: Route 5 Sevierville TN 37862 Office: Box 1030 Knoxville TN 37901

MOELLER, WALTER H., supt.schs.; b. Chester, Ill., Feb. 20, 1912; B.S., Central Mich. U., 1944; M.S., Wayne State U., 1953. Elementary prin. St. Pauls Lutheran Sch., Farmington, Mich., 1932-33; elementary tchr. St. Johns Sch., Bellwood, Ill., 1933-34, Trinity Lutheran Sch., Saginaw, Mich., 1934-46; prin., tchr., dir. Christian edn. Peace Lutheran Sch., Detroit, 1946-66; dir. Christian edn. and youth Grace Luth. Ch., Winter Haven, Fla., 1966-69, prin., 1969—. Chmn. parish edn. com. Fla.-Ga. Dist. Luth. Ch., 1966, now supt. schs. Mem. Luth. Edn. Assn., Phi Delta Kappa. Address: 1341 Av South NW Winter Haven FL 33880*

MOFFET, JOHN ANDREW, broadcasting co. exec.; b. Phila., July 22, 1915; s. Andrew and Jane (Oetter) M.; B.S., Swarthmore Coll., 1937; m. G. A. Elizabeth Morris, Dec. 19, 1942; children—Gwendolyn Ida, John Andrew II, William Morris. Vice-pres., chief engr. William L. Foss Inc., Washington, 1946-52; partner firm Silliman, Moffet & Kowalski, Cons. Radio & TV Engrs., Washington, 1952—. Mem. Assn. Fed. Communications Engrs. (pres. 1971-72, Soc. Broadcast Engrs., I.E.E.E., Kappa Sigma. Republican. Presbyn. Home: 2919 N Edison St Arlington VA 22207 Office: 711 14th St NW Washington DC 20005

MOFFETT, ANDERSON GRANT, state ofcl.; b. Belvoir, Va., May 8, 1919; s. Anderson Franklin and Lucy (Grant) M.; B.S. in Agrl. Edn., Va. Poly. Inst., 1941; postgrad. N.C. State Agr. Policy Inst., 1962, U. Richmond, 1963; m. Anne Fielding, Apr. 25, 1942; 1 son, Grant Lower. Tchr. vocational agr. pub. schs., Warrenton, Va., 1946-48; poultry marketing agt. Va. Dept. Agr., Richmond, 1948-49, supr. market expansion, 1949-63, asst. dir. div. markets and market devel., 1963—; dir. program devel. and field services Va. Farm Bur. Fedn., Richmond, 1968—. Adviser Va. Agr. Export-Import Com., 1963—. Mem. Va. World Trade Com., Shenandoah Community Assn. Bd. dirs. Va. Rural Health Assn., Richmond Met. Authority; mem. nursing liaison com. Va. Commonwealth U. Served to maj. AUS, 1941-46; PTO. Recipient Recognition award Va. Poultry Fedn., 1951, award Nat. Safety Council, 1954, U.S. Dept. Agr., 1965. Mem. Am. Marketing Assn., Alpha Zeta. Baptist. Rotarian. Home: 9400 Highgate Rd Richmond VA 23235 Office: Va Farm Bur Fedn 200 W Grace St Richmond VA 23220

MOFFETT, SAM(UEL) M(CKEE), educator; b. Madison, Ind., Jan. 23, 1916; s. Robert B. and Nellie (Elliott) M.; A.B. magna cum laude, Hanover Coll., 1938; Ph.D. in organic chemistry, Ohio State U., 1942; m. Janet Duncan Holt, June 16, 1942; children—Kenneth McKee, Douglas Elliott (dec.). Instr. chemistry Alma (Mich.) Coll., 1942-45, acting head dept. chemistry, 1944-45; asst. prof. chemistry Ohio Wesleyan U., Delaware, 1945-46; asst. prof. Park Coll., Parkville, Mo., 1946-51, acting head dept. chemistry, 1946-47, head dept. chemistry, 1947-51; asso. research chemist Midwest Research Inst., Kansas City, Mo., 1951-53, sr. research chemist, 1953-54; sr. research chemist John Deere Chem. Co., Pryor, Okla., 1954-57, research group leader, 1957-61; sr. research chemist Nitrogen div. Allied Chem. Corp., Hopewell, Va., 1961-64; prof. chemistry Va. Union U., Richmond, 1964-65; asso. prof. chemistry Va. State Coll., Petersburg, 1965-67, prof. 1967—, head dept. chemistry, 1969-71. Pres. Hopewell (Va.) Council on Human Relations, 1966; bd. dirs. Va. Council on Human Relations 1963—. Mem. Am. Chem. Soc., A.A.A.S., Sci. Research Soc. Am., Soc. for Social Responsibility in Sci., Am. Assn. U. Profs., Sigma Xi, Gamma Sigma Pi, Delta Epsilon, Phi Lambda Upsilon. Presbyn. Research on organic nitrogen compounds. Patentee nitrogen compounds. Home: 3001 W Riverside Av Hopewell VA 23860 Office: Va State Coll Petersburg VA 23803

MOFFITT, CATHERINE DYESS, psychologist; b. Claude, Tex., Dec. 30, 1908; d. Benjamin Cicero and Alice (McClellan) Dyess; B.S., Okla. A. and M. Coll. (now Okla. State U.), 1928; M.A., Furman U., 1952; m. James William Moffitt, Feb. 16, 1930 (dec. 1956). Faculty, S.W. Bapt. Coll., Bolivar, Mo., 1928-31, Okla. Bapt. U., Shawnee, 1931-36; tester Greenville (S.C.) City Schs., 1948-52; psychologist Guilford County Mental Health Center, High Point, Greensboro, N.C., 1952-69; dir. psychol. services Devel. Evaluation Clinic, Guilford County Health Dept., High Point, 1969-71; psychologist

Infant and Child Clinic, High Point, 1971—. Instr., High Point Meml. Hosp. Sch. Nursing, 1963-66, High Point Coll. Evening Sch., 1964-66. Asso. mem. Am., N.C. psychol. assns.; mem. N.C. Pub. Health Assn., N.C. Mental Health Assn., High Point Execs. Club, Phi Kappa Phi, Zeta Tau Alpha. Democrat. Baptist. Club: Altrusa. Home: 804 Woodrow Av High Point NC 27262 Office: 4015 W Wendover Av Greensboro NC 27470

MOFFITT, FRANKLYN MONROE, oil co. exec.; b. Lynbrook, N.Y., Aug. 24, 1914; s. John J. and Olive (Brower) M.; B.A., Duke, 1938; m. Nancy Webb, Apr. 21, 1937; children—Earle W., F. Brower. With Ashland Oil, Inc. (Ky.), 1940—, chemist, terminal mgr., Coraopolis, Pa., salesman, div. mgr., Pitts., sr. salesman, mgr. light oil sales, mgr. nat. account sales, 1940-57, v.p., 1957—, sr. v.p. Ashland Chem. Co. div.; v.p. R.J. Brown Co., St. Louis; dir. R.J. Brown Co. of Can., Ltd.; v.p., dir. JaRo-Chem. Inc. Bd. dirs. Ry. Progress Inst., Adhesive and Sealant Council. Served as lt. USNR, 1943-45. Mem. Nat. Petroleum Refiners Assn. (chmn. petrochem. div.), Q.M.'s Assn. U.S., Engrs. Soc. Western Pa., Ry. Club Pitts., Am. Petroleum Inst., Ky., Huntington chambers commerce, Newcomen Soc., Am. Coke and Coal Chems. Inst. (dir.), Sigma Phi Epsilon. Episcopalian. Clubs: Dunes Beach and Golf (Myrtle Beach, S.C.); Bellefonte Country (Ashland). Home: 2727 Algonquin Av Ashland KY 41101 Office: 1409 Winchester Av Ashland KY 41101

MOFFITT, ROY BRATTON, lawyer, engr.; b. Greensboro, N.C., Sept. 11, 1927; s. Royall Brower and Janet (Bratton) M.; B. Geol. Engring., N.C. State U., 1952, profl. degree in Ceramic Engring., 1957, B.S. in Chem. Engring., 1961; J.D. George Washington U., 1966; m. Hilda Marie Geide, July 8, 1967. With coal mine works U.S. Steel Co., Fairfield, Ala., 1952-54; instr. engring. N.C. State U., Raleigh, 1955-57, asst. prof. research, 1957-63; with Office Legislative Planning, U.S. Dept. Commerce, Patent Office, Washington, 1963-68; coordinator patent activities Superior Continental Corp., 1968-69, patent counsel, 1969—. Admitted to D.C. bar, 1967, N.C. bar, 1968; engring cons., 1957-63. Republican precinct capt., Birmingham, Ala., 1952. Served with USMC, 1946-47. Mem. Profl. Engrs. N.C., D.C., N.C., Catawoa bar assns. Kiwanian. Contbr. articles to profl. jours. Patentee in field. Home: Box 777 T Route 2 Hickory NC 28601 Office: Superior Continental Corp PO Box 489 Hickory NC 28601

MOFIELD, WILLIAM RAY, coll. adminstr.; b. Hardin, Ky., July 3, 1921; s. Kelzie E. and Zela (Irvan) M.; A.B., Murray State Coll., 1943; M.A., Columbia, 1958; Ph.D., So. Ill. U., 1964; LL.D., Ida. Christian Coll., 1962; m. Janie Belle Bloomingburg, July 24, 1953; 1 dau., Ruth Ann. Tchr., Vienna (Ill.) High Sch., 1944-45; with WPAD-AM-FM, Paducah, Ky., 1945-59, mgr., 1959; mgr. WCBL-AM-FM, Benton, 1959; dir. acad. affairs radio-tv dept. So. Ill. U., 1959-64; exec. pres. Murray (Ky.) State U., 1964-68, chmn. dept. communications, 1968—. Stringer, CBS News, 1945-64; sportscaster Ashland Oil Network, 1946-59; radio-tv mgmt. cons., 1945—; alternate mem. Ky. Commn. Higher Edn., 1965—. Bd. dirs. to Assn., Paducah, Ky., 1956-59; commr. Boy Scouts Am., 1965, 66—, bd. dirs., 1965—; bd. dirs. Benton (Ky.) Hosp., Ky. State Penitentiary, Eddyville. Served with USNR, 1942-43. Recipient Duke of Paducah Civic award Mayor Paducah, 1956; named Ky. Col. CBS Found. News fellow, 1958. Mem. Nat. Assn. Broadcasters, Am. Soc. Disk Jockey Newscasters, Sportscasters, Ky. Broadcasters Assn., Ky. Edn. Assn., Alpha Phi Omega, Alpha Phi Gamma, Sigma Delta Chi, Tau Kappa Alpha, Sigma Beta Gamma. Democrat. Mem. Ch. of Christ. Rotarian. Home: RFD 1 Hardin KY 42048 Office: Murray State U Murray KY 42071

MOGER, ALLEN WESLEY, educator; b. Nansemond County, Va., May 12, 1905; s. Lorenzo Dow and Martha (Johnson) M.; A.B., Randolph Macon Coll., 1927; postgrad. Johns Hopkins, 1927-28; M.A., Columbia, 1935, Ph.D., 1940; m. Marguerite Neale, June 19, 1936; children—Alice Neale, Esther. Instr. Latin, Va. Episcopal Sch., Lynchburg, Va., 1928-29; with Washington and Lee U., 1929—, successively instr., asst. prof. to asso. prof., 1929-51, prof. history, 1951—; vis. prov. prof. history U. Va., summer 1956, Columbia, summer 1958; vis. prof. history U. Va., 1957-58. Mem. Am., So., Va. hist. socs., Va. Social Sci. Assn. (pres. 1949), Phi Beta Kappa, Omicron Delta Kappa, Tau Kappa Alpha, Pi Gamma Mu. Presbyn. Author: The Rebuilding of the Old Dominion, 1880-1902, 1940; Virginia: Bourbonism to Byrd, 1870 to 1925, 1968. Contbr. articles to profl. jours. Home: 506 Jackson Av Lexington VA 24450

MOHR, JULIAN BOEHM, chem. mfg. co. exec.; b. Atlanta, Apr. 29, 1930; s. Samuel and Marian (Boehm) M.; B.A., Washington and Lee U., 1952; m. Teena Stern, June 24, 1956 (div. Aug. 1970); children—Julie Lin, Greg Eugene. With Momar, Inc., Atlanta, 1952—, treas., 1956—, pres., 1965—; v.p. Momar (Can.) Ltd., Toronto, 1961—, treas. Momar Export, Inc., Atlanta, 1960, pres. 1965—; v.p. J. &B. Enterprizes, real estate devel. and apt. mgmt. co.; dir. Cansa div. Momar South Africa, Capetown. Cons., Paris, France, 1967. Pres. exec. bd. Atlanta Civic Ballet, Inc., 1964-69. Jewish religion (trustee temple 1968—). Mem. B'nai B'rith. Clubs: Civitan of Atlanta, Toastmasters (pres. 1959). Home: Box 20224 Station N Atlanta GA 30325 Office: 1830 Ellsworth Industrial Dr NW Atlanta GA 30318

MOISY, CLAUDE, journalist. Chief, Washington bur. France Presse. Home: 5421 Duvall Dr Westmoreland Hills Washington DC 20016*

MOLAND, JOHN, JR., educator; b. Jacksonville, Fla., Mar. 24, 1926; s. John and Tular (Sudderth) M.; B.A., Fisk U., 1952, M.A., 1954; Ph.D. in Sociology, U. Chgo., 1967; m. Kathryn Gadson, Apr. 15, 1960; children—Jesse, John, Kathy. Asst. prof. sociology Fla. A. and M. U., Tallahassee, 1953-60; asst. prof. sociology Grambling (La.) Coll., 1960-61, prof. sociology, 1965-68; chmn. sociology dept. Fisk U., 1968-69; dir. social research Center Social Research, chmn. sociology dept. So. U., Baton Rouge, 1969—; research asst. Youth Studies Program, U. Chgo., 1961-63; research asso. Program Detached Workers, YMCA Met.-Chgo., 1964. Research cons. Wash. State U., Pullman, 1965. Chmn. housing com. Baton Rouge Goals Congrsss. Served with AUS, 1945-46. Mem. Am., So., Southwestern sociol. assns., La. Edn. Assn., Am. Assn. U. Profs., Soc. Study Social Problems, Ancient Mystical Order Rosae Crucis, Alpha Kappa Delta, Alpha Phi Alpha. Epicsopalian (treas.). Contbr. articles to profl. jours. Research in juvenile delinquency, 1962-66. Home: 2133 78th Av Baton Rouge LA 70807

MOLANDER, WILLIAM AUSTIN, electronic co. exec.; b. Boston, Mar. 23, 1926; s. William A. and Ellen (Baron) M.; B.S. in Elec. Engring., Tufts U., 1951; M.Elec. Engring., Stevens Inst. Tech., 1956; postgrad. Poly. Inst. Bklyn., 1951-54; m. Sally Ann Stone, Aug. 2, 1969; children—(from previous marriage) William A., Darlene. Engr., Curtiss-Wright Corp., Caldwell, N.J., 1951-54; mgr. computer br. Kearfott div. Gen. Precision, Inc., Clifton, N.J., 1954-62; dir. communication engring. Honeywell, Inc., Tampa, Fla., 1962-67; chmn. bd., pres. Fla. Communications & Electronics, Inc., Clearwater, 1967—. Registered profl. engr., Fla., N.J. Mem. Armed Forces Communications and Electronics Assn., Tau Beta Pi. Patentee hydraulic valve. Home: 1458 S Jefferson Av Clearwater FL 33516 Office: 800 Belleair Rd Clearwater FL 33516

MOLER, EDWARD HAROLD, lawyer; b. Oklahoma City, May 26, 1923; s. Harold Stanley and Rosemary (Callahan) M.; B.A., U. Okla., 1947, LL.B., 1948; m. Donna Cram, Sept. 12, 1964; children—John Frederick, Shelley Elizabeth, Christopher Bryan. Admitted to Okla. bar, 1948, since practiced in Oklahoma City; atty. Reynolds & Ridings, 1948-52; asst. city municipal counselor Oklahoma City, 1952-59, city municipal counselor, 1959-61; partner Barefoot, Moler & Claro, 1961—. Bd. dirs. Mummers Theatre. Served to 2d lt. USAAF, 1944-45. Mem. Oklahoma County Bar Assn. (pres., dir.), Phi Delta Phi, Phi Gamma Delta (pres., dir. Nu Omega Housing Assn.). Rotarian. Home: 2540 NW Grand Blvd Oklahoma City OK 73116 Office: City Nat Bank Tower Oklahoma City OK 73102

MOLES, HUGH SHERMAN, lumberman, farmer; b. Sneedville, Tenn., July 6, 1902; s. William Sherman and Mary (Williams) M.; student pub. schs.; m. Elsie Katherine Lawson, Dec. 26, 1926; 1 dau., Mary Jane (Mrs. William P. Goodman). Automobile dealer Moles and Livesay Chevrolet Dealer, Kyles Ford. Tenn., 1928-30; with Hugh S. Moles, gen. mdse. and produce, 1930-46; lumberman, farmer, Rogersville, Tenn., 1946—. Chmn. Hancock County Bd. Edn., 1934-38; Floterial rep. 70th gen. assembly, Hancock-Grainger Counties, 1937-39; mem. Hancock County Ct., 1944-46; mem. Rogersville Bd. Alderman, 1952; chmn. Rogersville Water Commn., 1956-62; mem. Tenn. Ho. of Reps. from Hawkins County, 1959-64. Served with U.S. Army, 1921-22. Republican. Baptist. Mason. Eagle. Address: 300 E Broadway Rogersville TN 37857

MOLETTE, CARLTON WOODARD, educator; b. Pine Bluff, Ark., Aug. 23, 1939; s. Carlton William and Evelyn Adelle (Richardson) M.; B.A., Morehouse Coll., 1959; M.A., U. Ia., 1962; Ph.D., Fla. State U., 1968; m. Barbara Jean Roseburr, June 15, 1960; children—Carla Evelyn, Andrea Rose. Asst. dir. Little Theatre Tuskegee Inst., 1960-61; tech. dir. Des Moines (Ia.) Community Playhouse, 1962-63; asst. prof. drama Howard U., 1963-64; with Fla. A. & M. U., 1964-69, asst. prof. speech and drama, 1964-66, asso. prof., 1967-69; asso. prof. drama Spelman Coll., 1969—, chmn. dept., 1971; theatre cons. Federal City Coll.; U. Neb.; Bowling Green State U.; Free So. Theatre; N.C. Speech and Drama Assn. Trustee Arts Festival of Atlanta. Recipient Ford Found. Early Admission scholarship; Carnegie Found. fellowship. Mem. Dramatists Guild, U.S. Inst. for Theatre Tech., Am. Theatre Assn., Nat. Assn. Dramatic and Speech Arts, Alpha Phi Alpha. Playwright Rosalee Pritchett, 1971; Dr. B.S. Black, 1969; editor Encore, 1965-71. Home: 3174 Mangum Lane SW Atlanta GA 30311 Office: Spelman Coll Box 579 Atlanta GA 30314

MOLHOLM, ALICE BURNS (MRS. HANS BARSO MOLHOLM), social worker; b. Glasgow, Scotland, Aug. 21, 1911; d. John Thomas and Alice Gallagher (Corcoran) Burns; came to U.S., 1924, naturalized, 1943; B.S., St. Xavier's Coll., 1932; M.A. (Univ. scholar) Loyola U. Sch. Social Work, 1935; m. Hans Barso Molholm, Feb. 6, 1949 (dec. June 1971); stepchildren John T. Thomas B. With Cook County Bur. Pub. Welfare, 1933-35; supr. field work, instr. advanced casework Loyola U. Sch. Social work, Chgo., 1935-42; dist. supr. home service dept. Chgo. chpt. A.R.C., 1942-44; dir. intramural service Chgo. State Hosp. for Mentally Ill, 1944-45; exec. dir. Forest Park Children's Center, St. Louis, 1945-47; asst. chief social service Inst. Juvenile Research Chgo., 1947-49; with East St. Louis Child Guidance Clinic, 1949; asso. prof. social work Washington U., St. Louis, 1950-54; ednl. dir. Columbus (O.) State Hosp. for Mentally Ill, 1954-57; dir. social services dept. Mental Health Inst., Independence, Ia., 1958; asst. dir. social service dept. U. Ark. Med. Center, Little Rock, 1957-65, 66-67, mem. child protection com., asso. prof. social work, 1966-67; asso. prof. social work U. Ark. Grad. Sch. Social Work, 1970—; dir. casework services Ark. State Hosp., Little Rock, 1967—. Cons. social work to various pub. pvt. instns., agys.; mem. task force Ark. Child Protection Com. Fellow Am. Orthopsychiat. Assn.; mem. Acad. Certified Social Workers, Nat. Assn. Social Workers, Child Study Assn. Am., Council Social Work Edn. Home: 7318 Ouachita Dr Little Rock AR 72205 Office: 4313 W Markham St Little Rock AR 72201

MOLL, WILHELM, educator; b. Vienna, Austria, June 2, 1920 (came to U.S., 1939, naturalized, 1945); s. Lopold and Marie (Schlesinger) M.; B.A., Denison U., 1943; J.D., U. Chgo., 1945; M.S. in Library Sci., Catholic U. Am., 1956; m. Margot Weith, Dec. 14, 1951; 1 son, Kenneth Carl. Polit. analyst War Dept., Frankfurt, Germany, 1945-49, fgn. affairs specialist, Bonn, Germany, 1949-51; research asso. war documents dept. Columbia U., N.Y.C., 1951-55; documents librarian Ind. U., Bloomington, 1956-60; asst. med. librarian Med. Center, U. Ky., Lexington, 1960-62; dir. med. library U. Va., Charlottesville, 1962—, asso. prof., 1962-70, prof., 1971—. Mem. Phi Beta Kappa. Contbr. to profl. jours. Home: 2217 Greenbrier Dr Charlottesville VA 22901

MOLONY, MICHAEL JANSSENS, JR., lawyer; b. New Orleans, Sept. 2, 1922; s. Michael Jassens and Marie (Perret) M.; J.D., Tulane U., 1950; m. Jane Leslie Waguespack, Oct. 21, 1951; children—Jane Leslie, Michael Janssens III, Megan, Kevin, Sara, Brian, Ian, Duncan. Admitted to La. bar, 1950; partner Molony & Baldwin, attys., 1950; asso. partner Jones, Flanders, Waechter & Walker, 1951-56; partner Jones, Walker, Waechter, Poitevent, Carrere & Denegre, New Orleans, 1956—; instr., lectr. Tulane U., 1953-59. Asst. sec.-treas. La. Law Inst., 1958-70. Mem. Eisenhower Legal Com., 1952; chmn. Gov.'s Task Force on Space Industry, 1971-72; chmn. Gov.'s Adv. Com. River Area Transp. and Planning Com., 1971-72; mem. Gov.'s Task Force on Natural Gas Requirements, 1971-72; mem. Mayor's Adv. Com. on City Charter; mem. goals found. council, ex-officio mem. goals found. Met. New Orleans Goals Program, 1969-72; vice chmn. ad hoc planning com. Goals for Met. New Orleans, 1969-72; vice chmn. Port of New Orleans Operation La. Impact Com., 1969-70; mem. Met. Area Com., New Orleans, 1970-72. Trustee, Pub. Affairs Research Council La., 1970-72; mem. corporate bd. Boys Clubs Greater New Orleans, 1969-71. Served from aviation cadet to staff sgt., AUS, USAAF, 1942-46, PTO. Mem. Am. (mem. anti-trust law com. 1968, mgmt. co-chmn. com. devel. law union adminstrn. and procedures 1969, mem. com. equal employment opportunity practice and procedure labor relations law sect.), La. (sec.-treas. 1957-59, gov. 1957-60, editor 1957-59), New Orleans (dir. legal aid bur. 1954, chmn. com. legislature 1968, vice chmn. standing com. pub. relations 1970-71), Fed. bar assns., Am. Judicature Soc., Internat. House, So. Inst. Mgmt. (a founder), U.S. (labor relations com. 1965, urban and regional affairs com. 1970-72, blue-ribbon com. lawyers for labor law reform), La. (dir. 1963-66), New Orleans Area (chmn. employer-employee relations council 1962-63, dir. 1963, v.p. bus. climate div. 1966-69), v.p. met. devel. and urban affairs 1969, pres. 1971, exec. com. bd. dirs. 1972) Chambers Commerce, Sigma Chi (pres. New Orleans alumni 1956). Roman Catholic. Clubs: Pickwick, Southern Yacht, Serra, Plimsoll, Bienville (New Orleans). Home: 3039 Hudson Pl New Orleans LA 70114 Office: 225 Baronne St New Orleans LA 70112

MONAGHAN, RICHARD PAUL, dentist; b. Port Arthur, Tex., July 9, 1909; s. Richard Vienne and Nancy Pearl (McClure) M.; student Tex. A. and M. Coll., 1927-28; D.D.S., Tex. Dental Coll., 1932; m. Laurene Lindsey, May 30, 1945; children—Susan (Mrs. Richard James Hockert), Janita (Mrs. Dee Lee Thomas). Practice dentistry, Overton, Tex., 1933—. Owner, Pemberton Co., Overton, Tex., 1966—; pres. TPM Co., Inc., Overton, 1962-67. Served with USNR, 1942-45. Mem. Am., Tex. dental assns., E. Tex. Dental Soc. (pres. 1958-59), Psi Omega. Democrat. Methodist. Rotarian. Named Outstanding Citizen Overton, C. of C., 1963. Patentee plastics. Home: 306 Lamar St Overton TX 75684 Office: PO Box 247 Overton TX 75684

MONAHAN, DAVID, supt. schs. Supt. schs. Catholic Diocese of Oklahoma City-Tulsa. Address: PO Box 512 Oklahoma City OK 73101*

MONBERG, LAWRENCE, architect; b. Copenhagen, Denmark, June 5, 1900; s. Lauritz C. and Anna (Theisen) M.; student Armour Inst. Tech., 1917-19; m. Evelyn Schold, June 21, 1937; children—Lawrence John, Bror Carl, Sven Helge. Came to U.S., 1909, naturalized (Act by Congress) 1909. Asso. Lawrence G. Hallberg, architects, 1921-33; own practice, 1934—; pres. Bay Islands Investments, Ltd., Nassau; designer Edgewater Hotel, Madison, Wis., Kungsholm Restaurant, Chgo., U. Wis. Extension Center, Kenosha, Carthage Coll. Sci. Library and Adminstrn. Bldg., Kenosha, and others. Served in U.S. Navy, 1917. Mem. A.I.A., Am. Legion, Navy League. Lutheran. Mason (32 deg.). Clubs: Maple Bluff Country (Madison, Wis.); Ill. Athletic (Chgo.). Home: 301 Spanish Trail SE Boca Raton FL 33432

MONCRIEF, EVERETTE WHITFIELD, JR., dentist; b. Montgomery, Ala., Nov. 8, 1930; s. Everette Whitfield and Ruth (Mathews) M.; student Emory U., 1948-50, Huntingdon Coll., 1950-51; D.M.D., U. Ala., 1955; M.P.H., U. N.C., 1968; m. Jane McFaden, July 18, 1953; children—Bonnie, Randall. Dental surgeon USAF, Alexandria, La., 1955-57; pvt. practice gen. dentistry, Montgomery, 1957-66; dental cons. Ala. State Health Dept., Montgomery, 1968—. Served with USAF, 1955-57. Recipient USPHS grant, 1967. Mem. Am. Dental Assn., Am. Assn. Pub. Health Dentists, Am., Ala. pub. health assns., Phi Delta Theta, Psi Omega. Home: 2420 Belcher Dr Montgomery AL 36111 Office: State Office Bldg Montgomery AL 36104

MONEY, JOHN MARSHALL, constrn. co. exec.; b. Carrollton, Miss., June 20, 1900; s. John Clark and Annie Laura (Marshall) M.; student Massey Bus. Coll., 1916-17, U. Va., 1918-21; m. Lorraine Lloyd, June 26, 1923; 1 dau., Betty Anne (Mrs. Robert Frances Arenz). With Hardaway Contracting Co., Columbus, Ga., 1921—, engr., 1921-25, supt., 1925-37, v.p., 1937-42, v.p. and gen. mgr., 1942-52, pres. 1952-69, chmn. bd., 1969—; chmn. bd. Internat. Incinerators, Inc., Atlanta; Cone Bros. Contracting Co., Tampa, Fla.; mem. adv. bd. First Nat. Bank. Served with AUS, 1918; Mem. Am. Soc. Civil Engrs. Meth. Clubs: Columbus Country, Atlanta Commerce. Home: 2222 Wildwood Av Columbus GA 31906 Office: 300 Eleventh St Columbus GA 31902

MONGAN, JAMES J., physician. Physician finance com. U.S. Senate. Address: 1507 28th St Washington DC 20007*

MONGET, HENRY SCHORTEN, dentist; b. Baton Rouge, May 1, 1899; s. Joseph William and Annie Elizabeth (Schorten) M.; D.D.S., Tulane U., 1925; m. Emma Jean Monget, Feb. 12, 1924; 1 dau., Jean (Mrs. A.M. Beveridge). Practice dentistry, specializing in anesthesia, Baton Rouge, 1935—. Mem. Nat., La., East Baton Rouge Parish dental socs., Internat. Assn. Anesthesiologists, Sigma Nu. Elk. Address: 1541 Ingleside Dr Baton Rouge LA 70808

MONINGER, WILLIAM HARVEY, beverage co. exec.; b. East Liverpool, O., June 27, 1916; s. Harvey J. and Minta (Huston) M.; student Harvard Bus. Sch., 1967-68; m. Kate Schmidt, June 16, 1956; children—Susan, David, William Harvey. Sales mgr. Wellsville China Co., 1934-50, pres., 1951-61; sales mgr. Coca Cola Bottling Co., Louisville, 1961—, v.p., 1966—. Bd. dirs. YMCA, Louisville. Served to capt. AUS, 1941-46. Mem. Louisville Power Squadron (comdr. 1968-69). Home: 508 Jarvis Lane Louisville KY 40207 Office: 1661 W Hill St Louisville KY 40210

MONK, GEORGE EDWARD, lawyer; b. Washington, July 18, 1907; s. John Edward and Anna (Tripp) M.; A.B., George Washington U., 1928, LL.B., 1930, LL.M., 1934; m. Mary Clark deLashmutt, Apr. 16, 1937; children—George Edward, Paul deLashmutt, David Hinton. Admitted to D.C. bar, 1930, Md. bar, 1939; practiced in Washington, 1930—; partner firm Hogan & Hartson, 1949—. Lectr. law George Washington U., Washington, 1947-67; dir. Woodward & Lothrop; gen. counsel D.C. Bankers Assn. 1967—. Served from capt. to lt. col., AUS, 1941-45; ETO. Mem. Am. Bar Assn., Bar Assn. D.C. (pres. 1969-70), Am. Soc. Internat. Law, Order of Coif. Delta Theta Phi. Lutheran. Rotarian. Clubs: Barristers, Nat. Lawyers, University, Columbia Country, Metropolitan (Washington). Home: 4020 Franklin St Kensington MD 20795 Office: Hogan & Hartson 815 Connecticut Av Washington DC 20006

MONK, JAMES FLOYD, banker; b. Moultrie, Ga., July 29, 1914; s. John Franklin and Rachel Matilda (Clark) M.; grad. high sch.; m. Mildred Harris, Jan. 15, 1942; children—Jamie Nell, Lynn Allison. Clerk, Friedlander's Dept. Store, Moultrie, Ga., 1932-33; sec. to prin. Moultrie High Sch., 1933-34; sec. to supt. Moultrie Pub. Schs., 1934-36; with Moultrie Banking Co., 1936-37; with Fla. Nat. Bank & Trust Co., Miami, 1937—, v.p., 1967—. Served with C.E., AUS, 1944-46. Mem. Hist. Assn. So. Fla. (treas. 1961-65), Fla. Anthrop. Soc. (pres. 1967), Fla. Hist. Soc., Soc. History of Discoveries, Nat. Hist. Soc., Nat. Aubudon Soc., Nat. Geog. Soc. Democrat. Presbyn. Home: 1960 S W 61st Court Miami FL 33155 Office: 169 E Flagler St Miami FL 33131

MONROE, DORIS DRIGGERS, editor, author; b. Mt. Pleasant, Tex., July 11, 1916; d. Samuel Wyatt and Leola (Harris) Driggers; student Mary-Hardin Baylor Coll., 1934-35, William Jewell Coll., 1935-37, Southwestern Bapt. Theol. Sem., 1937-38, So. Bapt. Theol. Sem., 1938-39, 44-45, George Peabody Coll., 1947-50; m. Edwin Ulys Monroe, Aug. 6, 1937; children—Leola Fran (Mrs. Dudley B. Burton), Billie Barbara (Mrs. William F. Hardy, Jr.). Music dir., pastor's asst. Bethany Bapt. Ch., Kansas City, Mo., 1945-47; asso. editor Story Hour Leader, Bapt. Sunday Sch. Bd., Nashville, 1947-50, editor Primary Leader, Every Day with Primaries, 1950-68, cons. Ch. Tng. Dept. Work with Exceptional Persons, 1968—. Mem. Nat. Assn. for Retarded Children, Am. Camping Assn., Am. Pen Women, Beta Lit. Soc. Author: When Marcia Goes to Church, 1966; The Come-and-Go Village, 1967; A Church Ministry to Retarded Persons, 1971. Co-author: The Primary Leadership Manual, 1957. Home: 2308 Donna Hill Ct Nashville TN 37214 Office: 127 9th Av N Nashville TN 37203

MONROE, ROBERT ALLAN, broadcasting exec.; b. Wabash, Ind., Oct. 30, 1915; s. Robert Emmett and Georgia Helen (Jordan) M.; B.A., Ohio State U.,; m. Mary Ashworth, Aug. 1950; children—Laurie, Maria. Writer, dir. radio programs, 1937-40; prodn. mgr. Donahue & Coe, advt., 1940-43; pres. Robert Monroe Prodns., radio program producers, 1946-49, RAM Enterprises 1950-54; sec.-treas., dir. Laury Assos., 1950-54; v.p. charge programming activities, dir. MBS, Inc., 1954-56; pres. Carolina Radio, Inc., 1958-62, So. States Radio Corp., 1961-65, Jefferson Cable Corp. Club:

Lambs (N.Y.C.). Home: Route 2 Box 66 Charlottesville VA 22201 Office: Box 1271 Charlottesville VA

MONSOUR, ANDREW R., dept. store exec.; b. Treveskyn, Pa., Aug. 28, 1915; s. Abe and Anise (Bitar) M.; student Duffs City Coll., 1932; m. Alyce Gayle Monsour, Apr. 6, 1940; children—Geoffrey, Andrea, Kriste, Trey. Dept. mgr. Wohl Shoe Co., Toledo, 1940, Cin., 1941, Wheeling, W.Va., 1946, Galveston, Tex., 1947; leased shoe dept. Eiband's Dept. Store, Galveston, 1949-64, owner store, 1964—, now pres., gen. mgr.; owner Monsour Shoes; pres. Geoffrey Shoes, Inc. Chmn. retail div. United Fund, 1969-70, mem. exec. bd., 1970—; vice chmn. Beach Park Bd., 1963-71. Bd. dirs. Family Service Bur.; mem. adv. bd. Goodwill Industries. Served to capt. AUS, 1941-46; ETO, PTO. Recipient Distinguished Service award Jr. C. of C., 1966; named Most Outstanding Citizen, 1966. Mem. Tex. Retail Fedn. (dir.), Galveston C. of C. (past pres., dir.), Galveston County Council C. of C. (past pres.), Am. Legion, Galveston County Research Council (dir.), So. Fedn. Syrian-Lebanese Am. Clubs (vice chmn. bd. dirs.). Mem. Greek Orthodox Ch. Rotarian (officer, dir.). Club: Galveston Country. Home: 62 Colony Park Circle Galveston TX 77550 Office: Central Plaza St Galveston TX 77550

MONTAG, LOUIS ADOLF, investment co. exec.; b. Atlanta, Nov. 18, 1903; s. Adolf and Helen Dora (Loeb) M.; B.S. in Econs., U. Pa., 1924; m. Jane Rich Myers, June 8, 1931; children—L. Anthony, James Lee. Treas., Montag Bros., Inc., Atlanta, 1924-40; asso. price exec., OPA, 1942-45; self employed investment counsel, Atlanta, 1945-56; sr. partner Montag & Caldwell, Atlanta, 1956-68, chmn. bd. Montag & Caldwell, Inc., Atlanta, 1968—; pres., chmn. bd., Alpha Fund, Inc., Atlanta, 1968—, Alpha Investors, Inc., 1970—; dir. Rich's Inc., mem. finance com. 1956—; dir. Am. Bus. Products, mem. exec. com., 1968—; adv. dir. Nat. Bank of Ga., mem. trust com., 1970—. Trustees Oglethorpe U.; lay trustee Marist Sch. Mem. Investment Counsel Assn. Am. (bd. govs. 1967-71), Atlanta Soc. Financial Analysts. Clubs: Commerce, Standard (Atlanta); (Hilton Head, S.C.). Mailing Address: 836 Northside Dr NW Atlanta GA 30305 Office: First Nat Bank Tower Atlanta GA 30303

MONTAGUE, DAVID NICHOLLS, lawyer; b. N.Y.C., Aug. 23, 1936; s. Edgar Sclater and Suzanne (Garrett) M.; B.A., U. Va., 1958, LL.B., 1961; m. Carolyn Stewart Day, June 21, 1958; children—Suzanne Stewart, David Nicholls. Admitted to Va. bar, 1961; mem. firm Montague, Cumming & Watkins, Hampton, Va., 1962-67, Montague & Montague, Hampton, 1967—. First vice chmn. Republican Party of Va., 1968—; chmn. Rep. Party of Hampton, 1968—. Served to 1st lt. AUS. 1958-62. Mem. Hampton Retail Mchts. Assn. (v.p. 1968—). Episcopalian (mem. vestry 1965—). Rotarian. Home: 29 Hampton Rds Av Hampton VA 23361 Office: 3 E Queen St Hampton VA 23369

MONTAGUE, ROBERT L., III, found. exec. Pres., dir. Hist. Alexandria Found. Address: 100 S Royal St Box 524 Alexandria VA 22314*

MONTALVO DURAND, ELADIO ALBERTO, physician; b. Mayaguez, P.R., Sept. 15, 1921; s. Miguel A. and Maria (Durand Castillo) Montavlo Toro; B.S., U. P.R., 1944; M.D., Nat. U. Mexico, 1952; m. Lydia Gonzalez, June 16, 1944; children—Miguel Angel, Lizetta Ileana (Mrs. Luis Lorenz), Alberto Eladio. Rotating intern Mexico Gen. Hosp., 1949-50, San Juan (P.R.) City Hosp., 1950-51; med. dir. Municipal Hosp., Corozal, P.R., 1951-52; resident obstetrics and gynecology Rodriguez Army Hosp., 1954-55; practice medicine specializing in obstetrics and gynecology, Rio Piedras, P.R., 1955—; mem. courtesy staff obstetrics and gynecology dept. Monteflores Hosp., 1956—, Auxilio Mutuo Hosp., 1956—, Tchrs. Hosp., 1956—, Drs. Hosp., 1956—, San Carlos Gen. Hosp., 1965—. Adviser P.R. Regional Med. program P.R. Sch. Medicine; cons. SSS, P.R., 1966—. Vice pres. Blue Shield Ins. Co., P.R. Served to capt., M.C., AUS, 1952-55. Mem. A.M.A., P.R. Med. Assn. (dir., exec. com. 1967, pres. pub. health council 1967-68, v.p. Credit Coop., mem. community activity com., pub. relations council, pres. elect 1969; named Dr. Citizen of Year 1967), P.R. Heart Assn. (pres. new mems. and credentials com; dir., mem. sci. com. 1967), Assn. Am. Physicians and Surgeons, Royal Soc. Health, Am. Legion, Am. Acad. Family Practice, Alpha Beta Chi, Phi Beta Pi. Home: 228 Tulipan St Rio Piedras PR 00928 Office: 1124 Ponce de Leon Av Rio Piedras PR 00925

MONTES, LEOPOLDO FELICIANO, physician, educator; b. Buenos Aires, Argentina, Nov. 22, 1929; s. Leopoldo A. and Celia (Gaztambide) M.; M.D., U. Buenos Aires, 1954; M.S., U. Mich., 1959; m. Maria Mercedes Pfeiffer, Nov. 25, 1961; children—Carolina, Mercedes, Ana, Leopoldo, Teresa. Came to U.S., 1955. Intern, City of Buenos Aires Hosps., 1954-55; resident dermatology Pa. Hosp.,Phila., 1955-56; resident U. Mich. Med. Center, Ann Arbor, 1956-58, instr. dermatology, 1958-60; practice medicine, specializing in dermatology, Buenos Aires, 1960-63, Houston, 1963-66, Birmingham, Ala., 1966—; asst. prof. dermatology Baylor U. Coll. Medicine, 1963-66; asso. prof. dermatology U. Ala. Med. Center and Med. Coll. Ala., Birmingham, 1966-69, prof. dermatology, 1969—, asso. prof. microbiology, 1968—. Recipient Research Career Devel. award USPHS, 1965-70. Fellow Am. Acad. Dermatology; mem. A.M.A., Am. Soc. Microbiology, Soc. Investigative Dermatology, Histochem Soc., Am. Soc. Cell Biology, A.A.A.S., Am. Fedn. Clin. Research, Am. Acad. Microbiology, Electron Microscopy Soc. Am., Internat. Soc. Tropical Dermatology (asst. sec. gen. 1969—), Sigma Xi. Home: 4319 Kennesaw Dr Birmingham AL 35213 Office: 1919 7th Av S Birmingham AL 35233

MONTGOMERY, A. DENBO, physician; b. Brookhaven, Miss., July 31, 1924; s. Charles Thaddeus and Elisibeth (Denbo) M.; B.S., Southwestern La. Inst., 1949; M.D., Tulane U., 1952; m. Ida Elizabeth Carter, June 10, 1952; children—Denbo Herbert, Anne Carter, James Marshall, Thomas Joseph, Elizabeth Leigh. Intern Charity Hosp. La., New Orleans, 1952; resident Tulane Service Charity Hosp., New Orleans, 1953-56; practice medicine specializing in otolaryngology, Lafayette, La., 1957—; mem. staffs Lafayette Gen., Our Lady of Lourdes, Charity hosps. (all Lafayette); surgeon Charity Hosp. La.; asst. prof. Tulane U., 1971—. Pres. Evangeline Area Guidance Center, 1959-60. Bd. dirs. U. Southwestern La. Found., Lafayette Gen. Hosp. Served with USAAF, 1944-46. Diplomate Am. Bd. Ophthalmology and Otolaryngology. Fellow Am. Laryngol., Rhinol. and Otol. Soc.; mem. A.M.A., Am. Acad. Ophthalmology and Otolaryngology, Am. Acad. Facial Plastic and Reconstructive Surgery, U. Southwestern La. Alumni Assn. (pres. 1960-61), Blue Key, Sigma Alpha Epsilon, Phi Chi. Home: 407 Girard Park Dr Lafayette LA 70501 Office: 225 Bendel Rd Lafayette LA 70501

MONTGOMERY, DOUGLAS MURRAY, coll. pres.; b. Los Angeles, Dec. 11, 1916; s. Harry and Hazel (Lindstrom) M.; A.B., U. Pa., 1938; LL.B., Harvard, 1941; M.A., Fla. State U., 1959, Ph.D., 1962; m. Jane Alys Robertson, Jan. 10, 1945; children—Carol Lynn, Sandra Jane. Commd. 2d lt. U.S. Air Force, 1941, advanced through grades to lt. col., 1961, ret., 1961; pres. East Central Jr. Coll., Decatur, Miss., 1962-66, Blue Ridge Coll., Weyers Cave, Va., 1966-69, Tidewater Community Coll., Portsmouth, Va., 1969-72; exec. Womble Realty Investment Virginia Beach, Va., 1972—. Pres. Tidewater council Boy Scouts Am. Mem. Sigma Alpha Epsilon. Home: 4500 Hermitage Rd Virginia Beach VA 23455 Office: Womble Realty Investment Virginia Beach VA 23462

MONTGOMERY, GILLESPIE V., congressman, gen. ins. agt.; b. Meridian, Miss. Mem. Miss. Senate, 1957-66; mem. 90th to 92d congresses from 4th Miss. Dist. Pres. Miss. Heart Assn., 1967. Mem. Am. Legion, V.F.W., 40 and 8, Miss. Nat. Guard Assn. (past pres.), Miss. State U. Alumni Assn. (past pres.), Kappa Alpha. Episcopalian. Mason (Shriner), Optimist. Home: Box 1009 Meridian MS 39301 also 2000 S Eads St Arlington VA 22202 Office: Ho of Reps Washington DC 20515

MONTGOMERY, JIM, newspaper reporter; b. Cleve., Oct. 30, 1927; s. Carl Tracy and Maude (Hainer) M.; B.S. in Journalism, U. Fla., 1953; m. Laura Florence Cunningham, Feb. 1, 1951; children—Karen, Mary. Bus., financial editor Atlanta Constn., 1953-69; staff reporter Wall Street Jour., 1969—. Served with AUS, 1945-47. Corecipient Pub. Service award A.P. of Ga., 1961. Nieman fellow Harvard, 1965-66. Mem. Soc. Nieman Fellows, Phi Gamma Delta. Home: 2718 Green Meadows Lane NE Atlanta GA 30319 Office: 55 Marietta St NW Atlanta GA 30303

MONTGOMERY, JOHN ALEXANDER, editor; b. Greeleyville, S.C., May 15, 1908; s. J. Alexander and Kate (Eaves) M.; A.B., Presbyn. Coll., 1928; m. Lottie Carter, June 29, 1940; children—Carole (Mrs. K. Frank Hunt), John Alexander, Carter. With The State (morning newspaper), Columbia, S.C., 1929-61, reporter, sports editor, city editor, 1929-41, mng. editor 1941-61; editor Columbia (S.C.) Record (afternoon newspaper), 1961—; instr. journalism U. S.C., 1945-46. Bd. dirs. S.C. div. Am. Cancer Soc., S.C. State Rehab. Agy. Mem. S.C. Press Assn. (pres. 1959), S.C. AP News Council (pres. 1952), So. Newspaper Pubs. Assn., Am. Soc. Newspaper Editors, S.C., Greater Columbia chambers commerce, Presbyn. Coll. Alumni Assn. (v.p. 1958), Sigma Upsilon, Sigma Nu. Democrat. Presbyn. Clubs: Palmetto, Forum, Cotillion (Columbia). Home: 2918 Delano Dr Columbia SC 29204 Office: PO Box 1333 Stadium Rd Columbia SC 29202

MONTGOMERY, JOHN DENNY, lawyer; b. Hobart, Okla., June 27, 1928; s. Robert Place and Theitis (Curreathers) M.; B.A., U. Okla., 1950, LL.B., 1955; m. Martha Carolyn Flow, June 9, 1950; children—John Denny, Mary Ann. Admitted to Okla. bar, 1955; since practiced in Hobart, Okla.; mem. firm Montgomery & Montgomery, 1955—. Pres., United Fund, Hobart, 1959; chmn. Kiowa County chpt. A.R.C., 1967—; sec. Hobart Planning Commn., 1964-65. Dir. S.W. Okla. Devel. Council, 1964, Hobart Industries, Inc., 1965. Served from ensign to lt. (j.g.) USNR, 1950-53; capt. Res. Mem. Am., Okla., Kiowa County (pres. 1960) bar assns., S.W. Okla. Bar Inst. (v.p. 1965), S.W. Okla. Legal Inst. (pres. 1966-67), Okla. Bar. Found. (trustee), C. of C. (pres. 1962), Kappa Alpha, Phi Alpha Delta. Republican. Presbyn. (elder). Rotarian (pres. 1958-59). Clubs: Hobart Country (pres. 1959), Quarterback (sec. 1965). Home: 107 E Dogwood St Hobart OK 73651 Office: Montgomery Bldg 325 S Main St Hobart OK 73651

MONTGOMERY, PAUL VAUGHAN, cons. actuary; b. Ft. Worth, Oct. 10, 1886; s. John Thirison and Sallie (Vaughan) M.; B.A., U. Tex., 1907; m. Mabel Chilton, Apr. 8, 1914 (dec. Aug. 19, 1971); children—Mary Vaughan (Mrs. Richard G. Fuller), Jean (Mrs. C.Z. Stevens III). Actuarial clk. Ft. Worth Life Ins. Co., 1907-09, v.p., actuary, 1914-23; actuarial clk., asst. actuary Southwestern Life Ins. Co., Dallas, 1909-14, v.p., actuary Southland Life Ins. Co., Dallas, 1923-49; cons. actuary, Dallas. 1949—. Dep. commr. Ins. div. Bur. War Risk Ins., Washington, 1918. Mem. town council, Highland Park, Tex., 1928-34, mayor, 1930-34. Fellow Conf. Actuaries Pub. Practice, Soc. Actuaries; mem. Acad. Actuaries, Kappa Sigma. Democrat. Episcopalian. Mason (32 deg.), Rotarian. Clubs: City, Dallas Country. Home: 4242 Lomo Alto Dr Dallas TX 75219 Office: Adolphus Tower Dallas TX 75202

MONTGOMERY, ROBERT PLACE, lawyer; b. Washington, Nov. 15, 1902; s. Denny and Cora (Johnson) M.; LL.B., U. Okla., 1925; m. Theitis Curreathers, July 6, 1927; children—John Denny, Robert Place. Admitted to Okla. bar, 1925; practiced in Hobart, Okla., 1925—; mem. firm Montgomery & Montgomery, 1955—; U.S. conciliation commr., 1934—; atty. City of Hobart, 1941-43; speaker Law Insts., Okla., 1940—; spl. justice Okla. Supreme Ct., 1964, 67. Dir. 1st Nat. Bank, Hobart. Dist. chmn. Boy Scouts Am., Hobart, 1941; chmn. Kiowa County chpt. A.R.C., 1940-46; co-chmn. Am. Cancer Soc., Hobart, 1948; adv. bd. Selective Service, 1940, 71— appeal agt., 1950-71; acting postmaster Hobart, 1927-28; chmn. Kiowa County Election Bd., 1928-34. Chmn., Kiowa County Republican Com., 1928-58, dist. chmn., 1934-58; del Rep. Nat. Convs., 1936, 44. Bd. dirs. Okla. Soc. Crippled Children, pres. elect, 1972; bd. dirs. Westminster Found., Okla.-Ark. Synod Found. Mem. Am., Okla. (central com. 1952—, exec. council 1951-53, v.p. 1954, asso. editor Jour. 1961) bar assns., Phi Delta Phi, Alpha Sigma Phi. Presbyn. Mason (32 deg.), Rotarian. Home: 126 W Dogwood St Hobart OK 73651 Office: 325 S Main St Hobart OK 73651

MONTGOMERY, WILDER PERCIVAL, physician; b. Washington, Aug. 10, 1910; s. Wilder Percival and Ethel Mineola (Pearson) M.; A.B., Dartmouth, 1931; M.D., U. Chgo., 1935; postgrad. U. Pa., 1936; m. Doris Mae Auter, July 4, 1942; children—Stephen Wilder, Gordon James. Intern Youngstown Hosp. Assn., resident Henry Phipps Inst. U. Pa.; practice medicine specializing in internal medicine, Washington, 1936—; mem. staff Freedmen's Hosp., Washington, Washington Hosp. Center, Rogers Meml. Hosp., Washington; asst. surgeon res. USPHS, 1946-41; attending physician Washington Chest Clinics, 1936-58; asst. clin. prof. medicine Med. Coll. Howard U., Washington, 1949—. Mem. Washington Bd. Police and Fire Surgeons, 1961-69; cons. appeals council Social Security Adminstrn., 1968—. Past bd. dirs. Washington Tb Assn., Diplomate Am. Bd. Internal Medicine. Fellow A.C.P.; mem. D.C. Med. Soc., Medico-Chirurgical Soc., D.C., D.C., Am. thoracic socs., D.C. Heart Assn., Phi Beta Kappa, Alpha Omega Alpha. Home: 1728 Shepherd St NW Washington DC 20011 Office: 2570 Sherman Av NW Washington DC 20001

MONTGOMERY, ZENO HART, accountant; b. Kingstree, S.C., June 1, 1935; s. Samuel John and Meta (Bookhardt) M.; B.S., U. S.C., 1957; m. Helen Runita Milling, Apr. 5, 1958; children—Michael Hart, Pamela Elizabeth. Sr. accountant McKnight, Frampton & McKnight, C.P.A.'s, 1957-63; comptroller So. Plastics Co., 1963-65; partner Kight, Beale & Montgomery, C.P.A.'s, Columbia, S.C., 1965-70, Finch, Kight & Jackson, C.P.A.'s, 1970-71; pvt. practice Z.H. Montgomery, C.P.A., 1972—. C.P.A., S.C. Mem. Am. Inst. C.P.A.'s, S.C. Assn. C.P.A.'s (chpt. pres. 1969-71). Presbyn. (ruling elder 1972—, trustee 1968—, ch. extension com. 1972—). Clubs: Richland Sertoma, Congaree Toastmasters (pres. 1965). Home: 158 Dorset Dr Columbia SC 29210 Office: 900 Elmwood Av Columbia SC 29201

MONTIN, JOHN ERNEST, refrigerating appliances co. exec.; b. Alexandria, Va., Aug. 3, 1918; s. Alfred Constance and Mary Marie (Ceppi) M.; B.S., Okla. A. and M. Coll., 1947; m. Lillian Stout, June 23, 1945; children—John, Jean, Robert, With Frigidaire Sales Corp., Oklahoma City, 1948-49; co-owner, v.p., dir. Refrigeration Sales & Engring. Co., Oklahoma City, 1950—; v.p. Mid Continent Constructors. Scoutmaster, Boy Scouts Am., 1956-62. Served with AUS, 1941-45; PTO. Decorated Legion of Merit. Registered profl engr., Okla. Mem. Am. Soc. Heating, Refrigerating and Air Conditioning Engrs., Nat. Soc. Profl. Engrs., C. of C., Okla. State U. Alumni Assn. Methodist. Mason, Kiwanian. Club: Oklahoma City Golf and Country. Home: 1400 Canterbury Pl Oklahoma City OK 73116 Office: 311 NW 6th St Oklahoma City OK 73102

MOOD, FRANCIS PALMER, JR., lawyer; b. Columbia, S.C., Feb. 4, 1938; s. Francis Palmer and Lula Sue (Rigby) M.; B.A., The Citadel, 1960; LL.B., U. Va., 1963; m. Jane Hammond McLaurin, Jan. 25, 1969; 1 son, Francis Palmer III. Admitted to S.C. bar, 1963; asst. trust officer, asst. v.p. Bankers Trust, 1966-67; asso. Boyd, Bruton, Knowlton, Tate & Finley, Columbia, 1967-70, partner, 1971—. Active United Fund. Served to lt. AUS, 1964-66. Mem. Am., S.C., Richland County bar assns., S.C. State Bar, Assn. Citadel Men. Republican. Presbyn. Clubs: Columbia Sertoma (v.p. 1970-72), Columbia Young Lawyers (v.p. 1969), Brigadier (dir.), Palmetto, Greater Columbia Citadel (v.p. 1970-71, pres. 1972), Forest Lake. Home: 4620 Furman Av Columbia SC 29206 Office: 1250 SCN Center Columbia SC 29201

MOODY, ADRIAN BRADLEY, assn. exec.; b. Munfordville, Ky., Apr. 28, 1935; s. Allen Hunter and Ethel (Sturgil) M.; B.S., Ky. Wesleyan Coll., 1957; postgrad. Springfield Coll., 1963; m. Frances Dillehay, June 1, 1957; children—Deborah, David, Stephanie. With YMCA, 1956—, asso. gen. sec., Augusta, Ga., 1959-64, gen. sec., Moultrie, Ga., 1964-69, exec. dir., Bristol, Tenn., 1969—. Exec. dir. United Funds of Colquitt County (Ga.), 1964-66. Recipient Outstanding Citizen's award for pub. service Pilot Club, Moultrie, Ga., 1968. Mem. Am. Camping Assn., Nat. Assn. Profl. Dirs., Tenn. Assn. Profl. Dirs. Baptist (deacon). Rotarian, Elk (mem. com. selection youth leadership awards 1964—). Club: Industrial Management. Home: 205 Earlway Rd Bristol TN 37620 Office: 400 Edgemont Av Bristol TN 37620

MOODY, ALFRED LEE, banker; b. Marysville, Tex., Nov. 9, 1936; s. Eligah Horace and Mildred Ethel (Shaw) H.; grad. high sch.; m. Lana Jane Sapp, June 18, 1966; children—Danny Todd, Craig David. Bookkeeper First State Bank, Bovina, Tex., 1955-61, cashier, 1961-68; v.p. Citizens Nat. Bank, Crosbyton, Tex., 1969—. Served with AUS, 1959-61. Mem. Crosby County Livestock Show Assn. Baptist (treas. 1970—). Lion. Club: Athletic Booster (Crosbyton). Home: 458 Box 540 S Ivy St Crosbyton TX 79322 Office: Box 529 Crosbyton TX 79322

MOODY, FRANK MCCORKLE, banker; b. Tuscaloosa, Ala., Sept. 25, 1915; s. Frank M. and Sarah (McCorkle) M.; grad. Episcopal High Sch., Alexandria, Va., 1933; A.B., U. Ala., 1937; postgrad. Rutgers U. Grad. Sch. Banking, 1939-40, Finance Sch., Duke, 1944; m. Louise Morrisette, May 8, 1941; children—Sarah, Louise, Jane, Frank McCorkle; m. 2d, Gloria N. Thomas, Sept. 13, 1969. With First Nat. Bank Tuscaloosa, 1937—, exec. v.p., 1954-56, pres., 1956-70, chmn. bd., 1970—; mem. adv. bd. Fed. Res. Bank, Birmingham, Ala., 1954-57; dir. Ala. Power Co. Chmn. Tuscaloosa County program U.S. Savs. Bonds, 1948—; mem. Civic Center Blue Ribbon Commn., 1970; co-chmn. bldg. fund drive Tuscaloosa County YMCA, 1955, 58, pres., 1959-62, mem. Nat. council, 1961—, bd. dirs. Tuscaloosa, 1956—; chmn. Tuscaloosa United Fund drive, 1956, pres., 1957, mem. finance and exec. coms., 1954—, chmn. Tuscaloosa A.R.C. drive, 1946, 47, chmn. Blood Bank, 1948-49; chmn. Tuscaloosa Acad. Bldg. Fund drive, 1968, United Negro Coll. Fund drive, 1970. Trustee Ala. Mental Health Bd., Druid City Hosp.; bd. dirs. Tuscaloosa Housing Authority, United Fund of Tuscaloosa County, Tuscaloosa Community Council. Served to capt. USAAF, 1941-45. Named Number One Boss, Tuscaloosa Bus. and Profl. Women's Club, 1957; recipient Citizen of Year award Civitan Club, 1958, Community Builder award, 1970. Mem. Am. (chmn. savs. bond com. Ala. 1950—, state v.p. 1971-72, Ala. (pres. 1966-67) bankers assns., Tuscaloosa (chmn. aviation com. 1948-51, pres. bd. dirs. 1950—), (v.p. new industries com. 1963), chambers commerce, Phi Delta Theta (pres. bd. trustees Ala. chpt. 1960-62). Episcopalian (vestryman). Clubs: Exchange1952-53), Tuscaloosa Country (dir. 1952-59, pres. 1955), Indian Hills Country 1961—) (Tuscaloosa). Home: PO Box 2028 Tuscaloosa AL 35401 Office: 1st Nat Bank PO Box 2028 Tuscaloosa AL 35401

MOODY, JAMES SHELTON, circuit judge; b. Plant City, Fla., Dec. 29, 1914; s. Thomas Edwin and Anna (Herron) M.; student Washington and Lee U., 1932-33; B.S. in Bus. Adminstrn. with honors, LL.B. with honors U. Fla., 1939; m. Irma Cone, Nov. 29, 1939; children—Carole Ann, James Shelton, William C. Admitted to Fla. bar, 1939; practice law Plant City, 1939-57; mem. Fla. Ho. of Reps., 1948-57; asst. atty. Hillsboro County, Fla., 1941-57; circuit judge, Tampa, Fla., 1957—, presiding judge 13th Jud. Circuit, 1963-65. Dir. 1st Fed. Savs. & Loan Assn., Plant City, Hillsboro Bank Plant City. Bd. dirs. East Hillsborough County Fair; chmn. Circuit Judges Conf. Fla., 1968-70; mem. Jud. Qualifications Commn. State Fla. Served with CIC, AUS, USAAF, 1943-46; ETO. Named Most Valuable Legislator, Allen Morris Poll, Most Valuable mem. of legislature St. Petersburg Times Poll, 1957. Mem. Am. (dir.), Tampa bar assns., Fla. Bar, Am. Legion, Pi Kappa Alpha, Phi Kappa Phi, Phi Delta Phi. Democrat. Presbyn. (elder). Elk. Club: Plant City Golf and Country (dir.). Home: 803 N Collins St Plant City FL 33566 Office: Ct House Tampa FL 33602

MOODY, JEPTHA EDWARD, JR., banking co. exec.; b. Scottsboro, Ala., June 30, 1926; s. Jeptha Edward and Ruby (Skelton) M.; student Yale U., 1944; B.S., Auburn U., 1949; m. Jeanne Adair Jacobs, June 29, 1953; children—Jane Adair, Jeptha Edward III, Jon Rice. Office mgr. Larkinsville Gin Co., Larkinsville, Ala., 1949-52; office mgr., Benham Underwear Mills, Scottsboro, Ala., 1952-56; with J.C. Jacobs Banking Co., Inc., Scottsboro, 1956—, v.p. and cashier, 1957, also dir. Trustee city bd. edn., Scottsboro. Served with AUS, 1944-46. Meth. Rotarian (treas. 1969-70). Club: Quarterback (Scottsboro, Ala.). Home: Roseberry Dr Scottsboro AL 35768 Office: PO Box 807 Scottsboro AL 35768

MOODY, JESSE, clergyman; b. Paducah, Tex., Aug. 19, 1925; s. Horace Frazier and Connie Valentine (Schrimsher) M.; B.A., Baylor U., 1948, postgrad., 1951; B.D., So. Bapt. Theol. Sem., 1956; D.D. (hon.), Campbellsville Coll., 1957; m. Doris Wade Cummins, July 4, 1949; children—Patrick Jess, Martha Kit. Ordained to ministry Bapt. Ch., 1944; preacher, Southwide Bapt. Youth Movement, Tex., 1945-50; So. Bapt. evangelist, Waco, Tex., 1950-56; pastor 1st Bapt. Ch., Owensboro, Ky., 1956-61, West Palm Beach, Fla., 1961—; pres. Palm Beach Atlantic Coll., West Palm Beach. Pres., S. Bapt. Pastors Conf., 1964-65. Bd. dirs. Bapt. Home Mission, So. Bapt. Theol. Sem.; mem. Christian Life Commn., 1964; gen. chmn. Bapt. Coll. Campaign, West Palm Beach, 1965; chmn. bd. trustees Fla. Bapt. Coll., 1967. Lead role motion picture Riding The Pulpit, winner oscar Evang. Film Festival, Phila., 1967. Author: You Can't Lose for Winning, 1965; Don't Miss It If You Can, 1965; A Drink At Joel's Place, 1967; The

Jesus Freaks, 1971. Home: 4515 S Flagler Dr West Palm Beach FL 33407 Office: 1101 S Flagler Dr West Palm Beach FL 33401

MOODY, NANCY PAXTON, lawyer; b. Austin, Tex., Sept. 20, 1932; d. Dan and Mildred (Paxton) Moody; student Sweet Briar Coll., 1950-51; B.A., U. Tex., 1956, LL.B., 1958; m. Hubert R. Hudson, Dec. 4, 1959 (div. Apr. 1968); stepchildren—Sarah Gibbs, William Parke Custis. Admitted to Tex. bar, 1958; asso. mem. Moody, Robertson &Moody, attys., Austin, 1958-59; pvt. practice law, Austin, 1960—. Parliamentarian, 56th legislature Tex. Senate, 1959; mem. Tex. Senate interim com. welfare reform, 1970. Trustee United Fund Brownsville, Tex., 1960-63; bd. dirs. Austin Child Guidance Center (formerly Austin Community Guidance Center), 1964-69. Mem. Tex. Hunter and Jumper Assn. (dir., pres. 1967-68), Am. Horse Shows Assn., Am. Bar Assn., State Bar Tex., Nat. Steeplechase and Hunt Assn., U.S. Pony Clubs (life), Phi Beta Kappa, Pi Beta Phi, Kappa Beta Pi, Pi Sigma Alpha. Episcopalian (parliamentarian ann. council Diocese of Tex. 1966—). Address: 2302 Woodlawn Blvd Austin TX 78703

MOODY, ROBERT REECE, JR., elec. engr.; b. Charlotte, N.C., Mar. 7, 1928; s. Robert Reece and Lola (Boyles) M.; B.S., Erskine Coll., 1949; B.E.E., N.C. State U., 1958; m. Martha Rosalind Bradley, Aug. 6, 1949; 1son, Robert Reece III. Indsl. engr. Swift & Co., Bartow, Fla., 1949-51; with TVA, 1958—, fgn. service inspecting and testing, Zurich, Switzerland, 1966-69, Cumberland City, Tenn., 1971—. State Vice Comdr. Dept. Ky., 1971—. Served with USMCR, 1951-54. Registered Profl. Engr., Ala. Mem. I.E.E.E., Am. Legion, V.F.W. Moose, Eagle. Home: 490 W 6th St Russellville KY 42276 Office: TVA Cumberland Steam Plant PO Box 2000 Cumberland City TN 37050

MOODY, WAYLAND PELTON, coll. pres.; b. Watt, Tex., Oct. 7, 1902; s. William McD. and Melissa (Wayland) M.; A.A., Westminster Coll., Tex., 1921; B.A., U. Tex., 1923. D.Ed., 1942; M.A., So. Meth. U., 1930; m. Lillian R. Pierce, Sept. 15, 1925; 1 son, Wayland Pierce. Instr. modern langs. Westminster Coll., 1923-28, dean, 1930-35; prin. Ferris (Tex.) High Sch., 1928-30; dean, bus. mgr. Lon Morris Coll., 1935-40; instr. U. Tex., 1940-42; adminstrv. asst., dean San Antonio Coll., 1947-55, pres., 1956—. Mem. U.S. Adv. Commn. on internat. edn. and cultural affairs, 1968-71. Served from 1st lt. to maj. USAAF, 1942-46; maj. Res. Mem. Am., So. (pres. 1957) assns. jr. colls., Assn. Higher Edn., Assn. Tex. Colls. and Univs. (pres. 1960-61), Phi Delta Kappa. Methodist. Mason, Kiwanian (pres. Alamo club 1957). Home: 415 W Ashby St San Antonio TX 78212

MOODY, WENDELL BRUCE, civil engr.; b. Tulia, Tex., Feb. 24, 1936; s. Alton and Camilla (Hansen) M.; B.S., Tex. Technol. Coll., 1958, M.S. in Civil Engring., 1961; m. Carolyn Loveless, June 29, 1957; 1 son, Steven Lee. Agrl. engr. Soil Conservation Service, U.S. Dept. Agr., Big Spring, Tex., 1958-60, civil engr., Ft. Worth, 1961-70, soil mechanics engr., Temple, Tex., 1970-72, asst. state conservation engr., Temple, 1972—. Registered profl. engr., Tex. Mem. Am. Soc. C.E., Am. Soc. Agrl. Engrs., Tex., Nat. socs. profl. engrs. Lutheran (pres. 1969, elder 1971—, chmn. elders 1967-68, steward 1963-64). Home: PO Box 1264 Temple TX 76501 Office: 1st Nat Bank Bldg Temple TX 76501

MOODY, WILLARD JAMES, lawyer, state senator; b. Franklin, Va., June 16, 1924; s. Willie James and May M. (Bryant) M.; pre law student Norfolk div. William and Mary Coll., 1946-47; LL.B., U. Richmond, 1952; m. Betty Glenn Covert, Aug. 21, 1948; children—Sharon Paige, Willard James, Paul Glenn. Admitted to Va. bar, 1952; asso. firm Dean & Perry, Norfolk, Va., 1952-54; practice law, Portsmouth, Va., 1955—; partner firm Moody, McMurran & Miller, and predecessor firm, 1968—; became mem. Va. Ho. of Reps., 1955; mem. Va. Senate, 1968—. Served with AUS, 1943-46. Named Outstanding Young Man of Yr., Portsmouth Jr. C. of C., 1959. Mem. Portsmouth C. of C. (dir. 1958-59), Portsmouth-Norfolk County Bar Assn. (pres. 1959-60). Clubs: Cosmopolitan (pres. 1958-59), Executive (Portsmouth). Home: 120 River Point Crescent Portsmouth VA 23707 Office: Profl Bldg Portsmouth VA 23219

MOOK, CONRAD PAYNE, meteorologist, ret. govt. ofcl.; b. Titusville, Pa., May 2, 1914; s. Raymond L. and Ella (Payne) M.; A.B., Coll. of Wooster, 1939; M.S., N.Y. U., 1943; m. Barbara Heer Held, Sept. 6, 1941; children—Patricia Ann (Mrs. Thomas J. Harris), Mary Ann (Mrs. William Douglas Barnum). Instr., N.Y. U., 1941-43; meteorologist U.S. Weather Bur., Washington, 1943-57; geophysicist Harry Diamond Labs., Washington, 1957-61; hurricane forecaster U.S. Weather Bur., Washington, 1961-62; Program mgr., space vehicle thermal control and vacuum tech. NASA Hdqrs., Washington, 1962-70; ret. Mem. Am. Meteorol. Soc., Am. Geophys. Union, Am. Inst. Aeros. and Astronautics. Home: 5222 26th Rd N Arlington VA 22207

MOON, FREDERICK DOUGLASS, ch. orgn. exec., assn. exec.; b. Fallis, Okla., May 4, 1896; s. Henry Clay and Polly (Twiggs) M.; B.S., Langston U., 1929; M.A., U. Chgo., 1938; L.H.D., Okla. Sch. Religion, 1961; m. Leeoshia Harris, Aug. 28, 1935; 1 dau., Freddye Lee (Mrs. Stanford Smith). Prin., Douglass Sch., Crescent, Okla., 1921-31, Douglass High Sch., Wewoka, Okla., 1931-40, Oklahoma City, 1940-61; exec. sec. Okla. Assn. Tchrs., Oklahoma City, 1947-70; exec. sec.-treas. Okla. Bapt. State Conv., Oklahoma City, 1961-70, dir. ednl. devel., 1970—. Prof. edn. Langston U., summers 1932-42. Pres., Oklahoma City Urban League, 1953-56; vice chmn. Oklahoma City Urban Renewal Authority; del. World Teaching Confedn., Turkey, 1955; mem. Adv. Commn. Civil Rights Okla., Okla. Tchr. Retirement Commn. Mem. Oklahoma City Bd. Edn. Bd. dirs., trustee Oklahoma City United Fund; chmn. bd. mgmt. YMCA, Oklahoma City, 1946-58. Named Prin. of Year, Crafts Pubs., New London, Conn., 1959; recipient citation Okla. Legislature, 1959; Distinguished Service citation U. Okla., 1964. Mem. Phi Delta Kappa, Alpha Phi Alpha, Sigma Pi Phi. Democrat. Baptist. Author: A Fifth Freedom for the Negro, 1945; Organization and Administration of High Schools for Negroes, 1938; Teacher Integration in Border States, 1957. Home: 1314 NE 8th St Oklahoma City OK 73117 Office: 501 NE 7th St Oklahoma City OK 73104

MOON, GRANT CAMP, govt. ofcl., mgmt. cons.; b. Malad., Ida., Oct. 13, 1918; s. William E. and Dessie (Camp) M.; certificate U. Ida., 1940; B.A., Brigham Young U., 1947; M.S. (Store Service scholar), N.Y. U., 1948; postgrad. U. Kan., 1949-50, U. Utah, summer 1952, 53, U. Mich., 1954-56; D.B.A., George Washington U., 1967; m. Ella Mae Richards, Apr. 26, 1945; children—Kathleen, William G., Richard L., Ronald R. Instr., U. Kan., 1948-50; asst. prof. U. S.D., 1950-51, asso. prof., head marketing dept., 1951-54; research asso., instr. U. Mich., 1954-56; chief research U.S. Army Logistics Mgmt. Center, Petersburg, Va., 1956-57; program dir. mgmt. course Am. Mgmt. Assn., Saranac Lake, N.Y., 1957-58; chief mgmt. devel. div. Small Bus. Adminstrn., Washington, 1958-64, dir. Office Bus. Adv. Services, 1964-67, spl. asst., dep. adminstr., 1967, spl. asst., asst. adminstr., 1967—, also dir. mgmt. planning and spl. projects. Asso. professorial lectr. George Washington U.; mgmt. cons. Hot Shoppes, Inc., Washington. Served with USAAF, 1944-45. Recipient Master M-Men award Young Men's Mut. Improvement Assn., 1945. Mem. Am. Marketing Assn., Midwest Econ. Assn., Nat. Council for Small Bus. Mgmt. Devel. (chmn. adv. bd.), Delta Phi. Co-author: Impact of Numerical Control on Small Business, 1971. Home: 5229 Yorktown Blvd Arlington VA 22207 Office: 1441 L St NW Washington DC 20416

MOON, JAMES E., hosp. adminstr.; b. Apr. 4, 1929; B.A. in Indsl. Arts, Ia. State Tchrs. Coll., 1951; postgrad. U. Houston, 1957-58; M.A. in Hosp. and Health Adminstrn., State U. Ia., 1960; m. 2 children. Adminstrv. resident Washington Hosp. Center, D.C. Gen. Hosp., 1959-60; asst. adminstr. Washington Hosp. Center, 1961-69; asso. adminstr. U. Ala. Hosps. and Clinics, Birmingham, 1969-71, adminstr., 1971—; asst. prof. Sch. Health Services Adminstrn., U. Ala., 1969—. Served with USAF, 1951-56. Fellow Am. Coll. Hosp. Adminstrs.; mem. Am. Hosp. Assn., Assn. Am. Med. Colls. (council teaching hosps.), Southeastern Hosp. Assn., Ala. Hosp. Assn. (mem. fiscal devel. com. 1971), Birmingham Regional Hosp. Council (dir. 1971, chmn. incentive reimbursement com. 1971, mem. central laundry com. 1970, pres. elect 1972), Birmingham Community Service Council (mem. community health planning commn. 1972), Md.-D.C.-Del. Hosp. Assn. (mem. council assn. devel. 1963, exhibit judging com. 1965, council hosp. services 1966, banquet com. ann. conf. 1968). Contbr. articles to profl. jours. Home: 3833 10th Av S Birmingham AL 35222 Office: 619 S 19th St Birmingham AL 35233

MOON, JESSE KENNETH, clergyman, educator; b. Callihan, Tex., Dec. 21, 1931; s. James Martin and Geneva Gertrude (Armstrong) M.; B.S., Southwestern Assemblies of God Coll., 1959; M.Divinity, Tex. Christian U., 1969, D.Ministry, 1972; m. Donna Faith Henegar, Jan. 7, 1950; children—Sheree Celeste, Glen Dean. Ordained to ministry Assemblies of God, 1959; minister churches in Frisco, Tex., 1957-58, Tyler, Tex., 1960-61, Dallas, 1971—; pres. State Youth Orgn., Assemblies of God, Waxahachie, Tex., 1961-66; prof., chmn. Christian ministry dept., coll. chaplain Southwestern Coll., Waxahachie, 1966—. Chmn. spl. fund raising plan Nat. Youth Missions Program, 1965-66; organizer, dir. tech. assistance to youth plan Youth Mission Program, 1962-66; judge Nat. Youth Talent Search and Quiz Program, 1964-65. Served with USAF, 1952-56. Mem. Am. Acad. Religion, Tex. Jr. Coll. Tchrs. Assn., Tex. Personnel Adminstrs. Assn., Tex. Guidance and Personnel Service Assn., Theta Pi. Contbr. articles profl. jours. Home: Rt 2 B Waxahachie TX 75165

MOON, JOSEPH KAY, physician; b. Chariton, Ia., July 28, 1934; s. Harold Leslie and Margaret Jane (James) M.; student Simpson Coll., 1952-53, U. Ia., 1953-55, U. Houston, 1957-58; B.S., Drake U., 1959, postgrad., 1959-63; M.D., U. Tex. at Galveston, 1967; m. Marybeth Blasdel, Apr. 2, 1958; children—Shari Kathleen, Tari Ann, Jodi Kay, Jacki Jo. Tchr. sci. and math. Irving (Tex.) Ind. Sch. Dist., 1959-60, Galveston (Tex.) Ind. Sch. Dist., 1961-63; intern Meml. Baptist Hosp., Houston, 1967-68; practice medicine specializing in gen. practice and surgery, Tomball, Tex., 1968-70, Houston, 1970—; mem. staff Pinewood, Meml. Baptist, Parkway, Tomball hosps.; chief staff Pinewood Meml. Hosp., Houston, 1970—; health officer, Tomball, Tex., 1968—. Mem. Tex. Polit. Action Com., 1967—. Am. Polit. Action Com., 1967—. Served with M.C., AUS, 1955-57. Mem. Am. Profl. Practice Assn., A.M.A., Tex. Med. Assn., Harris County Med. Soc., Am. Assn. Gen. Practice, Assn. Am. Physicians and Surgeons, Lambda Chi Alpha, Theta Kappa Psi. Methodist. Mason. Home: 711 Barbara St Tomball TX 77375 Office: 2801 Little York Rd Houston TX 77016

MOON, WILLIAM HAROLD, educator; b. Columbus, Ga., Oct. 4, 1931; s. John L. and Elizabeth (Lavender) M.; B.S., Auburn U., 1956; Ph.D., Fla. State U., 1962; m. Kay Thiel, Sept. 14, 1957; children—Alison, Brian Harold. Clin. psychology intern U. Tenn. Med. Sch. Memphis, 1961-62; clin. psychologist Lee County Mental Health Center, Opelika, Ala., 1962-64; mem. faculty Auburn (Ala.) U., 1964-71, asso. prof. psychology, 1967-71; prof., chmn. dept. psychology Augusta (Ga.) Coll., 1972—. Cons. psychologist E. Ala. Comprehensive Mental Health Center, Opelika, 1964-71, Ala. VA Hosp., Tuskegee, 1965-69. Mem. Ala. Bd. Examiners Psychology, 1968-71, vice chmn., 1969-71. Pres., Auburn Bi-racial Self Study Group, 1965. Served with AUS, 1952-54. Mem. Am., Southeastern, Ala. (editor newsletter 1964-67, sec.-treas. 1967-69, pres. 1970-71) psychol. assns., Am. Assn. U. Profs. (chpt. pres. 1968-69), Gerontological Soc., Lee County Mental Health Assn. (bd. dirs. 1967-70), Phi Kappa Phi, Psi Chi. Home: 3058 Westwood Ct Augusta GA 30904

MOONEY, PRENTISS, govt. ofcl.; b. McLoud, Okla., July 18, 1905; s. Jesse and Ella (Ridley) M.; student Okla. Bapt. U., 1923-25, U. Okla., 1925-28; m. Betty J. Robinson, Feb. 25, 1944; children—Gretchen F., Prentiss R. Newspaper reporter, editor, radio broadcaster, St. Joseph, Mo., 1936-42; dir. Mo. Div. Resources and Devel., Jefferson City, 1946-56; dir. Ohio Div. Econ. Devel. and Publicity, Columbus, 1956-59; dir. pub. relations Am. Motor Hotel Assn., Kansas City, Mo., 1959-63, exec. v.p., 1963-65; indsl. devel. specialist U.S. Bur. Indian Affairs, Washington, 1966-69, chief div. indsl. and tourism devel., 1969—. Recipient Young Man of Yr. award St. Joseph Jr. C. of C., 1941. Mem. Nat. Assn. Travel Orgns. (pres. 1955), Soc. Am. Travel Writers, Am. Indsl. Devel. Council, Discover Am. Travel Orgn. (dir.), Outdoor Writers Am., Sigma Chi. Presbyn. Mason, Lion. Clubs: Nat. Aviation (Washington); International Town and Country (Fairfax, Va.). Home: 3627 1st Rd S Arlington VA 22204 Office: US Bur Indian Affairs 1951 Constitution Av NW Washington DC 20242

MOOR, RALPH CARL, state ofcl.; b. Waycross, Ga., Dec. 18, 1912; s. Arthur Fisk and Eva (Frey) M.; B.S., Ga. State U., 1937; M.A., George Washington U., 1947; m. Ruth Sanders, July 10, 1937 (div. Oct. 1957); children—Ralph Carl, Larry Sanders; m. 2d, Nadine Penney, June 11, 1965. Dean, prof. econs. S.Ga. Coll., Douglas, 1948-51; educationist U.S. Office Edn., 1951-52; dep. dir. State Merit System Personnel Adminstrn., Atlanta, 1953—. Trustee, sec. Christian Ch. Counseling, Inc., Atlanta, 1968—; trustee Ga. State U. Found., 1969—. Served from 2d lt. to col. AUS; brig. gen. N.G. ret. Mem. Ga. State U. Alumni Assn. (dir. 1969—), Internat. Personnel Mgmt. Assn. (sec.-treas. So. region 1969-70, 2d vice chmn. 1970-71, 1st vice chmn. 1971-72, chmn. 1972-73). Home: 3649 Peachtree Rd NE Atlanta GA 30319 Office: 244 Washington St SW Atlanta GA 30334

MOORE, ALFRED, lawyer, banker; b. Hattiesburg, Miss., May 28, 1912; s. Henderson Alfred and Lucy (Currie) M.; student U. So. Miss., 1931-32; B.A., U. Miss., 1934, LL.B., 1936; m. Mary Cleo Barnes, June 16, 1946; children—Betty Barnes, Henderson Alfred III, Lucy Currie. Admitted to Miss. bar, 1936; since practiced in Hattiesburg; pros. atty. Hattiesburg, 1938-41, 47-49; judge Hattiesburg, 1941-42, city atty., 1949-53; mem. firm Moore & Jones, 1961—; exec. v.p., dir. First Fed. Savs. & Loan Assn., Hattiesburg, 1961-70, pres., 1970—. Mem. Gov.'s staff, 1964—; adv. com. personnel Miss. Employment Security Commn., 1962—. Bd. dirs. U. So. Miss. Found.; past pres. Miss. Savs. & Loan League; trustee S. Miss. Presbytery. Served to lt. USNR, 1942-46. Mem. Am., Forrest County bar assns., Miss. State Bar, Miss. Bar Found., Miss. Folklore Soc., Hattiesburg Bd. Realtors, Miss. Econ. Council, Hattiesburg Civic Assn. (past pres.), C. of C. (past pres.), Alumni Assn. U. So. Miss., Alumni Assn. U. Miss., Newcomen Soc., Phi Alpha Delta, Pi Kappa Alpha. Presbyn. (elder). Elk. Club: Hattiesburg Country. Home: 2312 Carriage Rd Hattiesburg MS 39401 Office: 130 W Front St Hattiesburg MS 39401

MOORE, ALVIN EDWARD, patent lawyer; b. Auburn, La., Sept. 3, 1904; s. William Absalom and Mahala (Scoggins) M.; student U.S. Naval Acad., 1921-24, George Washington U. Law Sch., 1925, John Marshall Law Sch., Atlanta, 1945; B.S. in History, Am. U., 1949, M.A. in History, 1958; postgrad. U. Fla., 1955-56, La. State U., 1958-61, Tulane U., 1961-62; m. Laura Belle Van Zandt, May 26, 1925. Seaman, U.S. Shipping Bd., 1924; nautical scientist U.S. Hydrographic Office, 1924; patrol insp. U.S. Border Patrol, 1926-27, immigration insp. U.S. Immigration Service, 1927-28; Am. vice consul, Guaymas, Mex., 1928-29; examiner U.S. Patent Office, 1924-25, 30-42, 45-49, 56-58; intelligence officer CIA, 1949-50, 53-56; admitted to Ga. bar, 1945, U.S. Ct. Customs and Patent Appeals bar, 1947; patent atty. Army Ordnance Missile Command, 1958-60; practice as patent atty., Waveland, Miss., 1960—. Co-founder Friends U.S. of Latin Am., 1950. Served with USN, 1921-24; from lt. to lt. comdr. USNR, 1942-46, comdr., 1950-53. Mem. Fed. Bar Assn., U.S. Naval Acad. Alumni Assn. Author: The World Republic, 1942; History of Hardy County, 1963. Contbr. articles, short stories, poems to various mags. Patentee in various fields. Address: 916 Beach Blvd Waveland MS 39576

MOORE, ANNE CORRIGAN (MRS. SIDNEY M. MOORE), economist, govt. ofcl.; b. Newark; d. George F. and Minerva (Patrick) Corrigan; B.S. magna cum laude in Finance, N.Y. U., 1932; A.M. in Econs., Columbia, 1933, postgrad., 1933-43; postgrad. Am. U. Sch. Internat. Service, 1961—; m. John T. Madden, Jan. 25, 1941 (dec. July 1948); m. 2d, Sidney M. Moore, June 29, 1957. Instr., asst. prof., chmn. dept. secretarial studies N.Y. U. Sch. Commerce, 1932-41; economist fgn. research div. Fed. Res. Bank of N.Y., 1944-45; with Dept. State, Washington, 1950-51; financial asst., asst. attache Am embassy, London, Eng., 1951-53; asst. prof. bus. adminstrn., chmn. dept. Pacific U., Forest Grove, Ore., 1955-56; asst. prof. bus. adminstrn. St. John Fisher Coll., Rochester, N.Y., 1956-57; vis. lectr. econs. and history U. Md., Paris, France, 1958-59; mgmt. cons. OEEC, Paris, 1958; vis. lectr. econs. Boston Coll., Chestnut Hill, Mass., 1959-60; internat. economist U.S. Dept. Commerce, Bus. and Def. Services Adminstrn., Bur. Internat. Commerce, Washington, 1960-65; financial economist Office Econ. Analysis, Small Bus., Adminstrn., Washington, 1965-67, financial analyst, program officer Office Financial Assistance, Washington, 1967-71, economist Office Planning, Research and Analysis, 1971—. Mem. Am. Econ. Assn., Assn. for Social Econs., Internat. Studies Assn., Am. Acad. Polit. and Social Sci., Am. Finance Assn., Am. Hist. Assn., Acad. Polit. Sci., Am. Assn. U. Women, Beta Gamma Sigma. Home: 4000 Massachusetts Av NW Washington DC 20016 Office: 1441 L St NW Washington DC 20416

MOORE, BERNICE MILBURN (MRS. HARRY E. MOORE), mental health cons., author; b. San Antonio, June 17, 1904; d. Ted Hatton and Carrie (Coley) Milburn; B.J., U. Tex., 1924, M.A., 1932; Ph.D., U. N.C., 1937; m. Harry Estil Moore, Nov. 27, 1924 (dec. July 1966). Reporter, Austin Am. and Statesman, 1924-26; dir. Child Welfare Survey Tex., Tex. Relief Commn., 1933-34; asst., Inst. Research Social Sci., U. N.C., 1934-37; asst. dir. Austin Regional Office, Profl. Projects, Work Projects Adminstrn. Tex., 1938-41; cons., Hogg Found. Mental Hygiene (name now Hogg Found. Mental Health), U. Tex., 1941-55, asst. to pres. community programs, 1955-72, exec. asso., 1972—, asso. dir. philanthropy in S.W., 1964-71; cons. home and family edn., counseling Tex. Edn. Agy., 1941-64, state adv. com. innovation and assessment edn., 1968—; cons. inter-disciplinary program Nat. Inst. Child Health and Human Devel., NIH, 1963-67. Task force on youth Joint Commn. Mental Health of Children; coordinator Tex. Coop. Youth Study; dir. seminars for chaplains in counseling human factors USAF, sponsored by Hogg Found. Mental Health, 1956-66; spl. cons. research utilization br. Nat. Inst. Mental Health, 1963-64; adv. bd. children Children's Bur., U.S. Office Health, Edn., and Welfare, 1963-66, ad hoc com. for youth services, 1968—. Recipient Nat. Headliner award Theta Sigma Phi, 1956; Spl. Service award Tex. Soc. Mental Health, also Ft. Worth-Tarrant County Soc. Mental Health; spl. merit award Am. Vocational Assn., 1963; Bernice Milburn Moore Scholarship established U. Tex. at Austin, 1970. Mem. Am. Sociol. Soc., Nat. Assn. Mental Health, Am. Home Econs. Assn., Southwestern Social Sci. Assn., Tex. Assn. Mental Health, Tex. Council Mental Health (past pres.), Tex. Council Mental Health Research, Future Homemakers Am. (nat. hon. mem.), Alpha Kappa Delta, Theta Sigma Phi, Delta Kappa Gamma, Phi Upsilon Omicron. Democrat. Mem. Disciples of Christ Ch. Author: (with Harry Estill Moore) Through Your Own Front Door, 1945; (with Dorothy M. Leahy) You and Your Family, 1948, rev. 1954; (with Robert L. Sutherland) Family, Community and Mental Health, 1950: Juvenile Delinquency, Research, Theory, Comment, 1959; (with W. H. Holtzman) Tomorrow's Parents, 1965; (with Robert L. Sutherland) Our Youngest Children, 1971; pamphlets and study guides on mental health and the family. Contbr. to edn. yearbooks. profl. jours. Home: 1215 W 22 1/2 St Austin TX 78705 Office: Hogg Found Mental Health Will C Hogg Bldg U Tex Austin TX 78712

MOORE, BESSIE H., educator, civic leader; B.A., State Coll. Ark.; M.A., U. Conn. Organizer county library, Pine Bluff, Ark., 1926; now dir. econ. and environmental edn. Ark. Dept. Edn.; exec. dir. State Council Econ. Edn. Dir. 1st Nat. Bank, Little Rock. Mem. adv. com. library services act U.S. Commr. Edn., 1954-59; mem. Ark. Library Commn., 1941—, chmn., 1949—; mem. U.S. com. Am. Library in Paris, 1970—; mem. Nat. Library Adv. Commn., 1967—; mem. Nat. Book Com.; mem. Gov.'s Adv. Com. on Status of Women, 1968—, Gov.'s Adv. Com. on Aging, 1968—; mem. adv. com. women in services Dept. Def. Mem. Ark. Democratic Com., 1932-36; del. Dem. Nat. Conv., 1936. Mem. Ark. Congress Parents and Tchrs. (life), A.L.A. (chmn. jury citation trustees 1969-70, chmn. trustees state libraries 1970), Am. Assn. U. Women, Little Rock C. of C. (mem. govtl. affairs com.), Delta Kappa Gamma. Office: Ark Dept Edn Little Rock AR 72201

MOORE, CARL LEE, physician; b. Dayton, Ky., Dec. 16, 1935; s. Louis Edward and Marie Anna (Knapp) M.; B.A., Hanover Coll., 1958; M.D., U. Cin., 1962; m. Mureen Foster, July 25, 1959; children—Judith Marie, Scot Edward, Steven Wayne. Intern, Mound Park Hosp., St. Petersburg, Fla., 1962-63, resident, 1963-64; practice medicine, St. Petersburg, 1964—. Chmn., Suncoast Tarpon Roundup, 1968-72. Mem. A.M.A., Fla., Pinellas County med. socs., Am., Fla. diabetic assns. Mason. Home: 7127 2nd Av S Saint Petersburg FL 33707 Office: 1609 Pasadena Av S Saint Petersburg FL 33707

MOORE, CHARLES GRAY, accountant; b. Franklin, Ky., July 7, 1916; s. Charles Thomas and Stella (Gray) M.; B.S., U. Ky., 1939; m. June Brown, June 21, 1953; children—Marcia Brown, Alan Gray. Auditor Dept. Revenue, Commonwealth of Ky., Frankfort, 1939-41; mem. exec. tng. program Sears, Roebuck & Co., Louisville and Chgo., 1946-48; auditor, mgr., partner Albert B. Maloney & Co., 1948-56; mgr. Ernst & Ernst, Murfreesboro, Tenn., 1956-63, Nashville, 1963—. Tchr. accounting Middle Tenn. State U., Murfreesboro, 1955. Treas. Murfreesboro Community Chest, 1955, Hillsboro High Men's Club, 1972. Bd. dirs. Goodwill Industries Nashville, 1968-69, treas., 1969, pres. elect, 1972. Served to lt. col. USAAF, 1941-46. C.P.A., Tenn. Mem. McMinnville Jr. C. of C. (sec. 1951), Nashville C. of C., Nat. Assn. Accountants (dir. Nashville chpt. 1969), Tenn. Soc. C.P.A.'s (chpt. treas. 1954-55, state treas. 1969-71, state council mem. 1972-74), Am. Accounting Assn., Nat. Soc. Accountants for Co-ops., U. Ky. Alumni Assn., Hon. Order Ky. Cols., Am. Inst. C.P.A.'s, Beta Gamma Sigma. Presbyn. (elder 1968-69). Rotarian (sec. Murfreesboro 1960-62; sec. Donelson club 1968-69, pres. 1970-71). Clubs: McMinnville Exchange (sec. 1953-54); Murfreesboro Stone River Country (sec. 1960-62, dir. 1960-62); Frankfort Wisemen's; Richland Country, Nashville City (Nashville); Stewart Air Force Base Officers (Smyrna, Tenn.). Home: 1605 Tynewood Dr Nashville TN 37215 Office: 315 Union St Nashville TN 37201

MOORE, CHARLES JACK, JR., textile mfg. co. exec.; b. Raleigh, N.C., Apr. 23, 1940; s. Charles Jack and Katherine (Ellis) M.; B.M.E., N.C. State U., 1962; m. Dorothea Yvonne Costin, June 24, 1960; children— Charles Jack III, Constance Faith. Application engr. Worthington Corp., Washington, 1962-63; plant engr. Chatham Mfg. Co., Elkin, N.C., 1965—. Mem. Regional Air Quality Control Bd., 1969-70; Town Commnr., Elkin, N.C., 1971—; vice-chmn. Elkin Pub. Housing Authority, 1969-71. Served to capt. AUS, 1963-65. Registered profl. engr., N.C. Mem. Nat. Soc. Profl. Engrs., Elkin Jr. C. of C. Methodist. Home: 223 Knollwood Dr Elkin NC 28621 Office: Main St Elkin NC 28621

MOORE, CHARLES LOUIS, natural resources cons.; b. Carlsbad, N.M., May 26, 1896; s. Charles William and Annie (D'Arcy) M.; m. Frances Pauline Dyer, June 20, 1920; children—Jessie P. (Mrs. William A. Brown), Ann E. (dec.), Vesta F. (Mrs. R.S. Keppler), Holmes S., Charles A., Oris W., Clark D. Civil engr. various locations, 1916-23; petroleum engr., Cal., 1923-44, Washington, 1944-49, 51—, Mexico, 1949-51; cons. historic patterns of exhaustible natural resources to industries, Seminole, Fla., 1968—. Mem. Am. Assn. Petroleum Geologists, Soc. Petroleum Engrs., Am. Inst. Mining, Metall., Petroleum Engrs. Contbr. numerous articles to profl. jours. Home: 8703 143d St N Seminole FL 33542 Office: Box 3336 Seminole FL 33542

MOORE, CHARLES ZIADY, pub. co. exec.; b. Lebanon, May 7, 1934 (came to U.S. 1955, naturalized); s. George K. and Mary J. (Nasr) Ziady; B.S., George Peabody Coll., 1959, M.A., 1960; Ph.D., U. R.I., 1968; m. Elaine D. Ortowski, Aug. 12, 1967. Asst. prof. North Park Coll., Chgo., 1961-63; research chemist Bristol Myers Co., Hillside, N.J., 1964-65; asst. prof. Middle Tenn. State U., 1969—. Mem. Am. Chem. Soc., Book Mfrs. Assn., Gamma Alpha. Office: 405 7th Av S Nashville TN 37203

MOORE, COYLE E., univ. ofcl.; b. Waterloo, S.C., Mar. 5, 1900; s. Sydney L. and Annie L. (Killingsworth) M.; B.S., The Citadel, 1920; M.S., U. N.C., 1925; Ph.D., U. Chgo., 1928; m. Mabel Boysworth, Sept. 1, 1928; 1 son, Coyle E. Athletic coach N.C. high schs., at Washington, Statesville, Rocky Mount; asso. prof. sociology and social work Fla. State U., 1928-41, prof. 1941-46, registrar, acad. counselor Tallahassee br., 1946-47, chmn. div. applied social scis., 1947-49, dean Sch. Social Welfare, 1949—. Served with U.S. Army, World War I. Mem. Fla. Bd. Social Welfare, 1933-37, Fla. Gov's Commn. on Social Legislature, 1936, Fla. Gov.'s Com. on Med. Care, 1954-56, Fla. Council Research and Tng. Mental Health, 1955—; pres. Fla. Conf. Social Work, 1936; mem. Nat. Council on Social Work Edn., 1946-56, Social Science Workshop, So. regional com. Social Sci. Research Council, 1936. Mem. Am., So. (sec. treas. 1940-47, pres. 1948) social socs., Am. Assn. U. Profs., Am. Assn. Social Workers, Nat. Conf. on Family Relations, Nat. Conf. Social Work, Am. A.A.A.S., N.E.A. Democrat. Methodist. Home: 2021 Mission Rd Tallahassee FL

MOORE, DAN KILLIAN, justice Supreme Ct. N.C.; b. Asheville, N.C., Apr. 2, 1906; s. Fred and Lela (Enloe) M.; B.S. in Bus. Adminstrn., U. N.C., 1927, postgrad. in law, 1927-28; m. Jeanelle Coulter, May 4, 1933; children—Edith (Mrs. Edgar Blanton Hamilton), Dan K. Admitted to N.C. bar, 1928; practiced in Sylva, 1928-46; solicitor Superior Ct., 20th Jud. Dist. N.C., Sylva, 1946-48, judge Superior Ct., 1949-58; counselor, asst. sec. Champion Papers, Inc., Canton, N.C., 1958-65; gov. N.C., 1965-69; partner Joyner, Moore & Howison, Raleigh, 1969; asso. justice Supreme Ct. N.C., 1969—. Dir. Wachovia Bank & Trust Co., Asheville, N.C., Durham Life Ins. Co.; dir. radio sta. WWIT, Canton. Vice chmn. N.C. Bd. Water Resources, 1959-65. Mem. N.C. Ho. of Reps., 1941-43. Bd. dirs. U. N.C. Law Found.; life trustee U. N.C.; trustee High Point Coll. Served with AUS, 1943-45. Mem. N.C. Bar Assn., U. N.C. Alumni Assn. (dir.) Phi Beta Kappa, Pi Kappa Phi. Democrat. Methodist. Mason, Rotarian. Club: Civitan (Canton). Home: 3621 E Anclote Arms Raleigh NC 27602 Office: Justice Bldg Raleigh NC 27602

MOORE, DANA CLIFTON, JR, lawyer; b. Shaw, Miss., Aug. 4, 1931; s. Dana Clifton and Malvina Yerger (Walker) M.; LL.B., U. Miss., 1957; m. Julia Gibert, Apr. 19, 1958; 1 dau., Julia Kilby. Admitted to Miss. bar, 1957, since practiced in Cleveland; mem. firm Cox & Moore, 1957—; mem. Miss. Ho. of Reps., 1964-71. Bolivar County youth counsellor, 1964—; chmn. Bolivar County Voters League, 1965-67; pres. Boliver County Cancer Soc., 1961-68. Past dir. Delta area council Boy Scouts Am.; pres. Episcopal Laymen Miss., 1972—; lay del. gen. conv. P.E. Ch., Louisville, 1973. Past dir. Miss. div. Am. Cancer Soc., bd. dirs. Cleveland Recreation Assn.; past dir. Bolivar County Conservation League. Mem. Am., Miss. Bolivar County (pres. 1969-70) bar assns., C. of C. (v.p. 1965, dir. 1962—), Phi Delta Theta, Phi Alpha Delta. Episcopalian (past sr. warden). Democrat. Rotarian (past dir., pres. 1968-69, treas.). Home: 806 Maple St Cleveland MS 38732 Office: 116 S Court St Cleveland MS 38732

MOORE, DANIEL KILLIAN, justice N.C. Supreme Ct.; b. Asheville, N.C., Apr. 2, 1906; s. Fred and Lela (Enloe) M.; B.S. in Bus. Adminstrn., U. N.C., 1927, postgrad. Law Sch., 1927-28; LL.B. (hon.), Elon Coll., 1965, U. N.C. at Chapel Hill, 1967, Wake Forest U., 1968, U. N.C., 1968; m. Jeanelle Coulter, May 4, 1933; children—Edith (Mrs. Edgar B. Hamilton, Jr.), Daniel Killian. Admitted to N.C. bar, 1928; practiced in Sylva until 1946; solicitor 20th Jud. Dist. N.C., Sylva, 1946-48; judge Superior Ct., Sylva, 1949-58; counsellor, asst. sec. Champion Papers, Inc., Canton, N.C., 1958-65; gov. N.C., Raleigh, 1965-69; partner firm Joyner, Moore & Howison, Raleigh, 1969; asso. justice N.C. Supreme Ct., Raleigh, 1969—. Dir. Wachovia Bank & Trust Co., Durham Life Ins. Co. Mem. N.C. Ho. of Reps., 1941; del. Democratic nat. convs., 1960, 64, 68; mem. N.C. Dem. Exec. Com. Vice chmn. N.C. Bd. Water Resources, 1959-64. Bd. dirs. U. N.C. Law Sch. Found.; life trustee U. N.C.; trustee High Point (N.C.) Coll. Served with AUS, 1943-45. Mem. N.C. Bar Assn., Phi Beta Kappa, Pi Kappa Phi. Methodist. Rotarian, Mason (Shriner). Club: Civitan. Home: 3621-E Anclote Arms Raleigh NC 27607 Office: Justice Bldg Box 1841 Raleigh NC 27602

MOORE, DAVE, assn. exec.; b. Pine Bluff, Ark., Jan. 28, 1920; s. William O. and Mary Lou (Wylie) M.; B.J., U. Mo., 1942; postgrad. Washington and Lee U., U. So. Cal., Northwestern U.; m. Martha Owen, Apr. 30, 1943; children—Marnee (Mrs. Pat Loftin), Becky, Davy, Mike. Asst. indsl. mgr. Little Rock C. of C., 1945-46; mgr. C. of C., Fordyce, Ark., 1946-47, Weslaco, Tex., 1947-49, Laredo, Tex., 1950-53, Borger, Tex., 1953-63; gen. mgr. Baytown (Tex.) C. of C., 1963—. Sec. adv. bd. Sterling Municipal Library, 1965-66, pres., 1966—. Served to capt. USAAF, 1942-45. Mem. Tex. C. of C. Mgrs. Assn. (past dir., past editor News), Sigma Alpha Epsilon. Methodist (lay speaker Tex. Conf.). Office: 2 W Texas Av Baytown TX 77520

MOORE, DAVID CLINTON, judge; b. Gladewater, Tex., June 7, 1922; s. Clinton Harvey and Alma (Wood) M.; B.S., North Tex. U., 1942; J.D., U. Tex., 1948; m. Billie Louise Newton, Oct. 12, 1942; children—David, James, Lynda. Admitted to Tex. bar, 1948. Fed. bar, 1950; asst. dist. atty. Gregg County, Longview, Tex., 1949-51, dist. atty., 1952-55; judge 124th Jud. Dist. Longview, 1955—. Dir. First State Bank, Gladewater, Gladwater Fed. Savs. & Loan. Active Boy Scouts Am., 1950—. Served as sgt. USAAF, 1942-46. Mem. Am., Tex. bar assns. Mason (32 deg.), Lion. Home: 308 E Commerce St Gladewater TX 75647 Office: Court House Longview TX 75601

MOORE, DON, JR., lawyer; b. Chattanooga, Nov. 27, 1928; s. Don M. and Frances (Wolfe) M.; student U. Chattanooga, 1948-49; J.D., U. Tenn., 1952; m. Sarah Mosley; children—Lisa Michele, Deidre Le Ayne. Admitted to Tenn. bar, 1953, Ga. bar, 1959; partner Crutchfield, Moore & Jenkins, attys. Partner Moore & Moore, contractors, 1966—; dir., gen. counsel Wright Systems Internat. Corp. Mem. Tenn. Ho. of Reps., 1956-58, 64-66, Tenn. Senate, 1966-68; chmn. fiscal rev. com. Tenn. Gen. Assembly, 1967-69. Served as staff sgt. U.S. Army Res., 1950-51. Named Legislative Conservationist of Yr., 1968. Mem. Am., Chattanooga bar assns., Am. Legion, Bar Assn. Tenn., Tenn. Trial Lawyers Assn. Democrat. Methodist. Mason (Shriner), Elk. Clubs: Chattanooga Flyers, Moccasin Flying, Brainerd Saddle. Home: 1802 Skyline Dr Chattanooga TN 37421 Office: 509 Cherry St Chattanooga TN 37402

MOORE, EDWARD RUSSELL, JR., physician; b. Camden, N.J., Oct. 3, 1931; s. Edward Russell and Dorothy Grace (Stowe) M.; student McNeese Jr. Coll., 1950; B.S., La. State U., 1953, M.D., 1959; m. Sherry Gail North, May 26, 1961; children—Martin Paul, Cathy Denise, Jon David. Intern, Charity Hosp., New Orleans, 1959-60; gen. practice medicine, Sulphur, La., 1960—; mem. staff West Calcasieu-Cameron, St. Patrick's hosps. Mem. A.M.A., La., Calcasieu Parish med. socs., Phi Beta Kappa, Phi Beta Pi. Republican. Episcopalian. Home: 2521 St Joseph St Sulphur LA 70663 Office: 2320 E Parish Rd Sulphur LA 70663

MOORE, ELLEN BRYAN, state ofcl., bus. exec.; b. Baton Rouge, Apr. 13, 1912; d. Alex Dunn and Louise (Rhodes) Bryan; B.A., La. State U., 1933, M.A., 1950; grad. student Tulane U., 1935; m. Darrow Haywood Moore, Jan. 27, 1944; children—Margaret L'Mell, Ellen Victoria. Tchr. pub. schs., Baton Rouge, 1933-40; builder, personal property mgmt., 1935—; register state lands State of La., 1952—. Vice chmn. La. Office Bldg. Corp. Mem. State Recreation and Park Commn., 1952; bd. dirs. Nat. Park Conf., 1953-60, 69-72; mem. State Park and Recreation Com., 1960—; chmn. La. Gov.'s Commn. Status of Women; rep. Bur. Outdoor Recreation Council; gov.'s rep. Pub. Land Law Commn.; state rep. Nat. Civilian Def. Women's Adv. Council, Washington, 1955. Area rep., bd. dirs. United Democrats La.; bd. dirs. Operation Crossroad (So. div.) Nat. Democratic Com. 1956. Bd. dirs. United Givers Fund, La. Hist. Assn., Capitol Region Planning Commn.; zone chmn. March of Dimes, 1957; mem. budget com. Community Services Council; pres. East Baton Rouge Lioness orgn., 1950-51; bd. dirs. Girl Scouts U.S.A., 1954-55, Camp Fire Girls, 1957. Served to capt. AUS, 1941-45. Hon. mem. Pelican Girls State. Mem. Nat. Assn. Real Estate Bds. (publicity dir. women's council), Am. Legion (del. nat. conv. 1953-54), Nat., La. edn. assns., Am. Assn. U. Women, Amvets, Am. Right of Way Assn., Nat. Conf. State Parks (membership chmn.), La. Council Music and Performing Arts (sec.), Bus. and Profl. Womens Club, Delta Zeta, Phi Lambda Phi, Psi Chi, Alpha Delta Kappa. Clubs: Pilot (pres. Baton Rouge 1940-41), Merry-Go-Round (past pres.). Home: 2222 Government St Baton Rouge LA 70806 Office: State Land and Resources Bldg Baton Rouge LA 70804

MOORE, FLOY JACK, physician; b. Moundsville, W.Va., May 25, 1924; s. William R. and May (Weaver) M.; A.B., U. W.Va., 1945; M.D., U. Pa., 1948; student Bethany Coll., 1943-44, Baylor U., 1953-55; m. Jacqueline VerBrugghen, Feb. 17, 1950; children—Adrian Ray, Kevin. Intern, Warren State Hosp., Pa., 1947, Pa. Hosp., Phila., 1947-48, Presbyn. Hosp., Chgo., 1948-49; resident Baylor U., 1951-53; practiced medicine, specializing in psychiatry and neurology, Jackson, Miss., 1956—; mem. staff VA Hosp., Univ. Med. Center; asst. instr., dept. psychiatry Baylor U., 1951-53, instr., 1953-55, asst. prof. physiology, 1955-56, asst. prof. psychiatry, 1955-56; prof. dept. psychiatry U. Miss., 1956—, chmn. dept., 1956-68. Served with USNR, 1943-45; to lt. M.C., USNR, 1948-51; now capt. M.C. Res. Fellow Am. Psychiat. Assn.; mem. Miss. Psychiat. Soc. (pres. 1959-60). Am. Electroencephalography Soc., So. Electroencephalographic Soc. (pres. 1958-59, council mem. 1959-62), A.M.A., Miss. State Med. Assn., Central Med. Soc. Miss., So. Profs. Psychiatry (chmn. 1962-63), So. Psychiatric Assn. (v.p. 1964-65), Am. Assn. for History of Medicine, Assn. Am. Med. Colls., Am. Acad. Psychoanalysis. Contbr. articles in field to profl. jours. Home: 2006 Cherokee Dr Jackson MS 39211 Office: 2500 N State St Jackson MS 39216

MOORE, FRANK HUGH, JR., dentist; b. Corpus Christi, Tex., June 10, 1940; s. Frank Hugh and Betty (Hedrick) M.; student U. Notre Dame, 1958-60; B.A., Tex. Christian U., 1963; postgrad. U. Tex., 1963-64; M.A., Southwestern Med. Sch. of U. Tex., 1966; D.D.S., Baylor U., 1969; m. Judy Ann Richter, Sept. 20, 1963; children—Frank Hugh III, Trevor Scott, Angie Catherine. Vice pres. Moores, Inc. and Moore's Saxet Center, Corpus Christi, 1965—; individual practice dentistry, Garland, Tex., 1971—. Served with USNR, 1969-71. Recipient Bernard Gottlieb Meml. award in oral pathology, 1969. Mem. Omicron Kappa Upsilon, Psi Omega, Sigma Chi. Republican. Roman Catholic. Home: 9824 Robin Hill Lane Dallas TX 75238 Office: 500 Eastgate Garland TX 75040

MOORE, GEOFFREY HOYT, economist, govt. ofcl.; b. Pequannock, N.J., Feb. 28, 1914; s. Edward H. and Marian (Leman) M.; B.S., Rutgers U., 1933, M.S., 1937; Ph.D., Harvard, 1947; m. Ella C. Goldschmid, July 12, 1938; children—Stephen, Peter, Kathleen, Pamela. Instr. agrl. econs. Rutgers U., 1936-42; mem. research staff Nat. Bur. Econ. Research, N.Y.C., 1939-68, asso. dir. research, 1948-64, dir. research, 1965-67, v.p. research, 1968; commr. labor statistics Dept. Labor, 1969—; asso. prof. econs. N.Y.U., 1947-48; vis. lectr. econs., Columbia U., 1953-54. Fellow Am. Statis. Assn. (pres. 1968); mem. Acad. Polit. Sci., Am. Econs. Assn., A.A.A.S., Conf. Bus. Economists, Nat. Assn. Bus. Economists, Phi Beta Kappa, Alpha Zeta. Club: Cosmos (Washington). Author: (with W.A. Wallis) A Significance Test for Time Series, 1941; Production of Industrial Materials in World Wars I and II, 1944; Statistical Indicators of Cyclical Revivals and Recessions, 1950; The Diffusion of Business Cycles in Economics and the Public Interest, 1955; Measuring Recessions, 1958; Business Cycle Indicators, 1960; Tested Knowledge of Business Cycles, 1962; (with J. Shiskin) Indicators of Business Expansions and Contractions, 1966; (with P. Klein) The Quality of Consumer Installment Credit, 1967; The Anatomy of Inflation, 1969; The Cyclical Behavior of Prices, 1971. Home: 2700 Virginia Av NW Washington DC 20037 Office: 441 G St NW Washington DC 20212

MOORE, GEORGE CARROLL, motel exec.; b. Van Buren, Ark., July 23, 1937; s. Nelson C. and Blanche (Hood) M.; student Ft. Smith Jr. Coll., 1959-61; m. Nola Diane Cress, June 14, 1963; children—Melinda Renee, George Kevin, Geoffrey Grant, Cindy Michelle. Desk clk. Holiday Inn, Ft. Smith, Ark., 1959, mgr., 1962-65; mgr. Holiday Inn, Colorado Springs, Colo., 1966-67; gen. mgr. Holiday Inn, Oklahoma City, 1967—. Adviser State Dept. Vocational and Tech. Edn., 1971; chmn. adv. bd. Hotel and Restaurant Sch., Okla. State U. Extension, 1971-72. Served with USAF, 1955-59. Mem. Oklahoma City Hotel and Motel Assn. (pres.), Okla. Lodging Assn. (dir.), Career Devel. Inst. (pres.). Kiwanian. Address: 801 S Meridian St Oklahoma City OK 73108

MOORE, GLENN EDWARD, chemist; b. Petersburg, Va., Jan. 23, 1930; s. George E. and Nell (Dance) M.; B.S., U. Richmond, 1961; m. Eloise Vick, Feb. 9, 1951 (dec. 1969); children—Glenn E., Thomas H., Cara E., m. 2d, Dorothy F. French, July 25, 1970; 1 stepdau., Pamela J. French. Chemist, Dan River Mills, Danville, Va., 1961-65; asst. dir. tech. service div. Va. Water Control Bd., Richmond, 1965—. Active Boy Scouts Am. Served with USMCR, 1950-51. Mem. Am. Assn. Textile Chemists and Colorists, Water Pollution Control Fedn., Am. Chem. Soc., Va. Water Pollution Control Assn. Mem. Christian Ch. Home: 302 Winston Av Colonial Heights VA 23834 Office: 4010 W Broad St Richmond VA 23230

MOORE, GLOVER, educator; b. Birmingham, Ala., Sept. 22, 1911; s. Glover and Maud (Mims) M.; B.A., Birmingham-So. Coll., 1932; M.A., Vanderbilt U., 1933, Ph.D., 1936. Teaching fellow Vanderbilt U., 1935-36; instr. history Miss. State U., 1936-38, asst. prof., 1938-46, asso. prof., 1946-53, prof., 1953—. Pres. Miss. Hist. Soc., 1970-71. Served with Adj. Gen.'s Dept., AUS, 1942-46. Mem. Am., So. hist. assns., Orgn. Am. Historians. Episcopalian. Author: The Missouri Controversy, 1819-1821, 1953; William Jemison Mims, Soldier and Squire, 1966. Home: 404 Myrtle St Starkville MS 39759 Office: Box 5326 State College MS 39762

MOORE, GORDON SIDNEY, accountant; b. Midlothian, Tex., Sept. 11, 1922; s. James Hayden and Eleanor (Rouse) M.; B.A., E.Tex. U., 1941; M.S., Tex. A. and M. U., 1943; m. Dorothy Geraldine Evans, Feb. 11, 1943; children—Robert E., Paul L. Instr., Tex. A. and M. U., 1942-43; revenue agt., regional analyst Internal Revenue Service, Dallas, 1946-55; partner Arthur Young & Co., Houston, 1955—. Served with AUS, 1943-46. Mem. Am. Inst. C.P.A.'s, Tex. Soc. C.P.A.'s, Houston Chpt. C.P.A.'s, Houston Bus. and Estate Planning Council. Clubs: Braeburn Country, Petroleum (Houston). Home: 8914 McAvoy Dr Houston TX 77036 Office: 4800 One Shell Plaza Houston TX 77002

MOORE, GRAY ELLESOR, JR., constrn. co. exec.; b. Greenwood, S.C., Dec. 17, 1942; s. Gray Ellesor and Ruth (Allen) M.; B.A., Wofford Coll., 1960-64; m. Cheryl Beattie, June 26, 1965; 1 dau., Ruth Elizabeth. With G.E. Moore Co., Inc., gen. contractor, Greenwood, 1964—, v.p., 1966—; v.p. Emerald Homes, Inc., Greenwood, 1970—. Chmn. adv. bd. constrn. Piedmont Tech. Edn. Center, Greenwood, 1971—. Bd. dirs. Neighborhood Playgrounds. Mem. Am. Inst. Constructors, Asso. Gen. Contractors Am. (bd. dirs. S.C., N.C. br. 1969—). Methodist (bd. dirs. 1968-70). Clubs: Greenwood Country, Greenwood Supper, Greenwood Metropolitan Dinner. Home: RFD 2 Box 469 Hodges SC 29653 Office: G E Moore Co Box 578 Greenwood SC 29646

MOORE, HARRY, banker; b. Sierra Blanca, Tex., Oct. 3, 1920; s. Harry and Alice (Yarbro) M.; student U. Tex., El Paso, 1937-40, Southwestern Grad. Sch. Banking, 1966-68; 1 dau., Charlotte (Mrs. Robert Fisk Mackin). Farmer, rancher, Hudspeth County, Tex., 1945-51; exec. v.p. El Paso Valley Cotton Assn., 1951-55; v.p. El Paso Nat. Bank, 1955—. Mem. Sheriff's Posse, 1960—, Better Bus. Bur., 1970—, Tex. Rangers Assn., 1959—. Served with USAAF, 1942-45. Decorated D.F.C., Air medal. Mem. W. Tex., El Paso chambers commerce. Kiwanian. Home: 4289 Canterbury St El Paso TX 79902 Office: PO Drawer 140 El Paso TX 79980

MOORE, HARVEY CLEAVER, educator; b. Port Penn, Del., Mar. 13, 1918; s. Harvey Enos and Lina (Bendler) M.; B.A., U. Del., 1938; Ph.D., U. N.M., 1950; m. Sarah Frances Morehead, Aug. 16, 1948. High sch. tchr., Del., 1938-42; asst. prof. anthropology Am. U., Washington, 1951-54, asso. prof., 1954-58, prof., 1958—, chmn. anthropology, 1965-69, asso. dean for grad studies and research Coll. Arts and Scis., 1970—. Research asso. Bur. Social Sci. Research, Washington, 1951-54; lectr. Johns Hopkins, 1953-56; vis. recognized scholar Inst. Social Anthropology, Oxford (Eng.) U., 1967-68. Served to 1st lt. AUS, 1942-46. Fellow A.A.A.S., African Studies Assn., Am. Anthrop. Assn., Am. Ethnol. Soc., Royal Anthrop. Inst.; mem. Anthrop. Soc. Washington (pres. 1959-61), Phi Beta Kappa, Phi Kappa Phi. Field research Navajo Reservation, 1951-54, 61, Sub-Saharan Africa, 1963. Author: Cumulation and Cultural Processes, 1954; Culture Change in a Navaho Community, 1967. Home: 1508 44th St NW Washington DC 20007

MOORE, HERBERT BELL, headmaster; b. Glen Cove, L.I., N.Y., July 30, 1926; s. Lewis Kingsley and Thelma Morton (Bell) M.; B.A., Bowdoin Coll., 1947; M.A., Boston U., 1953; Ed.M., Harvard, 1958; m. Martha Marie Fay, June 22, 1951; children—Jeffrey, Janice, Stephen, Susan, Elizabeth, Charles. Tchr. math., coach Berkshire Sch., Sheffield, Mass., 1947-51; tchr. history, coach, pub. relations dir., fund sec. Belmont (Mass.) Hill Sch. 1951-58; headmaster Tilton (N.H.) Sch., 1958-65, Holland Hall Sch., Tulsa, 1965—. Mem. governing bds. Nat. Assn. Episcopal Schs.; treas. Country Day Sch. Headmasters Assn.; regent Cum Laude Soc. Mem. Ind. Sch. Assn. of S.W. (past pres.). Home: 2532 E 26th Pl Tulsa OK 74114

MOORE, HERBERT MOFFETT, lumber co. exec.; b. nr. Waynesville, N.C.; B.S., Clemson Coll., 1930, postgrad. U. S.C., 1930-31; m. Virginia Sparks, Apr. 11, 1936. Lumber research, 1932-33; owner, operator Herbert M. Moore Hardwood Lumber Co., Morganton, N.C., 1933—. Served with USNR, World War II; PTO. Elk. Home: 101 Woodbine Terrace Morganton NC 28655 also (summer) Blowing Rock NC Office: Morganton NC 28655

MOORE, HOLLIS ANDREW, JR., coll. adminstr.; b. Peirce City, Mo., Apr. 3, 1923; s. Hollis Andrew and Kathleen Ruth (Jordan) M.; A.B., Baylor U., 1946; postgrad. Brown U., 1946-47; Ed.D., U. Tex., 1953; m. Mabel Marian Brown, Aug. 22, 1946; children—Hollis Andrew III, Michael Brown. Adminstrv. asst. Dallas Civic Fedn., 1948; tchr. social studies Fulmore Jr. High Sch., Austin, Tex., 1949-50; dean boys Austin High Sch., 1950-51; asso. editor Nation's Schs., 1952-55; exec. sec. Com. Advancement Sch. Adminstrn., 1955-60; dean edn. U. Ariz., 1960-64; dir. div. edn. W. K. Kellogg Found., 1964-65; v.p. acad. affairs George Peabody Coll., Nashville, 1965—. Vis. lectr. Northwestern U., 1953-55, U. Va., 1954-55, No. Ariz. U., 1956, U. Denver, 1957, Stanford, 1958-60, U. Neb., 1960. Bd. dirs. Citizens for Ct. Modernization, Inc., mem. Tenn. Adv.

Council Community Services and Continuing Edn., 1966—. Bd. dirs. Central Midwestern Regional Ednl. Lab., 1966—. Served with AUS, World War II: ETO. Decorated Purple Heart. Mem. N.E.A., Am. Assn. Sch. Adminstrs. (chmn. yearbook commn. 1960), Phi Delta Kappa (pres. Mu chpt. 1951). Democrat. Conglist. Kiwanian. Club: University (Nashville). Author: Studies in School Administration, 1957; contbg. author: Behavioral Science and Educational Administration, 1964; Perspectives on Educational Change, 1967; co-author: The Administrative Team and Long Range Planning, 1967. Home: 4804 Sewanee Rd Nashville TN 37220

MOORE, HOMER (GAIL), ret. petroleum geologist; b. Ava, Ill., Apr. 4, 1918; s. George Gail and Maidia (Carruthers) M.; student Kemper Mil. Sch., 1936-38; B.S. in Geology, U. Okla., 1941; m. Bobbe Jene Pace, Dec. 31, 1942; children—Melinda Gail, Patti Pace. Div. geologist Pan Am. Prodn. Co., Houston, 1946-51; chief geologist La. Land & Exploration Co., New Orleans, 1952-54; partner Dunnam & Moore, Houston, geologists, oil operators, 1954-68; pres., dir. Benquin Corp., 1969-72. Breeder registered Polled Hereford cattle, nr. Belle Rive, Ill., 1958—. Served as aviator USNR, 1941-45. Mem. Am. Assn. Petroleum Geologists, Houston Geol. Soc., Gulf Coast Assn. Geol. Socs. Mason (32 deg., Shriner). Clubs: Houston, Lakeside Country (Houston); Brazos River (West Columbia, Tex.). Home: 5854 Shady River Rd Houston TX 77027 Office: 1212 Main St Houston TX 77002

MOORE, JAMES ALFRED, lawyer; b. Madisonville, Ky., Oct. 20, 1915; s. Virgil Y. and Ina (Price) M.; A.B., U. Ky., 1936; LL.B., Harvard, 1939; m. Dorothy Marie Kelly, Sept. 27, 1941 (div. Oct. 1968); children—Marjorie Y., James Kelly, Kathleen; m. 2d, Lucile Carpenter, June 29, 1970. Admitted to Pa. bar, 1940; with Pepper, Hamilton & Schertz, Phila., 1939—, partner, 1951—; pres. Camelback Ski Corp., 1962—, Eagle Land Co., 1967—; dir. Selby, Battersby & Co., Phila. Iron Works Co., Ski Roundtop, Inc. Bd. dirs. Phila. Soc. for Crippled Children and Adults. Served from ensign to lt. comdr. USNR, 1942-45. Mem. Am. Bar Assn., Am. Law Inst. Clubs: Merion Cricket (Haverford, Pa.); Columbia Country (Chevy Chase, Md.). Home: 2450 Virginia Av NW Washington DC 20037 Office: 1701 Pennsylvania Av NW Washington DC 20006

MOORE, JAMES FRANCIS, educator, accountant; b. Paducah, Ky., July 16, 1925; s. Robert Allen and Robbie (Tatom) M.; M.B.A., Tulane U., 1948; B.S., Bowling Green Coll. Commerce, 1947; m. Sara Ann Swords, June 14, 1957; 1 son, John Craig. Reporter Park City Daily News, Bowling Green, Ky., 1942-45; instr. U. Fla., 1948-53, asst. prof. accounting, 1953-65; pvt. practice as pub. accountant, Gainesville, 1953—; partner Moore, Cobb, Cloud & Crippen, C.P.A.'s. Mem. Fla. Bd. Accountancy, 1967-71, chmn., 1968-71. Mem. Fla. Legislature SCOPE Com., 1967-71; Fla. pres. Nat. Muscular Dystrophy Research Found., Inc., 1954-60. Mem. Am., Fla. insts. C.P.A.'s, Nat. Assn. State Bds. Accountancy, U.S. Jr. C. of C. (Gainesville treas. 1958, bd. dirs. 1958; Jaybird editor 1959), Beta Alpha Psi, Alpha Kappa Psi. Republican. Baptist. Contbr. articles to profl. jours. Editor: Fla. C.P.A. Jour., 1960-65. Home: 1300 NW 6th St Gainesville FL 32601

MOORE, JAMES HERBERT, realtor; b. Charleston, W.Va., Dec. 22, 1911; s. Herbert Spencer and Alice (Hanson) M.; student U. Va., 1929-31; B.S., U. Miami (Fla.), 1934; m. Virginia Ashbrook Lee, Apr. 30, 1938; children—James H., Claudia A. (Mrs. Moore Kromer). Pres., Clinton Realty Inc., Cleve., 1937-50, James H. Moore Co., Oak Ridge, 1945—, Cardinal Point, Inc., Paducah, Ky., 1954—; gen. mgr. Mei Foo Investments, Ltd., Hong Kong, 1965-67; dir. Hamilton 1st Nat. Bank, Oak Ridge. Chmn., Oak Ridge chpt. A.R.C., 1948-50. Mem. S.A.R., Oak Ridge Real Estate Bd. (pres. 1964), Delta Chi. Republican. Presbyn. Mason (Shriner), Elk, Rotarian. Clubs: Key Biscayne (Fla.) Yacht; Royal Hong Kong Yacht, Hong Kong; Oak Ridge Golf and Country. Home: 422 Virginia Rd Oak Ridge TN 37830 Office: 315 Rutgers Av Oak Ridge TN 37830

MOORE, JAMES LEWIS, newspaper pub.; b. Greenwood, S.C., Feb. 16, 1908; s. James Walker and Minnie (Thompson) M.; student Brevard Coll., 1934-35, U. Mo., 1935; m. Betty Propst, Sept. 7, 1929 (dec. May 1963); m. 2d, Eloise Tucker Carriker, May 13, 1965. Pub. The Toweler, Kannapolis, N.C., 1927, The China Grove (N.C.) Press, 1930; pres., treas. Kannapolis Pub. Co., now chmn. bd.; pub. gen. mgr. The Daily Independent, Kannapolis. Trustee Independent Student Aid Assn. Mem. Kannapolis C. of C. Methodist. Author: Cabarrus Re-Born. Home: 205 East E St Kannapolis NC 28081 Office: 119-125 N Main St Kannapolis NC 28081

MOORE, JAMES WALLACE, educator; b. Birmingham, Ala., Feb. 19, 1923; s. Felix Tyre and Mary (Ingraham) M.; student Berea Coll., 1941-42; B.A., Tenn. Poly. Inst., 1951; M.S., U. Ky., 1952; Ph.D., Purdue U., 1962; m. Doris Jean Livingston, Sept. 3, 1948; children—Karen Sue, Joyce Ann, James Wallace IV. Project engr. Carbide and Carbon Chem. Co., South Charleston, W. Va., 1952-55; sr. project engr. Allison div. Gen. Motors Corp., Indpls., 1955-57; research asst. Purdue U., West Lafayette, Ind., 1958-62; sr. research engr. Jet Propulsion Lab., Cal. Inst. Tech., summers 1960-61; asso. prof. U. Va., Charlottesville, 1962-67, prof., 1967—, mem. univ. senate, 1967-71, U. Va. Sesquicentennial fellow, Barcelona, Spain, 1971-72. Co-chmn. Automatic Control Group, 1967—; cons. automatic controls NASA, Moorex, Inc., Phillip Morris; cons. machine design Datastrip Corp.; cons. automobile accident and failure analysis, various legal and ins. firms.; program chmn. Joint Automatic Control Conf., 1965. Pres., Woodbrook P.T.A., 1966. Mem. Albemarle County Republican Com., 1966—. Served with AUS, 1943, 45-46; USAF, 1944. Mem. Am. Soc. M.E. (chmn. exec. com. automatic control div. 1971, paper rev. chmn. automatic control div. 1965-67, mem. exec. com. automatic control div. 1967-72), Sigma Xi, Pi Tau Sigma, Tau Beta Pi. Baptist (deacon 1969-72). Contbr. articles to profl. jours. Patentee automotive safety screen, jet engine variable nozzle; research in reading machine for the blind, learning control and patterns. Home: 3409 Indian Spring Rd Charlottesville VA 22901

MOORE, JAMES YOUNG, mcht.; b. Florence, Ala., Jan. 24, 1913; s. Charles Wallace and Ada Jane (Young) M.; student U. Tenn., N.Y. U.; m. Elizabeth Lumpkin, Jan. 8, 1938; children—James Young, Mary Jane (Mrs. Timothy J. Cambias), Elizabeth Diane (Mrs. James D. Cone), Susan Wallace, Molly Ann. Mfg. rep. Schloss Bros., Balt., 1936-39; organizer, chmn. bd. Jim Moore Co., Lawrenceburg, Tenn., 1939—; organizer Quality Cleaners, 1940—; partner Moore & Myrick Farms, Ltd., 1958—; organizer Lawrence County Bank, Lawrenceburg. Rep. exec. seminar men's wear store mgmt. N.Y. U., 1967. Past Internat. dir. Boy Scouts Am.; past dir. Am. Cancer Soc.: exec. com. Citizens for Ct. Modernization. Presdl. elector at large for Tenn., 1936; nat. committeeman Young Republican Fedn., 1938-48; del. Rep. Nat. Conv., 1940; sustaining mem. Republican Nat. Com. Mem. Menninger Found. Mem. C. of C. (past nat. counselor, past dir.), Internat. Platform Assn., Farm Bur., Men's Wear Retailers Am., Tenn. Conf. to Improve Adminstrn. Justice, Delta Tau Delta (life). Mem. Ch. of Christ. Clubs: Lawrenceburg (Tenn.) Golf and Country; Wally Byam Caravan. Home: Jackson Hwy S Lawrenceburg TN 38464 Office: 39 NW Public Square Lawrenceburg TN 38464

MOORE, JAMIE, city ofcl.; m. children. With Birmingham (Ala.) Police Dept., 1936—, chief of police, 1956—. Mem. Internat. Assn. Chiefs of Police, Ala. Peace Officer's Assn., FBI Nat. Acad. Assos. Presbyn. Mason (32 deg., Shriner), Fraternal Order Police, Lion. Home: 752 S 85th St Birmingham AL 35206 Office: Birmingham Police Dept. City Hall Bldg Birmingham AL 35203

MOORE, JENNY MCKEAN, author; b. Boston, Mar. 12, 1923; d. Q.A. Shaw and Margaret (Sargent) McKean; B.A., Barnard Coll.; m. Nov. 26, 1944; children—Honor, Paul, Adelia, Rosemary, George, Marian, Daniel, Susanna, Patience. Author: The People On Second St., 1968. Address: 3319 Newark St NW Washington DC 20008

MOORE, JOHN BORTON, govt. ofcl.; b. Newcomerstown, O., Apr. 11, 1913; s. Craig and Sybil (Mugford) M.; B.S. in Accounting, Ohio State U., 1941; m. Marion Ellen Greegor, Nov. 21, 1941; children—John Borton, Pamela Ann (Mrs. Neal Waxman). With Konopah, Hurst & Dalton, C.P.A.'s, Toledo, 1941-42, Keller, Kirschner, Martin & Clinger, C.P.A.'s, Columbus, O., 1942-52; asst. treas. Cambridge Glass Co. (O.), 1953; audit mgr. U.S. Gen. Accounting Office, Dallas, 1953-62; comptroller U.S. sect. Internat. Boundary and Water Commn., El Paso, 1963—. C.P.A., Ohio. Mem. Am. Inst. C.P.A.'s, Ohio, Tex. socs. C.P.A.'s, Beta Alpha Psi. Home: 248 Northwind Dr El Paso TX 79912 Office: PO Box 1859 El Paso TX 79950

MOORE, JOHN HENRY, newspaper exec.; b. N.C., June 7, 1916; s. Odus Lee and Sue (Parker) M.; student Presbyn. Jr. Coll., 1934-35; student Wake Forest U., 1935-37; m. Carolyn Scudder Lindsay, June 1, 1946; children—Susan Lindsay, Karen Elizabeth, Carolyn Anne. With Laurinburg (N.C.) Exchange newspaper, 1937—, mgr. advt., 1937-41, mgr. bus., 1946-66, editor, pres., 1966—. Pres., chmn. campaign Scotland County United Fund, Laurinburg, 1965, 66. Chmn. Zoning Commn., Laurinburg, 1950-63. Bd. dirs. Scotland Meml. Hosp. Served to lt. (j.g.) USNR, 1944-45. Mem. N.C. Press Assn. (past officer), Laurinburg C. of C. (v.p. 1965). Baptist (bd. deacons). Lion (pres. Laurinburg 1965). Home: McLaurin Acres Laurinburg NC 28352 Office: The Laurinburg Exchange 214-18 Cronly St Laurinburg NC 28352

MOORE, JOHN HENRY, circuit judge; b. Atlantic City, Aug. 5, 1929; s. Harry Cordery and Gertrude (Wasleski) M.; B.S., Syracuse U., 1952; J.D., U. Fla., 1961; m. Joan Claire Kraft, Dec. 29, 1951; children—Deborah Joan, Katherine Louise. With U.S. Gauge div. Am. Machine & Metals, Inc., 1956-58; admitted to Fla. bar, 1961; partner Fleming, O'Bryan & Fleming, Fort Lauderdale, 1960-67; circuit judge 17th Jud. Dist., Fort Lauderdale, 1967—. Pres. Broward County Assn. Retarded Children, 1963-65. Served with USNR, 1952-56. Mem. Am. Arbitration Assn., U. Fla., Syracuse U. alumni assns., U.S. Navy League (council judge adv. 1969-71), U.S. Jr. C. of C. Clubs: Optimist (pres. 1965-66), Touchdown. Republican. Home: 1235 N Rio Vista Blvd Fort Lauderdale FL 33301 Office: Broward County Courthouse Fort Lauderdale FL 33301

MOORE, JOHN LAUTHLIN, judge; b. Porterville, Miss., Sept. 4, 1917; s. John Lauthlin and Jennie (Ware) M.; B.A., U. Miss., 1939; LL.B., U. Ala., 1942; m. Mary Anne Grieme, Dec. 14, 1950; children—Anne Grieme, John Lauthlin IV. Admitted to Ala. bar, 1942; pvt. practice law, Mobile, Ala., 1944-63; judge Probate Court, Mobile County, Mobile, Ala., 1963—; gen. counsel Ala. State Docks, 1963; spl. asst. atty. gen. State Ala., 1962-63. Del. Democratic Nat. Conv., 1948; mem. Ala. State Democratic Exec. Com., 1964-68. Mem. Ala. Probate Judges Assn. (pres. 1970), Ala. Bar Assn., Historic Mobile Preservation Soc., English Speaking Union, Ala. Hist. Assn., Kappa Alpha, Phi Delta Phi. Baptist. Clubs: Isle Dauphine Country, Athelstan. Home: 1363 Dauphin St Mobile AL 36604 Office: Probate Court Mobile County Mobile AL 36604

MOORE, JOHN PAUL, lawyer, state senator; b. Louisville, Miss., Aug. 4, 1930; s. Clinton and Birdie (Clay) M.; student Miss. State U., 1954-55; B.B.A., U. Miss., 1957, LL.B., 1959, J.D., 1969; m. Evelyn Jackson, Jan. 31, 1957; children—Teresa Ann, John Stuart, Bruce Alan, Ronald Scott. Admitted to Miss. bar, 1959; practiced in Columbus, Miss. 1959-60; with firm Carter & Van Evry, 1959-60; pvt. practice Starkville, 1960—; mem. Miss. Senate, 1968—. Lectr. Miss. State U., 1960-68; dir. Golden Triangle Savs. and Loan Assn., Starkville, Starkville Steaks, Inc. (Miss.). Served to sgt. USAF, 1950-54. Mem. Comml. Law League Am., Phi Alpha Delta. Club: Civitan International. Home: 205 Woodlawn St Starkville MS 39759 Office: 207 1/2 E Main St Starkville MS 39759

MOORE, JOHN ROBERT, cons. civil engr.; b. Kewanee, Ill., July 25, 1924; s. John Elmer and Alice (Twing) M.; B.S. with high honors in Civil Engring., U. Ill., 1948; m. Juanita Donnewald, Nov. 23, 1950; children—Kim, Robin, Gary, Lisa, Chris, Kamlin, Alison. With B.P. Thacker & Co., Waukegan, Ill., 1948-49; asst. supr. hwys. Clinton County (Ill.), 1949-50; with James G. Cooney & Assos., Carlyle, Ill., 1950-56; with Harland Bartholomew & Assos., Honolulu, 1956-57, Memphis, 1957—, asso. partner, 1958-66, partner, 1966—; exec. v.p., dir. Harland Bartholomew & Assos. Internat., Inc. 1966—. Mem. Nat. Def. Exec. Res., U.S. Dept. Transp. Adv. com. civil engring. curriculum U. Ill., 1968—. Served as lt. A.C., AUS, 1943-45. Fellow Am. Soc. C.E.; mem. Am. Water Works Assn., Nat. Soc. Profl. Engrs., Cons. Engrs. Council, Am. Ry. Engring. Assn., Hwy. Research Bd., Water Pollution Control Fedn., Am. Inst. Cons. Engrs., Chi Epsilon. Methodist. Rotarian. Home: 5401 Collingwood Cove Memphis TN 38117 Office: 188 Jefferson Av Memphis TN 38103

MOORE, JOHN STERLING, JR, clergyman; b. Memphis, Aug. 25, 1918; s. John Sterling and Lorena (Bounds) M.; student Auburn U., 1936-37; A.B., Samford U., 1940; Th.M., So. Baptist Theol. Sem., 1944; m. Martha Louise Paulette, July 6, 1944; children—Sterling Hale, John Marshall, Carolyn Paulette. Ordained to ministry Bapt. Ch., 1942; pastor in Pamplin, Va., 1944-48, Amherst, Va., 1949-57, Manly Meml. Bapt. Ch., Lexington, Va., 1957—. Mem. hist. commn. So. Bapt. Conv., 1968—; pres. Va. Bapt. Pastor's Conf., 1963. Chmn. Lexington Mayor's Com. Race Relations, 1962-65. Bd. dirs. Rockbridge Mental Health Assn., 1962—; bd. dirs. Stonewall Jackson Hosp., Lexington, 1967-71, pres., 1969-70. Mem. Soc. Bib. Lit. Mason. Contbr. articles to profl. jours. Editor, The Va. Bapt. register, 1972—; Va. editor Ency. So. Bapts., vol. 3, 1971. Home: 463 2444 30 Sellers Av Lexington VA 24450 Office: 463 4181 Main at Preston Sts Lexington VA 24450

MOORE, KENNETH BURT, lumberman; b. Red Oak, Tex., May 12, 1913; s. Alvah and Beulah (Russell) M.; student Trinity U., 1930-32, 35, night classes 4C Coll., Waco, Tex., 1938, So. Meth. U., 1943; m. Ruth Wilcher, Mar. 26, 1937; children—Kenneth B. II, William James. Tchr. pub. schs., 1935-37; tchr., prin. William Cameron & Co., Inc., Waco, Tex., 1937-48; part owner, pres. Simms-Moore Lumber Co., Carrollton, Tex., 1948—; pres. Redwood Lumber Co., Dallas; v.p. Wheat Lumber Co., Dallas, Builders Supply Co., Grand Prairie, Tex.; owner Simms-Moore Lumber, Dallas; part owner, v.p. Redwoods, Inc., Waco, Tex.; v.p. Hill Country Lumber, Kerrville, Blanco Lumber, Tex.; dir. Carrollton State Bank (Tex.). Mem. Lumbermans Assn. Tex. Mem. Christian Ch. Clubs: Dallas Athletic, Brookhaven Country, Royal Oaks Country (Dallas). Home: 5838 Belt Line Dallas TX 75240

MOORE, LARRY S, lawyer; b. Thomaston, Ala., Oct. 12, 1913; s. Samuel P. and Addie (Barkley) M.; LL.B., Wake Forest Coll., 1938; m. Dorothy Wallace, Sept. 9, 1939; children—Dorothy Barkley (Mrs. Numa Lee Absher, Jr.), Larry Wallace, Patricia Foster. Admitted to N.C. bar, 1940; since practiced in North Wilkesboro; claims mgr. Hartford Accident & Indemnity Co., Greensboro, N.C., 1941-45. Chmn., Wilkes County Bd. Elections, 1958-62. Mem. N.C. (dist. councilor 1965-68), 23d Jud. Dist. (pres. 1962) bar assns. Democrat. Baptist. Elk, Kiwanian. Office: Moore & Rousseau Bldg 311 9th St North Wilkesboro NC 28659

MOORE, LEE, dentist; b. Jenkins, Ky., Dec. 24, 1916; s. Harry Lee and Nellie (Kane) M.; student Eastern State U., 1933-34, U. Ky., 1935-36; D.M.D., U. Louisville, 1940. Pvt. practice dentistry, Whitesburg, Ky., 1940—. Chmn., Letcher County Health Bd., 1962-72. Mem. City Council, Whitesburg, Ky., 1955-72. Mem. Southeastern Health Planning Council (bd. dirs. 1966-72), Ky. River Health Planning Council (bd. dirs. 1965-72), Ky. Dental Assn. (bd. dirs., 1968-72), Blue Grass Dental Study Club. Republican. Presbyn. (elder 1947—). Mason, Kiwanian (pres. 1944), Lion (pres. 1945), Rotarian (pres., 1956). Home: 204 Harris St Whitesburg KY 41858 Office: Frazier Bldg Main St Whitesburg KY 41858

MOORE, LEE PERMENTER, agr. co. exec. mayor; b. Palmetto, Fla., Dec. 8, 1923; s. James Harrison and Lois (Permenter) M.; student U. Fla., 1946-48; m. Ann Leffler Wiggins, Sept. 7, 1946; children— Kathleen Lois (Mrs. Larry Lovell), Analee, Thomas Wiggins, Carolyn, Jere Elizabeth. Account exec. Goodbody & Co., Orlando, Fla., 1956-57; resident mgr. A.M. Kidder & Co., Winter Park, Fla., 1957-61, So. regional mgr., 1961-63; regional mgr. Reynold & Co., Winter Park, 1963-65; exec. v.p., gen. mgr. Chase & Co., Sanford, Fla., 1965—; mayor, Sanford, 1969—. Dir. Fla. State Bank, Sanford. Chmn. United Fund Seminole County, 1965, v.p., 1971; chmn. Seminole County Port Authority, 1968-69. Served to capt. AUS, 1942-46. Mem. Winter Park C. of C. (pres. 1961-62). Episcopalian. Mason, Rotarian. Home: 2456 Mellonville Av Sanford FL 32771 Office: PO Box 1697 Sanford FL 32771

MOORE, LUTHER WILLIAM, lawyer, accountant; b. Minden, La., Nov. 20, 1930; s. Luther Carter and Ida (Wallace) M.; B.S. cum laude, La. Poly. Inst., 1952; J.D., La. State U., 1957; m. Claire Drake, June 28, 1958; children—William Drake, Cynthia Claire. Admitted to La. bar, 1957; practice pub. accounting and law, Minden, 1957—; asst. prof. accounting and law La. Poly. Inst. Sec.-treas. Webbo, Inc. Chmn., Minden Municipal Fire and Police Civil Service Bd., 1965-67, Minden Heart Fund, 1966; pres., sec.-treas. La. Tech. Alumni Found.; pres. Minden Indsl. Devel. Corp. Served with AUS, 1953-55. Mem. Am. Inst. C.P.A.'s, La. Soc. C.P.A.'s, La., Webster Parish (sec.-treas.) bar assns., Tax Inst. Ark.-La.-Tex., Am. Legion (trustee post comdr.), Minden C. of C. (dir.), La. Tech. Alumni Assn. (exec. com.), Lambda Chi Alpha, Omicron Delta Kappa, Beta Gamma Sigma, Phi Kappa Phi. Methodist. Lion. Home: 1301 Drake Dr Minden LA 71055 Office: PO Box 896 Minden LA 71055

MOORE, MELTON HEWITT, pub. housing exec.; b. McComb, Miss., Mar. 11, 1918; s. John H. and Annie (Melton) M.; student Port Arthur Bus. Coll., 1938; m. Ophelia Price, Feb. 27, 1944; children—Nancy Ophelia (Mrs. William Thomas Hewitt), Mary Virginia. Exec. dir. McComb Housing Authority, 1968—; dir. Moore's Transfer, Inc., McComb, 1968—, First Fed. Savs. & Loan Assn., McComb. Served with AUS, 1941-45. Mem. United Comml. Travelers of Am., Am. Legion, V.F.W. Baptist. Rotarian. Home: 820 North St McComb MS 39648 Office: PO Box 469 McComb MS 39648

MOORE, MILTON BRITTAIN, JR., physician; b. Jacksonville, Fla., Sept. 2, 1930; s. Milton Brittain and Octavia (McNair) M.; student S. Ga. Coll., 1948-50; A.B., Emory U., 1951, M.D., 1956; m. Ann Martin, Aug. 9, 1953; children—Mary Martin, Laura Brittain. Intern, Atlanta VA Hosp., 1956-57; dir. venereal disease control Louisville-Jefferson County, Ky., 1957-59; resident dermatology Baylor U., Houston, 1959-62; dir. Veneral Disease Research Lab. Communicable Disease Center USPHS, 1962-64; pvt. practice medicine specializing in dermatology Watson Clinic, Lakeland, Fla., 1964—; mem. staff Lakeland Gen. Hosp. Cons. Center for Disease Control USPHS, 1964—. Pres., Am. Cancer Soc., Polk County, 1968-69. Served to sr. surgeon USPHS, 1957-64. Mem. A.M.A., Fla. Med. Assn., Am. Acad. Dermatology, Fla. Soc. Dermatology, Am. Venereal Disease Assn. (sec.-treas. 1967-70), S.E. Allergy Assn., Phi Chi, Sigma Alpha Epsilon, Alpha Omega Alpha. Contbr. articles to profl. jours. Home: 2327 Hawthorne Trail Lakeland FL 33803 Office: 1600 Lakeland Hills Blvd Lakeland FL 33802

MOORE, MILTON JASPER, engr.; b. Wilson County, N.C., Aug. 17, 1928; s. Callie Jasper and Cornelia (Massengill) M.; B.C.E., N.C. State U., 1951; m. Julia Doris Lancaster, May 24, 1952; children—Susan, Kathy. With Shell Oil Co., Charlotte, N.C., 1954—, sr. dist. engr., 1970—. Served with AUS, 1951-53. Registered profl. engr., N.C. Mem. N.C. Soc. Profl. Engrs. Baptist (chmn. deacon bd. 1970). Home: 7025 Foxworth Dr Charlotte NC 28211 Office: PO Box 17347 Charlotte NC 28210

MOORE, MITCHELL DAVID, lawyer; b. Osceola, Ark., May 22, 1922; s. David Michael and Susan (Moore) M.; LL.B., Cumberland U., Lebanon, Tenn., 1943; LL.B., Ark. Law Sch., Little Rock, 1947; m. Faye J. Trawick, Apr. 7, 1947; children—Carolyn (Mrs. Richard Kinley Impoden), Janet Kay, Bren Rae, Mitchell David. Admitted to Ark. bar, 1947; asso. Ark. Supreme Ct., 1946-47; practiced in Osceola, 1948—; city atty., Osceola, 1949—. Dir. J.T. Parsons Cabinet Co., Inc. Bd. govs. Mississippi County Hosps. Served with USMCR, World War II. Mem. Am., Ark., Mississippi County, Osceola bar assns. Kiwanian. Author: (with William H. Bowen) Workbook for Arkansas Estate Planners, 1969. Home: 1600 Erman Lane Osceola AR 72370 Office: 306 W Hale Av Osceola AR 72370

MOORE, NOLAN AUBREY, JR., banker; b. Wichita Falls, Tex., June 9, 1917; s. Nolan Aubrey and Fan (Wiley) M.; B.B.A., U. Tex., 1938; m. Frances Morgan, Oct. 26, 1940; children—Nolan Aubrey III, Danny Morgan, Tommy Wiley, Nancy Ann. With City Nat. Bank, Wichita Falls, 1940—, loan officer, 1971—, sr. v.p., 71—. Pres. United Fund Wichita Falls, 1967. Bd. dirs. A.R.C., 1969-71. Mem. Am. Inst. Banking (nat. v.p. 1963-64; nat. pres. 1964-65), C. of C. (dir. 1965-68). Lion. Named Outstanding Alumni Midwestern U., 1967. Home: 1401 Tilden St Wichita Falls TX 76309 Office: City Nat Bank 8th and Scott St Wichita Falls TX 76307

MOORE, (GEORGE) PAUL, educator; b. Everson, W. Va., Nov. 2, 1907; s. George Binney and Emma (Ayers) M.; A.B., W. Va. U., 1929; M.A., Northwestern U., 1930, Ph.D., 1936; m. Gertrude Conley, June 10, 1929; children—Anne Gertrude (Mrs. Peter Dooley), Paul David. Mem. faculty Northwestern U., 1930-62, asso. prof. communicative disorders, 1948-60, prof. voice pathology, 1960-62, lectr. otolaryngology Northwestern U. Med. Sch., 1952-62, dir. voice clinic, 1952-62, dir. voice research lab., 1936-62; dir. Gould Research Lab.

of Inst. Laryngology and Voice Disorders, Chgo., 1957-62; v.p., editor-in-chief Ellamac, Inc., Lang. Master Library, Chgo., 1952-62; prof., chmn. dept. speech, dir. communication scis. lab. U. Fla., Gainesville, 1962-—. Sr. civilian research staff, voice communications lab., USAAF, 1944-45; mem. sensory diseases study sect. NIH, 1959-63; mem. speech pathology and audiology adv. panel Office Vocational Rehab., 1962-64; mem. communicative disorders research tng. com. Nat. Inst. Neurol. Diseases and Blindness, NIH, 1964-68; mem. neurol. and sensory diseases adv. panel Division Chronic Diseases, Bur. State Services, Dept. Health, Edn. and Welfare, 1964-67; mem. communicative disorders program project rev. com. Nat. Inst. Neurol. Diseases and Stroke, 1969-72, chmn., 1971-72; mem. communicative disorders review com. NINDS, NIH, 1972-73. Recipient Merit award Am. Acad. Ophthalmology and Otolaryngology, 1962; Gould award, 1962, Barraquer Meml. award Smith, Miller and Patch, Inc., 1969. Fellow Am. Speech and Hearing Assn. (pres. 1961; chmn. publs. bd. 1963-66); mem. Internat. Assn. Logopedics and Phoniatrics (dir.), A.M.A. (spl. affiliate), Fla. Speech and Hearing Assn., So. Speech Communication Assn., Speech Communication Assn. (Golden Anniversary award 1969), Delta Tau Delta. Presbyn. Author book, articles, chpts. in books. Editor Central State Speech Jour., 1952-53; asso. editor Quar. Jour. Speech, 1948-50, Speech Monographs, 1939-41, Jour. Speech and Hearing Disorders, 1956-58; mem. editorial bd. Folia Phoniatrica, 1961-—. Mem. publ. bd. AMA Archives of Otolaryngology. Producer ednl. motion pictures on function normal and pathologic larynx as related to voice. Home: 2234 NW 6th Pl Gainesville FL 32601

MOORE, PAUL, JR., bishop; b. Morristown, N.J., Nov. 15, 1919; s. Paul and Fanny Weber (Hanna) M.; grad. St. Paul's Sch., Concord, N.H., 1937; B.A., Yale U., 1941; S.T.B., Gen. Theol. Sem., N.Y.C., 1949, S.T.D., 1960, D.D. 1964; m. Jenny McKean, Nov. 26, 1944; children—Honor, Paul III, Adelia, Rosemary, George Mead, Marian Shaw, Daniel Sargent, Susanna McKean, Patience. Ordained to ministry P.E. Ch., 1949; mem. team ministry Grace Ch., Jersey City, 1949-57; dean Christ Ch. Cathedral, Indpls., 1957-64; suffragan bishop, Washington, 1964-—. Lectr. St. Augustine's Coll., Canterbury, Eng., 1960; mem. commn. Delta Ministry Nat. Council Chs., 1964-67; mem. urban div., nat. exec. council Episcopal Ch., 1952-68; dep. to Gen. Conv., 1961, Anglican Congress, 1963. Fellow Yale Corp.; chmn. George W. Henry Found.; chmn. com. of 100, legal def. fund N.A.A.C.P.; mem. nat. bd. Nat. Recreation Bd.; chmn. Met. Ecumenical Tng. Center. Trustee Gen. Theol. Sem. Served as capt. USMCR, 1941-45; PTO. Decorated Navy Cross, Silver Star, Purple Heart. Mem. Urban League Washington (dir.). Author: The Church Reclaims the City, 1964. Home: 3400 Newark St NW Washington DC 20016 Office: Episcopal Church House Mt St Alban NW Washington DC 20016

MOORE, PAUL MEADOWS, lawyer; b. French Camp, Miss., June 24, 1914; s. Arthur Monroe and Nancy E. (Meadows) M.; LL.B., U. Miss., 1938; m. Mary Nell Sheffield, July 26, 1941; children—Nancy Elizabeth, Mary Sue, Barbara Kay, Paul M., Patricia Lynn, Jerry. Admitted to Miss. bar, 1938; practiced in Calhoun City, Miss., 1938-—. Vice pres., atty., dir. Bank of Miss., Tupelo, 1958-—; dir. 1st Fed. Savs. & Loan Assn., Grenada, Miss. Mem., past pres. bd. trustees Calhoun City Sch. Dist., 1950-58; mem., past pres. Pushmataha council Boy Scouts Am., 1948-68. Served with USAAF, 1942. Mem. Am., Miss., Calhoun County bar assns., Phi Alpha Delta. Democrat. Presbyn. Rotarian (past pres.). Home: 311 N Main St Calhoun City MS 38916 Office: NW Corner Pub Sq Calhoun City MS 38916

MOORE, PUGH CANNON, journalist; b. McKenzie, Tenn., Apr. 24, 1907; s. Richard Benjamin and May (Cannon) M.; ed. Vanderbilt U. widower. With A.P., 1930-55, state mgr., Ark., 1940-43, mgr. for Belgium, Luxembourg, Netherlands, 1945-46; pub. relations dir. Nat. Assn. Life Underwriters, 1955-60; financial editor Memphis Press-Scimitar, 1963-—. Recipient ETO Citation for Distinguished Service as war corr., World War II. Mem. Vanderbilt U. Alumni Assn. Met. N.Y. (pres. 1954-55), Alpha Tau Omega. Presbyn. Home: 135 N Montgomery St Memphis TN 38104 Office: Memphis Press-Scimitar Memphis TN 38101

MOORE, RAYMOND TILLETT, dentist; b. Mt. Holly, N.C., Nov. 23, 1920; s. Burmah Dixon and Marigold (Gallup) M.; B.S., Wake Forest Coll., 1941; D.D.S., Med. Coll. Va., 1946; m. Betty Palmer, Nov. 27, 1943; children—Mary Ellen (Mrs. Cyril Alfred Wright III), Betty Ann (Mrs. C. Eldridge Lee). Practice dentistry, Greenville, N.C., 1946-48, Mt. Holly, N.C., 1948-71; practice exodontia and denture prosthesis, Charlotte, N.C., 1971-—. Councilman, City of Mt. Holly, 1961-65, mayor, 1969-71. Served to lt. USNR, 1944-46, 51-53. Mem. Am. Dental Assn., N.C., N.C. Second Dist. dental socs., Am. Legion, Delta Sigma Delta. Democrat. Episcopalian. Mason (Shriner), Rotarian (past pres.). Home: 145 Oakland St Mount Holly NC 28120 Office: 921 Elizabeth Av Charlotte NC 28204

MOORE, REID FRANCIS, JR., lawyer; b. Chattanooga, Sept. 27, 1934; s. Reid Francis and Corinne (Milton) M.; B.A., Yale, 1956; LL.B., U. Va., 1959; m. Janice Griffin, July 20, 1963; children—Allyson, Ramsey, Carter. Admitted to Fla. bar, 1959; practiced in Palm Beach, 1959-—, West Palm Beach, 1965-—; mayor, West Palm Beach, 1967-68. Commr., West Palm Beach, 1965-69. Recipient Distinguished Service award West Palm Beach Jr. C. of C., 1965, Good Govt. award 1967. Mem. Am., Palm Beach County (chmn. law day com. 1962, 63) bar assns., Fla. Bar, C. of C. (dir.), West Palm Beach Jr. C. of C. (pres. 1963-64), Phi Alpha Delta. Episcopalian. Republican. Mason (Shriner), Kiwanian. Home: 139 N County Rd West Palm Beach FL 33405 Office: Paramount Bldg Palm Beach FL 33480

MOORE, RICHARD ANTHONY, govt. ofcl.; b. Albany, N.Y., Jan. 23, 1914; s. John Denis and Julia (Leader) M.; grad. Phillips Acad., Andover, Mass., 1932; B.A., Yale, 1936, LL.B., 1939; m. Jane Swift, Mar. 27, 1943; children—Richard A., Matthew S., Joseph F., Kate L., Samuel S. Spl. asst. to atty. gen., Washington, 1970; spl. counsel to Pres. Nixon, 1970-—. Served with USAAF, 1942-46. Decorated Legion of Merit. Home: 4917 Rockwood Pkwy Washington DC 20016 Office: The White House Washington DC 20500

MOORE, RICHARD LEE, dentist; b. Neame, La., Apr. 20, 1917; s. Wade Hampton and Sarah Frances (Sanders) M.; B.A., U. Tex., 1942, B.S. in Pharmacy, 1947, D.D.S., 1955; m. Allie Elizabeth Hanson, May 14, 1939; children—Richard, Michael, Stephen. Pharmacist, Gunning-Casteel, Inc., El Paso, Tex., 1947-51; pvt. practice orthodontics, El Paso, 1955-—. Served with USNR, World War II. Mem. Internat. Assn. Orthodontics (pres. 1971-72), Tex., Am. dental assns., Tex., Am. socs. dentistry for children, Psi Omega. Presbyn. Mason. Home: 4700 Louisiana St El Paso TX 79930 Office: 1200 Chesea St El Paso TX 79903

MOORE, RICHARD V., coll. pres.; b. Quincy, Fla., Nov. 20, 1906; B.E., Knoxville Coll., 1932, LL.D., 1950; M.Ed., Atlanta U., 1944; postgrad. N.Y.U.; LL.D., Edward Waters Coll., Jacksonville, Fla., 1948; m. Beauford J. Jones, 1934; 9 children. Tchr. social studies Pinellas High Sch., Clearwater, Fla., 1932-34; prin. Union Acad., Tarpon Springs, Fla., 1934-37, Rosenwald High Sch., Panama City, Fla., 1937-44, Washington High Sch., Pensacola, Fla., 1944-46; supr. Negro secondary schs., Tallahassee, 1946-47; pres. Bethune-Cookman Coll., Daytona Beach, Fla., 1947-—. Chmn. Daytona Beach Interracial Adv. Bd.; sec. Asso. Mid-Fla. Colls. Bd. dirs. United Negro Coll. Fund. Recipient medallion and citation for 25 yrs. service Fla. Tb and Health Assn.; certificate for meritorious services So. Recreation Assn.; many other awards. Mem. Statewide Negro Health Com. (past pres.), Interracial Commn. Daytona Beach (sec.), Am. Tchrs. Assn. (life), Fla. Tchrs. Assn., Fla. Citizen's Com. Edn., Nat. Ednl. Assn., So. Regional Council, Inc., Fla. Scholarship Com., Council Negro Coll. Presidents Fla., Alpha Phi Alpha, Sigma Pi. Mason (Shriner), Elk, K.P. Address: Daytona Beach FL

MOORE, ROBERT EDWARD, research co. exec.; b. Winsted, Conn., July 29, 1923; s. Alfred Edward and Elizabeth (Clark) M.; B.S. in Mech. Engring., U. Wis., 1948; m. Georgiana Muriel Moore, Dec. 22, 1946; children—Kathleen Mary, Brian Robert, John Craig. Chief insp. Rockwell-Standard Corp., Newark, O., 1948-51; sec.-treas. A.E. Moore Co., Oshkosh, Wis., 1951-53; v.p. John I. Thompson & Co., Washington, 1953-65; pres. Potomac Research, Inc., Baileys Crossroads, Va., 1965-—. Served with AUS, 1943-46. Registered profl. engr., D.C. Mem. Am. Soc. M.E. Republican. Episcopalian. Home: 3610 Bent Branch Ct Falls Church VA 22041 Office: 5821 Seminary Rd Baileys Crossroads VA 22041

MOORE, SAMUEL JAMES TILDEN, JR., lawyer; b. Deltaville, Va., Apr. 26, 1913; s. Samuel J.T. and Nettie (Powell) M.; A.B., Washington and Lee U., 1935; student U. Richmond Law Sch., 1936-39; m. Mary Frances Edmunds, Apr. 13, 1963; 1 son, Samuel J.T. III. Claim supr. Liberty Mut. Ins. Co., Boston, 1940-50, div. v.p., 1950-51; admitted to Va. bar, 1950; partner Sands, Marks & Sands, Richmond, Va., 1951-61, Shewmake & Gary, Richmond, 1960-—. Instr. history Richmond Profl. Inst., 1963-—. Mem. St. Peter's Ch. Restoration Assn., New Kent, Va., 1955, v.p., 1960-—; mem. adv. bd. Salvation Army, Richmond, 1958-—. Pres., Young Democratic Club, 1956-57. Mem. Am., Va., Richmond bar assns., Am. Judicature Soc., Internat. Assn. Ins. Counsel, Assn. Ins. Attys., Def. Research Inst. (v.p.), Va. Trial Lawyers Assn., Sons Confederate Vets. (Va. commdr. 1957-63), Richmond Civil War Roundtable (pres. 1956), Va. Hist. Soc., Va. Mus. Fine Arts, English Speaking Union, U.S. Naval Inst., Navy League, Am. Legion, Chesapeake Bay Yacht Racing Assn., Internat. Platform Assn., N.Am. Yacht Racing Union, U.S. Internat. Sailing Assn., Sigma Delta Chi, Sigma Alpha Epsilon. Episcopalian. Clubs: Fishing Bay Yacht (Deltaville, Va.); Capes Beach and Cabana (Virginia Beach, Va.); Virginia Boat, Bull and Bear, (Richmond). Author: The Jefferson Hotel-A Southern Landmark, 1940. Home: 2216 Park Av Richmond VA 23220 Office: 10 S 10th St Richmond VA 23219

MOORE, SHIRLEY THROCKMORTON (MRS. ELMER LEE MOORE), accountant; b. Des Moines, July 3, 1918; d. John Carder and Jessie (Wright) Throckmorton; student Ia. State Tchrs. Coll., summers 1937-38, Madison Coll., 1939-41; M.C.S., Benjamin Franklin U., 1944; m. Elmer Lee Moore, Dec. 10, 1946; children—Fay, Lynn Dallas. Asst. bookkeeper Sibley Hosp., Washington, 1941-42, Alvord & Alvord, 1942-46, bookkeeper, 1946-49, chief accountant, 1950-—, financial adviser to sr. partner, 1957-64; pvt. practice accounting, 1964-—; dir. Allen Oil Co. Mem. sch. bd. Takoma Acad. Bd. dirs. Washington Sanitarium and Hosp., Takoma Programs, Inc. Recipient Distinguished Grad. award Banjamin Franklin U., 1961, Distinguished Alumni award, 1964. C.P.A., Md. Mem. Am., D.C. insts. C.P.A.'s, Md. Assn. C.P.A.'s (county chmn. membership com. 1963-64, chpt. pres. 1968-69), Am. Women's Soc. C.P.A.'s, Am. Soc. Women Accountants (legislation chmn. 1960-62, nat. dir. 1952-53, nat. treas. 1953-54), Am. Accounting Assn., Internat. Platform Assn., Bus. and Profl. Women's Club, Benjamin Franklin U. Alumni Assn. (charter, past dir.), D.A.R. Mem. Seventh Day Adventist Ch. Contbr. articles to profl. jours. Home: 1007 Elm Av Takoma Park MD 20012 Office: World Center Bldg Washington DC 20006

MOORE, THOMAS ANDREW, wood preserving co. exec.; b. Spartanburg, S.C., July 1, 1915; s. Paul Vernon and Ethel (Seabrook) M.; B.S., U.S.C., 1938; m. Gerda Bengtson Sylvan, Sept. 9, 1939; children—Gerda Sylvan (Mrs. Moore Belknap), Ethel Elizabeth. With Taylor-Colquitt Co. (name now So. Wood Piedmont Co.), Spartanburg, S.C., 1941-—, v.p., 1961-—. Served with USNR, World War II. Mem. S.C. Agrl. and Mech. Soc. (dir.). Home: 609 Norwood St Spartanburg SC 29302 Office: 217 Main St Spartanburg SC 29301

MOORE, THOMAS JUSTIN, JR., utility co. exec.; b. Richmond, Va., Apr. 15, 1925; s. Thomas Justin and Carrie (Willingham) M.; A.B., Princeton, 1947; LL.B., U. Va., 1950; m. Mary Elizabeth Pearson, Oct. 22, 1954; children—Mary Elizabeth, Thomas Justin III. Admitted to Va. bar, 1949; asso. firm Hunton, Williams, Gay & Gibson, Richmond, 1950-54, mem. firm., 1955-67; asso. gen. counsel Va. Electric and Power Co., Richmond, 1958-67, sr. v.p., 1967-69, exec. v.p., 1969-70, pres., 1970-—, also dir.;Central Nat. Bank of Richmond, Universal Leaf Co. Vice Chmn. Va. Coll. Bldg. Authority, 1966-69; campaign chmn. v.p. Richmond United Givers Fund, 1962; counsel Va. Mus. Fine Arts, 1960. Mem. met. bd. Richmond YMCA; mem. adv. bd. First Fund Va., Inc., trustee Va. Found for Ind. Colls.; Colonial Williamsburg (Va.) Found., U. Richmond, Richmond Meml. Hosp. Served to lt. (j.g.) USNR, 1943-46; PTO. Mem. Am. (mem. council pub. utility law sect. 1968-—), Fed., Va. (chmn. exec. com. 1967), Richmond (pres. 1966) bar assns., Bar Assn. City N.Y., Phi Alpha Delta. Episcopalian. Clubs: Princeton, Knickerbocker (N.Y.C.); Metropolitan (Washington); Country of Va., Commonwealth, Downtown (Richmond). Home: Office: 700 E Franklin St Richmond VA 23219

MOORE, THORNTON BIDGOOD, govt. ofcl.; b. Mobile, Ala., Feb. 15, 1909; s. John Payne and Lucille (Bidgood) M.; B.S. in Bus. Adminstrn., U. Ala., 1930; m. Elizabeth Charlton, Apr. 8, 1966; 1 son (by previous marriage), Thornton Bidgood. Asst. dir. marketing research Appliance div. Westinghouse Electric Corp., Mansfield, O., 1930-36, 37-42; asst. dir. marketing Hearst Mags., N.Y.C., 1936-37; statistician consumer durable goods div. WPB, U.S. Navy, War Assets Adminstrn., U.S. Govt., 1942-48, Dept. Commerce, 1948-—, dep. dir. consumer durable goods div., 1953-57, asst. dir. Office Indsl. Moblzn., 1958-64, dir. gen. indsl. equipment and components div., 1965-68, dir. consumer products div., 1968-—. Exec. com. Greater Washington Tennis Assn., 1954-62, pres., 1956-59; exec. com. Middle Atlantic Lawn Tennis Assn., 1958-60; bd. dirs. Washington Area Tennis Patrons Found. Served as lt. USN, 1944-46. Recipient Meritorius Service award U.S. Dept. Commerce, 1959. Unitarian. Clubs: University, (Washington); Edgemoor (pres. 1955-57, bd. govs. 1951-57) (Bethesda, Md.). Home: 5508 Cornish Rd Bethesda MD 20014 Office: Main Commerce Bldg 14th and Constitution Av NW Washington DC 20230

MOORE, TOM M., lawyer; b. Pulaski, Tenn., June 20, 1911; B.A., Washington and Lee U., 1935; LL.B., Cumberland U., 1937. Admitted to Tenn. bar, 1938, U.S. Ct. Mil. Appeals bar, 1959, U.S. Supreme Ct. bar, 1959, U.S. Ct. of Appeals 6th Circuit bar, 1963; practiced in Pulaski, 1938-—; mem. firm Moore, Henry, Henry, Lewis & Cain. Dir. Union Bank, 1958-—; city atty., Pulaski, 1954-64. Trustee, gen. counsel Martin Coll., 1956-—; trustee Pulaski Cemetery Assn., Austin Hewitt Home. Mem. Am., Tenn., Pulaski bar assns., Blue Key. Office: 121 S 1st St Pulaski TN 38478*

MOORE, WALTER BELDING, editor; b. San Antonio, Jan. 19, 1909; s. Walter Lucian and Clara (Lamkin) M.; B.J., So. Methodist U., 1930; m. Mary Isabel Tomlin, Sept. 1, 1935; children—Tomlin Walter, Bertrand Stuart, John McKenzie. Asso. agrl. editor Dallas News, 1930-36; asso. dir., editorial service Nat. Cottonseed Products Assn., Dallas, 1936-52; editor Cotton Gin & Oil Mill Press, Dallas, 1952-61; editor Texas Almanac also asso. editorial page dir. Dallas Morning News, 1961-—. Recipient Freedom's Found. award, 1964, 70; Mark Francis award, 1970. Mem. Tex. Profl. Agrl. Workers Assn., Dallas Agrl. Club, Sigma Delta Chi. Clubs: SMU Dads'. Home: 2820 University Blvd Dallas TX 75205 Office: Dallas Morning News Communications Center Dallas TX 75222

MOORE, WALTER VOGLER, JR., lawyer; b. Richmond, Va., July 20, 1928; s. Walter Vogler and Josephine (Peacock) M.; grad. Woodberry Forest Sch. (Va.), 1947; student Hampden Sydney Coll., 1948-50; J.D., U. Richmond, 1954; m. Elizabeth Gilmer Evans, Aug. 28, 1954;children—Mary Easley, Walter W. II, Francis Hudson II. Admitted to Va. bar, 1954; since practiced in Orange; partner firm Somerville Moore & Joyner, 1956-—. Pres., sec., treas., dir. Orange Youth Improvement Assn; campaign chmn. March of Dimes; pres. March of Dimes County Found.; mem. Orange County Indsl. Devel. Corp. Mem. Va. State Bar, Va., Am. bar assns., Orange County C. of C. Presbyn. (past deacon, elder). Home: 135 Landon Lane Orange VA 22960 Office: Va Nat Bank Bldg Orange VA 22960

MOORE, WARREN NEWTON, med. adminstr.; b. Memphis, Oct. 26, 1934; s. Alexander Alfred and Alene (Langston) M.; A.B., LeMoyne Coll., 1962; postgrad. Interdenominational Theol. Center, 1962-63, Mennonite Bibl. Sem., 1963-64, U. Tenn., 1968-69; M.A., Scarritt Coll., 1970; postgrad. Vanderbilt U., 1970-71; m. Delores Del-Rio Jones, Aug. 7, 1954; children—Diane Renee, Warren, Ophelia, Kenneth. Race specialist Gen. Conf. Mennonite Ch., Newton, Kan., 1964-65; asst. dir. Memphis Urban League, 1965, Tenn. Commn. Human Devel., Nashville, 1965-67; exec. dir. Met. Human Relations Commn., Nashville, 1967-70, United Meth. Neighborhood Centers, Nashville, 1970-71; adminstr. Oncology Center, Meharry Med. Coll., Nashville, 1971-—. Instr. Scarritt Coll., Nashville, 1970-—; pres. Urban Projects, Inc., 1967; cons. S.E. region U.S. Civil Rights Commn., Office Econ. Opportunity, 1967-—; commr. Administrn. of Justice Commn., Nashville, 1967. Bd. dirs. Am. Civil Liberties Union Middle Tenn. Served with USAF, 1953-57. Recipient Key to city Memphis, 1965. Mem. Tenn. Conf. Social Welfare, Nat. Geog. Tchrs. Edn. Alliance for Met. Middle Tenn., Tchrs. of Afro-Am. Hisotry, Am. Soc. Pub. Adminstrn., Nat. Assn. Black Social Workers, Nat. Assn. Intergroup Relations Ofcls. Methodist. Home: 907 Sutton Hill Rd Nashville TN 37204 Office: Meharry Med Coll Nashville TN 37208

MOORE, WEST TABB, physician; b. Richmond, Va., July 5, 1933; s. Roderick Dunn and Virginia Underwood (Tabb) M.; B.A., U. Va., 1955; M.D., Johns Hopkins, 1959; m. Rosaline Lovett Nowland, Jan. 13, 1961; children—Jonathan Tabb, Ann Lovett. Intern Johns Hopkins, Balt., 1959-60, resident, 1960-61, 63-64; fellow endocrinology Mass. Gen. Hosp., Boston, 1961-63; practice medicine specializing in endocrinology, Washington, 1964-—; mem. staff Washington Hosp. Center. Clin. instr. George Washington U. Hosp., Washington, 1964-70, asst. clin. prof., 1970-—; dir. endocrine clinic Columbia Hosp. for Women, 1966-—. Trustee Johns Hopkins U., Balt., 1970-—. Diplomate Am. Bd. Internal Medicine. Fellow A.C.P. Clubs: University, Chevy Chase. Home: 5188 Palisades Lane NW Washington DC 20016 Office: 2001 Eye St NW Washington DC 20006

MOORE, WILLIAM EDGAR, educator; b. Bishopville, S.C., Mar. 20, 1908; s. Lorenzo William and Bertha (Thompson) M.; B.A., Furman U., 1928; M.A., Columbia, 1929; Ph.D., George Peabody Coll. Tchrs., 1946; fellow human devel., U. Chgo., 1944; m. Jane Crumrine, June 9, 1935; children—Jane Elizabeth, Sara Anne. Successively instr. English, asst. prof., acting univ. examiner U. Fla., 1930-44; prof. English, Ga. State Coll. Women, 1945-46; prof. humanities, student counselor Univ. Coll., U. Fla., also chmn. dept. comprehensive logic, 1957-—, dir. counseling, 1962-—. Mem. Am. Assn. Humanistic Psychology, Assn. Gen. and Liberal Studies, U.S. Power Squadron, Theta Chi. Democrat. Unitarian. Author: (with others) Applied Logic, 1955; Creative and Critical Thinking, 1967. Home: 1603 NW 10th Av Gainesville FL 32601

MOORE, WILLIAM LEE, physician; b. Somerset, Pa., Jan. 12, 1935; s. John Brown and Rebecca (Kaufman) M.; B.S., Washington & Jefferson Coll., 1956; M.D., Hahnemann Med. Coll., 1960; m. Isabel Carmen Fernandez, Sept. 18, 1966; children—Heidi Ann, William Lee II. Intern Bayfront Med. Center, 1961-62; practice as family physician, Saint Petersburg, Fla., 1965-—; chief of infection com. Palms of Pasadena Hosp., 1966-—; chief of gen. practice Saint Petersburg Gen. Hosp., 1969-—, exec. com., 1969-—. Served to lt. USNR, 1962-64. Mem. A.M.A., St. Petersburg C. of C., Phi Kappa Sigma Phi Chi. Republican. Episcopalian. Mason (Shriner), Rotarian. Clubs: Bath, Yacht (Saint Petersburg, Fla.). Home: 7211 4th Av S Saint Petersburg FL 33707 Office: 1232 66th St N Saint Petersburg FL 33710

MOORE, WILLIAM MICHAEL, civil engr.; b. Houston, July 31, 1934; s. A.B. and Mildred (Ankle) M.; B.S., Tex. A. and M. U., 1956, M.E., 1958, Ph.D., 1965; m. Randa Kunzman, Sept. 3, 1955; children—Gina Berniece, Michael Joseph, Lisa Anne, Randa Elizabeth, Patrick Alastair, Laura Jean, Alexander Ribiere. Grad. asst. Tex. A. and M. U., 1956-57, instr., 1957-61; asst. city engr. College Station, Tex., 1956-62; asst. research engr. Tex. Transp. Inst., 1962-67, asso. research engr., 1967-—; pvt. practice engring. cons., College Station, 1961-—. Served from 2d lt. to 1st lt., C.E., U.S. Army Res., 1956-64. Automotive Safety Found. fellow, 1961-62. Registered profl. engr., Tex. Mem. Sigma Xi; Phi Eta Sigma, Tau Beta Pi. Republican. Roman Catholic. Author research papers in pavement design and soil mechanics. Research in field. Home: 125 Lee St College Station TX 77840 Office: Pavement Design Dept Texas Transportation Institute Texas A and M Univ College Station TX 77843

MOORE, WILLIAM T(AYLOR), journalist; b. Rossville, Ill., Jan. 3, 1901; s. William Taylor and Jennie (Meridith) M.; student U. Chgo., 1924-28; m. Eloise Tasher, June 1, 1929. Feature writer Chgo. Herald and Examiner, 1924-36; mem. editorial staff Chgo. Tribune, 1936-66, mem. Washington bur., 1942-56, corr. Chgo. Tribune Press Service, Moscow, 1956-57, congl. corr., 1957-66; writer Ft. Lauderdale (Fla.) News, 1966-69; lectr. on Russia. Mem Phi Gamma Delta. Republican. Presbyn. Clubs: Cliff Dwellers (Chgo); University, Nat. Press, Arts (past pres.), City Tavern Assn. (Washington). Home: 125 Ocean Av Palm Beach Shores Singer Island FL 33404

MOORE, WOODVALL RAY, librarian; b. Flatwoods, Ky., May 19, 1942; s. Clyde Raymond and Erma (Gallion) M.; student U. Ky., 1960-62, Ashland Oil fellow, 1966-67; A.A., So. Bible Coll., 1964, B.S., 1965; M.S.L.S., U. Ky., 1972; m. Sarah Ellen Markham, Dec. 14,

1963; 1dau., Tamra Sheri. Head librarian So. Bible Coll., Houston, 1968—, asso. prof. Christian edn. dept., 1968-70; ordained to ministry Pentecostal Ch. of God of Am., 1969. Precinct chmn. Republican Party, 1969-70, 72—. Mem. A.L.A., Tex. Library Assn. Address: 10950 Beaumont Hwy Houston TX 77028

MOORHEAD, WILLIAM DAVID, mech. engr.; b. Lynchburg, Tenn., 1908; s. David F. Robertson and Sallie (Ashby) M.; student Ga. Sch. Tech., 1926-29, Vanderbilt U., 1941; m. Virginia Wood, Jan. 3, 1938; 1 son, William David III. Project engr. Manhattan Project, Tenn. Eastman Corp., Oak Ridge, 1944-46; div. engr. Kellex Corp., N.Y., 1948; pres. Atlas Engring. Co., Oak Ridge, 1951-53; chief of design Olin-Matheson Co., Balt., 1953-55; project engr. Arthur G. McKee Co., Cleve., 1955-58; supt. engring. Pan Am. World Airways, Patrick AFB, Fla., 1958-66; prin. engr. Bendix Corp., Kennedy Space Center, Fla., 1966—. Mem. Melbourne (Fla.) Planning and Zoning Bd., 1965—, chmn., 1971-72. Named Engr. of Year, Bendix, 1968; recipient commendation for work on Manhattan Project, Sec. War, 1946. Mem. Nat. Assn. Corrosion Engrs. Mason. Home: 2420 S Scenic Dr Melbourne FL 32901 Office: Kennedy Space Center FL 32899

MOORMAN, ROBERT WARDLAW, educator; b. Berwyn, Ill., Sept. 16, 1919; s. Thomas S. and Amanda (Clawson) M.; B.C.E., Clemson U., 1940; M.S., U. Ia., 1947, Ph.D., 1955. Naval architect Charleston (S.C.) Navy Yard, 1940-41; asst. prof. dept. engring. mechanics Clemson (S.C.) U., 1947—, prof. and head dept., 1957—. Served to maj. C.E., AUS, 1941-46; now col. Res. Decorated Bronze Star medal; ETO campaign with five battle stars. Registered profl. engr., S.C. Fellow Am. Soc. C.E.; mem. Am. Soc. Engring. Edn., Am. Acad. Mechanics, S.C. Soc. Engrs., Sigma Xi, Tau Beta Pi, Phi Kappa Phi. Rotarian. Club: Clemson Fellowship. Episcopalian. Home: 115 N Palmetto Blvd Clemson SC 29631

MOOSA, WILSON JOSEPH, owner automobile agy.; b. Eunice, La., Mar. 19, 1915; s. Theophile and Victoria (Mohana) M.; grad. high sch.; m. Hazel Manuel, May 10, 1952; stepchildren—Douglas, Jere, Jeffery; 1 son, Wilson Joseph. Owner Moosa Equipment Co., Eunice, 1945—, Moosa Pontiac-Buick, Eunice, 1947—, Wilson J. Moosa Ins. Agy., Eunice, 1947—. Chmn. Moosa Meml. Hosp., 1956-71, Eunice Indsl. Bdl., 1964—, Downtown Redevel., 1968—. Mem. city council City of Eunice, 1965-69, mayor, 1969-73. Named Outstanding Kiwanian, Eunice Kiwanis Club, 1962; recipient Capt. of Industry award La. Dept. Commerce and Industry, 1970. Mem. Nat. League Cities (mem. environmental com. 1969-71), 7th Congl. Dist. Municipal Ofcls. (v.p. 1971-72). K.C., Woodmen of World, Kiwanian (pres. 1953, lt. gov. 1959). Home: 450 Park Av Eunice LA 70535 Office: 1st and Vine Sts Eunice LA 70535

MOOSE, DALE HUBART, metals and plastic products mfg. co. exec.; b. Sulphur, Okla., Sept. 6, 1913; s. Adolphus Franklin and Sarah Olive (Sain) M.; student Murray State Coll., 1933-35; m. Myrtle Cooper, Aug. 18, 1935; children—Joanna Mae (Mrs. Dwayne Jacobs), Jurhee Anita (Mrs. Gary Ivy). Computer engr. United Geophys. Co., Cal., 1939-42; party chief N.Am. Geophys. Co., Tex., 1942-44; gen. mgr. Schaeffer Geophys. Co., Okla., 1944-49; pres. Gen. Engring. & Mfg. Co., Inc., Port Lavaca, Tex., 1949—. Democrat. Baptist. Mason. Patentee in field. Home: 110 Beachmont St Port Lavaca TX 77979 Office: 120 Juanita St Port Lavaca TX 77979

MOOT, ROBERT CLINTON, govt ofcl.; b. Orange, N.J., June 1, 1911; s. William W. and Helen (Budd) M.; grad. high sch.; m. Helen C. Helms, Jan. 4, 1952; children—Karen, Robert, Gregory. Comptroller, Bur. Supplies and Accounts Navy Dept., Washington, 1946-57; dep. adminstr. Small Bus. Adminstrn., Washington, 1966-67, adminstr. 1967-68; with Def. Dept., 1957-66, 68—, dep. asst. sec. Def. for logistics services, 1965-66, asst. sec. Def. (comptroller), 1968—. Served with AUS, 1943-46. Recipient Meritorious Civilian Service award Def. Dept., 1966. Distinguished Civilian Service award with bronze palm, 1969; Civilian Service, award Def. Supply Agy., 1963, Meritorious Civilian Service award, 1965; Distinguished Civilian Service award Small Bus. Adminstrn., 1968; Winthrop Rockefeller Pub. Service award; named Financial Mgr. of Year, Am. Soc. Mil. Comptrollers, 1971. Home: 4201 Woolls Pl Annandale VA 22003 Office: Asst Sec Defense Washington DC 20301

MOQUIN, JOSEPH CHARLES, aerospace co. exec.; b. Middleboro, Mass., July 7, 1924; s. Joseph Alfred and Sarah (Bump) M.; student Miss. State Coll., 1943-44; B.S., Washington U., 1949; postgrad., 1949-51; m. Margaret Jane Claiborne, Jan. 9, 1948; children—Michael James, Stephen Charles, Claiborne Lee, Margaret Mary, Sarah Jo, William Alfred, Paul Benedict, Thomas Joseph Ousley. Indsl. engr. Beltex Corp., St. Louis, United Wood Heel Co., 1949-50, Rice-Stix Co., 1950-52; program dir. ordnance mgmt. engr. tng. program Rock Island (Ill.) Arsenal, 1952-56; chief mgmt. services Army Ballistic Missile Agy., Redstone Arsenal, Ala., 1956-58; chief mgmt. engring. Army Ordnance Missile Command, 1958-59; exec. v.p. Brown Engring. Co., Inc., Huntsville, Ala., 1959-66, pres., 1966—. Bd. dirs. United Givers Fund, Huntsville and Madison County, Ala., 1962-70, pres., 1964—; bd. dirs. Madison County Council Community Orgns., 1959-65, Huntsville Indsl. Expansion Com., 1965-70; mem. local govt. study commn., 1971—; exec. bd. Huntsville Boys Club, Inc., 1956—, Tenn. Valley council Boy Scouts Am., 1970-72. Served to 1st lt. C.E., AUS, 1943-46. Mem. Ala. Soc. Profl. Engrs., Am. Inst. Indsl. Engrs., Assn. U.S. Army, Am. Ordnance Assn., Am. Inst. Aeros. and Astronautics (chmn. Ala. sect. 1965-66), C. of C. (dir. 1964-68), Sigma Nu. Kiwanian (pres.). Home: 1904 Chippendale Dr Huntsville AL 35801 Office: Research Park Huntsville AL 35807

MORABITO, ROCCO, newspaper photographer; b. Port Chester, N.Y., Nov. 2, 1920; s. Frank and Fortunata (Famma) M.; grad. high sch.; m. Sophie B. Rio, May 31, 1952; children—Tina, Anne. With Jacksonville (Fla.) Jour., 1930—, staff photographer, 1949—. Served with USAAF, 1943-45. Decorated Air medal with four oak leaf clusters, Bronze Star with four oak leaf clusters; recipient Pulitizer prize in spot news photography. Mem. Nat. Press Photographers Assn. Roman Catholic. Moose. Home: 3038 Gilmore St Jacksonville FL 32205 Office: 1 Riverside Av Jacksonville FL 32201

MORACK, JOHN F., coll. adminstr.; b. New Brighton, Pa., Sept. 1, 1931; s. Eugene James and Mary (Bosco) M.; Asso. Engring., Cleve. Inst. Engring., 1957; B.S. in Bus. Adminstrn., Geneva Coll., Beaver Falls, Pa., 1959; M.A. in Edn., Duquesne U., 1964; Ph.D., U. Pitts., 1970; m. Rose Marie Signore, May 7, 1955; children—Kathleen Ann, Daniel Eugene. Asst. to supt. for bus. Hopewell-Independence-Racoon Joint Schs., Aliquippa, Pa., 1958-66; dean financial affairs Community Coll. of Beaver County, Freedom, Pa., 1966-68; asst. to supt. for bus. North Hills Sch. Dist., Pitts., 1968-70; dean bus. affairs Broward Community Coll., Ft. Lauderdale, 1970—. Sec. study com. on sch. bus. Tri State Area Sch. Study Council, 1966-68; mem. com. for revision fed. handbook 2 Pa. Dept. Edn., 1969. Ednl. div. chmn. Lower Beaver County United Fund, 1965-67, bd. dirs. Central Beaver County, 1968; bd. dirs. Aliquippa Exchange Club, 1963. Treas. Hopewell Twp. Sch. Bd., 1959-66, Hopewell-Independence-Racoon Joint Sch. Bd., 1959-66. Served with USAF, 1949-52. Mem. Assn. Sch. Bus. Ofcls. of U.S. and Can. (mem. nat. nominating com. 1969), Pa. Assn. Sch. Bus. Ofcls. (pres. 1969-70), Western Pa. Assn. Sch. Bus. Ofcls. (co-founder program chmn. 1966-67), Pa. Sch. Bds. Assn. (adminstrs. adv. com. 1969-70), Am. Assn. Sch. Adminstrs. Home: 7201 NW 5th St Plantation FL 33313 Office: Broward Community Coll 3501 SW Davie Rd Fort Lauderdale FL 33314

MORA-FARIA, LUIS ENRIQUE, educator; b. Santurce, P.R., Oct. 10, 1937; s. Felipe N. Mora and Dolores L. Faria; B.S., Rensselaer Poly. Inst., 1959, Ph.D., 1964; M.S., Tex. A. and M. U., 1961; m. Belkis Antongiorgi, Mar. 18, 1960; children—Luis Mora-Antongiorgi, David Mora-Antongiorgi, Belkis Mora-Antongiorgi. Instr., U. P.R., 1959, asst. prof., 1964-67, asso. prof. civil engring., 1967—; lectr. Inter Am. U., 1962; pvt. practice cons. engr., 1964—. Pres. housing com. Popular Democratic Party, 1972. Served with P.R. N.G., 1953-57. Ford Found. grantee 1962. Mem. Am. Soc. C.E., Am. Soc. Engring. Edn., Am. Concrete Inst., Am. Assn. U. Profs., Sigma Xi. Chi Epsilon, Phi Eta Mu, Phi Iota Alpha. Rotarian. Home: 7 Santiago St San German PR 00753 Office: Civil Engring Dept U P R Mayaguez PR 00708

MORAGNE, EDWARD LEVERNE, research and devel. corp. exec.; b. Somerset, Tex., July 28, 1915; s. Clarence S. and Ruth (Penn) M.; B.S., Tulane U., 1938; M.S., Columbia, 1940, Ph.D. in Math., 1943, in Physics, 1945; m. Katheryn Elsik, Aug. 28, 1947; 1 dau., Yolanda Kay. Chief theoretical physics Fercleve, Oak Ridge, 1942-45; mgr. Midwest div. H.K. Ferguson Co., Houston, 1945-47; design engr. Fluor Corp., Houston, 1947-50; pvt. cons. petro-chems., Houston, 1950-55; organizer, pres., gen. mgr. Moragne Research and Devel. Corp., Moragne Machine & Mfg. Corp., Poly Perm Electrochem. Co. (all Houston), Clark Moragne Corp., Dehy Drex Corp. (both Freeport, Tex.), 1955—. Cons., NASA, AEC, Am. Coll. Research Scientists, Harris County Crime Commn. Provider 4 scholarships to boys from Boy's Town and Farley's Boys Ranch, annually 1955—; adminstr. Moragne Found., Yolanda Kay Moragne Trust. Bd. dirs. Robinson Found., Houston; partner, trustee Agate Hills Ranch Ltd., Sanderson, Tex. Served to comdr. USNR, 1941-42. Decorated D.S.C. Recipient Presdl. award AEC, 1945. Fellow Internat. Oceanography Found. (life); mem. Am. Mus. Natural History, Am. Coll. Research Scientists, Am. Inventors Assn., United Inventors and Scientists, Am. Astro-Phys. Soc., Am. Soc. Physics, Instruments Soc. Am., Houston C. of C., Nat. Fedn. Ind. Bus., Sheriff's Assn. Tex., V.F.W., Am. Legion, Order Purple Heart, Am. Petroleum Inst. Clubs: Houston Country, Houston Knife and Fork, Houston, Lakewood Yacht, Cork (Houston). Developer, patentee electromagnetic process making first atomic bomb possible; witnessed explosion at White Sands, N.M.; developer atomic pile Soldier's Field, Chgo., 1942. Over 300 patents in field. Home: 4723 Nenana Dr Houston TX 77035 Office: 3036 E Hwy 332 Route 2 Box 599A Freeport TX 77541

MORALES, CECILIO JOSE, banker; b. Buenos Aires, Argentina, Mar. 18, 1921 (came to U.S., 1952); s. Luis C. and Jacinta (Magliano) M.; student U. Buenos Aires, 1936-43; m. Ann M. Kiesewetter, Dec. 11, 1971; children—Cecilio Jose, Maria Helena, Christian Francis. Dir. pub. health statistics, Argentina, 1945-52; econ. counsellor Argentine Delegation to UN, N.Y.C., 1952-57; dir. econ. and social affairs OAS, Washington, 1959-61; tech. mgr. Inter. Am. Devel. Bank, Washington, 1962—. Mem. Am. Econ. Assn., Inst. Mgmt. Scis. Home: 5622 Massachusetts Av Washington DC 20016 Office: 808 17th St Washington DC 20577

MORALES, MARTIN MOONEY, banker; b. Houston, Apr. 20, 1928; s. Simone Mooney and Lena (Costa) M.; grad. pub. high sch.; m. Joan Marie Loverde, July 27, 1952; children—Martin Mooney, Janet, Richard, Marilyn. Runner Houston Nat. Bank, 1946-50; teller Univ. State Bank, Houston, 1952-57; asst. cashier Chimney Rock Bank, Houston, 1957-62; asst. v.p. North Side Bank, Houston, 1962-67; v.p. Fidelity Bank, Houston, 1967-69, also dir.; pres. Jacinto City Bank (Tex.), 1969—, also dir., chmn. exec. com. Served with USAAF, 1950-52. Mem. Am. Inst. Banking. Democrat. Roman Catholic. Club: Unico International (Houston). Home: 5914 Rutherglen Houston TX 77035 Office: PO Box 24117 Houston TX 77029

MORALES, RAFAEL, lawyer. Practice law, San Juan, P.R. Mem. P.R. Bar Assn. (exec. dir. 1970—, dir. 1971—). Home: 472 De Diego Av Rio Piedras PR 00923 Office: Box 1900 San Juan PR 00903*

MORALES-CABRANES, RAFAEL FORTUNATO, assn. exec.; b. Naranjito, P.R., May 27, 1942; s. Manuel F. Morales and Rafaela Cabranes; B.A., U. P.R., 1962, LL.B., 1965; m. Elsa Lopez-Oliver, Apr. 20, 1969. Admitted to P.R. bar, 1965; mem. firm. Goldman, Antonetti & Subira, San Juan, P.R., 1967-70; exec. dir. P.R. Bar Assn., San Juan, 1970—. Chmn. tournaments P.R. Volleyball Fedn., 1968, pub. relations officer, 1969-70. Served with AUS, 1965-67. Mem. Phi Sigma Alpha. Home: 472 De Diego Av Rio Piedras PR 00923 Office: PO Box 1900 San Juan PR 00903

MORALES-SANCHEZ, JULIO, lawyer, govt. ofcl.; b. Caguas, P.R., Oct. 11, 1940; s. Julio and Gladys (Sanchez-Diaz) Morales-Ortiz; B.A., U. P.R., 1962, LL.B., 1965; m. Ilia Miranda-Cassanova, Dec. 16, 1967; children—Gladymar Morales-Miranda, Julio Enrique Morales-Miranda. Admitted to P.R. bar, 1965; asst. atty. gen. for legislation Commonwealth of P.R., San Juan, 1965-66, chief legal counsel Communications Authority, 1966-69, spl. aide, atty. gen., 1969-70; asst. U.S. atty. Dist. of P.R., U.S. Dept. Justice, San Juan, 1970, U.S. atty., 1970—. Prof. comml. English, U. P.R., 1965-67. Recipient medal for excellence and leadership Nat. Exchange Club, 1962. Home: 206 Hija del Caribe Hato Rey PR 00918 Office: PO Box 3391 San Juan PR 00904

MORALES-SERRANO, EFRER, architect; b. Humacao, P.R., Jan. 21, 1928; s. Jose and Almedina (Serrano-McCormick) M.; B. Architecture, U. So. Cal., 1948; m. Anita Amaral de Morales, Dec. 16, 1951; children— Estela Maria, Efrer Jose, Juan Manuel. Architect I and II building design div. Dept. Pub. Works, San Juan, P.R., 1950-53; archtl. designer Toro-Ferrer architects, 1953-56; partner archtl. firm Amaral y Morales-Arquitectos, 1956-69; pvt. practice E. Morales-Serrano-Arquitecto, Hato Rey, P.R., 1970—; prof. design Sch. Architecture U. P.R., 1970—. Mem. A.I.A. (v.p. P.R. chpt. 1969), Sociedad Bolivariano de Arquitectos (hon.), Sociedad de Arquitectos de Guatemala, Instituto de Arquitectos de P.R. (pres. 1970), Colegio de Ingenieros, Arquitectos y Agrimensores de P.R. (bd. dirs. 1966-68). Lion. Home: 557 Abolicion St Baldrich Hato Rey PR 00918 Office: PO Box 395 Hato Rey PR 00919

MORAN, ABBY HARDY DUGGAN (MRS. JOHN STEPHEN MORAN), ret. librarian; b. Eagle Pass, Tex., Aug. 22, 1903; d. Malonc and Victoria Abby (Hardy) Duggan; B.A., Tex. Woman's U., 1952, M.L.S., 1953; student Radcliffe Coll., 1958, Am. U., 1963; m. John Stephen Moran, Jan. 22, 1923 (dec. 1969); children—John Stephen (dec.), Victoria Abby (Mrs. Willard Randolph van Liew, Jr.) (dec.), Brian Thomas. Indexer engring. library Gen. Dynamics Corp., Ft. Worth, 1954-57; head S.W. history and genealogy div. Ft. Worth Pub. Library, 1957-63. ret. 1963; free-lance research in fields of history, biography and genealogy, 1963—; book indexer for publs., 1964—; tchr. research methods Tarrant County Jr. Coll., Ft. Worth, 1970-72. Active A.R.C., 1941-47. Mem. Am. Cath. Hist. Assn., Tex. (charter), Ft. Worth (bd. mem.) geneal. socs., Tex. Hist. Assn., Tarrant County Hist. Soc., Hist. Soc. Pa., N.Y. Geneal. and Biographical Soc., Soc. Genealogists (London, Eng.). Democrat. Contbr. articles to profl. jours. Home: 5125 El Campo Av Fort Worth TX 76107

MORAN, J. ANTHONY, lawyer; b. Altoona, Pa., Sept. 8, 1920; s. Joseph and Josephine (Cuzzolina) M.; student St. Frances Coll., 1937-38, Dickinson Coll., 1938-40; LL.B., George Washington U., 1949, LL.M., 1950; LL.D. (hon.), Alliance Coll., 1968; m. Virginia Lee Carpenter, Aug. 14, 1968; children—Diane Narkunas, Helene Eckhart, Joseph S. Admitted to D.C. bar, 1949, since practiced in Washington; asst. to dep. adminstr. WAA, Washington, 1946-47; legal trainee Pub. Housing Adminstrn., 1948-49; legal cons. OPS, 1951, House Select Com. on Astronautics and Space Exploration, 1958-59; cons. to Vice Pres. Johnson, 1960-63, to Pres. Johnson, 1963-65; adviser to Vice Pres. Humphrey, 1966-68. Del., Democratic Nat. Conv., 1968. Served with AUS, 1942-46. Recipient Meritorious Pub. Service award Govt. D.C., 1966. Mem. Am., D.C. bar assns., Air Force Assn. Italian Execs. Am. (bd. govs.), Am. Legion, Delta Theta Phi. Roman Catholic. Club: Congressional Country. Home: 500 Coleridge Av Altoona PA 16602 Office: 2750 Q St NW Washington DC 20007*

MORAN, JOHN LAZARUS, JR., clergyman; b. Lumberton, Miss., Sept. 16, 1917; s. John L. and Evangeline (Austin) M.; B.A., Miss. Coll., 1942; Th.M., So. Bapt. Theol. Sem., 1945, Th.D., 1949; m. Fay F. Ferguson, July 10, 1943; children—Harriet Harvey, John Austin. Ordained to ministry Baptist Ch., 1941; asso. to minister chs. at Crystal Springs, Miss., 1941-42, Speed, Ind., 1943-44; pastor, Paint Lick, Ky., 1944-45, Brownstown, Ind., Richmond, Va., 1949-51, Churchland Bapt. Ch., Portsmouth, Va., 1954—; tchr. religious edn. extension div. U. Richmond, 1962-63. Pres. Community Concert Assn., Portsmouth, 1961-68. Mem. Chesapeake Library Bd., 1963, 1968, chmn., 1967-68; chmn. bd. dirs. Emily Green Home for Aged, 1967-70. Served as chaplain USNR, 1945-46, USN, 1951-54. Mem. Portsmouth Bapt. Ministers Conf. (pres. 1954-55), Portsmouth Bapt. Assn. (moderator 1955-57), Portsmouth Ministers' Conf., Bapt. Gen. Assn. Va. (Christian life com. 1958, mem. gen bd. 1969—). Portsmouth United Preaching Mission (chmn. 1960), Protestants and Other Americans (nat. adv. bd. 1948—), So. Bapt. Conv. (fgn. mission bd. 1965-71, rec. sec. 1967-71). Home: 3012 Oakley Hall Rd Portsmouth VA 23703 Office: Churchland Baptist Church Western Branch Blvd Portsmouth VA 23703

MORAN, JOHN MORGAN, bldg. materials co. exec.; b. Louisville, Nov. 7, 1923; s. William Augustus and Thelma Bridget (Kieley) M.; student Ga. Sch. Tech., 1943-44, U. Tenn., 1946-48; m. Alice Marie Thoman, June 14, 1948; children—John Morgan, Sudie Ann, Nancy Melissa, Bruce Howell. Salesman, Pitts. Plate Glass Co., Nashville, 1946-55; indsl. relations mgr. Hayes Internat. Corp., Birmingham, Ala., 1955-65; indsl. relations dir. Gary Aircraft Corp., San Antonio, Tex., 1965-66; v.p., asst. to pres. Geo. C. Vaughan & Sons, San Antonio, 1966—; also dir. lumber div.; dir. Schulenburg Industries, Vaughan Realty Co. Trustee George C. Vaughan & Sons Employees' Profit Sharing Trust. Served with USNR, World War II. Club: Canyon Creek Country (San Antonio). Home: 10907 Burr Oak St San Antonio TX 78230 Office: PO Box 1001 201 N St Marys St San Antonio TX 78294

MORAN, NEIL CLYMER, med. scientist, educator; b. Phoenix, Oct. 12, 1924; s. Francis Joseph and Ethel (Clymer) M.; student Long Beach City Coll., 1942-43, La. State U., 1943-44, U. Mo., 1944, Creighton U., 1945-46, U. Kan., 1946; A.B., Stanford, 1949, M.D., 1950; m. Charlotte Jean Davidson, June 19, 1948; children—Michael Neil, Margaret Lois, James Duncan. Intern, Stanford U. Hosps., Cal., 1949-50; Irving fellow in physiology, 1950-51; asso. prof. pharmacology Emory U., 1956-62, prof., chmn. dept. pharmacology, 1962—; vis. scientist Karolinska Institutet, Stockholm, Sweden, 1960-61. Mem. Am. Civil Liberties Union of Ga., Ga. Heart Assn. Served with AUS, 1943-46; served with USPHS, 1951-56. Fellow Am. Coll. Cardiology; mem. Am. Soc. Pharmacology and Exptl. Therapeutics, A.A.A.S., Am. Assn. U. Profs., Am. Heart Assn., Sigma Xi, Alpha Omega Alpha. Contbr. numerous articles in field to profl. jours. Editor, Jour. of Pharmacology and Exptl. Therapeutics, 1961-65; asso. editor Pharm. Reviews, 1966-69; mem. editorial bd. Circulation Research, 1968—. Home: 1802 E Clifton Rd NE Atlanta GA 30307 Office: Dept Pharmacology Emory U Atlanta GA 30322

MORAN, THOMAS MAURICE, oil co. exec.; b. Boston, Sept. 21, 1923; s. Luke and Julia (Spillaine) M.; B.S., Boston Coll., 1948; M.B.A., U. Mich., 1951; m. Louise Stepat, Sept. 13, 1958; children—Dona Marie, Thomas Maurice, Robert M., John M. Tech. rep. Shell Chem. Corp., N.Y.C., 1951-55; chem. rep. Eastern States Petroleum & Chem. Corp., 1955-58; dist. mgr. Signal Oil & Gas Co., Houston, 1958-60, asst. mgr. chem. sales, 1961-63, domestic sales mgr. petrochems. dept., 1963-66, gen. mgr. petrochems. dept., 1966-71; v.p. petrochem. sales Charter Internat. Oil Co., Houston, 1971—; pres., dir. Charter Export Co., 1971—; v.p. Ind. Petrochem. Corp., 1967-72, pres., 1972—. Served to lt. (j.g.) USNR, 1943-46. Mem. Nat. Petroleum Refiners Assn. (chmn. petrochems. com. 1970-72, dir.), Nat. Paint, Varnish and Lacquer Assn. Republican. Roman Catholic. Clubs: Champions Golf (Houston); Houston. Home: 12323 Tunbridge Houston TX 77024 Office: 8938 Manchester St Houston TX 77012

MORAN, WILLIAM EDWARD, JR., assn. exec.; b. Herkimer, N.Y., Jan. 8, 1916; s. William Edward and Esther Florence (Henry) M.; A.B., Syracuse U., 1937, LL.B., 1940; m. Phyllis Marie Duffy, May 17, 1941; children— William Edward III, Patricia Marie. Asst. dir. ECA Mission to Belgium, 1949-52; chief dependent overseas territories br. ECA, Mut. Security Agy., 1952-53; dir. Africa div. FOA, 1953-57; dep. dir. ICA Mission to Morocco, 1957-59; head Africa program Stanford Research Inst., 1959-62; dean Sch. Fgn. Service, Georgetown U., 1962-66; v.p., exec. dir. Internat. Econ. Policy Assn., Washington, 1966-68; pres. Population Reference Bur., Washington, 1968—. Fellow African Studies Assn.; mem. Population Reference Bur. (v.p.), Catholic Assn. for Internat. Peace (pres.), Council Fgn. Relations, Washington Inst. Fgn. Affairs, Phi Delta Phi. Co-author: Handbook on African Economic Development, 1962. Editor: Population Growth: Threat to Peace. Home: 4514 Hawthorne St NW Washington DC 20016 Office: 1755 Massachusetts Av NW Washington DC 20036

MORAN, WILLIAM THOMAS, gas co. exec.; b. Bellevue, Ky., May 14, 1899; s. Michael R. and Mary A.C. (Gannon) M.; student Notre Dame Acad., 1907-09; m. Louise Jarrett, Nov. 17, 1943; children—Betty Ann (Mrs. T.K. Franke), William Thomas, Marvin Joseph. Gas engr., supr. Ky. Gas Co., 1918-21; pres., dir. Moran Corp., Houston, 1925—; pres., dir. Moran Utilities Co., Glen Rose Corp., Canadian Moran, Ltd., Tex. Intrastate Gas Co.; dir. First City Nat. Bank of Houston. Mem. Houston Symphony, Mus. Fine Arts; bd. dirs. St. Joseph Hosp. Found. Mem. Am. Gas Assn., Tex. Ind. Producers and Royalty Owners Assn., Mid-Continent Oil and Gas Assn. Elk. Clubs: Petroleum, Ramada, Houston, International. Home:

Warwick Hotel Houston TX 77005 Office: Bank of S W Bldg Houston TX 77002

MOREAU, JAMES A., dist. councilman New Orleans. Address: City Hall New Orleans LA 70112*

MOREHEAD, ROBERT PAGE, physician; b. Lasker, N.C., Sept. 4, 1910; s. Robert Page and Dorcas Ann (Vernon) M.; B.S., Wake Forest Coll., 1931, M.A., 1932, B.S. in Medicine, 1934; M.D., Jefferson Med. Coll., 1936; m. Dorothy Ann Myers, May 18, 1946; children—Robert Page III, John Myers, Dorothy Ann. Teaching fellow biology Wake Forest Coll., 1931-32, instr. pathology, 1936-37, asst. prof. Pathology, 1938-41; asso. prof. pathology Bowman Gray Sch. Medicine, Winston-Salem, N.C. 1941-46, prof. pathology, chmn. dept., 1946—; chief pathology N.C. Bapt. Hosp., Winston-Salem, 1941—; pathologist Med. Center, Winston-Salem, 1963—. Recipient Bronze award Am. Soc. Clin. Pathologists, Coll. Am. Pathologists, 1960. Mem. Forsyth County Med. Soc., Med. Soc. N.C. (Best Sci. Exhibit award 1961), A.M.A., A.C.P., Coll. Am. Pathologists, Am, Soc. Clin. Pathologists, Am. Assn. Pathologists and Bacteriologists, Am. Assn. Cancer Research, Internat. Acad. Pathology, N.C.Surg. Assn., A.A.A.S., N.C. Soc. Pathologists, So. Med. Assn. Author: Human Pathology, 1965. Home: 1051 Arbor Rd Winston-Salem NC 27104 Office: Bowman Gray Sch Medicine Winston-Salem NC 27103

MORELAND, DONALD EDWIN, plant physiologist, educator; b. Enfield, Conn., Oct. 12, 1919; s. Albert Sinclair and Ruth (Cowan) M.; B.S., N.C. State Coll., 1949, M.S., 1950, Ph.D. (AEC fellow), 1953; m Verdie Stallings, Nov. 6, 1954; 1 dau., Donna Faye; step children—Frank C. Ziglar, Paul Ziglar. Plant physiologist State U. N.Y. Coll. Forestry, Syracuse, 1952-53; plant physiologist Agrl. Research Service, U.S. Dept. Agr., also asst. prof. N.C. State U., Raleigh, 1953-61, asso. prof., sr. plant physiologist, 1961-65, prof. botany and crop sci., prin. plant physiologist, 1965—. Mem. toxicology study sect. NIH, USPHS, 1963-67. Served from pvt. to 1st lt. AUS, 1941-46; PTO. Fellow A.A.A.S.; mem. Am. Soc. Plant Physiologists, Bot. Soc. Am., Weed Sci. Soc. Am., N.C. Acad. Sci., Sigma Xi, Phi Kappa Phi, Alpha Gamma Rho, Gamma Sigma Delta. Contbr. articles, revs. to sci. jours. Mem. editorial bd. Essays in Toxicology, 1968—, Pesticide Biochemistry and Physiology, 1970—. Home: 1508 Pineview Dr Raleigh NC 27606

MORELAND, LOIS BALDWIN (MRS. CHARLIE J. MORELAND, educator; b. Washington; d. Genis George and Fannie (Rives) Baldwin; B.A., Sarah Lawrence Coll., 1955; M.A., Howard U., 1957; Ph.D., Am. U., 1968; m. Charlie J. Moreland, Dec. 28, 1958; 1 dau., Lisa Carol. Grad. asst. Howard U., Washington, 1956-57, instr., 1958-59; regional field sec. N.A.A.C.P., N.Y.C., 1957-58, Atlanta, 1958; legal adv. Legislative Reference Service, Library of Congress, Am. Law Div., Washington, 1958-59; legislative asst. U.S. Senator, Washington, 1959; lectr. Spelman Coll., Atlanta, 1959-60, asst. prof. polit. sci., 1960-69, asso. prof., chmn. dept. polit sci., 1969—; acting dean instrn., 1970—. Ford Found. cons. for doctoral fellowships, 1970. Mem. Fulton County Jury Commn., 1969—, Fulton County Bd. of Elections, 1969—, Ga. Commn. on Status of Women, 1966—. Mem. Fulton County Democratic Exec. Com., 1966—; vice chmn. Democratic Party, 3d Ward, Atlanta, 1964. Ford Found. fellow, 1956-57. Mem. Am., So., Ga. polit. sci. assns., Am. Assn. U. Women, Am. Assn. U. Profs., Alpha Kappa Alpha, Pi Sigma Alpha, Home: 849 Woodmere Dr NW Atlanta GA 30318

MORELOCK, JONATHAN EDWARD, III, research co. exec.; b. Opelika, Ala., June 20, 1939; s. Jonathan Edward and Edna Ruth (Gass) M.; B.S., Auburn U., 1961; postgrad. Nashville Law Sch., 1962-63; m. Janet Landers, Dec. 17, 1960. Legal rep. Liberty Mut. Ins. Co., Nashville, 1962-65; contract adminstr. Boeing Co., Huntsville, Ala., 1965-66; contract adminstr. Wyle Labs., Huntsville, 1966-69, adminstrv. mgr., 1969—. Lectr., Calhoun Jr. Coll., 1971; adviser minority businesses. Head div. United Givers Fund, 1970-71; permanent Madison County chmn. U.S. Savs. Bond Program, chmn. Madison County payroll savs., 1968-71; mem. Huntsville Madison County Youth Leadership Program, 1969—, Huntsville Indsl. Expansion Com. Served with USAF, 1961-62. Recipient Merit citation Outstanding Service to Madison County, 1968-72; Patriotic Service award Treas. Dept., 1969-71. Mem. Auburn Alumni Assn., Huntsville Madison County C. of C., Madison Jr. C. of C., Nat. Contract Mgmt. Assn. (sec. 1971), Omicron Delta Kappa, Lambda Chi Alpha, Alpha Phi Omega. Elk. Clubs: Huntsville Quarterback, Huntsville Country, Madison County Auburn (pres. 1972—). Home: 824 Loukell Av SE Huntsville AL 35802 Office: 7800 Governors Dr W Huntsville AL 35807

MORENO, LEOPOLD SEGISMUNDO, physician; b. Corrientes, Argentina, Feb. 6, 1927; s. Leopoldo Sixto and Espectacion Blasia (Saling) M.; B.S., Colegio Nacional Gen. San Martin, 1944; M.D., Buenos Aires Med. Sch., 1951 chilren—Karen, L. Bryan, Mark. Came to U.S., 1952, naturalized, 1957. Practicante Adscripto, Hosp. Alvarez, Buenos Aires, 1950-51; practicante Hosp. Espanol, Buenos Aires, 1950-52; resident tng. Tampa (Fla.) Municipal Hosp., 1952, St. Marys Hosp., Troy, N.Y., 1953, Suffolk Sanatorium, L.I., N.Y., 1954, Jackson Park Hosp., Chgo., 1955, Lincoln (Ill.) State Sch., 1956; gen. practice medicine, Norfolk, Va., 1957—. Diplomate Am. Bd. Family Practice. Mem. A.M.A., Am. Thoracic Soc., Va., Norfolk County med. socs., Am., Tidewater (corr. sec.) acads. gen. practice, Am. Geriatric Soc., Va. Tb. Assn. Home: 7640 Gifford St Norfolk VA 23518 Office: 7927 Old Ocean View Rd Norfolk VA 23518

MORENO, RUBEN, dentist; b. Los Palos, Province of Havana, Cuba, Sept. 24, 1909; s. Gustavo Moreno and Consuelo (Piedra) M. Lanza; D.D.S., Loyola U. at New Orleans, 1933; m. Mirtha Garcia, Sept. 24, 1936; children—Mirtha (Mrs. S. Buster Agliano), Sonia (Mrs. Frank J. Costa), Ruben Joseph. Practice of dentistry, Tampa, Fla., 1933—. Mem. Brewster Research Dental Clinic. Mem. 1st city Election Bd., 1939. Served with AUS, 1942-46. Fellow Fla. State Dental Soc.; mem. Am. Dental Assn., Fla. State (life), West Coast Dist., Hillsborough County (pres. 1947-49) dental socs., Tampa Hist. Soc., Tampa Bay Art, Eta Phi Lambda Alpha (pres. 1931-33). Democrat. Roman Catholic. Home: 589 Luzon Av Tampa FL 33606 Office: 220 Madison St Tampa FL 33602

MORET, ANDRES MANUEL, physician; b. Arroyo, Puerto Rico, Apr. 23, 1935; s. Andres Antonio and Gervasia (Velazquez) M.; student Universidad de Puerto Rico, 1952-54, Marquette U., 1954-56; Licenciado in medicine and surgery, Universidad de Barcelona, 1964; m. Amalia Perez, Jan. 5, 1961. Rotating intern, Teacher's Hosp., Hato Rey, Puerto Rico, 1964-65; physician for San Juan City Hosp. and San Juan Municipal Govt., 1965-67; house physician San Jorge Hosp., Santurce, Puerto Rico, physician for Hilton Internat. Hotels of Puerto Rico, med. examiner John Hancock Life Ins. Corp., Equitable Life Ins. Corp., Great Commonwealth Life Ins. Corp., Ga. Life Ins. Corp., New England Life Ins. Corp. Served to capt., M.C., Puerto Rico Nat. Guard. Fellow Royal Soc. Health, Puerto Rico Med. Assn., Assn. of Military Surgeons of the U.S.A., Nat. Guard Assn. U.S.A. Democrat. Roman Catholic. Home: 256 Rosario St Santurce PR 00912 Office: San Jorge St Santurce Puerto Rico 00912

MORETZ, WILLIAM HENRY, surgeon, educator; b. Hickory, N.C., Oct. 23, 1914; s. Joseph A. and Elizabeth (Leonard) M.; B.S., Lenoir Rhyne Coll., 1935, D.Sc. (hon.), 1960; postgrad. Med. Sch. U. N.C., 1935-37; M.D., Harvard, 1939; m. Laura Thelma Schlums, Dec. 5, 1947; children—William Henry, John D., Robert L., Richard E., Elizabeth L., David L. Intern, also asst. resident surgery, resident surgery Strong Meml. Hosp., Rochester, N.Y., 1939-43; instr. surgery U. Rochester Sch. Medicine, 1944-47; asst. prof. surgery U. Utah Coll. Medicine, 1947-49, asso. prof., 1949-55; prof. surgery, chmn. dept. Med. Coll. Ga., Augusta, 1955-72, pres. coll., 1972—. Cons. surgery VA Hosp., Augusta, U.S. Army Hosp., Augusta, Ga. Served from lt. to capt. M.C., AUS, 1944-47. Fellow A.C.S.; mem. Soc. U. Surgeons, Western, Am., So. surg. assns., Soc. Surgery Alimentary Tract, A.M.A., Richmond County Med. Soc., Ga. Surg. Soc., Internat. Soc. Surgery, Internat. Cardiovascular Soc. Contbr. articles to surg. lit. Home: 2345 McDowell St Augusta GA 30904

MORGAN, ALBERT RUFUS, JR., elec. co. exec.; b. Rutherfordton, N.C., Sept. 22, 1916; s. Albert Rufus and Madeline Mahala (Prentiss) M.; B.A., U. S.C., 1937; B.S. in Civil Engring., Ga. Inst. Tech., 1940; m. Irene Elizabeth Mitchell, June 11, 1949; children—Albert Rufus III, Anna Chipman. Prin. naval architect Charleston (S.C.) Navy Yard, 1940-43; engr. Commonwealth and So. Corp., N.Y., 1946-49; depreciation engr. So. Services, Inc., Birmingham, Ala., 1949-63, asst. to tax adviser, 1963-65, asst. mgr. tax dept., Atlanta, 1965-71, mgr. depreciation accounting services 1971—. Treas., Christian Council of Met. Atlanta, 1968. Served to staff sgt. AUS, 1943-46; CBI. Recipient First prize student chapters S.E. Conf. Am. Soc. C.E., 1940; san. engr. summer fellowship W. K. Kellogg Found., 1940; Naval Architect Certificate, The Citadel, 1941. Mem. The Edison Electric Inst. (chmn. depreciation accounting com. 1966-67), Isaak Walton League (dirs.), Sigma Alpha Epsilon, Delta Phi Alpha, Omicron Delta Kappa. Home: 6558 Roswell Rd NW Atlanta GA 30328 Office: 64 Perimeter Center E P O Box 720071 Atlanta GA 30346

MORGAN, ANTONIA BELL (MRS. WILLIAM J. MORGAN), psychologist; b. London, Eng., Oct. 5, 1914; d. James Young and Jean (Macnair) Bell; B.A., U. Oxford, 1936, M.A., 1945; tchrs. diploma U. London, 1938; m. William James Morgan, Nov. 2, 1944; children—William James, Jean Elizabeth, Robert Macnair. Came to U.S., 1946, naturalized, 1948. Chmn. dept. classical studies St. Albans Sch., Hertfordshire, Eng., 1938-41; Walter Hines Page scholar, lectr. English-Speaking Union, 1941-42; lectr. Brit. Ministry of Information, 1942-43, asst. prin., India Office, 1943-45; sec. Aptitude Assos., 1946-49, asso. dir. 1949—; cons. ch. schs. Diocese Va.; lectr. mental health topics to civic groups, schs. Vice pres. No. Va. Mental Health Assn., 1959-61. Certified clin. psychologist, Va. Mem. A.A.A.S., Am. Personnel and Guidance Assn. Episcopalian. Author psychol. and projective tests, articles on edn. of gifted children. Home and office: 2816 Gallows Rd Vienna VA 22180

MORGAN, ARTHUR C., sculptor, sch. dir.; b. Ascension Parish, La., Aug. 3, 1904; s. H. Arthur and Cora (Carmene) M.; ed. pub. and pvt. schs.; pvt. study with Gutzon Borglum, 1920-21; student Beaux Arts Inst. Design, N.Y., 1921-23; m. Gladys Butler, Mar. 2, 1929; children—Diana, Cynthia (dec.). Sculptor, N.Y.C., 1923, New Orleans, 1924-26; dir. Centenary Coll., Shreveport, 1928-33; founder Southwestern Inst. Arts, dir., 1934—. Works include: heroic figure chief Justice Edward Douglas White, in U.S. Capitol; Morehead Meml., E. L. Kurth Meml. Hosp., Lufkin; E. K. Long momument, Winnfield, La.; basreliefs and monolith Civic Theater, Shreveport, Paul Gersler Meml., Berwick, monumental, archtl. garden and portrait sculpture; bust Judge Robert B. Butler, Ct. House, Houma, La. Henry Miller Shreve monument, Shreveport, La.; busts Paul M. Brown, Dr. George S. Sexton, Dr. John B. Entrikin, Centenary Coll.; marble bust Dr. James M. Owens, stone carving St. Mark's Episcopal Ch.; heroic stone carving Ch. Holy Rosary, Shreveport; Van Cliburn medallion; Henry Schuyler Thibodaux bust, Municipal Auditorium, Thibodaux; represented many pvt. collections. Mem. Nat. Arts Club, (N.Y.C.). Episcopalian. Rotarian. Writer, lectr. in field. Home: 657 Jordan St Shreveport LA 71101 Office: Southwestern Inst of Arts Shreveport LA 71101

MORGAN, CHARLES, JR., lawyer, assn. adminstr.; b. Cin., Mar. 11, 1930; s. Charles and Ethel (Mitchell) M.; B.S., U. Ala., 1953, J.D., 1955; m. Camille Walpole, Sept. 5, 1953; 1 son, Charles III. Admitted to Ala. bar, 1955; practiced in Birmingham, Ala., 1955-63; asst. gen. counsel Am. Assn. U. Profs., 1963-64; spl. counsel N.A.A.C.P. Legal Def. and Ednl. Fund, 1963-64; dir. So. regional office Am. Civil Liberties Union, 1964—. Instr. Am. econ. History U. Ala., 1954-55. Nat. committeeman Ala. Young Democrats, 1951-55; nat. committeeman Nat. Democratic Party of Ala., 1968-69; chmn. Kennedy-Johnson speakers campaign, 1960. Pres., Jefferson County Heart Found., 1963; bd. dirs. Ala. Assn. for Mental Health, 1958-63. Named Man of Yr., Utility Club N.Y., 1964; hon. fellow U. Pa. Sch. Law, 1964. Mem. Phi Alpha Delta, Delta Tau Delta (pres. chpt. 1951-52, v.p. So. region 1962-63). Author: A Time To Speak, 1964. Contbr. anthologies; writer for periodicals. Home: 820 Cardova Dr NE Atlanta GA 30324 Office: 52 Fairlie St NW Atlanta GA 30303

MORGAN, CLYDE NATHANIEL, physician; b. nr. Belton, Tex., Nov. 2, 1923; s. Xenophen William and Rhoda Ella (Deck) M.; B.S., Abilene Christian Coll., 1948; M.D., U. Tex., 1953; m. Birdie Joyce Palmer, Mar. 3, 1951; children—Clyde Nathaniel, Reinette, Nancy. Intern, Robert B. Green Meml. Hosp., San Antonio, 1953-54; resident Cook County Hosp., Chgo., 1967-68; practice gen. medicine, 1954-66, practice specializing in dermatology, Abilene, Tex., 1968—; asso. prof. biology Abilene Christian Coll., 1954-56; instr. Hendrick Meml. Hosp. Sch. Nursing, 1954-59. Chmn. Taylor County Republican Party, 1965-70; del. Rep. Nat. Conv., 1968. Served to 1st lt. USAAF, 1943-45; ETO. Recipient Med. Econs. award, 1963, Physicians Recognition award A.M.A., 1969. Mem. Tex. Dermatologic Soc., Ibero Latin Am. Coll. Dermatology, A.M.A., Tex., So. med. assns., Taylor-Jones County Med. Soc., Am., Tex. assns. gen. practice, Aircraft Owners and Pilot Assn., Abilene C. of C. Kiwanian. Author: (with others) The Forbidden Apple, 1965. Home: 1718 Cedarcrest St Abilene TX 79601 Office: 1166 Merchant St Abilene TX 79603

MORGAN, DAVID L., transp. co. exec.; b. High Point, N.C., May 24, 1935; s. David Early and Polly Anne (Whitley) M.; student Wake Forest Coll., 1962-63, U. N.C., 1966-68; m. Betty Jo Robinson, June 16, 1960; children—Michael David, Deborah JoAnn, Nancy Elizabeth, Joel Wesley. Sec.-treas. Buck Young Oil Co., Inc., Lexington, N.C., 1960-69, Maybelle Transport Co., 1969—; also dir. Bd. dirs. Buck Young Found. Served with USNR, 1956-60. Mem. Jr. C. of C. (Outstanding Mem. 1964), Indsl. Mgmt. Club (v.p. 1968). Mason. Club: Sertoma. Home: 504 Queens Rd Lexington NC 27292 Office: 1820 S Main St Lexington NC 27292

MORGAN, DONALD CLINTON, hosp. adminstr.; b. Salisbury, N.C., Aug. 14, 1927; s. Walter C. and Neta (Cranford) M.; A.B., Catawba Coll., 1950; certificate Charlotte Meml. Hosp. Sch. Adminstrn., 1954; m. Peggy Jean Wolfe, Aug. 14, 1951; children—Brad, Andrew, Jeffery. Asst. adminstr. Good Samaritan Hosp., Charlotte, N.C., 1951-52; asst. adminstr. Anderson Meml. Hosp., 1954-58; adminstr. C. J. Harris Community Hosp., Sylva, N.C., 1958—. Mem. regional adv. com. N.C. Med. Program. Bd. dirs. Fontana Regional Library, Jackson County Library. Served with AUS, World War II. Named Citizen of Year, Jackson County C. of C., 1970. Mem. Am. Coll. Hosp. Adminstrs., Am., N.C. hosp. assns. Presbyn. (deacon). Rotarian. Home: Fisher Creek Rd Sylva NC 28779 Office: 59 Hospital Rd Sylva NC 28779

MORGAN, EDWARD GREENE, food co. exec.; b. Amory, Miss., Aug. 14, 1914; s. Lucian B. and Maude M. (Walden) M.; grad. high sch.; m. Merle A. Holloway, Nov. 30, 1940; children—Edward Greene, John D., Janet M. With Household Paper Co., Memphis, 1935-37; office mgr. Cudahy Packing Co., Memphis, Vicksburg, Miss., 1937-46; v.p. Lykes Bros., Inc., Plant City, Fla., 1946—. Mason. Home: 4404 Sevilla St Tampa FL 33609 Office: Box 518 Plant City FL 33566

MORGAN, EDWARD P., writer, broadcaster; b. Walla Walla, Wash., June 23, 1910; s. Arthur H. and Pansy Eledice (Paddock) M.; B.A. cum laude, Whitman Coll., 1932, L.H.D., 1957; grad. student U. Wash., 1932-33; m. Jane Stolle, Dec. 31, 1937 (div. 1945); 1 dau., Linda; m. 2d, Katharine Burden Sohier, July 18, 1960. Reporter Seattle Star, 1932-34; corr. U.P.I., 1934-43, Chgo. Daily News Fgn. Service, 1943-46; corr., asso. editor Collier's Weekly, 1946-48; free lance writer Europe, 1948-50; corr. CBS, 1951-54, dir. news for radio and TV, 1954; news commentator ABC, Wash., 1955-67, 69—; newspaper columnist for Newsday Syndicate, 1966—; sr. corr. Pub. Broadcast Lab., 1967-69. Recipient Peabody award for radio news, 1956; Sidney Hillman Found. award for radio news analysis, 1959; Alfred I. du Pont award best broadcast commentary, 1960; George Polk Meml. award for outstanding radio reporting, 1965; Overseas Press Club citation, 1966; Capital Press Club Journalism Excellence award, 1966. Bd. overseers Whitman Coll.; trustee Howard U. Mem. Overseas Writers, Radio and TV Corrs. Assn. Wash. (pres.), Assn. Radio News Analysts, Am. Civil Liberties Union, Phi Beta Kappa, Sigma Delta Chi, Beta Theta Pi. Clubs: Federal City, Nat. Press (Washington); Century (N.Y.C.). Co-author: Candidates, 1960; The Press in Washington, 1966. Editor: This I Believe, vol. 1, 1952, contbg. author, vol. 2, 1954; Clearing the Air, 1963. Office: 1124 Connecticut Av NW Washington DC 20036

MORGAN, EDWIN BUFORD, hosp. adminstr.; b. Marlow, Okla., Dec. 11, 1918; s. William Pruitt and Sarah Elizabeth (Nevins) M.; student Ark. Tech. Coll., 1938-39, U. Okla., 1940; m. Mary Merle Arline, Sept. 30, 1944; children—Edwin Buford, Dennis Wayne, William Randolph. Asst. adminstr. Angus Hosp., Lawton, Okla., 1945-49; mgr. Double-Cola Bottling Co., Ardmore, Okla., 1949-51; adminstr. Lawton Clinic, 1951-66, John Buist Chester Hosp., also Chester Clinics, Dallas, 1966—; pres. Dallas Credit Consultants, Inc. Vice pres. Dallas Hosp. Council, 1971; pres., 1972; dir. Regional Health Planning Council of N. Central Tex. Council Govts. Mem. Dallas Fire Council, Dallas Health Planning Council. Served with USCG, 1941-44. Fellow Am. Acad. Med. Adminstrs.; mem. Tex. Hosp. Assn. (chmn. Blacklands div. 1971), Okla. Anthropol. Soc. (pres. S.W. chpt. 1961, 65-66), Southwestern Okla. Hist. Soc. (sec.-treas. 1963-66). Home: 1540 Driftwood Dr Dallas TX 75224 Office: 3330 S Lancaster St Dallas TX 75216

MORGAN, ERNEST, U.S. atty.; b. Dilley, Tex., Dec. 19, 1912; s. James Evan and Mary Jane (Hooks) M.; student Tex. State Coll., 1933-34; LL.B., U. Tex., 1938; m. Billie Hall, Nov. 30, 1940; children— Daniel Franklin, Marilissa. Admitted to Tex. bar; finance officer, area dir. Nat. Youth Adminstrn., 1938-41; practice in San Marcos, 1946-61; U.S. atty. Western Dist. Tex., 1961—. Dir. State Bank & Trust Co., San Marcos. Trustee San Marcos Ind. Sch. Dist. Served as officer, inf., AUS, 1941-46; ETO. Methodist (trustee). Home: 705 W San Antonio St San Marcos TX 78666 Office: Box 1701 San Antonio TX 78206

MORGAN, GARY L., pub. relations and assn. exec.; b. Nashville, Oct. 16, 1935; s. Alec L. and Alva Jane (Kington) M.; B.A., Vanderbilt U., 1959; m. Christine Binkley, July 7, 1953; 1 son, Gary L. With WSM Radio-TV, 1953-58; writer, producer, dir. WKGM-TV, 1959-60; writer, dir. and producer for TV, 1953—; founder Digne Enterprises, Nashville, 1960, Nashville Insta-Print, Inc., 1965; sec. Coronada Stone Co., Inc., 1970—, also dir.; exec. dir. Home Builders Assn. of Tenn., 1968—; chmn. bd. dirs. Image Devel. Assos., 1966—; pres. Association Services, 1970—. Served with AUS, 1958-60. Mem. Pub. Relations Soc. Am., Nat. Assn. of Home Builders (v.p. exec. officers council, 1971), Tenn. Soc. Assn. Execs. (v.p. 1972). Home: Rt 2 River Oaks Brentwood TN 37027 Office: Capitol Hill Bldg Nashville TN 37219

MORGAN, GEORGE EMIR, dentist; b. Waynesville, Mo., Jan. 28, 1895; s. John Bunyan and Ida Belle (Rollins) M.; student Southwest State Coll., 1911-13; D.D.S., Washington U., 1916; m. Lee Mary Burchard, Apr. 28, 1919; children—Dorothy Lee (Mrs. Claude S. Hayes), George Emir. Practice of pedodontics, Milw., 1918-60; prof. pedodontics Marquette U., 1929-49; hon. mem. med. staff Boca Raton Community Hosp., 1967—. Trustee, Boca Raton Community Hosp., 1967—, treas. exec. com., 1968—. Mem. Am. Dental Assn. (trustee 1935-41), Wis. State Dental Soc. (pres. 1935), Milw. County Dental Soc. (pres. 1926), Fla. Soc. of Dentistry for Children (life), Sturdy Oaks Bowling Club for Retired Men (founder 1963), Retired Physicians and Dentists Club (co-founder 1966), Delta Sigma Delta. Methodist (trustee 1970—). Mason. Club: Deerfield Country (Deerfield Beach, Fla.). Address: 632 SW 4th St Boca Raton FL 33432

MORGAN, GEORGE ROBERT, petroleum corp. exec.; b. Baton Rouge, Oct. 30, 1897; s. Thomas O. and Mattie H. (Joor) M.; student La. State U., 1920-21; m. Nell M. Boddeker, Aug. 5, 1925. Stenographer traffic dept. Gulf Coast Lines, 1916-17; chief clk. land dept. Sinclair Oil & Gas Co., 1918-19; clk.-stenographer Am. Petroleum Co., Tex., 1921-22, asst. sec., 1922—, dir., 1940—; asst. treas. Am. Republics Corp., 1932-51, chief communications div., 1951-56, ret., 1956. Democrat. Methodist. Home: RFD 4 Box 432 Baton Rouge LA 70805

MORGAN, HERMAN WILTON, educator; b. Brooksville, Fla., Apr. 13, 1925; s. Soloman Arleigh and Alice (Lee) M.; B.S., Fla. So. Coll., 1949; M.S., Fla. State U., 1958; m. Florence Harrison, Sept. 7, 1949 (dec. 1964); children—Laura Ann, Herman Wilton; m. 2d, Willette Phillips, Feb. 27, 1965. Linotype operator Dade City (Fla.) Banner, 1949-52; asso. editor Zephyrhills (Fla.) News, 1952-54; printing instr. Brewster Vocational Sch., Tampa, Fla., 1954-62; evening trade extension coordinator Evening Vocational Sch., Tampa, 1962-63; prin. Adult Tech. Sch., Tampa, 1963—. Pres., Printing Industry Tampa, 1960-62; bd. dirs. Printing Industries Fla., 1960-62. Served with USNR, 1943-46. Mem. Fla. Vocational Assn. (exec. bd. 1961-71, v.p. 1961-63, sec.-treas. 1963-66, 68-71, pres. 1967), Theta Chi, Phi Delta Kappa, Iota Lambda Sigma. Democrat. Methodist. Home: 410 Island Rd Temple Terrace FL 33617 Office: 105 W Ross Av Tampa FL 33602

MORGAN, HUBERT S., retail exec.; b. Henderson, Tenn., Jan. 18, 1918; s. Hubert A. and Leander (Holmes) M.; student Lambuth Coll., Jackson, Tenn., 1935-37, Union U., Jackson, 1937-38; m. Vivian Tucker, July 9, 1944. Owner Morgan Furniture Co., Henderson, 1940—, Morgan Funeral Home, Henderson, 1940—; dir. 1st State

Bank of Henderson. Active A.R.C. Treas. Chester County Dem. Com., 1968-70; hon. staff mem. Congressman Ray Blanton. Mem. Am. Legion (past post comdr.). Methodist. Mason, Lion. Club: Woodland Hills Country (Pinson, Tenn.). Home: 490 North Av Henderson TN 38340 Office: PO Box 294 Henderson TN 38340

MORGAN, JAMES E., museum curator. Curator La. Wildlife Mus., New Orleans. Office: 400 Royal St New Orleans LA 70130*

MORGAN, JAMES EARL, librarian; b. Wheeling, W.Va., June 30, 1941; s. James Harpfer Latel and Ethel Irene (Goodwin) M.; B.S., Ariz. State Coll., 1965; M.S., Fla. State U., 1966; m. Carman Hope Head, Dec. 23, 1966. Head pub. services Ga. Coll. Library, 1967-69; dir. pub. services U. Tex. Med. Br. Library, 1969—. Mem. A.L.A., Med., Tex. library assns., Am. Assn. U. Profs., Kappa Delta Pi, Phi Mu Alpha. Club: Sierra (Galveston). Home: 1021 19th St Galveston TX 77550 Office: University of Texas Medical Branch Library Galveston TX 77550

MORGAN, JO VALENTINE, JR., lawyer; b. Washington, June 26, 1920; s. Jo V. and Elizabeth Parker (Crenshaw) M.; A.B. magna cum laude, Princeton, 1942; LL.B., Yale, 1947; m. Norma Jean Lawrence, May 22, 1943; children—Carol Jo, Jo Lawrence, Susan Leigh. Admitted to D.C. bar, 1948, Md. bar, 1948; mem. firm Whiteford, Hart, Carmody & Wilson, Washington, 1948—, partner, 1953—; v.p., dir. Wesmond Bldg. & Investment Co., 1955—, also other corps. engaged in residential constrn.; dir., gen. counsel Chesapeake Instrument Corp. Chmn. Bethesda U.S.O., 1949-52; pres. Summer Citizens Assn., 1958-61, Westmoreland Citizens Assn., 1956-57. Bd. dirs. Internat. Soc. for Protection Animals; pres. Montgomery County Humane Soc., 1972—. Served from 2d lt. to capt., AUS, 1942-45; ETO. Decorated D.F.C., Purple Heart, Air medals (AAC). Mem. Am., D.C. (dir. 1958-60) bar assns., D. C. Lawyers Club, Order of Coif, Phi Beta Kappa. Democrat. Episcopalian. Clubs: Chevy Chase, Princeton, Barristers. Home: 5120 Westpath Way Sumner MD 20016 Office: 815 15th St Washington DC 20005 also 7942 Wisconsin Av Bethesda MD 20014

MORGAN, JOE LEE, librarian; b. nr. Marshall, N.C., May 14, 1931; s. Frank Woodard and Effie Mae (McDaris) M.; A.B. in History and Polit. Sci., Berea Coll., 1954; postgrad. No. Ill. U., 1955, U. Hawaii, 1956, U. Colo., 1957, 58, U. N.C., 1957-58, Asian Affairs Inst., Duke, summer 1959, E. Tenn. State U., summers 1960-63, 68-69, 71. Farmer, Marshall, 1945-71; tchr. pub. schs., West Brooklyn, Ill., 1954, Mendota, Ill, 1954-55, Charlotte, N.C., 1957-59, Hot Springs, N.C., 1959-60, Walnut, N.C., 1960-61, Mars Hill, 1961-63; librarian Mars Hill High Sch., 1963-65; head librarian Truett McConnell Coll., Cleveland, Ga., 1965-67; tchr. history Capt. Riverside Mil. Acad., Gainesville, Ga., 1967-69; librarian Vardell Hall Girls' Prep. Sch., Red Springs, N.C., 1969—. Regional rep. N.C. Sch. Performing Arts; mem. library council, chmn. adult lit. program French Broad Bapt. Assn., 1964-66, clk., 1965-69, contbr. minutes, 1965-69; Sunday Sch. sec., tchr., supt., librarian Peek's Chapel Bapt. Ch., Marshall, 1946-66; mem. Arts and Humanities Commn., Council So. Mountains, 1966-69, edn. commn., 1970-71; mem. Citizens Com. for Free Cuba; bd. policy of Liberty Lobby; mem. Am. Friends Vietnam, Inc.; mem. Civic Arts Council, Inc. Asheville, N.C., 1964-67; active A.R.C. Broadcasting bd. sponsors Radio Free Asia. Mem. Mecklenburg County Republican Exec. Com., 1958-59; temporary chmn. White County, Ga., Rep. Conv., 1966; 1st vice chmn. White County Rep. party 1966-67; del. Ga. congl. and state convs., 1958, 62, 64, 66, N.C., 1958, 62, 64, 70, 71; mem. United Reps. Am.; chmn. Robeson County Young Reps., 1970; chmn. community services com. N.C. Fedn. Young Reps., 1971, also mem. exec. bd.; chmn. Madison County Rep. Com., 1971—; mem. exec. com. N.C. Rep. Com., 1971—. Served with AUS, 1955-57. Mem. N.E.A., N.C. Edn. Assn., N.C. Librarians Assn., Korean Cultural and Freedom Found., Young Ams. for Freedom, N.C. Literary and Hist. Assn., RCA Victor Soc. Great Music (founding mem.), N.C. Farm Bur., Nat. Congress Parents and Tchrs., Western N.C., Roanoke Island (chmn. Madison County 1971—) hist. assns., N.C. Soc. Preservation Antiquities, U.N. Assn. U.S., Ashville (N.C.) Community Concerts Assn., Am.'s Future, Inc., Internat. Platform Assn. Author: A Librarian's Handbook, 1964; Reflection on the Scopes Evolution Trial, 1965; North Carolina and The Admission of Kansas, 1966. Contbr. to profl. publs. Home: Route 2 Marshall NC 28753 Office: Vardell Hall Red Springs NC

MORGAN, JOHN KNIGHTON, city ofcl.; b. Dallas, Oct. 28, 1913; s. Boniar Stewart and Clara Louise (Reynolds) M.; student San Antonio Jr. Coll., 1932; m. Josephine Alice Winslow, Dec. 25, 1935; children—John Knighton, Dale S. Asst. mgr. Dickason Goodman Co., Pawhuska, Okla., 1935-40; mgr. Peoples Furniture Co., Odessa, Tex., 1940-42; foreman Continental Motors, Inc., Garland, 1942-45; mgr. Murphy Automotive, Inc., 1945-48; v.p., gen. mgr. Rudy-Patrick Seed Co., 1948-61; city sec., City of Graham, Tex., 1961—. Mem. Internat. Inst. Municipal Clerks, Municipal Finance Officers Assn., Internat. Assn. Assessing Officers (sec. Red River chpt. 1962—), C. of C. Episcopalian (vestryman, treas.). Mason (32 deg., Shriner), Lion (sec. 1962-63). Home: 1411 Scenic Dr Graham TX 76046 Office: City Hall Graham TX 76046

MORGAN, JOSEPH FRANCIS, investment co. exec.; b. El Paso, Tex., Jan. 2, 1906; s. Joseph Edward and Margaret Mary (McCarthy) M.; student U. Ill., 1926-29; m. Mary Cecelia Fitzgerald, Apr. 26, 1932. Partner, J. E. Morgan & Sons, El Paso, Tex., 1929-66, J. E. Morgan & Sons Investment and Real Estate Rental Bus., 1966—; dir. El Paso Nat. Bank, 1945—. Alderman, El Paso City Council, 1939-41; pres. Goodwill Industries of El Paso, 1948-60, pres. United Fund, 1959; pres. Southwestern Sun Carnival, 1950; mem. initial com. preparing agreement of Chamizal Agreement Settlement with Mexico, 1962-64. Bd. devel. U. Tex., 1960-66; lay adv. bd. Hotel Dieu Hosp., 1958—; chmn. bd. trustees Sun Towers Hosp., 1966—; chmn. bd. dirs. St. Joseph's Hosp., 1971—; bd. dirs. El Paso Mus. of Art, 1969-70; council of adminstrn. Catholic Diocese of El Paso, 1966—. Served with C.E., AUS, 1941-45. Recipient Humanitarian award, Nat. Conference of Christians and Jews, 1968; Outstanding Citizen award, El Paso Realtors, 1969. Mem. C. of C. (pres. 1949). Roman Catholic. K.C., Lion. Home: 1127 Rim Rd El Paso TX 79902 Office: 1211 El Paso Nat Bank Bldg El Paso TX 79901

MORGAN, LEWIS RENDER, U.S. judge; b. LaGrange, Ga., July 14, 1913; s. William Ellington and Bettie (Render) M.; student U. Mich., 1930-32; LL.B., U. Ga., 1935; m. Sue Phillips, July 29, 1944; children— Parks Healy, Sue Ann. Admitted to Ga. bar, 1935; mem. firm Wyatt & Morgan, La Grange, 1935-61; U.S. judge No. Dist. Ga., 1961, formerly chief judge; judge U.S. Ct. Appeals, 5th Circuit, 1968—. Mem. Gen. Assembly Ga., 1937-39; exec. sec. Congressman A. Sidney Camp, 1939-42. Mem. Chi Psi, Phi Delta Phi. Presbyn. Home: Cameron Mill Rd LaGrange GA 30240 Office: Newnan GA 30263

MORGAN, LILLIAN S. (MRS. ODIS MORGAN), educator; b. Georginana, Ala., Mar. 2, 1915; d. R.L. and Mary (Wilson) Shell; B.S., Troy State Tchrs. Coll., 1953; m. Odis Morgan, Dec. 8, 1935. Tchr., prin., Brushey Creek Sch., Butler County Bd. Edn., 1935-62, Chapman Sch., 1962-65; tchr. Georgiana High Sch., 1965-70, headmistress Ft. Dale Acad., Greenville, Ala., 1970—. Named Outstanding Classroom Tchr. in Conservation, Ala. Wildlife Fedn. Govs. Conservation, 1962; recipient Outstanding Personalities award, 1967. Mem. Nat., Butler County edn. assns., Ala. Edn. Assn., Delta Kappa Gamma. Clubs: Junior Garden, Junior Conservation. Address: Fort Dale Academy Greenville AL 36037

MORGAN, MARIE GRIFFIN (MRS. LOY WESTON MORGAN), club woman, civic worker, ins. agt.; b. Hickox, Ga., Dec. 1, 1914; d. Raiford Avant and Carrie (Higginbotham) Griffin; certificate Abraham Baldwin Agrl. Coll., 1937; B.S. in Home Econs., U. Ga., 1939; postgrad. U. Kan., 1948; m. Loy Weston Morgan, Aug. 29, 1944; children—Raiford Gordon, Linda Marilyn, Patricia Marie. Tchr. home econs. Lockhart (S.C.) High Sch., 1939-40; asst. home mgmt. supr. FSA, U.S. Dept. Agr., Quitman, Ga., 1940, home supr. Farmers Home Administrn., Donalsonville, Ga., 1940-44, acting farm supr., 1944-46, home supr., Olathe, Kan., 1946; sec., receptionist U.S. Bur. Entomology and Plant Quarantine, Tifton, Ga., 1948-51; tchr. Omega (Ga.) High Sch., 1955-56; reporter for radio, news editor The News Examiner, Tifton, 1960-61; asst. women's news reporter Radio and News Examiner, Tifton, 1962-65; women's news reporter radio sta. WWGS and News Examiner, 1965-69; photographer Live Wire Press Assn.; owner, operator Red Oak Springs Farm; agt. Am. Nat. Ins. Co., 1971—. Mem. resource instrs. com. Tifton Jr. High Sch. Retarded Children's Class; v.p. Hillcrest Neighborhood Garden Club, Tifton, 1949-50, pres., 1951-52, social chmn., 1962-63, civil def. chmn., 1963-64, devotional chmn., 1970-71, publicity chmn., 1971-72; Tift County (Ga.) sec. Am. Legion Aux., 1955-57, 2d v.p., 1957-58, 1st v.p., 1958-59, pres., 1959-61, chmn. numerous coms., 1955—, unit 2d v.p., 1968-70, chmn. rehab. com., 1969-70, mem. unit fair com., 1962—, membership chmn. 1968-70, 2d. dist. historian, 1960-61, dist. chmn. nat. security com., 1962-63, dist. 1st v.p., 1963-64, Ga. chmn. community service com., 1961-62, mem. dept. radio-TV com., 1962-64, 2d dist. pres., 1964-65, chmn. dept. child welfare, 1965-66, dist. sec. and jr. activities chmn., 1968-69, communications chmn., 1969-70, chaplain, publicity, radio-TV, rehab. chmn., pres. unit 21, 1965-66, Dept. Ga. civil def. chmn., 1967-68, rehab. com. and field service vol. dir., 1968-69, communications chmn., 1969-70, dept. legislative chmn., 1970-71, dept. jr. activities chmn., 1971-72; sec. Annie Belle Clark P.T.A., Tifton, 1958-60, hospitality chmn., 1960-62; membership chmn. Tifton Jr. High Sch. P.T.A., 1961-62; chmn. bldg. and grounds com., 1962-64, publicity chmn., sec. Tift County High Sch. P.T.A., 1967-68; neighborhood cookie chmn. Girl Scouts; den mother Cub Scouts, Tifton 1957-60, mem. leadership tng. com., 1960-62; key woman Ga. Civil Def.; pres. Tift County Civil Def. Women's Activities Council, 1961-63; coordinator women's activities Civil Def., 1963-64, 67—, radiol. monitor, instr., 1964; charter mem. Scout Mothers Aux., Tifton, 1960-61, pres., 1962-64; councilor Bapt. Girls Aux. Jrs., Tifton, 1961-62, adviser, 1962-63; fund chmn. A.R.C., 1962, chpt. publicity chmn., 1962—; publicity chmn. Blood Bank Program, Tifton, 1961-62, adult leader 4-H Club, 1961-62; publicity chmn, VA Vol. Services Subcom., Thomasville, Ga.; chmn. courtesy and civil def. coms. Hillcrest Neighborhood Garden Club, 1961-62; mem. Tifton Music Assn., 1961-62; mem. com. of Tift County Gifted Children, 1968-70; mem. Ga. Youth and Children's Com.; chmn. 2d dist. Child Welfare Com.; chmn. Dept. Ga. Civil Def.; sec.-treas. Tift County Community Council, 1971—. Recipient longevity service awards Thomasville (Ga.) VA Domiciliary, Dublin VA Center; Baldwin Alumni Homemaker of Yr. award, 1963, Community Leader of Am. award, 1969. Mem. Confederate Hist. Soc. Eng., Book Browsers Club Am., Colonial Dames 17th Century (chpt. directory chmn., chmn. hist. restoration and marking sites com.), U.D.C. (chpt. pres. 1969-72; organizer, sr. chmn., adviser Children of Confederacy chpt. 1964, 2d v.p. chpt. 1966—, program chmn.; chmn. Ga. div. Jefferson Davis Meml. Park com., Ga. Chaplain), Internat. Platform Assn., D.A.R. (chmn. mag. com., vice regent 1966-68, sch. good citizen chmn. 1968-70, registrar 1968-70), Bus. and Profl. Womens Clubs (pres. 1970-71). Tift County Band Parents Assn. (sec., publicity chmn. 1969-70), Am. Forestry Assn., Tifton Art Assn. (publicity com.), Ga. Retarded Children's Assn., U. Kan., U. Ga., Abraham Baldwin Agrl. Coll. alumni socs. Baptist (asso. missionary So. Bapt. Radio and TV Commn.). Clubs: Twentieth Century Woman's (edn. chmn. 1970-72); Friends of the Library. Home: Route 3 607 Davis Rd Tifton GA 31794

MORGAN, OMAR JOHN, physician; b. Muskogee, Okla., June 19, 1933; s. Charles Grandison and Nannie Ruth (Freese) M.; student Okla. State U., 1951-52, Northeastern State Coll., 1952-54, 56-58; M.D., Okla. U., 1962. Intern, Wesley Hosp., Oklahoma City, 1962-63; gen. practice medicine, Tahlequah, Okla., 1963—; sch. physician Northeastern State Coll., 1968—; mem. staff Tahlequah (Okla.) City Hosp. Mem. bd. electors Okla. Athletic Hall of Fame, Served with USAF, 1954-56. Mem. A.M.A., Okla. Med. Assn., Am. Assn. Gen. Practice, Am. Coll. Sports Medicine, Cookson Hills Med. Soc. (pres., del. state conv.), Tahlequah C. of C., Okla. U. Sch. Medicine Alumni Assn., Kappa Sigma, Rho Theta Sigma, Phi Sigma Epsilon, Phi Lambda Chi. Republican. Episcopalian. Club: Muskogee Country. Address: 220 N Muskogee Av Tahlequah OK 74464

MORGAN, PAGE WESLEY, educator; b. Phoenix, Apr. 3, 1933; s. Guy W. and Page (Ikard) M.; B.S., Tex. A. and M. Coll., 1955, M.S., 1958, Ph.D., 1961; m. Joyce M. Broseh, June 3, 1955; children—Ronald Jay, Catherine Elaine, Randall Page. Range conservationist Soil Conservation Service, U.S. Dept. Agr., Claude, Tex., 1955-56; grad. teaching and research asst. Anderson-Clayton fellow, depts. range and plant scis. Tex. A. and M. Coll., College Station, 1956-60, asst. prof., 1960-66, asso. prof., 1966-69, prof. dept. plant scis., 1969—. Cons. Union Carbide Corp., Seadrift plant, 1969-70. Pres. College Station (Tex.) Little League, 1968-69. Served as 2d lt. Transp. Corps, AUS, 1956. Recipient Outstanding Teaching award, Standard Oil Ind., Tex. A. and M. U., 1968. Mem. Am. Soc. Plant Physiologists (vice-chmn., chmn., sec.-treas. So. sect. 1968-71), Sigma Xi, Alpha Zeta, Phi Kappa Phi. Home: 1903 Lawyer Pl College Station TX 77840

MORGAN, PHILIP WILLIAM, govt. ofcl.; b. Aberdeen, S.D., Nov. 8, 1921; s. William Henry and Julia Theresa (Connelly) M.; student St. Thomas Coll., St. Paul, Minn., 1940-42; B.S.C. cum laude, U. Notre Dame, 1947; J.D., Georgetown U., 1951. Admitted to S.D. bar, 1951; asst. U.S. atty. 4th Jud. Div., Dist. Alaska, Fairbanks, 1954-56; chief div. Alaskan affairs Office Territories, Dept. Interior, Washington, 1956-59; chief counsel Minority Senate Permanent Sub-com. Investigations, U.S. Senate Com. Govt. Operations, 1959—, chmn. intradepartmental com. on Alaskan rural devel. Served as 1st lt. USMCR, World War II; capt. Korean Emergency; now col. Res. Elk. Editor: Mid-Century Alaska, 1957. Home: 101 N Carolina Av SE Washington DC 20003 Office: 160 Old Senate Office Bldg Washington DC 20510

MORGAN, ROBERT BURREN, lawyer, state ofcl.; b. Lillington, N.C., Oct. 5, 1925; s. James Harvey and Alice (Butts) M.; B.S., E. Carolina Coll., 1947; LL.B., Wake Forest Law Sch., 1950; m. Katie Owen, Aug. 1960; children—Margaret Ann, Mary Elizabeth, Alice Jean (dec.); foster son, Rupert. Admitted to N.C. bar, 1950; clerk superior ct. Harnett County, N.C., 1950-54, judge probate, juvenile cts., 1950-54; since practiced in Lillington. N.C.; now mem. firm Morgan Jones; atty. gen. State of N.C., 1969—. Dir., v.p. Holden Beach Fishing Pier, Inc. (N.C.), 1959—; dir. Angier Devel. Corp. (N.C.), Home Savs. & Loan Assn., Dunn, N.C. Mem. N.C. Senate, 1955-68, pres. protem, 1965-68. Pres. bd. Harnett County Library; trustee E. Carolina Coll., chmn. bd., 1964—; dir. Justice Found. N.C. Served as ensign USNR, 1944-46, lt. comdr., 1952-53, Korea; lt. col. Res. Mem. E. Carolina Gen. Alumni Assn. (pres. 1956-59), Am., N.C. bar assns., Am. Trial Lawyers Assn., Am. Legion, V.F.W., Phi Alpha Delta, Phi Sigma Pi. Baptist. Mason, Rotarian (past pres.), Moose; mem. Order Eastern Star. Home: Morgan Dr Lillington NC 27546 Office: NC Dept Justice PO Box 629 Raleigh NC 27602

MORGAN, ROBERT LEWIS, research physicist; b. Fayetteville, Tenn., Jan. 6, 1932; s. Joseph and Clara (Looney) M.; B.S. in Physics, U. Tex., 1953; postgrad. Tex. Christian U., 1958; M.S. in Physics, U. Ala., 1971; m. Beverly Lou Hammersley, Sept. 20, 1957; children—Janet Claire, Robert David. Physicist, U.S. Naval Ordnance Test Sta., China Lake, Cal, 1953-56, Convair, Ft. Worth, 1956-60, Chrysler Corp., Huntsville, Ala., 1960-62; research physicist U.S. Army Missile Command, Redstone Arsenal, Ala., 1962—; dir. Norman & Assos., Inc., Huntsville. Bd. dirs., trustee Huntsville Scottish Rite Temple Corp. Mem. Am. Phys. Soc., Am. Inst. Physics. Presbyn. (elder 1967). Mason. Contbr. articles to profl. jours. Inventor nonlinear optimal control system for small missles, automatically controlled T.O.F. mass spectrometer. Home: 4511 Apt G Patton Rd Huntsville AL 35805 Office: AMSMIRRX Bldg 5411 Redstone Arsenal AL 35809

MORGAN, ROLAND REGINALD, ret. supt. schs.; b. Nealsville, N.C., Oct. 13, 1906; s. Jason Sidney and Emma Bertha (Cannon) M.; A.B., Berea Coll., 1928; M.A., U. N.C., 1940, Ph.D., 1955; m. Sarah Henrietta Wilkins, Apr. 22, 1934; 1 dau., Gretchen (Mrs. Thomas T. Downer). Postgrad. asst. Oberlin Coll., 1930-31; postgrad. asst. Northwestern U., 1931-32; tchr., coach, Thorsby, Ala., 1928-29, Tri-High, Caroleen, N.C., 1932-37; dist. supt. schs. Caroleen (N.C.) Pub. Schs., 1938-45, supt., Mooresville city schs., 1945-71; now ednl. cons. trustee N.C. Outward Bound Sch. Mem. N.E.A., Am. Assn. Sch. Adminstrs., N.C. Edn. Assn. (pres. div. supts. 1965), Mooresville C. of C. (past pres.), Phi Delta Kappa. Methodist (ofcl. bd., trustee). Mason (32 deg.), Elk Kiwanian. Author: The Status, Functions and Activities of School Board Members, 1955. Home: 716 Pineward Circle Mooresville NC 28115

MORGAN, RYALL STAPLETON, mfrs. agy. exec.; b. Savannah, Ga., Nov. 15, 1901; s. Wayland Berry, and Minnie (Stapleton) M.; student Mercer U., 1922-23, U. Cin., 1923-25; m. Jule Lester, Aug. 19, 1930. Office mgr. Gt. A & P Tea Co., New Orleans, 1929-38, sales mgr., 1938-43; exec. staff Research Inst. Am., N.Y.C., 1944-45; v.p. J. Wallace Paletou, Inc., New Orleans, 1946-48; So. regional mgr. Celotex Corp., New Orleans, 1949-54; pres. Acousti Engring. of Ala. Inc., Birmingham, Ala., 1955-58; prop. Ryall S. Morgan Sales Agy., Birmingham, 1959—; pres., dir. Found. Investment Service, Inc., Birmingham. Treas., Ala. Ballet Co., 1967. Mem. Ala., Nat. (pres. gen. 1972-73) socs. sons. Am. revolution, Ala. Soc. Colonial Wars (gov. 1969-70), Ga. Salzburger Soc., Ala. Hist. Soc. Republican. Kiwanian. Club: Downtown. Home: 16 Glen Iris Park Birmingham AL 35205 Office: PO Box 3205 Birmingham AL 35205

MORGAN, SHELDON LEGRANDE, banker; b. Thomasville, Ala., Oct. 9, 1929; s. Stevy Moore and Floy (Brasell) M.; student U. Ala., 1952-53; B.S., Auburn U., 1955, M.Ed., 1956; postgrad. Tulane U., U. Ga., U.N.C., U. Okla., 1958—; m. Joyce Hardwick Morgan, Jan. 31, 1957; children—Ann, Jane, Jack, Steven LeGrande. Adminstrv. trainee Ala. Docks Dept., Mobile, 1957, asst. dir. pub. relations, 1957-60; world trade mgr. Mobile Area C. of C., 1960-63, mgr. indsl. devel., 1963-72; mgr. indsl. devel. Merchants Nat. Bank Mobile Hon. consul of Nicaragua. Pres., Mobile Azalea Trail and Festival, 1961; sec. Sr. Citizens Services Ala.; chmn. Ala. Indsl. Devel. Conf. Adv. bd. Providence Hosp. Sch. Nursing; bd. dirs. Am. Jr. Miss Pageant, 1961, Mobile County Tb and Health Assn., 1960-63. Served with USAF, 1948-52. Mem. C. of C., Am., So. (dir.) indsl. devel. councils, Indsl. Developers Assn. Ala. (pres.), Phi Delta Kappa. Baptist. Kiwanian. Clubs: International Trade; Dauphin Island Country. Home: 4 Graf Ct Mobile AL 36606 Office: 408 Merchants Nat Bank Bldg Mobile AL 36601

MORGAN, THOMAS EUGENE, educator; b. Guthrie, Ky., Sept. 10, 1929; s. Eugene and Virginia (Lannom) M.; B.S., Austin Peay State U., 1951; M.S., U. Tenn., 1954, Ed.D., 1968; m. Marylou Johnson, July 15, 1954; children—Mary, Thomas Eugene, Patrick. Engr. Lou & Nash Railroad, Louisville, 1954-57; part time instr. in engring. graphics U. Louisville, 1956-57; instr. gen. engring. U. Ky., 1957-60, asst. prof. civil engring., 1960-66; research assc. U. Tenn., 1966-68; asso. prof. edn. and dir. ednl. planning services, Auburn (Ala.) U., 1968—; cons. in ednl. planning. Scoutmaster Boy Scouts of Am., 1963—. Mem. Council of Ednl. Facilities Planners, Internat. Soc. Ednl. Planners, Southeast Council of Ednl. Facilities Planners (bd. govs. 1970—, sec. treas. 1970—), Iota Lambda Sigma, Phi Delta Kappa. Mem. Disciples of Christ (deacon 1959—). Mason. Home: 913 Terrace Auburn AL 36830

MORGAN, W.H., educator. Dir., Water Resources Research Center, U. Fla. at Gainesville. Office: 220 Environmental Engring Bldg Univ Florida Gainesville FL 32601*

MORGAN, WILLIAM JAMES, psychologist; b. Rochester, N.Y., Apr. 30, 1910; A.B., U. Rochester, 1933; Ph.D., Yale, 1937; m. Antonia Mary Farquharson Bell, Nov. 2, 1944; children—William James, Jean Elizabeth, Robert Macnair. Chief clinician Vineland (N.J.) Tng. Sch., 1936-38; psychologist Bd. Edn., Rochester, N.Y., 1939-41; dir. Psychol. Test Bur., Rochester, 1941-42; dep. chief tng., chief psychol. assessment CIA, 1947-52; mem. Psychol. Strategy Bd., White House, 1952-53; pres. Aptitude Assos., Merrifield, Va., 1953—; mem. Army Research Com.; cons. Dept. Justice, Dept. Def., other agys. Mem. Va. Bd. Certification Clin. Psychologists. Served from pvt. to maj. AUS, 1942-47; OSS, ETO. Diplomate in clin. psychology Am. Bd. Examiners Profl. Psychology. Mem. Va. Psychol. Assn. (pres. 1957-58), Sigma Xi. Author: Spies and Saboteurs (Gollancs-London), 1955; The O.S.S. and I, 1957; numerous articles and tests. Home: 2816 Gallows Rd Vienna VA 22180

MORGENROTH, WILLIAM MASON, educator; b. Akron, O., May 21, 1915; s. Abraham Lee and Jeanette (Mason) M.; A.B. in Math., U. Mich., 1938, M.B.A. in Accounting, 1940; M.A. in Sociology, U. Colo., 1951; Ph.D. in Indsl. Mgmt., U. Pitts., 1962; m. Margaret Lillian Moellenbrock, Jan. 28, 1959; children—Virginia, Robert, Rebecca, William, Amy, Maria. Indsl. relations mgr. Westinghouse Electric Co., Irwin, Pa., 1951-56; asst. to pres. Mason Shaver & Rhoades, McKeesport, Pa., 1956-58; instr. indsl. mgmt. U. Pitts., 1958-61; asst. prof., then asso. prof. Ohio State U., Columbus, 1962-67; prof., head div. bus. econs. Cal. State Coll., Hayward, 1967; prof. indsl. mgmt. U. S.C., Columbia, 1968—, also holder Citizens and So. Nat. Bank chair in mgmt., dir. marketing programs. Bd. dirs. Am. Heart Assn., Pitts., 1955. Served with USNR, World War II. Mem. Am. Marketing Assn. (pres. Central Ohio 1966-67), Soc. Advancement Mgmt. (asso. regional dir. Pitts. 1959-62), Am. Econ. Assn., Alpha Kappa Psi. Mason (Shriner). Contbr. articles to profl. jours. Home: 2847 Kirkwood Dr Springdale SC 29169

MORGENSTERN, SHELDON, condr.; b. Cleve.; B.M., Northwestern U.; M.M., New Eng. Conservatory. Past asst. condr. New Eng. Conservatory Orch., now musical dir. (N.C.) Symphony Orch., also Eastern Music Festival; guest condr. orchs. U.S., Can., Europe. Address: 808 N Elm St Greensboro NC 27401*

MORIARTY, G. MARSHALL, govt. ofcl. Spl. asst. to sec. Dept. Health, Edn. and Welfare, Washington. Home: 325 Maryland Av NE Washington DC 20002 Office: 330 Independence Blvd SW Washington DC 20201*

MORIARTY, HERBERT BERNARD, JR., lawyer; b. Memphis, June 5, 1929; s. Herbert Bernard and Kathleen (Prindaville) M.; B.A., Vanderbilt U., 1950, LL.B., 1952; M.B.A., Memphis State U., 1967; m. Madeleine Hildreth Smith, Apr. 30, 1960; children—Herbert Bernard III, Kathleen Louise, Madeleine Patricia, Brian Donovan. Admitted to Tenn. bar, 1952; gen. practice, Memphis, 1954—; Shelby County ct. magistrate, 1960-66. Mem. Tenn. Ho. of Reps. 1959-60. Served to capt. USAF, 1952-54. Mem. Am., Tenn., Memphis, Shelby County, Fed. bar assns., Am. Trial Lawyers, Young Lawyers Assn., Sigma Chi, Delta Theta Phi. Democrat. Roman Catholic. Kiwanian. Home: 172 Green Glade Rd Memphis TN 38117 Office: Commerce Title Bldg Memphis TN 38103

MORITZ, WALLACE ALBERT, realtor; b. Milw., Apr. 21, 1913; s. Leopold and Theresa (Bauer) M.; student Marquette U., 1931; m. Ruth Kalle, Jan. 2, 1945; children—Judith (Mrs. James L. Freeman), Diana (Mrs. Dan R. Hill), Arthur Lee. Founder Wallace Labs. Inc., San Angelo, Tex., 1940, now dir.; pres. W. Tex. Bus. Music Co., San Angelo, 1953; owner Wallace A. Moritz and Assos., San Angelo, 1960—. Chmn. Nat. Wool Pageant, 1958-59; pres. Crippled Children's Center, San Angelo, 1958, United Fund, San Angelo, 1963, Lighthouse, San Angelo, 1965. Named San Angelo Citizen of Year, 1958. Mem. Tex. Assn. Realtors (dir. 1969, 1st v.p. 1972), San Angelo Bd. Realtors (pres. 1967). Presbyn. Mason, Kiwanian. Home: 166 Moritz Circle San Angelo TX 76901 Office: 1900 Sherwood Way San Angelo TX 76901

MORKOVSKY, JOHN L(OUIS), clergyman; b. Moulton, Tex., Aug. 16, 1909; s. Alois J(oseph) and Marie (Raska) M.; grad. St. John's Sem., San Antonio, 1930; student N. Am. Coll., Rome, Italy, 1930-36; S.T.D., Pontifical Gregorian U., 1936; A.M., Cath. U. Am. 1943; LL.D., St. Edward's U., 1958. Ordained priest Roman Cath. Ch. in Rome, 1933; asst. pastor St. Michael's, Weimar, Tex., 1936-39, St. Ann's, San Antonio, 1940; prof. canon law St, John's Sem, San Antonio, 1940-41; archdiocesan supt. of schs., 1941-56; pastor St. Leo's Parish, San Antonio, 1945-54, St. Mary Magdalen Parish, 1954-56; titular bishop of Hieron and aux. bishop of Amarillo, 1956-58, vicar gen., chancellor Amarillo, Diocese, 1956-58, bishop, Amarillo, 1958-63; coadjutor bishop, aostolic adminstr., Galveston-Houston, 1963—. Apptd. Papal Chamberlain with title of Very Reverend Monsignor, 1944, Domestic Prelate with title Right Rev. Monsignor, 1954. Judge, Archiocesan Tribunal, 1946-56; mem. Archdiocesan Bd. Consultors, 1947-56; pres. Tex. Conf. Chs., 1970-72. K.C. (4 deg.). Address: Catholic Chancery 1700 San Jacinto St Houston TX 77002

MORLAND, ALVIN WESLEY, assn. exec.; b. Birmingham, Ala., July 29, 1914; s. Howard Canon and Ethel May (Cowan) M.; B.S., Auburn U., 1937; postgrad. Inst. Orgn. Mgmt., U. N.C., 1954, Syracuse U., 1966, U. Notre Dame, 1972; m. Gretchen Bickelhaupt, Feb. 15, 1947; children—Douglas Verne, Timothy Easton. With U.S. Steel Corp., Birmingham, 1937-41, 46-47; adminstrv. asst. U.S. Congressman L.C. Battle, 1947-49; city mgr. Mountain Brook, Ala., 1949-51; mgr. trade devel. Birmingham C. of C., 1951-53; mgr. Dothan (Ala.) C. of C., 1953-55, Ft. Pierce (Fla.) C. of C., 1955-62; exec. v.p. Pompano Beach (Fla.) C. of C., 1963—. Served with AUS, 1941-46. Decorated Purple Heart, Bronze Star. Mem. Internat. City Mgrs. Assn., So. Assn. C. of C. Execs. (dir. 1971-72), Am., Ala. (dir. 1954), Fla. (pres. 1964-65) chambers commerce execs., Sigma Alpha Epsilon, Omicron Delta Kappa (pres. Auburn U. chpt. 1936-37). Republican. Rotarian (dir. Pompano Beach club 1967, officer, dir. 1969-71). Home: 2326 N E 29th St Lighthouse Point FL 33064 Office: Chamber of Commerce 2200 E Atlantic Blvd Pompano Beach FL 33062

MORLAND, RICHARD BOYD, educator; b. Huntsville, Ala., June 27, 1919; s. Howard Canon and Ethel May (Cowan) M.; A.B., Birmingham-So. Coll., 1940; M.Ed., Springfield Coll., 1947; Ph.D. (So. Fellowships Fund fellow 1957-58), N.Y. U. 1958; m. Jessie May Parrish, Mar. 17, 1949; 1 dau., Laura. Phys. dir. YMCA, Frankfort, Ky., 1940-41; dir. athletics, Fla. So. Coll., 1947-50; lect. in edn., N.Y. U., 1950-51; chmn. dept. phy. edn., Stetson U., Deland, Fla., 1952-60, asso. prof., 1958-63, prof., 1963—, chmn. grad. council, 1962-69, chmn. dept. edn., 1969—. Served to lt., USNR, 1941-45. Mem. Am. Assn. Higher Edn., Philosophy of Edn. Soc. (pres. region 1963-64), Am. Edn. Studies Assn., Omicron Delta, Phi Alpha Theta, Kappa Delta Pi, Kappa Alpha. Methodist. Contbr. articles to profl. jours. Home: 524 N McDonald St DeLand FL 32720

MORLEY, RICHARD E., coll. pres.; b. Nixon, Tex., May 30, 1915; s. Lester H. and D. Lee (Wingfield) M.; B.S., Trinity U., 1954, M.Ed., 1955; Ed.D., U. Houston, 1957; postgrad. U. Tex., Tex. A. and M. U., Fla. State U.; m. Ellenor Rooks, Aug. 13, 1943; 1 dau., Donna Ruth. Prodn. and pub. numerous Tex. weekly and daily newspapers including Nixon News, Gonzales Daily Inquirer, San Antonio Express-News, 1933-49; counselor, tchr. pub. schs., Houston, San Antonio, 1949-57; dean Pensacola (Fla.) Jr. Coll., 1957-60; pres. Gulf Coast Community Coll., Panama City, Fla., 1960—. Cons. psychol. services and mgmt. devel., 1950—; lectr. to clubs, chambers commerces, industry; auctioneer. Chmn. United Fund Drive. Served with USCGR, 1942-45. Named Outstanding Indsl. Tchr., State of Tex. Mem. Am. Council Higher Edn., Nat., Fla. auctioneer assns., Panama City C. of C., So. Assn. Colls. and Schs. (sec. commn. on colls. and univs., mem. exec. council), Internat. Platform Assn., Kappa Delta Pi, Iota Lambda Sigma, Phi Delta Kappa. Baptist (lay speaker). Rotarian (past pres. Panama City). Author: Can You Ask the Intelligent Question, 1967. Contbr. numerous articles to mags. and newspapers. Home: PO Box 13327 Mexico Beach Sta Panama City FL 32401

MORLEY, RONALD BRITTON, dentist; b. Albany, N.Y., July 19, 1935; s. Francis Britton and Anne Marie (Huth) M.; A.B., Maryville Coll., 1957; D.D.S., U. Md., 1961; m. Faith Browning Nollner, May 23, 1957; children—Lisa, Regina, Andrea. Commd. 1st lt. USAF, 1961, advanced through grades to maj., 1972; base dental surgeon Sewart AFB, Tenn., 1966-70; course supr. dental lab. tech. tng. Sch. Health Care Scis., Sheppard AFB, Tex., 1970—. Mem. Am. Dental Assn., Psi Omega. Home: 2304 Clarinda Wichita Falls TX 76311 Office: Sch Health Care Sciences Sheppard AFB TX 76311

MORLEY, STANLEY MALCOLM, lawyer; b. Cheyenne, Wyo., Jan 9, 1912; s. William and Marion (Stirrit) M.; student Georgetown U., 1930-32; LL.B., Cath. U. Am., 1937, B.C.S., 1940; m. Irene Helen Lipscomb, Jan. 18, 1935; children—Mary Jane (Mrs. Steven Joseph Conway), Betsy Anne (Mrs. John Gerard Swanhaus). Admitted to D.C. bar, 1937, U.S. Supreme Ct. bar, 1945; mem. firm Shannon & Morley, Washington, 1945—. Mem. Nat. Lawyers Club, Fed. Power (pres.), Am. bar assns., Bar Assn. D.C. Club: Congressional Country. Home: 6405 Garnett Dr Chevy Chase MD 20015 Office: 1700 K St NW Washington DC 20006

MORR, ALEXANDER, theater exec.; b. Cleve.; ed. Western Res. U., Free U Berlin. Stage mgr., dir. Cleve. Playhouse, 1958-59; mgr. Hanna Theater, Cleve., 1961-62, Mineola (N.Y.) Playhouse, 1962-64, Colonial and Wilbur theaters, Boston, 1964-72; gen. mgr. theater complex John F. Kennedy Center for Performing Arts, Washington, 1972—. Office: John F Kennedy Center for Performing Arts Washington DC 20566*

MORRIS, ALLEN COVINGTON, state ofcl., columnist, photographic archivist; b. Chgo., Dec. 3, 1909; s. Gustave Allen and Anna (Hunter) M.; student pub. schs.; m. Dorothy Elizabeth Hedley, Nov. 1, 1932 (dec.); children—Martha (Mrs. Kermit Bernard Marsh), David Allen; m. 2d, Joan Lee Perry, Dec. 28, 1966. Photographer, writer Miami (Fla.) News, 1925-33; corr. A.P., Miami, 1933-37; writer Miami (Fla.) Herald, 1937-43; free-lance polit. columnist, Tallahassee, 1943—; photographic archivist Fla. State U., 1951—. Vice-chmn. Fla. Advt. Commn., 1949; mem., sec. Jud. Council Fla., 1953-63; mem. Fla. Library Bd., 1963—; cons. procedure Fla. Ho. of Reps., Tallahassee, 1947—, clk., 1966—. Served to lt. (j.g.) USCGR, 1943-45. Mem. Spl. Libraries Assn., Legislative Corrs. Assn. (pres. 1947-49). Author: The Florida Handbook, 1947, rev. biennially; Florida Facts and Figures, 1954; Florida Business Handbook, 1956; Florida Business Year Book, 1961; Our Florida Government, 1961; Florida Industrial Case Book, 1963. Co-author: How To Win in Politics, 1948; Legal Background to the Government of Florida, 1961; Your Florida Government, 1965; Florida Business Profiles, 1965; The Speaker's Manual, 1965; Florida Under Five Flags, 1967. Home: 2015 E Randolph Circle Tallahassee FL 32303 Office: The Capitol Bldg Tallahassee FL 32304

MORRIS, BARTON W., JR., newspaper editor. Exec. editor Roanoke (Va.) Times and World-News. Office: 201-209 W Campbell Av Roanoke VA 24010

MORRIS, BENJAMIN HUME, lawyer; b. Louisville, Sept. 25, 1917; s. Ben F. and Mary B. (Hume) M.; J.D., U. Louisville 1941; m. Lacy Hibbs Abell, July 7, 1942; (div. 1968); children—Ben Hume, Lacy Wayne; m. 2d, Mary Fowler Gatlin, Nov. 9, 1968. Admitted to Ky. bar, 1940; mem. firm Doolan, Helm, Stites & Wood, Louisville, 1941-50; atty. Brown-Forman Distillers Corp., Louisville, 1950-55, resident counsel, 1955-59, resident counsel and asst. sec., 1959-64, v.p., mem. exec. com., 1964—; pres., dir. Canadian Mist Distillers, Ltd., 1971—; dir. Licensed Beverage Industries, Inc., 1966—, vice chmn. bd., 1968—. Chmn. adv. com. Jefferson County Social Service, 1961-64, mem., 1964-68. Bd. dirs. Distilled Spirits Inst., 1966—, chmn. exec. com., 1969-70, chmn. bd., 1971-72; bd. dirs. Assn. Canadian Distillers, 1971—; bd. dirs. Better Bus. Bur., Louisville, 1969—, sec., trustee W.L. Lyons Brown Found. Served from aviation cadet to capt., pilot AC, AUS, 1941-45; ETO; col. USAF Res. ret. Decorated Air medal (Army) with oak leaf cluster. Mem. Ky. C. of C. (dir. 1969—), Soc. Colonial Wars (registrar 1969—), Ky. Distillers Assn. (dir. 1966—, pres. 1969, chmn. 1970), Am., Ky. State, Louisville bar assns., Am. Judicature Soc., Ky. Hist. Soc., Louisville Health and Welfare Council, S.A.R. (pres. Thruston chpt. 1965-66), Kappa Alpha, Omicron Delta Kappa. Presbyn. (elder). Clubs: Filson, Louisville Boat, Midland Trail Golf. Home: 2005 High Ridge Rd Louisville KY 40207 Office: 850 Dixie Hwy Louisville KY 40210

MORRIS, CHARLES HILL, publisher; b. Augusta, Ga., May 31, 1938; s. William Shivers and Florence (Hill) M.; B.A., U. Ga., 1960; m. Rosalie Stone; children—Ruth Hightower, Matilda Reaney, Mary Haley. Pres., Morris Newspaper Corp., owners and operators newspapers, Key West and Deland, Fla., Murfreesboro, Tenn., Statesboro, Ga. Home: 18 Clarendon Rd Savannah GA 31404 Office: 31 W Congress St Savannah GA 31402

MORRIS, CHARLES JACOB, educator; b. Houston, Aug. 16, 1923; s. Joseph Lewis and Flora (Susnitsky) Moskowitz; student Rice Inst., 1940-42, U. Chgo., 1942-43, Washington and Lee U., 1943; A.B., Temple U., 1944; LL.B., Columbia, 1948; m. Thelma Minnette Fineglass, Mar. 8, 1952; children—Jeffrey Bruce, Jena Sue, Joseph Lewis, John Hunter. Admitted to Tex. bar, 1948; practiced in Dallas, 1948-66; with firm Mullinax & Wells, 1948-52; partner, Mullinax, Wells Morris, Mauzy, 1952-66; lectr. So. Meth. U,. 1964-66, vis. prof. law, 1966-69, prof. law, 1969—. Labor arbitrator. Research fellow Southwestern Legal Found., 1963-67. Served with AUS, 1943-46. Mem. Am. Bar Assn., Nat. Acad. Arbitrators, Internat. Soc. Labor Law and Social Legislation, Am. Judicature Soc., State Bar Tex., Labor Law Group Trust. Jewish religion. Author numerous articles in field for legal jours. Editor in chief The Developing Labor Law, 1971. Office: School of Law Southern Methodist U Dallas TX 75222

MORRIS, CHARLES ROBERT, educator; b. Houston, Nov. 21, 1924; s. Earl Luckett and Hazel (Hemphill) M.; student Southwestern U., Georgetown, Tex., 1942-44, 46; Columbia, 1944; D.D.S., U. Tex., 1950, postgrad. certificate oral surgery field, 1960; m. Evelyn Barbee Williams, Sept. 13, 1947; children—Charles Robert, Jane (Mrs. Lonnie E. Longmire), Margaret Ann, Claire Christine, Amy Frances, Earl Leslie. Commd. 2d lt. U.S. Air Force, 1950, advanced through grades to col., 1968; chief oral surgery Air Force Hosp., Wiesbaden, Germany, 1962-66; chief outpatient surgery Willford Hall Air Force Hosp., Lackland AFB, Tex., 1966-67, chief inpatient oral surgery, 1967-68; chief div. dentistry br. dental scis. div. Sch. Aerospace Medicine, Brooks AFB, Tex., 1968-71, dep. chief dental scis. div., 1969-71; ret., 1971; mem. faculty Dental Sch., U. Tex. at Houston, 1966-69, at San Antonio, 1968—, clin. prof. dept. diagnosis and radiology, 1970-71, prof., chmn. dept., 1971—. Cons. various depts. U.S. Air Force, 1960—. Active Boy Scouts Am., 1959—; pres. N.D. chpt. P.T.A., 1961-62, hon. life mem., 1962—. Decorated Legion of Merit; recipient certificate of achievement Surgeon Gen. Air Force, 1970. Diplomate Am. Bd. Oral Surgery. Fellow Internat. Assn. Oral Surgeons, Am. Coll. Dentists; mem. Am. Soc. Oral Surgeons, Tex., Am. dental assns., Internat. Assn. Dental Research, Western Germany Armed Forces, San Antonio Dist. dental socs., Am. Assn. Dental Schs., Kappa Sigma, Psi Omega. Baptist (deacon). Contbr. articles to profl. jours. Home: 3119 War Arrow Dr San Antonio TX 78238 Office: 7703 Floyd Curl Dr San Antonio TX 78229

MORRIS, CLIFTON HOWINGTON, JR., boat co. exec.; b. Ft. Worth, July 26, 1935; s. Clifton Howington and Lois (Woods) M.; B.B.A., U. Tex., 1958; m. Andrea Ruhl. With McCammon, Morris, Pickens & Mayhew, C.P.A.'s, Ft. Worth, 1958-61, Arthur Young & Co., C.P.A.'s, 1961-66; with Service Corp. Internat., Houston, 1966-71, financial v.p., 1970-71, also dir.; chmn. bd. Boat World, Inc., Houston, 1971—. Mem. Am. Inst. C.P.A.'s. Episcopalian. Home: 5616 Winsome Houston TX 77027 Office: PO Box 1312 Houston TX 77001

MORRIS, DAVID H., broadcasting exec. Pres. KQUE-FM, Houston. Office: P O Box 188 Houston TX 77001*

MORRIS, EARLE ELIAS, JR., banker, lt. gov. S.C.; b. Greenville, S.C., July 14, 1928; s. Earle Elias and Bernice (Carey) M.; B.S., Clemson Coll., 1949; children—Lynda Lewis, Carey M., Elizabeth, Earle E. III. Owner, operator Morris & Co., Inc., wholesale grocers, Pickens, S.C., 1949-56; v.p., dir. Pickens Bank, 1956—, Bankers Trust S.C., 1968—; pres. Gen. Ins. Agy.; sec. Carolina Investors, Inc.; partner Morris Realty Co., Pickens; dir. Brunswick Worsted Mills. Mem. S.C. Ho. of Reps., 1950-54, S.C. Senate, 1954-70. S.C. rep. So. Regional Council Mental Health. Mem. Crippled Children's Soc. S.C.; mem. S.C. Gov.'s Adv. Group Mental Health Planning; mem. Nat. Adv. Mental Health Council; mem. S.C. Interagy. Council Mental Retardation. Del. S.C. Democratic Conv., 1950, 52, 54, 56, 58, 60, 62, 64, 66, 68, 70, nat. conv., 1952, 56, 68; state chmn. S.C. Dem. Party. Mem. Jr. C. of C., S.C. Vocational Rehab. Assn. (v.p.), S.A.R., Blue Key, Phi Kappa Phi. Presbyn. Mason (32 deg., Shriner), Elk, Moose, Lion. Home: Route 3 Pickens SC 29671 Office: Bankers Trust Main St Pickens SC 29671

MORRIS, ERNEST LIDDELL, food broker; b. Frankford, Del., Aug. 20, 1908; s. Sherman A. and Viola (Hickman) M.; student U. Va., 1928, Southwestern U., 1929; m. Sally L. Curry, Feb. 14, 1935; children—Jacquelyn (Mrs. James E. Smith), Dean, Larry. With Colgate-Palmolive-Peet Co., 1942-51, Perkins Brokerage Co., 1951-57; exec. gen. mgr. Ferguson-Morris & Assos., Dallas, 1958-69, dir., cons., 1969—. Served with AUS, 1944-45. Mem. Dallas Food Brokers Assn. (pres. 1967). Episcopalian (mem. vestry 1964-67). Home: 301 S 38th No 102 Corsicana TX 75110 Office: 3030 Hansbord St Dallas TX 75224

MORRIS, EUGENE TAYLOR, city ofcl.; b. Albemarle, N.C., Dec. 23, 1919; s. Joe and Bessie Mae (Blaylock) M.; student Inst. Govt., U. N.C., 1953-55; m. Mary Hazel Underwood, Jan. 5, 1943; children—Barbara (Mrs. Edward Perrell), Kay (Mrs. Johnny Billings), Eugene Taylor. Vets. service officer Davidson County, N.C., 1951-53; mgr., 1953-60; city mgr., City of Lexington, N.C., 1960—. Chmn., Davidson County Bd. Elections, 1965-66; chmn. March of Dimes, 1954. Bd. dirs., YMCA. Served with AUS, 1940-46; lt. col. Res. Decorated Bronze Star medals (2); recipient Outstanding Public Service award Kiwanis Internat., 1968. Mem. Piedmont Electric Cities Assn. (treas. 1968-70), V.F.W. (comdr. 1951-52), Am. Legion (comdr. 1954-55). Kiwanian, Moose (gov. 1953), Mason (32 deg., Shriner). Home: 207 Woodhaven Dr Lexington NC 27292 Office: PO Box 649 Lexington NC 27292

MORRIS, FRED JOHN, research co. exec.; b. Chgo., Dec. 6, 1919; s. Harry and Lillium (Richardson) M.; B.S., Tex. A. and I., 1942; M.A., U. Tex. at Austin, 1944, Ph.D., 1951; m. Vera Walsh, Sept. 5, 1942; children—Nansi, Gary Kim. Instr. physics U. Tex. at Austin, 1946-51; pres., dir. research Electro-Mechanics Co., Austin, 1951—. Sci. adviser Joint Chiefs Staff, Washington, 1959; cons. Colgate U., 1951, research and engring. program Def. Dept., 1962. Served to lt. (j.g.) USNR, 1944-46. Mem. Am. Phys. Soc., Soc. Am. Mil. Engrs., Am. Geophys. Union, A.A.A.S., I.E.E.E., Optical Soc. Tex., Soc. Exploration Geophysicists, Sigma Xi, Sigma Pi Sigma. Rotarian. Contbr. articles to profl. jours. Patentee magnetic field measurement instruments. Home: Route 7 Box 718E Austin TX 78703 Office: PO Box 1546 Austin TX 78767

MORRIS, JACK AUSTIN, JR., art dir.; b. Macon, Ga., Sept. 29, 1939; s. Jack Austin and Mattie Wise (Elliott) M.; A.B. in Fine Arts, U.S.C., 1962; certificate arts adminstrn., Harvard, 1970; m. Mary Sylvia Emanuel, Mar. 31, 1961; children—Dana Lynn, Jack Austin III. Trainee Columbia (S.C.) Museum Art, 1962-63, lectr., 1963-64, asst. to dir., 1964-65; dir. Greenville County (S.C.) Museum Art, 1965—; founder, pres. Concept II, Inc., Greenville, S.C., 1969—; instr. art. Richland Art Sch., Columbia, 1962-65; lectr. Museum Sch. Art, Greenville, 1965—; juror art exhbns. S.C. chmn. Liberty Life scholastic art award, 1967—; chmn. Star Student Program Congl. Dist., 1969. Bd. dirs. Greenville Symphony, Greenville Civic Choral, S.C. Arts Commn. Mem. S.E. Museums Conf., Am. Assn. Museums, S.C. Craftsman's Council (mem. exec. bd. 1965—), Guild of S.C. Artists (pres. 1968), S.C. Fedn. Museums (founder 1970). Rotarian. Author: Contemporary Artists of South Carolina, 1970; William M. Halsey: Retrospective, 1972. Home: 22 Selwyn Dr Greenville SC 29607 Office: 106 DuPont Dr Greenville SC 29607

MORRIS, JACK RECTOR, ins. co. exec.; b. Kansas City, Mo., Sept. 12, 1909; s. Charles F. and A. Josephine (Rector) M.; A.B., U., Kan., 1931; m. Ada Norman, Sept. 21, 1941 (dec. Nov. 1965); children—Donna Kay (Mrs. Phillip Lassiter), Jack Ronald; m. 2d, Ernestine Wannamaker, Apr. 22, 1966. With Business Men's Assurance Co., Kansas City, 1932-56, v.p., dir. pub. relations, 1954; v.p., dir. pub. relations Republic Nat. Life Ins. Co., Dallas, 1956-63, sr. v.p. pub. relations div., 1963-68, sr. v.p., exec. dir. pub. relations, 1968—. Chmn. pub. information com. Am. Cancer Crusade, 1957. Mem. Pub. Relations Soc. Am., Life Ins. Advt. Assn. (pres. 1953-54), Life Ins. Agy. Mgmt. Assn. (pub. relations com. 1953-54), Health and Accident Underwriters Conf. (pub. relations com. 1953-54), Life Insurers Conf. (pub. relations com. 1953-54), Dallas Advt. Club (dir. 1956-57, chmn. advt. week 1957, pres. 1959-60), Newcomen Soc. N.Am., Sigma Delta Chi, Delta Upsilon. Author: So... You're Going to Run a Convention; So... You're Going to Produce an Annual Report; How To Survive A Convention-with or without your wife; How To Live With Your Wife's Arrogant Poodle. Home: 6335 W Northwest Hwy Dallas TX75225 Office: 3988 N Central Expressway Dallas TX 75204

MORRIS, JAMES ALLEN, engring. mgr.; b. Vienna, Ga., Jan. 18, 1929; s. Clyde Center and Gladys (Taylor) M.; student Ga. Mil. Coll., 1945-46, U.S. Naval Acad., 1946-49; B.S., Mass. Inst. Tech., 1952; postgrad U. Tenn., 1957-68; m. Annabel Cheney Trapp, Sept. 30, 1950; children—James Allen, Linda Carol, Glenn Perry. Tchr. advanced sci. Lanier High Sch., Macon, Ga., 1949-50; engr. Robins AFB, Ga., 1950-51; test engr. U.S. Naval Engring. Expt. Sta., Annapolis, Md., 1952-55; project engr. Ford Sci. Lab., Ford Motor Co., Dearborn, Mich., 1955-57; project engr. ARO, Inc. Arnold Engring. Devel. Center, Arnold Air Force Sta., Tenn., 1957-68; dept. mgr. Planning Research Corp., Huntsville, Ala., 1968—. Instr. steam engring. Tenn. Agrl. and Indst. State U., 1962-68; cons. propulsion, overall systems problems, systems engring. mgmt., advanced research and devel. on new aerospace and weapons systems. Served with USN, 1946-49. Registered profl. engr., Tenn. Asso. fellow Am. Inst. Aero. and Astronautics: mem. Am. Ordnance Assn., Am. Legion. Baptist (deacon). Contbr. articles in field to publs. Home: 8018 Navios Dr SE Huntsville AL 35802 Office: 7911 Charlotte Dr Huntsville AL 35802

MORRIS, JAMES ALOYSIUS, economist, educator; b. Lawrence, Mass., May 25, 1918; s. George Thomas and Elizabeth (Reardon) M.; B.A., Northeastern U., 1942, LL.D., 1968; A.M., Harvard, 1947, Ph.D., 1951; m. Marjorie Leila Frampton, May 30, 1942; children—Stephen Frampton, Elizabeth Harvey. Asst. prof. U. S.C., Columbia, 1947-51, asso. prof., 1951-56, prof. econs., 1956-68, dean Coll. Bus. Adminstrn., 1961-66, v.p. advanced studies and research, dean Grad. Sch., 1966-68; commr. S.C. Commn. Higher Edn., 1968-72; distinguished prof. econs. U. S.C., Columbia, 1972—; vis. prof. Oxford (Eng.) U., 1953-54. Spl. econ. adviser U.S. Mission to Turkey, 1956-57; former chmn. bd. dirs. Charlotte br. Fed. Res. Bank of Richmond; dir. Pioneer Steel Co. Mem. Gov.'s Adv. Council on Health Planning; bd. govs. So. Regional Ednl. Bd.; commr. Edn. Commn. of States. Bd. dirs. U. S.C. Ednl. Found., Nat. Lab. Higher Edn., S.C. Hosp. Service Plan; trustee, mem. exec. com. Voorhees Coll.; mem. corp. Northeastern U. Served to lt. col. AUS, 1940-41, 42-46; PTO. Mem. Am., So. econ. assns., Am. Arbitration Assn. (chmn. S.C. adv. com.), Nat. Acad. Arbitrators, Phi Kappa Phi, Beta Gamma Sigma, Omicron Delta Kappa. Episcopalian (lay reader). Rotarian (past local pres.). Club: Forum. Author: Woolen and Worsted Manufacturing in the Southern Piedmont. Contbr. articles to profl. jours., columns to newspapers. Home: 1117 Adger Rd Columbia SC 29205 Office: U SC Columbia SC 29201

MORRIS, JAMES RUSSELL, assn. economist; b. Lakeland, Fla., Nov. 27, 1922; s. Scott and Blanche Gladys (Dicus) M.; A.A., U. Fla., 1943; B.A., Oberlin Coll., 1945; M.B.A., U. Chgo., 1947, Ph.D., 1957; m. Grace Fanes, June 1946. Cons. economist, Chgo., 1953-57, Winter Haven, Fla., 1958-59, Gainesville, Fla., 1959-60; sr. economist Am. Enterprise Assn., Washington, 1960-61; cons. economist, Alexandria, Va., 1961-65; sr. asso. C. of C. U.S., 1965—; staff economist Task Force on Econ. Growth and Opportunity, Washington, 1965-70. Instr. U. Ill., Chgo., 1946-57; lectr. U. Chgo., winter 1950; asst. prof. U. Ark., Fayetteville, Ark., 1957-58. Mem. Am. Econ. Assn., A.A.A.S., Am. Acad. Polit. and Social Sci., Phi Eta Sigma, Beta Gamma Sigma. Episcopalian. Author: Employment Opportunities in Later Years, 1960; (with T. Johnson, J. Butts) Renewing America's Cities, 1962. Contbr. to econ. jours. Home: 2406 Nemeth Ct Alexandria VA 22306 Office: 1615 H St NW Washington DC 20006

MORRIS, JAMES TRAVIS, advt. co. exec.; b. Waxahachie, Tex., Aug. 18, 1915; s. James Arthur and Annie (Walden) M.; B.S., U. Tex., 1938; m. Dorothy Brookes, June 15, 1939; children—Arthur, David, Kenneth, Carl, Linda, Paul. Engr. Mission Mfg. Co., Houston, 1938-39; with Brennan Advt. Agcy., Houston, 1939-54, tech. copywriter, 1939-48, exec. v.p., 1948-54; pres. Morris & Co., Houston, 1954-55; research dir. Rives Dyke & Co., Houston, 1955-62; v.p. Don L. Baxter, Inc., Dallas, 1962-67; v.p., mgr. Albert Frank-Guenther Law, Dallas, 1967—. Served with USAAF, 1942-45. Mem. Am. Soc. M.E., Assn. Indsl. Advertisers, Dallas Advt. League. Methodist. Home: 5722 Mercedes St Dallas TX 75206 Office: 2020 Live Oak St Dallas TX 75201

MORRIS, JEAN AARON (MRS. JOE TERRY MORRIS), broadcasting sta. exec.; b. Athens; Ga., Feb. 11, 1929; d. Ralph Edward and Ruth (Llewallyn) Aaron; B.S., U. Tampa, 1959; M.A., U. South Fla., 1969; m. Joe Terry Morris, July 2, 1946; children—Jean Karen, Laura Susan, Teresa Ruth. Music dir. Sta. WFLA, Tampa, Fla., 1957-69, radio and TV talent scout Sta. WFLA Radio & TV, 1960-62, account exec., 1962-65, TV producer, 1962-65; broadcasting sta. exec. WGTO Radio Sta., Cypress Gardens, Fla., 1965; became account exec. Radio Sta. WALT, Tampa, Fla., 1965; formerly broadcast exec. WINQ Radio, Tampa; prodn. specialist for Ednl. TV Duval County Sch. Bd. at WJCT Community TV, Jacksonville, 1970; TV coordinator Hillsboro County Sch. System, Tampa, 1959-60. Bd. dirs. Tampa Jr. C. of C. Wives, 1961-62, Fla. West Coast chpt. Multiple Sclerosis Soc. Mem. Am. Women in Radio and Television (pres. Fla 1962-64), Council for Exceptional Children, Tampa Advt. Club (sec., dir.), Tampa U. Alumni Assn., Green Key Honor Club, Pi Delta Epsilon, Sigma Tau Delta. Clubs: Toastmistress (charter mem.); Forest Hill Junior Women's (v.p. 1962-63). Home: 1856 Challen Av Jacksonville FL 32205 Office: 2037 Main St Jacksonville FL 32206

MORRIS, JOHN BURNETT, clergyman; b. Brunswick, Ga., Feb. 10, 1930; s. Hervey Clark and Anne (Burnett) M.; B.A., Columbia, 1951; B.D., Va. Theol. Sem., 1954; m. Harriet Barnes Pratt, Aug. 25, 1952; children— Anne, Christopher, John Burnett, Ellen. Ordained priest Episcopal Ch., 1954; rector St. Barnabas' Ch., Dillon, S.C., 1954-58; founder, exec. dir. Episcopal Soc. for Cultural and Racial Unity, Atlanta, 1958-67; spl. asst. So. Regional Council, Atlanta, 1968-70; civil rights specialist Dept. Health, Edn., Welfare, Atlanta 1971—. Del., Democratic Nat. Conv., 1968. Recipient Bishop Lichtenberger Human Rights award Episcopal Diocese of Chgo., 1968. Editor: South Carolinians Speak, 1957. Contbr. articles to periodicals. Home: 4655 Jett Rd NW Atlanta GA 30327 Office: 680 W Peachtree St NE Atlanta GA 30323

MORRIS, JOSEPH WILSON, lawyer; b. Rice County, Kan., Apr. 28, 1922; s. J. Bertrand and Hazel Mary (Sluder) M.; B.A., Washburn U., 1943, LL.B., 1947; LL.M., U. Mich., 1945, S.J.D., 1955; m. Deane Conklin, Nov. 6, 1948; children—Jeffrey David, Marilyn, Cynthia. Admitted to Kan. bar, 1947, Okla. bar, 1949; staff atty. Shell Oil Co., Tulsa, and N.Y.C., 1948-60; asso. gen. counsel Amerada Petroleum Corp., Tulsa, 1960-67, gen. counsel, 1967-69, gen. counsel Amerada div. Amerada Hess Corp., 1969-71, v.p., asso. gen. counsel Amerada Hess Corp., 1971—; adj. prof. law Coll. Law U. Tulsa, 1950—. Mem. Okla. State Regents for Higher Edn., 1969—. Served to lt. (j.g.) USNR, 1944-46. Mem. Am. (council, natural resources law sect. 1970-73), Okla., Tulsa County (pres. 1971) bar assns., Phi Delta Theta, Delta Theta Phi. Republican. Episcopalian. Mason (32 deg. Shriner), Royal Order of Jesters. Contbr. articles in field to profl. jours. Home: 2154 E 31st Place Tulsa OK 74105 Office: PO Box 2040 Tulsa OK 74102

MORRIS, KENNETH WAYNE, dentist; b. Lynchburg, Va., Mar. 12, 1939; s. Ulysses Bernice and Louise Elvira (Adams) M.; B.A., U. Va., 1961; D.D.S., Med. Coll. of Va., 1965; m. Judy Faye Atkins, May 31, 1964; children—Jeffrey Wayne, Kenneth Christian. Gen. practice dentistry South Hill, Va., 1967—; mem. staff Community Meml. Hosp., South Hill, 1967—. Served to lt., USNR, 1965-67. Mem. Gideons Internat. (pres. S.Central camp 1969-72), Am., Va. dental assns., Southside Dental Soc., Alumni Assn. Med. Coll. Va., Alumni Assn. U. Va., South Hill C. of C. (dir. 1971—). Baptist (deacon, tchr. Sunday sch.). Club: Tanglewood Shores Golf and Country. Home: 509 Raleigh Av South Hill VA 23970 Office: 604 N Thomas St South Hill VA 23970

MORRIS, LEWIS SPEIGHT, textile co. exec.; b. Salisbury, N.C., Feb. 5, 1915 Vice pres., dir. Cone Mills Corp., Greensboro, N.C., 1959-65, pres., 1965—. Office: Cone Mills Corp 4th and Maple Sts Greensboro NC 27405

MORRIS, LOUISE ELIZABETH BURTON (MRS. HARRY JOSEPH MORRIS), author, editor, genealogist, heraldist, lectr., club woman; b. Arleston, Tex., Dec 6, 1905; d. Edgar and Myrtie Etoile (Black) Burton; student Oklahoma City U., 1922-24; spl. courses Okla. U., Samford U., Brigham Young U.; grad. Nat. Archives Inst. Geneal. Research, 1972; m. Harry Joseph Morris, Nov. 3, 1945. Factory rep. for U.S.A., Ohio Plastic Co., Frazeyburg, O., 1941; spl. rep. for Tex., Richard Hudnut Co,, N.Y.C., 1942; for 4 states, Coty, Inc., N.Y.C., 1944; factory rep. for 11 states Sharpe & Sheehan, N.Y.C., 1951; factory rep. for Cook County, Ill., H. H. Ayres div. Lever Bros., N.Y.C., 1953. Lectr. biography, genealogy, history, conducted geneal. forum, 1967, 69, 71, 72, at gathering Scottish clans, Salado, Tex. State chmn. Tex. Magna Charta Com.; ofcl. rep. State of Tex. and City of Dallas to 750th Anniversary of Magna Carta, Eng., 1965; chmn. administrv. com. Dallas County Hist. Survey Com.; liaison officer Goals for Dallas; lectr., mem. program com. World Conf. on Records and Genealogy, 1969; lectr., condr. geneal. seminars, other workshops. Trustee, permanent chmn. Library of Central Tex. Area Mus., Salado; hon. fellow Harry S. Truman Library Inst. for Nat. and Internat. Affairs, Independence, Mo. Recipient awards for geneal. publs., articles and essays. Fellow Tex. Geneal. Soc. (v.p.), Heraldic and Geneal. Studies Soc. (Eng.) (founding), So. Soc. Genealogists (founding); The Augustan Soc. (v.p.), D.A.R. (chpt. mag. chmn.; organizer and 1st regent, hon. life regent Capt. Thomas Black chpt.; Tex. and Ill. chmn. pub. relations), Nat. Soc. Children Am. Revolution (nat. and state promoter; soc. hon. life sr. pres.; hon. life E. Tex. colony gov.), Gen. Soc. Mayflower Descs. (dep. gov. gen. Tex., rec. sec. Tex.), Nat. Soc. Women Descs. of Ancient and Honorable Arty. Co. (organizer, 1st Tex. pres.; hon. life state pres.; nat. 1st v.p. 1962-65, nat. corr. sec. 1959-62, state parliamentarian), Nat. Soc. Magna Charta Dames (dir., state parliamentarian; 1st Tex. regent, hon. life state regent; hon. life colony regent; chmn. 6th ann. state parliament 1965), Dallas So. Meml. Assn., San Jacinto Descendants (1st v.p.; founder-pres. Dallas chpt.), Tex. Hist. Found., Nat., Tex. library assns., Central Tex. Geneal. Soc. (hon. mem.), Mesquite Geneal. Soc., Sovereign Order Alfred the Great (internat. dame of Grand Cross; grand genealogist-heraldist.), Ladies Hermitage Assn., Nat. Soc. New Eng. Women (organizer, and 1st Tex. pres., hon. life state pres., state parliamentarian), Nat. Soc. Daus. Am. Colonists (hon. life colony regent and state regent), Ams. Royal Descent (life), Colonial Order Crown (life), Plantagenet Soc. (life), Nat. Soc. Old Plymouth Colony Descs. (life; Tex. organizing pres.; hon. life state pres., state parliamentarian), Descs. Knights of Garter (asso.), Colonial Dames Am. Inc., Nat. Soc. Daus. Colonial Wars (state parliamentarian; state chmn. lineage research adviser program), Soc. Genealogists (London), Heraldry Soc. (London), Heraldry Soc. (Canada), Am. Soc. Heraldry, Nat. Trust for Hist. Preservation, Dallas County Heritage Soc. Brit.-Am. Soc. (life), Coastal Bend Area Geneal. Soc. (hon.), Soc. Friends of St. George's (life), Nat. Soc. Dames Court of Honor, Nat. Soc. U.S. Daus. 1812, U.D.C. (hon. life pres. Chgo. chpt.; Tex. state chmn. radio and TV; chpt. 1st v.p.), Daus. Republic of Tex. (state chmn. and editor lineage book com.; hon. life pres. chpt.; chpt. 1st v.p.), Order of Washington (life), Nat. Smithsonian Assos., Am. Assn. State and Local History, Ark.-La.-Tex., Permian Basin, Ala., E. Ala., Tenn., Lubbock, Ill., Okla., St. Louis, Ft. Worth geneal. socs., So. Genealogists Exchange, Tex., U.S. Capitol hist. socs., Nat. Soc. Arts and Letters Crockett Hist. and Genealogy Soc., Scottish Genealogy Soc., (Scotland), Dallas Local History and Geneal. Soc. (v.p., editor, dir.), New Eng. Hist. Geneal. Soc., Nat. Geneal. Soc., Dallas Council World Affairs, Nat. His. Soc., Dallas Woman's Forum (gen. chmn. civic com.; membership chmn. lit. dept.), Dallas Civic Opera Guild, Dallas Symphony Orch. League, Dallas theatre Center, Soc, Descs. King William I, The Conqueror And His Companions At Arms, London, Eng. (rep.-genealogist Tex.), Internat. Platform Assn., Geneal. Soc. Victoria, Western History Assn. U.S., Collector's Inst. (founding), Dallas C. of C. (tourism com.), Alpha Chi Omega (life). Methodist. Clubs: Knife and Fork, Public Affairs Luncheon (Dallas); Friends of Library (Dallas). Author: Primer of Genealogical Research 1965; Lineages and Genealogical Notes, 1967; Instant Historical Programs, 1968; also articles, book reviews, essays in various mags. Editor: The Local History and Genealogy Society Quarterly, 1963-65. Compiler, editor: Founder and Patriots of the Republic of Texas, 1963; Handbook of Seminars in Genealogical Research, 1964. Presented papers on heraldry 10th Internat. Congress Geneal. and Heraldic Scis., Vienna, Austria, 1970, 1st Internat. Seminar on Heraldry, Toronto, Canada, 1971, 11th Internat. Congress, Liege, Belgium, 1972. Home: Twin Oaks 4700 W Stanford Dallas TX 75209

MORRIS, MARTIN EUGENE, judge; b. Anderson, Ind., Mar. 2, 1929; s. James Minton and Inez (Clark) M.; B.A., U. South, 1949; LL.B., Wash. Coll. Law, 1959; m. Gwendolyn Strangways-Jones, Jan. 17, 1951; children— Carol Anne, Diane Lucile. Pub. relations asst. N.E.A., 1955-57; asst. to dir. pub. relations Am. Trucking Assns., 1956-59; admitted to Va. bar, 1959; atty. McLean, Va., 1959-67; judge, County Ct., Fairfax County, Va., 1967—. Sec., dir. Vega Precision Labs., Vienna, Va., 1964—. Served with AUS, 1951-53. Episcopalian (vestryman 1966-68). Home: 9117 Falls Run Rd McLean VA 22101

MORRIS, NAOMI, judge. Asso. judge U.S. Ct. Appeals, Raleigh, N.C. Home: 523 Wade Av Raleigh NC 27605 Office: 1 W Morgan St Raleigh NC 27601*

MORRIS, PAUL J., supt. schs. Ordained priest Roman Catholic Ch.; now supt. schs. Catholic Diocese of Memphis. Address: 1475 E Shelby Dr Memphis TN 38116*

MORRIS, ROBERT, univ. chancellor; b. Jersey City, Sept. 30, 1914; s. John Henry and Sarah (Williams) M.; A.B., St. Peters Coll., Jersey City, 1936; J.D., Fordham U., 1939; LL.D., St. Francis Coll., Bklyn., 1954; D.H.L., Fujen U., Taipei, China, 1971; m. Joan Russell Byles, Dec. 27, 1951; children—Robert, Paul Esdaile, Roger, Joan Byles II, William E., John Henry II, Geoffrey. Newspaper reporter 1934-36; tchr. Greek, Latin and govt. St. Peters Prep. Sch., Jersey City, 1936-39; admitted to N.Y. State bar, 1939, also U.S. Supreme Ct. bar, Tex. bar, 1962; asso. firm Hines, Rearick, Door & Hammond, N.Y.C., 1939-40; asst. counsel N.Y. State Investigating Com., 1940-41; sec. to Congressman F. R. Coudert, Jr., 1946-50; sec.-treas Monrovia Port Mgmt. Co. (Africa), 1947-49; with firm Hochwald, Morris & Richmond, N.Y.C., 1946-52; spl. counsel U.S. Senate Internal Security Subcom., 1951-53, chief counsel, 1953, 56-58; judge Municipal Ct., N.Y.C., 1954-56; counsel to U.S. senators Hickenlooper and Lodge on U.S. Senate Fgn. Relations Com., 1950; pres. U. Dallas, 1960-62; pres. U. Plano (Tex.), 1964-71, chancellor, 1971—. Editor, pub. Twin Circle, 1970—; dir., mem. exec. com. Schick Co. Candidate for U.S. Senate from N.J., 1958, 60, from Tex., 1964. Served to lt. comdr. USNR, 1941-46; comdr. Ret. Mem. Am., Dallas bar assns., Phi Delta Phi. Clubs: City (Dallas); University (N.Y.C.). Author: No Wonder We Are Losing, 1958; Disarmament, Weapon of Conquest, 1963; What Is Developmental Education1967; also articles. Home: 5415 Lobello Dr Dallas TX 75220 also 1237 Ocean Rd Mantoloking NJ Office: 29 Broadway New York City NY 10005 also Merc Dallas Bldg Dallas TX

MORRIS, ROBERT AUSTIN, petroleum engr.; b. Bloomington, Ind., June 12, 1930; s. William Robert and Marguerite (Vint) Reveal; B.S., Tex. Tech. Coll., 1964; m. Eva O. Blankenship, Dec. 19, 1953. Fallout shelter inspector Hasie & Green, Cons. Engrs., Lubbock, Tex., 1960-61; field engr. Dowell Div., Dow Chem. Co., Tex., Okla., Ark., 1964-66; prodn. engr. Ark. Western Gas Co., Fayetteville, Ark., 1966-67; chief engr. Dover Corp., Norris Div. SRO, Tulsa, 1967—. Served with USN, 1948-57. Registered profl. engr., Okla. Mem. Engrs. Soc. Tulsa, Am. Petroleum Inst., Am. Soc. for Metals, Am. Soc. M.E., Nat. Assn. Corrosion Engrs. Home: 429 S Allegheny Av Tulsa OK 74112 Office: Box 1496 Tulsa OK 74101

MORRIS, ROBERT CALDER, entomologist; b. Wellsville, O., May 28, 1912; s. William Llewellyn and Annie Bell (Davidson) M.; B.S., Coll. Forestry State U. N.Y., 1948; M.S., U. Fla., 1968; m. Ora Bee Stuckey, Apr. 4, 1943; children—Brian Deric, Ian David, Adrian Craig. Entomologist U.S. Agr. Dept., 1948-53, Gulfport, Miss., 1951, Panama Canal Zone, 1951-53; with U.S. Forestry Ser., Gulfport and Stoneville, Miss., 1953—, supervisory research entomologist, Stoneville, 1968-71, project leader so. hardwood and insect disease research, 1971—. Leader Delta area concil Boy Scouts Am., 1970, 4-H, Leland, Miss., 1965; mem. Leland (Miss.) Beautification Com., 1962—. Served with AUS, 1940-45. Decorated Combat Infantryman Badge. Recipient Best Insect Forestry Publ. award So. Forest Insect Work Conf., 1967. Mem. Entomol. Soc. Am., N.Y. Acad. Sci., Internat. Soc. Tropical Foresters, Internat. Poplar Commn. (mem. exec. com.), Miss. Archeol. Assn. (pres. 1966-67), Poplar Council Am. (sec.-treas., 1970—). Home: 205 Lakeview Dr Leland MS 38756 Office: Southern Hardwoods Lab Stoneville MS 38776

MORRIS, ROBERT DOUGLAS, assn. exec.; b. Hillsboro, Tex., June 25, 1929; s. Douglas and Virgie Mae (Gilstrap) M.; B.A., Tex. Wesleyan Coll., 1951; B.D., So. Meth. U., 1955; postgrad. U. Okla., Tex. A. and M.U.; m. Ruth Elizabeth Sprinkle, Dec. 19, 1947 (div.); children— Deborah Ruth, Stephen Douglas. Asso. prof., counselor Tex. Wesleyan Coll., 1953-56; fund raiser, bus. mgr. Meth. Ch., 1956-60; regional dir. Nat. Conf. Christians and Jews, 1960-66; exec. v.p., gen. mgr. Hurst-Euless-Bedford C. of C., Euless, Tex., 1966—; univ. lectr. Episcopalian. Mason (K.T., Shriner), Rotarian. Home: 3542 Av L Ft Worth TX 76105 Office: 1102 W Euless Blvd Euless TX 76039

MORRIS, ROBERT NELSON, banker; b. Glasgow, Ky., Sept. 5, 1926; s. Ralph P. and Myrtle (Gillock) M.; B.S., U. Ky., 1952, postgrad., 1953; m. Mary Elizabeth Galloway, June 3, 1953; children—Robert Michael, Marcus Allen, Timothy Ray. Tchr. Park City (Ky.) High Sch.; with Conservation Service. U.S. Dept. Agr., Lexington, Ky., 1953; asst. county agt. Fla. Agrl. Extension Service, Tampa, 1953-54; v.p. First Nat. Bank, Tampa, 1954-67; adminst. Fla. Soil and Water Conservation Bd., 1967—; dir., v.p. M. & M Supply Co. of Fla., Inc., 1961—; v.p. Exchange Nat. Bank of Tampa. Supr. Hillsboro Soil Conservation Dist., 1956-67; sec., dir. Hillsboro County Farm Bur., 1961-67. Mem. Fla. Assn. Soil Conservation Suprs. (pres. 1962-64), Hillsboro Cattlemens Assn. (dir. 1956-67). Home: 5622 Oakland Dr Tampa FL 33617 Office: PO Box 1809 Tampa FL 33601

MORRIS, ROBERT WESLEY, hosp. adminstr.; b. Pasadena, Cal., July 21, 1924; s. John W. and Esther (Brown) M.; B.A., LaSierra Coll., 1948; M.S., Northwestern U., 1961; m. Caroline M. Gibson, Mar. 9, 1968; children—James Olin, Esther Lynn, Constance Estelle, Cynthia Faye, Deborah Ann. Adminstrv. asst. Chgo. Wesley Meml. Hosp., 1957-59; adminstr. Madison (Tenn.) Hosp., 1960—. Treas., Edn. and Research Found., 1969—; v.p. Mid-Cumberland Health Planning Council, 1969—. Trustee, So. Missionary Coll., Madison Acad., Takoma Hosp., Riverside Hosp., Fla. Hosp. Corp. Served with AUS, 1946-47. Mem. Middle Tenn. Hosp. Council (pres. 1964-65), Tenn. Hosp. Assn. (trustee 1969—, pres. 1971-72), Am. Hosp. Assn., 7th Day Adventist Hosp. Assn. (pres. 1970-71), Am. Coll. Hosp. Adminstrs., C. of C. (pres. 1965). Rotarian (past pres.). Home: 225 Peeler Trail Madison TN 37115 Office: Madison Hosp Madison TN 37115

MORRIS, SAMUEL BARRY, supt. schs.; b. Horry, S.C., June 22, 1920; s. Samuel C. and Hattie Lee (Haynes) M.; diploma Ferrum Jr. Coll., 1941; A.B., Duke, 1943; M.A., U. N.C., 1950; postgrad. Fla. State U., 1959-61; m. Elizabeth M. Mullinix, June 24, 1949; children— John B., Robert H., David W., Lee Ann. Tchr. pub. schs., High Point, N.C., 1943-45, Honolulu, 1945-46; tchr. Armed Forces Inst., 1951-58; dir. audio visual edn. Durham County (N.C.) Schs., 1949-51, Asheville (N.C.) City Schs., 1951-58, Fla. Dept. Edn., 1958-62; asst. supt. Fairfax (Va.) County Schs., 1962-70, area supt., 1970—; faculty Appalachian State U., Boone, N.C., 1959, Fla. State U., 1960, U. Va. Sch. Gen. Studies, 1963—. Pres. Nat. Council Chief State Audio Visual Officers, 1961; investigator States Audio Visual Edn. Survey, 1962-63; mem. media specialists panel of advisers U.S. Office Edn., 1968—. Bd. mgrs. Fla. Congress P.T.A., 1961. Mem. Am. Assn. Sch. Adminstrs., Assn. for Edn. Communications and Tech., N.E.A. (life mem., adviser Ednl. Policies Commn. 1960-66, chmn. legislative comm. dept. audio visual instrn. 1962-65), N.C. Audio Visual Assn. (past pres., chmn. bd. dirs.), Assn. Sch. Bus. Ofcls., Va., Fairfax edn. assns., Nat. Acad. Sch. Execs. (dir.), Phi Delta Kappa. Home: 7408 Bull Run Dr Centreville VA 22020 Office: 2500 James Madison Dr Vienna VA 22180

MORRIS, SETH IRWIN, JR., architect; b. Madisonville, Tex., Sept. 1, 1914; s. Seth Irwin and Carrie (Holleman) M.; B.A., Rice Inst., 1935; m. Suzanne Kibler, Dec. 29, 1945; children—Mark Peter, Maria, David Kibler, Laura, John. Practice architecture, Houston, 1935—; partner Wilson, Morris, Crain & Anderson, 1954—; vis. lectr. architecture Rice Inst., 1957; prin. works include U.S. Post Office, Houston, 1968, World Trade Center, Houston, 1960. Western Nat. Bank, 1964, Southwestern Bell Telephone Co. Area Hdqrs., 1966, Harris County Domed Stadium, 1965, Houston Lighting & Power Co., 1967, Bd. dirs. Houston Museum Fine Arts, 1960-68, pres., 1967-68. Served to comdr. USNR, 1942-46. Decorated Legion of Merit; Order Cloud and Banner (China); recipient honor awards Tex. Soc. Architects; 5 Nat. awards, 16 awards Houston chpt. A.I.A. 2 awards. Fellow A.I.A. (pres. Houston 1961); mem. Tex. Soc. Architects, Houston C. of C. (dir. 1964-70), Presbyn. (elder). Home: 2 Waverly Pl Houston TX 77005 Office: 3465 W Alabama St Houston TX 77027

MORRIS, STEWART, lawyer, title co. exec.; b. Houston, Oct. 28, 1919; s. William Carloss and Willie (Stewart) M.; B.A., U. Tex., 1943; L.L.B., So. Meth. U., 1943; m. Joella Mitchell, July 17, 1943; children—Carlotta, Stewart, Caralisa. With Stewart Title Co., Houston, 1935—, pres., 1950— admitted to Tex. bar, 1943, since practiced in Houston; partner, Morris, Termini, Harris & McCanne, 1946—; dir. Nassau Bay Nat. Bank, First Nat. Bank of Stafford, Houston Bank & Trust Co., Stewart Title Guaranty Co., Stewart Title Co., Stewart Trust Co., Admiral Investment Co., Inc.; chmn. bd. Stewart Info Services, Holly Resources, Inc. Co-founder, chmn. bd. trustees Houston Bapt. Coll.; chmn. bd. trustees Space Center Meml. Hosp. Found.; trustee Star of Hope Mission; adv. bd. Nat. Trust for Historic Preservation; trustee Oldham Little Ch. Found. Served to lt. (j.g.), USNR, 1943-46; PTO. Fellow Tex. Bar Found.; mem. State Bar Tex., Delta Theta Phi, Alpha Tau Omega. Clubs: River Oaks Country, Sugar Creek Country. Home: 5 E Rivercrest Dr Houston TX 77042 Office: 1302 Rusk Av Houston TX 77002

MORRIS, THERESA LINTHICUM (MRS. HARRELL HOUSTON MORRIS), social worker; b. Wickliffe, Ky.; d. Charles P. and Ruby Regal (Ives) Linthicum; A.B., Oklahoma City U., 1927; M.S.W., Washington U. (St. Louis), 1947; m. Harrell Houston Morris, Aug. 4, 1934 (dec. June 1953). Social worker Pub. Welfare Agy., Oklahoma City, 1935-37; med. social worker Okla. Commn. for Crippled Children, 1937-55, dir. med. social work, 1955-59; supr. social work Dept. Pub. Welfare, Crippled Children's Unit, Oklahoma City, 1959-60; social worker Okla. State Dept. Health, Oklahoma City, 1959-63, 72—, coordinator State Information and Referral Service Project, 1963-67, head information and referral sect., 1967-72. Mem. Okla. City Council on Alcoholism, 1968—. Sec. bd. dirs. Okla. Council on Handicapped Children, 1959-63; mem. adv. com. Sr. Citizens Centers; bd. dirs. Towers Sr. Adults Center. Mem. Nat. Assn. Social Workers (mem. pub. relations com.), Okla. Assn.

Social Workers, Okla. Health and Welfare Assn. (dir. 1967—, pres. 1969-70), Am., Okla. pub. health assns. (editorial com. 1969—), Okla. Rehab. (sec. bd. dirs. 1961-68), Am. Okla. heart assns., Am. Pub. Welfare Assn., Oklahoma City U. Alumni Assn. (dir. 1960-64). Methodist. Home: 1604 Linwood Blvd Oklahoma City OK 73106

MORRIS, VIRGIL DIXON, clergyman; b. Little Rock, July 4, 1907; s. Luther Walter and Hattie (Dixon) M.; B.A., Hendrix Coll., 1929; B.D., Th.M., So. Meth. U., 1931; D.D., Centenary Coll., 1954; m. Fannie Elizabeth Emmerich, Sept. 6, 1930 (dec. 1953); children—Ouida Fae, Virgil Dixon; m. 2d. Marjorie Marie Minkler, Nov. 28, 1954. Ordained to ministry Meth. Ch., 1929; minister, Douglasville and Geyer Springs, Ark., 1927-29, Tioga and Gunther, Tex., 1929-30, Delta Circuit, La., 1931-34, Columbia, La., 1934-39, 1st Ch., Lafayette, La., 1939-42, Homer, La., 1942-44, Alexandria, La., 1948-52; dist. supt. Baton Rouge dist. Meth. Ch., 1944-48, New Orleans dist. Meth. Ch., 1952-58; pastor Trinity Ch., Ruston, La., 1958-60, Istrouma Meth. Ch., 1960; exec. dir. South Central Jurisdiction, United, Meth. Ch., 1960—, mem. gen. commn. structure Methodism overseas, 1956-72. Bd. trustees Meth. Seashore Assembly, Biloxi, Miss., 1952-60, Meth. Gulfside Assembly, Waveland, Miss., 1972—, La. annual conf. Meth. Ch., 1951-60; commr. The Ark.-La. Meth., Little Rock, 1950-60; del. gen. confs. Meth. Ch., 1944-60, jurisdictional conf., 1944-60; alternate del. Meth. Ecumenical Conf., Oxford, 1951; del. World Meth. Conf., Oslo, 1961, Conf., London, Eng., 1966, Denver, 1971, World Meth. Family Life Conf., London, 1966. Trustee Centenary Coll., 1949-61, Meth. Home Hosp., New Orleans, 1961—, St. Paul Sch. Theology, Kansas City, Mo., 1961—, Lydia Patterson Inst., El Paso, Tex., 1948—, Mt. Sequoyah Meth. Assembly; chmn. La. Conf. Bd. Missions, 1956-58. Mason (32 deg., Shriner, K.T.). Co-founder, asso. editor The La. Meth., 1949-50. La. Conf. trustee New Orleans Christian Advocate files, 1950—. Home: 2404 NW 19th St Oklahoma City OK 73107 Office: Bixler Bldg 2400 NW 23d St Oklahoma City OK 73107

MORRIS, WILLIAM COKE, editor; b. Columbia, S.C., Feb. 21, 1922; s. Robert F. and Frances G. (Green) M.; A.B., Emory U., 1948; m. Mary Walker Leatherwood, Oct. 11, 1949; children—Mary C., William B., Susan F. Publicity dir. Wofford Coll., Spartanburg, S.C., 1949-51; staff writer Greenville (S.C.) Piedmont, 1951-63, city editor, 1963-65, mng. editor, 1965—. Mem. bd. Greenville High Sch. P.T.A., 1966—; treas. Greenville County Mental Health Assn., 1962. Treas. Greenville Republican Com., 1963-64; mem. Greenville County Republican Exec. Com., 1956-65; del. S.C. Rep. convs., 1960, 62, 64, 66. Trustee, Greenville Rescue Mission, S.C. Methodist Center, Columbia, 1957-64; chmn. adv. bd. S.C. Methodist Adv., 1960-65. Served with AUS, 1942-46; ETO. Recipient awards for writing S.C. Press Assn., 1955, 56, 57, 58, 68. Mem. Alston Wilkes Soc. (dir. Greenville County chpt. (1968—, state dir.), Greenville Jr. C. of C., Sigma Delta Chi. Methodist (ofcl. bd.). Author series on survey of S.C. prison camps which resulted in law requiring state inspection all prisons, jails, 1967. Home: 132 Fernwood Lane Greenville SC 29607 Office: News-Piedmont Co PO Box 1688 Greenville SC 29602

MORRIS, WILLIAM SHIVERS, III, newspaper pub.; b. Augusta, Ga., Oct. 3, 1934; s. William Shivers, Jr. and Florence (Hill) M.; B.A. in Journalism, U. Ga., 1956; m. Mary Sue Ellis, Jan. 18, 1958; children—William Shivers IV, John Tyler, Susie Blackmar. Pres., pub., dir. Southeastern Newspapers Corp., Augusta Newspapers, Inc., 1956-60; v.p., dir. Savannah Newspapers, Inc., Savannah News-Press, Inc., 1960-63; v.p., dir. Southeastern Newspapers, Corp., Augusta, 1963-66, pres., pub. Augusta Chronicle, Augusta Herald, 1966—; pres. Banner-Herald Pub. Co., Athens, Ga., 1965—, Athens Daily News, 1967—; pres. Morris Communications Corp., dir. So. Co., Inc., Ga. Power Co., Atlanta. Co-chmn. Joint Ga.-Ga. Tech. Devel. Fund Campaign, Augusta area, 1964; chmn. Augusta Jr. Achievement Membership Campaign, 1965; campaign chmn. YMCA-YWCA expansion program, 1971. Bd. dirs. United Fund Augusta; trustee Augusta Coll. Found.; bd. regents U. System Ga. Served as capt. USAF, 1958. Mem. So. Newspapers Pubs. Assn. (dir.) Golden Quill Soc., Sigma Alpha Epsilon. Presbyn. (deacon, elder). Clubs: University (N.Y.C.); Commerce (Atlanta); Oglethorpe (Savannah); Pinnacle (pres. Augusta). Home: 3209 Wheeler Rd Augusta GA 30904 Office: News Bldg Broad St Augusta GA 30902

MORRISETTE, N. WELCH, JR., lawyer; b. Uniontown, Ala., Aug. 29, 1921; J.D., U. Ala., 1947. Admitted to Ala. bar, 1947, S.C. Supreme Ct. bar, 1950, U.S. Supreme Ct. bar, 1954; since practiced in Columbia, S.C.; U.S. atty. Eastern dist. S.C., 1953-61. Mem. city council, Columbia, 1970—. Mem. Am., Richland County, S.C., 4th Judicial Circuit (mem. judicial conf. 1958—) bar assns., Am. Judicature Soc. (vice chmn. 1969—, mem. state election commn.). Office: 1306 Main St Columbia SC 29201*

MORRISEY, NORMAN STEWART, petroleum service co. exec.; b. Quincy, Mass., Dec. 10, 1918; s. Alexander N. and Elizabeth (Millea) M.; Geol. Engr., Colo. Sch. Mines, 1942; postgrad. Mass. Inst. Tech., 1943, Stanford, 1946-47; M.S. in Geol. Engring., U. Tulsa, 1950; m. Mary Frances Morrisey, Nov. 25, 1950. Research geologist and geophys. coordinator Amoco Prodn. Co. (then Stanolind O & G Co.), Oklahoma City, 1947-54; tech. editor Oil and Gas Jour., Tulsa, 1954-58; advt. mgr. Am. Assn. Petroleum Geologists, 1959-61; with GeoData Corp., Tulsa, 1961—, v.p. acquisition and sales, 1965—; exec. v.p. Gulf Coast GeoData Corp., Houston; sec.-treas. GeoData Internat., Ltd., London. Sec. Fairgrounds Tennis Assn., 1971-72. Mem. adv.bd. YMCA, 1968—. Served to lt. USNR, 1942-46. Mem. Am. Assn. Petroleum Geologists, Soc. Exploration Geophysicists, Tulsa Geol. Soc., Oklahoma City Geol. Soc., Geol. Soc. Houston, Geophys. Soc. Tulsa. Club: Tulsa Ski (past pres.). Home: 6818 E 55th St Tulsa OK 74145 Office: Thompson Bldg Tulsa OK 74103

MORRISON, EDWARD WALTER, JR., milling co. exec.; b. Wichita, Kan., Feb. 22, 1921; s. Edward Walter and Myrtle (Lane) M.; B.S., N.Tex. State U., Denton, 1939; postgrad. Kan. State U., 1939-42; m. Virginia Ann Boydston, Aug. 21, 1965; 1 son, Edward Walter III. Pres. Morrison Milling Co., Denton, 1942—. Past pres., dir. Self Rising Flour and Corn Meal Program. Served with AUS, 1944-45. Mem. Millers Nat. Fedn. (dir.), Am. Corn Millers Fedn. (dir.), Denton C. of C. (past dir.), Alpha Mu. Mem. Christian Ch. (elder, trustee). Rotarian. Club: Denton Country (dir.). Home: 414 Mimosa St Denton TX 76201 Office: 319 E Prairie St PO Box 719 Denton TX 76201

MORRISON, HARRY, lawyer; b. Crawfordville, Fla., Sept. 21, 1917; s. Angus and Marie Walker) M.; grad. high sch.; pvt. study law; m. Estelle Mills, Apr. 23, 1953; children—James D., Harry, Angus II. Admitted to Fla. bar, 1940; spl. agt. FBI, 1940-47; gen. practice Tallahassee, 1947—; first asst. state atty., 2nd Jud. Circuit Fla., 1949—; pres. Penninsular Point, Inc., Beach Developers. Dir. Alligator Point Water Resources Dist. Mem. Am., Tallahassee (past pres.) bar assns., Fla. Bar (grievance com. mem. 2d circuit, 1957—), Soc. Former Spl. Agts. FBI (v.p. 1961). Democrat. Baptist. Mason (Shriner), Elk. Clubs: Capital City Contry. Home: 2011 E Randolph Circle Tallahassee FL 32303 Office: Midyette-Moor Bldg Tallahassee FL 32301

MORRISON, HERSCHEL JAMES, JR., conservationist; b. Rockwood, Tenn., Dec. 10, 1940; s. Herschel James and Grace (Nipper) M.; B.A. in journalism U. Ga. 1962; m. Nina Wynnette Park, June 3, 1962; children—Nina Lynn, James Robert. News reporter WBT Radio and WBTV-TV, Charlotte, N.C., 1962-63; informational asst. Ga. Game and Fish. Commn., Atlanta, 1963, chief information and edn., 1963-70, editor Ga. Game and Fish mag., 1966—; dir. pub. information Ga. Conservancy, Atlanta, 1970—; now program liaison specialist U.S. Dept. Interior Bur. Outdoor Recreation, Atlanta. Free-lance mag. writer and photographer. Chmn. Ga. Natural Resource Edn. Council, 1965-69. Recipient Conservation Communications of Year award Ga. Sportsmen's Fedn., 1967, Conservationist of Year award Nat. Wildlife Fedn., 1970. Mem. Outdoor Writers Am., Am. Assn. Conservation Information (dir. 1967) S.E. Game and Fish Commrs. Assn. (pres. information and edn. sect. 1967-68), Am. Assn. Conservation (dir.), 1967-69), Ga. Outdoor Writers Assn. Home: 4019 Woburn Dr Tucker GA 30084 Office: Candler Bldg Atlanta GA 30303

MORRISON, JULIAN KNOX, III, systems analyst cons.; b. New London, Conn., Aug. 22, 1929; s. Julian Knox and Drucilla (Hallam) M.; student George Washington U., 1947-48, 64-65, Am. U., 1965-70; B.A., (N ROTC scholar), U. Va., 1952; m. Helen Banks Adams, June 10, 1952; children—Drucilla, Helen, Julie Ann, Patricia. Weapon systems analyst Chance Vought Aircraft Co., Dallas, 1958-61; programs mgr., systems analyses Ling-Temco-Vought, Inc., Dallas, 1961-64; sr. staff mem. Research Analysis Corp., McLean, Va., 1964-69; exec. sec. Am. Revolution Bicentennial Commn., 1969-72, information and research coordinator, 1972—. Page, U.S. Supreme Ct., Washington, 1943-47; spl. cons. sec. Health, Edn. and Welfare, 1968-69; cons. NASA, 1968-69, Am. Revolution Bicentennial Commn., 1969. Served with USN, 1952-58. Mem. Operations Research Soc., Am. Polit. Sci. Assn., Acad. Polit. Sci., U.S. Naval Inst., Am. Acad. Polit. and Social Scis., Pi Sigma Alpha, Sigma Chi. Author: Notes on Social Reporting, 1969. Home: 4530 Lowell St NW Washington DC 20016

MORRISON, KATHRYN JAYDENE WALKER (MRS. MICHAEL HOWE MORRISON), educator; b. Cherokee, Okla., Aug. 22, 1933; d. Jay Frank and Kathryn (Johnson) Walker; B.S., Okla. State U., 1955, M.S., 1957; postgrad. U. Colo., 1965, Central State Coll., 1969; m. Michael Howe Morrison, Aug. 12, 1955; children—Jay Edward, Michael McCollough. Tchr. pub. schs., Cushing, Okla., 1955-57, Indpls., 1958-59; tchr. Helena (Okla.) Pub. Schs., 1965—, counselor, 1965—; spl. edn. tchr. Helena-Goltry Sch., 1969—. Recipient Masonic Tchr. of Year award, 1968. Mem. Am., Okla. (dist. 2 rep. 1971-72) personnel and guidance assns., N.E.A., Okla. Edn. Assn., Alfalfa County Tchrs. Assn. (pres. 1972-73), Okla. Sch. Psychologists, Okla. Div. Learning Disabilities. N.W. Dist of Okla. Counselors (pres. 1970-71, v.p. 1971-72), Chi Omega Alumni Assn, Chi Omega (chpt v.p. 1954). Mem. Disciples of Christ Ch. Home: Box 585 Helena OK 73741

MORRISON, KENNETH DOUGLAS, sanctuary dir.; b. Mpls., April 1, 1918; s. Kenneth Mortimore and Florence Myrtle (Sutton) M.; A.B., Carleton Coll., 1940; grad.study U. Miami, 1940-41, U. Minn., 1941; m. Helen Curtis, Feb. 25, 1943; children—Kenneth D., Sally, Steven C., Mary. Free lance writer, Mpls., 1941; editor publs. Minn. Dept. Conservation, 1942-47; Minn. rep. Nat. Audubon Soc., 1947-49; dir. pub. relations, editor Audubon mag., 1949-56, v.p., 1955-56; dir. Mountain Lake Sanctuary and Singing Tower, Am. Found., 1956—; Audubon tour lectr., 1958-63; interviewer naturalists Wildlife Unlimited, TV sta. WOR-TV, N.Y.C., 1951-52. Mem. Minn. Bird Commn., 1951-54; trustee Fla. Nature Conservancy, Fla. Conservation Found.; v.p., trustee Conservation 70's; mem. Gov. Fla. Natural Resources Com.; mem. nat. council Nature Conservancy. Recipient Gov. Fla. Wildlife Conservation award, 1960. Mem. Am. Ornithologists Union, Wilson Ornithol. Club, Wilderness Soc., Nat. Parks Assn., Cornell U. Ornithol. Lab., Fla. Audubon Soc. (pres.), Hawk Mountain Sanctuary Assn. (bd. sponsors), Pi Delta Epsilon. Methodist. Author: Favorite Birds of America, 1951; Favorite Animals of America, 1951; also articles nat. mags. Compiler: Where to Find Birds in Minnesota (with Mrs. M.E. Herz), 1950. Home: Babson Park FL 33827 Office: Mountain Lake Sanctuary Lake Wales FL 33853

MORRISON, MAMON L., pianist; b. Coffeyville, Kan., Jan. 8, 1933; s. Hilliard and Galatha (Morrison) M.; Mus.B. Edn., B.Mus., U. Colo., 1957; M.A., Western Res. U., 1958. Faculty, Cleve. Mus. Settlement, 1957-59; asst. prof., chmn. piano Fla. A. and M. U., Tallahassee, 1959-60; asso. prof., chmn. piano Va. State Coll., Petersburg, 1961—. Concert tour of Europe, 1967, 69; soloist Colo. Summer Symphony, 1957, Rochester Symphony, 1963, Va. Symphony, 1965. Served with AUS, 1953-55. Mem. Am. Assn. U. Profs., Phi Mu Alpha. Home: 20908 3d Av Ettrick VA 23803 Office: Va State Coll Petersburg VA 23803

MORRISON, RICHARD DAVID, coll. pres.; b. Utica, Miss., Jan. 18, 1910; s. John and Emma (Lee) M.; B.S., Tuskegee Inst., 1931; M.Ed., Cornell U., 1941; Ph.D., Mich. State U., 1954; m. Ethel B. Williams, Sept. 11, 1934. Tchr. vocational agr., Talladega County, Ala., 1932-37; dir. agr. Ala. A. and M. Coll., Normal, 1937-62, pres., 1962—. Charter mem. Fidelity Fed. Savs. & Loan Assn., Huntsville, Ala. Mem. Ala. adv. com. Farmers Home Adminstrn.; mem. adv. com. Marshall Space Flight Center; mem. adv. com. on cotton U.S. Dept. Agr., Washington; mem. joint com. on edn. for Govt. Service. Bd. dirs. Harris Home for Children, Ala. A. and M. Coll. United Fund Raising. Recipient Alumnus of Year award Tuskegee Inst., 1963. Mem. Am. Country Life Assn., Am., Ala. tchrs. assns., Am. Assn. U. Profs. Address: Ala A and M College Normal AL 35762

MORRISON, RICHARD LELAND, III, physician; b. Charleston, S.C., Apr. 25, 1935; s. Richard Leland and Dorothy Cornelia (Plumblee) M.; B.S., The Citadel, 1957; M.D., Med. Coll. S.C., 1961; m. Jackie Elizabeth Louigno, Sept. 9, 1961; children—Phyllis Elizabeth, Jackie Roxanne. Intern Columbia (S.C.) Hosp., 1961-62; practice medicine, Georgetown, S.C., 1964—; chief staff Georgetown County Hosp., 1968-70. Mem. Georgetown City Bd. Health. Campaign chmn. Girl Scouts Am., 1968; pres. Heart Fund Georgetown County, 1970—. Bd. dirs. Georgetown-Horry Mental Health Assn. Methodist (chmn. adminstrv. bd.). Rotarian. Home: 203 Bolick St Georgetown SC 29440 Office: 1530 Highmarket St Georgetown SC 29440

MORRISON, WALTON S., lawyer; b. Big Spring, Tex., June 16, 1907; s. M. H. and Ethel (Jackson) M.; student Texas A. and M. Coll., 1926-28; J.D., Texas U., 1932; m. Mary Bell, Dec. 19, 1932. Admitted to Tex. bar, 1932: asso. Morrison & Morrison, Big Spring, 1932-37; county atty. Howard County, Tex., 1937-39; county judge Howard County, 1941-42; pvt. practice, 1946-47; county judge Howard, 1947-48; partner Morrison & Morrison, 1949-53; pvt. practice, 1953—; city atty. Big Spring, 1949-58. Served with USAF, 1942-46. Mem. Am., state, local assns. Rotarian. Home: 1501 11th Pl Big Spring TX 79720 Office: 113 E 2d St Big Spring TX

MORRISS, JAMES TOLLEISON, IV, funeral dir.; b. Petersburg, Va., May 22, 1918; s. Charles L. and Sarah (Triplett) M.; student Randolph-Macon Coll., 1940; m. Sara Taylor, Feb. 27, 1943; children—James T., Kathy M. (Mrs. Kenneth R. Bell), Jane T. Pres., J.T. Morriss & Son, Inc., Petersburg, 1936—; sec.-treas., dir. C.F. Lauterbach's Sons, Inc., Petersburg, Pres., treas. Woodlawn Meml. Gardens, Inc., Norfolk, Va. Bd. dirs. Petersburg United Fund, Southside Va. Emergency Crew, YMCA. Served with USAAF, 1942-46. Mem. Va. Funeral Dirs. Assn. (past pres.), Va. Bd. Funeral Dirs. and Embalmers (past pres.), Central Dist. Funeral Dirs. Assn. (past pres.), Nat. Selected Morticians (past pres.), Petersburg C. of C. (dir.). Episcopalian. Mason. Clubs: Rotary (past pres.), Petersburg Country, Colonial. Home: 27 Belmead St Petersburg VA 23803 Office: Wythe and Adams St PO Box 1168 Petersburg VA 23803

MORROW, ALLEN, investment co. exec.; b. Kansas City, Mo., May 6, 1919; s. Allen E. and Lulu E. (Holiday) M.; student William Jewell Coll., 1936-38, Okla. U., 1938-39; B.B.A., Mo. U., 1941; m. Mary Ellen McCambridge, Jan. 19, 1948; children—Murrey, Allen Jeffrey, Matthew Joseph. With City Nat. Bank, Kansas City, Mo., 1946-49; account exec. Merrill Lynch Pierce Fenner & Beane, 1950-53, Stern Brothers & Co., Kansas City, Mo., 1953-57; regional rep. F. Eberstadt & Co., Milw., 1957-62; regional v.p. Eaton & Howard, Inc., Atlanta, Ga., 1963—. Served with USAAF, 1941-45; ETO. Decorated D.F.C., Air medal with four oak leaf clusters. Mem. Kappa Alpha. Democrat. Presbyn. Club: Commerce (Atlanta, Ga.). Home: 1191 Lake Hearn Dr Atlanta GA 30319 Office: 6057 Roswell Rd Atlanta GA 30328

MORROW, GLENN DAVIS, govt. ofcl.; b. Madisonville, Ky., Mar. 4, 1911; s. Charly and Willie (Hughes) M.; A.B., Murray State Coll., 1933; M.A., George Peabody Coll., 1940; postgrad. U. Ky., 1941-43, U. Chgo., 1966-67; m. Mary B. Folwell, Nov., 1943; 1 son, Dan F. Research asst. Bur. Bus. Research, U. Ky., Lexington, 1941-44, prof. Coll. Commerce, 1942-49; mem. Am. Finance Mission to Iran, Tehran, 1944-45; tax specialist U.S. Army Occupation Japan, Tokyo, 1949-51; spl. asst. to commr. Ky. Dept. Revenue, Frankfort, 1941-52, exec. asst. to commr. Dept. Finance, 1952-54; research asso. Commn. Intergovtl. Relations, Washington, 1954; cons. govt. survey and reorgn. commn. Republic Philippines, Manila, 1955-56; tax adminstrn. adviser ICA Mission to Korea, Seoul, 1957; social sci. analyst, finance studies Social Security Adminstrn., Washington, 1958-63; financial economist Office Econ. Adviser, Small Bus. Adminstrn., Washington, 1963-67, supervising economist Office Planning, Research and Analysis, 1967—. Cons. to mayor Louisville, 1953, Legislative Reference Service, Library Congress, Washington, 1954, Com. Econ. Devel., Washington, 1958. Recipient certificate Appreciation, Govt. Survey and Reorgn. Commn. Philippines, 1956. Mem. Beta Gamma Sigma. Club: University of Kentucky Research (Lexington). Contbr. articles to financial jours. Home: 4848 Chevy Chase Dr Chevy Chase MD 20015 Office: 1441 L St NW Washington DC 20416

MORROW, ROBERT MICHAEL, prosthodontist; b. Osceola, Mo., Feb. 22, 1931; s. Cornelous H. and Helene (Knight) M.; student Central Mo. State Coll., Warrensburg, 1948-51; D.D.S., U. Mo., 1955; postgrad. U. Tex., 1961-62; m. Wanita Maye Gilbert, June 12, 1953; children— Robert Michael, Audrey Jane. Commd. 1st lt. USAF, 1954, advanced through grades to col., 1971; gen. dental officer 5010 USAF Hosp., Eielson AFB, Alaska, 1955-58; prosthodontist USAF Hosp., Keesler AFB, Miss., 1961: resident prosthodontics Wilford Hall USAF Hosp., 1962-64, tng. officer for prosthodontic residents, research project officer, 1964-69, asst. chmn. for resident tng., research project officer, 1969—; asso. prof. U. Tex. Dental Br., Houston. Decorated Air Force Commendation medal. Diplomate Am. Bd. Prosthodontics. Fellow Acad. Plastic Research in Dentistry (nat. v.p. 1971), Internat. (Outstanding Contbn. to Dental Lit. award Tex. sect. 1967), Am. colls. dentists, Am. Acad. Maxillofacial Prosthesis, Am. Coll. Prosthodontists; mem. Internat. Assn. for Dental Research (v.p. San Antonio chpt.). Home: 303 Beard Av Honolulu HI 96553

MORROW, ROBERT PROSSER, JR., physician; b. Faunsdale, Ala., Jan. 11, 1916; s. Robert Prosser and Mary (McConnell) M.; B.S., Davidson Coll., 1936; M.D., Tulane U., 1940; M.S. in Urology, U. Minn., 1951; m. Lelia Henry Terry, Apr. 5, 1941; children—Lelia Terry, Robert Prosser III. Intern, Touro Infirmary, New Orleans, 1940-41, resident in urology, 1941-42, sr. and chief urology service, 1962—; fellow in urology Mayo Found., Rochester, Minn., 1948-51; practice medicine specializing in urology, New Orleans, 1951—; asst. prof. urology La. State U., New Orleans, 1946-58, asso. prof., 1961-68, prof., 1968—; asso. prof. urology Tulane U., New Orleans, 1958-61; vis. surgeon So. Bapt., Sara Mayo, Flint-Goodridge hosps.; sr. surgeon Charity Hosp; cons. in urology La. Cripple Children's Service, USPHS Hosp. Served to capt. M.C., AUS, 1941-46. Diplomate Am. Bd. Urology. Mem. Am. (Southeastern sect. exec. com., La. rep. 1964-67, chmn. sci. awards com. 1966-67, chmn. advancement sci. com. 1966-68, sec. 1967—, pres. 1971-72), La. urol. assns., A.C.S., Urologist Corr. Club, Pan-Am. (diplomate in urology), Orleans Parish med. socs., So. Med. Assn., New Orleans Grad. Med. Assembly, Am. Med. Soc. Vienna, Royal Soc. Health, Sigma Xi, Kappa Delta Phi, Omicron Delta Kappa, Nu Sigma Nu, Kappa Sigma. Presbyn. (elder). Contbr. articles to med. jours. Home: 1536 Webster St New Orleans LA 70118 Office: Med Arts Bldg 3439 Prytania St New Orleans LA 70115

MORROW, RUSSELL OLIVER, judge; b. Waterloo, Ia., Oct. 27, 1907; s. Bert Lincoln and Lulu (Bovee) M.; A.B., Washington and Lee U., 1931, LL.B., 1932; m. Victoria Dahlberg, Dec. 16, 1936. Admitted to Fla. bar, 1933; practiced in West Palm Beach, Fla., 1933; states atty., 1942; circuit judge, West Palm Beach, 1955—. Mem. Fla. Ho. of Reps., 1936-47, Fla. Senate, 1950-55. Served to capt. USNR, World War II. Mem. Am. Legion, V.F.W., Fla. Bar, Am. Bar Assn. Home: 1314 N Lakeside Dr Lake Worth FL 33466 Office: County Courthouse West Palm Beach FL 33401

MORSE, F. D., JR., dentist; b. Glen Lyn, Va., Apr. 5, 1928; s. Frank D. and Ida Estell (Davis) M.; B.S., Concord Coll., 1951; D.D.S., Med. Coll. Va., 1955; m. Patsy Lee Apple, Feb. 4, 1967; 1 son, Fortis Davis. Free lance photographer, 1950-56; practice dentistry, Pearisburg, Va., 1958—; mem. staff Giles Hosp., Pearisburg, 1958—. Served from asst. dental surgeon to sr. asst. dental surgeon USPHS, 1955-57; assigned to USCG, 1957-58. Mem. Am., S.W. Va. dental assns., Assn. Mil. Surgeons, A.A.A.S., Nat. Assn. Advancement Sci., Fedn. Dentaire Internat., Internat. Platform Assn., W.Va. Collegiate Acad. Sci., Beta Phi. Kiwanian. Home: 202 Poplar Lane Pearisburg VA 24134 Office: Giles Profl Bldg Pearisburg VA 24134

MORSE, GENEVIEVE FORBES (MRS. FREDERICK TRACY MORSE), club woman; b. New Rochelle, N.Y., June 8, 1905; d. James and Mabel (Sabin) Forbes; B.A., La. Poly. Inst., 1932; m. Frederick Tracy Morse, Jan. 1, 1926; 1 son Robert Frederick. Pres., U. Va. Hosp. Circle, 1947-49, bd. dirs., 1945-66; Va. corr. sec. D.A.R., 1953-56, editor Va. News Bull., 1953-59, vice regent, 1956-59, regent, 1959-62, v.p. gen. from Va., 1962-64, curator gen. nat. soc., 1965-68, adviser D.A.R. Museum, 1968—, state chmn. Va. Room, in Washington, 1968-71, mem. com., 1971—; Va. rec. sec. Daus.

Colonial Wars, 1953-56, chaplain, 1959-62, pres., 1956-59; nat. chmn. nat. def. com., 1959-62, nat. pres., 1962-65, nat. chmn. historic research and preservation com., 1968-71, chmn. by laws com., 1971—. Mem. Daus. 17th Century, Order of Crown, Daus. Am. Colonists, Daus. Barons Runnemede, Order Descs. Colonial Clergy, Hereditary Order Descs. Colonial Govs. (registrar gen. 1961-67, gov. gen. 1967-70), Soc. Descs. of William I, the Conqueror, Albermarle Hist. Soc., Nat. Soc. Am. Royal Descent, Nat. Trust Hist. Preservation, Ky. Hist. Soc., Sigma Tau Delta, Kappa Delta (nat. council 1953-67, nat. editor The Angelos 1953-59, pres. Alpha South province 1950-54, nat. pres. 1959-67, nat. historiographer 1970). Epsicopalian. Editor: Monticello Cook Book, 3d edit., 1950. Author: Through the Years, and Other Poems, 1945. Contbr. poetry to various anthologies. Home: Retreat Albermarle County Charlottesville VA 22902 Office: 3426 University Station Charlottesville VA 22903

MORTON, ANSELM HERBERT, JR., sales exec.; b. Cullman, Ala., June 17, 1910; s. Anselm Herbert and Florence (Felter) M.; B.S., Ala. Poly. Inst., 1945; m. Clara Crenshaw, June 6, 1935; children—Geralyn Crenshaw (Mrs. John G. Austin, Jr.), Anselm Herbert III; m. 2d, Magdalene Eck, Aug. 3, 1949; children—Elizabeth Ellen (Mrs. Robert Brasington III), John Eugene. San. engr. Ala. Health Dept., Montgomery, 1934-36; civil engr. ARMCO Steel Co., Atlanta, 1936-41; commd. 2d lt., USAF (Res.), 1934, advanced through grades to lt. col., 1945; ret., 1962; pres. Morton Sales Co., 1946-65; owner Herbert Morton, Sales Engr., Montgomery, 1965—. Dir. Montgomery Choral Soc., 1962-67; mem. Arts Council Montgomery, Montgomery County Bd. Revenue, 1964—. Vice chmn. Montgomery County Rep. Party, 1961-64, now sec. Registered profl. engr., Ala. Mem. Montgomery Bldg. Material Dealers Assn. (past pres.), Soc. Am. Mil. Engrs., Res. Officers Assn. Episcopalian. Lion (past pres.). Clubs: Auburn, Woodley Country (Montgomery). Home: 1605 E Fairview Av Montgomery AL 36106

MORTON, CHARLES BRINKLEY, clergyman, former state rep. and state senator; b. Meridian, Miss., Jan. 6, 1926; s. Albert Cole and Jean (Brinkley) M.; J.D. with distinction, U. Miss., 1949; M.Div. optime merens, U. South, 1959; m. Virginia Roseborough, Aug. 26, 1948; children—Charles Brinkley, Mary Virginia. Admitted to Miss. bar, 1949; practiced in Senatobia, Miss., 1949-56; mem. firm Thomas & Morton, 1952-56; ordained to ministry P.E. Ch. as deacon and priest, 1949; priest-in-charge Ch. of Incarnation, West Point, Miss., 1959-62; rector Grace-St. Luke's Ch., Memphis 1962—. Mem. Miss. Commn. Interstate Cooperation, 1952-56, Miss. State Hist. Commn., 1952-56, Miss. State Sovereignty Commn., 1955-56. Chmn. N. Miss. Polio Fund, 1954. Mem. Miss. House of Reps., 1948-52, Miss. Senate, 1952-56. Served with AUS, World War II, Korea; now lt. col., chaplain Res. Decorated Silver Star, Bronze Star medal with cluster, Purple Heart, Combat Inf. Badge; recipient Freedoms Found. Honor medal, 1967-68. Mem. Miss. State Bar (complaint commr. 1953), Internat. Soc. Bibl. Lit. and Exegesis, Mil. Order World Wars. Am. Legion (past post comdr.), Phi Delta Phi, Tau Kappa Alpha, Omicron Delta Kappa, Phi Delta Theta. Democrat. Rotarian. Contbr. articles law and hist. jours. Home: 246 S Belvedere Blvd Memphis TN 38104 Office: 1720 Peabody Av Memphis TN 38104

MORTON, JAMES HARRY, diversified industry exec.; b. Charlotte, N.C., Feb. 18, 1939; s. John Harry and Mary Elizabeth (Stikeleather) M.; grad. Am. Inst. Banking, 1964; m. Yvonne Marie Haigler, Nov. 14, 1958; 1 dau., Tina Marie. Staff accountant N.C. Nat. Bank, Charlotte, 1956-66; pub. accountant Conrad, Hoey, East & Co., Charlotte, 1966-69; controller, sec.-treas. Aabco Industries, Inc., Gaffney, S.C., 1969-71, pres. Accounting Assos. Bus. Services, 1971—, Gaffney Distbg. Co., Inc., 1971—, Morris Constrn. & Devel. Corp. (all Gaffney). Nat. v.p. pub. relations Distributive Edn. Clubs Am., 1955-57, pres. N.C. State, 1955-57, pres. N.C. Western Region, 1955-57. Chmn. bd. dirs. Gaffney Day Sch. Mem. Nat. Assn. Accountants. Methodist (mem. adminstrv. bd.). Club: Cherokee Sertoma (dir.). (Gaffney). Home: 219 Trenton Rd Gaffney SC 29340 Office: PO Box 1116 230 E Smith St Gaffney SC 29340

MORTON, RICHARD ALBERT DUNLAP, JR., physician; b. El Paso, Tex., Sept. 6, 1932; s. Richard Albert Dunlap and Julianne (More) M.; student Tex. Western Coll., 1950-53, U. Colo., 1952; M.D., Tulane U., 1957; postgrad. N.Y. U., 1959-61; m. Margaret A. Brown, Dec. 27, 1954; children—Priscilla, Richard Albert Dunlap III, Margaret and Maria (twins), Arthur and Andrew (twins). Intern, St. Vincent's Hosp., N.Y.C., 1957-58; resident otolaryngology Bellevue Hosp., N.Y.C., 1958-61; instr. otolaryngology N.Y. U. Coll. Medicine and U. Hosp., 1959-61; chief Eye, Ear, Nose and Throat Clinic, USAF Hosp., Maxwell Afb. Montgomery, Ala., 1961-63; cons. dept. hearing and speech N.M. State U., Las Cruces; cons. otolaryngology So. Pacific R.R., T. & P. R.R., Santa Fe R.R., Wm. Beaumont Army Hosp., 1963—; mem. active staff Providence Meml. Hosp., Hotel Dieu Hosp.; courtesy staff Southwestern Gen. Hosp., Sun Towers Hosp. Cons. ear, nose and throat USAF, Southeastern U.S., 1961-63, Holloman Air Force Base; chief, ear, nose and throat service Providence Meml. Hosp., 1964-65, Hotel Dieu Hosp., 1965-66, 69-70. Mem. Boy Scout Council, El Paso. Bd. trustees Pan Am. Tumor Inst.; chmn. alumni fund for excellence U. Tex. at El Paso, 1970; trustee El Paso Ind. Sch. Dist. Served to capt. USAF, 1961-63. Diplomate Am. Bd. Otolaryngology. Fellow Am. Acad. Ophthalmology and Otolaryngology; mem. Am., Tex., El Paso County med. assns., Tex. Otolaryn. Assn. (trustee 1966-68), A.C.S., Am. Cancer Soc. (chmn.), Phi Chi, Sigma Alpha Epsilon. Home: 5043 Montoya St El Paso TX 79922 Office: 1501 Arizona El Paso TX 79902

MORTON, T. BALLARD, JR., broadcasting exec. Pres., WAVE, Louisville. Office: 725 S Floyd St Louisville KY 40203

MORTON, THRUSTON BALLARD, banker, former U.S. senator; b. Louisville, Aug. 19, 1907; s. David Cummings and Mary Harris (Ballard) M.; student Woodberry Forest Sch., Orange, Va., 1922-25; B.A., Yale, 1929; m. Belle Clay Lyons, Apr. 18, 1931; children—Thruston Ballard, Clay Lyons. Held various positions with Ballard & Ballard, Louisville, 1929—, was chmn. bd.; mem. 80th to 82d Congresses, 3d Ky. Dist.; asst. sec. state for Congl. Relations. Dept. State, Washington, 1953-56; U.S. senator from Ky., 1957-69; vice chmn. Liberty Nat. Bank & Trust Co., 1969—. Dir. Brown Forman Distillers Inc., Louisville, Pillsbury Co., Mpls., Pittston Co., N.Y.C., Tex. Gas Transmission, Owensboro, Ky. Chmn. bd. Churchill Downs, Inc. Chmn. Nat. Rep. Senatorial Campaign Com., 1963-67. Trustee Frontier Nursing Service, Lincoln Inst. of Ky. Chmn. Rep. Nat. Com., 1959-61. Served as comdr. USNR, 1941-45. Mem. Order Cincinnati, Alpha Delta Phi. Republican. Episcopalian. Home: 1415 Willow Av Louisville KY 40204

MOSBY, JOHN SINGLETON, judge; b. Holly Springs, Miss., Aug. 4, 1903; s. Edward Littleberry and Alta Dandridge (Shackleford) M.; student Ark. Law Sch., 1925; m. Catherine Corinne Mellard, Apr. 8, 1938; 1 son, John Singleton. Admitted to Ark. bar, 1925, U.S. Supreme Ct. bar, 1936; city atty., Lepanto, 1925-63; Caraway, 1949-59, Tyronza, 1950-63; judge 2d jud. dist. Ark., 1963. Mayor, Lepanto, Ark., 1927-30; mem. Ark. Ho. of Reps., 1943-44; mem. senate, 31st Dist., 1945-49; bd. pub. utilities, Lepanto, 1961-65; commr., exec. sec. Lepanto Park Commn., 1953-65. Chmn. County Welfare Bd., 1943- 49; dir. Ark. Assn. for Crippled, 1957—; founder Lepanto Student Aid, Inc., 1956; chmn. City Planning Commn., 1960-64; sec. Lepanto Indsl. Devel. Corp., 1956—. Pres., Ark. Young Democrats Club, 1942-50. Named Lepanto Man of Year, 1964. Mem. Lepanto C. of C. (pres. 1959-62), Am., Ark., N.E. Ark. (pres. 1955-56), Poinsett County (pres. 1942-54) bar assns., S.A.R. (Ark. pres. 1972, chpt. pres. 1970—), Sons Confederacy. Methodist. Mason (K.T., Shriner). Clubs: Rivermont, Memphis Yacht, Summit (Memphis); Lions (pres. 1932-34), Rotary (pres. 1962-63). Home: 400 Berney St Lepanto AR 72354 Office: 111 Berney St Lepanto AR 72354

MOSCA, LOUIS, fire chief; b. Lake Charles, La., Aug. 21, 1925; s. Bernardo and Lucia (Saltaformaggi) M.; grad. high sch.; m. Mary Irona Fruge, Oct. 18, 1947; children—Paula Jane (Mrs. Kelley Vigo), Vincent Lee, Emelie E. With Fire Dept., Lake Charles, 1955—, driver, 1957-67, capt., 1967-68, chief, 1968—. Served with USAAF, 1943-46; PTO. Mem. S.W. La. Mut. Aid Soc. (pres.), Internat. Fire Chiefs Assn., La. Arson and Fire Prevention Assn., La. Firemens Assn. Home: 3434 Kingham Rd Lake Charles LA 70601 Office: PO Box 1703 Lake Charles LA 70601

MOSCOSO, TEODORE, govt. ofcl.; b. Barcelena, Spain, Nov. 26, 1910 (parents U.S. citizens); s. Teodoro and Alejandrina (Mora) M.; student Phila. Coll. Pharmacy and Sci., 1928; B.S., U. Mich., 1932; m. Gloria Sanchez Vilella, July 3, 1937; children—Margarita, Jose Teodoro. Gen. mgr. Moscoso Hno. & Co., Inc., Ponce, P.R., 1932-39; pres. Puerto Rican-Am. Drug Co., Inc., 1936-39; vice chmn., exec. dir. Ponce (P.R.) Housing Authority, 1938-42; pres., gen. mgr. P.R. Indsl. Devel. Co., 1942-50; adminstr. Econ. Devel. Adminstrn., P.R., 1950-60; ambassador to Venezuela, 1961-62; U.S. coordinator Alliance for Progress, 1962-64; spl. adviser to asst. sec. state for internat. affairs, 1964—. Chmn. bd. Commonwealth Oil Refining Co.; dir. Rexach Constrn. Co., Arthur D. Little, Inc., Banco de Ponce, Santurce, P.R. Trustee Manhattan Coll., Cath. U. P.R. Mem. Soc. Internat. Devel., Coll. Pharmacists P.R. (pres. 1938), Am. Soc. Pub. Adminstrn. (pres. P.R. chpt. 1952), Rho Chi. Mem. Popular Democratic Party. Clubs: Fifth Avenue, Hermitage, Casino de Puerto Rico, Bankers, U. Mich., A.F.D.A. Address: Palma Real Condominium 2 Madrid St San Juan PR 00907

MOSCOVITZ, ISADORE, editor pub.; b. Jacksonville, Fla., Sept. 15, 1911; s. Joseph H. and Anne (Zossman) M.; B.S., U. Fla., 1933; m. Ethel Katz, Oct. 7, 1934; children—Arlene (Mrs. Bernard J. Shainbrown), David, Howard. Editor, pub. So. Jewish Weekly, 1933—; owner Evergreen Press, 1945—. Served to maj. AUS, 1941-45. Mem. Zionist Orgn. Am. (v.p. Southeastern region), Phi Kappa Phi, Sigma Delta Chi. Democrat. Mem. B'nai B'rith. Club: Beauclerc Country. Home: 1320 Lakewood Rd Jacksonville 7 FL 32207 Office: 1836 Evergreen Jacksonville 6 FL 32206

MOSELEY, CARL MORRIS, JR., architect; b. Bessemer, Ala., Dec. 23, 1917; s. Carl Morris and Anneola (Bingham) M.; B.S. in Aero. Engring., U. Ala., 1941; B.Arch., Ga. Inst. Tech., 1948; m. Mary Florentine Schuyler, Aug. 1, 1940. With Glenn L. Martin Co., Balt., 1940-41, Bush-Brown, Gailey, Heffernan, Architects, Atlanta, 1947-48, Don. B. Schuyler, Architect, Tuscaloosa, Ala., 1948-49; pvt. practice architecture, Tuscaloosa, 1950—. Served to maj. C.E., AUS, 1941-45. Decorated Bronze Star. Mem. A.I.A., Phi Kappa Phi, Tau Beta Pi, Chi Epsilon. Mason (Shriner), Rotarian. Clubs: Tuscaloosa Country; Millwood (Sawyerville, Ala.). Prin. works include banks, schs. Home: 23 Beech Hills Rd Tuscaloosa AL 35401 Office: 817 21st Av Tuscaloosa AL 35401

MOSELEY, DONALD RAY, dentist; b. Ringgold, La., Oct. 19, 1933; s. Dayton Lee and Rose Ernestine (Smith) M.; student La. State U., 1952-55; D.D.S., Baylor U., 1959; m. Patricia Ann Lessard, Apr. 21, 1962; children—Donald Ray, Lee Charles. Practice of dentistry, Ringgold, La., 1961—; dir. Bank of Ringgold, pres. Ringgold Devel. Corp., 1968—. Alderman, Town of Ringgold, 1966—. Served to lt., Dental Corps, USNR, 1959-61. Mem. Am., Fourth Dist. dental assns., Kappa Sigma, Xi Psi Phi. Lion (pres. 1970-71). Home: Parkway Ringgold LA 71068 Office: Bienville Hwy Ringgold LA 71068

MOSELEY, GERALD MORSE, aerospace engr.; b. Tarrant, Ala., July 16, 1930; s. Malcolm Daniel and Nancy (Morse) M.; student Howard Coll., 1954-55; B.S. in Aero. Engring. Auburn U., 1957; m. Nellie Sue Thomas, Aug. 17, 1953; children—Gerald Morse Jr., Thomas, Susan, John. Flight test engr. Convair, Ft. Worth, Tex., 1957-60; research engr. The Boeing Airplane Co., Seattle, 1960-63; prin. engr. Teledyne-Brown Engring., Huntsville, Ala., 1963—. Mem. advancement com. Tenn. Valley council Boy Scouts Am., 1965-68, instnl. rep., 1964-69. Served with USN, 1948-52. Mem. Am. Inst. Astronautics and Aeros. Acoust. Soc. Am. Baptist. Mason. Club: Brown Engring. Mgmt. Home: 2004 Clubview Dr Huntsville AL 35810 Office: 300 Sparkman Dr Huntsville AL 35807

MOSELEY, JAMES ALAN, physician; b. Painesville, O., Oct. 31, 1931; s. John Wilber and Florence G. (Toomey) M.; student U. Fla., 1950, Ga. Tech., 1952-53; B.S., Mass. Inst. Tech., 1956; postgrad Canisius Coll., 1961, State U. N.Y., 1962-64; M.D., U. Miami, 1966; m. Barbara Joan Marshall Anderson, Sept. 16, 1955; children— James Alan, Jonathan Alden, Cameron Elizabeth. Asst. to tech. and research dir. Steel Founders Soc. of Am., Cleve., 1956-58; v.p. Altas Steel Castings Co., Buffalo, N.Y., 1962; intern Gorgas Hosp., Canal Zone, 1966-67; practice of gen. medicine, Boca Raton, Fla., 1967; mem. staff Boca Raton Community Hosp., sec., 1971-72. Pres. Found. for study of learning problems, Boca Raton, 1970—; adviser Alden Acad. for Learning Problems. Served with USNR, 1950-51. Mem. Fla., Palm Beach County med. socs. Editor: Research Jour., 1956-58. Home: 360 SW 6th St Boca Raton FL 33432 Office: 600 S Dixie St Boca Raton FL 33432

MOSELEY, VINCE, physician, educator; b. Orangeburg, S.C., Oct. 29, 1912; s. William Lawrence and Jessie George (Vince) M.; student Clemson Coll., 1929-31; A.B., Duke, 1933, M.D., 1936; m. Matilda Elizabeth Holleman, Oct. 11, 1938; children—Robert Dwight, Julia Caroline, Kelsey Elizabeth, William Vince, Matilda Raine, Esther Jane, Lawrence Holleman, Selma Jessica. Intern, Duke Hosp., Durham, N.C., 1937-38, resident, 1938-39; fellow, asst. Duke Sch. Medicine, 1939-40; fellow asso. U. Pa. Sch. Medicine, 1940-41; asso. Med. U. S.C. Coll. Medicine, 1947, asst. prof., 1947, asso. prof., 1948, prof. medicine, co-chmn. dept., 1949—, dean clin. medicine, 1960-65; chief med. service VA Hosp., Charleston, 1965-69; dir. div. continuing edn. Med. U. S.C., 1969—; coordinator S. C. Regional Med. Program, 1969—. Trustee Presbyn. Coll., Clinton, 1957-66; hosp. adv. council S.C. Bd. Health; chmn. bd. trustees S.C. Retarded Childrens Habilitation Center, 1963-69; mem. S.C. Commn. Mental Retardation, Govs. Adv. Council Vocational Rehab. Trustee Palmer Coll. Served from lt. to col. extended active duty, AUS, 1941-47. Fellow A.C.P. (gov. S.C. 1969) A.C.S.; mem. Am., S.C., So. med. assns., Soc. Exptl. Biology and Medicine, Am. Clin. and Climatol. Assn., Am., So. socs. clin. research, N.Y., S.C. acads. sci., A.A.A.S., Kappa Alpha, Alpha Omega Alpha, Phi Chi. Presbyn. Kiwanian. Home: 51 E Battery St Charleston SC 29401 Office: 80 Barre St Charleston SC 29401

MOSELEY, MRS. VINCE (MATILDA ELIZABETH HOLLEMAN MOSELEY), civic worker; b. Durham, N.C., Mar. 25, 1911; d. William Dunn and Alberta (Ratterree) Holleman; student Meredith Coll., 1927-29; A.B., Duke, 1931, R.N., 1934, B.S., in Nursing Edn., 1936; m. Vince Moseley, Oct. 11, 1938; children—Dwight, Julia, Kelsey, Vince, Raine, Esther, Lawrence, Selma. Surg. supr. Duke Hosp., 1936-38, asso. prof. nursing edn., 1942-45, prof. nursing arts, 1938-40; instr. English, Palmer Coll., Charleston, S.C. Pres. Charleston County Health Council, 1948-50, Charleston County Med. Aux., 1958—; sec. S.C. State Med. Aux., 1959; v.p. Charleston Community Chest, 1956—; bd. dirs. N.C. and S.C. United Fund, 1958—; treas. Mental Health Assn., 1959-61; mem. Salvation Army Bd., 1957—, Tb Assn. Bd., 1959-61; Am. Cancer Bd., 1957—; active Girl Scouts Am.; pub. relations chmn. League Women Voters, 1952, adv. bd. Juvenile Ct., 1958—; sec. Family Agy. Bd., 1954-58; commr. Housing Commn., Charleston, S.C., 1959-72; mem. bd. Free Kindergarten Assn., Jr. League Speech Sch.; sec. Florence Crittenton Home Bd., 1959-61; mem. Charleston County Planning Bd., 1958, Charleston County Charter Commn., 1969; bd. dirs. Charleston Symphony Bd., 1959—, Retarded Children's Council, 1964—; mem. Com. Vocational Rehab. Retarded Adults; mem. Soc. Preservation Old Dwellings. Vice pres. Charleston City Democratic Party. Trustee Charleston County Hosp. Named Woman of Year, Charleston Fedn. Women's Clubs, 1955; recipient service to mankind award Sertoma Club, 1965; youth appreciation award Optimist Club, 1965. Mem. Internat. Order Kings Daus. and Sons (pres. S.C. 1959-61), Am. Assn. U. Women (pres. 1957-58), U.D.C. (sec. 1949), Benevolent Soc., Carolina Art Assn. (mem. bd.), Charleston Hist. Soc., Sigma Theta Tau (charter), Beta Sigma Phi. Presbyn. Home: 51 E Bay St Charleston SC 29401

MOSELEY, WILLIAM WARD, architect; b. Lawrenceville, Va., Mar. 26, 1930; s. William Stuart and Anne Gray (Duke) M.; B.S., Va. Poly. Inst., 1952, postgrad., 1952; m. Jewel Mason Moncure, Aug. 22, 1959; children—William Ward, Robert Moncure. Project mgr. Merrill C. Lee, Richmond, Va., 1955-59; project mgr. Marcellus Wright & Son, Richmond, 1959-65; partner Marcellus Wright & Partners, 1965-70; prin. William Ward Moseley, architect-planner, Richmond, 1970-72; pres. Moseley-Henning Asso., Inc., Richmond, 1972—; faculty interior design dept. Va. Commonwealth U., 1970-71. Pres. Highland Hills Community Corp., Bon Air, Va., 1964-65. Served with USAF, 1952-54. Recipient Design award of merit for Richmond Residence, 1966. Mem. A.I.A., Am. Soc. Planning Ofcls., Constrn. Specifications Inst., Va. Citizens Planning Assn., Va. Assn. Professions, Va. Poly. Inst. Alumni Assn., Pi Delta Epsilon, Omicron Delta Kappa. Methodist. Club: Salisbury Country (Midlothian, Va.). Contbr. articles profl. jours. Home: 8410 Halidan Dr Bon Air VA 23235 Office: 2922 Hathaway Rd Richmond VA 23225

MOSER, LEROY CARROLL, ret. state ofcl.; real estate cons.; b. Boonsboro, Md., Sept. 27, 1908; s. Henry C. and Emma (Martz) M.; student U. Md., 1927-30; spl. real estate course Johns Hopkins U., 1959-61, Am. Inst. Real Estate Courses, 1959-62; m. Mary Julia Kirby, Jan. 3, 1929 (dec.); m. 2d, Delmar Amelia Dyott, Nov. 28, 1931; 1 son, Charles C. With Md. State Roads Commn., 1930-69, constrn. div., 1930-37, asst. chief right of way div., 1948-51, chief, right of way div., 1951-69. Mem. Howard County (Md.) Met. Commn., 1954-63; mem. land acquisition and control of hwy. access com. Hwy. Research Bd., 1957-69. Mem. Am. Assn. State Hwy. Ofcls. (chmn. right of way com. 1968), Am. Right of Way Assn (pres. Potomac chpt. 1957), Am. Soc. Appraisers (pres. Md. chpt. 1960-61), Soc. Real Estate Appraisers (pres. Balt. chpt. 1969-70), Real Estate Bd. Greater Balt., Md. Assn. Engrs., Am. Pub. Works Assn., Md. Real Estate Appraisal Council, Howard County Grand Jurors Assn. Mason (32deg., Shriner). Contbr. articles in field to profl. jours. Home: 10284 Monarch Dr Imperial Point Largo FL 33540

MOSES, WILLIAM HENRY, educator; b. nr. Richmond, Va., Aug. 20, 1901; s. William Henry and Julia (Trent) M.; B.S., Pa. State Coll., Pa. State Coll., 1933; student N.Y.U., 1939, Columbia, 1945; m. Julia Ann Mason, Aug. 15, 1935; children—William Henry III, Michael Lynn (Mrs. Frank B. Holland). Tchr. architecture Hampton Inst., Va., 1934-71, prof. emeritus, 1971—, chmn. dept. architecture, 1942-65, archtl. cons., 1969—. Cons. Bricks Sch., Enfield, N.C. Mem. N.A.A.C.P. (chpt. pres. 1960-62), Nat. Builders Assn., Nat. Tech. Assn., Am. Assn. U. Profs., Omega Psi Phi. Elks. Designer Whittaker Meml. Hosp., Newport News, Va.; Peoples Bldg. & Loan Assn., Hampton, Va., 1937. Author column A Dark Point of View, 1969—. Home: 2120 Garner Terrace Newport. News VA 23607 Office: Hampton Inst Hampton VA 23360

MOSLEY, ELLIS GREENLEE, educator; b. Mayflower, Ark., Jan. 30, 1901; s. Wiley Thornton and Maude (Greenlee) M.; A.B. magna cum laude, Hendrix Coll., 1923; B.D., Austin Theol. Sem., 1926; M.A., U. Tex., 1949; D.D., Ark. Coll., 1956; m. Mary Elizabeth Newton, May 19, 1926; children—James, Edward. Ordained to ministry Presbyn. Ch., 1926; minister, Hamilton, Tex., 1926-29, Clifton, 1929-30; asso. Wiley Mosley Bus. Interests, Faulkner County, Ark., 1931-46; tchr. Mayflower (Ark.) High Sch., 1946-48; faculty Ark. Coll., Batesville, 1948—, asso. prof. religion and social studies, 1953—, acting pres., summer 1952. Minister part time supply chs. E. Ark. Presbytery, 1948-67; commr. Gen. Assembly Presbyn. Ch. U.S., 1956; chaplain Ark. S.A.R., 1955-57. Recorder, Mayflower, 1940-47; mem. Ark. Gov.'s Citizen's Adv. Com., 1967—. Mem. Am. Acad. Polit. and Social Sci., Am. Acad. Religion, Am., Ark. hist. assns., Southwestern Sociology Assn., Ark. Acad. Sci., Independence County Hist. Soc. (pres. 1964-65). Democrat. Mason (Shriner). Home: 1950 Maple St Batesville AR 72501

MOSS, ALLEN MILLER, educator; b. Bethpage, Tenn., Aug. 31, 1923; s. Ulyses Duke and Ruth (Galloway) M.; A.B., Western Ky. U., 1950, M.A., 1962; Ph.D., U. Ala., 1968; m. Lucele Murphy, Aug. 5, 1950; children—Cheryl Anne, David Allen. Band master Shepherdsville (Ky.) Pub. Schs., 1950-51; price analyst Reynolds Metals Co., Louisville, 1951-55; tchr. math. Trigg County High Sch., Cadiz, Ky., minister United Methodist Ch., Ky., also Ala., 1955—; prof. psychology Florence State U., 1966—. Chmn. treatment com. for drug addiction Muscle Shoals Mental Health Assn. Served with AUS, 1945-47. Mem. Am. Assn. U. Profs., Ala., Nat. edn. assns., Phi Delta Kappa. Methodist. Home: 302 Park Lane Florence AL 35630 Office: Florence State U Florence AL 35630

MOSS, CHARLES BASIL, physician; b. Medicine Park, Okla., Sept. 13, 1925; s. Robert Frank and Lovie Vitula (Williamson) M.; B.S., Southwestern La. U., 1947; M.D., U. Okla., 1949; m. Pauline Joyce Montgomery, June 15, 1947; children—Paulette Cecila, Leslie Charlene, Anita Louellen. Intern, St. Joseph's Hosp., Fort Worth, 1949-50; gen. practice medicine, Lubbock, 1952—; mem. staff West Texas Methodist hosps. Med. dir., disaster program. A.R.C., 1970. Mem. City-County Child Welfare Bd., 1953-56. Del., Tex. Republican Convention, 1966, precinct chmn., fund raiser, 1966-67. Bd. dirs. W. Tex. Hosp. and Med. Arts Clinic, Lubbock, 1952—, Drug Crisis Center, 1970—, Parkdale Sick Children's Clinic, 1960—, Wesley Found., 1969, chmn., 1970—. Served with USNR, 1943-45, 50-52. Mem. Acad. Gen. Practice (pres. 1956), Sons of Republic of Tex. (pres. 1971). Club: Lubbock Riders. Methodist. Med. dir., panelist, prodn. 4 shows TV, 1968, panelist drug abuse, 1969, 71; lectr. sex edn.,

1955—. Home: 5508 Av T Lubbock TX 79412 Office: 1318 Broadway St Lubbock TX 79401

MOSS, EDWARD KIPER,, econ. affairs counsel; b. Lancaster, Pa., June 23, 1916; s. Lestre R. and Henrietta (Kiper) M.; student Culver Mil. Acad., 1930-34, Yale, 1934-35, George Washington U., 1939-40; m. Virginia Bennett Moore, Nov. 23, 1939 (div. 1951). Staff writer Atlantic City (N.J.) Evening Union, 1935-36, Atlantic City Press, 1936-37; South Jersey corr. Phila. Inquirer, Camden (N.J.) Courier, also A.P., 1937; pres. Edward K. Moss Asso. (pub. relations cons.), 1937-39; asst. chief analysis and reports div. Nat. Emergency Council, 1939-40; chief information sect. office govt. reports Exec. Office of Pres., 1940-42; dir. pub. relations Am. Mgmt. Assn., 1946-50; bd. dirs. Attitudes, Inc. (pub. relations cons.), 1948-50; asst. adminstr. in charge pub. information NPA, 1950-52; asst. adminstr. in charge pub. information DPA, 1951-53; chmn. Def. Prodn. Information Com. (inter-agency), 1951-53; pub., econ. affairs adviser to govts. Africa, Europe, Asia, U.S. Govt. agys. and industries, 1953—; mem. Nat. Def. Exec. Reserve, 1957—; pub. relations counsel U.S. John Marshall Bi-Centennial Commn., 1955, Woodrow Wilson Centennial Commn., 1956; dep. asst. dir. war on poverty U.S. Office Econ. Opportunity, 1965-66; pub. affairs adv. White House Conf. on Civil Rights, 1966; cons. cabinet com. Mexican-Am. Affairs, 1968. Served from ensign to lt. comdr. USNR, 1942-45, charge Combat Info. Center Sch., New Caledonia, 1942-43, air def., combat information corps, staff, Fleet Adm. W.F. Halsey, Jr., 1944-45, office of Chief of Naval Operations, Navy Dept., Washington, in charge navy electronics operational tng. Decorated Bronze Star with Combat V.; awarded Navy Unit commendation, Presdl. Unit citation. Mem. Am. Acad. Polit. and Social Scis., Acad. Polit. Sci., Assn. Electronic Res. Officers (exec. sec. 1946-51, bd. govs. since 1946), Pub. Relations Soc. Am. (research, edn. com., chmn. subcom. social sci. research), Soc. Internat. Devel., Asia Soc., African Studies Assn., Internat. Soc. Aviation Writers, Marine Hist. Assn. Clubs: Nat. Press, Yale (N.Y. City), Darien (Conn.) Five Mile River Canoe and Sailing (rear commodore 1949-50); Army and Navy (Washington). Founder Pub. Relations Index on Social Sci. Research. Address: 1600 Foxhall Rd NW Washington DC 20007

MOSS, JAMES MERCER, physician; b. Bradley, Ga., Dec. 15, 1917; s. Fred August and Rosa (Mercer) M.; M.D., U. Va., 1941; m. Rachel Scott Bybee, Sept. 6, 1941; children—James Marion, Fred Aubrey (dec.), William Wallace, Robert Edward. Intern U. Va. Hosp., 1941-42, resident medicine, 1947-49; fellow, instr. endocrinology Duke U., 1946-47; pvt. practice internal medicine, Alexandria, Va., 1949—; instr. clin. medicine Georgetown U., 1949-51, clin. asst. prof. medicine, 1952-56, clin. asso. prof., 1956-62, clin. prof., 1962—; dir. diabetic clinic Georgetown U. Hosp., 1949—, D.C. Gen. Hosp., 1950-55; active staff Circle Terrace Hosp., pres., 1965-68. Dir. City Bank & Trust, 1963-71, Circle Terrace, Inc., 1965— (all Alexandria, Va.). Treas. No. Va. Med. Com. Good Govt., 1960, 62. Chmn. Va.-Med. Polit. Action Com., 1966-67; chmn. Va. Physicians for Reelection of the President, 1972. Served from lt. to maj., M.C., AUS, 1942-46. Recipient awards for sci. exhibits. Fellow A.C.P., Am. Coll. Cardiology; mem. Am. (pharm. com.), Va. (pres. 1962-63) socs. internal medicine, Am. Heart Assn., Am., Va. (pres. 1971-72) diabetes assns., Endocrine Soc., So. Med. Assn., Med. Soc. Va. (pres. 1970-71), Diabetes Assn. D.C. (pres. 1956-57), Med. Council Washington Met. Area (pres. 1958-59), Heart Assn. No. Va. (pres. 1964-65), Am. Podiatry Assn. (hon.), Am. Med. Writers Assn., Alexandria Med. Soc. (pres. 1958-59), Med. Alumni Assn. U.Va. (pres. 1965-66), Phi Chi, ALpha Omega Alpha. Editorial bd. Va. Med. Monthly, 1961-70. Editorial cons. Am. Acad. Gen. Practice, 1969—, Author: Fundamentals of Diabetic Management. Contbr. articles to profl. jours. Home: 319 Mansion Dr Alexandria VA 22302 Office: 1707 Osage St Alexandria VA 22302

MOSS, JAMES THOMAS, devel. co. exec.; b. Youngsville, N.C., July 3, 1927; s. William Thomas and Lula (Wade) M.; B.S., N.C. State U., 1947, M.S., 1949; m. Margaret McLeod Bunn, Dec. 18, 1948; children— James Thomas, William Howard, David Bunn. Co-owner Mosswood Farms, Youngsville, 1949—; v.p. 1st Union Nat. Bank, Raleigh, N.C., 1968—, Pres. N.C. Found. Seed Producers, 1968, Mem. N.C. Banking Commn., 1966—. Pres. N.C. Soil and Water Conservation Dist., 1966, Youngsville Devel. Corp., 1967—. Mem. Sigma Xi, Alpha Zeta, Alpha Gamma Rho, Phi Kappa Phi. Mason, Lion. Home: PO Box 268 Youngsville NC 27596 Office: 1st Union Nat Bank Raleigh NC 27602

MOSS, JAMES WILLIAM, govt. ofcl.; b. Wilmar, Cal., Aug. 13, 1926; s. Dwight P. and Christine (Hagen) M.; A.B., San Jose State Coll., 1952, M.A., 1953; Ph.D., George Peabody Coll. Tchrs., 1958; m. Margaret Harrison, Apr. 16, 1949; children—Maike Sarah Ann, John Andrew. Research asso. San Francisco State Coll., 1959-60; asst. prof. U. Ill., 1960-63; asso. prof. Yeshiva U., 1963-64; dir. research Bur. Edn. for Handicapped, U.S. Office Edn., Washington, 1964—. Fellow Am. Assn. Mental Deficiency; mem. Am. Psychol. Assn., Council on Exceptional Children. Home: 2001 19th St NW Washington DC 20009 Office: 2010 Regional Office Bldg 7th and D Sts SW Washington DC 20202

MOSS, JOE ALBAUGH, oil co. exec.; b. Waco, Tex., July 26, 1925; s. Robert Edwin and Winnie (Hughes) M.; B.B.A., U. Tex., 1948, LL.B., 1950; m. Anna Lee Reese, May 30, 1947; 1 son, Joe David. Admitted to Tex. bar, 1950; practiced in Austin, 1950; atty. Tex. Bd. Hosps. and Spl. Schs., Abilene, 1950; sec., asst. gen. counsel Cosden Petroleum Corp., 1950-63; v.p., sec., chief counsel Cosden Oil & Chem. Co., Big Spring, Tex., 1963—; chief counsel Am. Petrofina, Inc., 1971—; dir., v.p., chief counsel Am. Petrofina Co. Tex., 1971—; dir., v.p., sec. Trust Pipe Line Co., 1956—; v.p., sec. River Pipeline Co., 1958—; dir., sec. Spencer & Co., 1959-64; sec. Cosden Pipe Line Co., 1961—. Vice chmn. Lone Star dist. Boy Scouts Am., 1961—; pres., trustee Big Spring Ind. Sch. Dist., 1961-71; trustee Permian Basin Petroleum Mus. Bd. dirs. W. Tex. Boys Ranch, Cosden Credit Union. Served with USNR, 1942-46, 50-52. Mem. Am., Tex., Howard County (past pres.) bar assns., Am. Petroleum Inst., Tex. Research League, Navy League U.S. Presbyn. (elder). Mason. Clubs: Big Spring Hunting and Fishing (trustee), Big Spring Country. Home: 5230 Royal Crest Dr Dallas TX 75229 Office: Mercantile Dallas Bldg Dallas TX 75221

MOSS, JOSEPH RODNEY, chief justice S.C. Supreme Ct.; b. York, S.C., July 15, 1903; s. James L. Sr. and Janie E. (Ford) M.; student Erskine Coll., 1920-23, LL.D., 1963; A.B., U. S.C., 1924, M.A., LL.B., 1927; LL.D., 1966, J.D., 1970; m. Rosa Dill, June 11, 1931 (dec. Dec. 1966). Admitted to S.C. bar, 1927; mem. firm Hart & Moss, York, 1927-48; judge 6th Circuit Ct. of S.C., 1948-56; asso. justice S.C. Supreme Ct., 1956-66, chief justice, 1966—. Mem. York County Democratic Exec. Com., 1933-48; mem. S.C. Senate, 1944-48. Presbyn. (elder). Home: PO Box 259 York SC 29754

MOSS, LAURENCE IRA, engr.; b. N.Y.C., June 3, 1935; s. Sydney I. and Dorothy (Candler) M.; B.S. in Chem. Engring., Mass. Inst. Tech., 1956, M.S. in Nuclear Engring., 1958; m. Anne Katherine Baker, July 17, 1971. Research engr. Atomics Internat. Div. N. Am. Rockwell Corp., Los Angeles, 1959-61, sr. engr., 1961-62; project engr., 1962-66, asst. project mgr., 1966-68; White House fellow U.S. Dept. Transp., 1968-69; exec. sec. com. pub. engring. policy Nat. Acad. Engring., Washington, 1969—. Mem. Am. Nuclear Soc., Am. Chem. Soc., A.A.A.S., Fedn. Am. Scientists (mem. council 1971—), Tau Beta Pi, Phi Lambda Upsilon. Club: Sierra (San Francisco) (dir. 1968—, v.p. 1972—). Home: 3241 N St NW Washington DC 20007 Office: Nat Acad Engring 2101 Constitution Av NW Washington DC 20418

MOSS, ROBERT SHERIFFS, lawyer; b. Milw., July 15, 1908; s. Roy M. and Cornelia M. (Sheriffs) M.; B.S., Northwestern U., 1929; J.D., U. Wis., 1932; LL.M., Georgetown U., 1964; m. Bernice M. Pfeifer, Aug. 24, 1946; children—Marilyn, Karen. Admitted to Wis. bar, 1932, D.C. bar, 1947; pvt. practice Milw., 1932-43, Washington, 1947—; counsel materials div. Office Gen. Counsel, Navy Dept., 1946-47; with Elmore, Moss & Moore, Washington, 1948-50; partner firm Hart, Moss & Tavenner, 1962-70; pvt. practice, 1970—; gen. counsel Graphic Arts Assn. Wis., 1936-43; lectr. Columbia U., 1950-54, Cath. U., 1945-55, Tax Practice Inst., 1955-58. Sec. Mayor's Adv. Council, Milw., 1936-37; pres. Milw. YMCA Toastmasters Club, YMCA Speakers' Bur. Mem. Am. (chmn. regional program com. 1965-67, chmn. pub. contracts com. 1953-55; mem. council, sect. pub. contract law 1968-71, sec. 1971—), Wis., Fed. (mem. nat. council 1968-69, 71—) bar assns., Bar Assn. D.C. (chmn. taxation com. 1954-55), Scribes, Phi Delta Phi. Clubs: University, Wranglers; National Lawyers. Author: Cases and Materials on The Law of Government Contracts; Flaherty's District of Columbia Practice; articles on law. Home: 8521 Doter Dr Waynewood Alexandria VA 22308 Office: 1815 H St NW Washington DC 20006

MOSS, WAYNE, broadcasting exec.; m. one child. Program dir., operations mgr. KAAY radio, Little Rock. Office: PO Box 1790 Little Rock AR 72203

MOSSMAN, MEREB ETHNA, educator; b. Winfield, Kan., Dec. 1, 1905; d. Frank E. and Zoa H. (Foster) Mossman; A.B., Morningside Coll., Sioux City, Ia., 1926, D.Lit.; A.M. U. Chgo., 1928, postgrad. 1935-36; L.H.D., Queens Coll. Social worker Chgo. Orphan Asylum, 1928-30; head sociology dept. Ginling Coll., Nanking, China 1930-35, 36-37; prof. sociol. Ala. Woman's Coll. summer 1936; prof. sociology U. N.C. Greensboro, 1937—, dean instrn., 1951-58, dean coll., 1958-63, dean faculty, 1963-69, vice chancellor for acad. affairs, 1969-71. Bd. dirs. Cone Hosp., 1954-59, Guilford County Dept. Pub. Welfare, 1950-56; v.p. So. Assn. Colls. Women, 1958-59, exec. com., 1959-61; cons. Am. Assn. Schs. Social Work, 1947, Nat. Council Social Work Edn., 1956, sec. 1960-62, mem. bd., 1959-63, 2d v.p., dir., 1965-71; mem. ho. of dels. and exec. com. 1965—; mem. bd. Guilford County Chronic Illness Found., 1960-65. Recipient Gardner award U. N.C., 1956. Mem. Am. Assn. U. Women (N.C. bd.), N.C. Conf. Social Service (v.p. 1956-57, pres. 1958-60), Am., So. sociol. socs., Council Social Agys., Greensboro (dir.), Am. Assn. Social Workers (past dir. N.C.), N.C. League for Nursing (dir. 1963-64), So. Assn. Colls. and Schs. (commn. on colls. 1963-68, exec. council), Greensboro Jr. League (hon.), N.C. Assn. Acad. Deans (past pres.), N.C. Council Women's Orgns., Delta Kappa Gamma (hon.), Alpha Kappa Delta. Home: 511 Audubon Dr Hamilton Lakes Greensboro NC 27408

MOSSNER, ERNEST CAMPBELL, educator; b. N.Y.C., Oct. 22, 1907; s. Gustave and Lillian (Campbell) M.; B.A., Coll. City N.Y., 1929; M.A., Columbia, 1930, Ph.D., 1936; m. Carolyn Walz, June 22, 1936; 1 son, David Campbell. Fellow, tutor, instr. English, Coll. City N.Y., 1929-37; asso. prof. English, Syracuse U., 1937-43, prof., 1943-47; prof. English, U. Tex., Austin, 1947-68, prof. English and philosophy, 1968—. Vis. prof. English summers Columbia, 1947, U. Colo., 1960; mem. editorial bd. Adam Smith bicentenary com. Glasgow U., 1965—. Served with AUS, 1943-45. Guggenheim fellow, 1939-40, 45-46; Am. Council Learned Socs. grantee, 1965; Fulbright research fellow Glasgow U., 1968-69. Mem. Internat. Assn. U. Profs. English, Modern Lang. Assn. Am., S.W. Modern Lang. Assn., Modern Humanities Research Assn., Nat. Council Tchrs. English, Milton Soc. Am., Augustan Reprint Soc., Tex. Inst. Letters (Best Biography award 1955), Tex. Assn. Coll. Tchrs., Phi Beta Kappa, Phi Kappa Phi, Delta Alpha. Club: Town and Gown (Austin). Author: Bishop Butler and the Age of Reason, 1936; The Forgotten Hume, 1943; The Life of David Hume, 1954. Editor: Justa Edovardo King, 1938; Bishop Butler: The Analogy of Religion, 1960; David Hume: Philosophical Essays on Human Understanding and Other Essays, 1962; Hume's Treatise, 1969. Co-editor New Letters of David Hume, 1954; A Letter from a Gentleman to his Friend in Edinburgh, 1745; A Pamphlet Hitherto Unknown by David Hume, 1967. Contbr. articles, chpts. to profl. jours. and books, encys; adv. editor Abstracts of English Studies, 1960-64; mem. editorial bd. Ency. of Philosophy, 1963-67; co-editor Texas Studies in Lit. and Lang., 1965—. Home: 3001 Glenview Av Austin TX 78703

MOSTILER, THOMAS WAYNE, dentist; b. Forest City, N.C., Feb. 27, 1941; s. Joe Thomas and Katherine (Page) M.; B.S., Wofford Coll., 1963; D.D.S., Med. Coll. Va., 1966; m. Barbara Ann Copenhaver, Oct. 20, 1961; children—Teresa Lynn, Thomas Wayne, Ann Catherine. Resident oral surgery Med. Coll. Va. Hosp., Richmond, 1966-69, chief resident oral surgery, 1969; chief dental service, chmn. dept. oral surgery U.S. Naval Hosp., Lemoore, Cal., 1969-71; pvt. practice oral surgery, Norfolk, Va., 1971—. Dir. dept. dentistry DePaul Hosp. Recipient A.D. Williams Scholarship award Med. Coll. Va., 1964-65, Psi Omega award, 1966. Diplomate Am. Bd. Oral Surgery. Mem. Atwood Wash Oral Surgery Soc., Am., Va. socs. oral surgeons, Am., Va. Tidewater dental assns., Psi Omega, Kappa Sigma, Sigma Zeta, Omicron Kappa Upsilon, Alpha Sigma Chi. Home: 224 Upperville Rd Virginia Beach VA 23462 Office: DePaul Med Bldg Norfolk VA 23505

MOSTOFI, FATHOLLAH K., physician; b. Teheran, Iran, 1911; M.D., Harvard, 1939. Intern St. Lukes Hosp., Bethlehem, Pa., 1939-40; house officer pathology Peter Ben Brigham Hosp., Boston, 1940-41; resident in pathology Boston Lying-In Host., Free Hosp. for Women, Brookline, Mass., Children's Hosp., Boston, 1942-43; asst. pathologist Mass. Gen. Hosp., Boston, 1944-45; cons. pathologist Mass. Eye and Ear Infirmary, Boston, 1945-46, Cancer fellow, 1947-48; cons. pathologisy Nat. Cancer Inst., Bethesda, Md., 1948-50; sci. dir. Am. Registery of Pathology, 1957-59, chief gen. and spl. pathology div., 1952—; chief genitourinary pathology br. Armed Forces Inst. Pathology, Washington, 1948—; clin.prof. pathology Georgetown U.; asst. prof. pathology Johns Hopkins. Served with M.C., AUS, 1944-47. Diplomate Am. Bd. Pathology. Fellow Coll. Am. Pathologists; mem. A.M.A., A.A.A.S., Am. Soc. Clin. Pathologists, Internat. Acad. Pathology (pres.), Am. Assn. Pathologists and Bacteriologists, Assn. Mil. Surgeons U.S., Am. Soc. Exptl. Pathology, Am. Assn. for Cancer Research, Internat. Urology Soc., Soc. Nuclear Medicine. Home: 7001 Georgia St Chevy Chase MD 20015 Office: Armed Forces Inst Pathology Washington DC 20305*

MOTHERSHED, GEORGE LLOYD, lawyer, oil co. exec.; b. Phoenix, June 12, 1943; s. Caldwell C. and Elizabeth Louise (Jagow) M.; B.S. in Econs. History, No. Ariz. U., 1965; J.D., U. Okla., 1968; m. Carrilee Abernathy, Apr. 11, 1963; 1 son, Robert Stuart. Vice pres. Post Oak Oil Co., Oklahoma City, 1966-72, pres., 1972—, also dir.; admitted to Okla. bar, 1968, since practiced in Oklahoma City; counsel Howell & Smith, Attys., Oklahoma City, 1968—; asst. sec. Big Chief Drilling Co., 1969-71; sec. Chiefs Corp. of Okla., Inc., 1971-72; sec., treas. Shaft Drillers, Inc., 1971— (all Oklahoma City); dir. Southwestern Bank & Trust Co., Oklahoma City, Big Chief Internat. Corp., Chieftain Petroleum, Inc. Oklahoma City. Bd. dirs. region 9 exploring com. Boy Scouts Am., chmn. exploring Last Frontier council, 1971—, mem. nat. exploring com., 1971—. Mem. Am. Petroleum Inst., Okla. Ind. Petroleum Assn., Ind. Petroleum Assn. Am., Am., Okla., Oklahoma County bar assns., N.A.M., Oklahoma City Zool. Soc., S.W. Legal Found., Okla. Heritage Assn. U.S. C. of C., Phi Alpha Delta, Delta Sigma Phi. Presbyn. (deacon). Clubs: Economics, Petroleum. Home: 1316 Brighton Av Oklahoma City OK 73120 Office: 2900 Liberty Tower 100 N Broadway Oklahoma City OK 73125

MOTHERSHED, SPAESIO WILLARD, librarian; b. Bloomburg, Tex., June 30, 1925; s. Charlie and Ollie (Johnson) M.; A.B., Jarvis Christian Coll., 1952; M.S., Syracuse U., 1954; postgrad. North Tex. State U., 1962-63; m. Juliene Craven, Aug. 20, 1961; children—Spaesio Willard, Willa Renee. Cataloger Mich. State Library, Lansing, 1954-60; head librarian Jarvis Christian Coll., Hawkins, Tex., 1960-66; dir. libraries Tex. So. U., Houston, 1966—. Resource cons. Model Cities Tng. Center, Houston, 1971. Served with USNR, 1943-46. Mem. A.L.A., Tex. Library Assn., Houston YMCA. Baptist. Home: 3515 Oakdale St Houston TX 77004 Office: 3201 Wheeler St Houston TX 77004

MOTLEY, GEORGE ALICE, supt. schs.; b. Frenchburg, Ky.; d. Oscar H. and Hettye (Wells) Motley; A.B., Morehead State U., 1947, M.A. (hon.), 1971. Supt. Menifee County Schs., Frenchburg, Ky., 1947—. Ky. Col. Mem. Ky. Hist. Soc., Am. Assn. Sch. Adminstrs., Kappa Delta Pi, Delta Kappa Gamma. Democrat. Home: US Rt 460 Frenchburg KY 40322

MOTLOW, TOM GREGORY, banker; b. Lynchburg, Tenn., May 19, 1877; s. Felix and Finettre (Domiel) M.; grad. Lynchburg Normal Sch., 1890; student South Central Normal Sch. and Bus. Coll., 1890-95; grad. Fall's Bus. Coll., Vanderbilt U., 1901. Cashier, Farmers Bank of Lynchburg, 1901-17, pres., 1907—. Chmn., U.S.A. Bond sales, Savs. Bonds Sales, Moore County. Col. on Gov.'s staff. Mem. Tenn. Bankers Assn. (past treas.), Phi Beta Kappa. Contbr. articles on local affairs to local newspapers. Home: Lynchburg TN 37352 Office: Farmers Bank Lynchburg TN 37352

MOTT, DOROTHY HALE WILLIAMS (MRS. GEORGE FOX MOTT), editor; b. Mpls., Oct. 3, 1910; d. Edward Hale and Margaret (Ladd) Williams; student Ginling Coll., Nanking, China, 1932-33; A.B., U. Minn., 1937; postgrad. Columbia, 1941; m. George Fox Mott, Feb. 12, 1944; children—David Edward Way, Jonathan Loren Gould. Librarian, tchr. social studies Marine Corps Children's Sch., Quantico, Va., 1941-43; adminstrv. asst. Mott of Washington & Assos., 1950-53, tech. writer, research asst., 1953-64, surpervising editor, 1964—. First v.p. Friends of D.C. Youth Orch., 1964—; treas. Chevy Chase Community Council, 1965—; mem. bd. Children's Theatre Washington, 1966—; bd. dirs. Noyes Sch. Rhythm Found.; dancer, tchr. Noyes Summer Sch., Portland, Conn., 1970—. Home: 3745 Kanawha St NW Washington DC 20015 Office: Dupont Circle Bldg Washington DC 20036

MOTT, GEORGE FOX, mgmt. cons.; b. Riverside, Cal., June 4, 1907; s. George Fox and Alice (Way) M.; A.B., Stanford, 1929, A.M., 1931; Ph.D., U. Minn., 1938; grad. Army Mgmt. Sch., 1959; m. Dorothy Hale Williams, Feb. 12, 1944; children—David Edward Way, Jonathan Loren Gould. Dean Jr. Coll., San Diego, Chgo., 1929-35; asst. to pres. Hancher Orgn., 1935-36; instr. U. Minn., 1936-38; dean N.M. A. & M. Coll., 1938-39; cons., asst. dir. Kansas City Sch. Survey, 1939: cons. Mayors Survey Coms., St. Louis, Houston, 1939-40; chief cons. analyst, adv. council War Assets Adminstrn., 1946-48; mng. partner, sr. cons. Mott of Washington &Assos., 1948—; chmn. Mott Research Group, 1952—; adj. prof. journalism and pub. relations Am. U. Founding dir. Am.-Korean Found.; internat. dir., also chmn. Greater Washington Council; united bd. Christian Higher Edn. in Asia. Commd. Arty., U.S. Army Res., 1928; served as col. AUS, 1940-46, with Insp. Gen.'s Office, 1941-44, insp. gen. combat units S.W. Pacific, 1944-45, Am. Forces-in-Korea, 1945-46, U.S. Army Res., 1946-63, detailed SSS, 1960-63. Decorated Bronze Star medal with cluster, Commendation medal, Distinguished Service citation (Korea), 1962. Mem. A.I.M. (pres.'s council), Am. Acad. Polit. Social Sci., Am. Polit. Sci. Assn., Nat. Def. Transp. Assn., Res. Officers Assn. (past pres. dept. Md., also dept. D.C.; nat. councilman D.C., past nat. councilman dept. Va., past chmn. nat. army affairs, nat. resolutions, nat. budget, nat. rules and finance coms.; nat. minuteman), Am. Rifle Assn., Mil. Order World Wars (editor hist. record, past chpt. comdr.), Mil. Order Fgn. Wars, Am. Legion (past dept. comdr.), Phi Delta Kappa. Elk. Club: Army and Navy. Author: San Diego Politically Speaking, 1932; History of Middle Ages, 1933, rev. 1958; Survey of Journalism, 1937; New Survey of Journalism, 1950, rev. 1959; Survey of U.S. Ports, 1951; Miami's Marine Destiny, 1955. Editor Transportation Renaissance, 1963. Editor, sr. author: Transportation Century, 1967. Editor: Urban Change and the Planning Syndrome, 1973. Home: 3745 Kanawha St NW Washington DC 20015 Office: Dupont Circle Bldg Washington DC 20036

MOTT, HUGH B., state ofcl.; b. Nashville, Aug. 14, 1920; grad. Marion Mil. Inst.; m. Mildred Latimer; 3 daus. Entered N.G., 1942, advanced through grades to maj. gen., 1968; comdr. 30th Armored Div., 1968—; adj. gen. State of Tenn., 1968—. Chmn. Wautauga Dist., Middle Tenn. council Boy Scouts Am. Mem. Am. Legion, 40 and 8. Mem. Christian Ch. Address: National Guard Armory Sidco Dr Nashville TN 37204*

MOTTER, DAVID CALVIN, govt. ofcl., economist; b. New London, O., Feb. 10, 1926; s. Doren M. and Bertha (Potter) M.; B.A., Baldwin-Wallace Coll., 1950; Ph.D., Vanderbilt U., 1958; m. Margaret Helen Malmfeldt, Aug. 12, 1950; 1 dau., Catherine Helen. Instr. econs. Franklin and Marshall Coll., 1954-56; research fellow Brookings Instn., 1956-57; lectr., then asst. prof. Wharton Sch., U. Pa., 1957-63; sr. economist Office Comptroller Currency, 1963-66; dep. comptroller currency for econs., 1966—. Mem. West Phila. Housing Com., 1960-63; pres. Regent Sq. Civic Assn., Phila., 1958-63. Bd. dirs. Fairfax Horsemen's Assn., 1968—. Served with USNR, 1944-46. Mem. Am. Econ. Assn., Am. Finance Assn., Am. Assn. U. Profs. Episcopalian. Author research studies. Home: Home: 1884 Beulah Rd Vienna VA 22180 Office: Dep Controller Currency Treasury Dept Washington DC 20220

MOTZ, ANNABELLE BENDER (MRS. JOSEPH W. MOTZ), sociologist; b. Milw., June 13, 1920; d. Alexander and Bertha (Wasserman) Bender; B.S., U. Wis., 1941; A.M., U. Chgo., 1943, Ph.D., 1950; m. Joseph W. Motz, Mar. 25, 1945; children— Alice Morine, Jay Sender. Instr., then asst. prof. U. Md., College Park, 1951-66; asso. prof. Am. U., Washington, 1966-68, prof., 1968—, dir. Inst. in Sociology for Secondary Sch. Tchrs., 1969—. Recipient grants U. Md. Research Bd., 1957-58, 63-64, USPHS, 1964-66, 66-69, NSF, 1968—. Fellow Am. Sociol. Assn. Home: 11306 Cushman Rd

Rockville MD 20852 Office: Dept Sociology Am U Washington DC 20016

MOUDY, JAMES MATTOX, univ. adminstr.; b. nr. Harlingen, Tex., July 18, 1916; s. Alvin Curtis and Helen (Sunderland) M.; B.A., Tex. Christian U., 1943. B.D., 1949; Ph.D. (Kearns fellow), Duke, 1953; LL.D., Atlantic Christian Coll., 1965; m. Lucille Lauritzen, July 24, 1943; children—Linda Rhea, Rosemary. Staff, Treasury Dept., Washington, 1933-39; ordained to ministry Christian Ch., 1943; dean Atlantic Christian Coll., Wilson, N.C., 1953-57, acting pres., 1953, 56; dean Grad. Sch., Tex. Christian U., 1957-64, vice chancellor acad. affairs, 1962-64, exec. vice chancellor, 1964-65, chancellor, 1965—. Exec. com. N.C. Coll. Conf.; pres. N.C. Conv. Christian Chs. Served as Capt., 406th Inf., Chaplains Corps, AUS, 1943-46. Decorated Bronze Star medal. Mem. Philos. Soc. Tex., Newcomen Soc. N.Am., Phi Beta Kappa, Pi Gamma Mu, Alpha Chi. Mem. Disciples of Christ Ch. (chmn. bd. higher edn. 1967, 68). Clubs: Ft. Worth, Colonial Country, Rotary; Rivercrest Country. Home: 2900 Simondale St Fort Worth TX 76109

MOUILLE, FRANCIS NORMAN, educator; b. Church Point, La., Feb. 19, 1938; s. Cleophas and Elsie Jewel (Higginbotham) M.; B.S., U. Southwestern La., 1959, M.Ed., 1961, Edn. Specialist, 1970; m. Katherine Irene Tabor, Dec. 28, 1961; children—Francis Norman II, Jean Cleophas, Katherine Jewel. Instr. sci.-math. Lafayette (La.) Parish Sch. Bd., Lafayette High Sch., 1959-63; supervising tchr. sci.-math. U. Southwestern La., 1961-63; tchr. sci.-math. Church Point (La.) High Sch., Acadia Parish Sch. Bd., 1963-65, prin., 1965—. Bd. advisers Acadiana Neuf, Inc., Lafayette; bd. govs. So. Educators Corp., chmn. Church Point Adv. Council. Recipient Am. Legion award, 1956. Mem. Church Point Jr. C. of C. (sec. 1963), N.E.A., La. Tchrs. Assn., Acadia Edn. Assn., Nat. Assn. Secondary Sch. Prins., S.A.R., Acadia Parish Adminstrs. Assn., La. Prins. Assn., Am. Assn. Sch. Adminstrs., Assn. Tchr. Educators, La. Assn. Supervision Curriculum Devel., Clay Family Assn., Sons Confederate Vets., La., New Orleans geneal. socs., La. High Sch. Athletic Assn., Lafayette Area Football Adminstrs. Assn. (exec. council 1968—), Lafayette Area Basketball Adminstrs. Assn., Attakapas Hist. Assn., Kappa Delta Pi, Kappa Mu Epsilon, Phi Kappa Phi, Phi Delta Kappa. Roman Catholic (lector 1964—). Home: PO Box 116 Church Point LA 70525

MOULTON, FRANK RAY, JR., petroleum co. exec.; b. Winthrop, Mass., June 17, 1924; s. Frank Ray and Mildred Pauline (Hendrickson) M.; student Northeastern U., 1942-43, Tufts Coll., 1943-44; B.S., Brown U., 1946; Geophys. Engr., Colo. Sch. Mines, 1951; m. Louise Pearl Kiser, May 10, 1952; children—Catherine Eugenie, Thaddeus Ray. Trainee, Superior Oil Co., Bakersfield, Cal., 1951, geophysicist, Andrews, Tex., 1952; geophysicist Carter Oil Co., Colo., Mont., 1952, Internat. Petroleum Co., Colombia, 1952-56; staff seismologist Petroleo Brasileiro (PETROBRAS) S.A., Rio de Janeiro, Brazil, 1956-60; staff asst. to mine mgr. Newgulf Tex. Gulf, Inc., 1961, sr. geophysicist, Houston, 1962-67, regional mgr. exploration, 1967-69, asst. gen. mgr. exploration, 1969-70, gen. mgr., 1970, v.p., 1971—, also officer various subsidiaries. Served to lt. (j.g.) USNR, 1943-48. Mem. Am. Assn. Petroleum Geologists, Geol. Soc. Am., Soc. Exploration Geophysicists, Sigma Nu, Tau Beta Pi. Conglist. Clubs: Houston, Petroleum (Houston); East India and Sports (London, Eng.). Home: 12643 Taylorcrest St Houston TX 77024 Office: 811 Rusk Av Houston TX 77002

MOULTRIE, JAMES YOUNG, JR., supt. schs.; b. Hillsboro, Ala., Apr. 21, 1921; s. James Young and Lula Ann (Smith) M.; B.S., Florence State U., 1943; M.A., George Peabody Coll., 1947, Ed.D., 1956; postdoctoral U. Ga.; m. Mollie Beth Darby, Aug. 12, 1944; children—Jimmy, Sherry Lynn (Mrs. Steve Birger). Tchr., Russellville, Ala., 1947-48; prin., Tusbumbia, Ala., 1948-49, Cullman, Ala., 1949-56; supt. edn., Scottsboro, Ala., 1956-57; asst. supt. edn., Columbus, Ga., 1957-64; supt. edn., Cordele, Ga., 1964-66; asso. supt. edn., Huntsville, Ala., 1966-68; supt. edn., Fitzgerald, Ga., 1968—. Mem. Ben Hill County Community Action Com. Served with USNR, 1943-46. Mem. N.E.A. (life), Ga. P.T.A. (life), Am. Assn. Sch. Adminstrs. Methodist (lay leader). Rotarian. Editor of Muscogiite, 1957-64. Contbr. articles to profl. jours. Home: Rt 2 Box 62 Fitzgerald GA 31750 Office: 515 Palm St Fitzgerald GA 31750

MOULTRIE, ROY DEAN, judge; b. Hamilton, Ga., Apr. 2, 1932; s. Alvah C. and Osie (Richardson) M.; terminal certificate West Ga. Coll., 1950; LL.B., Mercer U., 1953; m. Ann Williams, Feb. 1, 1959; children—Charles Dean, Elizabeth Ann. Admitted to Ga. bar, 1953; county atty. Harris County, Ga., 1958-62; owner Roy D. Moultrie Ins. Agy., 1958—; judge Ct. Ordinary, Harris County, Ga., 1957—; pres. Southern, Inc.; sec., treas. Harris County Realty, Inc. Treas. Chattahoochee Devel. and Planning Commn., 1965-67. Bd. dirs. Ga. YMCA, 1960-64. Mem. Am., Ga., Chattahoochee Circuit (pres. 1960-61) bar assns. Baptist. Mason (32 deg.), Lion (dep. dist. gov. 1962-63; devel. and retention chmn. dist. 18E 1963-64). Address: Courthouse Hamilton GA 31811

MOUNT, CHARLES LE MEAR, JR., physician; b. Holdenville, Okla., June 19, 1912; s. Charles Le Mear and Lela Evelyn (Roseboom) M.; B.S., U. Okla., 1935; M.D., Johns Hopkins, 1940; m. Susan Mae Berry, Jan. 13, 1968; children—Charles Le Mear III (dec.), Susan, Peter. House staff Johns Hopkins Sch. Medicine, 1940-43; asst. resident medicine Vanderbilt U. Hosp., 1944; resident medicine Johns Hopkins Hosp., 1945; chief of medicine and cardiology Winter Gen. Hosp., Topeka, 1946-50; pvt. practice medicine, specializing in internal medicine, Okla., 1951-54; indsl. cardiologist E.I. duPont de Nemours & Co., Charleston, W. Va., 1954-56; chief of geriatrics Central State Griffin Meml. Hosp., Norman, Okla., 1959—; instr. medicine Johns Hopkins Sch. Medicine; lectr. Kellogg Center Continuing Edn. U. Okla.; lectr. psychosomatic medicine and heart disease Winter Gen. Hosp., Menninger Psychiat. Inst.; lectr. geriatrics Okla. Dept. Mental Health; chief med. dir. Central Okla. Vets. Center; med. cons. State Nursing Home Assn.; cons. Southwestern Okla. Soil Conservation Commn. Served as maj. AUS, 1956-58. Mem. U. Okla. Alumni Assn., Balt., Johns Hopkins med. and surg. socs., Okla. Johns Hopkins Alumni Assn., Royal Soc. Health (London, Eng.), Am. Gerontol. Soc., Am. Psychiat. Assn. (hon.), Okla. Arts and Scis. Found., Phi Beta Kappa, Sigma Zi, Sigma Alpha Epsilon, Nu Sigma Nu. Home: 2610 Cypress St Norman OK 73069 Office: Box 151 Norman OK 73069

MOUNTAIN, CLIFTON FLETCHER, physician; b. Toledo, Apr. 15, 1924; s. Ira Fletcher and Mary (Stone) M.; A.B., Harvard, 1947, postgrad., 1946-47; M.D., Boston U., 1954; postgrad. U. Chgo., 1954-59; m. Marilyn Isabelle Tapper, Feb. 28, 1945; children—Karen Lockerby, Clifton Fletcher, Jeffrey Richardson. Dir. dept. statis. research Boston U., 1947-50; cons. research analyst Dept. Pub. Health, Commonwealth of Mass., 1951-53; intern U. Chgo. Clinics, 1954, resident, 1955-58, instr. surgery, 1958-59; practice medicine, specializing in surgery, Houston, 1959—; mem. staff M.D. Anderson Hosp. and Tumor Research Inst.; asst. prof. thoracic surgery U. Tex., 1960-63, chmn. program in biomath. and computer sci., 1962-64, asso. prof. surgery, 1963—; Mike Hogg vis. lectr. in S. Am., 1967. Mem. com. health, research and edn. facilities Community Council, Houston, 1964—; mem. Am. Joint Com. for Cancer Staging and End Result Reporting, 1966—; mem. NIH Working Party on Lung Cancer, 1971—, chmn. com. surgery, 1971—. Chmn. profl. adv. com. Harris County Mental Health Assn.; bd. dirs. Harris County chpt. Am. Cancer Soc. Served to lt. (j.g.) USNR, 1942-46. Diplomate Am. Bd. Surgery. Fellow Am. (j.g.) USNR, 1942-46. Diplomate Am. Bd. Surgery. Fellow Am. Coll. Chest Physicians (chmn. com. cancer 1967—), Inst. Environmental Scis., N.Y. Acad. Sci., A.C.S.; mem. A.A.A.S., Am. Assn. Cancer Research, Am., So. med. assns., Am. Thoracic Soc., Soc. Thoracic Surgeons, Soc. Biomed. Computing, Biomed. Information Processing Orgn., Am. Fedn. Clin. Research, Assn. Computing Machinery, Am. Radium Soc., Pan-Am. Med. Assn., Am. Congress Rehab. Medicine, Houston Surg. Soc., Southwest Cancer Chemotherapy Study Group, James Ewing Soc., Sigma Xi. Editorial bd. Yearbook of Cancer, 1960—. Contbr. articles to profl. jours. Editor: The New Physician, 1955-59. Home: 1612 South Blvd Houston TX 77006 Office: 6723 Bertner Av Houston TX 77025

MOURSUND, M. WADDELL, banker; b. San Antonio, Tex., Jan 31, 1919; s. Walter H. and Freda (Plate) M.; student Baylor U., 1936-39; B.B.A., So. Methodist U., 1940; m. Sue Mottley, May 31, 1947; children—Kay (Mrs. T. B. Ewbank), Rikke, Walter K. With Republic Nat. Bank, Dallas, 1939-41, N.Am. Aviation Co., 1942-43; asst. cashier Nat. Bank Commerce, Houston, 1943-50; partner Malsby Creamery, 1950-59; asst. v.p. Houston Bank & Trust Co., 1959-60, v.p., 1960-65, sr. v.p., 1965-71; pres., dir. Astro Bank, Houston, 1971—. Trustee St. Anthony Center. Home: 4021 Piping Rock Lane Houston TX 77027 Office: 8634 Kirby Dr Houston TX 77025

MOUSER, EDWARD MILNER, lawyer; b. Columbia, La., May 28, 1933; s. Vinson M. and Helen (Holmes) M.; B.A., La. State U., 1958, LL.B., 1959, J.D., 1968; m. Erma Del Jones, Aug. 24, 1958; children—Christopher Michael, Patrick Daniel. Admitted to La. bar, 1959; practiced in Oakdale, 1959-63, Kinder, 1963-69; mem. firm Mouser & Mouser, 1959-63; dist. judge 33d Jud. Dist., Allen Parish (La.), 1969—. Served with USMCR, 1954-56. Methodist. Rotarian. Address: PO Drawer AB Kinder LA 70648

MOUTON, GROVER ERNEST, III, architect, artist; b. Lafayette, La., Nov. 18, 1946; s. Grover Ernest, Jr. and Elaine Elizabeth Mouton; student U. Southwestern La., 1966-67, Skowhegan (Me.) Sch. Painting, 1969, Archtl. Assos. London (Eng.), 1970; B.Arch., Tulane U., 1971; fellow Am. Acad. Rome (Italy), 1971—. Exhibited one-man shows, New Orleans, 1968, Circle Gallery, New Orleans, 1970; exhibited in group shows U. Southwestern La., Lafayette, 1967, Dublin Nat. Print and Drawing Competition, Dublin Gallery of Art, Knoxville, Tenn., 1970. Recipient Prix de Rome, 1971. Mem. A.I.A., Kappa Sigma. Roman Catholic. Ind. research, design non-gravitational environment. Home: 140 Oakview Blvd Lafayette LA 70501 Office: Am Acad in Rome Via Angelo Masina 5 00153 Rome Italy

MOWLANA, HAMID, educator; b. Tabriz, Iran, Feb. 25, 1937; s. Karim S. Agha and Robab (Ibrahimi) M.; B.A., Northwestern U., 1959, M.S., 1960, Ph.D., 1963 Fgn. corr. Kayhan Newspapers, Iran and Sacramento Bee, 1957-62; editor-in-chief Kayhan Newspapers, Teheran, 1963-64; Washington commentator, cons. to USIA in Washington, fgn. affairs writer MacLatchy Newspapers in Cal., 1964-65; asst. prof. communication U. Tenn., 1965-68; asso. prof. internat. communication, chmn. univ. com. on communication Am. U., Washington, 1968-71, prof., dir. internat. communication program, 1971—. Asst. to dir. research Northwestern U. Sch. Journalism, 1960-62. Recipient awards U.S. State Dept., 1958, Brit. Fgn. Office, 1963, French Fgn. Ministry, 1963, German Govt., 1963, 68. Mem. Am. Acad. Polit. and Social Sci., A.A.A.S., Am. Polit. Sci. Assn., Assn. for Edn. in Journalism, Soc. for Journalist, Sigma Delta Chi. Author: Journalism in Iran: A History and Interpretation, 1963; International Communication: A Selected Bibliography, 1967; (with others) Expanding Horizons in African Studies, 1969; Handbook to the Middle East, 1971; International Communication-Media, Channels and Function, 1970; International Communication as a Field Study, 1970; The New Soldier, 1971. Contbr. articles to profl. jours. Home: 6420 Bradley Blvd Bethesda MD 20034 Office: Am U Washington DC 20016

MOY, HENRY KWOK LEONG, govt. ofcl.; b. N.Y.C., June 30, 1916; s. Kwon Kie and Moy Shee (Chin) M.; student Coll. City N.Y., 1934, Lingnan U., China, 1934-37; B.S., N.Y. U., 1939; M.S., Columbia, 1941; certificate Indsl. Coll. Armed Forces, 1962; m. Kathryn Choy Mui Kit, Nov. 17, 1947; children—Clifford Warren, Calvin Brian, Colin Stevenson. Economist, OPS, 1951-53. Bur. Labor Statistics, Labor Dept., 1955-56; statistician manpower and tng. Dept. Air Force, Washington, 1956-62, statistician sampling, 1962-66; economist, dep. chief staff for personnel, directorate personnel studies and research Dept Army, 1966-70, statistician, comptroller, directorate mgmt., rev. and analysis, 1970—. Treas., Wheaton council Nat. Capital Area, Boy Scouts Am., 1961-64. Served with AUS, 1942-45. Recipient Superior Performance award Dept. Air Force, 1962; Appreciation certificate Dept. Army, 1970. Mem. Am. Econ. Assn. Home: 13402 Lydia St Silver Spring MD 20906 Office: Comptroller Directorate Mgmt Rev and Analysis Dept Army Pentagon Washington DC 20310

MOYE, JAMES M., Republican nat. committeeman; b. Laurel, Miss., Feb. 9, 1921; ed. Jones County Jr. Coll., So. Coll. Optometry, Memphis; m. Mae Eleanor Moye, Feb. 5, 1944; children—Marilyn, Jamie. Mem. Republican Nat. Com., 1968—. Mem. State Bd. Examiners in Optometry, 1956-61. Mem. Am., Miss. optometric assns., Laurel C. of C. Presbyn. Address: 515 5th Av Laurel MS 39440

MOYER, PAUL KENNETH, financial exec.; b. Hamburg, Pa., May 29, 1936; s. Paul Frederick and Verna (Miller) M.; B.B.A., Tex. Luth. Coll., 1962; postgrad. U. Houston, 1966; M.B.A., So. Meth. U., 1971; m. Betty Louise Scheffer, Aug. 25, 1962; 1 son, Mark Kevin. Auditor Ernst & Ernst, C.P.A.'s, Houston, 1962-65; asst. to asst. treas. Gulf & Western Industries, Inc., N.Y.C., 1965-68, asst. treas., 1968-69; v.p., controller UCC Financial Corp., Dallas, 1969—. Served with USAF, 1954-58. C.P.A., Tex. Mem. Am. Inst. C.P.A.'s Nat. Assn. Accountants, Tex. Soc. C.P.A.'s. Home: 12515 Ruthdale Dr Dallas TX 75234 Office: PO Box 1771 Dallas TX 75221

MOYLE, JON, chmn. Fla. Democratic Exec. Com., Tallahassee. Office: Suite 858 Tallahassee Bank and Trust Bldg Tallahassee FL 32304*

MOYNAHAN, BERNARD THOMAS, JR., judge; b. Akron, O., Dec. 29, 1918; s. Bernard Thomas and Mayme (Turner) M.; A.B., U. Ky., 1935, LL.B., 1938; m. Mary Thomas Parks, Dec. 19, 1942; children—Mary Patricia, Bernard Thomas III. Admitted to Ky. bar, 1940; practice in Nicholasville, 1940-42, 54-61; county atty. Jessamine County, 1946-54; U.S. atty. Eastern Dist. Ky., 1961-63, U.S. dist. judge, 1963—. Served to 1st lt. USAAF, 1942-45. Home: 203 Richmond Av Nicholasville KY 40356 Office: Court Row Nicholasville KY 40356

MOZINGO, JAMES DELBERT, ednl. adminstr.; b. Toxey, Ala., Mar. 9, 1935; s. Lewis Weslen and Maggie (Burnham) M.; student Whitworth Coll., 1960-61; B.S., Livingston State Coll., 1967, M.Ed., 1969; m. Gracie Evelyn Hendrix, June 28, 1953; children—James Carlos, Dwight Delbert, Gerald Frank. Store operator, Butler, Ala. also Forest, Miss., 1953-60; bus. mgr. Whitworth Coll., 1960-61; minister Methodist Protestant Ch., Toxey, Ala., 1953-72, pres. Gen. Conf. Bd. Missions, 1965-67, treas. Miss. Conf., 1971-72; tchr. English, speech So. Choctaw High Sch., Silas, Ala., 1967-69; prin. Gilbertown (Ala.) Jr. High Sch., 1969—. Adviser Gilbertown council Boy Scouts Am., 1969-72. Mem. Choctaw County (pres. 1968-69), Am. (del. 1969) edn. assns., Pi Tau Chi, Alpha Rho Tau. Home: Drawer C Gilbertown AL 36908 Office: Drawer C Gilbertown AL 36908

MUDANO, FRANK ROBERT, architect; b. Winsted, Conn., Dec. 30, 1928; s. Sebastian and Marian (Bazzano) M.; B.S., Ga. Inst. Tech., 1952, B.Arch., 1952; m. Cornelia C. Crawford, July 20, 1966; children—Lisa Marian, Amy Elaine. Gen. Mgr. Southeastern Engrng. Co., Clearwater, Fla., 1958-64; self employed as architect, Clearwater, 1964—. Chmn. bd. Hytronics Corp., Pinellas Park, Fla., 1971-72. Pres. Fla. Gulf Coast Art Center, 1971—. Bd. dirs. Upper Pinellas YMCA, second v.p. 1971-72. Served with AUS, 1952-54. Mem. A.I.A. (chpt. pres. 1970-71; state treas. 1971-72; dir. 1970-71), Constrn. Specifications Inst. (chpt. v.p. 1969-70), Downtown Assn. Clearwater (founder). Club: Clearwater Breakfast Exchange. Home: 504 Pointsettia Rd Belleaire Clearwater FL 33516 Office: 1189 NE Cleveland St Clearwater FL 33515

MUDD, SISTER HILDA, librarian; b. New Haven, Ky.; d. Edward D. and Estelle (Howard) Mudd; A.B., St. Mary of the Woods, Ind., 1938; B.S. in L.S., Catholic U. Am., 1953; postgrad. Creighton U., 1970—. Tchr., librarian St. Charles High Sch., Lebanon, Ky., 1938-45; librarian Brescia Coll., Owensboro, Ky., 1949—. Mem. Am., Cath. Ky. library assns. Address: Brescia Coll 120 W 7th St Owensboro KY 42301

MUDD, JOHN PHILIP, lawyer, real estate exec.; b. Washington, Aug. 22, 1932; s. T. Paul and Frances M. (Finotti) M.; B.S., Georgetown U., 1954, J.D., 1956; m. Barbara E. Sweeney, Aug. 10, 1957; children—Laura, Ellen, Philip, Clare, David. Admitted to Fla. bar, 1964, Md. bar, 1956, Washington, bar, 1963; practice law, Upper Marlboro, Md., 1956-66; chief corporate counsel, Deltona Corp., Miami, Fla., 1966-68, chief corp. counsel, sec., 1968—, v.p., 1972—; dir. 1st Bank Deltona. Sec., Marco Island Devel. Corp., Miami, Fla., 1968—. Mem. internat. land devel. adv. com. N.Y. State, 1971—. Mem. Fla., Am., Dade County bar assns. Republican. Roman Catholic. Home: 1211 Hardee Rd Coral Gables FL 33146 Office: 3250 SW 3d Av Miami FL 33129

MUDD, ROGER HARRISON, news broadcaster; b. Washington, Feb. 9, 1928; s. Kostka and Irma Iris (Harrison) M.; A.B., Washington and Lee U., 1950; M.A., U. N.C., 1953; m. Emma Jeanne Spears, Oct. 28, 1957; children—Daniel H., Maria M., Jonathan Matthew M. Tchr., Darlington Sch., Rome, Ga., 1951-52; reporter Richmond (Va.) News Leader, 1953; news dir. radio sta. WRNL, Richmond, 1953-56; reporter radio and TV sta. WTOP, Washington, 1956-61; corr. CBS, 1961—. Bd. dirs. Citizens Scholarship Found. Am. Served with AUS, 1945-47. Mem. Radio-TV Corr. Assn. (pres. 1969-70). Club: Nat. Press (Washington). Home: 4025 Glenridge St Kensington MD 20795 Office: 2020 M St Washington DC 20036

MUDIE, JOHN HOWARD, banker; b. Hackensack, N.J., July 13, 1927; s. John A. and Rose C. (Schwager) M.; A.B., Dartmouth, 1949; M.B.A., U. Pa., 1951; Ph.D., U. Tex., 1960. Asst. prof. Tex. A. and M. Coll., College Station, 1954-55; with Govt. Devel. Bank for P.R., San Juan, 1956—, v.p., 1967—; prof. econs. and bus. adminstrn. Inter-Am. U. P.R., Hato Rey, 1968—. Served with AUS, 1946-47. Mem. Am. Econ. Assn., Soc. for Internat. Devel. Home: 83 Cervantes St Santurce PR 00907 Office: Box 4591 San Juan PR 00905

MUELLER, ALFRED JEROME, physician, county ofcl.; b. Worcester, Mass., Sept. 15, 1928; s. Alfred Don and Marie (Struve) M.; B.S., U. Tenn., 1950, M.D., 1952; m. Margaret Jo Coleman, Feb. 1, 1953; children— Daniel Jerome, Margaret Ann, William Don, Charles Gregory, Molly Marie. Intern, John Gaston Hosp., Memphis, 1952-53; resident obstetrics, gynecology Vanderbilt U. Hosp., Nashville, 1955-57, U. Ark. Med. Center, Little Rock, 1957-58; practice medicine, specializing in obstetrics and gynecology, Lexington, Ky., 1958-59; dir. Jackson-Madison County Health Dept., Jackson, Tenn., 1959—; Madison County health officer, 1960—; asst. Div. Preventive Medicine, U. Tenn., 1962—. Cons. preventive medicine and pub. health Jackson-Madison County Gen. Hosp., 1964—, mem. med. staff exec. com., 1970—; surgeon Cocks-Danuiels Post, V.F.W., 1962-70. Dir. V.F.W. Recreation Center, 1963—. Bd. dirs. Jackson YMCA, 1967-70, Goals for Jackson, 1970—. Served from 1st lt. to capt. M.C., USAF, 1952-55. Mem. Am., Tenn. (chmn. maternal-child health com. 1963, 64, 66; chmn. health officers' sect. 1967-68, pres. 1971-72) pub. health assns., Tenn. Med. Assn., Consol. Med. Assembly W. Tenn., Am. Assn. Pub. Health Physicians, Am. Legion, Alpha Epsilon Delta, Pi Kappa Alpha, Phi Chi, Alpha Omega Alpha. Methodist (adminstrv. bd.). Rotarian. Home: 137 Shadowlawn Dr Jackson TN 38301 Office: 745 W Forest St Jackson TN 38301

MUELLER, HERBERT JOACHIM, dentist; b. N.Y.C., Apr. 17, 1928; s. Willy Ernst and Milda Frieda (Ludwig) M.; B.S., St. Peter's U., 1950; D.D.S., Georgetown U., 1954; m. Sondra Lee Kerr, June 15, 1963; children—Debra Kerr, Jeffrey Stuart. Individual practice dentistry, Washington, 1958—; asso. clin. prof. Georgetown U. Dental Sch., 1958—. Served with USNR, 1954-57. Mem. D.C. Dental Soc. (chmn. com. on civil def. 1967), Omicron Kappa Upsilon, Psi Omega. Republican. Methodist (chmn. Met. Meml. pre-sch. 1970-72). Kiwanian (bd. dirs. Georgetown club 1969-72; treas. 1969—). Address: 4644 Verplanck Pl NW Washington DC 20016

MUELLER, JOHN FREDERICK, supt. schs.; b. Bucyrus, O., Apr. 21, 1911; s. John Simon and Frances Barbara (Faulhaber) M.; B.A., U. Dayton, 1932; S.T.L., Catholic U. Am., 1942; M.A., Columbia Tchrs Coll., 1950, Ed.D., 1953. Joined Soc. of Mary, 1928, ordained priest Roman Catholic Ch., 1941; tchr. religion, English, Latin and Spanish schs. in Ohio, Ia., N.Y. and P.R., 1932-48; supt. Catholic schs., P.R., 1953-61; pres. Catholic U. P.R., 1961-65; supt. Catholic schs. Archdiocese of San Juan, Arecibo and Caguas, P.R., 1966—. Bd. dirs. P.R.-V.I. council Boy Scouts Am., 1960—. Mem. Phi Delta Kappa. Author monograph. Address: Box 1967 San Juan PR 08903

MUELLER, ROBERT LOUIS, physician; b. Granite City, Ill., Sept. 2, 1929; s. Louis Jacob and Mildred (Fegley) M.; A.B. magna cum laude, Carthage Coll., 1951; M.D., U. Ill., 1955; m. Dorothy Jane Grant, Apr. 28, 1956; children—Deborah Jean, Mary Jane, Allan Louis, Catherine Grant. Intern Ill. Central Hosp., Chgo., 1955-56; resident obstetrics and gynecology U. Tenn. and City of Memphis Hosps., 1957-60; practice medicine, specializing in obstetrics and gynecology, Morristown, Tenn., 1964—; mem. staff Morristown Hamblen Hosp., chief staff, 1969-70. Served to maj. AUS, 1956-64. Diplomate Am. Bd. Obstetrics and Gynecology. Fellow Am. Coll.

Obstetrics and Gynecology; mem. A.M.A., Tenn., So. med. assns. Lutheran. Home: 1420 Doyal Dr Morristown TN 37814 Office: 705 McFarland St Morristown TN 37814

MUGGE, ROBERT H, sociologist; b. Tampa, Fla., Nov. 28, 1921; s. August Bremer and Dorothea (Schoel) M.; B.A., U. Fla., 1943, M.A., 1947; Ph.D., U. Chgo., 1957; m. A. Elizabeth Messersmith, June 14, 1947; children—Robert E., John A., Frances E., Paul R. Research asso. Commn. on Human Resources, Washington, 1951-52; dir. research and statistics N.C. State Bd. Pub. Welfare, Raleigh, 1952-59; chief demographic research group Bur. Family Services, U.S. Dept. Health, Edn. and Welfare, Washington, 1959-66, chief program research br., 1966-67, also mem. career service bd. for math. and statistics; acting dir. social and rehab. service Nat. Center Social Statistics, 1967-70; asst. to the dir. Nat. Center for Health Statistics, 1971—; asst. prof. sociology U. Md., College Park. Bd. social ministry Luth. Ch.-Mo. Synod, 1969—; mem. steering com. welfare services div. Luth. Council in U.S.A., 1966—. Bd. dirs. Wheat Ridge Found. Served to 1st lt., F.A., Aus, 1943-46; ETO. Recipient Superior Service awards U.S. Dept. Health, Edn. and Welfare, 1964, 65. Fellow Am. Sociol. Assn.; mem. Population Assn. Am., Am. Pub. Welfare Assn., Phi Beta Kappa, Phi Kappa Phi, Phi Gamma Delta. Home: 222 Hillsboro Dr Silver Spring MD 20902 Office: US Dept Health Edn and Welfare 5600 Fishers Lane Rockville MD 20852

MUHONEN, ELMER WILLIAM, govt. ofcl.; b. Duluth, Minn., Jan. 21, 1922; s. Alexander Gustave and Hilda (Huhtanen) M.; student Hibbing Minn. Jr. Coll., 1938-40, U. Pa., 1943-44; B.B.A., U. Minn., 1945; postgrad. Geo. Wash. U., 1953-54, 62; m. Clara Lee Silvea, Dec. 26, 1944; children—Linda (Mrs. David Lee), Mark Allen, Yvonne Marie. Jr. accountant, Haskins & Sells C.P.A.'s, Chgo., 1945-46; asst. dir. civil accounting and auditing div. U.S. Gen. Accounting Office, Washington, 1946-60; dir. audit U.S. Devel. Loan Fund, Washington, 1960-61; chief field operations staff Office Controller AID, Washington, 1961-64; dir. audit div. U.S. Housing and Home Finance Agy., Washington, 1964-66; dir. office audit U.S. Dept. Housing and Urban Devel., Washington, 1966—. Served with AUS, 1942-44. C.P.A., N.C. Mem. Am., D.C. insts. C.P.A.'s, Fed. Govt. Accountants Assn. Lutheran. Home: 1274 Palmer Rd Oxon Hill MD 20022 Office: 451 7th St SW Washington DC 20410

MUIJE, CORNELIUS SCHULF, tobacco co. exec.; b. Salt Lake City, July 18, 1925; s. Cornelis and Elisabeth (Schuif) M.; B.S. in Mech. Engring., U. Utah, 1956, postgrad., 1956-57; advanced mgmt. program Harvard Bus. Sch., 1971; m. Lilian Siebert, Oct. 22, 1946; 1 dau., Susan A. Supr. operations research, advt. dept. Procter & Gamble, Cin., 1957-64; dir. marketing research Brown & Williamson Tobacco Corp., Louisville, 1964—. Mem. Cin. World Front TV Com., 1961-64. Served with CIC, AUS, 1946-53. Mem. Am., Cin. (pres., 1962-64) philatelic socs., Nat. Indsl. Conf. Bd., Council Marketing Research Dirs., Am. Civil Liberties Union. Home: 4700 Trowbridge Terrace Louisville KY 40207 Office: 1600 W Hill St Louisville KY 40201

MUIR, HELEN, author; b. Yonkers, N.Y., Feb. 9, 1911; d. Emmet A. and Helen T. (Flaherty) Lennehan; student Yonkers pub. schools; m. William Whalley Muir, Jan. 23, 1936; children—Mary (Mrs. Frederick W. Burrell), William Torbert. With Yonkers Herald Statesman, 1929-30, 31-33, N.Y. Eve. Post, 1930-31, N.Y. Eve. Jour., 1933-34, Carl Byoir & Assos., 1934-35; syndicated columnist Universal Service, 1935-38, Miami Daily News, 1935-39; broadcaster stas. WIOD, WQAM, 1935, 42; columnist Miami Herald, 1941-42; woman's editor Miami Daily News, 1943-44; free lance mag. writer, Sat. Eve. Post, This Week, Nations Bus., Woman's Day, 1944—; children's book editor Miami Herald, 1949-56; drama critic Miami News, 1960-65. Trustee Coconut Grove Library Assn., Friends U. Miami Library. Trustee, Met. Dade County Library Bd. Recipient award Delta Kappa Gamma, 1960. Mem. Theta Sigma Phi. Club: Fla. Womens Press (award 1963). Author: Miami, U.S.A., 1954. Home: 3855 Stewart Av Miami FL 33133

MUIR, J LAWRENCE, geologist; b. Enid, Okla., Apr. 4, 1903; s. Alexander and Lillie (Vaught) M.; B.S., U. Okla., 1930, M.S., 1933; m. Hazel Munhall, Apr. 22, 1930; children—Vivian (Mrs. Leo C. Varian), Robert L., Carolyn (Mrs. Charles R. Gasaway), Gordon K. Geologist, Gulf Refining Co., Shreveport, La., 1930; geologist, then dist. geologist Amerada Petroleum Corp., 1933-48; chief geologist Champlin Refining Co., Enid, Okla., 1948-51, v.p. exploration and devel., 1951-54; cons. geologist, Enid, 1954-62; petroleum geologist SEC, Washington, 1962-68, chief petroleum geologist, chief sect. oil and gas, 1968—. Vis. asso. prof. petroleum geology U. Okla., 1955-56. Pres., U. Okla. Dad's Assn., 1957-58. Mem. Am. Assn. Petroleum Geologists, Am. Inst. Mining and Metall. Engrs., Geol. Soc. Am., Soc. Exploration Geophysicists, Soc. Econ. Paleontologists and Mineralogists, Phi Beta Kappa, Sigma Xi, Sigma Gamma Epsilon. Methodist. Home: 533 W Great Falls St Falls Church VA 22046 Office: Securities and Exchange Commn 500 N Capitol St Washington DC 20549

MUIR, JOHN ANDERSON, metal fabricating co. exec.; b. Springfield, Ill., Jan 24, 1926; s. John Anderson and Irene (Davis) M.; B.S., U. Ill., 1953; m. Sue Crawford, Aug. 1, 1945; children—Sherryl S. (Mrs. Morrow), Marcia S. Tool and die maker Sangamo Electric Co., Springfield, 1946-50, sales engr., 1953-55, plant mech. engr., Pickens, S.C., 1956-59, asst. plant mgr., 1959-62, plant mgr., 1962-64; pres. Metal Fabricators, Inc., Greenville, S.C., 1964—, also dir.; v.p. Gantt Mfg. Corp., Greenville, 1967—, also dir.; pres. Gantt Bldg., Inc., Greenville, 1967, now dir., v.p.; v.p. Golden Tye Corp., Pickens, 1967—, also dir.; sec., treas. Pickens R.R. Co., 1968—, also dir.; dir. Thermal Engring. Corp., Columbia, S.C. Chmn., Oconee County Republicans for Strom Thurmond, 1968. Served with USMCR, 1942-46. Methodist. Mason (Shriner). Clubs: Poinsett, Green Valley Country. Home: 129 Chisolm Trail Greenville SC 29607 Office: PO Box 1946 Greenville SC 29602

MUIRHEAD, JEAN DENMAN, lawyer; b. nr. Charleston, Miss., May 12, 1929; d. Joe M. and Eva (Bufkin) Denman; student Delta State Coll., 1945-47; LL.B., Jackson Sch. Law, 1967; children—Mike, Scott, Melissa. Legal sec. Office Atty. Gen., State of Miss., Jackson, 1947-50; legal sec. firm Overstreet, Kuykendall, Perry & Phillips, Jackson, 1962-64, Satterfield, Shell, Williams & Buford, Jackson, 1967; admitted to Miss. bar, 1967; pvt. practice in Jackson, Miss., 1967—; mem. Miss. Senate, 1968-72. First v.p. Hinds County Kidney Found.; mem. 1970 Assay Commn.; mem. Law Enforcement Assistance Regional Council No. 3. Bd. dirs. Hinds County Mental Health Assn. Mem. Am., Miss., Hinds County bar assns., Nat. Assn. Women Lawyers, Order of Women Legislators, Jackson Bus. and Profl. Womens Club (Woman of Achievement 1970). Home: Belvedere Manor Apt 411 Jackson MS 39212 Office: 506 S President St Jackson MS 39201

MUIRHEAD, SAMUEL JOHN, physician, hosp. adminstr.; b. Brazil, Feb. 11, 1913; s. Harold Harvey and Sarah Alyne (Guynes) M.; A.B., Baylor U., 1933, M.D., 1936; m. Ann Elizabeth Fry, June 9, 1936; children—Sue Ann, Robert Samuel, John William. Intern Shreveport Charity Hosp., 1936-37; resident North Little Rock (Ark.) VA Hosp., 1948-49; pvt. practice medicine, Garland, Tex., 1939-41; with VA, 1941—; psychiatrist in hosps. at Waco, Tex., and Los Angeles, 1941-42; chief continued treatment service, Sheridan, Wyo., 1942-44, 46-47; asst. dir. profl. edn., asst. chief profl. services, North Little Rock, 1948-52, dir. profl. services, Lebanon, Pa., 1952-55; mgr. VA Hosp., Salisbury, N.C., 1955-61; dir. VA Center, Temple, Tex., 1961—; advanced tng. hosp. adminstrn. Inter-Agy. Inst. for Fed. Hosp. Adminstrs., 1956. Bd. dirs. U.S.O. Temple. Served with AUS, 1938-39, 44-46. Diplomate Am. Bd. Psychiatry and Neurology. Fellow Am. Psychiatric Assn. (certified mental hosp. adminstr.); mem. A.M.A., Tex. Med. Assn., Bell County Med. Soc., So. Psychiat. Assn., Am. Legion. Presbyn. Mason (Shriner). Home: 3906 Las Cienega Blvd Temple TX 76501 Office: VA Center Temple TX 76501

MULHALL, LAWRENCE JOSEPH, wholesale co. exec.; b. Louisville, May 27, 1908; s. Joseph Horace and Elizabeth (Shea) M.; student U. Ky., 1927, U. Louisville, 1928, 29; m. Louise Gillespie, Sept. 13, 1936; 1 dau., Elizabeth (Mrs. Kenneth Allen Agee). Pres., dir. McWhorter Weaver & Co., Nashville, 1946—; pres., dir. Grayson Corp., 1958—. Chmn., Nashville Mayor's adv. com. Housing and Urban Devel., 1968-69; pres. Nashville Symphony Assn., 1969; chmn. adv. bd. St. Thomas Hosp., Nashville, 1970—. Served with USNR, 1942-45; ETO, MTO, PTO. Mem. Nashville Sales Exec. Counsel (pres. 1948), Nashville C. of C. (pres. 1957). Kiwanian (pres. 1947). Club: Belle Meade Country, Cumberland, Amateur Chefs Soc. (Nashville). Home: 1616 Chickering Rd Nashville TN 37215 Office: 1101 Menzler Rd Nashville TN 37210

MULLANEY, JOSEPH EDWARD, govt. ofcl.; b. Fall River, Mass., Mar. 22, 1933; s. Joseph Edward and Beatrice (Hancock) M.; A.B. magna cum laude, Holy Cross Coll., 1955; LL.B. magna cum laude, Harvard, 1958; m. Rosemary Woodman, June 22, 1957; children—Joseph Edward III, Brian. Sean, Maura. Admitted to Ohio bar, Mass. bar; with firm Jones, Day, Cockley & Reavis, Cleve., 1960-70, partner, 1966-70; gen. counsel Office Spl. Rep. for Trade Negotiations, Exec. Office of Pres., Washington, 1970—. Legal counsel to John Carroll U. Exec. com. Republican party Cuyahoga County, O., precinct committeeman, Cleve. Trustee Gilmour Acad. Served with AUS. Mem. Holy Cross Nat. Alumni Council (dir.), Mass. Bar Assn. Home: 10612 Gainsborough Rd Potomac MD 20854 Office: Room 725 1800 G St NW Washington DC 20506

MULLANEY, SISTER MICHAEL LEO, adminstr. St. Joseph's Hosp., Lexington, Ky. Address: 1400 Harrodsburg Rd Lexington KY 40504*

MULLEN, ANDREW JUDSON, physician; b. Selma, Ala., June 23, 1922; s. Andrew J. and Helen (Johnson) M.; A.B., Vanderbilt U., 1948; M.D., Jefferson Med. Coll., 1952; m. Elizabeth E. Sherman, Mar. 17, 1958; children—Tom S., J. Thomas, Michael B., Debbie, Gail, Andrea, Shawn, Connie, Beth. Intern, U.S. Marine Hosp., Galveston, Tex., 1952-53; resident Tex. Med. Center, Houston, 1954-57; chief neurology and psychiatry service VA Hosp., Jackson, Miss., 1957; dir. Mobile (Ala.) Mental Health Center, 1957-58; practice medicine, specializing in psychiatry and neurology, Shreveport, La., 1958—; chief female service Confederate Meml. Med. Center, 1959-63, bd. dirs., chmn. pub. relations com., 1964; med. dir. Shreveport Child Guidance Center, 1961—; cons. psychiatry and neurology Barksdale AFB, Methodist Children's Home, VA Hosp.; co-chief staff Brentwood Neuro-Psychiatric Hosp., Shreveport, 1970—; asst. clin. prof. psychiatry La. State U. Sch. Medicine, 1961—. Dep. coroner, cons., Caddo Parish, La., 1964; chmn. mental health com. Community Council, 1964—. Served with RCAF, 1941-42, AUS, 1942-45. Decorated Purple Heart with oak leaf cluster, Bronze Star. Diplomate Am. Bd. Psychiatry and Neurology (asst. examiner). Fellow Am., So. psychiat. assns.; mem. A.M.A., So. Med. Assn., Shreveport Med. Soc. (dir. 1971-72), Flying Physicians Assn., Alpha Tau Omega, Nu Sigma Nu. Episcopalian. Home: 333 Berkshire Pl Shreveport LA 71101 Office: 902 Olive St Shreveport LA 71104

MULLEN, ROBERT RODOLF, public relations exec.; b. Alamogordo, N.M., Nov. 24, 1908; s. Robert Gordon and Madeline (Rodolf) M.; student U. Wis., 1928-29, U. Denver, 1930-31; m. Edna Cummings, Mar. 13, 1936; children—Robert R., Jonathan, Christopher, Suzanne. Reporter, Rocky Mountain News, Denver, 1931-33; advt. mgr. Denver Park & Amusement Co., 1933-34; staff corr. Christian Sci. Monitor, Boston, 1934-37, asst. city editor 1937-40, editorial writer, 1940-42; U.S. mem. pub. relations com. U.S.-U.K. Combined Bds., 1943-45; asst. editor, editorial writer Life mag., N.Y.C, 1946-48; dir. information ECA, 1949-52; pub. relations chief Citizens for Eisenhower, 1952; exec. dir. Nat. Citizens Com. for Ednl. TV, 1953-55; chmn. Robert R. Mullen & Co., pub. relations, Washington and N.Y.C., 1956—. Chmn. pub. relations for Nixon/Agnew, 1968. Republican. Christian Scientist. Clubs: Metropolitan. Nat. Press (Washington); Overseas Press (N.Y.C.). Contbr. to periodicals. Home: 2510 Virginia Av NW Washington DC 20037 Office: 1729 H St Washington DC 20006 also 152 E 78th St New York City NY 10021

MULLEN, SANFORD ALLEN, physician; b. Tampa, Fla., Jan. 16, 1925; s. Earl and Edith (Allen) M.; student Mercer U., 1943-45; M.D., Columbia U., 1949; m. Minnie Lucille Woodall, Dec. 23, 1945; children—Sanford Allen, Henry Woodall, Michael Hill. Intern, Grady Meml. Hosp., Atlanta, 1949-50; resident anatomic pathology, 1950, 53-54; fellow clin. pathology U. Minn. Hosps., Mpls., 1954-56; practice medicine specializing in pathology, Jacksonville, Fla., 1958—; mem. staff Duval Med. Center, Bapt. Meml., St. Vincent's, Meml., Hope Haven Children's hosps.; chief med. staff Cathedral Health and Rehab. Center (all Jacksonville), Putnam Meml. Hosp., Palatka, Fla., Lake Shore Hosp., Lake City, Fla. Nat. bd. govs. Arthritis Found., 1963-64, pres. Duval County div., 1960-61, pres. Fla. chpt., 1963-64; chmn. Jacksonville Mayor's Citizens Adv. Com. on Water Pollution Control, 1968-70, United Fund Campaign; vice chmn. Jacksonville Water Quality Control Bd., 1971—; exec. v.p., med. dir. Jacksonville Blood Bank, 1970—; mem. various adv. coms. Fla. Bd. Health, Fla. Dept. Edn., Fla. Jr. Coll., Jacksonville; mem. adv. bd. Fla. div. Salvation Army, 1971—; pres. Civic Round Table, 1967-69; rep. Greater Jacksonville Econ. Opportunity, Inc., 1966-68. Bd. dirs. Jacksonville Symphony Assn., 1970—. Served with M.C., USNR, 1950-52; on loan to AUS in Korea; comdr. Res. Ret. Diplomate Am. Bd. Pathology. Fellow Coll. Am. Pathologists (gov. 1966-69, 70—, chmn. state legislative com. 1969—); mem. A.M.A. A.A.A.S., Jacksonville Acad. Medicine (pres. 1963, dir. 1966-68), Fla. Soc. Pathologists (pres. 1964-66, 72-73, v.p. 1966-67), Am. Soc. Clin. Pathologists (councilor Fla. 1962-66), Duval County Med. Soc. (chmn. legislative council 1968, exec. com., 1968), Fla. (ho. of dels. 1964—, chmn. com. on state legislation 1969—), So. (vice-chmn. sect. pathology 1967-68) med. assns., N.E. Fla. Heart Assn. (dir. 1967-71), Fla. (dir. 1968—, pres.-elect 1972—), Am. (state rep. for Fla. 1971—) assns. blood banks, Am. Cancer Soc., Fla. Med. Polit. Action Com. (dir. 1964-65), Jacksonville Area C. of C. (gov. 1966-68, 72—, chmn. pub. health com. 1965-66, v.p. membership affairs), Jacksonville Art Mus., Cummer Gallery Art, Ye Mystic Revellers, Blue Key, Sigma Mu, Gamma Sigma Epsilon, Phi Eta Sigma, Alpha Tau Omega (pres. Jacksonville alumni 1958-59). Episcopalian (vestryman 1967-69, sr. warden 1969). Rotarian (pres. Jacksonville 1970-71). Clubs: Seminole, Fla. Yacht, Timuquana Country, University, St. Johns Dinner (dir. 1967-70, pres. 1969-70), Torch (dir. 1968—, pres. 1971-72). Home: 5171 Yacht Club Rd Jacksonville FL 32210 Office: Box 2921 Jacksonville FL 32203

MULLENDORE, GEORGE PIERCE, agrl. extension agt.; b. Louisville, Miss., June 16, 1934; s. George Allen and Cornelia Ruth (Young) M.; B.S., Miss. State U., 1955, M.S., 1969, Ph.D., 1971; m. Marilyn Joyce McGehee, June 19, 1955; children—Deborah Faith, Karen Kay, George Michael. Salesman, Taylor Machine Works, 1955-56; asst. county agt. Miss. Extension Service, 1957-58, asso. county agt., 1958-62, asst. agronomist, 1962-63, asso. extension agronomist, Stoneville, Miss., 1963-70, asso. extension agronomist State College, Miss., 1970—; cons. agr., chem. industry, agrl. photographer. Served with AUS, 1956-57; ETO. Fellow Nat. Cotton Council; mem. Am. Soc. Agronomy, So. Weed Sci. Soc., Miss. Farm Bur., Miss. Weed Sci. Soc. (sec. treas. 1966-71), Cotton Disease Council, Cotton Physiology and Defoliation Council, Miss. Agrl. Chems. Council, Epsilon Sigma Phi, Gamma Sigma Delta, Rotarian, Mason (32 deg.). Presbyn. (deacon 1959—). Contbr. articles to publs. Home: 607 Sherwood Rd Starkville MS 39759 Office: Box 5425 State College MS 39762

MULLENS, RICHARD ARNOLD, lawyer; b. Cheyenne, Wyo., Apr. 15, 1918; s. Arnold R. and Ada (Brook) M.; B.A., U. Wyo., 1940, LL.B., 1942; m. Barbara Nelson, Apr. 5, 1942; children—Sherry, Joan, Elizabeth. Admitted to Wyo. bar, 1942, D.C. bar, 1954; atty. Internal Revenue Service, 1946-50, legal adv. staff Treasury Dept., 1953-54; asso. firm Hogan & Hartson, Washington, 1954-60; partner firm Silverstein & Mullens, Washington, 1960—. Trustee Nat. Cathedral Sch. for Girls, Washington. Served with AUS, 1942-46, 50-52. Mem. Am. Bar Assn. (com. adminstrv. practice, sect. on taxation 1954—), Wyo. State Bar, Bar Assn. D.C. Episcopalian. Asso. editor Tax Exec. mag., 1963-71. Home: 2710 36th St NW Washington DC 20007 Office: 1776 K St NW Washington DC 20006

MULLER, BERT, assn. exec.; b. Jersey City, Dec. 6, 1926; s. Albert and Sally (O'Gorman) M.; student U. Fla., 1960; m. Rita Jean Sebacher, Feb. 23, 1957; children—Leslie Jean, David Thomas, Christine Louise, Michele Lynn, Albert John. Pres., Muller Ins., Inc., St. Petersburg, Fla., 1952-63; exec. dir Pinellas Assn. for Retarded Children, Pinellas Park, Fla., 1963—, also mental retardation planning coordinator for Pinellas County; dir. Peter Pan Sch. for Retarded Children. Mem. Day Care Adv. Com., Fla. Dept. Pub. Welfare, 1965—; mem. Gov.'s Conf. of Dirs., Tallahassee, 1964-65, Gov.'s Adv. Council Mental Retardation, 1967—, Gov.'s Hire Handicapped Com. Served with USNR, 1944-46. Mem. Am. Assn. Mental Deficiency, Council Exceptional Children, Nat. Assn. for Pvt. Residential Facilities for Mentally Retarded, Fla. Assn. Retarded Children. Rotarian, Optimist. Contbr. articles to profl. jours. Author Fla. PKU legislation. Home: 7148 9th St S St Petersburg FL 33705 Office: 3100 75th St N St Petersburg FL 33710

MULLER, CHARLES JULIUS, architect; b. Commerce, Tex., Feb. 24, 1918; s. Charles Julius and Nora Bradley (Cockerham) M.; B.S., East Tex. State U., 1938; B.Arch., Mass. Inst. Tech., 1941; postgrad. U. Tex., 1939; M.Ed., East Tex. State U., 1962; m. Linda Moody, May 18, 1943; children—Charles Julius, Jamie (Mrs. H. Jack Lassiter). Gen. mgr. Muller Ice Co., Commerce, Tex., 1945-58; pvt. practice architecture, 1946—; dir. First Nat. Bank. Chmn., Commerce Bd. Adjustment, 1967—, Housing Authority of Commerce, 1949—. Served to maj. AUS, 1941-45. Mem. A.I.A., Tex. Soc. Architects. C. of C. (pres. 1951), E. Tex. State U. Alumni Assn. (bd. dirs. 1970—), Phi Delta Kappa. Episcopalian. Lion (pres. 1951). Home: 2505 Washington St Commerce TX 71428 Office: 2507 Washington St Commerce TX 75428

MULLIGAN, PETER JOHN, systems engr.; b. Bklyn., Aug. 1, 1936; s. John Vincent and Virginia (Body) M.; B.E.E., U. Fla., 1961, M.S., in Engring., 1967. With Gen. Electric Co., 1961—, design engr. communications products dept., Lynchburg, Va., 1961, engr. space power systems, missile and space vehicle dept., Valley Forge, Pa., 1961-62, product engr. neutron devices dept., St. Petersburg, Fla., 1962-63, engr. lunar module, Apollo systems dept., Daytona Beach, Fla., 1963-69, sr. engr. Apollo systems dept., Washington, 1969—, mem. quality reliability team Apollo Lunar Mission, 1969. Student guidance counselor engring. U. Fla., 1966-69. Served with USMC, 1954-57. Recipient NASA commendation award, 1966; Apolloneer award Apollo Systems Dept., 1967. Registered profl. engr., Fla. Mem. Am. Inst. Aeros. and Astronautics (treas. 1965, chmn. honors and awards 1966), I.E.E.E. (chmn. reliability chpt. 1967, chmn. honors and awards 1968), Phi Eta Sigma, Sigma Tau, Tau Beta Pi, Phi Kappa Phi, Alpha Pi Mu. Democrat. Roman Catholic. Home: 2500 N Van Dorn St Alexandria VA 22302 Office: 955 L'Enfant Plaza N SW Washington DC 20024

MULLINGS, WILLIAM NORMAN, ret. statistician; b. Gorman, Tex., July 10, 1909; s. Felix Wayne and Julia (Evans) M.; B.A., U. Tex., 1930; m. Dorothy Lucille Lindahl, Oct. 10, 1935; children—Norma Lucille (Mrs. Brevard Thomas Hunt), Eileen Adell (Mrs. Andrew M. Smith). Regional statistician Soil Conservation Service, 1937-47, PHA, 1947-48; statistician, program analyst Third U.S.Army, 1948-69; sec-treas. Regents, Inc., 1962—. Bd. dirs. Ft. McPherson Credit Union, 1952—, pres., 1953-69; treas. Sylvan Hills Civic Club, 1961—; bd. dirs. Swan Lake Estates, Inc., 1971—. Served with USNR, 1943-45. Mem. Am. Statis. Assn., Armed Forces Mgmt. Assn. Methodist. (treas.). Home: Route 4 Lakeshore Dr Stockbridge GA 30281

MULLINIX, BOBBY RAY, govt. ofcl.; b. Jamestown, Tenn., June 15, 1936; s. Fred Ottley and Orpha Hazel (Linder) M.; B.S. in Mech. Engring., Tenn. Tech. U., 1958, M.S. in Engring. Mechanics, 1969; Ph.D. in Engring. Mechanics, Va. Tech. and State U., 1972; m. Sandra Kay Bullock, Sept. 18, 1964; children—Benjamin Ray, Bret Allen, Kim Sheree. Mech. engr. U.S. C.E., 1958-64; aerospace engr. U.S. Army Missile Command, Redstone Arsenal, Ala., 1964—; cons. specific missile systems problems Project Mgmt. Offices, 1964—. Tech. rep. contracting officer Nashville, YMCA, 1959-61; active Civilian Welfare League, 1964-72. Registered profl. engr., Ala. Mem. Assn. U.S. Army, Am. Soc. M.E., Soc. Am. Mil. Engrs., Soc. Exptl. Stress Analysis (v.p. 1971-72), Tenn. Soc. Profl. Engrs. Baptist. Club: Castle Camera (Nashville). Research in fluid and fracture mechanics. Home: 11020 Jean Rd Huntsville AL 35803 Office: AMSMI RLA Bldg 5400 Redstone Arsenal AL 35809

MULLINS, DAVID WILEY, univ. pres.; b. Ash Flat, Ark., Aug. 11, 1906; s. Roscoe C. and Emma Matilda (Roberts) M.; B.A. cum laude, U. Ark., 1931; M.A., U. Colo., 1934; Ed.D., Columbia, 1941; LL.D., Hendrix Coll., Conway, Ark., 1965; m. Eula Elizabeth Harrell, Aug. 9, 1935; children—Carolyn Jeanne, David Wiley, Gary Eugene. Tchr. high sch. Williford (Ark.) Consol Schs., 1931-32, supt., 1932-35; supt. schs., Lepanto, Ark., 1935-41; asso. prof. Sch. Adminstrn. Ala. Poly. Inst., 1941-43, research prof. edn., 1946-47, acting dir. div. instrn., 1947-49, exec. v.p., 1949-60; pres. U. Ark., Fayetteville, 1960—. Mem. council on grad. edn. in agrl. scis. So. Regional Edn. Bd., mem., 1960—, mem. exec. com., 1966, pres., 1972-73, vice chmn., 1969—; mem. Ala. Study Com., 1957-59; mem. fed. relations commn. Am. Council on Edn., 1970—, bd. dirs., 1971—; mem. So. regional panel for selection White House Fellows; adv. com. Inst. Internat. Edn.; mem. Higher Edn. Adv. Com. on Wages and Prices, 1971—; mem. adv. panel R.O.T.C. Bd. dirs. Grad. Research Center S.W.; trustee Ark. Coll., 1970—. Served as lt. USNR, 1943-46. Named Ark. Man of Yr., Ark. Democrat newspaper, Little Rock, 1969. Mem. So. Assn. Land Grant Colls. and State Univs. (pres. 1962-63), Ark. Edn. Assn., Nat. Planning Assn. (nat. planning council), Internat. Assn. U. Presidents, N.E.A., Am. Assn. Sch. Adminstrs., Ark. C. of C. (dir. 1960-63), Nat. Assn. State Univ. and Land-Grant Colls. (exec. com. 1969—, com. on fed. legislation 1970—, pres. 1971-72), So. Univ. Conf. (pres. 1968), Atlantic Council, Ala. Edn. Assn. (pres. 1955-56), Phi Beta Kappa, Phi Kappa Phi, Phi Delta Kappa, Omicron Delta Kappa, Phi Eta Sigma, Kappa Delta Pi, Pi Mu Epsilon, Phi Alpha Theta. Democrat. Rotarian (dist. gov. 1950-51). Contbr. articles to profl. publs. Home: 531 N Sequoyah Dr Fayetteville AR 72701

MULLINS, JOHN WILLIAM, supt. schs.; b. Newport, Ark., Jan 17, 1921; s. John William and Trula Elnora (Mayfield) M.; student Ouachita U., 1940, N.E. Okla. State U., 1941; B.S., Ark. State U., 1949; M.A., Peabody Coll., 1953; advanced Adminstrs. certificate, U. Tenn., 1965; m. Mary Jane Foster, June 22, 1946; 1 dau., Patti Jo. Athletic dir. Illmo (Mo.) High Sch., 1949-50; coach, instr. history Corning (Ark.) High Sch., 1950-53; supt. Pucico (Mo.) Pub. Schs., 1953-55; supt. Portageville (Mo.) Sch. Dist., 1955-60; supt. Hayti (Mo.) Sch. Dist., 1960-62; supt. Newport (Ark.) Sch. Dist., 1962—. Pres. City Beautiful Com., Newport, 1968. Served with USAAF, 1942-45; ETO. Decorated Air medal, Purple Heart. Mem. Am. Assn. Sch. Adminstrs., Ark. Sch. Adminstrs. Assn. (pres.), Ark. (dir.), Newport (pres.) edn. assns., Area Methodist Men (pres.), Region 3AA Athletic Assn. (pres.), Dist. XII Activities Assn. (pres.), Phi Delta Kappa. Mason, Rotarian. Home: 4 Sue Circle Newport AR 72112 Office: Remmel Park Newport AR 72112

MULLINS, LESLIE MORRIS, lawyer; b. Coeburn, Va., Apr. 19, 1917; s. George Milburn and Willie (Boyd) M.; A.B., Emory and Henry Coll., 1940; J.D., U. Va., 1942; m. Dorothy Ann McGlothlin, June 24, 1943; children—Leslie Wayne, Michael Morris, Elizabeth Ann. Admitted to Va. bar, 1942; practiced in Norton, 1946—; mem. firm Greear, Bowen, Mullins & Winston, and predecessors, 1946—. Chmn. Eastern Wise County chpt. A.R.C., 1947-53. Served with USNR, 1942-46. Fellow Am. Coll. Trial Lawyers; mem. Am., Va. State bar assns., Am. R.R. Trial Lawyers Assn., Norton C. of C. (pres. 1949). Democrat. Methodist. Mason, Kiwanian, Club: Lonesome Pine Country. Home: 315 Henry St Norton VA 24273 Office: Law Bldg 7th St Norton VA 24273

MULLINS, LESLIE P., city ofcl.; b. Webbville, Ky., Aug. 10, 1909; s. Fleming Lewis and Sara Jane (Pennington) M.; student Ky. Christian Coll., 1932, Law Sch., U. Balt., 1934-35, W.Va. State Police Recruit Sch., 1938; m. Judy Elizabeth Clay, July 9, 1946; children—Jane (Mrs. Robert Stephen O'Rear). With Island Creek Coal Co., Holden, W.Va., 1929-38; with W.Va. State Police, 1938-60; chief of police, Ocoee, Fla., 1960-61, Lake City, Fla., 1961—. Mem. Fla. Gov.'s Council Criminal Justice. Bd. dirs., Goodwill Industries. Region 11, North Fla. Council, Boy Scouts Am., 1964-72, Keep Fla. Beautiful. Served with USNR, 1943-46; PTO. Mem. Internat. Chiefs of Police Assn., Fla. Police Chiefs Assn. (pres. 1971-72), Fla. Peace Officers Assn., W.Va. State Police Retired Members Assn., Columbia County Law Enforcement Assn., Am. Legion, Fraternal Order Police, V.F.W. Mason (32 deg., Shriner), Lion; mem. Order of DeMolay (hon.). Home: 1611 S Division St Lake City FL 32055 Office: 150 N Alachua St Lake City FL 32055

MULLINS, ROLAND THOMAS, educator; b. Gainesville, Ark., May 20, 1932; s. Ray Marshall and Mae Vella (McDaniel) M.; B.S., Ark. State Coll., 1956; M.B.A., U. Ark., 1957, Ph.D., 1960; m. Billie Ann Laffoon, Aug. 18, 1954; children—Joel Wayne, Gary Alan. Economist TVA, Chattanooga, 1959; chmn. dept. econs., finance Memphis State U., 1960-65; chmn. dept. gen. bus., econs. Ark. State U. at State University, 1965-69, prof. econs., finance, 1969—. Tchr., cons. bus. and banking groups, 19 —. Served to sgt., USMCR, 1951-52. Decorated Purple Heart, Bronze Star. Gen. Electric Corp. fellow U. Chgo., 1967. Mem. Am., So., Ozark (pres. 1965) econ. assns., Ark. Coll. Tchrs. of Econs. and Bus. (pres. 1967), Alpha Kappa Psi, Phi Gamma Mu. Lion. Home: 1000 Sylvan Hill Dr Jonesboro AR 72401

MULLIS, CAROL BEA, utility co. exec.; b. Charlotte, N.C., Oct. 6, 1923; s. John Ingram and Lula (Tarlton) M.; B.E.E., N.C. State U., 1950; B.A., U. N.C., 1969; m. Dorothy Margaret Martin, May 29, 1958; 1son, Nathaniel T. Maintenance engr. Duke Power Co., Charlotte, N.C., 1950-56, asst. elec. engr., 1956-60, asst. planning engr., 1960-69, economist, 1969—; adj. instr. elec. engring. Charlotte Coll., 1959-61; adj. instr. math. Central Piedmont Community Coll., 1967—. Mem. Mecklenburg County Republican Exec. Com., 1958—; mem. N.C. Social Scis. Adv. Com., 1958—; mem. S.C. Social Scis. Adv. Com., 1968—. Served with USAAF, 1942-46. Mem. I.E.E.E. (sec. Charlotte sect. 1966-67), Am. Legion. Republican. Methodist. Home: 2500 Hargett Dr Matthews NC 28105 Office: PO Box 932 Charlotte NC 28201

MUMFORD, LAWRENCE QUINCY, librarian; b. Ayden N.C., Dec. 11, 1903; s. Jacob Edward and Emma Luvenia (Stocks) M.; A.B. magna cum laude, Duke, 1925, A.M., 1928, Litt.D., 1957; M.L.S., Columbia, 1929; Litt.D., Bethany Coll., 1954, Rutgers U., 1956, Belmont Abbey Coll., 1963; LL.D., Union Coll., 1955, Bucknell U., 1956, U. Notre Dame, 1964, U. Pitts., 1964; H.H.D., Kings Coll., 1970; m. Permelia Catharine Stevens, Oct. 4, 1930 (dec. Apr. 1961); 1 dau., Kathryn; m. 2d, Betsy Perrin Fox, Nov. 28, 1969. Mem. staff Duke Library, 1922-28; acting chief reference and circulation, 1928; student asst. Columbia U. Library, 1928-29; staff N.Y. Pub. Library, 1929-45, gen. asst. charge dir.'s office, 1932-35, exec. asst., chief preparation div., 1936-43, exec. asst., coordinator gen. services divs., 1943-45; asst. dir. Cleve. Pub. Library, 1945-50, dir., 1950-54; dir. processing dept. Library of Congress, Washington, 1940-41, librarian, 1954—. Chmn. Fed. Library Com.; bd. advisers Dumbarton Oaks Research Library and Collection; mem. sponsors com. Papers of Woodrow Wilson; mem. adv. com. Edward R. Murrow Meml. Fund. of Overseas Press Club Found.; mem. Carolina Charter Corp.; mem. adv. commn. for publ. Papers of George Washington; chmn. ex officio Permanent Com. for Oliver Wendell Holmes Devise; mem., sec. ex officio Library of Congress Trust Fund Bd.; mem. ex officio adv. bd. Nat. Park Service's Historic Am. Bldgs. Survey; mem. ex officio Nat. Commn. Libraries and Information Sci.; mem. Sci. Information Council, Fed. Council on Arts and Humanities, Am. Revolution Bicentennial Comm., Nat. Hist. Publs. Commn.; mem. nat. adv. com. Am. Antiquarian Soc.; mem. U.S. com. for Am. Library Paris. Chmn. bd. visitors Duke U. Library; adv. bd. Cafritz Found.; bd. regents Nat. Library Medicine; trustee John F. Kennedy Center for Performing Arts, Woodrow Wilson Internat. Center for Scholars, Greater Washington Ednl. TV Assn.; hon. fellow Harry S. Truman Library Inst. for Nat. and Internat. Affairs. Benjamin Franklin fellow Royal Soc. for Encouragement of Arts, Manufactures and Commerce (London). Mem. Nat. Trust for Historic Preservation, U.S. Nat. Book Com., Brit. Mus. Soc., Mass. Hist. Soc. (corr.), Capitol Hill Hist. Soc. (hon. trustee), A.L.A. (pres. 1954-55), Ohio Library Assn. (pres. 1947-48), Manuscript Soc. (pres. 1968-70), D.C. Library Assn., Phi Beta Kappa, Omicron Delta Kappa, Beta Phi Mu. Clubs: Cosmos, International (Washington). Home: 3721 49th St NW Washington DC 20016 Office: Library of Congress Washington DC 20540

MUMFORD, LEE WARREN, banker; b. Harriman, Tenn., Jan. 18, 1941; s. John Phillip and Jane Eleanor (Becker) M.; student U. Va., 1964-66; B.S., Frederick Coll., 1964; m. Carol Mancuso, Aug. 28, 1965; children—Keith Warren, Christopher Lee. With Bank Ashland (Ky.), 1966—, v.p., 1971—. Mem. Ky. Citizens Commn. on Consumer Protection, 1970-71. Bd. dirs. Ashland (Ky.) Community Concert Assn., 1967. Served with USAF, 1960-61. Mem. Small Bus. Adminstrn. (regional adviser 1971—), Am. Inst. Banking (dir. Tri-State chpt. 1968-69), Ashland Jr. C. of C. (dir. 1967). Episcopalian (treas. 1971—). Home: 2709 Iroquois Av Ashland KY 41101 Office: 1416 Winchester Av Ashland KY 41101

MUMMA, ALBERT GIRARD, JR., architect; b. Long Beach, Cal., July 2, 1928; s. Albert Girard and Carmen (Braley) M.; B. Architecture, U.Va., 1951; Medal, A.I.A., 1951; m.; children—Eugenia Suzanne, Albert Girard III, Peter Brenaman. Designer, McLeod, & Ferrara, Architects, Washington, 1951-56; asso. Deigert & Yerkes, Architects, 1956-62; prin. Mumma & Assos., Washington, 1962—; cons. Carl. M. Freeman & Assoc., 1965—. Served with USMCR, 1945-47. Recipient Design award Washington Bd. or Trade, 1964. Mem. A.I.A. Presbyn. Prin. archtl. works include; Nat. Arboretum Headquarters Bldg., 1961, Finnmark Square, Silver Spring, Md., 1964, Post Office and Fed. Bldg., Elkins, W.Va., 1971, pvt. residences, Subdivision and Townhouse projects, Washington, Md., Va., Penn., 1962-71. Address: 1071 Wisconsin Av NW Washington DC 20007

MUMPHREY, ANTHONY, coll. dean; b. St. Rose, La., Oct. 9, 1921; s. Joseph and Lena (Yenni) M.; B.S., La. State U., 1943, M.S., 1949, Ph.D., 1956; m. Amelie Marie Robert, Apr. 26, 1948; children—Linda Marie, Peggy Jane, Joseph Scott, Robbie Ann, Ray Anthony, Terri Geralyn, Michael Louis, Robert Neil. Tchr. vocational agr., 1945-56; prin. Dutchtown (La.) High Sch., 1956-63; prof. La. State U., Baton Rouge, 1963-65; dean La. State U. at Eunice 1965—. World War II. Recipient hon. state farmer degree, 1965. Mem. Am., La. vocational assns., La. Tchrs. Assn., Nat. Vocational Agr. Tchrs. Assn., La. Agr. Tchrs. Assn., Future Farmers Am., Phi Eta Sigma, Alpha Tau Alpha, Alpha Zeta, Phi Kappa Phi, Kappa Phi Kappa. Rotarian, Lion. Co-author: Essential Aspects of Career Planning and Development. Home: Route 2 Box 73-B Eunice LA 70535

MUNCIE, DOUGLAS JENNINGS, physician; b. Bklyn., Oct. 8, 1916; s. Curtis Hamilton and Louise (Jennings) M.; student U. N.C., 1937-38; D.O., Kirksville Coll. Osteopathy and Surgery, 1942; M.D., Kansas City U., 1944; m. JoAnn Tenney, Dec. 22, 1966; children (by previous marriage)—Curtis Hamilton II, Douglas Newson. Intern, Orange Meml. Hosp., Orlando, Fla., 1944; practice medicine, specializing in deafness, Miami, Fla., 1946—; founder Muncie Inst. for Hearing, Miami, 1946. Served with AUS, 1945. Recipient Optimist Club award, Lakeland, Fla., 1958. Mem. Am. Acad. Osteo. Surgeons, Am. Acad. Medicine and Surgery, Dade County Osteo. Med. Soc., Am., Dade County osteo. assns. Research and publs. on treatment of deafness. Home and office: 150 NE 96th St Miami Shores FL 33138 Office: 1940 E Charleston St Las Vegas NV 89104

MUNDEN, KENNETH WHITE, archivist, editor; b. Elizabeth City, N.C., Feb. 16, 1912; s. Joshua Warren and Elizabeth Jane (White) M.; student Duke, 1929-31; A.B., Geoege Washington U., 1943; m. Lia Ghezzi, Aug. 24, 1946; children—Robin Ghezzi, Gordon Ghezzi. Statistician, War Dept., 1934-39; archivist Nat. Archives, 1939-43, 58-68; archivist Dept. Army, 1948-50, 52-57; archivist Fed. Civil Def. Adminstrn., 1958; editor Am. Film Inst., 1968—. Lectr. archival methodology Temple U., Am. U., 1951-68. Served with AUS, 1932-48, 51-52; lt. col. Res. ret. Recipient Waldo G. Leland prize Soc. Am. Archivists, 1963, Meritorious Achievement award Gen. Services Adminstrn., 1963; Meritorious Service award Civil War Centennial Commn., 1966; decorated Bronze Star. Mem. Internat. Council Archives, Soc. Am. Archivists, Am. Hist. Assn., Orgn. Am. Historians, Am. Assn. State and Local History, Soc. Cinema Studies. Author: Combined British-American Records of Mediterranean Theater of Operations in World War II, 1948; Preservation of Records Essential to Continuity of State and Local Government, 1958; (with H.P. Beers) Guide to Federal Archives Relating to the Civil War, 1967. Editor: Archives & The Public Interest: Selected Essays by Ernest Posner, 1967; The American Film Institute Catalog of Motion Pictures Produced in the United States: Feature Films 1921-30, 1971. Editor, The American Archivist, 1960-68. Home: 2673 N Upshur St Arlington VA 22207 Office: American Film Inst 1815 H St NW Washington DC 20006

MUNDT, LESLIE KROW, physician; b. Helena, Ark., 1912; M.D., Tulane U., 1937; M.S. in Dermatology and Syphilogy, U. Mich., 1941. Intern, U. Mich. Hosp., Ann Arbor, 1937-38, asst. resident in dermatology and syphilolgy, 1938-39, resident, 1939-40; sr. physician Touro Infirmary; sr. vis. physician Charity Hosp. of La., New Orleans; instr. U. Mich., 1940-41; clin. prof. dermotology and syphilology La. State U., New Orleans. Served to lt. col., M.C., AUS, 1941-45. Diplomate Am. Bd. Dermatology. Mem. A.M.A., So. Med. Assn., Am. Acad. Dermatology, Royal Soc. Medicine. Office: 1477 Louisiana Av New Orleans LA 70115*

MUNFORD, MRS. GEORGE L., dir. Rolfe-Warren House, Surry, Va. Address: Rolfe-Warren House Surry VA 23883*

MUNGER, ELMER LEWIS, civil engr., educator; b. Manhattan, Kan., Jan 4, 1915; s. Harold Hawley and Jane (Green) M.; B.S., Kan. State U., 1936, M.S., 1938; Ph.D., Ia. State U., 1957; m. Vivian Marie Bloomfield, Dec. 28, 1939; children—John Thomas, Harold Hawley II, Jane Marie. Rodman, St. Louis-Southwestern Ry., Ark., Mo., 1937-38; engr. U.S. Engr. Dept., Ohio, Neb., 1938-46; missionary engr. Philippine Episcopal Ch., 1946-48; engr. Wilson & Co., Salina, Kan., 1948; faculty Ia. State U., 1948-51, 54-58; engr. Corps Engrs., U.S. Army, Alaska, 1951-54; faculty, dean Norwich U., Northfield, Vt., 1958-69; prof. gen. engring. U. P.R. Mayaguez, 1969—. Registered profl. engr., Neb., Kan., Ia., Vt. Fellow Am. Soc. C.E.; mem. Soc. Am. Mil. Engrs., Am. Concrete Inst., Nat., Vt. socs. profl. engrs., Am. Assn. U. Profs., A.A.A.S., Am. Soc. Engring. Edn., Eastern Snow Conf., Izaak Walton League Am., Phi Kappa Phi, Sigma Tau, Tau Beta Pi. Episcopalian. Mason (Shriner). Author: (with C.J. Douglas) Construction Management. Home: Cesani Apts 61 Calle Mendez Vigo 53 Oeste Mayaguez PR 00708

MUNIZ, NICOLAS, shoe mfr.; b. Havana, Cuba, Sept. 21, 1927; s. Jose M. and Avelina (Rodriguez) M.; B.S. magna cum laude, Havana U., 1950, Ph.D. cum laude, 1960; m. Olga Arias, Apr. 9, 1961; children— Nicolas J., Antonio E., Carlos A., Beatriz C., Olga M. Came to U.S., 1965. Supr. accounting Caledonian Am. Ins. Co., Havana, 1950-52; head budget dept. Gen. Accounting Office of Cuba, 1952-58; tech. adviser, dir. Bank of Social Security of Cuba, 1959-60; supt. accounting Industrias y Confecciones, Madrid, Spain, 1962-65; v.p. finance Suave Shoe Corp., Hialeah, Fla., 1965-72; pres. Joy Footwear Corp., Hialeah, 1972—; prof. econs. Havana U., 1959-61. Mem. Cuban Delegation for Tax Treaty with U.S., 1955-58; mem. Commn. Tax Revision of Cuba, 1953-59; collaborator Tax Studies Inst. of Treasury Dept. of Spain, 1962. Recipient Prize Dean Cadenas, Cuban Inst. Pub. Accountants, 1960. Mem. Nat. Assn. Accountants. Club: Big Five (Miami). Author: Study of the Cuban Budgetary Revenues in 1952; The Social Security in Cuba, 1954; The Needless Taxes, 1955; The Tax Treaty Between Cuba and the United States of America, 1957. Home: 1401 W 81st St Hialeah FL 33014 Office: 440 W 27th St Hialeah FL 33010

MUNME, HENRY THEODORE, JR., dentist, naval officer; b. New Orleans, Sept. 22, 1921; s. Henry Theodore and Juanita Eleanore (Augustin) M.; D.D.S., Loyola U. South, New Orleans, 1945; m. Evelyn Rose Jordan, Dec. 26, 1946. Commd. ensign U.S. Navy, 1943-45, advanced through grades to capt., 1959; asst. dental officer Naval Tng. Center, Bainbridge, Md., 1945-47; pvt. practice dentistry, New Orleans, 1947-49; prosthodontist VA Hosp., New Orleans, 1949-50; sr. dental officer in U.S.S. Arcadia, 1960-61, in U.S.S. Grand Canyon, 1961-62; asst. dental officer Naval Air Sta., Pensacola, Fla., 1962-66; staff dental officer Naval Tng. Center, Kenitra, Morocco, 1966-68; asst. officer-in-charge Dental Detachment, Marine Corps Recruit Dept., Parris Island, S.C., 1968-71, officer-in-charge, 1971-72; dist. dental officer 8th Naval Dist., also sr. dental officer Naval Support Activity, New Orleans, 1972—. Mem. Am. Dental Assn., S.A.R., Psi Omega. Republican. Roman Catholic. K.C.; mem. Order of Alhambra. Home: 3641 Rue Colette New Orleans LA

MUNOZ-MARIN, LUIS, P.R. senator; b. San Juan, P.R., Feb. 18, 1898; s. Luis and Amalia (Marin) Munoz-Rivera; student Georgetown U., 1912-16; LL.D., Harvard, 1955, U. Kan., 1955, Bates Coll., 1957, Brandeis U., 1961, Columbia, 1963, Rutgers U., 1965; m. Muna Lee, July 1, 1919 (div.); children—Munita, Luis; m. 2d, Ines Maria Mendoza; children—Vivian, Victoria. Sec. to resident commr. for P.R. in Washington, 1916-18; editor La Revista de Indias (mag. devoted to Pan-Am. culture), 1918-19; active work in Pan-Am. labor movement and in movement for Latin-Am. unity; editor, pub. La Democracia, daily newspaper; elected gov. of P.R., 1948; mem. constl. assembly P.R., 1951; elected 1st gov. under constn. of Commonwealth of P.R., 1952, re-elected, 1956, 1960; senator Commonwealth of P.R., 1964—. Mem. gen. secretariat, Pan-Am. Conf., Havana; formerly econ. commr. P.R. in U.S.; elected senator-at-large, P.R., 1932. Founder, pres. Popular Dem. Party, 1938; pres. P.R. Senate, 1941-48; founder, editor El Batey, newspaper; spl. corr. Balt. Sun. Decorated Order de Vasco Nunez de Balboa Gran Cruz de la Orden del Sol (Peru); recipient Freedom House award, 1956, Murray Green award, 1962, Cardozo award, 1962, Distinguished Citizen award Caballeros de S.J. de Chgo., Presdl. Medal of Freedom, 1963, Author: Borrones, 1917; Madre Haraposa (in collaboration), 1917. Contbr. to Am. Mercury, Nation, New Republic, Fgn. Affairs. Address: Trujillo Alto Rd San Juan PR 00760

MUNROE, CLARK CAMERON, banker; b. Cherry Tree, Pa., Oct. 27, 1925; s. Thomas William and Alice Imogene (Cameron) M.; B.S., Tex. A and M. U., 1950; grad. Southwestern Grad. Sch. of Banking, So. Meth. U., 1971; m. Virginia L. Findley, July 28, 1956; children—Michael Cameron, Martha Elizabeth. Dist. supt., sr. engr. Southwestern Bell Telephone Co., Dallas, 1954-62; dir. personnel Tex. A. and M. U., College Station, 1962-67; dir. indsl. relations Albritton Engring. Corp., Bryan, Tex., 1967-69, also dir., 1967-69; sr. v.p. City Nat. Bank, Bryan, 1969—, also dir. Vice chmn. City Planning Commn., Bryan, 1968—; chmn. City Housing Commn., Bryan, 1968—; chmn. United Fund, 1968-69; committeeman Sam Houston Area Council, Boy Scouts Am., 1969—, dist. com., 1966-68. Bd. dirs. Brazos County Indsl. Found., Crestview Home for the Retired. Served with USNR, 1943-46; AUS, 1950-54. Decorated D.S.M., Bronze Star with oak leaf cluster, Purple Heart. Mem. Assn. of U.S. Army, C. of C. (dir. 1965-68). Presbyn. (elder 1968—). Author: A History of the Second Infantry Division in Korea, 1952. Home: 3502 Parkway Terrace Bryan TX 77801 Office: PO Box 913 Byran TX 77801

MUNSON, G. KIBBY, lawyer; b. Rochester, N.Y., May 15, 1893; s. George W. and Lena L. (Kibby) M; A.B., U. Rochester, 1914; LL.B. George Washington U., 1924; m. Grace L. Bulloch, Jan. 4, 1919; 1 dau., Marion Elizabeth (Mrs. William H. Webb, Jr.). Sec. to Rep. A. D. Sanders, 1917-27; engaged in active law practice, 1928—; spl. examiner in so-called sabotage cases before Mixed Claims Commn., U.S. and Germany (Black Tom and Kingsland fire cases), 1929-30; dep. asst. atty. gen. of Ga. to represent Ga. Pub. Service Commn. 1953-54; mem. firm Bird & Tansill, Washington. Dir. Va. Blue Ridge Ry. Served in USNRF, 7 mos. active duty, World War I. Mem. Am. Bar Assn., Bar Assn. D.C., Am. Judicature Soc., Internat. Platform Assn., Smithsonian Assos., Order of Coif, Phi Delta Phi, Delta Upsilon. Republican. Presbyn. Club: Columbia Country (Chevy Chase, Md.). Author legal and tech. articles. Home: 7500 Meadow Lane Chevy Chase MD 20015 Office: 1140 Connecticut Av NW Washington DC 20036

MURCHISON, CLINTON W., chmn. bd. Dallas Cowboys Profl. Football Team. Address: 5738 N Central Expressway Dallas TX 75205*

MURCHISON, JOHN TAYNTON, educator; b. Ft. Niagara, N.Y., Feb. 7, 1906; s. William Gaither and Lydia (Taynton) M.; A.B., U. Neb., 1927; M.A., U. Tex., 1930, Ph.D., 1933; m. C. Eleanor Carr, Aug. 25, 1932; children—John Taynton, Eleanor Susan (Mrs. Richard T. Fiala), William G. III, Mary Carolyn (Mrs. Roger M. Weed). Prof., head dept. chemistry North Tex. Agrl. Coll., Arlington, 1933-41; prof., head dept. chemistry U. Tex., Arlington, 1946-67, asst. dean sci., 1967-71, prof. chemistry, 1971—. Council pres. Girl Scouts Am. Arlington, 1948. Served as lt. col. Ordnance Dept., AUS, 1942-46. Fellow A.A.A.S., Tex. Acad. Sci., mem. Am. Chem. Soc., Res. Officers Assn., Ret. Officers Assn., Sigma Xi, Phi Lambda Upsilon, Alpha Chi Sigma. Presbyn. (deacon, elder, trustee). Author: Notes in General Chemistry, 1957, rev. edit., 1960. Home: 3207 Glasgow Terrace Arlington TX 76015

MURDOCK, ROBERT MEAD, mus. curator; b. N.Y.C., Dec. 18, 1941; s. Robert Davidson and Elizabeth (Mead) M.; B.A., Trinity Coll., 1963; M.A., Yale, 1965; m. Ellen Rebecca Olson, Apr. 22, 1967; children—Alison Mead, Anne Davidson. Ford Found. intern Walker Art Center, Mpls., 1965-67; mus. asst. Albright-Knox Art Gallery, Buffalo, summer 1963, curator, 1967-70; curator contemporary art Dallas Mus. Fine Arts, 1970—. Mem. Delta Kappa Epsilon. Home: 4534 Fairway Av Dallas TX 75219 Office: Dallas Museum Fine Arts Fair Park Dallas TX 75226

MURFF, CLARENCE YUALPA, JR., educator; b. Ft. Worth, Mar. 26, 1918; s. Clarence Yualpa and Evalyn (Rector) M.; student Tex. Christian U., 1935-36; D.D.S., Baylor U., 1940; m. Eldred Ferguson Wells, Jan. 17, 1945; children—Bruce Wells, Joclyn Dianne. Gen. practice dentistry, Seminole, Tex., 1940-42, Ft. Worth, 1945-47; served with USNR, 1942-45; commd. lt. comdr. U.S. Navy, 1948, advanced through grades to capt., 1955; instr. U.S. Naval Dental Technicians Sch., San Diego, 1948-50, officer-in-charge, Bainbridge, Md., 1951-54, San Diego, 1956-62, ret., 1964; asso. prof. operative dentistry Baylor U. Coll. Dentistry, Dallas, 1964. Fellow Am. Coll. Dentists; mem. Am., Tex., Dallas County Dental Assns., Delta Sigma

Delta, Omicron Kappa Upsilon (v.p.). Presbyn. (elder) Home: 9728 Lanshire Dr Dallas TX 75238

MURFF, SAMUEL HOUSTON, storage co. exec.; b. Hesterville, Miss., Apr. 4, 1906; s. Samuel Levi and Sarah Alice (Strahan) M.; student U. Miss., 1924-26; m. Georgie Lee Thornton, Dec. 30, 1928; children— Thelma Elizabeth, Samuel Thornton. With Aransas Compress Co., San Marcos and Corpus Christi, Tex., 1926-60, Cotton Warehouse, Lovington, N.M., 1960-61; mgr. North Plains Compress Co., Tulia, Tex., 1961. City commr. city of San Marcos (Tex.), 1940-44, City of Tulia (Tex.), 1966—. Methodist (steward 1934-68). Mason, Rotarian. Home: 300 Comanche Trail Tulia TX 79088 Office: Drawer 7 Tulia TX 79088

MURPH, BENJAMIN ELLERY, dentist; b. Greensboro, N.C., July 7, 1918; s. James Washington and Lillian Beatrice M.; B.S., S.C. State Coll., 1928; D.D.S., Meharry Med. Coll., 1935; m. Conoleta Gant, Dec. 6, 1940; children—Sandra (Mrs. David Davis), Janet (Mrs. Robert Waymer). Pvt. dental practice, Laurel, Miss., 1935—. Pres. Laurel N.A.A.C.P., 1948—, adviser youth council, 1956—; active Boy Scouts Am.; chmn. Community Fund, 1950-54; mem. Interracial Com. to Advise Sch. and Trustee Bd.; mem. Laurel Urban Renewal Commn. Trustee Campbell Coll. Mem. Laurel C. of C., Nat., Miss. (pres.) dental socs., Omega Psi Phi. Mem. A.M.E. Ch. (del. gen. conf.). K.P., Mason. Home: 118 Harrison Blvd Laurel MS 39440 Office: 205 S 4th Av Laurel MS 39440

MURPHEY, WILLIS HULL, dentist; b. Belleville, Ill., Mar. 10, 1910; s. Willis Phelps and Anastacia Agnes (O'Flaherty) M.; B.A., Howard Payne Coll., 1933; D.D.S., Baylor U., 1933; certificate Forsythe Dental Infirmary for Children, Boston, Mass., 1934; m. Elois Taylor, June 6, 1936; children—Willis Hull, Griffin Taylor. Practice dentistry specializing in orthodontics, Fort Worth, 1934-72. Del. Tex. Dental Leaders People to People Goodwill Mission to No. Europe, U.S.S.R., 1968; del. leader, So. Europe, U.S.S.R., 1970. Inter-relations adv. bd. Baylor U. Coll. Dentistry, 1970-71. Served to lt. comdr. USCG, 1942-45. Recipient distinguished alumnus award Howard Payne Coll., 1969, distinguished service award Fort Worth Dist. Dental Soc., 1971. Diplomate Am. Bd. Orthodontics. Fellow Am. Coll. Dentists, Internat. Coll. Dentists, Fedn. Dentaire Internationale; mem. Tex. Orthodontic Soc. (pres. 1969-70), Southwestern Soc. Orthodontists (pres. 1969-70), Tex. Dental Assn. (pres. 1968-69, adv. bd. 1971-72), Fort Worth Dist. Dental Soc. (pres. 1939-40). Home: 4211 Lone Oak Dr Fort Worth TX 76107 Office: 4901 Byers St Fort Worth TX 76107

MURPHY, ANDREW PHILLIP, JR., lawyer; b. Swampscott, Mass., Sept. 27, 1922; s. Andrew Philip and Irene Mary (O'Connell) M.; A.B., Harvard, 1943; LL.B., Boston U., 1949; m. Ann Marie O. Hagen, Feb. 13, 1954; children—Sean Francis, Andrew Philip, Chrystal Ann, James Byrne, Paul Clarke. Admitted to Mass. bar, 1949. D.C. bar, 1957; practiced in Lynn, Mass., 1949-50; with Econ. Stablzn. Agy., 1951-53, Office Chief Counsel, WSB, 1951, counsel R.R. and Airline Wage Bd., 1952, alternate mem., counsel Nat. Enforcement Commn., 1953; indsl. relations adv. Office Chief Ordnance, U.S. Army, 1954; labor relations dir. Nat. Assn. Home Builders, 1954-60; pvt. law practice, 1960—. Dir. Woodlawn Nat. Bank, Alexandria, Va. Alternate mem. Constrn. Industry Joint Conf., 1960-61; sec.-treas. U.S. Expn. Sci. and Industry, 1960—; alternate mem. Constrn. Industry Stblzn. Com., Washington, 1971—. Served as lt. (j.g.) USNR. Mem. Fed. Bar Assn. (treas. D.C. chpt. 1952-53, 2d v.p. 1953-54, nat. council 1954-59), U.S. C. of C. (labor relations com. 1955-59). Clubs: Harvard (N.Y.C.); Metropolitan (Washington); Belle Haven Country (Alexandria); Annapolis (Md.) Yacht; Farmington Hunt (Va.) Club. Editor in chief Fed. Bar Jour., 1952-59; co-editor Research and Development Procurement, 1958. Home: 1815 Edgehille Dr Alexandria VA 22307 Office: 1707 L St NW Washington DC 20006 also 40 Court St Boston MA 02109

MURPHY, BILLY JACK, football coach, athletic dir.; b. Lorenzo, Tex., Jan. 13, 1921; s. Ernest C. and Mattie Elizabeth (Fullingim) M.; B.A., Miss. State U., 1947; m. Elizabeth (Parrish), Feb. 14, 1947; children—Mike, Libby. Asst. football coach Memphis State U., 1947-52, head football coach, 1958—, athletic dir., 1966—; asst. football coach Miss. State U., 1952-54, U. Minn., 1954-58. Served with USMC, 1943-46, 51. Decorated Bronze Star. Named Coach of Yr., Detroit Sports Extra, 1963; recipient Memphis In-Print award Memphis Printing Industries, 1963; award for outstanding achievements in amateur athletics, 1967; named Mo. Valley Conf. Coach of Yr., 1969. Home: 5301 Pecan Grove Lane Memphis TN 38117

MURPHY, CHARLES EDMOND, nuclear engr.; b. Nashville, June 14, 1927; s. William Wesley and Ellamai (Grizzard) M.; B.S., Auburn U., 1948; postgrad. U. Tenn., 1950-51, Drexel Inst. Tech., 1962-65; m. Norma Jean Wootton, Aug. 20, 1955; children—Donna Jean, Charles Edmond, Carol Jane. Elec. engring. supr. Hiwassee Area Projects, TVA, Knoxville, 1949-54; elec. engr. Long Sault Dam, Uhl, Hall & Rich, Massena, N.Y., 1955-57; nuclear engr. Aircraft Carrier Enterprise, Westinghouse, Newport News, Va., 1957-60; nuclear plant supr. PM-1 Plant, Martin Co., Balt., 1960-65; staff engr. FPC, Washington, 1966-69, also tech. adviser; br. chief reactor test br. AEC, Atlanta, 1969—. Mem. Vice Pres.'s Com. on Environment, 1968-69. Served with USNR, 1945-46. Registered profl. engr., Ala., Ga. Mem. Am. Nuclear Soc., I.E.E.E., Nat., Ga. Socs. profl. engrs. Contbr. chpts. to Hydroelectric Power Evaluation, 1968; National Power Survey, 1970. Home: 5256 Fleur de Lis Ct Atlanta GA 30340 Office: 230 Peachtree St Atlanta GA 30303

MURPHY, CHARLES HAYWOOD, JR., oil co. exec., investor; b. El Dorado, Ark., Mar. 6, 1920; s. Charles Haywood and Bertie (Wilson) M.; student pub. schs., El Dorado and pvt. tutors; LL.D., U. Ark., 1966; m. Johnie Walker, Oct. 14, 1939; children—Michael Walker, Martha Wilson, Charles Haywood III, Robert Madison. Ind. oil producer, 1939-50; pres. Murphy Oil Corp., El Dorado, 1950-72, chmn. bd., chief exec. officer, 1972—; dir. 1st Tenn. Nat. Corp., 1st Nat. Bank El Dorado. Mem. Ark. Bd. Higher Edn. Bd. dirs. Oschner Found. Hosp., New Orleans; trustee Hendrix Coll.; bd. visitors Tulane U. Served with AUS, World War II. Mem. Am. Petroleum Inst. (exec. com., dir.), Nat. Petroleum Council. Home: Calion Rd El Dorado AR 71730 Office: Murphy Bldg 200 E Jefferson Av El Dorado AR 71730

MURPHY, EMILY JOHNSTONE MCCUTCHEN (MRS. WARREN MASON MURPHY), civic worker; b. Washington, Oct. 3, 1937; d. James Malcolm and Emily Strother (Dunovant) McCutchen; B.A., U.S.C., 1959; m. Warren Mason Murphy, July 6, 1963. Tchr. jr. high sch., Arlington County, Va., 1959-63. Mem. Service League No. Va.; county co-chmn. Mother's March of Dimes, Pulaski County, Ark., 1964-65; capt. Pulaski County Cystic Fibrosis, 1965-67, Heart Fund, 1965; capt. Easter Seals, 1966, maj., 1967-68, 70; mem. Cotillion (Va.), Jr. Assembly Arlington (Va.), Women's City Club, Little Rock. Recipient Mother's March of Dimes award, 1965, Ark. Soc. D.A.R. Outstanding Jr., 1967. Mem. D.A.R. (marshall 1966-68, state chmn, 1965-68, state finance com. 1968-72, state treas. 1968-70, state chmn. 1970-72, chpt. vice regent 1969-71, treas. state officers club 1970), Children Am. Revolution (sr. state pres. 1965-68, hon. sr. state pres. 1970), S.C. Hist. Soc. Episcopalian. Home: 102 Coronado Pl North Little Rock AR 72116

MURPHY, FREDERICK BRUNSON, dentist; b. Iredelle, Tex., Feb. 19, 1923; s. Frederick Brunson and Mary Annie (Cox) M.; student Auburn U., 1948-49; D.M.D., U. Ala., 1953; m. Cenus Corine Owen, Dec. 27, 1954; children—Frederick Brunson, Cenus Annie, Michele Madge. Pvt. practice dentistry, Tallassee, Ala., 1953—. Sec.-treas., dir. MMR Corp., Tallassee, 1971—; pres., dir. First Fed. Savs. & Loan Assn. Tallassee, 1962—. Finance and dist. chmn. Creek Nation dist. Boy Scouts Am., 1967-71. Served with C.E., AUS, 1942-46; CBI. Baptist (chmn. bd. deacons 1967-68). Mem. A.A.A.S., Am., Ala. dental assns., 2d Dist. Dental Soc., Jr. C. of C. (pres. 1955-56), Alpha Gamma Rho, Alpha Epsilon Delta, Psi Omega. Rotarian (pres. 1960-61), Mason (Shriner). Home: Box 637 Noble Rd Tallassee AL 36078 Office: Box 637 James St Tallassee AL 36078

MURPHY, GEORGE EDWARD, hosp. adminstr.; b. Conneaut, O., Dec. 17, 1910; s. Patrick Joseph and Grace Adell (Hill) M.; grad. hosp. adminstrn. program U.S. Army-Baylor U., 1951; m. Edna Marie Macht, Dec. 20, 1940; children—Judith Ann (Mrs. James R. Gibbs), David Arthur. Commd. 1st lt. Med. Adminstrv. Corps, U.S. Army, 1942, advanced through grades to col. Med. Service Corps, 1959; various adminstrv. assignments in U.S. Army hosps., 1931-44; exec. officer U.S. Army Hosp., Ft. Chaffee, Ark., 1944-45; dir. personnel Stark Gen. Hosp., Charleston, S.C., 1945; exec. officer 317th Sta. Hosp., Wiesbaden, Germany, 1946-47, med. sect. hdqrs. U.S. Forces in Austria, 1947-49, U.S. Army Hosp., Ft. Campbell, Ky., 1949-50; mgmt. officer, dir. personnel U.S. Army Hosp., Ft. Jackson, S.C., 1951-53; insp. gen. Valley Forge Gen. Hosp., Phoenixville, Pa., 1954-57; exec. officer U.S. Army Med. Group, Korea, 1957, med. sec. Hdqrs. 8th U.S. Army, Korea, 1957-58; exec. officer Gen. Leonard Wood Army Hosp., Ft. Leonard Wood, Mo., 1958-66; adminstr. Middlesboro (Ky.) Appalachian Regional Hosp., 1966—. Bd. dirs. Southeastern Ky. Regional Health Demonstration. Decorated Legion of Merit. Mem. Am. Coll. Hosp. Adminstrs., Ky. Hosp. Assn. Home: 208 Greenwood Rd Middlesboro KY 40965 Office: PO Box 340 Middlesboro KY 40965

MURPHY, GEORGE LAWRENCE, profl. engr.; b. Lineville, Ia., Jan. 24, 1928; s. George L. and Nellie (McClain) M.; B.S., Ia. State U., 1951; m. Margaret Hamer, Dec. 19, 1959; children—Mark Alan, Sherrie Ann. Television engr. WOI-TV, Ames, Ia., 1953; studio engr. WHO-TV, Des Moines, 1954; engring. dir. Auburn U. Ednl. TV, 1955-59; mgr. quality control operations Magnetic Tape div. Ampex Corp., Opelika, Ala., 1959-61, mgr., application engring. 1961-64, mgr. quality control, 1964-67, mgr. tech. services, 1967-69; corporate engring. mgr. Diversified Products Corp., Opelika, 1969, div. mgr. Ala. div., 1969-71; pres. Craftmaster, Inc., Opelika, 1971—. Served with USMCR, 1946-47; with USAF, 1951-53. Registered profl. engr. Ala. Mem. I.E.E.E., Ala. Soc. Profl. Engrs. (v.p. Auburn chpt. 1959, pres. 1960, state dir. 1961, state v.p. 1962-63, state pres. 1964), Soc. Motion Picture Television Engrs. Home: 1052 Terrace Acres Auburn AL 36830 Office: 902 Geneva St Opelika AL 36801

MURPHY, MARGARETTE CELESTINE EVANS (MRS. ROBERT H. MURPHY), educator; b. Chgo., June 25, 1926; d. Crawford and Ethel Hazel (Cartman) Evans; Ph.B., U. Chgo., 1945, A.M., 1949, postgrad., 1953, 54, 55; postgrad. Chgo. Tchrs. Coll., 1950, 51, Mundelein Coll., 1961; m. Robert H. Murphy, Sept. 25, 1949; 1 dau., Linda Michelle. Tchr., Willard Elementary Sch., Chgo., 1949-51; tchr. Spanish, French, freshman sponsor and counselor, sch. rep. P.T.A., McKinley High Sch., Chgo., 1951-54; tchr. Spanish, French, Crane Tech. High Sch., Chgo., 1954-55, 59; now tchr. Spanish, French, chmn. fgn. lang. dept., Harlan High Sch., Chgo.; attendance counselor, 1955-56, chmn. modern lang. dept., 1963—; spl. lectr. modern fgn. langs. Crane br. Chgo. City Jr. Coll., 1962; pvt. tutor French, Spanish, 1949—. Mem. Feminine League; donor various charitable, religious orgns. Mem. Ill. Edn. Assn., Ill. Assn. Modern Lang. Tchrs., Am. Council Fgn. Lang. Tchrs., Am. Assn. Tchrs. Spanish and Portuguese, Am. Assn. Tchrs. French, Brazilian Soc. Chgo., Pan Am. Bd. Edn., Interam. Inst. Pan Am. Bd. Edn., Pan Am. Assembly, Pan Am. Council of Chgo., Am. Assn. U. Women, Am. Council Fgn. Lang. Tchrs., Women's Share in Pub. Service, Internat. Platform Assn., Internat. Fedn. U. Women, Modern Lang. Assn. Am., U. Chgo. Alumni Assn. Entertainment fgn. visitors to Chgo. for Internat. Edn. Inst., U.S. Dept. State, 1962—. Home: 8214 S Evans St Chicago IL 60619 also 907 Polk Av Memphis TN 38104

MURPHY, MARY MARTHA, clin. psychologist; b. Peru, Ind., Oct. 14, 1909; d. Roscoe E. and June (Pence) Murphy; B.S., Northwestern U., 1930; M.A., U. Chgo., 1938, Ph.D., 1952; m. Leonard C. Lund, May 18, 1959 (dec. Mar. 1967). Tchr. remedial reading Hammond (Ind.) pub. schs., 1930-42; clin. psychologist Manteno (Ill.) State Hosp., 1945-51, So. Wis. Tng. Sch., Union Grove, 1952-53, VA Center, Bath, N.Y., 1954; chief psychologist State Colony, Woodbine, N.J., 1955-58, Kent-Sussex Mental Hygiene Clincs, Georgetown and Dover, Del., 1958-60, Southside area Mental Hygiene Clinic, Petersburg, Va., 1960-61; psychol. cons. Regional Tng. Center; mem. adv. com. U. Ala. Med. Center, Birmingham; instr. Richmond Profl. Inst. Coll. William and Mary, 1960-61; research psychologist S.E. La. Hosp., Mandeville, 1962-65; cons. St. Tammany Guidance Center, Covington, La., 1962-65; pvt. practice remedial reading and psychol. services, 1963—; chief psychologist dept. pediatrics Child Devel. Clinic, Sch. Medicine, U. Miss. Med. Center, Jackson, 1965—, asst. prof. dept. pediatrics, 1966—, mem. grad. edn. faculty, 1968—; asso. in psychology U. Miss., Oxford, 1967—. Fellow Am. Assn. Mental Deficiency; mem. A.A.A.S., Am., Miss., So. psychol. assns., Soc. Pediatric Psychology, Bus. and Profl. Women's Club, N.Y. Acad. Scis., D.A.R. Mem. Disciples of Christ Ch. Mem. Order of Eastern Star. Contbr. research studies to profl. jours. Home: 536 Woodbury Rd Jackson MS 39206 Office: Dept Pediatrics U Miss Med Center 2500 N State St Jackson MS 39216

MURPHY, PAUL B., engr.; b. Gateshead, Eng., Mar. 2, 1925; nat. diploma and higher nat. certificate in elec. and mech. engring. Rutherford Coll. Tech., Newcastle-upon-Tyne, Eng; postgrad. U. Cal. at Los Angeles; m. 1 child. Elec. apprentice A. Reyrolle & Co., 1940-45, with engring. and sales depts., 1945-47; constrn. engr. Anglo-Iranian Oil Co., 1947-52; constrn. engr. Canadian Comstock Co., 1952-55, project mgr. hydroelectric project, West Pakistan, 1955-57, mgr. br. office, Ottawa, Ont., Can., 1958; with Fischbach and Moore, 1958—, v.p., gen. mgr. dist. office, New Orleans, 1964-70, regional v.p., 1970—. Registered profl. engr., Cal., Province of Ont. Home: 422 Country Club Dr Lakewood South New Orleans LA 70124

MURPHY, PAUL HAMPTON, librarian; b. Nashville, Apr. 28, 1928; s. John Peter and Annie M. (Curran) M.; B.A., St. Ambrose Coll., 1952; M.A., George Peabody Coll., 1961, M.L.S., 1963. Clk. Guaranty Title Co., Nashville, 1955-58; asst. librarian So. Edn. Reporting Service, Nashville, 1961-63; reference librarian Joint Univ. Libraries, Nashville, 1964-66, sci. librarian, 1967—. Mem. Am., Southeastern, Tenn. library assns. Editor Tennessee Librarian, 1967—. Home: 107 Lea Av Nashville TN 37210 Office: Joint U Libraries Nashville TN 37203

MURPHY, REG, newspaper editor; b. Hoschton, Ga., Jan. 7, 1934; s. John Lee and Mae (Ward) M.; student Mercer U., 1950-54, (Nieman fellow), Harvard, 1959-60; m. Virginia Grace Rawls, Dec. 23, 1953; children—Karen Leigh, Susan Virginia. Reporter, Macon (Ga.) Telegraph, 1952-54; bur. chief Macon Telegraph and News, Atlanta, 1955-61; polit. editor Atlanta Constn., 1961-65, editorial page editor, 1968, editor, 1969—; freelance writer and cons., Atlanta, 1965-68. Recipient Pub. Service award A.P., 1963; Sigma Delta Chi award, 1962. Clubs: Atlanta Press, Commerce, Capital City (Atlanta). Author: The Southern Strategy, 1971. Home: 1325 N Decatur Rd Atlanta GA 30306 Office: 10 Forsyth St NW Atlanta GA 30302

MURPHY, ROSALIE, business exec.; b. Carthage, Tex.; d. Fletcher M. and Florence (Britton) Davis; high sch. grad.; m. Frank W. Murphy, Aug. 27, 1942; children—Joyce (Mrs. Finas W. Jackson), Patricia (Mrs. David H. Hudson), Frank W. Exec. v.p., sec., treas., dir. Frank W. Murphy Mfrs., Inc., Tulsa, 1941—, Magnetic Switches, Inc., Tulsa, 1959—, Controls Components Ltd., Tulsa, 1967—. Mem. Petroleum Club Tulsa, Tulsa Philharmonic. Club: Harvard (Tulsa). Home: 3614 E 48th Pl Tulsa OK 74135 Office: 3131 S Sheridan St Tulsa OK 74114

MURPHY, THOMAS S., broadcasting exec. Pres. KTRK-TV. Address: PO Box 12 Houston TX 77001*

MURRAH, ALFRED PAUL, judge; b. Johnston County, Okla., Oct. 27, 1904; s. George Washington and Nora (Simmons) M.; LL.B., U. Okla., 1927; LL.D., Oklahoma City U., 1954; m. Agnes Milam, June 29, 1930; children—Ann, Paul, Sue. Admitted to Okla. bar, 1928; judge U.S. Dist. Ct., 1937-40; became judge U.S. Circuit Ct. of Appeals 10th Jud. Circuit, 1940, now sr. judge, dir. Fed. Jud. Center, Washington. Trustee, So. Meth. U. Recipient Distinguished Service citation U. Okla., 1954; Hattom W. Summers award, 1954. Mem. Am., Okla. bar assns., Order of Coif, Lambda Chi, Phi Alpha Delta. Methodist. Mason (32 deg.). Address: Fed Bldg Oklahoma City OK 73101

MURRAH, WILLIAM FITZHUGH, lawyer; b. Brookhaven, Miss., Nov. 6, 1889; s. William Belton and Beulah (Fitzhugh) M.; A.B., Millsaps Coll., 1908, LL.D., 1959; M.A., Vanderbilt U., 1909, LL.B., 1912, J.D., 1969; m. Corinne Falls, Apr. 3, 1918; children—William Fitzhugh, Mary Fargason (Mrs. John J. Fitzmaurice), Corinne Falls (Mrs. Paul Preston Wilson). Admitted to Tenn. bar, 1912; asso. firm Fitzhugh & Biggs (later Fitzhugh, Murrah & Fitzhugh), Memphis, 1912-50; practiced in Memphis, 1950—; head trust and title guaranty depts. Fidelity Bank and Trust Co., 1925-29. Pres. Memphis Council Americanism, 1944-51; 1st v.p., dir. Memphis Pub. Library, 1954-70, pres., 1970—; pres. Memphis Community Council, 1946-48; pres. Memphis Community Chest, 1948-50. Bd. dirs. Shelby United Neighbors, 1959; trustee, v.p. Mid-So. Found., 1952. Served as capt. U.S. Army, 1917-19. Mem. Bar Assn. Tenn. (v.p. 1960-61), Am., Memphis, Shelby County (pres. 1957-58) bar assns., Am. Judicature Soc., C. of C. (dir. 1915), Am. Legion (post comdr. 1925), Mil. Order World Wars (chpt. comdr. 1944), Vanderbilt Law Alumni (v.p.), Alumni Millsaps Coll. (dir.), Kappa Alpha, Phi Delta Phi, Sigma Upsilon. Methodist (pres. bd. trustees). Home: 8830 Hwy 72 Germantown TN 38138 Office: Sterick Bldg Memphis TN 38103

MURRAH, WILLIAM NOLAN, JR., lawyer; b. Columbus, Ga., Oct. 27, 1934; s, William Nolan and Mary Lee (Huguley) M.; student U. Ga., 1952-55; A.B., Emory U., 1957, LL.B., 1957; postgrad. Harvard, 1957-58; m. Barbara Ann Greene, Sept. 7, 1955; children—William Nolan III, Lee Allan. Admitted to Ga. bar, 1957; law asst. to Justice J. D. Quillian, 1961; sec.-counsel Royal Crown Cola Co., Columbus, 1961-67, v.p., sec., gen. counsel, 1967—; dir. Royal Crown Bottlers of Gainesville, Inc., Royal Crown Bottlers of Orlando, Inc., Royal Crown Bottlers of Richmond, Inc. Chmn. 3d Dist. Republican Com. Served to capt., Judge Adv. Gen.'s Dept., USAF, 1958-61. Named Outstanding Young man of Columbus, 1969. Mem. Am., Ga. bar assns., Am. Judicature Soc., Phi Delta Phi, Sigma Alpha Epsilon. Contbr. articles to profl. jours. Home: 1829 Park Dr Columbus GA 31906 Office: 1000 10th Av Columbus GA 31901

MURRAY, GROVER ELMER, univ. pres.; b. Maiden, N.C., Oct. 26, 1916; s. Grover Elmer and Lucy (Lore) M.; B.S., U. N.C., 1937; M.S., La. State U., 1939, Ph.D., 1942; m. Nancy Beatrice Setzer, June 21, 1941; children—Martha, Barbara Elizabeth. Research geologist La. Geol. Survey, 1939-41; geologist Magnolia Petroleum Co., Jackson, Miss., 1941-48; prof. dept. geology La. State U., 1948-55, chmn. dept., 1950-53, Boyd prof. geology, 1955-66, v.p., dean acad. affairs, 1963-65, v.p. acad. affairs La. State U. System, 1965-66; pres. Tex. Tech U., Lubbock, 1966—, pres. Tex. Tech Sch. Medicine, 1969—. Vis. lectr. U. Tex., 1958; mem. Internat. Commn. on Stratigraphy; mem. Am. Stratigraphic Commn., 1957-63; vice chmn., sec. Am. Commn. Stratigraphic Nomenclature, 1960-62; mem. U.S. Nat. Com. on Geology, 1963-68, chmn., 1964-68; parttime cons. geologist, 1948—; dir. NSF project basic geologic studies in Northeastern Mexico, 1958-61; mem. marine resources adv. com. U.S. Dept. Interior, 1967-69; del. Internat. Geol. Congresses, 1956, 60, 64, 68, 72; del. Internat. Com. on History Geol. Scis., Yerevan, USSR, 1967. Bd. dirs. S.W. Center for Advanced Studies, Internat. Center for Arid and Semi-Arid Land Studies, United Health Founds., Nat. Sci. Bd., 1968—, Royal Resources Exploration, Inc., Western Information Network Assn., 1967—, WHO, 1966-70. Recipient Distinguished Alumnus award U. N.C., 1971. Fellow Geol. Soc. Am. (chmn. symposium on sedimentary vols. in Coastal Plain, U.S. and Mexico, 1951, program chmn. New Orleans Meeting 1955, councillor 1961-64, chmn. ann. meeting 1967, asso. editor 1963-68), World Acad. Art and Sci.; mem. Am. Assn. Petroleum Geologists (chmn. com. geol. names and nomenclature 1952-54, editor 1959-63, pres. 1964-65, chmn. medal awards com. 1968-69), Soc. Econ. Paleontologists and Mineralogists (editor Jour. Paleontology 1951-54, pres. 1963-64), Am. Geol. Inst., Paleontol. Soc., Orgn. Tropical Studies (dir. 1966-69), Gulf Univs. Research Corp. (dir. 1964-69, pres. 1966, chmn. bd. 1966-67, mem. exec. com. 1965-69), Nat. Assn. Geology Tchrs., Am. Arbitration Assn. (nat. panel arbitrators), Am. Soc. Oceanography, Australian Petroleum Exploration Assn., Soc. Exploration Geophysicists, Am. Inst. Profl. Geologists, Antarctican Soc., Am. Geophys. Union, Paleontol. Research Inst., Geol. and Mining Soc., Natural Fibers and Food Protein Com. Tex., Norsk Geologisk Forening (life), Asociacion Mexicana de Geologos Petroleros, Sociedad Geologica Mexicana, Sigma Xi, Sigma Gamma Epsilon, Omicron Delta Kappa. Author: Geology of Atlantic and Gulf Coastal Province of North America, 1961. Contbr. articles to ednl. and sci. jours. Home: 2909 19th St Lubbock TX 79410

MURRAY, JAMES EDWARD, govt. ofcl.; b. Bancroft, Ia., June 12, 1932; s. William A. and Elizabeth M. (McDonald) M.; B.A. cum laude, Notre Dame U., 1955, J.D. cum laude, 1956; m. Mary McNerney, Oct. 1, 1960; children—Kathleen M., Kerry E., William A., Susan A. Law clk. chief Judge Luther M. Swygert, Dist. Ct. No. Dist. Ind., 1956-57; asso. firm Hogarn & Harston, 1960-67, partner, 1967; v.p., gen. counsel Fed. Nat. Mortgage Assn., Washington, 1970—. Served with JAG Corps, AUS, 1957-60. Mem. Am., Ia., D.C. bar assns., Soc. Hosp. Atty.'s, Am. Judicature Soc. Home: 4706 Ft Sumner Dr Washington DC 20016 Office: Fed Nat Mortgage Assn 1133 15th St NW Washington DC 20005

MURRAY, JESSE GEORGE, author; b. St. Louis, Dec. 28, 1909; s. Peter George and Emma McCook (Marshall) M.; grad. Chaminade Coll., 1923; m. Virginia M. Suechting, Oct. 16, 1948; children—George Read, Peter George. Reporter, Chgo. Herald & Examiner, 1932-37; writer Rocky Mountain News, Denver, Toronto Star, Townsend Nat. Weekly, 1937-48; press attache U.S. Fgn. Service, Am. embassy, Vienna, Austria, 1948-53; columnist, writer Chgo. Am., 1954-71. Author: New Horizons, 1943; O'Malley, 1947; The Big Clout, 1949; History of the Rehabilitation of Austria, 5 vols., 1950; Virginia, 1956; The Madhouse on Madison Street, 1965; The Legacy of Al Capone, 1971; (plays) Off the Record, 1941, Johnny on a Spot, 1942. Home: Box 732 Route 2 Eureka Springs AR 72632

MURRAY, THOMAS LAVERNE, civil engr., govt. ofcl.; b. Jesup, Ga., Apr. 10, 1929; s. Thomas McKinley and Gladys (Horne) M.; B.S., Ga. Inst. Tech., 1958; m. Shirley Hayes, Feb. 20, 1953; 1 dau., Deborah Ann. Designer Ga. Hwy. Dept., Atlanta, 1953-64; prodn. rep. Housing Assistance Adminstrn., U.S. Dept. Housing and Urban Devel., Atlanta, 1964-70, program mgr. Columbia (S.C.) Area Office, 1970—. Served with USNR, 1948-52. Mem. Am. Soc. C.E. Mason. Home: 1135 Green Valley Lane Columbia SC 29210 Office: 1801 Main St Columbia SC 29201

MURRAY, WILLIAM DAVID, assn. exec.; b. Rocky Mount, N.C., Sept. 9, 1908; A.B., Duke 1931; m. Carolyn Kirby, 1930; children—Joy (Mrs. R. E. Whitman), Marilyn (Mrs. W. L. Donigan), Carol (Mrs. Marshal Happer). Coach, prin., dean boys Winston-Salem (N.C.) Children's Home, 1931-40, asst. supt., 1933-40; coach U. Del., 1940-51, dir. div. student health, phys. edn., athletics, 1945-51; football coach Duke, 1951-66; exec. dir. Am. Football Coaches Assn., 1966—. Pres. Middle Atlantic States Collegiate Athletic Conf., 1947-49, chmn. football com., 1945-47; mem. exec. council Eastern Coll. Athletic Conf., 1947-50; bd. dirs. Football Hall Fame, Named Coach of Year, Atlantic Coast Conf., 1952, 54, 60-62. Mem. Am. Football Coaches Assn. (dir. 1954-62, pres. 1962—, Amos Alonzo Stagg award 1972), Fellowship Christian Athletes (dir. 1963—, v.p. 1964-65, pres. 1967-69), Eastern Intercollegiate Football Assn. (exec. com.). Home: 3610 Hathaway Rd Durham NC 27707

MURRY, IKE, lawyer; b. Fordyce, Ark., May 8, 1913; s. Isaac Taylor and Pearl (Harris) M.; grad. high sch.; m. Catherine Samuel, Aug. 9, 1935; 1 dau., Ginger (Mrs. John Anderson McEntire). Admitted to Ark. bar, 1935; pvt. practice, Fordyce, 1935-42, Little Rock, 1952—; chief asst. atty. gen. Ark., 1942-48, atty. gen., 1948-52. Mem. Ark. Ho. of Reps. from Dallas County, 1937-42. Vice pres. Advt. and Promotion Commn., 1971-72. Served with USNR, 1943-45. Mem. Little Rock C. of C. (v.p. 1972). Mason (Shriner, Jester). Clubs: Little Rock (pres. 1972), Little Rock Country. Home: 31 Sherrill Heights St Little Rock AR 72207 Office: 1960 Union Nat Plaza Little Rock AR 72201

MUSE, MCGILLIVRAY, lawyer; b. Bridgeport, Tex., Apr. 26, 1909; s. Robert V. and Helen (Bailey) M.; A.B., Daniel Baker Coll., 1928; LL.B., U. Tex., 1931; m. Leona McKie, Nov. 9, 1935; 1 son, Marshall McKie. Admitted to Tex. bar, 1931; asso. with Judge R. E. Lee, in practice of law, Brownwood, Tex., 1931-34; mem. firm McCartney, McCartney & Muse, Brownwood, 1934-36; practiced in Brownwood, 1936-38, Dallas, 1945—; asso. firm Locke, Locke, Dyer & Purnell, Dallas, 1938-45; land owner in Limestone and Brown Counties, Tex., Atoka County, Okla. Pres. Daniel Baker Ex-Students Assn., 1932-33; bd. dirs. Brownwood C. of C., 1936-68, Dallas Big Bros., 1945-49. Mem. Am., Dallas bar assns., State Bar Tex., Beta Theta Pi. Presbyn. (elder). Mason (K.T.). Democrat. Lion. Club: Lancer. Author: Rights of Afterborn Children under Wills (12 Tex. bar jours). Home: 4400 Fairfax Dallas TX 75205 Office: 1st Nat Bank Bldg Dallas TX 75202

MUSGRAVE, JOHN CHARLES, economist; b. Springfield, Mo., Jan 2, 1939; s. John Reichert and Thelma (Peck) M.; B.A., U. Kan., 1961; M.A., U. Cal., 1962; postgrad. Am. U., 1962-65. Math. statistician Econ. Research and Analysis div. Bur. Census, 1962-65, Constrn. Statistics div., 1967-69, economist Nat. Income and Wealth div. U.S. Bur. Econ. Analysis, 1970—, OECD, Paris, France, 1966. Mem. Am. Statis. Assn., Am. Econ. Assn., Phi Beta Kappa, Pi Mu Epsilon, Omicron Delta Epsilon. Republican. Baptist. Contbr. articles to profl. jours. Home: 1831 N Herndon St Arlington VA 22201 Office: US Bureau of Economic Analysis Washington DC 20230

MUSGRAVE, STORY, astronaut; b. Boston, Aug. 19, 1935; B.S. in Statistics, Syracuse U., 1958; M.B.A., U. Cal. at Los Angeles, 1959; B.A. in Chemistry, Marietta Coll., 1960; M.D., Columbia, 1964; M.S. in Biophysics, U. Ky., 1966; m. Patricia Marguertie Van Kirk; children—Lorelei Lisa, Bradley Scott, Holly Kay, Christopher Todd, Jeffrey Paul. Surg. intern U. Ky. Med. Center, Lexington, 1964-65, U.S. Air Force postdoctoral fellow aerospace physiology and medicine, Nat. Heart Inst. postdoctoral fellow, 1965-67; part-time resident gen. surgery Denver Gen. Hosp., 1967—; part-time instr. dept. physiology and biophysics U. Ky. Med. Coll., 1967—; scientist-astronaut NASA, Houston, 1967—. Served with USMCR, 1953-56. Mem. Aerospace Med. Assn., Aircraft Owners and Pilots Assn., Air Force Assn., A.A.A.S., Am. Inst. Aeros. and Astronautics, A.M.A., Flying Physicians Assn., Nat. Aeros. Assn., Nat. Aerospace Edn. Council, Nat. Geog. Soc., Soaring Soc. Am., U.S. Parachute Assn. Office: NASA Manned Spacecraft Center Houston TX 78421

MUSHAWAY, GROVER LEE, mfg. exec.; b. Houston, July 11, 1919; s. Grover and Montez (Branch) M.; B.S. in Aero. Engring., Tex. A. and M. U., 1947; m. Kathleen Patricia Sheridan, Jan. 23, 1944; 1 son, Michael Grover. Design engr. Wyatt Metal & Boiler Co., 1947-49; maintenance engr. Eastern States Petroleum Co., 1949-50; chief engr. Wright Shipley Corp., 1950-52; sales engr. Kreiter Indsl. Supply Co., Houston 1952-57; founder, pres. Hi-Line Industries, Inc., Houston, 1954—. Scout master Boy Scouts Am., Houston, 1964-65; bd. dirs. Meyerland Civic Club, 1963. Served to capt. USAAF, 1941-45. Registered profl. engr., Tex. Mem. Nat. Soc. Profl. Engrs. Methodist. Mason (Shriner). Home: 1521 Sherwood Forest Dr Houston TX 77043 Office: 1138 W Belt Dr N Houston TX 77024

MUSSELMAN, RUTH, ednl. adminstr. Mem. Okla. Bd. Edn. Address: Okla Bd Edn State Capitol Bldg Oklahoma City OK 73105*

MUSSER, MARC JAMES, med. adminstr.; b. Terre Haute, Ind., July 3, 1910; s. Marc James and Margaret (Gallagher) M.; A.B., U. Wis., 1930, M.D., 1934; m. Sarah Ann Wiley, Sept. 23, 1933 (dec. 1944); children—Marc David, Barbara (Mrs. Frank Bilek); m. 2d, Gladys Norsetter, Feb. 22, 1946 (div. 1956); 1 son, Stephen K.; m. 3d, Alice Balcuns, Sept. 23, 1957; 1 son, William M. Intern Kansas City (Mo.) Gen. Hosp., 1934-35, resident internal medicine and neuropsychiatry Wis. Gen. Hosp., Madison, 1935-38; mem. faculty U. Wis. Med. Sch., 1938-58, prof. medicine, 1954-58; prof. medicine Baylor U. Coll. Medicine, 1958-59; with VA, 1957-66, dir. research service, asst. chief med., also dir. research and edn. in medicine, Washington, 1959-64, dep. chief med. dir., 1964-66; prof. medicine Duke U. Sch. Medicine, also exec. dir. N.C. Regional Med. Program, 1966—. Served to col., M.C., AUS, 1941-45; PTO. Decorated Legion of Merit, Fellow A.C.P.; mem. A.M.A., Central Soc. Clin. Research, Sigma Xi, Sigma Sigma, Alpha Omega Alpha, Psi Upsilon, Nu Sigma Nu. Home: 2756 McDowell Rd Durham NC 27705

MUSTAIN, CARL THOMAS, supt. schs.; b. Oologah, Okla., Aug. 12, 1911; s. John Franklin and Sally Jane (Munds) M.; B.S., Northeastern State Coll., 1940; M.S., Okla. State U., 1952; m. Eathel Tipton, Nov. 16, 1929; children—Thomas Andrew, Howard Ray, Janice (Mrs. Hugo Johnson), Eathel Eileen. Elementary tchr., Delaward County, Okla., 1934-42; shipping clk. Standard Oil Cal., Richmond, 1942-47; elementary prin. Beck, Delaware, County, Okla., 1947-51; supt. schs., Cleora, Okla., 1951-57, Big Cabin, Okla., 1957-60, Fairland, Okla., 1960-65, Commerce, Okla., 1965—. Mem. bd. edn. N.E. Okla. Area Vo-Tech. Sch. Dist. 11, 1969—. Mem. Okla. ho. of reps., 1955-57. Mem. N.E.A., Am. Okla. assns. sch. adminstrs., Okla. Edn. Assn., Ottawa County Edn. Assn. (pres. 1961). Mason, Lion. Home: 121 N Maple St Commerce OK 74339 Office: PO Box 10 Commerce OK 74339

MUSTIAN, MIDDLETON T., hosp. adminstr. Dir., Tallahassee Meml. Hosp. Address: Miccosukee Rd Tallahassee FL 32303*

MUTSCHER, GUS FRANKLIN, state legislator; b. William Penn Community, Tex., Nov. 19, 1932; s. G.F. and Gertie (Goeke) M.; student Blinn Coll., Brenham, 1950-52; B.B.A., U. Tex., Austin, 1956; m. Donna A. Axum, June 7, 1969. Field rep. Borden Co., Houston, 1959-61; mem. Tex. Ho. of Rep., 1961—, speaker, 1969—. Mem. So. Conf. adv. com. Council State Govts. Served to 1st lt. AUS, 1956-59. Named Outstanding Young Businessman of Harris County, 1959, One of Five Outstanding Young Texans, 1967, Distinguished Alumnus U. Tex., 1969. Mem. Gamma Delta. Home: 1805 Harrison Rd Brenham TX 77833 Office: Ho of Reps Austin TX 78711

MUTTERS, LEWIS EDWARD, city ofcl.; b. Ashland, Ky., Nov. 23, 1913; s. John Dixon and Ada Augusta (Leslie) M.; ed FBI Nat. Acad., 1963; m. Evelyn Katherine Colley, Sept. 25, 1937; 1 son, John Leslie. With Police Dept. Ashland, Ky., 1946—, detective sgt., 1958-63, chief, 1963—. Served with USMCR, World War II. Mem. Ky. Peace Officers' Assn. (pres. 1964), Ky. Law Enforcement Council (dir. 1966-72). Mason (32 deg.). Home: 4032 Southview Rd Ashland KY 41101 Office: City Bldg Ashland KY 41101

MYERS, BURTON KELLOCK, accountant; b. Wilmington, N,C., June 22, 1925; s. Burton Kellock and Elizabeth (Moore) M.; B.S. in Naval Sci., U.S. Mcht. Marine Acad. 1945; B.S. in Commerce, U. N.C., 1949; m. Margaret Glover, Sept. 8, 1949; children—Burton, Andrew, Worth, Nina, Gladys. C.P.A. bus. mgr. Am. Psychol. Assn., 1959-62; propr. Burton K. Myers & Co., C.P.A.'s, Falls Church, Va., 1962-72; treas. Accounting Supplies & Systems, Inc., 1962—; dir. Hamilton Bank & Trust Co. Prof. Am. Inst. Banking, George Washington U., Benjamin Franklin U. Treas., Lake Bancroft Civic Assn., 1968—; scoutmaster Boy Scouts Am., 1948-69. C.P.A., D.C., Va., Md. Mem. Am., D.C. insts. C.P.A.'s, Va. Soc. C.P.A.'s, Am. Accounting Assn. Home: 6364 Lakeview Dr Falls Church VA 22041 Office: 450 W Broad St Falls Church VA 22046

MYERS, CHARLES FRANKLIN, JR., corp. exec.; b. Charleston, W.Va., July 17, 1911; s. Charles Franklin and Elsie Bell (Smith) M.; student Woodberry Forest Sch., 1924-29; A.B., Davidson Coll., 1933; M.B.A., Harvard, 1935; m. Rebecca Brevard Wright, Sept. 23, 1941; children— Rebecca Brevard, Margaret Alexander, Susan Wright, Elizabeth Churchill. With Bank of N.Y., 1935-39; v.p., dir. Wachovia Bank &Trust Co., Charlotte, N.C., 1939-47; with Burlington Industries, Inc., Greensboro, N.C., 1947—, treas., 1953-62, exec. v.p., 1961-62, pres., 1962-68, chmn. bd., chief exec. officer, 1968—; dir. Chase R.J. Reynolds Industries, Inc., Wachovia Bank & Trust Co., Jefferson-Pilot Corp., U.S. Steel Corp. Mem. Bus. Council; trustee Research Triangle Found. N.C., N.C. Found. Ch.-Related Colls., Davidson Coll., Union Theol. Sem., Chatham Hall, U. Va. Grad. Bus. Sch. Sponsors; bd. visitors Harvard. Mem. Am. Textile Mfrs. Inst. (past pres.), N.Y. So. Soc., Sigma Alpha Epsilon. Presbyn. (elder). Clubs: Country (Greensboro); University, Links (N.Y.C.). Home: 2005 Granville Rd Greensboro NC 27408 Office: 3330 W Friendly Av Greensboro NC 27410

MYERS, DENYS P(ETER), JR., govt. historian; b. Boston, Apr. 23, 1916; s. Denys Peter and Ethel May (Johnston) M.; S.B., Harvard, 1940; postgrad. Fogg Art Mus., 1949-50; M.A., Columbia, 1948; m. Anne Buchonis, Aug. 24, 1940. Asst. reference dept. N.Y. Pub. Library, 1941-42, charge exhbns., 1942-43; instr. Hunter Coll., N.Y.C., 1947; dir. Art Inst., Zanesville, O., 1947-55; dir. Philbrook Art Center, Tulsa, 1955-58, Des Moines Art Center, 1958-60; asst. dir. Balt. Mus. Art, 1960-64; dir. No. Va. Fine Arts Assn., 1964-66; historian Nat. Park Service, U.S. Dept. Interior, 1966-68, prin. archtl. historian historic Am. bldgs. survey, 1968—; lectr. Cath. U. Am., 1966-67; vis. lectr. dept. fine arts Johns Hopkins, 1964. Ordained perpetual deacon Episcopal Ch., 1954. Served with AUS, 1943-46; monuments, fine arts and archives specialist. Mem. Soc. Archtl. Historians, Steamship Hist. Soc. Am. Democrat. Episcopalian. Home: 201 N Columbus St Alexandria VA 22314 Office: Office Archeology and Historic Preservation Nat Park Service 1100 L St NW Washington DC 20005

MYERS, DONALD BUFORD, social worker; b. Ardmore, Okla., Jan. 15, 1934; s. Thomas Buford and Clydie (Baggett) M.; B.S. in Psychology, Abilene Christian Coll., 1956; postgrad. U. Tex. Guidance and Counseling Inst., 1961, M.S. in Social Work, 1965; m. Carla Willis, June 17, 1955; children—Darla Lynn, Jerry Don, Terri Gwyn, Patricia Ann, John Richard, Merry Carol. Elementary sch. tchr., Corpus Christi, Tex., 1956-62; dir. social service Travis State Sch., Austin, Tex., 1967-68, High Plains Children's Home, Amarillo, Tex., 1968-71; instnl. licensing supr. Tex. Dept. Pub. Welfare, Amarillo, 1971-72, program dir., 1972—. Cons. adoption and foster home workshops; cons. inservice tng. N.W. Tex. Hosp. Sch. Nursing, Amarillo, 1968—; mem. council on youth Domestic Relations Ct., Amarillo, 1968—; vol. council State Center for Human Devel., 1968—; mem. adv. bd. Sch. Social Work, West Tex. State U., 1972—. Mem. sch. bd. Amarillo Christian Sch., 1969-70; bd. dirs. Damascus Christian Center for Drug Rehab. Agy. Mem. Nat. Assn. Social Workers, Acad. Certified Social Workers, S.W., Tex. assns. homes for children, Tex. Assn. Services for Children. Mem. Ch. of Christ. Home: 5313 Berget St Amarillo TX 79106 Office: 517 S Taylor St Amarillo TX 79105

MYERS, EDNA MILDRED, supt. schs.; b. Quinlan, Okla., Jan. 26, 1908; d. Charles P. and Laura (Duncan) Mock; A.B., Northwestern State Coll., Alva, Okla., 1949; M.Ed., Phillips U., Enid, Okla., 1953; postgrad. U. Colo., Okla. A. and M. Coll.; m. Ralph C. Myers, July 29, 1933. Tchr. pub. schs. (including rural area) 28 years; county supt. of schs. Woodward County, Okla., 1953—. Pres. county supt. dept. N.W. Dist. Okla. Edn. Assn., 1953-54, Audio-visual coordinator for 4-H Club camps, Carnegie Library Reading Programs, hosp. and adult edn., ch. schs. Organized Woodward County Future Tchrs. Club, Northwestern Okla. Pioneer Women, also Woodward County (Okla.) Tchrs. State dir. Okla. Heart Assn.; pres. Woodward County Tb Assn.; sec., dir. Mental Health Assn., 1962—; state rep. Spl. Unit on Aging; chmn. Survey for State Okla. Services to the Retarded; dir. N.W. Okla. Guidance Center, 1970—; pres. local br. Am. Cancer Soc.; treas. Woodward County Salvation Army; v.p. N.W. Okla. Regional Tb and Respiratory Disease Assn. Recipient Outstanding 4-H Leader award, 1951. Mem. N.E.A. (life), Am. Assn. of Sch. Adminstrs. (state membership chmn.), C. of C., Woodward Bus. and Profl. Women's Civic Club (past pres.), Dist. Five County Officers' Assn. (pres. 1960—), N.W. Vocational Rehab. Dept. (exec. bd.), Kappa Kappa Iota (past pres. Alpha Chi chpt.). Methodist. Mem. Rebekah, Royal Neighbor. Club: Toastmistress (pres. Woodward). Home: 512 16th St Box 907 Woodward OK 73801 Office: Courthouse 1600 Main St Woodward OK 73801

MYERS, EDWIN NELSON, electronic engr.; b. Sayre, Pa., Jan. 26, 1924; s. Everett Harding and Edith (Lane) M.; B.S., Okla. State U., 1956; M.S., Mass. Inst. Tech., 1961; m. Marian Louise Engler, Aug. 29, 1944; children—Metta Lou, Mari Anne. Commd. 2d lt. USAAF, 1944, advanced through grades to lt. col., 1963; with Continental Weather Wing, 1946-54, asst. chief systems engr. Air Research and Devel. Command, N.Y.C., 1956-59, research and devel. program mgr. Radar Techniques and Lasers, Pentagon, 1961-65; ret., 1965; staff specialist electronic devices and lasers Office Dir. of Def. Research and Engring., Office Sec. Def., 1965-70, staff asst. to asst. dir. electronics and computer scis., 1971—. Mem. I.E.E.E., Am. Radio Relay League, Mil. Affiliate Radio System, Sigma Xi, Phi Kappa Phi, Eta Kappa Nu, Pi Mu Epsilon. Home: 1010 Priscilla Lane Alexandria VA 22308 Office: Sec of Defense Washington DC 20301

MYERS, EUGENE EKANDER, art adminstr.; b. Grand Forks, N.D., May 5, 1914; s. John Q. and Hattye Jane (Ekander) M.; B.S. in Edn., U. N.D., 1936, M.S. in Edn., 1938; postgrad. U. Ore., summer 1937; M.A., Northwestern U., 1940; M.A., Columbia, 1947; advanced mgmt. program Harvard, 1953; certificate Cambridge (Eng.) U., 1958; postgrad. U. Md., 1958-61, Oxford (Eng.) U., 1964; diploma various mil. schs. Student asst. U. N.D., 1935-36, instr. summer sessions 1936, 37, asst., 1936-37; instr. N.D. Tchrs. Coll., 1938-40, Tchrs. Coll., Columbia, 1940-41; prof. U. Vt., summer 1941, 42; commd. 1st lt. USAAF, 1942, advanced through grades to col., 1951; dir. personnel plans and tng. Hdqrs. Air Force Systems Command, Washington, 1959-60, dir. personnel research and longrange plans, 1960-62, head dept. internat. relations Air War Coll., Air U., Maxwell AFB, Ala., 1962-63, dir. curriculum, dean, 1963-65, dir. res. affairs Hdqrs. Air Res. Personnel Center, Denver, 1965-66; dean Corcoran Sch. Art, Washington, 1966-69; v.p. Corcoran Gallery Art, Washington, 1970-72; art cons., vis. art dir., Palm Beach, Fla. and Washington, 1972—. Bd. dirs. World Arts Found., Columbia Sch. Art, Assos. Artists Equity. Mem. Nat. Soc. Study Communication (hon.), Speech Assn. Am., U. N.D. Alumni Assn. (pres. Washington 1959), Mil. Classics Soc., Co. Mil. Historians, St. Andrews Soc., Mil. Order of Carabao, Order of Lafayette (dir.), Delta Omicron Epsilon, Lambda Chi Alpha, Delta Phi Delta, Phi Delta Kappa, Phi Alpha Theta. Presbyn. Lion. Clubs: Curzon House (London, Eng.); Union (Manchester, Eng.); Army and Navy, Army and Navy Country, Nat. Aviation, Georgetown, City Tavern, Harvard Business School (Washington); Metropolitan, Salmagundi, Wings, Explorers (N.Y.C.); Minneapolis; Beach (Palm Beach, Fla.). Author: (with Paul E. Barr) Creative Lettering, 1938; (with others) The Subject Fields in General Education, 1939; Applied Psychology, 1940. Contbr. articles and reports in mags. and profl. publs. Address: 3320 Volta Pl NW Washington DC 20007 also 1 Royal Palm Way Palm Beach FL 33480

MYERS, FREDDIE RAY, banker; b. Stamford, Tex., July 30, 1939; s. Leonard Jackson and Lucille (Hart) M.; B.B.A., Sul Ross State U., 1961; m. Anita Stephenson, Aug. 22, 1959; 1 son, Stephen J. Vice pres. First Nat. Bank, Post, Tex., 1965—, adv. dir. Mem. Post City Council, 1970-71. Bd. dirs. Post Stampede Rodeo, 1962-71. Mem. Antelope Booster's Club (v.p., dir. 1970—). Mem. Christian Ch. Home: 107 Ridge Rd Post TX 79356 Office: 216 W Main St Post TX 79356

MYERS, IRA LEE, physician, state ofcl.; b. Monvoria, Ala., Feb. 9, 1924; s. Ira Willie and Azalea (Cobbs) M.; B.S., Howard Coll., 1945; M.D., U. Ala., 1949; M.P.H., Harvard, 1953; m. Dorothy Will Foust, Sept. 4, 1943; children—Martha Crystal, Ira Grady, Stephen Allen, Joanna Lynn. Intern, USPHS Hosp., Seattle, 1949-50; practice medicine, specializing in epidiomology, USPHS, 1950-55; adminstrv. officer Ala. Dept. Pub. Health, Montgomery, 1955-63, state health officer, Montgomery, 1963—; asst. prof. preventive medicine U. Ala. Med. Coll., Birmingham, 1958—. Sec. Ala. Bd. Med. Examiners, Montgomery, 1962—; chmn. Ala. Water Improvement Commn., Montgomery, 1963—; mem. govs. com. to White Ho. Conf. on Aging, Washington, 1960-61. Served to sr. surgeon USPHS, 1949-55. Diplomate Am. Bd. Preventive Medicine. Mem. Ala. (pres. 1963), Am. pub. health assns., Am. Assn. Pub. Health Physicians (pres. 1970), Ala. Thoracic Soc. (pres. 1960), Ala. Hosp. Assn., (hon.), Assn. Sanitarians (hon.), A.M.A., Med. Assn. Ala., Am. Acad. Gen. Practice. Baptist (deacon, trustee). Home: 925 Green Forest Dr Montgomery AL 36109 Office: 501 Dexter Av Montgomery AL 36104

MYERS, JACK EDGAR, biologist; b. Boyds Mills, Pa., July 10, 1913; s. Garry Cleveland and Caroline (Clark) M.; B.S., Juniata Coll., 1934, D.Sc., 1966; M.S., Mont. State Coll., 1935; Ph.D., U. Minn., 1939; m. Evelyn DeTurck, June 19, 1937; children—Shirley Ann, Jacquelyn, Linda Caroline, Kathleen. NRC fellow Smithsonian Instn., 1940-41; asst. prof. zoology U. Tex., 1941-45, asso. prof., 1945-48, prof. zoology, 1948—, prof. botany, 1955—. Guggenheim fellow, 1959. Mem. Soc. Gen. Physiologists, Am. Soc. Plant Physiologists, Bot. Soc. Am., Phycol. Soc., A.A.A.S., Tex. Acad. Sci., Sigma Xi. Author: (with F. A. Matsen and N. H. Hackerman) Premedical Physical Chemistry, 1947. Sci. editor Highlights for Children, 1960—. Contbr.: Algal Culture: from Laboratory to Pilot Plant, 1953; Proc. of the World Symposium on Applied Solar Energy, 1956. Contbr. articles to profl. jours. Home: Route 7 Box 514 Austin TX 78703

MYERS, JAMES FRANCIS, safety systems mfg. co. exec.; b. Plattsburg, Mo., Dec. 2, 1913; s. Frank Marion and Margaret (Glenn) M.; B.S. in Bus. Adminstrn., Mo. Wesleyan Coll., Cameron, 1935; m. Marjorie Anderson, Oct. 27, 1939; 1 son, James Lee. From oil field product trainee to v.p., gen. mgr. Black, Suvalls & Bryson, Inc. (name now B.S. & B. Safety Systems, Inc.), Tulsa. Served with USNR. Mem. Am. Inst. Chem. Engrs., Am. Petroleum Inst. (mem. mfrs. subcom.), Tulsa C. of C. Club: Petroleum (Tulsa). Patentee in field testing of valves with reverse buckling disc installed at valve inlet. Contbr. tech. papers to profl. jours. Home: 4870 E 68th St Apt 233 Tulsa OK 74136 Office: 7455 E 46th St Tulsa OK 74145

MYERS, KENNETH MORTON, state senator; b. Miami, Fla., Mar. 11, 1933; s. Stanley C. and Martha (Scheinberg) M.; A.B., U. N.C., 1954; LL.B., U. Fla., 1957; m. Ursula Wienholtz, 1969. Admitted to Fla.bar, 1957; practiced in Miami, 1957-65; mem. Fla. Ho. of Reps., 1965-69; mem. Fla. State Senate, 1969—, mem. ways and means com., chmn. health, welfare and insts. coms. Bd. dirs. Dade County Children's Psychiat. Center. Mem. Am., Dade County bar assns., Dade County Jr. Bar Assn., Miami-Dade C. of C. Home: 2451 Brickell Av Miami FL 33129 Office: 1150 SW First St Miami FL 33130*

MYERS, LAWRENCE, agrl. economist, mayor; b. Humboldt, Ia., July 14, 1898; s. George A. and Mary (Barrett) M.; B.S., U. Minn., 1922, postgrad., 1923-27; M.S., Ia. State Coll., 1923; m. Anne Cornelia Henkel, July 15, 1924; children—Margaret Mary (Mrs.

James J. Rast), Dorothy Helen (Mrs. James G. Sampas). Instr. agrl. econs. U. Minn., St. Paul, 1925-27; economist Bur. Agr. Econs., U.S. Dept. Agr., Washington, 1927-33; economist, div. dir.. A.A.A., Washington, 1933-39; div. dir. CCC, Washington, 1939-46; dir. textiles and raw materials UNNRA, Washington, 1946; asst. to sec. agr., Washington, 1946; dir. sugar div. U.S. Dept. Agr., Washington, 1947-63; chmn. bd. Nat. Molasses Corp., Washington, 1963-68; Washington rep. C. Brewer & Affiliates, 1968-71; econ. cons., 1972—. mayor City of Friendship Heights (Md.), 1965—. Chmn. Internat. Sugar Council, 1955. Served with U.S. Army, 1918. Recipient certificate of merit Dept. Agr., 3 times, Distinguished Service award, 1955. Republican. Clubs: Cosmos (Washington); Iron Bridge Hunt (pres. 1965-67) (Laurel, Md.); Potomac (Md.) Hunt. Home: 5530 Friendship Blvd Chevy Chase MD 20015 Office: 1001 Connecticut Av NW Washington DC 20036

MYERS, ORIE EUGENE, JR., coll. adminstr.; b. Hagan, Ga., Oct. 14, 1920; s. Orie Eugene and Betty (Shuman) M.; student Ga. Inst. Tech., 1937-38; A.B., Emory U., 1941, M.A., 1957; m. Margaret Elizabeth Nesbit, June 7, 1941; children—Orie Eugene III, Curtis Alan, Adrian Marvyn. Personnel asst. Atlanta Personnel Bd., 1940-41; personnel officer Nat. Youth Adminstrn., 1941-43, Office Emergency Mgmt., 1943-44, VA, 1946-48; dir. personnel Emory U., Atlanta, 1948-61, bus. mgr., 1961, dean adminstrn., dir. health services, 1961-64, v.p. bus., dir. Woodruff Med. Center, 1964—. Dir. DeKalb County Fed. Savs. & Loan Assn. Trustee, chmn. health com. Wesley Homes; chmn. bd. dirs. DeKalb County unit Am. Cancer Soc. Served to 1st lt., USAAF, 1944-46. Mem. Coll. and Univ. Personnel Assn. (past pres.), So. Assn. Coll. and Univ. Bus. Officers (v.p.), Sigma Nu. Democrat. Baptist. Home: 236 Mt Vernon Dr Decatur GA 30030 Office: Emory University Atlanta GA 30322

MYERS, PAUL FREDRICK, govt. ofcl.; b. Turtle Creek, Pa., Dec. 17, 1916; s. Joseph A. and Elizabeth (Reinkemeyer) M.; B.A. magna cum laude, U. Ala., 1941; postgrad. Am. U., 1946-48;; m. Alice Christine Fuls, Nov. 24, 1941; children—David, Christine. Chemist, E. I. du Pont de Nemours, Memphis, 1941-44; statistician, VA, Dept. Navy, U.S. Bur. Census, 1946-62; chief fgn. demographic analysis div. U.S. Bur. Census, Washington, 1962—. Served with AUS, 1943-46. Mem. Population Assn. Am., Internat. Union for Sci. Study Population, Am. Sociol. Assn., Am. Statis. Assn. Author: (with W. Parker Mauldin) The Population of the Federal Republic of Germany and West Berlin, 1952; (with Arthur A. Campbell) The Population of Yugoslavia, 1954. Home: 12811 Crisfield Rd Silver Spring MD 20906 Office: 2400 M St NW Washington DC 20230

MYERS, WILLIAM HUNTER, oceanographer; b. Cumberland, Md., June 28, 1922; s. Hunter Lee and Helen (Merrbaugh) M.; B.S., U. Md., 1943, M.S., 1948, postgrad., 1948-51. Oceanographer, U.S. Naval Oceanographic Office, Washington, 1951-60; oceanographer Nat. Oceanographic Data Center, Washington, 1961-62, dir. quality control div., 1962-67, dir. devel. div., 1968—. Served with AUS, 1944-46. Mem. Marine Tech. Soc., Oceanographical Soc. Japan, Washington Acad. Scis. Home: 125 4th St NE Washington DC 20002 Office: Nat Oceanographic Data Center Rockville MD 20852

MYKLESTAD, NILS OTTO, educator; b. Williston, N.D., Mar. 24, 1909; s. Nils and Augusta (Moller) M.; cand. polyt. Royal Tech. Coll., Copenhagen, Denmark, 1932; student U. Cal. at Berkeley, 1937-38; Ph.D., Cornell U., 1940; m. Dorothea Marie Gerisch, Dec. 21, 1941 (div. Nov. 1965); children—Ingrid, Nancy, Erik. Mech. engr. Westinghouse Co., Phila., 1932-34, Fairbanks Morse, Beloit, Wis., 1934-35, Atlas Diesel, Oakland, Cal., 1935-36, Standard Oil Co., San Francisco, 1936-37; teaching asst. U. Cal. at Berkeley, 1937-38; instr. Cornell U., 1938-40; asst. prof. Ill. Inst. Tech., 1940-42; research Cal. Inst. Tech., 1942-46; prof. U. Ill. 1947-52; prof. engring. Ariz. State U., 1961-67; prof. engring. mechanics U. Tex., Arlington, 1967—. Cons. Aerospace Industries, 1952-61, Bell Helicopter Co., 1967—. Mem. A.A.A.S., Am. Soc. M.E., Am. Soc. Engring Edn., Sigma Xi, Tau Beta Pi. Author: Vibration Analysis, 1944; Fund of Vibration Analysis, 1956; Engineering Mechanics, 1965; Statics of Deformable Bodies, 1966; Cartesian Tensors, 1967. Home: 406 Baylor Dr Arlington TX 76010

MYNARD, CHARLES ROBERT, accountant; b. Marshall, Tex., Sept. 29, 1923; s. Aubrey Green and Agnes (Vining) M.; B.B.A., U. Tex., 1951; m. Jacqueline Lee, Dec. 10, 1962; children—Randall, Lee, Melinda, Pamela, Cynthia. Chief accountant Corpus Christi (Tex.) Ind. Sch. Dist.; accountant Doughty & Co.; asst. treas., chief accountant Arnold Pipe Co., 1951-61; self-employed as C.P.A., Corpus Christi, 1961—. Treas., Cliff Maus Village Trust, Corpus Christi, 1969—. Served with USAAF, 1942-45. Mem. Am. Inst. C.P.A.'s, Tex. Soc. C.P.A.'s, Beta Alpha Psi, Beta Gamma Sigma. Episcopalian. Mason, Rotarian. Home: 2610 Linn St Corpus Christi TX 78410 Office: 3763 Leopard St Corpus Christi TX 78408

MYNATT, WILLIAM ATCHLEY, dentist; b. nr. Knoxville, Tenn., Apr. 7, 1927; s. William Howard and Anna T. (Sumter) M.; student U. Tenn., 1946-48, D.D.S., 1953; m. Lee Tickle, June 29, 1950; children—Rebecca Judson, William Atchley, Anne Elizabeth. With N.C. Dept. Oral Hygiene, 1954; pvt, dental practice, Asheville, N.C., 1955—. Dir. Asheville Country Day Sch., 1968-70. Served with USNR, 1945-46. Fellow Internat. Coll. Dentists; mem. Buncombe County (pres. 1962), N.C. 1st Dist. (pres. 1970), N.C., Chgo. dental socs., Am. Dental Assn., Delta Sigma Delta. Presbyn. (elder). Clubs: Biltmore Forest Country, Mountain City (Asheville). Home: 46 Hilltop Rd Asheville NC 28803 Office: 36 All Souls Crescent Asheville NC 28803

MYNETT, JACK WILLIAM, corp. exec.; b. Council Bluffs, Ia., Aug. 7, 1924; s. Charles William and Edna (Burke) M.; B.B.A., So. Methodist U., 1949, M.B.A., 1951; m. Jo Nell Stubblefield, Mar. 1, 1946; children—Judy Lynne, Charles William II. Dir. personnel Hartford Ins. Group, Dallas, 1951-63; v.p. planning, devel. and gen. services Gulf Ins. Group, Dallas, 1963-68; sr. v.p., dir. UCC Financial Corp., 1968-72; resident mgr. Boyden Assos., Inc., 1972—; dir. Gulf Computer Services, Inc. Active various community drives. Trustee, Amigos de las Ams., 1971—. Served with AUS, 1942-46. Mem. Adminstrv. Mgmt. Soc. (Diamond Merit award 1967, Mem. of Year Dallas chpt. 1965, internat. v.p.-treas. 1967-68, chpt. pres. 1964-65), Dallas Mgmt. Assn. (pres. 1963-64), Dallas Personnel Assn. (pres. 1963-64), So. Methodist U. Bus. Sch. Alumni Assn. (pres. 1957), Dallas C. of C. (pres., life mem. club 1965-66, Triple Life mem. 1962, 63, 67). Home: 4308 Alta Vista Lane Dallas TX 75229 Office: Suite 2060 One Main Pl Dallas TX 75250

NABERS, JANE PORTER (MRS. DRAYTON NABERS), civic worker; b. Birmingham, Ala., Nov. 16, 1913; d. James Devereux and Jennie (Pollard) Porter; A.B., Goucher Coll., 1934; m. Drayton Nabers, Sept. 22, 1936; children—Jane Porter (Mrs. Frank H. MCFadden), Drayton, Susan Porter (Mrs. Wyatt R. Haskell). Mem. Jr. League of Birmingham (Ala.), 1935—, treas., 1941-42, chmn. sustaining group, 1966-67; mem. citizens com. adv. bd. Juvenile and Domestic Relations Ct. Jefferson County, 1966—; mem. bd. Linly Heflin Unit, 1962—, treas., 1964-67, v.p., 1967-68, pres., 1968-69; rec. sec. Opera Guild Bd., 1964-66; trustee Birmingham Hist. Soc., 1947-70; bd. dirs. Bapt. Hosps. Found., Birmingham, 1967-71; mem. com. 100 Women Birmingham, 1964-67. Bd. dirs. Ala. Boys Indsl. Sch., 1952—, pres., 1960-68, v.p., 1968—; bd. dirs. Jefferson County chpt. A.R.C., 1969-72; trustee Children's Hosp., 1947—, 3rd v.p., 1961-63, 2d v.p., 1970—. Presbyn. (elder). Co-editor: Sketches of Alabama, 1970. Home: 6 Beechwood Rd Birmingham AL 35213

NABHOLZ, ROBERT DANIEL, contractor; b. Conway, Ark., Mar. 16, 1924; s. Emil A. and Mary Ann (Strack) N.; student State Coll. Ark., 1946-48, U. Okla., 1947-48; m. Barbara J. Harpe, June 13, 1949; children— Susan, Robert, David, Nancy, Tim, John. Founder, pres. Nabholz Constrn. Co., Conway, 1949—; founder, sec.-treas. Nabholz Supply Co., 1952—; sec., treas. NABCO Inc., 1959—; v.p. Conark Builders, Conway, 1961—; dir. First Nat. Bank, Conway, 1961—. Pres. Ark. Basin Assn., 1966-68; vice-chmn. Conway Devel. Corp., 1970-72. Served with AUS, 1943-46; ETO. Mem. Am. Inst. Constructors, Conway C. of C. (pres. 1962), Diocesan Council Cath. Men. Roman Catholic. Kiwanian. Home: Route 4 Conway AR 72032 Office: 610 Garland St Conway AR 72032

NABLE, RAYMOND DANIEL, dentist; b. Orlando, Fla., Apr. 21, 1934; s. Gustavus Raymond and Oradell Matilda (Raybon) N.; student U. Fla., 1952-54; D.D.S., Emory U., 1958; m. Mary Ann Austin, Apr. 8, 1961; children—Raymond Daniel, Richard Austin. Pvt. practice dentistry, Atlanta, 1961—; asst. prof. operative dentistry Emory U. Sch. Dentistry, 1962—; staff Ben Massell Dental Clinic, 1961—, mem. adv. bd., 1965—. Active High Mus. Art. Served with USNR, 1958-61. Mem. Am. Dental Assn., No. Dist. Ga. Dental Assn., Atlanta C. of C., Delta Sigma Delta. Methodist (steward 1964—). Club: Buckhead Mens Garden (Atlanta). Home: 472 Glencastle Dr NW Atlanta GA 30327 Office: 2970 Peachtree Rd NE Atlanta GA 30305

NABORS, OLLIE WILSON, senator, lawyer; b. Gadsden, Ala., July 1, 1926; s. Wallace Scott and Lola (Atkins) N.; LL.B., U. Ala., 1950; m. Leatha Jeanette Thornton, Dec. 18, 1949; 1 dau., Peggy Jeanette. Admitted to Ala. bar, 1950; practiced in Gadsden, 1950—; pres. Merit Hills, Inc., Gadsden, 1955-66; sec.-treas. Merit Corp., Gadsden, 1962-66. Tchr. polit. sci., real estate law U. Ala. Center in Gadsden, 1952-66. Mem. Ala. Ho. of Reps., 1962-66; senator, 1966—. Sec., Gadsden Indsl. Devel. Bd., 1962—. Served with USNR, 1944-46. Named Outstanding Freshman Legislator, Ala. Ho. of Reps., 1963, Outstanding Debator, 1965, Outstanding State Senator of Ala., 1967. Mem. Gadsden C. of C. (dir. 1959-62), Pi Kappa Phi, Omega Delta Kappa, Phi Eta Sigma. Mason, Rotarian. Club: Gadsden Country (bd. govs. 1964-67). Home: 108 Gwindale Rd Gadsden AL 35901 Office: 1st City Nat Bank 400 W Meighan Blvd Gadsden AL 35901

NABRIT, SAMUEL MILTON, fund exec.; b. Macon, Ga., Feb. 21, 1905; s. James Madison and Augusta (West) N.; B.S., Morehouse Coll., 1925, LL.D., 1960; M.S., Brown U., 1928, Ph.D., 1932, D.Sc. (hon.), 1962; D.Sc., Atlanta U., 1963, Howard U., 1963; LL.D., U. Ky., 1972; m. Constance Crocker, Aug. 8, 1927. Prof. biol. Morehouse Coll., 1925-31; prof., chmn. dept. biology Atlanta U., 1932-55, dean grad. sch., 1947-55; pres. Tex. So. U., Houston, 1955-66; commr. AEC, Washington, 1966-67; exec. dir. So. Fellowships Fund, 1967—. Coordinator Carnegie Grants-in-Aid program, 1948—; mem. com. higher edn. So. Regional Bd. Control, 1950—; mem. Corp. Marine Biol. Lab., 1948—, Nat. Com. on Research Sci. Edn., 1936—; mem. Nat. Sci. Bd., 1956—; mem. adminstrv. com. So. Fellowships Fund, 1954—; com. for tng. coll. tchrs. Am. Council Edn., 1952—, bd. dirs., 1961; bd. dirs. So. Edn. Found.; trustee Brown U., 1967—; mem. screening com. Fund for Advancement of Edn. Faculty Fellowships, 1950-54. Mem. A.A.A.S., Am. Soc. Zoologists, N.Y. Acad. Sci., Soc. Study Growth and Devel., Nat. Inst. Sci. (3d pres.), Sigma Xi, Phi Beta Kappa, Beta Kappa Chi, Omega Psi Phi, Sigma Pi Phi, Pi Delta Phi. Contbr. profl. jours. Home: 686 Beckwith St SW Atlanta GA 30314 Office: 795 Peachtree St NE Atlanta GA 30308

NACE, RAYMOND LEE, govt. scientist; b. Los Angeles, Oct. 13, 1907; s. Perley Frank and Alice (Carson) N.; B.S., U. Wyo., 1935, M.A., 1936; postgrad. Yale, 1939-41; Ph.D., Columbia U., 1960; m. Edna Helen Lane, July 31, 1935; children—Samuel L., Robert L. Part-time field geologist Geol. Survey of Wyo., 1934-36; instr. geology U. Wyo., 1937-39, Yale, 1939-41; geologist, hydrologist U.S. Geol. Survey, 1941—. Served with AUS, 1941-46, ETO. Fellow Geol. Soc. Am., A.A.A.S., Sigma Xi. Home: 9226 E Parkhill Dr Bethesda MD 20014 Office: 19th & F Sts NW Washington DC 20242

NADER, JEANETTE HELEN BALAGIA, home economist; b. Austin, Tex., Mar. 13, 1927; d. Tofie and Bertha (Johns) Balagia; B.B.A., U. Tex., 1946; m. Nesib Nader, Dec. 27, 1949; children—William, Michael, Linda, Rene. Accountant, Gem Jewelry Co., Austin, 1946-49, 1st. Nat. Bank, Shreveport, La., 1949-52; home economist 245 Wedgewood Dr., Shreveport, 1949—. Mem. Am. Legion Auxiliary, Am. Bar Assn. Auxiliary, U. Tex. Alumni Assn. Republican. Episcopalian. Clubs: Lebanon, Phoenician (Shreveport). Home and Office: 245 Wedgewood Dr Shreveport LA 71105

NADER, NESIB, lawyer; b. Shreveport, La., Aug. 14, 1916; s. Ike A. and Mamie (Monsour) N.; B.A., La. State U., 1940; law student Loyola U., 1947-48. Centenary Coll., 1950-53; m. Jeanette Balagia, Dec. 27, 1949; children—Billy Glenn, Michael Wayne, Linda, Rene. Admitted to La. bar, 1953, since in pvt. practice at Shreveport; asst. atty. gen. State La., 1960—. Mem. Gov.'s staff, 1956—. Vice chmn., adv. council Shreveport Youth Opportunity Center, Shreveport, 1967—. Bd. dirs. Caddo Democratic Assn. Served from pvt. to staff sgt. AUS, 1941-45. PTO. Decorated Bronze Star medal. Mem. Am., La., Shreveport bar assns., Am. Legion (post judge adv. 1961-62, mem. nat. com. membership and post activities, district comdr. 4th dist. La. 1966-67, mem. nat. counter-subversive activities com., chmn. sch. awards 4th dist.), D.A.V., V.F.W., So. Fedn. Syrian-Lebanon-Am. Clubs (pres., del. Nat. Fedn.). Episcopalian. Clubs: Optimist, Phoenician (pres. 1960-61), Louisiana (v.p. 1957). Home: 245 Wedgewood St Shreveport LA 71105 Office: Giddens Lane Bldg Shreveport LA 71105

NADLER, JOSEPH REXWOOD, mech. engr., co. exec.; b. Atlanta; s. Jacques and Berthe (Clerc) N.; B.S., Auburn U.; M.E., M.E.E., Cornell U.; postgrad. U. Cin., Robert Coll., Am. U., Istanbul, Turkey. Began as instr. engring. Cornell; with Ala. Power Co., later So. dist. mgr. Detroit Steel Products Co., Birmingham, Ala.; was asst. prof. engring. Robert Coll., Am. U., Instanbul; v.p. Binswanger & Co., Miami, Fla., and Richmond, Va., Montauk Constrn. Co.; pres., owner Investment Research, pub. lectr. Mem. adv. com. 350th Anniversary celebration, Jamestown, Va.; mem. Va. citizens com. on birthplace restoration and adv. com. for Woodrow Wilson Centennial Celebration, Staunton; pres. Richmond council, mem. state com. U.S.O. President Greater Richmond Republican Club; mem. Richmond Rep. com.; del. Nat. Rep. Conv,, 1956, 60. Dist. chmn, Cornell U. Alumni Fund. Civilian engr., asst, to chief engr. U.S. Army Transp. Corps, World War II. Registered mech. engr., Ohio. Mem. N.Y. So. Soc., Richmond Film Soc. (past officer), Richmond C. of C., Am. Contract Bridge League, Phi Kappa Phi (charter mem. 1st sec.). Unitarian (bd. stewards, chmn. finance com.). Mason (32 deg., Shriner), Lion. Clubs: Circus Saints and Sinners, Downtown, Bull and Bear (charter), Cornell of Virginia (pres.) (Richmond, Va.). Contbr. nat. mags. Home: 2606 Kensington Av Richmond VA 23220

NAESS, MICHAEL RAGNAR, shipping co. exec.; b. Edenbridge, Kent, Eng., June 18, 1939; s. Erling Dekke and Eleanore Frances (Clowes) N.; came to U.S., 1941, naturalized, 1947. B.A., Amherst Coll., 1961; M.B.A., Harvard, 1969; m. Katrin Julia Singer, June 8, 1968; 1 dau., Stephanie Katrin. Exec. v.p. Naess Shipping Co., Inc., N.Y.C., 1961-67; v.p. corp. devel. Southdown, Inc., Houston, 1969-70; exec. v.p., dir. Zapata Norness, Inc., Houston, 1970—; chmn. Anglo Norness Shipping Co., Ltd., Bermuda, 1970—, Boone County Coal Corp., Huntington, W. Va., 1970-71; dir. Fannin Bank, Houston. Served from ensign to lt. (j.g.) USNR, 1962-65. Mem. Am. Bur. Shipping, Nat. Coal Assn. Republican. Clubs: Forest, Coronado, Criterion (Houston). Home: 347 Westminster Dr Houston TX 77024 Office: Southwest Tower Houston TX 77002

NAGAY, JOHN ADAM, govt. ofcl.; b. Hazleton, Pa., May 12, 1918; s. Adam A. and Mary (Duchon) N.; B.S., U. Pitts., 1941, M.S., 1951; Ph.D., Am. U., 1964; m, Jeanne A. Kopp, Mar. 2, 1946. Project dir. Am. Insts. Research, Pitts., 1948-51; dir. group psychology programs Office Naval Research, Washington, 1966—, asst. head personnel and tng. research bur., 1951-65, liason scientist ONR, London, 1965-66. Served with USAAF, Mem. Am., D.C., Eastern, Midwestern psychol. assns., Research Soc. Am., Internat. Congress Applied Psychology, Psi Chi. Home: 3315 Barkley Dr Fairfax VA 22030 Office: Office Naval Research Arlington VA 22217

NAGEL, EUGENE LOUIS, educator, physician; b. Quincy, Ill., Aug. 12, 1924; s. Irwing G. and Zelda (Schwartz) N.; B. Elec. Engring., Cornell U., 1949; M.D., Washington U., St. Louis, 1959; m. Margaret Joan Kaeflein, Jan. 4, 1963; children—Linda, Dennis, Susan. Elec. engr. S.I. Edison Corp., 1949-52, V.A. Snyder Co., Inc., S.I., 1952-54; intern St. Luke's Hosp., St. Louis, 1959-60; resident Columbia-Presbyn. Hosp., N.Y.C., 1960-62; mem. staff Jackson Meml. Hosp., Miami, Fla., 1962—; asso. prof. anesthesiology U. Miami Sch. Medicine, 1962—. Mem. subcom. communications in emergency med. services NRC-Nat. Acad. Scis., 1971—. Served with AUS, 1943-46. Diplomate Am. Bd. Anesthesiology. Fellow Am. Coll. Cardiology; mem. I.E.E.E., Fla. Soc. Anesthesiologists (1st v.p. 1970—), N.Y. Acad. Scis., Am. Soc. Anesthesiologists (sect. vice chmn. 1971—), Sigma Xi. Contbr. articles to sci. jours. Home: 7741 SW 134th Terrace Miami FL 33156 Office: 1700 NW 10th Av Miami FL 31136

NAGEL, ROBERT HAMILTON, orgn. exec.; b. N.Y.C., Apr. 19, 1918; s. William C. and Christine (Hamilton) N.; B.S. in Civil Engring., Cornell U., 1939; M.S. in Civil Engring., U. Tenn., 1941; m. Ruth Lyman Davis, Nov. 25, 1939; children—Virginia (Mrs. David A. Culver), Robert D., Cynthia H. Engr. TVA, Knoxville, Tenn., 1939-43; asst. prof. civil engring. U. Tenn., Knoxville, 1943-44; bridge engr. So. Ry. Co., Knoxville, 1944-46; sec., treas., editor Tau Beta Pi Assn., Knoxville, 1947—; sec., treas. Internat. Assn. Torch Clubs, Knoxville, 1968—. Registered profl. engr., Tenn. Fellow A.A.A.S., Am. Soc. C.E.; mem. Nat., Tenn. socs. profl. engrs., Tech. Soc. Knoxville, Newcomen Soc. N.Am., Chi Epsilon, Alpha Kappa Mu. Home: 4406 Sunset Rd Knoxville TN 37914 Office: Box 8840 Univ Sta Knoxville TN 37916

NAGLEE, DAVID INGERSOLL, educator, clergyman; b. Somers Point, N.J., Sept. 15, 1930; s. Jacob Hann and Dorcas (Ingersoll) N.; B.A., Houghton Coll., 1953; postgrad. Temple Sch. Theology, 1956-58; B.D., Crozer Theol. Sem., 1959; M.A., Temple U., 1963, Ph.D., 1966; m. Elfriede Elsa Kurz, Sept. 6, 1952; children—David Stephen, Joanna Jane, Deborah Ruth, Miriam Louise, Joy Ann. Ordained to ministry Meth. Ch., 1959; pastor chs., Ellicottville, N.Y., 1953-56, Bridgeton, N.J., 1956-58, Port Norris, N.J., 1958-62, Bridgeton, 1962-64, Millville, N.J., 1964-66; asst. prof. religion and philosophy LaGrange (Ga.) Coll., 1966-67, asso. prof., 1967-71, Flora Glenn Candler prof. religion and philosophy, 1971—. Lectr. in religion and Bible Southeastern Jurisdiction United Meth. Ch., 1969; automotive cons., technician Norris/Harrington Racing Co., LaGrange, Ga., 1971; musician, cellist Columbus (Ga.) Symphony Orch., 1969-71. Dir. tutorial program for needy children, LaGrange, 1967-68; mem. Human Relations Council, LaGrange, 1966-71; adviser Maidee Smith Nursery, LaGrange, 1966-71. Served with USNR, 1948-49. Mem. Pi Gamma Mu. Mason. Author: The History of the Methodist Church at Port Norris, New Jersey, 1962. Composer: Hymn of Church Renewal, 1969; A Lenten Hymn, 1970; Contemporary Pilates, 1970; Man Come of Age, 1970. Contbr. news articles to newspapers. Home: 804 Piney Woods Dr LaGrange GA 30240

NAGLER, BENEDICT, physician; b. Czermowitz, Austria, Mar. 14, 1900; s. Samuel Oswald and Charlotte Josephine (Schorr) N.; M.D., U. Hamburg, 1925; m. Hilde Laub, Oct. 20, 1927; children—Ralph Lewis, Eva. (Mrs. Barron M. Hirsch). Came to U.S. 1935, naturalized, 1941. Intern, resident neurology, psychiatry, internal medicine, Hamburg and Berlin, 1924-31; practice medicine, specializing in psychiatry and neurology, Berlin, 1931-33, Tunis, N. Africa, 1934, Newark, 1935-43; chief Neurology-Psychiatry Service VA Hosp., Richmond, Va., 1946-53; chief neurology div. Psychiatry and Neurology Service VA, Washington, 1953-57; supt. Lynchburg Tng. Sch. and Hosp., 1957—; asst. prof. psychiatry and neurology Med. Coll. Va., 1946-67; asso. prof. clin. neurology Georgetown U., 1953-57, professorial lectr., 1957-67; lectr. dept. neurology and psychiatry U. Va., 1957-67; cons. Nat. Inst. Neurol. Diseases and Stroke. Bd. dirs. Partridge Schs. and Rehab. Center, Devel. Council Sweet Briar (Va.) Coll.; trustee Woodrow Wilson Rehab. Found. Served to maj. M.C., AUS, 1943-46. Recipient Nat. Brotherhood award Lynchburg chpt. Nat. Conf. Christians and Jews, 1970. Diplomate Am. Bd. Psychiatry and Neurology (asso. examiner 1953-66). Fellow Am. Psychiat. Assn. (del. 1968-71; Gold Achievement award 1962), Am. Epilepsy Soc. (past councillor), So. Psychiat. Assn. (life), Am. Acad. Neurology (past councillor, past chmn. com. on problems mental retardation), Am. Assn. on Mental Deficiency (past councillor, past chmn. com. internat. activities, past chmn. Mid-Eastern region); mem. A.M.A., Va. Med. Soc., Lynchburg Acad. Medicine, Va. Neuropsychiat. Soc. (past chmn. com. mental retardation), L'Alliance Francaise de Lynchburg (dir.), Mil. Order World Wars (past comdr. Lynchburg chpt.), So. Electroencephalographic Soc. (past pres.), Fedn. Am. Scientists, Assn. for Research Nervous and Mental Diseases, Am. Assn. Med. Supts. of Pub. Mental Hosps. (past councillor), Am. Acad. Mental Retardation (past pres.), Am. Med. EEG Soc., (asso. editor Clin. Electroencephalography 1968—), Internat. Assn. Sci., Study Mental Deficiency (past councillor, chmn. finance com.). Translator: (from German to English) Cerebral Function in Infancy and Childhood, 1963. Cons. editor: Am. Jour. Mental Deficiency, 1961-71; mem. editorial bd. Staff Am. Psychiat. Assn. Publ., 1964-67. Home: PO Box 1098 Lynchburg VA 24505 Office: Lynchburg Tng Sch and Hosp PO Box 1098 Lynchburg VA 24505

NAIDORF, CARROL PHILIP, physician; b. N.Y.C., May 1, 1904; s. Zelig and Sarah (Breslau) N.; student Syracuse U., 1921-23; M.D., Syracue U. Upstate Med. Center, 1927; m. Rose Mann, Apr. 19, 1931. Intern, Bronx (N.Y.) Hosp., 1927-28, resident, 1928-29; practice med., Bklyn., 1927-42, specializing in radiology, 1946—; radiologist Halloran VA Hosp., S.I., N.Y., 1949-50; chief radiologist Gen. Hosp., Ft. Hamilton, N.Y., 1948-62; chief grade radiologist U.S. VA Out

Patient Clinic, Bklyn., 1953-68, cons., 1968—; asso. vis. radiation therapist Downstate Med. Center, 1949—; clinician Chest Clinic, N.Y.C. Dept. Health, 1955-65; cons. 1st U.S. Army, 1951-52. Treas. Bklyn. Dr.'s Symphony Orch., 1954-56. Served to col. AUS, 1942-46. Mem. A.M.A., Am. Coll. Radiology, InterAm. Coll. Radiology, N.Y. State, Kings County (pres. 1963-66) radiol. socs., Radiol. Soc. N.-Am., N.Y. State, Kings County med. socs., Alumni Assn. Bronx Hosp., Assn. Mil. Surgeons U.S., L.I. Early Fliers, Silver Wings Frat., Phi Delta Epsilon. Mason. Contbr. articles to profl. jours. Address: 9700 E Bay Harbor Dr Bay Harbor Island Miami Beach FL 33154

NAIL, LOWELL THOMAS, banker; b. Rosedale, Okla., Nov. 22, 1913; s. Eli Thomas and Vera Lucretia (Dawson) N.; student accounting Hills Bus. Coll., 1935; m. Eulalie Ann Reid, Sept. 19, 1948; children—Cathy Marie, Paul Reid, Karen Ann. Bookkeeper First State Bank, Butler, Okla., 1936-39; teller First Nat. Bank, Guthrie, Okla., 1939-42; teller Security State Bank, Weatherford, Okla., 1946-50; head bookkeeper, head teller Roswell (N.M.) State Bank, 1950-52; cashier Rosedale State Bank, Kansas City, Kan., 1952-53; asst. cashier, loan teller First State Bank & Trust Co., Oklahoma City, 1953-55, First Nat. Bank, Yale, Okla., 1955-61; cashier, loan teller Security State Bank, Weatherford, Okla., 1961—. Mem. bd. city commrs., Yale, Okla., 1958-61. Served with USNR, 1942-45. Mem. Weatherford C. of C. Republican. Baptist. (dir. Sunday Sch. 1963-64). Mason. Home: 816 N Caddo St Weatherford OK 73096 Office: PO Box 71 Weatherford OK 73096

NAISMITH, JAMES SHERMAN, civil engr.; b. Lawrence, Kan., May 7, 1913; s. James and Maude Evelyn (Sherman) N.; B.S., U. Kan., 1933; m. Frances Pomeroy, Aug. 8, 1933 (dec. Jan. 1968); children—Frances Anne (Mrs. M.K. Boatright), James Pomeroy, Ian Alan; m. 2d, Katharine Wareham Holmes, Apr. 19, 1969. With Standard Oil of Ind., Lawrence, 1933-35; engr. Myers & Noyes, Cons. Engrs., Dallas and Corpus Christi, Tex., 1935-43, Corpus Christi, 1946-47; engr. Lee Aikin Constrn. Co., Corpus Christi, 1947-49; v.p. Blucher & Naismith, Inc., Cons. Engrs., Corpus Christi, 1949-60, pres., 1960-69; pres. Naismith Engrs., Inc., Corpus Christi, 1969—. Mem. Tex. Bd. Registration for Profl. Engrs., 1965-69. City councilman Corpus Christi, 1953-55. Served to lt. USNR, 1943-46. Recipient Engr. of Year award, 1966. Fellow Am. Soc. C.E.; mem. Nat., Tex. socs. profl. engrs. Home: 625 Ralston St Corpus Christi TX 78404 Office: 109 N Chaparral St Corpus Christi TX 78401

NAKA, FUMIO ROBERT, govt. ofcl.; b. San Francisco, July 18, 1923; s. Kaizo and Shizuno (Kamegawa) N.; B.S., U. Mo., 1945; M.S., U. Minn., 1947; Sc.D., Harvard, 1951, grad. Advanced Mgmt. Program, 1967; m. Patricia Ann Neilon, July 23, 1949; children—David Robert, Holly Louise, Michael Neilon, Peter Jeremy. With Mass. Inst. Tech. Lincoln Lab., Lexington, 1951-59, asso. group leader, 1954-56, group leader, 1956-59; dept. head MITRE Corp., Bedford, Mass., 1959-60, asso. tech. dir., 1960-62, tech. dir., 1962-68, chief scientist, 1968-69; dep. under sec. Air Force (space systems), Washington, 1969—. Mem. Space Program Adv. Council NASA, 1971—. Coach Lexington baseball team, 1962-66. Bd. dirs. Lexington chpt. A.R.C., 1956-69, fund chmn., 1957, vice chmn., 1956-58, chmn., 1958-61; bd. dirs. Community Nursery Sch., 1958-61, Chesterbrook-McLean (Va.) Little League; adv. council U. Mo. Coll. Engring., 1970—. Recipient Honor award for Distinguished Service in Engring. U. Mo., 1971; NRC-RCA predoctoral fellow, 1949-51. Mem. Sigma Xi, Tau Beta Pi, Omicron Delta Kappa. Conglist. (deacon 1965-68, 70—). Club: Harvard of Boston. Home: 977 Saigon Circle McLean VA 22101 Office: SAFUSS Room 4C1000 The Pentagon Washington DC 20330

NAKARAI, TOYOZO WADA, educator; b. Kyoto, Japan, May 16, 1898; s. Tosui and Wakae (Harada) N.; A.B., Kokugakuin U., Tokyo, 1920; A.B., Butler U., 1924, A.M., 1925; Ph.D. (fellow Sch. Religion), U. Mich., 1930, also post-doctorate studies; grad. student Nippon U., Tokyo, U. Chgo., Hebrew Union Coll., N.Y.U.; m. Frances Aileen Yorn, June 22, 1933; children—Charles Frederick Toyozo, Frederick Leroy. Came to U.S., 1923, naturalized, 1953. Instr. Tokyo Fourth High Sch., Sei Gakuin Mission Sch., Matsumiya Lang. Sch., Tokyo, 1920-23; instr. Coll. of Missions, Indpls., 1923-25; instr. Semitics, Butler U., Indpls., 1927-28, asst. prof., 1928-29, asso. prof., 1929-31, prof., head dept. Semitics, 1931-65, prof. emeritus, 1965—; vis. prof. Emmanuel Sch. Religion, 1965-67, prof., head dept. semitics, 1965-71, hon. prof. Old Testament, 1971—; profl. appointee Am. Sch. Oriental Research, Jerusalem, 1947-48, hon. asso., 1962-63; alumni lectureship Ky. Christian Coll., 1956, T. H. Johnson Meml. lectr. Manhattan Bible Coll., 1957; lectr. Sch. Ministry, Milligan Coll., 1957, 66; vis. prof. Tainan Theol. Coll., Formosa, 1963. Mem. Gov.'s Abraham Lincoln Commn. to Orient, 1960. Mem. Jerusalem Exam. Com. recipient Baxter Found. award, medal and scroll Internat. Order B'rith Abraham, Nat. Assn. Profs. Hebrew; J. I. Holcomb prize Butler U.; citation and scroll Histadrut Ivrit. Mem. Am. Assn. U. Profs., Am. Oriental Soc., Am. Sch. Oriental Research (chmn. cast investigation com. 1941-42), Am. Acad. Religion, Internat. Platform Assn., Soc. Sci. Study Religion, Soc. Bibl. Lit. (v.p. Midwest br. 1949-51, pres. 1951-52), Nat. Assn. Profs. Hebrew (pres. 1956-58), Israel Exploration Soc., Nippon Kyuyaku Gakkai, World Union Jewish Studies, Eta Beta Rho, Phi Kappa Phi, Theta Phi, Author: AStudy of the Kokinshu, 1931, Biblical Hebrew, 1951; (with others) To Do and To Teach, 1953; Shin Tosa Nikki, 1962; An Elder's Public Prayers, 1968. Asso. editor: Hebrew Abstracts; editorial com. Jour. Hebraic Studies; adv. mem. Marquis Biog. Library Soc. Home: Route 4 PO Box 240 Elizabethtown TN 37643 Office: Drawer Q Milligan College TN 37682

NAMAN, WILFORD WOLFIE, lawyer; b. Waco, Tex., Mar. 6, 1887; s. Jacob I. and Fannie (Cohen) N.; student Baylor U., 1903-05; A.B., Yale, 1908; grad. student N.Y.U., 1909-10; m. Isidora Levy, Feb. 12, 1923; 1 son, Jay I. Admitted to Tex. bar, 1911, since practiced in Waco; mem. firm Naman, Howell, Smith & Lee, attys., 1917—, now sr. partner; spl. judge 19th Dist. Ct., McLennan County, 1917; lectr. law Baylor U., 1948-50. Chmn. bd. KWTX Broadcasting Co., 1953-64. Chmn. Family Counseling and Child Welfare Com.; trustee Waco Community Chest; pres. McLennan County Assn. for Blind, 1946-49, Waco Legal Aid Clinic; dir. United Charities, Pub. Library; mem. Parks and Recreation Bd. of Waco. Vice pres. Bolton Found. Served from pvt. to 1st lt., F.A., U.S. Army, 1917-19. Fellow Am. Bar Found., Southwestern Legal Found., Am. Coll. Probate Counsel, Am. Coll. Trial Lawyers, Tex. Bar Found.; mem. Internat. Assn. Inst. Counsel, Nat. Planning Assn. (nat. council 1957—), State Bar of Tex. (chmn. bd. dirs. 1952-53), C. of C. (dir. 1939), McLennan County Bar Assn. (pres. 1935), Baylor U. Ex-Students Assn. (pres. 1938), Fedn. Ins, Counsel, Am. Judicature Soc., Internat. Assn. Ins. Counsel. Home: 3805 Castle Dr Waco TX 76710 Office: 1st Nat Bldg Waco TX 76701

NAMROW, ARNOLD, psychoanalyst; b. N.Y.C., Aug. 1, 1924; s. Samuel and Mary (Blecker) N.; student U. Fla., 1940-41; A.B., Washington U. (St. Louis), 1943, M.D., 1947; m. Lillian Coe, Dec. 2, 1950; children—James, Andrew, Laurel, David. Intern, St. Elizabeths Hosp., Washington, 1947-48; resident Perry Point (Md.) VA Hosp., 1948-49, VA Mental Hygiene Clinic, Washington, 1949-51; practice medicine specializing in psychiatry and psychoanalysis, Washington, 1953—; mem. staff Georgetown U., Sibley hosps., Washington; clin. asso. prof. psychiatry Georgetown U., 1968—; instr. Washington Psychoanalytic Inst., 1969—; cons. Glen Dale Tb Hosp., Hebrew Home for Aged, Jewish Social Service Agy. Served with USNR, 1943-45, 51-53. Diplomate Am. Bd. Psychiatry and Neurology. Fellow Am. Psychiat. Assn.; mem. Am. Psychoanalytic Assn., Washington Psychiat. Soc., D.C. Med. Soc. Home: 6406 E Halbert Rd Bethesda MD 20034 Office: 4501 Connecticut Av NW Washington DC 20008

NANCE, HOMER EUGENE, bus. machine mfg. co. exec.; b. Chadbourn, N.C., Sept. 16, 1925; s. Nathan H. and Nora (Brown) N.; B.S., Wake Forest U., 1951; M.A., E. Carolina U., 1959; m. Tilda Anne Arnette, Dec. 21, 1947; children—Neva Carol, Tina Lynn. Sales rep. regional sales mgr., gen. sales mgr., v.p. sales Universal Bus. Machines, Inc., Columbia, S.C., 1959-63; product sales mgr. Fairchild Davidson div. Fairchild Camera & Instrument Corp., Comack, L.I., N.Y., 1963-64, distbr. sales mgr., 1964-66; pres., chmn. Universal Bus. Machines, Inc., Columbia, 1966—, dir., 1966—, also treas. Served with USNR, 1943-46. Mem. Sigma Pi, Alpha Kappa Psi. Baptist. Mason. Home: G 101 Friars Pl Hunt Club Rd Columbia SC 29260 Office: PO Box 6616 13457 Percival Rd Columbia SC 29260

NANCE, JOHN WESLEY, physician; b. Greensboro, N.C., Dec. 19, 1920; s. Lindsey Edgar and Bessie Ann (Boone) N.; student Elon Coll., 1937-38; B.S., Wake Forest Coll., 1941; M.D., Bowman Gray Med. Sch., 1948; m. Doris Augusta Warner, Sept. 1, 1945; children—Susan, Deborah, Jean, John, William. Intern N.C. Bapt. Hosp., 1949, Pa. Hosp., Phila., 1949-51, individual practice medicine, Clinton, N.C., 1951—. Served with USAAF, 1941-45. Decorated D.F.C. with 1 cluster, 4 Air Medals. Diplomate Am. Bd. Family Practice. Mem. Sampson County Med. Soc., N.C. Acad. Family Practice, Bowman Gray Med. Sch. Alumni Council (pres.-elect 1972). Address: 403 Fairview St Clinton NC 28328

NANCE, JOSEPH TURNER, lawyer; b. Clarksville, Tex., Apr. 12, 1917; s. Kelce Turner and Mary Hettie (Bryarly) N.; B.B.A., So. Methodist U., 1950, J.D., 1953; m. Margrette Zuleika Grubbs, Aug. 23, 1945; children—John Joseph, Mary Carolyn. Service and inspection mgr. S.W. regional office Sears, Roebuck & Co., 1941-52; admitted to Tex. bar, 1953; practiced in Dallas, 1953—; asso. firm Jenkens, Anson, Spradley & Gilchrist, 1953-60, partner, 1960-67; v.p. law TCO Industries Inc., Dallas, 1967-70; v.p., gen. counsel Europe Holiday Inns Internat., 1970—; v.p., asso. gen. counsel Holiday Inns, Inc., 1970—; v.p. Holiday Inns Italiana, 1970—, dir. subsidiaries; dir., v.p. Hosps., Inc., 1957-61; sec. Dallas Realty Co., 1959-70; v.p. Northlake Corp., 1960-66; asst. sec. Kirby Petroleum Co., 1960-67; v.p. Henderson County Trading Co., 1962-67; asst. sec. El Paso-Venezuela Co., 1966-67, Caribbean Finance Co., 1965-67. Vis. leader grad. seminar in ethics and law So. Methodist U., 1962-67, admissions counselor Sch. Law, 1969— Govt. appeal agt. local bd. SSS, 1960-70; active various community drives; treas. Mus. Achievement Found., 1966-70; pres. Norrell Found., 1948; mem. adv. council Community Chest Trust Fund, 1969—. Bd. visitors So. Methodist U. Sch. Law, 1966-69; bd. dirs. Hillcrest Estates Assn. Served as 2d lt. USAAF, 1945-46. Mem. Am., Dallas (chmn. by-laws com. 1969-70) bar assns., State Bar Tex., Southwestern Legal Found., Dallas Chamber Music Soc., Dallas C. of C., So. Methodist U. Law Alumni Assn. (dir. 1966-69), Phi Alpha Delta, Alpha Sigma Lambda. Republican. Methodist (ofcl. bd. 1965-68. Kiwanian. Clubs: Northwood, Lancer's; Chateau Sainte-Anne (Brussels, Belgium). Editor: Southwestern Law Jour., 1953, hon. editor, 1954—. Home: 11525 E Ricks Circle Dallas TX 75230 Office: 3742 Lamar Av Memphis TN 38118 also Holidaystraat 1920 Diegem Belgium

NANCE, L(UTHER) CLAYTON, circuit judge; b. Savannah, Ga., Apr. 18, 1924; s. Marshall Edward and Etta (Floyd) N.; A.A., U. Cin., 1944; LL.B., U. Fla., 1953; m. Dorothy Aurelia Tinkler, May 13, 1950; children—Timothy Louis, Margo Beth. Admitted to Fla. bar, 1953; since practiced in Ft. Lauderdale, Fla.; mem. firm L. Clayton Nance & Assos., 1953-65; 1st pub. defender Broward County and 17th Jud. Circuit, 1953-65; judge 17th Jud. Circuit, Ft. Lauderdale, 1966—. Served with AUS, 1943-46. Mem. Am. Bar Assn., Fla. Bar, Nat. Legal Aid and Defender Assn. Democrat. Methodist. Mason (Shriner). Home: 3661 SW 23d St Fort Lauderdale FL 33312 Office: Court House Fort Lauderdale FL 33301

NANCE, PAUL KINT, coll. exec.; b. Perkins Okla., Nov. 20, 1917; s. Wilson Earl and Bertha (Kint) N.; student U. Okla., 1934-37, M.A., 1956; student Oklahoma City U., 1942-43; A.B., Okla. Bapt. U., 1945; postgrad. Columbia. summer 1948; m. Helen Pearl Lee, June 10, 1938; children—Joseph Earl, Paula Nelamari. Accountant Okla. Gas & Electric Co., 1938-43; bus. mgr. Okla. Bapt. U., 1944-48, treas., comptroller, 1949-55, financial v.p., 1956-62, v.p. univ., 1962-63; specialist coll. bus. administrn. U.S. Office Edn., 1963, acting chief bus. administrn. sect., 1964—, sect. chief fiscal and adminstrv. group, higher edn. studies br. 1966; v.p., treas. Furman U., 1964; bus. mgr. Gallaudet Coll., Washington, 1967—. Drive chmn. United Fund, 1960; pres. bd. Camp Fire Girls Am., 1961-62. Precinct chmn. Dem. party, 1957-60. Bd. dirs. B. B. McKinney Music Research Found. Mem. Okla. So., Central assns. coll. and univ. bus. officers, Nat. Assn. Ednl. Buyers, Nat. Fedn. Coll and U. Bus. Officers Assns. (pres. 1950), Washington C. of C., Beta Gamma Sigma. Baptist (pres. Men's Brotherhood 1960, deacon). Rotarian (pres. 1962). Co-author: Guide to College Business Management, 1964; Business Management in Selected Colleges and Universities. Contbr. articles profl. jours. Home: 6907 Churchhill Rd McLean VA 22101 Office: Gallaudet Coll 7th at Florida Av NE Washington DC 20002

NANCE, SAMMYE HAWKINS (MRS. THOMAS E. NANCE, SR.), realtor, contractor; b. Darlington County, Hartsville, S.C., Aug. 11, 1932; d. Harley E. and Pauline (Cassidy) Hawkins; student Carolina Coll. Commerce, 1957-59; student U.S.C., 1964-67, postgrad., 1968-69; m. Thomas E. Nance, Sr., Feb. 10, 1962; children by previous marriage—Darvin L., Dennis M., Sammye Darlene. Various positions, 1958-61; propr. Sanco Realty &Constrn., Hartsville, S.C., 1960—. Mem. Citizens Adv. Com., Hartsville, 1969—; troop leader Girl Scouts Am., Myrtle Beach, S.C., 1962-64; chmn. bus. div. Hartsville (S.C.) United Fund, 1969. Mem. Darlington County Bd. Realtors (pres. 1969-70), S.C. Assn. Realtors (dir.), Hartsville Bd. Realtors (pres. 1971-72), Nat. Home Builders Assn., Nat. Inst. Real Estate Bds., Shriners Jolly Jeepsterettes (pres. 1969-70), C. of C. (bd. dirs., Distinguished Service plaque 1971), Nat., S.C. fedns. bus. and profl. women's clubs. Baptist (Sunday sch. tchr. 1965-70). Home: 1411 Loring Dr Hartsville SC 29550 Office: Box 476 Hartsville SC 29550

NANES, ALLAN SAMUEL, govt. ofcl.; b. Bklyn., May 3, 1921; s. Philip and Belle (Hillman) N.; A.B. summa cum laude, Brown U., 1941; A.M., Harvard, 1947, Ph.D., 1949; m. Alice Kutzin, May 11, 1964; children—Erika Rachel, Bruce Preston. With State Dept., Office Intelligence Research, 1949-50; mem. faculty Hofstra Coll., 1950-51 instr. polit. sci. Bklyn. Coll., 1951-54 with Dept. Def., Office Internat. Security Affairs, 1965-66; with Legislative Reference Service, Library of Congress, Washington, 1955-65, specialist internat. devel., 1966—; editorial cons. Everyman's Internat. Ency. Served with USAAF, 1943-45; PTO, CBI. Mem. Soc. for Internat. Devel., Phi Beta Kappa. Contbr. to Current History, 1957-64, 67, 69; New Internat. Year Book, 1957-65; Standard Reference Ency. Year Book, 1969—. Home: 13004 Autumn Dr Silver Spring MD 20904 Office: Library of Congress Washington DC 20540

NANNEY, ALLAN DOUGLAS, constrn. co. exec.; b. Lincolnton, Ga., Oct. 22, 1918; s. Add Douglas and Marie (Stribling) N.; student U. N.C., 1935-37, King's Coll., 1937-38; m. Elizabeth Dellinger, Nov. 15, 1947; children—Allan Douglas, Jr., John Edward. Accountant, bus. mgr. Loftis Constrn. Co., Charlotte, N.C., 1938-42; sr. accountant E. B. Taylor, C.P.A., Charlotte, 1942-46; sec., treas. Dickerson, Inc., Monroe, N.C., 1946—, Contractors & Materials, Inc., Monroe, 1960—; v.p. Comml. Products, Inc., Monroe, 1952—. C.P.A., N.C. Mem. N.C. Assn. C.P.A.'s, Am. Inst. C.P.A.'s. Methodist. Mason (Shriner). Home: 6014 Preston Lane Charlotte NC 28211 Office: Box 400 Monroe NC 28110

NANNY, HUGH ROGERS, city ofcl.; b. Haskell, Tex., Nov. 15, 1935; s. Walter Lewis and Ruby Inez (Medford) N.; B.B.A. in Accounting, Tex. A. and M. U., 1958; m. Patricia Ann McWhorter, Jan. 31, 1959; children—Steven Matt, Mary LaNell, Michael Hugh. Accounting clk. Mobil Oil Co., Abilene, Tex., 1958-59; accountant Harris & Marsh, C.P.A.'s, Sweetwater, Tex., 1959-63; comptroller City of Sweetwater, 1963-71; dir. finance City of Big Spring, Tex., 1971—. Cons. accounting Community Action Program, Sweetwater, 1969-71; project dir. Nolan County Neighborhood Youth Corps, 1965-66; dir. civil service City Sweetwater, 1963-71. Co-chmn. spl. gifts div. Nolan County United Fund, 1966. Mem. Municipal Finance Orgn. U.S. and Can. (regional dir. 1965-66). Baptist (deacon 1967-71). Home: 610 Bucknell Av Big Spring TX 79720 Office: 4th and Nolan Sts PO Box 391 Big Spring TX 79720

NAPIER, HENDLEY VARNER, lawyer; b. Macon, Ga., Feb. 1, 1919; s. Hendley Varner, Jr. and Viola (Ross) N.; student Ga. Sch. Tech., 1937-38; A.B., Mercer U., 1941, J.D., 1943; m. Delores Ward, Jan. 21, 1956; 1 dau., Hannah Lee. Admitted to Ga. bar, 1943, since practiced in Macon; mem. firm Martin, Snow, Grant & Napier, 1943—. Pres., dir. St. Paul Apts., Inc. Mem. Macon Bar Assn. (pres. 1962-63), Macon (dir. 1946), Macon Jr. (pres. 1946) chambers commerce, Kappa Alpha. Episcopalian. Moose. Club: Exchange of Bibb County (pres.). Home: 1515 Briarcliff Rd Macon GA 31201 Office: Home Fed Bldg Macon GA 31201

NAPOLIELLO, EDWARD, indsl. devel. engr.; b. Phila., Oct. 2, 1916; s. Luigi and Teresa (Mattia) N.; student Girard Coll., 1934; B.S.C., Temple U., 1941; m. Adair Snyder, Dec. 11, 1944; children—Edward R., Steven G., Gale V. Machinist Heintz Mfg. Co., Phila., 1934-37; instr. machine shop Merle Dobbins Sch., Phila., 1942-44; sr. engr. Smith, Hinchman & Grylls, N.Y.C., 1944-45; instr. tool and die apprentice sch. Gen. Electric Co., Phila., 1946-49; with machine shop Burlington Industries, Inc., Riverside, N.J., 1950-54; industry adviser to ministry econ. affairs U.S. Dept. State, AID, Indonesia, 1954-55, indsl. mgmt. tng. adviser to indsl. devel. center div. Nat. Econ. Council, Phillippines, 1955-57, chief adviser industry and mines devel. center div. Ministry of Industry and Mines, Iran, 1957-59, devel. officer, El Salvador, 1959-66, dep. chief, econ. analysis and devel. staff and devel. officer, Guatemala, 1966-68, sr. investment officer, Washington, 1968-70; chief adviser to pres. Salvadorean Indsl. Devel. Corp., 1959-67; sr. adviser to ministry industry UN Indsl. Devel. Orgn., Mexico City, Mexico, 1971—. Bd. dirs. Am. Club, Teheran, Iran, 1957-59. Served with USN, 1966. Recipient Gold medal and Certificate of Merit for contbn. to pvt. enterprise devel. Assn. Industries, 1966. Mem. Girard Coll. Alumni Assn., Phila. Center City Residents Assn., Temple U. Alumni Assn. Home: 274 Palm Av Palm Island Miami Beach FL 33139 Office: UN Devel Program Mexico City Mexico

NAPP, RALPH RAYMOND VON TRESCKOW, educator; b. Bridgeport, Conn., Sept. 5, 1921; s. Emil A. and Helene (von Tresckow) N.; B.A., U. Ala., 1947; postgrad. U. Munich, 1951-57; M. Ed., Duke, 1960, Ed.D., 1964; m. Hannelore L. Rath, Mar. 15, 1952; children—Ralph R. von Tresckow, Winifred A. von Tresckow. Instr. sociology Walker Jr. Coll., 1947; lectr., discussion group leader USIA, State Dept., Germany, 1951-53; lectr. Am. history, Am. sociology Munich (Germany) Interpreter's Coll., 1952-53; instr. psychology U. Md. Overseas U.S. Armed Forces Inst., Munich, 1954, dir. Am. Youth Adminstrn., 1955-56, dir. religious edn., 1956-57; grad. asst. dept. sociology and anthropology Duke, 1958-59; asst. prof. sociology E. Carolina U., Greenville, N.C., 1957-64, asso. prof., 1964-69, headstart cons., poverty program cons., 1967-69; asso. prof. sociology Madison Coll., Harrisonburg, Va., 1969-71; prof., coordinator sociology Winston-Salem State U., 1971—. Guest lectr. U. Heidelberg (Germany), USIA State Dept., Germany, 1968. Mem. Pitt County Bi-racial Com., Greenville, 1967-69, Council on Human Relations, Harrisonburg, 1969—. Served with AUS, World War II. Mem. Am. Assn. U. Profs., So. Sociol. Soc., Am. Sociol. Assn., Alpha Kappa Delta, Kappa Delta Pi. Author: (with Reiner Rodenhauser) Breaking Down the Barrier, 1961. Home: 230 Flintshire Rd Winston-Salem NC 27104

NASH, BERNARD ELBERT, govt. ofcl.; b. Palmer, Mass., Nov. 7, 1922; s. Perlin Elbert and Leah (Berthiaume) N.; B.A. cum laude, U. Minn., 1953, M.S.W., 1953; postgrad. Fed. Execs. Inst., 1969; m. Marjorie Jean Rosenwald, Feb. 16, 1946 (dec. June 1968); children—Cynthia Jean, Debra Jane, David William; m. 2d, Mary Elizabeth Hobbs, July 5, 1969. Research asst. Community Council, Mpls., 1949-51; group worker with street gangs, St. Paul, 1951-52; program dir. Children's Instns., State of Minn., 1952-53; parole agt. Minn. Parole Bd., 1953-54; resident supr. parole Minn. State Prison, Stillwater, 1954-56; cons. children's instns. Minn. Dept. Welfare, 1956-57; exec. sec. Minn. Gov.'s Council on Aging, 1957-62; dir., chmn. dept. community devel., asso. prof. U. Mo., Columbia, 1962-65; nat. dir. Foster Grandparent Program, U.S. Adminstrn. on Aging, Dept. Health, Edn. and Welfare, 1965-66, dep. commr. on aging, 1966-69, asst. to U.S. Commr. on Aging, Washington, 1969—. Chmn., Career Devel. Bd. for Social Workers, 1968—; mem. Mo. Gov.'s Commn. on Children and Youth, 1963-65; cons. Com. on State Orgn., 1959-61; del. White House Conf. on Aging, 1961. Served with USNR, 1942-49. Recipient Citation for Organizing Foster Grandparent Program, 1968. Mem. Am. Gerontological Soc., Am. Pub. Welfare Assn. (adv. com. on aging), Am. Soc. for Pub. Adminstrn., Acad. Certified Social Workers, Nat. Assn. Social Workers, Nat. Conf. on Social Welfare, Internat. Soc. for Community Devel., Res. Officers Assn., Naval Res. Assn., Am. Assn. U. Profs. Episcopalian. Mason. Contbr. articles to profl. jours. Home: 7305 Konrad Dr Camp Springs MD 20031 Office: US Dept Health Edn and Welfare Washington DC 20201

NASH, CHARLES HENRY, physician; b. Union Parish, La., Mar. 14, 1934; s. Joseph Carl and Sally Odessa (Elkins) N.; B.A., La. Tech. U., 1958; M.D., La. State U., 1960; m. Patsy Rougon Foster, July 22, 1956; children—Joseph Craig, Regina Kaye. Intern, T.E. Schumpert Meml. Hosp., Shreveport, La., 1960-61; practice medicine specializing in family practice; partner Family Clinic, 1961-71; v.p. Family Clinic, Inc., 1970—; pres. staff Physicians and Surgeons Hosp.; city physician, Shreveport. Mem. Caddo Bossier Council Alcoholics Anonymous Assn. Mem. Am., La. acads. gen. practice, La. Fourth Dist., Shreveport med. socs., Shreveport C. of C. Home: 245

Pierremont Rd Shreveport LA 71102 Office: 838 Margaret Pl Shreveport LA 71101

NASH, EDITH ROSENFELS (MRS. PHILLEO NASH), educator; b. Oak Park, Ill., July 12, 1913; d. Irwin S. and Helen (Zuckerman) Rosenfels; student Vassar Coll., 1930-31; A.B., U. Chgo., 1934, postgrad., 1934-35; m. Philleo Nash, Nov. 2, 1935; children—Margaret Helen (Mrs. Eric C. Kast), Sally. Field worker in anthropology U. Chgo., Mescalero Indian Reservation, N.M. and Klamath Indian Reservation, Ore., 1935-36; research Library of Congress, Washington, 1942, O.W.I., Bur. Overseas Intelligence, Washington, 1943-44; asst. dir. Georgetown Day Sch., Washington, 1945-51; dir., 1961—. Bd. dirs. Woodley House, Washington, 1966-68. Mem. Assn. Ind. Schs. Greater Washington (sec.-treas. 1968-70, Am. Assn. Sex Educators and Counselors (v.p. 1972—). Home: 540 N St SW Washington DC 20024 Office: 4530 MacArthur Blvd Washington DC 20007

NASH, ETHEL MILLER HUGHES (MRS. ARNOLD SAMUEL NASH), educator; b. Liverpool, Eng., June 20, 1909; d. Edmund Miller and Lillian (Ellery) Hughes; B.A. with honours, U. Liverpool, 1931; spl. student Yale, 1939; M.A., U. N.C., 1949; m. Arnold Samuel Nash, July 1, 1933; children—A. E. Keir, David Charles. Came to U.S., 1939, naturalized, 1956. Psychologist, Toronto (Ont., Can.) City Schs., 1941-42; lectr. Assn. for Family Living, Chgo., 1946; lectr. dept. sociology, marriage counselor, U. N.C., Chapel Hill, 1949-53; asst. prof. preventive medicine, asso. in obstetrics and gynecology Bowman Gray Sch. Medicine, Winston-Salem, N.C., 1956-66; clin. asso. prof. obstetrics and gynecology U. N.C., 1966—, faculty U. N.C. Population Center; clin. asso. Psychiat. Assos. of Chapel Hill, Mem. Am. Sociol. Assn., Soc. for Study Social Problems, Soc. for Sci. Study Sex, Am. Orthopsychiat. Assn., Am. Assn. Marriage Counselors (dir. 1963-64 pres. 1965-66), Nat. Council on Family Relations (bd. dirs.). Author: With This Ring, 1942. Editor: Marriage Counseling in Medical Practice, 1964. Contbr. profl. publs. Home: Bowling Creek Rd Chapel Hill NC 27514

NASH, HENRY WARREN, educator; b. Tampa, Fla., Sept. 19, 1927; s. Leslie Dikeman and Mildred (Johnson) N.; B.S., U. Fla., 1951, M.B.A., 1951, Ph.D. (Loveman's Merchandising fellow), U. Ala., 1965; m. Frances Lora Venters, Aug. 20, 1950; children—Warren Leslie, Richard Dale. Grad. asst. U. Fla., 1950-51, Ind. U., 1951-53; salesman Field Enterprises, Inc., Chgo., 1953; asso. prof. bus. and econs. Miss. Coll., Clinton, 1953-57 faculty Miss. State U., State College, 1957—, prof., head dept. marketing, 1966—. Partner, Southland Cons. Assos., Starkville, Miss., 1968—. Bd. dirs., v.p. Govt. Employees Credit Union, Starkville. Served with USNR, 1945-46. Mem. Sales and Marketing Execs. (internat. chmn. educators com. 1969-71), Miss. Retail Mchts. Assn. (dir.), Am., So. marketing assns., Acad. Mgmt., Am. Acad. Advt., So. Econs. Assn., Pi Sigma Epsilon (nat. educator v.p. 1967-69) (nat. pres. 1969-71), Alpha Kappa Psi, Omicron Delta Kappa, Beta Gamma Sigma. Kiwanian (treas. Starkville 1969-70). Author: (with others) Principles of Marketing, 1961. Home: 8 Forest Hill Dr Starkville MS 39759 Office: PO Drawer N State College MS 39762

NASH , MARY BURT (MRS. WILLIAM NASH), lawyer; b. Little Rock, June 17, 1912; d. William Burt and Orriette (Morris) Brooks; B.S., Northwestern U., 1931; M.A., U. Ia., 1932; LL.B., Ark. Law Sch., 1934; m. William Nash, Jan. 7, 1937; children—David William, Morris Brooks. Admitted to Ark. bar, 1934; referee Pulaski County Juvenile Ct., 1956—. Vice chmn. Comm. on Crime and Law Enforcement, Ark. Trustee So. State Coll., Magnolia, Ark., 1952-63, sec. bd. trustees, 1961-63. Recipient Alumni award Little Rock U., 1952; Alumni Merit award Northwestern U., 1963; named Woman of Yr. Ark., 1964. Mem. Am. Bar Assn., Nat. Panhellenic Conf. (sec. 1959-61, chmn. 1961-63). Nat Council Juvenile Ct. Judges, Nat., Ark. (pres. 1966-68) assns. women lawyers, Nat. Assn. Women Deans and Counselors, Am. Assn. U. Women (legislative program com. 1955-61, past state pres.), Inter-fraternity Research and Adv. Council (trustee 1961-63), Daus. Am. Colonists (past state regent), D.A.R., Dames Ct. Honor (past state pres.), P.E.O., Altrusa, Delta Kappa Gamma, Alpha Xi Delta (past nat. pres.; nat. council 1951-71). Presbyn. Home: 410 Fairfax Av Little Rock AR 72205 Office: Juvenile Court Juvenile Adminstrn Center 3201 W Roosevelt Rd Little Rock AR 72204

NASH, MICHAUX, JR., banker; b. Dallas, Aug. 20, 1933; s. Michaux and Joel (Waggoner) N.; B.B.A., So. Methodist U., 1956, postgrad. Southwestern Grad. Sch. Banking; postgrad. Harvard, Sch. Bank Pub. Relations and Marketing, Northwestern U.; m. Margaret Eileen Ruebel, Oct. 19, 1956; children—Michaux III, Paige Eileen, Noble, Joel. With Empire State Bank (merged with Nat. Bank of Commerce, 1967), Dallas, 1958—, exec. v.p., 1967—, also dir.; dir. United Fidelity Life Ins. Co., Dallas. Mem. Zoning Commn., University Park, Tex., 1962-68; chmn. commerce and industry div. United Fund Dr., 1965-69; bd. dirs. Hope Cottage-Childrens Bur. 1960-69, treas., 1963-65, pres. 1967-68; bd. dirs. Dallas Zoo, 1964-67, Community Council, Dallas, Childrens Med. Center, Dallas Natural Sci. Assn., Tex. Com. on Natural Resources, Tex. United Community Services, Tex. United Funds; bd. mgmt. Park Cities-North Dallas YMCA, 1962-70, pres., 1967-68. Served to capt. USAF. Mem. Ind. Bankers Assn. Am., Sigma Alpha Epsilon (pres. 1965). Democrat. Episcopalian. Clubs: Terpsichorean, Lancers, Koon Kreek; Dallas Athletic, Sportsmen's of Dallas (pres. adv. com.), Dallas Gun, Dallas Country, Idlewild, Tex. Game Fishing, Ferndale Hunting and Fishing, Dallas Tornado Soccer, Dallas Woods and Waters (exec. v.p. 1967, pres. 1968). Home: 4400 McFarlin Blvd Dallas TX 75205 Office: 1525 Elm St Dallas TX 75201

NASH, PHILLEO, cons. anthropologist, assn. exec.; b. Wisconsin Rapids, Wis., Oct. 25, 1909; s. Guy and Florence Belle (Philleo) N.; A.B., U. Wis., 1932; Ph.D., U. Chgo., 1937; m. Edith Rosenfels, Nov. 2, 1935; children—Maggie Kast, Sally. Lectr. anthropology U. Toronto, 1937-41; mgr. Biron Cranberry Co., 1941-42, pres., 1946—;spl. asst. to dir. White House liaison O.W.I., 1942-46; spl. asst. The White House, 1946-52; adminstrv. asst. President of U.S., 1952-53; lt. gov. Wis., 1959-61; asst. to Asst. Sec. Pub. Land Mgmt., Dept. Interior, Washington, 1961, U.S. commr. Indian affairs Dept. Interior, 1961-66; research asso. Smithsonian Instn., Washington, 1968-70; treas. Am. Anthrop. Assn., 1968-70; adj. prof. anthropology Am. U., 1971—. Spl. cons. sec. war, 1943. Chmn. Dem. Party Wis., 1955-57. Mem. Soc. Applied Anthropology (pres. 1970-71). Club: Cosmos (Washington). Home: 540 N St SW Washington DC 20024

NASH, RICHARD JAMES, banker; b. Detroit, Aug. 8, 1930; s. Ernest John and Edna (Unverdros) N.; student Fla. So. Coll., 1949-50, La. State U., 1957-60; m. Jayne Kerr, May 11, 1951; children—Richard J., Kerin Jayne, Margaret Ann. Cashier Bank of Zephyr Hills (Fla.), 1953-61; exec. v.p. Citizens Bank, Frostproof, Fla., 1961—, also dir. Chmn. Frostproof Zoning Bd. Appeals, 1965—. Chmn. trustees Polk Jr. Coll., Winter Haven, Fla., 1970-71; trustee Lake Wales (Fla.) Hosp. Served with AUS, 1946-48. Mem. Frostproof C. of C. (pres.) Mason. Home: 311 3d St Frostproof FL 33843 Office: 7 Wall St Frostproof FL 33843

NASH, RONALD HERMAN, educator; b. Cleve., May 27, 1936; s. Herman and Violet (Pankratz) N.; B.A., Barrington Coll., 1958; M.A., Brown U., 1960; Ph.D. (fellow 1962-63), Syracuse U., 1964; m. Betty Jane Perry, June 8, 1957; children—Jeffrey Alan, Jennifer Anne. Instr. philosophy Barrington Coll., 1958-60, Houghton Coll., 1960-62, Syracuse U., 1963-64; mem. faculty Western Ky. U., Bowling Green, 1964—, prof. philosophy, head dept., 1966—. Lectr., Chgo., Phila., others, 1962—. Co-chmn. Ky. Tchrs. for Nixon-Agnew, 1968. Nat. Endownment for Humanities fellow, 1969; recipient Ann. Alumni Achievement award Barrington Coll., 1970. Mem. Am., Ky. (pres. 1969-70) philos. assns., Evangelical Theol. Soc. Republican. Baptist. Author: Dooyeweerd And The Amsterdam Philosophy, 1963; The New Evangelicalism, 1964; The Philosophy of Gordon Clark, 1968; Ideas of History, 1969; The Light of the Mind, 1969. Contbr. articles to profl. jours. Home: 638 Ridgecrest St Bowling Green KY 42101

NASH, WILLIAM WRAY, JR., educator; b. Bklyn., Nov. 25, 1928; s. William Wray and Janet (Fobes) N.; A.B., Harvard, 1950, M.City Planning, U. Pa., 1956, Ph.D., 1961; m. Dorothy Westerberg, Dec. 23, 1950; children—Meryl Elaine, Wendy Wray, Janet Amanda, Joseph Adamson. Planning analyst Phila. Urban Traffic and Transp. Bd., 1954-56; research analyst ACTION 1956-58, mem. faculty Harvard, 1958-71, prof. city and regional planning, 1966-71, chmn. dept., 1964-69, dir. Center for Environmental Design Studies, 1969-70; prof. urban life, asso. dir. Urban Field Service Ga. State U., Atlanta, 1971—. UN tech. adviser to Bandung (Indonesia) Inst. Tech., 1961-62; prin. Nash-Vigier, Inc., planning cons., 1966-71; vis. prof. U. Wis., 1968, Fla. State U., 1969, 70; cons. in field, 1958—. Mem. Gov. Mass. Adv. Com. Planning and Zoning Enabling Legislation, 1967-71; Cambridge Adv. Com. Restudy Inner Belt Hwy., 1967-68; faculty adviser Joint Center Urban Studies, Mass. Inst. Tech.-Harvard, 1965-69; planning adviser office Ga. Gov., 1971—. Bd. dirs. South End Community Devel. Corp., 1966-69. Served to 1st lt. AUS, 1950-53. Decorated Bronze Star medal. Mem. Am. Inst. Planners (dir. Boston sect. N.E. chpt. 1963-64), Am. Inst. Urban and Regional Affairs (pres. 1968-69), Am. Acad. Polit. and Social Scis., Sigma Xi, Tau Sigma Delta. Episcopalian. Author: Residential Rehabilitation; Private Profits and Public Policy, 1959, also articles. Editor: (with B. Frieden) Shaping and Urban America. Home: 4436 Lakeridge Circle SW Atlanta GA 30331 Office: Sch Urban Life Ga State U 33 Gilmer St SW Atlanta GA 30303 also Office State Planning Trinity-Washington Bldg Atlanta GA 30334

NASOU, JOHN PETER, physician; b. Cavalla, Greece, July 14, 1925; s. Peter A. and Eleni (Biblias) N.; (parents Am. citizens); student U. Md., 1943-45; A.B. magna cum laude, U. Minn., 1947, postgrad., 1947; M.D., George Washington U., 1952; m. Mary Frank, July 1, 1951; children—Eleni, Peter. Intern, resident George Washington U. and D.C. Gen. Hosps., 1952-58; fellow in medicine George Washington U., Washington, 1953-54, guest lectr. dept. health care adminstrn., asso. prof. Sch. Medicine, 1961—; officer USPHS, 1958-61; practice medicine, specializing in internal medicine, Washington, 1961—, Silver Spring, Md., 1970—; clin. asso. lab. clin. investigation Nat. Inst. Allergy and Infectious Diseases, NIH, 1958-60, attending physician, 1960-61, cons., 1961-62; chief med. officer outpatient div. D.C. Gen. Hosp., 1961-64, supt., chief of staff, 1964-70; faculty Childrens Hosp. D.C., Capitol City Sch. Nursing. Supr. tng. program U.S. Civil Service Commn., 1963. Served to lt. M.C., USNR, 1955-57. Recipient Melvin Hazen award as outstanding D.C. Govt. Employee, 1962, Superior Performance award Govt. of D.C., 1963. Diplomate Am. Bd. Internal Medicine. Mem. Am. Fedn. Clin. Research, A.M.A., Med. Soc. D.C., D.C. Pub. Health Assn., Rheumatism Soc. D.C., Am. Rheumatism Assn., Am.,D.C. socs. internal medicine, Am. Acad. Med. Adminstrs., George Washington U. Med. Alumni Assn., Am., Med.-Del.-D.C. hosp. assns., Nat. League Nursing, Phi Chi. Contbr. articles to profl. jours. Home: 9602 Culver St Kensington MD 20795 Office: School of Medicine George Washington University Washington DC 20005

NASSIKAS, JOHN NICHOLAS, govt. ofcl.; b. Manchester, N.H., Apr. 29, 1917; s. Nicholas John and Constantina (Gagalis) N.; A.B., Dartmouth, 1938; M.B.A., Harvard, 1940, J.D., 1948; LL.D., Notre Dame Coll., 1972; m. Constantina Andreson, Feb. 21, 1943; children—Constance (Mrs. John J. Hohenadel, Jr.), Mary (Mrs. Robert C. Hall), Elizabeth, John Nicholas III. Admitted to N.H. and Mass. bars, 1948, D.C. bar, 1968, also U.S. Supreme Ct., 1st Circuit Ct. Appeals, 1964, Tax Ct. U.S., 1964, also other fed. bars; with Pratt & Whitney div. United Aircraft, Hartford, Conn., 1941-42; with firm Warren, Wilson, Wiggin & Sundeen, 1948-50; asst., dep. atty. gen. N.H., 1950-53; sr. and mng. partner firm Wiggin, Nourie, Sundeen, Nassikas & Pingree, Manchester, N.H., 1953-69; chief counsel Republican minority U.S. Senate Com. Commerce, 1968-69; chmn. FPC, 1969—. Dir. No. R.R., 1965-69. Mem. Adminstrv. Conf. U.S. Rulemaking com., U.S. Nat. Com. of World Energy Conf.; mem. Water Resources Council; observer President's Cabinet Task Force on Oil Import Control; mem. Energy Subcommittee of Domestic Council, Pres.'s Joint Bd. Fuel Supply and Fuel Transport. Exec. adv. council Jr. Achievement Met. Washington; mem. corp. Madeira Sch.; mem. council Nat. Harvard Law Sch. Assn. Served to lt. USNR, 1942-46. Mem. Am., N.H., Mass., Fed. bar assns., Newcomen Soc. N.Am., Kappa Kappa Kappa. Republican. Mem. Greek Orthodox Ch. Clubs: Bald Peak Colony, Congressional Country. Home: 4512 Potomac School Rd McLean VA 22101 Office: 441 G St NW Washington DC 20426

NATCHER, WILLIAM HUSTON, congressman; b. Bowling Green, Ky., Sept. 11, 1909; s. J. M. and Blanche (Hays) N.; A.B., Western Ky. State Coll., Bowling Green, 1930; LL.B., Ohio State U., 1933; m. Virginia Reardon, June 17, 1937; children—Celeste, Louise. Admitted to Ky. bar, 1934, pvt. practice, Bowling Green, 1934—. Fed. conciliation commr. Western Dist. Ky., 1936-37; atty. Warren Co., 1937-49; commonwealth atty., 8th Jud. Dist., 1952-53; elected to 83d Congress (to fill unexpired term of Garrett L. Withers), 1953; mem. 84th to 92d Congresses, 2d Ky. Dist. Served as lt. USNR, 1942-45. Mem. Bowling Green Bar Assn. (pres.), Am. Legion, 40 and 8. Democrat. Odd Fellow, Kiwanian. Home: 638 E Main St Bowling Green KY 42101 Office: 414 E 10th St Bowling Green KY 42101

NATHAN, RICHARD PERLE, govt. ofcl.; b. Schenectady, Nov. 4, 1935; s. Sidney Robert and Betty (Green) N.; A.B., Brown U., 1957; M. in Pub. Adminstrn., Harvard, 1959; Ph.D., 1966; m. Mary McNamara, June 10, 1957; children—Robert Joseph, Carol Hewit. Legislative asst. to Sen. Kenneth B. Keating, 1959-62; dir. domestic policy research for Nelson A. Rockefeller, 1963-64; asso. dir. Nat. Adv. Commn. on Civil Disorders, 1967-68; research asso. Brookings Instn., 1966-69; asst. dir. U.S. Bur. of the Budget, Washington, 1969-71; dep. under sec. U.S. Dept. Health, Edn., Welfare, 1971—. Chmn. Nixon adminstrn. Transition Task Forces on Welfare and Intergovtl. Fiscal Relations, 1968. Mem. Phi Beta Kappa, Theta Delta Chi. Author: Jobs and Civil Rights, The Role of the Federal Government in Promoting Equal Opportunity in Employment and Training, 1969; editor: (with Harvey S. Perloff) Revenue Sharing and the City, 1968; also author chpts. in various books. Home: 7503 Cayuga Av Bethesda MD 20034 Office: Dept Health Edn Welfare Washington DC 20201

NATHANSON, LEONARD, educator; b. N.Y.C., Sept. 22, 1933; s. Morris Gerzog and Lena (Kelman) N.; B.A., Bklyn. Coll., 1954; M.A., Duke, 1955; Ph.D., U. Wis., 1959. Instr. English Northwestern U., Evanston, Ill., 1959-60; asst. prof. English U. Cin., 1960-66; asso. prof. English Vanderbilt U., Nashville, 1966—. Recipient Research Grant Taft Meml. Found., 1962. Mem. Modern Lang. Assn. Am., South Atlantic Modern Lang. Assn., Milton Soc. Am., Am. Assn. U. Profs. Phi Beta Kappa. Author: The Strategy of Truth: A Study of Sir Thomas Browne, 1967. Home: 4200 Harding Rd Nashville TN 37205

NATIELLO, THOMAS ANTHONY, educator; b. N.Y.C., Dec. 23, 1936; s. Charles Anthony and Rose (Ventura) N.; B.S., Mich. State U., 1959, M.B.A., 1963, Ph.D., 1966; m. Mary Delores Stewart, Dec. 31, 1960; children— Hilary Elise, Thomas Anthony. Electro-mech. designer Markite Corp., N.Y.C., 1955-56; research asso. Mich. State U., 1963-65, Ford Found. fellow, 1965-66; supr. mgmt. systems Apollo-Saturn V program Boeing Co., 1966; prof. mgmt. and marketing U. Miami (Fla.), 1966—. Cons. Office Econ. Opportunity, 1968—, Child Devel. Centers, 1969—. Mem. Community Relations Bd. Dade County, Fla., 1968—. chmn. Blue Ribbon Study Com., Coral Gables, Fla., 1969—; commr., chmn. equal employment and fair housing, Dade County, 1968—. Served with USNR, 1959-61. NSF grantee, 1967. Mem. Acad. Mgmt., So. Mgmt. Assn., Am. Marketing Assn., Profl. Soc. (v.p. 1954). Home: PO Box 8524 Coral Gables FL 33124 Office: U Miami Miami FL 33124

NATTRESS, JOHN ANDREW, educator; b. Lansdowne, Pa., June 16, 1920; s. Andrew and Sophia (Heinickle) N.; B.S., Drexel U., Phila., 1943; M.S., Ga. Tech., 1949; D.Eng., Embry-Riddle U., 1969; m. June Pinter, Dec. 8, 1943; children—Donald and Daniel. Instr., asst. prof., head indsl. technology dept., asso. prof. So. Tech. Inst., 1949-53; chief indsl. engr. Norwood Mfg. Co., Chgo., 1953-54; dir. Charlotte Tech. Inst., 1954-55; asst. prof. indsl. engring. N.C. State Coll., Raleigh, 1955-57; prof. Coll. Engring., U. Fla., 1957—, acting dean, 1966-68, asso. dean, 1968—; cons. in indsl. engring. Chmn. Alachua County Zoning Commn. Served to capt. AUS, 1943-47. Registered profl. engr., Fla. Mem. Am. Inst. Indsl. Engrs. (past regional v.p.), Fla. Engring. Soc., Nat. Soc. Profl. Engrs., Am. Soc. for Engring. Edn., Alpha Pi Mu, Sigma Tau, Tau Beta Pi. Contbr. articles in field to profl. jours. Home: 5960 SW 35th Way Gainesville FL 32601

NAUDAIN, GLENN GARNET, chemist; b. Algona, Ia., Oct. 31, 1894; s. William Eliason and Ella (Foster) N.; student Ia. State Coll., A. and M. Arts, 1913-15, B.S., 1917, M.S., 1922, Ph.D., 1923; student Occidental Coll., Los Angeles, 1915-16, Mellon Inst., U. Pitts., 1923-25; B.E., Kan. State Coll., 1926; student Columbia Peabody Coll., Harvard U. Md., U. Chgo., U. Cal. one summer each, also in France and Germany, summer 1937. M.A. in Coll. Adminstrn., N.Y. U., 1939; D.Sc., Academia de Sciencias E Arts of Rio de Janeiro, 1937; m. Lillian Gamrath, Sept. 15, 1921. Tchr. high sch., Oskaloosa, Ia., 1917-18; instr., Ia. State Coll. Agr. and Mech. Arts, 1919-23; fellow Mellon Inst., 1923-25; prof. Kan. State Coll., 1925-26; prof. chemistry, head of dept. Winthrop Coll., Rock Hill, S.C., 1926-50; pvt. cons. chemist, 1950—. Tchr. one summer, Purdue U. Served in World War I; served to col, CWS, AUS, 1942-44, aux. recruiting officer, 1948-52. Fellow A.A.A.S., Royal Soc. Arts, London; mem. Am. Chem. Soc. (councilor S.C. sect., 1945-48); S.C. Acad. Sci. (exec. council; pres. 1938-39; sec.-treas. 1940-41), Am. Acad. Polit. and Social Sci., Am. Assn. U. Profs., S.C. Edn. Assn., Mil. Order Fidelity, Am. Legion (past comdr.) 40 and 8, Res. Officers Assn. (pres. S.C. 1936-37, 41-46, nat. del. to Mpls., Memphis and Springfield, Mass.; New Orleans del., 1941, Washington del., 1942, Chgo. del. 1946, Phila. del. 1953; past pres. Rock Hill chpt.; past pres. 5th Congl. Dist.), Sigma Xi, Phi Kappa Phi, Phi Lambda Upsilon, Gamma Sigma Delta, Lambda Sigma Kappa, Alpha Gamma Tau, Zeta Alpha. Methodist. Mason (32 deg.). Elk. Clubs: Science, Rotary (del. internat. conv. Nice, France 1937, Chgo. 1955, sec. Rock Hill 1965—); Executive; sponsor Winthrop Coll. Chemistry Club. Author: Food and Physiological Chemistry 1928; also A Survey on Teaching of Chemistry in the Secondary Schools of South Carolina, and A survey of the Chloride Production in the U.S. for Chemical Warfare Service, Chemical Warfare Agents and Food Supplies. Editor: Rotary News, 1957—. Contbr. to Am. Food Jour.; also monographs on food chemistry. Home: 919 Charlotte Av Rock Hill SC 29730

NAUMER, HELMUTH JACOB, museum exec.; b. Santa Fe, May 7, 1934; s. Helmuth and Tomee (Reuter) N.; B.A., U. N.M., 1958; postgrad. U. Minn., 1959; m. Carolyn Lou Palmer, Oct. 9, 1966; children—Karina Anne, Helmuth Karl, Kyrsten Anne, Tanya. Marina mgr. Yellowstone Nat. Park Co., Lake, Wyo., 1958; gen. mgr. Twining Ski Corp., Taos Ski Valley, Taos, N.M., 1959; archaeologist in charge Town Creek Indian Mound, N.C. Dept. Archives and History, Raleigh, 1959-60; dir. Charlotte (N.C.) Childrens Nature Mus., 1960-62; exec. dir. Ft. Worth Mus. Sci. and History, 1962—. Mem. adv. bd. Ednl. Service Programs, New Haven 1968—; pres. Naumer Mus. Cons., Ft. Worth, 1963—. Pres., Tarrant County United Fund Execs., 1966; mem. exec. bd. Regional Sci. Fair, 1962-67. Recipient Elsie M.B. Naumburg award, 1968. Mem. Am. Assn. Youth Museums (pres. 1967-68), Tex. Mus. Assn. (pres. 1964, 66, 69-70), Am. Assn. Museums, Internat. Council Museums, Mountan-Plains Mus. Conf. (chmn. 1970). Republican. Contbr. articles to profl. jours., books. Home: 4600 Winthrop Av E Fort Worth TX 76116 Office: 1501 Montgomery St Fort Worth TX 76107

NAVE, JOHN THOMAS, city ofcl.; b. Mountain City, Tenn., Sept. 18, 1921; s. Luther Garfield and Sarah Elizabeth (Dyer) N.; student E. Tenn. State U., 1940-42, B.S., 1947; student U. Tenn., 1942-43; M.S., N.C. State Coll., 1953; m. Ella Erminie McKnight, Mar. 17, 1951; children—Thomas Bradford, Kathy Lynn, Deborah Ann. Tchr. N.C. Pub. Schs., 1955-56; chief pilot Abney Mills, Greenwood, S.C., 1956—; mayor, Greenwood, S.C., 1967-71. Active Boy Scouts Am., P.T.A. County chmn. Republican party, 1964-67, city chmn., 1962-64. Served to lt. col. USAF, 1943-46, 47-55; PTO. Decorated Air medal. Named So. Aristocrat, So. Airways, 1963. Mem. Aircraft Owners and Pilots Assn., Am. Legion, C. of C. (com. chmn. 1963-64). Presbyn. (deacon 1959—). Lion. Clubs: Metropolitan Dinner (Greenwood, S.C.); Terpsichorean Dance (Greenwood); Carillon Ball, Inc. (Columbia). Home: 606 Brooklane Dr Greenwood SC 29646

NAY, MARY SPENCER, artist, educator; b. Crestwood, Ky., May 13, 1913; d. Ben Franklin and Edna (Stringer) Nay; A.B., U. Louisville, 1941, M.A., 1960; student Art Center Assn. Sch., 1933-40; summer study Internat. Sch. Art, Mexico, 1946; m. Lou Block, Mar. 17, 1951; children—Malu Nay, Fayette. Fed. art project mural Louisville Pub. Library, 1934; N.Y.A. supr. art project, 1938-40; instr. Art Center Assoc. Sch., 1941-59; art prof. U. Louisville, 1959—; one-man show Ruth White Gallery, 1963; retrospective show, U. Louisville, 1967; represented in permanent collections Evansville Mus., J.B. Speed Art Mus., Ohio U., Athens, O., Ky. State Fair Exposition Center, Ashland Oil Co. and others. Dir. Children's Free Art Classes, 1951-55. Sec. bd. Jr. Art Gallery, 1950-55. Bd. dirs. Ky. Arts and Crafts Guild. Recipient bronze medal for contbn. to the arts from IBM, 1939; 4 annual purchase awards Ky. State Fair, 1954, 58, 60, 65, and others. Mem. Am. Assn. U. Profs., J. B. Speed Art Mus., Art Center Assn., Provincetown Art Assn. Democrat. Episcopalian. Club: Arts. Home: 207 S Galt Av Louisville KY 40206

NAYAR, JAI KRISHEN, entomologist; b. Kisumu, East Africa, Jan. 3, 1933 (came to U.S. 1958, naturalized 1968); s. Kishen Parshad and Harbans (Khosla) N.; B.S. with Honors, U. Delhi, India, 1954, M.S., 1956; Ph.D., U. Ill., 1961; m. Gisela Kathe Dora Hoelscher, Oct. 30, 1964; children—Veena, Karen, Gisela. Research asst. Indian Agrl. Research Inst., Delhi, 1956-58; NRC Can. post-doctoral fellow U. Man., Winnipeg, 1961-63; entomologist Entomol. Research Center, Vero Beach, Fla., 1963-—. Mem. Entomol. Soc. Am., Sigma Xi. Home: 2601 19th Pl Vero Beach FL 32960 Office: PO Box 520 Vero Beach FL 32960

NAYLOR, ROBERT ERNEST, coll. pres.; b. Hartshorne, Okla., Jan. 24, 1909; s. George Rufus and Mattie Mae (Ross) N.; A.B., East Central State Tchrs. Coll., Ada, Okla., 1928; Th.M., Southwestern Bapt. Theol. Sem., 1932; D.D. (hon.) Ouachita Coll., Arkadelphia, Ark., 1941; LL.D., Tex. Christian U., 1965; m. Goldia Geneva Dalton, Aug. 29, 1930; children—Robert Ernest Jr., Richard Dalton, Rebekah Ann. Ordained to ministry Bapt. Ch.; 1929 served at Nashville, Ark., 1932-35, Malvern, 1935-37, Arkdelphia, 1937-44, Enid, Okla., 1944-47, First Ch., Columbia, S.C., 1947-52; Travis Av. Baptist Ch., Fort Worth, Tex., 1952-58; pres. Southwestern Bapt. Theol. Sem., 1958—. Dir. Ouachita Coll. Campaign, 1940-41; pres. bd. trustees S.W. Bapt. Theol. Sem., Benedict Coll. (Columbia), S.C., Bapt. Hosp. Chmn. Ark. Bapt. Exec. Bd., 1943-44; mem. gen. bd. S.C. Bapt. Conv., 1952-53, mem. exec. bd. Tex. Bapt. Conv., 1953-58. Clubs: Rotary (Columbia), Kiwanis (Ft. Worth, Tex.). Author: Adult Sunday School Quarterly, 2 quarters, 1946, last quarter 1956; The Baptist Deacon, 1955. Contbr. publs. of Baptist Sun. Sch. Bd. Home: 1901 W Boyce St Fort Worth TX 76115

NAYLOR, THOMAS HECTOR, JR., state ofcl.; b. Lauderdale, Miss., Apr. 10, 1904; s. Thomas Hector and Myrtie (McConnell) N.; B.A., Millsaps Coll., 1925; postgrad. U. Ala., 1931, Peabody Coll., 1947; M.A., U. Miss., 1949; m. Martha P. Watkins, June 20, 1928; 1 son, Thomas Herbert. Tchr. math. and history Gulf Coast Mil. Acad., 1925; tchr. math., basketball coach Jackson Central High Sch., 1926-35; supt. edn. Hinds County, 1936-46; dir. sch. bldg. and transp. State Dept. Edn., 1947-57; cons. Miss. Ednl. Finance Commn., Jackson, 1954-57, exec. dir., 1957—. Pres. Interstate Sch. Bldg. Service, 1952-53; mem. exec. com. Nat. Council Schoolhouse Constrn., 1955-57. Trustee Hinds Jr. Coll. Recipient Alumni Citation, Millsaps Coll., 1967, award for distinguished service Lambda Chi Alpha, 1942. Mem. Council Ednl. Facility Planners (mem. long range planning com. 1967), Am., Miss. assns. sch. adminstrs., Miss. Edn. Assn., Southeastern States Sch. Bus Transp. Ofcls. (pres. 1956), Miss. Hist. Soc., Millsaps Coll. Alumni Assn. (pres. 1936, 53), Red Red Rose, Phi Delta Kappa, Lambda Chi Alpha, Omicron Delta Kappa. Methodist (mem. ofcl. bd. 1930-72). Lion. Home: 1404 St Ann St Jackson MS 39202 Office: Sillers Bldg Jackson MS 39201

NAZARETIAN, ANGELINE, educator; b. Fairfield, Ala., Apr. 29, 1928; d. O. Jeane and Alice (Yarchak) Nazaretian; B.S., Ala. Coll., 1950; M.A., U. Ala., 1958, also postgrad. Tchr. girls' phys. edn., sci. Graysville (Ala) Jr. High Sch., 1951-55; dir. girls' phys. edn. McAdory High Sch., McCalla, Ala., 1955-58; dir. health, phys. edn. Athens (Ala.) Coll., 1958-—. First aid, water safety chmn. Limestone County chpt. A.R.C., Athens, 1958—; active Girl Scouts Am.; organizer, 1st pres. Athens Humane Soc., Athens Beautification Program. Bd. dirs. Ala. Heart Assn.; chmn. Limestone County chpt. A.R.C. Recipient Honor award Ala. Assn. Health, Phys. Edn., 1968; named Alumnus of Year Ala. Coll., 1968, Community Leader Am., 1968. Mem. Jefferson County Tchrs. Assn., Am., Ala., Jefferson County assns. health phys. edn. and recreation, Ala. Edn. Assn., N.E.A., Jefferson County Classroom Tchrs. Assn., Am. Camping Assn., Am. Assn. U. Women (charter treas. Athens), Am. Assn. U. Profs., Athens Bus. and Profl. Women, So., Nat. assns. phys. edn. coll. Women, Delta Kappa Gamma. Pi Delta Epsilon, Kappa Delta Pi, Kappa Delta Kappa, Delta Psi Omega, Pi Tau Chi, Zeta Tau Alpha (chpt. founder). Presbyn. Mem. Order Eastern Star. Club: Athens Country. Home: 212 N Beaty St Athens AL 35611

NAZARIO, LUIS ADAM, dentist; b. Sabana Grande, P.R., Sept. 25, 1909; s. Antero and Ramona N.; B.A., Inter Am. U., 1930; B.Th., Evang. Sem. P.R., 1934; M.S.W., Tulane U., 1943; D.D.S., Loyla U., New Orleans, 1946; m. Rosaline Rodriguez Alonso, Oct. 27, 1936; children—Yolanda N. (Mrs. Ronald Goldman), Nilda N. (Mrs. Roger Maldonade). Pvt. practice dentistry, Santurce, P.R., 1947-—. Pres., founder Health Coop. P.R., 1960-65, Retirement City P.R., 1963-71; pres. bd. trustees Evang. Hosp. Assn. P.R., 1955-71; bd. dirs. Geriatric Commn. P.R., 1966-—; pres., founder Club Sebaneno P.R., 1953-60; pres. Gideons Internat. Assn. P.R., 1965-68; v.p. Council Chs. P.R., 1968-—. Served with AUS, 1943-44. Fellow Internat. Acad. Law and Sci.; mem. Coll. Dentists P.R., Am., Ohio dental assns. Presbyn. (elder 1955-—). Mason (32 deg., Shriner); mem. Order Eastern Star (Grand rep. 1970-—). Author: Principles of Dental Health, 1960; My Student Life in New Orleans, 1971. Contbr. articles to dental and cultural mags. Home: 168 Amatista St Golden Gate Guaynabo PR 00657 Office: (mailing) Box 6244 Loiza Sta Santurce PR 00914

NEAL, BILLY JAMES, city ofcl.; b. Hemphill, Tex., May 14, 1935; s. Arvie and Luciet (Williams) N.; grad. high sch.; m. Opal Sue Beard, Dec. 20, 1955; children—William Keith, Kristie Karen, Cindy Carol. Patrolman police force, Nederland, Tex., 1957-60, chief police, 1960-—. Vice pres. Jefferson County Law Enforcement Council, 1971. Recipient Distinguished Citizen award Bus. and Profl. Women's Club, 1971; Outstanding Law Enforcement award Sabine Chiefs Assn., 1966. Mem. Jefferson County Sheriff's Posse. Club: Optimist (bd. dirs. 1965-70; pres. 1970-71) (Nederland). Home: 1407 22d St Nederland TX 77627 Office: 1400 Boston St Nederland TX 77627

NEAL, FRANCES POTTER, librarian; b. Strong, Ark., Oct. 27, 1905; d. Finis and Lucy Letitia (Richardson) Potter; B.S. in Edn., U. Ark., 1945; M.A., U. Denver, 1949; m. Karl Neal, Apr. 25, 1931. Tchr. pub. schs., El Dorado, Ark., 1924-31; librarian Warren (Ark.) Elementary Sch., 1941-47; circulation librarian, reference librarian Ark. Library Commn., 1947-51, exec. sec., state librarian, 1952-—. Councilor Ark. Library Assn. to A.L.A., 1951-—. Recipient Progressive Farmer Woman of Year, Dem. award. 1957. Mem. A.L.A., Ark. (pres. 1950), Southwestern (dir. 1962-—, pres. 1964-66, program chmn. biennial conf. 1964) library assns., Am. Assn. U. Women. Bus. and Profl. Women's Club (2d v.p. Little Rock 1956, Pfeifer Cup 1957), Kappa Delta Pi, Delta Kappa Gamma. Home: 108 Brown St Little Rock AR 72205

NEAL, JAMES ARCHER, lawyer; b. Winston-Salem, N.C., Feb. 20, 1932; s. William Henry and Jeannette (Archer) N.; B.S., Davidson Coll., 1954; LL.B., U. N.C., 1964. Asst. to treas. Davidson Coll., N.C., 1955-57; supr. Security Life and Trust Co., Winston-Salem, 1957-61; admitted to N.C. bar, 1964; asst. solicitor Municipal Ct. Winston-Salem, 1964-68; gen. practice Winston-Salem, 1964-—. Mem. Am., N.C., Forsyth County bar assns., Pi Kappa Phi, Phi Mu Alpha. Democrat. Presbyn. Club: Winston-Salem Bachelors (pres. 1970). Home: 611 Gunston Ct Winston-Salem NC 27106 Office: Pepper Bldg Winston-Salem NC 27101

NEAL, JAMES EDWARD, hosp. adminstr.; b. Ooltewah, Tenn., Jan. 10, 1928; s. James Franklin and Arlzie (Parris) N.; B.S. in Commerce, U. Louisville, 1965; M. Hosp. Adminstrn., Med. Coll. Va., 1967; m. Birdie Summerhill, Jan. 8, 1928; children—Karen Sue, Teresa Ann, Edith Annette, James Edward, Jr. Asst. adminstr. High Plains Bapt. Hosp., Amarillo, Tex., 1967-69; adminstr. Berea (Ky.) Hosp., Inc., 1969-71, Wilbarger Gen. Hosp., Vernon, Tex., 1971-—. Bd. dirs. Madison County Mental Health, Richmond, Ky., 1969-71, mem. mental retardation bd., 1969-71. Served with C.E., AUS, 1946-48. Named Ky. Col. Mem. Am. Coll. Hosp. Adminstrs., Am. Coll. Nursing Home Adminstrs. Mason, Rotarian. Home: 3515 Paradise St Vernon TX 76384 Office: 920 Hillcrest Dr Vernon TX 76384

NEAL, JAMES F., lawyer; b. Tenn., Sept. 7, 1929; s. R.G. and Emma (Clendenning) N.; B.S., U. Wyo., 1952; LL.B., Vanderbilt U., 1957; LL.M., Georgetown U., 1960; m. Ellen Julie Neal, Jan. 2, 1954; children—James F., Julie Ellen. Admitted to Tenn. bar, 1957; asso. firm Turney & Turney, Washington, 1957-60; spl. asst. to atty. gen. U.S., Washington, 1961-64; U.S. dist. atty. Middle Dist. Tenn., 1964-66; partner firm Cornelius, Collins, Neal & Higgins, Nashville, 1966-71; sr. partner firm Neal, Karzon & Harwell, Nashville, 1971-—. Lectr. in law Vanderbilt U. Vice pres. Nashville Urban League. Served to capt. USMCR, 1952-54. Mem. Am., Tenn., Nashville Fed. (past pres. Nashville chpt.) bar assns., Order of Coif. Clubs: Nashville Exchange, University, Hillwood Country, Capital (Nashville). Contbr. articles to profl. jours. Home: 2225 Woodmont Blvd Nashville TN 37215 Office: 8th Floor 3d Nat Bank Bldg Nashville TN 37219

NEAL, JAMES WOODWARD, editor, actor; b. Lometa, Tex., Feb. 7, 1931; s. Roy Edwin and Iva Rue (Woodward) N.; B.A., N. Tex. State Coll., 1956; m. Patricia Ann Dulin, Apr. 17, 1954. Amusements editor Denton (Tex.) Record-Chronicle, 1954-60; Sunday and wire editor Ft. Worth Press, 1960-—; actor Tex. Gridiron Show, 1957-—, Casa Manana Theater, Ft. Worth, including Guys and Dolls, Lil Abner, Desert Song, Annie Get Your Gun, West Side Story, Fiddler on the Roof, others. Asst. instr. Denton (Tex.) Jr. Optimist Judo Club, 1959-60. Served with USNR, 1949-53. Mem. Actors Equity Assn., Sigma Delta Chi. Home: 5225 Camp Bowie Fort Worth TX 76108 Office: 507 Jones St Fort Worth TX 76101

NEAL, MAHLON STARK, banker; b. Mattoon, Ill., Dec. 21, 1927; s. Herman E. and Helen (Craig) N.; B.S., U. Ill., 1950; grad. Grad. Sch. Banking, U. Wis., 1968; m. Kathryn Collins, Nov. 12, 1958; children—Richard Neal, Lyn. With Boulder Bank & Trust Co., Tulsa, 1950-—, sr. v.p., 1967-69, pres., 1969-—, dir., 1959-—. Sec. treas. West of Main Improvement Assn., 1958. Chmn. bd., treas. Tulsa County Heart Assn., 1954-—; bd. mgmt. YMCA; asst. fund chmn. Tulsa Community Chest, 1969. Served with USNR, 1945-46. Mem. Chi Phi. Presbyn. Clubs: Kiwanis (dir. 1963), Tulsa Ski. Home: 3343 S Troost St Tulsa OK 74105 Office: 1437 S Boulder St Tulsa OK 74119

NEAL, MARCUS PINSON, JR., physician, educator; b. Columbia, Mo., Apr. 22, 1927; s. Marcus Pinson and Mathilde (Evers) N.; A.B., U. Mo.; 1949, B.S. in Medicine, 1951; M.D., U. Tenn., 1953; m. Gail S. Fallon, May 27, 1961; children—Sandra G., Marcus Pinson III. Intern Medical College Virginia Hospitals, Richmond, 1953-54; resident in radiology. U. Wis. Hosps., Madison, 1954-57, mem. staff, 1957-63; practice medicine, specializing in radiology, Madison, 1957-63; instr. dept. radiology U. Wis. Sch. Medicine, 1957-59, asst. prof., 1959-63; asso. prof. radiology Med. Coll. Va., Richmond, 1963-66, prof., 1966-—, dir. postgrad. courses dept. radiology, 1964-—, chmn. div. radiodiagnosis, 1965-68; asst. dean Sch. Medicine, Health Scis. div. Va. Commonwealth U., 1968-72, asst. v.p. for health scis., 1971-—, dir. continuing med. edn., 1969-—, dir. Grad. Med. Edn., 1969-72; radiologist Central Wis. Colony, Madison, 1959-63; cons. radiologist VA Hosp., Madison, 1961-63, Wis. Diagnostic Center, Madison, 1961-63, USAF, Truax Field, Madison, 1962-63, McGuire VA Hosp., Richmond, Va., 1963-—. Pres. Va. Council Health and Med. Care, 1971-73. Served with USNR, 1945-47. Diplomate Am. Bd. Radiology. Fellow Am. Coll. Radiology; mem. Assn. U. Radiologists, Am., So. med. assns., Radiol. Soc. N.A., Va. Med. Soc., Va., Richmond radiol. socs., Richmond Acad. Medicine, Brit. Inst. Radiology, Am. Roentgen Ray Soc., Am. Assn. U. Profs., Phi Beta Pi. Presbyn. Home: 2822 E Weyburn Rd Richmond VA 23235

NEAL, MARY JULIA, educator, author; b. Auburn, Ky., Aug. 15, 1905; d. Presley Taylor and Nettie Lou (Pace) Neal; student Bethel Womans Coll., 1923-25; B.S., Western Ky. U., 1931, M.A., 1933; postgrad. U. Mich., 1943-45, U. Denver, summer 1965, Syracuse U., summer 1967. Instr. English, Western Ky. U., Bowling Green, 1934-41, dir. Ky. Library and Mus., 1964-72; dean of residence Kingswood-Cranbrook, Bloomfield Hills, Mich., 1944-46; asso. prof. English, Florence (Ala.) State Coll., 1946-64. Mem. South Atlantic Modern Lang. Assn., Assn. Am. Archivists, Am. Studies, A.L.A., Sigma Tau Delta, Chi Delta Phi. Author: Shakers By their Fruits, 1947; The Journal of Eldress Nancy, 1963. Home: 1523 Park St Bowling Green KY 42101

NEAL, PERCY JONES, business exec., mfr.; b. Walnut Cove, N.C., Jan. 16, 1901; s. William Thomas and Ella (Carter) N.; student King's Coll. (Raleigh, N.C.), 1919; m. Grace Fag, June 18, 1932. Asso., Glen's Warehouse, Planter's Warehouse, 1926; real estate and ins. broker Phil R. Carlton, Inc., 1926-30; sec. Tomlinson of High Point, Inc., 1933-—, treas., 1943-—; dir. Phil R. Carlton, Inc.; v.p. Asso. Industries. Mem. C. of C., N.A.M. (tax com.), N.C. Indsl. Council (furniture mem.). Democrat. Methodist. Clubs: Civitan (High Point), Country (Emerywood); String and Splinter. Home: 220 Hillcrest Dr High Point NC 27262 Office: 305 High Av W High Point NC 27261

NEAL, PHIL HUDSON, JR., mfg. exec.; b. Birmingham, Ala., Nov. 17, 1926; s. Phil Hudson and Amy (Gross) N.; A.B., Duke, 1950; M.B.A., Harvard, 1952; m. Sarah Swift Britton, Sept. 19, 1959 children—Amy Brannon, Phil Hudson III, Samuel Abney Britton. Investment analyst 1st Nat. Bank, Birmingham, Ala., 1952-55; procedures analyst Gen. Electric Co., Hendersonville, N.C., 1955-58; with Ala. By-Products Corp., Birmingham, 1958-—, asst. mgr. nitrogen sales, 1962-63, mgr. indsl. nitrogen sales, 1963-68, asst. treas., 1964-68, treas., 1968-—; dir. Smokeless Fuel Co., Birmingham. Trustee Advent Episcopal Day Sch., 1967-—, pres., 1968-—; bd. dirs. Advent Episcopal Assn. for Edn.; trustee Ala. Found. for Hearing and Speech, 1967-—, v.p., 1968-69, pres., 1969-71. Served with USNR, 1945-46. Mem. Phi Beta Kappa, Sigma Nu, Phi Eta Sigma. Episcopalian. Rotarian. Clubs: Birmingham Country, The Club, Harvard (v.p. 1971-—). Home: 3336 Hermitage Rd Birmingham AL 35223 Office: PO Box 10246 Birmingham AL 35202

NEAL, WILLIAM COOK, iron and bridge works exec.; b. Asberrys, Va., July 6, 1931; s. William Frederick and Mattie Mae (Cook) N.; student Steed Coll., 1948-49; m. Bettie Tate Taylor, July 11, 1952; children—Stephen Allen, Regina Ann, Patricia Beth, Nancy Carol. Engrs. aide Va. Dept. Hwys., 1949-51; asst. dept. head Burlington Industries, 1955-57; dir. purchasing Roanoke Iron & Bridge Works (Va.), 1957-—. Served with USN, 1951-55. Mem. Nat. Assn. Purchasing Mgrs., Purchasing Mgmt. Assn. Old Dominion. Methodist (mem. adminstrv. bd.). Home: Route 5 Box 392B Roanoke VA 24014 Office: 338 Walnut Av SE Roanoke VA 24008

NEBERGALL, ROGER ELLIS, educator; b. Davenport, Ia., July 3, 1926; s. Ellis William and Hilda (Bruhn) N.; A.B., Augustana Coll., 1949; M.A., Bradley U., 1951; Ph.D., U. Ill., 1956; m. Nelda Lee Smith, Apr. 10, 1958; 1 dau., Madelon. Instr., asst. prof. speech Bradley U., 1951-54, 54-55; asst. prof. U. Okla., Norman, 1955-60, asso. prof. 1960-65, prof. speech, 1965-—, chmn. dept. speech, 1959-—. Exec. sec. Missouri Valley Forensic League, 1959-—. Served with AUS, 1946-47; PTO. Recipient Golden Ann. Prize Fund award Speech Assn. Am., 1966. Mem. Speech Assn. Am. (group chmn.), Central States, Okla. (pres.) speech assns., Nat. Soc. for Study Communication, Pi Kappa Delta, Pi Kappa Alpha, Gamma Alpha Beta. Republican. Author: (with W.R. Carmack) Communication and Supervision, 1960; (with others) Attitude and Attitude Change: The Social Judgment Involvement Approach, 1965. Editor: Dimensions of Rhetorical Scholarship, 1963; Central States Speech Jour., 1967-—. Contbr. articles scholarly jours. Home: 501 Trenton Rd Norman OK 73069

NEBLETT, WILLIAM EDWIN, lawyer; b. Lunenburg County, Va., June 1, 1896; s. William Edwin and Rosa Cabell (Hite) N.; student William and Mary College, 1915-17; LL.B., Washington and Lee U., 1922; m. Virginia Louise Akers, July 12, 1930; 1 dau., Virginia Akers (Mrs. Dan A. Jones). Admitted to Va. bar, 1922, since practiced Lunenburg; commonwealth atty., 1924-47. Served 12 months A.E.F., 1918-19. Mem. Am., Va. bar assns., Am. Legion, Kappa Sigma. Mason. Democrat, Episcopalian. Club: Kiwanis. Home: Lunenburg County VA 23952

NECESSARY, JAMES EDWARD, mech. engr.; b. Hot Springs, Ark., Jan. 1, 1939; s. James Martin and Saphronia (Elwell) N.; B.S., U. Ark., 1962; m. Marilyn Lewis, Oct. 24, 1959; children—Jeffrey Todd, Scott Andrew. Design engr. Remington Rand Office Machines, Searcy, Ark., 1962-63; project engr. Reynolds Metals Co., Arkadelphia, Ark., 1963-—; dir., sec. R.P. Patterson Fed. Credit Union, Arkadelphia, 1967-68. Mem. Arkadelphia Bd. Zoning Adjustment, 1966-—; mem. Arkadelphia Airport Commn., 1968-—, vice chmn., 1969-—. Registered profl. engr., Ark. Mem. Soaring Soc. Am. Mem. Ch. of Christ. Home: 119 Leewood Dr Arkadelphia AR 71923 Office: PO Box 520 Arkadelphia AR 71923

NEDDERMAN, WENDELL HERMAN, educator; b. Lovilia, Ia., Oct. 31, 1921; s. Walter Herman and Fern (Gray) N.; B.S., Ia. State Coll., 1943; M.S., Tex. A. and M., 1949; Ph.D., Ia. State U., 1951; m. Betty Ann Vezey, Dec 20, 1947; children—Howard, John, Jeff, Eric. instr. in civil engring. Tex. A and M U., 1947-49, asst. prof., 1951-52, asso. prof., 1952-57, prof., 1957-59; dean engring. Arlington (Tex.) State Coll., 1959-69; v.p. for research and grad. affairs U. Tex., Arlington, 1967-68, v.p. acad. affairs, 1968-—; cons. structural engr. in coastal and offshore structures in petroleum industry. Dir. Arlington Bank Commerce. Bd. dirs. Arlington (Tex.) Meml. Hosp.; chmn. bd. dirs. N.E. Tex. Information Network Assn.; chmn. coordinating com. Tarrant County Gen. Hosp. Served with AUS, 1943-46. Mem. Am. Soc. C.E., Am. Soc. for Engring. Edn., Am. Concrete Inst., Tex. Soc. Profl. Engrs., Sigma Xi, Phi Kappa Phi, Tau Beta Pi, Chi Epsilon. Republican. Home: 1802 Raydon St Arlington TX 76010

NEDIMYER, JOHN ADRIAN, ins. and mut. funds exec.; b. Flinton, Pa., Mar. 30, 1920; s. Rudolph J. and Mary S. (Gill) N.; grad. high sch.; m. Nadja U. Karachewski, Nov. 16, 1946; 1 dau., Lynn M. With Pa. Funds Corp., 1953-63; with Waddell & Reed, Inc., Washington, 1963-—, resident v.p., 1968-—. Served with AUS, 1942-46. Club: Washington Gas Light. Home: 3826 Bosworth Ct Fairfax VA 22030 Office: 7900 Westpark Dr McLean VA 22101

NEEDLES, ROBERT JOHNSON, physician; b. Atlantic, Ia., Mar. 31, 1903; s. Charles Wesley and Estelle (Murray) N.; Ph.G., State U. Ia., 1924, M.D., 1930; m. Helen Irene Swartz, Apr. 18, 1930; children—Eleanor Jane (Mrs. Leroy West Chapin), Susan Irene (Mrs. Glenn A. Schlecht). Intern Henry Ford Hosp., Detroit, 1930-31, asst. in pathology, 1931-32, asso. pathologist, 1934-35, asso. physician div. cardiorespiratory diseases, 1935-39; pathologist, asst. med. dir. Cia Ford do Brasil, Boa Vista, Para, Brazil, 1932-34; pvt. practice, St. Petersburg, Fla., 1939-42, 46-—. Founding mem. Citizens Charter Group, St. Petersburg, Fla., 1948-—. Served from capt. to lt. col. M.C., USAAF, 1942-46. Diplomate in cardiovascular disease Am. Bd. Internal Medicine. Fellow A.C.P., Am. Coll. Cardiology, Am. Soc. Clin. Pathologists; mem. Am. Heart Assn. (fellow council clin. cardiology), Assn. Am. Physicians and Surgeons (del. from Fla.), Am. Diabetes Assn., Am. Rheumatism Assn., Am., Fla. (pres. 1956-57) socs. internal medicine, Alpha Omega Alpha. Republican. Author: (with Edith Stoney) A Coronary Primer, 1958; Your Heart and Common Sense, 1964; also papers in field, essays various non-med. jours. Home: 1227 14th Av N St Petersburg FL 33705 Office: 615 11th St N St Petersburg FL 33705

NEEL, JACK FAGG, city ofcl.; b. Bluefield, W.Va., Apr. 19, 1930; s. Milton Fagg and Arie (Robey) N.; B.S. in Civil Engring., Va. Poly. Inst., 1952, M.S. in San Engring., 1956; m. Kathryn Strother Hale, July 22, 1950; children—Deborah, Kathryn, Joanne, Linda, Elizabeth. Asst. maintenance engr. Washington Suburban San. Commn., Hyattsville, Md., 1954-55; teaching fellow Va. Poly. Inst., Blacksburg, 1955-56; design engr. M. H. Connell and Assos., Miami, Fla., 1956-57; mgr. Town of Tazewell (Va.), 1957-59, City of Roxboro (N.C.), 1959-67. City of Albemarle (N.C.), 1967-—. Served to 1st lt., arty., AUS, 1952-54. Registered profl. engr., N.C., Va. Mem. Internat. City Mgmt. Assn., N.C. City and County Mgmt. Assn. (pres. 1970-71), Am. Water Works Assn. Lion (dir., v.p., pres. Roxboro, dep. dist. gov.). Address: City Hall Albemarle NC 28001

NEEL, RICHARD EUGENE, economist, educator; b. Bluefield, Va., Jan. 7, 1932; s. Charles Richard and Zell (Bowling) N.; diploma Bluefield Coll., 1952; B.S., U. Tenn., 1954, M.S., 1955; Ph.D., Ohio State U., 1960; m. Binnie Jo LeFever, June 10, 1961; children—Jeffrey Richard, Cynthia Jo. Asst. instr. Ohio State U., 1955-58, instr., 1958-60; research statistician Ohio Dept. Taxation, 1958-60; asst. prof. Coll. of William and Mary, 1960-61; adminstrv. specialist Ohio Dept. Natural Resources, summer 1961; asst. prof. U. S. Fla., Tampa, 1961-63, asso. prof., 1963-66, chmn. econs. and finance programs, 1964-66, acting chmn. grad. program Coll. Bus. Adminstrn., 1965-66; dir. instnl. planning Fla. Technol. U., Orlando, 1966-68, prof., chmn. dept. econs., 1968-69; prof. econs., asso. dean Sch. Bus. Adminstrn. Ga. State U., 1969-—. Mem. Am., So. econ. assns., Southwestern Social Sci. Assn., Phi Kappa Phi, Beta Gamma Sigma. Contbr. articles to profl. jours. Home: 58 Pheasant Dr Marietta GA 30062 Office: Ga State U 33 Gilmer St SE Atlanta GA 30303

NEEL, ROBERT GEORGE, meml. park exec.; b. Doe Run, Mo., Mar. 10, 1923; s. Robert R. and Nina (Vogt) N.; B.A., U. Mo.; m. Annette Yarnell Peter, Nov. 4, 1949; children—Asher, Robin, Nancy, David. Sales rep. H.O. Peet & Co., Kansas City, Mo., 1948-49; pres. Woodlawn Meml. Park, Orlando, Fla., 1949-—; dir. Orlando Bank and Trust Co. Pres. Orlando United Appeal, 1962-—. Served with AC USNR, 1943-46. Recipient Outstanding Citizen of Orlando award,

1963. Mem. Nat. Assn. Cemetaries (1st v.p.), Orlando C. of C. (pres. 1968), Sales and Marketing Execs. (past pres.) Mason (Shriner), Rotarian (dist. gov.). Contbr. articles to profl. jours. Home: 1415 Country Lane Orlando FL 32804 Office: PO Box 15641 Orlando FL 32808

NEEL, SAMUEL REGESTER, JR., jr. coll. pres.; b. Alderson, W.Va., May 15, 1914; s. Samuel Regester and Blanche (Smith) N.; B.A., Emory and Henry U., 1935; Ph.D., Duke, 1942; m. Adriana Vander Jagt, Aug. 11, 1938 (dec.); children—Helen V. (Mrs. Robert Younskevisius), Samuel Regester III; m. 2d, Eleanor P. Neel, May 17, 1971. Prof., Lambuth Coll., Jackson, Tenn., 1942-44, Fla. State U., Tallahassee, 1948-51, 1952-57; dir. Inter-Church Student Fellowship, Kalamazoo, Mich., 1946-48; founder, pres. Manatee Jr. Coll., Bradenton, Fla., 1957—. Pres. United Fund Manatee County, Bradenton, Fla., 1969-70. Served with AUS, 1944-46, 51-52. Decorated Bronze Star medals (2). Mem. Fla. Assn. Pub. Jr. Colls. (pres. 1961-62), Fla. Assn. Colls. and U. (pres. 1967-68), Omicron Delta Kappa, Phi Delta Kappa, Blue Key. Kiwanian. Author: Personal Development, 1953. Home: 5825 34th St W Bradenton FL 33507

NEEL, WILLIAM STEWART, lawyer; b. Mooresville, N.C., Nov. 25, 1922; s. Samuel Stewart and Bonte (Wiley) N.; A.B., U. N.C. at Chapel Hill, 1943, LL.B., 1949; m. Agnes Preston, June 19, 1947; 1 dau., Frances LaVaun. Admitted to N.C. bar, 1950, since practiced in Mooresville mem. firm Neel and Randall, 1966—; solicitor Recorder's Ct., Mooresville, 1952-62; judge Recorders Ct., 1963-70. Dir., chmn. bd. Carolina First Nat. Bank; dir. Citizens Savs. & Loan Assn., Mooresville Telephone, Inc. Dir., v.p. Lowrance Hosp., Inc. Served to lt. (j.g.) USNR, 1943-46. Mem. C. of C. (past pres.). Presbyn. (elder). Elk, Kiwanian (past pres.). Home: 173 Brookfield Circle Mooresville NC 28115 Office: 149 E Iredell Av Mooresville NC 28115

NEELY, J(AMES) WINSTON, plant breeder; b. Cotton Plant, Ark., Feb. 4, 1906; s. James William and Daisy (Holland) N.; B.S., U. Ark., 1928; Ph.D., Cornell U., 1935; m. Elsie Norris, June 13, 1935; 1 son, Eugene Trahin. Asst. in agronomy U. Ark., 1929-30, Cornell U., 1930-35; geneticist U.S. Dept. Agr., 1935-46; plant breeder Stoneville (Miss.) Pedigreed Seed Co., 1946-51; v.p., dir. plant breeding Coker's Pedigreed Seed Co., Hartsville, S.C., 1951-71, cons., 1971; exec. v.p. S.C. Soybean Assn., 1971—; adviser Clemson Coll., U.S. Dept. Agr., assns. and orgns. Fellow A.A.A.S., Am. Soc. Agr.; mem. Phi Kappa Phi, Sigma Xi. Methodist. Home: 301 Church Av Hartsville SC 29550

NEELY, ROBERT ALLEN, physician; b. Temple, Tex., Mar. 1, 1921; s. Jubal A. and Almeida (Fordtran) N.; B.A., U. Tex., 1942, M.D., 1944; postgrad. Washington U., 1951-52; m. Eleanor V. Stein, June 29, 1944; children—Byron D., Warren F. Intern Hermann Hosp., Houston, 1944-45; gen. practice medicine, 1946-51, specializing in ophthalmology, Bellville, Tex., 1955—, trustee Bellville Hosp., Inc. Dir. 1st Nat. Bank of Bellville. Mem. Bellville Ind. Sch. Dist. Sch. Bd., 1948-53; pres. Bellville Area United Fund; exec. bd. mem. Sam Houston Area council Boy Scouts Am., also mem. Nat. council. Served with USNR, 1943-46, 53-55. Mem. Am. Acad. Ophthalmology and Otolaryngology, A.M.A., Austin, Walter County, Austin-Grimes-Waller Counties (past pres.) med. soc., Tex. Med. Assn., Tex. Ophthal. Assn., Houston Ophthal. Soc., Bellville C. of C. Republican. Lutheran. Clubs: Bellville Golf (pres.), Champions Golf, Lions (past pres.). Home: 105 E Hacienda Lane Bellville TX 77418 Office: 24 N Bell St Bellville TX 77418

NEELY, SAM BOYD, lawyer; b. Hazel, Ky., June 20, 1915; s. Henry Irwin and Ava (Boyd) N.; B.S., Murray State U., 1937; J.D., U. Ky., 1942; m. Hays Ellen Kelsay, Jan. 26, 1947; children—Ellen (Mrs. Jerry Hurt), Sam Boyd, Bill. Admitted to Ky. bar, 1941; practiced in Mayfield, Ky., 1947—; mem. firms Martin & Neely, 1947-55, Martin, Neely & Reed, 1955-60, Neely & Reed, 1960-70, Neely, Reed & Brien, Mayfield, Ky., 1970—; atty., C.E., U.S. Govt., 1942-46; city atty., Mayfield, Ky., 1949—; dir. Liberty Savs. Bank, Mayfield. Bd. dirs. Indsl. Devel. Bd., 1955-65. Mem. Am., First Jud. Dist. (pres. 1966-67), Ky. State, Graves County (pres. 1964-65) bar assns., Phi Delta Phi, Woodmen of World. Baptist (deacon bd. chmn. 1951-54, 57-60, 61-64, 68-70). Home: 823 Pryor St Mayfield KY 42066 Office: 238 N 7th St Mayfield KY 42066

NEELY, WILLIAM JEWELL, author; b. Jane Lew, W.Va., Aug. 18, 1930; s. Walter and Madge (Bush) N.; B.A. in English, W.Va. Wesleyan, 1952; M.A. in English, W.Va. U., 1953; m. Martina Winemiller, Nov. 27, 1965; children—Michael, Jodi, Annamaria, Susan, Walter, III. Dir. pub. relations W.Va. Wesleyan Coll., 1952-56; mgr. racing pub. relations Goodyear Tire & Rubber, Akron, O., 1959-65; mgr. pub. relations Central region Humble Oil and Refining, Houston, 1966-69; author books Spirit of America, 1970, Grand National, 1971, A Closer Walk, 1972. Prof. English, pub. relations Robert Morris Jr. Coll., Pitts., 1956-59; dir. Crockett Enterprises, Medford, N.J. Chmn. United Fund Akron, 1962. Pres. Young Republican Club Pitts., 1957. Trustee Allegheny Gen. Hosp., Pitts. Mem. Kappa Alpha (province comdr. 1952-63). Mason. Editor film, writer script Nat. Press Photographers Assn., 1969. Contbr. articles to various mags. Address: 5911 Sewell St Pensacola FL 32504

NEELY, WOODFIN CARLISLE, textile co. exec.; b. Florence, S.C., June 15, 1910; s. Woodfin Cowan and Florence May (Smoak) N.; B.S. in Commerce, U. S.C., 1931; m. Helen Earle Lee, Aug. 19, 1937; children— Robert Carlisle, Joseph Frederick. Pub. accountant, Columbia, S.C., Greenville, S.C., 1931-37; accountant Clinton Mills, Inc. (S.C.), 1937-41, sec., 1941-70, v.p., treas., 1970—, also dir.; sec., dir. Clinton Mills Sales Corp., N.Y.C., 1948—; accountant Lydia Cotton Mills, Clinton, 1937-48, asst. sec., 1948-62, sec., 1962-64, dir., 1953-64; dir. M.S. Bailey & Son, Clinton, Llanelly Corp., Ft. Washington, Pa., Va. Corp., Clinton, South Land Co., Clinton, Dillard Boland, Jeweler, Inc., Clinton. Mem. Clinton Recreation Commn., 1946-51, Laurens County (S.C.) Bd. Edn., 1951-59, Clinton Planning Commn., 1967-70, Comprehensive Health Planning Com. Upper Savannah Devel. Dist., 1971—; mem. adv. com. Bailey Found., 1951—. Bd. dirs. Clinton Hosp. Dist., 1959—. Mem. Sigma Chi, Delta Sigma Pi. Clubs: Palmetto (Columbia); Lakeside Country (Laurens County); Clinton Cotillion. Home: 303 W Walnut St Clinton SC 29325 Office: 600 Academy St Clinton SC 29325

NEES, BERNARD JOSEPH, investment co. exec.; b. East Liverpool, O., Apr. 7, 1908; s. Bernard Martin and Agnes Elizabeth (Snyder) N.; LL.B., George Washington U., 1931; m. Emily Grace Fuller, May 19, 1932; 1 son, Bernard Horace. With Johnston Lemon & Co., Washington, 1929—, partner, 1936—; with Washington Mut. Investors Fund, Inc., Washington, 1952—, pres., 1967—. Mem. adv. bd. Suburban Trust Co., Hyattsville, Md., 1952; dir. Washington Bd. Trade. Mem. Investment Bankers Assn., Nat. Assn. Securities Dealers. Club: University (sec. 1968-72; bd. govs. 1969-72) (Washington). Home: 7007 Chansory Lane Hyattsville MD 20782 Office: Washington Mut Investors Fund Inc Southern Bldg Washington DC 20005

NEESE, C. G., U.S. judge; b. Paris, Tenn., Oct. 3, 1916; s. Charles Gentry and Anna Claire (Nunn) N.; student U. Tenn., 1936; LL.B., Cumberland U., 1937; m. Althea Debord children—Charles Gelbert III, Gerry Jan. Admitted to Tenn. bar, 1938; practice in Paris and Nashville, 1938-61; exec. asst. gov. Tenn., 1944; adminstrv. asst. Senator Kefauver, 1949-51; U.S. dist. judge Eastern Dist. Tenn., 1961—. Past sec., gen. counsel Capitol Life Ins. Co. Tenn.; past dir. Guaranty Savs. Life Ins. Co. Dir. primary campaigns Senator Kefauver, 1948, 54. A founder, original trustee, 1st pres. Family Clinic, Nashville. Mem. Am. Judicature Soc., Phi Delta Phi. Democrat. Mason. Home: Greene County TN 37080 Office: US Courthouse Greeneville TN 37080

NEESE, C.G., judge; b. Paris, Tenn., Oct. 3, 1916; s. Charles Gentry and Anna Claire (Nunn) N.; student U. Tenn., 1936; LL.B., Cumberland U., 1937; m. Althea DeBord; children—Charles Gelbert III, Gerry Jan. Admitted to Tenn. bar, 1938; practice in Paris and Nashville, 1938-61; exec. asst. gov. Tenn., 1944; adminstrv. asst. Senator Kefauver, 1949-51; U.S. dist. judge Eastern Dist. Tenn., 1961—. Past sec., gen. counsel Capitol Life Ins. Co. Tenn. Dir. primary campaigns Senator Kefauver, 1948, 54. A founder, original trustee, 1st pres. Family Clinic, Nashville. Democrat. Mason. Home: Greene County TN Office: US Courthouse Greenville TN 37743

NEFF, FRANK ROBINSON, JR., educator, clergyman; b. Phila., Sept. 4, 1907; s. Frank Robinson and Mary Printz (Mulliken) N.; A.B., Maryville Coll., 1933; Th.B. Princeton Theol. Sem., 1936, Th.M., 1938; postgrad. U. Pitts., 1939-40, 43-44; m. Isabelle Westwood Harrison, June 5, 1937; children—Mary Margaret (Mrs. Lewis Rothenberg), Elizabeth Anne (Mrs. Christian White Knudsen). Engrng. draftsman Charles A. Blatchley, cons. engr., Phila., 1926-29; ordained to ministry Presbyn. Ch., 1937; supply pastor S. Side Presbyn. Ch., Bethlehem, Pa., 1936-37; pastor 1st Presbyn. Ch., Pickford, Mich., 1937-38, Mt. Pleasant, O., 1939-42, Everglades (Fla.) Community Ch., 1942-46; asst. prof. Trinity U., 1946-52, asso. prof. religion 1952-68. Stated clk. Presbytery of Austin, 1951-57, permanent clk., 1957-60; permanent clk. Presbytery of Alamo, 1960-68; choirmaster Los Angeles Heights Presbyn. Ch., San Antonio, 1951-68, organist, 1956-68. Committeeman, Alamo Area council Boy Scouts Am., 1965-68. Bd. dirs. House of Neighborly Service, San Antonio, 1963-68. Mem. Nat., San Antonio (chmn. dept. Christian edn. 1954-59, 66, sec. 1960, dir.) council chs., Am. Assn. U. Profs., S.A.R., A.M. Guild Organists (sub-dean 1957-58), Ch. Service Soc. U.S.A., Am., Tex choral dirs. assns., Nat. Assn. Bibl. Instrs., Bibl. Instr. S.W. Democrat. Home: 139 Morningside Dr San Antonio TX 78209 Died Sept 1968

NEFF, HELEN MARGARET OSTERHOLM, writer, editor; b. Superior, Wis., Oct. 15, 1908; d. Albin N. and Ellen (Julien) Osterholm; student U. Neb., 1925-27, U. Cal., Berkeley, 1929-30; A.B., Washington U., St. Louis, 1933, Rensselaer Poly. Inst.-Tech. Writers' Inst., 1962; m. Carroll Forsyth Neff, Feb. 1, 1930, (div. 1957); children—Charlotte (Mrs. Walter R. Newman), Carroll Forsyth. Sch. reporter Omaha World-Herald, 1923-27; sec. Swedish Vice Consul, Omaha, 1927-29; case worker St. Louis Relief Adminstrn., 1935-36; med. writer dept. surgery Emory U. Sch. Medicine, Atlanta, 1951-55; writer-editor Center for Disease Control USPHS, Atlanta, 1955—, chief, editorial sect. Information Office, 1960—. Bd. dirs., editor newsletter Druid Hills Civic Assn., 1949-70. Mem. Am. Pub. Health Assn., A.A.A.S., Am. Med. Writers Assn. (nat. sec. 1967-70), League Women Voters, Internat. Platform Assn. Methodist. Contbr. articles to profl. jours. Home: 400 Princeton Way NE Atlanta GA 30307 Office: Center for Disease Control Atlanta GA 30333

NEFF, JOHN EARLE, JR., ins. co. exec.; b. Lake Charles, La., July 30, 1924; s. John Earle and Mary Edith (Bergstedt) N.; B.S., U. Tex., 1944, B.B.A., 1946, M.B.A., 1948; student So. Meth. U. Inst. Ins. Marketing, 1957, Life Ins. Agy. Mgmt. Assn., 1959; m. Barbara Louise Davis, Aug. 7, 1948; children—Nancy Louise, Barbara Gretchen, John Earle, III. Mem. home office staff Austin (Tex.) Life Ins. Co., 1950; pres. Am. Savers Life Ins. Co. (merger Am. Founders Life Ins. Co., 1967), San Antonio, 1963-67, sr. v.p., chmn. exec. com., Austin, Tex., 1967-68; pres., mem. bd. Am. Founders Life Ins. Co., Austin, 1968—. Mem. bd. Tex. Life Conv., 1966—; mem. bd. dirs. Lamar Savs. Assn., Austin, 1961; mem. bd. govs. Internat. Ins. Seminars, Inc., 1970-71; chmn. Ednl. KLRN Channel 9 TV, 1970-71. Pres. Austin High Sch. PTA, 1968-69. Served to lt. (j.g.) USNR, 1944-46. Mem. Tex. Legal Reserve Ofcls. Assn. (pres. 1970-71; mem. bd. 1969—), Nat. Assn. Life Cos. (mem. bd. 1970-71), Austin Jr. C. of C. (dir. 1952), Travis County Grand Jury Assn., Phi Gamma Delta (trustee 1951—). Episcopalian (sr. warden 1971—). Lion (dir. 1960-61). Clubs: Headliners, Citadel, Tarry House, Coronet, Admiral's (Austin, Tex.). Home: 1414 Wathen St Austin TX 78703 Office: PO Box 2068 6937 N Interregional St Austin TX 78767

NEFF, LUCINDA BELLE, genealogist; b. Colchester, N.Y.; d. Lewis Bennett and Jennie Lela (Rutherford) Neff; A.B., cum laude, Syracuse U., 1906. Tchr. pub. high schs., Middleburg, N.Y., 1906-08, Rockville Centre, N.Y., 1908-11, Muskogee, Okla., 1911-21; office mgr., law clk. Neff & Neff, Tulsa, 1925-63. Dep. gov. Gen. Soc. Mayflower Descs., 1957—, editor Mayflower Quar., 1961-64, acting sec. gen., 1962, Okla. sec., 1951—, editor Okla. Mayflower Newsletter, 1951—; organizing sec. Elder William Brewster Descs. Soc., 1963; Tulsa parliamentarian D.A.R., 1955-57, Okla. lineage research chmn., 1962-64; organizing pres. Okla. Ct. assts. Nat. Soc. Women Descs. Ancient and Hon. Arty. Co., 1964-65, nat. organizing sec., 1965-68; organizing sec. Oil Capitol unit Nat. Assn. Parliamentarians, 1956-58, pres., 1958-60. Recipient Mayflower cup for improving Mayflower Quar., 1963. Mem. Am. Assn. U. Women, Okla. Hist. Soc., New Eng. Hist. Geneal. Soc., Soc. Genealogists, Colonial Dames, Colonial Clergy, Magna Charta Dames. Research in Eng., Holland on Mayflower passenger, 1961-65. Home: 1316 S Trenton Av Tulsa OK 74120

NEFF, WILLIAM, JR., clergyman; b. Muskogee, Okla., May 22, 1925; s. William and Arnetas (Zink) N.; B.A., U. Tulsa, 1945; B.D., Garrett Bibl. Inst., 1947; m. Margie Fisk, June 19, 1946; children—William, Naomi, Jonathan, David. Ordained to Meth. ministry, 1947; pastor Sheridan Av. Ch., Tulsa, 1947-49, Pilgrim Presbyn. Ch., Vinita, Okla., 1949-55; St. Andrews Presbyn. Ch., Tulsa, 1955—. Chmn. dept. Christian edn., Tulsa Council Chs., radio-TV Tulsa Synod; chaplain Okla. legislature. Dept. Gov. Okla. Mayflower Soc. Mem. Soc. Mayflower Descs. (elder gen.), Descs. Colonial Clergy, Lambda Chi Alpha, Phi Gamma Kappa, Pi Gamma Mu, Pi Kappa Delta. Mason. Home: 10301 S Yale St Tulsa OK 74136 Office: 36th and Yale St Tulsa OK 74135

NEFF, ZELGEL WINSTON, govt. ofcl.; b. Salisbury, Mo., Apr. 17, 1916; s. Roy S. and Cordie Jane (Chrane) N.; A.B., S.W. Mo. State, 1939; LL.B., U. Mo., 1948; LL.M., Georgetown U., 1958; m. Margaret Joan Mirras, Dec. 21, 1941; children—Sandra Mary, Teresa Jane. Admitted to Mo. bar, 1948, D.C. bar, 1958; field atty. NLRB, 1948-49; law partner Judge D. W. Gilmore, 1949-51; asst. atty. gen. Mo., 1953-54; commr. U.S. Ct. Mil. Appeals, 1955-57; spl. asst. Judge Adv. Gen. Navy, 1957-58; mem. U.S. Navy Bd. Review, 1958-63; spl. asst., legal adviser Dep. Asst. Sec. Def. for Manpower, 1963-64; mem. U.S. Bd. Parole, 1964—, now chmn. youth correction div. Served with USNR, 1940-45, 51-55. Decorated Navy Cross, Air medal with 7 gold stars, Presdl. Unit citation with silver star. Mem. Judge Advocates Assn. U.S. (nat. sec.), Am., Fed. (exec. sec. mil. justice com. 1958) bar assns., Phi Delta Phi. Catholic. Home: 9424 Locust Hill Rd Bethesda MD 20014 Office: 101 Indiana Av Washington DC 20530

NEGLEY, GLENN, educator; b. Indpls., Nov. 5, 1907; s. Homer Hanway and Jessie Myrtle (Rhoades) N.; A.B., Butler U., 1930, M.A., 1934; Ph.D., U. Chgo., 1939; m. Julia Mary Henderson, July 7, 1939. Statistician, Van Camp Packing Co., 1930-32; legislative asst. State Senate of Ill.; instr. philosophy U. Okla., 1937-38, U. Ill., 1938-41, asst. prof., 1941-42; prof. philosophy Duke, 1946—, chmn. dept. philosophy, 1950-55; vis. prof. San Jose State Coll. summer 1957; Rockefeller research fellow, 1946; Ford Found. fellow, 1953-54; research fellow Newberry, Huntington libraries, 1964; staff observer Adminstrv. Staff Coll., Henley-on-Thames, Eng., 1960, 66; vis. prof. U. Tex., summers 1939, 1961. Served as maj. A.C., AUS, 1942-46. Mem. Am. Philos. Assn., Am. Polit. Sci. Assn., Am. Assn. U. Profs. Author: The Organization of Knowledge, 1942; Political Fact and Moral Judgment, 1965; The Duke University Library Utopia Collection, 1965; co-author: Democracy vs. Dictatorship, 1942; The Quest for Utopia, 1952. Contbr. chpts. to compilations; profl. jours. Home: 2330 Hilton Av Yorktowne Durham NC 27707

NEGRON-FERNANDEZ, LUIS, chief justice P.R. Supreme Ct.; b. Catano, P.R., Apr. 29, 1910; s. Ramon Negron-Flores and Joaquina (Fernandez); student Coll. William and Mary; law degree U. P.R., 1934; m. 2d, Aida Rodriquez; children—Luis, Victor, Antonio, Arturo. Dist. atty., Humacao, 1938-40; asst. prosecutor Supreme Ct. P.R., 1940-45, acting atty gen., asst. atty. gen., prosecutor, 1946-47, asso. Justice, 1948-57, chief justice, 1957—; 1st asst. gen. of P.R., 1945-46; atty. gen. of P.R., 1947-48. Substitute fed. dist. judge, 1949, 51. Adhonorem prof. Law Sch., U. P.R., 1965; chmn. Jud. Conf. P.R., 1957—, Jud. Conf. Ams., 1965—; mem. adv. com. Pres. U.S. on applicability fed. laws to P.R., 1948-49; chmn. Constl. Bd. for Revision Electoral Dists. P.R., 1962-64; v.p. Internat. Congress Jurists, Petropolis, Brazil, 1962; participant Washington Conf. on World Peace Through Law, 1965; mem. adv. com. on pvt. internat. law U.S. Dept. State, 1964—. Mem. Am. Judicature Soc. (hon. life; dir. 1962-66, v.p. 1966—), Am. Soc. Internat. Law, Am. Law Inst., Am. Acad. Polit. and Social Sci., Internat., Inter-Am. (chmn. spl. integral law of Am.), Am. (certificate of recognition 1965) bar assns., Inst. Jud. Adminstrn., Internat. Acad. Law and Sci. (pres. 1966-67, v.p. 1965, regent 1963-64, asso. editor jour.). Conf. Chief Justices U.S., Bar Assn. P.R. (ann. award 1959-60), Internat. Commn. Jurists, Am. Soc. Internat. Law, Acad. Arts and Scis. P.R. Roman Catholic. Address: PO Box 2733 San Juan PR 00903 Office: Supreme Ct Bldg San Juan PR 00936

NEHER, CLARENCE M., chem. co. exec.; b. Twin Falls, Ida., May 14, 1916; s. S.S. and Emma F. (Fike) N.; A.B., Manchester Coll., 1937; M.S., Purdue U., 1937, Ph.D., 1941; m. Eileen Byerly, June 9, 1939; children—James Dean, David M., Mary Janet, Nancy. With Ethyl Corp., 1941—, spl. problems dir., Baton Rouge, 1941-57, dir. comml. devel., 1957-63, v.p., gen. mgr. plastics div., 1964-69, sr. v.p., 1969—, also dir. Mem. Baton Rouge C. of C. (econ. devel. com. 1964), Am. Chem. Soc., Chem. Market Research Assn., Comml. Devel. Assn., Soc. Plastics Industries, Mfg. Chemists Assn. (chmn. plastics com., dir.), Sigma Xi. Methodist. Rotarian. Clubs: Camelot, Baton Rouge Country, City (Baton Rouge); Chemists, Sky (N.Y.C.). Contbr. articles to profl. jours. Patentee in field. Home: 861 Delgado Dr Baton Rouge LA 70808 Office: Ethyl Tower 451 Florida St Baton Rouge LA 70801

NEIL, ALICE VIRGINIA, librarian; b. Omaha, Sept. 29, 1910; d. Wesley N. and Alice (Camfield) Neil; Ph.B., U. Chgo., 1931; B.S. in Library Sci., Carnegie Library Sch., 1932; student German and history, Northwestern U., 1936-41; certificate Chgo. Sch. Filing and Indexing, 1932. Librarian, statistician, Infilco, Chgo., 1933-35; asst. librarian Ill. Inst. Tech., 1935-41; librarian Gen. Electric Research Lab., Schenectady, 1941-62; specialist Reference Information Center, Apollo Tech. Information Services, Gen. Electric Co., Daytona Beach, Fla., 1962-64, tech. librarian, Bay St. Louis, Miss., 1964-66; librarian Roy E. Crummer Sch., Rollins Coll., Winter Park, Fla., 1966—. Commr.'s com. reference, research library resources, N.Y. Dept. Edn., 1960; chmn. Model Library project Mainland Sr. High Sch., Daytona Beach. Mem. Spl. Libraries Assn. (pres. Western N.Y. chpt., 1949-50; chmn. engrng. sect., 1953-54; sec.-treas. sci.-tech. div., 1956-57, treas. div. 1957-58; mem. translations center commn., 1959-61, sec.-treas. La. chpt. 1965-66; dir. Fla. chpt. 1969-71) N.Y. State Hist. Assn., Am. Assn. U. Women, Hudson-Mohawk Library Assn. (pres. 1961-62), Schenectady County Hist. Soc., Am. Hist. Soc., S.E., Fla. library assns. Republican. Methodist. Editor: Documentation Digest of Sci.-Tech. News, 1961-62. Home: 1100 Delaney Av Orlando FL 32806

NEILAN, EDWIN PETER, banker; b. nr. Ludington, Mich., Oct. 24, 1905; s. Peter Andrew and Goldie Alice (Comstock) N.; student U. Omaha, 1923-24; B.A., Rice Inst., 1928; postgrad. So. Tex. Sch. Law, 1931-33, Grad. Sch. Banking Rutgers U., 1935-37; D.Sc. in Bus. Adminstrn. honoris causa, Bryant Coll., 1963; LL.D. honoris causa, Omaha U., 1964; m. Julia Ellen Motheral, July 20, 1929. With Houston Bank & Trust Co., 1928-33; chief trust examiner Fed. Res. Bank of Dallas, 1933-36; examiner Fed. Res. Bank of N.Y., 1936-37, Fed. Res. Bank of Phila., 1937-40; asso. trust officer Security Trust Co., Wilmington, 1940-42, v.p., sec., dir., 1946-52; exec. v.p., dir. Bank of Del. (formerly Equitable Security Trust Co.), Wilmington, 1952-56, pres., 1956-59, pres., chmn. bd., 1959-69, chmn. bd. 1969—; dir., chmn. finance Del. Econ. Devel. Bd., Inc.; dir. H. P. Cannon & Son, Inc. Chanslor-Western Oil and Devel. Co. Chmn. spl. budget com. to recommend fed. budgetry improvements to Pres. Kennedy, 1962-63. Bd. dirs., past pres., v.p., mem. exec. com. United Community Fund; bd. dirs., mem. exec. com. Greater Wilmington Devel. Council, Inc., chmn., 1961-63; dir. Del. Indsl. Found., Inc.; financial adviser YWCA; mem. Del. Research Found; v.p. finance, dir. Del. Safety Council; employer del., mem. governing body ILO, 1966—, employer v.p. 50th anniversary conf., 1969; trustee Found. Comml. Banks, 1965-66; mem. bus.-industry adv. com. OECD, 1967-68; mem. exec. com. Internat. Orgn. Employers, 1966—, jr. v.p., 1968-69, pres., 1970-71; mem. adv. com. bus. programs Brookings Inst.; mem. adv. com. Coll. Bus. and Econs. U. Del., Newark, 1968-69. Mem. bd. Internat. Centre Advanced Tech. and Vocational Tng., Turin, Italy, 1963—. Served from lt. to lt. comdr., USNR, 1942-46. Recipient gold medal S.A.R., gold medal West Side Assn. N.Y., 1963, Leonard Ayres award for leadership Rutgers U., 1964, Josiah Margvel award for service to Del., 1965; named Outstanding Citizen of Year Order of Ahrpa, Mgr. of Year Soc. Advancement Mgmt., Del., 1961. Mem. Am. Inst. Banking (pres. state bank div. 1964-65, dir. Wilmington), U.S. C. of C. (chmn. govt. operations and expenditures com. 1960-61, pres. 1963-64, chmn. bd. 1964-65, dir. 1959-70), Conf. Bd., Am. (pres. state bank div. 1964-65, dir.), Del. (past pres.) bankers assns., Beta Gamma Sigma (hon.). Kiwanian. Address: 62 Town House Lane Corpus Christi TX 78412

NEILL, FLOYD MILTON, bank exec.; b. Gary, Tex., Jan. 18, 1902; s. Joe Darby and Alta (Cleaveland) N.; student grade sch.; m. Birdie Lorene Bearden, Apr. 30, 1926; children—Billie Jo, Charles, Duran Altar, Ruth Leaih, Floyd Ann Minor. Rep. Marshall Prodn. Credit Assn., Marshall, 1936-56; exec. v.p. First State Bank, Lockney, Tex.,

1956-62, v.p., 1962; with First State Bank Marlin, Tex., 1962—, chmn. bd., 1962—; chmn. First State Bank, Marlin. Trustee Pine Hill Sch., Pine Hill, Tex., 1940-41. Democrat. Methodist. Mason (Shriner). Home: 425 E Main St Henderson TX 75652 Office: First State Bank 101 Liveoak St Box 720 Marlin TX 76661

NEILL, RAY, cartoonist Dallas Morning News. Home: 2115 Highwood St Dallas TX 75228 Office: Dallas Morning News Dallas TX 75222*

NEILL, THOMAS TAYLOR, govt. cons.; b. Washington, Dec. 4, 1903; s. Charles P. and Esther (Waggaman) N.; B.S. in Mech. Engring., Cath. U. Am., 1925; M.S., Mass Inst. Tech., 1926; m. Helen M. Mitchell, June 8, 1929; children—Agnes A., Hugh M. Mech. engr. aircraft engine research lab. Nat. Bur. Standards, Washington, 1926-39; ignition engr. AAC, Dayton, O., 1939-42; asst. to dir. research NACA, Washington, 1942-58; chief research adminstrn. div., office of dir. of advanced research programs, NASA, Washington, 1958-61, chief research and tech. reports div. Office Advanced Research and Tech., 1961-70; cons. Nat. Air and Space Mus. Smithsonian Instn., Washington, 1971—. Mem. Soc. Automotive Engrs. (v.p. aircraft 1953). Author articles in field. Patentee synchronized street traffic control system, 1924, rate of fuel consumption indicator, 1942. Home: 4520 Hawthorne St Washington DC 20016 Office: 900 Jefferson Dr SE Washington DC 20560

NELMS, JOHN KING, govt. ofcl.; b. nr. Oxford, N.C., Sept. 14, 1921; s. John Henry and Daisy (Hobgood) N.; B.Mech. Engring., N.C. State U., 1942; m. Mary Ruth Clark, Jan. 31, 1948; 1 son, John King. Owner, operator Oxford Auto Machine Co., 1945-53, John Motor Sales, 1953-63; exec. dir. Granville County-Oxford Planning Commn., 1963—; asst. sec., dir. Granville Indsl. Developers, Inc., 1963—. Exec. sec. Oxford Housing Authority, 1969—. Dir. Granville County Farm Bur., 1961-68, pres., 1962-64; chmn. Joint Granville-Oxford, Vance-Henderson Airport Authority, 1968; pres. Human Relations Commn., 1963-68. Bd. dirs. N.C. Farm Bur. Fedn., 1965-66, Durham Dairy Council, 1958-64. Served to maj. Aus, 1942-45. Decorated Bronze Star medal. Democrat. Baptist. Home: 126 Pine Cone Dr Oxford NC 27565 Office: 104 College St Oxford NC 27565

NELSON, ALVIN FREDOLPH, educator; b. Oakland, Neb., June 27, 1917; s. John N. and Bena (Anderson) N.; B.A., U. Neb., 1938, M.A. in Philosophy, 1939; Ph.D. in Philosophy, Ohio State U., 1942. Asst. prof. philosophy Wesleyan Coll., Macon, Ga., 1949-51; prof. edn., psychology Newberry (S.C.) Coll., 1951-53; acting chmn. div. edn. Berry Coll., Mt. Berry, Ga., 1953-54; Fiske prof. philosophy, psychology Yankton (S.D.) Coll., 1954-60; asso. prof. philosophy Tex. Christian U., Fort Worth, 1960-65, prof. philosophy, 1965—, acting chmn. dept. philosophy, 1971—. Mem. So. Soc. Philosophy and Psychology (sect. pres. 1952-53), Am., Southwestern, North Tex. (pres. 1969-70) philos. assns., Metaphys. Soc. Am., Am. Assn. U. Profs., Phi Beta Kappa. Author: Structure of Normative Ethics, 1943; (with D. L. Evans and W. S. Gamertsfelder) Elements of Logic, 1957; (with G.A. Ferre) Basic Philosophical Issues, 1962; Development of Lester Ward's World View, 1968, 2d. edition, 1970. Editor: Primary Questions - Historical Answers (A.E. Avey), 1968. Home: 3514B University Dr Fort Worth TX 76109

NELSON, ARNOLD FRANKLIN, clergyman; b. Union, Miss., Jan. 29, 1911; s. Sidney Franklin and Susie (Gordon) N.; student E. Central Jr. Coll., 1930, U. Miss., 1932-34; B.S., U. So. Miss., 1946; B.D., New Orleans Bapt. Theol. Sem., 1949, Th.D., 1952; m. Donnie C. Winstead, June 29, 1935; children—Dorothy Jean, Charlotte Ann. Tchr., coach, prin., pub. schs., Miss., 1934-42; ordained to ministry Bapt. Ch., 1946 student pastor McNeil, Johnston Station and Tylertown, Miss., 1946-52; pastor 1st Bapt. Ch., Thibodaux, La., 1952-61, Calvary Bapt. Ch., Slidell, La., 1961-63; field sec. La. Bapt. Conv., Mansfield, La., 1963—, mem. exec. bd., 1954-62, chmn. state missions com., 1958-62, mem. stewardship commn., 1966—. Bd. dirs. La. Moral and Civic Found. Served with AUS, 1943-46. Mason, Lion. Home: 106 Hope St Mansfield LA 71052

NELSON, BOWEN CRESTON, former mortgage banker; b. Birdsville, Ky., Aug. 19, 1900; s. Carson Marshall and Lavinia (Bowen) N.; LL.B., U. Ky., 1942; m. Hazel Fowler, Oct. 26, 1941; 1 dau., Creston Annette. Admitted to Ky. bar, 1924, Fla. bar, 1930; pvt. practice law Paducah, Ky. 1924-25, Miami, Fla. 1929-33; atty. Keswick Corp. (subsidiary Md. Casualty Co.), Miami, negotiator, field rep. Home Owners Loan Corp., 1933-35; abstractor N.Y. Title and Mortgage Co., Miami, Fla., 1935-37; formed Nelson Mortgage Co., Miami, 1937, inc., 1941, pres., 1941-69, ret.; dir. Smith Ins. Agy., Inc., Peoples Am. Nat. Bank. Mem. Small Bus. Adv. Council Fla. Mem. citizen's com. U. Miami, 1952—. Mem. Miami-Dade County C. of C., Mortgage Bankers' Assn. Greater Miami (pres. 1957-58), Mortgage Bankers Assn. Am. (mem. nat. policy coms., 1957-58, nat. membership com., 1961-69, mem. com. arranging program nat. conv. 1961), Execs. Assn. Greater Miami (rep. of mortgage cos.), Fla. Hist. Assn., Internat. Platform Assn., Sons of Confederacy. Vizcayans Soc. So. Families, Delta Chi. Democrat. Mem. Christian Ch. Clubs: Kiwanis (charter mem. Biscayne Bay chpt.); Coral Gables Country; Century (Coral Gables, Florida). Home: 10255 SW 53rd Av Miami FL 33156

NELSON, DAVID ANDREWS, clergyman; b. Shannon, Miss. Aug. 14, 1926; s. Charles and T. Willie (Grant) N.; student U. Ala., 1946, Samford U., 1949; B.D., So. Bapt. Theol. Sem., 1951, Th.D., 1955; m. Jo Griffin, June 8, 1950; children—David Andrews, Kathryn Brown. Ordained to ministry Bapt. Ch., 1949; pastor Vine St. Bapt. Ch., Louisville, 1949-55, Highland Bapt. Ch., Louisville, 1956-61, 1st Bapt. Ch., Owensboro, Ky., 1961—. Teaching fellow So. Bapt. Theol. Sem., 1951-53. Trustee Ky. So. Coll., 1960-68, Southeastern Bapt. Theol. Sem., 1963-68; pres. Ky. Bapt. Conv., 1965-66; bd. dirs. United Fund, Owensboro Chs. for Better Homes. Served with USAAF, 1944-45. Mem. Alpha Epsilon Delta. Rotarian (pres. 1968-69). Home: 2176 S Stratford Dr Owensboro KY 42301 Office: PO Box 656 Owensboro KY 42301

NELSON, DONALD SIEGFRIED, architect; b. Chgo., Feb. 10, 1907; s. August G. and Diana (Fredrickson) N.; student Mass. Inst. Tech., 1924-25, Ecole des Beaux Arts, Fountainebleu, France, 1925; postgrad. Ecole Nationale Superieur des Beaux Arts, Paris, France, 1927-30; m. Matilda Fowler, Sept. 17, 1929; 1 son, Donald Fowler. Partner firm Bennett, Parsons & Frost, Chgo., 1929-35; partner firm Broad & Nelson, Dallas, 1946—; works include govt. bldgs., office bldgs., memls., banks, hosps., schs. and libraries. Mem. Dallas Crime Commn., 1969—. Served to maj. C.E. USAAF, 1942-46. Winner 20th Paris prize Ecole des Beaux Arts, 1927-30; 2d prize Columbus Meml., 1931. Fellow A.I.A.; mem. Tec. Soc. Architects, Tex. Archtl. Found. (dir., sec. 1950-54), Archtl. League N.Y., Nat. Inst. Archtl. Edn., Dallas C. of C., Dallas Hist. Soc., Mass. Inst. Tech., Fontainebleau alumni assns. Mason (33, K.T.). Clubs: Dallas Athletic, Variety International, Optimists (Dallas). Patentee Air Force Wind computer, also patentee transp. field. Home: 4408 Mockingbird Pkwy Dallas TX 75205 Office: 626 Mercantile Dallas Bldg Dallas TX 75201

NELSON, ESTHER MARION, educator; b. Mpls.; d. Victor and Ellen (Martin) Nelson; B.S., U. Ore., 1926; M.A., Columbia, 1929, Ph.D., 1939, postdoctoral research, 1946-48; postgrad. U. Heidelberg, Germany, 1934; postdoctoral Harvard, summers 1940, N.Y.U., 1942. Instr. English, edn. State U. N.Y. Coll. Edn., Oneonta, 1931-43; educator U.S. Naval Operating Base, Guantanamo Bay, Cuba, 1948-50; from asso. prof. to prof. secondary edn. U. Houston, 1950—. Asso., Nat. Survey Edn. Tchrs. U.S., 1931-35; del. Christian Endeavor World Conv., Budapest, Hungary, 1935. Served in WAC, 1943-46. Recipient Internat. certificates of merit Dictionary of Internat. Biography, 1968, 72, Distinguished Achievement awards Two Thousand Women of Achievement, 1969, 70. Mem. Am. Assn. U. Women, Am. Assn. U. Profs., N.E.A., Nat Soc. for Study Edn., Assn. Higher Edn., Tex. State Tchrs. Assn., Acad. Polit. Sci., Nat. Council for Social Studies, Am. Legion, Nat. Audubon Soc., Nat. Wildlife Fedn., Wilderness Soc., Nat. Assn. Smithsonian Instn., Nat. Geog. Soc., Nat. Assn. Drs. in U.S.A., Internat. Platform Assn., Marquis Biog. Library Soc., Nat. Travel Club, Kappa Delta Pi, Pi Lambda Theta, Alpha Lambda Delta, Alpha Sigma Omicron. Republican. Presbyn. Author: Analysis of Content of Student Teaching Courses in State Teachers Colleges, 1939. Editor: FEASC Intelligence Bull., 1944-45. Contbr. to various ednl. publs. Home: 4432 Wheeler St Houston TX 77004

NELSON, GEORGE CARL EDWARD, librarian; b. N.Y. C., Aug 3, 1900; s. Charles and Christina (Gustafson) N.; B.S., Coll. City N.Y., 1925, M.S., 1926; Ph.D., Columbia, 1931; librarian certificate McGill U., 1932; m. Lillian Gleissner, July 5, 1935; m. 2d, Mary Baronowski, Feb. 18, 1966. Asst. N.Y. Pub. Library, 1917; library asst. Coll. City N.Y., 1921-25, instr. biol. sci., 1925-31, asst. librarian, 1928, asso. librarian, 1934-52; prof., librarian Fairleigh Dickinson U., 1952—, dir. grad. sch., 1954-55, dir. library, 1954—, dean libraries, 1958-60; dir. Instituto de Arte y Literature de Cuernavaca, 1961—, Centro Para Retirados Cuahnauac, A.C., 1966—. Mem. A.L.A., Spl. Libraries Assn., A.I.M., A.M. A., Am. Soc. for Quality Control, Am. Assn. U. Profs., Am. Philatelic Soc., Am. Topical Assn., Phi Delta Kappa, Omega Epsilon Phi (past nat. pres.). Republican. Conglist. Author: Introductory Biological Sciences in Liberal Arts Coll., 1931; Omega Epsilon Directory, 1932; Thomas Jefferson's Garden Book; Go Native in Mexico, 1958; Guide to Selected Research Tools and Source Materials for Graduate Students, 1958; Retire on 65 a Week in Mexico, 1967; Live It Up on 65 a Week in Sunny Mexico, 1968; Historical Dictionary of Mexico, 1970 Contbr. library and sci. jours. Home: Privada Las Quintas 10-12 Cuernavaca Mor Mexico

NELSON, GEORGE DALMAN, ins. agy. exec.; b. Junction City, La., Oct. 9, 1917; s. Noah W. and Birdie (Reynolds) N.; B.A., La. State U., 1938, LL.B., 1940; m. Nell Carolyn Querbes, Dec. 29, 1945; children— George Dalman, Carolyn Querbes. Admitted to La. bar, 1940; spl. agt. FBI, 1940-47; partner Querbes & Bourquin, ins. agts., Shreveport, La., 1947—; dir. La. Fire Ins. Co. of Baton Rouge. Sr. v.p. Council for Better La. Chmn. bd. trustees Centenary Coll. La. Mem. Am., La. bar assns., Omicron Delta Kappa, Phi Kappa Phi, Phi Eta Sigma, Mu Sigma Rho. Methodist. Clubs: Shreveport, Petroleum (Shreveport); Boston (New Orleans). Home: 2770 Fairfield Av Shreveport LA 71104 Office: 214 Milam St Shreveport LA 71102

NELSON, HARRY TRACY, lawyer; b. Clayton, Tex., May 30, 1895; s. Henry Calvin and Sudie Lorene (Davis) N.; grad. S.W. Tex. Tchrs. Coll., 1913; LL.B., Jefferson Sch. Law, 1930; m. Carrie Wright Marshall, Oct. 2, 1920; children—Harry Marshall, Virginia Wright. Tchr. pub. schs., Tex., 1914-15; U.S. revenue agt., 1919-20; partner Nelson & Nelson, C.P.A.'s, Dallas, 1926—; dir. Frito Co., Dallas. Counselor in astronomy Boy Scouts Am., 1944-55. Served with U.S. Army, 1917-18. Mem. Tex. Soc. C.P.A.'s (pres. 1937), Am. Bar Assn., Am. Inst. C.P.A.'s, Petroleum Club, Tex. Astron. Soc., Am. Assn. Atty. C.P.A.'s, Chautauqua Literary Soc., Navy League V.F.W., Phi Alpha Chi. Republican. Methodist. Author: Heavens and Earth Declare, 1934; newspaper column Todays Tax Talk, 1936—. Patentee in field. Home: 3545 Southwestern St Dallas TX 75225 Office: 1st Nat Bank Bldg Dallas TX 75202

NELSON, HAZEL FOWLER (MRS. BOWEN CRESTON NELSON), civic worker; b. Mulhall, Okla., May 16, 1905; d. Oscar Frederick and Belle Virginia (Lowe) Fowler; B.A., U. Okla., 1927; postgrad. U. Wis., 1928; m. Bowen Creston Nelson, Oct. 26, 1941; 1 dau., Creston Annette. Tchr. journalism, English, sponsor publs. Chickasha (Okla.) High Sch., 1927-30; reporter Norman (Okla.) Transcript, 1930-37; feature writer Oklahoma City Times, 1937-41; mil. editor Miami (Fla.) Herald, 1942-45; officer Nelson Mortgage Co., Inc., Miami, 1941-69, sec., dir., 1942-69. Mem. bd. Childrens Service Bur., Miami, 1952; pres. Franklin Bush chpt. U. Miami Women's Cancer Assn., 1969. Recipient silver award for assistance through newspaper series Miami's Fgn. War Brides, 1946. Mem. Vizcayans Soc. So. Families, Fla. Hist. Assn., Internat. Platform Assn., Theta Sigma Phi (pres. U. Okla. chpt. 1927, Miami chpt. 1952-53). Democrat. Mem. Christian Ch. Club: Coral Gables Country. Home: 10255 SW 53d Av Miami FL 33156

NELSON, HOWARD COLLINS, civil engr.; b. Milton, Fla., June 4, 1914; s. Erasmus Lenwell and Florie (Brooks) N.; B.C.E., U. Fla., 1946; m. Florence Lucille Finley, May 24, 1936; children—Peggy Lucille (Mrs. James G. Rogers), Jerry Jim and Terry Tim (twins). Resident hydrographer Internat. Boundary Com., USDS, 1937-40; pvt. practice as civil engr., 1946-48; with Soil Conservation Service, U.S. Dept. Agr., 1949—, design engr.-civil. Gainesville, Fla., 1967—. Owner, Ceil's Ceramics, Gainesville, 1968—. Mem. Martin County Planning and Zoning Bd., 1957-58. Served from 2d lt. to maj., arty. AUS, 1941-45, 50-52. Registered profl. engr., Fla. Mem. Am. Soc. C.E., NAOGE (nat. v.p. 1968—, Fla. chpt. pres. 1965—), Am. Soc. Agrl. Engrs. (sect. v.p. 1963-64), V.F.W., Phi Gamma Delta (mem. bd. chpt. advisers 1964—). Clubs: U.S. 441 Square Dance (pres. 1964-65), Swinging Squares Dance (pres. 1968-69). Home: 4118 NW 36th St Gainesville FL 32601 Office: PO Box 1208 Gainesville FL 32601

NELSON, JAMES RICHARD, educator; b. Norway, Mich., Feb. 27, 1929; s. Ernest Oscar and Hilma (Peterson) N.; student No. Mich. Coll. Edn., 1948, Art Inst. Chgo., 1949; M.F.A., U. Chgo., 1960; postgrad. Meadville Theol. Sem., summer 1967, Harvard Sch. Arts Adminstrn., summer 1971; m. Andrea Margaret Canavera, June 9, 1956; children—Elisa, Eric, Kirsten. Instr. art Huntingdon Coll., Montgomery, Ala., 1958-60, acting chmn. art dept., 1961-63, chmn. art dept., 1963—, asst. prof., asso. prof., 1960-65, prof. art dept., 1965—, chmn. dept. visual and performing arts, 1970—; exec. dir. Ala. High Sch. Fine Arts, 1972—. Guest lectr. Am. art Allied Officers Sch., Maxwell AFB, 1966-68; lectr. art Troy State U., 1969-70. Bd. dirs. Montgomery Mus. Fine Arts, Ala. Council on Arts and Humanities, State High Sch. for Fine Arts. Served with AUS, 1949-52. Mem. Southeastern Coll. Art Conf., Am. Assn. Museums, Nat. Soc. Arts and Letters (chpt. pres. 1967), Am. Assn. U. Profs. (chpt. pres. 1969-70), Ala. Art League (pres. 1964-66, 68). Home: 1620 Stonewall Dr Birmingham AL 35226

NELSON, JAMES THOMAS, judge; b. Daytona Beach, Fla., May 29, 1917; s. Frank J. and Katherine (Mitchell) N.; student Marion Mil. Inst., 1934-35, U. Ala., 1935-37; LL.B., Stetson U., 1941; m. Virginia Lee Hoysley, Jan. 23, 1947; children—Tommy, Frank, Kathy, Steve, Linda. Admitted to Fla. bar, 1941; practiced in Daytona Beach, 1945-64; judge Circuit Ct., State of Fla., Holly Hill, 1964—. Pres., co-owner Halifax Title Co., Daytona Beach, 1950-70. Served with USNR, 1941-45. Mem. Am. Bar Assn., Fla. Bar, Phi Alpha Delta. Democrat. Roman Catholic. Lion (pres. 1950). Home: 928 S Peninsula Dr Daytona Beach FL 32018 Office: Law Center Holly Hill FL 32017

NELSON, JOHN HOWARD, journalist; b. Talladega, Ala., Oct. 11, 1929; s. Howard Alonzo and Barbara Lena (O'Donnell) N.; student econs. Ga. State Coll., 1953-57; Nieman fellow Harvard, 1961-62; m. Virginia Dare Dickinson, Aug. 4, 1951; children—Karen Dare, John Michael, Steven Howard. Reporter, Biloxi (Miss.) Daily Herald, 1947-51, Atlanta Constitution, 1952-65; So. Bur. chief Los Angeles Times, Atlanta, 1965—. Served with AUS, 1951-52. Recipient Pulitzer prize for local reporting under deadline pressure. 1960; named one of ten outstanding young men in U.S., U.S. Jr. C. of C., 1960. Mem. Sigma Delta Chi. Author: (with Gene Roberts, Jr.) The Censors and The Schools, 1963. Home: 2158 Oregon Ct Decatur GA Office: 10 Forsyth St Atlanta GA 30302

NELSON, JOHN PETTIT, lawyer; b. Gulfport, Miss., Aug. 5, 1921; s. John P. and Stella (Foret) N.; student La. State U., 1938-40; B.S., Loyola U., 1947, LL.B., 1950; m. Marie Anna Murphy, June 5, 1946; children—Marie Anna, Jeanne, Cesyle, Stephanie. Admitted to La. bar, 1950; asso. Dodd, Hirsch & Barker, 1950-54; asst. dist. atty. Parish of Orleans, 1953-58; sr. partner Nelson & Nelson, 1958—. Served to capt. AUS, 1940-45. Decorated Silver Star, Bronze Star medal, Purple Heart. Mem. Am., La., New Orleans bar assns., Am. Legion, Nat. Cath. Conf. of Interracial Justice. Home: 2432 Jay St New Orleans LA 70122 Office: Medallion Towers New Orleans LA 70130

NELSON, JOSEPH CONRAD, mfg. co. exec., lawyer; b. Rochester, N.Y., Sept. 20, 1926; s. Joseph F. and Louise (Mairhuber) N.; A.B. with high distinction, U. Rochester, 1947; J.D., Harvard, 1949; m. Anita Elizabeth Rougol, May 19, 1945; children—Lynn Louise, Lisa Ann. Admitted to Mich. bar, 1949, ICC bar, 1950, Ill. bar, 1958, Mo. bar, 1966, Tex. bar, 1967, U.S. Supreme Ct. bar; atty. N.Y.C. R.R., 1949-52; lectr. Detroit Coll. Law, 1950-58; atty. Mich. Wis. Pipe Line Co., 1952-56; asst. sec. Am. La. Pipe Line Co., 1956-58; atty. Sears, Roebuck and Co., 1958-63, coordinator mdse. mgmt. com., 1963-65; sec., gen. counsel Kellwood Co., St. Louis, 1965-67; sec., dir. Stahl Urban Co., Brookhaven, Miss., 1966-67, Quilted Textiles Corp., Rossville, Ga., 1966-67; sec. Fashion Design of Kellwood, Inc., N.Y.C., 1965-67; sec., gen. atty. Tex. Industries, Inc., Dallas, 1967—, v.p., 1969—. Sec. Mich. R.R. Lawyers Assn., 1952. Mem. scholarship com. Telluride Assn., Detroit, 1956; legislative chmn. Birmingham (Mich.) PTA, 1957; chmn. Winnetka (Ill.) Cancer Crusade, 1964; chmn. Dallas regional admissions and scholarship com. U. Rochester, 1969—. Sec., dir. Pub. TV Found. for North Tex., 1969—; bd. dirs. Chgo.-North Shore unit Am. Cancer Soc., 1965, Dallas County unit Am. Cancer Soc., 1968—; trustee Dallas Symphony Assn., 1968—, mem. exec. com., 1969-71. Mem. Am., Tex., Dallas bar assns., Phi Beta Kappa. Presbyn. Club: Brookhaven Country. Home: 4610 S Lindhurst Av Dallas TX 75229 Office: 8100 Carpenter Freeway Dallas TX 75247

NELSON, KINLOCH, physician, educator; b. Richmond, Va., Mar. 12, 1903; s. John Garnett and Susie Rose (Morris) N.; B.A., U. Va., 1923, M.D., 1927; m. Alice Macgill Deford, July 26, 1936. Intern U. Minn. Hosp., 1927-28; asst. resident medicine Billings Meml. Hosp. Chgo. 1928-29 mem. faculty Med. Coll. Va., Richmond, 1929—, prof. medicine, 1958—, dean medicine, 1963-71, emeritus, 1971—; asso. chief of staff for edn. McGuire VA Hosp., 1971—. Served to maj. M.C. AUS, 1942-44. Mem. A.M.A., Med. Soc. Va. (speaker ho. dels. 1963-65), Richmond Acad. Medicine (pres. 1951), A.C.P. (gov. for Va.1959-65), Am. Soc. Internal Medicine. Episcopalian. Home: 1621 Hanover Av Richmond VA 23220 Office: McGuire VA Hosp Richmond VA 23219

NELSON, LLOYD ADRIAN, govt. ofcl.; b. Tioga, N.D., June 29, 1908; s. Albin F. and Anna (Egeberg) N.; B.C.S., Southeastern U., 1935; postgrad. U. Minn., 1935, Benjamin Franklin U., 1936, Am. U., 1966, Agr. Grad. Sch., 1950; m. Rachel Miller, June 30, 1934; children— Rodger, Richard, Susan. Statis. reviewer Census Bur., 1931-32; chief accountant Nat. Trade Assn., 1934-35; accountant Farm Security Adminstrn., 1935-42; auditor USN, 1942; chief accounting sect. Fgn. Econ. Adminstrn., 1942-45; chief accountant War Assets Adminstrn., 1945-48; asso. dir. Accounting Systems div., U.S. Gen. Accounting Office, Washington, 1948-56, asso. dir., civil div., 1956—. Com. mem., treas. troop Takoma Park (Md.) council Boy Scouts Am., 1949-59; citizen's assn. rep. Allied Civic Group, 1965-66; bd. mem. Fellowship Sq. Found., 1967-70, v.p., 1969-71; active P.T.A. C.P.A., Md. Mem. Fed. Govt. Accountants Assn. (mem. bd. Washington chpt. 1956-57, 66-67), Nat. Assn. Accountants (mem. bd. Washington chpt. 1946-47), Am. Accounting Assn., Am. Inst. C.P.A.'s. Republican. Lutheran. Home: 12200 Brookhaven Dr Silver Spring MD 20902 Office: 441 G St NW Washington DC 20548

NELSON, LOUIS EDWARD, educator; b. Cedar Rapids, Ia., May 2, 1920; s. Marshall Barr and Meta (Winkenwerder) N.; B.A., Coe Coll., 1948; M.Ed., Springfield Coll., 1951; Ed.D., Fla. State U., 1958; m. Janice F. Bissell, Nov. 25, 1948; children—Louis Edward II, Larry Edwin, Lester Evan. Boys' work sec. Davenport (Ia.) YMCA, 1948-50, membership, adult program sec., Aurora, Ill., 1952-54; instr. sociology E. Tenn. State U., 1956-59, asst. prof., 1959-62, asso. prof., 1962-64, chmn. social services, 1964—, prof., 1965—; pvt. practice marriage, family counseling, Johnson City, Tenn., 1959—. Served with AUS, 1942-45. Mem. Acad. Certified Social Workers, Am. Assn. Marriage and Family Counselors, Nat. Assn. Social Workers, Tenn. Conf. Social Welfare (dir. 1962—, 1st v.p. 1965-66, regional v.p., 1967-68, pres. elect 1972-73). Presbyn. Research YMCA family programming, social welfare regional topics, Contbr. articles to profl. jours. Home: 2901 Woodhill Rd Johnson City TN 37601

NELSON, PHILIP PAGE, constrn. co. exec.; b. Greensboro, N.C., June 8, 1912; s. Philip and Lily Todd (Woodard) N.; student Coll. William and Mary, 1928-30; B.S. in Civil Engring., Va. Mil. Inst., 1932; m. Bessie Mae White, July 27, 1935; children—William Howard, Leila Lee (Mrs. Jay P. Schwertfeger). Insp., Va. Dept. Hwys., 1932-38; constrn. supt. Williamsburg (Va.) Restoration, Inc., 1938-39, gen. constrn. supt., 1939-41; supt. Doyle & Russell, Norfolk, Va., 1942; constrn. mgr. Walter P. Chrysler, Jr., Warrenton, Va., 1946-47; owner, pres., gen. mgr. Nelson Constrn. Co., 1947—; pres. Central Concrete Products Inc., 1950—; pres., dir. Fauquier Savs. and Loan Assn., 1960—; mem. adv. dir. Marshall Nat. Bank & Trust Co., 1970—; dir. Sulphur Springs Investment Corp. Chmn. disaster relief com. Fauquier-Rappahannock chpt. A.R.C., 1955-67. Served with USNR, 1942-46. Decorated Bronze Star medal with Combat V. Mem. Am. Soc. C.E., Soc. Am. Mil. Engrs., Sigma Alpha Epsilon. Democrat. Episcopalian. Clubs: Fauquier, Fauquier Springs Country (Warrenton). Home: 204 Roebling St Warrenton VA 22186 Office: 85 Garrett St Warrenton VA 22186

NELSON, RICHARD FRANCIS, oil co. exec.; b. El Dorado, Ark., Jan. 26, 1927; s. Walter Francis and Floy C. (Madean) N.; B.S. in Mech. Engring., U. Kan., 1946; m. Phyllis Chancellor, June 20, 1949; children— Richard Francis, Jr., Marjorie, Walter, Stuart. With Shell Oil Co., 1947—, gen. mgr. offshore div., Metairie, La., 1968—; pres. Blue Dolphin Pipe Line Co., Metairie, 1970-71; vice chmn. Offshore Operators Com., 1971. Served to ensign USNR, 1944-47. Mem. Am. Inst. Mineral., Metall. and Petroleum Engrs., Am. Petroleum Inst., Mid-Continent Oil and Gas Assn., C. of C. Clubs: Metairie Country; Petroleum, Plimsoll (New Orleans). Home: 6011 Chatham Dr New Orleans LA 70122 Office: 2900 Veterans Memorial Blvd Metairie LA 70002

NELSON, RICHARD STANLEY, lawyer; b. Pitts., June 22, 1931; s. Ben and Minna (Blumer) N.; B.A., U. Mich., 1953; LL.B., U. Pitts., 1956; m. Inez Joan Krouse, Oct. 17, 1954; children—David Keith, Gary Robert, Linda Sari, Wendy Barbara. Admitted to Pa. bar, 1956; Ky. bar, 1961; practiced in Pitts., 1956; spl. agt. FBI, U.S. Dept. of Justice, Louisville, Covington, Ky., 1959-61; practiced in Covington, 1961—; judge protem, trial commr. Kenton County Ct., 1964-69; city atty. Ft. Mitchell, 1965—. Served with AUS, 1956-59. Mem. Am., Ky. (Ho. Dels.), Pa., Kenton County (pres. 1972) bar assns., Am. Arbitration Assn., Soc. Am. Magicians, Soc. Former Spl. Agts. FBI, Am., Ky. trial lawyers assns., Phi Alpha Delta. Democrat. Jewish religion. Home: 135 Thompson Av Fort Mitchell KY 41017 Office: 11 W 6th St Covington KY 41011

NELSON, RICHARD THURLOW, retail co. exec.; b. Waupaca, Wis., Feb. 23, 1932; s. Reuben Thorwaldt and Gertrude Elizabeth (Mason) N.; student U. Wis., 1950, Northwestern Prep. Sch., 1951; B.S., U.S. Naval Acad., 1955; m. Mary Lucile Delchamps, July 6, 1956; children—Richard T., Robert Frederick, Wayne Stewart. With Delchamps, Inc., Mobile, Ala., 1959—, asst. to v.p. service operations, 1960-65, dir. service operations, 1965-66, dir. personnel devel., 1966-68, v.p. personnel, 1968—. Pres. Children's Dental Clinic, 1967-68. Pres. Greater Gulf State Fair, 1965, Vis. Nurses Assn., 1968; gen. chmn. Am.'s Jr. Miss Pageant, 1967. Mem. Ala. Republican Exec. Com., 1968-71, chmn. 1st. dist. exec. com., 1970-71. Served as aviator USN, 1955-59. Mem. Mobile Jr. (v.p. 1962), Ala. Jr. (Ryan de Graffenreid Meml. award 1966; v.p. 1964) chambers commerce, Am. Soc. Personnel Adminstrs. Methodist (sec. adminstrn. bd. 1963). Club: Country (Mobile). Home: 4452 Winnie Way Mobile AL 36608 Office: PO Box 1668 Mobile AL 36601

NELSON, ROBERT BURWELL, physician, educator; b. Blacksburg, Va., Feb. 6, 1910; s. Robert Burwell and Sallie (Seddon) N.; B.A., U. Va., 1932, M.D., 1936; m. Susanne Richardson Wickes, May 21, 1958; children—Page Mershon, Susan Seddon, Robert Burwell III. Intern surgery Johns Hopkins Hosp., 1936-37; resident obstetrics Garfield Meml. Hosp., Washington 1937-39; resident gynecology N.Y. Postgrad. Hosp. 1939-40; pvt. practice obstetrics and gynecology, Washington, 1946—; sr. attending gynecology Washington Hosp. Center, vice chmn. dept. gynecology, 1959-64, chmn., 1964—, adminstrv. chmn., 1969-70, pres. med. staff, 1971-72; asso. clin. prof. obstetrics and gynecology George Washington U. Med. Sch., 1965—. Served to col., flight surgeon USAAF, 1940-45; mem. Res. Decorated Bronze Star medal. Diplomate Am. Bd. Obstetrics and Gynecology. Fellow Am. Coll. Obstetrics and Gynecology; mem. A.M.A., Washington Gynecol. Soc. (pres. 1968-69), Med. Arts Soc., Louis Mackall Med. Soc., Osler Soc., Clinico-Path. Soc. (past pres.), Med. Soc. D.C., Phi Beta Kappa, Alpha Omega Alpha. Episcopalian. Rotarian. Clubs: University (Washington); Chevy Chase (Md.). Author articles in field. Home: 7933 Deepwell Dr Bethesda MD 20014 Office: 916 19th St NW Washington DC 20006

NELSON, ROBERT MELLINGER, educator; b. Burlington, Ia., May 17, 1918; s. Harry Joseph and Grace S. (Mellinger) N.; B.A., U. Ia., 1940, M.S., 1941, D.D.S., 1950, M.S. in Orthodontics, 1951. Individual practice dentistry, Chgo., 1951-53; asst. prof. dept. orthodontics U. N.C., Chapel Hill, 1953—, chmn. orthodontic dept., 1965—. Lectr. orthodontics. Served with USNR, 1941-46. Mem. Jr. C. of C., Am. Dental Assn., Am. Assn. Orthodontists, So. Soc. Orthodontists, N.C. Orthodontic Soc., Am. Assn. Dentistry for Children, Am. Bd. Orthodontists, Psi Omega. Home: 903 Coker Dr Chapel Hill NC 27514

NELSON, ROBERT STUART, physician; b. Atlantic City, Apr. 7, 1911; s. Kent Nelson and Edith (Wills) N.; B.S., U. Minn., 1934, M.D., 1935; m. Mary Agnes Groves, July 11, 1936; children—Mary Sheila (Mrs. Jack Pearson), Patricia W. (Mrs. Scott L. Catlett), Roberta J. Internist, chief gastroenterology sect. dept. medicine M.D. Anderson Hosp. and Tumor Inst., Houston, 1956—; asso. clin. prof. medicine Baylor U. Coll. Medicine, 1961—; prof. medicine gen. faculty U. Tex., 1965—. Served to col., M.C., AUS, 1935-55. Fellow A.C.P.; mem. Am. Gastroent. Assn., A.M.A., Am. Assn. for Cancer Research, Am. Soc. for Gastrointestinal Endoscropy. Contbr. articles to profl. jours. Home: 1400 Hermann Dr Houston TX 77004 Office: 6723 Bertner Blvd Houston TX 77225

NELSON, ROLAND HILL, educator; b. Salisbury, Md., July 28, 1928; s. Roland Hill and Marian A. (Beauchamp) N.; A.B., Duke U., 1949; M.Ed., U. Va., 1955; Ed.D., Harvard U., 1960; m. Hazel Batte, Feb. 17, 1952; children—Rolanda, Deborah, Lisa. High sch. tchr. Stony Creek, Va., 1949-50; elementary prin. Albermarle County, Va., 1954-55; headmaster Metairie Park Country Day Sch., New Orleans, 1956-61; vis. asso. prof. edn. Tulane U., 1959-61 part-time; asst. dean arts and scis. and asso. prof. edn. U. Louisville, 1961-63; asso. dean Sch. Edn. and asso. prof. edn. Northwestern U., 1963-65; chmn. dept. edn. and prof. Duke U., 1965-67; pres. Richmond Profl. Inst., 1967—. Dir. Nat. Conf. Christians and Jews. Served to Capt. USMCR, 1951-53. Mem. Am. Assn. Sch. Adminstrs., Phi Delta Kappa, Kappa Delta Pi. Home: 910 W Franklin St Richmond VA 23220 Office: 901 W Franklin St Richmond VA 23220

NELSON, THOMAS WILLIAM, pub. co. exec.; b. Little Elm, Tex., June 22, 1906; s. James William and Nora (Robertson) N.; student Baylor U., 1924-27; m. Ilvy Jeanne Boulet, June 15, 1930; children—Thomas William, Ward Boulet, Virginia Ruth, David Ray, James Lee. With Gulf Pub. Co., Houston, 1927—, dist. rep., 1930-38, sales mgr., dir., 1938-55, overseas mgr., 1955-57, v.p.-gen. mgr., 1957-68, pres., 1968—. Mem. Am. Bus. Press, Am. Petroleum Inst., Assn. Indsl. Advertisers (organizer Houston chpt.), Nat. Oil Equipment Mfrs. and Dels. (past pres., regent), World Trade Assn., Houston Club Men's Forum. Baptist. Mason. Rotarian. Home: 3841 Overbrook St Houston TX 77027 Office: Gulf Pub Co PO Box 2608 Houston TX 77001

NELSON, WALLACE BOYD, educator; b. Oilton, Okla., Mar. 17, 1923; s. Frank and Notie (Ferguson) N.; B.S., So. Ill. U., 1947; M.A., State U. Ia., 1948, Ph.D., 1950; m. Merietta Josephine Lair, Sept. 1, 1942 1 son, Larry Frank. Asst. prof. to prof. econs. Kan. State U., 1950-61; prof. bus., head dept. bus. adminstrn. Arlington (Tex.) State Coll., 1961-65; prof. econs., dean sch. bus. U. Tex., Arlington, 1965—. Research fellow Claremont Men's Coll., Los Angeles, 1957. Served with USAAF, 1943-46, USAF, 1951-53. Mem. Am. Econ. Assn., Indsl. Relations Research Assn., Southwestern Social Sci. Assn., Am. Assn. U. Profs., Am. Arbitration Assn. (panel arbitrators 1961—), Arlington C. of C. (past chmn. edn. com.), Order of Artus (past pres.). Presbyn. (trustee). Rotarian (past local sec.). Contbr. articles in field to profl. jours. Home: 917 Sherwood Dr Arlington TX 76013

NELSON, WAYNE MALONE, corp. exec.; b. Kernersville, N.C., June 25, 1900; s. Romulus Shepard and Myrtle (Felts) N.; grad. high sch., Kernersville; m. 1 son, Philip Wayne. Office clk. So. Bell Telephone and Duke Power Co., Greensboro, N.C., 1917-20; builder, owner, mgr. radio sta. WNRC, Greensboro, 1925-34; builder, mng. radio sta. WMFR, High Point, N.C., 1936-40; builder, owner, mgr. radio sta. WEGO, Concord, N.C., 1941-49, radio stas. WWNF, Fayetteville, N.C., 1946-50, WAYN, Rockingham, N.C., 1946-64, WHIP, Mooresville, N.C., 1950—; pres., gen. mgr. Wayne M. Nelson Industries, Inc., Mooresville, N.C., 1950—. Mem. Am. Radio Relay League, Quarter Century Wireless Assn., Radio Club Am. Mem. Soc. of Friends. Kiwanian. Historian, collector early wireless equipment. Mailing address 414 S Union St Concord NC 28025 Office: PO Box 127 Concord NC 28025

NELSON, WILLARD HARRY, educator; b. Newawka, Neb., May 3, 1914; s. B. Harry and Selma (Johnson) N.; B.S., Neb. Wesleyan U., 1935; M.A., U. Neb., 1947, Ph.D., 1953; m. Anna Mae Botts, June 21, 1944; children—Ben Albert, David Wallace. Tchr., coach adminstr. pub. schs., Neb. and Mo., 1935-37, 41-42,46; counselor U. Neb., 1946-47, instr., 1948-51; dir. edn. Neb. State Reformatory, 1947-48; asst. prof. psychology Ala. Poly. Inst., Auburn, 1951-55, asso. prof., 1955-57; postdoctoral fellow U. Ill., 1958; asso. prof., dir. doctoral tng. program in sch. psychology Fla. State U., 1959-66; dir. research Broward County Schs., Ft. Lauderdale, Fla., 1966-69; prof., dir. Alexander D. Henderson U. Sch., Fla. Atlantic U., Boca Raton, 1969-70, prof., 1971—. Cons. to sch. systems, 1948—, Fla. State Dept. Edn., 1960—, Tri-county Mental Health Clinic, Thomasville, Ga., 1965-66. Served with USAAF, 1943-46. Mem. Fla. (mem. exec. council 1964-71), Am., So. (dir. insts. 1968—) psychol. assns., Am. Ednl. Research Assn., A.A.A.S., Kappa Sigma Pi. Contbr. research articles on ednl. and psychol. research to profl. jours. Co-founder, bd. dirs. Jour. Sch. Psychology, cons. editor, 1964-70; cons. editor Fla. Jour. Ednl. Research, 1970—. Home: 1040 SW 2d St Boca Raton FL 33432

NELSON, WILLIAM EUGENE, lawyer; b. Roland, Ia., Sept. 23, 1927; s. Samuel J. and Katherine (Coffey) N.; B.A., State U. Ia. 1950; J.D., Drake U., 1957; m. Sherlee M. Stanford, July 11, 1959; children—Anne Elizabeth, Kristin Stanford, William Coffey, Admitted to D.C. bar; atty. U.S. Dept. Justice, 1957—, now chief econ. stabilization sect. Served with USNR, 1945-46. Mem. Fed., Am. bar assns., State Bar Ia., Internat. Platform Assn. Order of Coif, Omicron Delta Kappa, Delta Theta Phi. Home: 4422 Ridge St Chevy Chase MD 20015 Office: Dept Justice Washington DC 20530

NEMECEK, PERRY LEE, banker; b. Oklahoma City, Dec. 4, 1944; s. Joe T. and Neva L. (Luper) N.; B.S., East Central State Coll., Ada, Okla., 1967; m. Glenda Rose, Aug. 1, 1964; children—Kelly Ray, Kerry Lee. Asst. cashier McClain County Nat. Bank, Purcell, Okla., 1967-69, cashier, 1970—. Chmn. bd., Wayne, Okla., 1966-72. Mem. McClain County Cattleman's Assn., Purcell C. of C. (chmn. pub. relations 1971-72), Young Farmers (sec. 1970-71), Future Farmers Am. (hon.). Lion. Clubs: Dance (dir. 1970—), Round Up, Flying (Purcell, Okla.). Home: Box 4 Wayne OK 73095 Office: 131 W Main St Purcell OK 73080

NEMETZ, GERALD EARL, elec. engr.; b. Mason City, Ia., May 8, 1925; s. Joseph and Rose B. (Vrba) N.; student Ia. State Coll., 1951-54; B.S. in Elec. Engring., U. Ky., 1955; postgrad. U. South Fla., 1965; m. Evelyn Amster Morgan, July 9, 1949; 1 son, Joseph D. Radio repairman Warwick Mfg. Co., Chgo., 1946-47; ground radio operator Trans World Airline, 1947-51; quality control analyst, gage, equipment engr. Gen. Electric Co., Louisville, 1955-60, inspection, facilities and test planner, advance quality control engr., St. Petersburg, Fla., 1960-65, quality control. engr., process engr., Lynchburg, Va., 1965—. Chmn. supervisory com. Credit Union, St. Petersburg, 1965. Served with USNR, 1943-46. Registered profl. engr., Fla. Mem. Lynchburg Soc. Engring. Sci., Am. Legion. Mason (32 deg., Shriner). Inventor, developer Pendulum Diffractometer. Home: 8202 Beechwood Dr Lynchburg VA 24502 Office: Gen Electric Co MRD Mountain View Rd Lynchburg VA 24501

NEMUTH, HAROLD ISAAC, physician; b. Norfolk, Va., Mar. 12, 1912; s. Marcus Cohen and Rose (Lasdan) N.; B.A., Columbia, 1934; M.D., Med. Coll. Va., 1939; m. Doreen Graham, Mar. 22, 1947; children—Mark Graham, Karen Lasdan, William Benson. Intern, Med. Coll. Va., 1938-39, Knickerbocker, N.Y., 1939-40; Sheltering Arms, Richmond, Va., 1940-41, St. Elizabeth Hosp., Richmond, 1941-42; practice medicine, Richmond, 1947—; asso. in medicine Med. Coll. Va., 1956—, asso. prof. preventive medicine, 1958—, acting chmn. dept. preventive medicine, 1959-62; chief of staff Sheltering Arms Hosp., 1956-67. Served with M.C., USNR, 1942-46. Mem. A.M.A., Med. Soc. Va. (v.p. 1970-71), Richmond Acad. Medicine (v.p. 1970-71), Am. Pub. Health Assn., Assn. Am. Med. Colls., Assn. Tchrs. Preventive Medicine, PanAm. Med. Assn., Am., Internat. gerontological socs. Jewish religion. Home: 5518 Riverside Dr Richmond VA 23225 Office: 2012 Monument Av Richmond VA 23220

NERDEN, JOSEPH TAFT, educator; b. Boston, Nov. 3, 1908; s. Jeremiah and Jeannette (Toff) N.; diploma mech. engring. Mass. Inst. Tech., 1928; B.S., Central Conn. State Coll., 1945; M.A., Yale, 1948, Ph.D., 1954; m. Lillian Ruth Gass, Aug. 18, 1931; children—Roberta (Mrs. Ernst Liebman), Cynthia (Mrs. Charles Krumbein). Mech. engr. Jones & Lamson Machine Co., Springfield, Vt., 1928-31; tchr. Boston Trade High Sch., 1925-28, Wilcox Regional Tech. Sch., Meriden, Conn., 1931-41; faculty, extension div. Central Conn. State Coll., New Britain, 1942-55; prof. indsl. and tech. edn. N.C. State U., Raleigh, 1964—. Mem. faculty Trinity Coll., Hartford, Conn., 1948, 49, 50; vis. cons., lectr. U.S. Office Edn. Leadership Devel. Insts. at various colls. and univs.; cons. audio-visual edn. Conn. Dept. Edn., 1941-53; cons. trade and indsl. edn. Conn. State Bd. Edn., 1953-57, chief bus. tech. insts., also chief bur. vocational-tech. schs., 1957-62, dir. div. vocational edn., 1962-64; mem. Nat. Com. for Evaluation of Vocational Edn., 1966—; cons. vocational edn. to various ednl. instns., govtl. agys. Named Outstanding Vocational Educator Am. Vocational Assn., 1971. Mem. Am. Assn. Sch. Adminstrs., Nat. Assn. Indsl. Tchr. Educators, Am. Tech. Edn. Assn. (trustee 1958-63, Am. life mem.; chmn. com. on evaluation and accreditation of vocational and tech. edn. 1964—), N.C. vocational assns. Mason. Home: 2201 Dixie Trail Raleigh NC 27607

NESBIT, PHYLLIS SCHNEIDER (MRS. PETER N. NESBIT), lawyer; b. New Kirk, Okla., Sept. 21, 1919; d. Vernon Lee and Irma Mae (Biddle) Schneider; B.S. in Chemistry, U. Ala., 1948, LL.B., 1958; m. Peter N. Nesbit, Sept. 14, 1939. Draftsman, Drydock & Shipbldg. Co., Mobile, Ala., 1942-45; tech. sec. B. F. Goodrich Co., Tuscaloosa, Ala., 1949-55; sec. Ala. Bus. Research Council, University, 1955-58; admitted to Ala. bar, 1958; partner firm Wilters, Brantley & Nesbit, Robertsdale, Ala., 1958—; judge Municipal Ct., Daphne, Ala. Sec., Daphne Civic Assn., 1962-66; auditor Joint Legislative Council Ala., 1970—, treas., 1972—. Mem. Ala. State Bar, Baldwin County Bar Assn. (pres. 1967-68), Nat. Assn. Women Lawyers, Ala. Women's Lawyers Assn. (pres. 1966-67), Ala. Municipal Judges Assn. (pres. 1970), Am. Judicature Soc., Gamma Sigma Epsilon. Methodist (steward, sec. 1960-64, sec. treas. 1965-68). Mem. Order Eastern Star (worthy matron 1963-64). Home: 411 Church St Daphne AL 36526 Office: Wilters Brantley & Nesbit Box 555 Robertsdale AL 36567

NESMITH, VERA COX (MRS. J. VERNON NESMITH), state ofcl.; b. St. Catherines, Ont., Can., Oct. 24, 1917; d. Ernest Henry and Edith (Rogers) Cox; came to U.S., 1921, naturalized, 1941; diploma Losey Secretarial Sch., 1937; certificate Orlando Jr. Coll., 1960; m. J. Vernon Nesmith, Dec. 3, 1966. Staff mem. Losey Secretarial Sch., 1937-38; with Fla. Div. Vocational Rehab., Orlando, also Winter Park, 1938—, dist. sec. to dist. dir., also in charge secs., 1948—, sec. II, DVR, sec. to dir. 1968—. Mem. Am. Assn. Med Assts. (program chmn. nat. conv. 1963, chmn., sec-treas.), Fla. (pres. 1961, del. nat. conv. 1961, 63, program chmn. state conv. 1964, membership chmn.; mem. past pres.'s council, med. Asst. of Year award 1965), Orange County (pres. 1959-61, dir. 1961-64, del. state conv. 1960, 61, rec. sec., Outstanding Mem. of Year award) med. assts. assns., Am. Acad. Med. Adminstrs. (chmn. legislative com.). Methodist. Home: 1912 Weber Av Orlando FL 32803 Office: 70 E South St Orlando FL 32801

NESTER, RUEL PAULLUS, agronomist; b. Marked Tree, Ark., July 8, 1921; s. William Henry and Madge Glynlin (Smith) N.; B.S. in Agr., U. Ark., 1953, M.S. in Agr., 1954; m. Norma Eloise Skelley, Nov. 12, 1949; 1 son, Paul Ruel. Seed buyer, seller, agriculturist Delta Seed Co., West Memphis, Ark., 1954-56; agriculturist, seed buyer, agrl. chem. sales Ark. Farmers Assn., Little Rock, 1956-57; research asst. U. Ark., Fayetteville, 1957-58; extension agronomist Agrl. Extension Service U.S. Dept. Edn., 1958—. Tchr. Ark. producers, 1958. Served with USAAF, 1940-45. Mem. Ark. Agrl. Pesticide Assn. (sec. 1969-71), Am., Ark. soybean assns., Alpha Zeta. Roman Catholic (finance chmn. 1966). K.C. (4 deg.). Author extension circulars. Contbr. articles to mags. and papers. Home: 1701 S Grant St Little Rock AR 72204 Office: 1201 McAlmont St Little Rock AR 72203

NETHERLAND, EDWARD RAY, community resource devel. specialist; b. Cambellsville, Ky., Oct. 14, 1931; s. Charles Neldid and Amy Gertrude (VanCleve) N.; B.S. in Agr., U. Ky., 1957, M.S. in Agr., (Grad. scholar 1961-62) 1963; m. Mary Lynn Miller, Dec. 22, 1954; children— Phyllis Carol, Linda Kay, Lora Lynn, Charles Russell. With U. Ky. Co-op. Extension Service, 1957—, 4-H club agt., Leitchfield, 1957-61, community resource devel. specialist, Princeton, 1962—. Chmn. Princeton (Ky.) Planning Commn., 1966-67. Served with AUS, 1953-55. Recipient Distinguished Service award Nat. Assn. County Agrl. Agts., 1971. Mem. C. of C., Community Devel. Soc. (founding mem. 1969). Democrat. Methodist (mem. bd. 1964—; dist. lay leader 1972—). Mason. Home: 103 Winchester Dr Princeton KY 42445 Office: PO Box 469 Princeton KY 42445

NETSKY, MARTIN GEORGE, educator; b. Phila., May 15, 1917; s. George Nathan and Clara (Sherman) N.; A.B., U. Pa., 1938, M.S., 1940, M.D., 1943; m. Helen Margaret Pease, Sept. 30, 1946. Intern, Hosp. of U. Pa., 1943, resident neurology, 1944; Arthur Weil fellow in neuropathology Montefiore Hosp., N.Y.C., 1946-47; lectr. neuroanatomy U.S. Naval Hosp., St. Albans, N.Y., 1948; asst. neuropathologist Montefiore Hosp., 1947-49; instr. Coll. Physicians and Surgeons, Columbia U., 1949-52, asso., 1952-55; asst. neuropsychiatry Montefiore Hosp., 1947-49, adj. attending physician, Div. Neuropsychiatry, 1949-52, asso. attending physician Div. Neuropsychiatry, 1949-52, asso. attending physician, 1952-55, asso. neuropathologist, 1950-55; cons. pathologist U.S. Naval Hosp., St. Albans, N.Y., 1950-55; asso. pathologist N.C. Bapt. Hosp., 1955-61, chief neurologic service, 1957-61; prof. neuropathology, asso. prof. neurology Bowman Gray Sch. Medicine, 1957-61, prof., chmn. dept. neurology, 1960-61, asso. physiology and pharmacology, 1958-61; prof. neuropathology U. Va. Sch. Medicine, 1962—; pathologist U. Va. Hosp., 1962—. Diplomate Am. Bd. Psychiatry and Neurology. Mem. Assn. for Research in Nervous and Mental Diseases, N.Y. County Med. Soc., A.M.A., Am. Acad. Neurology, Am. League Against Epilepsy, A.A.A.S., Am. Neurol. Assn. Forsyth County Med. Soc., Assn. Am. Med. Colls., Nat. Soc. for the Study of Edn., Am. Assn. U. Profs., Am. Assn. Pathologists and Bacteriologists, Am. Soc. for Exptl. Pathology, Siam Soc., Albemarle County Med. Soc., Internat. Coll. Pathology Alpha Omega Alpha. Contbr. articles in field to profl. jours. Home: Franklin RFD 7 Charlottesville VA 22901

NETTLES, BERT SHEFFIELD, lawyer; b. Monroeville, Ala., May 6, 1936; s. George Lee and Blanche (Sheffield) N.; B.S. U. Ala., 1958, LL.B., 1960; m. Elizabeth Duquet; children—Jane Elizabeth, Mary Katherine. Admitted to Ala. bar, 1960; asst. atty. gen., Ala., 1960-61; asso. firm Johnston, Johnston & Nettles, Mobile, Ala., 1961-64, partner, 1964-69; partner firm Nettles & Cox, 1970—. Asst. commr. Mobile Area council Boy Scouts Am., 1967-70. Vice chmn. Mobile County Republican Exec. Com., 1967-68; legal counsel Ala. Young Rep. Fedn., 1967; chmn. Ala. Rep. Conv., 1968; mem. Ala. Ho. Reps., 1969—. Bd. dirs. Mobile County chpt. A.R.C., 1967-70; bd. govs. Mobile Protestant Children's Home. Recipient Algernon Sydney Sullivan medallion U. Ala., 1958. Mem. Am., Ala. (chmn. young lawyers sect. 1966), Mobile (sec. 1965) bar assns., Ala. Def. Lawyers Assn. (dir. 1967—), Am. Right of Way Assn. (chpt. 1st v.p. 1971), U. Ala. Alumni Assn. (v.p. 1968), Omicron Delta Kappa, Alpha Tau Omega, Beta Gamma Sigma, Tau Kappa Alpha. Clubs: Bienville, Kiwanis, Episcopalian. Home: 136 Silverwood St Mobile AL 36607 Office: First National Bank Bldg Mobile AL 36602

NETTLES, EDWIN CARTER, JR., lawyer; b. Wakefield, Va., Mar. 5, 1936; s. Edwin Carter and Louis (Robertson) N.; B.S., Coll. William and Mary, 1958; LL.B., U. Richmond, 1961; m. Kathryn Lumpkin Chappell, July 19, 1958; children—Bryar Chappell, Kathryn Carter, Edwin Carter III. Admitted to Va. bar, 1961; practiced in Wakefield, 1961—; Commonwealth's atty., Sussex County, Va., 1963—; town atty., Waverly, Va., 1964—. Vice pres. Wakefield Equipment Co. Clk. Sussex County Planning Commn., 1967. Bd. dirs. U. Richmond Law Sch. Mem. Am., Va. trial lawyers assn., Va. State Bar Assn., Sussex County Bar Assn. (treas. 1964—), Assn. Preservation Va. Antiquities, Va. Farm Bur., S.A.R., Delta Theta Phi, Phi Kappa Tau, Beta. Democrat. Baptist. Rotarian. Clubs: Pheasant Pluckers Internat. (Franklin, Va.); Wakefield Sportsman, Wakefield Hunt; Homeville Hunt (Waverly). Home: Route 603 Wakefield VA 23888 Office: Wilson Av Wakefield VA 23888

NETTLES, JOHN BARNWELL, physician, educator; b. Dover, N.C., May 19, 1922; s. Stephen A. and Estelle (Hendrix) N.; B.S., U. S.C., 1941; M.D., Med. Coll. S.C., 1944; m. Eunice Anita Saugstad, Apr. 28, 1956; children—Eric, Robert, John Barnwell. Intern Garfield Meml. Hosp., Washington, 1944-45; research fellow in pathology Med. Coll. Ga., Augusta 1946-47; resident in obstetrics and gynecology U. Ill. Research and Ednl. Hosps., Chgo., 1947-51; instr. to asst. prof. obstetrics and gynecology U. Ill. Coll. Medicine, Chgo., 1951-57; asst. prof., asso. prof., prof. obstetrics and gynecology U. Ark. Med. Center, Little Rock, 1957-69; dir. grad. edn. Hillcrest [illegible]

Center, Tulsa, 1969—; prof. U. Okla. Med. Sch., 1969—; dir. Tulsa Obs. and Gynecol. Edn. Found., 1969—. Coordinator med. edn. for Nat. Def., Ark., 1961-69. Served as lt. (j.g.) M.C., USNR, 1945-46, as lt., 1953-54. Diplomate Am. Bd. Obstetrics and Gynecology. Fellow Am. Coll. Obstetricians and Gynecologists (dist. sec.-treas., dist. chmn. exec. bd. 1970—), A.C.S. (bd. govs. 1969-71); mem. Ark. Obstet. and Gynecol. Soc. (exec. sec. 1959-69), Central Assn. Obstetrics and Gynecology (exec. com. 1966-69, v.p. 1971-72), Internat. Soc. Advancement Humanistic Studies in Gynecology, Assn. Mil. Surgeons U.S., Am., Soc. med. assns., Okla., Tulsa County, Chgo. med. socs., Am. Assn. for Maternal and Infant Health, Assn. Am. Med. Colls., Am. Pub. Health Assn., Assn. Hosp. Med. Edn., Assn. Planned Parenthood Physicians, N.Y. Acad. Sci., Soc. for Gynecol. Investigation. Assn. Profs. Gynecology and Obstetrics, A.A.A.S., Am. Soc. for Study Fertility and Sterility, Internat. Soc. Gen. Semantics, Aerospace Med. Assn., So. Gynecol. and Obstet. Soc., Royal Soc. Health, Sigma Xi, Phi Rho Sigma; affiliate Royal Soc. Medicine. Lutheran. Research and main publs. on uterine malignancy, kidney biopsy in pregnancy, perinatal morbidity and mortality. Address: Hillcrest Med Center 1120 S Utica St Tulsa OK 74104

NETTLES, WILLIAM CARL, JR., agr. exec.; b. Anderson, S.C., Dec. 21, 1934; s. William Carl and Ruby Mae (Stevenson) N.; B.S., Clemson U., 1955, M.S., 1959; Ph.D. (Headlee fellow 1959-62), Rutgers U., 1962; m. Mary Patricia Maguire, May 27, 1967. Research entomologist U.S. Dept. Agr.-Agrl. Research Service, Baton Rouge, 1962—. Served with AUS, 1955-57. Mem. Entomol. Soc. Am., A.A.A.S., La. Entomol. Soc., Sigma Xi. Baptist. Club: Pelican Yacht (commodore 1967; sec., treas. 1965-66) Baton Route. Home: 565 Castle Kirk Baton Rouge LA 70808 Office: 4115 Gourrier St Baton Rouge LA 70808

NEU, HOWARD MITCHELL, lawyer; b. Chgo., Mar. 22, 1941; s. Maurice A. and Phyllis (Spector) N.; student U. Fla., 1958-61; B.B.A., U. Miami, 1962, J.D., 1968; m. Elinor Sontag, June 18, 1961; children—Carol Deborah, Wendy Joy. C.P.A., Weber, Thompson & Lefcourt, 1962-63, Morgan, Altemus & Barrs, 1963-68; admitted to Fla. bar, 1968; mem. firms William J. Goldworn, Miami, Fla., 1968-69, Goldworn & Neu, Miami, 1969-70; pvt. practice, 1970—. Asso. judge, North Miami, 1971—. Interim instr. U. Miami Sch. Law, 1969-70; instr. Miami Edn. Consortium, 1971—. Chmn., Metro-Dade County Library Adv. Bd., 1968-69; chmn. Fla. Library Devel. Council, 1971—. Bd. dirs. Abbey Hosp. C.P.A., Fla. Mem. Am., Fla. insts. C.P.A.'s, Greater Miami, Interama Area C. of C., Am. Fla., Dade County bar assns., Am. Arbitration Assn., Am. Assn. Atty. C.P.A., U. Miami Alumni Assn. Kiwanian; mem. B'nai B'rith. Jewish religion (temple choir dir. 1966—). Club: Tiger Bay Political (Miami). Home: 2180 NE 121st St North Miami FL 33161 Office: 1001 NE 125th St North Miami FL 33161

NEUFELD, DON HOWARD, chem. co. exec.; b. Enid, Okla., Jan. 21, 1924; s. Arthur C. and Eva (Wiens) N.; student Enid Bus. Coll., 1940-41, Eastern Ky. State U., 1942, Cin. U., 1943; B.S., Okla. State U., 1949; m. Janice Rose Hight, Aug. 28, 1948; children—Michael Howard, Doni Ramona. Plant controller Chem. div. Kaiser Aluminum & Chem. Corp., Cal. plants, 1949-64; asst. controller Kaiser Bauxite Co., Jamaica, W.I., 1953-58; controller Copolymer Rubber & Chem. Corp., Baton Rouge, 1964-65, v.p., sec.-treas., 1967—. Treas. Jr. Achievement, 1965—, chmn. planning com., 1970-71; mem. finance com. Cancer Radiation Center, 1970—; mem. La. Polit. Action Council, 1969—. Bd. dirs. Copolymer Found. Served with AUS, 1943-46; ETO. Decorated Bronze Star medal. Mem. Baton Rouge C. of C. (law enforcement and govtl. affairs coms. 1964—), Alpha Kappa Psi, Kappa Sigma. Republican. Presbyn. Club: Camelot and Sherwood Forest Country (Baton Rouge). Home: 1020 Woodhaven St Baton Rouge LA 70815 Office: PO Box 2591 Baton Rouge LA 70821

NEUMAN, ROBERT H., lawyer; b. N.Y.C., Oct. 14, 1936; A.B. magna cum laude, Harvard, 1958, LL.B., 1961. Ford Found. fellow, West Africa, 1961-62; admitted to N.Y. State bar, 1962, D.C. bar, 1962; atty. Office Legal Adviser, Dept. State, Washington, 1964-68, asst. legal adviser for Near Eastern and South Asian affairs, 1968-69, asst. legal adviser for politico-mil. and ocean affairs, 1969-70; mem. firm. Arent, Fox, Kintner, Plotkin & Kahn, Washington. Lectr. internat. law George Washington U., 1966-67; U.S. rep. to UN Conf. on Marine Pollution, 1969. Mem. Am. Soc. Internat. Law, Phi Beta Kappa. Address: 3408 34th Pl NW Washington DC 20016*

NEUMAN, SUSAN CATHERINE, pub. relations exec., editor; b. Detroit, Jan. 29, 1942; d. Paul Edmund and Elsie (Goetz) Neuman; A.B. in Am. Civilization, U. Miami, 1964. Reporter, columnist North Dade Hub, 1959-61; reporter, feature writer Miami Herald, 1962-64; reporter, columnist, photographer North Dade Jour., 1964-65; editor, exec. dir. publs. dept. Maimi-Dade County C. of C., Miami, Fla., editor Miamian mag., 1965-69; dir. communications Ferendino/Grafton/Pancoast, 1969-70; pres., editor Susan Neuman, Inc., pub. relations for bus. and industry, 1970—. Editor campus newspaper U. Miami, 1961-62; campus corr. Mademoiselle mag., 1960-64. Recipient various awards. Mem. Am. Assn. U. Women, Advt. Club of Greater Miami (bd. dirs. 1968-70, asso. editor yearbook 1968), Am. Assn. Commerce Publs. (bd. dirs.), Internat. Council Indsl. Editors, Fla. Mag. Assn., Bus. and Profl. Women's Club (v.p.), Mag. Pubs. Assn., Theta Sigma Phi (Headliner award 1964, chmn. employment com. 1966, chmn. Date with the Press 1970). Home: 4080 NW 165th St Miami FL 33054 Office: PO Box 975 Miami FL 33101

NEUMANN, HANS, accountant, auditor; b. Port Arthur, Tex.,July 15, 1923; s. Rudolf A. and Hedwig (Thiem) N.; student Tex. A. and M. U., 1942-43, 46; B.B.A., U. Houston, 1949, postgrad., 1955-57; m. Mildred M. Moerbe, Dec. 28, 1944; children—Margo Ann, Diana Lyn. Accountant A. O. Smith Corp., Houston, 1949-52; internal auditor The Fluor Corp., Ltd., Houston, Los Angeles, 1952-60; asst. comptroller Wyatt Industries, Inc., Houston, 1960-63; adminstrv. asst., project Mohole, Brown & Root, Inc., Houston, 1963-67 state auditor. systems analyst State of Tex., Austin, 1967—. Served with Signal Corps, AUS, 1943-46. C.P.A., Tex. Mem. Am. Inst. C.P.A.'s, Tex. Soc. C.P.A.'s, Tex. State Agy. Bus. Adminstrs. Assn. (pres. 1971-72). Home: Route 2 Box 258 Bastrop TX 78602 Office: PO Box 12067 Austin TX 78711

NEUMANN, JOHN EDWARD, SR., physician; b. Highland, Ill., Sept. 28, 1919; s. John G. and Stella (Litz) N.; student St. Louis U., 1937-40, Wis. U. summer, 1940; B.S., U. Ill., at Chgo., 1942; M.D., 1943; m. Idabelle Nischwitz, Sept. 22, 1943; children—Theodore Henry, Kathryn Sue, William Thomas, John Edward, Mary, Martha. Intern St. Louis City Hosp., St. Louis, 1944; resident in internal medicine Alexian Bros. Hosp., St. Louis, 1946-47, Kennedy VA Hosp., Memphis, 1947-49; practice medicine specializing in internal medicine Paris, Tenn., 1949—; staff mem. Rhea Clinic, Paris, Tenn., Henry County Gen. Hosp. Served from lt. (j.g.) to lt., M.C., USNR, 1944-46. Diplomate Am Bd. Internal Medicine. Fellow A.C.P., Am. Coll. Gastroenterology, Am. Coll. Chest Physicians; mem. Paris, Henry County C. of C. (named Man of Year 1968), W. Tenn. Heart Assn. (pres. 1961). Roman Catholic. Elks. Rotarian (Paris, Tenn.). Home: 501 Dunlap St Paris TN 38242 Office: 302 Caldwell St Paris TN 38242

NEUMANN, OTTO, trading stamps and redemption exec.; b. Winnipeg, Man., Can., Jan. 2, 1900; s. Henry and Amanda (Foote) N.; brought to U.S., 1902, naturalized, 1923; student U.S. Army Sch., Coblenz, Germany, 1920-21, U. Tenn., 1961-64; m. Jenny Ann Hartung, Jan. 21, 1923; 1 son, William Ashley; m. 2d, Beatrix L. Moody, Apr. 8, 1957; 1 dau., Colleene A. (Mrs. William A. Wilmoth). With Anaconda Co., Great Falls and Anaconda, Mont., 1917-18, 1939-44; auditor, controller Giesche Spolka Akcyjna, Katowice Poland, Anaconda-Harriman Interests, 1928-39; treas., asst. sec. Electromanganese Corp., Knoxville, Tenn., 1944-56; plant accountant Foote Mineral Co., Knoxville, 1956-58; controller Sea Island Co., Sea Island, Ga., 1959-60; staff accountant Timmons & Co., C.P.A.'s, Knoxville, 1961-65; with Consumers Res. Green Stamp Co., Inc., Knoxville, 1965—, v.p., gen. mgr., 1965—. Served with AUS, 1919-23. Mem. Nat. Assn. Accountants (emeritus life asso.), A.I.M. (mem. pres.'s council 1971), V.F.W. (post comdr. 1927). Elk. Home: 908 Cedar Lane Knoxville TN 37912 Office: 111 Patton St Knoxville TN 37917

NEUROTH, MILTON LOUIS, pharmacy educator; b. Ft. Wayne, Ind., Nov. 12, 1908; s. Charles E. and Emily (Hinkley) N.; B.S., Purdue U., 1935; M.S., 1940, Ph.D. 1946; m. H. Louise Jones, July 7, 1948; children—Grover C. III, Robert W. Jones (step-sons), Rhea Maureen (Mrs. John Baldino, Jr.). Control chemist Gen. Cable Corp., 1929-34; pharmacist Meyer Brothers Drug Co., 1935-36; instr. to asst. prof. pharmacy Ohio Northern, 1936-43; instr. pharm. chemistry, Purdue, 1943-44; asst. prof. pharmacy Med. Coll. of Va., 1946-47; asso. prof., 1947-49, prof., 1949—, chmn. pharmacy dept., 1949-72. Served with Ind. NG, 1934-37. Mem. Friends of Hist. Pharmacy (pres. 1969—), Am. Med. Writers Assn., Am., Va. pharm. assns., Va. Soc. Hosp. Pharm., Rho Chi (pres. 1954-56), Kappa Psi (nat. pres. 1957-59), Phi Lambda Upsilon, Sigma Xi. Mason. Club: Lions (pres. 1970-71). Contbr. chpts. in textbooks, also articles profl. jours. Home: 903 Woodberry Rd Richmond VA 23229 Office: 12th and Clay Sts Richmond VA 23219

NEUSTADT, DAVID HAROLD, physician; b. Evansville, Ind., Dec. 2, 1925; s. Mose and Leah (Epstein) N.; student DePauw U., 1943-44, 46-47; M.D., U. Louisville, 1950; m. Carolyn Jacobson, June 15, 1952; children—Susan Miriam, Jeffrey Bruce, Robert Alan. Intern Morrisania City Hosp., N.Y.C., 1950-51; resident Lenox Hill Hosp., N.Y.C., 1951-52, trainee in rheumatic diseases, 1952-53, resident, 1953-54; practice medicine, specializing in rheumatic diseases, Louisville, 1954—; chief arthritis clinic Louisville Gen. Hosp., 1960—; asst. prof. medicine U. Louisville Sch. Medicine, 1960-67, asso. prof. clin. medicine, 1967—, head sect. rheumatic diseases 1960—; chief dept. medicine Jewish Hosp., Louisville, pres. med. staff, 1966—; cons. in rheumatology VA, 1970—. Former chmn. med. sci. com. Ky. chpt. Arthritis Found. Served with AUS, 1944-46. Fellow Am. Med. Writers Assn.; mem. A.C.P., N.Y. Rheumatism Soc., Ky. (pres. 1956-57), Am. rheumatism assns., A.M.A., A.A.A.S., N.Y. Acad. Scis., Internat. Soc. Internal Medicine. Jewish religion. Mason (32 deg., Shriner). Elk. Author: The Chemistry and Therapy of Collagen Diseases, 1963. Editor: Arthritis Abstracts, References Indexes, 1970—. Contbr. numerous articles to profl. jours. Research on rheumatic diseases. Home: 216 Smithfield Rd Louisville KY 40207 Office: Med Towers Louisville KY 40202

NEUSTADT, WALTER, JR., petroleum co. exec.; b. Ardmore, Okla., Mar. 9, 1919; s. Walter and Doris (Westheimer) N.; B.S., Yale, 1940; M.S., Okla. U., 1941; m. Dolores Krasne, Aug. 7, 1951; children— Nancy Kay, Susan Lynn, Kathy Krasne. Geologist, Westheimer-Neustadt Corp., Ardmore, Okla., 1946-60, exec. v.p., 1960-65, pres., 1965—; dir. Dial Financial Corp., Des Moines, Exchange Nat. Bank, Ardmore. Pres., Ardmore United Fund, 1956-57, Ardmore Devel. Authority, 1968; mem. Okla. Dept. Libraries, 1965-69, chmn., 1965-67; v. p. Nat. Jewish Hosp., Denver, 1965—. Bd. regents U. Okla. Served to 1st lt. USAAF, 1942-45. Mem. Am. Assn. Petroleum Geologists, Soc. Econ. Paleontologists and Mineralogists, Ardmore C. of C. (pres. 1966), Sigma Gamma Epsilon, Omicron Delta Kappa. Republican. Jewish religion. Mason (33 deg.). Rotarian. Home: 1805 Stanley St Ardmore OK 73401 Office: Box 788 911 W Broadway Ardmore OK 73401

NEVILLE, CHARLES WILLIS, physician; b. Dalton, Kan., June 9, 1901; s. Charles and Henrietta Isabella (Randall) N.; A.B., Southwestern Coll., 1924; M.D., Vanderbilt U., 1928; m. Edna Mac Hatfield, Dec. 30, 1928; children—Charles Willis, Gordon H. Intern, Hillman Hosp., Birmingham, Ala., 1928-29; gen. practice medicine, Flat Creek, Ala., 1929-45, Birmingham, Ala., 1945—; mem. staff Carraway Meth. Hosp., Birmingham, Bapt. Hosp., Birmingham. Mem. bd. edn., Birmingham, 1964—. Mem. Am. Acad. Gen. Practice (pres. Ala. chpt. 1958), Jefferson County Med. Soc. (pres. 1966). Home: 4269 Overlook Dr Birmingham AL 35222 Office: 2714 31st Av N Birmingham AL 35207

NEVILLE, CHARLES WILLIS, JR., educator; b. Birmingham, Ala., May, 1931; s. Charles Willis and May (Hatfield) N.; B.A., Vanderbilt U., 1953, M.D., 1956; D.M.S., State U. N.Y., 1970; m. Martha Eugenia Wheeler, Mar. 21, 1957; children—Ann Elizabeth, John William, Paul Wheeler, Susan May, Nancy Jean. Intern Vanderbilt Hosp., 1956-57; resident psychiatry McLean Hosp., 1957-59, Beth-Israel Hosp., Boston, 1959-60; teaching fellow psychiatry Harvard Med. Sch., 1959-60; research tng. psychiatry D.M.S. Program, State U. N.Y. at Bklyn., 1962-64; asso. psychiatry Duke U. Med. Center, 1964-65, asst. prof. psychiatry, 1965-70, asso. prof., 1970—, med. dir. Highland Hosp. div. 1965—. Served to capt. AUS 1960-62. Diplomate Am. Bd. Neurology and Psychiatry. Fellow Am. Psychiatric Assn.; mem. Am., N.C. med. assns. A.A.A.S., N.Y. Acad. Sci., N.C. Neuropsychiat. Assn. (sec. 1969—), Asheville C. of C. Contbr. articles profl. jours. Home: 56 Woodbury Rd Asheville NC 28804

NEVILLE, JAMES FRANCIS, lawyer, govt. ofcl.; b. Harrison, N.Y., Sept. 10, 1907; s. Denis and Annie (Hanratty) N.; A.B., Georgetown U., 1932, J.D., 1938; m. Mary R. Gilroy, Nov. 8, 1935; children—James Francis, Thomas Joseph, Martha Ann, Gerald Denis, Kathleen Ann. Admitted to D.C. bar, 1938; with Dept. Agr., 1934-37; atty. legal div. FHA, 1938-46, asst. zone commr. western U.S., 1947-48, dep. asst. commr. field operations, 1948-51, zone commr. eastern U.S. 1951-54, regional dir. southwestern U.S., 1954-61, operations commr., 1961-68, dir. Internat. div., 1968-70, asst. adminstr. Farmers Home Adminstrn., 1971—; pres., dir. Indsl. Loan Corp. Va.; v.p. realty holding and constrn. corps. in Ohio; mgr. Navy Dept.-owned realty throughout world; dir. Capehart Housing Projects, 1958-59; dir. rental housing, mortgage finance Nat. Assn. Home Builders, Washington, 1959-61. Mem. faculty Practicing Law Inst. Recipient Merrick medal Georgetown U., 1932. Mem. Bar Assn. D.C., Gamma Eta Gamma. Club: Fairfax (Va.) Country. Co-Author: What Builders Should Know About Garden-Type Apartments; The Apartment Plan. Contbr. articles on mortgage financing to publs. Home: 3228 Juniper Lane Falls Church VA 22044 Office: Dept of Agr-FHA Independence Av SW WashingTon DC 20411

NEVILLE, JOHN, editor art, drama editor Dallas Morning News. Office: Dallas News-Communications Center Dallas TX 75222*

NEVILLE, WILLIAM VINKLEY, JR., lawyer; b. Montgomery, Ala., July 23, 1934; s. William V. and Mildred (Greene) N.; B.S., Ala. Polytech. Inst., 1956; LL.B., U. Va., 1959; m Anna Sigridur Gisladottir, Apr. 8, 1961; children—William Vinkley, III, Margaret Gudrun. Admitted to Ala. bar, 1959; since practiced in Eufaula, Ala., 1962—. Mem. Ala. Ho. of Reps., 1967-71. Soc., Eufaula Heritage Assn.; chmn. Hist. Chattahoochee Commn. Served with USAF, 1959-61. Mem. Phi Kappa Phi, Omicron Delta Kappa, Pi Kappa Alpha. Home: Country Club Rd Eufaula AL 36027 Office: Box 239 Eufaula AL 36027

NEVINS, ELLIOT HOWARD, broadcasting exec.; b. New Bedford, Mass., Feb. 4, 1933; s. Robert and Lillian Nevins; grad. N.Y.U., 1955; m. Rose Caparulo, Feb. 5, 1961; children—Michael Keith, Joshua Gregory. With WOV, N.Y.C., WKNY, Kingston, N.Y., WSKN, Saugerties, N.Y., WJET, Erie, Pa., WNHC Radio and TV, New Haven; air personality WIOD, Miami, Fla., also program dir.; pres. sta. WIOD-WIOD-FM, Miami. Mem. adv. com. United Fund Miami, Variety Childrens Hosp. Bd. dirs. Miami Pub. Library, City of Miami Beautification Com. Served with AUS, 1951-53. Decorated Purple Heart. Named Outstanding Personality of Year, Civitan Internat., 1963-64. Mem. Interam. C. of C. (dir.), Sigma Delta Chi. Home: 671 NE 57th St Miami FL 33137 Office: 1401 North Bay Causeway Miami FL 33138

NEW, WILLIAM LAFAYETTE, former telephone exec.; b. nr. Swainsboro, Ga., Mar. 20, 1901; s. William Madison and Daisy (Powell) N.; student Mercer U., 1921, 26; m. Minnie Lee Grant, Aug. 8, 1924; children— Elizabeth (Mrs. O. F. Loosier, Junior), Grant. Prof., Latin and algebra Lyons High Sch., 1926; auditor So. Bell Tel. & Tel. Co., Atlanta, 1927-35; bus. mgr. Thomaston Telephone Co. (Ga.), 1935-49; pres., owner Commerce Telephone Co. (Ga.), 1950-68, now ret. Lt. col. Gov's Staff, 1963—. Adv. council Ga. Recreation Com. Bd. trustees Brewton Parker Coll. Recipient certificate for distinguished service, Am. Legion, 1945; citizenship award Vets Fgn. Wars, 1962; recreation award Am. Legion and Ruritan Club, 1962. Mem. Knight of The Garter, Commerce C. of C. Baptist. Mason (Shriner). Kiwanian. Home: Altamonte Springs FL 32701

NEWBERGER, SETH AMOS, distbg. co. exec.; b. N.Y.C., Jan. 2, 1937; s. David William and Jane (Pollak) N.; student Cornell U., 1955-59; J.D., N.Y.U., 1962; m. Kaye Lynn Epstein, Oct. 13, 1963; 1 dau., Abigail. Admitted to N.Y. bar, 1963, practiced in N.Y.C., 1963-65; mem. firm Frim Fried & Mailmon, 1963-65; treas. Central Distbg. Co., San Antonio, 1965—, also dir. Mem. San Antonio Soc. Security Analysts. Club: Cornell (San Antonio). Home: 513 Mandalay Dr E San Antonio TX 78212 Office: PO Box 1229 San Antonio TX 78294

NEWBERN, CAPTOLIA DENT, educator; b. Dublin, Ga., Sept. 22, 1902; d. John West and Arnetta (Rozier) Dent; B.S., Paine Coll., 1925; Mus.B., Talladega Coll., 1937. M.S.W. (Porter Lee fellow), Columbia, 1942, Ed.D. (Intergroup Edn. scholar), 1954; m. Samuel Hiawatha Newbern, Dec. 2, 1939 (dec. Nov. 1949). Instr. English, Latin, history, high sch. dept. Paine Coll., Augusta, Ga., 1925-31, head music dept., 1931-34; instr. sch. music Calhoun (Ala.) Sch., 1935-36; dir. coll.-community extension program, instr. sch. music, dir. glee club, Drewry Practice High Sch., Talladega (Ala.) Coll., 1937-42; employee counselor War Dept., Ordanance Bur., Washington, 1942-46; exec. sec. East 5th St. br. YWCA, Plainfield, N.J., 1946-48; asst. prof. English Albany (Ga.) State Coll., 1948-49; dir. music and Christian edn. Williams Instl. Christian M.E. Ch., N.Y.C., 1952-58; exec. dir. Heart of Harlem Neighborhood Council, Protestant Council Greater N.Y., Inc., N.Y.C., 1956-58; adminstrv. asst., ednl. dir. 7th Episcopal dist. Christian M.E. Ch., 1958-62; chmn. dept. religion and philosophy, prof. religion Lane Coll., Jackson, Tenn., 1962—, tchr. social studies Upward Bound, Office Econ. Opportunity, 1966-67. Active various community drives. Mem. nat. com. Democratic party, 1968. Mem. Tenn. Commn. on Aging; bd. dirs. Jackson Mental Health Center; citizens adv. comm. Tenn. Jackson Madison County Dept. Pub. Welfare. Recipient plaque for Distinguished Service Lane Coll., 1967-68, Tchr. of Year, 1966-67; citation War Dept., 1946, Scroll of Honor Theta Iota chpt. Omega Psi Phi, 1966-67. Mem. N.A.A.C.P., Fed. Women's Clubs, Internat. Council Social Welfare, Nat. Conf. Social Welfare, Am. Acad. Religion, Hymn Soc. Am., Nat. Council Chs., Am. Assn. U. Profs., Religious Edn. Assn., Acad. Polit. Sci., Internat. Platform Assn., Top Ladies of Distinction, Tenn. Tchrs. Assn., Pi Lambda Theta. Author: Making the Missionary Society Work in the Local Church, 1956; Stewardess Manual of the Christian Methodist Episcopal Church, 1962; Tithing is the Answer, 1966. Home: 5833 Cobbs Creek Pkwy Philadelphia PA 19143 Office: Lane Coll Jackson TN 38301

NEWBERN, COPELAND DAVIS, food products co. exec.; b. Powells Point, N.C., Aug. 22, 1911; B.S. in Agr., U. Fla., 1933, postgrad., 1936-37; m. Edna Creekmore, Aug. 24, 1935; children—Caroline (Mrs. John Shepard), Nancy. Tchr. vocational agr., coach, Moyock, N.C., 1933-34; operator vocational agr. dept., Hernando County, N.C., Brooksville, 1935; agrl. agt., Hernando and Manatee County, 1938-45; pres., owner Newbern Groves, Inc., 1946—; pres., owner Fancy Fresh Farms, Inc., Tampa, Fla., 1967—; dir. Northside Bank Tampa, Universal Foods Miami (Fla.); pres. Newbern Truck Terminal, Inc., Tampa, 1955—. Mem. Stephens Coll. Dads' Com., 1967-69, mem. bd. curators, 1970—. Mem. Greater Tampa (bd. govs. 1970—), North Tampa chambers commerce, Fla. Fresh Citrus Shippers Assn., United Fresh Fruit and Vegetable Assn. (dir. 1972—). Clubs: Tampa Yacht and Country, Florida; University (Tampa). Home: 912 S Himes Av Tampa FL 33609 Office: Newbern Groves Inc PO Box 17237 Tampa FL 33612

NEWBOLT, LAWRENCE EDWARD, civil engr.; b. Shidler, Okla., Sept. 23, 1939; s. Clarence Dave and Helen (Ferguson) N.; B.S. in Civil Engring., Lamar State Coll. Tech., 1962; M.E. in Civil Engring., Tex. A. and M. U., 1970; m. Patsy Anne Smith, Aug. 26, 1961; children—Christine Renee, Elizabeth Anne. Project engr. U.S. C.E., Galveston, Tex., 1962—. Registered profl. engr., Tex. Methodist. Office: PO Box 1229 Galveston TX 77550

NEWBY, HI EASTLAND, physician; b. Del Rio, Tex., Dec. 8, 1929; s. Byron Elvel and Amanda (Eastland) N.; tudent Schreiner Inst., 1947-48; B.A., Baylor U., 1951, M.D., 1957; postgrad. Sul Ross State U., 1948, 51-52; m. Ona Darlene Northcutt, Apr. 25, 1959; children—Byron Edgar, Hi Eastland. Intern, Bexar County Hosp., Dist., San Antonio, 1957-58; practice family medicine, Del Rio, 1957—; chief staff Val Verde Meml. Hosp., Del Rio, 1968-69; med. cons. Tex. Rehab. Agy., San Antonio area, 1966—; examining physician, So. Pacific Co., 1959—. Mem. charter commn., City of Del Rio, 1966-67. Mem. Del Rio Ind. Sch. Dist. Bd., 1968-71, pres., 1969-71; pres. San Felipe Del Rio Consol. Ind. Sch. Dist., 1971-72; mem. Val Verde County Sch. Bd., 1972—. Diplomate Am. Bd. Family Practice. Mem. A.M.A., Tex. Med. Assn., Tex. Acad. Gen. Practice (dir. 1966-70), Tex. Acad. Family Physicians (chmn. membership and credential com. 1971-72). Mason (Shriner), Rotarian. Home: 201 Park Av Del Rio TX 78840 Office: 1011 E 7th St PO Box 1549 Del Rio TX 78840

NEWBY, JERRY BOWERS, petroleum geologist, engr.; b. Elk, Kan., Aug. 8, 1890; s. Hiram Warner and Ceoria Alice (Bowers) N.; A.B., U. Okla., 1912; student U. Chgo., 1912-13; m. Edna Cash, May 31, 1922; 1 dau., Mary Margaret (Mrs. Robert Lee Pierce). Geologist Gulf Oil Corp., Tulsa, 1913-17; cons. geologist, Tulsa, 1917-18, Oklahoma City, 1919-24; resident mgr. Petroleum Reclamation Co., Bradford, Pa., 1924-29; cons. geologist, engr., Oklahoma City, 1929-—. Served as pvt., F.A., U.S. Army, 1918. Mem. Am. Assn. Petroleum Geologists (a founder, hon. mem.), Inst. Mining, Metall. and Petroleum Engrs., Oklahoma City Geol. Soc. (hon. life mem.; pres. 1935), Am. Inst. Profl. Geologists (charter mem.), Sigma Chi, Gamma Alpha, Sigma Gamma Epsilon. Clubs: Petroleum, Men's Dinner, Engineering. Address: 1816 NW 23d St Oklahoma City OK 73106

NEWBY, JOHN SMITH, structural engr., govt. ofcl.; b. Burkesville, Ky., July 12, 1915; s. William H. and Beulah (Smith) N.; student Lindsey Wilson Coll., 1935-37; B.A., Berea Coll., 1939; B.S., U. Ky., 1947; m. Halliene Ramsey, June 30, 1947; children—John, Deborah, Carl, Hugh. Bridge design engr. State of Cal., Sacramento, 1947-52; bldg. design engr. U.S. Army C.E., Savannah, Ga., 1952-58; gen. engr. U.S. Army Ordnance, Huntsville, Ala., 1958-61; structural engr. Voice of Am., Washington, 1961-—. Pres. Tillinghurst Elementary Sch. P.T.A., Columbus, Ga., 1958; mem. Athens (Ala.) council Boy Scouts Am., 1960-61. Served to lt. col. USAAF, 1941-63. Registered profl. engr., Ky. Mem. Am. Soc. C.E., Meterol. Soc., Sigma Pi Sigma, Methodist. Home: 4133 Teton Pl Alexandria VA 22312 Office: 25 M St SW Washington DC 20547

NEWCOMB, CLAUDE LETCHER, automotive co. exec.; b. nr. Forest, Va., June 2, 1907; s. James Letcher and Mary Lelia (Wilson) N.; student pub. schs.; m. Hilda Mae Barton, Nov. 24, 1937; 1 son, Wayne E. Founder Lynchburg Battery & Ignition Co., Inc. (Va.), 1930, pres., treas., 1930-—; founder, pres. Newcomb Auto Parts, Farmville, Va., 1946-—; founder, sec. Newcomb, Inc., Lynchburg, 1971-—; dir. Bank Central Va., Lynchburg. Bd. suprs. Bedford County, Va., 1963; chmn. Equalization Bd., Lynchburg, Va., 1970. Methodist. Mason (Shriner), Elk. Lion. Home: 3015 Ravenwood St Lynchburg VA 24503 Office: 406 5th St Lynchburg VA 24505

NEWELL, CHARLES VANCE, pub. relations counselor; b. Denver, Jan. 23, 1914; s. Charles Haney and Grace (Vance) N.; B.A., Yale, 1935; m. Laura Bess Lee, Feb. 12, 1956; 1 son, Thomas Lee. Mem. editorial staff Houston Chronicle, 1935-50, 55-57; exec. Asso. En. Contractors Am., Austin, Tex., 1950-55, Max Jacobs Agy., Houston, 1957-60; partner firm Jacobs-Keeper-Newell, 1960-64; v.p. Keeper-Newell & Assos., 1964-67; pres., owner Vance Newell &Assos., Houston, 1967-—; dir. Louis Werner Saw Mill Co., 1968. Served with USAAF, 1942-45. Mem. Pub. Relations Soc. Am., Alpha Sigma Phi, Delta Sigma Phi. Democrat. Presbyn. (elder). Clubs: Houston Press; Yale of Southeastern Texas (past bd. dirs.). Home: 2301 Fountain View Houston TX 77027 Office: 3210 Marquart Houston TX 77027

NEWELL, EDWARD ALPHONSO, physician; b. Hyannis, Mass., Oct. 4, 1926; s. Alphonso Murat and Blanche E. (Sauter) N.; student Western Md. Coll., 1942-44; M.D., U. Md., 1948; m. Hannah Jo Parris, Oct. 1, 1962; children—Jo Anne, Kappa, Parris Layne. Intern, South Baltimore (Md.) Gen. Hosp., 1948-49, resident, 1949-50; resident Kings County Hosp., N.Y.C., 1950-51; otolaryngology fellow Lahey Clinic, Boston, 1951-52; practice medicine specializing in otolaryngology, Dallas, 1952-—; mem. staff Baylor U. Med. Center, Parkland Meml., St. Paul hosps., Children's Med. Center, Presbyn., VA hosps. (all Dallas); asso. otolaryngology prof. U. Tex. Southwestern Med. Sch., Dallas, 1952-—; pres. Dallas Speech and Hearing Center, 1955-58, Caruth Meml. Rehab. Center, Dallas, 1961-62; bd. govs. Northwood Inst., Dallas. Bd. dirs. Dallas Civic Opera, Dallas Civic Ballet. Fellow A.C.S., Internat. Coll. Surgeons; mem. Am. Hearing Soc. (dir., past v.p.), Pan Am., Tex. med. assns., Am., Dallas (past pres.) acads. opthalmology and otolaryngology, Am. Laryngol., Rhinol. and Otol. Soc., Pan-Am. Assn. Otorhinolaryngology and Bronchoesophogology, Tex. Otolaryn. Assn. (past pres.), Tex. Soc. Opthalmology and Otolaryngology, A.M.A., Dallas County Med. Soc., Dallas So. Clin. Soc. Home: 7225 N Jan Mar Dr Dallas TX 75230 Office: 3207 Turtle Creek Blvd Dallas TX 75219

NEWELL, HAROLD MOSLEY, constrn. co. exec.; b. nr. Montgomery, Ala., May 6, 1912; s. William Samuel and Barrie Bonham (Mosley) N.; student Ga. Inst. Tech., 1935; B.S., Birmingham So. U., 1936; m. Jimmie Louise Jacks, Dec. 29, 1946; children—Harold Jacks, Edwin Lee. Chemist Swan Chm. Co., Birmingham, Ala., 1936-37; supt. hwy. constrn. Newell Bros., Ala., Miss., S.C., 1938-42; engr. Pan Am. Airways, South Am., 1943-44; co-owner Newell Bros. Constrn. Co., Montgomery, 1945-—; pres. Newell Roadbuilders, Inc., Hull, Ala., 1958-—. Mem. Ga. Hwy. Contractors Assn., Theta Kappa Nu. Rotarian. Club: Arrowhead Country (Montgomery). Home: RD No 1 Hope Hull AL 36043 Office: Rt 1 U S Hwy 31 Hope Hull AL 36043

NEWELL, WARDEN JOHN, petroleum sales industry exec.; b. Carthage, Mo., Dec. 11, 1907; s. James Patton and Jessie Maude (Caffee) N.; B.S. magna cum laude, Princeton, 1929; m. Bonnie Ursula Boone, Jan. 8, 1933; children—Laurie, Warden John, Joanna, David, Thomas Van Auken (adopted). Geologist Brit. Govt. and Phillips Petroleum Co., 1929-32; sales exec. Gulf Oil Corp., 1932-38; with Newell Oil Co., Alpine, Tex., 1939-—, pres., 1939-—. Pres. Sirocco Devel. Corp., Alpine, 1952-—; sec., treas. Alpine TV Cable, Inc., 1961-—, Red House Ranch, Inc., Alpine, 1971-—. Mem. Tex. Good Neighbor Commn., 1961-62, Internat. Good Neighbor Council, 1958-—; chmn. Nat. Parks Devel. Com., 1970-—; Treas. Nat. Found., 1955-—. Councilman, Alpine, 1962-63. Recipient award most outstanding service to tourist devel. Gov. Tex., 1969, Award of Distinction Tex. Oil Jobbers Assn., 1970. Mem. Tex. Oil Jobbers Assn. (dir. 1948-—; pres. 1963), Alpine C. of C. (pres. 1941-43). Democrat. Episcopalian (Bishops warden 1957). Rotarian (pres. 1945-46). Author pamphlet series Newell-Gulf West Texas Road Logs, 1966. Home: 203 E Murphy St Alpine TX 79830 Office: Box 390 Alpine TX 79830

NEWELL, WILLIAM EDWARD, banker; b. Bridgeport, Tex., Sept. 18, 1907; s. John P. and Margaret (Campbell) N.; A.B., U. Tenn., 1929; postgrad. U. Wis., 1949; m. Mary Elizabeth Ferris, Nov. 6, 1931; children— Edward, John, David, Sarah. Admitted to Tenn. bar, 1931; practiced in Knoxville, 1929-31; asst. trust officer Fidelity Bankers Trust Co., Knoxville, 1931-41; sr. v.p. Hamilton Nat. Bank, 1941-58; pres., dir. 1st Nat. Bank of Sullivan County, Kingsport, Tenn., 1958-—, also chief exec. officer; dir. Gen. Shale Products Corp., Appalachian Nat. Life Ins. Co.; dir. Nashville br. Fed. Res. Bank, 1959-61. Mem. devel. council U. Tenn.; mem. com. of 100 Emory U.; mem. exec. council Tenn. Taxpayers Assn. Bd. dirs., mem. exec. com. Holston Valley Community Hosp. Mem. Am. (Tenn. v.p. 1965-66), Tenn. (pres. 1967-68, exec. council 1967-—) bankers assns., Kingsport C. of C. (pres. 1964), Sigma Nu. Clubs: Rotary, Ridgefields Country; Kingsport (Tenn.) Country: City (Knoxville); Bristol Country. Home: 1321 Linville St Kingsport TN 37662 Office: PO Box 889 Kingsport TN 37662

NEWFIELD, MAYER ULLMAN, lawyer; b. Birmingham, Ala., Apr. 5, 1905; s. Morris and Leah (Ullman) N.; A.B., Howard Coll., Birmingham, Ala., 1927; postgrad. Harvard Law Sch., 1928-29; LL.B., U. Ala., 1931; m. Bertha Lehman, June 8, 1938; children—Jane, Melanie. Admitted to Ala. bar, 1931, U.S. Supreme Ct. bar, 1941; mem. firm London, Yancey & Brower, Birmingham, 1931-34; supervising atty. Home Owners' Loan Corp., 1934-35; sr. trial atty. chief of litigation and enforcement sect., asst. regional adminstr. SEC; Atlanta, Washington, Phila., N.Y.C., 1935-47; asst. atty. City of Birmingham, 1948-56; gen. practice Birmingham, 1956-—; sec., v.p., dir. N. Ala. Mineral Devel. Co. Pres. Civic Opera Assn., 1964-66; nat. commr. Anti-Defamation League, 1956-—; Ala. co-chmn. Nat. Conf. Christians and Jews, 1964-—. Bd. dirs. Anti-Tb Assn. of Jefferson County, 1968-—, Leo N. Levi Hosp., Hot Springs, 1968-—, Jewish Children's Home, 1968-—; pres. bd. dirs. Jewish Community Center, 1970-71. Mem. Am., Ala., Birmingham bar assns. Democrat. Jewish religion. Mem. B'nai B'rith. Home: 2900 Thornhill Rd Birmingham AL 35213 Office: City Fed Bldg Birmingham AL 35203

NEWLIN, BOB J., pipeline co. exec.; b. Port Lavaca, Tex., Sept. 9, 1932; s. Carl Earnest and Catherine Elizabeth (Heinroth) N.; B.J., U. Tex., 1953; m. Constance Key Horine, Apr. 26, 1958; children—Christopher Michael, Kimberly Key. Asso. editor Houston Mag., Houston C. of C., 1956-57; asso. editor publs. Transcontinental Gas Pipe Line Corp., Houston, 1957, editor publs., 1958-69, asst. dir. publs., 1969-—. Mem. publ. information com. A.R.C., Houston and Harris County, 1959-70. Served with AUS, 1953-55. Mem. Internat. Assn. Bus. Communicators, Pub. Relations Soc. Am., Southeastern Gas Assn., Press Club Houston, Houston C. of C. (mem. information and publs. coms. 1958-69). Democrat. Presbyn. Home: 2606 Centenary St Houston TX 77005 Office: 3100 Travis St Houston TX 77006

NEWLIN, DIKA, composer, musicologist; b. Portland, Ore., Nov. 22, 1923; d. Claude Milton and Dorothy (Hull) Newlin; B.A., Mich. State U., 1939; M.A., U. Cal. at Los Angeles, 1941; Ph.D., Columbia, 1945; L.H.D., Upsala (N.J.) Coll., 1964. Instr. Western Md. Coll., 1945-46, asst. prof., 1946-49; asst. prof. fine arts Syracuse U., 1949-51; founder, prof. music, head music dept. Drew U., 1952-65; prof. music N. Tex. State U., Denton, Tex., since 1965-—. Fulbright fellow, Vienna, 1951-52; recipient Mahler Medal Honor, Bruckner Soc. Am., 1957, Silver medal French Minister Fgn. Affairs, Ring of Excellence, Sigma Alpha Iota. Mem. Am. Music Center, Am. Musicol. Soc., Broadcast Music, Inc., Pi Kappa Lambda, Sigma Alpha Iota, Phi Kappa Phi. Author: Bruckner-Mahler-Schoenberg, 1947. Editor, translator Schoenberg, Style and Idea, 1950; Rufer, The Works of Arnold Schoenberg, 1962; Werner, Felix Mendelssohn, 1963, others. Mem. editorial bd. Pan Pipes of Sigma Alpha Iota, 1947-68. Contbr. Book of Knowledge, New Cath. Ency., The Commonwealth of Music, Ency. Judaica. Home: Box 13288 N T Sta Denton TX 76203

NEWMAN, ANDREW LEO, JR., govt. ofcl.; b. Phillipsburg, N.J., Sept. 15, 1918; s. Andrew L. and Alice E. (Troxell) N.; A.B. summa cum laude, Lafayette Coll., 1940, A.M., Columbia U., 1941; postgrad. study Northwestern U., 1941-42, Ohio State U., 1942; m. Lois M. Gardner, Nov. 2, 1946; children—Lawrence Lee, Debra Loanne, Julie Lynn. State editor Morning Free Press, Easton, Pa., 1936-39; asst. dir. pub. relations Northwestern U., 1941; nat. dir. pub. relations, publs. Am. Vets. Com., 1946-48; asso. editor Army Times Pub. Co., 1948-49; information officer U.S.P.H.S., 1950; lectr., instr. Am. U. since 1950; dir. information Def. Solid Fuels Adminstrn. Dept. Interior 1951-53, div. information Office of Sec., 1954-55; asst. dir. information Dept. of Interior, 1955, dep. dir. information, 1956. Mem. Acad. Polit. Sci., Phi Beta Kappa. Contbr. World Book Ency. Home: 4647 N 38th Pl N Arlington VA 22207 Office: Dept of Interior Washington DC 20240

NEWMAN, CHESTER FRANK, life ins. co. exec.; b. Greenville, Ky., Dec. 8, 1915; s. Wyatt Black and Ida Rushie (Hudson) N.; student U.S. Navy Service Sch., 1944; m. Margaret Denham, Apr. 12, 1941; children—Mitchell Chester, Courtney. With Western and So. Life Ins. Co., Vanceburg, Ky., 1947-—, staff mgr., 1955-—; real estate appraiser, Vanceburg, 1953-—; dir. Citizens Deposit Bank, Vanceburg. Instr. life underwriters tng. class, Maysville, Ky., 1954-55. Mem. bd. Lewis County Fair, 1947-—. Mem. Lewis County Bd. Edn., 1956-60; life commr. Republican Party. Served with USNR, 1944-46. Methodist. Lion (pres. 1952-53). Home: Route 7 Vanceburg KY 41179 Office: 615 Forest Av Maysville KY 41056

NEWMAN, CYNTHIA STAIR, govt. ofcl.; b. Mpls., Mar. 24, 1922; d. John Stewart and Bernice (Barber) Dalrymple; grad. Smith Coll.; LL.B., U. Va., 1944; m. Carson Boru Newman, May 16, 1958; children—Robert Hamill, Nancy Stair, Pamela Barber (Mrs. Zimmerman), Tracy Stewart, Christopher Carson. Admitted to Va. bar, 1944; atty. UN Relief and Rehabilitation Adminstrn., 1944-45; nat. dir. Rep. Open Forums, 1946-48; asst. to chmn. Rep. Senate Com., 1948-50; pres. Waters Travel Service, 1963-72; mem. Rep. Nat. Com., Va., 1956-58, 68-—; finance chmn. Va. State Rep. Party, 1959-62, vice chmn., 1952-56, 62-68; sec. Commonwealth of Va., 1970-—. Bd. dirs. Met. Washington YMCA; mem. Nat. Tourism Resources and Review Commn. Mem. Am., Va. bar assns. Mem. Am. Soc. Travel Agts., Soroptimists. Unitarian. Address: 3535 Half Moon Circle Falls Church VA 22044

NEWMAN, DAVID, JR., musician; b. Corsicana, Tex., Feb. 24, 1933; s. David and Louise (Cavanaugh) N.; student pub. schs.; m. Esther Rae Peterson, Nov. 14, 1954; children—Elizabeth (stepdau.), Andre, Cadino, Benji. Performed with T-Bone Walker, Lowell Fulson; with Ray Charles band as tenor and alto saxophonist and flute player, 1954-64; rec. artist Atlantic Records, 1959-—; formed own group, 1966-—. Albums include: Ray Charles presents David Fat Head Newman, 1959, Straight Ahead, 1960; Fat Head Comes On, 1962; Cannonball presents David Newman and James Clay, 1962; House of David, Double Barrelled Soul, Newman and McDuff, 1968. Home: 2623 Downing Av Dallas TX 75216 Office: care B & B Booking Agy 1674 Broadway New York City NY 10019

NEWMAN, DONALD HERBERT, mfg. co. exec.; b. Bell, Cal., May 31, 1929; s. Herbert Stanley and Bessie Lois (Hixson) N.; B.S. in Gen. Agr., East Los Angeles Jr. Coll., 1949; B.S., U. Cal. at Davis, 1951; postgrad. Los Angeles State Coll., 1957; m. Bonnie Jean Smith, July 8, 1955; children—Sheryl, Michael, James, Wendy. Sr. accountant Snell & Co., Los Angeles, 1957-62; chief accountant Paul Hardeman, Inc., Stanton, Cal., 1964, Gibson Products Co., Seagonville, Tex., 1964-67; with Peerless Mfg. Co., Dallas, 1967-—, sec.-treas., 1969-—. Served with USAF, 1951-55. C.P.A., Cal. Mem. Am. Inst. Corporate Controllers, Dallas Mgmt. Assn. Presbyn. Home: 5266 Ponderosa Circle Dallas TX 75227 Office: 2811 Walnut Hill Lane Dallas TX 75220

NEWMAN, JAMES EARL, dentist; b. Greenville, Ky., Dec. 14, 1943; s. James Raleigh and Jane Frances (Quisenberry) N.; student Fla. State U., 1961-64; D.D.S., Emory U., 1968; m. Jolene Anne Anderson, Dec. 17, 1966; children—Cynthia Ann, James Earl. Gen. practice dentistry, Fairfax, S.C., 1968-—. Co-owner Ga.-Carolina Seafood, Ltd., Charleston, S.C., 1970-—; cons. dentistry Salkahatchie Community Action Council, 1968-—; affiliate dentist VA, 1968-—; mem. staff Allendale County Hosp., Fairfax, 1968-—. Mem. Fairfax Jr. C. of C. (Man of Year 1969-70, treas. 1970-71), Am., Coastal Dist. dental socs., Pi Kappa Phi, Psi Omega. Republican. Baptist. Address: PO Box 518 Fairfax SC 29827

NEWMAN, JOHN EDWARD, oil bus. exec.; b. Okmulgee, Okla., Dec. 30, 1914; s. William Campbell and Lena (Fuhrman) N.; B.S., Columbia, 1936; m. Florence Bell, June 22, 1945; children—John Edward, Nancy Jean. With Gulf Oil Corp., 1936-37, Prince Bros. Drilling Co., 1937, Parker Drilling Co., 1937-38; partner Newman Bros. Drilling Co., 1938-—; dir. Straus-Frank Co., San Antonio. Bd. dirs. San Antonio Pub. Service Bd. Mem. exec. bd. San Antonio Zool. Soc. Trustee S.W. Research Found. Served to capt. AUS, 1942-45. Clubs: Oak Hills Country, Argyle, San Antonio. Home: 231 W Lynwood St San Antonio TX 78212 Office: 1432 Milam Bldg San Antonio TX 78205

NEWMAN, JOHN WILBUR, chem. engr.; b. Ashland, Ky., Dec. 11, 1937; s. Clarence Mathew and Theresa (Tate) N.; Chem.E. (univ. scholar) U. Cin., 1961; m. Faye Louise Taylor, June 26, 1960; 1 dau., Karen Lynne. Supr. gas chromatography lab. Ashland Oil & Refining Co. (Ky.), 1961-64, research pilot plant engr., 1964-67, research project evaluator, 1967-69, research chem. engr., 1969-—. Mem. Am. Inst. Chem. Engrs., Am. Chem. Soc. (membership chmn. 1966-67), Am. Soc. Testing Materials, Alpha Chi Sigma. Democrat. Baptist. Patentee petrochems. Home: 2740 Jackson Av Ashland KY 41101 Office: 1409 Winchester Av Ashland KY 41101

NEWMAN, LEWIS WINFRED, educator; b. Corpus Christi, Tex., Oct. 4, 1919; s. Walter Winfred and Francis Elizabeth (Harrison) N.; student U. Corpus Christi, 1947-48; B.A., Baylor U., 1950, M.A., 1952; B.D., Southwestern Bapt. Theol. Sem., 1953, M.R.E., 1954, D.R.E., 1958;; m. Rhoda Spruce, Nov. 28, 1941; children—Michael Lewis, Spruce Lee. Ordained to ministry Bapt. Ch., 1948; pastor Burlington (Tex.) Bapt. Ch., 1950-56; asso. prof. U. Corpus Christi (Tex.), 1956-60, prof., adminstr., 1968-—, dir. div. humanities, 1968-—; adminstr. Bapt. Home Mission Bd., Atlanta, 1960-68. Mem. White House Conf. Beautifying Am., 1963-64; pres. Apache Cattle Corp., Hereford, Tex., 1971-—. Mem. adv. bd. Nat. Assn. Conservation Dists., 1960-68. Served with USAF, 1941-45. Mem. Am. Assn. U. Profs., Am. Acad. Religion, Southwestern Assn. Bapt. Tchrs. Religion. Club: Padre Isles Country (Corpus Christi). Author: Understanding Texas Baptist Life 1959, 64, 68; Church Development Ministry, 1963. Contbr. to Soil Stewardship in the Sixties, 1970. Home: 6050 Rio Vista St Corpus Christi TX 78412

NEWMAN, PAUL KENNETH, physician; b. Neptune, N.J., May 27, 1932; s. Edward Alston and Beatrice Emma (Burns) N.; B.S., Bucknell U., 1958; M.D., Temple U., 1962; m. Audrey Mae White, June 14, 1952; children— Linda Susan, Deborah Carol, Paul Kenneth. Inter, U.S. Naval Hosp., Jacksonville, Fla., 1962-63; resident anesthesiology U.S. Naval Hosp., Phila., 1963-65; chief anesthesiology U.S. Naval Hosp., Jacksonville, 1965-69; attending anesthesiologist Bapt. Meml. Hosp., Jacksonville, 1969-—, med. dir. dept. respiratory therapy, 1969-—. Served with USN, 1962-69. Diplomate Am. Bd. Anesthesiologists. Fellow A.C.P., Am. Coll. Anesthesiologists. Home: 2255 Miller Oaks Dr Jacksonville FL 32217 Office: 1453 Louise St Jacksonville FL 32207

NEWMAN, PHILLIP BARBOUR, III, food co. exec.; b. Louisville, May 31, 1932; s. Phillip Barbour and Frances Thompson (Powell) N.; B.E., Yale, 1956, B.S., 1957; m. Eleanor Griffith Tarrant, May 15, 1965; children—Phillip Barbour IV, John. Engr. Westinghouse Electric Corp., Balt., 1960-64; first v.p. mfg. Glenmore Distilleries Co., Louisville, 1964-—, dir., 1970-—. Dir. Bourbon Cooperage Co. Served with USNR, 1956-60. Mem. Ky. Distillers Assn. (chmn. 1972-73). Clubs: Country, Pendennis (Louisville); Yale (N.Y.C.). Home: 3760 Upper Valley Rd Louisville KY 40207 Office: Citizens Plaza Louisville KY 40202

NEWMAN, SANFORD BERNHART, sci. adminstr.; b. N.Y.C., July 26, 1914; s. Otto and Carrie (Bernhart) N.; B.S., Long Island U., 1936; M.A., George Washington U., 1941; Ph.D., U. Md., 1951; m. Dorothy Krall, Aug. 2, 1942; children—Martha, Carl. Trainee U.S. Patent Office, 1939-41; sci. adminstr. Nat. Bur. of Standards, Washington 1941-70, spl. asst. to the dir. for programs, 1970-—. Fellow Royal Microscopical Soc., Wash. Acad. Sci.; mem. Am. Soc. for Testing and Materials, Sigma Xi. Club: Cosmos. Contbr. articles in field to. profl. jours. Home: 3508 Woodbine St Chevy Chase MD 20015 Office: Adminstrn Bldg Washington DC 20234

NEWMAN, STEWART ALBERT, educator; b. Jermyn, Tex., Jan. 26, 1907; s. Virgil Albert and Willie Elnora (Bayless) N.; B.A., Hardin Simmons U., 1930, D.D., 1947; Th.M., Southwestern Sem., 1935, Th.D., 1939; m. Sara Evelyn Knupp, Aug. 15, 1930; children—Charles Virgil, Stewart, Jr., Harvey Knupp. Mem. faculty Southwestern Sem., Fort Worth, 1935-52, Southeastern Sem., Wake Forest, N.C., 1952-66; prof. philosophy Campbell Coll., Buies Creek, N.C., 1966-—. Mem. Town Council, Wake Forest, N.C., 1957-59. Trustee Am. Bapt. Sem., Nashville, 1956-64. Am. Assn. Theol. Schs. scholar, 1965-66. Mason, Rotarian. Author: (with Duke K. McCall) What is the Church, 1958; W. T. Conner, Theologian of the Southwest, 1964. Home: Buie's Creek NC 27506 Office: Campbell Coll Buie's Creek NC 27506

NEWMAN, TEDFORD COX, social work adminstr.; b. Camden, Ark., Jan. 2, 1937; s. Dewey Autry and Lola (Tedford) N.; B.S., So. State U., Ark., 1959; postgrad. U. Tenn., 1960-61; M.S.W., U. Okla., 1963; m. Delma Jean Hicks, Nov. 26, 1959; children—Michael Tedford, Alan William. Dir. social services and homemaker services Econ. Opportunity Agy. Pulaski County, Little Rock, 1966-67; with Ark. State Hosp., Little Rock, 1959-66, 67-—, dir. community mental health projects, 1969-71, dir. pub. service careers, 1971-72; planner Ark. Dept. Social and Rehab. Service, 1972-—. Cons. social work to pub. agys., instns.; spl. instr. sociology Little Rock U., 1963-—. Pres. Ark. Conf. on Social Welfare. Mem. Acad. Certified Social Workers, Nat., Ark. confs. social welfare, Nat. Assn. Social Workers (chpt. treas. 1964-—, chpt. vice chmn. 1965-—). Nat., Ark. assns. for mental health. Baptist. Lion. Home: 14 McGovern Dr Little Rock AR 72205 Office: 406 Nat Old Line Bldg Little Rock AR 72201

NEWMAN, WILLIAM RICHARD, III, ins. co. exec.; b. Jackson, Miss., May 10, 1939; s. William Richard and Elizabeth (Bentley) N.; B.B.A., U. Miss., 1960, M.B.A., 1961; m. Nancy Ray Mize, June 6, 1961; children—Nancy Amelia, William Richard IV. Officer Deposit Guaranty Nat. Bank, Jackson, 1961-64; pres., dir. Standard Life Ins. Co., Jackson, 1964-—; dir. Pine Investments, Inc., Guaranty Nat. Bank, Magna Corp. Bd. dirs. local Goodwill Industries, Boy Scouts Am., Boys' Club, YMCA, Jr. Achievement. Mem. Miss. Life Companies Assn., Sigma Chi. Baptist. Home: 3535 Hawthorn Dr Jackson MS 39216 Office: PO Box 1729 Jackson MS 39205

NEWPORT, LAMAR RICHARD, univ. adminstr.; b. Halls, Tenn., Jan. 26, 1909; s. William Emmett and Ida Lee (Richards) N.; B.A., Bethel Coll., 1932; M.S., U. Tenn., 1940; m. Elizabeth Callicott, Aug. 1, 1933; 1 son, William Lamar. Prin., sci. instr. Martin (Tenn.) High Sch., 1932-35; sci. instr. Chester County High Sch., Henderson,

Tenn., 1935-40; supt., Alamo (Tenn.) Schs., 1941; prof. phys. sci. Memphis State U., 1941-43, bus. mgr., 1943-49, acting pres., 1949-51, bus. mgr., 1952-68, dir. off-campus facilities, 1968—. Mem. exec. bd. Chickasaw council Boy Scouts Am., 1954-58; treas. Lions Sch. for Visually Handicapped Children, 1955—; mem. exec. com. Postal Forum, 1966—. Mem. Am. Assn. Sch. Adminstrs., Memphis Edn. Assn., Sigma Chi, Phi Delta Kappa, Chi Beta Phi. Democrat. Baptist. Mason. Home: 421 Colonial Rd Memphis TN 38117

NEWSOM, ANN JOHNSON DOUGLAS (MRS. L. MACK NEWSOM, JR.), journalist; b. Dallas, Jan. 16, 1934; d. J. Douglas and R. Grace (Dickson) Johnson; B.J. cum laude, U. Tex., 1954, B.F.A. summa cum laude, 1955, M.J., 1956; m. L. Mack Newsom, Jr., Oct. 27, 1956; children—Michael Douglas, Kevin Jackson, Nancy Elizabeth, William Macklemore. Gen. publicity State Fair Tex., 1955; advt. and promotion Newsom's Women's Wear, 1956-57; publicity Auto Market Show, 1961; lab. instr. radio-tv news-writing course U. Tex., 1961-62; local publicist Tex. Boys Choir, 1964-69, nat. publicist, 1967-69; pub. relations dir. Gt. S.W. Boat Show Dallas, 1966—, Family Fun Show, 1970-71, Horace Ainsworth Co., Dallas; asst. prof. dept. journalism, adviser yearbook and mag. Tex. Christian U., Fort Worth, 1970—. Mem. Assn. Edn. in Journalism, Theta Sigma Phi (nat. conv. treas. 1967, nat. pub. relations chmn. 1969-71), Delta Delta Delta, Mortar Bd. Alumnae. Baptist. Home: 4237 Shannon Dr Fort Worth TX 76116 Office: Horace Ainsworth Co 2001 Bryan Tower Dallas TX 75207

NEWSOM, DAVID DUNLOP, fgn. service officer; b. Richmond, Cal., Jan. 6, 1918; s. Fred Stoddard and Ivy Elizabeth (Dunlop) N.; A.B., U. Cal., 1938; M.S., Columbia, 1940; m. Jean Frances Craig, Nov. 17, 1942; children—John, Daniel, Nancy, David, Katherine. Pulitzer traveling scholar, 1940-41; pub. Walnut Creek (Cal.) Courier-Jour., 1946-47; 3d sec., information officer Am. Embassy, Karachi, Pakistan, 1948-50; 2d sec., vice consul Am. Embassy, Oslo, Norway, 1950-51; pub. affairs officer Am. Embassy, Baghdad, Iraq, 1952-55; officer-in-charge of the Arabian peninsula affairs Dept. of State, Washington, 1955-59; with Nat. War Coll., 1959-60; 1st sec. Am. Embassy, London, Eng., 1960-62; dep. dir. Office No. African Affairs, Dept. State, Washington, 1962-63, dir., 1963-65; U.S. ambassador to Libya, 1965-69; asst. sec. state for African affairs, 1969—. Served as lt. USNR, 1942-46. Recipient Commendable Service award, U.S.I.S., 1955, Dept. of State Meritorious Service award, 1958, Nat. Civil Service League award, 1971. Mem. U.S. Fgn. Service Assn. Presbyn. Home: 3308 Woodley Rd NW Washington DC 20008 Office: Dept of State Washington DC 20520

NEWSOM, DONZELLE ATLAS, retail co. exec.; b. Funston, Ga., Feb. 22, 1920; s. Daniel Atlas and Katherine Eugenia (Smith) N.; student pub. schs., Tampa, Fla.; m. Beatrice Helen Kovich, June 7, 1941; children— Donzelle Atlas, Crighton Dowd. Store supt. E.S. Levy & Co., Galveston, Tex., 1946-60; v.p. operations and planning Lichtenstein's, Inc., Corpus Christi, Tex., 1960—. Served with USNR, 1943-46. Presbyn. (trustee 1965-70, elder 1964-67). Mason (32 deg.). Home: 421 Ashland Dr Corpus Christi TX 78412 Office: 401 N Chaparral St Corpus Christi TX 78403

NEWSOM, EDWARD C., III, accountant; b. Jacksonville, Fla., Aug. 12, 1936; s. Edward C., Jr. and Frances (Mitchell) N.; B.S., Jacksonville U., 1961; m. Mary Jane Byrnes, June 14, 1957; children—Edward C., IV, Charles B., Carol F. Staff accountant James & Harris, C.P.A.s, 1961-63; individual practice accounting, 1963-67; controller, Universal Marion Corp., Jacksonville, 1969—. Instr., Jacksonville U., 1967—. Mem. Am. Accounting Assn., Nat. Assn. Accountants, Fla., Am. insts. certified pub. accountants, Inst. Internal Auditors, Alpha Kappa Psi. Home: PO Box 16216 Jacksonville FL 32216 Office: PO Box 4369 Jacksonville FL 32201

NEWSOM, ERLE THORNTON, JR., assn. exec.; b. Camilia, Ga., Dec. 2, 1915; s. Erle Thornton and Ethel (Perry) N.; B.S. in Forestry, U. Ga., 1938; m. Lois LaVerne Bell, Nov. 8, 1941; children—Laurie Ann, Elizabeth Jane. Forester Ga. Forestry Commn., Albany and Baxley, Ga., 1939-41; chief forester So. Pine Lumber Co., Diboll, Tex., 1941-42; land acquisition cruiser Ga. Kraft Co., 1945-47, chief forester, 1947-56, dir. Woodlands, 1956-68; field rep. Ga. Div., Inc., Am. Cancer Soc., 1968-69, state crusade coordinator, 1969-71; asso. dir. Ga. Heart Assn., 1971—. Mem. Ga. Bd. Registration for Foresters, 1957-68, chmn., 1960-62, vice chmn., 1965-68. Mem. steering com. U. Ga. Sch. Forestry; adv. com. N.C. State Sch. Forestry. Served with AUS, 1942-45, ETO. Decorated Presdl. Unit citation. Registered forester, Ga., Ala. Sr. mem. Nat. Soc. Fund Raisers, Soc. Am. Foresters (chmn. Ga. chpt. 1952), Ga. Forestry Assn. (dir., v.p.), Ga. Tree Farm Com. (chmn. 1957-61), Am Pulpwood Assn. Baptist. Elk. Club: Exchange (Rome, Ga.). Home: 5249 Fleur De Lis Ct Atlanta GA 30340 Office: 2581 Piedmont Rd Atlanta GA 30309

NEWSOM, ROBERT WESLEY, indsl. engr.; b. Winston-Salem, N.C., Feb. 4, 1920; s. Robert Wesley and Hattie (Carter) N.; B.Indsl. Engring., N.C. State U., 1943; m. Florence Abigail Sharp, Aug. 25, 1945; children—Susie Sharp, Robert Wesley III. Asst. engr. Am. S. African Steamship Lines, N.Y.C., 1943-46; with R.J. Reynolds Tobacco Co., Winston-Salem, 1946-68, chief indsl. engr., 1950-68; dir. indsl. engring. R.J. Reynolds Foods Co., N.Y.C., 1968-70; dir. material and engring. services Lorillard Co., Greensboro, N.C., 1970—, v.p. operations, 1971—; dir. N.W. N.C. Devel. Assn., 1965—. Pres. Goodwill Rehab. Center, 1964. Trustee N.C. Design Found. Served with U.S. Maritime Service, 1943. Fellow Soc. for Advancement Mgmt., Am. Inst. Indsl. Engrs. (pres. 1971-72); mem. Operations Research Soc. Am., Am. Statis. Assn., Soc. for Engring. Edn. Republican. Episcopalian. Rotarian. Home: 901 Fairgreen Rd Greensboro NC 27410 Office: Lorillard Co 2525 E Market St Greensboro NC 27420

NEWSON, HAROLD PAUL, lumber wood products assn. exec.; b. Niagara Falls, N.Y., Apr. 24, 1922; s. David John and Mary Francis (Welsh) N.; A.B. in English, Allegheny Coll., 1943; postgrad. N.Y. U., 1946-47, Catholic U., 1950, Am. U., 1951-55, Brown U., 1968; m. Patricia Mary Chagnon, Apr. 7, 1947; children—David, Ellen (Mrs. Darrell Wayne Grable Jr.), Stephen, Mark, Daniel. Market reporter, Oil, Paint and Drug Reporter, N.Y.C., 1946-47; asst. to mgr. advt., sales promotion Solvay Sales Corp., N.Y.C., 1947-48; dir. pub. information Allegheny Coll., Meadville, Pa., 1948-51; spl. asst. dir. Def. Supply Mgmt. Agy., Office Sec. Def., Washington, 1951-53; dep. dir. Nat. Security Indsl. Assn., Washington, 1953-59; dir. pub. relations Nat. Lumber Mfrs. Assn., Washington, 1959-65, Common Carrier Conf. Domestic Water Carriers, Washington, 1965-66; vice pres. pub. affairs Nat. Forest Products Assn., Washington, 1966—. Served with USMC, 1943-46. Mem. Pub. Relations Soc. Am., Am. Soc. Assn. Execs., Naval Inst., Soc. Am. Foresters, Phi Kappa Psi. Clubs: Columbia Country (Chevy Chase, Md.). Contbr. articles to various jours. Home: 7213 Delfield St Chevy Chase MD 20015 Office: 1619 Massachusetts Av NW Washington DC 20036

NEWTON, ADRIAN JEFFERSON, jud. ofcl.; b.nr. Thomasville, N.C., Sept. 30, 1901; s. Jefferson Davis and Martha (Mills) N.; LL.B., Wake Forest Coll., 1925; m. Lois Long Spaugh, Aug. 10, 1927; children—Mrs. William H. Wilson, Mrs. Richard L. Sommers, Adrian Jefferson, Thomas Long, Henry Williams. Admitted to N.C. bar, 1925; city clk., clk. Recorder's Ct., Thomasville, 1920; asst. clk. Superior Ct., Davidson County, 1922-24; practice law, Lexington, N.C., 1926-37; judge Davidson County Ct., 1928-34; gen. counsel N.C. Unemployment Compensation Commn., 1937-41; clk. Supreme Ct. N.C., Raleigh, 1941—; tendered post clk. World Ct., Tokyo, Japan, 1945. Chmn., Lexington chpt. A.R.C., 1928-34, bd. dirs. Wake County chpt.; bd. dirs. Raleigh YMCA, N.C. State U. Named Tar Heel of Week, Raleigh News & Observer, 1954. Mem. N.C., Davidson County, Wake County bar assns., Mayflower Soc., Order of Golden Bough, Omicron Delta Kappa, Kappa Sigma, Phi Delta Phi. Baptist (deacon 1942—, chmn. bd. 1942, 56). Kiwanian (pres. Raleigh Scholarship Found. 1949-54). Club: Torch (pres. Raleigh 1946-47). Home: 2506 Beechridge Rd Raleigh NC 27608 Office: Justice Bldg Raleigh NC 27602

NEWTON, DON ALLEN, indsl. developer; b. Laurel, Miss., Oct. 19, 1934; s. Wilfred L. and Mary (McMullan) N.; A.A., Meridian Jr. Coll., 1954; B.A., U. Ala., 1956; postgrad., U. N.C., summers 1960-62, U. Okla., summers 1963, 65; m. Coleta Farrell, Oct. 11, 1958; children—Don, Coleta Mary. Asst. mgr., Meridian C. of C. (Miss.), 1956; mgr., Winston County C. of C., Louisville, Miss., 1960-61; asst. dir. Delta Council Indsl. and Community Devel. Dept., Stoneville, Miss., 1961-62, dir., 1962-70; exec. v.p. Met. Devel. Bd., Birmingham, Ala., 1970—. Served to lt. USNR, 1957-60. Mem. Am. So., Ala. indsl. devel. councils, Regional Export Expansion Council, Sigma Delta Chi, Sigma Chi. Contbr. articles to profl. jours., newspapers. Home: 2541 Canterbury Rd Mountain Brook AL 35223 Office: PO Box 11004 Birmingham AL 35202

NEWTON, FRANK, ret. business exec.; b. Macon, Ga., Mar. 22, 1904; s. Arthur Fitzgerald and Sarah (Redwine) N.; E.E., Ga. Inst. Tech., 1925; LL.D., Samford U., 1967; m. Nelle Marie Bowen, Apr. 19, 1929; children—Nelle Marie (Mrs. Minor Read Rootes), Dorothy Claire (Mrs. Warren Guy Garrett). With So. Bell Tel. & Tel. Co., 1925-68, v.p., 1957-68; exec. v.p., dir. South Central Bell Telephone Co., Birmingham, Ala., 1968-69; dir. Exchange Security Bank, Birmingham. Chmn. steering com. Ala. Safety Council, 1965-66, bd. dirs., 1966-69; chmn. state citizenship com. Asso. Industries Ala., 1960-61; chmn. community affairs com. City of Birmingham, 1963-64; chmn. outlying div., United Appeal, Birmingham, 1961-62, co-chmn., 1962-63. Bds. dirs. Jefferson County (Ala.) Community Chest, Birmingham Centennial Corp. Named Man of Year, City of Birmingham, 1963. Mem. Ala. (dir. 1965-69), Birmingham Area (pres. 1964, chmn. bldg. com. 1969—, dir. 1960—, exec. com. 1966-68) chambers commerce, Ga. Inst. Tech. Nat. Alumni Assn. (trustee 1963-66), Sigma Nu, Tau Beta Pi, Beta Gamma Sigma. Methodist (chmn. bd. stewards). Rotarian (dir. 1960-62). Clubs: The Club (dir.), Relay House (dir.), Downtown, Birmingham Country (Birmingham); Athletic (Atlanta). Home: 3352 Faring Rd Birmingham AL 35223

NEWTON, JOEL DAVID, bank exec.; b. Cameron, Tex., Apr. 7, 1918; s. Walter Oliver and Mary (Jeter) N.; B.B.A., Baylor U., 1940; grad. Sch. Bank Adminstrn., U. Wis., 1957; m. Helen Awtrey, Mar. 29, 1941; 1 son, Joel David, II. With Citizens Nat. Bank Waco, Tex., 1939—, auditor, 1949-62, controller, 1962-66, v.p., 1966—, dir., 1967—; exec. v.p., dir. Citizens Fidelity Ins. Co., Waco, 1965. Served with Signal Corps AUS, 1941-45. Mem. C. of C., Jr. C. of C., Am. Inst. Banking (chmn. 1947), Tex. Bankers Assn. (sect. chmn. 1953), Bank Adminstrn. Inst. (pres. Central Tex. Conf. 1960-61, Nat. Alumni Assn. (pres. 1968-69). Episcopalian (sr. warden 1969). Clubs: Lake Waco Country (pres. 1947) Ridgewood Country (Waco). Home: 5205 Lockwood Dr Waco TX 76710 Office: Box 829 514 Austin Av Waco TX 76703

NEWTON, JOHN FRANCIS, lawyer, mfg. co. exec.; b. Chgo., Apr. 21, 1934; s. Thomas M. and Evelyn (Rooney) N.; B.S. Fordham U., 1956, LL.B., 1962; m. Carol Kleinsmith, June 16, 1962; children—Sarah Marie, Thomas Matthew. Tax rep. Price Waterhouse & Co., N.Y.C., 1962-66; v.p., financial planning, treas. Chestnutt Corp. and Am. Investors Fund, Inc., Greenwich, Conn., 1966-70; v.p. finance, dir. Peters, Griffin, Woodward, Inc., N.Y.C., 1970-71; treas. Union Carbide P.R., Hato Rey, 1971—. Admitted to Conn. bar, 1964. Served with USAF, 1956-59. CPA., Conn. Mem. Conn. Bar Assn., Conn. Soc. C.P.A.'s, Am. Inst. C.P.A.'s, Financial Execs. Inst. Clubs: Innis Arden Golf Old Greenwich, treas. dir.), Downtown Athletic (N.Y.C.); Bankers (P.R.). Home: San Geronimo Condominium San turce PR 00907 Office: Suite 1605 Pan Am Bldg Hato Rey PR 00917

NEWTON, JOSEPHINE BOND KEENE (MRS. JOHN F. NEWTON), cons.; b. Phila., July 16, 1926; d. Paul Farwell and Josephine (Hebron) Keene; A.B., Howard U., 1948; M.S.W., U. Pa., 1962; postgrad. U. Wis., 1946, Columbia, 1947, Temple U., 1965; m. John F. Newton, Sept. 17, 1950; children—Joann F., Paul G. Counselor, adviser Bklyn. (N.Y.) Training Sch. for Girls, 1949; adjustment investigator B. Altman & Co., N.Y.C., 1950-52; instr., teens counselor East Elmhurst Community Center, L.I., 1953-54; directoress Newton's Sch. Dance Edn., Pensacola, Fla., 1956-58, 64-67; caseworker Fla. Dept. Pub. Welfare, 1957-59, child welfare worker, 1960-61, 62-64; child welfare worker Philadelphia County Dept. Welfare, Phila., 1959-60, Children's Aid Soc., Phila., 1961-62; vis. tchr., sch. social worker Escambia County (Fla.) Bd. Pub. Instrn., Pensacola, 1964-71; cons. pupil personnel Fla. Dept. Personnel, Tallahassee, 1971—; dir. Escambia County Project Head Start, 1966—, mem. adv. com., 1969-71; adj. prof. U. W. Fla., 1970—. Dance instr. E.S. Cobb Recreation Center, Pensacola, 1967-69; W. Fla. area adoption worker Family and Children's Services, St. Petersburg, 1966-68; mem. sch. social workers guide com. Fla. Dept. Edn., 1968—. Troop cons. Girl Scouts U.S.A., Pensacola, 1963-66; Pensacola area coordinator Joint Action in Community Service, 1968—; mem. edn. com. Escambia County Mental Health Assn., 1968—, treas., chmn. finance com., bd. dirs. 1969-70; ex-officio mem. Title I Elementary and Secondary Edn. Act Adv. Com., 1968—; mem. Fla. State div. Family Service Task Force on Vol. Services in Escambia County, 1970-71; co-chmn. Greater Pensacola United Fund Task Force on Family and Children Services in Escambia County, 1970-71. Bd. dirs. Escambia County Mental Health Assn., Nat. Found. March of Dimes. Project Somebody, Tallahassee. Mem. Nat. Assn. Social Workers, Nat. Assn. Black Social Workers, Acad. Certified Social Workers, Internat. Assn. Pupil Personnel Workers, N.E.A., Fla. (mem. sect. finance com. 1969-70), Escambia (bldg. rep. 1968-69) edn. assns., Delta Sigma Theta (chpt. pres. 1967-68, chpt. corr. sec. 1968-69). Episcopalian. Contbr. articles to profl. publs. Home: 809 E Magnolia Dr Tallahassee FL 32301 Office: Fla State Dept Edn Knott Bldg Tallahassee FL 32304

NEWTON, PHILIP TOWNSEND, chem. co. exec.; b. Miami, Fla., May 6, 1927; s. George David and Eloise F. (Townsend) N.; B.B.A., U. Ga., 1950; m. Patricia Preston, Dec. 20, 1950; children—Philip, Preston, Patrick. Financial mgr. C. A. Trussell Motor Co., Athens, Ga., 1950-53; sec., treas. Townsend Bldrs. Supply, Whiteville, N.C., 1953-57; with Dixie-O'Brien Corp., Brunswick, Ga., 1957—, treas., 1961—, v.p., gen. mgr., 1971—, also dir. Parent Co. and subsidiares; dir. First Nat. Bank Brunswick; Pres. United Community Fund, 1970, dir., 1965-70, mem. exec. com., 1971; trustee YWCA, 1965—; mem. exec. com. Okefenokee Council Boy Scouts Am., 1971-72. Mem. Bd. Edn. Glynn County, 1970-73, chmn. finance com., 1970-73. Served with AUS, 1945-47. Named Boss of Year Nat. Assn. Secs., 1971. Mem. Nat. Paint, Varnish and Lacquer Assn. (chmn. 1970-72; speaker convs.), Nat. Credit Mgmt. Assn. (speaker convs.), Brunswick C. of C. (dir.). Baptist (chmn. finance com. 1971). Rotarian. Home: 2812 Wildwood Dr Brunswick GA 31520 Office: PO Box 864 Brunswick GA 31520

NEWTON, ROBERT JULIUS, JR., hosp. adminstr.; b. Greenville, S.C., Mar. 18, 1927; s. Robert Julius and Mary Eugene (Nichols) N.; B.A., Duke, 1949; m. Alice Patricia Calvert, Mar. 3, 1951; children—Janet, Marcia, Virginia, Catherine, Julia. Regional rep. Streitmann Biscuit Co., Charlotte, N.C., 1949-52; insp. Retail Credit Co., Charlotte, 1952-53; sales rep. Blue Diamond Coal Co., Charlotte, 1953-55; regional supr. Armored Motors Service, Va., N.C., S.C., and Ga., 1955-56; self-employed errand express and patrol service, Greenville, 1956-59; with program hosp. adminstrn. Duke Hosp., Durham, N.C., 1959-61; asst. adminstr. Cape Fear Valley Hosp., Fayetteville, N.C., 1961-64, adminstr., 1964-66; adminstr. St. Lukes Hosp., Bluefield, W.Va., 1966-67; adminstr. St. Francis Community Hosp., Greenville, 1967-71, exec. dir., mem. bd. mgrs., 1971—. Mem. adv. bd. Greenville Tech. Edn. Health Careers Center, 1968—. Mem. Greenville County Health Planning Council, 1971—; mem. ad hoc S.C. Regional Appalachian Policy and Planning Com., 1970-71. Served with AUS, 1944-46. Mem. Greenville C. of C., Am. Coll. Hosp. Adminstrs., Am., S.C., Cath. hosp. assns., Southeastern Hosp. Conf. Presbyn. Clubs: Country, Pelham Estates (Greenville). Home: 118 St Augustine St Greenville SC 29607 Office: Sumner St Greenville SC 29601

NEWTON, ROBERT PARK, JR., engring. co. exec.; b. Jackson, Ga., Oct. 25, 1913; s. Robert Park and Bessie (Powell) N.; B.S. in Chem. Engring., Ga. Inst. Tech., 1935; m. Elizabeth Edwards, Aug. 11, 1936; children—Nancy Elizabeth, Robert Park III, William Aris. Asst. chem. instr. Ga. Inst. Tech., 1936; research chemist Swann & Co., Birmingham, Ala., 1936-39; plant design engr. Naval Stores, Valdosta, Ga., 1940; exec. v.p. Wannamaker Chem. Co., Orangeburg, S.C., 1941-45; pres., treas. Applied Engring. Co., Orangeburg, 1946—; pres., treas. Dixie Laundry, Inc., Columbia, S.C., 1955—; dir. 1st Nat. Bank, Orangeburg. Regional trustee Orangeburg Hosp. Mem. Am. Chem. Soc., S.C. C. of C. (dir.), Phi Delta Theta, Tau Beta Pi, Alpha Chi Sigma. Rotarian. Clubs: Palmetto (Columbia); Orangeburg Country; Wildcat Cliffs Country (Highlands, N.C.). Inventor engring. devices. Home: 1120 Moss Av Orangeburg SC 29115 Office: 1525 Charleston Rd Orangeburg SC 29115

NEWTON, THOMAS VEACH, accountant; b. Houston, Nov. 4, 1933; s. Thomas Verch and Maybelle (Williams) N.; B.B.A., U. Houston, 1956; postgrad. S. Tex. Coll. Law, 1961; m. Zilpha Mae Cain, Apr. 15, 1961 children—Terry, Gary, Larry, Bobby, Sherry. Tax accountant Continental Oil Co., Ponca City, Okla., 1956-58; tax mgr. Crescent Corp., Tulsa, 1959; accountant Peat, Marwick, Mitchell &Co., Houston, 1960-63; partner Tom Newton & Co., Gonzales, Tex., 1964—. Treas., Gonzales County Republican party, 1967—. Mem. Tex. Soc. C.P.A.'s (chpt. pres. 1971-72, dir.), Hermann Sons. Baptist. Rotarian, Elk. Club: Safari. Home: Route 1 Box 32B Gonzales TX 78629 Office: Gonzales Bank Bldg Gonzales TX 78629

NEWTON, WILLIAM HARRISON, SR., chem. co. exec.; b. Ft. Worth, Jan. 25, 1917; s. Thomas Edward and Mae (Harrison) N.; B.A. in Bus. Adminstrn., Tex. A. and M. U., 1939; m. Barbara Helen West, Jan. 3, 1939; children—William H., Douglas W., Barbara Joan. Terminal mgr. Southwestern Greyhound Lines, Ft. Worth, 1939-43; buyer Gulfport Shipbldg. Corp., Port Arthur, 1945-50; buyer Tex. U.S. Chem. Co., Port Neches, 1950-51, purchasing supr., 1951—. Served to 2d lt. USAAF, 1943-45. Mem. Nat. Assn. Purchasing Agts., Aircraft Owners and Pilot Assn., Internat. Platform Assn., Izaak Walton League Am. (life mem.). Home: 3165 Gardendale Dr Port Neches TX 77651 also Sandy Pines Buna TX Office: PO Box 667 Port Neches TX 77651

NEY, RANDOLPH JEROME, retail co. exec.; b. Fort Smith, Ark., Aug. 27, 1937; s. Jerome Marshall and Ione (Sternberg) N.; grad. Choate Sch., Wallingford, Conn., 1955; B.A., Yale, 1959; m. DiAnn Smith, Jan. 27, 1961; children—Jennifer Diann, Marshall Smith. Mdse. mgr. Kerr's, Inc., Oklahoma City, 1960-61; with Boston Store Dry Goods Co., Fort Smith, Ark., 1962—, v.p., gen. mdse. mgr., 1962-70, exec. v.p., gen. mgr., 1970—, dir., 1962—. Dir. White House, Beaumont, Tex. Bd. dirs. Broadway Theater League, 1967—, Episcopal Sch., 1968—. Served with USAF, 1959-60. Mem. Fort Smith C. of C.; (div. pres. 1963-65; dir. 1968-70), Nat. Retail Mchts. Assn. (dir. div. 1969—), Whiffenpoofs, Beta Theta Pi. Home: 4701 E Valley Rd Fort Smith AR 72901 Office: 40 Central Mall Fort Smith AR 72901

NIBBELIN, DAVID ALLAN, engring. co. exec.; b. Peoria, Ill., Apr. 28, 1931; s. Clarence John and Muriel (Johnson) N.; B.S., Bradley U., 1953; postgrad. Ohio State U., 1955; m. Jeanette Beverly Barnes, July 30, 1949; children—Russell Allan, Stuart David, Gina Louise. Commd. 2d lt. USAF, 1954, advanced through grades to capt,, 1957; research and devel. engring., navigator, Air Force component and systems devel. for aircraft systems; ret. 1961; design specialist Gen. Dynamics Corp., Ft. Worth, 1961-68; v.p. research and engring. NRT Electronics Inc., Weatherford, Tex., 1968-70; pres., dir. Variable Acoustics Corp., Ft. Worth, 1967—. Instr., Tex. Christian U., Ft. Worth, 1965-67; cons. acoustical engr., 1967—. Pres., Ft. Worth Opera Chorus, 1966-67. Trustee Tex. Boys Choir. Mem. I.E.E.E., Acoustical Soc. Am., Nat., Tex. socs. profl. engrs., Am. Inst. Physics. Presbyn. (elder). Club: Texas Boys Choir Parents (pres. 1964-65). Home: 2540 Ridgmar Blvd Fort Worth TX 76116 Office: 2108 W Vickery Fort Worth TX 76102

NIBLING, BOYD, physician; b. San Angelo, Tex., June 5, 1909; s. George William and Jerre (Harrison) N.; B.S., U. Tex., 1936; M.D., U. Tex. at Galveston, 1937; m. Ollie Ruth Frazier, July 3, 1954; children—Iris Lynne, Edith Ann, Lisa Marie. Intern, Robert B. Green Meml. Hosp., San Antonio, 1937-38; resident W. T. Shannon Meml. Hosp., San Angelo, Tex., 1946-47; individual practice medicine, Beaumont, Tex., 1941-42, 47-49, McCamey, Tex., 1949-65; mem. med. and surg. staff Mexia (Tex.) State Sch., 1965-71; staff physician VA Hosp., Waco, Tex., 1971—. Served with AUS, 1942-46. Decorated Battle Star. Mem. Limestone County (pres. 1969), McLennan County med. socs., Tex., Am. med. assns., Nu Sigma Nu. Lion, Rotarian. Home: 9508 Teresa Circle Waco TX 76710 Office: VA Hosp Memorial Dr Waco TX 76703

NICHOL, CHARLES ADAM, pharmacologist, educator; b. Fergus, Ont., Can., May 3, 1922; s. Walter Laidlaw and Marianne (Wingate) N.; B.S., U. Toronto (Ont., Can.), 1944; M.S., McGill U. (Can.), 1946; Ph.D., U. Wis., 1949; m. Marion Aldred, Dec. 27, 1947; children—Paul, Catherine, Charles. Mem. faculty Western Res. U., 1949-53, Yale, 1953-56; research prof. State U. N.Y. Grad. Sch., also dir. dept. exptl. therapeutics Roswell Park Meml. Inst., Buffalo, 1956-69; dir. reserach Welkome Research Labs., Tuckahoe, N.Y., 1969-70, Research Triangle Park, N.C., 1970—; adj. prof. pharmacology and medicine Duke Sch. Medicine, 1970—. Cons.

Cancer Chemotherapy Nat. Service Center, 1957-61, Nat. Cancer Inst., 1967-68. Mem. Am. Soc. Biol. Chemists, Am. Assn. Cancer Research, A.A.A.S., Am. Chem. Soc., Am. Soc. Pharmacology and Exptl. Therapeutics, N.Y. Acad. Scis., Soc. Exptl. Biology and Medicine, Sigma Xi. Research and publs. on mode of action of antileukemic drugs and cellular basis of drug resistance. Home: 1508 Ward St Durham NC 27707 Office: Research Triangle Park NC 27709

NICHOL, H(UGH) GORDON, state ofcl.; b. Nashville, July 20, 1902; s. Henry Gifforn and India Lillian (Brinkley) N.; student Vanderbilt U.; m. Margarite Cathey, June 13, 1964; children—H. Gordon, Marcia (Mrs. David Burns), James Patrick. Mgr., Firestone Stores, Nashville, 1931-36; operator 7th Av. Garage, 1936-40; owner Gordon Nichol Tractor Co., 1940-58; dir. Social Security for Tenn., Nashville, 1958-—. Democrat. Mason, Lion, Elk. Home: 5025 Franklin Rd Nashville TN 37220 Office: Cordell Hull Bldg Nashville TN 37219

NICHOLAS, DOYNE JACKSON, educator, clergyman; b. Pollard, Ark., Nov. 5, 1932; s. Oran Jackson and Lorene (Pillow) N.; A.A., So. Bapt. Coll., 1953; B.S., Ark. State U., 1958; B.D., Southwestern Bapt. Theol. Sem., 1961; M.S., N. Tex. U., 1963, Ed.D., 1965; m. Martha Ann Williams, Aug. 29, 1954. Tchr. English, Gideon High Sch., Gideon, Mo., 1955-58; teaching fellow psychology N. Tex. State U., Denton, Tex., 1964-65; prof. psychology Cal. Bapt. Coll., Riverside, Cal., 1965-66; dean of students So. Bapt. Coll., Walnut Ridge, Ark., 1966-—, exec. v.p., 1967-70, chmn. dept. psychology, 1970-—; also pastor various Bapt. Chs., 1952-67. Mem. Am. Psychol. Assn., Phi Delta Kappa, Alumni Assn. So. Bapt. Coll. Baptist. Mason. Home: Southern Baptist Coll Walnut Ridge AR 72476

NICHOLAS, LOUIS THURSTON, educator; b. Trimble, Tenn., Oct. 2, 1910; s. Jeff Thurston and Lottie (Dunivant) N.; A.B., Southwestern at Memphis, 1934; postgrad. Memphis Coll. Music, 1934-38; M.Mus., U. Mich., 1939; diploma, Columbia, 1952; m. Sarah Elizabeth Lacey, Mar. 27, 1942; children—Joel Edward, David Paul, Kevin Lacey. Tchr. pub. schs., Dyer County, Tenn., 1928-30; tchr. pub. schs., Memphis, 1936-41; instr. music N.Tex. State Tchrs. Coll., 1941-44; asst. prof. music George Peabody Coll. for Tchrs., Nashville, 1944-51, asso. prof., 1951-68, prof., 1968-—; music editor and critic Nashville Tennessean, 1951-—; tenor soloist, dir. various chs. Bd. dirs. Nashville Community Concert Assn. Served with AUS, 1942-43. Mem. Nat. Assn. Tchrs. Singing (past pres.), Am. Acad. Tchrs. Singing, Music Tchrs. Nat. Assn., Music Educators Nat. Conf., Phi Mu Alpha, Omicron Delta Kappa. Democrat. Mem. Disciples of Christ Ch. Home: 207 Craighead Av Nashville TN 37205

NICHOLAS, PATRICIA ANN, educator; b. Norfolk, Va., Mar. 1, 1937; d. William Leroy and Margarette (Leary) Nicholas; B.S., Madison Coll., 1959; M.A., Eastern Mich. U., 1962. Tchr., Gar-Field High Sch., Prince William County, Va., 1956-61, Robichaud (Mich.) High Sch., 1962-63; dir. guidance Holland (Va.) High Sch., 1963-64; asst. prof. sociology Stratford Coll., Danville, Va., 1964-67, dean students, 1967-71, chmn. sociology dept., 1971-—. Mem. Va., Mich. edn. assns., Am. Assn. U. Profs., Am. Assn. U. Women, Nat. Assn. Women Deans and Counselors, Regional Assn. Women Deans and Counselors, Sigma Sigma Sigma. Methodist. Mem. Order Eastern Star. Home: 321 Starmont Dr Danville VA 24541

NICHOLAS, PAUL HARTMAN, chem., adhesive products co. exec.; b. Northampton, Pa., Dec. 25, 1918; s. Ezra Fred and Bertha Eliza (Hartman) N.; B.S. in Chemistry, Muhlenberg Coll., 1936-40; m. Louis Bertha Burns, Mar. 2, 1946; children—Holly (Mrs. Joseph Roper), Kathryn, Bruce, Paul, Nancy. Chemist, Lone Star Cement Corp., Nazareth, Pa., 1941-42, Union Paste Co., Boston, 1946-52, lab. dir., 1952-57; lab. group leader Interchem. Corp., Cambridge, Mass., 1958-60; lab. mgr. Upaco Adhesives, Inc., Boston, 1961-67, Upaco-So. Adhesives Corp., Richmond, Va., 1968-—. Dir., pres. Woodmont Recreation Assn., Richmond, 1970-71. Served to lt. col. AUS, 1942-46. Roman Catholic. Home: 10317 Jason Rd Richmond VA 23235 Office: 4105 Castlewood Rd Richmond VA 23234

NICHOLS, DONALD EUGENE, mech. engr.; b. Nashville, Aug. 21, 1923; s. William T. and Nannie (Sanders) N.; B.S. in M.E., Tenn. Tech. U., 1949; m. Ama Virginia Foster, Dec. 17, 1949; 1 dau., Barbara Ann. Engring. draftsman I.C. Thomasson & Assos., Inc., cons. engrs., Nashville, 1949-51, design engr., 1951-58, asso., 1958-65, sr. asso., sec.-treas., dir., 1965-71, exec. v.p., 1971-72, pres., 1972-—. Mem. Metro Nashville Gas Code Com., 1965-67; mem. engring. adv. com. Engring. Devel. Found., Tenn. Tech. U., 1968-—. Registered profl. engr., Tenn. Mem. Am. Soc. Heating, Refrigerating and Air Conditioning Engrs. (pres. Mid-Tenn. chpt. 1961-62, regional dir. 1969-72), Nat., Tenn. (chmn. fees and salary com. 1958) socs. profl. engrs., Tau Beta Pi. Mem. Christian Ch. (chmn. ch. bd. 1967, ch. elder). Mason (Shriner). Home: 5056 Kingsview Ct Nashville TN 37220 Office: 2120 8th Av S Nashville TN 37204

NICHOLS, DOUGLASS YOUNG, SR., banker; b. Austin, Tex., Nov. 12, 1924; s. James Routte and Anna Douglass (Young) N.; student U. Tex., 1942-43, 1946-49; m. Dorothy Estelle Faulkner, Aug. 19, 1950; children—Douglass Young, Carol Anna, James Russell. With Am. Nat. Bank, Austin, Tex., 1950-—, clk. proof dept., 1950-52, collection, exchange window teller, 1952-56, office mgr. trust dept., 1957-59, asst. v.p., 1963-69, v.p. in charge advt. and pub. relations, 1969-—. Instr. Am. Inst. Banking, 1959-69. Treas McCallum Sr. High Sch. P.T.A., 1971-72; treas. Austin chpt. Cystic Fibrosis, 1965-72. Bd. dirs. A.R.C., 1969-—, internat. hosp. com. U. Tex., 1966-71. Served with USNR, 1943-45. Mem. C. of C., U.S. Submarine Vets. (chpt. treas. 1956-69). Presbyn. (deacon 1956-60, elder 1961-64). Club: Admirals (Austin, Tex.). Home: 4713 Chiappero Trail Austin TX 78731 Office: 127 W 6th St Austin TX 78701

NICHOLS, H.E., judge; b. 1912; LL.B., Samford U. Admitted to Ga. bar, 1935; asso. justice Ga. Supreme Ct. Office: Judicial Bldg Atlanta GA 30334*

NICHOLS, HENRY LOUIS, lawyer; b. nr. McKinney, Tex., Nov. 7, 1916; s. Jess Cleveland and Leva (Stiff) N.; LL.B., So. Meth. U., 1940; m. Elaine Mary Guentherman, May 17, 1949; children—David, Martha. Admitted to Tex. bar, 1939; practiced in Dallas, 1951-—; asst. city atty., Dallas, 1946-50; mem. firm Saner, Jack, Sallinger & Nichols, Dallas, 1951-—. Dir. Richardson Heights Bank & Trust Co. Bd. dirs. Mary Taxis Found. Served to lt. col. AUS, 1941-46; Col. Res. ret. Southwestern Legal Found. research fellow. Mem. Dallas Bar Assn. (pres. 1963), Tex. Bar Found. Mason. Club: Lakewood Country (Dallas). Home: 3904 Euclid St Dallas TX 75205 Office: Republic Bank Bldg Dallas TX 75201

NICHOLS, JAMES RICHARD, civil engr.; b. Amarillo, Tex., June 29, 1923; s. Marvin Curtis and Ethel N.; B.S. in Civil Engring., Tex. A. & M. U., 1949, M.S. in C.E., 1950; m. Billie Louise Smith, Dec. 24, 1944; children—Judith Ann, James R., Jr., John M. Partner Freese and Nichols (name changed to Freese, Nichols and Endress 1956), Fort Worth, 1950-—, v.p., 1968-—. Farm operator Chisholm, Tex., 1969-—; dir. Continental Nat. Bank, Fort Worth. Bd. dirs. Panther Boys Club, Fort Worth, 1969-—. Served with AUS, 1943-46. Registered profl. engr., Tex., Okla., N.M. Mem. Am. Inst. Cons. Engrs., Cons. Engrs. Council, Am. Soc. C.E., Nat. Soc. Profl. Engrs. Democrat. Methodist. Mason, Rotarian. Clubs: Fort Worth (Fort Worth); Colonial Country (Fort Worth). Home: 3729 Arroyo Rd Fort Worth TX 76109 Office: 811 Lamar St Fort Worth TX 76102

NICHOLS, JAMES WALTER, communications co. exec.; b. Abilene, Tex., Nov, 14, 1927; s. Elmer Lee and Gladys (Williamson) N.; B.A., Abilene Christian Coll., 1947; postgrad., U. Ia., 1947-51; m. Bettye Elrod, Apr. 25, 1953; children—Mark Lee, Jay Matthew. Preacher, Central Ch. of Christ, Cedar Rapids, Ia., 1947-51; radio speaker Herald of Truth, 1951-54; gen. mgr. Chronicle Pub. Co., 1955-57; exec. v.p. Fidelity Enterprises, Abilene, 1957-66, pres., 1966-69; pres. Hallmark Group Cas., Inc., Dallas (merger Fiedity Enterprises, Inc. and Dynamic Theatre Networks, Inc.), 1969-—; chmn. bd. dirs. Pacific Western Mobile Estates, Hallmark Film Prodns., Hallmark Assos., Hallmark Communications Marketing, HFP Corp.; dir. U.S. Capital Corp., GDL Prodns., Inc. Mem. adv. bd. Abilene Christian Coll., 1955-—. Trustee Columbia Christian Coll. Mem. Am. Inst. Mgmt. Home: 6812 Midcrest St Dallas TX 75240 Office: 4230 LBJ Freeway Suite 208 Dallas TX 75234

NICHOLS, KATHERINE CAMERON (MRS. CARLILE NICHOLS), educator; b. Knoxville, Tenn., Jan. 18, 1915; d. Donald Field and Katherine (Knight) Cameron; B.S., U. Tenn., 1938, M.S., 1942; student Columbia, summer 1945; m. Carlile Nichols, June 24, 1950. Tchr., Leadwood (Mo.) High Sch., 1938-41; asst. prof. Flora McDonald Coll., Red Spring, N.C., 1942-45; asso. prof. home econs. Centre Coll., Danville, Ky., 1945-50, 54-63, dean women, asso. prof. art 1963-—. Head residental drives March of Dimes, 1955, United Community Fund, 1954, A.R.C., 1953. Bd. dirs. March of Dimes, 1954-60; bd dirs. Cancer Soc., 1953-60, treas., 1958-60. Mem. Am. Assn. U. Women, Nat., Ky. assns. women deans and counselors, Nat. Soc. Interior Designers, Ky. Hist. Soc., So. Coll. Personnel Assn. Clubs: Danville Garden, Amanda Rodes Book. Home: 141 N 5th St Danville KY 40422

NICHOLS, PHILIP, JR., judge; b. Boston, Aug. 11, 1907; s. Philip and Mabel (Gibson) N.; A.B., Harvard, 1929, LL.B., 1932;; m. Dorothy Jackson, Apr. 19, 1940; children—Donald, Patricia, Christopher. Admitted to Mass. bar, 1932, D.C. bar, 1954; practiced in Boston, 1932-38; atty. Lands div. Dept. Jutice, 1938-41; office of gen. counsel, WPB, 1942-43; counsel Navy Price Adjustment Bd., 1945-46, gen. counsel War Contracts Price Adjustmt. Bd., 1946; chief counsel Bur. Fed. Supply, Treasury Dept., 1946-48, asst. gen. counsel, 1948-51; gen. counsel Renegotiation Bd., 1951-54; pvt. practice 1954-61; commr. customs Treasury Dept., 1961-64; judge U.S. Customs Ct., 1964-66, U.S. Ct. Claims, 1966-—. Served from lt. (j.g.) to lt. comdr. USNR, 1943-46. Mem. Fed. Bar Assn. Home: 2801 New Mexico Av Washington DC 20007 Office: 717 Madison Pl Washington DC 20003

NICHOLS, ROBERT BARRY, civil engr.; b. Knoxville, Tenn., Aug. 15, 1911; s. Shade B. and Ethel (Hazelwood) N.; B.S., U. Tenn., 1935; m. Helen Marie Moore, Oct. 18, 1939; children—Barbara (Mrs. Andrew G. Smith, Jr.), Patricia (Mrs. Edward B. Brantly). Various civil engring. positions TVA, 1935-—, chief nav. engring. br., div. nav. devel., Knoxville, 1957-—. Observer 6th Internat. Tech. Conf. Lighthouses, Washington, 1960. Served to capt. AUS, 1941-45, lt. col. Res. ret. Registered profl. engr., Tenn. Fellow Am. Soc. C.E. (task com. on inland waterways ports and terminal facilities 1969-—); mem. Internat. Assn. Nav. Congresses, Phi Eta Sigma, Tau Beta Pi. Democrat. Roman Catholic. Club: Holston Hills Country. Home: 5500 Crestwood Dr Knoxville TN 37914 Office: Arnstein Bldg Knoxville TN 37902

NICHOLS, WEEDEN BENJAMIN, property mgmt. exec.; b. Horseheads, N.Y., Aug. 20, 1905; s. C. C. and Minerva (Rockwell) N.; ed. Rochester (N.Y.) Athenaeum, Mechanics Inst. Mgr., Smith-Young Tower, San Antonio, 1929-39, Hoblitzelle Properties, Dallas, 1939-46; mgr. comml. real estate dept. Interstate Circuit Inc., Dallas, 1947-50; v.p., gen. mgr. Republic Nat. Bank Bldg. Co., Dallas, 1950-71. Served as col., inf., AUS, 1940-47. Decorated Legion of Merit, Order Poa Ting. Mem. Nat. (past v.p. S.W.), San Antonio (past pres.), Dallas (past pres.) assns. bldg. owners and mgrs., Variety Clubs Internat., Boat Owners Assn. U.S., U.S. Power Squadron, Reserve Officers Assn., Nat. Assn. Real Estate Bds., Dallas Real Estate Bd. Office: PO Box 12841 St Petersburg FL 33733 Home: Yacht Eden Maximo Moorings Marina St Petersburg FL

NICHOLS, WILLIAM FLYNT, congressman; b. Amory, Miss., Oct. 18, 1916; s. William Francis and Daisey (Williams) N.; B.S. in Agr., Auburn U., 1939, M.S. in Agr., 1941; m. Carolyn Fenderburk, Jan. 30, 1942; children—Memory, Margaret, Flynt. Pres., Parker Gin Co.; v.p. Parker Fertilizer Co. (both Sylacauga, Ala.); mem. Ala. Ho. of Reps., 1959-62, Ala. Senate, 1963-66; mem. 92d Congress from 4th Ala. Dist., mem. armed forces com. Mem. Sylacauga Sch. Bd., Bd. govs. Nat. Bd., Bd. govs. Nat. Hall of Fame. Trustee Auburn University, 1968-—. Served to capt. AUS, 1942-47. ETO. Decorated Purple Heart, Bronze Star medal. Named Most Outstanding Mem. Ala. Senate, 1965, Man of Year in Agr. Progressive Farmer Mag., 1965. Mem. Am. Legion, V.F.W., D.A.V. Ala. Cattlemens' Assn., U. Auburn Alumni Assn., Ala. Farm Bur., Gamma Sigma Delta, Bluckey, Scabbard and Blade. Dem. Meth. (bd. stewards). Mason. Home: PO Box N Sylacauga AL 35150 Office: House Bldg Washington DC 20515

NICHOLSON, ALFRED OSCAR, banker; b. Shamrock, Tex., Apr. 29, 1906; s. Oscar T. and Mabel (Moore) N.; B.S. in Agrl. Adminstrn., Tex. A. and M. Coll., 1927; M.B.A., U. Tex., 1929; grad. Grad. Sch. Banking, Rutgers U., 1949; m. Sue Nelleen Robertson, Feb. 1930 (div. Apr. 1954); children—Betty Sue (Mrs. Fred A. Alexander), Dorothy Ann (Mrs. Ruel E. Walthall), Margaret Dale (Mrs. W.H. Black, Jr.); m. 2d, Marylea Thomas June 1955. Bank examiner State of Tex., 1929-34, Fed. Reserve Bank of Dallas, 1934-36, Fed. Deposit Ins. Corp., 1936-50; v.p. Merc. Nat. Bank at Dallas, 1950-60; pres. Farmers and Mchts. State Bank. Shamrock, Tex., 1955-68, chmn. bd., 1968-—. Served from 1st lt. to lt. col., Finance Corps. AUS, 1941-46; col., ret. Mem. S.A.R. Methodist. Mason (Shriner). Home: 800 S Madden St Shamrock TX 79079 Office: 109 E 2d St Shamrock TX 79079

NICHOLSON, DENNIS DEWITT, JR., coll. exec.; b. Union, Miss., May 18, 1921; s. Dennis Dewitt and Sudie (McDonald) N.; student George Washington U., 1958, Marine Corps Amphibious Warefare Sch., 1950; m. Julia Celeste Peeples, Jan. 22, 1942; children—Julia (Mrs. Keith Gordon Frey), Dennis, III, David Ross, Donald McDonald. Commd. 2d. lt. U.S. Marine Corps, 1942, advanced through grades to lt. col., 1957, ret., 1958; dir. pub. relations The Citadel, Charleston, S.C., 1960-65, exec. asst. to pres., 1965-70, v.p. for devel., 1970-—. Dir. Mini Parks, Inc. Mem. exec. bd. Coastal Carolina council Boy Scouts Am., 1967-—; 2d. v.p. U.S. Officers Christian Union, 1954-55; exec. dir. Civilian Adv. Panel on Draft, 1967; chmn. Charleston County Local Events Com., Tricentennial, 1970; mem. exec. com. Charleston Devel. Bd., 1971-—. Bd. dirs. Gibbes Art Gallery, Carolina Art Assn., Charleston unit Am. Cancer Soc. Decorated Bronze Star. Mem. Triden C. of C. (v.p. 1970). Baptist (deacon 1965-69). Contbr. articles to numerous mags. Home: 17 Eton Rd Charleston SC 29407 Office: The Citadel Charleston SC 29409

NICHOLSON, DOROTHY ANN, geographer; b. Phila., July 5, 1932; d. John Lewis and Amanda (Sykes) Nicholson; student Rhodes U. Coll., Grahamstown, Rep. S. Africa, 1950; B.S., Kent State U., 1954; M.A., Northwestern U., 1956. Jr. engr. Goodyear Aerospace Corp. (formerly Goodyear Aircraft Corp.), Akron, O., 1956-59, cartographic researcher Nat. Geog. Soc., Washington, 1962-—. Recipient St. Elizabeth's Hosp. Vol. Service Award, 1966. Carnegie Corp. scholar in African studies, 1955-56. Mem. Assn. Am. Geographers (sec.-treas. Middle Atlantic div. 1972), Am. Geog. Soc., A.A.A.S., Gamma Theta Upsilon, Gamma Phi Beta. Home: 5304 Worthington Dr Washington DC 20016 Office: 17th and M Sts NW Washington DC 20036

NICHOLSON, HENRY HALE, JR., surgeon; b. Statesville, N.C., June 22, 1922; s. Henry Hale and Haseltine (Miller) N.; B.A., Duke U., 1944, M.D., 1947; m. Freda Lewis Hyams, Sept. 24, 1956; children—Henry Hale III, T.D. Miller, J. Christie, Michael, Freda Amanda, William Stuart Cooper. Rotating intern Wis., Gen. Hosp., Madison, 1947-48, Ray Brook State Tb Hosp., Ray Brook, N.Y., 1947; resident surgery Med. Coll. Va., Richmond, 1948-49; fellow gen. surgery Alton Ochsner Med. Found., New Orleans, 1949-51, 53-54, inaugural fellow colon-rectal surgery, 1955-56; chief resident La. Charity Hosp., Tulane U., 1954-55; pvt. practice gen., colon and rectal surgery, Charlotte, N.C., 1956-—; dir. colon and rectal clinics Charlotte Meml. Hosp.; mem. surg. staff Presbyn., Mercy, Charlotte Rehab. hosps. (all Charlotte). Med. asso. dir. Mecklenburg County Red Cross Disaster Com., 1958-61; pres. Mecklenburg County div. Am. Cancer Soc., 1967-69. Served from pvt. to pfc., AUS, 1943-46, 1st lt. to capt., M.C., USAF, 1951-53, col. N.C. Air N.G. M.C. Diplomate Am. Bds. Gen. Surgery, Colon and Rectal Surgery. Fellow A.C.S., Am. Proctol. Soc.; mem. Piedmont Proctologic Soc., Am., So. med. assns., Southeastern Clin. Soc., Duke U. Alumni Assn. (pres. 1944, 60-65, rep. nat. council 1965-70), Alton Ochsner, Charlotte surg. socs., Aerospace Med. Assn., Flying Drs. Soc. East Africa, Mecklenburg County Med. Soc. (treas., mem. cabinet, pres. 1972), Alpha Tau Omega, Phi Chi, Omicron Delta Kappa. Methodist (bd. stewards). Mason (32 deg.). Clubs: Barclay Downs Swim and Racket (dir. 1961-64), Hazel Creek Trout, Robert Burns Soc. (past pres., Charlotte, N.C.), Maracas (Charlotte), Hound Ears (Blowing Rock, N.C.), Carolina-Caribbean (N.C. and V.I.). Home: 635 Manning Dr Charlotte NC 28209 Office: 1012 Kings Dr Charlotte NC 28207

NICHOLSON, HUBERT ALLIE, bank exec.; b. Decherd, Tenn., Nov. 30, 1917; s. Thomas Norman and Bessie (Foster) N.; B.S., U. Tenn., 1940; m. Mary James Lindsey, Apr. 23, 1942; children—Norma (Mrs. Michael Powers), Nancy. Pres. Comml. Nursery Co., Decherd, Tenn., 1953-—; with First Nat. Bank, Decherd, 1957-—, dir., chmn. bd., 1967-—. Vice chmn. Decherd (Tenn.) Housing Authority, 1968-—. Mem. support council U. Tenn. Space Inst., Tullahoma, 1968-—; trustee Meml. Hosp., Winchester, Tenn., 1965-70. Served with AUS, 1942-46, 51-52. Decorated Bronze Star. Mem. Am., Tenn. (pres. 1954), So. (pres. 1959) assns. nurserymen. Methodist (chmn. bd. trustees 1960). Mason. Home: Decherd TN 37324 Office: Box 487 Decherd TN 37324

NICHOLSON, JAMES HERMAN, II, dentist; b. Dallas, May 25, 1924; s. James Herman and Ruth (Chatfield) N.; student U. Houston, 1946-47; B.A., So. Meth. U., 1955; D.D.S., Baylor U., 1949; m. Melva Milatovich, Jan. 2, 1950; children—James Herman III, Melva, Mary. Pvt. practice dentistry, Dallas, 1959-—; instr. Baylor U. Coll. Dentistry, 1959-—, instr. gross anatomy and histology, 1959-62. Served from pvt. to 2d lt., inf., 1942-46, to capt., 1949-54. Mem. Am., Tex. dental assns., Flying Dentists Assn., Acad. gen. Dentistry, Assn. Am. Dentists, Dallas County Dental Soc. Republican. Club: Lakewood Country. Home: 7102 Lakewood Blvd Dallas TX 75214 Office: 511 Casa Linda Plaza Dallas TX 75218

NICHOLSON, JOHN THOMAS, dentist; b. Indpls., Nov. 30, 1933; s. M. Roy and Lois (Beahm) N.; B.S., Bridgewater Coll., 1956; D.D.S.,Med. Coll. Va., 1957; M.S. in Oral Surgery, Georgetown U., 1962; m. Nilda Rivera, Nov. 28, 1958; children—Teresa Maria, Ana Nilda, Thomas Roy, Rebecca Lois. Gen. practice dentistry, Aibonito, P.R., 1962-—; organized dental program, Anguilla, W.I., 1968. Mem. Christian Dental Assn. (dir. Carribean area, 1968-69), Internat. Fedn. Dentists (participant sci. program Tel-Avie, Israel 1966, Varna, Bulgaria 1968), Soc. Preservation Oral Health. Home: A-97 Reparto Robles Aibonito PR 00609 Office: 8 Jose Vazquez Aibonito PR 00609

NICHOLSON, LOUIS BENTLEY, bldg. contractor; b. Whiteville, Tenn., July 15, 1910; s. Clarence Linden and Birdie (Bentley) N.; student pub. schs.; m. Jamie Virginia Little, Jan. 20, 1935; children—Charles Louis, Macie Oneida. Cement finisher foreman Morgan-Hill Paving Co., Birmingham, Ala., 1927-29; constrn. insp., engring. dept. State of Tenn., 1930-32, gen. bldg. maintenance, dept. instns., 1935-42; finisher foreman Sanderson & Porter, engring., Pine Bluff Arsenal, Ark., 1942; concrete supt. constrn. rubber plant Lummus Co., 1943-45; concrete control engr. duPont Co., Wilmington, Del., 1946-47; owner L. B. Nicholson Bldg. Supply and Gen. Contracting Co., Nederland, Tex., 1948-—; v.p., dir. Nederland Pub. Co., 1949-66; dir. Nederland State Bank. Mem. Jefferson County Hwy. Constrn. Com., 1968-—; mem. bldg. code bd. appeals City of Nederland, 1955-71, city charter com., 1954; adv. bd. Nederland Ind. Sch. Dist., 1970-—. Bd. dirs. Little League, Babe Ruth League. Named Outstanding Sr. Citizen, Mid-County Jr. C. of C., 1954. Mem. Nederland C. of C. (dir. 1949-66, pres. 1949), Bd. Realtors (asso.). Mem. Ch. of Christ. Lion (1st v.p. 1952). Home: 227 30th St Nederland TX 77627 Office: 144 Twin City Hwy Nederland TX 77627

NICHOLSON, NELLIE RUTHRAUFF (MRS. GEORGE A. NICHOLSON), civic worker; b. Circleville, O., Apr. 24, 1884; d. John Mosheim and Sarah Ellen (Morrison) Ruthrauff; A.B., Wittenberg Coll., 1903; postgrad. Baker U., 1908-09; m. George Albert Nicholson, Jan. 30, 1907; children—George Albert, Ruth (Mrs. George Fox Trowbridge), Florence Isabelle (Mrs. Charles Overton Stillwell). Tchr., Ariz., Ill., 1904-06; sec., treas. Kusa, Okla. unit Okmulgee County Council Def., 1917-18; chmn. women's div. liberty loan No. half Okmulgee County, 1917-18; mem. Women's Community Council, Kansas City, Mo., 1921-22; treas. Kansas City Conservatory Music, 1923-24; chmn. women's golf com. Mission Hills Club, Kansas City, 1924-47; bd. dirs. YWCA, Kansas City, 1921-24; dir., sec., v.p. Consumers' League Kansas City, 1923-30; bd. dirs. Women's City Club, Kansas City, 1923-26; vice chmn. Daphne Recreation Bd. Pres., Daphne Republican study Club. Named Ala. Republican Woman of Yr., 1971. Mem. Am. Assn. N. Women (v.p., fellowship chmn.), D.A.R. (chpt. vice regent 1959-61), Kansas City Art Inst., Nat. Soc. Colonial Dames Am., Birmingham Hist. Soc., Birmingham Art Assn., Birmingham Opera Assn., Mobile Hist. Soc., Mobile Art Assn., Mobile Opera Guild, Met. Opera Guild, Mobile Symphony Aux., Eastern Shore Art Assn., Delta Delta Delta. Episcopalian. Clubs: Highland Book, Daphne Women's Study, The Club, Lakewood Golf, Mountain Brook. Home: 1019 O'Neal Rd Daphne AL 36526

NICHOLSON, RALPH, former newspaper publisher; b. Green Fork, Ind., Feb. 12, 1899; s. Florence C. and Fannie (David) N.; B.A., Earlham Coll., 1920, LL.D., 1962; M.A., Harvard, 1941; m. Jane

Elizabeth Blayney Harvey, Apr. 5, 1926; children—Blayney (Mrs. Allison Hodges Pell, Jr.), Martha (Mrs. Willoughby Brooke Beresford Fox). European corr. Phila. Pub. Ledger, 1920-21; v.p. Editorial Research Assn., N.Y.C., 1923-25; prodn. mgr. N.Y. Evening Post, 1925-27; gen. mgr. Japan Advertiser, also Trans-Pacific Advt. Agy., Tokyo, Japan, 1927-28; prodn. mgr. N.Y. Telegram, 1928-30, asst. bus. mgr. Pitts. Press., 1930; mgr. pub. relations dept. Gen. Motors Corp., 1930-31; gen. mgr. MacFadden Newspapers, N.Y.C., 1932; asst. to pub. N.Y. Daily Mirror, 1932-33; co-owner, gen. mgr., v.p., treas. Tampa (Fla.) Times Co., 1933-41, dir., v.p., 1933-51; owner, pres., pub. New Orleans Item, 1941-49; spl. cons. to sec. Dept Army, 1949-50; 1st dir. Office Pub. Affairs, U.S. High Commr. for Germany, 1949-50; owner, pres., pub. St. Petersburg (Fla.) Ind., 1950-52; pres., pub. Charlotte (N.C.) Observer, 1951-53; owner, pres., pub. Dothan (Ala.) Eagle, 1956-66, Troy (Ala.) Messenger, 1961-66, Brundidge (Ala.) Banner, 1962-66, Chronicle, Pascagoula-Moss Point, Miss., 1963-66. Aide, lt. col. gov.'s staff, Fla., 1941; a.d.c. gov.'s staff, La., 1943; hon. col. Ala. Militia, 1964. Del., Democratic Nat. Conv., 1944. Mem. Am. (chmn. postal com. 1959-64), So. newspaper pubs. assns., Am. Soc. Newspaper Editors, La.-Miss. Press Assn., Newcomen Soc., Nat. Def. Exec. Res., Sigma Delta Chi. Clubs: Harvard (N.Y.C.); Metropolitan, Nat. Press (Washington); Boston (New Orleans). Home: Route 1 Box 221 Tallahassee FL 32301

NICKELL, MAURICE CHESTER, dentist; b. Fayetteville, Ark., Oct. 10, 1934; s. Chester A. and Ola Ione (Moore) N.; B.A., Okla. Bapt. U., 1955; postgrad. U. Okla., 1956-59; D.D.S., U. Mo. at Kansas City; m. Mary Ann Tubbs, Dec. 22, 1955; children—Jennifer Ruth, John Clark, Samuel Aaron, Leslie Ann. Clin. instr. U. Mo. at Kansas City Dental Sch., 1963-64; practice dentistry, Midwest City, Okla., 1964—. Instr. dental hygiene program Oscar Rese Community Coll., Midwest City, 1970—; chmn. dental staff Midwest Meml. Hosp., 1964—. Mem. Am., Okla. dental assns., Okla. Bapt. U. Alumni Assn. (dir. 1968-70), Omicron Kappa Upsilon. Baptist. Optimist. Home: 109 Orchard St Midwest City OK 73110 Office: 2817 Parklawn St Midwest City OK 73110

NICKERSON, KENNETH STANFORD, psychologist, educator; b. Dartmouth, N.S., Sept. 11, 1930 (came to U.S. 1953, naturalized 1964); s. Stanford Morton and Ethel H. (Sanborn) N.; B.A., U. Kings Coll., Halifax, N.S., 1951; M.A., Dalhousie U., Halifax, 1952; Ph.D., Duke, 1959; m. Connie Brown, June 7, 1969 (div.); children—Kenneth Scott, Bruce Alan. Psychologist, N.S. Hosp., Dartmouth, 1954, 58-59, S.C. State Hosp., Columbia, 1959-65; partner Gertz, Nickerson & Jones, Columbia, 1961-62; lectr. U. S.C., Columbia, 1960-65; asso. prof. psychology U. N.C., Asheville, 1965-71; prof. psychology Clayton Jr. Coll., Morrow, Ga., 1971; chief psychologist Indian River Community Mental Health Center, 1971-72; prof. psychology and faculty adviser U. North Fla., Jacksonville, 1972—. cons. psychologist Lutheran Ch. in Am., 1961-71, Blue Ridge Community Mental Health Center, 1968-70. Bd. dirs. Mental Health Center, Asheville, N.C., 1967-68, Counseling and Consultation Service, Black Mountain, N.C., 1967-69, Circle Childrens Center, Asheville, 1967-70. Mem. Am., S.C., N.C., Ga., Fla., Southeastern psychol. assns., Inst. for Rational Living, Am. Personnel and Guidance Assn., Asso. in Ministry Studies, Sigma Xi. Office: Dept Psychology U North Fla PO Box 17074 Jacksonville FL 32216

NICKEY, LAURANCE NOYES, physician; b. Fort Worth, May 25, 1931; s. Laurance N. and Jennie Maye (Langston) N.; student Vanderbilt U., 1948, Tex. Western Coll., 1948-51; M.D., Baylor U., 1955; m. Ann Collins, Dec. 10, 1955; children—Deborah Ann, Laurance N., Donna Lynn, Stephen Harrison. Intern, Jefferson Davis Hosp., Houston, 1955-56 resident Baylor Med. Sch. Affiliated Hosps., Houston, 1956-58; practice medicine, specializing in pediatrics, El Paso, 1960—; mem. staff Providence Meml., Hotel Dieu, R.E. Thomason hosps. Pediatric cons. N.M. Crippled Childrens Hosp., 1960—. Chmn. El Paso Tb Assn., 1965, El Paso County Child Welfare Unit, 1965-66 pediatrician-in-charge Children's Tb Clinic, El Paso, 1960—. Served to capt. M.C., AUS, 1958-60. Diplomate Am. Bd. Pediatrics. Mem. Am. Acad. Pediatrics, Tex. Pediatric Soc. (v.p. 1971-72), Am., So., Southwestern (pres. 1968-70), Tex. (dist. pres. 1970-71), med. assns., El Paso County Med. Soc. (sec. 1965-66). Presbyn. Contbr. articles to profl. jours. Home: 901 Cincinnati Av El Paso TX 79902 Office: 1515 N Oregon St El Paso TX 79902

NICKS, R.S., chancellor U. Tenn. Office: University of Tenn Nashville TN 37203*

NICKSICK, THEODORE, JR., coll. pres.; b. Slovan, Pa., July 30, 1921; s. Theodore and Mary (Mattick) N.; B.S., Tex. Wesleyan Coll., 1948; M.S., N. Tex. State U., 1951; Ed.D., 1957; m. Bernice Stone, Apr. 21, 1946; children—Jana Cecile, Sarah Suzanne. Instr. edn., psychology N. Tex. State U., 1951-57; asso. dean students Austin (Tex.) Coll., 1958-59; pres. Ranger Jr. Coll., 1959-66, Wharton County (Tex.) Jr. Coll., 1966—. Bd. dirs. Tex. United Fund. Served with AUS, 1943-46. Fellow A.I.M.; mem. Phi Delta Kappa. Lion (mem. Tex. history com.). Home: 1424 Ladelle Wharton TX 77488

NICODEMUS, CHARLES, reporter, polit. columnist Washington bur. Chgo. Daily News. Office: care Washington bur Chgo Daily News Washington DC 20005*

NICOL, WILLIAM FRANKLIN, scale co. exec.; b. Dallas, Apr. 12, 1911; s. William Franklin and Myra (Herring) N.; B.B.A., So. Meth. U., 1955; m. Ivor Noreen Lewis, Aug. 1, 1937; children—Ivor Noreen, Myra Jean (Mrs. VanZandt Williams). Chief engr. Braniff Internat. Airways, Dallas, 1935-42; pres. Range Data, Inc., Dallas, 1937-42, Aero. Services, Inc., Washington, 1945-46; statistician Am. Airlines, Inc., Dallas, 1946-48; pres. Nicol Scales, Inc., Dallas, 1948—. Instr., Dallas Coll., So. Meth. U., 1964-69. Trustee Norrell Found. Served with USAAF, 1942-45, maj. Res., ret. Mem. So. Meth. U. Alumni Assn. (past v.p.), Nat. Scalesmen's Assn. (pres. 1962-63). Rotarian (pres. Dallas Club 1967-68 dist. gov. 1971-72). Author: Range Data, 1937; Broadcast Data, 1942. Home: 821 W Greenbriar Lane Dallas TX 75208 Office: PO Box 22288 Dallas TX 75222

NIEBALL, MARY LOUISE ROY, librarian; b. Odessa, Tex., Feb. 28, 1929; d. Tom and Angela Roy; A.A., Odessa Coll., 1956; B.S., Sul Ross State Coll, Alpine, Tex., 1959; M.L.S., Tex. Woman's U., 1963; post-grad. work Ariz. State U., Tex. Woman's U., Cal. Western U., San Diego; M.A., U.S. Internat. U., 1971; m. Paul R. Nieball, Aug. 19, 1950; children—Paul Jay, Jon Roy. Library clk. Ector County Library, Odessa, Tex., 1944-49; asst. librarian Odessa Coll. Library, 1950-51; librarian Shannon Sch. of Nursing, San Angelo, 1951-52; supr. asst. and audio visual librarian Ector County Library, 1953-58; serials clk. U. Tex. Library Sch., Austin, 1956; cataloguer Sul Ross State Coll. Library, Alpine, Tex., 1959; sch. librarian Sam Houston Elementary Sch., Odessa, 1959-62, Gonzales Elementary Sch., Odessa, 1963-64; asst. librarian Odessa Coll. Library, 1964-67, head librarian Odessa Coll. Library, 1967—; cons. on sch. libraries. Mem. Am. Assn. U. Women, League Women Voters, Odessa C. of C., Am., Southwest, Tex. library assns., Tex State Tchrs. Assn., Ector County Tchrs. Assn., Tex. Jr. Coll. Tchrs. Assn., Permian Hist. Assn., Phi Theta Kappa, Kappa Delta Pi, Sigma Tau Delta, Alpha Delta Kappa. Home: 3733 Dover Dr Odessa TX 79760 Office: PO Box 3752 Odessa TX 79760

NIEBEL, ROBERT JACK, pub. co. exec.; b. Canton, O., July 2, 1938; s. Jack Joseph and Winifred Vivian (Havener) N.; B.S. magna cum laude in Accounting, David Lipscomb Coll., 1960; m. Shirley Joyce Niebel, Dec. 13, 1957; children—Deborah Gay, Robert Jack Jr., John James. Staff auditor Ernst & Ernst, Canton, 1960-63; mgr. comml. cost accounting Aero Space Structures div. Avco Corp., Nashville, 1963-66; financial officer IKG Industries div. Harsco Corp., Nashville, 1966-69; sec.-treas. Royal Pub., Inc., Nashville, 1969—. C.P.A., Tenn. Mem. Nat. Assn. Accountants (recipient Top Accountant grad. award 1960), Tenn. Soc. C.P.A.'s. Mem. Ch. of Christ (deacon; treas.). Home: 4083 Marydale Dr Nashville TN 37207 Office: 405 7th Av S Nashville TN 37202

NIELSEN, OTTO R., univ. adminstr., psychologist; b. Omaha, Dec. 24, 1905; s. Peder and Marthina (Christiansen) N.; A.B., Tex. Christian U., 1933, B.D., 1937, A.M., 1940; grad. study U. Chgo., 1933, U. Minn., 1939; Ph.D., U. Tex., 1942; m. Martha Jane Butts, June 15, 1935; children—Elizabeth Carol, Patricia Jean, David Howard. Asst. prof. psychology Tex. Christian U., 1938-40, dean of men, 1933-40, dir. personnel, 1936-40; dir. research Hogg Fund, 1940-42; instr. ednl. psychology, asst. to dean Coll. Arts and Scis., U. Tex., 1940-42; prof. vocational guidance E. Tex. State Tchrs. Coll., summer 1942; dean, prof. psychology and personnel adminstrn. Tex. Coll. Arts and Industries, Kingsville, 1942-50; exec. v.p. Tex. Christian U., 1950-52, dean Sch. Edn., dir. tchr. edn., 1952-63; chief div. human resources devel. AID, Latin Am., 1962-67; exec. v.p., prof. psychology U. Americas, Mexico City, 1967—; vis. asso. prof. U. Chgo., summers 1947-48; cons. in field. Fellow Am. Psychol. Assn.; mem. Tex., (past bd. dirs.), Corpus Christi (past exec. com.) personnel assns., Tex. Soc. Mental Hygiene (past bd. dirs.), N.E.A., So. Conf. Acad. Deans (past pres.), Am. Assn. Higher Edn., So. Assn. Colls. and Secondary Schs., Tex. Assn. Coordinators Vets. Coll. Edn. (past exec. com.), Am. Coll Personnel Assn., Assn. Tex. Colls., Tex. Tchrs. Assn., Phi Delta Kappa Mem. Christian Ch. Clubs: Rotary (past bd. dir.) Golf (Ft. Worth). Address: care Univ Americas Puebla Mexico

NIELSEN, WALTER NASBY, steel co. exec.; b. Racine, Wis., Nov. 29, 1909; s. Christian and Birgitte (Jensen) N.; B.S. in Engring., U. Mich., 1932; m. S. Elizabeth Dillon, Aug. 6, 1936; 1 dau., Brenda Nancy. Trainee, Sloss-Sheffield Steel & Iron Co., Birmingham, Ala., 1933-36; utility engr. Woodward Iron Co., Birmingham, 1936; mgmt. engr. Neville, Brown & Walters, 1937-40; asst. supt., supt. U.S. Pipe & Foundry Co., 1940—. Candidate City Council, Birmingham, 1963; mem. Citizens Adv. com., Birmingham, 1963. Chmn. bd. North Birmingham Day Nursery. Mem. Iron and Steel Engrs., Am. Inst. Mining, Metall. and Petroleum Engrs., Tau Beta Pi. Baptist. Eagle. Home: 663 Idlewild Circle Birmingham AL 35205 Office: 3300 1st Av N Birmingham AL 35201

NIELSON, VEIGH JENSEN, petroleum co. exec.; b. Whitney, Ida., Feb. 1, 1921; s. Waldemar W. and Beatrice (Jensen) N.; B.S., U. Utah, 1942; M.B.A., Harvard, 1947; m. Janet Moyle, Jan. 19, 1949; children—Nadine, Veigh M., Henry M., David M., Janet Ann. Indsl. engr. Geneva Steel Co., Provo, Utah, 1947-49; indsl. relations analyst Arabian Am. Oil Co., 1949-50; employee relations mgr. and asst. to exec. v.p. Trans-Arabian Pipe Line Co., 1950-52; tng. dir. Phillips Chem. Co., Bartlesville, Okla., 1952-54, asst. to research and devel. mgr., 1954-59, adminstrv. div. mgr., research and devel. dept., 1959—. Mem. exec. com., chmn. safety com. Cherokee council Boy Scouts Am., 1967—. Served to lt. USNR, 1942-46. Mem. Ch. of Jesus Christ of Latter-day Saints (1st counselor Tulsa State presidency 1960-69, pres. 1970—). Kiwanian. Home: 2100 Skyline Dr Bartlesville OK 74003 Office: Phillips Petroleum Co Bartlesville OK 74003

NIERMAN, LEONARDO MENDELEJIS, artist; b. Mexico City, Mexico, Nov. 1, 1932; s. Chanel and Clara (Mendelejis) Nierman; B.S. in Physics and Math., U. Mexico, also degrees in Bus. Adminstrn., Music, and hon. degree, 1960; m. Esther Ptak, Feb. 16, 1957; children—Monica Daniel, Claudia. Exhibited one-man shows Proteo Gallery, 1958, 60, C.D.I. Gallery, 1956, Misrachi Gallery, 1964, Galeria Mer-kup, 1969, Mus. Modern Art, 1972 (all Mexico City), Galeria Sudamericana, N.Y.C., 1958, Hammer Galleries, N.Y.C., 1960, I.F.A. Galleries, Washington, 1959, 62, 65, 68, 71, Edgardo Acosta Gallery, Beverly Hills, Cal., 1961, Art Collectors Gallery, Beverly Hills, 1966, Main St. Gallery, Chgo., 1961, Dol & Richard Gallery, Boston, 1963, Pucker Safrai Gallery, Boston, 1969, El Paso (Tex.) Mus. Art, 1964, 71, Wolfard's Gallery, Rochester, N.Y., 1964, Pub. Library Rockville Centre, N.Y., 1964, Little Gallery, Phila., 1964, 70, Neusteters Gallery Fine Arts, Denver, 1965, Judah L. Magnes Meml. Mus., Berkeley, Cal., 1967, Galerie Katia Granoff, Paris, 1969, Alwin Gallery, London, Eng., 1970, Gallery Modern Art, Scottsdale, Ariz., 1971, Pan Am. Union, Washington, 1972, also mus., galleries, Haifa, Israel, Rome, Italy, Toronto, Ont., Can., Paris, France, Madrid, Spain, 1962—; exhibited group shows in museums in Caracas, Venezuela, 1958, Mexico City, 1958—, Havana, Cuba, 1959; Tokyo, Japan, 1963, Paris, France, 1961, Nagoya, Japan, 1963, Kyoto Japan, 1963, Osaka, Japan, 1963, Bogota, Colombia, 1963, Santiago, Chile, 1963, Buenos Aires, Argentina, 1963, Rio de Janeiro, Brazil, 1963, Costa Rica, 1963, Panama, 1963, Oslo, Norway, 1965, Warsaw, Poland, 1965, Madrid, Spain, 1965, Stockholm, Sweden, 1966, Brussels, Belgium, 1966 (also exhibited Expo 1958), also numerous museums and univs. Eastern and Western U.S. and Can., 1958—; executed murals Sch. Commerce University City, Mexico, 1956, San Francisco, 1965, physics bldg. Princeton, 1969; also executed stained glass windows Mexican temples, 1968-69; represented in permanent collections Mus. Modern Art in Mexico, Atlanta Mus., Mus. Modern Art Haifa, Mus. Fine Arts Boston, Meml. Art Gallery, Rochester, Inst. Fine Arts Mexico, Gallery Modern Art, N.Y.C., Phoenix Mus., Pan Am. Union, Washington, Museo de Ponce (P.R.), Santa Barbara (Cal.) Mus., Mpls. Inst. Art, other mus. and galleries. Recipient 1st prize Mexican Contemporary Art, Art Inst. Mexico, 1964, award Palme D'or Des Beaux Arts exhbn., Monaco, Silver medal Found. Tomasso Campanella, Italy, 1970, Royce medal, 1970. Life fellow Royal Soc. Arts (London). Home: Reforma 16-B San Angel Mexico City Mexico Studio: Nuevo Leon 160-701 Mexico City Mexico

NIGAGLIONI, ADAN, univ. ofcl.; b. Penuelas, P.R., Jan. 12, 1930; s. Luis and Felicita (Loyola) N.; B.S., U. P.R., 1950, M.D., 1954; m. Iraida Rivera, Sept. 25, 1954; children—Rafael Adan, Iraida, Carmen Cecilia, Adan E., Marie L. Intern Grad. Hosp., Phila., 1954-55; tng. internal medicine and gastroenterology, Phila., 1957-61; pvt. practice, San Juan, P.R., 1961-63; dean Med. Sch. U. P.R., 1963-66, rector med. scis., 1966—. Served with M.C., AUS, 1955-57. Fellow A.C.P.; mem. Am. Gastroent. Assn., P.R. Med. Assn. Home: Av Ponce de Leon Parada 3 Puerta de Leon PR 00928 Office: Univ Puerto Rico Med Campus San Juan PR 00905

NIGH, GEORGE PATTERSON, lt. gov. of Okla., former gov.; b. McAlester, Okla., June 9, 1927; s. Wilbur Roscoe and Irene (Crockett) N.; student Okla. Eastern A. and M. Coll., 1946-48; B.A., Central State Tchr.'s Coll., Ada, Okla., 1950; m. Donna Faye Skinner, Oct. 14, 1963; children—Mike, Georgeann. Tchr. history and polit. sci. McAlester High Sch., 1951-58; mem. Okla. Ho. of Reps., 1951-59; lt. gov. State of Okla., Oklahoma City, 1959-63, 67—, gov., 1963. Served with USNR, 1945-46. Recipient Distinguished Service awards McAlester Jr. C. of C., 1952, 54, 55. Mem. Am. Legion. Mason (32 deg., Shriner), Lion. Home: 8321 Picnic Lane Oklahoma City OK 73127 Office: State Capitol Bldg Oklahoma City OK 73105

NIHART, FRANKLIN BROOKE, mil. affairs writer; b. Los Angeles, Mar. 16, 1919; s. Claude Eugene and Vera (Brooke) N.; B.A., Occidental Coll., 1940; postgrad. George Washington U., 1953-55, Marine Corps Command and Staff Coll., 1956-57; m. Mary Helen Brosius, Feb. 11, 1945 children—Mary Catherine, Virginia Brooke. Commd. 2d lt. USMC, 1940, advanced through grades to col., 1957; various assignments 1940-51, bn. comdr. 1st Marine Div., Korea, 1951-52, duty hdqrs., Washington, 1953-56, staff Sec. Def. Adv. Com. on Prisoners of War, 1955-56, U.S. naval attache, Rangoon, Burma, 1959-61, regtl. comdr. 1st Marine Div., 1961-63, asst. dep. chief of staff Research and Devel., Washington, 1964-66; ret., 1966; sr. research analyst Georgetown Research Project, Atlantic Research Corp., Washington, 1966-68; staff asso. Hist. Evaluation and Research Orgn., McLean, Va., 1968-69; sr. editor Armed Forces Jour., Washington, 1970—. Pres., gov. Co. Mil. Historians, 1966-69, Trustee Am. Mil. Inst. Decorated Navy Cross, Bronze Star medal. Mem. Operational Research Soc. Am., Washington Operations Research Council, Inst. for Strategic Studies (London). Clubs: Army and Navy, Ends-of-the-Earth, Carabao. Contbr. articles to various encys., mil. jours. Editor: Almanac of World Military Power, Harrisburg, 1970. Home: 6208 Kellogg Dr McLean VA 22101 Office: 1710 Connecticut Av NW Washington DC 20009

NISBET, JOHN BYERS, JR., city ofcl., ins. agt.; b. Jacksonville, Ala., Nov. 21, 1931; s. John B. and Mattie M. (McCutchen) N.; student Davidson Coll., 1949-52; A.B., Jacksonville State U., 1956; m. Dorothy Jane Warren, June 8, 1956; children—John B. III, Nancy, Virginia. Ins. agt., real estate broker Nisbet Ins. Agcy., Jacksonville, Ala., 1952—. Instr., ins. Jacksonville State U., 1968—. Vice-pres., campaign dir. Calhoun County United Fund, 1967; scoutmaster Choccolocco council Boy Scouts Am., 1952-67. City councilman, Jacksonville, 1964-68, mayor, 1968—. Chmn. E. Ala. Regional Planning Commn., 1971—; pres. Ala. Assn. Regional Planning Commns., 1972. Bd. dirs., pres. Jacksonville Community Chest. Named Young Man of the Year Jacksonville News, 1955; recipient Silver Beaver award Boy Scouts Am., 1966. Mem. C. of C. (pres. 1953-55), Alpha Tau Omega. Presbyn. (elder 1953—). Clubs: Jacksonville Exchange (dist. gov. 1965-66). Home: 211 W Mountain Av Jacksonville AL 36265 Office: Pub Square Jacksonville AL 36265

NISBET, WALTER OLIN, III, investment counseling co. exec.; b. Charlotte, N.C., Mar. 18, 1940; s. Walter Olin and Rebecca Wise (Jones) N.; B.A., Davidson Coll., 1963; M.B.A., Harvard Bus. Sch., 1967; m. Marian Harvey McGowan, Aug. 11, 1962; children—Walter Olin IV, William McGowan. Mgr. syndicate and corporate finance Interstate Securities Corp., Charlotte, 1967-68, v.p., 1968-70, dir., mem. exec. com., 1968-70; pres. Nisbet, Inc., Charlotte, 1970—, dir. Conner Homes Corp., Mineral Research and Devel. Co., Manetta Mills, Comm-Sound, Mt. Mitchell Broadcasters, Inc. Active campaigns United Community Services. Served to 1st lt. AUS, 1963-65. Mem. Harvard Bus. Sch. Alumni Assn. (pres. Charlotte chpt. 1971), Episcopal High Sch. Old Boys' Council, Sigma Alpha Epsilon. Republican. Presbyn. Clubs: Charlotte Country, Charlotte City. Home: 4028 Ridgecrest Av Charlotte NC 28211 Office: 1616 Johnston Bldg S Tryon St Charlotte NC 28202

NISHIZAWA, LUIS, painter. Address: Galleria Plastica de Mexico Calle de Londres 139 Mexico City DF Mexico*

NISSEN, LOWELL ALLEN, educator; b. Fergus Falls, Minn., Jan. 10, 1932; s. Nanning Henry and Marie Caroline (Chell) N.; B.A. magna cum laude, U. Minn., 1954, M.A., 1958; Ph.D., U. Neb., 1962; m. Beverly Ann Chloupek, July 31, 1960. Instr. Concordia Tchrs. Coll., River Forest, Ill., 1960-61; instr. U. Ark., Fayetteville, 1963-65, asst. prof., 1965-70, asso. prof. philosophy of sci., 1970—. Served with AUS, 1954-56. Recipient Regent's fellowship, 1959-60. Mem. Am. Philos. Assn., Philosophy Sci. Assn., Phi Beta Kappa. Lutheran. Author: John Dewey's Theory of Inquiry and Truth, 1966; Reflective Thinking: The Fundamentals of Logic, 1968. Home: Route 3 Fayetteville AR Office: Dept Philosophy U Ark Fayetteville AR 72701

NISSLER, CHRISTIAN WILLIAM, III, constrn. co. exec.; b. Phila., Aug. 27, 1923; s. Christian William and Anna Haynes (Fitzgerald) N.; B.S., U. Mich., 1949; m. Sara Betty Kelly, May 13, 1961. Estimator Walter L. Couse &Co., Detroit, 1949-59, Dunn Constrn. Co., Birmingham, Ala., 1959-63; v.p., estimator Stuart Constrn. Co., Bay Minette, 1963—. Served with USNR, 1943-46, PTO. Recipient Honorable Mention in Sculpture, Spring Hill Coll., 1966. Fellow Am. Soc. C.E.; mem. Phi Delta Theta. Episcopalian (vestryman 1966-70). Club: Holly Hills Country (pres. 1969) (Bay Minette). Home: Rt 2 Chalet Ridge Bay Minette AL 36507 Office: PO Box 570 Bay Minette AL 36507

NITCHOLAS, MONTY CLIFFORD, city ofcl.; b. McKinney, Tex., Dec. 8, 1932; s. Charles Edward and Fayma Lee (Smith) N.; B.A., N. Tex. U., 1955; m. Bettie June Britton, Aug. 27, 1954; children—Monty Kent, Teresa Diane, David Lee, Mark Charles. Accountant, City of Garland, Tex., 1958; accountant Grinnen Mortgage Co., Dallas, 1959-60; dir. finance City of McKinney, Tex., 1961-64; county auditor Collin County, Tex., 1964-67; dir. finance city of Sherman, Tex., 1967—. Active United Fund, Austin Coll. Fund drive. Served to 1st. lt. USAF, 1955-58. Mem. Municipal Finance Officers Assn. (sec.-treas. Tex. chpt.), Jr. C. of C. (pres. 1963). Democrat. Roman Catholic. Clubs: Sherman Noon Optimist (v.p. 1969), Sherman Sports Booster (v.p. 1971). Home: 2401 Ridgewood St Sherman TX 75090 Office: PO Box 1106 Sherman TX 75090

NIVEN, HENRY DOWNS, banker; b. Matthews, N.C., Nov. 1, 1908; s. Edward Eugene and Theresa Jane (Downs) N.; student U. of N.C., 1926-27; m. Mary Lou Lowry, Sept. 17, 1931; 1 son, Edward Carl. With The Bank of Commerce, Charlotte, N.C., 1930-32 37—, exec. v.p., 1972—, also dir.; farmer, Matthews, N.C., 1932-35; with WPA, 1935-37. Served with AUS, 1944-46. Presbyn. (elder 1951—). Home: 1146 Andover Rd Charlotte NC 28211 Office: PO Box 1413 Charlotte NC 28201

NIX, ALICE PEARL, educator; b. Choestoe, Ga.; d. Columbus H. and Lillie (Henson) Nix; A.B., Piedmont Coll., 1940; M.Ed., U. Ga., 1946, Ed.D., 1959. Tchr., White County Schs., Cleveland, Ga., 1932-35, 36-45, cons., 1945-47; tchr. Hall County Schs., Gainesville, 1935-36; dir. guidance and tchr. edn. Truett-McConnell Jr. Coll., Cleveland, 1947-57; counselor U. Ga., Athens, 1958-59; faculty psychology W.Ga. Coll., Carrollton, 1959—, dir. psycho-ednl. services, 1967—. Chmn. social service com. Carroll County Mental Health Assn., 1964-66. Mem. Am. Assn. U. Profs. (chpt. sec. 1964-65), Am., Southeastern, Ga. psychol. assns. Nat., Ga. edn. assns., Assn. Higher Edn., League Women Voters (Carrollton pres. 1965-66, 68-70), Delta Kappa Gamma (chpt. pres. 1964-66, program chmn. 1968-70), Kappa Delta Pi. Baptist (tchr. adult class 1959—). Home: 229 Griffin Dr Carrollton GA 30117

NIX, JACK P., supt. schs.; b. Cleveland, Ga., Oct. 6, 1921; s. Harrison S. and Cora (Stansell) N.; B.S., U. Ga., 1943, M.A., 1952; postgrad. Piedmont Coll., Demorest, Ga., 1967, John Marshall Law Sch., Atlanta, 1967; m. Ruby Ash, Aug. 8, 1945; children— Phil, Phyllis. Vocational tchr., Habersham County, Ga., 1943-44; vocational tchr., Banks County, Ga., 1946-56, supt. schs., 1956-59; supr. tchr. certification Ga. Dept. Edn., 1959-60, state dir. vocational edn., 1960-65; supt. schs. State of Ga., Atlanta, 1966—. Dir., adviser on edn. Bankers Fidelity Life Ins. Co. Mem. Ga. Beta Club Council, Ga. Com. for Children and Youth; mem. hosp. adv. com. Ga. Dept. Pub. Health, Inter-Agy. Council Mental Health and Mental Retardation. Trustee Ga. Athletic Hall of Fame. Served to 1st lt., inf., AUS, 1944-46; PTO. Mem. Am. (life), Ga. vocational assns., N.E.A., Ga. Edn. Assn., Am. Assn. Sch. Adminstrs., Nat. Assn. State Dirs. Vocational Edn. (dir., exec. bd.), Ga. Edn. Improvement Council, Ga. Sci. and Tech. Commn., Ga. Higher Edn. Asistance Corp., Edn. Commn. of States. Home: 355 Riverhill Dr NW Atlanta GA 30328 Office: State Office Bldg Atlanta GA 30334

NIXON, CLARENCE HERBERT, banker; b. Nashville, Feb. 19, 1929; s. Clarence Hunt and Ossye (Young) N.; B.A., Vanderbilt U., 1951; postgrad. U. Wis., 1959. With 1st Am. Nat. Bank, Nashville, 1951—, asst. auditor, 1960-68, auditor, 1968—. Served with USNR, 1952-53. Mem. Sigma Nu. Mason (32 deg.). Club: Old Hickory Golf. Home: 4010 Ivy Dr Nashville TN 37216 Office: 326 Union St Nashville TN 37202

NIXON, DAVID ALLEN, retail trade co. exec.; b. Pine Bluff, Ark., Aug. 11, 1921; s. Coy M. and Willie B. (Mason) N.; student State Coll. Ark., 1941-43; B.S., U. Ark., 1948; m. Gloria Matthews, Apr. 11, 1953; children—David Allen, Ruth Van Lear. Dep. sheriff and collector Jefferson County, Ark., 1948-50, sheriff and collector, 1951-54; bank officer Simmons 1st Nat. Bank, 1955-57; v.p. E.C. Barton & Co., Jonesboro, Ark., 1957-67, pres., gen. mgr., 1967—. Bd. dirs. Craighead County Library. Mem. So. States Indsl. Council (v.p. 1969-71, pres.-elect 1971-72), Ark. C. of C. (v.p. 1968-71, dir. 1967-72). Democrat. Methodist (trustee 1970-71). Elk. Home: 2905 Mockingbird Lane Jonesboro AR 72401 Office: 241 Union St Jonesboro AR 72401

NIXON, EUGENIA FRANCES WALDEN (MRS. MAURY LEE NIXON), housing authority exec.; b. Booneville, Miss.; d. John Sidney and Effie (Mayo) Walden; grad. high sch.; m. Maury Lee Nixon, Oct. 22, 1939; 1 son, Maury Lee. Exec. dir. Housing Authority of Red Bay (Ala.), 1954—. Mem. edn. com. Bear Creek Watershed Assn., 1965—; active various community drives. Mem. P.T.A. (v.p. 1966-67). Baptist (supt. intermediate Sunday sch. dept. 1967-70). Clubs: Red Bay Garden (pres. 1955-57, 62-65, radio chmn. 1969-70, civic chmn. 1971-72), Redmont Ladies Luncheon (v.p. 1969-70). Home: PO Drawer L Red Bay AL 35582 Office: 6th Av N Red Bay AL 35582

NIXON, GRAHAM TOWNSEND, assn. exec.; b. Jacksonville, Ark., Mar. 24, 1913; s. Walter Watson and Hattie (Graham) N.; student U. Ark., 1938-39; B.S., State Coll. Ark., 1942; M.A., Peabody Coll., 1948; postgrad. Ind. U., 1950-51; m. Clara Vise, Nov. 14, 1943; children—Cheryl (Mrs. Weldon), Janice Joanne (Mrs. Craiglow). Technician, Soil Conservation Service, 1934-41; dir. pub. relations State Coll. Ark., Conway, 1946-58; exec. dir. Ark. Hosp. Assn., Little Rock, 1958—; vice chmn., dir. Bank of Cabot; mem. Ark. Senate, 1961-64. Trustee Ark. Tb Assn. Mem. Conway City Council, 1957-60. Served with Ordnance Dept., AUS, 1942-46. Mem. Am. Hosp. Assn. (council on govt. relations), Conway C. of C. (trustee), Phi Delta Kappa, Kappa Delta Pi. Democrat. Mason, Rotarian. Home: Austin AR 72007 Office: 601 Gaines St PO Box 2181 Little Rock AR 72201

NIXON, GWINN HUXLEY, lawyer; b. Augusta, Ga., Jan. 17, 1906; s. Gwinn H. and Eliza Huxley (Scott) N.; B.S., U. Ga., 1926, J.D., 1929; m. Nora Palmer Fortson, Apr. 30, 1930; children—Eleanora N. Hoernle, Sally N. Hand, Gwinn Huxley; m. 2d, Caroline Stavely Fortson, May 14, 1954; children—Nelson Alexander, John Maddox. Admitted to Ga. bar, 1929, since practiced in Augusta; mem. firm Cumming, Nixon, Yow, Waller & Capers; dir. First R.R. & Banking Co. Ga., First Ga. Devel. Corp. Pres. Augusta Citizens Union; co-chmn. Augusta Round Table, Nat. Conf. Christians and Jews; chmn. Com. for Good Govt., 1939-40, Augusta Pub. Forum, 1938-41. Dir. Augusta Library, pres. 1951-54; chmn. bd. trustees Gertrude Herbert Inst. Art.; bd. dirs. Augusta Opera Assn. Served with AUS, 1942-46; lt. col. O.R.C., 1953-66; lt. col. AUS, ret., 1966. Mem. Am., Ga., Augusta (pres.) bar assns., Judge Advocates Assn., U. Ga. Alumni Soc. (v.p. 1940-41), Am. Legion, 40 and 8, Res. Officers Assn., S.R., Phi Kappa Phi, Chi Psi. Democrat. Episcopalian (sr. warden; chancellor Diocese of Georgia, 1972—; lay dep. gen. conv. 1964). Elk, Kiwanian. Clubs: Art (pres. 1932-40; dir.), Augusta Sailing (commodore 1957, dir.), Augusta Country; Pinnacle. Home: 3285 Wheeler Rd Augusta GA 30904 Office: Ga Railroad Bank Bldg Augusta GA 30902

NIXON, JOHN WILLIAM, dentist; b. Homeland, Fla., Mar. 2, 1922; s. Will and Veivor (Robinson) N.; student Bethune-Cookman Coll., 1939-42, Fisk U., 1946-47; D.D.S., Meharry Med. Coll., 1951; m. Ethyl Commons, Apr. 12, 1963; children—John William, Karl Henry, Melba Haley. Practice dentistry, Birmingham, Ala., 1952—; instr. dept. dentistry U. Ala., 1971—. Dir. Citizens Fed. Savings and Loan Assn. Chmn. Concentrated Employment Program, 1968—; mem. Downtown Action Com., 1968—; mem. Operation New Birmingham, 1968—; pres. Ensley Neighborhood Credit Union, 1970—; mem. exec. com. Birmingham Area Manpower Resource Devel. Planning Bd., 1971—; chmn. outreach com. Birmingham chpt. Am. Nat. Red. Cross, 1970-71; mem. adv. bd. Mercy Hosp. Bd. dirs. Volunteer Bur., Greater Birmingham; apptd. rep. of pub. Southeastern Regional Manpower Adv. Com., 1971. Served with AUS, 1943-45. Mem. Ala. Dental Soc. (pres. 1963-64), Frontiers Internat. (pres. chpt. 1960), Kappa Alpha Psi. Baptist. Mason (Shriner), Elk. Author: (with C. A. Brown) Stepping Stones, 1961, God Smiles on aTroubled City, 1963. Home: RFD 6 Birmingham AL 35217 Office: 1728 20th St Ensley Birmingham AL 35218

NIXON, RICHARD MILHOUS, President of U.S.; b. Yorba Linda, Cal., Jan 9, 1913; s. Francis A. and Hannah (Milhous) N.; A.B., Whittier Coll., 1934; LL.B., Duke, 1937; m. Patricia Ryan, June 21, 1940; children—Patricia (Mrs. Edward Finch Cox), Julie (Mrs. Dwight David Eisenhower II). Lawyer Whittier, Cal., 1937-42; atty. with OPA, Washington, 1942; mem. 80th and 81st Congresses; Senator 1950-53; Vice Pres. of U.S., 1952, 56; nominated for Pres. of U.S., Rep. Party, 1960; 37th Pres. of U.S., 1969—. Counsel law firm Adams, Dugue & Hazeltine, Los Angeles, 1961-63; mem. firm Mudge, Stern, Baldwin & Todd, N.Y.C., 1963-64; partner firm Nixon, Mudge, Rose, Guthrie & Alexander, 1964-67, Nixon, Mudge, Rose, Guthrie, Alexander & Mitchell, 1967-68. Served with USNR, 1942-46. Mem. Order of Coif. Mem. Soc of Friends. Author: Six Crises, 1962. Home: The White House Washington DC 20500 also Key Biscayne FL San Clemente CA Office: The White House 1600 Pennsylvania Av NW Washington DC 20500

NIXON, THELMA CATHERINE PATRICIA RYAN (MRS. RICHARD MILHOUS NIXON), wife of President of U.S.; b. Ely, Nev., Mar. 16, 1912; grad. cum laude, U. So. Cal., 1937, L.H.D., 1961; m. Richard Milhous Nixon (37th Pres. of U.S.), June 21, 1940; children—Patricia (Tricia) (Mrs. Edward Finch Cox), Julie (Mrs. Dwight David Eisenhower). X-ray technician, N.Y.C., 1931-33; tchr. high schs., Cal., 1937-41; govt. economist, 1942-45. Promoter world-wide humanitarian service, volunteerism in U.S. Decorated grand cross Order of Sun (Peru), grand cordon Most Venerable Order of Knighthood of Pioneers of Republic of Liberia; named among most admired women George Gallup poll, 1957, 68, 69, 70, 71. Address: The White House 1600 Pennsylvania Av Washington DC 20500

NIXON, WALTER LOUIS, JR., U.S. judge; b. Biloxi, Miss., Dec. 16, 1928; s. Walter L. and Hazel (Kornman) N.; student Marion (Ala.) Mil. Inst., 1946-47, La. State U., 1947-48; LL.B., Tulane U., 1951; m. Darnell Holt, Aug. 3, 1949; children—Karen Adair, Walter Louis III. Admitted to La. bar, 1951, Miss. bar, 1952; gen. practice, Biloxi, 1952-68; judge U.S. Dist. Ct., So. Dist. Miss., 1968—. Served with USAF, 1953-55. Mem. Biloxi C. of C. (past pres., dir.), Order of Coif, Phi Delta Phi. Elk, K.C. Home: 1400 Porter Av Biloxi MS 39530 Office: US Dist Ct Biloxi MS 39533

NIZER, KATHRYN ANN, social worker; b. New Orleans, May 10, 1927; d. William T. and Imelda (Kenner) Nizer; B.S., U. Southwestern La., 1948; M.S.W., Tulane U., 1952. With La. State Dept. Pub. Welfare, 1947-65, med. social worker, 1963-65; med. social cons. La. State Dept. Pub. Health, New Orleans, 1965—. Bd. dirs. Westbank Assn. Retarded Children. Mem. Nat. Assn. Social Workers, St. Bernard Bus. and Profl. Women's Club. Roman Catholic. Home: 6408 Music St New Orleans LA 70122 Office: PO Box 60630 New Orleans LA 70130

NOAKES, EDMUND DUPREE, civil engr.; b. Chickasha, Okla., Dec. 30, 1932; s. Edmund Perry and Margaret Lee (Dupree) N.; B.S., Tex. Tech. U., 1956, B. Arch., 1963, M.S., 1971; m. Janet C. Lindley, Mar. 30, 1969; children—Valerie Leigh, Darla Renee and Diana Lynn (twins). Engr., Parkhill, Smith & Cooper, Inc., Lubbock, Tex., 1964-69; engr. and planner Forrest and Cotton, Inc., Dallas, 1969-72; chief civil engring. and planning div. CECI Cons. Engrs., 1972—; cons. in engring. Served with C.E., AUS, 1956-63. Registered profl. engr., Tex. Mem. A.A.A.S., Am. Soc. C.E., Soc. Am. Mil. Engrs., Tex. Soc. Profl. Engrs., A.I.A., Am. Inst. Planners. Contbr. articles to profl. jours. Home: 2230 Stafford Lane Mesquite TX 75149 Office: 11854 E NW Hwy Dallas TX 75218

NOBLE, CHARLES MACINTOSH, cons. engr.; b. Bushnell, Fla., June 10, 1896; s. Charles McIntosh and Mary Jewell (Taylor) N.; student Columbia, 1930-31; m. Kathryn Schubert, Aug. 21, 1917; children—Charles MacIntosh, Vaux Coffyn (Mrs. William Magnus Jamieson), Kathryn Schubarth Taylor (Mrs. Robert Carter Henry), Mary Ball (Mrs. Starling Loving Hanford). With A.F. Harley, Cons. Engr., also U.S. Engrs., Ala. Hwy. Dept., 1914-21; resident engr. Ky. Hwy. Dept., 1921-23, N.J. Hwy. Dept., 1923-25; engr. Port N.Y. Authority, N.Y.C., 1925-38; spl. hwy. engr. Pa. Turnpike Commn., 1938-41; hwy. engr. C.E., Arlington, Va., 1941-42; state hwy. engr. N.J. Hwy. Dept., 1946-49; chief engr. N.J. Turnpike Authority, 1949-57; dir. Ohio Dept. Hwys., 1957-59; adv. cons. civil engr., 1959—. Registered profl. engr., Fla., Md., N.J., N.Y., Ohio, Pa. Served with USNR, World War I, World War II. Decorated Legion of Merit, Bronze Star; recipient Clemens Herschel prize, 1937, Arthur Wellington prize, 1938, hon. award. N.J. Soc. Profl. Engrs., 1950, Theodore M. Matson award, 1962. Club: Ponte Vedra (Ponte Vedra Beach, Fla.). Contbr. articles profl. jours. Home: 895 Ponte Vedra Blvd Ponte Vedra Beach FL 32082 Office: PO Box 386 Ponte Vedra Beach FL 32082

NOBLE, MARVIN JACOB, physician; b. Houston, Feb. 3, 1935; s. Ben Zion and Esther (Littmann) N.; B.S., Tex. A. & M. U., 1957, M.S. in Biochemistry, 1957; M.D., U. Tex. Southwestern Med. Sch., 1961; m. Cyvia Yankuner, June 24, 1962; children—Sharon, Samuel Zion, Tamara. Intern Cleve. Met. Gen. Hosp., Cleve., 1961-62; resident anesthesiology Hosp. U. Pa., Phila., 1962-64; instr. anesthesiology U. Tex. Southwestern Med. Sch., Dallas, 1966-68; pvt. practice medicine specializing in anesthesiology, Dallas, 1968—; asst. clin. prof. anesthesiology U. Tex. Southwestern Med. Sch., Dallas, 1969—. Bd. trustees Hillel Found. Tex. A. and M. U., 1968—. Served with M.C., AUS, 1964-66. NIH Spl. fellow in Pharmacology and Anesthesiology, 1967-68. Diplomate Am. Bd. Anesthesiology. Fellow Am. Coll. Anesthesiologists; mem. A.M.A., Am. Soc. Anesthesiologists, Dallas County Anesthesiology Soc. (sec., treas. 1970—), Internat. Anesthesia Research Soc., Phi Delta Epsilon. Jewish religion (trustee temple 1968-71). Mem. B'nai B'rith. Home: 6511 Stichter St Dallas TX 75230 Office: 8210 Walnut Hill Lane Dallas TX 75231

NOBLE, ROBERT DALE, child care agy. exec.; b. Atlanta, Oct. 15, 1932; s. Walter Barns and Julia (Fendley) N.; student N.C. State U., 1954-57; B.S., U. N.C., 1958; M.S.W., 1963; m. Sylvia Allen, Apr. 21, 1951; children—Robert Dale, Paul Allen, Stephen Clements. Exec. sec. Community Chest Greater Anderson (S.C.), 1958-60; campaign dir. Charlotte (N.C.) United Appeal, 1960-61; exec. dir. Episcopal Child Care Services, Thompson Orphanage and Tng. Instn., Charlotte, 1961—. Bd. dirs. Group Child Care Cons. Services. Served with USNR, 1951-54; Korea. Mem. Nat. Assn. Social Workers, Acad. Certified Social Workers, N.C. Assn. Child Caring Agys. (past pres.), Southeastern Child Care Assn. (pres.). Republican. Episcopalian. Home: 2000 Sharon Lane Charlotte NC 28211 Office: 1130 E 4th St Charlotte NC 28204

NOBLES, HERBERT ALTON, nursing home exec.; b. Greenville, N.C., Sept. 29, 1929; s. Martin Luther and Huldah Louise (Albritton) N.; B.S., U. N.C., 1966; m. Peggy Jane Hartman, Sept. 4, 1954; children— Laura, William, John, Hubert. Staff accountant Peat, Marwick, Mitchell & Co., C.P.A.'s, Raleigh, N.C., 1966-69; v.p. and treas. Guardian Care, Inc., Rocky Mount, N.C., 1969—. Served with USAF, 1951-53. C.P.A., N.C. Mem. N.C. Assn. of C.P.A.'s, Am. Inst. C.P.A.'s. Home: 3504 Hawthorne Rd Rocky Mount NC 27801 Office: Sunset Av West PO Box 4305 Rocky Mount NC 27801

NOBLES, WILLIAM LEWIS, coll. pres.; b. Meridian, Miss., Sept. 11, 1925; s. Julius Sidney and Ruby Rae (Roper) N.; student Ursinus Coll., 1944-45; B.S. in Pharmacy, U. Miss., 1948, M.S., 1949; Ph.D., U. Kan., 1952; NSF postdoctoral fellow, U. Mich., 1958-59; m. Joy Ford, Aug. 29, 1948; children—Sandra Jeanne, Glenda Suzanne. Mem. faculty U. Miss., 1952-68, prof. pharm. chemistry, 1955-68, dean Grad. Sch., 1960-68; pres. Miss. Coll., Clinton, 1968—. Chmn. regional adv. group Miss. Regional Med. Program. Trustee New Orleans Baptist Theol. Sem. Served to lt. (j.g.) USNR, 1944-46. Fellow Am. Found. Pharm. Edn., 1949, Gustavus A. Pfeiffer Meml. Research fellow, 1955; recipient award for stimulation of research Am. Pharm. Assn. Found., 1966. Fellow A.A.A.S.; mem. Am. Chem. Soc., Acad. of Pharm. Scis. (chmn. medicinal chemistry sect. 1967-68), Am. Pharm. Assn., Sigma Xi, Phi Eta Sigma, Pi Kappa Pi. Baptist. Rotarian. Contbr. books. Home: Box 643 Clinton MS 39056

NOCK, WALTER JOHN, refining co. exec.; b. Mexico, D.F., Mexico, Oct. 13, 1906; s. Edwin Herbert and Emma (Pitt) N.; came to U.S., 1956, naturalized, 1961; S.B., Mass., Inst. Tech., 1928; m. Lela Marguerite Meleen, Aug. 28, 1937; 1 son, Walter Ronald. With Am. Smelting and Refining Co., 1928—, v.p. charge mining, milling and smelting operations in Mexico, 1960—; pres. Campania Minera Asarco, S.A., 1960-65; dir. gen. Asarco Mexicana, S.A., 1965—. Mem. Am. Inst. Mining, Metall. and Petroleum Engrs. Home: Augustin Ahumada 310-G Mexico DF 10 Mexico Office: Paseo de la Reforma 76 Mexico DF 6 Mexico

NOE, JAMES A., JR., pres. WNOE, New Orleans. Address: 529 Bienville St New Orleans LA 70130*

NOE, SAMUEL VANARSDALE, supt. schs.; b. Springfield, Ky., Apr. 26, 1901; s. James Richard and Cora (VanArsdale) N.; A.B., Centre Coll., Danville, Ky., 1922, LL.D., 1962; M.A., Columbia, 1928; student U. Mich., Harvard, Peabody Coll.; m. Elizabeth McDonald, Aug. 7, 1930; 1 son, Samuel VanArsdale. Prin., Eminence (Ky.) Sch., 1922-24, supt. schs., 1924-28; prin. elementary and high schs. in Louisville, 1928-50; adminstrv. asst. to supt. Louisville schs., 1950-60, supt. schs., 1960—; vis. prof. U. Louisville Grad. Sch., 1947-60. Past dir. Health and Welfare Council. Bd. dirs. Louisville Met. YMCA, Louisville chpt. A.R.C. Served to maj. AUS, 1943-46; Italy. Decorated Bronze Star; knight officer Order Crown Italy. Mem. Am., Ky. assns. sch. adminstrs., Nat. (life), Ky. (past officer, bd. mem.) edn. assns., Nat. Sch. Pub. Relations Assn., Louisville C. of C., Beta Theta Pi. Presbyn. (elder, clk.). Kiwanian (past pres., Louisville). Home: 414 Club Lane Louisville KY 40207 Office: 506 W Hill St Louisville KY 40208

NOEL, JAMES LATANE, JR., judge; b. Pilot Point, Tex., Oct. 28, 1909; s. James Latney and Ina (Bobbitt) N.; B.S. in Civil Engring., So. Methodist U., 1931, B.S. in Commerce, 1932, LL.B., 1937; m. Virginia Grubbs, Apr. 21, 1942; children—James Latane III, Carol Annelle, Edmund Orr, William David, Robert Cornelius. Admitted to Tex. bar, 1936; asst. budget officer, Dallas County, 1935-37, asst. dist. atty., 1937-38; asst. atty. gen. State of Tex., Austin, 1939-42, 45-46; partner firm Butler, Binion, Rice & Cook, Houston, 1946-53; pvt. practice 1953-61; U.S. dist. judge So. Dist. Tex., Houston, 1961—. Mem. U.S. Commn. on Govt. Security, Washington, 1956-58. Trustee Geol. Scis. and Petroleum Engring. Found., Tex. A. and M. U. Mem. Am., Houston bar assns., State Bar Tex. Democrat. Methodist. Clubs: Houston Petroleum, Houston Country; Idlewild (Dallas). Home: 2454 Pine Valley Dr Houston TX 77019 Office: US Courthouse Houston TX 77061

NOEL, JOHN ARMSTEAD, sch. supply co. exec.; b. Worthington, Ind., Jan. 4, 1920; s. William Bryan and Lorene (Calvert) N.; B.S. cum laude in Bus. Adminstrn., Butler U., 1941; m. Estelle Pullen, Oct. 3, 1943; children—Estelle (Mrs. Michael Morgan Mockbee, Jr.), John Armstead, Carol Carson; m. 2d Merelee Joplin, Oct. 20, 1967. Cost clk. Gen. Electric Co., Schenectady, 1941-42; jr. accountant Dick D. Quin & Co., Jackson, Miss., 1945-47; v.p., treas. Miss. Sch. Supply Co. and subsidiaries, 1947—, also dir. Mem. exec. com. Scoutmaster Andrew Jackson council Boy Scouts Am., 1953-57. Trustee Magnolia State Found., Missco Retirement Trust. C.P.A., Miss. Mem. Nat. Assn. Accountants, Am. Inst. C.P.A.'s, Miss. Soc. C.P.A.'s. Methodist. Club: Jackson Country. Contbr. articles profl. jours. Home: 242 Ashcot Circle Jackson MS 39211 Office: 4155 Industrial Dr Jackson MS 39205

NOEL, WILLIAM DOUGLAS, gas co. exec.; b. Ft. Worth, May 11, 1914; s. Earnest and Inez (Turnpaugh) N.; student U. Tex., 1935; m. Ellen Witwer, May 24, 1937; children—Sherwood (Mrs. John F. McGuigan), Ellen Melissa (Mrs. W. T. Speller). Chemist, Gulf Oil Co., Breckenridge, Tex., 1935-40; pres. Trebol Oil Co., McCamey, Tex., ind. oil operator, Odessa, Tex., 1940-63; pres. Odessa Natural Gasoline Co., 1947—; pres. West Tex. Gathering Co., El Paso Products Co.; co-owner, dir. Am. Bank of Commerce, Odessa, Citizens Nat. Bank of Lubbock (Tex.), San Angelo Nat. Bank (Tex.), First Nat. Bank, San Antonio. Mem. McCamey (Tex.) Sch. Bd., 1942-49; commr. Tex. Liquor Control Bd., 1961-69; sponsor Jr. League Baseball Team, Odessa Symphony, Permian Hist. Soc., Permian Playhouse, Crippled Childrens Clinic. Bd. dirs. Tex. Technol. Coll. Found. Named Man of Month Southwestern Petroleum News, 1963, Outstanding Man of Odessa, 1963. Mem. Tex. Ind. Gas Producers Assn., Permian Basin Petroleum Assn. U. Tex. Dads' Assn., West Tex. C. of C., Beta Theta Pi. Democrat. Presbyn. Club: President's. Home: Route 1 Box 498 Country Club Estates Odessa TX 79760 Office: PO Box 3986 Odessa TX 79760*

NOETZEL, GROVER A(RCHIBALD) J(OSEPH), educator; b. Greenwood, Wis., June 14, 1908; s. August Herman and Coralie Marie (Van Den Bossche) N.; A.B., U. Wis., 1929, Ph.D., 1934; certificate in econs., U. London, 1930, U. Geneva, 1936; fellow Social Sci. Research Council, 1935-36; m. Anna B. Dobbins, June 11, 1953. Instr. econ. U. S.D., 1930-32; instr. econ. U. Wis., 1934-35; economist Nat. Bur. Econ. Research, 1936-37; asst. prof. Temple U., 1937-40, asso. prof., 1940-46; pvt. cons. econ. and investment counselor, Phila. and N.Y.C., 1939-46; prof. econ. U. Miami, 1946-48, dean Sch. Bus. Adminstrn., 1948-61, prof. econs., cons. economist, 1961—. Dir., mem. finance com. bd. Am. Bankers Ins. Co. Fla.; dir. Fla. Nat. Bank at Coral Gables, Coral Gables Fed. Savs & Loan Assn., Security Trust Co., Miami, Hill Bros., Miami, First Equity Financial Corp. Bd. dirs. Goodwill Industries, Inc., Med. Service Bur. Miami. Mem. Am. Assn. U. Profs., Am. Acad. Polit. and Social Sci., Am. Finance Assn., Am., So. econ. assns., Econ. Soc. S. Fla. (dir., pres. 1956), Newcomen Soc., Phi Kappa Phi, Alpha Phi Omega, Alpha Delta Sigma, Delta Sigma Pi, Artus, Beta Gamma Sigma. Clubs: Rotary (Miami, Fla.); Coral Gables Country, Rivieria Country, Century (Coral Gables). Author: Recent Theories of Foreign Exchange, 1934; Cooperation Entre L'Universite et Les Milieux Economiques, 1956; Objectives of a Management Center, 1956; Decisions That Affect Profits, 1957; also articles in field. Home: 4990 SW 86th St South Miami FL 33143 Office: Sch Bus Adminstrn U Miami Coral Gables FL 33134

NOLAN, ARTHUR JOSEPH, govt. ofcl.; b. Jersey City, Aug. 14, 1923; s. Walter Francis and Gertrude (Flynn) N.; A.B., Columbia, 1949, M.A., 1952. Economist, U.S. Labor Dept., Washington, 1951-53; examiner U.S. Bur. Budget, Washington, 1954-59; asso. prof. Def. Mgmt. Center, Ohio State U., Columbus, Dayton, 1959-62; dir. Contract Mgmt. Inst., Washington, 1962-71; dep. chief research contracts Nat. Cancer Inst., Bethesda, Md., 1971—. Treas., Intercontinental Commerce, 1968-69; cons. govt. contract matters; lectr. on govt. contracts Oxford U., 1967. Served with USAAF, 1942-45; PTO. Author: Productivity and Output per Man Hour, Metal Containers, 1954; Incentive Contracting in the Aerospace Industry, 1966. Editor: The Budget of the Department of Defense, 1970. Home: 4163 S Four Mile Run Arlington VA 22204 Office: 9000 Rockville Pike Bethesda MD 20014

NOLAN, PAUL, educator; b. Boston, Jan. 31, 1919; s. Joseph J. and Fannie (Bransfield) N.; student U. N.H., 1941; Ph.D., Cath. U. Am., 1950, Ph.D., 1954. Instr. Cath. U. Am., 1953-59, asst. prof., 1959-65, asso. prof., 1965—; guest lectr. Georgetown U., 1956, 62, U. Md., 1957-59. Served to capt. AUS, 1945. Asso. editor Bull. Guild Cath.

Psychiatrists, 1957—. Home: 530 A St SE Washington DC 20003 Office: Cath U Am Washington DC 20017

NOLAN, RAYMOND PAUL, physician; b. Tullow, Ireland; s. Stephen John and Elizabeth (O'Brien) N.; came to U.S., 1923, naturalized, 1929; B.S., Columbia, 1948; M.D., N.Y.U., 1951; m. Mildred Geiger, Feb. 11, 1957; children—Robert Paul, Kenneth Joseph. Intern St. Vincent's Hosp., N.Y.C., 1951-52; resident Bellevue Med. Center, N.Y.U., 1952-56; practice medicine, specializing in obstetrics and gynecology, Hollywood, Fla., 1960—; asst. prof. obstetrics and gynecology N.Y.U. Coll. Medicine, 1957-60; attending obstetrician and gynecologist, chief dept. Meml. Hosp., Hollywood, Fla. Served with USAAF, 1943-46. Fellow A.C.S.; mem. Am., Fla., Broward County med. assns., Am. Coll. Obstetricians and Gynecologists, Fla., Broward County obstet. and gynecol. socs. Home: 4911 Madison St Hollywood FL 33021 Office: 3711 Garfield St Hollywood FL 33021

NOLAND, IVESON B., bishop; b. Baton Rouge, Sept. 10, 1916; s. Ives B. and Camille (Reynaud) N.; B.A., La. State U., 1937; B.D., Sewanee U., 1940, D.D., 1952; m. Nell Burden, Feb. 3, 1936; children— Iveson B. III, John Burden, Daniel Woodring. Ordained to ministry Episcopal Ch.; rector, Charlotte, N.C., 1946-50, Lake Charles, La., 1950-52; bishop Episcopal Diocese of La., Baton Rouge, 1952—. Mem. bd. exam. chaplains Diocese of N.C. Served as chaplain AUS, 1942-45; PTO. Mem. Scabbard and Blade, Phi Kappa Phi, Sigma Nu. Home: 7324 Bocage St Baton Rouge LA 70809 Office: 8833 Goodwood St Baton Rouge LA 70806

NOLAND, JAMES RUSSELL, govt. adminstr.; b. Paris, Ky., Jan. 10, 1924; s. James Russell and Christine (Haley) N.; A.B., Emory U., 1945; M.Div., Yale, 1948; postgrad. Columbia, 1951-52; M.A., N.Y. U., 1954; m. Mary Richerson, Dec. 22, 1945; children—James Russell III, Ellen Gay (Mrs. Robert Vernon), Mary Elise. Coordinator urban ch. dept. Nat. Council Chs., 1953-55; exec. dir. Protestant Charities Houston, 1955-67; asst. to pres. Prairie View A. and M. Coll., 1967-68; research sociologist Houston Bapt. Coll., 1968; asst. to dean U. Houston, 1968—, coordinator Farfel lectures, 1969. Pres., Value Guidance Systems, Inc., 1969—; dir. Tchr. Tng. Inst., U. St. Thomas, 1964—. Active Harris County United Fund, Planned Parenthood, Council on Human Relations (award 1964), A.R.C., Community Planning Assn. Trustee Childers Found. Served with USNR, 1942-46. Recipient Head Start award Houston Community Action Program, 1965; Merit Achievement award Protestant Charities of Houston, 1966; Distinguished Service award Houston Tchrs. Assn., 1968. Fellow Am. Sociol. Soc.; mem. Nat. Assn. Social Welfare, Acad. Certified Social Workers, Am. Bus. Writing Assn. Democrat. Episcopalian. Home: 13303 Havershire Houston TX 77024

NOLAND, THOMAS BENJAMIN, city govt. ofcl.; b. nr. Waynesville, N.C., May 12, 1915; s. Robert Long and Addie (Dehart) N.; B.S., U. Va., 1940; m. Annie Marie Choate, June 10, 1940; children—Sarah Jane (Mrs. Richard Wells Matthis), Thomas Benjamin. City mgr., Altavista, Va., 1947-50, Franklin, Va., 1950-56, Pulaski, Va., 1956-66, Martinsville, Va., 1966—. Mem. Com. to Study State Sch. Aid Formula, 1968-69. Pres. bd. dirs. YMCA. Served with C.E., AUS, 1943-46. Mem. Internat. City Mgmt. Assn., City-County C. of C. (dir.). Home: 1267 Lanier Rd Martinsville VA 24112 Office: PO Box 1112 Martinsville VA 24112

NOLD, WENDELIN JOSEPH, clergyman; b. Bonham, Tex., Jan. 18, 1900; s. Wendelin Joseph and Mary Elizabeth (Charles) N.; A.B., St. Mary's U., La-Porte, Tex., 1921; S.T.D., N.Am. Coll., Rome, Italy, 1925; LL.D., St. Edwards U., Austin, Tex. Ordained priest Roman Catholic Ch., Rome, Apr. 11, 1925; asst. rector Sacred Heart Cathedral, Dallas, 1925-41, consultor, 1934-48; pastor Christ the King Ch., Dallas, 1941-48; coadjutor bishop of Galveston, Tex., 1948-50; consecrated bishop 1948; bishop Galveston- Houston Diocese of Tex., 1950—. Decorated knight comdr. Knight of Holy Sepulchre. Home: 4206 S MacGregor Way Houston TX 77021 Office: Chancery 1411 Av I Galveston TX 77550

NOLEN, JOHN HENRY, lawyer; b. Spartanburg, S.C., July 9, 1919; s. John Henry and Mary (Fry) N.; A.B., Wofford Coll., 1940; LL.B., Duke, 1946; m. Eileen Nichols Ramabottom, July 11, 1942; children—John H., Eileen Esther. Admitted to S.C. bar, 1946; since practiced in Spartanburg; mem. firm Odom, Nolen & Foster, 1946—. Mem. S.C. Ho. of Reps., 1955-56; county solicitor, Spartanburg County, S.C., 1957-60; 7th Circuit solicitor, Spartanburg, 1960—. Served to capt. AUS, 1941—. Mason (Shriner), Lion. Home: 109 Sydnor Rd Spartanburg SC 29302 Office: 120 Walnut St Spartanburg SC 29301

NOLLEY, EUGENE DAVIS, physician; b. Nokesville, Va., Mar. 4, 1925; s. William Davis and Pearl Zena (Shaffer) N.; B.A., Bridgewater Coll., 1952; M.D., Med. Coll. Va., 1956; m. Doris Kathryn Bowman, Sept. 3, 1949; children—Ronald Eugene, Curtis Bowman, Dana Sue, Phillip Lee, Eric Wayne, Kevin Davis. Intern, Johnston-Willis Hosp., Richmond, Va., 1956-57; practice medicine specializing in family practice, Churchville, Va., 1957—; mem. staff King's Daus. Hosp., Staunton, Va. Mem. Va., County med. socs. Home: PO Box 104 Staunton VA 24421 Office: PO Box 100 Churchville VA 24421

NOLTE, EWALD VALENTIN, musician, educator; b. Utica, Neb., Sept. 21, 1909; s. William and Mamie (Schmidt) N.; student Concordia Tchrs. Coll., 1927-29, Bowling Green State U., 1935-36; Defiance Coll., 1937-38; Mus.B., Northwestern U., 1944, Mus.M., 1945, Ph.D., 1954; postgrad. Yale, 1950-51; m. Irene Schmidt, Aug. 12, 1931; children—Loren, Darla (Mrs. Clarence Koch). Elementary sch. prin., Lorain, also Napoleon, O., 1929-42; dir. music St. Paul's Luth. Ch., Melrose Park, Ill., 1942-44; mem. music faculty Northwestern U., Evanston, Ill., 1944-64; dir., editor-in-chief Moravian Music Found., Winston-Salem, N.C., 1964-72; prof. music Salem Coll., Winson-Salem, 1964—, vis. lectr. music U. N.C., Greensboro, U. Ill., U. Colo. Mus. dir. Forsyth County Singers Guild, 1965-67. Recipient Outstanding Tchr. citation Northwestern U., 1958. Mem. Am., Internat. musicological socs., Gesellschaft fur Musikwissenschaft, Pi Kappa Lambda, Phi Mu Alpha. Author: (with Frank Cookson) Creative-Analytical Theory of Music, 1948. Composer and arranger. Home: 1016 Willowlake Rd Winston-Salem NC 27106

NOONKESTER, JAMES RALPH, coll. pres.; b. Flatridge, Va., June 10, 1924; s. Reggie L. and Arcie (Parks) N.; B.A., U. Richmond, 1944; Th.M., So. Baptist Theol. Sem., 1947, Th.D., 1949; LL.D. (hon.), U. Richmond, 1968; m. Naomi Hopkins, June 10, 1947; children—Myron, Craig, Lila. Minister of edn. First Baptist Ch., Charlottesville, Va., 1950-52; prof., head div. religion and philosophy William Carey Coll., Hattiesburg, Miss., 1952-56, acad. dean, 1953-56, pres., 1956—. Chmn. bd. dirs. Miss. div. Am. Cancer Soc., 1966. Recipient award outstanding graduate English, U. Richmond, 1944; named Hattiesburg's Outstanding Young Man of 1956. Mem. Nat., Miss. edn. assns., Hattiesburg Concert Assn. (dir.), So. Assn. Bapt. Colls. and Schs. (pres.), Miss. Assn. Colls. (pres.), Hattiesburg C. of C. (pres. 1966), Phi Beta Kappa, Phi Delta Kappa, Chi Beta Phi, Omicron Delta Kappa. Kiwanian. Home: President's House William Carey Coll Hattiesburg MS

NOPPER, DAVID EUGENE, pub. relations exec.; b. Atlantic City, N.J., July 3, 1912; s. Charles G. and Charlotte (Schlissler) N.; student Balt. City Coll., 1929-31; A.B., St. John's Coll., 1935; m. Margaret Ann Kellam, May 17, 1947; 1 dau., Suzanne Shelton. Staff writer Washington Post, 1936, Balt. Sun, 1936-40; night editor A.P., Balt., 1940, bur. chief, Annapolis, Md., 1940-42; Eastern regional dir. pub. relations Am. Airlines, Inc., N.Y.C., 1945-49; spl. asst. ECA, Washington, 1949-54; pub. relations account exec. Bozell & Jacobs, 1953-58; mgr. pub. relations Ketchum, MacLeod & Grove, Inc., Washington, 1958—. Served with USMC, 1942-45. Mem. Pub. Relations Soc. Am., U.S. Power Squadron, Fed. Editors Assn., Govt. Information Orgn., Sigma Alpha Epsilon. Club: Nat. Press (Washington). Home: 5975 Wilton Rd Alexandria VA 22310 Office: 815 Connecticut Av NW Washington DC 20006

NORCROSS, ALVIN WATT, govt. ofcl.; b. Buffalo, Sept. 21, 1918; s. William Watt and Nettie (Alexander) N.; B.A., Baldwin Wallace Coll., 1940; postgrad. Ohio State U., 1940; M. Pub. Adminstrn., Harvard, 1948; m. Charlotte Anne Guptill, Oct. 23, 1948; children—David Lichty, Nancy Dayna. Employment mgr. Nat. Screw & Mfg. Co., Cleve., 1941-43; personnel officer Dept. Air Force, Washington, 1948-54, spl. asst. to dir. civilian personnel, 1954-58; asst. to dir. personnel Gen. Services Adminstrn., Washington, 1958-59, chief of employment, 1959-61; asst. dir. personnel Treasury Dept., 1961-67; dep. dir. Bur. Inspections, U.S. Civil Service Commn., 1967—. Del., Fairfax County Fedn. Civic Assns., 1957; pres. Vienna Hills Civic Assn., 1958; mem. personnel com. No. Va. council Girl Scouts U.S.A. Town councilman, Vienna, Va., 1959-65; mem. Vienna Civil Def. Com., 1960-62. Served with USAAF, 1943-46, lt. col. res. Recipient Air Force Superior Performance award, 1957, Treasury Meritorious Service award, 1966, Office of Sec. Treasury award, 1966, others. Mem. Am. Soc. Pub. Adminstrn., Soc. Personnel Adminstrn. (v.p. 1972), Pub. Personnel Assn. (past pres. Washington chpt.), Am. Soc. for Tng. and Devel. Club: Harvard (Washington). Home: 2038 Carrhill Rd Vienna VA 22180 Office: Dir Bur of Inspections US Civil Service Commn Washington DC 20415

NORDGULEN, GEORGE STERLING, educator; b. Fitchburg, Mass., Feb. 3, 1933; s. Ray Jeff and Lorraine Marguerite (Shandorf) N.; B.Th., N.W. Christian Coll., 1958; A.B. (Outstanding Student grantee), Phillips U., 1961, B.D., 1962; postgrad. U. Ore., 1962-63; Ph.D. (Lilly Found. grantee), Claremont U., 1966; m. June Marie Boyce, June 30, 1954; children—Eric Jon, Gary Scott, Kristi Jan. Asst. prof. religion and philosophy Drury Coll., Springfield, Mo., 1966-69; asso. prof. religion and philosophy Knoxville (Tenn.) Coll., 1969-72; asso. prof. religion Eastern Ky. U., Richmond, 1972—. Mem. Am. Acad. Religion, Metaphys. Soc. Am. Home: 104 Douglas St Berea KY 40403

NORDLINGER, GERSON, JR., investor; b. Washington, Feb. 2, 1916; s. Gerson and Camille (Bensinger) N.; B.A., George Washington U., 1935; B.C.S., Benjamin Franklin U., 1939. Head, Navy Dept. Bur. Aeros. Budget, 1946-50; treas. Nordlinger Investment Corp., Washington, 1955—; dir. Washington Real Estate Investment Trust, 1961—; sec. Drico, Inc., 1961—. Chmn., D.C. Arts Commn., 1965-67; v.p. Nat. Symphony Orch. Assn., 1953-59, 70-71, Nat. Ballet, 1966—; pres. Prevention of Blindness Soc., 1960-67; treas. Friendship House, 1951-69; vice chmn. D.C. Recreation Bd., 1960-67. Trustee Washington Performing Arts Soc., Opera Soc. Mem. state com. Republican party, 1952-64. Served to lt. comdr. Supply Corps, USNR, 1941-46; PTO. C.P.A., D.C. Mem. D.C. Inst. C.P.A.'s, Washington Bd. Trade. Jewish religion. Clubs: Army-Navy, Arts, International. Home: 2737 Devonshire Pl NW Washington DC 20008 Office: 1346 Connecticut Av Washington DC 20036

NORDWALL, CHARLES WILLIAM ALEXANDER, hosp. adminstr.; b. South Shields, Eng., Nov. 25, 1925; s. Charles William and Alice (Bridger) N.; brought to U.S., 1930, naturalized, 1935; B.S., Union Coll., 1950; M.S. in Hosp. Adminstrn., Columbia, 1955; m. Bernice Hilda Cotton, Aug. 21, 1949; children—Brian Lawrence, Deborah Gail. Adminstrv. resident Strong Meml. Hosp., Rochester, N.Y., 1954-55, adminstrv. asst., 1955-58, asst. adminstr., 1958; adminstr. Rochester Municipal Hosp., 1958-63, Monroe County Home and Infirmary, Rochester, 1963-65; dir. dept. hosps. Dade County, Fla., also exec. dir. Jackson Meml. Hosp., 1965—; past instr. hosp. adminstrn. U. Rochester; asso. prof. medicine U. Miami. Preceptor Washington U., St. Louis, George Washington U., Washington. Bd. dirs. Dade div. A.R.C., Dade County Blood Bank, Dade County Assn. Child Guidance Clinics, 1966. Served with USAAF, 1944-46. Mem. Am. Assn. Pub. Adminstrs., Assn. Am. Med. Colls., Dade County Med. Assn., Am., Fla. hosp. assns., Am. Coll. Hosp. Adminstrs. Unitarian. Mason. Home: 7201 SW 126th St Miami FL 33157 Office: 1700 NW 10th Av Miami FL 33156

NORDWALL, DARRELL ROBERT, wholesale exec.; b. Webster City, Ia., May 26, 1904; s. Alfred Edward and Beth (Woodruff) N.; student U. So. Cal., 1926; m. Rosita Elizabeth Hopps, Oct. 1, 1929; children—Sigrid (Mrs. Peter M. Wells), Elizabeth, (Mrs. William Jones). With Crane Co., Phoenix, 1932-37, Bridgeport, Conn., 1937-40, Boston, 1940-41; gen. sales mgr. Ohio Injector Co., Wadsworth, 1941-44; mgr. export sales Crane Co., N.Y.C., 1944-52, br. mgr., 1952-54, Los Angeles, 1954-56, Eastern dist. mgr., 1956-58, Pacific Coast dist. mgr., 1958, gen. sales mgr., Chgo., 1958-59; pres. Tucson Pipe & Supply Co., 1967—, Morrison Co., Santa Ana, Cal., Morrison Supply Co., Fort Worth, 1970—. Mem. Pacific Southwest Distbrs. Assn. (pres. 1963-64; dir. 1961-69), Am. Inst. (dir. 1962-68), Am. Supply Assn. Republican. Rotarian. Clubs: Colonial Country (Forth Worth); Santa Ana Country. Home: 346 Westview Terrace Arlington TX 76013 Office: PO Box 70 Fort Worth TX 76101

NORICK, JAMES HENRY, printing co. exec.; b. Oklahoma City, Jan. 23, 1920; s. Henry C. and Ruth (Coleman) N.; student Okla. Mil. Acad., 1938-40; m. Madalynne King, Mar. 25, 1940; children—Ronald J., Vickie L. Pres., Norick Bros., Inc., Oklahoma City, 1940—; v.p. Nobco, Inc., Oklahoma City, 1967. City councilman, Oklahoma City, 1951-55, mayor, 1959-63, 67-71. Served with USNR, 1942-45. Mason (Shriner). Home: 2909 Elmhurst St Oklahoma City OK 73120 Office: 3909 NW 36th St Oklahoma City OK 73112

NORICK, RONALD JAMES, printing co. exec.; b. Oklahoma City, Okla., Aug. 5, 1941; s. James H. and Madalynne (King) N.; B.S., Oklahoma City U., 1964; m. Carolyn K. Marshall, July 28, 1961; children—Allyson Lynne, Lance Marshall. With Norick Bros. Inc., Oklahoma City, 1961—, prodn. mgr., 1971—; pres. The House of Kawasaki, Inc., Oklahoma City, 1965—; owner Da-Con, Oklahoma City, 1965—; dir. Lunn Printing Co. Chmn. Oklahoma City Jr. C. of C. Invitational, 1969-72. Bd. dirs. Taft Stadium Bd. Recipient Key Man award Oklahoma City Jr. C. of C. 1967-68, 69-70. Mem. Printing Industry of Am., Printing Industry of Okla. (bd. dirs. 1969-71), All Sports Assn., Jr. C. of C. (pres. 1968-69, chmn. bd. 1969-70), Delta Sigma Pi. Mason (32 deg., Shriner). Home: 2304 Carlton Way Oklahoma City OK 73120 Office: PO Box 12073 Oklahoma City OK 73112

NORMAN, ALBERT GEORGE, JR., lawyer; b. Birmingham, Ala., May 29, 1929; s. Albert G. and Ila Mae (Carroll) N.; B.A., Auburn U., 1953; LL.B., Emory U., 1958; M.A., U. N.C., 1960; m. Catherine Marshall DeShazo, Sept. 3, 1955; children—Catherine Marshall, Albert George III. Admitted to Ga. bar, 1957; asso. Moise, Post & Gardner, Atlanta, 1958-60, partner, 1960-62; partner Hansell, Post, Brandon & Dorsey, Atlanta, 1962—. Served with USAF, 1946-49. Mem. Am., Ga., Atlanta bar assns. Clubs: Lawyers (Atlanta), Cherokee Town and Country. Home: 3381 Valley Circle NW Atlanta GA 30305 Office: First Nat Bank Bldg Atlanta GA 30303

NORMAN, HENRY ROBERT, cons. civil engr.; b. Carlton, Minn., Aug. 12, 1904; s. August R. and Anna (Ullman) N.; B.S. in Civil Engring., U. Minn., 1927, postgrad., 1930-31; m. Minda B. Rodal, May 21, 1929 (dec. Oct. 1963); children—John, Jerry; m. 2d, Doris J. Yawn, Dec. 22, 1964; stepchildren—Richard, Susan. Served from insp. to prin. engr. Milw., St. Paul and Galveston (Tex.) dist. offices, Upper Miss. Valley div. office, and chief engrs., Washington office C.E. U.S. Army, 1927-50; partner Norman Knappen Tippetts Engring. Co., Houston, 1950-51; transp. engr. KTA Engring. Co., Rangoon, Burma, 1951-53; cons. civil engr. Brown & Root, Inc., Houston, 1953-69, spl. water cons. City of Houston, 1960-69; asst. dir. Dept. Pub. Works, City of Houston, 1969—. Served to lt. col. AUS, 1942-46. Fellow Am. Soc. C.E.; mem. Am. Geophys. Union, Soc. Am. Mil. Engrs., Nat., Tex. socs. profl. engrs., Am. Ordnance Assn., Houston C. of C. (ports and waterways and water supply com.), Am. Soc. Oceanography (charter), Sigma Nu. Contbr. articles to profl. publs. Home: 2336 McClendon St Houston TX 77025

NORMAN, ISAAC WALKER, oil and gas co. exec.; b. Taylor, Tex., Oct. 11, 1925; s. Isaac and Winnie (Rickard) N.; B.S. (Scholarship 1942), U. Tex., 1948; postgrad. U. Houston, 1950; m. Frances Eileen Tyler, Apr. 10, 1948; children—Wynette (Mrs. James Weaver), Leigh, Patricia, Lisa, Howard. Geologist, Gulf Oil Corp., 1948-52; dist. geologist Drilling and Exploration Co., 1952-57, div. geologist, 1957-64, chief geologist, 1964-68; v.p., gen. mgr. oil and gas div. Highland Resources, Inc., Houston, 1968—; dir. Prodn. Systems Internat., Gas Turbine, Inc. Served to 2d lt. USAAF, 1943-46. Mem. Am. Assn. Petroleum Geologists, Soc. Exploration Geophysics, Houston Geol. Soc. Club: Houston. Home: 3832 Olympia St Houston TX 77019 Office: San Jacinto Bldg Houston TX 77002

NORMAN, JOHN ROYCE, dentist; b. Jamestown, Tenn., Oct. 19, 1934; s. Ambrosia and Imogene Catherine (Cruze) N.; B.S., U. Tenn., 1956, D.D.S., 1966; m. Andrea Carole Warren, Aug. 7, 1965; children—Carole Jean, John Andrew, Joseph David. Systems analyst Combustion Engring., Inc., Chattanooga, 1956-61; dentist N.C. Dept. Health, Surry County, 1967; gen. practice dentistry, Athens, Tenn., 1967—; mem. staff Epperson Hosp., Athens. Served with AUS, 1957-58. Mem. Am. Endodontic Soc., Am. Dental Assn., Athens C. of C., 3d Dist., Tenn. dental socs. Lion, Elk. Home: Route 2 Athens TN 37303 Office: 109 Park St Athens TN 37303

NORMAN, SUMMERS A., lawyer; b. Rusk, Tex., Aug. 25, 1905; s. Wyatt T. and Brunette (Summers) N.; LL.B., So. Meth. U., Dallas, 1929; m. Mary Nell Odom, Aug. 25, 1929. Admitted to Tex. bar, 1929; with firms Norman & Norman, 1929, Norman, Stone & Norman, 1937, Norman, Stone, Rounsaville & Hassell, 1948-59, Norman, Rounsaville, Hassell & Spiers, 1950—; v.p., dir. First State Bank, Wells; v.p. S-K Fixture & Church Furniture Co., Mid-Continent Church Furniture Co., S-K Cabinet Co.; dir. Nichols Industries, Inc., 1st Nat. Bank Jacksonville. Chmn. Tex. Liquor Control Bd., 1947-65; chmn. bd. trustees, dir. Nan Travis Meml. Hosp.; chmn. bd. dirs. Jacksonville Indsl. Found. Served as lt. comdr. USNR, Fellow Am. Judicature Soc., Southwestern Legal Found., Tex. State Bar Found.; mem. State Bar Tex. (bd. dirs.), C. of C. (past pres.), Pi Kappa Alpha. Presbyn. (elder, trustee). Mason (Shriner), Rotarian (past pres.). Clubs: Petroleum (Houston); Austin, (Austin); Dallas Athletic (Dallas); Cherokee Country. Home: 1212 Hillcrest Dr Jacksonville TX 75766 Office: First Nat Bank Bldg Jacksonville TX 75766

NORMENT, HARTWELL TALIAFERRO, pharm. co. exec.; b. Richmond, Va., July 14, 1922; s. Thomas Julien and Mattie Lee (Hudson) N.; student U. Richmond, 1939-40, Va. Commonwealth U., 1946-49; m. Lois Proffitt, June 29, 1946. With Wm. P. Poythress & Co., Inc., Richmond, Va., 1940—, analytical chemist, 1946-56, prodn. mgr., 1956-65, plant mgr., 1965—, corp. sec., 1969—, also dir. Served with AUS, 1942-45. Decorated with Purple Heart with two oak leaf clusters. Mem. Am. Chem. Soc. Home: 202 Hickory Dr Manakin VA 23103 Office: 16 N 22nd St Richmond VA 23261

NORRIS, BERRY EARLE, JR., engring. exec.; b. Wichita Falls, Tex., Nov. 8, 1927; s. Berry E. and Vera (Ferguson) N.; B.S., U. Houston, 1952, B.S., 1953, M.S., 1959; m. Sandra Suzanne Ellis, Apr. 22, 1965; 1 dau., Nathalie. Chemist, Shell Devel. Co., Houston, 1950-52; chem. engr. Houston Research Inst., 1952—, dir., treas., 1963—, pres., 1967—; v.p. operations Gulf So. Research Inst., Baton Rouge, 1968-69, v.p., gen. mgr., 1969—. Campaign mgr. Republican Senatorial candidate, 1964. Mem. Am. Inst. Chem. Engrs., Nat., Tex. socs. profl. engrs. Rotarian. Patentee in field. Home: 766 Rodney Dr Baton Rouge LA 70808 Office: 8000 GSRI Av Baton Rouge LA 70808

NORRIS, RICHARD LEE, computing co. exec.; b. Louisville, Feb. 20, 1934; s. Chester Lee and Anna Mae (Ballard) N.; B.S., Eastern Ky. U., 1956; postgrad. U. Louisville, 1957-61; m. Lois Samson, June 20, 1959; children—Andrea Kay, Scott Alan, Keith Wayne, Richard Lee, John David. Computer technique specialist in systems analysis Gen. Electric Co., Louisville, 1956-68; v.p., mgr. computation div. Metridata Computing, Inc., Louisville, 1968—. Mem. faculty Ballarmine Coll., Louisville, 1967-68. Served with AUS, 1959. Republican. Roman Catholic. Home: 6511 Downs Branch St Louisville KY 40228 Office: PO Box 21099 Louisville KY 40221

NORRIS, ROY HART, JR., coal co. exec.; b. Ariton, Ala., Sept. 18, 1902; s. Roy Hart and Martha (Shiver) N.; student Auburn U., 1920-22; m. Dorothy Davis Putnam, Aug. 15, 1942; children—Roy Hart III, Dorothy Putnam. Order, billing clk. Lamar Rankin Drug, Montgomery, Ala., 1922-23; bookkeeper Armour & Co., Montgomery, 1923-24; bookkeeper, mgr. Montgomery Abattoir, 1924-25; salesman V-C Chems., Richmond, Va., 1925-29; salesman Ala. By-Products Corp., Birmingham, 1929-43, asst. mgr. coal sales, 1943-46, mgr. coal sales, 1946-54, v.p. sales, 1954-68, sr. v.p., 1968—, dir., 1964—. Mem. Am. Coke and Coal Chems. Inst. (treas. 1967-71; pres. 1971-72), Nat. Plant Food Inst. (dir. 1966-69), Am. Foundrymen's Soc. (dir. 1957-58), Newcomen Soc. N.Am. Republican. Presbyn. Clubs: Vestavia Country, The Club, Relay House (Birmingham). Home: 1006 Euclid Av Crestline Birmingham AL 35213 Office: PO Box 10246 Birmingham AL 35202

NORRIS, SAMUEL HOLLIS, geologist; b. Glasgow, Ky., June 1, 1932; s. Hollis Franklin and Olga Elizabeth (Lane) N.; B.A., Vanderbilt U., 1954; postgrad., U. Ky., 1957-59; m. Anna Owen, Sept. 4, 1960; children—Steven, Nan, Jan, Timothy, Mary, Amy. Geologist Ky. Geol. Cons., Inc., Lexington, 1959-61; pres. Petroleum Drilling Co., Inc., Greensburg, Ky., 1961-62; sr. oil and gas insp., oil and gas div., Ky. Dept. Mines and Minerals, Glasgow, 1962—; pres. Glasgow

Marine, Inc., (Ky.), 1964—; dir. Citizens Bank and Trust Co. Councilman, Glasgow, Ky., 1962-68; mem. Glasgow Bd. Adjustments, 1968—; mem. Draft Bd., 1970—. Served with AUS, 1954-56. Address: Route 2 Glasgow KY 42141

NORRIS, WALTER LEWIS, architect; b. Mexia, Tex., Sept. 16, 1927; s. Robert Lee and Nona Merle (Ward) N.; B.Arch., Tex. A. and M. Coll., 1948; m. Billie Ann Ives, Nov. 10, 1950; children—Ann Norris, Susan, Diane. Archtl. draftsman H. C. Avery, Jr., architect, Midland, Tex., 1948-51; architect Walter L. Norris, architects, Midland, 1951-54; architect, partner Pierce, Norris, McCutchan, Pace & Assos., architects, Midland, 1954-56, Pierce, Norris, Pace & Assos., architects, Midland, 1956-70; architect, pres. Walter L. Norris Assos., Inc., architects and planners, 1970—. Mem. A.I.A., Tex. Soc. Architects. Mason (Shriner), Lion. Home: 1201 Cheyenne Pl Richardson TX 75080 Office: Stemmons Tower S Dallas TX 75207

NORTH, HERSCHEL I., state ofcl.; b. Fowlerton, Tex., Nov. 16, 1914; s. Herschel Ira and Lola (Cupples) N.; B.A., Abilene Christian Coll., 1934; M.B.A., U. Tex., Austin, 1939; m. Jane Atkinson, Aug. 3, 1940 (dec. Sept. 1962); 1 dau., Linda; m. 2d, Virginia O. Singleton, Nov. 1, 1966; stepchildren—Danny, Kenny, Larry, Kerry. Tchr. pub. schs., Sweetwater and Munday, Tex., 1934-37; auditor Arthur Anderson and Co., Houston, 1939; pvt. practice pub. accounting, San Angelo, Tex., 1940-41; accountant Lockheed Aircraft, Burbank, Cal., 1941-45; realtor H. I. North Co., San Fernando Valley, Cal., 1945-49; adminstrv. asst. Tex. Dept. Health, Austin, 1950-55, dir. finance 1955-59, asst. adminstr., 1959-64, exec. dir. adminstrn., 1964-65, exec. dir., 1965-69, dep. commr. health for finance, 1969—. C.P.A., Tex. Mem. Tex. Soc. C.P.A.'s, Tex. Pub. Employees Assn., Nat. Assn. Bus. Mgmt. in Pub. Health. Lion (sec. San Angelo 1940). Home: 7203 Shoal Creek Austin TX 78757 Office: 1100 W 49th St Austin TX 78756

NORTH, PHILLIP RECORD, investor; b. Ft. Worth, July 6, 1918; s. James Mortimer and Lottie Record (N.); A.B., U. Notre Dame, 1939; m. Janis Mary Harris, July 28, 1944; children—Phillip Kevin, Kerry Lawrence, Mairin Kathleen, Deirdre Aine. Exec. editor, v.p. Fort Worth Star-Telegram, Carter Publs., Inc., 1954-62; dir. Continental Nat. Bank, Ft. Worth, Tandy Corp., Ft. Worth. Vice pres. Ft. Worth Diocese Endowment and Devel. Fund Inc., 1971—; mem. adv. council U. Notre Dame, 1967—. Served to maj. AUS, 1940-46. Roman Catholic. Clubs: Fort Worth, Shady Oaks Country, Rivercrest Country (Ft. Worth). Home and office: 6141 Locke St Fort Worth TX 76116

NORTH, WILLIAM CHARLES, physician, educator; b. Chungking, China, Aug. 17, 1925; s. William Robert and Sarah Strohm (Shuey) N.; came to U.S., 1928; A.B., DePauw U., 1945; M.S. (Abbott fellow), Northwestern U., 1948, M.D., 1950, Ph.D., 1952; m. Arlene Boss, Sept. 15, 1945; children—W. Thomas, Gregg R., David K., Christopher P., Melinda R.; m. 2d, Joyce S. Pace, Oct. 7, 1971; children—B. Preston, Nancy L., Karen G., Elisa M. Intern, Chgo. Meml. Hosp., 1949-50; resident Chgo. Wesley Hosp., 1957-59; mem. faculty Northwestern U., 1948-59, asst. prof. pharmacology, 1954-59; mem. faculty Duke U., Durham, N.C., 1959-65, asst. prof. anesthesiology, 1959-62, asso. prof. anesthesiology, also pharmacology, 1963-65; prof. pharmacology, chmn. dept. anesthsiology, U. Tenn. at Memphis, 1965—. Served with USNR, 1943-46. Mem. A.M.A., Am. Soc. Anesthesiologists, Am. Soc. Pharmacology and Exptl. Therapeutics, Internat. Anesthesia Research Soc., Am. Coll. Anesthesiologists, Am. Assn. U. Profs., A.A.A.S. Home: 317 S Yates St Memphis TN 38117

NORTHEN, OSCAR EDWARDS, JR., architect; b. Charlottsville, Va., Jan. 8, 1931; s. Oscar Edwards and Francis Bernetta (Wagner) N.; asso. diploma Mars Hill Coll., 1950; B.S. in Architecture, U. Va., 1954; M.City Planning, Yale, 1960; m. Joan Dawn Morley, Dec. 20, 1952; children—Oscar Edwards III, Rebecca Kay, Stephanie Renee. Archtl. designer New Haven City Planning Dept., 1958-60; architect, chief planner Stonorov & Haws, Phila., 1960-64; partner firm Lynch & Northen, Lancaster, Pa., 1964-65; owner Oscar Northen, Architect, Virginia Beach, Va., 1965-67; partner firm McGorkle, Northen & Assos., Virginia Beach, 1967-70; owner Oscar Northen Assos., Architects and Planning Cons., Virginia Beach, 1970—. Pres. Va. Beach Civic Chorus, 1968-69; bd. dirs. Virginia Beach Civic Ballet, 1970—, Virginia Beach Experiment, Tidewater Young Life Com., v.p. Virginia Beach Friends of Music. Served with USAF, 1954-58. Mem. A.I.A., Am. Inst. Planners, Constrn. Specifications Inst. Presbyn. (deacon). Elk, Rotarian. Club: Cavalier Golf and Yacht (Virginia Beach). Home: 1601 Dendron Dr Virginia Beach VA 23451 Office: 633-D Independence Blvd Virginia Beach VA 23462

NORTHINGTON, LOUIS GUTHRIE, veterinarian, state ofcl.; b. Bandana, Ky., Oct. 11, 1918; s. Hiram W. and Lottie L. (Turner) N.; D.V.M., Ohio State U., 1940; m. Mary Lou Cosby, Dec. 6, 1940; children—Jerry W., Wade A., L. Ned. Practice vet. medicine, Graves County, Ky., 1940-68; state veterinarian, div. livestock sanitation Ky. Dept. Agr., Frankfort, 1968—. Mem. Ky. Bd. Vet. Examiners, 1958-66. Mem. Am., Ky. (pres. 1949, exec. com. 1950-65, named Veterinarian of Year 1969) vet. med. assns. Home: 110 Thistle Rd Frankfort KY 40601 Office: Capitol Annex Frankfort KY 40601

NORTHRUP, JACK RICHARD, city ofcl.; b. Waverly, N.Y., Apr. 10, 1935; s. Harold and Beatrice (Grant) N.; B.S., Ark. State U., 1964; m. Melba Jean Edwards, May 11, 1957; children—Tanya Kay, Jackie Lynn, Terri Jean. Social worker Ark. Dept. Pub. Welfare, Harrisburg, 1964, dir., Marianna, 1964-65; dir. Urban Renewal, Marianna, 1965-66; exec. dir. Housing and Urban Renewal, Marianna, 1967-72; city coordinator City of Olney, Tex., 1972—. Served with AUS, 1954-58. Mem. Nat., Ark. housing and redevel. ofcls., D.A.V., C. of C. (dir. 1969—). Lion (2d v.p. 1969—). Home: 604 W Oak St Olney TX 76374 Office: City Hall Olney TX 76374

NORTON, ETHELBERT B., coll. pres.; b. Jefferson County, Ala., June 5, 1902; s. Rev. Ethelbert B. and Grace (Myatt) N.; A.B., Birmingham-So. Coll., 1923, L.H.D., 1943; LL.D., Ala. Poly. Inst., 1942; m. Laura Cowart, Aug. 17, 1926; children—Mack, Bert, Betty. Tchr. sci., dir. athletics Pike Road High Sch., Montgomery County, Ala., 1924-27; prin. Rawls High Sch., Covington County, Ala., 1927-34, county supt. of edn., 1934-42; supt. edn. State of Ala., 1942-46; dir. sch. adminstrn. U.S. Office of Edn., Washington, June 1946, dep. commr., Nov. 1946-June 1948; exec. sec. Nat. Council Chief State Sch. Officers, June 1948-Dec. 1948; pres. State Tchrs. Coll., Florence, Ala., 1948—. Mem. adv. bd. State Nat. Bank Florence. Mem. exec. com. Am. Assn. of Coll. for Tchr. Edn., mem. commn. on accrediting, mem. commn. on safety edn. Ex-officio mem. bd. trustees Alabama Coll., Montevallo, Ala., Ala. Poly. Inst., Auburn, Ala., U. Ala., Tuscaloosa, Ala. (1942-46); chmn. finance com. 1st White House Conf. on Rural Edn., 1944; mem. U.S. Edn. Mission to Japan, 1946; chmn. Covington County chpt. Am. Red Cross, 1940-42; pres. Ala. Edn. Assn., 1939; past pres. Ala. Assn. Sch. Adminstrs.; bd. mgrs. Ala. Congress of Parents and Tchrs., 1934-46; mem. exec. and legislative coms. Nat. Council Chief State Sch. Officers, 1944-46; pres. So. Council Tchr. Edn., 1953-54. Mem. Phi Beta Kappa, Kappa Phi Kappa, Phi Delta Kappa, Omicron Delta Kappa. Past pres. Andalusia Rotary Club. Home: Florence AL

NORTON, HUGH STANTON, economist, educator; b. Delta, Colo., Sept. 18, 1921; s. Cecil A. and Olive (Stanton) N.; A.B., George Washington U., 1947, Ph.D., 1956; m. Miriam Jarmon, Dec. 17, 1949; children— Pamela, John. Instr., U. Md., College Park, 1948-54; economist U.S. Dept. Agr., Washington, 1954-57; asso. prof. econs. U. Tenn., Knoxville, 1957-60, prof., 1960-66; prof. econs. U. S.C., Columbia, 1966-68, D.H. Johnson prof. econs., 1968—, chmn. dept. econs., 1971—. Cons., sr. econ. adviser Wilbur Smith & Assos. Served with AUS, 1942-45. Mem. Am. Econ. Assn., Nat. Assn. Bus. Economists, Order of Artus. Club: Rockbridge Country (past pres.). Author: Modern Transportation Economics, 1963; Economic Policy, 1966; National Transportation Policy, 1968; Economist, Role in Government Policy Making, 1969; Economist in Business, 1969. Home: 3335 Overcreek Rd Columbia SC 29206

NORTON, JAMES JOSEPH, sch. supt.; b. Donora, Pa., May 18, 1914; s. Joseph J. and Sarah (Corbett) N.; student California (Pa.) State Coll., 1932-34; B.S., U. Miami, 1949; M.A., Columbia, 1950; m. Harriet R. Copenhaver, June 19, 1942. Tchr. elementary sch., Miami, Fla., 1948-53; elementary sch. prin., Miami, 1953-57; jr. high sch. prin., Coral Gables, Fla., 1957-62; high sch. prin., Coral Gables, 1962-66; dist. supt., Miami, 1966—. Served with USMCR, 1943-46. Mem. Phi Delta Kappa. Democrat. Roman Catholic. Kiwanian. Home: 7230 SW 53 Ct South Miami FL 33143 Office: 2201 SW 4th St Miami FL 33135

NORTON, MARVIN LEROY, JR., electronic engr.; b. North Wildwood, N.J., Oct. 27, 1935; s. Marvin Leroy and Elizabeth (Steelman) N.; B.S., Rutgers U., 1957; M.S., Newark Coll. Engring., 1962; M.S., Fla. Inst. Tech., 1968; m. Dorothea Johanna Petermann, June 29, 1958; children—Karl Eric, Jeannette Alyson, Joy Alicia, Brian Edward, Arthur Roy, Gail Elizabeth. Asst. engr. N.J. Bell Telephone Co., Newark, 1957-59 engr. Internat. Tel. & Tel. Fed. Labs., Nutley, N.J., 1959-65; engr. RCA Service Corp. Missile Test Project, Patrick AFB, Fla., 1965-66, analyst, 1966-69, leader, 1969—; pres. N.P. Research Corp., 1970—. Adj. instr. Fla. Inst. Tech. Commr., Boy Scouts Am., 1966-67, committeeman, 1968, leader, 1969. Registered profl. engr., N.J., Fla. Fellow Brit. Interplanetary Soc.; sr. mem. I.E.E.E., Fla. Engring. Soc.; mem. A.A.A.S., Nat. Soc. Profl. Engrs., Am. Geophys. Union, Marine Tech. Soc. (sect. councilor 1969, sec. 1970-71, vice chmn. 1971-72), Internat. Oceanographic Found. Republican. Lutheran. Home: 990 Sarazen Dr Rockledge FL 32955 Office: Mail unit 811 Patrick AFB FL 32935

NORTON, WADE ANDREW, computer exec.; b. Birmingham, Ala., Oct. 1, 1928; s. William Andrews and Ola Grace (Mason) N.; A.B., Birmingham-So. Coll., 1949; M.S., Auburn U., 1961; M.A., Peabody Coll., 1950; m. Ann LaVerne Holladay, June 7, 1958; children—William Andrew, Frances Ruth. Asst. state editor Birmingham Post-Herald, 1956-57; teaching fellow math. Auburn U., 1957-59; instr. math. West End High Sch., Birmingham, 1959-61, Howard Coll., 1961-64, U. Ala., 1967; mathematician Computer Center, So. Services, Inc., 1961-66, chief analyst, 1966-68, sr. analyst engring. group, 1968-69, sr. analyst computer systems support, 1969-71; systems mgr. U. Ala. Computer Center, Tuscaloosa, 1971—. Served with USAF, 1951-55. Mem. Data Processing Mgmt. Assn., Assn. for Computing Machinery (chpt. chmn. 1969), S.A.R. COMMON (exec. v.p. 1969), Kappa Phi Kappa, Phi Delta Kappa. Methodist (mem. ofcl. bd. 1964-66, sec. 1965-66). Editor: Common. Home: 4 Hillswood One Tuscaloosa AL 35401 Office: Box 2511 University AL 35486

NORVIEL, ANITA EVELYN TOWNSEND, hosp. exec. sec.; b. Chattanooga; d. Frank C. and Janie (Phillips) Townsend; student Okaloosa Walton Jr. Coll., 1967—; m. Donald L. Norviel, Sr., Oct. 7, 1939; children—Janie (Mrs. Bennie L. Stone), Bette (Mrs. Eugene V. Smith), Donald L. II. Sec. to neurosurgeon, Amarillo, Tex., 1960-61; sec. to registrar USAF Hosp., Amarillo, 1962-63; sec. to chief Air Ground Operations Sch., 1963-64; exec. sec. to chief hosp. services USAF Regional Hosp., Eglin Air Force Base, Fla., 1965—. Sec. Ft. Walton Beach Mus. Bd., 1965-67, Ft. Walton Beach Civic Improvement Assn., 1964-65; bd. dirs. Am. Cancer Soc., 1967-71; sec. civilian welfare fund bd. Eglin Air Force Base, 1966-72. Named sec. of year Nat. Secs. Assn., Ft. Walton Beach, 1965, 67. Mem. Nat. Secs. Assn. (pres. Fla. div.). Home: 26 Ferry Rd NE Ft Walton Beach FL 32548 Office: USAF Regional Hospital Eglin Air Force Base FL 32542

NORWOOD, JANET LIPPE, economist; b. Newark, Dec. 11, 1923; d. M. Turner and Thelma (Levinson) Lippe; B.A., Douglass Coll., 1945; M.A., Tufts U., 1946, Ph.D., 1949; m. Bernard Norwood, June 25, 1943; children—Stephen Harlan, Peter Carlton. Instr. Wellesley Coll., 1948-49; economist William L. Clayton Center of Fletcher Sch. Law and Diplomacy, 1952-58; economist Office Fgn. Labor and Trade of U.S. Bur. Labor Statistics, Washington, 1963-67, economist Office Prices and Living Conditions, 1967-70, chief Div. Consumer Prices and Price Indexes, 1970—. Mem. Am. Econ. Assn., Am. Statis. Assn., Nat. Economists Club. Home: 6409 Marjory Lane Bethesda MD 20034 Office: US Bur Labor Statistics Washington DC 20212

NORWOOD, NORMAN ROBERT, bldg. co. exec.; b. Fayetteville, Ark., Feb. 28, 1924; s. Norman and Maureen (Williams) N.; student Baylor U., 1960-61, U. Houston, 1961-66; m. Andrea Lee Ross, Aug. 25, 1962; children—Lauri Lee, Juli Andrea, Kristi Maureen. With Monarch Homes, Inc., Houston, 1962—, salesman, 1962-63, constrn. supt., 1964-67, salesman, 1967-68, sub-div. mgr., 1968-69, prodn. mgr., v.p., 1969-70, v.p., sales mgr., 1970, exec. v.p., 1970-71, pres., 1971—. Mem. Greater Houston Builders Assn. (mem. com. 1970-71). Baptist (deacon 1966—). Club: Tri-County Optimist (Katy, Tex.). Home: 2203 Saddle Horn Trail Katy TX 77450 Office: 8005 Dunlap St Houston TX 77036

NORWOOD, TRACY, football coach Northeastern State Coll., Tahlequah, Okla. Address: Athletic Dept Northeastern State Coll Tahlequah OK 74464*

NOTT, ERNEST CLAYTON, JR., hosp. adminstr.; b. Ocala, Fla., Apr. 12, 1924; s. Ernest C. and Hilda (Monroe) N.; B.S., Wake Forest Coll., 1945; M.H.A., Med. Coll. Va., 1957; m. Frances Belle Meggs, June 5, 1949; children—Marsha Leigh, Cynthia Marie, Terri Ann. Personnel dir. Baptist Hosp., Jacksonville, Fla., 1957-58; administrv. asst. Broward Gen. Hosp., Fort Lauderdale, Fla., 1958-60, administr., 1960-62; adminstr. Bapt. Hosp., Miami, Fla., 1962—. Bd. dirs. Blue Cross, Fla., Comprehensive Health Planning Council South Fla., Community Health, Inc. Served from lt. to capt., AUS, 1945-53. Mem. Am. Hosp. Assn., Am. Coll. Hosp. Adminstrs., S. Fla. Hosp. Council (pres. 1965-66), Fla. Hosp. Assn. (pres. 1970-71. Baptist (deacon). Kiwanian. Home: 8424 SW 78th St South Miami FL 33143 Office: 8900 N Kendall Dr Miami FL 33156

NOVAK, ALBERT JOHN WITTMAYER, electronics co. exec.; b. Grand Rapids, Mich., Mar. 30, 1921; s. Albert Joseph and Joan (Wittmayer) N.; A.B. in Physics magna cum laude, Harvard, 1941; postgrad. Mass. Inst. Tech., 1943-44, Case Inst. Tech., 1946-48; m. Patricia Mabel Henline, Mar. 25, 1950; children—Patricia Joan, Albert John Wittmayer, David Bruce, Loren Lee. Mfg. engr. RCA, Camden, N.J., 1941-42; sales mgr. Brush Electronics Div. Clevite Corp., 1946-54; div. mgr. Tex. div. Clevite Corp., Houston, 1955-57; sales mgr., engring. mgr. Ansonia Wire & Cable Co., Ashton, R.I., 1957-59; v.p., gen. mgr. Hoover Electronics Co., Timonium, Md., Pompano Beach, Fla., 1959-64; pres. Novatronics, Inc., Pompano Beach, 1965—, Novatronics of Can., Ltd., Stratford, Ont., 1969— ; dir. Pompano Beach Bank & Trust. Vice pres. Broward County (Fla.) Jr. Achievement, 1967—; vice chmn. Broward County Community Relations Commn.; pres. Ft. Lauderdale (Fla.) Symphony Orch. Assn., 1970; vice chmn. Broward Manpower Planning Council. Served from ensign to lt. comdr. USNR, 1942-46. Recipient Outstanding Service award Nat. Elec. Mfrs. Assn., 1967. Mem. Broward Mfrs. Assn. (pres. 1966-67, Industrialist of Year 1969), Sci. Apparatus Mfrs. Assn., Am. Mgmt. Assn., Am. Ordnance Assn., Fla. Def. Space Industries Assn. (pres. 1969-70), I.E.E.E., Navy League, Phi Beta Kappa. Kiwanian. Club: Harvard (Broward County). Home: 2220 NE 52d Ct Fort Lauderdale FL 33308 Office: 500 N Andrews Av Extension Pompano Beach FL 33061

NOVAK, ARTHUR FRANCIS, educator; b. Balt., Oct. 25, 1916; s. Frank C. and Anna Barbara (Hulka) N.; B.S., U. Md., 1937; M.S., U. Ala., 1939; Ph.D., Purdue U., 1947; postgrad, Johns Hopkins, 1939-40, U. Louisville, 1941-42, U. So. Cal., 1951-53; m. Mary Frances Miller, May 15, 1947; children—Katrina Marie, Stephen Francis. Supr. fermentation Seagram: Calvert, Louisville, 1940-47; prof. bacteriology and chemistry U. Fla., Gainesville, 1947-51; dir. research Nutrilite Products, Inc., Buena Park, Cal., 1951-54; prof., head dept. food sci and tech., prof. marine sci. La. State U., Baton Rouge, 1954—. Cons in foods and drugs, 1947—; cons. to state and fed. agys., 1949—; Ford Found. adviser oceanography and food sci. to Brazil, 1968-69; prof. physiology U. Sao Paulo (Brazil) Faculty of Medicine; tech. dir. Internat. Shrimp Council, 1967—. Mem. Internat. Tech. Assistance Com., 1960—. Bd. dirs. Boys Clubs So. Cal., pres., 1952-54. Fellow Am. Inst. Chemists; mem. A.A.A.S., Gulf Coast Inst. Food Technologists (pres. 1964-65), Am. Pharm. Assn., Am. Nuclear Soc., Oyster Inst. N.Am., Nat. Fisheries Inst., Nat. Shell Fisheries Assn., Am. Soc. Microbiology, Am. Chem. Soc., Marine Tech. Soc., Shrimp Assn. Ams., Shrimp Breeders and Processors Am. (tech. dir.), Nat. Fisheries Inst., So. Assn. Food and Drug Ofcls., Council Am. Bioanalysts, Am. Soc. for Heating, Air Conditioning and Refrigeration Engrs., Inst. Food Technologists (chmn. constn.) and by laws, also food quality control), Rho Chi, Gamma Sigma Epsilon, Phi Kappa Phi, Gamma Sigma Delta, Pi Tau Sigma, Lambda Tau, Phi Kappa, Omicron Delta Kappa. Author: Microbiology of Shellfish, 1962; Fundamentals of Food Science. Contbr. numerous articles to profl. jours. Patentee in field. Home: 656 College Hill Dr Baton Rouge LA 70808

NOVAK, EARL EDWARD, dentist; b. Spearman, Tex., Nov. 7, 1934; s. Frank F. and Frances (Nespor) N.; student Okla. State U., 1953-57; D.D.S., Baylor U., 1961; m. Barbara Fulkerson, Nov. 27, 1959; children—Hunter, Cinda. Partner farming enterprise, Hansford County, Tex., 1953-61; pvt. practice dentistry, Spearman, 1961—; farm ranch operator, Spearman, 1961—. Sec. med. staff Hansford Hosp., 1967, 69. Mem. Am. Acad. Gen. Dentistry, Panhandle Dental Study Club (sec.-treas. 1968), Baylor Odontological Honor Soc., Jr. C. of C., Alpha Zeta, Phi Eta Sigma, Alpha Gamma Rho, Psi Omega. Democrat. Mem. Christian Ch. (deacon 1966-68, 69). Rotarian. Home: Star Route 1 Box 67 Spearman TX 79081 Office: 712 S Roland St Spearman TX 79081

NOVAK, JOSEPH ROBERT, paper products co. exec.; b. Waco, Tex., Mar. 18, 1928; s. Alfons and Fannie Pearl (Hamby) N.; B.A., Baylor U., 1951; M.R.E., Southwestern Baptist Theol. Sem. (Tex.), 1955; m. Rynell Stiff, May 11, 1954; children—Robert David, Daniel Allan, Timothy Criswell, Rebekah, Elisabeth. Editorial asst. Bapt. Standard, Dallas, 1956-57; editor Bapt. Digest, Wichita, Kan., 1957-59; exec. editor Houston Mag., 1960-61; mgr. pub. relations Houston C. of C., 1961-64; pub. relations and devel. Meml. Bapt. Hosp. System, Houston, 1964-67; asst. mgr. Nat. Assn. Conservation Dists., League City, Tex., 1967-69; staff asst. Moore Bus. Forms, Bryan, Tex., 1969-71, staff asst. indsl. relations So. div., Denton, Tex., 1971—. Chmn., United Fund, 1963-64; v.p. League City vol. fire dept., 1968-69; chmn. dist. pub. relations and publicity P.T.A., 1971; tchr. adult edn. courses, 1963-64. Served with USNR, 1946-47, 51-52. Mem. Am. Soc. for Personnel Adminstrn., Toastmasters Internat. (pres. 1971), Am. C. of C. Execs., Pub. Relations Soc. Am., Tex. Bapt. pub. relations assns. Baptist (deacon 1961—). Rotarian. Home: 2120 Preston Pl Denton TX 76201 Office: PO Box 1369 Denton TX 76201

NOWAK, JEAN M., govt. ofcl.; b. Sheboygan, Wis.; d. Ramond Carleton and Leila (Stephen) McDuffie; student Lake Forest Coll., 1935-38; B.A., U. Wis., 1939; m. Francis Jefferson Nowak, Dec. 28, 1940 (div. Apr. 1966); children—Francis Jefferson, Nancy Jean, Robert Craig. Asso. editor North Chgo. Tribune, 1938-40; information specialist State of Ill., Springfield, 1940-41; free lance writer, pub. relations cons., Ill., Wis., 1941-51; radio-TV chief Am. Nat. Red Cross, Alexandria, Va., 1951-56, pub. edn. adviser, Washington, 1956-59; dir. information Indian Health Service, Dept. Health, Edn. and Welfare, Washington, 1959—. Mem. pub. relations com. Girl Scouts U.S.A., Met. Area Council, Washington. Recipient award USPHS, 1968. Mem. Am. Assn. U. Women (dir.), Am. Women in Radio and Television, Am. Newspaper Women's Club, Women's Nat. Press Club (dir.). Episcopalian. Home: 3223 Volta Pl NW Washington DC 20007 Office: 5600 Fishers Lane Rockville MD 20852

NOWELL, HARVEY REX, dentist; b. Headland, Ala., Nov. 8, 1933; s. Harvey Marvette and Katherine Ethelle (Wells) N.; student Auburn U., 1951-53; D.M.D., U. Ala., 1957; m. Marcia M. McKinney, Aug. 29, 1953; children—Mary Katherine, Donald Rex. Practice of dentistry, Marianna, Fla., 1959—. Vice chmn. Marianna Recreation Commn., 1968—. Trustee Jackson Hosp., Served to capt. Dental Corps, USAF, 1957-59. Mem. Fla. Dental Assn. (mem. ho. of dels. 1968-71), Jr. C. of C. (pres. 1962-63), Alpha Epsilon Delta, Phi Eta Sigma, Theta Chi, Delta Sigma Delta. Elk, Rotarian (pres. 1967-68). Home: 162 Watson Dr Marianna FL 32446 Office: 711 3d Av Marianna FL 32446

NOWELL, JOHN WILLIAM, educator; b. Wake Forest, N.C., Aug. 26, 1919; s. John William and Margaret (Edwards) N.; B.S., Wake Forest Coll., 1940; Ph.D., U. N.C., 1945. Sr. physicist Am. Cyanamid Research Labs., Stanford, Conn., 1944-45; mem. faculty Wake Forest U., Winston-Salem, N.C., 1945—, prof. chemistry, 1954—, chmn. dept. chemistry, 1963-72. Mem. Am. Chem. Soc. (sect. chmn. 1951), N.Y., N.C. acads. scis., Phi Beta Kappa, Sigma Xi, Omicron Delta Kappa, Kappa Alpha Order (nat. pres. 1961-65). Home: 4115 Student Dr Winston-Salem NC 27109

NOWELL, WESLEY RAYMOND, air force officer, entomologist; b. Oakland, Cal., Feb. 9, 1924; s. George Madison and Florence Alice (Sorrells) N.; A.B., Stanford, 1947, A.M., 1948, Ph.D., 1951; m. Maria Soledad Rael, Dec. 14, 1946; children—George W., Wayne A., Lawrence E., Roxanne T. Commd. 1st lt. USAF, 1951, advanced through grades to lt. col., 1965; cons. med. entomologist Far East, 1951-52, Europe, 1955-58; chief entomology service USAF Epidemiological Flight, Turkey, 1962-65; chief entomology br. USAF

Epidemiological Lab., Tex., 1965—, asso. chief biomed. scis. corps, 1968—. Instr. U. Tampa (Fla.), 1961-62. Served with USAAF, 1943-46. Decorated Bronze Star medal, Air medal. Mem. Entomol. Soc. Am., Am., Cal. mosquito control assns., Hawaiian Entomol. Soc., Sigma Xi. Home: 2722 Belvoir Dr San Antonio TX 78230 Office: USAF Sch. Aerospace Medicine Brooks AFB TX 78235

NOWLIN, NEWMAN RODEN, banker; b. Guntersville, Ala., Feb. 13, 1921; s. David McBroom and Bernice Mariah (Roden) N.; B.S., U. Ala., 1941; postgrad. Grad. Sch. Banking, Rutgers U., 1962; m. Lucy Mason Turner, Dec. 25, 1948; children—Yancey, Newman Roden, Charles Forrest, Lucy Mariah. Asst. nat. bank examiner Office Comptroller of Treasury, Atlanta, 1947-50; with Am. Nat. Bank, Gadsden, Ala., 1950—, sr. v.p., trust officer, 1968—, also dir. Pres. Etowah County Arthritis and Rheumatism Found., 1964. Served with USNR, 1942-46. Methodist (steward 1965—). Club: Golden Country. Home: 307 Turrentine Av Gadsden AL 35901 Office: PO Box 389 Gadsden AL 35902

NOWOTNY, GEORGE EDWARD, JR., geophysicist, state legislator; b. New Braunfels, Tex., Oct. 18, 1932; s. George E. and Margaret (Voight) N.; B.S., U. Tex., 1955; m. Lura Duff Elliston, Aug. 14, 1954; children— Edward Duff, George Edward, III, Addison Dance. Geophysicist, Standard Oil Co. N.J., 1955-60; partner Barton & Nowothy, Fort Smith, Ark., 1961-63; cons. oil, gas geologist Nowotny & Co., Fort Smith, 1963—; mem. Ark. Ho. of Reps., 1967—. Area disaster chmn. A.R.C., 1966-67, chmn. exec. bd., 1968; active United Fund; mem. State Health Planning Commn., 1968—; mem. natural resources com. Interstate Oil Compact Comm., 1968-71. Bd. dirs. Civil Air Patrol. Del. Republican Nat. Conv., 1972; state coordinator re-election Pres., 1972. Mem. Nat. Legislative Leader's Conf., C. of C., Nat. Soc. State Legislators, Am. Assn. Petroleum Geologists, Soc. Exploration Geophysicists, Am. Assn. Petroleum Landmen, Phi Beta Kappa, Delta Tau Delta. Home: 18 Berry Hill Fort Smith AR 72901 Office: First Fed Bldg Fort Smith AR 72901

NOWOTNY, LURA DUFF ELLISTON, civic worker, poet; b. Ft. Worth, July 20, 1933; d. Fred Addison and Lura Duff (Elliston) M.; student Duke, 1951-52, U. Tex., 1952-54; m. George Edward Nowotny, Jr., Aug. 14, 1954; children—Edward Duff, George Edward III, Addison Dance. Bd. dirs. Sebastian County Mental Health Assn., 1963-69, Ark. Assn. Mental Health 1966—; gov. Western Ark. Counciling and Guidance Center, 1969—; dir. Spark's Hosp. Guild, 1964-70, Community Concert Assn., 1968—; pres. Ft. Smith Affiliation of the Arts, 1968—; co-chmn. arts festivals, 1964, 65, 70; leadership cons. Nat. Assn. Retarded Children, 1968-69; mem. Retardation Com. State Health Planning, 1968-69. Committeewoman Rep. 3d Congl. Dist., 1962-64, 68-70; charter mem. County Rep. Women, 1961—; co-chmn. Rep. United Campaign, 1962; sec. Rep. State Conv., 1968. Life trustee Old Fort Museum, 1968—, pres., 1971-72; trustee St. John's Sch. for Children with Learning Disabilities, 1971—; mem. adv. bd. St. Edward's Mercy Hosp., 1967-69. Recipient first place award, Ark. Arts Festival, 1968; named one of outstanding young women of Am., 1966. Mem. Jr. League Ft. Smith, D.A.R., Delta Delta Delta. Episcopalian (pres. ch. women 1961-62). Author: New Look Trio, 1970. Founder, designer Ft. Smith Children's Museumobile, 1965; author vol. art enrichment program Ft. Smith Pub. Schs., 1969; design concept mini parks City of Ft. Smith, 1972. Home: 18 Berry Hill Fort Smith AR 72901

NOYA, CARLOS JOSE, dentist, educator; b. Santurce, P.R., Sept. 11, 1925; s. Emilio J. and Maria C. (Gonzalez) N.; student U. P.R., 1943-46; D.D.S., U. Md., 1946-50; m. Irmahe Murati, Feb. 14, 1953; children—Carlos, Laura, Diana. Practice of dentistry, Santurce, P.R., 1952—; prof. ethics, Sch. Dentistry, U. P.R., 1964—; cons. quality control Sequros de Servicio de Salud, 1969—; chmn. adv. com. to P.R. Sec. of Health on Medicaid, 1966-68. Served to capt. AUS, 1950-52. Fellow Am. Coll. Dentists, Internat. Coll. of Dentists; mem. Colegio Cirujanos Dentistas de Puerto Rico (pres. 1965), Am. (chmn. com. on rules and order 1969), P.R. (pres. 1965) dental assns., Psi Omega, Phi Eta Mu. Home: 667 McKinley St Santurce PR 00907 Office: 904 Jose Marti Santurce PR 00907

NOYES, CROSBY STUART, journalist; b. Washington, Mar. 2, 1921; s. Newbold and Alexandra (Ewing) N.; B.A., Yale, 1943; m. Letitia Hughson, Mar. 25, 1943; children—Annetje Noyes Jacobs, Josephine, Crosby Stuart, Letitia Ann. Reporter, Washington Evening Star, 1947-54; European corr. Washington Star, Paris, France, 1954-56, nat. editor, 1956-58, European corr., columnist, 1958-64, fgn. affairs editor, 1964—; columnist Washington Star Syndicate; dir. Evening Star Newspaper Co., Washington. Served as pilot USAAF, 1942-46. Decorated Air medal, D.F.C.; chevalier Legion of Honor (France). Mem. Phi Beta Kappa. Clubs: Metropolitan, Chevy Chase (Washington); Garrick (London, Eng.). Home: 5311 Elliott Rd Washington DC 20016 Office: Evening Star 2d St and Virginia Av SE Washington DC 20003

NOYES, JONATHAN HOWARD, securities co. exec.; b. Duluth, Minn., Sept. 6, 1920; s. Jonathan Alvan and Caroline Clark N.; B.S., Mass. Inst. Tech., 1942; LL.B., U. Tex., 1949; m. Earlene Katherine Jaster, Oct. 30, 1948; children—Timothy Alvan, Joan Elizabeth, Susan Carol, Jonathan Clark, Margaret Katherine. Engr. RCA, 1942-44; partner Terrell Bartlett Engrs., 1950-51, Russ & Co. and Muir Investment, San Antonio, 1953-58; owner Porter, Noyes, Inc., 1958-63; pres. Rowle, Winston, Rausher, Pierce, 1964-70; v.p. Eppler Guerin & Turner, Inc., Corpus Christi, Tex., 1961—; dir. Halm Instrument. Tchr. U. Tex., 1948-49. Vice-pres. Gulf Coast council Boy Scouts Am., 1964-65. Served with USNR, 1944-46. Kiwanian. Home: 930 Coral St Corpus Christi TX 78411 Office: 101 Guaranty Bank Plaza Corpus Christi TX 78401

NOYES, NEWBOLD, newspaperman; b. Sorrento, Me., Aug. 10, 1918; s. Newbold and Alexandra (Ewing) N.; B.A., Yale, 1941; m. Beatrice Spencer Baldwin, Dec. 12, 1944; children—Howard B., Newbold III, Alexandra E., Elizabeth S. Mem. staff Evening Star, Washington. 1941—, reporter, 1941-52; dir. Evening Star Newspaper Co., 1948—, various editorial assignments, 1952-63, editor, 1963—; dir. A.P. Mem. Pulitzer Prize Adv. Com. Bd. dirs. Am. Press Inst.; trustee Washington Journalism Center. Served as vol. ambulance driver, Am. Field Service, Near East and Italian campaigns, 1942-43; war. corr. ETO, 1943-45. Mem. Am. Soc. Newspaper Editors (pres. 1970-71), dir.). Clubs: Chevy Chase, Metropolitan. Home: 3015 Garfield St NW Washington DC 20016 Office: 225 Virginia Av SE Washington DC 20003

NUCKOLLS, THOMAS EARL, food products co. exec.; b. Paducah, Ky., Jan. 25, 1933; s. John Edward and Mary Suzan (Rohrer) N.; grad high sch.; m. Beverly Jane Greenwell, Apr. 18, 1933; children—Kathy Sue, Mary Jane. Salesman Bunny Bread Co., Paducah, 1955-61; salesman Colonial Baking Co., Paducah, 1961-63, supr., 1963-66, sales mgr., 1966-71, gen. sales mgr., 1971—, v.p., 1972—. Mem. Paducah C. of C. Lion. Home: 216 Calvert Dr Paducah KY 42001 Office: 3201 Cook St Paducah KY 42001

NUGENT, WESLEY OLIVER, welding and repair co. exec.; b. Lafayette, La., July 13, 1925; s. Alonza Lee and Essie Florence (Deare) N.; grad. high sch.; m. Mary Iris Segura, May 11, 1947; children—Robert Oliver, Patrick Matthew. Sales rep. Waukesha Pearce Industries, New Iberia, La., 1952-63; pres. Casting Welding & Repair, Inc., New Iberia, 1963—, mem. pension trust com., 1966—. Served with USNR, 1943-46. Mem. Am. Petroleum Inst., La. Sugar Cane Festival Assn., Mu Sigma. Clubs: Iberia Golf and Country, Sertoma (dir. 1965-68) (New Iberia). Home: 5307 Shoreline Dr New Iberia LA 70560 Office: 3536 Main St New Iberia LA 70560

NUNALLY, VAN DALEY, JR., asst. adj. gen. Tenn.; b. Baxter, Tenn., Mar. 9, 1917; s. Van Daley and Aline (Leftwich) N.; student U. Chattanooga, 1935-38; m. Frances Ditty, Dec. 4, 1942; children—Linda Frances (Mrs. Leon Moore), Ann Daley (Mrs. Ann Ford). Enlisted in U.S. Army, 1941, commd. 2d lt., 1942, advanced through grades to capt., 1944; served in France, Czechoslovakia, Germany, World War II; assigned Ft. Monroe, Va., 1948; mem. staff and faculty Armor Sch., Ft. Knox, Ky., 1950-54; joined Tenn. N.G., 1947, advanced through grades to brig. gen.; mem. staff adj. gen. Tenn., 1951—, now asst. adj. gen. Dir. Orgn. and Tng. Civil Disturbances, Tenn. Chmn. for Tenn. for Vets. Day, also Heart Fund drive; mem. exec. bd. Middle Tenn. council Boy Scouts Am. Mem. Adj. Gen. Assn. (exec. com.), Am. Legion (vice chmn. nat. security council), V.F.W., Alpha Lamda Tau. Methodist. Mason (Shriner). Home: 715 Graycroft Av Madison TN 37115 Office: Nat Guard Armory Sidco Dr Nashville TN 37204

NUNLEY, LEONARD JAMES, computer co. exec.; b. St. Louis, Oct. 22, 1933; s. Charles Spurgeon and Margaret Minna (Schmidt) N.; B.E.E., U. Fla., 1955; M.S., So. Meth. U., 1962; m. Lorene Weddington, June 7, 1957; children—Stephen, Angela. Design engr. Convair div. Gen. Dynamics, Ft. Worth, 1955-59; project engr. Nat. Data Processing Corp., Dallas, 1959-61; with Recognition Equipment Inc., Irving, 1961—, now sr. v.p. and chief tech. officer. Mem. I.E.E.E. Methodist. Patentee in field. Home: 3936 Shady Creek Lane Dallas TX 75229 Office: 2701 E Granwyler Rd Irving TX 75060

NUNN, GEORGE VIRGIL, supt. schs.; b. Waverly, Ala., Aug. 14, 1910; s. George Gillis and Susie Lloyal (Allen) N.; B.S., Auburn U., 1932, M.S., 1935; m. Maude Prescott Woodward, Dec. 27, 1938; children—Margaret Ann (Mrs. Thomas Hiram Todd, Jr.), Sheila Lynn (Mrs. Samuel Watson Moss), George Woodward. Tchr., Pickens County Bd. Edn., Gordo, Ala., 1932-34, Fairfield City Bd. Edn., 1934-36; prin. Fairfield Jr. High Sch., 1936-40; supt. Fairfield City Schs., 1946-70; supt. Homewood (Ala.) City Bd. Edn., 1970—. Served to col. AUS, 1940-45. Decorated Bronze Star medal. Mem. N.E.A., Am. Assn. Sch. Adminstrs., Ala. Edn. Assn., C. of C. (pres. 1961-62), Kappa Phi Kappa. Baptist (deacon 1968-69). Rotarian. Home: 333 Fair Oaks Dr Fairfield AL 35064 Office: 1903 29th Av S Homewood AL 35209

NUNN, LOUIE B., gov. of Ky.; b. Mar. 8, 1924; ed. Bowling Green Bus. U., U. Cin.; Law Degree, U. Louisville; m. Buela Cornelius Aspley; 5 children. Elected judge Barren County (Ky.), 1953; mgr. Eisenhower-Cooper-Morton campaign, 1956, Cooper and Morton campaigns, 1960, 62; now gov. State of Ky. Past pres. Glasgow (Ky.) PTA; past dist. pres. Ky. Welfare Assn. Del., Republican Nat. Conv., 1968. Served with AUS, World War II. Named One of 3 Outstanding Young Men of Ky., 1956. Mem. Am. Legion (past comdr.), C. of C. (past v.p.). Mason, Rotarian (past v.p.). Mem. Christian Ch. (chmn. bd. elders). Address: State Capitol Frankfort KY 40601

NUNN, STUART EVERETT, judge; b. Monticello, Ark., Nov. 12, 1912; s. Stuart Everett and Eva (McClintock) N.; grad. Texarkana Coll., 1932; student U. Tex., 1932-33; LL.B., Baylor U., 1936 Admitted to Tex. bar, 1936; practiced in Texarkana, 1936-40; judge City Ct., Texarkana, 1940-42, 47-55; county probate judge, 1955-61; dist. judge 5th Dist., Texarkana, 1961—. Chmn. A.R.C., 1948-49. Bd. dirs. Community Chest. Served with AUS, 1942-45. Mem. Texarkana Jr. C. of C. (pres.), Am. Legion. Mason (Shriner), Elk. Home: 2520 Olive St Texarkana TX 75501 Office: County Bldg Texarkana TX 75501

NUNN, WALTER HARRIS, polit. scientist; b. Monticello, Ark., Feb. 17, 1942; s. Wallace H. and Eileen (Wicker) N.; B.A. with honors, Hendrix Coll., 1964; M.A., U. Kan., 1966; m. Rosemary Smee, July 3, 1969. Research asst. Citizens Conf. on State Legislatures, Kansas City, Mo., 1966-67; sr. research asst. Ark. Constl. Revision Study Commn., Little Rock, 1967; dir. Constl. Conv. Adv. Commn., Little Rock, 1968; research dir. Ark. Constl. Conv., Little Rock, 1969-70; asst. dir. Arkansans for the Constn. of 1970, 1970; mgmt. information officer Little Rock (Ark.) Model Cities, 1970-72; govtl. affairs cons., 1972—. Tchr. U. Ark., Little Rock, 1969. Justice of the Peace, Pulaski County, 1969-70. Mem. Ark. Arts Center, Pulaski County Mental Health Assn., Nat. Municipal League. Home: 1705 S Taylor St Little Rock AR 72204 Office: 300 Spring Bldg Little Rock AR 72201

NUNNALLY, JEFF DORRIS, oil and gas co. exec.; b. Lapile, Ark., Dec. 15, 1917; s. Niles Henry and Nancy Evelyn (White) N.; student East Tex. Bapt. Coll., 1936-37, U. Tex., 1939-41; B.S., U. Okla., 1947; m. Nelva Eugenia Wyatt, May 31, 1942; children—James Jeffrey, Joseph Wyatt. Geologist, Gulf Oil Corp., 1947, exploration mgr., Houston, 1956-60; chief geologist Delhi-Taylor Oil Corp., Dallas, 1960-64, internat. cons., 1964-69; v.p. exploration Triton Oil & Gas Corp., Dallas, 1969—. Cons. Zululand Oil Exploration Co. Ltd., Union South Africa, 1966—. Served with USAAF, 1943-46. Decorated Air medal with two oak leaf clusters. Mem. Am. Assn. Petroleum Geologists, Dallas Geol. Soc., Dallas Petroleum Club. Republican. Baptist. Author: The Lower Cretaceous Geology of Mississippi, 1952. Home: 928 Chadwick Dr Richardson TX 75080 Office: Republic Bank Tower Dallas TX 75201

NUNNERY, MICHAEL YATES, educator; b. Camden, Tenn., Sept. 28, 1929; s. Joel and Mary Edith (Yates) N.; student Murray State U., 1947-49; B.S., Austin Peay State U., 1951; postgrad. George Peabody Coll., 1951-52; M.S., N.C. State U., 1956; Ed.D., U. Tenn., 1958; m. Barbara Ann Beddingfield, Nov. 5, 1955; children—Douglas, Marianna. Prin., Lavinia (Tenn.) Elementary and Jr. High Sch., 1951-52; teaching asst. U. Tenn., 1956-58, asst. prof. edn., 1958-59; asso. prof. edn., 1963-66, prof. edn., 1966-68; asst. prof. edn. Auburn U., 1959-63; prof. edn. U. Fla., Gainesville, 1968—. Mem. plenary session Univ. Council for Ednl. Adminstrn., 1965—. Served to USMCR, 1952-56. Mem. Am. Assn. Sch. Adminstrs., Am. Ednl. Research Assn., Nat. Conf. Profs. Ednl. Adminstrn., So. Regional Council Ednl. Adminstrn., Phi Delta Kappa, Phi Kappa Phi. Democrat. Presbyn. Co-author: Politics, Power, Polls, and School Elections, 1971. Editor research and psychology sect., mem. editorial commn. Ednl. Adminstrn. Abstracts, 1968—. Home: 1945 NW 22d St Gainesville FL 32601

NUSSBAUM, HANS, assn. exec.; b. Suhl, Germany, Oct. 21, 1908; s. Daniel and Jenny (Rosenthal) N.; student U. Frankfurt, 1927-28, U. Kiel, 1928; M.A., U. Cologne, 1930, Ph.D., 1932; m. Anne Kipnis, Aug. 15, 1943; 1 son, Sheldon Lawrence. Came to U.S., 1938, naturalized, 1943. Volontar Willy Rendsburg, paper wholesale, Hamburg, Germany, 1933-34; accountant Daniel Nussbaum, shoe wholesale, Suhl, 1934-38; shipping clk. Colonial Carpet Corp., N.Y.C., 1938-41; salesman Leventhal's Dept. Store, Washington, 1941-42; accountant Konsum Coop., Washington, 1942-43, Konsum Fed. Credit Union, Washington, 1942-43; accountant A.A.A.S., Washington, 1945-49, bus. mgr., 1949—, editor bull., 1963-71. Served with AUS, 1943-45. Fellow A.A.A.S. Home: 1526 Locust Rd NW Washington DC 20012 Office: 1515 Massachusetts Av NW Washington DC 20005

NUSSBAUM, MAX EHRLICH, newspaper pub.; b. Bainbridge, Ga., July 29, 1907; s. Max E. and Belle (Wise) N.; B.S. in Commerce, Ga. Inst. Tech., 1928; m. Frances Allen, Oct. 5, 1935; children—Helen Allen (Mrs. Nussbaum Kruger), Patricia Allen (Mrs. William Lies III). Engaged in life ins. sales, 1928-30; with Atlanta Georgian, 1931-32, Huntsville (Ala.) Daily Register, 1933; with Multrie (Ga.) Observer, 1934—, pres., 1950—, dir. A.P., 1960-69; treas., dir. Moultrie Community Trust Co., 1945—; dir. Miller Hydro Co., C. & S. Bank Colquitt County, Bainbridge, Brit. Miller Hydro Co., Ga. & Fla. Ry. Co. Chmn. Moultrie Appeal Rev. Bd., 1957-60, Moultrie United Fund drive, 1951; dir. Moultrie- Colquitt County Indsl. Devel. Corp. Democratic presdl. elector, 1956. Maj., Ga. State Guard, World War II. Mem. Ga. Newspaper Advt. Execs. Assn. (pres. 1937), So. Newspaper Pub. Assn. (dir. 1952-57), Ga. Press Assn. (bd. mgrs. 1954-56), Moultrie C. of C. (pres. 1960), Phi Epsilon Pi. Kiwanian. Home: 25 12th Av SE Moultrie GA 31768 Office: Moultrie Observer Moultrie GA 37168

NUTT, ZACK, food co. exec.; b. nr. Mt. Vernon, Tex., Apr. 21, 1905; s. John Paul and Jessie Brownie (Kilpatrick) N.; ed. Mt. Vernon (Tex.) High Sch., 1919-22; m. Elfleda Dale Martin, June 3, 1927. Store mgr. Brookshire Food Store, Longview, Tex., 1939-56, supr. Eastern dist., Longview, 1956-61, supr., v.p., hdqrs. Tyler, Tex., 1961—. Mem. Supermarket Inst., Tex. Grocers Assn., Nat. Assn. Food Chains, Tex. Mchts. Assn. Baptist. Kiwanian, Toastmaster. Home: 1401 LeDuke Longview TX 75601 Office: PO Box 1411 Tyler TX 75701

NUTTER, DALE EDWARD, mech. engr.; b. Borger, Tex., July 20, 1935; s. I. Earl and Martha (Crowell) N.; student Rice U., 1954-56; B.S. in M.E., Okla. State U., 1958; m. Mary Lou Chambers, May 12, 1962; children—Mark Edward, Michael Earl. Asso. engr. Douglas Aircraft Co., Santa Monica, Cal., 1958-60; sales engr. Nutter Engring. Co., Tulsa, 1960-63, v.p. sales, 1963-68; v.p. devel. Heat/Fluid Engring. Co., Tulsa, 1968—; dir., mem. tech. com. Fractionation Research Inc., Bartlesville, Okla. Registered profl. engr., Okla., Tex. Mem. Am. Inst. Chem. Engrs., Nat. Petroleum Refiners Assn. (supply men's finance chmn. 1968), Acad. Model Aeros. (contest bd. rep. 1965). Patentee in field. Home: 2498 E 49th St Tulsa OK 74105 Office: 2230 E 49th St Tulsa OK 74105

NYKAMP, HARRIS, aluminum co. exec.; b. Hamilton, Mich., May 21, 1934; s. Henry K. and Minnie (Terpstra) N.; student Chgo. Tech. Sch., U. Mich., U. Miami; m. Alma Joan Boers, Feb. 22, 1957; children—Diana Lynn, Cindy Lou, Dawn Renee, Thomas Lee. Design engr. Hart & Cooley Mfg. Co., Holland, Mich., 1951-56, asst. prodn. control mgr., 1959-61; mgr. adminstrn. Aluminaire, Inc., Miami, Fla., 1962-68, gen. mgr., 1968—. Served with USNR, 1957-58. Mem. Miami C. of C. Republican. Mem. Christian Reformed Ch. (elder). Home: 14570 English Rd Miami Lakes FL 33014 Office: 1600 NW 165th St Miami FL 33169

OAKES, CHARLES GEORGE, sociologist; b. San Francisco, Jan. 4, 1931; s. Marshall Johns and Gladys (Benedict) O.; A.B., U. Cal. at Berkeley, 1957, M.A., 1959; postgrad. Stanford, 1959-60; Ph.D., Emory U., 1966; m. Carolyn Bradley Lawrence, Dec. 23, 1961; children— Mark Odell, Bradley Benedict. Asst. prof., acting chmn. dept. sociology Southwestern U., Memphis, 1962-66; instr. preventive medicine U. Tenn. Coll. Medicine, Memphis, 1964-66; asst. prof. Converse Coll., Spartanburg, S.C., 1966, asso. prof., 1967—, chmn. dept. sociology, 1966-72; dir. div. planning and evaluation N.C. Regional Med. Program, Durham, 1972—; asst. prof. dept. community health scis. Duke U. Med. Center, 1972—; research asso. Sacramento State Coll., 1959-60. Cons., Ga. Dept. Health, Ga. Dept. Family and Children Services, Spartanburg County Health Dept., S.C. Dept. Pub. Welfare. Research asso. Donner Biophysics Lab., U. Cal. at Berkeley, 1958-59. Mem. Shelby County Planning Commn., 1960-62; bd. dirs. Spartanburg County Council on Alcoholism; chmn. com. on research, com. on aging Council for Spartanburg County 1966—. Served with USN, 1951-55. Mem. Am. Sociol. Assn., Soc. for Applied Anthropology, So. Sociol. Soc., Am. Acad. Social and Polit. Sci., N.Y. Acad. Scis., Sigma Xi, Pi Gamma Mu. Author: Walking Patients and The Health Crises. Editor: Our Elderly Americans: Challenge and Response; Foundations of Practical Gerontology; Functional Elements of Outpatient Services. Home: 326 Azalea Dr Chapel Hill NC 27514

OAKES, ROY BLUDWORTH, city ofcl.; b. Yoakum, Tex., Jan. 1, 1900; s. Roy Cleveland and Harriet Stella (Budworth) O.; student Harvard, 1917-18, U. Detroit, 1920-21, Rice Inst., 1921-22, Tyler Comml. Coll., 1922-23; LL.D., Houston Law Sch., 1931; m. Margaret Estell Hale, Apr. 18, 1931; children—Roy Hale, Margaret Hale, Jerry Hale, James Hale. With U.S. Shipping Port, 1921-26, Anderson Clayton Cotton Co., 1926-28, Humble Oil & Refining Co., 1928-41; with purchasing dept. City of Houston, 1941-45, city controller, 1945—. Mem. Local Draft Bd. 60, 1956-67. Served with USN, 1917-19. Mason. Home: 2511 Willowick No 201 Houston TX 77027 Office: City Hall 6th Floor Houston TX 77002

OAKES, THOMAS CLAYTON, supt. schs.; b. Groesbeck, Tex., May 13, 1914; s. William M. and Nettie (Sims) O.; A.A., Westminster Jr. Coll., 1932; B.A., S.W. Tex. State U., 1942; M.A., Baylor U., 1950, postgrad. 1956—; m. Bernice W. Slaughter, May 23, 1939; children—James C. Judith L. (Mrs. Richard P. Welch). Tchr. Fairoaks Elementary Sch., Groesbeck, 1934-35, prin., 1935-37; coach, prin. Fairoaks High Sch., Groesbeck, 1937-42, supt., 1943-51; supt. Wortham Pub. Schs., Wortham, Tex., 1951-55. Connally Pub. Schs., Waco, Tex., 1955—. Bd. dirs. McLennan Cancer Soc. Mem. Am., Tex. assns. sch. adminstrs., N.E.A., Tex. Tchrs. Assn. Baptist. Mason, Lion, Rotarian (sec. 1967). Home: 609 Theresa St Waco TX 76705

OAKLEY, CHARLES HERBERT, accountant, city ofcl.; b. Texarkana, Ark., Dec. 24, 1917; s. William H. and Mattie Ann (Dodgen) O.; student So. Ill. U., 1941-42, Murray (Ky.) State Coll., 1951-52; corr. course Internat. Accountants Soc., 1945-48; m. Maxine O. Thomas, June 7, 1935; children—Charles Herbert, Stephen Louis, Deborah Kay. Supt., Murray Electirc System, 1942-45; spl. partner McIntyre & Assos., C.P.A.'s, Nashville, 1945-50; propr. Charles H. Oakley, C.P.A., Paducah, Ky., Murray, 1950-61; finance dir. City of Oak Ridge, 1961-66; dir. adminstrn., finance City of Gainesville (Fla.), 1966—. Named Ky. col., 1954, Duke of Paducah, 1961; recipient Boss of Yr. award Oak Ridge chpt. Nat. Secs. Assn., 1962. C.P.A., Tenn., Ky. Mem. Am. Inst. C.P.A.'s, Tenn., Ky. socs. C.P.A.'s, Nat. Municipal Finance Officers Assn. Methodist. Lion (counsellor). Home: 1403 NW 31st St Gainesville FL 32601 Office: PO Box 490 Gainesville FL 32601

OAKLEY, MARY LOUISE, educator; b. nr. Lexington, Tenn., Mar. 26, 1909; d. Nuit Rush and Carlie (Page) Oakley; student Memphis State U., 1928-29; A.B., Union U., Jackson, Tenn., 1936; M.A., George Peabody Coll. Tchrs., 1945 postgrad. U. Tenn., summer 1947. Tchr., Henderson County Schs., Lexington, Tenn., 1927-35, supr., 1935-41; tchr. Memphis State U., 1941-42, vis. prof., 1943-45 supr. W. Tenn. Schs., 1942-46 tchr. Lexington City Schs., 1946-47 supr. Union City (Tenn.) Schs., 1947-52 cons. prodn. and use lang. arts material Birmingham Paper Co. (Ala.), 1952-54; dean women, prof. edn. Union U., 1954-55, vis. prof., summers 1947-52; supr. Madison County Schs., Jackson, 1955-63; tchr. corrective reading Shelby County Schs., Memphis, 1963-66, Humboldt (Tenn.) City Schs., 1966-67; instr. edn. Jackson State Community Coll., 1967-70, asst. prof., 1970—. Cons., devel. courses lang. arts, high sch. English, social studies various counties Tenn., Ky., Ala. Mem. N.E.A., Tenn. Edn. Assn., Nat. Council Tchrs. English, Assn. for Childhood Edn. Internat. (state pres.), Tenn. (pres.), W.Tenn. (pres.) suprs. assns., Assn. for Supervision and Curriculum Devel. (state rep. nat. bd.), Delta Kappa Gamma (pres. Theta, Omicron and state chpts.) Democrat. Baptist. Author: (with Lucille Rogers) Light From Many Candles, 1960. Lang. arts editor: The Instructor, 1953-58. Home: 682 Wilshire Dr Jackson TN 38301

OATES, JOHN FRANCIS, educator; b. Holyoke, Mass., Aug. 7, 1934; s. William Adrian and Lilian (Woods) O.; B.A., Yale, 1956, M.A., 1958, Ph.D., 1960; postgrad. (Fulbright fellow), Am. Sch. Classical Studies, Athens, Greece, 1956-57; m. Rosemary Walsh, June 27, 1957; children—Elizabeth, Emily, John Francis, Sarah. Instr. classics Yale, 1960-63, asst. prof. classics, 1963-67; hon. research asst. Greek, University Coll., London, Eng., 1965-66; asso. prof. ancient history Duke U., Durham, N.C., 1967-71, prof. ancient history, chmn. dept. classical studies, 1971—. Mem. Am. Philol. Assn., Archael. Inst. Am., Am. Hist. Assn., Am. Soc. Papyrologists (v.p. 1971—), Assn. Internationale de Papyrologues. Phi Beta Kappa. Democrat. Episcopalian. Author: (with A. E. Samuel and C. B. Welles) Yale Papyri in the Beinecke Library, 1967. Contbr. articles in field to profl. jours. Home: 1025 Dacian Av Durham NC 27001

OBENSHAIN, JAMES WARNER, supt. schs.; b. Eagle Rock, Va., July 19, 1916; s. Rufus Z. and Estelle (Honts) O.; B.S., Va. Poly. Inst., 1939; M.Ed., U. Va., 1960; m. Mary G. Makinney, June 23, 1944; 1 dau., Sandra Faye. Tchr. vocational agr. Fincastle (Va.) High Sch., 1941-53, prin., 1953-58; supr. Botetourt County (Va.) high schs., 1958-59, supt., 1959—. Mem. Nat., Va. edn. assns., Nat., Va. assns. sch. adminstrs. Baptist (trustee). Rotarian (pres. Fincastle 1945). Address: PO Box 101 Fincastle VA 24090

OBERDORFER, DONALD, JR., journalist; b. Atlanta, May 28, 1931; s. Donald and Dorothy (Bayersdorfer) O.; B.A. in Pub. and Internat. Affairs, Princeton, 1952; m. Laura Jane Klein, Apr. 24, 1955; children— Daniel, Karen Sue. Reporter, Charlotte (N.C.) Observer, 1955-58; Washington corr. Knight Newspapers, 1958-61, 65-68; staff writer Washington Post, 1968—; associate editor, contbg. editor Sat. Eve. Post, 1961-65. Served to 1st lt. AUS, 1952-54. Mem. Soc. Mag. Writers. Clubs: Nat. Press, Fed. City (Washington); Princeton (N.Y.C.). Author: Tet, 1971. Contbr. nat. mags. Office: Washington Post 1150 15th St NW Washington DC 20005

OBERHEU, VICTOR LOUIS, physician; b. Trivandrum, Travencore, South India, Mar. 14, 1933 (parents Am. citizens); s. Gerhard Carl Ferdinand and Nellie Elizabeth (Schlotthauer) O.; B.A., So. Ill. U., 1954; B.S., U. Ill., 1956, M.D., 1958; m. Jane Nugent Donoghue, July 11, 1959; children—David John, Daniel Lee, Martha Jane. Intern, St. Louis City Hosp., 1958-59, gen. practice resident, 1959-60; gen. practice medicine, Jerseyville, Ill., 1960-69; resident radiology Meth. Hosp., Memphis, 1969-72. Established Jersey-Calhoun Mental Health Clinic, 1966; pres. Jersey chpt. Am. Heart Assn., 1964-69; mem. Jersey County Pub. Health Dept., 1965-69; fund chmn. Ill. Valley Tb Assn., 1965-69; conducted weekly radio program, Jerseyville, 1962-69. Mem. A.M.A., Am. Coll. Radiology, Ill. State, Jersey-Calhoun med. socs., St. Louis City Hosp. Alumni Assn., Phi Rho Sigma. Lutheran (elder 1960-72, pres.). Home: 427 River Oak Dr Danville VA 24541

OBERMAN, ALBERT, physician; b. St. Louis, Feb. 9, 1934; s. Max and Helen (Schryer) O.; A.B., Washington U., St. Louis, 1955, M.D., 1959; M.P.H., U. Mich., 1966; m. Marian Kleg, June 20, 1954; children—Steven, David, Karen. Intern, Jewish Hosp., St. Louis, 1959-60, resident, 1960-62; staff physician heart disease control program USPHS, 1962-65; staff physician sub-com. criteria and methods Am. Heart Assn., Birmingham, Ala., 1966-67; prof. pub. health and epidemiology, asso. medicine U. Ala. Med. Center, Birmingham, 1967—; cons. Naval Aerospace Med. Inst., Pensacola, Fla., 1967—. Fellow A.C.P., Am. Heart Assn. (council epidemiology 1966—, com. on criteria and methods, nat. study group 1970-72); mem. Am. Pub. Health Assn. Home: 3585 Rockhill Rd Birmingham AL 35223

OBERMAYER, HERMAN JOSEPH, editor, publisher; b. Phila., Sept. 19, 1924; s. Leon J. and Julia (Sinsheimer) O.; student U. Geneva (Switzerland), 1946; A.B. cum laude, Dartmouth, 1948; m. Betty Nan Levy, June 28, 1955; children—Helen Julia, Veronica Levy, Adele Beatrice, Elizabeth Rose. Reporter, L.I. Daily Press, Jamaica, N.Y., 1950-53; classified advt. mgr. New Orleans Item, 1953-55; promotion dir. New Bedford (Mass.) Standard-Times, 1955-57; editor, pub. Long Branch (N.J.) Daily Record, 1957-71, No. Va. Sun, Arlington, 1963—. Bd. dirs. exec. council Boy Scouts Am., Monmouth (N.J.) council, 1958-71, Nat. Capital Council, 1971; bd. dirs. Arlington (Va.) Bicentennial Commn. Long Branch Community Adult Sch., Anti-Defamation League N.J. Regional Adv. Council. Trustee Twin Lights Hist. Mus., Highlands, N.J.; mem. Va. Alcoholic Beverage Control Study Commn., 1972; bd. dirs., asst. v.p. Monmouth (N.J.) Med. Center, 1958-71. Served with AUS, 1943-46; ETO. Recipient Friends of Scouting award, 1966. Mem. Am. Soc. Newspaper Editors, Am., So. (editorial com.) newspaper pubs. assns., Fairfax (Va.) C. of C. (mem. sr. council), Sigma Chi, Sigma Delta Chi. Jewish religion. Rotarian. Clubs: Dartmouth (N.Y.C.); National Press (Washington); Ocean Beach (Elberon, N.J.); Contbr. column Editor's Viewpoint to No. Va. Sun, articles to popular, trade mags. Home: 4114 N Ridgeview Rd Arlington VA 22101 Office: 3409 Wilson Blvd Arlington VA 22210

O'BERRY, CELIA MOLLY, pub. health nurse; b. Spring Lake, Fla., Mar. 12, 1900; d. Daniel Marion and Mary Ann (Nicks) O'Berry; R.N., St. Luke's Hosp. Tng. Sch., Jacksonville, Fla., 1922; student George Peabody Coll. Tchrs., 1930, 39, 40, 47, U. Mich., 1946, U. N.C., 1954, 61, 62. Office nurse, 1923-29; nurse A.R.C., 1930-33, Fed. Emergency Relief Program State Nursing Project, Fla., 1933-36; pub. health nurse, Escambia County, Fla., 1936-38, Gadsden County, 1938-39; pub. health nurse Lake County Health Dept., Tavares, Fla., 1940—, supr. pub. health nurses, 1944—. Mem. Am., Fla. pub. health assns., Nat. League Nursing, Am. Sch. Health Assn., Am., Fla. (dist. pres. 1954) nurses assns. Democrat. Methodist. Club: Pilot (charter mem.). Home: PO Box 944 Tavares FL 32778 Office: Lake County Health Dept Tavares FL 32778

OBERT, PAUL MICHAEL, physician; b. Apache, Okal., Apr. 25, 1924; s. Joseph M. and Mary (Fitter) O.; B.Sc., Stanford, 1944; M.D., U. Okla., 1947; m. Gene Salisbury, Apr. 27, 1947; children—Mary, Jeanne, Paul, Elizabeth. Catherine. Intern, St. Anthony Hosp., Oklahoma City, 1947-48; practice gen. medicine, Purcell, Okla., 1948-50, resident U. Hosp. Oklahoma City, 1950-52, cancer research fellow, 1951-52; practice medicine, specializing in pathology Victoria, Tex., 1956—; chief staff McCurdy Hosp., Purcell, Okla., 1949-50; asst. prof. pathology U. Okla. Sch. Medicine, Oklahoma City, 1952-56; attending pathologist VA Hosp., Oklahoma City, 1953-56; pathologist-in chief USPHS Hosp., Galveston, Tex., 1953-56; asst. prof. pathology U. Tex. Sch. Medicine, Galveston, 1954-57; chief pathologist, dir. labs. Citizens Meml., Calhoun County Meml. Victoria, Mauritz, Nightengale hosps., all 1956—; cons. pathologist Matagorda County, Huth Meml., Cuero, Burns, Wagner, Yorktown, Palacious City hosps., 1956—; dir. labs. Meml. Hosp., Beeville, Tex., 1963—; vis. pathologist M.D. Anderson Hosp., 1962—; dir. lab Matagorda Gen. Hosp. and Goliod County Hosp., 1963—, Kleborg Hosp., Kingsville, Tex., 1968—; forensic pathologist South Tex., 1968; bd. dirs. Victoria Med. Center, 1963—, pres., 1969—; bd. dirs. Tex. Rehab. Center, Gonzales, 1970—. Tex. dir. Cancer Soc. Trustee Victoria Ednl. Found.; bd. dirs. Victoria Fine Arts Assn. Served with AUS, 1943-46; comdr., USPHS, 1953-56. Diplomate Am. Bd. Pathology. Fellow Coll. Am. Pathologists, Am. Soc. Clin. Pathologists; mem. Am., Tex., Victoria-Calhoun-Coliad County med. assns., Internat. Acad. Pathology, Tex. Assn. Pathologists, N.Y. Acad. Scis., A.A.A.S., Soc. Exptl. Biology and Medicine, Am. Assn. Blood Banks. Roman Catholic. Clubs: Victoria Country, Serra (trustee). Contbr. articles to profl. publs. Home: 303 Tampa Dr Victoria TX 77901 Office: 2602 Houston Hwy Victoria TX 77901

OBERWARTH, CLARENCE JULIAN, architect; b. Frankfort, Ky., Mar. 1, 1900; s. Leo Louis and Ruth Buckner (Hawkins) O.; student U. of Ky., 1919-20; B.S. in Arch., Mass. Inst. of Tech., 1924; m. Lillian Murray Wiard, Nov. 28, 1935; children—Ann (Mrs. William J. Dennis), Lee Franklin (Mrs. Bruce E. King III), Julie (Mrs. Samuel P. Williams). Exec. dir. Ky. Bd. Examiners and Registration of Architects, 1966—; pvt. practice architecture, Frankfort, 1925—; prin. works include Frankfort Elementary Sch.; Arts and Crafts Bldg., Georgetown Coll.; student Union Bldg., dining Hall, Science and Class Room Bldg., Women's Dormitory, Library, Men's Dormitory, Fine Arts Bldg., all Ky. State Coll., Frankfort; several buildings at Kentucky Sch. for Deaf, Danville; restoration Dr. Ephriam McDowell Meml. and Constn. Sq., Danville, Ky.; replanning and reconstrn. Ky. State Capitol and Exec. Mansion, Rosenwald Lab. Sch., First Ch. of Christ Scientist, King's Daus. Hosp., State Police Barracks and Tng. Acad., Nat. Guard Armory, Frankfort Municipal Bldg., Franklin County Health Center, other pub. bldgs. Exec. dir. Ky. State Bd. Archtl. Examiners, 1966—. Served as seaman USNRF, 1917-18. Recipient Dist. Service award, Ky. Soc. Architects, 1968. Fellow A.I.A. (mem. bd. dirs. 1941-43; chmn. com. on wards and scholarships, 1943; chmn. com. on registration 1935-41; membership sec. and chmn. com. on membership, 1943-46, pres. Ky. chpt., 1933, recipient Honor award 1968); mem. Assn. Ky. Archs., Soc. of Tech. Archs., Am. Legion, Triglyph; hon. life mem. Ind. Soc. of Architects (elected, 1946). Episcopalian. Elk. Rotarian. Contbr. to profl. jours. Home: 116 W 4th St Frankfort KY 40601 Office: 323 Shelby St Frankfort KY 40601

O'BOYLE, PATRICK A., clergyman. Ordained priest Roman Cath. Ch., 1921; consecrated archbishop of Washington, Jan. 14, 1948, elevated to cardinal, 1967. Office: 1721 Rhode Island Av Washington DC 20036

O'BRIEN, ALLEN JOHN, lawyer; b. Minot, N.D., June 7, 1914; s. Thomas W. and Ellen (Malm) O'B.; student St. Johns U., 1935-37; LL.B., Catholic U., 1952; m. Maxine T. Schulte, Dec. 27, 1937; children—Michael, Mary Jane (Mrs. Kevin O'Neill). Various traffic positions Gt. No. Ry., Klamath Falls, Ore., 1937-42 traffic mgr. Mfrs. Express, New Haven, Conn., 1945-48; admitted to D.C. bar, 1952; traffic atty. USAF and Sec. of Def., Washington, 1948-57, Aerospace Industry Assn., Washington, 1957—. Served to capt. AUS, 1942-45. Mem. Nat. Indsl. Traffic League (dir. 1960—), Nat. Def. Transp. Assn. (chapt. dir. 1969). Contbr. articles in field to profl. jours. Home: 6757 N 27TH St Arlington VA 22213 Office: 1725 DeSales St NW Washington DC 20036

O'BRIEN, EDWARD JOHN, III, tobacco co. exec.; b. Louisville, Mar. 28, 1920; s. Edward John and Mary (Malone) O'B.; B.A., Princeton, 1942; m. Lucy Dickenson Scott, July 30, 1960; children—Edward John IV, Mary Scott. With Edward J. O'Brien Co., Louisville, 1946—, sec., 1955-70, v.p., sec., 1970—. Com. chmn., United Way, 1971; vice chmn. Louisville chpt. A.R.C., 1969—; civic com. Bellarmine-Ursuline Coll., 1960. Bd. dirs. Internat. Center, U. Louisville. Served to capt., AUS, 1942-46. Mem. Tobacco Assn. U.S. (v.p. 1970—), Burley Tobacco Dealers Assn. (pres. 1962-63; dir.), Burley Dark Leaf Tobacco Export Assn. Rotarian. Home: 406 Springwood Lane Louisville KY 40207 Office: 815 W Main St Louisville KY 40202

O'BRIEN, EDWARD WILLIAM, journalist; b. Palisades, N.Y., Oct. 29, 1916; s. Dennis and Julia (Scanlan) O'B.; B.B.A., Manhattan Coll., 1937; M.B.A., N.Y.U., 1942; m. Marian Louise Johnson, Sept. 17, 1949; children—Julia Louise, Theodore William. With Equitable Life Assurance Soc. U.S., 1937-44; asst. editor Newsweek mag., 1944-45, bur. chief, Detroit, 1946-47, bur. chief, Chgo., 1948-49; mem. Rep. Congl. Com., 1949-52, asst. dir. pub. relations, 1953-54; chief Washington bur. St. Louis Globe-Democrat, 1954—. Mem. White House Corrs. Assn. Clubs: Federal City, National Press (Washington); Gridiron. Home: 940 Peacock Station Rd McLean VA 22101 Office: 1750 Pennsylvania Av NW Washington DC 20006

O'BRIEN, LAWRENCE FRANCIS, investment banker, past chmn. Democratic Nat. Com.; b. Springfield, Mass., July 7, 1917; s. Lawrence Francis and Myra Theresa (Sweeney) O'B.; LL.B., Northeastern U., 1942; m. Elva Brassard, May 30, 1944; 1 son, Lawrence Francis III. Engaged in real estate and pub. relations, Springfield, 1943-60; active organizing polit. campaigns, 1938—; dir. orgn. Democratic Congl. campaigns 2d Dist. Mass., 1946, 48, 50; adminstrv. asst. to U.S. Rep. Furcolo, 1948-50; dir. orgn. Senator Kennedy's campaign, 1952, Mass. Dem. Com., 1956-57, Senator Kennedy's re-election campaign, 1958; nat. dir. orgn. Kennedy for Pres. campaign, 1959-60. Dem. Nat. Com., 1960-61, Kennedy-Johnson Presdl. campaign, 1960; spl. asst. to Pres. Kennedy for Congl. relations and personnel, until 1963; spl. asst. for congl. relations to Pres. Johnson, 1963-65; postmaster gen. of U.S., 1965-68; chmn. Dem. Nat. Com., 1969, 70-72; campaign mgr. McGovern for Pres. campaign, 1972—; pres. McDonnell & Co., Inc., investment bankers, N.Y.C. Served with AUS, World War II. Address: 2600 Virginia Av Washington DC 20037

O'BRIEN, RICHARD HAROLD, title co. exec.; b. Bklyn., Oct. 4, 1931; s. Harold Augustus and Gladys J. (Swanson) O'B.; B.S., Hofstra U., 1958. With Security Title & Guaranty Co., Mineola, N.Y., 1956-69, asst. sec., 1959-61, asst. v.p., 1961-63, v.p., 1963-69; v.p. Dist. Realty Title Ins. Corp., Washington, 1969—, also dir.; dir. Queens County Real Estate Brokers Assn., Inc. Mem. Washington Bd. Trade. Vice pres. Alden Terrace Civic Assn., 1947-48. Pres., Elmont Republican Recruits, 1948; v.p. Nassau County Council Rep. Recruits, 1950-51. Served with AUS, 1952-54. Recipient Gen. Dwight Eisenhower Pub. Service award, 1944; Nat. Service award, 1954. Mem. Met. Washington Home Builders Assn., Am., D.C. land title assns., Tamadachi. Lutheran. Lion, Elk. Club: Bethesda Country. Home: 11700 Old Columbia Pike Silver Spring MD 20904 Office: 1030 15th St NW Washington DC 20005

OBRIG, ELWOOD MANSFIELD, lawyer; b. Summit, N.J., Sept. 5, 1941; s. Elwood Mansfield and Dorothy (Bergman) O.; grad. Manlius Sch., 1959; A.B., U. Richmond, 1963; J.D., U. Miami (Fla.), 1966; m. Mary Elizabeth Coleman, June 15, 1963; children—Paige Elizabeth, Scott Coleman. Admitted to Fla. bar, 1966; research asst. State Atty.'s Office, Appellate Div., Dade County, Fla., 1965, 66; research asst. State atty. Gen.'s Office, Dade County, 1966; asst. state atty., Dade County, 1966-67; asst. city atty., Ft. Lauderdale, Fla., 1967-72; partner Andrews, Lubbers & Obrig. Profl. Assn., Ft. Lauderdale, 1968—. Served with AUS, 1967. Mem. Am., Fla., Broward County bar assns., Phi Delta Phi (past pres.), Phi Kappa Sigma (past v.p.). Republican. Presbyn. Home: 2100 NE 59th Ct Fort Lauderdale FL 33308 Office: 2601 E Oakland Park Blvd Fort Lauderdale FL 33306

O'BRYAN, MAUD (MRS. GEORGE NELSON RONSTROM), newspaper columnist; b. Sulphur Mine, La., June 28, 1914; d. F. Daniel and Annie Christina (Coldwater) O'Bryan; B.A. in Journalism, La. State U., 1932; m. George Nelson Ronstrom, Sept. 14, 1939. Daily columnist Times-Picayune, New Orleans, also New Orleans States-Item. Mem. Theta Sigma Phi. Contbr. articles to nat. mags., including Antiques, Am. Antiques, Jour., Hobbies. Home: 524 Esplanade Av New Orleans LA 70116 Office: Times-Picayune New Orleans LA 70140

O'BRYANT, ALBERT, ednl. adminstr.; b. Augusta, Ga., Dec. 16, 1926; s. Jack and Idell (Lyons) O'B.; B.S., Ft. Valley State Coll., 1951; postgrad. Nat. Defense Edn. Act. Inst., Atlanta U., 1961-62; M.A., Atlanta U., 1965; m. Frances Woodall, Dec. 18, 1951; children—Pamela, Albert, Franklin, Samuel, Lewyn. Tchr.-coach, counselor Taylor County Bd. Edn., Butler, Ga., 1953-61, prin., 1962—; tchr., cons. Paul Quinn Coll., Waco, Tex., 1969. Dir. Capitol Holding Co., Atlanta. Bd. dirs., organizer Head Start Programs, Taylor County, Ga. Served with USNR, 1943-45; ETO, PTO. Recipient Scholarship, Nat. Defense Edn. Act Inst., Atlanta U., 1961-62. Mem. N.E.A., Am. Assn. Sch. Adminstrs., Ga. Edn. Assn., Phi Beta Sigma. Democrat. Methodist (supt. Sunday Sch. 1967-72). Mason. Home: 1310 S Macon St Fort Valley GA 31030 Office: PO Box 428 Butler GA 31006

OCASIO-ESTEBAN, RAFAEL, constrn. co. exec.; b. San Juan, P.R., June 12, 1931; s. Perfecto and Carmen (Esteban) Ocasio; B.S.C.E., U. P.R., 1954; m. Angelina Carle, Sept. 4, 1959; children—Rafael A., Esteban L., Maria T., Jorge J. Staff engr. P.R. Planning Bd., 1956-57; with IBEC Housing Co., Inc., Rio Piedras, P.R., 1957—, chief engr., 1960-67, v.p., gen. mgr. operations, 1967-70, pres., 1970—; dir. RELBEC Corp., San Juan; adv. bd. Banco de Economias. Served to 1st lt. AUS, 1954-56. Mem. P.R. Inst. Engrs. and Architects, C. of C. of P.R., San Juan Bd. Realtors, Internat. Recreation Assn., Nat. Assn. Home Builders (bd. dirs. 1968-72), P.R. Home Builders Assn. (pres. 1970-71), Nu Sigma Beta. Club: Exchange. Home: 1833 Acacia St Santa Maria Rio Piedras PR 00927 Office: Box AX Rio Piedras PR 00928

OCH, LOUISE MARIA (MRS. JOSEPH L. H. OCH), tile co. exec.; b. Augsburg, Germany, Nov. 24, 1914; d. Martin and Maria (Schott) Scharz; came to U.S., 1928, naturalized, 1935; R.N., Cornell U., 1935; m. Joseph L. H. Och, July 10, 1940. Head nurse Cornell Med. Center, N.Y.C., 1935-38; supr. Alton Rd. Hosp., Miami, Fla., 1938-40; indsl. nurse charge first aid Opa Locka AFB, Miami, 1940-44; pub. health nurse Dade County Health Dept., Miami, 1946-49; v.p. Continental Tile Co., Miami, 1952—. Mem. Miami Opera Guild, Miami Mental Health Soc., Friends of Univ. Library, U. Miami, Miami Builders Exchange, Women in Constrn. Clubs: Run Away Bay (Miami); Jockey; Ocean Reefs (Key Largo, Fla.), The Vizcayans, Coral Reef Yacht (Miami). Home: 10343 NE 6th Av Miami Shores FL 33153 Office: 381 NE 61st St Miami FL 33137

OCHSNER, ALTON, surgeon; b. Kimball, S.D., May 4, 1896; s. Edward Phillip and Clara (Shontz) O.; A.B., U. of S.D., 1918, hon. D.Sc., 1936; M.D., Washington U., 1920; Sc.D., Brigham Young U., 1961, Loyola U., New Orleans, 1969; Doctor Honoris Causa, Universidad Libre de Nicaragua, 1946; LL.D., Tulane U., 1966, McNeese State U., 1972; m. Isabel Kathryn Lockwood, Sept. 13, 1923 (dec. Apr. 1968); children—Alton, John Lockwood, Mims Gage, Isabel; m. 2d, Jane Kellogg, Feb. 12, 1970. Intern, Barnes Hosp., St. Louis, 1920-21, Augustana Hosp., Chgo., 1921-22; exchange surg. asst., Kantons Hosp., Zurich, Switzerland, 1922-23, Staedtisches Krankenhaus, Frankfurt am Main, 1923-24; visited European and Am. clinics, 1924-25; instr. in surgery, Northwestern U. Med. School, 1925-26; asst. prof. surgery, U. of Wis., 1926-27; prof. surgery and chmn. dept. of surgery, Tulane U., 1927-56, prof. clin. surgery, 1956-61, emeritus prof. surgery, 1961—, William Henderson prof. surgery, 1938-56; dir. sect. on gen. surgery Ochsner Clinic, Found. Hosp., 1942-66, sr. cons. surgery, 1967—, sr. surgeon Touro Infirmary; cons. in surgery Charity Hosp., cons. in thoracic surg. USPHS Hosp., VA Hosp., New Orleans; cons. surgeon I.C. Hosp., New Orleans, U.S. Air Force Surgeon. Pres. Cordell Hull Found. for Internat. Edn.; pres. Internat. House, 1962. Decorated Order Vasco Nunez de Balboa, Cruz Eloy-Alfaro, Panama; Order of Al Merito, Republic of Ecuador; recipient Service award A.M.A., 1967; Cunningham Inter-Am. Relations award, 1967; Thomas F. Cunningham award Internat. House of New Orleans, 1968. Mem. com. on growth NRC. Diplomate Am. Bd. Surgery (a founder), Am. Bd. Thoracic Surgery (a founder). Fellow Royal Coll. Surgeons. Ireland (hon.), Royal Coll. Surgeons Eng. (hon.), A.C.S. (past pres., past regent), Am. Surg. Assn., So. Surg. Assn. (past pres.); mem. A.M.A., Am. Assn. Thoracic Surgery (past pres.), Internat. Surg. Soc. (pres. 1963), Soc. Clin. Surgery, Southeastern Surg. Assn. (past pres.), Orleans Parish Med. Assn., Soc. Exptl. Biology and Medicine, So. Med. Assn., Am. Cancer Soc. (dir., past pres.), Am. Acad. Orthopedic Surgs., Internat. Soc. Angiology (past pres.), Interstate Postgrad. Med. Assn. (past pres.), Soc. for Vascular Surg. (past pres.), Academia Mexicana de Cirugia (hon.). Internat. Soc. Surgery (pres.), Pan-Pacific Surg. Assn. (pres.), Delta Sigma Pi, Nu Sigma Nu, Alpha Omega Alpha, Sigma Xi, Omicron Delta Kappa. Phi Delta Theta. Clubs: Boston, New Orleans Country. Writer sect. on diseases of veins, Lewis' System of Surgery, monographs on varicose veins. Editor Internat. Surgical Digest; editor surg. sect. The Cyclopedia of Medicine, Surgery and Specialties; former co-editor of Surgery; asso. editor Lewis Practice of Surgery. Home: 1347 Exposition Blvd New Orleans LA 70118 Office: Ochsner Clinic 1514 Jefferson Hwy New Orleans LA 70121

OCHSNER, JOHN LOCKWOOD, physician; b. Madison, Wis., Feb. 10, 1927; s. Edward Alton and Isabel (Lockwood) O.; M.D., Tulane U., 1952; m. Mary Louise Hannon, Mar. 20, 1954; children—John Lockwood, Joby Hannon, Katherine, Frank Hannon. Intern U. Mich. Hosp., 1952-53, surg. resident, 1953-54; surg. resident

Jefferson Davis Hosp., Houston, 1956-59, chief resident, 1959; cardio-vascular resident Tex. Children's Hosp., 1960; surg. staff Baylor Med. Sch., 1960-61; staff Ochsner Clinic, New Orleans, 1961; clin. prof. surgery Tulane U. Sch. Medicine; chmn. dept. surgery Ochsner Clinic and Oschner Found. Hosp.; cons. cardiac surgeon La. Bd. Health; cons. gen. and thoracic surgery USPHS Hosp., New Orleans; cons. cardiovascular surgeon Lafayette (La.) Meml. Hosp.; vis. surgeon E.A. Conway Meml. Hosp. Mem. bd. Jefferson Heart Council, 1961. Served with M.C., USAF, 1954-56. Diplomate Am. Bd. Surgery, Am. Bd. Thoracic Surgery. Fellow A.C.S., Am. Coll. Chest Physicians; mem. Internat. Surg. Soc., Am., So. surg. assns., Internat. Cardiovascular Soc., Am. Assn. Thoracic Surgeons, A.M.A., La., Orleans Parish med. socs., So. Thoracic Surg. Assn., Am. Heart Assn., La. Thoracic Soc., So. Med. Assn., New Orleans Surg. Soc., Soc. for Vascular Surgery, S.E. Surg. Congress, Soc. Thoracic Surgeons, Beta Theta Pi, Nu Sigma Nu. Home: 84 Audubon Blvd New Orleans LA 70118 Office: Ochsner Clinic New Orleans LA 70121

O'CONNELL, STEPHEN CORNELIUS, univ. pres.; b. West Palm Beach, Fla., Jan. 22, 1916; s. Daniel Joseph and Nora (McKenna) O'C; B.S., J.D., U. Fla., 1940, LL.B., Jacksonville U., 1968, Notre Dame, 1969; Ed.D., Biscayne Coll., 1969; m. Rita Mavis McTigue, Nov. 6, 1946; children—Rite Denise (Mrs. Herbert Cumbie), Stephen C., Martin Robert, Ann Maureen. Admitted to Fla. bar, 1940, and practiced in Ft. Lauderdale, 1940-55; justice Supreme Ct. of Fla., 1955-67, chief justice, 1967; pres. U. Fla., Gainesville, 1967—. Dir. Fla. Nat. Banks. Chmn., Jud. Council, 1957-59; atty. Fla. Road Dept., 1953, Racing Commn., 1954; chmn. Fla. Citizenship Clearing House. Bd. dirs. Newman Found., UF Found. Served from 2d lt. to maj., USAAF, 1942-46. Recipient Annual Brotherhood award Nat. Conf. Christians and Jews, Man of Year award K.C., 1965; Liberty Bell award 8th Jud. Circuit, 1971; decorated Pro Eclesia et Pontifica medal Pope Paul, 1970. Mem. Am. Bar Assn., Fla. Bar, Phi Delta Phi, Phi Kappa Phi, Alpha Tau Omega. Elk. Home: 2151 W University Av Gainesville FL 36601

O'CONNOR, DANIEL J., clergyman, sec. for edn. Atlanta Archdiocesan Schs. Office: 320 Courtland NE Atlanta GA 30303*

O'CONNOR, E. JEROME, architect; b. White Plains, N.Y., Apr. 30, 1891; s. John and Mary (Baldwin) O'C.; B.Arch., Cornell U., 1912. Designer, W. Welles Bosworth, N.Y.C., 1912-15; pvt. practice, N.Y.C., 1920-41; exec. architect J. W. O'Connor, 1926-31; asso. architect Frank H. Hutton, 1935-37; co-ordinating architect Pentagon Bldg., Arlington, Va., 1941-42, field dir. airplane plants, 1942-44; designing architect Chem. Warfare plants, 1944-45; pvt. practice Alexandria, and Washington, 1945—; designer, architect Indsl. Mart, Washington; architect Nat. Grange Hdqrs. Bldg., Washington, Coll. Lab. Sch., Frostburg, Md. Registered architect, N.Y., N.J., Conn., Md., Va., D.C., Ky. Mem. Washington Bldg. Congress, N.Y. State Assn. Architects, Soc. Pentagon. A.I.A., Am. Standards Com. Indsl. Lighting, Constrn. Specifications Inst., Soc. Archtl. Historians. Club: Cornell. Address: 810 18th St NW Washington DC 20006

O'CONNOR, JEAN SMITH (MRS. GERALD FRANCIS O'CONNOR), author; b. nr. Hamlin, W.Va.; d. Oscar French and Florence (Adkins) Smith; grad. W.Va. Bus. Coll.; m. Gerald Francis O'Connor, Aug. 3, 1929; children—Joan Florence (Mrs. Alfred James Dickerson, Jr.), Peggy Frances (Mrs. Lanny J. Pixley), Geraldine Phyllis (Mrs. Philip James Barrons). Mem. editorial staff Echoes of W.Va., Charleston, 1952-56; v.p., sec.-treas. Line Creek Coal Corp., Charleston, 1962-66. Mem. W.Va. Poetry Soc. (state pres. 1967, 68-69), Nat. League Am. Pen Women (state pres. 1964-66, nat. poetry chmn. 1970-72), Cath. Daus. Am., Huntington Poetry Guild, Poetry Soc. Va. Democrat. Roman Catholic. Author: The Quiet Hills, 1963. Home: Plaza E 4300 N Ocean Blvd Fort Lauderdale FL 33308

O'CONNOR, JOHN ALBERT, JR., lawyer, business exec.; b. New Orleans, Apr. 10, 1913; s. John A. and Stella (Toledano) O'C.; A.B., Tulane, 1934, LL.B., 1936; m. Paula McKinney, Nov. 24, 1936; children—John A., Peter M., Paula T. (Mrs. Ben Smith III), Patricia M. Admitted to La. bar, 1936, Ark. bar, 1937; atty. Lion Oil Co., El Dorado, Ark., 1936-41; partner Knox, Keith & O'Connor, 1941-45, Crumpler, O'Connor & Wynne, 1945—; sec., dir. Radio Enterprises, Inc. (radio sta. KELD), 1946—; sec. Ocean Drilling & Exploration Co., 1955-66, dir., 1955—; pres., dir. Brook Tarpaulin Co., Inc., New Orleans, 1950- ; sec. Murphy Oil Corp., 1954-66, v.p., gen. counsel, 1958-66, former chmn. bd., now dir., chmn. exec. com. Pres. bd. dirs. El Dorado Sch. Dist. 15, 1949-50; pres. Community Chest, 1948-50. Served to lt. comdr. USNR, World War II. Mem. Am., La., Ark. bar assns., El Dorado C. of C. (dir., pres. 1950). Clubs: Eldorado Golf and Country; Boston, Internat. House, Plimsoll (New Orleans); National Lawyers, International (Washington). Home: 510 E Faulkner St El Dorado AR 71730 Office: Murphy Bldg El Dorado AR 71730

O'CONNOR, PATRICK REGAN, physician; b. Louisville, Mar. 5, 1937; s. Patrick John Regan and Blanche (Nageleisen) O'C.; B.A., Vanderbilt U., 1959, M.D., 1962; m. Donna Nelson, Aug. 1, 1959; children—Patrick Regan III, Kelly Nelson. Intern, U. Miss. Hosp., 1962-63; resident in ophthalmology U. Louisville, 1963-66, chief resident, 1966, asst. prof. ophthalmology, 1969-71, asso. prof., 1971—; dir. retinal service Ky. Lions Eye Research Inst., 1969—; cons. Louisville Gen. Hosp., Children's Hosp., Jewish Hosp., VA Hosp., Irland Army Hosp. Fellow Cornell U., 1968-69. Served to capt. M.C., USAF, 1966-68. Diplomate Am. Bd. Ophthalmology. Mem. Am. Acad. Ophthalmology, Louisville Acad. Ophthalmology, Jefferson County Med. Soc., Ky. Med. Assn., Retinal Soc. Am., Soc. Heed Fellows, Am. Coll. Surgs. Republican. Catholic. Club: Louisville Boat. Contbr. articles to med. jours. Home: 1021 Alta Vista Rd Louisville KY 40205 Office: 301 E Walnut St Louisville KY 40202

O'CONNOR, ROBERT DORMAN, JR., hosp. adminstr.; b. Vicksburg, Miss., Oct. 8, 1935; s. Robert Dorman and Rubye Austin (King) O'C.; student Hinds Jr. Coll., 1957-59; B.S., U. So. Miss., 1960, M.S., 1961; m. Barbara Ann Williams, June 5, 1959; children—Kimberly Wynne, Leigh Shannon. Asst. dean student affairs, instr. psychology Holmes Jr. Coll., Goodman, Miss., 1961-64; with div. Rehab., Miss. Dept. Edn., 1964-65; asst. adminstr. Hinds Gen. Hosp., Jackson, Miss., 1965-68; adminstr. Rankin Gen. Hosp., Brandon, Miss., 1968—; co-owner Contract Cars, Ltd., Jackson; asso. Malone & Asso., health planning cons., Jackson. Pres. Miss. Assn. Mental Health, 1972. Bd. dirs. Goodwin Industries, Jackson, 1966-69, Cleary Heights Assn., Cleary, Miss., 1970—. Served with AUS, 1954-57. Mem. Am. Coll. Hosp. Adminstrs., Rankin C. of C. (exec. com. 1971—). Mason, Rotarian. Contbr. articles to profl. pubs. Home: Route 3 Box 302 Florence MS 39073 Office: 350 Crossgates Blvd Brandon MS 39042

O'CONNOR, TRELYON WALDO, JR., gen. engr.; b. Clifton Forge, Va., Aug. 16, 1921; s. Trelyon Waldo and Lucy (Greene) O'C.; B.S., Va. Polytech. Inst., 1948; m. Dorothy Marie Rogers, July 6, 1952; children—Cynthia, Alice, Rosemary. Engr. Rural Electrification Adminstrn., U.S. Dept. Agr., Washington, 1948-50; engr. rep. Sears, Roebuck & Co., 1950-51; project engr. U.S. Army Mobility Equipment Research and Devel. Center, Ft. Belvoir, Va., 1953-56, chief Mech. Standards Sect. and Topographic Material Sect., 1956-66, dep. chief power engring. div., 1966-71, dep. chief electro tech. dept., 1971—. Mem. Brookland Estates Civic Assn. Panel mem. Bd. Civil Service Examiners for Scientists and Engrs., Mil. Dist. Washington. Served to capt. USAAF, 1942-46, USAF, 1951-53; lt. col. USAF Reserve. Decorated D.F.C., Air Medal with oak leaf clusters, Commendation medal. Registered profl. engr., Va. Mem. Am. Soc. Agrl. Engrs. (asso.), Va. Tech. Alumni and Student Aid Assns., Am. Contract Bridge League, Am. Standards Assn. (mem. sectional com. B-29 for power transmission chains and sprockets), Nat., Am. socs. profl. engrs., Soc. Am. Mil. Engrs., Res. Officers Assn., Am. Bowling Congress (pres. league 1966-67). Lutheran. Home: 5909 Pratt St Alexandria VA 22310 Office: 314 USA MERDC Fort Belvoir VA 22606

O'CONNOR, WILLIAM CHARLES, apparel co. exec.; b. Bowling Green, Ky., May 1, 1927; s. John S. and Mary (Schneider) O'C.; student Stevens Inst. Tech., 1945-46; B.S. in Accounting, Western Ky. U., 1949; LL.B., Nashville YMCA Evening Law Sch., 1958; m. Mary Margaret Campion, Apr. 7, 1951; children—Marianne, Margaret, Thomas. Staff accountant Osborn & Page, C.P.A.'s, Nashville, 1949-56; with Genesco, Inc., Nashville, 1956—, asst. v.p., 1965—; admitted to Tenn. bar, 1958. Served with USNR, 1945-46. Mem. Am., Tenn. bar assns., Serra Internat. K.C. Home: 117 Groome St Nashville TN 37205 Office: 111 7th Av N Nashville TN 37202

ODDO, PAUL CHARLES, pub. co. exec.; b. Bklyn., Feb. 9, 1915; s. Antonio and Pauline (Signorelli) O.; B.B.A., St. John's U., 1936; M.A., Columbia, 1937; m. Genevieve Grillo, Dec. 7, 1946; children—Paul, Charles, Warren. Tchr. pvt. schs., N.Y.C., 1936-40; with Grolier Soc., Inc., N.Y.C., 1942-58, v.p. sch. and library div., 1950-58; cons. to publishers, 1958-64; pres. Oddo Publishing, Inc., Fayetteville, Ga., 1964—. Served with USNR, 1942-46. Mem. A.L.A., Am. Booksellers Assn., Iota Alpha Sigma. Roman Catholic. Rotarian. Home: Beauregard Blvd Fayetteville GA 30214 Office: Box 68 Fayetteville GA 30214

ODELL, ARTHUR GOULD, JR., architect; b. Concord, N.C., Nov. 22, 1913; s. Arthur Gould and Grace (Patterson) O.; student Duke, 1930-31; B.Arch., Cornell U., 1935; student Atelier Debat-Ponsan, Ecole des Beaux Arts, Paris, France, 1935-36; m. Polly Robinson, Nov. 10, 1941 (div. 1950); children—William R., Alexandra; m. 2d, Mary Walker Ehringhaus, Oct. 30, 1951; 1 son, Charles Alexander; stepchildren—Carroll, Michael Ehringhaus. Prin. Odell Assos., Inc., Charlotte, N.C., 1940—; works include pub. schs., Charlotte Auditorium and Coliseum, 1955, Charlotte Pub. Library and Belk's Dept. Store, 1956, Charlotte Meml. Hosp., 1960, St. Andrews Presbyn. Coll. of Laurinburg, N.C., 1960, Whitaker Plant, Reynolds Industries, Winston-Salem, N.C., 1961, Balt. Civic Center, 1962, Spring Mills Offices, Lancaster, S.C., 1969, Hampton Rds. Coliseum, Va., 1970, Burlington Industries Hdqrs., 1971; vis. critic Cornell U. Coll. Architecture, 1955-56. Commr., Charlotte Planning Bd., 1951-53; chmn. Charlotte Bldg. Code Bd. Appeals, 1957, N.C. Bldg. Code Council, 1957-59. Chmn. Kerr Industries, Inc., Concord. Mem. various nat. archtl. award juries. Chmn., Potomac Planning Task Force, Dept. of Interior, 1965—; pres. Charlotte Community Concert Assn., 1952; pres. trustees Mint Museum Art, Charlotte, 1959-63; mem. council Cornell U., 1960-62, 65; mem. N.C. Emergency Resources Planning Com., 1963; bd. dirs. N.C. Archtl. Found., 1954—, Central Charlotte Assn., 1959—. Served to lt. col., C.E., AUS, 1941-45. Decorated grand ofcl. Orden del Sol del Peru; recipient of School Exec. design award, 1953, Progressive Arch. citation, 1955, 60, Copper and Brass Research Assn. design award, 1960, McGraw Hill Pub. Co. best plant competition award, 1962, Instns. Mag. award, 1964, and others. Fellow A.I.A. (com. Sch. bldgs. 1955-58, national dir. 1959-62, pres. N.C. chpt. 1953-55; award of merit 1954, 57, S. Atlantic award of merit 1956, N.C. chpt. award merit 1955, 56, 57, 61, 62, 68, 69, 71, nat. 2d v.p. 1962-63, 1st v.p. 1963-64, pres. 1964-65); mem. Charlotte C. of C. (dir. 1963-64, 66-68, dir. at large 1970), Philippines Soc. Architects, Alpha Tau Omega, L'Ogive, Scabbard and Blade. Methodist. Clubs: Charlotte Country, City (director 1958-61), Quail Hollow Country, Charlotte Athletic (Charlotte); Cabarrus Country (Concord). Home: 2149 Sherwood Av Charlotte NC 28207 Office: 102 W Trade St Charlotte NC 28202

O'DELL, JAMES WALTER, supt. schs.; b. Camden, Ark., Feb. 12, 1927; s. Clyde and Alma (Tate) O'D.; B.A., Henderson State Coll., 1950, M.S. in Edn., 1959; Ed.D., East Coast U., 1972; m. Vivian Tollifson, Nov. 25, 1948; children—Sharon, Elaine, Ginger, Scott. Tchr. pub. schs. Mena, Ark., 1950; prin. Tinsman (Ark.) Sch. Dist., 1951-57; supt. Thornton (Ark.) Sch. Dist., 1957—. Mayor Thornton, 1967—. Scoutmaster De Soto Area Council, 1958—. Served with AUS, 1945-47. Mem. Am. Legion (comdr., 1968—), N.E.A., Ark. Edn. Assn., Am. Assn. Sch. Adminstrs., Phi Delta Kappa. Lion. Home and office: School St Thornton AR 71766

ODEN, FARRIS COTTRELL, ins. co. exec.; b. Amity, Ark., June 30, 1905; s. Thomas B. and Sarah E. (Walker) O.; student Okla. U., 1927; m. Dorothy McCown, Nov. 5, 1927; children—Bob F., Richard Lee, Jon T., Rebecca Ann (Mrs. Jim Weatherall). Ins. agt. Panhandle Ins. Agy., 1930-51; exec. v.p. Western Nat. Life Ins. Co., Amarillo, Tex., 1952-59, pres., 1960-71, chmn. bd., 1971—; v.p., dir. Southwestern Investment Co., 1944—; dir. Security Fed. Savs. and Loan Assn. Pres., United Fund, 1967; pres. Llano Estacado council Boy Scouts Am., 1962-64; active YMCA. Trustee, McMurray Coll., Abilene, Tex., 1970-71. Mem. C. of C. (bd. dirs.; pres. 1969). Rotarian (pres. 1937-38). Club: Amarillo Country. Home: 2314 Harmony St Amarillo TX 79106 Office: Box 871 205 E 10 St Amarillo TX 79105

ODEN, KENNETH, lawyer; b. Yoakum, Tex., Sept. 5, 1923; s. J.D. and Lena (Upchurch) O.; student Kilgore Jr. Coll., 1941-42, U. Tulsa, 1943, Navarra Coll., 1946; A.B., LL.B., Baylor U., 1950; m. Frances Walker, May 29, 1948; children—Kenneth, Theresa Lynne, Patricia Marie. Admitted to Tex. bar, 1950, since practiced in Alice, Tex.; mem. firm Perkins, Davis, Oden & Warburton, 1960—. Sec.-treas., dir., mem. John G. and Marie Stella Kennedy Meml. Found., 1963—. Served to capt. USAAF, 1944-46; ETO. Decorated Air medal with 5 oak leaf clusters. Mem. Com. on Mexican-Am. Law Relations, Am., Coastal Bend (past pres.) bar assns., State Bar Tex. (past mem. prosecuting grievance com.), Am. Judicature Soc., Tex. Assn. Def. Counsel. Baptist. Home: 1821 Walker St Alice TX 78332 Office: 500 E Main St Alice TX 78332

ODEN, SYDNOR, mfg. co. dir.; b. Dallas, May 25, 1902; s. Charles and Sarah (Sydnor) O.; ed. pub. schs. Houston; m. Olga Poe, June 10, 1926; children—Marilyn (Mrs. Ben A. Brallier), Charles S. Clk., Anderson Clayton & Co., Houston, 1920-25; partner Lamar Fleming &Co., Milan, Italy, 1925-37; v.p., then exec. v.p. Anderson Clayton & Co., Houston, 1937-66. Mem. Am. C. of C. for Italy (pres. 1933-34), Am. Cotton Shippers Assn. (pres. 1953-54), Houston C. of C. (pres. 1952). Home: 3640 Willowick St Houston TX 77019 Office: PO Box 2538 Houston TX 77001

ODEN, WALDO TALMAGE, JR., lawyer; b. Altus, Okla., May 17, 1929; s. Waldo Talmage and Lily (Clark) O.; B.A., U. Okla., 1950, LL.B., 1952, J.D., 1970; m. Rebecca Jane Hazlitt, Mar. 25, 1951; children—Waldo Talmage III, Timothy Patrick, Amy Germaine, Jonathan Andrew. Admitted to Okla. bar, 1952. U.S. Supreme Ct. bar, 1960; practiced in Altus, 1952—; mem. firm Robinson & Oden, 1952-53, Oden & Oden, 1954-67; mng. partner Oden, Oden & Derryberry, 1967—; asst. atty. Jackson County, 1953-54. Dir. Farmers & Mchts. Bank. Instr. bus. law Altus Coll., 1956-59; instr. criminology Altus AFB, 1958; mem. Okla. Jud. Nominating Commn., 1967-71. Dir. Jackson County Civil Def., 1959-68; chmn. Kicking Bird dist. Boy Scouts Am., 1969—; del. Methodist Jurisdictional Confs., 1964, 66, 68, 70, Methodist Gen. Confs., 1964; 68; sec. exec. com. Methodist Series of Protestant Hour, 1968—; mem. exec. com. W.W. and Rosa Woodworth Estate; pres. U. Okla. Wesley Found., 1947, Okla. Methodist Student Movement, 1948. Campaign chmn. Jackson County Democratic Com., 1954-60. Trustee, Altus Library Bd., 1965-72. Mem. Am., Okla., Jackson County bar assns., Am., Okla. trial lawyers assns., Phi Delta Phi. Methodist (chmn. ofcl. bd. 1960-61. Mason, Rotarian (pres. 1959-60). Mem. staff Okla. Law Rev., 1950-52. Home: 913 E Elm St Altus OK 73521 Office: PO Drawer J 209 N Hudson St Altus OK 73521

ODLAND, LURA M(AE), coll. dean; b. Morgantown, W.Va., Nov. 22, 1921; d. Theodore E. and R. Elizabeth (Aamodt) Odland; B.S., U. R.I., 1943, D.Sc., 1969; M.S., U. Conn., 1945; Ph.D. (fellow 1947-50) U. Wis., 1950. Instr. foods and nutrition U. Conn., 1945; nutritionist com. on food composition, food and nutrition bd., NRC, 1945-47; asst. U. Wis., 1947-50; asso. prof. Mont. State Coll. and Agrl. Expt. Sta., 1950-55; adminstr. State Expt. Stas. div. U.S. Dept. Agr., Washington, 1955-59; dean Coll. Home Econs., U. Tenn., 1959—, dir. home sci. under ICA in India, 1959-62. Rep. of U.S. Dept. Agr. to Internat. Congress of Nutrition, 1957, 1966. Fellow A.A.A.S., Am. Pub. Health Assn.; mem. Am. Inst. Nutrition, Am. Chem. Soc., Am. Home Econs. Assn., Tenn. Edn. Assn., Am. Dietetic Assn., Tenn. Home Econs. Assn. (pres. 1964-66), Inst. Food Technologists, Sigma Xi (chpt. pres. 1965-66), Phi Kappa Phi, Omicron Nu. Author numerous tech. publs. Office: Coll Home Econs U Tenn Knoxville TN 37916

ODLE, JOE TAFT, religious assn. editor; b. West Frankfort, Ill., Aug. 19, 1908; s. Harry Logan and Mary Winona (Dillon) O.; A.B., Union U., 1930; postgrad. So. Baptist Theol. Sem., Louisville, 1935; D.D., Miss. Coll., 1949; m. Clara Mabel Riley, July 17, 1930; children—Joe Thomas (dec.), Sara Ann (Mrs. Roland Maddox). Ordained to ministry Baptist Ch., 1925; pastor Bapt. chs. in Orient, Ill., 1926, Gallaway and Rossville, Tenn., 1928-29, Barlow and Bandana, Ky., 1930-32, East Bapt. Ch., Paducah, Ky., 1932-43, First Bapt. Ch., Crystal Springs, Miss., 1943-47, Gulfport, Miss., 1947-56; asso. exec. sec. Miss. Bapt. Conv. Bd., Jackson, 1956-59, editor Bapt. Record, 1959—. Mem. So. Bapt. Conv. Annuity Bd., 1949-56, Bapt. Joint Com., Washington, 1963-69; v.p. Miss. Bapt. Conv., 1954. Mem. Asso. Ch. Press, So. Bapt. (pres. 1971), Evangelical press assns. Rotarian. Author: Church Member's Handbook, 1941; It's A Great Life, 1967; Is Christ Coming Soon, 1971; Why I Am a Baptist, 1972. Home: 1322 Robert Dr Jackson MS 39211 Office: PO Box 530 Jackson MS 39205

ODOM, ANDREW JACKSON, dentist; b. Enterprise, Miss., Mar. 17, 1899; s. William Thomas and Minnie Florence (Culpepper) O.; D.D.S., Tulane U., 1926; m. Frankie Kathryn Stumpe, June 6, 1934; children— Jackson Fred, Kathryn Phoebe (Mrs. Patrick Henry Phelan). Practice dentistry, Orange, Tex., 1926-31, Beaumont, 1931—. Active United Appeals, YMCA, Muscular Distrophy Assn., Tb Assn. Fellow Am. Coll. Dentists; mem. Am. Dental Assn, Tex. Dental Assn. (v.p. 1947-48), Sabine Dist. Dental Soc. (pres. 1936-37, 46-47), Occlusal Rehab. Seminar Southwest (pres. 1969-70), Pierre Fauchard Acad., Acad. Gen. Dentistry, L.D. Pankey Study Group., C. of C. Methodist (trustee 1950—). Rotarian. Clubs: Beaumont, Beaumont Country. Home: 620 21st St Beaumont TX 77706 Office: 515-16 Goodhue Bldg Beaumont TX 77701

ODOM, FRANK LEE, supt. schs.; b. Granby, Mo., Jan. 3, 1926; s. John Thomas and Florence Annie (Miller) O.; B.S., U. Ark., 1949, M.S., 1953; m. Janice Fern Turner, June 29, 1958; children—David Lee, Dana Arnold. Math. tchr. Gruver (Tex.) High Sch., 1954-56; supt. schs. Miami (Tex.) Ind. Sch. Dist., 1956-59; high sch. prin. Wellman (Tex.) Ind. Sch. Dist., 1959-66, supt. schs., 1966—. Served with AUS, 1944-45. Decorated Combat Inf. badge. Mem. Am., Tex. assns. sch. adminstrs., Tex. Tchrs. Assn. (pres. Terry County unit), Nat. Assn. Secondary Sch. Prins. Methodist. Lion. Home: PO Box 66 Wellman TX 79378 Office: PO Box 68 Wellman TX 79378

ODOM, FREDERICK MARION, JR., utilities exec.; b. Bastrop, La., Jan. 7, 1910; s. Frederic Marion and Emma Inez (Scogin) O.; A.B., Centenary Coll. La., 1929; student Tulane U., 1929-31; m. Betty Hugh Watkins, Sept. 20, 1941; children—Fred Marion III, Ellen Lacy, Mark Watkins. Stenographer, Supreme Ct. of La., New Orleans, 1931-36; with Pennzoil Co., subsidiaries and predecessor firms, 1936—, beginning as laborer, successively clk., sr. clk., sec. to pres., 1947-57, v.p., 1957—; v.p. United Gas Pipe Line Co., Pennzoil Producing Co., subsidiaries, Served as radio operator USAAF, World War II, Mem. Kappa Alpha. Baptist. Home: 5959 Creswell Rd Shreveport LA 71106 Office: 1525 Fairfield Av Shreveport LA 71101

ODOM, GUY LEARY, physician; b. New Orleans, May 20, 1911; s. Guy Leroy and Marion (Brown) O.; M.D., Tulane U., 1933; m. Suzanne Price, Aug. 19, 1933 (dec. Nov. 1965); children—Linda (Mrs. Wesley Cook), Carolyn (Mrs. Terry H. Little), Guy Leary; m. 2d, Mataline Nye, Dec. 29, 1968. Intern, resident E. La. State Hosp., Jackson, 1933-37; practice medicine, specializing in neurol. surgery, Montreal, Que., Can., 1937-42, New Orleans, 1942-43, Durham, N.C. 1943—; instr. Montreal Neurol. Inst., 1937-42; asso. in surgery La. State U., 1942-43; faculty Duke U. Med. Sch., 1943—, prof. neurosurgery, 1950—, chmn. dept. 1960—; cons. VA Hosp., Durham; cons. neurosurgery Watts Hosp., Durham, Womack Army Hosp., Ft. Bragg, N.C. Mem. Adv. Bd. Med. Specialists. Diplomate Am. Bd. Neurol. Surgery (sec.-treas. 1964-70, chmn. 1970). Mem. A.M.A., Pan Am. Med. Assn., N.C., Durham-Orange County med. socs., World Fedn. Neurol. Surgery, Am. Acad. Neurol. Surgeons (pres. 1967), Soc. Neurol. Surgeons (pres. 1970), Am. Surg. Assn., So. Neurol. Soc. (pres. 1968), Harvey Cushing Soc. (pres. 1971-72). Home: 2812 Chelsea Circle Durham NC 27707 Office: Duke U Med Center Durham NC 27710

ODOM, MRS. JAMES M. (ELLEN PAYNE ODOM), civic worker; b. Blossburg, Ala., July 5, 1906; d. Turner Ashby and Annie Ellen (Ancell) Payne; A.B. summa cum laude, Judson Coll., 1923-26; M.A., U. Ala., 1931; B.S., Howard Coll., 1932; m. James Malcolm Odom, Aug. 25, 1935. Tchr. French, Spanish, Italian, Judson Coll., 1926-30; U. Ala., 1930-31; head dept. romance langs. Norman Coll., Norman Park, Ga., 1933-35. Chmn. Colquitt County March of Dimes, 1953; sec. Colquitt County Civic Music Assn., 1959-65; mem. adv. bd. Ga. Extension Service, 1957-63; dir. Ga. Tb Assn. (mem. exec. com. 1963-66, sec. 1965-66), Moultrie YMCA; adviser 4-H Club, 1936—, state adviser, 1961-62; pres. Colquitt County Tb Assn., 1961-62. Mem. 2d Congl. dist. Ga. Democratic Exec. Com., 1965-66. Trustee Colquitt-Thomas Regional Library, 1963-71, mem. regional bd., 1964-71. Named Colquitt County Woman of Year, 1961. Mem. Friend of Library, League Women Voters, U.D.C. (Ga. div. v.p. 1968-70, parliamentarian 1970— div. exec. bd. 1948—), Huguenots (nat. corr. sec. 1948-49), D.A.R. Club: Woman's (pres. 1957-58). Research Colquitt County, Ga. A Field Lab. for Study and

Experiment in Intergovtl. Relations. Author: A History of the Library of Moultrie, Georgia, 1966. Home: Odomfarms RFD 5 Moultrie GA 31768

ODOM, JOEL MARTIN, dentist; b. Muskogee, Okla., July 1, 1936; s. Martin and Emma (Prater) O.; B.S., Southeastern State U., 1957; D.D.S., U. Tenn., 1960; m. Brenda Tabbytite, Sept. 10, 1969; 1 dau., Francine Melony. Pvt. practice dentistry, Okmulgee, Okla., 1961—. Mem. Am., Okla. dental assns., Eastern Dist. Dental Soc., Okmulgee C. of C. (past dir.), Tau Kappa Epsilon, Psi Omega. Home: 6102 S Fulton St Tulsa OK 74135 Office: 4720 E 51st St Tulsa OK 74135

ODOM, JOHN PERSHING, constrn. co. exec.; b. Rockingham, N.C., Jan. 7, 1918; s. Luther L. and Minnie (Allred) O.; student Brevard Coll., 1936-37; B.A., Furman U., 1947; m. Aileen Alewine, Mar. 30, 1941; 1 son, Taylor. Jr. accountant, sr. accountant S.D. Leidesdorf & Co., Greenville, S.C., 1947-53; chief accountant S.C. div. Daniel Constrn. Co., Greenville, 1953-64, asst. sec., controller, 1964-67, v.p. taxes, 1967—. Served with USNR, 1943-45. Baptist. Mason (32 deg., Shriner), Lion. Home: 203 Rosemary Lane Greenville SC 29607 Office: Daniel Bldg Greenville SC 29602

ODOM, ROY HARRIS, state ofcl.; b. Alexandria, La., Oct. 14, 1906; s. George Andrew and Mary Alma (Deaton) O.; student La. Tech. Coll., 1925-29, La. State U., 1941; m. Willie Mai Tolar, Oct. 10, 1934; children—Roy H., William McBride, Elsa (Mrs. G. W. West). Tech. reports editor State La., Baton Rouge, 1939-52; program dir. La. Forestry Commn., Baton Rouge, 1952—. Owner Gulf South Advt. Agy., Baton Rouge, 1947—. Vice pres. League Am. Wheelmen, 1970—; pres. Baton Rouge Cycle Club, 1969, 71—. Mem. State Information Reps. (pres. 1971), Advt. Splty. Sales Promotion Assn., Splty. Advt. Assn. Internat., Internat. Assn. Bus. Communicators, Pub. Relations Soc. Am. (accredited 1969—). Mason. Club: Press. Home: 558 Nelson Dr Baton Rouge LA 70808 Office: 5150 Florida St Baton Rouge LA 70815

O'DONNELL, PETER, JR., Republican nat. committeeman; b. Dallas, Apr. 21, 1924; s. Peter and Annette (Campbell) O'D.; B.S., U. of South, 1947; M.B.A., Wharton Sch. Finance, Pa.; m. Edith Jones, Nov. 22, 1952; children—Ann, Carol, Ruth. Precinct committeeman Republican party, 1956-59; chmn. Dallas County (Tex.) Rep. Com., 1959—, Tex. Rep. Com., 1962—; mem. exec. com. Rep. Nat. Finance Com., 1964—; chmn. So. Assn. Rep. State Chmn., 1965—; state chmn. Rep. Nat. Com. Trustee U. of South, So. Meth. U., Found. for Bus. and Econs.; adv. trustee U. Dallas. Served to lt. j.g., USNR, 1943-46. Mem. Dallas Assn. Investment Analysts, Phi Beta Kappa, Phi Delta Theta. Episcopalian. Home: 4300 St John's Dr Dallas TX 75205 Office: 4275 First Nat Bank Bldg Dallas TX 75202*

O'DONOGHUE, DON HORATIO, orthopaedic surgeon; b. Storm Lake, Ia., Nov. 13, 1901; s. James Horatio and Janet (Fairbairn) O'D.; student Buena Vista Coll., Storm Lake, Ia., 1919-20; B.S., Ia. U., 1923, M.D., 1926; D.S., Morningside Coll., 1944; m. Ragnhild Christensen, Jan. 4, 1928; 1 son, Donald Patrick. Surgery resident Ia. U. Hosps., 1926-27; orthopaedic surgery resident Okla. U. Hosp., 1927-30; gen. practice specializing in orthopaedic surgery, Oklahoma City, 1930—; prof., chmn. dept. orthopaedic surgery and fractures U. Okla. Med. Sch., 1948—, chmn. faculty bd., mem. bd. U. Hosp.; chief orthopaedics St. Anthony's Hosp., Vets Hosp.; mem. staff Presbyn., Mercy, Bapt. hosps. Chmn. profl. adv. com. Dept. Pub. Welfare; mem. health and hosp. planning Community Council. Bd. dirs. YMCA; trustee United Fund. Recipient Distinguished Service award U. Okla., 1969, U. Ia., 1971; named to Okla. Hall of Fame, 1970. Fellow Internat. Coll. Surgeons, Sicot, A.C.S.; mem. Am. Acad. Orthopaedic Surgeons, Am. Orthopaedic Assn. (pres.), A.M.A., So., Okla. State, Oklahoma County med. socs., Clin. Orthopaedic Soc., Western Surg. Assn., S.W. Surg. Congress, Pan-Pacific Surg. Soc., Mid-Central State Orthopaedic Soc., Am. Assn. for Surgery of Trauma, Am. Trauma Soc., (founding mem.), Am. Orthopaedic Soc. Sports Medicine (founding mem., first pres.). Author: Treatment of Injuries to Athletes, 1962, rev. edit., 1970; also articles in profl. jours. Editorial bd. Orthopaedic Review. Home: 1403 Glenwood Av Oklahoma City OK 73116 Office: 1111 N Lee Oklahoma City OK 73103

ODUM, EUGENE PLEASANTS, educator, ecologist; b. Lake Sunapee, N.H., Sept. 17, 1913; s. Howard Washington and Anna Louise (Kranz) O.; A.B., U. N.C., 1934, A.M., 1936; Ph.D., U. Ill., 1939; m. Martha Ann Huff, Nov. 18, 1940; 1 son, William Eugene. Instr., Western Res. U., Cleve., 1936-37; resident biologist Edmund Niles Huyck Preserve, Rensselaerville, N.Y., 1939-40; instr., asst. prof., asso. prof., prof. U. Ga., 1940-58, Alumni Found. distinguished prof., 1958—; instr. in charge marine ecology tng. program Marine Biol. Lab., Woods Hole, Mass., summers 1957-61; dir. Inst. Ecology, U. Ga., 1961—. NSF sr. postdoctoral fellow, 1958-59; recipient Michael award, U. Ga., 1945, Mercer award Ecol. Soc. Am., 1956; named Ga. Scientist of Year, 1968. Mem. Ecol. Soc. Am. (pres. 1964), A.A.A.S., Am. Soc. Limnology and Oceanography, Am. Ornithologists Union, Am. Soc. Mammalogists, Wildlife Soc., Soc. Study Evolution, Am. Naturalist Soc., Nat. Acad. Sci., Am. Soc. Zoologists, Sigma Xi. Author: Fundamentals of Ecology, 1953, 3d edit., 1971; Ecology, 1963; co-author: (with others) Birds of Georgia, 1945; (with H. H. Brimley) A North Carolina Naturalist, 1949; also many papers pub. sci. jours. Home: Beech Creek Rd Athens GA 30601

O'DWYER, THOMAS ALOYSIUS, elec. co. exec.; b. Texarkana, Ark., July 21, 1925; s. Thomas A. and Martha (Ryan) O'D.; B.S. in Engring., Texas A. and M. Coll., 1949; m. Jeanne B. Bird, Aug 2, 1950; children— Ann, Kay, Tom, George, Bill. Engr., Southwestern Gas & Electric Co., Texarkana, 1943-44; estimator Ling Electric (now Ling-Oliver-O'Dwyer Electric, Inc.), Dallas, 1949-51, v.p., 1952-57, pres., 1962—, dir., 1961—; pres., dir. Lone Star Beer Distbr.; dir. Republic Aluminum Co. (all Dallas), Richardson Heights Bank. Active Boy Scouts Am.; chmn. trustees Jesuit Prep. Sch., Dallas. Served with USNR, 1944-46. Mem. Tex. Mfrs. Assn., Constrn. Employers Council (past pres.), Young Pres. Orgn. Nat. Elec. Contractors Assn. (past pres., dir. N.E. Texas chpt.). Roman Catholic. K.C. (4 deg.). Club: Aggie (dir., exec. com.). Home: 3843 Shenandoah St Dallas TX 75205 Office: 727 S Central Expressway Richardson TX 75080

OEHLSCHLAGER, FREDERICK KEITH, physician; b. Kansas City, Mo., Apr. 16, 1911; s. Henry George and Lillie Marie (Kaltenbach) O.; A.A., Kansas City Jr. Coll., 1930; B.S., U. Kan., 1933; M.D., 1935; m. Helen Mae Poulson, May 10, 1935 (dec. 1960); children—Richard, Susan, Robert; m. 2d, Jimmie Nell Lietzow, Mar. 10, 1965; stepchildren—Cynthia, Matthew, Celeste, Colleen. Intern, U.S. Marine Hosp., New Orleans, 1935-36; pvt. practice Lees Summit, Mo., 1936, Yale, Okla., 1936-51, Odessa, Tex., 1951—; chief of staff Cushing Meml. Hosp., Okla., 1950-51; mem. staff Med. Center Hosp., Odessa, 1951—, chmn. dept. obstetrics and gynecology, 1962-63, 72-73; sec. Permian Basin Investment Corp.; founder, sec.-treas., med. dir. Permian Basin Life Ins. Co., 1954-63. Med. dir., mem. bd. Permian Basin Planned Parenthood, 1971—. Pres. Permian Playhouse, Inc., Odessa, 1962-64; dir. Permian Basin Ballet Assn., 1968-70, Midland-Odessa Symphony Assn., 1968-71; mayor City of Yale, Okla., 1948-50; chmn. Ector County-City of Odessa, Tex. Dept. Parks and Recreation, 1954-62; chmn. Ector County Child Welfare Bd., 1952-56; dir. Tri-County Group Foster Home Bd., 1951-57, A.R.C., 1954-57; pres. Permian Basin Civic Ballet Assn., 1969-70, Midland-Odessa Symphony Assn., 1969-70. Pres. Payne-Pawnee County Med. Soc. (Okla.), 1944. Mem. Am. Cancer Soc. (dir. 1955, Ector County pres. 1967-68, dist. dir. 1968—), Odessa C. of C., Am., Tex. med. assns., Andrews, Ector and Midland County Med. Soc., Pan-Pacific Surg. Assn., West Tex. Soc. Obstetrics and Gynecology, Am. Soc. Study Fertility, Internat. Fertility Assn., Internat. Soc. Obstetrics and Gynecology, Am. Hemercallis Soc., Am. Iris Soc., Bromeliad Soc., Cymbidium Soc., Indoor Light Gardening Soc., Nat. Chrysanthemum Soc., Am. Begonia Soc., Am. Daffodil Soc., Am. Orchid Soc., Am. Gesneriad Soc., Am. Camilla Soc. Methodist. Mason (Shriner). Clubs: Odessa Country, Rotary (pres. 1963-64), Knife and Fork, Men's Garden (pres. 1970-71). Home: 316 Casa Grande Odessa TX 79760 Office: Sherwood Med Center 42d and Everglade Sts Odessa TX 79762

OEHSER, PAUL HENRY, editor, writer, conservationist; b. Cherry Creek, N.Y., Mar. 27, 1904; s. Henry Christian and Agnes Theodosia (Abbey) O.; grad. Forestville (N.Y.) Free Acad., 1921; A.B., Greenville (Ill.) Coll., 1925; student U. Ia., 1924, Am. U., 1926-30; m. Grace Edgbert, Oct. 4, 1927; children—Gordon Vincent, Richard Edgbert. Asst. editor Bur. Biol. Survey, Dept. Agr., 1925-31; editor U.S. Nat. Mus., Smithsonian Instn., 1931-50, chief editorial and publs. div., 1950-66, research asso., 1966—; editor sci. publs. Nat. Geog. Soc., 1966—; mng. editor Jour. Washington Acad. Scis., 1939-59; editor Proc. 8th Am. Sci. Congress, Dept. State, 1941-43. Bd. dirs. Greater Washington Ednl. TV Assn., Inc., 1958-64, Horne of England, Ltd., 1967—; trustee Lake George (N.Y.) Hist. Assn., Westminster Sch., Annandale, Va. Fellow Washington Acad. Scis.; mem. Arlington County Hist. Soc. (editor mag. 1959-62), Philos. Soc. Washington, Am. Ornithol. Union, Biol. Soc. Washington, Wilderness Soc. (mem. council 1964—, asst. treas. 1965-70), History of Sci. Club (Washington), Thoreau Soc. Am. (pres. 1961), Washington Biologists' Field Club (v.p. 1962-64, pres. 1964-67), Columbia Hist. Soc., Literary Soc. of Washington. Clubs: Cosmos (sec. 1950-69, editor Bull. 1951-69), Palaver (Washington). Author: Sons of Science, the Story of the Smithsonian Institution and Its Leaders, 1949; Fifty Poems, 1954; the Smithsonian Institution, 1970. Contbr. articles, reviews and verse to mags., jours., encys., news publs. Gen. editor United States Encyclopedia of History, 1967-68. Home: 9012 Old Dominion Dr McLean VA 22101 Office: Nat Geog Soc Washington DC 20036

OESTERLE, RALPH EDWARD, accounting exec.; b. Flushing, N.Y.; Aug. 7, 1924; s. William Henry and Linda (Kraft) O.; B.A., U. Miami, 1949; postgrad. LaSalle Law Sch., 1949-50, N.Y. U. Inst. Fed. Taxation, 1963; m. Clara Rush, July 30, 1949; children— Jacquelyn, Patricia, Robin, Michael, Ralph Edward. Partner, Oesterle & Co., Accountants, Miami, Fla., 1946—; pres. Reoco, Inc., Miami, 1945—, Lake Lune Corp. (N.C.), 1964—; chmn., dir. Burger King Restaurants, Las Vegas, Nev., 1965—, Outer Limits Corp., Miami, 1967—, Worlds Beyond Inc., Key Largo, Fla., 1967—; dir. RPD, Inc., South Miami, 1962—. Oesterle Corp., Miami, 1966—. Served with USNR, 1941-45. Mem. Fla. Accountants Assn., Nat. Assn. Pub. Accountants, Internat. Soc. Tax Consultants (pres. 1955-67). Elk. Clubs: Ocean Reef, Coral Gables Country. Editor: Tax News, 1960-66. Home: 18500 Caribbean Blvd Miami FL 33157 Office: 5965 SW 8th St Miami FL 33144

OFELT, GEORGE STERLING, physicist; b. Washington, Jan. 22, 1937; s. George R. and Rowena (Horan) O.; B.S., Coll. William and Mary, 1957; Ph.D., Johns Hopkins U., 1962; m. Anne McQuade, July 7, 1962; children—Susan Anne, George William. Instr. Johns Hopkins U., Balt., 1962-63; asst. prof. Coll. William and Mary, 1963-67; asso. prof. Old Dominion U., Norfolk, Va., 1967—; cons., lectr. NASA, 1963—. Chmn. founding com. Kingspoint Community Assn., Williamsburg, Va., 1966-67. Mem. Optical Soc. Am., Phi Beta Kappa, Sigma Xi. Home: 824 St Clement Rd Virginia Beach VA 23455 Office: Old Dominion U Norfolk VA 23508

OFFIK, WOLFGANG GEORGE, engr.; b. Davos, Switzerland, May 31, 1913; s. Georg Victor and Frieda (Roth) O.; B.S. in Elec. Engring., Inst. Tech., Karisruhe, Germany, 1934; M.S., Inst. Tech., Stuttgart, Germany, 1939; m. Anna Wuerthner, May 26, 1939; children—Rainer, Karin Erika, Michael Wolfgang. Came to U.S., 1953, naturalized, 1959. Chief advanced design methods Gerhard Fieseler Werke Kassel, Germany, 1938-42; exec. v.p. engring. Bachem-Werk Waldsee, Germany, 1942-45; design engr. Lockeed Aircraft, Burbank, Cal., 1953-56; maj. project leader N.Am. Aviation, Inc., Columbus, O., 1956-60; chief tech. analysis sect. Martin Co., Denver 1960-63; sr. staff engr. advanced design Chrysler Corp., Huntsville operations, Huntsville, Ala., 1964-70; owner Gamco Products, Huntsville, 1970—. Asso. fellow Am. Inst. Aeros. and Astronautics; mem. Am. Astronautical Soc. (sr.), Am. Ordnance Assn., Air Force Assn. Registered profl. engr., Colo., Ala. Home: 2027 Wooddale Dr NE Huntsville AL 35801 Office: 704 Pratt Av Huntsville AL 35801

O'FLAHERTY, JAMES C., educator; b. Henrico County, Va., Apr. 28, 1914; B.A., Georgetown Coll., 1939; M.A., U. Ky., 1941; Ph.D., U. Chgo., 1950; m. 1936; 1 child. Instr. history and religion Georgetown Coll., 1939-41; instr. German, Wake Forest Coll., Winston-Salem, N.C., N.C., 1947-51, asst. prof., 1951-53, asso. prof., 1953-58, prof., 1958—, chmn. dept., 1961—, editor Hamann News-Letter, 1953-63. Beecher lectr. Amherst Coll., 1958; lectr. Kulturelles Wort Ser, Sudwestfunk, Baden-Baden, Germany, 1961; mem. adv. com. Fulbright Awards, 1962, chmn., 1963. Am. Philos. Soc. research grantee, Germany, 1958; Fulbright research fellow, Germany, 1960-61. Mem. Modern Lang. Assn., Am. Assn. Tchrs. Germany, Kierkegaard Soc. Copenhagen. Author: Unity and Lenguage: A Study in the Philosophy of Johann Georg Hamann, 1952. Research on Johann Georg Hamaan, philosophy of lang., philos. bases of lit. criticism. Office: Dept Langs Wake Forest College Winston-Salem NC 27109*

O'GARA, JOHN FRANCIS, govt. ofcl.; b. Providence, July 30, 1918; s. John Francis and Elizabeth C. (Kinnecom) O'G.; A.B. cum laude, Providence Coll., 1940; m. Norma Alice Bright, Sept. 20, 1941; children— Diane Frances (Mrs. Richard F. Brumme), Mary Louise. Mil. intelligence analyst, tech. cons. Office Asst. Chief Staff Intelligence, Dept. Army, 1946-61; asst. dir. spl. intelligence Office Dir. Def. Research and Engring., Office Sec. Def., 1961—. Served to capt. AUS, 1942-46. Roman Catholic. Home: 3435 Slade Run Dr Falls Church VA 22042 Office: ODDR—The Pentagon Washington DC 20301

OGBURN, CHARLTON, JR., writer; b. Atlanta, Mar. 15, 1911; s. Charlton and Dorothy (Stevens) O.; S.B. cum laude, Harvard, 1932; grad. Nat. War Coll., 1952; m. Mary C. Aldis, June 6, 1945 (div. 1951); 1 son, Charlton III; m. 2d, Vera Weidman, Feb. 24, 1951; children—Nyssa, Holly. Writer Alfred P. Sloan Found., 1937-39; book reviewer Book-of-the-Month Club, 1940-41; with Div. Southeast Asian Affairs, Dept. of State, 1946-50, polit. adviser, acting U.S. rep. com. good offices on Indonesia, UN Security Council, 1947-48, policy planning adviser Bur. Far Eastern Affairs, 1952-54, chief div. research Near East, S. Asia and Africa, 1954-57. Trustee Nat. Parks Assn. Served to capt., AUS, 1941-46; India-Burma. Recipient John Burroughs medal 1967. Club: Cosmos (Washington). Author: The White Falcon, 1955; The Bridge, 1957; Big Caesar, 1958; The Marauders, 1969; U.S. Army, 1960; The Gold of the River Sea, 1965; The Winter Beach, 1966; The Forging of Our Continent, 1968; The Continent in Our Hands, 1971. Co-author: Shakespeare: The Man Behind the Name, 1962. Contbr. mags. Home: 10710 Vale Rd Oakton VA 22124

OGDEN, JAMES NICHOLSON, railroad ofcl.; b. Quinnimont, W.Va., Sept. 1, 1907; s. Lucian Bryson and Georgiana Gilmore (McDonough) O.; LL.B., U. Miss., 1930, J.D., 1968; m. Beatrice Flowers, Aug. 18, 1933 (dec. 1948); m. 2d, Elizabeth Courtney Hammond, Feb. 12, 1949. Admitted to Miss. bar, 1930, Ala. bar, 1942; with G.M. & O. R.R., 1940—, v.p., gen. counsel, 1958—; gen. counsel New Orleans Great No. Ry. Co., 1957—; gen. counsel, dir. Gulf Transport Co., 1959—. Mem. Am., Miss., Ala., Mobile County bar assns. Home: 16 Hillwood Rd Mobile AL 36608 Office: 104 St Francis St Mobile AL 36602

OGDEN, JOHN BENNETT, mfg. co. exec.; b. Plainview, Tex., Jan. 2, 1911; s. Walter V. and Anna (Saunders) O.; LL.B., Cumberland U., 1933; m. Hazel Louise Smith, May 10, 1936; children—Harold L., Dorothy (Mrs. John Clark), Nancy Jean (Mrs. J. Barry Wilder). Admitted to Tex. bar, 1934; practiced in El Paso, Tex., 1934-36, Kermit, Tex., 1936-40, with Cameron Iron Works, Inc., Houston, 1941—, mgr. indsl. relations, 1948—, asst. sec., 1955—, v.p., 1959—, asst. treas. 1966—; dir., v.p. Cameron Iron Works Can. Ltd., Edmonton, Ala., 1960—, asst. sec., 1951—. Chmn., Harris County Com. Employment of Handicapped, 1966—. Mem. N.A.M., Am. Ordnance Assn., Tex. Mfg. Assn., Houston (ins. com. 1959—), Spring Branch chambers commerce. Methodist. Home: 1610 Lynnview St Houston TX 77055 Office: PO Box 1212 Houston TX 77001

OGDON, DONALD POTTER, psychologist; b. Oak Park, Ill., July 26, 1923; s. Glenn H. and Elizabeth (McDonald) O.; B.S., U. Ill., Urbana, 1949; M.A., U. Tex., 1950; Ph.D., U. Mo., 1955; m. Catherine Hatfield Ogdon, Jan. 15, 1966; children—Glenn Scott, Donald Gregory. Instr. psychologist U. Mo., 1953-54; psychologist Mo. State Sch., Marshall, Mo., 1954-55; asso. prof. William and Mary Coll., Richmond, Va., 1955-63; prof. Old Dominion U., Norfolk, 1963—, also chmn. dept. psychology; dir. dept. psychology Bayberry Hosp., Hampton, Va., 1966—. Served to 2d lt. USAAF, 1945-46. Fellow Soc. Personality Assessment; mem. Va. Psychol. Assn. (past pres.), Am. Psychol. Assn., A.A.A.S., Sigma Xi, Psi Chi. Contbr. articles to psychol. jours. Home: 1323 Sussex Pl Norfolk VA 23508 Office: Old Dominion Univ Norfolk VA 23508

OGG, TERRELL WILBUR, supt. schs.; b. Navasota, Tex., July 24, 1912; s. William Henry and Hettie (Ballard) O.; B.S., Stephen F. Austin State Tchrs. Coll., 1935; M.Ed., U. Tex., 1942; Ed.D., U. Houston, 1958; m. Evelyn Fay Linscomb, July 29, 1939; children—Sandra (Mrs. Dan H. Rose), Suzanne (Mrs. Stephen P. Harris). Tchr. pub. sch., Vidor, Tex., 1936-37, prin. high sch., 1937-41; asst. supt. schs., Orange, Tex., 1941-46; supt. schs. Brazosport (Tex.) Ind. Sch. Dist., 1946-57; group services dir. Bus. Assurance Co., Houston, 1957-58; supt. schs., Crockett, Tex., 1958-66, Mt. Pleasant, Tex., 1966—. Mem. Tex. Assn. Sch. Adminstrs. (pres. 1970-71). Baptist. Mason (dep. dist. gov. 1965), Lion. Home: 615 E Dogwood St PO Box 808 Mount Pleasant TX 75455 Office: PO Box 1117 Mount Pleasant TX 75455

OGILBY, JOHN JOSEPH, citrus processing co. exec.; b. Ft. Lauderdale, Fla., Oct. 24, 1926; s. Thomas and Felicia (Zerman) O.; B.S., U. Fla., 1950; m. Muriel Davies, Aug. 7, 1954; children—Jack, Karen. Accountant, Ernst & Ernst, Atlanta, 1950-56; v.p., treas., dir. Tropicana Products, Inc., Bradenton, Fla., 1956—. Pres., treas. Manatee County Blood Bank, 1962-68. Trustee, treas. St. Stephen's Episcopal Sch. Served with AUS, 1944-46. C.P.A., Fla. Mem. Fla. Inst. C.P.A.'s (pres. Gulf Coast chpt. 1963-64). Presbyn. (elder 1967—). Lion. Club: Country (pres., dir. 1969-70) (Bradenton, Fla.). Home: 403 N 31st St W Bradenton FL 33505 Office: PO Box 338 Bradenton FL 33505

OGILVIE, PHILIP SMYTHE, librarian; b. Savannah, Ga., Mar. 14, 1919; s. Philip Smythe and Mary Eva (Moore) O.; B.A., St. Mary's Sem. and U., Balt., 1944; B.S. in L.S., Cath. U. Am., 1947; postgrad. U. N.C., N.C. State Coll., Winthrop Coll., Loyola U. of South, Abraham Baldwin Agr. Coll.; m. Joan Marie Forshag, May 29, 1952; children—Elizabeth M., Patrick A., Henry A., Anne L., Joseph A., Jane K. Exec. sec. N.C. Cath. Layman's Assn., 1947-49; asso. editor N.C. Cath., 1947-49; exec. sec. Cath. Com. of the South, 1949-53; asst. librarian Rock Hill (S.C.) Pub. Library, 1953-54; dir. Albemarie Regional Library, Winton, N.C., 1954-56; organizer, 1st dir. Coastal Plain Regional Library, Tifton, Ga., 1956-58; dir. Roanoke (Va.) Pub. Library, 1958-61; dir. Jackson (Miss.) Pub. Library, 1961-63; chief Central Library, Tulsa, 1963-65; state librarian, Raleigh N.C., 1965—. Mem. Am., Southeastern, N.C., spl. library assns. Roman Catholic. Contbr. to publs. in field. Home: 308 Peartree Lane Raleigh NC 27610 Office: NC State Library Raleigh NC 27611

OGLESBEE, DWIGHT CONLAN, geol. engr.; b. Virgil, Kan., Jan. 1, 1929; s. Byrd S. and Thelma (Richard) O.; B.S., U. Kan., 1953; postgrad. U. Tulsa, 1962-63; m. Gailya Drue Bennett, Dec. 31, 1963; children— Dwight Byrd, Nelda Irene, Lori Ann, Shawn Adam. Mgr. tech. services Richards & Oglesbee Oil Co., Sedan, Kan., 1948-49; petroleum engr. Sinclair Oil & Gas Co., Independence, Kan., 1950-51; pvt. cons. engr., Lawrence, Kan. 1951-53; sales engr., mgr. Midland Parts & Bearings Co., Kansas City, Mo., 1953-54; engring. tech. asst. aviation gas turbine div. Westinghouse Electric Corp., Kansas City, Mo., 1954; v.p. Black Widow Uranium, Inc., Three Forks, Mont., 1954-55; pres. Oglesbee Oil Co., Sedan, 1955; with Skelly Oil Co., Sweetwater, Tex., also Tulsa, 1956—, advanced staff prodn. engr., 1965-67, sr. corrosion engr., 1967—. Cons. Plator Gra-Louise Can. Ltd., Atikokan, Ont., 1953; cons. geologist, petroleum engr., Sedan, 1954-56. Registered profl. engr., Kan. Mem. Am. Inst. Mining, Metall. and Petroleum Engrs., Am. Assn. Petroleum Geologists, Nat. Assn. Corrosion Engrs. (sect. chmn. 1964, mem. various coms., task groups 1962—), Am. Petroleum Inst. (various task groups, coms.). Mem. Ch. of Christ. Mason. Contbr. articles to profl. jours., bulls. Inventor deep groundbed anode assemblages, deep groundbed cathodic protection devices. Home: 611 N Main St Delaware OK 74027 Office: 1437 S Boulder St Tulsa OK 74102

OGLESBY, CLAIRE CRAIG, business exec.; b. Logansport, Ind., Oct. 20, 1917; d. Everard Granville and Clare (Fischer) Delgado; A.B. cum laude, Butler U., 1938; m. Robert Oglesby, Aug. 30, 1958. Translator in Spanish, asst. to mgr. S. Am. div. Eli Lilly & Co., Indpls., 1938-40; reservation and ticket mgr. Trans World Airlines, Indpls., 1940-46; founder, owner, pres., gen. mgr. Travel, Inc., Washington, 1946-61; regional v.p. Fugazy Travel Bur., Inc., 1961-66; owner Oglesby Enterprises, Inc., 1966-69; dir. tour and travel and govt. Southeastern div. Hiltons Hotels Corp., 1969—, cons. in travel to Quota Internat., Inc. Adm. of Am. Airlines. Mem. Nat. Assn. Life Underwriters, Nat. Fedn. Bus. and Profl. Women's Clubs, Chi Omega; ambassador mem. Trans World Airlines. Presbyn. Clubs: Quota (dir.)

(Washington, D.C.); Clipper of Pan American World Airlines, Nat. Association Executives of Washington. Author: Beginning Spanish, 1938. Home: 4201 Cathedral Av NW Washington DC 20016 Office: Hilton Hotels Corp Washington DC 20009

OGLESBY, HENRY RUBE, JR., mfg. co. exec.; b. Warrensburg, Mo., Nov. 23, 1914; s. Henry Rube and Mary Ann (Shouse) O.; B.S., Central Mo. State Coll., 1935; B.S. in Civil Engring., Ga. Inst. Tech., 1938; m. Ruth Keith, Aug. 6, 1938; children—Robert K., Robin Jane. With Municipal Service Co., Kansas City, Mo., 1946-61, v.p., 1950-61, gen. mgr., 1950-61; self-employed in field of real estate, mergers, cons., Palm Beach, Fla., 1961-70; sec. treas. Airtronics Internat. Corp., Ft. Lauderdale, Fla., 1970-72, chmn. bd., pres., 1972-—, also dir. Served with C.E., AUS, 1941-45. Registered profl. engr., Mo., Ill. Fellow Am. Soc. C.E. Mem. Am. Water Works Assn. Home: 130 Sunrise St Palm Beach FL 33480 Office: PO Box 212 Palm Beach FL 33480

OGLETREE, WILLIAM BEECHER, civil engr.; b. Little Rock, Dec. 8, 1928; s. Lee Scotty and Dora Elizabeth (Cunningham) O.; student North Tex. Agrl. Coll., 1946-48, North Tex. State Coll., 1951; B.S. in Archtl. Engring., U. Tex., Austin, 1954; m. Sharon Kay Jones, Aug. 29, 1953; children—Carrie Kay, Leslie Scott, William Bruce. Engr., Convair Aircraft Co., Ft. Worth, 1951; engr. Tex. Hwy. Dept., Austin, 1952; student employee dept. archtl. engring. U. Tex., Austin, 1953-54, research engr., 1958-59; engr. John Broad, Gen. Contractor, Austin, 1954; cons. engr. Walter P. Moore, Houston, 1954-57; engr. Continental EMSCO, Houston, 1957; owner William B. Ogletree, Cons. Engr., Corpus Christi, Tex., 1959-69; partner Ogletree & Gunn, Engring. Cons., Corpus Christi, 1969-—; instr. Del Mar Coll., Corpus Christi, 1960-61, asst. prof., 1961-63. Scuba instr. YMCA, 1962-—. Served with USNR, 1948-49, USAF, 1950-51. Mem. Nat., Tex. (past treas. Nueces chpt.) socs. profl. engrs., Am. Soc. C.E. (past pres. Corpus Christi br.), Soc. Am. Mil. Engrs. (past pres. Coastal Band post). Rotarian. Author: (with Turnbow) Energy Absorbing Characteristics of Air Bags, 1958; (with Jones) Air Delivery Sampling Net. Home: 610 Bradshaw St Corpus Christi TX 78412 Office: 1806 S Alameda St Corpus Christi TX 78404

OGLEVEE, CHRISTINE LOUISE, nurse educator; b. Clendenon, W.Va., Sept. 5, 1910; d. Edward R. and Rae Elizabeth (Curry) Oglevee; diploma Miami Valley Hosp., Dayton, O., 1932; B.S., U. Chgo., 1947, M.S., 1948. Ednl. dir. Dixon (Ill.) Pub. Hosp., 1935-38; dir. nursing Meml. Hosp., Springfield, Ill., 1938-41, Allegheny Valley Hosp., Tarentum, Pa., 1941-44; prof., dean Sch. Nursing, U. Miss., 1949-—. Mem. Med. Adv. Bd. on Ednl. Film Prodns., 1968-—; mem. profl. adv. com. Hinds County Mental Health Assn., 1969-—; mem. div. comprehensive health planning State Health Planning Adv. Council; mem. devel. com. U. Miss., 1969-—; mem. exec. com. Comprehensive Health Planning Council. Miss. rep. Volunteer Adv. Com. to SSS on selection physicians, dentists and allied specialists; Miss. rep. Def. Adv. Com. Women Services, 1961-64. Mem. Miss. Women's Cabinet of Pub. Affairs. Served to lt. (j.g.), Navy Nurse Corps, 1944-46. Named Woman of Achievement, Jackson Profl. Women's Club, 1968-69; recipient citation from Pres. U.S. Mem. Am. (vice chmn. ethical standards com. 1962-64), Miss. (pres. 1952-55), Miss. Dist. (pres. Oxford 1950-52) nurses assns., Nat., Miss. leagues for nursing, Am. Assn. U. Women (2d v.p. Miss. div. 1966-67, pres. Jackson br. 1967-69), Jackson Civic Arts Council. Home: 5412 Pine Lane Dr Jackson MS 39211

O'GORMAN, JUAN, architect, artist; b. Coyoacan, D.F., Mexico, July 6, 1905; s. Cecil Crawford and Encarnacion (O'Gorman) O'G.; Architect deg., Nat. U. Mexico, 1926; m. Helen Fowler, Aug. 7, 1940; one dau., Maria Elena O'Gorman, Aug. 31, 1956. With C. Obregon Santacilia and J. Villagran, architects, 1926-29; pvt. practice architecture, 1929-32; prof. sch. engring. Politechnical Inst., Mexico City, 1932-—; vis. critic in architecture Yale, 1967; head dept. architecture Secretariat of Pub. Edn., 1932-35. Works include murals for Mexico City Air Port, Patzcuaro (Mich.) Library, (3 frescos) Castle Chapultepec, (fresco) Banco Internacional S.A. (fresco) Center Social Studies Unidad Independencia (all Mexico City), (mosaic) Hotel Pasada de la Mision, Taxco, Guerrero, Mexico, (mosaic) Santiago, Chile; mosaics for the Library of the University City of Mexico, Secretariat Pub. Works and Communications bldgs., Convention Center Bldg., Hemisfair, 1968. One-man show of easel paintings, Palace of Fine Arts, Mexico City, 1950; paintings in permanent exhbn. Modern Mus. Art, N.Y.C., Mus. Modern Art Mexico City. Mem. Council of Superior Edn. and Sci. Investigation, Mexican Soc. Architects, Mexican Acad. Arts. Author booklets and mag. articles on art and architecture. Home: Jardin 88 San Angel Inn Mexico 20 DF Mexico

OGRAM, ERNEST WILLIAM, JR., univ. adminstr.; b. Hartford, Conn., June 29, 1928; s. Ernest William and Edith (Sickles) O.; B.A., Am. U., 1950; M.A., U. Conn., 1951; Ph.D., U. Ill., 1957; m. Antonia Santangelo, Dec. 26, 1953; 1 dau., Robbin Van Syckel. Asst. prof. Ga. State U., 1957-59, asso. prof., 1959-63, prof., 1963, dir. Inst. Internat. Bus., 1964-—. Chmn. Ga. Partners of the Americas Com., 1968-—. Bd. dirs. Atlanta Council for Internat. Visitors, Ga. Internat. Trade Assn., So. Consortium for Internat. Edn. Served to 1st lt. AUS, 1943-46. Recipient Atlanta C. of C. World Trade award, 1970. Mem. Am. Assn. U. Profs. (pres. Ga. chpt. 1968), Assn. for Edn. in Internat. Bus. Presbyn. (elder). Editor: Essays in International Business, 1967-69, Jour. of International Business Studies, 1970-—. Home: 1303 Middlesex Av Atlanta GA 30306

O'HANLON, ISAAC HAWLEY, bus. exec., former state legislator; b. Fayetteville, N.C., Sept. 5, 1911; s. George Adkins and Dora (Hawley) O.; student Wake Forest Coll., 1935; m. Emma Merle Sikes, Sept. 1, 1935; children—William Hawley, Edward Willkings. Clk., RFC, Washington, 1935-44; mgr. Orkin Exterminating Co., Fayetteville, N.C., 1945-55; owner Antex Exterminating Co. Inc., Fayetteville, 1955-—; mem. N.C. Ho. of Reps., 1953, 1955, 1963, 1965, 1967. Mem. N.C. State Structural Pest Control Commn., 1955-58, 1967-70. Dist. chmn. Boy Scouts Am., 1955; pres. Cumberland County (N.C.) Infantile Paralysis Assn., 1945-60, Methodist Coll. Found., Fayetteville. Exec. bd. trustees Vardoll Hall Red Springs N.C.; chmn. bd. dirs. Fayetteville YMCA, 1961. Trustee E. Carolina Coll., 1953-59. Mem. (hon.) Fayetteville Ind. Light Infantry. Kiwanian (pres. Fayetteville 1959, lt. gov. 4th div.). Home: 3605 Morgantown Rd Fayetteville NC 28304 Office: 406 Washington Dr Fayetteville NC 28301

O'HARA, GEORGE EDWARD, JR., ins. co. exec.; b. Norfolk, Va., May 26, 1920; s. George Edward and Margaret Eula (Dance) O'H.; student Va. So. Coll., 1948, So. Methodist U., 1950-51, Am. Coll. Life Underwriters, 1963-67; m. Louise Thompson, Apr. 26, 1952. Agt., Life & Casualty Ins. Co., Roanoke, Va., 1946-48; with Shenandoah Life Ins. Co., 1949-—, agy. sec., 1956-62, dir. spl. services, 1962-66, dir. promotion and advt., 1966-68, asst. v.p. adminstrn., 1968-—. Pres., Roanoke Citizens Assn., 1953-54. Bd. dirs. Roanoke Area Tb and Respiratory Assn., 1967-—. Served with USNR, 1942-46. Named Outstanding Nat. Chmn., U.S. Jr. C. of C., 1953, recipient Distinguished Service award Roanoke Jr. C. of C., 1956, C.L.U. Mem. Am. Soc. Chartered Life Underwriters (chpt. dir. 1969-70), Am. Advt. Fedn., Nat. Alliance Businessmen, Life Ins. Advertisers Assn., Advt. Club of Roanoke Valley, Pub. Relations Soc. Am. (chpt. pres. 1970), Roanoke Valley (dir. 1956-57, U.S. Jr. (nat. dir. 1953-54) chambers commerce, Beta Tau. Methodist. Mason (Shriner, Jester), Kiwanian (pres. 1970-71). Home: 1605 Wilbur Rd SW Roanoke VA 24015 Office: 2301 Brambleton Av SW Roanoke VA 24015

O'HARA, JAMES DONALD MICHAEL, textile co. exec.; b. Miami, Ariz., Sept. 6, 1936; A.B. (Jefferson Standard scholar), U. N.C., 1959; m. Francina Newkirk Dodd, Jan. 17, 1959; children—Mary, James. News editor The News Jour., Raeford, N. C., 1959-60; news editor WSOC-TV, Charlotte, N.C., 1961-63; pub. relations supr. Duke Power Co., Charlotte, 1964-66; mgr. community relations Collins & Aikman Corp., Charlotte, 1966-—. Pub. relations cons. Episcopal Child Care Services N.C., 1967-—. Dir. pub. affairs N.C. Rep. exec. com., 1963-64. Mem. Pub. Relations Soc. Am., Internat., South Atlantic councils indsl. editors (pres. 1968-69), Am. Assn. Indsl. Editors (dir. 1968-69), Alpha Phi Omega. Episcopalian. Home: 7024 Foxworth Dr Charlotte NC 28211 Office: 701 McCullough Dr Charlotte NC 28201

O'HARA, JOHN J., lawyer; b. Rocky Mount, N.C., Oct. 1, 1922; Ph.B., Xavier U., 1947; LL.B., U. Ky., 1949. Admitted to Ky. bar, 1949; commonwealth atty. 16th Jud. Dist. Ky., Covington, 1958-—. Mem. Am., Ky. (pres. 1971-72), Kenton County (v.p. 1956, pres. 1957) bar assns., Ky. Commonwealth Atty.'s Assn. (pres. 1964-65), Phi Alpha Delta. Address: Box 187 Covington KY 41011*

O'HARE, JOHN JOSEPH, research psychologist; b. Boston, Oct. 21, 1925; s. Michael J. and Catherine (Connolly) O'H.; B.S., Boston Coll., 1950; M.A., Cath. U. Am., 1952, Ph.D., 1957. Research psychologist med. research lab. USN, New London, Conn., 1953-59; human factors analyst Internat. Electric Corp., Paramus, N.J., 1959-61; head human factors dept., prin. scientist United Aircraft Corp., East Hartford, Conn., 1961-64; mem. tech. staff MITRE Corp., Arlington, Va., 1964-66; asso. prof. psychology, chmn. dept. Georgetown U., Washington, 1966-71; research psychologist Office of Naval Research 1971-—. Served with USNR, 1943-46. Mem. Am., Eastern psychol. assns., Human Factors Soc. (edn. com. 1969-71). Home: 301 G St SW Washington DC 20024

O'HAREN, JAMES FRANCIS, mfg. co. exec.; b. Shenandoah, Pa., July 21, 1930; s. James Francis and Elizabeth Margaret (Sauer) O'H.; B.S. cum laude, Mt. St. Mary's Coll., 1956; postgrad. Law Sch., U. Houston, 1962-63; m. Florence Virginia Civiletto, May 17, 1958; 1 foster son, Richard J. European comml. mgr. Tex. Butadiene & Chem. Internat., Ltd., Houston, 1956-59, N.Y.C., 1959-60, Lausanne, Switzerland, 1960-62; controller Maurice Pincoffs Co., Houston, 1963-65; controller, asst. sec. Marathon Mfg. Co., 1965-66, treas., controller, asst. sec., 1966-68, v.p., treas., asst. sec., 1968-71, sec., 1971-—; v.p., dir. Ericsson Chem. Services, Inc., 1962-—; sec., dir. Marathon LeTourneau Co., 1970-—; v.p., sec. Marathon Battery Co., 1969-—, Marathon Franke Co., 1969-—, Marathon Leasing Co., 1970-—, Marathon Metallic Bldg. Co., 1970-—, Marathon Warehouse Co., 1968-—, Marathon Tank Car Co., 1969-—, Kelven, Inc., 1968-—; v.p., asst. sec. Marathon Morco Co., 1968-—; sec. Marathon Shipbuilding Co., 1970-—, Marathon Carey-McFall Co., 1969-—, Handy Venetian Blind Corp., 1969-—. Served with AUS, 1949-50, 50-52; Korea. Mem. U.S. Lawn Tennis Assn., Financial Execs. Inst., Am. Soc. Corp. Secs. Republican. Roman Catholic. Clubs: Doering Place Civic (v.p. 1971), Petroleum, Houston Racquet, Inwood Forest Country (Houston), Admirals (N.Y.C.). Home: 59 Williamsburg Lane Houston TX 77024 Office: 801 Houston S Natural Gas Bldg Houston TX 77002

O'HARRO, MICHAEL GARY, assn. exec.; b. Hollywood, Cal., Dec. 26, 1939; s. Pat E. and Virginia (Gary) O.; student Los Angeles Valley Coll., 1958-59; B.S., U. Ariz., 1962. Founder Jr. Officers & Profl. Assn., Washington, 1964, pres., 1964-—; opener Gentlemen II Nightclub, Washington, 1967, Gentlemen II Nightclub, Balt., 1968, Montage Nightclub, Washington, 1969, Beowulf Nightclub, Washington, 1969; pres. Universal Singles Enterprises, Inc., Washington, 1970-—, Michael James, Inc., Washington, 1967-70, Club Mgmt., Inc., Arlington, Va., 1965-70, 1112 20th St. Inc., Washington, 1969-—; v.p. James Michael Enterprises, Ltd., Balt., 1968-71. Advance-man for Humphrey presidential campaign, Democratic Party, 1968. Served to lt. (j.g.) USNR, 1963-65. Mem. Alpha Delta Sigma, Alpha Kappa Psi, Alpha Tau Omega. Presbyn. Home: 3830 N 26th St Arlington VA 22207 Office: 3286 M St NW Washington DC 20007

O'HEARN, WILLIAM WILSON, judge; b. Memphis, Jan. 14, 1914; s. John Joseph and Mollie (Kehoe) O'H.; LL.B., So. Law U., 1941; m. Mary Ann Turley, Aug. 22, 1950 (dec. June 1972); 1 dau., Mary Ann. Admitted to Tenn. bar, 1941; Tenn. asst. dist. atty.-gen. 1946-48; partner O'Hearn and Keathley, Memphis, 1957-61, Doneson, Adams, O'Hearn, Grogan and Edwards, Memphis, 1961-64, Moriarty, Fuqua & O'Hearn, Memphis, 1965-66; judge circuit ct. 15th judicial dist. Tenn., Memphis, 1966-—. Pres. Memphis Pub. Affairs Forum, 1961-62; mem. sch. bd. St. Anne Sch., 1967-—. Trustee Ave Maria Home for Aged, Memphis, 1957-59. Served to maj. with AUS, 1941-45. Decorated Bronze Star medal. Mem. Am., Tenn., Memphis and Shelby County (bd. dirs. 1957-60, chmn. com. discipline and ethics 1963-64, sponsor judiciary com. 1958-59) bar assns., Reserve Officers Assn. (pres. W.Tenn. chpt. 1949-50), Mil. Order World Wars (treas. 1966-67, judge adv. 1959), Am. Legion (exec. com. Memphis chpt. 1948-49), St. Vincent DePaul Soc. (hon.), Serra Internat. (trustee 1967-68). Roman Catholic. K.C. Home: 4264 Rhodes Av Memphis TN 38111 Office: Courthouse Memphis TN 38113

O'HEERON, MICHAEL KINNEY, physician-urologist; b. Elvins, Mo., Aug. 31, 1908; s. John Kinney and Viola (Neely) O'H.; B.A., Culver-Stockton Coll., 1934; M.D., Washington U., 1935; m. Sharmayne Olson, Oct. 19, 1945; children—Michael Kinney, John Bingham, William Edward, Mark Cummings. Intern St. Louis City Hosp., 1935-36; resident in urology Presbyn. Hosp., Chgo., 1936-40; practice medicine, specializing in urology, Houston, 1940-—; clin. prof. urology Baylor U., Houston, 1949-66; chief urology sect. St. Joseph's Hosp., 1947-—; cons. urologist Methodist Hosp., Houston, 1947-—; sr. asso. urologist Jefferson Davis Hosp., Houston, 1946-62; area cons. in urology VA Hosp. Tex. and La., 1951-65; cons. urologist Brooke Army Hosp., 1955-68. Chmn. urology sect. Internat. Coll. Surgeons meeting, N.Y.C., 1953; chmn sci. exhibits com. South Central sect. Am. Urol. Assn., 1951-67; presented papers and demonstrations internat. meeting Internat. Coll. Surgeons, Sao Paulo, Brazil, 1954; chmn. sci. exhibits com. South Central section Am. Urol Assn., 1951-67. Diplomate Am. Bd. Urology. Fellow A.C.S.; mem. A.M.A., Am. Urol. Assn. (pres. S. central sect. 1969), So. Med. Assn., Internat. Coll. Surgeons (pres. U.S. sect. 1969), Southwestern Surg. Cong., Tex. Med. Assn., Harris County Med. Soc. Contbr. numerous papers and articles in medicine and urology to tech. jours. Home: 474 N Post Oak Lane Houston TX 77024 Office: St Joseph Profl Bldg Houston TX 77002

O'HIGGINS, PABLO, painter. Address: Xochiealtitla 52 Mexico City DF Mexico*

OHLIGER, GLORIA ANN, pub. information specialist; b. Brownsville, Tex., 1925; d. Frederick and Evangeline (Anzaldua) Ohliger; student George Washington U., 1945-46. Editor women's page Washington Daily News, 1963-70; pub. information specialist Bur. Mint, Dept. Treasury, 1970-—. Clubs: Washington Press, Am. Newspaper Women's. Home: 1330 New Hampshire Av NW Washington DC 20036 Office: Bur Mint Dept Treasury Washington DC 20220

OHM, ROBERT ERVIN, univ. dean; b. Sheboygan, Wis., Oct. 17, 1917; s. Frank B. and Elsie (Kaliebe) O.; B.S. cum laude, U. Wis., 1939, M.S., 1940; Ph.D., U. Chgo., 1962; m. Ruth Boettner, Mary 18, 1948; children—Susan, Ellen. Tchr. Midlothian (Ill.) Pub. Schs., 1941-42; asso. prof. edn., dir. lab. sch. Antioch Coll., 1946-55; asst. prof. edn., prin. lab. schs. U. Chgo., 1955-60; adminstrv. coordinator MAT program, asst. prof., 1960-61; asso. dir. edn. professions div., prof. ednl. adminstrn. U. Okla., Norman, 1962-67, dean Coll. Edn., dir. edn. professions div., 1967-—. Served to lt. comdr. USNR. Decorated Air medal with two stars. Mem. Am. Ednl. Research Assn., Am., Okla. assns. sch. adminstrs., Am. Soc. Pub. Adminstrn., Nat. Conf. Profs. Ednl. Adminstrn., Phi Delta Kappa. Author: Leadership Games: Secondary Principalship and Elementary Principalship, 1968. Editor: (with O. D. Johns) Negotiations in the Schools, 1965; (with W. G. Monahan) Educational Adminstration-Philosophy in Action, 1964. Contbr. articles to profl. pubs. Home: 712 Juniper Lane Norman OK 73069

O'KEEF, HERBERT EDWARD, JR., newspaper editor; b. Wilmington, N.C., July 23, 1908; s. Herbert Edward and Fannie K. (Corbett) O'K.; A.B., Duke, 1930; m. Margaret Wyatt Link, June 17, 1937; 1 dau., Sallie C. Reporter, Durham (N.C.) Herald-Sun, 1930-33, Asso. Press, Raleigh, N.C., 1933, News and Observer, Raleigh, 1933-34, Asso. Press., Balt., 1934-38, successively asst. city editor, city editor, feature editor News and Observer, 1938-57; editor Raleigh Times, 1957-—. Sec. Wake County Dem. Exec. Com., 1946-60. Served with AUS, 1942-45; PTO. Decorated Bronze Star medal. Mem. Am. Soc. Newspaper Editors, Nat. Press Club, Phi Beta Kappa. Democrat. Presbyn. (ruling elder), Kiwanian. Club: Raleigh City. Home: 907 Runnymede Rd Raleigh NC 27607 Office: Raleigh Times 215 S McDowell St Raleigh NC 27601

O'KEEFE, DANIEL FRANCIS, JR., lawyer, trade assn. exec.; b. Belmont, Mass., July 1, 1936; s. Daniel Francis and Helen (Chamberlin) O.; B.A., U. Va., 1957, LL.B., 1960; M.B.A., Harvard, 1963; m. Sandra McKee Smith, July 27, 1957; children—Vicki Elizabeth, Timothy Jude. Admitted to Va. bar, 1960, D.C. bar, 1961, U.S. Supreme Ct. bar, 1967; atty. U.S. Dept. Justice, Washington, 1960-61; atty. U.S. Dept. Commerce, Washington 1963-65, asst. gen. counsel, 1965-67; mgr. employee relations Allied Chem. Corp., N.Y.C., 1967-68; sec. Proprietary Assn., Washington, 1968-—, v.p., 1969-—. Bd. advisers 1st Nat. Bank Washington, 1969-—. Bd. dirs. Am. Cancer Soc., Alexandria, Va., 1966-67; trustee Nat. Coordinating Council on Drug Edn., 1970-—. Recipient Dept. Commerce Silver Medal award, 1966. Mem. Am., Va. bar assns., D.C. Bar, Am. Soc. Assn. Execs., Sigma Chi, Phi Delta Phi. Clubs: University, Harvard Business School, Army-Navy Country. Home: 625 Pulman Pl Alexandria VA 22305 Office: 1700 Pennsylvania Av NW Washington DC 20006

O'KEEFE, MICHAEL HANLEY, lawyer, state senator; b. New Orleans, Dec. 1, 1931; s. Arthur J. and Eleanora (Gordon) O'K.; LL.B., Loyola U., 1955; m. Jean Ann VanGeffen, June 18, 1955; children—Michael H., Erin Elizabeth. Admitted to La. bar, 1955; partner O'Keefe, O'Keefe & Berrigan, 1955-—; mem. La. Senate, 1957-—, Senate floor leader, 1964-—; pres. pro tem, 1971. Chmn. La. Commn. on Intergovtl. Relations; mem. Council State Govts.; chmn. Goals for La., v.p. Council for Music and Performing Arts, Archdiocesan Commn. on Housing and Community Life; mem. La. Commn. Status of Women; chmn. Gov.'s Com. Correctional Treatment and Rehab.; chmn. adv. com. La. Planning Office. Served from 2d lt. to 1st lt., AUS, 1955-57. Mem. C. of C., Am., La., New Orleans bar assns., Res. Officers Assn., Blue Key (hon.). Roman Catholic. K.C., Kiwanian. Home: 4 Gull St New Orleans LA 70124 Office: Am Bank Bldg New Orleans LA 70130

O'KEEFE, ROBERT EMMETT, govt. ofcl.; b. Detroit, Apr. 28, 1926; s. Thomas F. and Lou (Brenner) O'K.; B.S. in Econs., U. Detroit, 1949, postgrad. Law Sch., 1948-49, postgrad. econs., 1950-53; m. Lucille Eva Renuart, Apr. 25, 1953; children—Michelle, Sean, Patrick, Colleen, Laura, Terrence, Jeanne, Brian. Sales promotion mgr. Pabst Distbrs., Detroit, 1948-58, v.p., 1958-61; analytical statistician Internal Revenue Service, Washington, 1961-—. Recipient Cash award Treasury Dept., 1964. Mem. Am. Statis. Soc. Home: 436 Sherrow Av Falls Church VA 22046 Office: 1111 Constitutional Av Washington DC 20024

OKELL, GEORGE SHAFFER, SR., lawyer; b. Scranton, Pa., May 29, 1906; s. George Muir and Blanche (Shaffer) O.; LL.B., U. Miami, 1933, J.D., 1967; m. Evelyn Maude Pottymer, Feb. 8, 1926; children—George Shaffer, James Muir, Jean Ann (Mrs. Jake Cooper), Jo Byna. Admitted to Fla. bar, 1933, since practiced law in Miami. Trustee Nat. Children's Cardia Home, 1952-—; mem. bd. govs. Moosehaven, home for aged mems. Moose, 1952-—. Mem. Fla. Ho. of Reps., 1945-55; city atty., Miami, Fla., 1956-57; atty. Dade County League of Municipalities, 1957-58. Organizer Dade County Young Dem. Club, 1931, pres., 1934-36; pres. Young Dem. Clubs of Fla., 1944-45; nat. parliamentarian, mem. exec. com. Young Dem. Clubs of Am., 1939-40. Recipient plaque, S.E. Optometric Assn. of Fla., 1950. Methodist. Elk (past exalted ruler), Moose (past gov. local lodge, pres. Fla. assn. 1948-50), Lion (pres. Coral Gables 1945-46). Home: 1245 Andalusia Av Coral Gables FL 33134 Office: 1392 NW 36th St Miami FL 33142

O'KELLEY, HAROLD ERNEST, mfg. co. exec.; b. Jacksonville, Fla., Mar. 20, 1925; s. Edward Barber and Ida Bessie (Blackwell) O'K.; B.E.E., Auburn U., 1947; M.S. in Engring., U. Fla., 1948; m. Sarah Blanche Adcock, June 5, 1949; children—Sarah (Mrs. J. Preston Silvernail), Ellen B., Shannon K., Harold Ernest. Asso. prof. elec. engring. Auburn (Ala.) U., 1948-57; v.p., gen. mgr. Radiation, Inc., Melbourne, Fla., 1964-68; v.p. programs Harris Intertype Corp., Melbourne, 1968-72, v.p. composition equipment group, 1972-—. Bd. dirs. Central Fla. council Boy Scouts Am., 1971-72, United Fund, 1971-—; bd. govs. Brevard Hosp., Melbourne, 1968-—. Mem. Armed Forces Communications and Electronics Assn., I.E.E.E., Am. Mgmt. Assn., Am. Inst. Aeros. and Astronautics, Am. Ordnance Assn., Tau Beta Pi, Eta Kappa Nu. Club: Civitan (pres. 1954-55). Home: 910 S Magnolia Av Indialantic FL 32903 Office: PO Box 37 Melbourne FL 32901

O'KELLEY, THOMAS AUGUSTUS, educator; b. Macon, Ga., Jan. 28, 1918; s. Frederick Henry and Ethel Elizabeth (Peacock) O.; B.A. with honors, U. S. Fla., 1963; M.A. (grad. fellow), Fla. State U., 1964, Ph.D., 1968; m. Mildred Winifred Herrick, July 27, 1957; stepchildren—James Horace Blackmer, Julie Ann Blackmer. Switchman plant dept. So. Bell Tel. and Tel. Co., 1937-45; self-employed as photographer, Atlanta, 1945-60; prof. logic and philosophy St. Petersburg Jr. Coll., Clearwater, Fla., 1964—. Mem. Am., Fla. philos. assns. Home: 2231 Harn Blvd Clearwater FL 33516

O'KELLEY, WILLIAM CLARK, judge; b. Atlanta, Jan. 2, 1930; s. Ezra Clark and Theo (Johnson) O'K.; A.B., Emory U., 1951, LL.B., 1953; m. Ernestine Allen, Mar. 28, 1953; children—Virginia Leigh, William Clark. Admitted to Ga. bar, 1952, practiced in Atlanta, 1957-59; asst. U.S. atty. No. Dist. Ga., 1959-61; partner law firm O'Kelley, Hopkins & Van Gerpen, Atlanta, 1961-70; U.S. dist. judge No. Dist. Ga., Atlanta, 1970—. Corporate sec., dir. Gwinnett Bank & Trust Co., Norcross, Ga., 1968-70. Mem. exec. com., gen. counsel Republican Party Ga., 1968-70. Served as 1st lt. USAF, 1953-57; capt. Res. Mem. Am., Atlanta, Gwinnett bar assns., Ga. State Bar, Am. Judicature Soc., Gwinnett C. of C. (v.p. 1966), Sigma Chi, Phi Delta Phi, Omicron Delta Kappa. Baptist. Kiwanian (past pres.). Clubs: Atlanta Athletic, Lawyers of Atlanta; Berkeley Hills Golf (Norcross, Ga.); Commerce. Home: 550 Ridgecrest Dr Norcross GA 30071 Office: US District Court Old Post Office Bldg Atlanta GA 30301

OKES, IMOGENE ESTA, govt. ofcl.; b. Terre Haute, Ind.; d. Vernor J. and Ethlyn (Willis) Okes; B.S., Ind. State U., 1944; M.A., Am. U., 1960. Clk., editor, librarian U.S. Fgn. Service, China and Norway, 1945-52; groupworker, pub. relations rep. Internat. Inst., Fresno, Cal., 1955-56; research asso. Spl. Operations Research Office, Am. U., Washington, 1957-61, Inst. for Def. Analyses, Washington, 1962-63; adult edn. specialist U.S. Office Edn., Washington, 1965—. Guest lectr. Fgn. Service Inst., U.S. Dept. State, Washington, 1961-62; instr. Ginling Girls Coll., Nanking, China, 1947; co-chmn. for arrangements nat. meeting Assn. Asian Studies, Washington, 1964. Program chmn. YWCA Internat. Womens Club, Nanking, 1947. Mem. Am. Assn. U. Women (sec., mem. bd. Washington br. 1969-71), Inst. Mgmt. Scis. (editorial bd. Washington chpt. 1970—), Adult Edn. Assn. (dir. Washington br. 1971—), Assn. for Ednl. Data Systems, Am. Ednl. Research Assn., Assn. Instnl. Research, Operations Research Soc. Am., Am. Polit. Sci. Assn., Am. Acad. Polit. and Social Scis., Assn. Asian Studies, Internat. Studies Assn., Mongolia-Tibet Soc. Author: Psychological Operations-Afghanistan Project PROSYMS, 1961; Effective Communications by Americans with Thai, 1961; Participation in Adult Education, 1969; Initial Report, 1971. Home: 5480 Wisconsin Av Chevy Chase MD 20015 Office: US Office Edn Washington DC 20202

O'KEY, CLIFFORD WILLIAM, city ofcl.; b. Chgo., Nov. 15, 1922; s. Floyd M. and Grace (Poore) O'K.; B.A., Westminster Coll., Pa., 1949; M.A. (Samuel Fels scholar), U. Pa., 1951; postgrad. U. Chgo., 1964; m. Ruth E. Gilliand, Sept. 26, 1945; children—Jeffrey, Allisyn, Susan, Clifford, Christopher. Asst. dir. research Pa. Tax Equalization Bd., 1950-52; dir. finance, asst. mgr., Milford, Conn., 1952-55; city adminstr., Rahway, N.J., 1955-57; city mgr., Clayton, Mo., 1957-65, Norman, Okla., 1965-67, Little Rock, 1967-68, Miami Beach, Fla., 1969—; adviser to Turkey, aid, Dept. State, 1965. Recipient Time mag. awards, 1958, 60. First Place award competition for civic improvement Okla. C. of C., 1965. Mem. Internat., Fla. city mgrs. assns., Am. Soc. Pub. Adminstrn., Am. Soc. Planning Ofcls., Am. Pub. Works Assn., Nat. Municipal League, Municipal Finance Officers Assn., Nat. Assn. Accountants. Kiwanian. Home: 4345 Alton Rd Miami Beach FL 33140

OKNER, BENJAMIN ALLEN, economist; b. Chgo., Aug. 24, 1936; s. Hyman and Sylvia (Chertob) O.; B.S., Ill. Inst. Tech., 1957; M.A., U. Mich., 1960, Ph.D., 1965. Asst. study dir. Survey Research Center, U. Mich., 1957-60; fiscal economist Office Tax Analysis, U.S. Treasury Dept., 1961-63; mem. staff Council Econ. Advisers, 1965-66; asst. prof. dept. econs. Ohio State U., 1966-67; sr. fellow Brookings Instn., Washington, 1968—. Mem. Am. Econ. Assn., Nat. Tax Assn. Home: 1761 R St NW Washington DC 20009 Office: 1775 Massachusetts Av NW Washington DC 20036

OKRASKI, HENRY CARL, electronics engr.; b. Utica, N.Y., Jan. 22, 1936; s. Andrew J. and Helen (Dowiak) O.; student Mohawk Valley Tech. Inst., 1953; B.E.E., Clarkson Coll. Tech., 1958; postgrad. Hofstra U., 1964, George Washington U., 1965, N.Y. U., 1969; M.E., U. Fla., 1972; m. Patricia Turner, Feb. 3, 1962 children—Anna Kay, Joseph Anthony, Andrew Edward. Electronic engr. Link Div., Gen. Precision, Inc., Binghamton, N.Y., 1958-62; supervisory gen. engr. U.S. Naval Tng. Device Center, Orlando, Fla., 1962—. Registered profl. engr., Fla. Mem. Fla. Engring. Soc., Nat. Soc. Profl. Engrs., Clarkson Coll. Alumni Assn., Pi Kappa Phi, Karma. Democrat. Roman Catholic. Home: 2844 Will-o-th-Green Winter Park FL 32789 Office: Naval Tng Device Center Orlando Naval Base Orlando FL 32813

OKUN, JACK H., orthodontist; b. N.Y.C., Jan. 30, 1932; s. Louis and Rachel (Ziperstein) O.; B.S., N.Y. U., 1953, D.D.S., 1956; M.S., Northwestern U., 1961; m. Rosalind Yagman, Nov. 18, 1967; children—Louis Brian, Michael Scott. Trombone player, N.Y.C., 1948-56; practice dentistry specializing in orthodontics, North Palm Beach, Fla., 1961—. Guest lectr. orthodontics Palm Beach County Dental Research Clinic, 1968-69. Mem. adv. bd. U. Palm Beach, 1969—. Served as capt. USAF, 1956-58. Recipient short story prize USAF, 1957, Mgmt. Dental Corps, USAF, 1957; Founders Day award N.Y. U., 1956. Mem. Am., Fla. (dental edn. com. 1968-70) dental assns., Atlantic Coast, Palm Beach County (chmn. budget and audit com. 1964-69, chmn. sch. edn. com. 1967-70) dental socs. Phi Beta Kappa, Omicron Kappa Upsilon. Contbr. articles to profl. jours. Home: 110 Dory Rd N North Palm Beach FL 33408 Office: 849 Park Av Lake Park FL 33403

OLANSKY, SIDNEY, physician; b. Boston, Jan. 11, 1914; s. Samuel and Anna (Olans) O.; B.S., N.Y.U., 1934; M.D., Duke, 1940; m. Marian Elizabeth Freehafer, Oct. 13, 1945; children—Leann, Alan, David, Ad. Served to med. dir. Venereal Disease Research Lab., USPHS, Atlanta, 1950-55; asso. prof. dermatology Duke U. Sch. Medicine, 1955-59; prof. medicine Emory U., Atlanta, 1959—; intern Met. Hosp., N.Y.C., 1940-41; resident Duke U. Med. Center, 1946-48; practice medicine, specializing in dermatology, Atlanta, 1959—; mem. staff Emory U., Grady Meml., Henriett Egleston hosps. Served with USPHS, 1940-46. Home: 3275 Majestic Circle Avondale Estate GA 30002 Office: Emory U Clinic Atlanta GA 30322

OLBRICHT, THOMAS HENRY, educator; b. Thayer, Mo., Nov. 3, 1929; s. Benjamin Joseph and Agnes Martha (Taylor) O.; B.S., No. Ill. U., 1951; M.A., U. Ia., 1953, Ph.D., 1959; S.T.B., Harvard, 1962; m. Dorothy Jetta Kiel, June 8, 1951; children—Suzanne, Eloise, Joel, Adele, Erica. Head speech dept. U. Dubuque, 1955-59; asso. prof. Pa. State U., 1962-67; prof. philosophy and religion Abilene (Tex.) Christian Coll., 1967—. Kiwanian (sec. 1970-71, dir.). Author: Informative Speaking, 1968. Asso. editor: Speech Monographs, 1964-67, Quar. Jour. Speech, 1967-71, Jour. Philosophy and Rhetoric, 1968—, Restorative Quar., 1969—. Home: 1400 Compere Blvd Abilene TX 79601

OLDAKER, LAWRENCE LEE, educator; b. Norfolk, Va., Sept. 6, 1932; s. Emery Ralph and Edith Louise (Eason) O.; student Old Dominion Coll., 1950-51; B.S., Appalachian State U., 1954; M.Ed., Coll. William and Mary, 1958; postgrad. U. Ga., 1966, Ed.D., 1969; m. Syble Maynard, May 31, 1958; children—David Lee, John Edward. Grad. asst. Coll. William and Mary, 1957-58; tchr. Arlington County (Va.) Pub. Schs., 1958-61; supt. Marine Corps Air Sta. Grade Schs., Laurel Bay, S.C., 1961-70; asso. prof. Valdosta (Ga.) State Coll., 1970—. Mem. Beaufort Mental Health Assn., Air Sta. Youth Activity Council. Served with AUS, 1954-56. Mem. S.C. Elementary Prins. Assn., S.C. Edn. Assn., Am. Assn. Sch. Adminstrs., N.E.A., Council Ednl. Facilities Planners, Kappa Delta Pi, Phi Delta Kappa, Kappa Alpha. Club: Sertoma (dir. Beaufort 1967-69). Home 5 Dogwood Circle Valdosta GA 30601 Office: Sch of Edn Valdosta GA 30601

OLDFIELD, MARGARET JESCHKE (MRS. JOHN S. OLDFIELD, civic worker; b. Parris Island, S.C., Jan. 10, 1920; d. Richard Hall and Margaret (Devereux) Jeschke; student George Washington U., 1936-39; m. John S. Oldfield, Aug. 2, 1939; children—Devereux Ann, John Sherman, Baird Dewes. Nurse aide A.R.C., Alexandria, Va., 1939-43, grey lady, 1943-57, mem. staff, 1957—, chpt. dir., 1964-67, chmn. Ptomac Council, 1965-67, dir., 1967—. Corp. dir. Alexandria Hosp., 1967-70; dir. Navy Marine Residence Found., 1964-66. Mem. Pi Beta Phi. Republican. Roman Catholic. Home: 401 Woodland Terrace Alexandria VA 22302

OLDHAM, ARTHUR SEARS, judge; b. Athens, Ga., Nov. 12, 1906; s. Henry Jackson and Julie (Biship) O.; LL.B., U. Ga., 1926; m. Florrie Phillips, July 15, 1932; 1 son, Henry Nevel. Admitted to Ga. bar. 1926, since practiced in Athens; judge City Ct. Athens, 1940—. Mem. Ga., Western Circuit. Athens bar assns. Methodist. Home: 100 Old Princeton Rd Athens GA 30601 Office: Court House Athens GA 30601

OLDHAM, DORTCH, pub. co. exec.; b. Hartsville, Tenn., Aug. 26, 1919; s. N. E. and Sally Jane (Gregory) O.; student Cumberland U., 1936-38, U. Richmond, 1939-41; m. Lenore Heubner, Oct. 2, 1948; children—Dortch, Gregory, Peter, Daniel, Mark. Sales mgr. Southwestern Co., pub. co., Nashville, 1946-59, pres., 1960—; dir. First Am. Nat. Bank, Synercon, Inc., Nasco, Inc. Mem. Tenn. Indsl. and Agrl. Devel. Commn., 1971—. Trustee, Cumberland Coll., Montgomery Bell Acad. Served with USAAF, 1942-46. Mem. Nashville C. of C. (dir. 1971—), Theta Chi. Republican. Presbyn. (elder). Rotarian (dir. 1970—). Clubs: Belle Meade Country, Cumberland. Home: 4390 Chickering Lane Nashville TN 37215 Office: 2968 Foster Creighton Dr Nashville TN 37211

OLDS, LAWRENCE BRUCE, pub. relations exec.; b. Hudson Falls, N.Y., Feb. 22, 1922; s. Carlton Bruce and Ethel (Craig) O.; B.S., St. Lawrence U., 1944; m. Elizabeth Fagg, June 20, 1955; 1 dau., Cynthia Craig. Radio monitor Time mag., N.Y.C., 1944-47; audio editor FM & TV mag., Great Barrington, Mass., 1947-49; sr. illustrator Gen. Electric Co., Pittsfield, Mass., 1949-54; tech. writer McGraw-Hill, N.Y.C., 1955; tech. editor Abex Corp., N.Y.C., 1955-57; account exec. Dudley, Anderson, Nutzy, N.Y.C., 1957-62, Cunningham & Walsh, Inc., N.Y.C., 1962-63; dir. field services Am. Iron & Steel Inst., Washington, 1963—. Cons. pub. and community relations steel cos. U.S., Can., Mexico, 1965-70. Served with AUS, 1943. Mem. Pub. Relations Soc. Am., Woodland Trail Riders, Profl. Indsl. Communicators Assn., Alpha Tau Omega. Presbyn. Home: 5110 Rockwood Pkwy Washington DC 20016 Office: 1000 16th St NW Washington DC 20036

OLDS, VIRGINIA ESTHER NEWTON (MRS. LLOYD E. OLDS), social worker, educator; b. Binghamton, N.Y., July 20, 1931; d. G. Leslie and Mable (Yost) Newton; B.S., Greenville Coll., 1959; M.S.W., U. Okla., 1962; m. Lloyd E. Olds, Apr. 3, 1964; 1 son, Lloyd Edward II. Registered nurse Williamsport (Pa.) Hosp., 1953-57, dental surgeon, Williamsport, 1954-57; instr. Lycoming Coll., Williamsport, 1956-57; nurse Greenville (Ill.) Coll., 1957-59, Salvation Army, St. Louis, summers 1958-59, Deaconess Hosp., Oklahoma City, 1959-60, part-time 1960-62, social worker, 1962; social worker, instr. U. Okla. Med. Center, Oklahoma City, 1963-67, social worker, asst. prof., Norman, 1967—. Social work cons. Deaconess Hosp., Oklahoma City, 1967-68. Mem. Nat. Assn. Social Workers (chpt. chmn. 1968-69), Am. Nurses Assn., Okla. Health and Welfare Assn., Nat. Rehab. Assn., Nat. Assn. Social Work, Acad. Certified Social Workers, Council Social Work Edn. Democrat. Methodist. Home: 7020 Comanche St Oklahoma City OK 73132 Office: U Okla Sch Social Work Norman OK 73069

O'LEARY, FRANKLIN J., author, artist; b. Marfa, Tex., Feb. 1, 1922; s. John J. and Mary Helen (Hess) O'L.; m. Wanda Margaret Howard, Feb. 28, 1946; children—Cathleen Margaret, Patrick Howard. Free lance author, artist, El Paso, 1953—; author: Poke-A-Long, 1955; Cappy Cardinal, 1960; Biffy, 1962; Flap, 1968. Served with AUS, 1943-45; ETO. Decorated Bronze Star medal with cluster. Rotarian. Address: 3409 Memphis El Paso TX 79930

O'LEARY, VIRGINIA KYLE BOOTH (MRS. DANIEL B. O'LEARY), journalist; b. Wash. Jan. 8, 1928; d. Kyle and Helen (Sutton) Booth; student George Washington U., Washington, 1944-46; m. Philip Warren, Jr. (dec.); children—Joseph B., Virginia Kyle, Philip C.S., Timothy P.M., Mary M., Ruth N., Kathleen; m. 2d, Daniel B. O'Leary, Nov. 12, 1967. Reporter, Alexandria (Va.) Gazette, 1943-50, women's editor, religious ne-s editor, asst. city editor, 1961-64; columnist N. Va. Free Press, 1948-49; women's editor, city editor No. Va. Sun., 1964-66; pub. relations dir. Arlington Red Cross, 1966; pub. relations dir. Alexandria Hosp., 1966-67; spl. writer Alexandria (Va.) Gazette, 1969—. Dir. Nat. capital area chpt. March of Dimes, 1961-67. Mem. Nat. League Am. Pen Women, No. Va. News Assn., Chi Omega. Home: 428 Monticello Blvd Alexandria VA 22305

OLEHY, JAMES HOWARD, former govt. ofcl.; b. Catlin, Ill., Apr. 13, 1903; s. Charles M. and Minnie (Bendinger) O.; B.S. in Elec. Engring., U. Colo., 1927; m. Hazel B. Wathor, July 1, 1933; children—James F., Mary Anna (Mrs. Joseph Tyler). Engr., Continental Oil Co., Ponca City, Okla., 1929-49, mgr. engring., 1949-50, mgr. mfg., Houston, 1950-56, project mgr. ammonia plants, 1964-67; gen. mgr. mfg. Petroleum Chem., Inc., Lake Charles, La., 1956-59, v.p. mfg., 1959-63; v.p. mining, mfg. Agrico Chem. Co. div. Continental Oil Co., Memphis, 1967-68, cons., 1968-69; regional dir. U.S. Post Office Dept., Memphis, 1969-72, cons., 1972—. Registered profl. engr., Okla. Mem. La Chem. Assn. (dir. 1963), Am., La. (dir., treas. 1960-61, pres., dir. 1962) chem. socs., Am. Inst. Chem. Engrs. Home: 1210 Farrow Rd Memphis TN 38116

OLEJAR, PAUL DUNCAN, univ. adminstr.; b. Hazelton, Pa., Sept. 13, 1906; s. George and Anna (Danco) O.; A.B., Dickinson Coll., 1928; m. Ann Ruth Dillard, Jan. 6, 1933; 1 son, Peter. Dir. edn. W.Va. Conservation Commn., 1936-41; coordinator U.S. Fish and Wildlife Service, 1941-42; chief press and radio Bur. Reclamation, Dept. Interior, 1946-47; editor Plant Industry Sta. AGRI, 1948-51; chmn. spl. reports Agrl. Research Adminstrn., 1951-56; dir. tech. information Edgewood Arsenal, Md., 1959-63; chief, tech. information, plans and programs Army Research Office, Washington, 1963-64; chmn. chem. information unit NSF, Washington, 1965-70; dir. drug information program Sch. Pharmacy, U. N.C., Chapel Hill, 1970—. Served with AUS, 1942-46. Decorated Army Commendation medal. Mem. Am. Soc. Information Sci., Am. Chem. Soc., Drug Information Assn., Ravens Claw, Theta Chi, Omicron Delta Kappa. Methodist. Home: 604 Churchill Dr Chapel Hill NC 27514

OLER, WESLEY MARION, III, physician; b. N.Y.C., Mar. 8, 1918; s. Wesley Marion, Jr. and Imogene (Rubel) O.; grad. Phillips Andover Acad., 1936; A.B., Yale, 1940; M.D., Columbia, 1943; m. Virginia Carolyn Craemer, Dec. 8, 1951; children—Helen Louise (dec.), Wesley Marion IV, Stephen Scott. Intern, Bellevue Hosp., N.Y.C., 1944, resident, 1948-50; fellow Hosp. U. Pa., 1951; practice medicine, specializing in internal medicine, Washington, 1952—; sr. attending physician, vice chmn. dept. medicine Washington Hosp. Center, 1962-64, v.p. med. bd., 1971-72; clin. prof. medicine Med. Sch., Georgetown U. Founder, pres. Washington Recorder Soc.; bd. dirs. Am. Recorder Soc. Served to maj. M.C., AUS, 1944-47. Fellow A.C.P.; mem. Mensa, Osler Soc. Washington (past pres.), Republican. Episcopalian. Clubs: Metropolitan, Cosmos; Chevy Chase. Contbr. to jours. on old musical instruments. Home: 4800 Van Ness St NW Washington DC 20016 Office: 2141 K St NW Washington DC 20037

OLGES, DARRELL GENE, ednl. adminstr.; b. Louisville, Oct. 18, 1941; s. Louis John and Alma DeVera (Ray) O.; B.A., Johnson Bible Coll., 1963; M.A., U. Louisville, 1968; m. Joe Anne Justice, Aug. 12, 1962; children—Timothy Alan, David Alan, Todd Alan. Ordained to ministry, Christian Ch., 1963; newsroom cons., music critic asst. Louisville Times, 1963-68; instr. dept. humanities U. Louisville, 1965-68; acad. dean Ky. Christian Coll., Grayson, 1968—, organ instr., concert choir dir., 1969—. Mem. Am. Assn. Higher Edn. Republican. Mem. Christian Ch. Home: Ky Christian Coll Grayson KY 41143

OLIVE, DON HILLIARD, educator; b. Talco, Tex., Aug. 28, 1939; s. James Hilliard and Frances Dee (Ratcliff) O.; B.A., E. Tex. Bapt. Coll., 1960; B.D., Southwestern Bapt. Theol. Sem., 1964, Th.D., 1966; postgrad. Tulane U., 1971—; m. Linda Sue Pridgen, Aug. 28, 1959; children—Don Hilliard, James R., Jennifer Lee. Ordained to ministry Bapt. Ch., 1960; pastor, First Bapt. Ch., Willis, Okla., 1962-67, Coronado Bapt. Chapel, El Paso, Tex., 1967-68; prof. philosophy and religion Wayland Bapt. Coll., Plainview, Tex., 1968—. Tex. Bapt. Faculty Improvement fellow, 1971, Nat. Def. Edn. Act fellow, Tulane U., 1971. Mem. Am. Acad. Religion, S.W. Assn. Bapt. Tchrs. Religion, Alpha Chi. Baptist. Author: Wolfhart Pannenberg: Maker of Modern Theological Thought, 1972. Office: Wayland Baptist Coll Plainview TX 79072

OLIVER, BENJAMIN HUGHER, JR., telephone co. exec.; b. N.Y.C., Mar. 1, 1907; s. Benjamin Hugher and Margaret W. R. (Zoller) O.; M.E., Stevens Inst. Tech., 1928; student N.Y.U., 1930-31; m. Lillie M. Kuhnle, Nov. 24, 1932; children—Susan L., Mary Jane. With N.Y. Telephone Co., 1928-55, 58-62, v.p. upstate, Albany, 1958-62; asst. v.p. plant operations Am. Tel. & Tel. Co., 1955-58, dir. of govt. communications Long Lines Dept., Am. Tel. & Tel. Co., Washington, 1962-64, v.p. govt. communications Long Lines Dept., 1964-68, v.p. gen. depts. and Long Line dept. govt. communications, 1968—. Mem. internat. communications service com. Nat. Industry Adv. Com., 1962—. Bd. dirs. Council of Nation's Capitol, Girl Scouts U.S.A., Washington. Served from capt. to col., AUS, 1942-45. Mem. Armed Forces Communications and Electronics Assn. (nat. pres. 1958-61, 69—, permanent dir., mem. exec. com.), Am. Legion, Defense Orientation Conf. Assn., I.E.E.E. Clubs: Congressional Country, International, Army and Navy (Washington). Home: 9100 Burning Tree Rd Bethesda MD 20034 Office: 2055 L St NW Washington DC 20036

OLIVER, CHARLES DICKSON, ins. exec.; b. Ware Shoals, S.C., Jan. 10, 1909; s. Rueben Spencer and Annie (Dickson) O.; C.E., Cornell U., 1931; postgrad. in bus. adminstrn. U. Cin., 1950; m. Alice Thomas, Oct. 18, 1934 (dec. May 1967); children—Charles Dickson, Jr., James William, Nancy Jane; m. 2d, Anne Jones, Jan. 1, 1969. Salesman, Liberty Mut. Ins. Co., Newark, 1933-35, staff sales, Louisville, 1935-39, mgr., Cin., 1940-43, 46-53, regional mgr., East Orange, N.J., 1953-59, So. div. mgr., v.p., Atlanta, 1959—. Bd. dirs. Ga. Insurors' Insolvency Fund, Fla. Ins. Guaranty Fund; trustee Ga. State U. Ednl. Found. Served with USNR, 1943-46. C.P.C.U. Mem. Newcomen Soc. Clubs: Commerce (Atlanta); Pendennis (Louisville); Piedmont (Spartanburg, S.C.); Charlotte (N.C.) City; Commonwealth (Richmond, Va.). Home: 271A Lakemoore Dr NE Atlanta GA 30342 Office: 1718 Peachtree Rd NW Atlanta GA 30308

OLIVER, CLIFTON, JR., assn. exec.; b. Amarillo, Tex., Dec. 3, 1916; s. Clifton, Sr. and Laura Pearl (Hudson) D.; B.A. in Econs., Tex. Tech. Coll., 1937, M.A. in Econs., 1939. Tchr., lectr. Tex. Christian U., Ft. Worth, 1939-41; asso. prof. in bus. adminstrn. U. Fla., Gainesville, 1946-71, dir. mgmt. center Coll. Bus. Adminstrn., 1959-71, coordinator for off-campus bus. confs.; staff cons. Okla. Bankers Assn.; cons. W. T. Grant Co., N.Y.C., State Farm Ins. Co., Jacksonville, Fla., Convair div. Fla. Heart Assn., St. Petersburg, Fla. Served to 2d lt. Med. Adminstrn. Corps, AUS, 1943-46. Mem. Am. Soc. Personnel Assn., Am. Soc. Tng. Dirs., Acad. Mgmt., Am., Southeastern econs. assns., Panel Am. Arbitration Assn., Am. Assn. U. Profs., Alpha Chi, Pi Sigma Alpha, Kappa Kappa Psi, Pi Gamma Mu, Alpha Kappa Psi, Alpha Tau Omega. Elk, Kiwanian. Home: PO Box 1516 Oklahoma City OK 73102 Office: 611 Colcord Bldg Oklahoma City OK 73102

OLIVER, EARL PORTER, physician; b. Lamasco, Ky., Apr. 26, 1918; s. Earl F. and Beatrice B. (Burns) O.; B.S., U. Ky., 1940; M.D., U. Louisville, 1943; m. Margurette C. Fultz, Mar. 20, 1943; 1 dau., Margurette (Mrs. Larry B. Stovall). Intern, Louisville Gen. Hosp., 1943-44; practice medicine Halcomb and Oliver Clinic, Scottsville, Ky., 1946—; mem. staff Allen County War Meml. Hosp., 1952—; med. dir. Selective Service Bd., 1946—; mem. Allen County Health Bd.; adminstr., partner Graves Infirmary, 1946-52. Mem. Ky. Commn. on Aging, 1961—, chmn. 1967-69; mem. Mammoth Cave Comprehensive Health Care Council, 1970-72. Served to maj. M.C., AUS, 1944-46. Diplomate Am. Bd. Family Practice. Mem. A.M.A., Ky., So., Allen County med. assns., Am. Acad. Gen. Practice, Am. Soc. Anesthesiologists, Ky. Corps of Long Riflemen. Mason (Shriner), Rotarian. Home: RR 1 Gallatin Rd Scottsville KY 42164 Office: 217 W Main St Scottsville KY 42164

OLIVER, IVAN P(ROCTOR), govt. ofcl.; b. San Saba, Tex., June 5, 1903; s. William A. and Sarah Ellen (Oliver) O.; B.S., North Tex. State Coll., 1927; M.A., U. Colo., 1936; m. Lois Kathryn Johnson, Aug. 20, 1929; children—Margaret Ann, Sara Louise. Supt. schs., Jacksboro, Tex., 1933-41, Stephenville, Tex., 1941-45; dist. sales supr. Allis-Chalmers Mfg. Co., Dallas, 1945-50; prin. Stephen F. Austin Elementary Sch., Marshall, Tex., 1950-53; city mgr. City of Marshall, 1953-57, City of Victoria (Tex.), 1957-59, Gladewater, Tex., 1959-66; community programs specialist Dept. Housing and Urban Devel., Ft. Worth, now area rehab. loan and grant specialist, San Antonio. Mem. Internat., Tex., East Tex. (pres. 1964—) city mgrs. assns., Mid- Tex. Ednl. Assn. (pres. 1944-45), Tex. Tchrs. Assn., C. of C. Presbyn. Mason. Club: Lions (dist. gov. 1944-45). Home: 9418 La Rue St San Antonio TX 78217 Office: Dept Housing and Urban Devel 410 S Main St San Antonio TX 78204

OLIVER, JOHN, business exec.; b. Bartlesville, Okla., Oct. 14, 1912; s. Earl and Lytha (Schearer) O.; B.S., Okla. A. & M. Coll., 1935; M.A., U. Chgo., 1938; m. Josephine Hill, May 29, 1936; children—John Hill, Frances Elizabeth, James Robert. Adminstrv. staff mem. Okla. A. & M. Coll., 1935-41; adminstrv. officer Okla. State Regents Higher Edn., Oklahoma City, 1941-42; mem. budget staff TVA, Knoxville, Tenn., 1942-46, chief budget officer, asst. gen. mgr., 1946-51, gen. mgr. 1951-54; asst. to pres. Wheland Co., 1954-56; exec. v.p. Devel. & Resources Corp., N.Y.C., 1956-64, pres., 1964-69; asst. to pres., also dir. planning and corporate devel. N. Am. Royalties, Inc., Chattanooga, 1969—. Mem. Kappa Alpha, Phi Delta Kappa. Episcopalian. Clubs: Mountain City, Signal Mountain Golf and Country. Home: 113 Grayson Rd Signal Mountain TN 37377 Office: N Am Royalties Inc Chattanooga TN 37402

OLIVER, JOHN MOULTRIE, indsl. devel. engr.; b. Greeleyville, S.C., May 29, 1921; s. Samuel Peter and Bettie (Register) O.; A.B., U. N.C., 1942; m. Eva Kornegay Boatwright, May 27, 1944; children—John M., Eva Lynn, Elizabeth Boatwright. Agt., Equitable Life Assurance Soc., 1947-61; indsl. devel. engr. commerce and industry div. State of N.C., 1961-66; dir. indsl. devel. Richmond County, N.C., 1966-71; exec. dir. Halifax Devel. Commn., Roanoke Rapids, N.C., 1971—. Treas., Cumberland County United Fund, 1952-54. Bd. dirs. Richmond County YMCA. Served to capt. AUS, 1942-46; ETO. Mem. N.C. Indsl. Developers Assn., N.C. Soc. Engrs., Chi Phi. Presbyn. (chmn. bd. deacons). Rotarian. Clubs: Highland Country (Fayetteville, N.C.); Richmond County Country (Rockingham, N.C.). Home: 107 Tanbar Ct Roanoke Rapids NC 27870 Office: PO Box 246 Roanoke Rapids NC 27870

OLIVER, LEAVY WINSTON, educator; b. Marion, Ala., Dec. 6, 1919; s. Earnest and Bertha Oliver; A.B., Miles Coll., 1942; M.A., Ind. U., 1952, Ph.D., 1955; m. Edith Moutry, Aug. 2, 1964; children—Gloria Jane, Leavy Winston, Stephen Vincent. Vets. vocational coordinator Birmingham (Ala.) Bd. Edn., 1946-48; tng. officer U.S. Govt., Wright-Patterson AFB, O., 1951-52; faculty polit. sci. Miles Coll., Birmingham, Ala., 1952-53, chmn. div. social sci., 1960-64, prof. polit. sci., dir. community research, 1968—; vis. prof. Tuskegee (Ala.) Inst., 71-72; faculty polit. sci. Grambling (La.) Coll., 1953-58; prof. polit. sci. Ala. A. and M. Coll., Normal, 1958-60; chmn. dept. history and govt. St. Augustines Coll., Raleigh, N.C., 1964-67; chmn. dept. sociology Wilberforce (O.) U., 1967-68. Mem. Fairfield Civic League, Young Men for Democracy and Civic Action, Mem. Jefferson County Council for Democratic party. Served with AUS, 1942-46. Recipient Outstanding Service awards Sigma Pi Alpha, 1971. Mem. Am. Polit. Sci. Assn., Am. Sociol. Soc., Ala. State Tchrs. Assn., Am. Hist. Assn., Assn. Social Sci. Tchrs., Internat. Platform Assn., Alpha Phi Alpha (award 1971). Baptist. Contbr. articles to profl. jours. Home: 416 56th St Fairfield AL 35064 Office: Miles Coll Birmingham AL 35064

OLIVER, LOUIS CECIL, cotton exchange exec.; b. Galveston, Tex., Jan. 18, 1921; s. Louis Green and Cecil (Barker) O.; ed. pub. schs.; m. Julia Manell Lloyd, Dec. 14, 1940; children—Judith Ann (Mrs. James Alvin Hogan), Nancy Evelyn (Mrs. Charles E. Scott), Ellen Jane. Accountant, Todd Shipyards Corp., Galveston, 1941-44 chief clk. Galveston Cotton Exchange and Bd. of Trade, 1946-64, sec., 1965—; pres. Ford & Oliver Accounting Service, 1966—, Sloane & Oliver Enterprises, 1968—. Chief clk. Galveston Maritime Assn., 1946-63, sec., 1964-68; chief insp. so. delivery points N.Y. Cotton Exchange Inspection Bur., Galveston, 1967—. Served with USNR, 1944-46. Baptist (chmn. bd. 1955-61, chmn. trustees 1957-60, treas. Galveston County Bapt. Assn. 1967—). Mason. Home: 1031 Yupon Dr La Marque TX 77568 Office: 2102 Av C Galveston TX 77550

OLIVER, L(UCIEN) E., dept. store exec.; b. Union, Ore., Jan. 7, 1906; s. Charles Ervin and Edna E. (Remillard) O.; grad. U. Ida., 1926; m. Nava L. Woodard, July 13, 1929; children—Joyce (Mrs. B. Jorgensen), Carol (Mrs. Robert Price), Gayle (Mrs. R. W. Ide, III), Julie (Mrs. Paul Freudenstein). With J.C. Penney Co., 1925-29; store mgr. Montgomery Ward, 1929-33; pres. Western Industries, Monterey, Cal., 1932-33; joined Sears, Roebuck & Co., 1933, dist. sales mgr., 1937-40, nat. retail mdse. mgr., 1949-52, gen. mgr. N.Y.C. office, 1952-58, v.p., 1958—, dir., 1959—; pres. Henry Rose Stores, Inc. (subsidiary of Sears, Roebuck & Co., liquidated, 1955), 1952-55, chmn. bd., 1954-55; chmn. bd. Colonial Stores, Inc.; dir. Allstate Ins. Co., First Nat. Bank of Atlanta, L. & N. R.R. Co., West Point-Pepperell Co. Chmn. Atlanta Arts Alliance. Mem. C. of C. (dir.), Delta Chi, Eta Mu Pi (hon.), Beta Gamma Sigma (hon.). Clubs: Commerce, Piedmont Driving, Capital City, Peachtree Golf (Atlanta); N.Y. Athletic; International (Chgo.). Home: 2222 Mt Paran Rd NW Atlanta GA 30327 Office: PO Box 4358 Atlanta GA 30302

OLIVER, MARY WILHELMINA, law librarian, educator; b. Cumberland, Md., May 4, 1919; d. John Arlington and Sophia (Lear) Oliver; A.B., Western Md. Coll., 1940; B.S. in Library Sci., Drexel Inst. Tech., 1943; J.D., U. N.C., 1951. Asst. circulation librarian N.J. Coll. Women, 1943-45; asst. in law library U. Va., 1945-47; asst. reference, social sci. librarian Drake U., 1947-49; research asst. Inst. Govt., U. N.C., 1951-52, asst. law librarian, 1952-55, asst. prof. law, law librarian, 1955-59, asso. prof. law, law librarian, 1959-69, prof. law and library sci., law librarian, 1969—; admitted to N.C. bar, 1951. Mem. Am. Assn. Law Libraries (pres. elect 1971), Spl. Libraries Assn., Am., N.C. bar assns., Assn. Am. Law Schs., Am. Soc. Legal History, Law Alumni Assn. U. N.C., Inc., Internat. Assn. Law Libraries, Seldon Soc., Order of Coif. Home: Box 733 Chapel Hill NC 27514

OLIVER, PRISCILLA LOWELL FOOTE (MRS. KEITH OLIVER), civic worker, physician; b. Caldwell, N.J., Dec. 28, 1920; d. Lowell Sanborn and Grace (Allen) Foote; A.B., Vassar Coll., 1941; M.D., U. Rochester, 1945; m. Keith Millner Oliver, Sept. 4, 1948; children—Priscilla Hope, Nancy Allen, Faith Sanborn, Wendy Carol, Susan Millner, Keith Miller. Jr. lab technician Rochester Health Dept., 1941-42; intern Duke, 1945-46, asst. resident, 1946-48; gen. practitioner medicine, Purcellville, Va., 1948-50; clinician Loudoun County Health Dept. Leesburg, Va., 1967—; mem. staff Loudoun Meml. Hosp., Leesburg. Chmn. dept. health Jr. Women's Club, 1955; mem. adv. bd. Loudon County Guidance Clinic, 1958—; pres. Loudoun County Easter Seal Soc., 1960—; bd. dirs. Girl Scout Council, Washington, 1966-71; social chmn. vestry Madison Parish, Purcellville, 1969-72; cons. Girl Scouts U.S.A., 1965—, tng. coordinator, 1969—, outdoor trainer, 1971—, day camp dir., 1971-72. Mem. Alpha Omega Alpha. Home: Route 1 Leesburg VA 22075 Office: Loudoun County Health Dept King St Leesburg VA 22075

OLIVER, WILLIAM ALBERT, JR., paleontologist; b. Columbus, O., June 26, 1926; s. William Albert and Mary-Maud (Thompson) O.; B.S., U. Ill., 1948; M.A., Cornell U., 1950; Ph.D., 1952; m. Johanna L. Kramer, Sept. 1, 1948; children—Robert A., James A. Instr., asst. prof. geology Brown U., Providence, 1952-57; research geologist-paleontology U.S. Geol. Survey, Washington, 1957—. Served with USNR, 1944-46. Fellow Geol. Soc. Am.; mem. Paleontol. Soc. (councilor 1964-69, editor Jour. 1964-69), Palaeontol. Assn. (London), A.A.A.S. Contbr. articles to profl. jours. Home: 4203 McCain Ct Kensington MD 20795 Office: E305 Nat Mus Bldg Washington DC 20560

OLIVER, WILLIAM BURNS, food products mfg. exec.; b. Chateaugay, N.Y., Oct. 3, 1911; s. T. Arthur and Myrtle Viola (Burns) O.; B.S., Ind. U., 1934; m. Agnes Cluthe, Sept. 28, 1934. Auditor, Haskins & Sells, N.Y.C., also Atlanta, 1935-39; sec.-treas. Frito-Lay, Inc. (formerly H. W. Lay & Co., Inc.), Atlanta, 1939-42, v.p. sales, 1946-50, exec. v.p., 1950-61, exec. v.p., dir. Frito-Lay, Inc., Dallas, 1961-66, became pres., dir., 1966, now chmn. bd. 1967—; v.p., dir. Pepsi Co., Inc. Bd. dirs. State Fair of Tex.; past dir. Atlanta Freight Bur.; mem. budget com. United Fund, Atlanta; past dir. Jr. Achievement of Ga.; bd. dirs. Jr. Achievement of Dallas, United Fund Dallas; mem. exec. bd. Circle 10 council Boy Scouts Am.; mem. adv. bd. Salvation Army. Served to maj. USAAF, 1942-46. Mem. Internat. Potato Chip Inst. (past pres.), Lambda Chi Alpha. Presbyn. Mason (Shriner). Clubs: Peachtree Golf (Atlanta); Brook Hollow Golf, Preston Trail Golf (Dallas). Home: 3310 Fairmount St Dallas TX 75201 Office: Frito-Lay Tower Dallas TX 75235

OLIVER, WILLIAM HAYES, dentist; b. Smithfield, N.C., Oct. 29, 1920; s. Rayford Gaston and Lyda Edna (Holt) O.; student The Citadel, 1937-39; B.S., Wake Forest U., 1941; D.D.S., Emory U., 1949; m. Cora Rena Williams, Oct. 12, 1941; children—William Rayford, Frank Hayes. Gen. practice dentistry, Four Oaks, N.C., 1949-54, Smithfield, 1956—. Adv., N.C. Dental Assts. Assn., 1965—. Commr., Four Oaks, N.C., 1951-54, Smithfield, 1963-67; mem. Smithfield Johnston County Library Planning Bd., 1963-67; mem. Johnston County Bd. Health, 1958—. Mem. Smithfield Dist. Sch. Bd., 1962-65. Served with USAF, 1954-56. Fellow Am. Coll. Dentists; mem. Am., N.C., Johnston County (treas. 1968—) dental socs., Fourth Dist. Dental Soc. (pres. 1965-66), Am. Legion, Delta Sigma Delta. Mem. Disciples of Christ Ch. (deacon, elder, trustee, treas. 1965—). Mason (Shriner.) Contbr. articles to profl. pubs. Home: 807 Vermont St Smithfield NC 27577 Office: 714 Wilkins St Smithfield NC 27577

OLIVER, WILLIAM HUNTLEY, dentist; b. Nashville, Aug. 4, 1920; s. Oren A. and Floy L. (Huntley) O.; student Vanderbilt U., 1938-40; D.M.D., U. Louisville, 1943; m. Gray Moore, Nov. 27, 1943; children— William Huntley, Douglass M., Gray A., Floy A. Pvt. practice dentistry, specializing in orthodontics, Nashville, 1946—; vis. instr. orthodontics Washington U., U. Mo. at Kansas City, U. N.C., Meharry Med. Coll. Dir. United Savs. Life of Tenn. Mem. Tenn. Pub. Health Council, 1965—. Bd. dirs. Bill Wilkerson Speech and Hearing Center, 1960-66, Nashville Cancer Soc., 1965. Served with USNR, 1943-46. Ky. Col. Diplomate Am. Bd. Orthodontics. Fellow Am. Coll. Dentists, Internat. Coll. Dentists; mem. Nashville Dental Soc. (past pres.), So. Soc. Orthodontics (past pres.), Pierre Fauchard Acad., Phi Delta Theta. Presbyn. (elder). Mason (Shriner), Rotarian. Club: Belle Meade Country. Editor, pub. Orthodontic Directory of the World, 1965—. Home: 229 Deer Park Dr Nashville TN 37205 Office: 1915 Broadway Nashville TN 37203

OLIVERA, OTTO, educator; b. Pedro Betancourt, Cuba, Apr. 20, 1919; s. Jose Francisco and Gregoria (Ibarra) O.; Doctorado en Filosofia y Letras, U. Havana, 1945; M.A., La. State U., 1947; Ph.D., Tulane U., 1953; m. Ruth Ritchey, Dec. 27, 1950; children— Deborah Ann, Rebecca Ruth, Maria Elena. Came to U.S., 1946, naturalized, 1957. Faculty, Syracuse (N.Y.) U., 1954-65, asst. prof., 1954-58, asso. prof. Spanish, Portuguese, 1958-65, prof., 1965; prof. Tulane U., New Orleans, 1965—. Mem. Am. Assn. U. Profs. Modern Lang. Assn., Am. Assn. Tchrs. Spanish and Portuguese, Inst. Internat. Lit. Iberoamericana. Author: Breve Historia de la Literatura Antiliana, 1957; Cuba en su Poesia, 1965; (with A.M. Vazquez) La Prosa modernista en Hispanoamerica, 1971. Home: 6 Trianon Plaza New Orleans LA 70125

OLIVIERI-CINTRON, ELMER, univ. dean; b. Mayaguez, P.R., Feb. 24, 1929; s. Leonardo Olivieri and Rosa A. Cintron; B.S., U. P.R., 1952; M.S., Tex. A. and M., 1958; m. Milka Gonzalez, Sept. 30, 1950; children— Milka, Lauro, Gino. Instr. U. P.R., 1954-58, head materials lab., 1958-65, dean engring. 1965—. Field engr. Found. engring. 1952; cons. various engring. firms, materials, concrete, soils, 1958. Served to 1st lt. AUS, 1952-54. Mem. Am. Concrete Inst., Am. Soc. C.E., Am. Soc. Engring. Edn., Soc. Structural Engrs. of P.R., P.R. Assn. Engring. Architecture and Surveying, Sigma Xi, Tau Beta Pi, Phi Kappa Phi, Phi Delta Gamma. Rotarian. Contbr. articles to profl. jours. Home: College Station Mayaguez PR 00708

OLKIN, ALAN JAY, computer co. exec.; b. Rockaway Beach, N.Y., Dec. 31, 1940; s. Milton Victor and Josepha Amelia (Goldberg) O.; B.S.E.E., U. Miami, 1963; m. Joan Oppenheim, Nov. 24, 1963; children— Terry Michael, Jeffrey Craig. With Boeing Co., Seattle, Wash. and Huntsville, Ala., 1963-64; research and devel. engr. Systems Engring. Labs., Fort Lauderdale, Fla., 1964-67; v.p., co-founder Datacraft Corp., 1967—, also dir. Mem. Assn. for Computer Machinery. Club: Skylake Optimist (North Miami Beach, Fla.). Home: 19830 NE 19th Av North Miami Beach FL 33162 Office: PO Box 23550 Fort Lauderdale FL 33307

OLMO, JAIME ALBERTO, physician; b. Berceloneta, P.R., Aug. 28, 1930; s. Juan and Emilia (Gonzalez) O.; B.S., U. P.R., 1950; M.D. Santiago deCompostela (Spain), 1956; m. Joaquina Rivas, June 24, 1954; children—Jaime A., Carlos A., Rosa I., Javier A., Ruth de Lourdes (dec.). Intern Auxillo Mutuo Hosp., Hato Rey, P.R., 1956-57; med. dir. Municipal Hosp., Aibonito, P.R., 1957-58; resident Doctors Hosp., Santurce, P.R., 1958-59; practice gen. medicine, Rio Piedras, P.R., 1959—; mem. staff Doctors Hosp., Hosp. San Carlos (both Santurce), Auxilio Mutuo, Tchrs. hosps. (both Hato Rey). Treas. Assn. Antituberculosa San Juan, 1959-68, v.p., 1968-69; mem. Instituto Culture Hispanica, Madrid, Spain, 1963—; active P.R. council Boy Scouts Am., 1965—, pres. Dist. No. 2, 1971—; pres. P.T.A., Consuelo Escalona Sch., Carolina, P.R., 1969-71, now bd. dirs.; treas. Inst. Puertorriqueno de Cultura Hispanica, 1971—. Decorated knight Corpus Christi, Toledo, Spain, 1970; recipient Scouters Key, 1967, Pelican award, 1968, Guajataka award, 1970, Silver Beaver award, 1971, all Boy Scouts Am. Mem. P.R. Med. Assn. (pres. Eastern dist. 1971), Am. Acad. Gen. Practice, Asociacion Graduados Universdades Espanolas (pres. 1964), A.M.A., Assn. Physicians, Surgeons. Roman Catholic. Home: 920 Josefa Gil de la Madrid Rio Piedras PR 00924 Office: 923 Carmen Hernandez Rio Piedras PR 00924

OLMSTED, GEORGE BICE, former govt. scientist; b. Edinburg, Ind., Apr. 28, 1918; s. Walter E. and Maggie (Crook) O.; A.B., De Pauw U., 1939; postgrad. U. Wis., 1939-41; m. Lois Anne Martin, Mar. 5, 1949; 1dau., Nancy Anne. Physicist, Naval Ordnance Lab., White Oak, Md., 1941-48; asst. tech. dir. USAF Tech. Applications Center, Alexandria, Va., 1948-72, ret. Sci. adviser to Western Delegation at Conf. of Experts on nuclear test cessation, Geneva, Switzerland, summer 1958. Recipient exceptional civilian service awards USAF, 1955, 58. Mem. Am. Phys. Soc., Am. Geophys. Union, Sigma Xi, Phi Beta Kappa. Methodist (lay leader 1964, 65). Home: 1117 Westmoreland Rd Alexandria VA 22308

OLMSTED, JERAULD LOCKWOOD, credit co. exec.; b. Des Moines, Aug. 26, 1938; s. George Hamden and Virginia (Camp) O.; B.S., Ia. State U., 1961; m. Karen Autenrieth, June 28, 1962; children—Scott, Victoria, Jerauld Lockwood. With 1st Nat. Bank Washington, 1963-69, v.p., 1968-69; v.p. Intermediate Credit Corp, Washington, 1969—, also dir.; dir. Ia. Capital Corp., Washington, Financial Realty Corp., Washington, Universal Lockport Corp., Chgo. Served with AUS, 1961-63. Club: University (Washington). Home: 3712 N Woodrow St Arlington VA 22207 Office: 1701 Pennsylvania Av NW Washington DC 20006

OLSEN, MARVIN N., aircraft co. exec.; b. Duluth, Minn., Oct. 24, 1907; s. Matt and Sofie (Simonsen) O.; B.S., U. Minn., 1929; M.S., Ia. State U., 1946; postgrad. Cornell U., 1948, Harvard, 1950, Mass. Inst. Tech., 1951; m. Marjorie Wolfe, Dec. 28, 1931; children— Donna (Mrs. John Satterfield), Susan. Prof., Ia. State U., 1941-46; prof. Wells Coll., 1946-51; rocketry research mgr. Reaction Motors, Inc., Denville, N.J., 1951-58; tech. mgr. operations mgr. TRW, Inc. Aerospace, Cape Canaveral, Fla., 1958—; exec. dir. Retro, Inc. Pres., bd. dirs. Community Services Council, United Fund. Mem. Am. Assn. U. Profs., A.A.A.S., Am. Inst. Aeros. and Astronautics (sect. chmn.), Am. Phys. Soc., Mental Health Assn. Home: 577 Capri Rd Cocoa Beach FL 32931 Office: 7001 N Atlantic Av Cape Canaveral FL 32932

OLSON, ALLAN LEROY, economist; b. Grand Forks, N.D., Mar. 25, 1935; s. Mancur Lloyd and Clara (Fuglesten) O.; B.S., N.D. State U., 1957; M.A., U. Minn., 1962 Research asst., instr. U. Minn., 1957-61; supervisory enumerator U.S. Dept. Agr., St. Paul, 1961-62, marketing research specialist, Washington, 1962-65; economist Office Bus. Econs., U.S. Dept. Commerce, Washington, 1965—, Mem. Am. Econ. Assn., Am. Statis. Assn. Home: 1001 3d St Washington DC 20024 Office: 2400 M St Washington DC 20230

OLSON, BURNEY KATHARINE MCAULEY (MRS. RUSSELL H. OLSON), social worker; b. Holly Springs, Miss.; d. Angus Malcolm and Van Burney (Deaton) McAuley; student Superior State Tchrs. Coll., 1931-32, Miss. Synodical Coll., 1932-33; B.S., U. Minn., 1936; M.D. in Social Work, U. Tenn., 1957; m. Russell Howard Olson, Aug. 9, 1938. Caseworker Children's Bur., Memphis, 1953-56, 57-61; caseworker Hope Cottage, Children's Bur., Dallas, 1961-64, dir. child care services, Dallas, 1964—. Mem. Nat. Assn. Social Workers, Chi Omega. Presbyn. Home: 10564 Royal Club Lane Dallas TX 75229 Office: 2301 Welborn St Dallas TX 75219

OLSON, DELMAR WALTER, educator; b. Alden, Minn., June 23, 1909; s. Walter and Nina Dagmar (Christenson) O.; B.S. in Indsl. Arts, Ia. State U., 1934; M.A., Ohio State U., 1937, Ph.D., 1957; m. Irene Marie Mikulecky, Oct. 10, 1936; children—Jonny D., Marene Marie (Mrs. Joseph Weinraub). Prof. indsl. arts Stanford U., Philippines, 1957-59; prof. indsl. arts Kent State U., 1943-63, chmn. dept. indsl. arts and tech., 1963-67; coordinator grad. study in indsl. arts N.C. State U., Raleigh, N.C., 1967—; exec. dir. Epsilon Pi Tau, Inc., 1971—; ednl. cons. Mem. Stow (O.) Bd. Edn., 1951-54, Stow Community Council, 1951-54. Recipient Laureate and Honors citation Epsilon Pi Tau, 1959. Mem. Am. Indsl. Arts Assn. (pres. 1968-69), S.E. Indsl. Arts Conf. (pres. 1970-71), N.E.A., Newcomen Soc. Eng., Am. Council for Indsl. Arts Tchr. Edn., Am. Council for Elementary Sch. Indsl. Arts, N.C. Assn. Educators, Phi Kappa Phi, Phi Delta Kappa. Author: (with Federico Costales) Ceramics for Schools and Industry in Developing Countries, 1960, Comparative Crafts, South Pacific, 1970, Industrial Arts and Technology, 1963, Technology and Industrial Arts, 1958, Industrial Arts for the General Shop, 1967, Teoria Y Practica Del Taller Industrial, 1964, Woods and Woodworking for Industrial Arts, 1965. Home: 518 Dixie Trail Raleigh NC 27607

OLSON, EDNA HOWARD (MRS. LAWRENCE CARROLL OLSON), librarian; b. nr. Dawsonville, Ga.; d. William Stevens and Esty (Dooley) Howard; B.C.S., Ga. State U., 1950; M. Librarian, Emory U., 1955; m. Lawrence Carroll Olson, Mar. 4, 1939 (dec. Oct. 1953); children—Lawrence Howard, Wayne Carroll, Edna Margaret. Librarian, Ga. Agrl. Expt. Sta., 1949—. Trustee Flint River Regional Library, Griffin, Ga. Mem. Internat. Assn. Agrl. Librarians and Documentalists, Am., Southeastern, Ga. (sec. 1961-63) library assns., Am. Library Trustees Assn., Delta Mu Delta. Baptist. Home: 733 E College St Griffin GA 30223 Office: Ga Agrl Expt Sta Experiment GA 30212

OLSON, ENAR BUSTER, govt. ofcl.; b. San Diego, Cal., Feb. 10, 1914; s. Edward S. and Ida (Troback) O.; A.B. in Polit. Sci. and Econs. magna cum laude, Whitman Coll., 1937; M.S. in Pub. Adminstrn. (Rockefeller fellow in pub. adminstrn. 1937-39), Syracuse U., 1939; m. Frances E. Hoagland, Dec. 17, 1939; children—Bruce E., V. Kristine. With Soil Conservation Service, Dept. Agr., 1939-40; asst. dir. personnel WPB, 1941-42; mgmt. specialist Office of Sec., Dept. Commerce, 1946-48; orgn. and methods officer CAA, 1949-51, dep. dir. aero. center, Oklahoma City, 1951-54, dep. regional adminstr., Honolulu, 1954-56; dir. adminstrn. Northwest Orient Airlines, St. Paul, 1956-57; dep. dir. aero. center Oklahoma City, FAA, 1957-60; dir. Fed. Aviation Agy. Acad. Oklahoma City, 1960-64; exec. officer FAA, Southwest region, Ft. Worth, 1964—. Chmn. study group on orgn. U.S. Dept. Transp. Mayor, Silver Lake, 1961-63. Served to maj. USAAF, 1942-46, ETO. Recipient Meritorious award FAA. Mem. Am. Soc. Public Adminstrn., Phi Beta Kappa, Phi Delta Theta. Presbyn. (elder). Home: 107 Linda Lane Granbury TX 76048 Office: PO Box 1689 Forth Worth TX 76107

OLSON, JAY D., govt. ofcl.; b. Stromsburg, Neb., Nov. 2, 1925; s. Russell B. and Pearl (Nelson) O.; B.A., U. Tulsa, 1950, M.A., 1958; M.S.W., U. Okla., 1963; m. Jerrie Jean Rogers, Apr. 16, 1955; children—Bradley, Adrian. Probation officer Tulsa Juvenile Court, 1950-56, dir., 1956-61; juvenile ct. and probation cons. U.S. Dept. Health, Edn. and Welfare, Washington, 1963-69, juvenile delinquency program specialist, 1969-71, dep. dir. div. program devel. Youth Devel. and Delinquency Prevention Adminstrn., 1971—. Spl. cons., mem. Nat. Council on Crime and Delinquency. Served with AUS, 1944-46; ETO. Mem. Gov. of Md.'s Commn. on Law Enforcement and Adminstrn. of Justice, 1968—. Home: 13117 Tamarack Rd Silver Spring MD 20909 Office: US Dept Health Edn and Welfare 3d and Independence Sts Washington DC 20201

OLSON, ORDELL PENDOR, govt. ofcl.; b. Lisbon, N.D., Jan. 4, 1930; s. Jens M. and Clara (Munkeby) O.; B.S., N.D. State U., 1953; postgrad. (Fulbright scholar), U. Oslo, 1953-54; M.S., S.D. State U., 1959, Ph.D., 1963; m. Marjorie Sauer Ott, June 20, 1959; children—Jennifer, Mark. Faculty, N.D. State U., Fargo, 1954-61, Ore. State U., Corvallis, 1963-64, Monmouth (Ill.) Coll., 1964-69; bd. govs. Federal Res. System, Washington 1969—. Mem. Am., Midwest econ. assns., Phi Kappa Phi, Kappa Delta Pi. Home: 937 N VanDorn St Alexandria VA 22304 Office: 20th and Constitution Washington DC 20551

OLSON, ROBERT HOWARD, architect; b. Chgo., Jan. 13, 1928; s. Bernard and Edna (Karnett) O.; student Wilson Sch. Engring., 1950-53; m. Marie Boughman, June 12, 1948; children—Robert Bernard, Kenneth Edward, Eric Wayne, Jon Karnett. With Coffey &

Olson, architects, Lenoir, N.C., 1948-62; architect Olson Assos., 1962-67, Harrell Clark & Assos., Hickory, 1967-72, Folger-Olson &Asso., Morganton, N.C., 1972—. Instr., Caldwell Community Coll., Lenoir, N.C., 1969—; tchr. Caldwell County Schs., 1964-66. Mem. career ednl. com. Hickory City Sch. Adminstrv. Dept., 1971—. Served with AUS, 1946-48. Mem. A.I.A. (chpt. legal com. 1963-64), Catawba Valley Council Architects (dir. 1969), Western N.C. Council Architects (pres. 1964). Home: 409 Westview St Lenoir NC 28645 Office: 204 S Sterling St Morganton NC 28655

OLSON, WILLIAM ANDREAS, lawyer, city ofcl.; b. Waco, Tex., July 1, 1923; s. Ernest A. and Beth (Fuller) O.; LL.B., Baylor U., 1950; m. Virginia Malloy, Feb. 14, 1942; children—Suzanne (Mrs. Larry S. Waldrep), William Andresas, John F., Judy C. Admitted to Tex. bar, 1950; pvt. practice law, Waco, Tex., 1950-58; gen. counsel Tex. Municipal League, Austin, 1958-63; with firm Vinson, Elkins, Weems & Searls, Houston, 1963-64; pvt. practice law, Austin, Tex., 1964-65; city atty., Houston, 1966—. Mem. adv. bd. Center for Municipal Legal Studies, Southwestern Legal Found., Dallas; mem. Gov.'s Tex. Urban Devel. Commn., 1970—; bd. dirs. Tex. Municipal League. Served with AUS, 1942-46; ETO. Mem. State Bar of Tex. (mem. Tex. constn. com.), Tex. City Attys. Assn. (pres. 1968-69). Home: 9900 Memorial Dr Houston TX 77024 Office: 300 City Hall Bagby St Houston TX 77002

OLTMAN, FLORINE ALMA, librarian; b. Flatonia, Tex., Nov. 13, 1915; d. Louis B. and Almeda (Scarborough) Oltman; B.A., S.W. Tex. State Tchrs. Coll., 1937; B.S. in Library Sci., U. Denver, 1942. Tchr., librarian high sch., Eagle Lake, Weslaco and Port Neches, Tex., 1937-43; librarian U.S. Naval Air Sta., U.S. Naval Hosp., Pensacola, Fla., 1943-46; cataloger U.S. Air U. Library, Maxwell AFB, 1946-47; librarian USAF Spl. Staff Sch., Craig AFB, 1947-50; reference librarian Air U. Library, Maxwell AFB, 1950-55, librarian Air War Coll., 1955-58; chief bibliog. br. Air U. Library, Maxwell AFB, Ala., 1958-71, chief reference br., 1971-72, chief reader services div., 1972—. Mem. Am. Assn. U. Women (2d v.p. 1964), Ala. (sec. 1956), Southeastern library assns., Spl. Libraries Assn. (pres. Ala. chpt. 1956, sec. mil. library div. 1954, chmn. mil. library div. 1959-60, 2d v.p. 1961-62, pres. 1970-71), Partners for the Alliance, English-Speaking Union. Methodist. Club: Espanol. Home: 219 E Riding Rd Montgomery AL 36111 Office: Air U Library Maxwell AFB Montgomery AL 36112

OLTMAN, ROY EDWIN, hydraulic engr.; b. Mpls., Nov. 16, 1911; s. Charles Albert and Lucy Caroline (Hennings) O.; B.C.E., U. Minn., 1933; m. Evelyn C. Powell, June 20, 1939; children—Maria (Mrs. Herbert Barlow), Mark, Mary. With topographic div. U.S. Geol. Survey, 1934-35, with water resources div., 1938-43, 46—, asst. chief hydrologist for research and tech. coordination Washington, 1971—. Served with USNR, 1935-37, to lt. 1943-46. Recipient Distinguished Service award U.S. Dept. Interior, 1971. Fellow Am. Soc. C.E.; mem. Nat. Soc. Profl. Engrs., Am. Water Works Assn., Am. Soc. Photogrammetry, Am. Geophys. Union. Mason (32 deg.). Home: 1006 Parker St Falls Church VA 22046 Office: Room 2226 General Services Bldg 18th and E Sts NW Washington DC 20242

OLTMAN, RUTH MARIE, educator, psychologist; b. Cleve.; d. Rudolph Carl and Ida (Schroeder) Oltman; A.B., Oberlin Coll., 1934; M.A., Western Res. U., 1951, Ph.D., 1961. Contact rep. VA, Cleve., 1946-51 adminstrv. asst. (personnel) Navy Finance Center, Cleve., 1951-55; counselor, psychologist Vocational Guidance and Rehab. Services, Cleve., 1955-62; dean of women Baldwin-Wallace Coll., Berea, O., 1962-69; staff asso., higher edn. Am. Assn. U. Women, Washington, 1969—. lectr. in psychology Cleve. Coll. of Western Res. U., 1952-53, Baldwin-Wallace Co., 1962. Served as lt. WAVES, 1942-46. Mem. Am. Psychol. Assn., Nat. Assn. Deans Women, Am. Personnel and Guidance Assn., Zonta, Phi Delta Gamma. Methodist. Home: 3760 Persimmon Circle Fairfax VA 22030 Office: 2401 Virginia Av NW Washington DC 20037

O'MALLEY, CHARLES JOHN, ednl. adminstr.; b. Chgo., May 3, 1935; s. Charles Borremeo and Aurelia Helen (Wisniewski) O'M.; student Loyola U., Chgo., 1952-54; B.S., DePaul U., 1957; postgrad. Northwestern U., 1959, U. Miami, 1960-62, Barry Coll., 1961; M.S., Emerson Coll., 1964, Cath. U., 1969; m. Nancy Marie Paino, Feb. 1, 1969; children—Colleen Marie, Sean Michael. Tchr., coach Queen of All Saints Sch., Chgo., 1953-56, St. Giles Sch., Oak Park, Ill., 1957, St. Thomas Aquinas High Sch., Ft. Lauderdale, Fla., 1959-67; tchr. Immaculate Conception Sch., Highland Park, Ill., 1958-59; asst. supt. schs. Diocese of Miami, 1967-69. Playground supr. Chgo. Bd. Edn., 1951-58; mem. Archdiocese of Miami Sch. Bd., 1967-69; mem. Fla. Instructional TV Bd., 1967-69; mem. Title II adv. bd. Fla. Dept. Edn., 1967-69; mem. Broward and Palm Beach Counties Title I Bd., 1967-71, Leon County Title I Bd., 1970—. Mem. youth service steering com. Dade County chpt. A.R.C., 1967-69; mem. coordinating group Broward County Econ. Opportunity, 1967-69. Mem. Broward County Adult Edn. Bd., 1967-69. Served with Ill. N.G., 1958-59. Named one of 10 outstanding men Pompano Beach Jr. C. of C., 1963; recipient Voice of Democracy award V.F.W., 1964. Mem. Nat. Cath. Edn. Assn., Fla. Assn. Acad. Nonpub. Schs. (sec. 1970-72), Speech Assn. Am., New Eng., So., Broward County speech assns., Broward County Tchrs. Speech and English, Cath. Tchrs. Guild, Nat. Cath. Forensic League (pres. Diocese Miami 1963-64), St. Coleman Holy Name Soc. (v.p. 1963-64), Phi Alpha Tau. Republican. Elk. Clubs: Civitan (dir. 1963-64), (Pompano Beach); Leon Quarter Back, Seminole Tip-Off (mem. exec. bd. 1971-72) (Tallahassee, Fla.). Home: 1126 Brandt Dr Tallahassee FL 32303 Office: PO Box 1571 Tallahassee FL 32302

O'MALLEY, WILLIAM JOSEPH, JR., social worker; b. Scranton, Pa., July 7, 1934; s. William J. and Catherine (Culkin) O'M.; B.S., U. Scranton, 1956; M.S.W., Fordham U., 1958; m. Margaret Cleveland, Dec. 28, 1957; children—William Joseph III, Suzanne, Miriam, Richard, Lynne, Mark Scott. Caseworker, Lackawanna County Instn. Dist., Div. Child Welfare, Scranton, Pa., 1958-59; clin. social worker VA Hosp., Wilkes Barre, Pa., 1959-63; commd. ensign USPHS, USN, 1963, advanced through grades to comdr., 1967, dir. social services Spalding Rehab. Hosp., Denver, 1968-69, with Clin. Research Center, Nat. Inst. Mental Health, Lexington, Ky., 1969—, dep. chief Excelsior House, 1972—; chief edn. and tng. sects., 1972—. Mem. Nat. Assn. Social Workers, Commd. Officers Assn. USPHS. Address: Box 2000 Leestown Rd Lexington KY 40507

O'MARA, JOHN DAVID, pub. co. exec.; b. Dubuque, Ia., Dec. 24, 1917; s. David John and Alice Elizabeth (Dunn) O'M.; student Loras Coll., 1937-38; m. Mary N. Mattison, Sept. 5, 1945; children—Janet, Joan. With Telegraph Herald, Dubuque, Ia., 1936-41; with Anniston (Ala.) Star, 1946—, dir. advt., 1968—. Bd. dirs. YMCA, Anniston, 1969. Served with AUS, 1942-46. Mem. Internat. Newspaper Advt. Execs., Ga.-Ala. Newspaper Advt. Assn., Ga.-Ala. Newspaper Assn. (pres. 1967-68). Home: 505 Crestview Rd Anniston AL 36201 Office: 216 W 10th St Anniston AL 36201

O'MELIA, CHARLES RICHARD, educator; b. N.Y.C., Nov. 1, 1934; s. Charles James and Anne Frances (Dobbin) O'M.; B.C.E., Manhattan Coll., 1955; M.S., U. Mich. 1956, Ph.D., 1963; m. Mary Elizabeth Curley, Oct. 27, 1956; children—Kathleen, Mary, Charles, Anne, John, Michael. Asst. engr. Hazen and Sawyer Engrs., New york, 1956-57; asst. prof. Ga. Inst. Tech., Atlanta, 1961-64; fellow, lecturer Harvard U. Cambridge, Mass., 1964-66; asso. prof., U. N.C., Chapel Hill, 1966-70, prof. 1970—. Adviser Environmental Sci. and Tech. Jour., 1972—. Mem. Am. Chem. Soc., Am. Soc. C.E., Am. Water Works Assn., Water Pollution Control Fedn., Am. Soc. Limnology and Oceanography. Home: 607 Churchill Dr Chapel Hill NC 27514

OMER, GUY CLIFTON, JR., scientist, educator; b. Mankato, Kan., Mar. 20, 1912; s. Guy C. and Margaret (Callahan) O.; Ph.D. cum laude, Cal. Inst. Tech., 1947; m. Martha Grace Steer, Sept. 13, 1942; children— Guy C. III, Richard William. Asst. prof. U. Ore., 1949-50; asst. prof. U. Chgo., 1950-55; vis. asst. prof. U. Mich., summer 1953; prof. phys. sci., physics, astronomy U. Fla., Gainesville, 1955—, chmn. dept. phys. scis., 1967—; vis. prof. U. Cal. at Los Angeles, 1964-65. Author: (with Knowles, Mundy and Yoho) Physical Science: Men and Concepts, 1962; contbr. articles to profl. jours. Home: 1080 SW 11th Terrace Gainesville FL 32601

ONCKEN, WILLIAM, JR., mgmt. cons.; b. Buffalo, Apr. 26, 1912; s. William and Eva (Von Knorring) O.; B.S. with honors in Physics, Princeton, 1934; postgrad. Columbia, 1941; m. Margaret Ann Kallina, June 22, 1941; children—William F. III, Ingeborg, John. Dir. civilian tng. Dept. Army, Washington, 1953-56; dir. mgmt. devel. N.Y.C. R.R., N.Y.C., 1956-59; sr. asso. Richardson- Bellows-Henry & Co., N.Y.C., 1959-61; pres. William Oncken Co., Dallas, Seattle, Madison, Wis., N.Y.C., 1961—. Lectr. on ednl. television, Am. Mgmt. Assn., 1963—; prin. lectr. Pres.' Assn., Hamilton, N.Y.; lectr. mgmt. topics various univs., 1963—, Indsl. Coll. Armed Forces (hon. faculty mem.). Served to lt. comdr. USNR, 1942-46. Mem. Kappa Delta Pi. Clubs: Larchmont (N.Y.) Shore; Princeton of N.Y. Contbr. articles to profl., trade jours. Home: 3525 Turtle Creek Dallas TX 75219 Office: Turtle Creek Bldg Dallas TX 75219

O'NEAL, KIRKMAN, steel co. exec.; b. Florence, Ala., June 17, 1890; s. Emmet and Elizabeth (Kirkman) O'N.; student State Tchrs. Coll., Florence, 1905-09; B.S., U.S. Naval Acad., 1909-13; m. Elizabeth Paramore, Oct. 9, 1917; children—Emmett, Elizabeth (Mrs. David H. White). Commd. ensign U.S. Navy, 1913, resigned, 1913, recalled to serve as lt. (s.g.), 1917-19; prodn. engr. Chickasaw Shipbldg. Co., 1919-20, Ingalls Iron Works Co., 1920-21; founder, pres. O'Neal Steel, Inc., Birmingham, Ala., 1921—, now chmn. bd., Ga., Tenn., Fla. and Miss.; chmn. bd. O'Neal Steel, Inc., Del.; dir. Indsl. Paint Co. Bd. dirs. finance com. local chpt. A.R.C.; bd. dirs. Birmingham Civic Symphony, Jr. Achievement of Am.; chmn. bd. dirs. The Kirkman and Elizabeth O'Neal Found. Mem. U.S., Ala., Birmingham chambers commerce, Nat. Assn. Aluminum Distbrs., Am. Warehouse Assn., S. Structural Steel Bd. of Trade, Ala. Hist. Soc., Conf. Bd., N.A.M., Newcomen Soc. N.Am. Presbyn. Clubs: Relay House, Mountain Brook Country, Birmingham Country, Redstone, The Club. Home: 2500 Mountain Brook Pkwy Birmingham AL 35223 Office: 745 N 41st St Birmingham AL 35202

O'NEAL, MASTON EMMETT, JR., former congressman; b. Bainbridge, Ga.; s. Maston Emmett and Bessie (Matthews) O'N.; A.B., Davidson Coll., 1927; postgrad. Emory U. Law Sch.; m. Mary Charlotte Tyson, June 4, 1934; children—Susan Charlotte (Mrs. Jerry Montgomery Bowden), Maston Emmett III. Prin., Shellman High Sch., 1927-28; admitted to practice law, 1930; solicitor gen. Albany Jud. Circuit Ga., 1941-64; mem. 89th-91st Congress from 2d Dist. Ga. Ruling elder Presbyn. Ch. U.S., former moderator Presbytery S.W. Ga. Served to lt. USNR, World War II; PTO. Mem. Solicitors Gen. Assn. Ga. (past pres.), Pi Kappa Alpha. Mason. Home: 805 Alice St Bainbridge GA 31717

O'NEAL, ROBERT PALMER, marine corps officer; b. Tonapah, Nev., Sept. 20, 1912; s. Robert McWilliam and Aimee (Ford) O'N.; A.B., Occidental Coll., 1935, M.A., 1936; m. Nancy Monroe, June 10, 1935; children—Robert M., Nancy B. (Mrs. Thomas Arthur), Patricia M. (Mrs. Marvin Colyer), Peggy F. (Mrs. Ray Perry). Eastern sales mgr. Monroe Chem. Co., Manchester, Conn., 1937-41; insp. naval aircraft, engines Pratt & Whitney Aircraft Corp., East Hartford, Conn., 1941-43; joined USMC, 1944, advanced through grades to lt. col.; aircraft maintenance officer, Japan, 1958-59; material and aircraft maintenance officer, Cherry Point, N.C., 1959-62; mem. Atlantic Task Force Team, 1962-64; coordinator weapons demonstration SEATO reps., Kadena AFB, Okinawa, 1964, coordinator movements 1st Marine Jet Squadron in combat, South Viet Nam, 1965; prodn. officer Japan Aircraft Corp., Ltd., Atsugi, Japan, 1967-69; aircraft maintenance officer, Chu Lai, Viet Nam, 1969-70; Staff AWSS, Norfolk, Va., 1971—. Recipient Adm. Coates Outstanding award, 1966. Fellow Internat. Biog. Assn.; mem. Am. Chem. Soc., A.A.A.S., Soc. Am. Mil. Engrs., Am. Ordnance Assn., Engrs. Joint Council Inc., Am. Inst. Aeros. and Astronautics, Internat. Platform Assn., N.C. Acad. Scis., Am. Mgmt. Assn., Optimists Internat., Delta Upsilon. Office: FMFLANT Staff AWSS Norfolk VA 23511

O'NEAL, RUSSELL AUBREY, utility co. exec.; b. Wauchula, Fla., Dec. 6, 1919; s. Russell A. and Hyacinth May (King) O'N.; student Norman Jr. Coll., 1939-41, Ga. Sch. Tech., 1949-52, Atlanta U., 1966-67, Mass. Inst. Tech., 1944-45; m. Emma Elizabeth Hardin, June 29, 1941; children—Russell Aubrey, Mrs. Richard Jeffers, Patrick O. Mgr., Irwin County Electric Membership Corp., Ocilla, Ga., 1953-55; gen. mgr. Carroll Electric Membership Corp., Carrollton, Ga., 1955—. Technician City of Newman, Ga., 1948-53. Dir. Bankers Underwriters, Atlanta, W. Ga. Fair Assn., Carrollton; sec. Ga. Electric Membership Corp., 1967—; pres. Ga. Rural Electric Service Corp., Reynolds, 1965—. Carroll County commr. Chattahoochee-Flint Area Planning and Devel. Commn., 1967—. Served with USNR, 1942-45. Recipient Nat. Mgmt. Achievement award Nat. Rural Electric Coop. Assn., 1966, Outstanding Service citation Future Farmers Am.; named Outstanding Leader in Agrl. Bus., Farm Bur. C. of C., 1967, Hon. State Farmer, 4-H Clubs, 1963. Mem. Am. Legion, V.F.W., C. of C., Ga. Ruritans, Sportsmen Fedn., Nat. Rural Electric Coop. Assn. (nat. ins. and employee welfare com. 1965—). Lion (past pres.). Mason (Shriner). Home: 246 N Lakeshore Dr Carrollton GA 30117 Office: 523 Dixie St Carrollton GA 30117

O'NEAL, SAPIRO DELBRIDGE, supt. schs.; b. Middlesex, N.C., Dec. 7, 1920; s. A. D. and Rebecca (Narron) O'N.; B.A., Atlantic Christian Coll., 1946; M.A., E. Carolina U., 1952; m. Pauline Elizabeth Lewis, Aug. 5, 1941; children—Delbridge S., Emily E. Tchr., asst. prin. Wendell (N.C.) High Sch., 1946-48; prin. Union High Sch., Engelhard High Sch., N.C., 1948-53, Central High Sch., Elizabeth City, N.C., 1953-59, Plymouth (N.C.) High Sch., 1959-61; supt. Washington County Schs., Plymouth, 1961—. Sec. Tidewater Athletic Conf., 1955. Served with AUS, 1943-46. Mem. N.C. Edn. Assn. (past local pres.), N.E.A., Am. Assn. Sch. Adminstrs., Albermarle Sch. Masters Club (past pres.). Baptist (deacon). Rotarian (past pres.), Kiwanian. Club: Ruritan (Elizabeth City, N.C.). Home: 112 Crescent Dr Plymouth NC 27962 Office: PO Box 747 Courthouse Adam St Plymouth NC 27962

O'NEAL, WILLIAM BERNARD, lawyer; b. Covington, Ky., Oct. 18, 1913; s. William Bernard and Nancy (Callahan) O'N.; LL.B., U. Cin., 1937, J.D.; m. Jacqueline Ewan Wood, Dec. 27, 1942; 1 son, William Bernard III. Admitted to Ohio bar, 1937, Ky. bar, 1938; practice law, Cin., Covington, 1937-39; asso. Matthews & Matthews, Cin., 1939-42; enforcement atty. U.S. Govt., Cin., 1946-47; mem. firm Kilcoyne, O'Neal, Meier & Varnau, and predecessor firm, Cin.; sec. Putman Candies, Inc., Cin.; dir., sec., treas. Strathmore Press, Inc., Cin.; dir. Motch, Inc., Covington, Cin. Prosecutor, Covington, 1952-55; city solicitor, Covington, 1958-62; judge Covington Police and Traffic Ct., 1965—. Served to maj. USMCR, 1942-46. Mem. Marine Corps Res. Officers Assn., Christopher Gist (charter mem.), Ky. hist. socs., Ohio, Ky. Cin., Kenton County (pres. 1958) bar assns. Phi Delta Theta, Phi Delta Phi. Democrat. Episcopalian (vestryman). Clubs: University, Bankers (Cin.), Ft. Mitchell (Ky.) Country, Standard. Home: 2606 Eastern Av Covington KY 41014 Office: Central Trust Tower Cincinnati OH 45202

O'NEIL, SHIRLEY MAE, educator; b. Dover, N.H., Apr. 21, 1927; d. George J. and Marian (Gillis) O'Neil; B.S., U. N.H., 1949; M.S., U. Tenn., 1958; Ph.D., U. Mich., 1966. Tchr., Kents Hill (Me.) Prep. Sch., 1949-51, Old Orchard Beach High Sch., Kents Hill, Me., 1951-53, Farmington (Conn.) Jr.-Sr. High Sch., 1954-57; teaching asst. U. Tenn., Knoxville, 1957-58; supr. student teaching, supr. phys. edn. U. Mich., Ann Arbor, 1958-63; Longwood Coll., Farmville, Va., 1966—. Asst. dir. Girl Scouts Camp Plymouth, Vt., 1954, Camp Brady, N.Y., 1955. Recreation chmn. Heart Fund, Farmville, 1969-70; pub. edn. dir. Farmville exec. com. Humane Soc., 1972. Bd. dirs. Farmville Recreation Assn., 1968-70. Mem. A.A.H.P.E.R., Nat., So. assns. phys. edn. coll. women, So. Dist. Assn. Health, Phys. Edn. and Recreation, N.E.A., Va. Edn. Assn. Home: 2d Av Farmville VA 23901

O'NEILL, CHARLES EDWARDS, clergyman, educator; b. New Orleans, Nov. 16, 1927; s. John Henry and Mary Albion (Edwards) O'N.; A.B., Spring Hill Coll., 1950; S.T.L., Institut St. Louis, Chantilly, France, 1958; H.E.D., Gregorian U., Rome, 1963. Instr., Jesuit High Sch., New Orleans, 1951-54; ordained priest Roman Catholic Ch., 1957; instr. St. Charles Coll., Grand Coteau, La., 1964; asst. prof. Loyola U., New Orleans, 1965-67, asso. prof., 1967-71, prof., 1971—. Vice provincial edn. of Jesuits, New Orleans Province, 1970—. Decorated Palmes Academiques, 1968. Mem. Jesuit History Inst. (Rome), Orgn. Am. Historians, Am. Cath. Hist. Assn. Author: Church and State in French Colonial Louisiana, 1966; Catalogo de Documentos sobre Luisiana...Archivo General de Indias, 1968. Home: 6363 St Charles Av New Orleans LA 70118

O'NEILL, FRANCIS A(LOYSIUS), JR., govt. official; b. Bklyn., Apr. 3, 1908; s. Francis Aloysius and Elizabeth (Evans) O.; A.B., Fordham U., 1929, LL.B., 1932; m. Lillian C. Gerner, Sept. 16, 1939. Admitted to N.Y. State bar, 1933, and practiced law (with father), 1933-39; atty., N.Y. state Labor Relations Bd., 1939-41, trial examiner 1941-43, chief trial examiner, 1946-47; apptd. mem. Nat. Mediation Bd., 1947—, now chmn.; mem. R.R. Wage-Bd. Served USNR, 1943-45; labor relations officer, Cin., 1944-45. Mem. N.Y. County Lawyers Assn., Fordham U. Alumni Assn. Rep. Roman Catholic. K.C. Home: 2151 California St NW Washington DC 20008 also 314 E 41st St New York City NY 10017 Office: Nat Mediation Bd 1230 16th St Washington DC 20572

O'NEILL, JAMES WARD, lawyer; b. N.Y.C., Aug. 20, 1903; s. Charles Joseph and Sarah T. (Ward) O'N.; A.B., Fordham U., 1924, LL.B., 1929; m. Helen M. Foller, Sept. 23, 1933; children—James Ward, Theodore George, Charles Kenneth. Admitted to N.Y. bar, 1930, U.S. Supreme Ct. bar, 1953, numerous fed. cts.; practice in N.Y.C., 1930—; partner firm Haight, Gardner, Poor & Havens, 1947—; lectr. N.Y.U., 1953, Practicing Law Inst., N.Y.C., 1953—. Pres. Faller Devel. Corp., S.I., Moravian Holding Co., S.I. Chmn. Citizens Com. for Erection of Carle Place (N.Y.) High Sch. Bd. govs. Fordham U., 1955-59, Fordham U. Law Sch.; adv. com. Talbot Perkins Adoption Service, Bklyn., 1957—. Fellow Am. Coll. Trial Lawyers; mem. Am. Internat. bar assns., Maritime Law Assn. (exec. com.), N.Y. Law Inst., Average Adjusters Assn., Maritime Exchange Port N.Y., Guild Cath. Lawyers, Fordham Coll. Alumni Assn. (dir. 1953-58), Fordham Law School Alumni Assn. (dir.) Knights of Malta. Clubs: Produce Exchange Luncheon, Propeller (gov.), Downtown Athletic (N.Y.C.); Douglaston, Douglaston Yacht, Squadron, Trade Center, Circumnavigators. Home: 304 Shore Rd Douglaston NY 11363 Office: 80 Broad St New York City NY

O'NEILL, JOSEPH IGNATIUS, JR., oil co. exec.; b. Phila., Oct. 1, 1914; s. Joseph Ignatius and Helen Marie (Byrne) O'N.; B.S., in Commerce, U. Notre Dame, 1937, also postgrad.; postgrad. in law Temple U., 1937-39; m. Catherine C. Cummings, Nov. 26, 1940 (dec. July 1970); children—Helen (Mrs. Jon E. Hansen), Joseph Ignatius, Kevin Patrick, Michael Timothy; m. 2d, Mary Eaton Porter, Mar. 5, 1971. Clk., F.I. duPont & Co., Phila., 1938-39; clk. and spl. agt. Home Ins. Co. of N.Y., N.Y.C. and Atlanta, 1939-42; spl. agt. and supr. FBI, San Francisco and Los Angeles, 1942-46; sales mgr. Van Waters & Rogers, Inc., Los Angeles, 1946-48; owner O'Neill Co., oil operations and investments, Midland, Tex., 1948—; dir. Comml. Bank & Trust Co., Midland. Trustee, U. Notre Dame; bd. govs. Midland Meml. Hosp. Found., 1954-72, pres., 1953. Recipient Silver Goalposts, Sports Illustrated mag., 1961. Mem. Ind. Petroleum Assn. Am. (dir. 1966-68), Permian Basin Petroleum Assn. (1st pres. 1962), U. Notre Dame Alumni Assn. (pres. 1953-67, dir. 1958-72). Home: 22 Oaklawn Park Midland TX 79701 Office: 410 W Ohio St Midland TX 79701

O'NEILL, PAUL HENRY, govt. ofcl.; b. St. Louis, Dec. 4, 1935; s. John Paul and Gaynald (Irvin) O'N.; A.B., Fresno State Coll., 1960; postgrad. Claremont Coll., 1960-61, George Washington U., 1962-65; M.P.A. (Nat. Inst. Pub. Affairs fellow), Ind. U., 1965; m. Nancy J. Wolfe, Sept. 4, 1955; children—Patricia, Margaret, Julie, Paul. Office engr. Kinkaid & King, Anchorage, 1955; site engr. Morrison Knudsen, 1956-57; computer systems analyst VA, Washington, 1961-65; budget examiner Bur. Budget, Washington, 1967-70; chief, human resources programs div. Office of Mgmt. and Budget, 1970, asst. dir. Exec. Office of Pres., 1970—. Chmn. health-welfare coms. Fairfax Fedn. Civic Assns. Mem. Am. Econ. Assn. Home: 5522 Kings Park Dr Springfield VA 22151 Office: Office Mgmt and Budget Washington DC 20503

O'NEILL, WILLIAM F., engring. co. exec.; b. Pitts., Nov. 8, 1908; s. William F. and Christy (Grady) O'N.; grad. U. Pitts.; postgrad. Carnegie Inst. Tech.; m. Jean Perry, Aug. 14, 1934; children—Barbara (dec.), Jack. Mgr. engring. and constrn. Blaw Knox Co., Pitts; founder, pres. Tampa Bay Engring. Co., St. Petersburg, Fla., 1957—; dir. 1st Nat. Bank, Farmers Nat. Life Ins. Co., Columbia (Fla.) Nat. Life Ins. Co., Dynamet, Inc., Pitts. Past pres. St. Petersburg Jr. Achievement, now bd. dirs.; mem. Pinellas (Fla.) County Com. 100, chmn. air and water pollution control com.; chmn. new industries com. Fla. Council 100; bd. dirs. Bayfront Med. Center, All Children's Hosp. Corp., Pinellas County United Fund, Fla. Indsl. Exposition; trustee Sci. Found. Center St. Petersburg, Fla. Presbyn. Coll., St. Petersburg, Gulf Coast Tb and Respiratory Disease Assn. Served with C.E., AUS, World War II. Fellow Presidents' Council, Am. Inst. Mgmt.; mem. Am. Mgmt. Assn. Republican. Presbyn. (deacon). Mason (Shriner). Home: 1345 Snell Harbour Dr St Petersburg FL 33704 Office: Tampa Bay Engring Co PO Box 7236 1355 Snell Isle Blvd St Petersburg FL 33734

ONION, JAMES COLLINS, judge; b. San Antonio, Mar. 27, 1925; s. John Frank and Harriett (Collins) O.; student Trinity U., 1946-47; LL.B., Tex. U., 1950; m. Isabel Mangold, Sept. 1, 1951; children—Janet, James Collins, Robert Frank. Admitted to Tex. bar, 1950; asst. dist. atty., Bexar County, Tex., 1950-56, 1st asst. dist. atty., 1953-56; corp. ct. judge City of San Antonio, 1958-60; partner firm Foster Lewis Langley & Onion, San Antonio, 1960-64; partner Carter, Callender & Onion, San Antonio, 1964—; judge, 73d Dist. Ct., Bexar County, San Antonio, 1969—. Instr. Trinity U., 1960. Served with USMCR, 1944-46; PTO. Mem. Tex., Am., San Antonio (pres. 1968-69) bar assns., Lambda Chi Alpha (past pres.). Baptist. Democrat. Optimist. Home: 121 Aribe Dr San Antonio TX 78216 Office: 73d Dist Ct Bexar County Courthouse San Antonio TX 78204

OOTEN, HOMER ANDREW, univ. adminstr.; b. Oakdale, Tenn., Aug. 30, 1942; s. Clarence Esco and Viola (Hamby) O.; B.S., Tenn. Technol. U., 1963; postgrad. Fla. Inst. Tech., 1966; M.S. (Univ. fellow), Fla. State U., 1969, D.B.A., 1972; m. Pamelia Frances McKinney, June 23, 1961; children—Cynthia Darlene, Terry Bryan. Design engr. DuPont Co., Chattanooga, 1963-64, supr., 1964, project coordinator, 1964-66; project engr., altitude chamber test condr. Bendix Corp., Kennedy Space Center, Fla., 1966-67; aerospace systems analysis engr. Boeing Co., Cocoa Beach, Fla., 1967-69; Univ. fellow Fla. State U., Tallahassee, 1969-70, dir. phys. planning, 1970-72, dir. bus. services, 1972—. Cons. engring. Belefant Assos., Cocoa Beach, Utility Contractors, Titusville, Fla., 1969. Mem. Young Republican Club, Chattanooga, 1964. Registered profl. engr., Fla. Mem. I.E.E.E. (sec. 1969), Soc. Coll., Univ. Planners, Fla. Engring. Soc., Nat. Soc. Profl. Engrs., Tau Beta Pi, Kappa Mu Epsilon, Eta Kappa Nu, Sigma Iota Epsilon (past pres.). Republican. Presbyn. (deacon 1965). Home: 2320 Meath Dr Tallahassee FL 32303 Office: 201 Diffenbaugh Fla State U Tallahassee FL 32306

OPPE, GRETA, educator; b. Galveston, Tex.; d. Frederick and Amelia (Wilde) Oppe; grad. Sam Houston State Tchrs. Coll., 1913; B.A., U. Tex., 1921; M.A., N.Y.U., 1928; postgrad. Harvard, 1941, Syracuse U., 1946, U. Mich., 1952. Tchr. chemistry Galveston pub. schs., 1918-64; chmn. sci. dept. Ball High Sch., 1922-64. Vice pres. Hist. Found.; mem. Friends Rosenberg Library. Recipient Nat. Sci. Tchrs. award for distinguished service, 1954, citation Tex. Assn. Sci. Tchrs., Tex. Acad. Sci., 1957, Sci. Edn. Recognition award, 1964, Distinguished Service award Tex. State Tchrs. Assn., 1964. Fellow Am. Geog. Soc., A.A.A.S.; distinguished fellow Tex. Acad. Sci.; mem. Nat. Assn. For Research Sci. Teaching (life), N.E.A., Tex. Tchrs. Assn., Nat. Sci. Tchrs. Assn. (past So. v.p.), Jr. Acad. Sci. Tex. (past dir.), Tex. Assn. Sci. Tchrs. (life mem.), Tex. Congress Parents and Tchrs., Am. Assn. U. Women, Delta Kappa Gamma. Lutheran (Sunday sch. tchr.). Author: Chemistry, Worktext and lab. manual for high schs. Contbr. articles to profl. jours. Home: 3412 Av R Galveston TX 77550

OPPENHEIMER, JESSE HALFF, lawyer; b. San Antonio, Jan. 4, 1919; s. Jesse D. and Lillie (Halff) O.; student U. Tex., 1935-37; B.A. with honors, U. Ariz., 1939; J.D. cum laude, Harvard, 1942; m. Susan Julia Rosenthal, July 18, 1946; children—Jesse David, Jean Louise, Barbara Sue. Admitted to Tex. bar, 1946; mem. firm Oppenheimer, Rosenthal, & Kelleher, Inc. San Antonio. Former mem. bd. United Fund, Downtown Assn. San Antonio; mem. Steering Com. Met. San Antonio Urban Coalition, 1968-69. Past bd. dirs. Coll.-Community Creative Arts Center, Our Lady of Lake Coll., San Antonio, Symphony Soc. San Antonio, Santa Rosa Children's Hosp., Children's Service Bur., Ursuline Acad. San Antonio; past trustee Robert B. Green Hosp., San Antonio, v.p., trustee Marion Koogler McNay Art Inst., trustee San Antonio, St. Mary's Hall, Jesse H. and Susan R. Oppenheimer Found., Tex. Hosp. Council. Served to lt. col. AUS, 1942-46. Home: 400 Mandalay Dr East San Antonio TX 78212 Office: Suite 620 711 Navarro St San Antonio TX 78205

OPPENLANDER, ROBERT, airline exec.; b. Bklyn., May 20, 1923; s. Robert and Lillian (Ahrens) O.; B.S., Mass. Inst. Tech., 1944; M.B.A., Harvard, 1948; m. Jessie I. Major, Sept. 30, 1950; children—Kris, Robert Kirk, Tenley. With Metals & Controls Corp., Attleboro, Mass., 1948-53; prin. Cresap, McCormick & Paget, N.Y.C., 1953-58; comptroller, treas. Delta Air Lines, Inc., Atlanta, 1958—, v.p. finance, 1964-67, sr. v.p. finance, treas., 1967—, dir., 1968—. Served to lt. USNR, 1944-46. Mem. Financial Execs. Inst., Tau Beta Pi, Phi Kappa Sigma. Club: Capital City. Home: 3944 Powers Ferry Rd NW Atlanta GA 30342 Office: Delta Air Lines Inc Hartsfield Atlanta Internat Airport Atlanta GA 30320

ORCHARD, JAMES MADISON, hotel exec.; b. Chgo., May 6, 1919; s. Francis M. and Amy (Hunter) O.; student Hill Sch., Pottstown, Pa., 1937-39; B.A., Wesleyan U., 1943, M.A., 1947; m. Bette M. Pohle, Nov. 23, 1942; children—Virginia (Mrs. Chi Ming Tan), Barbara. Program mgr. Sta. WJAR-TV, Providence, 1948-49, Sta. KOTV, Tulsa, 1949-50; account exec. Paramount TV Prodns., N.Y.C., 1950-52, CBS-TV Films, N.Y.C., 1952-56, Sta. WABC-TV, N.Y.C., 1956-58, Lux Brill Films, N.Y.C., 1960-63; prodn. mgr. CBS Network, N.Y.C., 1958-63; marketing mgr. Grumman Aerospace Co., Bethpage, N.Y., 1963-70; mgr. Howard Johnson's Motor Lodge, Islamorada, Fla., 1971—. Served to lt. USNR, 1942-46. Home: 84775 Old Rd Islamorada FL 33036 Office: PO Box 224 Islamorado FL 33036

ORCI PESQUEIRA, LUIS, Mexican diplomat. Consul from Mexico, Houston. Office: World Trade Bldg Houston TX 77002*

ORCUTT, CARROL WARREN, former, newspaper editor; b. Aurora, Ill., Dec. 2, 1901; s. Eugene Grant and Emma (Allison) O.; student Wabash Coll., Crawfordsville, Ind., 1921-24; m. Noma Decker, 1945; children—William Decker, James Allison, Circulation mgr. LaPorte (Ind.) Herald, 1918-21; editor Lima (O.) Gazette, 1925-26; reporter, copyreader Chgo. Tribune, 1926-28; mng. editor Bloomington (Ill.) Pantagraph, 1928-35; news editor St. Louis Star-Times, 1935-46; mng. editor Knoxville (Tenn.) News-Sentinel, 1946-68, asso. editor, 1968-72, ret.; lectr. U. Tenn., 1950—, Knoxville Coll., 1968. Charter mem. A.P. Mng. Editors Assn.; mem. Knoxville C. of C. Clubs: Deane Hill Country, Senators Country (Knoxville). Home: 600 Hemlock Rd Knoxville TN 37919 Office: 204 W Church Av Knoxville TN 37901

ORDMAN, ARNOLD, govt. ofcl.; b. Somersworth, N.H., Feb. 16, 1912; s. Maurice J. and Anna (Pierce) O.; B.A., Boston U., 1933; LL.B., Harvard, 1936; m. Evelyn R. Sisson, Feb. 5, 1939; children—Edward Thorne, Alfred Bram. Admitted to Mass. bar, 1936; pvt. practice, Salem, Mass., 1937-42; with NLRB, 1946—, chief counsel to chmn., 1961-63, gen. counsel, 1962—. Served with USNR, 1942-45. Mem. Internat. Soc. Labor Law and Social Action (exec. bd.), A.A.A.S., Phi Beta Kappa. Home: 4701 Willard Av Chevy Chase MD Office: 1717 Pennsylvania Av NW Washington DC 20570

O'REILLY, DON, columnist, sportscaster; b. Attleboro, Mass., May 1, 1913; s. Dennis C. and Helen L. (Barden) O'R.; student pub. schs.; m. Edith L. Macomber, July 9, 1938; 1 son, Howard. Owner, Eagle Press, Plainville, Mass., 1930-35; reporter, photographer Attleboro Sun, 1935-40, New London (Conn.) Day, 1940-42; reporter Washington Post, 1945-47; editor, pub. Speed Age mag., Washington, 1947-53; dir. News Bur., Nat. Assn. for Stock Car Racing, 1954-56; syndicated columnist Inside Auto Racing, Fla., also editor Auto News Syndicate, 1956-59, Atlanta, Detroit, 1959—; broadcaster auto races NBC Radio Network Monitor, Northeastern, Southeastern U.S., 1956-59; dir. pub. relations Atlanta Internat. Raceway, 1959-64; broadcaster syndicated radio program Inside Auto Racing, 1963-65; mgr. automotive div. Dynamics Films. Inc. of N.Y.C., Atlanta, Detroit, 1964-69; broadcaster motor sports Mutual Radio Network, 1970—. Served with USCGR, 1942-45. Mem. Nat., Detroit, Indianapolis, Atlanta press clubs, Nat. Press Photographers Assn., Automotive Old Timers, Indpls. Motor Speedway Oldtimers Assn., Nat. Sportscasters and Sportswriters Assn., Ga. Assn. Broadcasters, Internat. Motor Press Assn., Nat. Motorsport Press Assn. (1st Pl. Broadcasting award 1965). Republican. Methodist. Variety. Home: 4586 Roswell Rd Atlanta GA 30342 Office: Carnegie Bldg Atlanta GA 30301

ORENTLICHER, HERMAN ISRAEL, lawyer, assn. exec.; b. Brockton, Mass., Oct. 26, 1910; s. George Harry and Yetta (Eiferman) O.; A.B., Harvard, 1933, J.D., 1936; m. Jeanette Adah Levin, July 3, 1938; children— John, Kay, George, David, Diane. Admitted to Mass. bar, D.C. bar, U.S. Supreme Ct. bar, practiced in Boston, 1936-37; counsel, chief briefs and opinions sect. U.S. Housing Authority, Washington, 1938-43, asst., acting gen. counsel HHFA, Washington, 1944-48; mem. faculty Nat. Law Center and Law Sch., George Washington U., Washington, 1949-60, prof., 1956-60; asso. sec., counsel Am. Assn. U. Profs., Washington, 1960-69, asso. gen. sec., counsel, 1969—. Vis. prof. Boston Coll. Law Sch., 1967-68; adj. prof. Va. Poly. Inst. and State U. Grad. Sch. Edn., 1972—; cons. in field; ex.-officio mem. Edn. Commn. of States, 1966-67. Mem. Phi Beta Kappa, Phi Delta Phi. Jewish religion (trustee, chmn. religious com.). Author: Tools of the National Housing Agency, 1944. Editor: (with William T. Fryer) Casebook, Legal Method and Legal System, 1968. Home: 5509 Huntington Pkwy Bethesda MD 20014 Office: Am Assn U Profs 500 1 Dupont Circle Washington DC 20036

ORLEANS, LEO A., govt. ofcl.; b. Russia, June 13, 1924; s. Anton J. and Susan (Agranovich) O. Came to U.S., 1939, naturalized, 1944; B.A., U. So. Cal., 1950; postgrad. in demography, econs., polit. sci. George Washington and Am. Univs., 1951-55; m. Helen Ruth Willis, Aug. 20, 1949; children—Nina, David. Sr. research analyst Library of Congress, Washington, 1951-65, China research specialist, 1966—, cons. NSF; asso. study dir. Office Econ. & Manpower Studies, NSF, Washington, 1965-66. Served with USAAF, 1943-46; PTO. Mem. Assn. for Asian Studies, Population Assn. Am. Author: Professional Manpower and Education in Communist China, 1961; Every Fifth Child: The Population of China, 1972. Contbr. articles to profl. jours. Home: 5301 Brinkley Rd SE Washington DC 20031 Office: Library of Congress Washington DC 20540

ORLEBEKE, CHARLES JOHN, govt. ofcl.; b. Grand Rapids, Mich., Oct. 27, 1934; s. Joe and Wilhelmina (Plekker) O.; B.A., Calvin Coll., 1957; M.A., Mich. State U., 1959, Ph.D., 1965; Fulbright scholar U. Sydney (Australia), 1960-61; m. Faith Irene Holtrop, Feb. 27, 1961; children—Evagren, Alison, Britany. Research asst. Romney for Gov. Com., Detroit, 1962; adminstrv. asst. on program devel. to Gov. George Romney, Lansing, Mich., 1963-66, exec. asst. planning and program devel., 1967-68; exec. asst. to Sec. Housing and Urban Devel., Washington, 1969-70, dep. undersec., 1970—. Home: 5215 Roosevelt St Bethesda MD 20014 Office: Department of Housing and Urban Devel Washington DC 20410

ORMES, ROBERT VERNER, editor; b. N.Y.C., Sept. 10, 1921; s. Ferguson Reddie and Mabrie (Verner) O.; A.B., Wabash Coll., 1943; postgrad. Columbia U.; m. Mary Ann Otto, Sept. 2, 1950; children—Julia C., Carolyn V., Margaret F. Instr. English, math. and contemporary civilization Wabash Coll., Crawfordsville, Ind., 1947-49; tech. writer, Cushing & Nevell, N.Y.C., 1954; editorial asst. Science, jour. of A.A.A.S., Washington, 1954-57, asst. editor, 1957-60, mng. editor, 1961—. Served to lt. (j.g.), USNR, 1943-46. Mem. A.A.A.S., Council Biology Editors, Beta Theta Pi, Phi Beta Kappa. Democrat. Home: 2810 Central Av Alexandria VA 22302 Office: 1515 Massachusetts Av NW Washington DC 20005

ORMES, WALTER MASON, JR., educator; b. Ronceverte, W.Va., Mar. 28, 1918; s. Walter Mason and Eulalia (Bower) O.; B.S., Sch. Pharmacy, Med. Coll. Va., 1939; D.D.S., Med. Coll. Va., 1947; m. Elizabeth Ashton Harrison, Feb. 14, 1942; children—Anne Harrison (Mrs. Charles Edward Beal, Jr.), Ashton Harrison. Pharmacist, Highland Park Pharmacy, Richmond, Va., 1940-42; pvt. practice dentistry, Richmond, 1947-48; asso. prof. Sch. Dentistry, Va. Commonwealth U., 1969—. Served with AUS, 1942-44; col. Res., ret. Decorated Legion of Merit. Mem. Am., Va. dental assns., Richmond Dental Soc., Va. Soc. Periodontists, Am. Acad. Periodontology, Assn. U.S. Army, Retired Officers Assn., Nat. Assn. Uniformed Services, Am. Assn. U. Profs., Am. Assn. Dental Schs., Kappa Psi, Psi Omega, Omicron Kappa Upsilon, Sigma Zeta, Alpha Sigma Chi. Home: 7733 Yorkdale Dr Richmond VA 23235

ORNE, JERROLD, librarian; b. St. Paul, Minn., Mar. 25, 1911; s. Benjamin and Gertrude (Black) O.; A.B., U. Minn., 1932, M.A., 1933; diplome, Sorbonne, Paris, 1934-35; Ph.D., U. Chgo., 1939; B.S., U. Minn., 1940; m. Catherine Lamont Bowen, June 14, 1939; children—Mary Lamont (Mrs. Bruce Cabot Law), Jonathan Bowen, Jean Lamont. Reference asst. St. Paul Pub. Library, 1927-36; language examiner U. Chgo., 1937-39; fellow in library science and romance langs. Library of Congress, 1940-41; librarian and prof. romance langs. Knox Coll., 1941-43; chief library div. Office Tech. Services, U.S. Dept. Commerce, 1946; dir. libraries Washington U., 1946-51; reference cons. Library of Congress, 1942, 1950; cons. U.S. Dept. of Commerce, 1947; dir. libraries Air U., Maxwell AFB, 1951-57; librarian U. N.C., 1957—. Cons. NSF, 1961, NASA, 1961, U.S. Army Missile Command, 1966. Served with USN, 1943-46. Recipient Award of Merit, Am. Soc. Information Sci., 1971. Mem. Assn. Southeastern Research Libraries (chmn. 1959-61), Am. (Melvil Dewey award 1972), N.C. Southeastern library assns., Spl. Libraries Assn., Am. Assn. U. Profs., Internat. Standards Assn. (U.S. rep., subcom. chmn.), Am. Standards Assn. (com. chmn.). Author: A Middle French Vocabulary Building Arts and Trades, 1941; Textbook for the Yeoman Striker (with K. W. Joy and H. K. Burrell), 1945; (with Grace Swift); Subject Heading list for Naval Research Libraries, 1946; Subject Headings for Technical Libraries (with Grace Swift), 1947; The Language of the Foreign Book Trade, 1949; El Futuro de la biblioteca en Cuba, 1950; Research Librarianship, 1971. Asso. editor: American Documentation, 1955-57; editor Southeastern Librarian, 1966-72; Education and Libraries, selected papers of L.R. Wilson, 1966. Contbr. profl. bulls. and other publs. Address: 516 Dogwood Dr Chapel Hill NC 27514

ORNISH, EDWIN PAUL, dentist; b. Dallas, Jan. 17, 1925; s. Louis and Hannah (Hoffman) O.; student So. Meth. U., 1941-43; D.D.S., Baylor U., 1946; m. Natalie Gene Moskowitz, Nov. 6, 1949; children—Laurel Ann, Dean Michael, Steven Andrew, Kathy April. Practice dentistry, Dallas, 1949—; pres. Natwin Co. Dallas, 1959—. Served to capt. Dental Corps, USAAF, 1946-48. Mem. Am., Tex. dental assns., Am., Tex. acads. gen. dentistry, Am., Tex. socs. dentistry for children, Dallas County Dental Soc., Alpha Omega (pres. 1946). Mason. Contbr. articles to profl. jours. Home: 7146 Currin Dr Dallas TX 75230 Office: 6031 Sherry Lane Dallas TX 75225

O'ROURKE, JAMES RALPH, librarian; b. Tuscaloosa, Ala., Mar. 16, 1913; s. Timothy R. and Sallie (Reese) O'R.; student Stillman Jr. Coll., 1935; B.L.S., Atlanta U., 1948; M.L.S., U. Ky., 1956; m. George Monroe Wright, Nov. 14, 1938; children—James Ralph, Reginald DeForest (dec.). Instr. history Stillman Jr. Coll., 1939, librarian, 1945-49; head librarian Ky. State Coll., 1949—, asso. prof. L.S., 1966—. Dir. summer L.S. workshops Ky. Dept. Libraries, 1961—; mem. Gov.'s Planning Com. on Libraries, 1967-68; exec. dir. Nat. Library Week in Ky., 1965-66. Dir. Lexington chpt. Nat. Conf. Christians and Jews, 1964-68; co-chmn. edn. com. Com. on Religion and Human Rights, Lexington, 1965-66; mem. Archives Commn. Ky., 1965-68; treas. West End Neighborhood Assn., 1966-68; mem. Govs. Planning Com. on Libraries, 1967-68. Bd. dirs. Lexington Assn. Religious Bodies, Emerson Center. Mem. Am., So., Ky. (sect. chmn. 1963-64) library assns., Ky. Negro Edn. Assn. (sect. chmn. 1952-53), Am. Assn. U. Profs., Ky. Edn. Assn., Omega Psi Phi. Democrat. Roman Catholic. K.C. (4 deg.). Home: 937 Waverly Dr Lexington KY 40505 Office: Ky State Coll Frankfort KY 40601

O'ROURKE, JOHN CASSUS, pump co. exec.; b. Oklahoma City, Jan. 4, 1928; s. John Edward and Anna Isabella (Fischer) O'R.; student Draughn's Bus. Coll., 1947; Asso. Diesel Tech., Okla. State U., 1953; m. Jeanne Carroll Thornton, Nov. 14, 1945; children—Kathryn Janelle, Theresa Mischelle, John Kevin. Plant engr. Reda Pump Co., Bartlesville, Okla., 1953-56, chief engr. plant prodn. and research and devel., 1956-69, mgr. engring., 1969—; v.p. engring., 1972—. Mem. Washington County Citizens Adv. Com., 1968-69, chmn., 1969. Served with USNR, 1945-46. Mem. Bartlesville Engrs. Club, (dir. 1968), Bartlesville C. of C. Republican. Roman Catholic. Elk. Clubs: Hillcrest Country, Toastmasters (adminstrv. v.p. 1966-67) (Bartlesville). Patentee in field. Office: 509 W Hensley St Bartlesville OK 74003

ORR, JAMES DUANE, indsl. devel. exec.; b. Hereford, Tex., Apr. 29, 1912; s. James Silas and Maude (Higgins) O.; B.S. in Civil Engring., Tex. Technol. U., 1933; m. Virginia Lynn Staggers, Nov. 22, 1936; 1 son, Don Duane. Engr., Tex. Hwy. Dept., 1933-37, 39, U.S. C.E., 1937, Tex. Reclamation Dept., 1937-39; with Port of Corpus Christi (Tex.), 1939—, dist. engr., dir. indsl. devel. and port planning, 1968—. Cons. engr. Pub. Grain Elevator, 1952—, Area Devel. Com., Corpus Christi, 1952—; alternate commr. Coastal Bend Regional Planning Commn., Corpus Christi, 1967—. U.S. del. Permanent Internat. Nav. Congress, 1968—, Named Top Salesman of Year of Corpus Christi, Corpus Christi Sales and Marketing Execs. Club, 1969. Registered profl. engr., Tex., Cal. Mem. Am. Soc. C.E., Am. Soc. Oceanography, Nat., Tex. socs. profl. engrs., C. of C. (mil. affairs and indsl. com. 1967—). Rotarian. Club: Corpus Christi Town. Home: 222 Leming St Corpus Christi TX 78404 Office: 222 Powers St Corpus Christi TX 78401

ORR, JAMES MILTON, dentist; b. Memphis, Tex., May 20, 1918; s. Milton Newton and Nannie Adalee (Vallance) O.; student Tex. Tech U., 1935-37; D.D.S., U. Tex., 1941; m. Elizabeth Hook, Nov. 22, 1941; children—Lynda (Mrs. Carol Joe Davis), Jane (Mrs. Tommy Glenn Thomas), Ann (Mrs. Lynn McLain). Instr. U. Tex. Dental Sch., 1941-45; practice dentistry, Wellington, Tex., 1945—; mem. staff Ollingsworth Gen. Hosp., Wellington. Dir. Wellington State Bank; sec. See More, Inc. Served to maj. USAF, 1953-55. Mem. Am. Dental Assn., Tex., Panhandle Dist. dental socs., Acad. Gen. Dentistry, Southwest Prosthetic Soc., Omicron Kappa Upsilon. Mason (32 deg.), Rotarian (pres. 1959), Kiwanian (pres. 1950). Home: 1700 Dalhart St Wellington TX 79095 Office: 916 West Av Wellington TX 79095

ORR, MARK TAYLOR, educator; b. Mt. Croghan, S.C., Apr. 20, 1914; s. Oliver H. and Jennie (Taylor) O.; student Mars Hill Coll., 1932-34; A.B., U. N.C., 1937, Ph.D., 1954; postgrad. U. Va., 1944, U. Mich., 1945; m. Katherine Wilkinson, Mar. 16, 1944; children—Karen Lee, Mark Taylor. Asst. dir. So. Council on Internat. Relations, Chapel Hill, N.C., 1937-41; instr. U. Tampa, 1941-42; chief edn. div. Gen. Hdqrs. Allied Powers, Tokyo, Japan, 1946-49; instr. U. N.C., 1949-51; coordinator Internat. Studies and Programs, asso. prof. U. S. Fla., Tampa, 1966—. Served with USAAF, 1941-46, to col. USAF, 1951-66. Mem. Japan Soc., Am. Polit. Sci. Assn., Am. Fgn. Service Officers Assn., Air Force Assn., Internat. Studies Assn., Assn. for Asian Studies, Nat. Assn. Fgn. Student Affairs. Author: (with Robert McAllen) Education in Japan, 1947. Editor: The South and World Affairs, 1937-41. Home: 2807 Samara Dr Tampa FL 33618

ORR, OLIVER HAMILTON, JR., historian; b. Brevard, N.C., Oct. 6, 1921; s. Oliver Hamilton and Jennie Lee (Taylor) O.; student Brevard Jr. Coll., 1938-40; A.B., U. N.C., 1942, Ph.D., 1958; m. Adriana Pannevis, Feb. 15, 1956. Library asst. U. N.C., Chapel Hill, 1945-56; instr. N.C. State U., Raleigh, 1959-61, asst. prof., dept. history, 1961-65; specialist Am. history Library of Congress, Washington, 1965-69, manuscript historian, 1969—. Served with AUS, 1942-45. Mem. Am., So. hist. assns., N.C. Literary and Hist. Assn., Hist. Soc. N.C., Soc. Am. Archivists, Orgn. Am. Historians, Forest History Soc., Wilderness Soc., Nat. Audubon Soc., Audubon Naturalist Soc., Am. Forestry Assn., Friends of Nat. Zoo, Smithsonian Soc. Assos., Am. Mus. Natural History, Nat. Fedn. Fed. Employees, U.S. Capitol Hist. Soc., Population Reference Bur., Council N.C., U. N.C. Alumni Assn. Democrat. Methodist. Club: Carolina Bird. Author: Charles Brantley Aycock, 1961. Home: 529 7th St SE Washington DC 20003 Office: Library of Congress Washington DC 20540

ORR, WILLIAM NEWTON, dentist; b. Memphis, Tex., Dec. 18, 1908; s. Milton Newton and Nannie (Vallance) O.; D.D.S., U. Tex., 1930; m. Leila Mae Brashear, Oct. 15, 1931; children—William Reed, Robert Lee. Practice dentistry, Shamrock, Tex., 1930-32, Littlefield, Tex., 1932-67; dir. Houston Dental Pub. Health, 1968—. Dist. chmn. Boy Scouts Am., 1935-47. Trustee Littlefield Ind. Sch., 1937-49. Named Littlefield Citizen of Year. C. of C., 1965. Fellow Am. Coll. Dentists, Tex. Dental Assn.; mem. Tex. State Assn. (v.p. 1960-61), S. Plains Dental Soc. (pres. 1945), Littlefield C. of C. (trustee 1961-68), U. Tex. Coll. Dentistry Alumni (pres. 1958). Methodist (finance chmn. 1945-54). Mason, Rotarian. Home: 10118 Hollyspring St Houston TX 77042 Office: 1115 N McGregor St Houston TX 77000

ORTNER, DONALD RICHARD, psychologist, educator; b. Bay City, Mich., Sept. 2, 1922; s. Richard J. and Caroline (Deuring) O.; B.A., Northwestern Coll., 1944; B.Mus., Ill. Wesleyan U., 1946; C.R.M., Wis. Luth. Sem., 1947; M.A., Eastern Mich. U., 1957; Ph.D., Mich. State U., 1964; m. Gertrude Martha Stoekli, June 29, 1947; 1 son, Stephen R. E. Ordained to ministry Luth. Ch., 1947; pastor Luth. chs., chaplain, univs., Toronto, Ont., Winnipeg, Man., Can., 1947-54; pastor St. John's Luth. Ch., Waltz, Mich., 1954-57; guidance counselor, tchr. Latin, St. Johns (Mich.) Pub. Schs., 1957-60; dir. counseling Morningside Coll., 1960-61; co-dir. Presbyn. Guidance Center, Hampden-Sydney (Va.) Coll., 1961-63, dean students, 1963-70, prof. psychology, chmn. dept., 1964—, coll. psychologist, 1970—; pastor-at-large English dist. Luth. Ch., 1964—. Mem. Am. Personnel and Guidance Assn., Nat. Vocational Guidance Assn., Am.

Sch. Counselor Assn., Am. Coll. Personnel Assn., Am. Psychol. Assn. (asso.), So. Soc. for Philosophy and Psychology, Royal Canadian Coll. Organists, Sigma Nu, Phi Delta Kappa, Phi Mu Alpha-Sinfonia. Democrat. Home: 1421 Gilliam Dr Farmville VA 23901

ORY, ROBERT LOUIS, biochemist; b. New Orleans, Nov. 26, 1925; s. Alfred A. and Louise (Gendron) O.; B.S., Loyola U., New Orleans, 1948; M.S., U. Detroit, 1950; Ph.D., Tex. A. and M. U., 1954; m. Mary Elizabeth Hobley, Dec. 27, 1948 (div. Feb. 1957); children—Barbara Ann, Mary Catherine. With U.S. Dept. Agr., 1954-68, 69—, head protein properties investigations, oilseed crops lab., New Orleans, 1969—; Fulbright research scholar Poly. Inst. Denmark, Lyngby, 1968-69; lectr. Mem. Am. Chem. Soc., A.A.A.S., Sci. Research Soc. Am., Am. Soc. Plant Physiologists, Am. Oil Chemists Soc., Am. Peanut Research Edn. Assn., Union of Holy Name Socs. New Orleans (dist. v.p. 1957-58), Men's Holy Name Soc. Parish Ch. (past pres., Outstanding Man of Year 1958), Sigma Xi. Served with USMCR, 1944-46. Contbg. author: Annual Review of Plant Physiology and Biochemical Preparations, 1963; also contbr. papers to profl. jours. Home: 3547 Roger Williams St New Orleans LA 70119 Office: PO Box 19687 New Orleans LA 70179

OSBORN, GLENN RICHARD, audio engr.; b. Los Angeles, Oct. 25, 1928; s. Glenn Litz and Nellie (Hoffman) O.; B.S. in Audio Engring., U. Hollywood, 1949; m. Joye Elise Hughes, Feb. 15, 1963; children—Eric William, John Howard. Head transmission engr., 1352 Motion Picture Squadron, Hollywood, 1953-60; head, sound dept., Sandia Corp., Albuquerque, 1960-65, supr. sound dept. A-V Corp., Manned Spacecraft Center, Houston, 1965—. Served with AUS, 1950-52. Mem. Audio Engring. Soc., Acoustical Soc. Am., Soc. Motion Picture and TV Engrs. Home: 2117 Willow Wisp Dr Seabrook TX 77586 Office: 2518 N Boulevard Houston TX 77001

OSBORN, JAMES EZRA, educator; b. Tuttle, Okla., Nov. 9, 1936; s. Roy Biel and Ida (Kuhlman) O.; B.S. (Nat. Def. Act fellow), Okla. State U., 1959, Ph.D., 1964; postgrad N.C. State U., 1962-64; m. Mary Ann Hardesty, Jan. 2, 1956; children—Nancy Kay, John Ezra. Grad asst. Okla. State U., 1959-62; research asst. N.C. State U., 1962-64; asst. prof. Auburn U., 1964-65; asso. prof. Tex. Tech. U., Lubbock, Tex., 1965-67, asso. prof., 1967—. Cons. in field. Chmn. bd. Child Care Center, Lubbock, 1968—; bd. dirs. W. Tex. Water Inst. Mem. Am., So., Western agrl. econs. assns., Tex. Assn. Coll. Tchrs., Sigma Xi, Alpha Zeta, Pi Gamma Mu, Omicron Delta Epsilon. Democrat. Methodist. Contbr. articles to profl. jours. Home: 6018 Norfolk St Lubbock TX 79413 Office: Dept Agrl Econs Tex Tech U Lubbock TX 79409

OSBORN, MALCOLM EVERETT, ins. co. exec.; b. Bangor, Me., Apr. 29, 1928; s. Lester Everett and Helen (Clark) O.; B.A., U. Me., 1952; postgrad. Harvard, 1952-54; J.D., Boston U., 1956, LL.M., in Taxation, 1961; m. Claire A. Franks, Aug. 30, 1953; children—Beverly, Lester, Malcolm, Jr., Ernest. Admitted to bars Me., 1956, Mass., 1956, N.C., 1965, U.S. Dist. Ct. Mass., Middle Dist., U.S. Tax Ct., U.S. Ct. Claims, I.R.S. Ct.; atty. tax counsel State Mut. Life Assurance Co. Am., Worcester, Mass., 1956-64; asst. gen. counsel Pan-Am. Life Ins. Co., New Orleans, 1964; 2d v.p., tax counsel Integon Corp., and other Integon group cos., Winston-Salem, N.C., 1964—. Bd. dirs., atty. Winston-Salem Swim Club, Inc., 1967—; bd. dirs. Integon Found., Inc.; trustee N.C. Council Econ. Edn. Mem. Worcester County, Forsyth County, N.C., Am. bar assns. Home: 3639 Kirkless Rd Winston-Salem NC 27104 Office: 420 N Spruce St Winston-Salem NC 27102

OSBORN, PRIME FRANCIS, III, lawyer, r.r. ofcl.; b. Greensboro, Ala., July 31, 1915; s. Prime Francis, Jr. and Anne (Fowlkes) O.; J.D., U. Ala., 1939; m. Grace Hambrick, Aug. 30, 1939; children—Prime Francis IV, Mary Anne. Admitted to Ala. bar, 1939, Ky. bar, 1952, N.C. bar, 1959, also Fed. Cts., ICC, U.S. Supreme Ct. bar; asst. atty. gen. Ala., 1939-41; atty. G., M.&O. R.R., 1946-51, commerce atty., 1950-51; gen. solicitor L. & N. R.R., 1951-57; v.p., gen. counsel, dir. A.C.L. R.R., 1957-67, S.C. Pacific R.R. Co., 1957—, Atlantic Land & Improvement Co., 1960—; v.p., dir. Columbia, Newberry & Laurens R.R. Co.; pres. Seacoast Transp. Co., 1961—; v.p. law Seaboard Coast Line R.R. Co., 1967-69, pres., 1970-72; pres. Louisville & Nashville R.R. Co., 1972—, Seaboard Coast Line Industries, Inc., 1970—; vice chmn. Alico Land Devel. Co., 1971—; dir. Winston-Salem Terminal Co., Winston-Salem Southbound Ry. Co., First Nat. Bank Louisville, L&N Railroad. Pres. North Florida council Boy Scouts Am., 1962-66, mem. nat. council; chmn. region 6 Boy Scouts Am., 1966-69; mem. exec. reserve program Office Emergency Transp. Trustee Sweet Briar Coll.; mem. nat. council provincial chmn. Episcopal Ch. Found. Served from 2d lt. to lt. col., arty., AUS, 1941-46. Decorated Bronze Star medal; named Man of Year, Duval County, 1962. Mem. Am., Ala., N.C. bar assns., Am. Judicature Soc., Jacksonville C. of C. (sr. v.p. 1970, bd. gov. 1969—, pres. 1971), Bar Assn. City N.Y., ICC Practitioners Assn. (past v.p.), Sons Confederate Vets., Newcomen Soc. N.A., Southern Soc. N.Y., Nat. Def. Transportation Assn., Episcopal Men of Ky. (past pres.), Episcopal Men of Ala. (past pres.), Scabbard and Blade, Jasons, Sigma Alpha Epsilon (pres.), Omicron Delta Kappa (v.p.), Tau Kappa Alpha. Democrat. Episcopalian (exec. counsel 4th Province 1963—, vestryman). Rotarian. Clubs: Pendennis (Louisville); Union League (N.Y.); Metropolitan (D.C.); Commonwealth (Richmond). Office: 908 W Broadway Louisville KY 40201

OSBORNE, COLIN PORTER, JR., dentist; b. Aberdeen, N.C., Jan. 15, 1921; s. Colin Porter and Marguerite Jessie (Brasington) O.; student Guilford Coll., 1938-41; D.D.S., Atlanta-So. Dental Sch., 1944; m. Frances Elizabeth Collins, Oct. 20, 1945; children—Colin Porter III, Pamela Jane, Rebecca Leigh, Margaret Elizabeth. Practice dentistry, Fayetteville, N.C., 1947, Lumberton, N.C., 1947—; chief dental services Robeson County Meml. Hosp.; cons. community colls. dept. N.C. Dept. Edn., 1966-70. Bd. dirs. N.C. Symphony Soc., 1949-54, Community Concert Assn., 1949—, Dental Found. N.C., 1960—, YMCA, Lumberton, 1960-66. Served with AUS, 1943-44, USNR, 1944-45, USMCR, 1945-46. Fellow Am. Coll. Dentists; mem. Am. Dental Assn., N.C., 4th Dist., Southeastern dental socs., Fedn. Dentaire Internat., Am. Soc. Dentistry for Children, Nat. Rehab. Assn., Flying Dentist Assn., Robeson Choral Soc., Delta Sigma Delta (nat. chmn. 1967-68). Democrat. Baptist (deacon). Kiwanian. Club: Music of Lumberton (pres. 1957). Home: 2405 Rowland Av Lumberton NC 28358 Office: Rowland Av at 27th St Lumberton NC 28358

OSBORNE, EARL T., judge; b. Benton, Ky., July 10, 1920; s. Willie C. and Dovie (Bradford) O.; LL.B., U. Ky., 1950; m. Helen Cooper, Nov. 17, 1942; children—William P., Thomas L., Phyllis J., Deborah J. Admitted Ky. bar, 1950; practiced in Benton, Ky. 1950-56; circuit judge 42d Jud. Dist. Ky., Benton, 1956-66; judge Court of Appeals of Ky. 1967—. Served with USAAF, 1940-46; ETO. Decorated Air Medal. Mem. Am., Ky. bar assns., V.F.W., Am. Legion. Democrat. Methodist. Contbr. to profl. jours. Lectr. on Constitution of Ky. Home: Route 1 Gilbertsville KY 42044 Office: Court of Appeals Capitol Bldg Frankfort KY 40601

OSBORNE, ERNEST LESLIE, ret. army officer, mgmt. cons.; b. Denver, Mo., June 15, 1889; s. Jerome Monroe and Flora (Harroun) O.; Ph.B., Yale, 1912; S.B., Mass. Inst. Tech., 1914; student Pace Inst., 1919-20; LL.B., La Salle Extension U., 1922; postgrad. Columbia, 1933-34; m. Gladys Maria Fogg, Jan. 1, 1920; 1 dau., Phyllis Marie (Mrs. Herbert Orville Whitten). Field engr. Pub. Service Commn., N.Y.C., 1914-15; engr. Gunn, Richards & Co., N.Y.C., 1915-16; partner Woodling & Osborne, N.Y.C., Newark, Boston, 1920-21; specialist charge merchandising and mgmt. research, and statistics, James W. Eadie Jr., Boston, 1921-29; controller Hahn Dept. Stores, Inc., N.Y.C., 1929-30; controller, sec., treas. Dictograph Products Co., Inc., N.Y.C., 1931-33; chmn. adv. group Nat. Recovery Adminstrn., also Dept. Commerce. Washington, 1934-36; econ. and statis. analyst ICC, Washington, 1936; sr. tech. adviser, mgmt. engr. Social Security Bd., Washington, 1936-41; mgmt. engr., col. Dept. Army, Washington, 1949-59; mgmt. counsellor, Washington, 1959—; cons. economist Research Council, Controllers Inst. Am., 1933-38. Served as lt. U.S. Army, 1912-13, major, 1916-19, col. AUS, 1941-49. Recipient Certificate Achievement, Dept. Army, 1959; Outstanding Service certificate Am. Soc. Mil. Comptrollers, 1957; Imperial Cross St. Nicholas. Mem. Am. Soc. Mil. Comptrollers (past sec., past pres. Washington, life mem. nat. council), U.S. Capitol Hist. Soc., S.A.R., Transp. Research Forum, Royal Statistical Soc. (London), Am. Soc. Mil. Comptrollers, Am. Legion, Assn. U.S. Army, Sigma Xi, Theta Tau, Phi Gamma Delta. Republican. Mem. Christian Ch. Clubs: Mass. Institute of Technology (v.p. 1957-59), Yale (Washington). Editor: Standard Accounting Guide, 1928. The Armed Forces Comptroller, 1956-57. Home: 3130 Wisconsin Av NW Washington DC 20016

OSBORNE, HARRY ALBERT, JR., banker; b. Winston-Salem, N.C., Mar. 23, 1936; s. Harry Albert and Louise (Kimbrough) O.; B.S., N.C. State U., 1958; M.B.A., U. N.C., 1962; m. Gladys Ann Rozier, June 8, 1963; 1 dau., Caroline Louise. Mgmt. trainee Wachovia Bank, Winston-Salem, 1962-63, br. mgr., lending officer loan adminstrn. officer, marketing officer, Goldsboro, N.C., 1963-67, v.p. corporate accounts dept., Winston-Salem, 1967—. Mem. admissions and budget com. United Fund, 1965-67; treas. Wayne County Heart Fund, 1966-67. Served as 1st lt. Signal Corps, AUS, 1958-60. Decorated Army Commendation medal. Lutheran (asst. treas. 1969—). Mason, Elk. Home: 570 Westoak Trail Winston-Salem NC 27104 Office: PO Box 3099 Winston-Salem NC 27102

OSBORNE, JOHN ARTHUR, accountant, univ. business officer; b. Denver, Feb. 7, 1931; s. Harold Humphrey and Erma (Allison) O.; A.A., Coffeyville (Kan.) Jr. Coll., 1954; B.S. with honors, U. Tulsa, 1956, law student, 1956-58; short course (scholarship student) U. Omaha, 1962. Accountant Pan. Am. Petroleum Corp., 1956-57; sr. accountant Frazer & Torbet, C.P.A., Tulsa, 1957-61; asst. sec.-treas. U. Tulsa, 1961—, comptroller, 1968—. Gen. chmn. Southwest Bus. Equipment Show of Tulsa, 1965; mem. planning com. Tulsa Conf. Accountants, 1965—, mayor's system study com., Tulsa, 1967. Served with USAF, 1951-52. C.P.A., Okla., 1959. Recipient Scholarship key Delta Sigma Pi, 1956; Gold medal award Okla. Soc. C.P.A.'s, 1956; certificate of merit Coll. Bus. Administrn., U. Tulsa, 1956, Merit award, Tulsa chapter Systems and Procedures Assn., 1967; named One of Outstanding Young Men in Am., 1966. Mem. Central Assn. Coll. and Univ. Bus. Officers (exec. com. 1963-64), Am. Inst. C.P.A.'s, Okla., Tulsa socs. C.P.A.'s, U. Tulsa Alumni Assn. (treas. 1960-70), Systems and Procedures Assn. (treas. Tulsa chpt. 1962-64, pres. 1965-66), Nat. Assn. Accountants (chpt. bd. dirs. 1971—), Am. Accounting Assn., Coll. and U. Personnel Assn., Assn. Ednl. Data Systems, Phi Gamma Kappa (treas.), Alpha Kappa Psi (charter mem. U. Tulsa chpt.). Episcopalian (stewardship com.). Club: University (incorporator, sec.-treas. 1963-69). Home: PO Box 4614 Tulsa OK 74104 Office: 600 S College St Tulsa OK 74104

OSBORNE, M. H., pres., gen. mgr. WWHO-FM, Jackson, Miss. Address: Box 1562 Jackson MS 39205*

OSBORNE, MRS. M. H., program dir. WWHO-FM, Jackson, Miss. Address: Box 22525 Jackson MS 39205*

OSBORNE, MILLARD HENRY, clergyman; b. Florence, S.C., June 23, 1922; s. Mark Rayburn and Dora Elizabeth (Bishop) O.; Certificate of Arts, Campbell Coll., 1943; B.A., Furman U., 1944; B.D., So. Bapt. Theol. Sem., 1947; m. Jacqueline Gasque Rouse, June 22, 1944; children—Jacqueline Elizabeth, Mary Catherine. Ordained to ministry Bapt. Ch., 1943; asso. pastor Pendleton St. Ch., Greenville, S.C., 1943-44; pastor Oak Grove Ch., Warsaw, Ky., 1945-46, Hardeeville Ch. (S.C.), 1947-49, Four Holes Bapt. Ch., Orangeburg, S.C., 1949-56, First Bapt. Ch., McColl, S.C., 1956-61; pastor Lakeview Bapt. Ch., Camden, S.C., 1961-65, Northgate Colonial Bapt. Ch., 1965-67, retired, 1967; cons. on hist. devel. S.C. Dept. Parks, Recreation and Tourism, 1967-71; asst. to gov. State of S.C., 1971—. Publicity dir., bd. dirs., exec. com., blood chmn. Orangeburg County chpt. A.R.C., now mem. regional coordination com.; seal sale chmn., dir., exec. com. Tb Assn. Marlboro County; mem. Kershaw County Pub. Welfare Commn.; dir. Cancer Soc.; sec. McColl Indsl. Devel. Bd.; sec. S.C. Legislative Study Com. for Travel, 1964—. Trustee, Furman U., 1950-60, alumni bd. dirs., 1972—. Recipient Distinguished Service award Am. Legion, 1963; Service award, Camden-Kershaw County C. of C., 1964. Mem. Camden Revolutionary War Assn. (pres. 1966), Colonial and Brit. Armies Am., Inc., (vice comdr. in-chief), Co. Mil. Historians and Collectors, Nat. Temple Hill Assn. N.Y., Camden Art Assn., Kershaw County Hist. Soc., C. of C. (historic com.). Kiwanian. Club: Horseless Carriage of Am. Author: Preliminary Archeological and Architectual Study of The Joseph Kershaw Magazine, 1777; also author weekly newspaper column Sights and Insights. Editor: Colonial and Brit. Gazette. Contbr. publs. Home: 207 Laurens St Camden SC 29020 Office: Office of Gov State House Columbia SC 29211

OSBORNE, RAY C., state ofcl.; b. Winston-Salem, N.C., Sept. 7, 1933; s. Rufus Charles and Maggie (Prevette) O.; B.S., N.C. State Coll., 1955; LL.B., U. N.C., 1961; m. Mary Thom White, Oct. 21, 1961; 1 dau., Molly Payne. Mem. Fla. State Ho. of Reps., 1964-68; alternate del. Rep. Nat. Conv., 1968; lt. gov. Fla., 1969—; practice law, Boca Raton, Fla. Mem. exec. com. Nat. Conf. Lt. Govs., 1969-. Served with AUS, 1955-57. Mem. Am. Bar. Assn., Am. Judicature Soc., Kappa Sigma, Phi Psi, Delta Theta Phi. Clubs: St. Petersburg Yacht, University, Dragon. Home: 1188 SW Walnut Terrace Boca Raton FL 33432 Office: PO Box X Boca Raton FL 33432

OSBORNE, W. C., cons. geologist; b. McGehee, Ark., Aug. 16, 1923; s. John Carroll and Lola (Mangum) O.; B.A., Centenary Coll. La., 1943; m. Dixie Tarver, Nov. 21, 1944; children—Janet Lee, John Carroll II. Area geologist Tide Water Assn. Oil, Midland, Tex., 1946-50, dist. geologist, 1950-51; dist. geologist Union Oil & Gas Corp. La., Midland, 1951-57; exploration mgr. Am. Trading & Prodn. Corp., Midland, 1957-69, gen. mgr. oil and gas div., 1969-70; partner Osborne & Jones Cons. Geologists, Midland, 1970-72; prin. W.C. Osborne Cons. Geologist, 1972—. Served with USNR, 1943-46. Mem. Am. Assn. Petroleum Geologists, W. Tex. Geol. Soc., Lambda Chi Alpha (past pres.). Republican. Mason (Shriner). Club: Midland Country. Baptist. Home: 2110 N I St Midland TX 79701 Office: 358 Mid America Bldg Midland TX 79701

OSBORNE, WEYMAR ZACK, scientist; b. Pampa, Tex., Nov. 6, 1932; s. Charles Woodman and Adelle (Williams) O.; B.S., U. Okla., 1954, M.S., 1957, Ph. D., 1961; m. Estelle Barbara Chodor, Dec. 18, 1959; children— Evan Woodman, David Matthew, Jason Andrew. Physicist Lawrence Radiation Lab. U. Cal. at Berkeley, 1963-65; asst. prof. physics dept. Ind. U., Bloomington, 1965-69; Nat. Acad. Scis.-NRC sr, research asso. NASA Manned Spacecraft Center, Houston, 1969—. Served to 1st lt. AUS, 1962-63. NSF fellow U. Okla., 1958-60, 61-62. Mem. Am. Phys. Soc., Delta Tau Delta. Home: 318 Shadow Creek Dr Seabrook TX 77586 Office: Manned Spacecraft Center TN2 NASA Houston TX 77058

OSGOOD, WILLIAM R., educator; b. Cambridge, Mass., Apr. 17, 1895; s. William Fogg and Therese (Ruprecht) O.; A.B. cum laude, Harvard, 1917; S.B., Mass. Inst. Tech., 1919; M.S., U. Ill., 1924, Ph.D., 1933. Asst. prof. structural engring. Cornell U., 1926-29; materials engr. Nat. Bur. Standards, 1929-46; sr. structural engr. David Taylor Model Basin, Washington, 1946-50; prof. mechanics, chmn. dept. mechanics Ill. Inst. Tech., Chgo., 1950-55; prof. mechanics, head dept. mechanics Rensselaer Poly Inst., Troy, N.Y., 1955-60, prof. emeritus, 1960—; prof. civil engring. Catholic U. Am., Washington, 1960-65, lectr., 1965-69. Fellow Am. Soc. C.E., Washington Acad. Scis.; mem. Am. Soc. M.E. (Tech. Achievement certificate 1970), Soc. Exptl. Stress Analysis, Am. Assn. U. Profs., Sigma Xi. Club: Cosmos (Washington). Editor: Residual Stresses in Metals and Metal Construction, 1954. Home: 2756 Macomb St NW Washington DC 20008

O'SHEA, H. WILLIAM, JR., librarian; b. Raleigh, N.C., Jan. 7, 1922; s. Horace William and Eleanor Mae (Dillon) O'S.; B.S., U. N.C., 1946, M.L.S., 1955; postgrad. Columbia, 1955-56. Salesman, Dillon Supply Co., Durham, N.C., 1946-54; jr. librarian Bklyn. Pub. Library, 1955-56; asst. librarian The Citadel, Charleston, S.C., 1956-60; dir. Rockingham County Pub. Libraries, Eden, N.C., 1960-66; dir. Wake County Pub. Libraries, Raleigh, N.C., 1966—. Named Young Man of the Year Durham, Durham Jaycees, 1953. Mem. N.C., Southeastern, Am. (dir. spl. libraries 1956-57) library assns. Rotarian. Clubs: Hope Valley Country, Pennrose Country, Raleigh City. Home: 1002 Cowper Dr Raleigh NC 27608 Office: 104 Fayetteville St Raleigh NC 27601

O'SHELL, VINCENT JOSEPH, orthodontist; b. Beaumont, Tex., May 10, 1927; s. Michael Vincent and Grace (Canizaro) O'S.; student Loyola U. of South, 1944-45, 46-47; B.S., Baylor U., 1949; D.D.S., U. Tex., 1953; M.S., U. Mo., 1954; m. Aphrodite Barbatis, June 28, 1954; children—Cynthia Graceann, Doria Maria, Michael Vincent. Practice orthodontics, Beaumont, 1954—. Served with U.S. Mcht. Marine, 1945-46; PTO. Mem. Am. Assn. Orthodontists, Tex. Tweed Orthodontic Soc., Tex. Soc. Dentistry for Children, Sabine Dist. Dental Soc., Beta Beta Beta, Xi Psi Phi. Republican. Roman Catholic. K.C. Home: 160 E Caldwood St Beaumont TX 77707 Office: 3325 Calder St Beaumont TX 77706

O'SHIELDS, WILLIAM THEODORE, automotive co. exec.; b. Van Buren, Ark., Nov. 11, 1922; s. Fay and Annie Mae (Johnston) O'S.; grad. high sch.; m. Edith Marie Packwood, Dec. 13, 1941; children—Gail (Mrs. Gerald Pope), William Theodore. With Crane Carrier Co. div. CCI Corp., Tulsa, 1949—, v.p. engring., 1957-61, v.p. mfg., 1961-68, exec. v.p., 1968-69, pres., 1970—. Served with USAAF, 1943-45. Decorated Air medal with three oak leaf clusters. Mem. Soc. Automotive Engrs., Am. Mgmt. Assn., Nat. Assn. Mfrs., Am. Welding Soc., Tulsa Mfrs. Club: Clubs: Meadowbrook Country, Coat of Arms (Tulsa). Patentee in field. Home: 1724 S Darlington St Tulsa OK 74112 Office: 1150 N Peoria St Tulsa OK 74104

OSIAS, RICHARD ALLAN, housing constrn. and real estate investment exec., city ofcl.; b. N.Y.C., Nov. 13, 1933; s. Harry L. and Leah (Schenk) O.; student Columbia; m. Alexandra Stuart Currey, Sept. 22, 1962; 1 dau., Alexandra Kimberly. Founder, Osias Orgn., Inc., N.Y.C., also Ft. Lauderdale, Fla., St. Clair, Mich., San Juan, P.R., 1953, chmn. bd. chief exec. officer, 1953—. Mem. North Lauderdale (Fla.) City Council, 1967—; police commr. North Lauderdale, 1967—. Served with USAF, 1953. Recipient Am. House award Am. Home Mag., 1962, Westinghouse award, 1968; named Builder of Year, Sunshine State information Bur., and Sunshine State Sr. Citizen, 1967-69. Mem. Ft. Lauderdale Better Bus. Bur., Lauderhill (Fla.) Fraternal Order Police Assn. (pres.), Fla., Margate, Ft. Lauderdale chambers commerce. Clubs: JocKey (Miami); Top of First (San Juan); Quater Deck (Galveston, Tex.), Landing Yacht. Prin. works include residential and apt. units, residential housing communities, shopping centers, country clubs, golf courses, hotel chains. Home: 31 S Compass Dr Ft Lauderdale FL Office: 801 W Oakland Park Blvd Ft Lauderdale FL 33304

OSIUS, LARRY CLARK, mag. editor; b. Detroit, Dec. 8, 1930; s. Walter Frederick and Ruth (Clark) O.; B.A. in Journalism, Okla. State U., 1952; m. Mary Ellen Gorman, Dec. 27, 1952; children—Mary Beth, Laura Lee. Sports and wire editor Ponca City (Okla.) Daily News, 1954-56; newsman A.P., Oklahoma City, 1956-61, Washington, 1961-65; with Copley News Service, Washington, 1965; mng. editor Elec. Contractor mag., Washington, 1965-71, editor, pub., 1972—. Served to 1st lt. AUS, 1952-54. Mem. Pi Kappa Alpha, Sigma Delta Chi. Democrat. Mem. Disciples of Christ Ch. Home: 6712 Greenview Lane Springfield VA 22152 Office: 7315 Wisconsin Av NW Washington DC 20036

OSOLNIK, RUDE, educator; b. Dawson, N.M., Mar. 4, 1915; s. Lukas and Rose (Penko) O.; B.S., Bradley U., 1937, M.S., 1950; m. Daphne Francis, June 7, 1938; children—Maureen, Michael J., Joseph Lee, Sharon Ann, David D. Export clk. Caterpillar Tractor Co., Peoria, Ill., 1937; instr. indsl. arts Berea (Ky.) Coll., 1937—, chmn. dept. 1941—, dir. woodcut industry; owner Osolnik Originals, Berea, 1956—. Cons. small industries and craft groups; exhibited in Mus. Sci. and Industry, Chgo., Southeastern Am. Craftsman Council Art Show Exhibit, Raleigh, N.C., Smithsonian Traveling Exhibit. Pres., treas. mem. bd. Berea Credit Union, 1948-62. Served to lt. (j.g.) USNR, 1943-46. Mem. Ky. Guild of Artists and Craftsmen (exec. sec. 1960—), So. Highland Handicraft Guild (pres. 1960-62, life mem.). Home: Scaffold Cane Rd Berea KY 40403

OSORIO, TRINIDAD, artist; b. Mexico City, Mexico, May 26, 1929; M.F.A., Nat. Sch. Plastic Arts at Nat. U. Mexico. Tchr. painting and graphic arts Nat. Sch. Plastic Arts, Nat. U. Mexico, 1954—; exhibited in 10 one-man shows in Mexico and one in U.S.; exhibited in group shows Mus. Modern Art, Paris, Mus. Modern Art, Kamakura, Japan, Library of Congress, Washington, Gulf-Caribbean Art exhbn. Mus. Fine Arts, Houston, Dallas Mus. Fine Arts, Inst. Contemporary Art, Boston, Munson-Williams Proctor Inst., Utica, N.Y., Colorado Springs Fine Arts Center, Barcelona (Spain) Biennial, Nat. Mus. Bogota (Columbia); exhibited paintings and drawings in China, Czechoslovakia, Poland, Brazil, Argentina, Cuba, Peru, Costa Rica, Haiti, Honduras, Panama; exhibited in Mexican Art Exhbn., Oslo, Norway, Rome, Italy, Ghent, Belgium, Stockholm, Sweden, Warsaw, Poland, London, Eng.; exhibited in Art Shows of the Cultural Program for the XIX Olympics, Mexico City, 1968. U. Mexico travel and study grantee, 1956.*

OSTAR, ALLAN WILLIAM, edn. assn. exec.; b. East Orange, N.J., Sept. 4, 1924; s. William and Rose (Mirmow) O.; certificate in Engring., U. Denver, 1943; B.S., Pa. State U., 1948; postgrad. U. Wis., 1949-55; LL.D., Colo. State Coll., 1968, Eastern Ky. U., 1972; m. A. Roberta Hutchison, Sept. 10, 1949; children—Karen, Rebecca, John. Dir. nat. pub. relations U.S. Nat. Student Assn., 1948-49; exec. asst. Commonwealth Fund, N.Y.C., 1952-53; asst. to dean extension div. U. Wis., 1949-52, dir. office communications services, 1954-58; dir. Joint Office Instl. Research, Nat. Assn. State Univs. and Land-Grant Colls., Washington, 1958-66; exec. dir. Am. Assn. State Colls. and Univs., Washington, 1966—. Cons. to govt. agys.; adv. com. higher Edn. Edn. Commn. of States. Chmn. higher edn. com. Md. Cong. Parents and Tchrs., 1969—; pres. Higher Edn. Group of Washington, 1968. Served with AUS, 1943-46. Decorated Bronze Star medal. Mem. Pa. State U. Alumni Assn. (mem. exec. bd. 1967—), Md. State P.T.A. (life), Sigma Delta Chi. Unitarian-Universalist. Home: 6322 Walhonding Rd Washington DC 20016 Office: 1 DuPont Circle Washington DC 20036

O'STEEN, CLAYTON ELWIN, hosp. adminstr.; b. Lakeland, Fla., Oct. 8, 1939; s. Clayton and Josephine Louise (Winn) O'S.; grad. Grady Meml. Hosp. Sch. X-Ray Tech., 1958; student U. Fla., 1959-61; B.S., Fla. So Coll., 1966; M.H.A., Med. Coll. Va., 1968; m. Helen Carol Sineath, Sept. 9, 1961; children—Jolene, Heather. Radiol. technologist Lakeland Gen. Hosp., 1961-66; spl. adminstrv. asst. Richmond (Va.) Meml. Hosp., 1968; adminstrv. asst. Columbia (S.C.) Hosp., 1968-69; adminstr. Jackson Hosp., Marianna, Fla., 1969—. Mem. licensed practical nurse adv. bd. Chipola Jr. Coll., 1970; active Am. Cancer Soc. Bd. dirs. Jackson County Guidance Center, 1969-70, v.p., 1971; bd. dirs. N.W. Fla. Mental Health Center, 1970-71; sec. N.W. Fla. Hosp. Council, 1971-72, bd. dirs., 1970-71. Mem. Am., Fla. (mem. pub. relations council) hosp. assns., Delta Sigma Phi. Elk, Rotarian. Home: 407 Russ St Marianna FL 32446 Office: 3d Av Marianna FL 32446

OSTEEN, WILLIAM L., U.S. dist. atty. for middle N.C. Home: 2322 N Elm St Greensboro NC 27406 Office: District Attorney's Office Greensboro NC 27402*

OSTER, RICHARD CHARLES, dentist; b. New Orleans, Jan. 20, 1922; s. Fred and Alvina Lenore (Waldmann) O.; student Valparaiso U., 1938-40; D.D.S., Loyola U., 1943; m. Lois Marie Wyneken, Feb. 5, 1944; children—Jean (Mrs. Walter Kretzmann), Barbara Ellen. Practice dentistry, New Orleans, 1946—. Cons. Aetna Ins. Co., New Orleans, 1969—; vis. lect. La. State U. Dental Sch., 1969—; dentist Bethlehem Orphan Home, 1947—, New Orleans Saints Profl. Football Team, 1968—. Sec. Vicksburg (Miss.) Luth. Hosp., 1951-53; chmn. St. John Luth. Sch. Bd., 1947-65. Bd. dirs. New Orleans chpt. Am. Leukemia Soc., Luth. High Sch.; trustee, mem. exec. com. Valparaiso U. Served to capt. Dental Corps, AUS, 1943-46; PTO. Named Toastmaster of Year, Toastmasters Club, 1954; recipient Appreciation award Optimist Club, 1966, Alumni Distinguished Service award Valparaiso U., 1970. Mem. Am., La. dental assns., New Orleans Dental Soc. (v.p. 1963), Delta Sigma Delta. Democrat. Lutheran (pres. St. John 1967-68). Clubs: Toastmasters (pres. 1953), Country (New Orleans). Home: 1224 Seville Dr New Orleans LA 70122 Office: 4219 Magnolia St New Orleans LA 70115

OSTERBIND, CARTER CLARK, JR., educator; b. Richmond, Va., July 24, 1913; s. Carter Clarke and Mary (Eakin) O.; B.S., Va. Poly. Inst., 1934, M.S., 1936; Ph.D., Am. U., 1953; m. Rosilie Stockard Hutcheson, June 14, 1939; children—Rosilie (Mrs. Louis Saffos), Ellen Amanda, Carter Clarke III. Dir. Center for Gerontology, U. Fla., Gainesville. Chmn., Fla. Commn. on Aging; mem. planning bd. 1971 White House Conf. on Aging. Trustee, Fla. Council on Aging. Fellow Gerontological Soc.; mem. So. Econ. Assn., Fla. C. of C. (mem. mil. affairs com.), Nat. Assn. State Units on Aging (dir.), Assn. Univ. Burs. Bus. and Econ. Research (dir., v.p.), Beta Gamma Sigma, Alpha Kappa Psi, Kappa Alpha. Home: 2105 NW 7th Lane Gainesville FL 32601 Office: 221 Matherly Hall U Fla Gainesville FL 32601

OSTERHAUS, LEO BENEDICT, educator; b. Fargo, N.D., Jan. 19, 1920; s. Bernard and Carolyn (Wiltz) O.; B.S., Kan. State U., 1942; M.S., Trinity U., 1961; Ph.D., U. Tex., 1966; m. Edna Reichie, Mar. 9, 1943; children—Susan (Mrs. Thomas O. Baldwin), Annette R. Commd. 2nd lt. U.S. Army, 1943, advanced through grades to lt. col., 1964; with Philippine Command Hdqrs., Manila, 1946-48; stationed Heidelberg, Germany, 1954-57; with Brook Army Med. Center, Med. Field Service Sch., Ft. Sam Houston, 1959-64; ret. 1964; asst. prof. hosp. adminstrn. Baylor U., San Antonio, 1959-64; teaching, adminstrv. asst. U. Tex. at Austin, 1964-66; asso. prof. bus. adminstrn. St. Edwards U., Austin, 1966-69, dir., dean., 1969-70, dir. Center Bus. Adminstrn., 1970—. Vis. prof. mgmt. U. Tex., 1966—. U. Md. European div., 1972-73. Cons. to industry and hosps. Recipient Gilbreth Mgmt. award U. Tex., 1966. Mem. Am. Mgmt. Assn., Acad. Mgmt., S.W. Social Sci. Assn., Austin Personnel Assn., Am. Accounting Assn., Sigma Epsilon. Contbr. articles to profl. jours. Home: 8307 Tecumseh Dr Austin TX 78753

OSTERMAN, FLOYD ARTHUR, physician; b. Seymour, Ind., May 20, 1919; s. John Carl and Elsa Katherine (Ortstadt) O.; B.S., U. Chgo., 1941; postgrad. U. Louisville, 1937-39; M.D., Northwestern U., 1945; m. Marie T. Rieder, June 10, 1944; children—Floyd Arthur, Lynda, Cynthia, Martina, Kristina. Intern, St. Joseph's Hosp., Chgo., 1944-45, resident internal medicine, 1945-46; fellow pathology Cook County Hosp., Chgo., 1948; resident internal medicine VA Hosp., Hines, Ill., 1949-51; practice medicine specializing in internal medicine, Fort Lauderdale, Fla., 1952—; mem. staffs Broward Gen., Holy Cross hosps. (both Fort Lauderdale); dir. First Bank of Plantation, (Fla.), Riverland Bank, Fort Lauderdale, Fla. Trustee, U. Miami, Coral Gables, Fla. Served with AUS, 1946-48. Diplomate Am. Bd. Internal Medicine. Mem. Phi Chi. Club: Lauderdale Yacht. Home: 860 E Tropical Way Fort Lauderdale FL 33314 Office: 1415 E Sunrise Blvd Fort Lauderdale FL 33304

OSTHAGEN, CLARENCE HILMANN, mgmt. and indsl. cons.; b. North Bergen, N.J., Apr. 9, 1911; s. Hilmann Marius and Elise (Ulricksen) O.; student Cooper Inst. Tech., 1920-25; B.S. in Engring., U. Ky., 1930; grad. student Columbia, 1930-31, George Washington U., 1934-37. Asst. to spl. rep. Allis-Chalmers Mfg. Co., 1920-25; indsl. engr. Henry L. Doherty Co., 1930-31; cons. engr., 1931-33; dep. adminstr. pub. utilities, also exec. asst. div. bus. coop. NRA, 1933-36; successively acting dir. project control. dir. adminstrv. operations, asst. dir. personnel, dir. employee mgmt. Fed. Works Agy., 1936-42, mgmt. engr., 1946-48; dep. asst. sec. (mgmt.) Dept. Air Force, 1948-50; acting under sec., also asst. sec. commerce Dept. Commerce, 1950-53; prin. mgmt. cons. Rogers, Slade & Hill, N.Y.C., 1953-56; v.p., exec. dir. Tidewater Va. Devel. Council, Norfolk, 1956-63; dir. mechanization div. Office Asst. Postmaster Gen., 1963-64; commr. Community Facilities Adminstrn., Housing and Home Finance Agy., 1964-66; dir. space and mechanization requirements Office of Asst. Postmaster Gen., 1966-69, spl. asst. to asst. postmaster gen. operations, U.S. Postal Service, 1969-71; now mgmt. and indsl. cons. Served to col. USAAF, World War II; col. Res. Decorated Legion of Merit, Commendation ribbon with 2 oak leaf clusters; recipient Exceptional Civilian Service decoration Dept. Air Force, 1950; Exceptional Service award Dept. Commerce, 1952; Meritorious Honor award P.O. Dept., 1968; Service award U.S. Postal Service, 1971; Centennial Dept. Centennial medallion, named Distinguished Alumni, named to Hall of Distinguised Alumni, U. Ky. Licensed profl. engr., N.J., Va., D.C., N.Y. Mem. Soc. Advancement Mgmt., Am. Soc. Pub. Adminstrn., Soc. Am. Mil. Engrs., Am. Inst. Indsl. Engrs., Nat., N.J. socs. profl. engrs., Am. Indsl. Devel. Council, Pub. Personnel Assn., Soc. Personnel Adminstrn., Air Force Assn., U. Ky. Alumni Assn., Nat. Sojourners, Rotary Internat. Sigma Chi, Omicron Delta Kappa. Mason (Shriner). Clubs: Virginia; Norfolk (Va.) Yacht and Country. Author mgmt. articles. Home: 1332 I St NW Washington DC 20005 also 302 Teaneck Av Ridgefield Park NJ 07660

OSTROFF, NATHAN, govt. ofcl.; b. New Haven, Apr. 27, 1910; s. Aaron and Sophie (Smirnoff) O.; B.A., Yale, 1932, LL.B., 1935; m. Ann Littman, Nov. 21, 1940; children—Peter, Robert, Aaron Daniel. With Solicitor's Office U.S. Dept. Agr., Washington, 1935-40; asst. to gen. counsel Fgn. Econ. Adminstrn.; gen. counsel Office Internat. Trade; asst. gen. counsel U.S. Dept. Commerce, 1951-61, dep. gen. counsel, 1961-63, chmn. departmental appeals bd., 1964—. Mem. War Agys. Protective Assn. (dir., cons.), Am. Acad. Polit. Sci., Soc. Internat. Law, Fed. Bar Assn. Club: National Press. Home: 2914 Kanawha St NW Washington DC 20015 Office: care US Dept of Commerce Washington DC 20230

O'SULLIVAN, BROTHER MALCOLM, coll. pres.; b. Limerick, Ireland; student in Paris, Rome, U. Madrid; B.A., Manhattan Coll.; M.A., Columbia U., Ph.D.; M.A., Fordham U.; postgrad. Harvard, 1971. Former tchr. journalism, Latin, English, religion; adminstr. secondary schs.; provincial adminstr. N.Y.-N.J.-Mich. area; faculty St. Joseph's Collegiate Sch., Buffalo, until 1970; with Christian Bros. Coll., Memphis, 1970—, pres., 1971—. Mem. exec. com. Tenn. Council for Pvt. Colls. Trustee, Sta. WKNO-TV. Rotarian. Office: Christian Brothers College 650 E Parkway S Memphis TN 38104*

OSWALD, HAROLD WILLIAM, JR., dentist; b. Algiers, La., Sept. 26, 1928; s. Harold William and Angeline Clottile (Guedry) O.; student La. State U., Baton Rouge, 1954-56; D.D.S., Loyola U. of the South, 1960; m. Lynette M. Braud, Sept. 5, 1956; children—Harold William III, Robert Mark. Individual practice dentistry, Reserve, La., 1960—. Served with AUS, 1952-54. Mem. Am., La., New Orleans dental assns., Alpha Sigma Nu, C. Victor Vignes Odontological Soc. Home: 121 Murray Hill Destraham LA 70047 Office: 402 James St Reserve LA 70084

OSWALT, JOHN MACON, clergyman; b. Fayette, Ala., Mar. 19, 1921; s. Andrew C. and Pearl (Patterson) O.; B.A., U. Ala., 1943; Th.M., Southwestern Bapt. Theol. Sem., 1945; m. Lois Elaine Thornton, June 16, 1943; children—Lynn Thornton, Lonn Macon, Lewis Earle, Lori Elaine. Ordained to ministry Bapt. Ch., 1942; student pastor, Royse City, Tex., Palestine, Tex., 1943-45; pastor Blanchard (La.) Bapt. Ch., 1945-50, Main St. Bapt. Ch., Bogalusa, La., 1950-54, 1st Bapt. Ch., Hammond, La, 1954—. Mem. Hammond United Givers Fund, 1971—; v.p. Tungipahon chpt. A.R.C., 1970-71. Trustee Baton Rouge Gen. Hosp., 1957-64; trustee La. Moral and Civic Found., 1957-64, 65—, 1st v.p., 1971. So. Bapt. Annuity Bd., 1962-68; pres. trustees S.E. Bapt. Assembly, Mandeville, La., 1967-68; mem. exec. bd. La. Bapt. Conv., 1971—. Mem. La. Bapt. Conv. (mem. exec. bd. 1956-63, chmn. pub. affairs com.), Dist. 11 Bapt. Conv. (pres. 1953-54, 59-60), La. Poetry Soc. Mason, Kiwanian (pres. 1957). Contbr. articles to profl. jours. Home: 108 College Dr Hammond LA 70401 Office: 200 S Pine St Hammond LA 70401

OSWALT, WILLIAM HENRY, III, business exec.; b. Jacksonville, Fla., Nov. 19, 1918; s. William Henry and Mary (Crayton) O.; B.S., Tex. A. and M. Coll., 1940; postgrad. So. Methodist U., 1941; m. Maulice Searcy, Aug. 31, 1941; children—Robert C., William Henry IV, Harryette. Engr. water dept., apprentice to city mgr. City of Dallas, 1940-42, engr. pub. works dept., 1946, asst. to city mgr., 1946-47; mgr. City of Jacksonville (Tex.), 1947-49, City of Midland (Tex.), 1949-54; v.p., dir. project devel. Southland Life Ins. Co., Dallas, 1954-60; exec. v.p. Exchange Park Co., Dallas, 1960-64, pres., 1964—; pres., dir. Diversa, Inc., 1969—, French Quarter Corp., Dallas, 1965—. Past mem. Nat. Com. Governmental Accounting. Registered profl. civil engr. Tex. Mem. Am. Soc. C.E., Newcomen Soc. N.Am., Nat., Tex. (pres. Permian Basin chpt. 1952-54) socs. profl. engrs., Internat. City Mgrs. Assn., Am. Pub. Works Assn., Am. Water Works Assn., Soc. Am. Mil. Engrs., Mil. Govt. Assn. Episcopalian (vestryman). Mason (Shriner), Rotarian. Club: Dallas Athletic. Contbr. numerous articles and bulls. to profl. publs. Home: 10203 Hollow Way Dallas TX 75229 Office: Frito-Lay Tower Exchange Park N Dallas TX 75235

OTIS, JACK, univ. adminstr.; b. N.Y.C, Feb. 13, 1923; s. Abraham and Esther (Goldberg) O.; B.A., Bklyn. Coll., 1946; M.S.W., U. Ill., 1948, M.Ed., 1955, Ph.D., 1957; m. Patricia Anne Stephens, Mar. 25, 1967; 1 dau., Alicia; children by prior marriage—Elizabeth, Erich, Marika, Marcus. Asso. prof. mental health U. Ill., Urbana, 1950-61; dep. dir. Pres.'s Com. on Juvenile Delinquency and Youth Crime, Washington, 1961-65; dean grad. sch. social work U. Tex., Austin, 1965—. Cons. Nat. Inst. Mental Health, 1966—, U.S. Dept. Justice, 1966—, U.S. Office Juvenile Delinquency and Youth Devel., 1966—; tng. staff Austin State Hosp., 1968—. Mem. Human Relations Commn., City of Austin, 1967—, Model Cities Program, 1968—; mem. bd. overseers Lemberg Center for Study of Violence, Brandeis U., 1965—. Served with AUS, 1943-46. Recipient awards U.S. Dept. Justice, 1967, Welfare Adminstrn. U.S. Dept. Health, Edn. and Welfare, 1966. Mem. Am. Assn. U. Profs., Am. Acad. Polit. and Social Sci., Am. Soc. Criminology, Council on Social Work Edn., Philosophy of Edn. Soc., Nat. Assn. Social Workers, Royal Soc. for Promotion of Health. Author: Corporate Society and Education, 1961; also articles. Home: 3635 W Lake Dr Austin TX 78746 Office: U Tex Austin TX 78712

OTIS, WILLIAM LYNAN, JR., lumber co. exec.; b. Columbia, S.C., Jan. 1, 1940; s. William Lynan and Nancy (Crouther) O.; B.S. in Econs., U. S.C., 1963; m. Alice VanYeverin Hopkins, July 29, 1966; children—William Lynan III, Thomas Porcher. Exec. v.p. Columbia Lumber & Mfg. Co., Inc., Columbia, S.C., 1963-69, pres., 1969—; dir. Home Fed. Savs. & Loan Assn. Chmn. adv. bd. Providence Hosp., 1971—; bd. dirs. Columbia Hist. Mus., 1967-70, Columbia Town Theater, 1968-71. Mem. Archtl. Woodwook Inst. Internat. (pres. 1971-72), So. Woodwork Assn. (pres. 1967-69), Carolina Lumber and Bldg. Material Dealers Assn. (dir. 1960-69). Clubs: Forest Lake Country, Palmetto, Pine Tree Hunt (Columbia). Home: 4535 Devereaux Rd Columbia SC 29205 Office: 500 Hampton St Columbia SC 29202

O'TOOLE, CHRISTOPHER JOHN, clergyman; b. Alpena, Mich., Oct. 1, 1906; s. Christopher and Margaret (McGrarry) O'T.; A.B., U. Notre Dame, 1929; LL.D., 1959; Ph.B., U. Louvain, 1939; M.A., Cath. U. Am., 1942, Ph.D., 1944; LL.D., U. Portland, 1951, St. Edwards U., 1960. Ordained priest Roman Catholic Ch., 1933; instr. philosophy dept. St. Edwards U., 1933-34, U. Notre Dame, 1934-36; master of novices, Dartmouth, Mass., 1936-38; superior Holy Cross Sem., Notre Dame, Ind., 1940; Holy Cross Coll., 1941-45; asst. provincial Ind. Province, 1945-50; supr. gen. congregation Holy Cross, Rome, Italy, 1950-62; superior Dist. of South, Austin, Tex., 1963-68; provincial supr. So. Province, Congregation of Holy Cross, 1968—; pres. Priests of Holy Cross, Dist. of Tex., Inc., Austin, 1963. Decorated knight Grand Cross Equestrian Order Holy Sepulchre. Mem. Nat. Cath. Philos. Assn. Home: 812 Audubon St New Orleans LA 70118

O'TOOLE, LELA, coll. dean; b. Thomas, Okla., Sept. 9, 1909; d. Edmund B. and Emma (Williams) O'Toole; B.S. in Edn., Okla. State U., 1935, B.S. in Home Econs. Edn., 1939, M.S. in Home Econs. Edn., 1941; Ph.D., Ohio State U., 1949. Elementary, secondary sch. tchr., Okla., 1929-34, 35-40; dist., state supr. home econs. edn., Okla., 1940-47; prof. home econs. edn. Okla. State U., Stillwater, 1949-50, dean div. home econs., 1951—. Program specialist home econ. edn. U.S. Office Edn., 1950-51; dir., tchr. first home econs. summer sch., Norway, 1954; leader ednl. study home econs., Pakistan, 1957, cons. Pakistan-Okla. Home Econs. Program, 1964—; v.p. Internat. Fedn. Home Econs.; mem. President's Nat. Council on Vocational Edn., 1967-68; group leader, speaker numerous confs. Recipient Centennial Achievement award Ohio State U., 1970. Mem. Nat., Okla. edn. assns., Am. (pres. 1969-70), Okla. home econs. assns., Mortar Bd., Phi Kappa Phi, Omicron Nu, Phi Upsilon Omicron, Kappa Delta Pi, Pi Lambda Theta, Delta Kappa Gamma. Baptist. Contbr. articles profl. jours., bulls. Home: 1820 Arrowhead Pl Stillwater OK 74074

OTT, AUGUSTUS LOUIS, III, architect; b. Camden, S.C., Aug. 30, 1928; s. Augustus Louis and Sadie (Haynes) O.; B.S., Clemson U., 1955; m. Barbara Ruth Bright, Dec. 23, 1951 (div. Feb. 1971); children—David Louis, Mary Barbara; m. 2d, Lucy Corder, Aug. 6, 1971. Draftsman, William Stork, Columbia, S.C., 1955-58; partner Stork & Ott, Columbia, 1958-62, Blume, Cannon & Ott, 1962—. Pres., Travler's Aid, 1968. Mem. Mayor's Com. for Handicapped, 1968. Served with USAF, 1951-52. Mem. A.I.A. (Outstanding Service award 1968, bd. dirs. 1966-68). Presbyn. Club: Sertoma (Richland). Home: 2153 Quail Run Apts Percival Rd Columbia SC 29206 Office: 2230 Devine St Columbia SC 29205

OTT, FRANKLIN BERNARD, physician; b. Newark, May 3, 1921; s. Frank B. and Jeanette (Haffert) O.; student Rutgers U., 1939-40; Seton Hall U., 1940-42; M.D., Loyola at Chgo., 1945; m. Claire M. Moriarty, Feb. 16, 1946; children—Richard, Paul, Jeffrey, David, Cindy. Intern St. Michael's Hosp., Newark, 1945-46; practice medicine, Irvington, N.J., 1945-58, Pompano Beach, Fla., 1958—; mem. staff Holy Cross Hosp., Ft. Lauderdale, Cypress Community Hosp., Pompano Beach. Instr. community medicine Med. Sch. U. Fla., Gainesville, 1970—. Mem. Bd. Edn. Archdiocese Miami, 1971—. Served to capt. M.C., AUS, 1946-48. Diplomate Am. Bd. Family Practice. Fellow Am. Acad. Family Physicians; mem. Am. Acad. Family Practice, Pan Am., So., Broward County, Fla. med. assns., Am. Geriatric Soc., A.M.A. Elk. Home: 4111 Bayview Dr Fort Lauderdale FL 33308 Office: 2 NE 26th Av Pompano Beach FL 33062

OTT, JULIAN A., motel and restaurant owner; b. nr. Orangeburg, S.C., Apr. 13, 1921; s. Ben Tillman and Florence (Myers) O.; student U. S.C., 1940-42; B.S., Clemson U., 1944; m. Mary Braswell, Apr. 6, 1947; children—Julian A., Rembert M., Timothy C., Melinda K. Farm owner, operator, 1946-60; pres. Julian A. Ott & Assos., Inc., operators Holiday Inns at Dunn, Elizabeth City and Smithfield, N.C., Rock Hill, Summerton and Santee, S.C., Turbeyville, S.C., Walterboro, S.C., Georgetown, S.C., Pocotaligo, S.C.; pres. Motel Assos., Inc., Investors Realty, Inc., CROW Assos., Inc., OWS & Assos., Inc., Santee Motor Inns, Inc., So. Motels, Inc., Waterboro Inns, Inc. v.p. SOW, Inc., ROW, Inc. Served with USNR, 1943-46. Mem. V.F.W., Am. Legion. Kiwanian, Elk. Club: Orangeburg Country. Home: Route 5 Box 10 Orangeburg SC 29115 Office: 178 Middlenton Orangeburg SC 29115

OTT, T. TRUETT, state senator; b. Osyka, Miss., Oct. 25, 1920; s. W.J. and Margaret Alexandria Ott; student Hinds Jr. Coll., 1937-39; LL.B., U. Fla., 1948; m. Anita Williams, Jan. 21, 1942; children—Sandra Ellen (Mrs. Gardner), Thomas William, Gary Truett, Hugh Justin. Admitted to Fla. bar; practiced in Tampa, 1948—; mem. Fla. Senate, 1966—. Mem. exec. bd. Gulf Ridge council Boy Scouts Am. Bd. dirs. Tampa YMCA, 1960-70. Served to Maj. USAAF, 1941-46; to lt. col. USAF, 1950-51. Recipient Outstanding Service award United Fund. Mem. Fla. Bar, Tampa-Hillsborough County Bar Assn. (dir. 1964-68), Am. Trial Lawyers Assn., Ye Mystic Krewe of Gasparilla, Phi Alpha Delta, Phi Delta Theta. Baptist. Mason. Home: 614 S Oregon St Tampa FL 33606 Office: 101 E Kennedy Blvd Tampa LF 33602*

OTTLEY, JOHN KING, JR., pub. relations exec.; b. Atlanta, Oct. 8, 1931; s. John King and Mary Henton (Harvey) O.; A.B., Davidson Coll., 1953; M.S., Columbia, 1954; m. Margaret Randolph Meriwether, June 22, 1966; 1 son, James Meriwether. Editorial trainee Charlotte Observer, 1958-59, reporter, 1959-60; reporter, Marietta (Ga.) Daily Jour., 1960-62, mng. editor, 1962-63; pub. relations mgr. So. Services, Inc., Atlanta, 1963-68; pub. relations account exec. Bell & Stanton, Inc., Atlanta, 1968—. Mem. adv. com. A.R.C., Atlanta, 1964—. Bd. dirs. Atlanta Mental Health Assn., Consumer Credit Counseling Service. Served with AUS, 1954-58. Mem. Pub. Relations Soc. Am., Ga. Conservancy, Appalachian Trail Conf., Ducks Unlimited, Reserve Officers Assn., Sigma Delta Chi. Clubs: Atlanta Press, Capital City (Atlanta). Home: 932 Glenbrook Dr NW Atlanta GA 30318 Office: Peachtree Center Bldg Atlanta GA 30303

OTTMAN, ROBERT WILLIAM, educator; b. Fulton, N.Y., May 3, 1914; s. Robert Noah and Lillian (Smith) O.; B.M., Eastman Sch. Music, 1938, M.M., 1943; Ph.D., N. Tex. State U., 1956; Mus.D., William Woods Coll., 1972; 1 dau., Ruth Elizabeth (Mrs. Donald Allen); m. 2d. Patricia Williams Martin, Aug. 26, 1967. Supr. music Groveland (N.Y.) Pub. Schs., 1938-42, supr. Akron (N.Y.) Pub. Schs., 1942-43; prof. music theory N.Tex. State U., Denton, 1946—. Served with AUS, 1943-46. Mem. Phi Mu Alpha Sinfonia, Pi Kappa Lambda. Kiwanian. Author: Music for Sight Singing, 2d edit., 1967; (with Paul Kreuger) Basic Repertoire for Singers, 1959; Elementary Harmony: Theory and Practice, 1961, 2d edit., 1970; Adv. Harmony: Theory and Practice, 1961, 2d edit., 1972; (with Frank Mainous) The 371 Chorales of Johann Sebastian Bach, 1966; (with Frank Mainous) Rudiments of Music, 1969. Home: 816 Edgewood Pl Denton TX 76201

OTTS, JOHN COAN, coll. dean; b. Spartanburg, S.C., Aug. 14, 1909; s. John Coan and Bertha Antoinette (Warren) O.; A.B., Wofford Coll., 1930; M.A. in English, Vanderbilt U., 1931; M.A. in Ednl. Adminstrn., Columbia U., 1941, Ed.D. (Alumni fellow 1955), 1955; m. Louise Bomar Smith, Dec. 21, 1940; children—Rebecca, Charlotte, Beverly, Sally. Tchr., prin. Spartanburg City Schs., 1931-45; prin. Central High Sch., Charlotte, N.C., 1945-55; asst. supt. Charlotte City Schs., 1955-60; asst. supt. Charlotte-Mecklenburg Schs., 1960-61; prof., head dept. edn. Queens Coll., Charlotte, 1961-62; prof. sch. edn. U. N.C. at Chapel Hill., 1962-65, acting dean, 1965-66; dean Coll. Edn. U.S.C., Columbia, 1966—. Recipient Distinguished alumnus award Wofford Coll., 1969. Mem. N.C. Edn.

Assn. (unit pres. 1949-51), Phi Delta Kappa. Presbyn. (elder 1946—). Home: 5 Granville Rd Columbia SC 29209

OTTS, LEE MACMILLAN, lawyer; b. Greensboro, Ala., May 21, 1922; s. Archie McEachin and Elizabeth (MacMillan) O.; A.B., U. Ala., 1943, LL.B., 1948; m. Mary Frances Byrd, Sept. 4, 1948; children— Harriett Byrd, Martha Frances, Elizabeth McEachin, Mary Lee. Admitted to Ala. bar, 1949; since practiced in Brewton, 1949—. Dir. First Nat. Bank, Brewton, Judge Inferior Ct., Escambia County, Brewton, 1951-53; Escambia County solicitor, 1953—, atty., 1960—. Mem. Ala. Regional Planning Com., 1968—. Mem. Brewton City Bd. Edn., 1961—, pres., 1967—; pres. City Housing Authority, 1966—. Bd. dirs. Ala. Assn. Sch. Bds. Served to capt., inf. AUS, 1943-46; ETO. Decorated Bronze Star medal, Purple Heart with oak leaf cluster. Mem. Ala. State Bar, Escambia County Bar Assn. (past pres.), C. of C., Am. Legion (past adj.), Phi Gamma Delta (past pres.), Phi Alpha Delta. Presbyn. (elder 1959—, clk of session 1965—). Rotarian (past pres. Brewton). Home: 1515 Poplar St Brewton AL 36426 Office: Jernigan Arcade Brewton AL 36426

OTWELL, RONNIE RAY, theatre, printing exec.; b. Carrollton, Ga., Aug. 13, 1929; s. William Clyde and Hazel (Helton) O.; student Ga. Inst. Tech., 1946-49; m. Mary Crawford Adams, Oct. 25, 1956; children—Ronnie Ray, Hazel Teresa, Timothy Lewis, Daniel Clyde. Mgr., Bremen Theatre (Ga.), 1950; dir. publicity, advt. Martin Theatres, Columbus, Ga., 1950-63; v.p., dir. Martin Theaters of Ga., Inc., 1963—, Martin Theatres of Ala., Inc., 1963—, dir. Martin Theatres of Columbus, Inc., 1963—, pres., dir. Columbus Prodns., Inc., 1966—. Mem. Nat. Assn. Theatre Owners Am., Nat. Assn. Theatres Owners Ga., Columbus C. of C., Columbus Mus. Arts and Crafts, Assn. U.S. Army. Methodist. Club: Columbus Country. Home: 2102 Garrard St Columbus GA 31906 Office: 1308 Broadway St Columbus GA 31902

OUALLINE, JUDD HAMNER, oil co. exec.; b. Conroe, Tex., Oct. 24, 1920; s. Ellis Augustus and Annie May (Hamner) O.; B.A., U. Tex., 1942, postgrad., 1946-47; m. Cynthia Shell Snell, Sept. 12, 1966; children—Judd Hamner, Catherine, Jennifer. Sr., div. staff geologist Stanolind Oil & Gas Co., Houston, 1947-52; dist. and div. geologist Skelly Oil Co., Houston, 1952-62, dist. exploration mgr., 1962-65, mgr. exploration dept., Tulsa, 1965-69, v.p. exploration and prodn. dept., 1969—; v.p., dir. Skelly Internat. Oil Co.; exec. v.p., dir. Skelly Oil Can., Ltd.; exec. v.p. Skelly Mozambique; v.p. Skelly Oil Co. Libya, Skelly Oil Co. of Gt. Britain, Ltd. Served to 1st lt. USAAF, 1943-46. Mem. Am. Petroleum Inst. (gen. com., div. 1968-70), Ind. Petroleum Assn. Am., Am. Assn. Petroleum Geologists, Soc. Exploration Geophysicists, Am. Inst. Mining, Metall. and Petroleum Engrs., Tulsa C. of C. (community devel. div. council 1970), Sigma Gamma Epsilon, Phi Sigma, Lambda Chi Alpha. Methodist (steward 1965-70). Home: 3732 S Utica St Tulsa OK 74105 Office: 1437 S Boulder St Tulsa OK 74102

OUBRE, SIDNEY JOSEPH, food co. exec.; b. Lutcher, La., Aug. 13, 1913; s. Joseph Telsmar and Eunice Marie (Rouillier) O.; grad. Soule Bus. Coll., 1935; m. Ruby Theresa Perret, Aug. 18, 1936; children— Lynn, Lynnelle (Mrs. John L. Lolley), Sidney Joseph, Wayne, Marsha. Cashier, bookkeeper Lutcher Wholesale Grocer Co., 1936-40; mgr. United Cash Grocery, New Orleans, 1940-42, Orleans Cash Grocery, 1942-44; buyer purchasing dept. Parent Co., 1944-46; mgr. Goodman & Beer Co., 1946-49; owner, operator retail grocery super market, Gramercy, La., 1949-59; internal auditor Consol. Companies, Inc., 1959-65; treas., dir. S.W. Food Suppliers, Inc., Lafayette, La., 1965—, mgr., 1965-67, gen. mgr., 1967—; v.p. Consol. Companies, Inc., 1967—; v.p. Rex Milling Co., New Iberia, La., 1968—; treas., dir. Tip Top Foods Inc., 1967—. Mayor, Town of Gramercy, 1950-54. Sec., dir. St. James Parish Hosp., Lutcher, 1955-62. Mem. Lafayette C. of C. Lion (pres. 1954), K.C. Club: Century (Lafayette). Home: 701 Brentwood Blvd Lafayette LA 70501 Office: 1617 S W Evangeline Thru Way Lafayette LA 70501

OUGHTERSON, WILLIAM ALEXANDER, lawyer; b. Nashville, Nov. 3, 1926; s. T.T. and Sarah (Sheppard) O.; student The Citadel, 1943-44, U. Miami, Coral Gables, Fla., 1944-45; B.A., LL.B., U. Fla., 1950; m. Leila Seay, July 13, 1949; children—William Scott, Lisa. Admitted to Fla. bar, 1950; practiced in Stuart, Fla., 1950—; mem. firm Oughterson, Oughterson & Prewitt, Stuart, 1950—; juvenile counselor Martin County, Fla., 1951-59, pros. atty., 1961—. Trustee, Lawyer's Title Guaranty Fund, 19th Jud. Circuit. Pres. Martin County Tb and Health Assn., 1956-57; disaster chmn. Martin County A.R.C., 1958, bd. dirs., 1957-62, chmn. bd., 1961-62. Served with USNR, 1944. Recipient Distinguished Service award Stuart Jr. C. of C., 1959. Mem. Martin County Bar Assn. (past pres.), Stuart C. of C. (chmn. membership drive 1961). Presbyn. (elder). Kiwanian (past officer Stuart; gov. Fla. dist. 1969). Home: 305 Pelican Dr Stuart FL 33494 Office: PO Drawer 86 Stuart FL 33494

OULD, EDWARD HATCHER, banker; b. Middlesboro, Ky., Sept. 13, 1907; s. Edward Hatcher and Ethel Stuart (Cole) O.; B.S., Washington and Lee U., 1929; grad. Grad. Sch. Banking, 1949; m. Madolyn Burruss Airheart, Oct. 21, 1933; children—Edward Hatcher III, Mary Robertson (Mrs. Frederic H. Sabin). With First Nat. Exchange Bank Va., 1936—, beginning as mgr. real estate and mortgage loan dept., successively asst. v.p., v.p., exec. v.p., 1936-56, dir., 1950—, pres., 1956—, chmn., 1964—; pres., chief exec. Dominion Bankshares Corp., 1967—; dir. Times-World Corp. Pres. Boanoke Pub. Library Found. Bd. dirs. Roanoke Symphony Soc.; trustee Roanoke Coll. Served as lt. USNR, World War II. Mem. Am. Bankers Assn. (v.p. for Va. 1955-56), Va., Roanoke (pres. 1949) chambers commerce, Kappa Sigma, Beta Gamma Sigma, Omicron Delta Kappa. Methodist (steward). Clubs: Shenandoah, German (Roanoke); Commonwealth (Richmond). Home: 3380 Peakwood Dr SW Roanoke VA 24014 Office: 201 S Jefferson St Roanoke VA 24011

OULLIBER, JOHN ANDREW, (JR.), banker; b. New Orleans, Feb. 24, 1911; s. John Andrew and Anna (Wirth) O.; LL.B., Loyola U., New Orleans, 1932; grad. Rutgers U. Grad. Sch. Banking, 1949; m. Gloria Yenni, Aug. 8, 1936; children—Sandra Adele, Judith Ann. Admitted to La. bar, 1933; atty. RFC, New Orleans, 1933-34; with Nat. Bank of Commerce, New Orleans, 1935—, exec. v.p., 1951-58, pres., 1958-69, chmn. bd. 1969—, also dir.; pres., dir. Gravier Improvement Co., Inc., New Orleans, 1950—; dir. Nat. Bank of Commerce, Jefferson Parish, La., Consol. Cos., Inc., New Orleans. Pres. New Orleans Clearing House Assn., 1964, 65. Mem. exec. com., dir. New Orleans Tourist Commn. Bd. dirs. Hotel Dieu Hosp., New Orleans, La.; dir. bd. regents Loyola U., New Orleans. Mem. Am. Bankers Assn., La., New Orleans bar assns., Blue Key, Beta Gamma Sigma. Clubs: New Orleans Country, Internat. House (director), Pickwick (New Orleans, La.). Home: 32 Lark St New Orleans LA Office: Nat Bank of Commerce Baronne and Common Sts New Orleans LA

OUREDNIK, RUDOLPH FRANK, wholesale trade co. exec.; b. N.Y.C., May 4, 1911; s. Gottlieb Frank and Marie (Pechkek) O.; student Sch. Commerce N.Y.U., 1929-30; m. Dorathy Andrews, Dec. 22, 1935; children— Rudolph Frank, Theodore, Marie (Mrs. Lebaron Scarlett). With Noland Co., various locations, 1930—, exec. v.p., Newport News, Va., 1968-70, pres., 1970—; also dir.; dir. Noland Credit Co., Newport News. Chmn. Human Relations Council, 1968-69. Bd. dirs. United Fund, 1968-69, Noland Found., 1968—; trustee Am. Inst. U., Washington, 1966-69. Served to lt. col., C.E., AUS, 1942-46. Mem. So. Wholesalers Assn. (pres. 1968-69), Am. Supply Assn. (v.p. 1971), Peninsula C. of C. (dir. 1970-71). Mason (Shriner). Clubs: James River Country, Huntington. Home: 15 Hilton Terrace Newport News VA 23607 Office: 2700 Warwick Blvd Newport News VA 23607

OUTLAR, JESSE, journalist; b. Finleyson, Ga., May 6, 1923; s. Jesse P. and Lois (Mangham) O.; B.S., U. Ga., 1943; m. Florence Beaton, Oct. 12, 1947; children—Jan Louise, Barry Thomas. Sports writer Atlanta Constitution, 1947-57, sports editor, 1957—. Home: 1731 Duke Rd Chamblee GA 30003 Office: 10 Forsyth St Atlanta GA 30302

OUTLAW, ARTHUR ROBERT, city ofcl.; b. Mobile, Sept. 8, 1926; s. George Cabell and Mayme (Ricks) O.; B.S. in Bus. Adminstrn., Spring Hill Coll., Mobile; m. Dorothy Smith, Nov. 23, 1949; children—Karen Ann, Arthur Robert, Mary Gay. Pub. accountant with Hollman, Childree & Ramsey, Mobile; asst. sec.-treas. Morrisons's, Inc., Mobile, now dir.; now city commr., Mobile. Mem. budget com. Mobile United Fund; mem. Sr. Bowl Com.; pres. Mobile Tb and Health Assn. Mem. lay adv. bd. Providence Hosp., Mobile; bd. dirs. Mobile Salvation Army. Served with USAAF, World War II. Mem. Mobile Area C. of C. (bd. dirs.), Nat. Assn. Accountants (past v.p. Mobile). Home: 250 Levert St Mobile AL 36607 Office: City Hall PO Box 1827 Mobile AL 36601

OUTTEN, JOSEPH FENDALL, dentist; b. Lynchburg, Va., Aug. 19, 1928; s. Clarence Fendall and Mary Jane (Wolf) O.; B.S., Va. Poly. Inst., 1949; postgrad. U. Richmond, 1949-50; D.D.S., Med. Coll. Va., 1954; m. Mildred Lacey Wright, Aug. 2, 1952; children—Joseph Fendall, Mary Cornelia, Samuel Wright, Thomas Hobson. Individual practice dentistry, Greenville, S.C., 1956—; pres. Hosa, Inc., Greenville, 1966—; sec.-treas. Composite Enterprises, Greenville, 1958-72. Bd. dirs. United Fund, Greenville, YMCA, Greenville. Served to capt. USAF, 1954-56. Recipient Service to Youth award YMCA, 1971. Mem. Dental Assos. of Greenville (sec.-treas. 1971-72), Am., S.C. dental assns., Am. Soc. Dentistry for Children, Southeastern Acad. Prosthetics, Greenville County Dental Assn. (pres. 1966-67), Piedmont Assn. (dir. 1968-69), Am. Legion, Theta Chi, Psi Omega. Mason. Clubs: American Business, Greenville Country (Greenville); Port Royal Country (Hilton Head, S.C.); Caroline Caribean Corp. (Banner Elk, N.C). Home: 130 Rockingham St Greenville SC 29607 Office: 10 Sevier St Greenville SC 29604

OUTTEN, L(ORA) M(ILTON), educator; b. Pocomoke City, Md., Aug. 17, 1913; s. L. P. and D. Elizabeth (Blades) O.; A.B., Western Md. Coll., 1934, M.A., 1937; M.S., Cornell University, 1950, Ph.D., 1956; postgrad. Ind. U., 1959, Harvard, 1961, Oxford (Eng.) U., 1967, Cambridge (Eng.) U., 1968, 71, U. Cal., 1969-71. Lab. asst. Western Md. Coll., 1933-34, 1936-37; tchr. pub. schs., Worcester County, Md., 1934-36, Ridgeway, Va., 1940-41, Buckingham, Md., 1943-44, Chincoteague, Va., 1944-46; instr. Mars Hill Coll., 1946-48, asst. prof., 1948-52, asso. prof., 1952-56, prof. biology, 1956—, also head dept. biology, 1967—. Fellow A.A.A.S.; mem. Am. Soc. Naturalists, Am. Soc. Zoologists, Am. Soc. Ichtyologists and Herpetologists, Ecol. Soc. Am., Soc. Systematic Zoology, Genetics Soc. Am., Soc. Limnology and Oceanography, N.C. Acad. Sci., Assn. Southeastern Biologists, Am. Inst. Biol. Scis., Internat. Soc. Limnology, Freshwater Biol. Assn. (Gt. Britain), Am. Fisheries Soc., Animal Behavior Soc., Am. Micros. Soc., Am. Nature Study Soc., Assn. for Tropical Biology, Gulf and Caribbean Fisheries Inst., Assn. for Edn. Tchrs. in Sci., Nat., N.C. edn. assns., Sigma Xi, Beta Beta Beta. Research in field. Contbr. articles to profl. jours. Home: Marshall Rd Box 722-C Mars Hill NC 28754

OVELMAN, ROBERT MAXWELL, airline co. exec.; b. Hagerstown, Md., Mar. 9, 1930; s. Robert George and Gay (Frye) O.; A.A., Hagerstown Jr. Coll., 1950; B.S., Va. Poly. Inst., 1953, M.S., 1954; m. Mary Lynn Morini. Chief designer Morton W. Noble, Architect, Washington, 1957-60; architect Am. Airlines, N.Y.C., 1960-63; chief of specifications U.S. P.O. Dept., Washington, 1963-65; sr. architect Eastern Airlines, N.Y.C., 1965-68; dir. facilities Allegheny Airlines, Pitts., also Washington, 1968—. Mem. Bldg. Code Appeals Bd., Alexandria, Va., 1963-67, Bldg. Site Selection Com., Leesburg, Va., 1963. Served with USAF, 1955-57. Recipient Archtl. Student award So. Brick and Tile, 1952; Best House Design in Va. award Am. Home Mag., 1959; FAME award Eastern Airlines, 1968. Mem. Soc. Am. Registered Architects, Tau Sigma Delta. Home: 113 Thornton Ct Culpeper VA 22701 Office: Washington Nat Airport Washington DC 20001

OVERBY, GEORGE ROBERT, educator; b. Jacksonville, Fla., July 21, 1923; s. Taylor Earl and Virginia (Hewitt) O.; B.A., Fla. State U., 1951, Ph.D., 1966; M.Ed., U. Fla., 1959, specialist in edn., 1963. Tchr., Lake Forest Hills Elementary Sch., 1956-59, Ribault Secondary Sch., 1961-64; prin. Jacksonville Christian Schs., 1959-61; asso. prof. Slippery Rock (Pa.) State Coll., 1966-68; asso. prof. Youngstown (O.) State U., 1968-71; chmn. dept. edn. Shelton Coll., Cape Canaveral, Fla., 1971—. Cons pvt., pub. edn., 1958—. Pres. bd. trustees Christian Enterprises, Inc., 1962-66; adv. bd. Am. Security Council. Served as aviator USNR, 1943-46. Fellow Intercontinental Biog. Assn. (life); mem. William Holmes McGuffey Hist. Soc., Am. Assn. Higher Ed. (life, charter), N.E.A. (life), Am. Assn. U. Profs., Assn. Childhood Edn. Internat., Nat. Council for Social Studies, Kappa Delta Pi (life), Phi Delta Kappa. Home: PO Drawer C Cape Canaveral FL 32920

OVERCASH, ANNIE JUANITA ROBERTS (MRS. H. HURSHEL OVERCASH), ednl. adminstr.; b. LaGrange, Ga., July 10, 1934; d. Olin Alvin and Annie Kate (Underwood) Roberts; certificate in secretarial sci., LaGrange Coll., 1957; m. H. Hurshel Overcash, Mar. 22, 1953; 1 son, Daryl Hurshel. Exec. sec. to dir. indsl. relations Callaway Mills Co., LaGrange, 1957-60; sec. to acad. dean LaGrange Coll., 1960-63, asso. registrar, 1963-66, acting registrar, 1966-68, registrar, 1968—. Mem. Am., Ga. assns. collegiate registrars and admissions officers. Baptist. Home: Pyne Rd LaGrange GA 30240

OVERGAARD, NEIL ALVIN, entomologist; b. Madera, Cal., July 24, 1929; s. Niels M. and Karen (Tommerstol) O.; student Fresno State Coll., 1947-49; B.S., U. Cal., 1951; m. Carol Dee, June 3, 1961; children— Karen Lynn, Trina, Christian, Craig. Agrl. insp. Tulare County, Visalia, Cal., 1953, Alameda County, Oakland, Cal., 1953-57; agrl. commr. Plumas County, Quincy, Cal., 1957-61; entomologist U.S. Forest Service, Alexandria, La., 1963—. Served with AUS, 1952-53. Decorated Bronze Star medal. Jehovah Witness. Home: 117 Arlington Dr Pineville LA 71360 Office: 2500 Shreveport Hwy Pineville LA 71360

OVERMYER, ROBERT FRANKLYN, astronaut; b. Lorain, O., July 14, 1936; s. Rolandus and Margaret (Fabian) O.; B.S. in Physics, Baldwin Wallace Coll., 1958; M.S. in Aeros., U.S. Naval Postgrad. Sch., 1964; m. Katherine Ellen Jones, Oct. 17, 1959; children—Carolyn Marie, Patricia Ann, Robert Rolandus. Commd. 2d. lt. USMC, 1958, advanced through grades to maj., 1970; completed aerospace research pilot sch. Edwards AFB, 1966; astronaut with Manned Orbiting Lab., 1966-69, NASA Manned Spacecraft Center, Houston, 1969—. Recipient Alumni Merit award Baldwin Wallace Coll., 1967. Mem. Soc. Exptl. Text Pilots (asso.), Sigma Xi. Home: 18510 Pt Lookout St Houston TX 77058 Office: NASA Manned Spacecraft Center Houston TX 77058

OVERSTREET, BONARO WILKINSON, author, lectr.; b. Geyserville, Cal., Oct. 30, 1902; d. Edward and Margaret Elizabeth (Bonar) Wilkinson; A.B., U. Cal., 1925, tchr.'s certificate, 1926; m. Harry Allen Overstreet, Aug. 23, 1932. Research asso. Am. Assn. Adult Edn., 1939-40; instr. adult edn. Claremont Co., Cal., summer, 1940, Mills Coll., Cal., summer, 1941, U. Mich. Extension Service, 1945-46, 49, U. Cal., extension div., 1948. Mem. Am. Assn. for Adult Edn., Sigma Delta Pi, Phi Beta Kappa, Theta Sigma Phi. Clubs: Nat. Press, International (Washington). Author: (books) Poetic Way of Release, 1931; Footsteps on the Earth, 1934; Search for a Self, 1938; Brave Enough for Life, 1941; (with H. A. Overstreet) Town Meeting Comes to Town, 1938; Leaders for Adult Education (Am. Assn. Adult Edn.), 1940; American Reasons, 1943; Courage for Crisis, 1943; Freedom's People, 1945; How to Think About Ourselves, 1948; Understanding Fear: in Ourselves and Others, 1951; The Mind Alive (with H. A. Overstreet), 1954; Hands Laid Upon the Wind, 1956; The Mind Goes Forth 1956; (with H.A. Overstreet) What We Must Know About Communism, 1958, The War Called Peace: Krushchev's Communism, 1961, The Iron Curtain, 1963, The Strange Tactics of Extremism, 1964, The FBI in Our Open Society, 1969. Contbr. to jours. Home: 3409 Fiddler's Green Falls Church VA 22044

OVERSTREET, N.W., lawyer; b. Jackson, Miss., Nov. 14, 1913; ed. Millsaps Coll.; LL.B., U. Miss., 1936. Admitted to Miss. bar, 1936; mem. firm Overstreet & Kuykendall, Jackson. Served with AUS, 1940-45. Fellow Am., Miss. (pres. 1963-65) bar founds.; mem. Am., Hinds County (pres. 1954-55) bar assns., Miss. State Bar (pres. 1967-68). Office: 829 Deposit Guaranty Bldg Jackson MS 39205*

OVERTON, ELEAZER C., optometrist; b. Birmingham, Ala.; D.Optometry cum laude, Ill. Coll. Optometry, 1948; m. Elizabeth Merring; 6 children. Former br. mgr. Southeastern Optical Co., Birmingham; pvt. practice optometry, Birmingham; mem. Birmingham City Council. Active Jefferson County Aid for Retarded Children, Birmingham Pub. Schs. Study Com., P.T.A., Found for Mentally Retarded and Handicapped Children. Served with USNR, World War II; PTO. Fellow Am. Acad. Optometry; mem. Ala. (past pres.), Jefferson County (past pres.) optometric assns., Am. Optometric Found. (life, state chmn. trustee), Ala. Acad. Sci. (past chmn. social sci. sect., v.p.). Baptist (deacon). Contbr. articles to profl. jours. Address: City Council City Hall 710 N 20th St Birmingham AL 35203*

OVERTON, HELEN PARKER (MRS. SAMUEL WATKINS OVERTON), civic worker; b. Memphis, Dec. 30, 1920; d. William and Pearl (Pinkston) Parker; m. Samuel Watkins Overton, Sept. 3, 1952; children—Helen Parker, Napoleon Hill. Exec. sec. Memphis State U., 1941-43, Chgo. and So. Air Lines, 1943-46, Memphis Bd. Edn., 1948-50; dir. women's program Sta. WHBQ-TV, Memphis, 1950-52. Pres., Beethoven Club, 1960-66, 72—; chmn. Tenn. Arts Commn., 1968-70; pres. Mid-South Opera Guild, 1966—; dir. auditions Mid-South region Met. Opera, 1961-71, mem. nat. council, 1961—. Bd. dirs. Memphis Acad. Arts, Memphis Opera Theatre, Arts Appreciation. Mem. Sigma Alpha Iota, Alpha Gamma Delta. Clubs: Memphis Country, Summit (Memphis). Home: 5476 Collingwood Cove Memphis TN 38117

OVERTON, JOSEPH ALLEN, JR., mining exec.; b. Parkersburg, W.Va., Apr. 17, 1921; s. Joseph Allen and Edith (Wharton) O.; J.D., Washington & Lee U., 1946; m. Bette Crosswhite, May 15, 1943; children—Joseph Allen III, Rebecca A., Mallory E. Admitted to W.Va. bar, 1947; mem. firm Handlan, Overton & Earley, Parkersburg, 1949-54; spl. asst. to gen. counsel Dept. Commerce, 1955-56, dep. gen. counsel, 1956-59; mem. U.S. Tariff Commn., 1959-62, vice chmn., 1959-60; adminstrv. v.p. Am. Mining Congress, Washington, 1962, exec. v.p., 1963-71, pres., 1972—, pub. Mining Congress Jour., 1963—. Mem. W.Va. Legislature, 1948-50; exec. dir. W.Va. Republican Exec. Com., 1951-54; spl. asst. to chmn. Nat. Citizens for Eisenhower, 1954-55. Served from pvt. to 1st lt. USAAF, 1941-46. Mem. Am., W.Va., Fed. bar assns., Am. Legion, 40 and 8, Phi Kappa Psi. Episcopalian. Elk. Home: 4677 N Dittmar Rd Arlington VA 22207 Office: Ring Bldg 18th St NW Washington DC 20036

OVERTON, NELSON TILGHMAN, judge; b. Newport News, Va., Feb. 7, 1928; s. Nelson Chilcoat and Lucile (Tilghman) O.; B.A., Va. Mil. Inst., 1949; LL.B., U. Va., 1952; m. Margaret Lee Payne, June 18, 1952; children—Nancy Chilcoat, Waverly Nelson, Margaret Lee. Admitted to Va. bar, 1952, practiced in Hampton, 1952-53, 55-64; judge 11th Jud. Circuit of Va., Hampton, 1964—. Served from 2d lt. inf. to 1st lt. Judge Advocates Gens. Corps, AUS, 1953-55. Mem. Va., Hampton bar assns., Order of Coif, Raven Soc., Kappa Alpha, Phi Delta Phi. Methodist. Home: 102 Congress Av Hampton VA 23369 Office: Circuit Ct Hampton VA 23369

OVERTON, STANLEY D., savs. and loan assn. exec.; b. Dickson, Tenn., May 2, 1928; s. Dallas Stanley and Ova (Dixon) O.; student Fall's Bus. Coll., 1948-49, Internat. Accountants Soc., 1950-52; grad. Savs. and Loan Sch., Ind. U., 1961-63; m. Betty Jo Womble, Aug. 31, 1948; children—Stanley D., James Stanton. With Fidelity Fed. Savs. & Loan Assn., Nashville, 1950—, exec. v.p., 1963-67, pres., 1967—, also dir.; dir. FLC Corp. Bd. dirs. local A.R.C., YMCA. Served with USNR, 1946-48. Mem. U.S. (dir.), Tenn. (past bd. dirs., pres. 1969-70) savs. and loan league, Am. Savs. and Loan Inst. (past pres. Nashville), Nashville Area C. of C. (bd. govs.). Mason (32 deg., Shriner), Kiwanian. Clubs: Hillwood Country (bd. dirs.), City (bd. dirs., pres. 1969-70) (Nashville). Home: 5908 Long Meadow Rd Nashville TN 37205 Office: 401 Union St Nashville TN 37219

OVERTON, WILLIAM WARD, JR., banker; b. Kansas City, Kan., Apr. 30, 1897; s. William Ward and Ella (Barnes) O.; student pvt. schs., Kansas City U., U. Tex.; m. Evelyn Lucas, June 10, 1924; children—Nancy (Mrs. Mark Lemmon), William T. (dec.), Thomas N. With W. W. Overton & Co., brokers, 1913—, pres. 1932-61, chmn. bd., 1961—; dir. Tex. Bank & Trust Co., Dallas, 1936—, chmn. bd., 1947-71, pres., 1961-65; adv. dir. Southland Corp.; dir. Dallas, Tex. Corp., Fishburn Cleaning & Laundry; pres. Dallas Clearing House Assn., 1962, 65, dir., 1967; dir. Beaver, Meade & Englewood R.R. Co. Hon. life mem. bd. dirs. Dallas chpt. A.R.C., past vice chmn. bd. govs., vice chmn. nat. fund, 1963, chmn. nat. conv., 1967; council mem. at-large Boy Scouts Am.; dir., exec. com. Tex. Research League; dir., chmn. finance com. Trinity Improvement Assn.; chmn. planning and research com. Dallas Central Bus. Dist. Assn., 1966-67, exec. com., 1965-66; bd. dirs., treas., adv. com., sec. treas., 1968-69, bd. dirs. 1968-70; Dallas Theater Center; trustee, finance com. Southwestern Med. Found.; trustee Tex. Research Found., trustee Tex. Safety Assn.; gov. Dallas Found.; bd. advisers Nat. Fund Med. Edn., 1966-67; dir. Dallas Council World Affairs, chmn., 1957-58; trustee, chmn. fund raising campaign S.W. Center for Advanced Studies, 1966—; exec. bd. Boys Club Dallas; chmn. youth study schs. service com. Council Social Agys. Dallas; adv. com. Dallas Pilot Inst. for Deaf; sponsor's com. Dallas Services for Blind, U. Dallas, 1959; mem. Robert Morris Assos.; dir. Dallas Citizens Council, Inc., Family Service, Dallas Zool. Soc.; dir., finance com. Dallas Crime Commn.; dir. Dallas Mus. Contemporary Arts, Citizens Traffic Commn.; past pres. and chmn. bd. Caruth Meml. Rehab. Inst.;

dir. Dallas County Campaign Screening Com., pres., 1962-65; dir; nat. council Met. Opera Bd. Dallas; v.p. Greater Dallas Planning Com., dir., 1966-67; adv. council Sch. Internat. Affairs, Columbia U.; adminstrv. com:, chmn. regional adv. council, life councillor, past trustee Nat. Indsl. Conf. Bd. chmn. bd. trustees, 1961-63; mem. Tex. Council State Fair Tex.; adv. bd. So. Meth. U. Grad. Sch. Banking, exec. com. bd. devel., sponsor dept. econs. doctoral program; adv. bd. League Women Voters, 1966-69; nat. council on good cities Action, Inc.; adv. com. Bus. Execs. Research Com., Charity Ball Found.; trustee St. Paul's Hosp.; adv. bd. Dallas Eye Bank.; nat. spl. gifts com. Nat. Conf. Christians and Jews; nat. emergency Com. Nat. Council Crime and Delinquency; dir. United Fund; mem. Tex. Emergency Resources Planning Com. Recipient Distinguished Service Plaque, Dallas County chpt., A.R.C.; Freedom Found. at Valley Forge award, 1962; Kudos Coll. award, Dallas; Testimonial Luncheon, Citizens Dallas. Served with U.S. Navy, World War I. Mem. Am. Bankers Assn. (exec. com., state chmn com. econ. edn. 1966-67), Internat. Mgmt. Congress (adv. bd.), Am. Acad. Polit. and Social Sci., Dallas Assos. Com. for Econ. Devel., Assn. Res. City Bankers (com. on corr. Bank Relations 1965-66), Nat. Planning Assn. (mem. nat. council), Dallas Hist. Soc. (trustee, finance com.), Tex. Hist. Soc. (dir.). Dallas C. of C. (past pres., dir. 1961-63, downtown Dallas com. 1966-67), Layman's Nat. Com. (nat. chmn. Nat. Bible Week 1962 chmn. spl. gifts com. 1963). U.S. C. of C (finance com., fgn. policy com.). Mason (33 deg., Shriner). Methodist (bd). Clubs: Brook Hollow Golf (past pres.), Dallas, City (Dallas); Little Sandy Hunting and Fishing (Hawkins, Tex., past pres.); Broadmoor Country, Garden of Gods (Colo. Springs, Colo.); Dallas Olympic Boosters; Rolling Rock (Ligonier, Pa.). Home: 4830 Cedar Springs, Dallas, TX 75219

OVERTON, MRS WILLIAM WARD, JR., civic worker; b. Dallas, Nov. 4, 1902; d. Thomas Madison and Josephine (Bradford) Lucas; grad. Smith Coll., 1924; m. William Ward Overton, Jr., June 10, 1924; children—Mrs. Mark Lemmon, Jr., William T., Thomas. Hon. chmn. S.W. hospitality bd. Dallas Met. Opera Assn., 1959-65, now chmn. adv. com., mem. bd.; mem. nat. council, patron mem. N.Y. Met. Opera Assn.; bd. mem. Dallas Symphony Guild, Guild Dallas Civic Opera; adv. com., womens bd. Dallas Civic Opera; adv. bd. Dallas Civic Ballet; adv. chmn. S.W. Hospitality Bd., 1969-70; mem. Gov. Tex. Preston Smith's Com. on Human Relations; mem. aux. bd. Rehab. Center, Dallas; mem. fine arts council So. Methodist U. Mem. Dallas Garden Center, Nat. Library League of Northwood Inst., Dallas Hist. Soc. Methodist. Clubs: Woman's Garden. Shakespeare (sec. 1960). Home: 4830 Cedar Springs Rd Dallas TX 75219

OWEN, AUSTIN EVERETT, III, lawyer; b. Norfolk, Va., July 21, 1924; s. Richard Clement and Judith (Berkley) O.; student Coll. William & Mary, Norfolk, Va., 1941-43, N.C. State Coll., 1943-44, U. Ky., 1944; J.D., U. Richmond, 1950; m. Edythe Virginia Dalton, July 22, 1950; children—Judith Claiborne, Elizabeth Dalton, Martha Berkley, Austin Everett IV. Admitted to Va. bar, 1950; asst. sec. Va. Alcoholic Beverage Control Bd., 1950-52; asst. U.S. Atty., Eastern Dist. Va., 1952-54; mem. firm Kellam & Kellam attys. at law, Norfolk, 1954-60; partner Owen, Guy, Rhodes & Betz, Virginia Beach, Va., 1961—. Pres. and dir. Commonwealth Bldg. Co., Virginia Beach, 1963-68, Virginia Beach Service Center, Inc., 1971—; commr. in chancery Circuit Ct., City of Virginia Beach, 1970—; dir. Bank of Va.-Tidewater, Virginia Beach; gen. counsel Tidewater Assn. Homebuilders, Norfolk, Va., 1964-67. Bd. dirs. Virginia Beach Tennis Patrons Assn., 1967-68, Health, Welfare, Recreation planning council, 1970—, United Community Fund, 1971—. Mem. Am., Va., Va. State, Norfolk-Portsmouth, Virginia Beach (pres. 1967) bar assns., Va. Trial Lawyers Assn., Delta Theta Phi. Democrat. Episcopalian (vestryman). Club: Princess Anne Country. Home: 3204 Sunnybrook Lane Virginia Beach VA 23452 Office: 281 Independence Blvd Virginia Beach VA 23462

OWEN, BEN, lawyer, state legislator; b. Columbus, Miss., July 12, 1921; s. Frank C. and Mary (Askew) O.; B.A., U. Miss., 1942, LL.B., 1947; m. Mary Jane Collins, June 12, 1949; children— Lydia, Frank, Marsha, David, Mary Jane, Judith. Admitted to Miss. bar, 1947, since practiced in Columbus; mem. Miss. Ho. of Reps., 1964-72. Served with AUS, 1942-46. Home: 2000 S 9th St Columbus MS 39701 Office: 2d Av N Columbus MS 39701

OWEN, DON, coll. pres.; b. Fletcher, Okla., Aug. 9, 1927; student Cameron Jr. Coll., 1946-48; B.S., Central State Coll., Okla., 1950; Ed.M., U. Okla., 1955, Ed.D., 1963; m. Audelle Lee Williams, Aug. 15, 1953;Shari, Andy, Flake. Tchr. math., Luther, Okla., 1950-51; tchr. math., sci., Fletcher, 1951-53; tchr. math., coach basketball, Lawton Okla., 1953-58; supt. Pioneer Schs., Chickasha, Okla., 1955-58; supt. schs., Arapaho, Okla., 1958-60, Clinton, Okla., 1960-66, Shawnee, Okla., 1966-69; pres. Cameron Coll., Lawton, 1969—. Chmn., Okla. State Textbook Com., 1969—. Mem. Am., Okla. (v.p. bd. dirs.) assns. sch. adminstrs., Nat., Okla. edn. assns., Lawton C. of C., Phi Delta Kappa. Mason (Shriner), Rotarian, Elk. Address: Cameron Coll Lawton OK 73501

OWEN, DONALD BRUCE, educator; b. Portland, Ore., Jan. 24, 1922; s. Floyd Nelson and Daisy (Stuart) O.; B.S., U. Wash., 1945, M.S., 1946, Ph.D., 1951; m. Ellen Adair Knox, Aug. 8, 1952; children—Mary Ellen, David, Matthew, Mark. Instr. math. U. Wash., Seattle, 1951-52; asst. prof. math. Purdue U., 1952-54; math. statistician Sandia Corp., Albuquerque, 1954-57, supr. statis. research, 1957-64; prof., head math. and stochastic systems div. S.W. Center for Advanced Studies, Dallas, 1964-66; prof. statistics So. Meth. U., Dallas, 1966—, chmn. dept. statistics, 1972—. Served with USAAF, 1942-43. Fellow Am. Statis. Assn., Inst. Math. Statistics, A.A.A,S.; mem. Am. Math. Soc., Biometrics Soc., Am. Soc. Quality Control, Internat. Assn. for Statistics in Phys. Scis., Am. Soc. Clin. Pharmacology and Therapeutics, Sigma Xi, Phi Beta Kappa. Author: (with G.J. Lieberman) Tables of the Hypergeometric Probability Distribution, 1961; Handbook of Statistical Tables, 1962. Contbr. articles to profl. jours. Editor: Selected Tables in Mathematical Statistics, 1970. Asso. editor Technometrics, 1965-71, Jour. Am. Statis. Assn., 1967-71. Home: 7614 Tophill Lane Dallas TX 75240 Office: So Meth U Dallas TX 75222

OWEN, EDGAR LYLE, educator; b. Kiowa County, Okla., July 25, 1906; s. Edgar and Stella Beatrice (Tibbets) O.; A.B., S.W. Mo. State Coll., 1927; M.A., U. Wis., 1928, Ph.D., 1937; m. Mary Vincent Kwapinski, Sept. 17, 1940 (div. Oct. 1961); children—Edgar Lauren, Robert Dale, Judith Irene. Teaching asst. econs. U. Wis., 1929-30; instr. econs. Carnegie Inst. Tech., 1930-38, asst. prof. econs. and govt., 1938-45; asso. prof. econs. U. Tulsa, 1945-47, prof. econs., 1947—, head dept. econs., 1945-69. Mem. Am. Assn. U. Profs., Am. Civil Liberties Union, Mo. Archaeol. Soc., State Hist. Soc. Mo., White River Valley Hist. Soc. Contbr. articles to profl. jours. Home: Route 1 Box 832 Branson MO 65616

OWEN, GUY, JR., author; b. Clarkton, N.C., Feb. 24; s., 1925 Guy and Margaret (Elkins) O.; B.A., U. N.C., 1947, M.A., 1949, Ph.D., 1955; m. Dorothy Jennings, 1953; children—William James, John Leslie. Tchr. U. N.C., Chapel Hill, Davidson (N.C.) Coll., Elon (N.C.) Coll.; now asso. prof. English, Stetson U., Deland, Fla. Served with AUS. Author: Cape Fear Country and Other Poems, 1958; Season of Fear, 1960; Journey for Joedel; White Stallion (poems); novels. Editor: So. Poetry Rev. Co.-editor: Southern Poetry Today, 1962; New Essays in Modern American Literature, 1962. Contbr. poems, revs., articles and short stories to numerous periodicals. Home: 15 Valencia Ct Deland FL 32720*

OWEN, HARRIS, program dir. KARK, Little Rock. Address: 10th and Spring Sts Little Rock AR 72203*

OWEN, JOE JEFFERSON, utilities exec.; b. Binger, Okla., Nov. 16, 1931; s. Glenn Lee and Lora Eller (Turney) O.; student Okla. State U., 1950-54; m. Eva Jean Bailey, Aug. 30, 1958; children—Glen, Mark, Dale, Lora, Mary. Salesman, Black Advt. Agy., 1954-55; salesman Bewley Mills, Dallas, 1955-56; jobber sales rep. E.Tex. and W.La., Flour Mills Am., 1956-57; rural sales rep. Okla. Gas & Electric Co., Ardmore, 1957-67, residential sales rep., 1967—. Sec.-treas. Ardmore Homebuilders Assn.; parliamentarian So. Okla. Water Corp., 1971—; cons. Town of Dickson, Okla. Chmn. res. div. Operation Pride, county chmn. Environmental Pride in Carter County, 1970-73; chmn. fund raising com. Dickson Area Fire Bldg., 1970; chmn. container div. Heart Fund Ardmore, 1962-63; area capt. March of Dimes, 1963-64. Democratic precinct chmn., 1965-70. Pres., United Comml. Travelers Am., 1969, now mem. exec. com.; bd. dirs. Sr. citizens Council Ardmore, Royal Ambassadors. Mem. Nat. Assn. Home Builders, Okla. State U. Alumni Assn., Carter County (dir., past pres.), Okla. Jr. (v.p.), Ardmore Jr. (pres., dir.), Ardmore (dir.) chambers commerce. Baptist (deacon). Clubs: Toastmasters (past v.p.), Okla. Gas and Electric Co. Mens (past pres.). Home: Route 1 Box 88 Ardmore OK 73401 Office: PO Box 129 Ardmore OK 73401

OWEN, JOHN PIPKIN, educator; b. Newport, Ark., Sept. 13, 1919; s. Henry M. and Alice C. (Pipkin) O.; B.A., La. State U., 1941, M.B.A., 1944, Ph.D., 1949; m. Yvonne M. Olinde, Aug. 16, 1947; children— Trina A., Yvonne T., Joan P., J. Elizabeth, John P. Instr. econs. La. State U., 1946-49; prof. econs., dir. grad. studies Coll. Bus. Adminstrn. U. Houston, 1949-67, chmn. dept. econs. and finance, 1949-66; dean Coll. Bus. Adminstrn., U. Ark., 1967—. Tex. mem. Econ. Stblzn. Planning Task Group. Recipient Small Bus. Adminstrn. research grant to Center Research, U. Houston, 1962. Mem. Am., So. econ. assns., Southwestern Social Sci. Assn., Southwestern Bus. Adminstrn. (pres. 1971-72), Indsl. Relations Research Assn., Sch. Banking of the South (sec. leader), Am. Arbitration Assn., Fed. Mediation and Conciliation Ser., Rotary Internat., Fayetteville C. of C., Phi Kappa Phi, Beta Gamma Sigma. Author: Syllabus and Workbook for Principles of Economics, 1952; What's Wrong With Workmen's Compensation, 1956; Adequacy of the Louisiana Unemployment Compensation Fund, 1949; Survey of Grievance and Arbitration Proceedings in The Houston Industrial Area, 1953; The Determination of Economic Feasibility of Multiple-Purpose Dams, 1957. Co-author: Mantrap; The Anatomy of a Workforce Reduction, 1967. Office: Coll Bus Adminstrn U Ark Fayetteville AR 72701

OWEN, KENNETH DALE, orthodontist; b. Charlotte, N.C., May 9, 1938; s. Olin Watson and Ruth (Watlington) O.; B.S., Davidson Coll., 1959; D.D.S., U. N.C., 1963, M.Sc. in Orthodontics, 1967; m. Lura Aven Carnes, Feb. 14, 1958; children—Kenneth Dale, Aven Anna. Individual practice orthodontics, Charlotte, 1966—. Asst. clin. prof. U. N.C. Sch. Dentistry, 1969-72. Served with Dental Corps, AUS, 1963-65. Mem. Am. Dental Assn., Am. Assn. Orthodontists, So. Soc. Orthodontists, N.C. Orthodontic Soc., N.C. (Jour. dist. editor 67-69; del. 1969-71), 2d Dist. (sec.-treas. 1971-72), Charlotte (chmn. various coms.) dental socs., U. N.C. Orthodontic Alumni Assn. (sec.-treas. 1971), Orthovista Orthodontic Study Group (pres. 1968; treas. 1972), Delta Sigma Delta (pres. N.C. grad. chpt.), Omicron Kappa Upsilon, Alpha Epsilon Delta. Methodist (steward 1968-69, adminstrn. bd. 1969-71). Home: 828 Longbow St Charlotte NC 28211 Office: 1201 E Morehead St Charlotte NC 28204

OWEN, LEONIDAS HORACE, JR., chem. co. exec.; b. Parkersburg, N.C., Mar. 6, 1932; s. Leonidas Horace and Nellie (Smith) O.; student Lamar Tech. Inst., 1959; m. Barbara Harris, Feb. 6, 1954; children—Ellen, Lee, Paul. Process operator Spencer Chems., Orange, Tex., 1955-60; start-up engr. Lummus Co., N.Y.C., C. & I. Girdler, Louisville, Ky., J.F. Prichard, Kansas City, Mo., 1960-66; plant supt. Green Valley Chem. Corp., Creston, Ia., 1966; prodn. supt. Terra Chem., Internat., Sergeant Bluff, Ia., 1966-68, mgr. operations, 1968-70, mgr. maintenance, 1970-71, plant mgr. Farmers Nat. Chem., Inc. Plainview, Tex., 1971—. Adult volunteer Sgt. Floyd council Boy Scouts Am., 1969. Served with USNR, 1949-53. Mem. Am. Soc. Mech. Engrs. Home: 1100 Itasca St Plainview TX 79072 Office: PO Box 1954 Plainview TX 79072

OWEN, MARTIN FREDERICK, mining co. exec.; b. Houston, June 26, 1932; s. William Frank and May Elizabeth (Spraull) O.; B.B.A., U. Tex., 1958, LL.B., 1959; m. Nancy Harwell, Aug. 30, 1957; children—Scott, Melissa, Steven. With Humble Oil & Refining Co., Houston, 1959-66; v.p. land and legal affairs Duval Corp., Houston, 1966—. Served with USMCR, 1952-54. Mem. Internat., Am., Tex. bar assns. Home: 6503 Fawnwood St Spring TX 77373 Office: 900 SW Tower St Houston TX 77002

OWEN, RAY, vice pres., gen. mgr. WAPA, Santurce, P.R. Address: 1304 Ponce de Leon Av Santurce PR 00905*

OWEN, RICHARD LACY, tobacco co. exec.; b. Richmond, Va., Nov. 18, 1928; s. Richard Dudley and Mabel E. (Britton) O.; B.S. in Civil Engring., Va. Mil. Inst., 1951; m. Jane Albert Royal, Nov. 20, 1954; children—Elizabeth Jane, Lynda Jean, Kathryn Rose. Asst. chief engr. Imperial Tobacco Group Ltd., Am. Leaf Orgn., Wilson, N.C., 1953-64, chief engr., 1964-68, v.p. engring., 1968—. Served to 1st lt. USAF, 1951-53. Methodist. Elk, Rotarian. Club: Wilson (N.C.) Country. Home: 1203 Waverly Rd Wilson NC 27893 Office: Box 1848 Wilson NC 27893

OWEN, RIPLEY PENDLETON, hosp. adminstr.; b. Lynchburg, Va., Mar. 27, 1936; s. William L. and Ester M. (Miller) O.; student U. Va., 1957-58, U. Wis., 1959-60, Internat. Accountants Soc., 1967-68; m. C. Jean Hardwick, Dec. 24, 1960; 1 dau., Patricia Hardwick. Indsl. engr. Babcock & Wilcox Co., 1956-60; prodn. engr. Reactive Metals, Inc., 1961-62; quality control mgr., dir. personnel Daystrom div. Schlumberger, 1963-66; adminstr. South Boston (Va.) Gen. Hosp., 1966—, treas., 1968—. Pres. Halifax County Mental Health Assn., 1969-70. Bd. dirs. Danville Area Clinic for Mental Health, 1968—, v.p., 1971-72. Served with USMCR, 1954-55. Recipient citation Halifax County Mental Health Assn., 1970. Mem. Am., Va. hosp. assns. Lion. Home: Route 2 Box 721 Halifax VA 24558 Office: N Main St South Boston VA 24592

OWEN, SAMUEL AUGUSTUS, clergyman; b. Stanton, Tenn., July 21, 1886; s. Henry Clay and Fannie (Ware) O.; A.B., Morehouse Coll., Atlanta, 1911, A.M., 1922; D.D., Roger Williams U., 1922; m. Mary Jane Wood, June 1, 1916; 1 son, Samuel Augustus. Ordained to ministry Baptist Ch., 1912; pastor chs. in Fla., 1913-20, Memphis, 1923—; pres. Tenn. Bapt. M. & E. Conv., 1936-65; moderator West Tenn. M. & E. Bapt. Assn., 1928-61; v.p. Nat. Bapt. Conv., Inc. Trustee LeMoyne-Owen Coll., Griggs Bus. Coll. Served to capt. AUS, 1941-44. Named Chattanooga ambassador of goodwill, 1966. Mem. Urban League, N.A.A.C.P., So. Christian Leadership Conf., Am. Legion, Phi Beta Sigma. Mason, K.P., Modern Woodman. Home: 1794 Netherwood Av Memphis TN 38114

OWEN, WILLIAM ABNER, educator; b. Elmira, N.Y., Aug. 1, 1925; s. Abner W. and Mary (Gordon) O.; B.A., Niagara U., 1949; M.A., Columbia U., 1951; Ph.D., Georgetown U., 1964; m. Myrta Sanoguet, May 26, 1964; children—William Abner, Maria, Grace, Myrta, Lawrence. Instr. U. P.R., Mayaguez, 1950—, dir. dept. humanities, 1964—. Served with AUS, 1943. Address: College Station Mayaguez PR 00708

OWEN, WILLIAM HAIGH, III, pub. co. exec.; b. Fayetteville, N.C., Aug. 18, 1934; s. William Haigh and Ethel Elizabeth (Harris) O.; student Fayetteville Tech. Inst. Electronics, 1967; grad. computer tech. Internat. Corr. Schs., 1970; m. Treva Ann Beck, Oct. 1, 1955; children—Cynthia Ann, Elizabeth Luann. Printer, mailer, machinist Fayetteville Pub. Co., 1952-65, composing room supt., 1965-66, prodn. mgr., 1966—; instr. Fayetteville Tech. Inst., 1969. Mem. N.C. N.G., 1952-60. Mem. N.C. Press Assn. Mech. Conf., So. Newspaper Pub. Assn. (exec. com. mech. div. 1971-74), Internat. Mgmt. Council. Democrat. Methodist (chmn. financial com. 1971). Club: Green Valley Golf and Country (Fayetteville). Home: 2517 Fordham Dr Fayetteville NC 28304 Office: 512 Hay St Fayetteville NC 28302

OWENDOFF, ROBERT SCOTT, navy officer; b. Washington, Mar. 16, 1945; s. Robert Albert and Vauda Mae (Paugh) O.; B.S., U.S. Naval Acad., 1968. Commd. ensign USN, 1968, advanced through grades to lt., 1971; staff officer U.S. Naval Oceanographic Office, Suitland, Md., 1968, student U.S. Naval Nuclear Power Sch., Bainbridge, Md., 1968-69, main propulsion asst. U.S.S. Page (DEG-5), Newport, R.I., 1969-70, engr. officer U.S.S. San Marcos (LSD-25), Norfolk, Va., 1970-71, engr. officer U.S.S. Thomaston (LSD-28), San Diego, Cal., 1971—. Recipient Award for Excellence in Research, Va. Acad. Sci., 1960. Mem. Antiquarian Horological Soc., Va. Acad. Sci. Home: 11156 Byrd Dr Fairfax VA 22030 Office: USS Thomaston (LSD-28) F P O San Francisco CA 96601

OWENS, ARTHUR NEAL, plastic surgeon; b. Heflin, Ala., Aug. 5, 1899; s. James Arthur and Laura (Neal) O.; B.S., U. Ala., 1924; M.D., Emory U., 1926; m. Georgia May Little, Sept. 30, 1931; children—Laura (Mrs. George Lewis), Lucile (Mrs. John C. Pryor), Alice (Mrs. Lee Johnson), Arthur Neal. Rotating intern Birmingham Baptist Hosp.; resident St. Agnes Hosp., Balt.; gen. surg. tng. with Dr. Joseph Bloodgood, Balt., 1928-31, also tng. plastic surgery; with Dr. John Stairge Davis, Balt., study plastic surgery with Dr. Harold Gillies, London, 1921; prof. plastic surgery Tulane U. Sch. Medicine; head dept., prof. plastic surgery Eye, Ear, Nose and Throat Hosp., New Orleans; cons. staff Touro Infirmary, Ill. Central R.R. Hosp., USPHS Hosp., Crippled Children's Hosp.; surg. staff Hotel Dieu, Mercy Hosp., Sara Mayo Hosp.; vis. surgeon of contour, surg. tub for treatment of burns and infected wounds, protection pressure dressing for wound treatment, surgical fabric, use of periosteal grafts. Pres., bd. dirs. Audubon Park Natatorium; mem. Audubon Park Commn. Served with USN, 1918. Recipient Honor award Am. Med. Writers. Diplomate Am. Bd. Plastic Surgery (past chmn.). Fellow A.C.S., Southeastern Soc. Plastic and Reconstructive Surgery (past pres.), Am. Surg. Assn., Internat. Coll. Surgeons (exec. council, v.p. U.S. sect., chmn. plastic surgery sect.); mem. Am. Assn. Plastic Surgeons (past pres., trustee), Am. Soc. Plastic and Reconstructive Surgeons (past pres.), A.M.A., So. Med. Assn., La., Orleans Parish med. socs., Am. Cancer Soc. (bd. dirs.), C. of C. (bd. dirs., mems. council), S.A.R., La. Soc., Internat. House, Sigma Chi, Phi Chi, Alpha Phi Omega. Clubs: Rotary, New Orleans Country; Metropolitan, Lotus (N.Y.C.); Lake Shore, Southern Yacht, Little Lake (pres.); Bohemian Club (San Francisco). Editor, Internat. Abstract Plastic and Reconstructive Surgery; year book on plastic surgery. Patentee Surg. dressings electric razor, land clearing blade. Home and Office: Apt 12-K The Carol 2100 St Charles Av New Orleans LA 70140

OWENS, BERYL HENRY, physician; b. Cawood, Ky., Nov. 17, 1926; s. Jessee Edward and Leota Frances (Ledford) O.; B.S magna cum laude, Lincoln Meml. U., 1950; M.D., U. Va., 1954; m. Mary Elizabeth Bray, Feb. 5, 1955; children—Courtney Beryl (dec.), Whitney Henry. Intern Fitzsimmon Army Hosp., Denver, 1954-55; gen. practice medicine Rose Hill, Va., 1955—; mem. staffs Middlesboro (Ky.) Hosp. and Clinic, Lee Gen. Hosp., Pennington Gap, Va. Med. adviser Lee County OEO, 1969, Lee County Draft Bd., 1966-72; mem. Adv. Com. on Health Occupations and Professions to State Council Higher Edn., 1971—. Chmn. Lee County Sch. Bd., 1969-71. Adminstr. Courtney Beryl Owens Meml. Scholarship Fund, 1969—. Mem. Lee County, Va. med. socs., A.M.A., Civitan Club (past pres. twice). Home: Box 98 Rose Hill VA 24281 Office: Box 193 Rose Hill VA 24281

OWENS, DEVEAUX LEGRAND, physician, banker; b. Limestone, Ark., July 28, 1897; s. James Newton and Grace Carroll (Ratcliffe) O.; M.D., U. Tenn., 1921; m. Edna Laura Stephenson, Dec. 19, 1921 (dec. June 1961); children—Doris (Mrs. Gaither C. Johnston), Laurel Joy (Mrs. Bill Burrette, Jr.); m. Glenna Jo Johnson, July 1, 1967. Intern, Little Rock City Hosp., 1921-22; gen. practice medicine, Harrison, Ark., 1922-66; mem. staff Boon County Hosp.; sr. v.p. 1st Nat. Bank, Harrison, Ark., 1946—, also dir.; v.p. Bank Credit Life Ins. Co., Harrison, Ark., 1958—, also dir. Bd. dirs. Boon County Hosp. Sec., bd. dirs. Ark. Bd. Med. Examiners, 1937-45; sec. Ark. Med. Council, 1928-47. Chmn., N.W. Ark. Dist. Examining Bd. and Appeals Bd., 1942-45. Mem. A.M.A., Mid South (v.p. 1958), Ark. (v.p. 1946), N.W. Ark. Dist. (pres. 1950), Boon County (pres. 1925) med. socs., Lion. Home: 406 N Ridge St Harrison AR 72601 Office: Box 875 Harrison AR 72601

OWENS, HUGH FRANKLIN, govt. ofcl.; b. Muskogee, Okla., Oct. 15, 1909; s. James Francis and Elizabeth (Turner) O.; A.B., U. Ill., 1931; LL.B., U. Okla., 1934; m. Louise Simon, Dec. 27, 1934; 1 dau., Julie (Mrs. William Charles Pickens). Admitted to Ill. bar, 1934, Okla. bar, 1934, U.S. Supreme Ct. bar; asso. firm Cummins, Hagenah & Flynn, Chgo., 1934-36. Rainey, Flynn, Green & Anderson, Oklahoma City, 1936-48; partner firm Hervey, May & Owens, Oklahoma City, 1948-51; div. atty. Superior Oil Co., Midland, Tex., 1951-53; gen. counsel Nat. Asso. Petroleum Co., Tulsa, 1953; practiced in Oklahoma City, 1953-59; adminstr. Okla. Securities Commn., Oklahoma City, 1959-64; commr. SEC, Washington, 1964—. Faculty, Oklahoma City U. Sch. Law, 1957-64. Bd. dirs. Salvation Army, Community Fund, Oklahoma City, 1938-41. Served as lt. comdr. USNR, World War II. Mem. Ret. Officers Assn., Okla., Kan. (hon. life) bar assns., U.S. Jr. C. of C. (past v.p.), Nat. Assn. Regulatory Utility Commrs. (exec. com.), Oklahoma City C. of C. (bd. dirs.), Phi Delta Phi, Sigma Chi (Significant Sig award). K.C. Democrat. Clubs: Men's Dinner (Oklahoma City); Metropolitan, Chevy Chase (Washington). Home: 4301 Massachusetts Av NW Washington DC 20016 Office: SEC 500 N Capitol St NW Washington DC 20549

OWENS, JACK VICTOR, rubber co. exec.; b. Charleston, S.C., Mar. 3, 1923; s. Samuel David and Emelyne (Wyndhan) O.; B.S., The Citadel, 1949; m. Thelma C. Heape, Mar. 7, 1952; children—Nancy, Jack Victor, Paul, Ronald, Richard. Lab. technician Raybestos-Manhattan, North Charleston, S.C., 1950-53, project dir., 1953-59, asst. dir. research and devel. rubber div., 1959—. Served with AUS, 1942-46. Decorated Purple Heart. Mem. Am. Chem. Soc., Charleston Chem. Engrs. Baptist. Home: 4948 Ashby Av North Charleston SC 29406 Office: Raybestos Manhattan North Charleston SC 29406

OWENS, JAMES CLARENCE, dentist; b. Roxboro, N.C., Feb. 19, 1916; s. Major and Lelia (Barnett) O.; B.S., Shaw U., 1938; postgrad. N.C. Coll., 1946; D.D.S., Meharry Med. Coll., 1950; m. Mary Lue Johnson, Feb. 10, 1941; children—Philip, James. Tchr., Person County Tng. Sch., 1938-42; practice dentistry, Roxboro, 1950—. Vice-chmn. Human Relations Commn., Roxboro, 1966-68, Roxboro Housing Authority, 1966-68. Mem. N.C. Democratic Exec. Com., 1970—; mem. Roxboro Council, 1968—, mayor pro-tem, 1971—. Bd. dirs. Roxboro United Fund, 1969-70. Served with AUS, 1943-46. Mem. Nat. Dental Assn. (mem. ho. of dels. 1968—), Old North State Dental Soc. (mem. exec. bd. 1958-59), Phi Beta Sigma. Baptist (chmn. bd. deacons 1967—). Home: 132 Trotter St Roxboro NC 27573 Office: 135 Gordon St Roxboro NC 27573

OWENS, JAMES MOFFATT, govt. ofcl.; b. Syracuse, N.Y., Feb. 15, 1917; s. James and Annie (Nicholson) O.; B.S., N.Y. State Coll., 1938; m. Marion Kiszonak, Oct. 8, 1942; children—Julie Ann, J. Michael. Assn. purchasing agt., Foreman U.S. Gypsum Co., Lisbon Falls, Me., 1938-39, asst. supt. fabrication plant, 1939-40, supt., 1940-42; tech. rep. on adhesives, plastics Am. Cyanamid Co., N.Y.C., 1946-47; plant supt. Fancher Furniture Co., Salamanca, N.Y., 1948-49; asso. prof. Coll. of Forestry, Syracuse, N.Y., 1950; asst. chief lumber, wood products OPS, Washington, 1951-53; head indsl. engring. Office Q.M. Gen., Washington, 1953; asst. dir. forest products div. Bus. and Def. Services Adminstrn., U.S. Dept. of Commerce, Washington, 1953-55, dep. dir., 1956-57, dir. 1957-61, dir. office indsl. materials, 1961-63, dir. office metals and minerals, 1963-68, dir. office basic materials, 1968—, v.p. credit union, 1963-67, pres., 1967—, also dir. U.S. Trade Mission to Yugoslavia, 1959. Mem. Pinerest Citizens Assn. (v.p. 1957). Served as capt. USAAF, 1944-45. Mem. Soc. Am. Foresters (chmn. Washington sect. 1959-60), Nat. Lumber Survey Com. (sec. 1954-63), Am. Inst. M.E. Contbr. numerous articles pub. in profl. jours. Home: 4315 Marionet St Alexandria VA 22312 Office: Dept of Commerce Washington DC 20230

OWENS, LOYD PARMER, agrl. extension agt.; b. Hopewell, Ala., June 2, 1925; s. Harvey Linvell and Lora (Harris) O.; student Jacksonville U., 1947-48; B.S., Auburn U., 1951, M.S., 1966; m. Dona McLendon, June 13, 1947; children—Ricky Lynn, Donna Gayle. Collection mgr. Sears Roebuck & Co., Anniston, Ala., 1952-54; asst. county agt. Extension Service Auburn U., Talladega, 1954-62, farm agt. Ashland, 1962-71, county extension chmn., Centreville, Ala., 1971—. Adv. Jr. Cattlemen Assn., 1967-71, Jr. Ham Radio Club, 1965-71; com. mem. Boy Scouts Am., 1958-62, scout master, 1963-65; pres. Ashland P.T.A., 1965-66; pres. Ashland Band Boosters Club, 1968-69; dir. and chmn. agr. div. Clay County United Givers Fund, 1968-70. Served with USNR, 1943-46. Mem. County Agrl. Agts. Assn., Mil. Affiliate Radio System. Methodist (adminstrv. bd. 1964-71). Rotarian (sec., v.p. 1968-71), Kiwanian (chmn. agr. and conservation com. 1971—). Home: 105 River Dr Centreville AL 35042 Office: County Extension Office Centreville AL 35042

OWENS, MACK LENSEY, JR., banker; b. West Monroe, La., Mar. 8, 1927; s. Mack Lensey and Gertrude (Kilpatrick) O.; B.S., Northeast La. U., 1952; M.B.A., La. State U., 1954, postgrad. Banking Sch., 1960; m. Dwana Byrd, June 7, 1957; children—Mark, Lensey Edwin. With Central Bank, Monroe, La., 1954—, mgmt. trainee, 1954-57, asst. cashier, 1957-58, asst. v.p., 1958-60, v.p., 1960-68, sr. v.p., 1968-70, chmn. exec. com., dir., 1970—. Mem. Ouachita Parish Sch. Bd., 1960-66, mem. finance com., 1964-66; active Boy Scouts Am., 1966-68, United Givers Fund, 1964-72, Salvation Army, 1964-66, Jr. Achievement, 1970-72, YMCA, 1970-71. Served with USNR, 1945-46. Mem. Banking Inst., Aircraft Owners and Pilots Assn. Baptist. Clubs: Bayou DeSiard Country, Lotus (Monroe); Highland Park Country (West Monroe). Home: 310 Marie Dr West Monroe LA 71291 Office: PO Box 4928 Monroe LA 71201

OWENS, RALPH EUGENE, realtor; b. Waxahachie, Tex., July 5, 1933; s. Elmer B. and Bennie Inez (Howard) O.; student Dallas Inst. Mortuary Sci., 1950-51, W. Tex. State U., 1961-63; m. Sydney Ann Finley, July 2, 1960; children—Doug Sidney, Connie Ann. Mortician, Gililland Funeral Home, 1960-63; pres. Ralph Owens & Assos., Inc., Hereford, Tex., 1963—; pres. Land & Homes, Inc.; sec. S.W. Feed Yards, Inc.; v.p. Hereford Grazing Corp.; dir. Tularosa Farms, Inc. Served with AUS, 1953-55. Mem. Nat. Assn. Realtors, Nat. Inst. Farm and Land Brokers, Tex. Assn. Realtors (state dir., 1971), Tex. Farm and Land Brokers (v.p. 1971-72), Hereford Bd. Realtors (pres. 1968, Man of Year 1969), U.S., W. Tex., Deaf Smith chambers commerce. Home: 234 Northwest Dr Hereford TX 79045 Office: 311 E Park Av Hereford TX 79045

OWENS, RICHARD C., librarian; b. Kennedy, Ala., Jan. 14, 1928; s. Walter Lurid and Connie Elizabeth (Dollar) O.; B.S., U. Ala., 1952. Librarian, Camp Chaffee, Ark., 1952-53, Aberdeen Proving Grounds, Md., 1953-54; hosp. librarian Ft. McClellan, Ala., 1954-55; post librarian, 1955-58; base librarian Columbus AFB, Miss., 1958—. Named Civilian of Year, SAC, Air Force Assn., 1964; recipient Superior Performance awards Civil Service, 1961, 64, 69. Mem. Am. (mem. civil service com. armed forces br. 1967-69), Miss. (chmn. spl. librarians sect. 1972—) library assns. Home: Route 2 Box 19 Kennedy AL 35574 Office: Base Library Columbus AFB MS 39701

OWENS, RUTH JOHNSON (MRS. WYATT OWENS), Democratic nat. committeewoman. Personal sec. to Gov. Folsom, Ala., 1955-58. Dem. nat. committeewoman, 1960—; del. Dem. Nat. Conv., 1968. Address: 1208 Vista Lane Birmingham AL 35203*

OWENS, WELDON, columnist Dallas Times-Herald. Address: 1101 Pacific St Dallas TX 75202*

OWENS, WILLIAM H., mining co. exec.; b. Denton, Tex., Aug. 16, 1893; s. James Madison and Jesse (McCutcheon) O.; student Schs., Hamilton Coll. Law, 1915; m. Elizabeth Sherburne, June 23, 1938; children—Virginia (Mrs. E.C. Meyer), Jeanne (Mrs. William Holcomb), William H. Pres. W. H. Owens Co., Tulsa, also Mexico, 1932—, Carribean Petroleum Co., Tulsa, also Panama, 1958—, Rosario Mining Co., Mexico, 1954—, Continental Mining Co., Mexico, 1955, Panama Exploration Co., 1936—, Western Hemisphere Trading Corp., 1947-59; v.p. Esterex de Mexico, 1945—; dir. all cos.; also dir. Cia-Hidro-Electrica del Amacuzac, S.A., Mexico; pres., chmn. bd. Casa FabMex, S.A., Distribuidora Diamonor, S.A. Home: 1705 E 36th St Tulsa OK 74105 Office: Av San Juan de Letran 21-911 Mexico City Mexico

OWINGS, WILLIAM JENNINGS BRYAN, ret. physician, surgeon; b. nr. Ashland, Ala., Feb. 25, 1908; s. Thomas Harvey and Josephine (Morris) O.; A.B., U. Ala., 1929, B.S., 1930; M.D., Tulane U., New Orleans, 1932; postgrad. Vanderbilt U., 1936; m. Lena Mae Thompson, Sept. 17, 1930; children—Clyde Lacy, William Orange, Joseph Lee, John and Alice (twins), Thomas Gene and Linda Kay (twins). Health officer Lamar Co., Ala., 1934-36; asso. USPHS, Hot Springs, Ark., 1940; dir. Bibb. Co. Venereal Disease Clinic, 1940-47, Bibb Co. Pediatric Clinic, 1940-47, Bibb Co. Prenatal Clinic, 1940-47; gen. practice medicine, Brent, Ala., 1936-63; owner, dir. Owings Clinic, 1940-63; sec. staff Bibb County Hosp., Centreville, Ala., 1959-60, v.p., 1962-63. Chmn. Bibb County Bd. Health, 1940-63, Bibb County Board Censors, 1937—; med. adviser local bd. Selective Service System, 1941-72; bd. dirs. East End Meml. Hosp., Birmingham, 1944-47; exec. bd. Black Warrior council Boy Scouts Am., 1943-63, v.p., 1946-50. Recipient Selective Service System medal, Wisdom award, 1972. Fellow Am. Inst. Chemists, (life), Royal Soc. Health (life), Am. Geriatric Soc., Am. Acad. Family Physicians; mem. Ala. Acad. Gen. Practice (pres. 1959, chmn. bd. dirs. 1960), Am., So. (asso. counsellor 1959-60, life mem.), Ala. (councillor 1941—) med. assns., Black Belt Med. Assn. (pres. 1953), Aero-Med. Assn., Am. Pub. Health Assn., Am. Acad. Gen. Practice (pres. elect 1958, pres. Ala. chpt. 1959-60), Mo. Pacific Hosp. Assn., Bibb County Med. Soc. (past pres.), Soc. (pres.), Phi Chi, Sigma Phi Epsilon. Baptist (deacon), Woodman World (council Comdr.), Mason (32 deg., Shriner), Elk. Clubs: Tuscaloosa Amateur Radio, Ala. Amateur, Civitan. Amateur radio operator. Home: PO Drawer A Brent AL 35034

OWSLEY, HARRIET FASON CHAPPELL (MRS. FRANK LAWRENCE OWSLEY), librarian; b. Waco, Tex.; d. Charles Arthur and Clementine (Fason) Chappell; student Birmingham-So. Coll., 1919-20, Vanderbilt U., 1921-22, 26-28, U. Chgo. summers 1920, 22, 23; B.A., George Peabody Coll., 1925; m. Frank Lawrence Owsley, July 24, 1920 (dec. Oct. 1956); children—Frank Lawrence, Margaret Chappell. Research asst. and collaborator with husband in several hist. articles, 1920-56; sr. archivist manuscript sect. Tenn. State Library and Archives, Nashville, 1958-64, dir. manuscript div., 1965-70. Laura Spellman Rockefeller fellow 1927-28, U. Ala. research fellow, 1956-59; Fulbright research fellow U.K., 1956-57. Mem. Soc. Am. Archivists (chmn. com. manuscripts and spl. collections 1963-66), Ladies Hermitage Assn., Assn. for Preservation Tenn. Antiquities, Tenn. Hist. Soc., So. Hist Assn. Editor: King Cotton Diplomacy (Frank L. Owsley), rev. edit., 1959; The South: Old and New Frontiers: Selected Essays of Frank Lawrence Owsley, 1970; Guide to Processed Manuscripts of the Tennessee Historical Society, 1969; asso. editor The Papers of Andrew Jackson, 1971-72. Contbr. articles to hist. jours. Home: 120 Mockingbird Rd Nashville TN 37205

OXLEY, PHILIP, oil and gas co. exec.; b. Utica, N.Y., Feb. 1, 1922; s. Chester Jay and Beatrice (Heller) O.; B.A., Denison U., Granville, O., 1943; M.A., Columbia, 1948, Ph.D., 1952; m. Patricia Jane Kienker, Aug. 27, 1946; children—Christopher, Jonathan, Timothy, Philip, Patricia. Grad. asst. geology Columbia, 1946-48; instr., asst. prof., chmn. dept. geology Hamilton Coll., Clinton, N.Y., 1948-53; geologist California Co., New Orleans, 1953-57; dist. geologist, div. exploration mgr. Tenneco Oil Co., Lafayette, La., 1957-61, geol. mgr., Houston, 1971—; div. exploration mgr., v.p., dir. domestic exploration Signal Oil & Gas Co., Los Angeles 1961-69, dir., 1967-69; exec. v.p., dir. Tex. Crude Oil Co., Inc., Houston, 1969-71. Served to lt. (j.g.) USNR, 1943-46; PTO. Fellow Geol. Soc. Am.; mem. Am. Assn. Petroleum Geologists, Sigma Xi, Phi Delta Theta. Contbr. articles to profl. jours. Home: 153 Hickory Ridge Houston TX 77024 Office: Tenneco Bldg Houston TX 77001

OYLER, EUGENE JOSEPH, journalist; b. Seattle, Feb 5, 1925; s. Joseph Eugene and Clara (Fox) O.; B.S., E. Tenn. State Coll., 1950; m. Betty Newsom, July 1, 1950; children—Eric Eugene, David Newsom. Sports writer, gen. reporter Press Chronicle, Johnson City, Tenn., 1947-53; telegraph editor Daily Jour., Tupelo, Miss., 1953-56; copyreader News and Courier, Charleston, S.C., 1956, Sunday editor, 1956-57, asst. news editor, 1957-58, asst. city editor, 1958-59, sr. asst. city editor, 1959-61, chief copy editor, 1961-67, exec. women's editor, 1967-68; exec. editor Standard and Review, Aiken, S.C., 1968-72; with Charleston Evening Post, 1972—; exec. editor Aiken Standard, 1968—. Mem. S.C. Asso. Press News Council (pres. 1970-72). Served with AUS, 1941-45. Home: 21 24th St Isle of Palms SC 29451 Office: 134 Columbus St Charleston SC 29451

OZELL, ALAN MUNCI, constrn. co. exec.; b. Izmir, Turkey, Aug. 26, 1917 (came to U.S. 1939, naturalized 1951); s. Cevat M. and Kadriye C. (Sakir) O.; B.S. in Civil Engring., Robert Coll., Istanbul, Turkey, 1939; M.S., U. Ill. at Urbana, 1941, Ph.D., 1944; m. Flo Nell Morris, July 11, 1945; children—Phillip, Camille, Tony, Timothy. Research asso. U. Ill. at Urbana, 1944-46; asso. prof. U. Okla., 1949-54; prof. U. Fla., 1954-61; cons. engr., Ankara, Turkey, 1946-49, Sarasota, Fla., 1961-65; with Mason & Hanger, Jacksonville, Fla., 1966-71; structural engr. Wilson & Asso., Jacksonville, 1971-72; now with firm Ozell, Baker, McGhin; & Padgett, Orange Park, Fla. Registered profl. engr., Fla., Ky., Tenn., La., Miss., Okla. Fellow Am. Soc. C.E.; mem. Am. Concrete Inst., Prestressed Concrete Inst., Welding Research Council. Contbr. articles to nat. and internat. jours. Home: 2446 La Mesa Dr Jacksonville FL 32217 Office: Ozell Baker McGhin & Padgett 2131 Kingsley Av Orange Park FL 32073

PACE, ARTHUR VIRGIL, JR., banker; b. Houston, Sept. 12, 1923; s. Arthur V. and Lucy (Hurst) P.; student N.M. Mil. Inst., 1940-42, U. Tex., 1942-45; B.B.A., U. Houston, 1946; grad. Southwestern Grad. Sch. Banking, Am. Inst. Banking, 1968; m. Barbara Curtin, Dec. 23, 1947; children—Lila Curtin, Arthur Virgil III, Henry Michael Curtin. Sales rep. W.H. Curtin & Co., 1947-51; br. office coordinator and rep. Am. Gen. Investors, 1951-55; customer mgr. McGill and Wareing Co., 1955-56; self-employed mortgage and investment finance, 1956-65; v.p. real estate Capital Nat. Bank, Houston, 1965-71; v.p., mgr. Wells Fargo Realty Advisors, Houston, 1972—. Mem. Am. Inst. Banking, U. Houston, U. Tex., N.M. Mil. Inst. alumni assns., Houston Bd. Realtors, Tex. Real Estate Assn., Houston Mortgage Bankers Assn., Edna Gladney Found., Tex. Mortgage Bankers Assn., Kappa Sigma. Episcopalian. Club: University (Houston). Home: 7606 Riverpoint Rd Houston TX 77042 Office: River Oaks Bank Bldg 2001 Kirby Houston TX 77019

PACE, BILLY JOE, univ. athletic dir.; b. Douthat, Okla., Feb. 14, 1932; s. Paul William and Helen (Wilson) P.; student Northeastern Okla. A. and M. Coll., Miami, 1950-52; B.A. in Bus., Wichita State U., 1954; m. Marjorie Joan Archer, Dec. 5, 1953; children—Sheri Lynn, Kim Diane, Asst. coach Wichita (Kan.) State U., 1954-55, Ark. U., 1957-58, 62-66, U. Kan., 1958-61; head coach Vanderbilt U., Nashville, 1966-71, athletic dir., head football coach, 1971—. Bd. dirs. Nashville YMCA. Served with AUS, 1955-57. Mem. Fellowship Christian Athletes, Nat. Football Coaches Assn. Methodist (mem. bd.). Home: 609 Lynnwood Blvd Nashville TN 37205

PACE, CHARLES MILLS, lawyer; b. Spartanburg, S.C., May 19, 1911; s. Otis Leroy and Amanda (Blackwood) P.; B.S., Clemson U., 1932; LL.B., U. S.C., 1935, J.D., 1969, Ph.D., 1970; m. June Cannington, July 23, 1966. Admitted to S.C. bar, 1935, practiced in Spartanburg, S.C., 1935-36, 71—; probate judge, Spartanburg, S.C., 1939-42; judge Superior County Ct., Spartanburg County, 1947-71. Mem. S.C. Ho. of Reps., 1937-38; mem. citizens com. Spartanburg County Council, 1963-66. Served from 2d lt. to maj. AUS, 1942-46; col. Res. ret. Mem. Am., S.C. (pres. county judges assn. div. 1969-70) bar assns., Pace Soc. Am. (1st v.p. 1963-68), Phi Delta Phi, Omicron Delta Kappa, Pi Kappa Alpha. Clubs: Spartanburg Country, Piedmont, Elks. Home: 1166 Woodburn Rd Spartanburg SC 29302 Office: 180 Library St PO Box 2413 Spartanburg SC 29302

PACE, ROCCO WILLIAM, architect; b. Boston, Sept. 13, 1932; s. Nicola and Leonia (Lippi) P.; B.S. in Archtl. Engring., U. Miami, 1960; postgrad. Royal Acad. Fine Arts, Stockholm, Sweden, 1961; m. Norma Lee Paisley, Apr. 26, 1963; children—Christopher Paisley, Bradford Hamilton. Draftsman, Stone & Webster Engring., Boston, 1951-52; design architect Bengt Hidemark, Arkitekt SAR, Stockholm, Sweden, 1957, 60-61, Dott Architetto Antonio Manzone, Ravenna, Italy, 1961-62; designer Watson, Deutschman & Kruse, Architects and Engrs., Miami, Fla., 1963-64; dir. archtl. dept. Greenleaf/Telesca Engrs., Architects and Planners, Miami, 1964-70; architect Rocco W. Pace, Architect, Coconut Grove, Fla., 1970—. Instr. basic design and planning U. Miami, 1965, 71; Cons. architecture Fla. Restaurateur and Purveyor News, 1971—. Trustee Sunrise Improvement Assn., Key Biscayne, Fla., 1966-68. Served with USAF, 1952-55. Recipient Hon. Mention award in town planning art Swedish Royal Acad., 1961. Mem. A.I.A. Home: 177 Ocean Lane Dr Key Biscayne FL 33149 Office: 3135 Commodore Plaza Coconut Grove FL 33133

PACE, WARREN M., ins. co. exec.; b. Glen Ridge, N.J., Apr. 14, 1920; B.S. in Bus., U. Richmond, Agt., Guardian Life Ins. Co. of N.Y., 1946-48, mgr., 1948-52, agy. dir., 1952-54; asst. v.p. Atlantic Life Ins. Co., 1954-56, agy. v.p. 1956-61; sr. v.p. charge Ordinary Agy. div. Life Ins. Co. of Va., Richmond, 1961-63, exec. v.p., 1963-65, pres., 1965—, also dir.; dir. State-Planters Bank of Commerce & Trusts. C.L.U. Mem. Richmond Life Underwriters Assn., Omicron Delta Kappa. Home: 9808 Kingsbridge Rd Richmond VA 23229 Office: 914 Capitol St Richmond VA 23219

PACETTI, ORRIN DAMON, JR., dentist; b. West Palm Beach, Fla., July 9, 1920; s. Orrin Damon and Lucille (Compher) P.; A.A., U. Fla., 1941; D.D.S., Northwestern U., 1945; m. Lee Hopkins, May 28, 1965; children— Lance, Bruce, Nanette, Carla. Gen. practice dentistry Miami, Fla., 1946—. Sec.-treas. Med. Service Bur. Dade County, Miami, 1961—. Capt. dental div. Community Chest, 1955-57; Bd. dirs. Am. Cancer Soc. Dade County, 1959-60. Served to lt. USNR, 1945-46, 52-54. Mem. Am. Dental Assn., Greater Miami Dental Study Group (pres., 1951), Miami (pres., 1959-60), E. Coast Dist. (exec. council, 1960-61), Fla. dental socs., Loyal Order Boar, Beta Theta Pi. Club: Viscayans. Home: 2301 S Miami Av Miami FL 33129 Office: 715 duPont Bldg 169 E Flagler St Miami FL 33131

PACKARD, MARJEAN PHILLIPS (MRS. CHARLES A. PACKARD), sch. adminstr.; b. New Vienna, O.; d. Harley M. and Nancy Ann (Johnson) Phillips; student Miami U., 1920-22; B.S., Wilmington (O.) Coll., 1944; M.Ed., U. Miami, 1954; m. Charles A. Packard, Sept. 7, 1927; 1 son, Charles Edgar. Tchr. Cin. pub. schs., 1922-27; saleswoman William Ruggles Real Estate, Evanston, Ill., 1936-38; tchr. Pine Crest Prep. Sch., Ft. Lauderdale, Fla., 1939-51; prin. Pine Crest Elementary Sch., 1951—. Pres. Broward County Panhellenic, 1947-48. Mem. bd. Broward County council Girl Scouts. Bd. dirs. Pine Crest Prep. Sch. Named Hon. Alumna, Pine Crest Sch. Mem. Nat., Fla. edn. assns., Assn. Supervision and Curriculum Devel., Assn. Childhood Edn. Internat., Internat. Reading Assn., Ft. Lauderdale Hist. Soc., P.E.O. (pres. chpt. X 1947-48), Nat., Fla. depts. elementary sch. prins., Internat. Platform Assn., Ft. Lauderdale Symphony Soc., Mus. Arts, Friends Library, Delta Kappa Gamma (pres. Xi chpt. 1959-62, state pres., chmn. courtesy internat. conv. 1960, S.E. regional dir. internat. bd.; state achievement award), Sigma Kappa. Presbyn. (deacon, trustee). Clubs: Zonta (v.p. Fort Lauderdale), Lauderdale Yacht. Contbr. to Jour. of Fla. Edn., Nat. Elementary Prins. Letter. Home: 124 Isle of Venice Box 2105 Fort Lauderdale FL 33301 Office: 1501 NE 62d St Fort Lauderdale FL 33308

PACKARD, MERLIN WADSWORTH, librarian; b. Portland, Me., Aprl 10, 1929; s. James Roy and Mary Esther (Wadsworth) P.; grad. Phillips Acad., Andover, Mass. 1946; B.A., Haverford Coll., 1950; postgrad. U. Munich, 1956-57, Columbia, 1960-64. Research analyst U.S. Dept. Def., Germany, 1950-56; with Dumbarton Oaks Research Library, Washington, 1964—, asst. to librarian, 1964-67, librarian, 1967—. Mem. Am. Hist. Assn., A.L.A., Mediaeval Acad. Am. Episcopalian. Office: 1703 32d St NW Washington DC 20007

PACKARD, ROBERT FREDERICK, former govt. ofcl.; b. Glen Ridge, N.J., Oct. 26, 1919; s. Frederick L. and Gertrude (French) P.; B.A., Amherst Coll., 1941; postgrad. Harvard, 1942; m. Jane L. Gold, July 17, 1943; children—Christine Louise, Frances Jane. With U.S. Dept. State, Washington, 1946-72, ret. Served to capt. AUS, 1942-46. Presbyn. Home: 2373 N Qunicy St Arlington VA 22207

PACKETT, LEONARD VASCO, JR., educator; b. Concord, Tenn., Feb. 22, 1932; s. Leonard V. and Lilly (Cooper) P.; B.S., Berea Coll., 1954; M.S., Tex. A. and M. U., 1956, Ph.D., 1958; m. Patty Sue Treadway, Apr. 14, 1954; children—Sandra Sue, Leonard Vasco III. Grad. asst. Tex. A. and M. U., 1954-58; Charles Pfizer Pharm. Co. summer fellow, Terre Haute, Ind., 1957; asst. prof. biochemistry Purdue U., 1958-66; NIH postdoctoral fellow Phila. Gen. Hosp., 1965-66; prof., chmn. dept. nutrition and food sci. U. Ky., Lexington, 1966—, acting dean Sch. Home Econs., 1968. Cons. in field, 1959—. Mem. Am. Chem. Soc., Am. Inst. Nutrition, Am. Assn. Animal Sci., Am. Home Econs. Soc., Sigma Xi. Contbr. articles on metabolism of nutrients to profl. jours. Home: 865 Rebecca Dr Lexington KY 40502

PACKO, JOSEPH JOHN, industrialist; b. Toledo, Mar. 9, 1925; s. Joseph Steve and Mary (Toth) P.; spl. student John Carroll U., U. N.C., 1943-44; B.S. in Physics, Math., Bus. Adminstrn., Bowling Green State U., 1948; Dr. Sc., Southeastern Mass. U., 1969; m. Bette Throne, July 10, 1948; children—Jo Anne, Mark. With J.J. Packo Industries, Ft. Lauderdale, Fla., 1953; pres. J.J. Packo Mortgage Corp., 1954-69, Packo Enterprises 1955—, South Fla. Asphalt Co., 1956-65; pres., chmn. Am. Dynamics Internat., Inc. 1969—. Mem. Trade Mission, West Berlin, 1965. Bd. dirs. Fla. chpt. Nat. Soc. Prevention Blindness, Holy Cross Hosp, A.R.C.; bd. dirs. Nova U. Alumnae Assn., v.p. 1966—; bd. dirs. Bowling Green State U. Alumnae Assn., 1972—. Served with USNR, 1943-45. Mem. Opera Guild Ft. Lauderdale, Young Presidents Orgn. (vice-chmn., sec.-treas. Fla. chpt. 1961—), Am. Mgmt. Assn., A.A.A.S., Asphalt Inst., Nat. Bd. Realtors, Nat. Mortgage Brokers Assn., Navy League, Sigma Chi. Patentee in field. Home: 28 Pelican Isle Fort Lauderdale FL 33301

PADDISON, RICHARD MILTON, neurologist; b. Rochester, N.Y., Aug. 20, 1919; s. Osborn Howard and Ruby (Rapp) P.; A.B., Duke, 1943, M.D., 1945; m. Josephine Butler Bowles, Dec. 18, 1943 (div. Aug. 1966); children—Richard Milton, Alice Jeannette, David Robert, Patricia Louise, Eileen Ruth, Wendy Anne; m. 2d, Vera Gay Davis, Nov. 20, 1966; children—Stephen Matthew, Diane Bell. Intern Duke Hosp., Durham, N.C., 1945-46; ward officer VA Hosp., Augusta, Ga., 1948; instr. neurology and neuro-anatomy U. Ga. Sch. Medicine, Augusta, 1948-49; resident neurology Jefferson Med. Coll., Phila., 1949-51; fellow psychiatry Pa. Hosp., Phila., 1951-52, fellow Psychiatry Inst., 1952-53; chief neuropsychiatric service Burlington County Hosp., Mt. Holly, N.J., 1953-54; attending psychiatrist Camden County Mental Hosp., Blackwood, N.J., 1953-54; asst. prof. neurology La. State U. Sch. Medicine, New Orleans, 1954-56, asso. prof., 1956-59, prof., 1959—, head dept. neurology, 1965—; vis. physician Charity Hosp. of La., New Orleans, 1954-55, sr. vis. physician, 1955—, chief electroencephalographic lab., 1968—; attending staff Hotel Dieu, Mercy Hosp.; chief electroencephalographic lab. So. Bapt. Hosp., 1956—; cons. neurologist State Colony and Tng. Sch., Pineville, La., 1954—, Crippled Children's Hosp., New Orleans, 1955—, Cerebral Palsy Center, 1955-57. Spl. cons. in neurol. scis. to surgeon gen. USPHS,

1966-70. Served from lt. to capt., M.C., AUS, 1946-48. Diplomate Am. Bd. Psychiatry and Neurology. Fellow A.C.P., Am. Psychiat. Assn., Am. Acad. Neurology, Am. Acad. Cerebral Palsy; mem. A.M.A., Orleans Parish, La. med. socs., N.Y. Acad. Scis., Assn. for Research in Nervous and Mental Disease, So. Electroencephalographic Soc. (pres. 1962-63), Soc. Clin. Neurologists (pres. 1969). Democrat. Home: 5435 Bellaire Dr New Orleans LA 70124 Office: 1542 Tulane Av New Orleans LA 70112

PADEV, MICHAEL ALEXANDER, journalist; b. Sofia, Bulgaria, Feb. 23, 1915; s. Dimitar and Catherine (Pavlov) P.; B.S., Am. Coll., Sofia, 1935; M.A., Sofia U., 1940; m. Antoinette Vazova, Jan. 7, 1968; 1 son, Danny G. Came U.S., 1956; naturalized, 1959. Reporter, parliamentary corr., dept. editor Slovo, Sofia, 1935-40; Sofia corr. London Times, 1939-41; editor Brit. Army Information Dept., Cairo, Egypt, 1941-42; news and polit. commentator BBC European Service, London, 1943-45; free-lance journalist, writer, lectr., London, 1945-54, also contbr. various periodicals; lectr. internat. affairs Dept. Air Force, Gt. Britain, 1950-54; scriptwriter Voice of Am., Munich, Germany, 1955; fgn. editor Indpls. Star and Ariz. Republic and Phoenix Gazette, 1956—. Club: Nat. Press (Washington). Author: What Happens to Communists, 1954; What is Foreign Aid; Three Faces of Russia, 1960. Home: 2121 P St NW Washington DC 20037 Office: Nat Press Bldg Washington DC 20004

PADGETT, JOE ALLEN, banker; b. Spartanburg, S.C., Sept. 8, 1937; s. Ellison Landrum and Ethel Marie (West) P.; B.S., U. S.C., 1959; m. Joy Elizabeth Ackerman, Apr. 23, 1960; children—Joe Allan, Scott Ackerman. With First Nat. Bank of S.C., Columbia, 1960—, asst. v.p., 1967-69, v.p., comml. loan officer, 1969—. Chmn. Central S.C. chpt. A.R.C., 1970-72; sect. chmn., div. chmn. Richland-Lexington United Fund, 1971-72; treas. March Dimes campaign, 1966-70; pres. Meadowfield Elementary P.T.A., 1970-71. Served with AUS, 1959-60. Mem. Am. Inst. Banking (chpt. pres. 1966-67, chpt. instr. 1967-71), S.C. Bankers Assn., Robert Morris Assos., U. S.C. Assos., Sigma Chi. Presbyn. Lion. Club: Forest Lake Country. Home: 126 Christopher St Columbia SC 29209 Office: 1208 Washington St Columbia SC 29201

PADRICK, COMER WOODWARD, JR., lawyer; b. Atlanta, Nov. 18, 1926; s. Comer Woodward and Doris (Harper) P.; A.B., Emory U., 1950, LL.B., 1953; m. Dorothy Rebecca South, June 7, 1953; children—Comer Woodward III, Martin Lydell, Tara Jeanne. Admitted to Ga. bar, 1952; mem. editoral bd. The Harrison Co., Atlanta, 1950-52; asso. atty. Sutherland, Asbill & Brennan, Atlanta, 1952-53; Jones, Williams, Dorsey & Kane, Atlanta 1956-59; asso. atty. Hansell, Post, Brandon & Dorsey, Atlanta, 1959-62, partner, 1962—; guest lectr. real estate law. Partner Peachtree Corner, Land Investors Assos., Winchester Apts. East. Mem. Dekalb Bd. Realtors. Active Atlanta Symphony Guild, Atlanta Legal Aid Soc. Served as 1st lt. with AUS, 1953-55. Recipient Medallion Inst. Continuing Legal Edn. in Ga. Mem. Am., Ga., Atlanta bar assns., Am., Atlanta mortgage Bankers assns., Old War Horse Lawyers, Am. Judicature Soc., Atlanta Real Estate Bd., Home Builders Assn. Met. Atlanta, Am. Bus. Law Assn., Emory U. Alumni Council, Internat. Platform Assn., Phi Beta Kappa, Omicron Delta Kappa, Pi Sigma Alpha, Phi Delta Phi. Episcopalian (vestryman). Clubs: Druid Hills Golf; Atlanta City, Lawyers (Atlanta); Civitan. Home: 3999 Beechwood Dr NW Atlanta GA 30327 Office: First National Bank Tower Atlanta GA 30303

PAESSLER, ALFRED H(ENRY), govt. ofcl.; b. Brenham, Tex., Apr. 6, 1916; s. Arno Oscar and Henriette (Schomburg) P.; B.Ch.E., U. Tex., 1939; m. Mildred Binebrink, Nov. 25, 1944; children—Sandra I., Karen M. Supt. water and sewage treatment City of Austin, Tex., 1939-44; exec. sec. State Water Control Bd., Commonwealth of Va., Richmond, Va., 1946—; instr. U. Tex., 1942-44, Va. Commonwealth U., 1966—. Mem. Engring. Com. Ohio River Valley Water Sanitation Commn., 1953—, chmn., 1956-58. Served with USNR, 1944-46. Recipient Conservationist of Year award, 1968. Mem. Water Pollution Control Fedn. (Sidney Bedell award 1971), Am. Pub. Health Assn., Water Resources Assn., Am. Water Works Assn. Roman Cath. Home: 7904 Dogwood Rd Richmond VA 23229 Office: PO Box 11143 Richmond VA 23230

PAFFORD, RAY WILSON, hosp. adminstr.; b. Justin, Tex., Apr. 30, 1900; s. Walter Fulkerson and Dora Ellen (Wilson) P.; student So. Meth. U., 1918-19, U. Tex., 1919-20; m. Alma Leona Perkins, May 13, 1922; 1 dau., Peggy Ellen (Mrs. Charles D. Johnson). With Acme Brick Co., Ft. Worth, 1921-59, ret., 1959; adminstr. Campbell Meml. Hosp., Weatherford, Tex., 1960—. Dir. First Nat. Bank, Weatherford. Capt. Parker County Sheriffs Posse, 1955; pres. Parker County United Fund, 1966. Mem. engr. adv. found. U. Tex., 1955. Fellow Am. Ceramic Soc. (pres. 1954-55); mem. Tex. Hosp. Assn. (chmn. Round-Up area 1971-72). Mason (32 deg., Shriner) (master 1932-33). Club: Green Oaks (Fort Worth). Home: Route 1 Box 64 Weatherford TX 76086 Office: 713 E Anderson St Weatherford TX 76086

PAGAN, RAYMOND, fgn. service officer; b. San Juan, P.R., May 23, 1914; A.B., Tufts U., 1937; spl. certificate German lang. and area study U. Pitts., 1944; LL.B., Am. Extension Sch. Law, 1959; m. Theresa Grace DeCarlo, Aug. 27, 1942; children—Daniel Leverett, Virginia Grace, Roxane Ruth. With Alexander Smith & Co., 1939-42; German publs. officer U.S. War Dept., 1945-47; dep. chief publs. div., chief publs. div. High Commr. of Germany, Wiesbaden, 1947-49; entered fgn. service U.S. State Dept., 1949, asst. editor Die Neue Zeitung, Berlin Germany, 1949-53; information officer Am. embassy, Cairo, Egypt, 1953-54, information specialist USIA, Washington, 1954-55, information officer FOA, ICA, Saigon, Vietnam, 1955-57, communications media officer ICA, Am. embassy, Beirut, Lebanon, 1959-60, asst. program officer, Kabul, Afghanistan, 1960-62, Afghan desk officer AID, 1962-67, program officer population, Washington, 1967—. Served with M.I., AUS, 1942-45. Office: care Agy for Internat Devel Dept of State Washington DC 20523

PAGAN, VICTOR JUAN, med. service exec.; b. San Juan, P.R., Oct. 9, 1922; s. Ricardo F. and Juanita (Fortiz) P.; B.S., U. P.R., 1947; M.D., Temple Med. Sch., 1951; m. Margot Ortiz Colon, May 24, 1942; children—Victor Juan, Myrna M. With Umbo Med. Service, Caparra Heights, P.R., 1951—, dir., 1962—; owner, operator UMBO Comml. Center, Rio Piedras, P.R., 1962—. Served to capt. AUS, 1941-46. Mem. Am. Legion, P.R. Med. Assn. (treas. 1969-70). Lion (pres. 1960-61), Mason (Shriner). Club: Yaucano (San Juan, P.R.). Home: 176 Violeta St Rio Piedras PR 00927 Office: Box V Caparra Heights PR 00922

PAGANINI, OTTO VICTOR, state ofcl.; b. Pitts., Sept. 15, 1911; s. Victor and Irene (Marcon) P.; B.S. in Petroleum Engring., U. Pitts., 1940; m. Mildred Wheeler, June 21, 1938; children—Jane Irene (Mrs. Thayer Draper, Jr.), Lee Ann (Mrs. Thomas J. Cullins). San. engr. Hidalgo County (Tex.), 1946-48; with Tex. State Health Dept., 1948—, chief engr. air pollution control services, Austin, 1956—. Served to san. engr. dir. USPHS, 1942-46; Res. Recipient Thanks badge local council Girl Scouts Am., 1960. Registered profl. engr., Tex. Diplomate Am. Acad. San. Engrs., Am. Indsl. Hygiene Bd. Mem. Air Pollution Control Assn., Nat., Tex. socs. profl. engrs., Am. Conf. Govtl. Hygienists (mem. air pollution com. 1963—), Am. Indsl. Hygiene Assn., Tex. Pub. Health Assn., Houston C. of C. (pub. health com. 1946-52). Mason. Contbr. articles to publs. Home: 6104 Shoalwood Av Austin TX 78757 Office: 1100 W 49th St Austin TX 78756

PAGE, DAVID P., editor, clergyman; b. Galway, Ireland, June 10, 1932; s. Thomas and Mary (Robinson) P.; came to U.S., 1958, naturalized, 1963; M.A., Cath. U. Am., 1962. Ordained priest Roman Catholic Ch., 1958; exec. editor Fla. Cath. Press, Inc., Orlando, 1965—. Pres. Orlando dist. Priest's Senate, 1969-70, 71-72. Mem. Fla. Fedn. Priests' Councils (pres. 1971-72). Home: PO Box 1868 Orlando FL 32802 Office: PO Box 3551 Orlando FL 32802

PAGE, GARLAND LEFTWICH, JR., civil engr.; b. Lynchburg, Va., Mar. 25, 1932; s. Garland Leftwich and Ruth Carlene (Matthews) P.; B.S. in Civil Engring., Va. Poly. Inst., 1953; m. Billie Anne Ogden, Sept. 6, 1952; children—Samuel Howard, Laura Ellen, Mary Garland, Anne Wingfield. Field engr. Wiley & Wilson, engrs., architects and planners, Lynchburg, Va., 1953-58, project mgr., 1958—, asso. mem. firm, 1963—, br. office mgr., Winston-Salem, N.C., 1969-71, asst. dir. bus. devel., 1971—. Served from 2d to lst lt. C.E., AUS, 1954-56. Registered profl. engr., Va., N.C. Mem. Nat., Va. (pres. Lynchburg chpt. 1962-63) socs. profl. engrs. Republican. Methodist (mem. ch. bd. 1958—). Kiwanian. Club: Oakwood Country (Lynchburg). Home: 1408 Northwood Circle Lynchburg VA 24503 Office: 2310 Langhorne Rd Lynchburg VA 24501

PAGE, GEORGE KEITH, savs. and loan assn. exec.; b. Rolling Prairie, Ind., July 7, 1917; s. Glenn Keith and Ruth (Mansfield) P.; ed. U. Ala., 1939; m. Vivian Marie Reed, Aug. 30, 1936; children—George Keith, Kay Louise, Susan Marie, John Michael. Asst. cashier Baldwin County Bank, Bay Minette, Ala., 1938-43; pres., dir. Baldwin County Savs. and Loan Assn., Robertsdale and Fairhope, Ala., 1943-58; pres., mng. officer, dir. 1st Fed. Savs. and Loan Assn., Sarasota, Fla., 1958—; dir. AMIC Corp., Raleigh, N.C. A founder, tchr. Greater Mobile Bay, Sarasota-Manatee chpts. Am. Savs. and Loan Inst. Gen. campaign chmn. United Appeal of Sarasota County, Inc., 1962-63, v.p., 1963-64, dir., 1963—, pres., 1964, also mem. spl. adv. council, chmn. advanced gifts com., 1970-71; gen. chmn. capital funds campaign Sarasota YMCA, 1969; past chmn. Sarasota Housing Authority; mem. bd. Met. YMCA of Sarasota-Manatee Counties. Served with USNR, 1944-45. Recipient certificate of honor City and C. of C., Fairhope, Ala., 1958; Silver Beaver award, Boy Scouts Am., 1949. Mem. Ala. (pres. 1956), Fla. (v.p., exec. com. 1962-64, pres. 1970-71), U.S. (pres. Southeastern conf. 1967-68) savs. and loan leagues, U. Ala. Alumnae Assn., Sarasota County C. of C. (dir., treas. 1964-65). Presbyn. Mason (32 1/2, Shriner). Rotarian (past pres., dir.). Clubs: Field (dir. 1968-71), Sara Bay Country, University (gov. 1969—). Office: 1st Fed Savs & Loan Assn of Sarasota PO Box 1478 Sarasota FL 33578

PAGE, HARRY ROBERT, educator; b. Milw., Mar. 22,, 1915; s. Harry Allen and Lydia (Rosendahl) P.; A.B., Mich. State U., 1941; postgrad. U.S. Army Command and Staff Coll., 1945-46, Indsl. Coll. of Armed Forces, 1958-59; M.B.A., Harvard, 1950; Ph.D., Am. U., 1966; m. Jeanne Tompkins, Apr. 1, 1945; children—Patricia Jeanne, Margaret Berenice. From 2d lt. to lt. col. U.S. Army, 1941-46, from lt. col. to col. USAF, 1946-61; exec. officer logistics directorate U.S. Joint Chiefs of Staff, Washington, 1959-61; asst. prof. bus. adminstrn. George Washington U., Washington, 1961-65, asso. prof., chmn. dept., 1965-69, prof., chmn. dept., 1969—. Cons., Advanced Study Program, Brookings Instn., Washington, 1966—; chmn. task group edn. and tng. Commn. Govt. Procurement, 1971. Active Boy Scouts Am. Bd. dirs., treas. Council of Chs. of Greater Washington, 1963-68. Decorated Air medal, Purple Heart, Legion of Merit. Mem. Am. Assn. U. Profs., Am. Mgmt. Assn., Harvard Bus. Sch. Assn., Air Force Assn., Nat. Parks Assn. (trustee), Alpha Phi Omega, Lambda Chi Alpha, Alpha Kappa Psi. Pi Sigma Alpha. Conglist. Author Church Budget Development, 1964; An Analysis of the Defense Procurement Program Decision-Making Process, 1966; co-author: Federal Contributions to Management, 1971. Home: 3612 N Glebe Rd Arlington VA 22207 Office: 710 21st St NW Washington DC 20006

PAGE, HENRIETTA MARIA, librarian; b. Queens County, L.I., N.Y., Dec. 6, 1900; d. William C. and Maria (Weinig) Wutz; student Queens Coll., Columbia, Drake Bus. Coll., Am. Inst. of Banking; m. Henry N. Page, Nov. 5, 1923 (dec.); children—Lois Ann (Mrs. Wendell E. Bennett), Natalie (Mrs. John F. Krause). With Guaranty Trust Co., 1921-23, 1927-33; research dept. Nat. Rep. Com., Washington, 1940-43. Office of Sec. of State, 1943-48; reporter, U.S. Delegation, UN, London, 1946; mil. intelligence research analyst, editor of publs. Air Def. Command, Ent AFB, Colorado Springs, 1949-56; organized Denver div. tech. library The Martin Co., 1956, organized research div., 1956; devel. div. AVCO, Corp., Wilmington, Mass., 1956, chief tech. library for corp., 1956-61; documentation engr. Itek Labs., Lexington, Mass., 1961-63; head library div. U.S. Naval Underwater Weapons Research and Engring. Sta., 1961-65; cons. Providence Pub. Library, 1965-66, Roger Williams Coll., 1965-68; library cons. Foxboro Co. (Mass.), 1967-70. Mem. Spl. Libraries Assn., Nat. Aeronautics Assn. Club: Pilot. Author: World Resources: The Fertile Crescent; The Moslem World; Treatise on Filing; (tng. manual) How to Do Research; Planning the New Library. Address: 747 Sommer Av NE Aiken SC

PAGE, JACK CULBERTSON, cons. co. exec.; b. Evanston, Ill., May 8, 1925; s. Philip P. and Alleyne (McCabe) P.; B.S., Mass. Inst. Tech., 1948; m. Imogene Spoerri, Nov. 21, 1951; children—Katherine H., Carter H., Philip J. Purchasing agt. Ekco Products Co., Wheeling, Ill., 1948-54; sales rep. Morris Paper Mills div. Fed. Paper Bd. Co., Montvale, N.J., 1954-56; v.p. Speed-Fam. Corp., Skokie, Ill., 1956-60; pres. Prodn. Lapping Co., Pasadena, Cal., 1960-61; v.p. Booz, Allen & Hamilton, Inc., Dallas, 1961—. Trustee Village of Riverwoods, Ill., 1965-66. Pres. Evanston Jr. C. of C., 1951-52; bd. dirs. Dallas Civic Opera; mem. corp. vis. com. for med. dept. Mass. Inst. Tech. Served with USNR, 1944-46. Clubs: Mass. Inst. Tech. (pres. Dallas), Northwood, Dallas, Dallas Petroleum, Tavern, Tres Vidas. Home: 4508 Hockaday Dr Dallas TX 75229 Office: Republic Bank Tower Dallas TX 75201

PAGE, JESSE BORING, educator; b. Loachapoka, Ala., Dec. 6, 1906; s. Robert Seldon and Lois (James) P.; B.S., Ala. Poly. Inst., 1927. M.S., 1929; m. Frances Whatley, Apr. 1, 1930; children—Frances Anne, Rebecca Jane. Teaching fellowship Ala. Poly. Inst., 1927-28; dir. athletics Langdale (Ala.) High Sch., 1928-29; prin. Smiths Station (Ala.) Consol. High Sch., 1929—. Active Smiths chpt. A.R.C., 1954—. Served from 1st lt. to capt., inf., AUS, 1942-45. Mem. N.E.A., Ala. Edn. Assn., Nat., Ala. (pres. 4th dist. 1964-65) assns. secondary sch. prins., Lee County Tchrs. Assn. (pres. 1934-36, dir. 1958—), Internat. Platform Assn., Kappa Delta Pi. Democrat. Methodist (ofcl. bd.). Club: Ruritan (Smiths, Ala.). Home: Smiths AL 36877

PAGE, RICHARD MICHAEL, food distbn. exec.; b. New Orleans, Sept. 8, 1910; s. Alfred F. and Eda (Richardson) P.; B.A. in Math., Tulane U., 1935; m. Nellie C. Curtis, Apr. 23, 1938; children—Richard Michael, Elizabeth C. With William B. Reily Co., Inc., New Orleans, 1935-42; prof. math. Tulane U., New Orleans, 1946-47; founder, pres. Arrow Food Distbrs., Inc., New Orleans, 1947—, also dir.; founder, treas., dir. Jefferson Cold Storage, New Orleans, 1953—; pres., dir. Frozen Food Forum, Atlanta, 1954—; treas., dir. Asso. Cold Storage, Baton Rouge, 1957—; reorganized New Orleans Shrimp Co., 1956, dir., exec. com., 1956-68; dir., pres. Sterling Foods, Inc., Universal Operations, Inc., Atlanta; v.p., dir. Oil Mop Inc., New Orleans, 1969—; dir. New Orleans Frosted Foods Creole Sales Co., Econo Meat Mart, Inc., New Orleans. Served from 2d lt. to capt. USAAF, 1942-46. Named to Royal Order Zerocrats Nat. Frozen Food Assn., 1957. Mem. Nat. (past pres.), Southwestern (founder, 1st pres.) frozen food assns., Nat. Assn. Wholesalers (trustee), Tulane U. Alumni Assn. (past pres., past mem. exec. com.), Phi Beta Kappa, Alpha Tau Omega. Clubs: Tulane T. (past pres.), New Orleans Athletic, Southern Yacht (New Orleans). Episcopalian (past sr. warden, chmn. sch. bd.). Home: 40 Hawk St New Orleans LA 70124 Office: 1405 Jefferson Hwy New Orleans LA 70121

PAGE, THORNTON LEIGH, astrophysicist; b. New Haven, Aug. 13, 1913; s. Leigh and Mary Edith Cholmondeley (Thornton) P.; B.S., Yale, 1934; D.Phil. in Astrophysics (Rhodes scholar for Conn. 1934-37), Oxford U. (Eng.), 1938; M.A. (hon.), Wesleyan U., Middletown, Conn., 1959; D.H.C. (hon.), U. Cordoba (Argentina), 1969; m. Helen Ashbee, Aug. 28, 1938 (div. 1944); 1 dau., Tanya; m. 2d, Lou Williams, Aug. 28, 1948; children—Mary Anne, Leigh II. Chief asst. Oxford U. Obs., 1937-38; from instr. to asst. prof. astronomy U. Chgo., 1938-50; physicist Naval Ordnance Lab., 1941-43; dep. dir. Operations Research Office, Johns Hopkins, 1950-58; prof. astronomy Wesleyan U., Middletown, 1958-72, dir. Van Vleck Obs., 1959-72; research asso. Manned Spacecraft Center, NASA, 1968-70; astrophysicist, Naval Research Lab., 1972—. Mem. operations research NRC, 1960-62; mem. research adv. com. United Aircraft Corp., 1959-72; Smithsonian research asso. Harvard Obs., 1965-67; Nat. Acad. Scis. sr. research asso., 1968-69. Served to comdr. USNR, 1943-46. Decorated Bronze Star, Legion of Merit. Fellow Royal Astron. Soc., A.A.A.S. (v.p. sect. D astronomy 1967-69), Am. Astron. Soc.; mem. Operations Research Soc. Am. (charter, editor, council, v.p.), Astron. Soc. Pacific, Am. Assn. Physics Tchrs., Internat. Astron. Union, Internat. Statis. Inst., Sigma Xi. Clubs: Cosmos (Washington); Appalachian Mountain. Author: Stars and Galaxies, 1962; Wanderers in the Sky, 1965; Neighbors of the Earth, 1965; Origin of the Solar System, 1966; Telescopes, 1966; Starlight, 1967; Evolution of Stars, 1967; Stars and Clouds of the Milky Way, 1968; Beyond the Milky Way, 1969. Astronomy editor Macmillan Co. Home: 18639 Point Lookout Dr Houston TX 77058 Office: Code TN NASA Manned Spacecraft Center Houston TX 77058

PAGE, MISS TONY, publisher, editor; b. Moscow, Ida., July 11, 1910; d. Clarence Mills and Ruby Ethyl (Slee) Edgett; ed. by tutors, grad. Mrs. Williams' Prep. Sch. for Young Ladies, Fort Worth, 1926; m. Holland Page, Jr., Mar. 1947 (div. June 1954). With Flight Mag., Dallas, 1940-45; aviation editor The Valley Times, San Fernando, Cal., 1945-47; writer Cross Country News, Austin, 1947-52, owner, 1952; owner Cross Country News, Ft. Worth, 1954—. Named Woman of the Year in Aviation, Woman's Aero. Assn., 1960, hon. chief Sycamore tribe Okla. Aeros. Commn., 1971; recipient James J. Strebig Meml. Trophy award Aviation Space Writers, 1962; Merit Certificate award Sherman Fairchild Internat. Air Safety Writing award, 1962, 63, 64, 65; Amelia Earhart Medal award Medal of Month Club, 1965. Mem. Aviation/Space Writers Assn., Nat. Aero. Assn., Hump Pilots Assn. (hon.), Women's Nat. Aero. Assn., The Whirly-Girls, Ninety Nines, Inc., Fort Worth Press Club. Club: OX-5 (hon. mem.). Author: Personal Please (poetry), 1957. Home: PO Box 9661 Fort Worth TX 76107 Office: Meacham Field Fort Worth TX 76106

PAGE, WILLIAM SPLANE, radio exec.; b. Detroit, Aug. 16, 1917; s. Blinn Stevens and Carlotta (Splane) P.; student Coll. de St., Germain-en-Laye, France, 1932-33; A.B., Cornell U., Ithaca, N.Y., 1940; m. Marie Sugg, June 26, 1943; children—William Splane, Mary Gayle (Mrs. Robert Grayson Shorkey). Civilian employee USAF, Washington and Trinidad, 1941-43; news editor radio stat. WKNS, Kinston, N.C., 1947-48; pres., gen. mgr. radio stat. WFTC, Kinston, 1949-54; pres. Farmers Broadcasting Service, WELS, Kinston, 1954—; pres. radio stat. WGOL, 1958-69; sec., dir. N.C. TV., Inc., WITN-TV, 1954—. Mem. Kinston Recreation Commn., 1954-59, Kinston Redevel. Commn., 1961—, chmn., 1963—, N.C. Good Neighbor Council, 1966-68; pres. Lamp, Inc., 1965-69. Alderman city of Kinston, 1954-59. Bd. dirs. Broadcasting Found. N.C., Greene Lamp, 1965-71. Served to lt. USNR, 1943-46. Recipient distinguished service award Kinston Jr. C. of C., 1949. Mem. N.C. Assn. Broadcasters (pres. 1955), Kinston Amateur Radio Soc. (pres. 1970), Kinston C. of C., (pres. 1953-54), Sigma Delta Chi (life mem.), Kappa Sigma. Episcopalian (sr. warden 1960-61, 68-70, lay dep. gen. conv. 1961, 64, 67, 69, 70, diocesan council 1961-63, 65-67, 71—, chmn. mutual responsibility commn. 1966—, vol. missionary Liberia, Siera Leone, Congo, 1968, Solomon Islands, 1965, New Hebrides Islands, 1965, 69, 70). Elk, Rotarian (pres. 1960-61). Home: 1105 Fairfield Av Kinston NC 28501 Office: 1312 W Vernon Av Kinston NC 28501

PAGE, WILLIS, condr.; b. Rochester, N.Y.; grad. with distinction Eastman Sch. Music, Rochster. With Boston Symphony Orch.; prin. bass Boston Pops; condr. Cecilia Soc. of Boston; organizer, condr. New Orchestral Soc. of Boston (name now Boston Festival Orch.); music dir.-condr. Nashville Symphony Orch., 8 years; asso. condr. Buffalo Philharmonic; condr. Yomiuri Nippon Symphony, Tokyo, Japan, 1962-63; prof. conducting Eastman Sch. Music, 1967-69; prof. conducting, dir. orchestral activities Drake U., Des Moines, 1969-71; condr. Jacksonville (Fla.) Symphony Orch., 1971—. Guest condr. with Boston Pops, Toronto, Rochester Civic, Eastman-Rochester, Denver, Muncie, Kol Israel orchs.; condr. all-state orchs. of N.Y., Ia., Ky., Tenn., Fla., also regional festivals. Ford Found. European travel award, 1967. Address: 46 W Duval St Jacksonville FL 32202*

PAGLIAI, BRUNO, bus. exec.; b. Modena, Italy, July 3, 1902 (came to U.S. 1921, Mexico 1939); m. 3d, Merle Oberon. Various positions Bank of Italy, San Francisco; established Hipodromo de las Americas race track, Mexico City, 1940, La Oceanica Ins. Co., (with others) Telefonos de Mexico, S.A., established TAMSA, seamless tube co., 1952, Aluminio, S.A., aluminum plant, Veracruz, 1963, Organization Editorial Novaro, S.A., Industria de Baleros Intercontinental, S.A., de C.V., Azufrera Intercontinental, S.A. de C.V., Lomas Verdes, S.A. de C.V.; dir. Asarco Mexicana, S.A., Capital Nat. Bank, Houston. Pres. Mexican Businessmen's Council. Trustee San Carlos Mus., U. Guadalajara; mem. vis. com. U. Cal. at Los Angeles Grad. Sch. Mgmt. Office: Calle Paris 15 Mexico 4DF Mexico

PAIEWONSKY, RALPH, gov. of V.I.; b. Charlotte Amalie, St. Thomas, V.I., Nov. 9, 1907; s. Isaac and Rebecca (Kushner) P.; B.S., N.Y.U., 1930; m. Ethel Heller, Aug. 11, 1930; 1 son, Bernard Hirsch. Research chemist, mgr. father's firm operated under name A.H. Rilse (est. 1838). Charlotte Amalie, 1930—; gov. of V.I., 1961—. Elected to local legislature, 1936, reelected, 1938, 40, chmn. municipal finance com., 1938; chmn. Municipal Council, 1940—; elected del. by Municipal Council to present needs of V.I. to Congress, 1939. Nat. Democratic committeeman for V.I., 1940-61; del. Nat. Dem Conv.,

Chgo., 1940, 44. Mem. V.I. Progressive Guide. Mason (32 deg.). Address: Charlotte Amalie St Thomas VI 00801

PAIN, CHARLES LESILE, lawyer; b. Austin, Tex., Apr. 26, 1913; s. William Francis and Ruby (Gates) P.; B.A., U. Okla., 1935, LL.B., 1935; m. Roberta Wilmoth, Mar. 27, 1942; children—Charles Laurence, William Francis, Glenn David. Admitted to Okla. bar, 1935; practiced in Okla., 1935—; partner firm Allen & Pain, Chickasha, Okla., 1946-51, Morris & Pain, Lawton, Okla, 1953-54, Barney & Pain, Anadarko, Okla., 1956-67; individual practice, Anadarko, 1967-70; partner Pain and Garland, Anadarko, 1970—; asst. atty. Southwestern Light & Power Co., Chickasha, Okla., 1935-40; exec. sec. Congressman Toby Morris, Washington, 1951-53. Mem. Okla. Bd. Bar Examiners, 1970—. Pres. Black Beaver Council Boy Scouts Am., 1971. Served with AUS, 1940-46; PTO; col. res., 1960. Mem. Am., Okla., Caddo County bar assns., Am. Legion, Res. Officers Assn., Anadarko C. of C., Order of Coif, Phi Beta Kappa, Phi Eta Sigma, Phi Alpha Delta, Sigma Chi. Democrat. Baptist. Lion (gov. dist. 3-L, Lions Internat., 1953-54). Home: 808 W Colorado Av Anadarko OK 73005 Office: 111 SW 2d St Anadarko OK 73005

PAINE, CLARENCE SIBLEY, librarian; b. Lincoln, Neb. June 9, 1908; s. Clarence Summer and Clara A. (Sibley) P.; A.B., U. Neb., 1936, A.M., 1937; B.L.S., U. Ill., 1937; m. Ena Ruth Moore, Dec. 24, 1937; 1 dau., Lucinda Kempton. Printer, 1922-26; retail merchandising advt., and personnel tng., 1926-333; asst. Neb. Hist. Library (part time), 1933-36; cataloger U. Ill. Library, 1937-38; vis. prof. U. Denver Coll. Librarianship, summer 1947; instr. history Army Air Crew Tng. Detachment, Beloit Coll., 1943-44; history research fellow Western Range Cattle Industry Study (Rockefeller Found.), summer 1944; dir. libraries 1938-47; dir. Oklahoma City Libraries 1947-59; chief librarian Lansing (Mich.) Sch. Dist. Libraries, 1959-65; now library bldg. cons.; pres. Red Plains Trading Post, Ltd., 1956-57; dir. Gt. Books Found., 1955-61; cons. on library personnel Office of Personnel, City of Madison (Wis.), 1944; cons. on library bldg. and planning. Spl. rep. Mobil Travel Guide. Chmn. county chpt. A.R.C., 1947, bd. dirs., 1948-50; mem. Alvord Meml. Commn., 1951-54. Mem. Am., Southwestern, Okla., Wis. (pres. 1943-44) library assns., Assn., Coll. and Reference Libraries (dir. 1946-47). Miss. Valley (exec. com., 1951-53), Beloit (pres. 1942-43) hist. assns., Westerners (Chgo. chpt.), Psi Chi. Episcopalian. Optimist, Rotarian (pres. 1947). Author: The Comedy of Manners, 1941; (with others) The Black Hills, 1952; Editor: Rev. Index, 1941-45. Contbr. articles and revs. to profl. and learned jours. Home: RFD 5 Box 192 Lenoir City TN 37771 Office: Box 10445 Knoxville TN 37919

PAINE, THOMAS FITE, JR., physician, educator; b. Aberdeen, Miss., Feb. 13, 1918; s. Thomas Fite and Mary Alice (Therrell) P.; B.A., Vanderbilt U., 1939, M.D., 1942; m. Grace Hillman Benedict, July 26, 1941; children—Thomas Fite III, George Carter, Anne Benedict, Grace Barrett. Intern, U. Rochester Strong Meml. Hosp., 1942-43; chief dept. bacteriology Mass. Gen. Hosp., asso. medicine Harvard Med. Sch., Boston, 1950-53; asso. prof. internatl medicine and bacteriology U. Mich., 1953-54; prof. medicine, chmn. dept. microbiology U. Ala., 1954-61; prof. medicine Vanderbilt U., chief med. service Nashville Gen. Hosp., 1961—; research fellow Harvard Thorndike Lab. at Boston City Hosp., 1946-48, Mass. Gen. Hosp., 1948-49, dept. biochemistry Cambridge U. (Eng.), 1949-50. Served to capt. MC, AUS, 1943-46. Diplomate Am. Bd. Internal Medicine. Mem. A.C.P., Am. Acad. Microbiology, Infectious Disease Soc. Am., Soc. for Exptl. Biology and Medicine, Sigma Xi, Alpha Omega Alpha. Contbr. articles to profl. pubs. Home: 4308 Iroquois Av Nashville TN 37205

PAINTER, FLOYD EUGENE, editor; b. Granite City, Ill., May 17, 1920; s. William D. and Bessie Florence (Andrews) P.; ed. pub. schs.; m. Katherine Weston Sewell, Dec. 25, 1942; children—Floyd Sewell, Pamela Kay, Deborah Roxanne. Formerly cave explorer, mountain climber, rodeo rider, constrn. worker, fruit picker, laborer archeol. projects in Mexico; successively advt. salesman, store clk., aircraft mechanic, shipyard machinist, 1946-48; archeologist Norfolk (Va.) Mus. Arts and Scis., 1955-69; editor assn. jour. Chesopiean Archeol. Jour., Norfolk, 1965—. Tchr. adult edn. classes Old Dominion U., Norfolk, 1971—; vol. lectr. archeol. topics to ch. and civic orgns. Served with USNR, 1941-46, AUS, 1948-55. Mem. Archeol. Soc. Va. (pres. 1958-60, asso. editor jour. 1956-63), Chesopiean Archeol. Assn. (pres. 1963-65). Asso. editor Anthropol. Jour. Can., 1965—. Contbr. articles to archeol. jours. Address: 7507 Pennington Rd Norfolk VA 23505

PAINTER, WILLIAM CALVIN, JR., engr., city ofcl.; b. Atlanta, Feb. 23, 1917; s. William Calvin and Ruby (Anchors) P.; B.S. in Indsl. Mgmt., Ga. Inst. Tech., 1938; m. Betty Claire Farmer, May 3, 1946; children— Betsy, Susan, Sally. With engring. dept. South-Eastern Underwriters Assn., Atlanta, 1938—, field engr., 1939-48, sr. field engr., 1949-52, staff engrs., 1953-62, div. engr., 1963-66, asst. chief engr., 1967-71, asst. chief engr. ins. services office, Southeastern regional office, 1972—. City commr., Decatur, Ga., 1962—. Served from 2d lt. to capt. Q.M.C., AUS, 1941-46; now col. Res. Decorated Legion of Merit. Registered profl. engr., Ga. Mem. Ga. Municipal Assn. (dist. pres. 1969—), Ins. Inst. Am. (asso.), Res. Officer Assn. U.S. (pres. Atlanta q.m. chpt.), Mil. Order World Wars, Am. Legion, Def. Supply Assn., Assn. U.S. Army, DeKalb County C. of C., Hon. Order Blue Goose, Pi Delta Epsilon, Phi Sigma Kappa. Baptist (deacon). Mason, Rotarian. Home: 217 Westchester Dr Decatur GA 30030 Office: 1577 Northeast Freeway NE Atlanta GA 30329

PAIR, HENRY TAZWELL, JR., banker; b. Atlanta, Mar. 30, 1928; s. Henry Tazwell and Dorris (Turner) P.; B.B.A., Ga. State U., 1961; m. Carolyn Holbrook, Aug. 19, 1950; children—Julie Lynn, Vann Henry. Mem. staff Citizens and So. Nat. Bank, Atlanta, 1946-68; v.p. Bank of Cumming, 1968—. Served with AUS, 1953-55. Mem. Forsyth County C. of C. (membership chmn. 1971-72). Baptist (chmn. deacons and finance com. 1958-62). Kiwanian (pres. 1970-71). Home: PO Box 35 Cumming GA 30130 Office: PO Box 267 Cumming GA 30130

PAJON, EDUARDO RODRIGUEZ, lawyer; b. Ciego de Avila, Camaquey, Cuba, Nov. 22, 1917; s. Francisco Rodriguez Ubals and Maria Luisa Pajon; J.D., U. Havana (Cuba), 1941, U. Miami, 1964; m. Olga M. Fernandez, Jan. 31, 1942; children—Olga (Mrs. Ignacio G. del Valle), Eduardo R. Came to U.S., 1959, naturalized, 1965. Admitted to Fla. bar, 1965; partner firm Helio R. Ecay, Havana, 1941-59, Salley, Barns, Pajon & Immer, Miami, 1967—; head legal dept., sec. Cuban subsidiaries The Cuban Am. Sugar Co. (name changed to N. Am. Sugar Industries, Inc. 1960), N.Y.C., 1952-60; sec., counsel Talisman Sugar Corp., Miami, 1965—; v.p., dir. Fla. Sugar Corp., Belle Glade, 1960-62, Sunshine Farms, Inc., South Bay, Fla., 1960—; dir. Republic Nat. Bank Miami. Mem. adv. bd. Fla. Meml. Coll., Miami, 1970—, endowment com. U. Miami, 1969—. Mem. Am., InterAm., Fla., Dade County bar assns. Republican. Roman Catholic. Clubs: Miami, LaGorce Country Surf (Miami Beach); Ocean Reef (Key Largo, Fla.); Jockey (North Miami, Fla.); American, Big Five (Miami). Home: 511 Bird Rd Coral Gables FL 33146 Office: Suite 700 loo Biscayne Blvd Miami FL 33132

PALEVEDA, ANNA MARY, printing co. exec.; b. Tampa, Fla., May 9, 1929; d. Nicholas Luke and Magdalen (Christ) Paleveda; A.A., Hillsborough Community Coll., 1971; now student U. South Fla. With Paleveda Printing Co., Inc., Tampa, 1954—, sec.-treas., 1963—; sec. Printing Industry of Tampa, 1956-63, treas., 1965-68; sec. Printing Industries of Fla., 1965-68. Sec. St. Joseph's Hosp. Aux., 1966-67, 1st v.p., 1968-69; 2d v.p. President's Round Table of Women's Clubs, Tampa, 1962-63. Democrat. Roman Catholic. Club: Altrusa (pres. Tampa 1962-63, editor dist. news 1964-68). Home: 4016 Seminole Av Tampa FL 33603 Office: 102 S Tampa St Tampa FL 33602

PALIK, EDWARD DANIEL, physicist; b. Elyria, O., Sept. 21, 1928; s. John and Christina (Dinga) P.; B.S., Ohio State U., 1950, M.S., 1952, Ph.D., 1955; m. Susan Elizabeth Young, Sept. 14, 1957; children—Ann Louise, Arthur John, Ted Ernest. Asst. prof. Ohio State U., 1955-56; NSF postdoctoral fellow U. Mich., 1956-57; Gen. Motors postdoctoral fellow Ohio State U., 1957-58; physicist Naval Research Lab., Washington, 1958—. Fellow Am. Phy. Soc.; mem. Optical Soc. Am. Research in magnetoptical studies of semiconductors. Home: 904 Pocahontas Dr Oxon Hill MD 20022 Office: Washington DC 20390

PALLAS, WILLIAM CHARLES, gynecologist, obstetrician; b. Jamestown, N.Y., Feb. 24, 1920; s. Chris and Magdaline (Plakas) P.; B.A., U. Rochester, 1942; M.D., L.I. Coll. Medicine, 1944; M.S. Obstetrics and Gynecology, U. Colo., 1950; m. Katherine Rigas, Aug. 29, 1951; 1son, Christopher. Intern, Queen of Angels Hosp., Los Angeles, 1944-45; resident surgery Fordham Hosp., N.Y.C., 1946; resident obstetrics and gynecology U. Colo., 1947-49; asst. instr., instr. dept. obstetrics and gynecology, U. Colo. Sch. Medicine, 1949-50; asst. prof. dept. obstetrics and gynecology U. Ark. Sch. Medicine, 1950-52; asst. prof. dept. anatomy Georgetown U. Sch. Medicine, 1954; med. dir., attending staff, former owner, operator Woman's Hosp.; owner, operator Woman's Clinic; pres., dir. Hosp. Realty Co., Inc.; courtesy staff Baroness Erlanger Hosp. Pres., dir. McCallie Realty Co., Inc., Athens TV Cable Co. Inc., McMinnville TV Cable Co., Harriman TV Cable Co., Rockwood TV Cable Co., Etowah TV Cable Co., Sparta TV Cable Co., Lookout Realty Co., Inc.; builder, owner comml. properties including Downtowner Motor Inn, Met. Life Ins. Co. and Burroughs; dir. Hosp. Affiliates, Inc., Western Empire Financial, Industry Fund Am., Mar-Search, Inc. Mem. med. adv. bd. Bio-Dynamics, Inc. Served as lt. M.C., USNR, 1945-46, in U.S.S. Hercules; lt. to lt. comdr., 1952-54, chief obstetrics Portsmouth Naval Hosp. Diplomate Am. Bd. Obstetrics and Gynecology. Fellow A.C.S., Am. Coll. Obstetrics and Gynecology, Southeastern Surg. Congress, Internat. Coll. Surgeons, Am. Coll. Abdominal Surgeons; mem. C. of C., Am., Tenn. med. assns., Chattanooga and Hamilton County Med. Soc., N.Y. Acad. Scis. Clubs: Lookout Mountain Golf, Signal Mountain Golf and Country. Author: Handbook of Obstetrics and Gynecology, 1949. Home: 10 Folts Circle Chattanooga TN 37415 Office: 859 McCallie Av Chattanooga TN 37403

PALLOT, RICHARD ALLEN, lawyer; b. Miami, Fla., July, 30, 1930; s. Moses M. and Julia (Marshall) P.; B.A., U. Fla., 1952, LL.B., 1956; m. Rosalind Brown Wedeles, Aug. 19, 1955; children—Joseph Wedeles, Melissa Aden. Admitted to Fla. bar, 1956, Fed. bar, 1956; practice, Dade County, Fla., 1956—; partner Pallot, Silver, Pallot, Stern & Proby, 1957—; counsel Inter Nat. Bank Miami, 1963—, dir., 1965—; pres., chief exec. officer Internat. Bank, Miami, 1969—; lectr. Fla. uniform comml. code, Fla. mechanics lein law, aspects of investment—corp. convertible debentures. Chmn. Fla. State Bd. Bus. Regulation. Co-chmn. benefactors com. Dade Family Opera. Trustee Opera Guild. Served to 1st lt. AUS, 1952-54. Mem. Am., Fla., Dade County bar assns., Pi Lambda Phi, Phi Alpha Delta. Mem. B'nai B'rith. Clubs: Kings Bay Yacht, Country, Symphony; Standard (Miami). Home: 12095 SW 63d Av Miami FL 33156 Office: Inter Nat Bank Bldg Miami FL 33135

PALLOT, WILLIAM LOUIS, lawyer, banker; b. Springfield, Mass., Nov. 9, 1912; s. Moses and Julia (Marshall) P.; LL.B., Cumberland U., 1939; m. Alberta Marie Tanenbaum, Dec. 25, 1939; children—Philip Roger, Barbara Stanli, Scott Marshall. Admitted to Fla. bar, 1940; practiced in Miami, 1940—; sr. partner firm Pallot, Stern, Proby & Adkins and predecessor, 1948—; chmn. Miami Nat. Bank, 1959-63; pres. Inter Nat. Bank of Miami, 1963-68, chmn. bd., 1968—; dir. NVF Corp., Wilmington, Del., Wilson Bros. Co., N.Y.C., Birdsboro Corp. (Pa.), DWG Corp., N.Y.C., Nat. Propane Corp., N.Y.C., Pa. Engr. Corp., New Castle, Sharon Steel Corp., Youngstown, O., Southeastern Pub. Service Corp., N.Y.C., No. Engring. Co., Detroit, Lectromelt Corp., Pitts., Barrington Industries, Inc., N.Y.C. Pres. Bd. Internat. Trade Greater Miami, 1971-72; pres. Internat. Center Greater Miami, 1972—. Mem. Pres.'s Regional Export Expansion Council, 1971—. Judge Municipal Ct., Coral Gables, Fla., 1948-52; city atty., Miami and North Miami, Fla., 1955-59; chmn. Pub. Works Authority, Miami, 1948-58; chmn. Miami Parking Authority, 1951-58; vice chmn. Planning Adv. Bd., Met. Dade County (Fla.), 1961-65; mem. Miami Beach Charter Bd., 1966—; mem. exec. com. Met. Miami Municipal Bd., 1953-55, Dade County Charter Bd., 1955-57; dir. Greater Miami Crime Commn., 1963-68; chmn. Fla. regional bd. Anti Defamation League, 1965-67; chmn. Dade County Criminal Justice Coordinating Council, 1972—. Trustee, Dade County United Fund; 1965—, mem. exec. com., 1969—, chmn. agy. operations com., 1969-70, treas., 1971; mem. citizens adv. bd. Fla. Meml. Coll., Miami, Biscayne Coll. for Men, Miami. Served with USNR 1942-46. Recipient Shield of Israel award, State of Israel, 1971; Sertoma Internat. Freedom award, 1972. Mem. Am., Fla. bankers assns., Am., Dade County bar assns., Fla. Bar, Am. Inst. Banking, Greater Miami Clearing House Assn. (pres. 1966), A.I.M. (pres.'s council), Hombres de Empresa Mason (Shriner, 32 deg.); mem. B'nai B'rith. Clubs: Progress, Standard, Palm Bay (Miami); Tiger Bay; Cuban-Am. Sertoma (v.p.) (Coral Gables); Propeller (v.p.). Home: 2300 Sunset Dr Sunset Island III Miami Beach FL 33140 Office: 627 SW 27th Av Miami FL 33135

PALMER, BRUCE BARTLETT, news dir.; b. Blue Earth, Minn., Nov. 26, 1908; s. Julian Manchester and Maud Edith (Bartlett) P.; student Cornell Coll., 1925-28; B.J., U. Mo., 1930; m. Leila Glen Eckles, Sept. 5, 1936; children—Bruce Laird, Sheila Glen. Reporter Okla. Pub. Co., Oklahoma City, 1930-32, editor, 1936-46; mem. staff Asso. Press, Mpls., 1932-36; news dir. WKY Radio, Oklahoma City, 1946-50, KWTV, Oklahoma City, 1953-66, Lowe Runkle Co., Oklahoma City, 1966—; information officer USIA, Colambo, Ceylon, 1951-53. Trustee Oklahoma City Gridiron Found., 1970-71. Served with AUS, 1943-45. Decorated Bronze Star. Mem. Radio TV News Dirs. Assn. (pres. 1965), Sigma Delta Chi. (chpt. pres. 1957). Mason. Home: 2316 Belleview Terrace Oklahoma City OK 73112 Office: 1800 Liberty Tower Oklahoma City OK 73102

PALMER, CHARLES EARL, ednl. adminstr.; b. Wiggins, S.C., Dec. 18, 1919; s. William David and Theodosia (Yarborough) P.; diploma Rice Bus. Coll., Charleston, S.C., 1937; student LaSalle Extension U., Chgo., 1941, U. Minn., 1944, The Citadel, 1949; D.C.S., Fort Lauderdale U., 1967; m. Rebecca Maull Palmer, Sept. 30, 1950; children—Barbara Faye, Charles Earl, John Clifford, Sarah Rebecca. Asst. to chief clk. Koppers Co., Charleston, S.C., 1937-41; post exchange mgr. Charleston Port of Embarkation, 1941-42; treasury rep. Orient region. Northwest Airlines St. Paul, 1947-49; owner Norfolk Coll., 1953-58, chmn. bd. trustees, 1958-60; pres. Palmer Coll., Charleston, 1949-72, pres. emeritus, 1972—; asso. exec. dir. for adminstrn. State Bd. Tech. and Comprehensive Edn., Columbia, S.C., 1972—; individual practice C.P.A., 1952—. Commr., Accrediting Commn. for Bus. Schs., Washington, 1961-65, chmn., 1964-65. Chmn. bd. trustees Ga.-Carolina Found., Inc., 1966—. Served to capt. USAAF, 1942-47. C.P.A., S.C. Mem. Charleston C. of C., S.C. Assn. C.P.A.'s, Am. Inst. C.P.A.'s, S.C. Assn. Bus. Colls. (past pres.), Southeastern Bus. Coll. Assn. (past pres.), Nat. Assn. and Council Bus. Schs. (past pres.), Am. Assn. Jr. Colls. (mem. commn. legislation 1967—), Charleston Trident C. of C. (dir. 1964-67). Rotarian (past pres., dist. gov. 1967-68). Co-author College Accounting Theory and Practice, 1963, 2d edit., 1968; Cost Accounting Theory and Practice, 1965, 2d edit., 1971; College Accounting Intermediate/Advanced, 1966; College Accounting for Secretaries, 1970. Contbr. articles to profl. publs. Home: 340 Brookshire Dr Whitehall Columbia SC 29210

PALMER, CHARLES FORREST, real estate exec.; b. Grand Rapids, Mich., Dec. 29, 1892; s. Walter Millard and Jeannette Hinsdill (Seymour) P.; student Dartmouth, 1914-15; LL.D., Emory U.; m. Laura Sawtell, Oct. 30, 1918; children—Margaret (Mrs. Earl C. Moses, Jr.), Laura (Mrs. T.W. Benedict), Jeannette (Mrs. Jacob M. Cath). Asso. with Wm. R. Staats Co., realtors, in Pasadena, Cal., Santa Barbara, Cal., San Diego, Chgo., 1912-17; owner C.F. Palmer Co., realtors, Santa Barbara, 1919-20; pres. Palmer, Inc., bus. real estate, Atlanta, 1921—; economist and lectr. at numerous univs. Organizer, Techwood Homes, first U.S. Slum Clearance, Atlanta, 1933, chmn. exec. com., 1934-38; chmn. Atlanta Housing Authority, 1938-40; def. housing coordinator Nat. Def. Commn. and Exec. Office of Pres., 1940-42; rep. of Pres. and head spl. housing mission to Gt. Britain, 1942; spl. asst. to Pres., 1943; chmn. Franklin D. Roosevelt Warm Springs (Ga.) Meml. Commn., mem. Nat. Council, Boy Scouts Am. Chmn. adv. com. grad. sch. city planning Ga. Inst. Tech. Nat. adv. council, Urban Am., Inc. Trustee Jesse Parker Williams Hosp., 1928-40. Mem. Atlanta adv. com. to comdg. gen. Third U.S. Army. Served as lt. Cavalry, U.S. Army, 1917-19. Awarded Mexican Campaign and Victory medals. Mem. So. Conf. of Bldg. Owners and Mgrs. (pres. 1923-24), Nat. Assn. Bldg. Owners and Mgrs. (pres. 1930-32), Housing Centre (London), Nat. Planning Assn., Atlanta Hist. Soc. (past v.p.; dir.), Council Fgn. Relations U.S.A., Am. Soc. Planning Ofcls., Nat. Housing and Town Planning Council (Eng.), Internat. Fedn. Housing and Town Planning (Netherlands), Nat. Assn. Housing Ofcls. (pres. 1940), Newcomen Soc., Atlanta C. of C. (pres. 1938), Am. Legion, Mil. Order of Fgn. Wars, English-Speaking Union, Ga. Writers' Assn. (trustee), Delta Kappa Epsilon. U.S. del., Internat. Fedn. for Housing and Town Planning, Mexico City, 1938; Hastings, Eng., 1946. Presbyn. Clubs: Capital City, Piedmont Driving, Rotary (Ga. Dist. gov., 1947-48), Warm Springs Golf; Burning Tree, Cosmos, Army-Navy (Washington); Dartmouth (N.Y.); Royal and Ancient Golf; St. Andrews' (Scotland). Author: Adventures of a Slum Fighter, 1955, also articles realty and housing publs. Home: 40 28th St NW Atlanta GA 30309 Office: Palmer Bldg 101 Marietta St NW Atlanta GA 30303

PALMER, FORREST CHARLES, librarian; b. Burlington, Wis., Oct. 17, 1924; s. Forrest Blaire and Marie Florence (Rubach) P.; student U. Pitts., 1943-44; B.A., Valparaiso U., 1948; B.S. in L.S., George Peabody Coll., 1949, M.S. in L.S., 1953; m. Lois Mae Davis, June 12, 1946; children—Forrest Charles, Beth Elaine, Janet Lorrayne. Head catalog dept. Janesville (Wis.) Pub. Library, 1949-50; serials cataloger N.C. State Coll., Raleigh, 1950-51, head serials dept., 1951-55; dir. libraries Miss. State U., 1955-62; librarian, head dept. library sci. Madison Coll., Harrisonburg, Va., 1962-70, librarian, prof. library sci., 1970—. Mem. library com. Va. Higher Edn. Study Commn.; mem. adv. com., exec. com. Va. Council Higher Edn.; Madison Coll. rep. Library Affairs Va. U. Center. Mem. edn. com. Starkville (Miss.) Youth Center, 1956; chmn. adv. bd. YMCA, State College, Miss., 1957-59. Served with Signal Corps, AUS, 1943-46. Mem. A.L.A., Southeastern (chmn. coll. sect. 1960-62), Miss. (chmn. standards and planning com. 1958-59, chmn. coll. sect. 1959-60) Va. (activities com. 1962-65, chmn. publs. com. 1963-65, v.p. 1968, pres. 1969) library assns., Pi Gamma Mu, Alpha Beta Alpha (adviser), Beta Phi Mu. Editor: Va. Librarian, 1963-65. Contbr. articles to profl. jours. Home: 60 E Weaver Av Harrisonburg VA 22801

PALMER, GEORGE, jewelry co. exec.; b. N.Y.C., Feb. 4, 1918; s. Harry and Rose (Gross) P.; B.S., Coll. City N.Y., 1938, M.S., U. Minn., 1939, Ph.D., 1943; M.S. in Metall. Engring., U. Tenn., 1966; m. Alice Katherine Herbst, Dec. 31, 1939; children—Alexandra Georgia (Mrs. Allen Rosen), Kenneth Howard. Jr. soil surveyor U.S. Dept. Agr., Lincoln, Neb., 1940-41; research chemist TVA, U. Tenn., 1942-44, 46-48; v.p. Alexander Herbst & Co., Knoxville, Tenn., 1948-66; pres. G & A Palmer Co., Knoxville, 1966—, Materials Applications, Inc., welding and metall. cons. in failure analysis. Served with AUS, 1944-46. Mem. Am. Soc. for Metals, Am. Inst. Mining and Metall. Engrs., N.Y. Acad. Scis., Sigma Xi. Contbr. articles to profl. jours. Home: 105 Westover Dr Knoxville TN 37919 Office: 514 Oxford Pl Knoxville TN 37902

PALMER, GEORGE JOSEPH, JR., govt. ofcl., b. New Orleans, Nov. 27, 1929; s. George Joseph and Juliette (Wehrmann) P.; B.B.A., Tulane U., 1952; postgrad. La. State U., 1954-55; Ph.D., Purdue U., 1958; m. Yolanda Manautou, Dec. 30, 1952; children—George Joseph III, Daphne. Asst. prof. indsl. psychology Tulane U., 1958-61; prof. indsl. psychology La. State U., 1961-62; research dir. Tex. Christian U., 1962-64; research scientist Human Scis. Research, McLean, Va., 1964-66, Century Research Corp., Arlington, Va., 1966-68; chief div. profl. manpower U.S. Dept. Transp., Nat. Hwy. Safety Bur., Washington, 1968-70, manpower program officer Nat. Hwy. Traffic Safety Adminstrn., 1970—. Cons. to utilities firm, 1962, Fasson Products, 1964, Nat. Hwy. Safety Bur., 1968, Diebold Asso., 1968. Served with USNR, 1952-54. Mem. Am. Psychol. Assn., A.A.A.S., Am. Statis. Assn., Internat. Union Psychol. Scis., Psychometric Soc., Sigma Xi. Home: 11205 Bellmont Dr Fairfax VA 22030 Office: Nat Hwy Traffic Safety Adminstrn Dept Transp 400 7th St SW Washington DC 20590

PALMER, HUBERT BERNARD, dentist, air force officer; b. San Antonio, Sept. 6, 1912; s. Hubert Victor and Rosemary (Garvey) P.; student St. Mary's U., 1931-34; D.D.S., Baylor U., 1938; postgrad. George Washington U., 1946-47, U. Md., 1950-53; m. Elizabeth Harriet McAlary, Aug. 16, 1945; children—Hubert Bernard II, Robert Leldon. Commd. 1st lt. USAAF, 1938, advanced through grades to col. USAF, 1969; chief dept. dental research U.S. Army, 1946-50; chief dept. exptl. dentistry, USAF, 1953-54, chief research dentistry div. 1954-56; command dental surgeon, 1958-59, 63-65, 65-68; dental staff officer, 1959-62, dir. dental services, 1968—. Decorated Legion of Merit, Commendation medal First Oak Leaf Cluster. Fellow A.A.A.S.; mem. Am. Dental Assn., Internat. Assn. Dental Research, Soc. Gen. Microbiology, Am. Soc. Microbiology, Omicron Kappa Upsilon. Contbr. articles to profl. jours. Research reduction decalcification tooth enamel. Home: 6115 Forest Timber San Antonio TX 78240 Office: USAF Hosp Keesler AFB MS 39534

PALMER, JACK SIDNEY, govt. researcher; b. Lubbock, Tex., Jan. 10, 1926; s. Henry Brewer and Rena (Key) P.; D.V.M., Tex., A. and M. U., 1946; M.P.H., U. Cal. at Berkeley, 1954; m. Lila Bertie Beard, Nov. 22, 1947; children—Jack Coleman, Scott Brewer, Grant Beard, Deanie Dee, Jo Beth. Vet. cons. UNRRA, Washington, 1946-47; practice vet. medicine, Sinton and Crystal City, Tex., 1947-49; dir. Vet. Pub. Health Utah, Salt Lake City, 1954-58; biol. sci. adminstr. Dugway Proving Ground, Utah, 1958-62; dir. VSR, Agrl. Research Service, U.S. Dept. Agrl., Kerrville, Tex., 1962—. Served with AUS, 1950-52; USPHS, 1957. Mem. Am. Tex. vet. med. assns., Am. Coll. Vet. Toxicologists. Democrat. Methodist. Mason (Shriner), Kiwanian (dir.). Contbr. articles to profl. publs. Home: 600 Overhill Dr Kerrville TX 78028 Office: PO Box 311 Kerrville TX 78028

PALMER, JAMES E., JR., lawyer; b. Laurel, Miss., July 17, 1913; s. James Ethel and Lela (Johnson) P.; A.B., Roanoke Coll., Salem, Va., 1935; M.A., Duke, 1936; LL.B., U. Va., 1940; m. Suzanne Kappler, Oct. 11, 1943; children—James E., III, Lela, Charles J., Carter (dec.), Suzanne. Admitted to Va. bar, 1939; engaged in pvt. law practice, Roanoke, Va., 1939-42; with Dept. of Justice 1942—, 1st asst. atty. general's lobbying survey, 1947-48, spl. asst. to atty. gen. Communist prosecutions, 1948-49; head Fines and Bond Collections Sect., Lands, 1948-54; staff Joint Com. on Def. Prodn. of Congress, 1956-59; mem. profl. staff Subcom. Housing, U.S. Senate, 1959—. Pres. Big Bros. of D.C., Inc., 1950-55, nat. dir., 1951-54. Served as lt., USCGR, World War II. Mem. Fed. (pres.), D.C., Va. bar assns., Am. Judicature Soc. Am. Acad. Polit. and Social Sci., Blue Key, Am. Legion, UN League of Lawyers (pres. Am. div.; internat. sec. gen. 1958—), Theta Chi, Sigma Nu Phi (nat. pres.), Pi Gamma Mu, Tau Kappa Alpha. Clubs: University, Jefferson Islands, Nat. Lawyers (gov.). Author of book: Carter Glass, Unreconstructed Rebel, 1939; editor: Federal Bar News, 1946—. Democrat. Episcopalian (vestryman). Mason (Shriner). Address: 406 23d St Virginia Beach VA 23451 also 3202 Klingle Rd NW Washington DC 20008

PALMER, JAMES EDWARD, educator; b. Yanceyville, N.C., Sept. 15, 1936; s. John Wesley and Vola Louise (Phillips) P.; student Grinnell Coll., 1955-57; B.S., Howard U., 1961, D.D.S., 1969. Instr. dept. pedodontics Howard U. Coll. Dentistry, Washington, 1969—. Served to capt. AUS, 1961-65. Mem. Robert T. Freeman Dental Soc. Home: 5001 5th St NW Washington DC 20011 Office: Dept Pedodontics Coll Dentistry 600 W St NW Washington DC 20011

PALMER, JANE JOLLIFFE (MRS. WADE H. PALMER), educator; b. Boyce, Va., Aug. 10, 1913; d. Thomas Powell and Effie (Shenk) Jolliffe; B.A., Coll. William and Mary, 1932; m. Wade Hampton Palmer, Dec. 5, 1936; children—Wade Hampton III, Janette Jolliffe (Mrs. Heilman). Tchr., prin. Shenandoah Sch., Clarke County, Va., 1932-33; tchr. math. Boyce High Sch., 1933-37; tchr. math. Round Hill (Va.) High Sch., 1940-41; tchr. math. Leesburg (Va.) High Sch., 1941-44, tchr. math., guidance dir., 1944-54; guidance dir. Loudoun County High Sch., Leesburg, 1954-63; sr. guidance counselor Loudoun Valley High Sch., Purcellville, Va., 1963—. Mem. Gov.'s Commn. on Status of Women, Citizens Com. on Status of Women in Va.; adv. bd. No. Va. Community Coll. Recipient Woman of Year award Loudoun County, Va., 1961. Mem. Loudoun County, Va. edn. assns., No. Va. Personnel and Guidance Assn., Dist. Guidance Assn. (pres. 1959-62), N.E.A., Am. Sch. Counselors' Assn., Nat. (dir. 1964-65, 70—), Va. (pres. 1964-65; pres. past pres.'s council 1965-66; scholarship chmn. 1966—) fedns. bus. and profl. women's clubs, Assn. Preservation Va. Antiquities, Soc. Alumni William and Mary, Va. Govtl. Employees Assn., Pi Sigma Rho, Delta Kappa Gamma. Home: Box 175 Purcellville VA 22132

PALMER, JESSE CLOWER, civil engr.; b. Cairo, Ga., Sept. 14, 1914; s. Clarence Eugene and Bessie Merle (Adams) P.; grad. structural engring. Internat. Corr. Schs., 1962; m. Audrey Vonceil Nunez, Jan. 7, 1939; children—Jesse Clower, George N., William E., Patricia. With Robert & Co., Atlanta, 1953-55, John J. Harte Co., Atlanta, 1955-57, Waldermor S. Nelson, New Orleans, 1957-58, E. M. Watkins, Tallahassee, 1958-59; proprietor Apalachee Engrs. & Land Surveyors, Inc., Tallahassee, 1959—; also Leon County surveyor Leon County, Fla., 1969—. Served to 2d lt. AUS. Registered profl. engr., Fla., Ga., Ala. Mem. Fla. Engring. Soc., Fla. Soc. Profl. Land Surveyors, Nat. Soc. Profl. Engrs. Elk. Clubs: Havana (Fla.) Golf and Country, Cairo Country. Designer main spillway and dispersion shoes Fontana Dam, N.C., 1943. Home: 2000 N Meridian Rd Tallahassee FL 32303 Office: PO Box 3163 Tallahassee FL 32303

PALMER, JESSE TAYLOR, educator; b. Lowell, Ind., Mar. 10, 1903; s. Martin Dewitt and Emma (Taylor) P.; B.S., U. Ill., 1928, M.S., 1931, Ph.D., 1936; m. Ruby Cloe Savell, July 20, 1953. Farm boy, Obsidian, Ida., 1910-23; tchr. elementary sch., Obsidian, 1923-25; farm mgr. United Fruit Co., Panama, 1928-30; econ. researcher U.S. Govt., 1936-53; econ. researcher State Cal., 1960-65; overseas cons. land reclamation and irrigation Justin & Courtney, Dacca, East Pakistan, 1966-67; prof. economics Miss. Valley State Coll., Itta Bena, since 1969—. Mem. Am., Midwest econ. assns., Internat. Assn. Agrl. Econs., Acad. Miss. Econs., Gamma Sigma Delta. Contbr. articles to profl. pubs. Home: 609 McLaurin Rolling Fork MS 39159

PALMER, JOHN DAVID, educator; b. Des Moines, Jan. 25, 1936; s. Cary Davis and Helen (McMillan) P.; B.B.A., Northwestern U., 1958; Ph.D., U. Tex., 1965; m. Robin Anne West, July 10, 1965; children—John David, Elizabeth McMillan. Asst. prof. polit. sci., research asso. Bur. Govtl. Research U. S.C., 1965-68; asso. prof. polit. sci. Ga. State U., Atlanta, 1968— asso. prof. urban life, 1970—; Nat. Assn. Schs. Pub. Affairs and Adminstrn. fellow Dept. Housing and Urban Devel., 1971-72. Cons. Project T Square, S.C. Econ. Opportunity Bd., summer 1967; mem. tech. adv. panel Resource Devel. Project So. Regional Edn. Bd., Atlanta, summer 1968, Resources Group Inc., Atlanta, 1969—. Mem. Housing Resources Com. City Atlanta, 1969, S.C. Polit. Party Platform Com., 1966, 68. Bd. dirs. U.S.O.; trustee United Community Services Columbia. Served with USN, 1958-60; comdr. Supply Corps Res. Recipient Outstanding Community Service award Columbia Record, 1967, Patriotic Civilian Service commendation U.S. Dept. Army, 1968; Spl. Certificate of Achievement, Dept. Housing and Urban Devel., 1972. Mem. Naval Res. Assn. (pres. Carolina chpt. 1966-68), Alston Wilkes Soc. (treas. 1968), Pub. Personnel Assn. (pres. Ga. chpt. 1969-70), Internat. Platform Assn., Am., So., Ga. polit. sci. assns., Soc. for Personnel Adminstrn., Am. Soc. Pub. Adminstrators, Nat. Civil Service and Municipal Leagues, Atlanta C. of C., U. Tex. Ex-student Assn. (pres. Atlanta chpt. 1970—); Am. Assn. U. Profs. Presbyn. (Sunday sch. tchr. 1968—). Contbr. articles, book revs. to profl. jours. Home: 2287 Bryn Mawr Dr NE Atlanta GA 30345

PALMER, JOHN DERWIN, govt. ofcl.; b. Desdemona, Tex., July 2, 1909; s. John Robert and Edna (Sporer) P.; grad. John Tarleton Coll., 1929; student U. Tex., 1930-31; B.S., Sul Ross State Coll., 1935; M.A., Hardin-Simmons U., 1938; Ph.D., Universdad Inter-americana (Mexico), 1962; m. Alene Moorman, May 10, 1930; children—Charles Robert, John Truett. Tchr., prin. various high schs., Canyon, Tex., Rochester, Tex., Goree, Tex., 1929-39; adminstrv. officer Social Security Adminstrn., Amarillo, Tex., 1939-40, Lufkin, Tex., 1940-41, Lubbock, Tex., 1941-43, Austin, Tex., 1941—, Alexandria, La., 1943-44, New Orleans, 1946-50, Dallas, 1950-53, Waco, Tex., 1953—; mgr. dist. office, San Antonio, 1953-66; asst. regional dir. information Dept. Health, Edn. and Welfare, Dallas; cons. Social Security to Republic of Costa Rica, Panama, Columbia, Peru, Chile, Guatemala, El Salvador, Nicaragua, Honduras, 1967-69. Pres. Bexar County chpt. Tex. Social Welfare Assn., 1956; mem. adv. bd. Community Services Div., St. Mary's U., 1955-66, cons. vocational counseling Div. Guidance and Placement, 1956-66; dir. Bexar County Tb Assn., 1957; mem. El Patronato, Universidad National de Mexico, 1960-67; C.S. Liaison officer to Instituto Mexicano del Seguro Socia., 1961-66; mem. adv. bd. Universidad Interamericana Saltillo, Coah, Mexico, 1962—; mem. exec. com. Tex.-Peru Partners in Alliance, 1964, Bd. dirs. Mexican Bapt. Children's Home; trustee Instituto Estudios IberoAmericanos, Saltillo, Mexico. Served with AUS, 1944-46. Recipient Boss of Year award, Nat. Secs. Assn., 1960; Pres.'s award Lions Internat., 1968, 69. Mem. San Antonio Council Presidents (pres. 1956), South Tex. Personnel and Guidance Assn. (pres. 1956), Nat. Ojce Mgmt. Assn. (pres. San Antonio chpt. 1955), Tex. Personnel and Mgmt. Assn., Am. Personnel and Guidance Assn., Nat. Vocational Guidance Assn. (profl. mem.), Council Internat. Relations (dir. 1957), San Antonio C. of C. (mem. com. 700 1960, mem. fgn. relations com. 1960-66), Hardins-Simmons Alumni Assn. (pres. 1959). Baptist (deacon, bd. tchr. Sunday sch.). Mason (past worshipful master, 32 deg., Shriner), Lion (past pres., dep. dist. gov.-at-large; gov. dist. 2-A2, 1963-64, internat. counsellor). Club: Press (Dallas). Author: El Seguro Social En Los Estados Unidos De America; Seguridad Social. Producer Spanish series Su Seguro Social. Home: 8416 Hunnicut Rd Dallas TX 75228 Office: 1114 Commerce St Dallas TX 75202

PALMER, JOHN RICHARD, coll. ofcl.; b. Lake Forest, Ill., Aug. 18, 1916; s. John Stephen and May (Sanders) P.; student Brothers Coll., Drew U., 1934-35; B.A., Dakota Wesleyan U., 1940, D.D. 1957; Th.M., Iliff Sch. Theology, 1945; LL.D., Rocky Mountain Coll., 1955; D.H.L., Westminster Coll., Salt Lake City, 1969; m. Ruth Sumner, Aug. 14, 1940 (div. 1969); children—Patricia Lorraine, Kathleen Ruth; m. 2d, Dorothy M. Richards, July 3, 1970. Ordained to ministry Meth. Ch., 1943; pastor, Lemon, S.D., 1935-36, Plankinton, S.D., 1936-40, Jefferson Av. Ch., Denver, 1940-41, Hanna, Wyo., 1941-44, Emmanuel Ch., Denver, 1944-52; pres. Westminster Coll., 1952-56, Morningside Coll., Sioux City, Ia., 1956-69; v.p. devel. Berea (Ky.) Coll., 1969—. Conf. youth dir. Colo. Ann. Conf. Meth. Ch., 1947-48; mem. bd. edn., gen. conf. Meth. Ch., 1964—, del. N. Central Jurisdictional Conf., 1960, 64, 68, del gen. conf., 1964, 68; pres. Nat. Assn. Schs. and Colls. of Meth. Ch., 1969. Chmn. Community Chest campaign, Arapahoe County, 1952; membership com. Denver YMCA. Trustee Westmar Coll., LeMars, Ia. Mem. Denver Council Chs., Denver Meth. Ministers Assn. (pres. 1951-52), N. Central Assn. Colls. and Secondary Schs. (commr. 1958-62). Mason (32 deg., Shriner), Rotarian. Clubs: Lions Englewood (Colo.); Kiwanis (Community Service medal Sioux City 1961). Home: 411 Jackson St Berea KY 40403

PALMER, LARRY GARLAND, educator; b. Warren, O., Nov. 13, 1938; s. Gerald L. and Esther Gertrude (Garland) P.; B.Mus., Oberlin Coll., 1960; M.Mus. (Nat. Def. Edn. Act fellow 1960-63), Eastman Sch. Music, U. Rochester, 1961, Mus.D., 1963; student Mozarteum, Salzburg, Austria, 1958-59, Summer Acad. Organ, Haarlem, Holland, 1964, 67. Chmn. dept. fine arts St. Paul's Coll., Lawrenceville, Va., 1963-65; prof. music Norfolk (Va.) State Coll., 1965-70; organist, choirmaster Trinity Luth. Ch., Norfolk, 1966-70; asso. prof. harpsichord and organ Meadows Sch. Arts, So. Meth. U., Dallas, 1970—; organist, choirmaster St. Luke's Episcopal Ch., Dallas, 1971—. Harpsichordist, mus. dir. Dallas Musica da Camera, 1971—; organist, harpsichordist concert tours, Europe, 1967, 69, 72; featured artist Nat. Conv. Am. Guild Organists, Dallas, 1972. Mem. Am. Guild Organists (dean chpt. 1968-70), Internat. Heinrich Schuetz Soc., Internat. Harpsichord Soc., Pi Kappa Lambda. Author: Hugo Distler and His Church Music, 1967. Editor harpsichord pages The Diapason, 1969—. Home: 10125 Cromwell Dr Dallas TX 75229

PALMER, LAUCHLEN SECORD, psychiatrist; b. Cleve., Nov. 1, 1908; s. Sterne Royal and Abigail (Secord) P.; student Washington and Lee U., 1927-30; M.D., U. Rochester, 1934; m. Catharine Mary Fleming, Sept. 1, 1934. Intern, Highland Hosp., Rochester, N.Y., 1934-35; psychiatrist N.Y. Dept. Mental Hygiene, 1935-68; dir. Chemung County Dept. Mental Health, 1958-63, individual practice psychiatry, Elmira, N.Y., 1958-64; dir. day treatment center VA Hosp., Miami, Fla., 1964-70; individual practice psychiatry; Lake Worth, Fla., 1970—. Asso. prof. psychiatry N.Y. State Med. U., 1952-58; clin. instr. psychiatry U. Miami Sch. Medicine, Miami, 1964-70; lectr. in field. Served with USNR, 1942-46. Diplomate Am. Bd. Psychiatry. Fellow Acad. Psychosomatic Medicine. A.C.P., Am. Psychiat. Assn.; mem. Am. Soc. Clin. Hypnosis, A.M.A. Asso. editor Acad. Psychosomatic Jour., 1961-69. Home: 8133 Pine Tree Lane West Palm Beach FL 33406 Office: 1710 4th Av N Lake Worth FL 33460

PALMER, MERLE, circuit ct. judge; b. Pontotoc County, Miss., Mar. 11, 1919; s. William Judson and Hesperia (Faulkner) P.; ed. U. Md. Admitted to Miss. bar; former municipal judge Miss., city atty., Pascagoula, Miss.; pros. atty. Jackson County (Miss.), 1948-52; mem. Miss. State Ho. of Reps., 1960-64; mem. Miss. State Senate, 1964-71, pres. pro tem, 1968-71; now judge 19th Circuit judge. Mem. World Travelers Assn., Ole Miss Alumni Assn., Am., Jackson County bar assns., Miss. State Bar, C. of C. Elk (past exalted ruler). Home: 1016 Cherubusco St Pascagoula MS 39567 Office: Box 59 Pascagoula MS 39567*

PALMER, OWEN THACKARA, JR., lawyer; b. Gulfport, Miss., July 15, 1920; s. Owen Thackara and Lula (Barksdale) P.; B.A., U. Miss., 1942, LL.B., 1947; m. Joanne Melton, Apr. 5, 1947; children—Jan Barksdale, Wawice Eugenia. Admitted to Miss. bar 1947; with firm Eaton & Cottrell, Gulfport, Miss.; 1947-48; individual practice law, Gulfport, 1948-64; sr. partner, Palmer & Stewart, Gulfport, 1965—. Asst. sec.-treas., Miss. Valley Petroleum Corp., Mississippi City, 1964-69; instr. Am. history U. Miss., 1947. Disaster, chmn., Gulfport chpt. A.R.C., 1949-51; coach, Gulfport Recreation dept., 1954-68. City pros. atty., asst. city atty., Gulfport, 1953-69; atty. Gulfport Municipal Separate Sch. Dist., 1957—. Dir., past pres. Gulfport-Harrison County Library, 1954-68; bd. dirs., 1st v.p., mem. exec. com. Miss. Safety Council, 1971—; past pres. Gulfport Little Theatre. Served with USNR. Mem. Miss. State Bar (chmn. traffic ct. com. 1962—), Am. (rep. State Miss. on adv. com. to traffic ct. com. 1966—), Harrison County (past pres.) bar assns., Am. Trial Lawyers Assn., Am. Judicature Assn., Delta Kappa Epsilon, Phi Delta Phi. Episcopalian. Rotarian. Club: Gulfport Yacht (past commodore). Home: 1308 E Beach St Gulfport MS 39501 Office: 2209 14th St Gulfport MS 39501

PALMER, RALPH THOMAS, clergyman, educator; b. San Diego, Mar. 18, 1926; s. Olaf Gideon and Dorothy (Decker) P.; B.A., Tex. Christian U., 1948, B.D., 1950; M.S. in Pub. Health, Yale, 1952; postgrad. Duke, 1956-57; m. Mary Maxine Jones, Aug. 30, 1948; children—Angella Marie, Carol Celeste. Ordained to ministry, 1947; pastor Cumberland Av. Christian Ch., Waco, Tex., 1947-50; spl. investigator New Haven Pub. Health Dept., 1950-51; research microbiologist Yale Med. Sch., 1951-52; with United Christian Missionary Soc., Indpls., 1952-70, missionary to Japan, 1952-57, exec. sec., 1957-70; dean Coll. of Missions, Indpls., 1957-70; sr. pastor 1st Christian Ch., Pampa, Tex., 1971—. Bd. dirs. Missionary Orientation Center, Agrl. Missions Inc., Japan Internat. Christian U., Layman's Overseas Service, Christian Med. Council; mem. organizing council Found. for Religious Studies, Inc. Bd. dirs. Suicide Prevention and Crisis Intervention of Pampa. Served with USNR, 1944-45. Mem. Ind. Archeol. Soc., Internat. Psychoanalytic Assn., Am. Pub. Health Assn., Am. Mgmt. Assn., Ind. Guidance Counsellors Assn., Am. Psychol. Assn., Pampa C. of C. Club: Knife and Fork (Pampa). Author: Framboesia (Yaws) in Jamaica, West Indies, 1952; co-author chpt. Minister's Own Mental Health, 1961. Contbr. articles on pub. health, missions, psychology to profl. publs. Home: 2404 Comanche St Pampa TX 79065 Office: First Christian Church 18th at Nelson Sts Pampa TX 79065

PALMER, RICHARD EUGENE, editor; b. Watertown, N.Y., July 7, 1920; s. Howard Welch and Pauline (Coulthart) P.; student Wesleyan U., Middletown, Conn., 1938-41; A.B., U. Mo., 1947; m. Elizabeth Winfield Lee, May 6, 1950; children—Melissa Lee, James Howard. Sports editor Portchester (N.Y.) Daily Item, 1941-42; news editor Daily Free Press, Kinston, N.C., 1947-48; editor Mid-York Weekly, Hamilton, N.Y., 1948-51; editor News-Herald, Willoughby, O., 1953-60; with State-Times and Morning Advocate, Baton Rouge, 1960—, asso. editor, 1965—, prodn. mgr., 1963—. Mem. adv. com. Research Inst., Am. Newspaper Publishers Assn., Easton, Pa., 1971—. Bd. mgrs. YMCA, Baton Rouge, 1966—, Salvation Army, Baton Rouge, 1965-71; trustee Newspaper Prodn. and Research Center, Oklahoma City, 1966—. Served to capt. AUS, 1942-46, 51-52. Mem. So. Newspaper Publishers Assn. (chmn. prodn. methods and labor com. 1970-71), So. Prodn. Program (bd. dirs. 1965—), Sigma Delta Chi. Mason. Home: 12363 E Millburn St Baton Rouge LA 70815 Office: 525 Lafayette St Baton Rouge LA 70821

PALMORE, JOHN STANLEY, JR., judge; b. Ancon, C.Z., Aug. 6, 1917; s. John Stanley and Antoinette (Gonzalez) P.; student Western Ky. State Coll., 1934-36; LL.B., U. Louisville, 1939; student Harvard Grad. Sch. Bus. Adminstrn., 1942-43; m. Eleanor Gertrude Anderson, July 31, 1938; 1 son, John W. Admitted to Ky. bar, 1938; asso. firm King & Flournoy, Henderson, Ky., 1939-42; chief legal br. Jeffersonville (Ind.) Q.M. Depot, 1946-47; partner firm Hunt & Palmore, Henderson, 1947-52, Palmore & Mitchell, Henderson, 1956-59; pvt. practice, 1952-56; Commonwealth's atty. 5th Jud. Dist. Ky., 1955-59; city atty. Henderson, 1954-55; pros. atty. Henderson, 1949-53; city atty. Sebree, Ky., 1954-59; judge Ct. Appeals Ky., 1959—, now asso. justice. Served to lt., Supply Corps, USNR, 1942-46, 51-52. Mem. Ky. Bar Assn. Democrat. Episcopalian. Home: Henderson KY 42420 Office: State Capitol Frankfort KY 40601*

PALMQUIST, EMIL EUGENE, govt. ofcl.; b. Otisco, Minn., Aug. 20, 1908; s. Axel G. and Hilma (Palm) P.; B.A., Gustavus Adolphus Coll., 1930; M.D., Northwestern U., 1937; M.P.H., U. Mich., 1942; m. Ingrid J. Ostrom, June 6, 1936; children—Kristin (Mrs. Walter Anton), Linda (Mrs. William M. Mason), Paula (Mrs. Norman Knoll), John. Intern Swedish Hosp., Seattle, 1936-37; practice gen. medicine, Seattle, 1937-38; pub. health officer, Yakima County, Clark County, Whitman County, Olympia Health Dist., Washington, 1938-44; dir. pub. health Seattle, King County, 1944-51; commd. surgeon USPHS, 1950, advanced through grades to asst. surgeon gen., 1970; chief health mission Point Four in Iran, 1951-53, asst. chief div. Internat. Health, USPHS, Washington, 1953-55; clin. prof. pub. health U. Cal. at Berkeley, also dir. pub. health, Berkeley, 1955-57; chief gen. health services USPHS, San Francisco, 1957-61; region III health dir. USPHS, Dept. Health, Edn. and Welfare, Charlottesville, Va., 1961-70, region IV health dir., Atlanta, 1970—; asst. clin. prof. pub. health U. Wash., 1947-51; lectr. Sch. Nursing, U. Wash., 1944-48, U. Cal. at Berkeley, 1957-61; vis. lectr. U. Tehran Med. Sch., Iran, 1951-53; teaching mission U.S. Dept. State to Ministry Health, Iran, 1950. Recipient Surgeon Gen.'s medal for meritorious service, 1964. Diplomate Am. Bd. Preventive Medicine. Fellow Am. Pub. Health Assn. (chmn. health officer's sect. 1959), Am. Coll. Preventive Medicine, Assn. Tchrs. Preventive Medicine; mem. A.M.A., Albemarle County Med. Soc., Phi Chi, Delta Omega. Contbr. articles on health adminstrn. to profl. jours. Home: 3460 Buford Hwy NE Atlanta GA 30329 Office: 50 N 7th St NE Atlanta GA 30323

PALMROS, ERIC KELVIN, accountant; b. Syracuse, N.Y., May 23, 1908; s. Alexander and Helen Frances (Snow) P.; student Tex. Christian U., 1947; m. Gladys Lucille Hedley, Aug. 25, 1930 (dec. Sept. 1966); children—Eric Kelvin, Alexander. Investment banker and broker, N.Y.C., 1928-41; accountant, auditor, 1941-43; auditor, chief cashier Montgomery Ward, 1943-45; bus. mgr. J.M. & O.P. Leonard, 1945-50; pub. accountant, Fort Worth, 1950—; officer, dir., owner several corps. and ventures; pres., T.O.L. Oil Co., 1950—, S.W. Investment & Devel. Co., 1964—. C.P.A., Tex. Mem. Nat. Assn. Accountants (chpt. pres. 1948-49), Am. Inst. C.P.A.'s, Am. Accounting Assn., Stuart Cameron McLeod Soc., Air Force Assn., Tex. Soc. C.P.A.'s (Ft. Worth chpt.). Episcopalian (vestryman, pres. men's club 1953-54). Mason (32 deg., Shriner). Office: Commerce Bldg Fort Worth TX 76102

PALS, CLARENCE HERMAN, assn. exec.; b. Meservey, Ia., July 10, 1907; s. Herman K. and Mintie (Rozeboom) P.; student Ia. State Tchrs. Coll., 1925; D.V.M., Ia. State U., 1932; m. Florence C. Cogswell, June 30, 1931; children—Calvan Herman, Helen Ruth (Mrs. William F. Kingsbury). Practice gen. vet. medicine, Thornton, Ia., 1932; with meat inspection div. U.S. Dept. Agr., Chgo., 1932-34, Washington, 1944-65, dir. U.S. Meat Inspection Service, 1960-65; cons. meat-packing industry, 1966—; exec. officer Nat. Assn. Fed. Veterinarians, Washington, 1969—. Mem. Ednl. Commn. for Fgn. Vet. Grads., 1971. Past chmn. Alexandria (Va.) dist. Boy Scouts Am., chmn. Alexandria dist. Eagle Bds. Rev., 1960—. Recipient Silver Beaver award Boy Scouts Am., 1957, Superior Service award U.S. Dept. Agr., 1955; named to Academie Veterinaire de France, 1964. Mem. World Assn. Vet. Food Hygienists (v.p. 1955-60, pres. 1960-67), Am. Vet. Med. Assn., U.S. Animal Health Assn., Orgn. Profl. Employees U.S. Dept. Agr., Nat. Assn. Fed. Veterinarians, Farm House frat., Phi Zeta. Methodist (lay leader). Mason (32 deg.). Editor The Fed. Veterinarian, 1968—. Home: 2338 S Ode St Arlington VA 22202 Office: National Association of Federal Veterinarians 1522 K St NW Washington DC 20005

PANAK, JOHN JESSE, research engr.; b. Hayden, Colo., Mar. 14, 1937; s. John and Alta May (Beezley) P.; B.S. in C.E., U. Colo., 1958; M.S. in C.E., U. Tex., 1968; m. Carolyn Ann Konz, Aug. 30, 1958; children—Mary, Jeffrey, David, Kathy. Jr. civil engr. Cal. Div. Hwys., Bishop, 1958-61; engr. III, Tex. Hwy. Dept., Austin, 1961-65; with U. Tex. Center for Hwy Research, Austin, 1965—, research engr. asso. IV, 1965—. Cons. prin. Austin Research Engrs., Inc., 1967—. Registered profl. engr., Tex. Mem. Am. Soc. C.E., Tex. Soc. Profl. Engrs., Am. Concrete Inst. Home: 6008 Shoal Creek Austin TX 78757 Office: Engring Sci Bldg Center for Hwy Research U Tex Austin TX 78705

PANKEY, FRANK LAWSON, ch. assn. ofcl.; b. Pamplin, Va., Jan. 29, 1925; s. Everette Leonard and Anne Powell (Hunt) P.; B.A., U. Richmond, 1948, D.D., 1971; B.D., So. Bapt. Theol Sem., 1951;

postgrad. Adult Edn. Inst. Ind. U., 1965, Presbyn. Sch. Christian Edn., 1969; m. Mary Alpha Rudasill, Aug. 19, 1950; children—David, Thomas, Susan, Elizabeth. Ordained to ministry So. Bapt. Ch., 1951; pastor Chesterfield and Skinquarter Chs., Moseley, Va., 1951-54; pastor Azalea Bapt. Ch., Norfolk, Va., 1955-64; asso. sec. tng. union dept. Va. Bapt. Gen. Bd., Richmond, 1965-67, acting sec., 1968-69; sec. dept. teaching and tng. Va. Bapt. Gen. Bd., 1970—. Dir. Sch. Christian Edn., Norfolk, 1958-62; pres. Norfolk Bapt. Pastors Conf., 1960-61. Mem. Va. Bapt. Religious Edn. Assn., U. Richmond Alumni Assn. (pres. luncheon 1958), Va. Alumni Group of So. Bapt. Theol. Sem. (sec. 1962), Va. Bapt. Hist. Soc. Home: 2916 Vesper Rd Richmond VA 23225 Office: POBox 8568 Richmond VA 23226

PANKEY, GEORGE ATKINSON, educator, physician; b. Shreveport, La., Aug. 11, 1933; s. George Edward and Annabel (Atkinson) P.; student La. Poly. Inst., 1950-51; B.S., Tulane U., 1954, M.D., 1957; M.S., U. Minn., 1961; m. Ann Adele Schillin, July 31, 1956; children— Susan Margaret, Stephen Charles, Laura Atkinson. Intern, U. Minn. Hosps., 1957-58, resident internal medicine, 1958-60, Mpls. VA Hosp., Mpls. Gen. Hosp., 1960-61; practice medicine, New Orleans, 1961—; partner Ochsner Clinic, New Orleans, 1968—; asst. vis. physician Charity Hosp. La., New Orleans, 1961-62, vis. physician, 1962—; cons. infectious diseases Ochsner Clinic and Found. Hosp., New Orleans, 1963—; instr. dept. medicine Div. Infectious Diseases Tulane U. Sch. Medicine, New Orleans, 1961-63, clin. instr., 1963-65; clin. asst. prof. medicine, 1965-68, clin. asso. prof., 1968—; clin. asso. prof. dept. oral diagnosis, medicine, radiology La. State U. Sch. Dentistry, New Orleans, 1970—. Pres. New Orleans Young Republican Club, 1969-71. Adv. bd. Angie Nall Sch. Hosp., Beaumont, Tex.; trustee Nall Found. for Children, Beaumont. Recipient certificate merit Am. Acad. Gen. Practice, 1970; certificate of award So. Med. Assn., 1970. Diplomate Am. Bd. Internal Medicine. Fellow A.C.P., Am. Coll. Preventive Medicine; mem. A.A.A.S., Internat. Platform Assn., Am. Assn. Contamination Control (chpt. pres. 1968-70), Am. Fedn. Clin. Research, Am. Heart Assn., Am., So. med. assns., Am. Soc. Internal Medicine (del. ann. meeting 1971-72), Am. Soc. Microbiology, Am. Thoracic Soc., Am. Venereal Disease Assn., La. Heart Assn., La. Soc. Internal Medicine (pres. elect 1972—), La. Med. Soc., La. Thoracic Soc. (chmn. program com. 1968), Musser Burch Soc., Orleans Parish Med. Soc., N.Y. Acad. Scis., Pan Am. Med. Assn. (diplomate mem. sect. internal medicine 1971), Internat. Oceanographic Found., Am. Mus. Natural Hist., Smithsonian Instn. Mason (32 deg., Shriner). Author: A Manual of Antimicrobial Therapy, 1969. Contbr. numerous articles to profl. jours. Bd. editors Patient Care, 1969—. Home: 4019 Alberta St Metairie LA 70001 Office: Ochsner Clinic 1514 Jefferson Hwy New Orleans LA 70121

PANKEY, GEORGE EDWARD, educator; b. Charlotte Court House, Va., Dec. 2, 1903; s. John Wesley and Cora Smith (Daniel) P.; B.A., U. Richmond, 1926; M.A., U. N.C., 1927; m. Annabel Atkinson, Mar. 6, 1931; 1 son, George Atkinson. Mem. faculty Ogden Coll. and Western Ky. State Tchrs. Coll., 1927-28, La. Poly. Inst., 1928-43; with land dept. Gulf Oil Corp., 1944-46; currently in research work. Mem. Huguenot Soc., S.A.R., Sigma Tau Delta. Baptist. Mason. Author: John Pankey of Manakin Town, Virginia and His Descendants, Vol. I, 1969, Vol. II, 1971; co-author: Five Thousand Useful Words, 1936. Address: PO Box 84 Ruston LA 71270

PANKEY, GEORGE STEPHEN, dentist; b. Durham, N.C., Dec. 3, 1922; s. Edwin Wilburn and Julia (Bender) P.; A.B., U. N.C., 1948; D.D.S., Emory U., 1954; m. Christina R. Curry, Jan. 17, 1959 (div. Feb. 1967); children—Julia Gay, Crista Merry; m. 2d, Diane Joy Flaim, Oct. 14, 1967; adopted children—Laura Jean, Julia Ann, George Stephen. Practice dentistry, Winter Garden, Fla., 1954-58, North Miami Beach, Fla., 1958-59, St. Cloud, Fla., 1959—; dir. Fla. United Investment, Inc. Served with AUS, 1943-46; ETO. Mem. Am. Dental Assn., Fla. State, Central Dist. dental socs., V.F.W., St. Cloud C. of C. (pres. 1961-62), Sigma Chi. Republican. Episcopalian. Mason (worshipful master 1965, Shriner), Rotarian (pres. 1962-63). Home: Pine Lake Estates St Cloud FL 32769 Office: 1216 10th St St Cloud FL 32769

PANNELL, CHARLES ADAM, SR., judge; b. Eton, Ga., June 19, 1911; s. Thomas Asbury, Sr. and Ila Catherine (Allen) P.; student Young Harris Coll., 1928-30, Mercer U. Law Sch., 1930-31, 35-36; LL.B., U. Ga., 1937; m. Ruth Ann Loughridge, Dec. 24, 1939; children—Charles Adam, James L., William A. Admitted to Ga. bar, 1937; tchr. history and math. pub. schs. Murray County (Ga.), 1931-35; practiced law, Chatsworth, Ga., 1937-63, city atty., 1942-50, county atty. Murray County, 1944-50, 58-60; judge Ga. Ct. Appeals, Atlanta, 1963—. Mayor, Eton, Ga., 1933-35; mem. Ga. Ho. of Reps., 1939-46, 48-50, 60-62; mem. Ga. Senate, 1946-48, 58-60, 63, floor leader, 1963; mem. Ga. Pardon and Parole Bd., 1950-55, chmn., 1953-55. Mem. Cherokee Bar Assn. (pres. 1958), Sigma Delta Kappa. Democrat. Methodist. Mason (Shriner), Odd Fellow, Lion (pres. Chatsworth 1960). Club: Atlanta Athletic. Home: 433 Chateau Dr Atlanta GA 30305 Office: 420 Capitol Square Atlanta GA 30324

PAPCUHIS, CHARLES JOHN, govt. ofcl.; b. Peabody, Mass., Dec. 22, 1925; s. John and Stella (Delivorias) P.; B.S. in Mech. Engring., Northeastern U., 1950; M.S., George Washington U., 1963; m. Stella Karapiperis, Jan. 15, 1950; children—John, Gary. Test engr., engr. Research & Devel. Labs., Ft. Belvoir, Va., 1950-55; asst. project engr. amphibians Bur. Ships, Washington, 1956-58; project engr. amphibians Naval Ship Systems Command, Navy Dept., Washington, 1958-68, dep. asst. project mgr., 1968-71, asst. project mgr., 1971—. Decorated Bronze Star medal. Registered profl. engr., Vt. Mem. Am. Ordnance Assn., Assn. Sr. Engrs. Naval Ship Systems Command, Order of Am. Hellenic Ednl. Progressive Assn. Greek Orthodox (pres., trustee). Home: 4 Saddlebrook Ct Silver Spring MD 20906 Office: Naval Ship Systems Command Washington DC 20360

PAPPAS, GUS JOHN, city ofcl.; b. Savannah, Ga., June 11, 1918; s. John and Calliope (Vatsios) P.; B.S., U. Ill., 1956; M.Engring. Adminstrn., George Washington U., 1959; m. Kathryn Mildred Avgerinos, Dec. 28, 1941; children—James, Mary Ellen, William. Elec. estimator Byck Electric Co., Savannah, 1937-40; commd. capt. U.S. Army, 1945; advanced through grades to col. U.S. Air Force, 1963; ret., 1969; with 118th F.A. Regt., 1940-42; officer C.E., 1942-48; civil engr. U.S. Air Force, 1948-69; cons. engr. Vollmer Assos., Washington, 1969-70; housing coordinator Met. Planning Commn., Savannah, Ga., 1970—. Pres. bd. dirs. Savannah (Ga.) Housing and Devel. Corp., 1970-71. Dist. commr. Coastal Empire council Boy Scouts Am., 1971—. Decorated Legion of Merit, Meritorious Service medal, Army Commendation medal, Air Force Commendation ribbon; recipient Distinctive Service award Soc. Am. Mil. Engrs., 1967. Registered profl. engr., Vt. Fellow Am. Soc. C.E.; mem. Soc. Am. Mil. Engrs. (pres. chpt. 1961-62, 67-68), Air Force Assn., Ret. Officers Assn. Mem. Greek Orthodox Ch. Lion. Home: 203 Devonshire Rd Savannah GA 31404 Office: 2 E Bay St Savannah GA 31401

PAPPAS, STEVE GEORGE, newspaper editor; b. Charlotte, N.C., Apr. 5, 1921; s. George T. and Jenny (Belios) P.; student La. State U., 1939-42; m. Katharine Kalas, June 12, 1947; 1 son, George. With news, sports depts. Charlotte News, 1945-50; with Daytona Beach (Fla.) News-Jour. Corp., 1950—; mng. editor Daytona Beach News-Jour., 1956—. Pres. Daytona Beach (Fla.) Symphony Soc., 1966-68. Served with USAAF, 1942-45. Mem. A.P. Assn. Fla. (pres. 1964-65). Democrat. Author weekly newspaper column, Purely Personal. Home: 548 N Halifax Dr Ormond Beach FL 32074 Office: 901 6th St Daytona Beach FL 32015

PAPPER, EMANUEL MARTIN, univ. adminstr., anesthesiologist; b. N.Y.C., July 12, 1915; s. Max and Lillian (Weitzner) P.; A.B., Columbia, 1935; M.D., N.Y.U., 1938; Dr. Med. (hon.), Univ. Uppsala (Sweden), 1964, U. Turin (Italy), 1969; m. Julia Fisher, Dec. 21, 1939; children—Barbara Ellen, Richard Nelson. Fellow medicine N.Y.U., 1938-39, fellow physiology, 1940, instr. anesthesiology, 1942-46, asst. prof., 1946-49, asso. prof., 1949; intern Bellevue Hosp., 1939-40, resident anesthesiology, 1940-42; prof. anesthesiology, chmn. dept. Columbia, also dir. anesthesiology service Presbyn. Hosp., 1949-69; dir. anesthesiology, vis. anesthesiologst Francis Delafield Hosp., 1951-69; v.p. med. affairs, dean, prof. anesthesiology, U. Miami, 1969—. Cons. div. med. scis. NRC. 1954-69, Huntington (N.Y.) Hosp., 1949-69; nat. cons. surgeon gen. USAF, 1963-70; mem. surgery study sect. NIH, 1958-62; civilian cons. First Army, USN; prin. cons. Nat. Inst. Gen. Med. Scis., 1965-66, chmn. project com. gen. med. research program, 1966-70; mem. nat. heart council NIH, 1962-66; hon. cons. Royal Prince Alfred Hosp., Sydney Australia; trustee Cedars of Lebanon, Mt. Sinai hosps. (both Miami). Served from 1st lt. to maj., M.C., AUS, 1942-46; chief anesthesiology sect. Torney, Dibble and Walter Reed hosps. Diplomate Am. Bd. Anesthesiology (dir. 1956-65, pres. 1964-65). Fellow Faculty Anesthesiologists Royal Coll. Surgeons, Royal Soc. Medicine; mem. N.Y. Acad. Medicine (1st pres. sect. anesthesiology), Am. Soc. Anesthesiologists (pres. 1967-68), N.Y. State Soc. Anesthesiologists (past pres.), NRC (chmn. com. anesthesia 1962-67), Am. Coll. Anesthesiologists, Am. Soc. Pharmacology and Exptl. Therapeutics, A.M.A., N.Y. Acad. Scis., N.Y. Co. Med. Soc., Am., N.Y. socs. anesthesiologists, A.A.A.S., Am. Assn. Thoracic Surgery, Harvey Soc, Am. Soc. Clin. Investigation, Am. Thoracic Soc., Assn. U. Anesthetists (co-founder, 1st pres.), Pan Am. Med. Assn., Assn. Anaesthestists Gt. Britain and Ireland (corr.), Swedish (hon.), Finnish (hon.), Israeli (hon.), Australian (hon.), N.Y. State (hon.), D.C. (hon.) socs. anesthesiologists, Halsted Soc. Phi Beta Kappa, Sigma Xi, Alpha Omega Alpha. Author sci. papers pub. in various med. jours., 3 textbooks. Home: Ocean Lane Dr Key Biscayne FL 33149 Office: Biscayne Annex Miami FL 33152

PAQUETTE, RADNOR JOSEPH, educator; b. Lake Linden, Mich., Feb. 2, 1902; s. Joseph Martin and Minnie (Kramer) P.; B.S., Met.E., Mich. Coll. Mining and Tech., 1927, M.S. in Mining, 1932; m. Katherine Frances Conway, Dec. 31, 1930; 1 dau., Julie Marie (Mrs. David Kenneth Smith). Mining engr. coal mines Corrigan McKinney Steel Co., Wolfpit, Ky., 1927-28; mining engr., supt. Fontana Mining Corp., 1928-30; office engr. Copper dist. Power Co., Ontonagon, Mich., 1930-31; engr. Mich. State Hwy. Dept., Lansing, 1933-48; asst. prof. civil engring., research engr. U. Fla. Engring. & Indsl. Expt. Sta., Gainesville, 1948-51; prof. civil engring. Ga. Inst. Tech. Sch. Civil Engring., Atlanta, 1951-69, prof. emeritus civil engring., 1969—, research asso. Engring. Expt. Sta., 1948-69. Cons., Met. Planning Commn., Atlanta. Registered profl. engr., Mich., Fla., Ga. Mem. Am. Soc. C.E., Am. Road Builders Assn. (pres. ednl. div. 1957-58), Am. Soc. Engring. Edn. (mem. hwy. research bd.), Ga. Engring. Soc., Theta Tau Beta, Chi Epsilon, Sigma Chi. Author: (with others) Highway Engineering, 1951, 2d. edit., 1960, 3d. edit., 1967; (with Ritter-Paquette) Engineering Materials, 1958; (with others) Transportation Engineering: Planning and Design, 1972. Home: 1875 Ardmore Rd NW Atlanta GA 30309 Office: 225 N Av Atlanta GA 30332

PARADISE, RICHARD ROBERT, lawyer; b. Quincy, Mass., Aug. 23, 1924; s. Alphonse J. and Anne (Larkin) P.; A.B. cum laude, Harvard, 1948; B.A. in Law (Harvard Fiske scholar), Trinity Coll., Cambridge U., Eng., 1950, M.A., 1955; postgrad. Acad. Internat. Law, The Hague, Netherlands, summers 1949, 51, N.Y. U. Sch. Law, 1953-55; m. Nancy Weld Burdick, Nov. 12, 1955 (dec. 1965); children— Allison, Mary. Legal dept. Monsanto Chems., Ltd., London, Eng., 1950-52; tchr. Berkshire Sch., Sheffield, Mass., 1952-53; law clk., asso. Hall, Haywood, Patterson & Taylor, N.Y.C., 1953-56; admitted to N.Y. bar, 1956; spl. partner Roberts & McInnis, Washington, 1956-65, McInnis, Wilson, Munson & Woods, Washington 1965-70; partner McInnis, Munson, Muzzall & Tansill, Washington, 1970-71. Mem. Alexandria (Va.) Republican City com., 1964-65. Served with AUS, 1943-46. Mem. Am. Bar Assn., Fed. Bar. Assn., Soc. Gray's Inn, London. Republican. Roman Catholic. Clubs: Potomac Boat, Harvard (London); Bunbury. Contbr. articles to profl. jours. Home: 4143 S Four Mile Run Dr Arlington VA 22204 Office: 1717 Pennsylvania Av NW Washington DC 20006

PARADY, WILLIAM HAROLD, ednl. assn. exec.; b. Waterbury, Conn., May 8, 1919; s. William Oliver and Frances (Campbell) P.; B.S., U. Ga., 1940; M.S., U. Fla., 1951; m. Eloise Deas, Sept. 11, 1943. Area supr., farm mechanics specialist Fla. Dept. Edn., Tallahassee, 1947-51; zone mgr., bus. mgmt. mgr. Fla. Ford Tractor Co., Jacksonville, 1952-64; exec. v.p. Growers Equipment Co., Miami, Fla., 1964; owner, mgr. Parady Ford Tractor Co., Griffin, Ga., 1965-66; coordinator Am. Assn. for Vocational Instructional Materials Agrl. Engring., U. Ga., Athens, 1967—. Served to maj. AUS, 1940-46. Decorated Croix de Guerre, Bronze Star medal. Mem. Am. Soc. Agrl. Engrs. (Fla. sect. chmn. 1964-65, Ga. sect. chmn. 1972-73), Phi Kappa Phi, Gamma Sigma Delta. Mem. Christian Ch. (chmn. bd. 1970-73). Rotarian. Contbr. articles to profl. jours. Home: 293 Cedar Creek Dr Athens GA 30601 Office: Am Assn Vocational Instructional Materials Agrl Engring Center U GA Athens GA 30601

PARCHER, JAMES VERNON, educator; b. Drumright, Okla., July 21, 1920; s. James Augustus and Pearl (Sharp) P.; B.S., Okla. State U., 1941, M.S., 1948; M.A., Harvard, 1967; Ph.D., U. Ark., 1968; m. Martha Hoff Ruckman, Aug. 7, 1943; children—Carol Susan (Mrs. Thomas H. Comegys), James Robert, David Loris, Dee Ellen, Kay Elaine. Maintenance engr. Remington Arms Co., Kings Mills, O., 1941-42; instr. Okla. State U., Stillwater, 1947-48, asst. prof., 1948-54, asso. prof., 1954-67, prof., 1967—, head Sch. Civil Engring., 1969—. Cons. in soil mechanics and founds., 1952—. Served with C.E., AUS, 1942-46, 50-52. Mem. Am. Soc. C.E., Am. Soc. Engring. Edn., Nat., Okla. socs. profl. engrs., Internat. Soc. of Soil Mechanics and Found. Engring., Sigma Xi, Phi Kappa Phi, Sigma Tau, Chi Epsilon. Author: (with R. E. Means) Physical Properties of Soils, 1962; (with R. E. Means) Soil Mechanics and Foundations, 1968. Home: 1024 W Knapp St Stillwater OK 74074

PARCHER, LORIS ALVIN, educator; b. Heartwell, Neb., Dec. 27, 1907; s. James Augustus and Pearl Lillian (Sharp) P.; B.S., Okla. State U., 1940, M.S., 1949; Ph.D., Tex. A. and M. U., 1955; m. Agnes Louise Ford, June 25, 1919; children—Linda (Mrs. Donald L. Kent), Diane (Mrs. Rodney V. Clark). Asst. prof. Okla. State U., Stillwater, 1940-55, asso. prof., 1955-61, prof. agrl. econs., 1962—; dean Coll. Agr., Imperial Ethiopian A. and M. Coll., Harrar, Ethiopia, 1955-57, pres., 1957-59. Served with AUS, 1943-45. Mem. Am., Okla. (pres. 1971-72) socs. farm mgrs. and rural appraisers, Am. Farm Econs. Assn., Phi Kappa Phi. Democrat. Methodist. Editor Current Farm Econs., 1946—. Home: 1108 S McFarland St Stillwater OK 74074

PARDEE, THOMAS HAUGHTON, pub. health ofcl.; b. Charlotte, N.C., Aug. 12, 1918; s. John Grove and Jane Hill (Haughton) P.; B.S., Davidson Coll., 1942; postgrad. U. N.C., 1946-47; m. Martha Cannon Means, May 22, 1949 (dec. 1967); 1 dau., Angela Cannon. Project engr. W. K. Dickson & Co., Charlotte, N.C., 1948-57; commd. officer USPHS, 1957, environmental health work in Va., 1960-66, S.C., 1966-67, Ala., 1967—, India, 1943-45, Liberia, 1957-60, P.R., 1964, area supr. Aedes Aegypti Program, Tuscaloosa, Ala., 1967-69, environmental health dir. Tri-County Dist. Health Service, Decatur, Ala., 1969—. Instr. Tubman Sch. Fine Arts, Monrovia, Liberia, 1958-60. Mem. President's sub-com. rural health, Republic of Liberia, 1958-60. Served with AUS, 1942-45. Registered land surveyor, N.C.; registered sanitarian, Ala. Mem. N.C. Water Works Operators Assn., Ala. Assn. Sanitarians, Ala. Pub. Health Assn. (chmn. environmental sect. 1971—), Parents Without Partners (pres. Decatur chpt. 1970—). Episcopalian. Club: Charlotte Engineers. Home: 705 Edgewood St SW Decatur AL 35601 Office: Tri-County District Health Service PO Box 850 Decatur AL 35601

PARDRIDGE, WILLIAM DEWEESE, pub. co. exec., economist; b. Chgo., Jan. 12, 1916; s. Clinton Edwin and Marie (DeWeese) P.; student U. Chgo., 1933-41, 64-65, U. Md., 1961-64; m. Muriel M. Morrissey, Feb. 28, 1944 (div. Aug. 1955); m. 2d; Kathleen M. Toon, June 15, 1960 (div. Oct. 1967); children—William Morrissey, Michael Morrissey. Editor, pub. Air Affairs, Washington, 1944-51; editorial dir., vice chmn. The Wealth of a Nation, Economic Inequities, Stanardsville, Va., 1965—; econ. analyst writer in 47 daily newspapers in 47 states, 1965—. Spl. research fellow U. Chgo., 1942-43. Served with USAAF, 1941-42, AUS, 1942-43. Mem. Am. Econ. Polit. Sci. and Sociology Assn. Republican. Home: PO Box 30198 Washington DC 20014 Office: Stanardsville VA 22973

PARDUE, DON CARSON, educator; b. Wilkesboro, N.C., Aug. 27, 1930; s. Eugene Forrest and Eva (Prevette) P.; student Mars Hill Jr. Coll., 1950; B.S. in Agr., Berea Coll., 1954; M.S. in Adult Edn., N.C. State U., 1970; m. Mary Carol Henderson, June 2, 1952; children—Eugene Forrest II, Lawrence, Joseph Daniel, Donna. Asst. county agt. Ky. Agrl. Extension Service, Berea, 1954-55, N.C. Agrl. Extension Service, Robbinsville, 1956, Burnsville, N.C., 1957-62; agt. N.C. State U., Agr. Extension Service, Asheville, N.C., 1963; farm bus. specialist N.C. State U. Agr. Extension Service, Raleigh, 1964—. Chmn. Yancey County Agrl. Workers Council, 1959-60. Served with USNR, 1948-49. Recipient grant N.C. Dairy Found., 1964-66. Mem. Nat. Farm Mgmt. Assn. (mem. subcom. 1965-67). Methodist (trustee 1960-62, mem. adminstrv. bd. 1966-70). Clubs: Burnsville (N.C.) Men's (treas. 1960); Cary (N.C.) Exchange (v.p. 1970). Developer of computer system for processing bus. records and analytical data N.C. farmers, 1964—. Contbr. articles to regional and nat. mags. Home: 914 Ralph Dr Cary NC 27511 Office: NC State U Raleigh NC 27607

PARDUE, ROBERT LEE, real estate cons., broker; b. Wilson, Okla., Apr. 6, 1924; s. Garland Victor and Ira (Wood) P.; student Tex. Tech. U., 1945-47; B.B.A., U. Tex., 1949; m. Diana Corzelius, Aug. 6, 1949; children—Diana Ruth, Frank M. C., Robert Lee, Melinda Gaye. Office mgr. Compania Minera De Huehuetenango, Guatemala City, Guatemala, 1949-51, dir., 1949-51; individual practice property tax cons., Ft. Worth, 1951-53, Houston, 1954-55 land mgr. West Securities Co., Houston, 1955-60; individual practice as real estate cons. and broker, Houston, 1960—; owner Pardue & Dark Interests, Houston, 1962—; chmn., founder R.L. Pardue & Co.; chmn., pres. PDL properties, Inc. Pres. Houston Bd. Realtors, 1971—. Served to 1st lt., USAF, 1942-45. Decorated D.F.C., Air medal (Army), Purple Heart. Mem. Nat. Assn. Real Estate Bds., Tex. Assn. Realtors (dir.), Delta Kappa Epsilon. Club: Exchange of Houston (past pres.). Home: 5676 Doliver St Houston TX 77027 Office: 2911 Brazos St Houston TX 77006

PAREDES, HELEN JEAN, utility co. exec.; b. Detroit, Aug. 9, 1919; d. Celestino P. and Honora (Waters) Paredes; B.A. in Econs., Berea Coll., 1941. Service rep. Mich. Bell & Telegraph Co., Detroit, 1941-42; service rep. So. Bell Tel. & Tel. Co., Miami, Fla., 1942-46, coach, 1946-47, unit supr., 1947-56, recruiting supr., 1956-65, employee relations supr., 1965—. Mem. Task Group on Rent control for Civil Def.; mem., com. chmn. Fla. Gov.'s Status of Women Commn. Mem. Bus. and Profl. Womens Club (state pres. 1963-64, chpt. pres. 1956-57, dist. dir. 1960-61), Personnel Assn. Greater Miami (sec. 1960-61), Am. Personnel and Guidance Assn., Am. Soc. Personnel Adminstrn., Miami C. of C. Address: PO Box 1471 Miami FL 33132

PARHAM, DONALD ALBERT, educator; b. Atoka, Okla., Apr. 3, 1930; s. Carl Albert and Louella (Mason) P.; student Eastern State Coll., Okla., 1948-50; B.S., Southeastern Okla. State Coll., 1952; M.S., Okla. State U., 1955; Ed.D., George Peabody Coll., 1959; m. Kay Baker, Dec. 26, 1954; children—David William, Brent Donald, Warren Gene. Asst. prof. phys. edn. So. Ark. State Coll., 1956-59; prof., chmn. dept. phys. edn., baseball coach Southeastern Okla. State Coll., Durant, 1959—, dir. athletics, 1970—. Chmn. Durant City Planning Commn., 1964—. Served with AUS 1952-54. Lion (past pres.). Home: 1221 Dixon St Durant OK 74701

PARHAM, GUY HENRY, JR., educator; b. Knoxville, Tenn., Oct. 4, 1913; s. Guy Henry and Rose (Morrison) P.; B.S., U. Cin., 1939; m. Dorothy Duggan, Oct. 11, 1939; 1 son, Guy Henry III. Faculty, U. Tenn., Knoxville, 1941-43, 46—; prof., 1947—; individual practice architecture, Fla., Tenn., 1945-46; lectr. safe boating Coast Guard Aux.; pres. Par-D Navigational Co., Knoxville, 1965—. Served with USAAF, 1943-45. Mem. U.S. Naval Inst., Inst. Navigation, Sigma Phi Epsilon, Omicron Delta Kappa. Author: Celestial Navigation, 1964; Oceanic Navigation, 1965; Map and Chart Reading, 1966; Star Identification, 1966; Advanced Celestial Navigation, 1967; Graphical Analysis of Navigation, 1969. Designer navigational computers. Home: 241 Hawthorne Av Knoxville TN 37920 Office: PO Box 2012 Knoxville TN 37901

PARHAM, ROY LEE, JR., environmental engr.; b. Tampa, Fla., Oct. 15, 1926; s. Roy Lee and Arta (Hendricks) P.; B.C.E., U. Fla., 1950; m. Mary Jane Blair, Dec. 22, 1951; children—Janet Irene, Susan Lee, Bonnie Josephine. Design engr. TVA, Knoxville, Tenn., 1950-51; asst. san. engr. N.Y. State Dept. Health, Albany, 1951-54 san. engr. Hillsborough County Health Dept., Tampa, 1954-55; chief san. engr. Watson & Co., Tampa, 1955-66; chief design engr. Coastal Engring. Co., Brooksville, Fla., 1966; dir. Environmental Engr. Div., Hillsborough County Health Dept., Tampa, Fla., 1966-72; head san. dept. Diaz, Seckinger's Assos., Inc., Tampa, 1972—. Served with AUS, 1945-46. Mem. Am. Soc. C.E., Am. Acad. Environmental Engrs., Sigma Tau. Home: 2112 W Hiawatha St Tampa FL 33604 Office: 800 W Buffalo Av Tampa FL 33603

PARIS, THOMAS LEE, govt. ofcl.; b. Macon, Ga., July 2, 1938; s. Cleo Eugene and Ena Louise (Barfield) P.; B. Indsl. Mgmt., Auburn U., 1960; m. Thelma Ollene Davidson, Nov. 24, 1960. Engr., Army Missile Command, Redstone Arsenal, Ala., 1963-68; Pershing engr. research, devel. and testing SAFEGUARD Ssytem Command,

Huntsville, Ala., 1968-69, chief resident office SAFEGUARD System Evaluation Agy., Huntsville, 1969—. Served with AUS, 1961-63. Decorated Army Commendation medal. Registered profl. engr., Ala. Baptist. Home: 712 Esslinger Rd SE Huntsville AL 35802 Office: SAFEGUARD System Command PO Box 1500 Huntsville AL 35807

PARIS, WILLIAM ANDREW, physician; b. Chattanooga, Mar. 20, 1924; s. Charles Thomas and Mary Ellen (O'Gravey) P.; student U. Chattanooga, 1944-45; B.S., U. Tenn., 1950, M.D., 1954; m. Frances Catherine McIsaac, June 2, 1951; children—William Andrew, Cathy, Chuck, Mary Ellen, Chris, Michael, John, David, Stephen. Intern, St. Joseph Infirmary, Atlanta, 1955-56; gen. practice medicine, Atlanta, 1955, Memphis, 1956, Lake Providence, La., 1957—; mem. staff East Carroll Hosp., chief staff, 1967, 71; pub. health cons., 1960-71; chmn. East Carroll Parish Cancer Soc. Coach, Dixie Youth Baseball, 1960; pres. St. Patrick's Sch. Bd., 1971-72. Served with AUS, 1947-49. Mem. Am., La. acads. gen. practice, Assn. Am. Physicians and Surgeons, Soc. Bariatrics. Roman Catholic. (council 1969—). K.C. Club: Quarterback (v.p. 1967-69) (Lake Providence). Home: Briarfield Terrace Lake Providence LA 71254 Office: 224 N Hood St Lake Providence LA 71254

PARISH, ARCHIE GALE, architect; b. Mpls., Jan. 5, 1898; s. Alfred and Sarah Elizabeth (Gale) P.; grad. Dunwoody Inst., 1918; extension student, U. Minn., 1919-20; grad. in reinforced concrete engring., Internat. Corr. Schs., 1922; m. Alma Louise Gravender, Nov. 18, 1919; children—James Gravender, Donald Gale, Nancy (Mrs. Charles V. Lair), Richard Archie. Draftsman, Clarence J. Brown, architect, 1918-20; engr. Farnum Constrn. Co., 1920-22; interior designer Wm. A. French Co., 1922-24; designer Woolpert & Brown, architects, 1924-26; partner Brown & Parish, 1926-28; owner A.G. Parish, architect, St. Petersburg, Fla., 1928-49, 57-65; mem. firm Parish, Merwin & Parish, St. Petersburg, 1965—; partner Parish & Crowe, 1950-57. Chmn. bldg. code com. St. Petersburg, 1950—; mem. materials bd. Bldg. Dept. St. Petersburg, 1935—; mem. Fla. Bd. Architecture, 1940-68. Recipient certificate award Nat. Council Archtl. Registration Bds., 1957. Fellow A.I.A. (Gold medal award Fla. Assn. 1968). Presbyn. (elder). Home: 145 Wildwood Lane SE St Petersburg FL 33705 Office: Rutland Bldg St Petersburg FL 33701

PARISH, NORMAN RAY, animal physiologist; b. Brady, Tex., Mar. 6, 1931; s. Henry E. and Edna M. (Hubbard) P.; B.S., Tex. A. and M. U., 1954; M.S., U Tenn., 1958; m. Seba A. Sutliff, June 8, 1957 children—Michelle, Elisabeth. Asso. prof. physiology of reprodn. U. Tenn., Oak Ridge, 1958-61; animal physiologist King Ranch, Inc., Kingsville, Tex., 1962—. Mem. governing bd. Agrl. Research Inst., 1972—. Mem. Am. Soc. Animal Sci., Costal Bend Agr. Bus. Council (v.p. 1968-69), Kleberg County C. of C. (chmn. agrl. com. 1971-72). Republican. Episcopalian. Kiwanian. Home: 1620 Santa Maria Kingsville TX 78363 Office: King Ranch Inc Kingsville TX 78363

PARISH, OVERTON L., JR., lawyer; b. Ballinger, Tex., Sept. 14, 1924; s. Overton L. and Lillie E. (Murphy) P.; LL.B., U. Tex., 1949; m. Martha Jo Reese, Oct. 31, 1942; children—Pamela Jo (Mrs. Wendell Underwood), Overton L., III. Admitted to Tex. bar, 1949; mem. firm Hathaway & Parish, Attys., Ballinger, Tex., 1949-53; atty. Runnels County Abstract Co., Ballinger, 1949-53, Runnels County, 1955—; pvt. practice law, Ballinger, Tex., 1954—. Dir. First Nat. Bank, Ballinger, Telephone Industries, Inc., Ballinger. Trustee Ballinger Ind. Sch. Dist., 1952-53. Served with AUS, 1943-45. Fellow Am. Coll. Probate Counsel; mem. State Bar Tex., U.S. Supreme Ct. Bar, V.F.W. Democrat. Methodist. Rotarian. Home: 802 Murrell St Ballinger TX 76821 Office: 704 Park Av Ballinger TX 76821

PARK, CURTIS JACKSON, dentist; b. La Grange, Ky., July 13, 1925; s. Curtis Field and Sara (Smock) P.; B.S., U. Ky., 1950; D.M.D., U. Louisville, 1953; postgrad. Dewey Sch. Orthodontia, 1960; m. Lucy Buckner Blanton, July 30, 1955; children—Curtis Jackson, Jane Clay, Harry Blanton. Gen. practice Dentistry, Paris, Ky., 1953—, orthodontia, 1960—. Cons. dentist Bourbon Heights, Inc., Paris, 1971; pres. Bourbon Farm Pain Co., Inc., Paris, 1961—. Chmn. Bourbon County Bd. Health, 1971-72; chmn. ins. com. Bourbon County 175th Anniversary Celebration, 1961. Served with USAAF, World War II. Mem. Am., Ky. dental assns., Bluegrass, Bourbon County (sec.-treas. 1971, v.p. 1972) dental socs., Internat. Acad. Orthodontics. Rotarian. Club: Stoner Creek Country. Home: 115 Houston Av Paris KY 40361 Office: 12 W 5th St Paris KY 40361

PARK, FRANCIS DE RONALD, civil engr.; b. Clarksville, Ark., Oct. 9, 1909; s. Merit Samual and Gladys Earl (Clark) P.; B.S., U. Ill., 1933; m. Helen Elisabeth Gates, July 8, 1933; 1 dau., Melinda Jane (Mrs. L.M. Burnett). With U.S. Army C.E., TVA, Tenn., Miss., Ark., White Rivers projects, 1933-46; asso. with John M. Rice, Pitts., 1947-48; water control engr., Dade County, Fla., 1949-60, chief engr. met. area pub. works, 1960-64, dir. water-control and coastal engring. met. area pub. works, 1964—. Bd. dirs. Fla. Shore and Beach Preservation. Recipient Certificate of Appreciation, Am. Soc. C.E., 1957. Registered profl. engr., Fla., Pa. Fellow Am. Soc. C.E., Fla. Engring. Soc. (engr. of year award 1972); mem. Soc. Am. Mil. Engrs., Nat. Soc. Profl. Engrs., Am. Pub. Works Assn., Soil and Crop Sci. Soc. Fla. Democrat. Methodist. Home: 4141 Raynolds Av Miami FL 33133 Office: Dade County Pub Works Dept Engring Div Justice Bldg 1351 NW 12th St Miami FL 33125

PARK, HARRY RAY, educator; b. Columbus, Ga., Aug. 12, 1921; s. Harry Lee and Annie (Seay) P.; B.S. in Econs., Trinity U., 1953; M.A. in Econs., U. Cal. at Berkeley, 1956; postgrad. N.Y.U., 1960—; m. Juanita Martin, Feb. 10, 1943 (div. 1965); children—Harry Ray, Alton Lee; m. 2d, Jean M. Masterson, Mar. 2, 1965; children—Melissa Lorien, Steven Craig. Served to maj. U.S. Air Force, 1940-57, ret.; air transport pilot, USAF, 1942-48; dir. adminstrn., Frankfurt, Germany, 1948-49; staff dir. adminstrn., San Antonio, 1949-51, dir. personnel, 1951-53; asst. dir. operations and tng., Cal., 1953-55; staff dir. operations and tng., Iceland, 1956-57; asso. prof., asst. dept. chmn. aerospace sci. N.Y.U., N.Y.C., 1959-62; supr. tng. div. Job Orientation in Neighborhoods, N.Y.C., 1963-67; asso. dir. Mgmt. Center, Inst. for Bus. and Community Devel., also asst. prof. U. Richmond (Va.), 1967—. Lectr. mgmt. Hofstra U., L.I., N.Y., 1963-64. Mem. Am. Econ. Assn., Am. Personnel and Guidance Assn., Am. Assn. U. Profs., Am. Mgmt. Assn., Am. Soc. Tng. and Devel., Am. Platform Assn., Am. Civil Liberties Union, Am. Humanist Assn. Home: 7617 Marilea Rd Richmond VA 23225

PARK, ISABELLE SPRINGER (MRS. DAVID EUGENE PARK), club woman; b. El Paso, Tex., Nov. 9, 1895; d. Thomas Hanson and Mary Louise (Rogers) Springer; certificate Ethical Culture Sch., N.Y.C., 1915; m. William J. Millard, June 9, 1917; children—William J., Mrs. Elizabeth Malley; m. 2d, David Eugene Park, Sept. 26, 1931; 1 son, David Eugene. Vice pres., sec. Am. Woman's Club, Buenos Aires, Argentina, 1932-36, v.p., Bogota, Colombia, 1937-38; charter mem. Campo Allegro Library, Caracas, Venezuela, 1939; pres. Am. unit Venezuela Red Cross, Caracas, 1940-42; mem. woman's com. Nat. Found. Poliomyelitis, N.Y.C., 1948-49; mem. bd. Harris County unit Am. Cancer Soc., Houston, 1958-62, sec.; mem. bd. Pan Am. Round Table, Houston, 1959-60; asso. state dir. Pan-Am. Round Tables Tex. Mem. Am. Inst. Mining, Metall. and Petroleum Engrs. Women's Aux. (dir. 1946-52, v.p.), D.A.R. (mem. chpt. bd. 1962-65), Daus. Republic Tex. Home: 2414 Inwood Dr Houston TX 77019

PARK, KWAN-BOO, dentist; b. Washington, Sept. 12, 1914; s. Chong Hyen and Yee Soon (Hong) P.; B.S., U. Hawaii, 1940; certificate orthodontics Columbia U. Dental Sch., 1954; D.D.S., St. Louis U. Sch. Dentistry, 1946; m. Kyong-Oak, July 12, 1948; children—Philip, Susan. Intern Guggenheim Dental Clinic, N.Y.C., 1947; asso. prof. operative dentistry Howard U. Sch. Dentistry, Washington, 1948-65; pvt. practice dentistry, Washington, 1965—. Vice pres. bd. Korean Student Fund, Washington, 1968—. One of founders Cafritz Hosp., Washington, 1960—, Diplomate Am. Bd. Orthodontics. Mem. Middle Atlantic Soc. Orthodontists, So. Md., Dist. dental socs. Methodist (deacon 1969—). Home: 9200 Cedar Lane Bethesda MD 20014 Office: 3230 Pennsylvania Av SE Washington DC 20020

PARK, LELAND MADISON, coll. librarian; b. Alexandria, La., Oct. 21, 1941; s. Arthur Harris and Jane Rebecca (Leland) P.; student McCallie Sch., 1957-59; A.B., Davidson Coll., 1963; M.L.S., Emory U., 1964; postgrad. Simmons Coll., 1968. Reference librarian Pub. Library of Charlotte and Mecklenburg County (N.C.), 1964-65; head of reference and student personnel Davidson (N.C.) Coll. Library, 1967-70, asst. dir., 1970—. Vis. lectr. Emory U., summer, 1972. Library cons. Mem. Wake County (N.C.) Citizens for Better Libraries; sec. com. library affairs Piedmont U. Center, 1969-70, chmn., 1970-72. Served to capt. AUS, 1965-67; now capt. Res. Mem. Am., Southeastern, N.C., Metrolina (pres. 1969-71), Mecklenburg County (treas. 1969-70) library assns., Soc. of Cin., S.A.R., Davidson Coll., McCallie Sch. alumni assns., Mil. Order World Wars, Jr. C. of C. (chmn. library com. 1965-67), Res. Officers Assn., Sigma Nu (chpt. alumni comdr. 1967—). Democrat. Episcopalian. Home: 418A Concord Rd PO Box 2201 Davidson NC 28036

PARK, ROBERT BENTON, lawyer; b. Hayward, Okla., Nov. 21, 1924; s. Charles Avery and Talley (Lord) P.; LL.B., Okla. U., 1949; m. Virginia Guest, July 24, 1948; children—Charles Weldon, Jane Alice. Admitted to Okla. bar, 1949, since practiced in Chickasha. Dir. 1st Nat. Bank & Trust Co., First Fed. Savs. & Loan Assn. Spl. justice Ct. Criminal Appeals; spl. commr. Supreme Ct. Bd. dirs. Jane Brooks Sch. for Deaf, Ambucs; bd. regents Okla. Coll. for Women (now Okla. Coll. Liberal Arts). Served with USNR, 1942-46. Fellow Am. Coll. Probate Counsel; mem. Am., Okla. (bd. govs.) bar assns., Am. Judicature Soc., Chickasha C. of C. (dir.), Delta Theta Phi. Home: 6 Circle Dr Chickasha OK 73018 Office: 118 N 4th St Chickasha OK 73018

PARK, SEI YOUNG, economist; b. Seoul, Korea, July 17, 1923; s. Chang Hyun and Yong In (Shin) P.; B.A., Chosun Christian U., Seoul, Korea, 1950; M.P.A., Harvard, 1955; m. Heisook Hong, Mar. 1, 1951; children—Eunhei Grace, Mihei Frances, Kihong Samuel, Jahei Virginia. Came to U.S., 1954. Sec. to Pres. Syngman Rhee, Republic of Korea, 1950-54; economist Internat. Bank for Reconstruction and Devel., Washington, 1958—, deputy div. chief, 1969—. Founding mem. Korean Student YMCA Fedn., 1947—. Bd. dirs. Am. Korean Found., Inc., N.Y.C., Korean Student Fund, Inc., Washington. Served with Republic of Korea Army, 1950-51. Decorated Bronze Star (U.S.). Mem. Am. Econ. Assn. Home: 6030 Sherborn Lane Springfield VA 22152 Office: 1818 H St NW Washington DC 20433

PARKER, ALTON BROOKS, JR., pub. relations exec.; b. San Antonio, Sept. 30, 1930; s. Alton Brooks and Hazel Florence (Lyons) P.; B.A., U. of South, Sewanee, 1957; postgrad. U. Tenn., Nashville, 1960-61; m. Anne Smith, July 30, 1959; children—Carrie, Malissa, Christopher, Alexander. With Ellis Shapiro Agy., San Antonio, 1955-56; research asst. U. of South, 1956-57; pub. relations supr. So. Bell Telephone Co., 1958-60; account exec. Robert H. Horsley Assos., 1960-63; v.p., dir. Buford Lewis Co., 1963-68; dir. Tenn. Health Careers Program, Nashville, 1968—; pub. relations cons. Nashville Symphony Assn., 1968; guest lectr. U. Tenn. Coll. Communications, Knoxville. Chmn. Met. Clean Up Week, Nashville, 1968. Vice pres. Tenn. Hosp. Edn. and Research Found., Inc.; bd. dirs. Jr. Bd. Printing Industry Nashville, Goodwill Industries of Middle Tenn. Served with USNR, 1951-53. Recipient grant Nat. Urban Coalition, 1972. Mem. Pub. Relations Soc. Am. (dist. chmn. 1969-70, nat. membership chmn. 1970—, nat. chmn.'s citation 1970, pres. Mid-Tenn. chpt. 1967), Nashville Area C. of C., Nashville Advt. Fedn. (past dir., editor, pub. affairs chmn.). Club: Nashville City. Home: 217 Lauderdale Rd Nashville TN 37205 Office: 210 Reidhurst Av Nashville TN 37203

PARKER, B. B., utility exec.; b. Monroe, N.C., Sept. 18, 1914; s. Henry F. and Kate (Hamilton) P.; B.S. in Elec. Engring., U. N.C., 1936; m. Virginia Osborn, July 25, 1941; children—Judith Lynn, Stephen Osborne. With Mill-Power Supply Co., Charlotte, N.C., 1936-62, asst. to pres., 1957-60, dir., 1957-65, pres., 1960-62; v.p. Duke Power Co., 1962, v.p. engring. and constrn., 1962-65, exec. v.p. power operations, 1965-71, exec. v.p., gen. mgr., 1971—, also dir. Cons. Def. Electric Power Adminstrn., Dept. Interior, 1951-52; vice chmn. Southeastern Electric Reliability Council; exec. council Nat. Electric Reliability Council. Pres. Jr. Achievement Charlotte, 1965; v.p. exec. council Boy Scouts Am., 1966-71; dir., v.p. N.C. United Community Service. Dir. Atomic Indsl. Forum: pres. N.C. Engring. Found., 1968, 69. Mem. Newcomen Soc. Methodist (adminstrv. bd.; mem. exec. bd. Meth. Home). Clubs: Cowansford Country; Engineers (dir. 1945), Myers Park Country (Charlotte). Home: 2414 Red Fox Trail Charlotte NC 28211 Office: PO Box 2178 Charlotte NC 28201

PARKER, BILLY JACK, rancher, realtor; b. Boaz, Ala., May 11, 1930; s. Newton Asbury and Jessie Virginia (Sanford) P.; student Snead Jr. Coll., 1949, U. Ala., 1950; D.M.C., U. Ala. Dental Sch., 1954; m. Annette Harwell, May 27, 1956; children—William Jeffrey, Leila Virginia. Pvt. practice dentistry, Brookhaven, Miss., 1956-57, Boaz, Ala., 1957-69, ret.; rancher, Nashville, Ark., 1969—; tchr. sci. Murfreesboro (Ark.) High Sch., 1969-70; realtor South Ark. Realty, Nashville, 1970—. Master Boy Scouts Am., 1961-62. Pres. Boaz (Ala.) Nursing Home, 1965-69, v.p., 1969—. Served to capt. USAF, 1954-56. Mem. Boaz (dir. 1960-62), Murfreesboro (dir. 1970—), chambers commerce, Am. Dental Assn., Nat. Assn. Real Estate Bds., Ark. Real Estate Assn. Mem. Ch. of Christ. Rotarian, Lion. Home: Route 4 Box 140 Highland Valley Ranch Nashville AR 71852 Office: First Nat Bank Bldg Nashville AR 71852

PARKER, CHARLES LEE, youth products co. exec.; b. Paducah, Tex., Sept. 30, 1933; s. Clarence M. and Hazel Louise (Probasco) P.; B.A., Tex. A. &M. U., 1955; M.B.A., Harvard Bus. Sch., 1963. Television newscaster WKY-TV, Oklahoma City, 1955-61; cost engr. Gen. Dynamics, Groton, Conn., 1963-65; gen. mgr. Herff Jones Co., Indpls., 1965-67; exec. v.p., dir. John Roberts, Inc., Austin, Tex., 1967—. Bd. dirs. Better Bus. Bur., Austin, 1970—. Trustee St. Andrews Episcopal Sch., Austin. Republican. Episcopalian. Author: Integrated Circuits, 1963. Office: 7500 S Interregional Austin TX 78767

PARKER, CHARLES SCOTT, oilwell servicing co. exec.; b. San Antonio, Aug. 27, 1935; s. Horatio Maxwell and Francis Page (Venable) P.; B.S. in Petroleum Engring., U. Tex., 1958; m. Barbara Joan Dresslar, Aug. 31, 1956; children—Jeffrey Scott, Gregory Maxwell. Area engr. Texaco, Inc., various locations, Tex., 1958-62; partner Poynor & Parker, Cons. Engrs., Liberty, Tex., 1962-65; v.p., gen. mgr. Bertman Well Service Co., Liberty, 1965-71; v.p. operations Bertman Gas & Oil Corp., Goodale Bertman & Co., Inc., Liberty, 1969-71; partner, v.p., sec., treas. Adkins-Parker Well Service, Inc., Liberty, 1971—. Sec. Liberty (Tex.) Zoning and Planning Commn., 1969—; chmn. Liberty Bd. Equalization, 1971. Served to 1st lt. C.E., AUS, 1959-60. Registered profl. engr., Tex. Mem. Liberty C. of C. (dir. 1969—), Am. Inst. Petroleum Engrs., Gulf Coast Assn. Oilwell Servicing Contractors (chmn. 1968-69), Order Alamo. Methodist (bd. stewards 1969-72). Rotarian (dir. 1972). Club: Megnolia Ridge Country (pres. 1969-72) (Liberty, Tex.). Home: 2415 Hollywood St Liberty TX 77575 Office: PO Box 1296 Liberty TX 77575

PARKER, CLARENCE COLCORD, govt. ofcl.; b. Gadsden, Ala., May 31, 1917; s. Andrew Leroy and Clara (Hogan) P.; B.S. in Mech. Engring., Ala. Poly. Inst., 1940; m. Sibyl Margaret McMahan, Aug. 17, 1942; children—Donna Jane, Bobbye Lou. Chief operations office Marshall Space Flight Center, NASA, 1960-62, asso. dir. adminstrn. and services Launch Operations Center, 1962-63, asst. dir. adminstrn. Kennedy Space Center, Fla., 1963-65, chief adminstrv. div., 1965-66, dep. dir. installation support, 1966—. Chmn., Project Stblzn. Bd., 1966. Bd. dirs. Titusville (Fla.) Hosp. Registered profl. engr., Ala. Mem. Am. Soc. M.E. Home: 1840 Hamlin Ct Titusville FL 32780 Office: KSC-NASA Kennedy Space Center FL 32899

PARKER, CLAUDE THOMAS, JR., county agrl. agt.; b. Rising Star, Tex., Apr. 17, 1922; s. Claude Thomas and Ethel Pansy (Nunnally) P.; B.S. in Agr., Tex. A. and M. U., 1944; m. Subil Marie Proctor, Jan. 27, 1945; 1 dau., Susan Ann. Livestock specialist Burrus FeedMills, Fort Worth, 1954-56; county agrl. agt., Bllinger, Tex., 1945-54, 1956—. Cons. Red Angus Assn. Am., 1959-67. Served with AUS, 1943-45. Recipient Distinguished Service award U.S. Dept. Agr., 1967, Certificate of Recognition, Fed. Land Bank, 1967, Soil Conservation Service award W. Tex. Assn. Soil Conservation Dirs., 1965; named Outstanding Citizen of Ballinger, 1960. Mem. Christian Ch. (speaker youth activities throughout state 1945—). Home: 400 6th St Ballinger TX 76821 Office: Box 658 Ballinger TX 76821

PARKER, DONALD LEON, educator; b. Dexter, Tex., Oct. 12, 1935; s. Jesse Raymond and Gladys (Ring) P.; B.A., N. Tex. State U., 1957, M.S., 1962; postgrad. Tex. A. and M. U., 1964-68 Ph.D., 1968; m. Doris Marie Dickerman, Nov. 4, 1955; children—Michael, Thomas, David, Catherine, Karen, Susan. Instr. physics N. Tex. State U., 1962-64; asst. prof. Lamar State U., 1967-68; vis. asst. prof. Tex. Tech. U., 1968-70; asst. prof. physics St. Mary's U., San Antonio, 1970—, chmn. dept., 1971—; sr. engr. Jet Propulsion Lab., summer 1970. Served with Armed Forces, 1958-61. Robert A. Welch Found. grantee, Tex. Natural Resources Found. grantee for research projects. Mem. Am. Assn. Physics Tchrs. (Tex. sect.), Sigma Xi. Home: 6321 Wigwam San Antonio TX 78238

PARKER, DOROTHY (DOROTHY BOTWEN APPEL), lawyer; b. N.Y.C., Jan. 30, 1916; d. Bernard Johnson and Clara (Landsman) Botwen; B.A., Barnard Coll., 1936; J.D., Columbia, 1938; m. Alexander Appel, Dec. 1, 1945 (dec. Apr. 1948); m. 2d, Benjamin M. Parker, Feb. 12, 1962. Admitted to N.Y. bar, 1938, D.C. bar, U.S. Supreme Ct. bar, 1961; gen. practice law, N.Y.C., 1938-41; cons. Office of Censorship, U.S. Govt., 1941-45; partner Alexander Appel, firm of Appel and Tannenbaum, Esquires, 1945-48; individual practice, N.Y.C., 1948—; chief adult and vocational edn. and research, office Gen. Counsel, U.S. Dept. Health, Edn. and Welfare, 1965-67, spl. asst. to asst. gen. counsel, edn. div., civil rights div., 1967-70, spl. asst. to dep. gen. counsel Office of Gen. Counsel, 1968-70; vice chmn. exchange visitor waiver rev. bd. U.S. Dept. Health, Edn. and Welfare; minority counsel, subcom. on Constl. amendments U.S. Senate Com. on the Judiciary, 1970—. Exec. dir. Ind. Citizens Com. to Re-elect LaGuardia, 1941. Mem. employment adv. com. Columbia Law Sch. Mem. D.C. Women's Bar Assn.; New York County Lawyers Assn., League of Women Voters, Hadassah, Am. Jewish Congress, Barnard Alumnae Assn., Columbia Law Alumni Assn. Jewish religion. Clubs: Columbia (Washington), Barnard College of Washington; Barnard College of N.Y. Home: 1600 S Joyce St Arlington VA 22202 Office: 200 Park Av New York City NY 10017 also 1600 S Joyce St Arlington VA 22202

PARKER, EDGAR TURNER, electronic engr.; b. Rossville, Ga., Dec. 29, 1938; s. Edgar Elliott and Ora (Turner) P.; B.S.E.E., U. Tenn., 1962; Ps.D., Coll. Divine Metaphysics, 1971; m. Lula Mae Clift, Apr. 12, 1963; children—Edgar Turner, Fredrick Boyd. Engring. trainee U.S. Army Ballistic Missile Agy., Redstone Arsenal, Ala., 1958-60; engring. trainee NASA, George Catlett Marshall Space Flight Center, Huntsville, Ala., 1960-62, aerospace technologist, 1962-67; with U.S. Army, 1967—; electronic engr. Missile Comd., Redstone Arsenal, 1967-68, Materiel Comd. Hdqrs., Washington, 1968-70, Computer Systems Comd. Hdqrs., Fort Belvoir, Va., 1970—. Certified Fallout Shelter Analyst; Registered Profl. Engr., Ala. Mem. Eta Kappa Nu, Tau Beta Pi. Mem. Free Will Baptist Ch. (Sunday sch. supt. 1969-70, deacon, trustee, clk. 1970-71). Home: 7013 Ben Franklin Rd Springfield VA 22150 Office: Bldg 2104 Black Rd Fort Belvoir VA 22060

PARKER, FLOYD LEE, banker; b. Rolla, Ark., Oct. 11, 1934; s. Fleix Dempsey and Nora Bell (Goodman) P.; student Henderson State Coll.; grad. Sch. Banking South, La. State U., 1964; m. Joyce Beason, June 2, 1956; children—Kyle Beason (dec.), Kristi Lee, Kara Suzanne. With Malvern (Ark.) Nat. Bank, 1953—, now exec. v.p. Pres. Malvern Boys Club, 1961-62, Malvern Little League, 1963-65; co-chmn. Hot Spring County Library Bd., 1970-72; chmn. adv. bd. Ouachita Vocational Tech. Sch., Malvern, 19——. Bd. dirs. West Central Ark. Econ. Devel. Dist., 1969-72, chmn. comprehensive planning com., 1970—; bd. dirs. Ouachita Area council Boy Scouts Am., 1970-71. Recipient Hot Spring County Leadership award Malvern C. of C., 1969, Leadership award Ark. Community Devel. Program, 1969. Mem. Ark. Bankers Assn. (chmn. com. 1971-72, pres. jr. bankers sect. 1966-67), Malvern C. of C. (pres. 1969, mem. com. 1969—). Mem. Assembly of God. Kiwanian (pres. 1967—). Home: 1214 Brownwood St Malvern AR 72104 Office: Main and Page Sts Malvern AR 72104

PARKER, FRANKLIN DALLAS, educator; b. Balt., Jan. 7, 1918; s. Milton Augustus and Josephine (Griffin) P.; student Roberts Coll., 1934-36; B.A., Greenville Coll., 1939; postgrad. Nat. U. Mexico, 1946, U. Ariz., 1947; M.A., U. Ill., 1949, Ph.D., 1951; m. Jennie Frances Borden, July 20, 1940; children—Virginia (Mrs. T. Joseph Collier), Jeannie (Mrs. Fred D. Blackwelder). Asst. prof. history Woman's Coll., U. N.C., 1951-59, asso. prof., 1959-64; prof. history U. N.C., Greensboro, 1964—. Mem. Latin Am. Studies Assn., Conf. on Latin Am. History, Sociedad de Geografía e Historia de Guatemala. Methodist. Author: Jose Cecilio del Valle and the Establishment of the Central American Confederation, 1954; The Central American Republics, 1964. Editor: Travels in Central America, 1970. Home: 2009 Wright Av Greensboro NC 27403

PARKER, GILBERT NORMAN, bank exec.; b. Kaatspan, N.Y., Oct. 19, 1902; s. Abram V. and Sarah (Marshall) P.; student, Hamilton Coll., 1922-23, Columbia, 1925-27, Columbia Grad. Sch. Bus.,

1952-53; m. Marjorie Anne Marshall, Nov. 30, 1930; children—Anne, William. Accountant Alaska Airlines, Anchorage, 1927-43; sec., treas. Alaska Airlines, N.Y.C., 1943-46; chmn. bd. Nat. Bank Sarasota, Fla., 1958—, pres., 1966-69; chmn. bd. Nat. Bank Gulf Gate, Sarasota, 1963—, pres., 1966—. Vice chmn. Sarasota County Pub. Housing Authority, 1959-69; chmn. Sarasota County Pub. Hosp. Bd., 1963-68, vice chmn., 1967; mem. Sarasota County Pub. Hosp. Bd., 1971—. Mem. C. of C., U.S. Coast Guard Aux., U.S. Power Squadron. Clubs: Yacht, Field (Sarasota). Home: 894 Freeling Dr Sarasota FL 33581 Office: Nat Bank Sarasota PO Box 5427 Sarasota FL 33579

PARKER, HAROLD TALBOT, educator; b. Cin., Dec. 26, 1907; s. Samuel Chester and Lucile (Jones) P.; Ph.B., U. Chgo., 1928, Ph.D., 1934; postgrad. Cornell U., 1929-30. Instr. history Duke, Durham, N.C., 1939-42, asst. prof., 1945-50, asso. prof., 1950-57, prof., 1957—. Served with USAAF, 1942-45. Mem. French Hist. Studies (pres. 1957), Am. Assn. U. Profs. (pres. Duke chpt. 1939, 60), Phi Beta Kappa (pres. Duke chpt. 1961). Episcopalian. Author: The Cult of Antiquity and the French Revolutionaries, 1937; Three Napoleonic Battles, 1943. Editor: (with Richard Herr) Ideas in History, 1965. Home: 1005 Demerius St Durham NC 27701

PARKER, HARRY JOHN, educator, psychologist; b. Sioux City, Ia., Jan. 18, 1923; A.B., Elmhurst Coll., 1947; M.A., Northwestern U., 1953, Ph.D., 1956, postgrad., 1958; postgrad. Roosevelt U., 1957-58. Counselor, Northwestern U. Counseling Center, Chgo., 1952-56, counseling psychologist, 1956-59, asst. dir., 1957-58, dir., 1958-59; pvt. practice counseling psychologist, Chgo., 1956-59, Okla., 1959-69; prof. edn. U. Okla., 1959-69; dir. manpower planning, regional med. program and Sch. Health Related Professions U. Okla. Med. Center, Oklahoma City, 1967-69, prof. preventive medicine and pub. health, 1966-69, prof. human ecology, 1969; asso. dean Sch. Allied Health Professions, U. Tex. Med. Sch. at Dallas, 1969—, prof. phys. medicine and rehab., 1969, prof. psychiatry, 1969—. Served with AUS, 1943-46. Licensed psychologist, Okla., Tex. Mem. Am., Southwestern, Dallas, Tex. psychol. assns., Am. Pub. Health Assn., Assn. Schs. of Allied Health Professions, Sigma Xi, Phi Delta Phi. Contbr. articles to profl. jours. Home: 3439 Salisbury Dr Dallas TX 75229 Office: U Tex Med Sch at Dallas 5323 Harry Hines Blvd Dallas TX 75235

PARKER, HENRY ALLEN, clergyman; b. Windom, Tex., June 17, 1913; s. Douglas R. and Minnie (Jones) P.; A.B., Howard U., 1936; Th.M., So. Sem., 1939; Th.D., So. Bapt. Theol. Sem., 1942; m. Virginia Reaves, June 1, 1937; children—Walter Allen, Sara Margaret (Mrs. Ross Davis), John David. Ordained to ministry Bapt. Ch., 1934; pastor 1st Bapt. Ch., Quincy, Fla., 1941-44, Allapattah Bapt. Ch., Miami, Fla., 1944-45, 1st Bapt. Ch., Dothan, Ala., 1945-52, Montgomery, Ala., 1952-56, Orlando, Fla., 1956—. Mem. Ala. Mission Bd., 1949-56; mem. Fla. Mission Bd., 1958-62, chmn., 1961-62; pres. Fla. Bapt. Conv., 1962-63; chaplain Orlando Jr. Coll., 1964-65; conducted USAF Protestant Religion Mission to Orient, 1964. Mem. Orlando Mayor's Bi-racial Com., 1966-67. Trustee Judson Coll. Marion, Ala., So. Bapt. Theol. Sem., Louisville, Stetson U., Deland, Fla. Mem. Orlando Ministerial Assn. (pres. 1964-65). Author: Special Day Sermons, 1966; Words to Live By, 1968; More Words to Live By, 1970; Peace in a Turbulent World, 1970. Radio broadcaster WDBO, 1959—. Rotarian (pres.). Home: 1050 Sweetbriar Rd Orlando FL 32801 Office: 100 E Pine St Orlando FL 32801

PARKER, JACK FLEMING, educator; b. Enid, Okla., July 27, 1925; s. Charles Alexander and Pauline Madonna (Fleming) P.; B.S., Northwestern State Coll., 1948; Ed.M., U. Okla., 1955; Ed.D., Tchrs. Coll., Columbia, 1958; m. Iris Emily Reid, Sept. 28, 1952; children—Karen Ann, Steven Lee, Alan Charles. Tchr. pub. schs., Cleveland, Okla. and Oklahoma City, 1948-56, Manhasset, N.Y., 1956-58; prin., asst. supt. pub. schs., Oklahoma City, supt., 1961-66; prof. edn. U. Okla., Norman, 1966—. Cons. numerous pub. sch. systems, 1966—; lectr., cons. various profl. and civic groups, 1959—. Mem. exec. com. Mid-Continent Regional Ednl. Lab., 1970—; Plenary rep. U. Council Edn. Adminstrn., 1967—. Served with USNR, 1943-45. Mem. Okla. Pub. Sch. Research Council (pres. 1955-66), Okla. Edn. TV Authority (chmn. 1967-68), Am. Assn. Sch. Adminstrs., Am. Assn. U. Profs., Nat. Soc. Study Edn., Phi Delta Kappa, Kappa Delta Pi. Democrat. Methodist. Home: 1911 Logan Dr Norman OK 73069

PARKER, JAMES ROSS, food co. exec.; b. Balt., Jan. 18, 1930; s. Thaddeus Cornelius and Catherine Marie (Ross) P.; B.S. in Commerce, The Citadel, 1952; m. Barbara June Wilson, Aug. 30, 1953; children—Karen, Jeffrey, Thaddeus. With Pepsi-Cola Bottling Co., Tampa, Fla., 1954—, asst. sales mgr., 1958-59, sales mgr., 1959-60, v.p. sales, 1960-61, pres., 1961—; v.p. sec., dir. Pinellas Bottling Co., St. Petersburg, Fla., 1965—; sec., dir. Service Leasing Co., 1971—; pres. P-S Enterprises, Inc., 1968—; dir. Exchange Bank Temple Terrace, Exchange Bank Tampa. Vice pres. Heart Assn., 1968; mem. Taxi Cab Commn., City of Tampa, 1969; mem. exec. com. U. So. Fla. Found., 1970-71. Bd. dirs., chmn. trust com. Jesuit High Sch. Found., 1968—, Holy Name Acad. Found., 1970—; trustee U. Community Hosp., St. Joseph Hosp. Found. Served to 1st lt. AUS, 1952-55. Mem. Tampa C. of C. (bd. govs. 1969-71), Tampa Chamber (mem. com. 1971), Pres.'s Round Table, Nat. Pepsi-Cola Bottlers Assn. (exec. v.p. 1971-72, chmn. com. 1970-71), Young Pres.'s Orgn. Home: 2821 Parkland Blvd Tampa FL 33609 Office: PO Box 17175 Tampa FL 33612

PARKER, JESSIE FRANK, hosp. adminstr.; b. Humboldt, Tenn., July 25, 1935; s. Frank B. and Alma Jo (Meals) P.; B.S., Memphis State U., 1967; m. Barbara A. Haynes, July 28, 1957; children—Geneen, Jessie. Teller, Bank Gibson (Tenn.), 1958-61, Citizens State Bank, Trenton, Tenn., 1961-62; adminstr. Gibson Gen. Hosp., Trenton, 1962—. Mem. W. Tenn. Hosp. Council, Kappa Sigma. Rotarian. Home: 305 Rosemont Dr Trenton TN 38382 Office: Gibson Gen Hosp Box 488 Trenton TN 38382

PARKER, JOHN ALBERT, city and regional planner; b. Kentville, N.S., Can., Mar. 27, 1909; s. Percy Nesbitt and Mary Kathleen (Smith) P.; student U. B.C., 1926-27; S.B. in Architecture, Mass. Inst. Tech., 1932, M.Arch., 1934, M. City and Regional Planning, 1946; m. Jane Elizabeth Curtis, Aug. 27, 1932; children—John Curtis, Robert Curtis. Naturalized, 1938. Worked in archtl. offices N.Y.C., Boston, 1932-35; dir. Lowthorpe Sch. Landscape Architecture, 1936-45; head div. planning R.I. Sch. Design, 1945-46; community planner TVA, 1946; head dept. city and regional planning U. N.C., Chapel Hill, 1946—, research prof. Inst. Research Social Sci., 1946-66. Cons. on planning edn. to Central Mortgage and Housing Corp., Ottawa, Ont., Can., 1949, AID, Chile, 1962, C. Am., 1963; cons. Nat. Capital Planning Commn., 1964, Office of Gov., 1964, Nat. Capital Parks and Planning Commn., 1965. Mem. Chapel Hill Town Planning Bd. 1947-50; vice chmn. State Capital Planning Commn., 1963-65; chmn. fellowship adv. bd. Dept. Housing and Urban Devel., 1968-69. Mem. Am. Inst. Planners (gov. 1953-55, chmn. membership com. 1954-55), A.L.A. (hon. mem. N.C. chpt.), Am. Soc. Planning Ofcls. (dir. 1961-64), Deutsche Akademie fur Statebau and Landesplanung. Sigma Nu. Author: Utilizing University Resources in the Education of Planners-Planning, 1948; A Permanent State Planning Board for North Carolina, 1949; Planning Education in Canada, 1950; The University as an Aid to Local Planning, 1952; co-author: Strategy for Development, 1964. Editor: Urban Research in the South, 1955. Contbr. Urban Growth Dynamics, Roles of the Planner in Urban Development, 1962. Project director Soviet Theory and Practice in City and Regional Planning, 1952-54; Postgrad. Planning Edn. in Chile, 1962. Home: 219 Ransom St Chapel Hill NC 27514

PARKER, JOHN WILLIAM, educator; b. Murfreesboro, N.C., Oct. 16, 1909; s. John Reuben and Brownie G. (Parker) P.; student Wake Forest Coll., 1926-27; B.A. in Edn., U. N.C., 1930, M.A. in Dramatic Art, 1936; m. Darice Lee Jackson, June 14, 1936; 1 son, Scott Jackson. Tchr., Four Oaks (N.C.) High Sch., 1930-31, High Point (N.C.) High Sch., 1931-34; prof. dramatic art U. N.C., Chapel Hill, 1934—; asso. dir. bus. mgr. Carolina Playmakers, 1936—; dir. Bur. Community Drama, 1946—, Jr. Playmakers, 1938—. Adviser on outdoor drama, 1939; exec. sec. Carolina Dramatic Assn., 1936—; gen. mgr. Lost Colony, Manteo, N.C., 1948-51; gen. mgr.-dir. Highland Call. Fayetteville, N.C., 1939-41; mem. Historic Murfreesboro Commn., 1968—. Bd. dirs. Meml. Recreation Forest of Eastern N.C. Served to capt. USAAF, 1942-46. Mem. ANTA, Am. Ednl. Theatre Assn., Roanoke Island Hist. Assn. (dir.), Inst. Outdoor Drama (dir.), Southeastern Theatre Conf. (past exec. sec.). Club: Faculty. Author: (plays) Sleep on Lemuel, 1932; Itchin' Heel, 1937. Editor: Caroline Stage 1936-40; Adventure in Playmaking, 1968. Home: 1 Brierbridge Lane Chapel Hill NC 27514

PARKER, JOSEPH MAYON, editor; b. Washington, N.C., Oct. 11, 1931; s. James Mayon and Mildred (Poe) P.; student Davidson Coll., 1949-51; B.A., U. N.C., 1953; postgrad. Carnegie Inst. Tech., 1955; m. Lauretta Owen Dyer, Mar. 23, 1957; children—Katherine Suzanne, Joseph Wilbur, James Dyer (dec.). Sec., mgr. comml. printing div. Parker Bros., Inc., Ahoskie, N.C., 1955—, mng. editor, 1961—, chief editorialist, 1963—, gen. mgr., 1971; pres. Roanoke Valley Pub. Co., Inc., 1971; dir. Tar Heel Bank & Trust Co. First Congl. Dist. chmn. Young Democrats, 1966-68. Treas., Chowan Graphic Arts Found. Bd. dirs. Ahoskie Projects, N.C. Civil Liberties Union. Served with AUS, 1953-55. Mem. Eastern N.C. Press Assn. (past pres.), N.C. Press Assn. (dir.), Sigma Phi Epsilon, Pi Sigma Alpha. Methodist. Kiwanian. Home: 310 Colony Av Ahoskie NC 27910 Office: 117-19 McGlohon St Ahoskie NC 27910

PARKER, JOSEPHUS DERWARD, limestone co. exec.; b. Elm City, N.C., Nov. 16, 1906; s. Josephus and Elizabeth (Edwards) P.; A.B., U. South, 1928; postgrad. Tulane U., 1928-29, U. N.C., 1929-30, Wake Forest Med. Coll., 1930-31; m. Mary Wright, Jan. 15, 1934 (dec. Dec. 1937); children—Mary Wright (Mrs. Mallory A. Pittman, Jr.), Josephus Derward; m. 2d, Helen Hodges Hackney, Jan. 24, 1940; children—Thomas Hackney, Alton Person, Derward Hodges, Sarah Helen. Founder, chmn. bd. J. D. Parker & Sons, Inc., Elm City, N.C., 1955—, Parker Tree Farms, Inc., 1956—; founder, pres. Invader, Inc., 1961-63; pres., dir. Brady Lumber Co., Inc., 1957-62; v.p., dir. Atlantic Limestone, Inc., Elm City, 1970—; owner, operator Parker Airport, Eagle Springs, N.C., 1940-62. Served to capt. USAAF, 1944-47. Episcopalian. Moose, Lion. Club: Wilson (N.C.) Country. Address: PO Box 405 Elm City NC 27822

PARKER, JULIUS FREDERICK, JR., lawyer; b. Tallahassee, June 24, 1937; s. Julius Frederick and Katy (Gold) P.; student Va. Mil. Inst., 1955-57, Duke, 1957-59; B.A., Fla. State U., 1960; J.D., U. Fla., 1962; m. Marie Estelle Giddings, Aug. 13, 1960; children—Jennifer Marie, Julius Frederick III, Kelly Kathryn. Admitted to Fla. bar, 1963; atty. Parker, Foster & Madigan, Tallahassee, 1963—, partner, 1967—. Chmn. bd. Hammons Asphalt Paving, Inc., 1966—; gen. counsel, dir. Tallahassee Bank North, 1969—; dir. Seminole Asphalt Refining, Inc., Tallahassee Bank & Trust Co. Mem. Fla. Bd. Regents, 1968—; pres. LeMoyne Art Found., 1965-66; mem. Fla. State U. Found., 1969—. Mem. Phi Delta Phi, Phi Kappa Phi. Home: 100 Bellac St Tallahassee FL 32303 Office: Brock Bldg PO Box 669 Tallahassee FL 32302

PARKER, KENNETH WHITTEN, oil corp. exec.; b. Conway, Ark., Feb. 20, 1929; s. Kelsey William and Daisy Henrietta (Saye) P.; B.A., Hendrix Coll., 1950; m. Charlene Lester, Jan. 16, 1953; children—Nancy, Mark, Mary Ruth. Reporter Ark. Gazette, Little Rock, 1950-51, asst. state editor, 1951-53, state editor, 1953-60; dir. pub. relations Ark. Valley Industries, Inc., Dardanelle, 1960-64; mgr. pub. relations Crossett (Ark.) div. Georgia-Pacific Corp., 1964-66; dir. pub. relations Murphy Oil Corp., El Dorado, Ark., 1966—. Mem. El Dorado (Ark.) Municipal Auditorium Commn., 1970—, chmn., 1972—. Bd. dirs. El Dorado Sch. Dist., 1972—, South Ark. Mental Health Center, El Dorado; mem. exec. bd. De Soto Area council Boy Scouts Am., 19. Mem. Pub. Relations Soc. Am. (dir. 1971—, chpt. pres. 1966). Methodist. Rotarian (pres. 1963-64, 72-73). Clubs: El Dorado Racquet; Arkansas Press, Top of the Rock (Little Rock). Home: 220 Chula Vista Rd El Dorado AR 71730 Office: 200 Jefferson Av El Dorado AR 71730

PARKER, LEE BRYAN, JR., physician; b. Dermott, Ark., May 10, 1929; s. Lee Bryan and Viola Lee (Rogers) P.; B.S., U. Ark., 1950, M.D., 1954; m. Beverly Edith Brosell, Dec. 23, 1951; children—Susan Leigh, Elizabeth Ann, Steven Lee, Edith Lynn. Intern Crawford Long Hosp., Atlanta, 1954-55; pvt. practice gen. medicine, Dermott, Ark., 1957-59, McGehee, Ark., 1959-67, Fayetteville, Ark., 1967—; mem. staff Washington County Hosp., City Hosp. Dir. dept. continuing edn. Sch. Medicine U. Ark., 1970—; mem. adv. bd. Ark. Regional Med. Program, 1966-70. Served with USAF, 1955-57. Recipient Distinguished Service award McGehee Jr. C. of C., Mem. Ark. Med. Soc. (2d. v.p. 1971-72), Ark. Acad. Gen. Practice (dir. 1961-67). Home: 1138 Glenn Lane Fayetteville AR 72701 Office: 241 W Spring St Fayetteville AR 72701

PARKER, LESLIE EVADINE, educator; b. Slaughters, Ky.; d. George E. and Leslie (Carlisle) Parker; B.S., Western Ky. State Coll., 1939; M.A., U. Ky., 1945. Tchr., Masonic Home Sch., Louisville, 1935-39; tchr. high schs., Mayslick, Ky., 1939-41, Auburn, Ky., 1941-42, Lexington, Ky., 1942-44; supervisory tchr. Western Ky. State Coll., 1941-42, U. Ky., 1942-44; tchr. Murray (Ky.) State Coll., 1944-48; asst. supr. home econs. dept. State Dept. Vocational Edn., Jefferson City, Mo., 1948-49; asst. prof. home econs. N.D. State U., Fargo, 1948-53, Western Ky. State U., Bowling Green, 1953—; vis. prof. Mont. State U., summer 1952. Chmn., Wartime Food Preservation Program, Fayette County, Ky., 1942-44. Hon. mem. Future Homemakers of N.D. Mem. Am. Assn. U. Women, Bus. and Profl. Women, Am. Vocational Assn., Ky. Vocational Home Econs. Tchrs. (pres. 1946-48), Am., Ky. (coll. chpts. adviser 1955-56) home econs. assns., Kappa Delta Pi, Phi Upsilon Omicron. Democrat. Methodist. Club: Altrusa (v.p. Bowling Green 1969-70, chmn. information com. 1970-71). Contbr. home econs. curriculum Ky. State Dept. Edn., 1971-72. Home: 2217 Grandview Dr Bowling Green KY 42101

PARKER, LILLA GRAY MALLARD, music educator; b. Winston-Salem, N.C.; d. O. R. and Anne Louis (Murphrey) Mallard; A.B., Salem Coll., 1909, Mus.B., 1912; diploma in voice, 1911; student Emory U., 1940-43; m Benjamin Franklin Parker, June 9, 1915 (dec. July 1946). Tchr. piano harmony Salem Coll., 1914-15; soloist in various chs., N.C., Ga., 1916-30; now pvt. piano tchr. and coach; faculty mem. Am. Coll. Musicians. Adjudicator Nat. Guild Piano Tchrs., 1950—; mem. faculty. Sustaining mem. Edward MacDowell Fund; active work Atlanta Community Funds; mem. Women's Assn. Atlanta Symphony Orch. Mem. Nat. Trust for Historic Preservation, Wilderness Soc., U.S. Capitol Hist. Soc. (supporting founding mem.), and other regional and nat. cultural orgns. Baptist. Home: 28 The Prado NE Atlanta GA 30309

PARKER, LOUIS WILLIAM, industrialist; b. Budapest, Hungary, Jan. 1, 1906 (came to U.S. 1923, naturalized 1931); s. Leslie and Emma (Mazur) Kolozsy; student Coll. City N.Y., 1940; Sc.D., Fort Lauderdale U., 1967, Nova U., 1970; m. Milla Barbara Etts, Nov. 23, 1966; children—Elsa, Raymond. Engr. various radio and television cos., 1923-44; sr. engr. Internat. Tel. & Tel. Co., 1944-47; pres. Parker Instrument Corp., Parker Found., Parker Ranch, Inc., Parker Electronics, Inc.; v.p. Parker Theatre, Inc. Trustee Nova U. Patentee in field. Home: 2408 Sunrise Key Blvd Fort Lauderdale FL 33304 Office: 2040 N Dixie Hwy Wilton Manors FL 33305

PARKER, MARY ANN GARDNER (MRS. MILTON LAWRENCE PARKER), city ofcl., civic worker; b. Waco, Tex., Nov. 4, 1916; d. Leslie Breckenridge and Netten (Wilkes) Gardner; student U. Colo., 1934-36, U. Tex., 1937-38; m. Milton Lawrence Parker, May 11, 1939; children—F. Gardner, Madeleine Leslie. Personnel clk. N. Am. Aviation, Waco, Tex., 1943-44; clk., tech. research dept. Tex. Co., N.Y.C., 1944; v.p. Andrews-Parker, Inc., Bryan, Tex., 1958-65; asso. mem. W. M. Sparks, Realtor Co., Bryan, 1963— v.p. M. L. Parker, Inc., 1965—. Sec. Boys' Clubs of Bryan, 1962—; pres. South Tex. Area council Boys' Clubs Am., 1963-64; sec. Bryan Coll. Sta. Real Estate Bd., 1963—; chmn. City of Bryan Parks and Recreation Bd., 1963-65; ann. chmn. Brazos County Clothing Drive; chmn. Tex. Gov.'s Brazos County Com. on Aging, 1965—; organizer, pres. Girls Club Brazos County, 1968-70; vice chmn. Brazos County com. on alcoholism, 1964—; city commr. Bryan (Tex.), 1969-71; mem. bldg. com. Brazos County Ind. Sch. Dist., 1969-71. Bd. dirs. Greater Bryan United Fund, Brazos County Community Council. Mem. Jr. League Waco, U. Tex. Brazos Valley Ex-Student Assn. (pres.), Woman's Civic League Bryan (sec.), Brazos County Council Social Agys., Kappa Kappa Gamma. Roman Catholic. Home: 810 N Rosemary Dr Bryan TX 77801 Office: 4301 Texas Av Bryan TX 77801

PARKER, MARY EVELYN (MRS. W. BRYANT PARKER), state ofcl.; b. Fullerton, La., Nov. 8, 1920; d. Racia E. and Addie (Graham) Dickerson; B.A., Northwestern State Coll., 1941; Dipl. Social Welfare, La. State U., 1943; m. W. Bryant Parker, Oct. 30, 1954 (dec. May 1965); children—Mary Bryant, Ann Graham. Social worker La. Dept. Pub. Welfare, Baton Rouge, 1941-42, chmn. State Bd. Pub. Welfare, 1950-51, commr. pub. welfare, 1956-63; personnel adminstr. U.S. War Dept., Camp Claiborne, La., 1943-47; editor Oakdale (La.) Jour., 1947-48; exec. dir. La. Dept. Commerce and Industry, Baton Rouge, 1948-52; with Mut. of N.Y., 1952-56; commnr. adminstrn. State La., Baton Rouge, 1964-67; treas. State La., 1968—. Chmn. White House Conf. on Children and Youth, 1960; pres. La. Conf. Social Welfare, 1959-61. Nat. Democratic committeewoman, 1948-52. Bd. dirs. Woman's Hosp., Baton Rouge. Baptist. Home: 2768 McCarroll Dr Baton Rouge LA 70809 Office: State Capitol Baton Rouge LA 70804

PARKER, OLIN GRIFFITH, educator; b. Plains, Kan., Feb. 28, 1922; s. Arthur R. and Ida L. (Griffith) P.; Mus.B., Bethany Coll., Lindsborg, Kan., 1947; Mus.M., U. Kan., 1949, Ed.D., 1961; m. Melba Joy Burwell, May 16, 1946; children—Craig Burwell, Michelle Joy. Music dir. Macksville, Kan., 1947-48; instrumental music dir. Leavenworth (Kan.) Pub. Schs., 1949-51; instrumental music dir., coordinator Salina (Kan.) Pub. Schs., 1953-64; mem. faculty U. Ga., Athens, 1964—, now chmn. music edn., mem. Faculty Woodwind Quartet, 1965-66. Served with AUS, 1942-46, 51-52. Decorated Bronze Star medal. Mem. Music Educators Nat. Conf., Ga. Music Educators Assn., Nat. Assn. Music Therapy, Nat. Band Assn., Pi Kappa Lambda, Phi Delta Kappa, Phi Mu Alpha Sinfonia (gov. province 36). Methodist. Home: 212 Fortson Dr Athens GA 30601

PARKER, RICHARD LANGLEY, govt. ofcl.; b. Manhattan, Kan., Apr. 5, 1929; s. Ralph Langley and Irene Diana (Gaskill) P.; B.S. in Biol. Scis. with Honors, Kan. State Coll., 1951, D.V.M., 1955; M. Pub. Health, U. Minn., 1963; m. Alma Mae Dodge, Mar. 23, 1956; children— Ryan L., Kirk W., Neil R., Suzy. Vet. office N.Y. State Health Dept., Albany, 1955-58; chief Midwest Rabies Investigations Sta., Poynette, Wis., 1959-61; vet. epidemiologist Minn. Health Dept., Mpls., 1962; dir. career devel. program Center Disease Control, U. Minn., Mpls., 1962-63; chief Border Rabies Control, El Paso, Tex., 1963-66; vet. cons. Pan Am. Health Orgn., El Paso, 1966-68; with Center for Disease Control, Atlanta, 1968—, chief Office Vet. Pub. Health Services, 1971—. Mem. Am. Vet. Med. Assn., Am. Pub. Health Assn., U.S. Animal Health Assn., Wildlife Soc., Wildlife Disease Assn. Home: 2478 Williamswood Ct Decatur GA 30033 Office: Center for Disease Control Atlanta GA 30333

PARKER, ROBERT ALLAN RIDLEY, astronaut; b. N.Y.C., Dec. 14, 1936; s. Allan Elwood and Alice (Heywood) P.; A.B., Amherst Coll., 1958; Ph.D., Cal. Inst. Tech., 1962; m. Joan Audrey Capers, June 14, 1958; children—Kimberly Ellen, Brian David Capers. NSF postdoctoral fellow U. Wis., 1962-63, asst. prof., then asso. prof. astronomy, 1963—; astronaut Manned Spacecraft Center, NASA, 1967—. Mem. Am., Royal astron. socs., Phi Beta Kappa, Sigma Xi. Home: 311 Cedar Lane Seabrook TX 77586 Office: Code CB NASA-MSC Houston TX 77058

PARKER, ROBERT PLEWES, clergyman coll. pres.; b. Covington, Va., June 13, 1917; s. W. Carlton and Mabel (Plewes) P.; A.B., Randolph-Macon Coll., 1938, D.D., 1960; B.D. magna cum laude, Yale, 1942; M.Ed., U. Va., 1966; m. Frances Joye Brantley, June 28, 1945; children— John Brantley, Robert Plewes II, Dana Carlton, Christopher Stewart. Instr., Randolph-Macon Coll., 1938-39, chaplain, 1948-52, asst. prof. Bible, 1949-51; ordained to ministry Methodist Ch., 1942; pastor, Middle Bedford, Bedford, Va., 1942-46, Danville, Va., 1946-48, Ashland, Va., 1948-52; pastor, Westover Hills, Meth. Ch., Richmond, Va., 1952-59; dir. Assn. Ednl. Instns., Richmond, 1959-65; pres. Randolph-Macon Acad., 1965-69, Shenandoah Coll. and Conservatory Music, Winchester, Va., 1969—. Dir. Va. Campaign for Higher Edn., 1961-65; dean Va. Meth. Conf. Pastors Sch., 1956-60. Merit badge examiner Boy Scouts Am., 1960-65. Bd. mgrs. Richmond YMCA, 1956-60. Mem. N.E.A., Nat. Assn. Secondary Sch. Prins., Phi Beta Kappa, Omicron Delta Kappa, Tau Kappa Alpha. Rotarian. Author: How to be a Dynamic Disciple, 1960; The Church on the Move, 1964; also weekly commentary Sunday sch. lessons, Va. Meth. Adv., 1953-65. Address: 524 Jefferson St Winchester VA 22601

PARKER, SIDNEY ARCH, elec. engr.; b. Austin, Tex., Mar. 3, 1929; s. Sidney L. and Adelaide (Lane) P.; B.S. in Elec. Engring., Tex. A. and M. U., 1955; m. Jo E. Snider, Dec. 19, 1953; 1 son, Robert Keith. Project engr. Tex. A. and M. Research Found., Tex. A. and M. U., 1954-55; project engr. Bryant Mfg. Co., div. Carrier Corp., 1955-59; mgr. research and devel. for air conditioning compressors

Lennox Industries, Inc., Ft. Worth, 1959—. Cons. engr. field of refrigeration. Served with USNR. Mem. Nat. Soc. Profl. Engrs., I.E.E.E., Am. Soc. Heating, Refrigerating and Air Conditioning Engrs. Contbr. articles in field of refrigeration to profl. jours. Patentee in field of refrigeration in U.S. and fgn. countries, in field bldg. constrn. in U.S. Home: 5820 Diamond Oaks Dr S Fort Worth TX 76117 Office: Hwy 121 at Maxine St PO Box 1839 Fort Worth TX 76101

PARKER, WILLIAM DALE, pub. relations exec.; b. Portsmouth, Va., Apr. 13, 1925; s. Otis Drurie and Eva Estelle (Dempsey) P.; student Coll. William and Mary, 1946; grad. Indsl. Engr., Internat. Corr. Schs., 1956; student U. Del., 1959-60, Cal. Western U. 1961-62, U. Cal., 1964; D.Sc., Jame Balmes U., Saltillio, Mex., 1968; Ph.D., E.R.I., 1971; m. Frances Ross Jennings, Feb. 2, 1946 (dec.); children—Frances Lea, Elizabeth Dale, Kim Carolyn Jane, Penny Jo Ann, Jacquelyn Susan; m. 2d, Boots Lee Farthing, 1968. Engr., Gen. Motors Corp., Wilmington, Del., 1949-59, asst. dir. salaried personnel pub. relations, 1959-61; engr., lectr. Gen. Dynamics/Astronautics, San Diego, 1961-64; dir. Internat. Inst. Human Relations, La Jolla, Cal., 1964—; aerospace scientist, mgmt. specialist Gemini and Expts. Program Office, Manned Spacecraft Center, NASA, Houston, 1964-67, program specialist Apollo application program, Cape Kennedy, Fla., 1967-69; family and marriage counselor, Titusville, Fla., 1967-69; pres. Service Corps of Retired Execs., 1969-72, Multiple Services, Inc., Titusville 1969—; dir. franchising Spangler Television, N.Y.C., 1969—; v.p. Travel Internat., Inc., Titusville, 1970—. Founder Monroe Park Civil Def. Orgn., 1951; mem. Wilmington council Boy Scouts Am., 1953-55; chmn. Varions Agy. Fund, 1954-60; co-chmn. Del. Dept. Civil Def. TV Shows, 1956-57; mem. Middle Atlantic States Conf. Correction, 1956-60; chmn. Del., Md., Pa. Tri-State Hosp. Com., 1957-58; mem. Wilmington Inner-City Study Commn., 1957-60; chmn. Del. Civil Def. Evacuation Commn., 1958-59, Del. Hwy. Safety Campaign, 1959-60; active P.T.A.; faculty adviser Mensa Coll. Bd. dirs. Boys and Girls Aid Soc. San Diego, 1962-64. Served with USCGR, World War II. Named Outstanding Young Man of Year, U.S., Wilmington, Jr. chambers commerce, 1957; recipient Silver award Del. Vol. Bur., 1957; ann. awards VA. Jr. Achievement Inc., 1959; speech award U.S. Jr. C. of C., 1960; Gemini award NASA, 1967; Internat. Distinguished Service to Humanity award 1969, Keys to City, Wilmington, Del., 1959, 61, 72, Titusville, Fla., 1970. Mem. Wilmington Jr. C. of C., Antique Automobile Club Am., Am. Legion (life), Wilmington Indsl. Mgmt. Club, Mensa Internat., Am. Inst. Indsl. Engrs., Monroe Park Civic Assn. (pres. 1952-53), Vols. Speakers Bur. (San Diego), Internat. Platform Assn., Fraternal Order Police. Mason, Elk. Clubs: Royal Oak Country, Mexican, S.Am. Turf. Author: Philosophy of Genius; American Values, Solutions to Family and Marriage Problems. Columnist, Sentinal Newspaper 1963-64, Campers Illustrated Mag., 1964-65, Star Adv., 1968, INSIGHT, 1969-72, Challenge, 1970—. Home: PO Box 1441 Titusville FL 32780 also PO Box 633 Portsmouth VA 23705 Office: 2323 S Washington Av Berkshire Bldg Titusville FL 32780

PARKES, ED, natural gas co. exec.; b. Bessemer, Ala., Nov. 22, 1904; s. William Jay and Myra (Huey) P.; B. Mech. Engring., U. Ark., 1925; m. Alice Washburn, Oct, 14, 1930; children—Ruth P. Bondurant, Myra P. Winder. Design engr. Ark. Power & Light Co., 1926-28; engr. United Gas Pipe Line Co. and predecessors, 1928-29, dist. supt., 1929-30, asst. gen. supt., 1930-37, gen. supt. field lines, 1937-47, v.p., dir., 1947-55, pres., 1956-67; also pres. Union Producing Co.; exec. v.p., dir. United Gas Corp., 1955-58, pres., dir. 1958-67, chmn. exec. com., 1967-68, dir., 1958-67; dir., chmn. exec. com. Pennzoil United, Inc.; dir. Atlas Processing Co., Duval Corp., Mid- Continent Oil & Gas Assn., First Nat. Bank Shreveport. Chmn. Shreveport Downtown Devel. Commn., 1967—. Trustee Miss. Found. Ind. Coll., 1959-65, Inst. Gas Tech., 1959-65. Mem. S.W. Research Inst. (trustee 1961—), Am. Petroleum Inst. (dir. 1956-68, exec. com. 1963-68), Am. Gas. Assn. (pres. 1964, chmn. natural gas reserves com. 1957—). Gulf South Research Inst. (trustee), Ind. Natural Gas Assn. Am., Ind. Petroleum Assn. Am., Tau Beta Pi. Clubs: Rotary; Boston (New Orleans); Shreveport (La.). Home: 5815 Creswell Rd Shreveport LA 71106 Office: 1525 Fairfield Av Shreveport LA 71101

PARKINS, ERVIN, city editor Raleigh Times. Address: 215 S McDowell St Raleigh NC 27601*

PARKINSON, JOAN LIDDELL (MRS. RALPH THOMAS PARKINSON), educator; b. Rockford, Ill., Oct. 2, 1926; d. Geroge Turner and Arlene (Pratt) Liddell; B.A., Maryville Coll., 1947; M.A., U. Ky., 1956; student George Peabody Coll., 1964, U. N.C. at Chapel Hill, 1965, 71-72; m. Ralph Thomas Parkinson, May 21, 1947 (dec. May 1955); children—Judith, Ralph Thomas. Tchr. pub. schs., Orange County, N.C., 1947-48, Limestone, Tenn., 1948-49, Washington, 1949-51, Berea Coll. Training Sch., Berea, Ky., 1956-57, Statesboro, Ga., 1958-60, Memphis, 1960-63; asst. prof. edn. Lenoir Rhyne Coll., Hickory, N.C., 1963—. Cons., Comprehensive Sch. Improvement Program, Burke County, N.C., Tchr. Aide Program, Shelby, N.C. Alumni bd. Maryville Coll. Mem. N.E.A., N.C. Edn. Assn. (chpt. pres. 1967-70), Assn. Childhood Edn. Internat., Am. Assn. U. Profs., Assn. Student Teaching, Delta Zeta (chpt. dir. 1965-69), P.E.O. Presbyn. Home: 717 5th Av NE Hickory NC 28601

PARKS, EDWIN J., chemist; b. Chgo., May 25, 1931; s. Olin and Alma (Olson) P.; student Kenyon Coll., 1951-52, Ohio State U., 1953-55; A.B., Gallaudet Coll. for Deaf, 1957; postgrad. Am. U., 1957—; m. Marjorie N. Tomei, July 19, 1958; children—Howard D., Genevieve A., Olin A., Gordon M. Gen. chemist Nat. Bur. Standards, Washington, 1957-65, research chemist, archival material sect., inst. applied tech., 1965—. Mem. Am. Chem. Soc., A.A.A.S. Home: 201 Brown St Washington Grove MD 20880 Office: Sect 41104 National Bur of Standards Washington DC 20234

PARKS, EVELYN AUGUSTA, trade assn. exec.; b. Pitts., Jan. 6, 1927; d. Ralph E. Wagner and Evelyn E. (Gettings) Gaudian; student Pa. State U., 1947-50, Ikeda U. Fine Art, Japan, 1953, 54, U. Nuremberg (Germany) Art, 1960-61, Inst. Orgn. Mgmt., Syracuse U., 1969; m. Robert H. Parks, Aug. 8, 1946 (div. Mar. 1963); children—Diane Renee, Martin Hill. With Nat. Assn. Cemeteries, Arlington, Va., 1961—, writer, asst. editor trade jour., office mgr., 1965—, exec. asst. to exec. v.p., 1968—. Mem. Fairfax Hunt, English Speaking Union, Hist. Soc. Fairfax County, Navy League U.S., S.C. Soc., Internat. Platform Assn., Ladies Oriental Shrine, Beta Sigma Phi. Episcopalian. Club: Arts (Washington). Home: 1240 Providence Terrace McLean VA 22101 Office: 1911 N Fort Myer Dr Arlington VA 22009

PARKS, JANITH FINLEY, advt. agy. radio and TV dir.; b. Detroit, Aug. 23, 1941; d. Benjamin Harrison and Yvonne (Lucas) Parks; B.A., Va. Union U., 1961; M.A., Wayne State U., 1965; postgrad. Houston Inst. Advanced Advt. Studies, U. Houston, 1969. Tchr., Richmond (Va.) Pub. Schs., 1961-67; instr. psychology Va. Union U., Richmond, nights and summer 1965-67; tchr. Houston Ind. Sch. Dist.-Pearl Rucker Elementary Sch., 1967-68; radio and TV dir. Gulf State Advt. Agy., Houston, 1968—. Star jazz show on radio sta. WENZ, Richmond, 1965-67. Mem. Am. Women in Radio and Television (rec. sec. Houston chpt. 1968—), Alpha Kappa Alpha. Home: 3411 Timmons Lane Houston TX 77027 Office: 2714 Southwest Freeway Houston TX 77005

PARKS, JEANUS BURRELL, JR., educator, orgn. exec.; b. Washington, Apr. 20, 1929; s. Jeanus B. and Ellen (Wilson) P.; student Howard U., 1947-50, LL.B., 1955; LL.M., Columbia, 1960; m. Jeanne Fields, Apr. 1, 1961; 1 son, John Brian. Admitted to D.C. bar, 1956; gen. practice, Washington, 1956-59; trial atty. Housing and Home Finance Agy., 1956-59; asst. prof. law Howard U. Sch. Law, 1960-63, asso. prof., 1963-66, prof. law, 1966—; exec. dir. Neighborhood Legal Services Program, 1968-69; exec. dir. United Planning Orgn., 1969—, also sec. bd. trustees. Founder mem., dir. United Community Nat. Bank, 1963-65. Mem. Community Police Alert Council, 1967, S.E. Neighbors; mem. nat. adv. bd. Legal Research and Services for Elderly; mem. nat. rev. com. regional Med. Programs Service, Dept. Health, Edn. and Welfare; mem. Bi-Centennial Commn. for D.C.; mem. Mayor's Adv. Com. Narcotics Addiction, Prevention and Rehab., Mayor's Econ. Devel. Com.; mem. Model Cities Commn. Trustee Family and Child Services, 1967-69; bd. dirs. Negro Community Council, Episcopal Center for Children, Nat. Assn. Community Devel., Met. Washington Urban Coalition; bd. organizers Nat. Conf. Black Lawyers. Served with AUS, 1950-52. Fellow Internat. Acad. Law and Sci.; mem. Am. Judicature Soc., Am., Fed. (mem. council community affairs), Inter-Am. (sr.), Nat., Washington bar assns., Am. Acad. Polit. and Social Sci., Am. Assn. U. Profs., Nat. Lawyers Club (founder mem.), Sigma Delta Tau. Contbr. articles to profl. jours. Home: 3347 Bangor St SE Washington DC 20020 Office: 1021 14th St NW Washington DC 20005

PARKS, JOHN LOUIS, univ. dean, physician; b. Muskogee, Okla., Jan. 4, 1908; s. John S. and Della N. (Northcutt) P.; B.A., U. Wis., 1930, M.S., 1932, M.D., 1934, postgrad. obstetrics and gynecology, 1935-37; m. Mary Dean Scott, Aug. 31, 1930; 1 son, John Scott. Intern U. Cin., 1934-35; instr. pathology U. Wis., 1937-38; chief med. officer obstetrics and gynecology Gallinger Municipal Hosp., 1938-44; prof. obstetrics and gynecology George Washington U., Washington, 1944—, dean Sch. Medicine, 1957-67, dean Univ. Med. Center, 1967-72, v.p. for health affairs, 1972, med. dir. hosp., 1957-65. Mem. Nat. Bd. Med. Examiners; cons. D.C. Gen. Hosp., Walter Reed Med. Center, NIH. Exec. com. Gorgas Meml. Inst. Trustee Greater Washington Ednl. TV, Inc. Decorated Eloy Alfaro Fundacion Internacional (Panama). Diplomate Am. Bd. Obstetrics and Gynecology (past dir.). Fellow A.C.S. (bd. govs. 1956-59, 69-72), Royal Coll. Obstetricians and Gynaecologists; hon. fellow Bklyn. Gynecol. Soc., Central, South Atlantic assns. obstetricians and gynecologists, S.W., Fla., Wash., Miami, Panama obstet. and gynecol. socs., Obstet. Soc. Phila., Soc. Obstetricians and Gynaecologists Can., La Societa Triveneta di Ostetricia e Ginecologia; mem. Am. Coll. Obstetrics and Gynecology (v.p. 1957), Assn. Am. Med. Colls. (pres. 1967-68, mem. exec. council), Insterstate Postgrad. Med. Assn. (pres. 1966), Med. Soc. D.C., Washington Gynecol. Soc., Smith-Reed-Russell Soc., Am. Gynecology Soc. (treas. 1955-59; pres. elect 1971-72), Am. Assn. Obstetrics and Gynecology (pres. 1961), Am., So. med. assns., Sigma Xi, Alpha Omega Alpha, Nu Sigma Nu, Alpha Delta Phi. Club: Cosmos (Washington). Contbr. to med. jours. Home: One Southgate Ct Annapolis MD 21401 Office: George Washington U Sch Medicine 1331 H St NW Washington DC 20005 Died July 5, 1972

PARKS, RICHARD HILL, hosp. supt.; b. Leechburg, Pa., Mar. 11, 1911; s. Clarence Carson and Zoe (Van Dyke) P.; A.B., Washington and Jefferson Coll., 1933; M.D., Jefferson Med. Coll., 1937; m. Mary Joy Alter, June 8, 1935; children—Clarence Carson II, Benjamin Riley, Richard Hill, Van Dyke. Intern Western Pa. Hosp., Pitts., 1937-38; psychiat. resident Warren (Pa.) State Hosp., 1938-40, psychiatrist, 1945-48; practice medicine specializing in psychiatry, McKeesport, Pa., 1948-62; staff psychiatrist South Fla. State Hosp., Hollywood, 1962-65, supt., 1965—; asst. clin. prof. U. Miami, 1965—. Served to maj., M.C., AUS, 1940-45. Decorated Bronze Star. Diplomate Am. Bd. Psychiatry and Neurology. Mem. A.M.A., Am. Psychiat. Assn., Alpha Kappa Kappa, Lamba Chi Alpha. Democrat. Mem. Christian Ch. Mason. Clubs: University (Pitts.); Univ. Miami Faculty; Country of Miami. Home: 19425 E St Andrews Dr Country Club of Miami Miami FL 33014 Office: 1000 SW 84th Av Hollywood FL 33023

PARKS, ROBERT DEE, accountant; b. Lawton, Okla., Aug. 11, 1932; s. D.C. and Rose Olin (Reed) P.; B.B.A., Okla. U., 1954; m. Evelyn June Jones, Nov. 22, 1953; children—Deanna June, Alyson Ann. With Ernst & Ernst, C.P.A.'s, Houston, 1954-58, Oklahoma City, 1958—, mgr., 1968-71; controller St. Mary's Hosp., Enid, Okla., 1971—. Served to capt. AUS, 1955-57. C.P.A., Okla. Mem. Am. Inst. C.P.A.'s, Okla. Soc. C.P.A.'s (legislative chmn. 1968—), Hosp. Financial Mgmt. Assn., C. of C. (life), Jr. Chamber Internat. Republican. Methodist. Clubs: Young Mens, Beacon, Quail Creek Golf and Country. Home: 704 W Randolph St Enid OK 73701 and 3012 Stonybrook Rd Oklahoma City OK 73120 Office: 305 S 5th St Enid OK 73701

PARKS, SAM LAWS, coll. adminstr.; b. Dover, Tenn., Jan. 9, 1916; s. Samuel Hume and Mary (Laws) P.; sci. diploma Athens Coll., 1950, B.S. in Bus. Adminstrn., 1950; postgrad. Peabody Coll., 1944-47, U. Ky., 1954-57; m. Esten Perry, Sept. 3, 1938; children—Barbara Lane (Mrs. Martin D. Jahn), Linda Ellen (Mrs. John R. Bourne). Accountant, asst. office mgr., order distbr. clk. Internat. Harvester Co., Chattanooga, Knoxville, Tenn. and Nashville, 1940-44; pub. accountant, dir. sales and advt. J. B. Cook Auto Machine Co., Nashville, 1944-47; tchr. accounting, bus. adminstrn., econs. Falls Bus. Coll., Nashville, 1947; bursar Athens (Ala.) Coll., 1948-51, tchr. Sch. Commerce, 1951; office, credit mgr. Quaker Oats Co., Decatur, Ala., 1951-54; bus. mgr.-treas., treas. bd. trustees Union Coll., Barbourville, Ky., 1954-57, 67-71, v.p., treas., 1971—; bus. mgr.-treas. Scarritt Coll., Nashville 1957-67. Dir., treas. Nashville Asbury Fed. Credit Union. Bd. dirs. Heart Fund, Barbourville, 1955-57, Easter Seals, Barbourville, 1955-57, Cumberland council Boy Scouts Am., 1955—. Mem. Nat. Assn. Accountants (v.p., dir.), N.E.A., Ky. Col., Knox County C. of C. (pres., dir.), Alt. Acad. Sci., Delta Nu Omega, Tau Delta Tau. Methodist (pres. adminstrn. bd.). Mason, Kiwanian (dir.). Club: Methodist Mens (pres.) (Barbourville). Author: Manual for Purchasing Colleges and Universities, 1955. Home: 112 College Park Dr Barbourville KY 40906

PARKS, SUZANNE LOWRY (MRS. PHILLIP HADDON PARKS), educator; b. Columbus, O., Feb. 29, 1936; d. Frank Carson and Mable (Brown) Lowry; B.S., Emory U., 1958, M.S., U. Md., 1959; m. Phillip Haddon Parks, July 20, 1963; children—Jennifer, Kristin, Gregory. Staff nurse Emory U. Hosp., Atlanta, 1958; instr. psychiat. nursing U. Va. Sch. Nursing, Charlottesville, 1959-60, asst. prof., 1960-61; instr. U. N.C., Chapel Hill, 1961-62, asst. prof., 1962-63; instr. med.-surg. nursing Rex Hosp. Sch. Nursing, Raleigh, N.C., 1963; asst. prof., dir. div. psychiat. nursing Duke Sch. Nursing, Durham, N.C., 1964-66, clin. specialist psychiat. nursing, 1966-67; clin. instr. psychiatry Emory U. Sch. Medicine, 1968—, crisis intervention therapist, 1968-71. Recipient Outstanding Faculty Mem. award U. N.C. grad. class nursing, 1963. Mem. Mental Health Assn., Am., N.C. nurses assns., Nat., N.C. leagues for nursing, Sigma Theta Tau. Home: 4331 Hickory Wood Lane Doraville GA 30340

PARLER, NETTIE PETTY (MRS. JAMES CARTER PARLER), educator; b. Pitts.; d. Floyd Hezekiah and Allie (Sims) Petty; A.B., Claflin Coll., 1936; M.A., Columbia U., 1944; Ph.D., N.Y.U., 1952; m. James Carter Parler, June 4, 1939 (dec. Jan. 1961); 1 dau., Janet Patricia. Tchr. English, Granard High Sch., Gaffney, S.C., 1936-39; tchr. elementary sch., Orangeburg (S.C.) City Schs., 1939-43; field worker S.C. Tb Assn., 1944; asso. prof. English, S.C. State Coll., Orangeburg, 1944-52, prof., 1952—, head dept., 1952-56, chmn. communications center, 1956—. Active Sunlight Club Community Center; mem. S.C. Com. for Humanities. Mem. Coll. Lang. Assn. (sec.), Nat. (state chmn. achievement awards program 1966—), S.C. (pres.) councils tchrs. English, Links (v.p. Orangeburg chpt. 1965—, pres.) S.C. Edn. Assn. (v.p. council dept. presidents), Conf. on Coll. Composition and Communication, Modern Lang. Assn., S.C. Assn. Depts. English (pres.) Am. Assn. U. Profs., Nat. Assn. Coll. Women, Alpha Kappa Mu, Delta Sigma Theta. Episcopalian. Mem. Order Eastern Star. Editorial bd. Coll. Lang. Assn. Jour.; editor Explorations in Edn. Home: Route 1 Orangeburg SC 29115

PARMLEY, LOREN FRANCIS, JR., physician, army officer; b. El Paso, Tex., Sept. 19, 1921; s. Loren Francis and Hope (Bartholomew) P.; B.A., U. Va., 1941, M.D., 1943; m. Dorothy Louise Turner, Apr. 4, 1942; children— Richard Turner, Robert James, Kathryn Louise. Intern Med. Coll. Va., Richmond, 1944; commd. 1st lt. M.C., U.S. Army, 1944, advanced through grades to col., 1962; resident medicine Brooke Gen. Hosp., San Antonio, 1947-48; resident, asst. prof. mil. sci., tactics U. Wis. Med. Sch., 1949-51; asst. army attache U.S. Embassy, India, 1954-56; chief cardiology Letterman Gen. Hosp., San Francisco, 1957-63, chief dept. medicine, 1962-63; chief dept. medicine Walter Reed Gen. Hosp., Washington, 1965-68; clin. asso. prof. medicine Georgetown U., 1967-68; asst. dean, clin. prof. medicine Med. Coll. S.C.; dir. med. edn. Spartanburg (S.C.) Gen. Hospital, 1968—; clin. prof. medicine Med. Coll. Ga. Cons. in field of medicine U.S. Army, Europe, 1963-65; Surgeon Gen., 1966-68; lectr. medicine U. Cal. Sch. Medicine, San Francisco, 1958-62. Decorated Legion of Merit. Diplomate internal medicine and cardovascular disease Am. Bd. Internal Medicine. Fellow A.C.P., Council Clin. Cardiology, Am. Coll. Chest Physicians, Am. Coll. Cardiology (gov. for S.C.), Am. Heart Assn.; mem. A.M.A., So. Med. Assn., Sigma Phi Epsilon, Phi Chi. Contbr. chpts. to textbooks. Address: 232 Beechwood Dr Spartanburg SC 29302

PARNELL, DAVID RUSSELL, retail co. exec.; b. Parkton, N.C., Nov. 16, 1925; s. John Quincy and Clelia (Britt) P.; B.S., Wake Forest U., 1949; m. Barbara Johnson, June 11, 1948; children—David Russell, Anne, Timothy. With J.Q. Parnell, Inc., Parkton, 1949—, mgr., exec. v.p., 1952—; mgr. Parnell Oil Co., 1954—, pres., 1961—; dir. First Union Nat. Bank, St. Pauls, N.C. Mem. Robeson County Indsl. Devel. Commn., 1964—, chmn., 1968; mem. N.C. State Hwy. Commn., 1969—, chmn secondary roads com., 1969-73. Democratic precinct chmn., Parkton, 1964-70. Served with AUS, 1945-46. Baptist. (treas. 1950—, deacon 1951—, chmn. bd. deacons 1961-70). Club: Parkton Ruritan (pres. 1954). Home: PO Box 190 Parkton NC 28371 Office: Parkton NC 28371

PARNELL, WALTER ALFRED, JR., coll. dean; b. Fort Lauderdale, Fla., Apr. 2, 1931; s. Walter A. and Daisy Louise (Williams) P.; B.A., U. Miami, 1957; M. Ed., U. Fla., 1962, Ed.D., 1971; m. Mary Rowena Pinner, Aug. 3, 1953; children—Walter Alfred III, David Lamont, Anthony Glenn. Supt. Sunset Plastering Co., Ft. Lauderdale, 1953-57; pres. Parnell Co., Fort Lauderdale, 1957-60; with Lake City (Fla.) Community Coll., 1962—, instr., 1962-71, dept. head, humanities, 1967-71, acad. dean, 1971—. Recipient Distinguished Tchr. award, Lake City Community Coll., 1967; Outstanding Educator award, 1970. Mem. Fla. Assn. Community Colls., So. Soc. Philosphy and Psychology. Mem. Ch. of God (mem. council 1971—). Home: Route 2 Box 75A5 Lake City FL 37055

PARR, EUGENE QUINCY, orthopedic surgeon; b. Erlanger, Ky., Aug. 4, 1925; s. Benjamin F. and Frances (Wright) P.; student Berea Coll., 1944-45, 46-48; M.D., U. Louisville, 1952; postgrad. Mayo Grad. Sch. Medicine, 1956-60; m. Joan Lykins, June 9, 1951; children—Eugene Quincy, Jeffrey Wright, Valerie. Intern, Barroness Erlanger Hosp., Chattanooga, 1952-53; practice medicine, Berea, Ky., 1953-56, specializing in orthopedic surgery, Lexington, Ky., 1960—; mem. staffs Central Capt. Hosp., Shriners Hosp. for Crippled Children, U. Ky. Med. Center, Good Samaritan, St. Joseph's hosps.; instr. orthopedic surgery U. Ky. Med. Sch., Lexington, 1962—. Trustee Berea Coll. Served with USNR, 1945-46. Diplomate Am. Bd. Orthopedic Surgery. Fellow Am. Acad. Orthopedic Surgeons; mem. A.M.A., So., Ky. State, Fayette County, Lexington med. socs., Lexington Orthopedic Soc. Phi Kappa Phi. Mason (32 deg., Shriner). Home: 3225 Tates Creek Rd Lexington KY 40502 Office: 2130 Nicholasville Rd Lexington KY 40503

PARR, GEORGE CHRISTOPHER, elec. engr.; b. Montgomery, Ala., Sept. 15, 1937; s. George Franklin and Mary Corinne (Polk) P.; B.E.E., Auburn U., 1960; m. Mayre Elizabeth Faucette, Mar. 14, 1964; children—Jeanne Marie, Christopher Lee. Jr. engr. Ala. Power Co., Birmingham, Ala., 1960-64, sr. engr. II, 1964-66, sr. engr. I, 1966-68, supr. system protection, 1968—. Vice pres. Security Planning Universal Inc., financial planning, Birmingham, 1970—. Served as 1st lt. AUS, 1961-63. Mem. I.E.E.E. (mem. power system relaying com. 1971—; chpt. chmn. Ala. sect. Power Engr. Soc. 1971-72). Tau Beta Pi, Eta Kappa Nu. Methodist (mem. ch. adminstrv. bd. 1967—). Home: 3521 Clayton Pl Birmingham AL 35216 Office: 600 N 18th St Birmingham AL 35203

PARR, WOLFGANG, educator; b. Ahlen, Germany, Nov. 7, 1937; s. Karl and Maria (Stieler) P.; B.S. in Chemistry, U. Munster, 1961; M.S., U. Tubingen (Germany), 1964, Ph. D., 1967; m. Brigitte Karola Wieneke, July 31, 1964; children—Martina and Sabine (twins), Susanne. Came to U.S., 1967. Research asso. U. Tubingen, 1965-67; postdoctoral fellow U. Houston, 1967-68, asst. prof. chemistry, 1968-72, asso. prof., 1972—. Robert Welch Found. fellow, 1968—; NSF grantee, 1970—. Mem. Am., German chem. socs., Rheno Chaltia, Sigma Xi. Home: 7918 Burning Hills Houston TX 77071 Office: Dept Chemistry University of Houston Houston TX 77004

PARRILL, I. BENJAMIN, hat co. exec.; b. N.Y.C., 1917; grad. Columbia U., 1937. Chmn., pres. Miller Bros. Hat Co., Dallas; chmn. Adam Hats, Inc., Tex. Miller Products, Inc., Wood Garment Mfg. Co.; pres., dir. Adam Hat Stores; v.p., dir. Tex. Miller Hat Corp., Miller Bros. Hat Sales Corp., Men's Hats, Inc. Home: 5047 Radbrook Pl Dallas TX 75220 Office: 2700 Canton St Dallas TX 75226*

PARRIS, ADDISON WILSON, govt. ofcl.; b. Balt., Nov. 30, 1923; s. Paul Southerland and Angela Addison (Wilson) P.; B.A., Tufts U., 1947; M.A., Fletcher Sch. Law and Diplomacy, 1949; student Miss. State U., 1943-44; postgrad. Columbia U. Grad. Sch. Bus., 1947-48; m. Judith Ann Heimlich, Oct. 12, 1968; children—(from a previous marriage)Susan Phipps, Addison Wilson. Asst. dir. internat. relations dept. N.A.M., N.Y.C., 1949-55; asst. mgr. finance div., Am. Mgmt. Assn., N.Y.C., 1955-57; internat. economist Com. for Economic Devel., Washington, 1957-61; dir. Office Financial and Comml. Policy, Bur. Internat. Commerce, U.S. Dept. Commerce, Washington, 1961-63; various positions U.S. Small Business Adminstrn.,

Washington, 1963—, dir. Office Planning and Program Evaluation, 1971—. Served with AUS, 1942-46. Mem. Am. Econ. Assn., Alpha Tau Omega. Methodist. Author: Foreign Travel-Dollar Earner for Foreign Countries, 1951; Topics of Current Interest in International Economic Relations, 1953; The European Common Market and Its Meaning to the United States, 1959; The Small Business Administration, 1968. Home: 3105 Northampton St NW Washington DC 20015 Office: 1441 L St NW Washington DC 20416

PARRIS, PORTER P., hotel exec.; b. Gilliland, Tex., Aug. 7, 1917; s. Samuel B. and Gertrude (Collier) P.; student North Tex. State Coll., 1934; grad. Tex. Technol. Coll., 1938; m. Mary Ross Edwards, Nov. 5, Various positions Hilton Hotels; 1935—, including El Paso, Tex., Long Beach, Cal., Lubbock, Tex., 1935-43; asst. mgr. Roosevelt Hotel, N.Y.C., 1943-44; gen. mgr. Dayton-Biltmore Hotel, Dayton, O., 1949-51; resident mgr. Conrad Hilton Hotel, Chgo., 1951-53, gen. mgr., 1962-68; gen. mgr. Hotel Plaza, N.Y.C., 1954-55; v.p., gen. mgr. Shamrock Hilton, Houston, 1955-62; v.p. Hilton Hotels Corp., 1962—; gen. mgr. Statler Hilton, Washington, 1968-69, Boston, 1969-70; mng. dir. Shamrock Hilton, Houston, 1970—. Bd. dirs. Greater Houston Conv. and Visitors Bur. Served as sgt. maj. inf., AUS, 1944-46. Mem. Hotel Assn. Washington, Am. Hotel-Motel Assn. (dir. 1972), Houston Hotel-Motel Assn. (pres.). Address: Shamrock Hilton PO Box 2848 Houston TX 77001

PARRIS, ROBERT, composer, educator; b. Phila., May 21, 1924; s. Louis and Rae (Oettinger) P.; M.S. in Music Edn., U. Pa., 1946; B.S. in Composition, Juilliard Sch. Music, 1948. Tchr. piano, theory State U. Wash., 1948-49; tchr. theory U. Md., 1960-63; tchr. theory George Washington U., 1963—; recording artist harpsichord Composers Recordings, Inc., N.Y.C., 1967—; performer harpsicord recitals, Washington, 1960. Mem. Am. Composers Alliance, Nat. Assn. Am. Composers and Condrs. Composer: Concerto for 5 Kettledrums and Orchestra, 1961; Lamentations and Praises, 1966; Fantasy and Fugue for Cello Solo, 1964, Sonata for Solo Violin, 1967. Home: 6515 Brookfield Rd Chevy Chase MD 20015 Office: 2023 H St NW Washington DC 20006

PARRISH, EDWARD, lawyer; b. Adel, Ga., Nov. 21, 1911; s. C. E. and Nona (Rountree) P.; grad. Young Harris (Ga.) Coll., 1930; m. Jeannette Crane. Admitted to Ga. bar, 1931, since practiced in Adel; county atty. Cook County, Ga., 1938-42; city atty. City of Adel, Ga., 1940-42, 46—, also city atty. Sparks, Ga.; solicitor-gen. Alapaha Jud. Circuit, 1949—. Dir. Cook-Berrien Service Corp., Cook County Fed. Savs. & Loan Assn., Adel. Served with AUS, 1942-45. Mem. Am. Legion, V.F.W., Woodmen of the World. Lion. Home: 201 E 8th St Adel GA 31620 Office: Sowega Bldg and County Ct House Adel GA 31620

PARRISH, FRANK JENNINGS, frozen foods co. exec.; b. Manassas, Va., Dec. 29, 1923; s. Edgar Goodloe and Alverda (Jennings) P.; student Va. Poly. Inst., 1942-43; m. Lorene Lomax, Feb. 11, 1944; children—Edgar Lee, Julia Lorene. Mng. partner Manassas Frozen Foods, 1946—; pres., mgr. Certified Food Buyers Service, Inc., 1953—; pres. First Nat. Acceptance Co., 1966—; dir. Manassas Ice & Fuel Co. Mem. bus. adminstrn. adv. com. No. Va. Community Coll. Served to maj. USAAF, 1943-46; CBI; col. Res. Decorated Air medal. Mem. Nat. Inst. Locker and Freezer Provisioners Am. (past pres.; Industry Leadership award 1968), Va. Frozen Foods Assn. (past pres., dir.), Hump Pilots Assn. Methodist (chmn. bd. trustees 1958-66). Kiwanian, Moose. Home: 9107 Park Av Manassas VA 22110 Office: 3150 Wilson Blvd Arlington VA also 9416 S Main St Manassas VA 22110 also Profl Arts Bldg Norfolk VA

PARRISH, HARRY JACOB, retail trade exec.; b. Fairfax County, nr. Manassas, Va., Feb. 19, 1922; s. Edgar Goodloe and Alverda Rita (Jennings) P.; B.A., Va. Poly Inst., 1944; postgrad. Wolford Coll., 1943; m. Mattie Hooe Cannon, Feb. 12, 1944; children—Judy (Mrs. Richard Jackson Ratcliffe), Harry Jacob, II. Mgr. Manassas Ice & Fuel Co., Inc., Manassas, Va., 1946-52, pres., 1952—. Dir. Peoples' Nat. Bank,. Mayor Town Manassas, Va., 1963—; pres. Va. Municipal League, 1970-71. Bd. dirs. Prince William Hosp., Manassas, Va., 1963—. Served with USAAF, 1942-46; served to col. USAF, 1946-71. Decorated D.F.C., Air medal with clusters, Air Force Commendation medal. Mem. Va. Petroleum Jobbers Assn. (pres. 1965-66), Nat. Oil Jobbers Assn. (dir. 1967-68), Am. Legion, V.F.W. Democrat. Methodist. Mason, Kiwanian. Home: 9307 Battle St Manassas VA 22110 Office: 9009 Center St Manassas VA 22110

PARRISH, JAMES RICHARD, free-lance writer; b. Moscow, Tex., Feb. 6, 1927; s. Winfrey Ottis and Ruth Estelle (Peebles) P.; B.S. in English-Journalism, Stephen F. Austin State U., 1950, M.A. in English, 1956; postgrad. U. Mo., 1963, So. Ill. U., 1964; m. Sylvia Ann Alexander; children—Patricia, Richard, Deborah, Mary, Kelly, Robert. Dir. pub. relations Stephen F. Austin State U., Nacogdoches, Tex., 1957-61; news bur. dir. Northeast (La.) State U., 1962-63; dir. publs. Southeastern La. State U., 1966-70; asso. prof. journalism Northwestern State Coll. La., Natchitoches, 1968-70; free-lance writer, Hattiesburg, Miss., 1970—. Chmn. com. recruitment Nat. Council Coll. Publs. Advisers, 1969. Served with AUS, 1945-46. Mem. Nat. Council Coll. Publs. Advisers, La. Press Assn., Pi Kappa Alpha. Methodist. Club: USM Golf (Hattiesburg, Miss.). Address: 108 Thompson St Hattiesburg MS 39401

PARRISH, JEMIMA BUCHANAN (MRS. A. LEONARD PARRISH), artist, poet; b. Jasper, Ala.; d. John H. and Anne (Tubb) Buchanan; student pub. schs.; m. A. Leonard Parrish, Aug. 17, 1926; 1 son, David Buchanan. Exhibited in group shows at Birmingham (Ala.) Art Mus., Buchanan Hall Gallery, Samford U. (Birmingham), Atlanta Art Assn., Fine Arts Center (Lynchburg, Va.), Dayton (O.) Art Inst., Emerson Mus. Art (Syracuse, N.Y.), Miami (Fla.) Mus. Modern Art, Smithsonian Instn., Norton Gallery (West Palm Beach, Fla.), Des Moines, Denver Art Mus., Municipal Art Gallery, Los Angeles; represented in permanent collections at Jackson, Miss., Ashville, N.C., Birmingham, Knoxville, Tenn. Mem. Nat. League Am. Pen Women (Ala. art chmn. 1968-70), Acad. Am. Poets, Ala. Writers Conclave, Ala. Poetry Soc. Club: Quill. Author: New American Poetry, 1945; Testament of Faith, 1942. Home: 1426 24th St N Birmingham AL 35234

PARRISH, JOHN RANDALL, ret. hosp. adminstr.; b. Pavo, Ga., Apr. 14, 1914; s. Lessie Newton and Nellie (Williams) P.; B.S., Auburn U., 1935, M.S., 1936; m. Isabel Webb, Aug. 28, 1935; children—Jannis (Mrs. John G. Parrish), Marjorie (Mrs. Gary F. Conklin). High sch. tchr., Atlanta, 1935-41; hosp. adminstr. with VA, 1946-71, dir. VA Hosp., Augusta, Ga., 1967-71. Served to lt. col. AUS, 1941-46. Fellow Am. Coll. Hosp. Adminstr. Home: 134 Leisureville Rd Boynton Beach FL 33435

PARRISH, LINWOOD G., utility exec., 1911; student U. Richmond Sch. Bus. Adminstrn.; m. 3 children. With Va. Electric & Power Co., 1928—, sec., 1968—, v.p. finance, sec., 1970—. Mem. Va., Richmond chambers commerce, Kiwanian. Home: 8215 Brookfield Rd Richmond VA 23227 Office: 700 E Franklin St Richmond VA 23209

PARRISH, RICHARD OWEN, food co. exec.; b. Dayton, O., June 20, 1931; s. Charles Martin and Bernice Louise (Stephenson) P.; B.S. in Advt., Journalism, Okla. State U., 1953; m. Joyce Elaine Prichard, Aug. 24, 1952; children—Pamela Jo, Deborah, Patti Beth, Melinda. Advt. specialist Gen. Electric Co., Schenectady, 1955-65; dir. advt., sales promotion Stitzel Weller Distillery, Louisville, 1965-72, v.p., 1971; mgr. mkt. Delmonico Food Co., Louisville, 1972—. Chmn. Oldham County Planning and Zoning Commn., 1969-70; mem. citizens com. Louisville Air Bd., 1970—. Served to lt. comdr. USNR, 1953-55. Mem. Alpha Tau Omega (pres. 1952). Optimist (dir. 1963-65). Home: 115 Central Av Pewee Valley KY 40056 Office: 2521 S Floyd Louisville KY 40210

PARRISH, WAYNE W., editor, publisher; b. Decatur, Ill., May 2, 1907; s. Roy Clifford and Frances Effie (Wayne) P.; ed. U. Ill.; B.Litt., Columbia U. Sch. Journalism, 1929, M.S., 1930; Pulitzer Traveling scholar, Europe, 1930-31; LL.D., Missouri Valley Coll., 1963; m. Frances Knight, Sept. 15, 1935. Reporter Decatur Herald, N.Y. Herald-Tribune; spl. corr., Christian Sci. Monitor, Chgo. Herald and Examiner, Literary Digest; editor Nat. Aeros. Asso. mag., 1935-37; founder, pres. Am. Aviation Publs., 1937, Am. Aviation mag., 1937—, Aviation Daily, 1939—, World Aviation Directory, 1940—, Who's Who in World Aviation, 1955—, Air Cargo mag., 1957—, Armed Forces Mgmt. mag., 1959—, Aerospace Daily, 1963—, World Space Directory, 1962—, Weekly of Bus. Aviation, 1965—, Internat. Aviation, 1966—. Recipient TWA award for excellence in aviation writing, 1938-40; award of merit, 1942, Indsl. Marketing bus. paper competition; 1st place TWA nat. competition for aviation writing, 1944; Strebig-Dobben Meml. award 1953; Diplome Paul Tissandier, Fedn. Aeronautique Internationale, Paris, 1956; award of achievemnet Nat. Aviation Club, 1967, Aero Club, 1967. Mem. Conquistadores del Cielo, Aviation Writers Assn. (pres. 1943), Sigma Delta Chi, Alpha Eta Rho. Clubs: Wings, University (N.Y.C.), Metropolitan, Nat. Aviation (pres. 1962-63), Internat., Aero. Nat. Press (Washington); American (London); Jupiter Island (Fla.). Home: 2221 30th St NW Washington DC 20008 Office: 1156 15th St NW Washington DC 20005

PARROTT, WILLIAM LAMAR, research entomologist; b. Fayetteville, Ga., Oct. 7, 1930; s. James Bartow and Willie Mae (Williams) P.; B.S., Purdue U., 1959, M.S., 1961; Ph.D., Miss. State U., 1967; m. Patricia May Dillman, June 28, 1953; children—Suzanne May, Diana Lynn, Stephen Lee. Instr. entomology Purdue U., Lafayette, Ind., 1959-61; research entomologist U.S. Dept. Agr., State College, Miss., 1961—; adj. asso. prof. entomology Miss. State U., 1969—. Served with USAF, 1950-54. Mem. Alpha Zeta, Gamma Sigma Delta, Sigma Xi. Mason. Home: 112 White Dr Starkville MS 39759 Office: Box 5367 State College MS 39762

PARSLEY, BRANTLEY HAMILTON, librarian; b. Balt., Oct. 15, 1927; s. Clarence Elroy and Florence Sally (Barnes) P.; A.A., Balt. Jr. Coll., 1950; B.A., U. Md., 1952; B.D., New Orleans Bapt. Theol. Sem., 1955, M.R.E., 1958; M.Librarianship, Emory U., 1965; m. Loyce Marie Franklin, Apr. 18, 1951; children—Linda Marie, Brantley Hamilton. Ordained to ministry Bapt. Ch., 1956; pastor Calvary Bapt. Ch., Albany, Ore., 1955-57; library asst. New Orleans Pub. Library, 1958-61; supt. night circulation and stacks Theology Library, Emory U., 1961-65; dir. library Campbellsville (Ky.) Coll., 1965—. Bd. dirs. Taylor County Community Concerts. Recipient Sch. award Am. Legion, 1947. Mem. Am., Southeastern, Ky. (chmn. coll. and research sect. 1970-71) library assns., Council Ind. Ky. Colls. (chmn. 1970—), Taylor County Hist. Soc. (bd. dirs. 1970), Taylor County Bapt. Assn. (bd. dirs. 1968-70), Taylor County Bapt. Sunday Sch. Assn. (supt. 1968-70). Home: 114 Longview Dr Campbellsville KY 42718

PARSLEY, ROBERT HORACE, lawyer; b. Erwin, Tenn., Apr. 9, 1923; s. Millard Fillmore and Daisy (Garland) P.; student East Tenn. State U., 1941-43, U. Tenn., 1946-47; LL.B., U. Va., 1949; m. Georganna Alice Strake, Apr. 11, 1953; children—Robert, Sharon, Brian, Sandra, Sally, David, John, Daniel, Jana. Admitted to Tex. bar, 1949; asso. Baker, Botts, Andrews & Parish, Houston, 1949-53; asso. Butler, Binion, Rice, Cook & Knapp, Houston, 1953-57, partner, 1957—. Dir. J.M. West Tex. Corp.; instr. law U. Va., Charlottesville, 1949, U. Houston, 1949-50, Tex. So. U., Houston, 1952-53. Bd. dirs. S.W. Law Inst., Strake Jesuit Coll. Prep.; trustee West Found. Served to 1st lt. USAAF, 1943-46. Mem. Am., Tex., Houston bar assns., Alpha Tau Omega, Phi Delta Phi. Rotarian. Clubs: Houston, Houston Country. Home: 5219 Shady River St Houston TX 77027

PARSON, RUTH BURNETTE (MRS. CHARLES H. PARSON), music educator; b. Omega, Okla.; d. Earl J. and Katie (Richert) Burnette; B.A., Northwestern State Coll., Okla., 1932; M.Ed., Howard Payne Coll., 1957; certification in supervision N. Tex. State Coll., Denton, 1958; m. Charles H. Parson, Dec. 4, 1933. Tchr., Arnett, Okla., 1930-31, High Sch., Gray, Okla., 1931-32, Boise City, Okla., 1932-33, Wilmore, Kan., 1934-35; tchr. vocal and instrumental music Lambert (Okla.) High Sch., 1936-38; English and music tchr. Capron (Okla.) High Sch., 1938-42; choral dir. Seymour (Tex.) High Sch., 1943-44, jr., sr. high schs., Vernon, Tex., 1945-56; asst. prof. edn. Howard Payne Coll., Brownwood Tex., 1956-57; coordinator music Abilene (Tex.) Pub. Schs., 1958—. Music cons. in Manhattanville Music Curriculum Program, 1967-70. Recipient Vernon Jr. C. of C. Distinguished Community Service award, 1948. Mem. N.E.A., Tex. State Tchrs. Assn., Assn. Childhood Edn., Music Educators Nat. Conf., Tex. Music Educators Assn., Bus. and Profl. Womens Club. Music Guild of Abilene (past pres.). Mem. Christian Ch. Home: 1648 Glenhaven Dr Abilene TX 79603

PARSONS, CHARLES HERBERT, architect; b. Evanston, Ill., Apr. 8, 1930; s. Harvey Dodson and Lillian (Eadie) P.; B. Arch. with honors, U. Fla., 1958; m. Freida Durrance, Mar. 17, 1951; children—Dale Herbert, Ray Charles, Keith Alan. Practice of architecture Charles H. Parsons, Kissimmee, Fla., 1961—. Pres., Kissimmee Boat-A-Cade, 1970-71. Served with AUS, 1952-54. Recipient Henry Adams award A.I.A., 1959. Mem. A.I.A., Kissimmee C. of C. (pres. 1967-68), Council Ednl. Facilities Planners. Elk, Rotarian (pres. 1965-66). Club: Tohopekaliga Yacht (Kissimmee). Prin. archtl. works include: City Hall, Kissimmee, 1965, City Hall, Sebring, Fla., 1969, Michigan Av. Elementary Sch., St. Cloud, Fla., 1971. Home: Route 1 Box 123-B Maitland FL 32751 Office: 1103 Main St Kissimmee FL 32741

PARSONS, DAVID LARRY, dentist; b. Charleston, W.Va., Apr. 3, 1943; s. Clarence Eugene and Ocie Mae (Hill) P.; student Duke U., 1961-63, Morris Harvey Coll., 1963-65; D.D.S., B.S. in Chemistry (Pfeiffer research fellow 1966-69), U. N.C., 1969; m. Carolyn Olivia Hackney, Aug. 31, 1963; children—Mary Ann, Christine Ruth, Charles David. Pvt. practice dentistry, Greensboro, N.C., 1969-71, Salisbury, N.C., 1972—, dentist David L. Parsons, D.D.S., Greensboro, 1971—; v.p. Triventures, Inc., Greensboro, 1970-72. Bd. dirs. Francisco Place Assn. Recipient Physics Achievement award Morris Harvey Coll., 1963-64. Mem. Nat., N.C., Guilford, Rowan County dental socs., Kappa Sigma, Psi Omega. Club: Epicureans (membership chmn. 1970-71) (Greensboro, N.C.). Home: 1304 Arden Dr Salisbury NC 28144 Office: 1917 W Innes St Salisbury NC 28144

PARSONS, FLOYD W., supt. schs.; b. Andice, Tex., Oct. 16, 1909; s. William Culberson and Ida A. (Davis) P.; B.A., U. Tex., 1935, M.A., 1945; m. Christina Fowler, Dec. 25, 1932; children—Lou Anne (Mrs. William Raymond Smoot), Floyd W., Paul. High sch. prin., tchr., coach Johnson City (Tex.) Pub. Schs., 1932-33; elementary prin., tchr. Orangedale (Tex.) Common Sch. Dist., 1933-36; supt. schs., Calallen, Tex., 1936-46, Bishop, Tex., 1946-52, Beeville, Tex., 1952-56, Big Spring, Tex., 1956-61, Little Rock Sch. Dist., 1961—. Instr. dept. sociology U. Tex., summer 1945; instr. Hardin-Simmons U., summer 1959; participant Columbia Workshop, summer 1958. Trustee Ark. State Tchrs. Retirement System; bd. dirs. Salvation Army, YMCA, United Fund, Pulaski County Assn. Mental Health, Boy Scouts Am. Mem. N.E.A. (life), Tex. Tchrs. Assn. (life), Tex. (life), Ark. (life) congresses parents and tchrs., Ark. Edn. Assn., Econ. Edn. Bd., Am. Assn. Sch. Adminstrs. (pres. 1972-73, exec. com.), Assn. for Advancement of Internat. Edn. (mem. bd.), Council of Ednl. Facility Planners, Horace Mann League U.S. (dir.), C. of C. (bd.), Phi Delta Kappa, Alpha Kappa Delta. Kiwanian (past pres. Little Rock). Home: 31 Nob View Circle Little Rock AK 72205 Office: W Markham and Izard Sts Little Rock AK 72201

PARSONS, JOE MAX, educator; b. nr. Lexington, Tenn., June 20, 1915; s. Cleff and Myrtle (White) P.; student U. Tenn. Jr. Coll., 1935-36, Union U., 1937-39, Syracuse U., 1942-44; B.S., George Peabody Coll. for Tchrs., 1947, M.A., 1948; m. Elizabeth Davis, Mar. 22, 1947. Tchr., sch. prin. Henderson County (Tenn.) pub. schs., 1936-42; instr. math. George Peabody Coll. for Tchrs., 1948, U. Tenn., 1948-52; chief instr. Tenn. Radio Service Sch., Knoxville, 1951-52; dean, head dept. math. Asheville-Biltmore Coll., 1952-63, dean of students, head dept. math., 1963-68, dean men, 1967-69; dean men, asso. prof. U. N.C., Asheville, 1969—. Bd. dirs. Humane Soc., Asheville, Buncombe County (N.C.) Dept. Pub. Welfare. Served to sgt. AUS, 1942-46. Mem. N.C. Coll. Conf., N.C. Edn. Assn. (v.p. div. higher edn. 1959—), Kappa Phi Kappa, Phi Delta Kappa. Democrat. Baptist. Lion. Clubs: School Masters of Western N.C. (pres. 1962), Asheville Executives, Asheville City. Home: 110 Stuyvesant Rd Asheville NC 28803

PARSONS, LARRY JIM, accountant; b. San Francisco, Nov. 2, 1929; s. Laurence E. and June (Mattson) P.; B.S., U. Tenn., 1952; student Weber Jr. Coll., 1947-49; m. Wanda Carolyn Swope, Apr. 25, 1953; children—Priscilla M., Laura L., Juliette. With Ernst & Ernst, C.P.A.'s, 1957—, asst. mgr., Albuquerque, 1957-61, mgr., N.Y.C., 1961-63, Dallas, 1963—, partner, 1966—. Served with AUS, 1950-51. C.P.A. Tenn., N.Y., Tex., N.M., La., N.C. Mem. Am. Inst. C.P.A.'s, Tex. (dir.), N.Y. socs. C.P.A.'s, Dallas Chpt. C.P.A.'s (dir.), Dallas Civic Opera Assn. (dir.). Kiwanian. Home: 6818 Velasco St Dallas TX 75214 Office: LTV Tower 1600 Pacific St Dallas TX 75201

PARSONS, RHEY BOYD, educator; b. Mayfield, Ky., Dec. 22, 1892; s. Jacob Fisher and Althea Willie (Hooker) P.; B.S., U. Chgo., 1917, M.A., 1923, Ph.D., 1935. Tchr. math., prin. elementary and high schs., Ky., Tex., 1913-23; prof. edn. Baylor Coll., 1923-26; asso. prof. edn. U. Tenn., 1926-33; asso. prof. edn., supt. demonstration sch. Fla. State Coll., 1935-38; prof. edn., dept. chmn. Central YMCA Coll., Chgo., 1939-45; civilian employee, br. chief Mil. Govt., Germany, 1945-46; prof. edn. Aurora Coll., 1946-48; prof. edn. Murray (Ky.) State U., 1948-63, prof. emeritus, 1963—. Fellow A.A.A.S.; mem. Phi Delta Kappa, Kappa Delta Pi, others. Mason. Home: 1013 Payne St Murray KY 42071

PARSONS, TARLTON FLEMING, II, military officer; b. Independence, Mo., Dec. 5, 1927; s. Tarlton Fleming and Elinor (Flournoy) P.; student U. Dela., 1945, Amherst Coll., 1946; B.S., U.S. Mil. Acad., 1950; M.B.A. with highest distinction Babson Coll., 1965; m. Joan Norwood Ferguson, June 10, 1950; children—Aileen Elinor, Tarlton Fleming III, Dawn. Entered U.S. Army, 1945, advanced through grades to lt. col., 1966; chief ammunition supply Continental Army Command, Va., 1961-64; exec. officer material requirements Army Materials Command, Va., 1968-70; asst. chief staff Yukon Command, Alaska, 1966-68; asst. chief logistics office, Vietnam, 1970-71; chief supply and maintenance, Mil. Dist. of Washington, 1971—. Lectr. econs. U. Alaska, 1966-68, mgmt. U. Md., 1970-71; dir. Huguenot Corp., Richmond, Va., 1958-63. Com. chmn. North Star council Boy scouts Am., 1966-68. Decorated Bronze Star medal with oak leaf cluster, Army Commendation medal with three oak leaf clusters, Royal Yugoslav War Cross, N.Y. State Conspicuous Service Cross; knight comdr. justice Order St. John of Jerusalem; Chevalier d'Honneur, Ordo Constantini Magni; knight Order St. Dennis of Zante; comdr. Orde St. Lazarus; recipient citizenship award Am. Legion, 1943. Fellow Soc. Antiquaries of Scotland, Augustan Soc.; mem. St. Andrews Soc. Washington. Mason (K.T.). Club: Army and Navy (Washington). Contbr. articles to profl. pubs. Home: 5349 Taney Av Alexandria VA 22304 Office: Headquarters AnLOG-SM Military Dist Washington Washington DC 20315

PARTEE, FRANK PAUL, govt. ofcl.; b. Hamilton, O., Apr. 23, 1937; s. Harvey Stephen and Theresa Mary (Dilling) P.; B. Chem. Engring., U. Cin., 1961; M.P.H., U. Mich., 1965; m. Alma Carol Rosso, July 23, 1966; children—Michael Curtis, Laura Ann. With Environmental Protection Agy., 1961-63, project engr. St. Louis Interstate Air Pollution Control Study, 1963-64, project officer St. Mary's, Fla. and Bernandina Beach, Fla., 1965-67, chief N.E. area, div. control agy. devel., Washington, 1967-69; tech. dir. Ky. Air Pollution Control Commn., Frankfort, 1969—; dir. div. air pollution control Ky. Dept. Health, 1969—. Served to maj. USPHS, 1961-69. Registered profl. engr., Ky. Community Found. scholar, Hamilton, O., 1955. Mem. Nat., Ky. socs. profl. engrs., Am. Pub. Works Assn., Air Pollution Control Assn. (mem. com. 1969—), State and Territorial Air Pollution Program Adminstrs. (bd. dirs. 1971), Phi Kappa Theta, Alpha Phi Omega. Home: 959 Brookhaven Dr Frankfort KY 40601 Office: 275 E Main St Frankfort KY 40601

PARTEE, WOODIE AUGUSTUS, JR., banker, lawyer; b. Washington, Ga., Oct. 3, 1921; s. Woodie Augustus and Edna (Chafin) P.; A.B., U. Ga., 1943; postgrad. Fletcher Sch. Law and Diplomacy, 1949-50; J.D., George Washington U., 1962; LL.M. in Taxation, Georgetown U., 1966. With Riggs Nat. Bank, Washington, 1951—, v.p. credit, 1970—; law clk. to Judge Marvin Jones U.S. Ct. Claims, 1962-63; admitted to D.C. bar, 1963. Served with Transp. Corps, AUS, 1945-49. Mem. Am., Fed. bar assns., Bar Assn. D.C., Robert Morris Assos., Order of Coif, Blue Key, Sphinx, Phi Beta Kappa, Phi Kappa Phi, Omicron Delta Kappa, Phi Eta Sigma, Phi Delta Phi, Sigma Chi. Club: Nat. Lawyers. Home: 2480 16th St NW Washington DC 20009 Office: 1503 Pennsylvania Av NW Washington DC 20005

PARTIN, WILLIAM, educator; b. Jacksonville, Fla., Aug. 10, 1924; s. James A. and Ada (Flowers) P.; B.A., Emory U., 1950, M.Ed., 1951; Ed.D., Peabody Coll., 1961; m. Betty Glass, Nov. 23, 1951; children— Betsy, Clyde, Keith Edward. Dean men Reinhardt Coll., Waleska, Ga., 1952-53; mem. faculty dept. phys. edn. Emory U., Atlanta, Oxford brs., 1951-52, 53—, asst. prof., Atlanta, 1961-65, asso. prof., 1965-66, prof., chmn. div. phys. edn., 1966—. Mem. Gov.'s Council on Phys. Fitness; active P.T.A., pres., 1960-61; v.p. Ga. Amateur Athletic Union, 1963-67. Served with USNR, 1942-45. Algeron S. Sullivan scholar, 1959. Recipient Distinguished Alumnus award George Peabody Coll., 1971. Fellow Am. Coll. Sports Medicine; mem. Ga. High Sch. Assn. (hon.), Am., Ga. (honor award 1967) assns. health, phys. edn. and recreation, Nat. Coll. Phys. Edn. Assn., N.E.A., Am. Sch. Health Assn., U.S. Soccer Football Assn. (4th v.p. 1971-72), Youth Am. Soccer League, Phi Kappa Phi, Phi Delta Kappa, Sigma Delta Psi, Sigma Nu. Methodist (ofcl. bd.). Rotarian. Home: 2881 Faraday Ct Decatur GA 30033 Office: 1380 S Oxford Rd Atlanta GA 30322

PARTINGTON, REX, artistic dir., mgr. Va. State Theater, 1972—. Office: Barter Theater Abingdon VA 24210*

PARVIN, MILLARD GYE, fishery exec., advt. co. exec.; b. Corinth, Miss., Sept. 28, 1920; s. Fred Gye and Callie Lane (Bratton) P.; student Biggersville Sch., 1926-33; m. Mary Ruth Loyd, Nov. 17, 1956; children—Barbara Gail (Mrs. Terrell Hatfield), Sherry Lynn. With Miss. div. King & Stanley Co., Inc., Corinth, 1946—, operations mgr., 1950—; partner Springwater Fish Farms, 1969—; lectr., cons. catfish farming, 1965—. Scoutmaster Boy Scouts Am., 1957—. Served with USMC, 1944-46. Decorated Purple Heart. Mem. Am. Legion, V.F.W., Catfish Farmers Am., Miss. Catfish Assn. (dir. 1968-69), Miss. Electric Sign Assn. Baptist. Mason. Clubs: Saddle (pres. 1964-67) (Corinth, Miss.); Boosters (Glen, Miss.). Inventor catfish brooder and automated catfish feeder, paint stripper. Home: Route 1 Glen MS 38846 Office: 119 W Linden St Corinth MS 38834

PASCAL, GERALD ROSS, psychologist, educator; b. Raritan, N.J., Aug. 3, 1907; s. Anthony and Mary (Ross) P.; A.B., U. Cal. at Berkeley, 1940; M.A., Harvard, 1942; Ph.D., Brown U., 1948; m. Lalla Vincent Sullivan, Sept. 14, 1964; children—Walther Gerald, Roy Darby, Lawrence Hiby, Christopher Biram. Chief psychologist Butler Hosp., Providence, 1946-49; lectr. Brown U., Providence, 1948; research psychologist, asso. prof. Western Psychiat. Inst., U. Pitts., 1949-51; prof. psychology, dir. Clin. Tng. U. Tenn., Knoxville, 1951-64; prof. psychiatry U. Miss. Med. Sch., Jackson, 1964—, dir. Pascal Clinic, 1966—. Profl. cons. Hinds County Mental Health Assn., Bapt. Childrens Village. Mem. bd. dirs. Goodwill Industries, 1969—. Served with USAAF, 1943-46. Diplomate Am. Bd. Examiners Profl. Psychology; Am. Bd. Examiners Psychol. Hypnosis. Fellow Am. Psychol. Assn.; mem. Am. Acad. Psychotherapists. Home: 3718 Kings Hwy Jackson MS 39216 Office: Med Tower Bldg Jackson MS 39216

PASCHAL, JERRY DREW, endl. adminstr.; b. Wewoka, Okla., Apr. 12, 1931; s. Arthur Gordon and Edna (Drew) P.; B.S., High Point Coll., 1956; M.S., U. N.C., 1959, advanced supts. certificate, 1962; Ph.D., Duke, 1971; m. Patricia Kornegay, July 4, 1954; children—Arthur Gordon, Joan Dee. Indsl. engr. Anvil Brand, High Point, N.C., 1956-57; tchr., prin., asst. supt. Jr. Order Children's Home, Lexington, N.C., 1957-59; prin., Eanes Elementary Sch., Lexington, N.C., 1959-60, Chadbourn (N.C.) Union Sch., 1960-61, Charles B. Aycock High Sch., Pikeville, N.C., 1961-64; asst. supt. Goldsboro (N.C.) City Schs., 1965-66, supt., 1966-72; asso. to vice chancellor Fort-Bragg-Pope AFB campus Fayetteville State U., 1972—. Pres., Pioneer Athletic Conf., 1962-63; mem. evaluation teams So. Assn. Coll. and Schs., 1962-69. Chmn. in edn. United Forces, 1967-68; mem. dist. exec. com. Tuscorora council Boy Scouts Am., 1968-70; mem. state com. Urban Studies Adv. Council, 1970—; mem. Commn. on Religion and Race, 1971—; mem. Mayor's Com. to Recognize Handicapped, 1969—. Bd. dirs. Wayne County Mental Health Assn., Wayne Sheltered Workshop, Boys' Club, Recreation and Parks Commn., Wayne Action Group for Econ. Solvency. Served with AUS, 1954-56. Mem. N.E.A., Am. Assn. Sch. Adminstrs., N. C. Assn. Educators (state dir. 1970-72), Nat. Council State Edn. Assns. (state pres. polit. action com. edn. 1970-72), Nat. Consortium for Humanizing Edn., Nat. Secondary Sch. Prins. Assn., Schoolmaster's Club (pres. 1961-62), Phi Delta Kappa, Kappa Delta Pi. Methodist (dir. 1964-65). Home: 606 S Claiborne St Goldsboro NC 27530 Office: PO Drawer 1997 Goldsboro NC 27530

PASCHALL, H. FRANKLIN, clergyman; b. Hazel, Ky., May 12, 1922; s. Cletus T. and Eva (Jones) P.; B.A., Union U., 1944; B.D., So. Baptist Sem., 1949, Th.D., 1951; m. Olga B. Bailey, June 4, 1944; children—Pam (Mrs. John Freeman), Sandra. Ordained to ministry Baptist Ch., 1941; pastor Hazel Bapt. Ch., 1941-51, 1st Bapt. Ch., Bowling Green, Ky., 1951-56, 1st Bapt. Ch., Nashville, 1956—. Pres. So. Bapt. Conv., 1966-68, mem. exec. com., mem. Tenn. exec. com., 1964—. Author: The Gospel for an Exploding World, 1967. Home: Bear Rd Nashville TN 37215

PASCHALL, J(OSHUA) E(RNEST), lawyer, state legislator; b. nr. Black Creek, N.C., Aug. 9, 1896; s. Joshua Walter and Sallie (Poole) P.; student U. N.C., 1917; A.B., Atlantic Christian Coll., 1918, LL.D., 1961; LL.B., Am. U., Los Angeles, 1926; m. Claire Hodges, Dec. 18, 1919; children—Julia Daly (Mrs. Charles W. Mauze), James E. With Branch Banking & Trust Co., Wilson, N.C., 1919—, asst. cashier, 1933-43, dir., 1943—, cashier, 1943-52, v.p. 1942-52, pres., 1952-64; dir. Wilson Savs. & Loan Assn., pres., 1944—; mem. N.C. Ho. of Reps., 1964—; engaged in law practice, Wilson, 1964—. Mem. Banking Commn. N.C., 1961-65. Vice chmn., bd. trustees, mem. exec. com., chmn. finance com. Atlantic Christian Coll.; bd. dirs. Coastal Plain Planning and Devel., assn. pres., 1965-66. Served with USNRF, 1918-19. Mem. Am., N.C., Wilson County bar assns., Newcomen Soc. N.Am., Nat. Soc. State Legislators, C. of C. (pres. 1945), Am. Legion (post comdr. 1935-36). Mem. Christian Ch. (ofcl. bd., trustee). Elk, Moose, Rotarian. Club: Wilson. Home: 1718 Wilshire Blvd Wilson NC 27893 Office: 113 E Nash St Wilson NC 27893

PASCUCCI, LUCIEN MICHELE, physician; b. Waterbury, Conn., 1909; M.D., Yale, 1934. Intern, Butler Hosp., Providence, 1934-35, New Haven Hosp., 1935-36; resident Fitchs Home and Hosp., Noroton Heights, Conn., 1937-38; resident in radiology Presbyn. Hosp., N.Y.C., 1938-41; dir. radiology Trudeau Sanitorium and Saranac Lab., Saranac Lake, N.Y., 1946-47; dir. radiology and phys. therapy St. Johns Hosp., Tulsa; cons. Bartlett Meml Hosp. Served to lt. col., M.C., AUS, 1941-46. Diplomate Am. Bd. Radiology. Fellow Am. Coll. Radiology; mem. A.M.A., Okla. Med. Assn. (pres. 1971-72), Radiol. Soc. N.Am., Am. Roentgen Ray Soc. Home: 2828 E 38th Blvd Tulsa OK 74105 Office: 1923 S Utica Av Tulsa OK 74104*

PASEWALK, HERBERT MACDONALD, ins. co. exec.; b. Mpls., Dec. 19, 1910; s. Herbert R. and Bertha S. (MacDonald) P.; B.C.S., Benjamin Franklin U., 1934, M.C.S., 1935; m. Mary Elisabeth Jester, Aug. 17, 1937. Night supt. Emergency Hosp., Washington, 1931-33; accountant Clyde B. Stovall & Co., 1934-36; property mgr. Mt. Vernon Mortgage Corp., 1936-42; pres., dir. Firemen's Ins. Co. of Washington, 1946—; exec. v.p., sec., dir. Howard & Hoffman, Inc., 1946—, Home Casualty and Surety Co., 1960—; dir. Howard & Hoffman Life Assos., Inc. Mem. Washington Bd. Trade. Served from 2d lt. to capt. USAF, 1942-45, now maj. res. Decorated Bronze Star medal. Mem. D.C. Assn. Ins. Agts. (past pres.), Air Force Assn., Order Blue Goose, Newcomen Soc. N.Am., Chevy Chase Citizens Assn., Benjamin Franklin U. Alumni Assn. (Distinguished Alumnus award 1971). Clubs: Nat. Press, Reciprocity (past pres.), Touchdown (Washington). Home: 6943 33d St NW Washington DC 20015 Office: 303 7th St NW Washington DC 20004

PASKINS, CLOYD WOODROW, educator; b. Mattoon, Ill., Sept. 30, 1914; s. Tilles Oratio and Sarah Jeanette (Sutton) P.; B.Ed., Eastern Ill. U., 1937; M.A., Duke, 1943; postgrad. (History fellow), La. State U., 1944-45, U. Cal. at Berkeley, 1940, U. Pitts., 1947, (Asian Student scholar) Syracuse U., 1956. Tchr., Fla. Secondary Schs., 1937-43; instr. Troy (Ala.) State U., 1943-44, asst. prof. history, sociology and comparative religions, 1958—; instr. East Central Jr. Coll., 1944-46; asso. prof. history, sociology Elon Coll., 1946-48; asso. prof. sociology Jacksonville State Coll., 1949-50; head social sci. dept. Ft. Myers (Fla.) High Sch., 1951-55; head social sci. dept. Palm Beach Jr. Coll., 1955-58; vis. prof. U. Miami, 1946; vis. sociologist Stephen F. Austin State Coll., 1949; Doctoral fellow Walden U., 1972-73. Pres., S.W. Fla. Council for Social Studies, 1953-55, Palm Beach County Council for Social Studies, 1956-58. Bd. dirs. Fla. Council for Social Studies, 1953-58. Fellow Am. Sociol. Assn.; mem. Am. Hist. Assn., Am. Assn. U. Profs., Nat. Council for Social Studies, Am. Civil Liberties Union. Home: 419 Collegedale Av Troy AL 36081

PASS, BOBBY CLIFTON, educator; b. Cleveland, Ala., Nov. 4, 1931; s Rufus Clifton and Alma Antionette (Payne) P.; student Snead Jr. Coll., 1949-50; B.S., Auburn U., 1952, M.S., 1960; Ph.D. (Alumni fellow), Clemson U., 1962; m. Ann Rutherford, Aug. 17, 1953; 1 son, Kevin Clifton. Salesman, U.S. Pipe & Foundry Co., Birmingham, Ala., 1955-57; research asst. Auburn (Ala.) U., 1958-60, Clemson (S.C.) U., 1960-62; asst. prof. U. Ky. at Lexington, 1962-67, asso. prof., 1967-68, asso. prof., chmn. dept. entomology, 1968-70, prof., chmn. dept. entomology, 1971—. Cons. Peace Corps, 1968. Served with AUS, 1953-55. Mem. Internat. Orgn. Biol. Programs, Entomol. Soc. Am., A.A.A.S., Ky. Acad. Sci., S.C. Entomol. Soc., Sigma Xi, Phi Kappa Phi, Gamma Sigma Delta. Contbr. articles to profl. jours. Home: 103 Tartan Dr Lexington KY 40503 Office: Dept Entomology U Ky Lexington KY 40506

PASSER, HAROLD CLARENCE, govt. ofcl.; b. Lakefield, Minn., Nov. 27, 1921; s. Clarence Walter and Esther (Nauman) P.; B.S. summa cum laude, Harvard, 1943, M.A., 1948, Ph.D., 1950; m. Astrid Anderson Thurber, Nov. 19, 1966; children—Christine L. Thurber, David C. Thurber, Jr. Asst. prof. econs. Princeton, 1950-52; economist Eastman Kodak Co., Rochester, N.Y., 1952-69; asst. sec. commerce for econ. affairs, Washington, 1969—; lectr. Cornell U., U. Rochester; mem. econ. adv. bd. U.S. Dept. Commerce, 1967-68. Treas., Genesee Region Council on Econ. Edn.; bd. dirs. N.Y. State Council on Econ. Edn. Served to lt. USNR, 1943-46. Mem. Am. Econ. Assn., Am. Statis. Assn., Nat. Assn. Bus. Economists, Conf. Bus. Economists, Nat. Econ. Club, Phi Beta Kappa. Republican. Presbyn. Club: Nat. Press. Author: The Electrical Manufacturers, 1953. Home: 3223 Garfield St NW Washington DC 20008 Office: US Dept Commerce Washington DC 20230

PASSMAN, OTTO ERNEST, congressman; b. nr. Franklinton, La., June 27, 1900; s. Ed. and Pheriby (Carrier) P.; grad. Comml. Bus. Coll.; m. Willie Bateman. Owner, Passman Equipment Co., Passman Investment Co., Monroe, La. Mem. 80th-92d Congresses, 5th La. Dist. Commd. lt. USN, 1942; material and procurement officer until 1944. Past state comdr. Am. Vets. World War II, Inc. Mem. Am. Legion. Democrat. Baptist. Mason (33 deg., Shriner, K.T., Scottish Rite, Red Cross of Constantine). Home: 120 Walnut St Monroe LA 71201 Office: House Office Bldg Washington DC 20515

PASSMORE, THELMA (JEAN) MIZELL (MRS. DAYMON PASSEMORE), educator; b. Arkadelphia, Ark., Oct. 24, 1922; d. William Harrison and Della L. (Scrivner) Mizell; B.A. summa cum laude, Ouachita Coll., 1943; M.Ed., S.W. Tex. State Coll., 1960; m. Daymon Passmore, Dec. 8, 1943 (dec. 1956); children—Leonard Harrison, Walter Jackson, Thelma Jean (Mrs. Terril Jay Wendt). Stock-farmer, Voca, Tex., 1956-59; tchr. English and speech Llano (Tex.) High Sch., 1957-59; tchr. world history, English, speech Rockdale (Tex.) High Sch., 1959-60; counselor Travis Jr. High Sch., McAllen, Tex., 1960-67, Comfort (Tex.) High Sch., 1967-68; counselor employment security div. Ark. State Employment Service, 1968-71; tchr. history Watson Chapel High Sch., Pine Bluff, Ark., 1971—; instr. freshman English, night class Pan Am. Coll., Edinburg, Tex., 1962-63. Mem. McCulloch County Library Bd., Brady, Tex., 1953-57. Mem. Tex. Tchrs. Assn., Internat. Assn. Personnel in Employment Security, Nat. Employment Counselors Assn., Am., Ark. personnel and guidance assns., Ark. Employment Counselors Assn., Ark. Personnel Employee Retirement Assn., Valley Guidance Assn., Am., Tex. personnel and guidance assns., Phi Theta Kappa, Pi Kappa Delta Presbyn. Mem. Order Eastern Star. Home: 3306 Miramar Dr Pine Bluff AR 71601

PASTORE, ARTHUR RALPH, JR., author; b. N.Y.C., Apr. 22, 1922; s. Arthur Ralph and Elvira (Frasca) P.; student Union Coll., 1940-41; B.A., Yale, 1947; M.S. in Journalism, Columbia, 1948; postgrad. U. Paris (France), 1950-51; M.A., U. Md., 1972; m. Evelyn Thomson, Feb. 24, 1951 (dec. Oct. 1965); m. 2d, Anna Brooks, Nov. 3, 1969. Staff writer, editor Fairchild Publs., N.Y.C., 1947-50; information specialist U.S. State Dept. Fgn. Service, Vienna, Austria, 1951-52; press attache Radio Free Europe, 1952-53, editor-writer Nat. Com. for Free Europe, N.Y.C., 1953-54; promotion mgr. European edit. Newsweek, Paris, France, 1954-56; staff writer Internat. News Service, Paris, 1956-57; dir. pub. relations N.Y.C. Commn. Human Rights, 1959-60; asst. pub. relations dir. N.Y.C. Housing Authority, 1960-62; asst. prof. journalism Duquesne U., Pitts., 1963-66; vis. asso. prof. journalism, broadcasting Am. U., Washington, 1966-67; asst. prof. English Montgomery Coll., Takoma Park, Md., 1967-68; resident lectr. U. Coll., U. Md., 1969; free-lance mag., newspaper journalist, Washington 1966—. Served with AUS, 1943-46; ETO. Pub. Relations Soc. Edn. and Research fellow, 1967; recipient Distinguished Broadcasting award WAMU, Am. U., 1967. Mem. Nat. Press Club, Assn. Edn. in Journalism, Soc. Am. Travel Writers, Am. Assn. U. Profs., Sigma Delta Chi, Kappa Tau Alpha. Author: Where to Eat in Europe, 1954; Mexico and Cuba on Your Own, 1954; Dynamite Under the Alps, 1963; Chatto & Windus, 1968. Address: 3410 38th St NW Washington DC 20016

PATCH, ETHEL LEE, ednl. adminstr.; b. nr. Richmond, Va., Jan 19, 1938; d. Ralph Lee and Alice (Winston) Patch; B.S., Radford Coll., 1960, M.S., 1965. Bus. tchr., guidance counselor James Wood High Sch., Winchester, Va., 1960-65; coordinator of guidance Frederick County Jr. High Sch., Winchester, 1965-67; counselor Central Va. Community Coll., Lynchburg, 1967-69, coordinator admissions and records, 1969—. Mem. Am., Va. personnel and guidance assns. Home: 1609A Wards Ferry Rd Lynchburg VA 14502

PATCH, NATHANIEL MAXWELL, educator; b. Geneva, N.Y., May 29, 1917; s. Maurice Byron and Mildred (Wheat) P.; Mus.B., Eastman Sch. Music, 1939, Mus.M., 1941; m. Gertrude Kendrick Lasseter, Aug. 20, 1949; children—Lauren, Ann. Asst. prof. music George Peabody Coll., Nashville, 1941-42, 46-49; asso. prof. music U. Ky., Lexington, 1949-53, prof. music, 1953—, head dept. piano, 1955—, head applied music, 1971—. Served to 1st lt. USAAF, 1943-45. Decorated Air Medal with oak leaf clusters (3). Mem. Am. Assn. U. Profs., Music Tchrs. Nat. Assn., Ky. Music Tchrs. Assn., Kappa Alpha, Phi Mu Alpha Sinfonia. Soloist, Louisville Orchestra, Nashville Symphony, Rochester Civic and Rochester Philharmonic, Lexington Philharmonic, Univ. Symphony and Band. Home: 228 Southport Dr Lexington KY 40503

PATE, ANNE (MRS. JAMES W. PATE), community worker; b. Hepzibah, Ga., Dec. 7, 1929; d. James Earle and Rhoda Lee (Stephenson); student Augusta Coll., 1946-47, U. Ga. Sch. Nursing, 1947-49; m. James W. Pate, Aug. 1, 1948; children—James W. II, Susan, Patricia. Del., Am. Cancer Soc., 1966-68; pres. Memphis Heart Assn. Aux., 1967—, chmn. fund raising, chmn. bd., 1970-71; active Duration Club Sch. for Mentally Retarded, 1967—; bd. govs., sec., exec. bd., chmn. fund raising Front St. Theatre, 1965-67; chmn. bd. Elias Lowenstein Home for Girls, 1966-67. Bd. dirs. Memphis Symphony League, Memphis Ballet Soc., Memphis Arts Council, Assn. for Preservation of Tenn. Antiquities, Tenn. Heart Assn. Clubs: Kennedy Wives (pres. 1958), U. Tenn. Faculty Women's (chmn. newcomers 1959), Mockingbird Garden (pres. 1960-62), LeLiversque, Nineteenth Century (bd. dirs., exec. bd. 1964—, jr. pres. 1964-65). Home: 6787 Satinwood Cove Memphis TN 38117

PATE, JAMES WYNFORD, surgeon, educator; b. Wedowee, Ala., Aug. 28, 1928; s. Wynford and Anne (Blount) P.; student Emory U., 1944-46; M.D., Med. Coll. Ga., 1950; m. Anne Stephenson, Aug. 1, 1948; children—James Wynford II, Susan Anne, Patricia Lee. Intern, Nat. Naval Med. Center, Bethesda, Md., 1950-51, resident, 1951-53; resident U. Ala. Med. Center, 1953-55; resident VA Hosp., Memphis, 1955-57, asst. chief thoracic surgery, 1957-59; with U. Tenn., 1959—, asst. prof. surgery, 1959-61, asso. prof., chmn. thoracic surgery, 1961-65, prof., chmn. thoracic surgery, 1965—, pres. faculty Coll. Medicine, 1965-66; chief thoracic and cardiovascular surgery City of Memphis Hosp., 1960—; cons. cardiac surgery VA Hosp., 1960—, Baptist Meml. Hosp., 1960—, Methodist Hosp., 1961—, West Tenn. Chest Hosp., 1966—, Naval Hosp., Memphis, 1961—, St. Joseph Hosp., 1961—, St. Jude Hosp., 1968—. Chmn., Memphis Regional Med. Program. Served with USNR, 1950-53. Fellow Am. Coll. Cardiology; mem. Memphis Heart Assn. (pres.), A.C.S., Am. Coll. Chest Physicians, Southeastern Surg. Congress, So. Surg. Assn., Soc. Vascular Surgery, Am. Assn. Thoracic Surgery, Dirs. Tng. Thoracic Surgery (pres. 1968-70), Am. Surg. Assn., Soc. Thoracic Surgeons, So. Thoracic Surg. Assn. (pres. elect 1971-73); Sigma Xi, Alpha Omega Alpha. Author: (with E. H. Storer, R.T. Sherman) The Science of Surgery, 1964. Contbr. numerous articles to med., sci. jours. Home: 6787 Satinwood Cove Memphis TN 38117

PATE, MARGERY, banker; b. Ft. Gaines, Ga., July 19, 1922; d. James Travis and Amy Estelle (Craft) Pate; grad. high sch. Clk., Baker County Bank, Newton, Ga., 1943-49, cashier, 1949-50; utility clk. First Nat. Bank & Trust Co., Macon, Ga., 1950-60; asst. cashier Ga. Bank & Trust Co., Macon, 1960-63, asst. v.p., from 1963, now v.p., asst. trust officer. Treas., Aid for Leukemia Stricken Children Am., Macon, 1960—; mem. service com. 7th div. Ga. Easter Seal Soc. Mem. Am. Inst. Banking, Nat. Assn. Bank Audit and Control (dir., 1962-63), Nat. Assn. Bank Women. Club: Quota (trustee 1961-65, treas., dir. 1963-65) (Macon). Home: 3089 Highpoint Dr Macon GA 31204 Office: 515 Mulberry St Macon GA 31202

PATE, MARIE M. MCDONALD (MRS. WALTER E. PATE), coll. dean; b. Evergreen, Ala.; d. John and Delunah (Williams) McDonald; B.S., U. Ala., 1952, M.A., 1957; postgrad. Auburn U., 1959-65; m. Walter E. Pate, May 23, 1926; children— Mary Evelyn (Mrs. Hubert T. Sullivan), Mildred Louise (Mrs. John T. Lee, Jr.), Patricia Ann (Mrs. Edward Baker). Tchr. elementary schs., Conecuh County, Ala., 1936-59, supr. instrn., 1959-65; acad. dean Jefferson Davis Jr. Coll., Brewton, Ala., 1965—. Pres. Conecuh County Mental Health Assn., 1963; chmn. Family Life Workshop, Conecuh County, 1963. Mem. Suprs. of Instrn. (state treas. 1967-69), Ala. Edn. Assn. (dist. pres. 1960), Delta Kappa Gamma. Home: Castleberry AL 36432 Office: Jefferson Davis Jr Coll Brewton AL 36426

PATE, PAUL ELBERT, architect; b. Ft. Smith, Ark., June 15, 1931; s. Otis Louis and Effie Lee (Parsons) P.; B.A., Baylor U., 1954; B. Arch., Harvard, 1962, M. Arch., 1962; M. Arch., Tex. A. and M. U., 1966; m. Sara Elizabeth Garrett, Apr. 10, 1952; children—Lady Jane, Sara Lee, Julie, Sharon, Paul Scot. Project architect Harrell & Hamilton, Dallas, 1962-63; asso. chmn. sch. architect Tex. A and M U., 1963-66; pres. Paul Pate Architect, College Station, Tex., 1966—; pres. Urban Inst., Inc., 1969—. Served with USNR, 1954-59. Mem. A.I.A. (pres. Brozos chpt. 1969-70), Soc. Coll. and Univ. Planners, Soc. U. Profs., Flying Architects. Home: 304 W Dexter College Station TX 77840 Office: 707 University Dr College Station TX 77840

PATE, WALLACE FENNELL, real estate developer; b. Greenville, S.C., Jan. 23, 1933; s. William Wilson and Alethea (Fennell) P.; student Davidson Coll., 1951-52, Furman U., 1952-53; B.B.A., U. Ga., 1955; m. Stella Hutchison Law, Aug. 21, 1953 (div. 1971); children—Stella Law, Wallace Fennell, Dorothy Parker, Alethea Beckham, John McDonald; m. 2d, Lucille Margaret Vanderbilt, Feb. 18, 1971. Vice pres. Wunda Weve Carpet Co., Greenville, 1957-59; pres. Litchfield Realty Co., Georgetown, S.C., 1959-63, Wallace-Pate Real Estate, Inc., Georgetown, 1959—; pres. DeBordieu Corp., Georgetown, 1969—; co-owner Holiday Inn., Georgetown, 1967-72; owner Nautica Marine Center, Georgetown, 1967-69. Chmn., Georgetown Housing Authority, 1968-69. Served to 2d lt. AUS, 1957-58. Mem. Nat. Assn. Real Estate Bds., Winyah Indigo Soc., C. of C. (dir. 1969-70), Ducks Unltd., Sigma Alpha Epsilon. Club: DeBordieu Colony (pres., dir.). Address: Arcadia Plantation Georgetown SC 29440

PATE, WILLIAM WILSON, mfr.; b. Bennettsville S.C., Aug. 17, 1900; s. William Walter and Willie (McElwee) P.; student Clemson Coll., 1918-19; m. Alethea Fennell, Nov. 20, 1928; children—William Wilson, Wallace Fennell. Vice pres. McAlister, Smith & Pate, Greenville, S.C., 1930-42, Convenience, Inc., also Star Cross, Inc., Greenville, 1942-48; pres. Belrug Mills, also Wunda Weve Carpet Co., Greenville, 1946-63, Patewood Corp., Byrd Furniture Co., Inc., 1964—. Campaign chmn. Greater Greenville Community Chest, 1945-46. Trustee Greenville County Hosp., 1953-59. Mem. S.C. Ins. Commn. Served with USN, World War I. Mem. Greenville C. of C. (pres.). Methodist (chmn. ofcl. bd.). Kiwanian (dir.). Clubs: Greenville Country (gov.), Green Valley Country (dir., charter mem.) (Greenville, S.C.); Biltmore (N.C.) Forest Country. Home: Route 10 Patewood Dr Greenville SC 29607 Office: Northwoods Indsl Park Greenville SC 29602

PATE, WOODROW WILSON, economist, educator; b. Murfreesboro, Ark., Feb. 11, 1913; s. Virgil Albert and Tula Etta (Smith) P.; A.B., Henderson State Tchrs. Coll., 1936; A.M., La. State U., 1938; Ph.D. (Gen. Edn. Bd. fellow), U. N.C., 1949; m. Helen Lee Timberlake, Dec. 26, 1938; children—Thomas Holloway, Judith Lee. Head dept. social sci. Ark. A. and M. Coll., 1938-43; asst. prof. econs. U. Okla., 1948-49; prof. econs. Centenary Coll. of La., Shreveport, 1949—. Econ. cons. Operations Research Office, 1952-53; pres. Conf. La. Colls. and Univs., 1967-68. Served with USNR, 1943-46. Mem. So. Econ. Assn., Southwestern Social Sci. Assn., Alpha Chi (nat. council 1967—). Home: 3823 Greenway Pl Shreveport LA

PATERSON, DONALD MICHAEL, interior decorator; b. Wilmington, Del., Feb. 8, 1929; s. Michael M. and Candida (Zelo) P.; student U. Del., 1946-48, Juillard Sch. Music, 1948-51, Columbia U., 1952, N.Y. Sch. Interior Design, 1952-54. Singer, profl., tv. and broadway shows, 1948-52; interior designer Michael Greer, Inc., N.Y.C., 1955-62; owner Donald M. Paterson, Inc., Palm Beach, Fla., 1962-—, N.Y.C., 1967-—. Mem. adv. com., interior design dept. Palm Beach Jr. Coll., 1970-—. Mem. Am. Inst. Interior Designers, Soc. of the Four Arts. Mailing address: 1208 Marine Way Old Port Cove North Palm Beach FL 33408 Office: 250 Worth Av Palm Beach FL 33480

PATMAN, WRIGHT, congressman; b. nr. Hughes Springs, Tex., Aug. 6, 1893; s. John and Emma (Spurlin) P.; LL.B., Cumberland U., 1916; m. Merle Connor, Feb. 14, 1919; children—Connor Wright, James Harold, William Neff. Cotton farmer, Tex., 1913-14; admitted to Tex. bar, 1916; practiced in Hughes Springs; asst. county atty. Cass County, Tex., 1916-17; dist. atty. 5th Jud. Dist., Tex., 1924-29; mem. 71st-92d congresses from 1st Tex. Dist. Mem. Tex. Ho. of Reps., 1921-24. Served with U.S. Army, 1917-19. Mem. Am. Legion, D.A.V. Democrat. Baptist. Mason (32 deg.). Club: Texas (pres. Washington). Home: 1205 Main St Texarkana TX 75501 also 500 23d St Washington DC 20037

PATO, MANUAL GONZALEZ, univ. athletic dir.; b. Ponce, P.R., 1913; B.S., La. State U., 1935, postgrad., 1935-37; m. 1941; 2 children. Tchr. pub. schs., P.R., from 1937; supt. community edn. Govt. of P.R., San Juan; faculty dept. phys. edn. Catholic U. P.R., Ponce, 1954-—, dir. athletics and recreation, 1966-—. Lectr., track and field coach P.R. nat. teams to World Olympics, Pan Am. games, Caribbean and C.Am. games, Iberian Am. games. Active Future Farmers Am., 4-H clubs, Boy Scouts Am., YNCA. Recipient awards for contbns. to youth of P.R. through phys. edn., sports and recreation from civic and ednl. orgns. Mem. P.R. (tech. com.), Caribbean and C.Am. (tech. com.) track and field fedns. Author textbooks on phys. edn., sports and recreation. Office: Catholic University of PR Ponce PR 00731*

PATRICK, CLIFFORD HOWARD, economist; b. Gaffney, S.C., Jan. 17, 1943; s. Claude Bryan and Sarah Frances (McCook) P.; student Limestone Coll., 1960-61, USAF Acad., 1961-65; B.A. magna cum laude, Clemson U., 1966; M.A. (NIH fellow), Duke, 1970, Ph.D., 1971; m. Diane Julian Mitchell, July 24, 1965; children—John Michael, Susan Dawn. Research cons. Manpower Improvement Through Community Effort Project, Durham, N.C., 1967; economist econ. research unit Fed. Deposit Ins. Corp., Washington, 1970-71; research economist Oak Ridge Nat. Lab., 1971-—; lectr. Sch. Bus., U. Tenn., 1972. Mem. Population Assn. Am., Am., So., Western (chmn. session on microeconomic theory 1971 meeting) econ. assns., Rocky Mountain Social Sci. Assn. Author: The Nonprofessional in a Rural Manpower Program, 1968; Some Aspects of the Demand for Children in the United States: An Economic Analysis of Household Reproductive Decisions, 1971; The Bank Holding Company Movement in Perspective, 1971; Changes in the Concentration of Manufacturing in Metropolitan Areas, 1972. Home: 100 Paine Lane Oak Ridge TN 37830 Office: Oak Ridge Nat Lab 4500 N K 244 PO Box X Oak Ridge TN 37830

PATRICK, JERRY HAMILTON, cosmetic co. exec.; b. Charlotte, N.C., Oct. 22, 1940; s. Earle Wilmore and Mary Evelyn (Jeter) P.; B.S., N.C. State U., 1963; m. Marion Lea Morris, Dec. 29, 1962; children— Kimberlea Marion, Jerry Hamilton. Personnel trainee Burlington Industries, Wake Forest, N.C., 1963-64; asst. personnel mgr., Raeford, 1964-65, asst. to div. personnel dir., Halifax, Va., 1965, personnel mgr., Raeford, N.C., 1965-66, Clarksville, Va., 1966-68; personnel mgr. Almay Cosmetics, Apex, N.C., 1968-—; mem. retirement com. Schieffelin & Co., N.Y.C., 1971-—. Town Commr., Apex, N.C., 1971-—; chmn. United Fund, 1971; mem. Triangle J Council Govt., 1972-—. Mem. Apex Jr. C. of C. (1st. v.p. projects 1969-70), Apex C. of C. (dir. 1968-71), Raleigh Wake Personnel Assn., Sigma Alpha Epsilon. Republican. Methodist (chmn. edn. 1970-72, v.p. council ministries 1970-71). Home: 1208 Maple Av Apex NC 27502 Office: Box 748 Almay Cosmetics Apex NC 27502

PATRICK, JOHN ACKERMAN, physician; b. St. George, S.C., Feb. 11, 1931; s. John Ackerman and Mary Elizabeth (Weeks) P.; A.A., North Greenville Jr. Coll., 1951; B.S., Furman U., 1953; M.D., U. S.C., 1957; m. Mildred Lucille Leopard, Aug. 3, 1954; children—Neva Karen, Shane Ackerman, Brian Timothy, Daniel Stephen. Intern medicine U. S.C. Teaching Hosps., Charleston, 1957-58; pvt. practice medicine, York, S.C., 1960-—; mem. staff York Gen., Divine Savior hosps., chief staff, 1962-63. Bd. dirs. Broad River Tb Assn., 1969-70. Served to capt. M.C., AUS, 1958-60. Mem. A.M.A., S.C., York County med. assns., York Jr. C. of C., Am. Legion. Democrat. Baptist (deacon 1963-66). Rotarian (dir. 1965, 68-69, pres., 1968-69). Home: 303 Woodland Dr York SC 29745 Office: 43 N Congress St York SC 29745

PATRICK, JOHN VERNON, JR., lawyer; b. Birmingham, Ala., May 7, 1931; s. John Vernon and Dorothy Gladys (Powell) P.; A.B. magna cum laude, Harvard, 1952, LL.B. magna cum laude, 1955; m. Sylvia Joyce Brown, May 22, 1965; children—Vera Kathryn, Virginia Gladys. Admitted to Ala. bar, 1955; law clk. to Justice Hugo L. Black, U.S. Supreme Ct., 1956-59; asso. White, Bradley, Arant, All & Rose, 1959-61, 63; spl. asst., loan officer Bur. for Near East and S. Asia, A.I.D., U.S. Dept. State, 1962; partner Vann & Patrick. 1963-65, Berkowitz, Lefkovits & Patrick and predecessor firms, 1965-—. Pres., Jefferson-Blount-St. Clair Mental Health Authority, 1969-—. Bd. dirs. Jefferson County Assn. for Mental Health (pres. 1967-68). Served to 1st lt. AUS, 1956-59. Mem. Am., Ala., Birmingham bar assns., Phi Beta Kappa. Democrat. Baptist. Clubs: Downtown, The Club, Mountain Brook Swim and Tennis. Contbr. articles to profl. jours. Home: 4140 Old Leeds Lane Birmingham AL 35213 Office: City Nat Bank Bldg Birmingham AL 35203

PATRICK, WALTER, lawyer; b. Harrodsburg, Ky., May 20, 1926; s. William L. and Martha (Shepherd) P.; J.D., U. Ky., 1951; m. Nancy Shinnick, Dec. 2, 1951; children—Tandy Carol, William Lewis. Admitted to Ky. bar. 1951, since practiced in Lawrenceburg; city atty., Lawrenceburg, 1952-72; circuit judge 53d Jud. Dist., 1972-—. Dir. Anderson Nat. Bank. Served to 1st lt., inf. AUS, 1944-46; PTO. Mem Am. Legion (comdr. 1954-55), C. of C. (pres. 1958-62), Phi Sigma Kappa, Phi Delta Phi. Democrat. Mem. Christian Ch. Rotarian (pres. 1957-58). Home: Route 2 Lawrenceburg KY 40342 Office: Gordon Bldg Lawrenceburg KY 40342

PATRICK, WILLIAM LEIGHTON, JR., city ofcl.; b. Meridian, Miss., Sept. 28, 1926; s. William Leighton and Mary Agnes (Joiner) P.; B.S., Miss. State Coll., 1948; m. Evelyn McCraw, Jan. 23, 1949; children—Deborah Patricia, Julia Leigh, Pamela Joiner. Owner, mgr. Patrick Radio Supply, 1953-69; mayor City of Laurel (Miss.), 1969-—; cons. elec. engr. Mem. exec. com. Miss. Municipal Assn., 1969-—, chmn. budget and finance com., 1971, chmn. pub. safety com., 1969-—; chmn. Nat. League of Cities, 1967-69; 1st chmn. Laurel Urban Renuewal Agy., 1967-69. Served with USNR, 1950-52; Korea. Mem. Miss. Law Enforcement Assn., Miss. Soc. Profl. Engrs. Republican. Presbyn. (elder 1965-—). Rotarian (pres. 1965), K.P. Clubs: Laurel Country, Dixie Golf (Laurel, Miss.). Home: 1315 18th St Laurel MS 39440 Office: City Hall Corner Oak St and 5th Av Laurel MS 39440

PATRICK, WILLIAM TILDEN, JR., dentist; b. Hampton, Va., Nov. 4, 1906; s. William Tilden and Sally Miller (West) P.; student U. Richmond, 1927-28; D.D.S., Emory U., 1933; m. Faith Crawford, Aug. 26, 1935. Practice of gen. dentistry and dental surgery, Hampton, 1933-—; mem. staff Dixie Hosp. Mem. Peninsula Dental Soc., Peninsula C. of C., Nat. Hist. Soc., Phi Gamma Delta, Phi Omega. Mason (32 deg., Shriner), Lion. Clubs: James River Country, Hampton Yacht, Huntington. Home: 1324 Chesapeake Av Hampton VA 23361 Office: 152 Chesterfield Rd Hampton VA 23361

PATTEN, IRA EUNICE BARRETT (MRS. GERLAND PAUL PATTEN), real estate and investment co. exec.; b. Greenville, Miss.; d. Ernest Arthur and Kittie Winfield (Walker) Barrett; student U. Ark., 1923, Nat. U. Mexico, 1960; m. Gerland Paul Patten, June 10, 1927; children—Gerald William (dec.), Yvonne Claire (Mrs. Yvonne Claire Law). With Western Union, 1924-27, HOLC, 1934-37; clk. U.S. Employment Security, 1942; head central files OPA, 1942-43; with U.S. C.E., 1943-60, cost accountant clk., 1943-60; sec.-treas., dir. Gerland P. Patten & Co., Little Rock, 1965-—; sec.-treas. Garland P. Patten Devel. Corp., 1972-—. Pres. Ladies Aux. of St. Vincents Infirmary, Little Rock, 1969-70, also vol.; treas. Girls Tng. Sch. Aux., Little Rock, 1965. Mem. Bookfellows (v.p. 1969-70, pres. 1971-73), Little Rock Musical Coterie, Ark. Assn. for Mental Health, Gaines House Aux. Methodist (treas. Womans Soc. Christian service, 1961-67, pres. 1972-73). Clubs: Fine Arts, Little Rock. Home: 8 Sunset Circle Little Rock AR 72207 Office: Nat Investors Life Bldg Little Rock AR 72201

PATTEN, ZEBOIM CARTTER, state senator, banker; b. Chattanooga, Feb. 2, 1903; s. Z.C. and Sarah (Key) P.; grad. Asheville Sch. for Boys, 1921; B.S., Cornell U., 1925; D.C.L., U. of South, 1962; m. Elizabeth Bryan, Aug. 19, 1931; children—Sarah (Mrs. Philip Haines Gwynn), Emma (Mrs. Beverly Allen Casey, Jr.), Zeboim Cartter III and W. A. Bryan (twins). Asst. treas. to v.p. Vol. State Life Ins. Co., 1928-39, now dir.; dir. Hamilton Nat. Bank; chmn. bd. First Fed. Savs. & Loan Assn. of Chattanooga. Mem. Tenn. Ho. of Reps., 1958-60, Tenn. Senate, 1961-—. Mem. Tenn. Hist. Commn. Trustee U. Chattanooga; chmn. bd. Bonny Oaks Sch. Served to lt. USCGR, 1942-44. Recipient Distinguished Service award Kiwanis Club, 1969; named Tenn. Conservationist of Year, 1970. Mem. Chattanooga Hist. Assn. (pres. 1949; treas. 1949-56). Episcopalian. Author: A Tennessee Chronicle, 1953; Signal Mountain and Walden's Ridge, 1962; So Firm a Foundation, 1968. Home: 406 N Palisades Dr Signal Mountain TN 37377 Office: 33 Patten Pkwy Chattanooga TN 37402

PATTERSON, ANDY JAMES, educator, composer; b. Gordon, Tex., Feb. 20, 1929; s. Andrew Ebenezer and Ida Kate (Fulferi) P.; B.A. in Music, Tex. Christian U., 1948, Mus.M., 1951; Mus.D., Fla. State U., 1969; m. Beverly Jane Shaw, Jan. 25, 1963; children—Andy James, Michael. Adminstrv. asst. to dean fine arts, instr. music Tex. Christian U., Ft. Worth, 1948-51, 53-56; grad. asst. music Fla. State U., Tallahassee, 1956-58; asst. prof. music Fla. A and M U., 1967-68; asst. prof. music Ga. Tchrs. Coll., Statesboro, 1958-59; mem. faculty Hardin-Simmons U., Abilene, Tex., 1959-—, asso. prof. music, 1959-69, prof., 1969-—, chmn. dept. theory and composition, 1959-—, also chmn. grad. studies in music. Served with AUS, 1951-53. Andy J. Patterson award named in his honor Theta Lambda chpt. Phi Mu Alpha-Sinfonia at Hardin-Simmons U.; recipient 1st place award orchestral composition Tex. Composers League Competition Contest, 1969. Mem. Am. Soc. U. Composers, Am. Music Center, Inc., Am. Assn. U. profs. (chpt. pres. 1964-66), Nat. Assn. Coll. Wind and Percussion Instrs., Southeastern Comosers League, Pi Kappa Lambda, Phi Mu Alpha-Sinfonia (province gov. 1962-66). Composer large works for orch., sonatas, songs and choral works, piano and organ works, concerti for various instruments, others. Home: 1642 Swenson St Abilene TX 79603

PATTERSON, ARCHIBALD OSCAR, civil engr.; b. Monroe, Ga., Dec. 26, 1908; s. Archibald Oscar and Katharine (Hensler) P.; B.S., Ga. Inst. Tech. 1929; m. Gwendolyn Maybelle Theiling, Sept. 2, 1933; children— Katharine Maybelle, James Archibald. Civil engr. Interstate Commerce Commn., Washington, 1929-30; hydraulic engr. U.S. Geol. Survey, Augusta, Me., 1930-32, Charleston, W.Va., 1932-35, Chattanooga, 1935, Lebanon, Tenn., 1936-37, Fayetteville, Tenn., 1937-38 Chattanooga, 1938-41, Knoxville, Tenn., 1942-47; dist. engr. Fla. dist., surface water br., Ocala, 1947-64; dir. div. water resources Fla. Bd. Conservation, Tallahassee, 1964-67; dir. Fla. Water Resources Research Center, prof. environmental engring. U. Fla., Gainesville, 1967-70; cons. engr., 1970-—. Recipient Meritorious Service award U.S. Dept. Interior, 1965. Fellow Am. Soc. C.E. (past pres. Fla. sect.). Presbyn. Mason. Home and office: 1444 SE 8th St Ocala FL 32670

PATTERSON, BENNETT BURR, lawyer; b. McCrory, Ark., Aug. 14, 1899; s. Marshall H. and Ethel E. (Lippman) P.; B.A., Hendrix Coll., 1918; postgrad. U. Ark., 1918; LL.B., Georgetown U., 1922; m. June Barbarin, Aug. 13, 1940; children—Sandra (Mrs. L.C. Woods), Kathleen June (Mrs. Wayne Merek). Admitted to Tex. bar, 1922, D.C. bar, 1922, U.S. Supreme Ct. bar, 1951; mem. firm Patterson & McDaniel and predecessor, Houston, 1922-48, sr. partner, 1948-—. Prof. Houston Sch. Law, 1926-34; spl. lectr. Rice U., 1956-57, U. Houston, 1957, 65-66. Bd. dirs. Houston Sch. for Deaf Children. Served with U.S. Army, 1918-19. Recipient 1st award Am. Acad. Pub. Affairs Los Angeles, 1956. Mem. Am., Tex. bar assns., Am. Judicature Soc., C. of C. Episcopalian. Mason (33 deg., Shriner). Clubs: Sertoma (past pres.) (Houston); Sagewood Country. Author: The Forgotten Ninth Amendment, 1955. Office: Houston 1st Savs Bldg 711 Fannin St Houston TX 77002

PATTERSON, CHARLES MEADE, geologist, author; b. Waynesburg, Pa., June 24, 1919; s. Robert Meade and Margaret (Milligan) P.; B.A., Coll. Wooster, 1940; M.A., Columbia, 1942; M.S., Cal. Inst. Tech., 1943; Ph.D., Columbia, 1947; m. Florence Arnelda Leach, June 16, 1943 (div. Jan. 1947); m. 2d, Constance Jacqueline Lawson, June 1947 (annulled 1950); m. 3d, Anna Marie Hibbs, Oct. 26, 1967. Geologist, Gulf Research & Devel. Co., Pitts., 1947-53; antique firearms specialist and staff editor Nat. Rifle Assn. Am., Washington, 1953-57; lime and calcium specialist Bur. Mines, Washington, 1957-63, sci. editor, 1964-67; marine geologist U.S. Naval Oceanographic Office, Washington, 1967-—. Hon. curator West Point Mus., 1952-58. Served to capt. USAAF, 1942-46. Fellow Co. of Mil. Historians; mem. Geol. Soc. Am., Am. Geophys. Union, Pa. Gun Collectors Assn. (pres. 1950-51), Research Soc. Am., Potomac (pres. 1955-57), Md. (pres. 1965-66) arms collectors assns. Author: (with Paul F. Kerr) Alteration of Santa Rita, N.M., Copper Mine, 1947; (with J.M. Kalman) A Pictorial History of U.S. Single Shot Martial Pistols, 1957. Sci. staff editor A Dictionary of Mining, Mineral and Related Terms, 1963-67; editor Gun Report, 1959-—. Home: PO Box 784 Hyattsville MD 20783 Office: US Naval Oceanographic Office Washington DC 20390

PATTERSON, DENNIS AUDEL, savs. and loan exec.; b. Newport News, Va., Nov. 24, 1925; s. Conway De Witt and Annie Eugenia (Brown) P.; diploma Hampton Inst., 1948; m. Frances R. Wright, Feb. 12, 1950; 1 dau., Lauren V. Sec., M.S.P. Enterprises, Inc., 1966-—, Sycamore Land Corp., 1967-—; v.p. Community Savs. & Loan Assn., Newport News, 1965-—; pres. Pat's Elec. Contracting, Inc., Newport News, 1948-—; dir. Bank of Newport News. Vice pres. bd. Newport News chpt. N.A.A.C.P., 1970-—. Mem. Democratic Exec. Com., 1969-—. Bd. dirs. Hampton Rhoads Boys Club. Served with AUS, 1943-46: PTO. Mem. Am. Inst. Mgmt., Nat. Bus. League (dir. 1970-72), Nat. Elec. Contractors Assn., Kappa Alpha Psi. Club: Dochiki Social. Home: 1336 26th St Newport News VA 23607 Office: 2704 Chestnut Av Newport News VA 23607

PATTERSON, DONIS DEAN, clergyman; b. Holmesville, O., Apr. 27, 1930; s. Raymond J. and Louella (Glasgow) P.; B. Sc., Ohio State U., 1952, postgrad., 1960-61; postgrad. Harvard Div. Sch., 1956, Coll. Preachers, 1959, Inst. Advanced Pastoral studies, 1960, U.S. Army Command and Gen. Staff Coll.; S.T.B., Episcopal Theol. Sch., 1957, M.Div., 1971; m. JoAnne Nida, Dec. 22, 1951; children—Christopher Nida, Andrew Joseph. Ordained to ministry Episcopal Ch., 1957; asst. Ch. Holy Nativity, South Weymouth, Mass., 1954-55, All Saints' Ch., Chelmsford, Mass., 1955-57; rector St. Andrew's Ch., Washington Court House, O., 1957-63; rector St. Mark's Episcopal Ch., Venice, Fla., 1963-70, headmaster Day Sch., 1963-70; rector All Saints Episcopal Ch., Winter Park, Fla., 1970-—. Chmn. armed forces div Episcopal Ch., 1958-63; moblzn. designee chief chaplains Dept. Army, 1959-—; chmn. div. evangelism Episcopal Diocese of South Fla., 1964-68, mem. exec. bd., 1964, 1965-69, chmn. div. Christian living, 1968-69, chmn. div. Christian edn., 1969-70; mem. bd. Episcopal Diocese of S.W. Fla., 1969-70; mem. Orlando Deanery Council, 1970-—; chmn. armed forces div. Episcopal Diocese of Central Fla., 1970-—; field rep. Anglican Fellowship of Prayer. Dist. chmn. Boy Scouts Am., 1960-63, instnl. rep., 1957-72, commr., 1958-60; chmn. clergy div. United Appeal, 1970-71. Bd. dirs., commr. Venice Housing Authority; bd. dirs. Sarasota (Fla.)-Manatee Guidance Center; trustee Fla. Episcopal Coll., 1970-—. Served with AUS, 1952-54; Korea; lt. col. Res. Recipient George Washington medal Freedoms Found. Valley Forge, 1965-71. Mem. Soc. Colonial Wars, S.A.R. (state chaplain), Mil. Order World Wars (chaplain) Am. Legion (chaplain), Res. Officers Assn., Fayette Ministerial Assn. (pres.), Lambda Chi Alpha. Rotarian (pres. 1966-67). Club: Venice Yacht (fleet chaplain). Contbr. articles to various publs. Home: 210 Trismen Terrace Winter Park FL 32789 Office: 338 E Lyman Av Winter Park Fl 32789

PATTERSON, DWIGHT F(LEMING), banker; b. Lanford, S.C., Nov. 19, 1907; s. William L. and Janie F. (Fleming) P.; A.B., Wofford Coll., 1929, LL.D., 1959; diploma Grad. Sch. Banking Rutgers U., 1940; m. Mary Smith, June 18, 1935; children—Dwight F., Lawrence Leon, Drayton Smith. Asst. cashier Palmetto Bank, Laurens, S.C., 1931-36, cashier, 1936-46, exec. v.p., dir., 1946-52, pres., 1952-—, chmn. bd.; dir. Laurens Indsl. Devel. Corp., Laurens Holding Co., Investors Nat. Life Ins. Co., Inc., Palmetto Spinning Corp., Laurens. Trustee Laurens City Schs., 1947-53, Laurens Co. Library, Laurens Sch. Dist. 55, 1963-—; sec. bd. trustees Columbia (S.C.) Coll., 1948-50; sec. bd. trustees Wofford Coll., 1948-68, chmn. bd., 1948-58, trustee 1968-—; mem. exec. council Methodist Coll. Found. S.C.; mem. bd. edn. Upper S.C. Conf. Methodist Ch., 1944-48. Mem. Ind. Bankers Assn. Am. (exec. council 1956-—), S.C. Bankers Assn. (pres. 1955-56), Blue Key, Phi Beta Kappa, Pi Kappa Phi. Methodist (steward). Kiwanian (past pres.). Club: Piedmont (Spartanburg S.C.). Contbr. articles on current banking to trade mags. Home: 701 W Main St Laurens SC 29360 Office: Pub Sq Laurens SC 29360

PATTERSON, EUGENE CORBETT, newspaper editor; b. Valdosta, Ga., Oct. 15, 1923; s. William C. and Annabel (Corbett) P.; student North Ga. Coll., Dahlonega, 1940-42; A.B. in Journalism, U. Ga., 1943; hon. degrees Emory U., Tuskegee Inst., Tusculum Coll., Oglethorpe Coll., Roanoke Coll., Mercer U.; LL.B. (hon.), Harvard, 1969; m. Mary S. Carter, Aug. 19, 1950; 1 dau., Mary A. Reporter Temple (Tex.) Daily Telegram and Macon (Ga.) Telegraph, 1947-48; mgr. for S.C., United Press, 1948-49, night bur. mgr., N.Y.C., 1949-53, mgr. London (Eng.) bur., chief corr. U.K., 1953-56; v.p., exec. editor Atlanta Jour. and Atlanta Constn., 1956-60; editor Atlanta Constn., 1960-68; mng. editor, Washington Post, 1968-71; prof. Duke U., 1971-72; editor, pres. St. Petersburg (Fla.) Times, 1972-—. Vice chmn. U.S. Commn. Civil Rights 1964-68. Served to capt. AUS, 1943-47; capt. Res. Decorated Silver Star, Bronze Star with oak leaf cluster; recipient Pulitzer prize for editorial writing, 1966. Mem. Am. Soc. Newspaper Editors (dir. 1966-71), Sigma Delta Chi. Lutheran. Home: 1967 Brightwaters Snell Isle St Petersburg FL 33704 Office: 490 1st Av S St Petersburg FL 33731

PATTERSON, FRANK WILLARD, journalist; b. Alva, Okla., July 6, 1907; s. Otis Harvey and Myrtle May (Holder) P.; B.A., Okla. Bapt. U., 1928; M.Th., Southwestern Bapt. Theol. Sem., 1932; M.A. in Spanish Lit., Nat. U. Mexico, 1940; D.Th., Central Bapt. Theol. Sem., 1957; m. Pauline Widner Gilliland, Sept. 7, 1933; children—Burton Harvey, Donald Ray Aldridge. Ordained to ministry Bapt. ch., 1926; pastor Bapt. chs., Okla., Ark., 1930-38; missionary, Mexico, 1939-40; bus. mgr. Bapt. Spanish Pub. House, El Paso, Tex., 1941-42, gen. dir., 1943-70; lit. rep. So. Baptist Fgn. Mission Bd. in Latin Am., 1971-72; editor Revista Evangelica, 1944-55, El Expositor Biblico, 1944-71. Cons. publ. work at seminars, confs., U.S., abroad. Mem. Commn. on Christian Teaching and Tng., Bapt. World Alliance, 1960-—. Recipient Outstanding Alumni Achievement award, Okla. Bapt. U., 1968, Distinguished Alumni award Southwestern Bapt. Theol. Sem., 1970. Author: El Plan Financiero de Dios, 1940; Sermones Selectos de Diez Evangelistas Famosas, 1946; Sermones Selectos de Diez Predicadores Eminentes, 1951; Manual de Finanzas para Iglesias, 1952; J.E. Davis, Printer for God, 1956; Evangelizando con el Espiritu Santo, 1958; Caribbean Quest, 1960; Manual para la Escuela Dominical, 1962; Impresor al Servicio de Dios, 1966; Como Escribir para Ser Entendido, 1972. Office: 7000 Alabama St Box 4255 El Paso TX 79914

PATTERSON, GEORGE ELLIOTT, JR., lawyer; b. East Orange, N.J., Oct. 24, 1916; s. George Elliott and Beatrice (Fair) P.; A.B., Dartmouth, 1939; LL.B., Cornell U., 1942; m. Maxine Webb, May 11, 1944; children— Caroline A. (Mrs. John M. Brumbaugh), Kathleen Fair. Admitted to Fla. bar, 1947; gen. practice law, Miami, Fla., 1947-—. Bd. dirs., sec. Dade County Citizens Safety Council, 1964-68. Served with AUS, 1942-46. Mem. Am., Fla., Dade County bar assns., Miami-Dade County C. of C. (pres. marine council 1962-64), Phi Delta Phi, Chi Phi. Club: Coral Reef Yacht (commodore 1968-69). Home: 8285 SW 54th Av Miami FL 33143 Office: Roberts Bldg 28 W Flagler St Miami FL 33131

PATTERSON, GRADY LESLIE, JR., govt. ofcl.; b. nr. Abbeville, S.C., Jan. 13, 1924; s. Grady L. and Claudia (McLain) P.; student Clemson U., 1942-43, U. Ala., 1943; LL.B., U.S.C., 1950; m. Marjorie Harrison Faucett, Dec. 22, 1951; children—Grady Leslie III, Steven G., Marjorie Lynne, Laura Anne, Amy Susan, Mary Beth. Admitted to S.C. bar, 1950, since practiced in Abbeville; service officer Abbeville County, S.C., 1950; legal and operations officer S.C. Air N. G., Columbia, 1952-58; asst. atty. gen. S.C., Columbia, 1959-66; treas., S.C., 1967-—. Asst. gen. counsel com. lending S.C. legislature, 1960, com. on penal system, 1961; speaker sta. ETV law enforcement tng. program, 1966, on eminent domain, trials, 1967. Sec., Columbia

United Fund drive, 1965, chmn. pub. employees div., 1970. Bd. dirs. N.C., S.C. Municipal Council. Served to maj. USAAF, 1943-46, USAF, 1950-52; Korea; USAF, 1961-62. Decorated Air medal with two oak leaf clusters. Mem. S.C. Bar Assn., U. S.C. Alumni Assn. (bd. dirs. 1965-67, chmn. ann. fund drive 1967), S.C. Employees Assn. (bd. dirs. 1965-66), Nat. Assn. State Auditors, Comptrollers and Treas. (treas. 1971; v.p. 1972), Am. Legion. Presbyn. (deacon, mem. bd., elder). Home: 3016 Petigru St Columbia SC 29204 Office: Office of State Treasurer 122 Wade Hampton Bldg Columbia SC 29201

PATTERSON, HUGH B(ASKIN), JR., publisher; b. Cotton Plant, Miss., Feb. 8, 1915; s. Hugh Baskin and Martha (Wilson) P.; student Henderson State Tchrs. Coll., 1933; m. Louise Caroline Heiskell, Mar. 29, 1944; children—Carrick Heiskell, Ralph Baskin. Sales dept. Smith Printing Co., Pine Bluff, Ark., 1933-36; asst. to sales mgr. Democrat Printing & Lithographing Co., Little Rock, 1936-38, promotion mgr., 1940-42; sales dept. Art Metal Constrn. Co., N.Y.C., 1938-39; planning and prodn. mgr. Rufus H. Darby Co., printers and pubs., Washington, 1939-40; with Ark. Gazette, 1946—, successively nat. advt. mgr., advt. dir., asst. bus mgr., publisher, 1948—; pres., treas. Gazette Pub. Co.; pres. Ark. Bldg. Co. Bd. dirs. Fgn. Policy Assn.; bd. visitors U. Ark. at Little Rock. Served to maj. AC, 1942-46. Gazette recipient Pulitzer Gold medal for pub. service, 1957, Freedom award Freedom House, 1958. Mem. Am., So. (pres. 1959-60) newspaper pubs. assns., Inter Am. Press Assn. (dir.), Council Fgn. Relations, Internat. Press Inst., Sigma Delta Chi. Democrat. Presbyn. Clubs: Overseas Press (N.Y.); Little Rock Country. Home: 24 Edgehill Rd Little Rock AR 72207 Office: 112 W 3d St Little Rock AR 72201

PATTERSON, JACKSON TAYLOR, ednl. adminstr.; b. Clarksville, Ark., Apr. 29, 1915; s. William N. and Clara (Burt) P.; student Coll. of Ozarks, 1934-35; grad. Draughon's Bus. Coll., 1937; m. Lucile Sanders, Dec. 24, 1937; children—Jack T., Clara Ann. Accountant, Allis Chalmers Mfg. Co., Dallas, 1937-41; N.Am. Aviation Co., Dallas, 1942-43; treas., bus. mgr. Coll. of Ozarks, Clarksville, 1943—. Mem. exec. bd. Westark council Boy Scouts Am. Mem. So. Assn. Coll. and Univ. Bus. Officers, Clarksville C. of C., Nat., Ark. edn. assns. Democrat. Presbyn. (elder). Mason (32 deg), Rotarian. Home: College Station Clarksville AR 72830

PATTERSON, JAMES NATHANIEL, JR., gen. contractor exec.; b. Wichita Falls, Tex., Mar. 10, 1927; s. James Nathaniel and Hal (Godley) P.; B.S., Tex. A. and M. U., 1948; postgrad. Mass. Inst. Tech., 1950; m. Lila Thrace Mathews, July 22, 1950; children—Debra Alice, James N. III, Jana Stone. Engr. Thos. S. Byrne, Inc., 1948-58, v.p., 1958-62, pres., 1962—. Served with AUS, 1951-53. Mem. Assn. Gen. Contractor of Am. (pres. Ft. Worth chpt. 1964-65). Home: 1724 Aztec Ft Worth TX 76112 Office: Ft Worth Nat Bank Bldg Ft Worth TX 76102

PATTERSON, JAMES NEVILLE, state justice; b. Monticello, Miss., Feb. 16, 1916; s. Edmund Burke and Irma (McEvoy) P.; LL.B., U. Miss., 1939; m. Catherine R. Stough, July 9, 1943; children—Martha Sue, Irma Catherine, James Neville. Admitted to Miss. bar, 1939; mem. firm Patterson & Patterson, Monticello, Miss., 1939-40, 45-47; atty. Fed. Land Bank, New Orleans, 1940-41; chancellor Chancery Ct., judge Youth Ct. div. 13th Miss. Jud. Dist., from 1947; asso. justice Miss. Supreme Ct. Served to capt. AUS, 1941-45; ETO. Mem. Miss. State Bar, Am. Legion. Democrat. Methodist. Office: Miss Supreme Ct Jackson MS 39205*

PATTERSON, JAMES R., architect; b. Dallas, Nov. 25, 1937; s. Jessie R. and Hassie (Altom) P.; B.Arch., Tex. A. and M. U., 1961; M.S. (McKim fellow), Columbia, 1962; m. Charlotte L. Burgess, Jan. 29, 1960; children—John Bradley, James Paul, Cayann. With Mario J. Ciampi, Architect, San Francisco, 1962, Harrell & Hamilton, Architects, Dallas, 1963; dir. Sch. Architecture Research and Grad. Center, Tex. A. and M. U., also dir. research projects in bldg., planning and constrn., 1963-69; pres. Internat. Bldg. Systems, Dallas, 1967—. Tech. assistance cons. Rehab. Services Adminstrn., Washington, 1968—; tech. cons. People to People Health Found., 1969—. William Kinne Fellows fellow Western Europe, 1962. Mem. Am., Tex. hosp. assns., Tau Beta Phi, Alpha Rho Chi. Contbr. articles to profl. jours. Home: 11515 St Michaels Dr Dallas TX 77230 Office: #900 3000 Diamond Park Dallas TX 75247

PATTERSON, JOHN MELVIN, physician; b. Nettleton, Miss., Dec. 16, 1925; s. John Lee and Melva (Black) P.; B.S., U. Miss., 1950; M.D., Jefferson Med. Sch., 1954; m. Maxine McDaniel, Aug. 24, 1952; children— Bettye Claire, Mary Lise, Patti Ann. Intern, Bapt. Meml. Hosp., Memphis, 1954-55; gen. practice medicine, Pontotoc, Miss., 1955—; mem. staff Pontotoc Community Hosp. Trustee Traceway Manor, Tupelo, Miss., Pontotoc Community Hosp. Served with USNR, 1944-47. Mem. Miss., N.E. Miss. med. socs., A.M.A., Am. Acad. Gen. Practice. Methodist (trustee) Lion. Home: 404 E Oxford St Pontotoc MS 38863 Office: 113 Washington St Pontotoc MS 38863

PATTERSON, JOSIE MILDRED LEE, educator; b. Levita, Tex., Aug. 18, 1927; d. Robert E. and Epsie Elizabeth (Simpson) Lee; B.A., S.W. Tex. State Coll., 1949; M.A., Baylor U., 1954, M.A., 1967; m. Jimmie Wyvon Patterson, May 20, 1952; children—Jimmy Dale, Pamela Jo. Tchr. pub. schs., Levita, Rochelle, Pearl, Paint Rock, Talpa, Bangs (all Tex.); 1946-57; asso. prof. English, Howard Payne Coll., Brownwood, Tex., 1962—. Recipient Outstanding Faculty Woman of Year award, Assn. Women Students, 1966, 68. Mem. Coll. Conf. Tchrs. English of Tex., Am. Assn. U. Women, Pacific Modern Lang. Assn., Dist. XI English Assn., Sigma Tau Delta. Club: Faculty Womens. Baptist. Home: 2201 11th St Brownwood TX 76801

PATTERSON, MILDRED L(UCRETIA), judge; b. Guthrie, Okla., July 30, 1912; d. Columbus W. and Lydia K. (Cash) Patterson; student Okla. City Coll. Law, 1941-45. Legal sec., bookkeeper, underwriter, 1931-51; admitted to Okla. bar, 1945; head law book dept. Co-Op. Pub. Co., Guthrie, 1951-54; asst. editor Ofcl. Session Laws of Okla., 1951, editor, 1953, 55, 57, 59, 61; asst. editor New Ins. Laws of Okla., 1951; county judge Logan County, Guthrie, 1955-69, asso. dist. judge, 1969—. Pres. bd. dirs. Guthrie Community Chest Fund, 1957-58; asso. mem. Gov.'s Com. on Furtherance of Employment for Physically Handicapped, 1957, 58—; mem. Pres.'s Com. on Handicapped; dir. Okla. Mental Health Assn. Trustee I.O.A. Ranch for Boys, Perkins, Okla.; mem. nat. council U.S.O. Mem. Okla. Council Juvenile Ct. Judges (sec.-treas. 1963-65), Am. Legion Aux., Nat. Council Juvenile Ct. Judges, Okla. Juvenile Officers Assn., Bus. and Profl. Women's Club (past pres.), Am. Life Assn. (dir.), Okla. Assn. Women Lawyers (state sec. 1948), Okla. County Officers Assn. (dist. pres.), Iota Tau Tau. Mem. Christian Ch. Mem. Order Eastern Star, Daus. of Nile. Home: 215 N Elm St Guthrie OK 73044 Office: Ct House Guthrie OK 73044

PATTERSON, PAUL STOYLE, advt. exec.; b. Mt. Vernon, O., July 1, 1904; s. James John and Mary Anna (Stoyle) P.; student Western Res. U., 1923, 25-26, U. Pitts., 1930; m. Susan Clark, Dec. 29, 1939; children—Virginia Ann (Mrs. Jesse Callahan Jr.), Jan Judge, James Reynolds. Advt. mgr. zone 5, Nat. Dairy Products Co., Pitts., 1942-53; dir. advt. Fla. Citrus Commn., Lakeland, 1953-57; v.p. Liller, Neal, Battle & Lindsey, Inc., Atlanta, 1957-69; advt. and promotion cons., 1969—. Mem. Active Voters Ga. (v.p. 1968), Brotherhood of New Hope, Atlanta (sec. 1967-68, v.p. 1969). Unitarian-Universalist (sec. 1959-60). Home and office: 496 Bryn Mawr Lane Atlanta GA 30327

PATTERSON, PHOEBE FRANCES BUMGARNER (MRS. ASHBY METCALFE PATTERSON), ch. and civic worker; b. Millers Creek, N.C.; d. George Washington and Mary Elizabeth (Nichols) Bumgarner; R.N., Baron Erlanger Hosp. Sch. Nursing, 1920; student U. Chattanooga, 1922, 36-37; m. Ashby Metcalfe Patterson, Dec. 27, 1926; 1 dau., Emma Elisabeth Metcalfe. Supr. patients Baroness Erlanger Hosp., 1920, night supt., 1922-23, record librarian, 1925-26; supt. nurses Newell Hosp., Chattanooga, 1924; pres., owner Phoebe's Antiques, Chattanooga, 1959—. Founder, Care and Share, Inc., 1959, pres., 1960-62, chmn. br., 1962—; pres. Garden Club of Riverview, 1939-41 (now hon. pres.), Chattanooga-Hamilton County Council Garden Clubs, 1941-43; v.p. Tenn. Fedn. Garden Clubs, 1943-45; a founder Chattanooga Rose Soc.; lectr. astronomy, 1945—, flower arranging and ornithology, 1938—; founder Chattanooga Early Am. Glass Club, 1963. Mem. Nat. Assn. Dealers in Antiques, Soc. Philatelic Ams., Nat. Early Am. Glass Club, Tenn. Poetry Soc. (councillor Chattanooga dist. and East Tenn.), Chattanooga Aubudon Soc. (a founder), Am. Numismatic Assn., Am. Poetry League. Methodist (pres. Woman's Soc. Christian Service 1944-46, 52-53). Contbr. poetry to various publs. Address: 1614 N Shady Circle Chattanooga TN 37405

PATTERSON, SANSON CORNELIUS, credit bur. exec.; b. McKeesport, Pa., Sept. 7, 1909; s. William Elmore and Lois Margaret (Close) P.; ed. pub. schs.; m. Mary Elizabeth Stroud, July 19, 1945; children—James Lane, Michael Anthony. Mgr., Beneficial Finance Co. Pa., Cal., Ore., Colo., 1930-40; mgr. Morr Loan Co., Pueblo, Colo., 1940-42; asst. credit mgr. May Co., Denver, 1942-43; credit mgr. Neustetter Co., Denver, 1943-50; gen. credit mgr. Winkelman Bros. Apparel, Inc., Detroit, 1950-58, J.C. Penney Co., N.Y.C., 1958-67; pres., chief exec. officer Nat. Found. Consumer Credit, Inc., Washington, 1967-69, also trustee; owner, pres. Credit Bur. New Haven, Conn., Inc., 1967-70; retail credit cons. 03-P-M Assos., 1969-70; pres. Credit Services Internat., Inc., 1971—. Mem. adv. com. to spl. com. Nat. Conf. Commrs. on Uniform State Laws, 1964—; chmn. spl. study group industry and labor on Non-Profit Commn. Debt Counseling Service, 1965-67; cons., truth in lending div. Fed. Res. Bd., Washington, 1968—. Mem. Nat. Retail Mchts. Assn. (bd. dirs. 1962-64, dir., chmn. credit mgmt. div. 1954-65), Detroit Retail Credit Men's Assn. (pres. 1953-54, dir. 1954-58), Asso. Credit Burs. Episcopalian. Mason (Shriner). Clubs: Houston, Warwick, Plaza (Houston); International (Washington). Contbr. articles in field to trade mags. Home: 831 Soboda Ct Houston TX 77024 Office: 6767 Southwest Freeway Houston TX 77036

PATTERSON, SHIRLEY DOBOS (MRS. BRADLEY HAWKES PATTERSON, JR.), govt. ofcl.; b. Oak Park, Ill.; d. Andrew and Hulda (Braese) DoBos; B.S., U. Chgo., 1943; M.A., George Washington U., 1965; m. Bradley H. Patterson, Jr., Dec. 26, 1943; children—Dawn Marie (Mrs. Ronald Jones), Bruce DoBos, Glenn Gilman, Brian Braese. Instr. child devel. and nutrition U. Md., College Park, 1954-56; field dir., camping adviser So. Md. council Girl Scouts U.S.A., Mt. Rainier, 1956-63, dir. camping Nations Capital council, Arlington, Va., 1963-64; pub. health analyst USPHS, Washington, 1964-70; staff coordinator White House Conf. on Children and Youth, 1970-71; with Am. Revolution Bicentennial Commn., Washington, 1971—. Fellow Am. Pub. Health Assn. (editor sch. health sect. newsletter 1967-69), Am. Sch. Health Assn.; mem. Phi Beta Kappa. Home: 6705 Pemberton St Bethesda MD 20034 Office: 736 Jackson Pl NW Washington DC 20276

PATTERSON, SOLON PETE, investment counselor; b. Atlanta, Nov. 11, 1935; s. Pete G. and Frances (Marinos) P.; B.B.A., Emory U., 1957, M.B.A., 1958; m. Marianna Reynolds, Oct. 29, 1960; children—John Solon, Joseph Peter. With Piedmont Adv. Corp., N.Y.C., 1958-62; v.p. Montag & Caldwell, Inc., Atlanta, 1962—; pres. Alpha Research Corp., Atlanta, 1968—; exec. v.p. Alpha Fund, Inc., Alpha Investors Fund. Trustee Gammon Theol. Sem. Named Atlanta's Outstanding Young Man of Year in Bus., 1968. Mem. Soc. Certified Financial Analysts, Atlanta Soc. Financial Analysts (pres.), Atlanta C. of C. Home: 1360 Barron Ct NW Atlanta GA 30327 Office: First Nat Bank Tower Atlanta GA 30303

PATTERSON, WAYNE, lawyer; b. Port Arthur, Tex., July 19, 1934; s. Herbert Ott and Mae Dell (Hollier) P.; B.S., Lamar State Coll. Tech., 1956; J.D., Baylor U., 1959; m. Judie Smith, May 6, 1968. Admitted to Tex. bar, 1959; asst. criminal dist. atty. Jefferson County, Tex., 1959-65; municipal judge, Port Arthur, 1965—; individual practice law, Port Arthur, 1965—. Mem. Am., Jefferson County (dir.), Port Arthur (pres. 1966-67) bar assns., Tex. Assn. Municipal Judges (dir.), Tex. Trial Lawyers Assn., Am. Judicature Soc., Phi Delta Phi. Elk. Contbr. articles to Baylor Law Rev. Home: 2895 Soloman St Port Arthur TX 77640 Office: 2300 Memorial Blvd Port Arthur TX 77640

PATTERSON, WILLIAM H., univ. dean; b. Charleston, S.C., April 10, 1913; s. William H. and Leacadia (Dawson) P.; A.B., U. S.C., 1934, M.A., 1949, Ph.D., 1952; summer student Columbia, U. Wis.; m. Frances Rhude Meetze, May 29, 1942 (div. Oct. 1970); m. 2d, Mary Alice Copeland, July 6, 1971. Draftsman FCA, 1934-37; topog. draftsman S.C. Hwy. Dept., 1937-40; archtl. engr. C.E., War Dept., 1940-43; instr. U. S.C., 1943-47, asst. prof. 1947-50, asst. to pres., 1950-52, dean adminstrn., bus. mgr. 1952-61, dean univ., 1961-66, sr. v.p., 1966-68, provost regional campuses, 1967-72, sec. bd. trustees, 1964—, provost, 1968—. Mem. Am., So., S.C. hist. assns., S.C. Soc. Engrs., Soc. History Tchr., Newcomen Soc. Eng. Episcopalian. Home: Senate Plaza Apts Columbia SC 29201

PATTESON, ALAN GUY, JR., radio sta. exec. operator, gin co. exec.; b. Jonesboro, Ark., Nov. 14, 1928; s. Alan Guy and Katherine Patricia (Carter) P.; B.S. in Agr., U. Mo., 1950; m. Carol Ann Busch, July 23, 1952; children—Christian, Lucia, Ellen, Guy, Dick. Partner, co-owner, operator Patteson Gin Co., Trumann, Ark., 1950—; co-owner, partner Patteson Bros. Farms, Trumann, 1950—; co-owner, partner, operator radio sta. KBTM AM-FM, Jonesboro, Ark., 1958—; dir. Merc. Bank, Jonesboro, 1968—; treas. Citizens Fed. Savs. & Loan, Jonesboro, 1964—. Chmn. bd. Ark. Council Human Relations, 1969-71; bd. dirs. Nat. Conf. Christians and Jews, Ark. Arts Center. Chmn. Ark. Library Trustees, 1972; treas. Eastern Ark. council Boy Scouts Am., 1960-67; chmn. Jonesboro Library Bd., 1961-70; trustee Ark. Library Commn. Ark. committeeman Republican party, 1970—. Recipient Silver Beaver award Eastern Ark. Area council Boy Scouts Am., 1971, Liberty Bell award Craighead Bar Assn., 1972. Mem. Am. Library Trustee Assn. (dir. 1971—), Jonesboro C. of C. (pres. 1965), Northeast Ark. Childhood Devel. Assn. (pres. 1966-68), Agrl. Council Ark. (mem. bd. 1954-65), Inst. Politics (dir. 1971—). Roman Catholic (chmn. parish edn. bd. 1965-67). Rotarian (pres. 1970-71). Home: 2801 Harrisburg Rd Jonesboro AR 72401 Office: 603 Madison St Jonesboro AR 72401

PATTESON, JOSEPH DRURY, JR., educator; b. Oklahoma City, Dec. 14, 1933; s. Joseph Drury and Verna June (Montooth) P.; student Baylor U., 1951, Okla. Bapt. U., 1952-54; B.A., Wheaton Coll., 1955; B.D., Southwestern Bapt. Theol. Sem., 1960, Th.D., 1965; M.A., U. Chgo., 1969; Dual fellow Rice U., 1962-63; m. Ida Mae Norris, June 14, 1958; children—Leah Renee, Jennifer Elyse. Jr. partner Patteson & Patteson, Homebuilders, Oklahoma City, 1957-69; part-time instr. philosophy and theology Judson Coll., Elgin, Ill., 1967; asso. prof. philosophy and religion Carson-Newman Coll., Jefferson City, Tenn., 1969—. Mem. Am. Acad. Religion, Am. Assn. U. Profs., Am. Philos. Assn. (Eastern div.), Phi Sigma Tau. Democrat. Baptist. Home: Box 65 Mill Springs Rd New Market TN 37820 Office: Box 2012 Carson Newman Coll Jefferson City TN 37760

PATTILLO, JOHN WALTHALL, librarian; b. Atlanta, Aug. 16, 1930; s. John Frank and Rosa Katherine (Morris) P.; B.A. in History, Emory U., 1951, M. Librarianship, 1955. Asst. gen. studies librarian Ga. Inst. Tech., Atlanta, 1956-59, acting gen. studies librarian, 1959-62, serials cataloger, 1962-64, inst. archivist, 1962-66, tech. processing librarian, 1964-66; dir. library So. Tech. Inst., Marietta, Ga., 1967—. Bd. dirs. Atlanta Civil War Roundtable. Served with AUS, 1951-54. Mem. Am., Ga., Southeastern library assns., Atlanta Hist. Soc., Delta Tau Delta. Presbyn. Home: 701 Martina Dr Atlanta GA 30305 Office: So Tech Inst Library Clay St Marietta GA 30060

PATTILLO, LEWIS CARL, civil engr.; b. Hartselle, Ala., Sept. 1, 1903; s. Marvin and Eulah (Echols) P.; B.S., Auburn U., 1925; m. Launa Freeman, Apr. 22, 1926; 1 dau., Nancy (Mrs. Richard W. Stoner). Pvt. practice as civil engr., No. Ala., 1925—. Chmn., Ala. Bd. Registration for Profl. Engrs., 1968—. Served with AUS, 1941-46. Decorated Legion of Merit with 2 oak leaf clusters, Bronze Star medal with 2 oak leaf clusters, Purple Heart; various fgn. decorations. Registered profl. engr., Ala., Ga., Tenn. Fellow Am. Soc. C.E.; mem. Ala. Soc. Profl. Engrs., Am. Congress Surveying and Mapping, Soc. Am. Mil. Engrs. Home: 610 High St Hartselle AL 35640 Office: 307 Franklin St Huntsville AL 35804

PATTISHALL, FRANKLIN DAVID, orthodontist; b. Burlington, N.C., Mar. 6, 1936; s. William Thomas and Bessie (Vincent) P.; student Elon Coll., 1954-57; D.D.S., U. N.C., 1961, M.S., 1969; m. Bennia Jo Carpenter, Dec. 19, 1959; children—Laura, Franklin David, Jane, Melissa. Pvt. practice dentistry, Morganton, N.C., 1965-67; pvt. practice orthodontics, Charlotte, N.C., 1969—. Served to lt. Dental Corps, USNR, 1961-63. Mem. Am. Dental Assn., Am. Assn. Orthodontists, So. Soc. Orthodontists, Psi Omega. Episcopalian. Club: Civitan (Charlotte, N.C.). Home: 6008 Bismark Pl Charlotte NC 28211 Office: 2301 Rama Rd Charlotte NC 28212

PATTISON, DAVID JOHN, govt. ofcl.; b. Hartford, Conn., May 4, 1937; s. William and Ruth (Anderson) P.; B.A., Am. U., 1959, J.D., 1961, M.A., 1965; m. Joyce Adams, June 13, 1959; children—Scott, Stuart, Sharon, Dwight. Corr. Fla. New Service, Washington, 1958-61; editor-reporter Bur. Nat. Affairs, Inc., Washington, 1961-63; asso. gen. counsel Nat. Assn. Life Underwriters, Washington, 1963-69; dir. liaison Office of Emergency Preparedness, Exec. Office of Pres., Washington, 1969-71, asst. to dir. for congl. and pub. affairs, 1971—. Mem. Fairfax County (Va.) Sch. Bd., 1968—, Fairfax County Juvenile Crime Study Commn., 1969. Republican candidate for Va. Ho. of Dels., 1967. Mem. Am., Va. bar assns., Va. Sch. Bds. Assn. Home: 3501 Prosperity Av Fairfax VA 22030 Office: Office of Emergency Preparedness Washington DC 20504

PATTON, ALTA CHAPMAN, legislative analyst; b. Livingston, Ala., Mar. 3, 1912; d. William Wayne and Anna (Chapman) Patton; student Livingston State Tchrs. Coll.; B.A., U. Ala., 1932; LL.B., Jones Law Sch., 1949. Social work, 1932-34; chief clk. Probate Office, Sumter County, Ala., 1935-38; stenographer State Dept. Agr., also State Atty. Gen.'s Office, 1939-46; accounts examiner VA, 1946-48; legislative analyst Legislative Reference Service, 1948—. Mem. Ala. Bar Assn., Women Lawyers Assn., Ala. Hist. Soc. English Speaking Union, Phi Mu. Democrat. Episcopalian. Home: 3010 Cloverdale Rd Montgomery AL 36106 Office: State Capitol Montgomery AL 36101

PATTON, DAVID, prof., chmn. dept. ophthalmology Baylor U. Coll. Medicine, Houston. Office: Baylor University College of Medicine Houston TX 77025*

PATTON, JAMES WELCH, educator; b. Murfreesboro, Tenn., Sept. 28, 1900; s. James Wesley and Elizabeth (Welch) P.; A.B., Vanderbilt U., 1924; A.M., U. N.C., 1925, Ph.D., 1929; m. Carlotta Dorothea Petersen, June 25, 1930; 1 dau., Emily Frances (Mrs. Sanders DeLuca). Prof. history Ga. State Woman's Coll., 1925-27; asso. prof. history The Citadel, 1929-30; asst. prof. history Wittenberg Coll., 1930-31; prof. history Converse Coll., 1931-42; prof., head dept. history and polit. sci. N.C. State Coll., 1942-48; prof. history U. N.C., 1948—, dir. So. Hist. collection, 1948-67. Mem. adv. council Civil War Centennial Commn., 1958—. Pres. S.C. Hist. Assn. 1938-39. Fellow Soc. Am. Archivists; mem. Am., So. (pres. 1956) hist. assns. Orgn. Am. Historians, Hist. Soc. N.C. (pres. 1966), English-Speaking Union (br. pres. 1966), Soc. Am. Archivists, N.C. Lit. and Hist. Assn. (pres. 1964), Phi Beta Kappa, Phi Kappa Phi, Sigma Chi. Democrat. Episcopalian. Author: Unionism and Reconstruction in Tennessee, 1934; The Women of the Confederacy (with Francis B. Simkins), 1936; editor: Minutes of the Greenville Ladies' Association in Aid of the Confederate Army, 1937; contbr. to Dictionary of Am. Biography, Dictionary of Am. History. Editor: Messages, Addresses, and Public Papers of Luther H. Hodges, Governor N.C., 1954-61, 3 vols., 1960, 62, 63. Home: 614 E Franklin St Chapel Hill NC 27514

PATTON, RAYMOND JAMES, supt. schs.; b. Harrison, Ark., Jan. 23, 1919; s. Walter G. and Fufa Belle (Pennington) P.; B.S., Central State Coll., Edmond, Okla., 1946; M.S., Okla. State U., 1950; m. Elsie Mae Morris, Mar. 8, 1939; children—James Edward, Billy Ray. Prin. high sch., Stroud, Okla., 1943-58; supt. schs., Shidler, Okla., 1958-61, Meeker, Okla., 1961-68, Chandler, Okla., 1968—. Served with AUS, 1944-45. Mem. Chandler C. of C., Am. Legion, Okla. Edn. Assn., N.E.A., Am., Okla. assns. sch. adminstrs., Okla. Sch. Bus. Ofcls. Lion. Home: 203 Moorman Dr Chandler OK 74834 Office: 15 Steele Av Chandler OK 74834

PATTON, ROBERT WILLIAM, judge; b. Wilmington, N.C., Feb. 6, 1911; s. Robert Evan and Ellinora (O'Keef) P.; student Duke, 1928-30; LL.B., U. Fla., 1933. Admitted to Fla. bar, 1933; practiced in St. Petersburg and Tampa, Fla., 1933-64; judge 13th Jud. Circuit of Fla., 1965—; asst. atty., Hillsborough County, Fla., 1959-63, county atty., 1964; dir. Real Estate Title Co., Tampa. Mem. Am., Tampa-Hillsborough County bar assns., Fla. Bar. Kiwanian. Home: 2904 Angeles St Tampa FL 33609 Office: Hillsborough County Ct House Tampa FL 33601

PATTON, ROGER DALE, banker; b. Olive Hill, Ky., June 16, 1933; s. Lon and Lula (King) P.; student Morehead U., 1954-57; m. Jenny Jo Tackett, Dec. 21, 1956; 1 son, Roger Michael. Lab. technician Gen. Refractories Co., Olive Hill, Ky., 1954-57; cashier Peoples Bank, Olive Hill, 1958-72, v.p., 1972—. Served with USAF, 1951-54. Mason. Home: Jordan Heights Olive Hill KY 41164 Office: Main St Olive Hill KY 41164

PATTON, STUART LYNN, newspaper publisher; b. Amsterdam, N.Y., Nov. 13, 1912; s. Walter Lynn and Ida (Johnson) P.; grad. Newark Sch. Fine Arts, 1932; student U. So. Cal., 1937; m. Elizabeth Prall, June 22, 1935 (dec.). Reporter, Honolulu Star-Bull., 1935-36. San Francisco News, 1936, San Francisco Chronicle, 1937; with art dept. Universal Pictures, Hollywood, Cal., 1937, asso. art dir., 1937-39; editorial, advt. work So. Cal. Assn. Newspapers, 1939-41; comdr. U.S. Maritime Commn., 1941-49, successively dir. West Coast pub. relations, editor MAST mag., exec. officer Pacific Coast operations; promotion dir. Bklyn. Eagle, 1949-55; pub. All Fla. mag., Ocala, 1955-60; pub. So. Arts Syndicate, 1960—. Recipient two citations Comdt. U.S. Maritime Commn., 1943. Mem. Nat. Newspaper Promotion Assn. (pres. N.Y. chpt. 1953-55). Author: 52 Important and Historical Florida Landmarks, 1967. Home: Lake Coronado Oklawaha FL Address: 121 Barcliff Av Chatham MA 02633

PATTON, VINCENT DION, state ofcl.; b. Pikesville, Tenn., Nov. 7, 1920; s. John A. and Sarah (Swafford) P.; B.Chem. Engring., U. Fla., 1949; M.S. in San. Engring., U. N.C., 1958; m. Sarah Bowyer, Sept. 2, 1950. Chem. engr. Fla. Citrus Commn., Lakeland, 1949-51, Hawkridge Metals Co., Boston, 1955-56; san. engr. Fla. Bd. Health, Jacksonville, 1956-62, dir. div. indsl. wastes, 1962-68; dir. Fla. Air and Water Pollution Control Commn., 1968-69; exec. dir. Fla. Air and Water Pollution Control Dept., 1969-71; exec. dir. Fla. Pollution Control Dept., 1971—. Sec. Fla. Air Pollution Control Commn. Served with AUS, 1942-45. Mem. Am. (chmn. Fla. sect.), Fla. planning and civic assns., Fla. Pollution Control Assn. (pres. 1969), Air Pollution Control Assn. (chmn. 1968), Delta Omega. Democrat. Episcopalian. Contbr. articles to profl. jours. Home: 1951 Meridian Rd Tallahassee FL 32303 Office: Bank Bldg Tallahassee FL 32301

PATZIG, GEORGE ALVIN, judge, lawyer; b. Carrollton, Tex., Dec. 27, 1935; s. Charles I. and Margie (Speer) P.; Asso. Sci., Arlington Jr. Coll., 1957; B.A., So. Methodist U., 1961, J.D., 1963; m. Janis A. Boedeker, Sept. 2, 1961; children—Michael Keith, Dina Kaylynn.Admitted to Tex. bar, 1963; practiced in Carrollton, 1963-67; city judge, Carrollton, 1968—. Vice pres., dir., gen. council Calfar Investments, Inc., Dallas, 1965—; dir. Ranchland Camps, Inc., Roanoke, Tex. Justice of peace, Dallas County, Tex., 1967—. Mem. Am. Bar Assn., State Bar Tex., Justice of Peace and Constables Assn. Tex. (dir. 1969-70). Methodist (trustee). Home: 1808 S Crest St Carrollton TX 75006 Office: 1411 W Beltline Rd Richardson TX 75080

PAUL, E(LL) GRADY, JR., lawyer; b. Montgomery, Ala., Oct. 7, 1918; s. E. Grady and Mamie (Blackburn) P.; student U. Richmond, 1939-41; LL.B., U. Va., 1948. Admitted to Va. bar, 1948; with Income and Estate Tax Dept., Internal Revenue Service, Richmond, Va., 1948-52; practiced in Richmond, 1952—; mem. firm Lane, Paul & Rudd, 1952-65. Served with USAAF, 1941-45. Decorated Silver Star, Purple Heart, Air medal. Mem. Am., Va. (past chmn. bd. govs.) bar assns., Va. State Bar, Theta Chi, Delta Theta Chi. Contbr. articles to profl. jours. Home: 104 E Franklin St Richmond VA 23220 Office: 830 E Main St Richmond VA 23219

PAUL, GEORGE, former v.p. personnel C. & N.W. Ry. Chgo.; now exec. v.p. adminstrn. So. Rys., Washington. Address: Southern Railways Bldg 920 15th St Washington DC*

PAUL, HANS FERDINAND, lawyer; b. Berlin, Germany, Mar. 17, 1930; s. Carl W. and Frida (Schrock) P.; came to U.S., 1935, naturalized, 1948; B.S. Clemson U., 1951; LL.B., U. S.C., 1955; m. Ernestine Rosalie Hill, June 8, 1951; children—Margaret Suzanne, Patricia Anne, Thomas Duane. Research pathologist McNair Seed Co., Laurinburg, N.C., 1951; admitted to S.C. bar, 1955; practiced in Charleston, S.C., 1955—; mem. firm Robinson, Paul & Belk; gen. counsel North Charleston Pub. Service Dist., 1962—; sec. Property Mgmt. Corp., 1962—. Pres. Charleston County Council Retarded Children; mem. Pollution Control Commn.; chmn. Charleston County Consol. Govt. Commn. Trustee Cancer Found. Served to 1st lt. AUS, 1951-53. Mem. Am., S.C., North Charleston (pres.) bar assns., Clemson Alumni Assn., Internat. Platform Assn. Democrat. Lutheran. Lion (pres. 1963; zone chmn. 1964). Home: 1784 Mosstree Rd North Charleston SC 29405 Office: 3370 Rivers Av Charleston Heights SC 29405

PAUL, HOMER, banker; b. Claremore, Okla., Sept. 14, 1932; s. Homer and Helen (Lafferty) P.; B.A., U. Okla., 1954, LL.B., 1959; m. Carol Ann Engleman, Aug. 23, 1958; children—Charles William, Lela Carol, Jamie Helen, Jennifer Jean. With Liberty Nat. Bank & Trust Co., Oklahoma City, 1959—, with trust dept., 1959-66, corr. dept., 1966-68, bus. devel. dept., 1968-69, v.p. comml. loan dept., 1969—. Bd. dirs. Okla. Mental Health Council. Served to lt. col. USMCR, 1954-56. Methodist (mem. ofcl. bd.). Home: 2905 Arrowhead Dr Edmond OK 73034 Office: PO Box 25848 Oklahoma City OK 73125

PAUL, ROBERT, lawyer; b. N.Y.C., Nov. 22, 1931; s. Gregory and Sonia (Rijock) P.; B.A., N.Y. U., 1953; J.D., Columbia, 1958; m. Arlene Naar, Feb. 2, 1953; children—Peter Franklin, Gina. Admitted to Fla. bar, 1958, N.Y. bar, 1959; partner Paul, Landy, Beiley & Bartel, Miami, 1964—, Morrison, Paul, Stillman &Beiley, N.Y.C., 1970—; counsel vice chmn. bd. dirs. Republic Nat. Bank Miami, 1968—; dir. Prime Equities, Inc., Clifton, N.J., All-Tech Industries, Inc., Miami Lakes, Fla., Amcourt Systems, Inc., Miami. Mem. Am., N.Y., Fla., Inter-Am. bar assns. Home: 700 Alhambra Circle Coral Gables FL 33134 Office: 150 SE 3d Av Miami FL 33131

PAULSON, FRANK OSCAR, cons. engr.; b. Clinton, Ia., Jan. 16, 1899; s. Carl and Hulda (Anderson) P.; B. S. in Mech. Engring., Ia. State U., 1924; m. Susan Imogene Dean, Dec. 11, 1924; children—Loree Alan Dean, Linda Elaine (Mrs. Chester Quillian Reeves). Asst. mech. engr. Atlantic Gulf & Pacific Co., N.Y.C., 1924-41; mech. engr. Norfolk Dredging Co. (Va.), 1941-45, Gahagan Dredging Corp., N.Y.C., Tampa, Fla., 1945-51; cons. engr. domestic and fgn. marine and dredging industry, Charleston, S.C., 1951—; pres. Paulson Engr. Services, Inc., 1951—, Paulson Dean Industries, 1967—, Woodward Paulson Engrs., 1966—. Mem. Am. Soc. Naval Engrs., Soc. Am. Mil. Engrs., Soc. Naval Architects and Marine Engrs., S.C. Soc. Profl. Engrs., Marine Tech. Soc. Methodist. Designer, inventor numerous machines for marine industry, hydraulic dredges for fgn. and domestic corps. Home: 308 Parkwood Estates Dr Charleston SC 29407 Office: Rice Mill Bldg Municipal Marina Charleston SC 29401

PAUTZ, MARTIN REINHARDT, librarian; b. Wisconsin Rapids, Wis., June 3, 1917; s. Reinhart F. and Ann E. (Mahnke) P.; student Concordia Coll., 1937; B.S., U. Wis., 1941; M.S. in L.S., U. N.C., 1968; m. Phyllis O'Hanlon, Sept. 14, 1942; children—Laura E., Andrew W., Anne E. Enlisted U.S. Army, 1941, U.S. Air Force, 1947, advanced through grades to lt. col., 1966; ret., 1966; instr. air Command and Staff Sch., 1953-59; prof. air sci. Coe Coll., 1959-68; dir. library Greenville (S.C.) Tech. Edn. Center, 1968-71; dir. Learning Resources Center, Clayton Jr. Coll., Morrow, Ga., 1971—. Mem. Am., So., Southeastern, S.C., Ga. library assns. Home: 2874 Priscilla Way Morrow GA 30260 Office: PO Box 285 Morrow GA 30260

PAV, PETER ANTON, educator; b. Berwyn, Ill., May 17, 1938; s. Anton and Blanche Augusta (Eichholze) P.; A.B. summa cum laude, Knox Coll., 1960; M.A., Ind. U., 1963, Ph.D., 1964; m. Yvonne Mae Tomasek, Aug. 13, 1960; children—Michael John, Anton Peter. Prof. philosophy Fla. Presbyn. Coll., St. Petersburg, 1966—. Pres., Lyric Opera Assn., St. Petersburg, 1968—. Served to capt., AUS, 1964-66. Danforth fellow, 1960; Nat. Def. Edn. Act fellow, 1960, NSF Grad. fellow, 1960, NSF Cooperative fellow, 1960. Mem. History Sci. Assn., Am. Sci. Affiliation (commr.), Philosophy Sci. Assn., Fla. Philos. Assn. (steering com., 1971—), Phi Beta Kappa. Home: 5032 41st St S St Petersburg FL 33711

PAWSON, DAVID LEO, mus. ofcl.; b. Napier, New Zealand, Oct. 5, 1938; s. Leslie Albert and Mary Alice (Wildermoth) P.; B.Sc., Victoria U., Wellington, New Zealand, 1960, M.Sc., 1961, Ph.D., 1964; m. Mary Tobin, Dec. 8, 1962. Came to U.S., 1964. Demonstrator zoology dept. Victoria U., 1960-62, teaching fellow, 1962-63, lectr., 1963-64; asso. curator marine invertebrates Smithsonian Instn., Washington, 1964-65, supr. div. echinoderms, 1965-71; chmn. dept. invertebrate zoology, 1971—; adj. lectr. George Washington U., Washington, 1966—; adj. asso. prof. U. Miami (Fla.). Mem. Soc. Systematic Zoology, Soc. Bibliog. Natural History, New Zealand Marine Scis. Soc., Royal Soc. New Zealand, Sigma Xi. Home: 1905 Memory Ct Vienna VA 22180 Office: Smithsonian Instn Washington DC 20560

PAXTON, FAY MURRAY, club woman; b. Fairview, Kan., May 23, 1889; d. Jacob M. and Friendly (Sewell) Murray; student Central Bus. Coll.; m. James C. Paxton, May 23, 1934 (dec. 1955). Tchr. shorthand and typing Centeral Bus. Coll., Kansas City, Mo., 1912-15; stenographer, bookkeeper, Bartlett Bros. Land & Loan Co., St. Joseph, 1915-20; stenographer, bookkeeper Quapaw Baths, Hot Springs, Ark., 1925-26, asst. mgr., 1928-34; pvt. sec. to Col. John R. Fordyce, Hot Springs, 1927; apt. house owner, Hot Springs, 1936—. Pres. Hot Springs Bus. and Profl. Women's Club, 1934; grey lady Army and Navy Hosp., 1947; mem. state exec. bd. Order Rainbow Girls, 1940-45, state mother adviser, 1945-46; helped organize Hot Springs Shrine Club Aux., 1949, pres., 1955-56; pres. Thinkers' Club, 1962-64; chpt. corr. sec. Phi Sigma Alpha, 1966; pres. Hot Springs Salvation Army Aux., 1968-70. Mem. Order Eastern Star (worthy matron 1943, 52). Home: 602 Quapaw Av Hot Springs AR 71901

PAXTON, WILLIAM FRANCIS, II, business cons.; b. Paducah, Ky., Apr. 30, 1907; s. William Percy and Flora (Dickie) P.; student Tulane U.; m. India Lang Watkins, Feb. 3, 1934 (dec. Jan. 1970); children—Barbaranelle (Mrs. Russell S. Shelton), William Francis III. With Claussner Hosiery Co. div. Indian Head Mills, Inc., 1927-65, pres., 1957-65; v.p., dir. So. Textile Machinery Co., Paducah, 1952—, Watkins, Inc., Paducah, 1937-67; sec., dir. Marvei Specialty Co., Paducah, 1937—; dir. Rubil Dry Goods Co., Paducah Newspapers, Inc., Burke & James Optical Co., Ace Mfg. Co., Paducah; business cons., 1965—. City commr., Paducah, Ky. until 1967. Mem. Paducah Bd. Edn., 1944-52; pres., dir. Paducah Community Chest, 1950; pres. Four Rivers council Boy Scouts Am., 1946-52, chmn. 1940-46, Del., Republican Nat. Conv., 1952, 64. Trustee W.P. Paxton Trust. Recipient Silver Beaver award Boy Scouts Am. Mem. Delta Tau Delta. Elk. Club: Paducah Country (pres. 1945-47, 51-52, dir. 1961-64). Home: 234 W Jefferson St Paducah KY 42202

PAYNE, BETTY LOU, educator; b. Edneyville, N.C., Oct. 3, 1935; d. John Franklin and Libby Viola (Russell) Payne; student San Diego State Coll., 1954-55; B.S., Fayetteville State U., 1958; M.A., Western Carolina U., 1967. Tchr. Rocky Mount (N.C.) City Schs., 1959-64, guidance counselor, 1965—. Active various community drives; troop leader Girl Scouts U.S.A. Mem. Am. Sch. Counselor Assn., Nat. Council on Crime and Delinquency, Am. Assn. U. Women (treas. Rocky Mount br. 1970-72), Am., N.C. personnel and guidance assns., N.E.A., N.C. Tchrs. Assn. (dist. pres., counselor div. 1968-70), Alpha Kappa Alpha. Episcopalian. Home: 712 Pennsylvania Av Rocky Mount NC 27801 Office: E Virginia St Rocky Mount NC 27801

PAYNE, BOBBIE LEE, oil co. exec.; b. Tulsa, Dec. 31, 1937; s. Harry Claude and Mabel Hazel (Woolsey) P.; B.S. in Petroleum Engring., U. Tulsa, 1960; J.D., U. Oklahoma City, 1967; m. Delores Kay Walton, Apr. 22, 1961; children—Angela, Andrew. Petroleum area research sr. engr. Union Oil Co. Cal., Oklahoma City, 1960-68; asst. to v.p. Amarillo (Tex.) Oil Co., 1968—, v.p., 1969—; dir. Amarillo Exploration, Inc. Mem. Randall County Republican Exec. Com., 1970—. Served with AUS, 1961. Registered profl. engr., Okla., Tex. Mem. Am., Okla., Tex. bar assns., Ind. Petroleum Assn. Am. (dir.), Panhandle Producers and Royalty Owners Assn. (dir., mem. exec. com. 1970—), Am. Assn. Mining, Metall. and Petroleum Engrs., Am. Petroleum Inst., Alpha Tau Omega. Republican. Baptist. Home: 6119 Calumet St Amarillo TX 79106 Office: PO Box 151 Amarillo TX 79105

PAYNE, BOBBY RAY, service co. exec.; b. Grandfield, Okla., June 21, 1928; s. Courtney Ray and Mildred Aluina (Gilger) P.; student Trinity U., 1947-48, U. Corpus Christi, 1954-55; m. Connie Jo Roper, Mar. 15, 1949; children—Deborah Dee, Julie Dianne, Robert Courtney. Mud engr. Milwhite Mud Sales, New Iberia, La., 1956-58; chief engr. Mission Mud Co., Corpus Christi, Tex., 1959-61; gen. mgr. Eagleban Mud Co., Robstown, Tex., 1961-63; pres. Mud Separators, Inc., Robstown, 1963-71, Payne & Harris Mfg., Robstown, 1969-71; operations mgr. drilling controls div. Milchem., Inc., Houston, 1971—. Served with USMC, 1945-47; PTO. Baptist. Club: National Aero. Address: 15109 Lakeview Dr Houston TX 77040

PAYNE, CHARLES WILLIAM, pub. relations exec.; b. Providence, Ky., Jan. 31, 1911; s. John Gammon and Beulah M. (Boyd) P.; student U. Evansville, 1928-29; B.A., Wittenberg U., 1932; postgrad. Northwestern U., 1947-49; m. Vera Mae Hierstein, Feb. 26, 1933; children— Marjorie L. (Mrs. George J. Kopp, dec.), Gammon W. Newsphoto editor AP, Washington, 1939-43; central div. mgr. Acme-N.E.A., Chgo., 1946-52; central div. newspicture mgr. UPI, Chgo., 1952-53; mgr., v.p. Selvage & Lee, Inc., Chgo., 1954-67; spl. asst. to gen. mgr. Ins. Information Inst., 1967, mgr. Washington govt. relations, 1967—. Pres. Mt. Prospect Park Dist., 1955-59, 1961-67, commr., 1955-60, 61-67. Chmn. C.H.O., Inc., charitable corp., 1969-71, co-treas., 1972; founder Navy Fleet Home Town News Center, Navy Journalist Sch. Served with USNR, 1943-46. Recipient George Washington Honor medal Freedoms Found. at Valley Forge. Mem. Pub. Relations Soc. Am., Nat. Press Club, Chgo. Press Club, Chgo. Press Photographers Assn., Sigma Delta Chi, Phi Gamma Delta. Mason (32 deg.). Home: 536 Marshall Rd SW Vienna VA 22180 Office: National Press Bldg Washington DC 20004

PAYNE, DAVID ALLEN, educator; b. Indpls., July 3, 1935; s. Carlyle Allen and Polly Dix (Smith) P.; student U. Mich., 1953-55; B.A., Hope Coll., 1957; M.A., Mich. State U., 1958, Ph.D., 1961; m. Mary Ann Vollink, Aug. 30, 1957; children—Michael, Steven, Jeffery, Karen. Instr., Mich. State U., 1961-62; asst. prof. Syracuse U., 1962-66, asso. prof., 1966-69; prof. ednl. psychology and curriculum and supr., U. Ga., Athens, 1969—. Dir. Ga. Ednl. TV Evaluation Project, 1969-70. Mem. Am. Psychol. Assn., Am. Ednl. Research Assn., Nat. Council Measurement in Edn., Inter-Assn. Council Test Reviewing (sec.-treas. 1970-72). Author: Educational and Psychological Measurement: Contributions to Theory and Practice, 1967; The Specification and Measurement of Learning Outcomes, 1968. Rev. editor Jour. Ednl. Measurement, 1968—. Home: 118 Spruce Valley Rd Athens GA 30601

PAYNE, DAVID LEBARRON, librarian; b. Gulfport, Miss., May 9, 1927; s. John Quincy Adams and Maybell (Franklin) P.; A.A., Perkinston Jr. Coll., 1948; B.S., Miss. State U., 1950, M.S., 1952; postgrad. Fla. State U., 1954; Ed.D., U. So. Miss., 1967; M.L.S., U. Ala., 1972; m. Lorraine Marling, Aug. 12, 1954; children—Robert, Debbie, John, Marlene. Asst. prof. Miss. State Coll. for Women, Columbus, 1967-68, dir. library, prof. L.S., 1969—; asst. prof. Northwestern State Coll. La., Natchitoches, 1968-69. Mem. Miss. Edn. Assn., A.L.A., Miss., Southeastern library assns., Nat. Council Social Studies, Nat. Soc. Study Edn., Am. Assn. Higher Edn., Phi Alpha Theta, Alpha Kappa Delta, Phi Delta Kappa, Kappa Delta Pi, Pi Gamma Mu, Alpha Beta Alpha, Lambda Chi Alpha. Democrat. Methodist. Mason (Shriner). Home: 131 Juanita St Columbus MS 39701

PAYNE, DAVID PEARSON, aviation co. exec.; b. Richmond, Va., July 11, 1905; s. Freemond Clifton and Mary Emma (Lewis) P.; student Drexel U., 1923-25; m. Florence Elizabeth Taylor, Oct. 2, 1936; children— David Pearson, John Taylor, Stephen Lewis. Elec. constrn. work, 1926-42; founder, pres. Aeroway, Inc., Richmond, 1947— (merged with Aero Industries), prin. owner, pres., 1958—. Mem. Gov.'s Commn. on Aeros., 1960-68. Served to lt. AC, USNR, 1943-45. Mem. Richmond C. of C. Episcopalian. Mason (32 deg., Shriner), Rotarian, Quiet Birdman. Home: 1704 Avondale Av Richmond VA 23227 Office: Exec Terminal Byrd Airport Richmond VA 23150

PAYNE, HENRY LELAND, travel agt.; b. Anderson, S.C., Oct. 12, 1916; s. Henry Leland and Essie (Simpson) P.; student Bombardier Sch., 1943, Radar-Nav. Sch., 1948; m. Mary Constance Brady, Mar. 4, 1946; children—Henry L. III, Melissa Ann. Funeral dir. Burney Funeral Home, Anderson, 1936-37; theatre mgr. Capitol Theatre, Asheboro, N.C., 1938; div. mgr. Sears-Roebuck Co., Anderson, S.C., 1939-40; joined USAAF, 1941, commd. lt., 1943, advanced through grades to maj., 1962; flew 29 missions ETO, 1944-45; master navigator, chief instr. USAF Nav. Sch., Salina, Kan., 1948-49; ret., 1962; owner Payne Cleaners & Laundry, Edinburg, Tex., 1962-69, Alley Shop, ladies' apparel, Edinburg, 1963-69; owner Payne's Travel Center, Edinburg, 1969—; founder, v.p. Nat. Services Investments, Inc., Oscoda, Mich., 1961-62; pres. Alliance Tours, Inc., Edinburg, 1969—. Vice pres. Am. Field Service, 1965, pres., 1966; mem. Airport Adv. Bd., 1968—; mem. Fiesta Hidalgo Com., 1967—; originator hist. Hidalgo Trail, 1968. City commr. Edinburg, 1964-68. Trustee Hidalgo County Mus. Decorated D.F.C., Air medal with 3 oak leaf clusters. Mem. Hist. Soc. (treas., pres. 1967-68, tour chmn.; pres. 1972), C. of C. (tourist com.; dir. 1972). Presbyn. (deacon 1964-67, treas. Men of Ch. 1964, pres. 1965). Rotarian (dir. 1963-66). Home: 1112 S 9th St Edinburg TX 78539 Office: 115 W Mahl St Edinburg TX 78539

PAYNE, KIRBY BOSWORTH, govt. ofcl.; b. Clarksburg, W.Va., June 3, 1916; s. John Bosworth and Eulainne Ashurst (Struve) P.; A.B., George Washington U., 1941; student Md. U., 1937; M.L.S., Cath. U. Am., 1954; m. Vivian Franklyn, Jan. 22, 1941; children—Vivian (Mrs. David Powell), Martha (Mrs. James R. Baldwin). Various positions D.C. Pub. Library, 1936-42; spl. agt. N.Y. Life Ins. Co., Washington, 1946-49; asst. dir. Nat. Agrl. Library, U.S. Dept. Agr., Washington, 1949-68; dir. FAA Library U.S. Dept. Transp., Washington, 1968-69, dir. Dept. Transp. Library, Washington, 1969—; guest lectr. Drexel Inst. Tech., 1960. Served with USNR, 1942-46. Mem. Am., D.C. library assns., Internat. Assn. Agrl. Librarians and Documentalists, Am. Inst. Aeros. and Astronautics, Spl. Libraries Assn., Amvets. Presbyn. (deacon 1960-65, ruling elder 1967-69). Lion. Home: 6524 35th Rd N Arlington VA 22213 Office: 400 7th St SW Washington DC 20590

PAYNE, LEO WILLIAM, ins. co. exec.; b. Houston, Okla., Aug. 25, 1934; s. Ted A. and Dora (Sinnett) P.; student Alvin Jr. Coll., 1955-57, Lee Coll., 1957; A.A., U. Houston, 1960; m. Joyce Marie Thurman, Sept. 15, 1952; children—Diane Lee, Leo William, Kenneth Joseph. Gen. agt. Nat. Western Life Ins. Co., 1964-67; pres. Pamco Corp., League City, Tex., 1959-67; gen. agt. Nat. Travelers Life Co., Houston, from 1968—; now pres., chmn. bd. Am. Travelers Life Ins. Co.; pres., dir. Sunscope Corp., Travelers Printing Corp.; dir. Tool Rentals, Inc. Named Man of Month, Nat. Western Life, 1965, Salesman of Year, Nat. Travelers Life, 1969. Mem. Nat. Assn. Life Underwriters. Elk. Club: Presidents. Home: 2001 Mariner Way Dickinson TX 77539 Office: 8330 Broadway Houston TX 77017

PAYNE, MARY LIBBY BICKERSTAFF (MRS. BOBBY RAY PAYNE), lawyer; b. Gulfport, Miss., Mar. 27, 1932; d. Reece O. and Emily A. (Cook) Bickerstaff; student Miss. State Coll. Women, 1950-52; B.A. cum laude, U. Miss., 1954, LL.B., 1955; m. Bobby Ray Payne, Dec. 20, 1955; children—Reece Allen, Glenn Russell. Admitted to Miss. bar, 1955; partner Bickerstaff & Bickerstaff, Gulfport, 1955-57; employee Guaranty Title Co., Jackson, 1957; asso. Henley, Jones & Henley, Jackson, 1958-61; free-lance research and brief writing, 1962-63; individual law practice, Brandon, 1963-68; exec. sec. Miss. Judiciary Commn., 1968-70; chief research and drafting div., ho. mgmt. com. Miss. Ho. of Reps., 1970—. Instr. bus. law Miss. Coll., Clinton, 1956-57; v.p., dir. First Finance Corp. of Rankin County, 1964-68; legislative draftsman Miss. Ho. of Reps., 1964-68. Chmn. Pearl-McLaurin Water Investigative Com., 1967; counsel Rankin County Christian Action Com., 1968. Mem. steering com. Rankin County campaign United Drys, 1966. Mem. Miss. State Bar (co-chmn. lawyers placement com. 1965, mem. bd. bar commrs. 1965-67, 71-72, Rankin County Bar Assn. (sec. 1965, v.p. 1966-67, pres. 1968), Am. Assn. U. Women (chpt. legislative chmn. 1956), P.T.A. (sec. Pearl-McLaurin 1966, parliamentarian 1967, pres. 1968, 69). Home: 3617 Wilcox Dr Jackson MS 39208 Office: New Capitol Bldg Jackson MS 39205

PAYNE, MELVIN MONROE, sci. and ednl. exec.; b. Washington, May 23, 1911; s. Julian R. and Jeanette V. (Perry) P.; student Nat. U., 1929-30; LL.B., Southeastern U., 1939; D.Sc., S.D. Sch. Mines and Tech., 1962; m. Ethel B. McDonnell, Sept. 1, 1938; children—Melvin Monroe (dec.), Frances, Nancy Jeanette. With N.Y. Sun, 1927; asst. to sec. Ry. Accounting Officers Assn., 1930-32; with Nat. Geog. Soc., Washington, 1932—, pres., chief exec. officer, from 1967, also trustee; admitted to D.C. bar, 1941. Adv. dir. Riggs Nat. Bank; dir. Equitable Savs. and Loan Assn., Inc., Ethyl Corp., Govt. Employees Ins. Co., Govt. Employees Life Ins. Co., Govt. Employees Corp., Criterion Life Ins. Co., Govt. Employees Financial Corp. Chmn. adv. bd. sec. interior Nat. Park System. Trustee, v.p. U.S. Capitol Hist. Soc. Mem. Am. Bar Assn., Am. Assn. Geographers, A.A.A.S. Clubs: Alfalfa, Nat. Press, Metropolitan, Cosmos (Washington); Chevy Chase (Md.); Burning Tree (Bethesda, Md.). Home: 8821 Burdette Rd Bethesda MD 20034 Office: 1145 17th St NW Washington DC 20036

PAYNE, ROBERT WAYNE, accountant; b. Appleton City, Mo., Oct. 4, 1929; s. Robert Fenton and Thelma Opal (Broadus) P.; B.S. in Bus. Adminstrn., Central Mo. State Coll., 1951; M.B.A., U. Denver 1957; m. Kathryn Margaret Eydt, Sept. 22, 1956; children—David Wayne, John Robert. C.P.A., Arthur Andersen & Co., St. Louis office, 1955-66, partner in charge Memphis office, 1966—. Bd. dirs. Jr. Achievement of Memphis. Served with USAF, 1951-55. C.P.A. Mem. Am. Inst. C.P.A.'s, Nat. Assn. Accountants. Methodist. Clubs: Chickasaw Country, Summit, Memphis Athletic. Home: 5527 Pecan Grove Lane Memphis TN 38117 Office: 165 Madison Av Memphis TN 38103

PAYNE, THOMAS ROBERT, banker; b. Charlotte, N.C., Jan. 4, 1922; s. William R. and Vanna (Simpson) P.; grad. The Citadel, 1940-43; LL.B., U. N.C., 1949; m. Hilda Elizabeth Owens, June 5, 1948; children—Shirley Elizabeth, Thomas Robert. Admitted to N.C. bar, 1949; with Comml. Nat. Bank, Charlotte, 1949-56; pvt. practice law, Charlotte, 1956-59; with N.C. Nat. Bank, Charlotte 1959—, sr. v.p., 1967—. Mem. Charlotte City Sch. Bd., 1959-62. Pres. St. Peters Hosp. Found., Charlotte, 1968; bd. govs. Thompson Orphanage,, Charlotte, 1966—, bd. dirs. Jr. Archievement Charlotte, 1965—, pres., 1967, chmn. bd., 1968. Served with inf. AUS, 1944-46. Episcopalian. Rotarian (sec. Charlotte 1962-63). Home: 2201 Pembroke Av Charlotte NC 28207 Office: 200 S Tryon St Charlotte NC 28202

PAYNE, WILLIAM ARCHIBALD, journalist; b. Greenville, Tex., Nov. 19, 1909; s. Oscar C. and Mittie (Baker) P.; B.A., Baylor U., 1931; m. Margaret Wilkerson, Apr. 23, 1932; children—William Archibald, Betty Carolyn. Mem. news dept. Dallas Dispatch, 1931-42; with Dallas News, 1946—, amusements editor, 1957—. Served with AUS, 1942-46. Home: 3509 Marquette St Dallas TX 75225 Office: Dallas News Dallas TX 75222

PAYNE, WILLIAM HOYT, asst. supt. schs.; b. Memphis, Mar. 19, 1935; s. Jack Allen and Roberta Catherine (Medaris) P.; B.S., William Carey Coll., 1957; M.Ed., U. Miss., 1960, Ed.D., 1969; m. Mary Edythe Bullock, Aug. 25, 1956; children—Mary Karen, William Hoyt. Tchr., coach pub. schs. Natchez, Miss., 1957-60; guidance tchr. pub. schs. Memphis, 1960—, asst. supt., 1971—. Instr. Sch. Edn. Memphis State U., 1969-70. P.T.A. scholar, 1962-63. Mem. Memphis, Tenn. edn. assns., N.E.A., Am. Assn. Sch. Adminstrs., Phi Delta Kappa. Home: 5457 Heritage St Memphis TN 38118 Office: 2225 James Rd Memphis TN 38127

PAYNE, WILLIAM MARCUS, profl. assn. exec.; b. Clyde, Kan., Jan. 13, 1930; s. Mose Francis and Julia Esther (Gram) P.; student Kan. State U., 1951-53, U. Houston, 1964-66, Tex. Christian U., 1970-71; m. Jo Ann Hudson, June 12, 1953; children—Marc, Julie, Greg, Jim, Bruce. With Tri County Refrigeration, Manhattan, Kan., 1950-53, Dick's Standard Service, Clay Center, Kan., 1953-55, Firestone Tire and Rubber Co., Salina, Kan., 1955-57; mgr. Stein's Men's Clothing, Wichita, Kan., Tulsa, Odessa, Tex., Natchez, Miss., 1957-64; mgr. Crane County (Tex.) C. of C., 1964-71; exec. v.p. Littlefield (Tex.) C. of C. and Agr. 1971—. Player agt. Crane County Little League, 1964-66, v.p., 1967-71; chmn. parents com. Crane County 4-H Club, 1967-68; chmn. local draft bd. 121, 1971; pres. Pee Wee Baseball, Crane, Tex., 1965-71. Served with USNR, 1947-50. Named Lion of Yr., Crane (Tex.) Noon Lions Club, 1965. Mem. Perman Basin C. of C. Mgrs. Assn. (pres. 1971), C. of C. Execs. Assn. (bd. dirs. 1966), Internat. Parks Hwy. US 385-85 Assn. (sec.-treas. 1965-66, Tex. div. pres. 1970—). Mason, Lion. Compiled, published It's Not All Glory, 1966. Home: 220 E 23d St Littlefield TX 79339 Office: Box 507 City Hall Littlefield TX 79339

PAYNE, WILLIAM THOMAS, oil well drilling contractor and producer; b. Tecumseh, Neb., Jan. 26, 1892; s. Thomas J. and Ellen (Meyer) P.; B.S. in Sci. and Lit., Okla. A. and M. Coll., 1915; m. Katheryne Bond, June 17, 1935; 1 son, Stephen Bond. Grad. asst. microbiology Mass. State Coll., 1916; chemist Digestive Ferments Co., Detroit, 1916-17; bacteriologist City of Detroit, 1917-18; oil scout N. Am. Oil Co., 1919-21; supt. W.H. Helmerich Co., 1921-26; v.p. Helmerich & Payne, 1926-36; pres. Big Chief Drilling Co., Oklahoma City, 1936-58, chmn. bd., 1958—; chmn. bd. Seneca Oil Co., 1961—; pres. Payne Petroleum Corp., 1945—; former dir. Liberty Nat. Bank & Trust Co.; dir. May Avenue Bank & Trust Co. Chmn. appeal board Western Fed. Jud. Dist. Okla., SSS, 1943-45, 48-67. Chmn. Vols. for Nixon-Lodge in Okla., 1960, Citizens for Eisenhower, Western Dist., Okla., 1956. Bd. dir. Oklahoma City United Fund. United Presbyn. Found.; exec. com. Okla. Med. Research Found. Served as 2d lt., San. Corps, U.S. Army, 1918-19. Recipient Horatio Alger award Am. Schs. and Colls. Assn., 1958; Outstanding Citizen award Oklahoma City United Fund, 1960; Alumni Hall of Fame award Okla. State U., 1959; Coll. Arts and Scis. award Okla. State U., 1962; Outstanding Service award Mercy Hosp., Oklahoma City, 1958; Okla. Med. Scis. Hall of Fame award, 1958; Silver Beaver award Boy Scouts Am., 1958, Silver Antelope award, 1958. Man with Heart award, 1960; Oil Man of Year award Okla. Petroleum Council, 1966; named to Okla. Hall of Fame, 1966. Mem. Ind. Petroleum Assn. Am. (dir.), Oklahoma City C. of C. (dir.), Am. Assn. Oilwell Drilling Contractors (pres. 1945), Mid-Continent (pres. Kan.-Okla. div. 1947-49), Gen. Mid-Continent (pres. 1950-51) oil and gas assns., Beta Theta Phi. Presbyn. (trustee). Clubs: Oklahoma City Golf and Country, Whitehall, Petroleum, Quail Creek Country, Beacon, Mens Dinner (Oklahoma City). Home: 6815 NW Grand Blvd Oklahoma City OK 73116 Office: 601 NE 63d St Oklahoma City OK 73114

PCHELKIN, HILDEGARD ELISABETH WOLFF (MRS. V. N. PCHELKIN), librarian; b. Oberstein, Nahe, West Germany, Jan. 8, 1914; d. Wilhelm and Elvira F. (Hahn) Wolff; diploma in philology Friedrich Wilhelm U., 1937; grad. library sci. Fla. State U., 1953; m. V. N. Pchelkin, Oct. 3, 1950; children—Richard B., Caspari. Came to U.S., 1938, naturalized, 1944. Library asst. Air U. Library, Maxwell AFB, 1944-48, information specialist, translator, 1948-50; tech. librarian Chemstrand Co. div. Monsanto Chem. Co., Pensacola, Fla., 1953-68; tech. librarian Textiles div. Monsanto Co., Pensacola, 1968—, head all Textiles Div. Tech. Libraries and Information Centers. Lectr. Pensacola Sci. Seminar for Superior Students, 1961—; established med. library Escambia Gen. Hosp., 1962-63. Mem. League Women Voters (Pensacola dir. 1961-62), Am. Assn. Textile Technologists, Fla. Library Assn., Spl. Libraries Assn., Am. Chem. Soc., Textile Information Users Council, Am. Soc. Fortesting and Materials. Home: 22 Highpoint Dr Gulf Breeze FL 32561 Office: Box 1507 Pensacola FL 32503

PEABODY, BREWSTER EARL, librarian; b. Plymouth, Mich., Oct. 18, 1934; s. Brewster Eldred and Emily Caroline (Weinmann) P.; B.A., U. Mich., 1956, M.A. in L.S., 1957, M.A. in History, 1958. Serials librarian U. Del., Newark, 1959-62; asst. librarian So. Ill. U., Edwardsville, 1962-66; library dir. Old Dominion U., Norfolk, Va., 1966—. Served with AUS, 1958-59. Mem. Am., Va., Southeastern library assns., Va. Hist. Soc., Light Rwy. Transport League. Home: 934 Amfield Circle Norfolk VA 23505 Office: Hampton at 48th St Norfolk VA 23508

PEACE, ALVARENE GREEN (MRS. JAMES FRANCIS PEACE), educator; b. Magnolia, Ark., June 5, 1922; d. George Edwin and Joanna (Rushton) Green; student So. State Coll., Magnolia, Ark., 1938-40; B.S., Oklahoma City U., 1942; diploma Southwestern Grad. Sch. Banking, So. Meth. U., 1964, M.B.A., 1967; m. James Francis Peace, Apr. 16, 1944; 1 dau., Mary Anna. Adminstrv. asst. regional office, Office of Sec. War, Civilian Personnel Div., Dallas, 1942-44; jr. economist regional office Bur. of Labor Statistics, Dallas, 1944-45; sec. office of V.S. Parham and Akoma Oil Co., Inc., 1946-48, 51-54; instr. bus. dept. So. State Coll., 1948-50; instr. bus. dept. So. State Coll., Magnolia, 1958-59, 65-68, asst. prof., 1968—; asst. sec. First Nat. Bank of Magnolia, 1959-64. Active Girl Scouts. Bd. dirs. South Ark. Symphony, 1962-65. Mem. Nat. Assn. Bank Women, Inc., Ark. Edn. Assn. Methodist. Clubs: Magnolia Music (pres. 1961-62), Ark. Fedn. of Music (rec. sec. S.W. dist. 1960-61). Home: 1007 Chestnut St Magnolia AR 71753

PEACE, BONY HAMPTON, JR., newspaper exec.; b. Greenville, S.C., Aug. 13, 1906; s. Bony Hampton and Laura Estelle (Chandler) P.; student Port Mil. Acad., 1921-23; A.B., Furman U., 1928; m. Dorothy Julia Pedrick, Dec. 24, 1929; children—Elizabeth Peace (Mrs. Edward Stall), Judith (Mrs. Norfleet Harte), Estelle (Mrs. Salters McClary), Bony Hampton III. Pres., mgr. radio sta. WFBC, Greenville, S.C., 1933-53; sr. v.p. Greenville News-Piedmont Co., 1958—, dir., 1934—; dir. Multimedia Broadcasting Co., now hon. chmn.; dir. Multimedia, Inc., Radio-TV (Greenville), Asheville (N.C.) Citizen-Times Pub. Co. Clubs: Greenville Country Green Valley Country, Poinsett (Greenville&y, Biltmore Forest Country (Biltmore, N.C.). Home: 119 Byrd Blvd Greenville SC 29606 Office: 305 S Main St Greenville SC 69601

PEACE, CORINNE, journalist; b. St. Augustine, Fla.; d. George and Lila (Capo) Peace; student McNeese State Coll., Lake Charles, La., 1962-68. Society editor, asst. editor Morgan City (La.) Rev. 1945-61; editor Focus mag., staff writer, food columnist Am. Press, Lake Charles, 1961—. Active Am. Cancer Soc.; bd. dirs., publicity chmn. Community Concert Assn., Morgan City; nat. chmn. Nat. Fedn. Press Women's Conv., New Orleans, 1970. Mem. La. Press Women (state pres. 1968-69), La., S.W. La. hist. assns., Art Assos. Lake Charles, Vis. Artists Group, France-Amerique of Lake Charles (rec. sec.), Council for Devel. French in La. (dir. Calcasieu chpt.). Club: Lake Charles Writers (pres.). Contbr. articles to profl. jours. Home: PO Box 577 Lake Charles LA 70601 Office: Box 2893 Lake Charles LA 70601

PEACE, VERONICA MILES CHMIELEWSKI, real estate broker; b. Glen Lyon, Pa., Jan. 21, 1915; d. Constance and Sophie (Wadzinska) Chmielewski; student U. Pa. Wharton Sch., 1941-43, U. Miami, 1953-55, Am. Savs. and Loan Inst., 1952-55; m. Paul Peace, Mar. 6, 1946 (div. Jan. 1956). Owner, operator Peace Real Estate, Coral Gables, Fla., 1957—; sec. Cat Cay, Ltd. (Bahamas), 1961—; owner, operator Peace Inn, Marathon, Fla., Atlantic Shores Motel, Marathon; real estate broker, accountant Coral Harbour, Nassau, Bahamas, 1958-59; gen. mgr., sales rep. 1st Savs. and Loan Assn., Nassau; cons. Bahama properties, 1956—. Mgr. Edgewood Pool Apt., Coral Gables. Republican candidate for state senate, 1966, 68; Rep. committee woman, 1971—. Mem. exec. com. Dade County (Fla.) Women's Club; sec. Belk's Physic Research Found., N.Y.C., First Savs. and Loan Assn., Nassau, Bahamas; mem. Metaphys. Research Found., N.Y.C.; active in little theatre groups. Mem. Miami Bd. Realtors, Nat. Spiritual Assn. (certified medium), Internat. Platform Assn., Nat. Assn. Appraisers. Republican. Mem. Order Eastern Star. Clubs: Polish American (Miami); Women's Welcome Wagon (S. Miami), Granada Women's Rep. Home: Box 297 7931 Overseas Hwy Marathon FL 33050 Office: 1809 Ponce de Leon Blvd Coral Gables FL 33134

PEACE, WILLIAM KITTRELL, librarian; b. Rusk, Tex., Mar. 25, 1925; s. George Wesley and LaVada May (Meltabarger) P.; B.A., Tex. Christian U., 1950; M.Ed., U. Tex., 1960; M.S. in Library Sci. (grad. fellow 1966-67), La. State U., 1964; certificate county and regional librarianship Rutgers U., 1954. Library asst. Fort Worth Pub. Library, 1948-49, U. Tex. Library, Austin, 1950-53; asst. legislative ref. librarian Tex. State Library, Austin, 1952-53, extension librarian, 1953-55, asst. state librarian, 1955-60, 1962-66, acting state librarian, 1960-62; librarian Lee Coll., Baytown, Tex., 1967—. Cons. Pub. Library Insts., Tex. State Library, 1954-66, library services Tex. Dept. Corrections for coll. programs, 1969-71. Served with USNR, 1943-46. Mem. Baytown C. of C., Tex. Library Assn. (dist. chmn. 1969), Am. Assn. U. Profs. (chpt. pres. 1968-69), Tex. Jr. Coll. Tchrs. Assn. (chpt. pres. 1969-71 sect. chmn. 1970). Author: History of the Texas State Library With Emphasis on the Period, 1930-59, 1959. Home: Box 356 Mount Belvieu TX 77580 Office: Box 818 Lee Dr Baytown TX 77520

PEAK, PAUL REED, JR., coast guard officer; b. Denver, Mar. 19, 1923; s. Paul Reed and Verl (Nicol) P.; student Tex. Mil. Coll., 1940-41; B.S. in Engring., U.S. Coast Guard Acad., 1944; postgrad. U.S. Naval Postgrad. Sch., 1948-49; M.S. in Physics, Ohio State U., 1951; m. Jane W. Worley, June 8, 1944; children—Roger W., Lucy N., Martha H. Commd. ensign U.S. Coast Guard, 1944, advanced through grades to capt., 1966; asso. prof. U.S. Coast Guard Acad., New London, Conn., 1957-61; chief readiness br. Coast Guard Dist. Staff, San Francisco, 1961-64; chief mil. liaison br. Office of Sec. of Transp., Washington, 1967-69; regional emergency transp. rep. U.S. Dept. Transp., San Francisco, 1969-71; chief inspection staff 8th Coast Guard Dist., New Orleans, 1971-72, chief staff, 1972—. Committeeman Boy Scouts Am., 1962—; leader Mariner Girl Scouts 1969-71; exec. sec. New Eng. Coll. Rifle League, 1960-61. Mem. Nat. Rifle Assn., Nat. Sci. Tchrs. Assn., Nat. Def. Transp. Assn., Am. Ordnance Assn., U.S. Naval Inst., Sigma Pi Sigma, Delta Nu Alpha. Unitarian (mem. bd. 1958-60). Clubs: Commonwealth, (San Francisco); Propeller, New Orleans Athletic, Southern Yacht, Traffic (New Orleans). Home: 13204 Delta Ct New Orleans LA 70127 Office: 8th Coast Guard Dist Custom House New Orleans LA 70130

PEARCE, BENJAMIN MCCOY, architect; b. Newberry, S.C., Feb. 7, 1936; s. James Chapman and Juanita (McEntire) P.; B. Arch., Clemson U., 1959; m. Susan Kirkpatrick Brown, June 28, 1969; 1 son, James Chapman II. Designer, Walter Hook Assos. Architects-Engrs., Charlotte, N.C., 1961-66; project mgr. Freeman-White Assos. Architects-Engrs., 1966—. Served with AUS, 1959-61. Mem. A.I.A., The Mint Mus. of Art. Presbyn. Mason. Prin. archtl. works include Onslow Meml. Hosp., 1970, Earth-Life Scis. Bldg., U. N.C. at Charlotte, 1971. Home: 2014 Hopedale Av Charlotte NC 28207 Office: 303 W Fourth St Charlotte NC 28202

PEARCE, CHARLES WELLINGTON, surgeon; b. Ballinger, Tex., Nov. 2, 1927; s. Francis Marion and Fannie (Brown) P.; student Rice U., 1945-46, 48-49, U. Tex., 1948; M.D., Cornell U., 1953; m. Dorothy Andree DeLorenzo, Apr. 2, 1955; children—Charles Wellington, Andrew F., Margaret E. Intern, resident N.Y. Hosp.-Cornell U. Med. Center, N.Y.C., 1953-55, 56-60; resident Charity Hosp., New Orleans, 1960-61; practice medicine specializing in cardiovascular and thoracic surgery, New Orleans, 1961—; mem. staff Touro Infirmary, So. Bapt. Hosp., Hotel Dieu, Mercy Hosp., Sara Mayo Hosp., West Jefferson Hosp., Methodist Hosp., East Jefferson Hosp., all New Orleans; mem. faculty Tulane U., New Orleans, 1960—, asso. prof. surgery, 1966-69, head sect. cardiovascular and thoracic surgery, 1967-69, asso. prof. clin. surgery, 1969—; vis. surgeon Charity Hosp., New Orleans, 1961—; cons. surgery Huey P. Long Charity Hosp., Pineville, La., 1961—, Lallie Kem Charity Hosp., Independence, La., 1961—, VA Hosp., Alexandria, La., 1961—, Keesler Air Force Hosp., Biloxi, Miss., 1967—; cons. cardiac sect. crippled children program La. Dept. Health. Served with AUS, 1946-48. Diplomate Am. Bd. Surgery, Bd. Thoracic Surgery. Fellow A.C.S., Am. Coll. Chest Physicians, Am. Coll. Cardiology; mem. Am. Assn. Thoracic Surgery, Soc. for Vascular Surgery, Am. Heart Assn. (established investigator 1962-65), A.M.A., Soc. Thoracic Surgeons, Internat. Cardiovascular Soc., Internat. Surg. Soc., So. Med. Assn., Soc. Mayflower Descs., S.A.R., Surg. Assn. La.; Phi Chi, Alpha Omega Alpha. Republican. Presbyn. Contbr. articles to profl. jours. Home: 4923 St Charles Av New Orleans LA 70115 Office: 1070 St Charles Av New Orleans LA 70130

PEARCE, CLIFFORD FORREST, stock yard co. exec.; b. Shelby County, Ky., Nov. 19, 1896; s. Robert Lee and Alice Esther (Harris) P.; grad. high sch.; m. Julia Hardy Robinson, Jan. 12, 1941; children—Luther W., Nell, Lisa, Carroll, Amy. Procurement mgr. milk Sealtest, 1927-62; pres., dir. Bourbon Stock Yard Co., Louisville, 1962—. Rotarian (pres.). Club: Agricultural (Louisville). Home: 11913 Old Shelbyville Rd Middletown KY 40243 Office: 1048 E Main St Louisville KY 40206

PEARCE, DAVE LAZARUS, state ofcl.; b. Gordon, La., Sept. 8, 1905; s. Logan B. and Ida (Christian) P.; student pub. schs.; m. Elizabeth Oldham, Mar. 21, 1928; children—Billie Jeane (Mrs. Joseph Lesley Fauntleroy), Ida Lee (Mrs. Glenn Gossett). Farmer, West Carroll Parish, 1928-52; engaged in merc. bus., Oak Grove, La., 1936-50; commr. agr. and immigration State of La., Baton Rouge, 1952-56, 60—; engaged in real estate bus., Baton Rouge, 1956-60. Pres. West Carroll Parish Farm Bur., 1941-43, 51-52; chmn. West Carroll Parish Prodn. and Marketing Adminstrn. Com., 1950-52. Chmn. La. Heart Fund, 1956-59. Mem. La. Ho. of Reps., 1940-48, chmn. agr. com., 1944-48. Recipient Hon. State Farmer Degree, La. chpt. Future Farmers Am., 1953; named Man of Year, Progressive Farmer, 1954; Extension 4-H Alumni award, 1954. Mem. Assn. So. Commrs. Agr. (past pres.), Gideon Soc. (past pres. Baton Rouge), Baton Rouge C. of C. Home: 9435 Goodwood Blvd Baton Rouge LA 70815 Office: State Capitol PO Box 4052 Capitol Station Baton Rouge LA 70804

PEARCE, DOROTHY ANDREE DE LORENZO, civic worker; b. N.Y.C., Mar. 22, 1927; d. Andrew John and Margaret (Robilotti) De Lorenzo; B.A., Barnard Coll., 1947; m. Charles W. Pearce, Apr. 2, 1955; children—Charles W., Andrew Francis, Margaret Elizabeth. Research asst. cardiac catherization lab. Bellevue Hosp., 1948-50, Cornell Med. Coll., 1950-55; exec. research librarian Shell Chem. Co., 1955-57. Thrift shop rep. Soc. N.Y. Hosp. Women's Aux., 1959-60; bd. govs. New Orleans Opera House Assn. Women's Guild, 1965—, social hostess, 1966—, historian, 1969—; chmn. uptown subscription com., 1967-69, mem. children's concerts com., 1964-66; mem. tour com. New Orleans Springs Fiesta Assn., 1966-67; mem. opera orientation com. New Orleans Opera House Assn., 1964—, registrar, hostess, 1965—; active New Orleans Symphony Previews, 1968—; mem. fund raising com. De Paul Hosp. Women's Aux., 1968—; vol. Crippled Children's Hosp. Guild, 1965-66; mem. La. Council for Performing Arts, 1967—; mem. Gallier Hall Women's Com., 1967; mem. bd. Community Concerts Assn., New Orleans; mem. fund raising com. Hotel Dieu Women's Aux., 1968—. Bd. dirs. Mercy Hosp. Women's Aux., 1965—, pres., 1970; bd. dirs. Sara Mayo Hosp. Guild, 1964—, chmn. hospitality com., 1967—; bd. dirs. Orleans Parish Med. Soc. Women's Aux., 1969—, chmn. A.M.A. edn. and research fund com., 1969—; bd. dirs. Vis. Nurses Assn. Mem. New Orleans Garden Soc. (chmn. Christmas decorations 1969—), Fgn. Relations Assn., Am. Assn. U. Women, La. Landmark Soc. Republican. Roman Catholic. Club: New Orleans Country. Home: 6145 St Charles Av New Orleans LA 70118

PEARCE, EDWIN MCKIGNEY, JR., lawyer; b. Atlanta, Apr. 25, 1908; s. Edwin McKigney and Ella (Pope) P.; student U. Va., 1925-26; LL.B., Emory U., 1931; m. Joanne Snelson, May 1, 1949; children—Anne, Virginia, Catherine, Edwin McKigney III. Admitted to Ga. bar, 1931, since practiced in Atlanta; partner firm Poole, Pearce & Cooper; regional price atty. Southeastern region OPA, 1944-45, regional price exec., 1946-47; lectr. law Emory U., 1941—. Dir., mem. exec. com. Ga. Life & Health Ins. Co., Ga. Investors, Inc., L.L. Antle & Co., Inc.; dir., trustee WRC Smith Pub. Co. Mem. Atlanta C. of C., Am. (mem. council, chmn. sect. labor relations), Ga. bar assns., Bryan Honor Soc., Sigma Alpha Epsilon, Phi Delta Phi. Baptist. Elk, Optimist, Clubs: Atlanta Athletic, Country, Commerce (Atlanta). Home: 1475 W Paces Ferry Rd NW Atlanta GA 30327 Office: National Bank of Ga Bldg Atlanta GA 30303

PEARL, MAURICE ALLEN, physician; b. Bklyn., Dec. 16, 1931; s. William Joseph and Rae (Weinblatt) P.; B.S., Tulane U., 1953, M.D., 1956; m. Rochelle Schreckinger, July 13, 1957; children—Michael, David, Richard. Intern, Mt. Sinai Hosp., N.Y.C., 1956-57; trainee Nat. Heart Inst., Tulane U., 1957-58, research fellow dept. medicine, 1961-63; resident internal medicine Charity Hosp. La., 1958-59; practice medicine specializing in internal medicine and nephrology, New Orleans, 1964—; mem. active staff So. Bapt. Hosp., 1970—, vice. chmn. sect. medicine, 1971—; mem. courtesy staff Touro Infirmary, 1964—; vis. physician Charity Hosp., 1961—; cons. renal diseases USPHS Hosp., New Orleans, 1961—; instr. dept. pathology Tulane U., 1957-58, dept. medicine, 1959-63, asst. prof. medicine, 1963-71, asso. clin. prof. medicine, 1971—. Trustee, chmn. med. adv. bd. Kidney Found. La. Served with USNR, 1959-61. Recipient Undergrad. award for med. research Borden Co., 1956. Diplomate Am. Bd. Internal Medicine. Fellow A.C.P.; mem. Am. Fedn. Clin. Research, A.M.A., Am. Soc. Internal Medicine, Am. Soc. Nephrology, Am., La. (dir. 1968-71) heart assns., La. State, Orleans Parish med. socs., La. Soc. Internal Medicine (pres. 1971-72), New Orleans Acad. Internal Medicine, New Orleans Kidney Soc. (pres. 1969-71), Alpha Omega Alpha. Contbr. articles to profl. jours. Home: 6309 Gladys St Metairie LA 70003 Office: 4303 Magnolia St New Orleans LA 70115

PEARSALL, DAVID MIDDLETON, chem. engr.; b. Rocky Mount, N.C., Mar. 22, 1937; s. Leon Moulton and Middleton (Trammell) P.; B.S., Davidson Coll., 1959; B.S. in Chem. Engring., Ga. Inst. Tech., 1961; m. Sally Heltzel, Sept. 7, 1963; children—Sally Ellen, Susan Middleton. Project engr. Internat. Paper Co., Mobile, Ala., 1962-67, sr. project engr., 1967-70, asst. pulp mill supt., 1970—. Served with AUS, 1961. Registered profl. engr., Ala. Mem. T.A.P.P.I., Am. Inst. Chem. Engrs., Mobile Jaycees (project chmn. 1970-71). Presbyn. (deacon 1969-72). Club: University of South Alabama Tip-Off (Mobile) (dir. 1971—). Home: 474 Pine Ct Mobile AL 36608 Office: Box 2448 Mobile AL 36601

PEARSALL, SAMUEL HAFF, diversified co. exec.; b. Guthrie, Ky., July 17, 1923; s. Samuel Haff and Claire (Miller) P.; B.E., Vanderbilt U., 1948, M.S., 1958; m. Isabelle Ikard, July 20, 1946; children—Samuel Haff III, Susan Claire, Sallie Mai, Timothy Hudson. Research and devel. staff WSM, Inc., Nashville, 1946-55; asso. prof. elec. engring. Vanderbilt U., 1955-63; v.p. R.W. Benson & Assos. Inc.,

Nashville, 1963-71, sec. of bd., 1963—; v.p. Bonitron, Inc., Nashville, 1965-71, sec. of bd., 1965-71; v.p. engring. Cutters Exchange, Nashville, 1971—; v.p., gen. mgr. Cutters Electronics Internat., 1971—; chief engr. Cutters Machine Co., 1971—. Mem. I.E.E.E. (sr. mem., chmn. Nashville sect. 1968), Sigma Xi. Mem. Christian Ch. (bd. dirs. 1968—). Patentee electronic instrumentation. Home: 118 Spring Valley Rd Donelson TN 37214 Office: 706 19th Av N Nashville TN 37203

PEARSON, BETSY DECELLE (MRS. WELTON DENNIS PEARSON), educator; b. Geromont, Liege, Belgium; d. Leon Gabriel and Camille Mignolet (Francois) DeCelle; student Sisters of Cross, Liege, Ecole Superieure de Demoiselles, Liege, Bus. Scis., Liege, Institut d'Education Physique, Liege; intern in re-edn. St. Laurent Mil. Hosp., 1943-44; M.Ed., U. Tenn., 1968; m. Welton Dennis Pearson, Apr. 24, 1946; 1 dau., Elisabeth Leone. Came to U.S., 1948, naturalized, 1964. Moniteur, Institut d'Education Physique, Liege, 1940-41, prof., 1942-43; asso. prof. Institut des Scis. Sociales, Liege, 1942-45; collaborator Laboratoire de Biometrie Experimentale, Liege, 1942-45, Sorbonne, 1962, N.D.E.A. Inst., 1965; now head lang. dept. Chattanooga High Sch. Vol. tchr. Talented Youth Program and Frey Inst.; mem. Opera Assn.; active Community Concerts, Heart Assn., United Fund, A.R.C.; treas. Newcomers Club. 1949; founder L'Amicale Francaise. Chattanooga, 1952. Served with Army of Liberation, 1940-45. Decorated Medaille de la Resistance (Belgium). Mieux Doues scholar, Liege, 3 years. Mem. Internat. Platform Assn., N.E.A., Am. Assn. Tchrs. French (pres. Tenn. 1967-68), Alpha Delta Kappa. Clubs: Music (dir. 1958-59), Metropolitan. Home: 938 McCallie Av Chattanooga TN 37403

PEARSON, CHARLS RICHARD, semioticist; b. Peru, Ind., May 31, 1932; s. Charles E. and Elizabeth (Wagner) P.; B.A., Ohio State U., 1955; M.S., U. Cin., 1962; postgrad. Rollins Coll., 1962, U. Houston, 1967, Ga. Inst. Tech.; m. Lois H. Polson, Jan. 24, 1953; children— Ann Elizabeth, Helen Margery, Charls Richard; m. 2d, Kathryn Diggs, Apr. 27, 1962; 1 dau., Sherilyn Joan. Mathematician N. Am. Aviation, Inc., Columbus, O., 1955-58; systems engr. Gen. Electric Co., Cin., 1958-59; group leader engring. computing Aeronca Mfg. Corp., Middletown, O., 1959-60; sr. systems engr. Martin Aircraft Co., Orlando, Fla., 1960-62; pres. Gen. Systems Assos., Orlando, 1962-63; chief systems engr. J.P. Stevens & Co., Inc., Wallace, S.C., 1963-67; sr. systems engr. Shell Devel. Co., Houston, 1967-68; project dir. Computone Information Systems, Inc. (formerly Computrol Systems, Inc.), Atlanta, 1968-69, research dir., 1969-70; research asso. Ga. Inst. Tech., Atlanta, 1970—. Mem. Good Govt. Atlanta. Asst. chmn. Orange County (Fla.) Democratic party, 1961-63. Mem. Assn. for Computing Machinery (past v.p. and founder Central Fla. chpt.), Instrument Soc. Am. (founder, past chmn. nat. tech. com. on computer systems instrumentation), Am. Assn. Textiles Chemists and Colorists. Democrat. Contbr. articles on computer systems instrumentation to tech. jours. Home: 2025 Peachtree Rd NE Apt 411 Atlanta GA 30309 Office: Ga Inst Tech Sch Information and Computer Sci Atlanta GA 30305

PEARSON, DAVID HENRY, pub. relations exec.; b. Bennington, Vt., May 3, 1932; s. Homer Colquitt and Elizabeth (Houran) P.; B.A., Emory U., 1958; m. Anne Stuart Bates, Nov. 5, 1960; children— Christopher, Margaret, Katherine. Corr., UPI, Montgomery, Ala., 1958-59; v.p. pub. relations Sea Pines Plantation, Hilton Head Island, S.C., 1959-63; dep. dir. information Peace Corps, Washington, 1963-65; v.p. pub. relations Bell & Stanton, Atlanta, 1965-66; pres. David Pearson Assos., Coral Gables, Fla., 1966—; dir. Sea Pines Plantation Co. Cons. Urban Land Inst., Washington, 1968, Fla. Bar, 1970, U.S. Justice Dept., 1966. Served with USCG, 1951-54. Recipient Pub. Service award Fla. Pros. Atty.'s Assn., 1971. Mem. Golf Writers Assn. Am. Democrat. Roman Catholic. Contbr. Sat. Rev., Pageant, Esquire. Home: 500 Hardee Rd Coral Gables FL 33146 Office: 312 Minorca Av Coral Gables FL 33134

PEARSON, GROSVENOR BENJAMIN, psychiatrist; b. Pitts., July 6, 1907; s. Eugene Oscar and Blanche (Righter) P.; B.S., U. Pitts., 1930, M.D., 1932. Intern, Med. Center, Pitts., 1932-33; resident Boston Psychopathic Hosp., 1933-36; practice medicine, specializing in psychiatry, Foxboro, Mass., 1936-42, Pitts., 1942-62, St. Petersburg, Fla., 1962—; dir. Western Psychiat. Inst. and Clinic, Pitts., 1942-49; psychiatrist Mental Health Clinic, VA Outpatient Service, St. Petersburg, 1962—; asso. prof. psychiatry U. Pitts. Med. Sch., 1942-62. Diplomate Am. Bd. Psychiatry and Neurology, Am. Bd. Clinic Hypnosis. Fellow (life) Am. Psychiat. Assn., Am. Soc. for Psychical Research, A.A.A.S.; mem. A.M.A., Am. Psychopath. Assn. (life), Western Pa. Soc. Clin. Hypnosis (hon.), Parapsychol. Assn. (asso. mem.), Order Ky. Cols., Nu Sigma Nu. Republican. Episcopalian. Club: Bath (St. Petersburg). Home: 10355 Paradise Blvd Treasure Island FL 33706 Office: Fed Bldg St Petersburg FL 33701

PEARSON, JOHN EARL, univ. adminstr.; b. Gilmer, Tex., Jan. 18, 1926; s. John Henry and Vera (Berry) P.; B.S., N. Tex. State U., 1948, M.S., 1948; Ph.D., Ind. U., 1956; m. Olga Bob Read, Aug. 31, 1947; children—John Read, Monte Lee, Eric Lynn. Prof. bus. statistics, chmn. div. gen. bus. N. Tex. State U., Denton, 1957-63; prof. bus. adminstrn., dir. Sch. Bus. Adminstrn., dean Coll. Bus. Adminstrn., Tex. A. and M. U., College Station, 1963—. First v.p., dir. Tereco Corp., Bryan, Tex.; dir. City Nat. Bank, Bryan, Tex.; statis., econs. cons. small bus. firms and pub. service agys. Chmn. Brazos County (Tex.) Heart Assn. campaign, 1964-65; bus. mgr. College Station Little League, 1969-70. Served with USAAF, 1943-45. Regional Faculty Research fellow in econs. Stanford U., 1960. Mem. Am. Econs. Assn., Am. Statistics Assn., Southwestern Social Sci. Assn., Tex. Commn. on Population Study, Dallas Mgmt. Assn., Bryan-College Station C. of C. (dir. 1969-71), Phi Kappa Phi, Beta Gamma Sigma, Sigma Iota Epsilon Author: (with O.J. Curry) Basic Mathmatics for Business Analysis, 1961; also monographs, articles. Home: 1100 Walton Dr College Station TX 77840

PEARSON, NELS R., judge; b. Chgo., May 8, 1934; s. Ragnar H. and Svea (Lilygren) P.; B.B.A., U. Miami, 1955, J.D., 1961; m. Patricia J. Thompson, Dec. 26, 1956; children—Wesley David, Darryl Thomas. Admitted to Fla. bar, 1961; spl. asst. atty. gen. Fla., 1961; city prosecutor, Fort Lauderdale, Fla., 1961-64, judge, 1964-67; judge of indsl. claims Fla. Indsl. Commn., Fort Lauderdale, 1967-68; judge Ct. Record, Broward County, Fort Lauderdale, 1968—. Bd. dirs. Broward County Lions Eye Found. Served with AUS, 1956-58. Mem. Delta Theta Phi. Mason. Club: Lions (pres. 1970-71). Address: Broward County Courthouse Fort Lauderdale FL 33301

PEARSON, ORRIN WALTER, dentist; b. Mpls., Nov. 7, 1917; s. Gustav Walter and Esther Marie (Bogren) P.; D.D.S., U. Minn., 1943; m. Mildred Mae Knox, Jan. 5, 1946; children—David Orrin, Marsha Elizabeth. Pvt. practice dentistry, Mpls., 1946-47; staff dentist VA Hosp., St. Cloud, Minn., 1947-51, Oklahoma City, 1951-64, asst. chief dental service, 1964-71, acting chief dental service, 1971—. Instr. dental surgery U. Okla. Sch. Medicine, 1961-66, asst. clin. prof. dental surgery, 1966—. Asst. scoutmaster, counselor Last Frontier council Boy Scouts Am., 1958-61; active Oklahoma City Symphony Soc. Opera Guild. Bd. dirs. VA Hosp. Fed. Credit Union, 1957-66. Served with USNR, 1943-46; PTO. Mem. Am. Dental Assn. Republican. Baptist. Mason. Home: 4928 N Pate Av Oklahoma City OK 73112 Office: 921 NE 13th St Oklahoma City OK 73104

PEARSON, PAUL CHESTER, physician; b. Arlington, Ill., July 31, 1901; s. Oscar Grant and Flora Mabel (Jones) P.; student William and Mary Coll., 1917-18, Randolph Macon Coll., 1927-28; M.D., Med. Coll. Va., 1933; m. Virginia Drewry McGeorge, Nov. 2, 1927; 1 dau., Patricia Cosette (Mrs. James Lee Hill). Intern, Christ Hosp., Jersey City, 1933-34; pvt. practice medicine, Aylett, Va., 1934-45, Warsaw, Va., 1945—; med. examiner Richmond County (Va.), 1946—; mem. staff Tappahaunaule Meml. Hosp., also now sec. Trustee King William County Sch. Electoral Bd., 1940, Mattaponi Indian Reservation, 1936. Served with USNR, 1920-28, Fellow Royal Soc. Health (fellow 1971); mem. Midtidewater (pres. 1940), No. Neck (pres. 1947) med. assns., Va. Thoracic Soc., Med. Soc. Va., So. Med. Soc. Mason. Home: Richmond Rd Warsaw VA 22572

PEARSON, WELTON DENNIS, prosthodontist; b. Jackson, Tenn., Oct. 20, 1906; s. Nedham B. and Elizabeth (Reid) P.; D.D.S., U. Tenn., 1936; postgrad. U. Pa., Ohio U., U. Mich., Tufts Coll., Northwestern U. Dental Sch., U. Ala. Sch. Dentistry, Marquette U. Sch. Dentistry; m. Betsy DeCelle, Apr. 24, 1946; 1 dau., Elisabeth Leone. Intern, M.C. Hosp., 1936-37; pvt. practice dentistry, Jackson, 1934-41, Chattanooga, 1947—; dir., mem. med. adv. bd. Chattanooga-Hamilton County Speech and Hearing Center; mem. staff Baroness Erlanger Hosp., 1949—; prosthodontist Siskin Rehab. Center for Physically Handicapped. Clinician nat. and internat. meetings; mem. regional cleft palate team Tenn. Health Dept. Served from 1st lt. to lt. col. Dental Corps, AUS, 1942-47; ETO. Diplomate Am. Bd. Prosthodontics. Mem. Fedn. Dentaire Internationale; Am. Coll. Prosthodontists, Am. Dental Assn., Tenn., 3d Dist. dental socs., Am. Denture Soc., So. Acad. Oral Surgery, Am. Soc. Dentistry Children, Royal Soc. Health London, Nat. Rehab. Assn., Assn. Mil. Surgeons U.S., Chgo. Dental Soc., Delta Sigma Delta. Presbyn. (elder). Mason. Contbr. articles in field. Prosthetics abstract editor Jour. of Tenn. Dental Assn. Address: 938 McCallie Av Chattanooga TN 37403

PEAVLER, BILL EUGENE, architect; b. Gotebo, Okla., June 1, 1923; s. Leonard Oscar and Florence (Swanson) P.; B.Arch., U. Okla., 1952; m. Charlotte Ann Lindsay, Mar. 19, 1949; children—Marcia Michael, Lindsay Kirk, Kristyn Ann, Sally Jeannee. Supt. constrn. Air Borne Engrs., Dutch New Guinea, Philippines, 1943-45; archtl. draftsman, engr. asst. Oklahoma City Bd. Edn., 1948-50; archtl. draftsman H-T-B & Assos., Oklahoma City, 1950-57; architect Hudgins-Thompson-Ball & Assos., Oklahoma City, 1957-60; gen. practice architecture, Oklahoma City, 1960—. Bd. dirs. Oklahoma City Community Counseling and Guidance Center. Served with AUS, 1943-45. Recipient Silver Beaver award Boys Scouts Am. Mem. A.I.A., Oklahoma City C. of C., U. Okla. Alumni Assn., Phi Kappa Sigma. Democrat. Methodist. Club: Oklahoma City Figure Skating. Office: 1010 Liberty Tower Oklahoma City OK 73102

PEAVY, JAMES EVERETT, JR., state ofcl.; b. Lufkin, Tex., Jan. 21, 1911; s. James Everett and Mamie (McClendon) P.; student Baylor U., 1927-30, M.D., 1935; M.P.H., Harvard, 1955; m. Frieda M. McNeal, July 28, 1936; children—Diane (Mrs. Cox), Janet Marie (Mrs. Prouse). Dir. health unit, Sweetwater, Tex., 1946-47; med. field cons. Tex. Dept. Health, 1947-55, dir. communicable disease div., 1955-59; commr. health Tex. Dept. Health, Austin, 1959—; lectr. Sch. Pub. Health, Houston. Adviser, U.S. delegation to 22d World Health Assembly, Boston, 1969. Served with M.C., AUS, 1942-46; PTO. Recipient Arthur G. McCormack award Am. Assn. Pub. Health Physicians. Diplomate Am. Bd. Preventive Medicine. Mem. A.M.A., Tex. Med. Assn., Am., Tex. pub. health assns., Am. Assn. Pub. Health Physicians, State and Territorial Health Officers (past pres.). Mason (Shriner), Rotarian. Contbr. articles to med. jours. Home: 11908 Oak Trail Austin TX 78753 Office: 1100 W 49th St Austin TX 78756

PECK, CECIL PAGE, psychologist; b. Lake Park, Minn., Feb. 16, 1922; s. George and Mabel (Barstad) P.; B.A., Concordia Coll., 1947; Ph.D., U. Ky., 1952; m. Joan Heinz, July 25, 1947; children—Lori Jo. Michael Page. Chief psychology service VA Hosp., Sheridan, Wyo., 1951-54; chief psychology tng. VA Hosp., Salt Lake City, 1955-56; chief cons. psychologist dept. medicine and surgery VA, Washington, 1956-61, chief psychology div., 1961—. Cons. mental health, rehab. to various fed. agys., states. Bd. dirs. Christ Ch. Child Center, Bethesda, Md. Served to capt. USAAF, 1942-46. Decorated Air medal with oak leaf cluster. Mem. Am. Psychol. Assn., A.A.A.S., Sigma Xi. Home: 9020 Honeybee Lane Bethesda MD 20034 Office: 810 Vermont Av Washington DC 20420

PECK, FELIX BREVARD, clergyman; b. nr. Concord, N.C., Feb. 1, 1897; s. Calvin Emanuel and Anna Beruna (Lentz) P.; A.B., Catawba Coll., 1919; B.D., Eden Theol. Sem., 1922; S.T.D., Wesley Theol. Sem., 1936; m. Annie J. Little, June 21, 1921; children—Howard Wayne, Larry Brevard. Ordained minister Evang. and Reformed Ch., 1922; pastor Clear Spring (Md.) Charge of Reformed Ch., 1922-27, St. Mary's Reformed Ch., Silver Run, 1927-38, Milton Av. Evang. and Reformed Ch., Louisville, 1938-44; asso. exec. sec. Dept. Ministry to Service Men, Ch. Fedn. Greater Chgo., 1944-46; dir. Ch. Extension Evang. and Reformed Ch., Chgo. area, 1946-49; pastor First Evang. and Reformed Ch., Charlotte, N.C., 1949-52; defense service minister Nat. Council Chs., Paducah, Ky., 1952-54; exec. dir. Council Chs., Yonkers, N.Y., 1954-62; acting pastor Mount Pleasant (N.C.) Charge of United Ch. of Christ, 1963-69. Pres. Md. Classis of Reformed Ch., 1926-27; chmn. stewardship com. Potomac Synod, Reformed Ch., 1936, del. Gen. Synod, 1932-38. Mem. Hist. Soc. Evangelical and Reformed Ch. (sec. So. chpt. 1962-69, v.p. So. chpt. 1969-72). Rotarian (pres. 1970-71). Home: R D 2 Gold Hill NC 28071

PECK, HARRY TEAL, concrete pipe co. exec.; b. Dallas, Feb. 6, 1923; s. Robert Thomas and Jimmie Mariah (Massey) P.; B.S., Tex. A. and M. U., 1948; m. Patsy Ruth Jones, Jan. 23, 1945; children—Sandra Jo, Janet K. (Mrs. Charles Precopia), Nancy Sue. Engr. research and devel. Twin Disc Clutch Co., 1948-53; v.p., gen. mgr. Gifford-Hill Pipe Co., Dallas, 1953—. Democratic precinct chmn., 1962—. Served to 1st lt. USAAF, 1943-45; ETO. Decorated Air medal with three oak leaf clusters, D.F.C. Registered profl. engr., Tex. Mason. Home: 1912 Elmhurst St Arlington TX 76012 Office: 2949 Stemmons Freeway Dallas TX 75247

PECK, JOSEPH COSGROVE, physician; b. Harerstraw, N.Y., Aug. 29, 1920; s. Joseph Cosgrove and Sophie Elizabeth (Lipinski) P.; B.S. in Chemistry, John B. Stetson U., 1949; M.D., Temple U. Med. Sch., 1953; m. Mary Bell Goode, Sept. 29, 1945; children—Susan (Mrs. Wyatt Bowman), Linda, Stephen. Intern, Temple U. Hosp., Phila., 1953-54; pvt. practice medicine, Galax, Va., 1954—; mem. staff Galax Gen. Hosp., bd. dirs., 1958—, chief staff, 1967, 72, med. dir. coronary care unit, 1970—; mem. staff Waddell Hosp., Galax. Served with AUS, 1942-46. Mem. Am., Va. acads. gen. practice, S.W. Va. Med. Soc., Va. Med. Soc., A.M.A. Elk. Home: Williams St Galax VA 24333 Office: 400 W Center St Galax VA 24333

PECK, MARY ANN EKSTROM (MRS. PAUL SANFORD PECK), designer, horse and dog breeder, civic worker; b. Hibbing, Minn., Apr. 12, 1920; d. Edwin Carl and Ethel Sophia (Solmonson) Ekstrom; grad. Hockaday Jr. Coll., 1939; degree in costume design and illustration Parson's N.Y. Sch. Fine and Applied Arts, 1939-42; m. Paul Sanford Peck, Feb. 14, 1943 (dec. Mar. 1964); children—Carl Sanford, Randal Nelson. Fashion coordinator coll. attire Neiman Marcus Co., Dallas, 1937-42; dir. Nuecces Transp. Co., Corpus Christi, Tex., 1945-64, exec. v.p., 1964-67; dir. Nueces Mack Truck Co., Nueces Truck & Equipment Leasing Co., 1950-64, exec. v.p., 1964-67; breeder saddle horses, showing and training Arabians, Am. Saddlebreds and Ponies, 1959—; owner Greyhound Equine and Canine Farms, Inc., Corpus Christi, 1964—. Donated (with father) and worked on building Carmelite Day Nursery, 1966; established perpetual fund for underprivileged boys YMCA, 1965; vol. work Jr. League, 1940-60; vol. decorator and designer for clubs and charities, 1945-53; pres. Charity League, 1960; charter mem. Gulf Coast Charity Horse Show, 1964, sec., 1964-65, v.p., 1967, v.p., sec., 1972. chmn. Buccaneer Day Parade, 1959. Named hon. dep. sheriff Nueces County, 1949, Friend of Ct., 1949. Mem. Am. Saddlebred Futurity Assn., Am. Horse Shows Assn., Nat. Coursing Assn., Las Donas de la Corte (charter), Order de Pineda (v.p. 1947, steering com. 1966). Democrat. Episcopalian. Clubs: Am. Cotillion (charter), Corpus Christi Country, Corpus Christi Town. Home: 401 Coral Pl Corpus Christi TX 78411

PECK, ROBERT FRANKLIN, educator, psychologist; b. Buffalo, Sept. 22, 1919; s. Charles R. and Jessie M. (Kelley) P.; B.Sc., U. Buffalo, 1941; M.Sc., Albany State Coll., 1942; Ph.D., U. Chgo., 1951; m. Tina Casillas, Apr. 9, 1946; children—Joan L., Brian C. Instr. to research asso. U. Chgo., 1947-54; cons. on exec. assessment Social Research, Inc., 1947-50; v.p. Worthington Assos., Inc., 1950-54; asso. prof. ednl. psychology U. Tex., 1954-59, prof., 1959—; dir. Personality Research Center, 1958—, Research and Devel. Center in Tchr. Edn., 1965—; dir. Mgmt. Devel. Services, Austin, Tex. and Chgo., 1957—. Vis. prof. Nat. U. Mexico, 1960. Mem. Am. Ednl. Research Assn., Internat. Assn. Sci. Psychology, Inter-Am. Soc. Psychology, Soc. Research Child Devel., Am. Psychol. Assn., Internat. Soc. for Study Behavorial Devel., Sigma Xi. Author: The Psychology of Character Development, 1960; research publs. on personality theory, personalizing edn., cross-cultural studies of coping skills and achievement. Home: 3304 Glen Rose Dr Austin TX 78731

PECK, T. T., JR., physician, oil investor; b. Poteau, Okla., Sept. 21, 1923; s. T.T. and Bonnie Louise (Patterson) P.; student Rice U., 1941-43; M.D., Baylor U., 1947-50; m. Ruby Rose Corley, Mar. 27, 1948; children—Larry Temple, Terry Rose. Intern, U.S. Naval Hosp., Pensacola, Fla., 1950-51; gen. practice medicine, Baytown, Tex., 1951-58; practice medicine, specializing med. hypnosis and psychosomatic medicine, 1958-62; NIH grantee, resident psychosomatic medicine, 1962; now in practice, Centerville, Tex.; chief staff Leon County Hosp., Buffalo, Tex. Adviser, Nat. Trainers Assn.; lectr. Pres. Birthdays, Inc.; city and county health officer. Mem. Centerville city council; pres. Leon County Devel. Corp.; participant 2d Congress Mental Health, Chgo., 1964. Served as lt. (j.g.), USNR, 1944-46: PTO; as lt. M.C., USNR: Korean War. Mem. Am. Soc. Clin. Hypnosis (life), A.M.A., Tex., Harris County med. assns., Am. Acad. Gen. Practice, Tex. Municipal League, Internat. Traders Assn., Oil and Gas Soc., Acad. Psychosomatic Medicine, Soc. Psychophysiol. Medicine, Brazos County Med. Soc., Royal Soc. Health (London, Eng.), Psychophysiol. Research Assn., Phi Beta Phi. Republican. Active in research with LSD-25, mescaline, psilocybin; study of Indians in Mexico using sacred mushrooms; co-inventor Lee Traction Shield; mem. Internat. Symposium on LSD-25 and Psychiatry, Princeton, 1959. Home: Camp NaJaha Centerville TX Office: Centerville Med Center Centerville TX 75833

PECKHAM, MORSE, educator; b. Yonkers, N.Y., Aug. 17, 1914; s. Ray Morse and Edith (Roake) P.; B.A., U. Rochester, 1935; M.A., Princeton, 1938, Ph.D., 1947. Asst. prof. The Citadel, Charleston, S.C., 1938-41; instr. Rutgers U., New Brunswick, N.J., 1947-48, asst. prof., 1948-49, U. Pa., Phila., 1949-52, asso. prof., 1952-60, prof. English lit., 1960-67, dir. Inst. Humanistic Studies for Execs., 1953-54, dir. U. Pa. Press, 1953-55; Distinguished prof. English and comparative lit. U. S.C., Columbia, 1967—. Served to lt. AUS., also USAAF, 1941-45. Decorated Bronze Star medal. Mem. Modern Lang. Assn., Soc. Archtl. Historians. Author: Charles Darwin's The Origin of Species: A Variorum Text, 1959; Humanistic Education for Business Executives, 1960; (with Seymour Chatman) Word, Meaning Poem, 1961; Beyond the Tragic Vision, 1962; Man's Rage for Chaos, 1965; Romanticism, 1965; Art and Pornography, 1969; The Triumph of Romanticism, 1970; Swinburne: Poems and Ballads and Atalanta in Calydon, 1970. Home: 6478 Bridgewood Rd Columbia SC 29206

PECKHAM, RUFUS WHEELER, JR., lawyer; b. N.Y.C., Jan. 25, 1928; s. Rufus Wheeler and Virginia (Selden) P.; B.S., Am. U., 1953; LL.B., Washington Coll. Law, 1957. Dep. clk. D.C. Municipal Ct., 1954-57; admitted to D.C. bar, 1958; Washington rep. Wine Inst., 1957-60; pvt. practice law, Washington, 1961—; spl. partner Shipley Ackerman Stein & Kaps, Washington, 1966—. Mem. D.C. Alcoholic Beverage Control Bd., 1970—. Mem. D.C. Republican Com., 1955-70, sec., 1968-70; field coordinator Republican Nat. Com., Washington, 1960-61. Served with USMC, 1946-48. Recipient Outstanding Service award D.C. Chief Police, 1969. Mem. Am., D.C. bar assns., Internat. Assn. Chiefs of Police, S.A.R., Alpha Tau Omega, Delta Theta Phi. Episcopalian. Clubs: Metropolitan, International of Washington (hon.). Home: 2501 Q St NW Washington DC 20007 Office: 1108 Nat Pres Bldg 529 14th St NW Washington DC 20004

PECKHAM, WILLIAM HENRY, III, lumber co. exec.; b. Houston, Mar. 11, 1929; s. Rufus Walter and Frances Mary (Jackson) P.; grad. high sch.; m. Mary Elizabeth Sparks, Jan. 2, 1968; children—Mary Lou Turner, Elizabeth Ann Rhemann, Joan Olive, Harriett Carlton, William Henry IV. Owner, West End Lumber Co., Houston, 1968—. Bd. dirs., founder R. W. Peckham Meml. Arboretum and Bot. Gardens. Mem. Quarter Horse Racing Guild (pres. 1965-67). Club: Houston Country Home: Route 2 Box 109 Richmond TX 77469 Office: 2704 North Blvd Houston TX 77006

PECOUL, JOHN ALBERT, JR., urban affairs specialist; b. New Orleans, Sept. 7, 1939; s. John Albert and Louella (Tardy) P.; B.A. with highest honor in Philosophy, Elmhurst Coll., 1961; certificate Internat. Fellows program Columbia, 1964; B.D. magna cum laude, Union Theol. Sem., 1964; M.A. in Polit. Sci., Temple U., 1967; m. Ellen Theodora Rasche, Aug. 18, 1963; children—Camille Sophia, Rachel Ellen. Resident dir. Ch. and World Inst., Temple U., Phila., 1964-66, teaching asst. dept. polit. sci., 1965-66; research asso. So. Regional Council, Atlanta, 1966-67; dir. community services and housing Urban League New Orleans, 1967-69, mem., 1970—; exec. dir. human relations com. city New Orleans, 1969—. Vis lectr. Xavier U., La., 1967—. Inst. Politics fellow Loyola U. of South, 1969-70. Mem. Am. Polit. Sci. Assn., New Orleans Coalition, Am. Civil Liberties Union La. Mem. United Ch. Christ. Author: To House A City (introductory handbook on housing in New Orleans), 1967. Home: 7614 Sycamore St New Orleans LA 70118 Office: City Hall 1300 Perdio St New Orleans LA 70112

PEDEN, JAMES ALTON, JR., lawyer; b. Gainesville, Fla., Apr. 24, 1944; s. James Alton and Frances Merle (Wilson) P.; B.A. summa cum laude, U. Miss., 1966, J.D. (Ford Found. Law fellow), 1970; postgrad.

(Fulbright scholar) U. Bristol (Eng.), 1966-67. Admitted to Miss., 1970; asso. firm Stennett, Wilkinson & Ward, Jackson, Miss., 1970—; staff asst. to Miss. lt. gov., 1972; reading clk. Miss. Senate, 1972. Staff asst. to Senator John C. Stennis, 1964, 65; asst. publicity dir. William Winter's campaign for Gov. Miss., 1967; mem. Hinds County Democratic Exec. Com., 1972—. Fellow Inst. Politics Miss., 1971-72. Mem. Am., Hinds Co., Jackson Jr. bar assns., Miss. State Bar, Miss. Hist. Soc., Beta Theta Pi, Omicron Delta Kappa, Phi Delta Phi, Phi Kappa Phi, Phi Eta Sigma, Phi Alpha Theta, Pi Sigma Alpha, Eta Sigma Phi. Baptist. Contbr. articles to legal jours. Home: 507 Merigold Dr Jackson MS 39204 Office: Suite 600 Barnett Bldg PO Box 673 Jackson MS 39205

PEDEN, KATHERINE GRAHAM, constrn. co. exec., industrialist; b. Hopkinsville, Ky., Jan. 2 1926; d. William E. and Mary (Gorin) Peden; grad. pub. schs. Ky. With radio sta. WHOP, Hopkinsville, Ky., 1944-64, v.p. 1957-64; pres. UNEX Bldg. Systems, Inc., Louisville. Mem. personnel bd. Commonwealth of Ky., 1960-63; commr. commerce, mem. Gov.'s Cabinet, 1963-67; President's Commn. on Civil Disorders, 1967-68. Mem. Democratic party Com. on Party Reform, 1969. Trustee Bus. and Profl. Women's Found., 1958-62. Recipient Woman of Year award Hopkinsville, 1951. Mem. Fedn. Bus. and Profl. Women's Clubs (pres. Ky. 1955-56, 1st nat. v.p. 1960-61, nat. pres. 1961-62), Am. Indsl. Devel. Council. Mem. Christian Ch. (deaconess 1956-59, 60-63). Home: 2118 S Virginia St Hopkinsville KY 42240 Office: 1400 S Western Pkwy Louisville KY 40211

PEDEN, MARIE MCKINNEY (MRS. RALPH HUTCHINGS PEDEN), editor; b. Greenville, S.C., Sept. 15, 1912; d. M. Ansel and Lillie (Barton) McKinney; B.A., Brenau Coll., 1932; m. Ralph Hutchings Peden, Oct. 19, 1934 (dec. 1969); children—Patricia Elaine, Ralph Hatchings. Bookkeeper Ivey's & Cabaniss-Gardner Co., Greenville, 1934-42; substitute tchr. city schs., 1953-54; asst. women's editor Greenville Piedmont, 1955-58, woman's editor, 1958—. Pres. local P.T.A., 1953-54; publicity chmn. local U.S.O. Vol. Corps, 1958-60, co-chmn. publicity, 1960-62. Recipient state awards in field, 1960-71; Greenville Bus. and Profl. Women's Career Woman of Year, 1963; Spl. award Nat. Fedn. Music Clubs, 1964, 68, spl. award of merit, 1971; Community Service award Salvation Army, 1965; Appreciation plaque from Gen. Hosp. for publicity service to community; named Newspaper Woman of Yr. S.C., 1967. Mem. S.C. Congress Parents and Tchrs. (life), Women in C. of C. (charter; community service award 1965), Delta Zeta. Presbyn. Clubs: Augusta Road Community (officer, com. chmn. 1952-58), Zonta (charter mem., v.p. 1961-62, Woman of Yr. 1972), Woman's (charter mem.) (Greenville). Home: 18 Tomassee Av Greenville SC 29605 Office: The Greenville Piedmont Box 1688 Greenville SC 29602

PEDEN, PHIL, judge; b. Ft. Worth, Sept. 14, 1916; s. Robert Franklin and Laura (Phillips) P.; A.B., Rice U., 1938; postgrad. Law Sch., George Washington U., 1940-42; m. Lois Lee Qualtrough, Apr. 20, 1941; children—Phil, Scott. Spl. agt. FBI, 1942-47; admitted to Tex. bar, 1946; practiced law, Houston, 1947-51; judge County Ct. at Law, Houston, 1951-57, Civil Dist. Ct., Houston, 1957-67; asso. justice Tex. 1st Ct. Civil Appeals, Houston, 1967—. Mem. Tex. Jud. Qualifications Commn. Mem. State Bar Tex. (past mem. exec. bd. jud. sect.), Soc. Former FBI Agts. (past chmn. Houston), Assn. Rice Alumni (past pres.), Phi Delta Phi. Episcopalian (past sr. warden). Home: 3727 Albans Rd Houston TX 77005 Office: Civil Courts Bldg Houston TX 77002

PEDEN, ROBERT F., JR., lawyer; b. Ft. Worth, July 26, 1911; s. Robert F. and Laura (Phillips) P.; LL.B., Cumberland U., 1933; m. Virginia LeTulle, May 25, 1939. Admitted to Tex. bar, 1934; practice law, Bay City, 1934—; city atty., Bay City, 1935-38, 65—; atty. Matagorda County, Tex., 1939-46, 50-54. Bd. dirs. Bay City Library Assn. Mem. State Bar Tex., Am., Matagorda (pres. 1961-62, v.p. 1967-68) bar assns., Am. Judicature Soc., Bay City C. of C. (dir. 1968-69), Lambda Chi Alpha. Democrat. Presbyn. (clk. session 1969-71). Rotarian (v.p. 1968-69, pres. 1969-70). Club: Knife and Fork (dir. 1968-69, pres. 1970-71). Home: 1916 Austin St Bay City TX Office: 1212 7th St PO Box 1245 Bay City TX 77414

PEDERSEN, HARALD ANSGAR, govt. ofcl.; b. Niagara, N.D., Jan. 16, 1911; s. Peder Hansen and Emilie (Anderson) P.; A.B., N.M. State U., 1939; M.A., La. State U., 1942; Ph.D., U. Wis., 1949; m. Edna Ross Strong, Dec. 14, 1945; 1 dau., Sidney Strong. Asst. prof. sociology Miss. State U., University Park, 1949-51, asso. prof., 1951-55, prof. 1955-57; community devel. adviser ICA, Pakistan, 1957-59; prof. sociology Mont. State U., Bozeman, 1959-63; statistician U.S. Bur. Census, Washington, 1962-63; cons. demography and research AID, Pakistan, 1963-70, with Office of Population, Washington, 1970—. Fulbright scholar, Denmark, 1954-55. Served with AUS, 1942-45. Fellow Am. Sociol. Assn.; mem. Population Assn. Am., Internat. Union for Sci. Study of Population. Address: AID Dept of State Washington DC 20005

PEDERSEN, RALPH, univ. athletic adminstr. Asst. athletic dir. Tulane U., New Orleans. Address: Athletic Dept Tulane U New Orleans LA 70118

PEDERSEN, THOMAS AUGUST, lawyer; b. Ribe, Denmark, Aug. 26, 1908 (parents Am. Citizens); s. Peder and Marie (Hahn) P.; A.B., U. Mich., 1932, J.D., 1934; m. Inez Smitherman, Apr. 28, 1940; children—Thomas Douglas, William Randolph. Admitted to Tenn. bar, 1935, since practiced in Knoxville; also admitted to U.S. Supreme Ct., U.S. Cts. Appeal for 4th, 5th, 6th dists.; Law clk. TVA, 1935, jr. atty., 1936-39, asso. atty., 1939, atty. 1940, sr. atty., 1941-48, prin. atty., 1948-53, asst. gen. counsel, 1953-69, solicitor, 1969-71. Mem. exec. bd., dist. chmn. Great Smokey Mountain council Boy Scouts Am., 1959. Served from pvt. to capt. CAC, C.E., AUS, 1942-46. Fellow Am. Coll. Trial Lawyers; mem. Fed., Am., Tenn., Knoxville bar assns. Rotarian, Elk. Club: Holston Hills Country. Home: 5801 Marilyn Dr Knoxville TN 37914 Office: TVA Law Div Knoxville TN 37902

PEEBLES, DICK, newspaper editor; b. Oil City, Pa., July 4, 1918; s. Herbert Lester and Sarah (Hagen) P.; student pub. schs., Erie, Pa.; m. Mary Theresa Holman, Nov. 7, 1950; children—Michael, Timothy. With Erie Dispatch-Herald, 1936-40, Sharon (Pa.) Herald, 1940-41, San Antonio Express, 1946-58; sports editor Houston Chronicle, 1958—. Served with AUS, 1942-46. Mem. Baseball Writers Assn. Am., Football Writers Assn. Am., Golf Writers Assn. Am., Delta Sigma Chi. Roman Catholic. Home: 9103 McAvoy Dr Houston TX 77036 Office: 512 Travis St Houston TX 77002

PEEBLES, GORDON ERVIN, architect; b. Raleigh, N.C., Aug. 1, 1923; s. Troy Herman and Lilly Belle (Council) P.; student N.C. State Coll., 1946-50; m. Lottie Lee Hight, Dec. 25, 1945; children—Gordon Ervin, Linda Anne, Patricia Diane. With L. Byron Burney, A.I.A., Raleigh, N.C., 1950; architect, engr. U.S. Govt., Fort Bragg, N.C., 1951-56; asso. architect W.L. Saunders, Fayetteville, N.C., 1956-59; pvt. practice architecture, 1959—. Served with USCGR, 1942-45. Decorated Purple Heart. Mem. A.I.A., N.C. Inst. Architects, Fayetteville C. of C. Baptist. Moose, Kiwanian. Home: 500 Glenville Av Fayetteville NC 28303 Office: PO Box 754 145 Rowan St Fayetteville NC 28302

PEEK, HAROLD FRED, constrn. co. exec.; b. Dallas, Feb. 6, 1939; s. Fred Nash and Ella Rae (Hugghins) P.; student Baylor U., 1957-58; B.B.A., So. Meth. U., 1961; m. Sarah Ann Eaker, Jan. 18, 1963; children—Melissa Ann, Harold Fred. Vice pres. constrn. Peek Enterprises, Inc., Dallas, 1961-65, exec. v.p. 1965-68, pres., chief exec. officer, 1969—; dir. BJSS, INC. Mem. Bldg. Code Bd. adjustment, plumbing Code Bd. Adjustment, Richardson, Tex., 1967-71. Active, United Fund, So. Meth. U. Sustentation Fund. Served with USAF, 1961-67. Mem. Home and Apartment Builders Assn. Met. Dallas (pres. 1971), Tex. Assn. Builders (bd. dirs.), Nat. Assn. Home Builders (bd. dirs.). Baptist. Clubs: Northwood, Mustang, Dervish, Salesmanship (all Dallas). 3611 Villanova Dr Dallas TX 75225 Office: PO Box 12146 Dallas TX 75225

PEEL, ELBERT SIDNEY, JR., judge; b. Williamston, N.C., Feb. 14, 1922; s. Elbert Sidney and Fannie (Manning) P.; student Va. Episcopal Sch., 1939-40; A.B., U. N.C., 1943, LL.B., 1949; m. Lucia Claire Hutchinson, Feb. 2, 1957; children—Lucia Claire, Sarah Margaret, Sydney Eldridge, Elizabeth Chase. Admitted to N.C. bar, 1949; mem. firm Peel & Peel, Williamston, 1949-63; resident judge 2d jud. dist. N.C., Williamston, 1963—. Chmn. Martin County (N.C.) Hosp. Com., 1960-63. Mem. N.C. Senate, 1959-61; mem. N.C. Ho. of Reps., 1961-63. Served to lt. (j.g.) USNR, 1943-46; served to capt. AUS, 1951-53. Mem. Williamston Jr. C. of C. (pres. 1955), Phi Beta Kappa, Zeta Psi. Democrat. Mem. Christian Ch. Kiwanian (pres. 1962). Home: Franklin St Williamston NC 27892 Office: Martin County Courthouse Williamston NC 27892

PEELER, ELIZABETH HASTINGS, librarian; b. Nashville, Apr. 5, 1914; d. John Thomas and Luna (Hastings) Peeler; B.A., Vanderbilt U., 1935, M.A., 1936; B.A. in L.S., Emory U., 1939; M.S. in L.S., Columbia, 1950. Tchr., Alvin C. York Inst., Jamestown, 1936-38; asst., acting librarian Southwestern at Memphis, 1939-42; asst. librarian Birmingham-So. Coll., 1942-44, Agnes Scott Coll. Decatur, Ga., 1944-46; head catalog dept. U. Miami (Fla.), 1946-60; sub-librarian, lectr. library sci. U. Ibadan, Nigeria, 1960-64; chief catalog sect. Dag Hammarskjold Library, UN, 1964-65; head catalog dept. State U. N.Y., Stony Brook, 1965-67; asso. dir. tech. services U. West Fla., Pensacola, 1967-71; internat. affairs librarian Fla. Internat. U., Miami, 1971—. Vis. lectr. div. librarianship Emory U., summer 1967, 70; vis. lectr. U. Denver Grad. Sch. Librarianship, summer 1969. Mem. Fla (pres. 1956-57), Dade County (pres. 1958-59) library assns., Spl. Libraries Assn., Am. Assn. U. Women, Sigma Kappa. Club: Zonta. Home: 822 Galiano St Coral Gables FL 33134 Office: Fla Internat University Miami FL 33144

PEELER, HERMAN RAY, textile co. exec.; b. Salisbury, N.C., Dec. 13, 1926; s. Paul A. and Mittie Frances (Shoe) P.; student Catawba Coll., 1943-44; m. Ermine Alberta Williams, Oct. 1, 1950; children—Irving Ray, Jeffrey Paul, Kim Leigh. Credit mgr. Norman's Furniture, Salisbury, N.C., 1952-56, mgr., 1957-63, gen. mgr. furniture div., Salisbury and Lumberton, N.C., 1959-63, sec., 1964—; asst. treas., credit mgr. Norman's Custom Draperies, 1956-61; sec.-treas. R.W. Norman Co., Inc., drapery and bed spread mfg., Salisbury, 1968—, dir., 1955—. Active bus. div. United Fund, 1962. Mem. Salisbury Spencer Furniture Dealers Assn. (pres. 1959). Lutheran (ch. council 1957-60). Home: 1221 Forestdale Dr Salisbury NC 28144 Office: 225-227 N Main St Salisbury NC 28144

PEELER, JAMES (JIMMY), state chmn. Dem. Com.; m. Mildred Peeler; children—Meredith, James III. Farmer, owner cotton gin; chmn. Democratic Com. Tenn.; Tenn. state chmn. Dem. Com. Mem. Am. Legion, V.F.W., C. of C. Home: 803 W Liberty Av Covington TN 38019 Office: Democratic Com Tenn Nat Hdqrs 1730 K St Washington DC 20002

PEELER, RAY DOSS, JR., lawyer; b. Bonham, Tex., May 4, 1929; s. Ray Doss and Opal (Porter) P.; B.A. with high honors, U. Tex., 1948, LL.B., 1951 children—William Bryan, Maribel Porter. Admitted to Tex. bar, 1951; practiced law, Bonham, 1953—, dist. and county atty., Fannin County, 1960-61; pres. Fannin Nat. Bank, Windom, Tex., 1963-70, chmn. bd., 1970—; dir. 1st Nat. Bank, Bonham, Fannin Properties, Inc., Bonham Mfg. Co. Del. Democratic Nat. Conv., 1960. Trustee S.B. Allen Meml. Hosp., Bonham, Wesley Found., East Tex. State U., Commerce. Served to capt. USAF, 1951-53. Mem. State Bar Tex., Am. Bar Assn., State Jr. Bar Tex. (v.p. 1959-60), Phi Beta Kappa, Phi Gamma Delta, Phi Alpha Delta. Mem. Christian Ch. Home: 1120 N Cedar St Bonham TX 75418 Office: Peeler Bldg Bonham TX 75418

PEELER, SAMUEL DAVID, office supply co. exec.; b. Dallas, July 17, 1913; s. Samuel H. and Elizabeth T. (Carnes) P.; student So. Meth. U., 1938-41; m. Frances E. Ross, Apr. 21, 1940; children—Samuel David, Nancy Ellen, Kathy Ann. With Stewart Office Supply Co., Dallas, 1932—, dir., 1965—; exec. v.p., 1970—. Mem. adv. council A. B. Dick Co., Chgo., 1964—. Bd. dirs. Sales and Marketing Execs., 1958-60. Mem. Ch. of Christ (deacon 1950-72, trustee 1971—). Mason (Shriner). Home: 1903 Marydale Dr Dallas TX 75208 Office: 400 Austin St Dallas TX 75202

PEEPLES, FRANK KOHLER, shipping agy. exec.; b. Savannah, Ga., Sept. 1, 1927; s. Homer F. and Marie (Purse) P.; B.Indsl. Engring., Ga. Inst. Tech., 1949; m. Elizabeth Clarke, Dec. 28, 1963; children—Marla S., Daryn S., Ashley B., Frank Kohler. Engr., Ga. Tin Plate Co., Savannah, 1949-50; sec. Quality Container Co., Savannah, 1952-54; pres. Stevens Shipping Co., Savannah, 1954-64; pres. Southeastern Maritime Co., Savannah, 1965—; dir. 1st Bank of Savannah. Bd. dirs. Savannah River Basin Devel. Commn. Served to 1st lt. AUS, 1950-52. Decorated Bronze Star medal. Mem. Am. Inst. Indsl. Engrs., Am. Soc. Safety Engrs. Episcopalian. Clubs: Whitehall (N.Y.C.); River (Jacksonville, Fla.); Chatham, Oglethorpe, Savannah Yacht. Home: Sylvan Island Savannah GA 31404 Office: 310 E Bay St Savannah GA 31402

PEEPLES, RODERICK LESLIE, feed mill exec.; b. Jasper, Fla., Aug. 27, 1922; s. Warren Leslie and Lillian Frances (Craig) P.; B.A., U. Fla., 1944; m. Ethel Marie Tucker, Jan. 12, 1948; children—Gary Leslie, Shirley Marie. Salesman, dairy speciality Jackson Grain Co., Tampa, 1948-61, Nutrena Mills, Tampa, 1961-62; br. mgr., nutritionist Hector Feed Mill, Deerfield Beach and Okeechobee, Fla., 1962-71; mgr. liquid feed div. Hughes Feed Mill, Okeechobee, 1971—. Served to 1st lt. AUS, 1943-45. Mason, Kiwanian. Home: 107 Sabal Lane Okeechobee FL 33472 Office: PO Box 835 Okeechobee FL 33472

PEET, RICHARD CLAYTON, lawyer, research co. exec.; b. N.Y.C., Aug. 24, 1928; s. Charles Francis and Florence L. (Isaacs) P.; J.D., Tulane U., 1953; m. Barbara Jean McClure, Mar. 17, 1956; children—Victoria Clementine, Alexandra Constance, Elizabeth Erica. Admitted to La. bar, 1955, also DC bar; law clk. Melvin M. Belli, San Francisco, 1954; The Cal. Co., Standard Oil of Cal., 1955; atty. appellate sect. Lands Div., Dept. Justice, Washington, 1956; asst. to dep. gen. counsel Dept. Commerce, 1957; mem. Rep. policy com. U.S. Senate, 1958, office of minority leader William F. Knowland, 1958; asso. counsel anti-trust subcom. House Judiciary Com., 1959-62; gen. practice law, Washington, 1962—; with Richard Clayton Peet & Assos., 1972—; pres., dir. Lincoln Research Center, 1965—. Served with AUS, 1946-47. Mem. Am., Inter-Am. bar assns., Internat. Inst. Space Law, Internat. Astronautical Fedn., Aviation-Space Writers Assn., Am. Inst. Aeros. and Astronautics, Phi Delta Phi, Pi Kappa Alpha. Republican. Clubs: National Space, Tulane Alumni of Washington. Author: Goals for a Constructive Opposition 1966; Challenge of the Seventies, 1967; Parties and Democracy, 1972. Composer song: Stand Up For America (recipient George Washington medal Freedom's Found. 1971), 1971. Patentee reclosable carton. Home: 4442 Hawthorne St NW Washington DC 20016 Office: 1629 K St NW Washington DC

PEFLEY, DOROTHY E. LITTLETON (MRS. WILLIAM R. PEFLEY), real estate broker; b. Swansboro, N.C., Dec. 2, 1924; d. Everett McClain and Zeta (Morton) Littleton; ed. pub. schs.; m. William R. Pefley, Dec. 6, 1942; 1 son, Charles Saunders. Real estate broker, Norfolk, Va., 1943—; sec. Will Sell Corp., Norfolk, 1953—co-organizer River Forrest Shores Shopping Center, Norfolk, 1955; co-owner Pioneer Camp Grounds, Inc.; co-developer Pefley's Beach on Saxis Island; sec. Shore Properties, Inc.; sec.-treas. Pefley, Inc., Lake Drummond Boat Tours, Inc. Home: Munden Point Farm Virginia Beach VA 23458 Office: 5711 Sellger Dr Norfolk VA 23502

PEFLEY, WILLIAM REGINALD, real estate developer; b. Detroit, Dec. 6, 1916; s. Norman and Rose (Harbaugh) P.; grad. high sch.; m. Dorothy Littleton, Dec. 6, 1942; 1 son, Charles Saunders. With Norfolk Naval Shipyard, Portsmouth, Va., 1939-47; real estate developer, ins. agt., builder, Norfolk, Va., 1947—, developer Eastern Park, 1952, Bradford Terrace, 1953, MacDonald Park, 1955, Gt. Neck Estates, 1957, River Forest Shores, 1958, Sect. II, 1960, Munden Beach South Mills Shores, 1964, Hidden Lake Retreat, 1965, Machipongo Shores, 1965-66, Pioneer Camp Grounds, Inc.; sec.-treas. Will-Sell Corp.; pres. Saxis Island Devel., Inc., River Forest Shores Shopping Center, Inc.; stockholder George Washington Hunt Club, Inc. Recipient medal for service during Jamestown (Pa.) Flood, 1936; commendation for civilian service World War II, Navy Dept. Mem. Tidewater Assn. Home Builders, Norfolk C. of C. Democrat. Episcopalian (vestryman). Mason (Shriner), Moose (life mem.), Optimist, Fraternal Order of Police. Home: Munden Point Farm Virginia Beach VA 23457 Office: corner Military Hwy and Sellger Dr Norfolk VA

PEIRCE, NEAL R., journalist; b. Phila., Jan. 5, 1932; s. J. Trevor and Miriam (Litchfield) P.; A.B., Princeton, 1954; postgrad. Harvard, 1957-58; m. Barbara von dem Bach-Zelewski, Apr. 18, 1959; children—Celia, Andrea, Trevor. Legislative asst. office Rep. Silvio O. Conte, 1959-60; polit. editor Congl. Quar. Service, Washington, 1960-69; contbg. editor Nat. Jour., Washington, 1969—. Alumni trustee South Kent (Conn.) Sch., 1968-71, Served with AUS, 1954-57. Woodrow Wilson Internat. Center for Scholars fellow, 1971-73. Mem. S.W. Neighborhood Assembly (chmn. 1963), S.W. Community Council (pres. 1963-65), Phi Beta Kappa. Episcopalian (chapel com. chmn. 1961-64). Clubs: Federal City, Author: The People's President, 1968; The Megastates of America, 1972; The Mountain States of America, 1972; The Pacific States of America, 1972. Home: 610 G St SW Washington DC 20024 Office: 1730 M St NW Washington DC 20036

PEIXOTTO, ERNEST DISHMAN, army officer; b. Ft. Leavenworth, Kan., July 24, 1929; s. Eustace Muduro and Catharine Augusta (Dishman) P.; B.S. in Civil Engring., U.S. Mil. Acad., 1951; M.S. in Civil Engring., Mass. Inst. Tech., 1957; postgrad. Nat. War Coll., 1969-70; m. Elizabeth Louella Smith, June 6, 1951; children—Vivian Elizabeth, Ernest Clifford. Commd. 2d lt. U.S. Army, 1951, advanced through grades to col., 1970; mil. asst. Office Dist. Engr., Vicksburg, Miss., 1954-55; project engr. U.S. AEC, Washington, 1957-59; engr., acad. adviser Vietnamese Nat. Mil. Acad., 1959-61; staff officer research and devel. Office Chief Engrs., Office Chief Research and Devel., Washington, 1961-64; area engr., Meshed, Iran, 1965-66; spl. asst. to chief engrs., Washington, 1966-68; commdg. officer 86th Combat Engr. Bn., Vietnam, 1968-69; dir. Engr. Waterways Expt. Sta., Vicksburg, Miss., 1970—. Decorated Legion of Merit with oak leaf cluster, Bronze Star medal, Army Commendation medal with oak leaf cluster. Registered profl. engr., Ala. Mem. Am. Soc. C.E., Soc. Am. Mil. Engrs. (pres. Vicksburg post 1970-71). Home: Quarters 4 US Army Engr Waterways Expt Sta Vicksburg MS 39180 Office: PO Box 631 Vicksburg MS 39180

PEJOVIC, ILIJA, hosp. supt.; b. Podgorica, Yugoslavia, 1919; s. Kosta and Zorka (Kazic) P.; M.D., U. Belgrade, 1944; m. Grace Ann Day, 1962; children—Vesna Bliss, Michele Lorraine. Came to U.S., 1953, naturalized, 1959. Intern Main Mil. Hosp., Belgrade, 1944-48; scholar cardiology, Paris, 1952-53; resident internal medicine, Atlanta and Houston, 1953-56; asst. med. dir. Tb Hosp., Decatur, Ala., 1957-58; mem. staff W.T. Edwards Tb Hosp., Tampa, Fla., 1958—, med. supt., 1966—. Served with Yugoslavian Navy, 1948-52. Mem. Am., So., Fla. med. assns., Am., Fla. thoracic socs., Gulf Coast Tb and Respiratory Disease Assn. Author papers. Office: 4000 Buffalo Av Tampa FL 33614

PELL, ALLISON HODGES, cotton mcht.; b. Richmond, Va., Feb. 25, 1901; s. Edward Leigh and Lucy (Hardison) P.; student U. N.C., 1917-19; m. Ellyn Dortch Gorham, Feb. 7, 1923; children—Allison Hodges, Ellyn Gorham (Mrs. James T. Tanner), Edward Leigh III. Asso. Bradshaw-Roberson Cotton Co., Greensboro, 1919-25; partner McIver & Pell, 1925-43; pres. Pell Cotton Co., 1943—, Pell Devel. Corp. (all Charlotte). Mem. N.Y., Memphis cotton exchanges; mem. cotton adv. com. Sec. Agr., 1955. Past chmn. bd. trustees Charlotte Country Day Sch. Mem. Atlantic Cotton Assn. (past pres.), Am. Cotton Shippers Assn. (past pres.). Methodist (trustee). Clubs: Charlotte Country, Charlotte City. Home: 2001 Carmel Rd Charlotte NC 28201 Office: 1221 Hawthorne Lane Charlotte NC 28201

PELLEGRINI, FRANK SAVERIO, physician, bank ofcl.; b. N.Y.C., Aug. 25, 1915; s. George and Filomena P.; B.S., L.I. U., 1935; M.D., Georgetown U., 1939; m. Gloria F. Masco, Sept. 7, 1940; children—Patria Ann (Mrs. Louis V. Kaufman), Phyllis Mary (Mrs. William Oetgen), Barbara Ann. Founder, past v.p., trustee, chief staff Cafritz Meml. Hosp.; founder, chmn. bd. So. Md. Bank & Trust Co. Served to maj. USAAF World War II. Recipient Alumni Achievement award Georgetown U., 1971. Mem. Provident Hosp. Alumni Assn. (founder, past pres.), Med. Soc. D.C. (pres.). Club: Oakcrest Country (founder, past pres.). Home: 12206 Braemer Circle Tantallon-on-Potomac MD 20022 Office: 3611 Branch Av SE Washington DC 20031

PELLETT, VERNON LLANO, agr. extension specialist; b. Viola, Wis., Apr. 13, 1924; s. Orval John and Freda (Buchanan) P.; B.S., Plattesville State U., 1948; M.S., U. Wis., 1966, Ph.D., 1970; m. Martha Jane Schroeder, Nov. 3, 1945; children—Steven, Pamela, Gary. County extension agt. Marathon and Portage counties (Wis.), 1948-66; asst. prof. dept. agr. and extension edn. U. Wis., 1966-67; health edn. specialist Tex. Agrl. Extension Service, College Station, Tex., 1969-72, adminstrv. asst., 1972—. Served with USAAF, 1942-45. Mem. Nat. Soc. Study of Edn., Adult Edn. Assn. U.S.A.

Home: 410 W Brookside Bryan TX 77801 Office: Systems Bldg Texas A and M College Station TX 77843

PELLEY, HARRY LAWRENCE, ednl. cons.; b. East Liverpool, O., July 14, 1923; s. Paul Leroy and Eliza Louise (Huddleston) P.; B.S. in Bus. Adminstrn., B.S. in Secondary Edn., Kent State U., 1949; M.Ed., Ohio State U., 1954; postgrad. Western Res. U., 1958-61; m. Colleen R. Brand, June 13, 1948; children—Ramona Louise, Michael Rex. Tchr., high sch. prin. Polk (O.) Local Sch. Dist., 1949-50; exec. head Sullivan (O.) Local Sch. Dist., 1950-52, Beach City (O.)-Wilmot Local Sch. Dist., 1952-54, N.W. Local Sch. Dist., Canal Fulton, O., 1954-58; sr. high sch. prin. Glenwood Sr. High Sch., Canton, O., 1958-61; exec. head W. Holmes Local Sch. Dist., Millersburg, O., 1961-65; ednl. cons. State Dept. Edn., Tallahassee, Fla., 1965-66; dir. ednl. facilities planning Fla. Dept. Edn., Tallahassee, 1966-72; ednl. cons., planner Eoghan N. Kelley Archtl. Firm. Sanford, Fla., 1972—. Chmn. edn. div. Stark County Fair, 1955; chmn. lit. com. Stark County, 1955-58; mem. accredation com. N. Central Assn. Secondary Schs. and Colls., 1958-62. Served with AUS, 1943-46. Recipient service citation Council Ednl. Facility Planners Internat., 1970. Mem. Am. Assn. Sch. Adminstrs., Council Ednl. Facility Planners Internat. (mem. communication com., editorial bd. jour. 1971—), Interstate Sch. Planners Assn., Ashland County Sch. Masters Assn. (chmn. 1952-53), Phi Delta Kappa. Mason (32 deg., Shriner). Elk. Author: Florida's New Look, 1970. Home: 112 Timbercove Longwood FL 32750 Office: Sanford Atlantic Bank Bldg Sanford FL 32771

PELOQUIN, GARRY WAYNE, hosp., nursing home adminstr.; b. Welch, La., Feb. 7, 1937; s. Joseph Lud and Dorlene (Langford) P.; B.S., U. Ala., 1964; m. Margaret Ann Nelson, Oct. 25, 1958; children—Garry L., Jerry W. X-ray technician U.S. Army Hosp., Heidleberg, Germany, 1956-58, Community Hosp., East Tallassee, Ala., 1959-62; dir. tng. technicians Druid City Hosp., Tuscaloosa, 1962-64; chief technologist, asst. dir. Bapt. Meml. Hosp. Sch. Radiology Technologist, Memphis, 1964-65; adminstr. Macon County Hosp., Tuskegee, Ala. 1965—, Magnolia Haven Nursing Home, Tuskegee, 1969—. Chmn. bd. Tuskegee Heart Fund Assn., 1970-72, Tuskegee Fund Ala. Soc. Crippled Children and Adults, 1969-72; pres. bd. Tuskegee Home Health Care Program, 1969-70, Tuskegee chpt. A.R.C., 1968-69. Served with AUS, 1955-58. Mem. Am., Ala. hosp. assns., Central Hosp. Council, State Ala. Hosp. Execs., Am. Coll. Hosp. Adminstrs., Ala. Soc. Radiol. Technologists, Am. Registry Radiol. Technology, Tenn. Soc. Radiologic Technologists (v.p. 1965), Am. Soc. Radiol. Technology, Southeastern Hosp. Conf., Ala. Civil Def. Assn. Rotarian (pres. 1970-71), Lion. Home: 739 S Main St Tuskegee AL 36083 Office: Macon County Hosp Lakeshore Dr Tuskegee AL 36083

PELOQUIN, ROBERT DOLAN, crime control mgmt. cons. exec.; b. Fall River, Mass., Jan. 9, 1929; s. Charles George and Margaret L. (Harpin) P.; B.S., Georgetown U., 1951, LL.B., 1956; m. Margaret Katherine Sheridan, June 28, 1952; children—Suzanne M., Robert Dolan, Charles, John, Mark. Admitted to Fed. bar, 1956; dep. chief security edn. div. Nat. Security Agy., Washington, 1955-57; trial atty. internal security div. Dept. Justice, Washington, 1957-58, area supervisory atty. organized crime and racketeering program, 1958-62, spl. asst. to atty. gen.; asst. house counsel, office of commr., profl. football leagues Am. Football League-Nat. Football League, New York, 1967-68; partner Hundley & Peloquin, Washington, 1968—; pres. Internat. Intelligence, Inc., 1970—. Trustee, De-Sales Hall Sch. Theology, Hyattsville, Md. Served from ensign to lt., USNR, 1951-55; comdr., 1966. Roman Catholic. Home: 6513 Tilden Lane Rockville MD 20852 Office: 839 17th St NW Washington DC 20006

PELOT, REUBEN NISBET, III, dentist; b. Crossville, Tenn., Mar. 18, 1935; s. Reuben Nisbet and Josephine Elizabeth (Powell) P.; student Ga. Inst. Tech., 1953-54, U. Tenn., 1954-59; m. Barbara Ann Bondurant, June 20, 1957; children—Lisa Maree, Laurie Ann, Lynda Carol, Reuben Nisbet IV. Pvt. practice dentistry, Knoxville, Tenn., 1961—; mem. staff dental dept. Tenn. Meml. Hosp. Mem. dist. council Smokey Mountain council Boy Scouts Am., 1965—. Served to capt., Dental Corps, AUS, 1959-61. Mem. Am., Tenn. State, Second Dist. dental assns., Sigma Nu, Xi Psi Phi. Republican. Methodist. Optimist. Home: 8437 Corteland Dr Knoxville TN 37919 Office: 6221 Kingston Pike Knoxville TN 37919

PELS, DONALD, pres. KAAY, Little Rock. Address: 1425 W 7th St Little Rock AR 72203*

PELTIER, HARVEY, lawyer; B.A., LL.B., La. State U.; m. May Ayo; children—5 children. Admitted to La. bar; practiced in Baton Rouge; v.p., dir. Citizens Bank and Trust Co., Thibodaux, La.; dir. Nat. Am. Bank of New Orleans; also engaged in oil, sugar, real estate, quarter horse bus. Vice pres. La. Bd. Edn. Mem. La. Ho. of Reps., 1924-30, La. Senate, 1930-40. Bd. suprs. La. State U. Address: La Bd Edn 626 N 4th St Baton Rouge LA 70802*

PELTIER, JAMES ROBERT, dentist; b. New Orleans, Sept. 15, 1930; s. Harvey Andrew and May (Ayo) P.; B.S., La. State U., 1950; D.D.S., Loyola U., New Orleans, 1954; m. Benita Ann Armstrong, Aug. 10, 1952; children—Jeanne Ellen, Robert James, David Charles. Intern Duke Hosp., 1956-57; resident Charity Hosp., New Orleans, 1957-59; practice oral surgery, Thibodaux, La., 1959—; chief dept. oral surgery St. Joseph Hosp., Thibodaux, La., 1959—; mem. courtesy staff Terrebone Gen. Hosp., Houma, La., 1959—; mem. courtesy staff St. Ann Gen. Hosp., Raceland, La., 1967—, La. State U. Div. Oral Surgery Charity Hosp. La., 1967—. Dir. Bay Drilling Corp.; pres. Boat Rentals, Inc., Caminada Corp.; v.p. Cane Machinery and Engring Co. Sec.-treas. Lefourche Assn. for Retarded Children, 1963—; rep. La. State U. Athletic Council, 1966-69; served S.S. Hope, Ceylon, 1968. Served to capt. USAF, 1954-56. Mem. La. State U. Alumni Assn. (pres. 1965), Thibodaux C. of C. (pres. 1971-72), V.F.W. (outstanding citizen's award 1970), Omicron Delta Kappa. Rotarian (past pres.). Contbr. articles to profl. jours. Home: Route 1 Box 570-A Thibodaux LA 70301 Office: 100 E 5th St Thibodaux LA 70301

PEMBROKE, CLAUDE GRAHAM, bank exec.; b. Weems, Va., May 25, 1911; s. Claude Augustine and Julia Van-Buskirk (Buck) P.; grad. Columbia Exec. Course, 1958; m. Grace Elizabeth Noblett, Dec. 23, 1933; children— Claude Graham, Albert Noblett. Truck driver Standard Oil Co., Esso, 1930-31, marketing petroleum clk. dist. office, 1931-33, plant agt., 1933, supt. oil burner, 1934; gen. salesman, 1934-40, indsl. salesman, 1940-43, dist. mgr., 1943-46, indsl. sales mgr. 1947-48, operations mgr., 1948-53, asst. mgr., 1953-63, mgr. W.Va.-Va. area, 1963-66; dir., exec. com. Bank of Lancaster, 1969—; dir. Sylvia Motor Co., Burgess, Va., 1971—. Bd. dirs. Central Va. Ednl. TV, 1964—, Richmond Meml. Hosp.; bd. dirs., chmn. finance com. Historic Christ Ch. Found., Irvington, Va., 1968—. Mem. Va. Mfrs. Assn., Va. Oilmen's Assn., Va. Hwy. User's Assn. Kiwanian. Clubs: Indian Creek Yacht and Country (commodore 1971) (Kilmarnock, Va.); Commonwealth, Forum (Richmond, Va.). Cons. Atlantic-Union Oil Co., Australia, 1957, Svenska Esso, Sweden, 1962. Address: PO Box 636 Kilmaronock VA 22482

PENA, FRANCISCO INOCENTE, physician; b. McAllen, Tex., Dec. 28, 1937; s. Abel N. and Josefa (Lopez) P.; B.A., U. Tex., 1960; M.D., U. Tex., 1962; m. Aurora Guerra, July 14, 1963; children—Maritza, Francisco I., Danellie. Intern, Martin Army Hosp., Fort Benning, Ga., 1962-63; gen. practice medicine with J.H. Trevino and Rafael Garza, McAllen, Tex., 1965—; mem. staff and sec., treas. staff McAllen (Tex.) Hosp., 1968-69. Dir., organizer Met. Nat. Bank, McAllen, Tex., 1970-72, Pub. Relations Bd., McAllen, Tex., 1971. Served with AUS, 1962-65. Decorated Air medal with four oak leaf clusters, Bronze Star medal, Purple Heart. Mem. McAllen C. of C., Cath. War Vets., V.F.W., Am. Legion. Mason, Kiwanian. Home: 512 S McColl St McAllen TX 78501 Office: 714 S Main St McAllen TX 78501

PENCE, FERN MCCOMB, state ofcl.; b. Fort Wayne, Ind., Oct. 27, 1908; d. Hubert James and Addie (Schorr) McComb; A.B., Ind. U., 1930; M.A. (Comonwealth fellow), U. Chgo., 1945; m. Robert G. Pence, Feb. 3, 1933 (div. Dec. 1941). Supr. pub. assistance cons. Ind. Dept. Pub. Welfare, Indpls., 1943-46; dir. social services St. Joseph County Dept. Pub. Welfare, South Bend, Ind., 1946-49, Cleve. Rehab. Center, 1952-56; exec. dir. Children's Day Care Assn., Fort Wayne, 1949-52; dir. welfare Am. Joint Distbn. Com., Casablanca, Morocco, 1956-58; supr. pub. assistance field staff Fla. Dept. Pub. Welfare, Jacksonville, 1959-61, fed. govt. program dir. to organize and direct U.S. Cuban refugee assistance program in Dade County, Miami, Fla., 1961-62, welfare program supr. for pub. assistance field service and Cuban refugee assistance program, Jacksonville, 1962-69; Fla. supr. sub-professionals, vols. Cuban Refugee Services, Jacksonville, 1970—. Pub. assistance cons. Greater Boston Health and Welfare Survey, 1948-49; cons., condr. insts. Child Welfare League Am., 1949-55; Nat. Soc. for Crippled Children speaker Nat. Conf. Social Work, 1951—; condr. grad. insts., pub. welfare adminstrn. Western Res. U. Sch. Applied Social Scis., Cleve., 1949-50, faculty med. social work dept., 1955; sec.-treas. Fla. Council on Aging, 1963-64, sec., 1967-69, 70—; trustee, 1969-70; citation for outstanding service, 1972. Recipient Scroll of Friendship, City of Miami, 1962. Mem. Nat. Assn. Social Workers, Acad. Certified Social Workers, Internat., Nat. confs. social work, Theta Sigma Phi, Phi Mu. Democrat. Episcopalian. Home: 479 Tabor Dr S Jacksonville FL 32216 Office: PO Box 2050 Jacksonville FL 32203

PENDALL, MAGDA GISLAINE, physician; b. Thorn, Netherlands, Oct. 30, 1912; d. Joseph A. and Marl (Palmen) Puppendahl; B.S., St. Louis U. 1937; M.D., Loyola U., Chgo., 1943; M.P.H., Columbia, 1954; m. Brian T. Shorney, Nov. 3, 1945 (div. 1958). Intern in dietetics St. Louis U. Hosps., 1937-38; chief dietitian St. Francis Hosp., Honolulu, Hawaii, 1938-39; surg. intern, resident Henry Ford Hosp., Detroit, 1943-46; med. dir. City Infirmary, Infirmary Hosp., St. Louis, 1946-48; asst. chief, then acting chief municipal physician, St. Croix V.I., 1948-51; pathology resident Sch. Tropical Medicine, San Juan, P.R., 1951; asst. prof. adminstrv. medicine Columbia Sch. Pub. Health and Adminstrv. Medicine, N.Y.C., 1954-59; part-time physician St. Barnabas Hosp. for Chronic Diseases, Bronx, 1954-59; 1 year study tour, Far and Near East, Europe, 1959-60; pvt. practice internal medicine St. Croix, V.I., 1961—. Fellow Am. Pub. Health Assn., Gerontol. Assn.; mem. Am. Hosp. Assn., Am. Coll. Hosp. Adminstrs., Am. Med. Women's Assn., Pan-Am. Women's Alliance, Flying Physicians Assn., V.I. Med. Soc. (pres. 1971). Address: Estate Orange Grove Christiansted St Croix VI 00820

PENDELL, LUCILLE HUNT, librarian, archivist; b. Hennessey, Okla., Jan. 17, 1902; d. Charles H. and Viola (Knox) Hunt; B.S., Okla. A. and M. Coll., 1925, M.A., 1930; B.L.S., Cath. U. Am., 1948; m. Elmer Pendell, Oct. 10, 1930; 1 dau., Martha Jane. Tchr. pub. schs., Sharon, Okla., 1919-21, Skiatook, Okla., 1922-23, Fort Supply, 1925-26; documents librarian Okla. A. and M. Coll., 1926-31; archivist war records office Nat. Archives, Washington, 1943-47; librarian Gallaudet Coll., Washington, 1947—, also asso. prof., chmn. dept. library sci. Dir., NDEA Inst., Library Service for Deaf, summer 1965, 66; asso. archivist U. Okla., summer 1949; Rockefeller fellow for achival research, 1950-51; chief librarian Mt. Alto VA Hosp., summer 1953; mem. adv. council Nat. Survey of Library Service to the Deaf, 1964—. Mem. A.L.A., Conv. Am. Instruction of Deaf, Am. Assn. U. Profs., D.C. Library Assn., Beta Phi Mu, Kappa Delta Pi, Delta Zeta. Methodist. Author several checklists of various records groups in Nat. Archives; contbr. articles relating to orgn. fed. documents in depository libraries, other library topics to profl. jours. Home: 25 E Oak St Alexandria VA 22301 Office: Gallaudet Coll Washington DC 20002

PENDERGRAFT, GRADON O'KELLY, JR., govt. ofcl.; b. Charleston, S.C., Dec. 4, 1934; s. Gradon O. and Maria (Burnett) P.; B.S. in Bus. Adminstrn., Va. Poly. Inst., 1960; m. Phyllis Morris, Sept. 30, 1961; 1 dau., Jimese Lynne. Tchr., Fishburne Mil. Sch., Waynesboro, Va., 1960; social worker, ct. probation officer, Waynesboro, 1962-65; supr. Reynolds Metal Co., Grottoes, Va., 1965-66; supt. Dept. Social Services, Waynesboro, 1967—. Cons., Waynesboro Mental Health Assn., Waynesboro Parents Without Partners Assn., 1969—; apptd. gov.'s commn. to study pub. assistance, 1971—; bd. dirs. Waynesboro Area Workshop Inc., Brethern Housing Assistance Corp.; chmn., regional conf. on illegitimacy Va. Council on Social Welfare, 1967; mem. dist. adv. council for Small Bus. Adminstrn. Served with AUS, 1955-57. Mem. Waynesboro Fish and Game Protective Assn., League Social Welfare Execs., Travelers Protective Assn. Republican. Mem. United Ch. (bd. dirs. nursery). Mason (Shriner, 32 deg.). Home: 1308 Crofton Av Waynesboro VA 22980 Office: 250 S Wayne Av Waynesboro VA 22980

PENDERGRAFT, PRESTON ALBERT, interior decorator; b. Tulsa, Oct. 23, 1931; s. Preston A. and Florence (Gillian) P.; B.S., Okla. State U., 1957; postgrad. U. Tulsa, 1957-58; m. Lois Schneiderman, Mar. 18, 1961; children—Lisa, Amy. Interior designer Douglas Aircraft, Tulsa, 1957, Palace Office Supply, 1957-59, Western Bank & Office Supply, Oklahoma City, 1959-60, House of Wren, 1960-61; self-employed interior decorator, Oklahoma City, 1961—. Mem. Oklahoma City Arts Council 1970—. Served with AUS, 1953-55. Mem. Am. Inst. Interior Designers (v.p. Okla. chpt. 1964—), Oklahoma City Design Professions (treas. 1970—), Pi Kappa Alpha. Home: 2045 N W 48th St Oklahoma City OK 73109 Office: 5609 Mosteller Dr Oklahoma City OK 73112

PENDERGRASS, EDWARD J(ULIAN), JR., bishop; b. Florence, S.C., Sept. 24, 1900; s. Edward Julian and Eula Ethel (Smith) P.; A.B., U. N.C., 1924; student Emory U., 1926; D.D., Fla. So. Coll., 1944; H.H.D., Rust Coll., 1968; LL.D., Millsaps Coll., 1969; m. Lois Mae Sheppard, June 26, 1929; children—Amy Katherine (Mrs. John Miller), Edla Ethel (Mrs. Burton R. Barnes), Edward Eugene. Ordained deacon Meth. Ch., 1932, elder, 1934; pastor, Ft. White, Fla., 1930-31, High Springs, 1931-32, Cross City, 1932-34, Ft. Pierce, 1934-38, College Heights, Lakeland, Fla., 1938-39, Seminole Heights, Tampa, Fla., 1939-43; dist. supt. Tallahassee dist., 1943-46; pastor First Meth. Ch., Tampa, 1946-52, Orlando, 1952-64; bishop Meth. Church, Jackson, Miss., 1964—. Sec. Bd. Missions Ann. Conf., sec. evangelism, 1943, 60; mem. bd. evangelism Gen. Conf., 1948, 52, 56, Jurisdictional Conf., 1948, 52, 56, 60, 64, Gen. Conf., 1952, 56, 60, 64, mem. Gen. Bd. Edn.; vice chmn. Gen. Bd. Evangelism. Trustee Children's Home, Fla. So. Coll., Meth. Hosp., Memphis, Meth. Home Hosp., New Orleans, Rust Coll., Lake Junaluska Assembly; v.p. bd. trustees Millsaps Coll. Mem. Alpha Tau Omega, Pi Gamma Mu. Mason, Kiwanian. Home: 4460 E Ridge Dr Jackson MS 39211 Office: Meth Bldg Jackson MS 39201

PENDERGRASS, FRANKLIN LEE, supt. schs.; b. Rutherford County, nr. Rutherford, N.C., July 27, 1928; s. Fred Lee and Viola Lillie (Briscoe) P.; A.A., Gardner Webb Jr. Coll., 1950; A.B., Catawba Coll., 1953; M.A., Appalachian State U., 1960; postgrad. U. N.C., 1963-65; m. Jean Carolyn Hames, Sept. 15, 1950; children—Steven Lee, George Robert. Tchr. city schs., Marion, N.C., 1953-59; prin. Manning Elementary Sch., Roanoke Rapids, N.C., 1959-65, Bailey (N.C.) High Sch., 1965-66; supt. Currituck County (N.C.) Schs., 1966—. Served with USNR, 1946-47. Mem. N.E.A., N.C. Assn. Educators, Am. Assn. Sch. Adminstrs. Club: Ruritan (Currituck). Home: Currituck NC 27929 Office: Currituck County Schs Currituck NC 27929

PENDLETON, ALFRED MOORE, cotton ginning engr.; b. Farmersville, Tex., Jan. 18, 1911; s. William Frederick and Mamie (Keller) P.; B.S., Tex. A. and M. U., 1932; m. Laurita Yeager, Feb. 11, 1934; 1 son, Fred A. Mgr., So. Gin Co., Terrell, Tex., 1932-43; cotton ginning specialist U.S. Dept. Agr., Dallas, 1943-62, cotton ginning engr., 1962—. Cons. all land grant univs. on cotton programs, 1962—. Mem. Am. Soc. Agrl. Engrs., Epsilon Sigma Phi. Baptist. Mason. Author (with others) Advances in Production and Utilization of Quality Cotton—Principles and Practices, 1968. Contbr. articles to sci. jours. Home: 3116 Beverly Dr Dallas TX 75205 Office: 1100 Commerce St Dallas TX 75202

PENDLETON, EDMUND E., JR., lawyer; b. St. Louis, June 8, 1922; s. Edmund E. and Katharine (Burum) P.; B.S. in Econs., U. Pa., 1942; J.D., Georgetown U., 1948; LL.M., George Washington U., 1951; m. Josephine Culbertson; 5 daus. Admitted to D.C. bar, 1948; confidential asst. to asst. sec. agr., Dept. Agr., Washington, 1955-57; counsel firm Leibman, Williams, Bennett, Baird and Minow, Washington. Vice pres. Leon Tempelsman & Son, Inc., 1970—. counsel for minority Subcom. on Nat. Policy Machinery, Senate Com. on Govt. Operations, 1960; cons. to U.S. delegation to 12th Internat. Conf. of Internat. Union Ofcl. Travel Orgns., 1957. Chmn., D.C. Republican Com. Served to lt. AUS, 1942-46. Mem. Bar Assn. D.C., Fed. Bar Assn. Office: 1156 15th St NW Suite 318 Washington DC 20005*

PENLAND, RUS, educator; b. Salem, Mo., Apr. 4, 1929; s. Carl Arthur and Annis (Petty) P.; B.F.A., Kansas City Art Inst. and Sch. Design, 1961; student U. Kansas City, 1961-62; M.A., U. Mo., 1964; m. Ruth Jacqueline Salveter, Aug. 17, 1953; children— Carl Edward, Dru Paul. Instr. art Paseo High Sch., Kansas City, Mo., 1962-63; instr. painting McNeese State Coll., 1964-66; asso. prof. art, head art dept. U. Corpus Christi (Tex.), 1966—. Served to sgt. maj. AUS, 1957-61. Decorated Bronze Star medal. Mem. Tex. Fine Arts Assn. (regional dir. 1969—), South Tex. Art League (pres. 1971-72), Coll. Art Assn. Am., Sculpture Soc. Corpus Christi. Democrat. Mem. Christian Ch. Home: 1322 Nile Dr Corpus Christi TX 78412

PENLEY, LARRY HOWARD, ednl. adminstr., clergyman; b. Collettsville, N.C., Jan. 13, 1922 Charles William and Laura (Raby) P.; A.B., Lenoir Rhyne Coll., 1947; B.D., So. Bapt. Theol. Sem., Louisville, 1952, M.Div., 1970; M.A., Applachian State U., 1964; D.Ed., Luther Rice Sem., 1969; m. Mildred Evelyn Winkler, Dec. 5, 1948; children—John Michael, Richard Wayne, Timothy Howard. Ordained to ministry Bapt. Ch., 1953; minister Mountain Grove Bapt. Ch., Hickory, N.C., Startown Ch., Newton, N.C., 1952-58; advt. mgr. Rutherford (N.C.) County News, 1959; editor Cleveland Times Newspaper, Shelby, N.C., 1959-60; dir. News Bur.-Alumni Affairs, Wingate, (N.C.) Coll., 1960-61; pub. information officer Appalachian State U., Boone, N.C., 1961-65; dir. adult and continuing edn. extension programs and pub. relations Catawba Valley Tech. Inst., Hickory, 1965—, acting dir. tech. and vocational program, 1966; interim minister Sweetwater Bapt. Ch., Hickory, 1967—, Corinth Bapt. Ch., Vale, N.C., 1968-69, Temple Bapt. Ch., Hickory, 1969, Mountain Grove Bapt. Ch., Hickory, 1970—, Temple Bapt. Ch., Stony Point, 1971—, Dudley Shoals Bapt. Ch., Granite Falls, 1971-72, Pooveys Grove Bapt. Ch., Granite Falls, 1972—. Active Boy Scouts Am. Bd. dirs. Community Coll. Adult Educators of N.C., Cleveland County Cancer Survey. Mem. Am., N.C. (dir., v.p. Southwestern dist., pres.) edn. assns., Nat. Assn. Pub. Sch. Adult Edn. (dir. N.C. unit), Am., N.C. vocation assns., Univ. Photographers Assn., Am. Alumni Council, So. Bapt. Pub. Relations Assn., Appalachian U. Alumni Assn. (pres. Catawba County 1965—), So. Appalachian Hist. Assn., Gamma Beta Chi, Alpha Psi Omega, Phi Delta Kappa, Alpha Kappa Omega. Democrat. Home: Route 8 Box 842 Hickory NC 28601

PENLEY, MILDRED E. WINKLER (MRS. LARRY HOWARD PENLEY), educator, club woman, religious worker; b. Hickory, N.C.; d. Thomas A. and Mamie (Jenkins) Winkler; student Wingate Coll., 1960-61, Catawba Valley Tech. Inst., 1968; m. Larry Howard Penley, Dec. 5, 1948; children—John Michael, Richard Wayne, Timothy Howard. Bookkeeper, sec. Cherokee Dairy, Louisville, 1950-52, Farmers Coop. Exchange, Boone, N.C., 1962-65; tchr. aide Mountain View Elementary Sch., Hickory, 1969—, substitute tchr., 1969-70. Mem. adv. youth council Theron Rankin Assn., Hickory, 1968—; vol. worker Aux. Catawba Meml. Hosp., Hickory, 1968—; pres. Bapt. Tng. Union, 19—. Mem. Womans Missionary Union (pres. 1967-69). Baptist. Clubs: Appalachian Garden (Boone) (sec. 1961-65); Mountain View Home Demonstration. Democrat. Home: Route 8 Box 842 Hickory NC 28601 Office: Mountain View Sch Route 1 Hickory NC 28601

PENN, CLARENCE NATHAN, city ofcl.; b. Rush Springs, Okla., Jan. 11, 1906; s. Nathan Jasper and Mattie (Beard) P.; grad. high sch.; m. Madeline Frenchette, May 14, 1949; 1 son, Nathan John. With Dallas Fire Dept., 1927—, fire chief, 1945—. Mason, Kiwanian (pres. Dallas). Home: 2528 Matland Dr Dallas TX 75237 Office: 2111 Main St Dallas TX 75201

PENN, CLARENCE PRESTON, JR., sch. prin.; b. Pulaski, Va., Aug. 4, 1941; s. Clarence Preston and Maria Penn (Lewis) P.; B.S., Bluefield State Coll., 1964; M.S. in Edn., Radford Coll., 1968; postgrad. U. Va., 1970—; m. Michaele Paulette Mitchell, Aug. 22, 1964; 1 dau., Michelle Paulette. Tchr., coach Park Central High Sch., Bluefield, W. Va., 1964-67; tchr., coach Randolph Henry High Sch., Charlotte Court House, Va., 1967-69; prin. Prince Edward County High Sch., Farmville, Va., 1969—. Mem. curriculum com. Va. Dept. Edn., 1971—; spl. cons. integration U. Va. Consultive Resource Center, 1971—. Mem. Va. Bd. Welfare and Instns., 1970-74; bd. dirs. Prince Edward County Recreation, 1970—, Central Piedmont Action Council, 1970—, Corbin br. Y.M.C.A. Recipient Outstanding Citizen award Sherrif's Dept., Prince Edward County, 1970. Mem. Nat., Va. edn. assns., N.A.A.C.P., Nat. Assn. Secondary Sch. Prins., Y.M.C.A., Voters League, Va. High Sch. League (regional chmn. 1969-71), vice chmn. James River dist. 1970-71), Alpha Phi Alpha. Elk, Mason (Shriner). Home: PO Box 45 Keysville VA 23947 Office: Route 3 Box 385 Farmville VA 23901

PENN, THOMAS AZOR, sch. admstr., former state senator; b. Lynn, Ark., Apr. 1, 1923; s. Joseph Richard and Pearl (Osburn) P.; B.A., Ark. State Coll., 1947; M.A., Peabody Coll., 1957; m. Mary Trice Dalton, June 7, 1947; children—Richard Lewis, Thomas Jackson. Tchr. pub. sch., Cave City, Ark., 1947-50; prin. pub. sch., Dalton, Ark., 1950-55; supt. schs., Blackrock, Ark., 1955-66, Cave City, 1966—. Mem. Ark. Senate, 1959-70. Served to 2d lt. USAAF 1943-45. Mem. Farm Bur., Ark. Edn. Assn., N.E.A. Mason (32 deg., Shriner), Lion. Address: Cave City AR 72521

PENN, THOMAS JEFFERSON, surgeon; b. Georgetown, Ky., May 25, 1923; s. L. Tandy and Dewey (Swinford) P.; A.B., U. Ky., 1945; M.D., U. Louisville, 1946; m. Kathleen Little, Dec. 1, 1956; children—Albert Tandy, Thomas J. III, William Robert. Intern, Good Samaritan Hosp., Lexington, Ky., 1947-48; pvt. practice Medicine, Nicholasville, 1948-51; resident surgery St. Joseph's Hosp., Lexington, 1953-56; pvt. practice medicine, specializing in surgery Grundy (Va.) Hosp., 1956-62; mem. surg. staff Somerset (Ky.) Hosp., 1964; chief surgery Grundy (Va.) Hosp., 1964—. Chmn. bd. March of Dimes, 1961. Served with AUS, 1943-46; as capt. M.C., 1951-53. Diplomate Am. Bd. Surgery. Fellow A.C.S. Southeastern Surg. Congress; mem. A.M.A., Va., Buchanan-Dickinson County med. socs. Methodist (dir.). Rotarian. Home: Grundy VA 24614 Office: Grundy Hosp Grundy VA 24614

PENNEBAKER, GORDON BENNETT, educator; b. Lovelaceville, Ky., June 13, 1899; s. Frederick Franklin and Izora (Cave) P.; student Murray (Ky.) State Coll., 1924; A.B., U. Ky., 1926, M.S., 1928; Ph.D., U. Wis., 1938; postgrad. Columbia, 1944; m. Dorothy Mayo Printz, June 6, 1926; children—Martha Lee, Judith Mayo. Prin. Providence (Ky.) Sr. High Sch., 1926-27; instr. Murray State State Coll., 1927-31, asst. prof., 1931-37, asso. prof., 1937-40; prof., dir. div. sci. Morehead (Ky.) State Coll., 1940-46, war tng. service, 1943-45; prof., head dept. biology, co-ordinator vets. affairs Tenn. Poly. Inst., Cookeville, 1946—, dir. Sch. Arts and Scis., 1948—. Active A.R.C.; mem. council Internat. Sci. Fair. Served with USN, 1918-21. Mem. Ky. (pres. 1944), Tenn. (treas. 1964—) acads. sci., Genetics Soc. Am., A.A.A.S., Sigma Xi, Phi Delta Kappa, Kappa Delta Pi. Baptist. Rotarian. Home: 641 Dixie Av Cookeville TN

PENNEBAKER, JOHN DAVID, mayor; b. Keesler Field AFB, Harrison County, Miss., Aug. 31, 1943; s. David M. and Cleo B. (Barkley) P.; B.A., Miss. State U., 1965; J.D., U. Miss., 1968; m. Dorothy Gwyndolyn McGee, Aug. 20, 1967. Admitted to Miss. bar, 1968; pvt. practice law, New Albany, Miss., 1968; mayor City of New Albany, 1969—. Served with Miss. N.G. 1967. Recipient Distinguished Service award U.S. Jaycees, 1970. Mem. Delta Theta Phi, Sigma Chi. Mason (Shriner), Rotarian. Address: PO Box 96 New Albany MS 38652

PENNEKAMP, JOHN DAVID, editor; b. Cin., Jan. 1, 1897; s. William Henry and Angela (Gluick) P.; student St. Francis of Assisi and pub. schs. Cin.; m. Irene R. McQuillan, Dec. 31, 1925; children—John David, Tom. Successively reporter, state editor, legislative corr., asst. city editor Cin. Post, 1916-18, asst. city editor, city editor, news editor, 1918-25; successively city editor, news editor, mng. editor Miami (Fla.) Herald, 1925-41, asso. editor 1941—. Mem. Fla. Parole Com., 1947; cons. U.S. Fish and Wildlife Service, Dept. Interior, 1954; mem. Fla. Bd. Parks and Hist. Memls., 1950-69, chmn., 1950-54; v.p., trustee Fairchild Tropical Gardens; mem. Fla. Cabinet's Com. on Seminole Affairs; mem. citizens bd. U. Miami; mem. Fla. Quadricentennial Commn.; dir. El Centro de las Americas. Served with U.S. Army, World War I; lt. ingelligence sect. USNR, 1927-39. Mem. Everglads Nat. Park Commn. Recipient conservation awards Nat. Audubon Soc., 1954, U.S. Dept. Interior, 1955, Sears Found., 1961. Mem. Am. Soc. Newspaper Editors. Home: 1710 Wa-Kee-Na Dr Miami FL 33133 Office: 1 Herald Plaza Miami FL 33101

PENNINGTON, BROOKS, state senator, seed co. exec.; b. Pennington, Ga., Oct. 21, 1925; s. Brooks Maddox and Lucile (Braswell) P.; student N. Ga. Mil. Coll., 1942-43; B.S., U. Ga., 1949; m. Jacquelyn C. Pennington, Aug. 14, 1953; children—Brooks III, Penny, Robert, Dan. Pres., Pennington Grain & Seed, Inc., Madison, Ga., 1950—; v.p. Piedmont Acid Delinting, Inc., Winder, Ga., 1960—; dir. Cotton Hybrid Research, Inc., Winder; mem. Ga. Senate, 1963—, chmn. agr. com. 1963—. Chmn. Morgan County Hosp. Authority, 1958-62; past chmn. Morgan County Bd. Commrs. bd. dirs. Agri-Bus. Council Ga., 1965—. Mem. Ga. Ho. of Reps., 1962-63, exec. com. Ga. Democratic party, 1963—. Served with USAAF, 1943-49. Mem. Ga. Seedsmen's Assn. (past pres.), So. Field Seed Council (past pres.), N.Ga. Coll. Alumni Assn. (pres. 1970-72). V.F.W. Methodist. Club: Morgan County Touch-Down (pres. 1955—). Address: PO Box 290 Madison GA 30650

PENNINGTON, CLAUDE LEE, physician; b. Macon, Ga., Nov. 20, 1927; s. Claude Lee and Evelyn (Adams) P.; B.S. in Medicine, Mercer U., 1952; M.D., Med. Coll. Ga., 1949; m. Betty Jean Weaver, Dec. 17, 1953; children—Evelyn Arlene, Claude Lee. Intern Macon Hosp., 1949-50; resident in otolaryngology Columbia Presbyn. Med. Center, N.Y.C., 1953-55; practice medicine, specializing in otolaryngology, Macon, 1956—; mem. staff Med. Center Central Ga., Middle Ga., Coliseum Park hosps. (all Macon); chmn. bd. dirs. Central Ga. Found. for Speech and Hearing, 1963-64, 67-68; chmn. adv. bd. otology Ga. Dept. Pub. Health, 1962-69. Served as officer M.C., AUS, 1951-52. Diplomate Am. Bd. Otolaryngology. Fellow A.C.S.; mem. Am. Laryngol., Rhinol. and Otol. Soc., Am. Acad. Opthalmology, Am. Acad. Otolaryngology, Am. Broncho-Esophagological Assn., Am. Council Otolaryngology (pres.-elect 1971, mem. otosclerosis study group), Am. Laryngol. Assn., Kappa Alpha. Republican. Episcopalian. Elk, Kiwanian. Club: Idle Hour Country. Author publs. in field. Home: 1161 Nottingham Dr Macon GA 31201 Office: 800 1st St Macon GA 31201

PENNINGTON, NEIL EDWARD, army officer, entomologist; b. Carnegie, Okla., May 10, 1932; s. James Cecil and Frances Leona (Burns) P.; B.S., Okla. State U., 1954; M.P.H., Tulane U., 1961; Ph.D., Okla. State U., 1971; m. Violet Alice Watkins, Dec. 5, 1952; children—John, Janeil, Diana, James. Commd. 2d lt. U.S. Army, 1954, advanced through grades to lt. col., 1968; med. entomologist Med. Service Corps, 1954—, Vietnam, 1971—. Recipient Army Commendation medal. Mem. Entomol. Soc. Am., Sigma Xi. Home: 3605 S Independence St Oklahoma City OK 73911 Office: US Army Med Command Vietnam APO San Francisco CA 96384

PENNINGTON, WALTER WILLIAM, III, librarian; b. Mobile, Ala., Nov. 12, 1942; s. Walter William and Juda Elizabeth (Wade) P.; A.A., North Fla. Jr. Coll., 1962; B.A., Fla. State U., 1965, M.S. (Master's fellow 1967-68), 1968; m. Barbara Anne Crockett, Aug. 8, 1969; 1 dau., Anne Elizabeth. Librarian Hamilton County High Sch., Jasper, Fla., 1965-67; dir. instructional materials center Univ. Sch., Fla. State U., Tallahassee, 1968—. Mem. Tallahassee Jr. C. of C., A.L.A., Assn. Ednl. Communications and Tech., Am., Fla. (bd. dirs. 1970—; editor Bookcase) assns. sch. librarians, Fla. Audio-Visual Assn. Home: 1806 Sunset Lane Tallahassee FL 32303 Office: Univ Sch Fla State U Tallahassee FL 32306

PENNINGTON, WILLIAM L., oil producer, operator; b. Erick, Okla., Apr. 2, 1923; s. William L. and Ona (McClinton) P.; B.S., U. Okla., 1949; m. Georgia Armstrong, Dec. 23, 1942; children—Paula Lynn, Patricia Anne, Denise. Geologist, Frank Wood, Wichita Falls, Tex., 1949-53, chief geologist, 1953-55; sr. geologist Texaco Inc., Wichita Falls, 1955-57; ind. cons. geologist, Wichita Falls, 1957-63; oil producer, operator, Wichita Falls, 1963—; pres. W. L. Pennington, Inc., 1964—, Brook Plaza, Inc., 1967—, Helix Oil Inc., 1967—; sole gen. partner Penpar Ltd., 1969— (all Wichita Falls). Served with AUS, 1946-47. Mem. Am. Assn. Petroleum Geologists, Am. Inst. Profl. Geologists, North Tex. Oil and Gas Assn., Tex. Ind. Producers and Royalty Owners Assn., Am. Inst. Mining, Metall. and Petroleum Engrs., Ind. Producers Assn. Am. (dir.), U. Okla. Alumni Assn., Sigma Gamma Epsilon. Clubs: Wichita, Wichita Falls Country, Lancers. Home: 4201 Cedar Elm Wichita Falls TX 76308 Office: Oil and Gas Bldg Wichita Falls TX 76301

PENNY, DONALD CHARLES, educator, artist; b. Atlanta, Oct. 5, 1935; s. Charles Leon and Catherine Doris (Stearns) P.; student Ga. Inst. Tech., 1953, 1957-58; B.B.A., Ga. State U., 1961; M.S., Fla. State U., 1963; postgrad. Penland Sch., 1965; m. Margaret Cheryl Burkhardt, Apr. 20, 1963; 1 son, Adam Nathan. Exhibited as ceramic artist in one-man shows: Miami Art Center, Ga. Southwestern Coll., Banks Haley Gallery, Valdosta State Coll., Le Moyne Found., Fla. State U., Fla. Atlantic U.; group shows: Signatore Shop, Ga. Designer Craftsmen, Fla. Craftsmen, Craftsmen U.S.A., Valdosta State Coll. Faculty Show, Atlanta Arts Festival; represented in pvt. and pub. collections Middle Tenn. State U., Le Moyne Found., Atlanta Meml. Arts Center; instr. art Palm Beach (Fla.) Jr. Coll., 1963-66; asso. prof. art Valdosta (Ga.) State Coll., 1966—; sr. lectr. fine arts Ahmadu Bello U., Zaria, Nigeria, 1972-73; Ga. rep. Am. Crafts Council, 1970-72. Served with AUS, 1954-57. Recipient 1st place St. Augustine Show, 1968, 69; Best in Show award Ga. Designer-Craftsmen, 1969. Penland Sch. grantee, 1971. Mem. Fla. Craftsmen (v.p., 1966), Ga. Art Edn. Assn., Ga. Designer-Craftsmen. Home: 5300 Essex Ct West Palm Beach FL 33405

PENNYCUICK, ELOUISE GERTRUDE WAGNER (MRS. ROY ALFRED PENNYCUICK), food co. exec., educator; b. Crystal City, Tex., June 5, 1918; d. Leander and Hedy (Erler) Wagner; B.S., U. Tex., 1940; postgrad. Trinity U.; m. Roy Alfred Pennycuick, June 27, 1937; 1dau., Janet Marguerite (Mrs. Karl Edward Bliss III). Supr., Fed. Rehab. Programs, Houston, 1940-43; supr. food service U.S. Dept. Immigration and Naturalization, Crystal City, Tex., Tex., 1943-46; corp. sec., treas. Erler-Pennycuick Food Co., San Antonio, 1946-69; mgr., operator Pennycuick Imports Co., San Antonio, 1962-70; tchr. P.F. Stewart Sch., San Antonio, 1968-70. Instr., Marie Gilbert Fashion Sch., 1960-70. Ex-officio mem. Zonta Found., 1968-69. Mem. Am. Classroom Tchrs., N.E.A., Tex. State Tchrs. Assn., San Antonio Tchrs. Council, San Antonio Conservation Soc., Gamma Phi Beta Alumni Assn. San Antonio (pres 1958-60). Club: Zonta (pres. 1968-69). Home: 542 Robinhood Pl San Antonio TX 78209 Office: 1950 Rigsby St San Antonio TX 78210

PENROD, KENNETH E(ARL), univ. adminstr.; b. Blanchester, O., Mar. 30, 1916; s. William F. and Josie Alma (Carman) P.; B.S., Miami (O.) U., 1938; Ph.D., Ia. State Coll., 1942; m. Virginia Hogue, June 29, 1942; children—Caroline Penrod, Bruce Hogue Penrod. Asst. prof. physiology Boston U. Sch. Medicine, 1946-50; asso. prof. physiology Duke U. Sch. Medicine, 1950-57, prof., 1957-59, asst. dean, 1952-59; v.p. med. affairs, prof. physiology W.Va. U., 1959-65; provost med. center, prof. physiology Ind. U., 1965-69; vice chancellor med. and health scis. State U. System Fla., Tallahassee, 1969—. Spl. cons. AID Latin Am. Served as 2d lt. to capt., USAAF, 1942-46; aviation physiologist. Mem. Am. Physiology Soc., Orgn. Univ. Health Center Adminstrs. (incorporator), Assn. Am. Med. Colls., A.A.A.S., Phi Beta Kappa, Sigma Xi, Phi Kappa Phi, Phi Kappa Tau, Alpha Omega Alpha. Presbyn. Editorial bd. Jour. Med. Edn., 1957-65. Office: 107 W Gaines St Tallahassee FL 32304

PENTON, HOWARD ALLEN, JR., state legislator, oil co. exec.; b. Wilmington, N.C., Aug. 5, 1931; s. Howard Allen and Marjorie (Willard) P.; student Davidson Coll., 1949, U. N.C., 1951; m. Clive Roi Malott, Oct. 8, 1960; children—Elizabeth Malott, Howard Allen III. Pres., Springer Coal & Oil Co., Inc., Wilmington, N.C., 1954—; dir. Wachovia Bank & Trust Wilmington, Nat. Devel. Corp., Long Beach, N.C., Peoples Savs. & Loan Assn. Wilmington, Quality Concrete, Inc., Wilmington; mem. N.C. Ho. of Reps., 1969—. Bd. dirs. Babies Hosp. Served with AUS, 1952-54. Named Man of Year Wilmington Jr. C. of C., 1964; Citizen of Year, Star News Newspaper, New Hanover County, 1965. Mem. Wilmington C. of C. (past pres.), Phi Gamma Delta. Democrat. Episcopalian. Rotarian. Home: 1119 Country Club Rd Wilmington NC 28401 Office: 620 Market St Wilmington NC 28401

PENUEL, RICHARD BYRON, pub. co. exec.; b. Watertown, Tenn., Sept. 13, 1932; s. Carmack Sneed and Mary Elizabeth (McCoy) P.; student Middle Tenn. State U., 1950-51, Memphis State U., 1952; B.S. in Bus., Union U., 1954; M.B.A. in Marketing, Ind. U., 1956; m. Ann Norris Shires, Apr. 20, 1968; 1 son, William Richard. Data processing sales trinee IBM, Cin., Lafayette, Ind., 1958; bookkeeper Southwestern Co., Nashville, 1958-60; with Southwestern Co., Nashville, 1960—, v.p., sec., treas., 1969—. Membership chmn. Better Bus. Bur., 1968-69, bd. dirs., 1969—, exec. com., 1970-71; bd. dirs. Nashville Jr. Achievement, 1968—, treas., 1970-71. Served with AUS, 1956-58. Mem. Sigma Alpha Epsilon. Presbyn. (bd. deacons 1968-70, vice chmn. 1969, treas. 1970). Home: 1956 Old Hickory Blvd Brentwood TN 37027 Office: 2968 Foster Creighton Dr Nashville TN 37211

PENWELL, HARVEY EUGENE, hosp. adminstr.; b. El Reno, Okla., May 8, 1934; s. Homer La Roy and Jessie Myrtis (Pickard) P.; student Okla. State U., 1952-54; B.A. in Journalism, U. Okla., 1958-61; M.S. in Hosp. Adminstrn., Washington U., St. Louis, 1967; m. Ethel Wynne Eaton Asbury, July 30, 1964; children—Harvey Eugene, Lee Jennings, Ethelwynne. Adminstrv. resident Jackson Meml. Hosp., Miami, Fla., 1966-67; bus. mgr. Bapt. Hosp. Miami, 1967-69; asst. adminstr. Morton Plant Hosp., Clearwater, Fla., 1969; adminstr. St. Joseph Hosp., Port Charlotte, Fla., 1969-71; adminstr. Lewisburg (Tenn.) Community Hosp., 1972—. Bd. dirs. Charlotte County Mental Health Assn., Charlotte County Health Dept., West Central Fla. Comprehensive Health Planning, Charlotte Sr. Citizen and Adult Edn. Assn.; lectr. Port Charlotte Adult Edn., Health Forum Series, 1970-71. Vice pres. bd. Charlotte County YMCA, 1970—; active United Fund Campaign, 1970-71. Served with USAF, 1954-58. Mem. Am. Coll. Hosp. Adminstrs., Am. Hosp. Assn., Fla. Hosp. Assn. (adv. council 1970-71), Am. Soc. Clin. Pathologists Med. Technologists. Kiwanian. Home: 715 Yell Rd Lewisburg TN 73091 Office: Ellington Pkwy Lewisburg TN 73091

PENZ, ANTON JACOB, educator; b. Cleve., Feb. 22, 1906; s. Stephen F. and Elizabeth (Prokosch) P.; B.S. in Elec. Engring., Cleve. State U., 1933; M.A. in Edn., Western Res. U., 1936; M.B.A., Northwestern U., 1942; Ph.D., Ohio State U., 1947. widower; children—Alton Jeffry, David Alan. Prof. Davis and Elkins Coll., 1937-40; lectr. Rennselaer Poly. Inst., 1944; asst. prof. La. State U., 1944-47; prof. accounting, head dept. U. Ala., University, 1947—. Distinguished vis. prof. U. Nev., spring 1972, U. Colo., 1973. Cons., lectr. AID, Lima, Peru, 1965-66. Mem. Nat. Assn. Accountants (Lybrand award 1951), Financial Execs. Inst., Am. Accounting Assn. (v.p. 1962-63), Beta Alpha Psi (pres. 1955-56, editor newsletter 1953-55). Author: Manual De Contabilidad Y Costos, 1966. Editor: Accounting Teachers Guide, 1953; Professional Developments: Accounting Teachers Guide, 1953; Accountancy, A Vocation and Profession, 1958; Guide to Accounting Instruction: Concepts and Practices, 1968; Introducing the Profession: A Guide to Accounting Instruction, 1968. Home: 25 Beech Hills Tuscaloosa AL 35401 Office: Box 3111 University AL 35486

PENZINER, BERNARD ALAN, hosp. adminstr.; b. Bklyn., June 19, 1926; s. Carl H. and Peggy (Cohn) P.; B.A., Antioch Coll., 1951; M.H.A., Cath. U. Am., 1959; m. Marjorie Greenberg, June 8, 1952; children— Andrew, Richard. Mgmt. analyst U.S. VA, Washington, 1951-63; budget analyst U.S. Bur. Budget, Washington, 1963-65; hosp. adminstrn. D.C. Dept. Health, Washington, 1965-67, Psychiat. Inst., Washington, 1967—. Served with USAAF, 1944-45. Mem. Am. Hosp. Assn., Am. Soc. Mental Health Adminstrs., Am. Coll. Hosp. Adminstrs., Pi Gamma Mu. Home: 1330 New Hampshire Av NW Washington DC 20036 Office: 1825 K St NW Washington DC 20006

PEOPLES, DAVID STUART, mfg. co. exec.; b. Morristown, Tenn., June 6, 1916; s. Jasper Hansel and Mary Louise (Stuart) P.; student King Coll., Bristol, Tenn., 1934-36; m. Twila Kathleen Cook, Jan. 26, 1945; children—Signe Kyle, David Stuart. With Ernst & Ernst, C.P.A.'s Winston-Salem, N.C., 1938-47; with R. J. Reynolds Tobacco Co., 1947-70, asst. comptroller, 1953-58, comptroller, dir., 1959-64, v.p., comptroller, dir., 1964-66, exec. v.p., dir., 1966-70, now dir.; pres., dir. R.J. Reynolds Industries, 1970—; dir. Wachovia Corp. Served to 1st lt. AUS, 1941-45. C.P.A., Tenn. Mem. Am. Inst. C.P.A.'s, N.C. Assn. C.P.A.'s, Am. Mgmt. Assn. Methodist. Club: Old Town Country. Home: 2700 Bartram Rd Winston-Salem NC 27106 Office: R J Reynolds Industries Winston-Salem NC 27102

PEOPLES, JOHN ARTHUR, JR., ednl. adminstr.; b. Starkville, Miss., Aug. 26, 1926; s. John Arthur and Maggie Rose (Peoples) P.; B.S., Jackson State Coll., 1950; M.A, U. Chgo., 1951, Ph.D., 1961; m. Mary E. Galloway, July 13, 1951; children—Kathleen, Mark Adam. Tchr. math. Froebel Sch., Gary, Ind., 1951-58; asst. prin. Lincoln Sch., Gary, 1958-62; prin. Banneker Sch., Gary, 1962-64; asst. to pres. Jackson (Miss.) State Coll., 1954-65, v.p., 1966-67, pres., 1967—; asst. to pres. State U. N.Y., Binghamton, 1965-66. Lectr. summers U. Mich., 1964, Tex. A. and M. U., 1967, Trinity U., 1968, U. Miss., 1968, U. Ga., winter 1972. Charter mem. Mississippians for Ednl. TV; mem. Task Force, Civil Disorders Tech. Assistance Unit, Law Enforcement Assistance Div.; mem. Miss. Econ. Council, commn. adminstrv. affairs Am. Council Edn., Task Force on Student Assistance Edn. Commn. U.S., adv. com. on accreditation and instl. eligibility U.S. Dept. Health, Edn. and Welfare. Mem. Jackson Citizen's Adv. Bd.; bd. dirs. Inst. for Service to Edn., Am. Council on Edn., mem. policy commn. So. Regional Edn. Bd.; bd. govs. Jackson Symphony Orch. Served with USMCR, 1944-47. Mem. Am. Assn. Higher Edn. (Southeastern regional council, dir.) Assn. for Higher Edn., N.E.A., Miss. Tchrs. Assn. (Outstanding Native Son award 1968), So. Assn. Colls. and Schs. (exec. council commn. on colls., chmn. nominating com.), Am. Assn. State Colls. and univs. (chmn. com. on studies), Assn. Am. Colls. (commn. on coll. adminstrn.), Jackson C. of C. Alpha Kappa Mu, Phi Delta Kappa, Omega Psi Phi (Man of Year, Alpha Chi chpt. 1962), Beta Beta Beta. Contbr. articles to profl. jours. Home: Jackson State College Jackson MS 39217

PEPPER, CLAUDE DENSON, congressman; b. Dudleyville, Ala., Sept. 8, 1900; s. Joseph Wheeler and Lena (Talbot) P.; A.B., U. Ala., 1921; LL.B., Harvard, 1924; LL.D., McMaster U., 1941, Toronto U., 1942, U. Ala., 1942, Rollins Coll., 1944; m. Irene Mildred Webster, Dec. 29, 1936. Instr. law U. Ark., 1924-25; admitted to Ala. bar, 1924, Fla. bar, 1925, practiced in Perry, Fla.; mem. Fla. Ho. of Reps., 1929; practiced in Tallahassee, 1930; mem. Fla. Board Pub. Welfare, 1931-32, Fla. Bd. Law Examiners, 1933; practiced in Washington, Miami, Tallahassee; U.S. Senator from Fla., 1936-51, mem. com. on small bus. and fgn. relations, coms. on mil. affairs, small bus., reorgn. of Congress, chmn. com. on inter-oceanic canals, chmn. middle east sub-com. of Senate fgn. relations com., 12 years; mem. 88th-89th congresses from 3d Fla. Dist., 90th-92d congresses from 11th Fla. Dist., 93d congress from 14th Fla. Dist., chmn. select com. on crime, rules com., internal security com. Officer, dir. Washington Fed. Savs. Loan Assn. Chmn. Fla. delegation Democratic Nat. Conv., 1940-44, alternate del., 1948, 52, 56, 60, 64. Mem. Am. Inter-Am., Internat., Tallahassee, Miami Beach, Coral Gables, Dade County bar assns., Fla. Bar, Assn. Bar City N.Y., Am. Legion, 40 and 8, Vets. World War I, Blue Key, Phi Beta Kappa, Omicron Delta Kappa, Phi Alpha Delta, Sigma Upsilon, Kappa Alpha. Baptist. Mason (Shriner), Moose, Elk. Clubs: Jefferson Island, Army-Navy (Washington); Harvard, Washington (Miami); Coral Gables (Fla.) Country; Miami Shores (Fla.) Country; Kiwanis (lt. gov. Western div. Fla.). Contbr. to periodicals. Home: 2121 N Bayshore Dr Miami FL 33137 also 402 Wilson Av Tallahassee FL also 4201 Cathedral Av Washington DC 20016 Office: 1701 Meridian Av Miami Beach FL also Cannon House Bldg Washington DC 20515

PEPPER, JACK WILSON, civil engr.; b. Yazoo City, Miss., Jan. 12, 1918; s. Jack Horton and Evie Louise (McRaven) P.; B.S. in Civil Engring., Miss. State U., 1939; m. Dorothy Heidel Luse, Mar. 23, 1946; 1 son, Jack Douglas. Hydraulic engr. U.S. Geol. Survey, Ocala, Fla., 1939-41; owner Pepper Engring. Co., Yazoo City, Miss., 1946-56; water engr. Miss. Bd. Water Commrs., Jackson, 1956—. Mem. adv. com. Coll. Engring., Miss. State U., 1969—. Mem. Miss. Air and Water Pollution Control Commn., 1966—; chmn.-elect So. Water Resources Conf., Council State Govts., 1970-71; mem. exec. com., chmn. intergovtl. relations com. Interstate Conf. Water Problems, Council State Govts., 1969—. Served to maj. AUS, 1941-46. Registered profl. engr., Miss., Ark., La. Mem. Am. Soc. C.E. (pres. Miss. sect. 1971-72), Miss. Soc. Profl. Engrs. (pres. elect 1972-73). Home: Route 1 Benton MS 39039 Office: 416 N State St Jackson MS 39201

PEPPER, ROBERT KENYON, editor; b. East Greenwich, R.I., Oct. 19, 1908; s. Ernest Tudor and Jennie (Rathbun) P.; A.B., Rollins Coll., 1930; m. Loretta Welch, Feb. 27, 1932; children—Robert Kenyon, Theo (Mrs. Kenneth Case), George Ernest; m. 2d, Kathryn Smith, June 29, 1961. Mgr., Miami Herald News Bur., Fort Myers, Fla., 1931-32; corr. U.P.I., Fort Myers, 1932-46; reporter Fort Myers News Press, 1933-35, news editor, 1935—. Spl. corr. Fla. area Wall St. Jour., 1948-51. Democrat. Episcopalian. Contbr. articles to profl. jours. Home: 1929 Braman Av Fort Myers FL 33931 Office: News Press Fort Myers FL 33931

PERAZA, HUMBERTO, sculptor, 1925 Works include bronze equestrian in Mexico City, death mask of bullfighter Arruza, abstract wrought in iron of bull, modern figure of a woman, figure honoring Jesus Garcia. Address: Pitagoras 523 Mexico City Mexico

PERCY, WALKER, author; b. Birmingham, Ala., May 28, 1916; s. Leroy Pratt and Martha Susan (Phinizy) P.; B.A., U. N.C., 1937; M.D., Columbia, 1941; m. Mary Bernice Townsend, Nov. 7, 1946; children—Mary Pratt, Ann Boyd. Intern Bellevue Hosp., N.Y.C., 1942; author, 1943—. Recipient Nat. Inst. Arts and Letters award, 1967. Fellow Am. Acad. Arts and Scis.; mem. Nat. Inst. Arts and Letters. Roman Catholic. Author: The Moviegoer (Nat. Book award 1962), 1961; The Last Gentleman, 1966; Love in the Ruins, 1972. Contbr. philos., critical and med. essays to jours. and mags. Address: Old Landing Rd Covington LA 70433

PERDUE, JAMES HOMER, JR., equipment leasing co. exec.; b. Roanoke, Va., Nov. 29, 1931; s. J. Homer and Maude (Rucker) P.; B.S., U. Tenn., 1957, postgrad., 1958; postgrad. Harvard, 1967; m. Parrielee Parks, Sept. 8, 1956; children—Parrielee Kirk, James Homer III, Joe Parks, Sarah Crockett. Cashier, 1st Nat. Bank, Mt. Pleasant, Tenn., 1957-59; asst. controller Mills Morris Co., Memphis, 1959-61; asst. credit mgr. Mohawk Rubber Co., Akron, O., 1961-63; gen. credit mgr. Berkline Corp., Morristown, Tenn., 1963-65; gen. credit mgr. Futorian Mfg. Corp. div. Mohasco Industries, New Albany, Miss., 1965-67; chief financial officer, controller NCC Industries, Inc., Memphis, 1967-68, regional sales mgr., 1969, v.p. marketing, 1969-71; v.p., dir. 1st Leasing & Capital Corp., Memphis, 1971—. Served with AUS, 1952-55. Mem. Data Processing Mgmt. Assn., Nat. Accountants Assn., Memphis Sales Execs. Club, Delta Sigma Phi. Club: Sertoma (Morristown v.p. 1963-65). Contbr. articles to profl. lit. Home: 5292 Dargen St Memphis TN 38118 Office: PO Box 125 Memphis TN 38101

PERDUE, RICHARD MASON, elec. products co. exec.; b. Hope, Ark., Dec. 4, 1921; s. Leo Douglas and Jessie Mason (Waddle) P.; B.A., Hendrix Coll., 1943; B.B.A., So. Meth. U., 1947; m. Mary Evelyn Adams, Nov. 16, 1947; 1 son, Mark Douglas. Asst. advt. mgr. Sears, Roebuck & Co., Dallas, 1947-50; mgr. advt. and pub. relations Browning Ferris, machinery distbr., Dallas, 1950-54, Ideco div. Dresser Industries, oil equipment mfg., 1954-59; mgr. pub. relations Tex. Instruments, 1959—. Instr. marketing So. Methodist U., part-time 1950-70. Mem. publicity staff and report drafting coms. Goals for Dallas, 1966—. Served with USNR, 1942-46. Mem. Pub. Relations Soc. Am. (dir. chpt. 1971-73, mem. nat. pub. relations com. 1969-72, mem. nat. awards com. 1970-73), Dallas Press (bd. dirs. 1968). Methodist (exec. com. 1966-69). Home: 3413 Villanova Dr Dallas TX 75225 Office: Mail Station 240 PO Box 5474 Dallas TX 75222

PERESS, MARUICE, symphony condr.; b. N.Y.,, 1930; ed. Mannes Sch. Music, N.Y.U.; m. Gloria Vanda, 1955; children—Paul, Loica, Anika. Orchestral asst. Mannes Sch. Music; dir. Washington Square Orch. and Chorus, N.Y.U.; asst. condr. N.Y. Philharmonic, from 1961; condr. Corpus Christi (Tex.) Symphony, 64—, Austin (Tex.) Symphony, 1970-72. Mus. dir. Joffrey Ballet inaugural season; condr. Mass (Bernstein), Kennedy Center for Performing Arts, Washington; orchestrates works of Monteverdi, Vivaldi, Duke Ellington, others; rec. artist for Columbia Records. Served with AUS. Address: Box 495 Corpus Christi TX 78403*

PEREZ, ANGEL PEREZ, utility co. exec.; b. Tampa, Fla., Sept. 8, 1908; s. Angel and Serafina (Perez) P.; B.S. in Elec. Engring., Auburn U., 1932; m. Carmen Torres, Jan. 8, 1945 (dec. 1968); 1 dau., Carmen Loretta. With Fla. Power Corp., 1936—, operations analyst, St. Petersburg, 1946-51; elec. design engr., 1951-60, v.p., 1960-67, pres., chief exec. officer, 1967—. Registered prof engr., Fla., Ga. Mem. Nat. Soc. Profl. Engrs., Fla. Engring. Soc., St. Petersburg C. of C., Am. Nuclear Soc., Pi Kappa Alpha. Democrat. Roman Catholic. Clubs: St. Petersburg Yacht; University (Tampa); University (Washington); Commerce of Pinellis County. Home: 331 61st St N St Petersburg FL 33710 Office: 101 S 5th St St Petersburg FL 33733

PEREZ, EUGENE REYES, surgeon; b. San Juan Bautista, Cal., Jan. 6, 1908; s. Frederick, P. and Christina E. (Rozas) P.; A.B., U. Cal. 1931; M.D., C.M., McGill U., Montreal, Que., Can., 1936; m. Evelyn E. Peterson, May 28, 1937; children—Teresa Dolores (Mrs. Albert Balz), Camila Ines (Mrs. Thomas Baumgartner). Postgrad. surg. tng. U. Cal. Hosp., San Francisco, 1936-37, 40-41; Letterman Gen. Hosp., San Francisco, 1938-40, Royal Victoria Hosp., McGill U., 1937-38; asst. chief resident surgeon U. Cal. Hosp., 1945-46; pvt. and indsl. surgery practice, San Jose, Cal., 1946-60; clin. instr. in surgery Stanford Sch. Medicine, 1958-60; dir. med. edn. and research Washington County Hosp., Hagerstown, Md., 1960-61; dir. med. edn. Williamsport (Pa.) Hosp., 1961-62; asst. supt., dir. profl. services and edn. Meadowbrook Hosp., L.I., 1962-63; med. dir. Rossmoor Leisure World Clinic, Walnut Creek, Cal., 1964-66; med. dir. Petersburg (Va.) Gen. Hosp., 1966-67; dir. Va. Regional Med. Program, also asst. prof. med. edn., Med. Coll. Va., 1967—. Vice pres. Va. League Nursing, 1970-72. Served as lt. col., M.C., AUS, 1941-45. Fellow A.C.S. (past pres. No. Cal. chpt.); mem. A.M.A., Pan Am. Med. Soc. (state dir.), A.A.A.S., Am. Assn. for History of Medicine, San Jose Surg. Soc. (pres. 1956-57), Am. Hosp. Assn., Assn. Am. Med. Colls., Assn. Hosp. Dirs. Med. Edn., Am. Soc. Abdominal Surgery, Va. Med. Soc., Richmond Acad. Med., Club: Bull and Bear. Office: VA Regional Med Program 700 E Main St Richmond VA 23219

PEREZ PIMENTEL, PEDRO, justice P.R. Supreme Ct.; b. Vieques, P.R., Apr. 1, 1904; s. Dionisio Perez Valles and Natividad Pimentel; LL.B., U. P.R., 1927; m. Margarita, Maria Margarita. Admitted to P.R. bar, 1927, practiced in Humacao, 1927-42; legal advisor of treas. of P.R., 1945-45; dist. judge, Guayama, P.R., 1945, Humacao, 1945-49, San Juan, 1949-52; asso. justice Supreme Ct. P.R., 1952—. Mem. Bar Assn. P.R. Rotarian. Home: Calle Travieso 1512 Santurce PR 00908 Office: Supreme Ct San Juan PR 00936

PEREZ-SOTO, ARMANDO, physician; b. Utuado, P.R., Feb. 12, 1936; s. Eduardo and Luisa (Soto) Perez-Ayala; B.S. cum laude, U. P.R., 1967. M.D., 1961; m. Ana L. Zabala, July 2, 1960; children—Armando L., Maria del Pilar, Roberto. Intern, Univ. Hosp., Rio Piedras, P.R., 1962; practice medicine specializing in internal medicine, Arecibo, P.R., 1966—. Served to capt. AUS, 1962-66. Mem. A.M.A., U. P.R. Med. Grads. Assn. Home: 54 Andres Garcia St Arecibo PR 00612 Office: 107 Hernandez Huertas St Arecibo PR 00612

PEREZ-VARELA, JOSE JULIO, educator; b. Havana, Cuba, Apr. 12, 1935; s. Jose and Avelina (Varela) P.; M.A., U. Granada (Spain), 1958, Ph.D., 1962; m. Delia Castellon, Aug. 17, 1967; 1 son, Joseph. Came to U.S., 1967. Prof., Cath. U., Caracas, Venezuela, 1962-67; prof. philosophy St. Joseph Coll., Jensen Beach, Fla., 1967—. Vis. prof. Javier U., Bogota, Colombia, 1964-65. Mem. Am. Cath., Fla. philos. assns. Home: 880 Solaz Av Fort Pierce FL 33450 Office: 720 S Indian River Dr Jensen Beach FL 33457

PEREZ-VERDIA, ANTONIO, JR., lawyer; b. Mexico City, Mexico, Apr. 4, 1917; Licentiate in Law, Nat. Autonomous U. Mexico, 1940. Admitted to Mexico bar, 1940; mem. firm Bufete Antonio Perez-Verdia, Jr., Mexico City. Hon. pres., bd. dirs. Inst. Social and Econ. Investigations. Mem. Mexican (dir. 1945-66), Internat. bar assns., Inter-Am. (dir.), Mexican (past pres.) assns. indsl. property, U.S. Trademark Assn., Internat. Fedn. Lawyers, Mexican Acad. Jurisprudence and Legislation, Barra Mexicana-Colegio de Abogados, Asociacion Mutualista de Abogados de Mexico, Ilustre y Nacional Colegio de Abogados de Mexico. Office: Rio Guadiana 23 7th and 8th floors Colonia Cuauhtemoc Mexico 5 DF Mexico*

PERKINS, ABNER LAVERNE, hwy. engr., land surveyor; b. Cairo, Ga., May 20, 1937; s. Thomas Abner and Mildred (Strickland) P.; student U. Okla., 1955-57, U. Ky., 1957; m. Inez Janet Worley, Mar. 1, 1959; children—Derwood Laverne, Melody Renee. Worker, mgr. Curry Furniture & Funeral Home, Chandler, Okla., 1953-55; worker Primrose Funeral Home, Norman, Okla., 1955-57; with Ky. Dept. Hwys., Lexington, 1957—, civil engr. asst., 1967, dist. program and planning engr., 1967—. Recipient certificate of service award Ky. Dept. Hwys., 1967. Registered profl. engr., Ky. Mem. Nat., Ky. socs. profl. engrs. Mem. Ch. of God. Designer, builder Ch. of God, Lexington, 1964. Home: 107 Sutton Pl Lexington KY 40504 Office: 763 New Circle Rd Lexington KY 40504

PERKINS, CARL D., legislator; b. Hindman, Ky., Oct. 15, 1912; s. J.E. and Dora (Calhoun) P.; grad. Jefferson Sch. Law, Louisville, 1935; m. Verna Johnson; 1 son, Christopher. Practice of law, Hindman, Ky., 1935; commonwealth atty. 31st Jud. Dist., 1939; mem. Ky. Gen. Assembly from 99th Dist., 1940; Knott County atty., 1941-48; counsel Dept. Hwys., Frankfort, Ky., 1948; mem. 81st to 92d congresses 7th dist. of Ky., chmn. house com. on edn. and labor, 1967—. Served with AUS, World War II: ETO; participated in battles No. France, Battle of the Bulge, Rhineland, Central Europe. Democrat. Home: Hindman KY 48122 Office: Rayburn Bldg Washington DC 20013

PERKINS, DONALD YOUNG, horticulturist, educator; b. Ponchatoula, La., June 27, 1923; s. Gerald and Louise (Young) P.; B.S., La., State U., 1950, M.S., 1951; Ph.D., Cornell U., 1954; m. Patricia Ruth Peifer, Jan. 28, 1956; children—Donald Young, Thomas William. Research asst. La. State U., Baton Rouge, 1950-51, Cornell U., Ithaca, N.Y., 1951-54; jr. olericulturist U. Cal. at Davis, 1954; asso. horticulturist La. State U., Baton Rouge, 1954-57; horticulturist, prin. horticulturist U.S. Dept. Agr., Washington, 1957-66; vis. asso. prof. Purdue U., Lafayette, Ind., 1964-65; head dept. horticulture, research Auburn U., Ala., 1966—. Served with AUS, 1943-45. Decorated Purple Heart with oak leaf cluster. Fellow A.A.A.S.; mem. Am. Soc. for Hort. Sci., Am. Genetic Assn., Am. Inst. Biol. Sci., Sigma Xi, Phi Eta Sigma, Phi Kappa Phi, Alpha Zeta. Home: 319 Singleton St Auburn AL 36830

PERKINS, GEORGE, research cons.; b. Lagrange, Ind., Mar. 20, 1917; s. Roy Isaac and Opal (Lovett) P.; B.S., Purdue U., 1937, Ph.D., 1940; M.S. in Social Work, U. Louisville, 1964; m. Helen M. Matsko, Apr. 25, 1940; children—George G., Gay Helen. With Standard Oil Co. (Ind.), 1941-42, Bohn Aluminum & Brass Co., Detroit, 1942-44; tech. adviser Reynolds Metals Co., Albany and N.Y.C., 1944-46, dir. tech. service, 1947-50, dir. products and applications, 1950-54, dir. product devel., Louisville, 1955-58; dir. Bellewood Presbyn. Home for Children, Anchorage, Ky., 1958-68; commr. Ky. Dept. Child Welfare, Frankfort, 1968-71; pres., exec. dir. Center for Devel. Human Potential, Inc., Anchorage, 1971—; chief social worker Bingham Child Guidance Clinic, Louisville, 1972—. Mem. bd. edn. Anchorage Sch. Dist., 1955-66. Bd. dirs. Presbyn. Home for Sr. Citizens, Louisville, 1954-68. Recipient Caleb Ballard Research award Kent. Sch., U. Louisville, 1964. Mem. Group Child Care Assn. y. (past pres.), Presbyn. Assn. Childrens Homes (past pres.), Sigma Xi, Tau Beta Pi, Phi Lambda Upsilon. Presbyn. (elder 1955—, synod moderator 1964-65). Home: 1003 Glenbrook Rd Anchorage KY 40223 Office: 601 S Floyd St Louisville KY 40202

PERKINS, HUEL DAVIS, coll. dean; b. Baton Rouge, La., Dec. 27, 1924; s. John Earl and Velma Valeria (Davis) P.; B.S., So. U., 1947; Mus.M., Northwestern U., 1951, Ph.D., 1958; m. Thelma Ovella Smith, Sept. 14, 1948; 1 son, Huel Alfred. Instr. Lincoln U., Jefferson City, Mo., 1948-50; asso. prof. music So. U., Baton Route, La., 1951-60, dir. music, 1960-68, dean Coll. Arts and Humanities, 1968—. Mem. Mayor's Commn. on Youth Activity, Baton Rouge, 1969-71; mem. vis. faculty Harvard, 1968. Bd. dirs. Bloundon Orphanage, Baton Rouge, 1970-71. Served with USNR, 1943-46. Danforth tchr. grantee, 1957. Mem. Alpha Kappa Mu, Phi Mu Alpha, Pi Kappa Lambda, Alpha Phi Alpha. Home: 1923 79th Av Baton Rouge LA 70807

PERKINS, JAMES NICHOLAS, publisher; b. Littleton, N.H., Aug. 9, 1933; s. Nicholas D. and Lucia (Tegu) P.; grad. Williston Acad., 1951; A.B., Dartmouth, 1955; postgrad. U. Md., 1958; m. Margaret Jennisch, Aug. 26, 1967; children—Susan, Karen, Elizabeth. Mng. editor Literary Guild, N.Y.C., 1960-61; v.p. Curtis Pub. Co., N.Y.C., 1963-64; v.p. Times Mirror, N.Y.C., 1967-69; pres. Times Mirror School Library Service, 1969-70; pres., chmn. bd. Fuller & Dees, Inc., Am. Community Publishers, Inc., Montgomery, Ala., 1969—, also dir. Served to capt. USAF, 1955-58. Decorated Commendation medal. Mem. Williston-Northampton Sch. Alumni (pres. 1970), Delta Kappa Epsilon. Clubs: Dutch Treat, Players (N.Y.C.). Contbr. articles to St. Eve. Post, Readers Digest, various other Profl. Pubs. Home: Corn Dance Farm Coosada AL 36020 Office: Box 3396 Montgomery AL 36109

PERKINS, JOSEPH RUSSELL, architect; b. Brookhaven, Miss., Dec. 25, 1925; s. James Martin and Gladys (Furr) P.; student engring. U. Miss., 1947; B.Arch., U. Okla., 1951; m. Mary Elizabeth Thames, Dec. 24, 1952; children—Pamela Elizabeth, Joseph Russell, Regina Ann, Mary Virginia, Beverly Furr. Designer, Mallett & Assos., Architects and Engrs., Jackson, Miss., 1951-54, Raymond Birchett, Architect, Jackson, 1954-56; self-employed Joseph Russell Perkins, Architect, Jackson, 1956-69; partner Benham and Perkins, Jackson, 1969—. Vice pres. Bienville Corp., Prentiss, Miss., 1964—. Rep. A.I.A. to Civics Arts Council, Jackson, 1965—. Served with AC, USNR, 1943-45. Recipient service award Am. Legion, 1960; Design award Miss. Pine Mfg. Assn., 1968; honorable mention award Miss. chpt. A.I.A., 1971. Mem. A.I.A. (v.p. 1966, dir. 1967). Prin. archtl. works include county office bldg., Prentiss, 1961; Battlefield Village Shopping Center, Vicksburg, Miss., 1966; Main Harbor Marina, Jackson 1967; Extended Facility Prentiss; Bailey & Bailey Office plaza, Jackson, Mainstream Mall Shopping Center, Greenville, Miss., 1971, adminstrn.-classroom bldg. Jackson State Coll., other univ. bldgs. Home: 1555 Lelia Dr Jackson MS 39216 Office: 3218 N State St Jackson MS 39216

PERKINS, MARCUS FRANKLIN, foam plastics mfg. exec.; b. Macon, Mo., Oct. 26, 1909; s. Walter Wingford and Anna (Reynolds) P.; student Ft. Lewis Coll., 1927-28, U. Utah, 1929-30; B.S., U. Okla., 1932; m. Oma Nicholson, Aug. 19, 1960; children—Delano, Gary, Douglas. Tchr. high sch., Colo., 1934-39; rancher, Dove Creek, Colo., 1934-60; operator El Rey Hotel, San Diego, 1947-61, Rogette Motel, Dove Creek, 1951-60; mfr. foam plastics, Fort Worth, 1958—. Mem. Sch. Bd., Dove Creek, 1940-52. Mem. Delta Sigma Phi. Patentee in amusement field. Home: 7320 Coronet St Fort Worth TX 76118 Office: 205 S Sylvania St Fort Worth TX 76111

PERKINS, MARGARET NELSON KAYE (MRS. WILLIAM ROBERTSON PERKINS, JR.), artist-painter; b. Topeka, Sept. 7, 1904; d. James Philip and Frances (Nelson) de Bevers Kay; student art, Florence, Italy, 1922-24; grad. N.Y. Sch. Fine and Applied Art, 1927; spl. student Randolph-Macon Woman's Coll., 1946-48; m. William Robertson Perkins, Jr., Oct. 1, 1938; 1 dau., Sarah Frances. One-man shows Lynchburg Art Club, 1961, Myrtle Beach, S.C., 1967; 2-man show Randolph-Macon Woman's Coll., 1948; exhibited in group shows Va. Mus. Fine Arts, Nat. Biennial Am. League Am. Pen Women, others. Recipient 1st prize Lynchburg Civic Art, 1949, 55, Va. Fed. Women's Clubs, 1955-58, Va. Biennial Nat. League Am. Pen Women, 1963. Mem. D.A.R., Archeol. Inst. Am., Assn. for Preservation Va. Antiquities, Historic Lynchburg Found., L'Alliance Francaise de Lynchburg, N.E. Hist Geneal. Soc., Am. Pen Women (v.p. Lynchburg br. 1966-67). Club: Garden of Virginia, Lynchburg Art. Illustrated booklet Christmas in Colonial Virginia, 1957. Home: 3116 Rivermont Av Lynchburg VA 24503

PERKINS, MARION MAY ZUELSDORF (MRS. DAVID LAVELLE PERKINS), dietitian; b. Markesan, Wis., May 9, 1921; d. George F. and Kathryn (Menke) Zuelsdorf; B.S., U. Wis., 1942; m. David Lavelle Perkins, July 16, 1947; children—Patricia Linda, Catherine Jean, Rebecca Ann. Dietetic intern U. Neb. Med. Center, 1942, Lincoln (Neb.) Gen. Hosp., 1943; dietitian Miami Valley Hosp., Dayton, O., 1943-44, U. Chgo. Clinics, 1944-47, VA Hosp., Jackson, Miss., 1950-55, U. Miss. Med. Center, Jackson, 1957; sch. lunch supr. Jackson (Miss.) Pub. Schs., 1958—. Tchr. sch. lunch workshops U. So. Miss., 1958—, U. Miss., 1967—. Served to 1st lt. AUS, 1944-46. Mem. Am. (del. to nat. conv. 1963-66), Miss. (exec. bd. 1958—, sec. 1968-70) dietetic assns., Am., Miss. (pres. 1966, exec. bd. 1964—) sch. food service assns., Miss. Nutrition Council. Home: 218 Carmel Av Jackson MS 39204 Office: PO Box 2338 Jackson MS 39205

PERKINS, PERCY HAROLD, JR., architect; b. Metter, Ga., Sept. 8, 1905; s. Percy Harold and Bertha Mae (Warwick) P.; student Ga. Sch. Tech., 1923-27; grad. The Infantry Sch., 1932, Command and Gen. Staff Sch., 1942, Gemological Inst. Am., 1966; m. Mary L. Martin, Nov. 5, 1933 (dec. June 1962); m. 2d, Estelle B. Bennett, Jan. 25, 1963; 1 stepson., James Gordon Bennett. Archtl. draftsman, 1927-33, Atlanta, 1936-41; asso. architect Barili & Humphreys, Atlanta, 1946-51; architect Percy H. Perkins Jr. & Assos., Atlanta, 1951—. Gemologist, 1966—; lectr. gems and gemology. Served from 2d lt. to capt., U.S. Army, 1933-36; from capt. to col., AUS, 1936-41. Aide-de-camp Gov.'s staff, 1971—. Decorated Bronze Star medal, Purple Heart; Czechoslovakia War Cross. Mem. Ga. Mineral Soc., Ga. Gem Soc., Res. Officers Assn. (past pres. Atlanta chpt.), Atlanta Hist. Soc., Atlanta Art Assn., Fulton County Grand Jurors Assn., Am. Legion (trustee), A.I.A. (past dir. Ga. chpt.), Ga. Archtl. and Engring. Soc. Presbyn. (elder). Mason (Shriner), Kiwanian. Writer newspaper column. Home: 5450 Peachtree-Dunwoody Rd NE Atlanta GA 30342 Office: 3110 Maple Dr NE Atlanta GA 30305

PERKINS, PETER BENTON, dentist; b. Batesville, Miss., Mar. 28, 1921; s. Marshall Louis and Annie Louise (Holmes) P.; B.S., U. Miss., 1942; D.D.S., U. Tenn., 1949; m. Jim Alice Cockrell, July 14, 1943; children—Ann (Mrs. Olen Cooper Bryant, Jr.), Peter Benton. Gen. practice dentistry, Hazlehurst, Miss., 1950—; dir. Mchts. and Planters Bank. Chmn. troop com. Choctaw council Boy Scouts Am., 1960-66; pres. Hazlehurst Youth Center, 1964-67; pres. Little League Baseball, Hazlehurst, 1962-65. Mem. Copiah County Sch. Bd., 1957-62, Hazlehurst Sch. Bd., 1966-69. Served to 1st lt. USAAF, 1942-45. Decorated Air medal. Fellow Am. Coll. Dentistry; mem. Acad. Gen. Dentistry, mem. Am. (alternate del. 1972), Miss. (pres. 1971-72) dental assns., Central Dist Dental Soc. (pres. 1970-71), Hazlehurst C. of C. (pres. 1954). Home: 405 S Extension St Hazlehurst MS 39083 Office: 206 W Green St Hazlehurst MS 39083

PERKINS, RICHARD BURLE, real estate broker; b. Rockville, Ind., July 1, 1923; s. Walter Mac and Olevia Maude (Vinson) P.; student Ball State U., 1941-42, Oberlin Coll., 1944-45, U. Mich., 1946; B.A., DePauw U., 1947; m. Mariam Catherine Jamail, Aug. 1, 1959; children—Richard Burle II, Mele Angelique. Territory mgr. P & G Edible Oils, Tex., La., Okla., 1947-53; dist. mgr. Southwest U.S. DCA Food Industries, spl. flours, mixes and machinery, Houston, Tex., 1953-62; pres. Gold Seal Donuts, Houston, 1962-63; div. mgr. Nat. Oats Co., Houston, 1963-68; mgr. apt. mng. systems Office Services, Inc., Houston, 1970—; owner Dick Perkins Co., developer subdiv., Houston, 1970—; registered securities rep. Waddel & Reed, Houston, 1970-71; gen. mgr. Seven-Up Bottling Corp., Houston, 1969. Chmn. orgn. and extension com. Sunset dist. Boy Scouts Am., 1970; com. chmn. Cub Scout Pack 855, 1968—; coach, sponsor Spring Branch Little League Baseball, 1967—. Served with USMCR, 1942-46. Mem. Pi Sigma Alpha. Club: Memorial Plaza Civic (pres. 1968) (Houston). Home: 5915 Havenwoods Dr Houston TX 77066 Office: 5903 Queensgate Dr Houston TX 77040

PERKINS, THEODORE EDISON, librarian; b. Goldsboro, N.C., Dec. 11, 1917; s. Isaac Thomas and Mamie (Aycock) P.; B.S., Western Carolina U., 1939; M. Div. Duke U., 1946; M.Ed., U. N.C., 1957, B.S. in L.S., 1957, M.S., 1962; m. Eugenia Mae Echerd, Nov. 3, 1946; children—Sarah Eugenia, David Theodore, Samuel Lee. Tchr., librarian pub. schs., N.C., 1939-43, 47-58; youth worker, pastor N.C. Yearly Meeting of Friends, 1943-54; librarian Elon (N.C.) Coll., 1958—. Ordained minister Religious Soc. Friends, 1945; presiding clk. Contentnea Quar. Meeting of Friends on Ministry and Counsel, 1950-52, New Garden Quar. Meeting of Friends, 1960-65, New Garden Quar. Meeting of Friends on Ministry and Counsel, 1966-70, Greensboro Monthly Meeting of Friends, 1970—. Mem. Am., Southeastern, N.C., Guilford (pres. 1967-68) library assns. Home: 128 Tate St Greensboro NC 27403 Office: Elon College Library Box 187 Elon College NC 27244

PERLIK, CHARLES ANDREW, JR., trade union ofcl.; b. Pitts., Nov. 13, 1923; s. Charles Andrew and Theresa (Kraft) P.; B.S. in Journalism, Northwestern U., 1949, M.S., 1950; m. Marion Virginia Ford, Jan. 3, 1948; children—Paul, Lesley, Stephen. Newsman, U.P., Pitts., Chgo., 1946-48; reporter Buffalo Evening News, 1950-52; internat. rep. Am. Newspaper Guild (now The Newspaper Guild 1971—), Buffalo, 1952-55, sec.-treas., Washington, 1955-69, pres., 1969—. Sec.-treas. Mellett Fund for Free and Responsible Press, 1964—. Served to 1st lt. USAAF, 1943-46. Mem. Sigma Delta Chi. Home: 2407 Barbour Rd Falls Church VA 22043 Office: care The Newspaper Guild 1126 16th St NW Washington DC 20036

PERLIS, LEO, labor ofcl.; b. Bialystok, Russia, Feb. 22, 1912; s. David and Anna (Hirsch) P.; came to U.S., 1923, naturalized, 1928; student pub. schs., Paterson, N.J.; m. Mimi Blatt, 1937 (dec. 1943); 1 son, Howard William; m. 2d, Betty Gantz; 1 son, Michael Fredrick. Nat. dir. CIO Community Services Com., 1945; dir. AFL-CIO community service activities, 1955—. Mem. labor adv. com. Office Econ. Opportunity, 1965; sec. Nat. Citizens Com. Pub. Schs.; cons. UN, 1947-48; v.p. U.S. Com. for UNICEF; sec. C.A.R.E., 1954; mem. adv. com. sheltered workshops Dept. Labor; hon. dir. Group Health Ins. Co.; mem. Pres.'s Citizens Adv. Com. Juvenile Delinquency and Youth Crime. Bd. dirs. Am. Heart Assn., Nat. Council Aging, Nat. Assn. Mental Health, United Community Funds and Councils Am., U.S.O., 1963-65, Nat. Assembly Social Policy and Devel.; bd. govs.

United Way Am.; adv. council Sch. Social Work, N.Y.U., Sch. Social Work, Hunter Coll.; trustee Nassau Community Coll.; asso. trustee U. Pa. Recipient Page One award Newspaper Guild, 1957; first award Council Social Work Edn., 1958; award Boys Clubs Am., 1968; Silver Beaver award Boy Scouts Am., 1970. Fellow Am. Pub. Health Assn.; mem. Health and Welfare Retirement Assn. (dir. 1968), Am. Nat. Council Health Edn. Pub. (dir.). Author articles in field. Home: 6101 16th St NW Washington DC 20011 Office: 815 16th St NW Washington DC 20006

PERLMAN, MATTHEW S., lawyer; b. Washington, Aug. 30, 1936; A.B. magna cum laude, Brown U., 1957; LL.B., magna cum laude, Harvard, 1960. Admitted to D.C. bar, 1960, Md. bar, 1960, U.S. Supreme Ct. bar, 1964, U.S. Ct. Claims bar, 1965; atty. Office Gen. Counsel, Dept. Air Force, 1960-65; mem. Armed Services Bd. Contract Appeals, 1965-67; gen. counsel President's Commn. on Postal Orgn., 1967; asst. gen. counsel Dept. Transp., 1967-69; mem. firm Arent, Fox, Kintner, Plotkin & Kahn, Washington. Mem. Am. (chmn. contract adjustment bd. com. pub. contract law sect. 1970-71), Fed. (vice chmn. govt. contracts com. 1969—) bar assns., Phi Beta Kappa. Editor: Harvard Law Rev., 1959-60. Office: Federal Bar Bldg Washington DC 20006*

PERLMUTTER, JEROME HERBERT, govt. ofcl., writer, editor; b. N.Y.C., Oct. 17, 1924; s. Morris and Rebecca (Shiffman) P.; A.B. cum laude, George Washington U., 1949; M.A., Am. U., 1957; m. Evelyn Lea Friedman, Sept. 19, 1948; children—Diane Muriel, Sandra Pauline, Bruce Steven. Chief editor service, prodn. editor N.E.A., Washington, 1949-50; editor in chief jour. A.A.H.P.E.R., Washington 1950-51, Rural Elec. News, Rural Electrification Adminstrn. USDA, Washington, 1951-53; publ. writer Agr. Research Service, 1953-56, chief, editor br. Office of Information, 1956-60, sec. Outlook and Situation Bd., chief econ. reports Econ. Research Service, 1960-62; chief div. pub. and reprodn. services U.S. Dept. State, Washington, 1962—. Writing instr., U. Md. Agr. Grad. Sch.; writing cons. Civil Service Commn., 1956, World Bank, 1967—, White House, 1969-70; coordinator Fed. Graphic Design Nat. Endowment for the Arts, 1972—. Served with USNR, 1943-46. Recipient Arthur S. Flemming award, 1963; Superior Service award Dept. State, 1966. Mem. Am. Assn. Agr. Coll. Editors, Fed. Editors Assn., Am. Farm Econ. Assn., Soc. Tech. Writers and Pubs., Phi Beta Kappa, Sigma Delta Chi, Phi Eta Sigma, Artus. Author: Practical Guide to Effective Writing. Contbr. articles in profl. jour. Home: 513 E Indian Spring Dr Silver Spring MD 20901 Office: US Dept State Washington DC 20520

PERLOFF, MAYER WILLIAM, lawyer; b. New Orleans, Sept. 2, 1926; s. Samuel and Rebecca (Mitchell) P.; B.S., U. Ala., 1949; LL.B., U. Md., 1953; m. Lottie Jewel Jordon, Oct. 16, 1961; children—Samuel Richard, Robert Jeffery, Johnathan Craig. Admitted to Md. bar, 1953, Ala. bar, 1957; pvt. practice law, Balt., 1953-56, Mobile, Ala., 1957—. Mem. Ala. Ho. of Reps., 1966—. Served with USNR, 1944-46. Mem. Mobile, Ala. bar assns., Comml. Law League Am. Democrat. Jewish religion. Mason (Shriner). Home: 3909 Radnor Av Mobile AL 36608 Office: 257 St Anthony St Mobile AL 36603

PERMENTER, ROY ARCH, supt. schs.; b. Joaquin, Tex., Jan. 15, 1913; s. James Archie and Mary (Childress) P.; B.S., Stephen F. Austin U., 1933; M.Ed., U. Houston, 1947; postgrad. U. Tex., U. Houston, 1960-65; m. Marianella Matlock, Aug. 18, 1935; 1 son, James Roy (dec.). Prin. high sch., Garrison, Tex., 1933-37; coach high sch., Chester, Tex., 1937-39; prin., coach high sch., Anahuac, 1939-42; prin. elementary sch., Beaumont, Tex., 1945-49; asst. supt. schs. South Park Schs., Beaumont, 1949-63; supt. schs. South Park Ind. Sch. Dist., Beaumont, 1963—, bus. mgr., 1951-60. Cons. ednl. adminstrn. Mem. N.E.A., Tex. Tchrs. Assn., Am., Tex. assns. sch. adminstrs., Jefferson County Adminstrs. Assn. Mason, Lion (pres. 1951-54). Home: 290 N Major Dr Beaumont TX 77706 Office: 1025 Woodrow St Beaumont TX 77706

PEROT, H. ROSS, electronics co. exec.; b. Texarkana, Tex., June 27, 1930; s. Gabriel Ross Perot; student Texarkana Jr. Coll; B.S., U.S. Naval Acad., 1953; m. Margot Birmingham, 1956; 3 daus., 1 son, H. Ross. Commd. ensign U.S. Navy, 1953, advanced through grades to lt., resigned, 1957; computer salesman IBM, Dallas, from 1957; founder Electronic Data Systems, Dallas, 1962, now pres. Founder Perot Found. Bd. dirs. United We Stand. Office: Electronic Data Systems Corp Exchange Bank Tower Dallas TX 75235

PERPALL, DOROTHY JEAN BELL (MRS. REX PERPALL), artist; b. Bellingham, Wash., July 15, 1901; d. Charles E. and Eugenia (Sterrett) Bell; student Coll. Western Wash., 1919-21, U. Ore., 1921-23; m. Rex Perpall, July 24, 1933. One-man shows, Gulf Coast Art Gallery, Palette Gallery; exhibited in group shows Lauguna Beach Art Gallery, Los Angeles County Mus., Port of Spain; represented in permanent collections U.S. Naval Hosp., Morton Plant Hosp., Fla. State Capitol. Tchr. art, history, pub. schs., Dunedin, Fla., 1926-33. Mem. Nat. League Am. Pen Women (br. pres. 1962-64, state pres. 1964-66, nat. corr. sec. 1966-68, nat. 3d v.p. 1968-70, nat. chaplain 1970-72), Nat. Soc. Arts and Letters (art chmn. 1965-66, local 1st v.p. 1970-71, 72—, local pres. 1972), Fine Arts Soc., Gulf Coast Art Center. Christian Scientist. Home: 1707 N Osceola Av Clearwater FL 33515

PERREN, JOHN THOMAS, laywer; b. nr. Villa Rica, Ga., Apr 22, 1932; s. Grady Bannister and Lilla (Newman) P.; LL.B., Atlanta Law Sch., 1951; m. Mildred Louise Byram, July 7, 1951; children—Lajuana Denise, Gale Renee, Marion John Thomas, Melanie Dee. Bookkeeper, Continental Ins. Co., Atlanta, 1948-52; claims adjuster Fidelity & Casualty Co. N.Y., Columbia, S.C., 1952-55; admitted to Ga. bar, 1951; gen. practice law, Dallas, 1955—; asst. solicitor gen. Tallapoosa Jud. Circuit, 1959-67, dist. atty., 1967—. Mem. Paulding County Bd. Edn. 1956-60. Named Young Man of the Year Paulding County, 1964. Mem. Am. Bar Assn., State Bar Ga. Baptist. Democrat. Mason (Shriner, K.T.). Home: 310 S Hardee St Dallas GA 30132 Office: Courthouse Dallas GA 30132

PERRIN, DONALD EMILIEN, social worker; b. New Orleans, July 14, 1932; s. Donald Stephen and Rose-Aimee (Fittere) P.; B.A., Tulane U., 1959, M.S.W., 1962; m. Nancy Ruth Hunley, Aug. 11, 1962; 1 dau., Vivienne Michelle. Family counselor Family & Childrens Services, Beaumont, Tex., 1962-64; exec. dir. Family Service Agy. Washington County, Md. Inc., Hagerstown, 1964-71; exec. dir. Florence Crittenton Services, Charlotte, N.C., 1971—. Pres. Washington County Mental Health Assn., 1966; dir. Washington County Community Action Council, 1967-71; mem. health adv. bd. Mental Health Adv. Com., 1967-71. Served with USAF, 1953-57. Mem. Nat. Assn. Social Workers. Club: Exchange. Address: 2118 Beverly Dr Charlotte NC 28207

PERRINE, RICHARD HOOKER, librarian; b. Bloomfield, N.J., Jan. 2, 1918; s. Stanley Moore and Beryl Raymond (Baldwin) P.; student Rutgers U., 1935; B.F.A., Yale, 1940; 2d Prix de Architecture, Fontainebleau, France, 1950; M. L.S., U. Tex., 1961. Draftsman, Warren, Knight & Davis, architects, Birmingham, Ala., 1946, Coca Cola Co., Atlanta, 1947; designer Raymond-Hegeman Co., The Lummus Co., Venezuela, 1948-50, DuPont Corp., Wilmington, Del., 1950, Kelley Corp., N.Y.C., 1951, The Lummus Co., Houston, 1952-53; v.p., gen. mgr. The Hawthorne Co., Houston, 1953-57; library asst. Rice U., Houston, 1958-60, reference librarian, 1961-67, asst. librarian for planning, 1968—. Library bldg. cons. for various colls. and univs. Served to 1st lt. C.E., AUS, 1941-46. Decorated Purple Heart. Mem. Am. (pres. reference services div. 1968-69), Tex. library assns. Author: Library Space Survey of Texas Colleges and Universities, 1970. Home: 2015 South Blvd Houston TX 77006

PERRITT, R. T., clergyman; b. Winnsboro, Tex., May 20, 1926; s. James Hogg and Clara (White) P.; A.A., Jacksonville (Tex.) Coll., 1948; B.D., Bible Bapt. Sem., Arlington, Tex., 1958; Th.M., Okla. Missionary Bapt. Inst. and Sem., 1960, Th.D., 1961; m. Betty Ruth Powell, Nov. 23, 1944; children—Robert Lynn, John Mark, Ruth Ann, James Lance. Ordained to ministry Bapt. Ch., 1945; pastor Calvary Missionary Bapt. Ch., Sherman, Tex., 1949-51, Liberty Missionary Bapt. Ch., Ft. Worth, 1951-56, Cavanaugh Missionary Bapt. Ch., Fort Smith, Ark., 1956-59, 5th St. Missionary Bapt. Ch., Marlow, Okla., 1959—; dean Okla. Missionary Bapt. Inst. and Sem., 1961-63, pres., 1963—; asst. moderator Bapt. Gen. Assembly Okla., 1970—. With Farm Security Adminstrn., Dallas, 1945-46. Pres., Cavanaugh Baseball Club, 1957-59. Served with U.S. Maritime Service and Mcht. Marine, 1944-45. Named Community Leader Am., 1969. Mem. Am. Bapt. Assn. (v.p., chmn. missionary com. 1966—). Democrat. Lion. Author: The Natural and the Spiritual, 1960; Kindling Fires for Church Growth, 1965; Mastery in Sorrow, 1969; also numerous religious tng. course quars. Home: 610 W Kiowa St Marlow OK 73055 Office: 415 W Cherokee St Marlow OK 73055 also 9th and Caddo Sts Marlow OK 73055

PERRODIN, ALEXANDER FRANK, educator; b. Wisconsin Rapids, Wis., Apr. 7, 1915; s. Alex F. and Rose M. (Jolly) P.; B.Ed., Central State Tchrs. Coll. Wis., 1935; Ph.M., U. Wis., 1941; Ed.D., Columbia, 1952; m. Patricia W. Haney, May 31, 1947; children—Catherine Elizabeth, Mary Susan. Tchr. elementary schs., Wis., 1935-41, prin., 1945-47; demonstration sch. tchr. LaCrosse (Wis.) State Tchrs. Coll., 1947-50; faculty Keene (N.H.) State Tchrs. Coll., 1951-53; prof. elementary edn. U. Ga. Coll. Edn., Athens, 1953—, asso. dean instrn., 1968—. Served from pvt. to maj. USAAF, 1941-45. Mem. Nat., Ga. edn. assns., Am. Ednl. Research Assn., Assn. of Tchr. Educators, Assn. Childhood Edn. Internat., Phi Delta Kappa, Phi Kappa Phi, Kappa Delta Pi. Methodist. Editor buls. Nat. Assn. for Student Teaching, 1964-68, Student Tchr.'s Reader, 1966. Contbr. articles to profl. jours. Home: 214 Davis Estates Rd Athens GA 30601

PERROT, JOHN DAVID, elec. products co. exec.; b. Saginaw, Mich., Dec. 1, 1934; s. David Lewis and Mary (Resseguie) P.; B.S., U. Miami (Fla.), 1960; M.S., Fla. Inst. Tech., 1969; m. Ethel M. Hasse, July 20, 1957; children—Mary Jane, Kimberly Sue, Deborah Lynn. Designer elec. and hydraulic system Jackson & Church Co., AuGres, Mich., 1952-59, v.p., 1968—; design engr., mem. Minuteman launch team Boeing Co., Cape Kennedy, Fla., 1960-63; launch complex operations mgr. Gen. Electric Co., Kennedy Space Center, Fla., 1963-68; pres. Jackson & Church Electronics Co., Melbourne, Fla., 1968—; v.p. Harbor City Office Supply, 1963—, Platinum Coast Industries, Inc., 1965—. Councilman, Satellite Beach, Fla., 1972—. Registered profl. engr., Fla., Mich. Mem. Fla. Engring. Soc. (sr. mem.), Nat. Soc. Profl. Engrs., Instrumentation Soc. Am. Mason (Shriner), Elk. Club: Eau Gallie (Fla.) Yacht. Contbr. articles to profl. pubs. Home: 650 Cinnamon Dr Satellite Beach FL 32937 Office: 436 S Neiman Av Melbourne FL 32901

PERRY, ANTHONY JOHN, former cons. engineer; b. Boston, Sept. 7, 1905; s. Anthony A. and Ellen M. (Connors) P.; A.B., Boston Coll., 1926; S.B., Mass. Inst. Tech., 1929. Civil and elec. engr. Bur. Reclamation, Dept. of Interior, specializing in design and constrn. hydro-electric power and high tension transmission, 1930-65. Cons. engr. electric generation and transmission; spl. assignment Point 4 program, Iran, Lebanon and Italy, 1952, ICA, Cambodia, 1958; cons. govts., Brazil, 1964, Republic Korea, 1966, Bolivia, 1967-68. Registered profl. engr., Colo., D.C. Fellow Am. Soc. C.E.; mem. Nat. Soc. Profl. Engrs. (life), Am. Ordnance Assn. Democrat. Roman Catholic. K.C. Address: 4000 Massachusetts Av NW Washington DC 20016

PERRY, BARBARA (MRS. OLIVER PERRY), artist; b. Yonkers, N.Y., Sept. 13, 1922; d. M. Stuart and Julia (Aldrich) Moon; student Rochester Inst. Tech., 1939-40, Syracuse U., 1940-42, Am. U., 1951-52; m. Oliver Hazard Perry, Dec. 14, 1946; children—Allison M., Laurel H. Staff asst. publicity, murals Am. Nat. Red Cross, overseas 1945-46; publicity pamphlet design Nat. Acad. Scis., 1951; research nuclear emulsions Brookhaven Nat. Lab., 1950-51; artist Princeton Packet Newspaper, 1956-59; chmn. ednl. TV art auction, Broward City, 1970; cartoons for Pompano Town News, Eagle Bull.-DeWitt Times; theatrical cartoonist; art work in pvt. collections; pub. relations U.S. Coast Guard Aux. Mem. Broward Art Guild, Art Guild Boca Raton. Address: 771 SE 7th Av Pompano Beach FL 33060

PERRY, CHARLES EDWARD, univ. pres.; b. Holden, W. Va., July 25, 1937; s. Lester and Ethel (White) P.; student Marshall U., 1956; B.A., Bowling Green State U., 1958, B.S., 1959, M.A., 1964, L.H.D., 1970; postgrad. U. Mich., 1964-67; LL.D., Bethune-Cookman Coll., 1969; m. Betty Eleanor Laird, Sept. 17, 1960; children—Thomas Edward, Lynnette Eleanor. Tchr., coach East Detroit (Mich). pub. schs., 1959; admissions counselor Bowling Green State U., 1959-61, dir. admissions, 1961-64, dir. devel., asst. to pres., 1964-67; spl. asst. to gov. for ednl. affairs, Tallahassee, 1967-68; vice chancellor State U. System Fla., Tallahassee, 1968-69; pres. Fla. Internat. U., Miami, 1969—. Chmn., Gov.'s Ednl. Adv. Council, 1967—, Council for Jr. Coll. Affairs, 1968-69; mem. Select Council on Post High Sch. Edn., So. Regional Edn. Bd., Southeastern Ednl. Lab., Fla. Edn. Council; mem. Fla. Commn. on Latin Am. Affairs, 1969—, Nat. Com. on Utilization of Ednl. TV, 1968—, Nat. Com. for Support of Pub. Schs., Council of 100 Edn. Com., 1968—; mem. U.S. Commn. to UNESCO, 1970—. Mem. Fla. Am. Revolution Bicentennial Commn. Bd. dirs. Fla. Internat. U. Found. Served with AUS, 1960, 61-62. Recipient Outstanding Young Man award U.S. Jr. C. of C., 1965, 66, Spl. Appreciation award for Outstanding Contbns. to State of Fla., 1968; named one of America's 10 Outstanding Young Men, 1971; named Outstanding Young Man of Bowling Green, 1966. Mem. Am. Assn. for Higher Edn., Am. Assn. State Colls. and Univs. (com. on internat. programs), Ohio Soc. N.Y., Fla., Greater Miami chambers commerce, Pi Sigma Alpha, Alpha Kappa Delta, Phi Delta Kappa, Sigma Nu. Methodist. Kiwanian. Clubs: Century, Kings Bay. Author: (with Cliff Boutelle) The Inauguration of a College President, 1964. Contbg. editor The State University--Creator or Conformist, 1965; exec. editor Education in Florida: Perspective for Tomorrow, 1967. Contbr. articles to profl. jours. Home: 1142 S Greenway Coral Gables FL 33134 Office: Fla Internat Univ Tamiami Trail Miami FL 33144

PERRY, CHARLES RUSSELL, ovt. ofcl.; b. Detroit, Mar. 14, 1939; s. Charles Russell and Dorothy Anne (McClure) P.; B.A. in Econs., U. Mich., 1960; M.B.A. (Woodrow Wilson fellow), U. Chgo., 1962, Ph.D., 1968. Asst. dean students Grad. Sch. Bus., U. Chgo., 1962-64, asso. dir. study collective action among pub. sch. tchrs., 1964-66; asst. prof. industry Wharton Sch. Finance and Commerce, U. Pa., 1966; spl. asst. to asso. dir. mgmt. Office Mgmt. and Budget, Washington, 1970-71, exec. asst. to dir., 1971—. Mem. Phi Beta Kappa, Beta Gamma Sigma. Author: The Impact of Bargaining in Public Education, 1970; The Negro in the Department Store Industry, 1971. Home: 8310 Tobin Rd Apt 24 Annandale VA 22003 Office: Office Mgmt and Budget Exec Office Pres Washington DC 20503

PERRY, HAROLD ROBERT, clergyman; b. Lake Charles, La., Oct. 9, 1916; s. Frank and Josephine (Petrie) P.; student Divine Word Sem., Bay St. Louis, Miss., 1930-36, novitiate, East Troy, Wis., Techny, Ill., 1936-38; D.D., Divine Word Coll., Rome, 1965; LL.D., St. Joseph's Coll., Collegeville, Ind., 1964; L.H.D., Canisus Coll., 1966. Joined Soc. Divine Word, 1938, ordained priest Roman Catholic Ch., 1944, bishop, 1966; asst. pastor chs., Lafayette, La., Pine Bluff, St. Martinville, La., Mound Bayou, Miss., 1944-52; founder, pastor St. Joseph's Ch., Broussard, La., 1952-58; rector St. Augustine's Maj. and Minor Sem., Bay St. Louis, 1958-64; titular bishop Mons ni Mauretania and aux. to archbishop New Orleans, 1965; vicar gen. Archdiocese of New Orleans, 1965—, vicar for religious, 1968, co-ordinator Higher Studies, also pastor Little Flower of Jesus Ch., New Orleans; aux. bishop of New Orleans, 1965, now bishop; rector Nat. Shrine of Our Lady of Prompt Succor, 1968; Provincial So. province Divine Word Soc., 1964—; nat. chaplain Knights and Ladies St. Peter Claver, 1956—; mem. Episcopal Com. of Pontificial Soc. of Propagation of Faith, 1965—. Bd. dirs. Nat. Catholic Conf. for Interracial Justice. Home: 2705 State St New Orleans LA 70118 Office: 7887 Walmsley Av New Orleans LA 70125

PERRY, J(AMES) LEE, lawyer; b. Atlanta, Aug. 3, 1935; s. Eddie Willis and Dorothy (Burk) P.; B.S., Ga. Inst. Tech., 1957; LL.B., Emory U., 1962; m. Carol Ann Brendel, July 28, 1962; children—Kevin Andrew (dec.), Steven Brian, Bruce Burke, Colin Brendan. Draftsman, Ga. Power Co., Atlanta, 1958-59; admitted to Ga. bar, 1961; law asst. to justice Supreme Ct. Ga., Atlanta, 1962-64; practiced in Atlanta, 1964-67; mem. firms Latimer & Allen, Latimer, Haddon & Stanfield, 1964-67; asso. atty. Bd. Edn. Atlanta, 1964-67; asst. atty. gen. State of Ga., Atlanta, 1968—. Instr., Atlanta Pub. Schs., 1967. Served with AUS, 1957. Mem. Am., Ga., Atlanta bar assns., Theta Chi, Phi Delta Phi. Methodist. Club: River Bend Gun. Home: 245 Glencourtney Dr Atlanta GA 30328 Office: 135 State Judicial Bldg Atlanta GA 30334

PERRY, JOHN ELLIOTT, physician, educator; b. Pecos, Tex., Aug. 24, 1931; s. John Knight and Leslie B. (Elliott) P.; B.A., Rice U., 1953; M.D., U. Tex., 1957; m. Carolyn Jane Aubert, Dec. 22, 1951; children—John Aubert, Sarah Beth, Lee Elliott, Christopher Knight. Intern, U. Tex. Med. Br. Hosps., 1957-58, resident internal medicine, 1958-60; fellow in medicine Johns Hopkins Sch. Medicine, 1960-62; pvt. practice medicine, specializing in internal medicine, Dickinson, Tex., 1969—; asst. prof. internal medicine U. Tex. Med. Br., 1962-67, asso. prof. internal medicine, preventive medicine and community health, 1957-59, chief div. infectious diseases, 1962-69, clin. asso. prof. internal medicine, preventive medicine and community health, 1969—. Med. cons. Manned Spacecraft Center, NASA, Houston, 1969-71. Recipient research and tng. grants Nat. Inst. Allergy and Infectious Diseases, 1962-69. Jeane B. Kempner scholar, 1960-62. Diplomate Am. Bd. Internal Medicine. Fellow A.C.P.; mem. Am., Tex. socs. internal medicine, Tex. Acad. Internal Medicine, A.M.A., Tex. Med. Assn., Galveston County Med. Soc. Republican. Episcopalian. Club: Dickinson Country. Contbr. articles profl. jours. Home: 2810 Colonial Dr Dickinson TX 77539 Office: 2602 Termini St Dickinson TX 77539

PERRY, JOHN HOLLIDAY, JR., oceanographer, newspaper exec.; b. Seattle, Jan. 2, 1917; s. John Holliday and Dorothy Lilly Perry; grad. Hotchkiss Sch., 1935; A. B., Yale, 1939; Harvard Sch. Bus. Adminstrn., 1940; m. Jeanne See, 1946 (div. 1966); children—John Holliday III, Henry A., Stanton See; m. 2d, Marina Rosati, Nov. 5, 1966; children—Christiana, Francesca, Alessandra. Pres. Higgins-McArthur/Longino & Porter, Inc., Palm Beach Cable TV, Perry Oceanographics, Inc., St. Lucie Cable Co., Inc., Perry Submarine Builders; chmn. bd. Underseas Engring., Inc., Bahama Pubs., Inc.; pres., chmn. bd. Martin County Cable Co., Inc. mem. Pres.'s Commn. on Marine Scis., Engring. and Resources; mem. Fla. Commn. Marine Scis. and Tech.; nat. asso. Boys' Clubs Am. Trustee Internat. Oceanographic Found.; pres. Nat. Dividend Found., Perry Found. Inc. Served to 1st lt. A.C., AUS, 1942-45. Mem. Zeta Psi. Presbyn. Clubs: Yale, Racquet and Tennis (N.Y.C.); Bath and Tennis, Everglades, Beach (Palm Beach, Fla.). Author: The National Dividend. Home: 240 Banyan Rd Palm Beach FL 33480 Office: Perry Oceanographics Inc 100 E 17th St Riviera Beach FL

PERRY, JOHN ROY, savings and loan exec.; b. Thomasville, N.C., Dec. 25, 1903; s. Thomas Gray and Martha Theodoshia (Clinard) P.; student High Point Coll., 1925-28; m. Imogene Lewis, Aug. 11, 1971; 1 son, John Roy. With Peoples Savs. and Loan Assn., Thomasville, N.C., 1929—, pres., treas., 1970—; with Ins. and Loan Co., 1935—, pres., 1971—; dir. N.C. Nat. Bank. Commr., Davidson County (N.C.), 1940-44. Bd. dirs. Community Found., 1952. Democrat. Methodist. Mason (Shriner), Lion (pres. 1943), Clubs: Colonial Country, Exchange (pres. 1941). Home: 110 Jones St Thomasville NC 27360 Office: 100 Salem St Thomasville NC 27360

PERRY, MARVIN BANKS, ednl. publishing co. exec.; b. Machen, Ga., Apr. 2, 1891; s. Edwin Fletcher and Varina Davis (Banks) P.; A.B., U. Ga., 1912; m. Elizabeth Mosby Gray, Aug. 16, 1917 (dec. 1951); children—Marvin Banks, John Mosby; m. 2d, Nelle Alexander, Sept. 10, 1953. Tchr. English, Univ. Sch. for Boys, Stone Mountain, Ga., 1912-13; acting prin. High Sch., Athens, Ga., 1913-14; so. rep. Am. Book Co., Atlanta, 1914-19; So. rep. D.C. Heath & Co., Atlanta, 1919-28, treas., Boston, 1928-46, dir. 1936—, pres., 1946—, chmn. bd., 1957—; trustee Newton Savs. Bank. Trustee Athens Regional Library, U. Ga. Found. Served as capt. F.A., U.S. Army, World War I. Mem. Am. Textbook Pubs. Inst. (pres.), U. Ga. Alumni Soc. (pres. 1962-63), Kappa Sigma. Democrat. Methodist. Mason. Club: Brae Burn (Newton); Algonquin (Boston); Athens Country. Home: 315 Beechwood Dr Athens GA 30601 Office: 125 Spring St Lexington MA 02173

PERRY, MARVIN LEE, JR., TV film and program dir.; b. Waldo, Ark., Dec. 2, 1924; s. Marvin Lee and Lillie M. (Harris) P.; student La. Tech. U., 1943-44, U. Ark., 1944-45; grad. M. Draughn Bus. Coll., 1946; m. Dorothy Ethel Sekora, Sept. 28, 1952; children—Marvin Lee III, Deborah Kay, Douglas. Control operator radio sta. KTBS, Shreveport, La., 1947-49, chief control and prodn. operator, 1949-55; film dir. KTBS-TV, 1955-67, film and program dir., 1967—. Mem. TV Programming Conf. Mem. Ark. Civil Air Patrol., 1944-45. Bd. dirs. N. La. chpt. Nat. Multiple Sclerosis Soc. Mem. Nat. Assn. TV Program Execs. Home: 3615 Elon St Shreveport LA 71109 Office: 312 E Kings Hwy Shreveport LA 71104

PERRY, RALPH PEREZ, pres. WKVM, San Juan, P.R. Address: PO Box 4189 San Juan PR 00903*

PERRY, REGINALD CARMAN, educator; b. Indian Islands, Nfld., Aug. 15, 1903; s. William and Mary (Horwood) P.; B.A., Mt. Allison U., 1930; M.A., Toronto U., 1936, Ph.D., 1945; postgrad. Harvard, 1951-54. Came to U.S., 1946. Tchr., Nfld. Schs., 1921-25, 27-28, prin., 1923-25, 27-28; pastor United Ch. Can., 1933-34, 36-41; instr. Syracuse U., 1946-48; asst. prof. Okla. A. and M. Coll., Stillwater, 1948-51; pvt. researcher in philosophy, Cambridge, Mass., 1954-65; asso. prof. humanities and philosophy Ark. A. and M. and Normal Coll., Pine Bluff, 1965—. Mem. Am., Ark. philos. assns. Home: 1015 N Cedar St Pine Bluff AR 71601

PERRY, ROBERT E., lawyer; b. Rienzi, Miss., June 16, 1916; B.Sc., U. Miss., 1937, J.D., 1939. Admitted to Miss. bar, 1939; mem. firm Perry, Phillips, Crockett, Peters & Morrison, Jackson, Miss. Chmn., Miss. Law Inst., 1951. Served to lt. USNR, 1943-46. Fellow Miss. Bar Found.; mem. Am., Hinds County, Jackson Jr. (pres. 1952-53) bar assns., Miss. State Bar, Miss. Oil and Gas Lawyers Assn., Phi Delta Phi. Address: Deposit Guaranty Nat Bank Bldg Jackson MS 39205*

PERRY, ROLAND WILLARD, clergyman; b. nr. Pittsboro, N.C., Oct. 22, 1924; s. William Crabtree and Lydia (Bryant) P.; A.B., Shaw U., 1961, B.D., 1964; D.D., Friendship Coll., 1972; m. Doris Ethel Burnette, Aug. 13, 1958; children—Teresa Darlene, Roland Willard II, Dexter Vincent. Ordained to ministry Baptist Ch., 1956; pastor Taylor's Chapel Baptist Ch., Sanford, N.C., 1955-59, New Light Bapt. Ch., Oxford, N.C., 1957-65, Syname Grove Bapt. Ch., Oxford, 1959-61, Mt. Sinai Bapt. Ch., Durham, N.C., 1961-63, Pleasant Grove Bapt. Ch., Clover, S.C., 1963-70, Shiloh Bapt. Ch., Henderson, N.C., 1972—; prof. Bible, Friendship Jr. Coll., Rock Hill, S.C., 1968—, acad. dean, 1969-70. A founder South Gastonia Community Service, Inc.; vice moderator Upper div. Sandy River Baptist Assn. Sec., Gastonia br. N.A.A.C.P., 1968—; pres. Joint Conv. York-Chester Counties (S.C.), 1968—. Bd. dirs. Gaston Community Action, Baptist Student Union of Friendship Coll. Mem. Shaw U. Theol. Alumni Assn. (sec. 1968—), Greater Gastonia Ministerial Assn., Interdenominational Minister's Alliance of Gaston County (pres. 1967-69). Mason. Home: 807 Memory Lane Gastonia NC 28052 Office: Shiloh Baptist Church 621 College St Henderson NC 27536

PERRY, RONALD JOSEPH, supt. schs.; b. Wilkes Barre, Pa., Sept. 12, 1927; s. Joseph Jude and Helen Lucille (Ranakowski) P.; B.S., Duquesne U., 1950; M.S., U. Scranton, 1957; Ed.D. (spl. grad. fellow 1960-62, Inst. for Devel. Ednl. Activities fellow 1967), U. Va., 1971; postgrad. Juillard Sch. Music, 1948, Davidson Coll., 1967, Bucknell U., 1968; m. Margaret Mary Hogan, Aug. 2, 1969; children—Ronald Joseph, Randall, Russell, Ellen, Margaret. Tchr. music, history, English Scranton (Pa.) pub. schs., 1950-62; prin. Hampton (Va.) pub. schs., 1962-65; supt. schs., Line Mountain, S.D., 1965-69; asst. prof. edn., coordinator higher edn. law enforcement adminstrn. U. Va., Charlottesville, 1969—; div. supt. schs. Prince Edwards County Pub. Schs., Farmville, Va., 1969-72; supt. Pascack Valley Regional High Sch. Dist., N.J., 1972—. Asst. prof. edn. U. Va., 1962-63, Coll. William and Mary, 1963-65, Hampton Inst., 1963-64, Fairleigh Dickenson U., 1972; bd. dirs. WVIA-TV, Wilkes-Barre, Pa., 19——, Guidance counselor Boy Scouts Am., 1952-60;; mem. Senator Spong Commn. Edn., 1961. Served with USNR, 1945-46. Shaeffer Meml. scholar, 1959; recipient Pacemaker award N.E.A., 1966. Mem. Am., Va., N.J. assns. sch. adminstrs., N.J. Sch. Bands Assn., Va. Edn. Assn., Farmville (chmn. 1966-69), Susquehanna Valley (chmn. edn. com. 1967-68) chambers commerce, Kappa Delta Pi. Kiwanian, Elk, K.C. Home: 110 Venable St Farmville VA 23901 Office: Box 429 Prince Edward County Pub Schs Farmville VA 23901

PERRY, ROTRAUD MEZGER (MRS. JOHN WILSON PERRY), lawyer; b. Berlin, Germany, Aug. 29, 1927; d. Fritz and Luise (Scheuerle) Mezger; A.B., Bryn Mawr Coll., 1948; L.B., U. Mich., 1952; m. John Wilson Perry, Sept. 9, 1950; children— Erik David, Julia Louise, Kathleen Anne, Duncan Gerrit, Ellen Eva. Accessioner, Library of Congress, 1947, translator German Aero. Collection, 1948, asst. librarian, 1949, acting head Am.-British Exchange, 1949, European Exchange Specialist, 1950; admitted to D.C. bar, 1954; admiralty lawyer for Mil. Sea Transp. Service of Navy Dept., 1955-56; gen. practice Washington, 1957—. Mem. Am. Soc. Internat. Law, Bar Assn. D.C., Am. Judicature Soc., Assn. Plaintiff's Trial Attys., Fgn. Law Soc., Women's Bar Assn. D.C., Internat. Platform Assn. Lutheran. Clubs: Bryn Mawr of Washington, Air Force Officers' Wives. Home: 5407 Ridgefield Rd Springfield MD 20016 Office: 501 D St NW Washington DC 20001

PERRY, R(UFUS) PATTERSON, univ. pres.; b. Brunswick, Ga., June 4, 1903; s. Harry P. and Nannie Alice (Williams) P.; B.A., Johnson C. Smith U., 1925, LL.D., 1956; M.S., U. Ia., 1927, Ph.D., 1939; m. Thelma Davis, Nov. 30, 1945; children—Margaret Maribeth, Dorothy Patricia. Chmn. natural sci. dept., also prof. and head dept. chemistry Prairie View (Tex.) A. and M. Coll., 1927-43, dir. div. arts and scis., 1939-43; adminstrv. dean, prof. chemistry, v.p. Langston U., 1943-57; pres. Johnson C. Smith U., Charlotte, N.C., 1957—. Pres. Perry Drug & Chem. Co., Oklahoma City, 1947—. Mem. exec. com. Council of Protestant Colls. and Univs., 1963-68; v.p. Presbyn. Coll. Union, 1965, pres., 1966; 1st v.p. N.C. Council Ch. Related Colls., 1965-66; dir. So. Fellowship Fund; mem. adv. council N.C. Commn. Higher Edn. Facilities; dir. United Arts Council; mem. bd. nat. missions United Presbyn. Ch. U.S.A., del. World Presbyn. Alliance, 1964. Fellow A.A.A.S., Okla. Acad. Sci.; mem. N.C. Acad. Sci., Am. Chem. Soc., Nat. Inst. Sci., Sigma Xi, Alpha Phi Alpha, Sigma Pi Phi. Democrat. Mason (32 deg.). Contbr. articles to profl. publs. Address: Johnson C Smith University Charlotte NC

PERRY, RUSSELL H., ins. exec.; b. Cornell, Ill., Nov. 8, 1908; s. Walter O. and Mabel (Hilton) P.; student N.Y. U., 1937; J.D. cum laude, Bklyn. Law Sch., 1940; m. Phoebe Sherwood, June 2, 1956. Clk., Chgo. Fire & Marine Ins. Co., 1925-32; underwriter Republic Ins. Co., N.Y.C., 1934-38, charge eastern dept. underwriting, 1939-42, asst. to v.p., 1942-43, spl. agt. for L.I. and Westchester, 1934-44., mgr. eastern dept., 1945-47, resident sec., 1947-49, v.p., 1949-59, exec. v.p., 1959-60; pres., dir. Republic-Vanguard, Blue Ridge Ins. Cos., 1961—, First Trans-Carribbean Corp., Republic-Vanguard Ins. Co. Ill.; pres. Republic-Vanguard Life Ins. Co., Vanguard Underwriters Ins. Co., Republic Underwriters; pres., dir. Republic Financial Services, Inc., 1961-71, chmn. bd., pres., 1971-72, chmn. bd., chief exec. officer, 1972—; dir Allied Finance Co., Indsl. Life Ins. Co. Lectr., Bklyn. Law Sch., 1946—. Bd. dirs. Greater Crime Commn.; mem. exec. com. Assn. Fire-Casualty Cos.; bd. dirs., chmn. Dallas Council on World Affairs; chmn. exec. com. Dallas Postal Customers Council; dir. Greater Dallas Planning Council; mem. Dallas Citizens Council, Citizens Coordinating Com. Dallas County; mem. council Boy Scouts Am.; adv. bd. Salvation Army, Dallas. Trustee Dallas Community Chest; bd. dirs. Dallas County unit Am. Cancer Soc., Texas Research League, Tex. Safety Assn. Mem. C. of C. N.Y., Philonomic Soc., Am., N.Y., Dallas bar assns., State Bar Tex., Tex. Good Roads Assn. (pres.), Newcomen Soc. N.Am., Dallas (chmn. central hyw. com.), N.Y., E. Tex. chambers commerce, Delta Theta Phi. Clubs: Lawyers of N.Y.; New York University; Insurance, Knife and Fork, Harper's Corner, Dallas Petroleum, Dallas Country, Rotary, Lancers (Dallas); Austin. Home: 4505 N Versailles Av Dallas TX 75205 Office: 2727 Turtle Creek Blvd Dallas TX 75219

PERRY, WILLIAM PAUL, broadcasting co. exec.; b. Chaplin, Ky., June 22, 1930; s. O.R. and Mary K. (Hawkins) P.; student U. Louisville; m. Nina June McMichen, Mar. 20, 1953; children—Nita K., Tanajo, Milton Briggs. Vice pres., gen. mgr. Mid-Am. Broadcasting Co., Louisville, 1955-69, Mission Central Broadcasting Co., San Antonio, 1969—. Mem. men's adv. bd. Santa Rosa Hosp. Served with USNR, 1952-54. Mem. Tex. Assn. Broadcasters, San Antonio Radio Broadcasters Assn., San Antonio C. of C. (publicity com.), San Antonio Advt. Club, San Antonio Sales Execs. Club, Sigma Delta Chi. Republican. Unitarian. Kiwanian. Home: 1502 Jackson-Keller St San Antonio TX 78213 Office: 317 Arden Grove San Antonio TX 78298

PERRY, WILLIE CLAYBORNE, univ. adminstr.; b. Hico, Tex., Aug. 16, 1910; s. Tom B. and Laura (Blackburn) P.; B.S., S.W. State Tchrs. Coll., San Marcos, Tex., 1937; student Tarleton State Coll., 1928-30; M.A., Baylor U., 1943, E.D., 1956; m. Ruby Oretta Partain, Aug. 22, 1931; children—Bobby Jack, Margie Belle. Tchr., Iredell, Tex., 1930-40; supt. schs., Walnut Springs, Tex., 1940-43, Meridian, Tex., 1943-52; dean men Baylor U., Waco, Tex., 1952-62, dean of students, 1962-68, v.p. for student affairs, 1968—. Co-organizer Big State Baseball Camp for Teenage Boys, Meridian, 1951; pres. bd. YMCA. Del., Tex. Democratic Conv., 1952. Mem. C. of C. (most useful citizen award 1945; past pres. Meridian), Am. Assn. U. Profs., Am. Assn. Sch. Adminstrs., Assn. Coll. and Univ. Housing Officers, Internat. Platform Assn., Bosque County Tchrs. Assn. (past pres.), N.E.A., Phi Eta Sigma. Baptist. Mason (32 deg.), Kiwanian. Home: 3820 Austin St Waco TX 76710

PERRYMAN, RAY WORTH, physician; b. Childress, Tex., Sept. 12, 1931; s. Eugene Clinton and Anna Bell (Slack) P.; B.A., N. Tex. State U., 1952; M.D., U. Tex., 1956; m. Sylvia Ann Hemphill, Aug. 27, 1955; children—Tom, David, John. Intern, St. Mary's Hosp., Saginaw, Mich., 1956-57; practice of medicine, Richardson, Tex., 1959—; pres. Arapaho Med. Corp., 1969—; mem. staff Richardson Gen. Hosp., Presbyn. Hosp., Dallas. Bd. dirs. Richardson Symphony Orch., Richardson Community Band. Served with USMCR, 1957-59. Diplomate Am. Bd. Family Practice. Mem. Am., Tex., Pan Am. med. assns., Dallas County Med. Soc. Home: No 4 Briarwood St Richardson TX 75080

PERSHING, RUTH WHIPPLE (MRS. IRVING KIMBALL PERSHING), occupational therapy educator; b. Saugatuck, Mich.; d. Harold Clifford and Leah (Durham) Whipple; student Mich. State U., 1947-49; B.S., Western Mich. U., 1953, M.A., 1957, postgrad., 1960-61, Specialist in Edn., 1969; postgrad. course in cerebral palsy Children's Rehab. Inst., 1953; m. Irving Kimball Pershing, Feb. 17, 1962; 1 dau., Bonnie Kimball. Chief occupational therapy Detroit Cerebral Palsy Center, 1953-56; asst. prof., asst. dir. Sch. Occupational Therapy, Tex. Woman's U., Denton, 1957-60, asso. prof., dir., 1961—. Mem. Ft. Worth Soc. for Crippled Children and Adults, Tex. United Cerebral Palsy Assn., Tex. Soc. for Crippled Children, Am. Legion, Am. Legion Aux., Am., Mich., Tex. occupational therapy assns., Am. Assn. U. Women, Am. Assn. U. Profs., Tex. Assn. Coll. Tchrs., Phi Theta Epsilon. Mem. Order Eastern Star. Club: Soroptimist. Home: Box 23718 TWU Station Denton TX 76204

PERSON, HARRY WILLIAM, mfg. co. exec.; b. Gallatin, Tenn., Apr. 21, 1925; s. Harry William and Prudie Winchester (Hitchcock) P.; student George Peabody Coll., 1948-50; B.S., U. Tenn., 1952. Chief time clk. Yale & Towne Mfg. Co., Gallatin, 1952-55; accountant Tenn. Prodn. & Chem. Corp., Nashville, 1955-58; comptroller Gallatin Aluminum Prods. Co., Inc., 1958—. Chmn. Sumner County Arts Council, 1967—; pres. Gallatin Community Theatre, 1965—. Served with USNR, World War II. Mem. Am. Legion, U. Tenn. Alumni Assn. (pres. 1965-66), Jr. C. of C. (sec. 1954-55), Delta Sigma Pi, Sigma Chi. Presbyn. (deacon). Kiwanian. Home: 519 S Water St Gallatin TN 37066 Office: Maple St Gallatin TN 37066

PERSONS, BENJAMIN STEPHEN, cons. engr.; b. Macon, Ga., Mar. 3, 1923; s. Ben. S. and Mary (Scandrett) P.; B.C.E., Ga. Tech. Inst., 1949; grad. advanced course Engr. Sch., Ft. Belvoir, Va., 1950; m. Frances Neisler, Dec. 29, 1946; children—Donna Maria, Benjamin Stephen, Robert Scandrett. Civil engr. with Charles Lee, San Francisco, 1950; engr., personnel mgr., asst. to exec. partner Dames & Moore, cons. engrs., San Francisco, Los Angeles, Chgo., 1950-54, partner, Atlanta, 1954—, mem. exec. com., 1961-62; dir. Coleman, Meadows, Pate Drug Co., Fairburn Rd., Inc. Engring. cons. Army Corps Engrs.; mem. Ga. gov.'s staff. Served from 2d lt. to capt., Engring. Corps., AUS, World War II; san. engr. USPHS Res. Decorated Silver Star, Bronze Star. Fellow Am. Soc. C.E. (dir. Ga. sect.); mem. Geol. Soc. Am., Cons. Engrs. Council (dir. 1958), Cons. Engrs. Assn. Ga. (pres. 1959), Am. Soc. C.E. (dir. Ga. sect.). Presbyn. (ruling elder 1952—). Author: Laterite, Genesis, Location, Use, 1970. Contbr. articles on civil engring. and related topics to profl. jours. Home: 1110 Mt Vernon Hwy NW Atlanta GA 30327 Office: 1314 W Peachtree St NW Atlanta GA 30309

PESEK, LEON FRANCIS, lawyer; b. Yoakum, Tex., Sept. 17, 1928; s. Emil Phillip and Annie (Benys) P.; LL.B., St. Marys U., 1951; m. Shirley Hutchins, June 26, 1954; children—Leon Francis, Phillip A., Catherine, Michael J. Admitted to Tex. bar, 1951; practiced in Texarkana, 1962—; county atty. Lavaca County, 1954-58; asst. atty. gen. Tex., 1958-62; partner Raffaelli, Keeney & Pesek, 1962-67; city atty., Texarkana, 1967-71, Hitt & Pesek, 1971—; gen. counsel Cath. Women Fraternal of Tex. Served to 1st lt., Judge Adv. Gen. Corps. AUS, 1952-54. Mem. State Bar of Texas. Rotarian. Home: 1311 Canadian St Texarkana TX 75501 Office: 2605 Texas Blvd Texarkana TX 75501

PETER, EMMETT BLACKSHEAR, JR., writer, editor; b. Leesburg, Fla., Nov. 19, 1919; s. Emmett Blackshear and Mary Ellen (Brown) P.; student Emory U., 1938-39, Stetson U., 1940-41; m. Marjorie Brown, June 10, 1944; children—Marcia (Mrs. B. Murray Tucker, Jr.), Melanie (Mrs. Lee A. Poole), Emmett III, Editor, pub. Eustis (Fla.) Lake Region, 1941-42; editor Leesburg Comml., 1946-47; reporter Tampa (Fla.) Tribune, 1947-50, Sunday editor, 1950-54; editor Daily Comml., Leesburg, 1955-60, editorial page dir., 1961-63; asso. editor Lakeland (Fla.) Ledger, 1964-68; sr. editorial writer Orlando Sentinel, 1969—. Owner, Peter Citrus Groves, Leesburg; founder, dir. Channel 24 pub. tv, Orlando, 1969—. Asso. editor Quill, Chgo., 1960-65. Mem. Fla. Bd. Forestry, 1959-66, v.p., 1963-65; mem. nat. adv. com. to sec. agr., 1965-69. Served with USAAF, 1942-45. Recipient Nat. Headliner and Sigma Delta Chi awards for pub. service, 1960; Brotherhood citation Nat. Conf. Christians and Jews, 1964. Mem. Fla. Soc. Editors (charter, pres. 1963-64), Sigma Delta Chi (pres. Central Fla. profl. chpt. 1960-61), Phi Delta Theta. Democrat. Methodist. Contbr. to The New Republic. Home: 320 Lakeview Apt 106 Orlando FL 32802 Office: PO Box 2833 Orlando FL 32802

PETER, JOHN EDWARD, architect; b. Oklahoma City, Dec. 23, 1934; s. Maurice Lyle and Claribel (Oldfield) P.; B.Arch., Okla. State U., 1958; m. Judith Louise Rice, Jan. 26, 1957; children—David Mark, Kevin Andrew, Anita Deborah. Chief draftsman Bignell-Fischer, Oklahoma City, 1961-62, ind. practice John E. Peter & Assos., Oklahoma City, 1962-67, Woodward, Okla., 1968—. Mem. diocese com. on architecture Episcopal Diocese Okla., 1964—, com. on clergy replacement; mem. bd. advisers Goodwill Industries Okla., 1964-68, Mayor's Com. for Hire Handicapped Oklahoma City, 1964-68; dist. commr. Boiling Springs dist. Boy Scouts Am., 1970; pres. Woodward Elks Rodeo, 1970-72. chmn. precinct, 1971-73. Pres. bd. Okla. N.W. Guidance Center, Okla. N.W., Inc. Registered profl. architect, Okla., Kan., Tex. Mem. Constrn. Specifications Inst., A.I.A., Mooreland C. of C., Laymen Inc., Woodward C. of C. Episcopalian (lay reader, treas. 1969-72). Rotarian, Elk. Club: Young Men's Skyhawk Flying. Home: 2426 Kansas Av Woodward OK 73801 Office: 1009 1/2 Main St Woodward OK 73801

PETER, LILY, plantation operator, writer; b. Marvell, Ark.; d. William Oliver and Florence (Mobrey) Peter; B.S., Memphis State U., 1927; M.A., Vanderbilt U., 1938; postgrad. U. Chgo., 1930, Columbia, 1935-36; L.H.D., Moravian Coll., Bethlehem, Pa., 1965. Owner, operator plantations, Marvell and Ratio, Ark., writer poetry, feature articles pub. in S.W. Quar., Delta Rev., Cyclo Flame, Etude, Am. Weave, others; mem. staff S.W. Writers Conf., Corpus Christi, Tex., 1954—, sponsor Ark. Writers' Conf. Chmn., Poetry Day in Ark., 1953—; chmn., sponsor music Ark. Territorial Sesquicentennial, 1969. Bd. dirs. Ark. Arts Festival, Little Rock, Grand Prairie Festival Arts; chmn. bd. Phillips County Community Center, 1969-71. Hon. trustee Moravian Music Found. Recipient Moramus award Friends of Moravian Music, 1964; Distinguished Alumni award Vanderbilt U., 1964; named Poet Laureat Ark., 1971; Democrat Woman of Year, 1971. Mem. D.A.R., (hon. state regent), Nat. League Am. Pen Women, Ark. Authors and Composers Soc., Poets' Roundtable Ark., poetry socs. of Tenn., Tex., Ga., Met. Opera Assn. (mem. nat. council), Sigma Alpha Iota. (hon.). Democrat. Methodist. Clubs: Pacaha (Helena, Ark.); Woman's City (Little Rock). Author: The Green Linen of Summer, 1964; The Great Riding, 1966. Home: Route 2 Box 39 Marvell AR 72366

PETERS, DOLORES SYLVIA (MRS. BELFORD E. PETERS), educator; b. New Bedford, Mass., Nov. 7, 1911; d. Julius V. and Mary Grace (Moniz) Sylvia; B.S., State Coll. Mass., 1958; postgrad. Radford Coll., 1959, U. Va., 1964; m. Belford E. Peters, Jan. 3, 1934; children—Virginia Lee, Randolph Brian. Nurse, various Tb and cancer hosps., Mass., 1936-44; tchr. Roanoke County Elementary and Cave Spring High Schs., Roanoke, Va., 1945—. Sponsor, leader 4-H Clubs, Roanoke, 1945-65; faculty rep. Exec. Bd. Roanoke County Edn. Assn., 1945—. Mem. Nat., Va., Roanoke County edn. assns., Va. Jr. Acad. Scis., Nat. Sci. Tchrs. Assn., Alpha Delta Kappa (chmn. state pres. council 1968-70). Home: Cedar Hill Route 4 Box 154 Floyd VA 24091 Office: Chaparral Dr Roanoke VA 24018

PETERS, GILBERT DEAN, realtor; b. Waskom, Tex., June 16, 1902; s. William Tremells and Mary (Gillen) P.; grad. high sch.; m. Edna Oswald, June 6, 1939; children—Frederick Dean, Eddie Joe Leslie. Owner, Gilbert D. Peters, Realtor, Shreveport, La., 1940—. Served with USN, 1918-19. Mem. Am. Legion (pub. relations dir.), 40 and 8, Exec. Sales and Marketing Club, Shreveport C. of C. Episcopalian. Mason (K.T.), Elk. Clubs: Petroleum, Ambassadors; Metropolitan Dinner. Home: 1815 Line Av Shreveport LA 71101 Office: 600 Ricou Brewster Bldg Shreveport LA 71101

PETERS, JACK ALLISON, hosp. adminstr.; b. Roanoke, Va., Dec. 14, 1928; s. James Mosley and Lois Rainly (Murphy) P.; B.B.A., Nat. Bus. Coll., 1957; B.B.A., Roanoke Coll., 1968; M. Hosp. Adminstrn., Va. Commonwealth U., 1970; m. Laira Faye Landers, July 28, 1956; children—Paul, Mary Allison, Mark. Cashier, Rainbo Bread Co., Roanoke, Va., 1951-55; controller Roanoke Coll., Salem, 1957-68; adminstr. St. Elizabeth's Hosp., Richmond, 1970—. Served with USMCR, 1947-51. Mem. Am., Va. hosp. assns., Central Va. Hosp. Council, Am. Coll. Hosp. Adminstrs., Hosp. Financial Mgmt. Assn., Richmond area Heart Assn., Inc., Capital area Comprehensive Health Planning Council, Va. Blood Bank, Inc. Home: 11711 Rexmoor Dr Richmond VA 23235 Office: 617 W Grace St Richmond VA 23220

PETERS, JAMES SOLOMON, banker; b. Nashville, Ga., Mar. 21, 1884; s. William Lot and Caroline (Walker) P.; student Emory U., 1905-06; LL.D., LaGrange Coll., 1961, Emory U., 1964; m. Mary V. Jones, Nov. 28, 1910; children—James Solomon, Mary Virginia (Mrs. S. I. Taylor); m. 2d, Mary Jane Hamruack, July 23, 1965. With Bank of Manchester (Ga.) 1910—, pres. 1934-58, chmn. bd. 1958—. Chmn Ga. Democratic Exec. Com., 1941-42, 1946-58, vice chmn., 1958—; chmn. Ga. delegation Dem. Nat. Conv., 1948, vice chmn., 1952; presdl. elector, Ga., 1952. Bd. regents State of Ga., 1941-42; mem., vice chmn. Ga. Bd. Edn., 1947-58, chmn., 1958—. Mem. Ga. Bankers Assn., (pres. 1923-24), Ind. Bankers Assn. Am. (pres. 1952-53). Methodist. Home: Manchester GA

PETERS, MARILYN WALKER (MRS. ROBERT LEE PETERS), artist; b. Columbus, O., Feb. 19, 1930; d. Edward Raymond and Ruby (Springer) Walker; grad. McBride Secretarial Sch., Dallas, 1947; B.S. with honors in Art, U. Tex., 1951; student Dallas Mus. Fine Arts, 1944-46, Odessa Coll., 1963, 65; m. Robert Lee Peters, Aug. 25, 1951;children—Lynn Ellen, Lee Edward, Steven Robert. Secretarial positions, 1949-51; clk.-typist Farmers Home Adminstrn., 1948; stenographer Dallas City Plan Commn., 1950-51; supr. advt. and personnel Newcomen Greeting Service, Pine Bluff, Ark., 1971—; free-lance art work, design, paintings, sketches, Odessa, Tex., 1951—; one-man shows Ector County Library, 1965, Sandhills Mus., Sandhills State Park, Monahans, Tex., 1966, Ector County Library, Odessa, 1968, 5 State Art Exhbn., Port Arthur, Tex., 1971, numerous Odessa Art Assn. group exhibits. Active fund drives; patroness N.Y. Debutante Assembly. Precinct sec. Ward 16, Democratic party, Odessa, 1956-62; del. Ector County Conv., 1956-60; ward chmn. various campaigns, 1958-61. Recipient 1st place award Permian Basin Art Show, 1963; awards Tex. Fine Arts Assn., 1965, 66, 67; Juror's Choice award, Circuit Merit award Tex. Fine Arts Assn., 1968; prizes in horticulture, Odessa flower shows. Mem. Tex. Garden Clubs, Inc., Council Odessa Garden Clubs (pres.), Casa Bella Gardeners (pres.), Symphony Assn., Civic Music Assn., Permian Playhouse, Odessa Art Assn. (dir. 1965-66), Tex. Fine Arts Assn. mem. regional coordinating com.), Internat. Platform Assn., Panhellenic, Women's Forum, Alpha Chi Omega. Methodist (mem. commn. missions). Clubs: Odessa Country, Odessa Country Women's Assn., Knife and Fork. Home: 3000 Eastover Dr Odessa TX 79760

PETERS, ROBERT WILLIAM, educator; b. Boyden, Ia., Sept. 3, 1921; s. William Joseph and Janet (Morris) P.; A.B., U. Minn., 1948; M.A., Ohio State U., 1950, Ph.D., 1953; m. Helen Abramson, Sept. 3, 1949; children—Colin, Sheila. Asst. prof., asso. prof. U. So. Miss., Hattiesburg, 1955-57, prof. speech, 1957-69, chmn. dept. speech, 1962-67, hearing sci., dir. Office Research and Projects, 1967-69; research asso. Ohio State U. Research Found., Columbus, 1953-55; prof. speech and hearing, prof. English, U. N.C., Chapel Hill, 1969—, dir. Inst. Speech and Hearing Scis., 1969—. Served with USAAF, 1943-46. Fellow Am. Speech and Hearing Assn.; mem. Speech Assn. Am., Am. Psychol. Assn., Accoustical Soc. Am., N.Y. Acad. Sci., Internat. Assn. Logopedics and Phoniatrics, NRC. Contbr. articles in field to profl. jours. Home: 312 Lone Pine Rd Chapel Hill NC 27514

PETERS, WARREN EDMUND, ednl. adminstr.; b. Belleville, Ill., Sept. 24, 1921; s. Fred W. and Emma (Echoff) P.; B.S., Trinity U., 1953; M.Ed., Bowling Green (O.) State U., 1963; m. Mary M. Dew, Dec. 25, 1945; 1 stepdau., Judith Ann Werner (Mrs. Howard Shifren); children—Jerry M., Nancy J., John W. Served as pvt. U.S. Army Air Force, 1940-45, commd. 2d lt., 1946, advanced through grades to lt. col. U.S. Air Force, 1964; chief program monitoring forces Hdqrs. U.S. Air Force in Europe, Wiesbaden, Germany, 1957-60; prof. aerospace studies, chmn. dept. Bowling Green State U., 1962-65; project officer, dep. chief staff for programs and resources Hdqrs. Dept. Air Force, 1965-68; distributive edn. coordinator Fairfax County Pub. Schs., Fairfax, Va., 1968—. Chmn. Wood County com. Boy Scouts Am. Mem. Air Force Assn., Arnold Air Soc., Am. Assn. U. Profs., Alpha Phi Omega. Mason (Shriner). Home: 8511 Queen Elizabeth Blvd Annondale VA

PETERSEN, DONALD JAMES, state ofcl.; b. N.Y.C., May 10, 1929; s. H. Clark and Anna (Fiorella) P.; student Wofford Coll., 1954-58, A.B. in Psychology, 1970; m. Thalia LaMona Ham, Mar. 27, 1954; children—Timothy S., Tamara A., Donald James III, Thalia LaMona. Med. service rep. A.H. Robins Co., Inc. Columbia, S.C., 1958-71; cons. on health facilities S.C. Bd. Health, Columbia, 1971—. Mem. steering coms. Stop Pollo Campaign, Columbia 1963-64, Anti-Tetanus Program, Columbia, 1964-65; pres. Satchelford Road Sch. P.T.A., 1964; coach and asst. coach Forest Baseball League, Columbia, 1965-69; asst. scoutmaster Congaree council Boy Scouts Am., 1969-70. Served with USN, 1946-51. Recipient Community Service award Stop Polio Campaign, 1963, 64. Mem. Palmetto Sertoma (pres. 1967-68), Sertoma Internat. (dist. gov. 1968-69, Distinguished Gov. award 1968). Methodist (mem. ch. bd.). Club: Gold Honor (pres. 1967). Home: 4661 Norwood Rd Columbia SC 29206

PETERSON, CHARLES BASCOM, JR., banker; b. Dallas, Nov. 27, 1913; s. Charles Bascom and Lida (Skillern) P.; grad. Rutgers U. Grad. Sch. Banking, 1952; student Inst. Mgmt., So. Methodist U., Nat. Indsl. Conf. Bd. Exec. Seminars; m. Helen Fair, Apr. 12, 1936; children—Sue Fair, Ann. With Tex. Bank & Trust Co., 1931-61, pres., 1958-61; exec. v.p. Republic Nat. Bank of Dallas, 1961—; dir. Frito Co., Employers Casualty Co., Sammon Enterprises, Inc. Instr. grad. courses Am. Inst. Banking. Mem. adv. bd. Salvation Army; treas. Circle Ten, Boy Scouts Am.; v.p. Boys' Club Dallas. Bd. dirs. Dallas A.R.C., chmn. membership and fund campaign, 1959; active Dallas Community Chest; trustee Methodist Hosp., Sci. Information Inst., Freeman Meml. Clinic, Tex. Research Found. Home: 5114 Royal Crest Dr Dallas TX 75229 Office: Republic Nat Bank of Dallas Dallas TX

PETERSON, DONALD H., astronaut; b. Winona, Miss., Oct. 22, 1933; s. Henry W. Peterson; B.S., U.S. Mil. Acad., 1955; M.S. in Nuclear Engring., Air Force Inst. Tech., 1962; m. Bonnie Love; children—Donald H., Jean M., Shari L. Commd. 2d lt. USAF, 1955, advanced through grades to lt. col.; flight instr., then mil. tng. officer Air Tng. Command, later nuclear systems analyst Air Force Systems Command; astronaut, 1969—; trainee manned space flights Space Shuttle Program. Office: NASA Manned Spacecraft Center 2101 Nasa Rd 1 Houston TX 76101

PETERSON, DONALD LEROY, dentist; b. Columbus, Kan., Dec. 6, 1908; s. Fred William and Myrtle Inez (Arnold) P.; D.D.S. cum laude, Loyola U., New Orleans, 1932; m. Mary Alma Bishop, Aug. 21, 1951; 1 son, Donald Leroy. Practice gen. dentistry, New Orleans, 1932—; mem. vis. staff Charity Hosp. La., New Orleans, 1932—, sr. vis. surgeon, 1945-61, mem. bd. adminstrs., 1956—, vice chmn., 1956-60, 64—, dental cons., 1961—; dental cons. Eye, Ear, Nose and Throat Hosp., 1947—, So. Bapt. Hosp., 1958—; instr. dept. physiology and chemistry Loyola U., 1933-34; asso. clin. prof. dept. oral surgery Dental Sch., La. State U., 1969—. Chmn. dental div. Greater New Orleans area chpt. A.R.C., 1950-51; mem. Greater New Orleans Cancer Assn., 1960—, pres., 1966-68. Sec. bd. dirs. Health Edn. Authority La., 1968—. Fellow Am. Coll. Dentists; mem. Am., La., New Orleans (dir. 1950-54; v.p. 1950), dental assns., Orleans Parish Med. Soc. (asso.), Kells Odontological Soc., New Orleans, U.S. power squadrons, Blue Key, Grand Isle Tarpon Rodeo (pres. 1956; dir. 1957-72), Psi Omega, Omega Kappa Upsilon. Roman Catholic. Clubs: Pendennis (dir. 1939—), Southern Yacht, New Orleans Big Game Fishing (New Orleans); Talley-Ho. Home: 1616 Mirabeau Av New Orleans LA 70122 Office: 711 Maison Blanche Bldg New Orleans LA 70112

PETERSON, GLENN APPLING, bldg. co. mgr., club woman; b. Luling, Tex., Sept. 2, 1918; d. Frank Lee and Nell A. (West) Appling; B.B.A., B.S., U. Tex., 1941; M.A. in Speech and Edn., W. Tex. State Coll., 1952; m. Leo John Peterson, Jr., Aug. 18, 1940 (div. May 1960); children—Leo John III, Terry Gay (Mrs. Ray George Eudy). Speech instr. W. Tex. State Coll., Canyon, 1951-58; gen. ins. agt. Cravens, Dargen & Co., Amarillo, Tex., 1951—, Cimarron County (Kan.), 1951—; life ins. agt. First Life Ins. Co., Fort Worth, 1960—; dir. sec. Amarillo Bowl, Inc., 1959-60; regional and spl. dep. Croft Ednl. Services of Vision, Inc., 1967-69; regional sales dir. Plan Inc., New Braunfels, Tex., 1969; mgr. ednl. marketing and research div. Monogram Industries, 1970-72; sales officer Lindal Cedar Homes of Tex., Dallas, 1972—. Chmn. children's theatre Jr. League, Amarillo, 1950-51; book reviewer Jr. Travel Study Club, Amarillo, 1950-56, bd. dirs., 1949—; athletic coach Kids, Inc., Amarillo, 1950-55, asso. 1949—; asst. den mother Cub Scouts Am., Amarillo, 1949-50; active A.R.C., Amarillo, 1948-54, Community Chest Drs., Amarillo, 1948-54, Am. Cancer Soc., Amarillo, 1950-51. Bd. dirs. YWCA, Amarillo, 1947-48, chmn. activities, 1952-55; bd. dirs. Girl Scouts U.S.A., Amarillo, 1949-51. Recipient pub. service award Amarillo News & Globe Times, 1954. Mem. Tex. Woman's Bowling Assn. (dist. dir. 1962-64), C. of C., Internat. Platform Assn., Tex. State Geneal. Soc., Zeta Tau Alpha, Democrat. Methodist (chmn. circle 1947-48). Club: Midland (pub. relations dir. 1964) (Tex.). Home: PO Box 111 Lake Dunlap New Braunfels TX 75130 Office: PO Box 34542 Dallas TX 78234

PETERSON, HAROLD BOYETTE, chemist; b. Dunn, N.C., May 5, 1924; s. Grady F. and Frances (Boyette) P.; B.S., N.C. State U., 1949; m. Clennis C. Stevens, May 4, 1949; 1949; 1 dau., Susan L. With Va. Chems., Inc., 1949-67, dist. mgr., Atlanta, 1965-67; with Am. Maize-Products Co., Atlanta, 1967—, now regional sales mgr. S. and W. coast. Mem. 4th Congl. Dist. adv. panel, 1966—. Served with USAAF, 1943-45; ETO. Decorated Air Medal with three clusters. Mem. Am. Chem. Soc., T.A.P.P.I., Atlanta Fgn. Trade Assn., Nat. Paper Industry Mgmt. Assn., Am. Assn. Textile Chemists and Colorists, Phi Psi, Tau Kappa Epsilon. Lion, Elk. Home: 2380 Pangborn Circle Decatur GA 30033 Office: 4 Executive Park Dr Atlanta GA 30329

PETERSON, HAROLD LEONARD, hosp. adminstr.; b. Willmar, Minn., May 15, 1910; s. Andrew and Ottillia (Engwall) P.; B.A., Gustavus-Adolphus Coll., 1931; M.S., Northwestern U., 1952; m. Doris Middlestadt, Dec. 26, 1936 1 dau., Judith Ann (Mrs. Henry P. Jewell). Mem. Minn. Ho. of Reps., 1936-40; sec.-organizer Farmer-Labor Party Minn., 1937-40; dir, safety Twin Cities Ordnance Plant, Mpls.-St. Paul, 1942-44; spl. asst. to 6-state zone adminstr. War Assets Adminstrn., Atlanta, 1946-48; suture cons. Ethicon Suture Labs., Buffalo, 1948-50; adminstrv. resident Baroness Erlanger Hosp., Chattanooga, 1951-52, asst. adminstr., 1952-54, adminstr., 1954—. Cons. hosp. adminstrn. to Govt. Venezuela for ICA, 1960; pres. Chattanooga Area Hosp. Council; mem. exec. com. Ga.-Tenn. Regional Appalachian Commn.; mem. Tenn. Bd. Nursing, Tenn. Health Planning Council. Pres., Tenn. Credit Union League; v.p. Chattanooga Area Heart Assn.; bd. dirs. Chattanooga chpt. Am. Cancer Soc., United Cerebral Palsy. Served to lt. comdr. USNR, 1944-46. Recipient Service to Mankind award Sertoma Club Chattanooga, 1968. Mem. Am. (Tenn. alternate del.), Tenn., (trustee, past pres.) hosp. assns., Am. Coll. Hosp. Adminstrs., Nat. Alumni Assn. Programs in Hosp. Adminstrn. (past pres.), Tenn. League Nursing (dir.), Soc. Advancement Mgmt., Chattanooga C. of C. (past chmn. health com.), Nat. League Nursing. Mason (Shriner), Kiwanian. Home and office: Baroness Erlanger Hosp 261 Wiehl St Chattanooga TN 37403

PETERSON, HARRY N., library cons.; b. Arendal, Norway, Sept. 27, 1907; s. Paul Christian and Nicoline (Terjesen) P.; B.S., N.Y. U., 1928; B.L.S., Columbia, 1934. Supervising asst. Mt. Vernon (N.Y.) Pub. Library, 1934-35; asst. librarian Yonkers (N.Y.) Pub. Library, 1935-38; librarian Fort Worth Pub. Library, 1939-47; dir. D.C. Pub. Library, 1947-70. Cons. on planning new central library bldgs. in numerous cities; surveyed pub. libraries, Fort Worth and Tarrant County, Texas, Lake Charles, La., Calcasieu Parish, La., Knoxville and Knox County, Tenn., Fort Lauderdale, Fla., Rock Island, Ill., others. Served to maj., AUS, 1942-46. Mem. A.L.A. (2d v.p. 1961, exec. bd. council), D.C. Library Assn. Methodist. Contbr. chpts. to books, articles to profl. jours. Office: 2000 Connecticut Av NW Washington DC 20008

PETERSON, JAMES HOWARD, dentist; b. Dothan, Ala., Sept. 22, 1917; s. John Alexander and Ella Virginia (McGehee) P.; student Howard Coll., 1939-41, U. Miami, 1945-46; D.D.S., Northwestern U., 1950; m. Vernell Louise Gillman, Aug. 23, 1943; children—James Howard, Linda (Mrs. Ray G. Hinze), Donald R., Robert A., William L., John E. Commd. 2d lt. U.S. Army, 1949, advanced through grades to lt. col., 1962; dental officer, Fort Knox, Ky., 1950-54; chief clinician Coleman Barracks Dental Clinic, Mannheim, Germany, 1954-57, Fort Dix, N.J., 1958-62, Korea, 1962-63; chief clinician Dep. Clinic, Fort Knox, 1964-67; pvt. practice dentistry, Radcliff, Ky., 1967—. Served with USNR, 1941-45. Baptist (deacon 1968). Optimist (pres. 1969-70). Club: Armored Center Officers (Fort Knox, Ky.). Home: 410 N Logsdon St Radcliff KY 40160 Office: 267 N Dixie Blvd Radcliff KY 40160

PETERSON, MEDEL LAZEAR, museum curator; b. Moore, Ida., Mar. 8, 1918; s. Hans Jordan and Fannie (Lish) P.; B.S. with honors, Miss. So. Coll., 1938; M.A., Vanderbilt U., 1940; grad. student Lowell Textile Inst., 1945-47; m. LaNelle Walker, July 5, 1937 (div. May 1962); children—LaNelle Hampton (Mrs. Gerald Spence), Mendel L.; m. 2d, Gertrude A. Auvil, Aug. 19, 1962; 1 dau., Anna Victoria. Camp edn. adviser Civilian Conservation Corps, 1939-42; div. merchandiser Montgomery Ward & Co. 1942-43; curator dept. history Smithsonian Inst., 1948-56, chmn. dept. armed forces history, 1956-69, dir. underwater exploration project, 1969—. Served from ensign to comdr. USNR, 1943—. Mem. A.A.A.S., Am. Inst. Archeology, Am. Numis. Assn., Internat. Oceanographic Found., Nautical Research Assn., Soc. South Pole, Co. Mil. Collectors and Historians, Internat. Inst. Conservation Historic and Artistic Works. Clubs: Explorers, Club de Exploraciones y Deportes Acuaticos de Mexico (hon. life). Author numerous articles in field. Home: 102 Westgate Dr Alexandria VA 22309

PETERSON, NEWTON CURTIS, JR., landscape architect; b. Lakeland, Fla., Aug. 23, 1922; s. Newton Curtis and Caroline Ellen (Smith) P.; student George Washington U., 1941-42, Fla. So. Coll., 1950-53; m. Ethel Lucille Schultz, Apr. 8, 1944; children—Newton Curtis III, Peter Karl. Foreman, Peterson's Nurseries, Lakeland, Fla., 1945-47, landscape supt., 1947—, landscape designer, 1948-53, landscape architect, 1953—, gen. mgr., 1954—, partner, 1958—. Ornamental horticulture rep. Agrl. Adv. Council, Fla. Dept. Agr., 1961—, sec.-treas. council, 1966-70; chmn., 1970—; mem. plant industry tech. com. Div. Plant Industry Fla., 1961—; nursery industry rep. Fla. Agrl. Tax Council; 1962—; pres., 1967-70; mem. Ornamental Horticulture DARE Com. Polk County, 1965—, Spreading Decline Ways and Means Com., 1966-68; mem. horticulture adv. com. Polk County Vocational Tech. Sch. Mem. Polk County Dem. exec. com., chmn. campaign com.; mem. Fla. Senate, 1972—. Bd. dirs. Polk County Assn. Retarded Children, 1963, v.p., 1971-72; bd. dirs. Agribus. Inst. Fla., 1971-72, Fla. Sheriff's Girls Villa, 1972—; sec.-treas. Fla. Clergy Econ. Edn. Conf., 1967-68; exec. committeeman Fla. Community Devel. Coordinating Council, 1967-68; mem. Lakeland Beautification Bd., 1965-68; cubmaster Boy Scouts Am., 1964-66; pres. Lakeland Conv. Bur., 1965-66; mem. horticulture adv. com. Polk Jr. Coll., 1964—. Served with USCGR, 1942-45. Named Fla. Nurseryman of Year, recipient Odenkirk Trophy, 1961. Mem. Am. Assn. Nurseryman, So. Nurseryman's Assn., Fla. Nurseryman and Growers Assn. (past pres.), Sigma Nu. Democrat. Baptist. Home: 1504 Warren Av Lakeland FL 33803 Office: 225 New Auburndale Rd Lakeland FL 33801 also PO Box 180 2034 S Combee Rd Eaton Park FL 33840

PETERSON, PAUL HAROLD, editor; b. Fairbury, Ill., Nov. 16, 1941; s. Harold Emanuel and Doreen (Christenson) P.; B.A., U Louisville, 1963. News editor Shively (Ky.) Newsweek, 1958-60; tit' examiner, asst. to pres. Lincoln Fed. Savs., Louisville, 1962; edit Cardinal Newspaper, Louisville, 1962-63; editor employee, dealer publs. Standard Oil Co., Louisville, 1963-68, advt. specialist, 1968—. Publicity dir. Miss Ky. Pageant; dir. Belknap Theatre; mem. pub. relations com. Ky. Derby Festival, 1972. Mem. Ky. Indsl. Editors (v.p. 1968), Internat. Editors (dir. internat. affairs 1968), Am. Council Indsl. Editors, Audubon Soc., Kentuckiana, Delta Upsilon Alumni Club (pres. 1966), Phi Delta Epsilon, Pi Sigma Alpha, Omicron Delta Kappa. Author: Standard Oil: Yesterday, Today and Tomorrow, 1967. Home: 2004 Peabody Ct Louisville KY 40220 Office: PO Box 1446 Louisville KY 40201

PETERSON, PETER G., sec. commerce U.S.; b. Kearney, Neb., June 5, 1926; s. George and Venet (Paul) P.; student Mass. Inst. Tech., 1944-45, B.S. summa cum laude, Northwestern U., 1947; M.B.A. with honors, U. Chgo., 1951; m. Sally Hornbogen, May 1953; children—John Scott, James S., David, Holly. Market analyst Market Facts, Inc., Chgo., 1947-49, asso. dir., 1949-51, exec. v.p., 1951-53; dir. marketing services McCann-Erickson, 1953, v.p., 1954-58, gen. mgr. Chgo. office, 1955-57, dir., asst. to pres. coordinating services regional offices, 1957-58; exec. v.p., dir. Bell & Howell Co., 1958-61, pres., 1961-63, pres., chief exec. officer, 1963-68, chmn. bd., chief exec. officer, 1968-70; asst. to Pres. for fgn. econ. policy, Washington, 1970-72, also exec. dir. Council on Internat. Econ. Policy; sec. of commerce, 1972—; dir. First Nat. Bank of Chgo., Ill. Bell Telephone Co. Chmn. planning com. Ill. Citizens for Eisenhower, 1952. Trustee Cancer Research Found., Salk Inst. Biol. Research, Brookings Instn., Com. Econ. Devel.; bd. dirs. Nat. Ednl. TV; chmn. council med. biol. research, trustee U. Chgo. Named outstanding young man of Chgo., Jr. C. of C., 1955. U.S., Jr. C. of C., 1961. Mem. Am. Mgmt. Assn., Am. Marketing Assn. Clubs: Chicago, Economics, Mid-America (Chgo.); Indian Hill (Winnetka, Ill.). Editor, contbr.; Readings in Market Organization and Price Policies, 1952. Office: Dept Commerce Washington DC

PETERSON, RUBY KETTLES (MRS. ARTHUR G. PETERSON), lawyer; b. Dalton, Ga., Mar. 20, 1910; d. Van F. and Lola (Harris) Kettles; student Ga. State Coll. Women; diploma in accountancy Internat. Accounts Soc., Inc., 1944; LL.B., Woodrow Wilson Coll. Law, 1947; postgrad. Benjamin Franklin Sch. Accountancy, U. Ga. Evening Sch.; m. Arthur G. Peterson, Feb. 1, 1953. Tchr. county elementary schs., 1928-36; admitted to Ga. bar, 1947, U.S. Supreme Ct. bar; with Internal Revenue Service, Washington, 1949—, spl. asst. to head rev. div. Chief Counsel's Office, 1956-59, staff asst. to chief counsel, 1959-61, chief corp. tax br., joint com. div., 1961-65; tech. asst. to chief counsel, 1965-69, Regional Counsel's Office, Jacksonville, Fla., 1969—. Treas. DeBary Arts and Crafts Club; parliamentarian DeBary Garden Club. Recipient Certificate of award Dept. Treasury, 1966, Superior Performance award, 1968, Albert Gallatin award, 1970; spl. Achievement award Internal Revenue Service, 1970. Mem. Am. Soc. Women Accountants (organizer D.C. chpt., 1950), Am., Ga., Fed., Whitfield County (first woman mem.) bar assns., Ga. Assn. Women Lawyers, Internat. Ikebana Club, Ikebana Ikenabo Club. Home: 16 Madera Rd De Bary FL 32713

PETERSON, SHAILER, univ. adminstr.; b. Albert Lea, Minn., Oct. 12, 1908; s. P. Augustus and Annie Christine (Olsen) P.; B.A., U. Ore., 1930, M.A., 1933; Ph.D. in Ednl. Psychology, U. Minn., 1943; m. Ella Cleone Devereaux, Nov. 1, 1935; 1 son, Devereaux Shailer. Instr., U. Minn., 1936-43; asso. prof. S.D. State Coll., 1944; asst. prof. U. Chgo., 1945-47; dir. ednl. measurements Council Dental Edn., Am. Dental Assn., Chgo., 1947-48, sec., 1948-61, asst. sec. ednl. affairs Am. Dental Assn., 1959-61; prof. dentistry, dean U. Tenn. Coll. Dentistry, Memphis, 1961-69; asso. dean, prof. U. Tex. Dental Sch., San Antonio, 1969—, prof. dental br., Houston, 1969—. Clin. asso. prof., guest lectr. Loyola U. Dental Sch., Chgo.; mem. dental tng. com. Nat. Instr. Dental Research; hon. mem. expert com. aux. dental personnel WHO; spl. cons. USPHS; cons. So. Regional Edn. Bd., Am. Dental Assn.; cons. to evaluation com. dental dept. Tenn. Pub. Health Dept.; chmn. com. dental student utilization USPHS. Fellow Internat., Am. (hon.) colls. dentists, A.A.A.S.; mem. R.D. and M. Deans' Odontological Soc. (hon.), Psychometric Soc., Memphis (hon.), Chgo. (hon.), N.C. (hon.), W. Va. (hon.) dental socs., N.E.A., Am. Psychol. Assn., Am. (asso.), Tenn. dental assns., Am. Statis. Assn., Am. Dental Hygenists Assn. (hon.), Am. Assn. Dental Examiners (hon.), Am. Ednl. Research Assn., Am. Pub. Health Assn., Am. Acad. Dental Medicine (hon.), Am. Acad. Gen. Dentistry (hon.), Am. Med. Coll. Assn., Internat. Assn. Dental Research, Am. Amateur Relay League, Sociedad Odontologaci Dominicana (hon.), San Antonio C. of C., Sigma Xi, Pi Mu Epsilon, Delta Sigma Delta (hon. life), Phi Delta Kappa, Omicron Kappa Upsilon. Club: Top of Hundred (Memphis). Author: How Well Are Indian Children Educated, 1945. Editor: Clinical Dental Hygiene, 1963, 4th edit., 1972; The Dentist and His Assistant, 1961, 3d edit., 1972; A Comprehensive Review for Dental Hygienists, 1965, 3d edit., 1973; Review and Test Manual for Dental Assistants, 1967. Home: 5511 Keystone Dr San Antonio TX 78229

PETERSON, SHERMAN BAXTER, educator; b. Melbourne, Ark., Nov. 13, 1930; s. W. W. and Lucy M. (Peterson) P.; B.A., Hendrix Coll., 1952; M.Ed., U. Ark., 1962, Ed.D., 1969; m. Jacque Floyd, June 12, 1954; children—Brent, Kimberly, Kevin, Scott. Coach, tchr. Charleston High Sch., 1957-61, Siloam Spring, Ark., 1961-64, sch. adminstr., 1964-66; grad. asst. U. Ark., 1966-68; dir. Model Sch., Monticello, Ark., 1968-69; asso. prof. edn. U. Ark., Monticello, 1969—. Mem. gov.'s adv. council on edn., 1968-71; adv. council, State Dept. Edn., 1971—. Served with USAF, 1952-57. NSF fellow; named Outstanding Young Educator, Siloam Springs (Ark.) Jaycees, 1965-66; Distinguished Educator Am., 1971. Mem. Am. Assn. Sch. Adminstrs., Ark. Edn. Assn., Ark. Edn. Devel. and Research Council, Phi Delta Kappa. Rotarian. Club: S.E. Ark. Schoolmasters. Home: Route 1 Box 313 Monticello AR 71655

PETERSON, VERNON LEROY, ednl. adminstr.; b. LaJunta, Colo., July 27, 1925; s. William Peter and Florence (Griffin) P.; B.A., Northwestern State Coll., 1949; M.Ed., Phillips U., 1951; Ed.D., Ohio Christian Coll., 1967; m. Katherine Virginia Simpson, July 31, 1946; children—Vernon Wayne, Gary Lynn, Sheryl Sue. Tchr., Woodward (Okla) Jr. High Sch., 1949-52; prin. high sch., Sharon, Okla., 1952-53; supt. schs., Fargo, Okla., 1953-61, Keyes, Okla., 1961-69, North Enid Pub. Schs., Enid, Okla., 1969—. Mem. Okla. Commn. for Ednl. Advancement. Served with USNR, 1943-46. Mem. Okla. Edn. Assn., N.E.A., Am. Okla. assns. sch. adminstrs., Okla. Assn. Sch. Bus. Ofcls. Lion (bd. dirs. 1970-72). Home: 3114 N Lincoln St Enid OK 73701 Office: Route 6 Enid OK 73701

PETRONE, ROCCO A., govt. ofcl.; b. Amsterdam, N.Y., Mar. 31, 1926; s. Anthony and Theresa (DeLuca) P.; B.S., U.S. Mil. Acad., 1946; degree in Mech. Engring., Mass. Inst. Tech., 1952; D.Sc. (hon.), Rollins Coll., 1969; m. Ruth Holley, Oct. 29, 1955; children—Teresa, Nancy, Kathryn, Michael. Devel. officer Redstone Missile Devel., Huntsville, Ala., 1952-55; mem. army gen. staff Dept. Army, Washington, 1956-60; mgr. Apollo program Kennedy Space Center, 1960-66, dir. launch operations, 1966-69; Apollo program dir., NASA, Washington, 1969—. Recipient D.S.M. with cluster NASA. Mem. Am. Inst. Aero. and Astronautics, Sigma Xi. Home: 1624 Golden Ct McLean VA 22101 Office: Hdqts NASA Washington DC 20546

PETROWITZ, HAROLD C., lawyer; b. Lansing, Mich., July 5, 1921; B.S., U. Mich., 1943; J.D., Georgetown U., 1950; LL.M., Columbia U., 1962. Admitted to D.C. bar, 1950, U.S. Ct. Claims bar, 1952, U.S. Supreme Ct. bar, 1953; mgr. govt. contracts White-Rodgers Co., St. Louis, 1954-56; asst. prof. law U. Denver Coll. Law, 1962-64; asso. prof., prof. Am. U., Washington, 1964—; mem. firm Ralph Becker, Washington. Cons., Senate Select Com. on Small Bus., Fed. Contract Law and Procurement Policy, 1965-69, architect of Capitol, 1966—, AEC, 1966—, Govt. Procurement Commn., 1970—. Mem. Am., Fed. bar assns. Contbr. articles to legal jours. Home: 3014 New Mexico Av Washington DC 20016 Office: Federal Bar Bldg West 1819 H St NW Washington DC 20006*

PETTENGILL, GEORGE EWALD, librarian; b. Cambridge, Mass., June 5, 1913; s. Ray Waldron and Rachel (Little) P.; A.B., Bowdoin Coll., 1933; B.S., Columbia U. Sch. Library Service, 1934, M.S., 1938; m. Margaret Elmira Williams, Aug. 16, 1940; children—Richard Little, Gail Ellen (Mrs. William D. Ellsworth). Reference asst. N.Y. Pub. Library, N.Y.C., 1935-37; reference librarian Reading (Pa.) Pub. Library 1937-45; asst. librarian Franklin Inst., Phila., 1945-51; librarian A.I.A., Washington, 1951—. Cons. Random House Dictionary, 1964—. Mem. A.L.A., A.I.A. (hon.), Spl. Libraries Assn. (pres. Phila. chpt. 1946, 47, Washington chpt. rec. sec. 1952-54), Bibliog. Soc. Am. Editor Arlington Hist. Mag., 1963-64. Office: 1785 Massachusetts Av NW Washington DC 20036

PETTINGER, WILLIAM A., physician; b. Cumberland, Ia., May 26, 1932; s. Adolph and Virginia (Lauhoff) P.; B.S., Creighton U., 1954, M.S., 1957, M.D., 1959; m. Margaret Carney, Aug. 12, 1961; children—Maria, Thomas, Elise, William. Intern, Med. Center, Jersey City, 1959-60, asst. resident, 1960-61; clin. investigator exptl. therapeutics, attending physician Nat. Heart Inst., Bethesda, Md., 1961-63; sr. asst. resident Yale U. Grace-New Haven Hosp., 1963-64; postdoctoral fellow, instr. medicine and pharmacology Vanderbilt U. Sch. Medicine, Nashville, Tenn., 1964-66, asst. prof., 1966-67; asso. dept. clin. pharmacology Hoffmann-LaRoche, Inc., Nutley, N.J., 1967-71, chief sect. cardiovascular pharmacology, 1969-71, research dir. clin. pharmacology unit Newark City Hosp., 1967-71; asso. prof. medicine N.J. Coll. Medicine, Jersey City; asso. prof. pharmacology and medicine, dir. clin. pharmacology Southwestern Med. Sch., U. Tex., Dallas, 1971—. Served with USPHS, 1961-63. Diplomate Am. Bd. Med. Examiners, Am. Bd. Internal Medicine. Mem. Am. Fedn. Clin. Research, Am. Soc. Pharmacology and Exptl. Therapeutics, Am., N.Y. acads. scis., So. Soc. Clin. Investigation. Contbr. articles to profl. jours. Home: 15432 Spring Creek Rd Dallas TX 75240 Office: 5323 Harry Hines Blvd Dallas TX 75235

PETTIS, ELIZABETH E. WADE (MRS. IRVING MCFARLAND PETTIS), health agy. exec.; b. Nappanee, Ind., Dec. 16, 1902; d. Raymond J. and Ella L. (Yarian) Wade; A.B., DePauw U., 1924; M.A., U. Chgo., 1926; postgrad. Northwestern U., 1928; m. Irving McFarland Pettis, Jan 28, 1933; children—Janet Louise (Mrs. Hunter Mason Morris), Robert Irving, Alan Wade. Caseworker, Family Welfare Assn., Evanston, Ill., 1926-28; dir. religious edn. 1st Methodist Ch., Evanston, 1928-29; exec. Family Welfare Assn., Evanston, 1930-32; chief social worker McLennan County Rehab. Center for Children and Adults, Waco, Tex., 1961-68; exec. dir. McLennan County Rehab. Center, Waco, 1968—. Vice pres. Waco Traffic Commn., 1951-52; mem. Citizens Charter Commn. Waco, 1957-70. Bd. dirs. Waco Council for Social Welfare, 1952-59, United Charities Waco, 1949-50, Waco Assn. Retarded Children, 1968-69. Mem. Nat. Assn. Social Workers, Acad. Certified Social Workers, Nat. Conf. Social Work, Nat. Easter Seal Execs. Assn., Am. Assn. U. Women, League Women Voters (state bd. 2d v.p. 1961-62), Alpha Chi Omega. Home: 2737 Cumberland St Waco TX 76707

PETTIT, MANSON BOWERS, hosp. adminstr., psychiatrist; b. Waco, Tex., May 26, 1902; s. Benjamin Franklin and Nancy (Phillips) P.; A.B., Trinity U., 1923; M.D., Vanderbilt U., 1928; m. Dagny Rudback, Mar. 26, 1930; children—Marjorie (Mrs. Carl Clifton James), John Whitney. Intern Methodist Hosp. So. Cal., 1928-29; resident in psychiatry St. Elizabeth's Hosp., Washington, 1930-33, staff psychiatrist, 1933-58, clin. dir., 1958-60; med. supt. State Hosp. No. 2, St. Joseph, Mo., 1960-66; supt. Southwestern State Hosp., Thomasville, Ga., 1966—; psychotherapist Washington Inst. Mental Hygiene, 1930-58; organizer Arlington County Mental Hygiene Center, 1947-60; lectr. mental health, hygiene, asso. clin. prof. psychiatry Georgetown U., 1941-60. Mem. St. Joseph Community Welfare Council, 1960-66. Diplomate Am. Bd. Psychiatry and Neurology. Fellow Am. Psychiat. Assn. (life); mem. Interprofl. Inst., A.M.A., Buchanan County Med. Soc., So. Med. Assn. (life mem.). Methodist. Mason (Shriner), Kiwanian. Contbr. to Biol. Abstracts; articles and book reviews to profl. jours. Home: 126 Tuxedo Dr Thomasville GA 31792 Office: Southwestern State Hosp Thomasville GA 31792

PETTUS, REGINALD HOFFMAN, legislator, lawyer; b. Hoffman, Keysville Va 23947 lawyer b. Keysville, Va., June 11, 1920; s. George Overton and Bertha (Hanmer) P.; J.D., Washington and Lee U., 1948; m. Anne Howard Early, Oct. 7, 1947; children—Pamela Kent, Regina Hanmer, Anne Tompkins, Thomas Richardson Randolph. Admitted to Va. bar, 1949, since practiced in Southside; pros. atty. Charlotte County (Va.), 1955-63; asso. county judge, 1963-69; mem. Va. Ho. of Reps., 1969-72. Chmn. bd. State Bank, Keysville, Va., mem. Va. Airports Authority, 1959; commr. of accounts, 1963—. Served with USAAF, 1942-45. ETO. Mem. Va. Bar Assn. (mem. council 1964-70). Democrat. Baptist. Address: Keysville VA 23947

PETTY, CHARLES SUTHERLAND, pathologist; b. Lewistown, Mont., Apr. 16, 1920; s. Charles Frederic and Mae (Reichert) P.; B.S., U. Wash., 1941, M.S., 1946; M.D., Harvard, 1950; m. Lois Muriel Swenson, Dec. 14, 1957; children—Heather Ann, Charles Sutherland II; children by previous marriage—Daniel S., Carol L. Intern, Mary Imogene Bassett Hosp., Coopertown, N.Y., 1950-52; resident pathology Peter Bent Brigham Hosp., Children's Med. Center, New Eng. Deaconess Hosp., Boston, 1952-55; instr. pathology La. State U. Sch. Medicine, 1955-56, asst. prof., 1956-58; asst. med. examiner State of Md., 1958-67; asst. prof. forensic pathology U. Md. Sch. Medicine, 1958-64, asso. prof., 1964-67; lectr., then asso. Johns Hopkins U. Sch. Hygiene and Pub. Health, 1959-67; dir. Balt. Regional A.R.C. Blood Program, 1959-67; prof. forensic pathology Ind. U. Sch. Medicine, Indpls., 1967-69; dir. lab. Ind. Commn. on Forensic Scis., 1967-69; chief med. examiner Dallas County, 1969—; prof. forensic scis., pathology U. Tex. Southwestern Med. Sch., Dallas, 1969—; also dir. Southeastern Inst. Forensic Scis., 1969—. Served from ensign to lt. comdr. USNR, 1941-45. Fellow Coll. Am. Pathologists, Am. Soc. Clin. Pathologists, A.C.P.; mem. Am. Acad. Forensic Scis. (pres. 1967-68), Sci. Research Soc. Am., Sigma Xi. Episcopalian. Home: 3964 Goodfellow Dr Dallas TX 75229 Office: 5230 Medical Center Dr Dallas TX 75235

PETTY, OLIVE SCOTT, geophys. engr.; b. Olive, Tex., Apr. 15, 1895; s. Van Alvin and Mary Cordelia (Dabney) P.; student Ga. Inst. Tech., 1913-14; B.S. in Civil Engring., U. Tex., 1917, C.E., 1920; m. Mary Edwina Harris, July 19, 1921; 1 son, Scott. Adj. prof. civil engring. U. Tex., 1920-23; structural engr. R.O. Jameson, Dallas, 1923-25; pres. Petty Geophys. Engring. Co., San Antonio, 1925-52, chmn. bd., 1952—; pres. Petty Geophys. Co., San Antonio, 1944-52, chmn. bd., 1952—; pres. Petty Labs., Inc., San Antonio, 1932-52, chmn. bd., 1952—; chmn. bd. Petty Geophys. Engring. Co. de Mex. S.A. de C.V., 1950—; also ranching, minerals, timber and investment interests. Sponsor San Antonio Symphony Soc.; patron San Antonio Art Inst.; mem. exec. com., founding mem. chancellor's council U. Tex. Served to 1st lt. engrs. U.S. Army, 1917-18; AEF in France. Recipient Distinguished Engring Grad. award U. Tex., 1962. Registered profl. engr., Tex. Fellow Tex. Acad. Sci. (hon. life); mem. San Antonio Livestock Assn. (life), Texas-Mid-Continent Oil and Gas Assn. (dir.), Am. Soc. C.E. (hon. life), Am. Inst. Mining, Metall. and Petroleum Engrs., Am. Assn. Petroleum Geologists, A.A.A.S., Am. Geophys. Union, Houston Geophys. Soc., S. Tex. Geol. Soc., Soc. Am. Mil. Engrs., Soc. Exptl. Geophysicists (hon. life and founding mem.), Newcomen Soc., Soc. 1st Div., 1st Officers Tng. Camp Assn., Tex., Tex. Heritage Found., Nat. Rifle Assn. (life), Tex. Soc. Profl. Engrs., Ind. Petroleum Assn. Am., Profl. Engrs. in Industry, Ex-Students' Assn. U. Tex. (life), Dads' Assn. U. Tex. (life), Tex. Sheep and Goat Raisers Assn., Tex. and Southwestern Cattle Raisers Assn., Nat. Wool Growers Assn., Am. Farm Bur., Nat. Wildlife Fedn., Chi Epsilon (hon. life), Theta Xi, Tau Beta Pi. Baptist. Clubs: San Antonio Country, Argyle, St. Anthony, (San Antonio). Patentee geophys. instruments, exploration methods. Home: 101 E Kings Hwy San Antonio TX 78212 Office: Tower Life Bldg San Antonio TX 78205

PETTY, SCOTT, JR., engring. co. exec.; b. San Antonio, Apr. 10, 1937; s. Olive Scott and Edwina (Harris) P.; B.S., U. Tex., 1960, M.S., 1961; m. Marie Louise James, June 10, 1959; children—Joan Louise, Susan Harris, James Scott. Asst. to pres. Petty Geophys. Engring. Co., San Antonio, 1961-63, v.p. 1963-65, dir., 1958—, pres., 1967—, also pres. and dir. subsidiaries, 1967—; pres. Petty Labs., Inc., 1965-67. Served to lt. AUS, 1959-60. Registered profl. engr., Tex. Mem. Tex. Soc. Profl. Engrs., Soc. Exploration Geophysicists, Am. Assn. Petroleum Geologists, Am. Inst. Mining, Metall. and Petroleum Engrs., Soc. Am. Mil. Engrs., Phi Gamma Delta, Sigma Gamma Epsilon, Tau Beta Pi. Home: 202 Lajara Blvd San Antonio TX 78209 Office: PO Drawer 2061 San Antonio TX 78206

PETTYJOHN, CHARLES STEPHENS, realtor; b. Denver, Aug. 30, 1910; s. Don C. and Myrtle (Stephens) P.; student Wis. Sch. Mines, 1929-33; B.S., Mich. Tech. Inst., 1934, postgrad. 1935; Petroleum Engr., Purdue U., 1937; postgrad. U. Chgo., 1940; m. Margaret A. Nekervis, July 26, 1937; children—Charles S. and Robert B. (twins). Research, inspection engr. Socony Vacuum Oil Co., East Chicago, Ill., 1936-47; engr., gen. mgmt. Standard Vacuum Petroleum, Mij, Palembang, Sumatera, 1947-58; sales finance Driggers Realty, Mount Dora, Fla., 1959-67; owner, realtor Asso. Realty Services, Mount Dora and Leesburg, Fla., 1967—. Commr. Planning and Zoning, Lake County, Fla., 1969—, chmn., 1971—. Trustee Waterman Meml. Hosp., Eustis, Fla. Named Realtor of Year Lake County, 1972. Mem. Nat. Assn. Real Estate Bds., Nat. Inst. Real Estate Brokers, Lake County, Leesburg bds. realtors, Mt. Dora C. of C. (pres. 1970). Kiwanian (past pres.). Home: Box 103 Fairview Point Tavares FL 32778 Office: 237 Eustis-Mt Dora Hwy 19A Mount Dora FL 32757

PEURIFOY, PAUL GARLAND, judge; b. Wortham, Tex., Aug. 9, 1906; s. Roy G. and Laura Pearl (Burton) P.; student U. Tex., 1923-26, So. Meth. U., 1926-27; m. Mary Jo Mouzon, Sept. 24, 1929; m. 2d, Audrey Posey, May 1, 1970. Admitted to Tex. bar, 1927; practiced in Dallas, 1941-42, 47-48; mem. firm Davis, Synnott & Hatchell, Dallas, 1927-29, Church, Read & Bane, Dallas, 1929-31, Hardy & Peurifoy Dallas, 1931-36; asst. dist. atty. Dallas (Tex.) County, 1937-41, presiding judge, 1958-59, 63-64; chmn. juvenile bd., 1957-58, 60-62; atty. OPA, 1945-47; judge County Ct. at Law 1, Dallas, 1948-52; dist. judge 95th Dist. Ct., Dallas, 1953—. Guest lectr. govt. So. Meth. U., 1948-51. Bd. dirs. Dallas Big Bros., 1947-53. Served with USAAF, 1943-45; MTO. Mem. Am., Dallas bar assns., State Bar Tex. Democrat. Methodist. Mason (32 deg., Shriner). Clubs: Dallas Athletic, Down-Town. Home: 10308 Stone Canyon Rd Dallas TX 75230 Office: Court House Dallas TX 75202

PEVLER, HERMAN H., r.r. exec.; b. Waynetown, Ind., Apr. 20, 1903; s. Chris and Bertha (Hoover) P.; B.S. in Civil Engring., Purdue, 1927; m. Roma H. Haines, June 6, 1931. Asst. engring. corps Pa. R.R., Phila., 1937, asst. supr. track Atlantic and Middle divs., 1927-29, supr. track Balt., Atlantic and Phila. divs., 1929-35, div. engr. St. Louis, Ft. Wayne and Pitts. divs., 1935-37, div. engr. gen. office, Phila., 1937-39, supt. Logansport div., 1939-40, supt. freight transp. Eastern region, Phila., 1940-42, supt. Phila. term. div., 1942, gen. supt. Eastern Pa. div., 1942-46, gen. mgr. Western region, Chgo., gen. mgr. Central region, Pitts., 1946-48, v.p. N.Y. zone, 1948-51, v.p. Western region, Chgo., 1951-55, v.p., regional mgr. Northwestern region, 1955-59, officer, dir. subsidiary cos., pres. Wabash R.R., 1959-63; officer, dir. subsidiary cos., pres. Norfolk & Western Ry., 1963-70, chmn., 1970—; dir. Dominion Bankshares Corp., Roanoke, First Nat. Exchange Bank of Va., A.E. Staley Mfg. Co., Decatur, Ill., Community Hosp. of Roanoke Valley Inc. Trustee Va. Found. Ind. Coll., Hampden-Sydney Coll.; bd. visitors Va. Mil. Inst. Mem. Assn. Am. Railroads (dir.). Clubs: Shenandoah, Roanoke Country, Hunting Hills Country (Roanoke, Va.); Crystal Downs Country (Frankfurt, Mich.); Bogey (St. Louis); Sky, (N.Y.C.); Coral Ridge Country (Boca Raton, Fla.). Home: 15 Cardinal Rd SW Roanoke VA 24014 Office: 106 N Jefferson St Roanoke VA 24011

PEVSNER, BARRY DAVID, pub. relations exec.; b. Memphis, Sept. 25, 1930; s. Bernard and Lucille (Joseph) P.; student U. Ill., 1948-51; m. Sandra Joy Sholdar, May 24, 1952; children—Joseph S., Naomi L., Sara E. Asst editor Chgo. Daily Law Bull., Assn. Ct. and Comml. Newspapers, Chgo., 1955-58; dir. employee communications Midwest territory Sears Roebuck and Co., Chgo., 1958-63, asst. press relations nat. publicity div., 1963-66, corporate publicity dir. S.W. territory, Dallas, 1966—, S.W. regional rep. Sears Roebuck Found., 1966—. Solicitor, Dallas Symphony, 1966—, Dallas County United Fund, 1966—; mem. State Fair Tex. com. Served with USNR 1951-55: Korea. Recipient citations indsl. journalism Internat. Council Indsl. Editors, 1959-64. Mem. Dallas Indsl. Editors Assn., Pub. Relations Soc. Am., Navy League, Internat. Assn. Bus. Communication. Jewish religion. Mason. Home: 7731 Royal Lane Dallas TX 75230 Office: Dept 703 SW 1000 Belleview Dr Dallas TX 75202

PEW, JOHN GLENN, oil co. exec.; b. Beaumont, Tex., May 14, 1902; s. James Edgar and Martha (Layng) P.; student So. Methodist U., 1921, Northeastern U., Mass. Inst. Tech., 1923-24, Cornell U., 1922; m. Roberta Haughton, June 27, 1929; children—John Glenn, Richard Haughton. With Sun Oil Co., 1924-67, v.p. charge prodn., 1946-60, sr. v.p., 1960-67, now dir., cons.; dir. MBS, Fidelity Union Ins. Co. Bd. dirs. Boys Clubs Am., Southwestern Med. Found., Wadley Insts. Molecular Medicine, Dallas Hist. Soc., Internat. Oil and Gas Ednl. Center, Southwestern Legal Found.; dir. sci. and tech. So. Methodist U. Mem. Am. Petroleum Inst. (hon., v.p. div. prodn. 1953-54; certificate of appreciation 1954), Mid-Continent Oil and Gas Assn. (dir. 1936; distinguished service award Tex. 1942), Am. Inst. Mining, Metall. and Petroleum Engrs., Psi Upsilon. Republican. Presbyn. Home: 3525 Turtle Creek Blvd Dallas TX 75219 Office: PO Box 2880 Dallas TX 75221

PEYTON, THOMAS GENE, hosp. adminstr.; b. Earlington, Ky., Jan. 4, 1924; s. William Thomas and Ruby (Foster) P.; B.A., U. Louisville, 1947, postgrad. Kent Sch. Social Work, 1947-48, U. N.C., 1948-49; m. Mary Elizabeth Metcalfe, Feb. 15, 1952; children—Ann Lee, William Dudley. Health program rep. USPHS, 1949-52; dir. outpatient services N.C. Meml. Hosp., Chapel Hill, 1952-57; adminstr. McPherson Hosp., Durham, N.C., 1957—. Bd. dirs. McPherson Hosp. Found. Served to 1st lt. USAAF, 1942-45; ETO. Decorated Air medal. Mem. Am. Coll. Hosp. Adminstrs. Home: 1502 Mason Farm Rd Chapel Hill NC 27514 Office: 1110 W Main St Durham NC 27701

PFAFF, WILLIAM SIEVERS, JR., newspaper exec.; b. New Orleans, July 5, 1919; s. William S. and Irene (Krummel) P.; student Soule Bus. Coll., 1936-40, Am. Acad. Art, 1947, Tulane U., 1968; m. Audrey M. Knecht, Dec. 26, 1942; 1 dau., Karol Ann. Advt. artist, copy writer Times-Picayune Pub. Corp., New Orleans, 1946-60, promotion mgr., 1960—, v.p., 1969—. Instr., Loyola U., New Orleans, 1966. Served with USAAF, 1942-45. Mem. Internat. Newspaper Promotion Assn. (pres. So. region 1964, Bronze award 1966), Advt. Club New Orleans (past dir.), Am. Marketing Assn. (past chpt. v.p.). Home: 3640 Post Oak Dr New Orleans LA 70114 Office: 3800 Howard Av New Orleans LA 70140

PFAUTSCH, LLOYD ALVIN, educator; b. Washington, Mo., Sept. 14, 1921; s. Walter and Ouida (Henselmeier) P.; B.A., Elmhurst Coll., 1943; B.D., Union Theol. Sem., 1946, M.S.M., 1948; D. Mus. (hon.), Elmhurst Coll., 1959; m. Edith Herseth, Sept. 7, 1946; children—Deborah, Eric, Peter, Jonathan. Mem. faculty Ill. Wesleyan U., 1948-58, prof. music, 1953-58; prof. music So. Meth. U., Dallas, 1958—. Vis. prof. U. Ill., 1956-57; guest lectr. univs. U.S. and Can. Organizer, mus. dir. Dallas Civic Chorus, 1960—. Mem. A.S.C.A.P., Am. Choral Dirs. Assn., Blue Key, Pi Kappa Lambda, Phi Mu Alpha, Phi Kappa Phi, Delta Omicron (nat. hon. patron). Author: Mental Warm Ups for the Choral Conductor, 1969; English Diction for the Singer, 1971. Composer, arranger numerous pub. songs. Home: 3710 Euclid Av Dallas TX 75205

PFEIL, WALTER JAMES MALONEY, ins. co. analyst; b. Buffalo, Sept. 20, 1945; s. Walter Fred and Mildred Agness (Maloney) P.; academia OAS, Quito, Ecuador, 1962; A.B. magna cum laude (George Catlin fellow, Nat. Def. Edn. Act fellow), Union Coll., Schenectady, 1968; M.A., U. Fla., 1969; m. Jane Elizabeth Hagans, Dec. 28, 1968. Mgr., Walter F. Pfeil Wholesale Lumber Co., Williamsville, N.Y., 1964-65; chief liaison officer minority enterprise small bus. investment cos. Small Bus. Adminstrn., Dept. Commerce, Washington, 1969-70; research analyst Prudential Ins. Co. Am., Jacksonville, Fla., 1971—. Pres., Help Them Learn Fund, Williamsville, N.Y., 1962-68. Mem. Am. Econ. Assn., U. Fla., Union Coll. alumni assns., Phi Beta Kappa, Beta Gamma Sigma, Phi Kappa Phi, Psi Upsilon. Republican. Episcopalian. Author: newspaper column Fire Facts, Clarence, N.Y., 1964-66. Home: 1034 Marvone Lane Neptune Beach FL 32233 Office: Planning and Analysis div Prudential Ins. Co Jacksonville FL 32207

PFOHL, JAMES CHRISTIAN, musician; b. Winston-Salem, N.C., Sept. 17, 1912; s. John Kenneth and Bessie (Whittington) P.; Mus.B., U. Mich., 1933, Mus.M., 1939, Mus.D. (hon.), Cin. Conservatory Music; m. Louise Nelson, June 11, 1934 (dec.); children—Alice Keith, James Christian, David Nelson; m. 2d, Carolyn Day, Aug. 16, 1968. Dir. music Davidson Coll., 1933-52; dir. Moravian Ch. Chorus, Winston-Salen, 1933-66; organist, choir dir. Myers Park Presbyn. Ch., Charlotte, N.C., 1941-61, founder, condr. Mint Mus. Art Orch., Charlotte, 1944-46; founder, dir. Transylvania Music Camp, Brevard, N.C., 1936-64, Reston (Va.) Music Center, 1966—; condr. No. Va. Youth Orch., 1967—; artistic dir. No. Va. Music Center, Reston, 1968; dir. choral music Robert E. Lee High Sch., Fairfax County, Va.; asst. dir. fine and performing arts Inter-Suburban Planning Project, Alexandria, Arlington, Falls Church sch. dists., 1966; music dir., condr. Brevard Music Festival Orch., 1946-64; condr. Charlotte Symphony, 1949-56. Charlotte Opera Assn., 1950-52, Jacksonville Symphony, 1952-61. Regional v.p. Am. Symphony Orchestra League. Mem. Am., N.C. bandmasters assns., Am. Guild Organists, Music Tchrs. Nat. Assn., N.C. Music Educators Assn., N.C. Orchestra Dirs. Assn., Reston Chorale and Mus. Soc. (founder, dir. 1966), N.C. Choral Dirs. Assn., Music Educators Nat. Conf., Fedn. Music Clubs: Scabbard and Blade, Delta Omicron, Phi Mu Alpha, Phi Kappa Phi, Omicron Delta Kappa, Phi Kappa Lambda, Sigma Chi. Mason, Rotarian. Home: Heron House 11400 Washington Plaza Reston VA 22070 Office: 1605 Washington Plaza N Reston VA 22070

PFOUTS, RALPH WILLIAM, educator; b. Atchison, Kan., Sept. 9, 1920; s. Ralph Ulysses and Alice (Oldham) P.; B.A., U. Kan., 1942, M.A., 1947; Ph.D., U. N.C., 1952; m. Jane Hoyer, Jan. 31, 1945; children—James William, Susan Jane, Thomas Robert, Elizabeth Ann. Research asst., instr. econs. U. Kan., 1946-47, U. N.C., Chapel Hill, 1947-50, lectr. 1950-52, asso. prof., 1952-58, prof., 1958—, chmn. grad. studies dept. econs. Sch. Bus. Adminstrn., 1957-62, chmn. dept. econs., 1962-68. Social Sci. Research Council fellow U. Cambridge, 1953-54; Ford Found. faculty research fellow, 1962-63. Served as deck officer USNR antisubmarine duty, 1943-46. Mem. Am., N.C. (pres. 1951-52) statis. assns., Am., So. (pres. 1965-66) econ. assns., Population Assn. Am., Econometric Soc., A.A.A.S., Phi Beta Kappa, Pi Sigma Alpha, Alpha Kappa Psi. Author: Elementary Economics: A Mathematical Approach, 1972. Editor So. Econ. Jour., 1955—. Editor, contbr. Techniques of Urban Economic Analysis, 1960, Essays in Economics and Econometrics, 1960. Mem. editorial bd. Metro Economica, 1961—. Contbr. articles profl. jours. Home: 502 Ransom St Chapel Hill NC 27514

PHARR, MARSHALL ALVIN, city ofcl.; b. Lubbock, Tex., Apr. 11, 1931; s. Homer Lee and Mabel (Chapman) P.; B.B.A., Tex. Technol. Coll., 1954, postgrad., 1957-58; postgrad. Wayland Baptist Coll., 1964-65; m. Edith Ann Standifer, June 17, 1955; children—Terri Annette, Mark Standifer, Denise Marie, Angela Kay. Mgr., Lubbock, Club, Inc., 1953-54; adminstrv. asst. City of Lubbock, 1957-59; city mgr. Andrews, Tex., 1959-64, Plainview, Tex., 1964—. Vice chmn. Haynes dist. Boy Scouts Am., 1965-67, chmn., 1967—, v.p. Southplains council; v.p. loyalty fund bd. Tex. Technol. Coll., 1960-64; mem. Wayland Law Enforcement Adv. Council, 1971—, Plainview Indsl. Contacts Team, 1972. Bd. dirs. Andrews Indsl. Found., 1962-64, Plainview Indsl. Found. Served to lt. USNR, 1955-57. Mem. Internat., Tex., (dir. 1965-66, 71—), Panhandle (pres.). West Tex. city mgrs. assns., Tex. Municipal League (dist. sec.), Plainview C. of C. (chmn. civic com.), Phi Delta Theta. Democrat. Methodist (pres. Methodist Men 1965-66, steward 1960-64, ch. sch. supt. 1961-64, chmn. finance campaign 1963-64). Mason, Rotarian (pres. Plainview and Andrews, dir.). Home: 2801 W 17th St Plainview TX 79072 Office: Box 520 Plainview TX 79072

PHELPS, ASHTON, newspaper exec., lawyer; b. New Orleans, Dec. 30, 1913; s. Esmond and Harriott K. (Barnwell) P.; grad. Woodberry Forest Sch., 1931; A.B., Tulane U., 1935, LL.B., 1937; student U. Mich. Law Sch., summer 1936; m. Jane C. George, Nov. 21, 1939; 1son, Ashton. Admitted to La. bar, 1937, since practiced in New Orleans; mem. firm Phelps, Dunbar, Marks, Claverie & Sims, 1946-67; pres., pub. The Times-Picayune Pub. Corp., New Orleans, 1967—, also dir. Mem. bd. Christian edn. Presbyn. Ch. U.S., 1958-61, also mem. com. wills and bequests; pres. bd. New Orleans Community Health Assn., 1945-49, Howard Meml. Library Assn., 1950—; chmn. adv. bd. Female Orphan Soc. New Orleans, 1946-59; bd. visitors Tulane U., 1953-55, v.p. bd. adminstrs., 1955-72, adv. adminstr., 1972—; trustee Mountain Retreat Assn., 1958-67; bd. dirs. New Orleans Pub. Library, 1948-62, New Orleans YMCA, 1954—, New Orleans chpt. A.R.C., 1954-60. Oschner Found. Hosp. Mem. Bd. of Liquidation City Debt, Sewerage and Water Board. Served from ensign to lt. (s.g.). USNR, 1942-45. Mem. Am. (spl. com. anti trust sect. on revision rules FTC), La., New Orleans bar assns., Assn. Bar City N.Y., Am. Law Inst., Am. Newspaper Pubs. Assn. (dir.), Order of Coif, Phi Beta Kappa, Delta Tau Delta, Phi Delta Phi, Omicron Delta Kappa. Clubs: Boston, Louisiana, New Orleans Country; City (Baton Rouge). Presbyn. (elder, trustee). Home: 1457 State St New Orleans LA 70118 Office: 3800 Howard Av New Orleans LA 70140

PHELPS, CLAUDIA LEA, club woman; b. Englewood, N.J., June 29, 1894; d. Sheffield and Claudia (Lea) Phelps; pvt. edn. Pres., S.C. Garden Club, 1935-38, chmn. conservation com., 1930-35; former v.p. S.C. Fedn. Women's Clubs; founder Girl Scouts Am., Aiken, S.C., 1920, capt., 1920—; head women's div. Aiken County Civil Def., World War II; vol. home service worker A.R.C., 1917-38, chmn. community service to camps and hosps., 1947-49; chmn.

1947-51; instr. U. Md. Overseas Program, Eng., 1955; grad. asst. U. N.M., 1955-56; asst., asso. prof. history Sul Ross State Coll., Alpine, Tex., 1956-60, prof. history, dean grad. div., 1962-71; asst. prof. Mankato (Minn.) State Coll., 1960-62; dir. baccalaureate programs coordinating bd. Tex. Coll. and Univ. System, Austin, 1971—. Chmn. bd. Wesley Found., Carlsbad Dist., 1962-66; v.p. Assn. Tex. Grad. Schs., 1967-69, pres., 1969-70. Mem. Am. Assn. U. Women, Am. Hist. Assn., Orgn. Am. Historians, N.M. Hist. Soc., N.E.A., Tex. Assn. Coll. Tchrs., Tex. Tchrs. Assn., Alpha Chi, Phi Kappa Phi, Phi Alpha Theta, Delta Gamma Kappa. Democrat. Methodist (mem. N.M. Conf. Bd. Edn., ch. ofcl. bd.). Research in Anglo-American relations, 1954-56, 1962. Home: 8700 Millway Dr Austin TX 78758 Office: Box 12788 Capitol Station Austin TX 78711

PHILLIPS, G. RICHARD, educator; b. Atlanta, Ill., Aug. 30, 1930; s. George W. and Frances W. (Hieronymus) P.; B.A., Th.M., Lincoln Christian Coll., 1952; B.D., Christian Theol. Sem., 1955; M.A., Butler U., 1958; Ph.D., Vanderbilt U., 1968; postgrad. U. Tenn., 1958-59, Columbia, 1968; m. Rebecca Brumett, Dec. 20, 1951; children—Richard W., Jane E. Ordained to ministry Christian Ch., 1956; pastor East Ridge Christian Ch., Chattanooga, Tenn., 1957-62; prof. philosophy Lincoln Christian Coll., 1962-67; prof. philosophy Milligan Coll. (Tenn.), 1967—. Served to maj. Ill. N.G., 1963—. Vis. faculty auditor intensive summer studies program Columbia U., summer 1968. Mem. Am. Acad. Religion, Disciples of Christ Hist. Soc., Am. Orchid Soc., Am. Assn. U. Profs. Home: 1808 Fairway Dr Johnson City TN Office: Box 267 Milligan Coll Milligan College TN 37682

PHILLIPS, GLYN RONALD, judge; b. nr. Clintwood, Va., Jan. 9, 1923; s. Robert A. and Rachel (Kiser) P.; A.B., Lincoln Meml U., 1946; student Carson Newman Coll., 1943, Northwestern U., 1944; LL.B., U. Va., 1948; postgrad. U. Nev., 1969; m. Rita Lambert, Oct. 7, 1950; children—Deborah Lee, Jennifer Lynn, Glyn Ronald. Admitted to Va. bar, 1948, practiced in Clintwood, 1948-56; atty. for Commonwealth of Va., 1956-60; judge 27th Jud. Circuit, Clintwood, 1967—. Vice pres. Wise (Va.) Appalachian Regional Hosp., 1968—, Cumberland Bank and Trust Co., Clintwood, 1972—. Mem. Va. Ho. of Dels., 1952-56; chmn. Dickenson County Democratic party, 1952-56. Bd. dirs. Johnston Meml. Hosp., Abingdon, Va. Served as lt. USNR, 1943-46: PTO. Mem. Am., Va. bar assns., Council on Ministries (chmn. 1969—). Methodist. Kiwanian (lt. gov. 1964). Address: Box 598 Clintwood VA 25228

PHILLIPS, GRACE BRIGGS, research center exec.; b. Mobile, Ala., Apr. 15, 1923; d. Grace Briggs and Annie Captoliz (Decell) P.; B.S., U. Md., 1954; Ph.D. (Founders Day award), N.Y.U., 1964; m. Clemmie Louise Butts, Dec. 29, 1951; children—Lee Briggs, Mary Louise, Robert Briggs. Asst. dir. indsl. health and safety Ft. Detrick (Md.), 194—66; with USPHS, Houston, 1966-67; dir. biol. safety and control Becton, Dickinson, Balt., 1967-69, dir. Research Center, Raleigh, N.C., 1969—; cons. NASA, USPHS. Served with Chem. Corps, AUS, 1943-46. Sec. Army Research and Study fellow, 1969. Fellow Am. Pub. Health Assn., Am. Acad. Microbiology; mem. Am. Assn. for Contamination Control (pres.). Author: Microbial Contamination Control Facilities, 1969. Contbr. articles to profl. jours. Home: Route 6 Springdale Estates Raleigh NC 27609 Office: PO Box 11276 Raleigh NC 27604

PHILLIPS, GUY BERRYMAN, JR., ins. co. exec.; b. Oxford, N.C., May 25, 1918; s. Guy B. and Annie (Craig) P.; B.S. in Commerce, U. N.C., 1938, postgrad. exec. program, 1958; m. Margaret Louise Anderson, May 24, 1941; children—Guy Berryman III, Patricia Anne. With Jefferson Standard Life Ins. Co., Greensboro, N.C., 1938—, mgr. premium notice div., 1947-51, planning supr., 1952, mgr. personnel div., 1953, asst. sec., mgr. personnel div., 1953-57, sec., 1957-60, 2d v.p., sec., 1960-64, v.p., sec., 1964—, asst. sec. Jefferson-Pilot Corp., 1968, sec., 1969. Active in local United Fund. Served from pvt. to maj., USAAF, 1942-46, USAF, 1951-52. Fellow Life Office Mgmt. Assn. Inst.; mem. Life Office Mgmt. Assn. (tchr., dir.), Greensboro C. of C. (dir.). Democrat. Methodist. Home: 3610 Dogwood Dr Greensboro NC 27403 Office: PO Box 21008 Greensboro NC 27420

PHILLIPS, GUY FRANK, beverage co. exec.; b. nr. Royston, Ga., May 24, 1923; s. James Rush and Flora (Adams) P.; A.B., Emory U., 1948; M.S., U. Tenn., 1949; m. Mary Virginia Grant, Aug. 30, 1946; children—Guy Frank, Rosemary Virginia. Chemist Nat. NuGrape Co., Atlanta, 1950-57; research chemist, dir. mfg. Royal Crown Cola Co., Columbus, Ga., 1957-64; mgr. research and quality control Dr. Pepper Co., Dallas, 1964—. Served with AUS, World War II; ETO. Mem. Inst. Food Tech. (nat. com. by-laws 1970-71), Am. Chem. Soc., Am. Waterworks Assn., Am. Soc. Microbiology, Soc. Soft Drink Tech. (dir. 1971—). Methodist. Kiwanian. Home: 7538 Woodstone Lane Dallas TX 75240 Office: PO Box 5086 Dallas TX 75222

PHILLIPS, HARMON, newspaper editor; b. Bellmont, Ill., Oct. 12, 1903; s. Charles R. and Minnie (Blair) P.; grad. high sch.; m. Lora Hutchinson, 1925; 1 son, Charles Robert. Reporter, Tulsa Tribune, 1927-37, city editor, 1937-44, mng. editor, 1944—, now exec. editor. Home: 119 S Indianapolis St Tulsa OK 74112 Office:315 S Boulder Av Tulsa OK 74103

PHILLIPS, HARRY, judge; b. Watertown, Tenn., July 28, 1909; s. Norman Cates and Bernice (Neal) P.; A.B., Cumberland U., 1932, LL.B., 1933, LL.D., 1951; m. Virginia Major, Nov. 26, 1936; children— Harriet (Mrs. Robert E. Scott), Rachel (Mrs. Sidney E. Eagles, Jr.), Caroline (Mrs. Robert M. Ligon), Martha. Admitted to Tenn. bar, 1933; practiced in Watertown, 1933-37; mem. firm Phillips, Gullett & Steele and predecessor, Nashville, 1950-63; asst. atty. gen., Tenn., 1937-43, 46-50; exec. sec. Tenn. Code Commn., 1953-63; judge U.S. Ct. Appeals, 6th Circuit, 1963-69, chief judge, 1969—. Mem. Tenn. Legislature, 1935-37. Served to lt. comdr. JAG, USNR, 1943-46. Recipient award merit Bar Assn. Tenn., 1960. Mem. S.A.R., Order Coif (hon.), Sigma Alpha Epsilon. Baptist. Clubs: University (Cin.); Cumberland, Exchange. Author: Phillips Family History, 1935; Phillips Prichard on Wills and Administration of Estates, 1955; (with others) History of Wilson County, Tennessee, 1962. Home: 2809 Wimbledon Rd Nashville TN 37215 Office: US Ct House Nashville TN 37203 also US Ct House Cincinnati OH 45202

PHILLIPS, HARRY LEWIS, govt. ofcl., educator; b. Indian Mills, W.Va., May 1, 1928; s. Walter McNutt and Nannie Hale (Spangler) P.; B.S. cum laude, Concord Coll., 1950; M.A., W.Va. U., 1954, Ed.D., 1968; m. Mildred Louise Shirey, Nov. 26, 1958; children—Cindy L., Debra A., Joan S. Tchr math. and sci. pub. schs., Monroe County, W.Va., 1952-55; instr. math. and physics Concord Coll., Athens, W.Va., 1955-58; supr. math. State Dept. Edn., Charleston, 1958-62; math. specialist office Branch and Div. Dir., U.S. Office of Edn., Washington, 1962—; adj. prof. Va. Poly Inst. and State U., 1971—. Pres., P.T.A., 1971-72. Served with Signal Corp, AUS, 1950-52. Recipient Superior Service award U.S. Govt., 1969. Mem. Nat. Assn. State Suprs. Math. (founder, pres. 1959-60), Am. Assn. Sch. Adminstrs. Contbr. articles in field to profl. jours. Home: 3201 N John Marshall Dr Arlington VA 22207 Office: Dir Div State Agency Cooperation U S Office of Education Washington DC 20202

PHILLIPS, HELEN DOROTHY BALL (MRS. MAX A. PHILLIPS), educator; b. Beaumont, Tex., Feb. 24, 1923; d. Vernis E. and Anita (Clotiaux) Ball; A.A., Lamar Jr. Coll., 1942; student Baylor U., 1942-43; B.A., Lamar State Coll. Tech., 1961; M.Ed., U. Houston, 1966, postgrad., 1967, 70; postgrad. McNeese State Coll., 1968, U. Colo., 1968, Tex. A. and M. U., 1971; m. Max A. Phillips, Mar. 21, 1942; 1 son, Max Allen II. With Alco Products, Inc., Beaumont, 1947-62; exec. sec., 1948-62; tchr. English, C.O. Wilson Jr. High Sch., Nederland, 1962-63, Forest Park High Sch., Beaumont, 1963-66; counselor Bridge City (Tex.) High Sch., 1966—; newspaper columnist. Mem. Lamar Septette, 1940-42; violinist Lamar Orch., 1940-42, Waco Symphony, 1942-43. Sec., Sabine area Indsl. Relations Assn., 1958-60. Named Outstanding Tchr., Beaumont A. and M. Club, 1964. Mem. N.E.A., Internat. Reading Assn., Sabine-Neches Sch. Bd. and Adminstrs. Assn., Nat., Tex. assns. for children with learning disabilities, Am., Tex. Sabine-Neches (charter, dir.) personnel and guidance assns., Am., Tex. sch. counselors assns., Assn. Measurement and Evaluation in Guidance, Nat., Tex. (charter) vocational guidance assns., Am., Tex. psychol. assns., Lamar Area Reading Council (charter), Am. Rehab. Counselors Assn., Tex., Orange County tchrs. assns., Mu Phi Epsilon, Phi Beta Mu, Delta Kappa Gamma. Baptist. Clubs: Desk and Derrick, Pilot. Home: 725 Cactus Dr Bridge City TX 77611

PHILLIPS, H(OWARD) M(ITCHELL), univ. adminstr.; b. Lumberton, N.C., June 27, 1910; s. Eli and Lydia Melissa (Byrd) P.; B.S., Wake Forest Coll., 1932, M.A., 1934, Sc.D., 1953; Ph.D., U. Va., 1938; postgrad. Inst. Coll. and Univ. Adminstrn., Harvard, summer 1958; m. Frances K. Dunn, June 2, 1934 (dec.); children—Howard Mitchell, Robert Neil; m. 2d, Caroline Martha Gregory, June 20, 1970. Teaching fellow Wake Forest Coll., 1932-34; research fellow U. Va., 1934-38; instr. Emory U., 1938-40, asst. prof., 1940-43, asso. prof., 1943-45, U.S. Navy V-12 Program, 1943-46, prof. biology, 1945-57, chmn. div. natural scis. and math., 1945-46, adminstrv. dep. div. natural sci. and math., 1946-48, chmn. dept. biology, 1948-52, dean Grad. Sch., 1952-57; prof. biology Ala. Coll., 1957-63, pres., 1957-63; pres. Birmingham-So. Coll., 1963-68; dean acad. affairs, dean Grad Sch., U. South Ala., Mobile, 1968-71, v.p. acad. affairs, 1971—. Chmn. com. on ednl. policies div. biology and agr. NRC, 1954-58; bd. dirs. Yerkes Labs. Primate Biology, 1955-57; mem. ednl. adv. bd. Nat. Acad. Scis.-NRC, 1956-58; vice chmn. council Oak Ridge Inst. Nuclear Studies, 1956-57, bd. dirs., 1959-64, v.p., 1963-65; bd. dirs. Oak Ridge Asso. Univs., 1965-70; adminstrv. com. So. Fellowships Fund, 1957-63; mem. Regional Adv. Council Nuclear Energy, 1957-59; cons., mem. panel bio.-med. facilities NSF, 1958-60, cons., mem. panel life sci. facilities, 1960-62, mem. adv. com. spl. projects sci. edn., 1960-64; sec.-treas. So. U. Conf., 1959-66; U.S. rep. Internat. Congress on Sci. Edn., Istanbul, Turkey, 1961; vice chmn. council chief acad. officers Ala. Commn. on Higher Edn., 1972—. Bd. dirs., mem. exec. com. Ala. Heart Assn.; bd. dirs. Birmingham Symphony Assn.; mem. exec. com. Ala. Consortium, Marine Environmental Scis., 1972—. Recipient Andrew Fleming prize in biology U. Va., 1938, Jefferson gold medal Va. Acad. Sci., 1938; Distinguished Service Alumni award Wake Forest Coll. Fellow A.A.A.S., Ga. Acad. Scis.; mem. Genetics Soc. Am., Am. Genetics Assn., Am. Assn. Anatomists, Am. Soc. Mammalogists, Soc. Study Evolution, Human Genetics Soc., Bot. Soc. Am. (chmn. Southeastern sect. 1947-48), Assn. Southeastern Biologists (pres. 1949-50, exec. com. 1950-51), Ala. Hist. Assn., Ala. Coll. Adminstrs. (pres. 1961-62), Ala. Edn. Assn. (v.p., exec. com. div. higher edn. 1959-60, pres. div. higher edn. 1960-61) Conf. So. Grad. Deans (pres. 1957-58), Council So. Univs. (sec. 1956-57), Assn. Am. Colls. (sci. faculty fellowship panel 1958, 60), Nat. Sci. Tchrs. Assn., Am. Inst. Biol. Scis., So. Assn. Colls. and Schs. (commn. colls. and univs. 1958—, chmn. com. on admissions sr. colls. 1960-63, trustee 1964-67), Mobile C. of C., Newcomen Soc., Phi Beta Kappa, Sigma Xi, Pi Kappa Alpha, Alpha Phi Omega, Phi Sigma, Omicron Delta Kappa, Beta Beta Beta. Kiwanian. Home: 4452 Airport Blvd Mobile AL 36608

PHILLIPS, HOWARD S., mag. editor. Editor, Mexican Life Monthly Rev. Office: Mexican Life Monthly Review Uruguay 3 DF Mexico

PHILLIPS, JAMES RANDOLPH, ednl. adminstr.; b. Aubrey, Tex., Dec. 8, 1916; s. Joseph Randolph and Berva (Barr) P.; B.B.A., North Tex. State U., 1939; M.Ed., So. Meth. U., 1952; student Columbia U. Tchrs. Coll., 1966; m. Reba Jane Boatler, June 15, 1941; children— Linda, Jimmy, Joe, Mark. Tchr., coach, prin. pub. schs., Seagoville, Tex., 1939-42, 1945-54; supt. Kaufman (Tex.) Ind. Sch. Dist., 1954—. Served with USNR, 1942-45. Mem. Kaufman C. of C. (dir. 1958-62, 64-67); N.E.A., Nat. Sch. Pub. Relations Assn., Tex. Assn. Tchrs. (legislative chmn. 1970-71, Tex., Dallas County (pres. 1952), Kaufman County assns. sch. adminstrs. (pres. 1956), Tex. U. Interscholastic League (chmn. 1971—). Methodist. Lion (pres. 1949). Home: 100 E 8th St Kaufman TX 75142 Office: 1000 S Houston St Kaufman TX 75142

PHILLIPS, JOHN TAYLOR, judge; b. Greenville, S.C., Aug. 20, 1921; s. Walter Dixon and Mattie Sue (Taylor) P.; student Glenville State Coll., 1949-52; LL.B., Mercer U., 1955; m. Elizabeth Parrish, Dec. 18, 1954; children—John Allen, Mary Susan, Linda Lea, Julia Taylor. Salesman, Brown & Williamson Tobacco Corp., Miami, Fla., 1941-47; W. Va. sales mgr. Penick & Ford Ltd., 1947-49; salesman Dan Williams Brokerage, Charleston, W.Va., 1949-50; admitted to Ga. bar, 1954; judge State Ct. Bibb County, 1964—; dir. trial practice and proc. Mercer U. Law Sch., 1968—. Bd. dirs. Bibb County Heart Fund; bd. dirs. United Cerebral Palsy, nat. v.p. of Reps., 1959-63, Ga. Senate, 1963-64. Served with USMC, Mem. Ga. Ho. 1942-45, 50-51. Decorated Purple Heart. Mem. Am., Ga., Macon bar assns. Methodist. Lion. Home: 1735 Winston Dr Macon GA 31206 Office: Courthouse Macon GA 31201

PHILLIPS, JOSEPH ROBINSON, psychiatrist; b. Clarksville, Tenn., Dec. 28, 1931; s. Fletcher P. and Elizabeth (New) P.; B.S., Tenn. A. and I. U., 1954, M.S., 1956; postgrad. U. Neb., 1955-56; M.D., Meharry Med. Coll., 1963; m. Sarah L. Wesley, May 31, 1956; children— Joseph Robinson II, De Natalie Christine, Vincent Wesley, De Lanie Maria. Acting chmn., instr. dept. biology Clark Coll., 1956-58; asst. prof. dept. anatomy Meharry Med. Coll., Nashville, 1959-68, instr. dept. psychiatry, 1968, asst. prof., 1970—, asso. grad. faculty in anatomy, 1969—; intern Hubbard Hosp., Nashville, 1963-64, resident, 1965-68; practice medicine specializing in psychiatry, Nashville, 1963—; cons. psychiatrist Nat. Inst. Mental Health, Matthew Walker Neighborhood Health Center; mem. adv. bd. Am. Sickle Cell Found. Bd. dirs. Big Bros. Agy. Am. Mem. Am., Tenn. psychiat. assns., Nat., So., Vol. State med. assns., R.F. Boyd Med. Soc., Nashville Acad. Medicine, Tenn. Med. Assn., Beta Kappa Chi, Omega Psi Phi. Home: 6512 Cornwall Dr Nashville TN 37205 Office: 1916 Patterson St Nashville TN 37203

PHILLIPS, LOYAL, newspaper exec.; b. Cullman, Ala., Apr. 11, 1905; s. Monroe and Lucy Ann (Bailey) P.; B.A., Howard Coll., 1928; m. Evelyn Caldwell, Apr. 8, 1928; children—Sharon Kay, Terry Lynn. Promotion mgr. Atlanta Georgian-Am., 1929; classified advt. mgr. Birmingham (Ala.) Post, 1930, Nashville Banner, 1931-32, Omaha World-Herald, 1933-34; classified advt. mgr. Washington Daily News, 1936, acting advt. dir., 1937-38; co-founder, partner, editor Parish-Phillips Newspaper Advt. Syndicate, Miami, Fla., 1939-43, also spl. cons. Tampa Times, Miami News, Washington Post; columnist Editor and Pubs. mag., N.Y.C., 1940; advt. dir. New Orleans Item, 1945-49; gen. mgr., treas. St. Petersburg Ind., Inc., 1950-59, editor, pub., sec., treas., 1952-59, pres., 1959-62; pres. Petersburg Newspaper Corp. (Va.) 1959-62; sec.-treas. Punta Gorda Herald and Clewiston News, 1953—; gen. mgr. S.W. Citizen; pres. Laurel (Miss.) Leader-Call, 1959-62, Independent, Inc., 1962—, WCCF radio sta., 1960; pub., v.p. Ocala (Fla.) Star-Banner, 1963-67; gen. mgr. Elizabeth City (N.C.) Daily Advance, 1967—; gen. mgr. Seabag Newspaper for Norfolk Navy Base, 1967—; asst. to pres. Dear Publ. & Radio, Inc., 1971-72; dir. Citizens Pub. Co. Active A.R.C., Goodwill Industries, Childrens Service Bur., Salvation Army, Boy Scouts Am.; treas. New Orleans Art Acad.; dir. Greater New Orleans, Inc.; chmn. Elizabeth City United Fund, 1969. Chmn. Fla. Gov.'s Traffic Safety Adv. Com., 1956. Served as lt. (j.g.) USNR, 1943-44; mem. res. adv. council 8th Naval Mgrs. 1947-49. Mem. Nat. Assn. Newspaper Classified Advt. mgrs. (v.p. 1933—), So. Newspaper Pubs. Assn. (dir., chmn. pub. relations), Sales Exec. Council, Assn. Commerce, Newspaper Advt. Execs. Assn., Internat. House, New Orleans Advt. Club (pres. 1945-46), Elizabeth City C. of C. (pres. 1971-72), Lambda Chi Alpha. Rotarian. Clubs: Metairie Country, Quarterback. Author: Newspaper Advertising, 1946; Fifty Successful Advertising Ideas, 1948. Home: 213 S Water St Elizabeth City NC 27909 Office: Daily Advance Elizabeth City NC 27909

PHILLIPS, MARCELLA LINDEMAN (MRS. JAMES F. PHILLIPS), physicist; b. Cumberland, Ia., Jan. 15, 1901; d. Frank and Marie (Marley) Lindeman; grad. Highland Park Coll., 1917; B.A., State U. Ia., 1921, M.S., 1922; m. James F. Phillips, June 27, 1927; children—Laura Marley, Frederica Lindeman (Mrs. Ulric Henry Weil). Asst. physicist State U. Ia., 1919-22; instr. Hunter Coll., N.Y.C., 1924-25; physicist Gen. Electric Co., Nela Park Lab., Cleve., 1925-27, Thomas and Hochwait Lab., Dayton, O., 1930-31; prof. physics Adamson U., Manila, 1937-39; physicist Carnegie Inst., 1940-42, Nat. Bur. Standards, Washington, 1942-51, Mass. Inst. Tech., 1951-53, cons. physicist, 1953—, also cos. including Am. Car & Foundry Industries, Electro-Physics Lab., Columbia, Md., Internat. Tel. &Tel., Comite Consultativ Internat.-Radio, Union Radio Sci. Internat., 1953—. Mem. Am. Phys. Soc., Am. Geophys. Union, Washington Philos. Soc., Acoustical Soc. Am., Washington Acad. Sci., I.E.E.E. (chmn. wave propagation com. 1956-62), Sigma Xi, Contbr. profl. publs. Address: Union Farm Mount Vernon VA 22121

PHILLIPS, NAT, JR., educator; b. Cleveland, Tenn., June 12, 1930; s. Nat and Grace Mayfield (Quinn) P.; B.A., Carson-Newman Coll., 1950; M.A., Vanderbilt U., 1961; B.D., Southwestern Bapt. Theol. Sem., 1955; postgrad. U. Tenn., 1964-67; m. Dolores Cornett, Dec. 26, 1950; children—Stephen Quinn, Dia Michele. Ordained to ministry Bapt. Ch., 1949; pastor Little Hope Bapt. Ch., Clarksville, Tenn., 1955-61; asso. pastor First Bapt. Ch., Balboa Heights, C.Z., 1961-63; pastor Fairview Bapt. Ch., Oak Ridge, 1961-67, Evang. Bapt. Ch., Weirton, W.Va., 1967-68; instr. philosophy dept. West Liberty State Coll., W.Va., 1967-68; prof. history and philosophy Tenn. Temple Coll., Chattanooga, 1968—. Mem. Am. Hist. Soc., Tenn. Edn. Assn., Columbian Literary Soc., Cumberland Assn. Baptists (moderator 1961). Editor Fairview (Baptist) Evangel, 1965-67. Home: 3701 Mary Ann Dr Chattanooga TN 37412 Office: 1901 Union Av Chattanooga TN 37404

PHILLIPS, ORIE LEON, judge; b. nr. Viola, Ill., Nov. 20, 1885; s. Edward and Susan (Thompson) P.; student Knox Coll. 1904-05; J.D., U. Mich., 1908, LL.D., 1935 E.D., Colo. Sch. Mines, 1940; LL.D., U. Denver, 1951, Colo. Coll., 1951, Knox Coll., 1955, Trinity Coll., 1955; m. Helen Mercedes Bissell, June 21, 1910 (dec. Feb. 1968). Admitted to N.M. bar, 1909, Fed. bar, 1912; practiced in Raton, N.M., 1910-23; asst. dist. atty. 8th Dist., N.M., 1912-16; majority leader N.M. Senate, 1923; U.S. Dist. judge, N.M., 1923-29; U.S. Circuit judge, 1929—; chief judge U.S. 10th Circuit, 1941-56. Vis. prof. law Northwestern U., 1936-37, U. Mich., 1939; commencement address Freedoms Found., 1951; council chmn. of Survey of Legal Profession of Am. Bar Assn. 1947—. Recipient medal, citation Am. Bar Assn., 1950. Mem. Am., Colo., N.M. bar assns. Author: Conduct of Judges. Home: Gulf Shore Colony Club Naples FL 33940 Office: PO Box 2210 Denver CO 30201

PHILLIPS, RAYMOND MCDONALD, former govt. ofcl.; b. Sylacuga, Ala., July 24, 1908; s. Bela Aterbide and Bessie Mae (McDonald) P.; B.S. in Elec. Engring., U. Ala., 1930; m. Patricia Margaret Lettice, June 27, 1942; children—Martha Mae, Margaret Ann, Sally Foster, Raymond McDonald. With Gen. Electric Co., 1930-31, Curtis Publ. Co., 1931-34; commd. lt. U.S. Army Res., 1930, advanced through grades to col., 1953; engr. Civilian Conservation Corp., 1935-38, engr., Eng., France, Germany, 1942-46; civilian engr., chief army engrs., Washington, 1941-42, 46-55; ret. 1960; civilian engr. U.S. P.O. Dept., Washington, 1955-71. Asst. to prof. physics U. Ala., Tuscaloosa, 1928-29, asst. to prof. elec. engring., 1929-30; rep. NRC, Washington, 1947—. Decorated Bronze Star medal (U.S.); Croix De Guerre with Star of Vermeil (France). Registered profl. engr., Ga. Mem. Nat., Va. socs. profl. engrs., U. Ala. Alumni Assn., Tau Beta Pi, Pi Mu Epsilon, Chi Beta Phi, Alpha Sigma Phi (past pres., sec.). Methodist. Club: Mt. Vernon Yacht (mem. organizing com. 1955, past dir., rec. sec.) (Alexandria, Va.). Home: 2710 S Inge St Arlington VA 22202

PHILLIPS, ROBERT EUGENE, advt. agy. exec.; b. Denver, June 8, 1933; s. Roy E. and Gloria (Loomis) P.; ed. pub. schs.; m. Bobbie Jean Teague, July 4, 1953 (div. Dec. 1967); children—Barney, Rex, Scott; m. 2d, Barbara Johnson Davenport, May 26, 1968. Various positions as comml. artist, designer, profl. singer, actor, musician in network tv and radio, films, also feature writer for Mystery Digest, Aviation News Illus., advt. photographer, N.Y.C., 1956-60; owner Phillips, Inc., Creative Services, Inc., Am. Sign Services, Inc., Intermarc Corp. (all Dallas), 1961—. Vol., United Fund, Heart Fund, other orgns., 1961—. Served with AUS, 1953-55. Recipient All Army Singing Contest award Freedom Found., 1955. Mem. Mystery Writers Am., Profl. Photographers Am., Advt. League, Am. Broadcasters Tex. Home: 5520 Emerson St Dallas TX 75209 Office: 2921 Fairmount Dallas TX 75201

PHILLIPS, ROBERT JAMES, chem. mfg. co. exec.; b. Mart, Tex., Aug. 25, 1922; s. William B. and Katie (Barrow) P.; B.S. in Chem. Engring., U. Tex., 1948; m. Mary Jo Bass, Dec. 27, 1944; children—Andrew Bass, Robert James II. Chem. engr. Humble Oil & Refining Co., Baytown, Tex., 1948-52; editorial dir. Gulf Pub. Co., Houston, 1952-53; with Howe-Baker Engrs., Inc., Tyler, Tex., 1955-70, v.p., 1955-60, pres., 1969-69, chmn. bd., 1970, dir., 1957-70; pres. Internat. Technovation, Inc., 1970-71; pres., chmn. bd. Amtech, Inc., 1971—; dir. Tyler Bank & Trust Co.; exec. v.p., dir. Tyler Savs. & Loan Assn., Peoples Life Ins. Co. Bd. dirs. Nat. Youth Found., 1961, United Community Fund, 1962, Salvation Army, 1964. Served to capt., USAAF, World War II. Mem. Am. Chem. Soc., Tex. Soc. Profl. Engrs., Am. Inst. Chem. Engrs., E. African Wild Life Soc., Tex. Council Higher Edn. Methodist (mem. ofcl. bd.). Mason (32 deg.). Clubs: Union League Chicago; Adventurers; Shikar-Safari, The Explorers, Houston, Willow Brook Country. Home: 2107 Parkway Pl Tyler TX 75701 Office: 3102 E 5th St Tyler TX 75701

PHILLIPS, SILAS BENT, JR., utilities exec.; b. Portland, Ore., Feb. 3, 1915; s. Silas Bent and May (Stevenson) P.; B.S., Harvard, 1937; m. Frances May Rau, Jan. 17, 1943; children—Dabney Carr, Elizabeth May, Jane Rowland, William Stevenson. Dist. mgr. West Tex. Utilities Co., Marfa, 1953-57, adminstrv. asst., Abilene, 1957-60, v.p., 1960-64, pres., dir., also chief exec. officer 1964-65; pres., dir. Central & S.W. Corp., Wilmington, Del., 1965—; pres., dir. CSR Services, Inc., Dallas, 1969—. Served from pvt. to maj. USAAF, 1941-46. Home: 4711 N Lindhurst Dallas TX 75229 Office: 300 Delaware Av Wilmington DE 19899 also 2828 One Main Pl Dallas TX 75250

PHILLIPS, WALTER RAY, lawyer; b. Democrat, N.C., Mar. 19, 1932; s. Walter Yancey and Bonnie (Wilson) P.; A.B., U. N.C., 1954; LL.B., Emory U., 1957, LL.M., 1962, J.D., 1970; postgrad. Yale, 1965-66; m. Patricia Ann Jones, Aug. 28, 1954; children—Bonnie Ann, Rebecca Lee. Admitted to Ga. bar, 1957, Fla. bar, 1958, Tex. bar, 1969, to practice before Supreme Ct. U.S.; with firm Jones, Adams, Paine & Foster, West Palm Beach, Fla., 1957-58; law clk. to chief judge U.S. Dist. Co., Atlanta, 1958-59; with firm Powell, Goldstein, Frazer & Murphy, Atlanta, 1959-60; referee in bankruptcy U.S. Cts., Atlanta, 1960-64; prof. law U. N.D., 1964-65; teaching fellow Yale, 1965-66; prof. law Fla. State U., 1966-68; prof. Tex. Tech. U., Lubbock, 1968-71; Distinguished Vis. prof. law Baylor U., 1971; atty. Commn. on Bankruptcy Laws of U.S., Washington, 1971—. Vice pres., dir. Killearn Estates, Inc. Bd. dirs. Lubbock Day Nurseries, now pres. Served with USAF, 1950. Mem. Am., Fed., Fla., Tex., Lubbock, Ga. bar assns., Am. Judicature Soc., Phi Alpha Delta (chief tribune). Baptist. Club: Belvedere Optimist of Decatur (dir. 1960-61). Author: Florida Law and Practice, 1960; Encyclopedia of Georgia Law, 1962; Seminar for Newly Appointed Referees in Bankruptcy, 1964; (with James William Moore) Debtors' and Creditors' Rights, Cases and Material, 1966; The Law of Debtor Relief, 1969, 2d edit., 1972; Rule 6, Moore's Federal Practice, 1969. Home: 9221 Graceland Pl Fairfax VA 22030

PHILLIPS, WAYNE A., supt. schs.; b. Marshall, Ark., Oct. 15, 1905; s. William Pinkney and Ara (LaVina) P.; student Tech. Coll. Russellville (Ark.), 1930; A.B., Northeastern State Coll., Okla., 1937; M.A., U. Okla., 1950; m. Eileen B. Billington, Dec. 29, 1929; 1 dau., Wanda Elaine. Tchr. elementary schs. Searcy County, Ark., 1924-29, Haskell County, 1929-44; supt. high sch. Onapa, 1944-46, Maud, Okla., 1946-57; supt. Webbers Falls (Okla.) High Sch., 1957-71; supt. schs. Muskogee (Okla.) County, 1971—. Bd. dirs. Okla. Heart Assn., 1965-71, Am. Heart Assn., 1965-71; instl. rep. Webbers Falls council Boy Scouts Am., 1970-71. Bd. dirs. County Cancer Assn., 1957. Hon. farmer Future Farmers Am. Mem. Okla. (treas. 1971—), Muskogee County (pres. 1964-65) edn. assns., Am., Okla. assns. sch. adminstrs, Ruritan Club (charter). Baptist. Mason (32 degree, Shriner). Home: 105 N Main St Webbers Falls OK 74470 Office: Court House Muskogee OK 74401

PHILLIPS, WILLIAM EARL, physician; b. Amory, Miss., July 16, 1939; s. Will J. and Lula (Dabbs) P.; student U. Miss., 1957-60, U. Vienna, Austria, 1958, Millsaps Coll., 1959, Tulane U., 1960-61; M.D., U. Tenn., 1964; M.P.H., U. Cal. at Los Angeles, 1967. Intern, City of Memphis Hosps., 1964-65; pub. health physician Memphis and Shelby County Health Dept., 1965, dir. Tb control, dir. chronic disease control, 1967-72, dir. disease detection, 1972—; asst. prof. U. Tenn. Coll. Medicine, 1972—. Mem. chest disease task force Tenn. Comprehensive Health Planning Council; mem. program com., bd. dirs. Community Action Agy. Memphis-Shelby County; mem. community service com., bd. dirs. Memphis Heart Assn.; mem. Memphis Area Council on Nutrition; program cons., bd. dirs. Planned Parenthood of Memphis, 1969—; adv. com. Memphis & Shelby County Medicare; Bd. dirs., program com. Memphis Tb and Health Assn. Recipient Community Service awards Memphis Area Council on Alcoholism, 1969, Memphis Heart Assn., 1972. Mem. A.M.A., So. Med. Assn., Tenn., Memphis and Shelby County med. socs., Am. Pub. Health Assn., Assn. State and Territorial Dirs. and Coordinators Research, Assn. Tchrs. Preventive Medicine, Am. Assn. Pub. Health Physicians, Memphis Heart Assn. (dir.), Soc. for Advanced Med. Systems, Phi Chi. Contbr. articles to profl. jours. Home: 1139 Stage Av Memphis TN 38127 Office: 814 Jefferson Av Memphis TN 38105

PHILLIPS, WILLIAM MILLER, editor; b. Pitts., Nov. 21, 1920; s. William Shannon and Elva (Miller) P.; B.S., U. Pitts., 1942; M.S., Columbia U., 1950; m. Marjorie I. Higgins, Oct. 20, 1944; children—Stacie M., William S., Shannon H. Editor, reporter Lake Charles (La.) Am. Press, 1948, Jamestown N.Y. Post Jour., 1949, Pitts. Post Gazette, 1949, St. Petersburg (Fla.) Times, 1950, Tampa (Fla.) Tribune, 1950, Miami Herald, 1951-65, also feature editor, Sunday editor, 1958-65; mng. editor Tallahassee Democrat, 1965—. Instr. U. Miami, 1960-65. Served with USNR, 1941-45: PTO. Mem. Sigma Delta Chi, Delta Tau Delta. Elk. Home: 3206 Brookforest Rd Tallahassee FL 32303 Office: 277 N Magolia Dr Tallahassee FL 32302

PHILLIPS, WILLIAM PERRY, food co. exec.; b. Spartanburg, S.C., May 6, 1933; s. Guion L. and Naomi T. (Phillips) P.; B.A., Wofford Coll., 1955; m. Mary Ann Reeves, Aug. 12, 1956; children—Shawn, Mary Ashley, Kelly Kathleen. Distbr. mgr. market applications group Cryovac div. W.R. Grace, 1955-69; v.p. operations franchise operator of Hardees Hamburger Restaurants, Spartan Food Systems, Spartanburg, S.C., 1969—. Active YMCA. Methodist. Club: Arrowhead Country (Montgomery, Ala.). Home: 15 Arrowhead Court Montgomery AL 36109 Office: Spartan Food Systems Spartanburg SC 29302

PHILLIPS, WILLIE EDWARD, govt. ofcl.; b. Clifton, Tenn., July 26, 1923; s. Cicero Buchanan and Willie (Hendrix) P.; B.S., Miss. State U., 1949, M.S., 1955; B.D., Emory U., 1951; Ph.D., Vanderbilt U., 1959; m. Maxie LaVoris Doddson, June 5, 1949; children—Martha Helen, Mary Katherine, Margaret Ann. Sec. YMCA, Miss. State U., 1951-54; research asst. Vanderbilt U., 1955-58; asst. prof. Tex. Tech. U., Lubbock, 1958-63, asso. prof., 1963-67; physicist Nat. Bur. Standards, Washington, summer 1966, and 1967—. Lectr., U. Md., also NBS Grad. Sch., 1967—; research participant Oak Ridge Nat. Lab., 1962; tech. staff Tex. Instruments, Dallas, summers 1964, 65. Served AUS, 1943-46. Recipient Gold Triangle award, 1948; Legion Merit award K.T., 1971. Mem. I.E.E.E. (sr., past sec. chmn.), Tex. Congress Parents and Tchrs. (hon. life), Am. Soc. for Testing and Materials, Blue Key, Sigma Xi, Tau Beta Pi, Eta Kappa Nu, Sigma Pi Sigma, Pi Kappa Delta, Omicron Delta Kappa, Lambda Chi Alpha. Methodist. Mason (32 deg., Shriner, K.T.). Research in field. Home: 6404 Queens Chapel Rd Hyattsville MD 20782 Office: Nat Bur Standards Washington DC 20234

PHILLIPS, WILLIS PAUL, dentist; b. Hale Center, Tex., Oct. 7, 1927; s. Clyde C. and Ada Erma (Stutzman) P.; B.S., Tex. Tech. Coll., 1947; postgrad. Tex. A. and M., 1948, Wayland Coll., 1962, West Tex. State U., 1963; D.D.S., Baylor U., 1967; m. Grace Holden, Apr. 6, 1950; children—Charles Vincent, Barbara Camille, Brenda Karen. Instr., Knox County Vocational Sch., Munday, Tex., 1948-50, Hale County Vocational Sch., Plainview, Tex., 1950-53; owner, oeprator dairy and farm, Hale Center, Tex., 1953-63; instr. Baylor U. Coll. Dentistry, Dallas, summer 1967; pvt. practice dentistry, Weatherford, Tex., 1967—; sec., dir. Preston Park Gas Coop., Hale Center, 1961-63. Mem. Planning and Zoning Bd. city of Weatherford (Tex.), 1969—. Mem. Am., Tex. dental assns., Fort Worth Dist. Dental Soc., Am. Soc. Dentistry for Children. Methodist (lay leader 1968-71). Mason, Rotarian (bd. dirs. 1969-71, pres. 1970). Patentee in field. Home: 603 Hilltop Dr Weatherford TX 76086 Office: 200 E Rentz St Weatherford TX 76086

PHILLIPS, YVONNE, educator; b. Newellton, La., Jan. 6, 1926; d. Jesse Moore and Jeanette (Hundley) Phillips; B.A., Northwestern State Coll. La., 1947; M.A., La. State U., 1950, Ph.D., 1953. Mem. faculty Northwestern State Coll., Natchitoches, La., 1947-69, prof. geography, 1958-69, head social sci. dept., 1954-67; dir., prof. La. Studies Inst., 1967-69; prof. geography Western Carolina U., Cullowhee, N.C., 1969—. Mem. Assn. Am. Geographers, Am. Geog. Soc., Southwestern Social Sci. Assn., La. Acad. Scis. (chmn. social sci. sect. 1955-56), Am. Assn. U. Profs., Am. Assn. U. Women, Phi Kappa Phi (chpt. treas. 1951-53), Phi Alpha Theta (chpt. pres. 1946-47), Kappa Delta Pi (chpt. pres. 1946-47). Editor La. Studies, 1962-69. Contbr. articles to publs. Home: PO Box 2141 Cullowhee NC 28723

PHILOON, WALLACE C., JR., chem. engr., educator; b. Mar. 19, 1923; B.S. in Chemistry, Bowdoin Coll., 1945; M.S. in Chem. Engring., Mass. Inst. Tech., 1947, Sc.D. in Chem. Engring., 1950; m. Ann Philoon. Asst. mgr. process devel. Uranium div. Mallinckrodt Chem. Works, Tulsa, 1957-61, project engr., 1961-64; mem. faculty U. Tulsa, 1964—, now assoc. prof. chem. engring. Mem. Phi Beta Kappa, Sigma Xi, Alpha Chi Sigma, Alpha Delta Phi. Home: 5636 S Quebec St Tulsa OK 74135*

PHILPOTT, ALBERT LEE, legislator, lawyer; b. Philpott, Va., July 29, 1919; s. John E. and Gertrude (Prillaman) P.; B.A., U. Richmond, 1941, LL.B., 1947; m. Katherine Spencer, Aug. 7, 1941; children—Judy (Mrs. Philip Steward Marstiller), Albert Lee. Admitted to Va. bar, 1947; practiced in Bassett, 1947-52, 58—; partner firm Philpott & McGhee, Bassett, 1958—; commonwealth's atty. Henry County (Va.), 1952-57; mem. Va. Ho. of Delegates, 1958—. Dir. 1st Nat. Bank, Bassett, Va., Patrick Henry Mental Health Clinic, Martinsville, Va. Served with USAAF, 1941-45. Mem. Am., Va., Martinsville, Henry County bar assns., Am. Legion, Lambda Chi Alpha. K.P., Moose, Elk. Home: Route 4 Bassett VA 24055 Office: Main St Bassett VA 24055

PHILPOTT, HARRY MELVIN, pres. univ.; b. Bassett, Va., May 6, 1917; s. Benjamin Cabell and Daisy (Hundley) P.; A.B., Washington and Lee U., 1938, LL.D., 1966; Ph.D., Yale, 1947; D.D., Stetson U., 1960; LL.D., U. Fla., 1969, U. Ala., 1970; m. Pauline Breck Moran, Sept. 15, 1943; children—Harry Melvin, Jean Todd, Benjamin Cabell II, Virginia Lee. Ordained to ministry Bapt. Ch., 1942; dir. religious activities Washington and Lee U., 1938-40; prof. religion U. Fla., 1947-52, v.p., 1957-65; dean, head dept. religion and philosophy Stephens Coll., 1952-57; pres. Auburn (Ala.) U., 1965—. Dir. 1st Nat. Bank, Montgomery, West Point Pepperell. Chmn. TV com. Am. Council on Edn., 1959-61; chmn. higher edn. div. Fla. Bapt. Conv., 1958-64; mem. So. Regional Edn. Bd., 1966—. Served to 1st lt., Chaplains Corps, USNR, 1943-46. Mem. Fla. Blue Key, Kappa Alpha, Omicron Delta Kappa, Kappa Delta Pi, Phi Eta Sigma. Kiwanian. Home: 430 S College St Auburn AL 36830

PHINNEY, CARL LAWRENCE, lawyer; b. Marble Falls, Tex., Oct. 22, 1904; s. C. D. and Lillie (Shugart) P.; student U. Tex., 1921-27; m. Louise Snow, Aug. 17, 1928; children—Louise Snow (Mrs. Josef Caldwell), Carl Lawrence. Admitted to Tex. bar, 1931; practiced in Dallas, 1931—; sr. partner firm Phinney, Hallman, Pulley & Livingstone, Dallas, 1939—. Mem. Tex. N.G., 1925-61, maj. gen. comdg. 36th Inf. Div., 1953-61. Decorated Silver Star, Legion of Merit (U.S.); Italian Cross of Officer cavalier Order of Sts. Maurizio and Lazzara. Mem. Mil. Order World Wars, Am., Tex., Dallas bar assns., Soc. Mayflower Descs., N.G. Assn. (past v.p.). Democrat. Methodist. Mason (33 deg., Shriner). Home: 4204 Shenandoah Av Dallas TX 75205 Office: First Nat Bank Bldg Dallas TX 75202

PHINNEY, R(OBERT) L(ORIN), govt. ofcl.; b. Marble Falls, Tex., Apr. 5, 1910; s. Charles DeWolfe and Lillie (Shugart) P.; student U. Tex., 1927-30; m. Helen Avery, Sept. 9, 1939; 1 dau., Susan. Dir. employment Dist. 9, WPA, Austin, Tex., 1935-40; postmaster, Austin, 1947-52; dist. dir. Internal Revenue Service, Austin, 1952—. Fed. area chmn. Crusade for Freedom Campaign, 1954—; mem. accounting adv. council U. Tex., Austin. Served to col. AUS, 1940-46. Decorated Bronze Star medal. Mem. Austin Fed. Exec. Assn. (president), Beta Alpha Psi. Democrat. Episcopalian. Clubs: Headliners, Citadel. Home: 1907 Exposition Blvd Austin TX 78703 Office: 800 E 8th St Austin TX 78701

PHIPPS, BENJAMIN KIMBALL, II, lawyer; b. Boston, Jan. 16, 1933; s. Benjamin Kimball and Bertha Elizabeth (Forsyth) P.; B.S. in Commerce, U. Va., 1955, LL.B., 1958; m. Phyllis Jarrett Anderson, Jan. 10, 1962; children—Lisa Jarrett, Christina Caroline. Admitted to Fla. bar, 1964; editor Municipal Code Corp., Tallahassee, 1964-65; practice law, Tallahassee, 1965—. Chmn. Historic Tallahassee Preservation Bd., 1970—; pres. Fla. Heritage Found., 1967. Counsel tax com. Fla. Ho. of Reps., 1966-70. Served to capt., airborne arty. AUS, 1958-64. Mem. Am., Fla. bar assns., Jefferson Soc., Sigma Alpha Epsilon, Phi Alpha Delta, Phi Delta Epsilon. Clubs: Cosmos, Exchange (Tallahassee). Contbr. articles in field. Home: Jubilee Thomasville Rd Tallahassee FL 32303 Office: PO Box 1351 Tallahassee FL 32302

PHIPPS, EDMOND CHARLES, music co. exec.; b. Leon, Ia., Oct. 31, 1925; s. William Floyd and Edith I. (McLaughlin) P.; grad. high sch.; m. Beatrice Lucile Graves, Dec. 27, 1943; children—Eddie Ray, Debbie Diane, Randall Richard, Linda. With Critchett Piano Co., Des Moines, 1946-49, King Music Co., Wichita, Kan., 1949-50, Rhodes Piano Co., Sioux City, Ia., 1950-52; pres. Phipps Piano Co., Duluth, Minn., also Birmingham, Ala., 1955-68; pres. Piano and Organ Land, Inc., Jacksonville, Fla., 1968-70; operator Phipps Piano Co., North Jacksonville Beach, Fla., 1970-71; dist. sales mgr. Grand Piano Co., Morganton, N.C., 1972—. Bd. dirs. Birmingham Symphony. Served with USNR, 1943-46. Mason (Shriner). Address: 1708 Indian Woods Dr Neptune Beach FL 32233

PHLEGAR, FREDERICK LEE, educator; b. Pearlsburg, Va., Feb. 6, 1929; s. Archie Stader and Madeline (Guthrie) P.; B.S., Va. Poly. Inst., 1951; M.A., Miami U., 1954; Ed.D., U. So. Cal., 1961; m. Barbara Lee Littler, June 12, 1953; children—Tomi Sue, Richard James, Kriste Ann, Randal John. Tchr. math. Long Beach (Cal.) Secondary Schs., 1954-59; sch. adminstr. Bonita High Sch., La Verne, Cal., 1959-61; sch. adminstr. Vandalia (O.) Pub. Schs., 1961-63; prof., chmn. dept. edn. Radford Coll., 1963—, cons. Va. Dept. Edn. Served with USAF, 1951-53. Mem. So. Assn. Colls. and Schs. (mem. Va. com. 1965-72), Phi Delta Kappa (sec. Radford chpt. 1971—). Presbyn. (deacon 1966-70). Kiwanian (dir. 1971-72). Home: 1303 Madison St Radford VA 24141 Office: Box 656 Radford Coll Radford VA 24141

PHOTIAS, NIKOS GEORGE, educator; b. Corinth, Greece, July 20, 1904; s. George N. and Katina G. (Kolokouri) P.; B.A. summa cum laude, U. Athens, 1922; M.B.A. summa cum laude, Handelshochschule, Koenigsberg, Germany, 1925; M.Pol.Sc. magna cum laude, U. Koenigsberg, 1926, Ph.D. cum laude, 1927; LL.D. cum laude, U. Berlin, 1928; postgrad. U. Paris, 1928; m. Anastasia Papadia, July 24, 1967. Came to U.S., 1946, naturalized, 1956. Asst. prof. Grad. Sch. Econs. and Bus., Athens, Greece, 1929-35, asso. prof., 1935-39, prof. bus. econs., 1939-54, pres., 1942-45, 51-53; vis. prof. Am. U., Washington, 1949-54, prof. bus. econs., 1954—, dir. Bus. Econs. Program, 1957—, asst. to dean, 1957-61, asst. dean, 1961-66, asso. dean Ph.D. Program, 1966-71, founder Doctoral Assn., 1965, also past rep. to Va., World Trade Conf. Mem. various govt. bds., Greece, 1930-46; del. UNRRA Conf., Geneva, 1946, mem. council, Washington, 1946-48; del. World Wheat Conf., Washington, 1947; econ. adviser UN, N.Y.C., 1947; mem. State Supply Mission, Washington, 1948-49. Bd. dirs. Fgn. Trade Program, 1956-61, Internat. Bus. Center, 1962-66. Served as lt. col. Greek Army, 1939-41. Recipient Gold medal Encyclopedia Hellanica, 1935; decorated Gold Cross, comdr. Royal Order Phoenix (Greece). Mem. Parnassus, Hellenic Soc. Econs., Atlantic Union, Atheneum, Am. Econs. Assn., Assn. for Edn. in Internat. Bus., Am. Assn. U. Profs., Am. Marketing Assn., Am. Accounting Assn., Soc. Internat. Studies. Hessiodosian, Rotarian. Author: Das System der Direkten Besteuerung in Griechenland, 1929; Introduction to Business Economics, 1935; Business and Industrial Organization, 1937, 2d edit., 1943; Economics of Enterprise, 1938; The Factors of Business Activity, 1939; Labor Management and Labor Relations, 1940, 2d edit., 1952; Business Economics and Management, 1953; Soviet Trade Resources and Foreign Trade Policies, 1961; others. Contbr. articles and chpts. to profl. publs. Home: 5161 Linnean Terrace NW Washington DC 20008

PICARDI, EGIDIO ALFRED, profl. engr.; b. N.Y.C., Mar. 6, 1922; s. Anthony S. and Marie (Guerriere) P.; B.S., Mass. Inst. Tech., 1947; m. Mary Elizabeth Long, Feb. 21, 1946; children—Mary Catherine (Mrs. Stephen B. Hilton), Anthony Charles, Alfred Phillip. Structural engr., various firms, Boston, 1947-51; asso. partner Bellman Gillett & Richards, Toledo, 1951-59, Skidmore, Owings & Merrill, Chgo., 1959-67; partner Perkins & Will Partnership, Washington, 1967—; v.p. Perkins & Will Corp., 1970—; partner Colin & Picardi, 1967—. Mem. Bd. Edn. Glenbrook Sch. Dist., Northbrook, Ill., 1965-66; mem. vis. com. in civil engring. Mass. Inst. Tech. Trustee Internat. Inst., Toledo, 1954-59, v.p., 1959. Fellow Am. Soc. C.E.; mem. Mass. Inst. Tech. Alumni Assn. (dir.). Clubs: Chesapeake (Irvington, Va.); University, Massachusetts Institute of Technology (Washington). Home: Rivendell White Stone VA 27578 Office: 1828 L St NW Washington DC 20036

PICCIONE, JOSEPH JAMES, lawyer; b. Lafayette, La., July 23, 1916; s. Sam and Mary (Mangiapane) P.; B.A., U. Southwestern La., 1937; LL.B., Tulane U., 1940, J.D., 1969; m. Wilma Kirkland, Dec. 17, 1946; children—Juanita, Jo Ann, Sylvia Beth, Cheryl Ann, James Kirk. Admitted to La. bar, 1940, since practiced law, Lafayette; partner Peter C. Piccione and Charles N. Wooten, 1952-71, sr. mem. Piccione, Piccione & Wooten, 1966—. Mem. Parish Mental Health Assn., pres. 1963-64; chmn. March of Dimes, 1956; chmn. Easter Seal sale, 1958; pres. Tb Assn., 1950-59; chmn. Crippled Children and Adults Assn., 1955-56; mem., acting chmn. Lafayette Capitol Improvement Com., 1965-70; mem. Cardinal Newman Forum, U. Southwestern La., chmn., 1965-67. Pres. bd. Cardinal Newman Found., U. Southwestern La., Lafayette, 1967-69. Served to capt. AUS, 1942-46. Recipient Medal Honor Am. Legion, 1935. Mem. Nat., La. trial attys. assns., Lafayette Parish (pres. 1958-59), 15th Jud. Dist. (pres. 1960-61), La. State (com. local bar assns.) bar assns., Am., La. trial lawyers assns., Judicature Soc., Order Coif. Kiwanian (pres. 1953). Club: Knife and Fork (pres. 1950). Bd. editors Tulane Law Review. Home: 2030 W St Mary Blvd Lafayette LA 70501 Office: 115 E Main St Lafayette LA 70501

PICHAL, HENRI THOMAS, electronics engr., inventor; b. Lambeth, London, Eng., Feb. 14, 1923; s. Henri T. and Mary (Conway) P.; student Internat. Corr. Schs., 1945-48; diploma Brit. I.R.E., London U., 1944; B.A., Masters in Psychology, Southend Tech. Coll., 1955; M.A., B.Sc., M.Sc., St. Petersburg Coll., 1963; student Alexander Hamilton Inst. Modern Bus., 1954-60; m. Eloise Vida Collum-Jones, Mar. 7, 1966; children by adoption-Christienne Conway, Henri Thomas III. Came to U.S., 1957, naturalized, 1962. Sr. staff Ekco Electronics, Southend on Sea-Essex, U.K., 1952-57; project engr. Gen. Dynamics/Electronics, Rochester, N.Y., 1957-59; program mgr. Electronic Communications, Inc., St. Petersburg, Fla., 1959-66; mem. staff Communications Devel. Center, Honeywell, Inc., St. Petersburg, 1966-70; chief engr. Fla. Communications, Inc., Clearwater, 1970-71; engring. mgr. time and frequency John Fluke Mfg. Co., Inc., Seattle, 1971—. Cons. in field. London County Council scholar, 1933, 37. Registered profl. engr., Fla. Mem. Am. Soc. Physics Tchrs., Inst. Physics, I.E.E.E. (sr.), Phys. Soc., Brit. I.R.E., TV Soc. Gt. Britain. Mason (32 deg. Shriner). Patentee in field. Home: 1759 Lakewood Dr S St Petersburg FL 33712 also 22015 99 Pl W Edmonds FL 98020

PICKARD, ANDREW EZRA, citrus grower; b. Toronto, Ont., Can., July 6, 1878; s. James and Mary Ann (Marquis) P.; came to U.S., 1890; ed. St. Cloud Tchrs. Coll., U. Minn., 1903; agr. and econs. courses U. Minn., 1905-10; m. Margaret Jane Armstrong, Aug. 30, 1903; children—Rowan Marquis, Jean (Mrs. Robert Scholer), Josephine (Mrs. Walt Killam), Elizabeth (Mrs. Julian Fishburne) m. 2d, Calla Marshall Shehyn, Sept. 3, 1954. Supt. city schs., Hinckley, Minn., 1903-12, Cokato, Minn., 1912-15; pres. Collegiate Bus. Inst., Mpls., 1915-26; citrus grower and processor, Orlando, Fla., 1926—; dir. Minute Maid. Pres. Citrus Sub-Exchange, 1934-44; dir. Lake Region Citrus Packing Assn., Orlando Citrus Growers, Citrus Mutual. Mem. Fla. Poultry Assn. (pres. 1936-40), Fla. Grape Growers (pres. 1940-50), Realty Bd. Orlando (pres. 1935), C. of C. (v.p. 1936). Republican. Methodist. Mason (32 deg., Shriner), Odd Fellow, Kiwanian (pres. Mpls. 1922, dist. gov. 1924). Author: Rural Education, 1915; Industrial Work for Boys; Industrial Work for Girls. Address: Jacaranda Route 3 Box 281 Winter Garden Rd Orlando FL 32802

PICKARD, JOSEPH ALLEN, supt. schs.; b. Tazewell, Ga., June 23, 1913; s. William Edwin and Clara E. (Hogg) P.; A.B., Mercer U., 1935; M.S., U. Ga., 1941; postgrad. Columbia U., U. Va., Auburn U., U. Ala. Elementary tchr. Edison, Ga., 1932-34, high sch. tchr., athletic coach, prin., 1935-36, supt., 1937-42; supt., Damascus, Ga., 1936-37; prin. jr. high sch., Lynchburg, Va., 1946-53, dir. instrn., 1953-57; supt. schs., Selma, Ala., 1957—. Dir., Am. Educators Ins. Co. Pres. United Community Services, 1967. Bd. dirs. Dallas County Scholarship Found., 1963—. Served with USAAF, 1942-46. Mem. Ala., Nat. edn. assns., Am. Assn. Sch. Adminstrs., Blue Key, Kappa Alpha, Phi Delta Kappa. Methodist. Home: 2019 Broad St Selma AL 36701 Office: PO Box F Selma AL 36701

PICKELL, CHARLES NORMAN, clergyman; b. Haddonfield, N.J., Dec. 18, 1927; s. William Norman and Ada Marie (Kelley) P.; B.A., Juniata Coll., 1949; B.D., Western Theol. Sem., Pitts., 1952; Th.M., Pitts.-Xenia Theol. Sem., 1957; postgrad. Harvard Div. Sch., 1959-60, Andover-Newton Theol. Sch., 1961-62; D.D., Sterling Coll., 1964; M.Div., Pitts. Theol. Sem., 1971; m. Christina L. Frazer, Mar. 11, 1972; children—Rachel Grace, Stuart Charles, Arthur John.

Ordained to ministry Presbyn. Ch. U.S.A., 1952; pastor Chelsea Presbyn. Ch., Atlantic City, 1952-55, 1st Presbyn. Ch., Monongahela, Pa., 1955-57, United Presbyn. Ch., Newton, Mass., 1957-63, Wallace Meml. United Presbyn. Ch., Hyattsville, Md., 1963-70, Vienna (Va.) Presbyn. Ch., 1970-—. Moderator, Presbytery of Boston, 1959, Synod of New Eng., 1960; chmn. ministerial relations Presbytery of Boston, 1961-63, chmn. nat. missions, 1962-63, chmn. evangelism Presbytery of Washington City, 1964-66, vice moderator, 1969, asst. stated clk., 1971; mem. Nat. Capital Union Presbytery, 1972-—; guest lectr. practical theology Gordon Div. Sch., Wenham, Mass., 1958-63, trustee, 1959-70. Incorporator, bd. dirs. Gordon-Conwell Theol. Sem., Hamilton, Mass., 1968-70; trustee Gordon Coll., Wenham, 1959-—, chmn. acad. affairs, 1965-—; trustee Westminster Coll., New Wilmington, Pa., 1957-61. Mem. Presbyn. Hist. Soc., Am. Soc. Ch. History, Fairfax County Council of Chs., Vienna-Oakton Ministerial Assn. Author: Preaching to Meet Men's Needs, 1958; Colossians, A Study Manual, 1965; Works Count Too, 1966; The Presbyterians, 1972. Editor, contbr.; Presbyterianism in New England, The Story of a Mission, 1962. Contbr. articles to religious publs., God.'s Minute, 1971. Office: Box 351 Vienna VA 22180 Home: 120 Park St NE Vienna VA 22180

PICKENS, ANDREW LEE, JR., mech. engr.; b. Greenville, S.C., Sept. 8, 1924; s. Andrew Lee and Belle (Meadors) P.; B.S. in Elec. Engring., U. S.C., 1949; postgrad. U. Tenn.; m. Anita Lee Stone, June 17, 1949; children—Anita Jane, Randi Ellen, Lisa Ann, Andrew Lee III. Draftsman, designer Buckeye Cotton Oil Co., Memphis, 1950-52, process engr., Cin., 1952-53; project engr. Buckeye Cellulose Corp., Foley, Fla., 1953-54, staff engr., 1954-72, mgr. design/engr. group, 1972-—. Mem. Big Bend Inland Naval Dist., Profl. Engrs. Conf. Bd. for Industry; mem. vis. com. U. Fla. Engring. Sch., 1967, 68, 69; adv. com. Fla. A. and M. U., 1968, 69, 70; mem. Pub. Relations Commn. for Engrs., 1971-—. Served with AC, AUS, 1942-46. Mem. Fla. Engring. Soc. (past pres.), Am. Soc. M.E., T.A.P.P.I., Water Pollution Control Fedn., Fla. Pollution Control Assn., Nat. Soc. Profl. Engrs., Phi Beta Kappa, Tau Beta Pi, Pi Kappa Alpha. Presbyn. Contbr. articles in field. Home: 121 Ridge Rd Perry FL 32347 Office: Perry FL 32347

PICKENS, CURTIS EDWARD, agr. co. exec.; b. Little Rock, Ark., July 28, 1931; s. Dallas and Hellen Irene (Birdsong) P.; B.S., Fla. So. Coll., 1957; m. Patricia Ellen Braymaire, Oct. 2, 1960; children—Kathey, Steven. Prodn. mgr. Roger Growers Coop, Winter Garden, Fla., 1957-—; exec. v.p. Citrus Helicopters Inc., 1966-—; pres. Winter Garden KOA Inc., 1970-—; pres. Citrus Grower Mgmt. Inc., Windermere, Fla., 1969-—; dir. West Orange Indsl. Park. Mem. Windermere Town Council, 1969-70. Bd. dirs. YMCA; trustee Endgewood Boys Ranch, 1971-—. Served with USNR, 1950-54. Recipient Outstanding Service award Fla. So. Coll., 1966. Rotarian (pres. 1969-70). Home: 618 Buller St Windermere FL 32786 Office: 279 Hwy 50 Winter Garden FL 32787

PICKENS, FRANKLIN ACE, legislator; b. Borger, Tex., Aug. 19, 1936; s. A.O. and Rhoda (Shaw) P.; B.B.A., U. Tex., 1958, J.D., 1962; m. Dianna Barnard, Dec. 17, 1966. Admitted to Tex. bar, 1962; asso. firm Shafer, Gilliland, Davis, Bunton & McCollum, Odessa; mem. Tex. Ho. of Reps., 1964-—. Dir. Ector County Abstract & Tile Co., Inc., Odessa, Tex.; incorporator Med. Center Devel., Inc., Odessa. Served with USNR, 1958-60. Named Outstanding Young Man of Odessa, 1969. Mem. Odessa C. of C., Odessa Jr. C. of C., State Bar Tex. (legislative com.), Delta Kappa Epsilon, Phi Alpha Delta. Democrat. Home: PO Box 1552 Odessa TX 79760 Office: First Nat Bank Odessa TX 79760

PICKENS, MARSHALL IVEY, trust adminstr.; b. Pineville, N.C., Jan. 23, 1904; s. Cornelius Miller and Emma (Watts) P.; A.B., Duke, 1925, M.A., 1926; LL.D. (hon.), Davidson Coll., 1962; m. Sarah Wakefield, Dec. 17, 1932; children—Lucinda Watts (Mrs. H. B. Lockwood, Jr.), Sarah Wakefield (Mrs. J. Worth Williamson, Jr.), Marshall Ivey. With The Duke Endowment, Charlotte, N.C., 1928-—, beginning as field rep., asst. sec., 1946-61, sec., 1961-66, asso. dir., 1948-50, dir. hosp. and child care sects., 1950-62, exec. dir. hosp. and child care sects., 1962-66, trustee, 1951-—, vice chmn. trustees, 1966-—; dir. Duke Power Co.; trustee Duke U. Past vice chmn. N.C. Med. Care Commn.; past pres. United Community Services, Charlotte, Mecklenburg County, N.C., Charlotte Social Planning Council; past pres., bd. mgrs. Meth. Home for the Aged; mem. bd. visitors Davidson (N.C.) Coll. Fellow Am. Coll. Hosp. Adminstrs. (hon.); mem. Am., N.C., S.C. hosp. assns., Am. Assn. Hosp. Cons., A.I.A. (hon. asso. mem.), Newcomen Soc., Omicron Delta Kappa, Pi Kappa Phi. Methodist. Clubs: Charlotte Country; Quail Hollow Country, Charlotte City. Home: 1730 Brandon Rd Charlotte NC 28207 Office: 200 S Tryon St Charlotte NC 28202

PICKETT, OWEN BRADFORD, legislator, lawyer; b. Richmond, Va., Aug. 31, 1930; s. Robert L. and Mary J. (Southworth) P.; B.S., Va. Poly. Inst., 1952; LL.B., U. Richmond, 1955; postgrad. U. Va., 1958-59; m. Sybil Catherine Kelly, Dec. 19, 1952; children—Laura Catherine, Karen Theresa, Mary Bradford. Admitted to Va. bar, 1955, D.C. bar, 1961; practiced in Richmond, 1955-56, Virginia Beach, 1965-—; practice pub. accounting, Richmond, 1956-58; asst. to v.p., treas. Tex. Utilities Co., Dallas, 1958-60; gen. counsel Gallant, Inc., Washington, 1960-63; controller Kettler Bros., Inc., Washington, 1964-65; mem. Va. Ho. Dels., 1972-—. Chmn. Virginia Beach City Democratic Com., 1967-71; mem. Dem. State Central Com. Va., 1968-—; mem. Hampton Rds. Area Com., 1969-70. C.P.A., Va. Mem. Am., Va., D.C., Virginia Beach bar assns., Va. Trial Lawyers Assn., Am. Inst. C.P.A.'s. Rotarian, Lion, Moose. Club: Ruritan (Princess Anne). Home: 321 Apasus Trail Virginia Beach VA 23452 Office: 2859 Virginia Beach Blvd Virginia Beach VA 23452

PICKETT, WILDA DOT PUMMILL (MRS. ORLIE WALTER PICKETT), educator; b. Winona, Mo.; d. Joseph Gilbert and Atlanta (Ware) Pummill; B.S., Central Mo., State Coll., 1932; M.A., Columbia, 1934, Ed.S., 1954, Ed.D., 1955; m. Orlie Walter Pickett, Jan. 1, 1941 (dec. Apr. 1951); 1 son, Joseph C.; 1 step-son, Richard O. Tchr. pub. schs., Winona, 1932-33, Kalamazoo, 1934-36, Dearborn, Mich., 1936-43; asst. prof. phys. edn. No. Ill. U., DeKalb, 1955-56; chmn. women's phys. edn. U. No. Ariz., Flagstaff, 1956-59; supr. student tchrs. Auburn U., Ala., 1959-62, U. Md., College Park, 1962-66; prof. edn., supr. student tchrs. Troy State U., Ala., 1966-70, chmn. health and phys. edn., prof. ednl. founds., 1970-—. Acad. coordinator Ala. Pvt. Sch. Assn. Mem. Delta Psi Kappa, Pi Lambda Theta, Delta Kappa Gamma, Kappa Delta Pi. Home: 128 Glenwood Av Troy AL 36081

PICKLE, CECYL LAMAR, lawyer; b. Jacksonville, Fla., June 8, 1925; s. Henry A. and Amanda (Houston) P.; student Fla. So. Coll., 1946-48; LL.B., U. Fla., 1951; m. Margot Reinburg, June 23, 1951; children—Jean Carol, Bruce Henry. Admitted to Fla. bar, 1951; claims adjuster U.S. Fidelity and Guaranty Co., Miami, Fla., 1951-53; practiced in Miami, 1953-—; asso. firm Fowler, White, Gillen, Yancey and Humkey, 1953-55, Knight, Underwood, Peters, Hoeveler and Pickle, 1955-—. Trustee, adv. council Bapt. Hosp., Miami, 1962-66. Served with USAAF, 1944-45. Mem. Fla. Bar (vice chmn. continuing legal edn. 1971), Am., Dade County bar assns., Internat. Assn. Ins. Counsel, Dade County Defense Bar (dir. 1965-66, 70, treas. 1971, pres. elect 1972), Phi Alpha Delta, Lambda Chi Alpha. Democrat, Baptist. Clubs: Coral Gables Country, Kiwanis (pres. 1965). Contbr. articles profl. jours. Home: 3401 Toledo St Coral Gables FL 33134 Office: Ingraham Bldg Miami FL 33131

PICKLE, J. J., congressman; b. Roscoe, Tex., Oct. 11, 1913; s. J. B. and Mary P.; B.A., U. Tex.; children—Peggy (Mrs. James Norris), Dick McCarroll and Graham McCarroll. Area dir. Nat. Youth Adminstrn., 1938-41; co-organizer Sta. KVET, Austin, Tex.; pub.relations and advt. bus.; dir. Tex. Democratic Exec. Com., 1957-60; mem. Tex. Employment Commn., 1961-63; mem. 88th-92d congresses 10th Dist. Tex. Served with USNR, World War II. Home: 3900 Watson Pl Washington DC 20016 Office: Cannon House Office Bldg Washington DC 20515

PICKRELL, KENNETH LEROY, plastic surgeon; b. Old Forge, Pa., June 6, 1910; s. Thomas and Anna May (Williams) P.; B.S., Franklin and Marshall Coll., 1931; M.D., Johns Hopkins, 1935; m. Katharine Council, June 11, 1935; children—Judith, Katharine Lee, Anna May, Elizabeth. Fellow surgery Johns Hopkins Hosp., 1935-36, successively instr. pathology, instr. neurosurgery, instr. plastic surgery, instr. gen. surgery, asso. surgery, 1936-44; asst. prof. plastic surgery Duke U. Sch. Medicine and Hosp., Durham, N.C., 1944-46, asso. prof. plastic surgery, 1946-50, prof. plastic and reconstructive surgery, 1950-—; cons. plastic surgeon VA hosps., Durham, Fayetteville, N.C., Womack Army Hosp., Ft. Bragg, N.C. Diplomate Am. Bd. Plastic Surgery (chmn. 1962-63), Am. Bd. Surgery. Fellow A.C.S., So. Surg. Assn.; mem. Soc. U. Surgeons, Am. Assn. U. Profs., Am. Soc. Surgery of Hand, Am. Soc. Plastic and Reconstructive Surgery (pres. 1960), Am. Assn. Plastic Surgeons, Am. Surg. Assn., Internat. Soc. Surgery, Japanese Soc. Plastic Surgeons. Contbr. sect. Principles and Practice of Surgery (Lea and Febiger), 1954. Contbr. articles to surg. jours., chpts. to books. Home: 3 Sylvan Rd Durham NC 27701 Office: Duke U Hosp Durham NC 27701

PICKRELL, THOMAS RICHARD, petroleum co. exec.; b. Jermyn, Tex., Dec. 30, 1926; s. Mont Bolt and Martha Alice (Dodson) P.; B.B.A., N. Tex. State U., 1951, M.B.A., 1952; postgrad. Ohio State U., 1954-55, Ind. U., 1967; m. Earline Bowen, Sept. 9, 1950; children—Thomas Wayne, Michael Bowen, Kent Richard, Paul Keith. Accountant, Hunt Oil Co., Dallas, 1952-54; instr. Ohio State U., 1954-55; internal auditor Continental Oil Co., Ponca City, Okla., 1955-61, dir. coordinating and planning, 1961-62, mgr. accounting, Houston, 1965-67, asst. controller, Ponca City, 1967-—; asst. prof. Pkla. State U., 1962-63; controller Douglas Oil Co., Los Angeles, 1963-65. Sr. lectr. U. So. Cal., 1964-65. Bd. dirs. Kay Guidance Clinic Found, Ponca City, Ponca City YMCA. Served with AUS, 1945-46; ETO. Mem. Financial Execs. Inst. (dir., pres.), Am. Inst. C.P.A.'s, Am. Accounting Assn., C. of C., Am. Petroleum Inst. (accounting research com. 1965-—), Beta Gamma Sigma, Beta Alpha Psi. Presbyn. Rotarian. Home: 2205 Meadowbrook St Ponca City OK 74601 Office: Box 1267 Ponca City OK 74601

PICO, ALBERTO A., nat. guard officer; b. Coamo, P.R., Aug. 23, 1918; s. Carlos and Eulalia (Leon) P.; student La. State U.; B.A., U. P.R.; m. Mignon Valls, May 9, 1942; 1 dau., Mignon (Mrs. Walter Vivaldi). Served to capt. AUS, 1940-45; to maj., 1950-53. Decorated Bronze Star, Mil. Cross Antonio Marino (Colombia). Mem. N.G. Assn. U.S., P.R. N.G. (adj. gen. for P.R. 1969-—), U.S. Custom Assn., Armor Assn. U.S., Assn. U.S. Army, Nat. Customs Service Assn., Phi Eta Mu. Clubs: Casino (Coamo); Deportivo de Ponce, Ponce Yacht and Fishing; P.R. Nat. Guard Officers. Address: Avenida Ponce de Leon Puerta De Tierra San Juan PR 00906*

PICOTT, J. RUPERT, assn. exec.; b. Suffolk, Va., Aug. 25, 1910; s. William M. and Mary V. (White) P.; A.B., Va. Union U., 1932, Ph.D., 1950; Ed.M., Temple U., 1940; m. Altia Hodges, June 19, 1937; children—J. Rupert, Hodges A. High sch. tchr., South Boston, Va., 1923-33; br. mgr. Jour. & Guide, Newport News (Va.), 1933-34; tchr. Huntington High Sch., Newport News, 1934-37; prin. John Marshall Sch., 1937-43; instr. Hampton Inst., 1943-44; exec. sec. Va. Tchrs. Assn., Richmond, 1944-67; nat. pres. Assn. Study Negro Life and History, Washington, 1967-70. Mem. Commn. Religion and Race, United Presbyn. Ch. U.S.A., also mem. permanent com. Christian relations. Mem. N.E.A. (asst. dir. div. membership devel.), Am. Tchrs. Assn. (pres. 1964), Richmond C. of C., Bus. and Profl. Men, Am. Assn. Sch. Admistrs., So. Conf. State Tchrs. Assns. (past chmn.), Frontiers Am., Nat. Alumni Assn. (past pres.), Alpha Phi Alpha. Democrat. Presbyn. Editor Va. Edn. Bull., 1944-67. Home: 800 Edge Hill Rd Richmond VA 23222 Office: 1201 16th St NW Washington DC 20036

PICOU, LEON ADAM, JR., lawyer; b. Garyville, La., Oct. 3, 1912; s. Leon Adam and Mary (Tufant) P.; B.A., Southwestern State U., Lafayette, La., 1936; J.D., La. State U., 1951; m. Orel Palmer, July 17, 1937; children—Saundra (Mrs. W. Lee Overton), Cynthia (Mrs. Stanley Excel Branton). High sch. tchr., Destrehan, La., 1936-40; dir. pub. welfare, Lafourche Parish, La., 1940-41; asst. mgr. Wesco Paints Inc., Good Hope, La., 1941-42; La. state parole and probation officer, 1942-44, 45-48; admitted to La. bar, 1951, since practiced in St. Francisville. Served with M.C., AUS, 1944-45. Mem. La. Municipal Assn. City Atty. (pres.), Holy Name Soc. (past pres.), Gamma Eta Gamma. Roman Catholic (chmn. cemetery com.). Lion. Home and office: Ferdinand St St Francisville LA 70775

PIERAS, JAIME, JR., Republican nat. committeeman, lawyer; b. San Juan, P.R., May 19, 1924; s. Jaime and Ines (Lopez-Cepero) P.; B.A., Catholic U. Am., 1945; LL.B., Georgetown U., 1948; m. Elsie Castaner, June 6, 1953; children—Awilda Ines, Jaime Roberto. Asso. Luis E. Dubon Law Office, 1949-52, Hartzell, Fernandez & Novas Law Office, 1953-59; partner Pieras & Torryella, 1959-—. Gen. counsel P.R. Tourism Bur., 1953. Mem. finance com. San Juan Electoral Campaign, 1960, chmn., 1964; alternate del. Rep. Nat. Conv., 1964, del., 1968, del., chmn. delegation, 1972; chmn. finance com. Statehood Rep. Party, P.R.; mem. polit. action com.; Rep. nat. committeeman, 1963-—; pres. P.R. Rep. Nat. Com., 1972. Served with AUS, 1946-47. Mem. Am., P.R. bar assns., Fed. Bar Assn. P.R., Cath. U. Am. Alumni Assn., Georgetown U. Alumni Assn., C. of C., K.C., Rotarian. Club: San Juan Country. Home: 1 Washington Av Condado San Juan PR 00907 Office: P O Box 507 Hato Rey PR 00919

PIERCE, ALLAN K., physician, educator; b. Houston, 1931; M.D., Baylor U., 1955. Intern, Univ. Hosps. of Cleve., 1955-56; resident Parkland Meml Hosp., Woodlawn Hosp., Dallas, 1958-61, fellow in chest diseases, 1961-62; prof. medicine U. Tex. Southwestern Med. Sch., Dallas, also chief pulmonary diseases. Served to capt., M.C., USAF, 1956-58. Mem. A.M.A., Am. Thoracic Soc. Home: 3537 Villanova St Dallas TX 75225*

PIERCE, ALLIN HUGH, fed. judge; b. Graceville, Minn., Jan. 18, 1897; s. Charles Sumner and Isabelle (Sanderson) P.; A.B., Swarthmore Coll., 1919; J.D., cum laude, U. Chgo., 1923; m. Florence Bennet, Aug. 15, 1938; children—Isabel Sanderson, Allin Hugh. Admitted to Ill. bar, 1923, N.Y. bar, 1937; practiced in Chgo., 1923-28; instr. Loyola U. Law Sch., Chgo., 1925; spl. atty. Bur. Internal Revenue, 1928-35; asso. Carter, Ledyard & Milburn, N.Y.C., 1936-43; mem. McDermott, Will & Emery, Chgo., 1943-45; pvt. practice, Chgo., 1946-55; judge Tax Ct. U.S., 1955-—; lectr. fed. taxation bar assns., univs., profl. assns. Served as aviation cadet US NRF, 1918. Mem. Am., Ill., Chgo. (chmn. com. fed. taxation 1949) bar assns., Assn. Bar City N.Y., Chgo. Fed. Tax Forum, Swarthmore Coll. Alumni Assn. (pres. 1939-40), Order of Coif, Delta Upsilon, Phi Delta Phi, Delta Sigma Rho. Republican. Methodist. Mason. Clubs: Columbia Country, Nat. Lawyers. Home: 3700 University Av Washington DC 20016 Office: Tax Ct US Washington DC 20004

PIERCE, ALVIN EDGAR, architect; b. Lampasas, Tex., Sept. 17, 1926; s. Julian Laural and Ruby Willa (Stewart) P.; student U. Tex., 1947-50; U. Houston, 1952-53; m. Bonnie Love Jobe, Oct. 3, 1969; children—Jan Denise, Bambi Gaye; step-children—James O. Bowling, Jr., Nancy Jolyn Bowling, David Lindsey Bowling. Draftsman, Brown & Root, Inc., Houston, 1951-54, Irving Klein, architect, 1954-57; sr. draftsman Boone Amyx, architect, 1957-58; sr. draftsman Am. Oil Co., New Orleans, 1958-60; sr. architect Champlin Petroleum Co., Ft. Worth, 1960-70, dir. design and constrn., 1970-—; practice architecture, Ft. Worth, 1967-—; cons. Served with AUS, 1945-46; ETO. Recipient Grand Prize in Architecture, Petroleum Industry, State of Okla., 1971. Registered architect, Tex. Mem. A.I.A., Tex. Soc. Architects, (chpt. chmn. continuing edn. and internship 1968-—). Republican. Mem. Christian Ch. Home: Route 2 Box 36 Aledo TX 76008 Office: 5301 Camp Bowie Blvd Fort Worth TX 76107

PIERCE, CHARLES EDWARD, newspaper editor; b. Augusta, Ga., May 24, 1920; s. John Walton and Ethel (Kalbfleisch) P.; student Atlanta Law Sch., 1940-41, U. Ga., 1946-47; m. Clyde McGiboney Boswell, July 2, 1943; 1 dau., Emily Rebecca. Staff photographer Atlanta Jour., 1947-51; mem. staff Miami (Fla.) News, 1951-59, asst. mng. editor, 1958-62, mng. editor, 1962-68; asst. mng. editor, dir. graphics Memphis Comml. Appeal, 1968-69; mng. editor Sarasota (Fla.) Herald Tribune, 1969-—. Active local United Fund, A.R.C. Served with AUS, World War II. Mem. Dade-Miami C. of C., Miami Press Photographers Assn. (past pres.), Fla. A.P. Mng. Editors (pres. 1967-68), Sigma Delta Chi (pres. 1967-68). Home: 2549 Colorado St Sarasota FL 33577 Office: 801 S Tamami Trail Sarasota FL 33577

PIERCE, CLEVELAND CARROLL, banker; b. Opp, Ala., Jan. 3, 1921; s. Grover Cleveland and Georgia B. (Carroll) P.; student Marion Inst., 1935-39; La. State U. Sch. Banking, 1960-62; m. Kathryn Eloise Mathews, Dec. 9, 1939; children—Caroline (Mrs. Roger F. Etheridge), Louise (Mrs. Rowayne Harper), Rebecca (Mrs. Ronald McLeod), George C. With First Nat. Bank Opp, 1939-—, asst. cashier, 1945-49, v.p., cashier, 1949-64, pres., dir., 1964-—. Treas. City of Opp Bd. Edn., 1971-—, Covington County Bd. Edn., 1971-—. Trustee Mizell Meml. Hosp., Opp, 1968-—; bd. dirs. Opp Hist. Soc., Covington County Mental Health Assn., Covington County Econ. Devel. Bd. Served with Transport Service, AUS, 1943-46; ETO. Mem. Ala., Am., Independent bankers assns. Mason (Shriner). Clubs: Civitan (dir. 1969-70), Country (Opp). Home: 204 E Ida Av Opp AL 36467 Office: PO Drawer A Opp AL 36467

PIERCE, CLIFFORD DAVIS, JR., lawyer; b. Memphis, Sept. 9, 1934; s. Clifford Davis and Isabelle (Curran) P.; B.A., Yale, 1956; LL.B., U. Va., 1961; m. Margaret Trumbull, Apr. 16, 1966. Admitted to Tenn. bar, 1961; partner law firm Pierce, Rice, Bratcher & Pierce, Memphis, 1961-—; mem. Tenn. Ho. of Reps., 1963-65; asst. city atty., Memphis, 1964-—. Bd. dirs. Tenn. Mental Health Assn., 1962-66; chmn. Civic Research Com., Inc., 1966-—. Served to lt. (j.g.), USNR, 1956-58. Mem. Am., Memphis, Shelby County bar assns., State Bar Tenn., Beta Theta Pi, Phi Alpha Delta. Democrat. Episcopalian. Home: 684 Center Dr Memphis TN 38112 Office: First Am Bank Bldg Memphis TN 38103

PIERCE, EARL BOYD, lawyer; b. Fort Gibson, Okla., Jan. 29, 1904; s. James M. and Nancy (Anderson) P.; LL.B., U. Okla., 1928; m. Ruth Clark, Aug. 26, 1923; 1 dau., Norma Jo (Mrs. Harry M. Shytles, Jr.). Admitted to Okla. bar, 1928, since practiced in Muskogee; asst. county atty. Muskogee County, 1931-33; state legal adviser NRA., 1933-34, litigation atty., Chgo., 1934-35; atty. Dept. Interior, 1935-36, Dept. Justice, Washington, 1936-37; prodn. specialist, expeditor Task Force Materiel, Ordnance Dept., U.S. Army, 1942-44; Cherokee tribal atty., 1948-62, gen. counsel Cherokee Nation, 1963-—. Bd. dirs. Five Civilized Tribes Mus., Cherokee Found., Hall of Fame for Famous Am. Indians. Mem. Am., Okla. bar assns., Okla. Hist. Soc. (dir.), Am. Trial Lawyers Assn., Cherokee Hist. Soc. Methodist. Mason (32 deg., Shriner). Club: Muskogee Country. Spearheaded successful judgements in favor of Cherokee Nation for treaty violations. Home: 1003 S Terrace Muskogee OK 74401 Office: PO Box 498 Fort Gibson OK 74434 also 1026 17th St NW Washington DC 20036

PIERCE, ELLA JANET, educator; b. Colerain, N.C.; d. Franklin and Anastasia (Garrett) Pierce; A.B., Meredith Coll., 1921; B.M.T., So. Baptist Theol. Sem., 1923; postgrad. Columbia, 1929, Harvard, summer 1937, 38; M.A., Cornell U., 1933, Ph.D., 1936. Mem. faculty Mars Hill Coll., 1925-65, chmn. dept. English, 1938-65; chmn. dept. English, Chowan Coll., Murfreesboro, N.C., 1965-—. Instr., Blue Mountain Coll., Miss., 1939, Wake Forest And Meredith, summer, 1936-37; counselor Y.W.A., 1926-29, dean women, 1930-36; counselor Vols. for Christ, 1936-65; faculty adviser Baptist Student Union, 1945-63, chmn. Honor Point System, 1937-40, chmn. library com. 1945-65. Mem. Nat. Council Tchrs. English (membership chmn. eastern div.), Murfreesboro Hist. Assn., Kappa Nu Sigma, Delta Kappa Gamma (v.p. Gamma chpt., chmn. scholarship, program com.). Home: 14 Liberty St Murfreesboro NC 27855

PIERCE, GEORGE CHESTER, communications co. exec.; b. Alexandria, Va., May 16, 1930; s. Chester Gaver and Jeanette (Cochran) P.; B.S. in Econ. and Engring., Mass. Inst. Tech., 1952; m. Lois Marie Bowden, Feb. 2, 1952; children—Rebecca (Mrs. Michael E. Bradley), Arnold, Stephen. Controller, Chesapeake Instrument Corp., Shadyside, Md., 1954-55; asst. to dir. EM div. Atlantic Research Corp., Alexandria, 1952-54, asst. dir., 1955-62, dir. Teleproducts div., 1962-64; chmn. bd., chief exec. officer, treas. Pulse Communications, Inc., Falls Church, Va., 1964-—; dir. Geotronics, Inc., Sci. Communication, Inc., Alexandria Amusement Corp. Mem. Washington Bd. Trade. Club: Mass. Inst. Tech. Alumni (sec. 1970-71) (Washington). Home: 3409 Sterling Av Alexandria VA 22304 Office: 5714 Columbia Pike Falls Church VA 22041

PIERCE, GEORGE FOSTER, JR., architect; b. Dallas, June 22, 1919; s. George Foster and Hallie Louise (Crutchfield) P.; student So. Meth. U., 1937-39; B.A., Rice U., 1942, B.Arch., 1943; diplome d'architecture, Ecoles d'Art Americaines, Ecole des Beaux-Arts, 1958; m. Betty Jean Reistle, Oct. 17, 1942; children—Ann Louise (Mrs. Robert G. Arnett), George Foster III, Nancy Reistle. Pvt. practice architecture, Houston, 1946-—; sr. partner G. Pierce, Goodwin & Flanagan; instr. archtl. design Rice U., 1945, preceptor in dept. architecture, 1962-67; projects include 8 bldgs. Rice U. Campus, So. Meth. U. Student Center, Houston Mus. Natural Sci. and Planetarium, 1st Nat. Bank of San Angelo, Houston Intercontinental Airport, S.W. Bell Telephone Co. office bldg., Petroleum Club of Houston, Houston State Psychiat. Inst., U. Houston Student Center, 500 bed teaching hosp. U. Tex. Med. Sch., Galveston, Two Houston

Center. Mem. exec. bd. Sam Houston area council Boy Scouts Am.; mem. Mayor's Com. on Zoning, 1961. Past pres., chmn. bd. trustees Contemporary Arts Mus., Houston, pres. Tex. Archtl. Found. Served as ensign USNR, World War II. Recipient Outstanding Young Texan award Jr. C. of C., 1954; also numerous nat., state, local archtl. awards for design. Fellow A.I.A. (past nat. chmn. com. on aesthetics, com. chpt. affairs), Sociedad Architectos Mexicanos (hon.); mem. Tex. Soc. Architects (past pres., v.p., sec. treas.), Houston Jr. C. of C. (past officer, dir.), Kappa Alpha. Methodist. Clubs: Houston Country, Petroleum (Houston). Home: 5211 Green Tree Rd Houston TX 77027 Office: PO Box 13319 Houston TX 77019

PIERCE, HARRY BROOKE, beverage co. exec.; b. Trion, Ga., Feb. 12, 1922; s. Harry Lewis and Vennie Mae (Greenwood) P.; B.S. in Edn., U. Ga., 1943; M.A., George Peabody Coll., 1959; m. Juanita Burkett, July 25, 1948; children—Cheryl Ann, Susan Lanier. Athletic dir., coach Summerville (Ga.) High Sch., 1946-50, Gordon Lee High Sch., Chickamauga, Ga., 1950-59; supt. Chickamauga City Schs., 1959-66; pres., co-owner Royal Crown Bottling Co., Chattanooga, 1966—, also dir. Served to capt. USMCR, 1943-46. Decorated Purple Heart. Mem. V.F.W. Democrat. Baptist (deacon). Lion, Mason. Club: Chickamauga Fly & Bait Casting (pres.). Home: 4416 Lilac Lane Chattanooga TN 37411 Office: 201 Broad St Chattanooga TN 37402

PIERCE, HUGH VERNON, banker; b. Jackson, Miss., Oct. 12, 1925; s. Hugh Victor and Effie (Sullivan) P.; B.S., Miss. State Coll., 1949; grad. Am. Inst. Banking, 1959, Sch. Banking of South, La. State U., 1965; m. Patricia Parker, June 20, 1953; children—Vernon, Celeste, James. With First Nat. Bank Jackson, 1949—, v.p. computer service dept., 1966—. Treas. Jackson Jr. C. of C., 1954. Treas. Hinds County chpt. Nat. Found., 1960; asst. treas. Middle Miss. council Girl Scouts U.S.A., 1965. Served with USAF, 1949. Mem. Am. Inst. Banking (pres. Jackson 1959, asso. councilman Miss., 1960-62), Nat. Assn. Bank Auditors, Comptrollers and Operations (pres. Jackson 1966), Nat. Assn. Accountants, Kappa Sigma, Alpha Psi Omega. Methodist (steward). Club: Capitol Civitan (treas. 1964) (Jackson). Home: 2209 Paden St Jackson MS 39204 Office: 248 E Capitol St Jackson MS 39205

PIERCE, JOHN EUGENE, educator; b. Hopewell, Va., Dec. 16, 1917; s. John Von and Della Louise (Smith) P.; B.A., U. Tenn., 1943, M.S., 1948; Ph.D. in Econs., U. Pa., 1956; m. Helen Elizabeth Harris, July 10, 1948; 1 son, Douglas Kyle. Supr., auditor U.S. Engr. Corps., N.Y.C., 1941-42; instr. econs. U. Tenn., 1947-48, U. Fla., Gainesville, 1950-55; asst. prof. bus. adminstrn. So. Meth. U., 1955; asst. prof. finance dept. U. Tenn., Knoxville, 1955-67, Faculty fellow, 1962-66; prof., chmn. dept. bus. adminstrn. Augusta (Ga.) Coll., 1967—. Served to lt. (j.g.) USNR, 1942-46. S.S. Huebner Found. for Ins. Edn. fellow 1948-56. Mem. Am. Econ. Assn., Regional, So. Regional sci. assns., Am. Finance Assn., Beta Gamma Sigma. Author: Development of Comprehensive Insurance for the Household, 1958; Structure of the Nashville Economy, 1969. Contbr. articles to profl. publs. Home: Apt F-5 Magnolia Villa Augusta GA 30904

PIERCE, MARGARET HUNTER, govt. ofcl.; b. Weedsport, N.Y., June 30, 1910; d. Thomas Murray and Ruby (Sanders) Hunter; B.A., Mt. Holyoke Coll., 1932; J.D., N.Y.U., 1939; m. John R. Pierce, Nov. 4, 1950 (div. May 1959); 1 dau., Barbara Hunter. Admitted to N.Y. bar, 1941, D.C. bar, 1958; atty. Office Alien Property Custodian, Washington, 1942-43, 45, Office Solicitor, Dept. Labor, 1943-45, NLRB, 1946, 47-48; atty.-adviser U.S. Ct. Claims, 1947-48, 48-59, reporter of decisions 1959-68; commr. U.S. Indian Claims Commn., 1968—. Mem. D.C. (ct. claims com., 1958—, mil. law com. 1967—), Fed. (Indian Law com. 1955—), Am., Womens bar assns. Presbyn. Mem. Order Eastern Star (ex-officio mem. Women's adv. com.). Club: Zonta (Washington). Home: 3829 Garfield St NW Washington DC 20007 Office: 1730 K Street NW Washington DC 20006

PIERCE, MARGARET K. (MRS. WALTER MORGAN PIERCE), club woman; b. Washington, Dec. 20; d. John Daniel and Ellen (O'Brien) Kelliher; student pub. and parochial schs.; m. Walter Morgan Pierce, Sept. 27, 1951; stepchildren—William N., Walter M., L. Staples. Sec. Morgan-MacNeal Co., Inc., Miami, Fla., 1959—. Past v.p. Miami chpt. Pearl S. Buck Found. Mem. Vizcaya, Young Patronesses of Opera (pres. 1962-63), Theatre Arts League (pres. 1960-62), Miami Opera Guild (trustee), chmn. Heart Ball, 1968, Ballet Ball, 1969, Opera Ball, 1970), Miami Ballet Soc. (dir.), Heart Assn. Miami (dir.), Miami Heart Inst. (women's aux.), Humane Soc. Democrat. Presbyn. Clubs: La Gorce Country (Miami Beach); Riviera Country (Coral Gables); Flamingo Dinner, Beach Colony, Palm Bay (Miami); Farmington Country (Charlottesville, Va.). Home: 900 SW 92d Av Miami FL 33156

PIERCE, THOMAS FLOYD, retail trade exec.; b. Bartlett, Tex., Feb. 2, 1916; s. Floyd Nunez and Ellen Gertrude (Wood); student U. Tex., 1934-38; m. Iris Eilers, Mar. 20, 1947; 1 son, Thomas Eilers (dec.). Partner, F.N. Pierce & Co., cotton mchts., Taylor, Tex., 1945-52; pres. Delta Constrn. Co., Taylor, 1952-64; partner Williamson County Equipment Co., Inc., retail farm equipment, automobiles, Taylor, 1943-69, chmn. bd., 1969—; dir. City Nat. Bank, Taylor. Mem. Sch. Bd., Taylor, 1964-70. Served with AC, USNR, 1942-45. Decorated D.F.C., Air medal. Presbyn. Home: 117 E 6th St Taylor TX 76574 Office: 1426 N Main St Taylor TX 76574

PIERCE, VIRGINIA ALLEN (MRS. KENDRICK E. PIERCE), banker; b. Monticello, Ark.; d. Andrew Emmett and Florence (Grisham) Allen; student Atlanta Bus. Coll., 1927; m. Kendrick E. Pierce, Nov. 8, 1936 (dec. Aug. 1960); children—William Allen, Jackson E. With Union Bank & Trust Co., Monticello, 1942—, asst. cashier 1945-58, v.p., 1958—. Chmn., Drew County Savs. Bonds, 1960-65; active various civic and philanthropic orgns. Mem. Nat. Assn. Bank Women, Drew County Hist. Soc., P.E.O. Presbyn. (elder). Home: 220 W Union St Monticello AR 71655 Office: PO Box 270 Monticello AR 71655

PIERCE, WALTER MORGAN, ins. exec.; b. Christiansburg, Va., May 19, 1898; s. William Luther and Julia (Baird) P.; B.S., Va. Tech., 1920; m. Margaret Marie Kelliher, Sept. 27, 1951; children—William N., L. Staples, Walter M., Jr. Elec. engr. Westinghouse Elec. Co., 1920-21; spl. agt. Aetna Life Ins. Co., 1921-24; propr. Walter M. Pierce Ins., Miami, Fla., 1924—; pres. Morgan-McNeal Corp. Mem. bd. of citizens bd. U. Miami; bd. dirs. Miami Heart Inst., Heart Assn. of Greater Miami; bd. advisers Drs. Hosp. Served with U.S. Army, 1918-19. Life mem. Million Dollar Round Table. Mem. Miami Life Underwriters (past pres.), Gen. Agts. and Mgrs. of Miami (past pres.), Gen. Agts. and Mgrs. Fla., Am. Legion, Nat. Conf. Christians and Jews, Miami Opera Guild (bd. trustees). Democrat. Presbyn. Clubs: Palm Bay (Miami); Kiwanis, Elks, Beach Colony (past pres.), Flamingo Dinner, LaGorce Country, Riviera Country, Rod and Reel, Surf (bd. dirs.), Farmington Golf and Country, South Miami Riding (pres.). Home: 5955 Pine Tree Dr Miami Beach FL 33140 Office: 2445 W Flagler St Miami FL 33135

PIERCE, WILLIAM FRANKLIN, dentist; b. Dyersburg, Tenn., July 1, 1936; s. William Franklin and Alma Louise (Switzer) P.; B.A., Vanderbilt U., 1958; D.D.S., U. Tenn., 1962; m. Mary Lucile Whelchel, Dec. 27, 1961; children—William Franklin IV, David Jordan, Mark Thomas. Extern, Tenn. Pub. Health, 1962; practice of dentistry, Dyersburg, Tenn., 1965—; mem. staff Parkview Hosp., 1965—. Vice pres. Community Concerts, 1969-71; vice chmn. Dyer County Bd. Edn., 1970—; pres. Dyer County Easter Seal, 1965-68. Served with USNR, 1962-65. Mem. Tenn. Council Dental Health, 7th Dist. Dental Soc. (sec., treas. 1970—), Dyersburg Jr. C. of C. (v.p. 1967-68), Am. Acad. Dentistry, Pierre Fauchard Acad. Kiwanian (bd. dirs.), Moose. Club: Dyersburg Country. Home: 2124 Morning Rd Dyersburg TN 38024 Office: 520 East Parkview St Dyersburg TN 38024

PIERRE, DALLAS, dentist; b. Charenton, La., June 9, 1933; s. Russell and Eva (Larry) P.; B.S., Prairie View A. and M. Coll., 1955; M.S., Tex. So. U., 1963; D.D.S., U. Tex., 1968; m. Carol Ann Yates, Aug. 27, 1960; 1 son, James Darian. Gen. practice dentistry, Lufkin, Tex., 1968—; dir. Nat. Security Bank, Tyler, Tex. Pres., Pub. Relations Orgn. for Community Laity Improvement, Lufkin, 1970—; chmn. adv. com. Manpower, Edn. and Tng. Center, Lufkin, 1971—. Bd. dirs. East Tex. Boy Scout Found., Angelina County Heart Fund, Lufkin Sheltered Workshop and Opportunity Center. Served with USAF, 1956-60. Mem. Nat. Platform Assn., U. Tex., Tex. Dental Br. alumni assns., Citizens C. of C. (bd. dirs. 1969—); Eastex Med. Dental Pharm. Assn. (pres. 1971—), Phi Beta Sigma. Baptist (deacon 1970—). Home: 106 McMullen St Lufkin TX 75901 Office: 809 Kurth Dr PO Box 1236 Lufkin TX 75901

PIERSON, JOSEPH HUNTER, banker; b. Natchitoches, La., July 31, 1925; s. Guthrie H. and Ruth (Williams) P.; student La. Poly. Inst., 1943-44; B.S., Northwestern State Coll., 1948; m. Margaret Helen Barnes, May 1, 1948; children—Margaret Ruth, Joseph Hunter, Robert Wade, Susan Fayre. Dep. sheriff Civil Dept., Natchitoches Parish (La.), 1948-49; asst. cashier City Bank & Trust Co., Natchitoches, 1949-59, v.p., dir., 1959—; dir. First Fed. Savs. & Loan Assn. Commr. finance City of Natchitoches, 1960—. Served to ensign USNR, 1943-46. Mem. Methodist (chmn. trustees 1968-71; treas. Natchitoches dist. 1971—). Rotarian. Home: 219 Whitfield St Natchitoches LA 71457 Office: PO Box 246 Natchitoches LA 71457

PIERSON, ROSCOE MITCHELL, librarian; b. Crenshaw, Miss., Sept. 21, 1921; s. Roscoe P. and Esther Virginia (Mitchell) P.; B.A., Centre Coll., 1947; M.A., U. Ky., 1950; postgrad. Lexington Theol. Sem. 1950-53; m. Dorothy McCowan, July 15, 1944; children—Eugenia (Mrs. Eugene Attkisson). Ordained to ministry Disciples of Christ Ch., 1955; librarian Lexington (Ky.) Theol. Sem., 1950—; instr. U. Ky., 1955-65; partner Erasmus Press, 1964-66. Served with USAAF, 1941-45. Decorated D.F.C., Air medal with three oak leaf clusters. Am. Theol. Library Assn. sr. librarian fellow, 1968. Mem. Am. Theol. Library Assn. (pres. 1966-67), Ky. Library Assn. (pres. 1964), Sigma Chi, Phi Beta Kappa. Contbr. articles in field to profl. jours. Home: 624 Seattle Dr Lexington KY 40503 Office: 631 S Limestone St Lexington KY 40508

PIGG, MARVIN E., accountant; b. Gunter, Tex., Sept. 7, 1920; s. John William and Eva (Etheridge) P.; student Murray State Coll., 1937-38, Freed-Hardeman Coll., 1938-39, Okla. U., 1939-41; m. Jeane Ann Bond, Jan. 24, 1943; children—John M., James. R., Marva Jean. Sr. accountant Billups, Wood & Champlin, C.P.A.'s, Oklahoma City, 1946-53; partner Champlin & Co., C.P.A.'s, Oklahoma City, 1953-56, Lingle, Pigg & Kraemer, C.P.A.'s, Oklahoma City, 1956—. Dir. Wheeler Evans Grain, Inc., Groom, Tex., Wheeler Evans Elevator Co., White Deer, Tex. Served with USNR, 1943-45. C.P.A., Okla. Mem. Am. Inst. C.P.A.'s, Okla. Soc. C.P.A.'s. Mem. Ch. of Christ. Mason. Home: 2628 NW 35th St Oklahoma City OK 73112 Office: Mayex Bldg 3022 NW Expressway Oklahoma City OK 73112

PIGGOTT, LUCILLE CORNELIA JOHNSON (MRS. BERT C. PIGGOTT), univ. ofcl.; b. Alton, Ill., Apr. 11, 1925; d. Cyrus Leroy and Jennie Cornelia (Keene) Johnson; B.S. in Bus. Edn. summa cum laude, N.C. Agrl. and Tech. State U., 1954; M.Ed. in Bus. Edn., U.N.C., Greensboro, 1964; m. Bert C. Piggott, Aug. 29, 1949; 1 son, Bert C., Jr. Statis. clk. Supreme Life Ins. Co., Chgo., 1945-49; stenographer Office of Pres. N.C. Agrl. and Tech. State U., Greensboro, 1954-60, sec. to dean acad. affairs, 1960-64, dean of women, 1964—, now asso. dean student affairs. Mem. Nat., N.C. (v.p. 1968-70, pres. 1970-72) assns. women deans and counselors, Jack and Jill Am., Inc., Holidays Inc., Alpha Kappa Alpha, Delta Pi Epsilon, Pi Omega Pi, Alpha Kappa Mu, Delta Kappa Gamma. Democrat. Presbyn. Home: 801 Cambridge St Greensboro NC 27406

PIGOTT, ARTHUR WILMAN, banker; b. McComb, Miss., Dec. 3, 1935; s. John Douglas and Patty Lou (Williams) P.; student S.W. Jr. Coll., 1954, Millsaps Coll., 1955; B.S., La. State U., 1957; m. Ruth Carlene Winborn, Feb. 28, 1959; children—Patty Wynn, Charles Martin, Kelli Leigh, Todd Brantley. Teller, Am. Bank and Trust Co., Baton Rouge, La., 1957-61; asst. v.p. Progressive Bank, Summit, Miss., 1961-63; v.p. Pascagoula-Moss Point Bank, Pascagoula, Miss., 1963-68; pres., chief exec. officer Bank of Prentiss (Miss.), 1968—. Sec. treas. Prentiss Christians Schs. Recipient Distinguished Service award Pascagoula C. of C., 1967; Outstanding Citizen award Jefferson Davis County (Miss.), 1968. Mem. Miss. Econ. Council (bd. dirs.), Miss. Bankers Assn., Miss. Art Assn., Miss. Bank Adminstrs. Inst. (sec. S.W. Miss. chpt.), Jeff Davis C. of C. (past pres.). Methodist. Rotarian. Club: Prentiss Country. Address: PO Drawer A Prentiss MS 39474

PIKAART, LEONARD, educator; b. Nutley, N.J., Jan. 4, 1933; s. Leonard Gascoigne and Janette (Hendrick) P.; student U.S. Naval Acad., 1952-55; B.A. with distinction, U. Va., 1959, M.Ed., 1960, Ed.D., 1963; m. Constance Natalie Headapohl, Nov. 6, 1954; children—Leonard Frederick, William Edward, Lori Janette, Lucinda Corinne. Research asst. div. ednl. research U. Va., Charlottesville, 1960-62, instr. math. Sch. Engring. and Applied Scis., 1961-63; asst. prof. math. edn. U. Ga., Athens, 1963-66, head math. edn. dept., 1966-69, asso. prof. math. edn., 1967-71, mem. grad. faculty, 1967—, prof. math. edn., 1971—. Bd. dirs. NSF In-service Math. Insts. in Ga., 1965-68. Served with AUS, 1956-58. Recipient Distinguished Achievement award Am. Assn. Colls. for Tchr. Edn., 1967. Mem. Nat., Ga. (pres. 1972—) council tchrs. math., Math. Assn. Am., Am. Assn. U. Profs., Am. Ednl. Research Assn., Phi Delta Kappa (chpt. pres. 1967, area coordinator 1969-71). Mem. editorial bd. The Arithmetic Tchr., 1967-70. Home: 180 Kings Rd Athens GA 30601

PIKE, ROBERT MERRETT, microbiologist; b. Hiram, Me., Apr. 5, 1906; s. John Bennett and Cora (Hubbard) P.; A.B., Brown U., 1928, M.A., 1930, Ph.D., 1932; m. Mary Brownell, June 17, 1932; children—Elizabeth (Mrs. Joe L. Dunlap), Mary Lu (Mrs. Ellery W. Sinclair), Robert B. Bacteriologist, Bassett Hosp. and Otsego County Labs., Cooperstown, N.Y., 1932-43; prof. microbiology U. Tex. Southwestern Med. Sch., Dallas, 1943—. Diplomate Am. Bd. Microbiology. Fellow Am. Acad. Microbiology; mem. Am. Soc. Microbiology, Am. Assn. Immunologists, Sigma Xi, Alpha Delta Phi. Research in med. bacteriology and immunology. Contbr. articles in field to profl. jours. Home: 5815 Elderwood Dr Dallas TX 75230 Office: 5323 Harry Hines Blvd Dallas TX 75235

PIKER, EVE SANDERS (MRS. HERBERT M. PIKER), editor, bus. exec.; b. Frankfort, Ind., Nov. 2, 1918; d. Fred and Mamye A. (Gwin) Sanders; student Franklin Coll.; m. James H. Heaney, Aug. 30, 1941 (killed in action 1942); 1 son, James Alfred; m. 2d, Herbert M. Piker, Oct. 30, 1970. Editor, Hendricks County Republican newspaper, Danville, Ind., 1942-46; continuity div. radio sta. WIBC, Indpls., 1946-47, WTHI, Terre Haute, Ind., 1947-49; account asst. Newman, Lynde & Asso. Advt. Agy., 1949-64, corp. sec., 1960-64; editor, bus. mgr. Jacksonville Mag., Jacksonville (Fla.) Area C. of C., 1964—. Active Camp Fire Girls; sec. Civic Round Table of Jacksonville, 1967—. Trustee Episcopal Child Day Care Centers. Mem. Am. C. of C. Execs., So. Assn. C. of C. Execs., Am. Assn. Commerce Publs. (pres.), Nat. League Am. Pen Women, Fla. Pub. Relations Assn., Gamma Alpha Chi (hon.). Episcopalian. Mem. Order Eastern Star. Home: Ca'd'Oro Villa 5039 Timuguana Rd Jacksonville FL 32210 Office: 604 Hogan St Jacksonville FL 32202

PILCHER, CRAWFORD LONG, former govt. ofcl.; b. Warrenton, Ga., Feb. 14, 1908; s. William Wyman and Kate (Burkhalter) P.; student Emory U.; m. Christine Lucille Einstein, Aug. 11, 1934; children—Edith Katherine (Mrs. Carr Glover Dodson), Suzanne (Mrs. Rhett L. Moody, Jr.). Admitted to Ga. bar, 1933; clk. City Council, Warrenton, Ga., 1934-36; mem. Ga. Ho. of Reps., 1937-43; asst. atty. gen., 1943-45; mem. Ga. Senate, 1949-53; pub. service commr. Ga., Atlanta, 1953-61, chmn., 1961-68. Mem. Chi Phi. Republican. Methodist. Home: 406 Johnson St Warrenton GA 30828 Office: 244 Washington St SW Atlanta GA 30334

PILCHER, JAMES BROWNIE, lawyer; b. Shreveport, La., May 19, 1929; s. James Reese and Mattie (Brown) P.; B.A., La. State U., 1952; J.D. summa cum laude, John Marshall U., 1955; postgrad. Emory U.; m. Frances M. Pettit, Jan. 28, 1951; children—Lydia, Martha, Bradley. Admitted to Ga. bar, 1955, since practiced in Atlanta; legal counsel to speaker Ho. Reps., Ga., 1961-64; asso. city atty., Atlanta, 1965-70. Prof. law, John Marshall U., 1955-59; pres. Brentwood Enterprises, Inc. Mem. Ga. Democratic exec. com., 1962-66; pres. Active Voters, 1966-69; chmn. Fulton County Dem. Com., 1969-71. Bd. dirs. Warren Meml. Boys Club, Atlanta Assn. UN; trustee Vanguard Housing Corp. Served with USNR, 1946-48. Named Outstanding Young Man of Atlanta in Community Affairs, 1962, Ga. 1963. Mem. Am., Ga., Atlanta bar assns., Am. Trial Lawyers Assn., Atlanta Jr. C. of C. (pres. 1961-62). Baptist. Kiwanian. Club: Young Democratic of Fulton County (Atlanta) (pres. 1964-65, Ga. 1965-66). Home: 434 Brentwood Dr NE Atlanta GA 30319 Office: William Oliver Bldg Atlanta GA 30303

PILCHER, PALMER CLYDE, educator; b. Syracuse, N.Y., Mar. 19, 1921; s. Edward and Lillian (Richards) Casey; B.A., Syracuse U., 1949, Ph.D., 1956; m. Thetis Miller Pilcher, Apr. 7, 1943; children—Bruce Francis, Scott Nugent. Asst. prof. govt. and pub. adminstrn. Am. U., 1952-55; asst. prof. pub. adminstrn. Wayne State U., 1955-58, asso. prof., 1958-65, asst. dean Grad. div., dir. Inst. for Regional and Urban Studies, 1956-64; dean acad. affairs, prof. govt. Fla. Atlantic U. at Boca Raton, 1964-67; v.p. acad. affairs U. Ark., Fayetteville, 1967—. Cons. effective citizenship program Ford Motor Co., Detroit, 1959-60; v.p. Nat. Ednl. Assos. for Research and Devel., Fort Lauderdale, Fla., 1965-68. Served with USCG, 1942-45. Mem. Am. Polit. Sci. Assn. Ednl. Data Systems, Fla. Ednl. Research Assn., Am. Soc. Pub. Adminstrn., Am. Council Engring. Edn. Lutheran. Co-editor: Management Science, 1959; Manpower and Local Government, 1963. Home: 1650 Applebury Dr Fayetteville AR 72701

PILGRIM, JAMES, curator Corcoran Gallery of Art, Washington. Address: 17th St and New York Av NW Washinton DC 20006*

PILGRIM, MARY ALICE GUNN (MRS. MANUEL R. PILGRIM), educator; b. Cuthbert, Tex., Oct. 11, 1918; d. Charles Henry and Julia (Burrus) Gunn; B.S., Tex. Woman's U., 1955, M.A., 1959; Ed.D., N. Tex. State U., 1965; m. Manuel R. Pilgrim, Dec. 17, 1943; 1 dau., Juliet Ann Bell. Clk., Lone Wolf Electric Coop., Colorado City, Tex., 1942-44, U.S. Army, C.E., Benicia (Cal.) Arsenal, 1944-45; sec., dir. placement Tex. Woman's U., Denton, 1954-55, exec. sec. to dean Coll. Edn., 1955-60; teaching fellow Sch. Bus. Adminstrn., N. Tex. State U., Denton, 1960-64; prof. div. bus. adminstrn. Tex. Wesleyan Coll., Fort Worth, 1964—. Evaluator bus. depts. various schs. So. Assn. Schs. and Colls., 1967-68. Mem. Nat., Tex. (reporter 1970—) bus. edn. assns., Internat. Soc. Bus. Edn., Tex. State Tchrs. Assn., Am. Assn. U. Profs., Soc. Automation in Bus. Edn., Delta Pi Epsilon (pres. 1967-68), Kappa Delta Pi. Home: 2419 Sheraton Rd Denton TX 76201 Office: Tex Wesleyan Coll Fort Worth TX 76105

PIMENTEL, DAVID, artist. Painter, Mexico City. Address: Galeria Romano Jose Maria Marroqui 5 Mexico City DF Mexico*

PINAJIAN, JOHN JOSEPH, chemist; b. Clifton, N.J., Oct. 31, 1921; s. Peter and Ruth (Nakashian) P.; student Columbia, 1947; B.S., Rutgers, The State U., 1949; M.S., Purdue U., 1954, Ph.D., 1955; postgrad. George Washington U., 1951-52; m. Harriet Jean Lorenzen, Feb. 5, 1949; 1 son, Cornelius John. Prof., research scientist U. Tenn., Oak Ridge, 1955-56; chemist Oak Ridge Nat. Lab., 1956-59, group leader, 1960-66, isotopes div. staff, 1967—; adj. prof. physics Vanderbilt U., Nashville, 1970—. Sci. expert Office Atomic Energy for Peace, Bangkok, Thailand, 1966-67; cons., guest scientist Cyclotron and Isotope Labs., N.V. Philips-Duphar, N. Holland, 1968-69, mgr., 1969. Served with USNR, 1942-46, 51-52. Fellow A.A.A.S., Am. Inst. Chemists; mem. Am. Chem. Soc., Am. Nuclear Soc., Am. Phys. Soc., Sigma Xi, Phi Lambda Upsilon, Rho Chi, Sigma Pi Sigma. Contbr. to Ency. of Physics, also articles to profl. jours. Home: 161 La Salle Rd Oak Ridge TN 37830 Office: Oak Ridge Nat Lab Oak Ridge TN 37830

PINARDI, NORMAN JOSEPH, banker; b. N.Y.C., June 16,, 1936; s. Marco and Adelle (Anselmi) P.; B.S., U. Fla., 1958; m. Bobby Jo Kight, June 8, 1957; children—Theresa Lynn, Robert Anthony. Dir. information Fla. Alcoholic Rehab. Program, Avon Park, 1961-65; dir. pub. relations Manatee County Com. of 100, Bradenton, Fla., 1965-67; v.p. pub. relations Inter City Nat. Bank, Bradenton, Fla., 1967—, also v.p. affiliate Bayshore State Bank, Bradenton, 1970—. Tchr. bank pub. relations Bank Adminstrn. Inst., 1970. Dir. pub. relations Manatee County LeRoy Collins for Senate Campaign. Publicity vol. United Fund, 1967. Bd. dirs. DeSoto Boys Club, Bradenton, 1967-70, United Fund, Bradenton, 1967—. Served with USAF, 1958-61. Mem. Manatee County C. of C., Pub. Relations Soc. Am. (v.p. 1971-72), Fla. Pub. Relations Assn. (pres. 1969). Rotarian. Club: Bradenton Country. Home: 5812 9th Av Dr W Bradenton FL 33505 Office: PO Box 771 Bradenton FL 33507

PINCKNEY, JOHN ADAMS, ret. bishop; b. Mt. Pleasant, S.C., Mar. 8, 1905; s. Francis Douglas and Mary Lee (Adams) P.; student Coll. Charleston, 1925-26, DuBose Meml. Sch., 1926-28; B.D., U. of South, 1931, D.D., 1964; m. Hilda W. Emerson, Oct. 8, 1931; children—Hilda Emerson (Mrs. William C. Ross), John Adams,

Francis Douglas. Ordained to ministry Episcopal Ch., 1931; minister Diocese of S.C., 1931-37, Ch. of Holy Cross, Tryon, N.C., 1937-39; rector St. Paul's Ch., Charleston, S.C., 1939-41; minister Holy Trinity Ch., Clemson, also chaplain Episcopal students Clemson Coll., 1941-48; rector St. James' Ch., Greenville, 1948-59; archdeacon Diocese of Upper S.C., 1959-63, bishop, 1963-72. Dir. youth confs. Kanuga Confs., Hendersonville, N.C., 1932-42, dir. confs. program, 1942-50; sec. Diocese of Upper S.C., also sec. Diocesan Exec. Council, 1954-63; dep. to Gen. Convs. and Provincial Synods. Mem. Newcomen Soc. Home: 307 Harrow Dr Columbia SC 29210 Office: PO Box 1789 Columbia SC 29202

PINE, DAVID ANDREW, judge; b. Washington, Sept. 22, 1891; s. David Emory and Charlotte (McCormick) P.; LL.B., Georgetown U., 1913, LL.D., 1954, postgrad., 1913-14; m. Elizabeth Bradshaw, Aug. 23, 1916 (dec.); 1 dau., Elizabeth Pine Dayton; m. 2d, Elenore E. Townsend, July 8, 1959. Admitted to D.C. bar, 1913; confidential clk. to U.S. atty. gen. Dept. Justice, Washington, 1914-16, law clk., 1916-17, asst. atty., 1919; spl. asst. to U.S. atty gen. in Western States, 1919-21; practiced in Washington, 1921-34; mem. firm Easby-Smith, Pine & Hill, 1925-29; chief asst. U.S. atty., D.C., 1934-37; U.S. atty. for D.C., 1938-40, judge U.S. Dist. Ct. D.C., 1940—, chief judge, 1959-61, sr. judge, 1965. Served from 1st lt. to capt. inf., U.S. Army, assigned to Provost Marshal Gen., World War I. Mem. Am. Bar Assn., Bar Assn. D.C. Democrat. Episcopalian. Clubs: Lawyers (past pres.), Barristers (past pres.); Metropolitan (Washington); Chevy Chase (Md.). Home: 3507 Lowell St NW Washington DC 20016 Office: US Ct House Washington DC 20001

PINEAU, ROGER, editor mus.; b. Chgo., Nov. 17, 1915; s. Auguste G. and Olga Constance (Erickson) P.; A.A., Flint (Mich.) Jr. Coll., 1940; B.A., U. Mich., 1942; grad. U.S. Naval Lang. Sch., 1943; J.D., George Washington U., 1954; m. Maxine Jessie Good, Nov. 4, 1942; children—Suzanne Lisette (Mrs. James Dulcan), Julienne Louise, Anthony Auguste, Antoinette Elizabeth. Far east intelligence officer Dept. State, 1957-61, social sci. officer, 1961-65; editor Smithsonian Instn., Washington, 1965—. Served with USNR, 1942-50; now capt. Res. Author: (with R. Sherrod) A Picture History of the Pacific War, 1952; (with M. Fuchida, M. Okumiya, C.H. Kawakami) Midway, The Battle that Doomed Japan, 1955; (with R. Inoguchi, T. Nakajima) The Divine Wind, 1958; (with T. Hara, F. Saito) Japanese Destroyer Captain, 1961; (with M. Ito, A. Kuroda) The End of the Imperial Japanese Navy, 1962. Editor: The Japan Expedition, M.C. Perry's personal diary, 1968. Contbr. articles to profl. pubs. Home: 9403 Holland Av Bethesda MD 20014 Office: Smithsonian Institution Washington DC 20560

PINGLETON, GEORGE GENE, ednl. adminstr.; b. Haileyville, Okla., Aug. 28, 1927; s. Julius Boss and Rachel Agnes (Hendricks) P.; B.S., U. Okla., 1950; M.S., Okla. State U., 1954, Adminstr.'s Certificate, 1956, 58 Ed. D., 1962; m. Nora Ruth Kirk, June 2, 1951; children—Jane Ann, Joan Ellen, Susan Gayle. Tchr., Ponca City (Okla.) Pub. Schs., 1950-56, elementary prin., 1956-60; dir. elementary edn. Oklahoma City Pub. Schs., 1961-66; supt. schs., Stillwater, Okla., 1966—. Pres., Okla. Commn. Ednl. Adminstrn., 1970-71. Active YMCA. Bd. dirs. Okla. Sci. and Arts Found., 1965, Payne County Health Bd., 1970, United Fund, 1969, Campfire Girls, Boy Scouts Am. Mem. Am. Assn. Sch. Adminstrs., N.E.A., Okla. Edn. Assn., Assn. for Supervision and Curriculum Devel., Stillwater C. of C., Phi Delta Kappa, Kappa Delta Pi. Presbyn. Rotarian. Home: 3023 W 27th St Stillwater OK 74074 Office: 314 S Lewis St Stillwater OK 74074

PINION, DWIGHT JAMES, lawyer; b. Neb., Mar. 12, 1911; s. Paul Andrew and Mabel (Anderson) P.; LL.B., Southeastern U., 1937; m. Kathryn Martin, Nov. 8, 1937; children—Carolyn (Mrs. Scott W. Elkins), Nancy (Mrs. James B. Stehman, Jr.), Pauline. Admitted to D.C. bar, 1937; atty. SEC, 1938-42; asst. counsel Office Legislative Counsel, U.S. Senate, 1942-66, legislative counsel, 1967-69; pvt. practice law, 1969—. Mem. Fed. Bar Assn. Baptist. Club: Nat. Lawyers (Washington). Home: 6910 Bright Av McLean VA 22101

PINKERTON, RICHARD SMITH, C. of C. exec.; b. Polo, Mo., Jan. 22, 1934; s. John Smith and Ethel (Hunt) P.; student Drake U., 1951-53; B.S., N.W. Mo. State U., 1958; m. Rolande Thompson, May 26, 1957; children— Sammi, Stacey. Tchr. pub. sch., St. Joseph, Mo., 1959-60, Faucett, Mo., 1960-64; asst. mgr. St. Joseph C. of C., 1964-67; exec. v.p. Sikeston (Mo.) C. of C., 1967-68; exec. mgr. Deland (Fla.) C. of C., 1968—. Served with AUS, 1953-55. Mem. So. Assn. C. of C. Execs., Am., Fla. C. of C. execs., U.S. C. of C., Soc. for Preservation and Encouragement of Barbershop Quartet Singing in Am. Mason (Shriner), Rotarian. Home: 31 Robin Ct Deland FL 32720 Office: PO Box 629 Deland FL 32720

PINKERTON, THOMAS ORVILLE, baking co. exec.; b. Gans, Okla., Dec. 12, 1910; s. Jess C. and Lila (Rogers) P.; grad. Draughon's Bus. Coll., 1929; m. Rosa Hatfield, Dec. 24, 1932; children—Lois Marie (Mrs. Robert Kaufman), Doris Mae (Eloyd J. Leger). Bookkeeper, Shipley Baking Co., Muskogee, Okla., 1929-31, sales dept., 1931-37, mgr. Muskogee plant, 1937-40, Ft. Smith, 1940; dist. mgr. Jackson Cookie Co., Oklahoma City, 1940-52, gen. sales mgr., Little Rock, Ark., 1952-55, gen. mgr., sec.-treas., 1955—. Mem. So. Cookie Assn. (pres. 1958-59), C. of C. Baptist. Rotarian, Mason (32 deg.). Home: 4619 Crestline Dr N Little Rock AR 72116 Office: 113 S Olive St N Little Rock AR 72115

PINKETT, FLAXIE MADISON, Democratic nat. committeewoman; b. St. Louis, Nov. 30, 1917; d. John Randolph and Flaxie (Holcombe) Pinkett; B.A., Howard U., 1936. Mem. pub. welfare adv. council D.C. Dept. Pub. Welfare, Washington, 1960-66; mem., chmn. Supt.'s Adv. Council, D.C. Pub. Schs., 1965-67; mem. adv. council Dept. Vocat. Edn. D.C., 1967-68; mem. Mayor's Com. on Employment of Handicapped, 1968, Mayor's Com. on Crime and Delinquency, Washington, 1969, Criminal Justice Co-ordinating Bd., 1969; div. Home Bldg. Assn.; exec. com. D.C. Bd. Realtors. Trustee D.C. Bd. Higher Edn., 1968; del. Democratic Nat. Conv., 1968; mem. Dem. Central Com. of D.C., 1968—, committeewoman from D.C., 1968—. Trustee, George Washington U.; gov. United Way. Recipient Alumni award Howard U., 1964; named Bus. Woman of Year State Fedn. Bus. and Profl. Women's Clubs, 1968; others. Mem. D.C. Health and Welfare Council (chmn.), Delta Sigma Theta. Author: Many Shades of Black, 1969; How to Succeed in Business by Really Trying. Episcopalian. Home: 4210 Argyle Terrace NW Washington DC 20011 Office: 1507 9th St NW Washington DC 20001

PINKSTON, J. W., JR., hosp. adminstr. Exec. dir. Grady Meml. Hosp., Atlanta. Office: 80 Butler St SE Atlanta GA 30303

PINNELL, RAYMOND A., JR., archtl. engr.; b. Wichita Falls, Tex., July 5, 1925; s. Raymond A. and Anna (Carter) P.; B.S., U. Tex. at Austin, 1950; m. Mary Waller, Mar. 23, 1947; children—Gary R., M. Angela. Jr. engr. R. Marvin Shipman Cons. Engrs., San Antonio, 1950-53; exec. v.p. Lift Slab Group & Research Co., Texstar Corp., 1953-55, pres., 1955-60; partner Freigenspan & Pinnell, cons. engrs., San Antonio, 1960—; pres. Prestressing Industries, 1958-60. Served with USNR, 1943-46. Recipient award of merit for outstanding engring. achievement for design of Palacio Del Rio Hotel, 1968. Mem. Nat., Tex. socs. profl. engrs., Am. Concrete Inst. Club: Alamo Heights Optimist (past treas.) (San Antonio). Prin. engring. designs include Tower of the Americas, San Antonio, 1968. Office: 335 W Sunset St San Antonio TX 78209

PINNEY, DON OVID, educator; b. Monmouth, Ill., Sept. 12, 1937; s. Merlyn Ovid and Violet Martha (Smith) P.; B.S., U. Ill., 1959; Ph.D. (Ralston Purina fellow), Okla. State U., 1963; m. Ruth Irene Watt, June 20, 1959; children—Martin Lee, Steven Don, Angela Dawn. Asst. prof. animal sci. U. Ky., 1963-66, Okla. State U., Stillwater, 1966—. Judge numerous nat. swine and beef livestock shows. Mem. Am. Soc. Animal Sci. (mem. several coms.), Internat. Intercollegiate Livestock Judging Coaches Assn. (pres. 1971-72), Alpha Zeta, Alpha Gamma Rho, Phi Eta Sigma, Gamma Sigma Delta. Contbr. articles to profl. pubs. Office: Dept Animal Sciences and Industry Oklahoma State U Stillwater OK 74074

PINSON, ANNA DOTSON (MRS. BLAKE PINSON), business exec.; b. Phelps, Ky., June 7, 1914; d. Paris W. and Allie (Dotson); student Pikeville Coll., 1932-34; B.S., Eastern State Coll., Richmond, Ky., 1936; M.A., Morehead U.; M.S., U. Louisville; Ph.D., Fla. State U.; m. Blake Pinson, June 7, 1936 (dec. June 1971); children—Anna Blake, Robert D. Tchr., Pike County (Ky.) Schs., 1936-40, sch. supr., 1940-43; office mgr. Pinson Motor Freight Co., Pikeville, also Huntington, W.Va., 1943-47; notary pub., 1947—; mgr., buyer Style Shop, Pikeville, 1947-50; mgr. Pinson Hotel; real estate broker Pinson Realty Co., 1950—; founder, mgr. Ann Pinson Interiors; pres. Pinson Ins. Agy., 1958—; v.p. L & P Contracting Co., Pikeville, 1955—; regional chmn. Heritage Life Ins. Co.; exec. v.p. Letcher Mfg. Co. Chmn., Small Bus. Service Center, 1965—; mem. Pikeville Library Bd., 1966—; mem. coms. on tourist promotion, edn., pub. relations, civic affairs Pikeville, 1963—; mem. Gov.'s Conf. on Edn., Louisville, 1956, Meth. Hosp. Guild, 1965—, Mental Health Assn., 1965—; active local P.T.A., band boosters assn., 1954—; mem. Children's Hosp., Louisville, 1963—; chmn. Model City neighborhood adv. council. Mem. Nat. Real Estate Bd. (mem. Women's Council), Am., Ky. hotel assns., Ky., Pikeville chambers commerce, Pikeville Coll. Alumni Assn. (pres. 1969—), Nat. Appraisers Assn. (charter mem.), Pikeville hist. socs., Internat. Platform Assn., Am. Assn. U. Women (publicity chmn.). Club: Pikeville Woman's. Home: 405 2d St Pikeville KY 41501 Office: Pinson Hotel Pike Av Pikeville KY 41501

PINSON, FURMAN BARRATT, JR., textile co. exec.; b. Tampa, Fla., Oct. 19, 1912; s. Furman Barratt and Nancy (Charles) P.; B.A., Presbyn. Coll., Clinton, S.C., 1933; m. Julia Ophelia Bailey, Feb. 24, 1940; children— Julianne Charles (Mrs. Stuart John Mahlin), Nancy Bailey. Purchasing agt. Slater Mfg. Co. (S.C.), 1934-39, Carter Fabrics Corp., Greensboro, N.C., 1939-41; mgr. purchasing J.P. Stevens & Co. Inc., Greensboro, 1946-62, v.p. purchasing, 1963—. Instr. purchasing Greensboro Evening Coll., 1948-49; purchasing cons. to Gov. of S.C., 1963-64. Trustee, Presbyn. Coll. Served to maj. AUS, 1942-45. Recipient Cross of Honor, U.D.C., 1964, Chmn.'s Cup, 1967. Mem. Carolinas-Va. Purchasing Agts. Assn. (pres. 1960, Thomas award 1962), Presbyn. Coll. Alumni Assn. (pres. 1968), Pi Kappa Phi. Presbyn. (ruling elder). Club: Starmount Forest Country (Greensboro). Home: 102 Beverly Pl Greensboro NC 27403 Office: 3511 W Market St Greensboro NC 27420

PINSON, WILLIAM MEREDITH, JR., clergyman, educator; b. Ft. Worth, Aug. 3, 1934; s. William Meredith and Ila (Jones) P.; B.A., North Tex. State U., 1955; B.D., Southwestern Sem., 1959, Th.D., 1963; postgrad. U. Edinburgh, Scotland, 1956-57, Tex. Christian U., 1957-58, Columbia U., Union Theol. Sem., Yale Div. Sch., Princeton Theol. Sem., San Francisco Theol. Sem., 1969-70; m. Bobbie Ruth Judd, June 4, 1955; children—Meredith Ann, Allison Ruth. Ordained to ministry Baptist Ch., 1956; preached in Scotland, Eng., Spain, Denmark, 1956-57; travel throughout Europe, 1956, Mexico, 1958, Bahamas, 1964; prof. ethics Southwestern Sem., Ft. Worth, 1963—; mem. Christian Life Commn., So. Baptist Conv. Named Outstanding Young Man in Am., Jr. C. of C., 1965. Mem. Am. Acad. Polit. and Social Sci., Am. Acad. Religion, Am. Soc. Christian Ethics. Author: How To Deal with Controversial Issues, 1966; Ambassadors and Christian Citizenship, 1963; Crisis in Morality, 1965; Out of Darkness, 1963; Resource Guide to Current Social Issues, 1967; Right or Wrong, 1971; Twenty Centuries of Great Preaching, 13 vols., 1971; Contemporary Christian Trends, 1972; Don't Blame The Game, 1972. Contbr. articles to profl. jours. Home: 3551 Binyon St Fort Worth TX 76133 Office: 2001 W Seminary Dr Fort Worth TX 76122

PIPER, ROY HERBERT, banker; b. Elgin, Ill., June 17, 1927; s. David Roy and Cleora Stuart (Greene) P.; B.A. with high honors, U. Ill., 1949; postgrad. U. N.C., 1950-51, Stonier Grad. Sch. Banking, 1967; m. Betty Eidson, Aug. 25, 1950; children—Phyllis, Catherine, David, Joseph. Secondary sch. tchr. Rutherford County, N.C., 1949-53; v.p. Ga. Railroad Bank & Trust Co., Augusta, Ga., 1953—. Instr. Am. Inst. Banking, 1961-70. Chmn. nat. essay contest Am. Soc. Personnel Adminstrn., 1968; mem. study com. Bd. Commrs. Richmond County, Ga., 1969; chmn. Merit System Commn., Richmond County, 1972—. Mem. Am. Soc. Personnel Adminstrn., Personnel Assn. Central Savannah River Area, Phi Alpha Theta. Home: 1334 Montego Pl Augusta GA 30904 Office: 699 Broad St Augusta GA 30902

PIPES, JOYCE ELMYRA GRAGG, educator; b. Boone, N.C., Nov. 27, 1927; d. William Roy and Myra (Shook) Gragg; B.S., Appalachian State U., 1948, M.A., 1962; postgrad. U. N.C., Greensboro, 1967-70; m. Charles Duane Pipes, Dec. 23, 1950 (div. Dec. 1961); 1 son, Richard Sherman. Tchr. various schs., N.C., Ariz., Mich., 1948-52, 53-54, 56-58, 59-60; grad. teaching fellow Appalachian State U., Boone, N.C., 1961-62; prof. phys. edn. Wingate (N.C.) Coll., 1962—. Mem. A.A.H.P.E.R., N.C. Assn. Health, Phys. Edn. and Recreation, Nat., So. (state membership chmn. 1963) assns. phys. edn. coll. women. Home: 206 Faculty Dr Wingate NC 28174

PIPKIN, JOHN B., II, banker; b. Greensboro, N.C., Feb. 8, 1935; s. Willis Benton and Ruth (Pringle) P.; B.A., Va. Mil. Inst., 1957; M.B.A., U. Va., 1961; m. Anne Hunter Baker, Nov. 1, 1958; children—Anne Hunter, Ruth Pringle. With N.C. Nat. Bank, 1961—, v.p., mgr. credit dept., 1963-69, v.p., dir. credit adminstrn. and services, 1969-71, v.p., sr. comml. loan officer, 1971-; dir. Knob Creek Morganton, Inc. Served with AUS, 1957-59. Mem. Nat. Assn. Accountants (Nat. Pub. Relations award 1969), Robert Morris Assos. Contbg. editor The Bankers Handbook, 1966. Home: 614 Ashworth Rd Charlotte NC 28211 Office: 200 S Tryon St Charlotte NC 28201

PIPKIN, MICHAEL BRUCE, librarian; b. Mena, Ark., Oct. 3, 1934; s. Compere Allen and Leyland (Chambers) P.; student Peabody Conservatory of Music, 1956-68; B.A., U. Md., 1961; M.L.S., U. N.C., 1952; m. Betty J. Jordan, Aug. 21, 1960; children—Michael, David, Christopher, Thomas. Librarian I, Free Library of Phila., 1962-64; base librarian Olmsted AFB, Pa., 1964-67; librarian City of Hampton (Va.), 1967—. Served with AUS, 1953-56. Mem. Am., Va., S.E. library assns., Va. Jr. Member's Round Table (chmn. 1969-70), Armed Forces Librarians Sect. (chmn. devel. com. 1965-66), Hampton Hist. Soc. (v.p. 1969-71), Archaeol. Soc. Va. (v.p. 1967-68). Club: Torch (Hampton Roads, Va.). Home: 137 O' Canoe Pl Hampton VA 23361 Office: 4205 Victoria Blvd Hampton VA 23369

PIPPEN, JOSEPH FRANKLIN, ins. co. exec.; b. Richmond, Va., Mar. 14, 1925; s. Icha Linwood and Margaret (Childress) P.; grad. Smithdeal Bus. Coll., 1946; m. Selma Browne Seay, July 5, 1944; children— Joseph Franklin, Bruce S. Clk., U.S. Govt., 1946-47; debit agt. Life of Va., Richmond, 1948-53, asso. mgr., Miami, Fla., 1953-54; with Atlantic Life Ins. Co. (merged with Southwestern Life Ins. Co. 1961), Richmond, 1954—, v.p. in charge combination div., 1961—, now v.p. Southwestern Life Ins. Co.; also sr. v.p., dir. Southwestern Gen. Life Ins. Co., Dallas, 1970—. Served with USMCR, 1943-45, 50-51. Republican. Methodist. Home: 7123 Briarmeadow St Dallas TX 75230 Office: PO Box 799 Dallas TX

PIPPIN, BASCUM C., educator; b. Britton, Okla., June 1, 1925; s. Bascum C. and Doris (Reid) P.; B.S., Central State U., 1948; D.D.S., U. Mo., 1952; m. Margaret Josephine Griffin, Dec. 26, 1948; children— Kris, Tra, Judy, Phil, John, Louis. Asst. prof. oral surgery Med. Sch. U. Okla., Oklahoma City, 1955-69, asst. prof. dental radiology, 1969—; cleft palate team speech and hearing dept., 1955—; staff oral surgery sect. Baptist Hosp., 1960—. Active YMCA. Served to corp. USMC, 1943-46. Mem. Am. Dental Assn., Delta Sigma Delta, Am. Acad. Dental Radiology. Democrat. Methodist (sec., treas. bd. dirs. 1955-60). Mason, Rotarian (pres. 1959-60). Home: 2825 Dorchester St Oklahoma City OK 73120 Office: 925 W Britton Rd Oklahoma City OK 73114

PIPPIN, WARREN FLOYD, research entomologist; b. Mulberry, Kan., Feb. 26, 1919; s. Arnold Golden and Nellie (Walthour) P.; B.S., Colo. State U., 1941; M.S., Okla. State U., 1958, Ph.D., 1968; m. Belle Dixson Porter, Dec. 8, 1942; children—Virginia, Warren, Donald. Served with AUS, 1942-46, quarantine insp. U.S. Dept. Agr., Nogales, Ariz., 1946-48, San Antonio, Tex., 1948-52; commd. capt. USAF, 1952, advanced through grades to lt. col., 1968; med. entomologist Army biol. lab., Ft. Detrick, Md., 1952-54; med. chief Entomology br. Ramey AFB, P.R., 1954-56; med. entomologist Air Force Inst. Tech., Okla. State U., Stillwater, 1956-58; chief, entomology br. Air Force Med. Service Sch., Gunter AFB, Ala., 1958-61; chief entomology br. 5th Epidemiological Flight, Japan, 1961-63, Philippine Islands, 1963—; asst. chief entomology br., epidemiological lab. Aerospace Med. Div., Lackland AFB, Tex., 1964-68, ret., research entomologist, 1968—; cons. Southwest Research Inst., 1969—. Mem. Entomol. Soc. Am., Am. Mosquito Control Assn., Nat. Sojourners, Sci. Research Soc. Am., Internat. Platform Assn., Sigma Xi, Phi Sigma, Alpha Zeta, Beta Beta Beta, Phi Kappa Phi. Republican, Presbyn. Mason (Shriner). Home: 227 Whitecliff Dr San Antonio TX 78227 Office: 227 Whitecliff Dr San Antonio TX 78227

PIPPIN, WILLIAM CLYDE, realtor, city ofcl.; b. Alexandria, Ala., Feb. 18, 1917; s. William Marion and Tannie Leola (Holland) P.; student Northwestern U., 1948; m. Frances Dickie, Dec. 23, 1939; children—Marian Ann (Mrs. Richard Bruce Nyman), Frances Dickie (Mrs. Robert S. Day, Jr.). Salesman, O.H. Parker & Co., Anniston, Ala., 1936-48; owner W.C. Pippin, realtor, Anniston; mgr. Hamilton & Co., Inc., Anniston, 1953-57; partner Pippin Agy., Anniston, 1957—; dir. Sunset Point Devel. Co., Inc., Anniston, P. & W. Devel. Co., Inc., Anniston, Anniston Enterprises, Inc., Anniston Hotels Co., Inc. Commr. City of Anniston, 1950-54, mayor, 1954, 1969—. Served with Seabees, 1944-46. Named Realtor of Yr., Ala. Real Estate Assn., 1960. Mem. So. Inst. Property Valuation., Internat. Real Estate Fedn., Nat. Inst. Real Estate Bds., Ala. Real Estate Assn. (pres. 1955). Mason (Shriner), Rotarian, Lion (pres. 1944). Home: 1212 Vine ST Anniston AL 36201 Office: 22 E 12th St Anniston AL 36201

PIRANIO, ANTHONY F., owner investment co.; b. Dallas, Dec. 15, 1918; s. Joseph T. and Lena (LaRoca) P.; certificate real estate So. Meth. U., 1962; m. Katherine Angelo, Nov. 27, 1946; children—Lynn Rose, Dana Louise, Gina Frances. Owner, operator A.F. Piranio Investments, Dallas, 1946—, A.F. Piranio Constrn. Co., Dallas, 1948—; sr. partner Piranio & Piranio Investments, Dallas, 1950—, Dal-Tex Builders, Inc., Dallas, 1955-57; co-owner PiLi Farms, Van Zandt County (Tex.), 1962—, P & L Cattle Co., 1969—. Cons. real estate, 1948—. Served with AUS, 1941-45; PTO. Home: 6705 Braeburn Dr Dallas TX 75214

PIRKEY, HENRY WARREN, JR., electric utility exec.; b. Annona, Tex., July 24, 1907; s. Henry Warren and Leilia (Giddens) P.; grad. Tyler (Tex.) Comml. Coll.; m. Addie Williams, July 2, 1928; children— Charles Warren (dec.), Leilia (Mrs. August C. Erickson). With Southwestern Electric Power Co., 1925—, exec. v.p., 1966. pres., 1966—, also dir.; dir. Central & S.W. Corp., 1st Nat. Bank Shreveport. Treas., Shreveport-Bossier City Econ. Devel. Found., 1967-69, dir., 1966-70; dir. Pub. Solicitation Rev. Council, Shreveport, 1967-70, v.p., 1971. Trustee Gulf South Research Inst., Southwest Atomic Energy Assos.; bd. dirs. Nat. Assn. Electric Cos., 1970—, Edison Electric Inst., 1971. Mem. Nat. Assn. Accountants (past pres. Shreveport chpt. past nat. v.p., dir.), Shreveport C. of C. (treas. 1958-62, bd. dirs. 1957-59, 67—, v.p., treas. 1969, pres. (1970), Mo. Valley Electric Assn. (pres. 1969-70), S.W. Electric Conf. (chmn. 1969-70). Home: 123 Ockley Dr Shreveport LA 71105 Office: 428 Travis St Shreveport LA 71102

PIRKLE, DAVID EUGENE, mech. engr.; b. Atlanta, Aug. 8, 1927; s. David Ambrose and Eugenia (Bragg) P.; B.S., Ga. Inst. Tech., 1952; m. Mildred Ransie Edgens, Jan. 31, 1959. Mech. engr. Lockheed Aircraft Co., Marietta, Ga., 1952-59; individual engring. practice, Atlanta, 1959-63, 70—; mech. engr. Atlanta Army Depot, Forest Park, Ga., 1963-70. Recipient award Lockheed Mgmt. Club, 1954; award for outstanding performance in engring. Dept. Army, 1966, 69. Registered profl. engr., Ga. Address: 2203 Polar Rock Pl SW Atlanta GA 30315

PIRKLE, MORGAN WRIGHT, govt. ofcl.; b. Buckhead, Ga., Dec. 12, 1911; s. Robert N. and Sarah Lou (Morrow) P.; B.S., Ga. Inst. Tech., 1934; M.S., U. Mich., 1938; m. Ellen Christine Carlsen, Nov. 26, 1948; 1 son, Randy Wright. Engr., Eastern Airlines, Atlanta, 1934-36, Ga. Dept. Health, 1936-41; civilian indsl. mgmt. USAF, Robins AFB, Ga., 1963—; dir. C & S Bank, Warner Robins, Ga.; real estate broker. Mem. Boy Scouts Am. Peach Belt Dist. Com. and Middle Ga. Regional Council, 1960-63. Served to col. USAF, 1941-63. Decorated Commendation medal (Army, Air Force), Bronze Star medal. Mem. Air Force Assn. (chmn. 1960-61, 69-71). Ret. Officers Assn., Ga. Tech. Alumni Assn., Ga. Tech. Found. Democrat. Episcopalian. Patentee in field. Home: 106 Chestnut Rd Warner Robins GA 31093 Office: Robins Air Force Base GA 31093

PIRRUNG, GILBERT R(OBINSON), business exec.; b. Columbus, O., July 12, 1911; s. Henry Casper and Catherine Manley (Robinson) P.; grad. Choate Sch., Wallingford, Conn., 1930; B.S., Yale, 1934; m. Lila Marshall Childress, 1937 (div. 1941); m. 2d, Joan D. H. Burgess, July 9, 1947; children—Lynette Robina, Clifford Mark, Henriette Christine, Timothy Burgess. Owner, mgr. Pirrung Racing Team, Indpls., 1934-36; prodn., sales depts. Gaylord Container Corp., St. Louis, 1936-39, budget dir., asst. to treas., 1939-41, dir., 1950-56; pres., owner, mgr. Aragon Farms, Bainbridge, Ga., 1950—; dir. Bank Cahokia (Ill.), 1962—. Trustee Aiken Prep. Sch.; mem. nat. exec. bd., nat. exec. com., internat. commr. Boy Scouts Am.; v.p., treas. bd. dirs. U.S. Found. for Internat. Scouting; pres. Interam. Scout Com.; mem. gen. council Presbyn. Ch. U.S., 1962-71, vice chmn., 1964-65, chmn.,

1966-68; chmn. Ga. Found. Ind. Colls., 1971—; trustee Ga. Conservancy, Inc., 1969—. Served as col. C.E., AUS, 1941-45. Decorated Silver Star, Bronze Star with 2 oak leaf clusters; Croix de Guerre; recipient Bronze Wolf award World Scout Conf.; Silver Beaver, Silver Antelope, Silver Buffalo awards Boy Scouts Am.; Silver Hawk award Boy Scouts Japan, Flor de Lis de Plata award Boy Scouts Paraguay. Presbyn. (elder). Clubs: St. Louis Country, Racquet (St. Louis); St. Anthony (N.Y.C.); Capital City (Atlanta); Little Harbor (Mich.); Home: Aragon Farms Bainbridge GA 31717

PIRTLE, GEORGE WILLIAM, geologist; b. Cecelia, Ky., Nov. 1, 1902; s. Thomas Louis and Laura (Shipley) P.; B.S., U. Ky., 1924, M.S., 1925; m. El Freda Taylor, July 16, 1928; 1 son, George William. Geologist, Ky. Geol. Survey, 1924-25; cons. geologist, partner Hudnall & Pirtle, Tyler, Tex., 1925-69; petroleum cons. Pirtle & Townsend, Inc., 1970—; dir. Peoples Nat. Bank, Gibraltar Life Ins. Co. Trustee Tyler Jr. Coll. Dir. South Central Region Boy Scouts Am., mem. nat. exec. bd. Recipient Silver Beaver, Silver Antelope, Silver Buffalo awards Boy Scouts Am.; named Tyler's Outstanding Citizen, 1962. Mem. Tex. Acad. Sci., Tyler C. of C. (past dir.), Geol. Soc. Am., Am. Assn. Petroleum Geologists, Mich. Acad. Sci., Am. Inst. Mining, Metall. and Petroleum Engrs., Sigma Xi, Omicron Delta Kappa. Methodist. Home: 115 E 2d St Tyler TX 75701 Office: 610 People Bank Bldg Tyler TX 75701

PIRTLE, IVYL LEORA FLEMING (MRS. J. MAX PIRTLE), educator, librarian; b. nr. Ottumwa, Ia., Jan. 11, 1906; d. Barton Earl and Lillie (Roberts) Fleming; student Ia. State Coll., 1931; B.A., U. Fla., 1944; M.A., Fla. State U., 1951; m. J. Max Pirtle, Sept. 17, 1938. Tchr. elementary schs., Ia., 1924-39; tchr. Grace Stern Pvt. Sch., Miami Beach, Fla., 1939-40; tchr. elementary schs., Indiantown, 1940-43; tchr. primary grades, Stuart, 1943-50; demonstration tchr. Fla. State U., Tallahassee, summer 1949; tchr. Palmetto Sch., West Palm Beach, 1950-55; supr. elementary edn. Palm Beach County, 1955-65, dir. library services, 1965-70. Mem. Fla. steering com. Nat. Def. Edn. Act, 1958-68. Trustee Jr. Mus. Palm Beach County, 1960-63. Recipient Certificate of Appreciation Fla. Dept. Edn., 1969. Mem. Assn. Childhood Edn. Internat. (br. pres. 1953-55, primary edn. com. 1954-56), Fla. Assn. Sch. Librarians (area chmn. 1959-62), N.E.A., Fla. Edn. Assn. (state chmn. dept. suprs. 1959-60, dept. supervisors citation 1968), Assn. Supervision and Curriculum Devel., Delta Kappa Gamma (chpt. pres. 1955-59), Kappa Delta Pi, Phi Kappa Phi. Club: Zonta. Contbr. articles profl. jours. Home: 340 Nottingham Blvd West Palm Beach FL 33405

PISARSKI, EDMUND PAUL, dentist; b. Chgo., May 25, 1936; s. Edmund Stanley and Marie Dorothy (Thomaszewski), P.; B.S., St. Procopius Coll., 1963; D.D.S., Loyola U. at Chgo., 1967, postgrad., 1967-68; m. Dolores Zych, June 10, 1961; children—Michelle Marie, Edmund Paul. Resident oral surgery Duval Med. Center, Jacksonville, Fla., 1968-70; practice oral surgery, North Palm Beach, Fla., 1970—; mem. staff St. Mary's Hosp., West Palm Beach, Good Samaritan, West Palm Beach, Palm Beach Gardens (Fla.) Hosp., Crippled Children's Hosp., West Palm Beach. Cons. staff Palm Beach County Jail, West Palm Beach, 1970—. Served with USNR, 1957-60. Mem. Am. Dental Assn., Ill., Chgo., Fla., Atlantic Coast, N. Palm Beach dental socs., Fla. Soc. Oral Surgeons. Elk. Home: 751 Tradewind Dr North Palm Beach FL 33404 Office: 531 US Hwy 1 North Palm Beach FL 33403

PISHKIN, VLADIMIR, educator, psychologist; b. Belgrade, Yugoslavia, Mar. 12, 1931; s. Vasili and Olga (Bartosh) P.; came to U.S., 1946, naturalized, 1951; B.A., Mont. State U., 1951, M.A., 1955; Ph.D., U. Utah, 1958; m. Dorothy L. Martin, Sept. 12, 1953; children—Gayle Ann, Mark Vladimir. Dir. research labs. VA Hosp., Tomah, Wis., 1959-62; chief research psychologist VA Hosp., Oklahoma City, 1962—; from asst. prof. to prof. dept. psychiatry U. Okla. Med. Sch., Oklahoma City, 1962—, prof. research psychology U. Okla. Med. Center, Oklahoma City, 1967—. Bd. dirs. Psychology Press. Served with USAF, 1952-54. Recipient Distinguished Service award Oklahoma City Jr. C. of C.; named Ambassador at Large, Oklahoma City, 1968. Mem. A.A.A.S., Am. Psychol. Assn. Mason (Shriner). Author: (with Mathis and Pierce) Basic Psychiatry, 1968. Asso. editor Jour. Clin. Psychology, 1969—. Contbr. articles to profl. jours. Home: 3113 NW 62 Oklahoma City OK 73112 Office: VA Hosp 921 NE 13th St Oklahoma City OK 73104

PISTOR, CHARLES HERMAN, traffic cons.; b. St. Louis, Aug. 23, 1901; s. Charles F. and Augusta (Reh) P.; LL.B., Benton Coll., 1925, LL.M., 1926; student Washington U., 1927-28; m. Virginia Grace Brown, Jan. 18, 1929; children—Charles Herman, Walter Brown, Virginia Reh. Stenographer, clk. Mobile & Ohio R.R., St. Louis, 1918-24; commerce clk., chief rate clk. M.-K.-T. R.R., 1924-28; with T. & P. Ry., 1928-67, successively clk., chief clk., asst. gen. freight agt., gen. freight agt., asst. freight traffic mgr., freight traffic mgr., 1928-53, gen. freight traffic mgr., 1953-60; asst. v.p. marketing, 1960-67; cons. Western Traffic Cons., Dallas, 1967—. Life mem. Jr. C. of C. of St. Louis, former dir. Mem. Am. Soc. Traffic and Transp., Nat. Freight Traffic Assn., Assn. ICC Practitioners, Dallas Knights of the Round Table (pres. 1945), Transp. Club of Dallas. Presbyn. (elder). Club: Dallas Athletic. Address: 7038 Currin Dr Dallas TX 75230

PITCHER, GRIFFITH FONTAINE, lawyer; b. Balt., Nov. 1, 1937; s. William Henry and Virginia Griffith (Stein) P.; grad. Gilman Sch., 1956; A.B., Johns Hopkins U., 1960; LL.B., U. Va., 1963; m. Virginia Kyle Badham, June 27, 1959; children—Virginia T., Lawrence B., William T.B., Margaret W. Admitted to Ala. bar, 1963, Fla. bar, 1971; asso. firm Bradley, Arant, Rose & White, Birmingham, Ala., 1963-71; mem. firm van den Berg, Gay, Burke & Dyer, Orlando, Fla., 1971—. Pres. Bessemer Plaza Hotel Corp. (Ala.), 1966-67. Mem. Internat. Platform Assn., Am., Ala., Fla. bar assns., Soc. Cincinnati, S.R., Soc. 1812, Desc. Lords of Md. Manors, Soc. Colonial Wars, Beaux Arts Krewe, St. Andrew Soc. (vice chancellor 1971), Ala. Aquarium Soc. (v.p. 1970), Order of Coif, Delta Phi. Republican. Episcopalian. Clubs: Mountain Brook (Birmingham); Emerald Valley Resort (Pinson, Ala.); Citrus (Orlando, Fla.). Editorial bd. Va. Law Rev., 1961-63. Home: 440 Henkel Circle Winter Park FL 32789 Office: 16 S Magnolia Av Orlando FL 32802

PITCHFORD, HARRIET DAY, librarian; b. Canton, Miss.; d. Sterling G. and Lidie (Hunnicutt) Pitchford; B.S., Miss. So. U., 1935; M.A., George Peabody Coll., 1959; postgrad. Columbia, summers 1961, 64, 66. Tchr. elementary sch., Miss., 1935-41; librarian Main Post Library, Camp Van Dorn, Miss., 1941-43, Camp Roberts, Cal., 1943-47, Camp Zama, Japan, 1947-49, Ft. Benning, Ga., 1949—, Vietnam 1970-71. Mem. Am. Assn. U. Women, UN Assn. of Am. Club: Altrusa (pres. 1967-68) (Columbus, Ga.). Home: 115 Matheson Rd Columbus GA 31903 Office: PO Box 1972 Ft Benning GA 31905

PITCOCK, LOUIS, JR., oil and gas co. exec.; b. Fort Worth, Tex.; s. Louis and Medora (Shepherd) P.; student N. Tex. State U., 1941-43, Dallas Coll. So. Methodist U., 1947; B.A., Southwestern U. Tex., 1949; m. Mary Ellen McFarlane, June 29, 1949; children—Ellen Shepherd (Mrs. Charles F. Morris), Louis III, Thomas Carl. With Pitcock Bros., concrete, Graham, Tex., 1949-56, Pitcock Drilling Co., oil well drilling, 1956-67; sec.-treas. Pitcock, Inc., oil and gas prodn., 1967—, v.p., 1969—. Pres. Graham area United Fund, 1965-66. Del., Tex. Democratic Convs., 1960—, precinct committeeman, 1958—. Bd. regents Midwestern U., acting chmn., 1968—; trustee Graham Pub. Library, chmn., 1966—; bd. dirs. Graham area Day Care Center, v.p., 1970—. Served with USAAF, 1943-46; CBI. Mem. North Tex., West Tex. oil and gas assns., Graham C. of C. (v.p. 1956-57, 69-70), Phi Delta Theta. Methodist (vice-chmn. central Tex. conf. bd. lay activities 1955-63, dist. bd. trustees 1956-68). Rotarian (pres. 1955-56, sec. 1953-55). Home: 813 Elm St Graham TX 76046 Office: PO Box 747 Graham TX 76046

PITTINGER, JAMES HOWARD, oil co. exec.; b. N.Y.C., Aug. 21, 1925; s. Henry Howard and Frankie Dot (Johnson) P.; Geol. Engr., Colo. Sch. Mines, 1949; m. Viola Nickel, Aug. 18, 1948; children—James E., Crystal A., Robert H., Lyndon F. With Shell Oil Co., 1949-66; pres. Shell Pipe Line, Houston, 1966-68; pres., chief exec. officer Apco Oil Corp., Oklahoma City, 1968—; dir. Liberty Nat. Bank and Trust Co., Oklahoma City. Recipient Distinguished Achievement medal Colo. Sch. Mines, 1968. Home: 8015 N Glenwood St Oklahoma City OK 73114 Office: Liberty Bank Bldg Oklahoma City OK 73102

PITTMAN, CHALMERS VAN ANGLEN, geophysicist; b. Trenton, N.J., July 25, 1904; s. Raymond Hill and Evanna Catherine (Van Anglen) P.; B.S., Haverford Coll., 1925; m. Margaret Ellen Hallett, Aug. 10, 1929; 1 dau., Janet McLellan. Geophysicist Geophys. Research Corp., Houston, 1927-30, Geophys. Service, Inc., Dallas, 1930-42; exec. v.p., geophysicist Geochem. Surveys, Dallas, 1942—, now chmn. bd. Bd. mgrs., Haverford Coll. Mem. Am. Assn. Petroleum Geologists, Soc. Exploration Geophysicists, Dallas Petroleum Club, S.A.R., Soc. Colonial Wars, Hereditary Order Descs. Colonial Govs., Corp. Haverford Coll., Nat. Huguenot Soc., Soc. Descs. Colonial Clergy. Mem. Soc. of Friends. Club: Dallas Country. Home: 3909 Miramar Av Dallas TX 75205 Office: 2505 Turtle Creek Blvd Dallas TX 75219

PITTMAN, DONALD ELI, banker; b. nr. Kershaw, S.C., Apr. 5, 1940; s. Eli C. and Annie Lee (Ogburn) P.; student U. Md., 1957-59, Perry Bus. Coll., 1960-61, Am. Inst. Banking, 1961-65, U. S.C., 1955, 67, U. Colo., 1970-71; m. Nelle Moore Jonas, June 27, 1964; children—Damon Kirk and Derek Kyle (twins). Mgmt. trainee S.C. Nat. Bank, Columbia, 1961-62, asst. cashier, 1961-65; cons. Gen. Electric Co., Charlotte, N.C., 1966-67; v.p. First Nat. Bank of S.C., Columbia, 1967—. Marketing cons. to smaller banks; mem. S.C. Bankers Marketing Com., 1970-71; sales instr. Am. Inst. Banking; advt. cons. to charitable orgns. Active United Fund drives. Served with AUS, 1957-59. Recipient Army commendation. Mem. Columbia Sales and Marketing Assn., Am. Inst. Banking, Bank Marketing Assn., Columbia Advt. Club. Baptist. Mason, Lion. Club: Lake Murray Day Sailer Fleet (fleet capt. 1970-71) (Columbia). Home: 1110 Slann Dr Cayce SC 29033 Office: 1208 Washington St Columbia SC 29202

PITTMAN, EDWIN LLOYD, lawyer, state senator; b. Hattiesburg, Miss., Jan. 2, 1935; s. Lloyd H. and Pauline (McCraney) P.; B.S., U. So. Miss., 1957; LL.B., U. Miss., 1960; m. Barbara Lucille Peel, Aug. 24, 1957; children—Melanie, Edwin Lloyd, Jennifer. Admitted to Miss. bar, 1960; practiced in Hattiesburg, 1960—; mem. Miss. Senate, 1964—. Vice chmn. Inter-State and Fed. Cooperation Commn.; mem. Miss. Bldg. Commn., Miss. Tele-Communications Commn. Pres. Forrest County Am. Cancer Soc.; bd. dirs. Forrest County chpt. A.R.C., Forrest County Salvation Army, Hub dist. Boy Scouts Am. Served with inf. AUS, 1957-58; capt. Miss. N.G. Mem. Am., Forrest County bar assns., Miss. State Bar, Hattiesburg Jr. C. of C. (pres.), Kappa Sigma. Democrat. Baptist. Lion. Home: 2101 Arcadia St Hattiesburg MS 39401 Office: Carter Bldg Hattiesburg MS 39401

PITTMAN, ISHAM WATSON, mfg. co. exec.; b. Turbeville, S.C., Feb. 19, 1913; s. Isham Watson and Alice Newell (Turbeville) P.; student Stokes Bus. Coll., Charleston, S.C., 1930; m. Katherine Mathis, Mar. 27, 1936; children—Katrina, John. Salesman Nat. Cash Register Co., Charleston, S.C., 1930-32, Nat. Life and Accident Ins. Co., Atlanta, 1933-36, Minn. Mining and Mfg. Co., 1937-48, Wm. and Harvey Rowland, Atlanta, 1948-53; pres., gen. mgr. Joint and Clutch Service, Charlotte, N.C., 1953-57; salesman William and Harvey Rowland of Ga., Inc., mfg. power transmission components for heavy duty trucks and equipment, Atlanta, 1949-68, asst. v.p., gen. mgr., 1968—. Baptist (pres. men's Bible class 1968, deacon). Mason. Clubs: Automotive Booster (pres. 1948), Druid Hills Golf (Atlanta). Home: 301 Heaton Park Dr Decatur GA 30030 Office: PO Box 43386 Atlanta GA 30336

PITTMAN, JAMES ALLEN, JR., physician; b. Orlando, Fla., Apr. 12, 1927; s. James Allen and Jean C. (Garretson) P.; B.S., Davidson Coll., 1948; M.D., Harvard, 1952; m. Constance Ming-Chung Shen, Feb. 19, 1955; children—James Clinton, John Merrill. Intern, asst. resident medicine Mass. Gen. Hosp., Boston, 1952-54; teaching fellow medicine Harvard, 1953-54; clin. asso. NIH, Bethesda, Md., 1954-56; instr. medicine George Washington U., 1955-56; chief resident medicine U. Ala. Med. Center, Birmingham, 1956-58, instr. medicine, 1956-59, asst. prof., 1959-62, asso. prof., 1962-64, prof. medicine, 1964-71, dir. endocrinology and metabolism div., 1962-71, co-chmn. dept. medicine, 1969-71, also asso. prof. physiology and biophysics, 1966-71; asst. chief med. dir. research and edn. in medicine U.S. Vets. Adminstrn., 1971—; prof. medicine Georgetown U. Med. Sch., Washington, 1971—. Mem. NIH pharmacology, endcrinology fellowships rev. cons., 1967-68. Fellow A.C.P. (life); mem. Endocrine Soc., Am. Thyroid Assn., N.Y. Acad. Scis. (life), Soc. Nuclear Medicine, Am. Diabetes Assn., Am. Chem. Soc., Wilson Ornithol. Club, Am. Ornithologists Union, Am. Fedn. Clin. Research (pres. So. sect., mem. nat. council 1962-66), So. Soc. Clin. Investigation, Phi Beta Kappa, Alpha Omega Alpha, Omicron Delta Kappa. Author: Diagnosis and Treatment of Thyroid Diseases, 1963. Contbr. articles in field to profl. jours. Home: 3456 Newark St NW Washington DC 20016 Office: 810 Vermont Av NW Washington DC 20420

PITTMAN, JAMES STUART, educator, geologist; b. Vicksburg, Miss., July 23, 1926; s. James Stuart and Marion (Dunn) P.; B.S., La. State U., 1949, M.S., 1952, postgrad., 1953-57; postgrad. U. Tex., 1968-70; m. Harriet Lou Maloney, Mar. 9, 1952 (dec. Sept. 1966); children—James Stuart III, Douglas Joel; m. 2d, Margaret Tillson, Sept. 18, 1968. Geologist, La. Geol. Survey, 1951-52; asst. prof. Miss. State Coll., 1952-53; jr. geologist Humble Oil & Refining Co., 1953; sr. exploration staff geologist Phillips Petroleum Co., Bartlesville, Okla., 1957-63; commr. Washington County (Okla.), 1965-68; chmn. County Bd. Health, 1966-68, Met. Area Planning Commn., 1966-68; instr. San Antonio Coll., 1970—. Mem. Bd. Washington County Community Action Found., Inc., 1967-70. Served with USNR, 1944-45, AUS, 1945-46. Mem. Am. Legion, Am. Assn. Petroleum Geologists, Geol. Soc. Am., Soc. Econ. Paleontologists and Mineralogists, Mineral. Soc., Geochemical Soc., Am. Inst. Profl. Geologists, Sigma Chi. Mason. Contbr. articles in field to profl. jours. Home: 10202 Desert Sands Apt 21K San Antonio TX 78216

PITTMAN, MALCOLM GALUSHA, JR., ins. co. exec.; b. Chgo., Aug. 25, 1924; s. Malcolm Galusha and Helen (Cottingham) P.; student Miami U., Oxford, O., 1943-44, Oberlin Coll., 1944-45; A.B., Central Meth. Coll., 1945; m. Norma June Matthews, Oct. 31, 1947; children—Malcolm Galusha III, Russell Warren III. Sr. underwriter Bus. Mens Assurance Co., Kansas City, 1946-51, Bankers Life Co., Des Moines, 1951-54; mgr. health underwriting Gulf Life Ins. Co., Jacksonville, Fla., 1954-61; underwriting v.p. Kennesaw Life & Accident Ins. Co., Atlanta, 1961-63; v.p., sec., dir. Ga. Life & Health Ins. Co., Atlanta, 1961—. Mem. Mensa, Sertoma Internat. (life). Home: 3655 Woodstream Circle NE Atlanta GA 30319 Office: 66 Luckie St NW Atlanta GA 30303

PITTMAN, RAY A., JR., petrochem. co. exec.; b. Amarillo, Tex., Sept. 12, 1917; s. Ray A. and Mary (Huff) P.; B.S. in Commerce, So. Methodist U., 1938, LL.B., 1940; m. Barbara Sue Rowan, Nov. 28, 1965; stepchildren—Patrick Rowan Laughlin, Erica Laughlin. Admitted to Tex. bar, 1940; practice law, mem. firm Robertson, Leachman, Payne, Gardere and Lancaster, Dallas, 1940; spl. agt. FBI, U.S., S.Am., 1940-45; atty., spl. asst. Tex. Co., Houston, N.Y., 1946-59; v.p. LR Devel., Ltd., Buenos Aires, Argentina, 1959-61, Argentina-cities Service Co., Buenos Aires, 1961-62; v.p. Union Tex. Petroleum Div., Houston, 1962—; v.p. Allied Chem. Corp. Internat., N.Y.C., 1966-67; pres. Allied Chem. Internat., Houston, 1967—; chmn. bd. Overbrook Properties, Inc., Houston, 1967—; dir. Central Nat. Bank, Houston. Mem. State Bar Tex., Blue Key, Kappa Sigma, Phi Alpha Delta, Alpha Kappa Psi. Home: 3640 Inwood Dr Houston TX 77019 Office: Post Oak Tower 5051 Westheimer St Houston TX 77027

PITTMAN, ROBERT HERBERT, ednl. adminstr.; b. Alexandria, La., Mar. 22, 1915; s. Jackson Boyd and Lillie (Davis) P.; student U. Wis., 1938; A.B., Northwestern State Coll. La., 1938; M.Ed., La. State U., 1949; Ed.D., U. Miss., 1961; m. Kathleen Higdon, July 17, 1950; children—Martha Joe, Kathleen Ann, Susan Elizabeth, Sharon Evelyn. Tchr. Rapides Parish Sch. Bd., Lecompte, La., 1938-42; tchr., coach LaSalle Parish Sch. Bd., Urania, La., 1942-48; vis. tchr. Jena, La., 1948-49; prin. Cameron Parish Sch. Bd., Grand Chenier, La., 1949-57; prof., head elementary edn., dir. ednl. research and services McNeese State Coll., Lake Charles, La., 1957-70, v.p., 1970—. Cons. sch. dists. and colls., Hurricane Audrey and Carla Disaster Studies; adminstr., coordinator Cameron Parish Police Jury for Hurricane Audrey Disaster, 1957-58. Mem. La. Tchrs. Assn., Nat. Acad. Sci., Assn. Supervision and Curriculum Devel., Assn. Student Tchrs., Phi Delta Kappa, Kappa Delta Pi. Baptist. Mason (Shriner). Author: (with others) The Social and Psychological Consequences of a Natural Disaster, 1963. Home: 314 University Dr Lake Charles LA 70601

PITTMAN, SILAS, supt. schs.; b. Cobbtown, Ga., Sept. 14, 1932; s. Jefferson Davis and Claudia (Coursey) P.; B.S., Valdosta State Coll., 1959; M.Ed., U. Fla., 1963; m. Jan Greer McColsky, Dec. 28, 1965; children—Alexis Greer, Daphne Elise. Tchr. pub. schs. Columbia County, Lake City, Fla., 1959-68, supt. schs., 1968—. Served with AUS, 1953-55. Recipient Valley Forge Freedom Found. award, 1968; named Columbia County Tchr. Year, Fla. C. of C., 1966, 67, 68. Mem. Fla. Edn. Assn. (past bd. dirs.). Elk. Home: 2065 W Duval St Lake City FL 32055 Office: PO Box 1148 Lake City FL 32055

PITTMAN, VIRGIL, judge. Dist. judge, Mobile, Ala. Office: US Courthouse Mobile AL 36602*

PITTS, CHARLES PHILIP, coll. pres.; b. Cleburne, Tex., Nov. 5, 1916; s. Charles P. and Lucy (Adams) P.; B.A., Howard Payne Coll., 1938, D.D., 1953; B.D., Southwestern Bapt. Theol. Sem., Ft. Worth, 1952; m. Johnny Lee Stephens, July 27, 1938. High sch. tchr., 1938-40; ordained in ministry Bapt. Ch., 1937; minister Bapt. Chs., Hebbronville, Tex., 1940, Laredo, Tex., 1941-42, Cleburne, 1946-54, Dallas, 1954-67; trustee Howard Payne Coll., 1952-63, Dallas Bapt. Coll., 1964-67, pres., 1967—. Mem. state exec. bd. Bapt. Gen. Conv. Tex., 1954-67; mem. So. Bapt. Conv. Annuity Bd., 1961-67. Served to col. AUS, 1942-46, 61-62. Recipient Silver Beaver award Boy Scouts Am., 1956. Democrat. Mason, Rotarian. Home: Wedgwood Apts 2511 Wedglea St Dallas TX 75211 Office: PO Box 21206 Dallas TX 75211

PITTS, JAMES EDWIN, educator; b. Louisville, Apr. 25, 1942; s. Alvord Clayton and Zelma Eunice (Bales) P.; B.S. (Atwood fellow), U. Ky., 1964, M.B.A., 1965, Ph.D. (Earhart fellow), 1968; m. Martha Lee DeMyer, June 24, 1967. Teaching asst. U. Ky., 1965-67, teaching fellow, 1967-68; asst. prof. Sch. Bus., Fla. State U., Tallahassee, 1968—; cons. Tallahassee C. of C. Pres. Maricord Records, Inc. Bd. dirs. Fellowship Christian Athletes, Fla. State U. NSF fellow, 1967. Mem. Am., So. econ. assns., Am. Inst. for Decision Sci. (mem. council, mem. editorial bd. Decision Scis., v.p. finance S.E. region), Beta Gamma Sigma Omicron Delta Epsilon, Delta Sigma Pi, Pi Kappa Alpha. Baptist (deacon). Contbr. articles profl. jours. Home: 1106 Shalimar Dr Tallahassee FL 32303

PITTS, LLOYD FRANK, oil co. exec.; b. Wesson, Miss., Oct. 7, 1910; s. John L. and Addie Mae (Sandifer) P.; student Copiah-Lincoln Jr. Coll., 1925-31, Northwestern U., 1932; m. Mary Martha McCann, Dec. 28, 1935; children—Lloyd F. (dec.), Linda (Mrs. William A. Custard). With Nu-Enamel Corp., 1931-48, pres., dir., 1939-48; pres., dir. Nu-Enamel Internat., 1947-48; owner Pitts Oil Co., Dallas, 1948—; v.p., dir. Star Oil Co., Dallas, 1946-60; pres., dir. Longhorn Prodn. Co., Dallas, 1960—; chmn. bd., chief exec. officer Exploration Surveys Inc., Dallas, 1961—, pres., 1967-71, dir., 1957-71; pres., dir. Computer Systems Corp., Dallas, 1967-70. Pres., Park Cities Rotary Club Found., Inc., 1967-68; mem. Baylor U. Devel. Council, Waco, 1966—, Golden Gate Sem. Devel. Council, Mill Valley, Cal., 1966—. Bd. dirs. Dallas Civic Opera, 1970—, v.p., 1972—. Mem. Am. Assn. Petroleum Landmen, Ind. Petroleum Assn. Am., Tex. Mid-Continent Oil and Gas Assn., Tex. Ind. Producers and Royalty Owners Assn. Baptist (deacon). Clubs: Park Cities Roatry (pres. 1966-67, dir.), Dallas Petroleum, Dallas, Brookhollow Golf, Preston Trails Golf. Home: 4938 DeLoache St Dallas TX 75220 Office: Meadows Bldg Dallas TX 75206

PITTS, ROY EUGENE, utility co. exec.; b. Dallas, May 8, 1912; s. John A. and Daisy (Daniel) P.; LL.B., Dallas Sch. Law, 1937; m. Agnes Maloney, July 13, 1935; children—Rosemary (Mrs. Burns), James Ray and John Robert (twins). Sec. legal dept. Lone Star Gas Co., Dallas, 1933-37, atty. legal dept., 1937-57, asst. gen. counsel, 1957-61, gen. counsel, 1961-67, v.p., gen. counsel, 1967-68, sr. v.p., gen. counsel, 1968-70, vice chmn., 1970-71, chmn. bd., 1971—; chmn. bd. Lone Star Gathering Co., Dallas, Lone Star Producing Co., N.pak, Inc., Lone Star Energy Co. Home: 4730 Chapel Hill Dallas TX Office: 301 S Harwood St Dallas TX 75201

PITTS, THOMAS REMFRY, furniture co. exec.; b. High Point, N.C., Oct. 2, 1918; s. Darrell Remfry and Mary Angeline (Powell) P.; ed. U. N.C.; m. Harriett Lawrence Harrison, June 19, 1960; children—William, Robert, Trent, Leslie, Brooke. Mason. Sales rep. Myrtle Desk Co., High Point, 1940-45, sales mgr., 1947-50, v.p., 1950-63, pres., 1963—; dir. Clarendon Industries, Inc., v.p., 1963—; dir. First Union Nat. Bank, Life of Carolina (both High Point). Chmn. N.C. adv. bd. Small Bus. Adminstrn., 1960-65. Trustee, Randolph Macon Acad., Front Royal, Va. Served with USAAF, 1942-45. Mem. Bus. Equipment Mfrs. Assn., Phi Gamma Delta. Democrat. Episcopalian. Club: Emerywood Country. Home: 1105 Forrest Hill

Drive High Point NC 27262 Office: Myrtle Desk Co Taylor and Millis Sts High Point NC 27261

PITZER, BENJIMAN FRANK, banker; b. Monahans, Tex., Sept. 20, 1943; s. Preston Knox and Vada Mae (Wylie) P.; student Howard County Jr. Coll., 1964-67; m. Mary Kay Wennik, Mar. 27, 1964. With State Nat. Bank, Big Spring, Tex., 1963-66; head teller Fairbanks State Bank, Houston, 1967, head note dept., 1968, asst. cashier, 1968, cashier, 1969-72, v.p., 1972-—; sec. Fairbanks Financial Corp., Houston, 1970-—. Served with AUS, 1966-67. Mem. Am. Inst. Banking, Am. Bankers Assn. (rep. 1969-—). Home: 8807 Langfield Houston TX 77040 Office: 13636 Hempstead Hwy Houston TX 77040

PIXLEY, JOHN SHERMAN, research co. exec.; b. Detroit, Aug. 24, 1929; s. Rex Arthur and Louise (Sherman) P.; B.A., U. Va., 1951; postgrad. Pa. State U., 1958-59; m. Peggy Marie Payne, Oct. 16, 1949; children—John Sherman, Steven, Lou Ann. Asst. cashier Old Dominion Bank, Arlington, Va., 1953-56; tech. dir. John I. Thompson & Co., research and engring. firm, Bellefonte, Pa., 1956-65; co-founder, exec. v.p. Potomac Research, Inc., Baileys Crossroads, Va., 1965-—. Mem. Fairfax County Republican Com., Annandale, Va., 1964-—; mem. finance com. for U.S. Rep. Joel T. Broyhill, Republican, Va., 1970-72. Served to 1st lt. AUS, 1952-53; maj. Res. ret. Decorated Army Commendation medal. Mem. I.E.E.E., Sleepy Hollow Woods Civic Assn. (v.p., pres. 1969-71). Presbyn. Club: Quantico (Va.) Flying (charter mem.). Home: 3711 Sleepy Hollow Rd Falls Church VA 22041 Office: 5821 Seminary Rd Baileys Crossroads VA 22041

PIZZITOLA, FRANK JOSEPH, internat. exec.; b. Holyoke, Mass., Aug. 21, 1923; s. Joseph F. and Veronica H. (Maloney) P.; A.B. cum laude, Brown U., 1949; M.B.A., Harvard, 1951; m. Elizabeth E. Bailey, Jan. 28, 1950; children—Linda A., Stephen F., Gregory M., Paul B. With Monsanto Co., St. Louis, 1951-56; v.p. Olin Mathieson Internat. Corp., N.Y.C., 1956-62; exec. v.p., dir. Celanese Corp., N.Y.C., 1962-69; pres., dir. Jim Walter Corp., Tampa, Fla., 1970-—, also chief operating officer. Served with USAAF, 1943-46. Clubs: Harvard (N.Y.C.); Westchester Country; Palma Ceia Golf & Country; Chicago. Home: 4937 Lyford Cay Rd Tampa FL 33609 Office: 1500 North Dale Mabry Tampa FL 33607

PIZZO, ANTHONY PAUL, wholesale importing co. exec.; b. Tampa, Fla., Sept. 22, 1912; s. Paul and Rosalie (Pizzolato) P.; student U. Fla., 1932-34; A.B., Stetson U., 1938; m. Josephine Acosta, July 14, 1941; children—Paul Rodger, Anthony Joseph. Pres. importing and distbg. Internat. Brands, Inc., Tampa, 1945-50; gen. sales and marketing mgr. Tampa Wholesale Liquor Co., Inc., 1950-—; sec.-treas. Midulla Importing Co., 1968-—. Charter v.p. Pan Am. Commn., Tampa, 1949-57; mem. U.S. Air force adv. com. 6th Congl Dist., 1970-72; mem. Tampa Round Table, 1966-67; chmn. Ybor City (Fla.) Redevel. Commn., 1950-56; mem. adv. bd. Hillsborough County Community Coll.; chmn. com. to establish Jose Marti Park, Tampa; mem. Tampa Zoning and Planning Bd., 1950-60; mem. adv. com. FHA, 1954-58. Bd. dirs. Hillsborough County Hist. Commns., U. Tampa Found. Served with AUS, 1942-43. Decorated by Cuban Govt.; Order Cavaliere Oficiale de Merito (Italy); named hon. mayor Ybor City, 1952, Tampa Man of Year, Tampa Civitan Club, 1956, Ybor City Man of Year, Optimist Club, 1953; recipient Good Neighbor of Year award Tampa Consular Corps, 1950, award Columbian-Pan Am. Soc. of Havana, 1957. Mem. Tampa Philharmonic Soc. (charter, v.p. 1954-56), Fla. (dir. 1970-—), Tampa (founding pres. 1971-72) hist. socs., Tampa Sales Execs. Club (founder), Greater Tampa C. of C., Internat. Platform Assn., Ye Mystic Krewe, Sigma Iota. Rotarian (founding pres. Ybor City 1948-49). Clubs: University, Tampa Yacht and Country (Tampa); Palma Ceia Golf and Country. Author: Tampa Town—The Cracker Village with a Latin Accent, 1968; History of Tampa Bay, 1971, also numberous hist. articles. Research on history of Tampa. Home: 451 Lucerne Av Tampa FL 33606 Office: 5515 Anderson Rd Tampa FL 33614

PLANAS, JUAN ENRIQUE, engring. co. exec.; b. Havana, Cuba, July 5, 1940; s. Juan I. and Leonor (Martinez) P.; B.S. in Civil Engring., U. Miami, 1963; m. Sylvia Novo, Sept. 15, 1962; children—Sylvia M., Juan E., Luis I., Lourdes M., Jorge M. Jr. engr. Connell Assos., Miami, Fla., 1962-64; engr. Meekins Prestress, Hallandale, Fla., 1964-66; sr. engr. Ross Assos., Miami, 1966-67; pres., cons. engr. Planas & Franyie Engrs., Inc., Miami, 1967-—; pres. Cauto Investment Corp., PFE Enterprises, Inc., Profl. and Constrn. Mgmt. Co. Part-time tchr. U. Miami, 1963-64, Broward Jr. Coll., Ft. Lauderdale, Fla., 1965-66; mem. Cons. Engrs. Council, Registered profl. engr., Fla. Mem. Nat. Soc. Profl. Engrs., Am. Soc. C.E., Am. Concrete Inst., Constrn. Specifications Inst., Fla. Engring. Soc., Cons. Engrs. Fla. Kiwanian. Home: 3300 SW 17th St Miami FL 33145 Office: 1825 Coral Way Miami FL 33145

PLANER, HAROLD ISADORE, textile co. exec.; b. Phila., Sept. 19, 1924; s. Benjamin Moris and Irene (Ween) P.; student Davidson Coll., 1941; B.S., N.C. State Coll., 1947; m. Mary K. Sellers, Dec. 23, 1946; children—Cynthia (Mrs. David Chavis), Geoffery A., Patricia L., Robert L. Self employed, retailing surplus mdse., Gastonia, N.C., 1947-49; with Gurney Industries, textile mfg., Gastonia, 1949-—, exec. v.p., 1970-—, sec., 1968-—, purchasing agt., 1968-—, dir., 1968-—. Served with AUS, 1941-44. Decorated Purple Heart. Home: 974 Sandswood Dr Gastonia NC 28052 Office: 201 E 5th St Gastonia NC 28052

PLANT, RICHARD, dentist; b. Madison, Fla., July 12, 1924; s. Clarence Mosley and Francis Marie (Garbutt) P.; B.S., U. Fla., 1949; D.M.D. U. Louisville, 1953; m. Renna Mae Pickens, Aug. 26, 1954; children—Rachel and Rebecca (twins). Intern, Fla. State Hosp., Chattahoochee, 1953-54; practice dentistry, Darlington, S.C., 1955-59, Tallahassee, 1962-—; asst. dir. Fla. Instl. Dental Service, 1960-62; sr. dental staff Tallahassee Meml. Hosp. Cons. Fed. Correctional Inst. Pres., Big Bend Tb and Respiratory Disease Assn., 1968-71. Served with USAAF, 1943-45. Mem. Am. Dental Assn. Methodist (asst. dist. lay leader 1967-—). Elk. Club: Toastmasters. Home: 808 Piedmont St Tallahassee FL 32303 Office: 1901 Miccosuke Rd Tallahassee FL 32303

PLANT, THOMAS WESLEY, banker; b. Dallas, Nov. 18, 1911; s. Charles T. and Clara (Schaeffer) P.; standard certificate Am. Inst. Banking, 1936; student Rutgers, 1950; m. Frances Dupree, June 3, 1938; children—Thomas W., Patricia Gayle (Mrs. Hugh E. Prather III). With Fed. Res. Bank Dallas, 1929-—, 1st v.p., 1968-—. Mem. Robert Morris Assos. Methodist. Rotarian. Home: 3320 Marquette St Dallas TX 75225 Office: 400 S Akard St Dallas TX 75222

PLASTERER, NICHOLAS NYLE, educator; b. Mt. Etna, Ind., Sept. 14, 1909; s. George Reynolds and Nellie (Jeffrey) P.; student DePauw U., 1927-28; B.A., Albion Coll., 1933; M.S. in Journalism, Northwestern U., 1940; J.D., U. Toledo, 1951; postgrad. U. Ia., 1963-64; m. Ruth Louise Blinn, May 28, 1937. Reporter Sturgis (Mich.) Daily Jour., 1928-30, 35-39, Parma (Mich.) News, 1933-35; reporter Ft. Wayne (Ind.) Jour.-Gazette, 1940-42, copyreader, city editor, 1952-55; copyreader Toledo Blade, 1946-52; mem. faculty Sch. Journalism, La. State U., Baton Rouge, 1955-—, asso. prof., 1960-69, prof., 1969-—. Served with USAAF, 1942-46. Mem. Ohio Bar Assn., Assn. for Edn. in Journalism, Am. Legion, Delta Theta Phi, Sigma Delta Chi. Republican. Presbyn. Author: Assignment Jonesville: A News Reporting Workbook, 1966, rev. edit., 1971. Home: 2404 Horace St Baton Rouge LA 70808

PLATNER, WALLACE EUGENE, hosp. adminstr.; b. Los Angeles, June 9, 1932; s. Wayne F. and Adele Gertrude (Jones) P.; B.A., Walla Walla Coll., 1954; M.B.A., U. Chgo., 1966; m. LaBreta Leal Logan, July 11, 1954; children—Cheryl Denise, Kevin Eugene, Beth Ann. With Hinsdale (Ill.) Sanitarium & Hosp. 1960-65, Loma Linda (Cal.) Univ. Hosp., 1966-68; adminstr. Meml. Hosp., Beeville, Tex., 1968-—. Sec. treas. Bee County United Fund, 1969. Bd. dirs. Tex. Hosp. Assn. Credit Union. Served with AUS, 1954-56. Rotarian. Home: Route 1 Box 41E Beeville TX 78102 Office: Memorial Hosp 1500 E Houston St Beeville TX 78102

PLATT, ALLAN, govt. ofcl.; b. Bayonne, N.J., Aug. 24, 1925; s. David and Jane (Shilkoff) P.; student Williamsport Jr. Coll., 1944, Bayonne Jr. Coll., 1946; B.M.E., Clarkson Coll. Tech., 1950; m. Ann Heryla, Aug. 2, 1958; children—Carlton Jay, Douglas Glenn. Insp. engr. Picatinny Arsenal, Dover, N.J., 1950-56, chief, quality assurance spl. munitions, 1956-59, mgr. ballistic missile and warhead sects. Army Munitions Command, 1959-64; dep. project mgr. guided missile system Army Missile Command, Redstone Arsenal, Ala., 1964-71, chief engring. div., 1971-72; plant mgr. Fed. Copper and Aluminum Co., 1972-—. Served with USAAF, 1943-45; with AUS, 1951-52. Recipient Meritorious Civilian Service award Dept. Army; Sr. Exec. award Army Missile Command. Profl. engr., Ala. Mem. Soc. Mfg. Engrs. Home: 8016 Craigmont Rd Huntsville AL 35802

PLATT, JOSEPH LAWSON, orthopaedic surgeon; b. Knoxville, Tenn., Jan. 19, 1913; s. Robert Baxter and Nette Blanche (Lawson) P.; B.S., Emory and Henry Coll., 1933; M.D., U. Va., 1941; m. Louise Amonette Davis, June 27, 1942; children—Katherine Ann, William Lawson, Robert Davis, Joseph Baxter. Intern, U. Va., 1941-42; resident orthopaedic surgery U. Pa. Hosp., Phila., 1946-49, fellow orthopaedic surgery, 1949-50; orthopaedic surgeon Penn Clinic, Knoxville, Tenn., 1950-51; gen. practice medicine, specializing in orthopaedic surgery, Lynchburg, Va., 1951-—; mem. staff Lynchburg Gen., Va. Bapt., hosps. Dir. Crippled Children's Clinic, Lynchburg and Bedford, Va.; pres. bd. Piedmont Orthopaedic Surgery Bldg., Inc., 1965-—. Served to lt. col. with AUS, 1942-46; ETO. Mem. Am., So. med. assns., Am. Assn. Orthopaedic Surgery, Va. Med. Soc., Eastern Orthopaedic Soc., Am. Rheumatism Assn., Sigma Xi. Methodist. Clubs: Boonsboro Country; The Piedmont. Patentee in field. Home: 3308 Woodridge Pl Lynchburg VA 24503 Office: 1914 Thomson Dr Lynchburg VA 24501

PLATT, LOIS IRENE, physician; b. Oil City, Pa., May 23, 1908; d. Hugh Ashley and Myrtle (Dolby) Platt; A.B., Goucher Coll., 1931; M.D., U. Md., 1946. Tchr. pub. schs., Baltimore County, Md., 1931-42; intern, resident Garfield Meml. Hosp., 1946-47; cancer trainee Nat. Cancer Inst., NIH, 1947-49; practice medicine specializing in pathology, Washington, 1949-—; clin. instr. pathology George Washington U., 1949-54, asst. prof., 1954-66, asso. prof., 1966-—; prof. biology Gallaudet Coll., 1966-—; cytologist Cancer Clinic, 1949-—; cons. VA; dir. Sch. Cytotech. dept. pathology George Washington U. Hosp., 1963-— dir. Employment and Counseling Service of No. Va., 1959-64. Trustee D.C. div. Am. Cancer Soc. Recipient Appreciation award Am. Cancer Soc. Mem. A.M.A., Am. Med. Women's Assn., Am. Soc. Cytology, A.A.A.S., N.Y. Acad. Scis., Smithsonian Instn. Assos. Episcopalian. Club: Soroptimist of Arlington (Va.). Contbr. articles to profl. pubs. Home: 3500 Perry St Fairfax VA 22030 Office: 2430 Pennsylvania Av NW Washington DC 20037

PLATTER, ALLEN ANDREW, educator; b. Houston, Dec. 9, 1921; s. George William and Leila (Martin) P.; B.F.A., U. Houston, 1947, M.L., 1948, Ed.D., 1961; m. Paula Leone Peterson, Sept 6, 1952; children—Candice Lee, Lance Lane. Instr., asst. prof. architecture U. Houston, 1947-52; instr. art Brazosport Sch. System, Freeport, Tex., 1954-61; asst. prof. art Colo. State Coll., Greeley, 1962-66; asst. prof. edn. Southeastern State Coll., Durant, Okla., 1966-67, chmn. dept. art, 1967-—, prof., 1967-—. Exhibited in group shows at Houston Mus. Fine Arts, Dallas Mus. Fine Arts, U. Houston, Colo. Coll., Colo. State Coll., So. Colo. State Coll., Central State Coll. (Edmond, Okla.), Southeastern State Coll. (Durant, Okla.). Served with inf., AUS, 1942-45. Decorated Bronze Star medal. Mem. Okla. Edn. Assn., Nat. Art Edn. Assn., Durant, C. of C., Phi Kappa Phi, Phi Delta Kappa, Kappa Delta Pi. Episcopalian (sr. warden 1970-72). Club: Durant Country. Rotarian (sec. 1967-68). Home: Briarwood Mead OK 73449

PLATZ, ADOLPH AUGUST, food co. exec.; b. Jersey City, Aug. 28, 1920; s. Leopold and Olga (Gietz) P.; B.S., N.Y. U., 1943, M.B.A., 1954, C.P.A., 1947; m. Anna L. Erlemann, Sept. 20, 1952; children—Frederick, Valerie, Stephanie, Irene. With Guaranty Trust Co., N.Y.C., 1937-40; ins. accountant Gen. Cover Underwriters Assn., 1940-42; auditor Ernst & Ernst, 1942-43, 45-52; chief accountant to asst. treas., then controller, treas. Eskimo Pie Corp., Richmond, Va., 1952-69, v.p., treas., 1969-—, also dir. Treas. bd. Ridgetop Recreation Assn., 1956-63, pres. assn., 1964-65. Served as warrant officer finance dept. Signal Corps, AUS, 1943-45. Mem. Am. Inst. C.P.A.'s, Nat. Accountants Assn., Systems and Proc. Assn., Financial Exec. Inst. Home: 513 Gardiner Rd Richmond VA 23229 Office: 530 E Main St Richmond VA 23212

PLEASANTS, JOHN EDWARD, oral surgeon, educator; b. Aberdeen, N.C., Dec. 17, 1916; s. Charles E. and Evelyn (Harrington) P.; student Presbyn. Jr. Coll., 1934-35; D.D.S., Emory U., 1939; postgrad. U. Tex., 1952-55; m. Anne Arrasmith, Dec. 26, 1941; 1 dau., Mary Evelyn Smith. Practice dentistry, Chapel Hill, N.C., 1939-42; commd. 1st lt. U.S. Army, 1942, advanced through grades to col., 1963; ret., 1965; oral surgeon U.S. Army Hosp. Ship Francis Y. Slanger, Atlantic, W.W. II; div. dental surgeon, Korean war; dir. dental edn., intern and residency tng. Ireland Army Hosp., Fort Knox, Ky.; asso. prof. surgery U. Tex., 1965-68, prof., 1968-—. Cons. oral surgery VA Hosp., USPHS, surgeon gen. U.S. Army. Decorated Bronze Star medal. Diplomate Am. Bd. Oral Surgery. Fellow Am. Coll. Dentists; mem. Am., Tex., Houston Dist. dental assns., Houston (sec.-treas.), Am. socs. oral surgeons, Omicron Kappa Upsilon, Xi Psi Phi. Contbr. articles in field to profl. jours. Home: 2536 Dryden Rd Houston TX 77025 Office: U Tex Houston TX 77025

PLEASANTS, WILLIAM SHEPARD, advt. co. exec., author; b. New Orleans, Apr. 2, 1898; s. George Joseph and Elizabeth (Toulmin) P.; m. Wilhelmina Woodville, Oct. 1, 1926; 1 son, William Shepard. Vice pres. Reese Advt. Agy., 1924-26; asst. advt. mgr. New Orleans Item, 1926-35, advt. mgr., 1935-44, advt.-bus. mgr., 1951-54; v.p., gen. mgr. Walker Saussy Advt. Agy., New Orleans, 1944-51; v.p., copy chief Bauerlein Advt. Agy., New Orleans, 1954-—. Served to 2d lt. AUS, World War I. Named Advt. Man of Year New Orleans, 1965. Mem. Advt. Club New Orleans (hon. life). Author: The Stingaree Murders, 1932. Home: 71 Versailles Blvd New Orleans LA 70125 Office: Hibernia Bank Bldg New Orleans LA 70112

PLEMMONS, WILLIAM HOWARD, coll. pres. emeritus; b. Buncombe County, N.C., June 11, 1904; s. Nelson and Eugenia (Silver) P.; A.B., Wake Forest Coll., 1928, LL.D., 1958; A.M., Duke, 1935; student U. Chgo., summers 1937, 39-41; Ph.D., U. N.C., 1943; m. Elizabeth Sparrow, Nov. 26, 1931. Tchr., Asheville (N.C.) City Schs., 1928-33; mgr. Jax-Pax Store, 1933-35; prin. Leicester Sch., 1935-36, Lee H. Edwards High Sch. (now Asheville High), Asheville, N.C., 1936-41; teaching fellow U. N.C., 1941-43, admissions officer, 1943-46, registrar, 1944-46, asso. prof. edn., 1946-49, prof. edn., 1949-55; exec. sec. N.C. Edn. Commn., 1947-49; pres. Appalachian State U., Boone, N.C., 1955-69, pres. emeritus, 1969-—. Dir. Northwestern Financial Corp. Past pres., dir. N.W. N.C. Devel. Assn.; former commr. Edn. Commn. States; exec. sec. N.C. State Adv. Com. Pub. Edn. Mem. So. Council Tchr. Edn. (past pres.), N.C. Assn. Colls. and Univs. (past pres.), N.E.A., N.C. Edn. Assn., Am. Assn. State Colls. and Univs. (past pres., dir., hon. mem.), Boone C. of C. (dir.), So. Appalachian Hist. Assn. (dir.), Phi Delta Kappa, Kappa Phi Kappa, Kappa Delta Phi. Democrat. Baptist. Rotarian. Home: Boone NC 28607

PLENTL, WILLARD GATHINGS, state ofcl.; b. Houston, Mar. 22, 1919; s. Adolph Hugo and Alliene (Gathings) P.; student U. Wichita, 1954, U. So. Cal., 1955, Air Force Command and Staff Sch., 1958; m. Gloria Belle Jones, Jan. 10, 1942; children—Willard Gathings, Joy Van (Mrs. Michael S. Hensley), John Patrick. Served with AUS, 1940-42; commd. 2d lt. USAF, 1943, advanced through grades to lt. col., 1960, ret., 1962; asst. dir. Va. Div. Aeros., Richmond, 1962-64, dir., 1964-—. Mem. Pres.' Adv. Commn. Aviation. Decorated D.F.C., Air medal with clusters. Recipient Meritorious Service awards FAA, 1965, Air Craft Owners and Pilots Assn., 1967; Distinguished Service award Flight Safety Found., 1968. Mem. Nat. Assn. State Aviation Ofcls. (past pres.), Air Force Assn. (past pres. Richmond chpt.). Mason (32 deg., Shriner), Rotarian. Home: 401 Kramer Dr Highland Springs VA 23075 Office: 4508 S Laburnum Av Richmond VA 23231

PLETCHER, ELDON LEE, editorial cartoonist; b. Goshen, Ind., Sept. 10, 1922; s. Arthur and Dora (Cripe) P.; student Chgo. Acad. Fine Arts, 1940-41, John Herron Art Sch., Indpls., 1946-47; m. Barbara Jeanne Jones, Jan. 29, 1948; children—Thomas Lee, Ellen Irene. Editorial cartoonist Sioux City (Ia.) Jour., 1949-66, New Orleans Times-Picayune, 1966-—. Represented permanent collections Syracuse U., So. Miss. U., Wichita State U., State Hist. Soc. Mo. Served with AUS, 1943-46. Recipient Christopher award, 1951; ten awards Freedoms Found. Mem. Assn. Am. Editorial Cartoonists. Presbyn. Home: 3435 Pittari Place New Orleans LA 70114 Office: 3800 Howard Av New Orleans LA 70140

PLOCKELMAN, CYNTHIA HOLLEY, librarian; b. West Palm Beach, Fla., June 22, 1938; d. Raymond Henry and Gracae (Holley) Plockelman; B.A., Fla. State U., 1960; M.A., Emory U., 1961. Spl. librarian Central and So. Fla. Flood Control Dist. Library, West Palm Beach, Fla., 1963-—. Vol. chmn. library Jr. League Palm Beaches, 1967-70; mem. Civic Music Assn., 1968-—. Bd. dirs. Nelle Smith Residence for Girls, 1971-—. Mem. Am. Assn. U. Women (treas. 1963-65), Am. Malacological Union, Cal. Malacozoological Soc., Internat. Graphic Arts Soc., Fla., Spl. (employment chmn. Fla. chpt. 1972) library assns. Episcopalian. Republican. Club: Palm Beach County Shell (editor Seafari 1965-70, exec. council 1963-64, 65-70). Home: 311 Franklin Rd West Palm Beach FL 33405 Office: PO Box 1671 West Palm Beach FL 33402

PLOG, ROSE MARIE (MRS. GERALD SCHNEIDER PLOG), civic worker; b. Gate City, Va., June 25, 1918; d. William T. and Lucinda (Jones) Bellamy; student U. Tenn. Sch. Nursing, 1938-40; m. Gerald Schneider Plog, Oct. 31, 1941; children—Michael Bellamy, Martha Ann. Dir. Martin First Fed. Savs. & Loan Assn. (Tenn.). Leader, Girl Scouts U.S.A., Martin, 1956-61; cub scout leader Boy Scouts Am., Martin, 1953-56; pres. Martin P.T.A., 1960-—. Mem. Am. Legion Aux., Zeta Tau Alpha. Methodist. Mem. Order Eastern Star (worthy matron 1962, grand com. mem. 1965). Home: 337 S McComb St Martin TN 38237

PLOSS, SIDNEY IRA, educator; b. Bklyn., Aug. 19, 1932; s. Reuben and Frieda (Buch) P.; B.A., Syracuse U., 1953; Ph.D., U. London (Eng.), 1957; m. Kaja Mirecka, June 24, 1966. Research specialist U.S. Dept. State, Washington, 1960-62; vis. research asso. Princeton (N.J.) Center Internat. Studies, 1962-64; asst. prof. polit. sci. U. Pa., Phila., 1964-66; asso. prof. internat. affairs George Washington U., Washington, 1966-71; research fellow Harvard U. Russian Research Center, 1971-72, USIA, 1972-—. Lectr. dept. govt. Howard U., Washington, 1967-69; cons. U.S. State Dept., 1972-—. Served to 2d lt. AUS, 1957. Mem. Phi Beta Kappa. Author: Conflict and Decision Making in Soviet Russia. A Case Study of Agricultural Policy 1953-63, 1965; The Soviet Political Process, 1970. Contbr. articles on Soviet politics to profl. jours. and newspapers. Home: 6116 Massachusetts Av NW Washington DC 20016

PLOWMAN, JOSEPH DAVID, cons. forester; b. nr. Albemarle, N.C., Jan. 8, 1934; s. Willis Smith and Nellie (Morton) P.; B.S., N.C. State Coll., 1959; M.F., N.C. State U., 1968; m. Carolyn Marie Wood, Dec. 23, 1954; children—Joseph Clark, Michael Sean. Timber mgmt. asst. U.S. Forest Service, McKenzie Ranger Dist., Willamette Nat. Forest, Ore., 1959-62; cons. forester J.D. Plowman, Mt. Gilead, N.C., 1964-—. Bd. dirs., v.p. Sandhills Community Action Program, 1970-—. Served with USMC, 1953-56. Land surveyor N.C. Mem. Soc. Am. Foresters (chpt. chmn. 1967), Assn. Cons. Foresters, Am. Soc. Photogrammetry, N.C. Soc. Cons. Foresters (sec.-treas. 1970, 71), N.C. Soc. Surveyors. Baptist. Address: Route 2 Box 126-A Mount Gilead NC 27306

PLUMB, MILTON MAX, pub. relations cons.; b. Detroit, Oct. 2, 1915; s. Milton Max and Florence (Perren) P.; student U. Chgo., 1933-37; m. Libbye Gould-Verschoyle, 1939; children—Richard, Shelley, Diane. Reporter, polo editor Detroit Free Press, 1929-36; mng. editor Detroit Daily Abendpost and asso. newspapers, 1937-39; information and publs. officer U.S. Library of Congress, Washington, 1939-51; dir. legislative information C.I.O., 1951-58; dir. pub. relations Ry. Labor Execs. Assn., 1958-65; pres. Milton Plumb & Assos., Pub. Relations Cons., 1965-—. Cons. Am. Inst. Free Labor Devel., 1965-—; sec. Joint U.S. Mex. Trade Union Com., 1953-—. Trustee Islands Research Found., 1943-—. Served to maj. AUS, 1930-37. Mem. Nat. Capitol Democratic Club. Mem. Am. Newspaper Guild, Pub. Relations Soc. Am., Indsl. Relations Research Assn., Nat. Council for Spanish Speaking, U. Chgo. Alumni Assn., Labor Press Assn., P.E.N., Soc. Internat. Devel., Highland County Farm Bur., Highland C. of C. Unitarian. Clubs: Homestead (Hot Springs, Va.); Internat., Nat. Press (Washington), Capitol Hill; Country of Stanton (Va.). Author: Railway Merger Mania, Its Causes and Cure, 1963. Contbr. articles to profl. jours. Home: 5404 Broad Br Rd NW Washington DC 20015 Summer Rancho de los Montes Monterey VA 24465 Office: Davis Bldg Washington DC 20006

PLUMBLEE, RALPH GLENN, lumber co. exec.; b. Greenville, S.C., Sept. 4, 1920; s. James Earnest and Lena (Jordan) P.; grad. Draughan's Bus. Coll., Greenville, S.C., 1958; m. Frances Hall, Sept. 24, 1949; children—Stephen Glenn, Terry Hall. With Georgia-Pacific Corp., Plymouth, N.C., 1946-—, mgr., 1964-—. Served with AUS,

World War II: ETO. Mem. Plymouth and Washington County C. of C. (pres.). Home: 314 Pettigrew Dr Plymouth NC 27962 Office: PO Box 487 Plymouth NC 27962

PLUMMER, A. Q., accountant; b. Moran, Tex., Dec. 23, 1921; s. John W. and Mittie (Gill) P.; B.B.A., U. Tex., 1947; m. Betty F. Cantrell, June 4, 1949; children—John Cantrell, Jim Mcclung, Betsy Beal. Accountant, The Tex. Co., Houston, 1947-55; tax accountant Tex. Gulf Producing Co., Houston, 1956-60, chief accountant, 1960-65, Libyan Am. Oil Co., Houston, 1960-65; sec.-treas. Barbers Hill Salt Water Co., Houston, 1960-65; pvt. practice C.P.A., Brenham, Tex., 1965—. Instr. accounting S. Tex. Coll., 1956-57; mem. Washington County Bluebonnet Trials Com., treas., 1961; mem. S.W. Houston Cub Scout pack Boy Scouts Am., Brazos Valley Estate Council. Bd. dirs. Bohne Hosp.; trustee St. Jude Hosp. Served with USAAF, 1943-45. C.P.A., Tex. Mem. Tex. Exec. Inst. (sec., treas. Houston), Tex. Soc. C.P.A.'s Washington County C. of C. Methodist (steward, auditor, sec. stewardship and finance commn.). Lion (sec.). Home: Plum Hill Brenham TX 77833 Office: 201 W Main St Brenham TX 77833

PLUMMER, MRS. MILDRED YATES, lawyer; b. Port Arthur, Tex., Feb. 21, 1921; d. Calder Emmet and Edith Olive (Coe) Yates; A.A., Lamar Coll., 1940; A.B. cum laude, Baylor U., 1942; LL.B., Tulane U., 1948, J.D., 1969; m. Herbert Aden Plummer, July 8, 1943; children—Pati Edith-Yates, Paula Coe-Yates. Tchr. English, Thomas Jefferson Sr. High Sch., Port Arthur, 1942-43; with Gulf Oil Corp., 1943-46; admitted Tex. bar, 1949, since practiced in Port Arthur, specializing real property, probate, collections, maritime, domestic relations law. Past pres. Port Arthur Symphony Club; past legislation chmn. Service League of Port Arthur; bd. dirs. Beaumont Civic Ballet. Recipient Outstanding Club Family award Tex. Fed. Women's Clubs, 1958. Mem. Daus. Republic Tex. (chpt. pres., state parliamentarian), Port Arthur Assn. Ins. Agts., D.A.R. (chpt. regent 1969-71), Bus. and Professional Women's Club Port Arthur (pres. 1969-70), Tex. Women's Club (pres. Magnolia dist. 1962-64), Tex. Fedn. Music Clubs (legislation chmn. 4th dist.), Beta Pi Theta, Kappa Delta Pi, Alpha Chi, Sigma Tau Delta, Pi Kappa Delta, Phi Delta Delta, Kappa Delta (pres. Sabine area 1962-63). Presbyn. Club: Department (past pres.). Home: 4200 Griffing Dr Port Arthur TX 77640 Office: 305 Dryden Pl Port Arthur TX 77640

PLUMMER, RALPH NEWTON, psychiat. social worker; b. Fort Collins, Colo., Apr. 8, 1907; s. Vernon Vincent and Louisa Margaret (Webb) P.; student Colo. State U., 1927-30; A.B., William Jewell Coll., 1945; Th.M., Central Bapt. Theol. Sem., 1948, Th.D. (Teaching fellow), 1952; M.S.W., Kan. U., 1960; m. Yvonne Marie Shaffer, Nov. 14, 1932. Ordained to ministry Bapt. Ch., 1940; pastor Wellington (Colo.) Federated Ch., 1939-42, Swift Av. Bapt. Ch., Kansas City, Mo., 1946-52, Temple Bapt. Ch., Kansas City, Mo., 1953-54, DeSota Bapt. Ch., 1955-58; counselor Christian Edn. for Blind, Fort Worth, 1960-61; psychiat. social work supr. Kan. Neurol. Inst., Topeka, 1961-63; psychiat. social worker Kay Guidance Clinic, Ponca City, Okla., 1963; chief psychiat. social worker Bi-State Mental Health Found., 1968—; pvt. practice psychiat. social work, Ponca City, 1963—. Mem. Pastors Conf., So. Bapt. Conv., 1946-55, Ponca City (Okla.) Ministerial Alliance, 1963—; regional chmn. Rehab. Survey, 1967-68; psychiat. social work cons. Chilocco Indian Sch., 1966-71, Wakita Health Center, 1969. Pres., Nat. Ch. Conf. for Blind, Inc., 1961-63; patron Ponca Play House, 1963—. Mem. Acad. Certified Social Work (chmn. social work practice com. 1967-68, chpt. Social Worker of Year award 1971), C. of C. Kiwanian. Home: 726 N 4th St Ponca City OK 74601 Office: 1600 N 6th St PO Box 951 Ponca City OK 74601

PLUMMER, YVONNE M. SHAFFER (MRS. RALPH N. PLUMMER), psychiat. social worker; b. Jamesport, Mo., Oct. 9, 1909; d. Sobeski Adolphus and Minnie A. (Blizzard) Shaffer; student Colo. State U., 1930-31; A.B., Wm. Jewell Coll., 1945; Th.M., Central Bapt. Theol. Sem., 1948; M.S.W., Kan. U., 1960; m. Ralph N. Plummer, Nov. 14, 1932. Psychiat. social worker Osawatomie (Kan.) State Hosp., 1958-59, Child Guidance Center, Kansas City, Mo., 1959-60, Family Guidance Service, Ft. Worth, 1960-61, Topeka State Hosp., 1961-63, Out-Patient and In-Patient Hosp. Service, Bi-State Mental Health Found., Ponca City, Okla., 1963—. Mem. Okla. State Planning Commn. Mental Retardation, 1966-67, Okla. State Bd. Registration and Social Workers, 1965-70. Mem. Am. Assn. U. Women, Nat. Assn. Social Workers, Okla. Health and Welfare Assn. (dir.), Okla. Mental Health Assn. Baptist. Home: 726 N 4th St Ponca City OK 74601 Office: Ponca City Hosp Ponca City OK 74601

POAGE, EDWIN FRANCIS, med. adminstr.; b. Des Moines, July 4, 1917; s. Allen Dwight and Miriam (Driscoll) P.; B.S., Drake U., 1936, M.A., 1938; M.H.A., U. Chgo., 1945; m. Irma Louise Weaver, Aug. 12, 1945. Asso. adminstr. VA div. hosps., Chgo., 1950-53, Ohio Dept. Mental Hygiene and Correction, 1953-55; asst. adminstr. St. Mary's Hosp., Passaic, N.J., 1958-61; adminstr. Rolling Hill Hosp. and Diagnostic Center, Elkins Park, Pa., 1961-62, Central State Hosp., Nashville, 1962-65, Adrian Hosp. Assn., Punxsutawney, Pa., 1965-66, Christian Hosp., Inc., Miami, Fla., 1966-70; cons. surgeon Bur. Hosp. Adminstrn., Dept. Army, 1959—. Mem. Gov. Pa. Council Mental Retardation, 1961—. Mem. pres.'s council WHO, 1963—. Bd. dirs. Econ. Opportunity Act region II, Western Pa., 1965—, Jefferson County chpt. Am. Cancer Soc., 1965—, Jefferson County chpt. Cerebral Palsy Assn., 1965—. Served as officer, Med. Service Corps, AUS, 1955-58. Fellow Am. Acad. Med. Adminstrs. (v.p. region III, 1964—), Royal Soc. Health, Am. Pub. Health Assn.; mem. Assn. Mil. Surgeons U.S., A.M.A., Cath. Hosp. Assn. U.S. and Can., Nat. Assn. Hosp. Purchasing Agts. (regional gov. 1964—). Roman Cath. Rotarian (chmn. bull. com. Punxsutawney). Author articles in field. Home: 1408 S Bayshore Dr Miami FL 33131

POAGE, SCOTT TABOR, educator; b. Waco, Tex., Dec. 5, 1931; s. Scott Allen and Robbie Lee (Tabor) P.; B.S. in Indsl. Engring., Tex. Technol. Coll., 1953; M.S. in Indsl. Engring., Tex. A. and M. U., 1957; Ph.D., Okla. State U., 1962. Prodn. control engr. rocket fuels div. Phillips Petroleum Co., McGregor, Tex., 1953; teaching fellow math. dept. Tex. A. and M. Coll., 1956, instr. indsl. engring. dept., 1957-59; asst. prof. indsl. engring. dept. Okla. State U., 1959-61; mem. faculty U. Tex., Arlington, 1961-67, head indsl. engring. dept. 1961-67, prof., 1962-67; prof., chmn. indsl. engring. dept. U. Houston, 1967—. Cons. various cos., govt. agys. Served to 1st lt. USAF, 1953-55. Recipient Danforth Found. award. Registered profl. engr., Tex., Okla. Mem. Am. Inst. Indsl. Engrs. (chpt. 1964-65, nat. v.p. 1965-67), Operations Research Soc. Am., Am. Soc. Engring. Edn. (chpt. vice chmn. 1958-59), Am. Soc. Quality Control, Nat., Tex. socs. profl. engrs., Houston Engring. and Scientific Soc., Sigma Xi (club sec. treas. 1964-65), Tau Beta Pi, Kappa Sigma, Phi Kappa Phi, Alpha Pi Mu. Democrat. Episcopalian. Mason. Clubs: Petroleum (Fort Worth), Rotary. Author: Quantitative Management Methods, 1970. Contbr. articles to publs. Home: 2828 Bammell Lane Houston TX 77006

POAGE, WILLIAM ROBERT, congressman; b. Waco, Tex., Dec. 28, 1899; s. William Alan and Helen Wheeler (Conger) P.; A.B., Baylor U., 1921, LL.B., 1924, LL.D., student U. of Tex., summer 1919, U. of Colo., summer 1923; m. Frances Cotton, Feb. 14, 1938. Farmer Throckmorton County, Tex., 1920-22; instr. geology Baylor U., 1922-24, instr. law, 1924-28; admitted to Tex. bar, 1924, since practiced in Waco; mem. firm Poage & Neff, 1928-35; mem. 75th to 92d Congress, 11th Tex. Dist., chmn. com. on agr. Am. del. tb Inter-Parliamentary Union, Cairo, 1947—. Served as apprentice seaman USNRF, 1918. Mem. Am. Legion. Democrat. Universalist. Mason. Home: 600 Edgewood Av Waco TX 76708 Office: Rayburn Office Bldg Washington DC 20515

POARCH, LEAR WILSON, JR., mag. editor; b. Petersburg, Va., Aug. 7, 1919; s. Lear Wilson and Estelle (James) P.; grad. high sch.; student Internat. Corr. Schs., 1949-50; m. Louise Parker, Mar. 27, 1946; 1 dau., Janice Louise. With Civilian Personnel Adminstrn., U.S. Dept. Army, 1955—, supervisory placement specialist, Alexandria, Va., 1962-66, mgmt. employee relations specialist, Ft. Belvoir, Va., 1970—. Mem. nat. awards com. Circus Hall of Fame, 1960—. Served to staff sgt. AUS, 1941-45. Mem. Circus Fans Assn. Am. (nat. pres. 1959-60). Baptist (deacon, trustee 1969-72). Editor So. Sawdust, circus publ., 1954—. Contbr. articles to circus programs, circus publs., newspapers. Collector circusiana. Home: 3706 N Rosser St Apt 202 Alexandria VA 22311 Office: Civilian Personnel Office USAEC&FB Bldg T-2318 Fort Belvoir VA 22060

POCKAT, DELMAR BENJAMIN, educator; b. Marion, Wis., July 15, 1927; s. Harry John and Irene (Pranke) P.; B.S., U. Wis., 1950, M.S., 1951, Ph.D., 1964; m. Mary Armaganian, Dec. 23, 1950; children—Richard John, Alison Ann. Tchr., Cudahy (Wis.) High Sch., 1951-53; adminstrv. asst. Waterloo (Wis.) Pub. Schs., 1953-55; prin. Mayville (Wis.) High Sch., 1955-57. Nicolet High Sch., Milwaukee County (Wis.), 1957-62; project asst. edn. finance studies U. Wis., 1962-64; asst. prof. Sch. Edn., U. S.C., 1964-66, asst. dean, 1966-69; prof., dean Sch. Edn., Middle Tenn. State U., Murfreesboro, 1969—. Mem. Bd. control YMCA, 1951-53. Bd. sch. trustees Richland County (S.C.), 1969. Served with AUS, 1945-46. Named Outstanding Faculty Mem., U. S.C., 1969. Mem. N.E.A. (life), Nat. Soc. Study Edn., Am. Assn. Sch. Adminstrs., Tenn. Edn. Assn., Phi Delta Kappa. Episcopalian (vestryman 1961-62, 70—). Mason, Lion. Author: (with others) Education and the Law in Tennessee, 1971. Adv. bd. Sch. Law Newsletter, 1971—. Home: 738 Cherokee Ct Murfreesboro TN 37130

POE, EDGAR ALLEN, newspaperman; b. Jasper, Ala., Feb. 12, 1906; s. Thomas W. and Dora (Gunter) P.; m. Frances Margaret Harwood, Nov. 16, 1929; children—Edgar Allen, Thomas Lea. Reporter, Birmingham (Ala.) News, 1928-30; mem. staff New Orleans Times-Picayune, 1930—, war corr. Pacific, World War II, Washington corr., 1947—. Mem. House and Senate Press Galleries. Recipient commendation U.S. Navy, 1945. Mem. White House Corr. Assn. (pres. 1972-73), Washington Overseas Writers (treas. 1961—), Sigma Delta Chi (past pres. Washington profl. chpt.) Club: Gridiron (pres. 1971-72) (Washington). Home: 2615 S Lynn St Arlington VA 22202 Office: Nat Press Bldg Washington DC 20004

POE, HAROLD WELLER, theatre dir.; b. Cin., May 21, 1932; s. Harold V. and Dorothy (Weller) P.; B.A., Beloit Coll., 1954; M.A., Fla. State U., 1957, Ph.D., 1967; m. Lydia Virginia Lind, Sept. 11, 1954; children—Michael Lind, David Harold, Timothy Claude. Designer, tech. dir., U. Southwestern La., Lafayette, 1956-64, asso. theatre dir., 1964-69, dir., 1969-72, asso. prof. speech, 1964-69, prof., 1969—, coordinator grad. studies in speech, 1969—; dir. Tea for Three Billion, and Reflections from Insects, World Univ. Theatre Festival, Nancy, France, 1967; actor Sarasota (Fla.) Asolo Theatre Festival, 1961, Last Days of Lincoln, Fla., 1962, Premiere of Long Night, Tallahassee, 1963, Ore. Shakespearean Festival, Ashland, 1967. Theatre cons. for design and constrn. Lafayette (La.) Municipal Auditorium, 1960. Mem. Speech Communications Assn., Nat. Collegiate Players, Tau Kappa Epsilon, Phi Kappa Phi. Author of plays: Gnista, 1965; Tea for Three Billion (with Martin J. O'Malley), 1967; The Little French Tailor, 1971; Hansel and Gretel from Lagniappe, 1972. Home: 402 Auburn Dr Lafayette LA 70501

POE, JAMES EDWARD, lawyer; b. Garfield, Ark., Feb. 21, 1935; s. Louis L. and Maude (Banta) P.; B.A., U. Tulsa, 1957, LL.B. cum laude, 1959; m. Virginia Gattis, Oct. 29, 1960; children—Jon Mark, Emily Diane, Edward Adrian. Admitted to Okla. bar, 1959; also fed. ct. bars; practice law, Tulsa, 1959—. Atty., adviser Okla. bd. govs. Registered Dentists of Okla., 1964—; atty. mem. City-County Appeal Bd., 1969-70; mem. Tulsa County Excise Bd., 1971—. Active Cub Scouts Am. Precinct chmn., dir. Republican Zone Com., 1964-71. Recipient Vernon Law Book Co. award for scholarship, 1959, also other scholarship awards. Mem. Okla. (del. 1969-70, mem. med.-legal relations com. 1970—), Tulsa County (sec. 1971) bar assns., Toastmasters Internat., Cum Laude Soc., Delta Theta Phi, Pi Gamma Mu, Phi Alpha Theta, Phi Gamma Kappa. Home: 5609 S Yorktown Pl Tulsa OK 74105 Office: Pythian Bldg Tulsa OK 74103

POE, WILLIAM EDWARD, lawyer; b. South Hill, Va., Dec. 18, 1923; s. William Dowd and Douglas (Thornton) P.; B.S., Wake Forest U., 1947; J.D., Harvard, 1950; m. Mary Warren, Aug. 26, 1948; children—William Edward, Stephen D., Kenneth W., Richard S., Michael D., Anne L. Admitted to N.C. bar, 1950; asst. dir. U. N.C. Inst. Govt., Chapel Hill, 1950-52; partner Grier, Parker, Poe, Thompson, Bernstein, Gage & Preston, Charlotte, N.C., 1952—. Mem. Charlotte-Mecklenburg Bd. Edn., 1964—, chmn., 1966—; pres., N.C. Sch. Bds. Assn., 1969-71; v.p. So. Region Sch. Bds. Assn.; bd. dirs. Charlotte Christian Rehab. Center. Trustee, Wake Forest U., N.C. Bapt. Children's Homes. Served with USAAF, 1943-46. Decorated Air medal. Mem. Am., N.C. bar assns., Charlotte C. of C. (bd. dirs.). Baptist. Democrat. Rotarian (bd. dirs.). Co-author: Motor Vehicle Law in N.C., 1952. Home: 2101 Coniston Pl Charlotte NC 28207 Office: Law Bldg Charlotte NC 28202

POFAHL, KIMBEL WILLIAM, utility co. exec.; b. Faribault, Minn., Nov. 1, 1917; s. Herman W. and Gertrude (Schwartz) P.; student U. Minn., 1938-41; m. Mary Ellen Roemer, Dec. 19, 1942; children—Judith Ellen (Mrs.Wayne Skinner), Kim Christine (Mrs. Steven Tuttle). With Mpls. Gas Co., 1946-53; v.p., gen. mgr. Gainesville Gas Co. (Fla.), 1953-63, pres., gen. mgr., 1963-69, pres., chief exec. officer, 1969—. Mem. Golden Valley Planning Commn., 1949; dir. Alachua County Tb Assn. Mem. Fla.-Ga. Gas Assn. (dir. 1954-61), (chmn. 1959-60), Fla. Nat. Gas Assn. (dir. 1962-68, pres. 1965-66), C. of C. (membership com.). Episcopalian. Kiwanian. Clubs: Century; University (Jacksonville, Fla.); Gainesville Golf & Country. Home: 2215 North West 9th Pl Gainesville FL 32601 Office: 530 W University Av Gainesville FL 32601

POFF, GEORGE WILLIAM, city ofcl.; b. Barberton, O., Apr. 14, 1932; s. George and Ruth Helen (Elliott) P.; student Ashland Coll., 1950, Arlington Bapt. Jr. Coll., 1957-61; m. Flossie I. Jones, Dec. 22, 1953; children—Vicky Sue, Ricky Ray, George Arthur, Cathy Marie. Dir. pub. service City of Grand Prairie, Tex., 1960—. Founder Litter Prevention Internat.; v.p. Beautify Tex. Council, 1968-71; dist. activities chmn. Circle Ten council Boy Scouts Am., 1968-71. Served with USNR, 1951-59. Recipient Pub. Service award Grand Prarie C. of C., 1962; Officer of Year award Grand Prarie Police Dept., 1963; Spl. Service award City and Grand Prarie C. of C., 1965; Zeus award Epsilon Omicron Sigma Alpha, 1966. Mem. Pub. Relations Soc. Am. (membership and standards com. 1969-71); Alpha Psi Omega (nat. adv. bd. dirs.). Baptist. Mason (Shriner). Clubs: Optimist (pres. 1968-69), Grand Prairie Country. Home: 413 NW 22d St Grand Prairie TX 75050 Office: 313 W Church St Grand Prairie TX 75050

POFF, RICHARD H(ARDING), congressman; b. Radford, Va., Oct. 19, 1923; s. Beecher David and Irene Louise (Nunley) P.; student Roanoke Coll., Salem, Va., 1943-43, LL.D., 1969; LL.B., U. Va., 1948; m. Jo Ann Ragan Topper, June 24, 1945; children—Rebecca Topper, Thomas R., Richard Harding. Admitted to Va. bar, 1947; mem. 83d-92d Congresses, 6th Cong. Dist. Va.; chmn. House Republican Task Force on Crime. Vice chmn. Nat. Com. Reform Fed. Criminal Laws. Named Outstanding Young Man 1954, Va. Jr. C. of C. Served with USAAF, 1943-45. Decorated D.F.C., Air medal. Mem. Am., Va. bar assns., C. of C. (pres.), V.F.W., Am. Legion. United Comml. Travellers Am., Grounding Club Am., Sigma Nu Phi. Mason, Moose. Club: Radford Lions. Home: 5001 Kingston Dr Annandale VA 22003 Office: House Office Bldg Washington DC

POGUE, FORREST CARLISLE, historian; b. Eddyville, Ky., Sept. 17, 1912; s. Forrest Carlisle and Frances (Carter) P.; A.B., Murray State Coll., 1931, LL.D., 1970; M.A., U. Ky., 1932; Ph.D., Clark U., 1939; Am. Exchange fellow, Inst. des Hautes Etudes Internationales, U. Paris (France), 1937-38; Litt. D., Washington and Lee U., 1970; m. Christine Brown, Sept. 4, 1954. Instr. Western Ky. State Coll., 1933; from instr. to asso. prof. Murray (Ky.) State Coll., 1933-42, prof. history, 1954-56; mem. hist. sect. U.S. Forces, ETO, 1944-46; with Office Chief Mil. History, Dept. Army, 1946-52; operations research analyst Operations Research Office, Johns Hopkins, Heidelberg, Germany, 1952-54; dir. George C. Marshall Research Center, Arlington, Va., 1956-64, George C. Marshall Research Library, 1964—, also exec. dir. George C. Marshall Research Found.; Mary Moody Northen vis. prof. history Va. Mil. Inst., 1972. Mem. adv. com. Chief Mil. History, Dept. Army, Dir. Naval History, Dept. Navy, U.S. Mil. History Research Collection, Carlisle Barracks; chmn. Am. Com. History World War II; mem. adv. com. publ. Eisenhower papers Johns Hopkins, publ. Roosevelt and Fgn. Relations series Roosevelt Library. Regent Omar N. Bradley Found.; mem. pres.'s council Clark U. Served with AUS, 1942-45; ETO. Decorated Bronze Star; Croix de Guerre (France); recipient Distinguished Alumnus award Murray State Coll., 1964; Distinguished Alumnus Centennial award U. Ky., 1965. Mem. Am., So. hist. assns., Orgn. Am. Historians, N.E.A., Am. Polit. Sci. Assn., Oral History Assn. (past pres.), Am. Mil. Inst. (v.p.), Am. Legion. Democrat. Presbyn. Author: The Supreme Command, 1954; George C. Marshall: Education of a General, vol. 1, 1963; George C. Marshall: Ordeal and Hope, 1939-42, vol. 2, 1966; George C. Marshall: Organizer of Victory, 1943-45, 1972. Co-author: The Meaning of Yalta, 1956. Contbr. to Command Decisions, 1960, Total War and Cold War, 1962, D-Day: The Normandy Invasion in Retrospect, 1971. Address: 1111 Army-Navy Dr Arlington VA 22202

POGUE, HENRY EDGAR, realtor; b. Maysville, Ky., Sept. 18, 1920; s. Henry Edgar and Mary Byrnes (Parker) P.; grad. Dartmouth, 1942; m. Susan Louise Cecil, Oct. 24, 1942; children—Susan (Mrs. David Hill), Catherine (Mrs. John Burt), Henry Edgar V. Pres., Covert Hills Inc., Ft. Thomas, Ky., 1946—, Winston Acres Inc., Ft. Thomas, 1958—, Ft. Thomas Enterprises Inc., 1960—, Campbell County Bus. Devel. Corp., Ft. Thomas, 1961—; dir. Ft. Thomas Bellevue Bank. Cons. to Office Emergency Planning, Exec. Office Pres., 1964—. Mem. Ky. Bd. Edn., 1955—, past chmn.; chmn. Ohio-Ky. Progress Com., 1972; v.p. Ky. Ind. Coll. Found. 1965—. Served to lt. USNR, 1942-45. Mem. Nat. Assn. Real Estate Bds. (past dir., exec. com., 1st v.p.), Ky. Assn. Realtors (dir. 1956—, pres. 1958), North Ky. C. of C. (past dir., pres. 1971). Republican. Episcopalian (past vestryman). Lion. Club: Highland Country. Home: 82 Henry Ct Fort Thomas KY 41075 Office: 11 S Ft Thomas Av Fort Thomas KY 41075

POGUE, JOSEPH EZEKIEL, petroleum cons.; b. Raleigh, N.C., June 6, 1887; s. Joseph Ezekiel and Henrietta (Kramer) P.; A.B., U. N.C., 1906; M.S., 1907; Ph.D., Yale, 1909; spl. student U. Heidelberg, 1911; Sc.D., U. N.C., 1963; m. Grace Needham, Apr. 17, 1919. Asst. curator div. mineralogy and petrology, Smithsonian Instn., 1909-13, mineral technologist div. mineral technology, 1917-18; asso. geologist, U.S. Geol. Survey, 1913-14; asso. prof. geology and mineralogy, Northwestern U., 1914-17; asst. dir. bur. oil conservation, U.S. Fuel Adminstrn., 1918; mgr. dept. econ. research, Sinclair Consol. Oil Corp., 1919-20; cons. engr., 1921-36; v.p. Chase Nat. Bank, 1936-49; cons., dir. Gulf Oil Corp., 1949-59. Acting chmn., petroleum econ. com. Fed. Oil Conservation Bd., 1930; mem. mineral adv. com. to Army & Navy Munitions Bd., 1939; spl. asst. to chmn. Petroleum Industry War Council, 1942; mem. Nat. Petroleum Council, 1946-61. Mem. Nat. Oil Policy Com., Petroleum Industry War Council, 1942-43. Fellow Geol. Soc. Am., Am. Statis. Assn.; mem. Am. Soc. M.E., Am. Inst. Mining and Metall. Engrs., Am. Econ. Assn., Am. Assn. Petroleum Geologists, Soc. Automotive Engrs., Am. Petroleum Inst., Nat. Assn. Bus. Econs., Phi Beta Kappa, Sigma Xi, Alpha Tau Omega. Clubs: University, Mining, Lake Placid, Mountain Lake. Author: Prices of Petroleum and Its Products During the War, 1919; The Economics of Petroleum, 1921; The Economic Structure of the American Petroleum Industry, 1939; Oil and National Policy, 1948; Oil in Venezuela, 1949; Oil in Canada, 1949; Oil in Brazil, 1951; Future Growth and Financial Requirements of the World Petroleum Industry, 1956. Co-author: The Energy Resources of the United States, 1919; America's Power Resources, 1921; Capital Formation in the Petroleum Industry, 1952. Wrote brochure The Turquoise. Contbr. numerous articles on tech. and econ. topics. Address: Mountain Lake Lake Wales FL 33853 Died Dec. 17, 1971

POGUE, WILLIAM REID, astronaut; b. Okemah, Okla., Jan. 23, 1930; s. Alex W. and Margaret (McDow) P.; B.S. in Secondary Edn., Okla. Bapt. U., 1951; M.S. in Math., Okla. State U., 1960; m. Helen Juanita Dittmar, Oct. 26, 1952; children—William Richard, Layna Sue, Thomas Reid. Commd. 2d lt., USAF, 1952, advanced through grades to lt. col., 1969; combat fighter pilot, Korea, 1953; gunnery instr., Luke AFB, Ariz., 1954; mem. acrobatic team USAF Thunderbirds, Luke AFB and Nellis AFB, Nev., 1955-57; asst. prof. math. USAF Acad., 1960-63; exchange test pilot Brit. Royal Aircraft Establishment, Ministry Aviation, Farnborough, Eng., 1964-65; instr. USAF Aerospace Research Pilots Sch., Edwards AFB, Cal., 1965-66; astronaut NASA, Manned Spacecraft Center, Houston, 1966—. Decorated Air medal with oak leaf cluster; Air Force Commendation medal. Mem. Soc. Exptl. Test Pilots, Sigma Xi, Pi Mu Epsilon. Baptist (deacon). Home: 306 Lakeshore Dr Seabrook TX 77586 Office: Code (CB) NASA-Manned Spacecraft Center Houston TX 77058

POITEVENT, EADS, banker; b. New Orleans, Nov. 16, 1919; s. Eads and Evelyn (Butts) P.; B.A., Tulane U., 1942; postgrad. Rutgers U.; m. Ginette Bertin; children—Eads, Edward, William Poitevent, Ralph Ducros, Louis Ducros. Trainee, Nat. Bank Commerce, New Orleans, 1946-50, asst. cashier, 1950-52, asst. v.p., 1952-54, v.p., 1954-56, sr. v.p., 1956-58; with Mid-Continent Investment Corp., 1958; pres. Nat. Am. Bank, New Orleans, 1958-62; pres., dir. Bus. Funds, Inc., Houston, 1962-65; chmn. bd., pres., chief exec. officer, dir. Internat. City Bank & Trust Co., New Orleans, 1965—; pres., chmn. bd. ICB Corp.; sr. partner Jung Hotel and subsidiaries; dir. J.F. Inglis Frozen Food Co., Modesto, Cal., United Foods, Inc. Nat. PMA Corp., Dallas. Mem., v.p. Bd. Commrs. Port of New Orleans; dir.

Internat. Trade Mart, Council for Better La. Former pres. New Orleans Area council Boy Scouts Am.; dir. La. Maritime Mus.; past nat. pres. Leukemia Soc. Am.; bd. dirs., mem. exec. com. Internat. Ho., New Orleans Philharmonic Symphony, Gulf South Research Inst., WYES Ednl. TV. Mem. Am., La. bankers assns., Am. Inst. Banks, Mortgage Bankers Assn., Res. City Banker, Bank Pub. Relations and Marketing Assn., Young Pres. Assn., New Orleans C. of C. (pres.). Home: 312 Timberlane St Gretna LA 70053 Office: 321 St Charles Av New Orleans LA 70130

POITEVINT, LOYD, feed mfg. co. exec.; b. Bainbridge, Ga., Oct. 16, 1918; s. James Henry and Mary (Martin) P.; B.S., U. Ga., 1947; m. Joyce Lynn, Aug. 26, 1940; children—Alex, Lynn. Poultry serviceman Flint River Mills, Inc., Bainbridge, 1942-44, dealer sales and service, 1947-55, nutritionist, 1955-65, marketing mgr., 1965-68, v.p., gen. mgr., 1968—; chmn. bd. Southeastern Minerals Co. Served with USNR, World War II. Rotarian (pres. elect 1972). Home: 731 Russ St Bainbridge GA 31717 Office: 1006 Dothan Rd Bainbridge GA 31717

POLAK, JACQUES JACOBUS, govt. ofcl.; b. Rotterdam, Netherlands, Apr. 25, 1914; s. James and Elisabeth F. (Polak) P.; M.A. in Econs., Amsterdam U., 1936, Ph.D. in Econs., 1937; m. Josephine Weening, Dec. 21, 1937; children—H. Joost, Willem L. Economist, League of Nations, 1937-43; with Netherlands embassy, Washington, 1943-44; asst. financial adviser, then econ. adviser UNRRA, Washington, 1944-46; with Internat. Monetary Fund, Washington, 1947—, dep. dir. research and statistics dept., 1954-58, dir. research dept., 1958—, econ. counsellor, 1966—; professorial lectr. in econs. Johns Hopkins, 1949-50, George Washington U., 1950-55. Fellow Econometric Soc.; mem. Am. Econ. Assn. Club: Cosmos (Washington). Author: Public Works as a Form of Business Cycle Policy (in Dutch), 1937; Economic Recovery of the Countries Assisted by UNRRA, 1946; The Dynamics of Business Cycles (with Jan Tinbergen), 1950; An International Economic System, 1953. Home: 3420 Porter St NW Washington DC 20016 Office: Internat Monetary Fund 19th and H Sts NW Washington DC 20431

POLANSKY, NORMAN ALBURT, educator; b. Carbondale, Pa., Oct. 22, 1920; s. Joseph Joel and Celia (Kaplan) P.; A.B., Harvard, 1940; postgrad. U. Ia., 1940-41; M.S. in Social Adminstrn., Western Res., 1943; Ph.D., U. Mich., 1951; m. Nancy Gale Finley, Feb. 7, 1964; children— Grace Rachael, Jonathan Rolfe. Case supr. VA, Mpls., 1947-48; research asso. Wayne State U., 1948-51, asso. prof., 1951-53; psychologist, Austen Riggs Center, Stockbridge, Mass., 1953-55; prof. social work and psychology Western Res., 1955-60; dir. social service Highland Hosp., Asheville, N.C., 1960-64; prof. social work and sociology U. Ga., Athens, 1964—. Pvt. practice psychotherapy, 1962—. Partner, Polansky & Polansky, Real Estate, 1967—. Served with AUS, 1943-46. Recipient citation Nat. Assn. Social Workers, 1960; Distinguished Alumnus award Western Res. U., 1966. Fellow Am. Psychol. Assn., Am. Orthopsychiat. Assn.; mem. Nat. Assn. Social Workers (chmn. social work research, mem. bd. dirs. 1961-63), Am. Sociol. Assn., Acad. Certified Social Workers. Democrat. Jewish religion. Author: (with others) Retrieval from Limbo, 1967; Ego Psychology and Communication, 1971; Child Neglect, 1972; Roots of Futility, 1972. Editor: Social Work Research, 1960. Editorial bd. Merrill-Palmer Quar., 1958—, Ga. Review, 1972—. Home: 440 West View Dr Athens GA 30601

POLITZ, HENRY ANTHONY, lawyer; b. Napoleonville, La., May 9, 1932; s. Anthony and Mary Virginia (Russo) P.; student Francis T. Nicholls Jr. Coll., 1950-51; B.A., La. State U., 1958, J.D., 1959; m. Jane Marie Simoneaux, Apr. 29, 1952; children—Nyle Anthony, Bennett Louis, Mark David, Angela Marie, Scott Thomas, Jane Geralyn, Michael Gerard, Henry Stephen, Alisa Marie, John Robert, Nina Virginia. Admitted to La. bar, 1959; asso. Booth, Lockard, Jack, Pleasant & LeSage, Shreveport, La., 1959-61, partner, 1962—. Bd. dirs. Caddo-Bossier Legal Aid Soc., Shreveport, 1964-66, vice chmn., 1965, chmn., 1966; bd. dirs. Holidays for Humanity, Shreveport, 1963—. Served with USAF, 1951-55. Mem. Am., La. State (outstanding young lawyer award 1971), Shreveport bar assns., Am., La. (bd. govs. 1964-65, 67-68, pres. 1970-71) trial lawyers assns., Air Force Assn. (La. wing treas. 1962-63), Am. Legion (judge adv. 1967-68, vice comdr. 1968-69), Order of Coif, Omicron Delta Kappa. Democrat. Roman Catholic. K.C. Club: Serra (sec. 1963-64). Home: 938 Linden St Shreveport LA 71104 Office: Mid South Towers Shreveport LA 71101

POLK, BAXTER, librarian; b. Santa Anna, Tex., Aug. 27, 1914; s. E.E. and Mayme (Baxter) P.; B.A. magna cum laude, Hardin-Simmons U., 1935; B.L.S. U. Okla., 1937; M.S., Columbia, 1952; m. Elizabeth S. Cram, Aug. 8, 1953 (dec. Nov. 1966); foster children—Judith S. Robinson, David W. Scudder. Head librarian U. Tex. at El Paso, 1936-71, dir. spl. collections, 1971—. Home: 716 Elmwood Dr El Paso TX 79932

POLK, ISAAC NEWTON, JR., research specialist; b. Cleburne, Tex., Nov. 19, 1919; s. Isaac Newton and Alberta (Hays) P.; student U. Tex., 1947-48; A.B. cum laude, Harvard, 1951; postgrad. U. Santa Clara, 1960-61; m. Patricia Nan Doyle, Apr. 5, 1954; children—Randolph Christopher, Nancy Elizabeth. Econ. analyst Creole Petroleum Corp., Venezuela, 1953-60; operations research Lockheed Aircraft Corp., Palo Alto, Cal., 1960-63; research specialist Gen. Dynamics Corp., Fort Worth, 1963—. Mem. adv. com. Cupertino (Cal.) Pub. Sch. Dist., 1962. Served with USAAF, 1942-45. Mem. Am. Econ. Assn. Presbyn. Contbr. articles to profl. jours. Home: 4416 Summercrest Ct Fort Worth TX 76109 Office: PO Box 748 Fort Worth TX 76101

POLK, JAMES AUSTIN, dentist; b. Monticello, Miss., Feb. 7, 1919; s. Zebulon Aaron and Mary Adeline (Hedgepeth) P.; D.D.S., Baylor U., 1950; m. Dorothy Mitchell, Aug. 24, 1940; children—James Donovan, Rodney Eugene, Anthony Gerald. Pvt. practice dentistry, Dallas, 1952—. Served with USAAF, 1943-46, USAF, 1950-52. Mem. N. Dallas C. of C. (chmn. flood control com. 1969, bd. dirs. 1970—), Am., Tex., Miss. dental assns., Dallas County Dental Soc. Baptist (tchr. Sunday sch. 1941—, spl. finance bldg. com. 1970—). Mason (Shriner), Club: Baylor Century. Home: 3744 Meadowdale Lane Dallas TX 75229 Office: 8016 Denton Dr Dallas TX 75235

POLK, WALTER BRASHEAR, chem. engr.; b. Vicksburgh, Miss., Dec. 9, 1920; s. Walter Howe and Mary (Brashear) P.; student Ark. A. and M. Coll., 1940-42; B.S. in Chem. Engring., Okla. State U., 1944; m. Martha Nelle Burton, May 27, 1949; 1 dau., Ann. Chemist, process engr., mech. design engr., Borger Refinery, Phillips Petroleum Co., Borger, Tex., 1945-50, chemist, process engr., Plains Plant, Borger, 1950-55, supr. process engring and maintenance, 1955-64, process design and cons. engring. div., Bartlesville, Okla., 1964-70, cons., environment control engr., 1970—. Instr., Frank Phillips Coll., Borger, 1957-63, coordinator and process cons. for design, constrn. N.V. Petrochim, London, Eng., 1965-66, Antwerp, Belgium, 1966-68. Registered profl. engr., Okla., Tex. Mem. Am. Chem. Soc., Am. Inst. Chem. Engrs. (founder Tex. Panhandle sect.), Sigma Tau, Phi Lambda Upsilon, Kappa Sigma Kappa, Blue Key. Club: American (Antwerp). Presbyn. (deacon, elder). Patentee in field. Home: 6025 SE Cornell Dr Bartlesville OK 74003 Office: Phillips Petroleum Co Bartlesville OK 74004

POLLAK, EDWARD, constrn. co. exec.; b. Houston, Dec. 3, 1916; s. Edward and Rose M. (Cohen) P.; student Rice U., 1933-37; m. Lillian B. Wiesenthal, June 30, 1940; children—Stephanie (Mrs. Allan Maierson), Fredell H. Engr., Harry L. Edwards Drilling Co., Houston, 1937-42; asst. project engr. U.S. C.E., Galveston, 1942-43; equipment mgr., asst. sec.-treas. Tellepsen Constrn. Co., Houston 1943—; v.p. Whitelak, Inc., Houston, 1962—. Mem. Soc. Automotive Engrs. Club: Internat. (Houston). Home: 3602 Aberdeen Way Houston TX 77025 Office: PO Box 2536 Houston TX 77001

POLLARD, BILLY MOORE, dentist; b. Gates, Tenn., Nov. 9, 1926; s. William Thomas and Alma Norma (Chisholm) P.; student Union U., 1946-48; D.D.S., U. Tenn., 1951; m. Mary Jean Riddle, June 6, 1948; children—Michael Thomas, Jean Michelle. Pvt. practice dentistry, Jackson, Tenn., 1953—. Cons. U. Tenn. Coll. Dentistry, Dept. Oral Diagnosis, Dean in Curricular Affairs, 1971. Commr. Jackson Housing Authority, 1971—; chmn. annual loyalty program L. G. Noel Meml. Found., 1971-72. Served with USNR, 1945-46, 51-53. Mem. Pierre Fauchard Acad., Acad. Gen. Dentistry, Am. Soc. Preventive Dentistry, Am., Tenn (trustee 1970-73) dental assns., So. Acad. Oral Surgery, Seventh Dist. Dental Soc. (pres.-elect 1972-73), Jackson Dental Study Club, Delta Sigma Delta, Alpha Tau Omega. Methodist. Mason, Kiwanian. Address: 1211 N Highland St Jackson TN 38301

POLLARD, FRED G., lawyer; b. Richmond, Va., May 7, 1918; A.B., U. Va., 1940, LL.B., 1942. Admitted to Va. bar, 1942; mem. firm Williams, Mullen & Christian, Richmond; mem. Va. Ho. of Dels., 1950-65; lt. gov. State of Va., Richmond, 1966-70. Mem. Am., Va. State, Richmond bar assns., Phi Delta Phi. Address: 510 United Va Bank Bldg Richmond VA 23219

POLLARD, ODELL, state chmn. Republican Nat. Com.; b. Union Hill, Ark., Apr. 29, 1927; s. Joseph F. and Beulah (Scantlin) P.; ed. Miss. Coll., Tulane U.; LL.B., U. Ark.; m. Sammy Lane Lewis, Feb. 8, 1953; children—Laura Lane, Paula Lynn, Mark. Mem. Ark. Rep. Exec. Com., 1960—, now state chmn.; del. Rep. Nat. Conv., 1968. Mem. Am., Ark., White County bar assns. Home: 407 W Race Av Searcey AR 72143 Office: P O Box 36 Searcey AR 72143*

POLLIN, ABE, builder; b. Phila., Dec. 3, 1923; s. Morris and Jennie (Sack) P.; student U. Md., 1941-44; B.A., George Washington U., 1945; m. Irene S. Kerchek, May 27, 1945; children—Robert Norman, James Edward. Engaged in home bldg. bus., 1945—; pres. Abe Pollin, Inc., Balt., 1962—; pres. Balt. Bullets Basketball Club, Inc., 1964—; dir. County Fed. Savs. & Loan Assn., Rockville, Md. Bd. dirs. United Jewish Appeal, Nat. Jewish Hosp., Jewish Community Center; bd. dirs., mem. adv. com. John F. Kennedy Cultural Center. Mem. Nat. Assn. Home Builders, Asso. Builders and Contractors Md., Washington Bd. Trade. Jewish religion. Home: 2 Goldsboro Ct Bethesda MD 20034 Office: 6101 16th St Washington DC 20011

POLLOCK, ELEANOR (MRS. ALBION HUGHES), profl. orgn. ofcl.; b. N.Y.C.; d. George E. and Alice (Pollock) Joseph; student Finch Jr. Coll., Gardner Sch., N.Y.C.: m. Albion Hughes, Mar. 28, 1956. Woman's editor Phila. Record, 1938-44; editor Cue mag., 1946-50; asso. editor Look mag., 1950-51; mag. editor Charm mag., 1951-53; editor Family Life mag., 1953; exec. women's editor Evening and Sunday Bull., Phila., 1955-64, spl. writer, 1964-65; White House liaison Project Head Start, Office Econ. Opportunity, 1965-66; dir. pub. affairs Nat. Endowment for Arts, 1966-67, Pres.'s Com. on Consumer Interests, 1967-69, Nat. Commn. on Product Safety, 1969—; dir. pub. affairs Nat. Commn. on Materials Policy, 1972—. Bd. govs. Fashion Group, Inc., 1946, 53, 64. Mem. Alliance Francaise, Philadelphia. Clubs: Washington Press (publicity chmn.). Contbr. articles to leading women's mags. Home: 2230 California St NW Washington DC 20008

POLOPOLUS, LEONIDAS, educator; b. San Bernardino, Cal., Aug. 8, 1933; s. Constantine and Irene (Bombolis) P.; B.S., U. Cal. at Davis, 1955; Ph.D., U. Cal. at Berkeley, 1960; m. Patricia Jones, Feb. 15, 1964; children—Michael, Margaret Irene, Eleni. Asst. prof. econs. La. State U., Baton Rouge, 1960-63, asso. prof., 1963-65; asso. prof. econs. U. Fla., Gainesville, 1965-69, prof., 1969—, asst. dean Grad. Sch., 1969—; research economist Fla. Citrus Commn., 1965-66, dir. econ. research dept., 1966-68. Recipient Outstanding Jr. Faculty award Gamma Sigma Delta, 1971. Mem. Am. Agrl. Econ. Assn., Am. Econ. Assn., Gamma Sigma Delta. Mason, Kiwanian (com. chmn. 1971—). Editor, Am. Jour. of Agrl. Econs., 1971—. Home: 1004 N W 34th St Gainesville FL 32601

POMERANCE, ROCKY, police chief; b. N.Y.C., May 20, 1927; s. Hyman and Mollie (Seiler) S.; grad. Coll. City N.Y., 1943, U. Miami, 1960; m. Hope Marie Nason, June 3, 1951; children—Kenneth Howard, James Gary, Victoria Ellen. Constable, Dist. 5, Dade County (Fla.), 1956-63; police chief Miami Beach, Fla., 1963—. Pres. Miami Beach Civic League, 1963; mem. adv. com. So. Eastern Inst. Criminal Justice, 1971, Biscayne Coll. Criminal Justice and Pub. Adminstrn., 1971. Coordinator security Republican Nat. Conv., 1968, 72, Dem. Nat. Conv., 1972. Served with AUS, 1945-46. Recipient Good Govt. award Jr. C. of C., 1960, First Community Service award Optimists Internat., 1964, Reverence for Law award Nat. Fraternal Order Eagles. Mem. Navy League, Internat. Assn. Chiefs Police (4th v.p. 1971), Dade Chiefs Assn. (pres. 1968-69), Fla. Police Chiefs Assn. (dir. 1971). Kiwanian. Author: (with Judge M. Goodman) You and the Law, 1965. Home: 4423 Alton Rd Miami Beach FL 33140 Office: 120 Meridian Av Miami Beach FL 33139

POMEROY, WILLIAM HENRY, JR., oil co. exec.; b. Tulsa, Oct. 4, 1912; s. William Henry and Norine (Wilson) P.; B.A., Amherst Coll., 1934; LL.B., Yale, 1937; m. Madeline Lewis, Feb. 1, 1944; children—William Henry (dec.), Barbara L. (dec.), Russell E., C. Renee, H. Suzanne. Admitted to Okla. bar, 1938; ind. oil operator, Midland, Tex., 1937-38, Evansville, Ind., 1938-41; v.p. Diamond Oil Well Drilling Co., Midland, Tex., 1946-58; v.p., Shoreline Oil and Gas Co. and Pearl Royalty Co., Tulsa and Midland, Tex., 1947-60, pres., 1960—. Bd. dirs. Community Theatre, pres., 1961-62; bd. dirs. Cancer Soc., pres., 1967-68; bd. dirs. Community Chest, treas., 1963-64; bd. dirs. A.R.C., v.p., 1963-64; bd. dirs. Symphony Assn. Trinity Sch. (all in Midland, Tex.). Served with AUS, 1941-42, 42-46. Mem. Ind. Petroleum Assn. Am., Okla. Bar Assn., C. of C. Presbyn. (elder, deacon). Clubs: Midland Country, Racquet (pres. 1962), Civitan (pres. 1953) (Midland, Tex.). Home: 1700 Princeton St Midland TX 79701 Office: 1226 Vaughn Bldg Midland TX 79701

PONDER, HENRY, educator, univ. adminstr.; b. Seminole, Okla., Mar. 28, 1928; s. Frank Jerry and Lille Mae (Edwards) P.; B.S., Langston U., 1951; M.S., Okla. State U., 1958; Ph.D., Ohio State U., 1963; m. Eunice Wilson, Nov. 22, 1952; children—Cheryl, Anna. Chmn. dept. agrl. econs. Va. State Coll., 1963-64; chmn. dept. bus. and econs. Ft. Valley State Coll., 1964-66; v.p. for acad. affairs Ala. A. and M. U., 1966—. Cons., Irving Trust Co., N.Y.C., summer 1968, Chase Manhattan Bank, summer 1969, U.S. Treasury Dept., Washington, summer 1970, Omaha Nat. Bank, summer 1971. Active United Givers Fund; lectr. consumer edn. Community Action Program, 1967—. Bd. dirs. Ala. A. and M. U. Found. Served with AUS, 1953-55. Mem. Am. Econ. Assn., New Farmers Am., Am. Farm Econ. Assn., Phi Gamma Mu, Gamma Sigma Delta, Alpha Phi Alpha. Mason (32 deg.). Home: 110 Chase Rd Huntsville AL 35811 Office: Ala A and M U Normal AL 35762

PONDER, SPEERS GORDON, educator; b. Gadsden, Ala., Dec. 23, 1911; s. William A. and Ellie (Rainwater) P.; student Madison Coll., 1930-33; B.S., N.C. State U., 1962, M.S., 1964; m. Lucy Edmonia Davis, Apr. 24, 1934; children—Gordon Edmond, Reginald Wallace, Patricia Elaine (Mrs. George Conrad Wilson), Betty-Lee (Mrs. Michael Eugene Stickler), Michael. With Victor Chem. Works, Mt. Pleasant, Tenn., 1933-41; commd. 2d lt. U.S. Army, 1941, advanced through grades to col., 1950; at Army Chem. Center, 1941-42, Air Proving Ground Command, 1942-45, Air Univ., 1946-47, Hdqrs. USAF, 1947-49, San Jose Project, 1949-50, Dugway Proving Ground, 1950-53, Korea, 1953-54, N.C. Mil. Dist., 1954-60; ret., 1960; faculty N.C. State U., 1963-65, Campbell Coll., Buies Greek, N.C., 1965-67, U. Richmond (Va.), 1967—. Decorated Legion of Merit. Mem. Am. Econ. Assn. Home: 8402 Glendale Dr Richmond VA 23229

PONDER, THOMAS C., editor; b. Tuckerman, Ark., Dec. 6, 1921; s. Harry Lee and Ruth Lee (Hopper) P.; B.S., U. Ark., 1948; m. Catherine Francis Cahill, Nov. 24, 1942; children—Thomas C., Stephen Cahill, Harry Lee. Process engr. PPG Industries, LakeCharles, La., 1948-51; project engr. Foster Wheeler Corp., Houston, 1951-54, Lummus Co., Houston, 1954-55; petrochems. editor Hydrocarbon Processing, Houston, 1955—. Served with USAAF, 1944-46. Mem. Am. Inst. Chem. Engrs., Am. Chem. Soc., Am. Assn. Cost Engrs. (nat. pres. 1965-66; award 1971). Contbr. articles to profl. jours. Home: 10227 Raritan Dr Houston TX 77043 Office: PO Box 2606 Houston TX 77001

PONDER, WILLIAM GRAHAM, publisher; b. Rutledge, Ga., Nov. 5, 1923; s. Paul Holloway and Mary (Graham) P.; student Emory U., 1943-44; B.S., Clemson U., 1948; postgrad. U. Ga., 1949; m. Adelaide Douglas Wallace, Apr. 24, 1948; children—Anne, Mary Graham, Adelaide Douglas, William Graham. Pub., The Madisonian, Madison, Ga., 1957—; pres. Madisonian Pub. Co., Inc.; sec.-treas., dir. Madison Investment Co., dir., sec.-treas. Greater Ga. Printers, Inc., 1969—; dir. Hardman & Stuckey Travel Investments, Inc., 1970—. Mem. City and County Planning Commns., 1960-62; mem. bldg. com. Ga. Press Found. Mem. City Council, Madison, 1958-62. Pres. Mental Health Assn.; chmn. bd. Morgan County Hosp. Authority. Served with USNR, 1944-47. Mem. Ga. Press Assn. (pres. 1965-66, com. chmn.), Atlanta Press Club (charter mem.), Sigma Nu, Sigma Delta Chi. Kiwanian (pres. 1970). Episcopalian. Home: 782 S Main St Madison GA 30650 Office: 131 E Jefferson St PO Box 191 Madison GA 30650

PONS, VICTOR MANUEL, JR., lawyer; b. Rio Piedras, P.R., Apr. 5, 1935; s. Victor Manuel and Carolina (Nunez) P.; diploma Hill Sch., 1952; student Swarthmore Coll., 1952-54; B.A. magna cum laude, U. P.R., 1956, LL.B. magna cum laude, 1959; m. Carmen Luisa Rexach, Feb. 26, 1960; children—Carolina Sofia, Carmen Luisa, Victor Manuel, Juan Antonio. Admitted to P.R. bar, 1959, since practiced in San Juan, P.R.; asso. firm Fiddler, Gonzalez & Rodriquez, 1959-62, partner, 1963-72. Ad honorem instr. U. P.R. Sch. Dentistry. Mem. Council on Higher Edn. P.R., 1966-71. Mem. Am., Inter-Am. bar assns., Colegio de Abogados de P.R., P.R. C. of C. (dir. 1971—). Home: GPO Box P San Juan PR 00936 Office: GPO Box 3507 San Juan PR 00936

POOL, JOHN CHARLES, banker; b. nr. Jasper, Tex., Feb. 15, 1940; s. Charles Cade and Lillie Ruth (Rainey) P.; B.B.A., U. Tex.; postgrad. Southwestern Grad. Sch. Banking, Dallas; m. Janet Gayle Messer, Feb. 20, 1964; 1 dau., Kendel. Exec. tng. program First Security Nat. Bank, Beaumont, Tex., 1964-65; vice chmn. bd. First State Bank, Jasper, Tex., 1971—. Served with AUS, 1966-69. Mem. Jasper C. of C. (dir.), Beta Theta Pi. Lion (past treas.). Home: 1307 Northwood Dr Jasper TX 75951 Office: PO Box 640 Jasper TX 75951

POOL, WILLIAM E., lawyer. exec. dir. Tex. Bar Assn. Address: Box 12487 Austin TX 78711*

POOLE, CHARLES PATTON, JR., physicist, educator; b. Panama City, Pa., June 7, 1927; s. Charles Patton and Irene (Hackett) P.; B.A., Fordham U., 1950, M.S., 1952; Ph.D., U. Md., 1958; m. Kathleen T. Walsh, Oct. 17, 1953; children—Kathleen Theresa, Charles Patton III, Michael Augustine, Mary Ellen, Elizabeth Irene. Devel. physicist Westinghouse Electric Corp., Bloomfield, N.J. and Balt., 1952-53; research physicist Gulf Research & Devel. Co., Pitts., 1958-64; asso. prof. dept. physics U. S.C., Columbia, 1964-66, prof., 1966—. Fellow Am. Phys. Soc.; mem. Albertus Magnus Guild, Groupement Ampere. Roman Catholic. Author: Electron Spin Resonance, 1967; (with others) Relaxation in Magnetic Resonance, 1971; theory of Magnetic Resonance, 1972. Editor five Russian sci. books, also jour. Magnetic Resonance Review. Home: 5716 Sylvan Dr Columbia SC 29206

POOLE, FRANK BURTON, JR., architect; b. Danville, Va., May 18, 1923; s. Frank Burton and Lenora (White) P.; student Rutgers, 1943; B.S. in Architecture, Va. Poly. Inst., 1947, M.S., 1949; m. Mae Sedalia Allen, Sept. 13, 1947; children—Susan L., Frank B., III. Archtl. designer, draftsman Stone & Pitts, Architects, Beaumont, Tex., 1948-50, Biberstein, Bowles & Meacham, Charlotte, N.C., 1950-52; partner Clark & Poole, Kingstree, S.C., 1952-57; asso. architect Merrill Lee & Assos., Richmond, Va., 1957-64; partner Lee King & Poole, Richmond, 1964—. Served with USAAF, 1943-46. Mem. A.I.A., Va. Assn. Professions, Tau Sigma Delta, Phi Kappa Phi. Baptist. Clubs: Rotunda, Downtown (Richmond). Home: 904 Penola Dr Richmond VA 23229 Office: Southern States Bldg Richmond VA 23219

POOLE, GEORGE GRAHAM, JR., real estate and loan exec.; b. Mullins, S.C., June 1, 1925; s. George Graham and Sarah Ally (Haltiwanger) P.; student Clemson Coll., 1942-43; m. Ruby Elizabeth Brant, July 1, 1946; children—Elizabeth Anne, George Martin. With George G. Poole Real Estate and Loans, Mullins, 1946—, owner-mgr., 1953—; dir. Davis Nat. Bank, Mullins. Mem. Marion County Bd. Commrs., 1959—; chmn. Mullins Pub. Housing Authority, 1968—; co-founder, chief Mullins Community Fire Dept., 1951; county rep. Clemson U. Iptay, 1965—, dist. dir., 1971—. Bd. dirs. Ind. Consumer Finance Assn. S.C. Served with C.E., AUS, 1943-46. Mem. Mullins C. of C. (pres. 1962-64), Am. Legion (vice comdr. 1948-49), V.F.W. Home: Poole Dr Mullins SC 29574 Office: 125 W Wine St Mullins SC 29574

POOLE, PIERRE PATILLO, physician; b. Cross Anchor, S.C., Sept. 8, 1917; s. Mack Collier and Kate (Holcombe) P.; B.S., John B. Stetson U., 1936; M.D., Duke U., 1940; postgrad. (Rockefeller fellow) Tulane Sch. Medicine, New Orleans, 1946-47; m. Elizabeth Porcher Gignilliat, Mar. 22, 1946; children—William Pierre, John Gignilliat. Rotating intern, Charity Hosp., New Orleans, 1940-41, resident medicine, 1941-42; instr. medicine Tulane Sch. Medicine, 1946-47; pvt. practice medicine, specializing in internal medicine and cardiology, Rocky Mount, N.C., 1947-50, Brownsville, Tex., 1950—; mem. staff, electrocardiographer Mount Mercy Hosp., Brownsville, Tex., chief dept. medicine, 1951-54, 56-57, 60-72, pres. staff, 1952; cons. internal medicine USPHS, Brownsville, 1960-72. Served to maj. AUS, 1942-46. Diplomate Am. Bd. Internal Medicine. Fellow Am. Coll. Chest Physicians, A.C.P.; mem. Am., Tex., heart assns., A.M.A., Cameron Willacy County Med. Soc. (pres. 1958), Am., Tex. socs. internal medicine, Tex. Acad. Internal Medicine, Am. Legion. Presbyn. Home: 205 Calle Jacaranda Brownsville TX 78520 Office: 44 E Levee St Brownsville TX 78520

POOLE, REID, musician; b. Toccoa, Ga., July 20, 1919; s. David Young and Jane Ann (Means) P.; B.A., U. Chgo., 1946, M.A., 1947; m. Doris Jane Wilson, Apr. 4, 1942; children—Christopher Howard, Deborah Doris. Instr. music Roosevelt U., 1947-49; mem. faculty U. Fla., 1949—. Asst. dir. bands, 1949-58, dir. bands, 1958-61, prof., chmn. dept. music, 1961—. Former treas. Fla. Arts Council. Served with AUS, 1941-45. Mem. Fla. Music Educators Assn. (past pres.), Assn. Coll. and Concert Mgrs. (bd. dirs., v.p.). Club: Torch. Editor: Fla. Music Dirs. Mag., 1965-71; mus. compositions and arrangements used by sch. and coll. bands. Home: 3706 SW 6th Pl Gainesville FL 32601

POOLE, RICHARD WILLIAM, educator; b. Oklahoma City, Dec. 4, 1927; s. William Robert and Lois (Spicer) P.; B.S., U. Okla., 1951, M.B.A., 1952; Ph.D., Okla. State U., 1960; m. Bertha Lynn Mehr, July 28, 1950; children—Richard William, Laura Lynne, Mark Stephen. Research analyst Okla. Gas & Electric Co., Oklahoma City, 1952-54; mgr. Sci. and Mfg. Devel. dept. Oklahoma City C. of C., 1954-58 asst. to pres. Frontiers of Sci. Found., 1955; mgr. Office of James E. Webb, Washington, 1957-58; instr. econs., asst. prof., asso. prof., prof., Okla. State U., 1960-65, dean Coll. of Bus., 1965-72, v.p. univ. relations and devel., 1972—. Cons. NASA, Midwest Research Inst. Mem. Gov's. gen. adv. com., tech. com. Statis. Standards, 1964—; mem. adv. exec. com. Nat. Govs. Conf., 1965. Bd. dirs. Stillwater Indsl. Found., 1967—, Stillwater YMCA, 1966. Mid-Continent Research and Devel. Council, 1965—, chmn., 1969; bd. dirs. Okla. Council on Econ. Edn., 1965—, mem. exec. council, 1965—. Served from pvt. to 2d lt., AUS, 1946-48. Mem. Am., So. econ. assns., Okla. (dir. 1965—), Stillwater (dir. 1965—, pres. 1968) chambers commerce, Regional Sci. Assn., Am. Assn. Collegiate Schs. Bus. (bd. dirs.), Southwestern Econ. Assn. (pres. 1968), Midwest Econ. Assn., Res. Officers Assn., Southwestern Bus. Adminstrn. Assn. (pres. 1972), Phi Eta Sigma, Beta Gamma Sigma, Pi Gamma Mu, Phi Kappa Phi, Omicron Delta Kappa. Lion. Contbr. articles to profl. jours. Home: 124 Georgia Av Stillwater OK 74074

POOLE, THOMAS CARL, JR., mfg. co. exec.; b. Leeds, Ala., Feb. 19, 1921; s. Thomas Carl and Grace (King) P.; B.S., Auburn U., 1948; postgrad. Coll. Advanced Traffic of Chgo. at Jacksonville State U., 1950-51; m. Mary Louise Miller, Oct. 7, 1960; children—Thomas Carl III, John Preston. Mgr. Traffic and shipping planning Dresser Mfg. div. Dresser Industries, Anniston, Ala., 1949—. Traffic cons. various firms, 1960—. Served with USAF, 1943. Mem. N.E. Ala. Traffic and Transp. Club (gov. 1960), Phi Kappa Tau. Home: Route 5 Box 567 Anniston AL 36201 Office: W 23d St Anniston AL 36201

POOLE, WILLIAM DANIEL, editor; b. Statesville, N.C., Nov. 3, 1932; s. William Oscar and Edna (Brewer) P.; B.A., Wake Forest Coll., 1955; m. Erika Kiene, Oct. 18, 1958. Reporter, Norfolk (Va.) Virginian-Pilot, 1955-57; reporter Washington Evening Star, 1957-61, real estate editor, 1961-71, features editor, 1971—. Recipient News Writing award Va. Press Assn., 1956, Real Estate Sect. award Nat. Assn. Home Builders, 1963, 69, Feature Writing award Nat. Assn. Real Estate Bds., 1965, 67, 69, Consumer Oriented Articles award Nat. Assn. Real Estate Editors, 1970. Mem. Nat. Assn. Real Estate Editors (dir. 1966-67, sec. 1968, treas. 1969, pres. 1971), White House Corrs. Assn., Newspaper Comics Council, Nat. Press Club, Am. Assn. Sunday and Feature Editors, Omicron Delta Kappa, Sigma Phi Epsilon. Home: 402 W Alexandria Av Alexandria VA 22302 Office: 225 Virginia Av SE Washington DC 20003

POOR, RICHARD LONGSTREET, utilities exec.; b. Summit, N.J., Dec. 28, 1910; s. Charles Longstreet and Mary L. (Austin) P.; B.S., U.S. Naval Acad., 1933; m. Margaret Kay English, July 12, 1934 (div. July 1940); children—Richard Longstreet, Austin E.; m. 2d, Elizabeth Louise Snavely, July 1942 (div. July 1962); 1 son, Earl S.; m. 3d, Elizabeth Maurey Salvesen, Oct. 17, 1963; stepchildren—Tina S., Jan S. Electric field supt. Beach Electric Co., Newark, 1946-48; electric insp. Fla. Power & Light Co., Miami, 1948-49, electric constrn. supt., 1949-50, asst. distbn. supr., 1950-52, comml. supr., 1952-53, asst. mgr. comml., 1953-55, asst. purchasing agt., 1955-60, asst. to v.p. operating, 1960—. Served with AC, U.S. Army, 1933-34; from ensign to comdr. USN, 1934-46. Decorated D.F.C. and Gold star, Air medal. Registered profl. engr., N.J., Fla. Mem. I.E.E.E., Nat. Soc. Profl. Engrs., Fla. Engring. Soc., Soc. Am. Mil. Engrs., Miami Beach C. of C. (zoning, bldg. com. 1953-54), Navy League, Greater Miami Aviation Assn. (edn. com. 1966—), Fla. Air Pilots Assn. Episcopalian. Rotarian. Club: Florida Aero (Miami). Home: 9011 N Bayshore Dr Miami FL 33138 Office: 4200 Flagler St Miami FL 33134

POORE, HOWARD LEE, aircraft mfg. co. exec.; b. Clayton, Dela., Apr. 8, 1915; s. Howard Griffin and Ethyl Virginia (Lee) P.; Aero. and Engring. license, Lincoln Aero. Inst., Lincoln, Neb., 1937; student Harvard Bus. Sch., 1958; m. Jeannette S. Stevenson, Nov. 23, 1939; children—Steven Lee, Griffin Craig. With Piper Aircraft, Pa., 1937-38, Bellanca Aircraft, Dela., 1938; with Lockheed Cal. Co., Burbank, 1939-51, supr., 1942-47, dept. foreman, 1947-51; with Lockheed Ga. Co., Marietta, 1951—, v.p., C-5 program mgr., 1967-69, exec. v.p., corp. v.p., 1969—. Mem. Soc. Automotive Engrs. (mem. aerospace adv. com. 1969—), Aerospace Industries Assn., Am. Mgmt. Assn. (mfg. council). Elk. Club: OX-5 (Atlanta). Home: 5075 Green Pine Dr NE Atlanta GA 30342 Office: 86 S Cobb Dr Marietta GA 30060

POPE, ANDREW JACKSON (JACK), JR., judge; b. Abilene, Tex., Apr. 18, 1913; s. A.J. and Ruth (Taylor) P.; B.A., Abilene Christian Coll., 1934; LL.B., U. Tex., 1937; m. Allene Nichols, June 11, 1938; children—A.J. III, Walter Allen. Admitted to Tex. bar, 1937; began practice of law in Corpus Christi, Tex., 1937, mem. firm Pope & Pope, 1937-44, Cannon, Pittman & Pope, 1946; judge Dist. Ct., 94th Jud. Dist., 1946-50; justice Ct. Civil Appeals, 4th Jud. Dist., San Antonio, 1950; now asso. justice Supreme Ct. Tex., Austin. Chmn. Tex. Judicial Sect., 1962. Pres. San Antonio YMCA, 1957. Served with USNR, 1944-46. Recipient Silver Beaver award Boy Scouts Am. Mem. Am. Judicature Soc., Am., Nueces County (pres. 1947), San Antonio, Travis County bar assns., State Bar Tex. Mem. Ch. of Christ. K.P. (grand chancellor Tex. 1948). Contbr. articles to profl. jours. Office: Supreme Ct Bldg Capitol Sta Austin TX 78711

POPE, EDWIN, newspaper editor. Sports editor Miami (Fla.) Herald. Office: 1 Herald Plaza Miami FL 33101

POPE, LARRY JACOB, librarian; b. Cin., Feb. 26, 1937; s. Jesse B. and Estelle M. (Moneyhon) P.; A.B., U. Ky., 1959, M.S., 1961; m. Genevieve Scott Johnston, July 10, 1965. Librarian, serials cataloger main library U. Ky., Lexington, 1961-64, head circulation librarian, 1964-66; asst. periodicals librarian Eastern Ky. U., Richmond, 1966-67, chief periodicals librarian, 1967—. Mem. Am., Southeastern Ky. library assns., Tech. Service Librarians (Ohio Valley group), Theatre Guild Soc. Am. Home: 112 Buckwood Dr Richmond KY 40475 Office: Crabbe Library Eastern Kentucky University Richmond KY 40475

POPE, ROY L(EON), accountant; b. Troup, Tex., Feb. 5, 1904; s. Charles Morse and Eugenia (McCuistion) P.; student U. Tex., 1923-27; m. Louise J. Roessler, Oct. 10, 1928; 1 son, Charles W. Sec. bd. dirs. Southwestern Engraving Co., Atlanta, 1927-30, San Antonio, 1930-35; pvt. accounting practice, San Antonio, 1935—; partner Howard & Pope, 1938-50, Roy L. Pope & Co., 1950-53; sr. partner Roy L. Pope & Spillers Co., 1953-69; partner Alexander Grant & Co., 1970—. C.P.A., Tex. Mem. Tex. Soc. C.P.A.'s, (past pres. state and local; state dir.), San Antonio C. of C. Unitarian. Mason (32 deg.), Rotarian. Home: 115 Arvin Dr San Antonio TX 78209 Office: 737 Travis Park West San Antonio TX 78205

POPE, THOMAS HARRINGTON, lawyer; b. Kinard, S.C., July 28, 1913; s. Thomas H. and Marie (Gary) P.; A.B., The Citadel, 1935; LL.B., U. S.C., 1938; LL.D., Newberry Coll., 1969; grad. Command and Gen. Staff Coll., 1951; m. Mary Waties Lumpkin, Jan. 3, 1940; children— Mary Waties, Thomas Harrington III, Gary Tusten. Admitted to S.C. bar, 1938, also U.S. Supreme Ct.; practice in Newberry, 1938—; spl. circuit judge Richland and Lexington counties, 1955-56; dir. Citizens and So. Nat. Bank S.C., Standard Savs. and Loan Assn., Am. Sentinel Life Ins. Co. Mem. S.C. Ports Authority, 1957-65, Jud. Council S.C., 1957—, S.C. Archives Commn., 1965—. S.C. Tricentennial Commn.; mem. adv. bd. Nat. Trust for Historic preservation, 1967—; chmn. Newberry County Sesqui-Centennial Commn., 1939. Mem. S.C. Ho. of Reps. from Newberry County, 1936-40, 45-50, speaker, 1949-50; chmn. S.C. Democratic Party, 1958-60; del. at large Dem. Nat. Conv., 1956, 60; pres. S.C. Dem. Conv., 1958, 62. Trustee, also chmn. S.C. Found. Ind. Colls., Newberry Coll., U. of South, 1965-69; bd. visitors The Citadel, 1939-40, 46. Served to lt. col. AUS, 1941-45; ETO. Fellow Am. Coll. Trial Lawyers; mem. Am., S.C. (pres. 1964, chmn. exec. com. 1956-58), Newberry County (pres. 1951) bar assns., Am. Law Inst., Am. Judicature Soc., Nat. Assn. R.R. Trial Counsel, Am., So. hist. assns., S.C., Newberry County (pres. 1966) hist. socs., Phi Beta Kappa, Omicron Delta Kappa, Phi Delta Phi, Alpha Tau Omega. Episcopalian (sr. warden 1963-65). Mason (grand master S.C. 1958-60; Albert Gallatin Mackey medal Grand Lodge S.C. 1965, Henry Price medal Grand Lodge Mass. 1960). Clubs: Newberry Country; Spring Valley Country, Forest Lake Country, Palmetto, Pine Tree Hunt (Columbia, S.C.); Army-Navy (Washington). Home: 1700 Boundary St Newberry SC 29108 Office: 1201 Boyce St Newberry SC 29108

POPE, VERLE A., state senator; b. Jacksonville, Fla., Dec. 12, 1903; ed. U. Fla.; m. Edith Taylor; 1 dau., Mrs. Richard O. Watson. Real estate and ins. broker; former mem. Dist. Welfare Bd.; former chmn. Bd. County Commrs., St. John's County (Fla.); mem. Fla. Senate, 1948—, pres., dir. Hastings Exchange Bank. Served with USAAF, World War II; ETO. Decorated European Air medal with eight clusters, Croix de Guerre. Mem. C. of C., Hist. Soc., Res. Officers Club, Am. Legion, V.F.W. Methodist. Mason, Kiwanian, Elk. Club: Arts. Address: PO Box 519 Saint Augustine FL 32084

POPE, WILLIAM BAKER, pub. relations cons.; b. Atlanta, Feb. 15, 1933; s. Arthur Bozeman and Juliette (Murray) P.; B.B.A., Emory U., 1955; m. Sarah Harper Anderson, Apr. 28, 1966; children—Juliette Rogers, Andrew Porter. Reporter, Dallas Morning News, 1957-59; state news editor Atlanta Constn., 1959-62; news editor Bahamas Ministry Finance and Tourism, Nassau, Hill & Knowlton, Inc., N.Y., 1963-66; self-employed as publicist and pub. relations cons., Atlanta, 1966—. Served with AUS, 1955-57. Mem. Pub. Relations Soc. Am., Am. Acad. Polit. and Social Sci., Alpha Tau Omega. Club: Doghouse (Nassau). Home: 1016 Farmington Lane NE Atlanta GA 30319 Office: PO Box 18787 Atlanta GA 30326

POPE, WILLIAM KENNETH, bishop; b. Hale, Mo., Nov. 21, 1901; s. William Mumford and Victoria (LaRue) P.; student Clarendon (Tex.) Coll., 1917-20; B.A., So. Meth. U., 1922, B.D., 1924, LL.D., 1964; postgrad. Yale, 1927-29; D.D. (hon.), Southwestern U., 1937, Hendrix Coll., 1961; m. Kate Sayle, Mar. 16, 1930; children—Katherine Victoria, Kenneth Sayle. Ordained ministry Meth. Ch., 1925, consecrated bishop, 1960; pastor in Milford, Tex., 1924-26, Breckenridge, 1929-33, Georgetown, 1933-36, Springfield, Mo., 1936-40, Austin, Tex., 1940-49, Houston, 1949-60; bishop Ark. area, 1960-64, Dallas, Ft. Worth area, 1964—. chmn. bd. trustees So. Meth. U., 1971—. Bd. Christian social concerns Meth. Ch.; chmn. bd. Western Meth. Assembly, Fayetteville, Ark., 1960-64; vis. lectr. Perkins Sch. Theology, So. Meth. U., 1949; del. World Conf. Life and Work, Oxford, Eng., 1937, World Meth. Conf., Oxford, 1951; vis. preacher Gen. Conf. Meth. Ch. in Mexico, 1946; rep. Meth. Ch. in U.S. to centennial celebration Methodism in India, 1956. Mem. Tex. Council Chs. (pres. 1968), Tex. Conf. Chs. (pres. 1969), Lambda Chi Alpha, Theta Phi, Tau Kappa Alpha. Club: Dallas Athletic. Contbr. to Christian Advocate, Adult Student, Prayer for Today. Home: 3131 Maple St Dallas TX 75201 Office: So Meth U Perkins Sch Theology Dallas TX 75205

POPE, WILLIAM ROBERT, lawyer, ex-state rep.; b. Mt. Mourne, N.C., Feb. 24, 1918; s. James Robert and Mary (Kelly) P.; grad. Brevard Jr. Coll., 1938; B.S., Davidson Coll., 1940; LL.B., U. N.C., 1948; m. Ina Amelia Barber, Sept. 16, 1946; children—William Robert, James Shuford, Charles Vance, Elizabeth Barber, Deborah, Caroline Amelia. Admitted to N.C. bar, 1948; pvt. practice, Mooresville, 1948—; judge Mooresville Recorder's Ct. 1952-63; gen. counsel, Piedmont Bank & Trust Co., Crescent Electric Membership Corp. Dir. Cornelius Devel. Co., Inc.; pres. Braco, Inc. Mem. N.C. House of Reps., 1951-52, 63-64. Chmn. adv. com. Iredell County Govtl. Complex. Mem. Lowrance Hosp., Inc. Served to lt. USNR, 1940-46. Decorated D.F.C. Mem. Am., N.C., Iredell County bar assns., Phi Delta Phi. Democrat. Presbyn. Mason, Elk, Rotarian. Home: US 21 Mooresville NC Office: PO Box 27 Mooresville NC

POPEJOY, LEE TARENCE, II, physician; b. Ada, Okla., June 17, 1935; s. Lee Tarence and Vivienne (Flowers) P.; student Tex. A. and M. Coll., 1953-54; B.S., Centenary Coll., 1957; M.D., La. State U., 1961; m. Judith Ann Rhodes, Oct. 27, 1956; children—Lauralee, Caroline Vivienne, Lee Tarence III, Augusta Susannah. Research asst. dept. anatomy La. State U., 1958-61; intern William Beaumont Army Hosp., El Paso, Tex., 1961-62; practice medicine specializing in gen. medicine, Jasper, Tex., 1964—. Vice pres. Mediplex Corp., Jasper, 1966—; pres. Mechanized Services Am., 1964—. Bd. dirs. M.E. Dickerson Hosp. Served to capt. M.C., AUS, 1961-64. Mem. Am., So., Tex. med. assns., Jasper C. of C. Presbyn. (elder). Rotarian. Contbr.: The Squirrel Monkey, 1969. Home: Bevilport Jasper TX 75951 Office: 1001 Dickerson Dr Jasper TX 75951

POPPENDIECK, ROBERT, govt. ofcl.; b. Carlstadt, N.J., Aug. 21, 1908; s. William and Etta (Prehn) P.; student Springfield (Mass.) Coll., 1926-28; A.B., Montclair (N.J.) State Tchrs. Coll., 1931; M.A., Tchrs. Coll., Columbia, 1934; Ed.D., Rutgers U., 1954; m. Gertrude Atkinson Pell, Aug. 19, 1934; children—Carol Ann, Gertrude Annsley (Mrs. Banks G. Prevatt), Janet Elizabeth (Mrs. John R. Kernodle, Jr.). Tchr. English, jr. high sch., Garwood, N.J., 1931-35; sec. YMCA, Mercer County, Trenton, 1935-37; tchr. English Jonathan Dayton Regional High Sch., Springfield, 1937-42, dept. head, 1938-42; personnel mgr. U.S. Hammered Piston Ring Co., Inc., Stirling, 1942-48; lectr. edn. Rutgers U., New Brunswick, 1948-54, asso. prof., 1954-58, dir. adminstrv. services Sch. Edn., 1954-58; specialist for tchr. edn. U.S. Office Edn., Washington, 1958—, acting chief tchr. edn. and devel. programs sect., 1962-63; dir. programs br. Tchr. Corps, 1966-68, dir. field services Bur. Ednl. Personnel Devel., 1968—. Cons., Ednl. Testing Service, Princeton, N.J., 1957; dir. adult sch. Jonathan Dayton Regional High Sch. Dist., 1957-58. Mem. East Hanover Twp. Bd. Edn., 1933-35; mem. Springfield Civil Def. Unit, 1942-45. Trustee, Albright Coll. Recipient Distinguished Alumni award Rutgers U. Sch. Edn., 1963. Mem. N.J. Personnel and Guidance Assn. (hon. life), Assn. Higher Edn., Assn. Field Services in Tchr. Edn., N.E.A. (life), Nat. Commn. Tchr. Edn. and Profl. Standards (liaison cons.), Phi Delta Kappa. United Methodist. Contbr. articles to profl. jours. and bulls. Home: 3112 Circle Hill Rd Alexandria VA 22305 Office: US Office Edn Washington DC 20202

PORCH, HARRY PILGER, JR., chem. engr.; b. Delair Park, N.J., Feb. 28, 1928; s. Harry Pilger and Florence Irene (Ridgway) P.; student Northampton Poly., London, Eng., 1951-56; higher nat. certificate in chem. engring., Grimsby (Eng.) Coll., 1961, postgrad., 1961-62; m. Vivienne Berenice Lomas, Oct 9, 1948; children—David Jonathan, Alison. Chem. engr. Eastern Gas Bd., London, 1950-57; with Brit. Titan Products Co. Ltd., Grimsby, 1957-65; chem. engr. Wellman-Lord, Inc., Lakeland, Fla., 1965-66, process mgr., 1966-72; supervising process engr. Dorr-Oliver Inc., Stamford, Conn., 1972—. Served with USNR, 1946-48. Registered profl. engr., Fla. Mem. Instn. Chem. Engrs., Eng. Lutheran (elder 1967—). Home: 1705 Petersburg Av Lakeland FL 33803 Office: 77 Havemeyer Lane Stamford CT 06904

PORRARO, RICHARD JOSEPH, dentist; b. Paterson, N.J., Feb. 1, 1937; s. Patsy and Natalina (Nigro) P.; D.D.S., St. Louis U., 1963; m. 2d, Joan Womble, Apr. 16, 1971; children—Lisa Maria, Richard Anthony, Patricia Marla, Kristina Maria, Kathleen McCulloch, Angus McCulloch. Dental Intern Fla. Sch. for Boys, Okeechobee, 1963-64; practice dentistry, Pompano Beach, Fla., 1964—. Vice pres. Young Republican Club North Broward County, Fla., 1969-70; dist. chmn. Fla. Fedn. Young Reps., 1969-70. Served with USNR, 1955-57. Mem. Am., Fla., Broward County dental assns., Nat. Rehab. Assn., Jr. C. of C. (pres. 1967-68). Roman Catholic. Home: 2532 SE 13th St Pompano Beach FL 33064 Office: 100 SW 6th St Pompano Beach FL 33060

PORRATA-DORIA-PATXOT, JOSE OSCAR, dentist; b. Naguabo, P.R., July 14, 1916; s. Oscar and Adriana (Patxot) P.; B.S., U. P.R., 1935; D.D.S., Med. Coll. Va., 1940; m. Margot Pietrantoni, July 3, 1943; children—Maria de Hourdes (Mrs. Carlos Grovas), Adriana Josefina, Viola Margarita (Mrs. Arturo Cortes). Practice dentistry, Santurce, P.R., 1941—; mem. staff Doctors Hosp. Mem. Am. Dental Assn., Dental Assn. P.R. (pres. 1954), Colegio de Cirujanos Dentistas de P.R., Hipodromo del Sur (dir. 1971—). A.F.D.A. Frat. (pres. 1967-69). Rotarian. Clubs: Caparra Country, Caribe Hilton Swimming and Tennis, San Juan Hotel Swimming and Tennis (San Juan). Home: 20 Washington St Santurce PR 00909 Office: 1107 Ponce de Leon Av Santurce PR 00908

PORTALES, CARLOS, dentist; b. Gonzales, Tex., Feb. 3, 1939; s. Joe and Cornelia (Diaz) P.; student Victoria Coll., 1957-59, Southwest Tex. State Coll., 1959; D.D.S., U. Tex., 1963; m. Irene Hernandez, June 16, 1963; children—Karen Irene, Charles Joseph, William Joseph. Intern oral surgery Fordham Hosp., Bronx, N.Y., 1963-64; resident oral surgery Bronx VA Hosp., 1964-66; practice dentistry specializing in oral surgery, San Antonio, 1968—. Served to capt. AUS, 1966-68; chief oral surgery U.S. Army Hosp., Ryukyu Islands. Mem. Am., Tex. dental assns., Southwest Soc. Oral Surgeons. Home: 5526 Chancellor St San Antonio TX 78229 Office: Nix Professional Bldg San Antonio TX 78205

PORTER, AUBREY L., lawyer; b. Mt. Pleasant, Tex., July 6, 1898; s. R. J. and Lavenia (Hall) P.; student E. Tex. Tchr's Coll., 1917-21; LL.B., Kent Coll. Law, Chgo., 1925; m. Hazel Harvey, Jan. 2, 1927; 1 son, Robert M. Admitted to Fla. bar, 1926, Circuit Ct., 1926, Fed. Ct., 1932, pros. atty. Wakulla Co., Fla., 1926-32; county judge, 1932-57; gen. law practice, 1957—; tree farming. Mem. Fla. Forest Fire Prevention Com., Wakulla County Forestry Com., Wakulla Co. Welfare Assn. Chmn. adv. com. Tallahassee Jr. Coll. Mem. Am. Legion, 40 and 8, Fla. Bar, 2d Jud. Circuit Bar Assn. (past pres.), Wakulla County C. of C. (past pres.). Democrat. Methodist (ofcl. bd. mem., past chmn.). Mason; mem. Order Eastern Star. Address: Crawfordville FL 32327

PORTER, CALVIN LINCOLN, journalist; b. Swan Quarter, N.C., Feb. 12, 1928; s. Leo and Pauline (Bowman) P.; B.A., Lynchburg Coll., 1951; m. Charlotte Andrews, Dec. 20, 1953; children—Stuart, Pamela, Lisa (dec.). Reporter, Rocky Mount (N.C.) Evening Telegram, 1952. Bertie Ledger-Advance, Windsor, N.C., 1952-53; news editor Mount Olive (N.C.) Tribune, 1952-60; city editor Sanford (N.C.) Herald, 1960-62; asst. city editor Lynchburg (Va.) News, 1962, sports writer, 1962-66, sports editor, 1966—. Instr. journalism Mount Olive Jr. Coll., 1958; press agt. Congressman L. H. Fountain, 1952. Pres. Madison (Va.) Young Republican Club, 1948. Mem. Va. Sportswriters and Sportscasters Assn. (v.p. 1967-68). Methodist. Home: 1131 Lindsay St Lynchburg VA 24505 Office: Church St Lynchburg VA 24505

PORTER, DUDLEY, JR., ins. co. exec.; b. Paris, Tenn., May 10, 1915; s. Dudley and Mary (Bolling) P.; student Murray State Coll., 1933-34; LL.B., Cumberland U., 1936; m. Mary Rhoda Montague, Oct. 21, 1950. Admitted to Tenn. bar, 1937; asst. atty. gen. State of Tenn., 1937-40; mem. firm Tyne, Peebles, Henry & Tyne, Nashville, 1940-49; mem. law dept. Nat. Life & Accident Ins. Co., Nashville, 1940-49; with provident Life & Accident Ins. Co., Chattanooga, 1949—, v.p., gen. counsel, sec., dir. 1966-70, sr. v.p., gen. counsel, sec., 1970-72, vice chmn. bd., gen. counsel, sec., 1972—; dir. Coca-Cola Bottling Co., Thomas, Inc., Chattanooga, Coca-Cola Bottling Corp., Cin. Mem. Hamilton County Juvenile Ct. Commn., 1958-64, chmn., 1963-64; mem. Tenn. Health Planning Council. Served with AUS, 1942-46; ETO. Mem. Am., Tenn., Chattanooga bar assns., Assn. Life Ins. Counsel (exec. com.), Am. Life Conv. (chmn. legal sect. 1958), Sigma Alpha Epsilon. Methodist. Clubs: Mountain City, Lookout Mountain Fairyland (Chattanooga); Belle Meade (Nashville). Home: Healing Springs Rd Elder Mountain Route 8 Chattanooga TN 37409 Office: Provident Bldg Fountain Square Chattanooga TN 37402

PORTER, FELIX NATHANIEL, banker; b. Caddo, Okla., Dec. 23, 1915; s. Hafford and Zelma (Porter) P.; B.S., Okla. State U., 1937; m. Jane Ward Harreld, Oct. 19, 1946. Exec. v.p. The First Nat. Bank and Trust Co., Oklahoma City, 1966, now pres.; dir. Am.-First title & Trust Co., Serivner-Boogaart, Inc., S.W. Property Mgmt. Corp.,

Northwest Bank, Am. Mortgage and Investment Co., First Data Mgmt. Corp., Mound City Trust Co.; v.p., dir. First Life Assurance Co., First Okla. Bancorp., Inc. Adv. dir. Founders Bank & Trust Co. Mem. bd. Baptist Meml. Hosp. Trustee Okla. Blue Cross. Served with AUS, 1941-46. Mem. C. of C. (v.p., dir.), Assn. Res. City Bankers, Pi Kappa Alpha, Alpha Kappa Psi. Democrat. Episcopalian. Clubs: Beacon, Economics, Men's Dinner, Municipal Bond of Oklahoma. Home: 3233 N Harvey Pkwy Oklahoma City OK 73118 Office: 120 N Robinson St Oklahoma City OK 73102

PORTER, GARLAND BURNS, editor, pub.; b. Dabney, N.C., June 3, 1897; s. William and Letitia (Cockerham) P.; A.B., U. N.C., 1922, M.A., 1923; m. Polly Wolff, June 22, 1925 (dec. Apr. 1941); children—Polly Jean (Mrs. V. Hugo Sewell), Garland Burns, David Darlington; m. 2d, Ruth Vail Selby, 1945 (div. Feb. 1951); 1 son, Joseph M. V.; m. 3d, Margaret McFarland, Feb. 1954; stepchildren—William Wyman, Margaret Tracy. Reporter, Atlanta Constitution, 1922; reporter-city editor Winston-Salem (N.C.) Jour., 1923-25; nat. advt. mgr. Atlanta Georgian, 1927-39; So. mgr. Hearst Advt. Service, 1934-40; mgr. N.C. News Bur., Raleigh, 1942-43; editor-gen. mgr. So. Advt. & Pub. Atlanta, 1949-64; editor, pub. So. Markets/Media, Atlanta, 1965-71; founder Porter Pub. Co., 1942; pub. So. Plastics Mag., 1945-46. Pres. N.C. Soc., Atlanta, 1930. Served to 2d lt. USMCR, 1918. Mem. So. Newspaper Pubs. Assn., Am. Advt. Fedn., Nat. Press Club, Sigma Delta Chi, Delta Tau Delta, Sigma Upsilon, Club: Poor Richard (Phila.). Contbr. articles to popular mags. Home: 69 Mobile Av NE Atlanta GA 30305

PORTER, GRANVILLE DWIGHT, telecommunications engr.; b. Ashtabula, Ohio, June 23, 1916; s. Jesse Wheeler and Lina (Dwight) P.; B.S.E.E., U. Miami, 1960; M.A., George Washington U., 1964; student U. Okla., 1969-73; m. Mary Jane Dicken, Apr. 19, 1943; children—Jane Shirley, Alma LaDue (Mrs. Richard Marshall Winfield III) (dec. Aug. 1970), Paul Dwight, Phyllis Elizabeth. Pvt. practice cons. engring., 1950-55 engr. Dade County, Fla., 1955-58 cons. engr., Miami, Fla., 1958-60; electronics engr. U.S. Navy, Washington, 1960-64; frequency engr. U.S. European Command, Paris, France, 1964-67; telecommunications engr. NASA, Marshall Space Flight Center, Ala., 1967—; cons. engr. Commnr. N.E. France dist. Boy Scouts Am., 1964-66. Served with USN, 1937-41. Registered profl. engr., Fla., Ala., D.C. Mem. A.A.A.S., I.E.E.E., Soc. Am. Mil. Engrs. Mason (32 deg., Shriner). Home: 1007 Willow Lane Madison AL 35758 Office: A & PS-MS-CE Marshall Space Flight Center AL 35812

PORTER, IRA JARED, banker; b. Caneyville, Ky., Nov. 20, 1896; s. Robert Brandon and Zilpha Angeline (Stone) P.; A.B., Georgetown (Ky.) Coll., 1920; LL.D., 1957; m. Mary Thompson, June 8, 1922; children— Maribeth (Mrs. Horace T. Hambrick), Robert J. With First State Bank, Pineville, Ky., 1920-25, dir., 1952—; with Guaranty Bank &Trust Co., Lexington, Ky., 1925-31, pres., 1929-31; with Louisville Trust Co., 1931—, vice chmn., 1962-67, now chmn. exec. com., also dir.; dir. Standard Printing Co., Mid-Land Warehouse Co., P. A. Vogel & Sons Co., Arcadia Realty Co., Stimpson Computing Scale Co. Chmn. Louisville chpt. A.R.C., 1960-62, 64-67, chmn. orgn. com. 1965 conv.; chmn. Ky. Blue Cross Hosp. Plan, 1963—. Mem. Louisville Med. Found.; bd. dirs. Ky. Ind. Coll. Found.; trustee So. Baptist Theol. Sem.; trustee, chmn. devel. com. Georgetown Coll. Served to ensign U.S. Navy, 1917-19. Recipient Layman's award merit Jefferson County (Ky.) Med. Soc., 1963; named Ky. col., 1955. Mem. Am. Bankers Assn. (exec. com. 1950-52). Baptist (deacon). Mason, Kiwanian (past pres. Louisville). Clubs: Pendennis, Big Spring Country (Louisville). Home: 11 Ridge Rd Louisville KY 40205 Office: PO Box 1619 Louisville KY 40202

PORTER, JAMES TINSLEY, textile co. exec.; b. Atlanta, Jan. 15, 1922; s. John Russell and Augusta (Tinsley) P.; B.S. in Chem. Engring., Ga. Inst. Tech., 1943, B.S. in Textile Engring., 1948; m. Catherine Tift, Dec. 7, 1944; children—Catherine, Pattie, James Tinsley, Thomas, Russell. Pres., Porter Carpet Mills, Inc., Cartersville, Ga., 1946—; v.p. Piedmont Cotton Mills, East Point, 1946—. Trustee Westminster Schs., Atlanta. Served to lt. USNR, 1943-45. Mem. Young Pres.'s Orgn. Presbyn. (elder 1958-64, 66—). Rotarian. Clubs: Piedmont Driving, Capital City, Peachtree Racket, University Yacht (all Atlanta); Union League (Chgo.). Home: 295 W Wesley Rd NW Atlanta GA 30305 Office: PO Box 688 Cartersville GA 30120

PORTER, JOSEPH ALEXANDER, clergyman; b. Talladega, Ala., Mar. 29, 1922; s. George Joshua and Cora (Yester) P.; student Emory U., 1940-43; B.A., Vanderbilt U., 1945; B.D., Yale, 1948; m. Lillian C. Kane, June 14, 1947; children—Joseph David, Thomas Alexander. Instr., Jr. Coll. Commerce, New Haven, 1946-48; ordained to ministry Meth. Ch., 1948 asso. dir. W.Va. U., Wesley Found., dir. U. Mich., Wesley Found., 1949-51; pastor 1st Congl. Ch., Marion, Mass., 1951-54; dean students staff N.C. State Coll., exec. dir. United Campus Ministry, Mich. State U., 1956-62; campus minister U. N.H., 1962-63; pastor 1st Congl. Ch. Ledyard, Conn., 1963-66, Congl. Ch., Tavares, Fla., 1967—. Moderator, N.E. Assn. Fla. Conf. United Ch. of Christ. Bd. dirs. Lake County Boys Ranch. Chaplain, Exchange Club, East Lansing, Mich., 1961-62. Chmn. renewal and outreach com. Fla. Conf. United Ch. Christ; mem. Fla. Council Chs. Commn. on Christian Life and Mission. Kiwanian (chmn. Key Club com.). Address: 122 St Clair Abrams Av Tavares FL 32778

PORTER, M. BAILEY, JR., physician. Pres., Tex. Bd. Edn. Address: 2402 Windsor Rd Austin TX 78703*

PORTER, MARTHA LEE TAYLOR (MRS. LLOYD J. PORTER), musician, educator; b. Ft. Lauderdale, Fla., Nov. 2, 1911; d. Charles Zell and Hulda Ann (Taliaferro) Taylor; student U. Chattanooga, 1929-30, Brenau Coll., 1930-31, Nat. Music Camp, 1929, 32; A.B., Carleton Coll., 1933; M.A., Columbia, 1942; postgrad. Appalachian State Tchrs. Coll., summer 1959, 60, 62; m. Lloyd Judson Porter, Oct. 15, 1942; children—G. Zell, Martha Carran. Instrumental instr. Cadek Conservatory, Chattanooga, 1929-30; dir. music Soddy (Tenn.) Sch., 1931-32; staff Nat. Music Camp, Interlochen, Mich. summer 1933, 38; supr. music Hamilton County Schs., Chattanooga, 1933-35; mem. staff Sweetbriar (Va.) Coll., summer 1934; dir. music, vocal, instrumental North and South Miami Beach (Fla.) Schs., 1935-42; home economist Fla. Power and Light Co., Coral Gables, summer 1935; dir. music Pine Crest Schs., Ft. Lauderdale, 1949-52, Bennet Sch., Ft. Lauderdale, 1952-56; prin. Hortt Sch., Ft. Lauderdale, 1956-58; dir. music Sunset Sch., Ft. Lauderdale, 1958-71; Sterling Sch., Hollywood, Fla., 1971-72. Clarinetist Nat. Orch. Eastern Tour, 1930, Carleton Symphony Band Tour, 1933, Nat. Music Camp Band, Worlds Fair, Chgo., 1933; dir. Dade County Music Festivals, Miami, 1939-42; European tour dir., 1956; chmn. children's concerts, Ft. Lauderdale, 1963; lectr. UNESCO sponsored schs. and other ednl. instns. in Middle East and Far East, 1965-66. Mem. Am. Assn. U. Women (pres. 1946-48), Panhellenic Assn. (pres. 1954-55), N.E.A., Fla., Broward edn. assns., Classroom Tchrs. Assn., Carleton Coll. Alumni Assn. (pres. 1955-57), Civic Music Assn., Ft. Lauderdale Symphony Soc., Broward County Elementary Music Tchrs. Assn. (pres. 1961-63), Alpha Delta Pi Alumni Assn. (pres. 1956-58). Presbyn. Club: Ridge Yacht. Office: 3980 SW 60th St Hollywood FL 33021

PORTER, RICHARD LISTER, educator; b. Omaha, Feb. 22, 1916; s. Elmer Raymond and Mary Catherine (Beck) P.; A.B., St. Louis U., 1939, M.A., 1942, Ph.D., 1952; postgrad., U. Cal. at Berkeley, 1950-51. Instr. social scis., St. Louis U. High Sch., 1942-44; instr. economics St. Louis U., 1951-54; asst. prof. econs. Rockhurst Coll., Kansas City, Mo., 1954-56; asso. prof. econs., chmn. dept. Creighton U., 1956-61; prof., chmn. dept. Marquette U., 1961-67; prof. econs. Okla. State U., Stillwater, 1967—. Recipient Kazanjian awards Joint Council on Econ. Edn., 1969, 70, 71, Ford Faculty Research fellow Mich. U., 1960-61. Mem. Am., Cath. (pres. 1969) econ. assns., Am. Hist. Assn., Royal Econ. Soc. Home: 1524 W University Av Stillwater OK 74074

PORTER, ROBERT, union ofcl.; b. East St. Louis, Ill., Aug. 11, 1927; s. Joseph and Lillian (Wells) P.; A.A., Belleville Jr. Coll., 1951; A.B., Washington U., St. Louis, 1953; postgrad. So. Ill. U., 1957, Oxford (Eng.) U., 1966; m. Patricia S. Penn, Aug. 29, 1952; children—Stephen, Paula, Rudolph. Tchr., Hancock (Mo.) Sch. Dist., 1953-54, Brentwood (Mo.) Sch. Dist., 1954-55, East St. Louis Sch. Dist., 1955-60; adminstrv. aide Am. Fedn. Tchrs., Washington, 1960-63, sec.-treas., 1963—. Mem. operating com. AFL-CIO, com. on polit. edn. Mem. A.L.A. (joint labor-library com.). Democrat. Lutheran. Home: 13511 Oriental St Rockville MD 20853 Office: 1012 14th St NW Washington DC 20005

PORTER, STANLEY PETAIN, accountant; b. Warren, Pa., Feb. 7, 1919; s. Ray Malcolm and Mabel (Hendrickson) P.; B.S., U. Kan., 1946; m. Bruce Finley biggs, May 8, 1944; children—Stanley Scott, Biggs Cunningham. With Arthur Young & Co., Dallas, 1946—, partner, 1955—, adminstrv. partner, 1959—, regional partner, 1969—, mem. mgmt. com., 1966—. Okla. chmn. U. Kan. Program for Progress, 1968-69; mem. adv. bd. Internat. Oil and Gas Edn. Center of Southwestern Legal Found. dir. Tulsa Boys Home, 1966-69; trustee U. Kan. Endowment Assn. Served with AUS, 1942-45. Decorated Bronze Star medal, Purple Heart. Mem. Am. Inst. C.P.A.'s, Nat. Assn. Accountants, Okla. State Bd. C.P.A.'s, Am. Accounting Assn., Am. Petroleum Inst. Methodist (deacon). Club: Southern Hills Country (bd. govs. 1965-69). Author: Petroleum Accounting Practices, 1965. Home: 5240 Royal Crest Dallas TX 75229 Office: Republic Bank Tower Dallas TX 75201

PORTER, WILLIAM J., U.S. ambassador; b. Eng., 1914; s. William and Sarah (Day) P.; ed. Thibodeau Bus. Coll., 1930-33; m. Eleanore Henry, Oct. 30, 1944; children—William, Eleanor. Pvt. Sec. to Am. Minister to Hungary, 1936-37; Am. vice consul, Baghdad, Iraq, 1937-41, Beirut, Lebanon, 1941-43, Damascus, Syria, 1943-45; legation attache, Damascus, 1945-46; Palestine desk officer, Dept. of State, 1946; vice consul., Jerusalem, Palestine, 1946, consul, 1947; established U.S. consulate at Nicosia, Cyprus, Apr. 1948-June 1949; assigned to Internat. Broadcasting div. Dept. of State, 1950; officer in charge Greek Affairs, Dept. of State, 1951; consul, Rabat, French Morocco, 1953, consul gen., 1954, established Am. embassy, Rabat, Morocco, 1956-57; dir. N. African affairs, 1957-60; assigned Fgn. Service Inst., Washington, 1960-61; consul gen. with rank of minister, Algiers, 1961-62; A.E. and P. to Algeria, 1962-65; dep. ambassador with rank of ambassador, Republic of Viet Nam, 1965-67; ambassador to Republic of Korea, 1967-71; chief U.S. delegation to Paris meetings on Viet-Nam with rank of ambassador, 1971—. Recipient Distinguished Honor award U.S. State Dept., 1966; Pres.'s award for Distinguished Fed. Civilian Service, 1967; Viet Nam Service medal, 1968. Address: care Dept State Washington DC 20521

PORTER, WILLIAM LUTHER, financial exec.; b. Washington, May 23, 1918; s. James A. and Anna (Foster) P.; B.S., Am. U., 1949, LL.B., 1954, J.D., 1968; m. Mae C. Hill, June 27, 1942. Accountant, auditor Smith &Davis, Washington, 1945-47; sr. partner Porter, Adams & Cramer, Washington, 1947-48; agt. Internal Revenue Service, Washington, 1948-59; sr. accountant M.B. Hariton & Co., Washington, 1959-66; commr. D.C. Pub. Service Commn., Washington, 1966-70; treas. Center for Community Change, Washington, 1970-72; prof. accounting Washington Tech. Inst., 1970-71; partner Lucas, Tucker & Co. C.P.A.s, Washington, 1971—. Financial adviser Jamaica Pub. Utilities Commn., Kingston, Jamaica, 1971—. Chmn. Southwest Neighborhood Assembly, Washington, 1968-70; bd. dirs. Washington Home Rule Com. Inc., Interracial Council Bus. Opportunity; bd. dirs. D.C. chpt. A.R.C. Mem. Democratic Central Com., 1964-66. Served with AUS, 1943-44. C.P.A., D.C. Mem. Am., D.C. insts. C.P.A.'s, Washington Bar Assn., Assn. Practicing C.P.A.'s, Urban League, Nat. Assn. Regulatory Utility Commrs., Met. Washington Bd. Trade, Brookings Instn., Omega Psi Phi. Club: Pigskin. Home: 907 6th St SW Washington DC 20024 Office: 1101 17th St NW Washington DC 20036

PORTERFIELD, AUSTIN LARIMORE, sociologist, educator; b. Salem, Ark., Oct. 16, 1896; s. John and Mary Emily (Rodman) P.; A.B., Oklahoma City U., 1923; B.D., Phillips U., 1926; A.M., Drake U., 1924; Ph.D., Duke, 1936; m. Rose Ella McCollum, Mar. 14, 1917; children—Frances Marie (Mrs. Clayton B. Willis), Vernon Eltinge, Rosella (Mrs. W. J. Chastant). Ordained to ministry Christian Ch.; pastor, Okmulgee, Okla., 1927-28; chmn. dept. sociology Southeastern State Coll., Durant, Okla., 1928-37, Tex. Christian U., 1937-67; prof. sociology U. of Americas, Mexico City, 1967—; vis. tchr. sociology Duke Summer Schs., 1938, 39, 42. Research cons. Ft. Worth Fed. Housing Authority, 1939; mem. exec. com. Ft. Worth Council Social Agys., 1939-44. Bd. dirs. Leo Potishman Found., 1946; trustee Jarvis Christian Coll. Mem. Nat. Probation and Parole Assn., Am. (exec. com. 1946-47), Southwestern (pres. 1948) sociol. socs., Southwestern Social Sci. Assn. Author: Creative Factors in Scientific Research, 1941; Youth in Trouble, 1946; Crime, Suicide, and Social Well-Being in Your State and City, 1948; Mid-Century Crime in Our Culture; 1954; Wait the Withering Rain, 1953; Mirror, Mirror: On Seeing Yourself in Books, 1957; Marriage and Family Living as Self-Other Fulfilment, 1962; Cultures of Violence; The Tragic Man in Society, 1965. Collaborator: The Urban South, 1955. Editor Jour. Health and Human Behavior, 1960—. Contbr. articles to sociol. jours. Address: U Americas PO Box 968 Mexico DF 1 Mexico

PORTERFIELD, HANCEL WAYNE, chemist, oceanographer, mgmt. cons.; b. McCaskill, Ark., Apr. 7, 1935; s. Jessie R. and Dorothy (Cunningham) P.; B.S., Henderson State Tchrs. Coll., 1956; postgrad. George Washington U., 1960, 64-65; m. Hariett Barbara McMillan, June 13, 1959; children—John Bradford, Johanna Beth. Chemist, Nat. Fireworks Co., Shumaker, Ark., 1956-57; test engr. SUBROC propulsion system Thiokol Chem. Corp., Elkton, Md., 1961-64; dir. ocean space systems dept. John I. Thompson & Co., Washington, 1964-66; engr., scientist-oceanology Tracor, Inc., Washington, 1966-67; mgr. Washington office research div. Western Co. of N.Am., 1967-68; pres. Environmental Research Internat., Inc., Washington, 1968—. Oceanographic cons. Marine Resources Commn., indsl. concerns. Served with USNR, 1957-61. Mem. Marine Tech. Soc. (charter, chmn. waste mgmt. com., co-chmn. econ. potential com.), Am. Geophys. Union, Water Pollution Control Fedn., Am. Ordnance Assn. Contbr.articles to profl. jours. Research in oceanography, explosives, pollution abatement, environmental quality monitoring. Home: 1232 Potomac St NW Washington DC 20007 Office: 1026 17th St NW Washington DC 20036

PORTERFIELD, JAY G., educator; b. Holton, Kan., July 1, 1921; s. Robert and Edythe Lillian (Gatewood) P.; B.S., Ia. State U., 1947, M.S., 1950; m. Vere Ernestine Spear, May 9, 1946; 1 dau., Edythe Jane. Instr., Ia. State U., 1947-49, asst. prof., 1949-51; service engr., Ia. Ford Tractor, 1949; asst. prof. Okla. State U., 1952-55, prof., 1955—. Served with USNR, 1943-46. Recipient NSF Faculty fellowship, Okla. Wondering of Engring., 1968. Registered profl. engr., Okla. Mem. Am. Soc. Agrl. Engrs., Alpha Zeta, Gamma Sigma Delta, Sigma Xi. Patentee in field. Home: Rt 1 Stillwater OK 74074

PORTEWIG, JAMES MILTON, architect; b. Richmond, Va., Feb. 3, 1913; s. John James and Maude (Hammond) P.; Archtl. Engring. degree McKinley Roosevelt Grad. Coll., 1942; m. Mary Jane Sweeten, June 29, 1964; children—Joyce (Mrs. William O. Williams), Janice (Mrs. Stephens Shepherd Hughes). Designer, Slaughter, Seville & Blackburn, Archtl. Engrs., Langley Field, Va., 1942-44; architect Merrill C. Lee, A.I.A., Richmond, 1944-65; in practice with own firm, Richmond, 1965—. Mem. A.I.A (mem. chpt. com. 1971—), Va. Assn. Professions, Retail Mchts. Assn. Greater Richmond, West Richmond Bus. Mens' Assn. Republican. Methodist. Mason. Clubs: Downtown, Press (Richmond). Home: 8603 Arran Rd Richmond VA 23235 Office: 405 E Laburnum Av Richmond VA 23222

PORTMAN, JOHN CALVIN, JR., architect; b. Walhalla, S.C., Dec. 4, 1924; student U.S. Naval Acad.; B.S. in Architecture, Ga. Inst. Tech., 1950; m. Joann Newton; 6 children. Formerly with Ketchum, Gina & Sharp, H. M. Heatly, Asso. Architects, N.Y. and Atlanta, also with 2 Atlanta archtl. firms, until 1953; opened own office, Atlanta, 1953; partner Edwards & Portman, Architects, Atlanta 1956-68; prin. John Portman & Assos., 1968—. Chmn. Atlanta Mdse. Mart; pres. Portman Properties; partner Peachtree Center Devel., Atlanta, Embarcadero Center, San Francisco. Bd. visitors Emory U., 1964. Trustee Atlanta Arts Alliance; sponsor Atlanta Symphony. Served with USNR, World War II. Recipient Southland Investment Corp. award, 1963; Ivan Allen award N. Ga. chpt. A.I.A., 1964; Annual award Ga. chpt. Pub. Relations Soc. Am., 1967; named Outstanding Young Man of Yr., Ga. Jr. C. of C., 1959. Registered architect, Ga. Mem. A.I.A. (chmn. profl. practice com. Ga. chpt. 1956), Architects and Engrs. Inst. (dir. 1960-61). Prin. works include: Regency Hyatt House (hotel), Atlanta Mdse. Mart, Atlanta Decorative Arts Center, Peachtree Center Office Bldg., Greenbriar Shopping Center, Peachtree Center South Bldg., Atlanta Gas Light Tower, Trailways Bus Terminal and Parking Decks (all Atlanta), Dana Fine Arts Bldg. at Agnes Scott Coll. (Decatur), Regency Hyatt House (O'Hare), Security Pacific Bank Bldg. (San Francisco), Blue Cross Bldg. (Chattanooga). Home: 5195 Northside Dr NW Atlanta GA 30305 Office: 1900 Peachtree Center South Bldg Atlanta GA 30303

PORTWOOD, THOMAS BRUCE, supt. schs.; b. Decatur, Tex., Aug. 27, 1893; s. William Bruce and Mattie (Payne) P.; B.S., Emporia State Tchrs. Coll., 1919; M.A., Columbia, 1922; Litt.D., Trinity U., San Antonio, 1947; m. Mary Elizabeth Meyers, June 24, 1920; children— Margaret Payne (Mrs. Don F. Tobin), Thomas Bruce, Richard Meyers. Prin. high sch., Atchinson, Kan., 1922-24, supt. schs., 1924-29; asst. supt. schs., San Antonio, 1929-46, supt. schs., 1946—. Mem. faculty U. Tex., 1935-36. Served as lt. U.S. Army, World War I. Decorated Silver Star. Mem. N.E.A., Am. Assn. Sch. Adminstrs. local and state tchrs. assns., Am. Legion, Phi Delta Kappa. Episcoplaian. Rotarian. Author: Our Nations; Our United States; Our Democracy; (with others) The Rise of Our Free Nation, Texas Government. Home: 2130 W Summit Av San Antonio TX Office: 141 Lavaca St San Antonio TX

POSEY, ABBIE RAYMOND, clergyman; b. Hereford, Tex., Nov. 13, 1908; s. Ellis B. and Luella Ivy (Fuqua) P.; B.A., Hardin Simmons U., 1942; Th.M., Southwestern Bapt. Theol. Sem., 1945, 52; m. Leau Ada Bowen, Aug. 1, 1928; children—Ellis B., Barbara Rae (Mrs. Ronnie Gandy). Cashier, First Nat. Bank, Hereford, Tex., 1937-39 ordained to ministry Bapt. Ch., 1939; pastor 1st Bapt. Chs., Chillicothe, Tex., 1945-48, Hamlin, Tex., 1948-51, Temple, Okla., 1952-54, Bapt. Temple Ch., Big Spring, Tex., 1954-62, Richland Heights Bapt. Ch., Richland, Wash., 1963-65, 1st Bapt. Ch., Sweet Home, Ore., 1965-68, Immanuel Bapt. Ch., Abilene, Tex., 1968—. Author: The New Testament Baptising Ones, 1966; Victory Over the Adversaries, 1972. Address: 1141 Cypress St Abilene TX 79601

POSEY, ELLIS BENTON, JR., educator; b. Hereford, Tex., Oct. 6, 1921; s. Ellis Benton and Louella Ivy (Fuqua) P.; B.S., Hardin-Simmons U., 1943, B.A., 1949, M.A., 1952; Ph.D., U. Tex., 1963; m. Martha Elizabeth Patton, Sept. 2, 1946. Tchr. pub. schs., Hereford, 1946, Sweetwater, Tex., 1947-54; high sch. prin., Baird, 1954-58; tchr. high sch., Austin, 1958-61; research asso. U. Tex., 1961-63; asminstrv. intern Tex. Edn. Agy., Austin, 1963; curriculum dir. pub. schs., Brownfield, 1963-67; asso. prof. edn., dir. tchr. certification West Tex. State U., Canyon, 1967—. Chmn. Am. Cancer Soc., Terry County, Tex., 1966-67; active United Fund drives, Brownfield, Tex. Served with AUS, 1943-46. Mem. Am., Tex. assns. sch. adminstrs., Tex. Tchrs. Assn., Tex. Assn. Coll. Tchrs., Phi Delta Kappa. Baptist. Rotarian (sec. 1971-72). Home: 1500 Creekmere Dr Canyon TX 79015

POSEY, WILLIAM THOMAS, rancher; b. Tehuacana, Tex., Apr. 19, 1910; s. Jonathan Reed and Bettha Mae (Bounds) P.; A.A., Westminster Jr. Coll., 1929; student Adrian Coll., 1929-30, Tex. A. and M. U., 1931-32; m. Julia Lelon Robbins, Dec. 25, 1932; children—Patsy Jean (Mrs. Bailey Earl Wheeless), Richard Thomas. Prin., Brandon Pub. Schs., Hill County, Tex., 1930-31; county agrl. agt. Extension Service, Tex. A. and M. U., Gilmer, 1934-35, Emory, 1935-38, Clarksville, 1938-41, Fort Stockton, 1941-66; rancher, Fort Stockton, 1967—. Mem. Sch. Bd., Emory Independent Sch. Dist., Rains County, Tex., 1936-38. Recipient award County Agts. Assn., 1949. Mem. County Agts. Assn. (bd. dirs. 1955-56), Am. Soc. Animal Sci., Tex. Beef Cattle Assn., Sigma Alpha Epsilon. Democrat. Methodist (chmn. bd. 1963-64). Mason, Kiwanian, Lion. Home: 105 S Rio St Box 1703 Stockton TX 79735 Office: Box 1015 Van Horn TX 29855

POSNER, BEN, govt. ofcl.; b. Tucson, Aug. 12, 1914; s. Phillip and Rose (Tsibula) P.; B.S. in Bus. Adminstrn. cum laude, U. Ariz., 1936; M.A. in Govt., George Washington U., 1942; Ph.D., Am. U., 1962; m. Selma E. Sheftelman, July 30, 1940; children—Richard Daniel, David Barnett. Teaching fellow U. Ariz., 1936-37; with Navy Dept., then NLRB, 1937-43; with U.S. Govt. burs., 1946—, asst. dir. for adminstrn. USIA, 1963-72; exec. dir. President's Study Commn. Internat. Radio Broadcasting, 1972—; spl. lectr. Royal-McBee Co., 1941-63; professorial lectr. George Washington U., 1962—. Mem. Com. on Efficiency and Economy, Montgomery County, Md., 1966—. Active local PTA., Boy Scouts Am. Served to 1st lt. AUS, 1943-46; PTO. Recipient Distinguished Service award USIA, 1961, Rockefeller 0,000 Pub. Service award, 1970. Mem. Am. Soc. Pub. Adminstrn., Fed. Govt. Accountants Assn. Mem. B'nai B'rith. Author articles in field. Home: 2405 Eccleston St Silver Springs MD 20902 Office: 1750 Pennsylvania Av NW Washington DC 20547

POSNER, MICHAEL LOUIS, newspaperman; b. Providence, Jan. 15, 1932; s. Eli and Minnie (Jacobson) P.; student U. Me., 1949-51; B.S., Boston U., 1953; m. C. Andrea Mattson, June 21, 1964. Mem.

staff U.P.I., 1956—, Congl. corr., Washington, 1959—; free-lance writer, 1953—; radio and TV panelist, 1959—. Served with inf. AUS, 1953-55. Mem. Am. Newspaper Guild, Wire Service Guild (nat. committeeman). White House Corr. Assn., Tau Epsilon Phi. Club: Nat. Press (Washington). Home: 2712 Wisconsin Av NW Washington DC 20007 also 6 Grasmere Rd Portland ME Office: Nat Press Bldg Washington DC 20004

POSS, WOODROW WILSON, dentist; b. Strathmore, Va., Nov. 19, 1916; s. Burton Wilner and Lillie Walker (Jacobs) P.; B.S., U. Va., 1940; postgrad. U. Richmond, 1945-46; D.D.S., Med. Coll. Va., 1950; m. Vivienne McCay Morrissette, Aug. 7, 1943. Quarterman, Newport News Shipbuilding and Dry Dock Co. (Va.), 1940-45; practice gen. dentistry, Gordonsville, 1950—. Chmn. Gordonsville Troop com. Boy Scouts Am., 1952-67. Mem. Orange County Sch. Bd., 1964-65. Fellow Va. Dental Assn. (dental edn. com. 1966-74, com. chmn., 1970—); mem. No. Va. Dental Soc. (past pres.), Gordonsville Bus. Men's Assn. (pres. 1952-53), Gordonsville C. of C. (pres. 1969-70). Presbyn. (trustee 1968—, clk. of session 1968—). Mason, Rotarian (pres. 1963-64). Clubs: Greene Hills Country, Woodberry Forest Golf. Home: PO Box 486 Gordonsville VA 22942 Office: P O Box 486 Gordonsville VA 22942

POST, ALLEN, lawyer; b. Newnan, Ga., Dec. 3, 1906; s. William Glenn and Rosa Kate (Muse) P.; A.B. summa cum laude, U. Ga., 1927; B.A. with first honors in Jurisprudence (Rhodes scholar), Oxford U., 1929, B.C.L., 1930, M.A., 1933; m. Mary Chastaine Cook, Dec. 27, 1934; 1 son, Allen. Admitted to Ga. bar, 1930; spl. atty. gen. Ga., 1933, 1935; asst. atty. gen. assigned Ga. Pub. Service Commn., 1934; partner Moise, Post & Gardner, Atlanta, 1942-61, specializing in bus. and corp. law; partner Hansell, Post, Brandon & Dorsey, 1962—; dir. Atlanta Gas Light Co. (exec. com.), First Nat. Bank Atlanta (exec. com.), Am. Cast Iron Pipe Co., Retail Credit Co. (exec. com.), numerous other corps.; also lectr., writer on legal subjects. Chmn. Navy Day, Atlanta, 1937-39; pres. Atlanta Estate Planning Council, 1960; trustee W.N. Banks Found., Howell Fund. Mem. State Democratic Exec. Com., mem. com. to rewrite election laws and revise primary rules of Ga., 1956; Dem. presdl. elector. Mem. Govs. staff; mem. State Com. to Revise Income Tax Laws of Ga., 1956; mem. Ga. Income Tax Study Commn. Served as lt. comdr., USNR World War II. Fellow Am. Coll. Trial Lawyers, Am. Coll. Probate Counsel; mem. Atlanta (exec. com., pres. 1956), Am., Ga. bar assns., Am. Judicature Soc., Atlanta Claims Assn., S.A.R., Navy League, Res. Officers Naval Services (1st pres. Atlanta chpt.), Mil. Order World Wars, Am. Legion (comdr.), Am. Assn. Rhodes Scholars, Sphinx, Phi Beta Kappa, Phi Kappa Phi, Phi Delta Phi, Kappa Alpha. Methodist. Clubs: Rotary, Capital City, Piedmont Driving, Lawyers (Atlanta); Old War Horse Lawyers (pres. 1962); Commerce. Home: 620 Peachtree Battle Av NW Atlanta GA 30327 Office: 1st Nat Bank Tower Atlanta GA 30303

POSTELL, WILLIAM DOSITE, librarian, educator; b. Plaquemine, La., Oct. 5, 1908; s. William Dazelle and Frances Clementine (Kleinpeter) P.; B.S., La. State U., 1930, M.S., 1932, B.S. in L.S., 1933; m. May Belle Andries, Aug. 11, 1937; children—Philip, Mary (Mrs. Joseph Davis), John, William Dosite, David. Asst. librarian Sabine Parish Library, Many, La., 1933-34; librarian Mansfield (La.) Pub. Schs., 1934-38; med. librarian, prof. med. bibliography La. State U. Sch. Medicine, New Orleans, 1938-59, Tulane U. Sch. Medicine, New Orleans, 1959—. Instr. various univs. and hosps. Pres., Pocket Parks Inc., New Orleans, 1971. Pres. Our Lady of Lourdes Sch. Bd., New Orleans, 1971-72. Served with USCGR, 1944-45. Recipient certificate of merit City of New Orleans, 1952, Marcia C. Noyes award Med. Library Assn., 1958. Mem. La. Tchrs. Assn. (pres. sect. 1934-35), La. (pres. 1950, Essee M. Culver awards 1972), Med. (pres. 1952-53) library assns., La. Hist. Assn., Am. Assn. History Medicine. Author: Introduction of Medical Bibliography 1951; Health of Slaves on Southern Plantations, 1951; Applied Medical Bibliography for Students, 1955; Classification for Med. Literature, 1966. Editor: Libraries of New Orleans, 1945. Editor bull. Med. Library Assn., 1945-49. Home: 1930 General Pershing St New Orleans LA 70115

POSTON, ERNEST EUGENE, coll. pres., clergyman; b. Chesnee, S.C., July 14, 1918; s. Summie A. and Minnie (Conner) P.; A.A., Gardner-Webb Coll., 1941-43; B.A., Wake Forest Coll., 1944; B.D., So. Bapt. Theol. Sem., 1947, Th.M., 1948, Th.D., 1950; m. Dorothy Elizabeth Jenkins, Jan. 28, 1939; children—Robert Stephen, Gloria Jean, Elizabeth Ann. Ordained to ministry Bapt. Ch., 1943; pastor Wise and Rock Springs chs. in Tar River Assn. N.C., 1943-44, Monterey, Swallowfield, Elk Lick and Dallasburg chs., Ky., 1944-50, Wallace (N.C.) Ch. 1951-57, First Ch., Jonesboro, Ga., 1958-59; head dept. religion Gardner-Webb Coll., Boiling Springs, 1959-61, pres., 1961—. Dir. Union Trust Co. Pres. N.C. Bapt. Pastor's Conf., 1956-57; moderator Wilmington (N.C.) Bapt. Assn. Chs. Del. White House Conf. on Children and Youth; active Boy Scouts Am. Bd. dirs. N.C. Conf. Social Service; sec. N.C. Found. Ch. Related Colls. Recipient Alumnus of Year award Gardner-Webb Coll. Alumni Assn., 1967. Mem. Am. Assn. U. Profs., Soc. Bibl. Lit. and Exegesis. Mason. Clubs: Exchange (Jonesboro, Ga.); Lions (Boiling Springs), Rotary. Home: Box 792 Boiling Springs NC 28017

POSTON, JERRY LEE, hwy. engr.; b. Walters, Okla., July 23, 1936; s. Harry and Ruby (Cowan) P.; B.C.E., U. Okla., 1959; m. Janice Marie Hanes, Sept. 4, 1956; 1 dau., Janice Lee. Hwy. engr. Ala. div. U.S. Bur. Pub. Rds., Montgomery, 1961-69, project engr., Kuwait, Kuwait, 1969-71; hwy. engr. Fed. Hwy. Adminstrn., Washington, 1971—. Served with AUS, 1960. Mem. Okla., Ala. socs. profl. engrs., Delta Upsilon. Baptist. Home: 6108 Sherborn Lane Springfield VA 22152 Office: 400 7th St SW Washington DC 20590

POSTON, JOHN PAUL, textile co. exec.; b. Johnsonville, S.C., Aug. 20, 1926; s. Mack Kenzie and Eulee (Greenwood) P.; A.B., Wofford Coll., 1953; m. Leta Tanner, June 12, 1948; children—Wayne, Anne, Stanley. Trainee, Deering Milliken Co., Hartsville, S.C., 1953-55, gen. overseer, 1956-63; asst. mgr. Springs Mills, Inc., Laurinburg, N.C., 1963-65, mgr., 1965-69, mgr., Biscoe, N.C., 1969—. Vice-pres., P.T.A., Laurinburg, 1966-67. Bd. dirs. Darlington County chpt. A.R.C., 1958-59; trustee Montgomery Meml. Hosp., 1971—. Served with AUS, 1945-47. Democrat. Methodist. (ofcl. bd. 1965-69, finance chmn. 1971-72). Mason (3 deg.), Lion (dir. 1970—). Clubs: Montgomery Country (Troy, N.C.), Optimist (dir. 1956-60). Home: P O Box 697 Candor NC 27229 Office: Springs Mills Inc Biscoe NC 27209

POSTON, RALPH R., steel erection co. exec., state senator; b. Miami, Fla., Jan. 2 1923; ed. U. Miami, U. Houston; m. Carolyn Davis; children— Ralph R., Dorothy Susan (Mrs. Barrier), Sheryl Lynne (Mrs. Harry Jordan. Founder, pres. Poston Bridge and Iron, Inc., Miami, 1950—; dir. Riverside Bank, Miami; mem. Fla. Ho. of Reps., 1964-66; mem. Fla. Senate, 1967—, chmn. transp. com., 1970—. Mem. Met.-Dade County Examining Bd.; advisor U. Miami Citizens Bd.; mem. adv. bd. Baptist Hosp.; chmn. standards implementation com. President's Nat. Hwy. Safety Adv. Com.; mem. Nat. Sch. Bus Safety Week Com. Bd. dirs. Goodwill Industries; trustee Southeastern Ironworkers Health and Welfare Com., Miami Ironworkers Pension Fund. Served with USNR, World War II. Mem. Nat. Erectors Assn. (pres. 1970-71), Steel and Ornamental Erectors Assn. South Fla. (past pres.), Asso. Gen. Contractors, Engring. Contracors Assn. (past dir.), D.A.V., Fla. (indsl. devel. com.), Miami-Dade (indsl. devel. council) chambers commerce, Fla. Road Builders, S.A.R. Methodist. Mason (Shriner), Kiwanian, Moose, Lion (past pres. Allapattah). Club: Tiger Bay. Home: 6282 SW 133d St Miami FL 33156 Office: 3103 NW 20th St Miami FL 33142*

POSTON, TALMADGE CHESLEY, banker; b. Valley Mills, Tex., Jan. 10, 1915; s. Dewitt T. and Molly Odell (Jones) P.; student Tarleton State Coll., 1934-35; m. Kathryn Velma Biggs, Oct. 12, 1936; children—Molly Alicia (Mrs. Alfred J. Berry), James T. Owner, Poston Feed Mill, Stephenville, Tex., 1940—; with Stephenville State Bank, 1947—, v.p., 1962—. Lion. Club: Tejas Country. Home: 1065 W Frey St Stephenville TX 76401 Office: 1020 N Graham St PO Box 146 Stephenville TX 76401

POTEAT, WILLIAM HARDMAN, educator; b. Kaifeng, Honan, China, Apr. 19, 1919; s. Edwin McNeill and Wilda (Hardman) P.; student Mars Hill Jr. Coll., 1936-37; A.B., Oberlin Coll., 1941; B.D., Yale Div. Sch., 1944; Ph.D., Duke, 1951; m. Marian Kelley, Sept. 8, 1943; children— Anne Carlyle, Susan Colquitt, Edwin McNeill III. Asso. sec. YMCA, U.N.C., 1944-46, acting sec., 1946-47, instr. dept. philosophy, 1947-50, asst. prof., 1950-54, asso. prof., 1954-57; Quin prof. philos. theology and Christian criticism Episcopal Theology Sem. of S.W., 1957-60; asso. prof. Christianity and culture Duke, 1960-66, prof., 1966-69, prof. religion and culture, 1969-71, prof. religion and comparative studies, 1971—, chmn. dept., 1972—. Vis. prof. Stanford U., 1970, U. Tex., 1971. Cons. spl. com. liberal studies Am. Assn. Colls., 1967; mem. Nat. Humanities Faculty, 1969—; mem. devel. bd. Lenoir Rhyne Coll., 1968—; mem. council grad. studies Danforth Found., 1967—; cons., lectr. World Student Christian Fedn., 1953-56; cons. research and devel. Gov. Terry Sanford, 1961-64; chmn. central com. Nat. Council for Religion and Higher Edn., 1954-55. Distinguished Humanities scholar Haverford (Pa.) Coll., 1969. Mem. Am. Philos. Assn., Am. Acad. Polit. and Social Sci., So. Soc. for Philos. and Psychology, Phi Beta Kappa. Democrat. Episcopalian. Contbr. articles in field to profl. jours. Co-editor, contbg. author Intellect and Hope: Essays in the Thought of Michael Polanyi, 1968. Home: 621 Greenwood Rd Chapel Hill NC 27514

POTEET, BRUCE COURTIN, architect; b. Kansas City, Kan., Oct. 19, 1936; s. Floyd Sargent and Millicent Ellen (Courtin) P.; B.S. in Architecture, U. Kan., 1960; m. Ellen Marie Venable, Aug. 14, 1965; 1 dau., Leslie Ellen. Architect, Terney & Biggs, Architects and Engrs., Kansas City, Mo., 1960-61, 62-64; archtl. systems cons., U.S. Gypsum Co., Chgo., 1964, Houston, 1964-66, Charlotte, N.C., 1966—; specalized pvt. archtl. practice, Charlotte, 1966—. Served with USAF, 1960-62; lt. Naval Res., 1962-72. Recipient awards Constrn. Specifications Inst., 1969, 71, 72. Mem. A.I.A., Constrn. Specifications Inst. (chpt. treas. 1971-72), Tau Kappa Epsilon. Republican. Methodist. K.C. Contbr. chpt. to Constrn. Specifications Inst. Handbook. Home: 1224 Worcaster Pl Charlotte NC 28211 Office: 1300 Baxter St Charlotte NC 28204

POTEET, MARK DEE, oil co. exec.; b. Olive, Mo., Sept. 16, 1920; s. G. W. and Nora U. (Salsman) P.; student Mo. U., 1937, Drury Coll., 1937-38, Draughons Bus. Coll., 1938-39; B.B.A., S.W. Mo. State U., 1954; m. Marjorie Elizabeth Potts, Jan. 31, 1939; children—James M., Cheryl (Mrs. Guy W. Stephenson), David W. Trainee Ajax & Interstate Pipe Line Co., Springfield, Mo., 1941-43, supt. materials, Springfield, Mo., Tulsa, Okla., 1946-54; coordinator employee devel. Cities Service Petroleum Co., Bartlesville, Okla., 1954-61; mgr. employee and pub. relations Skelly Oil Co., Tulsa, Okla., 1961—. Mem. Hillcrest Assos., Hillcrest Hosp., 1965—; mem. vis. com. Sch. Bus., U. Okla., 1968—. Chmn. Republican Dist. Com., 1960, precinct vice-chmn., 1970. Bd. dirs., pres. Skelly Oil Co. Found., Tulsa Target Area Action Group. Served with USMCR, 1943-46. Mem. Pub. Relations Soc. Am. (dir. 1965—). N.A.M. (mem. pub. affairs com. 1966—), Petroleum Club Tulsa, U.S. C. of C. (mem. pub. affairs com. 1965). Club: Hurricane (dir. 1963) (Tulsa). Home: 2149 S Fulton Pl Tulsa OK 74114 Office: 1437 S Boulder St Tulsa OK 74102

POTTER, ANDREW ELWIN, chemist; b. St. Petersburg, Fla., Nov. 29, 1926; s. Andrew E. and Lucille (Frisbie) P.; B.S., U. Fla., 1948; Ph.D., U. Wis., 1953; postgrad. U. Coll., London, 1960; m. Shirley Marie Barrett, July 7, 1952; children—Andrew Elwin III, Lloyd B., Thomas N. Research scientist NACA, Lewis Flight Propulsion Lab., Cleve., 1953-58; head combustion fundamentals sect. NASA, Lewis Research Center, Cleve., 1958-64, chief elec. energy sources br., 1964-68, staff scientist space physics div. NASA Manned Spacecraft Center, Houston, 1968-70, chief applied physics br., 1970—, mem. atmospheres subcom. space sci. steering com., 1960—. Served with USNR, 1944-45. Recipient jr. achievement award Cleve. Tech. Socs., 1962. Mem. Am. Chem. Soc., Am. Geophys. Union, Combustion Inst., Cosmos Club, Sigma Xi, Delta Tau Delta. Research on flame quenching, devel. thin-film solar cells, planetary atmospheres static electricity in spacecraft, earth observations from spacecraft. Home: 1714 Neptune Lane Houston TX 77058 Office: NASA Manned Spacecraft Center Houston TX 77058

POTTER, CLARKE JAMES, constrn. co. exec.; b. Denison, Ia., Dec. 7, 1915; s. Forrest J. and Beulah P. (Barrett) P.; B.S., Ia. State U., 1941; m. Marie Pautsch, Jan. 5, 1943; children—Clarke James II, Stephen B. With Ruby Constrn. Co., Louisville, 1950—, pres., 1964—; pres JFC Co., Louisville, 1965—, Ruby-Collins, Inc., Louisville, 1970—; pres. First Mut. Life Ins. Co., Lexington, Ky., 1970—, also dir. Mem. Air Pollution Control Commn. Louisville and Jefferson County, 1968-69, chmn., 1965-66. Mem. Am. Soc. C.E., Ky. Soc. Profl. Engrs., Hwy. Contractors, Inc. (pres. 1966, 67, Asso. Gen. Contractors (pres. Louisville, 1966), Asso. Gen. Contractors Ky. (dir. 1969-71), Nat. Asso. Gen. Contractors (nat. dir. 1971), Am. Rd. Builders Assn. (pres. 1961-62), Ky. Assn. Hwy. Contractors (2d v.p. 1971-72), Louisville C. of C. (mem. streets and hwys. com. 1966-67), Sigma Pi. Presbyn. (treas., deacon, elder). Clubs: Engineer and Architect, Big Spring Country (pres. 1970-71) (Louisville). Home: 3820 Washington Sq Louisville KY 40207 Office: 3837 Fitzgerald Rd Louisville KY 40216

POTTER, ERNEST ELLIS, bldg. constrn. exec.; b. Big Spring, Tex., Sept. 8, 1933; s. Ernest and Zola (Neil) P.; B.S. in Gen. Engring., U. S. Naval Acad., 1954; B.S. in Mech. Engring., Mass. Inst. Tech., 1959; M.B.A., Columbia U., 1960; m. Gayle Price, Dec. 22, 1954; children—Price Randall, Kimberly Anne, Kelly Sue. Market research and bus. analyst Humble Oil and Refinery Co., 1960-64; with Boise Cascade Corp., Boise, Ida., also Salem, Ore., 1964-66; gen. mgr., pres. So. Mouldings, Inc., Americus, Ga., 1966-69; v.p. marketing Mouldings, Inc., Marion, Va., 1969-70; pres., chmn. bd. Housing Supply Industries, Americus, 1970—. Served with USAF, 1954-57. Mem. Am. So. M.E. (dir. peak textiles 1970—), Ga. Mobile Home Assn. (chpt. sec., treas. 1971—). Elk. Home: 115 Clearview Circle Americus GA 31709 Office: PO Box 663 Americus GA 31709

POTTER, GORDON COOPER, civil engr.; b. Denver, Mar. 14, 1920; s. Cecil William and Sibley (Deshayes) P.; B.S. cum laude, U. Colo., 1943; postgrad. U. Chgo., 1944; m. Marilyn Elizabeth Oldland, June 25, 1949; children—Charles Edward, Anne Louise. Bridge designer Crocker & Ryan, Cons., Denver, 1946-49; with Humble Oil & Refining Co., Denver, Billings, Seattle, Houston, 1949—, tech. adviser, Houston, 1961—. Served with USAAF, 1943-46. Registered profl. engr., Colo. Mem. Tau Beta Pi. Presbyn. Home: 13502 Appletree St Houston TX 77024 Office: Humble Bldg Houston TX 77001

POTTER, I(RWIN) LEE, exec. dir. Republican Congl. Boosters Club; b. Tower City, Pa., Oct. 5, 1909; s. Harry Stewart and Emma (Wagner) P.; B.C.S., Southeastern U., 1943; m. Dulcie Horner, May 28, 1927; 1 son, Alan Lee. Apprentice printer Govt. Printing Office, 1928-32, printer, 1932-41; chief of printing Dept. Labor, 1941-46; partner constrn. firm MacPherson & Potter, 1946-53; spl. asst. Sec. Labor Mitchell, 1954-55; campaign mgr. Congressman Broyhill, Gen. Eisenhower, 1952; dir. personnel div. Rep. Nat. Com., 1955-57, spl. asst. to chmn., 1957-67; exec. dir. Rep. Congl. Campaign Com., 1967-70; chmn. bd. Frank R. Jelleff, Inc.; pres. Jelleff Assos., Inc.; gen. partner Crystal Assos., Lee-Hi Indsl. Park; dir. Am. Realty Trust, Arlington Trust Co. (Va.), Kimel Furniture, Inc. Former pres. Arlington Civic Symphony Assn. chmn. Republican County Com., chmn. 10th Dist. Va., chmn. Va. Rep. Com., 1956-62, mem. Rep. Nat. Com., 1956-62; mem. Rep. Nat. Com. for Va., 1964-72. Bd. dirs. Wolff Trap Found. for Performing Arts, 1969—. Clubs: Optimist, Capitol Hill, Washington Golf and Country (Washington). Home: 3120 N Wakefield St Arlington VA 22207 Office: Hotel Congressional Washington DC 20003

POTTER, PHILIP, journalist; b. Mpls., Nov. 14, 1907; s. William Ransom and Minnie May (Morgan) P.; B.A., U. Minn., 1934; m. Ruth Anne Benjamin, Jan. 23, 1932; children—John, Barbara, Susan. Mng. editor Rapid City (S.D.) Daily Jour., 1936-41; mem. staff Balt. Sun, 1942—, war corr. in CBI, 1945-46, in Palestine, 1947-48, in Korea, 1950-51, Washington and fgn. corr., 1951-63, chief bur., New Delhi, India, 1961-62, chief bur., Washington, 1964—. Decorated Purple Heart. Mem. White House Corr. Assn., Overseas Writers. Clubs: Federal City, Gridiron, Nat. Press (Washington). Contbr. to The Candidates, 1960. Home: 1011 Copley Lane Silver Spring MD 20904 Office: Nat Press Bldg Washington DC 20004

POTTER, RICHARD RALPH, electronic engr.; b. Lawrence, Kan., May 9, 1926; s. Earl and Geraldine (Hull) P.; B.S. in Elec. Engring. (Summerfield scholar), U. Kan., 1948, M.S., 1950; m. Doris Dean Edmiston, Feb. 21, 1950; 1 dau., Alexandra Amy. Jr. electronic engr. U.S. Naval Weapons Lab., Dahlgren, Va., 1949-50, electronic scientist, 1951-55, supervisory gen. engr., 1956-59, supervisory research electronic engr., 1959-64, asst. dir. Weapons Devel. and Evaluation Lab., 1965-68, research asso., 1969—. Served with USNR, 1945-46. Mem. I.E.E.E., Am. Ordnance Assn., Fed. Profl. Assn., Sigma Xi, Tau Beta Pi, Sigma Tau, Pi Mu Epsilon, Phi Delta Theta. Home: Route 2 Box 371 J King George VA 22485 Office: US Naval Weapons Lab Dahlgren VA 22448

POTTER, ROBERT ELLIS, librarian; b. Knoxville, Tenn., Mar. 16, 1937; s. Pollye Jack and Violet Belle (Walker) P.; B.S., U. Tenn., 1961; postgrad. U. So. Cal. at Los Angeles, 1963-64; m. Rosemary Byrd Lee, Dec. 28, 1963; children—Robert Ellis II, and Kenyon David (twins). Student asst. U. Tenn. Libraries, 1959-61; copyreader The Knoxville News-Sentinel, 1961-62; library asst. U. Tenn. Libraries, 1962-63; library aide Los Angeles County Library System, El Monte, Cal., 1963-65; reference librarian, bus. and sci. collection City of Hialeah Library div. Hialeah John F. Kennedy Library (Fla.), 1966—. Counselor, Trail Blazer's Camps, Inc., N.Y.C., 1958; chaplain's asst. U.S. Army Res., 1959-64. Mem. Mus. Sci. and Planetarium, Miami, Fairchild Tropical Garden, Miami. Served with AUS, 1959. Mem. Am., Fla., Dade County (pres. 1970-71) library assns., Internat Platform Assn., U. Tenn. Alumni Annual Giving Program, Hist. Assn. So. Fla., East Tenn. Hist. Soc., Sigma Delta Chi. Editor newsletter Dade County Library Assn., 1971—, bull. SORT, A.L.A., 1971—. Home: 258 W 46th St Hialeah FL 33012 Office: 190 W 49th St Hialeah FL 33012

POTTER, THEODORE, JR., art gallery dir.; b. Springhill, Kan., Dec. 6, 1932; s. Theodore and Blanche Ruth (Harris) P.; B.A., Baker U., 1954; postgrad. fine arts U. Kan., 1958-59, U. Cal., 1960; M.F.A., Cal. Coll. Arts and Crafts, 1961; m. Barbara Ann Palmer, June 18, 1968; 1 dau., Kelly Palmer. Dir. Shelby Galleries, Sausalito, Cal., 1966; art dir. Glide Found., San Francisco, 1966-67; dir. Gallery Contemporary Art, Winston-Salem, N.C., 1967—. Cons. N.C. Arts Council, Inc., 1971—, visual arts div. Nat. Endowment for Arts, 1971—; mem. adv. council N.C. Art Soc., 1970—. Served with AUS, 1957-58. Rotarian. One-man exhbns. at Vanderbilt U., Salem Coll., Davidson Coll., others. Home: 2149 Country Club Rd Winston-Salem NC 27104 Office: Gallery of Contemporary Art 500 S Main St Winston-Salem NC 27101

POTTINGER, J. STANLEY, lawyer, govt. ofcl.; B.A. with honors in Govt., Harvard, 1962, LL.B., 1965; m. Gloria Jean Anderson; children—Paul, Kathryn. Admitted to Cal. bar, 1965; asso. firm Broad, Khourie and Schulz, San Francisco, 1965-69; cons. Dept. Health, Edn. and Welfare, Washington, 1969-70, dir. Office for Civil Rights, also asst. to sec. for civil rights, 1970—. Past pres. Richmond Dist. Community Council, San Francisco. Past mem. bd. dirs. Lighthouse for Blind, San Francisco. Contbr. articles to profl. jours. Home: 2 Bay Tree Lane Bethesda MD 20016 Office: Dept Health Edn and Welfare Washington DC 20201*

POTTS, BENJAMIN FRANKLIN, JR., wood products co. exec.; b. Louisville, Oct. 28, 1920; s. Benjamin Franklin and Theresa Jane (Everard) P.; student U. Louisville, 1945; m. Elvina Catherine Stottman, Jan. 24, 1942; children—Marilyn (Mrs. Harold Silverman), Joan (Mrs. Kenneth Danner), Kathleen (Mrs. Patrick Welsh), Steven, John, Mark. Engring. draftsman E.I. DuPont Co., Charlestown, Inc., 1940-42; draftsman, estimator sales Kister Lumber Co., Louisville, 1945-62; v.p. sales Anderson Wood Products Co., Louisville, 1962—. Mem. scholarship Fund com. Catherine Spalding Coll., 1968-72. Served with USAAF, 1942-45. Decorated Air medal with 2 oak leaf clusters, 3 Bronze Stars. Roman Catholic. K.C. Clubs: Kenwood Optimist, Iroquois Civic, South Park Country (Louisville). Home: 920 Southview Rd Louisville KY 40214 Office: 1381 Beech St Louisville KY 40211

POTTS, DONALD CULLEN, stock broker; b. Dallas, Sept. 2, 1938; s. Cullen Floyd and Marie Elizabeth (Clayton) P.; B.B.A., N. Tex. State U., 1963; postgrad. So. Meth. U., 1963-64; m. Sara Sue Stone, Oct. 4, 1958; 1 dau., Kristi Dawn. Instl. salesman Merill Lynch, Pierce, Fenner & Smith, Inc., 1964-69; v.p., dir. instl. sales Walston & Co., Dallas, 1969—. Active Dallas Metropolitan Ballet Guild. Mem. Ins. Inst. Am., 500, Inc. (mem. exec. 1968-71). Iota Un Sigma (pres. 1961-63). Mason (Shriner). Club: Optimist (pres. 1966) (Dallas). Home: 6920 Joyce Way Dallas TX 75225 Office: 1510 Pacific St Dallas TX 75201

POTTS, ERWIN, newspaper exec. Vice pres., gen. mgr. Tallahassee Democrat. Home: 3053 Carlow Circle Tallahassee FL 32303 Office: Tallahassee Democrat 277 Magnolia Dr PO Box 990 Tallahassee FL 32301

POTTS, JOHN GARY, dentist; b. Salisbury, Md., Sept. 4, 1899; s. Reginald Harrell and Annie Christian (Moore) P.; student Randolph Macon Coll., 1917-20; D.D.S., Med. Coll. Va., 1924; m. Virginia Carter Tyree, June 19, 1929; children—Nancy Duval (Mrs. Jack Preston Weikel), Anne Elizabeth (Mrs. Edward Alan Heady). Pvt. practice dentistry, Lynchburg, Va., 1924—. Mem. Bedford County Sch. Bd., 1948-62; mem. Va. Sch. Bd. Assn., pres., 1957-58. Mem. Am. Va., dental assns., Lynchburg (pres.), Piedmont (pres.) dental assns., Kappa Alpha Order, Psi Omega. Methodist (chrm. bd. 1953-54). Kiwanian. Club: Ruritan. Home: 1517 Clayton Ave Lynchburg VA 24503 Office: Fort Early Bldg Lynchburg VA 24502

POU, JOHN WILLIAM, banker; b. Elmwood, N.C., July 8, 1917; s. William Clarence and Mary (Arey) P.; B.S. (Danforth fellow 1937) N.C. State Coll., 1938; M.S., U. Wis., 1947; Ph.D., Cornell U., 1951; Nat. 4-H fellow U.S. Dept. Agr., 1941; m. Margaretha Brinn Craig, May 2, 1942; children—John William, Constance Craig. Asst. county agt. Iredell County, Statesville, N.C., 1938-41; dairy extension specialist N.C. State Coll., 1946, head animal industry dept., 1953-58, also mem. faculty senate; extension dairyman U. Md., College Park, 1947-50, head dairy dept., 1951-53; dir. Ariz. Agrl. Extension, U. Ariz., 1958-61; v.p., mgr. agrl. dept. Wachovia Bank & Trust Co., Greenville, N.C., 1962-66, v.p., head Greenville offices, 1966-68, v.p. marketing N.E. div., 1968—. Dir. N.C. YMCA; coach Nat. Champion 4-H Dairy Cattle Judging team, 1950; mem. Ariz. Gov.'s Civil Def. Council, 1960-61; pres. Coastal Plains Planning and Devel. Commn., 1964-65, N.C. 4-H Devel. Fund, Inc., 1964, 65, Pitt County United Fund, 1965-66; dir. N.C. Home Econs. Found., Inc., 1964-65; mem. bd. dirs. 4-H Club Found. Served from 2d lt. to maj., AUS, 1942-45, PTO; lt. col. Res. Mem. Am. Dairy Sci. Assn. (chmn. type com., chmn. So. div. 1958-59), Western States Extension Dirs. (chmn. 1958-59), N.C. Bankers Assn. (chmn. agrl. com. 1963-64), Greenville C. of C. (pres. 1969), Assn. Agrl. Bankers (pres. 1970), Blue Key, Alpha Zeta, Phi Kappa Phi. Baptist. Kiwanian (chmn. agrl. and conservation com., N.C. 4-H Honor (4-H alumni award Iredell County), 1954), Rotarian (pres. Greenville 1970). Home: 1108 Greenville Blvd Greenville NC 27834 Office: Wachovia Bank & Trust Co Greenville NC 27834

POUCHER, DEAN JOSEPH, profl. assn. exec.; b. St. Petersburg, Fla., Sept. 3, 1935; s. Curtis Alman and Vivian (Bentley) P.; student U. S.C., 1953-57; m. Cecelia Ann Connelly, Feb. 19, 1971; children—by previous marriage Tina, Jay, Shannon. Writer, actor, producer, dir. WIS-TV, Columbia, S.C., 1953-57; free lance writer, 1957-60; operations mgr. WCCA-TV, Columbia, gen. mgr. WQXL Radio, Columbia, 1963-66; exec. v.p. Beaufort County C. of C. (S.C.), 1966—; v.p. Quave Poucher Enterprises, Inc., Columbia, 1962—. Com. chmn. Beaufort council Boy Scouts Am., 1967-69. Recipient Pub. Service award U.S. Treasury Dept., 1969, award Am. Bar Assn., 1963, Mem. Internat. Game Fish Assn., Internat. Oceanographic Found., Nat., S.C. wildlife fedns., S.C. C. of C., S.C. Saltwater Sportsfishing Assn. (dir. 1970—), Southeastern Outdoor Press Assn. (dir. 1970—), Outdoor Writers Am. Assn. Presbyn. Writer and producer numerous half hour dramatic series Alcohol, Tobacco and Firearms div. U.S. Dept. Treasury, 1963-72. Home: PO Box 169 Beaufort SC 29902 Office: Star Route 1 Box 1 Beaufort SC 29902

POULOS, RALEIGH ANEST, shopping center exec.; b. Galveston, Tex., Aug. 8, 1922; s. Anastasio Pete and Christine (Kalaboukidou) P.; student pub. schs.; m. Martha Panagos, Oct. 19, 1968. Mgr. D. Masus & Sons, Monroe La., 1945-52; gen. mgr. Palais Royal, specialty stores, Houston, 1952-67; gen. mgr. Town and Country Village, Houston, 1967—. Commr. Housing Authority, Monroe, 1950-52. Mem. bd. devel. YMCA, Houston, 1963-67. Served with AUS, 1942-45. Mem. Tex. Retail Fedn., C. of C. Mem. Greek Orthodox Ch. Home: 359 North Post Oak Lane Apt 328 Houston TX 77024 Office: Town and Country Village Houston TX 77024

POUNCY, MITCHELL LOUIS, librarian; b. Palestine, Tex., Apr. 3, 1930; s. Dee and Detroit (Denman) P.; A.B., Prairie View A and M. Coll., 1951; M.S. in Library Sci., Atlanta U., 1955; certificate La. Poly. U., 1970. With library So. U., Baton Rouge, 1955—, circulation librarian, 1961-65, catalog librarian, 1965—. Mem. Vis. Com. for Evaluation 3 High Schs. La., 1958-62. Mem. Community Assn. for Advancement of Sch. Children. Served as sgt. USMCR, 1952-54. Mem. A.L.A. Baptist. Office: Box 10031 So Br PO Baton Rouge LA 70813

POUNDS, HASKIN RICHARD, state ofcl.; b. Augusta, Ark., July 9, 1933; s. Ralph and Ruby (New) P.; B.S., Henderson State Coll., 1954; M.Ed., U. Ark., 1959, Ed.D., 1963; 1 dau., Roxanne. Tchr., Alma (Ark.) High Sch., 1957-58; prin. Paris (Ark.) Elementary Sch., 1958-60; supt. schs., Scranton, Ark., 1960-61; asst. prof. edn. U. Ark., 1963-65; asst. prof. edn. U. Ga., 1965-68, asst. vice chancellor Univ. System of Ga., Atlanta, 1968—. Served with AUS, 1954-56. Mem. Ga., Nat. edn. assns., Am. Assn. Sch. Adminstrs., Phi Delta Kappa. Rotarian, Lion. Author: Organizing, Supervising and Administering the Elementary School, 1969. Home: 1587 Creekford Way Stone Mountain GA 30083 Office: Bd Regents 244 Washington St SW Atlanta GA 30334

POUNDS, JAMES ARTHUR, cons. engr.; b. Pletcher, Ala., Nov. 25, 1920; s. Isham Frank and Minnie J. (Crane) P.; A.A., Pensacola Jr. Coll., 1961; student U. Md., 1951, U. Ala., 1953-55, U. Chgo., 1961-63.; m. Angela D. Rossetti, Feb. 9, 1950; 1 dau., Jeanette Angela. Lab. mgr. A.W. Williams Co., Mobile, Ala., 1954-55; supt. Sanitation div. City of Pensacola, Fla., 1956-63; gen. mgr. Econ. Utilities Corp., Orlando, 1963-64; supt. water div. City of Pensacola, 1964-68; city engr., dir. pub. works City of Auburn, Ala., from 1968; now cons. engr., Atlanta; partner James A. Taylor, Assos., Inc., Cons. Engrs., Tucker, Ga. Tchr. mil. sci. and tactics U. Me., 1949-51. Radiol. def. officer Escambia County (Fla.) Civil Def., 1957-67; bd. dirs. City Employees Credit Union, Pensacola, 1967. Served to capt. C.E., AUS, 1942-53. Decorated Bronze Star medal. Registered profl. engr., Ala., Miss., Ga., Me. Mem. Nat., Ala. socs. profl. engrs., Am. Pub. Works Assn., Am. Water Works Assn. (trustee), Fla. Water and Waste Water Operators Assn. (regional dir., mem. bd. examiners 1959-67), Fla. Engrs. Soc. Methodist. Home: PO Box 28634 Atlanta GA 30328 Office: 2246 Colledge Rd Tucker GA 30084

POVICH, SHIRLEY LEWIS, sports editor; b. Bar Harbor, Me., July 15, 1905; s. Nathan and Rosa (Orlovich) P.; student Georgetown U., 1922-24; m. Ethyl Friedman, Feb. 21, 1932; children—David, Maurice R., Lynn. Reporter, Washington Post, 1923-25, sports editor, 1926-33, columnist, 1933-45, war corr., PTO, 1945, now sports editor; columnist Washington Post & Times Herald, 1946—. Recipient citation for outstanding service as war corr., 1945, Nat. Headliners award, 1947, grand prize Best Sports Stories, 1956. Mem. Baseball Writers Assn. Am. (pres. 1955). Author: The Washington Senators, 1954. Contbr. articles to mags. Home: 1801 Sudbury Lane NW Washington DC 20012 Office: Washington Post & Times-Herald 1515 L St NW Washington DC 20005

POW, ALEXANDER SIMPSON, educator; b. Birmingham, Ala., Jan. 11, 1919; s. Alexander Simpson and Margaret Liston (Johnstone) P.; B.S., U. Ala., 1941; M.S., U. Denver, 1943; Ph.D., N.Y.U., 1960; m. Mary Elsie Deal, Dec. 21, 1942; children—Margaret Susan (Mrs. Clellon K. Baeder), William Alexander, Thomas Deal. Research asst. pub. adminstrn. U. Ala., Tuscaloosa, 1943, dir. arts, scis. extension services, asso. prof. polit. sci., 1953-55, dir. for contract, grant devel. office of pres., 1958-63, asso. prof. polit sci., 1958-60, prof., 1960-68, v.p. instl. devel., 1963-65, v.p. acad. affairs, 1965-68; pres. Western Carolina U., 1968-72, prof. polit. sci., 1968—; exec. legislative research asst. to Gov. Ala., Montgomery, 1943-45; dir. State of Ala. Legislative Reference Service, Montgomery, 1945-47; dir. U. Ala. Centers, Montgomery and Selma, 1947-53; domestic program supr., asso. dir., dir. N.Y.U.-Ankara Project, asst. to the dean grad. sch. pub. adminstrn. N.Y.U., 1955-58; mem. nat. core group Univ.-NASA relations, 1961; mem. gen. adv. group, spl. cons. to select com. on govt. research U.S. Ho. of Reps., 1963-65; mem. commn. on accreditation Council on Social Work Edn., 1970-71. Bd. dirs. Duke U. Center for So. Studies. Mem. Am. Assn. U. Profs., Phi Alpha Theta, Beta Gamma Sigma, Delta Sigma Pi, Delta Chi, Omicron Delta Kappa. Club: Waynesville North River Yacht. Editorial adv. panel Jour. of Edn. for Social Work. Home: 1905 7th St Tuscaloosa AL 35401

POWELL, ABNER RILEY, JR., lawyer; b. Andalusia, Ala., Mar. 21, 1916; s. Abner Riley and Gertrude (Deer) P.; LL.B., U. Ala., 1937; m. Jean Smith, June 8, 1937; children—Patricia (Mrs. Lomax Cassady), Annette (Mrs. C. Ward Hall, Jr.), Abner Riley III. Admitted to Ala. bar, 1937, since practiced in Andalusia; sr. partner Powell & Sikes, 1966—. Mem. Ala. Bar Commrs., 1942-43. Register Circuit Ct., 1938-66. Served with USNR, 1944-45. Mem. Am., Ala., Covington County (pres. 1961) bar assns., Ala. Def. Lawyers Assn. (dir. 1964-67), Phi Alpha Delta, Sigma Nu. Baptist (former deacon). Home: 122 Thames St Andalusia AL 36420 Office: 102 N Cotton St Andalusia AL 36420

POWELL, ANICE CARPENTER (MRS. ROBERT WAINWRIGHT POWELL), librarian; b. Moorhead, Miss., Dec. 2, 1928; d. Horace Aubrey and Celeste (Brian) Carpenter; student Sunflower Jr. Coll., 1945-47, Miss. State Coll. Women, 1947-48; B.S., Delta State Coll., 1961; m. Robert Wainwright Powell, July 19, 1948; children—Penelope Elizabeth, Deborah Alma. Librarian, Sunflower (Miss.) Pub. Library, 1958-61; instr. English, Isola (Miss.) High Sch., 1961-62; coordinator Sunflower County Library, 1962—. Mem. adv. council State Instl. Library Services, 1967-71; participant Inst. Library Service to Disadvantaged, U. S.Fla., summer 1971. Chmn. Miss. Heart Assn., Sunflower, 1963—. Mem. Miss. Library Assn. (sect. chmn. 1965, treas. 1970), Kappa Delta Pi. Methodist. Home: Box 387 Sunflower MS 38778 Office: Box 428 Sunflower MS 38778

POWELL, BENJAMIN EDWARD, librarian; b. Sunbury, N.C., Aug. 28, 1905; s. Willis Warren and Beatrice (Franklin) P.; A.B., Duke U., 1926; B.L.S., Columbia, 1930; Ph.D., U. Chgo., 1946; m. Elizabeth Graves, Mar. 6, 1940; 1 dau., Lisa Holland. Athletic dir. Bethel (N.C.) High Sch., 1926-27; asst. Duke U. Library, Durham, N.C., 1927-29, reference librarian and supt. circulation, 1930-34, 35-37, librarian, 1946—; librarian U. Mo. Library, 1937-46. Vis. prof. U. N.C. Sch. Library Science, 1961, 62, 68. Chmn. bd. trustees Durham Pub. Library; mem. James Madison Meml. Commn. Mem. A.L.A. (council 1947-54, v.p., 1958-59, pres. 1959-60, mem. exec. bd. 1956-58; chmn. com. cooperative microfilm project 1950-54, joint com. govt. publs. 1955-56, govt. documents 1956-59, spl. com. on reorgn. 1957), Assn. Research Libraries (dir. 1950-55, 62-64), Southeastern, N.C., Mo. (pres. 1938-39) library assns., Assn. Coll. & Reference Libraries (sec. 1940-44, v.p. 1947-48, pres. 1948-49), N.C. Literary and Hist. Assn., So. Hist. Assn., Bibliog. Soc. Am., Phi Beta Kappa, Sigma Nu. Democrat. Methodist. Rotarian. Clubs: Hope Valley Country, University (Durham, N.C.). Home: Hope Valley Durham NC

POWELL, BENJAMIN NEFF, educator; b. Montclair, N.J., Oct. 28, 1941; s. George Neff and Elsie Miriam (Davies) P.; B.A., Amherst Coll., 1963; M.A., Columbia, 1966, Ph.D., 1968; m. Susan Elizabeth Wolfe, Aug. 29, 1964. Research asso. Smithsonian Astrophys. Obs., Cambridge, Mass., 1969-70; asst. prof. geology, Rice U., Houston, 1970—. Recipient Nininger Meteorite prize, 1968. NASA lunar sample study grantee, 1971—. Fellow Meteoritical Soc.; mem. Geol. Soc. Am., Mineral Soc. Am., Geochem. Soc., Am. Geophys. Union, A.A.A.S., Nat. Wildlife Fedn., Sigma Xi. Contbr. articles to scientific jours. Home: 4114 Merrick St Houston TX 77025

POWELL, BENTON WIRT, banker; b. Aurora, Ind., July 25, 1899; s. Wirt Benton and Marguerite Katherine (Sohns) P.; student Ill. Wesleyan U., LaSalle Extension U., YMCA Central Coll., Northwestern U.; m. Virginia Marie Smith, May 21, 1950; 1 dau. by previous marriage, Aryls Justin (Mrs. John S. Odom). Pres. Palmer First Nat. Bank & Trust Co., Sarasota, Fla., 1933-64, chmn. bd., 1964—; pres. St. Armands Palmer Bank, 1962-67, chmn. bd., 1967—; chmn. bd. Siesta Key Palmer Bank, 1969—; v.p., dir. Palmer Fla. Corp., Chgo., 1940—, Palmer Properties, Inc., Chgo., 1940—; dir. Fla. Power & Light Co., Indsl. Devel. Corp. Fla., Orlando. Past pres. Sarasota County Pub. Hosp. Bd.; state dir. Orange Bowl Com., Miami, Fla.; trustee, treas. New Coll., Sarasota, Fla.; trustee Plymouth Harbor, Inc., Sarasota. Served as a pvt. U.S. Army, World War I; served to maj. AUS, World War II. C.P.A., Ill. Recipient Silver medal for scholastic achievement Ill. Soc. C.P.A.'s, 1928. Mem. Mil. Order World Wars, Adv. Council Naval Affairs, Fla. State C. of C. Presbyn. Home: 915 Pomelo Av Sarasota FL 33577 Office: Palmer First Nat Bank & Trust Co Sarasota FL 33579

POWELL, BOONE, med. adminstr.; b. Etowah, Tenn., July 15, 1912; s. N.C. and Savannah (Smith) P.; student U. Ga., 1931-33, U. Tenn., 1934-36; LL.D., Baylor U., 1958; m. Ruth Galloway, Nov. 30, 1935; children—Boone, Jerry Aileen, James Lawrence. Mgr. pub. services TVA, Norris, Tenn., 1936-41; asst. chief Govt. Project of War Housing, 1941; asst. regional dir. S.W. Region Fed. Works Agy., 1942-45; bus. mgr. Baylor U. Hosp., 1945-47, asst. adminstr., 1947-48, adminstr., 1948—, exec. dir. Baylor U. Med. Center, 1948—. Active Boy Scouts Am. Fellow Am. Coll. Hosp. Adminstrs. (past pres.); mem. Tex. Hosp. Assn. (past pres.), Dallas C. of C. Home: 6563 Blanch Circle Dallas TX 75214 Office: 3500 Gaston Av Dallas TX 75246

POWELL, BURRELL EDWIN, physician; b. Conroe, Tex., July 22, 1924; s. Albert Birg and Sybil (Matthews) P.; B.S., Sam Houston State Tchrs. Coll., 1952; M.D., Baylor U., 1952; m. Elsie Fern Funderburk, May 24, 1948; children—Alan Keith, Eugene Albert, Kathy Lynn; m. 2d, Beverly Ann Newton, Sept. 10, 1963; children—Brian Edwin, Julie Virginia. Intern Bapt. Meml. Hosp., San Antonio, 1952-53; practice medicine, Chillicothe, Tex., 1953-58, Conroe, 1958—; mem. staff Montgomery County Hosp., 1958—, chief staff, 1960, 70, sec. Bd. dirs. Montgomery County Cancer Soc., 1958—, United Fund, 1959—; pres. Montgomery County Heart Assn. 1958—. Served with USNR, 1943-46. Diplomate Am. Bd. Family Practice. Mem. Tex. Acad. Gen. Practice (chpt. pres. 1965-66; dir. 1968-71). Methodist. Mason (32 deg., Shriner, K.T.), Lion (pres. 1961). Home: 1210 N Thompson St Conroe TX 77301 Office: 401 W Davis St Conroe TX 77301

POWELL, CECIL CALVIN, grocery exec.; b. Trenton, Tenn., Apr. 4, 1920; s. Joseph Eli and Mary (Hicks) P.; student Draughn's Bus. Sch., 1940; m. Joyce Ann Parnell, July 11, 1970. Mgr., Kroger Co., Memphis, 1940-47; owner, operator restaurant, Newbern, Tenn., 1947-49; mgr. food div. Goldblatt Bros., Chgo., Joliet, Ill., 1949-53; store supr. Liberty Cash Grocery div., Memphis, 1953-59; owner, pres. Liberty Supermarkets, Martin, Tenn., 1956—; sole owner C.C. Powell Realty Co.; dir. Martin Bank. Chmn., Weakley County chpt. A.R.C., 1965. Served with USMCR, 1943-45. Mason, Rotarian. Home: 804 E Main Union City TN 38261 Office: Obion Square Shopping Center Union City TN 38261

POWELL, CHARLES KENNETH, lawyer, Republican nat. committeeman from S.C.; b. Greenwood, S.C., Aug. 11, 1939; s. Charles Willis and Gladys (Ouzts) P.; B.S., Clemson U.; LL.B., U. S.C., 1964; m. Edna Durant. Admitted to S.C. bar, 1964; practiced law, 1964-69; mem. firm Powell, Atria & Smith, Columbia, S.C., 1969—. Active Cub Scouts Am.; mem. S.C. Gov.'s Conf. on Youth. Chmn., Richland County Rep. Com., 1970, S.C. Rep. Com., 1971—; mem. Nat. Rep. Com., 1971—. Bd. dirs. Richland County br. Am. Cancer Soc. Mem. S.C. Bar Assn., Blue Key. Baptist. Mason (3 deg.). Club: Exchange. Home: 138 Cardiff St Columbia SC 29209 Office: 3012 Devine St Columbia SC 29205*

POWELL, CLAYTON PERRY, city ofcl.; b. Henrietta, N.C., June 26, 1931; s. Jesse Martin and Bertie Marie (Stacy) P.; B.A., Southwestern State Coll., Weatherford, Okla., 1970; postgrad. U. Ark.; m. Bessie Burlene Quinn, Aug. 11, 1951 (div. Aug. 1969); children—Richard D., Keith P., Sheila M.; m. 2d, Grace V. Barnes, July 16, 1971. Enlisted U.S. Air Force, 1950, advanced through grades to sgt., 1964; assigned to hdqrs. Strategic Air Command, 1957-59; recruiting duty, Greensboro, N.C., 1964-67; served in Vietnam, 1968-69; ret., 1970; intern city mgr. Fayetteville, Ark., 1970-71, dir. pub. works, 1971—. Owner, operator mobile vending ice cream products, Mountain Home, Ida., 1960-64. Decorated Air medal with oak leaf cluster. City Fayetteville scholar, 1970-71. Mem. Pi Sigma Alpha. Democrat. Baptist. Mason (K.T.), Elk. Home: 1501 Stubblefield Rd Fayetteville AR 72701 Office: PO Box F Fayetteville AR 72701

POWELL, EDWARD LEWIS, JR., dentist; b. Cumberland, Md., Nov. 24, 1941; s. Edward Lewis and Edith Redwood (Christian) P.; student Tulane U., 1961-62; B.A., U. Tex., 1965; D.D.S., Baylor U., 1969, M.S.D., 1971; m. Billie Sue Henna, June 15, 1963; children—Edward Lewis III, Catherine Christian. Practice dentistry, specializing in periodontics, San Antonio, 1971—; periodontal cons. Childrens Med. Center, Dallas, Denton (Tex.) State Sch. Recipient Merritt-Parks award in periodontology, clinic awards from Dallas Midwinter Clinics, Tex. Dental Assn., 1969-72. Mem. Am., Tex. dental assns., San Antonio Dist. Dental Soc., Am. Acad. Periodontology, S.W. Soc. Periodontology, Kappa Sigma, Delta Sigma Delta. Home: 3511 Fallen Leaf Lane San Antonio TX 78230 Office: 4118 McCullough St San Antonio TX 78212

POWELL, EPPIE CHARLES, physician; b. Holly Springs, N.C., June 10, 1910; s. Eppie Clifton and Annie (Knight) P.; B.S., U. N.C., 1931; M.D., U. Pa., 1935; postgrad. Columbia, N.Y.U., U. Tenn.; m. Eleanor Laura Bizzell, July 1, 1936; children—Eleanor Patricia, Charles Thomas. Intern Park View Hosp., Rocky Mountain, N.C., 1935-36; pvt. practice medicine Rocky Mountain, 1937-40, Goldsboro, 1946-70, mem. cons. staff, 1970—; chief staff Wayne County Meml. Hosp., 1952-54, chief obstetrics, 1955-70; chmn. dept. sci. Wayne Community Coll., Goldsboro, 1970—. Mem. Carolina Charter Tercentenary Commn.; mem. joint com. allied health edn. N.C. Bd. Higher Edn. Served from capt. to col. M.C., AUS, 1940-45, Decorated Bronze Star medal. Fellow Am. Coll. Obstetricians and Gynecologists; mem. Confederate Stamp Alliance, Nat. Guard Assn. U.S., Am. Ordnance Assn. (dir. Carolina post), Wayne County Hist. Soc. (dir.), A.A.A.S., Coastal Plains Obstet.-Gynecol. Soc., Assn. Mil. Surgs. U.S., Goldsboro Area Broadcasters, Nat. Sci. Tchrs. Assn., Nat. League Nursing, Citizens Band Radio Club N.C. Presbyn. (elder). Clubs: Goldsboro Country, Croda (pres.), Walnut Creek Country (bd. dirs.). Home: Walnut Creek Estates Goldsboro NC 27530 Office: Wayne Community Coll Goldsboro NC 27530

POWELL, JAMES ORMOND, editor; b. Andalusia, Ala., Oct. 24, 1919; s. Abner Riley and Gertrude (Deer) P.; B.A., U. Fla., 1942; m. Ruth Hogan, June 27, 1951; children—James Ormond, Lee Riley. Reporter, Ala. Jour., Montgomery, 1940; reporter, state capitol corr. Tampa (Fla.) Tribune, 1946-54; state capitol corr. Miami (Fla.) Herald, 1955; adminstrv. asst. Senator George Smathers, Washington, 1955-56; editorial writer, asso. editor Tampa Tribune, 1956-59; editor editorial page Ark. Gazette, Little Rock, 1959—. Exec. com. Gov.'s Council Human Resources, 1967-70; pres. Community Concert Assn. Little Rock, 1968; bd. dirs. Ark. Opera Assn., 1961-63. Served with AUS, 1941-45. Recipient Mrs. David Terry award Little Rock Council on Human Relations, 1971. Mem. Am. Soc. Newspaper Editors, Nat. Conf. Editorial Writers, Nat. Conf. Christians and Jews (dir. Ark. council 1964-65, recipient nat. editorial writing award 1969), Nat. Com. Support of Pub. Schs., Nat. Planning Assn., Sigma Delta Chi (chpt. v.p. 1965), Sigma Nu. Democrat. Baptist. Home: 311 Schoolwood Lane Little Rock AR 72207 Office: Ark Gazette 112 W 3d St Little Rock AR 72201

POWELL, JOHN ROLFE, accountant; b. Birmingham, Ala., Mar. 23, 1915; s. Bolling Raines and Marie (Arnold) P.; B.Accounts, Wheeler Bus. Coll., Birmingham, 1933; grad. LaSalle Extension U., 1936; m. Sarah Randolph Lacy, Apr. 15, 1939; children—Sarah Lacy (Mrs. Howard Peter Prudner, Jr.), Medora Braxton (Mrs. Dale Laverne Fahnestock), Marie Bolling, John Rolfe. Pub. accountant John Rolfe Powell, Montgomery, Ala., 1941—. Dir. Starke Bros. Realty Co., Inc., Oakwood Cemetery Annex, Inc. Chmn. budget and finance com. Montgomery Child Care Council, 1967-69. C.P.A., Ala. Mem. Ala. Soc. C.P.A.'s (chpt. pres. 1961-62), Ala. Assn. Pub. Accountants (chpt. pres. 1954), Nat. Assn. Accountants (chpt. pres. 1967-68), Am. Inst. C.P.A.'s. Episcopalian. Home: 1345 Glen Gratten Av Montgomery AL 36111 Office: 507 Executive Bldg Montgomery AL 36104

POWELL, LOYD WALTER, oil co. exec.; b. Smiley, Tex., June 22, 1900; s. Frank Robert and Margaret (Caraway) P.; student grade schs.; m. Reba Goudelock Perry, Nov. 24, 1943; children—Loyd Walter, Jr., Margaret Mary (Mrs. Zechariah Clifton Dameron, III). With Gulf Oil Co., Caddo Parrish, La., 1917-25, El Dorado, Ark., 1925-26; field mgr. El Dorado Gas., 1925-26; gen. supt. So. Crude Oil & Purchasing Co., El Dorado, 1926; prodn. foreman, supt. So. Crude Oil, Winkler County, Tex., 1926-32; owner Red Iron Drilling Co., Gladewater, Tex., 1932-36, Producers Oil Co., Gladewater, 1932-36, Victory Swabbing Co., Gladewater, 1936-48; chmn. bd. L.&M. Oil Co., Dallas, 1968—. Ind. oil producer, Tex., Okla., Ky., 1932—; rancher, farmer, St. Jo, Tex., 1958-71. Served with AUS, 1942-43. Club: Brookhaven Country (Dallas). Home: 4511 Isabella Lane Dallas TX 75229 Office: Exchange Bank Bldg Dallas TX 75235

POWELL, MINA JO, hotel exec.; b. Gainesville, Fla., Apr. 11, 1928; d. Caleb Allen and Josie Mae (Roberts) Powell; B.S. in Pub. Adminstrn., Fla. State U., 1950, M.S.W. (Mental Health scholar), 1963; postgrad. U. Houston, 1953-54. Med. sec. Prudential, Houston, 1958-59; pub. assistance social caseworker Pub. Welfare, Houston, 1959-61; psychiat. social worker N.E. Fla. State Hosp., Macclenney,

1963-64; with Holiday Inn, Thomasville, Ga., 1963-—, dir., 1963-—, pres., 1967-—. Vol. aux. Archbold Hosp., Thomasville, 1968-71. Sec. Thomas County Republican Party, 1970-71. Mem. Fla. Hotel Motel Assn. (mem. com. 1962), Fla. State U. Alumni Assn. Methodist. Club: Seminole (chmn. 1966-71) (Thomasville). Address: PO Box 1055 Holiday Inn Thomasville GA 31792

POWELL, ROY JAMES, ednl. adminstr.; b. Miami, Fla., Feb. 18, 1934; s. Ernest Everett and Edna Lodessa (Hand) P.; B.Ed., U. Miami, 1966; M.Ed., Fla. Atlantic U., 1967; Ph.D., U. Miami, 1971. Broadcast engr. radio station WRUF, Gainesville, Fla., 1958-59; communications technician City Miami, Fla., 1959-60; electronics tech. Eastern Airlines, Miami, 1960-64; sci. instr. Youth Manpower Tng. Program, 1964; curriculum writer Dade County Pub. Schs., 1965; electronics instr. Miami Sr. High Sch., 1965-66; researcher Dade County Pub. Schs., 1966-67; grad. asst. tchr. corps tng. program U. Miami, Coral Gables, 1967-68; research asso., dir. bus. affairs Fla. Migratory Child Survey Center, 1968-69; chmn. Dept. Elec. Engring. Techs., Miami-Dade Jr. Coll., 1969-—. Engring cons. Gemini Marine Research, Hialeah, Fla., 1965; sound cons. Ferendino Grafton Spillis Candela, Architects, Engrs. and Planners, Inc., Miami, 1971; audio cons. pvt. indvls., Miami, Fla., 1963. Served with USAF, 1952-56. Mem. Am. Assn. Sch. Adminstrs., Am. Tech. Edn. Assn., Am. Soc. Engring. Edn., Fla. Assn. Community Colls., Med. Electronic and Data Soc., Phi Delta Kappa. Author: Electronics Instructor's Guides, 1965. Editor and contributor Radio and Television Servicing Instructor's Guide and Electricity Instructor's Guide, 1965. Contbr. to Migrant Children in Florida, 1969. Home: 850 Palm Springs Mile Hialeah FL 33012

POWELL, RUSSELL HENRY, librarian; b. Windber, Pa., July 29, 1943; s. James Raymond and Judith Beatrice (Russell) P.; B.A., Juniata Coll., 1965; M.L.S., U. Pitts., 1966; m. Beverly Jean Ambrose, Aug. 25, 1965; children—Deborah Louise, Kimberly Jean. Sci. librarian Juniata Coll., Hunt, Pa., 1966-68; engring. librarian U. Ky., Lexington, 1968-—, instr. Coll. Library Sci., 1970-—. Mem. A.L.A., Spl. Libraries Assn., Am. Soc. Engring. Edn. (vice chmn. sect. 1969-71), Soc. for Preservation and Encouragement Barber Shop Quartet Singing Am. Home: 973 Stonewall Rd Lexington KY 40504

POWELL, THOMAS EDWARD, JR., biol. supply co. exec.; b. Warrenton, N.C., July 6, 1899; s. Thomas Edward and Clara (Bobbitt) P.; A.B., Elon Coll., 1919, Sc.D.(hon.), 1968; M.A., U. N.C., 1923; Ph.D., Duke, 1930; m. Maude Sharpe, July 22, 1922 (dec. Sept. 1944); children— Sophia Maude (Mrs. A. E. Wolfe), Thomas Edward III, James Bobbitt, John Sharpe; m. 2d, Annabelle Council, Aug. 31, 1945; children—William Council, Joseph Eugene, Samuel Christopher, Annabelle Council. Instr. Elon (N.C.) Coll., 1919-21, asst. prof., 1921-27, prof., head dept. geology and biology, 1927-32; pres. Carolina Biol. Supply Co., Burlington, N.C., 1932-—; dir. Wachovia Bank and Trust Co., Burlington, 1960-70. Mem. Alamance County Bd. Edn., 1934-61, N.C. Citizens Com. for Better Schs., 1957-59; pres. N.C. Sch. Bd. Assn., 1943-45. Bd. dirs. Va. Mil. Inst. Research Labs., 1963-69. Served to lt. U.S. Army, 1918. Named Alumnus of Year, Elon Coll., 1964; Paul Revere Patriot of Commonwealth Mass., 1965. Mem. A.A.A.S., Newcomen Soc., Soc. Protozoologists, Am. Inst. Biol. Scis., Assn. Scientists and Industrialists, Burlington-Alamance County C. of C. (dir. 1965-67). Methodist. Mason. Research primarily concerned with the life history and control of Lasioderma serricorne, the tobacco beetle. Address: 2400 York Rd Burlington NC 27215

POWELL, WILBUR LLOYD, accountant; b. Marquez, Tex., Mar. 14, 1912; s. Albert Lloyd and Mattie (McLean) P.; student Tex. A. and I. U., 1931-34; m. Virginia Jeroline Moore, June 30, 1934; 1 dau., Jennye Lou (Mrs. Frank L. Cannon, Jr.). Accountant, Benson & Co., 1938-41, Benson, Powell & Sparks, 1941-44, Benson & Powell, 1944-48, Benson, Powell & Morrison, 1948-55, W.L. Powell C.P.A., 1955-67, Powell & Donald, C.P.A.'s, Alice, Tex., 1967-71; prin. W.L. Powell C.P.A., 1971-—. Auditor, Jim Wells County, Tex., 1945-—. Mem. Am. Inst. C.P.A.'s, Tex. Soc. C.P.A.'s. Baptist. Home: 1900 Alta Vista Alice TX 78332 Office: 62 N Cameron Alice TX 78332

POWELL, WILLIAM ALLAN, educator; b. Wallace, N.C., May 28, 1921; s. Purvey Oglesby and Anna (Maynard) P.; B.S., Wake Forest U., 1942; postgrad. U. Pitts., 1947-48; Ph.D. (DuPont fellow), Duke, 1953; m. Edna Rae Bradshaw, Aug. 29, 1941; children—William Allan, Richard Bradshaw, Elizabeth Maynard. Asst. chief chemist Carolina Aluminum Co., Badin, N.C., 1942-46; indsl. hygiene chemist Aluminum Co. Am., New Kensington, Pa., 1946-48; instr. chemistry Wake Forest U., 1948-49, Duke, part-time 1949-51; asst. prof. chemistry U. Richmond (Va.), 1952-56, asso. prof., 1956-66, prof., 1966-—, chmn. dept. chemistry, 1959-—. Cons. Philip Morris Research Labs. Mem. Am. Chem. Soc. (chmn. Va. 1964, councilor 1970-—), Va. Acad. Sci. (chmn. chemistry sect. 1961), Phi Beta Kappa, Sigma Xi, Phi Lambda Upsilon, Omicron Delta Kappa, Delta Sigma Phi, Gamma Sigma Epsilon (nat. pres. 1954-58, nat. sec. 1958-66, editor Ray, 1958-71). Democrat. Baptist. Mason. Home: 6808 Lakewood Dr Richmond VA 23229

POWELL, WILLIAM DAVID, JR., educator; b. Birmingham, Ala., Feb. 10, 1917; s. William David and Lena Irona (Burks) P.; student Howard Coll., 1934-37; D.M.D., U. Ala., 1953; m. Doris Barbara Sanford, June 7, 1941; children—William David, III, Barbara Ann. Practice dentistry, Birmingham, 1953-67, part-time, 1967-—; asst. prof. Ala. Sch. Dentistry, Birmingham, part-time, 1953-67; prof. clin. dentistry U. Ala., Birmingham, 1967-—. Cons. VA, 1966, Army at Fort Benning, 1968. Fellow Internat. Coll. Dentists; mem. Am. Assn. Dental Schs., Am., Ala., Birmingham dental assns., Am. Acad. Restorative Dentistry, Omicron Kappa Upsilon, Psi Omega. Baptist (deacon 1947-—, chmn., 1957-58). Mason (Shriner). Home: 1300 Montgomery Hwy Birmingham AL 35216 Office: U Ala Med Center Birmingham AL 35233

POWELL, WILLIAM EDWARD, III, food scientist; b. Leroy, Ala., Mar. 29, 1944; s. William Edward, Jr. and Ina Cornelia (Etheredge) P.; B.S., Auburn U., 1966, Ph.D., 1970; m. Elizabeth Crawford, Sept. 9, 1967. Asst. prof. dept. animal sci. Auburn (Ala.) U., 1969-70, specialist in food sci. Coop. Extension Service, 1970-—, v.p. Student Body, 1965-66. First v.p. Nat. Red Angus Assn., 1971-—. Recipient Sigma Xi award for outstanding research, 1971; named Outstanding Grad., Sch. Agr., 1966. Pres. Danforth Summer Fellowship, 1965, Nat. Def. Edn. Act fellow. Mem. Am. Soc. Animal Sci., Am. Meat Sci. Assn., Sigma Xi, Phi Kappa Phi, Alpha Gamma Rho, Gamma Delta Zeta, Omicron Delta Kappa, Phi Eta Sigma. Methodist. Home: 706 Green St Auburn AL 36830

POWERS, DONALD ELROY, lawyer, judge; b. Tryon, Okla., Nov. 17, 1919; s. Floyd L. and Ethel L. (Barclay) P.; B.S., Central State Coll., Edmond, Okla., 1941; LL.B., U. Okla., 1948; m. Mary H. Mayes, Oct. 17, 1942; children—Donald ElRoy, James Edward. Admitted to Okla. bar, 1948; atty. Lincoln County, Chandler, Okla., 1949-50; sec. to Congressman Tom Steed, Washington, 1952-54; dist. judge 23d Jud. Dist., Chandler, 1955-—. Pres., Will Rogers council Boy Scouts Am., 1962-64. Chmn. bd. trustees Central State Coll. Alumni Found., 1965-66. Served to lt. USAAF, 1942-45; capt. Okla. N.G., 1950-52; Korea. Decorated D.F.C., Air medal with four oak leaf clusters; recipient Silver Beaver award Boy Scouts Am., 1961. Mem. Am., Okla. bar assns., Am. Judicature Soc., Nat. Assn. State Trial Judges, Okla. Jud. Conf. (pres. 1966), Central State Coll. Alumni Assn. (pres. 1967). Methodist. Lion, Mason; mem. Order Eastern Star. Home: 323 W 6th St Chandler OK 74834 Office: Court House Chandler OK 74834

POWERS, FRED JEROME, utility co. exec.; b. nr. Muncie, Ind., Sept. 20, 1914; s. Harlan Dent and Susie Minerva (Evans) P.; student pub. schs.; m. Mildred Lee Hendricks, Feb. 8, 1936; children—Carolyn Louise (Mrs. John Glauber), James Orville, Fred Jerome. With Ky. Utilities Co., Carrollton, Ky., 1947, mgr., Owenton, 1960-—. Chmn. Owenton Water Commn., 1967-71; pres. Student Loan Fund, Inc., Owenton, 1970-—. Mem. Owen County C. of C. (pres. 1969-70). Democrat. Baptist (treas. 1971-—). Mason, Rotarian (editor bull. 1971). Home: Sunset Dr Owenton KY 40359 Office: 125 W Seminary St Owenton KY 40359

POWERS, HUGH WILLIAM, newspaperman; b. Slaton, Tex., Dec. 20, 1926; s. James J. and Myrtle (Black) P.; student W.Va. U., 1944-47; m. Constance Cornwall, Aug. 30, 1952; children—Nan Margaret, Sarah Ann. Mng. editor Houston chpt. Asso. Gen. Contractors News Service, until 1957; with Houston Press, 1957-64, city editor, 1964; mem. staff Houston Chronicle, 1964-—, now asso. editor. Mem. bd. dirs. Houston Jr. C. of C. Mem. Phi Kappa Psi. Home: 10818 Hillcroft St Houston TX 77035 Office: 512 Travis St Houston TX 77002

POWERS, JACK E., indsl. relations exec.; b. Woodruff, S.C., Feb. 21, 1934; s. Boyce W. and Lydia (Stevens) P.; B.A., Furman U., 1956; m. Audrey May Turner, Nov. 19, 1955; children—Carol Lynn, Elizabeth Ann, Laura Lee. Mgmt. trainee, indsl. engr., asst. overseer Deering Milliken, Union, S.C., 1956-59; with Cryovac div. W.R. Grace & Co., Simpsonville, S.C., 1959-68, personnel mgr., 1963-67, indsl. relations mgr., 1967-68; mgr. employee and community relations Converted Plastics Group, W.R. Grace & Co., Duncan, S.C., 1968-—. Mem. adv. bd. Juvenile and Domestic Relations Ct., Greenville, S.C., 1965-68, chmn., 1966-68; mem. S.C. Pollution Control Authority, 1970-—; mem. S.C. Appalachian Adult Basic Edn. Com., 1969-71, Greenville County events com. S.C. Tricentennial, 1969; pres. Golden Strip YMCA, Simpsonville, 1968-—. Bd. dirs. Emergency Relief Fund Agy., Simpsonville, South Greenville Fair, Greater Greenville YMCA, Paladin Club of Furman U. Recipient Distinguished Service award Simpsonville Jr. C. of C., 1966, named Boss of Year, 1967. Mem. Greenville Area Personnel Assn. (bd. dirs.), Simpsonville C. of C. Baptist (deacon). Rotarian. Home: RD 1 Beechwood Dr Simpsonville SC 29681 Office: PO Box 464 Duncan SC 29334

POWERS, L. B., mining engr.; b. Frakes, Ky., July 18, 1932; s. Julius and Nona (Lambdin) P.; B.S., U. Ky., 1956. Asst. engr. Blue Diamond Coal Co., Knoxville, Tenn., 1957-65, mining engr., 1965-66, chief engr., 1966-67, asst. to the pres., 1969-—; gen. supt. Scotia Coal Co., 1967-68. Mem. adv. com. Appalachian Resources Project, U. Tenn. Served to lt. Signal Corps, AUS, 1956-57. Registered profl. engr., Ky., Tenn. Mem. Ky. Mining Inst., Ky. Coal Assn. (dir.), Hazard Coal Operators Assn. (dir.), Tau Kappa Epsilon. Republican. Baptist. Home: PO Box 10927 8039 Kingston Pike NW Knoxville TN 37919 Office: PO Box 10008 Knoxville TN 37919

POWERS, LEON GANO, chief of police; b. Itasca, Tex., Jan. 19, 1926; s. George and Birtamae (Burnett) P.; student FBI Nat. Acad., 1962; m. Maydel Curry, Sept. 12, 1946; children—Freddie, Jack. Patrolman, City of Irving (Tex.), 1956-57, Sgt., 1957-58, asst. chief, 1958-68; chief police City of Greenville (Tex.) 1968-—. Vis. instr. East Tex. State U., Commers, 1968. Served with USMC, 1944-46. Decorated Presdl. Citation; recipient Meritorious Service citation Am. Legion, 1970. Mem. Tex. Police Assn. (mem. exec. com. 1970-71), FBI Nat. Acad. North Tex. (pres. 1963), Tex. (sec., treas. 1971), North Tex. (pres. 1971) police chiefs. Mem. Ch. of Christ (elder 1971-—). Kiwanian (bd. dirs. 1960, 70-71; 1st v.p. 1961). Home: 617 Deer Dr Greenville TX 75401 Office: 2800 Washington St Greenville TX 75401

POWERS, ORMUND DEVERE, newspaper editor; b. Concordia, Kan., Sept. 26, 1914; s. Edward Ray and Clara (Peterson) P.; student U. Fla., 1932-34; m. Barbara Ann Griffin; children—Richard DeVere, James N., Leslie H., Amanda Lee. With Orlando (Fla.) Sentinel-Star, 1934-—, now editor editorial page. Mem. Fla. Soc. Editors (pres.). Episcopalian. Mason, Elk, Rotarian. Home: 1134 Western Way Orlando FL 32804 Office: 633 N Orange Way Orlando FL 32804

POYNTER, NELSON, editor, pub.; b. Sullivan, Ind., Dec. 15, 1903; s. Paul and Alice (Wilkey) P.; A.B., Ind. U., 1924, A.M., Yale, 1927; Litt.D., Stetson U., 1962, Fla. State U., 1970; m. Henrietta Malkiel, Aug. 8, 1942 (dec. 1968); m. 2d, Marion Knauss, May 4, 1970. Reporter Scripps-Howard, Washington, 1923; news editor Japan Times, Tokyo, 1924; bus. mgr. Washington Daily News; editor Ohio Scripps-Howard, 1935-37; editor, owner St. Petersburg (Fla.) Times, 1938-—; chmn. bd. Times Pub. Co., 1968-—; owner Evening Ind., 1962-—; editor, pres. Congl. Quarterly Publs., also Editorial Research Reports, Washington. Served as dep. dir. COI-OWI, 1941-44. Mem. Am. Soc. Newspaper Editors, Am. Newspaper Pubs. Assn., Phi Gamma Delta, Sigma Delta Chi (nat. hon. pres. 1970). Clubs: National Press, Metropolitan (Washington); Yacht, Bath (St. Petersburg). Author: Post War Jobs, 1945. Contbr. to Freedom of Press: Interpretations of Journalism. Office: Times PO Box 1121 St Petersburg FL 33731 also 1735 K St NW Washington DC 20006

PRADO, FRED TIMMINS, artist, cartoonist; b. Monterrey N.L., Mexico, Sept. 26, 1907; s. Herman Timmins and Jesusita (Morales) T.; brought to U.S., 1908; student artist Jose Arpa, 1928-31; m. Carmen Valdez, Dec. 17, 1933; 1 dau., Mary Evelyn (Mrs. Ralph Tibiletti). With art dept. San Antonio Light newspaper, 1927-—, chief artist, head editorial art dept., 1946-—. Mem. Coppini Acad. Fine Arts, Witte Mus. San Antonio, San Antonio Art League. Home: 6903 Dorothy Louise Dr San Antonio TX 78229 Office: 420 Broadway San Antonio TX 78205

PRASIL, ANTONE GEORGE, pub. utility exec.; b. Friendship, Wis., Aug. 24, 1922; s. Anton Mike and Anna (Burian) P.; B.S., U. Wis., 1946; B.S. in Chem. Engring., Harvard, 1968; m. Helen Ethel Smith, July 27, 1945; children—Antone George, Jr., Edward Joseph, Peggy Ann, Richard Alan, James Rupert. Dist. engr. Wis. Pub. Service, Oshkosh, 1946-51, staff engr., 1951-58; engr. So. Union Gas, Dallas, 1958-60, chief engr., 1960-—, v.p., chief engr., Southern Union Gathering Co., 1967-—. Dir. So. Union Energy, So. Union Internat., Asso. Pipelines. Mem. Council Boy Scouts Am., 1958-64, Camp Fire Girls U.S., 1959-62. Served with USNR, 1943-45. Registered profl. engr., Wis., Tex., Okla., Ariz., N.M., Colo. Mem. Am. Soc. Mech. Engrs., Am. Inst. Chem. Engrs., Nat. Assn. Corrosion Engrs. (pres. N. Tex. chpt. 1959-63), Profl. Engrs. Soc., Petroleum Engrs., N.E. Tex. Measurement Soc., Am. Gas. Assn., So. Gas Assn., Alpha Chi Sigma. Home: 10042 Coppedge St Dallas TX 75229 Office: Fidelity Union Tower Dallas TX 75201

PRASSEL, ALLEN WILLIAM, wholesale lumberman; b. New Orleans, Jan. 13, 1922; s. Bruno William and Lucille (Allen) P.; student Hinds Jr. Coll., 1940-41, Colo. State U., 1941-42 Pasadena City Coll., 1942, Stanford U., 1942-43; m. June Steagall, July 17, 1947 (div. 1954); children—Allen William, Suzanne; m. 2d, Peggy Buckley, Aug. 11, 1962;children—Tana Lyn, Bryan William. Owner, Prassel Co., Leesville, La., 1946-55; pres. Prassel Lumber Co., Jackson, Miss., 1957-—, Prassel Furniture & Boxwoods, Inc., Jackson, 1960-—, Prassel Enterprises, Inc., Jackson, 1961-—, Prassel West Coast & Pine Lumber Co., Jackson, 1963-—, Prassel Lumber Co. Ala., 1967-—, Allen Prassel Lumber Co. Tex., 1967-—, Prassel Investments, Jackson, 1967-—, Prassel Internat., Jackson, 1972; owner A-D Ranch, Raymond, Miss., 1966-—. Mem. Miss. Republican Finance Com., 1961-63. Served to 2d lt. AUS, 1941-45. Methodist. Address: Raymond Gardens Apts PO Box 8305 Battlefield Station Jackson MS 39204

PRATER, JESSE WALLACE, dentist; b. Ocala, Fla., Mar. 23, 1932; s. Jesse A. and Helen (Jones) P.; D.M.D., U. Louisville, 1962; m. Bettye Beam, June 15, 1952; children—Jesse W., Suzanne Beam. Practice dentistry, Tampa, Fla., 1962-—. Pres., Stat Inc., 1969-—, TRI ARC Prodns., 1970-—(both Tampa). Lectr. dental practice mgmt. and tech. dentistry. Faculty adviser Fla. Coll. Med. and Dental Assts.; cons. Fla. Dept. Health and Rehabilitative Services, Fla. Cripple Children's Soc. Served with AUS, 1953-55. Mem. Lauritzen (chmn. 1968-69), Hillsboro County dental research groups, Am. Soc. Preventive Dentistry (v.p. Fla. chpt. 1972-73), Fedn. Dentaire Internationale, Am. Dental Assn., Fla. W. Coast Dental Soc., Am. Acad. Dental Practice Adminstrn., Hillsboro County Dental Soc., Am. Equilibration Soc., Internat. Platform Assn., Nat. Rifle Assn., Psi Omega, Alpha Epsilon Delta. Mason (32 deg., Shriner). Club: Sertoma. Author: Book Ways to Better Days in Your Practice, 1970. Cons. editor Dental Mgmt. mag. Home: 12101 Lake Carroll Dr Tampa FL 33618 Office: 2630 W Water Av Tampa FL 33614

PRATT, CHARLES, chemist; b. Celina, Tex., Nov. 9, 1926; s. Jack and Anne (Sanders) P.; B.S., Langston U., 1951; M.S., U. Okla., 1958; Ph.D., 1962;; m. Lois Magness, Mar. 28, 1947; children—Michael Charles, Frederick Charles, Dian Charles. Tchr. sci. B.T. Washington High Sch., Cushing, Okla., 1951-56; asso. prof. chemistry Prairie View A. and M. Coll., Tex., 1960-61; became prof. chemistry Savannah (Ga.) State Coll., 1961; now seed program mgr. Am. Chem. Soc., Washington. Served with USMC, 1945-47. Recipient research grant NSF, 1962-66, U.S. Dept. Agr., 1965-68; U.S. Army Research Office, 1965-68. Mem. Am. Chem. Soc., Am. Oil Chemists Soc., Botanical Soc., Sigma Xi. Contbr. articles in field to profl. jours. Home: 555 Newcomb St SE Washington DC 20032

PRATT, EDWARD TAYLOR, JR., hotel co. exec.; b. Joplin, Mo., Aug. 12, 1923; s. Edward Taylor and Etner (Peek) P.; grad. high sch.; m. Billie Ruth Skelton, Aug. 27, 1941; children—Carolyn Sue (Mrs. Charles E. Hickey), Diana L. (Mrs. Richard Heisler), Edward Taylor, III, Sharon R. Mng. partner Pratt & Co., Dallas, developing Holiday Inns in Tex., Mexico and C. Am., 1960-—, Prattco, Inc., operating co. for Holiday Inns, 1969-—. Chmn. Mineral Wells (Tex.) Planning-Zoning Commn., 1967-—. Chmn. bd. Bristol Hosp., Dallas, 1962-—. Served with AUS, 1942-46. Mem. C. of C. (dir. 1962-69). Republican. Home: 908 Lakeview Dr Mineral Wells TX 76067 Office: Brazos Shopping Center PO Box 939 Mineral Wells TX 76067

PRATT, HARRY DAVIS, ret. govt. ofcl.; b. North Adams, Mass., Apr. 13, 1915; s. Harry Edward and Ethel (Davis) P.; B.S., Mass. State Coll., 1936, M.S., 1938; Ph.D., U. Minn., 1941; m. Caroline Georgine Kreiss, Apr. 13, 1944 (dec. May 1951); children—Harry Davis, Katherine Maria (Mrs. R. Neal Garrison), George Kreiss; m. 2d, Dora Belle Ford, Nov. 29, 1952. Entomologist, Malaria Control in War Areas, San Juan, P.R., 1942-46; chief med. entomology lab. Communicable Disease Center, Atlanta, 1946-53, chief vestor control tng., 1953-64, chief tng. br., Aedes Aegypti eradication campaign, 1964-68; chief insect and rodent control br. Bur. Community Environmental Mgmt., USPHS, 1968-72; asst. prof. microbiology Emory U., 1948-—. Recipient commendation medal USPHS, 1962; Gorgas medal Mil. Surgeons of U.S., 1964; Distinguished Service medal U.S. Dept. Health, Edn. and Welfare, 1971. Mem. Am. Mosquito Control Assn. (pres. 1967), Am. Soc. Tropical Medicine and Hygiene, Entomological Soc. Am., Am. Soc. Parasitologists. Published series insect and rodent control training manuals, 1946-—. Produced numerous motion pictures and film strips dealing with insect and rodent control. Home: 879 Glen Arden Way NE Atlanta GA 30306

PRATT, JOHN HELM, judge; b. Portsmouth, N.H., Nov. 17, 1910; s. Harold Boswell and Marguerite (Rockwell) P.; A.B. cum laude, Harvard, 1930, LL.B., 1934; m. Bernice G. Safford, Oct. 25, 1938; children— Clare, Lucinda (Mrs. Daniel D. Pearlman), John Helm, Patricia, Mary. Admitted D.C. bar, 1934, since practiced in Washington; partner firm Morris, Pearce, Gardner & Pratt, 1954-68; asst. counsel Boys Club Greater Washington, 1948-68; U.S. district judge, Washington, 1968-—. Chmn. Montgomery County (Md.) Housing Authority, 1950-53. Chmn. bd. trustees D.C. Legal Aid Agy., 1967-68. Served to capt. USMCR, 1942-46; PTO. Decorated Bronze Star medal, Purple Heart; recipient Army citation for civilian service in field prosthetics, 1948. Mem. Am. Bar Assn. (ho dels. 1963-64), Am. Bar Found., Bar Assn. D.C. (pres. 1963-64), Harvard Law Sch. Assn. (pres. Washington 1952-53), Asso. Harvard Clubs (pres. 1952-53), Marine. Res. Corps Officers Assn. (judge adv. gen. 1961-68). Democrat. Roman Cath. Clubs: Barristers (pres. 1959), Lawyers, Harvard (pres. 1949-51) (Washington); Chevy Chase; Metropolitan. Home: 4119 Rosemary St Chevy Chase MD 20015 Office: US Courthouse Washington DC 20001

PRATT, JOSEPH GAITHER, psychologist, educator; b. Winston-Salem, N.C., Aug. 31, 1910; s. Joseph Monroe and Mattie Elizabeth (Hauser) P.; A.B., Duke, 1931, M.A., 1933, Ph.D., 1936; m. Nellie Ruth Pratt, June 14, 1936; children—John Herman, Vernon Gaither, Joseph Marion, Ellen Wilson. Research asso., research staff parapsychology lab. Duke, 1937-63; insp. engr. Gen. Motors Corp., 1942-43; now asso. prof. psychiatry U. Va. Med. Sch., spl. research problem extrasensory perception. Pres., Psychical Research Found., Durham. Served to lt. USNR, 1944-46. Mem. Parapsychol. Assn. (pres. 1960, mem. council 1959, 64-72, editorial staff jour. 1942-63), Am. Soc. Psychical Research, Am. Psychol. Assn., Soc. Psychical Research (London, Eng.), Phi Beta Kappa, Sigma Xi, Omicron Delta Kappa, Tau Kappa Alpha. Author: (with others) Extrasensory Perception After Sixty Years, 1940; (with J. B. Rhine) Parapsychology: Frontier Science of the Mind, 1957; Parapsychology, An Insider's View of ESP, 1964; also numerous articles in field. Home: Route 1 Keswick VA 22947 Office: Box 152 U Va Hosp Charlottesville VA 22901

PRATT, JOSEPH NEAL, agronomist; b. Dallas, Apr. 14, 1932; s. Rogers Truett and Mary Lou (Boren) P.; B.S., S.W. Tex. State U., 1953, M.A., 1954; Ph.D., Mich. State U., 1961; m. Marjorie Ann Bryan, June 23, 1959; children—Mary Jean, Nancy Louise, Barbara Ann. Tchr. high sch. Indsl. Consol. Sch. Dist., Vanderbilt, Tex., 1954-55; area agronomist Tex. Agrl. Extension Service, Weslaco, Tex., 1960-64; agronomist Tex. Agrl. Extension Service, Tex. A. and M. U., College Station, 1964-—. Served with AUS, 1955-57. Recipient Recognition award U.S. Dept. Agr., 1970; certificate merit Am. Forage and Grassland Council, 1972; several county awards.

Mem. Am. Soc. Agronomy, Soil Sci. Soc. Am., Am. Soc. Animal Sci., Am. Forage and Grassland Council, Tex. Plant Food Inst., Sigma Xi, Gamma Sigma Delta, Epsilon Sigma Phi. Baptist (deacon). Contbr. profl. jours. Home: 1304 Leacrest St College Station TX 77840

PREER, GEORGE THOMAS, educator; b. Columbus, Ga., Dec. 7, 1906; s. George Thomas and Harriet Valentine (Young) P.; A.B., Davidson Coll., 1929; M.A., Brown U., 1930, postgrad., 1930; postgrad Harvard U., 1931; Ph.D (duPont sr. fellow 1932-33), U. Va., 1938; B.D. (Anna Whitner Meml. fellow), Columbia Theol. Sem., 1935; m. Gertrude Gardenhire Reiney, Aug. 24, 1937. Ordained to ministry Presbyn. Ch., 1937; student pastor Presbyn. Ch., U. Va., 1935-37; pastor Oakdale Presbyn. Ch., (La.) 1937-41, College Park Presbyn. Ch., (Ga.), 1941-44, Presbyn. Ch., Lafayette, La., 1944-50, Collins and McDonald Presbyn. Chs., Collins, Miss., 1950-54; minister to Presbyn. students U. So. Miss., 1954-60; prof. philosophy Belhaven Coll., Jackson, Miss., 1960—. Active Boy Scouts Am., 1950-54. Mem. So. Soc. Philosophy and Psychology, Miss. Philosophy Assn. Home: 313 N 25th Av Hattiesburg MS 39401

PREHN, WALTER LAWRENCE, JR., research inst. exec.; b. St. Louis, Apr. 15, 1920; s. Walter Lawrence and Lucille (Hille) P.; B.S., Rice U., 1943; M.S., Cornell U., 1946; m. Helen Grace Burkhart, Oct. 14, 1967; children—Katherine Rebecca, Laurel Lee, Elizabeth Anne, Walter Lawrence III; stepchildren—David James Terwey, Kathryn Grace Terwey, Emily Ruth Terwey. Pilot plant engr. Esso Labs., Baton Rouge, 1946-49; research engr., valuation engr. Atlantic Labs., Dallas, 1949-52; research engr. Stanford Research Inst., Menlo Park, Cal., 1954-58, mgr. S.W. Office, Phoenix, 1958-60, mgr. program devel., 1960-62; mgr. indsl. and comml. sales Del E. Webb Corp., Houston, 1962-63; dir. applied econs. S.W. Research Inst., Houston, 1964-71, dir. social and mgmt. scis., San Antonio, 1971—. Bd. dirs. Tex. Indsl. Devel. Council, 1966-67. Served with USNR, 1943-46, 52-53. Mem. Am. Inst. Chem. Engrs., San Antonio C. of C. Methodist. Rotarian. Clubs: Petroleum (Houston); Canyon Creek Country (San Antonio). Contbr. articles profl. jours. Home: 9210 Autumn Leaf Dr San Antonio TX 78217 Office: 8500 Culebra Rd San Antonio TX 78284

PREJEAN, JOHN MARSHALL, engring. corp. exec.; b. Scott, La., May 16, 1931; s. Louis Rousseau and Frances (Mouton) P.; student U. Southwest La., 1948-50; m. Mary Jane Trahan, June 1, 1952; children—Janae, Marsha, Renada. With Otis Engring. Corp., Dallas, 1953—, v.p., 1969—, also dir.; dir. Life Ins. Co. Southwest, Dallas. Served with USAF, 1950-53. Mem. Am. Inst. M.E. Democrat. Roman Catholic. Clubs: Nomads, Petroleum (Dallas). Home: 13581 Crestmoor St Dallas TX 75234 Office: PO Box 34380 Dallas TX 75234

PRENDERGAST, ALBERT JOHN, govt. ofcl.; b. Belfast, No. Ireland, Nov. 30, 1926; s. Joseph H. and Catherine (McQuillan) P.; B.S., Boston U., 1950, M.A., 1953; Ph.D., U. Tex., 1961; m. Joyce Riggin, June 6, 1951; children—Kathy, Tim. Sr. systems engr. for large-scale computers, IBM, 1955-61; commr. V.I. Dept. Commerce, St. Thomas, 1963—. Served with AUS, 1945-46; served to capt. USAF. Home: PO Box 2928 Saint Thomas VI 00801 Office: Dept Commerce Saint Thomas VI 00801

PRENDERGAST, JOSEPH, assn. exec.; b. Chgo., Mar. 27, 1904; s. Michael John and Lillian (Mallory) P.; grad. Phillips Exeter Acad., 1923; B.A., Princeton, 1927; postgrad., Balliol Coll., Oxford U. (Eng.), 1927-29; barrister-at-law, Inner Temple, London, 1927—; M.S. in Social Work, Columbia, 1947; LL.D., Springfield Coll., 1955; m. Amalyn Caroline Sartorelli, Dec. 21, 1932 (dec. Nov. 1969); m. 2d, Eugene Reed, May 29, 1971. Admitted to N.Y. bar, 1931, Fed. Cts., 1934; asso. Sullivan and Comwell N.Y.C., 1930-32, Osborn, Fleming and Whittlesey, 1933; U.S. atty. S. dist. N.Y., 1934-46; spl. asst. to U.S. atty. gen., 1937-42; instr. N.Y. U., 1939-40, Columbia, 1948-49; exec. sec. social welfare legislation information service N.Y. State Charities Aid Assn., 1948-49; exec. dir. Nat. Recreation Assn., 1950-65; exec. v.p. Nat. Recreation and Park Assn., 1965-66; exec. dir. Nat. Trust for Historic Preservation, 1967—. Mem. nat. citizens' adv. com. on Fitness Am. Youth, 1957-64, Pres.'s People-to-People Partnership Coms., 1957-61; chmn. Nat. Adv. Council to Keep Am. Beautiful, 1954-57; adv. com. on arts Kennedy Center Performing Arts, 1959-64; nat. adv. council Outdoor Recreation Resources Rev. Commn., 1959-62; nat. adv. council to AFL-CIO Community Services Com., 1959-65; nat. adv. com. for White House Conf. on Aging, 1961. Served to maj. AUS, 1942-46. Decorated Bronze Star medal, Purple Heart. Recipient certificate of Appreciation for services to White House Conf. on Children and Youth, 1960, spl. citation Am. Recreation Soc., 1961, award for Profl. Accomplishment N.Y. Recreation and Park Soc., 1965. Mem. Acad. Certified Social Workers. Address: Oak Hill Farm Aldie VA 22001

PRENDERGAST, THOMAS AIDEN, mfg. exec.; b. N.Y.C., Dec. 10, 1933; s. Thomas Aiden and Margaret (Dalton) P.; B.S., Fordham U., 1955; postgrad. U. Tex., 1957-60; m. Mary Alice Peinado, Aug. 4, 1956; children— Laura Ann, Elizabeth Jane. Accountant, Hurdman & Cranstoun, C.P.A.'s, N.Y.C., 1955; auditor El Paso (Tex.) Pub. Schs., 1957-61; C.P.A., El Paso, 1958-61; v.p. finance, dir. Farah Mfg. Co., Inc., El Paso, 1961-71; chmn. bd. Billy The Kid, Inc., El Paso, 1971—. Trustee El Paso Community Coll. Served to 2d lt. AUS, 1955-57. Home: 4252 Park Hill El Paso TX 79902 Office: 100 S Cotton El Paso TX 79987

PRENSNER, STEVEN, educator; b. Passaic, N.J.; s. Stephen and Susana (Nacsa) P.; grad. Newark State Normal, 1934; B.S., Sam Houston State Tchrs. Coll., 1938; M.Ed., U. Houston, 1950, Ed.D., 1971; m. Selma Ida Berger, July 4, 1936; children—Douglas S., Gary L., Steven R. Tchr. shop, drawing pub. schs., Brazoria and Galveston counties, 1934-48; prin. high schs., Friends Wood, 1948-54, Pearland, Tex., 1954-66; supt. Pearland Schs., 1966-68; research asst. U. Houston, 1968—. Active Boy Scouts Am., Eagle Scout, 1935. Mem. Nat., Tex. assns. secondary sch. prins., Tex. Tchrs. Assn., Am. Soc. Tool Engrs., Am. Assn. Sch. Adminstrs., Kappa Delta Pi, Phi Delta Kappa. Methodist. Rotarian (charter), Lion. Home: Box 503 Pearland TX 77581

PRESLEY, W. DEWEY, banker; b. Wills Point, Tex., May 26, 1918; s. Dewey and Myrtle (Threatt) P.; B.A., Baylor U., 1939; m. Virginia Shepperd, Nov. 22, 1940; children—Charlotte, Suzanne, Rachel. With Magnolia Oil Co. and Magnolia Pipe Line Co., 1939-42; spl. agt. FBI, 1942-52; with First Nat. Bank, Dallas, 1952—, sr. v.p., 1960-63, chmn. bd., mem. and chmn. exec. com., dir., 1963—, also pres.; dir. Southeastern Drilling, Inc. Bd. dirs. Baptist Found. Tex. C.P.A., Tex. Mem. Am. Inst. C.P.A.'s, Tex., Dallas socs. C.P.A.'s. Baptist. Home: 7715 Bryn Mawr Dr Dallas TX 75225 Office: 1401 Main St Dallas TX 75202

PRESSBURG, BERNARD SAMUEL, educator; b. Alexandria, La., Jan. 23, 1918; s. Henry and Jetty (Nelken) P.; B.S., La. State U., 1937, M.S., 1939, Ph.D., 1941; m. Gretchen Peiser, Aug. 12, 1947; children—Ellen, Jean Frances. Research fellow Dixie Pine Products Co., Hattiesburg, Miss., 1937-41, chief chemist, 1941; asst. prof. chem. engring. La. State U., Baton Rouge, 1941-42, 46-48, asso prof., 1948-55, prof., 1955—, acting dean Coll. Engring., 1964-65, asso. dean, 1965—; chem. engr. Humble Oil & Refining Co., summer 1950, Ethyl Corp., summers 1951-62. Served with AUS, 1942-46. Mem. Am. Inst. Chem. Engring., Am. Chem. Soc., Am. Soc. Engring. Edn., Sigma Xi, Phi Lambda Upsilon, Tau Beta Pi, Omicron Delta Kappa, Phi Kappa Phi. Jewish religion. Contbr. articles to profl. jours. Home: 1312 Ross Av Baton Rouge LA 70808

PRESSLY, WILLIAM L(AURENS), sch. adminstr.; b. Louisville, Ga., July 24, 1908; s. Paul and Lois (Moffatt) P.; A.B., Princeton, 1931; M.A., Harvard, 1947; Litt.D., Washington and Lee U., 1949; m. Alice Fletcher McCallie, Aug. 28, 1940; children—Paul Moffatt, William L. Head English dept. McCallie Sch., Chattanooga, 1936-44, asso. headmaster, 1944-49, co-headmaster, 1949-51; pres. Westminster Schs., Atlanta, 1951—. Trustee Nat. Assn. Ind. Schs., 1962-67, Coll. Entrance Exam. Bd., 1955-58, 61, 64, Edni. Testing Service, 64-68; chmn. Nat. Council Ind. Schs., 1957-59; trustee So. Assn. Colls. and Schs., 1957-60, 65-68, pres., 1967. Mem. Headmasters Assn. (pres. 1972-73), Country Day Sch. Headmasters' Assn. Presbyn. (elder). Home: 1424 W Paces Ferry Rd NW Atlanta GA

PRESTIDGE, JERRY ELMO, petroleum engr.; b. Earlsboro, Okla., Dec. 19, 1929; s. Marion Thomas and Lillie (Lemons) P.; A.A., Wharton Jr. Coll., 1953; B.S., Tex. A. and I. U., 1956; m. Mary Beth Anderson, Dec. 19, 1953; children—Jerry, Leigh Ellen, Terri Elizabeth. Gas engr. Texaco, Snyder, Tex., 1956-57; gas engr. Superior Oil Co., Alleyton, Tex., 1957-68, sr. design engr., 1970-71; mgr. Process Gas Devel., Union Tex. Petroleum, Houston, 1969—; cons., 1971—. Served with USMCR, 1948-49, 51-52. Registered profl. engr., Tex. Mem.Houston, Permian Basin gas men. Rotarian. Address: 27233 Lana Lane Conroe TX 77301

PRESTON, FRANK BROCKENBROUGH, JR., bank exec.; b. Buenos Aires, Argentina, June 3, 1927; s. Frank Brockenbrough and Margaret Erwin (Jones) P.; B.A. in Internat. Relations, Yale, 1951; J.D., U. Va. Law Sch., 1956; grad. Stonier Grad. Sch. Banking, 1966; m. Pauline Widen, Mar. 31, 1951; children—Frank Brockenbrough, Helen Margaret. With U.S. Govt., 1951-53; exec. trainee First Nat. Bank Boston, 1956-57, apoderado, Havanna, Cuba, 1957-60; asst. v.p., comml. loan officer First Nat. Bank Tampa, 1961-63, v.p., comml. loan officer, 1963-68; pres., dir. Ellis Nat. Bank Tampa, 1968-71; pres., dir. Internat. Bank Tampa, A Barnett Bank, 1971—. Dir. Bennett, Wallace, Welch & Green Ins., Inc., St. Petersburg, Fla., 1968—. Vice chmn. Tampa Port Authority, 1970—, treas., 1969-70; mem. Com. of 100, 1969—. Trustee St. John's Parish Day Sch., 1967—; bd. dirs. Easter Seal Soc. Crippled Children & Adults Hillsborough County, 1963—, pres., 1969; bd. dirs. Am. Cancer Soc. Hillsborough County, 1964—, campaign chmn., 1966—. Served with U.S. Maritime Service, 1945-47. Mem. Chi Phi, Phi Alpha Delta. Republican. Episcopalian (treas., vestryman 1971—). Toastmaster (past pres.), Krewe of Venus (dir. 1966—). Clubs: Tampa Yacht and Country (Tampa, Fla.); Republican Mens (dir. 1970—), Palma Ceia Golf and Country, University, Exchange (Tampa). Home: 5020 The Riviera St Tampa FL 33609 Office: 1570 Franklin St Tampa FL 33601

PRESTON, JOHN RONALD, mus. exec.; b. Seminole, Okla., Nov. 20, 1932; s. Ray S. and Lorena (Blanton) P.; B.S., Okla. State U., 1955; M.S., U. Ark., 1961; m. Sara R. Huggins, Nov. 25, 1952; children—Teresa R., Ron, Lora, Aaron. Curator, Fort Worth Mus. Sci. and Natural History, 1959-66; dir. Mid Fairfield County Mus., Westport, Conn., 1966-67; asst. dir. U. Ark. Mus., Fayetteville, 1967-69; dir. Mus. Sci. and Natural History, Little Rock, 1969—, dir. mus. spl. activity and ednl. programs. Mem. Am. Assn. Museums, Ark. Mus. Assn. (pres.), Soc. Am. Mammals, Nat. Audubon Soc. Home: 7914 W 29th St Little Rock AR 72204 Office: MacArthur Park Little Rock AR 72203

PRESTON, LOYCE ELAINE, educator; b. Texarkana, Ark., Feb. 25, 1929; d. Harvey Martin and Florence (Whitlock) Preston; student Texarkana Jr. Coll., 1946-47; B.S., Henderson State Tchrs. Coll., 1950; certificate in social work La. State U., 1952; M.S.W., Columbia U., 1956. Tchr. pub. schs., Dierks, Ark., 1950-51; child welfare worker Ark. Dept. Pub. Welfare, Clark and Hot Spring counties, 1951-56, child welfare cons., 1956-58; casework dir. Ruth Sch. Girls, Burien, Wash., 1958-60; asst. prof. spl. edn. La. Poly. Inst., Ruston, 1960-63; asst. prof. Northwestern State Coll., Shreveport, La., 1963—. Chpt. sec. La. Assn. Mental Health, 1965-67, Gov's. adv. council, 1967-70; mem. Mayor's Com. for Community Improvement, 1972—. Mem. Am. Assn. Univ. Women (dir. Shreveport br. 1963-69), Acad. Cert. Social Workers, Nat. Assn. Social Workers (del. 1964-65, pres. N. La. chpt., state-wide com. 1968-69), La Conf. Social Welfare, La. Fedn. Council Exceptional Children (pres. 1970-71), La. Tchrs. Assn. Home: 602 Pickwick Pl Shreveport LA 71108 Office: 2720 Hearne Av Shreveport LA 71103

PRESTON, NATHANIEL STONE, educator; b. Boston, Mar. 1, 1928; s. Jerome and Iva (Stone) P.; A.B., Boston U., 1950; M.A., U. Pa., 1951; Ph.D., Princeton, 1960; m. Ravida Duryee Kennedy, Nov. 22, 1958; children—Emily Duryee, Andrew Greeley, Sarah Ells. Instr., W.Va. U., 1953-55; lectr. Boston Coll., 1957; lectr. Tufts U., 1957-58; instr. Trinity Coll., Hartford, Conn., 1959-61; asst. prof. Am. U., Washington, 1961-63, asso. prof., 1963-66, prof., 1966—; dir. Washington Semester Program, 1962—. Corp. mem. Squam Lakes Sci. Center, Holderness, N.H., 1971—; dir. Squam Lakes Assn., 1972—. Trustee, Trinity Neighborhood House, Boston, 1958-59. Mem. Am., D.C. (past mem. council) polit. sci. assns., Phi Beta Kappa, Pi Sigma Alpha. Republican. Episcopalian. Author: Politics, Economics and Power: Ideology and Practice under Capitalism, Socialism, Communism and Fascism, 1967; Public Authorities, 1971. Editor: The Senate Institution, 1969. Home: 5212 Partridge Lane Washington DC 20016 Office: Am U Washington DC 20016

PRESTON, ROBERT ANDREWS, ednl. adminstr.; b. Richmond, Va., June 6, 1931; s. Joseph Martin and Mary Edyth (Andrews) P.; A.B., Belmont Abbey Coll., 1953; M.A., Cath. U. Am., 1958, Ph.D., 1960; m. Helen Solari, Sept. 6, 1958; children—Kathryn, Robert, Mary Frances, Margaret Helen, James Martin. Lectr. philosophy Cath. U. Am., 1959-60; asst. prof. philosophy John Carroll U., 1960-63, St. Louis U., 1963-66; asso. prof. Bellarmine Coll., Louisville, 1966-67, chmn. dept. philosophy, 1967-68, acad. dean, 1968—, pres. acad. affairs, 1969—. Served with AUS, 1953-55. Mem. Am. Assn. U. Profs., Am. Assn. Acad. Deans, Nat. Cath. Edn. Assn., Assn. Am. Colls., So. Assn. Acad. Deans, English Speaking Union (dir. Ky. chpt. 1969—). Home: 1869 Douglass Blvd Louisville KY 40205

PRESTON, WILL MANIER, lawyer, banker; b. Nashville, May 27, 1904; s. Robert Hatton and Dayse (High) P.; LL.B., Vanderbilt U., 1925; m. Eunice Lannom, Dec. 29, 1926; 1 dau. Dolores Clyntelle (Mrs. William H. Fields). Admitted to Tenn. bar, 1925, Fla. bar, 1926; practice in Miami, 1926—; mem. firm Scott, McCarthy, Preston & Steel, 1943-65; gen. counsel Everglades Nat. Park Assn., 1947; counsel Scott. McCarthy, Steel, Hector & Davis, 1965—. Chmn. bd., dir. Dade Nat. Bank, Miami, 1956-69; dir. Fla. Power and Light Co., Am. Bankers Life Assurance Co. Fla., Wackenhut Corp. Charter mem., past pres., dir. Orange Bowl Com. Mem. Am., Dade County (past pres.) bar assns., Fla. Bar. Lion (past pres. Miami), Kiwanian (past pres. Miami). Home: 710 Lake Rd Miami FL 33137 Office: First Nat Bank Bldg Miami FL 33131

PRESTWOOD, ROGER AUSTIN, lawyer; b. Andalusia, Ala., Oct 23, 1910; s. J. Morgan and Ellie (Snead) P.; student Emory U., 1930-32, U. Ala., 1932-33; LL.B., Atlanta Law Sch., 1938, LL.M., 1939; m. Catherine Maxwell, 1933; 1 dau., Elaine (Mrs. Sam A. Carmack, Jr.). Admitted to Ga. bar, 1936, Ala. bar, 1940, also Supreme Ct., U.S. Ct. Appeals, U.S. Dist. Cts. Ala.; practiced in Atlanta, 1936-43, Washington, 1947-54, Andalusia, 1954—; dist. atty. 22d jud. circuit, Ala., 1970—; atty., adviser office gen. counsel FHA, Washington, 1950; asso. gen. counsel Econ. Stabilization Agy., Washington, 1950, legislative counsel, 1951; co-founder, gen. counsel Equity Life Ins. Co., Andalusia, 1955-66. Mem. Ala. Govs. Indsl. Adv. Com., 1966. Served to comdr. USNR, 1942-47. Mem. Ala., Covington (pres. 1963-64) bar assns., Am. Judicature Soc., Dist. Attys. Assn. Ala., Kappa Sigma. Baptist. Home: 1000 Meadowbrook Dr Andalusia AL 36420 Office: PO Box 1 Courthouse Andalusia AL 36420

PREVITS, GARY JOHN JAMES, educator; b. Cleve., Oct. 23, 1942; s. Julius Albert and Lillian Marie (Guta) P.; B.S. in Bus. Adminstrn. magna cum laude, John Carroll U., 1963; M. Accounting, Ohio State U., 1964; m. Frances Ann Porubsky, Oct. 3, 1964; 1 son, Robert Jude. Staff accountant Haskins & Sells, Cleve., 1964-65, 67-68; asst. prof. bus. Augusta Coll., 1968-70; grad. instr., adminstrv. asst. U. Fla., 1970—, Arthur Andersen Doctoral fellow, 1972. Pres. Valley Park Recreation Assn., Augusta, Ga., 1968-70. Served to lt. AUS, 1965-67. C.P.A., Ohio. Mem. Am. Inst. C.P.A.'S, Ohio, Ga., Fla. socs. C.P.A.'s, Am. Accounting Assn., Ponderosa Internat., Inc. (adv. dir. 1970—). Home: 4725 NW 30th Terrace Gainesville FL 32601

PREWITT, TOM ORIN, JR., social worker; b. Jackson, Miss., Aug. 13, 1934; s. Tom Orin and Lois (Minor) P.; B.A., Millsaps Coll., 1956; M.S.W., Fla. State U., 1959; m. Patricia Morgan, June 30, 1956; children— Tom Orin III, Susan M. With Miss. Dept. Pub. Welfare, Jackson, 1957—, now dir. field services. Mem. Miss. Conf. Social Welfare (past pres.). Home: 705 Tanglewood St Clinton MS 39056 Office: PO Box 4321 Foudren Sta Jackson MS 39216

PREWITT, VERLON WAYNE, garment co. exec.; b. Ravenna, Ky., Oct. 17, 1935; s. William Roscoe and Elizabeth Belle (Hughes) P.; B.S., Eastern Ky. U., 1963, postgrad., 1968-69; m. Patricia Lee Tucker, Nov. 23, 1956; children—Christopher Wayne, William Gregory. Switchman, Louisville and Nashville R.R., Ravenna, Ky., 1957-64; plant engr. Carhartt, Inc., Irvine, Ky., 1964-69, plant mgr., 1969—. Scoutmaster Blue Grass council Boy Scouts Am., 1969—. Mem. Estill County Bd. Edn., 1969—. Mem. Am. Inst. Indsl. Engrs., Res. Officers Assn., Estill County C. of C. (pres. 1967-69). Club: Estill County Golf (dir. 1970—). Home: 117 Francis St Irvine KY 40336 Office: Box 88 Irvine KY 40336

PREYER, LUNSFORD RICHARDSON, congressman; b. Greensboro, N.C., Jan 11, 1919; s. William Yost and Mary Norris (Richardson) P.; grad. Woodberry Forest Sch., 1937; A.B., Princeton, 1941; LL.B., Harvard, 1949; m. Emily Irving Harris, May 11, 1946; children—Lunsford Richardson, Mary Norris, Britt Armfield, Jane Bethell, Emily Harris. Admitted to N.C. bar, 1950; with firm Silliman & Prowell, N.Y.C., 1949-50, Preyer & Bynum, Greensboro, 1951-56; judge N.C. Superior Ct., 1956-61, U.S. Ct. Middle Dist. N.C., 1961-64; mem. 91st-92d Congresses from 6th Dist. N.C. Trustee Woodberry Forest Sch.; chmn. trustees L. Richardson Meml. Hosp., Central Carolina Convalescent Hosp. Served to lt. (s.g.) USNR, 1941-45; PTO. Decorated Bronze Star medal. Fellow Am. Bar Assn.; mem. N.C. Bar Assn. Home: 603 Sunset Dr Greensboro NC 27408 Office: Federal Bldg Greensboro NC 27402

PRIBIC, NIKOLA R., educator; b. Rijeka, Yugoslavia, May 22, 1913; s. Radivoj I. and Olga (Zoric) P.; student (French Govt. fellow) U. Paris, 1939-40; M.A., U. Zagreb, Yugoslavia, 1939; Ph.D., U. Munich, Germany, 1948; m. Elizabeth Dufke, Mau 6, 1946; 1 son, Rado S. Came to U.S., 1961. Asst. prof. U. Zagreb, U. Belgrade, 1939-41; lectr. U. Munich, 1948-61; asso. prof. U. Tex., Austin, 1961-64; prof. Slavic langs. and lit., Fla. State U., Tallahassee, 1965—. Pres., Serbian Orthodox Ch. Community, Munich, 1946-52, editor Zivot i Rad, 1948-50. German Forschungsgemeinschaft fellow, 1956-58. Mem. Am. Assn. Advancement Slavic Studies Inc., Modern Lang. Assn., Sudosteuropagesellschaft, Am. Assn. South Slavic Studies (pres. 1971-72). Author: Beitrage zur Kenntnis des Binnenkroatischen Literarischen Barocks, 1961; Kleine Slavische Biographie, 1958; Goethe Talvj and the South Slavic Folk Songs, 1969; Talog in America, 1971. Home: 1940 Sageway Dr Tallahassee FL 32303

PRICE, BILL, automobile dealer; b. Burlington, N.C., Oct. 22, 1914; s. Mark Cordier and Ivie (Johnson) P.; E.E., N.C. State Coll., 1935; m. Helen Elizabeth Baker, Jan. 31, 1942; children—Bill II, Mark Edward, Elizabeth Baker, David Johnson. Pres., dir. Bill Price Buick, Burlington, N.C., 1945—, also dir.; partner Southeastern Roofing Distbrs., Morehead City, N.C., 1965—, Holly Hill Realty, 1967—; pres., dir. The Western Corp., 1968—; sec., dir. Bareco, Inc, 1966—; chmn. bd., treas. dir. Carteret Carolina Devel. Corp.; pres. Bill Price Aviation, Inc., 1963—; gen. partner Bill Price & Assos., Burlington. Mem. World Meth. Council, 1965-70, The Meth. Corp., 1964-68; pres. world service and finance commn. N.C. Conf. Meth. Ch., 1960-66. Vice chmn. bd. trustees Scarritt Coll., Nashville; trustee Greensboro (N.C.) Coll., 1968—; mem. gen. bd. Nat. Council Chs. Christ U.S.A., 1966—, also mem. gen. adminstrn. and finance com., chmn. donor support com.; bd. dirs., asso. industry com. Laymen's Nat. Bible Com., 1968—. Served to comdr. USNR, 1942-45. Home: Holly Hill Farm Rt 7 Burlington NC 27215 Office: Drawer 969 Burlington NC 27215

PRICE, C. JACK, hosp. dist. adminstr.; student Wingate Jr. Coll., 1938-39, 46-47; B.A., Catawba Coll., 1949; grad. hosp. adminstrn. course Meml. Mission Hosp., Asheville, N.C., 1951. Office mgr. Southeastern div. R.B. Tyler Constrn. Co., Monroe, N.C., until 1943; asst. adminstr. Meml. Mission Hosp., 1951-55; adminstr. Stanly County Hosp., Albemarle, N.C., 1955-62; asso. adminstr. Dallas County Hosp. Dist., Dallas, 1962-63, adminstr., 1963—. Vice pres. Dallas Hosp. Council, 1966, pres., 1967; mem. hosp. adv. com. North Central Tex. Council Govts., 1968-71; clin. prof. preventive medicine and pub. health U. Tex. Southwestern Med. Sch., 1963—, mem. med. faculty council, 1968—; mem. adv. hosp. council Tex. Dept. Health, 1965-70; cons. manpower div. USPHS, 1970-71; mem. Dallas County Spl. Drug Abuse Study Com.; mem., spl. cons. neurology program-project A com. Nat. Inst. Neurol. Diseases and Stroke, NIH, 1969—; mem. membership body Dallas County Health Planning Council, 1971—. Active numerous civic orgns. Bd. dirs. Vis. Nurse Assn., Dallas Area Respiratory Health Assn., Dallas Council on Alcoholism, 1968-71. Served with AUS, 1943-46. Fellow Am. Coll. Hosp. Adminstrs.; mem. Royal Soc. Health (London), Am. (com. on rehab. 1966-68), Tex. (trustee 1968-71, v.p. 1970-71, pres.-elect 1971-72, pres. 1972-73) hosp. assns., Dallas C. of C. (pub. health com. 1968-71). Methodist (past steward). Rotarian (past treas. Dallas). Club: Press (Dallas). Office: Dallas County Hospital District 5201 Harry Hines Blvd Dallas TX 75235*

PRICE, CHARLES EUGENE, educator; b. Apalachicola, Fla., Mar. 13, 1924; s. Charles P. and Lela (Joseph) P.; B.A., Johnson C. Smith, 1946; M.A., Howard U., 1949; LL.B., Am. Sch. Law, 1951: J.D., John Marshall Law Sch., 1967; postgrad. Johns Hopkins, 1951-52, Boston U., 1956; m. Lennie Florence Bryant, Nov. 25, 1946; 1 son, Charles Eugene (dec.). Tchr. high sch., Ga., 1947-48, Fla., 1948-49; asst. prof. history and polit. sci. Butler Coll., 1950-52, dean, 1952-53; asso. prof., dean Fla. Meml. Coll., 1953-55; field sec. N.A.A.C.P., 1955-57; asst. prof. Livingstone Coll., 1957-59; asso. prof. polit. sci. Morris Brown Coll., Atlanta, 1960-—, asst. dean, 1967-71. Mem. Dekalb Republican Exec. Com., 1964-68; mem. Fulton Rep. Exec. Com., 1972-—, ho. dist. chmn., 1972-—. Bd. dirs., treas. Dekalb Econ. Opportunity Authority. Recipient Sincere Leadership award N.A.A.C.P., 1966, Albert award DeKalb N.A.A.C.P., 1965. Mem. Am. Polit. Sci. Assn., Assn. Social Sci. Tchrs., N.A.A.C.P. (pres. Dekalb chpt. 1964-68), Alpha Kappa Mu, Sigma Rho Sigma, Alpha Phi Alpha. Home: 1480 Austin Rd Atlanta GA 30331

PRICE, CHARLES RILEY, advt. agcy. exec.; b. Asheville, N.C., Aug. 13, 1941; s. Charles R. and Duane (Thomas) P.; A.B., U. N.C., 1963; m. Charlene Haynes, Sept. 29, 1963; children—Charla Duane, Charles Riley III. Advt. salesman Asheville Citizen-Times, 1963-65; advt. specialist Olin Matheson Chem. Corp., 1965-67; pres. Price/McNabb Advt. Agcy., Asheville, N.C., 1967-—. Prof. advt., marketing, Western Carolina U., Cullowhee, 1968-69. Bd. dirs. Handi-Skills Workshop. Served with AUS, 1965. Mem. Asheville Sales Marketing Execs., Asheville Jr. C. of C., Sigma Delta Chi. Clubs: Asheville Country, Asheville City (gov.). Baptist. Home: 2 Deerview Lane Asheville NC 28804 Office: Northwestern Bank Bldg Asheville NC 28801

PRICE, DELTON EDISON, agrl. devel. agt.; b. Cove, Ark., Aug. 7, 1924; s. Daniel Fletcher and Birdie Esther (Phillips) P.; student So. State Coll., 1942-43; B.S. in Agr., U. Ark., 1950, M.S. in Agr., 1965; m. Betty Jean Woods, July 23, 1948; children—Nancy (Mrs. Boyce A. Drummond, III), Sharon, Blake, Grant Price. Asst. county agt. Yell County, Ark., 1950, Union County, Ark., 1951-52; county agt. Perry County, Ark., 1952-55, Franklin County Ark., 1955-66; area devel. agt. Western Extension Dist., Fort Smith, Ark., 1966-—. Operator beef cattle farm, Ozark, Ark., 1958-65; part owner Masonery Products Co., 1963-64. Chmn. Western Ark. Area Manpower Planning Bd., 1971. Mem. bd. Franklin County 4-H Found., 1962-66. Served with Signal Corps, AUS, 1943-46. Recipient Distinguished Service award Nat. County Agts. Assn., 1966. Mem. Fort Smith C. of C., Franklin County, Sebastian County farm burs., County Agts. Assn. (bd. dirs. 1955, 66), Epsilon Sigma Phi. Methodist (chmn. commn. edn. 1958-63, ofcl. bd. 1958-63). Home: 2016 S 69th St Fort Smith AR 72901 Office: PO Box 973 Agrl Extension Service Fort Smith AR 72901

PRICE, EDGAR HILLEARY, JR., citrus processing co. exec., ex-state senator; b. Jacksonville, Fla., Jan. 1, 1918; s. Edgar Hilleary and Mary (Phillips) P.; student U. Fla., 1937-38; m. Elise Ingram, May 24, 1947; 1 son, Jerald Steven. Gen. mgr. Terra Ceia Bay Farms, Inc., Palmetto, Fla., 1945-49; mgr. Fla. Gladiolus Growers Assn., Bradenton, 1949-55; exec. v.p. Tropicana Products, Inc., Bradenton, Fla., 1955-—, also dir.; exec. v.p., dir. Indsl. Glass Co., Inc.; dir. First Nat. Bank of Bradenton, Fla., Fla. Power and Light Co., Central Telephone Co. Fla.; mem. Fla. Senate, 1958-66. Adv. com. Fla. Citrus Manual; dir. Fla. Citrus Expn., 1958-—; chmn. Fla. Citrus Commn. Del. Democratic Nat. Conv., 1960. Mem. gov.'s com. employment of physically handicapped, 1960; chmn. bd. trustees Manatee County Sch. Dist., 1956-57; mem. Bradenton Housing Authority, 1951-57, commr., 1951-—; bd. dirs. Salvation Army, Bradenton, 1954-—; regional chmn. Crusade for Freedom, 1952-53; active A.R.C., Manatee County Crippled Childrens Soc., Boys Club, Blood Bank; commr. Census of 12th Jud. Circuit, 1957; mem. Fla. Bd. Control, 1957-58; mem. Fla. Plant Bd., 1957-58; chmn. Gov.'s Freeze Damage Survey Team, 1957-58; commr. Manatee County Indsl. Commn., 1956. Trustee Univ. S. Fla. Found., Fla. Investment Trust. Served from pvt. to sgt., M.C., AUS, 1941-43, to 1st lt. USAAF, 1943-45. Decorated Air medal with 4 oak leaf clusters; named outstanding freshman senator Fla. Legislature, 1959; recipient Distinguished Service award U.S. Jr. C. of C., 1949; Fla. Man of Yr. in Agr. Progressive Farmer mag., 1961; Good Govt. award Jr. C. of C., 1961; Allen Morris award most valuable mem. Fla. legislature, 1965; St. Petersburg Times award for most outstanding senator, 1965. Mem. Fla. (dir. 1956-—, pres. 1970-71, chmn. roads and bridges com. 1953-54, finance com. 1954-55, new bldg. com. 1955-56), Bradenton (dir.), Bradenton Jr. (past v.p.), Manatee County (pres. 1968) chambers of commerce, Com. of 100 (vice chmn.), Fla. State Fair Assn. (dir.), Future Farmers, Fla. Hort. Soc. (pres. 1967-68), Fla. Fruit and Vegetable Assn. (dir. 1968). Baptist (deacon, tchr. Sunday sch.). Kiwanian (past pres. Bradenton). Home: 3009 Riverview Blvd W Bradenton FL 33505 Office: 9th St and 13th Av W Brandenton FL 33505

PRICE, EUGENIA, author; b. Charleston, W.Va., June 22, 1916; d. Walter Wesley and Ann (Davidson) Price; student Ohio U., 1933-35, Northwestern U., 1935-38, D.Litt. (hon.), Alderson-Broaddus Coll., 1967. Scriptwriter NBC, Chgo., 1939-41, CBS, Chgo., 1942-44; owner Eugenia Price Prodns., Chgo., 1944-49; writer, dir. radio drama Unshackled Chgo., 1950-56; cons., speaker radio and TV workshops. Eugenia Price collection formed in her honor Mugar Library, Boston U., 1967. Mem. Coastal Ga. Hist. Soc. Author: Discoveries, 1953; The Burden is Light, 1954; Early Will I Seek Thee, 1956; Woman to Woman, 1958; Beloved World, 1961; The Beloved Invader, 1965; The Wider Place, 1966; Make Love Your Aim, 1967; Just As I Am, 1968; New Moon Rising, 1969; Lighthouse, 1971; many others. Home: Frederica Saint Simons Island GA 31522

PRICE, GEORGE RAYMOND, JR., architect; b. Greenwood, S.C., Nov. 30, 1925; s. George Raymond and Edyth Marion (Prince) P.; B.S. in Architecture, Clemson Coll., 1950; m. Jonnie Jo Ann Barton, Nov. 19, 1966. Architect J.B. Urquhart, Columbia, S.C., 1950-52, W.S. Stork, Columbia, 1952-54, Lyles, Bissett, Carlisle & Wolff, Columbia, 1954-57, Maynard Pearlstine, Columbia, 1960-62, Reid Hearn & Assos., Columbia, 1962-63; supt. George R. Price, Gen. Contractor, Columbia, 1957-60; asso. Califf, Geiger & Price, Columbia, 1963-65; chief architect Jones & Fellers, Augusta, Ga., 1965-68; owner George R. Price & Assos., Aiken, S.C., also Augusta, 1968-—. Partner George R. Price Constrn. Co., Columbia, 1950-62. Mem. dist. com. Boy Scouts Am., 1963; mem. Friends of Library, Aiken, S.C., 1968-—, Historic Augusta, Inc., 1970-—; mem. exec. com. Augusta Opera Assn., 1969-71; pres. Carolina Opera Guild, 1970-71; treas. Aiken Civic Ballet, 1970-71; founder Greater Aiken Arts Council, 1971. Served with inf. AUS, 1944-46. Decorated Combat Inf. medal, Purple Heart; recipient Scouters award, 1957, Order of Arrow, 1957, Scouting Wood Badge, 1959, Scouters Key, 1961. Mem. A.I.A., Constrn. Specifications Inst. (pres. 1970), Guild for Religious Architecture, C. of C. Greater Augusta, Alston Wilkes Soc., Richmond County Hist. Soc., V.F.W., D.A.V. Roman Catholic. K.C. Clubs: Sertoma (charter mem. Aiken), Aiken Quadrille, Fermata (Aiken); C.S.R.A. Scuba (Augusta); Columbia (S.C.) Museum Art; Lettermens (Clemsen U); Carillon Ball (Columbia). Co-inventor brick laying aide. Home: 110 Ellenton St Aiken SC 29801 107 Macartan St Augusta GA 30902 also 140 Newberry St Aiken SC 29801

PRICE, HARRY B., economist, educator; b. China; grad. Davidson Coll., Yale. Mem. faculty Yenching Coll., Peking, China; asst. dir. China Mission of UNRRA; cons., later br. chief ECA, Washington, from 1948; with UN, Nepal, 3 years; now chmn. dept. econs. Maryville (Tenn.) Coll. Author: The Marshall Plan and Its Meaning; Rural Reconstruction and Development: A Manual for Field Workers; co-author 3 vol. history of UNRRA, 1950. Office: Dept of Economics Maryville College Maryville TN 37801*

PRICE, HARVEY EARL, banker; b. Johnston County, N.C., Aug. 6, 1920; s. Moses Leon and Lettie (Wall) P.; grad. Sch. Commerce, Atlantic Christian Coll., Wilson, N.C., 1941; Carolinas Sch. Banking, Chapel Hill, N.C., 1946, 58; m. Eleanor Farmer Blow, Feb. 22, 1947; children—Harvey Craig, Stephen Russ. With accounting sect. Post Ordnance Dept., U.S. Army, Ft. Bragg, 1941-42; with First-Citizens Bank & Trust Co., Smithfield, N.C., 1942-—, auditor, 1950-—, now sr. v.p. and gen. auditor. Instr. auditing and comml. law, 1955-56. Pres., Smithfield P.T.A., 1965-66; dist. committeeman, financial chmn. Century Club, Boy Scouts Am., 1965-—; finance chmn. N.C. Symphony Soc., 1967-70. Bd. dirs. Johnston County Mental Health Assn., 1962-70. Mem. Nat. Assn. Bank Auditors and Comptrollers. Democrat. Baptist (sec. bd. deacons 1963-67, chmn. 1970-72, Sunday sch. tchr. 1962-—). Rotarian (pres. Smithfield 1964-65). Home: 805 Vermont St Smithfield NC 27577 Office: 241 E Market St Smithfield NC 27577

PRICE, HOLLIS F., TV exec.; b. Va. Pres., LeMoyne-Owen Coll., Memphis, 27 years.; now exec. officer Sta. WMC-TV, Memphis. Address: 825 Walker Av Memphis TN*

PRICE, HOWARD LEWIS, city ofcl.; b. Gaston, N.C., Aug. 17, 1934; s. Joseph Clarence and Ada (Thornburge) P.; A.B., Catawba Coll., 1957; m. Carol Joyce Carter, Aug. 17, 1957; children—Howard Lewis Jr., Courtney Leigh. Adminstrv. asst. City Gastonia, N.C., 1957-59; city mgr. Mt. Holly, N.C., 1959-64 city mgr. Lenoir, N.C., 1964-—. Served to lt. AUS. Mem. N.C., Lenoir, Caldwell County mgrs. assns., Internat. City Mgrs. Assn. Baptist. Rotarian. Home: 6107 Armstrong St Lenoir NC 28645 Office: 206 S Main St Lenoir NC 28645

PRICE, JAMES TRAVIS, lawyer, city ofcl.; b. Springfield, Tenn., Dec. 20, 1920; s. Belah Edward and Lora Ione (O'Brien) P.; A.A., George Washington U., 1950, LL.B., 1954; m. Martha Lois Driscoll, Jan. 1, 1943; children—Steven O'Brien, Emily Susan, Laura Wiley, Robert Andrew. Clerical worker First Nat. Bank, Clarksville, Tenn., 1939-41; civilian personnel position classifier VA, Washington, 1945-46; classifier Office of Sec. Navy, Washington, 1946; adminstrv. officer Judge Adv. Gen. of Navy, 1946-54; admitted to D.C. bar, Tenn. bar, 1954; since practiced in Springfield; mayor, Springfield, 1959-—. Pres. Mid Cumberland Council Govts. and Devel. Dist., 1970; chmn. Mid-Cumberland Emergency Med. Services Adv. Com., 1972-—. Active Boy Scouts Am., United Givers Fund, and others. Bd. dirs. Mid-Cumberland Comprehensive Health Planning Council. Served to 1st lt. M.C., AUS, 1942-45. Named Tenn. Mayor of Yr., Tex. Municipal League, 1966. Mem. Am., Tenn., Robertson County bar assns., Tenn. Municipal League (bd. dirs. 1965-71, pres. 1966-67), Am. Pub. Power Assn. (legal com.). Methodist (bd. stewards 1957-—), Mason (32 deg. Shriner), Lion. Home: 318 Garner St Springfield TN 37172 Office: 121 5th Av W Springfield TN 37172

PRICE, JIMMY RAY, banker; b. Dublin, Tex., Sept. 26, 1937; s. William Paul and Effie (Ovela) P.; B.B.A., Tex. Tech. U., 1963; postgrad. Am. Inst. Banking, 1965, U. Okla., 1970; m. Judith Rae Dennis, Aug. 26, 1957; children—Amy Gwyn, Elizabeth Ann. With First Nat. Bank, Sweetwater, Tex., 1954-59; with First Nat. Bank, Lubbock 1959-—, asst. cashier, 1964-66, asst. v.p., 1966-68, v.p., 1968-—. Pres. Lubbock Assn. Credit Mgmt., 1968; instr. Am. Inst. Banking, 1969-71; guest speaker Tex. Tech. U., 1964-71. Vice chmn. comml. div. United Fund, Lubbock, 1968; commr. Lubbock Urban Renewal Agy., 1969-—. Bd. dirs. YMCA, Lubbock, 1969, Goodwill Industries, 1969. Named Kiwanian of Yr. Lubbock Kiwanis Club, 1964; Top Ranch Boss, YMCA, Lubbock, 1969; recipient Distinguished Service award Lubbock Jr. C. of C., 1969. Mem. C. of C. (chmn. task force 1970), Phi Kappa Phi, Phi Alpha Kappa, Beta Gamma Sigma. Baptist (deacon 1970). Kiwanian (bd. dirs. 1964-68, pres. 1967). Home: 3501 78th Dr Lubbock TX 79413 Office: P O Box 1241 Lubbock TX 79408

PRICE, JOHN PRESSLEY, pharmacist; b. Louisville, Apr. 17, 1921; s. John Frank and Nannie Lou (Herndon) P.; student U. N.C., 1944-46; B.S., Mercer So. Coll. Pharmacy, 1951; m. Virginia Marie Mason, Aug. 17, 1946; children—Gloria, Jackie, Mason. Owner, Price Pharmacy, Chickamauga, Ga., 1955-64; pres., Price Pharmacy, Inc., Trenton, Ga., 1961-—; pres. Price Ringgold Drug, Inc., Ringgold, 1963-—; dir. Am. Consumers, Inc. Mem. Walker County (Ga.) Planning Commn., 1968-—; mem. City Council, Chickamauga, Ga., 1963-68. Served with USNR, 1940-46. Mem. Am., Ga. pharm. assns., Nat. Assn. Retail Druggists, Sigma Nu. Baptist (trustee 1957, chmn. bd. trustees). Address: Route 2 Kensington GA 30727

PRICE, J(OHN) WILLIAM, paper co. exec.; b. Quebec, Que., Can., June 23, 1927; s. John Herbert and Lorna (Macdougall) P.; student U. N.B., 1945-47, Bishops U., 1947-48; m. Helen Julia Stevenson, Jan. 15, 1954; children—Diana, John, David. Came to U.S., 1952. Asst. forestry engr. Powell River Paper Co., Vancouver, B.C., Can., 1948-50; adminstrv. asst. Bowaters Nfld. Pulp & Paper Co., 1950-52; serviceman Bowater Paper Co., N.Y.C., 1952, service mgr., 1953-54, salesman, 1954-55, dist. sales mgr., 1956-58, v.p. N. Am. sales, 1959-64; v.p., dir. Perkins Goodwin Co., Inc., N.Y.C., 1964-—, chmn. bd., 1970-—; dir. Southland Paper Mills, Inc. Clubs: Canadian (N.Y.C.); Winged Foot Golf (Mamaroneek, N.Y.); Preston Trail, Brookhollow (Dallas). Home: 5423 Meaders Lane Dallas TX 75229 Office: 1702 Adolphus Tower Dallas TX 75202

PRICE, LARRY EUGENE, educator; b. Little Rock, Aug. 16, 1934; s. Lew J. and Marcia (Stark) P.; A.A., Little Rock Jr. Coll., 1953; B.S. E.E., U. Ark., 1959, M.B.A., 1961, Ph.D. in Finance, 1966; m. Barbara Ann Parke, June 3, 1956; children—Jane Elizabeth, Carol Lynn, Steven Russell. Electronics engr. missile div. Bendix Aviation Corp., Mishawaka, Ind., 1956-58; instr. gen. bus. U. Ark., Fayetteville, 1960-63; asst. prof. sch. bus., Ga. So. Coll., Statesboro, 1963-67, asso. prof., 1968-71, prof., also chmn. finance dept., 1971-—. Mem. Regional Export Expansion Council, 1967-—. Mem. Am., So. econ. assns., Am., So. finance assns., Am. Assn. U. Profs., Beta Gamma Sigma, Omicron Delta Epsilon. Episcopalian. Club: Forest Heights Country. Home: 222 S Edgewood Dr Statesboro GA 30458

PRICE, LEE GEORGE, govt. ofcl.; b. Washington, Sept. 1, 1940; s. David George and Katharine (Blake) P.; student Washington and Lee U., 1959-60; A.A., George Washington U., 1961, A.B. in Govt., 1963; postgrad. Am. U., 1963-65; m. Janice Anne Kennard, Oct. 26, 1961; 1 dau., Deborah Lee. Clk. typist, student asst. various fed. govt. agys., Washington, 1959-63; adminstrv. asst. First Nat. Bank, Washington, 1964-66; mgmt. intern Internal Revenue Service, Washington, 1966; program analyst Office Comptroller of the Navy, Washington, 1967-—. Mem. Am. Soc. Mil. Comptrollers, Am. Soc. Pub. Adminstrn. Methodist (chmn. finance com.). Home: 2315 Ashboro Dr Chevy Chase MD 20015 Office: The Pentagon Washington DC 20350

PRICE, LEE OLIN, JR., judge; b. Athens, Ga., Apr. 6, 1914; s. Lee Olin and Nellie (Gardner) P.; A.B., U. Ga., 1947, J.D., 1936; m. Frances Sanders, Dec. 10, 1939; 1 dau., Cynthia (Mrs. James M. Kenney). Admitted to Ga. bar, 1937; since practiced in Athens; mem. Ga. Ho. of Reps., 1941-49; prof. polit. sci. U. Ga., Athens, 1946-50; judge Athens Municipal Ct., 1948-—; judge Clarke County Juvenile Ct., Athens, 1953-—. Pres. Ga. Council Juvenile Ct. Judges, 1964-65; mem. exec. com. Nat. Council Juvenile Ct. Judges, 1968-—. Active civic orgns. Pres. Young Democrats Ga., 1948-49, nat. committeeman, 1948. Served as 1st lt. inf. AUS, 1942. Named Citizen of Year, Athens Area Kiwanis Club, 1964. Mem. Ga. Recorder's Ct. Judges Assn. (pres. 1952-53), Ga. Municipal Assn., Western Circuit (pres. 1953-54), Athens (pres. 1955-56) bar assns. Democrat. Elk, Kiwanian. Home: 216 Morton Av Athens GA 30601 Office: 301 Courthouse Athens GA 30601

PRICE, LEW, city and county ofcl.; b. Lynchburg, Va., Jan. 3, 1922; s. Lewis E. and Virginia (Cooper) P.; grad., U. Miami, 1940-46; m. Marjorie Johnson, Sept. 17, 1946; children—Cindy Lou (Mrs. Michael Goldberg), Kerry, Scott, Patrick Michael. Pub. relations cons. Venn, Cole & Price, Miami, 1954-57; reporter, Miami Herald, 1942; dir. publicity and tourism City Miami and Dade County, 1957-—. Editor and columnist Florida Sun, 1950-52. Served as 1st lt. Inf. AUS, 1942-46; ETO. Recipient Silver Anvil, Pub. Relations Soc. Am., 1959, Personal Attainment award, 1965; People to People award, 1967; many others. Mem. Fla. Pub. Relations Assn. (pres. 1969-70). Club: Variety. Home: 15301 SW 88 Av Miami FL 33157 Office: 499 Biscayne Blvd Miami FL 33132

PRICE, MADISON RANKIN, dentist; b. Aiken, S.C., Dec. 29, 1933; s. Bruce Hays and Eva (Rankin) P.; B.A., U. Richmond, 1955; D.D.S., Med. Coll. Va., 1959; m. Dorothy Lee Stiff, Aug. 25, 1956; children— Robert Bruce, Thomas Madison, Leslie Britton. Research fellow Nat. Inst. Health, Richmond, Va., 1957-58; analytical chemist Naval Weapons Sta., Yorktown, Va., 1955-56; practice dentistry, Newport News, Va., 1961-—. Faculty pedodontics Va. Commonwealth U.-Med. Coll. Va. Sch. Dentistry, Richmond, 1970-—. Served to capt. Dental Corps, USAF, 1959-61. Fellow Acad. Gen. Dentistry; mem. Am., Va. State (exec. council 1971-—), Peninsula (pres. 1967-68) dental assns., Am. Soc. Dentistry for Children (Va. exec. council 1968-—), Fedn. Dentaire Internationale, Omicron Kappa Upsilon, Sigma Zeta, Delta Sigma Delta, Sigma Phi Epsilon. Baptist (deacon). Home: 7 Beverly Hills Dr Newport News VA 23606 Office: 367 Denbigh Blvd Newport News VA 23602

PRICE, MARK A., dentist; b. Bernice, La., Nov. 13, 1924; s. Mark A., Jr. and Mary (Moore) P.; student La. Tech. U., 1948; D.D.S., Emory U., 1956; m. Margie Nell Allen, June 7, 1946; children—Mary, John Marcus. Practice dentistry, specializing in orthodontics, Monroe, La., 1956-—. Served with USNR, 1943-46. Mem. Am. Assn. Orthodontists, Southwestern Soc. Orthodontists (sec.-treas.), Am. (del.), La. (1st v.p.), Fifth Dist. (past pres.) dental assns. Rotarian. Home: 3801 Deborah Dr Monroe LA 71201 Office: 1212 Stubbs Av Monroe LA 71201

PRICE, ORVILLE OLIVER, math. statistician; b.Greenbrier, Ark., Apr. 7, 1907; s. William and Emma (Webb) P.; B.S., State Coll. Ark., 1931; postgrad Am. U., 1948-51; m. Alice Elizabeth Love, Dec. 17, 1945; children—Barbara (Mrs. John R. Bridgeman), Orville O. Math instr., dean of boys Idabel (Okla.) High Sch., 1931-35; statistician U.S. VA, Washington, 1935-62; chief sampling staff Internal Revenue Service, U.S. Treasury Dept., 1962-67, cons. Office of Compliance, 1968-69; pvt. cons. math. statistics, 1969-—. Served with AUS, 1943-44. Mem. Am. Statis. Assn., Am. Soc. Quality Control. Contbr. articles to profl. jours. Address: 2270 NW 21st Av Gainesville FL 32601

PRICE, RAYMOND KISSAM, JR., govt. ofcl.; b. N.Y.C., May 6, 1930; s. Raymond Kissam and Beth (Porter) P.; B.A., Yale, 1951. With Crowell-Collier Pub. Co., 1955-57, asst. to editor Collier's mag., 1956-57, reporter Life mag., 1957, with N.Y. Herald Tribune, 1957-66, chief editorial writer, editor editorial page, 1964-66; asst. to Richard M. Nixon, N.Y.C., 1967-69, spl. asst. to Pres. Nixon, 1969-—. Served to lt. (j.g.) USNR, 1952-55. Mem. Aurelian Honor Soc., Skull and Bones. Clubs: Yale, Overseas Press (N.Y.C.); Metropolitan, Federal City (Washington). Office: The White House Washington DC 20500

PRICE, ROBERT DALE, congressman; b. Reading, Kan., Sept, 7, 1927; s. Ben F. and Gladys (Watson) P.; B.S., Okla. State U., 1951; m. Martha Ann White, June 7, 1951; children—Robert Grant, Benjamin Carl, Janice Ann. Rancher, near Pampa, Tex., 1955-66; mem. 90th-92nd congresses from the 18th Tex. Dist. Mem. bd. dirs. devel. bd. Wayland Bapt. Coll., Plainview, Tex. Served to 1st lt. USAF, 1951-55. Decorated Air medal. Mem. Top O'Texas Rodeo Assn. (dir.), V.F.W., Am. Legion, Sigma Alpha Epsilon. Mason, Kiwanian. Home: 2135 Charles St Pampa TX 79065 Office: Cannon Office Bldg Washington DC 20510

PRICE, WILLIAM ARCHER, govt. ofcl.; b. Selma, Ala., Nov. 30, 1910; s. Robert Watkins and Eilleen (Archer) P.; student Duke U., 1932-34; A.B., U. Ala., 1931, LL.B., 1935; m. Rosalie Pettus, Oct. 3, 1936. Admitted to Ala. bar, 1935; practiced in Birmingham, Ala., 1935-43; asst. dir. FHA, Birmingham, 1946-66, dep. dir., 1966-70; area counsel Dept. Housing and Urban Devel., Birmingham, 1970-—. Chmn. bd. dirs. Ala. Opera Assn.; bd. dirs. Birmingham Mus. Art, 1950-52, Birmingham Civic Opera Assn., 1959-—, Birmingham Symphony Assn., 1970-—, Birmingham Civic Ballet, 1970-—; pres. Birmingham Festival of Arts, 1964, Birmingham Music Club, 1970-72. Served as lt. USNR, 1943-46. Mem. Ala. Bar Assn., S.R. (Ala. pres. 1960), S.A.R., Soc. Colonial Wars, Birmingham Com. Fgn. Relations, Phi Delta Phi. Episcopalian. Kiwanian. Clubs: Birmingham Country, The Club. Home: 300 Windsor Dr Birmingham AL 35209 Office: 524 Daniel Bldg Birmingham AL 35233

PRICE, WILLIAM ERNEST, ret. educator; b. Macon, Ga., Oct. 31, 1902; s. David and Emma (Bowden) P.; A.B., Morris Coll., 1926; postgrad. Dickinson Law Sch., 1927-29, Atlanta Sch. Social Work, 1935-36, Ohio State U., 1950-56; M.A., Hampton Inst., 1944; Pd.D., Morris Coll., Sumter, S.C., 1965; m. Ada Lee Olive, Aug. 22, 1935. Prin., Cordele (Ga.) Bd. Edn., 1930-35, Jefferson County, Bartow, Ga., 1935-38, Dawson, Ga., 1938-40, Louisville (Ga.) Acad. Sch., 1940-72. Vis. prof. social studies Savannah State Coll., summer sch., 1946-49. City chmn. A.R.C., polio, cancer, and heart funds; chmn. survey com. on bldg. facilities, Jefferson County Sch. System. Mem. exec. com. Community Welfare; bd. dirs. Interracial Devel. Corp.; chmn. exec. com. Community Beautification Program, 1950-55; city chmn. Pub. Relations Program; lt. col., a.d.c. on Ga. gov.'s staff. Mem. Nat. Tchrs. Assn., Jefferson County Prins. Council (pres.), Ga. (trustee, dir., past regional dir.), Jefferson County (chmn. exec. com.) tchrs. and edn. assns., Louisville C. of C. (exec. bd.). Baptist (chmn. bldg. program, chmn. bd. deacons). Mason (chmn. bldg. fund). Club: Lakeview Country (chmn. bldg. fund). Home: 3155 Imperial Dr

Macon GA 31201 Office: Jefferson County High Sch PO Box 128 Louisville GA 30434

PRICE (MARION) WOODROW, journalist; b. Elizabeth City, N.C., Oct. 13, 1914; s. James Asa and Meddie (Divers) P.; student Wake Forest Coll., 1933-34; m. Mary Dudley Pittman, Aug. 31, 1940; children—Wiley, Dudley, Mary, Catherine. Reporter, Daily Advance, Elizabeth City, 1935-39, Raleigh (N.C.) Times, 1939-41; mng. editor Daily Ind., Kannapolis, N.C., 1941-42; reporter A.P., Raleigh, 1942-43; reporter News and Observer, Raleigh, 1946-57, mng. editor, 1957-72, outdoor editor, 1949—. Mem. Kerr Reservoir Devel. Commn., 1950-52, Cape Hatteras Seashore Commn., 1949-50; chmn. N.C. Outer Banks Park Commn., 1962-63, N.C. Seashore Commn., 1963-69, N.C. State Ports Authority, 1969—. Served with USAAF, 1943-45. Mem. A.P. Mng. Editors Assn., Outdoor Writers Am. Baptist. Home: 519 Dixie Trail Raleigh NC 27607 Office: 215 S McDowell St Raleigh NC 27602

PRICKETT, JOHN SAMUEL, JR., state ofcl.; b. nr. Bowdon, Ga., Jan. 26, 1910; s. John Sanford and Iula Permela (Hearn) P.; B.S., U. Ga., 1938, M.S., 1940; postgrad. N.Y. U., 1950; m. Burnell Faye Wright, June 20, 1931; children—John Sanford III, Betty Carole (Mrs. Robert J. Taggart), Lanny Asbury, Rebecca Nan (Mrs. Marshall Miller). Tchr., prin. Ga. schs., 1931-42; counselor vocational rehab. Ga. Dept. Edn., Atlanta, 1942-44, dist. supr., 1944-51, asst. dir., 1951-64, dir., 1964-67, asst. state supt. schs., 1967—. Pres., State Dept. Edn. Credit Union, 1961-64; mem. Joint Commn. on Correctional Manpower and Tng., 1967; adv. bd. Mental Retardation Inst., U. N.C., Butner, 1967—; mem. adv. com. to rehab. counseling program Fla. State U., 1967—, U. Ga., 1970—; mem. Manpower Adv. Council Coastal Plains Area, 1968. Pres., Ga. Tb Assn., 1964-65, mem. bd., 1957—; mem. adult vocational adv. bd. United Cerebral Assn., N.Y., 1952-63; mem. bd. Goodwill Industries Atlanta, Inc., 1968—, co-chmn. Gov.'s Com. for Arthritis, 1969-70. Trustee Atlanta Community Services for the Blind. Recipient Distinguished Service award Ga. Rehab. Assn., 1961. Mem. Nat. (nat. membership chmn. 1966-67, mem. bd. 1967—), Ga. (pres. 1959-60) rehab. assns., U. Ga. Alumni Assn. (pres. DeKalb County chpt. 1962), Kappa Phi Kappa. Methodist (chmn. ofcl. bd. 1962-64). Home: 1162 Berkeley Rd Avondale Estates GA 30002 Office: State Office Bldg Atlanta GA 30334

PRIDDY, ASHLEY HORNE, oil and gas co. exec.; b. Wichita Falls, Tex., Apr. 1, 1922; s. Walter Mason and Swannanoa (Horne) P.; student Rice U., 1939-41; B.B.A., U. Tex., 1949, B.S. in Petroleum Engring., 1949; m. Kathryn Amsler, Dec. 30, 1947; children—Hervey, Betty, Ann. With Sabine Royalty Corp., Dallas, 1949—, petroleum engr., 1949-55, v.p., 1958-68, pres., chief exec. officer, 1968—. Mem. council Town of Highland Park, (Tex.), 1966-70; mayor, Highland Park, 1970—. Bd. trustees Hockaday Sch., Dallas, Engring. Sch. Found. U. Tex. Served to lt. USNR, 1943-46; PTO. Mem. Beta Theta Pi, Tau Beta Pi. Clubs: Dallas Petroleum; Brook Hollow Golf (Dallas). Home: 4222 Arcady Av Dallas TX 75205 Office: Mercantile Bank Bldg Dallas TX 75201

PRIDDY, LOIE JEFFERY, surveyor; b. High Point, N.C., Sept. 1, 1938; s. Lester Jeffery and Carrie Beatrice (Stallings) P.; student Mil. Surveying Sch., 1955-57, Davidson Community Coll., 1969; m. Nancy Ellen Cecil, June 27, 1959; children—Crystal Lynn, Jeffery Allen. Party chief Guarino Engring. Co., High Point, 1960-67, land surveyor, 1967-70; chief engring. br., estuarine research surveyor N.C. Div. Comml. and Sports Fisheries, Morehead City, 1970—. Lectr. surveying ednl. instns., 1957, 70. Owner, operator Priddy's Coin-O-Wash, High Point, 1965-66; owner, operator Olympic Labs., High Point, 1968—. Performer music for local children's homes, VA hosp., civic orgn. fund-raising drives, 1960—. Served as computer and party chief Communications Engring. Squadron, USAF, 1955-59. Mem. N.C. Soc. Surveyors, Nat., Atlantic estuarine research socs., Consumers Union, High Point (N.C.) VHF Amateur Radio Club. Republican. Baptist. Research and publ. in field. Home: RFD 4 Box 161 High Point NC 27263 Office: 1600 Arendell St Morehead City NC 28557

PRIDGEN, THOMAS DUPREE, engring. exec.; b. Lakeland, Fla., July 31, 1925; s. High I. and Myrlene (Robinson) P.; B.C.E., U. Fla., 1949; postgrad. U. South Fla., 1964-69; m. Morag Gardner, Oct. 22, 1950; 1 dau., Julie Annette. Civil engr. Minerals Separation N.A.M. Corp., Lakeland, Fla., 1949-51; structural engr. H.K. Ferguson Co., Cleve., 1951-53; project engr. Minerals and Chem. Corp. of Am., Lakeland, 1953-55; chief design engr. Frank M. Murphy Assos., Inc., Bartow, Fla., 1955-63; mgr. design engring. Dorr-Oliver, Inc., Bartow, 1963-68; v.p., dir. Dorr-Oliver Engring., Ltd., Bartow, 1966-68; v.p., dir. Manzer-Pridgen Engrings., Inc., Lakeland, 1968-69; pres. Pridgen Engring. Co., Inc., Lakeland, 1969—, also dir. Mem. engring. adv. com. Com. of 100, Lakeland, 1964-65; mem. adv. com. for constrn. tech. Polk Jr. Coll., Winter Haven, 1964-68. Served with AUS, 1943-46. Decorated Purple Heart with oak leaf cluster. Registered profl. engr., Fla., La., Miss. Mem. Nat. Soc. Profl. Engrs., Fla. Engring. Soc. Methodist. Clubs: Lakeland Yacht and Country, Sertoma (Lakeland). Contbr. articles to profl. jours. Home: Route 1 Box 345 1203 Lake Point Dr Lakeland FL 33803 Office: PO Box 2084 Lakeland FL 33803

PRIEBE, ELDEN PAUL, business exec.; b. Chgo., Aug. 15, 1908; s. Paul R. and Myrtle F. (Prisk) P.; B.S. with honors, U. Ill., 1930; m. Jeanette F. Smallfeldt, Apr. 17, 1933; 1 dau., Janice M. (Mrs. John C. Windsor, Jr.). With Skelly Oil Co., 1933-40, 44-52, internal auditor, 1944-52; controller Spartan Aircraft Co., 1940-44; sec., treas. Bay Petroleum Corp., 1952-55; with Tenneco Inc., Houston, 1955—, controller, 1958-68, v.p., 1961—. C.P.A., Tex., Colo., Okla. Mem. Financial Execs. Inst., Am. Inst. C.P.A.s, Am. Petroleum Inst., Beta Alpha Psi, Phi Kappa Sigma, Beta Gamma Sigma. Episcopalian. Mason. Clubs: Houston, Panorama Country (Conroe, Tex.); Harvard Business School. Home: 10220 Memorial Dr Houston TX 77024 Office: PO Box 2511 Houston TX 77001

PRIEN, JOHN DANIEL, JR., engring. assn. exec.; b. Ord, Neb., Apr. 2, 1930; s. John Daniel and Elsie (Malottke) P.; B.S., U. Neb., 1953, J.D., 1958; m. Joanne Frances Eppard, June 21, 1953; children—Deborah Kay, Deanna Lynn, John Daniel III. Project engr. Kirkham-Michael & Assos., Omaha, 1958-59; chief civil engr. Lincoln AFB, Neb., 1959-62; contract adminstr. Pan Am. Airways, Cape Kennedy, Fla., 1962-66; acting data mgr. IBM Corp., Cape Kennedy, Fla., 1966-67; exec. dir. Ga. Soc. Profl. Engrs., Atlanta, 1967—. Cons. on environmental health Comprehensive Health Planning Council, Ga. Dept. Pub. Health; mem. Gov.'s Adv. Com. on Ga. Housing Code, 1971-72; mem. Dekalb County (Ga.) Housing Codes Adv. Com., 1971-72. Vice chmn. small bus. div. Heart Fund, Atlanta, 1969-70. Candidate, Ga. Ho. of Reps., 1972. Served with C.E., AUS, 1953-55. Registered profl. engr., Neb., Fla., Ga. Mem. Am., Neb. bar assns., Nat. (vice chmn. state soc. adminstrs. council 1970-72), Ga. socs. profl. engrs., Am. Soc. C.E., Ga. Soc. Assn. Execs. (pres. 1972-73). Editor: Ga. Profl Engr. mag., 1967—. Home: 3861 Foxford Dr NE Atlanta GA 30340 Office: 1375 Peachtree St NE Atlanta GA 30309

PRIEST, BILL JASON, ednl. adminstr.; b. French, Camp, Cal., Sept. 23, 1917; s. Jesse and Clarissa (Stubbs) P.; student Modesto Jr. Coll., 1934-35; A.B., U. Cal. at Berkeley, 1938, M.A., 1946, Ed.D., 1947; postdoctoral study Columbia, 1954-55; m. Marietta F. Shaw, Mar. 8, 1941; 1 son, Andy J. Profl. baseball player Phila. Athletics, 1938, Oakland Oaks, 1939; tchr., coach Modesto Jr. Coll., 1939-40, Mountain View High Sch., 1940-47; supr. Vallejo Jr. Coll., 1947-48; dean, asst. supt. Orange Coast Coll., 1948-55; supt., pres. Am. River Jr. Coll., 1955-64; dist. supt. Los Rios Jr. Coll. Dist., 1964-65; pres. Dallas County Jr. Coll. Dist., 1965-67, chancellor, 1967—. Past mem. bd. Nat. Commn. Accreditation; commr., mem. higher edn. adv. com. Edn. Commn. of States; Mem. Nat. Adv. Council Grad. Edn.; bd. dirs., exec. com. S.W. Ednl. Devel. Lab.; exec. com. of bd. trustees League Innovation in Community Coll.; edn. com. Commn. Environment Tex. Soc. Architects; regional adv. com. Regional Med. Program Tex. Exec. bd. Circle Ten Council Boy Scouts Am. Trustee Aerospace Edn. Found. Served to lt. comdr. USNR, 1941-46. Mem. Am. Assn. Jr. Colls., (bd. dirs., pres. 1966-67; rep. to edn. commn. states), Cal. Jr. Coll. Assn. (legislative chmn., past pres.), Internat. Chili Appreciation Soc., Phi Delta Kappa. Rotarian. Home: 7210 Twin Tree Lane Dallas TX 75214 Office: Main and Lamar Sts Dallas TX 75202

PRIEST, GERALD GORDON, chem. co. exec.; b. Little Rock, Nov. 23, 1930; s. August E. and Helen (Tyson) P.; B.S., Ark. State Tchrs. Coll., 1951; M.S., Auburn U., 1953; m. Peggy Probst, Sept. 30, 1950. Research fellow, instr. chemistry Auburn U., 1952; research engr. Humble Oil & Refining Co., Houston, 1953-58; v.p. research and devel. Dixie Chem. Co., Houston, 1958-72, pres., 1972—, also dir.; v.p., dir. Dixie Chem. Products, Inc., 1967—; dir. Dixie Chem. Service Co., Inc. Served with USN, 1945-47. Mem. Am. Chem. Soc., A.A.A.S., Tex. Mid-Continent Oil & Gas Assn., Sigma Xi. Methodist. Contbr. articles, patentee in field. Home: 2141 Stanmore Houston TX 77019 Office: 3635 W Dallas St at S Sheperd St Houston TX 77019

PRIEST, JAMES ROBERT, physician; b. Pontotoc, Miss., Oct. 18, 1939; s. John Robert and Rebecca Marie (Reinhardt) P.; student Northeastern State Coll., Tahlequah, Okla., 1957-60; M.D., U. Okla., 1964; m. Linda Kay Burrows, June 17, 1961; children—John Robert, Michael Vernon, William Richard. Intern, St. John's Hosp., Tulsa, 1964-64; practice medicine, specializing in family practice, Pawhuska, Okla., 1967—; mem. staff Pawhaska Med Clinic, 1967—; mem. staffs Pawhuska Hosp.; asso. preceptor Okla. U. Sch. Medicine, 1967—. Mem. Bd. Edn., Pawhuska, 1969—, pres., 1972. Served to capt. USAF, 1965-67. Recipient Air Force Commendation medal. Mem. A.M.A., Okla. Med. Soc., Osage County Med. Soc. (sec. 1968-71, v.p. 1971-72, pres. 1972). Phi Lambda Chi. Presbyn. (elder 1972—, deacon 1968—). Home: 203 E 11th St Pawhuska OK 74056 Office: 701 Leahy St Pawhuska OK 74056

PRIESTER, AMOS ULMER, III, hotel exec.; b. LaGrange, Ga., Aug. 13, 1933; s. Amos Ulmer and Rebekah (Herring) P.; B.S. in Secondary Edn., Clemson U., 1956; m. Peggy Cofield, Jan. 29, 1955; children—Amos Ulmer, IV, Peter G., Rebecah Jo. Athletic dir. Camden (S.C.) High Sch., 1963; innkeeper Downtowner Corp., Memphis, 1963-64, regional mgr., 1965-66, nat. tng. supr., 1966-67; gen. mgr. Blount Bros. Enterprises, Inc., Greensboro, N.C., 1967-69, pres., 1970; pres. Interstate Inns, Inc., Greensboro, 1970—. Served with AUS, 1956-58. Mem. N.C. Hotel and Motel Assn. (dir. 1968-69), Kappa Phi Kappa (pres. 1955). Baptist. Moose, Lion. Home: 3229 Edenwood St Greensboro NC 27406 Office: PO Box 5525 Greensboro NC 27403

PRIESTER, FRANCIS ALLEN, elec. engr.; b. Augusta, Ga., July 6, 1924; s. Wyman Jesse and Bessie Bell (Corley) P.; Jr. Coll. certificate, Middle Ga. Coll., 1947; B.E.E., Ga. Inst. Tech., 1949; m. Hazel Maxine Linnville, Apr. 22, 1950; children—Allen, Judy. Jr. engr. Gulf Power Co., Pensacola, Fla., 1949-51; elec. engr. U.S. Navy Mine Def. Lab., Panama City, Fla., 1951-60; elec. engr. inertial guidance and control lab. U.S. Army Missile Command, Redstone Arsenal, Ala., 1960-70, chief short range land combat br. maintenance engring. div., 1970—. Served with USNR, 1943-46. Registered profl. engr., Ala. Mem. Nat. Soc. Profl. Engrs., I.E.E.E. (past chmn. Huntsville chpt.), Am. Ordnance Assn., Assn. U.S. Army. Presbyn. (elder). Home: 3410 Euclid Circle Huntsville AL 35810 Office: AMSMI-NES Redstone Arsenal AL 35809

PRIGMORE, CHARLES SAMUEL, educator; b. Lodge, Tenn., Mar. 21, 1919; s. Charles H. and Mary Lou (Raulston) P.; A.B., U. Chattanooga, 1939; M.S., U. Wis., 1947, Ph.D., 1961; m. Shirley Melaine Buuck, June 7, 1947; 1 son, Philip Brand. Social caseworker Children's Service Soc., Milw., 1947-48; social worker Wis. Sch. for Boys, Waukesha, 1948-51; supr. tng. Wis. Bur. Probation and Parole, Madison, 1951-56; supt. Tenn. Vocational Tng. Sch. for Boys, Nashville, 1956-59; asso. prof. La. State U., 1959-64; ednl. cons. Council Social Work Edn., N.Y., 1962-64; Exec. Dir. Joint Commn. Correctional Manpower & Tng., Washington, 1964-67; prof. Sch. Social Work, U. Ala., 1967—, chmn. com. on Korean relationships; part-time cons. with four research projects, 1959-65; part-time tchr. U. Md., 1965—; frequent lectr. and workshop leader. Chmn. Ala. Citizens Environmental Action, 1971-72, Tuscaloosa Council Environmental Quality, 1970-72. Served to 2d lt. USAAF, 1940-45. Decorated Air medal with oak leaf cluster. Recipient Conservation award Woodmen of the World, 1971. Mem. Acad. Certified Social Workers, Am. Correctional Assn., Am. Assn. U. Profs., Am. Soc. Criminology, Am. Sociol. Assn., Council Social Work Edn., Nat. Assn. Social Workers, Nat. Council Crime and Delinquency, Royal Soc. Health, Tuscaloosa C. of C., Tuscaloosa Civitan Club, Alpha Kappa Delta, Beta Beta Beta. Author: Textbook on Social Problems, 1971. Editor 2 books. Contbr. articles in field to profl. jours. Home: 19 High Forest St Tuscaloosa AL 35401 Office: U Ala University AL 35486

PRIM, WILLIS GERALD, banker; b. Ridgeway, Tex., May 6, 1905; s. George Stevenson and Verna Mae (Stewart) P.; student E.Tex. State Coll., Commerce, 1921-23; m. Doris Robinson, Dec. 16, 1944; children— Mary Kathrine (Mrs. P. F. Bradley), Alice (Mrs. Don W. Bradley), Ruth Ann (Mrs. Charles Britton). With Ridgeway State Bank, 1924-27; dir., chief exec. officer Sulphur Springs (Tex.) State Bank, 1927—; dir. Sulphur Springs Loan & Bldg. Assn. Treas., Hopkins County Crippled Childrens Assn., Hopkins County Rural Progress Club. Presbyn. (elder). K.P., Rotarian. Club: Sulphur Springs Country (dir., past pres.). Home: 505 Jefferson St Sulphur Springs TX 75482 Office: 100 W Jefferson St Sulphur Springs TX 75482

PRINCE, DAVID HYDE, educator; b. Dunngannon, Va., Mar. 2, 1922; s. Walter Eugene and Mary Hunter (Palmer) P.; A.B., Wofford Coll., 1947, M.A., 1951; Ph.D., U. N.C., 1959; m. Jennie Theresa Cox, Aug. 21, 1948; children—David Hyde, Theresa Brooks. Athletic dir., tchr. Tryon (N.C.) High Sch., 1947-54, E. Mecklenburg High Sch., Charlotte, N.C., 1954-55; adminstrv. asst. continuation edn. U.N.C. Sch. Medicine, 1955-58; prof. edn. and psychology, chmn. edn. dept. Wofford Coll., Spartanburg, S.C., 1958—. Cons. indsl. psychology Butte Knitting Mills, Spartanburg, S.C., 1967, Learning Founds. of Carolinas, 1967-68; vis. prof. summer sch. Furman U., 1965-69. Served with AUS, 1943-46; ETO. Decorated Purple Heart; named Gold Honor Club Pres., Sertoma Club, 1969. Mem. S.C. Coll. Tchrs. Edn. (pres. 1960-61), N.E.A., S.C. Edn. Assn. Presbyn. Home: 225 Ponce de Leon Av Spartanburg SC 29302

PRINCE, JULIAN DAY, supt. schs.; b. Greenwood, Miss., Mar. 5, 1927; s. Julian Day and Lois (Jones) P.; B.S., Millsaps Coll., 1949; M.Ed., Emory U., 1953; m. LaVerne Carnell Baker, Jan. 22, 1949; children—Joanne, Julian, John, David. Tchr., McComb (Miss.) High Sch., 1949-52, prin. 1953-59; asst. supt. McComb Pub. Schs., 1959-60, supt., 1965—; supt. Corinth (Miss.) Pub. Schs., 1960-65; pres. Edn. Systems Devel. Corp., 1968—; mgr. manpower div. Miss. Research and Devel. Corp., 1969-70. Scoutmaster, Yocona Area council Boy Scouts Am., 1963-67; chmn. Community Fund Drive, Corinth, 1963-64; v.p. Miss. Council Pub. Sch. Systems, 1971; mem. Miss. Commn. on Hosp. Care, 1963—. Served with AUS, 1945-47; PTO. Ford Found. fellow, 1952-53. Mem. Am., Miss. assns. sch. adminstrs., Miss. Edn. Assn., Millsaps Coll. Alumni Assn. (dir. 1961—), Lambda Chi Alhpa. Methodist (ch. steward 1957—). Lion. Home: 647 Louisiana Av McComb MS 39648

PRINCE, WILLIAM HURSCHEL, JR., advt. agy. exec.; b. Brownwood, Tex., Mar. 28, 1922; s. William Hurschel and Ruth Grady P.; B.J., U. Tex., 1950; m. Mary Lois Pruitt, June 9, 1946; children—Mary Ann, Linda Jane. Editor, gen. mgr. Comanche Times (Tex.), 1950; program dir., asst. mgr., sales mgr. radio sta. KSTV, Stephenville, Tex., 1950-52 nat. advt. sales mgr. Nat. Future Farmer, Washington, 1952-56; asso. account exec. Campbell-Mithun, Inc., Mpls., 1956-57, account exec., 1957-58, account dir., 1958-59; merchandising mgr. Frito-Lay, Inc., Dallas, 1959-66; pres. Prestige Foods, Inc., Dallas, 1966—; founder, mng. partner Creative Guides, pub. relations and advt., Dallas; dir. Bahia-Mar Corp., Town Crier, Inc. Cons. Lew Williams & Assn. Mem. agrl. com. Mpls. C. of C., 1957-59; mem. membership com. Dallas Better Bus. Bur., 1961; adviser Jr. Achievement, 1964-65. Served with USNR, 1942-45. Recipient internat. Sales Promotion Man of Year award Sales Promotion Execs. Assn., 1965, Nat. Sales Leadership award Houston Sales Assn., 1965. Republican. Baptist. Home: 6727 Santa Anita St Dallas TX 75214

PRINDLE, RICHARD A(LAN), pub. health adminstr.; b. Mansfield, O., Dec. 28, 1925; s. Raymond and Georgia Anna (Richardson) P.; student, Centenary Coll., La., 1942-44; M.D., Harvard, 1948, M.P.H. cum laude, 1954; m. Susannah Budd Freeman, Mar. 17, 1951; children—Mark R., Timothy E. Research fellow epidemiology Harvard Med. Sch., 1948-51, research asso., 1951-54; commd. USPHS, 1951, now med. dir.; asst. chief poliomyelitis investigations USPHS, 1951-53; asst. chief health and sanitation div. ICA, Haiti, 1954-57; epidemiologist air pollution program USPHS, 1954-60, dep. chief div. air pollution, 1960-63, chief div. pub. health methods Office Surgeon Gen., 1963-66, asst. surgeon gen., 1964-71, chief Bur. State Services, 1964-66, dir. Bur. Disease Prevention and Environmental Control, 1966-68, spl. asst. to surg. gen., 1968-70. Vis. lectr. U. Pa., 1961-70; chief dept. Health and Population Dynamics Pan Am. Health Orgn., 1970—. Fed. Exec. fellow Center for Advanced Study, Brookings Instn.; mem. expert com. on air pollution WHO, 1963—; cons. adv. com. health statistics Pan Am. Health Orgn., 1964—. Bd. dirs. Phipps Inst., Phila., 1961-65; mem. adv. com. environmental scis. Nat. Colls. Art and Scis. Recipient Meritorious Service medal USPHS, 1963. Diplomate Am. Bd. Pub. Health and Preventive Medicine. Fellow A.A.A.S., Am. Coll. Preventive Medicine, Am. Pub. Health Assn.; mem. A.M.A., Royal Soc. Health, Assn. Tchrs. Preventive Medicine, Air Pollution Control Assn., (dir. 1962-63). Contbr. articles to profl. jours. Home: 4909 Cumberland Av Chevy Chase MD Office: 525 23d St NW Washington DC 20037

PRITCHARD, CLARENCE HUBERT, city ofcl.; b. Elizabeth City, N.C., Nov. 26, 1909; s. Miles Rufus and El Dora (Davis) P.; LL.B., Wake Forest Coll., 1932; m. Shelton Elizabeth Twiddy, June 20, 1931; children—William Miles, Charles Scott. Financial adminstr. Office of City Clk., Raleigh, N.C., 1955—. Mem. gen. bd. Bapt. State Conv., 1969-71. Mem. Municipal Finance Officers Assn., Delta Sigma Chi. Democrat. Baptist (deacon 1945-70). Club: Exchange (pres. 1954). Home: 3520 Bellevue Rd Raleigh NC 27609 Office: PO Box 590 Raleigh NC 27602

PRITCHARD, JOHN HAYES, architect; b. Indpls., May 5, 1905; s. John M. and Leona Dell (Hayes) P.; B.S. in Architecture, Ga. Sch. Tech., 1930; m. Charlie Lowe, June 10, 1930; 1 son, John Hayes. Archtl. designer, draftsman, Beaumont, Tex., 1928-34; designer rural farm communities U.S. Govt., Austin, 1934-36; asso. bd. govs. Fed. Res. System, Washington, 1937; chief architect Nat. Youth Adminstrn., Washington, 1938-40, so regional dir., Memphis, 1940-42; pvt. practice architecture, Tunica, Miss., 1946—; asso. Pritchard & Nickles, architects and engrs., Tunica, 1951—. Alderman, Town Bd., Tunica, Miss. Exec. com. Boy Scouts Am., 1947—, chmn. dist. com., 1948-59, mem. nat. council 1952—, mem. nominating com. Delta Area council Silver Beaver award, 1957. Served as maj., AUS, 1943-46. Decorated Bronze Star medal. Registered architect Miss., Tenn., Tex., Ark. Fellow A.I.A. (pres. Miss. chpt. 1950-51, mem. nominating com.; mem. nat. jud. bd.; nat. bd. examiners 1955-56; regional dir. Gulf States region; Miss. chmn. legislative com. 1963); mem. Miss. Archtl. Assn., Soc. Friends Tewkesbury Abbey (life), Soc. Archtl. Historians (Delta council coms., health com. ednl. policy com.) North Miss., Miss. archeol. assns., V.F.W., 40 and 8, Am. Legion, Sigma Phi Epsilon. Episcopalian (mission bd.). Rotarian (pres. 1950-51). Address: PO Box 236 Tunica MS 38676

PRITCHARD, WILLIAM SHELTON, JR., lawyer; b. Birmingham, Ala., Dec. 24, 1924; s. William Shelton and Catharine (Robinson) P.; A.B., U. Ala., 1947, LL.B., 1950; m. Ann Brooking Adams, Apr. 8, 1953; children— William Shelton III, Franklin Adams, Thomas McCoy. Admitted to Ala. bar, 1950; practiced in Birmingham, 1950—; mem. firm Prichard, McCall & Jones, 1955—. Dir., v.p. Home Fed. Savs. & Loan Assn.; mem. adv. bd. 1st Nat. Bank. Bd. dirs. Met. YMCA, Greater Birmingham Ministries; trustee U. Ala. Law Sch. Found. Served to lt. USNR, 1943-46, 50-52. Mem. Ala. State Bar, Am., Birmingham (exec. com.) bar assns., U. Ala. Alumni Assn. (past pres. local chpt.), Farrah Law Soc. (v.p.), Am. Legion (officer). Mem. Ch. of Advent (vestryman). Club: Monday Morning Quarterback (dir.). Home: 3805 Knollwood Lane Birmingham AL 35243 Office: Frank Nelson Bldg Birmingham AL 35203

PRITCHARTT, VAN, JR., newspaper editor. City editor Press-Scimitar, Memphis. Office: 495 Union Av Memphis TN 38101*

PRITZ, ROBERT WILLIAM, JR., dentist; b. Denver, Sept. 5, 1932; s. Robert William and Ann G. (Foster) P.; B.S., Denver U., 1960; D.D.S., Baylor U., 1964; m. Freda Gutschow, Sept. 15, 1954; 1 son, Robert William III. Practice dentistry, Plano, Tex., 1964—. Served with USAF, 1950-56. Mem. Plano Jr. C. of C. (pres., 1965), Am. Dental Assn., Tex. Dental Assn., Dallas County Dental Soc., Dallas Dento-Econ. Soc. (pres., 1969-70), S.W. Soc. Dental Analgesia (v.p., 1970-71). Home: 3017 Brookview St Plano TX 75074 Office: 1410 14th St Plano TX 75074

PRIVETT, REX, speaker Okla. Ho. of Reps., rancher; b. Maramec, Okla., May 28, 1924; s. Arnold Loyde and Muriel (Hauser) P.; B.A., Okla. State U., 1949; m. Patricia Ann Nichols, Aug. 8, 1947 children—Deborah Ann (Mrs. James R. Fletcher), Rex Nichols, Patricia Michelle. Rancher, Maramec, Okla., 1949—; mem. Okla. Ho. of Reps., 1957—, vice chmn. State Personnel Com., 1959-61, chmn. County, State and Fed. Govt. Com., 1961-63, speaker pro tempore, 1963-67, speaker Ho. Reps., 1967—. Mem. exec. com. Nat. Conf. State Legislative Leaders, 1969—; mem. exec. com. Council State Govt., 1969—, v.p., 1970; mem. exec. com. Nat. Legislative Council, 1969—, So. Conf. Council State Govts., 1969—. Committeeman Boy Scouts Am., 1965—, council mem. at large Will Rogers Council, 1967—; hon. mem. Pawnee Indian Tribe, 1967—. Mem. bd. dirs. Bi-State Mental Health Found. Mem. Ambassadors Corps. Served with AUS, 1943-46; PTO. Recipient Gold Watch, Pawnee C. of C., 1967. Mem. Pawnee County Cattlemen's Assn. (pres. 1953-57), Kappa Sigma (treas. 1946-49). Democrat. Methodist (chmn. ofcl. bd. 1954-55; lay speaker 1955—). Home: Route 1 Maramec OK 74045 Office: Speaker's Office Okla State Capitol Oklahoma City OK 73105

PRIVETTE, JAMES ATLAS, dentist; b. Wilson, N.C., June 12, 1933; s. James Edward and Lois (Motley) P.; B.S., Wake Forest Coll., 1955; D.D.S., U. N.C., 1964; m. Ruth Nelson Partin, June 4, 1955; children— James Atlas II, Julia Annette. Pvt. practice dentistry, Kinston, N.C., 1964—; part-time asst. prof. U. N.C. Sch. Dentistry. Mem. exec. com. E. Carolina council Boy Scouts Am., 1965—, finance chmn. Caswell dist., 1969; chmn. Lenoir County United Cerebral Palsy, 1966-67; crusade vice-chmn. Lenoir County unit Am. Cancer Soc., 1967, chmn. 1968, pres., 1970. Mem. Kinston C. of C. (dir.), Kinston Fedn. Ch. Sch. Men (pres. 1969-70), Am. Dental Assn., Am. Soc. Dentistry for Children, N.C. (asso. editor jour. 1969—), 5th Dist. (editor 1965-68, sec.-treas. 1968-72, pres. 1972—) dental socs. Republican. Presbyn. (chmn. bd. deacons 1968, elder 1969—). Home: 2104 St George Pl Kinston NC 28501 Office: 2201 N Herritage St Kinston NC 28501

PROCTER, JOSEPH WINSTON, drug co. exec.; b. Houston, Aug. 29, 1912; s. Doak Chambers and Lillian Ora (Pennick) P.; B.A., Southwestern U., Georgetown, Tex., 1935; postgrad. U. Wis., 1936; m. Jimmie Ruth Nixon, Jan. 29, 1941. Athletic coach Beaumont High Sch., (Tex.), 1935-36; owner Procter Sport Shop, Beaumont, 1937-42; pres. Jefferson Drug Co., Inc., Beaumont, 1960—; dir. First Fed. Savings & Loan Assn, Am. Nat. Bank (both Beaumont). Gen. chmn. United Fund Drive, 1963. Bd. regents com. Lamar U., Beaumont. Served with USNR, 1941-45. Mem. Nat. Wholesale Druggists Assn., Nat. Assn. Wholesalers, Beaumont C. of C. (pres. 1961), Phi Delta Theta. Rotarian. Clubs: Sales Executives (pres. 1960), Country (Beaumont), Beaumont. Home: 1255 19th St Beaumont TX 77706 Office: 950 Grand Av Beaumont TX 77701

PROCTER, REGINALD JARVIS, sch. prin.; b. Raleigh, N.C., Dec. 3, 1924; s. Ivan Marriott and Madeline Jane (Jones) P.; B.S., Wake Forest Coll., 1948; M.Ed., U. N.C., 1960; m. Earleen Virginia Humphreys, Sept. 17, 1955; children—Lucy Ann, Elizabeth Humphreys, Rebecca Battle. Tchr., Episcopal High Sch., Alexandria, Va., 1950-53; tchr. Fishburne Mil. Sch., Waynesboro, Va., 1953-55; counselor Hugh Morson Jr. High Sch., Raleigh, 1955-62, prin., 1962-64; prin. Charles B. Aycock Jr. High Sch., Raleigh, 1964—. Mem. Mayor's Drug Com., 1970-71; dist. commr. Occoneechee council Boy Scouts Am. Served with AUS, 1946-47. Recipient Silver Beaver award Boy Scouts Am., 1966. Mem. Nat. Assn. Secondary Sch. Prins., N.C. Assn. Educators. Methodist (mem. ch. bd. 1968-70). Club: Raleigh Kiwanis (dir. 1968-71). Home: 2217 Dixie Trail Raleigh NC 27607 Office: 128 Clarendon Crescent Raleigh NC 27610

PROCTOR, CHARLES LAFAYETTE, educator; b. nr. Collinsville, Okla., Feb. 28, 1923; s. Emory and Jessie (Rains) P.; B.S. in Mech. Engring., Okla. State U., 1951, Ph.D., 1963; M.S. in Mech. Engring., Purdue U., 1955. With Beech Aircraft Corp., 1951-53; instr. Purdue U., 1953-55; missile engr. McDonnell Aircraft Corp., 1955-56; asst. prof. mech. engring. U. Toronto, 1956-63; asso. prof. indsl. and systems engring. U. Okla., 1963-66; resident dir., prof. indsl. and systems engring. U. Fla., Daytona Beach, 1966-68, prof. U. Fla., Gainesville, 1969-70; resident dir. Grad. Engring. system U. Fla., West Palm Beach, 1970—. Cons. Apollo support dept. Gen. Electric Corp., 1967—; cons. Embry Riddle Aero. U., 1967—; also trustee. Bd. dirs. Volusia County (Fla.) Mental Health Assn. Served with USNR, 1942-46. Mem. Am. Soc. M.E., Am. Inst. Indsl. Engrs., Sigma Xi, Tau Beta Pi, Alpha Pi Mu, Pi Tau Sigma, Sigma Tau. Mason (Shriner), Rotarian. Author: Analysis of a Hydromechanical Control Element, 1955. Contbr. profl. jours. Home: 223 Atlantic Av Palm Beach FL 33480 Office: Grad Engring Edn System West Palm Beach FL 33401

PROCTOR, FRANK SCOTT, radio broadcasting co. exec.; b. Nashville, May 30, 1910; s. Robert Lee and Martha (Scott) P.; B.Engring., Vanderbilt U., 1932; m. Patty Brown Harvey, Dec. 2, 1936; 1 dau., Patty Harvey. With sales dept. Tenn. div. Standard Oil Co. La., 1932-36; refinery insp. Standard Oil Devel. Co., Linden, N.J., 1936-46; mgr. radio sta. WTJS, v.p., dir. Sun Pub. Co., Jackson, Tenn., 1946—; sec.-treas. Kelly Foods, Inc., Jackson, 1958—; dir. First Nat. Bank, Jackson. Pres., Jackson United Fund, 1961, YMCA, 1964. Mem. Jackson C. of C. (pres. 1950), Tenn. Assn. Broadcasters (pres. 1951), Tau Beta Pi. Presbyn. (elder). Rotarian (pres. 1952). Home: 410 Walnut Av Jackson TN 38301 Office: 255 W Lafayette St Jackson TN 38301

PROCTOR, JAMES THORNTON, psychiatrist; b. Blytheville, Ark., Nov. 20, 1922; s. Cloud Colbert and Hettie (Garrett) P.; A.B., U. Kan., 1943, M.D., 1946; m. Bobbie Lee Hilton, May 8, 1953 (dec. May, 1968); children—Kirk, Mark. Intern, Providence Hosp., Kansas City, Kan., 1946-47; resident VA Hosp., Denver, 1951-52, U. Colo. Sch. Med., 1952-53, New Orleans Guidance Center, 1953-54; pvt. practice psychiatry Tulsa, 1962—; mem. staff Children's Med. Center, St. John's, Hillcrest, St. Francis hosps., (all Tulsa), U. Hosp., Oklahoma City; asso. prof. child psychiatry U. N.C. Sch. Med., Chapel Hill, 1953-62; med., tng. dir. Children's Med. Center, Tulsa, 1962—; clin. prof. U. Okla. Med. Center, Oklahoma City, 1962—. Served to lt. (j.g.) M.C., USNR, 1947-50. Fellow Am. Psychiat. Assn., Am. Orthopsychiatric Assn., Am. Assn. Mental Deficiency; mem. Tau Kappa Epsilon, Nu Sigma Nu. Home: 2606 E 57th Pl Tulsa OK 74135 Office: 4818 S Lewis St Tulsa OK 74105

PROCTOR, JESSE VIRGIL, mech. engr.; b. LaGrange, Ky., Aug. 31, 1905; s. Richard and Leah (Tharp) P.; B.S., U. Ky., 1930; postgrad. Princeton and Mass. Inst. Tech., 1944; m. Elizabeth Hazlitt Hanson, Mar 28, 1932; children—James Virgil, Eleanor Hanson (Mrs. Alfred E. Coleman). Field engr. Ky-W.Va. Gas Co., 1930-35; engr. charge constrn. U. Ky., 1935-42; mech. disign engr. Wilson, Bell & Watkins, 1942-44; pres. Proctor-Ingels & Assos., Inc., Lexington, Ky., 1946—; dir. J.J. Tuttle & Assos., Inc.; pres. P.I.S.W., Inc. Served with USAAF, 1944-46; PTO. Recipient Medal of Freedom, Gen. Curtis E. LeMay, 1946. Mem. Cons. Engrs. Council Ky. (past pres.), Nat. Cons. Engrs. Council (dir. 1965). Episcopalian. Home: 210 Shady Lane Lexington KY 40503 Office: 915 Limestone St Lexington KY 40503

PROCTOR, JOHN HOWARD, scientist, research co. exec.; b. Bronx, N.Y., June 3, 1931; s. John Carol and Carolyn Elizabeth (Slade) P.; B.S., Davidson Coll., 1953; M.S., Purdue U., 1954, Ph.D., 1958; m. Emily Jayne Alexander, Dec. 28, 1956; children—Donna Lynn, Susan Carol, John Christopher, James Alexander. Cons., Humble Oil and Refining Co., 1957-58; dir. tng. and personnel research bleached bd. div. W.Va. Pulp & Paper Co., 1958-60; tech. staff Mitre Corp., 1960-64; sr. project dir. Data Dynamics Inc., 1964-66; gen. mgr. Eastern operations Mellonics div. Litton Systems Inc., 1966-70; pres., chmn. bd. Data Solutions Corp., Washington, 1970—, Mgmt. Information Systems, Inc. 1963—. Served with AUS, 1954-56. Mem. A.A.A.S., Am. Psychol. Assn., Soc. Gen. Systems Research (v.p. Fla. chpt. 1964-66), Sigma Xi. Mem. Disciples of Christ Ch. Mason (32 deg.), Elk. Author: (with W.M. Thornton) Training- A Handbook for Line Managers, 1961; Organizational Climate Audit, 1970. Contbr. articles to profl. jours. Developer controlled exercises (Contex) for U.S. Air Force, 1962; designer for Dept. Def. Computer Inst., 1964. Home: 505 Arnon Meadow Rd Great Falls VA 22066 Office: Suite 100 5272 River Rd Bethesda MD 20016

PROCTOR, MELVIN P(ORCH), constrn. co. exec.; b. Cisco, Tex., Aug. 8, 1928; s. Jess and Ima (Leveridge) P.; student Cisco Jr. Coll., 1945, 47, U. Houston, 1949-51; m. Rita B. Henderson, Apr. 28, 1950; children—Stephen Jeffrey, Donna Rae, Linda Diane, Gwen Ann. Salesman, Able Supply Co., Houston, 1950-56; v.p. Thorpe Insulation Co., 1956-60; v.p. J.T. Thorpe Co., constrn., 1960—; dir., sec.-treas. Thorpe Insulation Co., Corpus Christi, Tex., 1966—; dir., sec. Thorpe Realty Co., Houston, 1963-69. Active Boy Scouts Am. Served with AUS, 1946-47. Mem. Thermal Insulation Soc. (bd. dirs. 1959-61). Republican. Clubs: Glenbrook Valley Civic (bd. dirs. 1970-72), Golfcrest Country (Houston). Home: 7515 Rockhill St Houston TX 77017 Office: 6833 Kirbyville St Houston TX 77033

PROCTOR, SAMUEL, educator; b. Jacksonville, Fla., Mar. 29, 1919; s. Jack and Celia (Schneider) P.; B.A., U. Fla., 1941, M.A., 1942, Ph.D., 1958; postgrad. U. N.C., 1948, Emory U., 1949; m. Bessie Rubin, Sept. 8, 1948; children—Mark Julian, Alan Lowell. With U.S. Army Engrs., Miami, Fla., 1942-43; mem. faculty U. Fla., Gainesville, 1946—, prof. history and social scis., 1963—, dir. oral history program, 1968—; co-dir. Doris Duke Southeastern Indian Oral History Program; vis. prof. history Jacksonville (Fla.) U., summers, 1963-66. Historian Fla. Civil War Centennial Commn., 1960-65; historian, cons. Fla. Pub. Relations Hall of Fame Commn., 1961—; cons. Fla. Bd. Parks and Historic Memls., 1965—, Fla. State Mus., 1968—, Historic Pensacola Preservation Bd., 1968; mem. adv. commn. Fla. div. Archives History and Records Mgmt., 1970—; mem. Fla. Am. Revolution Bicentennial Commn.; mem. Fla. review com. Nat. Register Hist. Places, 1971—; mem. adv. com. Am. Assn. State and Local Hist. Bicentennial Publs. Mem. exec. com. Fla. Anti-Defamation League, 1957—; pres. Gainesville chpt. Multiple Sclerosis Soc., 1958-61. Bd. dirs. Fla. State Mus., Gainesville, Jacksonville River Garden Home for Aged. Served with AUS, 1943-46. Named Fla. Historian of Year, Peace River Valley Hist. Soc., 1967; recipient Outstanding Alumnus award Tau Epsilon Phi, 1971. Mem. Fla. (dir. 1951-53, 61—), So. hist. assns., Am. Assn. State and Local History, Nat. Oral History Assn. (mem. council 1971—), Fla. Anthrop. Soc., Fla. Blue Key, Tau Epsilon Phi (recipient service award key 1953, Michael C.C. Lilienfeld Nat. Distinguished Service award 1958), Pi Kappa Phi, Alpha Kappa Delta, Phi Alpha Theta, Pi Gamma Mu. Democrat. Jewish religion. Author: Napoleon Bonaparte Broward, Florida's Fighting Democrat, 1950; Florida Commemorates the Civil War Centennial, 1962; Florida a Hundred Years Ago, 1966; Florida Historic Preservation Planning, 1971. Editor, author introduction: Dickison and His Men: Reminiscences of the War in Florida, 1962; series editor Floridiana Facsimile Series, Fla. Bicentennial Monograph Series; editor Eighteenth Century Florida and Its Borderlands, 1972. Contbr. articles profl. publs. Asso. editor Fla. Hist. Quar., 1962-64, editor, 1964—. Home: 2235 NW 9th Pl Gainesville FL 32601

PROFFITT, JOHN ROSCOE, JR., textile co. exec.; b. Tifton, Ga., July 31, 1924; s. John R. and Floreid (Adams) P.; B.A., Emory U., 1944, M.A., 1948, Ph.D., 1950; m. Sybil Joyce Harrison, Mar. 13, 1948; children— John Roscoe III, William Terrell. Research chemist E.I. du Pont de Nemours, Waynesboro, Va., 1950-55, research supr., 1955-59; pres., dir. Proffitt Masters, Dalton, Ga., 1956—; exec. v.p., dir. Proffitt Textile Co., 1959—; pres., dir., Meat Seperator Corp., 1952—; treas., dir. Proffitt Sales Assn., Inc., 1971—; dir. Hardwick Bank and Trust Co., Dalton. Vice chmn. Bd. Edn., City of Dalton, 1961—; chmn. City of Dalton. Whitfield County Merger Commn., 1969-70. Bd. dirs. Jr. Achievement, Dalton, Big Bros., Dalton; bd. visitors Emory U. Served with AUS, 1944-56. Mem. Am. Chem. Soc., A.A.A.S., Am. Assn. Textile Chemists and Colourists, Sigma Xi, Phi Beta Kappa, Chi Phi. Democrat. Baptist. Club: Dalton Golf and Country. Patentee in field. Home: 1022 E Lakeshore Dr Dalton GA 30720 Office: Box 729 Dalton GA 30720

PROKOP, JULIUS JOSEPH, JR., accountant, retail sales co. exec.; b. Chgo., Apr. 4, 1936; s. Julius Joseph and Barbara (Novak) P.; B.A., Southeastern La. Coll., 1961; postgrad. La. State U., 1965-66; m. Helen O. Sykes, June 2, 1956; children—Julius Joseph III, Robert M., Edward J., Alexander S., Barbara V. Financial and mgmt. auditor U.S. Gen. Accounting Office, New Orleans, 1961-63; revenue agt., tax auditor Internal Revenue Service, Baton Rouge, 1963-66; individual practice accounting, Amite, La., 1966-70; comptroller A.E. Hood Cos., Amite, 1966-70; partner Prokop & Sykes, Hammond, La., 1971—. Trustee A.E. Hood Found. Served with USAF, 1954-58. C.P.A., La. Mem. Am. Inst. C.P.A.'s. Home: PO Box 408 Albany LA 70711 Office: 210 W Morris Hammond LA 70401

PROMISEL, NATHAN E., exec. dir. Nat. Materials Adv. Bd., Nat. Acad. Scis. Mem. Am. Soc. Metals (pres. 1971). Address: 12519 Davan Dr Silver Springs ME 20904*

PROTHRO, DUKE HAMILTON, dentist; b. Campti, La., Jan. 8, 1905; s. George Edmond and Mary Glenn (Hayes) P.; student N.W. La. State U., 1925, La. State U., 1926-27; D.D.S., Emory U., 1930; m. Edith Maureen Steele (dec. 1959); m. 2d Henri Dee Sneed Hamilton, Feb. 2, 1961; children—Kitty (Mrs. Keith Allan), Maureen; stepchildren—Hugh C. Hamilton III, Pattie (Mrs. Wesley Shamp), Robert C. Hamilton, Niki Hamilton. Pvt. practice dentistry, Zwolle, La., 1930-35, Shreveport, La., 1935—. Cons., instr. Dental Lab. Technitions, State La., 1957-58; asst. to chief oral surgery Confederate Meml. Hosp.; mem. staff Shreveport hosps. Served with USNG, 1922-23. Mem. Fedn. Dentaire Internationale, 4th Dist. Dental Soc. (com. chmn. 1940-41), Am., La. dental assns., Psi Omega, Pi Kappa Alpha. Democrat. Baptist. Elk. Clubs: Shreveport Country, Broadmoore Mens Golf, Met. Dinner (Shreveport). Home: 380 Albert St Shreveport LA 71105 Office: 6150 Line Av Shreveport LA 71106

PROTHRO, GEORGE WILLIAM, physician; b. Wesson, Ark., Dec. 29, 1920; s. Henry Bussey and Norma (Baker) P.; student Eastern N.M.U., 1938-40; B.S., U.N.M., 1942; M.D., Washington U. Med. Sch., 1945; M.P.H., Univ. of North Carolina, 1967; m. Anna Margaret Lark, Sept. 25, 1943; children—George Lark, Karen Ann. Intern Lincoln Gen. Hosp., Lincoln, Neb., 1945-46; pvt. practice pediatrics, Clovis, N.M., 1948-64; dist. health officer N.M. Dept. Pub. Health, Dist. 10, 1965-68; dir. Tulsa City-County Health Dept., 1968—; clin. asst. prof. U. Okla. Coll. Medicine and Health. Served as lt. (j.g.), M.C., USNR, 1946-47. Fellow Am. Pub. Health Assn., Am. Sch. Health Assn.; mem. A.M.A., Okla. Med. Soc., Tulsa County Med. Soc., Phi Kappa Phi, Phi Sigma, Kappa Mu Epsilon, Delta Omega. Methodist. Rotarian. Home: 5424 S 76th E Av Tulsa OK 74145 Office: 4616 E 15th St Tulsa OK 74145

PROTHRO, JOHNNIE WATTS, nutritionist; b. Atlanta, Feb. 26, 1922; d. John D. and Theresa (Young) Hines; B.S., Spelman Coll., 1941; M.S., Columbia, 1946; Ph.D., U. Chgo., 1952; m. Charles E. Prothro, Jr., Sept. 6, 1964; 1 dau., Darielle L. Instr., So. U., Scotlandville, La., 1946-47; asso. prof. Tuskegee Inst., Ala., 1952-64; prof. nutrition, 1968-72; program analyst nutrition program Center for Disease Control, Atlanta, 1972—; asso. prof. nutrition U. Conn. at Storrs, 1964-68. Mem. Am. Inst. Nutrition. Home: 919 Falcon Dr SW Atlanta GA 30311 Office: Center for Disease Control 1600 Clifton Rd NE Atlanta GA 30333

PROVEAUX, CURTIS LEROY, pub. health engr.; b. Jesup, Ga., Mar. 11, 1921; s. William Wesley and Mary (Croft) P.; B.S., U. Ga., 1948; M.P.H., U. Mich., 1958; m. Miriam Ruth Bufford, May 11, 1952; children— Sanford Bryan, Harlan Anthony. Pub. health engr. Athens-Clarke County (Ga.) Health Dept., 1948-56; dir. environmental health services dist. 14 (Ware, Clinch, Coffee, Atkinson counties), Waycross, Ga., 1956-70, dist. chief 14 counties, 1970—. Tchr. health edn. U. Ga. Off-Campus Center. Mem. community action com. Office Econ. Opportunity, 1967-72, mem. governing bd. Community Action Agy., 1969-72; radiol. def. officer Civil Def., 1958—; v.p. Waycross Civic Music Assn., 1967, Ware County Heart Assn., 1965, pres., 1966-70; dist. chmn. advancement Okefenokee Area council Boy Scouts Am., 1967-70, chmn. health and safety, 1969-70; v.p. Okefenokee Hist. Mus. Assn., 1968, pres., 1969-70. Trustee Cerebral Palsy Sch., Waycross. Recipient Outstanding Service award Lions Internat., 1964-65; 25-Year Service pin Ga. Health Dept., 1971; Service awards Ga. Heart Assn., 1968, 69. Registered profl. engr., Ga. Mem. Ga. Assn. Dist. Dirs. Environmental Sanitation (v.p. 1957-58, 69-70, pres. 1971), Ga. Soc. Profl. Engrs. (pres. Clarke County chpt. 1955, Ware chpt. 1963), Lambda Chi Alpha, Omicron Delta Kappa. Republican. Baptist (deacon, tchr., Sunday Sch. supt.). Elk. Home: 1504 Danora Dr Waycross GA 31501 Office: 1101 Church St Waycross GA 31501

PRUCINO, LAWRENCE JOSEPH, textile mill exec.; b. Wilmington, Del., June 9, 1925; s. Frank and Josephine (DeToro) P.; B.A., U. Del., 1947, M.S., 1948; Ph.D., Emory U., 1951; m. Marjorie Lowe, July 7, 1945; children—Linda, Tracey, Diane, Roger. Research chemist E.I. duPont de Nemours & Co., Deepwater Point, N.J., 1951-54; plant chemist Joseph Bancroft & Sons Co., Wilmington, Del., 1954-65; v.p., plant mgr. Holliston Mills., Inc., Kingsport, Tenn., 1965—; dir. Kingsport Nat. Bank. Pres. Jr. Achievment, Kingsport, 1969-70, bd. dirs., 1966-71; bd. dirs. Kingsport Sheltered Workhsop, 1966-71, Holston Valley Community Hosp., Kingsport, 1969-72. Served to lt. (j.g.) USNR, 1944-46. Mem. Am. Chem. Soc., Am. Legion. Presbyn. (elder). Rotarian. Club: Ridgefields Country. Home: 2964 Cliffside Rd Kingsport TN 37664 Office: PO Box 478 Kingsport TN 37662

PRUD'HOMME, ECK GABRIEL, JR., physician; b. Texarkana, Tex., Feb. 8, 1924; s. Eck Gabriel and Mary (Young) P.; student Tex. A. and M. U., 1941-43; B.S. in Physics, U. Chgo., 1948; postgrad. Rice Inst., 1946; M.D., U. Tex., 1952; m. Margaret Peavy Murray, Jan. 24, 1948; children—Ann Clark, Kay Eleanor. Intern Herman Hosp., Houston, 1952-53; gen. practice medicine, Winnie, Tex., 1953-57, Ft. Worth, 1957—; mem. staff St. Joseph Hosp., Ft. Worth, also v.p. medicine, 1970—. Vice pres., bd. dirs. Am. Civil Liberties Union, Fort Worth, 1968—, chmn. discrimination com., 1969—; founding pres. Ballet Concerto, Ft. Worth, 1969-70; moderator Great Books Group, Fort Worth, 1957—. Active campaigns Senator Yarborough, 1970-72, Eugene McCarthy, 1968. Chmn. bd. YMCA, Fort Worth, 1968-69; bd. dirs. Como Betterment Council, 1970-71. Served to 1st lt. USAAF, 1944-46; CBI. Roman Catholic. Kiwanian. Home: 6304 Genoa Rd Fort Worth TX 76116 Office: 5153 River Oaks Blvd Fort Worth TX 76114

PRUEFER, CLIFFORD HUEBNER, real estate exec.; b. Garfield, N.J., Mar. 4, 1915; s. Julius and Olga (Huebner) P.; B.B.A., U. Cin., 1937; M.A., U. Minn., 1939; m. Mary Carolyn Luther, June 11, 1953; children—Christina E. (stepdau.), Kent D., Catherine D. Instr. econs. U. Minn., 1938-40; classification investigator War Dept., 1941; economist OPA, 1941-42, 46-47; intelligence officer CIA, 1947-49; intelligence research specialist Air Force, 1949-63; dep. chief, coordination and integration group Def. Intelligence Agy., Dept. of Def., Washington, 1963-68, sr. civilian Eastern area office, 1968-70; now in real estate and politics. Vice chmn. Fairfax County Tenant Landlord Commn. Vice chmn. Providence Dist. Democratic Com. Served to lt. comdr. USNR, 1942-46; now capt. Res. Mem. Am. Legion, Beta Gamma Sigma, Tau Kappa Alpha, Omicron Delta Kappa, Phi Eta Sigma. Democrat. Presbyn. Club: Internat. Golf and Country. Home and office: 3407 Barkley Dr Fairfax VA 22030

PRUETT, HASKELL, educator; b. Mingus, Tex., June 16, 1897; s. Ozie D. and Minerva (Small) P.; B.S., Peabody Coll., 1926, M.A., 1930, Ph.D., 1933; M.S., U. Okla., 1930; m. Agnes Murray, July 28, 1920; children—Mildred, Dresslar. Sch. tchr., Greer County, Okla., 1917-20; county supt. schs., Greer County, 1920-23; state rural sch. supr. State Okla., 1923-26; dir. sch. bldgs. and transp. Okla. Dept. Edn., 1926-35; bus. mgr. Okla. State U., 1935-36, prof. ednl. 1936-48, head dept. photography, 1948—. Mem. Photog. Soc. Am., Profl. Photogs. Am., Phi Kappa Delta, Kappa Delta Pi. Baptist. Mason (32 deg.). Author articles on edn. and photography. Home: 155 S Redwood Dr Stillwater OK 74074

PRUETT, JEFFERSON WILLIAM, JR., soft drink co. exec.; b. Atlanta, Aug. 15, 1930; s. Jefferson W. and Marguerite (Smith) P.; B.F.A., U. Ga., 1952; m. Nancy Hart, June 7, 1958; children—Jefferson William III, Benjamin Hart. Indsl. editor Lockheed Aircraft Corp., Marietta, Ga., 1954-56; v.p. Conway Publs., Inc., Atlanta, 1956-59; dir. press relations Coca-Cola Co., Atlanta, 1959-63, mgr. pub. relations dept., 1963—; asst. v.p., 1971—. Served with AUS, 1952-54. Mem. Pub. Relations Soc. Am., Ga. Press Assn., Nat. Editorial Assn. Home: 1093 Blackshear Dr Decatur GA 30033 Office: 310 North Av NW Atlanta GA 30313

PRUETTE, CHURCHILL RAY, educator; b. Stokes, N.C., Oct. 3, 1917; s. Warner Miller and Gertrude (Hardy) P.; B.A., E. Carolina U., 1939; M.A., 1950; postgrad. Wake Forest Coll., 1946, U. N.C., Chapel Hill, 1960; m. Margaret Maria Allen, May 7, 1942. Sci. tchr. Edward Best High Sch., Louisburg, N.C., 1939-42, Mills High Sch., Louisburg, 1943-45, Franklinton (N.C.) Pub. Schs., 1945-49; mem. faculty Louisburg (N.C.) Coll., 1949—, prof. chemistry, physics, 1949—, chmn. sci. dept., 1958—. Pres., Franklin County unit Am. Cancer Soc., 1959, state dir. N.C. div., 1969—; chmn. Franklin County Library Bd., 1967—. White cane chmn. N.C. Assn. for the Blind, 1971-72. Fellow Am. Inst. Chemists; mem. N.C. Acad. Sci., Am. Assn. Physics Tchrs., Am. Chem. Soc., Phi Sigma Pi, Alpha Beta

Gamma. Democrat. Baptist. Lion (dist. gov. 1967-68). Home: 8 S Chavis St Franklington NC 27525 Office: Louisburg Coll Louisburg NC 27549

PRUNTY, MICHAEL NEAL, dentist; b. Jenkins, Ky., June 17, 1934; s. Marshall Erlo and Geneieve Carmel (Cordray) P.; B.A., U. Ky., 1957; D.D.S., Med. Coll. Va., 1962, M.S., 1968; m. Nancy Carroll Stapleton, Jan. 13, 1957; children—Michael Neal, Genevieve, Mark. Dir. children's clinic, instr. dept. periodontics Med. Coll. Va., 1964-66; practice dentistry, specializing in orthodontics, Lexington, Ky., 1968—. Mem. Lexington Bd. Health, 1970—. Mem. Young Republican Com. Served to capt. Dental Corps, AUS, 1962-64. Mem. Am., Ky. dental assns., So. Soc. Orthodontics, Am. Assn. Orthodontics, Kappa Alpha. Rotarian (chmn. entertainment com. 1970). Club: Pyramid. Home: 361 Queensway St Lexington KY 40502 Office: 540 E Main St Lexington KY 40508

PRYER, RONALD STANLEY, psychologist; b. Shreveport, La., July 1, 1930; s. Frank S. and Alberta Pryer; B.A., Centenary Coll., 1952; M.A., La. State U., 1956, Ph.D., 1959; m. Margaret Wakefield, Dec. 21, 1956. Coordinator mental health planning div. La. State Dept. Hosps., Baton Rouge, 1963-64; chief psychologist Central La. State Hosp., Pineville, 1964—; cons. State Indsl. Sch. for Girls, Pineville, La., 1960—; prof. psychology La. Coll., Pineville, 1960—. Mem. research review com. Nat. Inst. Mental Health, 1967-71; coordinator Hosp. Improvement Project, Pineville, La., 1964—; dir. Vocational Rehab. Center for Adolescents, Central La. State Hosp., Pineville, 1968—. Served with AUS, 1947-48, 50-51. Mem. Am., Southeastern, La. (pres. 1966) psychol. assns., La. State Bd. Examiners Psychologists (chmn. 1967-68). Contbr. articles to profl. jours. Home: PO Box 31 Pineville LA 71360

PRYOR, DAVID, congressman; b. Camden, Ark., Aug. 29, 1934; s. Edgar and Susie (Newton) P.; student Henderson State Coll.; B.A., U. Ark., 1957, grad. Law Sch., 1964; m. Barbara Lunsford; children—David, Mark, Scott. Founder, pub. Ouachita Citizen, Camden, 1957-61; admitted to Ark. bar, 1964; practiced as mem. firm Pryor & Barnes, Camden; mem. 89th to 92d Congresses from 4th Ark. Dist., mem. House appropriations com. Mem. Ark. Ho. of Reps., 1960-64; del. Democratic nat. conv., 1968. Mem. C. of C. (past dir. Camden), Jr. C. of C., Blue Key, Sigma Alpha Epsilon, Phi Alpha Delta, Delta Theta Phi. Democrat. Presbyn. Home: 3321 N Ohio St Arlington VA 22207 Office: Longworth House Office Bldg Washington DC 20515

PRYOR, PAUL, hosp. adminstr. Adminstr. Miss. Bapt. Hosp., Jackson. Office: 1190 N State St Jackson MS 39201*

PRYOR, R(OBERT) EMMET, mcht.; b. Troup, Tex., Sept. 1, 1909; s. Thomas Moore and Comfort (Fox) P.; student Officer Candidate Sch., Camp Barkley, Tex., 1943; m. Anna Josephine Jones, Apr. 11, 1931; 1 son, Robert Emmet. Salesman, Rolle, Jewett & Beck, Houston, 1927; traveling sales rep. Gerson & Kaplan, Houston, 1928-35, Reliance Mfg. Co., Chgo., 1935-38; sales supr. Stern, Slegman, Prins Co., Kansas City, Mo., 1938-62; owner Pryor Men's Store, Palestine, Tex., 1947—. Cons. Betty Rose Coats & Suits, 1962-66. Pres., Palestine Indsl. Found., 1968. Served to capt. AUS, 1942-46. Decorated Legion of Merit; named Ky. Col., 1962. Mem. Palestine C. of C. (dir.), Nat. Assn. Womens and Childrens Wear Salesmen, Men's Retailers Am., Am. Fashion Assn. (pres. 1942). Episcopalian (vestryman 1972—). Rotarian (pres. 1965-66). Club: Meadowbrook Country (past pres. Palestine). Home: 1204 E Brazos St Palestine TX 75801 Office: 217 W Main St Palestine TX 75801

PRYOR, WILLIAM A., educator. Now prof. chemistry La. State U., Baton Rouge, La. State U. Found. Distinguished Faculty fellow, 1970, Guggenheim fellow, 1970-71, special postdoctoral fellow NIH, 1970-71. Fellow Am. Inst. Chemists, Gerontological Soc. (mem. Edn. Research com.), Intra-Sci. Research Found.; mem. numerous profl. socs. Author: Free Radicals, 1966. Editor profl. jours. Contbr. to jours. in field. Office: La State U Coll Chemistry Physics Baton Rouge LA 70803*

PRYOR, WILLIAM LEE, educator; b. Lakeland, Fla., Oct. 29, 1926; s. Dahl and Lottie Mae (Merchant) P.; A.B., Fla. So. Coll., 1949; M.A., Fla. State U., 1950, Ph.D., 1959; postgrad. U. N.C., 1952-53; pvt. art study with Florence Wilde; pvt. voice study with Colin O'More and Anna Kaskas. Asst. prof. English, dir. drama Bridgewater Coll., 1950-52; vis. instr. English Fla. So. Coll., MacDill Army Air Base, summer 1951; grad. teaching fellow humanities Fla. State U., 1953-55, 57-58; instr. English, U. Houston, 1955-59, asst. prof., 1959-62, asso. prof., 1962-71, prof., 1971—, asso. editor Forum, 1967, editor, 1967—; vis. instr. English, Tex. So. U., 1961-63; vis. instr. humanities, govt. U. Tex. Dental Br., 1962-63; lectr. The Women's Inst., Houston, 1967—; originator, moderator weekly television and radio program The Arts in Houston on KUHT-TV and KUHF-FM, 1956-57, 58-63. Bd. dirs. Houston Shakespeare Soc., 1964-67; bd. dirs., program annotator Houston Chamber Orch. Soc., 1964—; bd. dirs., program annotator Music Guild, Houston, 1960-67, v.p., 1963-67, adv. bd. 1967-70; bd. dirs. Contemporary Music Soc., Houston, 1958-63; mem.-at-large bd. dirs. Houston Grand Opera Guild, 1966-67; mem. repertory com. Houston Grand Opera Assn., 1967—; bd. dirs. Houston Grand Opera; mem. cultural adv. com. Jewish Community Center, 1960-66; bd. dirs. Houston Friends Pub. Library, 1962-67, 1st v.p., 1963-67; adv. mem. cultural affairs com. Houston C. of C., 1972. Mem. Coll. English Assn., Modern Langs. Assn., L'Alliance Francaise, English-Speaking Union, Alumni Assn. Fla. State U., Am. Assn. U. Profs., S. Central Modern Lang. Assn., Coll. Conf. Tchrs. English, Phi Beta (patron), Phi Mu Alpha Sinfonia, Alpha Psi Omega, Pi Kappa Alpha, Sigma Tau Delta, Tau Kappa Alpha. Episcopalian. Contbg. author: National Poetry Anthology, 1952; Panorama das Literaturas das Americas, 4 vols., 1958-60. Home: 2625 Arbuckle St Houston TX 77005 Office: 3801 Cullen Blvd Houston TX 77004

PTACEK, CHARLES FRANK, paint corp. exec.; b. Chgo., Feb. 12, 1940; s. Charles William and Rose (Chroust) P.; student, Ga. State Coll., 1956-60; m. Sharon Kathleen Jackson; children—Charles Frank, Kimberly Rose, Michael Davey, Tammy Zee. With Precision Paint Corp., Atlanta, 1961—, v.p., 1962-65, exec. v.p., 1965-68, pres., chmn. bd., 1968—. Mem. Aircraft Owners and Pilots Assn. Club: Cherokee Town and Country. Home: 1555 Spalding Dr NE Atlanta GA 30338 Office: 5275 Peachtree Industrial Blvd Atlanta GA 30341

PUCCI, GERARD RICHARD, lawyer, mech. engr.; b. N.Y.C., Aug. 7, 1924; s. Santo and Mary (Principe) P.; B.S. in Mech. Engring., Va. Poly. Inst., 1944; J.D., George Washington U., 1949; m. Ruth Motz, July 20, 1955. Admitted to Fla. bar, 1949; patent engr. RCA, 1946-48; tool designer Douglas Aircraft Corp., 1950-51; patent atty. U.S. Navy Ordnance Test Sta., 1951-52; staff analyst, N.Am. Aviation, 1952-54; pvt. practice as atty. and engr., 1954—. Prof. aerospace dept. Miami-Dade Jr. Coll.-South Campus, 1966—. Chmn. Planning Bd. Coral Gables, Fla., 1959-63, mem. Zoning Bd., 1959-63; mem. dist. advancement com. Boy Scouts Am., S. Fla., 1967-70. Served as lt. (j.g.) USNR, 1944-46. Registered profl. engr., Fla. Recipient Old Guard award Am. Soc. M.E., 1944; George Washington award Freedoms Found. Valley Forge, 1963. Mem. Nat. Soc. Profl. Engrs., Fla. Engring. Soc., Tau Beta Pi, Pi Tau Sigma. Rotarian (sec., dir. S.W. Miami 1960). K.C. (4 deg.). Roman Catholic. Producer, Speaker own radio program on Am. Govt., Miami, 1962-65. Author: (textbook) Aviation Law-Fundamental Cases, 1970. Home: 35 Menores Av Coral Gables FL 33134 Office: 250 Bird Rd Coral Gables FL 33146

PUCKETT, JAMES RICHARD, metal products co. exec.; b. Anderson, Ind., Aug. 2, 1929; s. Jefferson Thomas and Wilma Inez (Funkhouser) P.; student U. Evansville, 1947-48; m. Patricia Ann Thornton, Aug. 30, 1949; children—Gary Michael, Neal Allen. Zone mgr. Airtex Products, Inc., Fairfield, Ill., 1951-62; regional mgr. A.P. Parts Corp., Toledo, 1962-67; sales mgr. Inca Metal Products Corp., Carrollton, Tex., 1967—; dir. Cisco Material Handling, Inc., Dallas. Swimming commr. Richardson Sports, Inc. (Tex.), 1966-67. Served with AUS, 1950-51. Mem. Automotive Warehouse Distbrs. Assn. (material handling com. 1972-73). Elk. Club: Braniff Internat. (Dallas). Home: 9953 Miller Rd Apt 1117 Dallas TX 75238 Office: P O Box 398 Carrollton TX 75006

PUCKETT, RUSSELL ELWOOD, elec. engr.; b. Ewing, Ky., Mar. 28, 1929; s. Ben and Nettie (Peach) P.; B.S., U. Ky., 1956, M.S., 1959; m. Dorothy C. Hoskins, Aug. 10, 1949; children—Malcolm Wayne, Stanley Allen, Janet Arlene, Owen Keith, Michael Edwin. Engr. U.S. Dept. Def., 1956-57; asst. prof. elec. engring. U. Ky., Lexington, 1957-66, research asso., 1967-68, asso. dir. office research Coll. Engring., 1968—, asso. prof. engring. tech., 1970—, chmn. div. engring. tech., 1972—; sr. research engr. Tex. Instruments, Versailles, Ky., 1966-67; pres., chmn. bd. REPCO, Inc. Cons. expert witness in patent infringement, trade secret lawsuits; mem. nat. com. electronic research Hwy. Research Bd. of Nat. Acad. Scis., 1964-70. Served with USAAF, 1946-49, with USAF, 1951-54. Registered profl. engr., Ky. Mem. I.E.E.E. (treas. Lexington sect. 1962-65, chmn. sect. 1969-70), Am. Soc. Elec. Engrs., Nat., Kan. (dir. Bluegrass chpt. 1971-73) socs. profl. engrs. Eta Kappa Nu, Tau Beta Pi, Phi Gamma Delta. Mason (32 deg.), Kiwanian. Patentee in field. Author: (with H. A. Romanowitz) Introduction to Electronics, 1968. Home: 1012 Lane Allen Rd Lexington KY 40504 Office: Anderson Hall U Ky Lexington KY 40506

PUGH, BURVIN EDMOND, ednl. adminstr.; b. Ashridge, Ala., Aug. 7, 1919; s. Arthur Thomas and Lula (Horton) P.; B.S., U. Ala., 1951, M.A. in Sch. Adminstrn. and Supervision, 1952; postgrad. U. So. Miss., 1953-54; m. Dorothy Sumrall, Jan. 26, 1947; children—Linda, Burvin Edmond, Tommy. Prin. Nicholson (Miss.) Elementary Sch., 1951-55; asst. prin. Columbia High Sch., Lake City, Fla., 1955-57; supervising prin. Walton High and Maude Saunders schs., DeFuniak Springs, 1957—, now prin. Gulf Breeze (Fla.) High Sch. Bd. dirs. Walton County (Fla.) Fed. Credit Union, 1960-64. Served with AUS, 1940-46. Recipient Bronze Indian Arrowhead Philippine Govt., 1944. Mem. N.E.A., Fla. Edn. Assn., Columbia County (pres. 1956-57), Walton County tchrs. assns., Northwest Fla. Athletic Assn. (pres. 1961-65). Baptist (chmn. bd. deacons 1966—, chmn. nomination com. 1967-68, asst. supt. Sunday sch. 1960—). Clubs: Kiwanis, Walton County Quarterback. Home: 27 Gilmore Dr Gulf Breeze FL 32561

PUGH, EDWARD NICHOLLS, social work adminstr.; b. Plaquemine, La., Aug. 3, 1914; s. John Howell and Mary Peace (Sprague) P.; student Notre Dame Sem., 1934-38; B.A., Loyola U. South, 1940; M.S.W., Cath. U. Am., 1942; m. Yvonne M. Duplantier, May 22, 1942; children— Kathleen (Mrs. John J. Griffin), Edward N. Jr., John Robert, Michael F., Dorothy E., Jacqueline A. Fieldworker La. Dept. Pub. Welfare, 1938-40; welfare officer UNRRA 1945-46; chief social work service VA Hosp., Gulfport, Miss., 1946-50, Waco, Tex., 1950—. Cons. social worker Action Planning Council, 1959; lectr. sociology and social welfare Baylor U., 1955-56; chmn. social welfare manpower devel. project Tex. State Dept. Pub. Welfare, 1968—. Mem. bd. dirs. Action Planning Council, 1953-66, v.p., 1963-65, pres., 1955-56; mem. bd. trustees United Fund, 1968-69, 70-73. Pres., St. Vincent de Paul Soc., 1953—. Served with USAAF, 1942-45. Recipient Community Service award U.S. Govt. Employees Union, 1962, Urban Service award Office Econ. Opportunity, 1968, Leadership award Caritas and Austin Diocese, 1972. Mem. Tex. Social Welfare Assn. (mem. bd. dirs. 1954-59; mem. exec. com. 1966-69), Nat. Assn. Social Workers (mem. bd. dirs. 1960-63; mem. social action commn. 1963-66), Tex. Council Nat. Assn. Social Workers (chpt. pres. 1956-58; chmn. social work edn. com. 1963—). Home: 2617 Pine Av Waco TX 76708 Office: VA Hosp Waco TX 76708

PUGH, MOFFETT LEONARD, geophysicist; b. Oreville, O., Feb. 16, 1916; s. John Paul and Elva (Cain) P.; B.S., Aero. Engr., La. State U., 1939; postgrad. Centenary Coll., 1954; m. Doris Robbins, Oct. 18, 1942; 1 son, John Thomas. Petroleum engr. trainee Pugh-Dekalb Co., Centralia, Ill., 1939-41; geophysicist Ark. Natural Gas Co., Shreveport, La., 1945-53; chief geophysicist Ark. La. Gas Co., Shreveport, 1953-70; chief geophysicist Amarex, Inc., Oklahoma City, 1970—. Dir. Caddo and Bossier parishes, dir. area II, Civil Def., 1954-61. Served with Ordnance Corps, AUS, 1941-46. Registered profl. engr., La. Mem. Soc. Exploration Geophysicists, Geophys. Soc. Oklahoma City. Club: Shreveport Petroleum. Designer spl. target abuttement to speed up testing and recovery of armorpiercing ammunition, 1942. Home: 4517 NW 32d St Oklahoma City OK 73122 Office: 2000 Classen Center Oklahoma City OK 73106

PUGH, OLIN SHARPE, educator; b. Prosperity, S.C., Mar. 6, 1923; s. J. E. and Martha (Counts) P.; B.S., U. S.C., 1948; A.M., Duke, 1951, Ph.D., 1956; m. Louise Ewell, Sept. 3, 1949 children— Catherine, Walter, Ernest. Instr. econs. dept. U. S.C., Columbia, 1949-52, asst. prof., 1952-57, asso. prof., 1957-61, prof. banking and finance, 1961—, acting dean Coll. Bus. Adminstrn., 1966-67, dir. grad. studies Coll. Bus. Adminstrn., 1967-71, dir. Bur. Bus. and Econ. Research, 1971—. Served with AUS, 1943-46. Mem. Am., So. econ. assns., Am., So. (pres. 1967-68) finance assns., Phi Beta Kappa, Beta Gamma Sigma. Author: Money, Banking and Monetary Policy, 1967. Contbr. articles to profl. jours. Home: 1502 Milford Rd Columbia SC 29206

PUIG, JOSEPH ALBERT, psychologist; b. San Juan, P.R., Apr. 27, 1923; s. Pedro A. and Dolores (Rios) P.; M.A. in Psychology, St. John's U., 1967, M.S. in Geology, N.Y. U., 1954; m. Elaine Bechtel, Apr. 12, 1958; children—Richard Allen, Robert Joseph, Carole Diane. Instr. geology Hofstra Coll., Hempstead, N.Y., 1950-51; geologist, mineralogist raw materials div. AEC, N.Y.C., 1951-54; engr. Fairchild Camera & Instrument Corp., Syosset, L.I., 1955-58; psychologist life scis. group Grumman Aircraft Engring. Corp., Bethpage, L.I., 1958-68; psychologist Dept. of Navy Naval Tng. Equipment Center, Orlando, Fla., 1968—. Served to lt. USNR, 1942-46; PTO. Mem. Human Factors Soc. Home: 1130 Willowbrook Trail Maitland FL 32751 Office: Dept of Navy Naval Tng Equipment Center Orlando FL 32813

PUJALS, HUMBERTO ANDRES, dentist, educator; b. Camaguey, Cuba, Nov. 30, 1920; s. Mario Santiago and Margarita (Garcia) P.; B.A., Camaguey Coll., 1939; D.D.S., Havana U., 1943; D.D.S., Georgetown U., 1963; m. Henrietta Ann Dias, Dec. 27, 1947; children—Margaret Rose (Mrs. Augusto Suarez), Humberto, Jr., David Mario. Came to U.S., 1944, naturalized, 1966. Intern, Forsyth Dental Inf. for Children, Boston, 1944, asst. instr., 1946; resident oral surgery dept. Boston City Hosp., 1944-46; oral surgeon-in-chief Camaguey Children Hosp., 1951-60; vis. oral surgeon, cons. Emergency and Gen. hosps., 1951-60; asso. prof. oral diagnosis, Georgetown U. Sch. Dentistry, Washington, 1965—. Pres., Soft Ball Catholic League, 1964—. Pres. Latin Am. Republican party, 1971—. Diplomate Dental Soc. P.R. Mem. Greater Washington, Southeastern, Middle Atlantic socs. oral surgeons, D.C. Dental Soc., Am. Cancer Soc., Pan Am. Med. Soc., Africare. Republican. Editor Spanish mag. Religion Y Patria, 1970—. Home: 2710 N Upshur St Arlington VA 22207 Office: 1726 Eye St NW Washington DC 20006

PULEO, JOHN RUDOLPH, microbiologist; b. Tampa, Fla., Nov. 27, 1930; s. Paul and Margaret (Parrino) P.; B.S., U. Fla., 1953, M.S., 1955; m. Evelyn Sapp, Aug. 24, 1952; children—Paul Douglas, Rudy Keith. Bacteriologist, asst. lab. officer U.S. Army Hosp., Ft. Polk, La., 1955-57; bacteriologist S.W. Fla. Tb Hosp., Tampa, 1957-59, S.W. Fla. Blood Bank, Tampa, 1959-61; microbiologist Germ-Free Life Research Center, Tampa, 1961-64; microbiologist USPHS, Phoenix-Cape Kennedy, Fla., 1965—. Served to 1st lt. AUS, 1955-57. Mem. Am. Soc. for Microbiology, Am. Assn. for Contamination Control. Democrat. Roman Catholic. Home: 136 W Gadsden Lane Cocoa Beach FL 32931 Office: Spacecraft Bioassay Unit Cape Kennedy FL 32920

PULIDO, MIGUEL LAZARO, chem. co. exec.; b. Havana, Cuba, Dec. 17, 1934; s. Jose F. and Maria (Perez) P. came to U.S., 1960, naturalized, 1969; A.E., Sugar Technologist, Havana U., 1956; M.S., La. State U., 1961, Ph.D., 1965; m. Maria M. Garcia, Oct. 4, 1957; children—Maria, Miguel. Mgr. east div. agrl. and indsl. devel. Bank of Cuba, 1956-59; tech. service ingeniero agronomo Productora de Superfosfatos, Havana, Cuba, 1959-60; grad. research asst. La. State U., 1962-65 asst. mgr. internat. tech. services Velsicol Chem. Co., Chgo., 1965-67; agrl. specialist Buckman Labs. Inc., Memphis, 1967-71, mgr. agrl. marketing, 1971—. Mem. Am. Phytopath. Soc., Am. Soc. Plant Physiologists, Am. Inst. Biol. Scis., Weed Sci. Soc. Am. (internat. affairs com. 1967—), Am. Cotton Disease Council, A.A.A.S. Editor: Fitopatologia, 1970—. Home: 5235 Boswell St Memphis TN 38117 Office: 1256 N McLean Blvd Memphis TN 38108

PULLEN, JOHN THOMAS, JR., mech. engr.; b. Covington, Tenn., Nov. 18, 1903; s. John Thomas and Thersa (Miller) P.; archtl. engring. degree U. Ill., 1926; m. Martha Frances Gragg, Aug. 21, 1928; children—Martha Jane (Mrs. Eugene Edward Tibbs), John Thomas III. Field engr. Gauger-Korsmo Constrn. Co., Memphis 1926-28; resident engr., designer W. F. Schulz, architect-engr., 1928-32; engr. charge bank protection party Corps Engrs., U.S. Army, 1932-38; staff engr. Firestone Tire & Rubber Co., Memphis, 1938-48; mech. engr. T. J. O'Brien Engring. Co., 1948-54; owner firm John T. Pullen, cons. engr., Memphis, 1954—. Air raid warden, 1941-46. Registered profl. engr., Ten., Mo., Ark., Miss. Mem. Am. Soc. Heating, Refrigerating and Air-Conditioning Engrs., Nat. Soc. Profl. Engrs., Engrs. Club Memphis. Democrat. Methodist. Mason. Club: Big Ten. Home: 3764 Gragg Av Memphis TN 38108 Office: Falls Bldg Memphis TN 38103

PULLEN, WILLIAM RUSSELL, librarian; b. Lexington, Va., Nov. 10, 1919; s. James Edward and Nettie Allen (Mays) P.; B.A., U. N.C., 1942, B.S. in L.S., 1947, M.A., 1948, Ph.D. in Polit. Sci., 1951; m. Pauline Purdin Evans, July 7, 1949; children—Linda Belle, Mark Evans. Asst. to dir. state records microfilm project Library of Congress, 1949-50; documents librarian, U. N.C. library, 1951-57, asst. librarian, 1957-58; librarian Ga. State Coll., Atlanta, 1959—. Fellow Carnegie Project Advanced Library Adminstrn., Rutgers U., 1958. Served with USAAF, 1942-45. Mem. Am., Southeastern, Ga. library assns., Alpha Kappa Psi. Methodist. Editor: Southeastern Librarian, 1961-64. Compiler: A Check List of Legislative Journals, 1955. Home: 2545 N Druid Hills Rd NE Atlanta GA 30329

PULLIAM, WALTER TILLMAN, pub., editor; b. Knoxville, Tenn., Nov. 5, 1913; s. James R. and Jennie Blanche (Badgett) P.; A.B., U. Tenn., 1936; m. Julia Brownlow; 1 dau., Mary Dorminy. Copy editor Knoxville Jour., 1936; reporter Knoxville News-Sentinel, 1936-42, polit. writer, 1946; nat. affairs reporter, asst. city editor Washington Post, 1947-49; editor, pub. Harriman (Tenn.) Today's News, also pres., gen. mgr. Record Printing Co., Inc., 1949—; pres. La Follette Press Inc., 1968—; pub. La Follette (Tenn.) Press, Jellico (Tenn.) Advance-Sentinel, Lake City (Tenn. Town Crier). Chmn. Indsl. Devel. Commn. Harriman. Mem. Harriman Pub. Library Bd. Served in inf. AUS, 1942-46; staff Mediterranean edit. Stars and Stripes. Mem. Tenn., Harriman businessmen's assns., Tenn. Press Assn. (past pres.), E. Tenn. Hist. Soc. Presbyn. (elder). Clubs: Nat. Press (Washington); Deane Hill Country (Knoxville); Rotary (dist. gov. 1972-73); Emory Golf and Country. Home: 413 Cumberland St Harriman TN 37748 Office: 512 Devonia St Harriman TN 37748

PULLIG, RICHARD MURPHY, physician; b. Old Aparta, La., Oct. 16, 1916; s. Wyatt Elmo and Lillian Bell (Murphy) P.; B.S., La. Poly. Inst., 1937; M.S. (Order Golden Microscope fellow 1937-39), La. State U., 1939, M.D., 1954; postgrad. Gradwohl Sch. Med. Tech., 1940-41; m. Rachael Virginia Jones, Dec. 26, 1943; children—Mary Lillian (Mrs. Edwin Frederick Schultz III), Rachael Virginia (Mrs. James Robert McDowell), Elizabeth Ann. Agt., U.S. Dept. Agr., New Orleans, 1938-39; instr. zoology La. Poly. Inst., 1939-42, asst. prof., 1942-47, asso. prof., 1947-50; intern Mercy Hosp., New Orleans, 1954-55; family practice medicine, Clinton, La., 1955—; head Green Clinic Lab., Ruston, La., 1945-50; tchr. Sch. Nursing, Charity Hosp., New Orleans, 1950-55; mem. staff Clinton Infirmary. Mem. Am. Med. Technologists (pres. 1954), Nu Sigma Nu. Baptist (deacon 1960—). Mason. Clubs: Los Amigos Social (Clinton, La.). Home: Box 365 Clinton LA 70722 Office: Clinton Infirmary Clinton LA 70722

PULS, WAYNE ELVIN, banker; b. Pueblo, Colo., Dec. 12, 1923; s. Fred William and Nora Malinda (Pulliam) P.; student U. Idaho, 1943, Central Coll., Fayette, Mo., 1944-45; B.A., U. Michigan, 1947; m. Sally Russell Robbins, Aug. 7, 1971; 1 dau., Susan Elaine. With Gen. Motors Acceptance Corp., several Fla. cities, 1948-60, mgr. br., Ft. Lauderdale, 1956-60; v.p., comml. loan officer First Nat. Bank, Orlando, 1960-65; pres. Central Nat. Bank, Jacksonville, 1965-67; sr. v.p. Barnett First Nat. Bank, Winter Park, 1967-71; pres., dir. Barnett Bank of Orlando, 1971; pres., dir. Barnett Bank Ft. Lauderdale (Fla.), 1971—; dir. Electone, Inc., Fern Park, Clarke Broadcasting Corp., Orlando.. Bd. dirs. Winter Park Community Chest, treas., 1971—; bd. dirs. Mid-Fla. Center for Alcoholics, Orlando, treas., 1969—; adv. bd. Salvation Army, Orlando, Fla. Served with USNR, 1942-46. Mem. Winter Park C. of C. (bd. dirs. 1970—, v.p., 1971—), Navy League (bd. dirs. 1970—). Clubs: Winter Park Racquet; Rotary (Maitland, Fla.); University (Winter Park, Fla.). Home: 5309 Buttonwood Ct Fort Lauderdale FL 33313 Office: 15 E Broward Blvd Fort Lauderdale FL 33302

PULVIRENTI, DOMENIC P., govt. ofcl.; b. Washington, Nov. 15, 1925; s. Domenic and Sara (Brocato) P.; student Va. Mil. Inst., 1943, Carnegie Inst. Tech., 1944; B.E.E., Catholic U. Am., 1950; postgrad. U. Md., 1951; m. Dolores M. Guido, Oct. 11, 1952; 1 son, Darren S. Radio engr. A.D. Ring & Co., Washington, 1950; electronics engr. Naval Ordnance Lab., White Oak, Md., 1950-54; supervisory gen.

engr. Bur. Naval Weapons, Washington, 1954-63, sr. systems engr., 1963-66; dep. weapon systems mgr. Naval Ordnance Systems Command, Washington, 1966—. Served with F.A., AUS, 1944-46. Mem. Am. Inst. Aeros. and Astronautics, Assn. Naval Weapons Engrs. and Scientists. Democrat. Roman Catholic. K.C. Club: Rock Creek Kay-Cee (past pres., Bethesda). Home: 9300 Parkhill Terrace Bethesda MD 20014 Office: Naval Ordnance Systems Command Washington DC 20360

PUMPHREY, NORMAN DEAN, state ofcl.; b. Sheridan, Ark., Feb. 19, 1932; s. Winfred and Ruby (Walker) P.; student U. Ark., 1950-51; m. Bobbye Jean Winbury, Sept. 9, 1951; children—Norman D., Gregory C., David L. Rodman, Ark. State Hwy. Dept. (part-time), 1946-50, instrument man, 1951-55; engr. asst. Short & Brownlee Constrn. Co., 1955-56; with Ark. State Hwy. Dept., Little Rock, 1957—, instrument man, 1957-59, acting resident engr., 1959-61, sr. resident engr., 1961-69, asst. constrn. engr., 1969—. Adviser constrn. tech. curriculum Southwest Inst. Tech., Camden, Ark., 1968-70. Mem. Ark. (Southwest chpt. pres. 1962-63 Outstanding Engr. award 1969), Nat. socs. profl. engrs., Ark. Assn. Registered Land Surveyors, Am. Congress Surveying Mapping. Baptist. Home: 5720 Chaucer Lane Little Rock AR 72209 Office: PO Box 2261 Little Rock AR 72209

PURCELL, GRAHAM BOYNTON, JR., congressman; b. Archer City, Tex., May 5, 1919; s. Graham Boynton and Della (Key) P.; B.S., Tex. A. and M. Coll., 1946; LL.B., Baylor U., 1949; m. Betty Smith, Jan. 29, 1943; children—Blaine Smith, Kirk Boynton, Jannie, Blake Elliott; m. 2d, Nancy Putty, 1970. Admitted to Tex. bar, 1949; practiced in Big Spring, 1949-51, Wichita Falls, 1951-55; judge 89th Dist. Ct., Wichita Falls, 1955-62; judge Juvenile Ct., Wichita County, 1955-62; mem. 87th to 92d Congress from 13th Tex. Dist.; mem. House Com. Agr., P.O. and Civil Service Com. Chmn. Juvenile Bd., Wichita County, 1959-60; mem. Child Welfare Bd., Wichita County, 1952-62. Dist. chmn. Boy Scouts Am., Wichita Falls, 1958-61, chmn. Cub Pack, 1953-58; coach Boys Club Football program, 1958-61, chmn., 1961; coach YMCA Kid Basketball program, 1959-61, chmn., 1961. Pres. N.W. Tex. chpt. Muscular Dystrophy Assn. Am.; bd. dirs. Wichita County Mental Health Assn., Sch. Listening Eyes Wichita Falls. Served to maj. AUS, 1941-45; lt. col. Res. Recipient Outstanding Citizen award Civilian Club, 1958, Altrusa Club, 1960. Mem. Am., Wichita County (past treas.) bar assns., State Bar Tex., Wichita Falls C. of C. (past chmn. ednl. com.). Democrat. Presbyn (deacon). Club: Y's Men. Home: Wichita Falls TX 76307 also 9026 Old Mt Vernon Rd Alexandria VA 22309 Office: House Office Bldg Washington DC 20515

PURCELL, THOMAS HECTOR, JR., aerospace engr.; b. Hope Mills, N.C., Sept. 11, 1920; s. Thomas Hector and Mabel Conrad (Pate) P.; B.Aero.Engring. with honors, N.C. State U., 1943; M.S.Aero. Engring., U. Mich., 1947; m. Mary Barbara Stevens, June 15, 1945; children—Barbara Katherine, Archie Thomas. Aerodynamicist, Fairchild Aircraft, Hagerstown, Md., 1948-50; chief design engr. Prewitt Aircraft, Clifton Heights, Pa., 1950-54; chief mech. engr. Missile and Electronics div. ESB Inc., Raleigh, N.C., 1966—; pres. Flight Dynamics, Inc., Raleigh, 1956—. Served with USAAF, 1943-48. Registered profl. engr., N.C. Mem. Exptl. Aircraft Assn. Presbyn. (elder, past ch. treas. and chmn. bd. deacons). Pioneer flyer manned flexwing aircraft off water, 1962; designer, builder, flyer Flightsail VII, amphibian, 1971; patentee aerospace designs. Home: 2709 Everett Av Raleigh NC 27607 Office: PO Box 5070 Raleigh NC 27607

PURCELL, WALTER LAMBUTH, financial mgmt. cons. firm exec.; b. Shady Dale, Ga., Mar. 26, 1922; s. William Edgar and Lillie (Neese) P.; A.A., Reinhardt Coll., 1941; B.S. in Math., Piedmont Coll., 1943, B.A. in Social Sci., 1943; LL.B., Emory U., Atlanta Law Sch., 1959; LL.M., Atlanta Law Sch., 1963; m. Dorothy Lanette Dimsdale, Jan. 17, 1947; children—Dorothy Cheryl (Mrs. Michael Perry Adams) and Melvyn Kenneth (twins). Dist. reporting and service mgr., also bus. cons., Dun & Bradstreet, Inc., 1947-62; dir. Dept. Community Services DeKalb County, Atlanta, 1962-64; pres. Purcell Cons. Assos., Inc., Decatur, Ga., 1964—. Lectr. various colls., univs.; instr. seminars; mem. faculty Grad. Sch. Arts and Scis., Emory U., Atlanta, 1965—; chmn. bd. Exec. Edn., Inc., Decatur, 1966—. Div. chmn. DeKalb unit Am. Cancer Soc., 1965—; mem. budget com. Atlanta Met. Community Chest, 1966—; bd. dirs. Met. area A.R.C., DeKalb County Heart Council, S.E. Region YMCA; pres. DeKalb Community Council, 1963-67; regional v.p. Inst. Mgmt. Cons. Named DeKalb County Citizen of Year, civitans of DeKalb County, 1964. Mem. So. Finance Assn., Atlanta Soc. Security Analysts, Pub. Relations Soc. Am., Ga. Pub. Relations Soc., Assn. Mgmt. Cons., Am. Pub. Health Assn., Ga. Hosp. Assn., So. Assn. Inst. Psychol. Services, Am. Recreation Soc., Ga. Recreation and Park Soc., Ga. Library Assn., Ga. Gerontology Soc., DeKalb County C. of C. (dir.), Delta Theta Phi. Methodist (pres. bd. trustees 1959—). Clubs: Atlanta Press, Kiwanis (Ga. dist. com. chmn. 1964-67), Toastmasters International (chpt. pres. 1952-53), Decatur Executive, Druid Hills Golf. Home: 1526 Rainier Falls Dr NE Atlanta GA 30329 Office: First Nat Bank Bldg Decatur GA 30030

PURDIE, DOUGLAS HAIG, ednl. adminstr.; b. Harrison, N.J., Oct. 27, 1916; s. William James and Charlottee (Taylor) P.; B.S., Ga. Eve. Coll., Atlanta, 1941; M.Ed., Emory U., 1949; postgrad. U. Hawaii, 1944, U. Ga., 1956; m. Frances Ethelyn Boswell, June 23, 1939; children—Ethelyn (Mrs. Robert Browning), Laura Joyce. Tchr., counselor Russell High Sch., East Point, Ga., 1941-52; vis. tchr. Fulton County (Ga.) Sch. System, 1952-55; counselor Hapeville (Ga.) High Sch., 1955-65, prin., 1965-70; adminstrn. asst. to dep. supt. Fulton County Sch. System, Hapeville, 1970—. Mem. Ga. Counseling and Testing Adv. Bd., 1961-63. Vol. worker Atlanta Area council Boy Scouts Am., 1945-65, Atlanta YMCA, 1945—; chmn. pensions bd. Fulton County Tchrs. Retirement Bd., 1960—. Bd. dirs. Annewaakee Found., Little Red School House for Exceptional Children. Served with USNR, 1943-45. Mem. Nat., Ga. edn. assns., Fulton County Tchrs. Assn., Ga. Assn. Sch. Counselors (pres. 1957), Audubon Soc. Presbyn. (elder 1948-72). Home: 4495 Danforth Rd SW Atlanta GA 30331 Office: 689 North Av Hapeville GA 30354

PURDOM, ELMER RAY, JR., ednl. adminstr.; b. DeKalb, Ill., Jan. 1, 1933; s. Elmer Ray and Fannie (Freeman) P.; A.B., U. Ky., 1957, M.A., 1958; m. Emmy Glo Davis, Dec. 26, 1953; 1 son, Mark Davis. Tchr. economics and history Lexington (Ky.) Baptist Coll., 1956-57; tchr. Henry Clay High Sch., Lexington, Ky., 1958-60, asst. prin., 1960-65; asst. supt. Lexington Pub. Schs., 1965-67; supt. Danville (Ky.) Pub. Schs., 1967—. Div. chmn. United Community Fund, 1966—; dir. Opportunity Workship for Handicapped, 1967—; mem. Danville Human Rights Commn., 1969—. Served with AUS, 1954-56. Named Ky. col., 1962. Mem. Danville C. of C., Nat., Ky., Danville edn. assns., Am. Assn. Sch. Adminstrs., UN Assn., Phi Delta Kappa. Baptist (deacon 1969-71). Home: 359 Proctor St Danville KY 40422 Office: Danville Bd Edn E Lexington Av Danville KY 40422

PURDY, HAROLD JOHN, clergyman; b. Newcomerston, O., June 14, 1914; s. Earle Edson and Mabel (Wilson) P.; student Alderson-Broadus Coll., 1932-34, Salem Coll., 1934-36, A.B., 1946; D.D., So. Bapt. Theol. Sem., 1942, B.D.; m. Virginia Elisabeth Burdette, Apr. 23, 1935. Ordained to ministry Bapt. Ch., 1935; pastor 1st Ch., Madison W. Va., 1935-39, Northview Ch., Clarksburg, W. Va., 1933-35; asso. pastor Deer Park Ch., Louisville, 1939-41; pastor 1st Ch., Madisonville, Ky., 1941-46, 1st Ch., Bowling Green, Ky., 1946-50, Belmont Heights Ch., Nashville, 1950-64, 1st Bapt. Ch., Madisonville, Ky., 1964—. Trustee Bapt. Sunday Sch. Bd., exec. bd. Ky. Bapt. Conv., 1964—, mem. hosp. commn., 1964—; mem. exec. com. So. Bapt. Conv., 1966—; pres. Tenn. Bapt. Conv., 1963, mem. ednl. commn., 1951-56, mem. exec. bd., 1960; moderator Nashville Bapt. Assn., 1962-63. Trustee Tenn. Bapt. Children's Home, 1951-63, Belmont Coll., 1953-64. Mem. com. alcohol studies State Tenn., 1952. Kiwanian. Contbr. ch. periodicals. Home: Greenville Pike Madisonville KY 42431 Office: 1st Baptist Ch 223 N Main St Madisonville KY 42431

PURDY, KENNETH RODMAN, educator; b. New Rochelle, N.Y., Oct. 16, 1933; s. Kenneth O. and Edna (Miller) P.; B. Mech. Engring., Ga. Inst. Tech., 1956, M.S., 1959, Ph.D., 1963; m. Nancy Berry Beam, Mar. 20, 1954; children—Linda Leigh, Kenneth Jeffrey. Asso. aircraft engr. Lockheed Aircraft Corp., Marietta, Ga., summer 1956; instr. Ga. Inst. Tech., 1956-59, asst. prof., 1959-64, research asso., 1957-64; asst. prof. Purdue U., 1964-66, asso. prof., 1966-68; prof. mech. engring. Tenn. Tech. U., Cookeville, 1968—. Cons., B. Offen & Co., Chgo., 1965, Design & Mfg. Corp., 1967-68, Frigidaire div. Gen. Motors, 1969-71, Oak Ridge Nat. Lab., 1970—. NASA-Am. Soc. Engring. Edn. fellow George C. Marshall Space Flight Center, summers 1966, 67. Mem. Am. Soc. M.E., Acoustical Soc. Am., Am. Soc. Engring. Edn., Sigma Xi, Pi Tau Sigma, Tau Beta Pi, Phi Kappa Phi, Sigma Phi Epsilon. Home: 1125 Mt Vernon Rd Cookeville TN 38501

PURDY, LAURENCE HENRY, educator; b. Miami, Ariz., Sept. 28, 1926; s. Laurence Henry and Winnie E. (Gibson) P.; student Mont. State U., 1944-45, 46-47; B.S., San Diego State Coll., 1949; Ph.D., U. Cal. at Davis, 1954; m. Barbara Ann Pershal, Feb. 14, 1948; children— Cynthia D., Laurence J., Timothy C., Paula E. Research plant pathologist Cereal Disease Research Lab., Cereal Crops Research Br., Crops Research div., U.S. Dept. Agr., Pullman, Wash., 1953-67; prof., chmn. dept. plant pathology U. Fla., Gainesville, 1967—. Served with AUS, 1945. Recipient Unit Superior Service award U.S. Dept. Agr., 1960. Mem. Am. Phytopath. Soc., A.A.A.S., Fla. State Hort. Soc., Sigma Xi, Sigma Alpha Epsilon. Home: 1519 NW 25th Terrace Gainesville FL 32601

PURDY, ROB ROY, univ. adminstr.; b. Pensacola, Fla., Feb. 11, 1914; s. William Wallace and Margaret (Mc-Lellan) P.; A.B., Davidson U., 1937; M.A., Vanderbilt U., 1938, Ph.D., 1946; postgrad. U. Grenoble, 1939; m. Frances Norine Edwards, June 15, 1939; children—Alan M., Rob, Frank C. Asst. prof. English, Florence (Ala.) State Coll., 1941-42; with Vanderbilt U., 1942—, successively instr., asst. prof., asso. prof., 1942-55, prof. English, 1955—, vice chancellor univ., 1959-66, sr. vice chancellor, 1966—, dir. Vanderbilt U. Press, 1957-59. Bd. di rs. United Givers Fund, Nashville; trustee Harpeth Hall Prep. Sch., Better Bus. Bur. Nashville-Middle Tenn. Inc. Served from ensign to lt. (j.g.) USNR, 1944-46. Am. Field Service fellow Inst. Internat. Edn., 1939-40. Mem. Modern Lang. Assn., Nashville C. of C. (bd. govs.), Omicron Delta Kappa. Presbyn. Rotarian (dir.) Editor: Fugitives Reunion, 1958. Contbr. articles publs. Home: 4305 Esteswood Dr Nashville TN 37215

PURKS, WILLIAM KENDRICK, physician; b. Greensboro, Ga., Sept. 1, 1905; s. James Harris and Lulie Carswell (Kinman) P.; B.S. cum laude, Emory U., 1926, M.D. with honor, 1929; m. Mary Helen Kemper, June 22, 1935; children—William Kendrick (dec.), Robert K. Intern, Grady Hosp., Atlanta, 1929-30; med. resident, 1929-30; asst. med. resident Peter Brent Brigham Hosp., Boston, 1931-34; practice medicine specializing in internal medicine, Vicksburg, Miss., 1934—; chief staff Vicksburg Hosp., 1962—, chief med. service, 1934—, pres. bd. dirs., 1962—; instr. medicine U. Miss. Med. Sch., 1956—. Mem. Vicksburg Sch. Bd., 1945-60, pres., 1955-60. Bd. dirs. YMCA, Vicksburg, pres., 1969-70; bd. dirs. Vicksburg Hosp. Med. Found., pres. 1962—. Fellow A.C.P. (gov. 1960-66); mem. Am., So., Miss. med. assns., West Miss. Med. Soc., Am. Fedn. Clin. Research, Am. Coll. Chest Physicians, Am. (bd. dirs. 1954-60), Miss. (pres. 1953) heart assns., Chi Phi, Phi Beta Kappa, Alpha Kappa Kappa. Kiwanian (pres. 1938). Contbr. articles to profl. pubs. Home: 1400 Baum St Vicksburg MS 39180 Office: 1600 Monroe St Vicksburg MS 39180

PURNELL, MAURICE EUGENE, lawyer; b. Dallas, Sept. 7, 1906; s. Charles Stewart and Ginevra (Locke) P.; A.B., So. Meth. U.; 1925; LL.B., Harvard, 1928; m. Marjorie Maillot, May 29, 1934; children—Marjorie Maillot, Maurice Eugene. Admitted to Tex. bar, 1928; asso. Locke, Locke, Stroud & Randolph, 1928, mem., 1934-39, Locke, Locke, Dyer & Purnell, 1939-45; sr. partner Locke, Purnell, Boren Laney & Neely, specializing corp. matters, financial planning and administrn. estates; dir. A.H. Belo Corp., Pioneer Natural Gas Co., Lomas & Nettleton Financial Corp., Mosher Steel Co., McAlester Fuel Co. Bd. dirs. Dallas Museum of Fine Arts (pres. 1956-59), Dallas Symphony Soc., Hockaday Sch. Mem. Am., Dallas bar assns., State Bar Tex., Am. Law Inst., English Speaking Union, Phi Beta Kappa, Sigma Alpha Epsilon. Clubs: Brook Hollow Golf (pres. 1958), Critic, Dallas, Koon Kreek, City, Petroleum (Dallas); Lawyers, University (N.Y.C.); Home: 4409 S Versailles Dallas TX 75205 Office: Republic Nat Bank Tower Dallas TX 75201

PURSELL, JOHN MACK, supt. schs.; b. Cashion, Okla., Oct. 22, 1933; s. John Russell and Neval Lorene (McKee) P.; student Central State U., 1951-53; B.S., Okla State U., 1956, M.S., 1957; postgrad. San Fernando Valley State Coll., 1959-66, U. Cal. at Los Angeles, 1960, Cal. Poly. Inst., 1963, Humboldt State Coll., 1964-66; m. Shirley Jean Walker, Sept. 18, 1954; children—John Mitchell, Kelly Shane, Timothy Sean. Tchr. agr. So. Kern Unified Sch. Dist., Rosamond, Cal., 1958-64, secondary prin., 1966-69; tchr. vocational agr. Arcata Union Sch. Dist., McKinleyville, Cal., 1964-66; supt. Medford (Okla.) Pub. Schs., 1969—. Mem. N.E.A., Okla. Edn. Assn. (mem. exec. com. 1971—), Medford C. of C., Phi Delta Kappa. Republican. Mem. Christian Ch. Kiwanian, Lion. Home: 223 N 5th St Medford OK 73759 Office: 300 N Main St Medford OK 73759

PURSELL, WALTER LEE, petroleum co. exec.; b. Alva, Okla., Dec. 13, 1910; s. Loran A. and Lois (Walton) P.; B.S. in Elec. Engring., Okla. A. and M. Coll., 1936, M.S. in Chemistry and Mech. Engring., 1937; postgrad. in mgmt. Kan. U., 1943-44, So. Meth. U., 1960; m. Edith Luceille Vogelman, June 14, 1940; children—Gerald Kent, Karen Sue. With Skelly Oil Co. Refinery, 1937—, chief process engr., 1945-50, chief engr., 1950-61, refinery mgr., 1961-64, spl. rep. engring. and constrn. dept., 1964-68, project mgr. project devel. dept., 1968—. Committeeman, Cub, Boy Scouts Am., El Dorado, 1957-60; safety chmn. P.T.A., El Dorado, 1960; mem. Kan. Gov.'s Emergency Resources Planning Com., 1962. Bd. dirs. Augusta-El Dorado Water Assn., Ark-Walnut River Basin Assn., Ark. Basin Devel. Assn. in Kan.; trustee Allen Meml. Hosp. Registered profl. engr., Kan., Okla. Mem. Am. Petroleum Inst., Soc. Automotive Engrs., Nat. Assn. Corrosion Engrs., Nat. Petroleum Refiners Assn., El Dorado C. of C. (dir. 1961-65), Phi Kappa Phi, Phi Lambda Upsilon, Sigma Tau. Methodist (steward). Rotarian. Club: El Dorado Country. Contbr. articles to profl. jours. Address: PO Box 1650 Tulsa OK 74102

PURSLEY, NORMAN B., physician, hosp. adminstr.; b. Griffin, Ga., Dec. 31, 1925; s. Frank Stewart and Willie (Brundage) P.; M.D., Med. Coll. Ga., 1948; m. Florence Ellen Morris, Sept. 30, 1948; children—Suzanne, Norman, George, Catherine, Claire, William, Louise, Elaine, Alice, June. Intern, Univ. Hosp., 1948-49; gen. practice of medicine, Hiawassee, Ga., 1949; sr. physician psychiatry, Milledgeville State Hosp., 1949-51; supt. Gracewood (Ga.) State Sch., and Hosp., 1951—; asst. clin. prof. pediatrics Med. Coll. Ga.; cons. Nat. Inst. Mental Health, Bethesda, Md. Bd. dirs. Ga. Assn. Retarded Children. Fellow Am. Assn. Mental Deficiency; mem. Am. Psychiat. Assn., Ga., So. med. assns., Richmond County Med. Soc. Methodist. Mason (Shriner). Address: Gracewood State School and Hospital Gracewood Ga 30812

PURSWELL, HENRY DOUGLAS, agrl. chem. co. exec.; b. Dothan, Ala., July 22, 1918; s. John Henry and Cynthia Audrey (Taylor) P.; B.S., Auburn U., 1942, M.S., 1947; m. Virginia Frances Martin, Apr. 16, 1944; children—Susan (Mrs. William Loy Woodruff), Beverly (Mrs. Robert P. Guarnella), Scott Douglas, Jeffrey Taylor. Asst. dir. Ga. Dept. Entomology, 1947-49; dir. agrl. chem. dept. Gold Kist, Inc., Atlanta, 1949—. Served to capt. AUS, 1942-45. Mem. Ga. Entomol. Soc. (pres. 1966-67), Ga. Weed Control Soc. (bd. dirs. 1969—, mem. exec. com. 1971—, So. Weed Soc., Entomol. Soc. Am., Southeast Agrl. Chem. Soc. Home: 534 Greenridge Circle Stone Mountain GA 30083 Office: 3348 Peachtree Rd N E Atlanta GA 30326

PURVIS, JOHN TAYLOR, neurol. surgeon; b. Morristown, Tenn., Feb. 4, 1929; s. Robert Averette and Katherine (Taylor) P.; student Carson-Newman Coll., 1948-49, U. Tenn., 1946-48, 50; M.D., U. Tenn., 1953; m. Patricia Ann Lane, Sept. 24, 1971; 1 son, Robert Henson; children (by previous marriage)—Katherine (Mrs. Alfred D. Sharp III), Elizabeth Harrison (Mrs. Gene Grace), John Taylor, Allyn Hunter, David Chilton. Intern, McGill U. Royal Victoria Hosp., Montreal, Que., Can., 1953-54; resident gen. surgery, neurol. surgery U. Va. Hosp., Charlottesville, 1956-60; commd. 1st lt. M.C., USAF, 1953, advanced through grades to maj., 1963; chief dept. neurol. surgery USAF Hosp., Wright-Patterson AFB, O., 1961-65; chief dept. neurol. surgery USAF Hosp., Clark Air Base, P.I., 1965-66; ret., 1966; pvt. practice medicine specializing in neurol. surgery, Birmingham, Ala., 1966-67, Richmond, Va., 1967-68, Knoxville, Tenn., 1968—; asst. prof. neurol. surgery U. Ala. Med. Center, 1966—; attending neurosurgeon St. Mary's Meml., Ft. Sanders Presbyn., E. Tenn. Baptist, E. Tenn. Childrens hosps. Clin. asso. prof. neurol. surgery U. Tenn., Knoxville. Diplomate Am. Bd. Neurol. Surgery. Fellow A.C.S.; mem. Am., Tenn. med. assns., Knoxville Acad. Medicine, Congress Neurol. Surgeons, So. Neurosurgical Soc., Am. Assn. Neurol. Surgeons, Assn. Air Force Mil. Surgeons, Phi Gamma Delta, Phi Ki. Methodist. Elk. Contbr. chpt. to book; papers to profl. jours. Home: Rt 2 Smith Rd Concord TN 37720 Office: Ft Sanders Profl Bldg Knoxville TN 37916

PURYEAR, ELMER LEE, educator; b. nr. Raleigh, N.C., Aug. 20, 1920; s. Rufus A. and Clohe (Strickland) P.; B.A. summa cum laude, Wake Forest U., 1943; M.A., U. N.C., 1947, Ph.D., 1954; m. Lois Bradley, Feb. 3, 1944; children—Paul, Leigh. Instr. history Wake Forest U., 1947-52; asst. prof. history W.Va. U., 1954-56; asso. prof. history Coll. of Charleston (S.C.), 1956-59, prof., 1959-62; prof. history, polit. sci. Greensboro (N.C.) Coll., 1962-71, dean, 1963-71; Graham A. Barden prof. govt. Campbell Coll., 1971—. Served with USNR, 1943-46; ETO. Mem. N.C. Hist. Soc. (sec., treas. 1965-69), Am., So. hist. assns. Rotarian. Author: (with others) Orange County, 1752-1952, 1953; Democratic Party Dissension in North Carolina, 1928-36, 1962. Contbr. articles to profl. jours. Home: 4013 Groometown Rd Greensboro NC 27407

PURYEAR, JOHN MOWERY, judge; b. Hartselle, Ala., July 13, 1918; s. William Miller and Esther Lee (Waldsmith) P.; student Marion Inst.; B.S. in Commerce, U. Ala., 1942, LL.B., 1948; m. Jane Katherin Binton, Aug. 23, 1946; children—Virginia Miller (Mrs. N.H. Mizedr), Jo (Mrs. Joe Macon, Jr.). Owner, operator The Corner, Tuscaloosa, Ala., 1946-68; probate judge Tuscaloosa County, Tuscaloosa, 1968—. Served with USAAF, 1942-45. Decorated Bronze Star medal. Home: RFD 1 Tuscaloosa AL 35401 Office: Box 67 Tuscaloosa AL 35401

PUSTER, FRANCES GARNETT (MRS. J. GREGG PUSTER), travel agy. exec.; b. Canon City, Colo., July 14, 1911; d. William Lacy and Persis (Briskey) Garnett; degree Rome Bus. Coll., 1930; student Internat. Corr. Schs., 1943; degree Am. Inst. Banking, 1955; student N.Y. Inst. Photography, 1959; m. J. Gregg Puster, July 10, 1972. Bookkeeper, Nat. City Bank, Rome, Ga., 1932-38, teller, 1939-47, head teller, 1948-59, head collection dept., 1960-68; owner-mgr. World Travel Agy., Rome, 1950—. Mem. Rome Symphony Orch., treas. 1950-56. Mem. Nat. Audubon Soc., Nat. Freelance Photographers Assn., Rome C. of C., Internat. Platform Assn., Photog. Soc. Am. Episcopalian. Office: World Travel Agy 486 Broad St PO Box 1393 Rome GA 30161

PUTMAN, DARRELL MILTON, oil co. exec.; b. Dickens, Ia., Mar. 14, 1903; s. Guy Myron and Cora Ann (Jones) P.; B.A., Colo. Coll., 1928; m. Margaret Ella White, Sept. 21, 1930; 1 dau., Margaret Ann (Mrs. Don Edward Schultz). Geologist, Producers & Refiners Corp., Okla. and Kan., 1929-31, Roy A. Godfrey, ind. oil producer, Madill, Okla., 1932-38; v.p., chief geologist Mack Oil Co., Duncan, Okla., 1939-70, dir., 1947—; dir. M&M Supply Co., Duncan, Thomas Drilling Co., Duncan, Fullwood Oil Co., Duncan. Lectr. extension course U. Okla., 1955-56. Surveyor, Summit County, Colo., 1928. Bd. dirs. Community Chest, Duncan, 1954-55. Mem. Duncan C. of C. (bd. dirs., 1949-57), Ardmore Geol. Soc. (hon. life), Am. Assn. Petroleum Geologists, Tulsa, Oklahoma City, Kan. geol. socs. Presbyn. (deacon, elder, trustee). Elk, Rotarian. Home: 1204 N 12th St Duncan OK 73533 Office: 1204 N 12th St Duncan OK 73533

PUTMAN, WILLIAM BENJAMIN, III, lawyer; b. Springdale, Ark., Aug. 23, 1923; s. William Benjamin and Maxine (Corbin) P.; B.A., U. Ark., 1947, J.D. with High Honors, 1953; m. Barbara Elizabeth Johnson, June 5, 1951; 1son, William Benjamin IV. With Stanolind Oil & Gas Co., 1948-51; practice law, admitted to Ark. bar, 1953; mem. firm Putman, Davis & Bassett, Fayetteville, 1953—. Lectr. in law U. Ark. Sch. Law, 1956—, pres. Ark. Law Sch. Found., 1966—; spl. justice Supreme Ct. of Ark., 1968, 70; mem. Ark. Bd. Law Examiners, 1959-64; mem. Ark. Supreme Ct. Com. on Jury Instrns., 1962—. Chmn., Washington County Democratic Central Com., 1957-61; mem. Washington County Bd. Election Commrs., 1957-61. Bd. dirs. Ark. Bar Found. Served with AUS, 1943-46. Decorated Purple Heart. Fellow Internat. Soc. Barristers; mem. Am., Ark. (spl. award 1966), Washington County bar assns., Am. Judicature Soc., Medico Legal Soc. London, Phi Alpha Delta, Omicron Delta Kappa, Sigma Alpha Epsilon. Editor, Ark. Law Rev., 1953. Home: 1547 Hope St Fayetteville AR 72701 Office: 28 S College Av Fayetteville AR 72701

PUTNAM, CARLETON, author, former air lines exec.; b. N.Y.C., Dec. 19, 1901; s. Israel and Louise (Carleton) P.; B.S., Princeton, 1924; LL.B., Columbia, 1932; m. 2d Lucy A. Chapman, Sept. 12, 1944 (div. 1956), m. 3d, Esther Willcox, 1956; one dau., Esther Louise. Founder, pres. Chgo. and Southern Air Lines, 1933-48, chmn. bd.,

1948-53; chmn. bd. Delta C & S Air Lines, 1953-54; dir. Delta Air Lines, 1954—. Mem. nat. labor-mgt. manpower policy com. ODM, 1953-61; mem. U.S. del., Internat. Civil Aviation Conf., Chgo., 1944 (advisor). Past gov. Nat. Aeronautic Assn., State of Mo.; past dir. Air Transport Assn. Am.; trustee Theodore Roosevelt Assn. Republican. Presbyn. Clubs: Cosmos, Chevy Chase (Washington); Princeton (N.Y.C.). Author: High Journey—A Decade in the Pilgrimage of an Airline Pioneer, 1945; Theodore Roosevelt, Vol. 1 The Formative Years, 1958; Race and Reason: A Yankee View, 1961; Race and Reality: A Search for Solutions, 1967; also numerous papers. Address: 1465 Kirby Rd McLean VA 22101

PUTNAM, FREDERICK WARREN, JR., bishop; b. Red Wing, Minn., June 17, 1917; s. Frederick W. and Margaret (Bunting) P.; B.A., U. Minn., 1939; B.D., Seabury-Western Theol. Sem., 1942, D.D., 1963; postgrad. State U. Ia., 1946-47; m. Helen Kathryn Prouse, Sept. 24, 1942; children—James Douglas, John Frederick, Andrew Warren. Ordained deacon, priest Episcopal Ch., 1942; pastor in Windom and Worthington, Minn., 1942-43, Iowa City, 1943-47, Evanston, Ill., 1947-59, Wichita, Kan., 1960-63; Episcopalian chaplain State U. Ia., 1943-47; suffragan bishop Episcopal Diocese Okla., 1963—; nat. chaplain Brotherhood St. Andrew, 1967—; v.p. Am. Commn. KEEP, 1961—. Pres. Okla. Conf. Religion and Race, 1963-67; v.p. Greater Oklahoma City Council Chs., 1966-67. Cons. St. Simeon's Episcopal Home, 1963—, St. Crispins Episcopal Conf. Center, 1963—, Casady Sch., 1963—, Holland Hall Sch., 1963—, Episcopal Theol. Sem. Southwest, 1966-69, Oklahoma City Community Relations Commn., 1967-70, Episcopal Soc. Cultural and Racial Unity, 1967-70. Recipient Distinguished Service award Evanston Jr. C. of C., 1952. Fellow Coll. Preachers, Oklahoma Camera Club; mem. Inst. Pastoral Care, Acad. Religion and Mental Health, Am. Civil Liberties Union, Asso. Parishes (pres. 1960-64), Assn. Clin. Pastoral Edn., Overseas Mission Soc., Assn. Am. Indian Affairs, Conf. Diocesan Execs. (pres. 1972—), Nat. Audubon Soc., Nat. Wildlife Fedn., U. Minn. Alumni Assn., Photog. Soc. Am., Phi Kappa Psi. Author articles. Editor, pub. Shareres mag., 1957-63. Home: 1704 Camden Way Oklahoma City OK 73116 Office: Box 1296 Oklahoma City OK 73101

PUTNAM, RICHARD JOHNSON, lawyer, judge; b. Abbeville, La., Sept. 27, 1913; s. Robert Emmet and Mathilde (Young) P.; B.S. cum laude, Springhill Coll., 1934; LL.B., Loyola U., New Orleans, 1937; m. Dorethea Gooch, Jan. 27, 1940; children—Richard Johnson, Claude Robert, Mary Stacy, Cynthia Ann. Admitted to La. bar, 1937, pvt. practice, Abbeville, 1937-54; dist. atty. 15th jud. dist., 1948-54; judge 15th Jud. Dist. Ct., 1954-61, U.S. dist. judge Western Dist. La., 1961—. Mem. Evangeline area council Boy Scouts Am. Served from ensign to lt. USNR, 1942-45. Mem. Dist. Atty. Assn. La., Nat. Assn. Dist. Attys., Dist. Judges Assn., Am., La. bar assns., Am. Judicature Soc., Am. Legion, V.F.W., C. of C., Delta Theta Phi. K.C. (4 deg.). Home: Windover 515 Lafitte Rd Abbeville LA 70510 Office: Post Office Bldg Lafayette LA 70501

PUTNAM, WILLIAM THOMAS, state ofcl.; b. Florence, S.C., July 30, 1926; s. Bluford Hugh and Lucy (Self) P.; B.S., U. S.C., 1948; m. Elizabeth Burch Harrell, July 14, 1951; children—William Thomas, Susan Elizabeth. Field auditor S.C. Tax Commn., Columbia, 1948-53, chief clk. income div., 1953-57, individual supr., 1957-61, dir. data processing div., 1961-66, asst. state auditor, 1966—. Served with USAAF, 1945-46. Baptist (deacon). Home: 109 Chartwell Rd Columbia SC 29210 Office: Wade Hampton Bldg Senate St Columbia SC 29202

PUTNEY, FLOYD JOHNSON, otolaryngologist; b. Easton, Md., 1910; M.D., Jefferson Med. Coll., 1934; postgrad. Harvard, 1939. Resident pathologist Jefferson Med. Coll., Phila., 1934-35, intern, 1935-37; asst. broncoscopist to physician, 1937-40; resident otolaryngologist Manhattan Eye, Ear, Throat Hosp., N.Y.C., 1940-41; attending otolaryngologist Med. U. S.C. Hosp., 1942—; cons. otolaryngologist VA Hosp., Charleston Naval Hosp., Charleston County Hosp. Prof. otolaryngology Med. Coll. S.C. Served to lt. col. M.C. AUS, World War II. Diplomate Am. Bd. Otolaryngology. Fellow A.C.S.; mem. A.M.A., Am. Laryngol. Rhinological Otol. Soc., Am. Broncho-Esophagological Assn., Am. Acad. Ophthalmology, Otolaryngology, Am. Laryngol. Assn., Am. Soc. Head and Neck Surgery. Address: 80 Barre St Charleston SC 29401*

PUTNEY, ROBERT HUBBARD, JR., physician; b. Elm City, N.C., Mar. 23, 1917; s. Robert Hubbard and Ruth Bedford (Jones) P.; A.B., U. N.C., 1939; M.D., Med. Coll. Va., 1943; m. Mildred Whitehead, June 6, 1942; children—Martha Witt (Mrs. R.B. Polhill, Jr.), Robert Hubbard III, Elizabeth Ruth, William. Intern, Park View Hosp., Rocky Mount, N.C., 1943-44, Brooke Gen. Hosp., San Antonio, 1944-45; family practice medicine, 1946—; mem. staff Wilson (N.C.) Meml. Hosp; owner Elm City Clinic, Elm City, N.C., 1946—; chmn. bd. Branch Banking and Trust Co., Elm City; pres. Ford Motor Co., Elm City, 1947-48. Chmn. bd. commrs. Town of Elm City, 1947; mem. Elm City Sch. Bd., 1947—. Mem. local com. Morehead Found. N.C. Served to capt. M.C. AUS, 1943-46. Mem. A.M.A., N.C., 4th Dist., Seaboard, So., Wilson County med. socs., Am. Legion, Sigma Delta, Lambda Chi Alpha, Phi Chi. Baptist (chmn. bd. trustees 1950—). Elk, Rotarian. Club: Country (Elm City). Home: Barnes St Elm City NC 27822 Office: Main St Elm City NC 27822

PUYAU, FRANCIS ALBERT, physician, educator; b. New Orleans, Dec. 1, 1928; s. Frank Albert and Rose Sue (Jones) P.; B.S., Notre Dame U., 1948; M.D., La. State U., 1952; m. Geraldine Sally Benedetto, June 6, 1951; children—Michael, Stephen, Jeane Marie, Julie, Melissa. Intern, Charity Hosp., New Orleans, 1952-53, resident fellow, 1955-57, staff radiologist, 1968—; mem. staff St. Tamman Hosp., Covington, La.; instr. pediatrics La. State U. Sch. Medicine, New Orleans, 1957-59, asst. prof. pediatrics, 1959-61, asso. prof., 1968-71, prof. pediatrics, radiology, 1971—, chmn. dept., 1972—; asst. prof. pediatrics Vanderbilt U., 1961-68; cons. VA Hosp., New Orleans. Served with USPHS, 1953-55. Diplomate Am. Bd. Pediatrics (mem. sub bd. 1961—), Am. Bd. Pediatric Cardiology, Am. Bd. Radiology. Fellow Am. Coll. Cardiology; mem. Am. Coll. Radiology, Orleans Parish Med. Soc. Contbr. articles to profl. jours. Home: 2104 State St New Orleans LA 70118 Office: 1542 Tulane Av New Orleans LA 70140

PYLE, HAROLD GIBSON, editor; b. Mineola, Tex., Apr. 19, 1902; s. Owen P. and Mildred Susie (Gibson) P.; m. Helen Howard, Jan. 15, 1939; 1 dau., Adelaide Marcella (Mrs. Michael R. Darnell). Editor, Belton (Tex.) Jour., 1921-25, Brownwood (Tex.) News, 1925-26; with Houston Chronicle, Houston Post., Galveston News, 1926-29; with Houston Chronicle, 1929-67, chief editorial writer, 1936-67, asso. editor, 1950-67; editor Houston Tribune, 1967—, pres., 1972—. Pres., Sam Houston Meml. Assn.; mem., past chmn. Harris County Hist. Survey Com. Recipient Christopher award, 1956; Freedoms Found. award, 1958. Republican. Roman Catholic. Home: 9025 Sandringham Houston TX Office: 4901 Richmond Av Houston TX 77027

PYLE, JOHNNIE AUGUSTUS, insulation co. exce.; b. Crockett, Tex., Oct. 16, 1914; s. Otis Augustus and Mary Bell (Richardson) P.; student pub. schs.; m. Iola McKnight, Dec. 1, 1945; children—Billy G., Shirley (Mrs. Lewis Watts, Jr.), Bobbie (Mrs. Edward Schiller), Linda (Mrs. Charles McNatt). Warehouseman, B & B Engring & Supply Co., Houston, 1945-46, purchasing agt., 1947-55, mgr. purchasing, 1956-70; v.p. B & B Insulation, Inc., Houston, 1971—. Served with USNR, 1945. Eagle. Home: 2006 Chaparrel St Houston TX 77043 Office: 6250 W Park St Houston TX 77027

PYLE, RICHARD ALDEN, lawyer; b. Eufaula, Okla., Apr. 16, 1931; s. Luther Alden and Margaret Catherine (Turner) P.; B. A., Central State U., 1964; LL.B., U. Okla., 1966; m. Forrest Marjorie Busha, Aug. 23, 1952; children—Traci Lou, Trent Alden. Admitted to Okla. bar, 1966; practiced in Eufaula, 1966-69; U.S. atty. for Eastern Dist. Okla., Muskogee, 1969—. Served with AUS, 1950, 52. Mem. McIntosh County (pres. 1970), Muskogee County, Fed. bar assns., Delta Theta Phi. Republican. Home: 206 Broadway St Eufaula OK 74432 Office: 333 Fed Bldg Muskogee OK 74401

PYLES, CHARLES BOYKIN, educator; b. North Little Rock, Ark., July 17, 1925; s. Noah Thornton and Martha (Sharp) P.; B.S., U. Ark., 1948, M.A., 1955; Ph.D., U. Ga., 1967; student George Washington U., 1956-60; m. Nelda Keith Burrows, June 25, 1949; children—Karen Ann, Charles David. Caseworker, Ark. State Bd. Health, Little Rock, 1948-50; vocational appraiser Little Rock (Ark.) Jr. Coll., 1950-51, bus. mgr., 1951-56; asst. prof. Ga. Inst. Tech., Atlanta, 1961-67; asso. prof. polit. sci. Ga. State U., Atlanta, 1967-70, prof., 1970—, chmn. dept. polit. sci., 1971—. Treas., Pub. Operations Research & Cons., Atlanta, 1969-72. Research asst. Gov's. Commn. on Efficiency and Economy in Govts., 1963-67. Served with USNR, 1943-46. Mem. Am. Polit. Sci. Assn., Ga. (pres. 1969-70), So. polit. sci. assns., Am. Assn. U. Profs., Pub. Personnel Assn., Am. Soc. for Pub. Adminstrn. (chpt. pres. 1969-70). Office: 33 Gilmer St SE Atlanta GA 30303

QUALLS, ROBERT L., banker; b. Burnsville, Miss., Nov. 6, 1933; s. Wes E. and Letha (Parker) Q.; B.S., Miss. State U., 1954, M.S., 1958; postgrad. La. State U., 1959-61; m. Mildred Daphne Ward, Nov. 5, 1966. Prof., chmn. div. econs. and bus. Belhaven Coll., Jackson, Miss., 1962-66, asst. to pres., 1965-66; asst. prof. finance Miss. State U., State College, 1967-69; sr. v.p. marketing Bank of Miss., Tupelo, 1969—; cons. First Fed. Savs. &Loan Assn., Jackson, 1963-68, dir. marketing, 1968-69; marketing cons. Ill. Central Industries, Chgo., 1964. Mem. 4-H adv. council, 1969; active Boy Scouts Am. Served to lt. AUS, 1954-56. Found. for Econ. Edn. fellow, 1964; Ford Found. faculty research fellow, 1963-64. Mem. Bus. and Profl. Group of Am. (dir. 1969), Newcomen Soc., Blue Key, Omicron Delta Kappa, Delta Sigma Pi, Sigma Phi Epsilon. Rotarian. Contbr. articles to profl. jours. Home: 1401 Fillmore St Tupelo MS 38801 Office: 201 Main St Tupelo MS 38801

QUARLES, GILFORD GODFREY, govt. ofcl.; b. Charlottesville, Va., Dec. 24, 1909; s. Charles H. and Carolynn (Payne) Q.; B.S. in Elec. Engring., U. Va., 1930, M.S. in Physics, 1933, Ph.D. in Physics, 1934; m. Mary Ethel Kase, Mar. 24, 1934 (div.) m. 2d, Betty Jane Haugh, Sept. 2, 1961. Tchr. physics Mercer U., 1934-35, U. Ala., 1935-41, Furman U., 1941-44; research asso. Harvard, 1944-45; prof. engring. research Pa. State U., 1945-58, dir. Ordnance Research Lab., 1952-58; tech. cons. comdg. gen. Army Ballistic Missile Agy., 1956-58; chief scientist Army Ordnance Missile Command, 1958-59, C.E., U.S. Army, 1959-60; dir. long range mil. planning Bendix Corp., 1960-61; chief sci. adviser C.E., U.S. Army, 1961—. Mem. Am. Phys. Soc., I.E.E.E., A.A.A.S., Assn. U.S. Army, Am. Soc. Engring. Edn., Sigma Xi, Theta Tau, Tau Beta Pi. Author: Elementary Photography, 1948; also articles electro-optics, acoustics, vibrations, space tech. Home: 1913 Earldale Ct Alexandria VA 22306 Office: Office Chief of Engrs Washington DC 20315

QUARLES, ROBERT JABE, banker; b. nr. Richmond, Va., Mar. 29, 1926; s. Harry F. and Hannah (Keith) Q.; student Coll. William and Mary, 1946-47; Roanoke Coll., 1948-49, U. Va., 1949-50; m. Betty Brillhart, Oct. 29, 1948; children—Barry Allen, Karen Leigh. File Clk. U.S. Employment Service, 1946-47; with Halfiegh & Co., 1947; with Bank of Va., Richmond, 1949—, now sr. v.p. Served with USAAF, 1944-46. Mem. Bank Adminstrn. Inst. (dir. Va.), Am. Inst. Banking. Baptist (trustee). Club: Downtown (Richmond). Home: 2546 Penrose Dr Richmond VA 23235 Office: 800 E Main St Richmond VA 23214

QUARM, JOAN HELANA PHELAN, educator, critic; b. Bristol, Eng.; d. Samuel George and Mary (O'Phelan) Phelan; B.A. Edn., Portsmouth Coll., U. Reading (Eng.), 1940; M.A., San Francisco State Coll., 1966; m. Thomas Quarm, 1949 (div. 1964); children—Susanna Rosemary Summ (Mrs. Terry Gardner), Michael, Robin, Christopher, Nicholas. Came to U.S., 1946, naturalized, 1948. Tchr., A.S. Neill's, Summerhill, Eng., Lisbon, Portugal, 1943, with Brit. Council, Peru, 1949-51, Cerro de Pasco Co., Central Africa, 1956; faculty U. Tex., El Paso, 1958—, asst. prof. English, 1967—; drama and music critic El Paso Herald-Post, 1962—. Co-founder The Theatre, El Paso, 1962, Festival Theatre, 1964, dir., 1965—. Recipient personal grant to found a bilingual theatre in El Paso from Nat. Found. Arts and Humanities and Tex. Fine Arts Commn., 1969. Mem. Am. Assn. U. Profs., Nat. Soc. Arts and Letters, Tex. Womens Press Assn. Home: 1520 Upson Av El Paso TX 79902

QUARTERMAN, GEORGE HENRY, clergyman; b. Poughkeepsie, N.Y., Aug. 12, 1906; s. Frederick George and Elizabeth Jane (Brown) Q.; A.B., St. Stephen's Coll., 1928; S.T.D., Gen. Theol. Sem., 1931; D.D., U. South, 1947; S.T.D., Ch. Div. Sch. of Pacific, 1959; m. Ruth Grace Spahr, Aug. 21, 1931; children—George Henry, William Edward, Ann Dorothy. Ordained to ministry Protestant Episcopal Ch., 1931; rector St. Phillip's Ch., Ardmore, Okla., 1931-46, St. Andrew's Ch., Amarillo, Tex., 1946; bishop Dist. N. Tex., 1946-48; bishop Diocese N.W. Tex., 1958-72, ret. Trustee U. of South, 1946—. Mason (32 deg.). Address: 1520 Bryan St Amarillo TX 79102

QUATTLEBAUM, CHARLES ALBERT, author, govt. ofcl.; b. Ridge Spring, S.C.; s. Charles Albert and Julia (Barr) Q.; A.B., U. Ga., 1933; M.A., George Washington U., 1940; postgrad. Northwestern U.; m. Marguerite Vogeding, June 1, 1941. Sch. adminstr., tchr. English, S.C. and Ga., 1925-35; spl. writer U.S. Treasury Dept., 1935-37; specialist edn. legislative reference service Library of Congress, 1937—. Mem. Am. Ednl. Research Assn., Higher Edn. Group, Am. Polit. Sci. Assn., Fed. Profl. Assn., Nat. Fedn. Fed. Employees, Soc. Advancement Edn., Kappa Delta Pi. Baptist. Author: Development of Scientific Engineering, and Other Professional Manpower, 1957; Government Programs in International Education, 1959; Federal Educational Policies, Programs and Proposals, 3 vols., 1960; The Historic and Current Federal Role in Education, 1961; Federal Legislation Concerning Education and Training, 1962; Proposed Federal Promotion of Shared Time Education, 1963; Enactments by the 89th Congress Concerning Education and Training, 1961; Federal Educational Policies, 3 vols., 1968; also govt. reports, articles ednl. field. Contbr. to Ency. American, other reference, text books, ednl. jours. Home: 1022 S 26th Rd Arlington VA 22202 Office: Library of Congress Washington DC 20540

QUATTLEBAUM, WALTER EMMETT, JR., telephone co. exec.; b. Midville, Ga., Dec. 22, 1922; s. Walter Emmett and Eva (Bagley) Q.; student Murrey Vocational Sch., 1941, U. Hawaii, 1943; m. Dorothy Evelyn Clewis, Oct. 22, 1946; children—Walter Emmett III, Amalia Ann. Former owner Fla. Telephone Exchange, Sneads, 1948—, Cottondale, 1954—, Grand Ridge, 1954—, Bonifay, 1955—, Westville, 1957—, Seagrove Beach, 1958—; past pres., chmn. bd. dirs. Tri-County Telephone Co., Bonifay; v.p., dir. Seminole Telephone Co., Donalsonville, Ga.; now investment analyst. City councilman, Sneads, 1950-52, pres. City Council, 1953. Served with AUS, 1944-46. Mem. Fla. Telephone Assn. (dir.), Telephone Pioneers Am. Methodist. Address: Bonifay FL 32425

QUATTLEBAUM, WILLIAM CASPER, dentist; b. Cullman, Ala., Aug. 19, 1924; s. Samuel Oscar and Lillie Cordelia (Hines) Q.; A.A., St. Bernard Coll., 1947; D.M.D., U. Ala., 1952; m. Virginia Ruth Houston, Nov. 16, 1946; children—Kenneth Wesley, Jane Lori, Samuel Oscar. Pvt. practice dentistry, Ozark, Ala., 1952—. Served with AUS, 1943-45. Mem. Am. (del. 1959-68), Ala. dental assns., 3d Dist. Dental Soc. (v.p. 1960, pres. 1961), Ozark C. of C. Baptist. (deacon 1956—, pres. trustees 1964—). Kiwanian (sec. 1955). Home: 441 E Broad St Ozark AL 36360 Office: 317 James St Ozark AL 36360

QUENG, JOSE T., allergist; b. Fukien, China, Sept. 20, 1933; M.D. (cum laude), U. Santo Tomas, Philippines, 1958; m. Theresa P. Chan. Rotating intern, Kings County Hosp. Center, Bklyn., 1958-59; resident in pediatrics Beth-El Hosp., Bklyn., 1959-60; asst. in pediatrics Baylor U. Coll. Medicine, Houston, 1960-64, resident in pediatrics, 1960-62, fellow in pediatric allergy, 1962-64, clin. asst. prof. pediatrics, 1969—; asst. prof. pediatrics Far Eastern U. Inst. Medicine, Manila, Philippines, 1965-67; clin. asst. prof. allergy, U. Tex. Grad. Sch. Bio-Med. Scis., Houston, 1970—; chief, pediatric allergy clinic Children's Med. Center, Quezon City, Philippines, 1964-67; St. Luke's Hosp., Quezon City, 1966-67; St. Joseph's Hosp., Houston, 1969—; now practice medicine specializing in allergies, Houston; mem. staff Tex. Children's Hosp., Bayshore Gen. Hosp.; cons. in allergy Rosewood Gen. Hosp. Lectr. on allergies. Recipient Mead Johnson Travel grant Am. Coll. Allergists, 1963. Diplomate Am. Bd. Pediatrics. Fellow Am. Acad. Allergy, Am. Coll. Allergists, Internat. Soc. Certified Allergists; mem. Internat. Corr. Soc. Allergists, Philippines Pediatrics Soc, A.M.A., Tex. Med. Assn., Harris County Med. Soc., So. Med. Assn., Tex. Pediatric Soc., A.A.A.S., Sigma Xi. Office: McGovern Allergy Clin 6655 Travis St Houston TX 77025*

QUESENBERRY, WILLIAM FITZHUGH, food broker; b. Jacksonville, Fla., Dec. 3, 1922; s. William Fitzhugh and Caroline (Kittrell) Q.; B.A., U. of South, 1943; m. Mary Belle Gardner, Apr. 13, 1946; 1 dau., Mary Belle (Mrs. Robert McIntyre). With Quesenberry & Catlin, Miami, Fla., 1946—, salesman, 1946-49, partner, 1949-53, sr. partner, 1953—. Bd. dirs. Muscular Dystrophy Soc. Fla.; trustee U. of South; bd. advisors Fla. Meml. Coll. Served to lt. comdr. USNR, 1943-46. Mem. Miami (pres. 1951-52), Nat. (dir. 1966-67) food brokers assns., Fla. Frozen Food Assn. (dir.), Hist. Soc. Fla., Traffic Club of Greater Miami (v.p. 1951-52), Phi Gamma Delta. Episcopalian (sr. warden 1970-71). Kiwanian (v.p. Miami 1971-72). Clubs: Riviera Country, Coral Gables Country. Home: 4102 Monserrate St Coral Gables FL 33146 Office: 735 NW 22d Av Miami FL 33135

QUEST, CHARLES FRANCIS, artist, educator, lectr.; b. Troy, N.Y., June 6, 1904; s. Charles F. and Ann (Hogan) Q.; student Washington U. Sch. Fine Arts, 1924-29, courses edn., 1938-39; Paris, France, 1929; m. Dorothy Johnson, Sept. 7, 1928. Executed murals pub. bldgs. libraries, and several large chs., 1930-45; instr. drawing and art analysis Washington U. Sch. Fine Arts, St. Louis, 1945, now asso. prof. Print maker wood engravings, wood cuts, etchings, copper engraving; painter oil, watercolor, tempera; sculptor; crafts stainglass, mosaic. Works purchased by Met. Mus. N.Y., Mus. Modern Art N.Y., Chgo. Art Inst., Phila. Art Mus., Library of Congress, St. Louis Art Mus., Bklyn. Mus., Brit., Victoria and Albert Mus., London, Bibliotheque Nationale, Paris, Nat. Mus. Stockholm, Nat. Mus. Jerusalem, Nat. Gallery Australia, others; exhibited in 90 mus. and galleries in U.S., France, Germany, Italy; represented in permanent collections 38 museums, also oil painting Still Life With Flowers at U.S. State Dept. Art in the Embassies Program. Exhibit color woodcuts Am. embassy, Paris, followed by year's tour of France, 1951; one-man show Smithsonian Inst., U.S. Nat. Mus., 1951, Maryville Coll. Mus., 1966, Am. Fedn. Arts, 1966; exhibited at Boston Mus. Art, Detroit Inst. Art, Cleve. Mus. Art, Fogg Mus. Harvard; two-man show Phila. Print Club (wood engravings and woodcuts), 1951; alter painting for Old Cathedral St. Louis, 1960. Recipient 51 prizes, 1923—. Mem. Soc. Am. Graphic Artists, Inc., Phila. Color Print Soc., So. Vt. Artists, Inc., Painters Gallery. Club: St. Louis (life). Home: 200 Hillswick Rd Tryon NC 28782

QUICK, CLARENCE CARL, pharmacist; b. Round Rock, Tex., Aug. 19, 1908; s. Oscar Edward and Caroline (Ericson) Q.; B.S. in Biology, U. Detroit, 1933; B.S. in Pharmacy, U. Tex., 1938; m. Alice Eudora Magee, Feb. 18, 1942; children—Marilyn (Mrs. Joe Richardson, Jr.), Linda (Mrs. Joe Carriere, Jr.), Barbara. Pharmacist, Skillern's Drug Store, Dallas, 1942; partner Quick Pharmacy, Round Rock, Tex., 1945-61, owner, Dayton, Tex., 1961—. Sec. Round Rock High Sch. Bd., 1950-57. Served to lt. USNR, 1942-45. Mem. C. of C. (pres. 1970-71). Methodist. Kiwanian, Rotarian. Club: Athletic (Dayton, Tex.). Home: 12 Sherwood St Dayton TX 77535 Office: 309 N Main St Dayton TX 77535

QUIJADA, FRANCISCO, Venezuelan diplomat. Consul gen. from Venezuela, New Orleans. Office: 1006 Internat Trade Mart 2 Canal St New Orleans LA 70130

QUILLEN, HOWARD EUGENE, dentist; b. nr. Gate City, Va., July 16, 1920; s. Hobart McKinley and Cora Mae (Vermillion) Q.; B.A., Emory and Henry Coll., 1950; postgrad. E. Tenn. State U., 1951, 57-58; D.D.S., Med. Coll. Va., 1962; m. Grace Jacqueline Broadwater, Dec. 31, 1949; children—Jacqueline Ann, Howard Eugene. Coach, Washington County Sch. Bd., 1948-50, Scott County Sch. Bd., 1950-53, Tazewell County Sch. Bd., 1953-57; pvt. practice dentistry, Gate City, Va., 1962—. Served with AUS, 1942-46. Recipient Deleware Valley Outstanding Student award Med. Coll. Va. Dental Sch., 1962. Mem. Am. Hist. Soc., Am., Va. State (mem. ethics com. 1971-72) dental assns., Smithsonian Assos., Am. Legion, Am. Heritage Soc., Nat. Hist. Soc., A.A.A.S., V.F.W. Republican. Methodist (mem. finance com. 1971—). Rotarian. Home and Office: PO Box 482 Gate City VA 24251

QUILLEN, JAMES H(ENRY), congressman; b. Wayland, Va., Jan. 11, 1916; s. John A. and Hannah (Chapman) Q.; ed. high sch.; LL.D. (hon.), Steed Coll., Tech., 1963; m. Cecile Cox, Aug. 9, 1952. With Kingsport Press, 1934-35, Kingsport Times, 1935-36; founder, pub. Kingsport Mirror, 1936-39; founder, pub. Johnson City Times, 1939-44, converted to daily, 1940; founder Kingsport Devel. Co., owner, pres., 1946—; pres. (inactive) Model City Investment Corp., Kingsport Devel. Co. Ins., Inc., Kingsport Devel. Co. Real Estate-Loans, Inc., Kingsport Devel. Co. Gen. Contractors, Inc.;

chmn. Johnson City Ins. Agy., Inc., Wofford Bros., Inc., Johnson City; dir. Kingsport Nat. Bank; mem. Tenn. Ho. of Reps., 1954-62, legislative council, 1957-59, 61; mem. 88th-92d Congresses 1st Tenn. Dist., mem. house rules com., house com. standards of ofcl. conduct. Bd. dirs. Sullivan County Tb Assn., past state dir.; past dir. Kingsport chpt. A.R.C. Served to lt. USNR, 1942-46. Recipient Young Man of Yr. award Johnson City Jr. C. of C., 1942. Mem. Kingsport Real Estate Bd. (dir., past pres.), Am. Legion, V.F.W., C. of C., Comml. Travelers. Republican. Methodist. Elk, Moose, Lion. Club: Ridgefield Country (Kingsport). Home: 1601 Fairidge Pl Kingsport TN 37664 Office: Cannon Bldg Washington DC 20515

QUILLIAM, WILLIAM REED, JR., lawyer, educator; b. Beaumont, Tex., Jan. 21, 1929; s. William Reed and Gladys (Harned) Q.; B.A., U. Tex. at Austin, 1949, B.B.A., 1951, LL.B., 1953; L.L.M., Harvard, 1969; m. Myrna Corinne Simmons, June 6, 1953; children—Mary Corinne, Kathryn Harned, William Reed III. Admitted to Tex. bar, 1953; asst. prof. Tex. Tech. U., 1955-56, prof. law, 1969—; trust officer Am. State Bank, 1959-60; pvt. practice law, Lubbock, Tex., 1956-58, 60-68; pres. Lubbock Lands, Inc., 1966—. Mem. Tex. Ho. Reps., 1961-69. Named Outstanding First-Term House Mem., U.P.I. poll, 1961, Outstanding prof. Tex. Tech. U., 1971. Served at lt. (j.g.) USNR, 1953-55; now lt. comdr. Res. Mem. State Bar Tex., State Jr. Bar Tex. (dir. 1957-59), Theta Xi, Phi Alpha Delta. Presbyn. Club: Lubbock. Home: 5703 Geneva St Lubbock TX 79413 Office: Sch Law Tex Tech U Lubbock TX 79409

QUILLIAN, WILLIAM FLETCHER, JR., coll. pres.; b. Nashville, Apr. 13, 1913; s. William Fletcher (D.D.) and Nonie (Acree) Q.; A.B., Emory U., 1935, Litt.D., 1959; B.D., Yale, 1938, Ph.D. (Day fellow, Rosenwald fellow), 1943; postgrad. U. Edinburgh (Scotland), 1938-39, U. Basel (Switzerland), 1939; LL.D., Ohio Wesleyan U., 1952, Randolph-Macon Coll., 1967; m. Margaret Hannah Weigle, June 15, 1940; children—William Fletcher III, Anne Acree, Katherine, Robert. Student asst. Stamford (Conn.) Presbyn. Ch., 1936-38; del. to gen. com. World Student Christian Fedn., Bievres, France, 1938; discussion leader World Conf. Christian Youth, Amsterdam, Holland, 1939; pastor Claredon (Vt.) Community Ch., summer 1940; ordained to ministry Methodist Ch., 1942; asst. prof. philosophy Gettysburg (Pa.) Coll., 1941-43, prof., 1943-45; prof. philosophy Ohio Wesleyan U., 1945-52; pres. Randolph Macon Woman's Coll., Lynchburg, Va., 1952—. Tchr., Garrett Bibl. Inst., summer 1951. Mem. univ. senate Methodist Ch., 1952—. Bd. dirs. Lynchburg Gen. Hosp. Mem. Va. Found. Ind. Colls. (pres. 1958-61), Assn. Va. Colls. (past pres.), So. Univ. Conf. (pres. 1967-68), So. Assn. Colls. Women (pres. 1956), Am. Philos. Assn., Nat. Council Religion Higher Edn. (central com. 1945-48, chmn. 1947-48), Nat. Assn. Bibl. Instrs., Am. Assn. U. Profs., Phi Beta Kappa, Omicron Delta Kappa, Alpha Tau Omega. Author: The Moral Theory of Evolutionary Naturalism, 1945; Evolution and Moral Theory in America; Evolutionary Thought in America, 1950. Contbr. articles to philos. and religious jours. Home: 2460 Rivermont Av Lynchburg VA 24503

QUIMBY, FREEMAN HENRY, physiologist; b. Battle Creek, Mich., June 11, 1915; s. Lyle Edward and Chloe (Eisenhood) Q.; B.A., Andrews U., 1938; M.S., Northwestern U., 1941; postgrad. Mich. State U., 1940; Ph.D., U. Md., 1947; m. Juanita Lenore Artress, Nov. 10, 1949; children—Kelvin, David, Carole. Mgr., Penny-a-dish cafeteria, Battle Creek, 1935-36; prof. biology Columbia Union Coll., 1941-48; head physiology br. Office Naval Research, San Francisco, 1948-56, chief scientist, 1956-59; chief research analysis Army Research Office, Arlington, Va., 1959-60; chief exobiology br. NASA, Washington, 1960-66; specialist life scis. Library of Congress, Washington, 1966—. Cons. Operations Research Office, U.S. Army. Mem. Fedn. Am. Soc. Exptl. Biology, A.A.A.S., Am. Phys. Soc., Wildlife Fedn., Wilderness Soc., Am. Acad. Polit. Social Scis., Sigma Xi. Author: Search for Extraterrestrial Life, 1963, The Participation of Federal Agencies in International Scientific Programs, 1967; Medical Experimentation on Human Beings, 1968; The State of Technology in Nonlethal Guns, 1968; Chemical and Biological Weapons, 1969; Flouridation: A Modern Paradox in Science and Public Policy, 1970; The Politics of Global Health, 1971. Contbr. articles to profl. jours. Home: 3926 Rickover Rd Silver Spring MD 20902 Office: Library of Congress Washington DC 20540

QUINN, CORBETT LATIMER, physician, mayor; b. nr. Pink Hill, N.C., Oct. 6, 1926; s. Corbett L. and Ina (Turner) Q.; B.A., U. N.C., 1949, certificate in medicine, 1951; M.D., U. Md., 1953; m. Ruth Arlene Montgomery, May 26, 1953; children—Corbett Latimer, Risa Teresa. Rotating intern Mercy Hosp., Balt., 1953-54, resident, 1954-55; gen. practice medicine, Magnolia, N.C., 1955—; pres., chief staff Duplin Gen. Hosp., 1955—; mayor, Magnolia, 1961—. Dir. Br. Banking & Trust Co., Warsaw, N.C. Mem. med. com. for driver evaluation N.C. Dept. Motor Vehicles, 1964—; mem. med. adv. com. James Sprint Inst., 1966—; rep. to Duplin County Cystic Fibrosis Soc., 1968—; civil def. dir., Magnolia, 1958—; surgeon 30th Inf. div. N.C. Army N.G., 1971—. Mem. Magnolia Town Bd. Commrs., 1957-61, mem. adv. com. on mental health, 1969—. Chmn. Duplin County Republican Party, 1970—. Chmn. Magnolia Community Meml. Found. Served with AUS, World War II, Res., 1957—. Diplomate Am. Bd. Family Practice. Mem. Am. Acad. Gen. Practice, Am. Geriatric Soc., A.M.A., So. Med. Assn., N.C., Duplin County (past pres.) med. socs., Duplin County Tb Assn. (past pres.), Duplin County Cancer Soc. (dir.) Address: Railroad St PO Box 128 Magnolia NC 28453

QUINN, EMILY HOTCHKISS, educator; b. Pitts.; d. Leonard B. and Thelma (Jennings) Hotchkiss; B.S., Ga. State Coll. for Women, 1948; M.S., U. Wis., 1962, Ph.D., 1964; m. Robert Earl, Aug. 25, 1955 (div. June 1958); 1 son, David Michael. Extension home economist U. Ga., Athens, 1955-56, U. Ariz., Tucson, 1956-61; fellow U. Wis., Madison, 1961-63; asso. prof. edn. N.C. State U., Raleigh, 1964-67, prof. edn. and state leader tng., 1967-71; dean Sch. Home Econs. U. Ga., 1971—. Mem. Adult Edn. Assn. of U.S., Ga. Adult Edn. Assn., Am., Ga. home econs. assns., So. Assn. Home Econs. Adminstrs., Phi Upsilon Omicron, Omicron Nu, Delta Kappa Gamma. Author: (with E. J. Boone, E. H. Quinn) Curriculum Development In Adult Basic Education, 1967. Cons. editor Adult Edn. jour. Home: 350 Ashton Dr Athens GA 30601

QUINN, JAMES WADE, JR., food co. exec.; b. Osceola, Ark., June 9, 1936; s. James Wade and Jean (Fisher) Q.; student Memphis State U., 1954-57; m. Edris Johanna Gooch, Apr. 18, 1964; children—James Wade III, James Thomas. Asst. mgr. Food Center Tenn., Memphis, 1957-58, Weingarten's, Memphis, 1959; mgr., owner Time Saver, Inc., Memphis, 1959-64, Pic'n'Sac, West Memphis, 1963-69, Jr. Food Stores, 1965—; pres. Quinn Wholesale Co. (name changed to J. Wade Quinn Inc.), Jonesboro, Ark., 1969—, dist. mgr. Brevoni Hosiery, 1970—. Mem. Jonesboro Bd. Adjustments, 1968-70. Methodist. Lion, Elk. Club: Jonesboro Country. Home: 2515 S Culberhouse Rd Jonesboro AR 72401 Office: 2515 S Culberhouse Rd Jonesboro AR 72401

QUINN, OLIN BYRON, banker; b. Long Leaf, La., Sept. 30, 1917; s. Willie W. and Elizabeth (Alexander) Q.; B.S., La. State U., 1949, M.S., 1951; m. Hazel Hogan, Dec. 21, 1941; children—Laura E., Julianne I. Research staff La. State U. 1951-52; asst. treas. Fed. Intermediate Credit Bank, 1952-59; treas., sr. v.p. Fed. Land Bank of New Orleans, 1959-68, pres., 1968—. Served to lt. USNR, 1941-46. Democrat. Methodist. Kiwanian (dir.). Home: 308 Crystal St New Orleans LA 70124 Office: PO Box 50590 New Orleans LA 70150

QUINN, TOM RAY, athletic coach; b. Beckley, W.Va., Mar. 19, 1930; s. Thomas and Charlene (Allison) Q.; A.B., Marshall U., 1954; M.A., U. Fla., 1955; m. Doris R. Smith, Aug. 23, 1960; children—Stephanie Rebecca, Thomas Ray. With Armed Forces Security Agy., Washington, 1950; basketball coach Cocoa (Fla.) High Sch., 1955-58; head basketball coach Newberry Coll., 1958-61; coach High Point Coll., 1961-65; basketball coach East Carolina U., Greenville, N.C., 1965—. Bd. dirs. Greenville Boys Club. Served with USAAF, 1946-49. Named S.C. Coach of Year, 1960, So. Conf. Coach of Year, 1969, Athlete of Top 100, W.Va. Centennial, 1965. Mem. Nat. Assn. Basketball Coaches, Pi Kappa Alpha. Rotarian. Home: Stratford Arms Greenville NC 27834

QUINONES, SEGISMUNDO, JR., broadcasting exec.; b. Santurce, P.R., Apr. 17, 1934; s. Segismundo and Juanita (Lores) Q.; B.S. in Bus. Adminstrn., Georgetown U., 1951-57; postgrad. Harvard Grad. Sch. Bus., 1963; m. Maria Eugenia Ramirez de Arellano, June 26, 1956; children—Segismundo, Jorge Arturo, Carlos Manuel, Maria Eugenia. Asst. mgr. WAPA Radio, San Juan, P.R., 1957-58; owner, gen. mgr. P.R. Music Services, WPRM-FM, San Juan, 1959-66; pres., gen. mgr. Radio Tiempo, Inc., San Juan, 1966—; v.p., treas. Computer, Inc., 1964-66. Mem. San Juan Mayor's Adv. Com., 1969—; mem. exec. com. World Congress, 1958; mem. adv. council to archbishop on social use of mass communication media, 1967—. Mem. San Juan Jr. C. of C., P.R. Broadcasters Assn. (FM dir. 1966—), Phi Eta Mu. Roman Catholic. Home: Calle A Esquina Palos Grandes Garden Hills Bayamon PR 00619 Office: 401 Ponce de Leon Ave Puerta de Tierra Station San Juan PR 00906

QUIREY, WILLIAM OXLEY, ret. army officer, educator; b. Princeton, Ky., Dec. 16, 1918; s. William Oxley and Mabel (Hopewell) Q.; A.B. in Polit. Sci., U. Ky., 1940; M.A., George Washington U., 1963; M.A., U. So. Fla., 1971; m. Virginia Irvine, Nov. 25, 1948; children— William Oxley, Marguerite Hopewell. Commd. 2d lt. U.S. Army, 1940, advanced through grades to brig. gen., 1967; dep. chief staff for personnel 7th Army, 1957-58; spl. asst. to Asst. Sec. for Def. Manpower, 1959-62; comdg. officer 52d Arty. Brigade, 1963-64; asst. chief of staff for plans and operations Allied Land Forces, S.E. Europe, 1964-66; dep. dir. Combat Operations Center, Vietnam, and comgd. gen. I Field Force Arty., Vietnam, 1966-67; dir. studies Dept. Army's Office Chief of Staff, 1968-69; ret., 1970. Active Boy Scouts Am., 1959-63. Decorated Legion of Merit with 2 oak leaf clusters, Air medal; named distinguished alumnus U. Ky., 1967. Mem. U.S. Power Squadron, Mil. Order World Wars, Am. Acad. Polit. and Social Sci. Address: 2056 Iowa Av NE St Petersburg FL 33703

QUITTMEYER, CHARLES LOREAUX, coll. dean; b. Peekskill, N.Y., Dec. 23, 1917; s. Ernest M. and Edith G. (Loreaux) Q.; student Wesleyan U., Middletown, Conn., 1935-37; A.B., Coll. William and Mary, 1940; M.B.A., Harvard, 1947; Ph.D. (fellow), Columbia, 1955; m. Maureen J. Rankin, June 2, 1956; children—Peter Charles, David Rankin, Andrew Robert, Jane Loreaux. Analyst, Century Indemnity Co., Boston, 1941-42; jr. economist Bur. Investigation and Research, Washington, 1942; group annuity contract writer Conn. Gen. Life Ins. Co., Hartford, Conn., 1947-48; asst. prof. bus. adminstrn. Coll. William and Mary, Williamsburg, Va., 1948-62, prof., head dept., 1962-68, dean Sch. Bus. Adminstrn., 1968—; lectr., asst. prof. marketing U. Buffalo, 1954-57; research asso., asso. prof. commerce U. Va., 1957-61; sr. scientist Tech. Operations, Inc., 1961-62; Pres. Williamsburg Community Council, 1964-65; chmn. Williamsburg Citizens Adv. Com. on Plan for Central Area, 1967, Indsl. Devel. Authority James City County, 1969; bd. suprs. James City County, 1969—; bd. dirs. Va. Peninsula Indsl. Com., 1969—. Mem. bd. Peninsula Community Mental Health Service. Served to capt., F.A. and M.I., AUS, 1942-46. Mem. Williamsburg-James City County bd. dirs. 1968-70, exec. com. 1969-70), Va. chambers commerce, Acad. Mgmt., Am., So. Econ. assns., Newcomen Soc. N. Am. Phi Beta Kappa, Beta Gamma Sigma, Kappa Delta Pi. Episcopalian (past sr. warden vestry). Rotarian. Club: Harvard of Va. Author: The Marketing of Virginia Seafood, 2 vols., 1950; The Virginia Travel Trade, 2 vols., 1951; The Potential Development of Steel-Making Industry in Virginia, 1957; The Economic Impact of the Ports of Virginia, 1958; (with others) Some Economic Consequences of a Channel to Richmond, 1963; Sufficiency Requirements for Future Combat Units, 1963; The Chesapeake Bay Fisheries of Maryland, 1966; The Virginia Travel Industry, 1966; Hampton Waterfront Economic Study, 1967; The Seafood Industry, A Local Analysis, 1968; James City County's Form of Government (with others), 1970; also papers in field. Home: 210 Kingswood Dr Williamsburg VA 23185

RABEL, FANNY, artist. Address: Galeria Plastica de Mexico Calle de Londres 139 Mexico City DF Mexico*

RABORN, HUBERT HARDIN, oil co. exec.; b. New Harp, Tex., Sept. 8, 1905; s. Oscar Orville and Emma Jane (Griffin) R.; student William Jewell Coll., 1925-26, St. Louis U., 1943-45; grad. exec. program bus. adminstrn., Columbia, 1953; m. Gladys Floyd Starnes, June 20, 1927; children—Hubert Hardin, Maynette (Mrs. Richard D. Whitworth). Bookkeeper, First Nat. Bank, El Dorado, Ark. 1925-29; accountant Imperials Refineries, Little Rock and St. Louis, 1929-43; with Touche, Niven, Bailey and Smart, C.P.A.'s 1943-50, resident mgr., Houston, 1948-50; v.p. Triangle Refineries, Inc., Houston, 1950—, sec., 1950-62; treas. Kerr-McGee Corp., Oklahoma City, 1957-61, v.p., gen. mgr. marketing, 1961-63, v.p. Marketing-Pipeline-Refining div., 1963-65; sr. v.p., 1967—; with Kerr-McGee Chem. Corp., 1966—, pres., dir., 1966-67, sr. v.p. of finance and adminstrn., 1967—; v.p. Hubbard-Hall Chem. Co., 1966—; v.p., dir. Kerr-McGee Bldg Corp., 1966—. Dir. Oklahoma City Better Bus. Bur. Mem. bus. adv. com. Okla. U., 1959; dir., v.p. Bapt. Laymen's Corp., Oklahoma City, 1960-67; chmn. governing bd. Golden Age Homes, Oklahoma City, 1966, dir. Bapt. Found, Okla.; mem. governing bd. Bapt. Meml. Hosp.; mem. annuity bd. So. Bapt. Conv., bd. dirs. found., 1967—. Mem. Arkansas N.G., 1923-25, C.P.A., Tex., Mo. Mem. Am. Petroleum Inst., Mid-Continent Oil and Gas Assn., Am. Inst. C.P.A.'s Tex., Mo. socs. C.P.A.'s, Oklahoma City C. of C. Baptist (deacon, Sunday sch. supt.). Clubs: Men's Dinner, Golf and Country, Petroleum (Oklahoma City); Houston. Home: 7501 Country Club Dr N Oklahoma City OK 73116 Office: Kerr-McGee Bldg Oklahoma City OK 73102

RACE, GEORGE WATSON, cons. structural engr.; b. Darlington, S.C., Apr. 14, 1905; s. Henry Charles and Mary Eleanor (Watson) R.; B.S., in Civil Engring, Ga. Tech. Inst., 1926, C.E., 1935; postgrad. U. Fla., 1932; m. Willie Stewart, June 16, 1928. With A.C.L. RR, 1929-30; structural engr. N.Y. State Archtl. Div., Albany, 1930-32; bridge designer Ga. Hwy. Bd., Atlanta, 1932-36; bldg. designer Sirrine Co., Greenville, S.C., 1936-41, 1946-48; prin. mem. archtl.-engring. firms, 1949-57; cons. engr. George Watson Race, Greenville, 1958—. Mem. Charities, Inc., Greenville, 1950-63; pres. Bd. Appeals, City Bldg. Commn., Greenville, 1960—; pres. County Rehab. Bd., Greenville, 1955-57. Served to col. AUS, 1941-46; ret. 1965. Registered profl. engr., S.C., N.C., Fla. Mem. Nat. Rifle Assn., Officer Res. Corps., Nat., S.C. socs. profl. engrs., Sigma Phi Epsilon. Methodist. Kiwanian. Clubs: International Torch (Greenville); Greenville Country. Author: (with R. J. Jones) Orientation, 1942; Race-Jones Method, 1941. Contbr. articles to profl. jours. Home: 103 Trails End Greenville SC 29607 Office: Box 5121B 252 S Pleasantburg Dr Greenville SC 29606

RACHAL, WILLIAM MUNFORD ELLIS, mag. editor; b. Marlinton, W.Va., June 20, 1910; s. Adolphe Sylvestre and Elvira Munford (Ellis) R.; B.S., Davidson Coll., 1933, Litt.D., 1972; M.A., U. Va., 1938; m. Maria Spady Fraser, Apr. 16, 1955; children—Ann Fraser, William Munford Ellis. Tchr., Alleghany County, Va., 1933-36; tchr. R.E. Lee Jr. High Sch., Lynchburg, Va., 1936-42; historian Va. World War II History Commn., Charlottesville, 1946-50, Va. State Library, Richmond, 1950-53; editor Va. Mag. History and Biography, Va. Hist. Soc., Richmond, 1953—. Served with AUS, 1942-46. Mem. Am., So. hist. assns., Presbyn., Va. hist. socs., Va. Social Sci. Assn. (pres. 1961-62), Phi Delta Kappa, Sigma Chi. Democrat. Presbyn. (elder 1948—). Club: Colonnade (Charlottesville). Editor: A Tour Through Part of Virginia, in the Summer of 1808 (John E. Caldwell), 1951; (with Henry Brimm) Yesterday and Tomorrow in the Synod of Virginia, 1962; (with William T. Hutchinson) The Papers of James Madison, vols. I-VII, 1962—. Editor Albemarle County Hist. Soc. Papers, 1947-50. Home: 3912 Sterling St Richmond VA 23221 Office: PO Box 7311 Richmond VA 23221

RACHELS, WILLIAM HOLLAND, mgmt. services co. exec.; b. Memphis, Jan. 11, 1926; s. William Franklin and Lonnie Massey (Holland) R.; student Northwestern U., 1946, U. Tenn., 1943, Memphis State U., 1947; D.D.S., U. Tenn., 1951; m. Betty Jean Wunderlich, Dec. 20, 1949; children—William Holland, Scott Wunderlich, Elizabeth Holland. Pvt. practice dentistry, Memphis, Tenn., 1951-56; agy. v.p. Nat. Trust Life Ins. Co., 1954-58, exec. v.p., chief adminstrv. officer, 1958-69; pres. Consol. Mgmt. Services, 1969—; pres. Limousine Services, Inc., 1971—; chmn. bd. Memphis and Chattanooga funeral homes, 1970—; dir. Service Corp. Internat.; pres. Memphis Indsl. Gardens, 1970—; vice chmn. bd. Protector Products Co., 1971—. Chmn. economic devel. study com. State of Tenn., 1971-72. Bd. dirs. YMCA, Memphis Area Young Life; pres. bd. dirs. LeBonheur Children's Hosp., 1968-72; bd. dirs. Chickasawy council Boy Scouts Am. Mem. Mid South Med. Center Council (chmn. alcohol and drug abuse com. 1972—), Memphis C. of C. (bd. dirs. 1972-73), Kappa Sigma, Zi Si Phi. Presbyn. (deacon 1972—). Club: University (Memphis). Home: 124 E Cherry Dr Memphis TN 38117 Office: 5625 Poplar Av Memphis TN 38117

RACHMEL, LEO, educator; b. N.Y.C., Aug. 31, 1919; s. Jack and Sarah (Winter) R.; B.B.A., Coll. City N.Y., 1940; M.S., U. Richmond, 1964; Ed.D., Laurence U., 1972; m. Carolyn Hentschel Miller, June 12, 1943; children—Lee Winter, Sandra Rae (Mrs. David Ellis Evans). Commd. 2d lt. U.S. Army, 1942, advanced through grades to lt. col., 1961; asst. prof. N.C. State U., 1949-53; instr. U.S. Army Logistics Mgmt. Center, Fort Lee, Va., 1962-67, logistics research analyst, 1967-69, chmn. research, devel., test and evaluation dept., 1969-71, dir. intern tng., 1971—; asst. prof. Sch. Bus. Adminstrn. Va. State Coll., Petersburg, 1966—. Instr. econs. Richard Bland Coll., Petersburg, Va., 1965-66, Coll. William and Mary, Williamsburg, Va., 1965-68; chmn. combined fed. campaign U.S. Army Logistics Mgmt. Center, Ft. Lee, Va., 1971. Mem. Nat. Def. Exec. Res. Office Pres. U.S., 1972. Decorated Army Commendation medal with oak leaf cluster, Bronze Star medal. Recipient Outstanding Performance award U.S. Civil Service, 1967. Mem. Soc. Logistics Engrs. (chmn. nat. edn. com. 1966-68), Am. Assn. U. Profs., Am., So. econs. assns., Amateur Athletic Union U.S. (bd. mgrs. Va. assn. 1960-62), Va. Bus. Edn. Assn. Home: 2123 Armistead Av Petersburg VA 23803 Office: Bus Adminstrn Dept Sch Bus Adminstrn Va State Coll Petersburg VA 23803

RACKLEY, ROBERT HUNTER, dentist; b. Millen, Ga., Apr. 3, 1922; s. Floyd Lawson and Katie (Hunter) R.; grad. Middle Ga. Coll., 1941; D.D.S., Emory U., 1944, postgrad., 1954-55; postgrad. U. Pa., 1957; m. Frances Harwell, Dec. 30, 1950; children—Robert Hunter, Lawson, Jan, Allison, Scott and Stewart (twins). Practice dentistry, Tampa, Fla., 1946-47, Millen, 1948—. Vice pres., dir. 1st Fed. Savs. & Loan Assn., Sylvania, Ga., 1963—; dir. Baker & Co., Atlanta; lectr. Med. Coll. Ga., Augusta, 1968—. Chmn., Ft. Lawton-Little Buckhead Creek Weatershed Project, 1960—, Jenkins County Bd. Edn., 1969; city councilman Millen, 1950-54. Bd. dirs. Youth, Inc. Mem. Ga. Bd. Dental Examiners, 1970—. Served with USNR, 1944-46. Fellow Am. Coll. Dentists; mem. Ga. Acad. Dental Practice (pres. elect 1969), Am., Eastern Dist., Ga. (pres. 1966-68) dental assns., So. Acad. Periodontology, Southeastern Acad. Prosthodontics, Am. Soc. Dentistry for Children, Internat. Platform Assn., Am. Coll. Dentists, Ga. Acad. Dental Practice. Rotarian. Club: Jenkins County Quarterback (past pres.). Home: Midville Rd Millen GA 30442 Office: 309 E Winthrope Av Millen GA 30442

RADCLIFFE, HAROLD, cons. engr.; b. New Bedford, Mass., Apr. 5, 1919; s. James and Emma (Moss) R.; B.S., Mass. Inst. Tech., 1941; m. Alice Isherwood, Oct. 4, 1941; 1 dau., Alyson. Sr. engr. Tuscarora Oil Co. Ltd., Harrisburg, Pa., 1946-53; sr. staff engr. Glace & Glace, Inc., Harrisburg, 1953-57; exec. v.p. Glace Engring. Corp., St. Petersburg, Fla., 1957-63, pres., 1963-68; pres. Glace & Radcliffe, Inc., St. Petersburg, 1968—. Chmn. zoning commn. Town of North Redington Beach, 1972—. Served to maj. AUS, 1941-46. Registered profl. engr. Fla., Pa., Conn., La. Mem. Am. Pub. Works Assn., Nat. Soc. Profl. Engrs., Fla. Engring. Soc. (chpt. treas. 1969), Fla. Pollution Control Assn., Air Pollution Control Assn. Episcopalian. Home: 401 Bath Club Blvd S North Redington Beach FL 33708 Office: 6727 1st Av S St Petersburg FL 33707

RADDON, HENRY ELIJAH, JR., hotel exec.; b. Laurel, Miss., Aug. 28, 1929; s. Henry Elijah and Carrie (Nelson) R.; A.S., Marion Mil. Inst., 1949; student Western Res. U., 1949-50, Miss. State Coll., 1950-51. Asst. mgr. J.C. Penney Co., Columbus and Brookhaven, Miss., 1952-59; innkeeper Holiday Inn., McComb, Miss., 1960-71; pres. Pike Investments, Inc. holding co. for Holiday Inn, McComb, 1971—. Served to 2d lt. inf. AUS, 1951-53. Recipient Top 8— awards Holiday Inn, 1962, 70. Mem. A.I.M. (pres.'s council), Miss. Innkeepers Assn. (dir.), S.W. Miss. Art Assn. (pres.). Episcopalian. Home: Lawrence St Summit MS 39666 Office: Holiday Inn Delaware Av McComb MS 39648

RADEBAUGH, CUSHMAN SHELTON, beef cattle rancher; b. Union City, Tenn., Aug. 3, 1903; s. Otis Barclay and Lalla B. (Shelton) R.; LL.B., Vanderbilt U., 1925; m. Adelma Giles, June 7, 1927; children—Cushman Shelton, James Giles, LeRoy Neil, Nancy (Mrs. Hans Grosklos). Admitted to Tenn. bar, 1925, Fla. bar, 1929; practice in Orlando, Fla., 1925-50; chmn. bd. Cushman S. Radebaugh & Sons, Inc., beef cattle and citrus fruit, Orlando, 1925—. Pres. Central Fla. Cattlemens Assn., 1942-46, Fla. Cattlemens Assn., 1951-52, Am. Nat. Cattlemens Assn., 1962-64; mem. Nat. Beef Cattle Legislative Com., 1950-62; dir. Fla. Farm Bur., 1942-48; mem. com. to revise Fla. Agrl. Dept., 1957-58. Trustee Fla. So. Coll. Served with USN, 1920-21.

Mem. Delta Theta Phi, Phi Kappa Psi, Sigma Phi Omega. Methodist (chmn. bd. trustees). Home: 902 Lake Davis Dr Orlando FL 32806 Office: PO Box 1928 Orlando FL

RADENTZ, WILLIAM HENRY, JR., dentist; b. St. Louis, July 7, 1927; s. William Henry and Alice Cathrine (Bauer) R.; student Mo. U., 1947-48; A.A., Harris Jr. Coll., 1950; D.D.S., St. Louis U., 1955; M.S., Baylor U., 1963; m. Kathleen Carmel Johnson, Sept. 7, 1951; children—Stephanie, Diana, Sydney, William, Stephan. Commd. lt. U.S. Army, 1954, advanced through grades to col., 1971; dental surgeon, Ft. Gulick, Panama, 1955-59; chief, Ft. Leonardwood, Mo., 1959-61; periodontist, Alaska, 1963-67; chief periodontics, asst. dir. residency program, chief Craven Dental Clinic, Ft. Knox, Ky., 1970—. Bd. mem. Old Ky. Home council Boy Scouts Am., 1970—. Diplomate Am. Acad. Periodontics. Mem. Am. Acad. Periodontology, Internat. Assn. Dental Research, Am. Dental Assn., Kappa Alpha, Psi Omega. Lutheran. Club: Hunt (bd. mem. 1969—) (Ft. Knox). Home: 9222 N Dixie Hwy Radcliff KY 40160 Office: US Army Dental Co Ft Knox KY 40121

RADER, FRANK, accountant; b. Buda, Tex., Jan. 7, 1919; s. George Franklin and Henrietta (Millard) R.; student U. Tex., 1940-41, Dallas Coll., So. Meth. U., 1950-65; m. Elizabeth Riley Thompson, Feb. 26, 1948; children—Lawrence Frank, Russell Ernest, Elizabeth Jane. Vets. rep. War Assets Adminstrn., Louisville, 1946-47; accountant Tex. Pub. Service Co., Austin, 1948-49; accountant So. Union Gas Co., Dallas, 1949-55, accounting mgr., 1955-67, asst. controller, 1967—. Served to capt. AUS, 1941-46. Mem. Am. Inst. C.P.A.'s, Am., So. gas assns. Methodist (trustee). Home: 3332 Ivy Dr Mesquite TX 75149 Office: Fidelity Union Tower Dallas TX 75201

RADER, FRANKLIN KEARNS, JR., gas transmission co. exec.; b. Lewisburg, W.Va., Nov. 21, 1919; s. Franklin Kearns and Carolyn (Brown) R.; B.S., So. Meth U., 1941; LL.B., Harvard, 1948; m. Letitia Doble, Nov. 8, 1943; children—Letitia Carolyn, Stephanie Hamilton. Gas contract rep. Shell Oil Co., 1948-51; with Tex. Gas Transmission Corp., 1952—, sr. v.p., 1961-66, exec. v.p., dir., 1967-68, pres. 1968—. Served to lt. (s.g.) USNR, 1941-46. Mem. N.A.M. (dir.), Phi Delta Theta, Alpha Kappa Psi. Republican. Presbyn. Home: Stone Creek Park Owensboro KY 42301 Office: 3800 Frederica St Owensboro KY 42301

RADER, LLOYD EDWIN, state ofcl.; b. Bridgeport, Okla., Aug. 30, 1906; s. Otis Zimmerman and Bedia Sarah (Boston) R.; student Southwestern State Coll., 1924-26; LL.B., Oklahoma City U., 1956; m. Ruth Schreiner, Sept. 30, 1930; 1 son—Lloyd Edwin. Asst. sec. Bldg. and Loan, also in ins., real estate, Weatherford, Okla., 1925-31; county relief dir. Custer County, Okla., 1932-33; chief auditor sales tax div. Tax Commn., Oklahoma City, 1933-35, dir. gen. enforcement div., 1935-39; in hardware, lumber, implement, constrn. bus., also ranching, Okla., 1939-51; dir. pub. welfare Okla., Oklahoma City, 1951—. Mem. Exec. Council State Welfare Dirs., 1953—; sec. Okla. Capitol Improvement Authority, 1959—; mem. adv. bd. Children's Convalescent Hosp., Bethany, Okla., 1959—; mem. Okla. Mental Health Planning Commn., 1965—; mem. Pres.'s Panel on Mental Retardation, 1966—. Elected to Okla. Hall Fame, 1966. Mem. Am. Pub. Welfare Assn. (treas. 1965-67), Okla. Health and Welfare Assn., State Welfare Dirs. and Commrs. Assn., Nat. Assn. Tng. Schs. Democrat. Mem. Disciples of Christ. Ch. Mason. Home: 6413 N Harvard Av Oklahoma City OK 73132

RADER, LOUIS T., educator; b. Frank, Can., Aug. 24, 1911 (came to U.S., 1934, naturalized 1940); s. Italo and Louise (Bonamico) R.; B.S., U. B.C., 1934; M.S. in Elec. Engring., Cal. Inst. Tech., 1935, Ph.D. in Elec. Engring., 1938; m. Constance Wayland, Sept. 10, 1938; children—Louis Albert, John Newton. With Gen. Electric Co., 1937-45, 64-69, 1947-59, engr., 1937-45, gen. mgr. splty. control div., 1951-59, v.p., gen. mgr. indsl. process control div. 1964-69; v.p., dir. Internat. Tel. & Tel. Corp., N.Y.C., 1959-61; group v.p. U.S. Comml., 1961-62; pres. Univac div. Sperry Rand Corp., 1962-64; prof., head dept. elec. engring. Ill. Inst. Tech., 1945-47. prof. elec. engring., chmn. dept., prof. bus. adminstrn. Grad. Sch. Bus., U. Va., 1969—. Dir. Smith's Transfer Corp., Staunton, Va. Dir. Rinfret Fund, N.Y.C., Macke Co., Cheverly, trustee HumRRO, Human Relations Research Orgn., Inc., Alexandria, Va. Mem. adv. com. on engring. LaFayette Coll., Easton, Pa.; trustee Robert A. Taft Inst., N.Y.C.; trustee Interuniv. Communications Council; vis. com. div. Engring. and Applied Sci. Cal. Inst. Tech. Recipient Alumni Distinguished Service award Cal. Inst. Tech., 1966. Fellow Am. Inst. E.E.; mem. Nat. Acad. Engring., Am. Assn. U. Profs., Am. Soc. Engring. Edn., U.S. C. of C. (mem. com. on communications), Newcomen Soc., Sigma Xi, Tau Beta Pi, Eta Kappa Nu. Club: University (N.Y.C.). Home: 1200 Boxwood Circle Waynesboro VA 22980 Office: Thornton Hall Univ of Va Charlottesville VA 22903

RADFORD, GARLAND, banker; b. Monroe, Ga., May 30, 1907; s. John Robert and Mary Eugenia (Brown) R.; B.B.A., Emory U., 1929; m. Vera Waller Kamper, Sept. 9, 1930; children—Vera (Mrs. Edmund W. Hughes), Mary (Mrs. Donald B. Hawkins), Nancy (Mrs. John P. Kokko), Garland Radford. Jr. accountant Joel Hunter & Co., Atlanta, 1929-31; with Standard Brands, Inc., Atlanta, 1931-33, Birmingham, Ala., 1933-34, 46-52, Cleve., 1934-43, N.Y.C., 1943-46; exec. v.p., dir. Nat. Bank, Monroe, 1952-63, pres., trust officer, 1963—; dir. Monroe Walton Co., Citizens & So. Fiduciary Stock Fund, Inc. Chmn., City of Monroe Housing Authority, 1969—. Trustee, chmn. bd. Walton County Hosp. Mem. Am., Ga. bankers assns., Walton County C. of C. (dir.), Phi Delta Theta. Democrat. Methodist (trustee). Kiwanian. Club: Monroe Golf and Country. Home: 146 Pine Crest Dr Monroe GA 30655 Office: 100 N Broad St Monroe GA 30655

RADFORD, ROBERT THOMAS, educator; b. Dallas, Aug. 8, 1932; s. Robert Leslie and Jewelle Link (Hardy) R.; B.A., Baylor U., 1954, M.A., 1959; Ph.D. (Univ. fellow), U. Tex., 1970; m. Nevalee Jones, Mar. 18, 1960; children—Robert G., Patricia. Tchr., Charlestown (Ind.) Twp. Schs., 1957-58; instr. humanities Caney Jr. Coll., Pippa Passes, Ky., 1958-60; teaching asst. philosophy U. Tex., Austin, 1960-62; asst. prof. philosophy Okla. State U., Stillwater, 1963—. Mem. Am. Assn. U. Profs., Am. Philos. Assn., Southwestern Philos. Soc., Mountain-Plains Philos. Conf. (exec. com. 1965-67, 69-70). Home: 823 S McFarland St Stillwater OK 74074

RADIN, ARTHUR, physician; b. Pitts., Jan. 6, 1916; s. David and Rose (Harris) R.; B.S., U. Pitts., 1941; M.D., U. Miami, 1957; m. Elizabeth A. Barnishin, Jan. 12, 1941; children—Patricia (Mrs. Milton J. Wallace), Dorothy, Rebecca. Intern, Mt. Sinai Hosp., Miami Beach, Fla., 1957-58; pvt. practice medicine, Hialeah, Fla., 1958-59; owner Century Med. Offices, Miami, 1959—; med. dir. Wilson Nat. Life Ins. Co., 1963—; mem. staff Bapt. Hosp., Miami; personnel physician Dade County, 1963-67. Mem. adv. bd. Dade County Pub. Health. Served with AUS, 1941-46. Decorated Purple Heart. Mem. A.M.A., So., Fla., Dade County med. socs., Century Alumni U. Miami, Phi Delta Epsilon. Home: 5825 SW 82d Av Rd Miami FL 33143 Office: 7890 Coral Way Miami FL 33155

RADIS, RICHARD ALAN, judge; b. New Haven, June 26, 1937; s. Louis R. and Hilda (Weissman) R.; A.B., St. Lawrence U., 1959; LL.B., Washington and Lee U., 1962. Admitted to Fla. bar, 1964; practiced in Ft. Lauderdale, Fla., 1965-69, 73—; juvenile judge Broward County, Ft. Lauderdale, Fla., 1969-73. Mem. Fraternal Order Police Assos. Mason (32 deg., Shriner). Home: 1271 N Rio Vista Blvd Ft Lauderdale FL 33306 Office: 111 SE 6th St Ft Lauderdale FL 33301

RADMAN, WILLIAM PAUL, dentist; b. St. Louis, Oct. 6, 1932; s. Fred E. and Mary (Zucker) R.; A.B., Washington U., St. Louis, 1955; D.D.S., St. Louis U., 1958; m. Elizabeth Simmons, May 21, 1966; children— Susan Marcia, David Michael, Sheryl Ann, Elizabeth Susann, Russell Paul. Intern, Jefferson Davis Hosp., Houston, 1958-59; practice dentistry specializing in endodontics, Dallas, 1959—; clin. instr. oral surgery U. Tex. S.W. Med. Sch., 1969—; clin. instr. endodontics Baylor Coll. Dentistry, 1969—. Vice pres. Dallas Symphony Orch. Guild, 1968-69, pres., 1971-72; bd. dirs. Dallas Civic Music Assn., 1971—; trustee Dallas Symphony Orch. Served with USAF, 1951-53. Mem. Am. Acad. Oral Medicine, S.W. Soc. Oral Medicine (pres. elect), Am., Tex., Dallas County dental assns., Fedn. Dentaire Internationale, Am. Assn. Endodontists, S.W. Soc. Endodontists (past pres.). Home: 5808 Lupton Dr Dallas TX 75225 Office: 8226 Douglas St Dallas TX 75225

RADOFF, LEONARD IRVING, librarian; b. Houston, Jan. 9, 1927; s. Morris and Jennie (Goldberg) R.; B.A. (Hoenthal scholar 1948) Rice U., 1949; M.L.S., U. Tex., 1965; m. Lisel Ruth Ephraim, July 25, 1953; 1 dau., Lesley. Tchr., Houston Ind. Sch. Dist., 1949-53; silk screen operator Rustproof Sign & Metal Co., 1953-59; tchr. Aldine (Tex.) Ind. Sch. Dist., 1959-61, sch. librarian, 1961-63; asst. to dir. Grad. Sch. Library Sci., U. Tex., 1963-64; pub. service librarian Abilene Pub. Library, 1964-65; dir. Pasadena Pub. Library, 1966-70; chief br. services Houston Pub. Library, 1971—. Vice pres. Pasadena South Houston Neighborhood Centers Assn., 1970; pres. Houston Great Books Council, 1970-72. Served with USNR, 1945-46. Nat. Def. Edn. Act scholar, 1960. Mem. Am., Southwestern, Tex. (dist. vice chmn. 1969-70, dist. chmn. 1970-71). library assns. Home: 2302 Colquitt St Houston TX 77006 Office: 3102 Center St Houston TX 77007

RADY, JOSEPH JAMES, civil engr.; b. N.Y.C., Oct. 4, 1899; s. Jacob J. and Rose (Swarz) R.; C.E., Cornell U., 1921; m. Bettye M. Clark, June 9, 1928. Owner, Joe J. Rady & Co., Ft. Worth, 1924—, now pres., chmn. bd. Rady & Assos., cons. engrs. Bd. dirs. Panther Boys Club. Served with U.S. Army Engrs., World War I. Named Engr. of Year Ft. Worth, Tex. Soc. Profl. Engrs., 1957. Fellow Am. Soc. C.E. (hon., pres. Tex. sect. 1964), Am. Water Assn., Nat. Soc. Profl. Engrs., Chi Epsilon. Rotarian. Clubs: Fort Worth, Colonial Country (dir.) (Fort Worth). Home: 2626 Simondale Dr Fort Worth TX 76109 Office: Continental Life Bldg Fort Worth TX 76102

RADZEWICZ, PAUL ANTHONY, oil co. exec.; b. nr. Hudson County, N.J., Apr. 7, 1920; s. Anthony Radzewicz and Helen (Lewicki) R.; grad. Fort Trumble Maritime Acad., 1944; student Millsaps Coll., 1950-51; LL.B., Jackson Sch. Law, 1951; m. Ethel Odel Cole, Sept. 15, 1949; children—Gene Anthony, Maureen Ethel. Instr. nav. machinery USN, Pearl Harbor, Honolulu, Hawaii, 1941-43; organizing sec., chief engr. internat. S.S. Line, Long Beach, Cal., 1947-49; pres. Starboard Oil Co., Jackson, Miss., 1949—; pres. Anthony's Yachts Co., Jackson, 1968—. Served with U.S. Maritime Service, 1943-46; PTO. Mem. Am. Petroleum Inst. (pres. Miss. chpt. 1968), Jackson Power Squadrons, Ind. Petroleum Assn. Am., Internat. Oil Scouts Assn., Marine Engrs. Benefit Assn., Internat. Assn. Petroleum Landmen, Miss. Landmen's Assn. Clubs: Gulfport (Miss.) Yacht; Patio (Jackson), Jackson Yacht, Jackson Country Capital City-Petroleum. Home: 1802 Eastover Dr Jackson MS 39211 Office: Deposit Guaranty Nat Bank Bldg 200 E Capitol St Jackson MS 39201

RAE, R(AYMOND) WILLIAM, operations research analyst; b. Kuru, Finland, Sept. 5, 1916; s. Anton and Impi (Makinen) R.; B.A., U. Toronto, 1938, M.A. in Physics, 1939, M.A. in Meterology, 1940; m. Dorothy Hurd Bladen, Nov. 29, 1968; children—(by previous marriage) Beverley Ann (Mrs. G. P. Hill), Constance Margaret (Mrs. R. Scott); step-children—Charles W., James B., Andrew J. Came to U.S., 1963, naturalized, 1969. Airway meterologist Meteorol. Service of Can., Toronto, Ont., 1940-47; officer-in-charge Canadian-U.S. Joint Arctic Sta., Resolute, N.W.T., 1947-49; head Arctic Sect. Meteorol. Service of Can., 1949-53; research officer Canadian Army Operational Research Establishment, Def. Research Bd., Ottawa, Ont., 1953-57, dep. dir., 1957-62, dir., 1963; dir. Research Analysis Corp. Field Office, Bangkok, Thailand, 1964-66; dep. dept. head Research Analysis Corp., McLean, Va., 1966—. Mem. Operations Research Soc. Am. Clubs: USAF Ski, Lake of the Woods Golf and Country. Home: 7805 Foxhound Rd McLean VA 22101 Office: Research Analysis Corp McLean VA 22101

RAE, ROBERT STIFFLER, assn. exec.; b. Newark, Dec. 26, 1902; s. George and Alice (Stiffler) R.; grad. Burdett Coll., 1925; B.C.S., Northeastern U., 1930; m. Ida Vose Stedman, Jan. 1, 1924; children—Marjorie, Virginia, Barbara, Roger W. Owner, White Owl Resort, Laconia, N.H., 1945-54; pres. Seminole (Fla.) C. of C., 1964-65, exec. sec., 1969—. Clk., City of Seminole, 1970-71. Served with USCGR, 1943-45. Conglist. Mason, Rotarian (past pres.). Home: 10005 Bay Pines Blvd St Petersburg FL 33708 Office: PO Box 3337 Seminole FL 33542

RAFFA, FREDERICK ANTHONY, economist; b. Liberty, N.Y., Feb. 19, 1944; s. Anthony and Helen Louise (Scobell) R.; B.S., Fla. State U., 1965, M.B.A., 1966, Ph.D., 1969; m. Jean Alyda Benedict, June 15, 1964; 1 dau., Juliette Louise. Instr. dept. econs. Fla. State U., Tallahassee, 1967-69; asst. prof. dept. econs. Fla. Tech. U., Orlando, 1969—. State dir. Fla. Clergy Econ. Edn. Council, 1969—; cons. E. Central Fla. Regional Planning Council, Dept. Health, Edn. and Welfare, Project RETRO. Recipient Distinction in Teaching award Fla. State U., 1969. NSF Summer Trainee fellow, 1968. Mem. Am., So. econs. assns., Omicron Delta Epsilon, Delta Sigma Pi. Episcopalian. Author: (with R.E. Hicks, W.J. Klages) Economics: Myth, Method or Madness, 1971. Home: 2901 Lolissa Lane Maitland FL 32751 Office: Dept Econs Fla Tech U Orlando FL 32816

RAFFEL, SHERMAN CARL, psychologist, educator; b. Ashland, Ky., Oct. 7, 1925; s. Louis and Rosa (Lipschitz) R.; A.B., George Washington U., 1948; M.A., U. Tenn., 1951, Ph.D., 1953; m. Marilyn Jean Berlin, June 5, 1949; children—Linda Marie, Michele. Chief clin. psychologist. Ft. Leonard Wood, Mo., 1953-56; dir. Montgomery County Mental Health Center, Montgomery, Ala., 1956-59; asst. to asso. prof. psychiatry and pub. health U. Ala. Med. Center, Birmingham, 1959—, also project coordinator Cerebrovascular Disease Project. Chmn. Bd. Examiners in Psychology, Ala., 1966—. Bd. dirs. Jefferson County Mental Health Assn. Served with AUS, 1944-46, 53-56; lt. col. Res. Diplomate Am. Bd. Profl. Psychology. Fellow Am. Orthopsychiat. Assn.; mem. Am., Southeastern, Ala. psychol. assns., Am. Assn. U. Profs. (pres. Ala. Conf.). Contbr. articles profl. jours. Home: 1107 Thornwood Dr Birmingham AL 35209 Office: 1919 7th Av S Birmingham AL 35233

RAFFERTY, HAROLD J., computer systems co. exec.; b. Bixby, Okla., Dec. 14, 1924; s. Clyde Dallas and Margaret Lona (Edwards) R.; student U. Tulsa, 1950-51, Okla. Sch. Bus., 1952-55; m. Margaret Colvin, June 30, 1951; children—Susan, Michael, Jeannine. Data processing mgr. Deep Rock Oil Corp., Tulsa, 1952-55; marketing rep. Univac, Tulsa, 1956-57; br. mgr. Barry Wright Corp., Tulsa, 1958-60; marketing rep. IBM, Tulsa, 1961-64; founder, dir. Data Processing Assos., Tulsa, 1964-68, merged into Affiliated Computer Systems, 1968, v.p., 1968—. Asst. scoutmaster Boy Scouts Am. troop 166, 1970—. Served with USNR, 1945-49. Recipient Scouters Tng. award, 1970. Mem. Nat. Assn. Accountants (v.p. 1961—). Mason, Rotarian. Home: 7043 E 59th St Tulsa OK 74145 Office:9105 E Pine St Tulsa OK 74115

RAFTERY, WILLIAM JOSEPH, accountant; b. Balt., Oct. 19, 1931; s. William Joseph and Carrie Lavinia (Calvert) R.; B.S., Loyola of East, 1956; LL.B., U. Balt., 1965; m. Leona Irene Clark, Sept. 4, 1954; children— Maureen Patricia, Timothy Patrick. With Ernst & Ernst, Balt., 1956-59; asst. to treas. Samuel Kirk & Son, Balt., 1959-61; controller Nat. Jewelry Stores, Inc., Balt., 1961-64; tax analyst Kerr-McGee Corp., Balt., Oklahoma City, 1964-67; with Peat, Marwick Mitchell & Co., Oklahoma City, 1968—. Instr. accounting Oklahoma City U. Sch. Bus., 1967-68, Sch. Law, 1968. Founder, pres. Taxpayers' Interest League, Balt., 1963-66. Mem. exec. com. Republican party Oklahoma County, 1969-72; Republican committeeman 5th congl. dist., 1971—. Served with Finance Corps, AUS, 1950-52. C.P.A., Md., Okla. Mem. Am. Inst. C.P.A.'s, Md. Assn. C.P.A.'s, Okla. Soc. C.P.A.'s, Nat., Okla. rifle assns. Lutheran. Club: Oklahoma City Gun. Home: 5704 NW 31st Terrace Oklahoma City OK 73122 Office: First Nat Bldg Oklahoma City OK 73102

RAGAN, COOPER KIRBY, lawyer; b. Newton, Tex., June 15, 1905; s. Daniel J. and Leila (Lee) R.; B.A., U. Tex., 1925, LL.B., 1928; m. Susan Menefee Wilson, June 6, 1945. Admitted to Tex. bar, 1928; with Ragan, Russell & Rorschach and predecessor firm, Houston, 1928—. Chmn., Tex. Civil War Centennial Com. 1959-63. Bd. dirs. The Jefferson Davis Assn. Served from lt. to lt. comdr. USNR, 1942-45. Mem. State Bar Tex., Am., Houston bar assns., Am. Law Inst., Philos. Soc. Tex., Tex. (pres. 1970-71), E. Tex. hist. assns., Chancellors, Phi Delta Phi. Mason (32 deg.). Clubs: Houston, River Oaks Country. Author articles in hist. field. Home: 3708 Inwood Dr Houston TX 77019 Office: Esperson Bldg Houston TX

RAGSDALE, FRANK VICTOR, constrn. engr.; b. Aurora, Mo., Oct. 18, 1891; s. Henry Elizer and Idella (Money) R.; B.S., U. Mo., 1912; m. Gladys Williams, Mar. 11, 1917; 1 dau., Anne (Mrs. James Irby Seay, Jr.). Asst. to city engr., Columbia, Mo., 1912; engr. Memphis dist. U.S. Army C.E., 1912-19; sales engr. Pidgeon-Thomas Iron Co., also Ingalls Iron Works Co., 1919; v.p., chief engr. Estes-Williams-Ragsdale Co., Memphis, 1919-26; propr. F.V. Ragsdale Co., Memphis, 1926—. Chmn. Traffic Adv. Commn. Memphis, 1950-60, Mayor's Com. Bus. Transp., 1955; mem. transit com., 1956, chmn., 1957-60; pres. Memphis Transit Authority, 1961—; mem. Memphis (Tenn.) and West Memphis (Ark.) Met. Area Joint Commn., 1961-71; cons. bus. transp. riders problems; chmn. governing bds. publicly owned transit systems U.S., Can., 1967-68. Trustee Engring. Found., U. Mo., 1955—; chmn. Memphis 3d U.S. Army Adv. Com., 1955—. Served from lt. col. to col., AUS, 1942-46. Decorated Legion of Merit. Mem. Am. Soc. C.E. (past pres. Mid-South sect.), Soc. Am. Mil. Engrs. (past pres. San Francisco), Engrs. Club Memphis (past pres.), Memphis C. of C. Presbyn. Rotarian (pres. Ednl. Found., Memphis 1957-58). Address: 1762 Autumn St Memphis TN 38112

RAGSDALE, SILAS BAGGETT, pub. co. dir.; b. Brownwood, Tex., Sept. 15, 1896; s. Paul Carter Calhoun and Maggie (Baggett) R.; B.A., U. Tex., 1918; m. Sadie Marie Jones, Apr. 4, 1923; children—Silas Baggett, Joan Marie (Mrs. Pat M. Baskin). Reporter, Brownwood Bull., 1915; city editor Galveston (Tex.) News, 1918-19, news editor, 1919-23, mng. editor, 1923-43; sec., dir. News Pub. Co., Galveston, Tex., 1923-43, dir., 1961-63; mng. editor Galveston Tribune, 1926-43, Oil Weekly, Houston, 1920-21, 44-47, Petroleum Refiner, Houston, 1947-54; editorial dir. Hydrocarbon Processing (formerly Petroleum Refiner), 1955-66; ret., 1966; dir. Gulf Pub. Co., Houston, 1955—. Mem. Nat. council YMCA, 1935-38; life mem. adv. council U. Tex. Sch. Communication, 1950—. Mem. U. Tex. Ex-Students Assn. (life), S.A.R., Sons Republic Tex., Delta Tau Delta, Sigma Delta Chi. Presbyn. Mason (32 deg., Shriner), Rotarian (past pres. Houston R club). Home: 1636 North Blvd Houston TX 77006

RAIFORD, WILLIAM HARRISON, mag. editor; b. Memphis, Aug. 8, 1935; s. Yancey Blackwell Massey and Virginia (Brown) Raiford; student U. Okla., 1955-56; B.S. in Journalism, Memphis State U., 1963; m. Carol Drake, June 6, 1964; children—Yancey Drew, Kenneth Farrow. Editor, DeSoto County News, Hernando, Miss., 1963-64; editor, pub. Suburban Press, Olive Branch and Southaven, Miss., 1964-67; editor So. Motor Cargo mag., Memphis, 1967—. Served with AUS, 1959-61. Mem. Asso. Transp. Club Memphis (pres. 1971), Am. Trucking Assn. (maintenance com. Regular Common Carrier Conf.), Soc. Automotive Engrs. (transp. and maintenance activity), Sigma Delta Chi (treas. mid-South profl. chpt. 1969), Alpha Tau Omega. Episcopalian. Club: Scenic Hills Recreation (Memphis). Home: 2915 Falkirk Rd Memphis TN 38128 Office: 1509 Madison Av Memphis TN 38104

RAILSBACK, BERNICE HICKMAN (MRS. JAMES ERNEST RAILSBACK), educator; b. Mountain Home, Ark.; d. Charles Isaac and America Maria (Lewis) Hickman; student Mountain Home Coll., 1927, 29, Ark. State Coll., summers 1930-31; B.S., Tex. Tech. Coll., 1941, M.S., 1951; m. James Ernest Railsback, June 9, 1932; children—Norman Leighton, Charles Hickman, Phyllis Elaine (Mrs. George A. Carlton). Tchr. pub. schs., Buford, Ark., 1927-28; tchr., girls coach Salem (Ark.) pub. schs., 1929-32, McClung Sch., Slaton, Tex., 1933-34; tchr. Hodges Sch., Levelland, Tex., 1939-41; tchr. jr. high sch. math. and reading Levelland Pub. Schs., 1947-54, dir. elementary edn., 1954-70, cons., 1970—. Mem. study com. tchr. certification Tex. Edn. Agy. Bd. dirs. Hockley County div. Am. Heart Assn., v.p. Tex. affiliate; bd. dirs. Tex. Com. for Pub. Edn. Recipient poetry award S. Plains Writers Assn., 1964, 65; named Woman of Year, Levelland C. of C., 1969. Mem. Assn. Supervision and Curriculum Devel. (Tex. rep. nat. bd. 1962-67, state pres. 1966-67, 69-70), Tex., W. Tex. (regional pres. 1966-67) assns. for supervision and curriculum devel., Tex. Assn. Instrnl. Suprs. (state pres. 1959-60), Am. Assn. U. Women, Tex. Congress Parents and Tchrs. (life), Internat. Platform Assn., Poetry Soc. Tex., S. Plains Writers Assn., Tex. Assn. for Improvement of Reading, Internat. Reading Assn., Tex. Assn. Edn. Young Children (dir.), Marigolds, Delta Kappa Gamma. Mem. Order Eastern Star (past worthy matron). Clubs: Matrons Study, Levelland Music. Contbr. to various publs. Home: 707 17th St PO Box 156 Levelland TX 79336

RAINER, DAVID LEE, supt. schs.; b. Livingston, Ala., Jan. 21, 1936; s. Richard Porter and Avis (Sellers) R.; B.S., Livingston U., 1958; M.Ed., U. Ga., 1963; Edn. Specialist, 1971; m. Yvonne Peeples, June 1, 1959; children—Alan, David. Tchr., Kingsland (Ga.) Elementary Sch., 1958-61, prin. 1961-65; supt. schs., Camden

entertainment and instrn. VA hosps., 1949-52, dir., 1948-53, 60—; chmn. Phelps Found., 1949—. Recipient award A.R.C., 1946; 1st woman named to Field Trial Hall of Fame. Home: 215 Greenville St Aiken SC 29801

PHELPS, DAVID SUTTON, archaeologist, educator; b. Gatesville, N.C., July 25, 1929; s. David Sutton and Jeannette (Costen) P.; student N.C. State U. Design, 1953-57; B.A., U. N.C., 1960; Ph.D., Tulane U., 1964;; m. Peggy Joann Sisson, Aug. 1, 1953. Archaeologist-in-charge Town Creek Indian Mound State Site, N.C., 1958-59; instr. anthropology Tulane U., summer 1963; asst. prof. anthropology Fla. State U., Tallahassee, 1964-68, asso. prof., 1968-70; asso. prof. anthropology East Carolina U., Greenville, N.C., 1970—. Served with USAF, 1948-52. Fellow Am. Anthrop. Assn.; mem. Soc for Am. Archaeology, A.A.A.S., Fla. Anthrop. Soc. (editor 1967-70), Southeastern Archaeol. Conf., Sigma Xi. Office: Dept Sociology and Anthropology East Carolina University Greenville NC 27834

PHELPS, FLORENCE LOUISE HARLLEE (MRS. JOHN C. PHELPS, JR.), social worker; b. Dallas; d. Norman Washington and Florence (Coleman) Harllee; A.B., Howard U., 1925; M.S.W., Atlanta U., 1949; M.Ed., N. Tex. State U., 1958; postgrad. summers, 1954, 64, U. Ill., 1959, So. Meth. U., 1963; m. John C. Phelps, Jr.; children—Norma Belle (Mrs. George Barratt), Lucy Pearl (Mrs. Albert Simeon Patterson). Social worker City County Dept. Pub. Welfare, Dallas, 1936-41; sch. social worker Dallas Ind. Sch. Dist., 1941-71; asst. prof. U. Tex. Grad. Sch. Social Work at Arlington, 1971-72. Instr., acting dir. Wiley Coll. Extension Sch., Dallas, 1955; cons. spl. case and adoptions Hope Cottage, Children's Bur., summer 1961. Mem. Goals for Dallas Task Force, 1968—; chmn., Community Round Table on Social, Health and Welfare Problems, 1962-64. Bd. dirs. Dallas Opportunities Industrialization Center, CEMA-Financial Corp. Mem. Nat. Assn. Social Workers, Acad. Certified Social Workers, Vis. Tchrs. Assn. Tex., Tex. Social Welfare Assn., League Women Voters, Wesleyan Service Guild (v.p. 1962), Internat. Platform Assn., Alpha Kappa Alpha. Home: 2804 Magna Vista Dr Dallas TX 75216

PHELPS, JONATHAN BAILEY, JR., synthetic fibers co. exec.; b. Texarkana, Tex., June 17, 1916; s. Jonathan Bailey and Patty (Holman) P.; student Hendrix Coll., 1932-34; B.S. in Chem. Engring., U. Tex., 1936, M.S., 1938; m. Roberta Otting, Jan 28, 1939; 1 son, Bailey Preston. Devel. engr. Lion Oil Co., El Dorado, Ark., 1938-41; process supt. Phillips Petroleum Co., Borger, Tex., 1941-46; asst. div. mgr. Celanese Corp., Corpus Christi, Tex., 1946-59; exec. v.p. Fiber Industries, Inc., Charlotte, NC., 1959—, also dir.; pres., dir. Duofil, Inc., Cleveland, Tenn., dir. Milhaven Fibers, Ltd. (Canada). Mem. Gov.'s Council for Econ. Devel., 1967-72; dist. chmn. Boy Scouts Am., 1963-66. Bd. dirs. Jr. Achievement; bd. advisers Gardner Webb Coll. Mem. Am. Inst. Chem. Engrs. Republican. Presbyn. (elder 1965-68). Rotarian, Kiwanian. Office: PO Box 10038 Charlotte NC 28201

PHELPS, JOSEPH WILLIAM, banker; b. nr. Richmond, Ky., Jan. 6, 1927; s. Ben and Hannah (Blunschi) P.; student pub. schs.; m. Mary Margaret Culton, Jan. 2, 1954; children—Melanie Jean, Joseph William. Nat. bank examiner U.S. Treasury Dept., 1950-58; asst. cashier Liberty Nat. Bank & Trust Co., Louisville, 1958-59, asst. v.p., 1959-62, v.p., 1962-67, head corr. bank dept., sec. to bd., exec. com., 1967-68, sr. v.p., 1968-70, exec. v.p., 1971—, dir., 1970—. Mem. exec. bd. Old Ky. Home council Boy Scouts Am. Served with AUS, 1945. Mem. Ky. C. of C., Am. Bankers Assn. (regional v.p.), Louisville C. of C., English Speaking Union, Am. Inst. Banking, Filson Club. Episcopalian (vestryman). Clubs: Pendennis, Big Spring Country (Louisville). Home: 5015 Dunvegan Rd Louisville KY 40222 Office: 416 W Jefferson St Louisville KY 40202

PHELPS, RICHARD RUSSELL, civil and san. engr., educator; b. Evansville, Ind., Jan. 21, 1931; s. Russel R. and Mildred (Rice) P.; B.S., Tex. A. and M. U., 1953; B.S. in Civil Engring., Lamar U., 1960; M.S. in Civil Engring., U. Colo., 1969; m. Margaret Swickheimer, Sept. 7, 1957; children—Linda Margaret, Laura Elizabeth. Jr. engr. George J. Schaumburg, cons. engr., Beaumont, Tex., 1957-59; civil engr., project mgr. Pitts, Phelps, White & Saxe, architects and engrs., Beaumont, 1959-68; san. engr., project mgr. Henningson, Durham & Rickardson, cons. engrs., Dallas, 1969-71; asst. prof. civil and environmental engring. U. N.C. at Charlotte, 1971—. Served to lt., Civil Engring. Corps, USNR, 1953-57. Registered profl. engr., N.C., Tex. Fellow Am. Soc. C.E.; mem. Nat. Soc. Profl. Engrs., Am. Water Works Assn., Am. Soc. for Engring. Edn., Water Pollution Control Fedn. Methodist. Rotarian. Home: 9201 Joyce Kilmer Dr Charlotte NC 28213

PHELPS, RICHARD THOMAS, JR., chem. co. exec.; b. Trinidad, Colo., Aug. 13, 1921; s. Richard Thomas and Helen Sindorf (Wardenburg) P.; B.S., Tex. Tech. Coll., 1948; postgrad. U. Va., 1961; m. LaVerne Pollard, Sept. 10, 1945; children—Beverly Ann (Mrs. Glen Schailey), Barbara Lyn, Richard Thomas III, Deborah Jean. Maintenance supt. DuPont Co., Belle, W. Va., 1948-52, Monsanto Co., Pensacola, Fla., 1952-56, plant engr., 1956-63, mfg. supt., 1963-66, plant mgr., Greenwood, S.C., 1966—. Chmn. bd. Cerebral Palsy, Greenwood, S.C., 1971-72; active YMCA, Jr. Achievement, Community Chest. Adv. bd. S. C. Nat. Bank, Greenwood, 1966—. Served to capt. USAAF, 1941-45. Methodist (bd. dirs. 1968—). Moose, Rotarian. Clubs: Industrial Management (top adv. com. 1967—), Greenwood Country. Home: Route 6 115 Crescent Dr Greenwood SC 29646 Office: PO Box 1057 Greenwood SC 29646

PHIFER, JOSEPH RUTLEDGE, dentist; b. Houston, Sept., 30, 1935; s. James Judson and Mamie Allien (Baskett) P.; B.A., U. St. Thomas, 1957; D.D.S., U. Tex., 1963. Pvt. practice dentistry, Houston, 1963—; pres. J. Rutledge Phifer, D.D.S., Inc., Houston, 1970—. Mem. Am., Tex. dental assns., Houston Dist. Dental Soc., Delta Sigma Delta. Episcopalian. Home: 111 W Hambrick Houston TX 77037 Office: 4501 Airline Dr Houston TX 77022

PHILIPS, ARTHUR MCCRINDELL, orgn. adminstr.; b. Richmond, Va., July 6, 1910; s. Harry Hunter and Maude (Livesay) P.; student Yale, 1933-34; postgrad. William and Mary Coll. Sch. Social Work, 1935-38. Exec., Community Chest, Raleigh, N.C., 1938-42, campaign dir., Atlanta, 1949-50; exec. dir. United Fund, Portland, Me., 1950-57; exec. dir. United Appeal, Oklahoma City, 1957—. Served with AUS, 1942-45. Decorated Legion of Merit. Mem. Nat. Assn. Social Workers, Acad. Certified Social Workers. Rotarian. Home: 4904 NW 26th St Oklahoma City OK 73127 Office: 312 Park Av Oklahoma City OK 73102

PHILIPSON, ALBERT, lawyer; b. Ossining, N.Y., Feb. 23, 1910; s. Henry and Rose (Arnson) P.; A.B., Columbia, 1931; LL.B., 1933; m. Edna Gumenick, Apr. 3, 1938; children—Romlee J. (Mrs. Allan J. Weinstein), Lorrin G. (Mrs. Kenneth Rosenbaum). Admitted to N.Y. bar, 1933, D.C. bar, 1944, U.S. Supreme Ct., 1946; with FCA, 1934-35; pvt. practice law. Westchester County, N.Y., 1936-41, Washington, 1946—. Vice pres., Calvert Homes, Inc., Chesapeake Ranch Club, Inc., Chesapeake Ranch Water Co., 1960—. Officer, trustee Nat. Found. for Research in Medicine, Albert and Edna Philipson Found. Served to maj. Q.M.C., AUS, 1942-46. Decorated Legion of Merit. Mem. Bar Assn. D.C. (chmn. corp. law com. 1953-57, 63-67), Fed., Am. bar assns., Beta Sigma Ro. Democrat. Jewish religion. Contbr. articles to law jours. Home: 3731 Fessenden St NW Washington DC 20016 Office: 1775 K St NW Washington DC 20006

PHILLEO, ROBERT EUGENE, govt. ofcl.; b. Spokane, Wash., Aug. 21, 1923; s. Archibald Marvin and Helen Mar (Slater) P.; B.S. in Civil Engring., Carnegie Inst. Tech., 1946; m. Margaret Guthrie, Apr. 3, 1948; children—Diane, Barbara, Margaret, Paul. Research engr. Portland Cement Assn., Chgo., 1946-58; chief concrete branch Office Chief Engrs., Directorate of Civil Works, Washington, 1958—. Lectr. Northwestern U., 1951-57; cons. concrete materials and constrn., 1967—. Pres., Broyhill Crest Citizens Assn., Annandale, Va., 1966. Served with AUS, 1943-46. Mem. Am. Concrete Inst. (v.p. 1971-72), Am. Soc. Testing and Materials (com. chmn. 1957-72), Hwy. Research Bd. (com. chmn. 1957-72), Joint Internat. Commn. Statis. Quality Control of Concrete Quality. Author: (with J.J. Waddell) Concrete Construction Handbook, 1968. Asso. editor: Cement and Concrete Research, an internat. jour., 1970-72. Home: 7420 Annanwood Court Annandale VA 22003 Office: Office Chief Engineers Attention DAEN-CWE-C Washington DC 20314

PHILLIPS, A(NDREW) CRAIG, ednl. adminstr.; b. Greensboro, N.C., Nov. 1, 1922; A.B., U. N.C., 1943, M.A., 1946, Ed.D. in Sch. Adminstrn., 1956; m.1943; 4children. Tchr., asst. supt. Winston-Salem (N.C.) City Schs., 1946-55, supt. schs., 1957-62; supt. Charlotte-Mecklenburg (N.C.) Schs., 1962-67; adminstrv. v.p. Richardson Found., 1967-68; supt. pub. instrn. State of N.C., Raleigh, 1969—. Mem. steering com. N.C. Gov.'s Com. To Study N.C. Pub. Sch. System, 1967-68; mem. Nat. Citizens Com. on Pub. Television, 1968, President's Commn. on Mental Health for Children. Mem. N.E.A., N.C. Assn. Edn., N.C. Edn. Assn., Am. Assn. Sch. Adminstrs. (dir., nat. acad. sch. exec. 1969), So. Assn. Colls. and Schs. Home: 2200 Barfield Ct Raleigh NC 27609 Office: State Dept Public Instruction State Capitol Raleigh NC 27602*

PHILLIPS, A(USTAVE) P(AUL), JR., advt., public relations and travel agy. exec.; b. Atlanta, May 30, 1903; s. A. P. and Kate (Faith) P.; student Washington and Lee U., 1920; B.S., U. Ala., 1925; m. Medda Euphemia Highleyman, May 5, 1926. Pres., owner A. P. Phillips Co., Orlando, Fla., 1925—, Phillips Internat. Travel Hdqrs., Orlando and Jacksonville; editor, pub. Forward Orlando, 1926-37, Orlandoan, 1926-42; dir. Gulf Life Ins. Co. Del. Democratic Nat. Conv., 1928, 32, 36. Served as maj. USAAF, 1942-46; now lt. col. Res. ret.; dep. dir. information Res. Forces, Scott, AFB, Ill., 1960-63. Decorated 10 battle stars, Bronze Star, 2 Presdl. Citations, Air Medal; donor Advt. Achievement awards to Fla. univs. and colls. Mem. Orlando (founder, pres. 1927), U.S. (v.p., dir. 1926-32), Internat. (senator) jr. chambers commerce, Internat. Pub. Relations Assn. (del. world congress 1958, 61, 64, 67), Am. Soc. Travel Agts., Pub. Relations Soc. Am. (nat. dir. 1956-57, dist. v.p. 1956, So. area dir. 1958-62, assembly del. for Fla. 1960-63, assembly del. N.-Central Fla. chpt. 1963-67, Fla. pres. 1955, S.E. dist. chmn. 1963-64), World Marketers, Advt. Fedn. Am. (dist. gov. 1950), Advt. Club Orlando (pres. 1949), Orlando Area Advt. Club (pres. sr.council 1966-68), Res. Officers Assn. (dept. pres. 1951, mem. nat. air force affairs com.), Mil. Order World Wars (regional comdr. 1956-60, mem. gen. staff at large 1960-67, comdr. Central Fla. 1955, mil. affairs com. 1964—), Orlando Area C. of C. (mil. affairs com. 1968—), Am. Legion (comdr. post 1948, vice chmn. nat. pub. relations com. 1955-56), 40 and 8, Newcomen. Soc. N.Am., Fla. Pub. Relations Assn. (chmn. pub. relations ednl. standards com. 1966-67), D.A.V., V.F.W., Air Force Assn. (v.p. 1962-66), Interallied Confedn. Res. Officers, Ret. Officers Assn., Order Lafayette, S.C.V., Alpha Delta Sigma. Methodist. Elk, Mason (Shriner). Clubs: University (Winter Park and Jacksonville, Fla.); Country, Citrus (Orlando); River, Skal (Jacksonville, Fla.). Author: Spirits of the Free, 1957; Communications, A Matter of Survival, 1958; Action-A Blueprint for Freedom, 1960; The Rightful Challenge of Public Relations, 1964; Our Heritage Under God, 1965; Our Heritage and the Challenge of Life, 1966; Our Future, A Reflection of the Past, 1970; Our Heritage, Men of Good Faith, 1971; Our Precious Heritage, These Things We Hold Most Dear, 1971. Home: 1354 Ivanhoe Blvd S Orlando FL 32804 Office: 1045 Legion Pl Orlando FL 32801 also 220 W Monroe St Jacksonville FL 32202

PHILLIPS, BARRY, lawyer; b. Valdosta, Ga., Feb. 16, 1929; s. William Otis and Beatrice (Mercer) P.; A.B., U. Ga., 1949, LL.B., 1954; m. Grace Greer, Aug. 3, 1957; children—Mary Grace, Barry, John Greer, Quinton Braddock. Admitted to Ga. bar, 1951; practiced in Atlanta, 1954—; mem. firm Kilpatrick, Cody, Rogers, McClatchey & Regenstein, 1954—; dir. Auto-Soler Co., Atlanta. Mem. Fund Appeals Rev. Bd., Atlanta, 1962-65. Served to 1st lt. AUS, 1951-53. Decorated Air medal. Mem. Am., Ga., Atlanta bar assns., Exec. Assn. Atlanta, Atlanta Soc. Investment Analysts, Phi Beta Kappa, Phi Kappa Phi, Pi Kappa Alpha, Phi Alpha Delta, Omicron Delta Kappa. Methodist. Clubs: Lawyers, Commerce, Piedmont Driving. Home: 4574 Meadow Valley Dr NE Atlanta GA 30305 Office: Hurt Bldg Atlanta GA 30303

PHILLIPS, BEEMAN NOAL, educator; b. Boonville, Ind., May 4, 1927; s. Bishop N. and Carrie D. (Dreves) P.; B.A., Evansville Coll., 1949; M.S., Ind. U., 1950, Ed.D., 1954; m. Sarah A. Haworth, Aug. 22, 1952; children—Gregory, Richard, Kathryn. Dir. div. research Ind. Dept. Pub. Instrn., Indpls., 1954-56; asst. prof., asso. prof., dept. edn. psychology U. Tex., Austin, 1956-67, prof., 1968—, dir. Nat. Inst. Mental Health Sch. Psychology Tng. Program, 1965—. Served with AUS, 1944-46. Diplomate Am. Bd. Professional Psychology. Fellow Am. Psychology Assn.; mem. Tex. Psychology Assn. (pres. 1969-70), S.W. Psychology Assn., A.A.A.S., Am. Ednl. Research Assn., Phi Delta Kappa, Sigma Xi. Contbr. articles in field to profl. jours. Home: 3303 Live Oak Circle Austin TX 78731

PHILLIPS, CECIL RANDOLPH, JR., mgmt. cons.; b. Birmingham, Ala., July 30, 1933; s. Cecil Randolph and Alberta (Smith) P.; B.S., Ga. Inst. Tech., 1955, M.S., 1960; postgrad, Fed. Inst. Tech., Zurich, Switzerland, 1955-56; m. Sara Lee Kirby, Aug. 25, 1956; children—Taylor Cy, Leslie Hope, Daniel Lee. Tech. editor advt., sales promotion dept. Gen. Electric Co., Schnectady, 1956-58; project leader Operations Research, Inc., Silver Springs, Md., 1960-62, asst. tech. dir., Atlanta, 1962-63; exec. v.p. Mgmt. Sci. Atlanta, Inc., 1963-67; mgr. Kurt Salmon Assos., Inc., Atlanta, 1967—. Bd. dirs. Ga. Inst. Tech. YMCA. Mem. Am. Inst. Indsl. Engrs., Operations Research Soc. Am., Inst. Mgmt. Scis., Systems and Procedures Assn., ANAK Soc., Am. Prodn. and Inventory Control Soc., Ga. Conservancy, Big Bros. Assn. of Atlanta, Omicron Delta Kappa, Alpha Tau Omega, Alpha Pi Mu. Author: (with Joseph J. Moder) Project Management With CPM and PERT, 1964, 2d edit., 1970. Contbr. articles to profl. jours. Home: 1711 Timberland Rd NE Atlanta GA 30345 Office: 1422 W Peachtree St NW Atlanta GA 30309

PHILLIPS, CECIL VERNON, elec. engr.; b. Hutchinson, Kan., Nov. 24, 1914; s. Charles Ezra and Ina (Boone) P.; student Hutchinson Jr. Coll., 1933-35; B.S. in Elec. Engring., Kan. State U., 1939; m. Mary Elizabeth Nolder, July 2, 1939; children—Inabelle Marlene (Mrs. John R. Wright), Roger Vernon. Div. engr. Kan. Power & Light Co., Hiawatha, 1939-43; utility engr. State Commn. Revenue and Taxation, Topeka, 1943-50; electronic engr. telephone div. Rural Electrification Adminstrn., Washington, 1950-52; elec. engr. USAF, Washington, 1952—. Instr. engring. sci., mgmt. war tng. program U. Kan., 1942-43. Scoutmaster, Sunflower council Boy Scouts Am., 1946-47. Recipient Outstanding Performance award Dept. Air Force, 1968. Mem. Nat., Kan. socs. profl. engrs., Am. Legion, Soc. Am. Mil. Engrs., Kappa Eta Kappa. Presbyn. (deacon 1954-57, ruling elder 1964-67). Home: 2001 Columbia Pike 306 Arlington VA 22204 Office: Hdqrs USAF (AFPRE) Washington DC 20330

PHILLIPS, CHANNING EMERY, clergyman, housing exec.; b. Bklyn., Mar. 23, 1928; s. Porter W. and Dorothy A. (Fletcher) P.; student U. Utah, 1945-46; A.B., Va. Union U., 1950; B.D., Colgate Rochester Div. Sch., 1953; postgrad. Drew U., 1953-56; m. Jane Celeste Nabors, Dec. 22, 1956; children—Channing Durward, Sheilah Nahketah, Tracy Jane, Jill Celeste, John Emery. Ordained to ministry United Ch. of Christ, 1952; instr., Howard U., 1956-58; sr. minister Lincoln Temple, Washington, 1961-70; pres. Housing Devel. Corp., Washington, 1967—. Chmn. D.C. delegation Nat. Democratic Conv., 1968; D.C. Dem. Nat. committeeman, 1968—. Bd. dirs. Washington Urban League, Center for Community Change. Served with USAAF, 1945-47. Mem. Alpha Phi Alpha. Home: 3801 Jennifer St NW Washington DC 22015 Office: 1010 Vermont Av NW Washington DC 20005

PHILLIPS, CHARLES FRANKLIN, JR., mayor, educator; b. Geneva, N.Y., Nov. 5, 1934; s. Charles Franklin and Evelyn (Minard) P.; B.A., U. N.H., 1956; Ph.D., Harvard, 1960; m. Marjorie Hancock, June 22, 1957; children—Charles Franklin III, Susan Hancock, Anne Davis. Asst. prof. econs. Washington and Lee U., Lexington, Va., 1959-62, asso. prof., 1962-65, prof., 1965—; mayor, Lexington, 1971—. Cons. utility cos. including Am. Tel. & Tel. Co., N.Y. Stock Exchange, S.C. Electric & Gas Co., Lee Telephone Co., Va. Electric and Power Co., Westinghouse Electric Corp., banking markets sect. bd. govs. Fed. Res. System. Mem. Lexington City Council, 1967-71; pres. Lexington-Rockbridge Boys' Club, 1969-73; mem. adv. bd. 1st Nat. Exchange & Bank Lexington; chmn. Central Shanandoah Planning Dist., 1971—. Bd. dirs. Rockbridge (Va.) Cancer Soc. Trustee, Hebron Acad. Mem. Am. Soc. econ. assns., Am. Marketing Assn., Phi Beta Kappa, Beta Gamma Sigma, Omicron Delta Epsilon (v.p.), Omicron Delta Kappa, Pi Sigma Alpha, Pi Gamma Mu. Kiwanian (past pres.). Author: Competition in the Synthetic Rubber Industry, 1963; The Economics of Regulation, 1965, rev. edit., 1969; also contbr. articles to profl. jours. Home: 414 Morningside Dr Lexington VA 24450

PHILLIPS, DAVID EUGENE, editor; b. Columbia City, Ind., Mar. 16, 1938; s. John Gilbert and Emma Jean (Young) P.; student Franklin Coll., 1956-57, Ind. State U., 1959-60; m. Sharon Lee Myers, Oct. 10, 1960; 1 son, Joel David. Writer Indpls. Times, 1956-57; newspaperman Columbia City Post, 1958-59; copy editor Oklahoman, 1968; copy-editor Ky. Post & Times Star, Covington, 1968-69; editor-pub. Bluegrass Basketball mag., Erlanger, Ky., 1969; editor Display World mags., Cin., 1969—; cons. in field. Served with USAF, 1959-68. Mem. Sigma Alpha Epsilon. Lutheran (elder). Club: Toastmasters. Home: 3018 Lindsey Dr Ft Mitchell KY 41017 Office: 407 Gilbert Av Cincinnati OH 45202

PHILLIPS, DORIS JEAN STURGIS (MRS. CAREY W. PHILLIPS, JR.), physician; b. Birmingham, Ala.; d. Franklin and Bethel (Crow) Sturgis; A.B., Samford U., 1946; M.D., Med. Coll. Ala., 1950; postgrad. Washington U., St. Louis, 1952-54; m. Carey W. Phillips Jr., Sept. 14, 1951; children—Anne Sturgis, Paula Beth, Jean Carey. Intern, Univ. Hosp., Birmingham, 1950-51; resident St. Louis Children's Hosp.; practice medicine specializing in pediatric allergy, Birmingham; mem. staff Children's Hosp., Birmingham; asso. clin. prof. pediatrics Med. Coll. Ala., Birmingham, 1954—. Mem. Women's Aux. Birmingham Symphony, Arlington Hist. Soc., A.M.A., Ala., Jefferson County med. socs., So. Med. Assn., Am. Acad. Pediatrics, Am. Coll. Allergists, Am. Acad. Allergy, Jefferson County Pediatric Soc., Med. Progress Assembly, D.A.R., Delta Zeta. Home: 2930 Carlisle Rd Birmingham AL 35213 Office: 942 S 8th St Birmingham AL 35205

PHILLIPS, EUGENE, pub. relations cons.; b. Canon, Ga., Nov. 26, 1917; s. M.D. and Minnie (Phillips) P.; A.B.J., U. Ga., 1939; m. Nadine Barnts, Dec. 29, 1941; 1 son, Thomas Eugene Barnts. Corr., reporter Atlanta Jour., 1938-39; dir. pub. relations Long-Bell Lumber Co., Longview, Wash., 1939-40; reporter, feature writer Milw. Jour., 1945-46; news editor A.P., New Orleans, 1947; U.S. Govt. information posts, Germany, France, Burma, 1948-52; editor Washington (Ga.) News-Reporter, 1952-53; pub. relations Delta Air Lines, Inc., Atlanta, 1954-60; asso. dir. pub. information, dir. Washington office Aerospace Corp., 1960-65; mgmt. cons. pub. relations Atlanta and Washington, 1966—. Served with AUS, 1939-45; brig. gen. Res. ret. Decorated French Croix de Guerre; Legion of Merit (U.S.). Mem. Res. Officers Assn. U.S. (life), Nat. Aviation Club, Aero Club Washington, Nat. Press Club, Pub. Relations Soc. Am., Sigma Delta Chi. Baptist. Home: Route 1 Box 58 Royston GA 30662 Office: 2 Peachtree St NW Atlanta GA 30303 also 1629 K St NW Washington DC 20006

PHILLIPS, EWING LAKIN, educator, psychologist; b. Higginsville, Mo., Apr. 29, 1915; s. Charles Brown and Martha (Lakin) P.; M.A., U. Mo., 1939; Ph.D., U. Minn., 1949; m. Gloria Twilla Liebner, Apr. 30, 1949; children—Charles William, Piper Jeanne, Nonie Elizabeth, Kirk Lakin. Asst. prof. psychology George Washington U., 1948-52; clin. psychologist Arlington (Va.) Mental Hygiene Clinic, 1949-55; clin. psychologist, cons. Nat. Orthopaedic and Rehab. Hosp., Arlington, 1952—; cons. govt., pvt. schs., agys., 1952—; prof. psychology, dir. Psychol. Clinic, George Washington U., Washington, 1962—. Mem. Am., Eastern, D.C., Southeastern psychol. assns., Va. Acad. Sci., Washington Soc. Clin. Psychologists, A.A.A.S. Author: Psychotherapy: A Modern Theory and Practice, 1956; (with James F. Gibson) Psychology and Personality, 1957; (with D.N. Wiener and N.G. Haring) Discipline, Achievement and Mental Health, 1960; (with N.G. Haring) Educating Emotionally Disturbed Children, 1962; (with D.N. Wiener) Short-Term Psychotherapy and Structured Behavior Change, 1966. Home: 11416 Vale Rd Oakton VA 22124 Office: 718 21st St SW Washington DC 20006

PHILLIPS, FERMAN, assn. exec.; b. Carney, Okla., Aug. 4, 1907; student Okla. Baptist U., LL.D., 1954; B.A., Southeastern State Coll., Durant, Okla.; M.A., Okla. State U.; m. Eula Mae Phillips. Supt. schs., Savanna, Okla., Atoka, Okla.; asst. to exec. sec. Okla. Edn. Assn., Oklahoma City, 1946-48, exec. sec., 1948—. Mem. Okla. Ho. of Reps., 6 years, Okla. Senate, 8 years. Served with AUS, World War II. Mem. Nat. Assn. Secs. State Tchrs. Assns. (pres. 1960). Office: Okla Edn Assn 323 E Madison St Oklahoma City OK 73105*

PHILLIPS, FRANCES MARIE, univ. ofcl.; b. Hale Center, Tex., Nov. 8, 1918; d. Clyde C. and Ada (Stutzman) Phillips; B.A., West Tex. State Coll., 1940, M.A., 1946; Ph.D. (Univ. fellow), U. N.M., 1956; postgrad. (Fulbright scholar), U. London, 1954-55. Tchr. pub. schs. Channing, Miami, Tex., Palisade, Colo., Tucumcari, N.M., 1940-46; supr. State Tchrs. Coll. Campus High Sch., Wayne, Neb.,

County, Ga., 1965—. Mem. Ga. Assn. Educators, Ga. Assn. Sch Supts. Home: Box 435 Kingsland GA 31548

RAINER, LAMAR SIDNEY, JR., banker; b. Troy, Ala., Jan. 19, 1925; s. Lamar Sidney and Violet (Dantzier) R.; student U. Vt., 1944; B.A.A., Auburn U., 1949; m. Helen Joyce Braswell, Oct. 21, 1950; children—Beverly Lynn, Lamar Sidney III. Advt. sales promotion Sears, Roebuck & Co., Columbus, Ga. and Tuscaloosa, Ala., 1950; with Gen. Ins. Co., Elba, Ala., 1951-54; home office mgr. claims and underwriting dept. Nat. Security Ins. Co., Elba, 1955-59; pres. Emergency Aid Ins. Co., Elba, 1959-62; organizer Peoples Bank, Elba, 1963, chmn., pres., 1964—; organizer, dir. 1st Fed. Savings & Loan Assn., Enterprise, Ala. City councilman, Elba, Ala., 1956-60; bd. dirs., mem. program com. Ala. Council on the Arts and Humanities, 1968—; mem. exec. bd. S.E. Ala. Council, Boy Scouts Am., Dothan, Ala., 1964-67. Treas., bd. dirs. Indsl. Bd. City of Elba, 1962—; vice chmn. bd. dirs. Water Works and Electric Bd., City of Elba, 1956-60, 63—; charter mem. Citizens Conf. on Ala. State Cts., 1966—, sec.-treas., 1969—; chmn. Elba Hosp. Assn., 1965-70; organizer, dir. Elba Little Theatre. Served with USAAF, 1943-45. Mem. V.F.W., Am. Legion, Elba C. of C., Phi Kappa Phi. Democrat. Methodist. Home: 579 E Davis St Elba AL 36323 Office: 304 Simmons St Elba AL 36323

RAINER, REX KELLY, educator; b. Montgomery, Ala., July 17, 1924; s. Kelly Kenyon and Pearl (Jones) R.; B.S., Auburn U., 1944, M.S., 1946; Ph.D., Okla. State U., 1967; m. Betty Ann Page, Aug. 28, 1945; children—Rex Kelly, John Kenyon. Asst. engr. L. & N. R.R. Co., Cin., 1944-45; design engr. Polglaze & Basenberg, Cons. Engrs., Birmingham, Ala., 1945-51; pres., chmn. Rainer Co., Inc., Orlando, Fla., 1951-62; prof. Auburn (Ala.) U., 1962-67, prof., head civil engring., 1967—; cons. to ins. cos., constrn. engring. firms. Mem. Municipal Planning Bd., 1963-65, Indsl. Park Devel. Bd., 1968—. Served with AUS, 1943. Fellow Am. Soc. C.E. (sec.-treas. Ala. sect. 1970, vice-chmn. Constrn. Research Council 1970—); mem. Asso. Gen. Contractors Am. (past dir. Central Fla.), Am. Soc. Engring. Edn., Phi Kappa Phi, Tau Beta Pi, Chi Epsilon. Baptist. Kiwanian. Contbr. articles profl. jours. Home: 1096 Terrace Acres Auburn AL 36830

RAINES, ERNEST RUDOLPH, supr. schs.; b. Breaks, Va., Apr. 30, 1921; s. Joseph and Dana (Sutherland) R.; B.A., Berea Coll., 1948; postgrad. William and Mary Coll., summer 1961; M.A., E. Tenn. State U., 1970; m. Shirley Estep, Aug. 3, 1945; children—Ernest Gary, James Howard, David Gregory, Lisa Carol. Tchr. high sch., Buchanan County Schs., Grundy, Va., 1948-55, prin. elementary sch., 1955-63, elementary supr., 1963-64, gen. supr., 1964—; chmn. com. for evaluation and planning, 1968—. Cub scoutmaster, 1955-57. Treas., Buchanan County Democratic Com., 1963-65; mem. Buchanan County Planning Commn., 1967-70; dir., coordinator Transp. Services for Civil Def. Buchanan County, 1967—. Served as staff sgt. USAAF, 1942-45. Decorated Purple Heart. Mem. Nat., Va., Buchanan (pres. 1954-56, chmn. profl. standards com. 1956-64) edn. assns., C. of C., Va. Assn. Supervision and Curriculum Devel., S.W. Regional Sch. Suprs. (program chmn. 1968-69), P.T.A. (life). Home: Breaks VA 24607 Office: Buchanan County School Board Grundy VA 24614

RAINEY, CLAUDE GLADWIN, hosp. adminstr.; b. Enloe, Tex., Apr. 21, 1923; s. Claude C. and Pauline (Whitlock) R.; student Pub. Health and Adminstrv. Medicine, Columbia, 1961-62; m. Peggy Ballard, July 27, 1947; children—Kathy Suzanne, David Claude, Mark Jeffery, Joel Allen, Peggy Jan, Susan Elise. Med. adminstr., officer VA Dept. Medicine & Surgery, Temple, Tex., 1946-51, Muskogee, Okla., 1951-56; med. adminstr. Fite Clinic, Lakeland Med. Center, Muskogee, 1956-59; hosp. adminstr. M.-K.-T. R.R. Employees Hosp. Assn., Denison, Tex., 1959-62, also sec., treas., trustee; hosp. adminstr., cons. Denison Hosp. Authority, Meml. Hosp., 1962-66; adminstr. Seton Hosp., Austin, Tex., 1966—. Pres. Am. Cancer Soc., N. Grayson County, 1960-66, dir. Tex., 1961—. Served with USNR, 1942-46. Mem. Am., Tex. hosp. assns., Am. Coll. Hosp. Adminstrs. Home: 4000 Edgerock Dr Austin TX 78731 Office: 600 W 26th St Austin TX 78705

RAINEY, EDWARD CARR, banker; b. Covington, Ga., Apr. 22, 1913; s. William Nathaniel and Ann Cureton (Carr) R.; certificate radio engring., Ga. Inst. Tech. 1938; student Rutgers U. Grad. Sch. Banking, 1948-50; grad. Advanced Mgmt. Program, Harvard, 1958; m. Lillian B. Sams, Nov. 30, 1938; children—Edward Carr, Linda Diane. With Fed. Res. Bank Atlanta, 1932—, v.p., mgr. Birmingham (Ala.) br., 1963-68, sr. v.p. Jacksonville (Fla.) br., 1969—; instr. Am. Inst. Banking, 1957, 60, 61. Bd. dirs. Indsl. Health Council Birmingham, 1963-68. Home: 4641 Arlon Lane Jacksonville FL 32210 Office: 515 Julia St Jacksonville FL 32203

RAINS, ALBERT, banker, lawyer; b. DeKalb County, Ala., Mar. 11, 1902; ed. pub. schs., student Snead Sem., State Tchrs. Coll., U. Ala.; m. Allison Blair, Dec. 29, 1939. Admitted to Ala. bar, 1928, mem. firm Rains & Rains, Gadsden, Ala.; chmn. bd. 1st City Nat. Bank, Gadsden; dep. sol. Etowah County, Ala., 1930-35; city atty. Gadsden, 1935-44; mem. Ho. of Reps., Ala. legislature, 1942-44; mem. 79th to 87th Congresses, 5th Ala. Dist., mem. 88th U.S. Congress at large; chmn. housing sub-com.; mem. banking and currency com., joint com. def. prodn.; now committeeman from Ala. nat. Democratic party. Home: 221 Alpine View Gadsen AL 35901 Office: 1st City Nat Bank Bldg Gadsen AL 35901

RAINS, GEORGE PAUL, utility co. exec.; b. Williamsburg, Ky., Dec. 16, 1940; s. John and Hattie (Jones) R.; student Cumberland Coll., 1958-59; B.C.E., U. Ky., 1963; m. Jo Eileen Patrick, Nov. 12, 1965; children—Paula Faye, Stephen J. Resident engr. Ky. Hwy. Dept., 1963-65; chief engr. T.C. Young Constrn. Co., Williamsburg, 1965-67; gen. mgr. Corbin (Ky.) Utilities Commn., 1968—, dir., 1967—. Mem. Corbin C. of C. (dir. indsl. devel. 1970-71). Mason. Home: 1219 Reasor St Corbin KY 40701 Office: 901 S Main St Corbin KY 40701

RAINWATER, CRAWFORD VEAZEY, bottling co. exec.; b. Atlanta, Apr. 23, 1916; s. Charles Veazey and Blanche (Edmondson) R.; B.B.A., Emory U., 1937; m. Betty Gregg, Oct. 29, 1938; children—Elizabeth Adair (Mrs. Kenneth H. Woolf), Crawford Veazey, Nancy Gregg. Employed with Hygeia Coca-Cola Bottling Co., Pensacola, Fla., 1937—, pres., dir., 1961—. Pres. Gulf Coast council Boy Scouts Am., 1958-60, chmn. region V, 1962-66, mem. Nat. Exec. Bd., 1962—; pres. Pensacola United Fund, 1963-64. Trustee Escambia County 4-H Timber Grazing and Game Project, 1941—; Pensacola Jr. Coll. Found., Inc., U. West Fla. Found., Inc. Served with USNR, 1943-46. Recipient Silver Beaver, Silver Antelope awards Boy Scouts Am.; Outstanding Citizens award Pensacola Kiwanis Club, 1956. Mem. So. Golf Assn. (dir. 1966), Am. Bottlers Carbonated Beverages Assn. (exec. bd.), Chi Phi. Episcopalian (vestry). Rotarian (pres. 1956). Clubs: Pensacola Country, Scenic Hills Country (Pensacola). Home: 777 W Lakeview Av Pensacola FL 32501 Office: 1625 N Palafox St Pensacola FL 32501

RAIT, ROBERT ALEXANDER, petroleum co. exec.; b. Lincoln, Neb., Mar. 10, 1911; s. Alexander Hamilton and Ida (Hoffman) R.; B.S. in Civil Engring., U. Neb., 1933; m. Sybil Frances Smith, June 11, 1939; with Humble Oil & Refining Co., Corpus Christi, Tex., 1944—, tech. adviser design, constrn. gas facilities, 1971—. Registered profl engr., Tex. Fellow Am. Soc. C.E. (pres. Houston br. 1956, past chmn. exec. com. pipeline div.); mem. Tex., Nat. socs. profl. engrs., Am. Inst. Mech. Engrs., Pi Mu Epsilon. Home: 702 Monette St Corpus Christi TX 78412 Office: Wilson Tower 520 N Caranchua Corpus Christi TX 78401

RAITERI, JOSEPH MARK, computer co. exec.; b. Memphis, Apr. 23, 1940; s. Charles T. and Virginia Estella (Lowe) R.; B.Mech. Engring., Ga. Inst. Tech., 1963; m. Carol Lynn Goforth, Aug. 15, 1964; children— Gavin Marc, Anthony Kent. Engr., So. Bell Telephone Co., Nashville, 1963-68; sr. system analyst Beaunit Corp., Raleigh, N.C., 1968-69, lab. mgr., 1969-70; gen. mgr. Compucolor div. Asystance Corp., Research Triangle Park, N.C., 1970—. Mem. Pi Tau Sigma. Home: 1600 Beechwood Dr Raleigh NC 27609 Office: Box 12012 Research Triangle Park NC 27709

RAKENTINE, LLOYD WILLIAM, comptroller; b. E. Rutherford, N.J., Jan. 26, 1915; s. William and Sarah (Niebling) R.; student Internat. Corr. Schs., 1946-47, Dallas Night Sch., 1951-55; m. Viola Ethel Varga, Sept. 11, 1942; 1 child, G. Ilona. Salesman, Crucible Steel Co. Am., N.Y.C., 1931-46; with purchasing dept. Celanese Corp. Am., N.Y.C., 1946-50; asst. sec.-treas., comptroller Tears Engrs. Inc., Dallas, 1950—; dir., comptroller Hunnicut Corp., 1958—; sec.-treas. Ford, Bacon & Davis Tex., Inc., 1966—. Served with USAAF, 1942-45. Mem. Nat. Assn. Accountants, Am. Legion. Methodist. Republican. Home: 6624 Hialeah Dr Dallas TX 75214 Office: 2908 National Dr Garland TX 75040

RAKESTRAW, BRYAN LAVERN, banker; b. Snyder, Okla., Dec. 5, 1910; s. Elias Vern and Ella Adella (Fry) R.; A.B., U. Okla., 1933; LL.B., 1939; LL.M., Georgetown U., 1949; grad. Okla. Bankers Assn. Intermediate Sch. Banking, 1968; m. Arthur Lory Morris, Jan. 19, 1942; children—Ella Kay (Mrs. Richard T. Yery), Don William, Lee Franklin. Asst. collector Internal Revenue Service, Okla., 1939-40; admitted to Okla. bar, 1940; commd. 1st lt. U.S. Army, 1940, advanced through grades to col., 1951; with Judge Adv. Gen.'s Dept., Washington, 1946-51, staff judge adv. Tng. Command, Tactical Air Command, U.S. Air Force in Europe, 1961-65; ret., 1966; v.p. Fidelity Nat. Bank Nat. Assn. and Trust Co., 1966—. Pres., Langley AFB Youth Assn., 1960; pres. Wildewood Devel. Assn., 1968; pres. United Cerebral Palsy of Greater Oklahoma City, Inc., 1970-72. Decorated Legion of Merit with oak leaf cluster; recipient award United Cerebral Palsy Assn., Oklahoma City, 1969. Mem. Am., Okla., Oklahoma County bar assns., Methodist. Mason (Shriner, 32 deg.). Club: Whitehall. Contbr. articles to profl. publs. Home: 5717 N Everest St Oklahoma City OK 73111 Office: Fidelity Bank NA Robert S Kerr and Robinson Sts Oklahoma City OK 73102

RALEY, BUN, ins. co. exec.; b. Valley Mills, Tex., Sept. 20, 1901; s. William C. and Celia Ellen (Taylor) R.; student N. Tex. Coll., 1921-22; m. Alkie Smallwood, July 12, 1922 (dec.); children—Mrs. Werner H. Barth, Russell C. (dec.); m. 2d Lucile Williamson, Aug. 29, 1942 (dec.). Vice pres. Tex. Rural Letter Carriers Assn., 1940-41, pres., 1942-43; legislative rep., 1944-46, now legislative rep. also chmn. rd. com.; editor Texas Carrier, 1944-45; exec. com. Nat. Rural Letter Carriers Assn., 1947, v.p., 1950, pres. 1951; legislative rep. Nat. League Postmasters, 1960-64, also exec. sec.; dir. rural appointments br. Bur. Operations, P.O. Dept., Washington, 1964-66; v.p. Am. Income Life Ins. Co., Waco, Tex., 1966—. Bd. dirs. Nat. Farm Rds. Found., 1953. Mem. Am., Tex. Rural (organizer) road builders assns. Methodist. Mason (Shriner). Clubs: Bosque County Sportsman (pres.); Lions. Author articles jours , newspapers. Home: 4101 Grim St Waco TX 76710 Office: Box 208 Waco TX 76703

RALEY, JOHN WESLEY, JR., lawyer; b. Bartlesville, Okla., May 23, 1932; s. John Wesley and Helen (Thames) R.; A.B., Okla. Bapt. U., 1954; J.D., U. Okla., 1959; m. Mary Layne Perry, Dec. 20, 1958; children—John Wesley III, Robert Thames. Admitted to Okla. bar, 1959; practice law, Oklahoma City, 1959-69, Ponca City, Okla., 1969—; asst. U.S. atty. Western dist. Okla., Oklahoma City, 1961-69; mem. firm. Northcutt, Northcutt, Ellifrit & Raley, Ponca City, Okla., 1969—. Drive chmn., pres. United Fund, 1971-72; asst. dist. chmn. Boy Scouts Am., 1970-71. Bd. dirs. United Fund Ponca City, Ponca City YMCA; trustee Okla. Bapt. U., Shawnee, Okla. Served to comdr. USNR, 1954-56. Mem. Am. state chmn. Law Day 1972, Okla bar assns., Ponca City C. of C. (dir.), Okla. Assn. Def. Counsel, Res. Officers Assn., Am. Legion, Navy League (pres. Ponca City 1971-72), Phi Alpha Delta, Omicron Delta Kappa. Democrat. Baptist. Mason, Kiwanian. Home: 2721 Canterbury St Ponca City OK 74601 Office: Security Bank Bldg Ponca City OK 74601

RALLS, MANTON, oil co. exec.; b. Comanche, Okla., July 1, 1906; s. Eustace Manton and Sarah Ann (Atkins) R.; student Okla. State U., 1924-26; m. Helen Bristow, Oct. 20, 1929; children—Anne Green, Rosemary (Mrs. Rosemary Fair), Robert M. Asst. cashier 1st Nat. Bank, Comanche, 1926-31; v.p., loan officer Okla. Nat. Bank, Duncan, 1931-45; sec.-treas. Mack Oil Co., Duncan, 1945—, also dir. Methodist. Kiwanian, Elk. Home: 1202 N 12th St Duncan OK 73533 Office: 1202 N 10th St Duncan OK 73533

RALLS, RAWLEIGH HAZEN, educator, cons.; b. Oklahoma City, Dec. 12, 1932; s. Rawleigh Hazen and Rosemary Thelma (Sprigg) R.; B.S., U.S. Mil. Acad., 1955; M.S., U.S. Naval Postgrad. Sch., 1964; D.B.A., George Washington U., 1971; m. Anne Byram Singer, June 7, 1955; children—Elizabeth Anne, Devon Anne, Rawleigh Hazen IV. Commd. 2d lt. arty. U.S. Army, 1955, advanced through grades to maj., 1965; various assignments, 1955-66, chief arty. systems group Office Army Chief of Staff, Washington, 1966-67, prof. operations research U.S. Army Mgmt. Sch., Fort Belvoir, Va., 1967-68; asso. prof. quantitative mgmt. sci., also coordinator statistics Coll. Bus. Adminstrn., U. Ark., Fayetteville, 1968—. Gen. partner Edn. & Research Assos., Alexandria, Va., 1968; pvt. cons. mgmt. and decision sci., Fayetteville, 1969—; pres. Edn. and Research Assos., Inc., 1970—. Trustee Whitney Scholarship Fund. Fellow A.A.A.S.; mem. Operations Research Soc. Am., Am. Econ. Assn., Am. Inst. for Decision Sci., Mensa. Episcopalian. Home: 412 Assembly Dr Fayetteville AR 72701

RALSTON, CARL CONRAD, constrn. co. exec.; b. Owensboro, Ky., Nov. 1, 1927; s. Carl C. and Elizabeth (Little) R.; Asso. B.B.A., Ky. Bus. Coll., 1949; B.A., Ky. Wesleyan Coll., 1956; m. Gerrie Henning, May 28, 1947; 1 dau., Pamela Kay. Pub. accountant, 1956; chief accountant, estimator Mills & Jones Inc., 1957-60, project mgr., 1960-65; v.p. Mills & Jones Constrn. Co., St. Petersburg, Fla., 1965—. Pres., Cross Bayou Little League, Seminole, Fla., 1959-61; treas. Seminole Lake Civic Assn., Seminole, 1959-62. Trustee Southeastern Ironworkers' Health and Welfare Fund. Served with USAAF, 1945-47. Mem. Am. Mgmt. Assn., Assn. Gen. Contractors (chpt. dir. 1969-70). Club: Seminole Lake Country (gov. 1964-67, chmn. bd. 1967-68). Home: 8499 Pelican Lane Seminole FL 33540 Office: 400 23d St S St Petersburg FL 33731

RAMAZANI, ROUHOLIAH KAREGAR, educator; b. Tehran, Iran, Mar. 21, 1928 (came to U.S. 1952, naturalized, 1961); s. Ali and Khadijeh (Sultani) R.; LL.M., U. Tehran, 1951; S.J.D., U. Va., 1954; m. Nesta Shahrokh, Feb. 22, 1952; children—Vaheed, David, Jahan, Sima. Lectr. fgn. affairs U. Va., 1954-57, research asso. Soviet Fgn. Econ. Relations Project, 1956-59, asst. prof. fgn. affairs, 1957-60, asso. prof., 1960-64, prof. govt. and fgn. affairs, 1964—, Edward R. Stettinius prof. govt. and fgn. affairs, 1972. Aga Khan vis. prof. Islamic studies Am. U., Beirut, 1967-68. Trustee, v.p. Am. Inst. Iranian Studies. Research Council grantee, 1967; Fulbright Research grantee, 1968. Recipient prize Am. Assn. for Middle Eastern Studies, 1964. Mem. Am. Soc. Internat. Law, Am., So. polit. sci. assns., Middle East Inst., Middle East Studies Assn. N.Am., Shaybani Soc. Internat. Law, Am. So. Polit. Sci. Assn. Author: The Middle East and the European Common Market, 1964; The Northern Tier: Afghanistan, Iran and Turkey, 1966; The Foreign Policy of Iran, 1500-1941: A Developing Nation in World Affairs, 1966; The Persian Gulf: Iran's Role, 1972; contbg. author Soviet Foreign Relations and World Communism, 1965; The Search for World Order, 1971. Home: Box 232 RFD 3 Charlottesville VA 22901

RAMER, WARREN CARLTON, physician; b. Jackson, Tenn., July 14, 1914; s. Dan and Annie (Pankey) R.; B.S., Union U. (Jackson, Tenn.), 1936; M.D., U. Tenn., 1937; m. Katherine Stark, Oct. 1, 1939; children— Warren C., Henry Stark. Intern, John Gaston Hosp., Memphis, 1938-39, U.S. Marine Hosp., Memphis, 1939; county health officer Tenn. Dept. Pub. Health, 1939-44; practice medicine, specializing in family practice, Lexington, Tenn., 1944—; mem. staff Lexington-Henderson County Gen. Hosp., former chief of staff; county physician Henderson County 1944-60. Mem. bldg. com. Lexington-Henderson County Gen. Hosp., 1958-64. Trustee Lambuth Coll., Jackson. Charter diplomate Am. Bd. Family Practice. Mem. A.M.A. (recipient Physicians Recognition award 1970), Consol. Med. Assembly W. Tenn. (past pres.), Tenn. Med. Assn. (past councilor), Am. Acad. Family Practice. Methodist (mem. ofcl. bd., bldg. com.). Rotarian. Clubs: Lexington Golf and Country, Pine Tree County (Lexington). Home: 468 N Broad St Lexington TN 38551 Office: 47 N Broad St Lexington TN 38351

RAMEY, ESTELLE R. (MRS. JAMES T. RAMEY), physiologist, educator; b. Detroit, Aug. 23, 1917; B.A., Bklyn. Coll.; M.A., Columbia U., 1940; Ph.D. in Physiology (Mergler scholar, USPHS fellow), U. Chgo., 1950, also doctorate in medicine; m. James T. Ramey, 1941; 2 children. Lectr., U. Tenn., 1942-47; instr. physiology U. Chgo., 1951-54, asst. prof., 1954-58; asst. prof. endocrinology Georgetown U. Sch. Med., Washington, 1956-60, asso. prof., 1960-66, prof., 1966—. Mem. Am. Physiol. Soc., Am. Chem. Soc., Soc. Exptl. Biology and Medicine, Endocrine Soc., Am. Diabetes Assn., Am. Acad. Neurology. Research on adrenal function and insulin action. Office: Georgetown University Sch Medicine Washington DC 20007*

RAMIREZ, MARIANO HECTOR, jurist; b. San Juan, P.R., Feb. 11, 1905; s. Mariano Ramirez and Irene (Bages); LL.B., Cornell U., 1927; m. Alicia T. Benet, Sept. 6, 1933; children—Alicia Irene, Marion Louise, Mariano Hector. Admitted to P.R. bar, 1927; practice in San Juan and Mayaguez, 1927-29; chief Latin Am. sec. div. comml. law Dept. Commerce, 1929-34; territorial counsel HOLC, 1934-36; counsel P.R. Reconstrn. Adminstrn., 1936-42; v.p., gen. counsel, sec. P.R. Indsl. Devel. Co., 1942-50; exec. asst., gen. counsel Econ. Devel. Adminstrn., 1950-54; gen. counsel P.R. Indsl. Devel. Co., also Econ. Devel. Adminstrn, 1954-62; asso. justice Supreme Ct. P.R., 1962—. Mem. U.S. Rationing and Draft Bds., 1942-62. Lion (past sec.-treas. dist. 51). Clubs: Casino, Berwind (San Juan). Author numerous pamphlets. Home: Laguna Terrace Condominium 6 Joffre St Condado PR 00907 Office: Supreme Ct PR San Juan PR 00901

RAMIREZ, MARIO EFRAIN, physician; b. Roma, Tex., Apr. 3, 1926; s. Efren Manuel and Carmen (Hinojosa) R.; student U. Tex., 1942-45; M.D., U. Tenn., 1948; m. Sarah B. Aycock, Nov. 25, 1949; children—Mario, Patricia Anne, Norman Michael, Jaime Eduardo, Roberto Luis. Intern, Shreveport (La.) Charity Hosp., 1948-49, resident, 1949-50; gen. practice medicine, Roma, Tex., 1950—; health officer Starr County, 1952-69; owner, med. dir. Manuel Ramirez Meml. Hosp., Roma, 1958—. Vice chmn. S. Tex. Devel. Council, 1971—; chmn. Tri-County Bd., Community Action Council, 1971—. Judge Starr County, 1969—. Served to capt. USAF, 1955-57; Japan. Recipient spl. citation for work done during Hurricane Beulah from surgeon gen. 1967; citation Tex. Acad. Gen. Practice, 1953. Diplomate Am. Bd. Family Practice. Mem. A.M.A., Tex. (Distinguished Service award 1972), Hidalgo-Starr County med. assns., Am., Tex. acads. family practice, C. of C., K.C., Rotarian, Lion. Built pvt. hosp. to serve Roma area, 1958. Address: Box 188 Roma TX 78584

RAMIREZ DE ARELLANO, ALFREDO, broadcaster, banker; b. San German, P.R., Feb. 10, 1916; s. Alfredo and Josefa (Bartoly) R. de A.; B.S. in Chem. Engring., U. P.R., 1937; m. Esther Del Valle, Jan. 28, 1939; children—Alfredo III, Gloria, Josie. Pres. Western Sugar Refining Co., Mayaguez, P.R., 1946-55, 61—, Radio Ams. Corp., 1948—, Voice P.R., Inc., Ponce, P.R., 1952—, Quality Telecasting Corp., Mayaguez, 1954—, Quality Broadcasting Co., San Juan, P.R., 1960—, Mayaguez Enterprises Corp., 1964—, Banco Commercial De Mayaguez, 1968—; dir. Puerto Rican and Am. Ins. Co.; mem. adv. bd. to bd. dirs. Banco Popular de P.R., 1966-67. Pres. campaign Mayaguez chpt. Boy Scouts Am. Pres. YMCA, Mayaguez P.R., 1955-59; mem. President's Council Inter-Am. U., 1966—, bd. dirs., 1967—. Served from 1st lt. to maj. AUS, 1941-45. Named Citizen of Year Mayaguez, 1970. Mem. Assn. de Ingenieros. Republican. Roman Catholic. Rotarian (pres. Mayaguez, 1950, gov. dist. 403, 1952). Home: Las Mesas K2 H3 Mayaguez PR Office: Banco Commercial Bldg Mayaguez PR 00708

RAMIREZ QUEZADA, JAIME A., Honduran diplomat; Ph.D. in Chemistry and Pharmacy; m. Ofelia Ochoa; 4 children. Consul gen. for Honduras, New Orleans. Mem. Nat. party; personal rep. to ex-pres. Gral. Tiburcio Carias. Home: 6369 Canal Blvd New Orleans LA 70124 Office: Internat Trade Mart New Orleans LA 70130

RAMIREZ-RIVERA, JOSE, physician, educator; b. Mayaguez, P.R., June 26, 1929; s. Juan C. and Maria Nieves (Rivera) Ramirez-Quiles; B.A., Johns Hopkins, 1949; M.D., Yale, 1953; m. Leila Suner, May 14, 1971; children—Frederico, Jose Steven, Sally Graciela, Juliette Marie, Matasha Nieves. Intern, Univ. Hosp., Balt., 1953-54, resident, 1957-60; mem. staff VA Hosp., Balt., 1960-68, asst. chief med. service, 1962-68; asso. chief staff for research and edn., 1963-68; asst. prof. medicine U. Md. Sch. Medicine, 1963-68; instr. medicine Johns Hopkins Sch. Medicine, 1963-68; asso. prof. medicine Duke U. Med. Center, 1968-70; staff mem. in pulmonary diseases and asst. chief med. service VA Hosp., Durham, N.C., 1968-70; chief of medicine, dir. edn. and clin. research Med. Center, Mayaguez, 1970—. A.C.P. Blaine Brover traveling scholar, 1967. Diplomate Nat. Bd. Med. Examiners, Am. Bd. Internal Medicine. Mem. A.M.A., Am. Fedn. Clin. Research, A.C.P., Am. Thoracic Soc., P.R. Med. Assn. Rotarian. Clubs: Casino de Mayaguez, Deportivo del Oeste, Hilton Swimming and Tennis. Home: 166 E Betances St Mayaguez PR 00708 Office: Centro Medico Mayaguez PR 00708

RAMM, H(ANS) HENRY, lawyer; b. Chgo., Dec. 2, 1905; s. Ernst Ludwig and Elisa Magdalen (Fornebo) R.; A.B. magna cum laude, U. Minn., 1926; LL.B., Harvard, 1929; m. Katherine Shelor Gravely, Oct. 27, 1934; children—Peter Henry, Katherine Elizabeth. Admitted to N.Y. State bar, 1931, N.C. bar, 1947; practice law, N.Y.C., 1931-46; solicitor and asst. to chmn. bd. R.J. Reynolds Tobacco Co., 1946-55, gen. counsel, 1955-70, v.p., 1957-70; chmn. exec. com., sr. v.p., gen. counsel R.J. Reynolds Industries, Inc., 1970, also dir.; chmn., pres. Council for Tobacco Research, U.S.A., Inc., 1971—. Trustee N.C. Blue Cross and Blue Shield, Inc., Mem. Am., N.C. and Forsyth County bar assns., Phi Beta Kappa, Episcopalian. Clubs: Old Town City, Twin City. Home: 714 Oaklawn Av Winston-Salem NC 27104

RAMON, EDNA LYDIA RAMIREZ (MRS. FELIPE VICTOR RAMON), dietician; b. Edinburg, Tex., June 28, 1925; d. Rafael R. and Emilia (Schunior) Ramirez; student Edinburg Jr. Coll., 1942-43; B.S., U. Tex., 1946; m. Felipe Victor Ramon, Sept. 4, 1948; children—Victor Jose, Rebecca Emilia, Edna Isabel, David Alfonso. Instr. home econs. Roma (Tex.) Pub. Sch., 1946-47; tchr. Monte Alto (Tex.) Schs., 1947-48; mgr. Piggly Wiggly Food Store, Rio Grande City, Tex. 1948-66; editor Rio Grande Herald, 1952-67; dietician Ramirez Meml. Hosp., Roma, Tex., 1967—; cafeteria dir. Rio Grande City Consol. Ind. Sch. Dist., 1969—. Crusade chmn., service chmn. Am. Cancer Soc., 1952—; county coordinator Tip of Tex. council Girl Scouts of Am., 1962-64. Mem. Gen. Fedn. Women's Clubs (state chmn. internat. news bull. 1966-68, Inter-Am. affairs div. 1968-70, internat. affairs dept. 1970—, valley chmn. awards com. 1970—), Am. Assn. U. Women, Pan Am. Round Table, Nat. Council Catholic Women. Roman Catholic. Club: Rio Grande City Woman's (pres. 1964-65). Home: 613 W 2d St Rio Grande City TX 78582 Office: PO Box 188 Roma TX 78584

RAMOS, HAROLD SMITH, physician, educator; b. Atlanta, July 20, 1928; s. Ralph C. and Louise (Price) R.; A.B., Johns Hopkins, 1948; M.D., Med. Coll. Ga., 1954; m. Catherine Vonetta Wise; children— Catherine, Ralph, Steven. Intern, Walter Reed Army Hosp., Washington, 1954-55, resident, 1955-58; with Md. Dept. Health, 1949-51; asst. prof. medicine Emory U. Sch. Medicine, Atlanta, 1963-66, asso. prof., 1966—, asst. dean, 1972—; chief of medicine Crawford W. Long Meml. Hosp., 1963, dir. med. edn., 1963—. Served from 1st lt. to maj. USAF, 1954-63. Fellow in hematology-renal disease, 1958-59. Mem. A.C.P., A.M.A., Assn. for Hosp. Med. Edn. Home: 1095 Mt Paran Rd NW Atlanta GA 30327

RAMOS, LIBERTO, govt. ofcl.; b. Cayey, P.R., Apr. 11, 1922; s. Emiliano and Maria (Lopez) R.; B.A., U. P.R., 1953, LL.B., 1960; m. Margaret Rose Pinkson, Dec. 12, 1964; children—Diana (Mrs. Jacinto Latorre), Liberto, Ruben Emilio, Fernando, Edna Carmen. Mem. Municipal Assembly, 1947-49; mem. Ho. of Reps. Commonwealth P.R., 1956-60; asso. mem. Labor Relations Bd., 1961-68; sec. to electoral affairs Municipal Com. Puerto Rican Independence Party, Cayey, 1971—. Sec. bd. dirs. Our Lady of Asumption Community Hosp., Cayey. Served with inf. AUS, 1942-46. Roman Catholic. Rotarian. Club: Associate Salesmen (Cayey). Home: 110 S Sanchez St Cayey PR 00633 Office: 108 S Munoz Rivera Av Cayey PR 00633

RAMOS YORDAN, LUIS ERNESTO, physician, P.R. legislator; b. Ponce, P.R., Feb. 2, 1915; s. Federico Ramos Antonini and Felicita (Yordan) R.; B.S., Lincoln U., 1941; M.D., Nat. U. Mexico, 1947; M.P.H., Columbia U., 1954; m. Lenabelle Smith, Mar. 13, 1943; children—Harry Luis, Lysa Lee. Prof. pub. health U. P.R. Coll. Pharmacy, 1948-50; med. dir. Arroyo City Hosp., 1949-51, Arecibo Dist. Hosp., 1951-53; pres., hosp. dir. Ramos-Yordan, Inc., 1957—; pres. Lenabelle & Burhans Lab., Inc., 1957—, Ramos & Smith Realty, Inc., 1964—; cons. indsl. medicine and safety P.R. Ho. of Reps., 1967-68, mem. and Popular Democratic Party floor leader, 1969—. Cons. indsl. medicine and occupational health P.R. Dept. Labor, 1955-56, P.R. Dept. Health, 1958-59; v.p. Internat. Congress Indsl. Accidents, Brussels, Belgium, 1958; bd. dirs. Internat. Congress for Study Better Living and Working Conditions, Cannes, France, 1956; mem. permanent com. occupational medicine Internat. Congress Occupational Med Assn., 1968. Served from capt. to maj., M.C., AUS, 1956-58. Mem. Indsl. Med. Assn., P.R. Med. Assn. Roman Catholic. Home: 40 SO and De Diego Av La Riviera PR 00921 Office: PO Box 10847 Caparra Heights Station PR 00922*

RAMPTON, FRANCIS ROBERT, orthodontist; b. Mason City, Ia., Sept. 29, 1919; s. Frank Cyras and Effie (Van Note) R.; student Mason City Jr. Coll., 1937-39; B.A., State U. Ia., 1941, D.D.S., 1946, M.S., 1949; m. Esther Marie Kehl, Mar. 22, 1942 (div. 1966); children—Linda Kehl, Steven Robert, Nancy Ellen, Frank Cyrus. Pvt. practice gen. dentistry Manly, Ia., 1946-48, orthodontics Jacksonville, Fla., 1952—. Pres. Ramco Mining, Inc., Cia. Minera Rosario Ltd. First v.p. Camp Fire Girls, 1955-56; bd. dirs. Jacksonville Opera and Choral Soc., 1960-61, dental div. United Fund, Jacksonville, 1972. Served with AUS, 1943-44; with USAF, 1950-52, lt. col. Res. Mem. Fla. Dental Soc. (del. exec. council 1963-65), Am. Assn. Orthodontists, Am. Dental Assn., Fla. Orthodontic Soc., Fedn. Dentaire Internat. Office: 3958 Oak St Jacksonville FL 32205

RAMPUTI, SAMUEL ALFRED, city ofcl.; b. N.Y.C., Feb. 15, 1928; s. Erminio and Margaret (Rossi) R.; student Broward Community Coll., 1970; m. Catherine Halleran, Sept. 15, 1951; children—Samuel Arthur, Steven, Gregory, William. With Police Dept., Miramar, Fla., 1957—, police chief, 1961—. Hon. life mem. N. Massapequa Fire Dept., 1956—. Served with AUS, 1945-47. Mem. Am. Legion, Police Benevolent Assn. (pres. 1959-61), Broward County (pres. 1969-70), Fla., Internat. police chiefs assns. Home: 3002 SW 68th Av Miramar FL 33023 Office: 6700 Miramar Pky Miramar FL 33023

RAMSAUR, EDMUND ADAMS, newspaper exec.; b. Greenville, S.C., Apr. 9, 1925; s. Claud and Dorcas (Lott) R.; student Davidson Coll., 1942-43, U. S.C., 1946-47; B.A., U. Va., 1949; m. Dorothy Ann Peace, Sept. 4, 1947; children—Edmund Adams, Etca Ann. Research analyst U.S. Def. Dept., Washington, 1949-52; polit. reporter Greenville (S.C.) News, Washington, 1952-54; Columbia, S.C., 1954-55, state editor, Greenville, 1955-58, asso. editor, 1959-66; v.p., asst. pub. Greenville News-Piedmont Co., 1966-68, dir., asso. pub., exec. v.p., gen. mgr., 1968—; v.p. Multimedia, Inc., Greenville, 1968—, dir., 1968—; dir. Peoples Nat. Bank, Greenville. Vice pres. United Fund, Greenville County, 1967; commr. S.C. Dept. Parks, Recreation and Tourism, 1967—; chmn. bd. Red Shield Boys Club, 1964. Served with USNR, 1943-46. Mem. So. Newspaper Pub. Assn., S.C. Press Assn., Greater Greenville C. of C. (pres. 1966), Sigma Delta Chi, Sigma Alpha Epsilon. Presbyn. Club: Greenville Country. Home: 1 Rockingham Rd Greenville SC 29607 Office: Box 1688 Greenville SC 29601

RAMSAY, JOHN ERWIN, architect; b. Salisbury, N.C., Sept. 23, 1915; s. John Ernest and Elizabeth (Craige) R.; B.A., U. N.C., 1938; B.F.A., Yale, 1941; m. Jean Anne Ferrier, Oct. 1, 1945; children—Anne Ferrier (Mrs. Frank L. Saunders, Jr.), John Erwin II, Kerr Craige, George Bard Ferrier. Pvt. practice architecture, Salisbury, 1946-55; pres. John Erwin Ramsay & Assos., Inc., Salisbury, 1955—. Mem. N.C. Bd. Architecture, 1954-64, pres., 1958-64; 2d v.p. Nat. Council Archtl. Registration Bds., 1965-66. Pres. N.C. Symphony Soc., 1967-68, Rowan Civic Music, 1950—; chmn. troop com., scoutmaster Uwharrie council Boy Scouts Am. Served as lt. USNR, 1942-46. Registered architect, N.C., S.C., Va. Fellow A.I.A. (pres. N.C. chpt. 1951); mem. Guild Religious Architects, Am. Assn. Sch. Administrs., Am. Theatre Assn., Soc. Coll. and Univ. Planning, N.C. Assn. Professions. Presbyn. Prin. works include: Farm Colony Bldg., Morganton State Hosp.; furniture display Center Am. of Martinsville, also chs., residences. Home: 119 Pine Tree Rd Salisbury NC 28144 Office: 625 W Innes St Salisbury NC 28144

RAMSEY, CLAUDE SWANSON, JR., mfg. co. exec.; b. Asheville, N.C., Feb. 6, 1925; s. Claude Swanson and Nell Grace (Hendon) R.; B.S. in Textiles, N.C. State Coll., 1949; M.S. in Retailing, N.Y.U., 1950; m. Kay Kemp; children—Kay, Scott, Steven. With Am. Enka Corp. (N.C.), 1950-70, v.p., 1962-65, exec. v.p., 1965-67, pres., chief exec. officer, 1967-70, also dir., chmn. exec. com.; pres., chief exec. officer Akzona, Inc., successor co. to Am. Enka Corp., 1970—, also chmn. exec. com., chmn. bd., dir.; dir. Amstar Corp., 1971—. Trustee, Asheville-Biltmore Coll., 1963-68; dir. N.C. Engring. Found., 1964-69, N.C. Textile Found. Mem. Econ. Club N.Y. Clubs: Union League (N.Y.C.); Biltmore Forest Country, Mountain City (Asheville); Morristown (Tenn.) Country; Country of N.C. (Pinehurst); Grandfather Golf and Country (Linville, N.C.); Hound Ears (N.C.). Home: 9 Fairway Pl Biltmore Forest Asheville NC 28803 Office: Akzona Inc Asheville NC 28802

RAMSEY, JERRY WARREN, chemist; b. Springfield, Ill., June 30, 1932; s. Herman Eugene and Eleanor (Luttrell) R.; student U. Ill., 1950-51; B.A., Ill. Coll., 1956; M.S., A. and M. Coll. Tex., 1958; m. Elizabeth Joanne Huffman, Nov. 27, 1952; children—Katherine Julia, Warren Howard, Ellen Marie. Instr., Tex. Western Coll., El Paso, 1958-59, Pa. State U., Pottsville, 1959-62, Pottsville Gen. Hosp., 1961-62; chemist Anthracite Research Center, U.S. Bur. Mines, Schuylkill Haven, Pa., 1962-64, research chemist, 1964-65, research chemist Laramie (Wyo.) Petroleum Research Center, 1965-67, program mgr. Office of Dir. Petroleum Research, Washington, 1967-70, asst. to the chief div. Shale Oil, 1970—. Chmn. troop com. Nat. Capital Area council Boy Scouts Am., 1970—. Trustee Ill. Coll. Alumni Assn. Served with C.E., AUS, 1952-54. Elected to Order of the Arrow, Boy Scouts Am. Mem. Am. Chem. Soc., N.Y. Acad. Scis., Washington Soc. Ill. Coll. (past pres.), Sigma Xi, Phi Alpha. Methodist (chmn. council on ministries 1972—). Contbr. articles to profl. jours. Home: 7718 Ontario Rd Gainesville VA 22065 Office: US Bur Mines Washington DC 20240

RAMSEY, OTTO BRYANT, educator; b. Sparta, Tenn., Feb. 7, 1909; s. George Washington and Arabelle (Watson) R.; A.B., Howard U., 1931; M.A., Columbia, 1940, Deans scholar Tchrs. Coll., spring 1945; postgrad. Nat. U. Mexico, summer 1947; Spanish Cultural Inst. exchange scholar U. Madrid (Spain), 1951-52; Ph.D. in Spanish, Universidad Interamericana, Saltillo, Mexico, 1966. Instr., dir. remedial reading clinic Xavier U., New Orleans, 1945-47; asst. prof. Spanish, Tex. So. U., Houston, 1948-51, asso. prof. Spanish, 1952-70, prof., 1970—, head dept. fgn. langs. and lits. Bd. dirs. La Universidad Interamericana de Saltillo, Coahuila, Mexico, 1969—, Inst. Hispanic Culture, Houston, 1970-72. Mem. Am. Assn. U. Profs., Am. Assn. Tchrs. Spanish and Portuguese, La Sociedad Nacional Hispanica, Sigma Delta Pi. Author: The Development of Reading Rate and Comprehension in Spanish; A Simplified Spanish Guide; Revised Edition, Parts 1, 2, 3, 1972. Home: 3134 Southmore Blvd Houston TX 77004

RAMSEY, RALPH HEYWARD, JR., lawyer; b. Wedgefield, S.C., Apr. 7, 1900; s. Ralph Heyward and Una Elizabeth (Wells) R.; B.S., U. S.C., 1921, M.A., 1923, LL.B., 1924; m. Mary Dick Alford, Aug. 27, 1926; children—Mary Ann, Ralph Heyward III, Gayle Edward, Sarah Martha. Admitted to S.C. bar, 1924, N.C., 1926; mem. firm Purdy & Ramsey, Sumter, S.C., 1924-26; practice of law, Hendersonville, N.C., 1926, Brevard, N.C., 1926—; sr. mem. firm Ramsey, Hill, Smart & Ramsey and predecessor firm, 1961—. Mayor, Town of Brevard, 1931-33, city atty., 1933-53; county atty. Transylvania County, N.C., 1939-60, 64—; state senator 32d dist. of N.C., 1935-37; dir., sec. Gay Valley Camp, Inc., Keystone Camp, Inc., Golf Club Estates, Inc., Round Hill Estates, Inc., Evergreen Devel. Co. (also treas.), Hogback Lakes, Inc.; asst. sec. Connestee Falls Devel. Corp., H. & R. Devel. Co. Mem. N.C. Sch. Commn., 1941-43, Commn. on Solicitorial and Jud. Dists., 1945-47, N.C. Gen. Statues Commn., 1946-49; N.C. Med. Care Commn., 1953-56; Western N.C. Regional Planning Commn., 1956-61. Trustee Transylvania Community Hosp. (chmn.), Mars Hill Coll., 1962-66, 68—, vice chmn., 1966, chmn. exec com., 1971—; chmn. Lyday Meml. Hosp., Brevard, 1933-40. Mem. C. of C. (dir.), Am. Legion, Brevard Music Found. (mem. bd. trustees 1947-60). Am., 18th Jud. Dist. (pres. 1945), Transylvania County, N.C. bar assns., N.C. State Bar (council 1962—, chmn. grievance com. 1968-71, 2d v.p. 1971-72, Am. Judicature Soc., Internat. Platform Assn., Pi Kappa Phi. Democrat. Baptist. Clubs: Kiwanis (sec. 1928-30, pres. 1930, dir. 1931-48, lt. gov. N.C. Dist. 1965), Lake Toxaway Country, Sapphire Valley Golf. Author: (booklet) Economic and Social Survey of Sumter County, 1923; (articles) Indians of Sumter County, The Old Village of Manchester. Home: High Meadows Rt 1 Brevard NC 28712 Office: Legal Bldg Brevard NC 28712

RAMSEY, RICHARDENA, librarian. Asst. dir. Birmingham (Ala.) Pub. Library. Address: 2020 7th Av Birmingham AL 35203*

RAMSEY, ROBERT DEWEY, JR., govt. ofcl., engr.; b. Algood, Tenn., Dec. 14, 1924; s. Robert Dewey and Byrnie (Phillips) R.; student U. Wis., 1943-44; B.S., Tenn. Poly. Inst., 1949; postgrad. U. Tenn., 1950; m. Bobbie Mai Manning, Feb. 4, 1946; children—Robert Dewey III, James Roger, Nancy Jane, Sarah Elizabeth, Mary Ellen, Margaret Sue. Lab. asst., instr. Engring. Sch., Tenn. Poly. Inst., 1948-51; design engr. Arnold Engring. Devel. Center, C.E., Tullahoma, Tenn., 1951-60; facilities design, mgmt. engr. George C. Marshall Space Flight Center, Huntsville, Ala., 1960—, chief design br., facilities and design office, 1963-69, chief engring. dir. facilities office, 1969—. Served to 2d lt., C.E., USAAF, 1943-46. Recipient Outstanding Performance award Tullahoma Dist. C.E., 1960. Registered profl. engr., Tenn. Fellow Am. Soc. C.E. (past v.p. Huntsville); mem. Soc. Am. Mil. Engrs. (past pres. Tullahoma, dir. Huntsville), Nat. Soc. Profl. Engrs. Methodist. Home: 2905 Mallory Av Huntsville AL 35810 Office: George C Marshall Space Flight Center Huntsville AL 35812

RAMSEY, ROGER ALAN, solid waste mgmt. co. exec.; b. Houston, June 25, 1938; s. Theo Adolph and Madeline Esther (Anderson) R.; B.S. cum laude, Tex. Christian U., 1960; m. Gayle Etta Garbs, Jan. 27, 1957; children—Roger Craig, Christopher Alan, Carrie Gayle, Curtis Theo. Tax mgr. Arthur Andersen & Co., Houston, 1960-69; v.p., dir. ARS, Inc., 1969, dir., 1969—; v.p. finance Browning-Ferris Industries, Inc., Houston, 1969—; dir. Fannin Group, Inc., Environmental Equipment Corp. Trustee Tex. Benevolent Found. Mem. Am. Inst. C.P.A.'s, Tex. Soc. C.P.A.'s, Houston Chpt. C.P.A.'s, Sigma Alpha Epsilon, Beta Gamma Sigma. Methodist. Club: Houston Yacht. Home: 380 Blalock Houston TX 77024 Office: Fannin Bank Bldg Houston TX 77025

RAMSEY, SALLY ANN SEITZ, state ofcl.; b. Columbus, O., Feb. 15, 1931; d. Albert Blazier and Mildred (Dodson) Seitz; B.A., Ohio State U., 1952, M.A., 1955, postgrad. 1963-66; postgrad. St. Mary Coll., Xavier, Kan., 1962; m. Edward Lewis Ramsey, Apr. 11, 1953 (div. Aug. 1962); children—Edward Lewis, Sylvia Ann. Research engr., then sr. research engr. N.Am. Aviation, Inc., Columbus, O. and Downey, Cal., 1962-67; legislative intern State of Ohio, 1964-65; research and information officer Ohio Dept. Urban Affairs, Columbus, 1967-68; adminstrv. specialist Ohio Dept. Devel., Columbus, 1968; asso. planner Div. State Planning, Fla. Dept. Adminstrn., Tallahassee, 1968—. Gray Lady, A.R.C., 1961-62; den mother Cub Scouts Am., 1964-65. Congl. campaign cons., 1966. Mem. Am. Polit. Sci. Assn., Am. Soc. Pub. Adminstrn., Kappa Kappa Gamma, Pi Sigma Alpha. Home: 2112 Faulk Dr Tallahassee FL 32303 Office: 725 S Bronough St Tallahassee FL 32304

RANCK, NATHAN HOOVER, mgmt. cons.; b. Bellevue, Pa., May 3, 1913; s. James Marsh and Lou Alice (Hoover) R.; student U. Tex., 1934-36; B.S., U. Md., 1952; m. Noralee Castle, May 6, 1938; 1 son, Kendall Castle. Commd. 2d lt. U.S. Army Air Force, 1938, advanced through grades to lt. col., 1944; wing operations officer, China; exec. for res. forces legislation Hdqrs. USAF; dep. comdr. Iceland Air Def. Force; ret., 1958; mgr. airline sales Borg Warner Corp., Bedford, O., 1958-60; supt. plannet-pert sect. Pan Am. World Airways, Air Force Eastern Test Range, Cape Canaveral, Fla., 1960-65; mgr. support control systems Trans World Airlines, Kennedy Space Center, Fla., 1965—; sr. engring. planning specialist Xerox Corp., Rochester, N.Y., 1969—. Cons. mgmt., lectr., 1969—; corporate planner, treas. Energy Systems, Inc., Melbourne, Fla., 1970-71, pres., dir., treas., 1971-72. Loaned exec. Brevard County (Fla.) United Fund, 1968; mem. Pres.'s Nat. Def. Exec. Res., 1959—. Decorated D.F.C., Air medal, Bronze Star Medal. Sr. mem. Am. Inst. Indsl. Engrs. Originator Vis-a-Plan mgmt. control technique. Address: 401 Orlando Blvd Indialantic FL 32903

RANDALL, CAREY WOODSON, marketing mgr.; b. Charlotte, N.C., Oct. 13, 1931; s. Carey Enoch and Ollie Bond (Bonderant) R.; B.S. in Elec. Engring., U. S.C., 1954; postgrad. indsl. engring. Ia. State U., 1964; M.B.A. in Marketing, Ga. State U., 1970; m. Marianne Brown, July 27, 1957; children—Carey Woodson II, Michael Cain, Deena West. Engr., So. Bell Tel. & Tel. Co., Columbia, S.C., 1954-64, staff engr., Atlanta, 1964-66, supr. marketing staff, 1966—. Bd. govs. Carolina Carrilon, parade marshall, 1962. Served with USAF, 1954-56, 61-62; maj. Res. Recipient Distinguished Community Service award City of Greenville, S.C., 1962. Registered profl. engr., Ala. Home: 4115 Rue D'Artagnan Stone Mountain GA 30083 Office: 848 Merchandise Mart Atlanta GA 30303

RANDALL, CLIFFORD WENDELL, educator; b. Somerset, Ky., May 1, 1936; s. William Lesbert and Geneva (James) R.; B.S., U. Ky., 1959, M.S., 1963; Ph.D., U. Tex., 1965; m. Phyllis Mae Amis, Aug. 15, 1959; children— Andrew Amis, William Otis. Asst. prof. civil engring. U. Tex., Arlington, 1965-68; asst. prof. civil engring. Va. Poly. Inst., Blacksburg, 1968-69, asso. prof., 1969-72, prof., 1972—. Research specialist aerobiology Southwestern Med. Sch., Dallas, summer 1966; research project dir. sludge drying San Antonio (Tex.) River Authority, summer 1967; tng. grant cons. Environmental Protection Agy., 1970-71; waste treatment cons. United Piece Dye Works, 1969—, E.I. duPont de Nemours & Co., Inc., Martinsville, Va., Hercules, Inc., Radford, Va., Mead Corp., Lynchburg, Va., 1970-71, Belding Corticelli, Bedford, Va., 1971—, R. Stuart Royer & Assos., Richmond, Va., 1969-70. Camp sec. Gideons Internat., Blacksburg, Va., 1970-72, v.p., 1972—; chmn., project dir. Upper Occuquan Monitoring Com., Manassas, Va., 1972—. Served to lt. U.S. Coast and Geodetic Survey, 1959-62. USPHS traineeship radiol. health, U. Tex., 1963-65. Mem. Am. Soc. C.E. (Meritorious tech. paper award, 1969), Water Pollution Control Fedn., Am. Assn. Profs. San. Engring., Am. Water Works Assn., Am. Soc. Engring. Edn., Am. Mus. Natural History (asso.), Sigma Xi, Phi Kappa Phi, Chi Epsilon. Baptist (deacon). Contbr. articles to profl. jours. Home: 1302 Crestview Dr SE Blacksburg VA 24060

RANDALL, HENRY PETTUS, publisher; b. Selma, Ala., Aug. 23, 1911; s. H. Pettus and Mary Bell (Reddick) R.; LL.B., U. Ala., 1936; m. Ettie Beeland Rogers, July 24, 1936; children—Annette (Mrs. George Spigener, Jr.), Ettie Beeland (Mrs. Brian Birthright), Henry Pettus III, Frank Culver and Jim Allen (twins). Pres. Colonial Creamery, 1946-50, Randall Pub. Co., 1934—, Miniature Museums, Inc., 1963—, Randall Printing Co., 1938—; dir. City Nat. Bank, Tuscaloosa. Mem. adv. council Small Bus. Adminstrn., 1961—; treas. Tuscaloosa Black Warrior council Boy Scouts, 1937-38; chmn. local fund drives. Mem. Nat. (dir. 1941), Ala. (pres. 1941), Tuscaloosa (dir. 1941) jr. chambers commerce, Sales Execs. Club. Delta Kappa Epsilon. Clubs: Exchange, Quarterback (pres. 1963-64). Home: 10 Central Highlands Tuscaloosa AL 35403 Office: 1700 26th Av Tuscaloosa AL 35401

RANDALL, J. MALCOLM, hosp. adminstr.; b. East St. Louis, Ill., Aug. 9, 1916; A.B., McKendree Coll., Lebanon, Ill., 1939; postgrad. U. Minn., 1950; M. Hosp. Adminstrn., St. Louis U., 1956; grad. Exec. Devel. Program, U. Chgo., 1957; postgrad. U. Wis., 1963, Milw. Inst. Tech., 1964. Asst. to athletic dir. McKendree Coll., 1939; supr. So. Ill. dist. WPA, 1939-42; adminstrv. officer br. office VA, St. Louis, 1946-49; asst. area dir. spl. services St. Louis Med. Area office VA, 1949-53; adminstrv. analyst Office Controller, Dept. Medicine and Surgery, Washington, 1953; spl. asst. to dir., chief spl. services VA Hosp., St. Louis, 1953-56; asst. dir. VA Hosp., Spokane, Wash., 1956-57; asst. dir. VA Research Hosp., Chgo., 1957-58, VA Hosp., Indpls., 1958-60, VA Center, Wood, Wis., 1960-64; dir. VA Hosp., Miles City, Mont., 1964-66, VA Hosp., Gainesville, Fla., 1966—; asso. prof. health and hosp. adminstrn. U. Fla., 1966—, mem. pres.'s community-campus council, mem. council J. Hillis Miller Health Center, 1966—, mem. adminstrv. council, 1966—; lectr. grad. program hosp. adminstrn. St. Louis U., 1955-56; preceptor dept. health care adminstrn. George Washington U., 1968—. Chmn. Nat. Com. to Assess Ednl. Capacity of VA System; mem. exec. bd. N. Central Fla. Health Planning Council; mem. nat. health related professions edn. com. VA System; chmn. Nat. Panel to Select Career VA Employees for Placement in Grad. Programs in Health Care Adminstrns.; mem. nat. research site visit panel to rev. research programs VA System; mem. adv. group hosp. dirs. to Chief Med. Dir., VA; dep. chmn. Naval Res. Mgmt. Study Group, 1970; mem. nat. adv. coms. nation computer policies and applications, nationwide cost reduction program, mgmt. improvement program VA; chmn. bd. Inter-Agy. Bd., U.S. Civil Service Examiners Fla. Chmn. Alachua County Employment Opportunities Council. Bd. dirs. United Fund Gainesville and Alachua County, North Central Fla. Regional Planning Council; mem. Fla. adv. group Fla. Regional Med. Program; mem. Fla. Health Planning Council, Community Health Adv. Council, Com. to Establish Center Vol. Action. Served with USN, 1942-46; capt. Res. Fellow Am. Coll. Hosp. Adminstrs. (mem. council regents; mem. Am., Fla. (chmn. council edn.) hosp. assns., Am. Soc. Pub. Adminstrn., Assn. Am. Med. Colls., Res. Officers Assn., Naval Res. Assn., Navy League (chmn. Gainesville council), Fed. Ofcls.

Assn., Am. Legion. Rotarian, Elk. Contbr. articles in field to profl. jours. Office: VA Hosp Archer Rd Gainesville FL 32601

RANDALL, M. T., stage legislator; b. Ft. Myers, Fla., Nov. 15, 1924; B.S.F., U. Fla., 1950; m. Mary Elizabeth Bunnell; children—Elizabeth, Wallace Frank, Laura Fair. Mem. Fla. Ho. of Reps., 1964—. Dir. Am. Bank Ft. Myers. Bd. dirs. Lee County Assn. Retarded Children, YMCA. Served with AC, AUS, World War II. Mem. Am. Ordnance Soc., Audubon Soc., Farm Bur., C. of C. Mason (32 deg.), Kiwanian, Woodmen of World. Episcopalian (vestryman, past jr. warden). Home: 1452 Lynwood Av Fort Myers FL 33901 Office: PO Box 1668 Fort Myers FL 33902*

RANDALL, PAUL K., advt. agy. exec.; b. Irvington, N.Y., Dec. 1, 1928; s. Paul K. and Katherine (Patteson) R.; grad. Hackley Sch., Tarrytown, N.Y., 1946; A.B., Hamilton Coll., 1950. Advt. mgr. Mfrs. Marketing Co., 1950-56; with Batten, Barton, Durstine & Osborn, Inc., 1956—, account exec., N.Y.C., 1957-61, San Francisco, 1961-62, Chgo., 1962-63, Dallas, 1963-65, regional mgr., Dallas, 1965—, v.p., 1967—. Mem. exec. com. Dallas council Boy Scouts Am. Mem. Am. (gov., vice chmn. S.W. council 1971), Southwestern (v.p., dir. 1968-70) assns. advt. agys., Assn. Broadcast Execs. of Tex., Dallas Advt. League, Dallas C. of C. (chmn. communications com.), Dallas Tennis Assn. (pres. 1972), 500 of Dallas. Club: Dallas Racquet (pres. 1968-69). Home: 4055 Bluffview St Dallas TX 75219 Office: 1810 Commerce St Suite 1125 Dallas TX 75201

RANDALL, ROBERT STANLEY, educator; b. Ferris, Tex., June 17, 1928; s. Robert Fillmore and Gladys (Gressett) R.; B.A., Howard Payne Coll., 1957; postgrad. summers Sul Ross State Coll., Alpine, Tex., 1958-59, Tex. Western Coll., El Paso, 1960; M.Ed., U. Tex., 1963, Ph.D., 1964; m. Billie Sue Funderburgh, May 5, 1948; children—Robert Stanley, Billy Michael, Rebekah Ann, Norma Sue, Cynthia Lee. Clk., Western Union, Dallas, 1945-46; lineman Dallas Power & Light Co., 1948-52; worker-gang boss Asso. Pipeline Contractors N.D., summer 1953, Mont., Minn., Tex., 1954; salesman Century Metalcraft Corp., Dallas, 1954-57; tchr. math. Norton (Tex.) Pub. Schs., 1957-58; high sch. prin., Ft. Hancock, Tex. 1958-61; research asso., instr. math. U. Tex., 1962-64; asst. prof. Tex. A. and M. U., 1964-66; dir. research and evaluation S.W. Ednl. Devel. Lab., Austin, Tex., 1966—. Cons. pub. schs., N.Y.C., Phila., Los Angeles. Pres., Founds. in Ednl. Adminstrn., 1964. Served with USNR, 1946-48; PTO. Mem. Tex. A. and M. Area Council Tchrs. Math. (past pres.), Am. Ednl. Research Assn., Nat. Council on Measurement in Edn., Am. Assn. U. Profs., Am. Civil Liberties Union, Phi Delta Kappa. Democrat. Unitarian. Contbr. articles to profl. jours. Home: 2606 Stratford Dr Austin TX 78764 Office: 800 Brazos Austin TX 78701

RANDALL, WILLIAM MADISON, educator; b. Belleville, Mich., Aug. 16, 1899; s. Will M. and Emma Adele (Henry) R.; A.B., U. Mich., 1921, A.M., 1924; Ph.D. summa cum laude, Hartford Theol. Sem., 1929; Litt.D. (hon.), U. N.C., 1971; travelling fellow Gen. Edn. Bd., 1935, Am. Assn. Learned Socs. (Middle East), 1938; m. Myldred Randolph Cady, June 21, 1924;children—William David, Duncan Peter; m. 2d, Mary Johnson McGee, 1954. Asso. prof. library sci. U. Chgo., 1929, prof., 1931, asst. dean of students, 1938; v.p. Snead & Co., Orange, Va., 1946; dir. libraries, student affairs U. Ga., 1947; capt. US Maritime Service; acad. dean U.S. Mcht. Marine Acad. 1948-51; dean Wilmington (N.C.) Coll., (name changed to U.N.C. at Wilmington 1969), 1951-58, pres., 1958-68, pres. emeritus, prof. modern langs., 1968—. Pres. Wilmington chpt. N.C. Symphony Soc., 1957-60. Mng. editor Library Quarterly, 1931-42; cons. Carnegie Corp. of N.Y., 1929-32; active in ednl. survey work, Gen. Edn. Bd., Meth. Bd. Edn., N. Central Assn., 1929-39; dir. Nat. Conf. Christians and Jews; chmn. county chpt. Nat. Found. Infantile Paralysis. Mem. legislative com. So. Assn. Jr. Colls.; sec.-treas. N.C. Jr. Coll. Athletic Conf., 1955-63. Mem. commn. sent to reorganize Vatican library, Carnegie Endowment for Internat. Peace, 1928. Served to lt. col. USAAF, 1942-45, with War Dept. Intelligence, stationed Cairo, Egypt, Casablanca, Morocco. Mem. N.C. State Community Coll. Com. 1952. Mem. A.L.A., N.E.A., Phi Sigma. Democrat. Episcopalian. Clubs: Rotary, Executives. Author: The College Library, 1932; (with F. L. D. Goodrich) Principles of College Library Administration, 1935; Acquisition and Cataloging of Library Materials, 1941. Home: 4622 Mocking Bird Lane Wilmington NC 28401

RANDOLPH, JOHN HAGER, JR., savs. and loan assn. exec.; b. Fredericksburg, Va., July 27, 1921; s. John Hager and Grace (Lee) R.; B.S., Va. Mil. Inst., 1942; m. Rebecca Meem, Sept, 7, 1946; children—Beverly Langhorne, Rebecca Hutter. With First Fed. Savs. & Loan Assn., Richmond, Va., 1945—, pres., 1955—; partner So. Ins. Agy.; v.p. So. Title Ins. Corp., Germantown Ins. Co., Phila., Va. Indsl. Devel. Corp., Fed. Home Loan Bank, Cecil Waller Co. Pres. Richmond Better Bus. Bur.. 1968. Bd. dirs., finance chmn. Commonwealth council Girl Scouts Am., 1966-67; Va. chmn. U.S. Savs. Bond program, 1968. Served with USAAF, 1942-45. Mem. U.S. Savs. and Loan League (v.p.). Episcopalian. Rotarian. Clubs: Country of Va., Commonwealth (Richmond). Home: 6327 Ridgeway Rd Richmond VA 23226 Office: First Fed Savs & Loan Assn Richmond VA 23219

RANDOLPH, KENNETH VINCENT, coll. pres.; b. Masontown, W.Va., Apr. 14, 1915; s. Russell Burton and Maude Gay (Vincent) R.; student W.Va. U., 1933-35; D.D.S., U. Md., 1939, B.S. in Edn., 1951; m. Elizabeth Virginia Bachman, Aug. 3, 1940; children—Janice Lee, Kenneth Vincent. Fellow operative dentistry U. Md., 1939-40, instr., then asst. and asso. prof. operative dentistry, 1940-46, prof., head dept., 1946-57; asso. dean, head dept. operative dentistry W.Va. U., 1957-58, dean, prof., 1958-68; prof., dean Coll. Dentistry, Baylor U., 1968-71, pres., also dean, 1971—. cons. VA Hosp., Dallas. Mem. council Nat. Bd. Dental Examiners, 1966-71, chmn., 1970-71. Trustee Am. Fund Dental Edn., 1967-72. Mem. Am. Coll. Dentists, Am. Dental Assn. (ho. dels. 1965-68), Tex., Dallas County dental socs., Am. Acad. Gen. Dentistry (hon.), Am. Acad. Gold Foil Operators, Phi Kappa Psi, Sigma Phi Alpha, Xi Psi Phi, Phi Delta Kappa, Omicron Kappa Upsilon. Democrat. Methodist. Home: 9533 Fieldcrest Ct Dallas TX 75238 Operators,

RANDOLPH, LUCIAN MENDLESSOHN, sch. adminstr.; b. Hurtsboro, Ala., July 25, 1917; s. Lawrence and Lucretia R. (Dunn) R.; B.S., Ala. A. and M. U., 1947; M.Ed., Ala. State U., 1950; m. Cleopatra Williams, Mar. 21, 1938; children—Alfred M., Gwendolyn L. Prin., Central Girard Elementary Sch., Phenix City, Ala., 1947-58; prin. Lewis Adams Sch., Tuskegee, Ala., 1958—. Instr., Columbus (Ga.) br. Albany State Coll., 1950-62; cons. S.E. region Community Action Program, 1970—. Mem. Beat 8 (Democratic com.), Macon County, Ala., 1968—. Mem. Ala. Congress P.T.A., v.p., 1968-70. Served with USNR, 1943-46. Mem. A.M.E. Ch. (lay leader 1968, mem., chmn. ch. stewards bd., budget com.). Mason (33 deg., Shriner). Home: PO Drawer RR Tuskegee Institute AL 36088 Office: Lewis Adams Sch PO Drawer RR Tuskegee Institute AL 36088

RANDOLPH, PHILIP LEE, scientist; b. Casper, Wyo., Feb. 25, 1931; s. Joseph Guy and Mary Alice (Hitshew) R.; B.S., U. Wash., 1952, Ph.D., 1958; m. Lillian Louise Larson, Nov. 12, 1952; children—Marcus Philip, Andrew Leland. Asso. div. leader nuclear explosive devel. Lawrence Radiation Lab., U. Cal. at Livermore, 1958-68; mgr. nuclear group energy resource devel. El Paso Natural Gas Co. (Tex.), 1968—. Mem. steering com. Atomic Indsl. Forum Com. on Indsl. Plowshare Applications, 1970—. Mem. Am. Phys. Soc., Am. Nuclear Soc. (mem. exec. com. tech. group for nuclear explosion engrng. 1969—). Home: 3040 Pierce St El Paso TX 79930 Office: PO Box 1492 El Paso TX 79978

RANDOLPH, THOMAS ALEXANDER, supr. schs.; b. Elk Horn, W.Va., Mar. 25, 1908; s. John Peter and Rose Ella (Butler) R.; B.S. in Edn., Bluefield State Tchrs. Coll., 1932; M.Ed., U. Va., 1969; m. Lauramer Autherine Williams, June 12, 1946; 1 son, Thomas Alexander. Tchr., Henry County, Va., 1932-33, elementary supr. Henry County Schs., Martinsville, Va., 1933—. Mem. Drug Use and Abuse Workshop, Radford Coll., 1970, 71. Chmn., Algonquian dist. Boy Scouts Am., 1960. Mem. Assn. for Supervision and Curriculum Devel., Va., dist. and local edn. assns. Home: PO Box 672 Fieldale VA 24089 Office: PO Box 511 Martinsville VA 24112

RANDQUIST, BOBBY WAYNE, sch. supt.; b. Cordell, Okla., Sept. 11, 1928; s. Carl Martin and Gladys Marie (Brown) R.; B.S., S.W. State Coll., Weatherford, Okla., 1951; M.Ed., U. Okla., 1957, Ed.D., 1970; m. Ruby Nell Crouch, Dec. 31, 1949; children—Robert Martin, Kathryn Annette. Prin., Davenport (Okla.) High Sch., 1960-62; supt. Oney Pub. Schs., Albert, Okla., 1962-64, Carnegie (Okla.) Pub. Schs., 1968—; asst. supt. Anadarko (Okla.) Pub. Sch., 1964-68. Cons. Indian Edn. Workshops, 1969—, Indian Edn. Curriculum Materials, 1969—. Mem. bd. Anadarko City Library, 1966-68. Served with AUS, 1946-47; PTO. Mem. N.E.A., Okla. Edn. Assn., Am. Assn. Sch. Adminstrs., Caddo County Tchrs. Assn. (pres. 1967-68). Baptist (tng. union dir. 1964-66). Rotarian (pres. 1970-71). Home: 26 Carol St Carnegie OK 73015 Office: Box 159 Carnegie OK 73015

RANGE, ROBERT LOUIS, electric co. exec.; b. Cuero, Tex., May 20, 1933; s. Louis Henry and Laura May (Mills) R.; B.B.A., S.W. Tex. State U., 1957; m. Laurie Lorraine Creel, Nov. 1, 1957; children—Robin Lynne, Robert Lee. Asst. sec. Central and S.W. Corp., Wilmington, Del., 1969—, asst. treas., 1969—, asst. to pres., 1970—; treas. CSR Services, Inc., Dallas, 1969—. Served with AUS, 1953-55. C.P.A., Tex. Mem. Am. Inst. C.P.A.'s, Tex. Soc. C.P.A.s. Home: 9635 Crestedge St Dallas TX 75238 Office: 2828 One Main Pl Dallas TX 75250

RANKIN, EDWARD LEE, JR., textile co. exec.; b. Chattanooga, May 12, 1919; s. Edward Lee and Gladys (Narramore) R.; A.B. in Journalism, U. N.C., 1940; m. Frances Wallace, June 12, 1948; children—Jane Elizabeth, Ann Wallace, Edward Lee III. Reporter, Salisbury (N.C.) Post, 1940-41, Raleigh (N.C.) News & Observer, 1941; night editor A.P., Charlotte, N.C., Columbia, S.C., 1946; dir. pub. relations State Hwy. & Pub. Works Commn., Raleigh, 1946-47; press sec. U.S. Sen. William B. Umstead, Washington, 1947-48; pub. relations exec. Burlington Mills, Greensboro, N.C., 1948-53; pvt. sec. to Gov. N.C., Raleigh, 1953-59; v.p. John Harden Assos., pub. relations firm, Raleigh, 1960-65; dir. State Dept. Administrn., Raleigh, 1965-67; exec. v.p. N.C. Citizens Assn., 1967-71; dir. pub. relations Cannon Mills Co., Kannapolis, N.C., 1972—. Bd. trustees Meredith Coll. Served to lt. USNR, 1941-46; U.S.S. LST 355 (comdg. officer), and 356, N. Africa, Sicily, Salerno, Normandy. Named Tar Heel of Week, News &Observer, Raleigh, 1959. Mem. Pub. Relations Soc. Am. Democrat. Baptist. Clubs: Sphinx, Sandwich, Watauga, Cabarrus Country. Home: 301 N Cannon Blvd Kannapolis NC 28081 Office: Cannon Mills Co Kannapolis NC 28081

RANKIN, JAMES, journalist; b. Lakeworth, Fla., Sept. 26, 1923; s. John Munro and Grace (Crews) S.; A.B., U. N.C., 1949; m. Sallie Lynwood Baber, June 6, 1953; 1 son, William Lynn. Reporter, Raleigh (N.C.) News & Observer, 1949-51; city editor Raleigh Times, 1953-56; copy editor, reporter Louisville Times, 1956-60; night city editor Atlanta Constn., 1960-66, editorial writer, columnist, 1966-68, city editor, 1968-70, asst. mng. editor, 1970—. Served with USNR, 1943-46, 51-53. Mem. Atlanta Press Club. Democrat. Episcopalian. Home: 391 Golfview Rd NW Atlanta GA 30309 Office: 10 Forsyth St Atlanta GA 30302

RANKIN, J(AMES) M(ATTHEW), wheat farmer; b. Rockdale, Tex., Oct. 19, 1892; s. Jackson M. and Sarah Alice (Mayfield) R.; student U. Tex., U. Grenoble (France); B.A., Tex. Tech. Coll., 1929, M.A., 1932; m. Maude E. Benton, May 12, 1920; children—Jean M., Joe D. (twins). Pub. Sch. adminstr., 1914-38; supt. Ralls (Tex.) pub. schs., 1931-38; editor, pub. Slaton Statonite, 1938-41; staff columnist Ralls Banner and Lorenzo Tribune, 1941—; farm mgr., Ralls 1941—; judge Crosby County, 1950-54. Sec.-treas. Crosby County chpt. A.R.C., 1950—. Bd. dirs. Plains Cotton Growers; Crosby County rep. Boll Weevil Control. Mem. Selective Service Bd. Served 1st div., U.S. Army, World War I. Decorated Purple Heart, Silver Star. Mem. Am. Legion. Baptist. Mason (32 deg.), Rotarian (past pres. Ralls). Address: Sect Nine Farms Box 190 Ralls TX 79357

RANKIN, JOE DAVID, coop. exec.; b. Ralls, Tex., May 8, 1929; s. James Matthew and Maude (Benton) R.; B.A., Tex. Technol. U., 1951; m. Emily Elizabeth Brasfield, Aug. 22, 1954; children—Joe David, Robin, James Matthew II. Dir., Plains Coop. Oil Mill, Lubbock, Tex., 1964—, pres., 1970—; dir. Farmer Coop. Compress. Served with USAF, 1951-54. Mem. Plains Cotton Coop. Marketing Assn. (dir.), Tex. Farmers Union (dir.). Rotarian. Home: Box 190 Ralls TX 79357 Office: 2901 Av A Lubbock TX 79404

RANKIN, JOHN WATKINS, hosp. adminstr.; b. Concord, N.C., May 11, 1919; s. Samuel Wharton and Louise Evans (Watkins) R.; A.B., U. N.C., 1939; certificate in Hosp. Adminstrn., Duke, 1941; fellow hosp. administrn., W. K. Kellogg Found., 1942; m. June Williamson, Apr. 20, 1967; children—John Robert, Samuel Martin, Juliann, Louise Watkins, John Watkins. Regional hosp. officer Office Civilian Def., USPHS, Atlanta, 1942-43; supt. Tuomey Hosp., Sumter, S.C., 1943-46; dir. James Walker Meml. Hosp., Wilmington, N.C., 1946-52; dir. Milwaukee County Instns. and Depts., 1952-61; dir. Charlotte (N.C.) Meml. Hosp., 1961—. Pres. Greater Milw. Hosp. Council, 1955, S.C. Hosp. Assn., 1946, Wis. Hosp. Assn., 1958, Tri-State Hosp. Assembly, 1959, Medi-Data, Inc. Fellow Am. Coll. Hosp. Adminstrs.; mem. Am. Hosp. Assn. (past del.), Am. Pub. Welfare Assn., Am. Pub. Health Assn. Presbyn. Rotarian. Home: 2832 Wheelock Rd Charlotte NC 28211 Office: Charlotte Meml Hosp Charlotte NC 28201

RANKIN, RICHARD EUGENE, physician; b. Mount Holly, N.C., Apr. 21, 1921; s. Frank Biasaner and Oneta (Battley) R.; B.S., Davidson Coll., 1943; postgrad. U. N.C., 1948; M.D., U. Va., 1950; m. Julia Wilson Pancake, June 16, 1950; children—Julia Hill, Kathleen, Richard Eugene. Intern, Tripler Gen. Hosp., Honolulu, 1950-51; practice gen. medicine, Mount Holly, 1951—; owner Rankin Clinic, Mt. Holly, 1951—; mem. staff Presbyn., Mercy, Meml. hosps., Charlotte, N.C. Served with USAAF, 1943-46. Mem. A.M.A., World Med. Assn., N.C., Gaston County (pres. 1965) med. socs. Presbyn. (elder 1954—). Club: Gaston County Country (Gastonia, N.C.) Home: Mount Holly Belmont Rd Mount Holly NC 28120 Office: Rankin Clinic Oakland St Mount Holly NC 28120

RANKIN, THOMAS LEE, farmer; b. Danville, Ky., Nov. 5, 1919; s. Jonathan David and Mary Eliza (Holtzclaw) R.; grad. high sch.; m. Josephine Cotton, Jan. 2, 1940; children—Jerry Thomas, Billy Joe. Farmer, Boyle County, Danville, 1940—; co-owner Farmers Tobacco Warehouse, Danville, 1960—; dir. Citizens Nat. Bank Danville. Magistrate Boyle County, 1969—. Named Ky. col. Mem. Boyle County Livestock Assn. (dir. 1968—). Democrat. Baptist. Club: Rockcastle County Saddle. Home: Route 1 Danville KY 40422 Office: PO Box 273 Danville KY 40422

RANKIN, WALLACE MURRAY, steel co. exec.; b. Howard Lake, Minn., Feb. 6, 1920; s. Joseph E. and Helena (Barron) R.; student U. Wis., 1938-40; m. Jean Thomas, Aug. 31, 1941; children—Sharyn Lee, Shelley Ann. With Armco Steel Corp., 1948—, asst. works mgr., Kansas City, Mo., 1958-62, Houston, 1962-63, works mgr., 1963—. Dir. A.O. Smith of Tex. Pres. Tax Research Assn., 1968-69. Bd. dirs. Jr. Achievement, Tex. Research League. Served with USNR, 1944-46. Presbyn. Clubs: Lakeside Country, Petroleum (Houston). Home: 12331 Mossycup Dr Houston TX 77024 Office: PO Box 1367 Houston TX 77001

RANNE, JOHN CLINTON, med. lab. exec.; b. McKinney, Tex., Oct. 29, 1924; s. Marion Clinton and Ada (Templeman) R.; student USN Hosp. Corps Sch., San Diego, 1942-43; m. Myrna Louise Erisman, July 25, 1960; children—Jerry Leon, Jo Ann, Janice Belle, Linda Louise, Kyle Ray. Owner, Med. Center Clin. Lab., Dallas, 1946—. Served with USNR, 1942-45; PTO. Recipient Distinguished Achievement award Tex. Soc. Am. Med. Technologists, 1959. Mem. Tex. Assn. Clin. Labs., Am. Assn. Bionalysts, Am. Coll. Med. Technologists, Am., Tex. socs. med. technologists, A.A.A.S., Tex. Soc X-Ray Technicians. Democrat. Home: 2855 Bay Meadows Circle Farmers Branch TX 75234 Office: 2703 Lawn Av Dallas TX 75219

RANNEY, J. BUCKMINSTER, health sci. adminstr.; b. Brattleboro, Vt., Dec. 26, 1919; s. Jonathan Harris and Agnes H. (Follensby) R.; student U. Vt., 1937-40; B.A., N.Y.U., 1946, M.A., 1947; Ph.D., Ohio State U., 1957; postgrad. Johns Hopkins, 1962-63; m. Joy Chisholm, Nov. 2, 1943; children—John, Bruce William, David. Instr., Syracuse U., 1946-48; asst. prof. Ohio No. U., 1948-57; dir. Speech and Hearing Clinic, Auburn U., 1957-69; chief audiology, speech pathology service VA Center, San Juan, P. R., 1966-67; exec. sec. communicative disorders tng. com. Nat. Inst. Neurol. Disease and Stroke, Bethesda, Md., 1969—. Cons. audiology and speech pathology Ala. Sch. for Deaf, VA Hosp. Candidate Ohio Assembly, 1954. Served to capt. USAAF, 1942-45. Fellow Am. Speech and Hearing Assn. Editor: SHAA Letter, 1963-66. Home: 2318 Tanglevale Dr Vienna VA 22180 Office: NINDS-EP NIH Westwood Bldg Bethesda MD 20014

RANSOM, HARRY HUNTT, former univ. chancellor; b. Galveston, Tex., Nov. 22, 1908; s. Harry Huntt and Marion Goodwin (Cunningham) R.; A.B. U. of South, 1928; A.M., Yale, 1930, Ph.D., 1938; student Harvard, 1929-30; Litt.D., U. of South, 1958, U. N.D., 1970, U. Dallas, 1971; LL.D., Baylor U., 1958, Trinity U., 1963, Tex. Christian U., 1963; L.H.D., Austin Coll., 1966, So. Meth. U., 1972; D.Eng., Colo. Sch. Mines, 1972; m. Hazel Louise Harrod, Aug. 11, 1951. Instr. English and journalism State Tchrs. Coll., Valley City, N.D., 1930-32, 33-34; instr. English and history Colo. State Coll., 1934-35; instr. English, U. Tex. at Austin, 1935-38, asst. prof., 1938-42, asso. prof., 1946-47, prof., 1947—, asst. dean Grad. Sch., 1951-53, asso. dean, 1953-54, dean Coll. Arts and Scis., 1954-57, v.p., provost, 1957-60, pres., 1960-61, chancellor U. Tex. System, 1961-71, chancellor emeritus, 1971—. Dir. Southwestern Bell Telephone Co., 1967—. Trustee Carnegie Found. for Advancement of Teaching, 1962-71; past mem. Commn. on Colls. and Univs. of the So. Assn. Past chmn. hist. commn. Internat. Copyright League; past mem. Commn. on White House Fellows, Pres.'s Commn. on Patent System, Nat. Adv. Commn. on Libraries, Nat. Adv. Council for Edn. in Health Professions; mem., pres. Internat. Commn. for Library Devel., 1965—, mem. com. on profl. sch. and world affairs, 1965-67; mem. permanent com. Oliver Wendell Holmes Devise, 1964-72, Nat. Com. on Accrediting Bd. Commrs., 1966-70; mem. commn. on acad. affairs Am. Council Edn., 1966-70. Served to maj. USAAF, 1942-46. Decorated Legion of Merit. Fellow Tex. Hist. Assn.; mem. Modern Lang. Assn., Grolier Club, Tex. Philos. Soc., Tex. Inst. Letters, Phi Beta Kappa, Kappa Sigma. Episcopalian. Author: Bibliography of English Copyright History, 1948; Notes of a Texas Book Collector, 1950; The First Copyright Statute, 1955. Editor: (With J. Frank Dobie and M. C. Boatright) Texas Folklore Publications, XIV, XV, XVI, XVII. Asso editor Tex. Folklore Soc., 1938-41, Southwest Hist. Quarterly, 1952-56; English Copyright Cases, 1660-1775, 1956. Editor Texas Quarterly, 1958—. Home: 1610 Watchill Rd Austin TX 78703

RAO, BADRI S.R.N., internat. orgn. exec.; b. Madras, India, Mar. 26, 1916 (came to U.S. 1945); s. Srinivasa and Kamala Rao; B.A. with honors, Annamalai U., India, M.A., M.L.H., 1941; postgrad. Harvard, 1946-47; m. Saroja Savkoor, May 27, 1951; children—Madhukar, Hemalatha. Confidential asst. fgn. and polit. dept. Govt. India, 1941-42; accounts officer Kolhapur Govt., 1943-43; confidential asst. fgn. and polit. dept. Eastern States Agy., 1943-44; econ. investigator finance dept. Govt. India, 1944-45; economist Internat. Bank for Reconstrn. and Devel., Washington, 1947—. Govt. of India fellow, 1947. Author: Road-Rail Transport in India, 1941; Recent Trends in the External Public Indebtedness of Latin American Countries, 1963. Home: 3322 Military Rd NW Washington DC 20015 Office: 1818 H St NW Washington DC 20433

RAPER, CHARLES ALBERT, cement co. exec.; b. Charleston, W.Va., Aug. 18, 1926; s. Kenneth B. and Louise (Williams) R.; student Okla. State U., 1945; B.S., U. Ill., 1949; m. Margaret Ann Weers, Dec. 26, 1947; children—Kathleen, Josephine, Charles. Sales mgr. Meyer Furnace Co., Peoria, Ill., 1949-54; v.p. marketing Master Consol., Inc., Dayton, O., 1954-61; mgmt. cons. McKinsey & Co., Inc., Chgo., 1961-67; v.p. marketing Gen. Portland Cement Co., Dallas, 1967-69, pres., 1969—, also dir. Charter mem. Sales Execs. Group, Peoria, 1954. Coordinator, Tomorrow's Am. Citizens Today Program, Dallas, 1969-71. Bd. dirs., v.p. Dallas C. of C.; bd. dirs. Portland Cement Assn. Served with USNR, 1944-46. Mem. Phi Gamma Delta. Club: Northwood (Dallas). Home: 7029 Gateridge St Dallas TX 75240 Office: PO Box 324 Republic Nat Bank Tower Dallas TX 75221

RAPETTI, VINCENT ANTHONY, librarian; b. Floral Park, N.Y., Jan. 26, 1926; s. James Vincent and Lucille Florence (Antonacchio)R.; A.B., Rollins Coll., 1950; M.A. in L.S., U. Mich., 1952, A.M. in History, 1952. Librarian, Soc. of the Four Arts, Palm Beach, Fla., 1952-57; adminstrn. asst. tech. services and extension Orlando (Fla.) Pub. Library, 1957-61; head cataloger, dept. dir. library system Nassau, N.Y., 1961-63; chief librarian LTV/Service Tech. Corp., J.F. Kennedy Space Center, Fla., 1964-71, project mgr., chief librarian New World Services, Inc., 1971—. Served with USAAF, 1944-46. Home: 1116 Glen Arden Way Altamonte Springs FL 32701 Office: J F Kennedy Space Center Library Kennedy Space Center FL 32899

RAPIER, THOMAS GWYNNE, lawyer; b. New Orleans, Apr. 27, 1933; s. Edward D. and Ana Marie (Alverez) R.; B.B.A., Tulane U,, 1959, LL,B., 1962; m. Marianne Hebert, Oct. 2, 1964;

children—Marguerite Walshe, Susan Walshe, Marianne Walshe, Edward Desforges, Gwynne Ann. Admitted to La. bar, 1962, since practiced in New Orleans; partner law firm Jones, Walker, Waechter, Poitevent, Carrere & Denegre. Dir. Med. Profl. Bldg. Corp., Day Minerals, Inc., Austin & 5th Corp. Mem. Am. Bar Assn. Home: 2219 Pine St New Orleans LA 70118 Office: 225 Baronne St New Orleans LA 70112

RAPPELET, ALBERT OTTO, contractor, state ofcl.; b. New Orleans, Sept. 18, 1910; s. Rene S. and Evelina (Terrebonne) R.; grad. high sch.; m. Velvina Vegas, June 10, 1950; children—Charles, Geraldine, Sharon, Rene. Pres., La. Constrn. & Material Co., Inc., Galliano, 1943-—; owner Creole Kitchen, Boutte, La., 1945-—, Home Ins. Agy., Galliano, 1956-—, Larose Lumber Co. (La.), 1967-—; mem. La. Ho. of Reps., 1968-—. Organizer, Internat. Found. for Exceptional Children, 1960, chmn. bd., 1960-63; pres., chmn. bd. Greater Lafourche Port Commn., 1960-—. Mem. La. Senate, 1948-52, 56-64. Recipient awards including Nicholls Alumni Fedn. award, 1969. Mem. La. Bldg. Material Dealers Assn., State Contractors Assn. Democrat. Methodist. Lion. Club: Young Men's Business (South Lafourche). Address: PO Box 217 Galliano LA 70354

RAPPS, ELMORE M., accountant; b. Union Mo., Aug. 3, 1919; s. Arthur John and Mary (Herberholz) R.; student Tex. Christian U., 1947-51; m. Ava Cecile Magill, Jan. 3, 1945; children—Mrs. William D. Gordon, Mrs. A.B. Cassinelli, Jr., Mrs. Robert Polk. Jr. partner Leatherwood & Ward, C.P.A.'s, Ft. Worth, 1951-63; controller Central Security Life Ins. Co., Ft. Worth, 1963-65, Esco Elevators, Inc., Ft. Worth, 1965-—, also sec.-treas., dir. Served with Armed Forces, 1941-46. Mem. Nat. Assn. Accountants (chpt. pres. 1964-65, nat. dir. 1965-66), Am. Inst. C.P.A.'s, Tex. Soc. C.P.A.'s, Nat. Assn. Accountants, Stuart Cameron McLeod Soc. Home: 5425 Woodway Lane Fort Worth TX 76133 Office: PO Box 445 Fort Worth TX 76101

RARDIN, WILLIAM GLEN, state ofcl.; b. Ravenswood, W.Va., Apr. 26, 1905; s. William DeWitt and Amy (Cox) R.; A.B., Lynchburg Coll., 1929; postgrad. U. Ill., 1933; m. Nell Mae Jack, Apr. 3, 1936. History tchr., dir. athletics, coach Randolph-Macon Acad., Bedford, Va., 1929-33; dir. athletics, asso. prof. phys. edn., coach Lynchburg (Va.) Coll., 1933-41; claims rep. div. war vets. claims Va. Dept. Law, Roanoke, 1945-51, asst. dir., 1951-—. Treas., Roanoke Valley Enterprises, Inc., 1965-—; counselor Am. Legion Boys State of Va., Inc., 1946-52, asst. dir., 1953-54, dir. 1955-—, mem. dept. Boys State com., 1948-53. Bd. dirs. Roanoke County Fair. Served with USNR, 1943-45. Recipient Hobbs Achievement award Lynchburg Coll., 1958, Citizenship award Am. Legion, Va., 1956. Mem. Am. Legion (hon. life mem.), V.F.W., D.A.V., Nat. Service Officers. Mason. Club: Roanoke Country. Home: 2751 Richelieu Av Roanoke VA 24014 Office: 211 W Campbell Av SW Roanoke VA 24012

RARICK, JOHN R., congressman; b. Waterford, Ind., Jan. 29, 1924; student Ball State Tchrs. Coll., 1942, 44-45, La. State U., 1943-44; J.D., Tulane U., 1949; m. Marguerite Pierce; three children. Admitted to La. bar, 1949; formerly judge 20th Jud. Dist. La.; mem. 90th-92d Congresses 6th Dist. La. Past bd. dirs. Audubon council Girls Scouts; past mem. sponsoring com. St. Francisville Boy Scout Troop. Served with AUS, World War II; ETO. Decorated Bronze Star medal, Purple Heart. Mem. D.A.V., V.F.W., Am. Legion. Democrat. Mason (32 deg., Shriner); mem. Order Eastern Star. Clubs: Civitan (past pres. St. Francisville, past internat. judge adv.), Toastmasters Internat. (past pres.). Office: 1525 Longworth House Office Bldg Washington DC 20515

RAS, FLORENCE ANN, educator; b. Chgo.; d. Andrew C. and Frances (Lechart) Ras; B.A., Barat Coll.; M.A., Northwestern U., 1962; postgrad. Fla. Atlantic U., 1964-—. Tchr., Ft. Lauderdale (Fla.) Oral Sch., 1958-—, asst. dir., 1962-64, dir., 1964-—. Instr., Confraternity of Christian Doctrine, 1963-64; tchr. deaf children, West Palm Beach, Fla., 1961. Leader, Girl Scouts U.S.A., Chgo., 1946-47; vol. worker A.R.C., Chgo., 1948-49; chmn. speech reading classes for adults, Broward County, Fla., 1966; mem. adv. com. for workshops and facilities State Dept. Edn. Div. Vocational Rehab., 1967-68. Bd. dirs., adviser Young Deaf Adult Club, Ft. Lauderdale, 1967-68. Mem. Alexander Graham Bell Assn., Conv. Am. Instrs. of Deaf, Am., Fla. Broward County (dir. 1965-67, pres. bd. 1967-68) speech and hearing assns., N.E.A., Barat Coll., Northwestern U. alumni assns. Home: 3124 NE 42d Ct Ft Lauderdale FL 33308 Office: 3100 SW 8th Av Ft Lauderdale FL 33315

RASBERRY, CHARLES LOREL, broadcasting co. exec.; b. Brookland, Ark., Sept. 14, 1934; s. Roy H. and Nellie (Schockney) R.; B.S., Ark. State U., 1956; M. TV, U. Ill., 1961. Announcer, newsman sta. KDRS, Paragould, Ark., 1953-56; newsman, sta. WILL and WILL-TV, Urbana, Ill., 1960-61; dir. broadcasting Ark. State U., Jonesboro, 1961-—, dir. closed-circuit TV system, 1967-—; gen. mgr. radio sta. KASU, Jonesboro, 1961-—. Dir. Ark. State U. Indian Sports Network, 1961-—, chmn. div. radio-TV, journalism, printing, 1969-—. Served with USNR, 1956-60. Mem. Nat. Assn. Profl. Broadcasting Edn., Nat. Assn. Ednl. Broadcasters (bd. dirs.), Kappa Tau Alpha, Pi Gamma Mu, Kappa Kappa Psi, Sigma Delta Chi. Methodist. Home: 208 Pekin St Jonesboro AR 72401 Office: Radio-TV Bldg Ark State Univ Jonesboro AR 72401

RASCOE, RALPH LAURENCE, city ofcl.; b. nr. Wallonia, Ky., Nov. 4, 1933; s. A.J. and Lucille E. (Gray) R.; accounting certificate Spencerian Bus. Coll., 1957; student Ky. Wesleyan Coll., 1957-61; m. Jane Marilyn Munday, Nov. 23, 1957; children—Lisa Jane, Karen Marie, Jeffrey Wayne. With A.B.C. Bookkeeping Service, Owensboro, Ky., 1957-59; accountant City of Owensboro, 1959-63, fir. finance, 1963-—. Nat. judge Jr. Achievement Conf., 1969; pres. Owensboro area Personnel Assn., 1968-69. Served with AUS, 1954-55. Named Boss of Year Am. Bus. Women Assn., Owensboro, Ky., 1967. Mem. Ky. Municipal Finance Assn. (pres. 1967), Ky. Finance Assn. (v.p., bd. dirs. 1970-71). Baptist (deacon 1963-71). Kiwanian. Home: 1125 Castlewood St Owensboro KY 42301 Office: PO Box 513 Owensboro KY 42301

RASKIN, MARCUS G., inst. exec.; A.B., U. Chgo., 1954, J.D., 1957. Legislative asst. to 12 congressmen, 1958; disarmament adviser to Pres. Kennedy; dep. asst. to McGeorge Bundy; co-founder, co-dir. Inst. for Policy Studies, Washington, 1963-—. Founder, New Party. Author: (with Bernard Fall) The Viet-Nam Reader, 1965; (with Arthur Waskow) The Call To Resist Illegitimate Authority, 1967; Being and Doing: From Deliberation to Liberation, 1971. Office: inst for Policy Studies 1520 New Hampshire Av NW Washington DC 20036*

RASMUSSEN, WAYNE DAVID, govt. ofcl.; b. Cushman, Mont., Feb. 5, 1915; s. Anton and Ethel (Bassett) R.; student Eastern Mont. State Coll., 1932-33; B.A., U. Mont., 1937; M.A., George Washington U., 1939, Ph.D., 1950; m. Marion Hollingworth Fowler, Dec. 27, 1939; children—Paul Wayne, Karen Ellen, Linda Marion. Records mgmt. U.S. Dept. Agr., Washington, 1937-40, agrl. historian, 1940-—, chief agrl. history br., 1961-—, lectr. Grad. Sch., 1950-—. Lectr. U. Md., 1963-—. Served with AUS, 1943-46. Mem. Agrl. History Soc. (exec. sec. 1952-62, 65-—; pres. 1965), Am. Hist. Assn., Orgn. Am. Historians, Econ. History Soc. Club: Cosmos (Washington). Author: History of the Emergency Farm Labor Supply Program, 1943-47, 1951; Readings in the History of American Agriculture, 1960; (with others) Century of Service, The First 100 Years of the United States Department of Agriculture, 1963; (with Gladys L. Baker) United States Department of Agriculture, 1972. Home: 3907 Ridge Rd Annandale VA 22003 Office: US Dept Agr Washington DC 20250

RASOR, MAC ROY, pub. relations exec.; b. Austin, Tex., Nov. 11, 1918; s. Roy Jonathon and Mattie (Chapman) R.; B.J., U. Tex., 1941; m. Reba Claire Graham, Dec. 24, 1946; children—John Graham, Daniel Lee, Nancy Claire. Reporter, sports editor, editor Austin Dispatch, 1936, 38-39; amusements editor Austin Statesman, 1940-41; reporter Ft. Worth Press, 1941; newswriter-editor, state capital bur. A.P., 1945-55; pub. relations cons., Austin, 1955-61; v.p. Bus. Research Corp. Tex., Austin, 1956-61; exec. sec. Texas Legal Res. Ofcls. Assn., 1955-61; dir. pub. relations Southwestern Life Ins. Co. Dallas, 1961-63, 2d v.p., pub. relations dir., 1963-67; v.p. for pub. relations, 1967-—; vis. instr. journalism U. Tex., 1956. Dir. pub. relations Tex. Democratic Presdl. campaigns, 1956, 60. Served with USMCR, 1941-45; PTO; to maj. Res. Mem. U. Tex. Journalism Ex-Students Assn. (past pres.), Pub. Relations Soc. Am. (past pres. N. Tex. chpt.), Dallas Advt. League, Life Ins. Advertisers Assn., Life Ins. Pub. Relations Council, Sigma Delta Chi (past state pres.). Mem. Christian Ch. (deacon). Club: Dallas Press. Home: 5650 Meadow Crest Dr Dallas TX 75230 Office: 1807 Ross Av Dallas TX 75201

RASSMAN, EMIL CHARLES, lawyer; b. Indpls., July 27, 1919; s. Fred Wolf and Helen (Leming) R.; A.B., Washington and Lee U., 1941; LL.B., U. Tex., 1947; m. Annie DeMontel, Jan. 31, 1943; children—Laura Helen (Mrs. Edward E. Bates, Jr.), James Neal. Admitted to Tex. bar, 1947; practiced in Midland, 1948-—; with Rassman, Gunter & Boldrick. Dir. Comml. Bank & Trust Co., Midland, Universal Resources Corp., Dallas. Mem. Tex. Civil Jud. Council, 1958-61. Trustee Stratford Coll., Danville, Va., 1967-—, Midland Ind. Sch. Dist., 1958-61; regent State Sr. Colls. Tex., 1961-—, pres., 1967-69. Campaign chmn. Midland County Community Chest, 1956, pres., 1957; chmn. Midland County chpt. A.R.C., 1971-—. Served to capt. AUS, 1941-46. Fellow Am. Coll. Trial Lawyers, Internat. Acad. Trial Lawyers, Am. Coll. Probate Counsel; mem. Internat. Assn. Ins. Counsel, Fedn. Ins. Counsel, Am. (fellow found.), Tex. (fellow found.), Midland County (pres. 1960) bar assns., State Bar Tex. (dir. 1972-—), West Tex. C. of C. (pres. elect 1972), Phi Delta Phi, Delta Tau Delta. Democrat. Episcopalian. Mason (32 deg., Shriner). Contbr. articles to profl. jours. Home: 2805 Lockheed Dr Midland TX 79701 Office: Midland Tower Bldg Midland TX 79701

RATCLIFF, ROBERT CURTIS, govt. ofcl.; b. Alexander, N.C., Aug. 26, 1929; s. LaFollette Dilly and Maude (Cook) R.; student Mars Hill Coll., 1948-49, 56, U. N.C., 1957-58; m. Gladys Juanita Westmoreland, Aug. 15, 1959; children—Dennis Dean, Donna Jean. Prodn. foreman Am. Enka Corp., Enka, N.C., 1958-66; clk. Superior Ct., judge Probate Ct., Buncombe County (N.C.), Asheville, 1966-—. Mem. exec. com. Republican Party, Buncombe County, 1962-—. Served with USNR, 1950-54. Home: Route 1 Alexander NC 28701 Office: PO Box 7315 Courthouse Sta Asheville NC 28807

RATH, R. JOHN, historian, educator; b. St. Francis, Kan., Dec. 12, 1910; s. John and Barbara (Schauer) R.; A.B., U. Kan., 1932; A.M., U. Cal. at Berkeley, 1934; Ph.D., Columbia, 1941; m. Isabel Jones, June 26, 1937; children—Laurens John (dec.), Isabel Ferguson. Instr. history U. Ark., 1936-37; pre-doctoral field fellow Social Sci. Research Council, in Austria and Italy, 1937-38; head dept. history and polit. sci. Lindenwood Coll., St. Charles, Mo., 1939-41; asso. prof. history Miss. State Coll. for Women, 1941-43; chief Bur. Documentary Evidence, UNRRA Bur. Documents and Tracing, U.S. Zone, Germany, 1945-46; asst. prof. history U. Ga., 1946-47; asso. prof. history, asso. editor Jour. Central European Affairs, U. Colo., 1947-51; prof. history U. Tex., 1951-63; chmn. dept. history and polit. sci. Rice U., 1963-68, Mary Gibbs Jones prof. history, 1968-—. Vis. prof. U. Ark., summer 1947, U. Wis., fall 1955-56, U. Colo., summer 1958, Duke, 1963; Guggenheim fellow in Italy, 1956-57; U.S. rep. Study Center Central and East European Cultures, 1970, 72; mem. sci. commn. Theodor Koenner Found. to study history 1st Austrian Republic, 1971-—. Served from pvt. to sgt. AUS, 1943-45. Recipient Austrian Honor Cross For Arts and Sci., 1963. Mem. Am. (exec. com. modern history sect. 1963-66, com. internat. hist. activities 1961-66), So. (chmn. European sect. 1961-62) hist. assns., Am. Assn. U. Profs., Soc. Italian Hist. Studies (nat. adv. bd.), Conf. Central European History (nat. exec. bd., chmn. 1970, exec. sec. com. Austrian history 1957-68), Austrian Acad. Scis. (corr.), Southwestern Social Sci. Assn. (chmn. history sect. 1972-—, mem. exec. bd. 1972-73), Phi Beta Kappa. Presbyn. Author: The Fall of the Napoleonic Kingdom of Italy, 1941; The Viennese Revolution of 1848, 1957; The Provisional Austrian Regime in Lombardy Venitia (1813-1815), 1969; also articles in profl. jours. Contbr.: Nationalism and Internationalism (edited by Edward Mead Earle), 1950; United States Diplomacy in Central and Eastern Europe (edited by Stephen Kertesz), 1956; European History in the South, 1959; Die Aufloesung des Habsburgerreiches, 1970; Native Fascism in the Successor States, 1971; Ency. Brit., Jr., World Book, Americana Ency., World Scope Ency.; East Central Europe and the World, 1962. Bd. editors Jour. Central European Affairs, 1960-64; editor Austrian History Newsletter, 1960-63, Austrian History Yearbook, 1964-—. Home: 7811 Fairdale St Houston TX 77042

RATHMAN, RICHARD FIELDING, educator; b. Detroit, Sept. 24, 1912; s. George A. and Mabel I. (Fielding) R.; A.B., Stanford, 1935, A.M., 1938; postgrad. San Jose State Coll. 1939-40; doctorat Universite de Paris (France), 1951; postgrad. Mills Coll., summer 1946, Laval U. (Que., Can.), summer 1947, U. So. Cal., summer 1952, Deutsche Sommerschule am Pazifik, Portland, Ore., 1962; m. Ruth Ann Holper, June 13, 1964; children—David Nathaniel Holper, Arthur Louis, Daniel George Paul; stepchildren—Stanley William, Steven Robert, Robin James Mason. Clk., C.E., San Francisco, 1940, So. Pacific Co., San Francisco, 1940-41; tchr. high sch., Hamilton City, Cal., 1942-43, Santa Clara, Cal., 1943-44, Dorris, Cal., 1944-45, Vanport City, Ore., 1945-46; tchr. Napa (Cal.) Jr. Coll., 1946-48, Douglas County (Nev.) High Sch., 1951-52, Livingston (Cal.) High Sch., 1952-53; clk. Los Angeles Dept. Water and Power, 1953-55; tchr. Minot (N.D.) High Sch., 1955-56; asso. prof. French, German and Spanish Bethel Coll., McKenzie, Tenn., 1959-64; asst. prof. French, Morehead (Ky.) State U., 1964-66; asso. prof. French, MacMurray Coll., Jacksonville, Ill., 1966-68; asst. prof. French, Morris Brown Coll., Atlanta, 1968-70, asso. prof., 1970-—; founder Franco-Usatian Enterprises, Los Angeles, 1953. Asst. scoutmaster Boy Scouts Am., Dorris, 1943-44, Paris, 1948-51, Atlanta, 1968-69; mem. symphony orch., Palo Alto, 1933-41, Modesto, Cal., 1952-53, Jackson, Tenn., 1961-64, Jacksonville, Ill., 1966-68. Mem. Modern Lang. Assn., N.E.A. (life), Nat. Assn. Tchrs. French, Am. Assn. U. Profs., South Atlantic Modern Lang. Assn., Coll. Lang. Assn., Nat. Geog. Soc., Tenn. Philol. Assn., Stanford Alumni Assn., Pi Delta Phi, Kappa Delta Pi. Republican. Presbyn. Editor: Deux Patries, 1938-42. Composer oratorios, cantatas, marches, concerto. Home: 4054 Pepperdine Dr Decatur GA 30034 Office: Morris Brown Coll Atlanta GA 30314

RATLIFF, CHARLES RAY, biochem. lab. exec.; b. Robertsdale, Ala., July 28, 1926; s. Otis Clay and Lucy (Matthews) R.; student Samford U., 1946-50, 52-53, B.S. in Chemistry, 1954; M.S., Birmingham-So. Coll., 1960; Ph.D., U. Ala., 1965; m. Mary Edith Conner, Feb. 17, 1951; children—Charles Ray, John Howell, Leslie Jane. Lab. supr. Peoples Hosp., Jasper, Ala., 1954-57; lab. mgr. Birmingham (Ala.) Bapt. Hosps., 1957-64, head parasitic disease lab., 1965-68, head clin. chemistry automated labs., 1966-68; instr. Walker Coll., Jasper, 1956-68; asst. prof. U. Ala. Coll. Gen. Studies, Birmingham, 1966-68, Med. Coll. U. Ala., 1966-68; chief sect. biochemistry, dir. clin. biochemistry Scott & White Clinic, Temple, Tex., 1968-—. Cons. Santa Fe Hosp., VA Center (both Temple, Tex.), Bioregional Reference Lab., San Antonio, Data-Med. Assos., Arlington, Tex. Bd. sci. advisers Meml. Inst. Pathology, Birmingham. Troop committeeman Boy Scouts Am., Birmingham, 1967-68. Served with USNR, 1944-46; PTO; with USAF, 1950-52; Korea. Recipient Achievement award Daniel Payne Coll., 1967. Fellow Am. Inst. Chemists, Am. Coll. Gastroenterology, Am. Chem. Soc.; mem. A.A.A.S., Am. Assn. Clin. Chemists, Am. Soc. Tropical Medicine and Hygiene, Am. Soc. Clin. Pathology, Digestive Disease Found., Am. Soc. Med. Technologists (Kimble research award 1961), Tex. Inst. Chemists. Contbr. articles on clin. chemistry, biochemistry, microbiology to profl. jours. Home: 3710 Indian Grove Dr Temple TX 76501 Office: Scott & White Clinic Temple TX 76501

RATLIFF, DAVID WADE, state senator, radio sta. exec.; b. Decatur, Tex., Apr. 20, 1912; s. Lemuel David and Myra Texas (Pace) R.; student Austin Coll., 1930-31, N. Tex. State Coll., 1932-34; m. Priscilla Albertine Gladish, July 17, 1931; children—David L., Lynnora Ann, Mary Jane, John A. Sec. Tex. R.R. Communa., Kilgore, Tex., 1935-39; clk. FCA, Dallas, 1939-40, Tex. Employment Commn., 1941-42; area supr. OPA, Ft, Worth, 1942-46; owner, operator radio sta. KDWT, Stamford, Tex., 1946-58; mem. Tex. Ho. of Reps., 1950-54; mem. Tex. Senate, 1954-—, pres. pro tem, 1961; acting gov. state Tex., June 30, 1961. Area chmn. Boy Scouts Together campaign. Mem. C. of C. (dir. 1950-—), S.A.R., Sons Confederacy. Clubs: Exchange (past pres.), Rotary (Stamford). Address: 1005 Wells St Stamford TX 79553

RATLIFF, JAMES EDWIN, dentist; b. Kingston, W.Va., Jan. 22, 1941; s. Hertaux and Lily Marie (Potter) R.; B.A., U. Louisville, 1962, D.M.D., 1966; m. Shirley Ellen Hamlin, Jan. 26, 1962; children—Tametha Lee, James Edwin II, Michael Todd. Pvt. practice dentistry, Salyersville, Ky., 1969-—. Served with AUS, 1966-69. Decorated Army Commendation medal. Mem. Am., Ky., Ky. Mountain dental assns., Delta Sigma Delta. Home: 1 Cardinal Ct Salyersville KY 41465 Office: Med Clinic Salyersville KY 41465

RATLIFF, JOHN WALTER, coal co. exec.; b. Wolfpit, Ky., Jan. 17, 1924; s. Roy Thomas and Olba (Raitliff) R.; student pub. schs.; m. Flora Jean Stiltner, Dec. 29, 1948; children—John Walter, Alecia Jean. With Harmon Coal Co.; owner Marrowbone Coal Co. (Ky.), 1943-54; owner Black Diamond Coal Co., Inc., Grundy, Va., 1954-67; owner Ratliff Farms, 1968-—, BeLibe Coal Co.; v.p. Internat. Coal Co.; exec. dir. Grundy Nat. Bank. Served with AUS, 1942-43. Ky. col. Mem. U.S. C. of C., A.I.M. Home: Route 1 Box 136 Tazewell VA 24651

RATLIFF, WILLIAM DURRAH, JR., lawyer; b. Gainesville, Tex., Nov. 17, 1921; s. William Durrah and Fay (Tippit) R.; B.B.A., U. Tex., 1943, LL.B., 1948; m. Barbara Jeanne Warner, June 20, 1947;children—William Durrah III, Robert Warner, Bryan Prichard, Barbara Louise, Edwin Brent, Dorothy Jeanne. Admitted to Tex. bar, 1948; practiced in Ft. Worth; mem. firm Kelly & Morris, 1948-49; pvt. practice, 1950-51; mem. firm Simon, Jones & Ratliff, 1951-54, Simon & Ratliff, 1954-62, Simon, Crowley, Wright, Ratliff & Miller, 1962-68, Shannon, Gracey, Ratliff & Miller, 1968-—. Dir. Aztec Mfg. Co. Served with USNR, 1943-46. Fellow Tex. Bar Found.; mem. Alpha Tau Omega. Presbyn. Clubs: River Crest Country, Fort Worth, Fort Worth Boat. Home: 5820 El Campo St Fort Worth TX 76107 Office: Continental Nat Bank Bldg Fort Worth TX 76102

RATTAN, GARLAND WARD, supt. schs.; b. Lamesa, Tex., June 15, 1933; s. Andy Ward and Vernie Pearl (Scott) R.; B.S., West Tex. State U., 1954, M.Ed., 1962; m. Shirley Jim Porter, Dec. 17, 1953; children— David Ward, Christopher Jerome. Tchr., asst. coach, prin. high sch., Matador, Tex., 1955-56, Boys Ranch, 1956-62; supt. schs., Boys Ranch Ind. Sch. Dist., Cal Farley's Boys Ranch, Boys Ranch, Tex., 1962-—. Recipient Distinguished Service award Tex. Vocational Agr. Tchrs. Assn., 1965. Mem. Tex. Tchrs. Assn., N.E.A., Am., Tex. Assns. sch. adminstrs., Fellowship Christian Athletes, Red Red Rose, Phi Delta Kappa. Baptist. Mason, Lion; mem. Order Eastern Star. Address: Boys Ranch TX 79010

RAUCH, HENRY E., textile exec.; b. Boston, Sept. 21, 1902; s. Carl and Louise (Roisener) R.; grad. Bentley Coll., Waltham, Mass.; m. Alice Atkins, June 20, 1929; children—Elizabeth R. Ferris, Dudley Atkins. Controller Am. Thread Co., N.Y.C., 1938-42, exec. v.p., 1942-50, dir., 1951-52; pres. Peterzell & Gelles, Inc., 1950-51, mgmt. cons., 1951; with Burlington Industries, Inc., 1952-—, sr. v.p., controller, 1961-62, chmn. bd., 1968-69, chmn. exec.-finance com., 1969, chmn. finance com., 1969-70, ret., 1970. Vice chmn. bd. trustees, mem. investment com., chmn. med. center bd. Duke; charter trustee, chmn. bd. trustees Bentley Coll. Club: Greensboro (N.C.) Country. Home: 504 Country Club Dr Greensboro NC 27408 Office: Wachovia Bldg Greensboro NC 27401

RAUCH, MARSHALL ARTHUR, textile co. exec.; b. N.Y.C., Feb. 2, 1923; s. Nathan A. and Tillie (Wohl) R.; student Duke, 1940-43; m. Jeanne Girard, 1946; children—John, Ingrid, Marc, Peter, Stephanie. Chmn. bd., treas., dir. Pyramid Mills Co., Inc., Bessemer City, N.C., 1954-—, Pyramid Dye Corp., Bessemer City, 1956-—, Homeside Yarn, Inc., Bessemer City, 1960-—, Nile Star, Inc., Woodmere, N.Y., 1961-—, Gastonia Dyeing Corp. (N.C.), 1968-—; treas., dir. E.P. Press, Inc., Gastonia, 1965-—; dir. Darby Chem. Co., Charlotte, N.C., So. Investment Corp., Charlotte, Sedgefield Realty Corp., Gastonia, Majestic Ins. Financing Corp., Gastonia, Advance Investment Fund, N.Y.C.; mgr. Narco Molding Co., Bessemer City. Chmn. Gaston Jewish Welfare Fund, 1958-62, 68-70; 1st v.p. N.C. Assn. Jewish Men, 1966; mem. nat. council Am. Jewish Joint Distbn. Com., 1968-70; mem. Gov.'s Good Neighbor Council, 1963-—; chmn. Gastonia Human Relations Com., 1964-67; chmn. N.C. Com. on Population and Family, 1968-—; mem. N.C. Jail Study Commn., 1968; pres. Asso. Industries, 1964-65; chmn. Employ the Handicap Com., 1964-65; mem. N.C. Citizens Com. for Dental Health, 1968; sr. adviser Gastonia Boys Club, 1947-63; mem. cons. commn. Pioneer council Girl Scouts U.S.A., 1968-69; pres. Gaston County YMCA, 1972. Mayor pro tem City of Gastonia, 1952-54, 61-63, mem. city council, 1952-54, 61-65; mem. N.C. State Senate, 1967-68, 68-69. Bd. dirs., treas. Rauch Found.; bd. dirs. N.C. United Jewish Appeal Cabinet, 1968-70, Gaston Skills, 1964-66, Salvation Army Boys Club, 1963-—, United Fund, 1963-67, Gaston Boys Club, 1964-—, Carolina Amateur Athletics Union, 1951-53, Gaston Mus. Natural History, 1963-64, Holy Angels Nursery, Belmont, N.C., 1960-—, Planned Parenthood and World Population, N.Y.C., 1968-69, Gaston Community Action, 1966, Gaston-Cleveland Tb Assn., 1968; bd. govs. N.C. Jewish Home for the Aged, 1968-70; mem. adv. council

N.C. Com. for Children and Youth, 1968-69; bd. dirs. Gastonia YMCA, 1959-62, 67-69, v.p., 1968-70; v.p., bd. dirs. Community Concert Assn., 1960-61; mem. top mgmt. adv. com. Gaston County Indsl. Mgmt. Club, 1963-65; bd. advisers Gardner Webb Coll., 1969-70; trustee U. N.C., 1969-70; mem. adv. com. N.C. Vocational Textile Sch., 1970-71. Served with AUS, World War II; ETO. Decorated Combat Infantry Badge; recipient Nat. Recreation citation Nat. Recreation Assn., 1965; Brotherhood award Nat. Council Christians and Jews, 1969; named Man of Yr., Gastonia Jaycees, 1957, Gastonia Jr. Women's Club, 1964, Gaston County chpt. Omega Psi Phi, 1966, N.C. Health Dept., 1968, Gastonia Red Shield Boys Club, 1970. Mem. Duke U. Alumni Assn. (pres. Gaston chpt. 1961-62). Jewish religion (pres. temple 1962-64, tchr. Sunday sch. 1951-56). Mem. B'nai B'rith. Home: 1121 Scotch Dr Gastonia NC 28052

RAULSTON, JIMMY RAY, entomologist; b. Shamrock, Tex., Feb. 2, 1941; s. Cleburne Texas and Obenetta (Chandler) R.; B.S., Eastern N.M. U., 1965; M.S., N.M. State U., 1967; m. Virginia Anne Reeves, Nov. 24, 1961. Grad. research asst. entomology N.M. State U., Las Cruces, 1965-67; research entomologist Entomology Research div. U.S. Dept. Agr., Brownsville, Tex., 1967—. Recipient Merit award U.S. Dept. Agr., 1968; Certificate of Merit, U.S. Dept. Agr., 1970; Sec. Mgmt. Improvement award U.S. Dept. Agr., 1970. Mem. Entomol. Soc. Am., Profl. Entomologists Assn., Beta Beta Beta, Gamma Theta Upsilon. Home: 4 Honey Dr Brownsville TX 78520 Office: PO Box 1033 Brownsville TX 78520

RAULT, JOSEPH MATTHEW, JR., petroleum co. exec.; b. New Orleans, Feb. 24, 1926; s. Joseph M. and Calista (Morgan) R.; student Georgetown U., 1948; B.S., Mass. Inst. Tech., 1948; LL.B., Tulane U., 1950 children—Catherine delavergne, Joseph Matthew III. Pres., Joseph M. Rault, Jr., Inc., New Orleans, 1959—. Rault Petroleum Corp., New Orleans, 1962—, Continental Rigs Internat., S.A. of Panama, 1960—, Rault Petroleum Corp. Venezuela, 1963—; dir. Constructora Otila, S.A. of Mex. Exec. chmn. Internat. Relations Com., City New Orleans, 1964-66; gen. chmn. U.S. Savs. Bond 25th Anniversary, New Orleans, 1966; mem. Miss. River Pkwy Commn., 1965-68, Chmn. bd. New Orleans R.R. Terminal; bd. regents Loyola U., New Orleans. Served to lt. with USNR, 1943-46. Mem. La. Soc. for Promotion of Music and Performing Arts. Home and office: 1111 Gravier St New Orleans LA 70112

RAUM, ARNOLD, judge; b. Lynn, Mass., Oct. 27, 1908; s. Isaac and Ida (Ross) R.; A.B. summa cum laude, Harvard, 1929, LL.B. magna cum laude, 1932; postgrad. (Sheldon fellow) Cambridge U. (Eng.), 1932; m. Muriel Leidner Slaff, Jan. 26, 1944 (div.); m. 2d, Violet Gang Kopp, Apr. 26, 1957; stepchildren—Robert E., Elizabeth A., Katherine F. Admitted to Mass. bar, 1932, U.S. Supreme Ct. bar, 1935, D.C. bar; atty. R.F.C., 1932-34; spl. asst. to U.S. atty. gen., 1934-50; spl. asst. to U.S. atty., Eastern Dist. La., 1939; asst. to U.S. solicitor gen., also acting solicitor gen., 1939-50; directed litigation all Fed. tax cases, also other cases U.S. Supreme Ct., 1939-50; judge Tax Ct. U.S., Washington, 1950—; lectr. taxation Yale Law Sch., 1937-38; mem. faculty Harvard Law Sch., 1947. Served as lt. comdr. USCGR World War II. Mem. Bar Assn. D.C. (hon.), Fed. Bar Assn. (hon.), Am. Law Inst., Phi Beta Kappa. Club: Cosmos, Harvard (Washington). Editor Harvard Law Rev., 1930-32. Home: 2622 31st St NW Washington DC 20008 Office: Tax Court US 1111 Constitution Av NW Washington DC 20044

RAUNBORG, JOHN DEE, petroleum co. exec.; b. Waco, Tex., Dec. 16, 1926; s. John Oscar and Grace Geraldine (Duckworth) R.; student Rutgers U., 1945; B.S., La. State U., 1949; postgrad. U. Tex., 1949-50; m. Flora B. Ewart, Aug. 26, 1946; children—Sharon Lynn, Ronald Ryan, Rhonda Ruth, Randell Ralph. Staff auditor Arthur Andersen &Co., 1950-57; mgr. internal auditing Kerr-McGee Corp., Oklahoma City, 1957-59, asst. to controller, 1960-62, controller oil and gas div., 1962-67, asst. controller, 1968, controller, 1969—. Served with AUS, 1944-47. C.P.A., Tex. Mem. Am. Inst. C.P.A.'s, Financial Execs. Inst., Am. Petroleum Inst., Ind. Petroleum Assn. Am., Oklahoma City C. of C. Methodist. Home: 7037 N Independence St Oklahoma City OK 73116 Office: Kerr-McGee Bldg Oklahoma City OK 73102

RAUPE, BUELL CRAIG, airlines exec.; b. Granbury, Tex., Sept. 19, 1925; s. Carl Bryan and Lottie Eula (Morris) R.; student So. Meth. U., 1948; B.A. in Econs. and Govt., North Tex. State Coll., 1950, M.A. in Polit. Sci., 1950; postgrad. U. Wis., 1950-51, Am. U., 1957-58; m. Joyce Adkins, June 5, 1948; children—Carl B., Joel C. Prin., Vega (Tex.) Sch., 1951-52; instr. civics Abilene (Tex.) High Sch., 1952-53; instr. econs. and history Weatherford (Tex.) Coll. 1953-54; adminstrv. asst. to U.S. Congressman Wright, 1954-60; with AID and Alliance for Progress, and predecessors, 1960-64, dir. Congl. relations, 1961-64; v.p. Eastern Air Lines, Washington and Miami, Fla., 1965—. Served with USNR, 1942-46; mem. U.S. Army Res. Mem. Am. Polit. Sci. Assn. Unitarian. Mason. Club: Burro (v.p. 1955) (Miami). Home: 7105 S W 109th Terrace Miami FL 33143 Office: Miami Internat Airport Miami FL 33148

RAUSCHER, JOHN H., JR., business exec. Pres., treas. Rauscher Pierce Securities Corp., Dallas. Home: 4328 Lorraine Av Dallas TX 75205 Office: Mercantile Dallas Bldg Dallas TX 75201*

RAUTH, GLEN EUGENE, agrl. engr.; b. Boonville, Ind., Nov. 19, 1928; s. Louis F. and Nora (Bierbaum) R.; B.S., Purdue U., 1950; m. Betty J. Higgins, Jan. 20, 1951; children—Carol Ann, Jane Virginia, Gene Alan. Prodn. mgr. farming Flavor Pict Coop., Delray Beach, Fla., 1951-62; chief engr. FMC Corp., Ocoee, Fla., 1962-69; asst. dir. grove operations citrus prodn. Foods div. Coca Cola Co., Auburndale, Fla., 1969—. Bd. dirs. Central Fla. Lions Sight Clinic. Served with AUS, 1952-54. Mem. Am. Soc. Agrl. Engrs., Fla. Hort. Soc., Citrus Industry Harvesting Com. (exec. com. 1969-71), Alpha Zeta. Presbyn. (elder 1959-71). Lion. Patentee in field. Home: 519 S Lake Florence St Winter Haven FL 33880 Office: PO Box 247 Auburndale FL 33823

RAUTH, LOUIS FREDRICK, agr. co. pres.; b. Boonville, Ind., Nov. 14, 1900; s. John George and Barbara (Roth) R.; student Ohio State U., 1919; m. Norma Emma Bierbaum, Aug. 28, 1927; children—Glen E., Robert G., Ruth (Mrs. Donal S. Rusk), Marie (Mrs. Lewis W. Currier, Jr.). Partner, Rauth Bros., Boonville, 1918-34, owner, 1934—; developer Vine Ripe Tomato Industry, 1952—; pres. Flavor Pict Co-Op, Delray Beach, Fla., Flavor Pict, Inc., Delray Beach, both 1967—. U. Fla. appointee Dare Com., Share Com., 1967-71. Named So. Ind. Bean King Ind. Farmers Guide, 1952, Palm Beach County Family of Year, 1963; recipient Efficiency award vegetable crops Nat. Ford Farm, 1963. Mem. Fla. Fruit and Vegetable Assn. (vice chmn. competition and marketing com. 1965—), Fla. Tomato Com. (chmn. 1959-68). Mem. United Ch. of Christ (trustee). Pioneer work in home freezer, 1938. Home: 314 NW 7th St Delray Beach FL 33444 Office: PO Box 1810 Delray Beach FL 33444

RAVENHOLT, REIMERT THOROLF, epidemiologist, govt. ofcl.; b. Milltown, Wis., Mar. 9, 1925; s. Ansgar B. and Kristine (Petersen) R.; B.S., U. Minn., 1948, M.B., 1951, M.D., 1952; M.P.H., U. Cal. at Berkeley, 1956; m. Mildred Evelyn Froysland, June 19, 1948; children—Janna, Mark, Lisa, Dane. Intern, USPHS Hosp., San Francisco, 1951-52; with epidemic intelligence service Communicable Disease Center, USPHS, 1952-54; dir. communicable disease div. Seattle-King County Health Dept., Seattle, 1954-61, epidemiology cons. European area USPHS, Am. Embassy, Paris, France, 1961-63; asso. prof. preventive medicine Sch. Medicine. U, Wash., Seattle, 1963-66; with AID, Washington, 1966—, dir. Office of Population, Washington 1969—. Recipient John J. Sippy Meml. award Western br. Am. Pub. Health Assn., 1961; Sesquicentennial award U. Mich., 1967. Diplomate Am. Bd. Preventive Medicine. Fellow Am. Pub. Health Assn. (sec. epidemiology sect. 1964-67). Royal Soc. Medicine; mem. A.A.A.S., Population Assn. Am., Soc. Study Evolution, Delta Omega. U.S. del. to Colombo Plan Conf., Karachi, 1966; U.S. adviser World Health Assembly, 1969, U.N. Population Commn., Geneva, 1969. Contbr. articles to profl. publs. Home: 7057 Wolftree Lane Rockville MD 20852 Office: Office of Population AIDWashington DC 20523

RAVESON, BETTY RICH (MRS. SHERMAN H. RAVESON), columnist; b. Schenectady, June 16, 1913; d. Edwin L. and Florence (Nutree) Rich; A.B., Columbia, 1934; m. Sherman H. Raveson, Apr. 26, 1932. Eastchester editor Herald Statesman, Yonkers, N.Y., 1940-42; night bur. mgr. U.P. Assn., Albany, 1942-43; Delray editor, columnist Palm Beach (Fla.) Illustrated, 1959-62; columnist Palm Beach Daily News, Delray Beach News-Jour., 1962-69, Boynton Beach News-Jour., 1966-69, Franklin (N.C.) Press, 1967—; feature writer Palm Beach Life mag., 1962-69, TV commentator, 1964—, exec. editor Palm Beach Voice, 1969-70; editor Mountain Living mag., 1970—. Pub. relations dir. Delray Beach Playhouse, 1959-61. Mem. N.C. Press Assn., Bus. and Profl. Women's Club. Presbyn. Clubs: Fla. Women's Press; Fla. Gold Coast Press (Outstanding Achievement award 1963) (Delray Beach); Quills (Palm Beach); Atlanta Press. Home: Wayah Valley Rd Franklin NC 28734 Office: PO Box 290 Franklin NC 28734

RAVESON, SHERMAN HAROLD, artist; b. New Haven, June 11, 1907; A.B., LL.B., Cumberland U. Art editor, Vanity Fair mag., 1929-34, Life mag., 1935, Esquire mag., 1936; with Pettingell & Fenton, 1937-41; v.p., art dir. Sterling Advt. Agy., N.Y.C., 1951-55; one-man shows Assn. Am. Artists, 1941, Grand Central Art Gallery, N.Y.C., 1955, 56, Carriage House Studios, Phila., 1956; works represented in collections numerous racetracks, U.S. Editor: Classified Boating Directory of Fla. East-West Coast, 1967—, Palm Beach Shopping Guide to Worth Av., 1967—. Home: Wayah Valley Rd Franklin NC 28734*

RAVLIN, JAMES NEGUS, tobacco co. exec.; b. Saskatoon, Sask., Can., Dec. 1, 1913; s. John Hanchett and Mary (Negus) R.; student Grinnell Coll., 1930-32; A.B., U. Minn., 1936, LL.B., 1939; m. Mary Morrow, Sept. 14, 1944; children—Mark Morrow, Juliet. Admitted to Minn. bar, 1939, Ky. bar, 1953; asst. to gen. counsel RFC, also sec. commerce, 1939-42; exec. sec. Ind. Air Freight Assn., 1946; tax legislative and facilities counsel Am. Airlines, Inc., 1947-50; counsel, del. Internat. Air Transp. Assn., Northwest Orient Airlines, Inc., 1950-53; asst. gen. counsel, sec. Brown & Williamson Tobacco Corp., Louisville, 1953—. Bd. dirs. Louisville Philharmonic Soc. Served with USNR, 1942-45. Mem. Am., Inter-Am., Fed., Ky., Louisville bar assns., Am. Judicature Soc., Am. Soc. Corp. Secs., Assn. Bar City N.Y., Louisville Com. Fgn. Relations, Nat. Tax Assn., Phi Delta Phi. Clubs: Louisville Beagle; Nat. Lawyers. Home: 4300 Talahi Way Louisville KY 40207 Office: 1600 W Hill St Louisville KY 40201

RAWALAY, SURJAN SINGH, educator; b. Langar Chhanni, India, Mar. 4, 1933; s. O. Mehan Singh and Kartar (Kaur) R.; B.Sc. Punjab U. (Chandigarh, India), 1956; M.Sc., Ohio State U., 1959, Ph.D., 1962; m. Parmesri Saroa, Jan. 26, 1953; children—Mohindar Kaur, Chhindar Kaur, Balwinder Kaur. Came to U.S., 1957. Asst. prof. biochemistry Punjab Agrl. U., Ludhiana, India, 1963-64; research chemist B.C. Research Council, Vancouver, Can., 1964-65; asst. prof. chemistry West Liberty State Coll. (W. Va.), 1965-68; prof. Voorhees Coll., Denmark, S.C., 1968—. Named Prof. of Year, West Liberty State Coll., 1967-68. Mem. Am. Chem. Soc., W. Va., S.C. acads. sci., Am. Inst. Chemists. Home: 1500 Voorhees Dr Denmark SC 29042 Office: Dept Chemistry Voorhees Coll Denmark SC 29042

RAWL, PAUL THOMAS, supt. schs.; b. Gaston, S.C., Nov. 10, 1938; s. Otis and Carrie Nea (Bodie) R.; A.B., U. S.C., 1959, M.A., 1966, postgrad. 1971—; m. Lynda Robinson, Sept. 10, 1960; children—Paul Thomas, Stanley Lewis. Coach, tchr. high sch., Aiken, S.C., 1960, Salem, S.C., 1960-61, North High Sch., Hopkins, S.C., 1961-65; sch. adminstr. Lower Richland High Sch., Hopkins, 1965-68; prin., dist. supt. Lexington (S.C.) High Sch., 1968—. Capt., United Fund, Lexington, 1970-71; mem. Lexington-Richland Drug Abuse Council; mem. tech. adv. group Columbia Area Transp. Study, 1968-71. Bd. dirs. S.C. Tb. Assn. Named outstanding young educator Lexington Jr. C. of C., 1970. Mem. Nat., S.C. (life mem., publs. com. 1968-71), Lexington County, Richland County (chmn. publicity com. 1966-67) edn. assns., Am. Assn. Sch. Adminstrs., Secondary Prins. Assn., Lexington County Supts. (chmn. 1969-71), Lexington C. of C. (dir. 1969-71, chmn. edn. com. 1969-71), Elementary Secondary Edn. Act Adminstrs. (audit com. 1969-70), Vietnam Prisoners of War. Lion (dir. 1969-71). Home: 618 N Lake Dr Lexington SC 29072 Office: PO Box 218 Lexington SC 29072

RAWLES, JAMES WHITE, banker; b. Richmond, Va., Oct. 30, 1907; s. Benjamin Watkins and Sarah Anne (White) R.; B.A., U. Va., 1928; M.B.A., Harvard, 1930; postgrad. Rutgers U., 1938-40; m. Georgina Olivia Marraccini, June 7, 1947; children—Marika Archbell, James White, Elizabeth Whittall, Georgina Offley, Benjamin Watkins III. With J. & W. Seligman & Co., N.Y.C., 1930-33; with United Va. Bank / State-Planters Richmond, 1933—, v.p., 1946-61, sr. v.p., 1961-66, exec. v.p., 1966—; dir. United Va. Bankshares, Inc. Chmn. for Richmond U.S. Savs. Bonds, 1965-67; Va. state chmn. U.S. Savs. Bonds, 1968—. Bd. dirs., past pres., past chmn. Va. div., del. Am. Cancer Soc.; past treas., bd. dirs. Richmond Area Community Chest, Richmond chpt. A.R.C.; v.p., trustee Valentine Mus.; trustee Hannah More Acad., Reisterstown, Md. Served from capt. to lt. col. Finance Dept., AUS, 1942-46. Mem. Assn. Res. City Bankers, Va. Bankers Assn. (past dir., past pres.), Am. Bankers Assn. (past mem. exec. Council), Soc. Colonial Wars in State Va. (lt. gov.), Assn. for Preservation Va. Antiquities (chmn. adv. com., dir.), U.S. C. of C. (past mem. com. on consumer issues Soc. Cin., The Richmond German, Richmond Hundred, Soixante Plus. Episcopalian. Clubs: Commonwealth; Country of Va.; Deep Run Hunt; Princess Anne Country. Home: 5001 Cary St Rd Richmond VA 23226 Office: 900 E Main St Richmond VA 23214

RAWLEY, JAMES WILLIAM, oil co. exec.; b. Palestine, Tex., Apr. 26, 1911; s. Walter Fleming and Mable Dean (Hallett) R.; grad. advanced mgmt. program Harvard, 1956; m. Carolyn Johnson, Feb. 7, 1937; 1 dau., Sarah Nan. With Seaboard Oil Co., Dallas, 1933-58, v.p., mgr. div., 1955-58, v.p., mgr. domestic div., 1958; asst. gen. mgr. domestic producing div. Texas Co. Houston, 1958-69; mgr. domestic producing div. Texaco, Tulsa, 1959-61, mgr. div., New Orleans, 1962-67, gen. mgr. Eastern U.S., Houston, 1967-71, v.p. S.E. region, New Orleans, 1971- —. Mem. Mid-Continent Oil and Gas Assn. (bd. dirs. 1960-72), Am. Petroleum Inst., Am. Assn. Petroleum Landmen. Home: 919 Topaz St New Orleans LA 70124 Office: 1501 Canal St New Orleans LA 70112

RAWLEY, PARKER HALLETT, investment co. exec.; b. Palestine, Tex., June 22, 1913; s. Walter Fleming and Mabel Dean (Hallett) R.; student Nixon Bus. Coll., 1933-34; m. Ann Marie Bachert, Nov. 14, 1936; 1 son, Paul Hallett. Salesman, Liggett-Meyers Tobacco Co., Galveston, Tex., 1934-36; S.W. div. mgr. Johnson & Johnson, surg. supplies, Dallas, 1936-53; regional sales mgr. Hazel Bishop Cosmetics, Dallas, 1954-65; owner retail drug stores, San Antonio, 1954-55, Dallas, 1955-65; pres. Redson Sales, Inc., Dallas, 1965—, Preston Forest Investment Co., Dallas, 1965—; dir. N. Dallas Bank & Trust Co. Active United Fund, Heart Assn. Mem. Drug Travelers State of Tex., Houston Drug Travelers (v.p. 1945-46), Dallas Sales Execs. Club. Republican. Episcopalian. Clubs: Brookhaven Country (Dallas). Home: 4325 Forest Bend Dallas TX 75234 Office: 5925 Forest Lane Dallas TX 75230

RAWLINGS, PAUL C., lawyer; b. Cave City, Ark., June 21, 1928; s. Otha A. and Leona (King) R.; grad. Little Rock Jr. Coll.; LL.B., U. Ark., 1950; m. Catherine Terral, Mar. 3, 1951 (div.); children—William Anthony, Rebecca Ann, Neal Anderson; m. 2d, Erma Martin, June 20, 1971. Admitted to Ark. bar, 1950, since practiced in Little Rock; partner Terral, Rawlings, Matthews & Purtle and predecessor firm, 1962—. Asst. atty. gen. State of Ark. Bd. dirs. Ark. Enterprises Blind. Served with AUS, 1950-52. Mem. Am., Ark., Pulaski County bar assns. Methodist (past chmn. bd. stewards, chmn. bd. trustees). Mason, Lion (past pres.). Home: 10617 David O Dodd Rd Little Rock AR 72201 Office: 300 Spring Bldg Little Rock AR 72201

RAWLINSON, KARL RICHARD, banker; b. Prattville, Ala., Dec. 31, 1931; s. Dayton and Thelma Marie (Chambliss) R.; B.S., U. Ala., 1954; m. Elizabeth Anne Smitherman, Aug. 10, 1954; children—Richard, Beverly, Barbara. Owner, farms and timberland, Prattville, 1956-59; with income tax div. Ala. Revenue Dept., Montgomery, 1959-60; bank examiner Fed. Deposit Ins. Corp., Atlanta, 1960-63; v.p. Bank Prattville, 1963—. Chmn. drive A.R.C., 1964. Served with AUS, 1954-56. Mem. Delta Chi. Methodist. Club: Prattville Country. Home: 1145 Perrydale Loop Prattville AL 36067 Office: 124 W Main St Prattville AL 36067

RAWLS, GEORGE CLIFFORD, utility exec.; b. McComb, Miss., Apr. 14, 1903; s. Christopher C. and Etta Victoria (Felder) R.; B.S., Miss. State Coll., 1923; postgrad. study Columbia, 1924-26; m. Marvel Elree Cato, Oct. 2, 1927; 1 dau., Gloria Fay (Mrs. Henry Forrest Askew). With Bell Telephone Labs., Inc. N.Y.C., 1923-26; groundman, meterman, local mgr., then div. mgr. Miss. Power & Light Co. (formerly Miss. Central Power Co.), 1926-39; operating mgr. La. Power & Light Co., 1939, v.p. operations, dir., now chmn. bd. 1968—. Reg. elec. and mech. engr., La. Mem. Tau Beta Pi. Home: 104 Woodland Pl New Orleans LA Office: 142 Delaronde St New Orleans LA

RAWLS, J. LEWIS, JR., lawyer, peanut oil co. exec.; b. Suffolk, Va., Dec. 7, 1923; s. J. Lewis and Azzie (Gatling) R.; student Va. Mil. Inst., 1942-43, Duke, 1943-44; LL.B., U. Va., 1950; m. Mary Helen Macklin, Oct. 4, 1947; children—John Lewis III, Rebecca Macklin, Frank Macklin. Admitted to Va. bar, 1950; gen. counsel Taylor Cos., 1952-57; individual law practice, Suffolk, 1950-52, 57-63; partner Rawls & Bagnell, Suffolk, 1963—; mem. Va. Ho. of Dels., 1962-70. Pres., chief exec. Suffolk Oil Mill, Inc., 1969—; dir., sec.-treas. Old Dominion Investors Trust, Suffolk, 1967—; dir. Tidewater Group, Norfolk, Va.; mem. Suffolk bd. Va. Nat. Bank; chmn. bd. Atlantic Nat. Life Assurance Co. Pres., March of Dimes, Suffolk, 1951-52. Served with USNR, 1945-46. Mem. Am., Va. bar assns. Mason, Elk, Rotarian. Home: 603 Dumville Av Suffolk VA 23434 Office: PO Box 1458 Suffolk VA 23434

RAWLS, JOSEPH LEONARD, JR., food co. exec.; b. Rocky Mount, N.C., June 14, 1931; s. Joseph L. and Lallah (Mizzel) R.; student U. N.C., 1949-51; B.C.S., Benjamin Franklin U., 1953; postgrad. U. E. Carolina, 1953-54; m. Nancy Lee Williams, Dec. 21, 1951; children—Vivian Lee, Joseph Leonard III. Partner, Luper & Rawls, C.P.A.'s, 1958-61; chmn., pres. Hardee's Food Systems, Inc., Rocky Mount, 1961—; dir. Planters Nat. Bank & Trust Co., Bus. Found. N.C. Mem. adv. bd. N.C. Zool. Commn., 1971; sec. N.C. Med. Found. Trustee N.C. Wesleyan Coll., Woodward Acad., Rocky Mount. Acad. Served with AUS, 1954-56. Recipient Distinguished Alumni award Woodward Acad., 1971. C.P.A., N.C. Mem. Am. Inst. C.P.A.'s, Am. Mgmt. Assn., Young Presidents Orgn., Silver Spoon Soc., Rocky Mount C. of C. (dir.), Phi Gamma Delta. Republican. Episcopalian (layreader 1958-71). Rotarian. Home: 508 Wildwood Av Rocky Mount NC 27801 Office: 1233 N Church St Rocky Mount NC 27801

RAWLS, LINWOOD LEE, surveyer; b. nr. Ahoskie, N.C., Nov. 7, 1931; s. Earl Robert and Annie Joseph (Hoggard) R.; student Carolina Sch. Commerce, 1958-60, N.C. State Coll., 1964, 70; m. Louise Jean Wiggins, Apr. 7, 1954; children—Linwood Lee, Deborah Lynn. With N.C. Hwy. Commn., Ahoskie, 1950-54; engr., Elizabeth City, Manteo, 1956-61, asst. dist. engr. and surveyor, Ahoskie, 1961—. Served with Judge Adv. staff AUS, 1954-56. Registered surveyor, N.C. Mem. E. Carolina Engrs. Soc. Mason (32 deg.). Home: Pine Ridge Drive Ahoskie NC 27910 Office: 220 Mitchell St Ahoskie NC 27910

RAWLS, WALTER CECIL, JR., lawyer, bus. exec.; b. Richmond, Va., Sept. 13, 1928; s. Walter Cecil and Ella (Freeman) R.; A.B., U. Mo., 1951; J.D., Washington U., St. Louis, 1958; m. Sheila Daphne Kirsch; children—James David, Richard Wayne. Agt. for France, Am. Trust Life Ins. Co., Wichita Falls, Tex., 1953-54; admitted to Fla. bar, 1958, since practiced in Jacksonville; mem. firm Ragland, Kurz, Toole, 1958, Marks, Gray, Yates, Conroy, Gibbs, 1959; pvt. practice, 1960-63, 1969—; partner Thomas & Rawls, 1963-67, Ogier, Stubbs & Rawls, 1967-69, RAWB & Co.; treas., dir. Ga.-Fla. Oil Co.; dir. F.I.D. Internat. Mem. adv. council Washington U. Law Sch., St. Louis. Served with AUS, 1951-53. Mem. Internat., Am., Jacksonville bar assns., Fla. Bar, Am. Soc. Internat. Law, Am. Judicature Soc., Am. Legion, S.A.R., Sons Confederate Vets., English Speaking Union, Am. Trial Lawyers Assn., Am. Arbitration Assn. (arbitrator), Internat. Platform Assn., Am. Philatelic Soc., Com. of 100, Jacksonville C. of C., Phi Delta Theta, Delta Theta Phi. Republican. Conglist. Clubs: Capitol Hill (Washington); Republican, Metropolitan Dinner (officer, mem. orgn. com.) (Jacksonville, Fla.). Home: 6962 Almours Pl Jacksonville FL 32217 Office: Fla Nat Bank Jacksonville FL 32202

RAWSON, WILLIAM SHERARD, educator; b. Abbeville, S.C., Mar. 31, 1935; s. Clarence Weaver and Annie Sherard (Wilson) R.; B.S., Davidson Coll., 1956; M.A., Vanderbilt U., 1963; Ph.D., Duke, 1967; m. Joanne McBride, Sept. 12, 1964; children—Sherard Anne William Stewart. Mgmt. trainee Union Carbide Corp., Charlotte, N.C., 1956-59; asst. prof. econs. and bus. adminstrn. Shorter Coll., Rome, Ga., 1960-63; asst. prof. dept. econs. U. S.C., Columbia, 1967—. Grad. econs. fellow Duke, 1964-65. Mem. Am. Finance Assn., Am., So. econs. assns., Omicron Delta Epsilon, Sigma Alpha Epsilon. Presbyn. Home: 3214 Derereaux Rd Columbia SC 29205

RAY, CHARLES ALBERT, accountant; b. Ft. Worth, Dec. 26, 1935; s. Joseph Berry and Hattie (Kitchell) R.; B.B.A., N. Tex. State U., 1957; M.B.A., U. Houston, 1963; m. Patsy Grimes, Sept. 8, 1956; children— Bruce Edwin, Charles Keith. Jr. accountant Tenn. Gas Transmission Co., Houston, 1957-60; field agt. Internal Revenue Service, Houston and Ft. Worth, 1960-64; tax sr. Alexander Grant & Co., C.P.A.'s, Dallas, 1964-65; instr. accounting U. Tex., Arlington, 1965-67; accountant C.A. Ray, C.P.A., Arlington, 1966-70; partner Ray, Long & Co. C.P.A., 1970-71; prin. Charles A. Ray C.P.A., 1971-72; partner Ray, Hoyle, Kiblinger & Co., 1972—. Active Boy Scouts Am. Bd. dirs. YMCA, Arlington, 1970—, treas., 1971, 72. Mem. Tex. Soc. C.P.A.'s (dir. Ft. Worth chpt. 1971—), Am. Inst. C.P.A.'s. Rotarian. Baptist. Home: 2618 Brentwood Circle Arlington TX 76010 Office: 600 E Abram Arlington TX 76010

RAY, DEWITT TALMAGE, banker; b. Tex., Nov. 22, 1894; s. James Hooten and Louise (Miller) R.; student Am. Inst. Banking, Dallas, 1926, South Tex. Sch. Law, Houston, 1930-33, grad. sch. banking Rutgers U., 1939; m. Mary Adelia Harris, June 28, 1923; children—DeWitt Talmage, Marilyn Harris, Nancy Jane. Gen. v.p. Republic Nat. Bank of Dallas, 1954—; treas., dir. Guardian Savs. & Loan Assn., 1944—; chmn. bd., exec. com. Lomas & Nettleton Financial Corp.; finance com., dir. Pan Am. Sulphur Co.; dir. 1st Nat. Bank, Pueblo, Volk Bros. Co., Colo., Comml. Bank, Colorado Springs, Volk Realty Co., Exchange Nat. Bank, Colorado Springs. Dir. Trinity Improvement Assn. Treas. Tex. Heart Assn.; treas., exec. com. Dallas chpt. Am. Cancer Soc.; bd. dirs. Dallas Civic Theatre; mem. Greater Dallas Planning Com. Pres., trustee Meth. Hosp., Dallas. Mem. Dallas C. of C. (dir., chmn. budget, finance com.), Dallas Citizens Council, Dallas Symphony Soc. (dir.), Am. (fed. legislative com., v.p. for Tex. 1943-46), Tex. (pres. 1946-47) bankers assns., Assn. Res. City Bankers, Nat. Assn. Mfrs. (Southwestern regional adv. com.), Tex. State Hist. Assn., Dallas Clearing House Assn. (pres. 1948-49), Houston Fiduciary Assn. (pres. 1937-38). Methodist (steward). Mason (Shriner). Clubs: Brook Hollow Golf, Country, City, Athletic (Dallas). Home: 4215 Beverly Dr Dallas TX 75205 Office: Republic Nat Bank Bldg Dallas TX 75201

RAY, EDGAR WAYNE, newspaper editor; b. Macon, Ga., Apr. 9, 1911; s. Edgar Leonard and Ada Wayne (Massey) R.; student Mercer U., 1929-31; m. Mary Dee Smith, Mar. 9, 1931; children—Elizabeth Lynn, Edgar Wayne. Mem. sports dept. Macon Telegraph, 1925-31, sports editor, 1931-33; sports editor Tampa (Fla.) Times, 1933-35, mng. editor, 1935-49; exec. editor Orlando (Fla.) Sentinel-Star, 1949-53, Johnson City (Tenn.) Press-Chronicle, 1953; exec. editor San Antonio Express and News, 1953-58, editor, 1958-60; mng. editor Houston Press, 1960-64; mng. editor Memphis Press-Scimitar, 1964—. Former pres. Tampa Urban League; speaker racial amity. Active A.R.C., Community Chest, U.S.O. Bd. dirs. Salvation Army, United Fund; bd. govs. St. Mary's U.; past vice chmn., gov. Orange County (Fla.) Meml. Hosp. Named Outstanding Young Tampan, Tampa Jr. C. of C., 1943. Mem. Houston C. of C. (bd. dirs.) A.P. Mng. Editor's Assn., Fla. A.P. Assn. (past pres.), Tex. A.P. Mng. Editors, Fla. Daily Newspaper Assn. (past dir.), Tenn. Press Assn. (dir.), Tex. U.P. Internat. Assn. (past pres.), Sigma Delta Chi. Presbyn. (elder). Home: 287 N White Station Rd Memphis TN 38117 Office: 495 Union Av Memphis TN 38101

RAY, H(OSEA) M(ANFRED), U.S. atty.; b. Rienzi, Miss., Aug. 9, 1924; s. Thomas Henry and Isabelle (Dunlap) R.; LL.B., U. Miss., 1949, J.D., 1968; m. Merle Burt, Nov. 28, 1953; children—Howard Manfred, Mark Andrew. Admitted to Miss. bar, 1949; practiced law, Corinth, 1949-61; pros. atty. Alcorn County, Miss., 1956-57, 58-61; U.S. atty. No. Dist. Miss., Oxford, 1961—. Treas., dir. Corinth Machinery Co., Am. Sawmill Machinery Co., Corinth, 1957-58. Chmn. Corinth Alcorn County Airport Bd., 1959-61. Mem. Miss. Ho. of Reps., 1948-51, author Miss. Workmens' Compensation Act, 1948. Served with USAAF, 1943-45, with USAF, 1951-53. Recipient Young Man of Distinguished Service award Corinth Jr. C. of C., 1958. Mem. Miss. State Bar, Am., Fed. bar assns., Delta Sigma Pi, Sigma Chi. Democrat. Presbyn. Mason, Kiwanian (lt. gov., dir. Miss., La., W. Tenn. dist. 955). Home: Colonial Rd Oxford MS 38655 Office: 1107 Jefferson Av Oxford MS 38655

RAY, JACK LEROY, banker; b. Gadsden, Ala., Jan. 1, 1928; s. John L. and Mary Lou (Allday) R.; student Tenn. Mil. Inst., 1945; A.B., Duke, 1949; m. Lugenia Morgan, Feb. 17, 1949; children—John Richard, Harold Daniel, William Allen. Salesman, Dowd Press, Charlotte, N.C., 1949-50, Mut. Life Ins. Co. of N.Y., Protective Life, 1950-54; pres. Ray Constrn. Co., Gadsden, 1954—; pres., chmn. bd. 1st State Bank, Altoona, Ala., 1959—; vice chmn. bd., dir. Exchange Bank, Attalla, Ala.; pres., dir. Gadsden Corp., Attalla Trust Co.; vice chmn. bd., dir. Trustee Life Ins. Co., Gadsden. Mem. Am., Ala., Ind. bankers assns., Home Builders Assn. Etowah County (pres. 1957), Beta Theta Pi. Baptist. Lion (pres. Gadsden 1958-59). Home: 2917 Scenic Hwy Gadsden AL 35901 Office: 1st State Bank Altoona AL 35952

RAY, JOHN E., physician; b. Rienzi, Miss., 1922; M.D., Northwestern U., 1947. Intern Cook County Hosp., Chgo., 1946-47; fellow gen. surgery Ochsner Clinic, New Orleans, 1950-53; chief resident in surgery Conway Meml. Hosp., Monroe, La., 1953-54; staff surgeon Found Hosp.; vis. surgeon Charity Hosp.; clin. asso. prof. surgery Tulane U. Served to capt. M.C., AUS, 1947-49. Diplomate Am. Bd. Colon and Rectal Surgery. Fellow A.C.S.; mem. A.M.A., Am. Proctologic Soc. (sec. 1968—, pres. elect), Southeastern Surg. Congress, So. Med. Assn. Address: 1514 Jefferson Hwy New Orleans LA 70121*

RAY, JOHN WILLIAM, football coach; b. Detroit, June 4, 1926; s. Marion A. Ray; student Notre Dame U., 1944-47; A.B., Olivet Coll., Mich., 1950; m. Barbara Fuller, June 18, 1945; children—Jeff, Kathy, Debora, Chris. Coach, Sturgis (Mich.) High Sch., 1950-51, Three Rivers (Mich.) High Sch., 1952-54; asst. coach U. Detroit, 1955-58; head coach John Carroll U., Cleve., 1959-63; asst. coach Notre Dame (Ind.) U., 1964-66, asst. head coach, 1967-69; now football coach U. Ky. Hon. chmn. St. Joseph County Heart Assn., 1967. Served with AUS. Mem. Nat. Coaches Athletic Assn. Club: Touchdown. Contbr. articles to nat. periodicals. Address: Univ. Ky Lexington KY 40506

RAY, MOSES ALEXANDER, dentist; b. Clinton, N.C., Sept. 25, 1920; s. Moses and Carrie Estelle (Beamon) R.; B.S., Shaw U., 1941; D.D.S., Howard U., 1945; m. Helen Bettina Jones, June 15, 1944; children— Shelia Anne, Ernest Alexander. Pvt. practice dentistry, Tarboro, N.C., 1946—; mem. staff Edgecombe Gen. Hosp., Tarboro. Pres., founder Panola Heights Housing Devel. Corp., Inc., 1970—; dir. Nash Edgecombe Econ. Devel. Corp., Tarboro Edgecombe Econ. Devel. Corp. Pres., East Tarboro Citizen's League, 1965—; councilman, Tarboro, 1967—; mem. N.C. Gov.'s Council Occupational Health, 1968-71. Trustee Edgecombe Econ. Devel. Corp. Served with USAF, 1951-53. Mem. N.C. Dental Soc., Am. Dental Assn., Omega Psi Phi. Democrat. Baptist. Mason. Home: 704 Panola St Tarboro NC 27886 Office: 409 Panola St Tarboro NC 27886

RAY, ROBERT SIDNEY, physician; b. Noonday, Tex., July 1, 1922; s. Lewis Edwin and Nellie (Armstrong) R.; certificate graduation, Tyler Jr. Coll., 1941; student U. Tex., 1941-42; B.A., U. Colo., 1948; M.D., U. Tex. at Galveston, 1954; m. Nancy Frances Waits, Apr. 21, 1945; children—Robert Sidney, Sally Louise, Gregory Francis. Intern, Brackenridge Hosp., Austin, 1954-55; resident in radiology Bexar County Hosp., San Antonio, 1969-71; practice gen. medicine, Seguin, Tex., 1956-69; staff radiologist Guadalupe Valley Hosp., Seguin, 1972—. Pres., sec. MedSur, Inc., Seguin, 1959-69; sec. Placid Heights, Inc., Seguin, 1966—. Chmn., Seguin Home Rule Charter Commn., 1971. Mem. Seguin Ind. Sch. Dist., 1966-72. Served with USNR, 1942-45. Mem. A.M.A., Guadalupe County, Tex. med. assns., Alamo, Tex., Am. acads. family practice, Radiol. Soc. N.Am., Am. Coll. Radiology, Seguin-Guadalupe County C. of C. (1st v.p. 1965). Home: 702 E College St Seguin TX 78155 Office: 702 E College St Seguin TX 78155

RAY, WILLIAM I(SAAC), JR., newspaper exec.; b. Johnson City, Tenn., May 31, 1914; s. William Isaac and Mabel Scarlett (Essensa) R.; B.J., U. Ga., 1935; m. Katherine Elizabeth Knox, Feb. 8, 1946. With Johnson City (Tenn.) Chronicle, Staff-News, 1931-35; editor, bus. mgr. The Red and Black, U. Ga., 1934-35; sports writer Atlanta, 1935-39, asst. sports editor, 1937-38, asst. news editor, 1938-39; promotion mgr. Atlanta Jour., 1940, asst. sports editor, 1940, news editor, 1946, asst. mng. editor, 1947-50, mng. editor, 1950-60; exec. editor, The Atlanta Jour., Constitution, 1960-67; v.p. Atlanta Newspapers, Inc., 1963-69, asst. to pres., 1968-70, exec. v.p., gen. mgr., 1970—, dir., 1970—, Mem. civilian adv. bd. 3d U.S. Army; mem. bd. mgrs. Atlanta YMCA; juror Pulitzer Prize, 1968-69. Served as maj. CID, AUS, 1943-46. Mem. Sigma Delta Chi, Alpha Lambda Tau, Omicron Delta Kappa, Scabbard and Blade. Presbyn. Clubs: Capital City (Atlanta); Nat. Press (Washington). Home: 1882 Anjaco Rd NW Atlanta GA 30309 Office: Box 4689 Atlanta GA 30302

RAY, WILLIAM KIRK, hosp. exec.; b. Ackerman, Miss., Aug. 21, 1936; s. Jessie Elmer and Nevie Mae (Oswalt) R.; B.A., Miss. State U., 1963; m. Charlotte Ann Carroll, Nov. 28, 1963; children—Robin Ray, Keri Ray. Asst. adminstr. Choctaw County Hosp., Ackerman, 1960-63; exec. dir. Coaldoma County Hosp., Clarksdale, Miss., 1964—. Vice chmn. Miss. Comprehensive Health Planning Commn., 1971—. Served with USMCR, 1955-59. Recipient Distinguished Service award Jr. C. of C., 1968-69. Mem. Miss. Hosp. Assn. (dir.), C. of C. (dir.), Am. Coll. Hosp. Adminstrs. Mason, Rotarian (v.p. 1970-71). Home: 281 Westover Dr Clarksdale MS 38614 Office: PO 1218 Hospital Dr Clarksdale MS 38614

RAYBURN, WILLIE RAY WRENN, educator; b. Nashville, Mar. 16, 1927; d. William Anderson and Ethel (Ray) Wrenn; B.S., George Peabody Coll. Tchrs., 1948, M.A., 1949; postgrad. Mont. State Coll., 1961; m. Mathew McCauley Rayburn, Sept. 11, 1951; 1 son, William Elbert. Instr., George Peabody Coll. Tchrs., 1948-49, summers, 1949, 50, 62; instr. Ark. Jr. Coll., Beebe, 1949-50; asso. prof. sci. Martin Coll., Pulaski, Tenn., 1950-69; asso. prof. phys. scis. Aquinas Jr. Coll., Nashville, 1969—. Tenn. chmn. Health Edn. Commn. Fellow Tenn. Acad. Sci.; mem. Tenn. Jr. Acad. Sci. (regional adviser), Am. Chem. Soc., A.A.A.S., Phi Theta Kappa (adviser), Kappa Delta Pi, Beta Beta Beta. Club: The Magazine (pres. 1956-58). Home: Route 1 Box 200 A Thompson Station TN 37179 Office: Aquinas Jr Coll 4210 Harding Rd Nashville TN 37205

RAYMER, ELWYN CARLOS, religious editor; b. Louisville, Apr. 17, 1935; s. Oscar and Edna (Christian) R.; B.A., Georgetown Coll., 1957; M.S.M., So. Sem. Sch. Sacred Music, Louisville, 1959; m. Flora Elizabeth Jacobs, Feb. 12, 1954; children—Kimbel Lee, Craig O. Minister of Music, First Bapt. Ch., Arkadelphia, Ark., 1959-63, First Bapt. Ch., Waco, Tex., 1963-66; instr. music dept. Baylor U., 1963-66; editor, youth-adult music Baptist S.S. Bd., Nashville, 1966—. Bd. dirs. Community Concerts Assn., Nashville; mem. exec. council So. Bapt. Ch. Music Conf. Republican. Lion. Contbr. articles in field to profl. jours. Home: 688 Brewer Dr Nashville TN 37211 Office: 127 9th Av N Nashville TN 37203

RAYMER, JACK MILTON, aerospace co. exec.; b. Chgo., Mar. 6, 1928; s. Milton Peter and Dorothy (McCorkhill) R.; B.S., U. Ill., 1951; m. Thelma Mae Dowler, Nov. 8, 1952; children—Patricia, Carolyn, Diane, Cheryl. Research engr. Wright-Paterson AFB, Dayton, O., 1951-52; with Avco Lycoming, 1954—, chief materials engring., Stratford, Conn., 1962-66, mgr. materials engring., 1966, mgr. engring., Charleston, S.C., 1966-68, dir. engring., 1968-71; mgr. advanced products Large Gas Turbine Operation, Gen. Electric Co., Greenville, S.C., 1971—. Mem. USAF-Am. Soc. for Metals Joint Com. for Writing and Pub. Aerospace Design Handbook, 1965—. Bd. visitors Clemson U., 1968—. Served with AUS, 1952-54. Methodist (chmn. finance and stewardship commn. 1967-71, pres. adult Sunday sch. 1967-68, mem. adminstrv. bd. 1967-71, mem. chancel choir 1966—). Home: 401 Foxcroft Rd Greenville SC 29607 Office: Gen Electric Co Large Gas Turbine Operation Box 648 Greenville SC 29602

RAYMOND, JOHN FRANCIS, editor, author; b. Findlay, O., Sept. 25, 1925; s. John F. and Cathleen (Cunniff) R.; A.A., Belmont Abbey Coll., 1950; B.A., U. N.C., 1952; m. Anne Stewart Raymond, Aug. 31, 1958. Sports editor Gainesville (Ga.) Daily Times, 1952-54; reporter Macon (Ga.) Telegraph, 1954-60; staff artist WMAZ-TV, Macon, 1960-64; book rev. editor Atlanta Jour., 1964—. Served with USNR, 1943-48. Author: Buffalo River, 1963; The Marvelous March of Jean Francois, 1965. Home: 1439 Stephens Dr NE Atlanta GA 30329 Office: 10 Forsyth St Atlanta GA 30302

RAYMOND, JOHN MARSHALL, JR., utility exec.; b. Boston, Nov. 19, 1923; s. John Marshall and Grace Huntington (Teel) R.; student Universite de Grenoble, France, 1945-46, Peterhouse, Cambridge U., 1946-47; B.A., Princeton, 1949. Asst. advt. staff Washington Gas Light Co., 1949-57, asst. advt. mgr., 1957-60, asst. to dir. sales, 1960-61, mgr. community affairs, 1961-64, dir. pub. relations, 1964—. Dep. comdr. Nat. Capital Wing, Civil Air Patrol, 1951-61; dir., mem. exec. com. A.R.C., Washington, 1969—. Served to maj. AUS, 1942-45; maj. Res. Decorated Bronze Star; recipient Golden Eagle award of Council Internat. Non-theatrical Events, 1966; Gold Cup, Australian Cine Soc., 1965. Mem. Am. Gas Assn. (chmn. com. 1968—), Pub. Relations Soc. Am., Met. Washington Bd. Trade. Republican. Home: 737 11th St NW Washington DC 20001 Office: 1100 H St NW Washington DC 20005

RAYMOND, RICHARD EVERETT, utility co. exec.; b. Montclair, N.J., Sept. 5, 1915; s. William Everett and Louise (Cook) R.; B.S., U. Fla., 1939; m. Betty Sue Elder, July 2, 1949; children—Ellen, William. With Fla. Power Corp., St. Petersburg, 1939-41, 46—, chief engr. operations, 1964, v.p. system operations, 1964-69, sr. v.p. system operations, 1969-70, sr. v.p. system engring. and operations, 1970—, also dir.; dir. Suncoast City Bank St. Petersburg, City Bank and Trust Co. St. Petersburg. Mem. indsl.-constrn. div. United Way Pinellas County Campaign Cabinet, 1972. Mem. exec. bd., Sec. Com. 100, Pinellas County, Inc. Served from 1st lt. to maj. arty. AUS, 1941-46; ETO. Registered profl. engr., Fla. Mem. Nat. Soc. Profl. Engrs., Am. Nuclear Soc., I.E.E.E. (sr.), Edison Electric Inst. (past chmn. safety subcom.), Southeastern Electric Exchange (vice chmn. engring. and operation div. 1968-69, chmn. 1970), Am. Right of Way Assn. (past chmn. utility liaison com.), St. Petersburg Area C. of C., Newcomen Soc. N. Am., Oil Users Assn. (dir.). Methodist (ofcl. bd. 1964—). Rotarian. Clubs: St. Petersburg Yacht, Lakewood; Commerce Pinellas County. (dir.). Home: 3935 Bayshore Blvd NE St Petersburg FL 33703 Office: PO Box 14042 St Petersburg FL 33733

RAYMOND, STAN, broadcasting exec. Pres. WAOK, Atlanta. Office: 110 Edgewood Av NE Atlanta GA 30303*

RAYNOR, STANLEY, govt. ofcl.; b. N.Y.C., Apr. 5, 1924; s. Morris and Fan (Spinner) R.; student Bklyn. Coll., 1941-43, Columbia, 1943-44; D.D.S., N.Y.U., 1948; m. Muriel Goldstein, July 3, 1948; children—Gene Seth, Jill Lesley, Elise Mara. With USPHS, Bur. Prisons, 1948—, dental officer Fed. Correctional Inst., Ashland, Ky., 1948—, dental officer Fed. Reformatory, Chillicothe, O., 1952-56, sr. dental officer Fed. Penitentiary, Lewisburg, Pa., 1956-64, chief dental services, dental dir. Bur. Prisons, Washington, 1964—, ed. Health Services Newsletter, 1961—. Served with USNR, 1941-46. Recipient Meritorious Service medal USPHS, 1969. Mem. Am. Dental Assn., Commd. Officers Assn. USPHS, Clin. Soc. USPHS, Alpha Omega. Contbr. articles to dental jours. Established Central Dental Lab. for tng. dental technicians. Home: 7420 Leahy Rd New Carrollton MD 20784 Office: Bureau of Prisons US Public Health Service 101 Indiana Av Washington DC 20537

RAYNSFORD, ROBERT WAYNE, economist; b. Neptune, N.J., July 13, 1935; s. Robert Wayne and Maud Marshall (Mason) R.; B.A. in History (Tyng scholar), Williams Coll., 1957; M.A. in Econs., Harvard, 1963, Ph.D., 1966; m. Irmela Ellen Erdmut Reichelt, Apr. 23, 1964; 1 son, Anthony Wayne. Economist, Metallgesellschaft AC, Frankfurt Main, West Germany, 1963-66; economist Econ. Devel. Adminstrn., Commerce Dept., Washington, 1966-68; economist Office Mgmt. and Budget, 1968-72, asst. chief statis. policy div., 1972—. Served with USAF, 1957-60. Woodrow Wilson fellow, 1960. Mem. Am. Econ. Assn., Am. Statis. Assn., Phi Beta Kappa, Delta Psi. Contbr. articles profl. jours. Home: 3850 Tunlaw Rd Washington DC 20007 Office: Statistical Policy Div US Office Mgmt and Budget New Executive Office Bldg Room 10208 Washington DC 20503

RAYSON, JACK HENRY, educator; b. Gonzales, Tex., July 22, 1931; s. Jack Henry and Florence M. (Zint) R.; student, U. Tex., 1949-53, D.D.S., 1957; m. Donna Marie Thornton, Oct. 19, 1957; children—Susan, Scott, David. Pvt. practice dentistry, San Antonio, 1961-62; asst. prof. prosthodontics Baylor U. Coll. Dentistry, Dallas, 1962-66; asst. prof. prosthodontics U. Ky. Coll. Dentistry, Lexington, 1966-69; mem. faculty La. State U. Sch. Dentistry, New Orleans, 1969—, asso. prof., head dept. prosthodontics, 1969—. Cons. VA Hosp., New Orleans, 1970—, Biloxi, Miss., 1970—. Served with USAF, 1957-61. Mem. Am., New Orleans, La. dental assns., Am. Prosthodontics Soc., Southeastern Acad. Prosthodontics, Omicron Kappa Upsilon, Xi Psi Phi. Home: 5012 Tartan Dr Metairie LA 70003 Office: 1190 Florida Av New Orleans LA 70119

RAYWID, ALAN, lawyer; b. Washington, Aug. 9, 1930; s. Leo and Vivian (Thrift) R.; A.B., Duke, 1952; LL.B., U. Mich., 1957. Admitted to D.C. bar, 1957; trial atty. Dept. Justice, Washington, 1957-66; asso. Nixon, Mudge, Rose, Gurthrie, Alexander & Mitchell, Washington, 1966-67; partner Cole, Zylstra, Raywid, Washington, 1967—. Pres., Community Assistance, Washington, 1967—; chmn. Duke Alumni Adv. Admissions Com., Washington, 1964—. Nat. chmn. Cable TV Campaign for Humphrey/Muskie, 1968. Served with USNR, 1952-54. Unitarian. Home: 4535 Windom Pl Washington DC 20016 Office: 2011 Eye St NW Washington DC 20006

RAZZANO, MICHAEL RICHARD, dentist; b. Patchogue, N.Y., Sept. 11, 1939; s. Vincent M. and Mary F. (Fedumn) R.; B.S., U. Fla., 1962; D.D.S., U. Md., 1966; m. Georgia L. Hodges, Sept. 7, 1962; children—Lisa, Michael, Vincent. Pvt. practice dentistry, Ocala, Fla., 1969—; mem. staff, cons. Monroe Meml. Hosp., Ocala. Chmn., Walk for Mankind, Fla. Jr. C. of C., 1970; mem. Marion County Gov.'s Adv. Com., 1971-74; regional coordinator Project Concern, 1970—. Served with USPHS, 1966-69. Recipient Harry E. Kelsey award, Harry B. Schwartz award U. Md., 1966. Mem. Am., Fla. dental assns., Marion County Dental Soc., Royal Soc. Health, Jr. C. of C. (Tommy Thompson award 1971, pres. 1971—), C. of C., Psi Omega, Omicron Kappa Upsilon. Elk. Contbr. articles to profl. pubs. Home: 4818 SE 7th Place Ocala FL 32670 Office: 1301 SW 1st Av Ocala FL 32670

REA, JOHN EDWARD, JR., engring. firm exec.; b. Los Angeles, Mar. 17, 1917; s. John Edward and Catherine (Wagner) R.; B.S. in Civil Engring., U. N.M., 1941; m. Reva Alka, Sept. 7, 1940; children—Nancy Lee (Mrs. D. Lee Jacobs), John Edward III, Thomas H. Hydraulics engr. U.S. Bur. Reclamation, Oklahoma City, 1941-42, 46-47; stress and liason engr. Douglas Aircraft Co., Oklahoma City, 1942-44; engr. Phillips & Stong Engring. Co., Oklahoma City, 1947-48; partner, engr. Rea Engring. Co., Oklahoma City, 1948-62; pres. Rea Engring. & Assos., Inc., Oklahoma City, 1962—, Rea Bignell, Fischer & Moore, architects, engrs., 1969—; dir. Southwestern Bank & Trust Co., Oklahoma City. Mem. exec. bd. Last Frontier council Boy Scouts Am., 1969-70. Served to lt. (j.g.) USNR, 1944-46. Registered profl. engr., Okla. Mem. Cons. Engrs. Council Okla. (pres. 1966), Pub. Works Council Okla. (pres. 1965), Nat., Okla. socs. profl. engrs., Am. Pub. Works Assn., Am. Water Works Assn., Kappa Sigma. Republican. Episcopalian. Rotarian (South Oklahoma City pres. 1963). Home: 3816 Waverly Ct Norman OK 73069 Office: 1133 SW 74th St Oklahoma City OK 73139

REA, JOHN WILLIAM, sch. supt.; b. Randolph, Miss., Apr. 24, 1909; s. James Thomas and Modena (Gardner) R.; B.S., Ark. State U., 1949; M.Ed., U. Miss., 1951; m. Zola Lucille Beshears, Jan. 11, 1937; children—Patricia (Mrs. Joe Ray Price), William L. Prin., Center Elementary Sch., Wynne, Ark., 1941-48, McCrory (Ark.) High Sch., 1948-55, Crawfordsville (Ark.) High Sch., 1955-56; supt. Gosnell Sch., Blytheville, Ark., 1956—. Mem. Ark Edn. Assn., Am., Ark. assns. sch. administrs., Nat. Sch. Bd. Assn. Methodist. Mason (Shriner); mem. Order Eastern Star, Kiwanian (bd. dirs.). Home: Route 4 Box 565 Blytheville AR 72315

READ, A. LOUIS, broadcasting exec.; b. New Orleans Oct. 12, 1914; A.B., Loyola U., 1937; m. Nathalie Doris Owings; children—Michael Owings, Susan Louise (Mrs. E. Douglas Johnson, Jr.), Carolyn Mary (Mrs. Edward Simmons), Stephen Louis. Mem. sales staff Blue Plate Foods, 1937-38; comml. mgr. radio sta. WWL, 1938-41, 45-47; advt. dir. Wembley, Inc., 1947-48; gen. mgr. WABB, Mobile, Ala., 1948-49; commr. mgr. WDSU, WDSU-TV, New Orleans, 1949-65, pres., 1965—; exec. v.p., dir. Royal St. Corp.; v.p., treas. Interchange Realty Co., Inc., operators Oakwood Shopping Center; v.p. Royal St. Investment Corp.; exec. v.p., dir. Starwood Land Corp., Aspen, Colo.; dir. Bank New Orleans. Chmn. NBC-TV Affiliates, 1963-67; chmn. bd. TV Stations, Inc., 1968-69; dir. TV Bur. Advt., 1958-62, chmn., 1961; mem. exec. com. U.S. Broadcasters for UN; chmn. S. Atlantic dist. Broadcast Pioneers Campaign Fund. Mem. Nat. Adv. Council on Supplemental Centers and Services, 1968-70; mem. com. on communications U.S. Catholic Conf., 1968; sr. v.p. Met. Area Com. New Orleans, mem. exec. com., 1967—; mem. task force on transp. Goals for La. program; mem. policy and information com. Council for

Better La.; mem. community action and crime prevention com. La. Commn. Law Enforcement and Adminstrn. Criminal Justice. Charter mem. Goals Found. Met. New Orleans; past trustee Greater New Orleans Area United Fund, gen. campaign chmn.; mem. exec. com. New Orleans Tourist and Convention Commn.; bd. dirs. Better Bus. Bur., Met. New Orleans Safety Council, Internat. Trade Mart, Internat. House, Christopher Homes, Catholic Human Relations Commn., Adult Edn. Center, Internat. Radio and TV Found.; mem. adv. council Loyola Coll. Bus. Adminstrn.; bd. govs. Tulane Med. Center; mem. pub. relations com. U. Notre Dame; bd. lay regents Xavier U., New Orleans; trustee St. Mary's Dominican Coll., 1965-71. Served as lt. comdr. USNR, World War II. Named La. Broadcaster of Yr. La. Assn. Broadcasters, 1968; recipient F. Edward Hebert award as outstanding alumnus Jesuit High Sch., 1968. Mem. Navy League, Nat. Assn. Broadcasters (chmn. TV bd. 1971-72, chmn. TV information com., chmn. bd. radio advt. bur.), Soc. TV Pioneers. Office: 520 Royal St New Orleans LA 70130

READ, CLARK PHARES, educator; b. Ft. Worth, Feb. 4, 1921; s. Clark P. and Helen (Chaudoin) R.; student Tulane U., 1943-45, U. Tex., 1945-46; B.A., M.A., Rice U., 1948, Ph.D., 1950; m. Leota A. Wolff, Oct. 23, 1944; children—Jo Hanna (Mrs. Stephen S. Tobias), Victoria Helen, Thomas Jefferson, Cathleen Eliot. AEC fellow Rice U., 1949; asst. prof. zoology U. Cal. at Los Angeles, 1950-54; asso. prof. pub. health Johns Hopkins, 1954-59; prof. biology, chmn. dept. Rice U., 1959—; prof. epidemiology Baylor U. Sch. Medicine, 1961-65; research prof. Tex. A. and M. U., 1963—. Chmn. tropical medicine study sect. USPHS, 1960-65. Chmn. Houston br. Am. Civil Liberties Union, 1968-70. Mem. adv. bd. Tex. Sch. Pub. Health, 1967—, Martin L. King Found., 1968—; trustee Marine Biol. Lab., 1966-70. Served with USNR, 1941-45. Guggenheim fellow, 1959-60 USPHS grantee, 1954-58. Mem. Am. Soc. Parsitologists (Henry B. Ward medal 1959), Soc. Gen. Physiologists, Am. Soc. Tropical Medicine, Soc. Protozoologists, Sigma Xi. Democrat. Unitarian. Author: Introduction to Parasitology, 1961, Parasitism and Symbiology, 1968; also sci. papers. Home: 1819 Dunstan Rd Houston TX 77005

READ, DUNCAN HICKS, bank dir.; b. Rye, N.Y., Oct. 30, 1896; s. William Augustus and Caroline Hicks (Seamen) R.; A.B., Harvard, 1919; m. Aldona Smoluchowska, Aug. 8, 1932; children—Pamela (Mrs. J. Gregory Peck), Caroline (Mrs. J. Wilbur Smith). With Dillon Read & Co., N.Y.C., 1920-32; with Fiduciary Trust Co., N.Y.C., 1932-43, dir., 1946—; pres. Middleburg Nat. Bank (Va.) 1946-58, dir., 1946—; dep. adminstr. Small Bus. Adminstrn., Washington, 1958-60. Lectr. astronomy. Served with USN, 1917-18; to capt. USNR, 1941-46. Address: Box 43 Route 2 Middleburg VA 22117

READ, EMERSON BRACKETT, real estate broker, ins. agt.; b. N.Y.C., Aug. 9, 1925; s. Thomas C. and Helen E. (Emerson) R.; student U. Pitts., 1944, Coll. Charleston, 1946; B.S. in Civil Engring., The Citadel, 1950; m. Doris E. Boyd, Dec. 2, 1950; children—Anne Standish, Elizabeth Emerson, Susan Lee, Emerson Brackett. Proprietor, Read & Read, realtors, Charleston, S.C., 1947-50, 65—; salesman Carleton Dooley, realtors, Miami, Fla., 1950-54, gen. sales mgr., 1954-55, sales exec. v.p., 1955-56; sales sr. asso. Keyes Co., Miami, 1956-61, exec. v.p., gen. sales mgr., 1961-65. Lectr. real estate exchanging and taxation U. S.C. Realtors Inst. Served with USAAF, 1943-45. Mem. Am. Legion, Charleston Real Estate Bd. (pres. 1972), Nat. Assn. Real Estate Bds., Charleston Bd. Ins. Underwriters, Nat. Assn. Ind. Fee Appraisers (sr. mem.), S.A.R., S.C.V., Huegenot Soc. Episcopalian (past vestryman). Club: Carolina Yacht (Charleston). Home: 19 King St Charleston SC 29401 Office: 37 Broad St Charleston SC 29401

READ, LOUIS JOHN, physician; b. Richmond, Va., Apr. 7, 1922; s. Arthur A. and Mary E. (Parchini) R.; student Lynchburg Coll., 1950-52; B.S., Med. Coll. Va., 1955, M.D., 1956; m. Jane Watkins, Sept. 4, 1954; children—Louis John, Cynthia J., Robert W. Intern, Meml. Hosp., Danville, Va., gen. practice medicine, Lynchburg, Va., 1957—; mem. active staff Va. Bapt. Hosp.; chief medicine, mem. adv. com. emergency room Lynchburg (Va.) Gen. Hosp. Med. examiner Lynchburg Tng. Sch. and Hosp. Active YMCA; mem. com. Lynchburg Drug Abuse Program, 1970-72. Served with AUS, 1942. Mem. Am. Acad. Family Practice, Nat. Med. Examiners, So., Tri-State med. assns., Va. Soc. Medicine, Piedmont, Lynchburg acads. medicine, Piedmont Heart Assn., Central Va. Tb Assn., Lynchburg C. of C., Chi Beta Phi, Theta Kappa Psi. Episcopalian (vestry 1970—). Elk, Lion. Club: Boonsboro Country (Lynchburg). Home: 3616 Sherwood Pl Lynchburg VA 24502 Office: 4847 Fort Av Lynchburg VA 24502

READ, WILLIE HAROLD, univ. adminstr.; b. Central City, Ky., Apr. 24, 1908; s., Clemon Thompson and Willie Mae (Brown) R.; B.S.C., U. Tenn., 1930; M.B.A., Northwestern U., 1935; m. Virgie Lee Lewis, Oct. 20, 1934; 1 dau., Bobby Jo (Mrs. B. J. Jones). Mem. faculty U. Tenn., 1930—, prof. accounting, 1946—, exec. asst. to pres., 1959—, v.p. finance, 1961—; lectr. accounting Northwestern U., 1940-41; finance and accounting cons., 1932—. Bd. dirs., pres. Univ. Concerts. Served to col. AUS, 1942-46. Decorated Legion of Merit. C.P.A., Tenn. Mem. Am. Inst. C.P.A.'s (editorial bd. Jour. Accounting), Tenn. Soc. C.P.A.'s, Am. Accounting Assn., Phi Kappa Phi, Beta Gamma Sigma, Pi Kappa Phi, Delta Sigma Pi, Omicron Delta Kappa. Episcopalian (vestry). Rotarian. Author: Accounting Manual for Tennessee Counties, 1938; Local Government Accounting, 1940; Minimum Accounting Standards for Tennessee Municipalities, 1940; Manual for Accounts for Tennessee Municipalities (with W. R. Snodgrass), 1951. Home: 2024 E Velmetta Circle Knoxville TN 37920

REAGAN, BARBARA BENTON (MRS. SYDNEY CHANDLER REAGAN, JR.), educator; b. San Antonio, May 31, 1920; d. Loren William and Cora (Martin) Benton; student Mary Baldwin Coll., 1937-38; B.S. with honors in Home Econs., U. Tex., 1941; M.A. in Statistics, Am. U., 1946; Ferguson fellow Harvard, 1947-49; M.A. in Econs., Harvard, 1949, Ph.D. in Econs., 1952; m. Sydney Chandler Reagan, Jr.; children—Patricia Benton, Sydney Chandler III. Home economist Bur. Home Econs., U.S. Dept. Agr., Washington, 1942, agrl. economist Farmers Home Adminstrn., Cin. and Washington, 1943-44; agrl. economist farm population and rural welfare Bur. Agrl. Econs., Washington, 1945-47; sr. project leader Agrl. Research Service, 1949-55; prof. home mgmt. and family econs. research Tex. Woman's U., Denton, 1959-66, mem. grad. council, 1960-66; prof. econs. So. Meth. U., Dallas, 1968—. Mem. agrl. econs. research adv. com. U.S. Dept. Agr., 1965-70; mem. adv. com. Agrl. Policy Inst., N.C. State U., 1965-69; mem. Nat. Adv. Food and Drug Council, 1968-71; mem. agrl. adv. com. to bd. dirs. and pres. Tex. A. and M. U., 1967-69. Mem. adv. bd. YWCA, So. Meth. U., 1960-72; bd. dirs. Women for Change, 1971—, League for Ednl. Advancement in Dallas, 1972—. Named Outstanding Tchr., So. Meth. U., 1972; recipient Outstanding Univ. Service award So. Meth. U., 1972. Mem. Am. Econs. Assn. (mem. com. status of women in econs. 1972—), Am. Statis. Assn., Am. (program of work com. 1961-64), Tex. (chmn. family econs. and home mgmt. sect. 1960-62; v.p. 1961-62; treas. 1962-64) home econs. assns., Southwestern Social Sci. Assn., Am. Assn. U. Profs., Tex. Agrl. Workers Assn. (dir. 1961-63; exec. com., program com. 1961-63), P.E.O., Mortar Bd., Orange Jackets, Phi Beta Kappa, Omicron Nu, Kappa Alpha Theta. Methodist (ofcl. bd. 1952-53). Club: University Women's of Southern Methodist University (v.p. Dallas 1962-63). Contbr. articles to profl. jours. Home: 6815 Prestonshire Lane Dallas TX 75225

REAGAN, RAWLEIGH TERRELL, constrn. co. exec.; b. Charleston, S.C., May 2, 1942; s. Royce Jennings and Ruby Pauline (Smith) R.; B.A., Baylor U., 1963; B.S., U. Tex., 1966. Vice pres. R.J. Reagan Co., Inc., Waco, Tex., 1960—; project engr. R.M.K.-B.R.J., Manila, Philippines, 1966-69; pres. Stahr & Gregory, Inc., Temple, Tex., 1969—; pres. Republic Roofing Corp., Austin, Tex., 1970—, Air Systems Engring., 1972—; v.p. Holley Reagan Constrn. Co., Waco. Pres. bd. dirs. Temple Civic Theatre. Recipient Cost Reduction award Dept. Navy, 1969; named Outstanding Civitan, 1971. Mem. Am. Inst. Physics, Am. Math. Assn., Am. Soc. M.E., Am. Soc. Archtl. Engrs., Am. Soc. C.E. Republican. Mem. Ch. of Christ. Club: Civitan (Temple). Home: 1300 N 11th Temple TX 76501 Office: Box 186 Temple TX 76501

REAGAN, SYDNEY CHANDLER, JR., educator, economist; b. Ft. Smith, Ark., Jan. 7, 1916; s. Sydney Chandler and Ollie (Wood) R.; B.B.A., U. Tex., 1937, J.D., 1941; M. Pub. Adminstrn., Harvard, 1949, Ph.D., 1954; m. Barbara Ruth Benton, June 8, 1940; children—Patricia, Sydney III. Economist, statistician U.S. Dept. Agr., Washington, 1941-55; prof. real estate and regional sci., chmn. real estate and regional sci. dept., dir. Inst. Urban and Environmental Studies. So. Meth. U., Dallas, 1955—. Econ. cons., gen. counsel Southwestern Peanut Shellers Assn., 1955—. Mem. Am. Econ. Assn., Regional Sci. Assn., Am. Farm Econ. Assn., Southwestern Social Sci. Assn., Nat. Bus. Economists Assn., State Bar Tex., Dallas Real Estate Bd. (hon.), Am. Real Estate and Urban Econs. Assn. Club: Dallas Economists. Contbr. articles to profl. jours. Home: 6815 Prestonshire Lane Dallas TX 75225

REAMS, WILLIAM DINWIDDIE, JR., judge; b. Culpeper, Va., Apr. 24, 1929; s. William Dinwiddie and Flora (Hudson) R.; student U. Md., 1948-49; B.A., U. Va., 1955, LL.B., 1958; m. Nancy Jane Walker, Aug. 6, 1955; children—William D. III, Laura Daniel, Gilbert Walker. Admitted to Va. bar, 1958; commonwealth atty. Culpeper County, Culpeper, 1958-68; judge Culpeper County Ct., 1968—. Mem. bd. dirs. Culpeper County Soc. Crippled Children and Adults, 1967—. Served with USMC, 1950-52. Mem. Culpeper Bar Assn. (pres. 1968). Mason, Kiwanian (dir. 1969—). Home: RFD 1 Box 464 Culpeper VA 22701 Office: W Davis St Culpeper VA 22701

REAMY, RODNEY WADSWORTH, utility exec.; b. Potomac Mills, Va., June 4, 1911; s. Charles J. and Frances (Dickinson) R.; student William and Mary Coll., 1928-29, Strayer Bus. Coll., Washington, 1930-31; m. Ada May Elrod, Nov. 25, 1934. With Washington Gas Light Co., 1931—, asst. sec., 1957-64, sec., 1964—. Bd. dirs. Washington YMCA, 1967—, Washington United Givers Fund, 1967—. Recipient Distinguished Service award United Givers Fund, 1967. Mem. Am. Gas Assn., Am. Soc. Corporate Secs., Met. Washington Bd. Trade, Mantua Citizens Assn. (past pres.). Presbyn. Elk, Lion (dir. Washington Hosts club). Home: 8913 Colesbury Pl Fairfax VA 22030

REAP, CHARLES AUGUSTUS, JR., dentist; b. Albemarle, N.C., Nov. 24, 1931; s. Charles Augustus and Mildred (Bostian) R.; student Duke, 1948-51, Catawba Coll., 1953-54; D.D.S., U. N.C. Sch. Dentistry, 1958; m. Betty Efird Taylor, May 6, 1956; children—Ellen, Cynthia, Linda, Charles, III, Hunter. Clin. instr. U. N.C., Chapel Hill, 1958-59; pvt. practice dentistry, Chapel Hill, 1958—; clinician various dental groups, 1964—. Pres. bd. dirs. YMCA; bd. dirs. N.C. Cancer Soc. Served with USAF, 1951-53. Named City Father of Year, Chapel Hill C. of C., 1968. Mem. Orange-Durham (pres. 1969), 3d Dist. N.C. (v.p. 1971) dental socs., Jr. C. of C. (pres. 1967-68). Methodist (mem. ofcl. bd. 1962-65). Rotarian (treas. 1970-71, sec. 1971-72). Club: Civitan (v.p. 1963-64) (Chapel Hill). Author: Handbook for Dental Secretaries, Assistants and Hygienists, 1973. Contbr. articles to profl. jours. Home: 2305 Honeysuckle Rd Chapel Hill NC 27514 Office: 861 Willow Dr Chapel Hill NC 27514

REASON, JOSEPH H(ENRY), librarian; b. Franklin, La., Mar. 23, 1905; s. Joseph and Bertha (Peoples) R.; B.A., New Orleans Coll., 1928; A.B., Howard U., 1932; A.M., U. Pa., 1933; B.S., Columbia, 1936; Ph.D., Catholic U. Am., 1958; m. Bernice P. Chism, June 24, 1931; children—Barbara, J. Paul. Tchr. langs. Gilbert Acad., New Orleans, 1928-29, Fla. A. and M. Coll., 1929-31, 34-35, chief librarian, 1936-38; reference librarian Howard U., 1938-46, univ. librarian, 1946-57, dir. univ. libraries 1957—; library adviser U. Rangoon, Burma, (Ford Found. grant with A.L.A.) 1961-62; exec. sec. Assn. Coll. and Research Libraries, 1962-63. Mem. A.L.A. (2d v.p. 1966-67), Assn. Coll. and Reference Libraries, D.C. Library Assn., Am. Dialect Soc., Internat. Arthurian Soc. Home: 1242 Girard St NE Washington DC 20017

REASONOVER, WILLIAM SUMTER, coll. pub. relations ofcl.; b. Camden, S.C., July 22, 1927; s. Marvin M. and Olive Z. (Rhame) R.; B.S. in Agrl. Econs., Clemson U., 1947. Dir. pub. relations Farmers Mut. Exchange, Durham, N.C., 1947-48; nat. advt. mgr. The Robesonian, Lumberton, N.C., 1949-57; dir. community and pub. relations Alaska Meth. U., Anchorage, 1957-58; dir. pub. relations Pfeiffer Coll., Misenheimer, N.C., 1958—. Sec. Richfield Park Com., 1971—. Bd. dirs. Stanley County Community Concert Assn. Mem. Albemarle-Stanley County C. of C. (v.p., dir. 1967—), Charlotte Pub. Relations Soc. (dir. 1966—), Coll. News Seminar Carolinas (pres. 1964; dir. 1968—) Am. Alumni Council, N.C. Civitan Youth Leadership Conf. (chmn. bd. govs. 1965-67), Pub. Relations Soc. Am., Am. Coll. Pub. Relations Soc. Methodist (lay speaker 1960—; mem. commn. communications 1968—). Club: Civitan (Richfield N.C.). Editor: Pfeiffer College Bull., 1960—. Contbr. articles to newspapers, mags. Home: 2 James Apartment Misenheimer NC 28109 Office: Drawer D Pfeiffer Coll Misenheimer NC 28109

REAVES, LEE, radio sta. exec.; b. Warren, Ark., Dec. 10, 1909; s. B.A. and Ellie (Martin) R.; A.B., Ark. A. and M. Coll., 1934; M.S., U. Ark., 1947; m. Glenda Pittman, Feb. 21, 1942; children— Glenda Anne (Mrs. Robert W. Downs, III), Robin Lee (Mrs. J.F. Hawkins, Jr.). Instr., Sch. for Blind, Little Rock, 1931-33; tchr. pub. schs., Warren, 1934-36; supt. schs., Hermitage, Ark., 1936-51; adminstr. Bradley County Meml. Hosp., Warren, 1951-53; part owner, operator Radio Sta. KWRF, Warren, 1953-59; v.p. Ark. A. and M. Coll., Monticello, 1959-63; dir. Ark. Ednl. TV Commn., Conway, 1963—. Mem. Ark. Senate, 1939-55, sec. senate, 1961—; chmn. Bradley County Democratic Com., 1945-49; mem. Ark. State Dem. Com., 1947-55. Mem. War Meml. Stadium Commn., 1948-63; chmn. Warren Planning Bd., 1957-59; mem. Warren Sch. Bd., 1953-59, Bradley County Sch. Bd., 1957-59. Mem. Warren C. of C. (dir. 1954-59, pres. 1956-58). Methodist (vice chmn. bd. stewards). Rotarian (v.p. Warren 1951-59). Author: Rule Book for the Arkansas Senate, 1943. Home: Hillman and Mitchell Sts Conway AR 72032 Office: 350 S Donaghy St Conway AR 72032

REBOZO, CHARLES GREGORY, banker; b. Tampa, Fla., Nov. 17, 1912; s. Francis Matias and Carmen (Sarmiento) Rebozo. Pres. Monroe Land Title Co., Key West, Fla., 1959—, Washwell, Inc., Miami, Fla., 1959—, Fisher's Island, Inc., Miami, 1956—, Key Biscayne Bank and Trust Co. (Fla.), 1964—. Pres., Jr. Achievement, Greater Miami, 1959-60; pres. Boys Clubs of Greater Miami, 1954-58. Kiwanian (pres. 1958). Clubs: Coral Gables Country, Riviera Country (Coral Gables, Fla.,); Key West Country (Fla.); Key Biscayne Yacht (commodore 1961). Home: 490 Bay Lane Key Biscayne FL 33149 Office: 95 W McIntire St Key Biscayne FL 33149

REBSAMEN, RAYMOND H., corp. exec.; b. Lancaster, Tex., Apr. 8, 1898; s. William Frederick and Edna Mae (Miller) R.; student U. Ark. (Distinguished Alumnus citition 1960); Litt.D. (hon.), Subiaco Coll.; C.P.A., Am. Inst. Accountants; m. Martha Jane Dickinson; children—Ruth Elizabeth (Mrs. Roland R. Remmel), Frederick Raymond. Organizer, chmn. Rebsamen & Assos., Inc., Little Rock, 1928—; dir. Ark. La. Gas Co., Shreveport; chmn. bd. Fed. Res. Bank, St. Louis, 1963-66. Served as pvt. U.S. Army, 1918; lt. col. Ordnance Corps, AUS, 1942-45. Mem. Sigma Alpha Epsilon. Presbyn. Mason (33 deg.). Clubs: Little Rock Country; University (St. Louis); Hunt and Polo, Memphis Country (Memphis). Home: 2500 N Jackson St Little Rock AR 72207 Office: Tower Bldg Little Rock AR 72201

RECHHOLTZ, ROBERT AUGUST, tobacco co. exec.; b. N.Y.C., Mar. 29, 1937; s. August Bruno and Frances (Wirth) R.; B.S., U. N.C., 1958; m. Caroline Morton Osborne, May 2, 1959; children—Laurie, Jennifer, Kristen. Marketing asst. Procter & Gamble Co., Cin., 1958-59, asst. copy supr., 1959-60; account supr. Bradham & Co., Greensboro, 1960-61; with R.J. Reynolds Tobacco Co., 1961—; marketing mgr., 1967-70, v.p., marketing mgr., Winston-Salem, N.C., 1970—, also dir.; dir. Westfall Prodns., ABC. Dir. Assn. Nat. Advertisers, Am. Advt. Fedn. Bd. dirs. Winston-Salem YMCA. Served with AUS, 1958, 61-62. Mem. Phi Beta Kappa. Republican. Episcopalian. Clubs. Winston-Salem Tennis, Forsyth Country (Winston-Salem). Home: 3315 Paddington Lane Winston-Salem NC 27106 Office: RJ Reynolds Tobacco Co 4th and Main Sts Winston-Salem NC 27102

RECHTIN, EBERHARDT, govt. ofcl.; b. Orange, N.J., Jan. 16, 1936; s. Eberhardt Carl and Ida (Pfarrer) R.; B.S. in Engring., Cal. Inst. Tech., 1946, Ph.D., 1950; m. Dorothy D. Denebrink, June 10, 1951; children—Andrea, Nina, Julie Anne, Erica, Mark Eberhardt. From research engr. to asst. dir. tracking and data acquisition Jet Propulsion Lab., Cal. Inst. Tech., 1949-67; dir. Adv. Research Projects Agy., Dept. Def., 1967-70; prin. dep. dir. def. research and engring. Dept. Def., 1970-72; sec. def. for telecommunications, 1972—. Fellow Am. Inst. Aeros. and Astronautics, I.E.E.E., Nat. Acad. Engring. Address: 6904 Old Gate Lane Rockville MD 20852*

RECK, ANDREW JOSEPH, educator; b. New Orleans, Oct. 29, 1927; s. Andrew Gervais and Catherine (Mangiaracina) R.; B.A., Tulane U., 1947, M.A., 1949; Ph.D., Yale, 1954; postgrad. (Fulbright scholar) U. St. Andrews, Scotland, 1952-53, U. Paris, 1962, 64. Instr. philosophy Yale, 1955-58, asst. prof. Tulane U., New Orleans, 1958-61, asso. prof., 1961-64, prof. philosophy, 1964—, chmn. dept., 1969—. Suarez lectr. Spring Hill Coll., Mobile, Ala., 1971. Served with AUS, 1953-55. Grantee Am. Council Learned Socs., 1961, Am. Philos. Soc., 1972; Howard Found. fellow, 1962-63. Mem. Metaphys. Soc. Am. (councillor 1971—), Southwestern Philos. Soc. (mem. exec. com. 1966-68, v.p. 1971—), So. Soc. Philosophy and Psychology (treas. 1968-71). Author: Recent American Philosophy, 1964; Introduction to William James, 1967; New American Philosophers, 1968; Speculative Philosophy, 1972. Editor: Selected Writings (George Herbert Mead), 1964. Home: 732 Cherokee St New Orleans LA 70118

RECORD, JAMES RALPH, county ofcl.; b. New Market, Ala., Dec. 27, 1918; s. John Raymond and Lillie Belle (Fisk) R.; student U. Ala., 1960-62; B.S., Cramwell U., 1963; m. Lillian Aho, June 15, 1946 (dec. Feb. 1963); children—Carole Denise, James. Partner, Huntsville (Ala.) Accounting Services, 1958—; owner Record Pub. Co., Huntsville, 1958—. Past vice chmn. Ala. Dept. Pensions and Security, 1958-72. Mem. adv. bd. Ala. Civil Def. Dept., 1959, League Women Voters; bd. dirs. Ala. Tb Sanitorium, Friends of Library. Mem. Ala. Senate, 1961-62; chmn. bd. county commrs. Madison County, 1962—. Served with USAAF, 1942-46. Mem. Huntsville C. of C. (dir.), V.F.W., Am. Legion, Ala. Hist. Soc., Madison County Farm Bur., Ala. Assn. County Commrs. (pres.). Baptist. Woodmen of World, Elk. Home: 9107 Hogan Dr Huntsville AL 35802 Office: Courthouse Huntsville AL 35804

RECORD, PHILLIP JULIUS, newspaper editor; b. Fort Worth, Jan. 12, 1929; s. Phillip Cross and Frances (McElwee) R.; B.A. in Journalism, U. Notre Dame, 1950; m. Patricia Ann Edwards, Sept. 29, 1954; children— Phillip Christopher, Gregory Edwards, Timothy James. Gen. reporter Lubbock (Tex.) Avalanche Jour., 1950-54; copy editor, reporter Fort Worth Star-Telegram, 1954-67, asst. city editor, 1967-68, city editor, evening edit., 1968—. Free-lance mag. writer. Mem. Fort Worth-Tarrant County (Tex.) Civil Def. Policy and Adv. Com.; troop committeeman Boy Scouts Am. Bd. dirs. Fort Worth Opera Assn., Catholic Social Services. Served with inf. AUS, 1950-52. Recipient 17 journalism awards for writing, photography and headline writing. Mem. Press Club of Fort Worth (past v.p.), Sigma Delta Chi (dir., v.p. local chpt.). Democrat. Roman Catholic. Home: 5533 Wheaton Dr Fort Worth TX 76133 Office: 400 W 7th St Fort Worth TX 76102

RECTOR, WILLIAM LEE, physician; b. Shawnee, Okla., Nov. 30, 1919; s. William Lee and Mary Elizabeth (Reese) R.; B.S., Okla. State U., 1940; M.D., Okla. U., 1943; m. N. Jane Fielder, May 3, 1943; children—Nancy Jane, Lee Anne. Intern, Ia. Lutheran Hosp., Des Moines, 1944-45; resident Scott and White Clinic, Temple, Tex., 1947-50; practice medicine specializing in internal medicine, Med. and Surg. Clinic, Wichita Falls, Tex., 1950—; cons. internal medicine Wichita Falls, State Hosp., 1951—. Mem. regional health adv. com. Health, Edn. and Welfare, 1970—; mem. census adv. com. on privacy and confidentiality U.S. Dept. Commerce, 1972—. Chmn. Tex. Republican Task Force Human Rights Responsibilities, 1967—, chmn. Rep. State Conv., 1970, mem. state exec. com., 1964—; del. Rep. Nat. Conv., 1968, 72. Trustee, chmn. bd. Community Center Mental Health-Mental Retardation. Served to capt. M.C., AUS, 1945-47. Recipient award for pub. service Altrusa Club, 1963. Mem. A.C.P., A.M.A., Tex., Wichita County (pres. 1964) med. assns. Baptist. Home: 4021 Taft St Wichita Falls TX 76308 Office: 1518 10th St Wichita Falls TX 76301

RED, WALTER SCOTT, lawyer; b. Houston, July 9, 1909; s. Samuel Clark and George (Plunkett) R.; B.A., U. Tex., 1933; LL.B., South Tex. Sch. Law, 1939; m. Ruth Pilkenton, Dec. 3, 1941; children—Walter Scott, Samuel Clark III. Admitted to Tex. bar, 1940; atty. First Nat. Bank Houston, 1942-56; practiced in Houston, 1940-42, 56—; mem. firm Boyles, Billingsley & Red, 1955-56, Billingsley & Red, 1956—; head law firm W. Scott Red, 1956—; gen. counsel Blume Systems Tree Experts, Past pres. Wier Homes, Inc., Houston, The Pladium, Inc., Houston. Chmn. law sect. Family and Child Welfare; patron Gilbert and Sullivan Soc. Houston, All City Symphony Orch., Young Audiences, Inc., Houston; pres. Briargrove Elementary Sch. P.T.A.; mem. Harris County Child Welfare Bd.; chmn. attys. unit United Fund, 1965—; mem. adv. com. Tanglewood

Homes Assn. Bd. dirs. Houston Community Council, Homes of St. Mark; past mem. exec. bd., legal counsel Houston Symphony Soc. Fellow State Bar Tex. Endowment; mem. Am. Trial Lawyers Assn., Nat. Legal Aid and Defenders Assn., Am., Houston (v.p. 1959-60) bar assns., State Bar Tex., Am. Judicature Soc., Tex. Assn. Plaintiff's Attys., Am. Legion, Houston C. of C. (chmn. edn. com.), S.A.R., Sons Republic Tex. (pres. 1961-62), Delta Theta Phi, Kappa Alpha. Presbyn. (clk. session). Kiwanian (dir.) Club: Knife and Fork. Pres. South Tex. Law Jour., 1963-64. Home: 903 Wild Valley Houston TX 77027 Office: 215 Guaranty Nat Bank Bldg 7500 Bellaire Blvd PO Box 36735 Houston TX 77036

REDDELL, WILLIAM JENNINGS, newspaper editor; b. Rule, Tex., Oct. 24, 1915; s. William C. and Bess (Roberts) R.; student Kan. City Art Inst., 1935, Baylor U., 1936-40; m. Martha Peay, Dec. 25, 1940 (dec. Aug. 1947); children—Jean, Judy; m. 2d, Cynthia Wiggins, Aug. 20, 1950; 1 dau., Molly. Reporter San Antonio Tex. Express, 1941-43, asst. city editor, 1943-47, Rio Grande Valley news bur. chief, 1947-51, city editor, 1951-52, columnist, 1952-55, asso. editor, 1955-56, editor editorial page, 1956-—. Trustee Baylor U., 1957-68, Bapt. Hosp. System, San Antonio, 1971-—. Mem. Sigma Delta Chi. Home: 134 Knibbe Rd San Antonio TX 78209 Office: Av E and 3d St San Antonio TX 78209

REDDEN, KENNETH ROBERT, lawyer, author, educator; b. N.Y.C., July 15, 1917; s. Vincent and Anna (Pulanska) R.; LL.B., U. Va., 1940; m. Hebe Mary Ruggieri, Sept. 11, 1943; children—Louis Rowen, Bianca Maria, George Jonas, Francesca Blakely, Kenneth Robert. Admitted to N.Y. bar, 1941; practice of law, Burlingame, Norse & Pettit, N.Y.C., 1940-42; law clk. U.S. Circuit Judge, 1942-44; prof. law U. Va. 1944-—, lectr. legal medicine U. Va. Med. Sch., Med. Coll. of Va., 1944-58; mem. summer faculty George Washington U., Ind. U.; mem. US-Internat. Coop. Adminstrn., Team, Turkey, 1955-57; prof. law Haile Selassie U., Addis Ababa, Ethiopia, 1964-66. Mem. U.S. Nat. Def. Exec. Res., 1959-—; mem. Fed. Meditation and Conciliation Service. Author: Law in Our Civilization, 1946; Cases on Equity, 1946; Virginia and West Virginia Jurisprudence, 1948; So You Want to be a Lawyer, 1950; Career Planning in the Law, 1950; Law Student's Form Book, 1950; Lawyer's Investment Manual, 1952; The Mining Law of Turkey, 1955; The Petroleum Law of Turkey, 1956; Legal Education in Turkey, 1957; Bar Association Activities in Turkey and the U.S., 1958. Editor: Lawyer's Medical Cyclopedia (6 vols.), 1959. Editor of Virginia Law Review, 1942-45, Va. Bar News, 1954-55; coordinating editor An Introduction to The Uniform Commercial Code, 1964; Journal of Ethiopian Law, 1965; Ethiopian Legal Formbook, 1966; The Law Making Process in Ethopia, 1966; The Legal System of Ethiopia, pub. 1968. Contributor articles to legal publs., Ency. Brit. Home: Shadwell VA 22970 Office: U Va Law Sch Charlottesville VA 22204

REDDICK, THOMAS LEONARD, educator; b. Springfield, Mo., Apr. 29, 1938; s. Leonard L. and Josephine L. (Campbell) R.; B.A., Drury Coll., 1960; M.Ed., U. Mo., 1963; Ph.D., U. Miss., 1967; m. Donna Mae Montgomery, Apr. 20, 1962; children—Kurt Erich, Karissa Jadonna. Tchr. Central Sr. High Sch. and Med. Center for Fed. Prisoners, Springfield, Mo., 1961-65; ednl. research analyst U. Miss., University, 1965-67; spl. asst. to asso. commr. U.S. Office Edn., Washington, 1967-68; mem. faculty Tenn. Technol. U., Cookeville, 1968-—, asso. prof. profl. edn. 1970-—. Cons. Tenn. Appalachia Ednl. Coop., various sch. systems, 1968-—; cons. expert U.S. Office Edn., 1968-69. Mem. Am. Assn. Sch. Adminstrs., Am. Ednl. Research Assn., N.E.A., Tenn. Edn. Assn., Phi Delta Kappa, Kappa Delta Pi, Phi Alpha Theta, Pi Gamma Mu, Sigma Delta Pi, Phi Kappa Phi. Episcopalian. Author: (with Edell M. Hearn) Simulated Behavioral Teaching Situations, 1971. Contbr. articles to profl. jours. Home: 1315 Maddux Av Cookeville TN 38501

REDDICK, W(ALKER) HOMER, social worker; b. River Junction, Fla., Mar. 26, 1922; s. Walker H. and Lillian (Anderson) R.; B.S., Fla. State U., 1951, M.S.W., 1957; m. Anne Elizabeth Hardwick, Sept. 7, 1947; children—Walker Homer, Andy Hardwick (dec.). Chief juvenile probation officer Muscogee County Juvenile Ct., Columbus, Ga., 1952-53; sr. child welfare worker Floyd County Dept. Pub. Welfare, Rome, Ga., 1955-56; chief social worker Montgomery County Dept. Pub. Health, Montgomery, Ala., 1957-59; dir. social services Ala. Bapt. Childrens Home, Troy, 1959-64; casework supr. Youth Devel. Center, Milledgeville, Ga., 1964-71; counselor Family Counseling Center, Macon, Ga., 1972-—. Mem. Ala. State Adv. Com. on Children and Youth, 1961-64. Served with AUS, 1940-43. Fellow Royal Soc. Health; mem. Nat. Assn. Social Workers, Acad. Certified Social Workers. So. Bapt. Social Service Assn. Baptist. Mason. Contbr. articles to profl. jours. Address: PO Box 21 Milledgeville GA 31061

REDDING, EARL WALLACE, educator; b. Randleman, N.C., June 26, 1932; s. Dallas Lester and Rachel (Dennis) R.; B.A., Guilford Coll., 1957; M.A., U. Miami (Fla.), 1963, Ph.D. (Nat. Def. Edn. Act fellow), 1969; postgrad. Nat. U. Mexico, Mexico City, 1966; m. Helen Virginia Duke, Aug. 11, 1954; children—Neal Wallace, Richard Alton, Virginia Grace, Kay Elizabeth. Pastor Piney Woods Friends Meeting, Belvidere, N.C., 1957-59, 10th Av. Friends Meeting, Miami, 1959-61; dir. Cuban refugee resettlement program Ch. World Service, Miami, 1961-63; acting dean students Guilford Coll., Greensboro, N.C., 1963-64, asst. prof. philosophy, 1963-71, asso. prof., 1971-—. Served with AUS, 1950. Mem. Soc. of Friends (mem. exec. com., gen. bd. Friends United Meeting). Home: 825 Rosecrest Dr High Point NC 27260 Office: Dept Philosophy Guilford Coll Greensboro NC 27410

REDDY, WILLIAM J., biochemist, educator; b. Boston, Aug. 10, 1926; s. Neil and Margaret (Doherty) R.; A.B., Harvard, 1949, M.S., 1957, D.Sc., 1960; m. Elizabeth Enaire, Jan. 1, 1955; children—Margaret, Elizabeth, Ann William. Chemist, Peter Bent Brigham Hosp., Boston, 1949-60, asso. staff, 1960-68; research asso. Harvard Med. Sch., Boston, 1960-64, asso. in biol. chemistry, 1964-68; dir. chem. dept. St. Vincent Hosp., Worcester, Mass., 1968-70, also cons.; prof. medicine and biochemistry U. Ala. Sch. Med., 1970-—. Pres. Boston chpt. Muscular Dystrophy Assn. Am., 1965-69, mem. exec. com., 1963-69. Mem. Am. Soc. Biol. Chemists, Am. Chem. Soc., Am. Physiol. Soc., Endocrine Soc., A.A.A.S. Contbr. articles in field to profl. jours. Home: 4147 Stone River Rd Birmingham AL 35213 Office: 1919 7th Av Birmingham AL 35233

REDFEARN, NORVEL EUGENE, real estate exec.; b. Mt. Pleasant, Tex., Sept. 28, 1931; s. Everett Bennitt and Mildred Eugena (Young) R.; B.S., East Tex. U., 1954; m. Ann Lilly Patrick, Oct. 27, 1956; children— Kelly, Scott, Pat. Sales mgr. Redfearn Bakery, 1957-64; engaged in oil and gas leasing, 1964-65; partner Buford-Redfearn Real Estate Co., 1965-— (all Mt. Pleasant); dir. Guaranty Bond State Bank; pres. Norcharart, Inc., 1971-—, Cypress Ranch, Inc., 1969-—, Norvel Redfearn Land Co., Inc., 1971-—. Pres. Mt. Pleasant Indsl. Found., 1971-—. Served to 1st lt. USAF, 1954-57. Mem. Mt. Pleasant C. of C. (dir. 1971-—). Methodist (trustee 1969-—). Clubs: Country (dir. 1960-63), Civitan (pres. 1957-58) (Mt. Pleasant). Home: PO Box 485 Mt Pleasant TX 75455 Office: 415 N Jefferson St Mt Pleasant TX 75455

REDFERN, JOHN JOSEPH, III, petroleum co. exec.; b. Oklahoma City, Jan. 9, 1939; s. John Joseph, Jr. and Rosalind (Kapps) R.; B.A. in Math., U. Tex., 1961, M.B.A., 1964; m. Doris Jean Purcell, Jan. 25, 1963; children—Mary Randall, John Joseph IV. Financial analyst Redfern Devel. Corp., Midland, Tex., 1964; security analyst trust dept. investment sect. Ft. Worth Nat. Bank, 1964-66; sec., treas. Flag-Redfern Oil Co., Midland, 1966-—. Mem. Houston Soc. Financial Analysts, Midland C. of C., Phi Gamma Delta. Home: 2506 Sinclair St Midland TX 79701 Office: PO Box 23 410 Wall Towers West Bldg Midland TX 79701

REDIKER, JOHN MICHAEL, lawyer; b. N.Y.C., Feb. 20, 1942; s. Norris and Lorol Roden (Bowron) R.; A.B. magna cum laude, Princeton, 1964; J.D., Harvard, 1967; m. Susan Elizabeth Walter, Oct. 11, 1969. Admitted to Ala. bar, 1967; asso., Cabaniss, Johnston, Gardner & Clark, attys. at law, 1967-69; partner, Ritchie & Rediker, attys. at law, Birmingham, Ala., 1970-—; sec., dir. Dixon Powdermaker Furniture Co., Jacksonville, Fla., 1967-—; dir. Rucker Industries, Inc. Lectr. Law U. Ala. Law Sch., 1969-—. Bd. dirs. Birmingham Jr. C. of C. Found., Positive Maturity, Inc., Community Service Council, Central Ala. chpt. Nat. Multiple Sclerosis Soc. Served with AUS, 1963. Mem. Am., Birmingham bar assns., Ala. State Bar, Birmingham Jr. C. of C. (dir. 1967-69). Clubs: Mountain Brook, Downtown (Birmingham); Princeton (N.Y.C.). Home: 3400 N Woodridge Rd Birmingham AL 35223 Office: First National-Southern Natural Bldg Birmingham AL 35203

REDMAN, JAMES LUTHER, lawyer, state legislator; b. Plant City, Fla., Jan. 19, 1932; s. James William and Madeline (Miller) R.; B.S.B., U. Fla., 1953, LL.B., 1958; m. Ruby Jean Barker, Aug. 9, 1957; children—Susan, Pamela, Jeanne. Admitted to Fla. bar, 1958, since practiced in Plant City; partner Trinkle, Trinkle & Redman, 1960-63, Trinkle, Redman, Clawson & Peavyhouse, 1965-—; asso. city judge Plant City, 1960-65; mem. Fla. Ho. of Reps., 1966-—. Mem. Hillsborough County Democratic Exec. Com., 1962-66; mem., sec. Hillsborough County Fair, 1965; active United Fund. Chmn. bd. dirs. S. Fla. Bapt. Hosp. Served with USAAF, 1954-55. Mem. Am., Hillsborough County bar assns., Plant City C. of C. Baptist. Home: Keen Rd Plant City FL 33566 Office: 306 W Reynolds St Plant City FL 33566

REDMAN, MANVILLE, lawyer; b. Oklahoma City, Aug. 17, 1925; s. Manville R. and Minnie (Lasby) R.; B.A., U. Okla., 1947, LL.B., 1949; m. Deanna K. Porter, Dec. 25, 1962; children—Tamara J., Sharon M., John N., Jennifer K. Admitted to Okla. bar, 1949; practiced in Lawton, 1950, 57-—; asst. county atty. Comanche County, 1951-53, county atty., 1953-57; partner Newcombe, Redman & Doolin, 1963-—. Mem. Okla. Ho. of Reps., 1960-62. Pres. Lawton Camp Fire Girls; chmn. adv. bd. Salvation Army, 1960. Served with AUS, 1943-47; lt. col. Res. Named Outstanding Young Man of Lawton, 1955. Mem. Okla., Comanche County bar assns., Lawton Jr. C. of C. (pres. 1954), Phi Alpha Delta, Phi Gamma Delta. Methodist. Kiwanian (pres. 1958). Home: 325 N 35th St Lawton OK 73501 Office: Security Bank Bldg Lawton OK 73501

REDMOND, JOHN, JR., environmental engr.; b. Grove Hill, Ala., Nov. 7, 1918; s. John and Sibyl (Calhoun) R.; B.C.E., Ala. Poly. Inst., 1940; M.P.H., U. Minn., 1950; grad. U.S. Army Command and Gen. Staff Coll., 1958; m. Sara Lee Davis, June 7, 1941; children—John III, Dianna (Mrs. Andrew Poynter). San. engr. Ala. Health Dept., 1940-42; commd. 2d lt. Med. Service Corps, U.S. Army, 1943, advanced through grades to col., 1966; assigned hdqrs. 7th Army, 1958-61, hdqrs. 6th Army, 1961-66; chief environmental engring. Office Surgeon Gen., Dept. Army, also asst. chief Med. Service Corps, 1966-70; chmn. environmental pollution control com. Def. Dept., 1969-70; ret., 1970; profl. asso. Nat. Acad. Scis., Washington, 1970-—. Decorated Army Commendation medal, Joint Service Commendation medal, Legion Merit. Diplomate Am. Acad. Environmental Engring. Fellow Am. Soc. C.E., Fed. Water Quality Assn.; mem. Am. Water Works Assn., N.Y. Acad. Scis., Nat. Soc. Profl. Engrs., Air Pollution Control Assn., Soc. Am. Mil. Engrs., Assn. Mil. Surgeons U.S., Conf. Fed. Environmental Engrs., Chi Epsilon. Home: 6202 Nethercombe Ct McLean VA 22101 Office: Nat Acad Scis 2101 Constitution Av Washington DC 20418

REECE, ALFRED THOMAS, JR., banker; b. Gate, Okla., Dec. 22, 1932; s. Alfred Thomas and Ila Maurine (Steel) R.; B.B.A., U. Okla., 1957; m. Mary E. Elmore, Mar. 1, 1971; children by previous marriage—Michael Dean, Gary Lynn, Stephen Wayne. Pres., Bankers Investment Co., Hutchinson, Kan., 1957-61; v.p. Fidelity Bank, Oklahoma City, 1961-—; pres. Reece Investment Co., Oklahoma City, 1965-—. Mem. Okla. Bankers Assn. Clubs: Civitan (dir. 1967-68), Quail Creek Country. Home: 3021 Brookhollow Rd Oklahoma City OK 73120 Office: PO Box 24128 Oklahoma City OK 73124

REECE, CLAUDE JEFFERSON, JR., elec. engr.; b. Waynesville, N.C., Mar. 20, 1936; s. Claude Jefferson and Nora (Massie) R.; B.S.E.E., Clemson U., 1957; m. Judith Mary Wasgatt, May 14, 1960; children—Caroline, Charles. Cons. engr. Jeff Reece Engrs., Waynesville, N.C., 1962-—. Chmn. Waynesville Townlift Commn. Served to capt. USAF, 1958-60. Registered profl. engr., N.C., Fla. Mem. I.E.E.E. (chmn. Western N.C. sect. 1964-65), Nat. Soc. Profl. Engr. N.C. Soc. Engrs., Profl. Engrs. in Pvt. Practice, Instrument Soc. Am. (sr. mem.), Illuminating Engring. Soc. Methodist (chmn. bd.). Mason (Shriner). Club: Mountain Valley Golf (pres., past sec.-treas). Home: 204 Grimball Dr Hazelwood NC 28738 Office: Box 540 Waynesville NC 28786

REECE, DORIS VIOLET CORNELIUS (MRS. ESTILL CARL REECE), club woman; b. Bradford, Pa., Dec. 6, 1907; d. William La Verne and Alice May (Saverline) Cornelius; R.N., Hardy Sanitarium, 1926-29; L.H.D. (hon.), Internat. Acad., Alfredian Order Eng., 1969; m. Estill Carl Reece, Feb. 28, 1929; 1 dau., Juanita Williams (Mrs. Earl Woffard). Charter regent Tex. Soc. Magna Charta Dames, 1960-62, organizing regent, 1960-62, state vice regent, 1960-62, state herald, 1962-64, hon. life vice regent, hon. life colony regent; chpt. chmn. nat. def. D.A.R., 1960-63, chmn. new citizens com., 1963-—, librarian, 1963-—; sec.-treas. Midland Ladies Oriental Shrine N.A., 1955-59, trustee, 1962-63; chpt. vice regent Daus. Am. Colonists, 1964-—; state chmn. nat. def. New Eng. Women, 1962-64; U.S. mem. geneal. staff, cons. Auguston Soc.; mem. bd. Odessa Beautiful Assn.; officer Women's Soc. Christian Service. Decorated Dame of Grand Cross, Alfredian Acad., 1969, comdr. Hon. Naval Command. Fellow Augustan Soc. Cal.; mem. Colonial Order Crown, Descs. Knights Garter, Ams. Royal Descent, Daus. Union Vets., Ladies Grand Army Republic, Colonial Dames Am., Daus. Colonial Wars, Order of Washington in Phila., Somerset Barons (asso. mem.; Eng.), Plantagenet Soc. Phila., Royal Soc. St. George (London), Nat., Tex. geneal. socs., Internat. Geneal. Research Found., The Brit.-Am., United Poets Laureate Internat., Poetry Soc. Tex., Poetry Book Soc., Lancashire Authors Assn., Phi Sigma Alpha (charter mem., pres. 1965-—), Epsilon Delta Chi. Methodist. Mem. Order Eastern Star. Clubs: Polyantha Garden (v.p.); Bards (Mich.); Geneva (Switzerland) Arts. Author poetry appearing in nat. mags. Home: 813 W 15th St Odessa TX 79761

REECE, ERROL KEMP, securities co. exec.; b. Jonesville, N.C., Sept. 12, 1922; s. John Edgar and Clyde (Holcomb) R.; B.S., Wake Forest U., 1943; m. Mildred Frances Hayworth, May 8, 1953; children—Anne Clyde, Errol Kemp. Vice pres., resident mgr. Interstate Securities Corp., Greensboro, N.C., 1964- . Vice pres. Y Mens Club, 1947-48; Hi Y adviser, 1948-49; scoutmaster Boy Scouts Am.; mem. N.C. Civil War Round Table, 1963-—; pres. Greensboro Sports Council. Vice pres. bd. dirs. Jr. C. of C.; bd. dirs. Guilford County Tb. Assn. Served with USNR, 1943-46. Recipient Internat. Sales Producers award, 1954. Mem. Investment Bankers Assn., Nat. Securities Traders Assn., Newcomen Soc., Am. Legion (past adj.). Methodist. Mason (32 deg., Shriner), Kiwanian (pres.). Clubs: Greensboro Country, Cedarbrook Country, Red Shield Boys (dir.), Guilford Wildlife (dir.); Wake Forest U. Deacon (pres.). Home: 1816 St Andrews Rd Greensboro NC 27408 Office: 119 N Elm St Greensboro NC 27401

REECE, MONROE FRANKLIN, govt. ofcl.; b. Carnegie, Okla., Aug. 27, 1926; s. M. F. and Lucile (Kimbrough) R.; B.S., Okla. State U., 1949; M.S., Okla. U., 1966; m. Jan Harman, Aug. 2, 1952; children—Karen, Nancy. Sanitarian Payne County (Okla.) Health Dept., Stillwater, 1949-54; milk control supr. Tulsa City-County Health Dept., 1954-63, chief environmental health div., 1963-—. Mem. Okla. Bd. Registration for Profl. Sanitarians. Served with AUS, 1946-47. Mem. Internat. Assn. Milk and Food Sanitarians, Nat. Assn. Sanitarians, Am. Pub. Health Assn. Lion. Home: 5628 S 77th E Av Tulsa OK 74145 Office: 4616 E 15th St Tulsa OK 74112

REECE, ROGER ALAN, pub. relation counselor; b. Columbus, O., Mar. 5, 1938; s. Harold Victor and Beatrice May (Beckford) R.; B.A., U. Miami, 1959; m. Sandra Lee Ragan, Nov. 7, 1970; children—Mina Ragan, Tammy Lynn, Jodie Ann, Tracy Alan. Newscaster, producer WGBS-Radio, Miami, Fla., 1958-60; account exec. Everett A. Clay &Assos., Miami, 1960-68; v.p. Newman/Schulte/Reece, Inc., Miami, 1968-—. Served with USMCR, 1954-62. Mem. Miami Jr. C. of C. (pres. 1966-67), Pub. Relations Soc. Am. (chpt. pres. 1971-72), Iron Arrow, Sigma Delta Chi (chpt. dir. 1969-71), Omicron Delta Kappa, Alpha Sigma Epsilon. Office: 10815 N Kendall Dr Miami FL 33156 Office: 5810 Biscayne Blvd Miama FL 33137

REECE, WILLIAM HOWARD, JR., garment co. exec.; b. Haleyville, Ala., Apr. 25, 1934; s. William Howard and Martha (Glenn) R.; B.S., U. Ala., 1957, M.B.A., 1959; m. Sibyl Alene Dobbs, Sept. 9, 1957; children— Karen Leigh, Sandra Kay, Martha Susanne. Tchr., Winston County High Sch., Double Springs, Ala., 1959-61; indsl. engr. Vanity Fair Mills, Atmore, Ala., 1961, asst. sewing foreman, 1962, sewing foreman, 1963; research and devel. Kayser Roth Lingerie, Haleyville, Ala., 1963-66; plant mgr. Winston Uniform Corp., Double Springs, 1966-67, gen. mgr., 1968-71, v.p., 1969-71; sales mgr. Garment Corp. Am., 1971-—. Republican. Baptist. Mason, Lion. Home: 3750 Newburg Rd Haleyville AL 35565 Office: PO Box 296 Double Springs AL 35553

REED, BEVINGTON ARNOLD, state ofcl.; b. Nimrod, Tex., Sept. 23, 1915; s. Joel Seaborn and Mildred (Harris) R.; student Randolph Jr. Coll., 1932-34; B.S., Daniel Baker Coll., 1937; M.A., Tex. Tech. Coll., 1947, Ph.D., 1952; m. Autalee Notgrass, July 4, 1942; 1 son, Joel Bevington. Tchr. pub. schs., Tex., 1934-41; field scout exec. Boy Scouts Am., Lubbock, Tex., 1941, 46; prin. Vaughn (N.M.) High Sch., 1947-50; teaching fellow Tex. Tech. Coll., Lubbock, 1950-52; asst. prof. govt. San Angelo (Tex.) Coll., 1952-53; asst. prof. Sul Ross State Coll., 1953-56, coll. dean, 1956-61; acad. dean Mankato State Coll., 1961-64; exec. dir. Minn. State Coll. Bd., St. Paul, 1964-65, chancellor, 1965-67; asst. commr. sr. colls. and univs. Coordination Bd. Tex., 1967-68; commr. of higher edn., Tex., 1968-—. Served to capt. USMCR, 1941-46; maj. Res., 1951-57. Mem. N.M. Edn. Assn. (pres. East Central dist. 1949-50), Alpha Pi Omega, Pi Sigma Alpha. Mem. Christian Ch., Mason. Home: 5006 Westview Dr Austin TX 78731 Office: Sam Houston Office Bldg Austin TX 78731

REED, CARL EUGENE, ednl. adminstr.; b. Amity, Me., Feb. 28, 1913; s. Hubert John and Nellie (Vail) R.; B.S., Ricker Classical Inst., Colby Coll., 1935; M.Ed., Boston U., 1951; Ed.D., U. Houston, 1955; m. Eleanor Eldora Shaw, July 9, 1934; children—Terence John, Sandra Darling. Prin., Somerset Acad., Athens, Me., 1935-38, Island Falls (Me.) High Sch., 1938-41; tchr. Bangor (Me.) High Sch., 1941-43; tchr. sci. Winchester (Mass.) High Sch., 1946-51; princ. Kinkaid (Tex.) High Sch., 1951-64; headmaster Bolles Sch., Jacksonville, Fla., 1964-—. Served with AUS, 1943-46; lt. col. Res. Mem. Fla. Council Ind. Schs. (pres. 1971-—), Jacksonville C. of C. (com. of 100, 1968-—), Phi Delta Kappa. Republican. Conglist. Rotarian. Clubs: St. Johns Dinner, University (Jacksonville). Editor: Disaster Control, 1962-63. Home: 7378 San Jose Blvd Jacksonville FL 32217 Office: 7400 San Jose Blvd Jacksonville FL 32217

REED, CHARLES HANCOCK, textile distbg. co. exec.; b. Richmond, Va., Dec. 25, 1900; s. Charles Clinton and Lyllian (Hancock) R.; student U. Va., 1918; B.S., U.S. Mil. Acad., 1922; grad. Command and Gen. Staff Sch., 1941, Cav. Sch., 1932; m. Janice Cannon, Dec. 27, 1924. Commd. 2d lt. U.S. Army, 1922, advanced through grades to col., 1943; comdr. 2d Armored Cav. Regt., ETO, 1944-47; sec. Gen. Army Field Forces, 1947-49; ret., 1949; treas. Williams & Reed, Inc., Richmond, 1949-50, pres., 1950-—; pres. George W. Delks Co., Smithfield, Va., 1950-—, Fosters, Mathews Co., 1950-—; dir. Bank of Va. Woodstock Corporation, Va. Skyline Corp., all Richmond. Pres. Va. Fair, 1965-—. Bd. visitors Va. Poly. Inst., 1949-59; vice rector Radford (Va.) Coll., 1950-—. Decorated D.S.C., Silver Star with clasp, Bronze Star, Purple Heart, Legion of Merit; Croix de Guerre with palms, chevalier Legion of Honor (France). Mem. Nat. Assn. Textile and Apparel Wholesalers (pres. 1965-66). Democrat. Home: Foundry Pl Midlothian VA 23113 Office: 3703 Carolina Av Richmond VA 23220

REED, CLARKE THOMAS, industrialist; b. Alliance, O., Aug. 4, 1928; s. Lyman Harlan and Kathryn (Reynolds) R.; grad. Columbia Mil. Acad., 1946; B.S., U. Mo., 1950; m. Julia Clements Brooks, Sept. 27, 1957; children—Julia Evans, Clarke Thomas, Reynolds Crews. Pres., Reed Joseph Co., 1953-—; pres. Republic Towing Co. and affiliates in barge transp., 1960-—; propr. delta farms. Appt. commr. Am. Revolution Bicentennial Commn., 1969-—. State finance chmn. Miss. Republican Com., 1966, state chmn., 1969; mem. Rep. Nat. Com., 1966-—, chmn. Miss. delegation Rep. conv., 1968. Served with USAF, 1953-55. Mem. Young Presidents Orgn., Phi Gamma Delta. Presbyn. (bd. deacons). Club: Greenville Country (past pres.). Home: Bayou Rd Greenville MS 38701 Office: PO Box 894 230 Main St Greenville MS 38701

REED, DANIEL JOHN, govt. ofcl.; b. Springfield, Ill., July 19, 1922; s. John Patrick and Laurine Anne (Burger) R.; B.S., St. Louis U., 1947, M.A., 1948; Ph.D., U. Chgo., 1958; m. Helen M. DeMars, May 15, 1945; six children. Instr., St. Louis U., 1947-49; instr. U. Detroit, 1950-53, dir. libraries, 1953-59; asst. chief manuscript div. Library of Congress, Washington, 1959-65; historian Nat. Portrait Gallery, 1965-68; asso. dir. Nat. Adv. Commn. on Libraries, 1967; asst. archivist for presdl. libraries Nat Archives, GSA, 1968-—. Mem. adv. bd. Archives Am. Art, 1967-—, Am. History and Life, 1970-—.

Served with USCGR, 1942-45. Mem. Am. Hist. Assn., Am. Assn. for State and Local History (mem. council), Soc. Am. Archivists, Orgn. Am. Historians. Author: Portraits of Presidents, 1968. Home: 130 N Jackson St Arlington VA 22201 Office: Office Presidential Libraries Room 104 Nat Archives Bldg Washington DC 20408

REED, DONALD UPHAM, news service exec.; b. Fresno, Cal., Nov. 17, 1926; s. Clyde Edgar and Grace (Hunter) R.; B.A., Fresno State Coll., 1950; m. Marcia Jean Snyder, Aug. 10, 1947; children—Hal, David, Richard. With U.P.I., 1950—, mgr. Fresno (Cal.) Bur., 1954-62, intermountain news editor, Salt Lake City, 1963-66, mgr. San Francisco bur., 1966-69, news editor S.W. div., Dallas, 1969—. Served with USNR, 1944-46; PTO. Mem. Press Club Dallas, Delta Sigma Phi, Sigma Delta Chi. Home: 6537 Lafayette Way Dallas TX 75230 Office: 1606 Patterson St Dallas TX 75201

REED, ERBIE LOYD, dentist; b. Chesterfield, Tenn., Oct. 11, 1920; s. Erbie Lester and Mary Velt (Blankenship) R.; student Memphis State U., 1946; D.D.S., U. Tenn., 1949; m. Marcille Duke, Dec. 12, 1942; children—Linda Faye (Mrs. Frank McCalla), Mark Loyd, Kevin Duke. Mgr., Reed's Saw Mill, 1936-41; farmer, Chesterfield, 1936-41; postmaster, Chesterfield, 1941-42; owner, operator Reed's Grocery & Gen. Store, Chesterfield, 1941-42; pvt. practice dentistry, Millington, Tenn., 1949—. Mem. Millington Recreation Com., 1950-56; mem. Millington Housing Authority, 1960-68; sec. Millington Biracial Com., 1967—. Sec. Millington Bd. Zoning Appeals, 1953—. Served with USNR, 1942-45. Mem. Pierre Fauchard Dental Acad., Am., Tenn. dental assns., Memphis Dental Soc., Millington C. of C. (pres. 1970-71). Baptist (treas. 1951—). Lion, Rotarian. Home: 4890 2d Av Millington TN 38053 Office: 4770 Easley St Millington TN 38053

REED, FORREST FRANCIS, book co. exec.; b. Fulton, Miss., Sept. 11, 1897; s. Charles Nathaniel and Alma (Gregory) R.; LL.B., Andrew Jackson U., 1940; m. Katherine Mueller, Dec. 17, 1925; children—John Martin, Martha (Mrs. M. Thomas Collins, Jr.). Mgr., Ark. Book Co., 1930-35; organizer, pres. Tenn. Book Co., Nashville, 1935-65; owner Reed & Co., pubs., Nashville, 1965—. Pres. Tenn. Conv. Christian Chs., 1957. Bd. dirs. Coll. of Bible, 1954-60, Disciples of Christ, Hist. Soc., 1952—, chmn. bd., 1962-66, endowed the soc.'s Forrest F. Reed Lectures, 1965. Mem. Am. Booksellers Assn., Tenn. Edn. Assn., A.L.A., Tenn. Hist. Soc., U.S. C. of C., S.A.R., Tenn. Businessmen's Assn. (pres. 1961). Club: Civitan (local pres. 1951). Home: 5115 Hillsboro Rd Nashville TN 37215 Office: Wilson-Bates Bldg Nashville TN 37215

REED, GEORGE JOSEPH, govt. ofcl.; b. Haigler, Neb., May 31, 1914; s. Edwin W. and Cleo (Randall) R.; A.B., Pasadena Coll., 1938, LL.D., 1953 Eastern Nazarene Coll., 1957; postgrad. U. So. Cal., 1948; m. Lois C. Goetze, Oct. 10, 1938; 1 son, George C. Probation officer Los Angeles County (Cal.), 1938-43; field rep. Cal. Youth Authority, Sacramento, 1946-49; dep. dir. Minn. Youth Correction Dept., 1948-53, chief div. delinquency prevention and parole, 1949-53; mem. U.S. Bd. Parole, 1953-65, chmn. bd., 1957-61; chief Parole and Probation of Nev., Carson City, 1965-67; dir. Lane County Juvenile Dept., Eugene, Ore., 1968-69; chmn. U.S. Bd. Parole, Washington, 1969—. Adminstr. Interstate Compact Nev., 1965-67; mem. Commn. Model Code for Administering State Correctional System, 1966—. Served with USNR, 1942-46. Fellow Am. Soc. Criminology, Am. Acad. Criminology; mem. Nat. Parole Council (chmn. 1960-64), Nat. Council Crime and Delinquency (trustee, mem. profl. council 1950—), Am. Congress Corrections, Am. Law Inst. (mem. model criminal code com. 1958—). Club: Nat. Exchange (com. chmn. 1959—). Contbr. chpts. to textbooks, articles to profl. publs. Home: 4201 Cathedral Av NW Washington DC 20016 Office: 101 Indiana Av NW Washington DC 20001

REED, GUY DEAN, osteo. physician; b. Kirksville, Mo., Nov. 4, 1922; s. Arthur Guy and Lena (Murphy) R.; student Wentworth Mil. Acad., 1939-41, Tulane U., 1942-43, Okla. State U., 1941-42, 1945-46; D.O., Kansas City Coll. of Osteopathy and Surgery, 1949; m. Elizabeth Marguerite Matheson, Oct. 20, 1957. Intern Okla. Osteo. Hosp., Tulsa, 1949-50; practice osteo. medicine, specializing in surgery, New Lexington O., 1950-55, Newark, O., 1955-57, Tulsa, 1957—, Owasso, Okla., 1958—; mem. staff Okla. Osteo. Hosp. Pres., chmn. bd. Owasso Devel. Corp., Sheridan Village Med. Clinic, Tulsa, Willow Dale Mobile Home addition, Owasso, Owasso Coin Op Car Wash, Utotem Grocery Store, Broken Arrow, Okla., Rally Dodge Co., Tulsa, Mingo Valley Shopping Center, Inc., Owasso; chmn. bd. Clover Leaf Shopping Center, Inc., Tulsa, Rally Chrysler-Plymouth, Muskogee, Okla. Served with M.C., AUS, 1942-45. Decorated Silver Star medal, Bronze Star medal with oak leaf cluster, Purple Heart. Mem. Am. Coll. Gen. Practitioners in Osteopathy and Surgery, Am., Okla., Ohio, Tulsa Dist. osteo. assns., Tulsa, Owasso (pres. 1959-60) chambers commerce. Mason, Lion. Home: 6775 S Atlanta Av Tulsa OK 74136 Office: 6109 E Admiral Pl Tulsa OK 74115 also 19 S Main St Owasso OK 75044

REED, LUTHER MCCLELLAN, lawyer, city ofcl.; b. nr. Clay, W.Va., June 19, 1908; s. L. James and Adora V. (Steorts) R.; student Marshall U., 1927-29; LL.B., W.Va. U., 1933; m. Nancy Ellen Flannagan, Nov. 25, 1932; 1 dau., Nancy Anne (Mrs. William S. Cate, Jr.). Admitted to W.Va. bar, 1933, Cal. bar, 1938, Tenn. bar, 1947; practiced in Clay, 1933-38, Pasadena, Cal., 1938-43, Oak Ridge, 1945—; with FTC, Treasury Dept., Washington, 1943-45. Dir. Synaflex Mica Corp., Oak Ridge. Asst. dist. atty. gen. Tenn., 19th Jud. Circuit, 1958; city atty., Oak Ridge, 1959—; mem. Anderson County Republican Exec. Com., 1954—; past pres. Oak Ridge Rep. Club. Mem. Am. Tenn., Anderson County (past pres.) bar assns., Oak Ridge Council Civic Clubs (past pres.), Nat. Inst. Municipal Law Officers. Methodist (trustee). Optomist (past pres.). Home: 119 E Magnolia Lane Oak Ridge TN 37830 Office: 253 Main St E Oak Ridge TN 37830

REED, MURRAY O., judge; b. Fulton, Miss., Jan. 27, 1899; s. Charles Nathaniel and Alma (Gregory) R.; student Ark. Law Sch.; m. Ellen Vineyard, Apr. 23, 1922; 1 dau., Meralen (Mrs. David A. Ruffin). Admitted to Ark. bar, 1920, practiced in Little Rock, 1921-56; mem. Ark. Ho. of Reps., 1930-32; dep. pros. atty. 6th jud. dist., 1934, 42, 46; asst. bank commr. Ark., 1937-41; chancery judge 2d Div., 1st Chancery Dist. Ark., 1948-49; gen. counsel Ark. Hwy Commn., 1949-52; municipal judge City of Little Rock, 1955-56; judge Chancery Ct. 1st Div., 1st Chancery Circuit Ark., 1957—. Pres., Jud. Council Ark., 1969-70. Pres. Little Rock Bd. Edn., 1940-41. Mem. Am., Ark., Pulaski County bar assns., Am. Judicature Soc. Democrat. Mem. Christian Ch. Kiwanian. Home: 4920 Lakeview Rd North Little Rock AR 72116 Office: Office Court House Little Rock AR 72201

REED, NATHANIEL PRYOR, govt. ofcl.; b. N.Y.C., July 22, 1933; s. Joseph Verner and Permelia (Pryor) R.; grad. Deerfield Acad. (Mass.), 1951; B.A., Trinity Coll., 1955; m. Alita Weaver, Jan. 9, 1965 children— Nathaniel Pryor, Alita Weaver, Adrian William Pryor. Vice pres. Hobe Sound Co. (Fla.), 1960-71; spl. asst. to Gov. Fla., Tallahassee, 1966-71; asst. sec. for fish, wildlife and parks Dept. of Interior, Washington, 1971—. Chmn., Dept. Air and Water Pollution Control, Tallahassee, 1969-71. Mem. Fla. Audubon Soc. Clubs: Jupiter Island, Links, Anglers Seminole. Home: Jupiter Island Hobe Sound FL 33455 also 2900 Woodland Dr Washington DC Office: Dept of Interior Washington DC

REED, O.M., dentist; b. Belfield, N.D., Nov. 17, 1920; s. George Allison and Edna Reid (Kane) R.; B.A., U. Cal., Berkeley, 1943; D.D.S., U. Cal., San Francisco, 1949; m. Evelyn Campbell, June 25, 1945; 1 son, Mark Allison. Practice dentistry, San Antonio, 1950—; dental research asso. S.W. Found. for Research and Edn., San Antonio, 1962—; cons. Migrant Workers Dental Health Edn., 1969. Served to 1st lt. USAAF, 1942-45. Decorated Air Medal with 5 oak leaf clusters, D.F.C. Recipient Nat. Inst. Dental Research grants, 1965-72. Fellow Am. Coll. Dentists; mem. Am. Assn. Anatomists, Internat. Assn. Dental Research, Am., Tex., San Antonio Dist. (pres.) dental assns., Psi Omega. Contbr. articles profl. jours. Home: 302 Cardinal St San Antonio TX 78209 Office: 1017 Shook Av San Antonio TX 78212

REED, PHILIP BYRON, psychiatrist; b. Waukon, Ia., Apr. 19, 1906; s. Philip Byron and Maude (Starr) R.; B.S., Ind. U., 1928, M.D., 1930, M.D. cum laude, 1932; certificate U. Pa. Grad. Sch. Medicine, Neurology, Psychiatry, 1940; m. Genevieve Pickrell, Jan. 2, 1934; children—Ann Starr, Philip Byron IV. Intern, Indpls. Gen. Hosp., 1930-31, resident, 1932-34, asst. supt., 1932-34; resident Norways Hosp., Indpls., 1935-36; practice medicine specializing in psychiatry and neurology, Indpls., 1937-65, St. Petersburg, Fla., 1969—; cons. Ind. U. Med. Center, Marion County Gen. Hosp.; asso. prof. psychiatry Ind. U. Sch. Medicine, 1950-69; asso. prof. psychiatry U. Fla. Sch. Medicine, 1969—; med. dir. Adult Mental Health Clinics, Clearwater and St. Petersburg, Fla., 1969—. Gen. sec. Norways Found. Diplomate Am. Bd. Psychiatry and Neurology. Fellow A.C.P., Am. Psychiat. Assn. (v.p. 1968-69), mem. Central Neuropsychiat. Hosp. Assn. (pres. 1952), Nat. Assn. Pvt. Psychiat. Hosps. (pres. 1956-57), Central Neuropsychiat. Assn. (pres. 1962), A.M.A., Sigma Chi, Scabbard and Blade, Nu Sigma Nu. Contbr. articles to med. jours. Home: 10124 Tarpon Dr Treasure Island FL 33706 Office: 6170 Central Av St Petersburg FL 33707

REED, ROBERT ALTON, ret. clergyman; b. Henderson, Tex., June 4, 1906; s. Will Z. and Annie (Smith) R.; B.A., Baylor U., 1927; student So. Bapt. Theol. Sem., 1927-30, U. Louisville, 1930; D.D., East Tex. Bapt. Coll., 1959; m. Helen Baker, Jan. 15, 1930; children—Carolyn (Mrs. David Wicker III), Annelle (Mrs. John M. Burton). Ordained to ministry Bapt. Ch., 1926; pastor, Dallas, 1932-34, 40-47, Henderson, Tex., 1934-37, Wichita Falls, Tex., 1937-40; radio-pub. relations dir. Tex. Bapt. Conv., 1947-53; asso. exec. sec. Annuity Bd., So. Bapt. Conv., 1953-55, exec. sec., 1955, pres., chief exec. officer to 1972, pres. emeritus, 1972—; pres. interagy. council, 1963, 64. Pres., Nat. Pensions Conf., N.Y.C., 1960-61. Pres., chmn. bd. Park Towers, Inc., 1966-68. Mem. Bapt. Pub. Relations Soc., Nat. Office Mgrs. Assn. Clubs: Dallas Athletic, DAC Country, Woodvale Fishing (pres. 1971-72), Five Eleven Investment (pres.). Home: Park Towers 3310 Fairmount St Dallas TX 75201

REED, ROBERT GEORGE, III, oil co. exec.; b. Cambridge, Mass., Aug. 9, 1927; s. Robert George and Marjorie (Furber) R.; grad. Phillips Andover Acad., 1945; B.A., Dartmouth, 1949; m. Barbara Bee, July 14, 1951; children—Sandra, Valerie, Jonathan. With Robert G. Reed Co., Boston, 1949-57; asst. gen. mgr. marketing Tidewater Oil Co., 1957-64; v.p., dir. Flying A Realty Co., 1958-64; v.p. Tide Water Realty Co., 1958-64, Veedol Realty Co., 1960-64; mgr. retail marketing Cities Service Oil Co., Tulsa, 1964-67, v.p., gen. mgr. marketing, 1967—, also dir.; dir. Nat. Oil Fuel Inst. Vice chmn. oil industry group Community Chest, Tulsa; vice chmn. oil div. United Dr. campaign, 1967. Republican committeeman, Marshfield, Mass.; county chmn. Rep. party, Plymouth County, Mass. Bd. govs. Boston Coll. Center Study Franchise Distbn. Mem. Am. Petroleum Inst., Chi Phi. Home: 4141 Oak Rd Tulsa OK 74105 Office: Cities Service Oil Co Box 300 Tulsa OK 74102

REED, ROBERT WENDELL, elec. engr.; b. Caroleen, N.C., Sept. 10, 1925; s. Martin Robert and Viola Mae (McDaniel) R.; B.E.E., N.C. State U., 1951; m. Montrose Katherine Beam, Dec. 23, 1948; children—Robert Russell, Allyson Wendella. With So. Bell Telephone Co., Charlotte, N.C., 1946-48, 51—, jr. engr., 1951-55, engr., 1955-66, project engr., 1966-68, supervising engr., 1968-72, equipment engr., 1972—; on loan Western Electric Co. to assist Def. Communications Agy., S. Vietnam, 1966-67. Served with USNR, 1943-45. Registered profl. engr., N.C. Licensee amateur radio, radiotelephone. Home: 426 Boyce Rd Charlotte NC 28211 Office: PO Box 240 Charlotte NC 28201

REED, STANLEY FOSTER, editor and pub.; b. Bogota, N.J., Sept. 28, 1917; s. Morton H. and Beryl (Turner) R.; student George Washington U., 1939-40, Johns Hopkins, 1940-41; m. Stella Swingle, Sept. 28, 1940; children—Nancie, Beryl Ann, Alexandra. With Bethlehem Steel Corp., Balt., 1940-41; cons. engr., 1942-44; founder, pres. Reed Research, Inc., Washington, 1945-62; pres. Reed Research Inst. Creative Studies, Washington, 1951—; Founder, chmn. LogEtronics, Inc., Washington, 1955; founder, pres. Tech. Audit Corp., Washington, 1962; editor, pub. Mergers & Acquisitions, The Jour. Corp. Venture, 1965; dir. Books, U.S.A., Hayden Pub. Co.; lectr. Union Theol. Sem., Prescott Coll., George Washington U., U. Pa., Pa. State U., U. Colo., Am. U., Claremont Coll. Registered profl. engr., D.C. Mem. Soc. Naval Architects and Marine Engrs., I.E.E.E., Northeast Coast Inst. Engrs. and Shipbuilders (Brit.), Am. Econ. Assn., Soc. Internat. Devel., Aspen Inst. Humanistic Studies (vice chmn. Aspen East). Clubs: Washington Golf and Country; N.Y. Yacht; International. Contbr. articles to leading jours.; chpts. in books. Patentee in field. Home: 1621 Brookside Rd McLean VA 20006 Office: RCA Bldg 1725 K St NW Washington DC 22101

REED, STEVE, mcht., county ofcl.; b. Plettenberg, La., May 20, 1904; s. Stevenson and Edna (McGehee) R.; student Millsaps Coll.; m. Marguerite Farr, Jan. 10, 1926; children—James F., Marguerite, Merwin, Bill H. With Mchts. Bank & Trust Co., Jackson, Miss., 1923-33; mem. Bd. Suprs. Wilkinson County, Pinckneyville, Miss., 1935—, pres., 1960—. Dir. Miss. Econ. Council, 1965-66; mem. Miss. Agrl. and Indsl. Bd., 1963-67; pres. S.W. Miss. Devel. Dist., 1966-67. Mem. Miss. Assn. County Suprs. (pres. 1968-69), Wilkinson County Farm Bur. (pres. 1945). Episcopalian. Address: Pinckneyville MS 39658

REED, THEODORE HAROLD, govt. ofcl.; b. Washington, July 25, 1922; s. Ollie William and Mildred Marie (Body) R.; D.V.M., Kan. State Coll., 1945; m. Mary Elizabeth Crandall, Apr. 20, 1945; children—Mark Crandall, Mary Alyce. Practice of vet. medicine, Ceylon Minn., also Caldwell, Ida., Ashland and Portland, Ore.; vet. Nat. Zool. Park, 1955-57, acting dir., 1956-58, dir., 1958—. Mem. Internat. Waterfowl Assn., Am. Assn. Zool. Parks and Aquariums, Internat. Union Dirs. of Zool. Gardens, Fauna Preservation Soc. (Eng.), Wildfowl Trust (Eng.), Avicultural Soc. (Eng.), E. African Wildlife Soc., Washington Biologists Field Club. Club: Cosmos. Home: 5005 Baltimore Av Washington DC 20016 Office: Nat Zool Park Washington DC 20009

REED, THOMAS BEAVERS, JR., banker; b. Iaeger, W.Va., Apr. 5, 1918; s. Thomas Beavers and Lexye Linda (Clifton) R.; student LaSalle Extension U., 1936-39; m. Grace E. Gullatt, June 1, 1940; children—Linda (Mrs. John R. McNally), Dianne (Mrs. Neil V. Spillane), Vikki, Thomas Beavers III, David. Asst. treas. Comml. Credit Corp., Charleston, W.Va., 1939-44, Macon, Ga., 1945-53; mgr. finance Gen. Acceptance Corp., Atlanta, 1953-55; sr. v.p. Pan Am. Bank, Miami, Fla., 1955-59; v.p. Walter Heller Co., Chgo., 1959-60, asst. to pres., 1959-60; sr. v.p. Union Trust Nat. Bank, St. Petersburg, Fla., 1960—. Tchr. consumer lending Am. Inst. Banking, 1955-58, mem. com. Boy Scouts Am., 1960—; v.p. No. Fla. Eye Bank, 1970-71; chmn. Council Govs., 1969-70. Bd. dirs. Fla. Found. for Blind. Served with AUS, 1945. Mem. C. of C. (asso.), Consumer Bankers Assn. (mem. membership com., Am. Bankers Assn. (mem. govt. relations com. of adv. bd.), Fla. Bankers Assn. (chmn. credit div. 1970-71; chmn. installment credit com. 1969-70), Group IV Installment Bankers Assn. Lion (dist. gov. 1969-70, pres. 1965-66; chmn. adv. council Bur. for Blind Services 1971-72), Mason. Clubs: Commerce, Lake Seminole Country (St. Petersburg). Address: 2349 Woodlawn Circle E St Petersburg FL 33704 Office: Central Av at 9th St St Petersburg FL 33701

REED, TRAVIS DEAN, newspaperman; b. Trinity, Tex., Sept. 27, 1930; s. Travis and Alma (Rains) R.; student Tex. A. and M. Coll., 1948-51, U. Houston, 1951-53; m. Caroline Mae McDonald, June 15, 1957; children—Anne McDonald, Lisa Gayle. Reporter, Houston Post, 1951-53; Washington bur. corr. McGraw-Hill Pub. Co., 1955-61. Boston Herald-Traveler, 1961-62; with Newhouse News Service 1962—, chief corr., 1964-67, editor 1967—. Served to 1st lt. AUS, 1953-55. Clubs: Nat. Press, Federal City (Washington). Home: 1304 Oberon Way McLean VA 22101 Office: 1750 Pennsylvania Av NW Washington DC 20006

REEDER, HAROLD LEE, social worker; b. Asheboro, N.C., Aug. 15, 1940; s. James Walter and Mozelle (Williams) R.; B.A., High Point Coll., 1961; M.S.W., U. N.C., 1965; m. Linda Louise Hartley, June 20, 1965. Caseworker, Rowan County Dept. Social Services, Salisbury, N.C., 1961-63; social work supr. Mecklenburg County Dept. Social Services, Charlotte, N.C., 1965-71; chief social worker Randolph Clinic, Charlotte, 1971—. Mem. Charlotte Police Community Council, 1967-69; mem. steering com. Big Bros. Orgn. of Charlotte, 1970-71. Bd. dirs. Alexander Children's Center. Mem. Nat. Assn. Social Workers (rec. sec. 1967-69), N.C. Social Service Assn. (vice chmn. chpt. 1970-71). Home: 6606 Sunview Dr Charlotte NC 28210 Office: 100 Billingsley Rd Charlotte NC 28211

REEDER, JAMES ARTHUR, lawyer; b. Baton Rouge, June 29, 1933; s. James Brown and Grace (Britt) R.; B.A., Washington and Lee U., 1955; postgrad. So. Meth. U., 1957-58; LL.B., U. Tex., 1960, La. State U., 1961; m. Leone Guthrie, Dec. 30, 1958; children—Mary Virginia, James A., Elizabeth Colby. Admitted to La. bar, 1961, since practiced in Shreveport; asso. firm Pugh & Schober, 1961, Booth, Lockard, Jack, Pleasant & LeSage, 1961-64, partner, 1964—. Participant Nat. Security Forum, Air War Coll., 1971. Active United Fund, Boy Scouts Am.; bd. dirs. Goodwill Industries, pres., 1972; pres. Holiday-in-Dixie, 1969. Served with AUS, 1955-57. Named Shreveport's Outstanding Young Man of Year, 1968; La. Outstanding Young Man of Year, 1968; La. Outstanding Young Lawyer of Year, La. Bar Assn., 1969. Mem. Am. (exec. council young lawyers sect. 1965-66, dir. young lawyers), La., Shreveport bar assns., State Bar Tex., La. State Jr. Bar (chmn. 1965-66), So. Meth. U. Alumni Assn. (past pres. Shreveport). Roman Catholic. Home: 419 Janie Lane Shreveport LA 71106 Office: PO Drawer 1092 Shreveport LA 71163

REEL, DONALD CHARLES, dentist; b. Greeneville, Tenn., Feb., 1935; s. Eugene Rankin and Hattie Martisha (Hashe) R.; student Tusculum Coll., 1952-54; D.D.S., U. Tenn., 1957; m. Shirley Virginia Hurt, Sept. 21, 1958. Staff dentist USPHS Outpatient Clinic, N.Y.C., 1958; officer in charge Mobile Dental Unit 5, U.S. Coast Guard, Portsmouth, Va., 1958-61; dep. chief dental service, Outpatient Clinic, Washington, 1961-68, Clin. Research Center, Nat. Inst. Mental Health, Lexington, Ky., 1970—; resident periodontics U. Ky. Coll. Dentistry, 1968-70, clin. instr. dept. periodontology, 1970—. Mem. Am. Dental Assn., Am. Acad. Periodontology, Delta Sigma Delta. Methodist. Home: 2025 Fontaine Rd Lexington KY 40502 Office: PO Box 2000 Lexington KY 40507

REES, PHILIP ADRIAN, librarian; b. Manitowoc, Wis., Oct. 19, 1931; s. Thomas Hugh and Winifred Agnes (Flatman) R.; B.A., Denison U., 1954; M.S. in L.S., Case Western Res. U., 1955; m. Margaret Louise Stamm, May 23, 1970. Reference librarian Union Coll., Schenectady, 1955-58; librarian Museum of City of N.Y., N.Y.C., 1959-62; readers' services librarian Sarah Lawrence Coll., Bronxville, N.Y., 1962-68; art librarian U. N.C., Chapel Hill, 1968—. Mem. Soc. Archtl. Historians, Victorian Soc. Am., Nat. Trust for Historic Preservation. Episcopalian. Home: Box 423 Chapel Hill NC 27514 Office: Ackland Art Center U NC Chapel Hill NC 27514

REESE, ADDISON H(ARDCASTLE), banker; b. Baltimore County, Md., Dec. 28, 1908; s. Gordon Lippencott and Edith Octavia (Ford) R.; grad. Marston's U. Sch., Riderwood, Md., 1926; student John Hopkins, 1926-29; LL.D., U. N.C., 1968; m. Gertrude Craig, Apr. 22, 1936. Asst. nat. bank examiner Treasury Dept., 1932-36, nat. bank examiner, 1936-40; v.p., dir. Nicodemus Nat. Bank, Hagerstown, Md., 1941-47; pres., chmn. bd. County Trust Co. of Md., Balt., 1947-51; exec. v.p. Am. Trust Co., Charlotte, N.C., 1951-54, pres. 1954-60; pres., dir. N.C. Nat. Bank, 1960-67, chmn. bd., 1967—; dir. Ruddick Corp., Speizman Industries, Duff-Norton Co. Chmn., Found. U. N.C. Bd. dirs. Mercy Hosp., N.C. Citizens Assn., N.C. Textile Found.; trustee U. N.C., Bus. Found. of U. N.C. Served from lt. to maj. USAF, 1942-45. Mem. Am. Bankers Assn. (chmn. exec. com. deposits div. 1971—), Assn. Res. City Bankers (dir., past pres.), Alpha Delta Phi. Episcopalian. Clubs: Charlotte Country, Quail Hollow Country, City (Charlotte); Sankaty Head Golf (Nantucket); Elkridge, Bachelors Cotillion (Balt.). Home: 441 Eastover Rd Charlotte NC 28207 Office: Box 120 Charlotte NC 28201

REESE, JESSE TIMOTHY, JR., real estate, ins. co. exec.; b. Columbia, S.C., Jan. 16, 1913; s. Jesse Timothy and Mary Hill (Mobley) R.; B.A., The Citadel, 1934; m. Aimee Gibbes Urquhart, Oct. 14, 1936; children—Aimee (Mrs. John D. Kornegay), Judith (Mrs. John Nye), Jesse Timothy, III, Mary (Mrs. Richard N. Burnside). With Jesse T. Reese, Inc., Columbia, S.C., 1934—, pres., 1967—; dir. Palmetto Wholesale, Columbia, 1950—; Calhoun Life, Columbia, 1950—; Palmetto Metal Products, Columbia, 1953—; Consol. Ins. Co., Columbia, 1954—. Pres. Columbia Real Estate Bd., 1950-51. Chmn. Bd. Assessors, 1946-50; chmn. Election Commn., Richland County, 1950-59; mem. city council, 1968—. Served with AUS, 1941-46; ETO. Mem. Nat. Assn. Real Estate Bds., Assn. Citadel Men (life), Hugenot Soc. (life). Democrat. Episcopalian. Mason (Shriner). Clubs: Forest Lake, Spring Valley (Columbia). Home: 2803 Canterbury St Columbia SC 29204 Office: 1319 Pickens St Columbia SC 29202

REESE, JIMMY MALCOLM, savs. and loan exec., mayor; b. Columbus, Ga., July 31, 1928; s. Clyde Bowden and Ora (Webb) R.; student Auburn U., 1945-46; grad. U. N.C. Southeastern Inst. for Orgn. Execs., 1957, U. Ind. Grad. Sch. for Savs. and Loan, 1960; m. Ann Stewart, Aug. 9, 1949; children—Joseph Bowden, James Malcolm. Head teller Columbus Bank & Trust Co., 1947-53; exec. sec., treas., mng. officer, dir. Fitzgerald Fed. Savs. & Loan Assn. (Ga.), 1953-60; mng. officer, dir. Security Fed. Savs. & Loan Assn., Perry, Ga., 1960—, pres., 1962—; mayor city Perry, 1970—. Pres., dir. Ben Hill Enterprises, Inc., Fitzgerald, 1958—; dir. Houston Halls, Inc., Houston Lake Devel., Inc., Fed. Home Loan Bank Atlanta, Secura Corp., Equity Mortgage Corp. Vice pres. Central Ga. council Boy Scouts Am. Pres., dir. Perry Club Council; mem. Fitzgerald Planning and Zoning Commn., 1956-60, Perry Municipal Planning Commn., Fitzgerald, 1958-59. Named One of Ga.'s 5 Outstanding Young Men, Ga. Jr. C. of C., 1960, Outstanding Young Man, Perry Jr. C. of C., 1960. Mem. U.S. (dir.), Ga. (dir. 1956-61, pres. 1961) savs. and loan leagues, Am. Savs. and Loan Inst. (gov. 1963-64), Soc. Savs. and Loan Controllers, Perry C. of C. (pres. 1963-67-68), Soc. Real Estate Appraisers. Kiwanian, Elk. Home: 1417 Baker St Perry GA 31069 Office: 916 Main St Perry GA 31069

REESE, MELVIN LEROY, city mgr.; b. Hazelton, Pa., Apr. 6, 1907; s. Evan D. and Mary (Dietz) R.; B.S., Stout Inst., 1930; M.S., U. Wis., 1931; m. Dorothy K. Kubits, June 23, 1934; children—Evan David, Thomas Simpson. With Wis. Bd. Vocational Edn., 1931-37; pres., gen. mgr. Quaker Dairy, Appleton, Wis., 1937-39; gen. mgr. Simpson-Parker Constrn. Co., Appleton, 1939-42; asst. exec. sec. WPB, Washington, 1942-45; dir. disposal policy War Assets Adminstrn., Washington, 1945-50; dir. adminstrn. Renegotiation Bd. Washington, 1950-55; county mgr. Montgomery County, Md., 1955-60; city mgr. Miami (Fla.), 1960—. Recipient award Valley Forge Freedom Found., 1961; Meritorious award C. of C. Americas, 1962. Mem. Internat. City Mgrs. Assn., Am. Soc. Pub. Adminstrn., Am. Pub. Works Assn., Am. Soc. Planning Ofcls., Nat. Assn. County Ofcls., Am. Mgmt. Assn., A.I.M., Nat. Tax Assn. Episcopalian (vestry). Mason (32 deg., Shriner). Clubs: Rotary, Com. 100 (Miami Beach), Miami. Home: 2401 SW 4th Av Miami FL 33129 Office: Dinner Key City Hall Miami FL 33133

REESE, PAUL MICHAEL, II, air freight and charter service exec.; b. New Orleans, Feb. 17, 1942; s. Paul Michael and Cathryn (Carter) R.; student La. State U., New Orleans, 1961, Tulane U., 1962-64; m. Elizabeth Saunders, Apr. 23, 1965; 1 son, Paul Michael III. With Gulf Oil Corp., New Orleans, 1964-69; owner Newton Printing Co., New Orleans, 1969-71; part owner Vanguard Airways, New Orleans, 1971—; diver, free lance under water photographer; Luger editor Guns and Ammo Mag., Los Angeles, 1970—; staff editor Nat. Diver Mag. Served with USMCR, 1960-68. Author: U.S. Trials/1900 Luger, 1970; Collectors Guide to Luger Values. Designer Charl III Diver's Companion Knife. Home: 3619 State St Dr New Orleans LA 70125 Office: PO Box 52364 New Orleans LA 70152

REESE, ROBERT LUTHER, bldg. corp. exec., city ofcl.; b. nr. Garysburg, N.C., Sept. 25, 1909; s. Robert Luther and Willie (Harris) R.; student High Point Coll., 1926; m. Elizabeth Ross, June 13, 1936; children—Sara Elizabeth (Mrs. Eugene Clark Cook), Robert. Vice pres., gen. mgr. Hedgecock Builders & Supply, Asheboro, N.C., 1946—; mayor City of Asheboro, 1963—. Dir. Randolph Savs. & Loan, First Nat. Bank. Mem. Asheboro City Sch. Bd., 1956-61. Bd. dirs. Randolph Hosp. Served with A.C., AUS, 1944-46. Democrat. Elk, Kiwanian (div. pres. 1956; div. lt. gov. 1961). Home: 625 Holly St Asheboro NC 27203 Office: 251 Ross St Asheboro NC 27203

REESE, THOMAS DEAL, indsl. distbn. co. exec.; b. Nacogdoches, Tex., Sept. 25, 1913; s. James Early and Laura (King) R.; student Stephen Austin State U., 1931-33, U. Tex. at Austin, 1935-36; m. Virginia Elizabeth Jackson, Apr. 9, 1938; children—Thomas D., J. Mark, Jamie Elizabeth. With Gulf Consol. Service, Inc. (Gulf Supply Co., Inc., Nunn Electric Supply Corp., Bay Supply Co., Inc., Reichardt Electric Co., Inc., Island Supply Co., Inc.), Houston, 1947—, v.p., 1971—, also dir. Mem. adv. council indsl. distbn. Tex. A. and M. U., Houston, 1970—. Episcopalian (mem. exec. bd.; dep. Gen. Conv., 1961, 64, 67, 70, 73). Clubs: Houston, Champions Golf (Houston). Home: 29 Colony East-Champions Houston TX 77069 Office: 7220 N Loop East Houston TX 77028

REESE, WEIMAN HERMAN, geophs. co. exec.; b. Lake Charles, La., Aug. 16, 1921; s. John Ira and Alma (Jessen) R.; student McNeese Jr. Coll., 1939-41; B.S., La. State U., 1943; m. Dorothy Meyer, Sept. 11, 1945; children—Cheryl (Mrs. Richard Nordin), Randy (Mrs. J.M. Duhon), Vicki (Mrs. James Mayfield), Edward. With Nat. Geophys. Co., Dallas, 1943-47, Geophys. Assos., Houston, 1947-55; v.p. McCollum Exploration (merged into Ray Geophys. 1959, then Mandrel Industries 1960), Houston, 1955-59; v.p. Mandrel Indus tries, Houston, 1960—. Served to lt. (j.g.) USNR, 1944-46. Mem. Soc. Exploration Geophysicists, Houston Geophys. Soc. Clubs: Houston; Explorers (N.Y.C.). Address: 584 Trianon St Houston TX 77024

REEVE, JOSEPH EDWIN, govt. ofcl.; b. Kendallville, Ind., Dec. 2, 1907; s. Frederick Edwin and Ruth (Conlogue) R.; B.A., Amherst Coll., 1929; postgrad. London Sch. Econs., 1929-30; Ph.D., U. Chgo., 1939; m. Betty Washburn, Dec. 30, 1938; children—Deborah (Mrs. Alfred McCray), Ruth (Mrs. Harrison Weed, Jr.). Instr. econs. Marietta Coll., 1931-33, Carleton Coll., 1935-36, Wayne U., 1937-38; economist Fed. Deposit Ins. Corp., Washington, 1939-41; asst. chief commerce and finance U.S. Bur. Budget, 1942-64, dir. monetary and credit analysis, 1964-70, cons. Office Mgmt. and Budget, 1970—. Exec. sec. Pres.'s Com. Fed. Credit Programs, 1962-63, Pres.'s Com. Financial Assets, 1966, Pres.'s Com. to Reappraise Fed. Credit Programs, 1969. Mem. Montgomery County (Md.) Library Bd., 1952-64, chmn., 1956, chmn. planning com., 1957-64; chmn. welfare com. Montgomery County Civic Fedn., 1960-64. Trustee, Pilgrim Fund. Recipient Exceptional Service award Bur. Budget, 1966. Mem. Am. Econ. Assn., Am. Finance Assn. Democrat. Mem. United Ch. Christ (dir. Central Atlantic conf. 1966-69). Club: Cosmos (Washington). Author: Monetary Reform Movements, 1943; (with others) Government Component in National Wealth, 1950; ann. spl. analyses of Fed. Credit Programs in Pres.'s budget, 1952-70. Home: 7171 E Brentwood Rd Fort Myers FL 33901 Office: Office of Management and Budget Washington DC 20503

REEVE, RAYMOND TOWNER, broadcasting co. exec.; b. Niagra Falls, N.Y., Apr. 25, 1901; s. Amos Gillette and Adilade (Campbell) R.; student Dartmouth, 1919-23; m. Marguerite Pierce, Sept. 20, 1941; children—Margot Towner, Sarah Michelle (Mrs. Wayne Underhill), Raymond Towner. Salesman, Oneida Ltd., 1923-31; announcer Radio Sta. KGMB, Honolulu, 1931-35, Radio Sta. KJBS, San Francisco, 1935-37, Teleflash Inc., N.Y.C., Balt. and Washington, 1937-39; sports dir. Capitol Broadcasting Co., Inc., Raleigh, N.C., 1939—; night mgr., sports dir. WRAL TV, 1956-71. Served with USNR, 1918-19. Named Hall of Fame N.C. Sports, 1967. Hall of Fame, Assn. Broadcasters, 1971. Home: 1607 Canterbury Rd Raleigh NC 27608 Office: PO Box 12000 Raleigh NC 27605

REEVES, ALVIN, JR., accountant; b. Pauls Valley, Okla., Jan. 12, 1944; s. Alvin G. and Delia Mae (Barnett) R.; B.A., Central State U., 1967; m. Thelma Jo Manning, Aug. 28, 1965; children—Daniel Todd, Dale Alan. Mem. staff Peters & Chandler, C.P.A.'s, Oklahoma City, 1967-69, Harold W. Spradlin, C.P.A., 1969-70, partner, Spradlin &Reeves, 1970-71; officer, dir. Spradlin, Lyle & Reeves, Inc., Oklahoma City, 1971—; asst. controller Sequoyah Industries, Inc., 1972—. C.P.A., Okla. Mem. Okla. Soc. C.P.A.'s, Am. Inst. C.P.A.'s, Capitol Hill C. of C., Tau Kappa Epsilon, Republican. Methodist (trustee ch.). Home: 605 SW 70th St Oklahoma City OK 73139 Office: 5201 S Western St Oklahoma City OK 73109

REEVES, BEN CHAPMAN, lawyer; b. Eufaula, Ala., Feb. 2, 1936; s. Malcolm McNab and Virginia (Chapman) R.; B.S., U. Ala., 1957, LL.B., 1960; m. Charlotte Adams, Aug. 22, 1959; children—Benjamin Chapman, Eleanor Virginia. Admitted to Ala. bar, 1960; dist. atty. 3d Jud. Circuit Ala., Eufaula, 1963—; dir. Guardian Savs. Investment Co. Trustee Lakeside Sch. Served to 1st lt. AUS, 1960-62. Mem. Nat. (dir.), Ala. (pres. 1967-68) dist. attys. assns., Barbour County Bar Assn. (pres. 1963), Eufaula C. of C. (pres. 1964), Phi Delta Theta, Beta Gamma Sigma, Omicron Delta Kappa. Rotarian. Episcopalian (ch. sch. supt.). Home: 1st St Francis Point Eufaula AL 36027 Office: Broad St Eufaula AL 35027

REEVES, BENJAMIN FRANKLIN, govt. ofcl.; b. Bowling Green, Ky., May 7, 1922; s. Ben Peden and Marguerite (Harvison) R.; A.B. in Journalism, U. Ky., 1949, postgrad. in Polit. Sci., 1951; m. Mavis Andree Mann, Sept. 15, 1956; 1 dau., Andree Elizabeth. Instr. journalism Richmond Profl. Inst. Coll. William and Mary, Richmond, Va., 1949-50; reporter Evansville (Ind.) Press, 1951; reporter Courier-Jour., Louisville, 1952-59, asst. mng. editor, 1959-61, mng. editor, 1961-65; Washington corr. Louisville Courier-Jour. and Louisville Times, 1965-66; asst. to chmn. House Com. on Edn. and Labor, 1967—. Intership to study Congress. Am. Polit. Sci. Assn., Washington, 1953-54. Served with USNR, 1942-46. Mem. Am. Polit. Sci. Assn., Phi Beta Kappa. Unitarian. Home: 5601 Wood Way Washington DC 20016 Office: Rayburn House Office Bldg Washington DC 20515

REEVES, BLAIR, county judge; b., 1924; LL.B., St. Mary's U., San Antonio. Now judge Bexar County, Tex. Address: 313 Country Hill Lane San Antonio TX 78209*

REEVES, CHARLES MERCER, JR., finance co. exec.; b. Sanford, N.C., Feb. 14, 1919; s. Charles Mercer and Suzanne Easten (Purvis) R.; B.S. in Bus. Adminstrn., U. N.C., 1940; m. Sarah Frances Crosby, Oct. 12, 1940; children—Charles Mercer III, David Crosby, Suzanne (Mrs. James Marion Parrott IV), John Mercer II. Pres., chmn. bd. Safeway Suburban Lines, Inc., Sanford, Dunn, Reidsville, N.C., 1946-49; pres. 1st provident Co., Inc., Sanford, 1949—, Brown's Auto Supply Co., Sanford, 1959-69; pres., chmn. bd. Atlantic & Western Ry., Sanford, 1968—; dir. Carolina Bank; pres., chmn. So. Provident Life Ins. Co., Phoenix. Partner, Rich Mountain Assos., Boone, N.C., Cape Lookout Assos., Morehead City, N.C. Mem. N.C. Banking Commn., 1954-61, 69—. Mem. N.C. Higher Bd. Edn., 1961-62; dist. exec. com. Boy Scouts Am., 1964—. Commr., Lee County, 1953-55. Served with AC USNR, World War II. Mem. Beta Theta Pi. Methodist. Rotarian. Home: Reeves Ridge Farm Sanford NC 27330 Office: 132 S Moore St Sanford NC 27330

REEVES, EDNA MABEL, state ofcl.; b. Castleberry, Ala., June 30, 1907; d. James Edward and Anna (Barrwo) Reeves; grad. Ga. Carolina Sch. Commerce, 1926. Various clk.-stenographer positions, Brewton, Ala., 1926-29, Montgomery, Ala., 1929-41, Maxwell Field, Ala., 1941-49; supr. U.S. Property and Disbursing Office, Montgomery, 1949-51; adminstrv. asst. social security div. Ala. Sec. of State (now social security div. State of Ala.), Montgomery, 1951-60, dir., 1960-61; dir. State Agy. for Social Security, 1961—. Chmn. legislative com. Nat. Conf. State Social Security Adminstrs., 1966—; legislative reporting rep. Commerce Clearing House, Inc., N.Y.C., 1951—. Mem. Montgomery Joint Legislative Council, 1962-71, chmn. legislative com., 1967-68. Mem. Pilot Club Montgomery (chmn. patriotic emblems com. 1962, 66-68, 70-71, chmn. Community Services Com. 1969-70, sec. 1965, chmn. edn. and internat. com. 1963, mem. joint legislation com. 1963—). Democrat. Mem. Ch. of Christ. Club: Pilot (sec. Montgomery 1965, chmn. community services com. 1969-70). Home: 3163 Norman Bridge Rd Montgomery AL 36106 Office: Pub Safety Bldg Montgomery AL 36104

REEVES, GARTH, newspaper exec. Publisher, Miami (Fla.) Times. Mem. Nat. Newspaper Pubs. Assn. (pres.). Office: One Herald Plaza Miami FL 33101*

REEVES, GLENN WILLARD, educator; b. Munday, Tex., Aug. 20, 1925; s. James Ely and Elizabeth (Perry) R.; B.Elec. Engring., Ga. Inst. Tech., 1946; B.D., So. Baptist Theol. Sem., 1949, Th.M., 1957, Th.D., 1963; m. Frances Elizabeth Smith, July 23, 1949; children—Glenn Willard, Samuel Ray. Tchr. Buckner Children's Home, Dallas, 1949-50; ordained to ministry Bapt. Ch., 1949; student pastorate New Washington (Ind.) Bapt. Ch., 1956-59; dir. religious activities Cumberland Coll., Williamsburg, Ky., 1963-65, prof., head dept. religion, 1964—, also chmn. div. religion, bib. langs. and philosophy. Scoutmaster, Blue Grass council Boy Scouts Am., 1965-66. Served with USNR, 1943-46, 51-55. Mem. Soc. Bibl. Lit., Am. Acad. Religion. Home: PO Box 429 Williamsburg KY 40769 Office: PO Box 520 Cumberland College Sta Williamsburg KY 40769

REEVES, H. REEVES, educator; b. Scott County, Ky., June 6, 1912; s. L.H. and Ada (Roberts) R.; A.B., U. Ky., 1933, M.A., 1934; M.S., Syracuse U., 1935; m. Emerin S. Bradley, Sept. 7, 1942; children—Edward Bradley, Hazel O'Rear. Asso. prof. polit. sci. U. Ky., 1941-42, prof. econs., part-time, 1949-50; asst. to pres. Stephens Coll., Columbia, Mo., 1954-56; tchr. grad. class bus. adminstrn. U. La., evenings 1962; pres. Ky. Ind. Coll. Found., 1960-63; exec. v.p. for Huntsville affairs U. Ala., 1963-69; prof. polit. and adminstrv. scis. U. Ala. in Huntsville, 1964—; mem. Ala. Edn. Study Commn., 1968-69; cons. in field. Gen. mgr. Louisville Transit Co., 1946-48; v.p. Bankers Life and Casualty Co., Chgo., 1952-54, also dir.; pres. State Ins. Co. Ky., 1956-63. Spl. asst. to U.S. Commr. Edn., 1935-36; dir. research and statistics Ky. Dept. Revenue, 1936-38, commr. Revenue, 1938-42, 48-52; state co-campaign dir. Ky. Heart Assn., 1951-52; exec. cons. Ky. Fair and Exposition Center, 1956-60. Bd. dirs. Huntsville Indsl. Expansion Com., 1965-69. Served with USCG, 1942-45; comdr. Res. ret. Mem. Nat. Assn. Tax Adminstrs. (pres. 1941-42), Nat. Tax Assn. (pres. 1952-53), Am. Soc. Pub. Adminstrn. (mem. council 1969—). Home: 2303 Annandale Rd SE Huntsville AL 35801

REEVES, HUBERT LISBON, economist; b. Little Rock, Sept. 30, 1904; s. Alfred Randolph and Jency (Hubert) R.; B.A., Morehouse Coll., 1924; postgrad. Northwestern U., 1926-28; M.A., Am. U., 1950; postgrad. N.Y.U., 1950-51; m. Stella Elizabeth Jones, Sept. 3, 1938. Economist, War Manpower Commn., Washington, 1942-45, U.S. Dept. Labor, Washington and N.Y.C., 1947-54; asso. internat. labor specialist U.S. Dept. Labor, Washington, 1955, economist, 1956-62, manpower devel. specialist, 1962-64, manpower research analyst, 1964-67; lectr. econs. Savannah State Coll., 1968—; econ. cons. Sociometrics, Inc., Silver Spring, Md., 1971—. Bd. dirs. Bethle-Community Center. Recipient Superior Performance award Dept. Labor, 1966. Mem. Am. Econ. Assn., Internat. Assn. Personnel in Employment Security, Alpha Phi Alpha. Conglist. Club: Pigskin (Washington). Contbr. articles to profl. jours. Home: 901 E 32d St Savannah GA 31401

REEVES, JAMES JERAULD, lawyer; b. Troy, Ala., Oct. 11, 1938; s. David Chester and Goldie Elaine (Jerauld) R.; student Pensacola Jr. Coll., Fla. State U.; LL.B., Stetson U., 1962; m. Lelia Frances Weaver, Apr. 10, 1963; children—Carl Michelle, James Jerauld, Rachel Suzanne. Admitted to Fla. bar.; partner firm Hopkins, Hanh & Reeves, Pensacola, Fla., 1962-64, Hahn, Reeves & Shimek, Pensacola, 1964-69, Hahn & Reeves, Pensacola, 1969-70, Hahn, Reeves & Barfield (formerly Hahn, Reeves & Atwell), Pensacola, 1970—. Mem. Fla. Ho. of Reps., 1966——. Bd. dirs. Pensacola Zool. Soc., Children's Home Soc. Fla.; bd. govs. Fiesta Five Flags, Pensacola Sports Assn. Served with USMCR. Recipient Distinguished Service award for outstanding young man Escambia County, Pensacola Jr. C. of C., 1966-67. Mem. Am., Fla. bar assns., Am. Trial Lawyers Assn., Soc. Bar 1st Jud. Circuit, Navy League (dir.). Democrat. Presbyn. Toastmaster. Home: 2300 Osceola Pensacola FL 32501 Office: 98 E Garden St Pensacola FL 32501

REEVES, JAMES WILLARD, univ. dean; b. Covington, La., Oct. 31, 1931; s. Leon R. and Julia (Sirmon) R.; B.S., La. State U., 1952, M.S., 1959; Ph.D., U. Ariz., 1970; m. Clara Ruby Robicheaux, Aug. 30, 1958; children—Karen Tracy, Christine Suzanne. Engr., Chance Vought Aircraft Co., Dallas, 1952-53; design engr. La. Dept. Pub. Works, Baton Rouge, 1956-57; chief engr. George Covert & Assos., cons. engrs., Baton Rouge, 1957-59; asso. prof. civil engring. U. Southwestern La., Lafayette, 1959-71, dean Coll. Engring., 1971—. Vice chmn. adv. com. La. Coastal Commn., 1970—. Served to lt. USNR, 1953-56. Recipient Halliburton Edn. Found. award for excellence in teaching, 1971. NSF Faculty fellow, 1967-68. Registered profl. engr., La. Mem. Am. Soc. C.E. (faculty adviser 1965-67), Am. Soc. Engring. Edn., La. Engring. Soc., Sigma Xi. Club: Lafayette Organic Gardening. Author: The Evaluation of Silicones for Use With Concretes, 1966; Design of Thick Walled Cylindrical Pressure Vessels, 1966; Nonlinear Analysis of Axisymmetric Circular Plates, 1970. Home: 104 Kim Dr Lafayette LA 70501

REEVES, MARVIN COKE, pharm. co. exec.; b. Mt. Airy, N.C., Dec. 29, 1911; s. Marvin Coke and Sarah Myrtle (Spaugh) R.; B.A., Westminster Coll., 1933; m. Lynne Elizabeth Martin, June 16, 1951; children—Marvin Coke III, Mary Lynne, Sarah Elizabeth, Virginia Louise. Civil engr. So. Mapping & Engring. Co., Greensboro, N.C., 1941-44; partner Western Wood Products Co., Houston, 1947-50; pres. Bentex Pharm. Co., Houston, 1950-71; v.p. pharm. group Internat. Chem. and Nuclear Corp., Houston, 1969—. Served to lt. USNR, 1944-47. Mem. Mensa, Phi Delta Theta. Home: 2105 Dryden Rd Houston TX 77025 Office: 12936 Player St Houston TX 77045

REEVES, WILLIAM AUBREY, supt. schs.; b. Haskell, Tex., June 26, 1914; s. Wyatt Wylie and Annie (Easterling) R.; B.A., Howard Payne Coll., 1935; M.A., Tex. A. and I. U., 1951; postgrad. U. Tex., 1952-56; m. Wilma Carole Miller, Aug. 16, 1938; children—Patsy (Mrs. W. Bruce Reaves), Linda, William Miller. Secondary sci. tchr., coach, prin. Holding Inst., Laredo, Tex., 1935-42; tchr., prin., coach Woodsboro (Tex.) Ind. Sch. Dist., 1942-44, 47-51, supt. schs., 1951—. Inst. Devel. Edn. Activities fellow, 1969. Mem. Nat. Edn. Assn., Am. Tex. assns. sch. adminstrs., Tex. Tchrs. Assn. Baptist. Lion (pres. 1956). Home: 708 Johnson St Woodsboro TX 78393 Office: 704 Locke St Woodsboro TX 78393

REGAN, TERRY MALCOLM, environmental engr.; b. Lexington, Ky., Mar. 18, 1935; s. Herman Daniel and Gladys Mae (Butler) R.; B.S. in Civil Engring., U. Ky., 1957; m. Phyllis Jean McCann, Dec. 21, 1957; children—Kathleen Dawn, Kelly Anne, Kevin McCann. Design and resident engr. Howard K. Bell, cons. engrs., Lexington, 1957-61; civil engr., asst. dir. Dept. Water Pollution Control, City of Lexington, 1962-70, acting dir., 1970—; pres. T.M. Regan, Inc., water quality control services, Lexington, 1970—. Instr., cons. environmental tng. courses for colls. and govt. agys. Mem. Ky. Bd. Certification for Water and Sewage, 1968—, chmn., 1968-71. Trustee Woodland Trust Fund. Served to capt. Inf., AUS, 1957, 61-62. Recipient C.E. Alumni award U. Ky. Coll. Engring., 1969. Registered profl. engr., Ky. Mem. Nat., Ky. (mem. registration com.; recipient Outstanding Young Engr. award 1971; pres. Bluegrass chpt. 1972) socs. profl. engrs., Water Pollution Control Fedn. (recipient William D. Hatfield award 1968, chmn. certification study com. 1971—), Am. Pub. Works Assn. (pres. Ky. chpt. 1968-69), Ky.-Tenn. Water Pollution Control Assn. (chmn. Ky.-Tenn. 1970-71), Am. Water Works Assn., Inst. Municipal Engrs., Inst. Solid Wastes, Ky. Hist. Soc., U. Ky. Alumni Assn., Delta Tau Delta. Mem. Christian Ch. (trustee 1971—). Home: 666 Montclair Dr Lexington KY 40502 Office: 386 Waller Av Lexington KY 40504

REGGIE, EDMUND MICHAEL, lawyer, judge; b. Crowley, La., July 19, 1926; s. Fred and Victoria (Andraous) R.; B.A., Southwestern La. Inst., 1946; LL.B., Tulane U., 1949; m. Doris Anne Boustany, June 17, 1951; children—Edmund Michael, Victoria Anne, Denis Andrew, Gregory F., Mariam, Raymond. Admitted La. bar, 1949; asso. Denis T. Canan, Crowley, 1949-50; judge, City Ct. of Crowley, 1950—. Sec., dir. Huval Baking Co., Inc., 1954—; v.p., dir. Western Investment Corp., 1954—, Frany Holding Corp., 1953—; chmn. bd. Acadia Savs. & Loan Assn., 1957; vice chmn. bd. La. Bank & Trust Co.; dir. Plant Industries, Inc. Specialist to Lebanon, Syria, Jordan, Egypt, Saudi Arabia, for U.S. Dept. State, 1961. Commr. Pub. Welfare of La. until 1965; mem. La. State Mineral Bd., 1964-66. La. chmn. Nat. Library Week, 1964. Del. Dem. Nat. Conv., 1956, 60, 64, 68; Dem. presdl. elector La., 1960; mem. Dem. state Central Com., 1956-60. Mem. bldg. com. Internat. Rice Festival, 1957, pres., 1960; chmn. Acadia Parish Polio Fund, 1953, 54, Acadia Paish A.R.C., 1953; pres. St. Vincent de Paul Conf., 1953; counsellor Boy Scouts Am.; exec. dir. La. Commn. Extension and Continuing Edn., 1967—; mem. Pub. Affairs Research Council; mem. La. Council for Music and Performing Arts; mem. La. Council Govtl. Reorgn., La. Conf. Children and Youth Com.; exec. com. La. delegation to Pres.'s White House Conf. Children and Youth. Bd. dirs. S.W. La. Rehab. Center, Nat. Rehab. Assn., Crowley Mental Health Assn., La. Conf. Social Welfare; trustee Williston-Northampton Sch. Named La.'s Distinguished Dem., Young Dems. La., 1963; Cardinal Newman award for S.W. La., 1963. Pres. Cardinal Newman Found. Mem. Nat. Assn. Municipal Ct. Judges, Am. Pub. Welfare Assn., Am., La., Acadia Parish (sec. 1955-56) bar assns., Am. Judicature Soc., La. Conf. Juvenile Correctional Workers, Nat. Council Juvenile Ct. Judges, La. City Judges Assn. (pres. 1971), La Societe du Droit Civile, Am. Trial Lawyers Assn., Am. Pub. Welfare Assn., Crowley Mental Health Assn., Nat. Rehab. Assn., Acadia Assn. Retarded Children, Crowley C. of C., Am. Acad. Polit. and Social Sci., N. Am. Judges Assn. Roman Catholic. K.C. (4 deg.). Clubs: Town, Kiwanis (dir. 1950-53, v.p. 1950-54), Bayou Bend Country; Nat. Capitol Democratic, Federal City. Home: 400 W Northern Av Crowley LA 70526 Office: Reggie Bldg Crowley LA 70526

REGISTER, NORMAN P., tax cons.; b. Shreveport, La., Aug. 10, 1909; s. Norman A. and Jane (Thornton) R.; grad. high sch.; m. Marjorie Sears, Dec. 2, 1942. With Tax Dept., City of Dallas, 1929-69, tax appraiser, 1932-46, chief tax appraiser, 1946-49, asst. assessor-collector, 1949-51, assessor and collector, 1951-53, dir. revenue and taxation, 1953-69; dir. revenue and taxation emeritus, City of Dallas, 1969—; now tax cons. Instr. property taxation for in-service tng. schs. Tex. Assn. Assessing Officers and U. Tex. Served with USAAF, World War II; PTO. Mem. Internat. (Most Valuable Mem. award 1955, pres. 1957-58, award 1965, hon. life mem. 1966—, author several pamphlets), Tex. (pres. 1952-53, 60-61, Achievement award 1962, hon. life mem. 1968—, award for meritorious service 1969) assns. assessing officers, Inst. Certified Tex. Assessors (chmn. bd. 1962). Author: Assessment of Banks, Insurance Companies, Savings and Loan Associations and Other Financial Institutions, 1959. Home: 6626 Yosemite Lane Dallas TX 75214 Office: Empire Central Bldg Dallas TX 75247

REGNIER, LOUIS A., property mgr., real estate developer; b. Cranston, R.I., June 27, 1927; s. Louis A. and Delia (MacPhail) R.; student U. Denver, 1951-52; m. Carol Jean Hall, Aug. 25, 1951; children— Stephen Dean, Lynn Ann, Christine Ann. Salesman, U.S. Radiator, Chgo., 1947-48, Clark-Babbitt Industries Boston, 1948; founder Contractors' Insulation Co., Providence, 1948-51; treas. Regnier-Laurienzo & Co., Inc., 1952-63; pres. Exec. House, Providence, 1961—, Louis A. Regnier Asso., Inc., 1963—, Lynn Investment Corp., 1962—; treas. Reservoir Investment Corp., 1961—; real estate investment cons. Bd. dirs. Beachpond Camp of Escoheag, Exec. Office Park, Apt. Owners and Mgmt. Assn. Served with USNR, 1945-46, USAF, 1952. Mem. Inst. Real Estate Mgmt., Nat. Assn. Realtors, Continental Varnums, Providence C. of C., Aircraft Ouners and Pilots Assn., Urban Land Inst., Am. Hereford Assn., Houston Apt. Assn., Builders Assn. Houston. Roman Catholic. Clubs: Greenwich, East Greenwich Yacht. Home: Fletcher Rd North Kingston RI 02852 also 5300 Woodhollow Dr Houston TX 77008 Office: 1145 Reservoir Av Cranston RI 02920 also Fannin Bank Bldg Houston TX 77025

REGULUS, HOMIE, librarian; b. Roberta, Ga.; d. Northern and Lucille (Lockett) R.; A.B., Clark Coll., 1938; B.S., Atlanta U., 1946, M.S., 1953. Tchr., Elberton (Ga.) Colored High Sch., 1938-42; asst. librarian Fort Valley State Coll., (Ga.), 1946-48, librarian, 1948—. Mem. Citizenship Edn. Commn. Trustee Thomas Pub. Library, Fort Valley, Mem. Southeastern, Ga. library assns., A.L.A., Ga. Assn. Educators, Alpha Kappa Alpha (south Atlantic regional dir. 1970-72). Democrat. Methodist. Home: 1209 Beverly St Fort Valley GA 31030

REHDER, HARALD ALFRED, zoologist; b. Jamaica Plain, Boston, June 5, 1907; s. Alfred and Anneliese (Schrefeld) R.; A.B., Bowdoin Coll., 1929; M.S., Harvard, 1933; Ph.D., George Washington U., 1934; m. Lois Fleming Corea, Oct. 15, 1938; children—Anne Fleming, Alfred Luis. Sci. aid, div. mollusks U.S. Nat. Museum, Smithsonian Instn., 1932-34, asst. curator, 1934-42, asso. curator, 1942-46, curator 1946-66, sr. zoologist, 1966—; mem. Smithsonian-Bredin expdns. to French Polynesia, 1957. Yucatan, 1962; Pacific Sci. Board Expdn. to Jaluit, Marshall Islands, 1960; expdns. to South Pacific, 1963, 64, 65, 67. Del. Am. Sci. Congress, 1940. Fellow A.A.A.S., Cal. Acad. Sci.; mem. Am. Malacological Union (pres. 1941), Washington Acad. Sci., Biol. Soc. Wash., Paleontological Soc., Soc. Systematic Zoology, Malacological Soc. London Club: Cosmos (Washington). Author: (with P. Bartsch) Marine Pelecypod Mollusks of Hawaiian Islands, 1938; also sci. papers. Editor Jour Washington Acad. Scis., 1944-46; co-editor Indo-Pacific Mollusca, 1959—. Home: 5620 Ogden Rd Springfield MD 21784 Office: Nat Mus Natural History Smithsonian Instn Washington DC 20560

REHM, GERALD STETSON, bus. exec., city ofcl.; b. W. Palm Beach, Fla., Mar. 10, 1927; s. Fred G. and Rose (Delfoe) R.; B.S., U.S. Merchant Marine Acad., 1948; postgrad. Hofstra Coll., 1950-56; m. Frances M. Smeja, Nov. 7, 1948; children—Gregory, Pamela, Scott. Deck officer Waterman S.S. Corp., N.Y.C., 1948-50; planning exec. Sperry Rand Corp., Great Neck, N.Y. and Clearwater, Fla., 1950-66; comptroller Bruce Taylor, Inc., Realtor-Insuror, Clearwater, 1967-69; organizer, pres. Experience Unlimited, Inc., Clearwater, 1969—; exec. dir. Eckerd Found., 1971—; v.p., gen. mgr. Screens Unltd., 1971—; also mayor city Dunedin, Fla., 1966—. Co-founder Dunedin Youth Festival; mem. Pinellas area council Boy Scouts Am. Mem. Alumni Assn. U.S. Merchant Marine Acad. (past nat. officer), Bd. Realtors. Republican. Roman Catholic (lay leader). Kiwanian (pres. 1962). Founder Caladesi Island State Park, Pinellas County, Fla., 1965-67. Home: 2228 Webb Av Dunedin FL 33528 Office: PO Box 4689 Clearwater FL 33518

REHM, JEROME GREGORY, dentist; b. Ste. Genevieve, Mo., Sept. 1, 1917; s. Henry Simon and Caroline Cora (Schaaf) R.; D.D.S., Washington U., St. Louis, 1940; m. Mary Catherine Hughes, Sept. 23, 1940; children—Catherine (Mrs. James Sidney Kohn), Thomas Jerome. Gen. practice dentistry, Jackson, Mo., 1940-42, Charlotte, N.C., 1946—. Served to maj. Dental Corps, AUS, 1942-46. Mem. Am. Dental Assn., Charlotte (pres. 1964-65), 2d Dist. dental socs., Omicron Kappa Upsilon, Xi Psi Phi. Home: 6200 Gothic Ct Charlotte NC 28210 Office: 1012 Kings Dr Charlotte NC 28207

REHNQUIST, WILLIAM HUBBS, U.S. Supreme Ct. justice; b. Milw., Oct. 1, 1924; s. William Benjamin and Margery (Peck) R.; B.A., M.A., Stanford, 1948, LL.B., 1952; M.A., Harvard, 1949; m. Natalie Cornell, Aug. 29, 1953; children—James, Janet, Nancy. Admitted to Ariz. bar; law clk. to former justice Robert H. Jackson, U.S. Supreme Ct., 1952-53; with firm Evans, Kitchel & Jenckes, Phoenix, 1953-55; mem. firm Ragan & Rehnquist, Phoenix, 1956-57; partner firm Cunningham, Carson & Messenger, Phoenix, 1957-60; partner firm Powers & Rehnquist, Phoenix, 1960-69; asst. atty.-gen. office of legal counsel Dept. of Justice, Washington, 1969-72; asso. justice U.S. Supreme Ct., 1972—. Mem. Nat. Conf. Commrs. Uniform State Laws, 1963-69. Served with USAAF, 1943-46; NATOUSA. Mem. Fed., Am. Maricopa (Ariz.) County bar assns., State Bar Ariz., Nat. Conf. Lawyers and Realtors, Phi Beta Kappa, Order of Coif, Phi Delta Phi. Republican. Lutheran. Contbr. articles law jours., nat. mags. Home: 7004 Arbor Lane McLean VA 22101 Office: Dept of Justice Washington DC 20530

REHRER, MERVIN, judge; b. Pine Grove, Pa., Mar. 16, 1913; s. Ottis and Cora R. (Zerbey) R.; A.B., Gettysburg (Pa.) Coll., 1939; postgrad. Dickinson Law Sch., Carlisle, Pa., 1940-41; J.D., Stetson Law Sch., DeLand, Fla., 1948; m. Catherine E. Swanson, Feb. 11, 1956; children—Marcia Jo Davis, James C., Laurie Diane. Visitor, Pa. Dept. Pub. Welfare, 1939-40; clk.-supr. U.S. Air Force, Middletown, Pa. and Newark, 1941-45; audit clk. Internal Revenue Service, Phila., 1949-51; auditor Army Ordnance, Phila., 1951-52; admitted to Fla. bar, 1948; practiced in Avon Park, 1953-57; city atty., Avon Park, 1953-57; judge Highlands County, Sebring, Fla., 1957—. Founder, trustee Youth Care, Inc. Mem. Am., Fla. bar assns., Fla. County Judges Assn., Nat., Fla. councils juvenile ct. judges. Lutheran (trustee). Rotarian, Elk. Home: 219 E Camphor St Avon Park FL 33825 Office: Court House Sebring FL 33870

REICH, DAVID LEE, librarian; b. Orlando, Fla., Nov. 25, 1930; s. P.F. and Opal Katherine (Wood) Reichelderfer (now Reich); Ph.B. magna cum laude, U. Detroit, 1961; A.M. in L.S., U. Mich., 1963; m. Kathleen Johanna Weichel, Aug. 2, 1954 (div. Sept. 1964); 1 son, Robert Weichel. Tchr. English, Jefferson Davis Jr. Sch., San Antonio, 1961-62; dir. engring. library Radiation Inc., Melbourne, Fla., 1963-64; asst. to dir. libraries Miami-Dade Jr. Coll., Miami, Fla., 1964-65; dir. learning resources Monroe County Community Coll., Monroe, Mich., 1965-68; dep. dir. Dallas Pub. Library, 1968—. Library cons. Macomb County Community Coll., Warren, Mich., 1967; chmn. adv. com. to library tech. asst. program El Centro Coll., Dallas, 1969-71. Mem. Inter-Task Working Group, Goals for Dallas, 1968-70; mem. Dallas Area Library Planning Council, Goals for Dallas, 1970—. Served as sgt. AUS, 1952-55. Carnegie L.S. Endowment scholar U. Mich., 1963; William B. Calkins Found. scholar, Orlando, 1963. Mem. Am. Assn. Jr. Colls., A.L.A. (council mem.-at-large 1968-72), Tex., Fla. (sec.-treas. coll. and spl. libraries div. 1965) library assns., Assn. Coll. and Research Libraries (sec. jr. coll. libraries sect. 1968-69). Contbr. articles to library jours. Home: 4262 Holland Av Dallas TX 75219 Office: Dallas Public Library 1954 Commerce St Dallas TX 75201

REICH, DON, broadcasting exec. Sta. mgr. WUNI, Mobile, Ala. Office: 1257 Springhill Av Mobile AL 36604*

REICHER, LOUIS JOSEPH, clergyman; b. Piqua, O., June 14, 1890; s. Jacob and Marie (Krebsbach) R.; student St. Jerome's Coll., Kitchener, Can., 1911; St. Mary's Sem., Cin., 1911-12; St. Mary's U., LaPorte, Tex., 1918; LL.D., St. Edward's U., Austin, Tex., 1944. Ordained priest Roman Catholic Ch., St. Mary's Cathedral, Galveston, Tex., 1918; chancellor Galveston diocese, 1918-48; vicar for religious and adminstrv. council, 1918-48; founded and built St. Christopher's parish, Houston, 1923-41; apptd. Domestic Prelate, 1935, Protonotary Apostolic, 1940; consecrated bishop of Austin, 1948. Address: 1205 Nueces St PO Box 637 Austin TX 78767

REICHERT, WALTER STEWART, lab. technician; b. Louisville, Aug. 8, 1929; s. Sauter Frank and Alice (Buschmann) R.; student U. Louisville, 1947-50; m. Ella Carolyn Ross, Feb. 9, 1952; children—Walter Stewart, Carolyn Jean, Paul Frank, David Lawrence. Lab. technician E.I. Du Pont Co., Louisville, 1950—; mem. Ky. State Senate, 1966—. Mem. Ky. Ho. of Reps., 1964-66. Served with USAF, 1950-53. Mem. Engrs. and Architects Soc. Louisville, Amvets. Republican. Home: 4909 E Manslick Rd Louisville KY 40219 Office: Box 1378 Camp Ground Rd Louisville KY 40201

REID, AMOS LAMAR, lawyer; b. Birmingham, Ala., July 10, 1925; s. Amos Lamar and Pauline Freeman (Kinney) R.; student Birmingham-So. Coll., 1942-43; LL.B., U. Ala., 1949; m. Martha Frances Smyer, Sept. 7, 1946; children—Martha Patricia, Amos Lamar III. Admitted to Ala. bar, 1949; practiced in Birmingham, 1949—; partner Smyer, Smyer, White & Reid, 1949-55; agy. mgr. Protective Life Ins. Co., Birmingham, 1955-58; partner Smyer, White, Reid & Acker, 1959—. Dir. State Security Life Ins. Co., Kokomo, Ind., Lincoln Life Ins. Co., Ariz., Jefferson Nat. Equities Corp., Ala., Jefferson Memory Co., Ala. Chmn. Jefferson County Democratic Exec. Com., 1953-55. Served to 1st lt. Inf., AUS, 1943-46. Mem. Farrar Order Jurisprudence, Phi Delta Phi, Sigma Alpha Epsilon. Mason (Shriner). Home: 2720 Cherokee Rd Birmingham AL 35216 Office: Title Bldg Birmingham AL 35203

REID, JAMES CUTLER, biochemist; b. Akron, O., Apr. 17, 1918; s. Lloyd George and Louise (Cutler) R.; B.S., U. Pa., 1939; M.S., Pa. State U., 1940; Ph.D., U. Cal. at Berkeley, 1944. Instr. chemistry Bowling Green State U., 1940-42; mem. staff Radiation Lab., U. Cal. at Berkeley, 1946-49, research asso. dept. chemistry, 1944-46; mem. research staff Nat. Cancer Inst., NIH, Bethesda, Md., 1949—. Mem. chemistry panel Interagy. Bd. Examiners, U.S. Civil Service Commn., 1967—. Fellow A.A.A.S.; mem. Am. Chem. Soc., Am. Soc. Biol. Chemists, Phi Beta Kappa, Sigma Xi. Author: (with Melvin Calvin and others) Isotopic Carbon, 1949; (with David Greenberg and others) Amino Acids and Proteins, 1951. Home: 4 Wyoming Ct Washington DC 20016 Office: Bldg 10 NIH Bethesda MD 20014

REID, JOHN CLIFTON, cons. mech. engr.; b. Fredericksburg, Va., May 2, 1932; s. Purcell Timberlake and Anne Louise (Patterson) R.; student George Washington U., 1953-55; B.S. in Mech. Engring., Va. Poly Inst., 1959; m. Ann Louise Downer, Feb. 14, 1953; children—Karen Lynn, Gretchen Dianne, Ashley Ann, Kevin Daniel. Asso., Wiley & Wilson, cons. engrs., Richmond, Va., 1959-69; asso. Hankins & Anderson, cons. engrs., Richmond, also Boston, 1969—. Served with AUS, 1952-55. Registered profl. engr., Va., N.C., Mass., N.Y., D.C., Md. Mem. Am. Soc. M.E., Am. Soc. Heating, Refrigerating and Air Conditioning Engrs., Nat. Soc. Profl. Engrs., Va. Assn. Profls., Am. Numis. Assn., Pi Tau Sigma, Tau Beta Pi. Methodist. Home: 8208 Chipplegate Dr Richmond VA 23227 Office: 2117 N Hamilton St Richmond VA 23230

REID, LESLIE MERLE, educator; b. Niagara Falls, N.Y., May 4, 1929; s. James Leslie and Ariel (Dunn) R.; B.S., Mich. Tech. U., 1951; M.S., Mich. State U., 1955; Ph.D., U. Mich., 1963; m. Dorothy Jean Cattell, Aug. 26, 1950; children—Michelle Elaine, John Leslie Campbell. Landscape forester City of Wyandotte, Mich., 1950-52; city forester, adminstrv. asst. parks Topeka, 1955-56; instr., asst. prof. park adminstrn., dept. resource devel. Mich. State U., East Lansing, 1957-65; prof., head recreation and parks dept. Tex. A. and M. U., College Station, 1965—. Collaborator, Nat. Park Service, 1970—. Served with Signal Corps, AUS, 1952-54. Mem. Nat. Recreation and Park Assn., Soc. Am. Foresters, Soc. Park and Recreation Educators (v.p. 1968-69, pres. 1969-70), Tex. Acad. Scis., Tex. Recreation and Park Soc., Phi Kappa Phi, Gamma Sigma Delta. Mason, Rotarian. Home: 1202 Pershing Av College Station TX 77840

REID, LESLIE WOODS, fruit co. exec.; b. Detroit, May 19, 1913; s. Richard John and Violet Wilhemina (White) R.; student U.S. Army Officer's Candidate Sch., 1954, Lakeland Bus. Inst., 1960; m. Margaret Ann Branam, June 6, 1952; children—Leslie Scott, Rhonda Frances, Mary Anna, Amy Lea. Commd. 2d lt. U.S. Army, 1944, advanced through grades to maj., 1952; q.m. Ft. Bragg, N.C., 1949-50; I Corps, Korea, 1950-52; A.J. Sch., Ft. Benjamin Harrison, Ind., 1953-54; SETAF-Italy, 1954-57; ret., 1957; office mgr. Coca-Cola Bottling Co., Lakeland, Fla., 1960-62; office mgr. Hardee Mfg. Co., Plant City, Fla., 1962-64; treas., dir. Carter Fruit Co., Lakeland, Fla., 1964—; dir. Carter Groves, Inc., Carter Realty Co., C & C Mgmt. Co. Mem. Am. Legion. Elk. Home: 1344 Edgewood Dr Lakeland FL 33803 Office: 201 1/2 E Lemon St PO Box 884 Lakeland FL 33802

REID, MILES ALVIN, sch. prin.; b. West Point, Va., Oct. 23, 1931; s. William Ensley and Cecelia Olymphia (Whiting) R.; B.A., Morgan State Coll., Balt., 1953; M.A., Hampton (Va.) Inst., 1968; postgrad. Va. State Coll., 1958-63, U. Va., 1969-70, Va. Commonwealth U., 1970-71; m. Alice Lee, Aug. 14, 1966; 1 dau., Alicia Mia. Social studies tchr. Central High Sch., King and Queen, Va., 1957-64; prin. King and Queen Elementary Sch., Shanghai, Va., 1964-72. Mem. West Point Bi-Racial Com., 1969—, West Point and Vicinity Community Action Group, 1971—. Mem. West Point Bd. Zoning Appeals, 1971—; mem. King William County Dem. Com., 1967—. Bd. dirs. West Point Area Improvement Assn., vice chmn., 1970-71; bd. dirs. West Point Centennial Corp., 1970. Mem. King William County Lit. Union (program chmn. 1970), Nat., Va. (pres.-elect dept. elementary sch. prins. dist. C, 1971), King and Queen edn. assns., N.A.A.C.P. Baptist (gen. supt. ch. sch. 1964—, mem. Pamunkey Bapt. Assn. and Ch. Sch. Conv., instr. Bapt. Gen. Conv. Va. Inst. 1964—). Home: 216 16th St West Point VA 23181 Office: Hamilton-Holmes Elementary Sch King William VA 23086

REID, PAUL APPERSON, coll. pres.; b. Vade Mecum Springs, N.C., Aug. 10, 1902; s. William Henry and Margaret (Apperson) R.; A.B., U. N.C., 1929, M.A., 1938; Litt.D., High Point Coll., 1956; m. Magdalene Fulk, Dec. 20, 1924 (dec. Mar. 1955); m. 2d, Nettie Dockery Haywood, Nov. 10, 1956. Elementary sch. tchr., prin., Pilot Mountain, N.C., 1923-27; bus. mgr., asst. supt. schs., Roanoke Rapids, N.C., 1929-35, prin. jr.-sr. high schs., 1935-38; prin. Needham Broughton High Sch., Raleigh, N.C., 1938-41; supt. pub. schs., Elizabeth City, N.C., 1941-44; controller N.C. Bd. Edn., 1944-49; pres. Western Carolina Coll., Cullowhee, N.C. 1949-56, 57—, now pres., emeritus; served as asst. dir. higher edn., N.C., 1956-67. N.C. rep. edn. adv. com. Appalachian Regional Commn. Mem. N.C. Hist. Sites Commn.; mem. Jackson County-Sylva Planning Bd.; exec. com. Raleigh-Wake County Community Chest. Mem. N.E.A., Am. Assn. Sch. Adminstrs., N.C. Hist. and Lit. Soc., N.C. Edn. Assn. (pres. Western dist. higher edn. div., past pres. N.E. dist.), N.C. City High Sch. Prins. Assn. (past pres.), Western N.C. Schoolmasters Club, Western N.C. Asso. Communities (dir., past pres.), N.C. Children's Home Soc. (dir.), N.C. League Crippled Children (dir.), Wake County Tb Assn. (dir.) Methodist (steward). Kiwanian (past pres.); Rotarian. (pres.). Home: Box 637 Pilot Mountain NC 27041

REID, PRESTON HARDING, educator; b. Akron, Colo., Nov. 15, 1923; s. William Preston and Elizabeth (Kircher) R.; B.S., Colo. State U., 1949; M.S., N.C. State Coll., 1951, Ph.D., 1956; m. Marianne Doherty, June 21, 1948; 1 dau., Jeralee Susanne (Mrs. Timothy Douglas Sigley). Research prof. N.C. State U., Raleigh, 1949-69; prof., scientist-in-charge Va. Poly. Inst. and N.C. State U.'s Tidewater Research Sta., Holland, Va., 1969—; dir. soil testing div. N.C. Dept. Agr., Raleigh, 1964-69; cons. Internat. Basic Economy Corp., Lima, Peru, 1966. Served with AUS, 1942-46. Mem. Am. Soc. Agronomy, Soil Sci. Soc. Am. (chmn. soil testing and plant analysis com. 1968), Va. Soil Fertility Assn., Assn. So. Agrl. Workers (chmn. expt. sta. supts. div. 1971), Sigma Xi, Beta Beta Beta. Contbr. articles to profl. jours. Home: 1204 West Point Dr Suffolk VA 23434 Office: PO Box 98 Holland VA 23391

REID, RALPH W(ALDO) E(MERSON), mgmt. ofcl.; b. Phila., July 5, 1915; s. Ralph Waldo Emerson and Alice Myrtle (Stuart) R.; student Temple U., 1932-34; B.S., Northwestern U., 1936; M.A., U. Hawaii, 1938; Ph.D., Harvard, 1949; m. Ruth Bull, Dec. 7, 1946; 1 son, Robert. Asst. to v.p. Northwestern U., 1938-40; chief municipal govt. br., spl. asst. govt. sect. Supreme Comdr. Allied Powers, 1946-47; spl. asst. under sec. army, 1948-49; chief Far Eastern affairs div. Office Occupied Areas, chief econs. div. Office Civil Affairs and Mil. Govt., Dept. Army, 1950-53; asst. to dir. Bur. Budget, 1953-55, asst. dir., 1955-61; resident mgr. A. T. Kearney & Co., 1961—. Mem. planning bd. NSC, 1954-61. Served from ensign to comdr., USNR, 1941-46. Decorated Dept. Navy Commendation Ribbon; recipient Dept. Army Exceptional Civilian Service award. Mem. Am. Oriental Soc., Am. Polit. Sci. Assn., C. of C. U.S. (com. govt. operations and expenditures, com. improvement fed. budget, adv. task force financing state and local govts.). Clubs: Union League (Chgo.); Capitol Hill, Cosmos (Washington). Home: 412 Monticello Blvd Alexandria VA 22305 Office: 1725 K St NW Washington DC 20006

REID, ROGER DELBERT, educator; b. Lamont, Ia., July 31, 1905; s. George Sawyer and Florence (McCormack) R.; A.B., U. S.D., 1927; M.S., Pa. State U., 1931, Ph.D., 1935; m. Erma House, June 7, 1933; children—Donald H., Barry H. Tchr., prin. Gann Valley (S.D.) High Sch., 1927-29; tchr. sci. U. S.D. High Sch., Vermillion, 1929-30; asst. prof. Pa. State U., 1931-36, U. Ida., 1936-37; instr. bacteriology Sch. Medicine, Johns Hopkins, 1937-46; biology researcher Hynson, Westcott & Dunning, Inc., Balt., 1946-48; head microbiology br. Office of Naval Research, Washington, 1948-57, dir. biol. scis. div., 1957-67, prof. microbiology U. West Fla., Pensacola, 1968—. Served with AUS, 1941-46. Recipient Outstanding Civilian Service award U.S. Navy, 1967, Barnett Cohen award Md. br. Am. Soc. Microbiology, 1965. Fellow A.A.A.S., Am. Soc. Microbiology; mem. Sigma Xi, Phi Sigma, Lambda Chi Alpha. Mason (32 deg.). Author: (with M.J. Pelczar) Microbiology, 3d edit., 1972. Research on penicillin and other antibiotics. Home: 6219 Vicksburg Dr Pensacola FL 32503 Office: Dept Microbiology U West Fla Pensacola FL 32504

REID, SILAS BOYD, furniture mfg. co. exec.; b. Centrahoma, Okla., Sept. 12, 1918; s. Samuel Elmer and Lela Esther (Campbell) R.; student Internal. Corr. Schs., 1957; m. Thelma Irene Reed, Sept. 24, 1938; 1 son, Gary Boyd. Laborer, Ward Furniture Mfg. Co., Ft. Smith, Ark., 1936-43; pattern maker, designer Douglas Aircraft Co., Oklahoma City, 1943-44; plant mgr. Okla. Furniture Mfg. Co., Guthrie, 1946—. Mgr., dir. PeeWee Ball Club, 1951-54; dir. Am. Legion Ball Club, 1954-59. Served with USNR, 1944-46. Mem. Am. Legion. Baptist (deacon). Mason, Kiwanian. Home: Route 3 Box 194 Guthrie OK 73044 Office: 400 W College St Guthrie OK 73044

REID, STEWART FOLEY, mortician; b. Manassas, Va., Dec. 14, 1930; s. William Cledford and Germaine (Tetar) R.; student Coll. William and Mary, 1949, 50; grad. mortuary sci. and mgmt. Pitts. Inst. Mortuary Sci., 1956; m. Janet Virginia Shumaker, Nov. 20, 1965; 1 dau., Laura Denise. Funeral dir., embalmer Baker Funeral Home, Manassas, 1956-68; partner, pres., treas. Crew & Clayton Funeral Home, Inc., Ashland, Va., 1969—. Chmn. Hanover County chpt. A.R.C., 1969-70, v.p. Richmond chpt., 1971; mem. Town and Gown Council (Town of Ashland-Randolph-Macon Coll.), 1970—; mem. Hanover Med. Services Com., 1970—. Bd. dirs. Va., Hanover mental health assns. Served with AUS, 1951-53. Mem. Ashland C. of C. (pres. 1970—), Va. (dir. 1971—), Central Dist. funeral dirs. assns. Club: Ashland Lions. Home: 300 Virginia St Ashland VA 23005 Office: PO Box 326 Ashland VA 23005

REID, SYDNEY AUGUSTUS, educator; b. Jamaica, May 17, 1926; s. Walter Charles and Mabel (Grant) R.; diploma Jamaica Sch. Agr., 1946; B.S., Cornell U., 1955, M.S., 1956, M.P.A., 1960; Ph.D., U. Mass., 1964; m. Leslene V. McDonald, Sept. 10, 1960; children—Karl Sydney, Dane Correli Sydney. Came to U.S., 1965, naturalized, 1969. Extension officer Govt. Jamaica, Spanish Town, 1946-53; research asso. State U. N.Y. Research Found., Bklyn., 1963-65; asso. prof. polit. sci. Va. State Coll., Petersburg, 1965-66, prof., head dept., 1966-69; prof., chmn. dept. Fla. A. and M. U., Tallahassee, 1969—. Mem. A.A.A.S., Am., So. polit. sci. assns., Am. Soc. Pub. Adminstrn., Am. Acad. Polit. and Social Sci., Am. Mgmt. Assn., N.A.A.C.P., Urban League. Episcopalian. Home: 3005 Lyndon Dr Tallahassee FL 32304

REIFF, JOHN CECIL, elec. engr.; b. Muskogee, Okla., Oct. 5, 1921; s. Cecil K. and Dorothy (McCloud) R.; B.S., Okla. U., 1947; M.S., Okla. A. and M. Coll., 1950; m. Marjorie Louise Jenry, May 8, 1943;

1 son, John Cecil. Instr. elec. engring. dept. U. N.M., 1947-51; research, devel. engr. missile systems Western Electric Co.-Bell Telephone Labs., 1951-54; research and devel. engr. White Sands Missile Range, N.M., 1954-68, supervisory missile systems engr., 1968—; pres. CJC Enterprises, Inc. Instl. rep. Cub Scouts Montgomery dist. Boy Scouts Am., 1955-58. Served with F.A., AUS, 1943-46, to capt., 1951-54; now col. Res. Registered profl. engr., Tex. Mem. I.E.E.E., Tex. Soc. Profl. Engrs., Phi Delta Theta. Baptist. Home: 9809 Gschwind St El Paso TX 79924 Office: SSEA Bldg 1400 White Sands Missile Range NM 88002

REIFF, WILLIAM HENRY, physician; b. Muskogee, Okla., July 24, 1918; s. Cecil K. and Dorothy Ellen (McCloud) R.; B.S., U. Okla., 1939, M.D., 1941; m. Maxine Ruth Hoffer, Feb. 20, 1942; children—William C., Kaethe M. (Mrs. Daniel F. Stella), Patricia A. (Mrs. John F. Moore). Intern, U. Mich. Hosp., 1941-42, asst. resident internal medicine, 1945-46, resident, 1946-48; practice medicine specializing in internal medicine, Oklahoma City, 1948—; mem. staff St. Anthony, Bapt. Meml., Deaconess hosps.; asst. prof. internal medicine U. Okla. Regent Oral Roberts U., Tulsa. Served with AUS, World War II. Decorated Bronze Star medal, Combat Med. badge, French Croix de Guerre with palm; recipient Pfizer Co. award for civil def., 1964. Diplomate Am. Bd. Internal Medicine. Fellow A.C.P.; mem. Soc. Nuclear Medicine, A.M.A., Okla. Med. Assn., Oklahoma County Med. Soc., Phi Chi, Phi Delta Theta. Home: 2505 NW 42d St Oklahoma City OK 73112 Office: 3015 NW 59th St Oklahoma City OK 73112

REIFSNYDER, CHARLES FRANK, lawyer; b. Ottumwa, Ia., Sept. 6, 1920; s. Charles L. and Lena (Emery) R.; A.B., George Washington U., 1944, LL.B., 1946; m. Sally Ann Evans, Dec. 27, 1948; children—Daniel Alan, Jeremy Evans; m. 2d, Nancy Lee Laws, Mar. 4, 1960; 1 son, Frank Laws. Admitted to D.C. bar, 1945; sec. Judge T. Alan Goldsborough, U.S. Dist. Ct., Washington, 1945; law clk. Chief Judge Bolitha J. Laws, U.S. Dist. Ct., 1946-47; asst. U.S. atty., Washington, 1947-51; spl. asst. to Atty. Gen. U.S., 1950-51; asso. Hogan & Hartson, Washington, 1951-58, partner, 1959—. Trustee Legal Aid Agy. D.C. (now Pub. Defender Service D.C.), 1960-67. Chmn. personnel security rev. bd. AEC, Washington. Fellow Inst. Jud. Adminstrn., 1967-68. Mem. Nat. Coll. State Judiciary (dir. 1968-70), Am. Bar Assn. (chmn. spl. com. coordination judicial improvements, chmn. sect. jud. adminstrn. 1967-68, mem. spl. com. atomic energy law, mem. ho. dels. 1968-69, nat. vice chmn. Jr. Bar Conf. 1955-56), Fed., Fed. Power (chmn. com. natural gas 1967-68) bar assns., Am. Arbitration Assn., Bar Assn. D.C. (dir. 1955-56), Phi Delta Phi, Sigma Nu. Episcopalian. Clubs: University, Barristers, National Lawyers, Metropolitan, Lawyers (Washington); Annapolis Yacht, Severn Sailing Assn. (Annapolis, Md.); Farmington Country (Charlottesville, Va.). Home: 10605 Stable Lane Potomac MD 20854 Office: 815 Connecticut Av Washington DC 20006

REILLY, CHARLES FRANCIS, JR., newspaper editor; b. Norfolk, Va., Nov. 4, 1910; s. Charles Francis and Mary (Miney) R.; student Norfolk div. Coll. William and Mary, 1930, U. Va., 1960; m. Dorothy L. Minton, Nov. 16, 1937. With Norfolk Ledger-Star, 1929—, news editor, 1958-61, mng. editor, 1961—. Pres. for Va., A.P., 1967. Served to capt. USCGR, 1942-46. Mem. Va. Press Assn. (bd. dirs.). Home: 1046 N Lexan Crescent Norfolk VA 23508 Office: 150 W Brambleton Av Norfolk VA 23501

REILLY, EDWARD JOSEPH, govt. ofcl.; b. N.Y.C., Oct. 13, 1920; s. Anthony Joseph and Theresa May (Clancy) R.; A.B., Rutgers U., 1947; M.A., N.Y.U., 1955; m. Olga Antuck, Jan. 28, 1950; 1 dau., Nina Marie. News and spl. events staff NBC, N.Y.C., 1941-42; govt. relations adviser Arabian-Am. Oil Co., Dhahran, Saudi Arabia, 1947-48; univ. relations counsel Ivy Lee & T.J. Ross, Public Relations, N.Y.C., 1948-51; dir. tech. liaison Army Engrs., Washington, Cal., N.Y., 1951-61; dir. information Army Transp., N.Y.C., 1961-62; pub. relations counsel Internal Revenue Service, N.Y.C., 1962-69, information specialist field service, Washington, 1969—. Organizer Am. Legion Jersey Boys State, Rutgers U., 1947. Trustee D.A.V. Hosp. Fund N.J. Served with USMCR, 1942-45; PTO. Decorated Bronze Star, Purple Heart. Mem. D.A.V., Am. Legion, Am. Mil. Engrs., Rutgers Alumni, Pub. Relations Soc., Zeta Psi. Contbr. articles to profl. jours. Home: 1842 Foxstone Dr Vienna VA 22180 Office: Nat Office Internal Revenue Service 1111 Constitution Av NW Washington DC 20224

REILLY, FRANK WARD, JR., mfg. exec.; b. Chattanooga, Dec. 13, 1928; s. Frank Ward and Margaret (White) R.; B.Indsl. Engring., Ga. Inst. Tech., 1953; m. Lenda Catherine Gay, Jan. 9, 1954; children—Frank Ward III, Lenda Gay. With Sherman & Reilly, Inc., Chattanooga, 1954—, dir., v.p., 1959-67, pres., 1967—. Bd. dirs. Chattanooga Girls Club. Served with USAF, 1953. Mem. I.E.E.E., Am. Ordnance Assn., Phi Delta Theta. Republican. Episcopalian. Kiwanian. Clubs: Lookout Mountain Golf, Lookout Mountain Fairyland (Tenn.); Blue Springs Hunting (Chattanooga). Home: 9 Bartram Rd Lookout Mountain TN 37350 Office: 1st and Broad Sts Chattanooga TN 37402

REILLY, TERRENCE EDWARD, banker; b. Providence, Sept. 5, 1920; s. Michael and Flora (DePine) R.; B.S., Bryant Coll., 1948; grad. U. Va. Sch. Consumer Banking, 1965; m. Virginia Mary Durham, Jan. 8, 1949; children—Katherine A., Terrence M., Stephen V., Thomas J., J. Kevin. Office mgr. Comml. Credit Corp., Providence, 1948-53; times sales rep. Indsl. Nat. Bank, Providence, 1953-57; asst. cashier Broward Nat. Bank, Ft. Lauderdale, Fla., 1957-58; v.p. Coral Ridge Nat. Bank, Ft. Lauderdale, 1958—. Tchr. Am. Inst. Banking, 1965. Served to maj. USAAF, 1942-46. Rotarian. Home: 529 SW 10th Av Ft Lauderdale FL 33312 Office: 2626 E Oakland Park Blvd Ft Lauderdale FL 33306

REILY, WILLIAM BOATNER, JR., coffee co.exec.; b. Morehouse Parish, La., Dec. 31, 1887; s. William Boatner and Estelle (Weaks) R.; student Tulane U., 1904-07; m. Elaine Pujo, Feb. 10, 1915; 1 son, William Boatner III. With Reily-Taylor Co., New Orleans, 1907-1916; organizer Standard Coffee Co., New Orleans, 1916; exec. v.p. Wm. B. Reily &Co., Inc., New Orleans, 1924-42, pres., 1942-68, chmn. bd., 1968—; executor Killarney Plantation, Collinston, La., 1940—. Founder, guarantor Tulane U. Sch. Bus. Adminstrn., 1914. Founder mem. Bur. Govtl. Research New Orleans; founder dir. Pub. Affairs Research Council La.; founder mem. La. Civil Service. Served to ensign USNRF, 1917-21. Mem. S.A.R., Sigma Alpha Epsilon. Clubs: Boston, Louisiana, Round Table (New Orleans); Little Lake (Lafitte, La.). Home: 2221 Prytania St New Orleans LA 70130 Office: 640 Magazine St New Orleans LA 70130

REIMER, RUDOLPH EDWARD, ret. mfg. exec.; b. Cincinnati, May 9, 1904; s. Frank and Bessie (Umbach) R.; Com. Engr., U. Cin., 1928; m. Cleone M. Brooks, Sept. 1, 1934; children—J. Brooks, Ross Alan. Controller, Dresser Mfg. Div., mfrs. pipe line coupling and accessories, Bradford, Pa., 1929-32. treas., 1932-43; sec.-treas. Dresser Industries, Inc., 1943-47, v.p., sec.-treas., 1947-58, exec. v.p., 1958-69, also dir.; officer, dir. subsidiary and affiliated corps.; sr. v.p., dir. Panoil Co., 1969—. Mem. Pi Kappa Alpha, Alpha Kappa Psi. Republican. Methodist. Mason (32 deg.). Clubs: Brook Hollow Golf, Dallas Petroleum. Home: 7408 Wellcrest Dr Dallas TX 75230

REINDORP, REGINALD CARL, educator; b. Alamogordo, N.M., June 3, 1907; s. Cecil Reginald Carl and Maude (Ketchum) R.; B.A., U. N.M., 1931, M.A., 1933; Ph.D., U. Tex., 1949; m. Trugen Williamson, May 26, 1961; children—Elizabeth Schuster, Evangeline Falcon, Carl, David. Tchr. N.M. pub. schs., 1932-37; chief field party U.S. Tech. Assistance Progarm, Latin Am., 1943-48, UN Tech. Assistance, Ecuador, 1952-53; prof., chmn. dept. fgn. langs. East Central State Coll., Ada, Okla., 1961-62; prof., chmn. div. langs., lit. and speech Fort Hayes (Kan.) State Coll., Hays, 1962-65; prof., chmn. dept. fgn. langs. Wesleyan Coll., Macon, Ga., 1965—. Dir., Inst. Latin Am. Studies, also adviser and sponsor Latin Am. students U. So. Miss., 1953-61; Latin Am. corr. Wood Products Co., Purvis, Miss., 1956-61. Pres., Fgn. Student Corp., U. Ark., 1949-51. Decorated by Republic of El Salvador, 1948; Pan Am. Union research grantee, 1966. Mem. Am. Assn. U. Profs., Phi Kappa Phi (pres.-elect 1971-72), Phi Delta Kappa, Phi Sigma Iota. Mason, Rotarian. Author: Spanish American Customs, Culture and Personality, 1968; (with E.R. Craine) The Chronicles of Michoacan, 1970; numerous others. Home: 641 Hathaway Dr Macon GA 31204

REINECKE, JOHN ALFRED, educator; b. New Orleans, Jan. 28, 1931; s. Joseph Alfred and Mariette (Sarrat) R.; B.B.A., Loyola U. of South, 1951; M.B.A., Tulane U., 1953; Ph.D., U. Ill., 1959; m. Gladys E. Aleman, Feb. 20, 1954; children—Thomas A., Elizabeth M., Margaret R., Paul S., Peter G., Helen F., Susan H. Instr., Loyola U., New Orleans, 1955-56; grad. asst. U. Ill., 1956-59; asst. prof. marketing La. State U., New Orleans, 1959-63, asso. prof., chmn. dept. mgmt. and marketing, 1963-66, prof. marketing, 1966—, dir. Internat. Marketing Inst., 1968-70; cons. Social Security Adminstrn., Nat. Council on Aging. Served from ensign to lt. (j.g.) USNR, 1952-55. Union Oil Corp. fellow in bus., 1963. Mem. Am. Marketing Assn. (past chpt. pres.), Am. Assn. U. Profs. (past pres.), Blue Key, Beta Gamma Sigma, Alpha Sigma Nu. Home: 1552 Pressburg St New Orleans LA 70122

REINFELDS, JURIS, educator; b. Riga, Latvia, Apr. 1, 1936; s. Nikolais and Irma (Kaulins) R.; B.Sc., U. Adelaide, S. Australia, 1959, Ph.D., 1962; m. Lauma Petersons, Sept. 15, 1962; children— Peteris Maris, Ivars Valdis, Martins Nikolajs. Came to U.S., 1965. Imperial Chem. Industries postdoctoral research fellow Tait Inst. Math. Physics, Edinburgh, Scotland, 1961-64; research asso. U. Adelaide (S. Australia), 1964, Nat. Acad. Scis., Huntsville, Ala., 1965-66; asst. prof. statistics Computer Center, U. Ga., Athens, 1966—. Member Association Computing Machinery, Am. Phys. Soc. Co-editor: Interactive Systems for Exptl. Applied Mathematics, 1968. Office: U Ga Computer Center Athens GA 30601

REINL, HARRY CHARLES, govt. ofcl.; b. Muttersdorf, Germany, Nov. 13, 1932 (parents Am. citizens); s. Carl and Angela (Plass) R.; B.S., Fordham U., 1953; postgrad. Columbia; A.M., George Washington U., 1968; grad. spl. summer program Mass. Inst. Tech., 1972. Jr. observer Sperry Rand Corp., N.Y.C., 1958-62; labor economist Office of Manpower Adminstr., U.S. Dept. Labor, Washington, 1962—. Mem. nat. bd. sponsors Inst. Am. Strategy. Served to 1st lt. AUS, 1953-55. Mem. Am. Security Council, Taxation with Representation, Am. Econ. Assn., Internat. Platform Assn. Club: Shenandoah Shores. Home: Shenandoah Shores Front Royal VA 22630 Office: 1730 M St Washington DC 20025

REINSCH, JAMES LEONARD, radio and TV exec.; b. Streator, Ill., June 28, 1908; s. Henry Emil and Lillian (Funk) R.; B.S., Northwestern U., 1934; m. Phyllis McGeough, Feb. 1, 1936; children—Penelope Luise (Mrs. E. William Bohn), James Leonard. With radio sta. WLS, Chgo., 1924; mgr. radio sta. WHIO, Dayton, O., 1934-39, exec. dir., 1942-64, mgr. WSB, Atlanta, 1939-42, exec. dir., 1942-64, exec. dir. WIOD, Miami, 1942-64; pres. Carolina Broadcasting Co., 1959-64; pres. Cox Broadcasting Corp., 1964—; chmn. Cox Cable Communications, 1966—; dir. Concept Industries, Atlanta, 1st Nat. Bank, Atlanta. Radio adviser to White House, 1945-52; former chmn. U.S. Adv. Commn. Information. Radio dir. Democratic Nat. Conv. and Presdl. Campaign, 1944; radio-TV adviser Dem. Nat. Com., 1952—, gen. mgr., 1956, exec. dir., 1960, 64, cons., 1968, radio-TV dir. 1952, Dem. presdl. campaign, 1960. Mem. Internat. Radio and TV Soc., Broadcast Pioneers. Clubs: Peachtree Golf (Atlanta); Burning Tree (Washington). Author: Radio Station Management, 1948, rev. edit., 1960. Home: 3671 Northside Dr NW Atlanta GA 30305 Office: 1601 W Peachtree St NE Atlanta GA 30309

REIS, HAROLD FRANK, lawyer; b. N.Y.C., July 22, 1916; s. Bernard and Rose (Frank) R; B.S.S., Coll. City N.Y., 1937; LL.B., Columbia, 1940; m. Ruthanne Abram; children—Alan B., Kate Susan (Mrs. Grogan), Deborah. Admitted to N.Y. bar, 1941, D.C. bar, 1953, also U.S. Supreme Ct.; atty. Dept. Justice, 1941-42; counsel P.R. Transp. Authority, 1942-43; with Office Alien Property Custodian, also Dept. Justice, 1943-67; now partner firm Newman, Reis & Axelrad; exec. asst. to atty. gen., 1964-67. Recipient Rockefeller Pub. Service award, 1964. Mem. Am., Fed. bar assns. Home: 3330 Stephenson Pl NW Washington DC 20015 Office: 1100 Connecticut Av NW Washington DC 20036

REISING, KEITH L., broadcasting exec. Pres., WKRX, Louisville. Office: PO Box 606 Louisville KY 40201*

REISS, EDMUND ALLAN, educator; b. Bklyn, Oct. 12, 1934; s. Edmund Lewis and Mabel Catherine (Curfman) R.; A.B., Pa. State U., 1955; M.A., 1956; Ph.D., Harvard, 1960; m. Louise Horner, July 17, 1964; children—Kathryn Lynn, Geoffrey Scott. Asst. prof. English, Western Res. U., 1960-63; asso. prof. English and comparative lit., coordinator comparative lit., 1963-64; asso. prof. English, Pa. State U., 1964-67; prof. English, Duke, Durham, N.C., 1967—; vis. prof. Harvard, summers, 1969-70. Cons. Project English Demonstration Center, Euclid, O., 1963-64. Dexter travelling fellow Harvard, 1959; grantee Am. Philos. Soc., 1962, 70, Am. Council Learned Socs., 1964, Huntington Library, 1965; Am. Council Learned Socs. fellow, 1966-67. Mem. Modern Lang. Assn., Mediaeval Acad. Am., Early English Text Soc., Dante Soc. Am., Internat. Arthurian Soc. Author: Sir. Thomas Malory, 1966, Elements of Literary Analysis, 1967, The Art of the Middle English Lyric: Essays in Criticism, 1972. Editor: Mark Twain's Mysterious Stranger and Other Stories, 1962, Mark Twain's Connecticut Yankee in King Arthur's Court, 1963; co-editor The Chaucer Review, 1966-70; asso. editor Jour. Medieval and Renaissance Studies, 1970—; bibliographer, sect. head Publs. Modern Lang. Assn., 1966—. Home: Route 1 Box 183-F Hillsborough NC 27278 Office: 502 Perkins Duke U Durham NC 27706

REISS, HOWARD ROBERT, physicist, educator; b. N.Y.C., July 29, 1929; s. Edward and Fannie (Metz) R.; B. Aero. Engring., Poly. Inst. Bklyn., 1950, M. Aero. Engring., 1951; Ph.D., U. Md., 1958; m. Gwendoline Agnes Heales, Dec. 15, 1951; children—Stephanie Jane, John Eden. Research fellow Poly. Inst. Bklyn., 1950-51; physicist U.S. Naval Ship Research and Devel. Center, Carderock, Md., 1951-55; physicist U.S. Naval Ordnance Lab., Silver Spring, Md., 1955-58, chief radiation physics div., 1958-69, cons., 1969-71; cons. Naval Research Lab., Washington, 1971-72. Lectr. dept. physics and astronomy U. Md., College Park, 1959-63; adj. prof. dept. physics Am. U., Washington, 1967-69, prof., 1969—. Served with USNR, 1951. Mem. Am. Phys. Soc., Washington Philos. Soc., Sigma Xi, Phi Kappa Phi, Sigma Pi Sigma, Tau Beta Pi. Home: 5245 Nebraska Av NW Washington DC 20015 Office: Am Univ Washington DC 20016

REISTLE, CARL ERNEST, JR., petroleum engr.; b. Denver, June 26, 1901; s. Carl E. and Leonara I. (McMaster) R.; B.S., U. Okla., 1922; student Harvard Sch. Bus. Adminstrn., 1948; D.Sc., U. Tulsa, 1966; m. Mattie A. Muldrow, June 23, 1922; children—Bette Jean (Mrs. Geo. F. Pierce), Mattie Ann, (Mrs. James Tracy Clark), Nancy L. (Mrs. Wilson Hayes Holliday), Carl Ernest III. Petroleum chemist U.S. Bur. Mines, 1922-29, petroleum engr., 1929-33; chmn. East Tex. Engring. Assn., 1933-36; with Humble Oil & Refining Co., 1933-66, successively engr. in charge, chief petroleum engr., gen. supt. prodn., mgr. prodn. dept., dir. mgr. prodn. dept., dir. charge prodn. dept., 1951-55, v.p. charge prodn. dept., 1955-57, exec. v.p., 1957-61, pres., 1961-63, chmn. bd. and chief exec. officer, 1963-66, cons., 1966—; dir. Eltra Corp., Olincraft, Inc., Reed Tool Co. Nat. dir. Jr. Achievement, Inc.; trustee Houston Mus. Natural Sci. Recipient Anthony Lucas medal, 1958; Engr. of Year award Nat. Soc. Profl. Engrs., 1966. Mem. Mining and Metall. Soc. Am., Am. Petroleum Inst. (dir.), Am. Inst. Mining and Metall. Engrs. (pres. 1956), Sigma Xi, Tau Beta Pi, Sigma Tau, Alpha Chi Sigma. Clubs: Petroleum, Ramada, River Oaks Country, Anglers of N.Y. Contbr. tech. articles to profl. jours. Home: 3196 Chevy Chase Houston TX 77019 Office: 2605 Humble Bldg Houston TX 77002

REISTRUP, JAMES, composer, pianist, educator; b. Racine, Wis.; s. James and Dorthea (Hansen) R.; Mus.B., Morningside Coll., 1936; student Chgo. Mus. Coll., 1925, 34; postgrad. U. Wis., 1947; m. Laura Jeanne Moss, July 23, 1931; children—Paul Hansen, John Valdemar. Head piano dept. Morningside Coll., 1915-50; dean Campbell Sch. Music, Washington, 1951-53; dir. Reistrup Studios, Washington, 1953—. Guest tchr. U. Wis., 1947; lectr. lit., music to clubs; recitals N.Y.C., N.H., Ia., N.J., Washington. Recipient awards for compositions; Nat. Inst. Arts and Scis. fellow, 1945. Mem. Nat. Assn. Composers and Conductors, Am. Assn. U. Profs., D.C. Fedn. Music Clubs (pres. 1954-58), Washington Music Tchrs. Assn. (v.p. 1953-54), Phi Mu Alpha Sinfonia (life). Contbr. articles in field to profl. jours. Composer: Suite of Eight Piano Pieces, 1942; Tommelise, 1942; The Brook, Sunday Morning, 1947; Etude, 1948; Ostinato, 1957; Canzonetta, 1968. Nat. judge compositions Nat. Guild Piano Tchrs., 1956-66. Address: 3701 Connecticut Av NW Washington DC 20008

REISTRUP, JEANNE MOSS (MRS. JAMES REISTRUP), interior designer; b. Glasgow, Mo., Aug. 11, 1905; d. Samuel and Jennie (Easley) Moss; student U. Ill., 1923-27; study in Europe, 1931; m. James Reistrup, July 23, 1931; children—Paul H., John V. Head bur. interior decorating Davidson Bros., Sioux City, Ia., 1928-31; owner firm Jeanne Moss Reistrup Interiors, 1933—; tchr. interior decorating YWCA; also lectr. Active United Givers, Symphony fund drs. and civic work. Recipient Woman of Achievement award, Sioux City, Ia., 1946. Fellow Am. Inst. Interior Designers (chmn. nat. conf. 1953, exhibit Nat. Housing Center 1959; mem. nat. by-laws com.; chmn. bd. govs., corr. sec. D.C. chpt.; mem. nat. nominating com. for govs.; chmn. chpt. relations D.C., chmn. lecture com. D.C. chpt. 1971-72); mem. Ia. State Soc. (v.p. 1963-65), Pan Am. Liaison Com. Women's Orgns. (corr. sec. 1959-60), P.E.O., Delta Zeta. Clubs: Fortnightly (past pres.), Morningside Coll. Faculty Women's (past pres.). Author articles in field. Home: 3701 Connecticut Av NW Washington DC 20008

REITER, EUGENE ANTHONY, banker; b. Chgo., Jan. 17, 1922; s. John Frederick and Barbara (Servais) R.; student Collegiate Bus. Coll., N.Y.C., 1947-49, Sch. Banking, Hofstra U., 1952; m. Gina Victoria Catanese, June 10, 1946; children—Eugene Anthony, Charles, John. Mgr. auto loan dept. Franklin Nat. Bank, Rockville Centre, N.Y., 1954-57; asst. v.p. Nat. Bank of Long Beach (N.Y.), 1957-59; v.p. 1st Va. Bank, Falls Church, Va., 1964—. Served with USNR, 1943-46. Mem. Consumer Bankers Assn. Club: St. Johns Bridge (McLean, Va.). Home: 1714 Linwood Place McLean VA 22101 Office: 6400 Arlington Blvd Falls Church VA 22042

REITH, CARL JOSEPH, super market co. exec.; b. Peoria, Ill., Jan. 11, 1914; s. Joseph and May (Kolb) R.; ed. high sch.; m. Jennie S. Habbinga, Apr. 3, 1936; 1 dau., Joyce Elaine. Sales, office staff Peoria Creamery Co. (Ill.), 1932; with Kroger Co., 1934-60, successively asst. br. accountant, office mgr., accountant, Terre Haute, Ind., also Atlanta, adminstr., coordinator tng. and mgmt. devel. programing Gen. Offices, Cin., gen. merchandising mgr. St. Louis br., br. mgr., Indpls., br. mgr., Cin., 1934-57, v.p., 1957-60; pres., chief exec. officer Colonial Stores, Inc., 1960-67, also dir.; pres. Oxford Industries, 1967—; dir. Fulton Nat. Bank Atlanta, Atlanta and West Point R.R., Cox Broadcasting Co. Adv. bd. Salvation Army, Atlanta; mem. adv. com. on bus community relations Emory U. Bd. dirs. Atlanta Symphony Guild; trustee Atlanta Art Assn. Mem. Nat. Assn. Food Chains (dir., exec. com.), Mo., Indiana (pres., v.p., 1951-55) chain store councils, Ind. (bd. 1954-55), Indpls. (bd. 1950), Ga. (indsl. devel. council) chambers commerce. Mason (Shriner), Rotarian. Clubs: Meridian Hill Country (Indpls.); Kenwood Country, Queen City (Cin.); Capital City, Peachtree Golf (Atlanta). Office: Atlas Industries Inc Atlanta GA 30312

RELPH, ROSS, civil engr.; b. Minco, Okla., Jan. 24, 1921; s. Tom and Geneva (Ross) R.; student U. Kan., 1939-41; m. Kaye Horner, June 19, 1947; children—Gene Ellen, Rosalind Kaye, Mary Eleda. Partner, sec.-treas. Lowrie-Relph-McNett & Assos., Oklahoma City, 1960—. Chmn. Oklahoma City Street Adv. Commn., 1965-66. Served with AUS, 1942-45. Registered profl. engr., Okla., N.M., Kan. Mem. Am. Soc. C.E., Nat., Okla. socs. profl. engrs., Oklahoma City C. of C., Capitol Hill C. of C. Home: 8401 Lakehurst Dr Oklahoma City OK 73120 Office: City National Bank Tower 200 N Robinson Oklahoma City OK 73102

REMEIN, QUENTIN ROBERT, govt. ofcl.; b. Rochester, N.Y., Sept. 5, 1919; s. Harry J. and Florence (Noland) R.; A.B., Calvin Coll., Grand Rapids, Mich., 1945; postgrad. U. Mich., 1946, Am. U., 1948-49; m. Harriet A. Kuipers, Apr. 3, 1944; children—Quentin Robert, Kathryn H., Teresa F. Statistician, venereal disease div. USPHS, Washington, 1946-54, chief statistician chronic disease program, 1954-57, asso. chief operational research, chronic disease program, 1957-62, chief program planning and evaluation Nat. Center for Chronic Disease Control, 1962-69; spl. asst. for planning and program coordination Dept. Health, Edn. and Welfare, Washington, 1969—. Served to 2d lt. AUS, 1941-44; PTO. Decorated Purple Heart; recipient Superior Service award Dept. HEW. Mem. Am. Pub. Health Assn., Am. Statis. Assn., N.Y., Acad. Scis., Washington Christian Sch. Soc., Am. Acad. Health Adminstrn. Mem. Christian Reformed Ch. (elder). Contbr. articles on pub. health and chronic diseases to sci. jours. Home: 18 Wynkoop Ct Bethesda MD 20034 Office: Office Asst Sec for Health and Sci Affairs Dept Health Edn and Welfare Washington DC 20201

REMINES, HAROLD PRESTON, dentist; b. Williamson, W. Va., Feb. 21, 1932; s. Harold Milton and Eva Emaline (Mullins) R.; student Va. Poly. Inst., 1951-54; D.D.S., Med. Coll. Va., 1958; m. Linda Kay Mercer, May 1, 1970; children—Charles Preston, Christy

Mercer, Rebecca Joan, Eva Jane. Pvt. practice dentistry, St. Paul Va., 1958—. Mem. Wise County Sch. Bd., 1971—. Mem. Southwest Va. Dental Soc., Va., Am. dental assns., Omicron Kappa Upsilon, Psi Omega. Lion. Home: St Paul VA 24283 Office: Phillips Bldg St Paul VA 24283

REMINGTON, CHARLES EMMETT, assn. exec.; b. Meridian, Ida., Feb. 12, 1905; s. Guy Amos and Josephine Patterson (Hill) R.; student U. Ida., 1923-27; B.S., Ore. State U., 1929; m. Cleda Raynor, May 29, 1930; children—Richard, Delbert. Engr., Ida. Hwy. Dept., Boise, 1931-35; with U.S. Forest Ser., 1935-61, asst. regional engr., Portland, Ore., 1954-59, regional engr., Denver, 1960-61; chief engr. Bur. Land Mgmt., Interior Dept., Washington, 1961-67; treas. Washington Soc. Engrs., 1969—. Served to lt. col. AUS, 1940-46; 51-54. Decorated Legion Merit; recipient Distinguished Service award Interior Dept., 1968. Mem. Am. Soc. C.E., Soc. Am. Mil. Engrs., Soc. Am. Foresters, Am. Congress Surveying and Mapping. Democrat. Methodist. Mason, Acacian. Home: 2005 Columbia Pike Arlington VA 22204

REMMEL, ROLAND ROWE, bldg. products exec.; b. Little Rock, Sept. 26, 1917; s. Augustus C. and Ellen Lucy (Cates) R.; student Washington and Lee U., 1935, 37, Va. Mil. Inst., 1937; B.S. in Bus. Adminstrn., U. Ark., 1940; m. Ruth Elizabeth Rebsamen, Apr. 8, 1948; children—Ruth Ellen, Mary Elizabeth, Emily Karen, Raymond Roland. Co-founder, chmn. bd. Southland Bldg. Products Co., Little Rock, 1948—; pres. Compass Co., Fixed Assets Leasing Co.; chmn. Little Rock br. St. Louis Fed. Res. Bd. Active Quapaw Area council Boy Scouts Am. Bd. mgmt. YMCA; chmn. Salvation Army. Served to capt. USAAF, 1941-45. Mem. Nat. Plywood Distbrs. Assn. (past pres.; mem. Plywood Hall of Fame), Ark. C. of C. (dir.), Ducks Unltd. (Ark. chmn.; nat. trustee), Sigma Chi. Methodist (steward). Rotarian. Clubs: Little Rock Country, Little Rock, Top of the Rock, Razorback. Home: 14 Edgehill Rd Little Rock AR 72207 Office: 1800 Cantrell Rd Little Rock AR 72203

RENAS, STANLEY RUBEN, educator; b. nr. Ferndale, N.Y., Sept. 17, 1924; s. Maurice and Bertha (Nevins) R.; B.S., Columbia, 1949; certificate in Psychol. Warfare Studies, Georgetown U., 1952; M.A., Ga. State U., 1967, D.B.A., 1970; m. Gladys Green, Oct. 25, 1945; children—Stephen G., Susan. Owner, mgr. Chem. Specialty Co., Atlanta, 1953-65; researcher Bur. Bus. and Econ. Research, Ga. State U., 1965-67; asst. prof. bus. adminstrn. Augusta Coll., 1967-70; asso. prof. bus. adminstrn. Middle Tenn. State U., Murfreesboro, 1970-72; asso. prof. marketing Sch. Bus. Auburn (Ala.) U., 1972—. Served with USAF, 1951-53. Mem. Acad. Mgmt., So. Marketing Assn., Am. Inst. Decision Scis., Am. Mgmt. Assn., Am. Econ. Assn., Beta Gamma Sigma, Alpha Kappa Psi. Club: Torch (Augusta). Contbr. articles profl. jours. Home: 1079 Burton Dr NE Atlanta GA 30329 Office: Sch Bus Auburn U Auburn AL 36830

RENAZCO, ANTONIO JOSE, Nicaraguan diplomat; b. Managua, Nicaragua, Oct. 9, 1926; s. Antonio Jose and Esmeralda (Guerrero) R.; E.E., Worcester Poly. Inst., 1951. With engring. dept. Buffalo Forge Co., 1951-52; chief engr. Technomat CA, Caracas, Venezuela, 1952-62; chief engr. air conditioning dept. Creole Petroleum Corp., Caracas, 1962-65; consul gen. of Nicaragua in New Orleans, 1965-69, in Houston, 1969—. Treas. New Orleans Consular Corps. Decorated Order of Malta; named Hon. Citizen Jackson, Miss. and New Orleans, 1967. Mem. Am. Soc. Heating, Refrigerating and Air Conditioning Engrs., Inst. Hispanic Culture, Theta Chi. Clubs: New Orleans Country, Plimsoll, Playboy (New Orleans). Home: 11315 Valley Spring Dr Houston TX 77043 Office: 1925 So W Fairway Houston TX 77006

RENDLEMAN, DAVID ATWELL, JR., physician; b. Salisbury, N.C., Dec. 15, 1919; s. David Atwell and Grace Gertrude (Aaron) R.; A.B., Catawba Coll., 1941; M.D., Emory U., 1944; m. Dorothy Lee Vernon, July 15, 1943; children—David Atwell, Dorothy (Mrs. Harvey F. Kline), Daniel, Paul. Intern, Meth. Hosp., Peoria, Ill., 1944-45; family practice medicine, Salisbury, N.C., 1947—; mem. staff Rowan Meml. Hosp., Salisbury. Served with AUS, 1945-47. Mem. N.C., Rowan-Davie County (sec.-treas. 1950) med. socs., Salisbury-Rowan Mchts. Assn., V.F.W. Republican. Moose. Club: Country (Salisbury). Home: 703 W Council St Salisbury NC 28144 Office: Wallace Bldg Salisbury NC 28144

RENEGAR, HORACE CALVIN, mgmt. cons.; b. Huntsville, Ala., Nov. 1, 1903; s. James Calvin and Mary Agnes (Meechan) R.; student Birmingham (Ala.)-So. Coll., 1921-24; children—Jeannette (Mrs. Robert Cornelius Smith), James Calvin. Reporter, editor A.P., 1924-29; mgr. news bur. Tulane U., 1929-41, dir. pub. relations, 1941-66, asst. to pres., 1960-66; spl. asst. to pres. Dillard U., 1967-69, dir. devel., 1969—; partner Renegar, Phillips & Vetter, mgmt. devel. cons., Horace Renegar and Assos. Mem. pub. relations adv. com. U.S. Office Edn., 1948. Mem. Pub. Relations Soc. Am. (dir., v.p.; Distinguished Service citation 1952), Am. Coll. Pub. Relations Assn. (past pres., recipient award for outstanding achievement 1954), Omicron Delta Kappa, Kappa Delta Phi. Democrat. Episcopalian. Author: (with another) College Publicity Manual, 1948. Home: 1545 Henry Clay Av New Orleans LA 70118

RENFRO, HAROLD BELL, geologist, petroleum engr.; b. Lufkin, Tex., Jan. 16, 1915; s. P. D. and Ruby (Hines) R.; student Lamar Inst. Tech., 1930-31, U. Houston, 1931-33; B.S. in Petroleum Engring., U. Tulsa, 1939; M.S. in Geology, U. Wis., Ph.D. in Geology, 1947; m. Joan Arden Ross, Feb. 1, 1942; children—Robert Bruce, Janet Arden (Mrs. James R. Elder); m. 2d, Alma Chastain Hutchings, Sept. 28, 1963; step-children—Gertrude, Sally, William S. Prof. geology U. Tulsa, 1946-48; dir. exploration and engring. Stoddard Oil Co., Dallas, 1948-53; organized H. B. Renfro and Co., Dallas, 1953—; asso. McGhee Prodn. Co., Dallas, 1954-57; organized, chmn., bd. dirs. Neches Petroleum Corp., 1963-70; dir., exec. com., prin. agt. Petroleum Reserves, Inc., N.Y.C., Houston, Dallas, 1955-58; cons. Ling-Temco-Vought, Inc., Hudson Inst., Harmon, N.Y., Lawrence Radiation Lab., Livermore, Cal., Lockheed Aircraft Corp., MITRE Corp. Bd. dirs. Dallas Council World Affairs, Southwestern Engring. Found., Dallas; bd. dirs. Community Guidance Service, Dallas, 1950-60, chmn., 1955-57. Served to lt. USNR, 1942-46. Mem. Am. Assn. Petroleum Geologist (co-compiler geol. hwy. map U.S.), Am. Inst. Mining, Metall. and Petroleum Engrs., Soc. Petroleum Engrs., Council Sci. Socs. Dallas-Ft. Worth Area (pres. 1960), Community Opera Guild (pres. 1957), Dallas Geol. Soc. (pres. 1966), Sigma Xi, Gamma Alpha, Lambda Chi Alpha, Pi Epsilon Tau. Baptist. Clubs: Engineers (pres. Dallas 1958), Petroleum Engineers (pres. Dallas 1952); Research on Lower Pennsylvania sedementary rocks Northeastern Okla., stratigraphy and structural geology of Wilmington oil field, application nuclear explosives to natural resources. Home: 4235 Bordeaux Dallas TX 75205

RENFRO, HARRY KEETON, broadcasting co. exec.; b. St. Louis, Mar. 19, 1916; s. Harry J. and Mabel (Keeton) R.; B.S., St. Louis U., 1938; m. Margaret Lydon, Mar. 30, 1940; 1 dau., Patricia K. With radio sta. KXOK, St. Louis, 1938-52, asst. gen. mgr., until 1952; v.p. charge radio and TV, D'Arcy Advt. Co., St. Louis, 1952-66; v.p. Calcasieu TV and Radio, Inc., Lake Charles, La., 1964-66, pres., 1966—; pres. Mo. Broadcasting, Inc., St. Louis, 1966—; v.p., dir. Radio Thirteen Eighty, Inc., St. Louis, 1966—. Bd. dirs. Better Bus. Bur., Lake Charles, 1967—, Calcasieu United Fund, 1967—, La. bd. Mental Health Assn., 1967—. Served with USMCR, 1941-46, 50-52. mem. La. Broadcasters Assn., Advt. Club St. Louis. Clubs: Lake Charles (La.) Country; Stadium (St. Louis). Home: 14 Hill Dr St. Louis MO 63122 Office: 320 Division St Lake Charles LA 70601

RENG, CARL R., univ. pres.; b. Sioux Rapids, Ia., May 13, 1910; s. John G. and Anna Marie (Severson) R.; A.B., Buena Vista Coll., 1932, LL.D., 1952; M.S., Drake U., 1940; Ed.D., U. Mo., 1948; m. Ruby I. McLaughlin, Aug. 15, 1935; children—Marilyn Ann, Barbara Diane. High sch. prin., coach, Cooper, Ia., 1932-35; supt. schs., Huxley, Ia., 1935-40, Dunlap, Ia., 1940-43; prof. edml. adminstrn. U. Ark., 1948-51; pres. Ark. State U., Jonesboro, 1951—. Served as lt. comdr., USN Coll. V-12 program, 1943-46. Mem. Am. Assn. Sch. Adminstrs., N.E.A., Ark. Edn. Assn., Phi Delta Kappa, Kappa Delta Pi. Methodist. Mason, Rotarian. Home: 110 College Dr Jonesboro AR 72401 Office: State College Dr Jonesboro AR 72401

RENICK, RALPH APPERSON, journalist; b. N.Y.C., Aug. 9, 1928; s. Ralph Apperson and Rosalie (Dwyer) R.; A.B., U. Miami (Fla.), 1949; m. Elizabeth Jane Henry, June 5, 1949 (dec. July 1964) children—Patricia, Kathryn, Ralph A., Susan, Pamela, Michele. News dir. TV Sta. WTVJ, Miami, 1950-58, v.p. for news, 1958— v.p. Wometco Enterprises, Miami, 1959—; instr. TV news reporting U. Miami, 1952-58. Mem. Dade County Mental Health Bd.; chmn. Dade County Library Devel. Council; mem. Fla. Library Devel. Council. Regional bd. govs. Nat. Conf. Christians and Jews; Barry Coll.; trustee United Fund Dade County, bd. dirs. Boystown of Fla. Recipient Radio-TV Mirror award, 1967. Mem. Radio Television News Dirs. Assn. (nat. pres. 1958-59), Nat. Press Club. Radio-TV Corrs. Assn., Miami-Dade C. of C., Iron Arrow, Sigma Delta Chi, (chpt. pres. 1958-59), Kiwanian. Home: 14040 NW 3d Av Miami FL 33168 Office: 316 N Miami Av Miami FL 33130

RENICK, RICHARD RANDOLPH, state legislator; b. Bronx, N.Y., Oct. 14, 1930; s. Ralph Apperson and Rosalie Marie (Dwyer) R.; ed. U. Miami; m. Valerie E. Phillips, Oct. 12, 1968; children—Deborah Kathleen, Karen Valerie. Television film dir. WTVJ, Miami, Fla., 1950-59; with Renick Prodns., 1960-69; mem. Fla. Ho. of Reps., 1965—. Mem. Miami State Employees Local, Internat. Photographers Local, Am. Legion, Jaycees. Kiwanian, K.C., Moose. Home: 13440 SW 80th Av Miami FL 33156 Office: 7500 Red Rd S Miami FL 33143*

RENNEKER, FREDERICK WEYMAN, JR., architect; b. Charleston, S.C., Oct. 9, 1908; s. Fred W. and Blanch A. (DeLorme) R.; B.Arch., Auburn U., 1931; m. Jean Battle Walker, Oct. 1, 1937; children—Frederick Weyman III, William. Draftsman, Miller & Martin, architects, Birmingham, 1931-33; in charge repair and maintenance foreclosed property Equitable Life Assurance Soc., Birmingham, 1933-44; partner Shaw & Renneker, architects, Birmingham, 1946-58; practice architecture Fred Renneker, Jr., Birmingham, 1958-68, Fred Renneker, Jr. and Assos., Inc., 1968—. Mem. Met. Bd. YMCA, 1950—, chmn. Birmingham Downtown YMCA, 1954-55. Mem. Jefferson County Zoning Bd. Adjustments, 1970—. Bd. dirs. Carraway Meth. Hosp. Served from pvt. to 2d lt. C.E. AUS, 1944-46. Licensed architect, Ala., Ga. Recipient (with Shaw) Highest Honor award for design Ensley br. Birmingham Pub. Library, Gulf States Regional Archtl. Conv., 1955, award for design Iron & Steel Workers Credit Union Bldg., Birmingham Festival of Arts competition, 1957, award for design Guaranty Savs. and Loan Assn. Bldg., 1958; recipient various other awards, including Merit award 1970 State Conv. Ala. council A.I.A., 1970, 1968 Conf. Ala. council. Mem. A.I.A. (pres. Birmingham chpt. 1966). Methodist (past Sunday sch. supt., chmn. ofcl. bd.). Kiwanian (past sec., pres.). Club: Civic. Home: 3201 Fernway Rd Birmingham AL 35223 Office: 2201 Arlington Av Birmingham AL 35205

RENNINGER, FREDERICK AUGUST, geologist; b. N.Y.C., Nov. 8, 1936; s. Frederick A. and Ada (Hadler) R.; B.S., Rensselaer Poly. Inst., 1958; postgrad. George Washington U., 1960-61; m. Anne Marie Hoffmann, June 25, 1960; children—David Frederick, Helen Rachel, Daniel Howard. Asst. mgr. Upstate Loan Co., Kingston, N.Y., 1958-59; technician Mt. Alto VA Hosp., Washington, 1959; dir. tech. services Nat. Crushed Stone Assn., Washington, 1959—; geology cons. Registered engr., Vt.; certified profl. geologist. Mem. Am. Soc. for Testing and Materials, Am. Inst. Mining, Metall. and Petroleum Engrs., Am. Inst. Profl. Geologists, Hwy. Research Bd., Am. Concrete Inst., Air Pollution Control Assn., Zeta Psi. Presbyn. (deacon). Contbr. articles in field to profl. jours. Home: 6806 Lynbrook Dr Springfield VA 22150 Office: 1415 Elliot Pl NW Washington DC 20007

RENO, RAMON, ret. supt. schs.; b. Afton, Okla., Jan. 14, 1907; s. William Lewis and Alma (Smith) R.; B.S., Okla. State U., 1933, M.S., 1937; m. Ruby Fisher, Aug. 24, 1934; children—Dana Darlene, Rodney Llewyn, Sherry Gayle. Prin. high sch., Ketchum, Okla., 1933-35; prin. high sch., Westville, Okla., 1935-40, supt. schs., 1940-48, Barnsdall, Okla., 1948-56, Stigler, Okla., 1956-69, Jay, Okla., 1969-71. Mem. Stigler C. of C. (pres. 1964), Phi Delta Kappa, Iota Lambda Sigma. Democrat. Mason (32 deg., Shriner), Rotarian (pres. Barnsdall 1955), Lion (pres. Stigler 1962), Odd Fellow. Home: Rural Route 2 Grove OK 74344

RENSHAW, JOHN CHARLES, TV exec.; b. Pitts., Oct. 22, 1928; s. David E. and Alice (Glover) R.; student Carnegie Inst. Tech., 1945-46; B.S. in Journalism, So. Meth. U., 1950, B.A. in Speech, 1950; m. Nita Faye Payne, Aug. 19, 1961; 1 son, John Charles. Writer, dir. WFAA-TV, Dallas, 1951-53; program dir. KRBC-TV, Abilene, Tex., 1953-54; program dir., v.p. KSLA-TV, Shreveport, La., 1954—. Founder, pres. Gas Light Players, Shreveport, 1959; conductor, dir. Shreveport Savoyards, 1963—; asso. amusements critic Shreveport Jour., 1960—. Mem. C. of C. (cultural affairs com.), TV Programming Conf. (past pres.), Gilbert and Sullivan Soc. Shreveport and N.Y., D'Oyly Carte Opera Trust, Sigma Delta Chi. Republican. Episcopalian. Home: 464 Irving Bluff E Shreveport LA 71107 Office: Box 92 KSLA-TV Shreveport LA 71102

RENZ, JAMES HENRY, librarian; b. Columbus, O., Oct. 23, 1928; B.A., Ohio State U., 1953; M.A. in L.S., U. Mich., 1957. Fla. collection librarian Miami (Fla.) Pub. Library, 1957-60; acquisition librarian Coll. William and Mary, Williamsburg, Va., 1960-62, asst. librarian, 1964-66, acting librarian, 1966, asso. librarian, 1966—, also faculty adviser; v.p. family-owned bus., Ft. Myers, Fla., 1963-64. Vis. lectr. Richmond Spl. Libraries Inst., 1965, 67. Served to capt. USAF, 1953-55. Mem. A.L.A., Va. (chmn. coll. and univ. sect. 1966), Southeastern, Fla. library assns., Delta Phi Alpha, Beta Phi Mu. Author: Richard Wagner and the Music Drama, 1967; Sources for the Music Dramas of Richard Wagner, 1969. Home: Heritage Inn Suite 3D 1324 Richmond Rd Williamsburg VA 23462*

REPASS, FRED GREENE, oral surgeon; b. Richlands, Va., Sept. 2, 1903; s. James Albert and Jennie Belle (Greene) R.; student U. Richmond, 1923-24; D.D.S., Med. Coll. Va., 1928; M.S., Northwestern U., 1938; m. Hazel Gaye Wiles, Aug. 3, 1933; children—Fred Greene, James Albert, John Scott, Thomas Hurt. Instr. dept. oral surgery Med. Coll. Va. Dental Sch., 1928-30; gen. practice dentistry, Bedford, Va., 1930-37, specializing in oral surgery, Roanoke, Va., 1938—; mem. staff Roanoke Meml. Hosp., Community Hosp. Roanoke Valley; cons. oral surgery VA Hosp., Roanoke, 1938—. Served from lt. (j.g.) to lt. USNR, 1930-38. Mem. Am. (life), Va. (life) dental assns., Piedmont, Roanoke dental socs., Am., Southeastern, Va. socs. oral surgeons, Theta Chi, Psi Omega, Omicron Kappa Upsilon. Republican. Methodist. Elk. Clubs: Roanoke Country; Hickory Lake. Contbr. articles profl. jours. Home: 1936 Tucker Lane Salem VA 24153 Office: Med Ars Bldg Roanoke VA 24011

RESOR, ROBERT REUBEN, pub. relations exec.; b. N.Y.C., May 1, 1921; s. Reuben Perry and Jeannette (Hummerstone) R.; B.S., Harvard, 1943; m. Julie Houstoun Harper, July 31, 1948; children—Randolph Richardson, Holly Amanda, Roberta Elizabeth, Hope Margaret. Reporter Voice of Am., Washington, 1946-47; mem. staff various pub. relations firms, N.Y.C., 1947-49; with Bozell & Jacobs, Inc., N.Y.C., 1949-68, sr. v.p., 1961-62, adminstrv. v.p., 1963-66, exec. v.p., 1966-68; spl. asst. labor Assn. Am. Railroads, Washington, 1968-70; dir. office of information services Occupational Safety and Health Adminstrn., U.S. Dept. of Labor, 1971; v.p. marketing Creative Systems, Inc., Washington, 1972—. Served to 1st lt. USAAF, 1943-46. Decorated Air medal (Army). Mem. Pub. Relations Soc. Am. (mem. com. on standards of profl. practice 1966-68), R.R. Pub. Relations Assn. Episcopalian. Clubs: Harvard (N.Y.C. and Washington); Nat. Press (Washington), Congl. Country (Bethesda, Md.). Author: The Communications Challenges in the Decade of the 60's, 1962. Contbg. editor Trusts and Estates mag., 1962-67. Home: 7307 Burdette Ct Bethesda MD 20034

RESSLER, PARKE E(DWARD), lawyer, accountant; b. Lancaster, Pa., Aug. 21, 1916; s. Parke H. and Sadie (Weiser) R.; B.S., U. Pa., 1947; B.B.A., Baylor U., 1947, LL.B., 1952, J.D., 1969; M.B.A., U. Houston, 1949; m. Margaret B. Tucker, June 3, 1944; children—Nancy Parke, Margaret Anne. Agt. Internal Revenue Service, 1947-50; part time instr. Baylor U., 1950-65; admitted to Tex. bar, 1952, since practiced in Waco; asso. firm Angus McSwain. Mem. Am. Inst. C.P.A.'s, Tex. Soc. C.P.A.'s, Am., Tex., McLennan County bar assns., Am. Assn. Atty.-C.P.A.'s, Phi Alpha Delta, Delta Sigma Pi. Mem. Christian Ch. Rotarian. Clubs: Ridgewood Country, Hedonia, Ridgewood Yacht, Baylor Bear. Home: 2209 Arroyo Rd Waco TX 76710 Office: 3201 Franklin Av Waco TX 76710

RESTON, JAMES BARRETT, author, newspaperman; b. Clydebank, Scotland, Nov. 3, 1909; s. James and Johanna (Irving) R.; brought to U.S., 1910; student Vale of Leven Acad., Alexandria, Scotland, 1914-20, B.S., U., Ill., 1932; Litt.D., Colgate U., 1951, Oberlin Coll., 1955, Rutgers U., 1957, U. Md., 1967, Willimas Coll., 1968, Harvard, 1970; LL.D. (hon.). Dartmouth Coll., 1959; LL.D., N.Y.U., 1961, U. Ill., 1962, Boston Coll., 1963, Brandeis U., 1964; D.H.L., Kenyon Coll., 1962, Columbia U., 1963, U. Mich., 1965, Harvard, 1970; m. Sarah Jane Fulton, Dec. 24, 1935; children—Richard Fulton, James Barrett, Thomas Busey. With Springfield (O.) Daily News, 1932-33, Ohio State U., 1933; publicity dir. Cin. Base Ball Club, 1934; reporter A.P., N.Y.C., 1934-37, London, 1937-39; reporter New York Times, London bur., 1939-41, Washington bur., 1941—, chief Washington corr., 1953-64, asso. editor, 1964-68, exec. editor, 1968-69, v.p., 1969—; owner, pub. Vineyard Gazette, Martha's Vineyard, Mass. Mem. Pulitzer prize bd. Columbia, 1969—. Recipient Pulitzer Prize for nat. corr., 1945, nat. reporting, 1957; Overseas Press Club award for interpretation internat. news. 1949, 51, 55; George Polk Memorial award for National Reporting, 1953; U. Mo. medal, 1961; J.P. Zenger award, 1964; Legion d'Honneur, Order St. Olav (Norway), Order of Merit (Chile). Clubs: Century (N.Y.C.); Metropolitan (Washington). Home: 3124 Woodley Rd NW Washington DC 20008 Office: New York Times Washington DC 20036

RESWEBER, JOE GAUTHIER, county ofcl.; b. St. Martinville, La., Nov. 9, 1913; s. Joseph and Odile (Gauthier) R.; tchr. tng. certificate U. Southwestern La., 1932; LL.B., Houston Law Sch., 1939; m. Inez Sammons, May 3, 1945; children—Judith Ann, Betty Jo. Fire marshal City of Houston, 1939-46, councilman, 1949-57; county atty. Harris County (Tex.), Houston, 1957—. Served with USNR, 1942-45. Elk, Eagle, Lion. Home: 302 Fairbanks St Houston TX 77009 Office: 301 San Jacinto St Houston TX 77002

RETAN, J. WALDEN, physician; b. Syracuse, N.Y., Oct. 30, 1930; s. H. Walden and Dorothy Eleanor (Brooks) R.; student Hamilton Coll., 1948-50, Mass. Inst. Tech., 1950-51; M.D., State U. N.Y., Syracuse, 1957; m. Carol D. Maynard, Feb. 22, 1955; children—Christopher, Nancy, Brian. Intern, Peter Bent Brigham Hosp., Boston, 1957-58, research fellow Cardiorenal Lab., 1958-61; dir. renal div. Wayne State U. Coll. Medicine, Detroit, 1961-63; mem. renal div. U. Ala. Med. Center, Birmingham, 1963-66, mem. pediatric renal div., 1967—; practice medicine specializing in internal medicine & renal diseases, Birmingham, 1967—; mem. staff Baptist Med. Center (Montclair), St. Vincents, Children's hosps.; dir. med. div. Freedom House, Birmingham, 1970—. Served with USAF, 1951-53. Mem. Alpha Omega Alpha. Home: 3105 Warrington Rd Birmingham AL 35223 Office: 1701 9th Av S Birmingham AL 35205

RETI-FORBES, JEAN, pianist, educator; b. Saltcoats, Sask., Can., 1911; d. G.W. and Clara (Boyle) Sahlmark; student U. Toronto, 1929-31; grad. Royal Acad. Music London, 1933; m. Rudolph Reti, July 3, 1943 (dec. 1957) m. 2d, W. Stanton Forbes, Nov. 15, 1963. Came to U.S., 1940, naturalized, 1964. Faculty, Sarah Lawrence Coll., 1947-48; played first performance of Reti's piano concerto with Detroit Symphony, 1948; after death of Reti prepared for publ. his Tonality-Atonality-Pantonality and Thematic Patterns in Sonatas of Beethoven; concertized and lectured throughout U.S. and Europe, 1959—; asso. prof. U. Ga., Athens, 1964—, also charge Olin Downes Papers U. Ga. Library. Vice pres., trustee Jay Hambidge Art Found. Rabun Gap, Ga. Can. Council grantee for work on Reti manuscripts, 1962. Mem. Am. Musicol. Soc., Kappa Lambda. Home: 552 Cobb St Athens GA 30601 also Tallulah Falls GA 30573

REUBEN, ODELL RICHARDSON, coll. pres.; b. Silverstreet, S.C., June 18, 1918; s. James J. and Matilda (Stewart) R.; A.B., Benedict Coll., Columbia, S.C., 1942, B.D., 1945, Dr. Pedagogy, 1961; B.D. Oberlin (O.) Coll., 1946, S.T.M., 1947; postgrad. Duke, 1966; LL.D., Allen U., Columbia, 1955; m. Anna Mays Daniels, Sept. 20, 1945; children—Wilhelmenia Matilda, Lucy Jeanette, Anna Marie, Odell Richardson, Jayne and Janice (twins). Ordained to ministry Baptist Ch., 1943; pastor in Allendale, S.C., 1943-48, Ware Shoals, S.C., 1946-49; instr. theology and social studies Morris Coll., Sumter, S.C., 1947-48, pres., 1948—. Bd. dirs. Community Hosp., Sumter, S.C. Council Human Relations. Mem. N.E.A., Am. Tchrs. Assn., S.C. Palmetto Assn., S.C. Christian Action Council, N.A.A.C.P., Am. Acad. Polit. Sci. Mason. Address: Morris Coll Sumter SC 29150

REUDELHUBER, FRANK OTTO, petroleum engring co. exec.; b. Toledo, Jan. 18, 1924; s. George Gildemus and Caroline Elizabeth (Lupfer) R.; B.S., U. Okla., 1948; m. Mary Doris Rountree, Feb. 9, 1950; children— Daniel, Timothy, Margaret. Field engr. Atlantic Refining Co., 1947, 51; mgr. reservoir fluid dept. Core Labs., Dallas,

1951-56, mgr. Francorelab, S.A., Paris, 1959-65, mgr. research and tech. service, 1965-68, asst. to pres., 1968—. Mem. exec. com. Boy Scouts Am., 1970-71. Served with AUS, 1943-46. Decorated Bronze Star medal, Purple Heart with oak leaf cluster. Mem. Am. Inst. Mining, Metall. and Petroleum Engrs. (chmn. L. C. Uren award com. 1971-72). Club: Oak Cliff Country (Dallas). Contbr. articles to profl. jours. Home: 2026 Matagorda St Dallas TX 75232 Office: PO Box 10185 Dallas TX 75207

REUE, JOHN WILLIAM, assn. exec.; b. Brenham, Tex., Oct. 19, 1908; s. Charles and Johanna (Weghorst) R.; grad. Blinn Meml. Coll., 1929, Inst. Orgn. Mgmt., U. Colo.; m. Ella Jahnke, July 31, 1938; children—Jo Ellen (Mrs. Timothy Carter), Sue Ann (Mrs. James M. Broome), Bobbie Jane (Mrs. Chester Dale West). Salesman Gulf Oil Corp., 1930-31, Washington Nat. Ins., 1931-33, salesman J. C. Penney Co., Brenham, 1933, asst. mgr. Brenham, 1933-40, Greenville, 1940-45, mgr., Floydada, Tex., 1945-55; owner dept. store, 1955-60; mgr. C. of C. Floydada, 1960—; sec.-treas. Floydada Devel. Co. Exec. dir. Housing Authority City of Floydada, 1960—; registrar Selective Service, 1959—. Active Boy Scouts Am. Mem. Tex. C. of C. Mgrs., Am. C. of C. Execs., Internat. Platform Assn. Mason, Rotarian (past chpt. pres.), Lion. Toastmaster (past pres.). Home: 811 W Cedar St Floydada TX 79235 Office: 302 E Tennessee St Floydada TX 79235

REUS-FROYLAN, FRANCISCO, bishop; b. San Juan, P.R., Apr. 14, 1919; s. Esteban and Carmen (Froylan) Reus; B.A., U. P.R., 1946, postgrad., 1954; L.Th., DuBose Sem., 1942; S.T.D., Gen. Theol. Sem., 1965; D.D., U. of South, 1968; S.T.D., Interam. U. P.R., 1969; m. Mary Doreen, Apr. 21, 1945; children—Pamela, Sandra, Carolyn. Ordained deacon Episcopal Ch., 1942, priest, 1943, bishop, 1964; curate St. John's Cathedral, 1942-43; curate St. Andrews Ch., 1943-44; rector St. Mark's Ponce, 1944-45; rector Atonement Ch., Ponce, 1945-48; tchr., chaplain St. Just Sch., 1948-54; rector, dean St. John's Cathedral, 1954-64; bishop, Santurce, P.R., 1964—. Bd. dirs. Episcopal Cathedral Sch., 1954-64, Instituto Sicologico of P.R.; chmn. bd. St. Luke's Episcopal Hosp., Sch. Nursing. Vice pres. P.R. council Boy Scouts Am., 1954-70. Bd. dirs. local A.R.C., 1967-70; trustee Good Samaritan Found.; chmn. bd. trustees Sem. of Caribbean; mem. exec. council Episcopal Ch., 1970—. Home: Ashford Av 1313 Santurce PR 00908 Office: Canals 309 Santurce PR 00908

REUTHER, JAMES RICHARD, optometrist; b. Starksville, Miss., Dec. 13, 1907; s. William Franklin and Alma (Johnson) R.; D. Optometry, No. Ill. Coll. of Optometry, 1939; m. Ruth Elizabeth Huffaker, Jan. 26, 1941; 1 dau., Alma Grace. Pvt. practice optometry, Gainesville, Tex., 1940-57; dr. in charge Mast Optical Co., Wichita Falls, Tex., 1958—. Past program dir., sec., treas. Gainesville Community Circus; past nat. chmn. Circus Fans Photography Conv. Served from pvt. to pfc., Med. Service Corps, AUS, 1944-46. Mem. Circus Fans Assn. Baptist. Mason (Shriner, K.T.), mem. Order Eastern Star. Club: Lions. Amateur Magician; chalk artist. Home: 4450 Phillips Dr Wichita Falls TX 76308 Office: 822 Indiana Av Wichita Falls TX 76301

REVELEY, WALTER TAYLOR, coll. pres.; b. Knoxville, Tenn., Feb. 11, 1917; s. Robert Jennings and Marguerite Emily (Grayson) R; B.A., Hampden-Sydney Coll., 1939; B.D., Union Theol. Sem., Va., 1942; Ph.D., Duke, 1953; LL.D., Southwestern at Memphis (Tenn.), 1966; m. Marie Gary Eason, Aug. 20, 1941; children—Walter Taylor Reveley, III, Caroline Christian (Mrs. Robert Barrie). Ordained to ministry, Presbyn. Ch., 1942; minister in Churchville, Va., 1942-44, Richmond, Va., 1946; mem. faculty Southwestern at Memphis, 1946-63, prof. Bible and Christian edn., 1957-63, dean admissions and records, 1961-63; pres. Hampden-Sydney Coll., 1963—; vis. prof. Presbyn. Faculty Fellowship, fall 1956-57; mem. Lilly Found. seminar Duke, summer 1957; mem. Grad. Workshop Bib. Lands, N.Y.U., summer 1960. Served as chaplain AUS, 1944-46. Mem. Omicron Delta Kappa, Chi Beta Phi, Pi Kappa Alpha. Lion. Author: The Way of a Student, 1963. Home: Presidents Home Hampden-Sydney Coll Hampden-Sydney VA 23943

REVELL, WALTER JONES, physician; b. Louisville, Ga., Aug. 10, 1916; s. Samuel Thompson Regrave and Lettie (Jones) R.; B.S., U. Ga., 1937; M.D., U. Md., 1941; m. Jean Eleanor Hunt, Jan. 3, 1948; children—Walter Jones, Jean Hunt, William Samuel, Harry Duff. Intern, U. Md. Hosp., Balt., 1941-42, City Hosp. of Balt., 1947; gen. practice medicine, Louisville, 1946—; mem. staff Jefferson Hosp., Louisville, 1946—. Chmn. Jefferson County Bd. Health, 1950—. Mem. Louisville City Council, 1960—, also mayor pro-tem., 1966—. Served with USNR, 1942-46. Diplomate Am. Bd. Family Practice. Mem. A.M.A., Ga., 10th Dist., Jefferson County med. assns., Nu Sigma Nu. Democrat. Presbyn. (elder). Mason, Kiwanian. Home: 815 Walnut St Louisville GA 30434 Office: 107 W 8th St Louisville GA 30434

REVELS, PERCY BURTON, judge; b. McCra, Fla., Dec. 16, 1901; s. William R. and Alice (Tyre) R.; student U. Fla., 1923-27; LL.B., Southeastern U., 1944; LL.D., Bethune-Cookman Coll., 1966; m. Bernice Hardy, June 20, 1929; children—Joan Dell (Mrs. John F. Gaines), Percy Burton. Admitted to Fla. bar, 1930, U.S. Supreme Ct. bar, 1944; practiced law in Palatka, Fla., 1930-51; atty. Putnam County (Fla.), 1933-51; judge 7th Jud. Circuit Fla., Palatka, 1951—; dean Fla. Meth. Sch. of Christian Mission, 1970-72. Exec. sec. Young Democratic Club Fla., 1939-40, pres., 1941, county del. state exec. com., 1940-48. Trustee, rec. sec., mem. exec. com. Bethune-Cookman Coll. Served to capt. USMCR, 1942-44. Recipient Good Govt. award Palatka Jr. C. of C., 1961; named Citizen of Year, Alpha Phi Alpha, 1965. Mem. Am. (nat. com. to draft model jud. legislation), Fla., Putnam County bar assns., Am. Judicature Soc., Putnam County Hist. Soc., Am. Camellia Soc., Nat. Assn. State Trial Judges (Fla. del. 1967, nat. com. 1968-69), Am. Legion (comdr. post), Putnam County C. of C., Phi Kappa Tau. Methodist (chmn. ofcl. bd. 1951-54, chmn. bd. Christian social concerns Fla. Ann. Conf., mem. Fla. Conf. Council). Vice-chmn. editorial staff Trial Judge's Jour., 1963—. Contbr. articles to profl. jours. Home: 1703 Laurel St Palatka FL 32077 Office: Courthouse Palatka FL 32077

REVERCOMB, EVERETT EUGENE, assn. exec.; b. Washington, Jan. 28, 1914; s. Luke Woodward and Effie (Davis) R.; A.B., Duke, 1935; m. Dorothy Elouise Faidley, Sept. 29, 1940; children—Everett Eugene, Steven Lee. Auditor, Nat. Assn. Broadcasters, 1935-43, asst. treas., 1946-50, sec.-treas., 1956—; adminstrv. asst. George Washington U., 1950-52; comptroller Nat. Assn. Home Builders, 1952-56. Active Boy Scouts Am.; past pres. McLean (Va.) Civic Assn. Served to lt. USNR, 1943-46. Lion, Mason. Home: 6523 Ridge Rd McLean VA 22101 Office: 1711 N St NW Washington DC 20006

REX, CHARLES HENRY, elec. engr.; b. Lexington, Mo., Jan. 12, 1903; s. Cleveland Alonzo and Addie (Wilker) R.; B.S., U. Ill., 1926; m. Alice Letatia Doherty, Nov. 25, 1935; children—Diane (Mrs. Denis G. Cain), Gartland Charles, Kathleen Alice, Michael Richard. Exchange installer Western Electric Co., Kansas City, 1923-24; with Gen. Electric Co., Chgo., Lynn, Mass., Hendersonville, N.C., 1926—, spl. rep., 1935-42, design, devel. engr., 1942—, ret., 1968. Mem. night visibility com., hwy. research bd., NRC, 1956. Registered profl. engr. Mass., N.C. Fellow Illuminating Engring. Soc. (bd. fellows, 1960-61); mem. Illuminating Engring. Soc., Internat. mem. (C.I.E.) Commn. on Illumination, Inst. Traffic Engring., I.E.E.E. Club: Hendersonville Country. Patentee various roadway lighting devices. Contbr. numerous articles to profl. jours. Address: Box 2 Route 3 Hendersonville NC 28739

REX, C(HARLES) WALTON, real estate exec.; b. Marietta, O., Sept. 24, 1902; s. John Walter and Vinnie (Waterman) R.; B.C.S., Washington and Lee U., 1925; m. Lottie Autrey, Sept. 15, 1927; 1 son, C. Walton. Sec., treas. Rex-McGill Investment Co., 1926-38, pres., 1938; dir. Fla. Orange Marketers, Inc., Trust Co. Fla. Mem. Central Fla. Devel. Com. Econ. Value Citrus Groves, 1961, Fla. Citrus Commn., 1941-42. Served as lt. USNR, 1942-45. Mem. Fla. Assn. Farm Mgrs. and Rural Appraisers, Fla. (past v.p.), Greater Orlando chambers commerce, Am. Inst. Real Estate Appraisers (orgn. mem., pres. Fla. chpt.), Navy League U.S., Ret. Officers Assn., V.F.W., Fla Citrus Mut. (past pres.), Orlando Bd. Realtors (past pres.), Soc. Residential Appraisers, Pi Kappa Phi, Alpha Kappa Psi, Pi Delta Epsilon. Presbyn. (elder). Kiwanian. Clubs: Citrus, Country of Orlando, University. Home: 1600 Spring Lake Dr Orlando FL 32804 Office: 1501 W Colonial Dr Orlando FL 32804

REYES SPINDOLA, ALBERTO, consul gen. of Mexico, New Orleans. Address: Internat Trade Mart New Orleans LA 70130*

REYNOLDS, CHARLES MCKINELY, JR., banker; b. Thomasville, Ga., Jan. 11, 1937; s. Charles McKinley and Johnnie (Hadley) R.; student Morehouse Coll., 1954-56; mortuary sci. certificate Wayne State U., 1962; postgrad. Atlanta U., 1965-66; m. Estella Mary Henry, Aug. 19, 1956; children—Eric Charles, Gregory Preston. Tchr. Southside Jr. High Sch., Albany, Ga., 1962-65; nat. bank examiner U.S. Treasury Dept., Atlanta, 1965-71; exec. v.p. Citizens Trust Co., 1971, pres., 1971—; treas. Pathways, Inc.; exec. sec. Temporary Devel. Agy., Albany, Ga., 1963-65, Atlanta Leadership Inst., 1966-67. Asst. commr. Central dist. Boy Scouts Am., Atlanta, 1969—; mem. Atlanta Coalition on Current Community Affairs; mem. housing task force Gov.'s Goals for Ga. Program; mem. Met. Rapid Transit Authority Commn.; pres. West Manor PTA, Atlanta, 1968-69. Bd. dirs. A.R.C., Atlanta Model Cities Housing Devel. Corp., Butler St. YMCA, United Appeal. Served with USAF, 1956-60. Mem. Ga., Albany (v.p. 1965—) tchr. and edn. assns., Social Sci. Work Study Group (pres. 1964-65), Atlanta C. of C. (housing and redevel. com.), Nat. Bus. League, Alpha Phi Alpha, Epsilon Nu Delta, Gamma Omicron Lambda (chpt. asst. sec. 1964-65). Clubs: Criterion (sec. 1963-65), Morehouse College Alumni. Home: 752 Lynn Circle SW Atlanta GA 30311 Office: 175 Houston St NE Atlanta GA 30303

REYNOLDS, DANA DRUMMOND, cons.; b. Flemington, W.Va., Nov. 22, 1908; s. Wayland Fuller and Inez (Brchard) R.; A.B., W.Va. U. 1930; postgrad. George Washington U., 1943, 46, Am. U., 1948; m. Lorna Woollacott Murphy, Sept. 12, 1933; children—Winifred W. (Mrs. R. Garcia), Deirdre A. (Mrs. Chester Eugene Peters), Lorna Jean, John Dana. Editorial asst. Agr. Extension Service, W.Va. U., 1927, asst. editor, 1928, acting editor, 1929; staff office information Dept. Agr., 1930-33, 36-43, 46-48; staff President's Inter-Agy. Com. for Upper Monogahela Valley, acting sec. for preparation of report, 1934-35; liaison agrl. information Dept. Agr.-ECA, 1949-50; food and agrl. specialist ECA-Mut. Security Agy., 1951-52; chief agr. instns. br. FOA-ICA, 1953-58; adv. com. sci. communications service Inter-Am. Inst. Agrl. Scis., Turrialba, 1955-58; dep. food and agr. officer U.S. Operations Mission to Libya, 1958-60, extension tng. adviser to Afghanistan, 1960-63; cons. AID, other orgns., 1963-68; pvt. cons. internat. devel. strategy, 1968-70; pres. Internat. Center for Dynamics of Devel., 1971—. Weekly agrl. news report ABC Network, 1947-48; bd. dirs. Washington Coop. Forum. Served from seaman to lt., USNR, 1944-45. Mem. Soc. for Internat. Devel., Kappa Tau Alpha. Editor symposium papers Popular Participation in Nat. Devel. Address: 4201 S 31st St Arlington VA 22206

REYNOLDS, DAVID PARHAM, metal products mfg. exec.; b. Bristol, Tenn., June 16, 1915; s. Richard Samuel and Julia Louise (Parham) R.; grad. Lawrenceville Sch.; student Princeton, 1938; m. Margaret Harrison, Mar. 25, 1944; children—Margaret Allis, Julia Parham, Dorothy Harrison. With Reynolds Metals Co., 1937—, salesman, asst. mgr. aircraft parts, 1937-44, asst. v.p., 1944-46, v.p., 1946-57, exec. v.p., 1958—, gen. mgr., 1969—; dir. Reynolds Metals Co., United Va./State Planters Bank, Reynolds Aluminum Sales Co., Reynolds Internat., Inc., Reynolds Aluminum Co. Can., Eskimo Pie Corp., Reynolds Jamaica Mines, Ltd. Mem. Prime Aluminum Products Industry Adv. Com., Fed. Govt., 1951—. Trustee Lawrenceville Sch., Foxcroft Sch. Presbyn. Home: 8905 Tresco Rd Richmond VA 23229 Office: 6601 Broad St Rd Richmond VA 23261

REYNOLDS, DONALD W(ORTHINGTON), publisher; b. Ft. Worth, Sept. 23, 1906; s. Gaines Worlie and Anna Louise (Elfers) R.; B.J., U. Mo., 1927. Pub. Southwest-Times Record, Ft. Smith, Ark., Okmulgee (Okla.) Times, 1940—, Bartlesville (Okla.) Examiner 1947—, Las Vegas (Nev.) Rev. Jour. 1949—, Ely (Nev.) Times and Carson City (Nev.) Appeal, 1950—, Blackwell (Okla.) Jour. Tribune and Rogers (Ark.) News, 1955—, Chickasha (Okla.) Express, 1956—, Guthrie (Okla.) Leader, 1958—, Hawaii Tribune-Herald of Hilo, 1961—, Pawhuska (Okla.) Daily Jour.-Capital, 1964—, Guymon (Okla.) Daily Herald, 1966—, Montclair (Cal.) Bonita Pub. Co., The Daily Report, Ontario, Cal., Pomona (Cal.) Progress-Bull., Frederick (Okla.) Daily Leader, Pauls Valley (Okla.) Daily Democrat, Wewoka (Okla.) Daily Times, 1967—, Red Bluff (Cal.) Daily News, 1968—, Bonneville (Ark.) Democrat, 1968—; pres. Donrey Outdoor, Inc.; owner and operator of radio sta. KFSA, Ft. Smith, 1946—, KBRS, Springdale, Ark., 1949—, KORK, Las Vegas, and KOLO, Reno, 1955—; owner operator TV stas. KFSA-TV, Ft. Smith, Ark., 1953—, KOLO-TV, Reno, 1954—; KORK-TV, Las Vegas, 1955—, KGNS-TV, Laredo, 1958—, Nev. Network, Reno, Las Vegas, Carson City, Ely, Winnemuca (Nev.), 1956—. Hon. disch. major M.I., 1945. Awarded Legion of Merit, Bronze Star, Purple Heart, 5 combat stars. Mem. Nat. Assn. Radio-TV Broadcasters, Am. Soc. Newspaper Editors, Am., So. newspaper pubs. assns., Am. Legion, Sigma Delta Chi, Pi Kappa Alpha. Clubs: Overseas Press (San Francisco); Hillcrest Country (Bartlesville); Tulsa, Dallas Athletic; Hardscrabble Country (Fort Smith); Prospector's (Reno); Pacific (Honolulu); Jonathan (Los Angeles); Metropolitan (N.Y.). Home: 1111 W Bonanza Las Vegas NV 89101 Office: Southwestern House 920 Rogers Av PO Box 1359 Ft Smith AR 72902

REYNOLDS, FRANK RUSSELL, physician; b. Wilmington, N.C., 1920; M.D., U. Pa., 1944. Intern, Med. Coll. Va. Hosp., Richmond, 1944-45; resident in pediatrics Childrens Hosp., Phila., 1945-46, asst. chief resident, 1949-50; resident in pediatrics James Walker Meml. Hosp., Wilmington, 1948-49, now vis. staff; practice medicine specializing in pediatrics, Wilmington; staff pediatrician Babies Hosp., Wrightsville Sound, N.C., Community Hosp., Wilmington. Served to capt., M.C., AUS, 1947-48. Diplomate Am. Bd. Pediatrics. Mem. A.M.A., Am. Acad. Pediatrics (dist. chmn.). Office: 1613 Dock St Wilmington NC 28401*

REYNOLDS, H. LESTER, state ofcl.; b. Tyner, Ky., Sept. 22, 1911; s. Walker R. and Mary (Jones) R.; B.S. in Civil Engring., U. Ky., 1939; m. Edith Waldroff Pennington, Feb. 1, 1958. With Rural Electrification Adminstrn., 1939-40, 41-42; with Jackson County (Ky.) Rural Electrification Commn., 1940-41, 46-47; airport lighting engr. CAA, Ill., 1947-49; with U.S. Naval Facilities Engring. Command, 1949-69, dir. utilities divs. 9ND, 12ND, 1949-61, head utilities dept., Guam, 1961-63, pub. utilities specialist, dir. utilities div., Ches. div., 1963-69; exec. dir. Ky. Bd. Registration for Profl. Engrs. and Land Surveyors, Lexington, 1969—. Served to comdr. USNR, 1942-46. Mem. Soc. Am. Mil. Engrs., Nat. Assn. Govt. Engrs., I.E.E.E., Nat., Ky., Va. socs. profl. engrs., Naval Res. Assn., Res. Officers Assn., Armed Forces Mgmt. Assn. (exec. council 1966-69), U. Ky. Alumni Assn., Toastmasters Club (charter pres. 1955-56). Methodist (ofcl. bd. 1966-71). Home: 131 Jesselin Dr Lexington KY 40503 Office: University Station Box 5075 Lexington KY 40506

REYNOLDS, HERBERT HAL, univ. adminstr.; b. Frankston, Tex., Mar. 20, 1930; s. Herbert Joseph and Avanell (Taylor) R.; B.S., Trinity U., 1952 M.S., Baylor U., 1958, Ph.D., 1961; Joy Myrla Copeland, June 17, 1950; children—Kevin Hal, Kent Andrew, Rhonda Sheryl. Commd. 2d lt. U.S. Air Force, 1948, advanced through grades to col., 1966; retired, 1968; personnel officer, 1948-54, mem. adv. group to Japanese Air Self Def. Force, 1954-56, asst. prof. air sci. Baylor U., 1956-59, grad. fellow Baylor U., 1959-61, chief comparative psychology Aero. Med. Lab., Holloman AFB, N.M., 1961-65, dir. research and dep. dir. Aero. Med. Lab., 1965-68, interim. dir. Air Force Human Resources Lab., Brooks AFB, Tex., 1968; prof. psychology, exec. v.p. Baylor U., Waco, Tex., 1969—. Mem. A.A.A.S., Am. Assn. U. Profs., Am., N.M., Tex. psychol. assns., Sigma Xi. Contbr. articles in field to profl. jours. Office: Baylor U Waco TX 76703

REYNOLDS, JIMMY, state ofcl.; b. Malakoff, Tex., Sept. 16, 1939; s. Walter and Julia Irvin (Pelham) R.; B.S. in Agrl. Engring., Tex. Tech. U., 1963; m. Erma Campbell, Apr. 25, 1964; children—Pamela Kay, Polly Kathleen. Hydraulic engr. Interior Dept., Houston, 1963-65; civil engr. U.S. Dept. Agr., Amarillo, Tex., 1965-66; with Tex. Dept. Agr., insp., Eustace, Tex., 1969—; owner Reynolds Merc. Co., Eustace, Tex., 1966—; engring. cons., Eustace, 1966—. Mem. P.T.A., 1966—; sponsor Circle 10 council Boy Scouts Am., 1969—. Trustee Eustace Sch. Bd., 1967-71; fire chief, Eustace, 1969-71, fire marshal, 1971. Bd. dirs. Am. Cancer Soc. Mem. Am. Soc. C.E., Am. Soc. Agrl. Engrs. Address: PO Box 98 Eustace TX 75124

REYNOLDS, JOHN ARCHIBALD SEABROOK, dentist; b. Lenoir, N.C., Feb. 16, 1933; s. Archibald Seabrook and Eva Mae (Craven) R.; student The Citadel, 1951-54; D.D.S., U. N.C., 1958; m. Jeanne Kathleen Fleming, July 5, 1958; children—Kathleen Fleming, Mary McLeod, Patricia Lynn. Pvt. practice dentistry, Charlotte, N.C., 1960—. Instr. dental interne program Charlotte Meml. Hosp., 1960—; cons. dental asst. program Community Coll., Charlotte, since 1962. Adviser, Explorer Scouts, 1968. Served with Dental Corps, USNR, 1958-60; now comdr. Res. Mem. Am. Dental Assn., N.C. (chmn. ethics com. 1971-72), 2d Dist., Charlotte dental socs., Citadel Alumni Assn., Omicron Kappa Upsilon, Xi Psi Phi. Episcopalian (vestryman 1964-67, lay reader 1958-72). Clubs: Myers Park Country, Lake Norman Yacht, Optimist. Home: 3022 Ferncliff Rd Charlotte NC 28211 Office: 1944 Brunswick Av Charlotte NC 28207

REYNOLDS, JOHN JOSEPH ALOYSIUS, JR., govt. ofcl.; b. Providence, Jan. 11, 1910; s. John Joseph Aloysius and Emma Frances (Ahearn) R.; B.A., Providence Coll., 1932, LL.B., Georgetown U., 1937; m. Mariantha Cotsonas, June 21, 1939; children—John Joseph Aloysius III, Tara L. (Mrs. Jerry Surratt), Kathleen. Admitted to D.C. bar; chief assessment div. FDIC, Washington, 1939-42; spl. agt. Office Alien Property Custodian, Chgo., 1942, N.Y.C., 1943; spl. asst. to pres. Solventol Chem. Products, Inc., Detroit, 1943-46; field atty. NLRB, Balt., 1947-51; spl. asst. enforcement div. OPS, Washington, 1951-53; spl. asst. to dir. Office Indsl. Personnel Security, Office Def., Washington, 1955-56; with NLRB, Balt., Cin., Winston-Salem, N.C., N.Y.C., 1956-60, regional dir., Memphis, 1960—. Recipient Outstanding Performance awards NLRB, 1962, 68. Home: 4159 Chicksaw Rd Memphis TN 38117 Office: 167 Main St Memphis TN 38103

REYNOLDS, JULIAN LOUIS, metals co. exec.; b. Winston-Salem, N.C., May 3, 1910; s. Richard and Julia Louise (Parham) R.; student Wharton Sch. Finance, U. Pa., 1928-29, Duke, 1929-30; m. Glenn Parkinson, Jan. 25, 1941; 1 dau., Glenn Parkinson Martin. With Reynolds Metals Co., Richmond, Va., 1933—, successively mgr. export div., mgr. seal and label div., v.p. and gen. sales mgr., v.p. charge operations, 1948-56, exec. v.p. operations, 1959—, dir., 1936—; chmn. chief exec. officer Reynolds Internat., Inc., 1959—; pres., dir. Metals Co., Louisville, 1933-34, salesman, 1934-36, export mgr., 1936-40, Reynolds Internacional de Mexico 1945—; v.p. Eskimo Pie Corp., 1942-53, pres., 1953—; pres., dir., chmn. Reynolds Aluminio, S.A.; pres. Reynolds Aluminum Co., Reynolds Aluminum Co. of Can., Ltd.; dir. Brit. Aluminum Co., Ltd., Canadian Brit. Aluminum Co., Ltd., Am. Fidelity Life Ins. Co. Presbyn. Clubs: Commonwealth, Country of Va. (Richmond); Athletic (N.Y.C.). Address: Richmond VA 23201

REYNOLDS, LESLIE B(OUSH), JR., physician; b. Lakeland, Fla., Aug. 16, 1923; s. Leslie Boush and Verna (Powell) R.; B.S., Randolph-Macon Coll., 1949 M.S., Ga. Inst. Tech., 1951; Ph.D., Med. Coll. S.C., 1941; M.D., Northwestern U., 1966; m. Alma Carter, Oct. 24, 1947; children—Alma Mary, Margaret Mary. Engr., E.I. du Pont de Nemours & Co., Inc., Kinston, N.C., 1951-53, group leader, 1954-55, lab. supr., 1956-57; asst. prof. physiology Northwestern U. Med. Sch., Chgo., 1961-64, research asso. medicine, 1964-66; intern St. Joseph Hosp., Chgo., 1966-67; practice medicine specializing in pulmonary disease, Memphis, 1968—; mem. staff City of Memphis Hosp., Bapt. Hosp.; asst. prof. medicine U. Tenn., 1967-71, asso. prof. medicine, 1971—, asso. prof. physiology and biophysics, 1967—, acting chmn. dept. physiology and biophysics, 1968-69. Served with USNR, 1942-46. Mem. Am. Physiol. Soc., A.M.A., Am. Thoracic Soc., Am. Coll. Chest Physicians, Am. Med. Writers Assn., A.A.A.S., Sigma Xi, Phi Lambda Upsilon. Research in respiratory reflexes, treatment of respiratory diseases. Home: 1601 Old Hickory Rd Memphis TN 38116 Office: 22 N Pauline St Memphis TN 38105

REYNOLDS, MERRILL SHELBY, bank dir.; b. Milton, W.Va., Dec. 21, 1919; s. Shelby Jackson and Mary Ellen (Nichoels) R.; student pub. schs.; m. Leah Katherine Baroff, June 15, 1941; children—Diane (Mrs. Ronnie Dallas Tury), Pamela (Mrs. Daniel Raymond Hair), Kerry Shawn. Glass designer Dunbar Glass Corp. (W.Va.), 1937-41; chem. insp. Union Carbide, South Charleston, W.Va., 1941-55; co-owner Dari Delite, Clearwater, Fla., 1955-57; salesman Tarpon Chevrolet, Tarpon Springs, Fla., 1956-66; pres. Caladesi Auto Sales & Service Co., Inc., Dunedin, Fla., 1966—; dir. Caladesi Nat. Bank, Dunedin. Mem. C. of C., Automobile Dealers Assn. Mason (Shriner), Elk. Home: PO Box 217 Dunedin FL 33528 Office: 553 Causeway Blvd Dunedin FL 33528

REYNOLDS, MILTON, pen mfg. exec., round-world record flyer, explorer; b. Albert Lea, Minn., July 10, 1892; s. Simon and Rose (Vehon) R.; student pub. schs. Quincy, Ill.; m. Edna Loebe, Oct. 19, 1917 (dec. Apr. 1958); children—Marjorie Jeanne, James Milton; m. 2d, Manolita Salas, Apr. 15, 1961. Chmn. Reynolds Pen Co., also Reynolds Printasign Co.; dir. Syntex Co. Mem. Mexican Geog. Soc. Clubs: Circumnavigators; Adventurers; Mexico City Country, Club de Golf Mex.; Pierre Marques Country (Acapulco). Invented the ball pen. Explorer, adventurer, round-the-world record flyer, air exploration of Chinese Tibet high mountains. Author: Hasta La Vista, 1944; Rocketing Round the World, 1946. Address: Av San Buenaventura 181 Tlalpam DF Mexico

REYNOLDS, RANDALL O., state legislator, dentist; b. nr. Chatham, Va., Oct. 19, 1907; s. Booker J. and Rowena (Mahan) R.; student U. Richmond, 1925-26; D.D.S., Med. Coll. Va. Sch. Dentistry, 1930; m. Billie Jean Wheeler, 1963; children—Elizabeth, Mary, Jean; 1 dau. (by previous marriage), Jane Rowe (Mrs. John B. Murray). Practice dentistry, Chatham, 1930—; mem. Va. Ho. of Dels., 1956—. Pres. Planters Bank & Trust Co., 1948-52, dir., 1938—; pres. Rex Motor Co., Inc., 1956—; pres. Gretna Finance Services, Inc., 1971—. Mayor, Chatham, 1948-50; mem. council Town of Chatham, 1938-48. Trustee Hargrave Mil. Acad., 1945—, sec. bd., 1950—. Mem. Am. Dental Assn., Va., Piedmont dental socs., Pierre Fauchard Dental Hon. Soc., Farm Bur., Farmers Union, Psi Omega. Baptist. Mason, Lion (past local pres.). Club: Cedars Country. Home: Peach St Chatham VA 24531 Office: Main St Chatham VA 24531

REYNOLDS, RICHARD CLYDE, physician, educator; b. Saugerties, N.Y., Sept. 2, 1929; s. Thomas Watson and Myrtle (Myer) R.; B.S., Rutgers U., 1949; M.D., Johns Hopkins, 1953; m. Mary Jane Beck, July 7, 1954; children—Karen Sue, Stephanie Ann, Wayne Thomas. Intern, Johns Hopkins Hosp., Balt., 1953-54, resident, 1954-55, fellow in medicine, 1957-59; practice medicine specializing in internal medicine, Frederick, Md., 1959-68; asso. prof. medicine U. Fla., Gainesville, 1968-71, prof. medicine, prof. community health and family medicine, 1971—, asst. dean Coll. Medicine, 1970—. Served to sr. asst. surgeon USPHS, 1955-57. Diplomate Am. Bd. Internal Medicine. Fellow A.C.P.; mem. A.M.A., Am. Acad. Family Practice. Home: 2015 NW 26th St Gainesville FL 32601

REYNOLDS, RICHARD S., JR., bus. exec.; b. Winston-Salem, N.C., May 27, 1908; s. Richard S. and Louise (Parham) R.; student Davidson Coll.; B.S., U. Pa., 1930; m. Virginia Sargeant; children—Richard S., Sargeant (dec.). Mem. N.Y. Stock Exchange, 1930—; partner banking co. Reynolds & Co., N.Y.C., 1930; asst. to pres. Reynolds Metals Co., Richmond, Va., 1938, treas., 1938-48, v.p., 1944-48, pres., 1948-63, chmn. bd., chief exec. officer, 1963-71, chmn. bd., pres., 1971—; chmn. bd. Robertshaw Controls Co., 1955—, chmn. exec. com., 1957-59, chmn., 1959—; dir. Mfrs. Hanover Trust Co., British Aluminum Ltd., Central Nat. Bank of Richmond. Mem. Aluminum Assn. (past pres.). Presbyn. Clubs: Brook (N.Y.C.); Metropolitan (Washington); Country of Va., Commonwealth (Richmond); Farmington Country; Deep Run Hunt. Home: 4509 Sulgrave Rd Richmond VA 23221 Office: Richmond VA 23261

REYNOLDS, ROBERT JACKSON, mfg. co. exec.; b. Joplin, Mo., May 5, 1910; s. Roy Randolph and Roberta Katherine (Taulbee) R.; student Mo. U., 1926-28; m. Anne Kenney Prewitt, July 2, 1931; children—Elizabeth (Mrs. Richard Carr), Robert Jackson. Civil engr. Ky. Hwy. Dept., 6th Dist., 1928-41; engr. Hercules Powder Co., Pulaski, Va., 1941-42, Bechtel, McCone & Parsons, Birmingham, Ala., 1942-43, Stone & Webster, Oak Ridge, Tenn., 1943, Mason & Hanger Co., Bamboo, Wis., 1943-45; pres., dir. Hwy. Concrete Pipe, Inc., Mt. Sterling, Ky., 1949—, Hwy. Drainage Pipe, Inc., 1954—, Mt. Sterling Broadcasting Corp., 1956—. Mem. Ky. Senate, 1950-58; chmn. Montgomery County Democratic Exec. Com., 1960—. Mem. Am. Soc. C.E., Ky. Soc. Profl. Engrs. Mem. Christian Ch. Democrat. Odd fellow. Club: Mt. Sterling Golf and Country. Home: Route 2 Mt Sterling KY 40353 Office: 13 N Bank St Mt Sterling KY 40353

REYNOLDS, VICTOR GEORGE FASSETT, publisher; b. Laceyville, Pa., Oct. 11, 1905; s. Hallock Solomon and Rubie Ann (Fassett) R.; B.S., Dartmouth, 1927; m. Lucille McCall, Sept. 5, 1936. With coll. dept., Ronald Press Co., N.Y.C., 1927-34, F. S. Crofts, N.Y.C., 1934-37; coll. dept. sales, sales promotion dir. The Macmillan Co., N.Y.C., 1937-43; univ. pub., mem. faculty Cornell U. and mgr. Cornell U. Press, 1943-63; dir. U. Press of Va., Charlottesville, 1963-69; editor, pub. U. Press New Eng., Hanover, N.H., 1970—; dir. Franklin Publs., Inc. Dir. Am. Book Pubs. Council, 1952-54; sec.-treas. Assn. Am. U. Presses, 1951-53, pres., 1953-55. Chmn. exec. com. Friends of the Datmouth Library, 1955-57. Life mem. Am. Hist. Assn., Hist. Soc. Pa., Pa. Hist. Assn., Va. Hist. Soc. Ind. Democrat. Home: 2 Tyler Rd Hanover NH 03755

REZNY, ARTHUR ADOLPH, educator; b. Chgo., Sept. 16, 1910; s. Martin B. and Helen M. (Pikas) R.; B.S., U. Ill., 1932, M.S., 1939; Ph.D., U. Mich., 1958; m. Sally Ann Matthews, June 22, 1935; children— Marilyn (Mrs. Gerald Hahn), Carolyn (Mrs. Lonnie Benson). Tchr. pub. schs., Elmwood Park, Ill., 1934-37, Ann Arbor, Mich., 1937-49, Royal Oak, Mich., 1949-52; faculty U. Wis., Milw., 1953-71; prof. ednl. adminstrn. Ark. State U., State University, 1971—. Vis. dean student affairs Northland Coll., Ashland, Wis., 1963-64; cons. various sch. dists., Wis., Mich. Served to lt. comdr. USNR, 1942-45. Mem. Mich. Edn. Assn., Am. Legion (post chmn. 1953), Phi Kappa Phi, Phi Delta Kappa. Methodist. Rotarian. Club: Optimist (dist. lt. gov. Mich. 17th Dist. 1952-53). Author: A Schoolman in the Law Library, 1962, rev., 1968. Editor-in-chief Legal Problems of School Boards, 1966. Contbr. articles to various publs. Home: 1904 Munos Lane Jonesboro AR 72401

REZSETAR, MARY ALICE HEDGE (MRS. STEPHEN WALTER REZSETAR), legislative cons.; b. Jacksonville, Fla., Sept. 22, 1941; d. George Oliver and Eloise (Burner) Hedge; grad. Winthrop Coll., S.C. Coll. for Women, 1963; m. Stephen Walter Rezsetar, Nov. 29, 1969. Exec. sec. to Congressman Charles E. Bennett, Washington, 1965-67; adminstrv. officer White House Nat. Adv. Commn. on Libraries, 1967-68; free lance legislative cons., 1969-71; asso. dep. dir., adminstrv. officer Nat. Commn. on Libraries and Information Sci., 1971—; asso. dir. Duke U. Library and Information Sci. publ. project, 1968-69; rep. City Jacksonville and State Fla. at N.Y. World's Fair, N.Y.C., 1964-65. Pianist, violinist Jacksonville Jr. Symphony, 1950-55. Named Miss Smile Jacksonville, 1963. Mem. Fla. State Soc., Pa. State Soc., Nat. Hist. Soc., Smithsonian Assos., Internat. Platform Assn., Nat. Wildlife Fedn., Sierra Club, Common Cause. Democrat. Methodist. Home: 217 Magnolia St Neptune Beach FL 32050 also 1024 Wisconsin Av NW Washington DC 20007

RHEA, IRA ELIZABETH HAY (MRS. CREIGHTON RHEA), physician; b. Eagleville, Tenn., Oct. 11, 1933; d. Ira James and Alice (Pettus) Hay; B.S. summa cum laude, Middle Tenn. State Coll., 1955; M.D., U. Tenn., 1958; m. Creighton Rhea, May 5, 1961. Intern, City of Memphis Hosps. and U. Tenn. Sch. Medicine, 1958-59, resident in radiology, 1959-61; practice medicine specializing in radiology, Murfreesboro, 1963—; mem. staffs DeKalb Gen. Hosp., Smithville, Tenn., Lady Ann Meml. Hosp., Livingston, Tenn.; radiologist White County Meml. Hosp., Sparta, Tenn.; staff physician VA Hosp., Murfreesboro, 1970—. Dealer, Tenn. Securities, Inc., Nashvillé, part-time 1968—. Mem. A.M.A., Tenn. Med. Assn., Stones River and Rutherford County Acad. Medicine, League Women Voters (local sec. 1966-69), Nat. Assn. Securities Dealers, Charity Circle of Murfreesboro, Alpha Omega Alpha. Clubs: Stores River Country, Smyrna Country, Oakland Assn. Women's. Address: 2610 Loyd St Murfreesboro TN 37130

RHEA, KARL BYINGTON, physician; b. Somerville, Tenn., Feb. 2, 1931; s. Howard Matthew and Wilhelmina (Litterer) R.; student Southwestern U., 1949-51, Memphis State U., 1951; M.D., U. Tenn., 1954; m. Mary Elizabeth Borum, June 11, 1959; children—Karl Byington, Robert Howard, William Scott. Intern, Confederate Meml. Hosp., Shreveport, La., 1954-55; with Tenn. Pub. Health Service, 1955-56; resident surgery Kennedy VA Hosp., Memphis, 1958-59; practice gen. medicine, Somerville, 1959—; adminstr. Morris Clinic and Hosp., Somerville, county med. examiner, Fayette County, 1961—, county coroner, 1961—. Former mem. Fayette County Democratic Exec. Com. Bd. dirs. Fayette Acad. Served with USPHS, 1956-58. Diplomate Am. Bd. Family Practice. Mem. W. Tenn. Consol. Med. Assembly, A.M.A., Am. Acad. Gen. Practice, Am. Assn. Physicians and Surgeons, Phi Chi, Kappa Sigma. Democrat. Presbyn. (chmn. bd. deacons). Club: Somerville Country. Home: Oak Rd Somerville TN 38068 Office: 138 Market St Somerville TN 38068

RHEAY, MARY LOUISE, librarian; b. Montgomery, Ala., Mar. 8, 1920; d. Ross Smith and Maria (Cunningham) Rheay; A.B., Ala. Coll., 1940; A.B. in Library Sci., Emory U., 1941, M.L.S., 1959. Library asst. Atlanta Pub. Library, 1941-42, supr. sch. work, 1942-53, asst. head, 1953-56, head children's dept., 1956-63, asst. dir., 1963—; part-time instr. Ga. State Coll., 1960—, Emory U. Library Sch., 1960-68. Named Atlanta Woman of Year in Professions, 1962. Mem. Am. (mem. Newberry Caldecott award com. for children's services div. 1962), Southeastern (acting chmn. sch. and children's sect. 1963-64, chmn. pub. library sect. 1968-69), Ga. (chmn. children's and young people's sect. 1949-51, 1st v.p., pres. elect 1971-73), Metro Atlanta (pres. 1964-65) library assns., Zonta Internat. (sec. 1969-70, v.p. 1971, 72), Delta Kappa Gamma (pres. 1966-68). Home: 4555 Meadow Valley Dr Atlanta GA 30305 Office: 126 Carnegie Way NE Atlanta GA 30303

RHEIN, FRANCIS BAYARD, clergyman; b. Phila., Jan. 5, 1915; s. John Henry Wallace and Elizabeth (Kane) R.; B.S., U. Va., 1938; M.Div., Va. Theol. Sem., 1942, S.T.M., 1971; m. Jane Alice Foster, Sept. 12, 1942; children—Patricia (Mrs. Robert Turner), Eliz (Mrs. Terence Collins), Peter, Jane. Ordained to ministry Episcopal Ch., 1942; rector St. James Ch., Montrose, Va., 1942-43, St. John's Ch., Warsaw, Va., 1946-48, Emmanuel Ch., Newport, R.I., 1948-50, Christ Ch., Millwood, Va., 1950-54, St. Peter's Ch., Phila., 1954-56; asso. prof. Bibl. lit and philosophy Madison Coll., 1956-66; rector Emmanuel Ch., Harrisonburg, Va., 1956-66; rector, Trinity Ch., Upperville, Va., 1966—. Prof. history Foxcroft Sch., 1966-69. Served with USNR, 1943-46; PTO. Episcopalian. Mason. Author: An Analytical Approach to the New Testament, 1966; A Simplified Approach to the New Testament, 1968. Home: Box 127 Upperville VA 22176 Office: Box 127 Upperville VA 22176

RHEM, DURWARD DUDLEY, pub. co. exec.; b. Florence, S.C., Aug. 22, 1927; s. Durward Dudley and Muriel (Williams) R.; B.A., Coll. William and Mary, 1952; m. Jane Patricia Odom, July 9, 1955; children—Durward Dudley IV, Patricia Anne, Jennifer Leah. Mgr. publs. Radiation, Inc., Melbourne, Fla., 1954-61; v.p. Soroban Engring., Palm Bay, Fla., 1961-68; pres. Brevard Graphics, Inc., Palm Bay, 1961—. Served with M.C., AUS, 1945-47. Mem. Am. Mgmt. Assn., Civitan. Mason. Clubs: Century, Eau Gallie Yacht. Home: 311 Palm Ct Indialantic FL 32901 Office: 829 New Haven Av Melbourne FL 32901

RHEM, SAMUEL DUNN, III, physician; b. Memphis, Aug. 28, 1937; s. Samuel Dunn and Mary (Nolan) R.; M.D., U. Tenn., 1961; J.D., South Tex. Coll. Law, 1971; m. Sharon Jenkins, Feb. 9, 1963; children—Samuel Dunn IV, Marcus. Intern, St. Thomas, Vanderbilt hosps., Nashville; practice medicine specializing in legal medicine, Pasadena, Tex., 1963—; chief staff Southmore Hosp. Fellow Acad. Clin. and Exptl. Hypnosis; mem. Harris County Med. Soc. (sec. S.E. br.), Am., So. (mem. postgrad. assembly) Tex. med. assns., Am. Acad. Gen. Practice, Am. Acad. Legal Medicine. Home: 2204 Perez St Pasadena TX 77502 Office: 906 E Southmore St Pasadena TX 77502

RHINEHART, FORREST H., dentist; b. Iowa County, Ia., Oct. 4, 1901; s. Homer Hampton and Mary Elizabeth (Bever) R.; D.D.S., U. Neb., 1926; m. Hope Hanson, Feb. 15, 1925; children—Marjorie Lee (Mrs. Harold H. Kemp), Donald Forrest. Practice gen. dentistry, Benkelman and Grand Island, Neb., 1926-42, Tulsa, 1946—. Served with AUS, 1942-46. Mem. Am., Okla. State, Tulsa dental assns., Xi Psi Phi. Episcopalian. Mason (32 deg.), Elk. Home: 235 N Yukon St Tulsa OK 74127 Office: Pythian Bldg Tulsa OK 74103

RHOAD, WILLIAM OTTERBEIN, clergyman; b. Pinegrove, Pa., Aug. 17, 1903; s. Hiram F. and Annie (Houser) R.; B.A., Lebannon Valley Coll., 1925; student Bonebrake Theol. Sem., 1925-26; Th.B., Princeton Theol. Sem., 1928; Th.M., Westminster Theol. Sem., 1944; Th.D., Central U., 1940; m. Myrtle Iva Dymond, Nov. 23, 1931; children—Priscilla (Mrs. Jack Pleasants), William Otterbein, John Calvin, Rebecca. Ordained ministry Presbyn. Ch., 1931; minister Kensington and Freetown Chs., P.E.I., Can., 1931-41, Ashfield and Ripley Chs., Ont., Can., 1941-49, Maryland Av. Ch., Balt., 1949-54, McDowell (Va.) Ch., 1954-61, Cedar Creek, Cedar Cliff, Mt. Hope chs., 1961-66, Keysville (Va.), Briery (Va.), Meherrin (Va.) Presbyn. chs., 1968—. Moderator Presbytery P.E.I., 1936, clk., 1937-41; moderator Maitland Presbytery, 1944, Huron-Maitland, 1947, Lexington 1957. Home: J St Keysville VA 23947 Office: Box 16 Keysville VA 23947

RHOADES, EDD DARREL, govt. engr.; b. Geronimo, Okla., May 26, 1919; s. Jacob Lee and Ada (Bull) R.; A.S., Cameron Coll., 1939; B.S., Okla. State U., 1942, M.S., 1951, postgrad. 1964-66; m. Erma Rae Embry, Aug. 28, 1946; children—Edd Darrel, Lynda, John. Ordnance engr. U.S. War Dept., 1942-44; agrl. engr. U.S. Soil Conservation Service, Sulpher, Okla., 1946-52; civil engr. U.S. Navy, McAlester, Okla., 1952-57; research agrl. engr. Agrl. Research Service, U.S. Dept. Agr., Chickasha, Okla., 1957—. Teaching fellow Okla. State U., 1949-50. Active local civic affairs, Chickasha. Served to lt. (j.g.) USNR, 1944-46. Mem. Soil Conservation Soc. Am., Am. Soc. Agrl. Engrs. Contbr. articles to profl. pubs. Home: 2400 S 12th St Chickasha OK 73018 Office: PO Box 400 Chickasha OK 73018

RHOADES, EVERETT RONALD, physician; b. Lawton, Okla, Oct. 24, 1931; s. Lee Joseph and Dorothy Apasha (Rowell) R.; student Lafayette Coll., 1949-52; M.D., U. Okla., 1956; m. Bernadine Herwona Toyebo, Sept. 28, 1953; children—Lee Charles, Melanie Cheryl, Melinda Sue, Dorothy Alison, Lisa Patricia. Intern, Gorgas Hosp., Ancon, C.Z.; resident U. Okla. Med. Center, Oklahoma City, 1957-61; chief infectious disease Wilford Hall USAF, Hosp., 1961-66; asst. prof. medicine and microbiology U. Okla. Med. Center, 1966-67, asso. prof., 1967-71, prof., 1972—, chief infectious disease, 1967—. Cons. U. Saigon Med. Sch., Western Okla. Tb Sanatarium; adv. council NIH, 1972—. Mem. Kiowa Tribal Bus. Com., 1967-70, Inter Tribal Land Use Com., 1967-70. Served to maj. USAF, 1957-66. Recipient fellowship John Hay Whitney Found., 1952, outstanding achievement award VA, 1958, 59. Mem. Nat. Congress Am. Indians, Assn. Am. Indian Physicians (founder 1971, pres. 1971-72), Nat. Council Minority Bus. Enterprise, Assn. Am. Indian Affairs (bd. dirs. 1970—), Kiowa Ton Kon Gaut Soc., Phi Beta Kappa, Alpha Omega Alpha, Sigma Xi. Home: 1808 Dorchester Dr Oklahoma City OK 73120 Office: 921 NE 13th St Oklahoma City OK 73104

RHOADES, RALPH SHORT, govt. ofcl.; b. Hugo, Colo., Nov. 27, 1926; s. Ralph and Lucille (Miller) R.; student Washington U., 1944-45; B.A., U. Tulsa, 1950; m. Shirley Barton, Mar. 28, 1950; children—Barton R., Brettley V. Pub. relations and advt. mgr. Okla. Blue Cross and Blue Shield Plans, 1950-66; v.p., head pub. relations div. Whitney Advt. Inc., 1966, pres. pub. relations counselors, 1966-67; pres. The Ralph Rhoades Co., advt., pub. relations, Tulsa, 1967—, spl. asst. Ozarks regional commn. U.S. Dept. Commerce, Washington, 1969—. Mem. Okla. Ho. Reps., 1962-64; mem. Okla. Senate, 1964-66. Served with AUS, 1945-47. Mem. Tulsa C. of C., Tulsa Advt. Fedn. (dir.), Tulsa U. Alumni Assn., Okla. Press Assn. (asso.), Pub. Relations Soc. Am., Tulsa press Club. Episcopalian. Author profl. articles and short stories. Home: 3733 E 45th Pl Tulsa OK 74135 Office: US Dept Commerce 2099 B Washington DC 20230

RHOADS, JAMES BERTON, archivist; b. Sioux City, Ia., Sept. 17, 1928; s. James Harrison and Mary (Keenan) R.; student Southwestern Jr. Coll., 1946-47, Union Coll., Lincoln, Neb., 1947-48; B.A., U. Cal. at Berkeley, 1950, M.A., 1952; Ph.D., Am. U., 1965; m. S. Angela Handy, Aug. 12, 1947; children—Cynthia Patrice, James Berton, Marcia Marie. With Gen. Services Adminstrn.-Nat. Archives and Records Service, Washington, 1952—, asst. archivist for civil archives, 1965, dep. archivist U.S., 1966-68, archivist U.S., 1968—; chmn. Archives Adv. Council; chmn. Nat. Archives Trust Fund Bd.; chmn. adminstrv. com. Fed. Register; chmn. Nat. Hist. Publs. Commn.; mem. Am. Revolution Bicentennial Commn., Fed. Fire Council. Trustee Woodrow Wilson Internat. Center for Scholars; bd. dirs. Harry S. Truman Library Inst. for Nat. and Internat. Affairs; adv. com. Eleutherian Mills-Hagley Found. Recipient Meritorious and Distinguished Service awards Gen. Service Adminstrn., 1966-68. Fellow Soc. Am. Archivists (mem. council); mem. Am. Hist. Assn., Internat. Council Archives (v.p.), Orgn. Am. Historians, Am. Assn. State and Local History, Am. Antiquarian Soc., Phi Alpha Theta, Phi Kappa Phi. Home: 6502 Cipriano Rd Lanham MD 20801 Office: Nat Archives Bldg Washington DC 20408

RHOADS, MAX NOLAN, city ofcl.; b. nr. Owensboro, Ky., Oct. 29, 1926; s. Meredith N. and Frances L. (Garrison) R.; student U. Ohio, 1943, U. Ky., 1947-48; B.S., Evansville Coll., 1950; m. Gloria England, Sept. 1948; children—Mike, Leigh Ann. With Owensboro Nat. Bank, 1953-56; finance dir. City Owensboro, 1956-59, city mgr., 1959—. Chmn., United Fund, 1967; lay mem. Brescia Coll., Owensboro, 1965—. Served to capt. AUS, 1944-46, 51-53. Mem. Am. Acad Polit. and Social Sci., Ky. (past pres.), Internat. city mgrs. assns., Ky. Municipal League (past bd. dirs., sec.), C. of C., Am. Pub. Works Assn. (Ky. dir.). Kiwanian. Home: 2930 Delaware Dr Owensboro KY 42301 2930 Delaware Dr Owensboro KY 42301 Office: City Hall 4th and St Ann St Owensboro KY 42301

RHODES, CLARENCE ALBERT, JR., elec. engr.; b. Winston-Salem, N.C., May 10, 1924; s. Clarence Albert and Evy Bell (Johnston) R.; B.S., Va. Poly. Inst., 1949; postgrad. Wake Forest U., 1968-69; m. Peggy Rose Reid, Apr. 11, 1953; children—William Edward, Sarah Weatherington, Ann Taylor, Elizabeth Shepherd. Elec. engr., asso. partner Lashmit, James, Brown & Pollock, architects and engrs., Winston-Salem, 1949-63; cons. elec. engr. C.A. Rhodes, Jr., Winston-Salem, 1963—; cons. engr. Housing Authority Winston-Salem, Old Salem, Inc., Winston-Salem Found. Instr. radiol. monitoring Civil Def. Tng. Program, 1965. Served with AUS, 1943-46. Registered profl. engr., N.C., S.C. Mem. A.A.A.S., Tau Beta Pi, Eta Kappa Nu. Methodist. Kiwanian. Home: 1780 Robinhood Rd Winston-Salem NC 27104 Office: Wachovia Bldg Winston-Salem NC 27101

RHODES, DONALD HENRY, lawyer; b. Norfolk, Va., Mar. 17, 1933; s. Early Clemons and Ivy Mae (Harris) R.; B.S. in Edn., U. Va., 1955, LL.B., 1961; postgrad. Pa. State U., 1955-56; m. Anna Margaret Young, June 13, 1959; children—Donald Henry, Chester Clemons. Admitted to Va. bar, 1961; dir. field services and summer rehab. center Va. Soc. Crippled Children and Adults, 1956-58, bd. dirs. Va. Beach, 1958—; asst. city atty. Norfolk (Va.), 1961-62; asso. Kellam & Kellam, attys., Virginia Beach, Va., 1962-66, partner, 1967-68; partner Owen, Guy, Rhodes & Betz, Virginia Beach, 1969—. Pres. Thalia Civic League Virginia Beach, 1967; mem. Virginia Beach City Council, 1970—, mayor, 1970—. Bd. dirs. Tidewater Mental Health Assn. Virginia Beach, 1965—. Mem. Men's Democratic Club Virginia Beach. Mem. Va., Virginia Beach, Norfolk-Portsmouth bar assns., Va. State Bar, Delta Theta Phi, Phi Kappa Psi, Clubs: Y.M.C.A. Men's Princess Anne Ruritan, Virginia Beach Sertoma (v.p. 1964-67, pres. 1967-68), Cavalier Golf and Yacht. Home: 621 Heron Point Circle Virginia Beach VA 23452 Office: 281 Independence Blvd Virginia Beach VA 23462

RHODES, EDWIN FRANKLIN, mfg. co. exec.; b. Mishawaka, Ind., Oct. 24, 1919; s. Edward R. and Edna (Arnold) R.; B.S., N.C. State U., 1940; m. Helen Hickman, Sept. 29, 1952; children—Charles, Mary Lisa, Christopher, Thomas, Cynthia, Priscilla, Eric, Stephanie. Installationist engr. Otis Elevator Co., 1940-41; tchr. pub. schs., Mishawaka, 1941-42, engr., tool engr., spl. project engr., specialist, purchasing agt. Dodge Mfg. Co. div. Reliance Electric, Mishawaka, 1942-58, mgr. purchases, 1958-69; mgr. operations controls Baldor Electric Co., Fort Smith, Ark., St. Louis and Columbus, Miss., 1969—; dir. N. Am. Foundry; mng. dir. Southwestern Die Casting. Mem. C. of C. Methodist. Mason (32 deg., Shriner). Home: 4112 S 35th St Fort Smith AR 72901 Office: Baldor Electric Co Fort Smith AR 72901

RHODES, ERIC FOSTER, editor, pub.; b. Luray, Va., Feb. 5, 1927; s. Wallace Keith and Bertha (Foster) R.; A.A., George Washington U., 1949, A.B., 1950, M.A., 1952, Ed.D., 1967; m. Barbara Ellen Henson, Oct. 19, 1946; children—Roxanne Jane, Laurel Lee; m. 2d, Lorraine Endresen, July 29, 1972. Tchr. high sch., Arlington, Va., 1950-52; counselor Washington Lee High Sch., Arlington, 1952-53, dir. publs., 1953-54, chmn. dept. English, 1954-55; exec. sec. Arlington Edn. Assn., 1952-53, Montgomery County (Md.) Edn. Assn., 1955-57; lectr. edn. George Washington U., 1955-60; salary cons. N.E.A., Washington, 1957-58, asst. dir. membership div., 1958-60, dir. N.Y. regional office, N.Y.C., 1960-64; ednl. cons. Ednl. Research Services, White Plains, N.Y., 1964-65; pres. Ednl. Service Bur., Inc., Arlington, 1965-72, chmn. bd., 1972—; pres. EFR Corp., 1972—. Cons. Va. Dept. Community Colls., 1965—; lectr. edn. Frostburg (Md.) State Coll., 1967; vice chancellor Va. Community Coll. System, 1970-71. Mem. Civil Rights Commn., Franklin Twp., N.J., 1962-64; mem. Franklin Twp. Bd. Edn., 1964-65; mem. adv. bd. Keep Am. Beautiful, 1964—, nat. chmn., 1968. Served with AUS, 1945-47. Mem. Am.

Assn. Sch. Adminstrs., N.E.A., Edn. Press Assn., Phi Delta Kappa (chpt. pres. 1959-60), Fed. Schoolmens Club, N.Y. Schoolmasters Club. Lion. Author: Negotiating Salaries. Editor: Adminstrv. Leadership, Salary and Merit. Home: 6631 Wakefield Dr Alexandria VA 22307 Office: 610 Madison St Alexandria VA 22314

RHODES, FRED BURNETT, JR., govt. ofcl.; b. Washington, Dec. 17, 1913; s. Fred Burnett and Florence (Shuffle) R.; A.B., Colgate U., 1936; LL.B., U. Md., 1941; m. Winona Henderson, Dec. 25, 1956. Claims adjuster Md. Casualty Co., 1936-41; admitted to Md. bar, 1941; exec. dir. Joint Com. Atomic Energy, 1947-49; liaison officer CIA, 1949-50; chief counsel armed services com. U.S. Senate, 1953-55; pvt. practice law, Washington, 1955-60; gen. counsel VA, 1960-62; minority counsel com. appropriations U.S. Senate, 1962-64, sec., staff dir. Republican policy com., 1964-69; dep. adminstr. VA, 1969-—. Vice pres. D.C. Bapt. Conv., 1962-64, pres., 1964-65; exec. com. So. Bapt. Conv., v.p., 1970-—. Served to maj. AUS, 1941-47, 51-53. Mem. Am., Fedn., D.C. bar assns. Baptist. Clubs: Army-Navy Country (Arlington); Potomac Appalachian Trail. Home: 3101 N Peary St Arlington VA 22207 Office: 810 Vermont Av NW Washington DC 20420

RHODES, JACK ALVIN, state ofcl.; b. Oklahoma City, Apr. 24, 1920; s. Ivan A. and Lola M. (Bradley) R.; student Kan. State Tchrs. Coll., 1939-40; B.A., Okla. U., 1943; M.P.A., Harvard, 1945; postgrad. (Fulbright fellow) Sidney Sussex Coll., Cambridge U., 1949-50; m. Lois N. Hopper, Aug. 29, 1952; 1 dau., Lois Ann. Instr., U. Okla., 1945-46, Wellesley (Mass.) Coll., 1946-47; teaching fellow, tutor Harvard, 1947; asst. dir. Okla. Legislative Council, Oklahoma City, 1947-49, dir., 1950-—. Pres., Nat. Legislative Conf., 1965-66. Home: 412 NW 21st St Oklahoma City OK 73103 Office: State Capitol Oklahoma City OK 73105

RHODES, ROBERT GRANT, petroleum co. exec.; b. Caney, Kan., Mar. 23, 1917; s. Charles William and Stella Susan (Toner) R.; B.S., U. Tex., 1939; m. Nellie Foldine Martin, Aug. 20, 1942; children—Cheryl Susan, Mary Rebecca, Robert William. With Phillips Petroleum Co., 1939-—, mgr. fertilizer and plastics plant, Pasadena, Tex., 1952-58, mgr. petrochem. div. mfg. dept., 1963-69, alternate mem. operating com., 1965, mgr. operations chem. and refining, 1969-72, gen. mgr. rubber chems., 1972-—; prodn. mgr. Phillips Chem. Co., Bartlesville, Okla., 1958-63; dir. Phosphate Chem. Inc. Mem. adv. bd. Salvation Army, Pasadena, 1952-58 mem. Civil Def. Commn., Houston; indsl. advisor U. Tex., 1966-—; pres. Nat. Little League Baseball, 1971, Am. Little League Baseball, 1972. Registered profl. engr., Okla. Mem. Nat., Okla. socs. profl. engrs., Am. Inst. Chem. Engrs., Nat. Petroleum Refiners Assn. (mem. mfg. com. 1971), Ind. Petroleum Producers Am. (asso.), Bartlesville Ambassador C. of C. Presbyn. (deacon). Club: Governors. Rotarian. Home: 1721 Cherokee Pl Bartlesville OK 74003 Office: Phillips Petroleum Co Bartlesville OK 74003

RHODES, THOMAS BENNET, editor, pub.; b. Monroe, La., Feb. 14, 1926; s. Deryl W. and Almena (Bennett) R.; grad. high sch.; m. Joyce Baker Jasper, Oct. 6, 1946; children—Linda (Mrs. B.J. Ward), D. Ladd, M. Kevin, Dona Kim, Rebeca Jo. Advt. mgr. Billups Western, New Orleans, 1946-50; account exec. H.S. Benjamin Assos., advt., Baton Rouge, 1950-52; owner Rhodes Pub. Co., Baton Rouge, 1952-—, editor, pub. Contractors mag., 1952-—. La. Motor Transport News, 1952-—, pub. Fun mag., 1972-—; pres. Boure Pub. Corp., 1972-—. Cons. La. Motor Transport Assn., Inc. Served with AUS, 1944-46. Methodist. Home: 1619 Carolyn Av Baton Rouge LA 70815 Office: 1724 Dallas Dr Baton Rouge LA 70815

RHONE, RAYMOND DOUGLAS, banker; b. Mt. Pleasant, Tex., May 24, 1918; s. Edgar and Alma Myra (Cope) R.; student Fed. Inst. Bus. Coll., 1936, Southwestern Grad. Sch. Banking, 1967-69, So. Methodist, 1967-69; m. Minnie Evelyn Miller, Dec. 3, 1939; children— Shirley (Mrs. Braxton Cowan), Raymond Douglas. Clk. transp. dept. St. Louis Southwestern Ry. Lines, Tyler, Tex., 1936-48; with Tyler Bank & Trust Co. (Tex.), 1949-—, sr. v.p., 1969-—. Served with USAAF, 1943-46. Mason (Shriner), Lion. Home: 2318 Pollard St Tyler TX 75701 Office: PO Box 2009 Tyler TX 75701

RHYNE, CHARLES HOWARD, social worker; b. McEwen, Tenn., Nov. 6, 1927; s. Howard L. and Ethel (Fitz-gerald) R.; B.A., Trevecca Nazerene Coll., Nashville, 1955; postgrad. Peabody Coll., summer 1955; M.S.W., U. Tenn., 1962; m. Hilda Louise Curtis, July 2, 1947; 1 dau., Melissa Jane. Fitter, Nashville Bridge Co., 1948-51, supr., 1957-61; tchr. State Tng. Sch. for Boys, Jordonia, Tenn., 1955-57; asso. dir. Community Chest and Council, Mobile, Ala., 1962-—. Cons. Careers in Social Work, U. Fla., 1968, Community Planning Workshop, Gulfport (Miss.) Planning Council, 1969. Chmn., Com. on Rural Resources to Guatemala-AID, 1965. Mem. Nat. Assn. Social Workers, Acad. Certified Social Workers, Ala. Conf. Social Work (past sec.). Contbr. to Jr. C. of C. Forum, 1964-66. Baptist. Home: 5201 Maudelayne Dr Mobile AL 36609 Office: 204 St Francis St Mobile AL 36602

RIANO, MANUEL, physician; b. Havana, Cuba, Sept. 5, 1913; s. Agapito and Maria J. (Jauma) R.; M.D., U. Havana, 1942; postgrad. U. Miami, Fla., 1963; m. Belen Dobal, June 1931; 1 son, Manuel J. Came to U.S., 1962. Intern, U. Havana Sch. Medicine, Univ. Hosp., 1942-43; resident Municipal Emergency Hosp., Havana, 1943-46; gen. practice medicine, Havana, 1942-62; head div. hosps. and pub. health services Ministry Pub. Health, Havana, 1948-50; med. dir. Saturnino Lora Gen. Hosp., Santiago de Cuba, Oriente, 1949-50; supt. Nat. Mental Hosp., Mazorra, Havana, 1950-52; internal medicine cons. Out-Patient Clinic, Ministry Pub. Health, Service of Hygiene and Pub. Health, 1946-48; mem. psychiat. staff Wichita Falls (Tex.) State Hosp., 1964-—; asst. prof. parasitology and tropical diseases U. Havana Sch. Medicine, 1940-42, instr., 1942-44. Gen. inspection pub. health services Ministry Pub. Health, Havana, 1952-60. Mem. exec. bd. Nat. Coll. Medicine, Havana, 1944-48, 54-60, Havana Coll. Medicine, 1942-44. Mem. Am. Assn. Hosps., A.M.A., Tex. Med. Assn., Wichita County Med. Soc., Centauro (hon. pres.). Address: Box 300 Wichita Falls TX 76307

RIBEIRO, LENOR DE SA, physician, hosp. adminstr., educator; b. Soa Goncalo, Brazil, Sept. 25, 1919; s. Americo J. Ribeiro and Coneicao S. Corres de Sa; B.A., Peter Second Coll., Rio de Janeiro, Brazil; B.S., Juruena Inst. Rio De Janeiro, Brazil, 1941; M.D., U. Rio de Janeiro, 1947; m. Maria J. Aguiar, Nov. 4, 1949; children— Silvia, Roberto, Elizabeth, Monica. Naturalized U.S. citizen, 1963. Intern St. John's Hosp., Lowell, Mass., 1951-52; resident physician, Tewksbury (Mass.) Hosp., 1953-54; resident pathologist St. Elizabeth Hosp., Youngstown, O., 1954-56; from staff physician to med. dir., clin. dir., asst. supt. and supt. Nashville Met. Bordeaux Hosp., 1956-—; asst. prof. medicine U. Rio de Janeiro, 1949-51; faculty dept. medicine Vanderbilt U. Hosp., Nashville, 1965-—. Chmn. Health and Safety Com. Middle Tenn.; active dist. health and safety com. Middle Tenn. council Boy Scouts Am.; bd. dirs. Council on Aging. Recipient Outstanding Civil Servant award Nashville Real Estate Bd., 1965. Mem. Am. Acad. Med. Adminstrs., Am., So., Tenn. med. assns., Am. Psychiat. Assn., Nashville Acad. Medicine, Middle Tenn. Hosp. Council, Am. Coll. Hosp. Adminstr., Pan-Am. Assn. Tenn. (pres. 1968-69). Address: County Hosp Rd Nashville TN 37218

RICARDS, HAROLD ANDREW, JR, oil co. exec.; b. Balt., June 21, 1917; s. Harold A. and Annette (Simpson) R.; B.E. in Chem. Engring., Johns Hopkins, 1939; M.S. in Chem. Engring., Mass. Inst. Tech., 1941; postgrad. U. Cal. at Berkeley, 1964; m. Eleanor Mae Connor, Dec. 25, 1943; children—Andrea Lee, Nancy Ellette. Unit head research div. Standard Oil Devel. Co., Linden, N.J., 1941-48; sect. mgr. process div. Esso Research & Engring. Co., Linden, 1948-56, mgr. distbn. and engring. research Esso Standard Oil, N.Y.C., 1957-60, asst. mgr. marketing econs., 1960; mgr. planning and evaluation Humble Oil & Refining Co., Houston, 1961-68, adminstrv. mgr. central region, Memphis, 1968, sales mgr. central region, 1969-—. Lectr., Pa. State U., 1952-57. Served with USAAF, World War II; ETO. Mem. Am. Quarter Horse Assn., Civil War Round Tables, Sigma Xi, Kappa Sigma, Omicron Delta Kappa, Pi Delta Epsilon. Contbr. articles to profl. jours. Patentee in field. Home: 1228 Brookfield Rd Memphis TN 38117 Office: PO Box 367 Memphis TN 38101

RICE, ATWOOD LUMBERD, JR., marine supply co. exec.; b. New Orleans, Apr. 30, 1918; s. Atwood Lumberd and Carrie Moore (Hayward) R.; student Loyola U. South, 1936-37; m. Nancy Barrier Stubblefield, Dec. 22, 1945;children—Atwood L., III, John Barrier. With Hibernia Nat. Bank, New Orleans, 1935-41; co-founder, partner Byrne & Rice Supply Co., New Orleans, 1946-60, pres. Byrne, Rice & Turner, Inc., 1960-—, pres. La. Air Pollution Controls div.; 1969-—; v.p. Rio Hondo Oil & Devel. Corp. La., 1960-71; sec., 1965-71. Pres. Orleans Neighborhood Centers, 1949-50; pres. New Orleans Sportsmen's League, 1970; mem. Met. Area Com., Council for a Better La., Pub. Affairs Research Council; pres. Valencia, Inc., 1971-—. Served to capt. AUS, 1941-45; ETO. Decorated Bronze Star. Mem. La. (co-founder, pres. 1948-49), New Orleans (co-founder, pres. 1939-41) junior chambers commerce, S.R. (pres. 1965-67), Mil. Order Fgn. Wars (comdr. La. 1964-66), Soc. Colonial Wars (gov. La. 1972). Episcopalian (treas. ch. 1968-72, chmn. Young Life New Orleans 1969-—). Clubs: Louisiana, New Orleans Country, Pendennis, Pickwick (New Orleans); Lake Shore (Slidell, La.); Avoca Duck (Morgan City, La.). Home: 1220 Philip St New Orleans LA 70130 Office: 1150 Camp St New Orleans LA 70130

RICE, CHARLES OLIVER, banker; b. Shreveport, La., May 9, 1933; s. Ollie Charles and Linna (Hart) R.; A.A., Allen Mil. Acad., 1954; B.B.A., U. Houston, 1956; certificate, Southwestern Grad. Sch. Banking So. Meth. U., 1967; m. Farolyn Ivey Shaw, Dec. 6, 1958 (div. Oct. 1967); 1 son, Charles O.; m. 2d, Micaela Garibay, Oct. 9, 1970. With Tex. Commerce Bank, Houston, 1956-—, asst. cashier, 1961-63, asst. v.p., 1963-65, v.p., 1965-—. Served with AUS, 1967. Mem. Houston C. of C., Mus. Fine Arts. Methodist. Home: 5331 Beverly Hill Houston TX 77027 Office: 712 Main St Houston TX 77027

RICE, CLARENCE IRWIN, electronics co. exec.; b. Rice Lake, Wis., Nov. 3, 1918; s. Chris Nilson and Ingeborg (Haug) R.; B.S. in E.E., U. Wis., 1943; B.S., St. Paul Coll. Law, 1950; m. S. Elaine Spurrier; children—Karen (Mrs. Lawrence O. Larson), Carol Jean, David Alan. Supr. aircraft radio engring. N.W. Airlines, St. Paul, 1946-51; staff engr. Aero. Radio, Inc., Washington, 1951-53; aviation sales mgr., gen. mgr. Bendix Avionics div., Balt., 1953-62; pres. Sunbeam Electronics, Inc., Ft. Lauderdale, Fla., 1962-66; v.p. Nova U., Ft. Lauderdale, Fla., 1966-68; sr. v.p. Collins Radio Co., Dallas, 1968-—. Bd. dirs., v.p. Fort Lauderdale Symphony Orch. Assn., 1964-68. Served to lt. comdr. USNR, 1943-46. Registered profl. engr., Minn., D.C. Mem. I.E.E.E., Am. Mgmt. Assn., Broward Mfrs. Assn. (v.p., dir. Fort Lauderdale 1964-68), Greater Fort Lauderdale C. of C. (v.p., dir. 1964-68). Republican. Presbyn. (elder 1960-—). Mason (32 deg., Shriner). Clubs: Wings (N.Y.C.); Nat. Aviation (Washington); Prestonwood Country (Dallas). Home: 5833 Copperwood Lane Dallas TX 75240 Office: Arapaho Rd Dallas TX 75080

RICE, CLARENCE W., sch. dist. ofcl.; b. New Braunfels, Tex., July 20, 1906; s. Charles Willard and Mathilda (Dannheim) R.; B.A., S.W. Tex. State Tchrs. Coll., 1929; M.A., U. Tex., 1937; postgrad. law, St. Mary's U., San Antonio, 1951; m. Melba Alves, Aug. 21, 1929 (dec. Dec. 1960); children—Shirley (Mrs. Lester C. Hahn), Kim A.; m. 2d, Edythe B. Porter, Sept. 15, 1962. Tchr. English, New Braunfels Sr. High Sch., 1926-31, head social studies, 1931-46; county judge Comal County, Tex., 1947-67; attendance investigator Austin (Tex.) Ind. Sch. Dist., 1967-—; real estate broker. Served as 1st lt. USAAF, 1943-45. Recipient Silver Beaver award Boy Scouts Am., 1953. Mem. S. Tex. County Judges and Commrs. Assn. (pres.), Texas Safety Assn. (hon. dir.), Nat., Tex. assns. county ofcls. Elk, Lion. Address: 4006 Edgerock Dr Austin TX 78731

RICE, DAVID FLEMING, state ofcl.; b. Hawkinsville, Ga., Aug. 30, 1907; s. Alexander John and Janie (Fleming) R.; B.S. in Civil Engring., Ga. Inst. Tech., 1929; m. Erlyne Lanier, July 22, 1934; children—David Lanier, Robert Fleming; m. 2d, Anagene P. Bartram, Jan. 29, 1966. Dept. head Sears Roebuck & Co., Atlanta, 1929-37; owner, operator Ellen Rice Restaurant, 1937-48, Town House Restaurant, 1948-54; apt. builder; officer various corps. Mem. Ga. Bd. Edn., Atlanta, 1961-—, vice chmn., 1970-—; bd. regents Univ. System Ga., Atlanta, 1954-61. Mem. Am. Assn. Sch. Adminstrs. (mem. mission to study edn. in Soviet Union 1969-—), Am. Vocational Assn., N.E.A., Ga. Edn. Assn., Navy League U.S., Atlanta Restaurant Assn. (pres. 1945-46, 52), Internat. Platform Assn., Nat. Assn. State Bds. Edn. (v.p. 1966-67, 67-68), Pi Delta Epsilon, Sigma Nu. Episcopalian. Clubs: Rotary, Atlanta Athletic. Address: 1175 W Conway Rd NW Atlanta GA 30327

RICE, DOWNEY, lawyer; b. Washington, Apr. 13, 1913; s. Fred J. and Agnes (Downey) R.; J.D. Cath. U., 1935, LL.M., 1936; m. Ellen Cushing Smith, Oct. 12, 1937; children—Michael Downey, Ellen Sue (Mrs. William C. Potter, Jr.). Admitted to D.C. bar, 1935; spl. agt. FBI, 1936-45; gen. practice Washington, 1945-—; spl. counsel to U.S. Atty., Washington, 1948; asso. counsel to com. investigate organized crime U.S. Senate, 1950-51, spl. counsel to preparedness com., 1952, chief counsel to commerce com., 1953; spl. counsel to anti-trust and monopoly sub-com. judiciary com., 1957, cons. to govt. operations com. McClellan rackets com., 1961. Mem. Washington Criminal Justice Assn. (bd. mem.), Soc. Former Spl. Agts. FBI, Am. Bar Assn., Am. Judicature Soc. Roman Catholic. Clubs: University, Nat. Press, Washington Athletic. Home: 3244 Aberfoyle Pl NW Washington DC 20015 Office: 1744 R St NW Washington DC 20009

RICE, FIDELIS, clergyman; b. Berwick, Me., Dec. 8, 1908; s. Patrick J. and Elizabeth A. (Burns) R.; student Holy Cross Sem., 1924-28. Ordained priest Roman Cath. Ch., 1936; priest Roman Cath. chs., Jamaica, N.Y., 1937-38, Rome, Italy, 1939-41, Scranton, Pa., 1941-44, Balt., 1944-53, West Springfield, Mass., from 1953; founder-producer weekly internat. radio program Hour of the Crucified, Crossroads; now retreat master Our Lady of Fla. monastery, North Palm Beach, Fla.; producer weekly radio program This Mixed World. Mem. Cath. Broadcasters Assn., Cath. Homiletic Soc. Home: 1300 US Hwy 1 North Palm Beach FL 33408

RICE, GEORGE FENTON, city ofcl.; b. Providence, Oct. 6, 1921; s. Lon V. and Ethel (Saalfelder) R.; B.S., U. R.I., 1946; M.S. in Social Work, U. N.C., 1948; postgrad. U. Pa., 1949-50; m. Jane B. Eddy, Sept. Service Soc., Wilmington, Del., 1949-54; exec. dir. Travelers Aid Soc., Norfolk, Va., 1955-57; exec. sec. Met. Health-Welfare-Recreation Planning Council of Norfolk, East Chesapeake and Virginia Beach (Va.), 1958-—. Mem. met. adv. com. USPHS, 1966-—; mem. program planning adv. bd. Norfolk Model City Program, 1968-—; project dir. Tidewater (Va.) Assembly on Family Life, 1967-—; coordinator Met. Study on Urban Life, Norfolk, Chesapeake, Virginia Beach, 1967-—; project dir. Neighborhood Diagnostic Social Survey, Norfolk, 1969-—; mem. com. law and order Southeastern Va. Dist. Planning Commn., 1969-—; exec. cons. 2d congl. dist. Va. Mental Health Study Commn., 1964-65; exec. dir. Hampton Roads (Va.) Health Information and Referral Planning Center, 1965-—; mem. nat. com. planning execs. United Community Funds and Councils Am., 1963-—, Southeastern conf. sec. exec. com. 1969-—, asso. trustee, 1968-—; bd. dirs. United Community Funds and Councils Va., 1962-—, Norfolk Urban Coalition. Fellow Am. Assn. Social Scis.; mem. Nat. Assn. Social Workers (chpt. pres. 1956-58), Nat. Conf. Social Work, Va. Bd. Registration of Social Workers, Va. Council Social Welfare (treas. state bd. dirs. 1961-62), Am. Pub. Health Assn., Jr. C. of C. (mem. exec. bd. 1952-53). Home: 1624 Arrowhead Point Virginia Beach VA 23455 Office: Royster Bldg Norfolk VA 23510

RICE, HOMER CRANSTON, univ. athletic adminstr.; b. Bellevue, Ky., Feb. 20, 1927; s. S.C. and Nancy Grace (Wilson) R.; A.B., Center Coll., Danville, Ky.; B.S., also M.Ed., Eastern Ky. State U.; m. Phyllis Wardrup, Aug. 12; children—Nancy Kathryn, Phyllis Wardrup, Angeles. Coach Spring City (Tenn.) High Sch., 1952-53, Highland High Sch., Ft. Thomas, Ky., 1954-61; head offensive football coach U. Ky., 1962-65, U. Okla., 1966; head football coach U. Cin., 1967-68; dir. athletics U. N.C., 1969-—; lectr. in field. Mem. Nat. Collegiate Athletic Assn. TV Com.; pres. Triangle chpt. Nat. Football Found. and Hall of Fame. Bd. dirs. YMCA, Centre Coll. Alumni. Served with Armed Forces, World War II. Named Ky. Col., Hon. Tex. Citizen. Methodist (lay speaker; mem. adminstrv. bd.). Author: How to Organize Football Practice, 1962; The Explosive Short-T, 1963. Contbr. articles to athletic jours. Home: 349 Tenney Circle Chapel Hill NC 27514

RICE, JACK VAUGHAN, hotel exec.; b. Lexington, Miss., Nov. 19, 1937; s. James Watford and Grace Wirt (Vaughan) R.; B.B.A., U. Miss., 1959. Mem. marketing research staff Plough, Inc., Memphis, 1960-62; exec. asst. to pres. Holiday Inns, Inc., Memphis, 1962-70, exec. asst. to vice chmn. bd., 1970-—; dir. Medicenters Am., Inc., Memphis, Alodex Corp., Memphis, Manor Care, Inc., Silver Spring, Md., Wallace E. Johnson Enterprises, Memphis. Trustee Sam Houston Meml. Hosp., Houston, Wallace E. Johnson-E.B. McCool Found., Memphis. Served with AUS, 1960. Mem. Sigma Chi. Club: University. Home: 4952 Devonshire St Memphis TN 38117 Office: 3742 Lamar St Memphis TN 38118

RICE, RALPH MARION, supt. schs.; b. nr. New Braunfels, Tex., Aug. 26, 1908; s. Charles Williard and Matilda (Dannheim) R.; B.A., S.W. Tex. State U., 1934, M.A., 1947; m. Mary Jo Alexander, July 19, 1930; children—Ralph Marion, Charles A., John Alan. Prin., tchr. Comel County Schs., Tex., 1927-32, Guadalupe County, 1932-41; prin., coach Gonzales Ind. Sch. Dist., 1941-44, 46; supt. schs. Boerne County Line Ind. Sch. Dist., 1947-52, Stockdale Ind. Sch. Dist., 1952-57, Austwell-Tivoli Ind. Sch. Dist., 1957-62, Devine Ind. Sch. Dist., 1962-—. Chmn. various charitable drives including Polio Assn., A.R.C., Boy Scouts Am. Served with USNR, 1944-45. Mem. Tex. Tchrs. Assn., Tex., Am. assns. sch. adminstrs. Baptist (deacon). Mason, Lion. Home: 610 Mockingbird St Devine TX 78016 Office: PO Drawer I Devine TX 78016

RICE, THELMA AUSTIN, educator; b. Montgomery, Ala.; d. Simuel Stakely and Henrietta (Wade) Austin; B.S., Ala. State Coll., 1937, M.Ed., 1946; postgrad. U. Minn., 1949-50, 51, 54, U. Kan., 1961-62, U.Wis., summer 1964; m. Louis Dexter Rice, Aug. 16, 1939. Tchr. pub. schs., Mobile, Ala., 1937-45, asst. prin., 1942-45; instr. Ala. State U., Montgomery, 1945-52, asst. prof., 1952-54, asso. prof., 1954-—, chmn. dept. math., 1954-63, NSF fellow, 1961-62. Math. cons. Mem. Am. Math. Soc., Math. Assn. Am., Am., Ala. tchrs. assns., Ala. Council Math. Tchrs., Nat. Council Women, Internat. Platform Assn., Beta Kappa Chi, Delta Sigma Theta. Baptist. Mem. Order Eastern Star. Home: 2935 Tyler Rd Montgomery AL 36110 Office: Ala State Univ PO Box 271 Montgomery AL 36101

RICE, WILLIAM RODERICK, banker; b. Little Rock, Ark., Oct. 27, 1930; s. Roderick John and Mattie Virginia (Thurman) R.; B.S. highest honors, U. Ark., 1952; m. Jean Pendleton, Aug. 31, 1951; children—David W., Carol E. Vice pres. The Twin City Bank, North Little Rock, Ark., 1954-58; v.p., cashier Mchts. and Planters Nat. Bank, Sherman, Tex., 1958-65; pres., chief exec. officer 1st Nat. Bank, Magnolia, Ark., 1965-69, 1st Am. Nat. Bank, North Little Rock, 1969-—. Mem. bd. regents Memphis Sch. Banking, 1971-—; faculty Sch. Basic Banking, Ark. Bankers Assn., 1969-—. Southwestern Grad. Sch. Banking, So. Meth. U., Dallas, 1969-—. Served to 1st lt. AUS, 1952-54. Mem. Blue Key, Beta Gamma Sigma, Phi Eta Sigma, Alpha Kappa Psi, Sigma Chi. Rotarian. Home: 40 Heritage Park Circle North Little Rock AR 72116 Office: 2nd and Main P O Box 5761 North Little Rock AR 72119

RICE, WILLIAM THOMAS, railroad exec.; b. Hague, Va., June 13, 1912; s. John and Elizabeth Conway (Snow) R.; B.S. in Civil Engring., Va. Polytech. Inst., 1934; LL.D., Stetson U., 1959; m. Jaqueline Johnston, Sept. 14, 1935; children—John Thomas, Jacqueline Norma. With Pa. R.R., 1934-42; joined Richmond, Fredericksburg & Potomac R.R. Co., 1946, pres., dir., 1955-57; pres., dir., exec. com. Atlantic Coast Line R.R. Co., 1957-67; pres., chief exec. officer Seaboard Coast Line R.R. Co., 1967-70, chmn. bd., chief exec. officer, 1970-72, chmn. bd., pres., 1972-—; chmn. bd., chief exec. officer Seabord Coast Line Industries, Inc., 1970-—, also dir., mem. exec. com.; dir. subsidiary and affiliated lines and stas.; chmn. bd., chmn. exec. com., dir. Alico Land Devel. Co.; dir. Chem. Bank N.Y. Trust Co., Graniteville Co., First & Mchts. Nat. Bank of Richmond, Fla. Nat. Bank of Jacksonville, Home Ins. Co., Borden Co., Ethyl Corp., Commonwealth Nat. Gas Co. Richmond. Trustee P.E. Theol. Sem. Va., Alexandria. Served from 1st lt. to lt. col. AUS, 1942-46. Decorated Legion of Merit with 2 oak leaf clusters. Mem. Am. Soc. C.E., Am. Ry. Engring. Assn., Am. Assn. R.R. Supts., Assn. Am. R.R.'s (dir.), Assn. Southeastern R.R.'s, Am. Soc. Traffic and Trnsp., Va. Poly. Inst. Alumni Assn., Transp. Assn. Am., Nat. Def. Transp. Assn. (life), Nat. Freight Traffic Assn., Newcomen Soc., Omicron Delta Kappa, Tau Beta Pi. Episcopalian. Clubs: Augusta (Ga.) Nat.; Sky, Union League (N.Y.C.); Metropolitan (Washington); Country of Va., Commonwealth (Richmond, Va.); River, Timuquana Country (Jacksonville, Fla.); Rotary. Home: 8739 Riverside Dr Richmond VA 23225 Office: 3600 W Broad St Richmond VA 23230 also 500 Water St Jacksonville FL 32202

RICE, WILLIAM VAUGHN, JR., air force officer; b. Hiawassee, Ga., Dec. 5, 1926; s. William Vaughn and Anne Julia (O'Quinn) R.; B.S., U.S. Mil. Acad., 1949; M.B.A., USAF Inst. Tech., 1958; Ph.D., La. State U., 1972; m. Claire L. Mikulin, Aug. 24, 1950; children—Michael D., William Vaughn III, Tamara Anne. Commd. 2d lt. USAF, 1949, advanced through grades to lt. col., 1967; air crew mem. SAC, 1950-57; ednl. adviser Republic of Korea Air Acad., Seoul, 1958-59;

asst. prof. aerospace studies La. State U., 1960-66; sr. instr. Acad. Instr. Sch., Air U., Montgomery, Ala., 1967-68, chief, labor-mgmt. relations div., 1969—; instr. econs. Troy State U. Adult Edn. Program, 1966—. Mem. Am., So. econ. assns., Am. Assn. U. Profs., Air Force Assn., Omicron Delta Epsilon. Mason. Author: Introduction to Air Force Labor Relations, Vol. I, 1971; The Evolution of EO 10988 and Its Impact on USAF Labor Relations, 1971. Home: 3516 Lancaster Lane Montgomery AL 36106 Office: Air U IPD-M Maxwell Air Force Base AL 36112

RICH, FRANK HART, mcht.; b. Washington, Apr. 13, 1921; s. Herbert J. and Rosa (Frank) R.; B.S., Lehigh U., 1942; postgrad. Harvard, 1943; m. Anadel Seidman, Mar. 15, 1959; children—Frank Hart, Polly Alice, Elizabeth Hart, Ned Swope, Abby Dee. Customer service mgr. The Hecht Co., Washington, 1946-49 v.p. Rich's Shoe Stores, Washington, 1949-56, pres., 1956—. Lectr., Am. U., 1957-58; pres. Metro-Washington Urban Coalition, 1969-71, bd. dirs., 1971—; mem. urban renewal council, D.C., 1959-66; mem. D.C. Health and Welfare Council, 1958-65; mem. Mayor's Econ. Devel. Com., 1970—; mem. Human Rights Commn., Washington, 1971—; chmn. Mayor's Adv. Com. on Narcotics, 1971—. Bd. dirs. Washington Area Council on Alcoholism, 1965-71, United Planning Orgn., Washington; trustee United Givers Fund, Washington, 1955-57. Served from pvt. to maj., AUS, 1942-46, CBI; served as lt. col. USAF, 1951-53. Decorated Bronze Star medal. Mem. Chevy Chase Center Mchts. Assn. (pres. 1957-60), Nat. Shoe Retailers Assn. (dir., pres. 1971—), Washington Bd. Trade. Jewish religion. Rotarian (Community Service award 1972). Club: Nat. Press (Washington). Home: 5001 38th St NW Washington DC 20016 Office: 1321 F St NW Washington DC 20004

RICH, GILES SUTHERLAND, judge; b. Rochester, N.Y., May 30, 1904; s. Giles Willard and Sarah Thompson (Sutherland) R.; S.B., Harvard, 1926; LL.B., Columbia, 1929; m. Gertrude Verity Braun, Jan. 10, 1931 (dec.); 1 dau., Verity Sutherland (Mrs. Alan D. Grinnell); m. 2d, Helen Gill Field, Oct. 10, 1953. Admitted to N.Y. bar, 1929; registered to practice U.S. Patent Office, 1934; practice law, N.Y.C., 1929-56, specializing patent and trademark law; partner Williams, Rich & Morse, 1937-52, Churchill, Rich, Weymouth & Engel, 1952-56; asso. judge U.S. Ct. Customs and Patent Appeals, 1956—; lectr. patent law Columbia, 1942-56, N.Y. Law Sch., 1952; adj. prof. Georgetown U. Law School. Recipient Jefferson medal, N.J. Patent Law Assn., 1955; Kettering award Patent, Trademark and Copyright Inst. George Washington U., 1963; Freedman Found. award Am. Inst. Chemists, 1967; Founders Day award George Washington U. Patent and Trademark Inst., 1970; Eli Whitney award Conn. Patent Law Assn., 1972. Mem. Assn. Bar City N.Y., Am. Bar Assn., Am., N.Y. (pres. 1950-51) patent law assns., Nat. Lawyers Club (hon.). Clubs: Harvard, Cosmos (Washington). Author articles in field. Home: 4949 Linnean Av NW Washington DC 20008 Office: US Court Customs and Patent Appeals Washington DC 20439

RICH, HELEN WALL (MRS. ARTHUR L. RICH), educator; b. Chester, S.C., May 4, 1912; d. George Addison and Georgia (Hardin) Wall; student Queen's Coll., 1930-32; B.S. summa cum laude, Catawba Coll., 1934 diploma in piano Juilliard Sch. Music, 1938; diplomas Christiansen Choral Sch., 1950, 51; m. Arthur Lowndes Rich, July 26, 1934; children—Arthur Lowndes, Ruth Anne. Instr. music Catawba Coll.; Salisbury, N.C., 1934-43; organist Mercer U., Macon, Ga., 1944-50, asst. prof. music, 1950—; organ recitalist throughout Southeast; v.p. Tudor Apts., Atlanta, 1960-68; sec.-treas. Richelieu Apts., Macon, 1955-68, Mem. Federated Music Clubs (chmn. scholarship contest), Ga. Piano Tchrs. Guild, Nat. Assn. Schs. Music (asso.), Am. Coll. and U. Concert Mgrs. Assn. (asso.), Cardinal Key Soc. Mercer U. (hon.), Delta Omicron. Club: Morning Music (dir.) (Macon). Home: 369 Condler Dr Macon GA 31204

RICH, LINVIL GENE, univ. dean; b. Pana, Ill., Mar. 10, 1921; s. Orville Cadel and Lillian Murle (Watkins) R.; B.S., Va. Poly. Inst., 1947, M.S., 1948, Ph.D., 1951; m. Peggy Jane Burton, June 17, 1944; children—Linvil Burton, Graham Watkins. Asso. prof. san. engring. Va. Poly. Inst., 1951-55; with USPHS, Bolivia, 1955-56; prof. san. engring. Ill. Inst. Tech., Chgo., 1956-61; dean engring. Clemson (S.C.) U., 1961—. Spl. cons. USPHS, Dept. Interior, Environmental Protection Agy. Served with AUS, 1942-46. Diplomate Environmental Engring. Intersoc. Bd. Fellow Am. Soc. C.E.; mem. Sigma Xi, Chi Epsilon, Tau Beta Pi, Phi Sigma, Phi Lambda Upsilon, Phi Kappa Phi. Author: Unit Operations of Sanitary Engineering, 1961; Unit Processes of Sanitary Engineering, 1963. Contbr. articles to profl. jours. Home: PO Box 1185 Clemson SC 29631

RICHARD, JOHN BENARD, librarian; b. Gulfport, Miss., Nov. 2, 1932; s. John Jesse and Helen Lucille (Schott) R.; student Perkinston Jr. Coll., 1950-52; B.S., Miss. So. Coll., 1954; M.S. in Library Sci., La. State U., 1959; m. Sandra E. Davis Mosley, Dec. 19, 1970; children—Brian Davis Mosley, John Blake. Preparations librarian La. State U., Baton Rouge, 1959-60; head librarian, La. State U., Alexandria, 1960—. Chmn. La. Coll. Conf. Library Sect., 1967-68; exec. dir. La. Nat. Library Week Program, 1968; mem. La. Bd. Library Examiners. Bd. dirs. Central La. Art Assn., Kent House Found. Served with AUS, 1954-57. Mem. Am. (rep. 1970—), La. (pres. 1969-70), Southwestern library assns., Conf. Academic Library Adminstrs. La. (chmn. 1967), Beta Phi Mu. Roman Catholic. Rotarian (pres. 1962). Contbr. articles to profl. jours. Home: PO Box 364 Lecompte LA 71346 Office: La State U Alexandria LA 71301

RICHARD, ROBERT DAY, SR., physician; b. Buies Creek, N.C., Feb. 6, 1929; s. George Greer and Ruth (Bass) R.; B.S., Va. Poly. Inst., 1950; M.D., Med. Coll. Va., 1954; m. Narvie Price Adams, Aug. 13, 1949; children—Lora Lea, Robert Day. Intern, Roanoke (Va.) Meml. Hosp., 1954-55; practice medicine specializing in family practice, Wilson, N.C., 1958—; mem. staff Wilson (N.C.) Meml. Hosp. Chmn. Wilson County Bd. Edn., 1969—. Bd. dirs. Wilson County Tech. Inst. Served with USNR, 1955-58. Diplomate Am. Bd. Family Practice. Mem. Am. Acad. Family Physicians, A.M.A., So. Med. Assn., Med. Soc. State N.C., Wilson County Med. Soc. (pres. 1964-65). Home: Route 1 Sims NC 27880 Office: Route 2 Wilson NC 27893

RICHARDS, ARTHUR A., coll. adminstr.; b. V.I., Sept. 8, 1924; s. Claude J. and Evelyn (DuBois) R.; B.S., Howard U., 1948; M.A., Hampton Inst., 1961; Ed. D., N.Y.U., 1965; m. Myrna Todmann, Apr. 2, 1955; children—Anthony, Pamela, Duane. Tchr., V.I., 1949-51; prin., V.I., 1951-61; dep. commr. edn. V.I., St. Croix, 1961-63, asst. commr., 1963-66, commr., 1966-69; provost, dean Coll. of V.I., St. Thomas, 1969—. Recipient Founders Day award, Service award N.Y.U., 1964. Mem. Kappa Delta Pi, Phi Delta Kappa. Research, publs. on devel. linear programming as an instrument for decision-making and as an instrn. aid. Home: PO Box 482 Charlotte Amalie St Thomas VI 00801 Office: Coll of VI St Thomas VI 00801

RICHARDS, BENJAMIN BILLINGS, II, librarian; b. Dubuque, Ia., Mar. 24, 1917; s. Clarence Whitaker and Lora Emma (Lindenberg) R.; student Loras Coll., 1934-36; A.B., U. No. Ia., Cedar Falls, 1939; B.S. in L.S., Case Western Res. U., 1941; M.A., Claremont (Cal.) Grad. Sch., 1951; postgrad. U. Chgo. Grad. Library Sch., 1952-56; m. Alice Louise Nagy, June 17, 1942; 1 dau., Janet Alden. With purchasing dept. Revere Copper & Brass Co., Inc., Chgo., 1936-38; jr. librarian Ia. Traveling Library, Des Moines, 1939-40; librarian Knox Coll., 1946-58; faculty U. Okla. Sch. Library Sci., summer 1958; prof., chmn. div. library edn. and service Kan. State Tchrs. Coll., Emporia, also librarian William Allen White Meml. Library 1959-63; librarian Chatham Coll., Pitts., 1963-69, Tex. Woman's U., Denton, 1969—. Sec.-treas. Kan. Friends of Libraries; chmn. adminstrv. com. William Allen White Childrens Book Award. Served to lt. USNR, 1941-45; PTO. Mem. Am., Tex. library assns., Assn. Coll. and Research Libraries, Tex. Assn. Coll. Tchrs., Am. Assn. U. Profs., Sigma Tau Delta, Beta Phi Mu. Episcopalian. Editor: The Stepladder, poetry quar., 1952-58; California Gold Rush Merchant: The Journal of Stephen Chapin Davis, 1849-52, 1956. Home: 714 Mimosa Dr Denton TX 76201

RICHARDS, CLYDE RICH, govt. ofcl.; b. Paris, Ida., June 9, 1921; s. Clyde Randall and Myrtle (Rich) R.; B.S., Utah State U., 1943; M.S., Cornell U., 1949, Ph.D., 1950; postgrad. U. Cal. at Davis, 1966-67; m. Carrol Maughan, July 18, 1946; children—Russell, Keith, Debra. Grad. asst. Cornell U., 1946-50; lectr. animal breeding Superior Sch. Agr., Athens, Greece, 1950-51; asst. prof., asso. prof. U. Del., 1951-61; prin. animal nutritionist Coop. State Research Service, Dept. Agr., Washington, 1961-71, dep. asst. adminstr., 1971—. Served with USNR, 1943-46. Mem. Am. Inst. Nutrition, Am. Dairy Sci. Assn., Am. Soc. Animal Sci., A.A.A.S., Sigma Xi. Mem. Ch. of Jesus Christ of Latter-day Saints. Home: 6409 Adelphi Rd Hyattsville MD 20782 Office: Coop State Research Service Dept Agr Washington DC 20250

RICHARDS, EDWARD EARL, dentist; b. Bronx, N.Y., May 2, 1932; s. H. Edward and LeOris (Pate) R.; B.A., Atlantic Union Coll. (Mass.), 1954; D.D.S., Loma Linda U., 1958; M.P.H., U. Mich., 1967; m. Ann Celestine Smart, May 29, 1960 children—Edward Earl, David Andre, Joi Celeste. Pvt. practice dentistry, Atlanta, 1958-66 clin. dentist Fulton County (Ga.) Health Dept., 1958-66; resident dental pub. health Ga. Dept. Pub. Health, 1967-68; dental dir. Atlanta Southside Comprehensive Health Center, 1968-71, project dir., 1971—; asst. prof. community dentistry Sch. Dentistry, Emory U., 1968—, asso. prof. preventive medicine and community health Sch. Medicine, 1971—; mem. staff Ben Massell Dental Clinic, 1959. Mem. Choral Guild Atlanta, 1964-66, Atlanta Health Council, 1965-66. Recipient Vol. Service award YWCA, 1959; certificates of appreciation Atlanta Pub. Schs., 1961, Am. Heart Assn., 1962. Mem. Am., Ga. (recipient citation 1963) dental assns., Am. Pub. Health Assn., No. Dist., N.Ga. (past pres., chaplain) dental socs. Seventh-day Adventist. Home: 2725 Veltre Pl SW Atlanta GA 30311 Office: 1039 Ridge Av SW Atlanta GA 30315

RICHARDS, GEORGE LEROY, gas co. exec.; b. El Paso, Tex., July 18, 1926; s. George Eaton and Mamie (Oden) R.; B.S. in Geology, Tex. Coll. Mines and Metallurgy, 1948; m. Ann Carlin, Sept. 3, 1948; children— Julie Ann, Jack Carlin. With Standard Oil Co. Tex., 1948-64; with Coastal States Gas Producing Co., Corpus Christi, Tex., 1964—, v.p., 1969—. Served with USNR, 1944-46. Mem. Am. Assn. Petroleum Geologists, Corpus Christi Geol. Soc. (mem. ho. of dels. 1969-72). Presbyn. Home: 502 Grant Pl Corpus Christi TX 78411 Office: Box 521 Corpus Christi TX 78403

RICHARDS, JAMES MCDOWELL, theol. sem. pres.; b. Statesville, N.C., Nov. 6, 1902; s. Charles Malone and Jane Leighton (McDowell) R.; grad. McCallie Sch., Chattanooga, 1918; B.A., Davidson (N.C.) Coll., 1922, D.D., 1933; M.A., Princeton, 1923; B.A., Oxford U. (Eng.), 1925, M.A. (Rhodes scholar), 1930; B.D., Columbia Theol. Sem., Decatur, Ga., 1928; LL.D., King Coll., 1956; m. Mary Evelyn Knight, Dec. 31, 1929; children—James McDowell, Mary Makemie, Charles Malone II. Ordained to ministry Presbyn. Ch., 1928; pastor successively at Clarkesville, Nacoochee and Helen, Ga., 1928-31, 1st Ch. Thomasville, Ga., 1931-32; pres. Columbia Theol. Sem., prof. practical theology, 1932-71, pres. emeritus, 1971—. Mem. permanent com. on Christian relations, chmn. com. on Negro work Presbyn. Ch. U.S., 1947-50, chmn. bd. ch. extension, 1950-56; moderator Presbyn. Ch. U.S. (So.), 1955—, mem. bd. world missions; v.p. Fed. Council Chs. Christ Am., 1942-44 (mem. exec. com.); mem. gen. bd. Nat. Council Chs., 1950-52. Pres. bd. trustees Davidson Coll., 1940-66, also mem. exec. com.; bd. dirs. Presbyn. Ministers Fund, Phila. Mem. Phi Beta Kappa, Kappa Alpha, Omicron Delta Kappa. Democrat. Rotarian. Editor: Soli Deo Gloria, 1968; mem. editorial bd. Theology Today. Home: 532 Kirk Rd Decatur GA 30030

RICHARDS, JAMES WILLIAM, steamship co. exec.; b. Bennettsville, S.C., Dec. 24, 1908; s. Ernest Vincent and Minnie (Pearce) R.; student bus. adminstrn. Tulane U., 1929-31; m. Sylvia Alice Williams, Sept. 4, 1934; 1 dau., Minnie Louise (Mrs. Herbert J. Griener). Accountant, Fed. Land Bank, New Orleans, 1932-33, Weinberger S.S. Corp., New Orleans, 1935-37; with Delta S.S. Lines, New Orleans, 1938-47, 63—, purchasing agt., operations asst., 1938-47, exec. asst., 1963—; partner Schofield Trading Co., 1947-57, pres., 1957-62; adv. com. Bank La., New Orleans. Bd. dirs. Internat. House, New Orleans, 1955-57, Seamen's Town House, New Orleans, 1970—, La. Maritime Mus., 1970—. Acting consul, Paraguay, New Orleans, 1970. Clubs: Export Managers, Plimsoll, So. Yacht, Propeller (v.p. 1972—) (New Orleans). Home: 210 Betz Pl Metairie LA 70005 Office: 1700 Internat Trade Mart New Orleans LA 70150

RICHARDS, KARL FREDERICK, educator, artist; b. Youngstown, O., June 14, 1920; s. Edwin John and Agnes Ann (Johnston) R.; diploma Cleve. Inst. Art, 1944; B.S. in Edn., Western Res. U., 1944; M.A. (Univ. scholar 1946-47), State U. Ia., 1947; Ph.D. (Univ. fellow 1954-56), Ohio State U., 1956; m. Sylvia June Pelt, Oct. 23, 1962; daus., Karen, Kelli. Asst. prof. art Bowling Green State U., 1947-56; prof. art, Tex. Christian U., 1956-71, chmn. dept., 1956-70; prof. art, chmn. div. art Ark. State U., 1971—; one man exhbns., include Cleve. Inst. Art, 1944, Contemporary Arts Gallery, St. Petersburg, Fla., 1955, Ohio State U., 1956, Arlington (Tex.) State Coll., 1962, San Angelo (Tex.) Coll., 1964; numerous group exhbns., 1940—, latest being USIS in S.Am., Far East, Europe and Near East, 1956-58, Dallas Mus. Fine Arts, 1958, Park Galleries, Dallas, 1962-63, Ft. Worth Art Center, 1958, 59, 64, 68, Lubbock Art Center, 1964, Dallas Pub. Library, 1966, Tex. Christian U., 1969, 70, State U. Colls. Central N.Y., 1969, Ark. Arts Center, Little Rock, 1972. Home: 108 E College Circle State University Jonesboro AR

RICHARDS, LLOYD FRANCIS, pub. health ofcl., educator; b. Royal Oak, Mich., Jan. 20, 1908; s. Lyman H. and Emma (King) R.; A.B., Albion Coll., 1929; D.D.S., U. Mich., 1934; M.P.H., U. Cal. at Berkeley, 1949; m. Jane Elizabeth Barringer, Oct. 5, 1945; children—Stephen Lloyd, Pamela Jane. Children's dentist Children's Fund, Detroit, 1934-36; individual practice, Detroit, 1937-43; supr. dental services Oakland (Cal.) pub. schs., 1949-51; pub. health officer div. dental health Cal. Dept. Pub. Health, Berkeley, 1951-52, chief, 1952-67; asso. prof., chmn. dept. dental health Baylor U., Coll. Dentistry, Dallas, 1967-70; also dir. Dallas dental health program, 1967—. Lectr. U. Cal. Sch. Pub. Health, Berkeley, 1954-67, U. So. Cal. at Los Angeles, 1952-60. Mem health panel Commnunity Council Greater Dallas, 1968—. Served to maj. with Dental Corps, AUS, 1943-47; ETO. Diplomate Am. Bd. Dental Pub. Health. Fellow Am. Coll. Dentists, Am., Tex. (chmn. dental sect. 1968, governing council 1968-71) pub. health assns., Am. Sch. Health Assn. (governing bd. 1950-57, 60-63, 63-66), A.A.A.S. (v.p., chmn. dental sect. 1965); mem. Am., Cal., Tex., Berkeley, Dallas County dental assns., Am. Assn. Pub. Health Dentists (exec. council 1961-63, 64-67), Cal. sch. Health Assn. (past pres.), Assn. State and Territorial Dental Dirs. (pres. 1965-67), Am. Soc. Dentistry for Children (pres. No. Cal. unit 1958), Dallas C. of C., Tau Kappa Omega. Home: 300 W Shore Dr Richardson TX 75080 Office: 2001 McKinney Av Dallas TX 75219

RICHARDS, PAUL RAPIER, profl. baseball club exec.; b. Waxahachie, Tex., Nov. 21, 1908; s. Jesse Thomas and Sarah (McGowen) R.; m. Margie McDonald, Feb. 14, 1932; 1 dau., Paula Del. Baseball player with Bklyn. Dodgers, N.Y. Giants, Phila. Athletics and Detroit Tigers, 1926-36, 43-46; mgr. Atlanta Baseball Club, 1938-42, Buffalo Baseball Club, 1947-49, Seattle Baseball Club, 1950, Chgo. White Sox Baseball Club, 1951-54; gen. mgr., field mgr., Balt. Orioles Baseball Club, 1955-59, field mgr., 1960-61; gen. mgr. Houston Colt 45s Baseball Club (now Houston Astros), 1962; then gen. mgr. Atlanta Braves, Inc., now v.p. baseball operations; served as mgr. Am. League All Stars team, 1961. Part-owner Waxahachie Daily Light, 1935-47. Bd. dirs. Assn. Profl. Ball Players Am. Named to Tex. Hall of Fame, 1960, Southwesterner of Yr., 1961, Texan of Yr., 1961. Baptist. Author: Modern Baseball Strategy, 3d edit., 1951. Home: Midlothian Rd Waxahachie TX 75165 Office: care Atlanta Braves Atlanta GA 30301

RICHARDS, ROY, business exec.; b. Carrollton, Ga., Apr. 11, 1912; s. Thomas Wiley and Ida (Stovall) R.; B.S. in Mech. Engring., Ga. Inst. Tech., 1935; m. Alice Coyner Huffard, Jan. 25, 1958; children— Roy, James Case, Nancy Huffard, Lee Wiley, Elizabeth Kemper, Robin Anne. Propr., Roy Richards Constrn. Co. (now Richards & Assos., Inc.), Carrollton, 1936-39, pres., 1935—; pres. Richards Motor and Equipment Co., Villa Rica, Ga., 1946—, Roy Richards Realty Corp., Carrollton, 1950—, Southwire Realty Co., Carrollton, 1950—, Southwire Internat. Corp., San Juan, P.R., 1952—, Nat.-Southwire Aluminum Co., Hawesville, Ky., 1968—; chmn. bd. Peoples Bank, Carrollton, 1970—, Southwire Co., Carrollton; dir. 1st Nat. Bank Atlanta, 1st Nat. Holding Corp., Atlanta, Ranchers Exploration & Devel. Corp., Albuquerque, Munford, Inc., Atlanta. Chmn. bd. Carroll City-County Hosp. Authority, 1946-72; bd. dirs. Tanner Meml. Hosp. Served from lt. to capt. AUS, 1942-45. Mem. Nat. Soc. Profl. Engrs. Episcopalian. Home: Box 400 Carrollton GA 30117 Office: PO Box 1000 Carrollton GA 30117

RICHARDS, WARREN NEWTON, supt. edn.; b. Phenix City, Ala., June 12, 1918; s. Warren Newton and Thelma (Turner) R.; B.S., U. Ga., 1942; M.Ed., Auburn U., 1961; m. Elyane Dron, July 27, 1946; children— Warren Newton IV, Monique, Elyane, Colette, Nicole. Tchr., Phenix City Bd. Edn., 1950-55, asst. prin., 1955-57, asst. supt. 1957-62; supt. edn. Russell County (Ala.) Bd. Edn., Phenix City, 1962—. Active Russell County A.R.C., United Givers Fund. Served with AUS, 1942-47. Mem. N.E.A., Ala. Edn. Assn. (v.p.), Am., Ala. assns. sch. adminstrs., V.F.W., Am. Legion, Phi Delta Kappa. Methodist. Rotarian. Home: 4002 Lakewood Dr Phenix City AL 36867 Office: PO Box 908 Phenix City AL 36867

RICHARDS, WILLIAM GEORGE, savs. and loan exec.; b. Lockhart, Tex., Feb. 20, 1920; s. Cyrus F. and Gussie (Baldridge) R.; LL.B., U. Tex., 1948; m. Winnifred Adams, Nov. 23, 1940 (dec. May 1969); children— Betty Ann, Mark Andrew. Admitted to Tex. bar, 1948; practiced law with father, Lockhart, 1948-55; v.p., atty., dir. Lockhart Savs. & Loan Assn., 1948-55; exec. v.p. Benjamin Franklin Savs. &Loan Assn., 1955-64, pres., 1964—; trustee Savs. & Loan Found., Inc., 1957-59. Mem. Tex. Ho. of Reps., 1947-50; mayor of Lockhart, 1954-55. Mem. Nat. League Insured Savs. Assns. (exec. com. 1962-66), Houston C. of C. (dir. 1966, 68—), Tex. Savs. and Loan League (dir. 1953-63, 63—; pres. 1967-68), Phi Delta Phi. Democrat. Episcopalian. Club: Houston. Home: 3620 Tartan Lane Houston TX 77025 Office: 720 Travis at Rusk Houston TX 77002

RICHARDSON, ALVAH BARTON, ins. co. exec.; b. Pine Bluff, Ark., Feb. 10, 1908; s. Alvah Barton and Martha Viroque (Clark) R.; B. Philosophy, Emory U., 1929; m. Alice Eley McDonald, June 26, 1937; 1 dau., Bonnie Alice (Mrs. Anthony DePinna Armer). Reporter Atlanta Georgian, 1929-36; ed. Newsview mag., Columbia, S.C., 1936; reporter, editor AP, Atlanta, 1937-44; So. rep. Aero. Tng. Soc., Washington, 1945; cons. pub. relations and advt., Atlanta, 1946; dir. pub. relations Life Ins. Co. Ga., Atlanta, 1946-56, v.p., 1956—; also dir. Vice pres. Atlanta Community Chest, 1959, 60, 66, 67; v.p. United Way Atlanta, 1972—. Bd. dirs. Atlanta Community Chest, 1969-71. Recipient Printer's Ink Man of Year in Atlanta silver medal Advt. Fedn. Am., 1959. Mem. Atlanta Advt. Club (bd. dirs. 1954-58), Atlanta Advt. Inst. (chmn., 1956), C. of C. (pub. relations and advt. com., 1969-70), Pub. Relations Soc. Am. (chpt. pres. 1958-59), Life Ins. Advertisers Assn. (pres. 1955-56), Life Insurers Conf. (exec. com. 1966-68), Inst. Life Ins. (pub. relations council 1962—), Sigma Delta Chi, Omicron Delta Kappa, Sigma Upsilon, Pi Delta Epsilon, Sigma Delta Chi, Alpha Delta Sigma. Presbyn. Club: Commerce of Atlanta. Home: 92 26th St NW Atlanta GA 30309 Office: 600 W Peachtree St NW Atlanta GA 30308

RICHARDSON, ANNE WORSHAM (MRS. MARVIN DIBBLE RICHARDSON), artist, ornithologist; b. Turbeville, S.C., Oct. 22, 1922; d. George Talbert and Jessie (Phillips) Worsham; student pub. and pvt. schs.; m. Marvin Dibble Richardson, Jan. 27, 1942; 1 son, Marvin D. One-man shows at Charleston Mus., Ga. Ornithol. Soc., Berkshire Mus., Turbeville Anne Worsham Richardson Day Exhibit, Gibbes Art Gallery, Columbia Museum Art, Kennedy Galleries, Harbour Town Mus., Hilton Head, S.C., Spartanburg Art Gallery, Sumter Art Gallery, others; exhibited in group shows at Charleston Artist Guild, Telfair Acad., S.C. Artist Guild, Carolina Art State Show, Bob Jones U., Medway Art Festival, Cal. Mus. Sci. and Industry, 1970 others; represented in permanent collections at Albert Leeberg collection, Gibbes Art Gallery, Charleston Mus.; bird paintings pub. by Nat. Wildlife Fedn., 1967, 68. Recipient 1st prize Summerville Artist Guild, 1959; 1st prize Coastal Carolina Art Exhibit, Charleston, S.C., 1967; Hughes fellow, 1970. Bd. dirs. YWCA, 1965—. Mem. Carolina Art Assn., Charleston Artist Guild (treas. 1953-57, pres. 1968-71, dir. 1962—), Guild S.C. Artists (sec. 1963-64), Am. Ornithol. Union, Wilson Ornithol. Soc., Charleston Natural History Soc. (dir. 1962, 65-66). Nat. Audubon Soc. Clubs: Carolina Bird; Carolina Wren with Yellow Jessamine, 1969. Published Birds from Coastal Gardens, 1967. Home: 7 Arcadian Park Charleston SC 29407

RICHARDSON, CARL NEWTON, textile co. exec.; b. Honey Grove, Tex., Sept. 18, 1908; s. John Tal and Katie Jo (Newton) R.; student Ga. Inst. Tech., 1926-27; m. Winifred Darsey, Apr. 29, 1932; 1 son, Carl Newton. Vice pres. Rushton Cotton Mills, Griffin, Ga., 1928—. Chmn. Griffin Spalding County Hosp. Authority, 1963—. Trustee Ga. Hosp. Assn. Mem. Ga. Textile Mfrs. Assn. (dir. 1968-72), Ga. Bus. and Industry Assn. (v.p. 1960-68). Baptist. Elk, Moose. Club: Lambs (N.Y.C.). Home: 1099 Pine Valley Rd Griffin GA 30223 Office: PO Box 97 Griffin GA 30223

RICHARDSON, CARLTON DUQUESNE, financial exec.; b. West Brookfield, Mass., Oct. 5, 1935; s. Milton C. and Charlotte R. (Brooks) R.; B.B.A., U. Mass., 1957; m. Lois Luke, Dec. 23, 1970; children—Christine Dorothy, Carla Duquesne; children by previous marriage—Linda Ann, Craig David. Sr. auditor Arthur Anderson & Co., C.P.A.'s, N.Y.C., 1957-64; audit mgr. Manual Cole & Co., C.P.A.'s, Hartford, Conn., 1964-66; audit supr. C.E., Inc., Windsor, Conn., 1966-67, controller, Chattanooga, 1967—; dir. Milton C. Richardson, Inc. Served with Ordnance Corps, AUS, 1961-63. C.P.A., N.J., Tenn. Mem. Am. Inst. C.P.A.'s, N.J., Conn. socs. C.P.A.'s, Financial Execs. Inst. (sec.-treas. 1972-73). Home: 8123 Holly Crest Dr Chattanooga TN 37421 Office: 911 W Main St Chattanooga TN 37401

RICHARDSON, CLAY VANCE, hosiery mfg. exec.; b. nr. Star, N.C., Dec. 27, 1899; s. John W. and Mary Lou (Parks) R.; student pub. schs.; m. Elsie Presnell Richardson, May 22, 1922 (dec. 1943); children—Emma Louise (Mrs. Jack M. Hartley), Ann Marie (Mrs. C. C. Winstead, Jr.), Joseph E.; m. 3d, Lola Monroe, Dec. 27, 1944; children—Clay Vance, John Monroe. Retail furniture bus., 1924-31; pres. Clayson Knitting Co., Inc., 1931-65, Star Indsl. Corp.; owner, v.p. V. & M. Furniture Mfg. Corp., 1965—. Vice pres. Montgomery Meml. Hosp., Troy, N.C., 1950—, chmn. bd., 1950-65. Mayor Town of Star, N.C., 1963-65. Mem. co-founders club Sch. Medicine, U. N.C., Chapel Hill; mem. adv. bd. N.C. Zool. Soc. Methodist. Rotarian. Address: PO Box 39 Star NC 27356

RICHARDSON, DAVID DURHAM, physician; b. Louisville, Miss., Sept. 6, 1921; s. Elbert Leach and Edna Earl (Triplett) R.; B.S., Miss. State U., 1943; postgrad. Miss. Coll., 1949; M.D., Tulane U., 1953; m. Alma Elizabeth Carl, Aug. 24, 1947; children—David Durham, Beth, Carl Donovan, Richard Laird. Intern, McLeod Infirmary, Florence, S.C., 1953-54; gen. practice medicine, Louisville, Miss., 1954—; chief staff Winston County Community Hosp., Louisville, Miss. Pres., Winston Acad., Louisville, Miss., 1967-70. Lewis Winston Found., 1967-70. Trustee Winston County Community Hosp. and Med. Center. Served to lt. USNR, 1943-46. Mem. Am. Acad. Gen. Practice, Am. Assn. Physicians and Surgeons, A.M.A., Miss., E. Miss. med. assns., Sigma Chi, Alpha Kappa Kappa. Baptist. Mason. Home: 106 Richardson Rd Louisville MS 39339 Office: 307 W Main St Louisville MS 39339

RICHARDSON, DON ARNOLD, physician; b. Anderson, S.C., Mar. 4, 1927; s. Kenneth and Frances (Riley) R.; B.S., Coll. of Charleston, 1950; postgrad. Clemson U., 1950-51; M.D., Med. Coll. S.C., 1955; m. Eleanor Mae Ballenger, Aug. 8, 1957; children—Frances Elizabeth, Emil Ann, Jeff Webb. Intern, Indpls. Gen. Hosp., 1955-56; gen. practice medicine, Seneca, S.C., 1956—; chief medicine Oconee Meml. Hosp. Bd. dirs. Oconee Assembly. Served with USNR, 1945-46. Mem. A.M.A., Am. Assn. Gen. Practice, Am. Heart Assn. (clin. council cardiology), S.C. Med. Assn., Oconee Med. Soc., Oconee Meml. Profl. Assn. (pres.), Alpha Kappa Kappa, Pi Delta Kappa, Alpha Chi Sigma. Republican. Presbyn. (deacon 1970—). Club: Oconee Country. Home: Robbin Dr Seneca SC 29678 Office: PO Box 1174 Seneca SC 29678

RICHARDSON, EARL LEROY, chemist, govt. ofcl.; b. Lebanon, Mo., Mar. 21, 1917; s. Jesse Gaford and Hassie (Lawson) R.; B.S. cum laude, Drury Coll., 1938, M.S., Okla. A. and M. Coll., 1939; Ph.D., Rutgers U., 1948; student N.Y.U., 1939-40; m. Virginia Van Middlesworth, Mar. 21, 1942; 1 son, Kenneth Earl. Control chemist Procter & Gamble Co., Kansas City, Kan., 1939; research chemist Am. Cyanamid Co., Bound Brook, N.J., 1940-42; sr. project chemist Colgate-Palmolive Co., Jersey City, 1942-47, group leader, 1947-50; research dir. Whitehall Labs., Elkhart, Ind., 1951-58, Hammonton, N.J. 1958-66; head technical services for cosmetic chems. Union Carbide Corp., Tarrytown, N.Y., 1967-71; project mgr. div. colors and cosmetics Food and Drug Adminstrn., Washington, 1972—. Mem. Am. Chem. Soc., Am. Pharm. Soc., Soc. Cosmetic Chemists, Acad. Pharm. Scis., Sigma Xi, Phi Lambda Upsilon, Conglist. Author articles profl. jours. Patentee in field. Home: 2309 Cheshire Lane Alexandria VA 22307 Office: 200 C St SW Washington DC 20204

RICHARDSON, EDWIN LELAND, lawyer; b. Magnolia, Ark., Mar. 9, 1904; s. Edwin Sanders and Zenobia (Longino) R.; student George Washington U., 1923-26; J.D., Georgetown U., 1930; m. Olive Maurine Adams, Dec. 31, 1932, 1 dau., Olive Maurine (Mrs. Robert L. Modjeski). Admitted to D.C. bar, 1929, La. bar, 1931; sec. Congressman John N. Sandlin, 1923-31; mem. firm Drew & Richardson, Minden, La., 1931-34; asst. atty gen. La., gen. counsel Dept. Revenue, Baton Rouge, 1934-41; atty. Gov. La., atty. dir. nat. gas conservation, 1943-48; mem. Dale, Richardson & Dale, Baton Rouge and Vidalia, La., 1941-67, Dale, Owen, Richardson, Taylor &Matthews, Baton Rouge, 1968—. Mem. La. Revenue Code Commn., 1946-48; 1st vice chmn. Interstate Oil Compact Commn., 1946-48, mem. legal com., 1947-48, La. rep., 1945-48. Mem. Am., La. (bd. govs. 1938-40, mem. com. draft La. formulary 1952-57) bar assns., Internat. Assn. Ins. Counsel, Assn. Ins. Attys., Internat. Bar Assn., Am. Coll. Trial Lawyers, Phi Delta Phi, Kappa Sigma. Democrat. Methodist. Mason (32 deg., Shriner), Rotarian. Clubs: City (pres. 1970), Baton Rouge Country, Baton Rouge Assembly, Camelot (Baton Rouge); Boston, Plimsoll (New Orleans); Nat. Press (Washington). Author: History of Conservation of Oil and Gas in Louisiana, 1934-48, 1949. Home: 7815 Highland Rd Baton Rouge LA 70808 Office: Reymond Bldg Baton Rouge LA 70801

RICHARDSON, ELLIOT LEE, govt. ofcl.; b. Boston, July 20, 1920; s. Dr. Edward P. and Clara (Shattuck) R.; A.B., Harvard, 1941, LL.B., 1947; LL.D., Emerson Coll., Harvard, Lowell Tech. Inst., Ohio State U., Springfield Coll., U. N.H., U. Pitts., Yeshiva U.; L.H.D., Brandeis U., Mass. Coll. Optometry, Whittier Coll.; m. Anne Francis Hazard, Aug. 2, 1952; children—Henry, Anne Hazard, Michael. Admitted to Mass. bar, 1950; law clk. Judge Learned Hand, 1947-48, Justice Felix Frankfurter, 1948-49; asso. Ropes, Gray, Best, Coolidge & Rugg, Boston, 1949-53, 54-56; lectr. law Harvard, 1952; asst. to Senator Leverett Saltonstall, 1953-54; asst. sec. for legislation U.S. Dept. Health, Edn., and Welfare, 1957-59; U.S. atty., Mass., 1959-61; spl. asst. to atty. gen. of U.S., 1961; partner law firm of Ropes and Gray, Boston, 1961-64; lt. gov. Mass., 1965-67, atty. gen. Mass., 1967-69; under sec. U.S. Dept. State, 1969-70; sec. Health, Edn. and Welfare, 1970—. Past dir. New Eng. Trust Co., Boston. Vice pres., dir. Mass. Bay United Bay. Bd. dirs. World Affairs Council Boston, United Community Services, Boston; bd. overseers Harvard; trustee Cambridge Drama Fest.; past trustee Brookline Pub. Library, Mass.; mem. Harvard overseers coms. to visit Harvard U. Press and Grad. Sch. of Pub. Adminstrn. First lt., 4th Inf. Division AUS, 1942-45. Decorated Bronze Star medal, Purple Heart. Mem. Am., Mass., Boston bar assns., Am. Acad. Arts and Scis., D.A.V., Am. Legion. Home: 1100 Crest Lane McLean VA 22101 Office: Dept Health Edn and Welfare Washington DC 20520

RICHARDSON, FRANCIS JOSEPH, III, banker; b. New Orleans, Mar. 22, 1943; s. Francis Joseph, Jr. and Stella (Schulze) R.; B.B.A., Tulane U., 1965, postgrad. Law Sch., 1969—; M.B.A., Loyola U., New Orleans, 1970; m. Carolyn Mary Bienvenu, Apr. 17, 1971. Jr. mech. engr. Boeing Aerospace-Saturn Launch Systems br.-Michoud, New Orleans, 1964-66; systems trainee, computer operator, computer sci. asst. Field Systems Center-Computer Datacenter, IBM Corp., New Orleans, 1966-71; investment service rep. First Nat. Bank of Commerce, New Orleans, 1971—; pres. Alfa Enterprises. Mem. Republican state Central Com. for 1st Rep. Dist., 1969-70. Bd. dirs. Museums Com.-Jeuness D'Orleans and La. Council. Recipient James C. Kraus award Young Mens Bus. Club, 1968. Mem. Am. Inst. Banking, Fgn. Relations Assn., Am. Econ. Assn., Operations Research Soc., Am. Mgmt. Assn., Young Mens Bus. Club Greater New Orleans (past dir.), Navy League U.S., New Orleans Jr. C. of C. (dir.), La. Poetry Soc., Met. New Orleans Safety Council, Tulane Assn. Bus. Alumni, New Orleans Geneal. Research Soc., Thackeray Soc. New Orleans (founding), La. Geneal. and Hist. Soc., Financial Analysts New Orleans, S.A.R. (treas. La. Soc. 1972), Phi Delta Phi (treas. Tulane 1970). Clubs: Internat. House, Round Table, Pendennis (New Orleans). Home: 6330 St Charles St New Orleans LA 70118 Office: 210 Baronne St New Orleans LA 70112

RICHARDSON, GEORGE, JR., judge; b., 1918; LL.B., U. Miami, 1935. Judge, Broward County, Fla. Office: County Court House Fort Lauderdale FL 33301*

RICHARDSON, H. B., vice pres., gen. mgr. Houston Astros profl. baseball team. Address: Astrodome Old Spanish Trail and Main St Houston TX 77022*

RICHARDSON, HERSCHEL ELROY, physician; b. Georgetown, Tex., July 3, 1914; s. Herschel Elroy and Mary Anderson (Mann) R.; B.A., Southwestern U. of Tex., 1935; M.D., Vanderbilt Med. Sch., 1939; postgrad. Naval Sch. Aviation Medicine, 1943, Cornell U. Sch. Medicine, 1946-47, U. Pa. Sch. Medicine, 1954-55; m. Suzanne Marie Ahern, Sept. 4, 1943; children—Dennise Marie (Mrs. Richard H. Browne), Mary Jean (Mrs. David A. Glasgow). Commd. lt. (j.g.) USN, 1939, advanced through grades to capt., 1956, ret., 1961; intern U.S. Naval Hosp., San Deigo, 1939-40, resident, 1953-54; resident Bellevue Hosp., N.Y.C., 1947; chief medicine U.S. Naval Hosp., Corpus Christi, Tex., 1947-50, U.S. Naval Hosp., Quantico, Va., 1950-51, U.S. Naval Hosp., Yokosuka, Japan, 1951-53, U.S. Naval Hosp., Phila., 1960-61; asst. chief medicine U.S. Naval Hosp. Nat. Naval Med. Center, Bethesda, Md., 1956-60; asso. med. dir. Prudential Ins. Co. Am., Houston, 1962—. Clin. instr. medicine George Washington U. Sch. Medicine, 1957-60; naval guest lecturer Hahnemann Med. Coll., Phila., 1960-61; instr. Maumee Valley Hosp., Toledo, 1961-62, Toledo Hosp., 1961-62. Diplomate Am. Bd. Internal Medicine. Mem. Coll. Physicians Phila., A.C.P., Am., So., Tex. med. assns. Cons. editor Medical, Annals of D.C., Washington, 1958-60. Home: 205 Mayerling St Houston TX 77024 Office: 1100 E Holcombe St Houston TX 77025

RICHARDSON, J.D., oil well contractor; b. Morton, Miss., Sept. 26, 1928; s. Thomas Emmit and Leola (Region) R.; student Internat. Detective Tng. Sch., 1950-60; m. Neva LaRue McKinney, July 27, 1948; children—Linda Kay, Stevie, Sam Holmes, Glinda Lea. Unit operator Williamson Well Service, Odessa, Tex., 1953-62; owner J.D. Richardson, Inc., Crane, Tex., 1962—; supt. C.M. Bell Oil Co. Served with USAF, 1946-53. Mem. Crane C. of C. (dir.). Lion. (tail twister, dir., Crane). Home: 507 E 6th St Crane TX 79731 Office: Box 208 Crane TX 79731

RICHARDSON, JAMES MILTON, clergyman; b. Sylvester, Ga., Jan. 8, 1913; s. James Milton and Pallie (Stewart) R.; A.B., U. Ga., 1934; B.D., Emory U., 1936, M.A., 1942; postgrad. Va. Theol. Sem., 1938, D.D., 1965; LL.D., John Marshall Law Sch., 1948; D.D., Episcopal Theol. Sem. Ky., 1960, U. South, 1961; m. Eugenia Preston Brooks, June 14, 1940; children—James Milton, Eugenia (Mrs. James R. Nash), Joan Stewart, Preston Brooks. Ordained to ministry Episcopal Ch., 1938; rector St. Timothy's Ch., Atlanta, 1938-40; asst. rector St. Luke's Ch., Atlanta, 1940-43, rector, 1943-52; dean Christ Ch. Cathedral, Houston, 1952-65; bishop Episcopal Diocese Tex., Houston, 1965—. Chmn. bd. trustees St. Stephen's Episcopal Sch., 1965—, Episcopal Theol. Sem. of S.W., 1967—; pres. St. Luke's Episcopal Hosp.; trustee Ch. Pension Fund, Episcopal Radio-TV Found., U. South. Mem. Blue Key, Phi Beta Kappa, Phi Kappa Phi, Omicron Delta Kappa, Alpha Tau Omega (worthy grand chaplain 1945-52, 56—, nat. pres. 1952-56). Home: 14 Shadowlawn Circle Houston TX 77005 Office: 520 San Jacinto St Houston TX 77002

RICHARDSON, JEROME JOHNSON, restaurant co. exec.; b. Spring Hope, N.C., July 18, 1936; s. George and Mary (Williams) R.; B.A., Wofford Coll., 1959; m. Rosalind Sallenger, Jan. 31, 1959; children—Jerome Johnson, Mark Sallenger, Ashley. Player, Balt. Colts, 1959-60; agt. Equitable Life Assurance Co., Spartanburg, S.C., 1961; exec. v.p. Spartan Food Systems, Inc. (formerly Spartan Investment Corp.), Spartanburg, 1961-69, pres., 1969—. Mem. Spartanburg County Adv. Bd. Higher Edn., 1967; coach Midget Football and Baseball, 1967. Served with AUS. Named Balt. Colts Rookie of Yr., 1959. Mem. Wofford Coll. Alumni Assn. (pres. 1970), Wofford Coll. Council of Assos. Methodist. Home: 360 Lake Forest Dr Spartanburg SC 29302 Office: PO Box 3168 Spartanburg SC 29302

RICHARDSON, JOSEPH THOMAS, educator; b. Mount Pleasant, Tenn., Oct. 20, 1926; s. Mark Schultz and Lillian (Brown) R.; D.D.S., Middle Tenn. State U., 1947-48; D.D.S., U. Tenn. Coll. Dentistry, 1948-51; M.A. in Teaching, The Citadel, 1972; m. 1950 children—Steve, David; m. 2d, Agnes Bailey Richardson, Jan. 20, 1971; children—Earle, Olivia. Gen. practice dentistry, Columbia, Tenn., 1954-70; asst. prof. crown and bridge Coll. Dental Medicine, Charleston, S.C., 1970—; mem. dental staff Maury County (Tenn.) Hosp., 1954-70. Resident dentist Tenn. Orphans Home, Spring Hill, Tenn., 1958-70. Mem. Maury County Bd. Health, 1966-70, chmn., 1968-70. Served with U.S. Mcht. Marines, 1945-46; served with USNR, 1952-54. Mem. 6th Dist. Dental Soc. (pres. 1962-63; alternate del. 1970), Am. Legion, Psi Omega. Home: 444 Wade Hampton Dr Charleston SC 29412 Office: 80 Barre St Charleston SC 29401

RICHARDSON, KENNETH WAYNE, physician; b. Eustis, Fla., Sept. 10, 1933; s. Ivan Elmer and Annie (Goodson) R.; student Emory U., 1951-54; M.D., U. Miami (Fla.), 1958; m. Betty Jo Minshew, Dec. 26, 1953; children—Deborah, Kenneth, Thomas, Mark. Intern The Med. Center, Columbus, Ga., 1958-59; practice gen. medicine, Apalachicola, Fla., 1959-60, as partner Thompson Clinic, Chattahoochee, Fla., 1960—. Mem. Chattahoochee City Council, 1962—. Mem. A.M.A., So., Fla., Pan Handle med. assns. Methodist. Club: Seminole Bass (Chattahoochee). Home: 743 Magnolia St Chattahoochee FL 32324 Office: PO Box 67 Chattahoochee FL 32324

RICHARDSON, PATRICK WILLIAM, lawyer; b. Huntsville, Ala., Oct. 5, 1925; s. Schuyler Harris and Suzanne (Smith) R.; B.S., U. Ala., 1947, LL.B., 1948; m. Martha Alice Holliman, Dec. 23, 1949 (div. Jan. 1969); children—Schuyler Harris III, James Holliman; m. 2d, Mary McAlpine Moore, Oct. 9, 1970. Admitted to Ala. bar, 1948; partner firm Bell, Richardson, Cleary, McLain & Tucker, predecessor firms, Huntsville, 1948—. Dir. Bank of Huntsville, 1963-64. Bd. dirs. Huntsville Indsl. Expansion Com., 1962—. Pres. U. Ala. Huntsville Found., 1962—, bd. dirs. Law Sch. Found., 1965—. Trustee, Randolph Sch., 1959—. Mem. Ala. (1st v.p. 1968-69, pres. 1969-70), Am., Huntsville-Madison County (pres. 1966-67) bar assns., Ala. Motorists Assn. (bd. dirs., v.p. 1948—), Nat. Assn. R.R. Trial Counsel, Nat. Conf. Bar Presidents, Am. Counsel Assn., Am. Judicature Soc., Ala. Law Inst. (council 1969—), Internat. Assn. Ins. Counsel, Kappa Sigma, Beta Gamma Sigma, Phi Alpha Delta. Rotarian. Home: 1708 Drake Av SE Huntsville AL 35802 Office: 408 Franklin St SE Huntsville AL 35801

RICHARDSON, ROBERT RICHMOND, lawyer; b. Atlanta, July 29, 1927; s. Leaver and Virginia (McLane) R.; student Ga. Inst. Tech., N.C., State Coll.; LL.B., Emory U.; m. Mary Anne Wagstaff, June 10, 1947; children— Robert Richmond, Mark Wagstaff, Laine Vaughan. Asso. firm Gambrell, Harlan, Russell, Moye & Richardson, from 1950, partner, until 1964; partner firm Hurt, Hill & Richardson, Atlanta, 1964—. Dir. United Security Holding Co. Instr. Ga. State U., 1952-58. Chief staff Gov. Carl E. Sanders, 1963-67; del. Democratic Nat. Conv., 1960, 64, mem. platform com., 1964. Bd. dirs. Atlanta-Fulton County Recreation Authority, 1964. Served with AUS, 1944-47. Mem. Ga. Young Lawyers (pres.) Am. Judicature Soc. (dir.), Am. Bar Assn. (dir.), Sigma Alpha Epsilon, Phi Delta Phi. Clubs: Piedmont Driving, Commerce, Atlanta Country (Atlanta). Home: 3781 Tuxedo Rd NW Atlanta GA 30305 Office: 614 William-Oliver Bldg Atlanta GA 30303

RICHARDSON, RUPERT NORVAL, educator; b. nr. Caddo, Tex., Apr. 28, 1891; s. Willie Baker and Nannie (Coon) R.; A.B., Hardin-Simmons U., Abilene, Tex., 1912; Ph.B., U. Chgo., 1914; A.M., U. Tex., 1922, Ph.D., 1928; m. Pauline Mayes, Dec. 28, 1915; 1 son, Rupert Norval. Prin. high sch., Cisco, Tex., 1914-16, Sweetwater, 1916-17; prof. history Hardin-Simmons U., 1917—, dean students, 1926-28, v.p., 1928-38, exec. v.p., 1938-40, acting pres., 1943-45, pres., 1945-53, pres. emeritus, prof., 1953-67, Piper prof., 1963—, Distinguished prof., 1967—; asso. prof., prof. hist. U. Tex. 8 summers, also 1940-41. Mem. So. Bapt. Edn. Commn., 1952-55; mem. Tex. Hist. Survey Com., 1953-67, pres., 1961-63. Served 2d lt. U.S. Army, 1918. Recipient Cultural Achievement in Lit. award West Tex. C. of C., 1967. Fellow Tex. State Hist. Assn. (pres. 1969-70); mem. Am., Miss. Valley hist. assns., Southwestern Social Sci. Assn. (adv. editor 1929-31, pres. 1936-37), Tex. Philos. Soc. (pres. 1962-63). Baptist. Mason. Lion (past pres., dist. gov.). Author: The Comanche Barrier to the South Plains Settlement, 1933; (with C. C. Rister) The Greater Southwest, 1934; Texas: the Lone Star State, 1943; Adventuring with a Purpose, 1952; The Frontier of Northwest Texas, 1963; Colonel Edward M. House: The Texas Years, 1964; Famous Are The Halls: Hardwin-Simmons University as I Have Seen It, 1964; Caddo, Texas: The Biography of a Community, 1966; Along Texas Old Forts Trail, Abilene, 1972. Editor: West Tex. Hist. Assn. Yearbook, 1929—. Contbr. to hist., ednl. publs. Home: 2220 Simmons Av Abilene TX 79601

RICHARDSON, THOMAS PURDIE, cons. engr.; b. Anson County, N.C.; s. Thomas P. and Sally (Wall) R.; B.S., N.C. State U.; m. Mildred Land, July 25, 1930; 1 dau., Mildred Purdie (Mrs. Donald Walker Shuman, Jr.). Engr., Carolina Power & Light Co., Raleigh, N.C., 1928-31; distbn. supt. Tenn. Power Co., Murfreesboro, 1931-34; dist. mgr. Fed. Works Program, Elizabeth City and Charlotte, N.C., 1934-40; mgr. Colonial Mica Corp., Asheville, N.C., 1943-46; owner mgr. Richardson Engring. Service, Asheville, N.C., 1946-60; prvt. cons. engr., Asheville, 1960—. Mem. Roanoke Colony Meml. Assn. (hon.), Nat. Soc. Profl. Engrs., N.C. Profl. Engrs., N.C. Assn. Professions. Address: 320 Montford Av Asheville NC 28801

RICHBURG, WILLIAM E., justice of the peace. Address: 410 S Beckley Dallas TX 75203

RICHERT, EARL HARVEY, newspaper editor; b. Deschutes, Ore., Sept. 20, 1914; s. Phil A. and May (Lawyer) R.; B.S. in Edn., Okla. A. and M. Coll., 1936; m. Margaret A. Vincent, Sept. 11, 1937; children— Bonnie Ruth, Carol Jean. Reporter Okla. News, Oklahoma City, 1936-39; polit. writer Indpls. Times, 1939-44; Washington corr. Scripps-Howard Newspapers, 1944-51; editor Evansville (Ind.) Press, 1951-59, Scripps-Howard Newspaper Alliance, Washington, 1959-69; editor-in-chief Scripps-Howard Newspapers, 1969—. Clubs: Congressional Country, Internat., Gridiron, Nat. Press. Home: 5214 Farrington Rd Washington DC 20016 Office: 1013 13th St NW Washington DC 20005

RICHESON, JAMES PETE, mech. engr.; b. Russellville, Ala., Sept. 29, 1930; s. James G. and Eathel (Hovater) R.; B.S. in Mech. Engring., Auburn U., 1953; B.S. in Bus. Adminstrn., Athens Coll., 1962; m. Julia Ann Lea, July 2, 1961; children—James Jeffrey, Robin Lea. Mech. draftsman James B. Clow, Birmingham, Ala., 1951-52; mech. engr. TVA, Chattanooga, 1953-54; supr. engring. Monsanto Co., Decatur, Ala., 1956-70; pres., gen. mgr. Sandek Engring. Inc., Guntersville, Ala., 1970—. Mem. City Council, Trinity, Ala., 1964—. Served with AUS, 1954-56. Registered profl. engr., Ala. Mem. Am. Legion. Democrat. Baptist. Mason (Shriner). Patentee in field. Home: Route 6 Guntersville AL Office: PO Box 596 Guntersville AL 35976

RICHMOND, ROBERT ALAN, city ofcl.; b. Cold Spring, N.Y., Oct. 29, 1922; s. W.L. and Elizabeth (Groeger) R.; B.B.A., U. Miami, 1956, J.D., 1960; m. Dolores Marie Dorak, Nov. 26, 1949; children—Robert Alan, Carole Anne (Mrs. Donald Gibbs), Linda Carole, William Edward, April Faith. Mem. City of Miami (Fla.) Civil Service Bd., 1957-58, examining supr., 1958-61, personnel asst. to city mgr., 1961-63, personnel dir., 1963—. Chmn., Local Bd. SSS, 1958—. Bd. dirs. Miami Navy League Cadet Program. Served with USAAF, 1943-45; PTO. Decorated D.F.C., Air medal with three oak leaf clusters. Mem. Pub. Personnel Assn. Home: 10353 SW 116th St Miami FL 33156 Office: PO Box 708 Dinner Key Miami FL 33133

RICHTER, CARL ARPAD, food standards and research exec.; b. Budapest, Hungary, Dec. 12, 1917; s. John and Irene (Mathes) R.; came to U.S., 1936, naturalized, 1942; student Trade Sch. for Cooks, Bucharest, Romania, 1931-34, U. Bucharest, 1935-36; m. Frances Regina Brady, Feb. 16, 1943. Chef Casino at Hecules Bad, 1934-35; pvt. chef to wife of Premier of Romania, 1935-36; with Racquet Club, Phila., also Strawbridge & Clothier and Slater System, Phila., 1936-41; with Slater System, Balt., 1946-49; v.p. food standards and research Servomation, Inc., Balt., 1950—; cons. chef; dir. spl. food seminars for chefs and mgrs.; judge culinary art shows; guest speaker. Served with AUS, 1941-45. Recipient silver and gold medal, Profl. Inst. Chefs of Am., 1966, gold medal, Am. Acad. Chefs. 19—. Mem. Chef de Cuisine Assn. Chgo., Balt. Culinary Art Assn. (pres. 1964-66), Profl. Inst. Chefs (nat. v.p. 1964-65). Home: 13800 NE 12th Av Miami FL 33161 Office: 803 Gleneagles Ct Baltimore MD 21204

RICHTER, HORACE EDWIN, lawyer; b. Cairo, Ga., May 31, 1919; s. Eugene Paul and Lola (Harper) R.; LL.B., Mercer U., 1942; m. Dorothy Anita Pope, Nov. 19, 1944; children—Dorothy Ellen (Mrs. Freddie Link), Horace Pope, Lee Roy. Admitted to Ga. bar, 1942; practiced in LaGrange, Ga., 1946—; mem. firm Richter & Birdsong, LaGrange, 1955—; city atty., LaGrange, 1946-71. Dir. Peoples Bank LaGrange, chmn. bd., 1965—. Served to 1st lt. Judge Adv. Gen. Corps AUS, 1942-46. Mem. Am., Ga. (pres. 1946-71), Troup County bar assns. Baptist. Lion, Mason, Elk, Moose. Club: Highland Country (LaGrange). Home: 405 Ridgecrest Rd LaGrange GA 30240 Office: Peoples Bank Bldg PO Box 508 LaGrange GA 30240

RICHTER, IRVING, educator; b. N.Y.C., Oct. 3, 1911; s. Nathan and Rose (Brenner) R.; B.A., U. Wis., 1934; M.A., Cambridge (Eng.) U., 1966; m. Jeanne Dishong, Aug. 5, 1963; children—Lora, Charles, David, James, Bradley, Niles, Lance. Asst. dir. WPA, Washington, 1934-37; sr. economist Labor Dept., 1938-43; legislative rep., polit. dir. U.A.W.-C.I.O., 1943-47; pres. Orgn. Services, Inc., Detroit, 1948-63; vis. lectr. Mt. Holyoke Coll., 1966-68; asso. prof. Fed. City Coll., Washington, 1968-—. Mem. Indsl. Relations Research Assn., Am. Assn. U. Profs. Club: Jewish Community Center Greater Washington. Author: Trade Union Political Purpose, 1972. Contbr. articles to profl. jours. Home: 3807 Everett St Kensington MD 20795 Office: 1317 H St NW Washington DC 20003

RICHTER, SHERRY (MRS. BERNARD RICHTER), TV broadcaster; b. Hamlet, N.C., Mar. 28; d. Joe and Gladys (Blacker) Levine; student U. N.C., 1946-47, Cath. U., 1949; m. Bernard Richter, Dec. 24, 1950; children—Lloyd, Benjamin. With Lost Colony, 1946; fashion commentator DuMont TV, Washington, 1948-49; in charge children's program WUQW, Charlotte, N.C., 1949-—, Sunday Bible program, 1949; program on WSOC-TV, 1957, WB-TV; free-lance programming, Chanels 3 and 9, 1959; program WBTV, 1959-—; fashion dir. Autom Fashion Show. Active Mint Mus. of Art, Charlotte Little Theatre, Children's Theatre, Mecklenburg County Girl Scouts. Mem. Am. Women in TV and Radio. Club: Junior Woman's (Charlotte, N.C.). Home: 1030 Huntington Park Charlotte NC 28207 Office: 1 Jefferson Pl Charlotte NC 28207

RICKARD, HENRY CHARLES, educator; b. Newport, Tenn., Jan. 3, 1930; s. Chesley C. and Mary (Alexander) R.; B.A., U. Tenn., 1954, Ph.D., 1959; m. Barbara Lynn Wallace, Sept. 1, 1954; children—Kathryn Marie, Jeanne Elise, Debra Lynn, Timothy Charles. Staff psychologist VA Hosps., 1959-61; mem. faculty U. Ala., University, 1961-—, prof. psychology, 1969-—, coordinator clin. tng., 1966-—. Cons. VA Hosps., Ala. State Mental Health Clinic; co-dir. Camp Ponderosa, Mentone, Ala., 1963-—. Served with AUS, 1950-52. Mem. Am., Southeastern psychol. assns., Sigma Xi. Home: 13 Idlewood St Tuscaloosa AL 35401 Office: Psychology Dept U Ala University AL 35486

RICKARD, JOSEPH CONWAY, psychologist, educator; b. Weatherford, Tex., July 16, 1926; s. Joe Smith and Mattie Mae (Wright) R.; A.A., San Angelo Coll., 1948; Ph.D., U. Chgo., 1955; m. Dorothy June Wilson, May 29, 1948; children—Miles, Janis, Robert, Martha, Sarah. Clin. psychologist VA Center, Temple, Tex., 1955-60, chief psychology service, 1960-—; individual practice clin. psychology, 1965-—. Instr., U. Tex., 1956-59, 60-62, 66-67, Temple Jr. Coll., 1965-66; asso. prof. Mary Hardin-Baylor Coll., 1966-—; cons. Bell County Rehab. Center, 1956-61, Temple Sch. System, 1965-—, Killeen (Tex.) Sch. System, 1971-—. Cubmaster, Heart O'Tex. council Boy Scouts Am., 1959-62, scoutmaster, 1962-65. Bd. dirs. Bell County Soc. for Crippled Children, Bell County Alcoholism Commn. Served with USAAF, 1945-46. Fellow Soc. for Projective Techniques; mem. Am., Southwestern, Tex., Central Tex. (pres. 1972) psychol. assns., Bell County Research Soc., Sigma Xi. Home: 3302 Oaklawn Dr Temple TX 76501 Office: VA Center Temple TX 76501

RICKELTON, DAVID, air conditioning co. exec.; b. Glasgow, Scotland, Nov. 8, 1916; s. John and Catherine (Simpson) R.; student Bklyn. Poly. Inst., 1940, Pratt Inst., 1942; m. Virginia Thompson, Nov. 29, 1942 (dec.); children—David Kendall, John Thompson; m. 2d, Geneva Y. Brown, June 19, 1968. Came to U.S., 1923, naturalized, 1929. With Buensod-Stacey Corp. (now Aeronca Inc. Environmental Control Group), Charlotte, N.C., 1940-—, successively draftsman, engr., cons., 1940-65, v.p., 1965-—. Served from pvt. to lt. AUS, 1942, served to capt., 1944-46. Registered profl. engr., N.C. Mem. Am. Soc. Heating, Refrigeration and Air Conditioning Engrs. (v.p., dir.), Nat. Soc. Profl. Engrs. Mem. Ch. of Christ (elder). Home: 3413 Highview Rd Charlotte NC 28210 Office: PO Box 688 Pineville NC 28134

RICKETTS, ARTHUR SAMUEL, librarian; b. Dansville, N.Y., Oct. 6, 1926; s. Glenn B. and Minnie (Holden) R.; Mus.B., Eastman Sch. Music, Rochester, N.Y., 1950; B.A., U. Okla., 1954; M.L.S., 1957; m. Martina F. Myers, Jan. 28, 1961; 1 dau., Robin Stacey. Mem. Oklahoma City Symphony Orch., 1950-57; with Louisville Free Pub. Library, 1957-64, head circulation dept., 1957-60, asst. dir., 1960-64, 66-—; asst. dir. Pasadena (Cal.) Pub. Library, 1964-65; dir. Mesa Pub. Library, Los Alamos, N.M., 1965-66. Served with USNR, 1944-46. Mem. Sierra Club (sec., treas. Ky. sect. 1967-68), Am., Southeastern Ky. library assns., Am. Ornithologists Union, Ky. Ornithology Soc. Contbr. reviews to lit. jours. Home: PO Box 127 Prospect KY 40059 Office: Louisville Free Pub Library 4th and York Sts Louisville KY 40203

RICKEY, HARRY WYNN, educator; b. Clinton, La., Apr. 9, 1899; s. Harry Wigginton and Octavia (Wynn) R.; B.A., Tulane U., 1922, M.A., 1924; Docteur de L'; Universite de Bordeaux, 1932; m. Sara Brandon, Sept. 10, 1924; children—Sara Wynn (Mrs. Alex B. Lundsteen), Gerard. Head dept. romance langs. La. Coll., Pineville, 1924-36; head dept. modern langs. Miss. State Coll., 1936-67; chmn. dept. French, So. Meth. U., 1937-64, also H. M. Munger prof. French until 1964; chmn. dept. fgn. langs. Ala. Coll., Montevallo, 1964-69; v.p., Univ. of Plano (Tex.), 1969-—. Sgt. U.S. Army, 1918-19; AEF; maj. to col. AUS, 1941-45. Decorated Officer d'Academie, Officer d' Instruction Publique; Franco-Am. scholar, 1929, Field Research fellow, France, 1931. Mem. Modern Lang. Assn., South Central Modern Language Assn. (pres. 1963), Societe des Professours Francais en Amerique (asso.), Am. Asst. Tchrs. French, Phi Beta Kappa, Pi Delta Phi (pres. 1959), Sigma Pi, Pi Kappa Delta. Clubs: Town and Gown, French Circle of Dallas (pres.). Author: Musset Shakespearien, 1932. Co-editor: Tresor Nobel, 1963; (with M. Shriver) Carmen, 1964. Home: 3404 Caruth Blvd Dallas TX 75225

RICKEY, HORACE BUSHNELL, JR, contractor; b. New Orleans, July 2, 1924; s. Horace Bushnell and Marjorie (Bouvier) R.; student Tulane U., 1940-42, 45; B.S. in Civil Engring., U. Wyo., 1947, B.S. in Archtl. Engring., 1948; postgrad. U. Cal. at Los Angeles, 1958; m. Jewel Katherine Seybold, Aug. 15, 1947; children—Sharon, Marjorie, Priscilla Gail. Vice pres., dir. Horace B. Rickey Inc., Lafayette, La., 1948-50, sec.-treas., 1950-67, pres., chmn. bd. dirs., 1967-—; pres. S.W. Materials Inc., Lafayette, 1950-—, S.W. Homes Real Estate & Ins., Lafayette, 1961-—; v.p., dir. Union Fed. Savs. & Loan Assn., Lafayette, 1958-—; sec.-treas. Motor Lodges Lafayette, 1966-—; treas. Twp. Developers; dir. Petroleum Data Consultants. Mem. nat. ins. com. Operators Council Howard Johnson, 1968-—. Chief, Lafayette St. Planning Commn., 1964-—; chmn. Lafayette United Gift Fund campaign, 1969-70; mem. adv. bd. Salvation Army, Lafayette, 1966-69; commr. Lafayette Midget Football League, 1963-—. Chmn. Republican Parish Municipal Exec. Com., 1954-68, sec. La. Central Com., 1956-61, del. nat. conv., 1956. Bd. dirs. Indsl. Found., Lafayette, U. Southwestern La.; bd. dirs. Lafayette council Girl Scouts U.S.A., 1962-—, v.p. to pres., 1967-70. Served with AUS, 1943-46; ETO. Decorated Combat Inf. Badge. Mem. Lafayette C. of C. (dir. 1958-61, 69-71). Asso. Gen. Contractors, Am. Soc. C.E., Am. Concrete Inst., Prestressed Concrete Inst. Presbyn. (deacon, elder, commr. gen. assembly). Kiwanian. Clubs: Century (U. Southwestern La.), Lafayette Town House. Home: 301 River Dr Lafayette LA 70501 Office: PO Box 3567 Lafayette LA 70501

RICKS, JAMES RALPH, III, physician; b. Oklahoma City, Dec. 29, 1939; s. James Ralph and Evelyn Frances (Murdock) R.; B.S. (Pres.' honor roll) in Pharmacy, Southwestern State Coll., 1963; M.D., Okla. U., 1967; m. Karen Cabaniss, Sept. 7, 1962; children—Robyn Renee, Julie Janae, Kristi Kathleen. Rotating intern Hillcrest Med. Center Hosp., Tulsa, Okla., 1967-68; gen. practice medicine specializing in internal medicine, Watonga, Okla., 1968-—; mem. staff Watonga (Okla.) Municipal Hosp. County Supt. Health, 1971, chmn. coronary care unit; cons. physician Geary Nursing Home, 1970-71, USPHS, 1968-71. Recipient Physicians Recognition award A.M.A., 1968-71. Diplomate Am. Bd. Family Practice. Mem. A.M.A., Am. Acad. Gen. Practice, Am., Okla. pharm. assns., S.A.R., Descendents Colonial Clergy, Okla. Thoracic Soc., Okla. Med. Assn., Blaine County Med. Assn., C. of C., Kappa Psi, Rho Chi. Democrat. Baptist. (deacon 1970-—, trustee 1970-—). Home: 833 Kelli Dr Watonga OK 73772 Office: 405 N Hook St Watonga OK 73772

RICKS, LEE EDWARD, banker; b. Pleasanton, Tex., June 26, 1904; s. Fletcher Bumpass and Annie Lee (Smith) R.; student U. Tex., 1923-24, Southwestern U., 1924-25; m. Mamie Ware, June 3, 1930; 1 son, Lee Edward. Mgr., Ricks Co., Pleasanton, 1926-49, chmn. Ricks Co., Inc., 1951-—; dir. 1st Nat. Bank, Pleasanton. Mem. Pleasanton Sch. Bd., 1945-55, pres., 1955; dir. Nueces Valley Water Dist., 1935-50. Bd. dirs. Mercy Hosp., Jourdanton, Tex., 1960-70. Methodist. Mem. Sigma Chi. Rotarian. Home: 620 W Oaklawn Rd Pleasanton TX 78064 Office: 201 N Main St Pleasanton TX 78064

RICKS, THADDEUS BENTON, pub. relations cons.; b. Tunica, Miss., Aug. 20, 1920; s. Thaddeus Benton and Lou Ollie Belle (Crosthwait) R.; student Baylor U., 1936-39; B.Journalism, U. Mo., 1941; m. Martha Ann Mills, Dec. 29, 1950; 1 dau., Lise. Reporter, copy reader, editor Temple (Tex.) Telegram, 1941, Columbus (Ga.) Enquirer, 1941, Galveston (Tex.) Tribune, 1942, Longview (Tex.) News Jour., 1947-48; Memphis Comml. Appeal, 1948-49; dir. pub. relations and advt. State Fair Tex., 1950-65; cons. pub. relations, Dallas, 1965-69; dir. pub. relations Tex. Industries, Inc., Dallas, 1969-71; project dir. Community Service Bur. Inc., Dallas, 1972-—. Served with USAF, 1942-46. Mem. Pub. Relations Soc. Am., Sigma Delta Chi. Democrat. Methodist. Club: Press (Dallas). Home: 7220 Lehigh St Dallas TX 75214 Office: 505 N Ervay Dallas TX 75201

RIDDICK, FLOYD MILLARD, parliamentarian; b. Trotville, N.C., July 13, 1908; s. John Bembry and Helen (Blanchard) R.; B.A., Duke, 1931, Ph.D., 1935; M.A., Vanderbilt U., 1932; m. Marguerite Louise Faerber, Feb. 24, 1940; children—Johanne Marjorie (Mrs. William E. Betsch), John Lindsay, Carol Dianne (Mrs. Panos Spiliotakos). Statis. analyst Fed. Govt., 1935-36; instr. polit. sci. Am. U., 1936-39; asso. Congl. Intelligence, Inc., Washington, 1939-43; legislative research dept. law and govt. Columbia, 1942-43; legislative analyst U.S. C. of C., 1943-47; editor Senate sect. Daily Digest of Congl. Record, 1947-51; asst. parliamentarian U.S. Senate, Washington, 1951-64, parliamentarian, 1965-—; instr., professorial lectr. George Washington U., 1944-70. Spl. research project and study U. Berlin, Germany, 1937. Author: Congressional Procedure, 1941; (with George H. E. Smith) Congress in Action, 1948; U.S. Congress: Organization and Procedure, 1949; (with Charles L. Watkins) Senate Procedure, 1958, 64. Contbr. articles profl. jours. Office: US Capitol Washington DC 20510

RIDDICK, FRANK ADAMS, JR., physician; b. Memphis, June 14, 1929; s. Frank Adams and Falba (Crawford) R.; B.A. cum laude, Vanderbilt U., 1951, M.D., 1954; m. Mary Belle Alston, June 15, 1952; children—Laura Elizabeth, Frank Adams III. Intern, Barnes Hosp., St. Louis, 1954-55, resident medicine, 1957-60; fellow in metabolic diseases Washington U. Sch. Medicine, St. Louis, 1960-61; practice medicine, specializing in internal medicine, New Orleans, 1961-—; med. staff Ochsner Clinic, Ochsner Found. Hosp., 1961-—, asst. med. dir., 1968-—; vis. physician Charity Hosp.; clin. asso. prof. medicine Tulane U. Sch. Medicine. Trustee St. Martin's Protestant Episcopal Sch., Metairie, La., Am. Soc. Internal Medicine Socio-econ. and Research Found. Served from 1st lt. to capt., M.C., U.S. Army, 1955-57. Recipient Young Internist award Am. Soc. Internal Medicine, 1969, Teaching award Alton Ochsner Med. Found., 1969. Mead Johnson scholar A.C.P., 1959-60. Fellow Endocrine Soc.; mem. Am. (trustee), La. (past pres.) socs. internal medicine, A.M.A., A.C.P., Am. Diabetes Assn., Phi Beta Kappa, Alpha Omega Alpha, Kappa Sigma, Phi Chi. Episcopalian. Home: 4820 Cleveland Pl Metairie LA 70003 Office: 1514 Jefferson Hwy New Orleans LA 70121

RIDDICK, WINSTON WADE, state ofcl.; b. Crowley, La., Feb. 11, 1941; s. Herbert Hobson and Elizabeth (Wade) R.; B.A. (T.H. Harris scholar, Joel L. Fletcher fellow), U. Southwestern La., 1962; M.A. (Woodrow Wilson fellow), U. N.C., 1963; postgrad. (NASA fellow), Columbia, 1963-65, La. State U. Law Sch., 1969-—; m. Patricia Ann Turner, Dec. 25, 1961; 1 son, Winston Wade. Asst. prof. govt., dir. Inst. Govt. Research, La. State U., Baton Rouge, 1966-67; instr. Hunter Coll., N.Y.C., 1965, Rutgers U., New Brunswick, N.J., 1964-65; dir. La. Higher Edn. Facilities Commn., Baton Rouge, 1967-72; exec. asst. Supt. edn. La. Dept. Edn., 1972-—. Cons. La. Joint Legislative Economy Com., 1966-67, La. Commn. on Extension and Continuing Edn., 1966-67, East Baton Rouge Parish Planning and Zoning Commn,, 1969-—; election analyst WBRZ-TV, Baton Rouge, 1966-67, ABC, 1964-68, spl. asst. Gov. John J. McKeithen, 1966; sec. Gov's. Efficiency Com., 1966; exec. dir. La. Commn. on Extension and Continuing Edn., 1966; mem. Gov's. Capital Outlay Budget Com., 1969, tech. adviser, 1968. Mem. East Baton Rouge Parish Plan of Govt. Study Com., 1969. Bd. dirs. So. Regional Edn. Bd., Policy Commn., Inst. for Equal Ednl. Opportunity in South, 1968-—. Recipient Alumni award U. Southwestern La., 1962. Mem. Assn. Exec. Dirs. Higher Edn. Facilities Commns. (mem. exec. council 1969-—, v.p.), Am. Soc. Pub. Adminstrs., Acad. Polit. Sci., Soc. Coll. and Univ. Planning, Am., So. polit. sci. assns., S.W. Social Sci. Assn., Blue Key, Circle K, Sigma Tau Delta, Phi Alpha Theta, Pi Kappa Delta, Pi Lambda Beta. Home: 1563 Oakley Dr Baton Rouge LA 70806 Office: State Dept Edn Box 44064 Capital Sta Baton Rouge LA 70804

RIDDLE, HAROLD JOE, architect; b. Lakeland, Fla., Nov. 4, 1922; s. Wilber Marion and Dora Ethel (Lentz) R.; B.S., Clemson U., 1949; m. Dorothy LaUna Cook, Jan. 20, 1951; children—Edward Neal, Keith Lentz, Celeste Jean. Trainee, J.N. Pease & Co., Charlotte, N.C., 1949-53; asso. William A. Faust, Architect, Myrtle Beach, S.C., 1953-55; partner Faust & Riddle, Myrtle Beach, 1955-57; prin. Harold J. Riddle, Architect, Myrtle Beach, 1957-66; pres. Harold J. Riddle & Assos., Myrtle Beach, 1964-66; pres. Riddle & Wilkes Architects, Inc., Myrtle Beach, 1966-—. Mem. Planning and Zoning Commn., Mrytle Beach, 1966-—. Served with USAAF, 1942-46. Mem. A.I.A. (pres. 1966, bd. dirs. 1962-67). Presbyn. (deacon). Clubs: Dunes Golf and Beach, Pine Lakes International Country. Architect Coastal Carolina Regional campus, U. S.C., Conway, 1965. Home: Lake Dr Dunes Cove Myrtle Beach SC 29577 Office: PO Box 806 511 Kings Hwy N Myrtle Beach SC 29577

RIDDLE, JAMES DOUGLASS, clergyman; b. Austin, Tex., Oct. 8, 1933; s. Prebble Elmer and Jewel Lee (Nalley) R.; B.A., Southwestern U., 1958; S.T.B., Boston U., 1962, postgrad., 1962-65; m. Marilyn Brown Moore, Sept. 8, 1956; children—Mary Elizabeth, Margaret Allison, Charles Douglass. Dir. youth activities Tex. Christian Rural Overseas Program, Tex. Council Chs., 1954-55; ordained to ministry Methodist Ch., 1963; pastor First Meth. Ch., Granger, Tex., 1956-68; pastor Meth. Parish, Biddeford, Me., 1958-62; co-minister First Parish Ch., Lincoln, Mass., 1963-67; minister Community Ch. of Chapel Hill, N.C., 1967-—; teaching fellow, lectr. human relations Boston U. Sch. Bus., 1960-64; mem. staff study of structure and mgmt. Mass. Conf., United Ch. of Christ, 1967. Chmn. Clergy Consultation on Problem Pregnancies N.C., 1968-72; mem. exec. bd., chmn. Commn. on Unity N.C. Council Chs., 1968-—, mem. commn. on faith and order, 1970-—, mem. gen. bd. Nat. Council Chs., 1969-—; chmn. United Ch. of Christ Commn. on Christian Unity and Ecumenical Study and Service, 1969-—, chmn. com. on social action So. Conf., 1968-70; del. Uniting Conf., World Alliance Reformed Chs. and Internat. Congl. Council, Nairobi, Kenya, 1970; mem. United Ch. Christ Council for Christian Social Action, 1971-—. Co-chmn. housing com., bd. dirs. Chapel Hill-Carrboro Inter-Ch. Council for Social Service, 1967-—; chmn. Assn. Community Agys. Orange County, 1969-—; pres. N.C. Legal Def. Fund, 1969-—; sec. Triangle Meml. and Funeral Soc., 1969-71. Del. Democratic State Conv., 1970. Mem. Soc. Sci. Study of Religion, Acad. Religion and Mental Health, Religious Edn. Assn., N. Am. Acad. Ecumenists, Pi Kappa Alpha, Pi Delta Epsilon. Address: Damascus Church Rd Box 507 Chapel Hill NC 27514

RIDDLE, JAMES EGBERT, brick co. exec.; b. Gray Court, S.C., July 18, 1926; s. Egbert Mayor and Ida (Burns) R.; B.S. in Ceramic Engring. cum laude, Clemson U., 1959; m. Sara Vernelle Cooper, Feb. 14, 1948; children—James Brian, Stephanie Lizette (dec.). Ceramic engr. Harrop Ceramic Service Co., Columbus, O., 1959-60, Miller Equipment Co., Salisbury, N.C., 1960-61; ceramic engr. The Moland-Drysdale Corp., Hendersonville, N.C., 1961-—, asst. to pres., 1964-—. Tchr. math. Spartanburg County (S.C.), Greenville (S.C.) tech. edn. centers, part-time 1966-67. Registered profl. engr., S.C., N.C., Ohio. Mem. Am. Ceramic Soc., Nat. Assn. Accountants, Nat. Soc. Profl. Engrs., Am., N.C. (pres. 1967-68) socs. safety engrs., Hendersonville Jr. C. of C. (v.p. 1961-62). Baptist. Rotarian (bd. dirs.), Elk. Home: 1161 Woodmont Dr Hendersonville NC 28739 Office: PO Drawer 2150 Hendersonville NC 28739

RIDDLE, LINDSEY GRANT, broadcasting co. exec.; b. Preston, Mo., Aug. 11, 1910; s. Joseph Grant and Jessie (Lindsey) R.; grad. pub. high sch.; m. Edwina Giles Barthe, Sept. 3, 1951; 1 dau., Martha (Mrs. Gary Bankson). Studio supr. WHB Broadcasting Co., Kansas City, Mo., 1933-46; chief engr. Stephens Broadcasting Service, Inc. (name changed to WDSU Broadcasting Corp., 1950), New Orleans, 1946-48, chief engr., 1949-66, v.p., chief engring. Royal St. Corp., WDSU-TV Inc., New Orleans, 1966-—. Mem. tech. adv. com. Delgado Coll., New Orleans, 1970-—; chmn. services subcom. La. Indsutry Adv. Com., 1967-—; mem. Lakewood Property Owners Assn. New Orleans, 1961-—. Registered profl. engr. La. Mem. Nat. Assn. Broadcasters (tech. com.), Assn. Broadcast Engring. Standards (tech. com.), I.E.E.E. (sr. mem.), Assn. Fedn. Communications Consulting Engrs., Nat. Soc. Profl. Engrs., La. Engring. Soc., Armed Forces Radio Services, New Orleans Engring. Club, New Orleans C. of C., Young Men's Bus. Club New Orleans, Royal Radio Club (pres.), Delta DX Amateur Radio Club (license W5JG), Am. Radio Relay League. Democrat. Methodist. Contbr. profl. jours. Home: 5646 Bellaire Dr New Orleans LA 70124 Office: 520 Royal St New Orleans LA 70130

RIDDLE, WILLIAM THEODORE, educator; b. Banty, Okla., Dec. 18, 1927; s. Marion G. and Nannie E. (Smith) R.; B.S., Southeastern State Coll., 1954; M.A., George Peabody Coll. 1958; Ed.D., Tex. Tech. Coll., 1961; student U. Miami (Fla.), spring 1955; m. Joan C. Benn, May 25, 1956; children—John Marion, Julie Anne, Jane Marie, Joan Janette. Tchr. pub. schs., Hobbs, N.M., 1955-56; reading specialist Lovington (N.M.) Municipal Schs., 1956-58; teaching fellow Tex. Tech. Coll., 1959-61; prof. edn. and psychology Northeastern State Coll., 1961-66, prof. spl. edn., dir. spl. edn., 1966-—. Cons., State Dept. Edn., Bur. Indian Affairs; vis. prof. S.W. Tex. State Coll., summer 1966. Bd. dirs. Osage County Spl. Edn. Services, Pawhuska, Okla. Mental Health Assn. Served with USAF, 1946-49. Mem. Okla. Edn. Assn., N.E.A., Nat. Soc. for Study Edn., Phi Delta Kappa. Presbyn. Kiwanian. Contbr. articles to profl. jours., seminars. Home: Box 438 Tahlequah OK 74464

RIDEN, THOMAS HARDWICK, educator; b. Bostwick, Ga., Oct. 29, 1918; s. Claude Franklin and Anna (Adair) R.; B.S., Piedmont Coll., 1940; M.Ed., U. Ga., 1953; m. Martha Agnes Brown, Dec. 31, 1944; children—Julianna (Mrs. William R. Howard), Martha Carole. Coach, Lexington (Ga.) High Sch., 1940-41; prin., coach Jefferson (Ga.) High Sch., 1941-42, 45-46; prin., coach Buford (Ga.) High Sch., 1946-60; prin. Morgan County High Sch., Madison, Ga., 1960-—. Mem. Gov.'s Staff, 1956-—; mem. Gov.'s Commn. on Youth, 1965-68; chmn. Buford Youth Center, 1948-60, Morgan County Recreation Commn., 1962-—, Morgan County Hosp. Authority, 1966-—; chmn., pres. Morgan County chpt. Ga. Heart Assn., 1961-70, dist. dir., 1964-68. Served with USNR, 1942-45. Named Tchr. of Year, 1953-54, Coach of Year, 1947, 50, 55, 58, 59. Mem. Ga. Edn. Assn. (pres., del.), Dist. Prins. Assn. (past pres.), Ga. High Sch. Assn. (past region pres.), Piedmont Coll. Alumni Assn. (area chmn.), Am. Legion. Baptist (deacon). Mason, Lion, Kiwanian. Home: 921 S Main St Madison GA 30650 Office: Morgan County High School Madison GA 30650

RIDEOUT, HAROLD WADE, fiberglass, plastic products mfg. co. exec.; b. St. Louis, Okla., Dec. 6, 1932; s. Henry Guy and Lula (Jacobs) R.; B.B.A., Tulsa U., 1964; m. Frieda Jean Short, Nov. 26, 1958; children—Mark Steven, Kevin Wade, Pamela Gayle, Cassandra Faye. Personnel mgr. Unit Rig & Equipment Co., Tulsa, 1964-65; mgr. personnel and tng. Fibercast Co., Tulsa, 1965-—; spl. adv., lectr. Tulsa Area Vocational Tech. Center; lectr. Tulsa U. Mem. adv. bd. Sand Springs (Okla.) Salvation Army, 1969-70; cubmaster, com. mem. Indian Nations council Boy Scouts Am., 1969-72. Served with USAF, 1951-55. Mem. Tulsa Personnel Assn. (dir. 1970-71), McArthur PTA, Indsl. Relations Assn., Sand Springs C. of C. (dir.). Democrat. Home: 7769 E Skelly Dr Tulsa OK 74129 Office: 101 S Lincoln St Sand Springs OK 74063

RIDGE, CHARLES HOUSTON, physician; b. Hearne, Tex., Mar. 14, 1931; s. George Washington and Troy Inez (Street) R.; student Howard Payne Coll., Brownwood, Tex., 1948-50; B.A., Hardin-Simmons U., Abilene, Tex., 1955; M.D., Southwestern Med. Sch., Dallas, 1959; m. Mildred Elizabeth Newkirk, June 7, 1956; children—Doris Elaine, Mildred Denise, Linda Diane, Ronald Dean. Intern, Methodist Hosp., Dallas, 1959-60; gen. practice medicine, Victoria, Tex., 1960-63, Nixon, Tex., 1963-65, Stockdale, Tex., 1965-—; instr. electronics Marine Corps Inst., Washington, 1954-55. City health officer, Stockdale, 1965-—; chmn. Wilson County Bd. Health, 1969-—. Served with USMCR, 1952-55. Mem. A.M.A., Tex. Med. Assn., Am., Tex. acads. gen. practice. Address: PO Box 98 Stockdale TX 78160

RIDGEWAY, LANNY ERVIN, hosp. adminstr.; b. Greenville, S.C., June 11, 1942; s. Otis Ervin and Elizabeth (McWhorter) R.; student Furman U., 1960-61, Duke, 1970-71; m. Mary Linda Sessoms, June 29, 1962; children— Deborah Kay, Lanny Ervin. Ordained to ministry Bapt. Ch., 1962; interviewer, adjuster Citizens & So. Bank S.C., Greenville, 1960-61; asst. adminstr. Beaufort County Hosp., Washington, N.C., 1961-68; adminstr. Medicenter of Am., Spartanburg, S.C., 1968-69, Alexander County Hosp., Taylorsville, N.C., 1969—. Chmn., A.R.C. Bloodmobile, 1969-71. Mem. Piedmont Council Govt., 1971—; mem. Govs. Com. Aging, 1971. Trustee Regional Health Council Eastern Applachia, 1968-70. Mem. North State Football Ofcls. Assn., N.C. High Sch. Athletic Assn., N.C. Hosp. Assn. (dist. sec., treas. 1966-68), Am. Assn. Hosp. Accountants (dir. 1967-68). Baptist (deacon 1969—). Home: 314 3d St SW Taylorsville NC 28681 Office: 313 3d St SW Taylorsville NC 28681

RIDOUT, WILLIAM JAMES, JR., utility exec.; b. LaCrosse, Va., Dec. 1, 1918; s. William James and Marie (Dunn) R.; B.S., Va. Poly. Inst., 1939; m. Mary Alice Muse, Dec. 23, 1939; children—William James III, Robert Sterling, Gary Lee. Rural service engr. Ky. Power Co., Pikeville, 1939-41; power sales engr. East Tenn. Light & Power Co., Bristol, 1941-43; rural elec. specialist S.C. Extension Service, Clemson Coll., 1943-44, N.C. State Coll., 1945-47; rural service mgr. Edison Electric Inst., N.Y.C., 1947-50; editor Electricity on the Farm mag., N.Y.C., 1950-55, pub., 1955-61; dir. agrl. devel. Carolina Power & Light Co., Raleigh, N.C., 1961-63, dir. mgmt. devel., 1963-65, gen. marketing mgr., 1965-67, v.p., group exec., 1968-72, sr. v.p., 1972—. Vice-pres., mem. exec. bd. Occoneechee council Boy Scouts Am.; bd. dirs. United Fund of Raleigh, N.C. Served with USNR, 1944-45. Mem. Farm Electrification Council (dir. 1969—), Elec. Heating Assn. (dir. 1970—), I.E.E.E., Am. Soc. Agrl. Engrs. Mason, Kiwanian. Home: 2319 Beechridge Rd Raleigh NC 27608 Office: 336 Fayetteville St Raleigh NC 27602

RIECKEN, WILLIAM EMIL, JR., physician; b. Deleware, O., Feb. 16, 1931; s. William Emil and Alma (Gollner) R.; B.S., Millsaps Coll., 1952; M.D., Tulane U., 1956; M.P.H., U. N.C., 1968; m. Bobbie Jeanenne Pridgen, June 7, 1954; children—Jeanne Lynn, Leigh Ann, William Edward. Intern Miss. Bapt. Hosp., Jackson, 1956-57; health officer Miss. Bd. Health, Attala County, Kosciusko, 1959-67, Leake Co., Carthage, 1959-67; resident in pub. health U. N.C., 1968-70; cons. local health services Miss. Bd. Health, Jackson, 1968-70, dir. family planning project, 1969-72, asst. dir. gen. health services, 1970—; cons. Assn. State and Territorial Health Officers Health Program Reporting System, 1971—. Med. liaison officer AEC-USPHS Radiol. Network, Miss., 1961-67; cons. preventive medicine Montefort Jones Hosp., Kosciusko, 1959-67. Bd. dirs. Central Miss., Inc., 1965-67. Mem. com. health and safety. Attala County Boy Scouts Am., 1960-65, exec. bd. Andrew Jackson council, Jackson, 1961—, commr. Mataleho dist., 1962-66. Served with USAF, 1957-59; lt. col. Miss. Air N.G. Recipient Walter Reed medal for sr. thesis in preventive med., 1956. Mem. Am., Aerospace med. assns., Central, N. Central (sec. 1964, pres. 1965, sec. 1966, 67) med. socs., Am., Miss. pub. health assns., Millsap Coll. Alumni Assn. (v.p. 1965-66), Theta Kappa Psi, Pi Kappa Alpha. Methodist (bd. stewards 1962-67; adminstrv. bd. 1972—; certified lay speaker; Sunday sch. tchr.; asst. choir dir.; Layman of Year 1965; dist. bd. lay activities 1966-67, chmn. commn. missions 1965-67). Home: 780 Woodhill Dr Jackson MS 39206 Office: Miss Bd Health Jackson MS 39205

RIEDER, RUDOLPH CHARLES, sheet and tube co. exec.; b. Saginaw, Mich., Dec. 12, 1915; s. Floyd J. and Lenore (Otto) R.; B.S. in Mech. Engring., U. Mich., 1937; grad. Gen. Electric Bus. Tng. Sch., 1939; m. Marion V. Fitzgerald, Sept. 10, 1938; 1 dau., Suzanne. Office mgr., cost accountant Gen. Electric Co., Niles, O., 1939-41; indsl. and mgmt. engr. Goodyear Aircraft Corp., Akron, O., 1941-46; v.p., works mgr., dir. Baker Perkins, Inc., Saginaw, 1946-61; v.p. engring. and mfg. Continental-Emsco Co. div. Youngstown Sheet and Tube Co., Dallas, 1961-63, exec. v.p., 1963-64, pres., chief exec. officer, 1964—, v.p. parent co., 1964-71, sr. v.p. mfg., 1971—, dir. parent co., 1970—, pres. Fibercast div., 1964—; pres., dir. Continental-Emsco Co., Ltd., Continental-Emsco Co., C.A., Venezuela, 1965—; pres. Timberline Equipment Co., 1965—; exec. v.p., dir. Nippon-Conemsco Co., Ltd. (Japan), 1972—; dir. Lykes-Youngstown Corp. Mem. Am. Petroleum Inst., Ind. Petroleum Assn., Mid-Continent Oil and Gas Assn. (dir.), Petroleum Equipment Suppliers Assn. (dir., past pres.), Dallas Citizens Council, Dallas Art Assn., Sigma Phi. Republican. Conglist. Clubs: Brook Hollow Golf; Dallas Petroleum. Home: 7106 Currin Dr Dallas TX 75230 Office: Mercantile-Continental Bldg Dallas TX 75201

RIEDERER, ROBERT EDWARD, physician; b. Rozel, Kan., Sept. 17, 1916; s. John Henry and Blanche Elizabeth (LaBounty) R.; A.B., U. Kan., 1938, M.D., 1942; m. Sarah Josephine Demsey, Oct. 30, 1942; children— Robert Neven, Bruce Fullerton. Intern, U. Kan. Hosps., Kansas City, 1942-43; practice medicine specializing in family practice, Olathe, Kan., 1946-61, 68-69; chief profl. tng. VA Central Office, Washington, 1961-62; staff physician Lovelace Clinic, 1962-68; physician, State Sch. Deaf, 1954-61; staff physician Jefferson Health Found., Birmingham, Ala., 1969—; mem. staff St. Mary's Hosp., Kansas City, Mo., Olathe (Kan.) Community Hosp., Bataan Meml. Meth., Presbyn. hosps., Albuquerque, S. Highlands Hosp., Birmingham, Ala. Pres. Bd. Edn., Olathe, Kan., 1957-61. Served to lt. USNR, 1943-46; PTO. Fellow Royal Soc. Health; mem. Am. Acad. Family Practice, So. Med. Assn., Phi Beta Kappa, Alpha Omega Alpha, Delta Tau Delta, Nu Sigma Nu. Clubs: Four Hills (Albuquerque); Green Valley Country (Birmingham, Ala.). Home: 1714 Somerset Circle Birmingham AL 35213 Office: 1500 6th Av S Birmingham AL 35205

RIEDL, JON MARTIN, mining co. exec.; b. Munich, Germany, Nov. 18, 1935; s. John A. and Rose T. (Lechleiter) R.; brought to U.S., 1936, naturalized, 1946; B.S. in Chemistry, Coll. City N.Y., 1959; m. Marianne Thomiszer, Apr. 29, 1966. Sales mgr. Naftone-Bayer Co., N.Y.C., 1961-69; exec. v.p. Am. Vermiculite Corp., Atlanta, 1969—, dir., 1972—. Served as 2d lt., C.E., AUS, 1959. Mem. Vermiculite Assn. (mng. dir. 1969—). Contbr. articles to tech. jours. Home: 255 I Winding River Dr Atlanta GA 30338 Office: American Vermiculite Corporation 52 Executive Park S Atlanta GA 30329

RIEFENBERG, JOHN ALAN, social worker; b. Omaha, Sept. 30, 1931; s. Elmer August and Cassie Lila (Williams) R.; A.A., Del Mar Jr. Coll., 1952; B.B.A., Tex. Coll. Arts and Industries, 1954; M.S.S.W., U. Tex., 1961; m. Janette Irene Meyer, June 3, 1961; children—Paul Alan, Erica Lynn. Pub. assistance field worker Tex. Dept. Pub. Welfare, Spur, 1957-58; caseworker Children's Services, Corpus Christi, Tex., 1959-60, Family and Children's Services, Shreveport, La., 1961-65; psychiat. social worker Children's Med. Center, Tulsa, Okla., 1965-68; pvt. practice counseling, Tulsa, Okla., 1966-68; exec. dir. Family Counseling Service, Corpus Christi, Tex., 1968-70; chief psychiat. social worker Child Guidance Clinic of Forsyth County, Winston-Salem, N.C., 1970—. Mem. Nat. Assn. Social Workers, Acad. Certified Social Workers, Am. Group Psychotherapy Assn., Am., N.C. assns. marriage and family counselors, Nat. Geog. Soc. Mem. Disciples Christ Ch. Home: 216 Capistrano Dr Winston-Salem NC 27106 Office: 1200 Glade St Winston-Salem NC 27104

RIEHM, CARL LEE, sch. supt.; b. Norfolk, Va., Jan. 23, 1929; s. Andrew Nelse and Nellie (Fitchett) R.; A.B., Citadel, 1952; M.Ed., U. Va., 1957 D.Ed., U. Fla., 1969; m. Barbara Hilton, June 15, 1952 1 son, Andrew Russell. Tchr., elementary sch. Norfolk, 1953-60, prin., 1960-66; dir. adjustive services Norfolk City Schs., 1967-69; dir. elementary edn. Prince William County, Manassas, Va., 1969-71, asst. supt. for instruction, 1971—. Extension tchr. U. Va., Hampton Roads Center, 1968-69. Served with USNR, 1947-48. Mem. N.E.A., Assn. Supervision and Curriculum Devel., Nat. Soc. Study Edn., Council for Exceptional Children, John Dewey Soc., Internat. Reading Assn., Va. Ednl. Assn., Kappa Delta Pi, Phi Delta Kappa. Methodist. Office: Prince William County Sch Bd Independent Hill Manassas VA 22110

RIES, EDWARD RICHARD, petroleum geologist; b. Freeman, S.D., Sept. 18, 1918; s. August and Mary F. (Graber) R.; student Freeman Jr. Coll., 1937-39; A.B., U. S.D., 1941; M.S., U. Okla., 1943, Ph.D. (Warden-Humble fellow), 1951; postgrad. Harvard, 1946-47; m. Amelia D. Capshaw, Jan. 24, 1948 (div. Oct. 1956); children—Rosemary Melinda, Victoria Elise; m. 2d, Maria Wipfler, June 12, 1964. Asst. geologist Geol. Survey S.D., Vermillion, 1941; geophys. interpreter Robert Ray Inc., Oklahoma City, 1942; jr. geologist Carter Oil Co., Mont., Wyo., 1943-44, geologist Cutbank, Mont., 1944-49; sr. geologist Standard Vacuum Oil Co., India, 1951-53, sr. regional geologist, Indonesia, 1953-59, geol. adviser for Far East and Africa, White Plains, N.Y., 1959-62; geol. adviser Far East, Africa, Oceania, Mobil Petroleum Co., N.Y.C., N.Y., 1962-65; geol. adviser for Europe, Far East, Mobil Oil Corp., N.Y.C., 1965-71, sr. regional explorationist Far East, Dallas, 1971—. Grad. asst., teaching fellow U. Okla., 1941-43, Harvard, 1946-47. Served with AUS, 1944-46. Mem. Am. Assn. Petroleum Geologists, Am. Geol. Inst., A.A.A.S., Nat. Audubon Soc., Nat. Wildlife Fedn., Wilderness Soc., Am. Legion, Sigma Xi, Phi Beta Kappa, Phi Sigma, Sigma Gamma Epsilon. Republican. Mennonite. Club: Harvard (Greenwich, Conn.). Home: 6009 Royal Crest Dr Dallas TX 75230 Office: 8303 Elmbrook Dr Dallas TX 75247

RIESENBERG, SAUL HERBERT, museum curator; b. Newark, Aug. 28, 1911; s. Jacob and Leah (Rothman) R.; A.B., U. Cal. at Los Angeles, 1932, Ph.D., at Berkeley, 1950; m. Mildred Rose Rand, Dec. 19, 1942; children—Jared Rand, Daniel Nicholas, Thomas Lee. Asst., then asso. prof. anthropology U. Hawaii., 1949-57; staff anthropologist U.S. Trust Ter. Pacific Islands, 1953-54, Govt. Am. Samoa, 1955-56; curator Pacific anthropology U.S. Nat. Mus., Smithsonian Instn., 1957—; summer tchr. U. Cal. at Berkeley, 1951, San Francisco State Coll., 1951; vis. research fellow Australian Nat. U., Canberra, 1970-71; spl. research Pacific ethnology. Served to capt. USAAF, 1942-45. Field trips to Ponape, 1947-48, 63, Samoa, 1955-56, Puluwat, 1967; del. 2d South Pacific Conf., Noumea, 1953, 8th Pacific Sci. Cong., Manila, 1953, 10th Pacific Sci. Congress, Honolulu, 1961, 5th Internat. Cong. Anthropology and Ethnol. Scis., Moscow, 1964. Pacific Sci. Bd. of NRC grantee, 1947, Wenner-Gren Found. grantee, 1949, 70, Carnegie Corp. grantee, 1955, NSF grantee, 1963. Fellow Am. Anthrop. Assn. mem. Polynesian Soc., Current Anthropology (asso.), Am. Ethnol. Soc., Anthrop. Soc. Washington (past pres.), Sigma Xi. Author articles, books, monographs. Home: 10105 Kinross Av Silver Spring MD 20901 Office: Smithsonian Instn Washington DC 20560

RIETH, CHESTER MARTIN, accountant; b. New Orleans, July 29, 1914; s. Anthony and Mary (Price) R.; B.S., Loyola U., 1937; m. Audrey Cecile Melancon, June 21, 1939; children—Marc Chester, Christopher Anthony, Gayvonne Claire, Virginia Louise, Justin Dennis, Kevin Amadeus. Accountant, Barton, Pilie & Sere, New Orleans, 1937-40; auditor State La., 1941; ofcl. City New Orleans, 1942—, asst. sec. bd. liquidation City Debt, 1951-63, sec., 1963—. Vice pres., chmn. prodn. com. New Orleans Opera House Assn., 1957—. K.C. Home: 750 Filmore Av New Orleans LA 70124 Office: 1300 Perdido St New Orleans LA 70112

RIFE, V.C., banker; b. Bentonville, Ark., Dec. 13, 1922; s. Vern Columbus and Lena Mae (Keeler) R.; student La. State U. Sch. Banking of the South, 1966; m. Adabelle Ford, June 18, 1944; children—Jon Michael, Thomas Gregory. Owner, Rife Grocery & Market, Bentonville, 1946-53; v.p. loans Bank of Bentonville, 1953—. Mem. Bentonville City Council, 1955-62. Treas. Benton County Fair, 1965-71. Served with USAAF, 1943-45; CBI. Decorated Air Medal. Mem. Ark. Jr. Bankers (exec. bd. 1960), V.F.W., Am. Legion. Democrat. Methodist. Kiwanian. Home: 2006 Oakwood St Route 4 Bentonville AR 72712 Office: Box 449 Bentonville AR 72712

RIGANTO, MAURY FRANK, auctioneer; appraiser; b. Norfolk, Va., Jan 22, 1913; s. Frank and Angelina (Chinchello) R.; student Coll. William and Mary, 1934; m. Grace Truman White, Dec. 3, 1942; 1 son, Maury Frank III. Sole owner Maury's, 1932-70; pres., treas. Norvair Aviation Corp., 1945-55, So. Yacht Marina Corp., 1946-65, Maury Riganto Auction Co.; founder Va. Pacific Corp.; dir. 1st Commonwealth Corp., Equity Mortgage Corp. Appraiser U.S. Bankruptcy Ct., Eastern Dist. Va. Chmn. Norfolk Parking and Traffic Commn., 1949-63; chmn. Virginia Beach Recreation Commn. Bd. dirs. Norfolk Sports Club Ednl. Found., 1950-60. Named Sportsman of Yr., Norfolk, 1950. Mem. Nat. Trust. Episcopalian (vestryman). Clubs: Princess Anne (Va.) Ruritan (past pres.); Norfolk Sports (past pres.); Commodore Country, Capes Beach and Cabana. Home: Rollingwood Route 2 Box 2011 Virginia Beach VA 23456 Office: PO Box 657 Norfolk VA 23501

RIGAU, MARCO ANTONIO, judge; b. Ponce, P.R., Mar. 5, 1919; s. Juan M. and Carmen (Gaztambide) R.; B.A., U. P.R., 1940, LL.B. cum laude, 1942; M.A. in Govt., Harvard, 1947; m. Alice Jimenez, Dec. 16, 1942 (div. Apr. 1968); children—Alma Carmen, Marco Antonio, Maria Alicia; m. 2d, Lucy Torres, Nov. 2, 1968. Admitted to P.R. bar, 1945; asst., atty. gen. P.R., 1947; legislative counsel Legislative Assembly P.R., 1948-49; spl. asst. to gov. P.R., 1949-51, exec. asst., 1951-58; partner firm Rigau, Goldman & Santiago, San Juan, 1959-61; asso. justice Supreme Ct. P.R., 1961—. Mem. adv. bd. Marquis Biograph. Soc. Served to capt., inf., AUS, 1942-45. Decorated Bronze Star medal, Combat Inf. Badge. Mem. P.R. Bar Assn., Am. Judicature Soc., Harvard Alumni Assn., Internat. Law Assn., Am. Soc. Internat. Law. Home: 1309 Magdalena Av Condado San Juan PR 00907 Office: Supreme Court Bldg San Juan PR 00902

RIGBY, FRED DURNFORD, univ. ofcl.; b. Missoula, Mont., Sept. 11, 1914; s. George Fred and Hypatia Mignonia (Durnford) R.; B.A., Reed Coll., 1935; M.S., State U. Ia., 1938, Ph.D., 1940; m. Vera Catherine Lenon, Aug. 26, 1937; children—Eloise Alice, Fred Alan. Instr. math. Tex. Tech. Coll., Lubbock, 1940-43; with Office Naval Research, 1943-63, dep. research dir., 1962-63; dean Grad. Sch. of Tex. Tech. U., Lubbock, 1963-68; asso. v.p. for acad. affairs, 1968—, also prof. math. Served to lt. comdr. USNR, 1943-46. Mem. Am. Math. Soc., Math. Assn. Am., Inst. Math. Statistics, Econometric Soc., A.A.A.S., Sigma Xi. Editor Naval Research Logistics quar., 1954—. Home: 3822 53d St Lubbock TX 79413

RIGBY, WILLIAM LAWSON, sch. supt.; b. Collins, Miss., June 27, 1909; s. William Lawson and Elsa (Watson) R.; B.S., Millsaps Coll., 1932; M.A., Peabody Coll., 1949; m. Mamie Lou Downing, Nov. 24, 1933; children—Clifford L., Wilna (Mrs. T.M. Stewart), Ruth (Mrs. Larry Sappington). Tchr. sci., coach Mendenhall (Miss.) High Sch., 1932-36; supt. Kilmichael (Miss.) Consol. Schs., 1936-41; pres. French Camp Acad., French Camp, Miss., 1941-43; prin. Utica (Miss.) Consol. Sch., 1945-49; prin. Gulfport (Miss.) High Sch., 1949-51, asst. supt., 1951-53, supt., 1953—. Chmn. adv. council Harrison County Youth Ct., 1957-64; pres. Council Pub. Schs. System, 1965-66; pres. Gulfport area Boy Scouts Am., 1952-53; regional coordinator Miss. Congress P.T.A., 1960. Mem. Miss. Edn. Assn. (pres. 1967-68), Am., Miss. assns. sch. adminstrs., Gulf Sch. Edn. Assn., White House Conf. Edn. Presbyn. (elder 1942—). Home: 915 2d St Gulfport MS 39501 Office: 2010 15th St Gulfport MS 39501

RIGGAN, WILSON BUTLER, agrl. economist; b. Waverly, Va., Sept. 15, 1914; s. Jesse Thomas and Ellia (Butler) R.; B.S. with honors, Va. Poly. Inst., 1950; Ph.D., N.C. State U., 1966; m. Edna Irene Downs Joyner, Aug. 8, 1953; children—Wilson Butler, Jesse Edmund. Asst. agrl. economist N.C. State Coll., 1955-57, instr., 1957-58; asst. prof. agrl. econs. and econometrics, grad. prof. U. Fla., 1958-64, supervisory statistician, biometry sect. ecol. research br., div. health effects research Nat. Air Pollution Control Adminstrn., Durham, N.C., 1964-66, chief biometry sect., 1966-67, asst. chief ecol. research br., 1967-71, asst. dir. for research operations, div. health effects research, 1971—. Served with U.S. Mcht. Marine, 1942-46. Mem. Am. Farm Econs. Assn., Am. Statis. Assn., Econometric Assn., Am. Econ. Assn., Am. Acad. Polit. and Social Sci., Biometric Assn., Am. Pub. Health Assn., Phi Kappa Phi, Alpha Zeta, Gamma Sigma Delta. Methodist. Home: 3609 Westover Rd Durham NC 27707 Office: Nat Environmental Research Center Environmental Protection Agy Research Triangle Park NC 27711

RIGGS, CARL D(ANIEL), educator, curator; b. Indpls., Dec. 7, 1920; s. Joseph M. and Margaret Helen (Schleicher) R.; B.S., U. Mich., 1944, M.S., 1945, Ph.D., 1953; m. Patricia Bynum, June 1, 1952; children— Margaret Clare, Carl Daniel, Jeffery Bynum, Catherine Elinor. Grad. asst. dept. zoology U. Mich., 1944-45, teaching fellow, 1945-47; field biologist Ind. Dept. Conservation, summers 1944-46, 48; instr. dept. zoology U. Okla., 1948-49, asst. prof., 1949-54, asso. prof., 1954-62, prof., 1962—, dean Grad. Coll., 1965—, v.p. grad. studies, 1966—; dir. Okla. Biol. Survey, 1949—, dir. U. Okla. Biol. Sta., 1950-69, curator zoology div. U. Okla. Mus., 1954-66; cons. constrn. and mgmt. lakes and ponds. Mem. panel for facilities and spl. programs, biol. and med. sci. Nat. Sci. Found. Mem. Norman City Commn. Chmn. Cleveland County chpt. Heart Fund, 1959-60; bd. dirs. Cleve. County chpt. A.R.C., Okla. Research Inst. Served with USAAF, World War II. Mem. Okla. Acad. Sci. (pres. 1967) Southwestern Assn. Naturalists (past pres.), Am. Fisheries Soc., Am. Soc. Ichthyologists and Herpetologists, Wilson Ornithol. Soc., Am. Inst. Biol. Scis., Phi Beta Kappa. Presbyn. Lion (pres. 1958-59). Author papers on North Am. fishes. Home: 2706 Walnut St Norman OK 73069

RIGGS, MYRTLE CRAVER BRADHAM (MRS. LARRY T. RIGGS), motel exec.; b. Newberry, S.C., Mar. 28, 1920; d. William Everett and Myrtle (Ivey) Craver; student Converse Coll., 1936-38, Furman U., Coll. Charleston, 1943-46; m. Richard Bradham, May 27, 1940 (dec. Oct. 1963); 1 dau., Helen (Mrs. Robert Lindley Furnans); m. 2d, Larry T. Riggs, June 26, 1966. Owner, operator Mount Vernon Motel, Charleston, S.C., 1950—; v.p., treas., dir. Superior Motels Inc. Chmn., St. Andrews Playground Commn., 1960—; pres. St. Andrews High Sch. PTA, 1956-58; mem. Gov.'s Com. on Edn., 1958-60; v.p. Charleston Safety Council, 1969; mem. Charleston County Zoning Bd., 1971—; charter mem., pres. Trident chpt. Nat. Multiple Scelerosis, 1971-73. Sec., Club 4 St. Andrews Parish Democratic Com., 1954-64. Bd. dirs. United Fund, Florence Crittendon Home, Progress Found.; bd. commrs. Oak Grove Orphanage; bd. dirs., v.p. Charleston County Cancer Soc.; mem. steering com. Faculty-Alumni Center, Coll. Charleston. Named Charleston Woman of Year, 1958; recipient Hospitality mag. Hall of Fame award, 1969, Distinguished Service award Superior Motels Inc., 1969, Mary Mildred Sullivan award Converse Coll., 1970. Mem. Coll. of Charleston Alumni Assn. (v.p. 1968), Converse Coll. Alumnae Council, Charleston Fedn. Women's Clubs (named to Hall of Fame 1971), Nat. Fedn. Women's Clubs (S.C. chmn. Am. Revolution com. 1972—), Wesley Service Guild (pres.), Soroptimists (gov.), Preservation Soc., Trident C. of C. of Charleston (women's div. bd.), Alliance Francaise, S.C. Innkeepers Soc. Home: 1265 Camerton St Charleston SC 29407 also 2826 Marshall Blvd Sullivan's Island SC 29482 Office: Mount Vernon Motel US 17 Charleston SC 29407

RIGGS, STUART, physician; b. Port Arthur, Tex., Sept. 23, 1928; s. Thomas Elton and Katherine (McKlemie) R.; M.D., U. Tex., 1953; m. Harriett Lee Davis, Dec. 21, 1951; children—Robert, Stuart, David Thomas, John William. Intern, U. Ia., 1953-54; resident internal medicine U. Ia. Hosps., 1954-57; research fellow infectious diseases U. Tex. Southwestern Med. Sch., 1961-62; practice medicine, specializing in infectious diseases, Houston, 1969—; attending physician John Sealy Hosp., Galveston, Tex., 1959-61, Parkland Meml. Hosp., Dallas, 1961-62, Ben Taub Gen. Hosp., Houston, 1962—, Meth. Hosp., Houston, 1967—, St. Luke's Hosp., Houston, 1969—; cons. infectious diseases VA Hosp., Houston, 1964—; head sect. infectious diseases Med. Service, Ben Taub Gen. Hosp., Houston, 1966-69, supr. clin. microbiology lab., 1966-69; supr. clin. microbiology lab. Kelsey-Seybold Clinic, Houston, 1969—; instr. U. Tex. Med. Br., Galveston, 1959-61; asst. prof. medicine Baylor U. Coll. Medicine, Houston, 1962-67, asst. prof. microbiology, 1966-69, asso. prof. medicine, 1967-69, clin. asso. prof. medicine, 1969—, adj. asst. prof. microbiology, 1969—. Served to lt., M.C., USNR, 1957-59. Diplomate Nat. Bd. Med. Examiners, Am. Bd. Internal Medicine. Fellow A.C.P.; mem. Am. Fedn. Clin. Research, Am. Soc. Microbiology, A.A.A.S., A.M.A., Tex. Med. Assn., Harris County Med. Soc. Methodist (mem. ofcl. bd. 1963-72). Home: 5259 Birdwood St Houston TX 77035 Office: 6624 Fannin St Houston TX 77025

RIGGS, WILLIAM WEBSTER, physician; b. Memphis, May 10, 1934; s. W. Webster and Mary (Norman) R.; B.S., U. Tenn., 1955, M.D., 1958; m. Helen Sands Turner, Dec. 22, 1956; children—Rollin, Russell, Ryan. Intern Bapt. Hosp., Nashville, 1958-59; resident Meth. Hosp., Memphis, 1961-63; chief resident Boston Children's Hosp., 1965; practice medicine specializing in radiology, 1964—; mem. staff City Memphis Hosps., 1964—; dir. radiology Le Bonheur Children's Hosp., Memphis, 1968—; asso. prof. radiology U. Tenn., Memphis, 1966-68. Served to capt. M.C., AUS, 1959-61. Diplomate Am. Bd. Radiology. Mem. Soc. Pediatric Radiology, Sigma Alpha Epsilon, Alpha Epsilon Delta. Home: 7 Belleair Dr Memphis TN 38104 Office: 848 Adams St Memphis TN 38103

RIGLER, FRANK CLEMENT, ret. educator; b. Keosauqua, Ia., Oct. 5, 1906; s. Charles George and Oria (Boyer) R.; B.J., U. Tex., 1930, M.J., 1932; m. Jewell LaVerne Gaddy, Mar. 10, 1928; 1 dau., Julie Faye (Mrs. James F. McMahon, Jr.). Faculty dept. journalism Tex. Woman's U., Denton, 1931-70, prof., chmn. dept., 1952-70; writer Tex., nat. newspapers, 1924—. Sponsor, Tex. High Sch. Press Assn., 1952-70. Mem. Denton Civil Service Bd., 1954-58. Bd. dirs., sec. Denton County chpt. A.R.C., 1958-70. Mem. Southwestern Journalism Congress (pres. 1950), Newspaper Advt. Execs. Assn. Presbyn. (deacon). Rotarian. Research Indian depredations of 1860's, also family genealogy. Home: 901 Jessie St Austin TX 78704

RIGSBY, CHESTER L., lawyer; A.B., U. Cin., 1929; LL.B., U. Louisville, 1931, J. D., 1969; m. (wife dec.); 4 children. Admitted to Ky. bar, since practiced in Louisville; asst. atty. Jefferson County; police judge Louisville; pros. atty. Louisville; now chmn. Ky. R.R. Commn. Home: 1927 Newburg Rd Louisville KY 40205 Office: Ky Home Life Bldg Louisville KY 40202

RIGSBY, MARGUERITE LORENE SPIEGLE (MRS. GILBERT L. RIGSBY), librarian; b. Ensley, Ala.; d. Alonzo D. and Lena S. (Higgins) Spiegle; B.S., Auburn U., 1951; postgrad. Peabody Coll., 1965; m. Gilbert L. Rigsby, Apr. 25, 1934; children— Gilbert Lynn, Marguerite Lorene (Mrs. David Gerald Parsons), Charles Owen. Tchr., Cullman County (Ala.) Sch. System, 1931-44, sch. prin., 1944-51; tchr. Cullman City Sch. System, 1952-62; adminstr. Cullman County Pub. Library, 1962—. Bd. dirs. Music Concert Series, 1965-67. Mem. Ala. Library Assn. (chmn. publicity pub. libraries div. 1964-65, sec. div. 1967-68, v.p. div. 1970-71, chmn. membership com.), Cullman Fedn. Garden Clubs (civic project chmn. 1964-65), Ch. Women United (pres. 1967), Cullman County Hist. Assn. (charter), Ala. Writers Conclave, Delta Kappa Gamma (pres. 1962-64), Alpha Beta Alpha. Mem. Christian Ch. (stewardess 1963-64, sec. bd. 1964-65, dir. youth groups 1947-54, choir dir., 1951-68). Club: Green Earth Garden (pres. 1963-65). Home: 212 12th NE Cullman AL 35055 Office: 200 Clark St Cullman AL 35055

RILEY, BOB COWLEY, lt. gov. of Ark., educator; b. Little Rock, Sept. 18, 1924; s. Columbus Allen and Winnie Mae (Craig) R.; B.A., U. Ark., 1950, M.A., 1951, Ed.D., 1957; m. Claudia Zimmerman, May 26, 1956; 1 dau., Megen. Broker, Freeling Ins. Agy., Little Rock, 1951; instr. Little Rock U., 1951-55; prof. history and polit. sci. Ouachita Baptist U., Arkadelphia, Ark., 1955—, chmn. dir. social sci., 1960—, chmn. dept. polit. sci., 1960—; past solicitor fire and casualty ins. Ark. Ins. Dept.; mem. Ark. Ho. of Reps., 1948-50, parliamentarian, 1969—; lt. gov. State of Ark., Little Rock, 1971—. Cons., Mitchellville Community Devel. Project, 1968. Founder, pres. U. Ark. Young Democrats Club; mem. Arkadelphia City Council, 1960-64, fire commr., mayor, 1965-66; del. Dem. Nat. Conf., 1968. Bd. dirs. Internat. Services for Blind. Served with USMCR, 1941-45; PTO. Recipient Distinguished Service award Ark. Municipal League. Mem. Am. Polit. Sci. Assn., Nat. Council Social Studies, Am. Assn. U. Profs., Am. Inst. Parliamentarians, Blinded Vets. Assn. (Nat. Achievement award 1963), D.A.V., Blue Key, Phi Eta Sigma, Phi Alpha Theta, Phi Delta Kappa, Psi Chi, Alpha Phi Omega, Sigma Chi. Baptist. K.P., Eagle, Moose, Rotarian, Knights Korassan. Author: They Never Came Back, 1959; The Party that Almost Was, 1960; The Reorganization of the Arkansas State Legislature, 1969. Home: 1076 Presidents Circle Arkadelphia AR 71293 Office: State Capitol Room 300 Little Rock AR

RILEY, FAY CARPENTER (MRS. ROBERT LAFAYETTE RILEY), educator; b. Plant City, Fla.; d. Miles Jonathan and Missouri Jane (Brown) Carpenter; extension student U. Fla., 1931-35; B.S., Fla. So. U., 1941, M.A., 1947; m. Robert Lafayette Riley, June 24, 1923; 1 son, Robert Lafayette. Tchr. elementary pub. schs., Hillsborough County, Fla., 1921-26, prin. Keysville Elementary Sch., 1930-36, tchr. English, speech secondary schs., 1941-51; tchr. Twin Lakes Elementary Sch., Tampa, 1951-55, asst. prin., 1955-68; prin. Citrus Park Sch., Tampa, 1968—. Mem. Am. Assn. U. Women (pres. Tampa br., 1st v.p. Fla. div.), Hillsborough County Elementary Sch. Prins. Assn. (sec. 1962-63), Nat., Fla., Hillsborough County edn. assns., Nat., Fla. prins. assns., Internat. Platform Assn., Am. Legion Aux., Kappa Delta Pi (v.p. 1967-68, pres. Tampa Bay alumni chpt. 1968, counselor alumni chpt. 1970-72). Baptist. Contbr. articles to profl. jours. Contbr. poetry to anthology. Home: 10505 Lake Carroll Way Tampa FL 33618

RILEY, JEANNIE C. STEPHENSON (MRS. MITCHELL E. RILEY), vocalist, entertainer; b. Stamford, Tex., Oct. 19, 1945; d. Oscar W. and Nora (Moore) Stephenson; grad. high sch., Anson, Tex.; m. Mitchell E. Riley, Dec. 20, 1963; 1 dau., Kim Michelle. Vocalist, recording artist popular music; TV appearances include Bob Hope, Hollywood Palace, Joey Bishop, Am. Bandstand, Happening '68, Upbeat, Top of Pops (Eng.) shows. Rec. Harper Valley P.T.A. voted no. 2 single, recipient gold record Recording Industry Assn. Am., 1968, also recipient gold record for Harper Valley P.T.A. Album, 1968; Harper Valley P.T.A. voted no. 1 Country and Western single Country Music Assn., 1968; voted most promising female vocalist pop field Record World Poll, 1968 and Cash Box Poll, 1968; recipient Gold Cartridge award. Mem. Country Music Assn., Nat. Acad. Rec. Arts and Scis. Address: 806 16th Av S Nashville TN 37203

RILEY, JOHN ROBERT, utility co. exec.; b. Dunn, N.C., July 5, 1913; s. John Manley and Mona (Phillips) R.; grad. in journalism, U. N.C., 1933; m. Neta Lee Townsend, Mar. 10, 1945; children—John Randolph, Lewis Cooper, Neta Vernessa. Reporter, Dunn Dispatch, 1932-33; editor, The Graphic, Nashville, N.C., 1933-37; capital reporter, columnist, Sunday editor The News and Observer, 1937-50; prof. journalism U. N.C., 1950-51, also bd. govs. U. Press and faculty mem. Publs. Bd.; joined Carolina Power & Light Co., Raleigh, N.C., 1951, publicity dir., 1951-63, asst. dir., pub. relations dept., 1963-64, v.p. pub. affairs, 1964—. Pres., Raleigh Concert Music Assn., 1958-60; pres. Wake County Tb Assn., 1958-60. Bd. dirs. So. States Indsl. Council. Served to maj. USMCR, 1942-46; PTO. Mem. U.S. C. of C. (agrl. com.), Nat. Assn. Mfrs. (pub. affairs com.). Club: Raleigh Executives (pres. 1961-62). Mem. Christian Ch. (bd. chmn. 1960-61; tchr. Sunday sch. 1946-69; elder). Home: 611 Smedes Pl Raleigh NC 27605 Office: 336 Fayetteville St Raleigh NC 27602

RILEY, JOSEPH (JOE) PATRICK, ins. co. exec.; b. Charleston, S.C., Apr. 11, 1912; s. Andrew J. and Mary (Oliver) R.; student U. S.C., 1932; LL.D., The Citadel, 1966; m. Helen Schachte, Nov. 1939; children— Joseph P., Suzanne (Mrs. Keith Emge), Mary (Mrs. Chambers), Jane (Mrs. Gerard S. Stelling). Salesman Investor syndicate Co., Charleston, 1933; agt. Life Ins. Co. Va., Charleston, 1934-37; pres. Joseph P. Riley Real Estate & Ins. Co., Charleston, 1937—; pres. Cooper Corp., Charleston, 1954—, East Oak Forest Corp., Charleston, 1948—; dir. First Fed. Savs. & Loan Assn., Charleston; mem. adv. bd. Citizens & So. Nat. Bank of S.C., Charleston, 1945—. Chmn. Charleston Municipal Auditorium Dedication Week, 1968, Charleston Tricentennial Parade Com., 1970, chmn. fund drives United Fund, 1955, Cancer Crusade, 1965; chmn. Azalea Fest., Inc., 1949—; treas. St. Francis Hosp. Devel. Found., 1965—; mem. Charleston Devel. Bd., 1950-70, Commandants Adv. Council on Nav. Affairs, 6th Nav. Dist., 1960—, Citadel Ednl. Found., 1954—, German Friendly Soc., 1935—, Hibernian Soc. Charleston, 1934—, study com. Nat. Naval Mus.; organizer, permanent sec. Mendel Rivers Monument Com., 1971—. Mgr., treas. campaigns Mendel Rivers for Congress, 1939-71. Bd. dirs. S.C. Port Authority, Coll. of Charleston Found., also chmn. fund-raising com.; bd. dirs. Merchants Housing Corp. of Charleston County, A.R.C., Coastal Carolina council Boy Scouts Am., Found. Modern Liquor Regulations and Controls. Recipient Meritorious Pub. Service citation Sec. Navy, 1968, Navy League award, 1966. Mem. Charleston (chmn. urban redevel. com. 1945—), S.C., U.S. (bd. dirs. 1954-58) chambers commerce, U.S. Navy League (bd. dirs.), New Eng. Soc., S.C. Soc., Charleston County Navy League (pres.), Charleston Bd. Ins. Underwriters, Charleston Bd. Realtors, S.C. Assn. Ins. and Casualty Underwriters, S.C. Bldg. and Loan Assn., (chmn. 9th dist. legis. com.). Lion, K.C. Clubs: Charleston Yacht, Charleston Propeller. Home: 74 Murray Blvd Charleston SC 29401 Office: 13 Broad St Charleston SC 29401

RILEY, JULIUS ELWOOD, hosp. adminstr.; b. Sayre, Okla., Dec. 12, 1918; s. Aubrey Ivan and Mattie May (Davis) R.; B.S. in Edn., U. Okla., 1947, M.Ed., 1954; m. Wanda Marie Inman, July 21, 1940; children— Gary Benton, Peggy Lynne, (Mrs. Larry Gene Girton). Prin. South Side High Sch., Elmer, Okla., 1946-49; supt. schs., 1949-53; supt. schs. Gotebo (Okla.) High Sch., 1953-57; dist. rep. Nat. Educators Life Ins. Co., Fort Worth, 1957; supt. schs. Shattuck, Okla., 1958-60; admistr. Newman Meml. Hosp., Shattuck, Okla., 1960—. Mem. State Okla. Textbook Commn., 1958-60; mem. Okla. High Sch. Athletic Assn. Bd. Control, 1958-60; mem. govs. adv. bd. Okla. Dept. Pub. Health for Okla. Nursing Homes, 1964-70. Precinct chmn. Democratic Party, Shattuck, Okla., 1960-67. Served with USNR, 1944-46. Mem. Jackson County Sch. Mens Assn. (pres. 1952), Okla. Hosp. Assn. (v.p. 1969-70, pres. 1971-72), Am. Coll. Hosp. Adminstrs., Purchasing Agts. Am. (asso.), Am. Hosp. Assn., Shattuck C. of C. (pres. 1960), Am. Legion, Phi Delta Kappa. Methodist. Mason; mem. Order Eastern Star; Lion. Home: 605 E 7th St Shattuck OK 73858 Office: 919 S Main St Shattuck OK 73858

RILEY, MAX LEROY, oil co. exec.; b. Shamrock, Okla., Apr. 10, 1917; s. Fred Leroy and Mae (McIlroy) R.; B.S., U. Okla., 1940; m. Maxine Koelling, July 3, 1938; 1 son, Max Leroy. Petroleum engr. Anco Gas Corp., Palestine, Tex., 1940-47; chief engr. S.W. Gas Producing Co., Monroe, La., 1947-49, chief engr., asst. mgr., 1949-54, v.p., gen. mgr., 1954-66, exec. v.p., 1966-71, pres., 1971—, also dir.; pres. Commonwealth Gas Corp., N.Y.C., Monla Gas Co., Inc., Monroe, Carbons Consol., Inc., Monroe, Ouachita Nat. Bank, Monroe, Natural Gas Processors Assn. Mem. natural gas com. Monroe Utilities Commn. Pres., Twin Cities YMCA, 1955-56, chmn. bldg. fund campaign, 1966-67; Monroe area chmn. United Givers Fund Campaign, 1967; mem. biracial com. sch. affairs, 1971. Bd. dirs. YMCA, Monroe, 1957-57, 60-62. Recipient award B'nai B'rith, Monroe, 1958. Mem. Am. Petroleum Inst., Am. Inst. Mining, Metall. and Petroleum Engrs., Monroe C. of C. (v.p. 1965-67, dir. 1956-58, 65-67). Mem. Ch. of Christ (elder 1967—). Home: 1306 Speed Av Monroe LA71201 Office: 1309 Louisville Av Monroe LA 72101

RILEY, WILLIAM WHITCOMB, pipe co. exec.; b. Tyler, Tex., May 28, 1932; s. Eugene Benton and Cathelene (Porter) B.; A.A., summa cum laude, Tyler Jr. Coll., 1968; B.B.A., East Tex. U., 1970; m. Mary Kathryn Malone, Mar. 30, 1950; children—Laura Ann, William Benton, Melissa Lynn, Kevin Lee. Store mgr., Butler, Inc., Atlanta, 1951-56; sales rep., Armour and Co., Ft. Worth, 1956-58; dir. purchasing inventory control Tyler Pipe Industries, 1958—. Mem. Am. Foundrymen's Soc., Am. Prodn. and Inventory Control Soc., Alpha Chi. Home: 8237 Columbia Dr Tyler TX 75701 Office: PO Box 2027 Tyler TX 75701

RING, ALFRED A., economist. Formerly chmn. dept. real estate and urban land studies U. Fla.; now with Noram Secured Income N.V. (Netherlands); economist Zinder Assos., Washington. Mem. adv. bd. Brit. Am. Investment Fund. Bd. dirs. Long Cove Point Assn. Mem. Fla. Assn. Realtors (life), Am. Inst. Real Estate Appraisers, Soc. Real Estate Appraisers. Author: Valuation of Real Estate, 2d edit., 1970; Real Estate Principles and Practices, 7th edit., 1972; Real Estate Questions and Problems, 3d edit., 1972; Real Estate Study Guide, 1969. Home: 1717 NW 23d Blvd Gainesville FL 32601

RINGEL, FRED MORTON, lawyer; b. Brunswick, Ga., July 19, 1929; s. Phil S. and Louise (Pfeiffer) R.; A.B., U. Ga., 1950; LL.B magna cum laude, Harvard, 1955; m. Toby Markowitz, Mar. 18, 1962; children— Andrew Franklin, Douglas Eric, Michael Stanley. Research asst. Am. Law Inst., Columbia Law Sch., N.Y.C., 1955-56; admitted to Fla. bar, 1955; asso. firm Carvath, Swaine & Moore, N.Y.C., 1956-59; atty. W. R. Grace & Co., N.Y.C., 1959-60; mem. firm Rogers, Towers, Bailey, Jones & Gay, Jacksonville, Fla., 1961—. Bd. govs. Fla. Nature Conservancy, 1962-69; exec. bd. Duval County Audubon Soc., 1965-69. Served to lt. USAF, 1951-53. Mem. Am., Ga., N.Y. bar assns., Fla. Bar, Phi Beta Kappa. Contbr. articles to profl. jours. Home: 4478 Craven Rd W Jacksonville FL 32217 Office: Fla Title Bldg Jacksonville FL 32202

RINGER, BARBARA ALICE, lawyer, govt. ofcl.; b. Lafayette, Ind., May 29, 1925; d. William Raimond and Gladys (Wells) Ringer; A.B. with distinction, George Washington U., 1945, M.A., 1947; LL.B., Columbia, 1949. Admitted to D.C. bar, 1949, U.S. Ct. Appeals bar, 1949, U.S. Supreme Ct. bar, 1968; examiner U.S. Copyright Office, Washington, 1949-51, head renewal and assignment sect. exam. div., 1951-56, asst. chief exam. div., 1956-60, acting chief, 1960-61, chief, 1961-63; asst. register copyrights for examining, 1963-66, asst. register copyrights, 1966—; on leave as dir. copyright div. UNESCO, Paris, France, 1972—; adj. prof. law Georgetown U., Washington, 1964-72. Recipient Library of Congress Superior Accomplishment award, 1951, Superior Service award, 1958; William A. Jump Meritorious award for achievement in pub. adminstrn., 1958. Mem. Am., Fed., D.C. bar assns., Am. Assn. U. Women, Copyright Soc. U.S. Author: Bibliography of Design Protection, 1955; Renewal of Copyright, 1960; Unauthorized Duplication of Sound Recordings, 1960; Notice of Copyright, 1960; Copyrights, 1963, rev., 1965. Contbr. articles to profl. publs. Home: 6 rue Eugene Delacroix Paris 16 France also 5102 Fairglen Lane Chevy Chase MD 20015

RINGOLD, ANTHONY FORMAN, lawyer; b. Tulsa, Aug. 6, 1931; s. Murray and Ida (Forman) R.; A.B., U. Mich., 1953, LL.B., 1955; M.A., U. Tulsa, 1972; m. Francine Leffler, June 7, 1955; children—Leslie Beth, John Stephen, James Andrew, Suzanne. Admitted to Okla. bar, 1955; practice law, Tulsa, 1957—; mem. Rosenstein, Livingston, Fist & Ringold, 1965—; sec., dir. CCI Corp., Tulsa, 1958-71; Selco, Ins., Tulsa, 1970—. Adj. prof. law U. Tulsa, 1960—. Counsel, bd. dirs. Planned Parenthood Assn. Tulsa, 1963—. Served with inf. AUS, 1955-57. Mem. Am., Okla., Tulsa County bar assns. Home: 122 E 25th St Tulsa OK 74114 Office: McFarlin Bldg Tulsa OK 74103

RINHART, FLOYD LINCOLN, author; b. Newark, N.J. Sept. 24, 1915; s. William Edward, Sr. and Elizabeth (Nodwell) R.; student Randolph Macon Coll., 1931-33; m. Marion Rebecca Hutchinson, Mar. 3, 1935; children— Joan (Mrs. Bernard N. Johnson), George Robert. With Lindsley Lumber Co., Miami, Fla., 1949-65, sales mgr., 1952-65; author, Melbourne Beach, Fla., 1963—. Cons. Am. pioneer photography, 1967—. Mem. Royal Photog. Soc. (London). Author: American Daguerreian Art, 1967; American Miniature Case Art, 1969; America's Affluent Age, 1971. Contbg. editor New Daguerreian Jour., 1971—. Home: Route 3 Box 340 Melbourne Beach FL 32951

RINK, JOHN FELIX, publ. co. exec.; b. Salisburg, N.C., Feb. 7, 1927; s. Hillery Hudson and Carrie (Fleming) R.; B.A., Catawba, Coll., 1949; m. Emily Anne Honeycutt, Aug. 14, 1949; children— Jennifer Anne, John Felix. With Post Publ. Co., Salisbury, N.C., 1943—, gen. mgr., 1968-70, gen. mgr., 1971—. Active Heart Fund, United Fund. Served with USNR, 1945-46. Named Lion of Year, 1969. Mem. Mid-Atlantic Circulation Mgrs. Assn. (pres. 1967-68), So. Newspaper Pubs. Assn., So. Prodn. Program. Democrat. Methodist. Lion (bd. dirs.), Elk. Home: 203 Maupin Av Salisbury NC 28144 Office: 131 W Innes St Salisbury NC 28144

RINKER, RICHARD NEWTON, clergyman; b. New Britain, Conn., Feb. 17, 1929; s. William Melvin and Helen Dorothy (Dix) R.; B.A., U. Conn., 1952; M.Div., Hartford Theol. Sem., 1955; m. Edna Jane Glidden, Aug. 22, 1953; children—Mark Craig, Cindy Jane, Sharon Jeanne. Pastor Bloomfield Congl. Ch., Pitts., 1955-59; minister of Christian edn. Pa. Conf. Congl. Christian Chs., Milroy, 1959-62, So. Conf. United Ch. Christ, Burlington, N.C., 1962—. Author: East Burlap Parables, 1969. Home: Route 7 Box 46DDD Burlington NC 27215 Office: PO Box 2410 Burlington NC 27215

RINTA, EUGENE FRIDOLPH, C. of C. council exec.; b. Fairport Harbor, O., Oct. 7, 1912; s. Michael and Maria (Saari) R.; B.S., Ohio U., 1938; m. Saga H. Lindberg, Dec. 18, 1946; children—Kerstin G., Karen M., Michael K. Spl. agt. FBI, Atlanta, N.Y.C., Cleve., Washington, 1938-46; fiscal analyst Council State C. of C., Washington, 1949-52, research dir., 1953-59, exec. dir., 1959—; dir. Vega Precision Labs. Inc.; also writer fed.-fiscal affairs. Mem. Nat. Tax Assn., Govt. Research Assn., Soc. Former Spl. Agts. FBI, Ohio U. Alumni Assn. (dir., nat. pres.), Beta Theta Pi. Lutheran. Home: 113 River Forest Lane Washington DC 20022 Office: 1028 Connecticut Av NW Washington DC 20036

RIOPELLE, ARTHUR JEAN, psychologist, educator; b. Thorp, Wis., Apr. 22, 1920; s. Wilfred G. and Ann Marie (Schroeder) R.; B.S., U. Wis., 1941, M.S., 1948, Ph.D., 1950; m. Mary Jane Astell, May 2, 1942; children—Mary Ann, James, Jean. Asst. prof., asso. prof. Emory U., 1950-57; dir. psychology div. U.S. Army Med. Research Lab., Ft. Knox, Ky., 1957-59; dir. Yerkes Labs. Primate Biology, Orange Park, Fla., 1959-62; dir. Delta Regional Primate Research Center, Tulane U., Covington, La., 1962-72; prof. La. State U., 1972—. Served with AUS, 1942-46. Mem. Am., So. psychol. assns., Am. Physiol. Soc., Soc. for Neurosci., Internat. Primatology Soc., Gerontol. Soc., Am. Inst. for Biol. Sci., A.A.A.S., Am. Assn. Phys. Anthropologists, Am. Assn. for Lab. Animal Sci., Sigma Xi. Home: Riverside Dr Covington LA 70433

RIPANDELLI, JOHN SIMON, actuary; b. N.Y.C., Oct. 1, 1918; s. Francesco and Ida (Gimma) R.; B.A., Columbia, 1940; m. Eleanor Weer Richards, Mar. 4, 1943; children—Carol, Joan, Diane. Cons. actuaries Miles M. Dawson & Son, Inc., N.Y.C., 1941-42; actuarial asst. Jefferson Standard Life Ins. Co., Greensboro, N.C., 1946-51 chief examiner and actuary, Ins. Commrs. Office, Tallahassee, 1953-59, chief actuary, 1965-66; pub. cons. actuary, Tallahassee, 1959-64, 1966—. Served to 1st lt. AUS, 1942-46, ETO. Fellow Conf. Actuaries in Pub. Practice; mem. Casualty Actuarial Soc., Nat. Soc. Pub. Accountants, Fraternal Actuarial Assn., Fla. Consumers Assn. (pres. 1969—), Internat. Assn. Cons. Actuaries, Am. Acad. Actuaries. Elk. Home: 3201 Springdale Dr Tallahasse FL 32303 Office: PO Box 3552 Tallahassee FL 32303

RIPLEY, KENNETH CLAY, physicist; b. Winchester, Ind., Apr. 17, 1904; s. Giles E. and Harriet L. (Marsh) R.; B.M.E., U. Ark., 1927; M.Sc., U. Pitts., 1932; m. Ellen Kearns, Dec. 28, 1949; 1 dau., Margaret M. Asst. engr. Research Labs., Westinghouse Electric & Mfg. Co., 1927-31; instr. machine design Purdue U., 1935; asst. physicist Naval Research Lab., 1936-39; asst. engr., asso. physicist, physicist, research group Bur. Ships, 1939-49; staff, comdr. Joint Task Force ONE (Operation Crossroads), 1946; sr. physicist (fluid dynamics) sci. sect. Bur. Ships, 1949-60; cons. on roll stblzn. of ships John J. McMullen Assoc., Inc., naval architects, N.Y.C.; self-employed fluid mechanics physicist, inventor, 1960—. Mem. Am. Phys. Soc., Tau Beta Pi. Methodist. Author: (with Dr. O.G. Tietiens) Air Resistance of High-Speed Trains and Inter-urban Cars. Home: 3058 Harrison St NW Washington DC 20015

RIPLEY, S(IDNEY) DILLON, D, zoologist, museum dir.; b. N.Y.C., Sept. 20, 1913; s. Louis Arthur and Constance Baillie (Rose) R.; grad. St. Paul's Sch., 1932; B.A., Yale, 1936, M.A., 1961; Ph.D., Harvard, 1943; D.H.L., Marlboro Coll., 1965, Williams Coll., 1972; D.Sc. (hon.), George Washington U., 1966, Catholic U., 1968, U. Md., 1970; LL.D. (hon.), Dickinson Coll., 1967, Hofstra U., 1968; m. Mary Moncrieffe Livingston, Aug. 18, 1949; children—Julie Dillon, (Mrs. Robert S. Ridgely), Rosemary Livingston, Sylvia McNeill. Staff, Acad. Natural Sci., Phila., 1936-39; vol. asst. Am. Mus. Natural History of N.Y., 1939-40; teaching asst. Harvard, 1941-42; asst. curator bds. Smithsonian Instn., Washington, 1942, sec., 1964—; lectr., asso. curator Yale, 1946-52, asst. prof., 1949-55, curator, 1952-64, asso. prof. zoology, 1955-61, prof. biology, 1961-64; expdns. to South Pacific, S.E. Asia, India, Nepal; dir. Peabody Mus. Natural History, 1959-64. Dir. Am. Security & Trust Co. Trustee Henry Francis du Pont Winterthur Mus., Conservation Found., White Meml. Found.; pres. Internat. Council of Bird Preservation; bd. dirs. World Wildlife Fund. Served as civilian with OSS, 1942-45. Decorated Order White Elephant, Freedom Medal (Thailand). Fulbright fellow, 1950, Guggenheim fellow, 1954; NSF fellow, 1954; recipient Gold medal N.Y. Zool. Soc., Royal Zool. Soc. Antwerp. Fellow A.A.A.S., Nat. Acad. Scis., Am. Ornithologists Union, Zool. Soc. India; mem. Council Fgn. Relations, Am. Naturalists Soc., Brit. Ornithol. Union, French (corr.), Argentine (corr.), S. African, New Zealand, Copper ornithol. socs., Soc. Systematic Zoology, Bombay Natural History Soc., Soc. Study Evolution, Wilson Soc., Internat. Wild Waterfowl Assn., Sigma Xi. Author: Trail of the Money Bird, 1942; Search for the Spiny Babbler, 1952; A Paddling of Ducks, 1957; (with L. Scribner) Ornithological Books in Yale Library; Synopsis Birds Indian and Pakistan, 1961; Land and Wildlife of Tropical Asia, 1964; (with Salim Ali) A Handbook of Indian Birds, 6 vols., 1968—; The Sacred Grove, 1969. Home: 2324 Massachusetts Av NW Washington DC 20008 also Litchfield CT 06759

RIPLEY, THOMAS HUNTINGTON, govt. ofcl.; b. Bennington, Vt., Nov. 18, 1927; s. Robert M. and Sue (Huntington) R.; B.S., Va. Poly. Inst., 1951, Ph.D., 1958; M.S., U. Mass., 1954; m. Anne Cabel Browning, June 16, 1948; children—Elizabeth, James, Constance. Grad. fellow U. Mass., Amherst, 1951-53; leader research project Mass. Div. Fisheries and Game, Marstons Mills, 1953-56; instr. biology Va. Poly. Inst., Blacksburg, 1956-57; leader research project Va. Commn. Game and Inland Fisheries, Blacksburg, 1957-58; with U.S. Forest Service, 1958-69, asst. dir. Southeastern Forest Expt. Sta., Asheville, N.C., 1965-67, asst. to dept. chief, Washington, 1967-69; dir. Forestry, Fisheries and Wildlife div. TVA, Norris, Tenn., 1969—. Adj. prof. Va. Poly. Inst., Blacksburg, 1965—, Sch. Forestry, N.C. State U., Raleigh, 1964—; mem. curriculum adv. com. Sch. Forestry, U. Fla., Gainesville, 1964—; mem. Pres.'s Recreation Adv. Study Com. on Measurement of Outdoor Recreation, Washington, 1965-68. Served with USNR, 1946-47. Mem. Soc. Am. Foresters, Am. Soc. Range Mgmt., Wildlife Soc., Am. Fisheries Soc., Sigma Xi, Phi Sigma, Alpha Zeta, Phi Kappa Phi, Omicron Delta Kappa. Episcopalian. Home: 7134 Cheshire Dr Knoxville TN 37919 Office: TVA Norris TN 37828

RIPPER, CARL HAROLD, coll. dean; b. Denver, June 14, 1905; s. Karl J. and Jessie L. (Baxter) R.; A.B., Coll. Emporia (Kan.), 1938; M.A., U. Wichita, 1942; Ph.D., State U. Ia., 1951; m. Opal Edith

Wheeler, June 30, 1928; children—Marice, Nadene Richards, Darlene Graves, Joyce Page, Leroy. Ordained to ministry Ch. of Nazarene, 1930; pastor in Colo. and Kan., 1930-42; mem. faculty Bethany Nazarene Coll., Bethany, Okla., 1942—, prof. psychology, 1944-46, dean Coll., 1946-67, academic v.p., 1967—. Mem. dist. bd. orders and relations N.W. Okla. Dist. Ch. of Nazarene, 1950—; treas. Oklahoma Assn. Pub. Trusts, 1964-68; mem. Okla. Commn. Tchr. Edn., 1953-55, planning and rev. com., 1956-58; Pres. Okla. Municipal League, 1960, bd. dirs., 1958-62; pres. Bethany Pub. Works Authority, 1960-69, Bethany Hosp. Trust, 1967-69; mem. Okla. County Library Commn. Councilman, Bethany, 1944, mayor, 1958-68. Mem. Nat., Okla. edn. assns., Assn. Student Teaching, Bethany C. of C., Phi Delta Lambda (nat pres. 1956-60). Kiwanian. Home: 4501 N Willow St Bethany OK 73008

RIPPY, WILSON CRUNK, JR., physician; b. Tampa, Fla., Dec. 11, 1926; s. Wilson Crunk and Ollie (Lankford) R.; student Ga. Sch. Tech., 1944-45, Emory U., 1946-48, B.S., 1949, M.D., 1952; m. Betty Joan Cross, Dec. 22, 1951 (div.); children—Douglas Wilson, Alice Joan, Elizabeth Ann. Intern medicine VA Hosp., Atlanta, 1952-53, resident medicine, 1953-54; asst. resident neurology and psychiatry U. Va. Hosp., Charlottesville, 1954-56; resident child psychiatry N.C. Meml. Hosp., Chapel Hill, 1956-57, fellow child psychiatry, 1957-58; clin. dir. Childrens Psychiat. Unit, Murdoch Center, Butner, N.C., 1958-63; gen. practice child psychiatry, Tampa, Fla., 1963—; clin. asst. prof. child psychiatry U. Fla. Coll. Medicine, 1964—; asst. prof child psychiatry Coll. Medicine, U. South Fla., 1972—; staff Tampa Gen. Hosp., 1964—, St. Joseph Hosp., 1965—; dir. child-adolescent psychiat. service St. Elizabeth Hosp., Tampa. cons. Fla. Div. Vocational Rehab., 1966—, Guidance Center of Hillsborough County, 1966—, MacDill Air Force Hosp., 1966—. Bd. dirs. Hillsborough County Mental Health Assn.; profl. adv. com. MacDonald Found., Tampa; bd. dirs. Donald S. Hendrick Found., Tampa. Served with USNR, 1945-46. Diplomate in psychiatry and child psychiatry Am. Bd. Psychiatry and Neurology. Fellow Am. Acad. Child Psychiatry, Am. Orthopsychiat. Assn.; mem. Am., Fla., Hillsborough County med. assns., Am. Psychiat. Assn., N.Y., N.C., Fla. acads. sci., A.A.A.S., Am. Acad. Polit. and Social Sci., Assn. Advancement Psychotherapy, Fla. Psychiat. Soc. Home: 13518 N Florida Av Tampa FL 33612 Office: 13518 N Florida Av Tampa FL 33612

RIPS, SERGE, econ. cons.; b. Minsk, Russia, Feb. 28, 1907; s. Jack and Raissa (Muravin) R.; student Royal Athenaeum and high course polit. and econ. sci., Antwerp, 1921-27. Came to U.S., 1941, naturalized 1944. Asso. with newspaper Neptune and Midi, Belgium, also mgr. ins. co., 1926-40; employed U.S. Govt., O.W.I., Bd. Econ. Warfare, Fgn. Econ. Adminstrn., 1942-45; econ. adviser to Greece, Washington 1946; adviser to Royal Thai Govt., spl. asst. on wartime financial problems to Ministry of Fgn. Affairs of Thailand, 1947-55; spl. asst. to the Pres. of Haiti, 1955; econ. cons. Washington, 1946—. Decorated officer Order Legion of Honor (France); knight comdr. Order of White Elephant (Thailand); knight comdr. Order Sacred Treasure (Japan); knight of Isabel the Cath. (Spain); knight Order of Crown (Italy); officer Order of Crown (Rumania); Order of Jade, Order of Golden Ear (China). Mem. Siam Soc. (Bangkok), Japan-Am. Soc. Club: Internat. of Washington. Home: 2801 New Mexico Av NW Washington DC 20007

RISENHOOVER, CARMEL CREDILLE, editor, pub.; b. Broken Bow, Okla., June 18, 1936; s. Carmel C. and Viola B. (Simpson) R.; student La. Coll., 1959-61; B.A., Baylor U., 1963, M.A., 1972; m. Rosemary Miller, Aug. 16, 1959; children—Robert Paul, Elizabeth Lynne, John Timothy. Reporter, Jacksonville (Tex.) Daily Progress, 1958; writer KALB-TV, Alexandria, La., 1959-61; news dir., baseball coach Houston Bapt. Coll., 1963-64; asso. pub. relations dir. Bapt. Gen. Conv. Tex., Dallas, 1965-66; dir. pub. relations Baylor U., 1967-71; editor, pub. Am. and Tex. Outdoorsman Mags., Wago, Tex., 1970—. Pres. Risenhoover, Inc., Waco, 1970—, Tex. Outdoorsman, Inc., Waco, 1970—, Pace Sports, Inc., Austin, 1971—. Optimist Boys Football League, Waco. Mem. Pub. Relations Soc. Am., Bapt. Pub. Relations Assn. Republican. Baptist. Home: 720 Dickens St Waco TX 76710 Office: 920 N Valley Mills Waco TX 76710

RISHER, JAMES FRANKLIN, ednl. adminstr.; b. Hampton, S.C., Nov. 26, 1889; s. Julius and Susie (Youmans) R.; B.Sc., The Citadel, 1911, LL.D., 1968; LL.D. Atlanta School Law; m. Ella Ida McTeer, 1915 (dec.); children—James Franklin, Sarah Helen; m. 2d, Emma Jane Varn, Apr. 14, 1926; children—William Rhett, Lanning Parsons, Mary, Eugene Varn. Tchr. pub. schs., Colleton County, S.C., 1911-12; supt. high school, Smoaks, S.C., 1913-14, 17-21, Ehrhardt, S.C., 1922-24; with Carlisle Sch., Bamberg, S.C., 1924-58, instr. until 1928, headmaster, 1928-58; pres. Carlisle Mil. Sch., Bamberg, also Camden (S.C.) Mil. Acad., 1958—. Mem. Bd. Edn. of Colleton County, 1917-21. Served as 1st lt. Co. K, 3d S.C. Inf., N.G., 1912-15; duty in World War with Liberty Loan and War Savs. campaigns, and as speaker and canvasser. Mason (Grand Master of S.C.). K.P. Democrat. Methodist. Inventor submarine escaping apparatus. Home: Bamberg SC 29003

RISINGER, BURTON RONALD, coll. dean; b. Lillie, La., Apr. 7, 1913; s. George Larkin and Louisa Anne (Burton) R.; A.B. cum laude, La. Poly. Inst., 1935; M.B.A., La. State U., advanced grad. student, 1937-40; m. Beatrice Wade, Dec. 31, 1932; children—Burton Ronald, Vance, Troy. Asst. La. State U., 1935- 37; instr., 1937-45; asst. dean Coll. Commerce, 1939-42, purchasing agt., 1942-45; dean Coll. Bus. Adminstrn., La. Tech. U., 1945—, acting bus. mgr., 1947-48; dir. Lincoln Securities Corp., Lincoln Bank & Trust Co.; pres. Ruston Investment Corp. Mem. Beta Alpha Psi, Phi Kappa Phi, Beta Gamma Sigma, Pi Gamma Mu, Omicron Delta Kappa, Delta Sigma Pi, Sigma Iota Epsilon. Democrat. Baptist. Lion. Home: Vienna LA 71270 Office: Tech Station Ruston LA 71270

RISKIND, REUBEN SAUL, banker; b. Eagle Pass, Tex., Mar. 28, 1919; s. Michael and Rachel (Edelstein) R.; student U. Tex. at Austin, 1937-41; m. Esther Swirce, July 6, 1941; children—David Herschel, Miriam Judith, Dan Joel. With M. Riskind, Inc., Eagle Pass, 1945—, v.p., 1945—, pres. subsidiaries The 21 Shop, 1964—, Coed Shop, 1967—; dir. 1st Nat. Bank Eagle Pass. Pres. Internat. Fiesta Assn., 1959-60, Maverick Planned Parenthood, 1969-70; chmn. Tri-County OEO, 1964-66, Jewish Welfare Bd., 1966-70, United Jewish Appeal, 1954-71. Bd. dirs. Maverick County United Fund, 1970-71; mem. bd. Eagle Pass Pub. Housing Commn., 1969-70; chmn. Eagle Pass Planning and Zoning Commn., 1969—. Del. Tex. Democratic Conv., 1960. Served with USAAF, 1941-45: CBI. Mem. Maverick County Hist. Soc., Eagle Pass C. of C. (pres. 1962-63), Sigma Alpha Mu. Democrat. Jewish religion. Home: 1919 Olive St Eagle Pass TX 78852 Office: 364 Main St Eagle Pass TX 78852

RISLEY, BURT LEROY, state ofcl.; b. San Antonio, Nov. 26, 1919; s. Clyde H. and Alice (Dillon) R.; B.B.A., U. Tex., 1948, M.B.A., 1949; postgrad. U. Colo., 1949. Supervisory tng. specialist div. extension U. Tex., Austin, 1950-52; field personnel mgr. Southeastern Drilling Co., Dallas, 1952-53; coordinator adult edn. for petroleum industry Odessa Coll., 1953-54; owner investment co., Austin, 1954-64; mem. Tex. Commn. for Blind, Austin, 1964—. Mem. Nat. Citizens Adv. Com. on Vocational Rehab., 1966-68; mem. Nat. Adv. Com. on Vocational Rehab., 1970—. Served with USAAF, 1940-44. Mem. Nat. Rehab. Assn., Am. Assn. Workers for Blind, Ex-Student's Assn. U. Tex., Blinded Vets. Assn. Clubs: Headliners (Austin); St. Anthony (San Antonio). Home: PO Box 12313 Capitol Station Austin TX 78711 Office: Sam Houston State Office Bldg Austin TX 78701

RISTROPF, PAUL LUCIEN, ret. traffic engr.; b. New Orleans, Sept. 18, 1908; s. Paul and Josephine L. (Meibaum) R.; certificate, Baton Rouge Bus. Coll., 1926; B.E.E., La. State U., 1930; certificate in Traffic Engring., Harvard, 1938; m. Irma Celestine Heard, Sept. 18, 1939; children—Paul L., Robert M., John H. Research engr. New Orleans Pub. Service, Inc., 1931-33; mass transit traffic engr., 1939-40, 47-54; first traffic engr. City New Orleans, 1936-40, 1947; traffic analyst Fed. Works Agy., Washington, 1939; dir. Civil Def. New Orleans, 1950-53; dir. utilities City New Orleans, 1953-65, dir. streets, 1965-71. Founding mem. Met. New Orleans Safety Council. Served with U.S. Army, 1933-36, AUS, 1940-46. Mem. Nat. Inst. Traffic Engrs. (past dir.), Am. Pub. Works Assn. (past dir. New Orleans chpt.), Engrs. Club New Orleans, Tau Beta Pi, Phi Kappa Phi. Roman Catholic. Club: Young Men's Bus. (New Orleans). Author: Army Staff Officers Field Manual 101-15, Traffic Circulation and Control. Home: 3337 De Saix Blvd New Orleans LA 70119

RITCHEY, DAN ARCHIE, JR., realtor, appraiser, insuror, counselor; b. De Ridder, La., Oct. 7, 1917; s. Dan Archie and Lottie (Donlon) R.; student spl. comml. courses U. Southwestern La., 1936-38; grad. Realtors Inst.; m. Cecilia Kelly, Aug. 31, 1941; children—Christine Cecile, Ronald James, Susan Marie. Real estate clk., Lafayette, La., 1935-40; salesman real estate Mike Donton, Realtor, 1947-56; fee appraiser, counselor, Lafayette, 1954—; owner, operator Dan A. Ritchey, Realtor, Insuror, Lafayette, 1956—. Cons. evaluation in condemnation City of Lafayette, also various attys.; mem. Bishop's Adv. Com. Real Estate Evaluation, Lafayette, 1963—; mem. Lafayette Bd. Adjustment for Zoning, 1963—; organizer, 1st chmn. Lafayette Planning Commn., 1953-57. Dir. Civil Def. for 8 La. parishes, 1961-63. Bd. dirs. Cath. Youth Orgn., Lafayette Pub. Bldgs. Corp., United Givers. Served to maj. inf. AUS, 1940-46; ETO. Decorated Bronze Star medal; named Realtor of Yr., Lafayette Bd. Realtors, 1960. Mem. Nat., La. (past pres.), Lafayette bds. realtors, Nat. Assn. Real Estate Bds., La. Realtors Assn. (dir.), Am. Right of Way Assn. (sr.), Nat. Assn. Sr. Ind. Fee Appraisers (pres. Lafayette chpt. 1964-65), Am. Soc. Appraisers (sr.), Mgmt. Inst., La. Nat. Guard Assn. (life, past pres.). Kiwanian (past pres.). Home: 223 Beverly Dr Lafayette LA 70501 Office: 311 W University Av Lafayette LA 70501

RITCHEY, SANFORD JEWELL, educator; b. Columbia, Miss., Feb. 6, 1930; s. Sanford M. and Lillian (Stewart) R.; B.S., La. State U., 1951; M.S., U. Ill., 1956, Ph.D., 1957; m. Elizabeth A. Agnew, Sept. 7, 1957; children—Kenneth, Eric, Julia. Postdoctoral fellow Tex. A. and M. U., College Station, 1957-59, asst. prof., 1959-63; asst. prof. human nutrition and food Va. Polytech. Inst., Blacksburg, 1963-66, prof., head dept., 1966—. Served with AUS, 1951-53. Mem. Inst. Food Technologists, Am. Inst. Nutrition, Am. Chem. Soc., N.Y. Acad. Sci., Am. Home Econ. Assn. Home: 612 Piedmont St Blacksburg VA 24061

RITCHIE, CHARLES WILLIAM, civil engr.; b. Louisville, May 25, 1938; s. William Coleman and Minnie (McCallum) R.; B.C.E., U. Louisville, 1962; m. N. Louise Goad, July 9, 1966; 1 son, Craig Coleman. Design engr. Hazelet & Erdal, cons. engrs., Louisville, 1962-67; chief engring. services Ky. Dept. Mental Health Frankfort, 1967—. Mem. West Point (Ky.) Vol. Fire Dept., 1956-66, sec.-treas. 1958-62. Served with AUS, 1968-69; capt. Res. Decorated Bronze Star medal. Mem. Am., Ky. (corr. sec. 1970-72) socs. civil engrs., Nat., Ky. socs. profl. engrs., Am. Soc. Hosp. Engrs., Am. Concrete Inst. Methodist (trustee 1969—). Home: 209 Pin Oak Pl Frankfort KY 40601 Office: PO Box 678 Frankfort KY 40601

RITCHIE, ERIS ALTON, JR, coll. adminstr.; b. Athens, Ala., Apr. 18, 1935; s. Eris Alton and Mary Ethel (Tackett) R.; B.S. cum laude, Abilene Christian Coll., 1957, M.Ed., 1961; m. Annita Hartsell, July 29, 1960; children—Matthew Eris, Robin Annette. Band dir. Trent (Tex.) Pub. Schs., 1957-59, Cisco (Tex.) Pub. Schs., 1959-68; pub. relations dir., band dir. Cisco Jr. Coll., 1968—, one of 15 bands appearing in Macy's Thanksgiving Day Parade, N.Y.C., 1971. Dir. Cisco Jr. Music Festival, 1960—; adjudicator for band and twirling contests, West, Central, N. Tex., 1965—; dir. summer camp clinics for baton twirlers, drum majs., cheerleaders, girls' drill teams, 1960—. Bd. dirs. Cisco Community Chest. Mem. Cisco Jr. C. of C., Cisco C. of C. (pres. 1970-71, Outstanding Young Citizen award 1964, Outstanding Citizen 1968). Mem. Ch. of Christ. Rotarian. Home: 1307 Park Dr Cisco TX 76437

RITCHIE, REEVES ESTES, utility exec.; b. Amarillo, Tex., July 8, 1914; s. Robert Estes and Mary (Reeves) R.; student bus. adminstrn. U. Ark., 1933-34, George Washington U., 1934-35; m. Gladys M. Cook, Jan. 31, 1936; children—Robert Estes II, Nancy Marie. With Ark. Power & Light Co., Little Rock, 1936—, v.p., dir. personnel, 1960-62, exec. v.p., 1962, pres., 1962—; dir. Middle South Utilities, Inc., Middle South Services, Inc., Systems Fuels, Inc. Mem. Ark. Council on Econ. Edn., Ozark Folk Cultural Center Commn. Bd. dirs. Little Rock Unltd. Progress, Edison Electric Inst.; bd. dirs., past pres. Southeastern Electric Exchange. Mem. Little Rock (dir., past pres.), Ark. (dir., past pres.) chambers commerce. Mem. Christian Ch. Mason (Shriner). Clubs: Little Rock, Capital, Little Rock Country, Pleasant Valley Country (Little Rock); Manhattan, Metropolitan (N.Y.C.); Boston (New Orleans). Home: Westriver Apts Little Rock AR 72202 Office: Ark Power & Light Co 9th and Louisiana Sts Little Rock AR 72203

RITCHIE, ROBERT BROOKE, contracting co. exec.; b. Pitts., July 5, 1918; s. Thomas C. and Elizabeth (Brooke) R.; B.A., Va. Mil. Inst., 1940; m. Irene Gilliam, Mar. 31, 1944; children—Jean Elizabeth, Kathryn Louise, Robert Brooke. Partner, Abbott & Ritchie, gen. contractors, Richmond, Va., 1947-56; owner, mgr. R.B. Ritchie, gen. contractor, Richmond, 1956-62; pres. Contractors, Inc., Richmond, 1962—, Empire Inns, Inc., Richmond, 1966-68, Auctioneers, Inc., 1969—; dir. Va. Preferred Land Ltd., 1970—; exec. v.p. Va. Telecasters, Inc., Richmond, 1966—; owner, mgr. Ace Realty Co., Richmond, 1960—; partner Breezewood Motel, Williamston, N.C., 1967-68; chmn. bd. Peoples Bank of Hanover County, Mechanicsville, Va. Served to lt. col. AUS, 1940-46. Decorated Silver Star medal, Legion of Merit, Bronze Star medal, Purple Heart with oak leaf cluster. Mem. Nat., Va. (dir.) auctioneers assn., Motel Assn. Am., So. InnKeepers Assn., Richmond Bd. Realtors. Home: 600 Pagebrooke Dr RFD 2 Richmond VA 23233 Office: 1400 Patterson Av PO Box 4657 Richmond VA 23229

RITTENBERG, LEON HIRSCH, JR, lawyer; b. New Orleans, May 17, 1934; s. Leon H. and Katherine (Polack) R.; LL.B., Tulane U., 1959; B.S. in Econs., U. Pa., 1956; m. Cynthia Neuwirth, May 30, 1965; children—Leon Hirsch III, Andrew Philip, Babette. Admitted to La. bar, 1959; practiced in New Orleans, 1959—; partner Polack, Rosenberg & Rittenberg, New Orleans, 1964—. C.P.A., La. Mem. La., New Orleans, Am. bar assns., Am. Judicature Soc., U. Pa. Alumni Club La. (pres. 1964—), U. Pa. Alumni Clubs (nat. exec. com.). Jewish religion (v.p. synagogue). Contbr. articles to profl. jours. Home: 5300 Marcia Av New Orleans LA 70124 Office: Hibernia Bank Bldg New Orleans LA 70112

RITTER, JACK FRANCIS, JR., lawyer; b. Austin, Tex., Dec. 19, 1933; s. Jack Francis and (Hulen) R.; B.B.A., U. Tex. at Austin, 1955, LL.B., 1960; m. Mary Carroll, Dec. 30, 1966; 1 dau., Cheryl Ann; children by previous marriage—Diane, Susan. Admitted to Tex. bar, 1960; mem. firm Coffee, marriage—Ritter & Goldston, Austin, 1961-71; owner firm Jack Ritter Jr., Austin, 1971—; v.p. Jack Ritter Sales Co., Austin; dir. Lamar Savs. & Loan Assn., Austin. Mem. Nat. Council YMCA's, 1968-70. Mem. Tex. Ho. of Reps., 1962-63; candidate for U.S. Congress, 10th dist. Tex., 1963. Served to comdr. USNR. Mem. State Bar Tex. (mem. pub. relations com. 1972), Am. (mem. econs. of law practice com. 1972—), Travis County bar assns., Am., Tex. (dir.) trial lawyers assns., Knights of Symphony Austin, Sigma Alpha Epsilon. Episcopalian. Home: 2802 Pecos St Austin TX 78703 Office: Brown Bldg Austin TX 78701

RITTER, JAMES WILLIAM, JR., city ofcl.; b. High Point, N.C., Mar. 22, 1910; s. James William and Maud (Jenkins) R.; student pub. schs.; m. Catherine Luck, Dec. 26, 1939; children—James William III, Ann Robin. Civil engr. Chesapeake & O. Ry., 1929-32, Va. Dept. Hwys., 1935-42, U.S. Engrs., 1942-43, So. Ry., 1943-48; town mgr. Manassas, Va., 1948-51, Marion, Va., 1951-63, Leesburg, Va., 1963—. Mem. Internat. City Mgrs. Assn., C. of C. Baptist. Mason, Kiwanian. Address: Town Hall Leesburg VA 22075

RITZMAN, DEAN FRANKLIN, educator; b. Gratz, Pa., July 25, 1915; s. Joseph Franklin and Ruth Claudine (Pinkterton) R.; B.A. magna cum laude, Franklin and Marshall Coll., 1948; M.A., U. Chgo., 1949; M.S., Columbia, 1967; m. Daisy Evelyn Moore, May 23, 1943; children— Darlene Frances (Mrs. Phillip Craig Oakley), Danny Franklin. Free-lance musician, 1932-41; prof. history Upsala Coll., East Orange, N.J., 1949-69, dir. libraries, 1967-69; dir. learning resources Edison Community Coll., Ft. Myers, Fla., 1969—. Condr. pvt. tours Gettysburg (Pa.) Battlefield, 1953-69. Served with AUS, 1941-45. Recipient citation N.J. Civil War Centennial Commn., Lindback Found. award for distinguished teaching Upsala Coll., 1965. Martin Luther fellow, 1956; faculty fellow Upsala Coll., 1961, 64; service award Upsala Coll. Alumni Assn., 1962. Mem. Am., So. hist. assns., Orgn. Am. Historians, Fla. Assn. Pub. Jr. Colls., Am. Assn. U. Profs., Am. Studies Assn., Fla. Library Assn., Civil War Round Table No. N.J. (founder 1960, pres. 1960-63), Phi Beta Kappa, Phi Alpha Theta, Sigma Gamma Mu, Phi Delta Kappa. Editor: Crossed Flags, publ. Civil War Round Table No. N.J., 1960-66. Contbr. to various publs. Home: 1624 Hanson St Fort Myers FL 33901

RIVENBARK, REMBERT REGINALD, shipbldg. exec.; b. St. Paul, S.C., Sept. 9, 1912; s. Reginald Vernon and Kathleen Frances (Fussell) R.; grad. Goldsboro (N.C.) High Sch.; m. Marie Barbour, July 20, 1932; children—Patricia (Mrs. Dewey H. Pate), Rembert Reginald, Herbert William Barbour. Foreman bottling dept. Coca Cola Bottling Co., New Bern, N.C., 1927-32; with Barbour Boat Works, New Bern, 1932—, successively bookkeeper, office mgr., gen. mgr., v.p., gen. mgr., 1945-57, pres., 1957-71, chmn. bd., 1957—; chmn. bd., pres. Marine Trading Corp., New Bern, 1948—; dir. Ocean Scallops, Inc. Bd. dirs. United Fund. Mem. Am. Boat Builders and Repairers Assn. (pres. 1963), Am. Boat Builders and Engine Mfrs. Assn., N.C. Med. Assn. (hon.), Am. Mgmt. Assn., U.S. C. of C., Am. Ordnance Assn., Crippled Childrens Assn. (life), N.C. Wildlife Assn., N.C. Fisheries Assn. (dir.). Methodist (ofcl. bd., chmn. commn. on stewardship and finance). Mason (Shriner), Elk, Rotarian. Club: East Carolina Yacht (charter). Home: Trent Shores Dr New Bern NC 28560 Office: 522-525 Tryon Palace Dr New Bern NC 28560

RIVENBARK, WILBURN HARLEY, educator; b. Burgaw, N.C., Apr. 11, 1915; s. Wilburn Harley and Scenie Raven (McLendon) R.; student U. Richmond, 1932-33; B.A., Stetson U., 1951, M.A., 1957; m. Nettie Carter Bridges, Oct. 6, 1935; children—Wilburn Harley III, Kenneth Forrest, Patricia Anne, Randi Dianne. Tchr., coach Mary Persons High Sch., Forsyth, Ga., 1951-52, Murphy High Sch., Atlanta, 1953-57, Seabreeze High Sch., Daytona Beach, Fla., 1957-64; prof. Daytona Beach (Fla.) Community Coll., 1963—. Mem. N.E.A., Fla. Assn. Pub. Jr. Colls., Fla. Edn. Assn. Democrat. Baptist. Home: 13 Cobblestone Village Daytona Beach FL 32016

RIVERA, CARLOS, educator; b. El Paso, Tex., Mar. 24, 1916; s. Tomas H. and Maria (Herrera) R.; B.A., U. Tex. at El Paso, 1938, M.A., 1947; diploma Sorbonne U., France, 1946; postgrad. Johns Hopkins U., 1947-48. U. Pa., 1948-49; m. Evangelina Bernal, Jan. 1, 1939; children—Carlos Antonio, Victor Xavier. Tchr. Spanish, Presidio (Tex.). Ind. Schs., 1938-39; tchr. English, Austin (Tex.) pub. schs., 1939-40; chmn. Spanish dept. Bowie High Sch., El Paso, 1940-42; with Censorship Office, Dept. Army, El Paso, 1942-44; instr. fgn. lang. U. Tex. at Austin, 1946-47, Goucher Coll., Balt., 1947-48, U. Pa., Phila., 1948-49; supr., coordinator Spanish and English, El Paso pub. schs., 1950-71; asst. supt. dir. Mexican-Am. edn., 1971-72; West area Supt. El Paso Pub. Schs., 1972—; dir. Bilingual Inst., N.M. Western Coll., summers 1952, 53; dir. Bilingual Inst., N.M. Western Coll., summers 1952, 53; dir. Bilingual Workshops, Tex. Tech. Inst., Lubbock, summers 1954-56; dir. lang. workshop U. Colo., Boulder, summers 1956-58; cons. in bilingual and migrant edn. programs Tex., summers 1959-67, West Tex. Workshop Migrant Edn. program, 1971, Tex. Child Migrant program, 1971. Bd. dirs. El Paso Day Care Nursery, now pres. Served with AUS, 1944-46. Mem. Tex. State Tchrs. Assn., Am. Assn. Tchrs. Spanish and Portuguese, Tchrs. English as Second Lang., Nat. Assn. Arts and Letters, El Paso County Assn. Educators de la Raza (gen. chmn.), Phi Delta Kappa. Roman Catholic. Kiwanian. Author: Para Mis Ninos, 1966, Spanish in Our Times, 1964. Contbng. author manuals, translations from Spanish to English, 1966-67. Home: 3231 Sacramento Av El Paso TX 79930 Office: 100 W Rio Grande St El Paso TX 79999

RIVERA, CARMEN LUCILA, educator; b. Vega Alta, P.R., Aug. 20, 1908; s. Leon and Juanita (Rivas) R.; B.A., U. P.R., 1941; M.A., Fla. State Coll. Women, 1947; D.Philos. and Let., U. Salamanca (Spain), 1963. Tchr. English, field asst. Govt. P.R., 1941-43; interpreter Fed. Govt., Miami, Fla., 1943-44; instr. Spanish, dir. Spanish House, Fla. State U., 1945-52; asst. prof. Spanish U. Rochester, 1952-55; instr. Spanish, dir. Spanish House, Mary Washington Coll., U. Va., 1955-61, asst. prof., 1961-65, asso. prof. 1965-68, prof., 1968—. Recipient 1st Grellet C. Simpson award, 1972. Mem. S. Atlantic Modern Lang. Assn., Modern Lang. Assn., Internat. Assn. Hispanists, Sigma Tau Delta, Sigma Delta Pi, Phi Sigma Iota. Democrat. Roman Catholic. Home: 914 William St Fredericksburg VA 22401 Office: Box 1221 College Sta Fredericksburg VA 22401

RIVERA-BISBAL, MIGUEL A., civil engr.; b. Arecibo, P.R., Feb. 25, 1925; s. Ramon RiveraVinas and Dolores Bisbal; B.S., U. P.R., 1944; M.S., U. Mich., 1946, postgrad. 1957; m. Esther Avila, June 6, 1952; children—James, Frank, Ted. Civil engr. P.R. Health Dept., San Juan, 1946-48, P.R. Aqueduct Authority, 1948-57; project civil engr. Tippetts, Abbett, McCarthy, Stratton, San Juan, 1957-61; environmental engr. U.S. Navy, San Juan, 1961-70; project mgr. Tippetts, Abbett, McCarthy, Stratton, San Juan, 1970—. Instr. civil engring. U. P.R., 1945. Registered profl. engr. P.R., Mich. Fellow Am.

Soc. C.E.; mem. Am. Acad. Environmental Engrs., Colegio de Ingenieros P.R., Phi Kappa Phi. Contbr. profl. jours. Home: 36 Palermo St Rio Piedras PR 00924 Office: Fomento Bldg Hato Rey PR 00919

RIVERA-COLON, LUCAS, constrn. co. exec.; b. Morovis, P.R., 1918; grad. U. P.R., 1940. Controller, asst. sec.-treas. Rexco Industries, Inc., San Juan, P.R.; asst. sec.-treas. P.R. Aggregates Co., Rexach H RH Constrn. Corp., P.R. Marble Industry, Inc., Floor Finishing Co., Canteras Carolina, Inc., Rex Metal Industries, Inc., Tubular Containers, Inc., P.R. Plastic Products Co., Rico P Plastics, Inc., Monteverde Constrn. Co., numerous others. Home: 598 Abolican St Hato Rey PR 00918 Office: 1500 Roosevelt Av San Juan PR 00918*

RIVERS, ARTHUR B., state welfare dir.; b. Mt. Croghan, S.C., Mar. 21, 1898; s. William A. and Roxana (Burch) R.; A.B., Wofford Coll., 1919, L.H.D. (hon.), 1961; m. Ida Maie Stafford, Oct. 2, 1920; 1 son, Robert S. Mcht., planter, 1919-33; adminstr. Chesterfield County (S.C.) Emergency Relief Adminstrn., 1933-35; asst. state procurement officer U.S. Treasury, 1935-42; state dir. Dept. procurement officer U.S. Treasury, 1935-42; dir. S.C. Dept. Pub. Welfare, Columbia, 1942—. Mem. S.C. Ho. of Reps., 1927-30; mayor, Mt. Croghan, 1924-25. Trustee Mt. Croghan High Sch. Dist., 1923-32, Chesterfield County Bd. Edn., 1934-38. Bd. dirs. S.C. Hosp. Service Plan, 1956-57, Carolinas United Red Feather Services, 1952-57, Nat. Publicity Council Health and Welfare, 1954-57, S.C. Health Assn.; ofcl. del. Nat. Conf. Children and Youth, 1950-60; del. White House Conf. Aging, 1961; mem. profl. adv. com. S.C. Soc. Crippled Children and Adults, 1959—; mem. Gov.'s Ofcl. Traffic Safety Adv. Com., Gov.'s Com. Personnel Adminstrn., State Coordinating Com. Coop. Area Manpower Planning System, S.C. Interagy. Council Aging, S.C. Adv, Council Comprehensive Health Planning, S.C. Econ. Opportunity Bds., Inc.; ex-officio mem. S.C. Appalachian Health Policy and Planning Council. Recipient commendation for pub. welfare services S.C. Gen. Assembly, 1962. Mem. S.C. Hosp. Assn. (hon.), S.C. Tb Assn. (mem. bd. 1948-58), Nat. Council State Pub. Assistance, Welfare Adminstrs. (exec. com.), S.C. Conf. Social Work (past pres.), Am. Pub. Welfare Assn. (exec. bd.; 1st v.p.; chmn. welfare policy com. 1955-57; dir. at large 1959-60), S.C. State Employees Assn. (dir. 1949-52, 58-61), Phi Kappa Phi. Democrat. Methodist. Modern Woodman, Lion. Home: 106 S Saluda Av Columbia SC 29205 Office: Rutledge Bldg 1429 Senate St 29201

RIVERS, BILL FLOYD, city ofcl.; b. Powderly, Tex., Oct. 19, 1936; s. Otis Dee and Edith Pearl (Foster) R.; student La. Poly. Inst., 1956-57, U. Southwestern La., 1958-59, U. Tex., 1965-66; m. Nancy Marie Granander, Nov. 25, 1960; 1 dau., Paula Gay. With Rady & Assos., Inc., Ft. Worth, 1964-68; constrn. and design engr. municipal pub. works projects City of Mineral Wells, Tex., 1968—, dir. pub. works, 1968—, asst. city mgr., 1970—. Mem. codes com. N. Central Tex. Council of Govts., 1971—. Bd. dirs. Mineral Wells Girls Club. Served with AUS, 1967-69. Registered profl. engr., Tex., N.M. Mem. Internat. City Mgrs. Assn., Inst. Municipal Engrs., Nat., Tex. socs. profl. engrs., Am., Tex. (chmn. membership com. 1970-71) pub. works assns., Tex. City Mgrs. Assn. Lion. Contbr. articles to profl. jours. Developer computer program for hydraulic analysis. Home: 3402 NE 10th St Mineral Wells TX 76067 Office: PO Box 216 Mineral Wells TX 76067

RIVERS, ERNEST W., lawyer; b. Corbin, Ky., July 31, 1923; student Cumberland Coll.; LL.B., U. Ky., 1951. Admitted to Ky. bar, 1951; atty. Ky. Bd. and Dept. Health, 1951-53; 1st asst. U.S. dist. atty., 1962-65; U.S. dist. atty. for Western Dist. Ky., Louisville, 1965-70; mem. firm Melton and Rivers, Paducah, Ky. Mem. Am., Fed., Ky., Louisville, McCracken County bar assns., Phi Delta Phi. Mem. editorial staff Ky. Law Jour., 1949-51. Office: Suite 234 Katterjohn Bldg Box 1407 Avondale Sta Paducah KY 42001*

RIVERS, ERSKINE HAROLD, clothing co. exec.; b. Gamble Mines, Ala., Dec. 3, 1921; s. Malcolm Lou and Lois (Wiggins) R.; B.A., Birmingham So. Coll., 1950; postgrad. U. Tenn., 1953-54, U. Va., 1957-58; m. Frieda Lee Bonds, Sept. 21, 1946; 1 son, Erskine Harold. With Dun & Bradstreet, Inc., 1946-61, 61-65, mgr., Birmingham, Ala., 1946-51, Knoxville, Tenn., 1952-57, Washington, 1957-61, Raleigh, N.C., 1961, account exec., Phila., 1961-64, Atlanta, 1964-65; loan rev. officer Small Bus. Adminstrn., Washington, 1961; credit mgr. Sewell Mfg. Co., Bremen, Ga., 1965—, dir., 1966—, pres., dir. Sentry Suit Centers Am., Bremen, 1970-72; cons. Exec. Edn., Inc., Decatur, Ga., 1967—. Trustee Bremen Gen. Hosp. Served with USAAF, 1942-45. Decorated Air medal with oak leaf cluster, Purple Heart with oak leaf cluster. Mem. Nat. Assn. Credit Mgmt., V.F.W., Phi Beta Kappa. Methodist. Rotarian (treas. Bremen 1971-72). Home: 517 Knollwood Dr Bremen GA 30110 Office: 113 Atlantic Av Bremen GA 30110

RIVES, ALBERT GORDON, lawyer; b. Birmingham, Ala., Apr. 12, 1901; s. John R.T. and Mamie Lillian (Gordon) R.; LL.B., U. Ala., 1924; m. Hester Maude Burchfield, May 22, 1926 (dec. Aug. 1963); m. 2d, Margaret Gordon Crawford. Asst. dir. athletics U. Ala., 1924; admitted to Ala. bar, 1925, since practiced in Birmingham; sr. partner firm Rives, Peterson, Pettus, Conway & Burge, 1958—. Served to lt. comdr. USNR, World War II. Mem. Am., Ala., Birmingham bar assns., Internat. Assn. Ins. Counsel, S.A.R., Sons Confederate Vets., Ala. Hist. Soc., Phi Alpha Delta, Sigma Chi. Baptist (chmn. bd. trustees). Mason (Shriner). Clubs: Bath and Tennis (Palm Beach, Fla.); Vestavia Country, Relay House, The Club (Birmingham). Home: 3415 Pine Ridge Rd Mountain Brook Birmingham AL 35213 Office: 2121 8th Av N Birmingham AL 35203

RIVES, GREEN, JR., trailer co. exec.; b. Mansfield, La., Sept. 18, 1921; s. Green and Kathleen (Long) R.; B.S. in Bus. Adminstrn., Washington and Lee U., 1942; m. Betty Gordon Smith, May 14, 1948; 1 son, Green III. Chief accountant W. C. Nabors Co., Mansfield, La., 1945-59; treas. Nabors Trailers, Inc., Mansfield, La., 1959-65, v.p., treas., 1965—, also dir.; pres., treas. Bayou Acceptance Corp., Mansfield, La., 1962—; dir. First Nat. Bank, Mansfield, La. Mem. DeSoto Parish exec. com. Democratic party, 1947—. Bd. dirs. DeSoto Hosp. Assn., Mansfield, La., 1947-56, pres., 1949-50. Served with USAAF, 1942-45. Mem. DeSoto Parish C. of C. (pres. 1949). Methodist (mem. ofcl. bd. 1951—). Rotarian. Club: Golf and Country (Mansfield). Home: 104 Julian St Mansfield LA 71052 Office: Mouton St Mansfield LA 71052

RIVES, HARRY CLAYTON, roofing co. exec.; b. Birmingham, Ala., Oct. 8, 1920; s. Harry Monroe and Lena Catherine (Dean) R.; Diploma in Bookkeeping, Southwest Pub. Co., 1939; student Jones Law Sch.; m. Lena Ruth Archibald, Oct. 6, 1945; children—Harriet (Mrs. Larry Brooks), Mollyanna (Mrs. John Schrefer), Clay, Nancy, Jim. Field office mgr. Acme Roofing Co., Montgomery, Ala., 1940-43; sec., treas. Standard Roofing Co., Inc., Montgomery, 1945—. Bd. dirs. South YMCA. Served with C.E., AUS, 1943-45. Methodist (chmn. council ministers 1969-71, mem. ofcl. bd. 1950-71). Lion (chmn. com. 1967-60; treas. 1963, tail twister), Mason. Home: 2406 Hermitage Dr Montgomery AL 36111 Office: 516 N McDonough St Montgomery AL 36102

RIVES, JAMES ALLEN, civil engr.; b. Norfolk, Va., Dec. 16, 1914; s. James Allen and Catherine Holly (Drewry) R.; student Old Dominion U., 1934-36; B.S. in Civil Engring., Va. Poly. Inst., Blacksburg, 1938, M.S. in San. Engring., 1940; m. Ethel Maxine Burks, Sept. 6, 1947; children—James Allen, Frank Burks. Supt. constrn. R.R. Richardson & Assos., Norfolk, 1938-39, 41-42; san. engr. Kellogg Found., Allegan, Mich., 1940; asso. prof. civil and san. engring. Va. Poly. Inst., 1946-51, head dept. san. engring., 1949-51; cons. engr. McGaughy, Marshall & McMillan, Norfolk, 1951—. Past pres. Va. Bd. for Exam. and Certification Architects, Profl. Engrs. and Land Surveyors; past dir. N.E. Zone, Nat. Council State Bds. Engring. Examiners. Sec. Norfolk Democratic Exec. Com., 1969—. Pres. Larchmont-Edgewater Civic League, 1968, Naval Base Little League. Served from ensign to comdr. CEC, USNR, 1942-46. Fellow Am. Soc. C.E. (past pres. Va. sect.); mem. Va. Soc. Profl. Engrs. (past pres., recipient certificate for outstanding service), Va. Water Pollution Control Assn. (past pres.), Am. Pub. Works Assn., Am. Water Works Assn., Solid Wastes Inst., Chi Epsilon, Alpha Phi Omega. Mem. Legion Honor, Order DeMolay; Kiwanian. Contbr. articles profl. jours. Home: 5401 Argall Av Norfolk VA 23508 Office: 220 W Freemason St Norfolk VA 23510

RIVES, RALPH HARDEE, educator; b. Rocky Mount, N.C., Nov. 24, 1930; s. Ralph Cooper and Lossie Day (Hardee) R.; B.S., East Carolina U., 1952, M.A., 1953; Ed.D. in Rhetoric, U. Va., 1960; certificate Oxford U. (Eng.), 1958. Asst. prof. to asso. prof. English, East Carolina U., Greenville, N.C., 1960—. 1st pres. Halifax County (N.C.) Hist. Assn., 1966-71; program chmn. Pitt County (N.C.) Hist. Soc.; v.p. commn. archives and history N.C. ann. conf. United Meth. Ch., 1972—. Served with AUS, 1953-55. John Gilbert Winant Lecture fellow, U.K., 1962. Mem. N.C. Lit. and Hist. Assn., Va. Hist. Soc., Orgn. Am. Historians, Ga., Miss., Nat. hist. socs., Nat. Trust Historic Preservation, N.C. Soc. County and Local Historians, Friends Hist. Edenton, Nash County (N.C.) Hist. Assn., Order Founders and Patriots Am., Soc. of Cincinnati, Soc. of War of 1812 in N.C. (pres. 1971—), English-Speaking Union U.S. (pres. Northeastern N.C. br. 1971—), S.A.R. (pres. N.C. Soc. 1972—), S.C.V., Order Stars and Bars. Republican. Methodist. Contbr. to regional newspapers, profl. jours. A compiler Ency. of World Methodism. Home: 307 W Burnette Av Enfield NC 27823 also Little Longwood 309 Lewis St Greenville NC 27834 Office: Dept English East Carolina U Greenville NC 27834

RIVES, RICHARD TAYLOR (REVZ), judge; b. Montgomery, Ala., Jan. 15, 1895; s. William Henry and Alice Bloodworth (Taylor) R.; student Tulane U., 1911-12; studied law in office of Hill, Hill, Whiting and Stern, Montgomery; LL.D., U. of Notre Dame, South Bend, Ind., 1966; m. Jessie Hall Dougherty, July 23, 1918; children—Richard Taylor, Callie Dougherty Smith. Admitted to Ala. bar, 1914; practice in Montgomery; judge Fifth Circuit, U.S. Ct. of Appeals, 1951-59, chief judge, 1959-60, judge, 1960-66, sr. U.S. circuit judge, 1966—. Del. Democratic Conv., Chgo., 1940. Served in N.G. Mexican Border, 1915-16, served as 1st lt. Signal Corps, A.E.F., 1918-19. Mem. Montgomery (former pres.), Ala. (pres. 1939), Am. bar assns., Am. Legion, Order of Coif (hon.). Presbyn. Mason. Home: 902 Park Av Montgomery AL 36106 Office: Federal Bldg Montgomery AL 36104

RIVKIND, LEONARD MELVIN, lawyer; b. Phila., Sept. 24, 1926; s. Samuel A. and Mae E. (Polishner) R.; B.B.A., U. Miami, 1950, J.D. magna cum laude, 1954, M.L., 1971; m. Hope E. Tanenbaum, June 20, 1948; children—Teri, Mark, Brett. Admitted to Fla. bar, 1954, since practiced in Miami Beach; now partner firm Rosen & Rivkind; spl. asst. state atty.; spl. asst. atty. gen. Chmn. adv. com. to combat pornography City of Miami Beach. Served as sgt. AUS, 1945-47. Mem. Miami Beach Bar Assn. (pres. 1966), Omicron Delta Kappa, Nu Beta Epsilon, Tau Epsilon Phi. Mason. Clubs: Massachusetts of Miami (pres. 1965) (Miami Beach); Optimist (pres. 1961-62). Home: 4180 Nautilus Dr Miami Beach FL 33139 Office: 420 Lincoln Rd Miami Beach FL 33139

RIXSE, CHARLES EVERETT, JR., city ofcl.; b. Little Rock, Sept. 29, 1929; s. Charles E. and Myrtle (Brewer) R.; B.A., U. Ark., 1951; m. Patricia Rawls, May 29, 1948; children—Donna, Sharon, Andra. Reporter, Ark. Democrat, 1953-55, reporter, night city editor Ark. Gazette, 1955-58; mng. editor North Little Rock Times, 1958-60; sales promotion dir., sec. Southland Security Life Ins., 1960-62; mgr. Little Rock Conv. Bur., 1962-65; exec. dir. Hot Springs (Ark.) Conv. Bur., 1965-70; exec. dir. Little Rock City Advt. and Promotion Commn., 1970—, Little Rock Bur. Convs. and Visitors, 1970—, Pulaski Visitors Council, 1970—, Little Rock Conv. Center, 1970—; sec.-treas. Heart of Ark. Travel Assn., 1970—. Served with AUS, 1951-53. Mem. Internat. Assn. Conv. Burs. (dir.), Internat. Assn. Auditorium Mgrs., Am. Soc. Assn. Execs. Home: 12640 Southridge Dr Little Rock AR 72207 Office: 501 Continental Bldg Little Rock AR 72201

RIZK, JAMES VINCENT, television exec.; b. Jacksonville, Fla., Dec. 11, 1928; s. Joseph and Mary (Rahaim) R.; student Jacksonville Jr. Coll., 1952-54; B.S., U. Fla., 1954-56; m. Ruth Mary Seiger, Aug. 22, 1954; children—Donna, Mark, Karen. Accountant, Duval Engring., Jacksonville, 1956-57; controller WFGA-TV, Jacksonville, 1957—. Served with AUS, 1942-52. Roman Catholic. Club: Spa (Jacksonville). Home: 3105 Ila Lane Jacksonville FL 32211 Office: 1070 E Adams St Jacksonville FL 32202

RIZK, JOSEF SALEEM, TV tech. exec.; b. Orlando, Fla., Mar. 24, 1917; s. Saleem K. and Wadeeha (Fatooch) R.; B.E.E., U. Fla., 1940; postgrad. Northwestern U., 1940, Mass. Inst. Tech., 1943; m. Mary V. Rizk, Feb. 8, 1947; 1 dau., Melinda Mary. Chief engr. Gibbs Marine Electronic Lab., Jacksonville, Fla., 1946-47; dir. instns. Inst. Radio and TV, 1947-50; pres. Southeastern Electronics, Inc., 1950-51; tech. dir. sta. WJXT-TV, Jacksonville, 1951—. Cons. U. Fla., 1952-57, Fla. State U., 1952-57. Served from ensign to lt. comdr., 1940-46. Registered profl. engr., Fla. Mem. Fla. Engring. Soc., Nat. Soc. Profl. Engrs., Soc. Am. Mil. Engrs. Home: 5821 San Juan Av Jacksonville FL 32210 Office: 1851 Southampton St Jacksonville FL 32207

RIZK, WADE SALEEM, physician; b. Jacksonville, Fla., Mar. 25, 1903; s. Saleem Kaleel and Wadeeha (Fisher) R.; B.S., Georgetown U., 1927, M.D., 1929; postgrad. radiology U. Pa., 1945-46; m. Lois Greiner, Nov. 3, 1933; children—Roger Wade, Norman Wade, Katherine Wade. Commd. lt. (j.g.) M.C., U.S. Navy, 1929, advanced through grades to comdr., 1943, intern U.S. Naval Hosp. Bklyn., 1929; ret., 1945; resident Louisville Gen. Hosp., 1946-47, Bellevue Hosp., N.Y.C., 1947-48; dir. dept. radiology St. Luke's Hosp., Jacksonville, 1950-60; practice medicine, specializing in radiology, Jacksonville, 1960—; mem. staff Univ. Hosp., Meth. Hosp., Bapt. Hosp., Meml. Hosp., all Jacksonville. Dir. Joe Berg Sci. Seminars for High Sch. Students; pres. N.E. Fla. Regional Sci. Fairs, 1967-68. Diplomate Nat. Bd. Med. Examiners, Am. Bd. Radiology. Fellow Am. Coll. Radiology; mem. Fla. Radiology Soc. (pres. 1969-70), Am. Radium Soc., Radiol. Soc. N.Am., A.M.A., Fla., So. med. assns., Fla. Thoracic Soc., Duval County Med. Soc. (pres. 1966-67), A.A.A.S. Kiwanian (pres. 1959). Club: Ortega School Dad's (pres. 1956-57). Contbr. articles to profl. jours. Home: 3861 Ortega Blvd Jacksonville FL 32210 Office: 1471 San Marco Blvd Jacksonville FL 32207

RIZLEY, ROSS, dist. judge; b. Beaver, Okla., July 5, 1892; s. Robert Martin and Arabella Narcissus (McCown) R.; LL.B., U. Kansas City, 1915; m. Ruby Elaine Seal, June 18, 1916; children— Merriam Elaine, Hortense (Mrs. G. Paul Barrere), Roscoe Quentin, Robert Seal, Leota LaMoyne, Max Devon, Jerry Wallace. Admitted to Okla. bar, 1915, since practiced Oklahoma City; atty., Beaver County, Okla., 1919-20; solicitor P.O. Dept., 1953; asst. sec. agr., 1953-54; chmn. CAB, 1955; now dist. judge Western dist. Okla. Mem. Okla. Senate, 1931-35 mem. 77th-80th Congresses from 8th Okla. dist., 1941-49. Mem. Guymon C. of C. (past dir.), Am., Okla. bar assns. Republican. Methodist. Mason (32 deg., Shriner), Lion. Club: Oklahoma (Oklahoma City). Address: 810 NW 15th St Oklahoma City OK 73106

ROACH, JACK WEDDINGTON, oil co. exec.; b. Guymon, Okla., Apr. 24, 1913; s. Dee and Osie (Hickman) R.; B.S., U. Tex., 1936; m. Betty LeeCason, Nov. 2, 1940; children—Robert Kiernan, James Michael, David Dee, Thomas Lea. With Phillips Petroleum Co., 1936-46; chief project engr. Stanolind Oil and Gas Co., Tulsa, 1946-49, div. gas supt., Ft. Worth, 1949-52; mgr. operations, refinery div. Kerr-McGee Corp., Oklahoma City, 1952-55, mgr. operations operations div., 1955, v.p., asst. to pres. Deep Rock Oil Co. subsidiary, 1955-56, v.p. refinery tech. services, 1956-59, v.p., asst. to pres, Kerr-McGee Corp., Inc., 1959-60, v.p. personnel, 1960-66, v.p. chems., 1966-68, v.p. hydrocarbon devel., 1968—. Mem. Petroleum Club, Am. Soc. M. E., Am. Chem. Soc., Am. Petroleum Inst., Mid-Continent Oil and Gas Assn., Am. Soc. for Personnel Adminstrn., Soc. for Advancement Mgmt., Phi Kappa Psi. Presbyn. Democrat. Lion. Home: 1401 Glenwood St Oklahoma City OK 73116 Office: Kerr-McGee Bldg 133 Robert S Kerr Av Oklahoma City OK 73102

ROACH, THOMAS ALBERT, farmer; b. Deport, Tex., Jan. 2, 1918; s. Thomas Abner and Lillie (Gunter) R.; student Freed-Hardeman Coll., 1936-38, E. Tex. State U., 1943-44; m. Ruby Terry Edwards, Nov. 24, 1938; 1 dau., Terry Ann (Mrs. Robert Nim Voelkle). Farmer, rancher, Paris, Tex., 1939—; chmn. bd. Paris Milling Co. Mem. Tex. Soil and Water Conservation Bd. Bd. dirs. Christian Coll. of S.W. Recipient Tex. Bank & Trust Co. Area award, 1959; Hoblitzelle award for contbn. to advancement of rural life, 1964; named hon. Lone Star farmer, 1960. Mem. Paris C. of C. (past dir.). Mem. Ch. of Christ (elder). Lion. Home: 2940 Abbott Lane Paris TX 75460

ROACH, WILLIAM LESTER, high sch. prin.; b. Ashland, Miss., Aug. 29, 1911; s. Julius P. and Nannie (Kidd) R.; B.S., George Peabody Tchrs. Coll., 1937; M.S., Miss. State Coll., 1945; M.E., U. Miss,, 1953; postgrad. U. Tex., summer 1937, Miss. State U., summer 1970; m. Ethye D. Young, Nov. 21, 1945; children—William Lester, Ruby Nan. Tchr. sci., coach Egypt (Miss.) High Sch., 1937-38, Noxapater (Miss.) High Sch., 1938-41; prin. elementary sch., coach high sch., Carthage, Miss., 1941-42; prin. Columbia (Miss.) Grammer Sch., 1942-46, Brookhaven (Miss.) High Sch., 1946—. Mem. Miss. Accrediting Commn., 1952-58, chmn., 1957-58; chmn. conf. steering com. Big Eight Athletic Conf., 1963—; col. gov.'s staff, 1960-68; mem. Miss. Ednl. Finance Commn., 1972—; mem. supt.'s adv. com. Y-Teens and Hi-Y. Trustee Lincoln County Hosp., 1960—. Recipient Distinguished Profl. Service certificate Nat. Assn. Secondary Sch. Prins., 1957. Mem. Nat., Miss. (chmn. high sch. sect. 1953-54), Brookhaven edn. assns., Big Eight Prins. Orgn, (chmn. 1955-58), Nat. Assn. Secondary Sch. Prins., Miss. Assn. Sch. Adminstrs., Miss. Assn. Secondary Sch. Prins. (chmn. 1957-58), Miss. High Sch. Activities Assn. (sec. dist. 7, 1950—, mem. state council 1966-68, 72—, mem. Miss. exec. com. 1968-72), Henry Boswell Soc. (trustee 1950—. pres. 1954-59), Red Red Rose, Phi Delta Kappa, Kappa Delta Pi. Baptist. Mason (Shriner), Lion (past sec.). Contbr. articles on discipline to profl. jours. Home: 505 Pine Dr Brookhaven MS 39601 Office: High Sch E Monticello St Brookhaven MS 39601

ROACHE, BONNARD ERNEST, constrn. co. exec.; b. Pelzer, S.C., Apr. 25, 1931; s. Ernest Augustus and Lillie Mae (Galloway) R.; student Furman U., 1947-48; B.S., Newberry Coll., 1952; postgrad. Clemson U., 1954-57; m. Linda Locke, Dec. 31, 1971. Tchr. sci. Belton (S.C.) High Sch., 1954-55, Anderson (S.C.) Schs., 1955-59; owner Roache Builders and Williamston Constrn. Co., 1957—; dir. So. Bank & Trust Co. Chmn. Williamston Planning and Devel. Bd., 1970—, Williamston Planning Commn., 1971—. Bd. dirs. Williamston Recreation Center. Served with AUS, 1952-54. Mem. Home Builders Assn. Anderson, Carolinas Assn. Mut. Ins. Agts., Anderson Area C. of C. Home: 1211 Dickens Av Williamston SC 29697 Office: 104 Greenville Dr Williamston SC 29697

ROAF, CLIFTON GEORGE, dentist; b. Pine Bluff, Ark., Feb. 10, 1941; s. Arthur Lee and Charlotte (Boughton) R.; B.S. in Zoology, Mich. State U., 1963; D.D.S., Howard U., 1969; m. Andree Yvonne Layton, July 6, 1963; children—Phoebe, Mary, William, Andrew. Practice dentistry with W.L. Molette, Pine Bluff, 1969—; mem. staff Jefferson Hosp., Pine Bluff, U. Ark. Med. Center, 1971—. Mem. Pine Bluff Planning Commn., 1971—; v.p. Interested Citizens for Voter Registration, 1970—. Mem. Pine Bluff Inter-Faith Council, 1971—; mem. adv. bd. Emergency Sch. Assistance Program, 1971—. Bd. dirs. Jefferson Comprehensive Care Clinic, S.E. Ark. chpt. A.R.C. Mem. Nat., Am. dental assns., Ark. Med., Dental and Pharm. Assn., Alpha Phi Alpha. Home: 3 Bonnie Park Dr Pine Bluff AR 71601 Office: 817 S Cherry St Pine Bluff AR 71601

ROANE, WALTER HOUSTON, geophys. cons.; b. Cleveland County, Okla., Dec. 7, 1902; s. James Henry and Rachael (Henry) R.; B.A., Okla. U., 1929; m. Alta Mae Boyd, July 4, 1931; children—Nina Mae (Mrs. Gerald W. Spotts), Sam Houston, James Boyd, Marvin Dickey (dec.). Chief computer Geophys. Research Corp. (Amerada), 1929-33; computer, Phillips Petroleum Co., 1933-37, party chief, 1937-43, dist. geophysicist, 1943-63, supr., 1951-57, ret., 1963; geophys. cons. Glover Hefner Kennedy Oil Co., Oklahoma City, 1966—. Cons. geophysics Phillips Petroleum Co., others, 1963-66. Precinct chmn. Republican party, 1955-72. Mem. Nat. Soc. Exploration Geophysicists, Oklahoma City Geol. Soc., Nat. Honor Soc. Home: Route 2 Box 326 Norman OK 73069

ROARK, GARLAND, author; b. Groesbeck, Tex., July 26, 1904; s. James and Mona Lee (Davidson) R.; grad. high sch.; m. Leola Burke, Sept. 14, 1939; children—Sharon Leigh (Mrs. David Garland), Wanda Louise (Mrs. James G. Ledbetter). Retail advt., Tex., 1921-46, Chgo., 1929; novelist, 1939—; writer feature hist. articles Houston Chronicle, 1960-64; oil paintings in permanent collection Sam Houston Room, Nacogdoches, Tex. Mem. Tex. Inst. Letters, Colo. Authors League, East Tex. Hist. Assn. Republican. Presbyn. Author: Wake of the Red Witch, 1946; Fair Wind to Java, 1948; Rainbow in the Royals, 1950, Slant of the Wild Wind, 1952; The Wreck of the Running Gale, 1953; Star in the Rigging, 1954; The Outlawed Banner, 1956; The Cruel Cocks, 1957; Tales of the Caribbean, 1959; The Lady and the Deep Blue Sea, 1958; Should the Wind Be Fair, 1960; The Witch of Manga Reva, 1962; The Coin of Contraband, 1964; Bay of Traitors, 1966; Hellfire Jackson, 1966; Angels in Exile, 1967; Drill A Crooked Hole, 1968; (Western novels under pseudonym George Garland) Doubtful Valley, 1951; The Big Dry, 1953; Apache

Warpath, 1959; Bugles and Brass, 1964; The Eye of the Needle, 1970. Address: 1323 N Fredonia St Nacogdoches TX 75961

ROBARDS, FRANK BENJAMIN, JR., banker; b. Henderson, N.C., Dec. 11, 1929; s. Frank Benjamin and Alice Milam (Thomas) R.; B.S., The Citadel, 1951; grad. Stonier Grad. Sch. Banking, Rutgers U., 1965; m. Mildred Kenyon Roberts, Sept. 28, 1957; children—Frank Benjamin III, James Roberts, Mary Kenyon. Asst. trust officer, asst. cashier Citizens & So. Nat. Bank, Augusta, Ga., 1955-62; asst. v.p. Citizens Bank & Trust Co., Henderson, 1962-64, v.p., 1964-66; exec. v.p. Rock Hill Nat. Bank (S.C.), 1966-69, pres., 1969—. Bd. dirs. United Fund, YMCA; trustee Catawaba Acad., Inc., York County Library. Served to capt. USAF, 1951-54; Mem. S.C. Bankers Assn. (dir. 1971—), Assn. Citadel Men, Rock Hill C. of C. Club: Country (Rock Hill). Home: 2057 Eakle Dr Rock Hill SC 29730 Office: PO Box 112 Rock Hill SC 29730

ROBARTS, HARRY JULIAN, indsl. developer; b. Gainesville, Fla., Aug. 17, 1926; s. George Washington and Ruth (Hunter) R.; B.S., Fla. So. Coll., 1949; m. Makonja Helena Faryna, May 25, 1947; 1 son. Scott. Editor, Lake Wales (Fla.) Highlander, 1949; Lake Wales News, 1950-51; sports editor Orlando (Fla.) Star, 1951-54; polit. writer, columnist Tampa (Fla.) Tribune, 1954-61; dir. pub. relations Henry Quednau Advt., Tampa, 1961; dir. pub. relations Hillsborough County Schs., Tampa, 1962; dir. Suwannee River Authority, Live Oak, Fla., 1963; indsl. developer Fla. Dept. Commerce, Tallahassee, 1964—, editor Indsl. Devel. News, 1967—. Free-lance writer, 1950—. Served with USNR, 1944-45. Recipient 2d place award A.P. ann. awards, 1960; 2d pl. award So. Indsl. Devel. Council, 1968. Mem. Tampa Jaycees, Am. Legion, V.F.W., Theta Chi. Elk. Clubs: Havana (Fla.) Golf and Country; Fla. Southern College Press (charter mem., sec. 1946-49) (Lakeland, Fla.). Home: 1015 Browning Dr Tallahassee FL 32303 Office: 107 W Gaines St Tallahassee FL 32304

ROBB, FELIX COMPTON, assn. exec.; b. Birmingham, Ala., Dec. 26, 1914; s. Felix Compton and Ruth (Nicholson) R.; A.B. summa cum laude, Birmingham-So. Coll., 1936; M.A., Vanderbilt U., 1939; student George Peabody Coll., 1939-40; Ed.D., Harvard, 1952; D.Ped., W.Va. Wesleyan Coll., 1968; LL.D., Mercer U., 1968. Tchr. jr. high sch., Irondale, Ala., 1936-37; tchr. Ensley High Sch., Birmingham, 1937-38; instr. English, Birmingham-So. Coll., 1940-42, successively alumni sec., registrar, 1946; asst. to pres. Peabody Coll., 1947-51, acting dir. Library Sch., 1947-48, acting dean coll., 1948-49, asso. prof. higher edn., 1950-53, prof., 1953-66, acting dir. surveys and field services, summer 1951, dean instrn., 1951-61, pres. coll., 1961-66; dir. So Assn. Colls. and Schs., Atlanta, 1966—; coordinator edn. project in Korea, 1956-58. Dir. Carnegie fellowships in teaching, 1950-60, Peabody Bldg. Fund Campaign, 1958; chief staff The Study of Coll. and Univ. Presidency, 1958-60; mem. Tenn. Adv. Council Tchr. Edn. and Certification, 1954-58; case writer Inst. Coll. and Univ. Adminstrs., Harvard, 1955; nat. selection com. Fulbright awards, 1955-57; dir. workshops in TV, ednl. TV program series, Nashville; chmn. gov.'s conf. edn. beyond high sch., 1958; mem. com. specialized personnel Dept. Labor, Tenn. Commn. Human Relations, 1964-66; exec. com. Met. Action Commn., 1965-66; chmn. S.E. Manpower Adv. Com., 1965-68; mem. bd. So. Edn. Reporting Service, 1961-69; pres. So. Council Tchr. Edn., 1956-57; mem. scholarship com. Presser Found.; mem. Cleve. Conf., Higher Edn. Colloquium, Commn. Non-Traditional Study. Served to lt. USNR, 1943-46. Mem. N.Y. So. Soc., Am. Assn. Sch. Adminstrs., Omicron Delta Kappa, Phi Delta Kappa, Kappa Phi Kappa, Pi Gamma Mu, Kappa Alpha, Kappa Delta Pi. Methodist. Rotarian. Home: 2520 Peachtree Rd NW No 216 Atlanta GA 30305 Office: 795 Peachtree St NE Atlanta GA 30308

ROBB, LESTER HARRY, assn. exec.; b. Cin., Dec. 18, 1911; s. Charle F. and Mary (Rigdon) R.; A.B., U. Cin., 1933, M.A., 1935; m. Louise E. Coffey, Oct. 25, 1935; children—Mary Louise (Mrs. Harold V. Tidwell), Pamela (Mrs. Barclay D. Wilson), Charles Lester. Sr. social worker City Cin., 1935-37; dir. Neighborhood Councils for Community Chest and City Cin., 1937-41; exec. sec. Council Community Forces, Chattanooga, 1941-43; exec. sec. Community Chest, Lexington, Ky., 1946-49, Nashville, 1949-54; chief exec. officer United Givers Fund, Nashville, 1954—. Served to lt. USNR, 1943-46. Mem. S.E. Conf. United Funds and Councils (past pres.), Blue Ridge Inst. Community Service Execs. (past pres.), Tenn. Conf. Social Welfare (past pres.), United Community Funds and Councils Am. (bd. dirs. 1962-68). Episcopalian. Rotarian. Home: 308 Walnut Dr Nashville TN 37205 Office: 404 James Robertson Pky Nashville TN 37219

ROBB, ROGER, judge; b. Bellows Falls, Vt., July 7, 1907; s. Charles Henry and Nettie May (George) R.; A.B., Yale, 1928; LL.B., 1931; m. Mary Ernst Cooper, 1932; 1 son, Charles Cooper; m. 2d, Lillian Nordstrom, 1943. Admitted to D.C. bar, 1931; asst. U.S. atty., D.C., 1931-38; practice law, Washington, 1938—; partner Robb, Porter, Kistler & Parkinson, and predecessor firms, 1951-69; judge U.S. Ct. Appeals for D.C., 1969—. Asso. counsel spl. Ho. com. investigate NLRB, 1939-40; counsel AEC Personnel Security Bd., 1954; mem. com. on admissions and grievances U.S. Dist. Ct. for D.C., 1953-69; spl. hearing officer U.S. Dept. Justice, 1956-58. Trustee Legal Aid Agy. D.C., 1960-68, chmn. bd., 1965-67. Fellow Am. Bar Found., Am. Coll. Trial Lawyers; mem. Am., D.C. (v.p., 1953-54) bar assns., Phi Beta Kappa. Clubs: Georgetown, Chevy Chase (Washington); Yale (N.Y.C.). Home: 1700 Hoban Rd Washington DC 20007 Office: US Courthouse Washington DC 20001

ROBBERSON, GUY EDWARD, supt. schs.; b. Gainesville, Tex., Feb. 27, 1917; s. John Wesley and Pearl (Hampton) R.; B.S., Central State Coll., Edmond, Okla., 1938; M.Ed., Okla. State U., 1946; postgrad. Okla. U., 1965; m. Zelda M. Combs, June 1, 1941; children—John Howard, James Kent. Tchr. math., sci., Bixby, Okla., 1938-41; supt. schs., Keystone, Okla., 1941-43, Hydro, Okla., 1946-49, Lindsay, Okla., 1949—; prin., sci. tchr., Bixby, 1943-45. Vice chmn. Black Beaver council Boy Scouts Am., 1968-72, acting chmn., 1972. Served with USNR, 1945-46. Recipient Most Useful Citizen's award Lindsay, Okla., 1956, Distinguished Former Student's award Central State Coll., 1965, Outstanding Service award P.T.A., 1963. Mem. N.E.A. (life), Okla. Edn. Assn. (dir. 1956-58, 61-63), Am., Okla. (dir. 1960-63) assns. sch. adminstrs., Lindsay C. of C. (dir. 1955-67). Methodist (asso. dist. lay leader). Rotarian (past pres.). Home: 923 W Creek St Lindsay OK 73052 Office: 302 SW 8th St Lindsay OK 73052

ROBBIE, JOSEPH, lawyer, profl. football exec.; b. Sisseton, S.D., July 7, 1916; s. Joseph and Jennie (Ready) R.; student No. States Tchrs. Coll., Aberdeen, S.D., 1953-58; A.B., U. S.D., 1943, LL.B., 1946; m. Elizabeth Lyle, Dec. 28, 1942; children—Diane, David, Janet (Mrs. John Glode), Joseph Michael, Deborah, Lynn, Timothy, Brian, Danny, Kevin. Admitted to S.D. bar, 1946; practiced in Mitchell, S.D., 1946-51, Mpls., 1953—; regional counsel OPS, 1951-52, regional dir., 1952-53; founder, pres., gen. mgr. Miami Dolphins, Ltd., profl. football team, 1965—. Asst. prof. econs. Dakota Wesleyan U., 1946-48; debate coach, instr. speech Coll. St. Catherine, 1953-54. Nat. v.p. Am. Lebanese Syrian Assn. Charities, 1964—; chmn. Miami Easter Seal campaign, 1969. Trustee Biscayne Coll.; bd. govs., chmn. budget com. St. Jude Children's Research Hosp., Memphis; bd. dirs. Community Relations Bd., Dade County, Fla., Crippled Children's Soc. Miami. Served with USNR, 1941-45. Decorated Bronze Star medal. Mem. Am. Bar Assn., Am. Judicature Soc., Am. Trial Lawyers Assn. K.C. Home: 339 W Elmwood Pl Minneapolis MN 55419 also 1301 NE 100th St Miami Shores FL Office: 904 Cargill Bldg Northstar Center MN 55402 also 330 Biscayne Blvd Miami FL 33132

ROBBINS, ERIC PATTERSON, physician; b. Wall, Tex., Dec. 12, 1909; s. Guy Thomas and Sara Isabella (Patterson) R.; B.S., U. Miss., 1931; M.D., Vanderbilt U., 1933; m. Celeste Jamerson, Sept. 29, 1949. Rotating intern Nashville Gen. Hosp., 1933-34; with Sayers Clinic, Nashville, 1934-35; asst. resident L.I. Hosp., Boston, 1936-37; with Miss. State Sanatorium, Sanatorium, 1937-39; gen. practice medicine, Brookhaven, Miss., 1939-41; mem. staff Kings Daus. Hosp., Brookhaven. Served with M.C., AUS, 1941-46, 65-66. Presbyn. (deacon 1956—). Mason (Shriner). Address: PO Box 598 Brookhaven MS 39601

ROBBINS, EVELYN WALL (MRS. HOMER ERWIN ROBBINS, JR.), musician; b. Lake City, S.C., Oct. 21, 1914; d. Victor Sterling and Ella Lou (Able) Wall; A.B., Agnes Scott Coll., 1937; m. Homer Erwin Robbins, Jr. Mar. 4, 1950. Asst. voice dept. Agnes Scott Coll., 1937-40; organist, dir. Decatur (Ga.), 1st Bapt. Ch., 1937-40, Meth. Ch., Atlanta, 1940-42; minister music Peachtree Rd. Meth. Ch., Atlanta, 1947-50; organist Larchmont Av. Ch., N.Y.C., 1950, Summerfield Meth. Ch., Port Chester, N.Y., 1951-52, St. John's Meth. Ch., New Rochelle, N.Y., 1952-54; minister music Salem United Ch. of Christ, Allentown, Pa., 1954-67; organist-dir. music St. James Meth. Ch., Atlanta, 1967-71, Druid Hills United Meth. Ch., Atlanta, 1972—; tchr. organ Cedar Crest Coll., Allentown, 1955-58. Mem. Am. Guild Organists (past dean Lehigh Valley chpt.), Meth. Musicians, Atlanta Music Club. Home: 7362 Cardigan Circle NW Atlanta GA 30328

ROBBINS, HARRY COOLIDGE, real estate exec.; b. Blowing Rock, N.C., Jan. 10, 1925; s. Grover Cleveland and Lena (Miller) R.; student Davidson (N.C.) Coll., 1945-46; m. Revalle Byrd, Nov. 20, 1948; children—Wendy Lee, Christopher Brooke, John Kevin, Mark Byrd. Exec. v.p., sec., asst. treas., dir. Carolina Caribbean Corp., Banner Elk, N.C., 1965-70, pres., chief exec. officer, dir., 1970—, chmn. bd., 1971—; pres., chief exec. officer Hound Ears Lodge & Club, Inc., Tweetsie R.R., Inc., Univ. Village, Inc., Carolina Mill & Lumber Co., Inc., Dominican Caribbean Corp. Crusade chmn. Am. Cancer Soc., 1971. Trustee Blowing Rock Hosp.; bd. visitors Davidson Coll., Appalachian State U., Lees McRae Coll. Served with USNR, 1942-45. Clubs: Bal Harbour; Hound Ears (Blowing Rock); Indian Creek Country (Miami, Fla.); Blowing Rock Country; Carolina Caribbean (Banner Elk). Home: Meadow Lane Blowing Rock NC 28605 also 228 Bal Cross Dr Bal Harbour FL 33154 Office: Box 227 Banner Elk NC 28604

ROBBINS, JAMES ARTHUR, assn. exec.; b. Mohawk, N.Y., Apr. 23, 1908; s. Arthur G. and Mary (McGovern) R.; student Syracuse U., 1928-29; B.C.S., Columbus U., 1947; m. Casilda Trujillo, Aug. 19, 1969; 1 son, Arthur G. Clk., A.A.A., 1933-38; chief accounting systems and procedures PHA, 1946-48, spl. asst. to comptroller, 1948-50; asst. dir. internal audit Gen. Services Adminstrn., 1950-52; chief internal audit Dept. Army, 1952-56, asst. chief for audit operations U.S. Army Audit Agy., 1956-60, dep. chief U.S. Army Audit Agy., 1960-67; ret., 1967 (all Washington); mgmt. cons., 1967-69; exec. dir. Fed. Govt. Accountants Assn., Arlington, Va., 1969—. Hon. mem. faculty Army Command Mgmt. Sch., 1954-67, Army Logistics Mgmt. Sch., 1954-69; research cons. Financial Mgmt. Inst., U.S. Civil Service Commn., 1954-67. Bd. councilors Federal City Coll., 1971—. Served with AUS, 1943-46; ETO. Decorated Purple Heart; recipient Meritorious Civilian Service award Dept. Army, 1961, Exceptional Civilian Service award, 1962. Mem. Fed. Govt. Accountants Assn. (nat. pres. 1961-62, Distinguished Leadership award 1966). Home: 1600 S Eads St Arlington VA 22202 Office: 727 S 23d St Arlington VA 22202

ROBBINS, JERRY HAL, educator; b. De Queen, Ark., Feb. 28, 1939; s. James Hal and Barbara I. (Rogers) R.; B.A. in Math, Hendrix Coll., 1960; M.Ed., U. Ark., 1963, Ed.D., 1966. Tchr. math., music Clinton (Ark.) Pub. Schs., 1960-61; prin. Adrian (Mo.) High Sch., 1961-63; exec. sec. Ark. Sch. Study Council, Fayetteville, 1963-65; mem. faculty U. Miss., University, 1965—, prof. ednl. adminstrn., 1970—, chmn. dept. ednl. adminstrn., 1970—. Mem. C. of C., N.E.A., Miss. Edn. Assn., Am. Assn. Sch. Adminstrs., Council Ednl. Facilities Planners, Nat. Assn. Secondary Sch. Prins., So. Regional Council Ednl. Adminstrn. (pres. 1970-71), Phi Delta Kappa, Kappa Delta Pi. Methodist. Club: Exchange (Oxford, Miss.). Author: (with S.B. Williams, Jr.) Student Activities in the Innovative School, 1969, School Custodian's Handbook, 1970, Administrator's Manual of School Plant Administration, 1970. Home: 216 Colonial Rd Oxford MS 38655 Office: Edn Bldg University MS 38677

ROBBINS, MARVIN RUSSELL, life ins. exec.; b. Rocky Mount, N.C., Jan. 16, 1897; s. Spencer and Mary Lucinda (Worsley) R.; A.B., U. N.C., 1918; m. Marion Erwin Hines, Nov. 14, 1923; 1 dau., Erwin MacEntyre (Mrs. Edward Stephen Blackburn). Field underwriter, also dist. mgr. Mut. Life Ins. Co. of N.Y., 1922—; pres. Rocky Mount TV System, Inc.; dir. Planters Nat. Bank & Trust Co., Citizens Sav. & Loan Assn. Trustee Rocky Mount Sch. Bd., 1930-36; civil def. dir. Rocky Mount, 1950-56. Pres. Robbins Found.; trustee Salem Acad. and Coll., 1952-56, Park View Hosp., 1931—, Braswell Meml. Library, 1940-50; bd. dirs. YMCA, 1927; mem. U.S.S. N.C. Battleship Commn., 1961-65. Cadet, student officer Naval Aviation, USNRFC, 1918; air controller, fleet tng. officer, comdr. USNR, 1941-45. Decorated Medalha de Guerra (Brazil); Cross of Mil. Service, U.D.C.; named Mut. of N.Y. Man of Yr., 1949. Mem. Million Dollar Round Table, Rocky Mount C. of C. (past pres.), So. Soc. N.Y., S.A.R., Am. Legion (past comdr.), Soc. of Cin., Pi Kappa Alpha. Democrat. Presbyn. Mason, Elk, Kiwanian (past pres.). Clubs: Bankers (N.Y.C.); Carolina Cotillion (past pres.), Benvenue Country. Home: 306 S Grace St Rocky Mount NC 27801 Office: Peoples Bank Bldg Rocky Mount NC 27801

ROBBINS, ROBERT MORRILL, hosp. adminstr.; b. Brookline, Mass., Sept. 25, 1918; s. Julius and Rose (Morrill) R.; A.B. cum laude, Harvard, 1940; m. Sascha Newman, Jan. 7, 1942 (div. Apr. 1962); children— Jay N., Patricia C. Vice pres., treas. Globe Plan, Inc., Boston, 1940-58; Fla. corr. James Talcott, Inc. Factors, Miami, 1959-62; v.p. Mill Factors Corp., Miami, 1962-69; pres. Am. Resources Corp., 1969—, Fla. Broadcasting System, Inc., 1970—; exec. dir. Miami Dade Gen. Hosp., 1971—. Served with USNR, 1942-46. Clubs: Harvard (Boston, N.Y.C., Miami). Home: 1408 SE Bayshore Dr Miami FL 33131 Office: 10 Biscayne Blvd Miami FL 33132

ROBBINS, WARREN M., museum curator; b. Worcester, Mass., Sept. 4, 1923; M.A. in History, U. Mich., 1949; B.A. in English, U. N.H., 1945. Tchr. secondary sch. U.S. Dependents Sch. System, Germany, 1949-50; vis. expert U.S. Cultural Program for Germany, USIA, 1950-51; edn. adviser U.S. High Commn. to Austria, USIA, Vienna, 1951-55; cultural officer Southwestern Germany, USIA, 1955-57, consul, pub. affairs officer for Southwest Germany, 1957-58; cultural attache, chief USIS Cultural Program for Germany, Am. embassy, Bonn, 1958-60; mem. staff U.S. Adv. Commn. Ednl. and Cultural Relations, Dept. State, 1960-61, asst. to dep. asst. sec. state for ednl. and cultural relations, 1961-62, course chmn. Fgn. Service Inst., 1962-63; founder, dir. Museum of African Art and Frederick Douglass Inst. Negro Arts and History, Washington, 1963—. Home: 530 6th St SE Washington DC 20003 Office: 316-318 A St NE Washington DC 20002

ROBERSON, ADRIAN L., civil engr., constrn. co. exec.; b. Hornbeak, Tenn., June 24, 1916; s. George S. and Minnie (Deane) R.; B.S., U. Tenn., 1941; m. Elaine Miller, June 22, 1946; children—Patricia Elaine, Len David, Margaret Ann. Pres., Roberson Constrn. Co., Columbia, S.C., 1946—, Indsl. Devel. Corp., Columbia, 1962—, Roberson Internat., Austin, Tex., 1969—. Cons. constrn. engr. Bd. govs. U. Tenn. Served as lt. col. C.E., AUS, 1941-46. Mem. Asso. Gen. Contractors, Columbia Contractors Assn. (past pres.). Club: Sertoma (past dir.). Home: 1728 Bannockburn Dr Columbia SC 29206 Office: 801 Pepper St Columbia SC 29290

ROBERSON, DAVID ALBERT, elec. engr.; b. Etowah, Tenn., Apr. 6, 1921; s. Richard Arthur and Ruth (Walker) R.; B.S., U. Tenn., 1943; m. Elizabeth Mae Allen, Sept. 5, 1943; children—Arliss Jean (Mrs. Robert Harris Turner), David Albert. Elec. engr. Tenn. Eastman Corp., 1943-46, Monsanto Chem. Co., 1946-47, Ebasco Services, Inc., 1947-55; mgr. elec. br. ARO, Inc., Arnold Air Force Sta., Tenn., 1955—. Cons. elec. engring., 1960-64; instr. elec. courses ARO Apprenticeship Sch., 1964-68. Recipient Outstanding Service award Tullahoma Lions club, 1958. Registered profl. engr., N.Y., Tenn., Fla. Mem. I.E.E.E. (Outstanding Service award Middle Tenn. sect. 1961; dir. 1957), U. Tenn. Alumni Assn. (dir. 1962), Nat. (dir. 1967), Tenn. (Outstanding Service award Tullahoma chpt. 1969; pres. 1968; presdl. citation 1970) socs. profl. engrs., Tau Beta Pi, Pi Kappa Phi. Baptist (deacon). Home: 113 Oak Park Circle Tullahoma TN 37388 Office: ARO Inc Arnold Air Force Station TN 37389

ROBERSON, FRED MCRAE, physician; b. Camden, Ark., Apr. 9, 1938; s. Fred Milton and Mary Jane (Gann) R.; B.S., La. Tech. U., 1960; M.D., La. State U., 1964; m. Jo Ellen Talley, July 2, 1960; children—Fred McRae, Jr., Scott Eldred, Mary Catherine. Intern, Confederate Meml. Med. Center, Shreveport, La., 1964-65; practice medicine, specializing in family practice, Vivian, La., 1965, Linden, Tex., 1967—; chief staff Linden Municipal Hosp. Cons., Cass County Family Planning Clinic, 1969—; mem. adviser Cass County Selective Service, 1969—; health officer Cass County, 1970, Linden, 1971—. Served to capt. AUS, 1965-67. Decorated Legion of Merit, Bronze Star, Air Medal with oak leaf cluster. Mem. Linden C. of C. (pres. 1968-69), Cass-Marion Med. Soc. (sec., treas. 1970-71), Tex. (mem. edn. com. 1971—), N.E. Tex. (pres. 1969-72) acads. gen. practice, A.M.A., Am. Acad. Family Physicians, Tex. Med. Assn., Nat. Rifle Assn., Am. Orchid Soc., Kappa Sigma, Phi Chi. Democrat. Baptist. Home: Hwy 59 North Linden TX 75563 Office: PO Box 780 Linden TX 75563

ROBERSON, JAMES HOLLIS, ins. co. exec.; b. Delphos, N.M., June 28, 1922; s. James Lafayette and Lola Mae (Howell) R.; B.S., Florence State Coll., 1950; M.S., Auburn U., 1955; m. Annie Myrl Hendon, Feb. 2, 1944; children—Nancy Myrl (Mrs. John W. Jones), Stefini Lynn (Mrs. Harry E. Greer, III). Ordained to ministry Ch. of Christ, 1941; minister Ch. of Christ, Fritch, Tex., 1944-54; instr. Auburn U., 1954-55, U. Ala., 1955-56; exec. v.p. Cotton States Life Ins. Co., Tuscaloosa, Ala., 1955-62; chief adminstrv. officer TranSouth Life, Dalton, Ga., 1962-65; pres. Atlantic Am. Life Ins. Co., Atlanta, 1965—, also dir.; pres. Apollo Nat. Life Ins. Co., Carbondale, Ill., 1970-71; v.p., dir. Atlantic Am. Corp., Atlanta, 1968—. Vice pres. Tuscaloosa Better Schs., 1960-61. C.L.U. Fellow Life Mgmt. Inst., Life Office Mgmt. Assn.; mem. S.E. Actuarial Club, Tuscaloosa C. of C. (v.p. 1961-62). Mason (32 deg.). Clubs: Civitan (pres. 1962) (Tuscaloosa); Acturial, City (Atlanta). Home: 6755 Wright Rd NE Atlanta GA 30328 Office: 90 Fairlie St NW Atlanta GA 30303

ROBERSON, OPAL FARRIS, govt. ofcl.; b. Batavia, Ark.; d. Thomas Alonzo and Martha Elizabeth (Officer) Farris; student Sam Houston State Tchrs. Coll., 1921-23; m. William Nathan Roberson, Dec. 30, 1942 (dec. 1955). Postmaster Daisetta, Tex., 1925-43, Temple, Tex., 1947—; tchr. pub. schs., Baytown, Tex., 1923-25. Del. equal Employment Opportunity Conf., Washington, 1967, sec. Temple Pub. Library Bd., 1963-71; mem. Temple Indsl. Found., 1965-71, Central Tex. Area Mus. 1964-71; meml. chmn. Am. Cancer Soc., 1963-71; chmn. woman's div. United Fund, bd. dirs., sec., 1960-71. Bd. dirs. Bell County Assn. Retarded Children, 1967-68, Bell County Tb. Assn., U.S.O.; trustee Central Tex. Area Mus. Recipient superior accomplishment award Nat. Assn. Postmasters, 1957, DMAA Distinguished Service award, 1971; named Outstanding Woman of Year, Temple, 1960. Mem. Nat. Assn. Postmasters (exec. com. 1951-54, sec.-treas. Tex. chpt. 1950-71), United Nat. Assn. Post Office Clks. (life), Bus. and Profl. Women's Club (past pres., dist. dir.), City (past pres.), Tex. (chmn. civic improvement com. Capitol Dist. 1967-68) fedns. women's clubs, Temple C. of C. (chmn. women's div. 1970-71), Triangle Forum (pres. 1967-69). Episcopalian (chmn. altar com. 1930-68). Mem Order Eastern Star (past matron). Home: Kyle Hotel Temple TX 76501 Office: PO Box 401 N Main St Temple TX 76501

ROBERT, WILLIAM PAUL, city ofcl.; b. New Orleans, Dec. 30, 1911; s. William Paul and Ella (Nick) R.; student Tulane U., 1929-31; m. Dorris McCarthy, May 4, 1938; children—William P., Lawrence M. Asst. to wharf supt. W.L. Richerson & Sons, Inc., New Orleans, 1938-40, wharf supt., 1940-48; v.p. E.J. McCarthy, Inc., New Orleans, 1948-54; pres. Continental Sheet Metal Co., Inc., New Orleans, 1954-58; aide to mayor New Orleans, 1961-64, exec. sec. to mayor, 1964—. Sec., Affiliated Council Democratic Orgns., 1966—. Clubs: Young Mens Business, New Orleans Athletic. Home: 6844 Canal Blvd New Orleans LA 70124 Office: City Hall New Orleans LA 70112

ROBERTS, AARON GENE, chemist, govt. ofcl.; b. N.Y.C., June 12, 1912; s. Louis Leroy and Fannie (Grodenski) R.; B.S. in Chemistry, U. Richmond, 1933; student Nat. Bur. Standards Grad. Sch., 1947-52; m. Honora Ann Mattare, Nov. 6, 1948; children—Timothy L., Sharon L., Norma A., Maureen L. Chief chemist casing dept. Sylvania Indsl. Corp., Fredericksburg, Va., 1934-41; lab. supr. ordnance dept. War Dept., Radford (Va.) Ordnance Works, 1941-43; project leader organic coatings Nat. Bur. Standards, Washington, 1946-67, phys. scientist, head test method devel. tire systems sect. Office Vehicle Systems Research, 1967-71; mgr. tire dynamics Safety Systems Lab., Research Inst., Nat. Hwy. Traffic Safety Adminstrn., 1971—. Served with USNR, 1943-46. Recipient Bronze Medal award Dept. Commerce, 1967. Mem. Am. Chem. Soc., Am. Soc. Testing and Materials, Washington Paint Tech. Group (pres. 1960-61, hon.). Contbr. articles on organic coatings, adhesion, abrasion resistance to profl. jours. Inventor jet abrader, electronic averaging device, dip-coating device. Author: Organic Coatings-Properties, Selection, and Use. Home: 9711 Braddock Rd Silver Spring MD 20903 Office: Code 43-20 NHTSA Washington DC 20590

ROBERTS, BARON GEORGE, sr. v.p. Liller Neal Battle & Lindsey, Inc. Home: 2170 Street DeVille Atlanta GA 30345 Office: Life of Ga Tower Atlanta GA 30308

ROBERTS, BOB LEE, petroleum engr.; b. Broken Bow, Okla., Oct. 3, 1924; s. John A. and Ruby (Howell) R.; B.S., U. Tulsa, 1953; m. Irene N. Beavers, Aug. 15, 1942; children—John Paul, Kirk Lee, Leah Ann. Project engr. Sunray Oil Corp., 1953-54; project engr. Aurora Gasoline Co., 1954-55; tech. sales rep. Wolverine Tube div. Calumet & Hecla, Inc., 1955-58; mgr. process equipment sales Yuba Heat Transfer Corp., 1958-63; organizer Marfab Co. (formerly Mafab Co.), 1963, v.p., dir., 1963-66, marketing mgr., 1963-69; mgr. engring., prodn. Copes Internat., Inc., Tulsa, 1969—. Served with USMCR, 1943-46. Registered profl. engr., Okla. Mem. Am. Soc. M.E. (power test code com. on air cooled heat transfer equipment 1961—), Am. Inst. Chem. Engrs., Pi Epsilon Tau. Home: Star Route 1 Box 115 B Pryor OK 74361 Office: PO Box 51306 Tulsa OK 74151

ROBERTS, BONNY K., judge; b. Sopchoppy, Fla., Feb. 5, 1907; s. Thomas and Florida (Morrison) R.; LL.B., U. Fla., 1928; LL.D., U. Miami, 1954; m. Mary Newman, Aug. 20, 1937; children—Mary Jane, Thomas Frederick. Admitted to Fla. bar, 1928; practice law, Tallahassee, 1928-49; justice Supreme Ct. Fla., 1949—; chief justice, 1953-54, 61-63, 71-72. Bus. exec., 1928—; past res. Capital Lincoln-Mercury Inc., Shoppicenter, Inc.; v.p. Tallahassee Bank & Trust Co., 1948-49; chmn. Jud. Council of Fla.; mem. Fla. Constn. Revision Com., 1966-67. Mem. bd. counselors Fla. Presbyn. Coll. Mem. Fla. Improvement Commn., 1949; U.S. shipping commr. Port of Jacksonville, 1943-45. Pres. Fla. State U. Found.; past pres. Fla. Heritage Found. Served as lt. comdr. USCG, 1942-45. Recipient Juror award Freedoms Found. Valley Forge, 1962; Distinguished Citizen award Stetson Law Coll., 1962. Mem. Am. (mem. com. internat. jud. cooperation, ofcl. ct. rep. meeting London 1957), Internat., Tallahassee (past pres.), Inter-Am. bar assns., Fla. Bar (past v.p.), Am. Law Inst., Am. Judicature Soc., Newcomen Soc. Eng. in N. Am., Am. Legion, Alpha Kappa Psi, Blue Key, Phi Alpha Delta, Delta Chi. Mason (Shriner), Elk, Odd Fellow, Kiwanian. Home: Meridian Pl Tallahassee FL 32303 Office: Supreme Ct Florida Tallahassee FL 32304

ROBERTS, BRAMLETT, lawyer; b. Oxford, Miss., May 4, 1907; s. William Isaac and Letitia (Wilson) R.; LL.B., U. Miss., 1930; m. Doris Allen, Aug. 9, 1936; children—Pama Lou (Mrs. Charles S. Pendleton), John Charles. Admitted to Miss. bar, 1930; gen. practice Oxford, 1930—; asst. prof. law U. Miss., parttime, 1946-64. Pros. atty. City of Oxford, 1933-60, atty. City of Oxford 1934-37, 56-60. Served with USNR, 1942-45. Mem. Am. Bar Assn., Miss. State Bar. Baptist. Home: 415 Longest Rd Oxford MS 38655 Office: 115 1/2 N Lamar Oxford MS 38655

ROBERTS, BRUCE DAN, data systems exec.; b. Lorain, O., Nov. 22, 1939; s. Dan Norman and Genevieve (Hancock) R.; B.S., St. Lawrence U., 1961; M.Systems Engring., U. Fla., 1966; m. Betsy Bancroft Barratt, Mar. 6, 1965; children—Kenneth Lee, Kathryn Ann. Analyst, Gen. Electric Co., Syracuse, N.Y., 1961-65, reliability engr., Daytona Beach, Fla., 1965-67, systems engr., 1967-69, mgr. engring. information systems and data processing, Cape Canaveral, Fla., 1969-70, mgr. engring. information and data systems, 1970—. Coach, Daytona Beach Cath. Basketball League, 1965-69, 70—, v.p., 1968. Mem. I.E.E.E., Operations Research Soc. Am., Phi Beta Kappa, Sigma Pi Sigma, Sigma Chi, Pi Mu Epsilon. Home: 235 Ormwood Dr Ormond Beach FL 32074 Office: Apollo Park Gen Electric Co PO Box 2500 Daytona Beach FL 32015

ROBERTS, CECIL ALBERT, JR., univ. adminstr., computer co. exec.; b. Waco, Tex., Oct. 17, 1931; s. Cecil Albert and Anna Betty Roberts; B.A., Baylor U., 1953; B.D., Southwestern Sem., 1956, Th.D., 1960; m. Dolores Mae Patterson, Feb. 28, 1953; children—Caren, Camille, Cynthia. Ordained to ministry Baptist Ch., 1956; minister First Bapt. Ch., Altus, Okla., 1957-62, First Bapt. Ch., Tallahassee, 1962-67; postdoctoral vis. scholar Harvard, 1967-68; adminstrv. asst. dept. athletics Rice U., Houston, 1971—; pres. Ch. Systems, Inc., Houston. Cons. Success Motivation Inst., Waco, Tex., 1967-71, Computer Demensions, Inc., Dallas, 1972—. Pres. So. Bapt. Pastor's Conf., 1967. Chaplain Fla. Ho. of Reps., 1962-65. Recipient Gold Key award Fla. State U., 1965; named Tallahassee Man of Year, 1963, Fla. Man of Year, 1964. Mem. Am. Acad. Religion, Am. Assn. U. Profs. Author: This Way To the Cross, 1966; A Life Worth Living, 1966. Home: 2807 W Pebble Beach Missouri City TX 77459 Office: Church Systems Inc 6065 Hillcroft St Houston TX 77036

ROBERTS, CHALMERS MCGEAGH, reporter b. Pitts., Nov. 18, 1910; s.; Franklin B. and Lillian B. (McGeagh) R.; A.B., Amherst Coll., 1933, L.H.D., 1963; m. Lois Hall Roberts, Sept. 11, 1941; children—David H., Patricia E., Christopher C. Reporter, Washington Post, 1933-34; reporter A.P., Pitts. bur., 1934-35, Toledo News-Bee, 1936-38, Japan Times, Tokyo, 1938-39; asst. mng. editor Washington Daily News, 1939-41; Sunday editor Washington Times-Herald, 1941; staff OWI, London, Washington, 1941-43; staff Life mag., 1946-47, Washington Star, 1947-49; with Washington Post, 1949—, reporter local and nat. news, 1949-53, fgn. affairs reporter, 1953-59, chief nat. news, bur., 1959-65, columnist, 1971—. Served from pvt. to capt., USAAF, 1943-46. Recipient Sigma Delta Chi award, 1953; Washington Newspaper Guild nat. news award, 1954, 60; citation Overseas Press Club, 1955; Washington Newspaper Guild Front Page grand prize, 1957, 60; Raymond Clapper Meml. award, 1957. Mem. Am. Newspaper Guild. State Dept. Corrs. Assn. (pres. 1958-59). Club: The International (Washington). Author: Washington Past and Present, 1950; Can We Meet the Russians Half Way 1958. Contbr. articles to popular mags. Home: 6699 MacArthur Blvd Washington DC 20016 Office: 1515 L St Washington DC 20005

ROBERTS, CHARLES TRUMAN, govt. ofcl.; b. Winnsboro, Tex., Apr. 26, 1912; s. Charles Luin and Carrie Jane (Turner) R.; B.A., E. Tex. State Tchrs. Coll., 1936; M.A., U. Colo., 1947; postgrad. summers, U. So. Cal., 1948, Columbia, 1951, 52; Ed.D., U. Tex., 1960; m. Connie Virginia Dickens, May 5, 1937; children—Charles Truman II, Connie Debra. Tchr., Muleshoe (Tex.) Elementary Sch., 1930-34; prin. Quitman (Tex.) Elementary Sch., 1934-37; tchr. Texas City Jr. High Sch., 1937-40; prin. Heights Elementary Sch., Texas City, 1940-46; prin. Robstown (Tex.) High Sch., 1946-49; supt. Wellington (Tex.) Schs., 1949-54; teaching fellow U. Tex., 1954-56; dir. planning Tex. Edn. Agy., Austin, 1956-61; specialist planning Office of Edn., Health, Edn. and Welfare, Washington, 1961-64, dir. statis. systems Nat. Center for Edn. Statistics, 1964—; stock broker, Washington, 1969—. Pres., Ednl. Cons., Washington, 1968—, Computer Credit Systems, Washington, 1969—. Mem. Am. Assn. Sch. Adminstrs., Nat. Council Sch. Planners, N.E.A., Washington Met. Bd. Trade, Austin C. of C., Phi Delta Kappa. Home: 8326 Wagon Wheel Rd Alexandria VA 22309 Office: 400 Maryland Av SW Washington DC 20202

ROBERTS, CHARLES WERTH, JR., elec. engr.; b. Augusta, Ga., Mar. 29, 1933; s. Charles Werth and Lucile Lyle (Williams) R.; B.S. in Elec. Engring., Auburn U., 1955; m. Frances Melanie Walthall, Aug. 4, 1955; children—Charles Werth III, Melanie Walthall, Susan, Carol Lynn, Thomas Arthur. Engr., Gen. Electric Co., Schenectady, 1955-56, Pittsfield, Mass., 1956-58; engr. Ala. Power Co., Montgomery, 1958-62, dist. supt., Demopolis, 1962—. Trustee Bryant Whitfield Meml. Hosp., Demopolis. Registered profl. engr., Ala. Mem. Sigma Alpha Epsilon. Episcopalian (jr. warden 1971—). Club: Demopolis Country (pres. 1971—). Home: 1814 Marengo Dr Demopolis AL 36732 Office: Box 819 Demopolis AL 36732

ROBERTS, CHARLES WESLEY, editor; b. Huntington, W.Va., Dec. 19, 1916; s. Charles Wesley and Bessie Bright (Clack) R.; student Northwestern U., 1935-36; B.A., U. Minn., 1940; m. Mary Stewart, Nov. 10, 1945; children—Judith (Mrs. Richard Getrich), Jill. Reporter, Evanston (Ill.) News-Index, 1934-35, Mpls. Jour., 1936, City News Bur., Chgo., 1940, Chgo. Tribune, 1941, Chgo. Sun, Sun-Times, 1946-50, Chgo. Daily News, 1951; Chgo. bur. chief Newsweek, 1951-53, asso. editor, N.Y.C., 1953-54, chief White House corr., 1954-69, contbg. editor, Washington, 1969—. Served to lt. USNR, 1941-45. Recipient Page One award Chgo., 1951, Excellence in Reporting awards Ill. Press Assn., 1935, Pi Delta Epsilon, 1939. Mem. White House Corrs. Assn., Nat. Press Club, Grey Friars, Phi Delta Theta. Episcopalian. Clubs: Federal City; Kenwood Country (Bethesda). Author: LBJ's Inner Circle, 1965; The Truth About the Assassination, 1967. Home: 8400 Fenway Rd Bethesda MD 20034 Office: 1750 Pennsylvania Av NW Washington DC 20006

ROBERTS, CLARENCE EUGENE, dentist; b. Coats, N.C., Apr. 4, 1916; s. Harry Clay and Edna (Thomas) R.; student Wake Forest U., 1936-39; D.D.S., Emory U., 1943; m. Vivian Anne Johnson, July 18, 1953; children—Jane, Clarence Eugene, Thomas Clay, Dan Johnson. Pvt. practice dentistry, Dunn, N.C., 1947—. Vice pres. First Fed. Savs. & Loan Assn., Dunn, 1959—. Chmn. Harnett County Bd. Health, 1964—. Served with AUS, 1943-46. Mem. Am. Dental Assn., N.C. Dental Soc., Dunn Jr. C. of C. (pres. 1950), Am. Legion. Baptist. Mason, Kiwanian. Home: 1000 W Pope St Dunn NC 28334 Office: 208 N Wilson Av Dunn NC 28334

ROBERTS, ELIOT COLLINS, educator; b. Camden, N.J., Apr. 25, 1927; s. Benjamin Jenkins and Ruth (Collins) R.; B.S., U. R.I., 1950; M.S., Rutgers U., 1952, Ph.D., 1955; m. Beverly Mae Cruickshank, June 30, 1951; children—Eliot Collins, Mary Alice, William Cruickshank. Asst. prof., asso. prof. U. Mass., 1954-59; asso. prof., prof. Ia. State U., 1959-67; prof., chmn. dept. ornamental horticulture Inst. Food and Agrl. Scis., U. Fla., Gainesville, 1967—; asso. Western States Landscape Assos. Served with USNR, 1945-46. Mem. Am. Soc. Hort. Sci., Weed Soc. Am., Am. Soc. Agronomy. Rotarian. Home: 3535 NW 14th Av Gainesville FL 32601

ROBERTS, ELMER A., banker; b. Crawford, Tex., Oct. 13, 1921; s. Clyde Howell and Ninnie Lou (Hay) R.; student Baylor U., 1939-41; m. Annette Stewart, Dec. 9, 1945; 1 dau., Nancy. Dep. clk. McLennan County, 1945-50; mgr. County Title Co., 1951-54; controller City of Waco (Tex.), 1954-58, dir. finance, 1958-64, city mgr., 1964-71; v.p. First Nat. Bank, Waco, 1971-72, pres., 1972—; v.p. S.W. Sprayer & Chem. Co., 1964; dir. S. Amsler Co. of Crawford, Inc. Bd. dirs. YMCA, United Fund, A.R.C., Baylor Stadium. Served with USAF, 1942-45. Named Outstanding Pub. Ofcl., Waco Jr. C. of C., 1960. Mem. Internat. City Mgrs. Assn., Waco C. of C. (dir.), Municipal Finance Officers Assn. U.S. and Can. Mason. Home: 2007 LaPorte Dr Waco TX 76710 Office: PO Box 1370 Waco TX 76703

ROBERTS, EMMETT S., state ofcl.; b. Clearwater, Fla., June 23, 1913; B.S., U. Fla., 1940; m. Jenlaura Geer; children—Anna Maria, Patricia Jane. Ins. agt., mortgage broker; past vice chmn. Central and So. Fla. Food Control; now dir. Fla. Dept. Pub. Welfare, Jacksonville. Past pres. Palm Beach County Resources Devel. Bd.; area chmn. March of Dimes. Mem. Fla. Ho. of Reps., 1954-66. Served with AUS. Mem. V.F.W., Am. Legion, C. of C. (past dir.), Sigma Phi Epsilon. Episcopalian (vestryman; trustee). Mason (Shriner), Elk, Lion (past dist. gov. So. Fla.). Home: 636 SE 2d St Belle Glade FL 33430 Office: PO Box 2050 Jacksonville FL 32203*

ROBERTS, FRANCIS ARCHIBALD, geophysicist; b. Jeanerette, La., Aug. 13, 1915; s. John Pierce and Bella (Hargis) R.; B.A. in Sci. and Math., La. State U., 1934, M.S. in Math., 1937; m. Ernestine Billie Browning, Mar. 6, 1942; children—Lindalee Marie. Geophys. exploration for various affiliates Standard Oil Co. (N.J.) in N.Am., S.Am., Asia, Europe and Africa, 1937—; research asso. Esso Prodn. Research Co., Houston, 1969—. Active drives for United Fund and Bus. Industry Activity Com. Mem. Soc. Exploration Geophysicists, Am. Assn. Petroleum Geologists, Am. Geophys. Union, Am. Soc. for Oceanography, Nat. Geog. Soc. Republican. Methodist. Home: 12327 Broken Bough Dr Houston TX 77024 Office: 3120 Buffalo Speedway Houston TX 77027

ROBERTS, GARLAND HENRY, county ofcl.; b. Lynchburg, Va., July 21, 1925; s. Elford Huitt and Nellie (Goode) R.; B.S., Va. Poly. Inst., 1951; m. Mary Catherine Newland, Sept. 12, 1 48; children—Garland Henry, Micheal Douglas, Lawrence Allen. With Va. Dept. Hwys., 1951-66, resident engr., 1960-66; chief field engr. Prince William Engring. Co., Woodbridge, Va., 1966-67; dir. flood plains and maj. drainage Dept. Pub. Works Fairfax County, Va., 1967; exec. sec., county engr. Hanover County, Hanover, Va., 1967—. Served with USNR, 1943-46. Kiwanian. Club: Ruitan (pres. 1965-66). Home: Route 1 Box 623 Ashland VA 23005 Office: Hanover Courthouse Hanover VA 23069

ROBERTS, GRADY LEON, research chemist; b. Wheeler, Tex., May 26, 1926; s. Wiley Lee and Letha (Williams) R.; student Miss. Coll., 1944-45; A.B. in Chemistry, Duke, 1947; M.A. in Phys. Chemistry, U. Tex., 1950; m. Mary Lee Mays, Nov. 22, 1949; children—Rowena Lisa, Jerry Leon. Teaching fellow U. Tex., Austin, 1947-49; analytical chemist Cities Service Refining Co., Lake Charles, La., 1949-51; research chemist Monsanto Chem. Co., Texas City, Tex., 1951-57; group leader, 1957-64, process specialist, 1964-67, sr. process specialist, 1967—. Adviser various youth groups. Served with USN, 1944-46. Mem. Am. Chem. Soc., A.A.A.S., Am. Soc. Testing and Materials (com. mem.), N.Y. Acad. Sci., Soc. Applied Spectroscopy, S.W. Catalyst Soc., Internat. Platform Assn. Research on applications of spectroscopy and gas chromatography to analytical problems. Home: 1109 Mainland Dr Texas City TX 77590 Office: care Monsanto Chem Co Texas City TX 77590

ROBERTS, HARRY F., retail drug co. exec., b. 1929; student U. Ga.; grad. Draughton's Bus. Coll.; m. Pres., Jack Eckerd Corp., Jack Eckerd Drug Co., Clearwater. Office: 2120 US 19 S Clearwater FL 33518*

ROBERTS, HERBERT RAY, congressman; b. McKinney, Tex., Mar. 28, 1913; s. Roy Clifton and Margaret Emma (Burton) R.; student Tex. A. and M. Coll., 1930-31, N. Tex. State U., 1931-32, Tex. U., 1932-35; m. Elizabeth Bush Kelly, Nov. 12, 1946; 1 stepdau., Kathryn Ann Kelly (Mrs. Tom Murray II). Dist. dir. Nat. Youth Adminstrn., Tex., 1935-40; mem. secretarial staff speaker Sam Rayburn, U.S. Ho. of Reps., 1941-42; engaged in real estate devel., McKinney, 1956—; mem. Tex. Senate, 1955-62; elected to U.S. Ho. of Reps. from 4th Dist., Tex. to fill term of Sam Rayburn, 1962; mem. 89th to 92d Congresses 4th Dist. Tex. Served to capt. USNR, 1942-45; MTO. Democrat. Home: 509 Tucker St McKinney TX 75069 Office: House Office Bldg Washington DC 20515

ROBERTS, HYMAN JACOB, physician; b. Boston, May 29, 1924; s. Benjamin and Eva (Sherman) R.; M.D. cum laude, Tufts U., 1947; m. Carol Antonia Klein, Aug. 9, 1953; children—David Barry, Jonathan Stuart, Mark Elliott, Stephen, Scott F., Pamela Beth. Intern Boston City Hosp., 1947-48, resident, 1948-49; resident Municipal Hosp., Washington, 1949-50; fellow in medicine Lahey Clinic, Boston, 1950-51; instr. in medicine, research fellow Tufts U. Med. Sch., Boston, 1948-49, Georgetown Med. Sch., Washington, 1949-50; pvt. practice medicine, West Palm Beach, Fla., 1955—; mem. cons. staff St. Mary's Hosp., Good Samaritan Hosp.; cons. endocrinology Gables Acad., Broward Acad.; 1st Eugene Dibble ann. lecture Tuskegee Inst., 1967; dir. Palm Beach Inst. for Med. Research. Trustee Am. Physicians Fellowship for Israel Med. Assn. Served from lt. (j.g.) to lt. USNR, 1943-45, 51-54. Recipient Fla.'s Outstanding Young Men award Jr. C. of C., 1959. Diplomate Am. Bd. Internal Medicine. Fellow Am. Coll. Angiology, Royal Soc. Health, Am. Coll. Chest Physicians; mem. Am. Fedn. Clin. Research, Endocrine Soc., Am. Assn. Study Headaches, Am. Soc. Internal Medicine, N.Y. Acad. Scis., A.C.P. (asso. mem.), Am., Fla. heart assns., Am. Diabetes Assn., A.A.A.S., Internat. Assn. for Accident and Traffic Medicine, Am., So., Fla. med. assns., Assn. for Psychophysiol. Study Sleep, Physicians for Automotive Safety, Am. Assn. for Automotive Medicine, Fla. Thoracic Soc., Alpha Omega Alpha. Mem. B'nai B'rith (v.p. 1958-59). Rotarian (charter mem., dir. 1956-58) (West Palm Beach, Fla.). Author: Difficult Diagnosis; A Guide To The Interpretation of Obscure Illness, 1958; The Causes, Ecology and Prevention of Traffic Accidents, 1971; An Inquiry Into the Safety of Vasectomy, 1973, also numerous sci. papers. Home: 6708 Pamela Lane West Palm Beach FL 33405 Office: 300 27th St West Palm Beach FL 33407

ROBERTS, JACK, judge, b. 1910; LL.B., U. Tex. 1933. Admitted to Tex. bar, 1933; now dist. judge Austin, Tex. Address: U.S. Courthouse Austin TX 78711*

ROBERTS, JAMES ELTON, banker; b. Terrell, Tex., Nov. 24, 1910; s. Henry Oscar and Ida Olivia (Phillips) R.; B.S., Tex. A. and M. U., 1933, M.S., 1947; m. Virgia L. Wileman, Oct. 4, 1935; 1 son, James Elton. Tchr. vocational agr., Mt. Vernon, Tex., 1933-34, Van, Tex., 1934-37, Denton, Tex., 1937-38; supt. Tex. Agrl. Expt. Sta., 1938-54; farms mgr. farms service dept. Tex. A. and M. U., 1954-68; v.p., dir. 1st Nat. Bank, Bryan, Tex., 1968—. Ford Found. cons. to Dominican Rep., 1962. Drive chmn. College Station United Chest, 1965. Mem. College Station C. of C. (dir. 1947-49). Mason (32 deg., Shriner). Clubs: Bryan-College Station Knife and Fork (past pres.), Van Lions (past pres.). Home: 840 S Rosemary St Bryan TX 77801 Office: 120 N Main St Bryan TX 77801

ROBERTS, JERRY LAMAR, banker; b. nr. Hogansville, Ga., July 21, 1941; s. Elihu Dee and Edna (Thompson) R.; student Ga. State Coll., W. Ga. Coll., 1961-64, grad. U. Ga. Banking Sch., U. Ga., 1964, Banking Sch. of South at La. State U., 1968; m. Joyce Tidwell, June 18, 1961; 1 son, Weston Lamar. Asst. v.p. Mfrs. Nat. Bank, Newnan, Ga., 1960-65; v.p., cashier Dixie County State Bank, Cross City, Fla., 1966-71, pres., 1971—. Treas. Sawanee Valley Ins. Agy. Inc. Mayor, Cross City, 1969-70; pres. Town Council, 1971-72. Bd. dirs. Lake City Community Coll. Found. Mem. C. of C. (past pres.). Baptist. Rotarian. Home: PO Box 643 Cross City FL 32628 Office: PO Box A Cross City FL 32628

ROBERTS, JOHN CARROLL, civil engr.; b. Frankfort, Ky., Apr. 15, 1934; s. Bowen Henry and Mayme (Burchfield) R.; B.S., U. Ky., 1960; m. Roberta Bow Miller, Apr. 14, 1956; children—Kathryn Miller, John Carroll, Patricia Jane. Sales rep. Atlas Chem. Industries, Inc., Wilmington, Del., 1960-62; chief engr. Geoghegan & Mathis, Inc., Bardstown, Ky., 1963-66; v.p., treas. Ky. Materials Co., Frankfort, 1961—; pvt. practice civil engring., 1964—, pres. Morehead Ho., Inc., 1967—; treas. D B Grugin Oil Co., 1964—; v.p. Geoghegan & Mathis, Inc., Bardstown, Ky., 1968-71; chief engr. Bush Contracting Co., Frankfort, 1971—. Chmn. Frankfort Municipal Sewer Bd., 1967—; mem. Capital Plaza Authority, 1970—; pres. E. Elkhorn PTA, 1969-70. Served with USNR, 1955-57. Mem. Nat., Ky. socs. profl. engrs., Am. Soc. C.E. Mem. Christian Ch. Rotarian, Elk. Club: Frankfort Country. Home: 300 Ute Trail Frankfort KY 40601 Office: 326 W Main St Frankfort KY 40610

ROBERTS, JOHN DAVID, profl. football coach; b. Oklahoma City, Oct. 24, 1932; s. William Edward and Mildred Elizabeth (Bianchi) R.; B.S. in Edn., U. Okla., 1955; m. June Hill, Feb. 8, 1958; children—Gregory, Rebecca, Melinda, Mark, Neil. Asst. coach football U. Denver, 1957, U. Okla., 1958-59, U.S. Naval Acad., 1960, Auburn (Ala.) U., 1961, U. Houston, 1962-64; asst. coach New Orleans Saints, profl. football team, 1967-68, head coach, 1970—; head coach Richmond (Va.) Saints, 1969-70; head coach South Squad, Sr. Bowl, 1972. Served with USMCR, 1955-57. Mem. A.F.T.R.A. Contbr. sports articles to nat. mags. Host weekly TV show Sta. WDSU-TV, New Orleans, daily radio sports show Sta. WDSU. Office: 6928 Saints Av Metairie LA 70003

ROBERTS, JOHN ELGIN, mag. editor; b. Shelby, N.C., Sept. 14, 1926; s. John Ellis and Annie (Spake) R.; diploma Gardner-Webb Jr. Coll., 1947-49; B.A., Furman U., 1951, LL.D., 1972; M.A., George Peabody Coll. Tchrs., 1952; D.Litt., Bapt. Coll. at Charleston, S.C., 1971; m. Helen E. Goodwin, Sept. 8, 1950; children—Wayne, Mark, Glenn, Jonna, Jill, Julie. Tchr. Gastonia (N.C.) City Schs., 1951-54; dir. pub. relations Gerdner-Webb Coll., 1954-60; dir. pub. relations, editor Charity and Children Bapt. Children's Homes of N.C., Thomasville, 1960-65; editor, bus. mgr. The Bapt. Courier, Greenville, S.C., 1966—. Mem. So. Bapt. Editors Conf., So. Bapt. Inter-Agy. Council; bd. advisers New Orleans Bapt. Theol. Sem.; instl. rep. Boy Scouts Am.; mem. Thomasville (N.C.) Bd. Edn., 1963-65. Served with AUS, 1945-46. Mem. So. Bapt. Pub. Relations Assn. (pres. 1956—), Bapt. World Alliance Commn. on Teaching and Tng. Baptist (deacon). Rotarian. Home: 106 Trinity Way Greenville SC 29609 Office: 100 Manly St Greenville SC 29602

ROBERTS, LA RUE, dentist; b. Hyden, Ky., Nov. 23, 1908; s. William B. and Armenta (Stamper) R.; B.A., Georgetown Coll., 1933; D.M.D., U. Louisville, 1941; m. Beatrice Botner, Mar. 28, 1936; children— Lana Rue (Mrs. Paul Braden), William Stacy. Tchr. math Bell County Schs., 1934-36; pvt. practice dentistry, Pineville, Ky., 1941—; mem. staff Pineville Community Hosp. Dir. First Fed. Loan, Pineville. Exhibited in one-man show, Louisville, 1970; exhibited in group shows at Harlan, Ky., 1969, 70, Middlesboro, Ky., 1969, 70, Lexington, Ky., 1971, Cumberland Coll., 1969. Pres. Tenn. Rose Soc., 1960-62. Mem. Southeastern Dental Soc. (pres. 1949-50), Lambda Chi Alpha, Gamma Sigma Epsilon. Baptist. Rotarian (pres. 1951-52), Mason (master 1957-58). Home: 534 Kentucky Av Pineville KY 40977 Office: Box 206 Pineville KY 40977

ROBERTS, MARCUS LAFAYETTE, JR., ednl. adminstr.; b. Altoona, Ala., Dec. 7, 1926; s. Marcus L. and Meade (Fant) R.; A.B., Jacksonville State U., 1947, B.S., 1947; M.A., U. Ala., 1951; m. Edith Lynn Harper, June 30, 1957; children—Marcus L. III, Melanie Lynn.

Pub. sch. tchr. Tuscaloosa, Ala.; chmn. dept. bus. edn. Tuscaloosa Sr. High Sch., 1947-54; asso. prof. edn. U. Ala., University, 1954—, dir. student services, 1960-70, asst. dean Coll. Edn., 1970—, head area of curriculum and instruction Coll. of Edn., 1971—. Cons. sch. systems Calhoun, Jefferson, Madison, Montgomery, Tuscaloosa counties, Mountain Brook, Ala., 1955—; pres. Ala. Credit Union, U. Ala., 1967. Mem. Nat., Ala. edn. assns., Nat., So., Ala. bus. edn. assns., Kappa Delta Pi, Phi Delta Kappa, Pi Tau Chi. Democrat. Methodist. Club: Tuscaloosa Exchange. Contbr. articles to profl. jours. Home: 204 32d Pl E Tuscaloosa AL 35401 Office: Box R University AL 35486

ROBERTS, MARKLEY, labor ofcl.; b. Shanghai, China, Sept. 3, 1930 (parents Am. citizens); s. Donald and Frances (Markley) R.; A.B., Princeton, 1951; Ph.D., Am. U., 1970; m. Jeanne Addison, Feb. 19, 1966. Reporter, Washington Star newspaper, 1952-57; legislative asst. Senator Hubert Humphrey, Washington, 1958-61; legislative asst. AFL-CIO, Washington, 1962—; dir. research Project Build, Washington, 1969-70. Lectr., U. Md., 1967—; asst. profl. lectr. George Washington U., 1969. Mem. D.C. Democratic Central Com., 1966-68. Mem. Am. Econ. Assn., Am. Polit. Sci. Assn., Am. Pub. Welfare Assn. Home: 4931 Albemarle St NW Washington DC 20016 Office: 815 16th St NW Washington DC 20006

ROBERTS, MORTON SPITZ, astronomer; b. N.Y.C., Nov. 5, 1926; B.A., Pomona Coll., 1948; M.S., Cal. Inst. Tech., 1950; Lick Obs. fellow, U. Cal., 1956-57, Ph.D. in Astronomy, 1958. Asst. prof. physics Occidental Coll., 1949-52; physicist underwater ordnance U.S. Naval Ordnance Test Sta., 1952-53; jr. research astronomer U. Cal., 1957-58, NSF fellow, 1958-59, lectr. astronomy, asst. research astronomer Radio Astron. Lab., 1959-60; lectr. astronomy, research asso. obs. Harvard, 1960-64; scientist Nat. Radio Astronomy Obs., Charlottesville, Va., 1964—. Mem. Am. Astron. Soc., Royal Astron. Soc. Research in galaxies, galactic structure, radio astronomy, star clusters. Address: Nat Radio Astronomy Obs Edgemont Rd Charlottesville VA 22901*

ROBERTS, PEARCE, JR., dentist; b. Weaverville, N.C., Sept. 16, 1919; s. Pearce and Mattie (Morgan) R.; student Mars Hill Coll., 1938; D.D.S., Med. Coll. Va., 1942; m. Camille Evans Stone, Jan. 21, 1947; children—Pearce III, James Stone, Camille Evans. Intern, Walter Reed Gen. Hosp., Washington, 1942-43; pvt. practice dentistry, Asheville, N.C., 1947—. Served from 1st lt. to maj. Dental Corps, AUS, 1943-46. Fellow Internat. Coll. Dentists; mem. Am. Acad. Dental Practice Adminstrn., Am. Acad. Restorative Dentistry, Am. Dental Assn. (N.C. del. 1969—), N.C. (pres. 1965-66), 1st Dist. (pres. 1953-54), Buncombe County (pres. 1950) dental socs., Psi Omega. Presbyn. Club: Biltmore Forest Country (Asheville). Home: 7 Lone Pine Rd Asheville NC 28801 Office: Doctors Bldg Asheville NC 28802

ROBERTS, RALPH RITCH, JR., dentist; b. Temple, Tex., June 6, 1932; s. Ralph Ritch and Ellen Louise (Orand) R.; B.A., Baylor U., 1954, D.D.S., 1958. Practice dentistry, Temple, 1959-60, Euless, Tex., 1960—. Bd. dirs. Euless Youth Assn., Hurst, Euless and Bedford Retardation Assn. Mem. Amegos Internat., Psi Omega. Baptist (deacon). Lion. Clubs: Assemblage, 500 (Dallas). Home: 1903 Summit Ridge Euless TX 76039 Office: 800 N Industrial Blvd Euless TX 76039

ROBERTS, RAY, congressman; b. Collin County, Tex., Mar. 28, 1913; s. Roy C. and Margaret (Burton) R.; student Tex. A. and M. Coll., N. Tex. State Coll., U. Tex.; m. Elizabeth Bush, Nov. 12, 1946; 1 dau., Kay (Mrs. Tom Murray III). Mem. staff U.S. Ho. of Reps. Speaker Rayburn, 1940-42; mem. Tex. Senate from 9th Dist., 1955-62; elected 87th Congress to fill unexpired term of Speaker Rayburn, 1962; mem. 88th-91st Congress 4th Dist. Tex. Served to capt. USNR, World War II. Democrat. Home: 509 Tucker St McKinney TX 75069 Office: Rayburn Office Bldg Washington DC 20515

ROBERTS, RICHARD DAVID, broadcasting exec.; b. Quincy, Mass., June 15, 1934; s. Cecil Austin and Helen Catherine (Knebel) R.; B.S., U.S. Naval Acad., 1956; M.B.A., Harvard, 1963; m. Shirley Phyllis Hanson, Aug. 3, 1957; children—Catherine, Helen, Caroline. Research dir. WTAR Radio-TV Corp., Norfolk, Va., 1963-64; research dir. Landmark Communications, Norfolk, 1964-65, asst. to pres., 1965-68, sec., 1967—; v.p. operations, sec., dir. TeleCable Corp., 1968—; dir. 16 TeleCable subsidiaries. Pres. Portsmouth Girls Club, 1970, dir., 1965—. Served with USNR, 1956-61. Presbyn. (elder). Moose, Lion (1st v.p., dir.). Home: 115 Snead Fairway Portsmouth VA 23701 Office: 740 Duke St Norfolk VA 23501

ROBERTS, R(ICHARD) RAY, postal ofcl.; b. Greentop, Mo., Dec. 4, 1918; s. John Henry and Nancy (Hall) R.; A.B., B.S. in Edn., N.E. Mo. State Coll., 1940; M.A. in Edn., George Washington U., 1957, Ed.D., 1964; m. Margaret Snow Linebarger, Aug. 22, 1959. Clk., Census Bur., 1940-42, City P.O., Washington, 1942-43, 46-50, Postal Inspection Service, 1950-51; writer Navy Tng. Pub. Center, 1950-61; editor Naval Tng. Bull., 1960-61; sch. relations asst. Bur. Naval Personnel, 1963-66; dir. Navy Edn. and Tng. Devel. Div., 1967; employee devel. officer U.S. Postal Service, Washington, 1967—. Lectr., George Washington U., 1960-61. Served from ensign to lt. USNR, 1943-46. Mem. Adult Edn. Assn., Am. Soc. Tng. and Devel. (award 1966), Naval Inst. (asso.), George Washington U. Sch. Edn. Alumni Assn. (chmn. 1968-69), Gen. Alumni Assn. George Washington U. (bd. govs. 1968-72), Phi Delta Kappa. Home: 3309 Rocky Mount Rd Fairfax VA 22030 Office: US Postal Service Mgmt Inst Bethesda MD 20014

ROBERTS, RICHARD VALGENE, ednl. adminstr.; b. Ocilla, Ga., Nov. 22, 1927; s. John William and Mary (Smith) R.; B.S., Ga. Tchrs. Coll., 1951; M.Ed., U. Ga., 1953; m. Daisy Branch, Sept. 12, 1953; children—Robbie Jean, Richard Valgene Jr. Prin., Ashburn (Ga.) Elem. Sch., 1962-66; prin. Montgomery County High Sch., Mt. Vernon, Ga., 1967-68; supt. Irwin County Schs., Ocilla, Ga., 1969—; mem. Irwin-Ben Hill Vocational Sch. Bd., 1968-72. Mem. Irwin County Health Bd., 1968-72. Mem. Irwin County Ednl. Assn., Ga. Assn. Educators, N.E.A., Ga. Supt. Assn., 8th Dist., Nat. supts. assns. Mason (Shriner), Rotarian. Home: 712 W 3d St Ocilla GA 31774 Office: Box 225 Ocilla GA 31774

ROBERTS, ROBERT EARL, food service co. exec.; b. Crawfordville, Ga., Sept. 3, 1932; s. Charles Stakley and Lettie (Denny) R.; B.S., U. Ga., 1954; m. Mary Arnold, Sept. 11, 1953; children—David Earl, Mark Arnold, Stuart Elliott. Asst. plant mgr. Kinnett Dairies, Columbus, Ga., 1956-57; creamery mgr. U. Ga., Athens, 1967; mgmt. cons. Am. Dairy Queen Corp., 1965-67, dir. field services, quality control Southeastern div., 1967-68, operations mgr. So. region, Atlanta, 1968-71; dist. mgr. Krystal Co., Atlanta, 1971—. Mem. adv. com. Sch. Bd., Clarke County, Ga., 1967-68. Served to 1st lt. with AUS, 1954-56. Mem. Atlanta Dairy Tech. Soc. (exec. sec. 1966—), Am. Dairy Sci. Assn. (sect. chmn. 1967), Res. Officers Assn. Army (chpt. v.p. 1965). Baptist (deacon). Kiwanian (pres. 1964). Home: 3612 Prestwick Dr Tucker GA 30084 Office: Krystal Co Suite 310 2220 Parklake Dr NE Atlanta GA 30345

ROBERTS, ROLAND DOUGLAS, JR., architect; b. Tulsa, Jan. 8, 1937; s. Roland Douglas and Cortez (Williamson) R.; B.Arch., Rice U., 1960; postgrad. Okla. U., 1962-63; m. Nancy Ray Carman, June 18, 1966. Designer, Grayson Gill, Inc., Dallas, 1961; tchr. U. Tex., Arlington, 1963-64; designer Smith & Warder, Grand Prairie, Tex., 1964-65; architect Leman H. Wilson, Tulsa, 1965-67, Brush, Hutchison & Gwinn, Nashville, 1967-70, owner archtl. firm Bledsoe-Roberts & Assos., Nashville, 1970—. Fallout shelter analyst. Served with USAF, 1960-61. W.W. Watking traveling fellow in architecture, recipient Nat. Council Archtl. Registration Bds. certificate. Registered profl. architect, 19 states. Mem. Nashville Jr. C. of C., Am. Concrete Inst., A.I.A., Tenn. Soc. Architects, Illumination Engring. Soc., Guild for Religious Architecture, Constrn. Specifications Inst. Archtl. works include: Highland Hosp., Portland, Tenn., Calvary Bapt. Ch., Winston-Salem, N.C., Buchi Plumbing Co., Nashville, Ch. of Christ, Belpre, O., Moffitt Rd. Bapt. Ch., Mobile, Ala. and numerous comml. structures. Home: 254 Cathy Jo Dr Nashville TN 37211 Office: 2814 Granny White Pike Nashville TN 37204

ROBERTS, RUFUS WINSTON, physician, educator; b. Birmingham, Ala., Aug. 9, 1916; s. R. Winston and Thelma (Guilford) R.; M.D., Duke, 1940; m. Patricia L. Moore, May 13, 1944; children—Patricia, Shelley, Judson. Intern, Duke Hosp., Durham, N.C., 1940-41, resident Duke Hosp. and N.C. Baptist Hosp., 1945-48; practice medicine, specializing in ophthalmology, Winston-Salem, N.C., 1948—; chief ophthalmology N.C. Baptist Hosp., 1948—; dir. ophthalmology Bowman Gray Sch. Medicine, 1948—, prof., 1956—, Mem. Pub. Sch. Curriculum Revision Com., 1960-62. Bd. dirs. N.C. Soc. for Prevention Blindness. Served to capt., M.C., USAAF, 1941-45. Decorated Silver Star Medal, Air Medal, Purple Heart. Diplomate Am. Bd. Ophthalmology. Mem. Am. Acad. Ophthalmology and Otolaryngology (instr.), A.M.A., N.C. Med. Soc., N.C. Ophthalmology Soc., Eye Study Club, Pan Am. Ophthalmology Assn., Sigma Alpha Epsilon. Republican. Methodist. Clubs: Old Town Country (Winston-Salem); Grandfather Country (Linnville, N.C.). Contbr. sect. to The Older Patient, 1960. Contbr. articles to profl. jours. Home: 271 Canterbury Trail Winston-Salem NC 27104

ROBERTS, S. OLIVER, psychologist, educator; b. Alexandria, Va., May 21, 1910; s. George and Esther (Ragland) R.; A.B., Brown U., 1932, A.M., 1933; postgrad. U. Chgo., summer 1941; Ph.D., U. Minn., 1944; m. Marion Taylor, Jan. 2, 1942; children—Esther (Mrs. Lillard Ashley, Jr.), Barbara (Mrs. Bert Stone), Kay. Instr., Atlanta U., 1933-36; research asst. U. Minn., Mpls. 1937-38; asso. prof. psychology and edn. Ark. Agrl. Mech. and Normal Coll., Pine Bluff, 1939-42; acting dean Dunbar Jr. Coll., Little Rock, 1942-43, dean of students, 1944-45; lectr. Meharry Med. Coll., Nashville, 1945—; asst. prof. psychology Fisk U., Nashville, 1945-46, asso. prof., 1946-50, prof., chmn. dept., 1950—. Mem. Met. Action Commn., 1964-70, vice chmn., 1967-68. Fellow Am. Psychol. Assn., Am. Ednl. Research Assn., Soc. for Research Child Devel. Home: 1806 Morena St Nashville TN 37208

ROBERTS, SYLVESTER, social worker; b. Aucilla, Fla., Dec. 3, 1930; s. Roma and Hattie Mae (Brooks) R.; B.S., Fla. A. and M. U., 1960; M.A., Atlanta U., 1961; M.S.W., Howard U., 1965; m. Margaret E. Ricks, Aug. 30, 1968. Tchr. social studies Grambling (La.) Coll., 1961-62; classification officer D.C. Dept. Correction, Washington, 1964; probation officer, social worker D.C. Juvenile Ct., Washington, 1965-70; supervisory social worker D.C. Dept. of Corrections, Washington, 1970—. Served with USAF, 1952-56. Mem. Nat. Assn. Social Workers, Acad. Certified Social Workers, Sigma Rho Sigma, Alpha Kappa Delta. Home: 6103 Balfour Dr Hyattsville MD 20782 Office: 614 H St NW Washington DC 20001

ROBERTS, THOMAS HEYM, govt. ofcl.; b. Cleve., Jan. 28, 1928; s. Burke Brockway and Charlotte Margaret (Heym) R.; B.S. in Civil Engring., Case Inst. Tech., 1950; M.Regional Planning, U. N.C., 1952; m. Jacquelyn Faye Kline, June 4, 1950; children—Judith, Mark, Holly, Tod, Sr. planner Youngstown (O.) City Planning Commn., 1952-54; sr. planner Charleston County (S.C.) Planning Bd., 1954-56; with Atlanta Region Met. Planning Commn., 1956-66, community planner, 1956-57, chief regional planner, 1957-58, asst. planning dir., 1958-59, planning dir., 1959-66; dir. regional planning Met. Washington Council of Govts., 1966-69; exec. dir. Am. Inst. Planners, Washington, 1969—. Pres. AIP Found., 1971—. Mem. Am. Inst. Planners (dir. Ga. sect. 1959, mem. exec. com. Nat. Capital area chpt., 1966-69), Am. Soc. Planning Ofcls., Soc. Preservation and Encouragement Barbershop Quartet Singing in Am. (pres. Atlanta chpt. 1960), Blue Key, Case Honor Key, Beta Theta Pi, Theta Tau, Lambda Alpha, Pi Delta Epsilon. Home: 8122 Lilly Stone Dr Bethesda MD 20034 Office: 917 15th St NW Washington DC 20005

ROBERTS, VAN MITCHELL, advt. agy. exec.; b. Cisco, Tex., Aug. 8, 1916; s. Gideon A. and Charlie (Mitchell) R.; student McMurry Coll., 1933-35; m. Margaret Belle Roberts, May 19, 1946; children—Teena Gale, Karen Elizabeth, Van Mitchell. Motion picture theatre publicist, mgr. Interstate Circuit, Inc., Abilene, Tex., 1933-37, Tyler, 1937-41, Wichita Falls, 1941, Dallas, 1941-42, Amarillo, 1942-43, theatre mgr., Dallas, 1951-53; theatre mgr. Jefferson Amusement Co., Beaumont, 1947-50, I.B. Adelman Theatres, Ft. Worth, 1946, Dallas, 1949-50, Tulsa, 1951; officer trainee Highland Park State Bank, Dallas, 1953-54; account exec. Ray Beall Advt. Agy., Dallas, 1954-55; owner Van Roberts Advt., Dallas, 1955—. Served with AUS, 1943-45. Mem. Dallas Advt. Club (dir. 1964-67, 71—, sec.-treas. 1966-67), Am., Dallas (v.p. 1969, 70) rose socs., Southwest Assn. Advt. Agys. (dir. 1971—), Dallas C. of C., Dallas Advt. League (dir. 1971—). Presbyn. (elder). Clubs: Variety of Tex., Lancers. Home: 5222 Meadow Crest Dr Dallas TX 75229 Office: 211 N Ervay Bldg Dallas TX 75201

ROBERTS, VERNELL RAYMOND, dentist; b. Pelham, Ga., May 4, 1920; s. Charles and Indiana (Williams) R.; B.S., Fla. A.& M. Coll., 1943; D.D.S., Howard U., 1951; m. Arneatha Jones, Mar. 18, 1961; children—Vernell, William, Emmie Denise. Pub. health dentist Va. State Health Dept., Richmond, 1951-56; dental officer D.C. Govt., Washington, 1956—; pvt. practice dentistry, Washington, 1956—. Served with AUS, 1943-45. Mem. Dist. Dental Soc., Nat., Am. dental assns., Robert T. Freeman Dental Soc., Phi Beta Sigma. Club: Century (Washington). Home: 384 N St SW Washington DC 20024 Office: 5503 Georgia Av NW Washington DC 20011

ROBERTS, WARREN AUSTIN, oil co. exec.; b. Pitts., Nov. 28, 1915; s. Warren Austin and Laura H. (Dennis) R.; B.S. in Chem. Engring., Carnegie Inst. Tech., 1937; m. Margaret E. Fry, Mar. 19, 1942; children—Warren Austin, III, Margaret Ann. With Phillips Petroleum Co., 1937—, dist. supt., Hobbs, N.M. and Los Angeles, 1953-60, div. mgr., Oklahoma City, 1960-63, vice chmn. operating com., Bartlesville, Okla., 1963-66, chmn. operating com., 1966-68, v.p. exploration and prodn. dept., 1968-69, sr. v.p., 1969-71, exec. v.p., 1971—, also dir.; dir. Pacific Petroleum Co. Ltd. Mem. nat. council, pres. Cherokee area council Boy Scouts Am.; nat. bd. dirs. Camp Fire Girls; chmn. industry liaison com., deep sea drilling project Scripps Inst. Oceanography; mem. Nat. Acad. Sci. panel on drilling technique Project Mohole, 1958-64; mem. Okla. Air Pollution Council, 1967—. Served from 2d lt. to maj. C.E., USAAF, 1942-46. Registered profl. engr., Okla. Mem. Okla. Petroleum Council (pres. 1965-66; Distinguished achievement award 1962), Nat. Soc. Profl. Engrs., Oklahoma City C. of C. (chmn. oil and gas div. 1962, 63), Bartlesville C. of C. (chmn. hwy. com. 1964-68; dir. 1970—). Home: 1208 Swan Dr Bartlesville OK 74003 Office: Phillips Bldg Bartlesville OK 74003

ROBERTS, WILBURN R., religious orgn. exec.; b. Mt. Olive, Miss., Apr. 9, 1910; s. James and Martha (Arender) R.; B.S., U. So. Miss., 1937; m. Nellie Mixon, Feb. 24, 1934; children—Kathleen (Mrs. Klaus B. Striegler), Wilburn R., John Mixon. Supt. schs., Petal, Miss., 1933-40, Silver Creek, Miss., 1940-44; with Miss. Bapt. Conv. Bd., Sc. Bapt. Conv., 1944—, annuity sec. Miss., Jackson, 1958—. Mem. stewardship commn. So. Bapt. Conv., 1967—. Trustee Bapt. Meml. Hosp., Memphis. Baptist (deacon). Mason. Home: 156 S Denver St Jackson MS 39209 Office: Bapt Bldg PO Box 530 Jackson MS 39205

ROBERTS, WILLIAM HENRY, textile co. exec.; b. Winfield, Ala., June 19, 1916; s. Walter Lee and Sarah (Smith) R.; student Internat. Corr. Sch., 1936-40; m. Annie Beth Perry, Oct. 2, 1937; children—Billie Anne (Mrs. Charles Leonard Simpson), Walter Perry. Supr. Ala. Mills Inc., Winfield, Ala., 1938-46, supt., 1946-56, supt. Ala. Mills div. Dan River Mills Inc., 1956-59; plant mgr. Moultrie Textiles div. Moultrie Cotton Mills (Ga.), 1960—. Mem. Winfield City Sch. System, 1951-55. Mason (Shriner). Lion, Kiwanian (dir. 1952). Club: Moultrie Sunset Country. Home: 1340 4th St SW Moultrie GA 31768 Office: PO Box 70 11th St SW Moultrie GA 31768

ROBERTS, WILLIAM JOHN, chem. co. exec.; b. Phila., June 5, 1918; s. William G. and Olive (Schoppe) R.; A.B., U. Pa., 1942, M.S., 1944, Ph.D., 1947; m. Eleanor Florence Kennedy, Oct. 2, 1948; children—John William, Wendy Eleanor. With Pa. Indsl. Chem. Corp., Chester, 1946-57, dir. research, 1955-57; dir. research Summit Research Labs., Celanese Corp., Summit, N.J., 1957-64; v.p., tech. dir. Celanese Fibers Co., Charlotte, N.C., 1965—. Fellow Am. Inst. Chemists; mem. Am. Chem. Soc., Soc. Chem. Industry, Textile Research Inst., Fiber Soc., Sigma Xi, Pi Mu Epsilon. Clubs: Chemists (N.Y.C.); Lake Norman Yacht. Home: 1031 Huntington Park Dr Charlotte NC 28211 Office: PO Box 1414 Charlotte NC 28201

ROBERTS, WILLIAM PHILIP, JR., dentist; b. St. Joseph, La., Apr. 22, 1907; s. William Philip and Effie Irene (Albritton) R.; student La. State U., 1924-26; D.D.S., Loyola U., New Orleans, 1930; m. Myra Louise Geary, Sept. 12, 1930; children—Carolyn (Mrs. Charles Austin Barber III), Marcia (Mrs. Lynn F. Wade). Intern, USPH Hosp., New Orleans, 1930-31; pvt. practice dentistry, Hot Springs, N.M., 1934-39, Baton Rouge, 1939-72. Served with USPHS, 1931-34. Mem. Am., La., Sixth Dist. (pres. 1943) dental assns., Psi Omega (pres. 1929), Omicron Kappa Upsilon, Sigma Chi. Episcopalian. Club: Camelot (Baton Rouge). Home: 1519 Ingelside Dr Baton Rouge LA 70808

ROBERTS, WILLIAM TALMAGE, judge; b. Atlanta, Feb. 28, 1925; s. William Harvard and Florence (Adams) R.; student Ga. Mil. Coll., 1942-43, Biarritz U., France, 1945; LL.B., U. Ga., 1950; m. Rosa Deal, Oct. 22, 1950; children—Connie, Angie. Admitted to Ga. bar, 1950, practice, Montezuma, 1950—; county atty. Macon County, 1950—; solicitor State Ct. of Macon County (Ga.), 1952-71; judge State Ct. Macon County, 1971—. Dir. Citizens Nat. Bank, Montezuma. Mayor pro-tem City of Montezuma, 1960; commr. Bd. Industry and Trade, State of Ga., 1963-67. Served with AUS, 1943-46. Decorated Purple Heart, Bronze Star medal. Mem. Gridiron Soc., Phi Delta Theta, Phi Alpha Delta. Democrat. Methodist. Mason, Kiwanian (past pres.). Home: 311 Leon Av Montezuma GA 31063 Office: 202 S Dooly St Montezuma GA 31063

ROBERTSHAW, JAMES, lawyer; b. Greenville, Miss., May 19, 1916; s. Frank Newell and Mary (Aldridge) R.; B.S., Miss. State U., 1937; J.D. Harvard, 1940; m. Sylvia Yale Schively, Apr. 28, 1956; children—Mary Nicholson, Sylvia Yale, James, Frank Paxton. Admitted to Miss. bar, 1940; gen. practice, Greenville, 1946—; partner Robertshaw, Merideth & Swank, 1964—. Charter bd. dirs. Washington County Ednl. Found., 1965—. Mem. Miss. Ho. of Reps., 1953-46. Mem. Community Relations Com.; v.p. Greenville Indsl. Found. chmn. Greenville Airport Commn. Served to col. AUS, 1941-46. Decorated Legion of Merit; Croix de Guerre (France). Mem. Am., Washington County (past pres.) bar assns., Miss. State Bar. Episcopalian (jr. warden). Clubs: Greenville Golf and Country, University, Lions (past pres.); Refuge Hunting (dir.). Home: 844 Arnold Av Greenville MS 38702 Office: Woolworth Bldg Greenville MS 38702

ROBERTSON, ADRIAN ANDREW, dentist; b. Moneta, Va., Apr. 16, 1939; s. Dan Field and Elsie (Moles) R.; student Ferrum Jr. Coll., 1958-59, U. Richmond, 1959-61; D.D.S., Va. Commonwealth U., 1965; m. Doris Elizabeth Joyner, July 26, 1964; children—Nicholas Andrew, Jennifer Joy. Pvt. practice dentistry, Newport News, Va., 1967—; dental cons. Patrick Henry Hosp. Counselor, Augsburger Crusade, 1970, Harrington Crusade, 1971. Bd. dirs. Peninsula Youth for Christ; trustee Youth for Christ, 1970-71. Served with USNR, 1965-67. Baptist (deacon 1969-70, dir. Sunday sch. 1970-72, chmn. nominating com. 1969-72, pulpit com. 1970, mem. finance com. 1969-70). Mason, Kiwanian (dir. 1969-71). Home: 104 Peirsey Pl Newport News VA 23602 Office: 559 Denbigh Blvd Newport News VA 23602

ROBERTSON, BERNICE TALMADGE BELL (MRS. RICHARD DALE ROBERTSON), hosp. adminstr.; b. Pittsburg, Tex., Mar. 25, 1920; d. Barney Arthur and Letha Bernice (Gautney) Bell; student Columbia U., 1962-63; m. Richard Dale Robertson, Dec. 23, 1938; children—Sherry (Mrs. Will Edd Grimes), Genie (Mrs. Cecil Boren, Jr.). PBX operator, adminstrv. clk. Desha County Hosp., Dumas Ark., 1952-55, bookkeeper, 1955-56, bookkeeper, adminstrv. asst., 1956-59, adminstr., 1959-65; surveyor, insp. State Health Dept., Little Rock, 1966; adminstr. McGehee Desha County Hosp., McGehee, Ark., 1966—. Sec., McGehee Ecology Commn., 1970—; pres P.T.A., Dumas, 1952-53, Desha County Health Adv. Council, 1969—; mem. area adv. council State Ark. Dept. Edn. Div. Vocational, Tech. and Adult Edn., 1971—; coordinator Candy Stripers, 1967—; treas. Grady Soc. Christian Service, 1958—. Bd. dirs. Areawide Health Adv. Council, 1969—. Mem. Women's C. of C., Am. Hosp. Assn., Am. Hosp. Financial Assn., Ark. Adminstrs. Forum (sec. 1961-62), Southeast Ark. Hosp. Council (pres. 1961-62, 1969-70, sec. 1971-72), Am. Coll. Hosp. Adminstrs. Methodist. Club: Women's Civic (pres. 1970-71) (McGehee). Home: Jefferson St McGehee AR 71654 Office: Green Meadow Addition McGehee AR 71654

ROBERTSON, BILLY PERKINS, cons.; b. Bangs, Tex., July 23, 1915; s. Nicholas Perkins and Addie May (Schulze) R.; B.S., U. Tex., 1942; postgrad. Northwestern U., 1964; m. Ida Elizabeth Gilliland, Dec. 29, 1943; children—Brian Paul, Elizabeth Jan. Research engr. Westinghouse Electric Corp., Pitts., 1942-47; sales engr. Humble Oil & Refining Co., Houston, 1947-49, mgr. sales engring., 1949-53, supt. spl. products mfg., 1955, dist. mgr., 1956-57, region mgr. gen. office, consumer sales, 1958-65, new products coordinator, 1965-72; now with Bus. Counselors, cons. firm, also Hompark Realty. dir. Humble

Leasing Co. Bd. dirs. Bellaire Presbyn. Day Sch.; trustee Brazos Presbyn. Homes. Recipient certificate commendation Am. Soc. M.E., 1957, Council award, 1959. Registered profl. engr., Tex. Mem. Tex. Mfrs. Assn., E. Tex., Houston chambers commerce, Houston Engring. and Sci. Soc. (v.p., dir.), Pi Tau Sigma. Presbyn. (deacon, elder). Contbr. articles to profl. Jours. Patentee in field. Home: 5819 Queensloch Houston TX 77035 Office: Humble Bldg PO Box 2180 Houston TX 77001

ROBERTSON, CARY, journalist; b. Louisville, Apr. 18, 1902; s. Archibald T. and Ella (Broadus) R.; student Wake Forest Coll., 1920-22, U. Va. 1922-25; Nieman fellow, Harvard, 1945-46; m. Priscilla Smith, May 26, 1934; children—Charlotte, Harry, Cary. With Louisville Courier-Jour., 1925—, reporter, 1925-27, day city editor, 1927, makeup editor, 1928, Sunday editor, 1930-68, book editor, 1968—; Ky. corr. Newsweek mag. 1950—; lectr. univs. Mem. Orgn. com. Assn. Chamber Music Players, N.Y.C., 1948—. Dir. George Rogers Clark Heritage, Inc. (chmn. 1966); trustee Louisville Chamber Music Soc., pres., 1964, 65. Mem. Am. Assn. Sunday and Feature Editors (v.p. 1964, pres. 1965), Locally Edited Mag. Editors Assn. (chmn. 1950), Anchorage Trails (pres. 1961), Sigma Delta Chi. Club: Owl Creek Country (Anchorage, Ky.). Home: Anchorage KY 40223 Office: Louisville Courier-Jour 525 W Broadway Louisville KY 40202

ROBERTSON, CLAUDE KELLER, lawyer; b. Nashville, Jan. 31, 1932; s. Elmer Sutton and Claudia (Keller) R.; J.D., U. Tenn., 1958; m. Irma Joyce McCollum, Sept. 25, 1953; children—Claudia Kay, DeAnna Joyce. Admitted to Tenn. bar, 1959; partner firm Fowler, Rowntree, Fowter & Robertson, attys. Bd. dirs. Knoxville United Fund, 1964, Knoxville Travelers Aid Soc., 1965—; bd. dirs., pres. Presbyn. Homes Tenn., 1963-68. Campaign mgr. Republican Howard Baker for Senate, 1964, 66; chmn. Tenn. Rep. State Exec. Com., 1967-69; del. Rep. Nat. Conv., 1968; mgr. Tenn. campaign Nixon for Pres., 1968; candidate for gov. of Tenn., 1970. Served with USAF, 1951-54. Mem. Am., Knoxville (pres. jr. bar sect. 1962) bar assns., Bar Assn. Tenn., Phi Delta Phi. Presbyn. (elder). Home: 211 Hartford Dr Knoxville TN 37920 Office: Hamilton Bank Bldg Knoxville TN 37902

ROBERTSON, IDA ROBERTS (MRS. SAMUEL THOMPSON ROBERTSON), home economist; b. Shawboro, N.C., Mar. 8, 1918; d. James M. and Ida C. (Perkins) Roberts; B.A., East Carolina U., 1939; postgrad. Woman's Coll., U. N.C. (now U. N.C. at Greensboro), 1948, 62; m. Samuel Thompson Robertson, June 30, 1949. Faculty pub. high sch., Kenansville, N.C., 1939-40; home mgmt. supr. county Farmer's Home Adminstrn., Raleigh, N.C., 1940-46; vocational home econs. tchr., high sch., Williamston, N.C., 1946-48; tchr. English high sch., Woodsdale, N.C., 1954-55; asst. dir. Dairy Council Richmond (Va.), 1957-62. Mem. Am., Richmond (v.p. 1958-60, publicity chmn. 1960-62, membership chmn. 1963-66, treas. 1965-67), home econs. assns., Va. (chmn. ways and means com. 1959-61), Richmond home economists in bus., Currituck County Hist. Soc., East Carolina Alumni Assn. (life mem., sec.-treas. Richmond area 1963-70), Richmond Agrl. Grange, Phi Sigma Alpha (pres. 1967-68, named Woman of Year 1968, extension officer, 1971—). Democrat. Methodist. Home: 5710 W Franklin St Richmond VA 23226

ROBERTSON, JAMES GREGORY, plastic surgeon; b. Carrollton, Ga., July 23, 1917; s. James Gregory and Eva (Crawford) R.; B.S., Emory U., 1941, M.D., 1942; m. Lorna Ann Dooling, Aug. 21, 1952; children—Bonnie Kay, Kim Evelyn, Sue Lynn, James G. Intern, Grady Meml. Hosp., Atlanta, 1942-43; surg. resident MacDill Sta. Hosp., Tampa, Fla., 1943-44; chief surg. resident City Hosp., Winston-Salem, N.C., 1946-47; gen. practice surgery, Atlanta, 1947-49; chief resident Coney Island Hosp., 1950-51; chief resident plastic surgery N.Y. Hosp., 1951-52; pvt. practice specializing in plastic and reconstructive surgery, Miami, Fla., 1952—; clin. instr. plastic surgery U. Miami Med. Sch., 1954—; chief of plastic surgery Coral Gables (Fla.) Hosp.; attending staff plastic surgery Bapt. Hosp., Miami; attending staff Jackson Meml. Hosp., Variety Children's Hosp., Mercy Hosp., South Miami Hosp. Trustee Opera Guild Greater Miami, v.p. men's opera group. Served with AUS, 1943-46. Decorated Bronze Star medal. Diplomate Am. Bd. Plastic Surgery. Fellow A.C.S.; mem. Fla., Dade County med. assns., Internat. Coll. Surgeons, Am., Southeastern, Fla. (past pres.) socs. plastic and reconstructive surgeons. Clubs: Surf, Coral Reef Yacht, Rod and Reel, Islandia Yacht, Surf, Ocean Reef, Com. of 100, Jamestown (pres.). Contbr. articles to profl. jours. Home: 570 Arvida Pkwy Coral Gables FL 33133 Office: Ingraham Bldg Miami FL 33131

ROBERTSON, JAMES MEBANE, physician; b. Olin, N.C., Aug. 4, 1906; s. William Lee and Augusta (Weisner) R.; B.A., U. N.C., 1928, postgrad., 1929-30; M.D., Temple U. Med. Sch., 1932; m. Ann Jones, Mar. 2, 1934; 1 son, James Mebane, Jr. Intern Hamot Hosp., Erie, Pa., 1932-33; pvt. practice gen. medicine, Harmony, N.C., 1933—; mem. staff Iredell Meml. Hosp., Statesville, N.C. Mayor, Harmony, N.C., 1971—. Mem. A.M.A., Iredell County Med. Soc., Am. Acad. Gen. Practice, Phi Rho Sigma. Democrat. Presbyn. (elder 1945-72). Mason (Shriner), Elk, Moose. Club: City (Statesville, N.C.). Home: 25 N Main St Harmony NC 28634 Office: 10 Union Grove Rd Harmony NC 28634

ROBERTSON, JOHN LOVELL, banker; b. Marietta, O., Aug. 14, 1919; s. Benjamin Harrison and Alice (Lovell) R.; grad. high sch.; m. Geneva P. White, Nov. 9, 1940; children—Susan W., John W. Engaged in cattle ranching, Okla. and Tex., 1938-42, 45-53; with First Nat. Bank and Trust Co., Tulsa, 1953—, exec. v.p., 1961-67, pres., chmn. exec. com. 1967—, also adv. dir.; sec. Fifth & Boston Corp. Pres., Tulsa Clearing House Assn.; dir., treas. Industries for Tulsa; mem. Tulsa Airport Authority; mem. sr. sdv. council Okla. Cattlemens Assn.; mem. Mayor Tulsa Com. Human Relations in Industry. Vice pres., dir. St. Francis Hosp.; bd. dirs., v.p., Tulsa Philharmonic Soc., Tulsa County div. A.R.C. Served with USAAF, 1942-46. Mem. Tulsa C. of C. (vice chmn. indsl. dept.). Methodist. Clubs: Tulsa, Tennis, Southern Hills Country (pres., dir.) (Tulsa). Home: 2469 E 33d St Tulsa OK 74105 Office: First Nat Bank & Trust Co Tulsa OK 74103

ROBERTSON, RICHARD BOYD, govt. ofcl.; b. Richmond, Va., Nov. 14, 1936; s. Walter G. and Annie (Boyd) R.; B.S., Va. Mil. Inst., 1958; hwy. traffic certificate Yale, 1961; M. in Regional Planning, U. N.C., 1964; m. Patricia Jean Atkinson, Aug. 29, 1959; children—Elizabeth Bruce, Richard Boyd. With Va. Dept. Hwys., Richmond, 1958-67, hwy. traffic engr., 1964-65, transp. planning engr., 1965-67; exec. dir. Richmond Regional Planning Dist. Commn., 1967-70; dir. Office of Transp. Planning, Div. of State Planning and Community Affairs, Office of the Gov., Commonwealth of Va., 1971; regional transp. planner Appalachian Regional Commn., Washington, 1972—. Mem. Am. Inst. Planners, Inst. Traffic Engrs., Am. Soc. C.E., Am. Polit. Sci. Assn., Regional Sci. Assn., Am. Soc. Pub. Adminstrn., Am. Acad. Polit. and Social Sci. Club: Va. Mil. Inst. (Richmond). Home: 7725 Canal Ct McLean VA 22101 Office: Appalachian Regional Commn 1666 Connecticut Av NW Washington DC 20008

ROBERTSON, ROBERT NELSON, civil engr.; b. Bay City, Tex., Nov. 26, 1933; s. John Houston and Madge (Clement) R.; B.S. in Archtl. Engring., U. Tex., 1956, M.S. in Civil Engring., 1961; m. Carol Beth Villarreal, June 7, 1958; children—Marta Elaine, Steven Michael, Douglas Arthur, Robert Carroll. With Walter Kidde, engrs., S.W., Houston, 1956-57, W. Clark Craig, engrs., Austin, Tex., 1957-58, Tex. Hwy. Dept., Austin, 1958-61; with Lockwood, Andrews & Newnam, Inc., Houston, 1961—, dept. head structural div., 1972—. Registered profl. engr., Tex. Mem. Am. Soc. C.E. (chmn. structural com. Tex. sect. 1969), Am. Inst. Steel Constrn., Am. Concrete Inst., Tex. Soc. Profl. Engrs., Assn. Iron and Steel Engrs., Phi Eta Sigma, Chi Epsilon. Presbyn. (elder 1969-70). Home: 8311 Burning Hills Houston TX 77071 Office: 1010 Waugh Dr Houston TX 77019

ROBERTSON, ROLAND BURLSON, JR., physician; b. Taylorsville, Miss., Feb. 17, 1934; s. Roland Burlson and Nellie (Vowell) R.; B.S., U. So. Miss., 1955; M.D., U. Tenn., 1958; m. Anita Jane McKelvey, Apr. 14, 1957; children—Katherine Ann, John David Roland. Intern, John Gaston Hosp., Memphis, 1958-59; gen. practice medicine, Taylorsville, Miss., 1959-61; resident in internal medicine U. Miss. Med. Center, 1963-66; practice medicine, specializing in internal medicine, Meridian, Miss., 1966-67; staff physician VA Hosp., Jackson, Miss., 1967—, asst. chief med. service, 1970—; asst. prof. medicine U. Miss. Med. Center, 1967—. Served with USAF, 1961-63. Mem. Central Med. Soc., Miss. State, Am. med. assns., Am. Coll. Physicians, Miss. (pres. 1971-72), Am. thoracic socs., Jackson Acad. Medicine, Alpha Omega Alpah. Episcopalian (warden 1970-72). Home: 541 Woodson Dr Jackson MS 39206 Office: 1500 E Woodrow Wilson Jackson MS 39216

ROBERTSON, STOKES V., JR, justice Miss. Supreme Ct.; b. Hattiesburg, Miss., Nov. 9, 1912; s. Stokes Vernon; student Millsaps Coll.; B.A., U. Miss., 1933, LL.B., 1935; m. Una L. Caldwell; children—Stokes V. III, David G., Helen C. Admitted to bar, 1935; practiced law in Jackson, 1935-55; Chancellor 5th (Miss.) dist., 1955-65; justice Miss. Supreme Ct., Jackson, 1966—. Served with Q.M.C., AUS, 1940-45, 51-52. Mem. Miss. State Bar (past 2d v.p.), Hinds County Bar Assn. Presbyn. (elder). Kiwanian. Home: 2246 N Cheryl Dr Jackson MS 39211 Office: Miss Supreme Ct Jackson MS 39205

ROBERTSON, THOMAS JAMES, banker; b. Columbia, S.C., Dec. 16, 1897; s. Edwin W. and Evelyn (Perkins) R.; grad. Hotchkiss Sch., Lakeville, Conn., 1917; A.B., Yale, 1921; m. Mary Martin, Oct. 20, 1923; children—Edwin Wales II, Mary Ravenel; m. 2d, Mary McN. Milling, Aug. 16, 1948. Began with Nat. Loan & Exchange Bank, Columbia, 1921, becoming pres. in 1927; now chmn. bd. First Nat. Bank of S.C., Columbia; pres. Columbia Real Estate & Trust Co. Served as comdr. U.S. Navy, World War II. Served as ensign Naval Aviation, U.S. Navy, World War I. Mem. Alpha Delta Phi, Scroll and Key (Yale). Presbyn. Clubs: Forest Lake, Palmetto, Pine Tree Hunt. Address: First National Bank Columbia SC 29201

ROBERTSON, THOMAS PASCHE, airline exec.; b. Austin, Tex., Mar. 14, 1915; s. Walter Lee and Gertrude (Pasche) R.; B.B.A., U. Tex., 1938; m. Agness Francis Foster, Mar. 24, 1941; children—Thomas Ross, Sharon Anne (Mrs. Duval F. Moss III). Accountant, Fed. Land Bank of Houston, 1939-42; indsl. relations analyst Lockheed Aircraft Corp., Dallas, 1942-43; statis. analyst Douglas Aircraft Corp., Oklahoma City, 1943-46; with Braniff Airways, ~~Inc.~~, Dallas, 1946—, v.p., 1967—. Mem. Newcomen Soc., Nat. Economists Club, Dallas Economist Club (past pres.), Delta Sigma Pi. Home: 6220 Royalton Dr Dallas TX 75230 Office: PO Box 35001 Dallas TX 75235

ROBERTSON, WALTER LOUIS, newspaper editor; b. Dallas, June 24, 1926; s. Ivan C. and Flora Mae (Russell) R.; B.S. in Journalism, So. Meth. U., 1950; m. Janice Darolyn Comegys, July 29, 1950; children—Louis Alan, Rebecca Eileen, Russell Caeson, Lisa Beth, Lauri Gail. Sports reporter Dallas Morning News, 1950-57, asst. sports editor, 1958-60, sports editor, 1961—. Co-chmn., Tex. Sports Hall of Fame, 1962—. Served with AUS, World War II; ETO. Mem. Football Writers Am., Basketball Writers Am., Tex. Sports Writers Assn. (v.p.), Dallas C. of C. (athletic com.). Democrat. Presbyn. Home: 2521 Beechmont Dr Dallas TX 75228 Office: Dallas Morning News Communications Center Dallas TX 75222

ROBERTSON, WILLIAM BERNARD, govt. ofcl.; b. Roanoke, Va., Jan. 31, 1933; s. Irvin W. and Rebecca (Roberts) R.; B.S., Bluefield State Coll., 1954; M.S., Radford Coll., 1965; m. Johnnie Lucille Early, Nov. 6, 1953; children—William Allen, Bernice Victoria. Tchr. pub. schs., Roanoke, Va., 1956-65, elementary supr., 1965-69; spl. asst. to Gov. Va., Richmond, 1970—; moderator Your Community Speaks program WTOY, Roanoke, 1968-69; moderator Valley Views program WRFT-TV, 1968-69. Pres. Southwest Va. Community Devel. Fund, 1968-69; mem. speakers bur. Roanoke Fine Arts Center, 1967-69; mem. Pres.'s Com. on Mental Retardation, 1970—, Pres.'s Adv. Com. Sickle Cell Anemia, 1971, Nat. Motor Vehicle Safety Adv. Com., 1972—. Trustee Roanoke Valley United Fund; bd. dirs. Catholic Family and Childrens Service of Roanoke, Family Service-Travelers Aid, Va. State Mental Health, Juvenile and Domestic Relations Ct., King-Kennedy Found. Mem. Roanoke, Va., Nat. edn. assns., Omega Psi Phi. Roman Catholic. Home: 5548 C Pony Farm Dr Richmond VA 23227 Office: Gov's Office State Capitol Richmond VA 23219

ROBERTSON, WILLIAM EDWARD, JR., research co. exec.; b. Carteret, N.J., Dec. 15, 1916; s. William E. and Beneva (Roy) R.; B.A., Bucknell U., 1938; m. Dorothy Mary Dunn, Sept. 21, 1940 (div.); children—William E. III, Malcolm B., Douglas A.; m. 2d, Regina E. Gallagher, Nov. 24, 1971. Reporter, editorial writer Courier-News, Plainfield, N.J., 1938-42; asst. to pub. Harpers Mag., N.Y.C., 1946-50; asso. pub. dir. U.S. News & World Report, Washington, 1950-69; chmn. bd. Communications Marketing, Inc., Washington, 1970-72, also dir.; v.p. Benson & Benson, Inc., Princeton, N.J., 1972—; dir. Meredith S. Conley, Inc., N.Y.C. Served to capt. AUS, 1942-46, 51-52. Mem. Nat. Press Club, Am. Marketing Assn., Am. Assn. Pub. Opinion Researchers, Assn. Indsl. Advertisers, Internat. Newspaper Promotion Assn., Izaak Walton League, Nat. Assn. Execs. Club, Washington Soc. Assn. Execs. Republican. Episcopalian. Clubs: Kenwood Golf and Country (Bethesda, Md.); National Capitol Gun (Washington). Home: 1600 S Eads St Arlington VA 22202 Office: 1629 K St NW Washington DC 20006

ROBERTSON, WILLIAM HARRIS PETERMAN, editor; b. New Orleans, July 22, 1920; s. John G.W. and Eleanor (Peterman) R.; B.S., U.S. Naval Acad., 1942; m. Arden Marion Bullock, Sept. 5, 1953; children—Caroline, Zaring, Winter. With Thoroughbred Record, Lexington, Ky., 1952—, mng. editor, 1955-63, editor, 1963—; pres. Record Pub. Co., Lexington, 1964-71, chmn., 1971—. Served with USN, 1942-52. Clubs: Thoroughbred Am., Iroquois Hunt, Spindletop Hall, Ryland Lakes Country. Author: History of Thoroughbred Racing in America, 1964. Home: Briar Hill Pike Route 4 Lexington KY 40505 Office: Thoroughbred Record 904 N Broadway Lexington KY 40505

ROBERTSON, WILLIAM THOMAS, SR., farm exec.; b. Greenville, Miss., Oct. 17, 1920; s. Thomas Dotson and Irene (Cooke) R.; B.S., Miss. State Coll., 1943; m. Frances Scott Bostick, June 3, 1943; children—William Thomas, Edna Kirk (Mrs. Henderson Alfred Moore III), Alexander Bostick. Partner, Holly Ridge Planting Co. (Miss.), 1943—, Holly Ridge Ranch, 1951—, Husbandville Plantation Farming Operations, Chatham, Miss., 1958—; pres. Holly Ridge Gin Co., Inc., 1958—, Kan. Plantation, Inc., Inverness, Miss., 1962—; dir. Valley Chem. Co., Yazoo Valley Oil Mill, Inc., Planters Bank & Trust Co., Ruleville, Miss., First Savs. & Loan, Indianola, Miss., Bell, Inc., St. Rest Plantation, Inc. Trustee Cotton, Inc. Served with AUS, World War II. Mem. Miss. Soybean Assn., Miss. Econ. Council, Delta Council, Sunflower County Farm Bur. Methodist (steward), Rotarian. Home: Holly Ridge MS 38749 Office: PO Box 95 Holly Ridge MS 38749

ROBESON, VERNON SCOTT, mech. engr.; b. Tama, Ia., Sept. 1, 1921; s. Scott Carlyle and Blanche Irene (Coe) R.; student Dana Coll., 1940; B.S. in M.E., U. Neb., 1949; postgrad. U. Ala. at Huntsville, 1960-64; m. Nina Mildred Peck, Sept. 27, 1941; children—Vicki Joan (Mrs. Dan Williams Nash), Philip Scott. Engr., Boeing Co., Seattle, 1949-50; chief engr. Kelly Ryan Farm Equipment Co., Blair, Neb., 1952-56; mech. engr. Omaha Dist. C.E., 1956-59; staff specialist, supr. facilities planning staff office Army Ballistic Missile Agy., Redstone Arsenal, Ala., 1959-63, value engring. mgr. Lance Missile System Project Office, 1963—. Served with AUS, 1943-46; ETO. Decorated Combat Infantryman's badge; recipient Outstanding Value Engr. award Army Missile Command, 1965; named One of Ten Top Stock Car Drivers, Washington County, Neb., 1956. Registered profl. engr., Ala. Mem. Huntsville Art League, Sigma Tau, Pi Tau Sigma. Painter oils and portraits; Neb. State champion model airplane flyer, 1948. Home: 8500 Camille Dr Huntsville AL 35802 Office: Lance Project Office Redstone Arsenal AL 35809

ROBEY, HARRY RUSSELL, coll. treas.; b. Buena Vista, Va., Sept. 30, 1895; s. William Thomas and Susan (Connor) R.; grad. Dunsmore Coll. Accounting, 1917; Washington and Lee U., 1918; m. Margaret Durham, Sept. 12, 1922. Cashier Kingsport Pulp Corp. (Va.), 1918-19; treas. Farmers & Mchts. Mills, Buena Vista, Va., 1920-22; treas., bus. mgr., partner So. Sem. and Jr. Coll., Buena Vista, Va., 1922—. Mem. Buena Vista City Council, 1934-50; mem. Buena Vista Planning Commn., 1936-50; chmn. Buena Vista United Fund, 1968-72; organizer Buena Vista Health Dept., City Recreation Dept. Served with USNR, 1917-19. Episcopalian (mem. exec. council 1970-72). Mason. Clubs: Farmington Country, Shenandoah, Tri-Brook Country. Home: 2156 N Chestnut Av Buena Vista VA 24416 Office: Southern Seminary & Jr Coll Buena Vista VA 24416

ROBEY, KATHLEEN MORAN (MRS. RALPH WEST ROBEY), club woman; b. Boston, Aug. 9, 1909; d. John Joseph and Katherine (Berrigan) Moran; B.A., Trinity Coll., Washington, 1933; m. Ralph West Robey, Jan. 28, 1941. Actress appearing in Pride and Prejudic, Broadway, 1935, Tomorrow is a Holiday, road co., 1935, Death Takes a Holiday, road co., 1936, Left Turn, Broadway, 1936, Come Home to Roost, Boston, 1936; pub. relations N.Y. Fashion Industry, N.Y.C., 1938-43. Mem. Florence Crittenton Home and Hosp., Women's Aux. Salvation Army, Gray Lady, D.C. chpt. A.R.C.; mem. Seton Guild St. Ann's Infant Home. Mem. Internat. Platform Assn. Republican (mem. League Rep. Women D.C.). Roman Catholic. Club: City Tavern, Cosmos (Washington); Springdale Hall (Camden, S.C.). Home: 4000 Cathedral Av NW Washington DC 20016

ROBIE, CARROLL H., JR., physician; b. Danville, Ky., Nov. 21, 1923; s. Carroll H. and Myrtle (Baker) R.; A.B., U. Ky., 1946; M.D., Ohio State U., 1949; m. Barbara Jean Brooks, Sept. 17, 1949; children—Marilyn Baker, David Brooks. Intern, Jefferson Med. Coll. Hosp., Phila., 1949-50; resident Henry Ford Hosp., Detroit, 1952-56; practice medicine specializing in internal medicine, Louisville, 1956—; asst. clin. prof. medicine U. Louisville Sch. Medicine, 1968—; mem. active staff Ky. Baptist, Methodist Evangelical, St. Anthony hosps.; mem. courtesy staff Jewish, St. Joseph, Norton Infirmary hosps. Mem. Ky. Health Facilities Council, 1971-73. Served with AUS, 1943-46, USAF, 1951-52. Fellow A.C.P.; mem. A.M.A., Am. Soc. Internal Medicine, Am. Coll. Chest Physicians, Ky. Med. Assn. (v.p. 1971-72), Louisville Soc. Internists (pres. 1969). Mem. Christian Ch. (deacon 1960-72). Optomist. Clubs: Jefferson, Filson (Louisville). Home: 2556 Seneca Dr Louisville KY 40205 Office: 1169 Eastern Pkwy Louisville KY 40217

ROBIN, VINCENT JOSEPH, III, corp. exec.; b. Larose, La., Mar. 4, 1918; s. Vincent Joseph and Edverine (Savoie) R.; student Internat. Corp. Sch., 1943-45, Internat. Corr. Schs., 1965; m. Erline E. Chaisson, June 1, 1935; children—Joel P., Marian (Mrs. Russell DiMarco), Donald J., Vincent Joseph IV. Owner, exec. pres. Robin Boat Rental Service, Inc., Robin, Inc., Offshore Cresboats, Inc., Erline E., Inc., Marine Taxis, Inc., Marian Ann, Inc., Robin Internat. Marine Towing Corp., Robin Marine Corp., Robin Towing Corp., Robin Cresboat Corp., Harvey, La., 1947—. Rotarian, K.C. Clubs: Krewe of Bacchus, Young Man's Business (New Orleans). Home: 4000 Westbank Expressway Marrero LA 70072 Office: 440 Pailet St PO Box 526 Harvey LA 70058

ROBINETTE, CARSON LINDSEY, ednl. adminstr.; b. Blackwater, Va., Apr. 9, 1913; s. Amos Oscar and Dettie (McPherson) R.; A.B., Lincoln Meml. U., 1936; M.A., Peabody Coll., 1952; m. Irene Eugenie Shoun, Oct. 10, 1936; children—Sammie Laura, Ramond Schmitt. Prin., Lee County (Va.) schs., 1936-60, dir. instrn. Lee County Sch. Bd., Jonesville, 1960—. Pres., Lee County Tchrs. Assn., 1950. Jury commr., 1961-62, mem. Grand Jury, 1971. Campaign mgr. Dem. congl. campaign, 1963. Mem. Meth. Library Bd., 1969. Mem. Va. Edn. Assn. Methodist. Lion (pres. Jonesville 1958), Mason (Shriner). Home: 142 Church St Jonesville VA 24263 Office: Lee County School Board Main St Jonesville VA 24263

ROBINETTE, DAVID PRESTON, govt. ofcl.; b. Kingsport, Tenn., Feb. 7, 1935; s. T. and Kathleen Alice (Necessary) R.; B.S., Va. Poly. Inst., 1959, M.Ed., 1965; m. Margaret E. Dutton, June 24, 1961. Tchr. vocational agr., 1959-64; prin. Allegheny Dist. High Sch., 1965-67; extension agt. Va. Polytech. Inst. and State U., Blacksburg, 1968—. Mem. Nat., Va. extension agr. assns., 4-H Extension Agts. Assn. Lion. Clubs: Ruritan (pres. 1966), Civitan (Abingdon). Home: Route 1 Box 228-C Meadowview VA 24361 Office: Federal Bldg Abingdon VA 24210

ROBINETTE, JOHN ZACK, project engr.; b. Racolet, S.C., Aug. 29, 1925; s. John Zack and Marie (Byars) Robinette; B.S. in Mech. Engring., Clemson A. and M. Coll., 1947; m. Edith Juanita Hames, Dec. 27, 1946; children—John Hames, Russell Conrad. Mgr. Robinette Motor Co., Pacolet, S.C., 1947-51; jr. engr. Deering Milliken Service Corp., Spartanburg, S.C., 1951-52, engr., 1954-56; plant engr. Gayley Mill Corp., Marietta, S.C., 1952-54; project engr. Lockwood Greene Engrs., Spartansburg, S.C., 1956-64, Fabric Services, Inc., Orangeburg, S.C., 1964-65, Woodside Mills, Inc., Greenville, S.C., 1965—. City engr., Pacolet, S.C., 1960-64. Served with USAAF, 1944-45. Registered profl. engr., S.C., Tenn., Ala., Ky. Mem. S.C. Soc. Profl. Engrs., C. of C. Home: 133 Fernbrook Circle

Spartanburg SC 29302 Office: 260 S Pleasantburg Dr Greenville SC 29607

ROBINS, E. CLAIBORNE, pharm. mfr.; b. Richmond, Va., July 8, 1910; s. Claiborne and Martha (Taylor) R.; student McGuire's U. Sch.; A.B., U. Richmond, 1931, LL.D., 1960; B.S., Med. Coll. Va. Sch. Pharmacy, 1933, D. Pharm. Sci., 1958, LL.D., 1960, D.Sc. in Pharmacy (hon.), Mass. Coll. Pharmacy; m. Lora McGlasson, June 24, 1938; children—Lora Elizabeth (Mrs. Mayer), E. Claiborne, Ann Carol (Mrs. John Cheves Haskell, Jr.). Chmn. bd., chief exec. officer A.H. Robins Co., Inc., Richmond; pres. A.H. Robins Co. of Can., Ltd., A.H. Robins de Mexico, S.A. de C.V., A.H. Robins Inter-Am. Corp., Whittier Labs, Monroe-Prestwould Corp.; dir., exec. com. Central Nat. Bank, Va.; dir. Thalhimers Bros., Inc., Ethyl Corp., Va. Electric & Power Co., Chesapeake & Potomac Telephone Co., Richmond Corp. Trustee Richmond Meml. Hosp., United Givers Fund, Crippled Childrens Hosp.; chmn. exec. com., trustee U. Richmond, past pres. alumni council. Recipient Distinguished Service award U. Richmond 1960, Dean M. McCann award Pharm. Wholesalers Assn., 1968, Hugo H. Schaefer medal Am. Pharm. Assn., 1969, Liberty Bell award Richmond Bar Assn., 1970; Sertoma Club award, 1970; Thomas Jefferson award Pub. Relations Soc. Am., 1970; named Pharmacist of Year, Va. Pharm. Assn., 1967, Bus. Leader of Year, Sales & Marketing Execs. Richmond, 1969, Medal of Honor, Virginians of Md., 1971, Distinguished Service award Va. C. of C. Mem. Pharm. Mfrs. Assn. (past chmn.), N.A.M., Va. Mfrs. Assn., Va. Pharm. Assn., Newcomen Soc. N.A., Richmond C. of C. (past pres.), Med. Coll. Va. Alumni Assn. (past pres., dir.), Phi Beta Kappa, Alpha Kappa Psi, Omicron Delta Kappa, Phi Delta Chi, Kappa Psi, Lambda Chi Alpha, Beta Gamma Sigma (honoree 1971). Baptist (mem. bd. adminstrn.). Clubs: Rotary (past dir.), Commonwealth Forum, Country of Va., Rotunda, Princess Anne. Home: Clear View River Rd Richmond VA 23226 Office: 1407 Cummings Dr Richmond VA 23220

ROBINS, EDWIN MORING, trucking co. exec., editor; b. Greensboro, N.C., Dec. 20, 1929; s. Marmaduke and Mary Elizabeth (Sussdorff) R.; A.B. in Journalism, U. N.C., 1951; m. Annemarie Sophie Elion, June 25, 1955; children—Thomas Daniel, Edwin Leonard, John Elion. Editor, Henry County (Va.) Jour., 1955; reporter Winston-Salem Jour. and Twin City Sentinel, 1955-64, copy editor, 1955-64; employee communications mgr. McLean Trucking Co., Winston-Salem, N.C., 1964—, editor Trek, 1964—. Served with USCGR, 1952-55. Recipient Best Newspaper award for trucking industry Am. Trucking Assns., 1966, 67, 68, 70. Mem. S. Atlantic Council Indsl. Editors (v.p., dir. 1969-70, pres. 1970-72, recipient Best Newspaper award 1966, 68, 70), Trucking Industry Pub. Relations Coordinating Com. (program chmn. 1970). Kiwanian. Home: 2961 St Claire Rd Winston-Salem NC 27106 Office: 617 Waughtown St Winston-Salem NC 27106

ROBINSON, ADELBERT CARL, lawyer; b. Shawnee, Okla., Dec. 13, 1926; s. William H. and Mayme (Forston) R.; student Okla. Baptist U., 1944-47; LL.B., Okla. U., 1950, J.D., 1970; m. Marilyn Ruth Stubbs, Dec. 28, 1963; children—William, James, Schuyler, Donald, David, Nancy, Lauri. Admitted to Okla. bar, 1950; practiced in Muskogee, 1956—; with legal dept. Phillips Petroleum Co., 1950-51; adjuster U.S. Fidelity & Guaranty Co., 1951-54, atty., adjuster-in-charge, 1954-56; partner Fite & Robinson, 1956-62; partner Fite, Robinson & Summers, 1963-70, Robinson & Summers, 1970-72, Robinson, Summers & Locke, 1972—; police judge, 1963-64; municipal judge, 1964-70. Chmn. Inter-Organizational Relations Com., 1960-63; chmn. Muskogee County Law Day, 1963; chmn. Muskogee Area Redevel. Authority, 1963; chmn. Muskogee County chpt. Am. Cancer Soc., 1956; chmn. Profl. Cooperation Com., 1965-69. Pres., bd. dirs. Muskogee Community Council; bd. dirs. Muskogee Community Concert Assn., Muskogee Tourist Information Bur., 1964-68; bd. dirs., gen. counsel United Cerebral Palsy Eastern Okla., 1964-68. Served with inf. AUS, 1945-46. Mem. Okla. (chmn. uniform law com., past regional chmn. grievance com.), Muskogee County (pres. 1971, mem. exec. council) bar assns., Okla. Assn. Def. Counsel (dir.), Okla. Assn. Municipal Judges (dir.), Muskogee C. of C., Delta Theta Phi. Methodist. Rotarian (pres. 1971-72). Home: Route 3 Box 141 Muskogee OK 74401 Office: 213 N 3d St P O Box 87 Muskogee OK 74401

ROBINSON, A(LICE) CHESTER, educator; b. Vidalia, Ga., July 29, 1921; s. Arthur E. and Rosa (Murdock) R.; B.S., Savannah State Coll., 1948; M.P.H., N.C. State Coll., 1949; postgrad. N.Y. U., 1954-55, Ind. U., 1958, U. Miami, 1963; LL.D., 1969; m. Verna L. Armstrong, June 7, 1948; children—Danitra Jo, Donna Alicia. Chmn. dept. health phys. edn., coll. supr. student tchrs. Ft. Valley State Coll., 1948-69, dir. health and temperance workshop, 1958-68; dir. Sch. Health Workshop, Atlanta U., 1958; chmn. dept. phys. edn. Fla. Meml. Coll., Miami, 1969—, dir. implementation self study, 1970. Cons. State Dept. Edn., 1968-69. Mem. Ga. Regional Med. Bd., 1969; mem. adv. bd. regents U. Ga., 1967-68. Bd. dirs. Ga. Respiratory and Tb Assn., Dade County Mentally Retarded Assn., Ch. of Open Doors. Served with AUS, 1942-46. Mem. A.A.H.P.E.R., Southeastern Athletic Assn. (corr. sec. 1970-71), Ga. Coaches Ofcls. Assn., Phi Beta Sigma (Plaque award 1969, state dir. 1966-69, Plock award 1972), Phi Delta Kappa. Home: 10700 NW 12th Ct Miami FL 33167

ROBINSON, AUBREY EUGENE, JR., U.S. dist. judge; b. Madison, N.J., Mar. 30, 1922; s. Aubrey Eugene and Mabel (Jackson) R.; A.B., Cornell U., 1943, LL.B., 1947; m. Sara E. Payne, Dec. 31, 1946; children—Paula, Sheryl. Admitted to N.Y., D.C. bars, 1948; practice with law firms, Washington, 1948-65; asso. judge Juvenile Ct. D.C., 1965-66, U.S. Dist. Ct. D.C., 1966—. Gen. counsel Am. Council Human Rights, 1953-55, dir., 1955; mem. D.C. Commr.'s Com. Child Placement Regulations, 1954-62. Mem. D.C. Pub. Welfare Adv. Council, 1963-65; mem. Washington Urban League Adoption Project, 1959; mem. membership steering com. Health and Welfare Council D.C., 1961-66; mem. budget steering com. Health and Welfare Council Nat. Capital Area, 1963-66; mem. exec. com. Interreligious Com. Race Relations, 1966-67; exec. com., bd. dirs. D.C. Citizens Better Pub. Edn., 1964-66. Trustee United Planning Orgn. D.C., 1963-66, Washington Center Met. Studies, 1967—; bd. dirs. Family and Child Services Washington, 1954-63, v.p., 1958-61; bd. dirs. Family Services Assn. Am., 1958-68, Washington Action for Youth, 1962-64, Barney Neighborhood Settlement House, 1962-64, Eugene and Agnes E. Meyer Found., 1969. Served with AUS, 1943-46. Mem. Am., Nat., D.C., Washington bar assns. Home: 1796 Sycamore St NW Washington DC 20012 Office: US Ct House Washington DC 20001

ROBINSON, AUBREY GLASS, dentist; b. Montgomery, Ala., Sept. 12, 1923; s. Aubrey Bradley and Rena Leigh (Glass) R.; D.V.M., Auburn U., 1946; grad. student U. Houston, 1957-58; D.D.S., U. Tex., 1962, M.S. in Dentistry, 1964; m. Ann Marie Stinson, June 29, 1950; children—Bruce Aubrey, Craig Stinson, Celia Ann. With Bur. Animal Industry, Mexico, 1946-50; pvt. practice vet. medicine, Ft. Walton Beach, Fla., 1950-57; teaching fellow U. Tex. Dental Br., Houston, 1962-64, asst. prof. pedodontics, 1964-66; pvt. practice pediatric dentistry, Clearwater, Fla., 1966—. Served with AUS, 1943-45. Diplomate Am. Bd. Pedodontics. Mem. Am., Fla. dental assns., West Coast Dental Soc., Am., Fla. Southeastern socs. dentistry for children. Home: 7 Leeward Island Clearwater FL 33515 Office: 430 Pinellas St Clearwater FL 33516

ROBINSON, BETTE GIGUETTE (MRS. STANLEY T. ROBINSON JR.), statistician; b. Pasadena, Cal., Apr. 11, 1922; d. Curtis and Mary T. (Proctor) Giguette; B.A., Marymount Coll., Los Angeles, 1942; student Immaculate Heart Coll., Los Angeles, 1942-43; m. Stanley T. Robinson, Jr., Aug. 20, 1949; children—Curtis B. Postel, Suzanne E., Michael T. Research asst. Bd. Govs. Fed. Res. System, Washington, 1961-66. Wishing Well chmn. Los Angeles League Crippled Children, 1940-49; decoration chmn. Los Angeles Jr. Guild, 1941-49; AEC hospitality chmn. Sandia Base Women's Club, Albuquerque, 1953-59; sec.-treas., show sec. Albuquerque Rabbit Breeders Assn., 1954-57; sec. Nat. Capitol Rabbit Breeders Assn., 1959-61; sec.-treas. Free State Rabbit Breeders Assn., 1961; active League Women Voters, Fairfax, Va., 1965-69. Clubs: River Bend Golf and Country (chmn. women's golf assn. 1969-71, tournament chmn. women's golf assn. 1971—) (Great Falls, Va.), McLean (Va.) Women's (safety chmn. 1970-71). Home: 10103 Sanders Ct Great Falls VA 22066

ROBINSON, BRYAN WRIGHT, physician, educator; b. Thomasville, Ga., Dec. 11, 1929; s. Alfred Green and Frances (Wright) R.; B.S., Davidson Coll., 1952; M.D., Emory U., 1956; m. Julia Hill Willingham, Aug. 23, 1953; children—Bryan David, Carol Susan, Stephen Kirk, Margaret Hill. Intern, U. Rochester (N.Y.), 1956-57, asst. resident psychiatry, 1957-58; research asso. neurophysiology NIH, 1958-63; resident, spl. fellow neurology, Stanford, 1963-65; practice medicine, specializing in neurology, Atlanta, 1965-68; chief lab. neurophysiology Yerkes Primate Center Emory U., 1965-68, asst. prof. medicine (neurology), research dir., asso. prof. phys. medicine Sch. Medicine, 1965-68; prof. psychology Fla. State U., Tallahassee, 1968-70; asst. prof. medicine (neurology) U. Fla., 1970—; mem. staff Tallahassee Meml. Hosp.; cons. neurologist Archbold Meml. Hosp., Thomasville, Ga. Mem. bus. adv. bd. Tallahassee Bank & Trust Co. Bd. dirs. LeMoyne Art Found. Served with USPHS, 1948-63. Mem. Phi Beta Kappa, Kappa Alpha, Omicron Delta Kappa. Regional editor: Physiology and Behavior, 1962—. Contbr. articles to profl. jours. Home: 613 Piedmont Dr Tallahassee FL 32303 Office: 1328 N Magnolia Dr Tallahassee FL 32303

ROBINSON, BUEFORD EDDIE, textile exec.; b. Valdese, N.C., Feb. 10, 1929; s. Jeff Logan and Flossie (Coffey) R.; B.A., Lenoir Rhyne Coll., 1956; m. Jewell Deanna Wilson, June 18, 1955; children—Timothy Mark, Donna Marie. Accounting clk. Valdese Mfg. Co., 1956-64, controller, 1964-67, corporate sec., 1967—, sec. co. found. Chmn., United Fund, Valdese, 1967. Mem. Valdese Sch. Bd., 1966—, chmn. bd., 1968-69. Served with USAF, 1948-52. Mem. Catawba Valley Exec. Club. Baptist (deacon). Rotarian (treas. 1969-70). Home: 600 Carolina St Valdese NC 28690 Office: PO Drawer 10 Valdese NC 28690

ROBINSON, DAVID HUNTER, engring. co. exec.; b. Blackstock, S.C., Aug. 5, 1911; s. David Walter and Beatrice (Hunter) R.; B.S. in C. E., Clemson U., 1941; M.S., U. Mo., 1952; m. Maimi Marie Osteen, Sept. 5, 1942; children—Melanie Marie, Rosalie Hunter. Asst. prof. mechanics and hydraulics dept. Clemson U. (S.C.), 1947-52; owner, chief exec. officer Robinson Engring. Service, Anderson, S.C., 1952—; pres. Avon Devels., Inc., Seneca, S.C., 1957-67; cons. land devel., sanitation-waste treatment. Chmn. profl. div. United Fund, Anderson, 1959; treas. Anderson Community Concerts Assn., 1958—. Served to maj. AUS, 1941-46; ETO. Decorated Bronze Star. Registered profl. engr., S.C., Ga. Mem. Am. Soc. C.E., Am. Soc. Profl. Engrs., S.C. Soc. Profl. Engrs., (past bd. dirs.), Anderson C. of C. (dir. 1971-72), Am. Water Works Assn., Ind. Telephone Pioneer Assn., Assn. Communication Engrs., Water Pollution Control Fedn. Rotarian. Home: 505 Woodland Way Anderson SC 29621 Office: 821 N Main St Anderson SC 29621

ROBINSON, DAVID WRIGHT, mech. engr.; b. Great Falls, Mont., Dec. 13, 1923; s. Fred Hilton and Alice (Brooks) R.; B.S. in M. E., Mont. State Coll., 1950; m. Jean Mohr Kearney, Nov. 24, 1951; children—Polly, Alice, Meg, Mark. Quality control engr. Zonolite Co., Libby, Mont., 1950-52, research engr., 1952-62; research engr. Zonolite div. W.R. Grace, Libby, 1962-69, sr. projects engr. constrn. products div., Travelers Rest, S.C., 1969-70, process engr., 1970—; dir. Grogan Robinson Lumber Co., Great Falls, 1962-70; pres. Lincoln County Broadcasters, Inc., 1966-69; dir. Kootenai Winner Sports, Inc., Libby, 1963-67. Pres. Swim Team Parents Assn., Libby, 1967, 68. Served to 1st lt. AUS, 1943-46. Decorated Purple Heart, Combat Inf. Badge. Registered profl. engr., Mont. Mem. Am. Ceramic Soc., Am. Soc. Heating, Air-Conditioning and Refrigeration Engrs., Clay Minerals Soc., Mont. Soc. Profl. Engrs., Sigma Chi. Episcopalian. Elk, Lion. Club: Cabinet View Country (Libby). Patentee in field. Home: 9 Pilgrims Point Rd Greenville SC 29607 Office: P O Box 517 Travelers Rest SC 29690

ROBINSON, DONALD LOUIS, govt. ofcl.; b. Ottawa, Ill., Dec. 8, 1936; s. Arthur and Louise (Freebury) R.; B.A., Northwestern U., 1958, M.A., 1959; Ph.D., American U., 1963; m. Sara Moore, Aug. 4, 1962; children—Marshall, Margaret. Adminstrv. asst. to U.S. Rep. Henry S. Reuss, Washington, 1963—; democratic co-chmn. bi-partisan intern program Ho. of Reps., Washington, 1969-70; Democratic co-chmn. bipartisan intern program Congress of U.S. Washington, 1971—; asso. prof. polit. sci. George Washington U., Washington, 1964—. Mem. Americans for Dem. Action; Am. Civil Liberties Union, co-chmn. nat. speakers bur. Young Citizens for Johnson-Humphrey, 1964. Served to lt. USNR, 1959-62. Mem. Alpha Tau Omega, Phi Mu Alpha, Pi Sigma Alpha, Phi Alpha Theta, Pi Gamma Mu, Alpha Phi Omega. Home: 1817 Kenyon St NW Washington DC 20010 Office: 2159 Rayburn House Office Bldg Washington DC 20515

ROBINSON, ENDERS ANTHONY, geophys. co. exec.; b. Boston, Mar. 18, 1930; s. Edward Arthur and Doris (Goodale) R.; B.S., Mass. Inst. Tech., 1950, M.S., 1952, Ph.D., 1954; m. Eva Arborelius, Sept. 9, 1962; children—Anna, Erik Arthur, Karin. Dir. Mass. Inst. Tech. Geophys. Analysis Group, 1952-54; asso. prof. U. Wis., 1958-62; dep. prof. Uppsala (Sweden) U., 1960-64; v.p., dir. Digicon, Inc., Houston, 1965—. Served to 2d lt. Ordnance Dept., AUS, 1950-51. Recipient medal Soc. Exploration Geophysicists, 1969. Author: Random Wavelets and Cybernetic Systems, 1962; Statistical Communication and Detection, 1967; Multichannel Time Series Analysis, 1967. Home: 8119 Augustine St Houston TX 77036 Office: 3701 Kirby Dr Houston TX 77006

ROBINSON, FEROL MACON, univ. ofcl.; b. Jewett, Tex., June 1, 1918; s. Bob and Cloud (Speer) R.; B.S., Sam Houston State U., 1942, M.A., 1947; D.Ed., U. Mo., 1953; m. Mary Creed Engledow, Jan. 27, 1946; children—Pamela, Patricia. Mem. faculty Sam Houston State U., Huntsville, Tex., 1946—, prof., dir. journalism, dir. information, 1953-71, v.p. univ. services, 1971—. Alderman, Huntsville, 1968-72. Served with AUS, 1942-46. Mem. Huntsville C. of C., Sigma Delta Chi, Phi Kappa Delta, Kappa Delta Phi, Pi Kappa Alpha. Methodist (mem. bd. stewards 1960—). Home: 1528 Pin Oak Dr Huntsville TX 77340

ROBINSON, G.L., state ofcl. Dir. Fla. Civil Def. Office: 1045 Riverside Av Jacksonville FL 32204

ROBINSON, HAROLD, govt. ofcl.; b. Springfield, Mass., Nov. 13, 1908; s. John and Ida (Mag) R.; B.A., Yale, 1929, LL.B. (editor law Jour.), 1931; m. Ruth Beinish, July 29, 1956; 1 dau., Adele. Regional counsel New Eng., U.S. Housing Agys., 1937-48; dir. Citizens Housing and Planning Council N.Y., 1948, Mass. Housing Program, 1948-51; housing cons., 1951-52; chief housing div. U.S. Operations Adminstrn., Israel, 1954-56, Chile, 1957-59; chief regional projects ICA, Africa, 1959-62; regional housing adviser Bur. Latin Am. Affairs, AID, 1962-64, chief housing and urban devel., 1964—. Sec., Mass. Housing Council, 1948-50. Served to capt. AUS, 1943-46. Clubs: Army-Navy, Yale (Washington); Yale (N.Y.C., Israel and Chile). Author articles in field. Home: 5 Winterberry Ct Bethesda MD 20034 Office: AID State Dept Washington DC 20025

ROBINSON, HARRY ENGLISH, brick co. exec.; b. Atlanta, Apr. 25, 1914; s. James Dixon and Emily Alexander (English) R.; A.B., Va. Mil. Inst., 1936; postgrad. Harvard Grad. Sch. Bus. Adminstrn., 1936-37; m. Ermine Dupont Cater, Dec. 14, 1937; children—Harry English, Peyton Cater. Account exec. Clement A. Evans, Courts & Co., 1946-54; exec. v.p. Chattahoochee Brick Co., Atlanta, 1954-57, pres., 1957-70, chmn. bd., chief exec. officer, dir., 1970—; pres., dir. Chattahoochee Land Mgmt. Co.; dir. First Nat. Bank of Atlanta, Southeastern Capital Corp. Mem. adv. bd. Ga. State Coll. Served to lt. col. AUS, 1940-46. Decorated Army Commendation medal. Mem. Soc. Colonial Wars, Atlanta Hist. Soc. Presbyn. Clubs: Piedmont Driving; Commerce; Capital City; University Yacht; Nine O'Clocks; Homosassa Fishing. Home: 3633 Dumbarton Rd NW Atlanta GA 30327 Office: P O Box 39158 Bolton Sta Atlanta GA 30318

ROBINSON, HERBERT WILLIAM, corp. exec., economist; b. Hull, Yorkshire, Eng., Jan. 2, 1914; s. Herbert and Mary Elizabeth (Ellis) R.; B.Sc. (London), U. Coll. of Hull, Eng., 1935; Ph.D., London Sch. Econs., 1937; D.Phil., Balliol Coll., Oxford U., 1939; m. Elsie Caroline Roenfeldt, May 8, 1948; children—Denise Patricia, Keith Brian. Came to U.S., 1943, naturalized, 1948. Sr. lectr. math. statistics, econ. theory, trade cycle theory, indsl. orgn. U. Coll., Hull, Eng., 1939; asst. to Lord Cherwell, 1939-42; asst. to Lord Layton, 1942-43; Brit. staff mem. Combined Prodn. and Resources Bd., U.S., U.K., Can., 1943-44; dep. dir. statistics, econ. and statistics div. Ministry Agr. and Fisheries, 1945; chief econ. trends VA, 1948; chief operational analysis div. UNRRA Mission to Poland, 1946-67; loan and econs. depts. Internat. Bank Reconstrn. and Devel., 1947-51; dep. div. dir. Office Program and Requirements, Def. Prodn. Adminstrn., 1951-53; pres. Council Econ. and Industry Research, Inc., Washington, 1954-57, pres. renamed corp. C-E-I- R, Inc., 1958-67, chmn. bd., 1954—, pres., 1966-67, also chief exec. officer; v.p. Control Data Corp., 1968-70; exec. cons., 1970—. Trustee Washington Tech. Inst., 1967—. Fellow Assn. Inc. Statistician Royal Statistical Soc. (mem. of council 1943, 44); mem. Am. Soc. for Cybernetics (dir. 1967—), Am. Econ. Assn., A.A.A.S., Inst. Mgmt. Scis., Am. Statis. Assn., Operations Research Soc., Econometric Soc., Soc. Indsl. and Applied Math., Nat. Acad. Econ. and Polit. Sci., Lambda Alpha, Alpha Kappa Psi. Clubs: Congressional Country, Cosmos (Washington). Author articles, reports on econ. subjects. Home: 7830 Persimmon Tree Lane Bethesda MD 20034 Office: 1015 18th St NW Washington DC 20036

ROBINSON, JACK EDWARD, trading stamp co. exec.; b. Paris, Tex., July 31, 1922; s. Clarence Edwin and Louise (Purvis) R.; B.S., So. Methodist U., 1949; m. Nell Jewell McMannis, Dec. 25, 1946; children— Shari Lou (Mrs. Robert Gibson), Jack Edward. Account exec. pub. relations Watson Assos., Dallas, 1949-51; asst. dir. pub. relations U.S. Steel Co., 1951-52; mgr. pub. relations East Tex. C. of C., 1952-53; asso. dir. pub. affairs Am. Petroleum Inst., 1954-59; legislative affairs Tex. Midcontinent Oil and Gas Assn., 1959-62; regional dir. govt. relations Sperry & Hutchinson Co., Dallas, 1962—. Trustee Sigma Delta Chi Meml. Scholarship Fund. Served with USMCR, 1941-45. Mem. Pub. Relations Soc. Am., Royal Order Gored Ox, Dallas Press Club, Sigma Delta Chi. Mason (32 deg., Shriner). Club: Brookhaven Country (Dallas). Home: 4024 Rocky Rd Dallas TX 75234 Office: 1700 Oaklawn St Dallas TX 75207

ROBINSON, JAMES, mayor of Montgomery; b. Columbus, Ga., Aug. 23, 1929; m. Dorothy Wells; children—Donald James, Vickie Lynn. Pres. paper co.; mayor City of Montgomery (Ala.), 1971—. Baptist (deacon, finance com.). Office: Office of Mayor City Hall 127 N Perry St Montgomery AL 36102*

ROBINSON, JAMES J., chief of police Mobile. Address: Police Bldg 51 Government St Mobile AL 36602*

ROBINSON, JAMES MILTON, pub. co. exec.; b. Savannah, Ga., Oct. 25, 1919; s. Arthur Maurice and Bertha (Giddens) R.; grad. high sch.; m. Elsie Ruth Young, Dec. 16, 1938; children—James M., Thomas Y. With Albany Herald Pub. Co. (Ga.), 1936—, exec. editor, 1958—, v.p., 1966—; v.p., dir. Gray Communication Systems Inc., Albany. Trustee Albany Pub. Library. Recipient several profl. awards. Chmn., Easter Seal Soc., 1957-58; adv. bd. Salvation Army, 1962—; mem. Bishops Council, Ga., 1961-63. Recipient several profl. awards. Mem. Am. Soc. Newspaper Editors, Ga. A.P. News Council (co-founder, past chmn., Sigma Delta Chi. Democrat. Episcopalian. Club: Doublegate Country (Albany). Home: 1813 Lullwater Rd Albany GA 31705 Office: 138 Pine Av Albany GA 31702

ROBINSON, JAMES THEODORE, city ofcl.; b. Natchez, Miss., Mar. 2, 1925; s. John Edward and Minnie Lee (Rascoe) R.; grad. high sch.; m. Donna K. Allred, Nov. 2, 1968; children by previous marriage—Teddy, Carl, Gwen, Terry, Jeri. Patrolman, Natchez, Miss., 1947-60, dep. sheriff, 1960-62, chief police, 1962—. Served with USMC, World War II. Mem. Internat. Assn. Chiefs Police, Nat. Narcotics and Dangerous Drugs Assn., Am. Legion, D.A.V., Miss.-Tenn. Peace Officers, Miss. Law Enforcement Officers, Am. Rifle Assn. (life), Miss. Assn. Chiefs Police, Frat. Order Police (past pres.). Home: 107 Gayosa Av Natchez MS 39120 Office: PO Box 133 Natchez MS 39120

ROBINSON, JAMES WILLIAM, chemist, educator; b. Kidderminster, Eng., July 12, 1923; s. James W. and Eva (Lane) R.; B.Sc. with honors, U. Birmingham, Eng., 1949, Ph.D., 1952; m. Winifred G. M. Nixon, Jan. 8, 1946; children—James W., Linda J., Sandra J.S. Sr. sci. officer British Civil Service, Eng., 1952-55; sr. chemist Esso Research, Baton Rouge, 1955-63; tech. adviser Ethyl Corp., 1963-64; prof. chemistry La. State U., Baton Rouge, 1964—, chmn. internat. analytical symposium, 1964—, chmn. analytical div. chemistry dept., 1967—. Mem. adminstrv. grant com. Environmental Protection Agy., 1969—. Served with R.A.F., 1941-46. Asso. Royal Inst. Chemistry; mem. Am. Chem. Soc., Soc. Applied Spectroscopy (pres. Southeast sect. 1967-68, chmn. nat. meeting 1970), Sigma Xi, Alpha Xi Sigma. Author: Atomic Absorption Spectroscopy, 1966; Undergraduate Instrumental Analysis, 1970. Asst. editor Analytica Chimca Acta, 1960—, Applied Spectroscopy, 1968—; editor Spectroscopy Letters, 1967—, Environmental Letters, 1970—. Home: 375 Amherst Dr Baton Rouge LA 70808

ROBINSON, JAY MILTON, ednl. adminstr.; b. Bakersville, N.C., May 8, 1928; s. Fred Herbert and Geneva (Jarrett) R.; student Mars Hill Jr. Coll., 1945-46; B.S., Appalachian State U., 1950; postgrad. E. Tenn. State U., 1951; M.Ed., U. N.C., 1956; m. Elizabeth Lamay Holland, July 25, 1951; children—Deborah Kay, Jay Milton. Tchr., coach Odell Sch., Concord, N.C., 1950-54; tchr., coach, prin. Winecoff Sch., Concord, 1954-62; prin. S. Stanley High Sch., 1962-63; asst. supt. Cabarrus County Schs., Concord, 1963-64, supt., 1965—. Chmn. Cabarrus County Bd. Health, 1969-70. Served with USAF, 1946-48. Mem. Nat. Assn. Secondary Sch. Prins., Am. Assn. Sch. Adminstrs., Nat. Acad. Sch. Execs., N.C. Assn. Educators (pres. Piedmont div. supts. 1969-70), N.C. High Sch. Athletic Assn. (pres. 1970-71, dir. 1967—). Lion, Rotarian. Home: 371 Hatley Circle Concord NC 28025 Office: 660 Hwy 29 N Box 388 Concord NC 28025

ROBINSON, JEWEL ESELENE PATTERSON, home economist; b. nr. Lott, Tex.; d. Claud W. and Laura (Smith) Patterson; B.S., Mary Hardin Baylor Coll., 1935; M.S., Tex. Tech. Coll., 1963; m. John W. Robinson, Oct. 24, 1941 (div. Jan. 1951); children—James William, Judy Jean (Mrs. Jerry Dan Prothro), Jerry Pat. Tchr. pub. schs., Falls County, 1933-35; home demonstration agt., McCulloch County, 1936-38, Wise County, 1939-41, Dickens County, 1948-49, Hockley County, 1949—; lunch room supr. Montaque County, Tex., 1941-42. Cons. dietetician South Plains Hosp., Levelland, Tex.; mem. Tex. Nutrition Council, 1960—, sec., 1968; mem. adv. bd. South Plains Mus., Levelland. Sec. county Easter Seal Soc., 1970. Recipient Distinguished Service award Nat. Assn. Extension Home Economists, 1971. Mem. Am., Tex. home econs. assns., Home Demonstration Agts. Assn. (dist. dir. 1969-70). Home Demonstration Agts. Assn., Epsilon Sigma Phi. Club: Rose Garden (Levelland). Home: 801 17th St Levelland TX 79336 Office: Court House Annex Levelland TX 79336

ROBINSON, JOHN GREER, geol. co. pres.; b. Phila., May 8, 1920; s. Harold McAfee and Mary Greer (Wiley) R.; A.B., Lafayette Coll., 1942; m. Patricia Ann Johnson, June 30, 1951; 1 son, Harold McAfee III. Chief computer Seismograph Service Corp., Tulsa, 1943-45; dairy farmer, Lovell, Me., 1945-50; engring. insp., field engr., Smith & Gillespie, Jacksonville, Fla., 1951, City Coral Gables, Fla., 1955-56, M.H. Connell, Miami, Fla., 1956-58, M.B. Harris, Miami, 1958-59, Hart-Reynolds, Miami, 1959-60; pres. Geotec, Inc., West Palm Beach, Fla., 1960—. Cons. geologist Gibbs Corp., Santo Domingo, 1955; asst. resident engr. Arthur G. Keller, Inc., Baton Rouge, 1965. Vice chmn. Fla. Sanitarians Registration Bd., 1968—. Mem. campaign coordinating com. Republican party, Palm Beach County, 1968-69. Served with USMCR, 1941, USNR, 1941-42. Mem. Water Pollution Control Fedn., Internat. Oceanographic Found., Inst. for Certification Engring. Technicians, Theta Xi. Presbyn. (deacon). Home: 530 Iris Circle Lake Park FL 33403 Office: 175 N Military Trail West Palm Beach FL 33406

ROBINSON, JOHN PAUL, physician; b. Sarepta, La., Dec. 5, 1924; s. Samual Cecil and Valera (Browning) R.; B.S., Centenary Coll., 1948; M.D., La. State U., 1951; m. Edith Haggard, July 13, 1942; children—James Lee, Constance Sue (Mrs. Charles Norman Huggs), Carol Ann, Mark Clinton. Intern, Santa Rosa Hosp., San Antonio, 1951-52; resident ophthalmology Confederate Meml. Med. Center, Shreveport, La., 1957-60, now mem. staff; practice medicine, Shreveport, 1953-57, specializing in opthalmology, 1960—; mem. clin. staff La. State U. Med. Sch., Shreveport, 1968—; mem. staff T.E. Schumpert Sanitarium, Highland, P. & S., Drs., Willis Knightin, Bossier Gen. hosps. Pres., Men's Art Guild, Shreveport, 1966-67. Served with USNR, 1943-46. Diplomate Am. Bd. Ophthalmology. Mem. Am., So. med. assns., La. Med. Soc., Ark.-La.-Tex. Ophthalmology and Otolaryngology Soc. (pres. 1964-65), Contact Lens Assn. Opthalmologists, Am. Assn. Physicians and Surgeons, Alpha Kappa Kappa. Episcopalian. Mason. Home: 850 Margaret Pl Shreveport LA 71106 Office: 850 Margaret Pl Shreveport LA 71101

ROBINSON, KLYDE, lawyer; b. Charleston, S.C., Mar. 13, 1922; s. Mitchel and Eva (Karesh) R.; student The Citadel, 1940-43, A.B., 1946; J.D., Harvard, 1949; m. Claire Zuckernik, Mar. 5, 1950; children—Amy Beth, Eve D. Admitted to S.C. bar, 1949; gen. practice law, Charleston, 1950-57; atty. for Charleston County, S.C., 1957-61; 1st asst. U.S. atty. Eastern dist. S.C., 1961-67, U.S. atty., dist. S.C., 1968-69; partner firm Robinson, Paul & Belk, Charleston Heights, S.C., 1969—. Chmn., Legislative Com. on Hwy. Safety, 1969—. Served with AUS, 1943-45. Mem. S.C. Bar Assn. (circuit v.p. 1962), S.C. Trial Lawyers Assn. Jewish religion (dir. temple). Mason, Elk. Home: 105 S Battery St Charleston SC 29401 Office: 3370 Rivers Av Charleston Heights SC 29405

ROBINSON, LEWIS WILLIAM, JR., city ofcl.; b. Dallas, Nov. 29, 1909; s. Lewis William and Mary (Roane) R.; B.S. in Civil Engring., U. Fla., 1933; m. Mary Whitmyer, Aug. 14, 1946; 1 dau., Ann Lucretia. Bldg. insp. City of Coral Gables (Fla.), 1939-42, supt. pub. works, 1946-54, city clk., finance dir., 1954-58, city mgr., 1959—; with C.E., U.S. Army, Trinidad, W.I., 1943-45. Pres. Coral Gables Municipal Credit Union, 1949—. Recipient Good Govt. award Coral Gables Jr. C. of C., 1960, Hendrick award, 1970-71. Mem. Internat., Fla. (pres. 1963-64), Dade County (pres. 1966-67) city mgrs. assns. Mason (Shriner, Jester), Lion. Home: 1228 Av Placetas Coral Gables FL 33146 Office: 405 Biltmore Way Coral Gables FL 33134

ROBINSON, LUTHER DABNEY, psychiatrist; b. Tappahannock, Va., Dec. 22, 1922; s. William Harvey and Fannie (Pollard) R.; B.S., Va. State Coll., 1943; M.D., Meharry Med. Coll., 1946; postgrad. George Washington U., 1959-60; m. Betty Gay Boyd, Mar. 18, 1950; children—Jan Turso, Barry Boyd, Vance Dabney. Intern Mercy Hosp., Phila., 1946-47; asst. physician Lakin (W.Va.) State Hosp., 1947-49; practice gen. medicine, Richmond, Va., 1952-53; resident psychiatry Freedmen's Hosp., Washington, 1953-54, St. Elizabeth's Hosp., Washington, 1954-55; mem. staff St. Elizabeth's Hosp., 1955—, clin. dir., 1964-68, 1st asst. physician, 1968-69, acting supt. hosp., 1969-72, supt. hosp., 1972—; mem. faculty Howard U., Washington, 1956-68, Gallaudet Coll. for Deaf, Washington, 1968—. Mem. profl. adv. com. D.C. Mental Health Assn., 1968—. Served with AUS, 1943-46, to capt. M.C., 1949-52. Recipient Superior Service award Dept. Health, Edn. and Welfare, 1966, Superior Work Performance award St. Elizabeth's Hosp., 1968. Diplomate Am. Bd. Psychiatry and Neurology. Fellow Am. Psychiat. Assn.; mem. A.M.A., Nat. Med. Assn., Med. Soc. St. Elizabeth's (pres. 1965-66), Washington Psychiat. Soc., Internat. Platform Assn. Baptist. Address: Staff Residence 4 St Elizabeths Hosp 2700 Martin Luther King JrAv Washington DC 20032

ROBINSON, LYLE MURRAY, utility exec.; b. Burns, Miss., July 7, 1920; s. Sylvester E. and Hattie (Burns) R.; student N.C. State Coll., 1944, Okla. State U., 1950-52; m. Katherine Nummy, Aug. 16, 1941; children—Cynthia Kay (Mrs. Carl Elwyn Hulett), Debra Lea, (Mrs. Dennis Hardee), Donna Marie. With Rural Electric Coop., McCombs, Miss., 1941, Stillwater, Okla., 1950-58; design engr. J.B. Payne & Assos., Enid, Okla., 1953-59; gen. mgr. Swisher Electric Coop., Tulia, Tex., 1959—; instr. tech. tng. Okla. State U., 1950-52; dir. 1st State Bank, Tulia, Tex. Cons. on rural electrification through co-op. work U.S. AID, Colombia, 1963, Viet Nam, 1965, India, 1966, 69-71. Chmn., Sch. Study Group, 1966. Bd. dirs. High Plains Research Found., Halfway, Tex., Tex. Partners of Alliance, Austin. Served with USAAF, 1942-46. Decorated Air medal. Mem. C. of C., Am. Legion. Methodist. Club: Toastmaster. Home: 44 Crockett Dr Tulia TX 79088 Office: 401 SW 2d St Tulia TX 79088

ROBINSON, MARTHA ANNA GOODWIN, librarian; b. Raleigh, N.C., Feb. 26, 1907; d. Ernest Harris and Mattie (Utley) Goodwin; student Pineland Coll., 1925-27, Emory U., 1948-49, Wake Forest Coll., 1954-55, N.Y. Sch. Interior Design, 1955-56; m. Bert DeLeon Robinson, Nov. 5, 1932 (dec. July 1956); children—Bert DeLeon, Martha (Mrs. Bob Steele Hastings), William Bradford. Art instr. High Point (N.C.) Coll., 1937-38, Jenkins Jr. High Sch., Spartanburg, S.C., 1942-43; art substitute tchr. Arlington (Va.) Pub. Schs., 1949-54; craft shop dir. N.C. State Coll., Raleigh, 1956-59, D.H. Hill Library, N.C. State Coll., 1959-62, librarian, 1964—; designer, decorator Kitchen Creations of Raleigh, 1962-64. Pres., High Point Art Center, 1937, Aeolian Music Club, Spartanburg, 1940-42, Spartanburg Art Club, 1945; emergency ambulance driver A.R.C., 1948-52; initiator Fine Arts Festival N.C. State Coll., 1957. Lifetime scholar Emory U. for fine arts work Decatur and Atlanta Woman's Clubs, 1948. Mem. D.A.R. (N.C. chmn. Am. heritage 1967-72, co-chmn. N.C. conf. 1970, N.C. custodian flags 1967—, organizing regent 4th sr. chpt., state organizing sec. 1972—), N.C. Hillsboro hist. socs., Nat. Trust for Hist. Preservation, Internat. Platform Assn. (art com.), N.C. Mus. Art. Democrat. Episcopalian. Decorator sec. state's office N.C. State Capitol, Raleigh, 1968. Home: 1020 W Peace St Raleigh NC 27605 Office: DH Hill Library NC State Univ Raleigh NC 27607

ROBINSON, MARY LOU (MRS. ALBERT JAMES ROBINSON), lawyer, judge; b. Dodge City, Kan., Aug. 25, 1926; d. Gerald J. and Frances Aynn (Pierce) Strueber; student Amarillo Coll., 1944-46; B.S., U. Tex., 1948, LL.B., 1950; m. Albert James Robinson; children—Rebecca, Diana, Matthew. Admitted Tex. bar., 1950; mem. firm Robinson & Robinson, Amarillo, 1950-55; judge county ct. law, Potter County, Tex., 1955-59, 108th Dist. Ct. 1961—. Mem. Amarillo Bar Assn., State Bar Tex. Presbyn. Home: 5302 Berget St Amarillo TX 79106 Office: Potter County Court House Amarillo TX 79101

ROBINSON, N(OBLE) ALLEN, state ofcl.; b. Hannabal, Mo., Aug. 19, 1926; s. Allen Green and Louise (Noble) R.; B.A., Culver Stockton Coll., 1949; m. Claudia Garrett Taylor, Apr. 11, 1950 (div. Dec. 1968); children—Roger Taylor, Allen Wayne, Kevin Blair; m. 2d, Marie Ann Greenlaw, May 30, 1970. Salesman, Hannabal (Mo.) Courier-Post, 1949; mgr., writer Okaloosa News Jour., Crestview, Fla., 1949-55; promotion specialist, writer Fla. Devel. Commn., Tallahassee, 1955-57; exec. v.p. Pub. Relations of Fla., Inc., Tallahassee, 1957-59; bur. chief Pensacola (Fla.) News Jour., 1959-66, also newscaster sta. WJSB; tourist dir. State Fla., Tallahassee, 1966—. Vice pres. Sampsell Funeral Home, Crestview, Fla., 1952-55, Crest Lake Colony Estates, Crestview, 1961-64; pub. relations cons. Crestview Bank, 1950-68; dir. Discover American Travel Orgn., 1967—; vice chmn. So. Travel Dirs. Council, 1968—. Pres. Little League, Crestview, 1959-62; mem. Northwest Fla. council Boy Scouts Am., 1960-61; bd. dirs. Old Spanish Trail Festival, Okaloosa County Ann. Celebration. Pres. Young Democrats Club Okaloosa County, 1960-62; area coordinator Republican com., 1966—. Served with USNR, 1944-46. Mem. Fla. Pub. Relations Assn., Fla. Travel Council, Am. Soc. Travel Agts., Assn. Execs. Club: Northwest Fla. Press. Home: 2411 20 Jackson Bluff Rd Tallahassee FL 32304 Office: 107 W Gaines St Tallahassee FL 32304

ROBINSON, P.H., utility exec., b. 1904 married. With Houston Lighting & Power Co., 1928—, v.p. operations, 1951-58, exec. v.p., 1958-62, pres., chief adminstrv. officer, 1962-65, pres., chief exec. officer, 1965-70, chmn. bd., prin. exec. officer, dir., 1970—. Home: 410 Fall River Rd Houston TX 77024 Office: 900 Fannin St Houston TX 77002*

ROBINSON, PAUL BAINBRIDGE, headmaster; b. Marysville, O., Apr. 16, 1911; s. John Clyde and Charlotte (Bainbridge) R.; B.S., Tenn. Poly. Inst., 1935; M.A., U. So. Miss., 1958; L.H.D. (hon.), Judson Coll., 1967; m. Vera Judd, July 31, 1934; children—Charlotte Ann, John Arnold, Paul Matthew, David Johnson (dec.), Joseph Melvin. Instr., coach Moore County High Sch., Lynchburg, Tenn., 1935-37; instr., coach, dean boys Warren County Central High Sch., McMinnville, Tenn., 1937-42; instr., coach, comdr. cadets Sewanee (Tenn.) Mil. Acad., 1942-40; asso. supr. Gulf Coast Mil. Acad., Mississippi City, Miss., 1948-49; instr., comdt. Marion (Ala.) Mil. Inst., 1949-52, pres., 1959—; supr. U. Mil. Sch., Mobile, 1952-59. Adv. com. higher edn. Ala. Bd. Edn. Mem. Nat. Council Ind. Schs. (So. rep. 1956-58), So. Assn. Ind. Schs. (pres. 1957-58), Ala. Assn. Jr. Colls. (pres. 1962-63, chmn. athletic affairs com.). Assn. Ala. Coll. Adminstrs. (dir. div. higher edn. 1962-63), Assn. Mil. Colls. and Schs. U.S. (pres., exec. com.). Phi Delta Kappa, Presbyn. (elder). Club: Marion Golf. Home: 110 Brown St Marion AL 36756

ROBINSON, PREZELL RUSSELL, coll. pres.; b. Batesburg, S.C., Aug. 25, 1922; s. Clarence and Annie (Folks) R.; diploma Voorhees Jr. Coll., 1946; M.S., Cornell U., 1951, Ed.D., 1956; m. Lulu Harris, Apr. 9, 1950; 1 dau. Prof. social sci. French, Bettis Jr. Coll., Trenton, S.C., 1946-48; prof. social sci., registrar Voorhees Jr. Coll., Denmark, S.C., 1948-51, prof. social sci., acting dean, 1952-53; dir. adult edn., prof. sociology, exec. dean St. Augustine's Coll., Raleigh, N.C., 1956, now pres. Dir. Wachovia Bank and Trust Co. Mem. N.C. Human Relations Council, Mayor's Community Relations Com; exec. com. Ochoneechee council Boy Scouts Am.; mem. exec. com. Wake County chpt. A.R.C.; spl. com. United Fund of Raleigh; mem. Gov.'s Adv. Bd. Higher Edn. Trustee Voorhees Coll., Denmark, S.C. Fulbright fellow to India, 1965. Served with AUS, 1942. Mem. Raleigh Citizens Assn., Assn. Social Sci. Tchrs., A.A.A.S., Nat. Assn. Collegiate Deans and Registrars, Am. Acad. Polit. and Social Sci., Acad. Polit. Sci., Am. Sociol. Assn., Phi Delta Kappa, Omega Psi Phi, Phi Kappa Phi. Home: St Augustine's College Raleigh NC 27602

ROBINSON, RALPH ROLIN, physician; b. Nashville, Kan., July 7, 1913; s. Walter S. and Mary (Inslee) R.; B.S. in Indsl. Arts, Okla. A and M, 1935; M.D., U. Wash., 1951; m. Mona R. McGraw, Mar. 28, 1953; children—Kim, Mark, Nancy, Ralph Rolin II, Katherine. Engr., Vornado Corp., Stillwater, Okla., 1934-41, Boeing Co., Seattle, 1941-51; intern Okla. U. Hosp. 1951-52, resident 1952-55; practice medicine, specializing in obstetrics and gynecology, Oklahoma City, 1951-55, Middlesboro, Ky., 1955—; asso. prof. U. Okla., 1955. Pres., Creative Ornament Co., Edmond, Okla.; v.p. R. K. Odor Research Co., Oklahoma City. Pres. staff Miners Meml. Hosp., Middlesboro, 1958. Chmn. Safety Com. Okmulgee County, 1956. Fellow A.C.S.; mem. Am. Coll. Obstetrics and Gynecology, Am. Soc. Abdominal Surgery, Phi Kappa Phi. Author: Endocrine Therapy for Gynecology, 1957. Co-inventor Vornado airplane, 1935; inventor contoceptor. Home: 322 Englewood Rd Middlesboro KY 40965 Office: 2024 Cumberland Av Middlesboro KY 40965

ROBINSON, REGINALD EDWARD, JR., civil engr.; b. Summerville, S.C., July 29, 1933; s. Reginald Edward and Luren (Knight) R.; C.E., Ga. Inst. Tech., 1957; M.S. in Engring. Adminstrn., So. Meth. U., 1967; m. Nancy Helen Grooms, Aug. 10, 1957; children—Susan Lynn, Kenneth Braden. Coop engring. student Charleston Naval Shipyard (S.C.), 1951-56; test engr. Chance Vought Aircraft Inc., Dallas, 1957-60; test engr. Martin Co., Orlando, Fla., 1960-62; engring. splst. LTV Aerospace Corp., Dallas, 1962—. Served to 2d lt. AUS, 1958. Mem. Tex. Soc. Profl. Engrs. (treas. Mid-Cities chpt. 1968), Soc. Exptl. Stress Analysis (pres. North Tex. sect. 1972-73) Chi Epsilon. Home: 1021 S Gloucester St Irving TX 75062 Office: PO Box 5907 Dallas TX 75222

ROBINSON, ROBERT DENHAM, golf co. exec.; b. Geneva, Ill., Oct. 11, 1927; s. Reginald and Florrie (Denham) R.; student No. Ill. State U., 1948-50; m. Wanda Mae Dool, Jan. 16, 1959; children—Brad Denham, Wendy Dool. Golf equipment salesman Wilson Sporting Goods Co., Chgo., 1952-59; nat. sales and promotion dir. Walter Hagen Golf Co., Grand Rapids, Mich., 1959-62; v.p., gen. mgr. Arnold Palmer Golf Co., Chattanooga, 1962—. Served with AUS, 1946. Clubs: Chattanooga Golf and Country, Signal Mountain Golf Country. Home: 507 S Palisades Dr Signal Mountain TN 37377 Office: 81 Tremont St Chattanooga TN 37405

ROBINSON, ROBERT HOWARD, physician; b. Verda, La., Jan. 21, 1919; s. Robert Lee and Florence (Courtney) R.; B.S., La. State U., 1938, M.D., 1942; m. Marguerite Barbara Boudreaux, July 7, 1943; children— Robert Stanley, Thomas Warren, Mary Katharine. Intern Tri-State Hosp. Shreveport, La., 1942-43; teaching fellow and clin. instr. in dermatology La. State U. Sch. Medicine, 1947-53; pvt. practice St. Martinville, La., 1945-47; dermatologist, pvt. practice, Lafayette, 1949—; owner, dir., Lafayette Skin and Skin Cancer Clinic, 1957—; cons. physician dermatology Lafayette Meml. San., Our Lady of Lourdes, Lafayette Charity hosps.; dep. comdr. and wing surgeon La. Wing Civil Air Patrol, 1954—. Med. examiner FAA. Served as med. officer AUS, 1943-45. Decorated Purple Heart. Fellow Acad. Internationale of Medicine; mem. A.M.A., Am. Acad. Dermatology, La., Lafayette Parish med. socs., La. State Dermatology Soc., Aero Space Med. Assn., Lafayette C. of C. (chmn. aviation com.), Royal Order of Scotland, Sheriff Flying Squadron (maj., head Lafayette parish 1968—). Episcopalian. Mason (32 deg., K.T., Shriner); mem. Order of Eastern Star. Home: 119 Girard Woods Rd Lafayette LA 70501 Office: 1144C Coolidge St Lafayette LA 70501

ROBINSON, ROBERT LEWIS, assn. exec., editor; b. Richfield Spa, N.Y., Jan. 1, 1915; s. Lewis Henry and Alice Ethel (Fisk) R.; B.S., St. Lawrence U., 1936; M.A., Fletcher Sch. Law and Diplomacy, 1937; postgrad. N.Y. State Tchrs. Coll., 1940-41; m. Anna Marion Weir, July 16, 1940. With U.S. Dept. Commerce, Washington, 1946-48; dir. pub. affairs Am. Psychiat. Assn., Washington, 1948—, editor Psychiat. News, 1966—. Vis. lectr. colls. and univs. Trustee, Woodley House, Washington. Served to capt. AUS, 1941-46. Mem. Am. Pub. Health Assn., Nat. Assn. Sci. Writers, A.A.A.S., A.M.A. (affiliate). Club: Cosmos (Washington). Cons. editor Psychiatry and Medical Education, 1952; Training the Psychiatrist to Meet Changing Needs, 1964; other books and jours. Home: 3721 Livingston St NW Washington DC 20015 Office: American Psychiatric Association 1700 18th St NW Washington DC 20009

ROBINSON, ROBERT WILLIAM, realtor; b. Lancaster, S.C., Dec. 1, 1917; s. Redic Earl and Myrtle (Beckham) R.; B.S. in Textile Chemistry, Clemson Coll., 1938; m. Carolyn J. Crews, May 29, 1938; children—Joan C., Robert W. Partner, E. Robinson Laundry, 1938-41, pres., 1946-51; pres. Robinson Realty Co., Columbia, S.C., 1951—; pres. E. Robinson Laundry & Dry Cleaning Co., Inc., Robinson Realty & Ins. Co., Inc., Robinson Laundry & Cleaners Machinery Co., Inc., 1961—, Robinson Holding Co., Inc., 1961—, E & M, Inc., 1962—; v.p. Robinson, Inc., 1960—, Matco, Inc., 1968—, New Lighthouse Co., Inc., 1970—. Served as capt. USAAF, 1942-46. Baptist. Lion. Club: Summerwood on the Gulf (v.p. 1970—). Home: 4314 Converse St Columbia SC 29206 Office: 2549 Forest Dr Columbia SC 29204

ROBINSON, ROSLYN QUINBY, virologist; b. Wolfeboro, N.H., Aug. 26, 1928; s. Harry Weeks and Evelyn (Ward) R.; B.S., U. N.H., 1950, M.S., 1952; Ph.D., U. Md., 1954; postgrad. World Influenza Center, London, 1960; m. Jane Camille Garner, Apr. 14, 1956; 1 dau., Damon Ann. Commd. in USPHS, 1956, advanced through grades to scientist, dir. grade; acting chief, 1958-60, chief, 1960-65, duty asst. chief respiratory disease unit, 1956-58, at Nat. Communicable Disease Center, Montgomery, Ala., 1956-60, Atlanta, 1960-65, dep. chief virology sect., 1965-66, acting chief virology sect., 1966, chief virology sect., 1966-68, asst. chief lab. program, 1968-69, dep. dir. lab. div., 1969—; dir. Internat. Influenza Center for Americas, WHO, 1958-70, Regional Reference Lab. for Respiratory Diseases, 1960-70. Mem. panel respiratory viruses NIH; asso. mem. commn. influenza U.S. Armed Forces Epidemiological Bd.; mem. standards and exams. com. Pub. Health and Med. Lab. Virology, Am. Bd. Microbiology. Served to 1st lt. USAF, 1954-56. Diplomate Am. Acad. Microbiology. Mem. Research Soc. Am., Conf. State and Provincial Health Lab. Dirs., Am. Pub. Health Assn., Commd. Officers Assn. USPHS. Research and pubis. in field of bacteriology and virology. Home: 2844 Glade Springs Dr Atlanta GA 30329 Office: Center for Disease Control Atlanta GA 30333

ROBINSON, SPOTTSWOOD WILLIAM, III, judge; b. Richmond, Va., July 26, 1916; s. Spottswood William, Jr. and Inez (Clements) R.; student Va. Union U., 1932-36, LL.D., 1955; LL.B. magna cum laude, Howard U., 1939; m. Marian Bernice Wilkerson, Mar. 5, 1936; children— Spottswood William IV, Nina Cecelia (Mrs. Oswald G. Govan). Admitted to Va. bar, 1943, U.S. Supreme Ct. bar, 1948; faculty Howard U., 1939-48, asso. prof. law, 1945-48, prof., dean Law Sch., 1960-63; mem. firm Hill & Robinson, Richmond, 1943-44, Hill, Martin & Robinson, 1944-55; sole practitioner, Richmond, 1955-60; legal rep. for Va. N.A.A.C.P. Legal Def. and Ednl. Fund, 1948-50, Southeast regional counsel, 1951-60; v.p., gen. counsel Consol. Bank & Trust Co., Richmond, 1963-64; judge U.S. Dist. Ct. D.C., Washington, 1964-66, ct. appeals D.C. circuit, 1966—. Mem. U.S. Commn. on Civil Rights, 1961-63. Named to Richmond Afro-Am. Honor Roll, 1946; recipient ann. alumni award in law Howard U., 1951, ann. non-mem. citizenship award Beta Gamma Lambda chpt. Alpha Phi Alpha, 1951, social action achievement award Phi Beta Sigma, 1953, citation Beta Theta Sigma chpt. Delta Sigma Theta, 1954, citation Richmond chpt. Frontiers of Am., 1954, award Md. Conf. N.A.A.C.P., 1959. Mem. Am., Nat., Va. (jud. mem.), Old Dominion, D.C. (hon.) bar assns., Nat. Lawyers Club (hon.). Episcopalian. Home: 5400 30th St NW Washington DC 20015 Office: US Courthouse Washington DC 20001

ROBINSON, THOMAS LEE, lawyer; b. Memphis, June 11, 1906; s. Thomas and Mabel (Hurt) R.; diploma Christian Bros. Coll., Memphis, 1926; student U. Memphis Law Sch., 1927-28; LL.B., Cumberland U., 1929; m. Lina Margaret Dunlap, October 24, 1929; children— Peggy Lee (Mrs. George R. Parker, Jr.), Patricia Claire (Mrs. George W. Sneed, Jr.). Admitted to Tenn. bar, 1929; with firm Poston & Polk, Memphis, 1929-32, Brode & Cohen, Memphis, 1932-33; partner firm Robinson & Robinson, Memphis, 1934-61; U.S. atty. Western Dist. Tenn., 1961-68; practice law, Memphis, 1968—. Dir. Mid-South Fair, Memphis, 1933-35. Mem. Am., Memphis and Shelby County bar assns. (dir. 1959-61), Bar Assn. Tenn., Irish Soc., Alumni Assn. Christian Bros. Coll. (pres. 1950-51), Delta Theta Pi,

Sigma Alpha Epsilon. Democrat. Elk. Clubs: Colonial Country (dir., atty. 1950-51), Tennessee (dir. 1963-64) (Memphis). Home: 2115 Hallwood Dr Memphis TN 38107 Office: 243 Adams Av Memphis TN 38103

ROBINSON, WALTER MCLAREN, JR., lawyer, ins. co. exec.; b. Louisville, Mar. 13, 1923; s. Walter McLaren and Emma (Hagerty) R.; B.A., Vanderbilt U., 1942; LL.B., Harvard, 1948; m. Margaret Ann Craig, Oct. 4, 1949; children—Ann Craig, Emmie Bridges, Elizabeth Wade, Walter McLaren III. Admitted to N.Y. State bar, 1948, Tenn. bar, 1950; asso. firm Cravath Swaine & Moore, N.Y.C., 1948-50; with Nat. Life & Accident Ins. Co., Nashville, 1950—, asst. gen. counsel, 1953-61, asso. gen. counsel, 1961-65, v.p., gen. counsel, 1965-71, sr. v.p., gen. counsel, 1971—, dir., 1968—; v.p., sec., treas., dir. WSM, Inc., Nashville, 1967—; sec.-treas. NLT Corp., Nashville, 1968—. Mem. exec. com. Mid-Cumberland Comprehensive Planning Council. Bd. dirs. Vanderbilt U. Med. Center. Served from pvt. to 1st lt. F.A., AUS, 1942-46, 66-68; ETO. Mem. Am., Tenn., Nashville bar assns., Am. Life Conv. (chmn. legal sect. Chgo. 1968), Assn. Life Ins. Counsel, Nashville Area C. of C. (gov. 1967-69), Phi Beta Kappa, Omicron Delta Kappa. Episcopalian (sr. warden 1962, 67). Clubs: Belle Meade Country, Cumberland, Coffee House, Exchange (pres. 1964-65) (Nashville). Home: 15 White Bridge Rd Nashville TN 37205 Office: Nat Life Center Nashville Tenn 37203

ROBINSON, WAYNE AUSTIN, journalist; b. Clinton, Okla., Aug. 13, 1937; s. Theodore Ralph and Minnie Elizabeth (Pryor) R.; Th.B., Southwestern Coll., 1959; B.A., Oklahoma City U., 1961; M.Th., So. Meth. U., 1967; m. Sharon Lee Cook, Mar. 30, 1963; children—Laura Beth, Brett. With Oral Roberts Assn., Tulsa, 1967-71, editor-in-chief publs. (Daily Blessing, Abundant Life, Outreach), 1967-68, v.p. communications, 1968-69, exec. producer Oral Roberts Presents and Contact TV shows, 1969-70, communications cons., 1970-71; v.p. pub. affairs Oral Roberts U., Tulsa, 1971-72, pub. relations cons., 1972—; exec. editor Forum House, Atlanta, 1972—. Producer, moderator Symposium '71, Oklahoma City U.; cons. World Neighbors, Oklahoma City, Inst. Ch. Renewal, Atlanta. Democrat. Methodist (elder 1968—). Author: What's a Nice Church Like You Doing in a Place Like This, 1972. Editor The Okla. Meth., 1969-70. Home: 6309 Connaught Ct Oklahoma City OK 73132 Office: 7777 S Lewis Av Tulsa OK 74136

ROBINSON, WILLIAM POWELL, educator; b. Butler, Okla., Nov. 28, 1910; s. William Winfred and Annie (Simpson) R.; student Vanderbilt U., 1928-29; B.A., U. Okla., 1933; M.A., U. Chgo., 1938; m. Frances Lois Baldwin, July 23, 1928; children—Lamyra R. (Mrs. Court), William B., John T. Tchr., prin. Purcell (Okla.) High Sch., 1933-39; tchr. Central High Sch., Tulsa, 1939-43, Western Mil. Acad., Alton, Ill., 1943-45; dir. pub. relations Tulsa schs., 1945-47; prin. Tulsa elementary schs., 1947—. Spl. writer Tulsa schs., 1945-60; ghost writer, 1947—; lectr. 1955—. Vice chmn. Profl. Practices Commn., 1965-66, chmn., 1966-69, 70-72. Recipient Sequoyah Book award, 1964. Mem. Tulsa Elementary Prins. Assn. (pres.), Armed Forces Writers League (past mem. editors jury), N.E.A., Okla. Reading Council, Phi Delta Kappa. Democrat. Presbyn. (ruling elder). Author: (with C. X. Dowler) Now, Wait A Minute, 1950; Where the Panther Screams, 1961. Home: 424 S 74th East Av Tulsa OK 74112 Office: 209 S Lakewood St Tulsa OK 74112

ROBINSON, WILLIAM RONALD, educator; b. Steubenville, O., Oct. 21, 1927; s. Jacob Lederer and and Ethel Teresa (McGuire) R.; B.A., Ohio State U., 1952, M.A., 1956, Ph.D., 1962; m. Mina Jeanine Shumway, June 10, 1952; children—Monica, Christopher, Teresa, Keenan. Instr., U. Va., Charlottesville, 1962-64, asst. prof., 1964-67; asso. prof. English dept. U. Fla., Gainesville, 1967-71, prof., 1971—. Served with AUS, 1946-47. Author: Man and the Movies, 1967; Edwin Arlington Robinson: A Poetry of the Act, 1967. Home: 2125 NW 7th Lane Gainesville FL 32601 Office: English Dept U Fla Gainesville FL 32601

ROBINSON, WOODROW WILSON, supt. schs.; b. Washington County, Va., Apr. 20, 1912; s. Ben Franklin and Bertha Mae (McClelland) R.; B.A., King Coll., 1932, Ed.D. (hon.), 1961; postgrad. Duke, summers, 1938-42; m. Marily Virginia McGhee, Nov. 26, 1942; children— Martha Jean (Mrs. Sylvio Zaidan), Barbara Anne (Mrs. Martin L. Slavin). Tchr. pub. schs., Washington County, Va., 1932-34, prin. high sch., 1934-37; tchr. Tazewell (Va.) High Sch., 1937-38; asst. prin. Marion (Va.) High Sch., 1938-42, Virginia High Sch., Bristol, Va., 1943-45; prin. Radford (Va.) High Sch., also supr. student teaching for Radford Coll., 1945-53; supt. county schs., Floyd County, Va., 1953-56, Shenandoah County, 1957—; mem. summer faculty Radford Coll., 1945-53. Mem. McMath Commn., 1968. Recipient Distinguished Service award Woodstock C. of C., 1968. Mem. N.E.A. (life), Am. Assn. Sch. Adminstrs., Va. Edn. Assn. (dist. pres. 1939-41, 51-55; pres. 1961, treas. 1955-61), Woodstock C. of C. Presbyn. (elder). Rotarian, Kiwanian (pres. Radford). Club: Ruritan (pres. 1956). (Floyd). Home: 259 Summit Av Woodstock VA 22664 Office: Court St Woodstock VA 22664

ROBISON, CLARENCE, surgeon; b. Tecumseh, Okla., Dec. 9, 1924; s. Clarence and Irene (Buzzard) R.; student U. Okla., 1942-43, Stanford, 1943-44; M.D., U. Okla., 1948; m. Patricia Antoinette Hagee, May 27, 1951; children—Timothy Dwight, John David, Paul Douglas, Rebecca Antoinette. Intern Good Samaritan Hosp., Portland, Ore., 1948-49; resident surgery VA Hosp., Oklahoma City U. Okla. Med. Center, 1953-57; teaching fellow pathology U. Okla., 1949-50, fellow in oncology, 1950-51; surgeon, clin. asst. VA. Hosp., Oklahoma City, U. Okla. Med. Center, 1957; pvt. practice med. specializing in surgery, Oklahoma City, 1957—; mem. staff Mercy, St. Anthonys, Bapt. Meml., Presbyn., University, Deaconess hosps., all Oklahoma City; asst. prof. surgery U. Okla., 1957—. Dir., pres. Rockwell-Britton Corp., Oklahoma City. Mem. adv. bd. Salvation Army, Oklahoma City; bd. dirs. Sr. Citizens, Inc., Oklahoma City, 1961; pres. Oklahoma County unit Am. Cancer Soc., mem. exec. com. Okla. chpt. Served with AUS, 1943-46; served from 1st lt. to capt., USAF, 1951-53. Diplomate Am. Bd. Surgery. Fellow A.C.S., Am. Coll. Angiology, Southwestern Surg. Congress; mem. Osler Soc., Okla. Surg. Assn., Am., Okla. (sec.-treas. 1966-68), So., Okla. County (dir.) med. assns., Oklahoma City Surg. Soc. (pres. 1967), Aircraft Owners and Pilots Assn., Phi Chi. Presbyn. (elder). Mason, Kiwanian; mem. Order Eastern Star. Clubs: Petroleum; Faculty House; Chandelle; Sportsman's. Home: 2309 Tall Oaks Trail Edmond OK 73034 Office: 5700 NW Grand Blvd Oklahoma City OK 73112

ROBLES, MARCO A., pres. Panama, b. 1906. Minister govt. and justice, Panama, 1960-64; pres. of Panama, 1964—. Mem. Union Nacional de Oposicion. Home: Palacio del Gobierno Panama City Panama

ROBSON, MAYNARD ALLEN, ednl. adminstr.; b. Yates Center, Kan., Oct. 8, 1914; s. Alonzo and Ruth Fae (Belew) R.; student Okla. Bapt. U., 1937; M.S., Okla. State U., 1949, Ed.D., 1965; m. Elma Iles, July 5, 1941; 1 son, Joe Allen. Math. tchr., coach, Cherokee, Okla., 1937-39, Fairview, Okla., 1939-41, Wagoner, Okla., 1941-42, 45-49; dir. spl. services, coach, Ponca City, Okla., 1949-61; prin. West Jr. High Sch., Ponca City, 1961-65; supt. schs., Ponca City, 1965—. Gen. council Okla. Bapt. U. Athletic Assn., 1971—. Served with USNR, 1941-46; ETO. Mem. N.E.A., Am., Okla. assns. sch. adminstrs., Okla. (chmn. policy commn. 1970—), No. Okla. (v.p. 1965), Ponca City (pres. 1951) edn. assns., C. of C. (dir. 1971—), Am. Legion, Phi Delta Kappa. Methodist. Lion. Club: Ponca City Country. Author: A Comparative Study of the Teaching of Algebra I, 1965. Home: 3013 Canterbury St Ponca City OK 74601 Office: Drawer 271 Ponca City OK 74601

ROBUCK, JOHN BENTON, power light co. exec.; b. Helena, Tex., May 1, 1907; s. Charles H. and Anna (Daughtrey) R.; student Southwestern U., 1924-26; B.S. in Elec. Engring., U. Tex., 1929; m. Josephine Hurt, June 30, 1930; children—Eva, Marvin Womack, Joel Henry. With Tex. Power & Light Co., 1929—, successively student engr. Hillsboro, engr., dist. operator, Sherman, electrician, McKinney, asst. div. engr., engr. Dallas, asst. supt. transmission, substa. engr., system engr., adminstrv. asst., 1959-61, asst. chief engr., 1961-68, chief engr., 1968-69, v.p. in charge engring., 1969—. Registered profl. engr., Tex. Fellow I.E.E.E.; mem. Tex. Soc. Profl. Engrs., Tau Beta Pi, Eta Kappa Nu. Methodist. Mason. Home: 1519 Matagorda Dr Dallas TX 75232 Office: Box 6331 Dallas TX 75222

ROCA, RAFAEL ANGEL, ins. exec.; b. Yauco, P.R., Aug. 11, 1928; s. Gaspar G. and Luisa (Natali) R.; B.S. in Econs., Wharton Sch., U. Pa., 1949; student Advanced Multiple Line Underwriting Course, Am. Ins. Group, Newark, N.J., 1950. Trainee, Am. Ins. Co., Newark, 1950-51; casualty underwriter Anglo-Porto Rican Ins. Agys., Inc., San Juan, P.R., 1951-54; asst. sec. Puerto Rican-Am. Ins. Co., San Juan, 1954-58, sec., 1958-60, asst. v.p., 1960, exec. v.p., 1960-61, pres., 1961—, dir., 1954—, mem. exec. com., 1962—, mem. finance com., 1954—; pres. Puerto Rican Reins. Agy., Inc., 1962—, also dir.; chmn. Nat. Life Ins. Co., 1969-71; pres., mem. exec. and finance coms. Preferred Risk Ins. Co., 1968—, also dir.; v.p. Santa Barbara Corp., 1964-65; dir. Banco Commercial de Mayaquez; chmn. J. Walter Thompson Co. Caribbean, 1968—. Mem. adv. ins. bd. Commonwealth P.R., 1964-68; mem. governing bd. Internat. Ins. Seminars, 1967—; mem. exec. com. P.R. Inspection and Rating Bur., 1966—, vice chmn. exec. com., 1971—, chmn. finance com., 1971; mem. P.R. casualty com. Nat. Bur. Casualty Underwriters; chmn. P.R. ins. information com. Ins. Information Inst., 1969—; chmn. adv. com. ins. matters Sec. Treasury P.R., 1972. Fellow Ins. Inst. P.R. (dir., bd. govs. lectr. Sch. Ins.); mem. Ins. Soc. N.Y., Am. Ins. Assn. (chmn. P.R. adv. com. 1965—), Assn. Casualty & Surety Cos. (pres. P.R. adv. com. 1963-64), Navy League U.S., Young Pres.'s Orgn., Bankers Club P.R. Rotarian. Home: 6 Joffre St Condado Santurce PR 00907 Office: PO Box 112 San Juan PR 00902

ROCHELL, CARLTON CHARLES, librarian; b. Lawrenceburg, Tenn., Nov. 2, 1933; s. William Frank and Mae (Crews) R.; B.S. in Math., George Peabody Coll., 1959; M.S. in L.S., Fla. State U., 1961; m. Rebecca Anne Ridley, Sept. 9, 1961; children—Carlton Charles, Anne Leslie. Reference librarian, spl. asst. to dir. Nashville Pub. Library, 1957-60; dir. Hattiesburg (Miss.)-Forrest County Pub. Library, 1961-63, Pub. Library Anniston and Calhoun County (Ala.), 1963-65, Pub. Library Knoxville and Knox County (Tenn.), 1965-68; Atlanta Pub. Library, 1968—; library service and bldg. cons., 1965—. Mem. exec. bd. Community Action Com., Anniston, 1963-65; mem. Model Cities Tech. Adv. Bd., Atlanta. Served with USNR, 1953-57. Recipient spl. citation City Anniston, 1965. Mem. Am. (standards com.), Tenn. (treas. 1966), Southeastern (pres. pub. library div. 1970), Ala. (past v.p., pres. elect pub. library div. 1965) library assns., Atlanta C. of C. (edn. com.). Democrat. Episcopalian. Home: 248 The Prado NE Atlanta GA 30309 Office: Atlanta Pub Library 126 Carnegie Way NW Atlanta GA 30303

ROCHESTER, MORGAN COLUMBUS, educator, economist; b. Salem, S.C., Dec. 6, 1907; s. Paul Sloan and Annie Lenora (Tucker) R.; B.S., Clemson U., 1931; M.S., U. Fla., 1933; Ph.D., U. Wis., 1946; postgrad. Case Inst. Tech., 1954; m. Susan Eureka Harbin, June 9, 1937; children—Penelope Sue (Mrs. Charles Claude Nicholson), David Patrick. Instr. U. Fla. at Gainesville, 1932-33; tchr. vocational agr. pub. schs., Fountain Inn, S.C., 1934; cooperative researcher U.S. Dept. Agr. and Clemson (S.C.) U., 1935-37; economist Extension Ser., Clemson U., 1937-72, prof. agrl. econs. and rural sociology, 1972—. Mem. S.C. Soc. Farm Mgrs. and Rural Appraisors (sec., treas.), Epsilon Sigma Phi, Gamma Sigma Delta. Baptist. Kiwanian. Contbr. feature articles to farm mags. Home: 116 Folger St Clemson SC 29631 Office: Clemson U Clemson SC 29631

ROCK, DAVID MIGUEL, environmental engr.; b. Havana, Cuba, Aug. 9, 1921; s. David Thomas and Olga Maria (Moenck) R.; B.S. in Chem. Engring., Mass. Inst. Tech., 1944, M.S., 1946; m. Cira Ruiz, Jan. 15, 1966; 1 dau., Anne-Marie. Came to U.S., 1962, naturalized, 1968. Teaching asst. Mass. Inst. Tech., Cambridge, 1944-45; process and product control supr. Ind. Consolidadas de Matanzas, Cuba, 1946-53, resident mgr., 1953-59, tech. dir., 1959-60; tech. mgr. Rayon Said Ind. Quim., Chile, 1960-62; rayon research leader Am. Enka Co., Enka, N.C., 1962-65, project engr., 1965-70, environmental engr., 1970—, project coordinator Environmental Protection Agy. research and devel. grant, 1968-70. Mem. Am. Inst. Chem. Engrs. (vice chmn. water quality engring. symposium 1971), Am. Chem. Soc., Sigma Xi, Tau Beta Pi, Alpha Chi Sigma. Club: Enka Lake. Home: PO Box 6 Enka NC 28728 Office: Central Engineering Dept American Enka Company Enka NC 28728

ROCK, JEROME IRWIN, dentist; b. Brooklyn, N.Y., Sept. 4, 1928; s. Louis A. and Ethel G. (Resnik) R.; B.A., Bklyn. Coll., 1946-50; D.D.S., N.Y. U., 1955; m. Margaret Felton, July 8, 1956; children—Melanie Ann, Robin Elizabeth. Pvt. practice dentistry, Montego Bay, Jamaica, W.I., 1957-61, Falls Church, Va., 1961—, Middleburg, Va., 1963—. Served to capt. AUS, 1955-57. Mem. Am., N. Va. dental assns., Fairfax County Dental Soc. Clubs: Middleburg Tennis, Orange County Hunt. Home: Box 126 Middleburg VA 22117 Office: Seven Corners Med Arts Bldg Falls Church VA 22044

ROCKEFELLER, WINTHROP, state ofcl.; b. N.Y.C., May 1, 1912; s. John D. Jr., and Abby Greene (Aldrich) R.; ed. Lincoln Sch. (N.Y.C.), Loomis Sch., Windsor, Conn., 1928-31, Yale, 1931-34; LL.D. (hon.), U. Ark., Coll. William and Mary, Hendrix Coll., Coll. Ozarks; Dr. Civl Law (hon.) Southwestern U. at Memphis; L.H.D., N.Y.U.; H.H.D., U. St. Francis Xavier; m. Barbara Sears, Feb. 14, 1948 (div. 1954); 1 son, Winthrop; m. 2d, Jeannette Edris, June 11, 1956 (div. 1971). With Humble Oil & Refining Co. (Tex.), 1934-37, Chase Nat. Bank, 1937-38; exec. v.p. Greater N.Y. Fund, 1935; fgn. dept. Socony-Vacuum Oil Co. 1939-41, 46-51; dir. Rockefeller Center, Inc. Chmn. bd. Colonial Williamsburg Found.; mem. Republican Nat. Com. Ark., 1961—; gov. of Ark., 1967-71; chmn. Ark. Museums and Cultural Commn., 1971—. Chmn. Ark. Indsl. Devel. Commn., 1955-64; trustee Nat. Urban League, 1940-64. Trustee Rockefeller Bros. Fund, Loomis Inst., Vanderbilt U. Served from pvt. to lt. col. AUS, 1941-46; with 77th Inf., invasion Guam, Leyte, Okinawa. Decorated Bronze Star Medal with oak leaf cluster, Purple Heart. Mem. Santa Gertrudis Breeders Internat. Assn. (past pres., dir.), Delta Kappa Epsilon. Baptist. Clubs: Yale, Links, (N.Y.C.); Little Rock, Little Rock Country; Pleasant Valley Country. Home: Winrock Farms Route 3 Morrilton AR 72110 Office: 450 Tower Bldg Little Rock AR 72201

ROCKWELL, REUBEN LUCIER, paper co. engr., computer analyst; b. Fairhope, Ala., May 7,, 1916; s. Reuben Linley and Helenbell (Lucier) R.; B.S., U. Ala., 1943, postgrad., 1956-57; m. Ruth Elizabeth Battey, Apr. 16, 1938; children—Ruth Anne (Mrs. Roy B. Zweidinger), Kenneth Lucier, Paula Louise. Test engr. Gen. Electric Co., Schenectady, 1944-45; sr. distbn. engr. Ala. Power Co., Mobile, 1946-56; asst. prof. elec. engring. U. Ala., Tuscaloosa, 1956-57; project engr., elect. and computer analyst Internat. Paper Co., Mobile, 1957—; partner Rockwell Mfg. Co., Fairhope, Ala., 1949-52. Bd. mgrs. Sch. of Organic Edn., 1959-61; mem. exec. council Fairhope Single Tax Corp., 1954-56. Registered profl. engr., Ala. Mem. I.E.E.E. (sect. sec.-treas. 1961-62, pres. 1962-63, exec. bd. 1964-66), Nat., Ala. socs. profl. engrs. Mem. Soc. of Friends. Clubs: Fairhope Yacht; Civitan (bd. govs. 1967) (Fairhope). Home: 703 Bellangee Fairhope AL 36532 Office: PO Box 2328 Mobile AL 36601

RODDENBERY, ROBERT SAMUEL, JR., lawyer; b. Bainbridge, Ga., Sept. 6, 1897; s. Robert S. and Lucy (Parker) R.; B.S., Ga. Mil. Coll., 1916; LL.B., Mercer U., 1919; m. Lucie Bland, July 1, 1920; 1 son, Thaddeus Hall. Admitted to Ga. bar, 1918, Fla. bar, 1926; practice, Albany, Ga., 1922-26, Orlando, Fla., 1926-30, Moultrie, Ga., 1919-22, 30—. U.S. commr., Albany, 1924-26; judge, Small Claims Ct. of Colquitt County, 1961—. Served to 2d lt. U.S. Army, 1918; served as 1st lt. Corps Mil. Police, AUS, 1942-44. Ky col. Mem. Am. Legion, (past post comdr.), Fla. Bar, Am., Ga. bar assns., Sigma Alpha Epsilon. Elk, Moose, Kiwanian. Author: Genesis of Cairo, 1965; also articles in field. Home: 605 S Main St Moultrie GA 31768 Office: 20 S Main St Moultrie GA 31768

RODENBURG, CARL EDWARD, dentist, army officer; b. Hackensack, N.J., Aug. 7, 1933; s. Carl Euler and Ann Irving (McIntosh) R.; A.B., U. Pa., 1955; postgrad. N.Y.U., 1956; D.D.S., Columbia, 1961; m. Helma Kumme, Mar. 25, 1961; children—Richard Robert, Cynthia Maria, Carl Robert. Commd. 1st lt. Dental Corps, U.S. Army, 1961, advanced through grades to lt. col., 1972; chief crown and bridge Ft. Campbell, 1961-64; chief crown and bridge, exec. officer 47th Med. Detachment, Ft. Wainwright, Alaska, 1964-68; chief crown and bridge Dental Clinic No. 2, resident, dir. Dental Clinic No. 4, chief prosthodontics dept. Dental Clinic No. 4, Ft. Bragg, N.C., 1968—. First aid instr. A.R.C. Mem. Am. Dental Assn., Fedn. Dentaire Internat., Nat. Rifle Assn. (life), Theta Xi, Psi Omega. Mason (Shriner); mem. Order Amaranth (royal patron), Order Eastern Star. Club: Friendship CB Radio (pres.) (Ft. Bragg). Home: 6 Nijmegen St Fort Bragg NC 28307 Office: Dental Activities (MEDDAC) Fort Bragg NC 28307

RODERICK, DORRANCE DOUGLAS, publisher; b. Brooklyn, Ia., Dec. 24, 1900; s. Tallesin Evan and Mary (Dorrance) R.; A.B., U. Okla., 1922; m. Olha Burnett, Aug. 14, 1922; children—Frances Rozelle, Dorrance Douglas. Reporter, Tulsa World, 1918; asst. editor A.P., Oklahoma City, 1922; with advt. dept. Wichita (Kan.) Eagle, 1923; advt. and bus. mgr. Lubbock (Tex.) Jour., 1924-25, pub., 1926-29, Lubbock Avalanche, 1926-29, El Paso (Tex.) Herald, 1929-31; pub. El Paso Times, 1929—; pres. El Paso Times, Inc., Newspaper Printing Corp., Newspaper Realty Corp.; chmn. bd. Times Enterprises, Inc., Mesa Vista, Inc.; dir. Avalanche-Jour. Pub. Co., Lubbock, Fed. Res. Bank, El Paso, 1945-51, chmn. bd., 1948-51; dir., mem. exec. com. El Paso Nat. Bank; v.p. Coronado Devel. Corp. Mem. El Paso Indsl. Bd., Tex. Good Neighbor Commn., 1943-57. Bd. dirs. United Fund El Paso, Armed Services Y.M.C.A., U. Tex. El Paso Adv. Council, Providence Meml. Hosp., El Paso Symphony Assn., pres. 1930-63, chmn. bd., 1963—. Served to maj. AUS, 1943-45. Mem. Tex. Daily Press League (dir.), El Paso Hist. Soc. (trustee), V.F.W., El Paso C. of C. (dir.), Phi Gamma Delta (trustee ednl. found.), Sigma Delta Chi, Phi Mu Alpha, Phi Alpha Tau. Episcopalian (vestryman). Mason (33 deg., Shriner), Kiwanian (dist. gov. 1935). Clubs: El Paso Country, International, Ormsbee (pres. 1934-36), Knife and Fork (pres. 1938-39), El Paso Country, International, Coronado Country, El Paso, Pioneers. Home: 4601 Cumberland Circle El Paso TX 79903 Office: The El Paso Times El Paso TX 79999

RODGERS, ALICE MARIE REYNOLDS, educator; b. Conway, Ark., Jan. 18, 1915; d. Cyrus Carl and Lydia Ellen (Bowen) Reynolds; B.S. in Edn., Ark. State Tchrs. Coll., 1936; postgrad. U. Ark., 1943; M.A., George Peabody Coll., 1948, postgrad., 1953, 68, 71; m. Norman Eugene Rodgers, Nov. 26, 1943 (dec. Feb. 1966); 1 dau., Rebecca Jane (dec.). Tchr. social studies Watson (Ark.) High Sch., 1936; tchr. English, Dyess (Ark.) High Sch., 1937-40; tchr. English, high sch. prin. Shawnee Consol. Schs., Joiner, 1940-46; instr. English, Potomac State Coll. of W.Va. U., Keyser, 1947-51, asst. prof., 1960-66; asst. prof. English, State Coll. Ark., Conway, 1966—. Recipient 1st place award one-act playwriting contest W.Va. Fedn. Women's Clubs, 1958, 59. Mem. Am. Assn. U. Women (br. v.p. 1952-53), N.E.A., Ark. Edn. Assn., Am. Assn. Higher Edn., Nat. Council Tchrs. English, Ark. Assn. Tchrs. English, Ark. Hist. Assn., Conf. on Coll. Composition and Communication, Kappa Delta Pi. Methodist. Contbr. articles and poems to various mags. and newspapers. Home: Box 341 Grandview Heights Conway AR 72032

RODGERS, EARL HAMILTON, banker; b. Eagle Lake, Tex., Sept. 23, 1922; s. Earl Houston and Dale (Simpson) R.; student S.W. Tex. State Tchrs. Coll., 1941-42, U. Tex., 1946-47; m. Annette Seaholm, May 21, 1948; children—Larry Hamilton, Ernest Earl. With Shell Oil Co., 1947-48; cashier First Nat. Bank, Eagle Lake, 1948, v.p., 1970—, also dir.; owner A.B. Store, 1949-70. Served with USNR, 1942-45. Mem. Eagle Lake C. of C. (pres. 1955), Tex. and Southwestern Cattle Raisers Assn., Nat. Rifle Assn. (life). Presbyn. (deacon). Mason (Shriner), Rotarian (pres. 1958-59). Home: 503 N Walnut St Eagle Lake TX 77434 Office: First Nat Bank Eagle Lake TX 77434

RODGERS, FANN ISABEL MATTHEWS (MRS. ALLEE THURMON RODGERS), educator; b. Livingston, Tenn., Aug. 29, 1913; d. George LaFayette and Louise (Walker) Matthews; B.S., Memphis State U., 1954; M.S. in Aerospace Edn., U. Tenn., 1956, postgrad., 1960; postgrad. Miami U., Oxford, O., 1957-58, Middle Tenn. State U., 1959; m. Allee Thurmon Rodgers, Nov. 16, 1934; 1 dau., Kathryn Louise (Mrs. Lewis McLaurine Abernathy). Tchr. elementary schs., Tenn., 1932-34, 49—, Germantown Elementary Sch., 1967—. Staff mem. aerospace edn. workshop U. Tenn., 1955-56, 60, Miami U., 1957-58, Middle Tenn. State U., Murfreesboro, 1955; aerospace edn. officer Tenn. wing Civil Air Patrol, 1957-65. Recording sec. Center Hill (Miss.) Cemetery Assn., 1965-68. Mem. N.E.A., Tenn. Edn. Assn. (del. legislative assembly), Internat. Platform Assn., Shelby County Tchrs. Edn. Assn., Assn. Childhood Edn. Internat. (state chmn. internat. affairs com. 1963-66), Assn. Childhood Edn. (br. pres. 1963-65 br. 1st v.p. 1971-72), Nat. (alternate del. to gen. conv. 1947), Tenn. (dist. chmn. internat. relations 1948-49, recording sec. 1950-51) fedns. women's clubs, Alpha Delta Kappa (parliamentarian chpt., pres. chpt. 1971-72). Clubs: Holmes Road Garden (charter, pres. 1950-52), Lamplighter Women's (1st v.p. 1971-72), Lunch Forum (Memphis, rec. sec. 1948-50), Germantown Women's (organizer 1947, pres. 1947-49, hon. life), Germantown Business and Professional Women's (pres. 1971-72). Co-author: Curriculum Guide for Aviation Education, 1958. Home: 7633 Holmes Rd Germantown TN 38038

RODGERS, GORDON ALEXANDER, JR., dentist; b. Anniston, Ala., Oct. 28, 1915; s. Gordon Alexander and Fannie Mamie (Lewis) R.; B.A., Talladega Coll., 1937; D.D.S., Meharry Med. Coll., 1941; m. Agnes Elizabeth Durrah, Feb. 29, 1951; children—Gordon, III, Cheryl, Beverly, Michelle. Pvt. practice dentistry, Anniston, Ala., 1946—. Mem. Anniston City Council, 1969—. Bd. dirs. Choccolocco council Boy Scouts Am., 1969—, Ala. Mental Health Assn., 1965—. Served with Dental Corps, AUS, 1941-46. Mem. Nat. Dental Assn., Ala. Dental Soc., Am. Legion, N.A.A.C.P. (br. pres. 1954-55), Omega Psi Phi. Home: 1001 Claxton St Anniston AL 36201 Office: 1616 Cooper St Anniston AL 36201

RODGERS, HENRY LEE, justice Miss. Supreme Ct.; b. Philadelphia, Miss., Apr. 6,, 1903; s. H. H. and Ettie Lee (Brantley) R.; student Miss. Coll., 1920-22. Cumberland U., 1922-24; LL.B., U. Miss., 1927; m. Leola Edwards, May 18, 1929. Admitted to Miss. bar, 1927, practiced in Louisville, until 1951; dist. atty. 5th Dist. Miss., 1946-51; circuit judge 5th Dist. Miss., 1951-61; asso. justice Miss. Supreme Ct., Jackson, 1961—. Mem. Miss. N.G., 1929-35; served with AUS, 1943-44. Mem. Miss. State Bar, Sons Confederate Vets., Am. Legion, 40 and 8. Methodist. Mason (Shriner). Author articles. Home: 432 N Spring Av Louisville MS 39339 also 751 N President St Jackson MS Office: Supreme Ct Bldg Jackson MS 39205

RODGERS, HILLMAN PHILLIP, planter, paper salesman; b. Lexington, Miss., Nov. 28, 1899; s. William Clay and Sarah Phillip (Eubank) R.; student Freed-Hardeman Coll., 1916-18; m. Frances Ellen Davies, Dec. 21, 1932; foster children—Sarah B. Gandy, Frances Gandy, Eiba Gandy, Mary Gandy (Mrs. Burnell Dwight), Hardee. Salesman, Southland Paper Co. Memphis, 1931-72; mill rep. Crown Zellerbach Corp., also Duro Paper Mfg. Co., 1972—; sales asso. Ike L. Myers Paper Co., 1972—. Mem. Memphis Retail Drug Club, Shelby County Livestock Assn. (past pres.), Shelby County Farm Bur. (dir.), Shelby County Soil Erosion Control Assn. (dir.), Memphis Agrl. Club, S.A.R. (registrar Shelby chpt. Brunswick, Tenn., state and nat. promoter CAR), Sons of Confederacy. Democrat. Episcopalian. Mason (Shriner). Club: Holly Hills Country. Home and Office: Davies Plantation Brunswick TN 38014

RODGERS, JACK, coll. pres.; b. Bogata, Tex., July 29, 1911; s. William Charles and Stella (Welch) R.; B.A., East Tex. State Coll., 1933; M.A. U. Tex., 1935, Ph.D., 1956; m. Ruth Tyer, June 6, 1939. Adminstrv. positions, county schs. of East Tex., 1929-34, Bogata, Tex., 1934-36; elementary, secondary sch., classroom teaching Odessa pub. schs., 1936-38, prin. Goldsmith Sch., 1938-41, coordinator Odessa Pub. Schs., 1941-45, prin. jr. high sch., 1945-49; dean, registrar Odessa Coll., 1949-60, v.p., 1952-60, pres., 1960—. Named Outstanding Man of Odessa, 1968. Mem. Am. Assn. Jr. Colls. (commn. instrn.), Tex. Pub. Jr. Coll. Assn., Tex. Jr. Coll. Tchrs. Assn., Tex. State Tchrs. Assn., Assn. Tex. Colls., Tex. Interscholastic League (regional dir.), Tex. Safety Assn. (regional sch. and safety dir. 1961), Phi Delta Kappa. Mason (32 deg., Shriner). Rotarian (pres. Odessa 1965, dist. gov. 1968-69). Club: Sportsman of Texas. Home: 1501 E 18th St Odessa TX 79760

RODGERS, JAMES FRANKLIN, dentist; b. Charlotte, N.C., June 11, 1927; s. John Boyce and Ella Graymo (Cornelius) R.; student The Citadel, 1944-45, Duke, 1945-46; B.S., Davidson Coll., 1950; D.D.S., U. N.C., 1956; m. Dorothy Louise Herring, Dec. 27, 1955; 1 son, John Herring. Pvt. practice dentistry, Statesville, N.C., 1956-67; mem. staff N.C. State Bd. Health, Statesville, 1967—. Served with USNR, 1945-46. Mem. Am. Dental Assn., N.C. Dental Soc., Delta Sigma Delta. Presbyn. (elder). Rotarian. Home: 412 Ridgeway Av Statesville NC 28677 Office: PO Box 182 Statesville NC 28677

RODGERS, JAMES JACOB, surgeon; b. Knoxville, Tenn., May 7, 1906; s. William Thomas and Eula (Hunter) R.; student Western Ill. U., 1924-26; B.S., U. Ill., 1928, M.D., 1930; m. Vivian Louise Edwards, Nov. 18, 1933; children—Nancy (Mrs. W. Charles R. Smith), Robert Hunter, James Steven, William Thomas. Intern, resident St. Louis City Hosp., 1930-33; asso. surgeon Riegal Hosp., Trion, Ga., 1934-38; practice gen. medicine, surgery Dayton, Tenn., 1938—; chief staff Rhea County Hosp., Dayton, 1964-66. Med. examiner Rhea County, 1965—; mem. Bd. Health Rhea County, 1950—. Mem. draft bd. Rhea County, 1941—; mayor Dayton, 1952-60. Trustee William J. Bryan Coll., Dayton. Recipient Silver Beaver award Boy Scouts Am., 1958. Mem. Tenn., Chattanooga-Hamilton County med. socs., A.M.A., Alpha Kappa Kappa. Methodist (chmn. ofcl. bd.). Lion, Rotarian. Home: 808 N Market St Dayton TN 37321 Office: 227 N Market St Dayton TN 37321

RODGERS, MARY VASTINE LUNN, educator; b. Jefferson Twp., O., Oct. 28, 1895; d. Benjamin Vastine and Mary Ella (Rankin) Lunn; student White's Bible Sch., 1922; B.Sc. in Home Econs., Ohio State U., 1922, B.A., 1922; postgrad. U. Guanajuato (Mexico), 1944; M.A. in Spanish, N. Tex. State U., 1948; m. Samuel Clark Rodgers, Jan. 16, 1924 (dec. Jan. 1946); children—Samuel Lunn, Mary Vastine (Mrs. John Thomas Easton). Various positions, 1914-20; tchr. Colegio Juarez, Guanajuato, 1924, dir., 1925-27, cons., 1933-35; tchr. Laura Temple Sch., Mexico City, 1923, dir. vocational home econs. dept., 1932, cons., 1933-35; prof. English U. Guanajuato and State Normal Sch., 1942-44; tchr. Bowie High Sch., El Paso, Tex., 1944-46; mem. faculty N. Tex. State U., 1946-48, Hardin-Simmons U., Abilene, 1954-55, 58-69, asso. prof. fgn. lang. dept., 1967-69, ret. Named hon. asso. prof. Carlsbad (N.M.) Pub. Schs., 1956. Mem. Modern Lang. Assn., S. Central Modern Lang. Assn., Tex. Library Assn., Am. Assn. Tchrs. Spanish and Portuguese, Womens Soc. Social Service (charter), Am. Assn. U. Women (chpt. historian 1961-72), D.A.R. (regent 1959-61, rec. sec. 1970-72), Daus. Am. Colonists (regent 1971-73), Huguenot Soc., Alphi Chi, Delta Kappa Gamma, Kappa Phi, Alpha Mu Gamma (nat. v.p.), Pi Gamma Mu, Phi Alpha Theta, Sigma Delta Pi. Club: University Women's (sec.-treas. 1951-53). Home: 1801 University Blvd Abilene TX 79603

RODGERS, ROBERT KAY, bank exec.; b. Cane Hill, Ark., Dec. 21, 1895; s. William F. and Mary Ellen (Reed) R.; dr. bus., Coll. Ozarks, 1958; m. Bessie Howard, Nov. 22, 1913; children—Wilma Faye (Mrs. B.T. Blevins), Roberta Kay (Mrs. Ed Pevehouse). Pres., Checkered Transfer and Storage Co., Ft. Smith, Ark., 1935—, Fort Smith Stockyards Co., Inc., 1950—, Rodgers Furniture Co., Ft. Smith, 1947—; pres. First Fed. Savs. and Loan Assn., 1954-67, chmn. bd., 1967—; pres. Modern Meat Processing Co., Inc., 1957-70; dir. First Nat. Bank, Ft. Smith Gas Co. Bd. dirs. Westark. area council Boy Scouts Am., until 1972, pres., 1946-47; chmn. Community Chest, 1948-49; pres. Sparks Meml. Hosp., 1949-65; bd. dirs. Ark.-Okla. Livestock Show, 1946-71, Ark. Livestock Show. Served from pvt. to sgt., Signal Corps, 1917-18. Recipient Golden Deed award Exchange Club, 1961. Mem. C. of C. (pres. 1941). Democrat. Mason (33 deg.; venerable master Western Ark.; Shriner), Kiwanian. Club: Noon Civic (Ft. Smith). Home: 5601 Park Av Fort Smith AR 72901 Office: First Fed Bldg Fort Smith AR 72901

RODGERS, VERNON LEON, restaurant exec.; b. Hot Springs, Ark., May 18, 1928; s. Oran A. and Hazel N. (Perry) R.; M.E., Little Rock Jr. Coll., 1956; student U. Tex., 1956-57, U. Ark., 1957-58; m. Dorothy Ward, May 18, 1946; children—Tracy Lynn, Lisa Anne. Dist. warehouseman Tex. Eastern Transmission Co., Little Rock, 1953-56; salesman, kitchen designer Dixie Equipment Co., Little Rock, 1960-63; salesman Master Bldg. Co., Cleve., 1963-65; v.p. Minute Man Am., Little Rock, 1965—. Served with USAF, 1951-53. Mem. Pulaski County Bus. Men's Assn. Baptist (mem. finance com. 1970-72, bldg. fund com. 1970-71). Home: 6816 Canna Rd Little Rock AR 72209 Office: 8112 W Markham St Little Rock AR 72205

RODGERS, WALTER M., lawyer; b. Greenwood, S.C., Mar. 26, 1915; B.S. in Elec. Engring., Clemson U., 1937; J.D., George Washington U., 1947. Admitted to D.C. bar, 1947, U.S. Ct. Customs and Patent Appeals bar, 1949, Ga. bar, 1953, U.S. Supreme Ct. bar, 1965; practiced in Atlanta. Served to maj. USAAF, 1941-45. Registered profl. engr. Mem. Am. (patent, trademark and copywright sect.), Atlanta bar assns., State Bar Ga. (chmn. sect. patents, trademarks and copyrights 1969-70), Am. Patent Law Assn. (com. on relations with Patent Office 1961), Am. Judicature Soc., Blue Key, Tau Beta Pi. Club: Lawyers (Atlanta). Office: 1918 Gaslight Tower 235 Peachtree St NE Atlanta GA 30303*

RODGERS, WILLIAM PAUL, JR., lawyer; b. St. Augustine, Fla., Aug. 9, 1933; s. William Paul and Margaret (Jones) R.; A.B., Mercer U., 1955; LL.B., 1957; m. Barbara Jean Broadrick, July 1, 1955; children— Stephen Paul, Marsha Lyn, Mary Elizabeth. Admitted to Ga. bar, 1956, U.S. Supreme Ct. bar, 1961, D.C. bar, 1968; atty. legal dept. Atlanta Gas Light Co., 1957-60; asst. atty. gen. Ga., 1960-65; gen. counsel, adminstrv. dir. Nat. Assn. Regulatory Utility Commrs., Washington, 1965—. Served with AUS, 1957. Mem. Am., D.C., Ga., Fed. Communications, Fed. Power bar assns., Phi Alpha Delta, Sigma Nu. Prepared original draft Ga. Election Code which became law, 1964. Contbr. Title on Elections to Ency. Ga. Law, 1965. Contbr. articles in utility and transp. fields to profl. jours. Home: 1329 Portia Pl McLean VA 22101 Office: ICC Bldg 12th St and Constitution Av NW Washington DC 20004

RODILOSSO, PHILIP THOMAS, physician; b. N.Y.C., Aug. 10, 1932; s. Santo and Mary (Rodilosso) R.; B.A., Cornell U., 1954; M.D., Georgetown U., 1958; m. Rosanne S. Lammers, June 14, 1958; children—Thomas, Maria, Carla. Intern Georgetown U. Hosp., Washington, 1958-59; resident Dist. of Columbia Gen. Hosp., Washington, 1959-60; heart disease control officer USPHS, Atlanta, 1960-62; med. resident Dist. of Columbia VA Hosp., Washington, 1962-64; practice medicine, specializing in internal medicine, Arlington, Va., 1964—; clin. instr. medicine Georgetown U., 1964-69, clin. asst. prof., 1969—; chief of medicine service Nat. Orthopedic Hosp., Arlington, Va., 1971. Sec.-treas. Beacon Hill Corp., 1969-70, v.p., 1970-71, pres. 1971. Diplomate Am. Bd. Internal Medicine. Mem. A.C.P., Am., Va. socs. internal medicine, No. Va. Acad. Internal Medicine, Arlington County, Va. med. socs., Am. Soc. Geriatrics, Alpha Epsilon Delta, Alpha Omega Alpha. Home: 6625 Beacon Lane Falls Church VA 22043 Office: 1400 S Joyce St Arlington VA 22202

RODMAN, TASKER NEWTON, physician; b. Newark, Ark., Jan. 13, 1919; s. Thomas Newton and Ethel (McGee) R.; student Ark. Coll., Batesville, 1936, Ark. State Tchrs. Coll., Conway, 1937-39; M.D., U. Ark., 1943; m. Geneva Geraldine Arnold, Feb. 8, 1941; children—Tasker N., II, Lynda, Rita (Mrs. Jerry Lee Hitt). Intern, Mo. Meth. Hosp., St. Joseph, 1943-44; postgrad. in obstetrics and gynecology, Washington U., St. Louis, 1946; practice medicine, Grays Hosp., Newport, Ark., 1946; gen. practice medicine, Leachville, Ark., 1946—; owner Rodman Clinic and Hosp., 1947—. Dir., Leachville State Bank. Participant preceptorship program U. Ark. Med. Sch., 1954—. A founder Little League Baseball, Leachville, 1954, coach, 1954-61; scoutmaster N.E. Ark. council Boy Scouts Am., 1955-58; mem. Leachville Sch. Bd., 1962—, pres., 1966, 72. Served with AUS, 1944-46; ETO. Decorated Bronze Star medal. Recipient Man of Year award Leachville C. of C., 1955. Mem. A.M.A., Am. Acad. Gen. Practice, Ark. Med. Soc., Mississippi County Med. Soc., Leachville P.T.A. (hon. life), Sigma Tau Gamma, Phi Beta Pi. Methodist (trustee). Mason (32 deg.). Club: Big Lake Country (Manila, Ark.). Home and office: PO Box 260 Leachville AR 72438

RODRIGUEZ, CLAUDIO CEFERINO, dentist, physician; b. Alajuela, Costa Rica, Aug. 26, 1904; s. Eloy and Elena (Arce) R.; B.Humanities, Instituto Alajuela, 1921; postgrad. Columbia, 1927, U. Richmond, 1927-28; D.D.S., Med. Coll. Va., 1932, M.D., 1938; m. Louise Henrietta Berger, June 14, 1939; children—Norman A., Helena O. (Mrs. Alexander Doohovskoy), Claude E., Carl R. Came to U.S., 1927, naturalized, 1941. Practice dentistry, Leesburg, Va., 1932-34, gen. practice medicine and dentistry, Norfolk, Va., 1941—; intern Med. Coll. Va., 1937-38, Elizabeth Burton Hosp., Newport News, Va., 1938-39; resident St. Vincents de Paul Hosp., Norfolk, 1939-41; mem. staffs Leigh Meml., Norfolk Gen., DePaul hosps. (all Norfolk). Mem. Am., Va., Norfolk County dental socs., A.M.A., Va., Norfolk County med. socs., Fedn. Dentaire Internationale, Omicron Kappa Upsilon, Alpha Omega Alpha. Lutheran. Composer short piano pieces. Home: 9415 Norfolk Av Norfolk VA 23503 Office: 9551 Granby St Norfolk VA 23503

RODRIGUEZ-HERNANDEZ, JESUS M., hosp. adminstr.; b. Quebradillas, P.R., Apr. 25, 1930; s. Jesus Maria and Maria Luisa (Hernandez) Rodriguez; B.S., U. P.R., 1952; M.S., Columbia, 1957; m. Maria Teresa Estevez, May 1, 1954; children—Jesus M., Maria Teresa. Hosp. adminstr. Humacao (P.R.) Health Center and Hosp., 1954-55; asst. exec. dir. Ponce (P.R.) Dist. Hosp., 1957-58, Arecibo (P.R.) Dist. Hosp., 1958-59, asst. dir. adminstrv. services no. health area Dept. Health, 1959-69; adminstr. San Juan (P.R.) Municipal Hosp., 1969-71, Presbyn. Community Hosp., San Juan, 1971—. Dist. chmn. Boy Scouts Am., 1958-60, A.R.C. campaign, 1960; dist. supr. Cancer Campaign, 1959; mem. Indsl. Com. Arecibo. Bd. govs. Girl Scouts Am.; bd. dirs. Nat. Assn. Crippled Children and Adults, Blue Cross of P.R., Employees City of Arecibo; trustee Dept. Health Coop., P.R., 1959-61; pres. finance com. San Antonio Abad Coll., 1972. Served as lt. AUS, 1952-54. Mem. Am. Hosp. Assn. (trustee P.R. chpt. 1960-61), Tb Assn., Navy League U.S., Hosp. Adminstrs. Assn. P.R., P.R. Hosp. Assn. (dir.), P.R. Hosp. Adminstr. Assn. (dir.), Chamber of Arecibo (v.p. Key Mem. Yr.), Phi Eta Mu (pres. supreme council 1961). Roman Catholic. K.C. Clubs: Rotary, Arecibo Country. Home: 559 Independencia St Baldrich Hato Rey PR 00919 Office: Presbyn Hosp 1451 Ashford Av Condado San Juan PR

RODRIQUEZ, JUAN GUADALUPE, entomologist acarologist, educator; b. Espanola, N.M., Dec. 23, 1920; s. Manuel D. and Lugardita (Salazar) R.; B.S., N.M. State U., 1943; M.S., Ohio State U., 1946, Ph.D., 1949; m. Lorraine Ditzler, Apr. 17, 1948; children—Carmen, Teresa, Carla, Rosa. Asst. to state entomologist N.M. State Coll., 1941-43; grad. asst. Ohio State U., research asst. O. Agrl. Expt. Sta., Wooster, 1946-49; asst. entomologist U. Ky., Lexington, 1949-55, asso. entomologist, 1955-61, prof. entomology, 1961—; adviser entomology Universidad de San Carlos, Guatemala, 1961; vis. scientist Warsaw U., Poland, 1971. Del. Internat. Congress Entomology, Vienna, Austria, 1960, Moscow, 1968, 1st Internat. Conf. Insects and Diseases of Coffee, San Jose, Costa Rica, 1965, 1st Internat. Congress Acarology, Ft. Collins, Colo., 1963, 2d Internat. Congress, Nottingham, Eng., 1967, 3d Internat. Congress, Prague, Czechoslovakia, 1971, 1st Nat. Congress Acarology, Ithaca, 1962. Bd. dirs. Lexington chpt. Nat. Conf. Christians and Jews. Served with inf. AUS, World War II. Recipient Univ. Ky. Alumni Assn. award for distinguished research, 1963; Thomas Poe Cooper award U. Ky. Coll. Agr., 1972. Mem. Am. Inst. Biol. Scis., Ky. Acad. Sci., A.A.A.S., entomol. socs. Can., Ont., Am. (br. sec.-treas. 1963-65; br. com. man-at-large 1968—), Ky. Research Club, Hon. Order Ky. Cols., Sigma Xi, Alpha Tau Alpha, Gamma Alpha, Gamma Sigma Delta. Roman Catholic. Contbr. numerous sci. and tech. publs. Researcher ecology and nutritional physiology of acarina, axenic arthropoda. Home: 1550 Beacon Hill Rd Lexington KY 40504

RODRIQUEZ, MARIO SANTOS, educator; b. Pasay City, Philippines, Nov. 16, 1932 (came to U.S. 1966); s. Jose Domingo and Josefa (Santos) R.; B.S. in Chemistry, U. Philippines, 1954, D. Dental Medicine, 1958, M.S. in Dental Materials, 1960; Ph.D. in Biochemistry, Georgetown U., 1964; D.D.S., Loyola U. of South, 1969.; m. Edna Laurel Del Rio, Nov. 24, 1961; children—Regina Josefa, Nancy Edna, Maria Louisa, Jose Mario. Research asso. Am. Dental Assn., Chgo., 1959-60; guest worker dental research div. Nat. Bur. Standards, Washington, 1959-63; research asso. Georgetown U., Washington, 1960-63; chmn., asst. prof. dental materials and biochemistry Loyola U., New Orleans, 1963-67; asso. prof., 1967-69; asst. prof. periodontology La. State U., 1969—. Mem. A.A.A.S., Am. Dental Assn., Internat. Assn. Dental Research, Am. Chem. Soc., Philippine Am. Profl. Assn. La. (pres. 1969-70). Home: 1190 Florida Av New Orleans LA 70122 Office: La State U New Orleans LA 70112

RODRIQUEZ, RUBEN RODRIQUEZ, supt. schs., Ponce, P.R. Address: Ponce Board Edn Ponce PR 00731

RODWELL, PERCY CREIGHTON, JR., dentist; b. Orangeburg, S.C., Aug. 6, 1920; s. Percy Creighton and Sue Goodrich (Walker) R.; student Wake Forest Coll., 1937-40, Northwestern U., 1940-41; D.D.S., Emory U., 1944; m. Mildred Ann Mayer, June 28, 1942; children—William David Creighton, Carol Sue. Practice dentistry, Orangeburg, 1947—. Served with Dental Corps, AUS, 1944-47. Mem. Am., S.C. dental assns., Coastal Dist. Dental Soc. Rotarian. Home: 305 Brookside Dr Orangeburg SC 29115 Office: PO Box 714 Orangeburg SC 29115

ROE, DAVID, pub. co. exec.; b. Oak Park, Ill., Jan. 3, 1936; s. Victor D. and Mildred Marie (Sindler) R.; B.S. in Journalism, Northwestern U., 1958, M.S., 1959; m. Judith Anne Weigand, Apr. 8, 1961; children—Kevin Scott, Mark and Matthew (twins). With Hollister Newspapers, Wilmette, Ill., 1959-69, asso. editor, 1960, mng. editor, 1960-63, pub., 1963-69, v.p., 1964-69, dir., 1965-69; mgr. spl. projects, Washington Post, 1970, prodn. comptroller, 1970-71, asst. to gen. mgr., 1971, asst. to pres., 1972—; pres., dir. Post-Trib Corp., 1972—. Instr., Medill Sch. Journalism, Northwestern U., 1958-64. Served with USMCR, 1959-60. Mem. YMCA. Lutheran. Rotarian. Home: 3822 N Roberts Lane Arlington VA 22207 Office: 1150 15th St NW Washington DC 20005

ROE, DONALD WINSTON, educator; b. Catlettsburg, Ky., Jan. 22, 1932; s. Lorenzo Dow and Myrtle (Rowland) R.; student Duke, 1949-51; B.S., Marshall U., 1955, M.S., 1956; postgrad. U. Tenn., 1956-57; Ph.D., W.Va. U., 1961; m. Betty Jo Bailey, Dec. 31, 1960; children—Sara Nell, Daniel Winston. Control chemist C. & O. R.R., Huntington, W.Va., 1955-56; AEC fellow U. Tenn., 1956-57; NSF fellow W.Va. U., 1959-60; research chemist Nat. Steel Corp., Weirton, W.Va., 1960-62; engr. RCA, Lancaster, Pa., 1962-68; acting chmn., asst. prof. U. Tampa (Fla.), 1968-70, asso. prof., 1970—, chmn. dept. chemistry, 1970—; chem. cons. SCI-CON Corp., Maitland, Fla., Conservation Consultants, Palmetto, Fla., 1970—, Intersci. Research & Engring. Corp., Tampa, 1971—. Fellow Am. Inst. Chemists; mem. Am. Chem. Soc., Sigma Xi, Phi Lambda Upsilon. Methodist. Contbr. articles profl. jours. Patentee in field.Home: 7018 W Pocahontas Dr Tampa FL 33614 Office: 401 W Kenneday Blvd Tampa FL 33606

ROE, ROY ARLINGTON, ednl. adminstr.; b. Wild Cherry, Ark., Sept. 27, 1919; s. Charles Edward and Sarah Elizabeth (Ducker) R.; B.A., Harding Coll., 1940; M.S., U. Ark., 1951; m. Wanda Jeraldean Finley, Dec. 25, 1940; children—Ramona, Roy Arlington II. Supt., Hardy (Ark.) Schs., 1946-51, Hartford (Ark.) Schs., 1951-55, Yellville (Ark.) Schs., 1955-65, Fountain Lake Sch., Hot Springs, Ark., 1965-68, Foreman (Ark.) Pub. Schs., 1968—. Served with USNR, 1944-46. Mem. N.E.A., Am. Assn. Sch. Adminstrs., Ark. Edn. Assn., Schoolmasters Club (pres. S.W. Ark. dist. 4), Ark. Ofcls. Assn., V.F.W., Phi Delta Kappa. Democrat. Mason (32 deg., Shriner), Kiwanian (pres.). Club: Ark. Traveler Antique Auto (Little Rock). Address: PO Box 280 Foreman AR 71836

ROE, THOMAS ANDERSON, bldg. supply co. exec.; b. Greenville, S.C., May 29, 1927; s. Thomas Anderson and Leila (Cunningham) R.; B.S., Furman U., 1948; diploma bus. mgmt. LaSalle Extension U., 1956; m. Bette Verner Bain, Oct. 14, 1950; children—Elizabeth Overton, Thomas Anderson III, Philip Stradley, John Verner. Cancer research asst. Furman U., Greenville, S.C., 1947-48; with Builder Marts of Am., Inc., Greenville, 1948—, asst. mgr., 1948-58, mgr., 1958-61, pres. 1961-69, now chmn. bd., chief exec. officer; chmn. bd. First Piedmont Corp., First Piedmont Bank & Trust Co. Mem. Greenville Civil Def. Council, 1956-60; air insp. Civil Air Patrol, Greenville, 1949-50; pres. Greenville Housing Found., 1971-72; mem. Greenville County Redevel. Authority. Vice chmn. S.C. Republican Com., 1963-64, mem. state budget and orgn. com., 1963-64, mem. party rules and forms com., 1963-64, state finance chmn., 1963-64; mem. Nat. Rep. Finance Com., 1963-64; state committeeman Greenville County Rep. Com., 1962-64; hon. asst. sgt. at arms Rep. Nat. Conv., Chgo., 1960. Bd. dirs. Greenville United Cerebral Palsy, 1959-63; bd. dirs. Greenville chpt. A.R.C.; trustee Christ Ch. Episcopal Sch. Named Greenville Builder of Yr., Greenville Home Builders Assn., 1962 Mem. Nat. Assn. Home Builders, Greenville Home Builders Assn. (dir. 1961-64, v.p. 1962-63), Nat. Lumber and Bldg. Material Dealers Assn. (alt. dir. 1965-66), Carolina (pres. 1965-66), Greenville (past pres.) bldg. material dealers assns., Greenville C. of C. (dir., chmn. legislative com. 1962, pres. 1970). Episcopalian. Clubs: Players (pres. 1951), Sertoma (local pres. 1960-61, Distinguished Service award 1959, Superior Leadership award 1961), Green Valley Country, Altamount dir.), Poinsett. Office: 1600 Daniel Bldg Greenville SC 29602 Home: Altamount Rd Paris Mountain RFD 7 Greenville SC 29609

ROEBUCK, TOMMY GIBBS, dentist; b. Dumas, Ark., Sept. 4, 1937; s. Carmel Clifton and Ollie Myrtle (Knight) R.; student Ark. A. and M. Coll., 1959 D.D.S., U. Tenn., 1963; m. Mona Jean McAdams, Aug. 26, 1956; children—Donna, Keri, Tommy Wade. Pvt. practice dentistry, Arkadelphia, Ark., 1965—. Served with Dental Corps, AUS, 1963-65. Recipient Distinguished Service award for outstanding community service Jr. C. of C., 1966. Mem. Am., Ark. State dental assns., Southwest Ark. Dist. Dental Soc. (pres. 1972), Arkadelphia C. of C. (dir.), Alpha Chi, Xi Psi Phi. Baptist (deacon 1967—). Kiwanian (pres. club 1971). Home: 1538 Pine Manor Dr Arkadelphia AR 71923 Office: 626 Caddo St Arkadelphia AR 71923

ROEDEL, GERHARD WILHELM EDWARD, German diplomat; b. Berlin, Germany, Nov. 8, 1908; s. Eugen Georg and Frida (Gertler) R.; Doctorate in Law, U. Marburg (Germany), 1932; m. Jenny Marie

Agnes Brodmeyer, Jan. 27, 1940; 1 son, Nikol. Legal adviser Deutsche Rentenbank, Berlin, 1936-39; asst. Germany embassy, Rome, Italy, 1941-42; head sect. German Ministry for Food, Agr. and Forestry, 1943-45; govt. ofcl. State of Schleswig-Holstein, dir. Parliament, 1945-53; joined German Fgn. Office, 1953, head Berlin sect., 1954-57, dep. permanent observer to UN, N.Y.C., 1957-60, ambassador to Guatemala, 1964-66, consul gen. German consulate gen., New Orleans, 1967—. Served with German Air Force, 1939-41. Decorated officer's cross Order of Merit (Germany), grand cross Order of Quetzal (Guatemala). Mem. German Soc. for Fgn. Politics. Rotarian. Home: 2228 Lake Oaks Pkwy New Orleans LA 70122 Office: 319 John Hancock Bldg 1055 St Charles Av New Orleans LA 70130

ROEDER, MARTIN, biologist, educator; b. Long Branch, N.J., Aug. 19, 1925; s. Herbert Julian and Selma (Hurwitz) R.; B.S., Queens Coll., N.Y.C., 1948; M.S., U. N.M., 1951; Ph.D., U. N.C., 1954; m. Rachel Shively Haralson, Aug. 11, 1957; children—Renee, Karl Martin. Grad. asst. U. N.M., 1949-51; U.S. AEC fellow U. N.C., Chapel Hill, 1951-53, asst. prof. chemistry U. N.C., Greensboro, 1954-56, asst. prof., asso. prof. biology, 1956-64; asso. prof. biol. sci. Fla. State U., Tallahassee, 1964—, asst. dean Coll. Arts and Scis., 1966-69, asso. dean, 1969—. Precinct chmn. Democratic Party N.C., 1963-64. Served with AUS, 1943-46. Fellow A.A.A.S.; mem. Am. Soc. Zoologists, Soc. Gen. Physiology, Assn. S.E. Biologists, Am. Inst. Biol. Scis., Sigma Xi. Home: 121 Ridgeland Rd Tallahassee FL 32303

ROEMER, JOSEPH SHULTZ, research engr., ret. air force officer; b. Bowling Green, Ky., Aug. 31, 1924; s. Adolph and Ola (Shultz) R.; student Western Ky. State Coll., 1946-47, U. Ky., 1947-48; B.S., U. Ill., 1957 Transmitter engr. Radio Sta. WLBJ, Bowling Green, 1949-51; enlisted as tech. sgt., USAF, 1951, advanced through grades to maj., 1967; chief engring. div. 6936 Communications Security Depot Group, USAF Security Service, San Antonio, 1962-63, chief maintenance USAF Cryptologic Depot, 1963-64; program support officer, dep. for program support Hdqrs. Air Force Eastern Test Range, Patrick AFB, Fla., 1964-67, ret. USAF, 1967; research engr. Boeing Co., 1967-69; sr. elec. engr. facilities maintenance dept. Litton Ship Systems, Pascagoula, Miss., 1969—, also mgr. elec. shop, 1970—. Served with USNR, 1943-46. Mason. Home: 123 W El Bonito Dr Ocean Springs MS 39564 Office: Pascagoula MS

ROEMER, WILLIAM CHARLES, assn. ofcl.; b. Kenosha, Wis., Oct. 7, 1931; s. Richard William and Margaret Elizabeth (Davidson) R.; B.S. in Pharmacy (Am. Found. Pharm. Edn. scholar), U. Wis., 1954; M.S. in Pharmacy (Grad. fellow), Purdue U., 1961; J.D., U. San Diego, 1969; postgrad. Food and Drug Law Inst., George Washington U. Law Center, 1970-71; m. Louise Catherine Bird, June 11, 1955; children—Marie Catherine, Kimberly Catherine. Instr., U. Ariz. Coll. Pharmacy, Tucson, 1961-63; exec. sec. Acad. Pharm. Scis., Washington, 1969—. Vol. atty. Am. Civil Liberties Union, Washington, 1970—, Friends of Juvenile Ct., Washington, 1970—. Served with AUS, 1955-59. NSF fellow, 1962-63. Fellow A.A.A.S., Am. Pharm. Assn.; mem. Sigma Xi, Rho Chi, Phi Lambda Upsilon, Kappa Psi, Phi Delta Phi. Contbr. articles on food and drug law to profl. jours. Home: 6102 Hibbling Av Springfield VA 22150 Office: 2215 Constitution Av NW Washington DC 20037

ROESLER, ROBERT HARRY, newspaper editor; b. Hammond, La., Oct. 5, 1927; s. Albert N. and Hilda (Schwartz) R.; student Tulane U.; m. Cloe Alferez, May 7, 1955; children—Kim, Bob, Toby. Mem. sports staff Times Picayune, New Orleans, 1949-67, sports editor, 1964—. Served with USNR, World War II, Korean conflict. Mem. Football Writers Am., Basketball Writers Assn., Am. Legion. Club: Press (pres. New Orleans 1959-60, sports writing awards). Home: 6958 Colbert St New Orleans LA 70124 Office: Times Picayune 3800 Howard Av New Orleans LA 70125

ROESSLER, PAUL ALBERT, govt. ofcl.; b. Buckman, N.M., Oct. 8, 1920; s. Joseph H. and Perfecta M. (Torrez) R.; B.S. in Fgn. Service, Georgetown U., 1949, postgrad., 1949-51; postgrad., U. Md., 1965—; m. Ann E. Collier, May 20, 1946; children—Paul, Elizabeth, Richard, Barbara, Mary Frances, Nancy, Timothy, Eric, Christina. Field rep. War Claims Commn., Washington, 1949-51, legislative analyst, 1951-52, Philippine liaison officer, 1952-53; fgn. liaison officer Fgn. Claims Settlement Commn., Washington, 1953-56 asst. attache AEC, Japan, 1957-61, fgn. affairs officer, 1961-63; asso. program dir. NSF, Washington, 1963-65; internat. economist Dept. of Army, Washington, 1965-70, fgn. affairs officer, 1970—. Cons. Am. Indsl. Consultants, Inc., 1961—. Exec. sec. Nat. Delta Phi Epsilon Found., 1967-68. Served with AUS, 1941-46. Mem. Nat. Economists Club, Soc. Govt. Economists, Internat. House of Japan, Soc. Internat. Devel., V.F.W., Am. Legion, D.A.V., Am. Defenders Bataan and Corregidor, Delta Phi Epsilon. Contbr. to American Prisoners of War, 1948. Home: 6731 Greentree Rd Bethesda MD 20034 Office: Dept of Army Pentagon Washington DC 20310

ROESSNER, ROLAND GOMMEL, architect, educator; b. Terre Haute, Ind., Nov. 19, 1911; s. Elmer George and Florence Carol R.; B. Arch., Miami U., Oxford, O., 1935; M. Arch., U. Cin., 1942; m. Virginia Gail Humberger, Nov. 17, 1943 (dec. Oct. 1955); 1 son, Roland Gommel. Asso. Grunkeymeyer & Sullivan and Assos., Clin., 1935-42; designing architect; pvt. practice architecture schs., pvt. residences R. Gommel Roesener A.I.A., St. Petersburg, Fla., 1945-47, Austin Tex., 1947—; asso. Creer and Roessner, cons. architects, Austin, 1958—; prof. architecture U. Tex. Sch. Architecture, Austin, 1947—, chmn. design com., 1954—, mem. grad. faculty, 1958—, also acting dir. chmn. architecture scholarship com., bd. dirs. Univ. Coop. Soc., 1958-62, 64-68, mem. athletic council, 1960-65, Mem. univ. bldg. com., 1972—. Profl. adviser community standards com. U.S. Dept. Commerce; mem. naval scholarship com. U. Tex., also mem. Naval Reserve research unit; adviser design State (Tex.) Bd. Archtl. Registration; mgr. Little League, Austin; mem. exec. com. Wesley Found. Recipient numerous honor awards, citations in Am., fgn. pubns. for architecture design excellence. Registered architect, Ohio, Fla., Tex. Fellow A.I.A. (Honor award 1965); mem. Am. Concrete Inst., Am. Mil. Inst., Tex., Ohio, Fla. assn. architects, Nat. Council Archtl. Registration Bds., Univ. Co-op. Soc. (chmn. bd. dirs.), Am. Legion. V.F.W., Delta Phi Delta, Delta Upsilon, Alpha Rho Chi. Methodist (trustee). Clubs: Optimist, Westwood Country, 40 Acres, Headliners, Tarryhouse Club. Contbr. articles on sch. design profl. publs. One-man shows, Cin., Austin, St. Petersburg, Fla. Home: 3414 Foothill Terrace Austin TX 78731

ROGALL, EDWARD MYRON, city ofcl.; b. Bklyn., Feb. 20, 1911; s. Benjamin and Rose (Elias) R.; student Coll. City N.Y., 1928-31; m. Pearl N. Goldstein, Sept. 1, 1933; children—Elisabeth (Mrs. Stephen A. Weseley), Stephanie. Partner, Lopin-Rogall Property Mgmt. Co., N.Y.C., 1931-60; pres. Eldorado Hotel Corp., St. Petersburg, Fla., 1954—; chmn. Housing Authority St. Petersburg, 1964—. Treas. Southeastern region Nat. Jewish Welfare Bd., 1969—; pres. Jewish Community Council, St. Petersburg, 1965-67, Jewish Community Center, 1967-69. Bd. dirs. Nat. Housing Conf. Mem. Nat. Assn. Housing and Redevel. Ofcls., Ceres Union, Phi Epsilon Pi. Clubs: Pasadena Golf (St. Petersburg). Home: 2150 Pelham Rd St Petersburg FL 33710 Office: 325 9th St S St Petersburg FL 33705

ROGERS, ALBERT RENE, citrus farmer; b. Shawnee, Kan., Aug. 20, 1912; s. Alfred and Emma (DeBouver) R.; bus. degree, Edinburg Jr. Coll., 1936; m. Dorothy Clare Haven, Nov. 11, 1937; children—David R., Linda (Mrs. James E. McGurk), Michael A. Mgr., gen. supt. Reising Constrn. Co., Edinburg, Tex., 1936-56; mgr. Crow Gravel Co., Edinburg, 1956—; citrus grower, Edinburg, 1938—; sec. Crow Iron & Supply Co. 1942-56, mgr., 1956—, pres., 1971—; dir. Tex. Citrus Exchange, Edinburg, 1969—; dir. 1st Nat. Bank, Edinburg. Mem. Edinburg (dir.), Tex. citrus assns., Valley C. of C. (dir.), Edinburg Farm Bur., Asso. Gen. Contractors Assn. Democrat. Roman Catholic. Rotarian (dir. 1971—), K.C. Home: 1325 S 15th St Edinburg TX 78539 Office: 1220 N Closner St Edinburg TX 78539

ROGERS, ALLAN DARROW, mfg. co. exec.; b. Mt. Kisco, N.Y., June 26, 1928; s. George Franklin and Grace (Allan) R.; B.S. in Elec. Engring., Clarkson Coll. Tech., 1951; m. Florence Elisabeth Browns, Aug. 28, 1951; children—Karen Anne, Robin Lynn. With Morganite, Inc., Long Island City, N.Y., 1953-65, Dunn, N.C., 1965—, v.p. mfg., 1970—, also dir.; dir. Morganite Modmor Inc., Costa Mesa, Cal. Served with U.S. C.E., 1951-53. Mem. Am. Mgmt. Assn., Am. Powder Metallurgy Inst. Mason. Club: North Ridge Country (Raleigh, N.C.). Home: 4008 Colby Dr Raleigh NC 27609 Office: 401 N Ashe Av Dunn NC 28334

ROGERS, BRUCE GEORGE, educator; b. Houston, Feb. 20, 1925; s. Ernest Bruce and Linda Hulda (Leissner) R.; B.S., U. Houston, 1957; M.S., U. Ill., 1958, Ph.D., 1961 Surveyor, geophysicist Robert H. Ray Co., Houston, 1946-52; engr. Tex. Hwy. Dept., Houston, 1952-56; teaching asst., instr. U. Ill. at Urbana, 1957-61; mem. faculty Lamar U., Beaumont, Tex., 1961—, asso. prof. civil engring., 1964-67, prof., 1967—. Mem. Jefferson County Econ. Opportunity Commn. Bd., 1970—. Served with USAAF, 1942-45. Mem. Am. Soc. C.E., Nat. Soc. Profl. Engrs., Am. Concrete Inst., Soc. Exptl. Stress Analysis, Am. Soc. Testing and Materials, Phi Kappa Phi, Tau Beta Pi. Unitarian. Registered profl. engr. Tex., La., Ill. Home: 4257 Maddox St Beaumont TX 77705

ROGERS, CHARLES FRANKLIN, JR., dentist; b. Tahlequah, Okla., Jan. 13, 1924; s. Charles Franklin and Allie Ethel (Stephens) R.; student Northeastern State Coll., Tahlequah, 1941-44; D.D.S., U. Mo., 1948; m. Betty Bradfield, May 17, 1943. Practice dentistry, Muskogee, Okla., 1948-50, Wagoner, Okla., 1950—. Mem. Wagoner City Council, 1965-69; chmn. Wagoner County Democratic Party, 1971-72. Served with AUS, 1942-43. Mem. Am. Dental Assn., Sports Car Club Am. Methodist. Home: 1100 S McQuarrie St Wagoner OK 74467 Office: PO Box 345 Wagoner OK 74467

ROGERS, CHARLES MCPHERSON ADUSTON, III, banker; b. Mobile, Ala., Nov. 10, 1932; s. Charles McPherson Aduston and Elisabeth (Benson) R.; B.A., Williams Coll., 1954; LL.B., U. Ala., 1959; m. Gail Whitehurst, June 19, 1954; children—Anne Aduston, Charles McPherson Aduston IV, Bradshaw Aduston. Admitted to Ala. bar, 1959; asso. McCorvey Turner Johnstone Adams & May, attys., Mobile, 1959-64, partner, 1964-67; v.p., trust officer Am. Nat. Bank & Trust Co., Mobile, 1967-71, exec. v.p., 1971—. Hon. consul of Belgium, 1970—. Pres. Mobile Symphony and Civic Music Assn., 1966-68. Mem. Ala. Ho. of Reps., 1960-66. Trustee St. Paul's Episcopal Day Sch., Mobile. Served to 1st lt. USAF, 1955-57. Mem. Am., Ala. bar assns., Mobile Area C. of C. (dir. 1969—), Phi Delta Theta, Phi Delta Phi, Omicron Delta Kappa. Episcopalian. Clubs: Athelstan (Mobile); Country of Mobile (Ala.). Home: 4010 Old Shell Rd Mobile AL 36608 Office: 130 St Joseph St Mobile AL 36602

ROGERS, DAVID WILLIAM, SR., ednl. adminstr.; b. Greensboro, N.C., May 29, 1925; s. Archibald Alexander and Mattie Belle (Straughan) R.; A.A., Campbell Coll., 1952; B.A., Wake Forest Coll., 1954; M.Ed., Duke, 1958, Ed.D., 1964; m. Rosa Christine Slaughter, Feb. 19, 1949; children—Joan Marie, Gloria Jean, David William. Elementary sch. tchr., prin., Coswell County, N.C., 1954-57; secondary sch. tchr., 1957-59; asst. prof. Furman U., 1960-61; dir. instrn. Lumberton (N.C.) City Schs., 1961-63; asso. supt. Burke County Schs., Morganton, N.C., 1963-67; asso. supt. Person County Schs., Roxboro, N.C., 1967—. Mem. exec. bd. Cherokee council Boy Scouts Am., 1968—; mem. family life com. N. Central Area Devel. Corp., 1969—; mem. adv. com. Mars Hil Coll., 1967-69. Trustee Piedmont Tech. Inst., Roxboro, N.C. Served with USAAF, 1943-46. Mem. N.E.A., Am. Assn. Sch. Adminstrs., N.C. Assn. Educators, Phi Delta Kappa, Kappa Delta Pi. Baptist (ordained pastor 1956). Rotarian. Club: Optimist (Morganton). Home: Route 2 Box 382 Roxboro NC 27573 Office: Box 1078 Roxboro NC 27573

ROGERS, DONALD LEE, trade assn. exec.; b. E. Steubenville, W. Va.; s. Mark Whittaker and Virginia (Campbell) R.; A.B., Miami U., Oxford, O., 1951; J.D., Ohio State U., 1953; m. Helen E. Long, 1960. Admitted to Fed. bar, 1957, Ohio bar, 1953; asst. counsel U.S. Senate Com. on Banking and Currency, Washington, 1953-54, counsel, 1955-58; exec. dir. Assn. Registered Bank Holding Cos., Washington, 1958—. Mem. Am. (banking com.), Fed., Ohio bar assns., Order of Coif. Methodist. Clubs: Capitol Hill, Nat. Press, Exchequer (pres.), City Tavern (Washington). Home: 4201 Cathedral Av NW Washington DC 20016 Office: 730 15th St NW Washington DC 20005

ROGERS, EDGAR CARLTON, former govt. ofcl.; b. Galena, Md., Jan. 3, 1903; s. Marcus Edgar and Anna Maude (Ringgold) R.; student Beacom Bus. Coll., Wilmington, Del., 1921-23, U. Md., 1937-40; m. Sara Louise Bristow, July 28, 1934; children—Patricia M., Gloria B. Sec. engr. Md. State Aviation Commn., 1939-42; hwy. engr. Md. State Rds. Commn., 1925-42; dep. chief flight insp. div. CAA, 1942-59; dep. chief flight insp. div. FAA, 1959, chief data control br., 1959-63, chief nat. flight data center FAA, 1963-69. Mem. Nat. Soc. Profl. Engrs., Md. Assn. Engrs., Am. Mil. Engrs., Am. Congress on Surveying and Mapping, Am. Soc. Photogammetry. Home: 320 S Ivy St Arlington VA 22204

ROGERS, ERNEST P(AUL), lawyer; b. nr. Duluth, Ga., Sept. 10, 1903; s. Raymond Clifford and Ora (Bloodworth) R.; student Darlington Sch., Rome, Ga., 1917-21; LL.B., U. Ga., 1926; m. Mary Weems, June 18, 1932; children—Mary Ann Rogers Hammaker, Ronald Weems, Michael Clayton, Ernest Paul. Admitted to Ga. bar, 1927; atty. legal staff Coca-Cola Co., Atlanta, 1927-35; asso. Harold Hirsch & Marion Smith, Atlanta, 1935-39; mem. firm Kilpatrick, Cody, Rogers, McClatchey & Regenstein, 1939—. Pres., Scripto Pencil Co., 1945-46, dir., mem. exec. com., 1936—; pres., dir. Laow Investment Co., Inc.; dir. Colonial Stores, Inc. Trustee Darlington Sch.; permanent trustee, treas. Atlanta Lawyers Found., Inc. Mem. Am. Judicature Soc., Am., Ga., Atlanta bar assns., Kappa Sigma, Phi Delta Phi. Methodist. Kiwanian. Clubs: Lawyers (past pres.), Executives Assn. (past pres.), Piedmont Driving, Capital City, Commerce (Atlanta). Home: 2933 Andrews Dr NW Atlanta GA 30305 Office: Equitable Bldg Atlanta GA 30303

ROGERS, GLENN EDWIN, librarian; b. Ft. Scott, Kan., Oct. 9, 1923; s. Earl Allen and Margaret Lillian (Williams) R.; B.S., John Brown U., 1953; M.Ed., U. Ark., 1955; M.L.S., U. Okla., 1961; m. Vineta M. Pryor, Dec. 8, 1945; children—Russell Gordon, Rita Jean. Dean of men John Brown U., Siloam Springs, Ark., 1953-56, asst. librarian, dir. audio-visual services, 1957-69, librarian, 1959—. Served with AUS, 1943-46; ETO. Mem. Ark. Library Assn. Mem. Ch. of God. Kiwanian. Home: Route 4 Box 289 Siloam Springs AR 72761

ROGERS, HAROLD, cleaners co. exec., city ofcl.; b. Paris, Ark., Oct. 25, 1928; s. Albert N. and Daphane (Kirkland) R.; certificate in bus. mgmt. West Ark. Coll., 1967; m. Dorothy Jane Bidiler, Dec. 22, 1947; children—Ronald Dean, Marilyn Jane. Owner, Rogers Cleaners, Paris, 1953—. Fire commr. City Paris, 1962—; mem. Logan County Redevel. Commn., 1963—; mem. Paris City Council 1962—. Dir., Ozarka Regional Devel. Assn., Paris, 1964—; mem. rev. bd. Boy Scouts Am., Paris, 1960-65, com. chmn. Explorer Scouts, 1960-66; dir. Boys Club, 1965-66. Named Outstanding Civic Leader, Paris, 1967. Mem. Paris C. of C. (v.p. 1964-65; pres. 1966-67; dir.). Rotarian (past pres.; dir. Paris). Home: 816 S Roseville St Paris AR 72855 Office: 121 E Main St Paris AR 72855

ROGERS, IDA ADRIAN RICE (MRS. GEORGE P. ROGERS), artist, educator; b. Calico Rock, Ark.; d. Alex and Edna (Cotheran) Adrian; B.A. in Art, Hendrix Coll., 1954; M.A., U. Ark., 1955; postgrad. Leyden U., 1960-61; m. John J. Rice, Apr. 1, 1926 (div. Jan. 1932); children—Sammie L., George J. (dec.), Sue; m. 2d, George P. Rogers, Feb. 26, 1943. Faculty, Little Rock U., 1957—, asst. prof. art, 1958—, chmn. visual arts dept., 1957—. Exhibited in shows at LaScala Gallery, Florence, Italy, 1971, Ark. Art Center, 1971, Ark. Dept. Edn., 1971; portraits represented in pvt. collections; archaeologist throughout Middle East, 1960-66. Tchr. arts, crafts Little Rock Boys Club, 1942—; art chmn. one-man shows Ark. Art Festival, 1962-63. Recipient Medal Merit for service in arts, scis. Centro Studi E Scambi, Rome, 1970. Mem. Am. Artists League N.Y. (state chmn. Am. art week 1959-60), Nat., Ark. (art chmn. 1963) socs. arts and letters, Internat. Platform Assn., Am. League Pen Women, Delta Kappa Gamma. Author: (poems) Thoughts of the Wanderer, 1971. Home: 2409 W 16th St North Little Rock AR 72114 Office: 33d and University Av Little Rock AR 72204

ROGERS, JAMES GAMBLE, II, archtl. engring. co. exec.; b. Chgo., Jan. 24, 1901; s. John A. and Elizabeth (Baird) R.; student Dartmouth, 1921-24; m. Evelyn Claire Smith, Sept. 28, 1929; children—James Gamble IV, John Hopewell. Established archtl. engring. firm Rogers, Lovelock & Fritz (formerly Jas. Gamble Rogers, II, Winter Park, Fla., 1935—, chmn. bd. trustees retirement fund, 1961—. Dir. Orlando (Fla.) Fed. Savs., 1964—, Chelynia, Inc., Deland, Fla., 1965—, Republic Service Corp., Orlando, 1970—. Cons. and authority on jail design Fla. Assn. Architects, 1935—, Nat. Jail Assn., 1958-65. Named Architect of the Year, Bldg. Stone Inst., 1963; recipient certificates of appreciation, Sec. Army, 1959, Chief of Engrs., 1959. Mem. Fla. Bd. Architecture 1935-44, pres., 1940-44. Fla. Mem. A.I.A. (pres. central chpt. 1938-42, chmn. Fla. regional judiciary com. 1963), Archtl. League N.Y., Soc. Am. Mil. Engrs., Am. Hosp. Assn., Ch. Archtl. Guild Am., Nat. Jail Assn., Orlando Art Assn., Archtl. League N.Y., Hispanic Inst. Presbyn. Club: University (Winter Park); Lake Beresford Yacht (Deland). Contbr. articles to profl. jours., popular mags. Executed Fla. Supreme Ct. Bldg., Tallahassee, 1949; county courthouse Orlando, 1958, courthouse Fort Pierce, Fla., 1960; mil. work in U.S. and fgn. countries including launching platforms at Cape Canaveral (Fla.), guidance towers Cape Kennedy and Antigua Island; hops. Fla. A and M. Coll., Tallahassee, 1949, hosp. MacDill AFB, Tampa, 1971, student union Stetson U., Deland, 1956; academic bldgs. Fla. State U., Tallahassee, 1959-62, Orlando Jr. Coll., 1954-65, Rollins Coll., Winter Park, 1951-68, addition Hillis Miller Health Center, Gainesville, Bush Science Center, Rollins Coll., 1969. Home: 1290 Palmer Av Winter Park FL 32789 Office: 145 Lincoln Av Winter Park FL 32789

ROGERS, JAMES LAWTON, publishing co. exec.; b. Morris, Ala., Jan. 16, 1908; s. Thomas Snow and Rosa Ella (James) R.; A.B., Howard Coll., 1927; m. Minnie Bauerlein, Mar. 24, 1931; children—Ava Ann (Mrs. Billy J. Wilson), James Lawton. With Progressive Farmer Co., Inc., Birmingham, Ala., 1930—, v.p., 1954—, dir., 1959—, dir. circulation, 1946—. Pres. Eastern Community Council, 1967-68, East End Civic Club, 1964, Wahouma-East Lake Youth Athletic Assn., 1963; Ala. state dir. Little League Baseball, 1965; dir. Wahouma Boys Baseball, 1964—; sec., trustee Lee McBride White Spastic Found., 1955-65. Named good citizen of year, East Lake Civitan Club, 1966-67. Mem. Internat. Agrl. Circulation Mgrs. Assn. (pres. 1969-70), Birmingham C. of C., Lambda Chi Alpha. Democrat. Baptist. Club: Eastern Area Civitan. Home: 7718 8th Av S Birmingham AL 35206 Office: 821 N 19th St Birmingham AL 35202

ROGERS, JAMES LLOYD, coll. adminstr.; b. Reger, Mo., May 11, 1903; s. John William and Cora (Ford) R.; B.S. in Edn., Northeast Mo. State Tchrs. Coll., 1927; M.A., U. Mo., 1930; Ph.D., State U. Ia. 1935; m. Mary Ruth Waller, Aug. 12, 1924; 1 son, James L. Tchr., supt., prin. pub. schs. Mo. also Ia. 1920-36; with Southwest Tex. State U., San Marcos, 1936—, prof. edn., 1941—, chmn. dept. edn. and psychology, 1957-67, dean sch. edn., 1965—; conducted TV series for Tex. Edn. Agy., WOAI, TV, San Antonio, 1957-58; chmn. Tex. Edn. Assn. Commn. on Profl. Edn., 1963-64. Mem. San Marcos Charter Commn., 1951. Served to maj. Adj. Gen. Dept., AUS, 1942-46. Mem. N.E.A., Tex. State Tchrs. Assn., Tex. Soc. Coll. Tchrs. Edn., (pres., 1957), Kappa Delta Pi. Methodist. Kiwanian (pres., San Marcos, 1948). Author: (with Gray, Votaw) General Achievement Tests, 1962. Contbr. Tex. Outlook, Ednl. Forum, W. Tex. Hist. Assn. Yearbook. Home: 909 W Hopkins St San Marcos TX 78666

ROGERS, JOHN, lawyer; b. Wheatland, Mo., Apr. 4, 1890; s. Pleasant Jasper and Nancy Frances (Dent) R.; LL.B., U. Okla., 1914; LL.D., U. Tulsa, 1958, John Brown U., 1966; L.H.D., Philips U., 1958, So. Meth. U., 1969; m. Hazel M. Beattie, Feb. 19, 1921; 1 son, John. Admitted to Okla. bar, 1914; atty. McMan Oil Co., Tulsa, 1915-17, atty., v.p. McMan Oil & Gas Co., 1919-31; receiver Superior Oil Corp., 1930-33, pres., 1933-35; atty. Chapman & McFarlin Interests, 1930—; dean, sch. law U. Tulsa, 1948-57; dir. Home Fed. Savs. & Loan Assn. Dir. Okla. Med. Research Found., pres., 1947-67; mem. State Regents for Higher Edn., 1941-59, pres., 1958-59; trustee U. Tulsa; regent U. Okla., 1924-31, 40-41; pres. YMCA, 1931-36, Tulsa Council Social Agys., 1941-42, Tulsa Community Chest, 1945; trustee John Brown U.; bd. dirs. Holland Hall Sch., Tulsa, 1959-66. Selected as Man of Yr. in Tulsa, 1945; recipient distinguished service citation U. Okla., 1956. Fellow Am. Bar Found.; mem. Am., Okla. bar assns., Am. Soc. Internat. Law, Am. Judicature Soc., Okla. Hist. Soc., Tulsa C. of C. (pres. 1938), Beta Theta Pi, Phi Delta Phi, Delta Sigma Rho. Mem. Disciples of Christ Ch. Club: Tulsa. Home: 3727 S Xanthus St Tulsa OK 74105 Office: Box 3209 Tulsa OK 74101

ROGERS, JOHN, state ofcl.; b. Clinton, Okla., Aug. 15, 1928; s. John Marvin and Annette (Jaworsky) R.; student U. Okla., Oklahoma City U.; m. (div.); children—John III, Mary Annette. Sec. state Okla., Oklahoma City, 1967—. Served with USMCR, 1946-48; with inf., AUS, 1953-55. Office: State Capitol Oklahoma City OK 73105

ROGERS, JOHN CICERO, JR., ednl. adminstr.; b. Alto, Tex., June 17, 1912; s. John Cicero and Katye Gertrude (Banks) R.; B.A., Stephen F. Austin U., 1932; M.A., U. Tex., 1940; m. Mary Nixon

Stephens, June 17, 1937; children—John Stephen, Mary Jean (Mrs. Arnim Vernis Haynes). Tchr., Canton (Tex.) Pub. Schs., 1932-34; tchr., coach Nat. Consol. Schs., Nacogdoches, Tex., 1934-35. Hearne (Tex.) Pub. Schs., 1935-38; tchr., coach, prin., supt. Columbia-Brazoria Schs., West Columbia, Tex., 1938-63; supt. Lamar Consol. Schs., Rosenberg, Tex., 1963-—. Mem. Tex. State Textbook Com., 1954; regional chmn. exec. com. Ednl. Service Center, 1970-71; chmn. Tex. Adv. Com. Data Processing, 1972-—. Mem. Tex. Tchrs. Assn. (dist. pres. 1964). Methodist. Rotarian, Mason. Home: 1028 Lindsey Dr Rosenberg TX 77471 Office: Sch Adminstrn Bldg Rosenberg TX 77471

ROGERS, JOHN RICHARD, lawyer; b. Ashburn, Ga., June 30, 1924; s. Edwin A. and Ella Mae (Evans) R.; LL.D., U. Ga., 1949; m. Reginald Ann Cox, Aug. 6, 1953; children—Sylvia, Dawn, Starr. Admitted to Ga. bar, 1949; gen. practice, Ashburn, 1949-—. Pres. Monroe Mall Corp., 1965-—; pres. First Fed. Savs. & Loan Assn. of Turner County. Served to 1st lt. AUS, 1944-46. Mem. Turner County C. of C. (pres., past dir.), Am., Tifton Circuit bar assns., Am. Trial Lawyers Assn., Am. Judicature Soc., Phi Eta Sigma, Sigma Chi, Phi Alpha Delta. Home: Madison Av Ashburn GA 31714 Office: Rogers Plaza Ashburn GA 31714

ROGERS, JOHN SEABORN, physician; b. Buena Vista, Ga., May 11, 1938; s. Joseph Maulk and Mary Josaphine (Zachary) R.; M.D., Emory U., 1963; m. Lydia Penelope Herrington, July 4, 1958; children—Daniel Joseph, Cynthia Penelope. Intern, Med. Center, Columbus, Ga., 1963-64, resident, 1964-66; gen. practice medicine Buena Vista, 1966-—; mem. staff Marion Meml. Hosp., Buena Vista, chief staff, 1967-—. Adviser explorers Chattahoochee council Boy Scouts Am., 1969-—. Served with AUS, 1956. Redipient Explorer adviser award Boy Scouts Am., 1970. Mem. Muscogee County Med. Soc., Med. Assn. Ga., A.M.A. Elk. Home: Oliver St Buena Vista GA 31803 Office: Box 155 Buena Vista GA 31803

ROGERS, JOHN THOMAS, JR., state ofcl.; b. Cleburne, Tex., Oct. 20, 1927; s. John Thomas and Lonnie (Wilbanks) R.; grad. Gulf Coast Sch. Bus. Adminstrn., 1948, Tex. Hwy. Patrol Tng. Acad., 1951; m. Juanita Elizabeth Shelley, Dec. 24, 1945; children—Linda Susan. Hwy. patrolman Tex. Dept. Pub. Safety, 1951, stationed in Houston, 1951-57, sgt., Brenham, Tex., 1957-61, dist. radar operator, photographer, police instr., counselor Tex. Dept. Pub. Safety Tng. Acad., 1961, 68-69; sgt. hwy. patrol, Area 1, Hdqrs. Region 2, Houston, 1961-—; spl. agt. La. State Police; adviser Washington County Civil Def., 1957-61. Active Merit Badge work Boy Scouts Am., Brenham, 1957-61; mem. Washington County Traffic Safety Commn., 1958-60; safety chmn., mem. exec. com. Brenham P.T.A., 1959-60. Mem. Nat. Rifle Assn., Tex. Police Assn., Conn. Assn. Chiefs of Police (hon.). Mem. Ch. of Christ (past deacon, tchr., supr. Sunday sch. dept.). Mason (past master); Rotarian (dir. Brenham 1960-62). Home: 4515 Briar Hollow Pl Apt 320 Houston TX 77027 Office: 10110 Northwest Freeway PO Drawer D Oak Forest Sta Houston TX 77018

ROGERS, JOSEPH BROWN, physician; b. New Albany, Miss., Oct. 18, 1911; s. Joe L. S. and Effie (Brown) R.; Ph.C., U. Miss., 1932, B.S., 1941; M.D., Northwestern Med. Sch., 1944; m. Carolyn McMillan, June 23, 1937; children—Joseph B., Warren K. Intern, Johns Hopkins Hosp., 1944, resident, 1944-45; resident Balt. City Hosp., 1945-46; practice medicine specializing in ophthalmology, Oxford, Miss.; 1948-—; mem. staffs Oxford-Lafayette County Hosp. Instr. ophthalmology U. Miss. Med. Sch., 1948-—; dir. Miss. Blue-Cross-Blue Shield, 1954-—. Mem. exec. com. Adv. Health Planning Council for Comprehensive Health Planning, Miss., 1968-69. Served to capt. AUS, 1946-48. Diplomate Am. Bd. Ophthalmology. Fellow La.-Miss. Ophthal. and Otolaryn. Soc. (past pres.), Am. Acad. Opthalmology Otolaryngology, Pan-Am. Ophthal. Soc., Soc. Cryo-Ophthalmology, Wilmer Resident's Assn., Johns Hopkins Med. and Surg. Soc.; mem. Internat. Platform Assn., North Miss. Med. Soc. (pres. 1964-65), Am. (alternate del. 1969-72, del. 1973-—), Miss. (pres. 1968-69), So. med. assns., Kappa Psi, Phi Chi. Methodist (steward 1953-—, trustee). Rotarian. Clubs: Oxford Country, Holly Hills Country (Memphis); Carolina Caribbean Country (Banner Elk, N.C.). Home: 109 College Hill Rd Oxford MS 38655 Office: 512 Van Buren Av Oxford MS 38655

ROGERS, JULIAN RICHARD, dentist; b. Wilmington, N.C., Nov. 19, 1932; s. Luther Thomas and Annlea (Rutherford) R.; D.D.S., U. N.C., 1959; m. Elizabeth Clark, June 19, 1954; children—Emmalee, Amelia Lucile, Christine Clark, Julian Richard, Neill Darrow. Individual practice dentistry, Greensboro, N.C., 1959-—; mem. dental staff Wesley Long Hosp., Greensboro, 1960-—. Gen. chmn. Greater Greensboro Open Golf Tournament, 1968; mem. adv. council explorer Explorer Scouts, 1969-—, adv. staff Greensboro Headstart, 1969-—. Recipient Distinguished Youth New Hanover County award Wilmington Police Benevolent Assn., 1951; Roy Carey award, 1968. Mem. Am. Dental Assn., Guiford, Dist. (chmn. pub. dental edn. 1969) dental socs., Greensboro Jr. C. of C. (life, past dir.) Psi Omega. Democrat. Presbyn. Rotarian. Club: Breakfast Optimist (Greensboro). Home: 3305 Charing Cross Rd Greensboro NC 27410 Office: 601 Walter Reed Dr Greensboro NC 27403

ROGERS, KING WALTER, JR., grocery stores exec.; b. Dyersburg, Tenn., Aug. 19, 1912; s. King Walter and Essie (Martin) R.; B.A., U. Tenn., 1934; postgrad. Harvard Bus. Sch., 1934-36; m. Mildred Hampton Moss, May 23, 1943; children—King Walter III, Robert Moss. Exec., Pennel-Edenton Wholesale Grocery, Dyersburg, 1936-39; with K.W. Rogers & Son, Inc., Dyersburg, 1939-—, pres., dir., 1943-—; pres. Nehi Bottling Co., Dyersburg; Ardmore Tel. Co. (Tenn.); dir. Holiday Inns, Dyersburg, United Tel. Co., Chapel Hills, Tenn., Crockett Tel. Co., Friendship, Tenn., First Citizens Nat. Bank Dyersburg, First Fed. Savs. & Loan Assn., Dyersburg; pres. Tipton County Utilities Inc., Dyersburg. Chmn., U. Tenn. Devel. Council, 1969-70; mem. Tenn. Planning Commn., 1970; mem. exec. com. Hosp. for Crippled Adults, Memphis, 1961-70. Bd. dirs. West Tenn. Area council Boy Scouts Am.; bd. mgrs. Meth. Hosp., Memphis. Served with AUS, 1942-45. Recipient Boy Scouts Silver Beaver award. Mem. Tenn. Retail Mchts. Council (pres. 1967), Nat. Piggly Wiggly Operators Assn. (pres. 1964-65). Methodist (trustee Memphis conf. 1953-56). Rotarian (dist. gov. 1960-61). Home: 950 Troy Av Dyersburg TN 38024 Office: 408 W Court St Dyersburg TN 38024

ROGERS, LEONARD R., mayor; b. Cordova, Tenn., Nov. 19, 1912; B.S., Coll. Agr., U. Tenn., 1937; m. Mary Will Webb, Sept. 26, 1935; children—Mrs. Fred Lewis, Mrs. Morgan Hall. Formerly with Security Mills, Inc., mfrs. poultry and livestock feeds, successively advt. mgr. wholesale seed div., gen. advt. mgr., sales promotion mgr., East Tenn. sales mgr.; also mgr. dairy and poultry farm; mayor City of Knoxville, 1965-—. Formerly sec.-mgr. Tennessee Valley Agrl. and Indsl. Fair, until 1965. Formerly mem. Tenn. Stream Pollution Control Bd.; past pres. Tenn. 4-H Club Found.; past pres., sec. E. Tenn. Community Devel. Com.; mem. emergency com. Tenn. River Valley Assn., Tenn. Law Envorcement Planning Agy. Former mem. Knoxville City Council. Past bd. dirs., also past pres. Southeastern Community Devel. Assn.; bd. dirs. exec. com. East Tenn. Bapt. Hosp., Boys Clubs of Knoxville, Knox County br. Arthritis Found. Am.; mem. exec. bd. Gt. Smoky Mountain council Boy Scouts Am.; mem. governing bd. Children's Hosp.; bd. dirs., also past pres. Tenn. Municipal League. Mem. Internat., (past dir.), Tenn. (past pres.) assns. fairs, Nat. (past mem. agrl. com.), Knoxville (past chmn. agrl. com., past chmn. U. Tenn. support com., past pres.) chambers commerce, Alumni Assn. U. Tenn. Coll. Agr. (past pres.). Baptist (deacon). Rotarian (past pres. Knoxville). Office: City Hall Knoxville TN 37902

ROGERS, LON B(ROWN), lawyer; b. Pikeville, Ky., Sept. 5, 1905; s. Fon and Ida (Brown) R.; B.S., U. Ky., 1928, LL.B., 1932; m. Mary Evelyn Walton, Dec. 17, 1938; children—Marylon Walton, Martha Brown, Fon II. Admitted to Ky. bar, 1932; practiced law in Lexington, 1932-38, Pikeville, 1939-—; dir. East Ky. Beverage Co., Pikeville, 1950-—. Mem. Pikeville City Council, 1951; mem. local bd. SSS, 1958-69; mem. Breaks Interstate Park Commn., Ky.-Va., 1960-68, chmn., 1960-62, 64-66, vice chmn. 1966-68; chmn. Community Services Commn. Pikeville Model Cities, 1969-71; mem. Ky. Arts Commn., 1965-—, Ky. Travel Council, 1967-70; pres. Ky. Mountain Laurel Festival Assn., 1971-72. Chmn. bd. trustees Presbytery Ebenezer, U.S.A., 1950-71, Pikeville Coll., 1951-72, Bd. Nat. Missions, United Presbyn. Ch. Am., 1954-66; trustee Appalachian Regional Hosps., Inc., 1963-67; trustee Ky. Ind. Coll. Found.; bd. dirs. Meth. Hosp. of Ky., 1966-—. Mem. Ky. C. of C. (regional v.p. 1962-64, 69-—), Ky. Hist. Soc., S.A.R., Sigma Alpha Epsilon, Phi Delta Phi. Republican. Presbyn. (elder). Clubs: Kiwanis (past lt. gov.); Filson, Green Meadow Country, Blue Grass Automobile (pres. 1971-—, dir.). Home: 501 5th St Pikeville KY 41501 Office: PO Box 181 Rogers Bldg Pikeville KY 41501

ROGERS, LUTHER RAYFORD, ednl. adminstr.; b. Roopville, Ga., Apr. 13, 1934; s. Luther Guy and Vesta (Kent) R.; B.S., West Ga. Coll., 1959; M.A., Auburn U., 1960; Ed.D., U. Fla., 1969; m. Betty Arrington Rogers, Dec. 22, 1955; children—Daryl Lance, Melba Jean, Douglas Wesley. Tchr. Buchanan (Ga.) Elementary Sch., 1957-58; grad. asst. Auburn (Ala.) U., 1959-60; with Brevard County sch. system, Titusville, Fla., 1960-—, area supt. North Dist., 1969-71, asst. supt. personnel services div., 1971-—. Asso. dir. Gainesville component Southeastern Ednl. Lab., 1966-68, field rep. for Central Fla., 1968-69; cons. project IDEALS, Fla. Ednl. Research and Devel. Council, Coll. Edn., U. Fla., Gainesville, 1968-69, adj. prof. edn., 1970-—; adj. prof. Stetson U., Deland, Fla., 1971-—. Mem. adv. bd. Goodwill Industries, 1971-—; commr. Brevard County Parks and Recreation Commn., 1969-71. Served with AUS, 1955-57. Mem. Am. Assn. Sch. Adminstrs., Nat. Assn. Secondary Sch. Prins., Assn. Supervision and Curriculum Devel., Nat. Sch. Pub. Relations Assn., Fla. Ednl. Research Assn., Phi Kappa Phi, Phi Delta Kappa. Home: 2415 DeWitt Dr Titusville FL 32780 Office: 3205 S Washington Av Titusville FL 32780

ROGERS, NATHANIEL SIMS, banker; b. New Albany, Miss., Nov. 17, 1919; s. Arthur L. and Elizabeth (Bouton) R.; A.B., Millsaps Coll., 1941; M.B.A., Harvard, 1947; m. Helen Elizabeth Ricks, July 3, 1942; children—Alice, John, Lewis. With Deposit Guaranty Bank & Trust Co., Jackson, Miss., 1947-—, 1st v.p., 1957-58, pres., dir., 1958-69; pres. First City Nat. Bank, Houston, 1969-—; pres. First City Bancorp. Tex., Inc. 1971-—; dir. Am. Gen. Bond Fund, Standard Life Ins. Co., lectr. Sch. Banking of South, La. State U., 1957-60. Chmn. Jackson United Givers Fund, 1957, pres., 1959, bd. dirs., 1958-61; pres. Andrew Jackson area council Boy Scouts Am., 1962. Trustee Miss. Found. Ind. Colls., 1959-—, Lon Morris Coll., Meth. Hosp., Houston, Piney Woods Country Life Sch., Found. for Full Service Banks; bd. dirs. Millsaps Coll.; bd. visitors U. Tex. M.D. Anderson Hosp. and Tumor Inst.; mem. adv. bd. Meml. Hosp., Houston. Served to lt. USNR, 1942-46. Nemed Outstanding Young Man of Year, 1955, Jackson Jr. C. of C. Mem. Miss. (pres. jr. banker sect. 1952-53, pres. 1964-65), Am. (pres. 1969-70) bankers assns., Robert Morris Assos. (pres. S.E. chpt. 1954-55, nat. dir. 1959-62), Jackson C. of C. (pres. 1962), Young Pres. Orgn., Millsaps Coll. Alumni Assn. (pres. 1955-56), Newcomen Soc., Omicron Delta Kappa, Kappa Alpha. Methodist (chmn. ofcl. bd.). Clubs: Ramada, River Oaks Country, Houston, Plaza (Houston). Home: 1833 Sharp Pl Houston TX 77019 Office: 100 Main Houston TX 77002

ROGERS, OSCAR ALLAN, JR., coll. pres.; b. Natchez, Miss., Sept. 10, 1928; s. Oscar Allan and Maria (Jackson) R.; Sr.; A.B., Tougaloo Coll., 1950; S.T.B., Harvard, 1953, A.M. in Teaching, 1954; Ed.D., U. Ark., 1960; m. Ethel Lee Lewis, Dec. 20, 1950; children—Christopher, Christian, Christoff. Ordained to ministry of Congl.-Christian Ch., 1953, Bapt. Ch., 1954; asst. pastor St. Mark Congl.-Christian Ch., Roxbury, Mass., 1951-54; dean-registrar Natchez Jr. Coll. (Miss.), 1954-56; pres. Ark. Bapt. Coll., Little Rock, 1956-59; dean of students, prof. social sci. edn. Jackson (Miss.) State Coll., 1960-—, dean grad. studies, 1969-—; pastor Asbury Meth. Ch., Bolton, also Kingly Chapel, Edwards, Miss., 1962-—. Mem. exec. bd. Little Rock Urban League, 1957-59. Served with USN, 1946-47. Mem. Am. Assn. U. Profs., Alpha Phi Alpha, Phi Delta Kappa, Kappa Delta Pi. Home: 1510 School View Dr Jackson MS 39213

ROGERS, PAUL (GRANT), congressman; b. Ocilla, Ga., June 4, 1921; s. Dwight L. and Florence (Roberts) R.; B.A., U. Fla., 1942, J.D., 1948; m. Rebecca Bell, Dec. 15, 1962; 1 dau., Rebecca Laing. Admitted to Fla. bar, 1948, since practiced in West Palm Beach; mem. 84th-92d congresses, 9th Dist. Fla. Served as maj. F.A., AUS, 1942-45; ETO. Mem. Fla. bar (bd. govs. jr. sect. 1952-53), Am., Palm Beach County bar assns., Maritime Law Assn., U.S., Phi Delta Phi, Phi Delta Theta. Methodist. Kiwanian. Home: 2800 N Flagler Dr West Palm Beach FL 33407 Office: Rayburn Bldg Washington DC 20515

ROGERS, PAUL MCKENDRY, food broker; b. Morrison, Tenn., Mar. 2, 1906; s. Mack H. and Nancy (Browne) R.; student U. Chattanooga, 1925-27, Tex. Western Coll., 1930; m. Sidney Rice, Nov. 28, 1935; 1 son, Paul McKendry. Office sec. YMCA, El Paso, Tex., 1929-37; salesman Nat. Biscuit Co., El Paso, 1937-51; founder, owner Paul M. Rogers Co., food broker, 1951-—, now partner. Mem. Nat., El Paso food brokers assns., C. of C. Methodist. Mason (Shriner, 32 deg.). Club: 20-30 (past pres.) (El Paso). Home: 1817 E Robinson Av El Paso TX 79902 Office: 711 N Walnut St El Paso TX 79903

ROGERS, RALPH B., chmn. bd. KERA-TV, Dallas. Office: 3000 Harry Hines Blvd Dallas TX 75201

ROGERS, RICHARD RAYMOND, cosmetic co. exec.; b. houston, Apr. 15, 1943; s. Julius Ben and Mary Kay (Wagnor) R.; student North Tex. State U., 1961-63; m. Linda Ann Provenzano, June 11, 1963; children—Terri Kay, Richard Raymond, II. Gen. mgr. Mary Kay Cosmetics, Inc., Dallas, 1963-65, v.p., 1965-69, pres., 1969-—. Co-trustee Marylyn R. Reed Family Trust, 1968-—. Served with USMCR, 1961. Named Marketing Man of Year, North Tex. chpt. Am. Marketing Assn., 1968. Home: 5618 Briar Dr Houston TX 77027 Office: 8900 Carpenter Freeway Dallas TX 75247

ROGERS, STANFIELD, cancer researcher, educator; b. Dyersburg, Tenn., Nov. 14, 1919; s. Charles Clifton and Floreta S. (Stanfield) R.; B.S., Duke, 1942, M.D., 1944; m. June H. Herzberg, May 8, 1946; children—Jane, Floreta, Clifton. Intern, Duke U. Hosp., Durham, N.C., 1943-44; resident John Gaton Hosp., Memphis, 1947; asst. Rockefeller Inst., 1947-52; asst. prof., asso. prof. Duke U., 1952-58; dir. U. Tenn. Meml. Research Center, 1958-64; head carcinogenesis program Oak Ridge Nat. Lab., 1964-72; prof. biochemistry U. Tenn. Med. Units, 1972-—. Bd. dirs. Tenn. div. Am. Cancer Soc., 1964-67. Served with AUS, 1945-47. Recipient Parke-Davis award in exptl. pathology, 1959; named Ky. col., 1960. Fellow N.Y., Soc. Health; mem. Am. Soc. Exptl. Pathology, Am. Soc. Pathologists and Bacteriologists, Soc. Cell Biology, A.A.A.S., Am. Assn. Cancer Research, Am. Chem. Soc. Home: 3418 Waynoka Av Memphis TN 37803

ROGERS, THELMA THARP (MRS. LOUIS ROGERS), mem. Rep. Nat. Com.; b. Elkin, N.C., Mar. 4, 1904; d. Noah W. and Alice (Council) Tharp; student Winthrop Coll.; m. Louis G. Rogers, Oct. 14, 1924; children—Catherine (Mrs. Alexander C. Buchanan), Louise G. Active Republican Party, 1940-—; mem. N.C. Rep. Exec. Com., 1956-—; mem. Rep. Nat. Com. for N.C., 1956-—; mem. arrangement com. nat. conv., 1960, 64, 68, 72, mem. nat. conv. reform com., 1967, 68, platform com., 1956, 60, 64, conv. rules com., 1972. Del. White House Conf. on Aging, 1961, mem. nat. adv. com., 1959-61; asso. mem. Gov. N.C. Coordinating Com. Aging, 1959-61; mem. Gov.'s Com. Status Women, 1964. Methodist. Address: Route 3 Box 251 Charlotte NC 28201

ROGERS, W.D., broadcasting exec., former mayor; b. Waco, Tex.; ed. Baylor U.; m. Edith Tighe; children—Kerry (Mrs. Sam Caddell), Kay, Karol. Founder sta. KEYL-TV (now sta. KENS-TV), San Antonio, 1949, operator, 1949-51; founder Tex. Telecasting, Inc., 1951; founder sta. KDUB-TV, Lubbock, Tex., 1952; established West Tex. TV Network, 1956, operator, 1956-61; now pres. Rogers Broadcasting Co., Lubbock, Rogers Capital Corp., Lubbock; chmn. bd. Champion Life Ins. Co., Dallas, also dir.; mayor, Lubbock, 1966-70. Co-founder, past chmn. bd. TV Bur. Advt., N.Y.C., now chmn. emeritus; founder TV Stas., Inc., N.Y.C. organizer Automatic Program Logging for TV stas. to IBM. Mem. Tex. Council Higher Edn.; mem. adv. bd. Tex. Tourist Devel. Council; past chmn. Lubbock Auditorium-Coliseum and Civic Center, Inc.; past chmn. Citizens Adv. Com. City of Lubbock. Past. bd. dirs. Salvation Army, Lubbock, Tex. United Fund, Lubbock United Fund, Caprock council Girl Scouts Am.; past mem. adv. bd. Lubbock Christian Coll.; past trustee, chmn. pub. relations and devel. com. Meth. Hosp., Lubbock. Decorated Order Republic of Chad; named to Am. Hall of Fame, 1969; recipient Legion of Honor Order DeMolay, Outstanding Community Salesman award, 1970. Mem. Nat. Assn. Broadcasters (founder predecessor TV Assn. Broadcasters; past chmn. bd.), Soc. TV Pioneers (pres. 1957-—), Assn. Broadcasting Execs. Tex., Young Pres. Orgn., Lubbock C. of C. (past pres.; past chmn. indsl. and econ. devel. com.), So. Plains Assn. Govts., Tex. Assn. Mayors, Councilmen and Commrs., Sales Execs. Club, Kappa Kappa Psi, Alpha Delta Sigma. Mem. Christian Ch. (deacon). Lion (mem. League for Crippled Children). Address: 1103 8th St Lubbock TX 79401

ROGERS, WARREN, civil engr., govt. ofcl.; b. Kittery, Me., Apr. 5, 1920; s. John Alexander and Anne (Larrabee) R.; B.S., U.S. Mil. Acad., 1943; M.S. in Civil Engring., Ia. State Coll., 1947; m. Nancy Ellen McCann, Nov. 10, 1945; children—Cathryn, Michael, Patrick, Peter. Commd. 2d lt. C.E., U.S. Army, 1943, advanced through grades to lt. col., 1965, ret., 1965; stationed in PTO, Guam, Iwo Jima, Germany, Korea; dir. logistics Engr. Sch., Europe, 1952-55; prof. mil. sci. engr. br. Mass. Inst. Tech., 1955-58; operations officer 34th Engring. Group, Ft. Ord, Cal., 1958-60; chief program budget div. Korean Mil. Adv. Group, 1960-62; post engr. Army Aviation Center, Ft. Rucker, Ala., 1962-65; project engr. Miss. test support dept. Gen. Electric Co., Bay St. Louis, 1965-66; chief depot facilities Atlanta Army Depot, Forest Park, Ga., 1966-68, dep. dir. for services, 1968-—. Com. chmn. Ala.-Fla. council Boy Scouts Am., 1962-65, mem. com. Greater Atlanta council, 1966-71, scoutmaster, 1969-71. Decorated Purple Heart. Registered profl. engr., Ala. Mem. Soc. Am. Mil. Engrs. (dir. Atlanta chpt. 1971-72), Nat. Soc. Profl. Engrs., Def. Supply Assn. Designer builder cantonment areas Hunter Ligget Mil. Reservation Cal., 1959; developed and implemented initial 5 year constrn. program for Korean Army, 1961; coordinated design, constrn. expanded helicopter aerial gunnery facilities Ft. Rucker, 1963-65. Home: 2442 Clifton Springs Manor Decatur GA 30034 Office: Bldg 101 Atlanta Army Depot Forest Park GA 30050

ROGERS, WILLIAM BRITTON, JR., lawyer; b. Carlsbad, N.M., Sept. 18, 1930; s. William Britton and Mabel (Patrick) R.; grad. N.M. Mil. Inst. 1949; B.A., U. Okla., 1951, LL.B., 1955; m. Joanne Harper, Aug. 30, 1955 (div. Jan. 1959); 1 son, Kevin Patrick. Admitted to Okla. bar, 1957; law clk. to A.P. Murrah, 10th Circuit Ct. Appeals, Oklahoma City, 1957-58; practiced in Oklahoma City, 1958-—; mem. firm Ames, Daugherty, Byrun, Black, Ashabramner & Rogers, 1958-—. Vice pres., dir. Harden Mortgage Loan Co., Oklahoma City, 1964-66, Western Paving Co., Oklahoma City, 1964-66, Oklahoma City Pub. Market, 1964-66; dir. Central Cenetry Co. of Ill., Chgo., Keller-Williams Furniture Mfg. Co., Oklahoma City, Haggards, Inc., Oklahoma City. Asso. prof. law Oklahoma City U., 1964-—. Trustee Rose Hill Burial Park; dir. Sigma Nu Corp. of Okla. Served to 1st lt. USAF, 1955-57. Mem. Am., Okla., N.M. bar assns., Am. Judicature Soc. Democrat. Episcopalian. Home: 7004 N Roff St Oklahoma City OK 73116 Office: 219 Couch Dr Oklahoma City OK 73102

ROGERS, WILLIAM CURRAN, editor; b. Commerce, Ga., Apr. 23, 1927; s. Amory Audrey and Marion (Rogers) R.; B.A., Emory U., 1949; M.A., U. Ga., 1950; m. Virginia Irene Kesler, Nov. 25, 1950; children—William C., Thomas Hamilton, Audrey Anne, Richard Wade. Advt. mgr. Calhoun (Ga.) Times, 1950-54; asst. dir. pub. relations Central of Ga. Ry., Savannah, 1954-55; editor True Citizen, Waynesboro, Ga., 1955-59; editor, pub. Swainsboro (Ga.) Forest-Blade, 1959-—. Mem. Swainsboro Bd. Edn., 1960-—. Served with USNR, 1945-47. Recipient Quill award Atlanta chpt. Sigma Delta Chi; named Outstanding Young Man of Swainsboro, 1964. Mem. Ga. Press Assn. (treas. 1967-69, pres. 1969-70), Swainsboro C. of C. (dir. 1965-—). Methodist (ofcl. bd., sec., lay leader). Kiwanian (dir. 1965-—). Home: 107 Price Av Swainsboro GA 30401 Office: 206 S Green St Swainsboro GA 30401

ROGERS, WILLIAM PIERCE, sec. state; b. Norfolk, N.Y., June 23, 1913; s. Harrison Alexander and Myra (Beswick) R.; A.B. Colgate U., 1934; LL.B., Cornell U., 1937; m. Adele Langston, June 27, 1936; children— Dale, Anthony Wood, Jeffrey Langston, Douglas Langston. Mem. editorial bd. Cornell Law Quar., 1935-37; admitted to N.Y. bar, 1937, D.C. bar, 1950; asst. dist. atty., N.Y. County, 1938-42, 46-47; counsel Senate War Investigating Com., 1947, chief counsel, 1947-48; chief counsel Senate Investigations Sub-Com. Exec. Expenditures Com., 1948-50; mem. firm Dwight, Royall, Harris, Koegel & Caskey, N.Y.C. and Washington, 1950-53; dep. atty. gen. U.S., 1953-57, atty. gen., 1957-61; partner firm Royall, Koegel & Rogers, N.Y.C. and Washington, 1961-69; sec. state, 1969-—. U.S. rep. 20th Gen. Assembly, UN, 1967, UN Ad Hoc Com. on South Africa, 1967; mem. Pres.'s Commn. Law Enforcement and Adminstrn., 1965-67. Served as lt. comdr. USN, 1942-46. Fellow Am. Bar Found.; mem. Bar Assn. City N.Y., Am., N.Y. State, D.C. bar assns., Am. Law Inst., Order of Coif, Sigma Chi. Clubs: Burning Tree, Country (Bethesda, Md.); Sky, Racquet and Tennis (N.Y.C.); Chevy Chase (Md.) Golf. Home: 7007 Glenbrook Rd Bethesda MD 20014 also 870 UN Plaza New York NY 10017 Office: Dept State Washington DC 20520

ROGET, EINAR LEONARD, govt. ofcl.; b. Superior, Wis., Mar. 12, 1926; s. John E. and Elsie (Carlson) R.; student Superior State Tchrs. Coll., 1946-47; B.S. in Forest Mgmt., Utah State U., 1950 M. Pub. Adminstrn., Harvard, 1960; m. Marjorie Jane Greenberg, Sept. 3, 1946 1 dau., Janet Louise. Mem. work unit Soil Conservation Service, U.S. Dept. Agr. El Centro, Cal., 1952-56; watershed planning specialist, Riverside, Cal., 1956-59; area and asst. State conservationist State of N.M., 1960-65, state conservationist, 1966-68; Ark. state conservationist Soil Conservation Service, Little Rock, 1968—. Served with USMCR, 1944-46. Mem. Soil Conservation Soc. Am. (pres. 1970), Soc. Am. Foresters. Home: 11127 Yosemite Valley Dr Little Rock AR 72207 Office: 5401 Fed Office Bldg Little Rock AR 72201

ROGOVIN, CHARLES HOWARD, pres. Police Found., Washington. Office: 1015 18th St NW Washington DC 20036

ROHAN, ALEXANDER JOHN, labor union ofcl.; b. Haverstraw, N.Y., Feb. 2, 1911; s. Alexander John and Bridget (Manton) R.; student Columbia, 1928-29; m. Margaret Cavanaugh, Feb. 5, 1934; children—Sandra (Mrs. Domonic Pisciotta), Carol Ann (Mrs. Wayne Cannon), Kevin Sean. With Fred F. French Co., 1926-31; with Turner Press, Yonkers, N.Y., 1931-37; pressman E.F. Merkle Press, Washington, 1937-43, foreman pressroom, 1946-51; rep. Internat. Printing Pressmen and Assistant's Union N.Am., Washington, 1951-53, v.p., 1953-61, sec.-treas., 1961—; vice chmn. Citizens Union Bank, Rogersville, Tenn. Bd. dirs. Community Services Com. AFL-CIO. Served with AUS, 1943-46. Democrat. Roman Catholic. Club: Touchdown (Washington). Home: 7604 Allman Dr Annandale VA 22003 Office: 1730 Rhode Island Av NW Washington DC 20036

ROHAN, JEROME JOHN, ednl. adminstr.; b. Hobson, Tex., Sept. 11, 1921; s. John A. and Agnes (Malik) R.; B.S., S.W. Tex. State U., 1949, M.Ed., 1954; m. Eunice Lorene Sommerlatte, May 29, 1947; children— Sylvia Ann, Geraldine E. (Mrs. Malcolm Morgenroth). Math. and sci. tchr. Alice (Tex.) Ind. Sch. Dist., Pawnee (Tex.) Ind. Sch. Dist., 1949-53, Hallettsville (Tex.) Ind. Sch. Dist., 1953-57; supt. LaVernia Ind. Sch. Dist., 1957-66. Poth Ind. Sch. Dist., 1966-71, Kenedy (Tex.) Ind. Sch. Dist., 1971—. Served with AUS, 1942-45. Mem. Am., Tex. assns. sch. adminstrs., Tex. Tchrs. Assn., C. of C. Lion, Rotarian. Home: 113 Sunnyside Dr Kenedy TX 78119 Office: PO Box 149 Kenedy TX 78119

ROHRBACH, PETER THOMAS, author, editor; b. N.Y.C., Feb. 27, 1926; s. James Peter and Kathryn (Foley) R.; A.B. in Philosophy, Cath. U. Am., 1951, M.A. in Edn., 1953; m. Sheila Ann Sheehan, Sept. 21, 1970. Author: Conversation With Christ, 1956; A Gentle Fury, 1959; A Girl and Her Teens, 1959; Bold Encounter, 1960; The Search for Therese, 1961; The Photo Album of Therese, 1962; The Art of Dynamic Preaching, 1965; Journey to Carith, 1966; The Disillusioned, 1968; editor Spiritual Life Mag., Washington, 1966-70; book editor City Mag., Washington, 1970—. Tchr. Georgetown U., Cath. U. Am., other colls., 1956-66. Editorial cons. govt. agys., 1968—. Contbr. articles to lit. mags. Home: 4000 Massachusetts Av NW Washington DC 20016 Office: City Magazine 2100 M St NW Washington DC 20037

ROHRER, JAMES VERNON, ednl. adminstr.; b. Wadsworth, O., Aug. 23, 1928; s. Samuel Dayton and Ella Mae (Rohrer) R.; student Eastern Mennonite Coll., 1946-48, Madison Coll., 1949; B.A., Goshen Coll., 1949; M.Ed., U. Va., 1956; m. Mary June Turner, Aug. 28, 1949; children—Jennifer, James, Jordan, Jane. Tchr., Bergton (Va.) Sch., 1949-52; prin. Broadway (Va.) Elementary Sch., 1952-64; prin. John C. Myers Intermediate Sch., Broadway, 1964-67; supr. instrnl. materials Rockingham County Schs., Harrisonburg, Va., 1967—. Mem. Ch. of Brethren. Home: Route 2 Timberville VA 22853 Office: 2 S Main St Harrisonburg VA 22801

ROIG, SALVADOR T., govt. ofcl.; b. Yauco, P.R., Nov. 9, 1907; s. Juan and Angela (Marietti) R.; B.S.A., U.P.R., 1931; grad. FBI Nat. Acad.; m. Aida Mejia Mattei, Dec. 23, 1936; children—Salvador, Angel Rafael, Juan Antonio. Agronomist various agys. govt. P.R.; supt. Camp Augustin Stahl Forest Service; chief of police P.R., supt., now adj. gen. P.R.; with P.R. Office Civil Def., 1952. Served with P.R. Nat. Guard, 1926-45; active duty from capt. to col., 1940-45; ETO. Decorated Bronze Star medal; named All Am. Skeet Shooting champion 1954; named to P.R. Hall of Fame. Mem. Internat. Assn. Chiefs of Police, Assn. Police Mems., Olympic Com. P.R. (del.) Coll. Agronomists, Nat. Skeet Shooting Assn., P.R. Fedn. (pres.). Clubs: Police Shooting; Met. Shooting; Ponce Yacht and Fishing; Deportive de Ponce. Home: 8-1 Av Ramirez de Arellano Torrimar PR 00619 Office: Pda 3 Ponce de Leon Av San Juan PR 00904

ROLAND, CHARLES PIERCE, educator; b. Maury City, Tenn., Apr. 8, 1918; s. Clifford Paul and Grace (Paysinger) R.; student Freed-Hardeman Jr. Coll., 1934-36; B.A., Vanderbilt U., 1938; postgrad. George Washington U., 1947; Ph.D., La. State U., 1951; m. Allie Lee Aycock, Jan. 23, 1948; children—John Clifford, Karen Jean, Charles Franklin. Tchr., Alamo (Tenn.) High Sch., 1938-40; hist. technician Nat. Park Service, Washington, 1940-42, 46-47; asst. to chief historian of the Army, Dept. Army, Washington, 1951-52; instr. history La. State U., Baton Rouge, 1950-51; with dept. history Tulane U., New Orleans, 1952-70, instr., 1952-53, asst. prof., 1953-57, asso. prof., 1957-60, prof., 1960-70, head arts and scis. history dept., 1963-67, chmn. dept., 1967-70; alumni prof. history U. Ky., 1970—; mem. adv. com. U.S. Civil War Centennial Commn., 1959-65; mem. adv. council Office Mil. History, Dept. Army, 1965-69. Served to capt. AUS, 1942-46. Decorated Bronze Star, Purple Heart. Recipient La. Lit. Award, La. Library Assn., 1957. Guggenheim Found. fellow, 1960-61. Mem. Am., So., La. hist. assns., Orgn. Am. Historians. Author: Louisiana Sugar Plantations During the American Civil War, 1957; The Confederacy, 1960; Albert Sidney Johnston: Soldier of Three Republics, 1964; (with Francis Butler Simkins) A History of the South, 1972. Home: 814 Sherwood Dr Lexington KY 40502

ROLEY, ROLF WIGHT, cons. engr.; b. Pana, Ill., Apr. 14, 1918; s. Paul Wight and Eula (Neal) R.; B.S. in Mech. Engring., U. Mo., 1940; E.M., 1952; D.Sc., Marlowe U., 1968; Ph.D., Ill. Christian Coll., 1968; m. Mary F. Brown, Aug. 5, 1939; 1 son, Robert D. Gen. engr. Ill. Hwy. Dept., 1934-40; with various mining and constrn. cos., 1940-52; with Reynolds Metals Co., Little Rock, 1952-62; pres. Roley Engrs., Inc., Roley Forensics, Kennesaw, Ga., 1962—. Cons in safety accident studies, forensic sci., 1948—; asso. prof. civil engring. Ga. Inst. Tech., 1962-68. Mem. Ark. Republican Com., 1954-60. Registered profl. engr., Ga., Ill., Wyo. Mem. A.A.A.S., Nat., Ga., Cobb County (dir.) socs. profl. engrs., Nat. Soc. Forensic Consultants, Nat. Fire Protection Assn., U.S., Ga. cons. engrs. councils, Nat. Oceanographic Soc. Club: Explorers (N.Y.C.). Contbr. articles to profl. jours. Home: Marrol House Madison GA 30650 Office: Shiloh Hills Kennesaw GA 30144

ROLL, WILLIAM GEORGE, JR., parapsychologist; b. Bremen, Germany, July 3, 1926 (parents Am. citizens); s. William George and Gudrun (Agerholm) R.; B.A., U. Cal. at Berkeley, 1949; B.Litt., Oxford U., 1960; m. Muriel Gold, June 22, 1950; children—Lise Renata, Leif Agerholm, William George III. Louis K. Anspacher fellow in parapsychology, parapsychology lab. Duke, 1957-58, research asso., 1958-60, project dir., 1960; project dir. Psychical Research Found., Inc., Durham, N.C., 1961—. Mem. Underground Danish Resistance Forces, 1943-45. Mem. A.A.A.S., Parapsychology Assn. (council 1957-60, 62-65, pres. 1964), Soc. Psychical Research London, Am. Soc. Psychical Research, Oxford U. Soc. Psychical Research (pres. 1952-57). Editor: Jour. Parapsychology, 1958-60, Theta, 1963—, P.A. Proceedings, 1964—. Contbr. articles to profl. jours. Home: 3509 Rugby Rd Durham NC 27707 Office: Duke Station Durham NC 27706

ROLLAND, E.O., state ofcl. Exec. dir. Fla. Bd. Adminstrn. Office: Carlton Bldg Tallahassee FL 32304*

ROLLER, HERBERT ALFRED, zoologist, chem. co. exec.; b. Magdeburg, Germany, Aug. 2, 1927; s. Alfred H. and Elfriede (Wartner) R.; B.S., Humanistisches Gymnasium, Halle, Germany, 1946; Ph.D., U. Gottingen (Germany), 1962; m. Manuela R. Buresch, Dec. 20, 1957. Came to U.S., 1962. Project asso. zoology U. Wis., 1962-65, asst. prof. pharmacology, 1965-66, research asso. zoology, 1966-67, asso. prof., 1967-68; prof. biology Tex. A. and M. U., 1968—; v.p. Zoecon Corp., Palo Alto, Cal., 1968—; mem., research dir. Internat. Centre Insect Physiology and Ecology, Nairobi, Kenya, 1970—. Mem. Am. Inst. Biol. Scis., A.A.A.S., Am. Assn. U. Profs., Entomol. Soc. Am., Tex. Acad. Sci., Am. Soc. Zoologists, Sigma Xi. Home: 1000 E 30th St Bryan TX 77801

ROLLINGS, HARRY EVAN, physician; b. Hattiesburg, Miss., July 23, 1920; s. Robert Evan and Emma (Siebe) R.; B.S., U. So. Miss., 1939; med. certificate U. Miss., 1941; M.D., Tulane U., 1943; m. Irma Lee Pittman, Jan. 12, 1945; children—Cynthia, Carol, Pamela, Janet, Ellen, Robert. Intern, Phila. Gen. Hosp., 1943-44; resident medicine Tulane U. service Charity Hosp., 1944-46; chief med. resident, 1945-46, instr. medicine Sch. Medicine, 1944-48; staff internist Ochsner Clinic and Ochsner Found. Hosp., Touro Infirmary, 1946-48; practice internal medicine, Savannah, Ga., 1948-51, 53—; chief of staff, trustee Warren A. Candler Hosp., Candler Central Hosp., Candler Telfair Hosps.; cons. staff St. Josephs Hosp.; courtesy staff Meml. Hosp., all Savannah. Cons. internal medicine USAF Hosp., Hunter AFB, Ga.; sr. med. examiner FAA. Dir. Colony Mortgage Co., Savannah. Served to capt. AUS, 1951-53; col. M.C., USAF Res. Diplomate Am. Bd. Internal Medicine. Fellow A.C.P., Internat. Coll. Physicians, Am. Coll. Chest Physicians; mem. Med. Assn. Ga., Ga. Med. Soc., Internat., Am. assns. internal medicine, Am. Diabetes Assn., Am. Geriatrics Assn., A.M.A., So. Med. Assn., Internat. Congress Internal Medicine, Aircraft Owners and Pilots Assn., Flying Physicians Assn., Air Force Assn., Am. Heart Assn. Methodist (ofcl. bd.). Clubs: Savannah Yacht, Savannah Golf, Windsor Forrest Golf. Contbg. author Communicable Disease, 1948; also articles. Home: 514 Arlington Rd Savannah GA 31406 Office: 100 E Park Av Savannah GA 31401

ROLLINGS, OLLIE EARL, III, dentist; b. Birmingham, Ala., Apr. 11, 1942; s. Ollie Earl, Jr. and Hazel E. (Huggins) R.; B.S., Auburn U., 1964; D.M.D., U. Ala., 1968; m. Cecilia Jane Brooks, June 20, 1964; children—Robert Brooks, Christy Lillian. Practice dentistry, Cape Coral, Fla., 1968—. Served to lt. USNR, 1968-70. Mem. Am., Fla. dental assns., West Coast Dental Soc., V.F.W., Cape Coral C. of C., Psi Omega, Pi Kappa Alpha. Republican. Baptist (deacon). Club: Tarpon Hunters (Cape Coral). Home: 1625 SE 41st St Cape Coral FL 33904 Office: 4408 Del Prado Pkwy Cape Coral FL 33904

ROLLINS, ALBERT WILLIAMSON, cons. engr.; b. Dallas, July 31, 1930; s. Andrew Peach and Mary (Williamson) R.; B.S. in Civil Engring., Tex. A. and M. Coll., 1951, M.S. in Civil Engring., 1956; m. Martha Ann James, Dec. 28, 1954; children—Elizabeth Ann, Mark Martin. Engring. asst. Tex. Hwy. Dept., Dallas, 1953-55; dir. pub. works City of Arlington (Tex.), 1956-63, city mgr., 1963-67; partner Schrickel, Rollins & Assos., land planners-engrs., Arlington, 1967—. Mem. Tarrant County Planning Commn.; chmn. Tex. Mass Transp. Commn. Bd. dirs. Tex. Turnpike Authority. Served as 1st lt. AUS, 1951-53. Registered profl. engr., Tex., La. Mem. Internat. City Mgrs. Assn., Nat. Soc. Profl. Engrs., Am. Soc. C.E., Am. Water Works Assn., Water Pollution Control Fedn., Sigma Xi, Phi Eta Sigma, Tau Beta Pi, Phi Kappa Phi. Contbr. articles to profl. jours. Home: 3004 Yellowstone Dr Arlington TX 76013 Office: 604 Av H East Arlington TX 76011

ROLLINS, ANDREW PEACH, JR., army officer; b. Gettysburg, Pa., Aug. 2, 1918; s. Andrew P. and Mary (Williamson) R.; B.S. in Civil Engring., Tex. A. and M. Coll., 1939; M.S., Cal. Inst. Tech., 1948; m. Suzanne Smith, Dec. 23, 1947; 1 dau., Suzanne Edna. Rodman, Tex. Hwy. Dept., 1939; jr. engr. Internat. Boundary Commn., San Benito, Tex., 1939-40; served with AUS, 1940; commn. 2d lt., C.E., U.S. Army, 1941, advanced through grades to maj. gen., 1968; dist. engr. Kansas City (Mo.) Dist., 1960-63; mil. constrn. dir. Office Chief Engrs., Washington, 1963-65; asst. for NASA Support, 1965-66, dir., 1966-67; commdg. gen. 18th Engr. Brigade, Vietnam, 1967; dir. constrn. Hdqrs. Mil Assistance Command, 1967-68; comdg. gen. Ft. Leonard Wood, Mo., 1968-69; pres. Miss. River Commn., also div. engr. Lower Miss. Valley div., Vicksburg, 1969-71; dep. chief of engrs. Dept. Army, Washington, 1971—. Decorated Legion of Merit, Bronze Star, Silver Star, Legion of Merit. Registered profl. engr., Tex., Mo. Fellow Am. Soc. C.E. (past mem. com. on engrs. in pub. practice); mem. Soc. Am. Mil. Engrs. (past local post pres.). Baptist. Home: Quarters 54 Fort Belvoir VA 22060 Office: Office Chief of Engineers Washington DC 20314

ROLLINS, ERNEST WILLIAM, JR., educator; b. Woodruff, S.C., July 3, 1932; s. Ernest William and Agnes (Wingo) R.; B.A., Wake Forest Coll., 1959; M.A., Ind. U., 1961; Ph.D., Vanderbilt U., 1968. Asst. prof. German, Stetson U., DeLand, Fla. 1962-68; asst. prof. N.C. State U., Raleigh, 1968-72, asso. prof., 1972—. Served with USAF, 1954-58. Mem. Modern Lang. Assn., Am. Assn. Tchrs. German, Am. Assn. U. Profs. Author: Men of Dialogue: Martin Buber and Albrecht Goes, 1969. Home: 602 B Smithdale Dr Raleigh NC 27606

ROLLINS, O. WAYNE, broadcasting exec.; b. Keith, Ga., 1912. Chmn., pres. Rollins Inc.; pres. WRAP, Norfolk, Va.; partner, Rollins Bros.; dir. Rollins Leasing Corp., Vendor S.A. de C.V., Dettelbach Chem. Corp., Dwoskin Inc., Orkin S.A. de C.V.; pres., dir. Rollins Realty Corp., Rollins Investment Corp., Rollins Telecasting Inc., Rollins Broadcasting of Del. Inc., Continental Broadcasting, Inc., WCHS-TV Corp., Rollins Outdoor Advt. Inc., Orkin Exterminating Corp., Kinro Advt. Co., Orkin Acceptance Corp. Office: PO Box 598 Norfolk VA 23501*

ROLLINS, ROBERT LEROY, JR., hosp. supt.; b. Farmville, N.C., Feb. 16, 1932; s. Robert LeRoy and Hope (Ward) R.; A.B., U. N.C., 1952; M.D., Duke, 1956; m. Janet Ruth Stansill, June 19, 1955; children—Martha Hope, Robert Scott. Intern Meml. Hosp., Charlotte, 1956-57; resident psychiatry Topeka VA Hosp., 1957-59, Meml. Hosp., Chapel Hill, N.C. 1959-60; pvt. practice psychiatry, Tampa, Fla., 1963-64, Wilmington, N.C., 1964-66; supt. Dorothea Dix Hosp., Raleigh, N.C., 1966—; clin. asso. prof. psychiatry U. N.C., 1968—; adj. asso. prof. sociology and anthropology N.C. State U., 1966—. Sec. New Hanover (N.C.) County Med. Soc., 1965; mem. Eugenics Bd. N.C., 1967—. Served to capt. USAF, 1960-62. Diplomate Am. Bd. Psychiatry and Neurology. Fellow Am. Psychiat. Assn.; mem. N.C. (chmn. sect. neurology and psychiatry), Wake County med. socs., N.C. Neuropsychiat. Assn. (v.p. 1971-72, pres. elect 1972—), Am. Pub. Health Assn., Am. Acad. Psychiatry and the Law, Am. Civil Liberties Union, Common Cause, N.C. State Employees Assn., Phi Beta Kappa. Home: 501 Spring Valley Dr Raleigh NC 27609 Office: Dorothea Dix Hosp Raleigh NC 27611

ROLLINS, STEED, newspaper exec.; b. Durham, N.C., Nov. 28, 1916; s. Edward Tyler and Bessie (Steed) R.; ed. Fishburne Mil. Sch., 1930-34; A.B., Vanderbilt U., 1938; m. Mozette Riggsbee, Dec. 30, 1944; children—Amy Elizabeth, Steed. Reporter for the Durham Morning Herald, 1938, lit. editor and asst. editorial writer, 1939-40, mng. editor, 1940-41, editor since 1950; exec. editor Durham Herald-Sun Papers, now pres.; v.p. Herald-Sun Papers, 1947—; dir. Home Savs. and Loan Assn., Durham Investment Corp., Durham Indsl. Devel. Corp. Trustee N.C. Symphony Soc.; chmn. Recreation Adv. Com., Durham, 1948-52; bd. dirs. Durham United Fund, Durham Com. of 100, Durham Mchts. Assn.; mem. N.C. Bd of Corrections & Training; bd. dirs. Journalism Found. of N.C. Served U.S.A.A.F., 1941-45. Rotarian. Club: N.C. Associated Press (pres. 1951). Home: 33 Oak Dr Durham NC 27707 Office: Durham Herald-Sun Papers Durham NC 27702

ROMAN, JAMES RUDOLPH, JR., educator; b. Jamestown, N.Y., Feb. 10, 1936; s. James Rudolph and Violet (Nyholm) R.; B.S., Bucknell U., 1957; M.B.A, U. Md., 1960, postgrad. 1960-63; D. Bus. Adminstrn., George Washington U., 1970; m. Nancy Ann Kelley, June 17, 1961. Instr., U. Md., 1959-63, U. Del., 1959-63; instr. George Washington U., 1963-66, asst. prof., 1966-70, asso. prof., 1971—. Lectr., mgmt. cons. in traffic, transp. bus. mgmt.; mem. adv. council Small Bus. Adminstrn. Mem. Am. Accounting Assn., Am. Assn. U. Profs., Soc. Advancement Mgmt., Am. Econs. Assn., Assn. Edn. in Internat. Bus., USCG Aux., Beta Gamma Sigma, Delta Sigma Pi, Tau Kappa Alpha, Delta Nu Alpha. Clubs: Traffic; Tantallon Country; Chautauqua Lake Yacht, Chautauqua Yacht, Ft. Washington Yacht and Tennis, George Washington University. Contbr. to Americana Ency. Ann., also profl. jours. Home: 12201 Holly Bank Dr Tantallon-on-the-Potomac Washington DC 20022 also 209 Gustavus Av Jamestown NY 14701 Office: 710 21st St NW Washington DC 20006

ROMAN, NANCY G(RACE), astronomer, govt. ofcl.; b. Nashville, May 16, 1925; d. Irwin and Georgia Frances (Smith) Roman; B.A. (Joshua Lippincott Meml. fellow), Swarthmore Coll., 1946; Ph.D., U. Chgo., 1949; D.Sc., Russell Sage Coll., 1966, Hood Coll., 1969, Bates Coll., 1970 Asst., Sproul Obs., Swarthmore Coll., 1943-46; asst. Yerkes Obs., U. Chgo. at Williams Bay, Wis., 1946-48, research asso., 1949-52, instr. stellar astronomy, 1952-55, asst. prof., 1955; research asso. Warner and Swasey Obs., Case Inst. Tech., Cleve., summer 1949; physicist radio astronomy br. U.S. Naval Research Lab., Washington, 1955-56, astronomer, head microwave spectroscopy sect., 1956-58, astronomer cons., 1958-59; head observational astronomy program Office Space Flight Devel., NASA, Washington, 1959-60, chief astronomy and solar physics, geophysics and astronomy programs, 1960-64, chief astronomy programs, physics and astronomy programs, 1964—. Recipient Fed. Woman's award, 1962, Pub. Service citation Colo. Woman's Coll., 1966, 90th Anniversary award Woman's Union, 1967, NASA Exceptional Sci. Achievement award, 1969. Mem. Am., Royal astron. socs., Internat. Astron. Union (editor symposium 1956, 58), Astron. Soc. Pacific, Internat. Sci. Radio Union, Am. Assn. U. Women. Contbr. articles to sci. periodicals. Research on stellar clusters, high velocity stars, radio astronomy. Office: NASA Hdqrs 400 Maryland Av SW Washington DC 20546

ROMANUS, CHARLES FRANKLIN, govt. ofcl.; b. Decatur, Ill., July 6, 1915; s. Charles Henry and Lulu Lucille (Crail) R.; student Blackburn Coll., 1932-34; A.M., U. Ill., 1937; postgrad. La. State U., 1937-41; m. Annie A. Armstrong, Aug. 12, 1940; children—Kathleen (Mrs. David William Smith), Charles Franklin, Charlene Ann. With Office of Chief Mil. History, Dept. Army, Washington, 1945—, chief gen. reference br., 1962—. Served to capt. AUS, 1943-46. Author: Stillwell's Mission to China, 1953; Stilwell's Command Problems, 1956; Time Runs Out in C.B.I., 1959. Home: 9022 Leesburg Pike McLean VA 22101 Office: 2d and R Sts SW Washington DC 20315

ROMERO BARCELO, CARLOS, lawyer; mayor; b. San Juan, P.R., Sept. 4, 1932; s. Antonio Romero and Josefina Barcelo; grad. Phillips Exeter Acad., Exeter, Mass., 1949; B.A., Yale, 1953; LL.B., U.P.R., 1956; m. Kathleen Donnelly, Jan. 2, 1966; children—Carlos, Andres, Juan Carlos, Melinda. Admitted to P.R. bar, 1956, since practiced in San Juan; asso. firm Rivera Zayas, Rivera Cestero & Rua, 1956-62, partner, 1962-63; mem. firm Segurola, Romero & Toledo, 1963-68; mayor, San Juan, 1968—. Pres., Citizens for Statehood, 1965-67; pres. polit. edn. and evaluation com. Statehood Republican Com.; a founder United Statehooders Group; afounder New Progressive Party, 1967, v.p., 1967; 1st v.p. New Progressive Party, 1971. Named Young Man of Yr., Jr. C. of C., 1968. Office: City Hall San Francisco St San Juan PR

ROMERSTEIN, HERBERT, govt. ofcl.; b. N.Y.C., Aug. 19, 1931; s. Philip and Rose (Alpert) R.; student Bklyn. Coll., 1950-51, 54-55; m. Patricia Cole, Oct. 10, 1961; children—Shari, David, Victoria, Rebecca. Cons. to various fed. and state agys., 1954-64; investigator N.Y. State Legislature, 1954-56; investigative cons. Waterfront Commn. N.Y. Harbor, 1962-63; investigator N.Y. State Senate, 1964; investigator com. on un-Am. activities U.S. Ho. of Reps., N.Y.C., 1965-69, investigator com. on internal security, 1969-71, chief investigator (minority staff) com. on internal security, 1971—. Mem. Suburban Jewish Center, Linden, N.J., 1966—. Served with AUS, 1952-53. Mem. Civil War Token Soc. Jewish religion. Republican. Author: Communism and Your Child, 1962; (monograph) The Communist International Youth and Student Apparatus, 1963; (with Grover Criswell) The Official Guide to Confederate Money and Civil War Tokens, 1971. Office: Cannon House Office Bldg Room 111 Washington DC 20515

ROMINE, BENJAMIN WALTER, physician; b. Valdosta, Ga., Mar. 13, 1936; s. Benjamin Houston and Sarah (Patrick) R.; student Carson-Newsome Coll., 1954-57; M.D., Med. Coll. Ga., 1962; m. Peggy Lois Tarvin, June 21, 1958; children—Carolyn Ann, Patricia Ann, Benjamin Walter. Intern Phoebe-Putney Meml. Hosp., Albany, Ga., 1962-63; gen. practice medicine, Quitman, Ga., 1963—. Mem. Bd. Health Brooks County, 1965—, Bd. Edn. Brooks County, 1966—. Mem. A.M.A., Ga., Thomas-Brooks med. assns., Alpha Kappa Kappa. Baptist (deacon). Rotarian. Home: Pine Circle Quitman GA 31643 Office: 907 N Culpepper St Quitman GA 13643

ROMINE, JOSEPHINE LACKEY (MRS. HARRY A. ROMINE), educator; b. Roseberg, Ore., Oct. 16, 1893; d. William Joseph and Lou Ella (Reynolds) Lackey; student S.W. State Tchrs. Coll., Weatherford, Okla., 1908-13; A.B., Oklahoma City U., 1924; postgrad. U. Chgo., 1924, U. Cal. at Los Angeles, 1927, Columbia, 1938, U. Miami,

1955-56; M.S., U. Okla., 1929; m. Harry A. Romine, May 31, 1920 (dec. 1971). Tchr. pub. schs., Okla., 1913-20, Oklahoma City, 1921-55; directing tchr. for interns U. Miami (Fla.), 1955-71. Tchr. reading Tchrs. Coll., Durant, Okla., summer 1955; counselor Camp Waldmer (Tex.), 1930, Cheley's Camp, Estes Park, Colo., 1934-35; owner, dir. Romine Camps, Oklahoma City, 1942, 54—. Guardian, Campfire Girls Am., Oklahoma City, 1925-34; vol. A.R.C. Mem. Am. Assn. U. Women, Nat., Okla., Fla. (life) edn. assns., Bus. Women's Club, Miami C. of C. (women's div.), Assn. Childhood Edn. Internat., Kappa Delta Pi, Alpha Delta Kappa. Presbyn. (supt. primary dept. Sunday sch.). Mem. Order Eastern Star. Home: 901 NW 25th St Oklahoma City OK 73106

ROMINGER, ELBY ELBERT, advt. agcy. exec.; b. Gove City, Kan., Nov. 20, 1908; s. Oscar and Flora (Fay) R.; student Omaha U., 1929-31; m. Eleanor Dean Robbins, May 7, 1932; children—Barton Dean, Judith Ann (Mrs. Dayle Casey). Reporter, advt. rep. Omaha Bee-News, 1926-29; account exec. Bozell & Jacobs Advt. Agcy., 1929-48; chmn. bd. Rominger Advt. Agy., Inc., Dallas, 1948—. Chmn. pub. relations com. Dallas Community Chest, 1950. Bd. dirs. Caruth Rehab. Center, Republican. Episcopalian. Club: Dallas Press Club (dir. 1964-67). Home: 7265 Kenny Lane Dallas TX 75230 Office: 2900 Turtle Creek Plaza Dallas TX 75219

ROMNEY, CARL F., seismologist; b. Salt Lake City; B.S. in Meteorology, Cal. Inst. Tech.; Ph.D., U. Cal. Seismologist, U.S. Dept. Air Force, 1955—. Tech. adviser to U.S. reps. in negotiations Test Ban Treaty; mem. U.S. delegation Geneva Conf. Experts, 1958, Conf. on Discontinuance Nuclear Weapons Tests, 1959, 60. Recipient President's award for distinguished fed. civilian Service, for outstanding contbs. to devel. of control system for underground nuclear tests, 1967. Contbr. articles to tech. jours. Address: HQ USAF (AFTAC/TD-1 Alexandria VA 22313

RONE, WILLIAM EUGENE, JR., editor; b. Atlanta, Nov. 7, 1926; s. William Eugene and Marguerite (Kellett) R.; A.B., Wofford Coll., 1949; LL.B., U.S.C., 1951; m. Margaret Louise Banks, July 17, 1953; 1 son, James Kellett. With The State, newspaper, Columbia, S.C., 1950—, city editor, 1962-65, asso. editor, 1966-69, editorial page editor, 1969—. S.C. corr. So. Edn. Reporting Service, Nashville, 1962-68; columnist Raleigh (N.C.) News & Observer. Organizer, chmn. S.C. Athletic Hall of Fame, Columbia, 1957-61. Served with USNR, 1945-46. Recipient S.C. A.P. award for best reporting in depth, 1962. Mem. Am. Soc. Newspaper Editors, Nat. Conf. Editorial Writers, Kappa Sigma, Phi Delta Phi. Episcopalian. Author: Biography of Max Hirsch, 1956. Home: 726 Fairway Lane Columbia SC 29210 Office: Box 1333 Columbia SC 29202

RONEY, RAYMOND GEORGE, librarian; b. Phila., July 26, 1939; s. Wallace and Rosezell (Harris) R.; B.A., Central State U., Wilberforce, O., 1963; M.L.S., Pratt Inst., 1965; postgrad. Catholic U., 1967—; m. Ruth A. Westgaph, Apr. 4, 1970. Asst. br. librarian Queens Borough Pub. Library, Jamaica, N.Y., 1964-65; supr. reference dept. Howard U. Library, Washington, 1965-66; dir. libraries Nat. League of Cities/U.S. Conf. Mayors, Washington, 1967-70; dir. library Washington Tech. Inst., 1970—. Cons. D.C. Pub. Schs.-Model Schs. Innovative Team, Washington. Mem. S.W. Washington Edn. Community Com., 1969-70. Recipient Outstanding Achievement award Bright Hope Baptist Ch., Phila., 1963. Mem. Am. Polit. Sci. Assn., Am. Acad. Polit. and Social Sci., Met. Washington Area Urban Studies Libraries, N.E.A. Home: 1521 Kalmia Rd NW Washington DC 20012 Office: 4100 Connecticut Av NW Washington DC 20008

RONEY, ROBERT KELLY, III, educator; b. Newbern, Tenn., Jan. 20, 1935; s. Robert Kelly and Grace Edris (Craddock) R.; student U. Tenn., 1953-55; A.B., Duke, 1957; M.A., Memphis State U., 1964; Ed.D., U. Tenn., 1970; m. Martha Anne Meek, June 14, 1957; children—Robert Kelly IV, Lisa Claire. Tchr., Martin (Tenn.) High Sch., 1959; tchr., Memphis City Schs., 1959-61, personnel asst., 1961-66; dir. instl. research U. Tenn. System, 1968-70; dir., asso. prof. ednl. adminstrn. U. Tenn. Memphis State U. Grad. Center, Memphis, 1970—. Cons., Richmond (Va.) Pub. Schs., 1968, Memphis City, Shelby County, Tipton County pub. schs., 1971. U.S. Office Edn. Grad. Research Tng. fellow U. Tenn., 1966-68. Mem. Am. Assn. Sch. Adminstrs., Am. Assn. Higher Edn., Am. Assn. Sch. Personnel Adminstrs., Am. Ednl. Research Assn., N.E.A., Tenn. Edn. Assn., Phi Delta Kappa. Democrat. Methodist. Home: 3051 Woodhills Dr Memphis TN 38128 Office: 711 Jefferson Av Memphis TN 38105

ROOD, NATHAN BARNETT, utility co. exec.; b. Odessa, Russia, Sept. 16, 1902 (came to U.S. 1905, naturalized 1920); s. Morris and Paula (Zlatopolski) R.; A.B., Columbia, 1924, LL.B., 1930; postgrad. Harvard, 1925, Mexico City Coll., 1958; m. Roddy Crossman, May 29, 1937; children—Judianne (Mrs. Sydney S. Traum), Ginger (Mrs. Steven B. Jacobs). Admitted to N.Y. bar, 1931, practiced, Peekskill, 1932-42; pres. City Constrn. Co., Miami, Fla., 1946-50, Rood Constrn. Co., 1950—, Atlantic Utilities Corp., 1961-66; pres., dir. North Dade Water Co., 1953-61, North Lauderdale Corp., Miami, 1960—, Atlantic Gas Corp., Miami, 1961-66; v.p., dir. South Broward Water Co., Ft. Lauderdale, Fla., 1953-67; chmn. bd. Great Am. Mgmt. & Research Co. Ltd., 1965-66; pres. U.S. Mgmt. Corp., 1969-70, chief exec. officer, 1970; chmn. bd. Pan Am. Bank Hialeah N.A., 1966—, Constrn. Research, Inc., 1971—, First Internat. Realty Securities Fund Ltd., 1969—; dir. Pan Am. Bancshares, 1969—. Mayor, North Lauderdale, Fla., 1963-69. Mem. citizens bd. U. Miami; adv. bd. Fla. Meml. Coll.; trustee Cedars of Lebanon Hosp.; bd. govs. Miami Jewish Fedn.; mem. nat. exec. bd., past pres. Miami chpt. Am. Jewish Com. Served from capt. to lt. col. AUS, 1942-46; col. Res. Mem. Fla. Water and Sewage Assn. (pres. 1960-63), Archaeol. Soc., Soc. Internat. Devel., Zool. Soc., Inst. Mayan Studies Econ. Soc. Miami. Clubs: Kings Bay Yacht and Country; Calusa Country; Standard; Bankers, Jockey. Home: 2451 Brickell Av Miami FL 33129 Office: 5850 Biscayne Blvd Miami FL 33137

ROOKER, ALBERT ALBIN, univ. ofcl.; b. Ennis, Tex., May 31, 1924; s. Jesse Clair and Margaret (Jennings) R.; B.S. in Phys. Edn., U. Tex., 1948, M.Ed. 1950; m. Jo Pearl Bass, Nov. 27, 1947; 1 son, Michael Scott. Asst. dir. intramural sports for men U. Tex., Austin, 1948-59, dir. intramural sports for men, 1959—. Dir summer camp Camp Son-Ro, 1956-57; owner S.W. Recreation Service, Austin, 1956—. Lifesaving and water safety instr. A.R.C., 1947-63; scoutmaster Circle Ten council Boy Scouts Am., 1940-42; mem. Tex. Gov.'s Adv. Com. on Phys. Fitness, 1970; exec. dir. Tex. Commn. Phys. Fitness, 1971—. Served to 1st lt. USAAF, 1943-45. Mem. Nat. Intramural Assn. (pres. 1967, cons. 1969—), Am., Tex. assns. health, phys. edn. and recreation, Coll. Phys. Edn. Assn., Hotel Sales Mgrs. Assn., N.E.A., Omicron Delta Kappa. Methodist. Mason. Home: 2811 W 50th St Austin TX 78731

ROOSA, STUART A., astronaut; b. Durango, Colo., Aug. 16, 1933; student Okla. State U., U. Ariz.; B.S. with honors in Aero. Engring., U. Colo.; grad. aviation cadet program Williams AFB, Ariz.; LL.D. (hon.), U. St. Thomas, Houston, 1971; m. Joan C. Barrett; children—Christopher A., John D., Stuart Allen, Rosemary D. Commd. 1st lt. U.S. Air Force, 1953; advanced through grades to lt. col.; successively fighter pilot Langely AFB, Va., chief service engring. Tachikawa Air Base; flight test pilot Olmstead AFB, Pa., 1962-64; student Aerospace Research Pilots Sch., 1964-65; exptl. test pilot Edwards AFB, Cal., 1965-66; astronaut NASA, Houston, 1966—. Decorated D.S.M.; recipient Distinguished Service medal NASA, 1970, Superior Achievement award Manned Spacecraft Center, 1970; John F. Kennedy award Arnold Air Soc., 1971; Gold medal City of N.Y., 1971. Mem. Soc. Exptl. Test Pilots (asso.). Address NASA Manned Spacecraft Center Houston TX 77060

ROOSEVELT, EDITH KERMIT, journalist; b. N.Y.C., Dec. 19, 1927; d. Archibald Bulloch and Grace (Lockwood) Roosevelt; B.A., Barnard Coll.,1948; m. Alexander Gregory Barmine, Sept. 8, 1948 (div.); 1 dau., Margot. Reporter, feature writer U.P.I., San Francisco, Los Angeles, Washington, 1950-55; feature writer, asso. editor Spadea Syndicate, N.Y.C. 1956-59; reporter, rewrite Newark Star Ledger, 1959-62; syndicated newspaper columnist, Washington, 1962—; Washington corr. for Manchester Union Leader, Vt. Sunday News, St. Alban's Messenger, Conn. Sunday Herald, N.H. Sunday News; lectr. in field. Contbr. to popular mags. Home: 272 M St SW Washington DC 20024

ROOSEVELT, ELLIOTT, JR., oil co. exec.; b. Ft. Worth, July 14, 1936; s. Elliott and Ruth (Googins) R.; grad. Phillips Acad., Andover, Mass., 1954; B.S. in Agr., Colo. State U., 1958; m. Jo Anne McFadden, Jan. 24, 1959; children—Laura, Elliott III, Elizabeth, David. Dist. landman Ambassador Oil Corp., Denver, 1960-64; pres. Gen. Petroleum Corp., Dallas, 1954—, Tex. Interstate Oil and Gas Co., Dallas, 1967-69, Prudential Minerals Explorations Corp., Dallas, 1969-71; v.p. Shenandoah Oil Corp., Ft. Worth, 1971—. Served to capt. AUS, 1959. Episcopalian. Office: 1500 Commerce Bldg Fort Worth TX 79902

ROOT, JOHN BERNARD, ret. educator; b. Strafford, Vt. May 7, 1889; s. Jethro B. and Abigail (Hatch) R.; B.S., Boston U., 1919; S.T.B., Harvard Sch. Div., 1922; A.M. cum laude, Stetson U., 1943; Th.D. magna cum laude, So. Sch. Div., 1959; m. Ethel Frances Whitmore, Aug. 31, 1922; children—Ethel Gladys (Mrs. James L. Henderson), John Bernard II. Tchr., Bryant and Stratton Bus. Coll., Manchester, N.H., 1913-14; ordained to ministry Congl. Ch., 1922; minister First Ch. of Christ, Lynn, Mass., 1922-26, Congl. Christian Ch., Sanford, Fla., 1926-59; head English dept. Seminole High Sch., 1945-59; head English dept. Piedmont Coll., Demorest, Ga., 1959-65, chmn. humanities div., 1963-65, ret. Served with U.S. Army, World War I. Mem. Nat. Tchrs. Assn., Vets. World War I, Sigma Alpha Epsilon. Mason (32 deg.), Kiwanian, Contbr. articles to papers and mags. Address: 1181 W Wellington Dr Deltona FL 32763

ROOT, NORMAN, economist; b. Mountaindale, N.Y., Feb. 4, 1923; s. Max Aaron and Sadie (Lees) R.; B.A., Rutgers U., 1948; M.A., St. Francis Coll., Loretto, Pa., 1963; m. Helen Kirsch, Sept. 27, 1947; children—Abby (Mrs. Neil Levy), Elisa, Mark. Various retail and sales positions, 1948-63; chief research, occupational safety and health statistics Bur. Labor Statistics, Dept. Labor, Washington, 1963—; guest lectr. Georgetown U.; tech. adviser White House Conf. on Children and Youth, 1970. Served with USNR, 1943-46. Mem. Am. Econ. Assn., Indsl. Relations Research Assn. Contbr. to Dept. Labor Occupational Outlook Handbook, 1964. Home: 11629 Lockwood Dr Silver Spring MD 20904 Office: Dept Labor 441 G St NW Washington DC 20212

ROPER, JOHN LONSDALE, III, shipyard exec.; b. Norfolk, Va., Jan. 19, 1927; s. John Lonsdale and Sarah (Dryfoos) R.; B.S. in Mech. Engring., U. Va., 1949; B.S. in Naval Architectures, Mass. Inst. Tech., 1951; m. Jane Harman Preston, Sept. 29, 1951; children—John Lonsdale IV, Susan S., Sarah P., Jane H., Katherine Hayward. Asst. supt. Norfolk Shipbldg. & Drydock Corp., 1951-67, v.p., asst. treas., asst. gen. mgr., 1967-69, exec. v.p., gen. mgr., 1969—, also dir.; pres., dir. Maritime Terminals, Inc.; dir. John L. Roper Estate, Inc., Lonsdale Corp., Cruise Internat., Norfolk Fed. Savs. & Loan Assn., Botetourt Corp., United Va. Bank Internat. Commr. Norfolk Port and Indsl. Authority, 1969—. Mem. president's adv. council Va. Wesleyan Coll. Bd. dirs. Norfolk chpt. A.R.C., Jr. Achievement, Norfolk Gen. Hosp., Va. Coll. Fund, United Community Fund; trustee Norfolk Acad. Served with USCGR, 1945-46. Mem. Am. Legion (past post comdr.), Norfolk C. of C., Soc. Naval Architects and Marine Engrs. (past sect. chmn.), Sigma Xi. Episcopalian. Clubs: Norfolk Yacht and Country, Norfolk German, Virginia, Harbor (Norfolk), Princess Anne Country (Virginia Beach, Va.); Propeller of U.S. Home: 8005 Blanford Rd Norfolk VA 23505 Office: PO Box 2100 Norfolk VA 23501

ROPP, THEODORE, educator; b. Hollywood, Ill., May 22, 1911; s. Irwin and Margaret (Esh) R.; A.B. summa cum laude, Oberlin Coll., 1934; A.M., Harvard, 1935, Ph.D., 1937; m. Elizabeth S. Chapman, Sept. 8, 1937; children—Stephen C., Frederick, Paul T. Instr. history Harvard, 1937-38, vis. lectr., 1947-48; faculty Duke, 1938—, prof. history, 1959—; Ernest J. King prof. U.S. Naval War Coll., 1962-63; spl. research compulsory mil. service and mil. conscription in Brit. Commonwealth; mem. Hist. Adv. Com. to sec. of army, 1962-65; dir. policy adv. com. Hist. Evaluation and Research Orgn., 1963—, chmn. bd. 1965—. Trustee Am. Mil. Inst., 1961—, pres., 1968—. Social Sci. Research Council fellow, 1958-59. Mem. Am., So. hist. assns., Am. Assn. U. Profs. (pres. No. Carolina conf. 1959-61, mem. council 1964-67). Author: (with Harold T. Parker) Historical Background of the World Today, 1947; War in the Modern World, 1959. Contbr. Makers of Modern Strategy, 1943. Home: 302 Woodridge Dr Durham NC 27707

ROREX, MARY EVELYN, architect; b. Panhandle, Tex., Dec. 29, 1931; d. Joe and Lydia (Lill) Rorex; student West Tex. State Coll., 1949-50; B.Arch., Tex. Technol. Coll., 1995. Draftsman, designer to campus landscape architect Tex. Technol. Coll., 1953-55; draftsman, designer Parks and Recreation Dept., Lubbock, Tex., 1953-55, Atcheson, Atkinson and Cartwright, architects and engrs., Lubbock, 1955-71; partner Atcheson, Atkinson, Cartwright and Rorex, architects and engrs., Lubbock, 1971—. Registered architect, Tex. Mem. A.I.A. (corporate; Outstanding Grad. Student award Panhandle chpt. 1955, treas. 1970), Alpha Chi. Democrat. Methodist. Designs include Swisher Meml. Hosp., Tulia, Tex., Big Spring (Tex.) High Sch. Home: Route 1 Box 610 Lubbock TX 79408 Office: 1214 14th St Lubbock TX 79401

RORRER, LAWRENCE NEAL, wholesale supply co. exec.; b. Bassett, Va., July 3, 1929; s. Kyle G. and Ada (Ballies) R.; B.S., Va. Poly. Inst., 1955; m. Martha Long, Aug. 3, 1956; children—Kyle Gordon, Elisa Renee, Kathryn Neal. Agt.-audit Internal Revenue Service, 1955-57; staff auditor E.J. Sapp, C.P.A., 1957-58, William Z. Ford, C.P.A., 1958-60; sr. auditor Burlington Industries, 1960-63; C.P.A., Martinsville, Va., 1963-69; Harrison, 1969—, v.p. Clear-Bullock Elec. Co., Inc., Martinsville, 1969—, in charge Ark. operations under name Jones Supply Co., Harrison, Batesville, Russellville, Springdale, 1969—. Served with USAF, 1947-52. C.P.A., Va. Mem. Am. Inst. C.P.A.'s. Republican. Baptist. Rotarian. Club: Exchange (pres. Martinsville 1966). Home: 5 Ocoee Cove Harrison AR 72601 Office: Hwy 62-65 N Harrison AR 72601

RORSCHACH, HAROLD E., lawyer, engr.; b. Parsons, Kan., Mar. 21, 1896; s. Emil and Emma (Roush) R.; student Tulsa U., 1929-32, Okla. Sch. Bus., 1922-24; m. Margaret Hermes, Aug. 25, 1919; children—Robert Louis, Harold E., Richard G. Constrn. and cons. engr., 1916-25; admitted to Okla. bar, 1932, U.S. Supreme Ct. bar, 1935, 9th and 10th Circuit Cts. Appeal, Ct. Claims of U.S., also U.S. Tax Ct., Gen. Accounting Office; pres., dir. Panhandle Producing Co., Ajax Investment Co.; pres., gen. counsel Colonial Royalties Co., sec. Nemaha Investment Corp.; counsel Transwestern Mining Co. Registered profl. engr., Okla. Mem. Am. (life), Okla. bar assns., Nat. Rifle Assn. (endowment mem.), Am. Inst. Mining, Metall. and Petroleum Engrs. (life), Ind. Petroleum Assn. Am., Okla. Ind. Petroleum Assn. (dir., chmn. legislative com.), Mem. Christian Ch. Mason (Shriner). Contbr. articles to engring. and legal publs. Home: 2544 S Norfolk St Tulsa OK 74114 Office: Resource Sciences Center Tulsa OK also Niels Esperson Bldg Houston TX also Fisk Bldg Amarillo TX 79102

ROSAMOND, WILLIAM IRBY, architect; b. Memphis, Nov. 4, 1912; s. William Irby and Lucy May (Pope) R.; B.S., Ga. Inst. Tech., 1936; m. Lilla Pratt, Oct. 10, 1939; children—William Henry, Lilla Merrill. Asso. archtl. firms, Miss., Tenn., 1936-39; v.p. Investment Banking & Mortgage Loan Co., Memphis, 1939-41; pvt. archtl. practice, Columbus, Miss., 1939-41, 46—; pres. Columbus Reprodn. Co., Inc., Willa Corp.; v.p. 1112 Main Corp.; prin. William I. Rosamond & Assos., Columbus, Miss.; dir. First Columbus Nat. Bank, Columbus Savs. & Loan Assn. Pres. Columbus-Lowndes County Community Fund, 1963. Mem. City Planning Commn., Columbus, 1947-48. Bd. dirs., sec. bd. State YMCA. Recipient certificate of award Gulf State Regional Dist. A.I.A., 1957. Mem. A.I.A. (pres. 1957), V.F.W., Am. Legion, Newcomen Soc. N.Am., Miss. Econ. Council, Beta Theta Pi. Mason (32 deg., Shriner), Rotarian. Clubs: Columbus Country, Lowndes County Chowder and Marching, Magowah Gun and Country (Columbus). Home: 423 3d Av N Columbus MS 39701 Office: 1112 Main St Columbus MS 39701

ROSBOROUGH, ROBERT FRANKLIN, oil co. exec.; b. Marshall, Tex., Dec. 24, 1904; s. James Craig and Hazel (Bonham) R.; B.S., Tex. A. and M. U., 1926; m. Marie Watson, Aug. 5, 1933; 1 dau., Gail (Mrs. Henri A. Meis, Jr.). Owner, Rosborough & Byrne Ins. Agy., 1929-44; v.p. Marshall Fed. Savings & Loan Assn., 1955-67; owner Rosborough Oil Co., Marshall, Tex., 1952—; dir. Peoples State Bank. Pres., Community Chest, 1949; co-chmn. Bond drive, 1965; mem. Citizens Com., 1965. Trustee Marshall Meml. Hosp. Served to capt. USAAF, 1942-46. Mem. Tex. A. and M. U. Ex-Students Assn. (regional dir. 1956-58). Methodist (steward 1947—). Mason, Rotarian. Club: Marshall Country (pres. 1939). Home: 402 Miller Dr Marshall TX 75670 Office: 505 E Travis St PO Box 356 Marshall TX 75670

ROSCOE, GEORGE BOGGS, editor; b. Washington, Ia., Jan. 3, 1907; s. George C. and Mary (Boggs) R.; A.B., U. Kan., 1928; m. Anne Marie Johnson, Apr. 7, 1944. Editor, Kansas City Post, 1928; corr. U.P., Kansas City, Mo., 1928, night bur. mgr., Dallas, 1928-29, state bur. mgr., Oklahoma City, 1929-33, div. news editor, Kansas City, Mo., 1933-39, N.Y.C., 1936, day editor, Washington, 1939-41; exec. asst. N.A.M., Washington, 1941-43; editor, pub. Nat. Elec. Contractors Assn., Inc., Washington, 1945—, editor Elec. Contractor (formerly Qualified Contractor) mag., 1945—. Exec. asst. Smaller War Plants Corp., 1943-44; exec. sec. Mech. Splty. Contracting Industries, 1952-61; mem. Postmaster Gen.'s Tech. Adv. Com., 1962-72. Mem. Pres.'s Com. Employment Phys. Handicapped, 1955—; pres. Columbia Pines Citizens Assn., 1951-52. Served as lt. USNR, 1943-45. Mem. Pub. Relations Soc. Am., Am. Soc. Assn. Execs., Soc. Nat. Assn. Publs. (founding pres., life dir.), Sigma Delta Chi. Clubs: Washington Golf and Country, Jefferson Islands (Washington). Home: 6609 Rosecroft Pl Falls Church VA 22043 Office: 1730 Rhode Island Av NW Washington DC 20036

ROSE, BENJAMIN LACY, clergyman, educator; b. Fayetteville, N.C., Dec. 12, 1914; s. Charles Grandison and Irene (Lacy) R.; A.B., Davidson Coll., 1935; B.D., Union Theol. Sem. in Va., 1938, Th.M., 1950, Th.D., 1955; postgrad. Columbia, Union Theol. Sem., N.Y.C., Princeton Theol. Sem.; D.D., King Coll.; m. Anne Claiborne Thompson, June 23, 1938; children—Anne Claiborne (Mrs. J. Michael Vosler), Margaret Rockwell (Mrs. J. Robert Day), Lucy Atkinson, Benjamin Lacy. Ordained to ministry Presbyn. Ch. in U.S., 1938; pastor in Chinquapin, Bethel, Beulaville, N.C., 1938-41, Central Presbyn. Ch., Bristol, Va., 1946-55, 1st Presbyn. Ch., Wilmington, N.C., 1955-56, Lake Waccamaw (N.C.) Presbyn. Ch., 1969-70; Benjamin Rice Lacy profl. pastoral leadership and homiletics Union Theol. Sem. in Va., Richmond, 1956—, also trustee. Chmn. Bd. Nat. Ministries, Gen. Assembly Presbyn. Ch. U.S.; moderator 111th Gen. Assembly, So. Presbyn. Ch., 1971—. Past trustee Peace Coll., Raleigh, N.C., St. Andrews Presbyn. Coll., Laurinburg, N.C. Served with AUS, 1941-46; ETO; col. Res. Decorated Bronze Star medal, Legion of Merit. Mem. Assn. Sem. Profs. in Practical Fields (past sec.-treas.). Author: Confirming Your Call. Editor Questions Column, Presbyn. Survey mag. Office: Union Theological Seminary 3401 Brook Rd Richmond VA 23227*

ROSE, CHARLES ALEX, lawyer; b. Louisville, June 14, 1932; s. Hector Edward and Mary (Shepard) R.; B.A., U. Louisville, 1954, J.D., 1960; m. Patricia Lechleiter, Apr. 24, 1954; children—Marc Alexander, Craig Allen, Lorna Jean, Gordon Curtis. Admitted to Ky. bar, 1960, since practiced in Louisville; mem. firm C. A. Rose, 1960-63, Jones, Ewen, MacKenzie & Peden, 1963-65, Curtis & Rose, 1965—. Served with USAF, 1954-56. Mem. Ky., Louisville, Am. bar assns., Nat. Ry. Hist. Soc. (dir.), Pi Kappa Phi, Phi Alpha Delta, Omicron Delta Kappa. Republican. Episcopalian. Clubs: Wildwood Country; Pendennis. Home: 3019 Whiteway Louisville KY 40205 Office: Marion Taylor Bldg Louisville KY 40202

ROSE, CHARLES ALLEN, city ofcl.; b. Orlando, Fla., Oct. 5, 1930; s. Allen Cecil and Flora (Peek) R.; student Ga. Inst. Tech. Night Sch., 1955, Ga. State Coll. Bus. Adminstrn., nights 1954; m. Carolyn McKelvey, June 25, 1950; children—June, Ricky, David, Tony. With traffic engring. dept. City of Atlanta, 1950-64, City of Chattanooga, 1964-65; traffic engr. Hensley-Schmidt Inc., 1965; city coordinator City of Chattanooga, 1965-69, commr. dept. pub. works, streets and airports, 1969—. Served with USNR, 1948-49; USMCR, 1950-51. Mem. Inst. Traffic Engrs. Baptist. Mason, Kiwanian. Home: 705 Davis Av Chattanooga TN 37411 Office: City Hall Chattanooga TN 37402

ROSE, DAVID SHEPHERD, bishop; b. Nashville, Mar. 10, 1913; s. Charles Solon and Amy (Payne) R.; B.A., U. of South, 1936, B.D., 1938, D.D., 1959; D.D., Va. Episcopal Sem., 1959; m. Frances Lewis Luce, Jan. 6, 1947; 1 son, Hill Luce. Ordained to ministry P.E. Ch., 1938; rector in Memphis, 1938-39, Pensacola, Fla., 1939-42; asst. to bishop of Fla., 1946-48; rector, Corpus Christi, Tex., 1948-58; suffragan bishop Diocese of So. Va., 1958-64, bishop coadjutor 1964-71, bishop, 1971—. Trustee Va. Theol. Sem., U. of South, St. Paul's Coll., Lawrenceville, Va. Served to maj., chaplain, AUS, 1943-46. Home: 6603 Caroline St Norfolk VA 23505 Office: 600 Talbot Hall Rd Norfolk VA 23505

ROSE, HOWARD VANCE, JR., lawyer, assn. exec.; b. Nashville, Oct. 25, 1930; s. Howard Vance and Charlotte (Jackson) R.; B.B.A. U. Tex., 1952, LL.B., 1953; m. Patsy Ann Patteson, June 26, 1954; children—Amanda, Howard Vance III, Julie Gay. Admitted to Tex. bar, 1953; asso. firm Stubbeman McRae Sealy & Laughlin, 1957-62, partner, 1964-67; exec. asst. to Gov. John Connolly, Austin, Tex., 1963-64; partner firm Brown, Maroney, Rose, Baker and Barber, Austin, 1967—. Mem. Tex. Water Quality Bd., 1964-69; Tex. rep. Interstate Oil Compact Commn., 1963-68. Served with AUS, 1954-57. Mem. Phi Delta Phi, Kappa Sigma. Democrat. Presbyn. Home: 3401 Southill Circle Austin TX 78703 Office: Brown Bldg Austin TX 78701

ROSE, JAMES MCKINLEY, JR., lawyer, govt. ofcl.; b. N.Y.C., Aug. 8, 1927; s. James McKinley and Helen (Goodwin) R.; grad. Phillips Exeter Acad., 1946; A.B., Princeton, 1951; LL.B., Harvard, 1954; m. Anne Louise Bourne, Aug. 19, 1960; children—Anne Clark, Louise Barnes. Admitted to N.Y. bar, 1954; atty. Dewey, Ballantine Bushby, Palmer & Wood, N.Y.C., 1954-57; asst. U.S. atty. So. Dist. N.Y., 1957-61; legal asst. to pres. Atlantic Mut. Ins. Co., Centennial Ins. Co., N.Y.C., 1961-66, sec., 1966-68, sec., counsel, 1968-71; asst. fed. ins. adminstr. Fed. Ins. Adminstrn., U.S. Dept. Housing and Urban Devel., 1971—. Served with AUS, 1946-47. Mem. Down Town Assn. Mem. P.E. Ch. (rector's council). Republican. Club: Union. Home: 4913 Rodman St NW Washington DC 20016 Office: US Dept Housing and Urban Devel Washington DC 20410

ROSE, JOHN DANIELS, JR., tobacco co. exec.; b. Henderson, N.C., May 14, 1919; s. John Daniels and Frances (Abbitt) R.; student U. N.C., 1937; m. Anne Whitehurst Mills, June 21, 1941; children—John Daniels III, David M., Cindy Claire. Foreman, J.P. Taylor Co., Henderson, 1938, tobacco buyer, 1948-54, br. mgr., 1954-56, dist. purchasing supr., Richmond, Va., 1957-61, v.p., 1959; v.p. Southwestern Tobacco Co., 1960, Universal Leaf Tobacco Co., Inc., Richmond, 1970—; pres. Rose Gin Supply Co., Henderson, 1966—. Trustee Maria Parham Hosp., Henderson. Served to 1st lt. AUS, 1942-45. Baptist. Club: Henderson Country. Mailing Address: 327 Lakeview Dr Henderson NC 27536 Office: Hamilton St at Broad St Richmond VA 23260

ROSE, JOHN WALTER, basketball coach; b. Ripley, Tenn., Sept. 5, 1935; s. Walter M. and Helen (McIntyre) R.; B.S., Union U., 1958; M.S., George Peabody Coll., 1961; m. Sherry Linda DeLoach, Aug. 30, 1959; children—John Walter, William Mark. Head track coach, asst. basketball coach, tchr. Union U., Jackson, Tenn., 1958-63; head track coach, asst. basketball coach Ark. State U., University, 1963-69, head basketball coach, 1969—. Lectr. sports clinics. Mem. Nat. Basketball Coaches Assn., Alpha Tau Omega. Baptist. Clubs: Jonesboro Country, Exchange (Jonesboro, Ark.). Home: 203 Scott St Jonesboro AR 72467 Office: Box 816 State St University AR 72467

ROSE, WARREN LEE, investment co. exec.; b. Richmond, Va., Nov. 19, 1939; s. John Herbert and Irma Lee (Reid) R.; student U. Richmond, 1957-60; m. Barbara Marie McDonnell, Mar. 5, 1960; children— Warren Lee, Joseph Lee, Frank Lee, Barbara Marie. With Davenport & Co., mems. N.Y. Stock Exchange, Richmond, Va., 1957-63; mgr. municipal bond dept. Investment Corp. of Va., mems. N.Y. Stock Exchange, Norfolk, 1963—, v.p., sec., dir., 1968—. Mem. Bond Club Va. (dir.), Nocturnal Adoration Soc. (pres. Norfolk chpt.). Roman Catholic. Clubs: St. Pius X Mens (pres.); Virginia (dir.). Home: 1672 Sheppard Av Norfolk VA 23518 Office: 5 Main Plaza E Norfolk VA 23518

ROSE, WESLEY HERMAN, music pub.; b. Chgo., Feb. 11, 1918; s. Fred and Della (Braico) R.; B.S. in Accounting, Walton Sch. Commerce, 1939; m. Margaret Erdelyan, Nov. 16, 1940; 1 dau., Scarlett (Mrs. John Neil Brown). Accountant, Standard Oil of Ind., 1944-45; gen. mgr. Acuff-Rose Pub., Inc., Nashville, 1945-51, partner, 1951—; with Hickory Records, Inc., Nashville, 1953—, pres., 1961—; pres. Fred Rose Music, Inc., Nashville, 1961—, Acuff-Rose Far East, Inc., Nashville, 1966—, Acuff Rose Internat., Inc., Nashville, 1966—, dir. fgn. affiliated firms; dir. 1st Am. Nat. Bank. Mem. med. bd. Vanderbilt U. Named Country Music Man of Yr., Billboard mag., 1963; Metronome award Mayor Nashville, 1967. Mem. Country Music Assn. (founding mem., dir. 1958—; chmn. bd. 1959, 60, 63, v.p. 1968), A.S.C.A.P. (bd.), Nat. Music Pubs. Assn. (bd.), Nat. Assn. Rec. Arts and Scis. (nat. trustee; pres. 1971-72), Country Music Assn. (dir.), Nashville area C. of C. (gov. 1969—). Club: Friar's. Lion. Home: Belle Harbor Dr Hendersonville TN 37075 Office: 2510 Franklin Rd Nashville TN 37204

ROSE, WILLIE PERRY (MRS. EDWIN A. ROSE), educator; b. West Blocton, Ala.; d. William Walter and Alice (Woods) Perry; A.B., Samford U., 1937; M.A., U. Ala., 1958; postgrad. Columbia; m. Edwin A. Rose, Sept. 17, 1930 (dec. 1960); children—Ann Rose Humphreys (Mrs. Robert L. Humphreys), Edwin A. Tchr. pub. schs., Birmingham, Ala., 1937-57, supr. speech arts, 1957—, dir. poetry reading festival. Bd. dirs. Women's Com. of 100, Birmingham Civic Ballet, Children's Theatre; bd. dirs. Birmingham Festival Arts, v.p. edn., 1972-73; bd. dirs. Birmingham Civic Opera, Freedom Ednl. Found., Birmingham. Recipient Merit certificate A.R.C., 1938, Freedoms Found. Valley Forge award, 1964; Festival Arts Silver Bowl award in Drama, 1971. Mem. Ala. (sec.-treas. 1958-62), So. speech assns., Ala. Edn. Assn., Birmingham Women Symphony League, Birmingham Art Mus., Women's C. of C., D.A.R., Altrusa Internat. (past v.p., dir.), Delta Kappa Gamma (pres. 1967-72), Kappa Delta Pi, Kappa Delta Epsilon (pres. 1966-67). Presbyn. Author: Auditorium Activities, 1958; Story of the Slogans of the Birmingham Public Schools, 1965; co-author: Speech Arts Curriculum Guide, 1968; Speech Arts Handbook, 1969. Participant ednl. TV programs. Home: 2326 Court R Birmingham AL 35218 Office: 2015 7th Av N Brimingham AL 35202

ROSELAND, PAUL LUTHER, furniture co. exec., artist; b. Viroqua, Wis., May 11, 1917; s. Luther M. and Alida B. (Anderson) R.; student Augsburg Coll., 1935-37; B.A., U. Minn., 1941; M.F.A., U. So. Cal., 1960; postgrad. U. Mexico, 1937, U. Cal. at Los Angeles, 1959; m. Evelyn Marie Sandberg, Aug. 30, 1942; children—Nancy Lynn, Paul Luther. Exhibited one-man show at Tex. Woman's U., 1962; exhibited two man show at U. So. Cal., 1960; exhibited group shows at Ball State Coll., 1961, Beaumont Art Mus., 1961, S.W. Am. Painting and Sculpture, Okla., 1962; represented in permanent collections at City of Los Angeles, also pvt. collections; regional mgr. Knoll Internat., N.Y.C., 1945-49; mgr. Western states Herman Miller Inc., Zeeland, Mich., 1949-59; asso. prof. art Tex. Womens U., 1961-67; prof. art Tex. Technol. U., Lubbock, 1968-71; mgr. ion div. Am. Desk Mfg. Co., Temple, Tex., 1972—. Vis. prof. design Ohio U., 1967-68. Served from ensign to lt., USNR, 1942-45. Mem. Am. Inst. Interior Designers. Lutheran. Home: 2114 S 5th St Temple TX 76501

ROSEMOND, KEN, basketball coach; b. Hillsborough, N.C., Oct. 3, 1930; student Appalachian State Tchrs. Coll., Boone, N.C.; B.A., U. N.C., 1957; m. Barbara Ballenger; children—Kenneth, Kevin. Coach freshman basketball U. N.C., 1957-58, asst. to head coach, 1959-61; coach basketball U. Ga., 1965—; asst. coach U. S.C., 1958-59. Hon. chmn. Clarke County chpt. Leukemia Soc. Am.; chmn. hall of fame com. dist. 3 Nat. Assn. Basketball Coaches. Bd. dirs. Clarke County chpt. Am. Cancer Soc., Ga. Tb and Respiratory Disease Assn. Address: Athletic Dept U Ga Athens GA 30601

ROSEN, IRVING LOUIS, physician; b. New Orleans, Mar. 28, 1928; s. Ulrich and Jeanette Blanche (Cohen) R.; B.S., Tulane U., 1947, M.D., 1949; m. Carol Lise Brenner, Mar. 9, 1957; children—Elizabeth Lynn, Edith Louise. Intern, Touro Infirmary, New Orleans, 1949-50; resident, 1950-54, staff mem., charge electrocardiographic research lab., 1955-62; resident Charity Hosp., New Orleans, 1950-54; practice medicine specializing in internal medicine and cardiology, New Orleans, 1955—; partner Fisher Rabin Med. Center, New Orleans; asst. clin. prof. La. State U. Sch. Medicine. Bd. dirs. La. Heart Assn. Served to capt., M.C., USAF, 1951-52. USPHS research grantee, 1960-62. Fellow A.C.P., Am. Coll. Chest Physicians, Am. Coll. Cardiology. Jewish religion (trustee temple). Contbr. articles to profl. jours. Home: 500 Audubon St New Orleans LA 70118 Office: 4015 Jefferson Hwy New Orleans LA 70121

ROSEN, JACK, audiologist, speech pathologist; b. N.Y.C., Jan. 18, 1913; s. Louis and Mollie (Pentasky) R.; student City Coll. N.Y., 1930-36; A.B., Stanford U., 1951, M.A., 1953, Ph.D., 1962; m. Nedda N. Eisman, Dec. 1, 1945. Teaching asst. Stanford Counseling and Testing Center, 1951-52; research dir. San Francisco Hearing and Speech Center, 1952-56; dir. audiologic services Cleve. Hearing and Speech Center, 1956-59; asst. prof. Western Res. U., 1956-59; exec. dir. New Orleans Speech and Hearing Center, 1959—. Mem. profl. services bd. Am. Bds. Examiners in Speech Pathology and Audiology; speech and hearing cons. La. div. Vocational Rehab., La. Bd. Health, Delgado Vocational Rehab. Center. Bd. dirs. Cottage Sch.; mem. Workshops and Rehab. Facilities Com. Served with USNR, 1943-45. Mem. Am., La. (pres.) speech and hearing assns., Acoustical Soc. Am., A. G. Bell Assn. for Deaf, Gerontol. Soc. Am., Acad. Rehab. Audiology, Council Exceptional Children, La. Assn. Children with Learning Disabilities, New Orleans Neurol. Soc. (pres. elect). Research in galvanic skin response audiometry, auditory disorders of Rh children, speech perception of nerve-deafened, and others. Home: 6818 Canal Blvd New Orleans LA 70124 Office: 1636 Toledano St New Orleans LA 70115

ROSEN, MORRIS D., lawyer; b. Charleston, S.C., Oct. 21, 1919; B.S., Coll. of Charleston, 1942; LL.B., U. S.C., 1947. Admitted to S.C. bar, 1947; practiced in Charleston; corp. counsel City of Charleston, 1959—. Mem. S.C. Bd. Law Examiners, 1960—. Mem. Am., S.C., Charleston County (pres. 1963-64) bar assns., S.C. Municipal Attys. Assn. (pres. 1964), Wig and Robe. Office: 45 Broad St Charleston SC 29402*

ROSEN, SEYMOUR MICHAEL, govt. ofcl.; b. N.Y.C.; s. Harry Francis (stepfather) and Sonia (Sarakowska) Dwyer; A.B., Brown U., 1950; M.A., Columbia, 1952, certificate Russian Inst., 1952; m. Elizabeth Henrietta Meyer, June 6, 1950; children—Edith Vivien, Kenneth Adlai, Julie Ann. Research analyst Soviet area U.S. Dept. State, Washington, 1953-56; sr. social sci. research analyst Library of Congress, Washington, 1957-59; specialist in comparative edn. for USSR and Eastern Europe, Office Edn., U.S. Dept. Health, Edn., and Welfare, Washington, 1960—. Vis. lectr. Fgn. Service Inst., U.S. Dept. State, 1963-65, Am. U., 1963, Loyola Coll., Balt., Md., 1963, Mich. State U., 1963, McGill U., Montreal, Que., Can., 1964; chmn. U.S. delegation to study Soviet edn. system, U.S.S.R., 1963. Served with USNR, 1942-46. Mem. Am. Assn. Advancement Slavic Studies, Comparative and Internat. Edn. Soc. Author: Higher Education in the USSR, 1963; Part-time Education in the U.S.S.R.; Evening and Correspondence Study, 1965; Education and Modernization in the USSR, 1971; also articles. Editor: Soviet Edn., 1968-69. Home: 9801 Culver St Kensington MD 20795 Office: 400 Maryland Av SW Washington DC 20202

ROSENBAUM, CORNELIUS LOUIS, JR., motel mgr.; b. Meridian, Miss., Jan. 1, 1927; s. Cornelius Louis and Ruth (Tatum) R.; B.A., U. Miss., 1951; m. Lela Carolyn Williams, Oct. 17, 1954; children—Cornelius Louis, Ruth Laurie, Charles Leigh. Owner, prin. R & M Tire Co., Inc., 1951-61; mgr. Holiday Inn, 1961-64; gen. mgr. Ramada Inn, 1965— (all Meridian). Sec. treas. Lauderdale County Heart Assn., 1960-70; mem. Pres.'s Nat. Com. for Hiring Handicapped, 1970-71; chmn. Citizens' Adv. Com., Meridian, 1967-70. Mem. exec. com. Gov. Waller campaign, 1960. Bd. dirs. A.R.C., Meridian, Meridian Symphony. Served with USNR, 1944-46. Mem. Miss. Innkeepers Assn., Hotel-Motel Assn. Am., Alpha Tau Omega. Democrat. Methodist. Mason, Kiwanian. Home: 1834 36th St Meridian MS 39301 Office: PO Box 5537 Meridian MS 39301

ROSENBAUM, LAWRENCE JEROME, educator; b. Newton, Kan., Nov. 19, 1933; s. Morris and Anna (Bonus) R.; student Drake U., 1952-54; B. Music, U. Ariz., 1958; M. Music, U. Ark., 1960; m. Jeanne Maureen Vincent, Jan. 28, 1960; children—Rachel Ann, Kristin Brock. Dir. choral activities Wash. State U., Pullman, 1960-61, Auburn (Ala.) U., 1961-66, prof. music, asst. to dean Sch. Architecture and the Arts, 1966—. choral and vocal clinician, adjudicator, throughout U.S., 1960—; cons. music curricula ednl. systems Ala., 1965—; music dir., condr. Auburn Community Chorus, 1966—, First Methodist Ch., Opelika, Ala., 1965—; adviser Ala. Gov.'s Council on the Arts, 1967-68, mem., 1968-69. Trustee Opelika Arts Assn., 1967-69. Served with 25th Div. Band, AUS, 1954-56. Mem. Am. Choral Dirs. Assn., Nat. Assn. Tchrs. Singing, Music Educators Natl. Conf., Auburn Chamber Music Soc. (trustee 1971—), Phi Mu Alpha. Methodist (pres. Men's club 1970-71). Home: 229 Singleton St Auburn AL 36830

ROSENBERG, ADOLPH, editor, publisher; b. Albany, Ga., Aug. 14, 1911 Aaron Leon and Anna (Bercovicci) R.; A.B., U. Ga., 1932. Editorial staff Albany Herald, 1931-32, U.S. Daily, Washington, 1932-33, Atlanta Jour., 1934-40, Atlanta Constn., 1941-42; editor So. Israelite, Atlanta, 1940-42, 45—, pub. 1951—; pres. Star Printing Co., 1954—. Served with USAAF, 1942-45. Mem. Am. Jewish Press Assn. (treas., sec., pres. bd. dirs.), Zionist Orgn. Am., Am. Jewish Com., Jewish War Vets., Atlanta Hist. Soc., Ga. Scholastic Press Assn. (pres. 1929), Sigma Delta Chi, Phi Kappa Phi. Deocrat. Mason (32 deg.); mem. B'nai B'rith. Club: Atlanta Press. Home: 1301 Juniper St NE Atlanta GA 30309 Office: 390 Courtland St NE Atlanta GA 30303

ROSENBERG, ELIAS WILLIAM, physician, educator; b. Phila., Mar. 11, 1930; s. Jacob Engel and Rose (Grossman) R.; B.S., Franklin and Marshall Coll., 1952; M.D., U. Pa., 1956; m. Evelyn Izenberg, June 1, 1958; children—Larisa, Jessica, Jonathan. Intern, Phila. Gen. Hosp., 1956-57; resident in dermatology Mass. Gen. Hosp., Boston, 1957-59; fellow U. Miami (Fla.), 1959-60; practice medicine specializing in dermatology, Memphis, 1962-67; prof. dermatology U. Tenn. Coll. Medicine, Memphis, 1967—; cons. VA Hosp., Memphis, U.S. Naval Hosp., Memphis, 1962—. Fellow A.C.P.; mem. Soc. Investigative Dermatology, Am. Dermatol. Assn. Home: 6055 Sweetbriar Cove Memphis TN 38138

ROSENBERG, MARCUS ABRAHAM, food co. exec.; b. Bardejov, Czechoslovakia, Nov. 6, 1923; s. Salamon L. and Ann (Tannenbaum) R.; student high sch.; m. Ann Pattenheim, July 28, 1956; children—Helen, Steven, Margot, Elizabeth, Sherri. Came to U.S., 1950, naturalized, 1955. Pres., Arrow Food Products, Inc., Dallas, 1950—, Ark. Charcoal Co., Paris, Ark., 1958—. Pres., Preston Hollow Day Sch.-Akiba Acad., 1962. Club: Columbian (Dallas). Home: 7122 Currin Dr Dallas TX 75230 Office: PO Box 34489 Dallas TX 75234

ROSENBERGER, HOMER TOPE, historian, personnel tng. cons.; b. Lansdale, Pa., Mar. 23, 1908; s. Daniel Hendricks and Jennie Kulp (Markley) R.; grad. Albright Coll., 1929, LL.D., 1955; M.A., Cornell U., 1930, Ph.D., 1932; m. Gertrude Pauline Richards, July 14, 1934; children—Arley Jane (Mrs. Harry C. Furminger), Lucretia Hazel (Mrs. Patrick Robert Myers). Tchr. history Tidioute (Pa.) High School, 1930-31; tchr. Adult Night School, Lock Haven, Pa., 1933-35; prof. history and govt. Susquehanna U., summer 1933; ednl. research and adminstrn. U.S., Office Edn., 1935-42; supr. tng. U.S. Bur. Prisons, 1942-57; chief tng. br. Bur. Pub. Rds., Dept. Commerce, 1957-65; mem. steering com. Tng. Officers Conf., U.S. Govt., 1947-67, chmn., 1949-50, 55-57, chmn. com. preparation Tng. Specialists' Directory, 1948-49, exhibits com., 1947, 49; mem. com. on tng., mem. subcom. tng. policy and legislation Fed. Personnel Council, 1949-51; trustee Nat. Inst. for Reading Improvement, 1953-54; mem., vice chmn. Pa. Bd. Pvt. Corr. Schs., 1957-72, chmn., 1972—. Mem. adv. com. on career counseling U.S. Dept. Agr. Grad. Sch., 1965-66; cons. mgmt. Inst. Pub. Adminstrn., N.Y.C., 1963-64; cons. personnel mgmt. United Hosps., Newark, 1960-69, Pa. Dept. Hwys., Pa. Civil Service Commn., State N.Y. Dept. Civil Service. Organizer, moderator Rose Hill Seminars, 1963—; study tour govtl. mgmt. recommendations Western Nigeria, Africa, 1963-64. Mem. Pa. Com. on Correctional Staff Tng., 1955-57; mem. exec. com. corrections sect. United Community Services Washington, 1954-55; dir. Bur. Rehab. Nat. Capital Area, 1951—, pres., 1958-61, mem. exec. com., 1967-71; mem. Civilian Conservation Corps Safety Council, 1938-42; organizer Pa. Hist. Junto, 1942, pres. 1942-46, 54-56, exec. com., 1942—, chmn. program com., 1946-49; editorial bd. Social Studies Tchrs. Adminstrs., 1949—. Mem. Pa. Hist. Assn. (mem. governing body 1945—, chmn. membership com., 1943-45, chmn. pubs. com., 1946-48, 51-67, chmn. program com., 1947; pres. 1967-69), Pa. German Soc. (dir. 1949—, v.p. 1952-57, chmn. citation com. 1954-56, pres. 1957-69), Pa. Prison Soc. (exec. com. 1949-65, chmn. award com. 1952-64), Howard League Penal Reform (London), Columbia Hist. Soc. Washington (bd. mgrs. 1953—, 1st v.p. 1959-68, chmn. program com., chmn. exec. com., pres. 1968—. Am. Peace Soc. (exec. com. 1961-64, chmn. com. publ. monographs 1963-65), Phi Alpha Theta, Alpha Pi Omega, Phi Delta Kappa, Pi Gamma Mu. United Methodist. Club: Cosmos (hist. com.). Author: What Should We Expect of Education, 1956; Letters from Africa, 1965; The Pennsylvania Germans, 1891-1965, 1966; Adventures and Philosophy of a Pennsylvannia Dutchman, 1971; Man and Modern Society: Philosophical Essays, 1972. Editor: Pennsylvania's Contributions to the Professions, 1964; Intimate Glimpses of the Pennsylvania Germans, 1965; Pennsylvania's Contributions to Art, 1967; contbg. editor Pa. History mag., 1943—. Contbr. articles to profl. jours. and mags. Author visual edn. and guidance materials, employee tng. courses and occupational tests. occupational tests. Office: 1307 New Hampshire Av NW Washington DC 20036

ROSENBERGER, STANLEY EUGENE, educator; b. Micanopy, Fla., Jan. 2, 1923; s. Eugene David and Lillian (Bauknight) R.; B.S. in Agr., U. Fla., 1947, M.Agr., 1949, Ph.D., 1962; postdoctoral study Purdue U., 1968-69; m. Marian Alvarez, July 1, 1951; children—Carol, Jean. Mem. faculty Inst. Food and Agrl. Sci., U. Fla., Gainesville, 1949—, asso. prof. agrl. econ., 1957-65, prof., 1965—; vis. prof. Purdue U., Lafayette, Ind., 1968-69. Served with USAAF, 1942-46. U. Fla. Profl. Devel. grantee, 1968-69; recipient appreciation award Fla. Retail Grocers Assn., 1963, service award Okla. State U., 1964. Mem. Am. Agrl. Econ. Assn., Produce Marketing Assn., Food Distbn. Research Soc., Fla. Seedsman and Garden Supply Assn. (hon.), Gamma Sigma Delta, Epsilon Sigma Phi, Alpha Gamma Rho. Home: 2905 NW 14th Pl Gainesville FL 32601

ROSENBLUTH, MORTON, periodontist; b. N.Y.C., Sept. 28, 1924; s. Jacob and Eva (Bigeleissen) R.; B.A., N.Y.U., 1943, grad. program in periodontia, oral medicine, D.D.S., 1946; m. Sylvia Fradin, July 2, 1946; children—Cheryl Bonnie, Hal Glen. Intern Bellevue Hosp. N.Y.C., 1946-47, resident 1947; pvt. practice dentistry N.Y.C., 1947-59; pvt. practice periodontia North Miami Beach, Fla., 1960—; periodontist Mt. Sinai Hosp., N.Y., Polyclinic Hosp. and Med. Sch. N.Y., Mt. Sinai Hosp., Miami Beach, Fla., Parkway Gen. Hosp.; chief dental dept., North Miami Gen. Hosp.; co-chmn. periodontia sect. Dade County Research Center. Lectr. throughout U.S.A., Israel, Mexico, Rome, Teheran, Bangkok, Hong Kong, Tokyo, Honolulu, Jamaica, Paris, London, Sicily, Budapest, Berlin, Luxembourg, and others; vis. lectr. U. Tenn. Dental Coll., N.Y.U. Dental Coll.; cons. VA Hosp., Miami; mem. profl. adv. bd. North Dade Childrens Center, Hope Sch. for Mentally Retarded Children; mem. sci. adv. com. United Health Found. Chmn. Dental div. United Fund of Dade County, Combined Jewish Appeal; nat. chmn. Hebrew U. Sch. Dental Medicine; bd. dirs. Health Planning Council S. Fla. Served with AUS, 1943-44; served as capt. USAF, 1951-52. Diplomate Am. Bd. Periodontology. Fellow Am. Coll. Dentists; Mem. Am. Acad. Periodontology, Am., Fla. socs. periodontists, Am. Assn. Hosp. Dental Chiefs, Am. Acad. Dental Medicine, Am. Soc. Advancement Gen. Anesthesia in Dentistry, Am. Dental Assn., Northeastern Soc. Periodontists, Fla., Miami, Miami Beach, East Coast (sec.-treas. 1968, pres. 1971-72), North Dade (pres. 1963-64) dental socs., Fedn. Dentaire Internationale, Fla. Acad. Dental Practice Adminstrn., Alpha Omega (pres. 1967-68). Jewish religion (trustee congregation 1961-64). K.P., Mason, Kiwanian (dir. 1965). Clubs: Nocoma (pres. 1958-60), N.Y.U. Century (local chmn.). Contbr. articles to profl. jours. Home: 2030 NE 197th Terrace North Miami Beach FL 33160 Office: Profl Center 1100 NE 163d St North Miami Beach FL 33162

ROSENFELD, LOUIS, surgeon; b. Nashville, June 18, 1911; s. David and Minnie (Lowenstein) R.; B.A., Vanderbilt U., 1933, M.D., 1936; m. Helen Werthan, Mar. 7, 1949; children—Roger Werthan Cohn (foster son), Robert Louis. Intern Vanderbilt Hosp., 1936-37, asst. resident, resident surgeon, 1939-42; asst. resident surgeon Beth Israel Hosp., Boston, 1937-39; gen. practice surgery, Nashville, 1946—; prof. clin. surgery Vanderbilt Med. Sch., 1963—; cons. surgeon Thayer VA Hosp., 1947—. Pres. Davidson County unit Am. Cancer Soc., 1965—. Served with AUS, 1942-45. Decorated Bronze Star medal. Diplomate Am. Bd. Surgery. Fellow A.C.S.; mem. Nashville Surg. Soc. (past pres.), Nashville Acad. Medicine (pres. 1969), Soc. Univ. Surgeons, So. Surg. Assn., Soc. Head and Neck Surgeons, Southeastern Surg. Congress. Contbr. articles to profl. jours. Home: 4434 Tyne Blvd Nashville TN 37215 Office: 1211 21st Av S Nashville TN 37212

ROSENFIELD, SAM JULIUS, shoe retail chain exec.; b. Galveston, Tex., Sept. 15, 1919; s. Joseph Levy and Helen (Gittelsohn) R.; student U. Tex., 1937-40; m. Annette Leff, Oct. 21, 1942; children—Phyllis (Mrs. Phillip Stoup), Joseph Levy, Sandra. With Kruger Jewelry Co., Austin, Tex., 1940-57, supr., 1946-50, v.p., 1950-57; pres. Pay-Less Shoe Stores, Austin, 1957—; pres. 34 other corps.; dir. Bank Austin. Mem. Grand Jury Assn., 1966—; v.p., chmn. fund raising United Jewish Appeal, 1969-70. Bd. dirs. Hillel Found., 1963-67, Travis County Sch. for Blind, Austin, 1970. Chmn. bldg. com. Temple Beth Israel, 1971-72. Mem. Two-Ten Assn., Jewish Chatauqua Soc. Democrat. Jewish religion. Mem. B'nai B'rith. Home: 3400 Westledge Circle Austin TX 78731 Office: 2835 Real St Austin TX 78722

ROSENTHAL, HAROLD, govt. ofcl.; b. Bklyn., May 25, 1924; s. Samuel and Anne (Weinstein) R.; B.A., George Washington U., 1949; postgrad., Am. U., 1949-52; m. Maye Feuerstein, Jan. 18, 1948; children— Diana Mikel (Mrs. Francis Daniel Purcell, Jr.), Jean Sylvia. Various fed. positions, 1949-66; chief information services div. Information Center, U.S. Office Econ. Opportunity, 1966-69; asst. dir. statis. reports and analysis staff Office of Dep. Under-sec., U.S. Dept. Housing and Urban Devel., Washington, 1969—. Statis. cons. pvt. firms. Served with AUS, 1943-46. Mem. Am. Statis. Assn. Home: 6130 31st St NW Washington DC 20015 Office: 451 7th St SW Washington DC 20410

ROSENTHAL, HERBERT MARTIN, psychiatrist; b. Giessen, Germany, Jan. 22, 1913; s. Siegfried and Sophie (Mayer) R.; student Geneva U., 1932, Frankfurt U., 1933; Ph.D., Naples U., 1936; Diploma, London Imperial Coll. Sci., 1937; Ph.G., U. Basel (Switzerland), 1939, M.D., 1946; grad., Am. Inst. Psychoanalysis, 1963; m. Irmgard Helen Busenhart, Feb. 7, 1946; 1 dau., Victoria Anne. Came to U.S., 1946, naturalized, 1954. Research biochemistry Basel U., 1939-46; rotating intern Jewish Meml. Hosp., N.Y.C., 1946-47; resident Crownsville (Md.) State Hosp., 1947, Croton Manor Sanitarium, Croton-on-Hudson, N.Y., 1948, Central Islip (N.Y.) State Hosp., 1948-52; supervising psychiatrist Manhattan State Hosp., N.Y.C., 1952-54; asso. psychiatrist U. Consultation and Treatment Center, Bronx, 1952-56; adjunct psychoanalyst Karen Horney Clinic, N.Y.C., 1954—; asso. med. dir. Jamaica Center Psychotherapy, N.Y.C., 1956—; dir. Woodstock Center Psychotherapy, 1962-69; asso. attending adolescent and children's div. Roosevelt Hosp., 1967—. Pres. Fedn. Mental Health Center, Inc., 1960-65, exec. dir., 1965-67, asso. attending adolescent and childrens div., 1967—; cons. psychiatrist Gateway Industries, Kingston, N.Y.; dean Advanced Inst. Analytic Psychotherapy. Fellow Assn. Med. Group Psychoanalysts; mem. A.M.A., Am. Psychiat. Assn., Kings County Neuropsychiat. soc., Virchow Soc., World Fedn. Mental Health, Am. Acad. Psychoanalysis, Assn. Advancement Psychoanalysis. Jr. editor Ars Medici, 1940-45. Home: Roundtop Carter's Bridge Charlottesville VA 22901 Office: 30 W 60th St New York City NY 10023

ROSENTHAL, JACOB, journalist; b. Tel-Aviv, Palestine, June 30, 1935; s. Manfred and Rachel (Kaplan) R.; came to U.S., 1938, naturalized 1943; A.B., Harvard, 1956; m. Marilyn Wayne Silver, April 6, 1963; children—John, Ann. Engaged as sports reporter with the Portland (Ore.) Oregonian, 1950-57, news reporter, copy editor, 1957-59; editorial writer, reporter Portland Reporter, 1959-61; asst. dir. pub. information U.S. Dept. Justice, Washington, 1961-64, spl. asst. to atty. gen., dir. pub. information, 1964-66; spl. asst. to undersec. state, 1966-67; Kennedy fellow Harvard Inst. Politics, 1967-68; nat. urban corr. Life mag., 1968-69; urban corr. N.Y. Times, Washington, 1969—. Served with AUS, 1958. Recipient Ruder and Finn award Am. U., 1966. Democrat. Jewish religion. Gen. Ed. Nat., Adv. Commn. Civil Disorders, 1968. Home: 3704 Huntington St NW Washington DC 20015 Office: 1920 L St NW Washington DC 20036

ROSENTHAL, JULIAN BERNARD, lawyer, assn. ofcl.; b. N.Y.C., July 4, 1908; s. Alex Sidney and Katherine (Goodman) R.; student Columbia U., 1925-26; LL.B., Fordham U., 1929; m. Francis Stone, Nov. 14, 1941; children—Brian, John L. Admitted to N.Y. State bar, 1931, since practiced in N.Y.C.; now mem. firm Javits & Javits. Mem. Air Force Assn., 1945—, life mem., 1946—, sec., 1946-59, chmn. bd. dirs., 1959-60, chmn. constn. committee, 1946—, permanent bd. dirs., 1960—, treas. Iron Gate chpt., 1971-72, recipient Man of Year award, 1953. Govt. appeal agt. SSS, 1943-44. Mem. motion picture div. Democratic Nat. Com., 1940. Nat. sec. Aerospace Edn. Found.; past treas., bd. dirs. Lydia M. Morrison Found.; formerly v.p., treas., bd. dirs. Vanguard Found.; trustee, sec., chmn. bd. Aerospace Edn. Council, N.Y.C. sec., bd. dirs. Herbert and Shirley C. Rosenthal Found. Served with USAAF, 1944-45. Mem. Am. Bar Assn., N.Y. County Lawyers Assn., Assn. Bar City N.Y., Fordham U. Alumni Assn. Home: 93 Willowick Dr Decatur GA 30034 Office: 1345 Av of the Americas New York City NY 10019

ROSENTHAL, SOL, architect; b. New Orleans, July 25, 1892; s. Jonas U. and Adele (Weil) R.; B. Arch., Tulane U., 1913. Architect. Rosenthal & Grosz, 1915-17. Rosenthal & Vanos, 1919-21; pvt. practice architecture, New Orleans, 1921—; asso. Jack J. H. Kessels, Ernest W. Jones, 1939—, Charles E. Ammen on work in La., 1950—; chief architect Calliope St., Lafitte Av. housing projects, Bienville Homes, Naval Hosp., Naval Air Base, other army and navy bases, 1942-44; vis. lectr. Sch. Architecture, Tulane U., 1949—, mem. Pres.'s Adv. Com. to Sch. Architecture, 1959—; spl. cons. arch. to La. fire marshal, 1942—; arch. numerous bldgs. for schs., univs. Mem. city fire prevention com., 1944-49; mem. civil, archtl., structural engrng. br., engrng. pub. works sect., tech. div. New Orleans Civil Def., 1951. Served as sgt. U.S. Army, 1917-18. Recipient W.R. Irby prize Arts and Crafts Club competition, New Orleans, 1922. Fellow A.I.A. (emeritus fellow 1962—, mem. nat. unification com. 1947-49, pres. La. 1948-51; award New Orleans chpt. 1951, chmn. Gulf States regional judiciary com. 1957-59); also mem. of La. Architects Assn. (pres. 1945-47), Soc. Am. Mil. Engrs., Am. Cryptogram Assn., New Orleans Art Assn., Delgado Mus. Art of New Orleans Athletic. Author: Public Schools of Jefferson Parish, Louisiana A Survey Report; A Community Survey of Educational Needs (Charles R. Colbert, Asso.); also articles. Contbr. archtl. publs. U.S. and fgn. countries. Home: The Claiborne New Orleans LA 70112 Office: 2515 Canal St New Orleans LA 70119

ROSENTHAL, WARREN WEIL, restaurant exec.; b. Paducah, Ky., Sept. 20, 1923; s. Govriel L. and Lucille (Weil) R.; B.S., U. Ky., 1947; m. Betty Lee Markhoff, Aug. 30, 1946; 1 dau., Carol Lee. Sec., treas. Rubel Dry Goods Co., Paducah, Ky., 1947-48; sec., treas. Jerrico, Inc., Lexington, Ky., 1948-57, exec. v.p., 1957-63, pres., 1963—. Vice pres. Thoroughbred council Boy Scouts Am., 1971-72; mem. gov's. com. Econ. Devel. Commn., 1969-72; mem. bd. Ky. Travel Council, 1965—; pres. Lexington chpt. Jr. Achievement, 1970-71. Bd. curators Transylvania U., Lexington, Ky., 1971—. Served with Signal Corps, AUS, 1943-46. Named Man of Year, Multi-Unit Food Service Operators, 1971. Mem. Internat. Franchise Assn. (pres. 1971), Ky. Restaurant Assn. (pres. 1967-68), Ky. C. of C. (mem. bd. 1965-68). Home: 751 Cottage Grove Lexington KY 40502 Office: 1949 Nicholasville Rd Lexington KY 40503

ROSIN, MORRIS, mfg. co. pres.; b. San Antonio, Feb. 21, 1924 Berco and Leia (Dupchansky) R.; student Tex. A. and M. U., 1943, St. Mary's U., 1948-50; m. Ethel Rosenberg, Dec. 15, 1965; children—Susan, Charles, Lindsay. Sec.-treas. Bimbi Mfg. Co., 1949-67; pres. Bimbi Shoe Co. div. Athlone Industries, San Antonio, 1970—; v.p. Athlone Industries, Parsippany, N.J., 1967—; pres. Ardo Pro, San Antonio, Yoakum Bend Corp., San Antonio, 1968—; sec.-treas. R & R Corp., San Antonio, 1970—. Served with USAAF, 1942-45. Mason (32 deg., Shriner). Home: 7500 Callaghan Rd Apt 150 San Antonio TX 78229 Office: PO Box 2680 San Antonio TX 78299

ROSOFSKY, ROSE GERTRUDE, govt. ofcl.; b. Middletown, N.Y., Sept. 22, 1915; d. Jacob L. and May (Shapiro) Rosofsky; B.A. cum laude, Bklyn. Coll., 1938; postgrad. New Sch. Social Research, N.Y.C., 1939-42. Economist, Bur. Employment Security, U.S. Dept. Labor, Washington, 1942-43, Nat. War Labor Bd., Washington, 1943-46, Bur. Labor Statistics, U.S. Dept. Labor, Washington, 1946, Nat. Income div. U.S. Dept. Commerce, Washington, 1946-49; chief br. learner regulations and interpretations, wage and hour and pub. contracts U.S. Dept. Labor, Washington, 1949-62, specialist Manpower, Automation and Tng. Office, Washington 1962—. Mem. exec. bd. Govt. div. United Jewish Appeal, 1960—. Mem. Washington Assn. Workers' Edn., Indsl. Relations Research Assn., Am. Fedn. Govt. Employees, Bklyn. Coll. Alumni Assn. Home: 530 N St NW Washington DC 20024 Office: US Dept Labor Washington DC

ROSS, AUBREY C., dist. dir. Internal Revenue Service, Atlanta. Address: 275 Peachtree St NE Atlanta GA 30303*

ROSS, BILLY IRVAN, educator; b. Murray, Ky., Jan 21, 1925; s. Enoch Herman and Mary (Ward) R.; student Murray State Coll, 1942-43; B.J., U. Mo., 1948; M.A., Eastern N.M. U., 1952; Ph.D., So. Ill. U., 1964; m. Avis Riedlinger, Nov. 26, 1949; 1 son, Randall Irvan. Advt. mgr. High Plains Jour., Dodge City, Kan., 1948-51; dir. publicity Ky. Wesleyan Coll., Owensboro, 1952-55; head advt., dept. Journalism U. Houston, 1955-63; pub. partner Galena Park (Tex.) Reporter, 1955-60; prof. advt. Tex. Tech. U., Lubbock, 1964—, chmn. dept. mass communications, 1970—. Mem. fund raising com. Houston Mus. Natural Sci. and Planetarium, 1962; coordinator Don Belding Internat. Grant-in-Aid Fund, 1967—. Served with AUS, 1943-46; col. Res. Mem. Am. Acad. Advt. (nat. pres. 1960-61), Am. Marketing Assn., Assn. Edn. in Journalism, Am. Advt. Fedn., Assn. U.S. Army, Res. Officers Assn., Alpha Delta Sigma (nat. pres. 1963-67, 6th degree key 1967), Sigma Delta Chi, Kappa Tau Alpha. Methodist. Rotarian. Author: Advertising Education, 1965; (with others) Toward Professionalism in Advertising, 1969. Contbr. to profl. jours. Home: 3429 55th St Lubbock TX 79413

ROSS, CHARLES LEE, educator; b. Rogersville, Tenn., Apr. 2, 1914; s. Charles B. and Ida Lee (Wilson) R.; A.B., Tusculum Coll., 1937; M.A., Peabody Coll., 1953; Ed.D., U. Tenn., 1963; m. Nancy Evans, Aug. 3, 1939; children—Charles E., James K. Tchr., coach Bulls Gap (Tenn.) High Sch., 1937-40; tchr. Morristown (Tenn.) Jr. High Sch., 1940-42, prin., 1942-43; wholesale salesman Myers Dry Goods, Morristown, 1946-49; prin. Rose Elementary Sch., Morristown, 1949-53, Morristown High Sch., 1953-55; supt. Morristown City Schs., 1955-63; prof. ednl. adminstrn. Eastern Ky. U., Richmond, 1963—. Served with AUS, 1943-46. Mem. N.E.A., Am., Ky. assns. sch. adminstrs., Ky. Edn. Assn., Phi Delta Kappa. Presbyn. (elder). Mason (Shriner). Home: Box 240 Route 2 Berea KY 40403 Office: Eastern Ky U Richmond KY 40475

ROSS, DAVID FRANCIS, educator; b. Ann Arbor, Mich., Nov. 27, 1925; s. Francis Ellsworth and Faith (Mullett) R.; student Mich. State U., 1943, U. Mich., 1946-48; A.B., Harvard U., 1950, M.A., 1951, Ph.D., 1956; m. Elizabeth Ann Bloomstrom, June 25, 1949; children— Betsy, Eric. Instr. econs. U. P.R., 1952-54, Cuttington Coll., Suakoko, Liberia, 1964-67; economist Commonwealth of P.R., San Juan, 1954-57; asso. prof. econ. Fla. State U., 1957-59; prof. econ. Bethany Coll., 1959-61, dean faculty, 1961-64; asso. prof. econs. U. Ky., Lexington, 1967—. Ordained priest Episcopal Ch., 1968; vicar St. Andrew's Episcopal Ch., Lexington, 1968—. Chmn. bd. trustees Margaret Hall Sch. Served with AUS, 1943-46. Mem. Am. Econ. Assn., Soc. for Internat. Devel., Union for Radical Polit. Econs., Latin Am. Studies Assn., Union Radical Latin Americanists, Assn. Evolutionary Econs., Phi Beta Kappa, Omicron Delta Epsilon. Episcopalian (vicar St. Andrew's 1968—). Author: The Long Uphill Path, 1966; author (with others) Honduras: A Problem in Economic Development, 1960. Editor: Growth and Change, 1971—. Home: 565 Hill-n-Dale Rd Lexington KY 40503

ROSS, DELOY CORNELIUS, food and beverage co. exec.; b. Leesville, La., Mar. 27, 1925; s. William Cornelius and Josey (Chance) R.; grad. high sch.; m. Louise Burna Lenahan, Sept. 23, 1951; 1 son, Richard Deloy. Owner, W. C. Ross & Son, Anacoco, La., 1940-68; pres., mng. dir. Ross Continental Motor Lodge, Leesville, La., 1965—, Continental Services, Inc., Leesville, La., 1967—; pres. Ross Investment Corp., Leesville, La., 1968—; dir. Mchts. & Farmers Bank, Leesville, La. Mem. Fort Polk Community Relations Council, 1965—. Served with USMCR, 1943-45. Decorated Purple Heart (2). Mem. C. of C. Democrat. Baptist. Lion. Home: Box 83 171 Hwy Anacoco LA 71446 Office: Box 1447 Leesville LA 71446

ROSS, ELWOOD, advt. exec.; b. Bklyn., June 14, 1918; s. Louis and Josephine (DeGorter) R.; student N.Y. U., 1936-38; m. Gwendolyn Faye Durant, Jan. 15, 1964; children—Nan, Alan. Salesman, Sparkes Mfg. Co. Ltd., N.Y.C., 1946-49; owner Ross Distbrs., Dallas, 1949-53; salesman Axel Bros. Inc., Jamaica, N.Y., 1953-60; pres. Pyramid Products Inc., Dallas, 1960-64; pres. Product Promotions, Inc., Dallas, 1964—, Ross Agy., Inc., Dallas, 1967—. Sales cons., various cos.; contbg. columnist Lewisville Leader. Dir. information Town of Flower Mound, 1968-71. Served with USAAF, 1942-45. Mem. Dallas C. of C., Dallas Better Bus. Bur., Dallas Advt. League, Nat. Fedn. Ind. Bus., Dallas All Sports Assn. Clubs: Brookhaven Country, Admirals, Sportsmen's of Texas. Home: Route 3 Roanoke TX 76262 Office: Products Promotions Bldg 11338 Emerald St Dallas TX 75229

ROSS, GRADY LEE, oral surgeon; b. Earl, N.C., May 10, 1897; s. Landrum Beatty and Amanda Ola (Shuford) R.; D.D.S., Vanderbilt U., 1923; postgrad. Columbia, 1935-36; m. Robbie Lee Gillis, Oct. 7, 1925; 1 dau., Robbie Lee (Mrs. Ross Andrews). Pvt. practice oral surgery, Charlotte, N.C., 1923—. Served with USNR, World War I. Mem. Fedn. Dentaire Internationale, Am., N.C. (pres. 1958) socs. dental anesthesiology, Am., Southeastern (pres. 1967), N.C. (pres. 1959) socs. oral surgeons, Am. Dental Assn., N.C., Charlotte (pres. 1924), Second Dist. dental socs., Delta Sigma Delta, Omicron Kappa Upsilon. Baptist. Mason (32 deg., Shriner). Clubs: Goodfellows, Charlotte (N.C.) Country, Red Fez, Mecklenburg County Wild Life (pres.), Providence Road Hunting, Mecklenburg County Waterfowl (Charlotte). Home: 2138 Sherwood Av Charlotte NC 28207 Office: 1961 Randolph Rd Charlotte NC 28207

ROSS, JAMES MILLER, physician; b. Knoxville, Tenn., July 19, 1938; s. Robert Marshall and Alma (Miller) R.; B.S., East Tenn. State U., 1961; M.D., U. Tenn., 1963; m. Johnnie Sue Vest, Sept. 29, 1961; children—Ann Elizabeth, James Miller, Robert Charles. Intern Martin Army Hosp., Ft. Benning, Ga., 1964, Hickory (N.C.) Meml. Hosp., 1965, now staff mem.; gen. practice medicine, Claremont, N.C., 1966—; mem. staff Catawba Meml. Hosp., Hickory, N.C. Dir. Mar-Loc Corp., Claremont, Sun World Broadcasting Co., Orlando, Fla. Mem. Claremont Zoning Bd., 1971—. Bd. dirs. Lov-N-Care Day Care Center, Newton, N.C. Served to capt., M.C., AUS, 1964-65. Diplomate Am. Bd. Family Practice. Mem. A.M.A., N.C., Catawba County med. socs, mem.), Alpha Kappa Kappa, Phi Sigma. Republican. Methodist (steward). Club: Catawba Country (Hickory). Home: E Main St Claremont NC 28610 Office: PO Box 508 Claremont NC 28610

ROSS, JIM BUCK, state ofcl.; b. Pelahatchie, Miss., Aug. 14, 1917; s. E.N. and Emma (Jones) R.; ed. Miss. State U., Jackson Sch. Law; m. Margaret Spann, Sept. 28, 1941; children—James Hal, Mary Gwendolyn. Admitted to Miss. bar; farm equipment dealer, cotton grower Rankin County, Miss., 1945-57; mayor, Palahatchie, 1955-59; mem. Miss. Senate, 1964-68; Miss. commr. agr., Jackson, 1968—. Mem. Miss. Econ. Council. Served to 1st lt. AUS, 1944-46; PTO. Mem. Nat., So. assns. state depts. agr., Gamma Sigma Delta. Methodist. Home: Pelahatchie MS 39145 Office: PO Box 1609 Jackson MS 39205

ROSS, JOEL ELMORE, educator; b. Clinton, S.C., Sept. 23, 1922; s. Joel Elmore and Cora (Cox) R.; A.B., Yale, 1946; M.B.A., 1959, D. Bus. Adminstrn., 1961; grad. U.S. Naval War Coll., 1962; m. Carol Ann Piscitelli, Nov. 23, 1946; children—Joel Elmore, Beverly, Gregory, Mary, Susan. Commd. ensign U.S. Navy, 1946, advanced through grades to comdr., 1962; dean sch. bus. Merrimack Coll., Lowell, Mass., 1963-64; prof., chmn. mgmt. and marketing Fla. Atlantic U., Boca Raton, 1964—; pres. Gen. Edn. Systems, Boca Raton, 1967-70. Mem. Acad. Mgmt., Am., So. econ. assns., Soc. Mgmt. Information Systems. Author: Management by Information Systems, 1970; Management Systems: Concepts and Practices, 1970. Contbr. articles to profl. jours. Home: 2767 Spanish River Rd Boca Raton FL 33432 Office: Dept Bus Fla Atlantic U Boca Raton FL 33432

ROSS, JOHN JOSEPH, lawyer; b. St. Johns, N.Y., Apr. 6, 1929; s. John J. and Anna Marie (Heatherton) A.; B.S., Va. Mil. Inst., 1951; LL.B., Georgetown U., 1956; m. Marie B. Katch, July 5, 1954; children—Terence P., Brendan S., Maura A., Kara A. Admitted to D.C. bar, 1956; asso. firm Hogan & Hartson, Washington, 1956-64, partner, 1964—. Dir. Jewell Ridge Coal Sales Co., Tazewell, Va., 1965-66. Chmn. P.L.I. Equal Employment Compliance Program, N.Y.C. and Atlanta, 1972. Panelist Practising Law Inst., N.Y.C., 1966. Bd. dirs., pres. Waynewood Assn., Alexandria, Va., 1964-67; mem. personnel com. Wash. Hosp. Center, 1967. Served to maj. USMCR, 1951-54. Decorated Navy Cross, Silver Star. Mem. Am. Fed., D.C. bar assns., Am. Judicature Soc., Am. Acad. Polit. Sci., Newcomen Soc. Clubs: Army-Navy, Belle Haven Country, Metropolitan. Author: Special Problems in the Protection of Trade Secrets in Dealing with the Government, 1966. Home: 7021 Marlan Dr Alexandria VA 22307 Office: 815 Connecticut Av NW Washington DC 20006

ROSS, JOHN TURNER, JR, steel co. exec.; b. Riddlesburg, Pa., Feb. 4, 1918; s. John Turner and Mable (Barnett) R.; B.A., Franklin and Marshall Coll., 1940; postgrad. U. Pa., 1940-41; m. Jeannette Scudder, June 7, 1947; children—George Ann, Leslie Jane, Susan Turner, Elizabeth Lee. With observer corps, U.S. Steel Co., Homestead, Pa., 1947-48; pipe sales Bethlehem Steel Co. (Pa.), 1948-51; mgr. tubular sales Edgcomb Steel Co., Phila., 1951-66; exec. v.p. Johnson City Foundry & Machine Works, Inc. (Tenn.), 1966—, also gen. mgr. Bd. dirs. United Fund, Johnson City. Served to capt. USNR. Mem. Am. Soc. Metals, Nat. Foundry Assn., Am. Ordnance Assn., Am. Foundry Soc., Am. Legion, C. of C. (dir. 1968), Blue Key, Phi Kappa Sigma. Republican, Episcopalian. Mason (Shriner), Rotarian, Elk. Club: Johnson City Country. Home: 705 E Holston Av Johnson City TN 37601 Office: 920 W Walnut St Johnson City TN 37601

ROSS, JOSEPH COMER, educator; b. Tompkinsville, Ky., June 16, 1927; s. Joseph M. and Annie (Pinckley) R.; B.S., U. Ky., 1950; M.D., Vanderbilt U., 1954; m. Isabelle Nevins, June 15, 1952; children—Laura Ann, Sharon Lynn, Jennifer Jo, Mary Martha, Jefferson Arthur. Instr. Ind. U. Sch. Medicine, 1958-60, asst. prof., 1960-62, asso. prof., 1962-66, prof., 1966-70; prof., chmn. dept. medicine Med. U. S.C., 1970—, mem. cardiovascular study sect. Nat. Inst. Health, 1966-70, program-project com., 1971—. Bd. dirs. S.C. Tb & Respiratory Disease Assn. Served with AUS, 1945-47. USPHS Research fellow, 1957-59, Research grantee, 1961—. Mem. Am. Coll. Chest Physicians (gov. S.C. 1970—), A.C.P., Am. Fedn. Clin. Research (chmn. Midwest sect. 1968-69), Am. Physiol. Soc., Am. Soc. for Clin. Investigation, Assn. Am. Physicians, Assn. Profs. Medicine, Central Soc. Clin. Research, Soc. Clin. Investigation, Am., S.C. med. assns., Am. Thoracic Soc., Sigma Xi, Phi Beta Kappa, Alpha Omega Alpha. Contbr. numerous research and clin. articles to sci. jours. Home: 433 Greenbriar Lane Charleston SC 29412 Office: Med U of SC Charleston SC 29401

ROSS, JOSEPH MURPHY, city planning cons.; b. Newport News, Va., Mar. 10, 1928; s. Joseph Gerhart and Annie (Murphy) R.; B.C.E., Ga. Inst. Tech., 1953; m. Evelyn Marie Williford, Feb. 26, 1949. Trainee plant operations Texaco, Inc., Atlanta, 1953-55; with Harland Bartholomew & Assos., Atlanta, 1955—. asso. partner, 1961—. Resident planner, Charlottesville, Va., 1956-58, Birmingham, 1958-61. Served with USMC, 1946-48, 1950-51. Mem. Am. Inst. Planners, Am. Soc. C.E. Home: 4047 Shannon Mill Rd NE Atlanta GA 30319 Office: 1700 Commerce Dr NW Atlanta GA 30318

ROSS, LEDYARD ELREE, orthodontist; b. Stokes, N.C., July 12, 1925; s. Ledyard Elree and Mildred Celia (Dupree) R.; Jr. Accountant, Hardbargers Bus. Coll., 1946; B.S., East Carolina Coll., 1949; D.D.S., Northwestern U., 1953; M.S. in Orthodontics, U. N.C., 1959; m. Elsie Martiel Congleton, Aug. 1, 1964; children— Dennis Paul, Kathryn Lynn, Jody Martiel, Cindy Beth. Gen. practice dentistry, Ayden, N.C., 1953-54, Greenville, N.C., 1954-57; practice orthodontics, Greenville, 1959—; v.p. Jaro Corp., New Bern, N.C., 1966—; dir. Urban Builders, Norfolk, Va. Served with USMCR, 1943-46. Mem. Am. Dental Assn., N.C., 5th Dist., Pitt and Beaufort County dental socs., Am. Assn. Orthodontics, N.C. Orthodontic Soc., Eastern N.C. Orthodontic Study Club (pres. 1963-64), Begg Orthodontic Soc. Methodist (dir. 1961-62, 70-72). Mason, Elk, Kiwanian. Home: 217 Churchill Dr Greenville NC 27834 Office: 602 E 10th St Greenville NC 27834

ROSS, MARGARET DEANE SMITH (MRS. EDWIN LEE ROSS), historian, newspaper columnist; b. North Little Rock, Ark., Aug. 24, 1922; d. Cecil Byron and Myrtle (Gibson) Smith; student Ark. Poly. Coll., 1939-41, U. Ark., 1941-42; m. Edwin Lee Ross, Sept. 7, 1942 (dec. July 1944); 1 son, Edwin Lee. Research asst. Ark. History Commn., Little Rock, 1954-57; curator J. N. Heiskell Collection of Arkansiana, Ark. Gazette, Little Rock, 1957—, columnist Chronicles of Ark., 1958-68. Mem. adv. com. Quapaw Quarter Assn. Recipient Award of Merit, Am. Assn. State and Local History, 1965, 71. Mem. Ark. Hist. Assn. (asso. editor Ark. Hist. Quar. 1953—, dir. 1968—), Pulaski County Hist. Soc. (editor Rev. 1953-57), Ark. Pioneers Assn., Delta Gamma. Baptist. Club: Ark. Press. Author: Arkansas Gazette: The Early Years 1819-1866, 1969. Home: 1600 Fair Park Blvd Little Rock AR 72204 Office: Ark Gazette Box 1821 Little Rock AR 72203

ROSS, NATHANIEL, city ofcl.; b. N.Y.C., Jan. 28, 1918; s. Herman and Henrietta (Krausse) R.; B.B.A., U. Cin., 1949; M.B.A., U. Chgo., 1952; m. Louise Katherine Couch, Nov. 13, 1943; children—Sandra (Mrs. Johnnie Lee Webb), Kevin T. Accounting supr. Kroger Co., Chgo., 1949-52, budget mgr., Cin., 1952-53, div. accountant, Roanoke, Va., 1953-56, treas.-controller, 1956-59, grocery merchandiser, Shreveport, La., 1959-61; budget dir. City of Tulsa, 1962-63; finance dir. Oklahoma City, 1964-71, city mgr., 1971—. Sec., Richardson Endowment Fund, 1966—; trustee Oklahoma City Municipal Improvement Authority, Oklahoma City Airport Trust, Oklahoma City Devel. Trust, Central Okla. Transp. and Parking Authority. Served from 2d lt. to capt., AUS, 1941-46; ETO. Mem. Municipal Finance Officers Assn. (state chmn. 1967-71), Internat. City Mgmt. Assn., Okla. Zool. Soc., Phi Eta Sigma, Beta Gamma Sigma, Alpha Kappa Psi. Presbyn. (elder 1960, 69-72). Mason (32 deg., Shriner), Rotarian, Kiwanian. Home: 4609 NW 31st Pl Oklahoma City OK 73122 Office: City Hall 200 N Walker St Oklahoma City OK 73102

ROSS, RONALD DUDLEY, editor; b. Fargo, N.D., Apr. 19, 1921; s. Earle Dudley and Ethel (Newbecker) R.; B.S., Ia. State U., 1943; m. Dorothy Ann Klein, Dec. 24, 1943; children—Ronald Dudley Jr., Elizabeth (Mrs. David Monroe Miller), Karl M. News editor, staff writer Sci. Service, Washington, 1946-49; Washington corr. McGraw-Hill Washington bur. Elec. World, 1949-51; mng. editor Pub. Power, Am. Pub. Power Assn., Washington, 1951-65, editor, 1965—. Served with USNR, 1943-46. Mem. Soc. Nat. Assn. Publs. (pres. 1968-69), Nat. Assn. Sci. Writers, Am. Soc. Bus. Press Editors, Sigma Delta Chi. Democrat. Unitarian. Club: Nat. Press. Home: 1201 N Evergreen St Arlington VA 22205 Office: 2600 Virginia Av NW Washington DC 20037

ROSS, SANFORD G., lawyer; b. St. Louis, Oct. 9, 1931; B.A., Washington U., St. Louis, 1953; LL.B., Harvard, 1956. Admitted to Cal. bar, 1957, N.Y. State bar, 1959, D.C. bar, 1969; teaching fellow, research asst. internat. program in taxation Harvard Law Sch., 1957-58; with Office Tax Legislative Council, Treasury Dept., 1961-63, asst. tax legislative counsel, 1962-63; prof. law N.Y.U., N.Y.C., 1963-69, adj. prof., 1969—; mem. firm Caplin & Drysdale, Washington; staff asst. White House, 1967-68; gen. counsel Dept. Transp., 1968-69. Exec. dir. President's Nat. Adv. Panel on Ins. in Riot-Affected Areas, Nat. Adv. Commn. on Civil Disorders, 1967-68; cons. UN, 1970—. Mem. Am., Fed. bar assns., State Bar Cal., Order of Artus, Phi Beta Kappa, Phi Eta Sigma, Phi Sigma Alpha. Editor: Harvard Law Rev., 1954-56. Home: 2914 33d Pl NW Washington DC 20008 Office: Caplin and Drysdale 1101 17th St NW Washington DC 20036*

ROSS, THOMAS BERNARD, newspaper corr.; b. N.Y.C., Sept. 2, 1929; s. Henry M. and Evelyn (Timothy) R.; B.A., Yale, 1951; postgrad. (Nieman fellow) Harvard, 1963-64; m. Gunilla Ekstrand, Nov. 2, 1963; children—Maria, Anne, Kristina. Reporter, Internat. News Service, Atlanta 1955-56, Hartford, Conn., 1956-57, Washington, 1957-58; reporter U.P.I., Washington, 1958; reporter Chgo. Sun-Times, Washington, 1958-68, fgn. corr., Beirut, Lebanon, 1968-69, Paris, France, 1969-70, Washington bur. chief, 1970—. Served to lt. (j.g.) USNR, 1951-54. Recipient Marshall Field award, 1961, 71. Roman Catholic. Author: (with David Wise) The U-2 Affair, 1962; The Invisible Government, 1964; The Espionage Establishment, 1967. Home: 2911 P St NW Washington DC 20007 Office: 1366 Nat Press Bldg Washington DC 20004

ROSS, THOMAS LLEWELLYN, cardiologist; b. Pretoria, Ga., Dec. 31, 1907; s. Thomas L. and Helen (Roberts) R.; B.S., Mercer U., 1926; M.D., Emory U., 1930; m. Rachel Johnson, Aug. 29, 1936; children—Susan (Mrs. Jerry Sawyer), Helen (Mrs. Julian Tolbert). Intern, Cin. Gen. Hosp., 1930-31, resident, 1931-33; practice medicine specializing in cardiology, Macon, Ga., 1935-69; chief cardiology Macon Hosp., 1946-69; asso. dir. Ga. Regional Med. Program, Macon, 1969—; mem. staffs Macon, Middle Ga. hosps. Cons. cardiology Dublin U., 1949-69; founder Macon Heart Clinic, 1948, chief clinic, 1948-69. Served to lt. col. M.C., AUS, 1942-46. Recipient Citizenship award Am. Legion, 1959, Award of Merit Am. Heart Assn., 1968. Diplomate Am. Bd. Internal Medicine. Fellow A.C.P. mem. Am. (dir. 1962-68), Ga. (pres. 1952-53, chmn. bd. dirs. 1957-58) heart assns., A.M.A., Med. Assn. Ga. Rotarian (pres. 1965). Home: 944 Nottingham Dr Macon GA 31201 Office: 707 Pine St Macon GA 31201

ROSSELLO, JUAN ANTONIO, educator; b. San Juan, P.R., Dec. 30, 1913; s. Pedro J. and Jacobina (Matanzo) R.; M.D., U. Md., 1938; m. Iris Gonzalez, Aug. 8, 1942; children—Pedro, Jacqueline, Jeannette, Ivette. Intern, Presbyn. Hosp., 1938-39; prof. psychiatry, head dept. U. P.R. Sch. Medicine, San Juan, 1958—; supt. State Psychiatric Hosp., San Juan, 1959—; dir. mental health program, P.R., 1960-69, sub. sec. mental health, 1969—; cons. Caribbean Fedn. Mental Health; Mem. Nat. Training Labs., Washington. Served with USPHS, 1944-45. Mem. P.R. Med. Assn., Pan Am. Med. Assn. (council sect. psychiatry), Assn. So. Profs. Psychiatry, Am. Psychiatric Assn. Author: Tratado General de Psiquiatria, 1962; Psicologia de las Organizaciones, 1967; Manuel de Psiquiatria Social, 1968; also papers on group dynamics. Editor: Jour. Psychiatry and Mental Health, 1969—. Address: GPO Box 61 San Juan PR 00936

ROSSIDES, EUGENE TELEMACHUS, lawyer, govt. ofcl.; b. Bklyn., Oct. 23, 1927; s. Telemachus and Anna (Maravel) R.; A.B., Columbia, 1949, LL.B., 1952; m. Elinor Burcham, Apr. 1, 1950 (div. Sept. 1956); 1 dau., Gale Daphne; m. 2d, Aphrodite Macotsin, Dec. 30, 1961; children— Michael Telemachus, Alexander Demetrius, Eleni Ariadne. Admitted to D.C. bar, 1953, N.Y. State bar, 1954; criminal law investigator N.Y. County Dist. Atty.'s Office, N.Y.C., 1952; asso. firm Royall, Koegel & Welis, and predecessors, N.Y.C., 1954-56, 61-65, partner, 1966-69; asst. atty. gen. State of N.Y., N.Y.C., 1956-58; spl. asst. to undersec. U.S. Treasury Dept., Washington, 1958-61; asst. sec. treasury, 1969—. Served with USAF, 1952-53. Mem. Am., Fed., N.Y. State bar assns., Nat. Football Found. (N.Y.C. chpt.), Am. Polit. Sci. Assn., N.Y. Dist. Attys. Assn., Cyprus Fedn. Am., Columbia Coll. (dir.), Columbia Law Sch. alumni assns. Clubs: Columbia University, Hellenic University, Touchdown (dir.), Columbia Varsity (N.Y.C.). Home: 6120 32d St NW Washington DC 20015 Office: Treasury Dept Washington DC 20220

ROST, DUANE DELBERT, business exec.; b. Hartley, Ia., Mar. 13, 1921; s. Alfred C. and Emma (Centner) R.; student Yale, 1943; B.S. in Econs., Wharton Sch., U. Pa., 1947; student Harvard Bus. Sch., 1945; m. Patricia J. Brooks, Dec. 6, 1945; children—Wendy, Mark, Randall. With Chicopee Mfg. Corp., New Brunswick, N.J., 1947-67, asst. controller, 1955-58, controller, 1958-64, treas., 1964-65, financial v.p., 1965-67, also dir.; v.p. accounting and adminstrn. Dresser Industries, Inc., Dallas, 1967—. Served with USCGR, 1942-44, to ensign USNR, 1944-46. Methodist. Home: 7317 Spring Valley Rd Dallas TX 75240 Office: Republic Nat Bank Bldg Dallas TX 75201

ROSTHAL, ROBERT BERNARD, educator; b. N.Y.C., Oct. 16, 1923; s. James and Antoinette (Limansky) R.; B.A., U. Wis., 1944; diploma Washington and Jefferson Coll., 1944; postgrad. U. Paris, 1948-51, Columbia, 1953-54; M.A., U. Chgo., 1954; Ph.D. (fellow), U. Mich., 1959; m. Marianne Heineberg, Mar. 8, 1952; 1 son, Andrew. Instr. N.Y.U., 1953-54, Bklyn. Coll., 1954-55, U. Mich., 1958-59; vis. lectr. Ohio State U., Columbus, 1959-60; asst. prof. Kenyon Coll., Gambier, O., 1960-61; asst. prof. U. N.C., Greensboro, 1961-64, asso. prof. philosophy, 1965—, head dept. philosophy, 1969—. Committeeman, N.C. Democratic Com., 1970—. Served with AUS, 1943-46; ETO. Decorated Purple Heart. Ford Found. grantee, 1964-65; N.C. research grantee, 1965. Mem. Am. Philos. Assn., Am. Assn. U. Profs., So. Assn. Philosophy and Psychology, Metaphys. Soc. Am., Am. Soc. Aesthetics. Home: 4810 Starmount Dr Greensboro NC 27410

ROTERUS, VICTOR, govt. ofcl.; b. Cloquet, Minn., July 20, 1907; s. Julius and Aleina (Somerin) R.; Ph.B., U. Chgo., 1930, M.S., 1931; m. Florence Ayres, Sept. 8, 1934; children—Julie, Mary (Mrs. John M. Ankele). Instr. geography Wash. State Coll., Pullman, 1931-35; regional planner TVA, Knoxville, Tenn., 1936-40; planning technician Nat. Resources Planning Bd., Washington, 1940-42; chief economist WPB, Washington, 1942-44; chief research sect. Cin. Planning Commn., 1944-46; resident dir. Social Sci. Research project U. Mich., Ann Arbor, 1946-48; with Dept. Commerce, Washington, 1948-67, dir. Office Area Devel., 1954-61, asst. dir. Area Redevel. Adminstrn., Econ. Devel. Adminstrn., 1961-67; spl. asst. Upper Great Lakes Regional Commn., Washington, 1967-69, cons., 1969—. Cons. prof. U. Md. at College Park, 1951-65; vis. prof. U. Ariz., Tucson, 1970-72. Recipient Merit citation Nat. Civil Service League, 1956. Mem. Assn. Am. Geographers (Meritorious Contbn. award, 1956). Author: Economy of the Cincinnati Metropolitan Area, 1946; Economic Development Atlas: Recent Changes in Regions and States, 1950. Home: 5611 Overlea Rd Washington DC 20016 Office: US Dept Commerce Washington DC 20230

ROTH, JACK, broadcasting co. exec.; b. San Antonio, July 17, 1926; s. Eugene J. and Dorothy (Schaffer) R.; B.S., Trinity U., 1952; m. LaVerne Whitehead, Dec. 14, 1948; children—John, Nancy, Lee, Julie. Pres., Mission Broadcasting Co., San Antonio, 1959—; pres., owner Mission Central Co., stas. KONO and KITY-FM, San Antonio, 1967—, Mission East Co., stas. WWOK and WIGL-FM, Miami, Fla., 1966—; pres. Mission Broadcasting Co., Nev., 1967—, Mission Advt. Co., San Antonio, 1960—, Fononews, Inc. of Tex., San Antonio, 1956—, Mission Charlotte Co. (N.C.), sta. WAME, 1968—, Mission Denver Co., sta. KERE, 1971—. Bd. dirs. Alamo Area council Boy Scouts Am., A.R.C. Served with USNR, 1944-46. Mem. Tex. Assn. Broadcasters (pres. 1963), San Antonio Zool. Soc. (dir.). Home: 136 Cas-Hills St San Antonio TX 78213 Office: PO Box 2338 San Antonio TX 78298

ROTH, ROBERT, journalist; b. N.Y.C., Nov. 11, 1901; s. Abraham Lincoln and Sophie (Hafer) R.; student Amherst Coll., 1919-21; m. Katherine Lennehan, July 22, 1928 (dec. July 1958), m. 2d, Edith R. Brill, Oct. 16, 1959. Reporter various newspapers, 1925-33; editor Mt. Vernon (N.Y.) Daily Argus, 1934-42; reporter Phila. Record, 1943-44, Washington corr., 1945-47; reporter, spl. writer Phila. Bull., 1947-49, chief Washington corr., 1954—. Mem. Sigma Delta Chi. Clubs: Nat. Press, Cosmos, Gridiron (Washington). Home: 2500 Q St NW Washington DC 20007 Office: Nat Press Bldg Washington DC 20004

ROTH, ROBERT HAROLD, educator; b. New Castle, Ind., Aug. 20, 1941; s. Robert Harold and Genevieve (Leavell) R.; A.B., Purdue U., 1963; M.A., Duke, 1965, Ph.D., 1967. Asst. prof. sociology Ohio State U., Columbus, 1967-71, dir. lab. studies sect. Disaster Research Center, 1967-71; asst. prof. Am. U., 1971—. Nat. Def. Edn. Act fellow, 1964-66; James B. Duke fellow, 1963-64. Mem. Am. Sociol. Assn., Am. Assn. U. Profs., So. Sociol. Soc., English-Speaking Union of Commonwealth. Office: Dept Sociology Am U Washington DC 20016

ROTHBARD, EDWARD, distbg. co. exec.; b. Camden, N.J., Apr. 20, 1909; s. Maurice Edward and Hanah (Elster) R.; grad. high sch.; m. Mary E. Cooper, Apr. 10, 1937; children—Lila J., Robert J. Pres., Liro Textile Co., Inc., Albany, N.Y., 1932—; pres. Am. Foam Rubber Distbg., Inc., Hialeah, Fla., 1960—, Am. Factors Co., Hialeah, 1960—; dir. Fidelity Nat. Bank, Miami. Chmn. Bonds for Israel campaign, 1953-56. Bd. dirs. Jewish Family and Childs Welfare, Miami. Served with USNR, 1967. Mem. chambers commerce Kings Bay, Sky Lake. Elk. Home: 800 Sky Lake Dr N North Miami Beach FL 33162 Office: 630 W 20th St Hialeah FL 33010

ROTHERMEL, JAMES DOUGLAS, educator; b. Burton, Tex., Aug. 20, 1918; s. Bailleux Edvin and Nathalie (Ponfick) R.; B.S., S.W. Tex. State Coll., 1949, M.Ed., 1952; student Blinn Coll., 1945-47, U. Houston, 1965—; m. Dorothy Ann Hodde, Aug. 24, 1947; children—James Douglas, Donald Henry. Constrn. painter, Corpus Christi, Tex., 1938-42; instr. bus. administrn. Brenham (Tex.) Ind. Sch. Dist., 1949-52; prin. high sch. Schulenburg (Tex.) Ind. Sch. Dist., 1952-57. Ganado (Tex.) Ind. Sch. Dist., 1957-64; instr., chmn. dept. bus. adminstrn. San Jacinto Coll., Pasadena, Tex., 1964—. Cons. small businessmen Brenham and Schulenburg, Tex. Served with USNR, 1942-45. Mem. Tex. State Tchrs. Assn., Tex. Jr. Coll. Tchrs. Assn., Am. Bus. Law Assn., Am. Legion (dist. comdr. 1961-63), Tex. (pres. dist IV 1970-71), Houston bus. edn. assns. Lutheran. Home: 1709 Blackburn Dr Pasadena TX 77502

ROTHFIELD, IRA, dentist; b. N.Y.C., Feb. 22, 1931; s. Leonard Edward and Bess Elizabeth (Rifkin) R.; B.S., Queens Coll., 1952; D.D.S., N.Y.U., 1956; m. Wendy Reiss, Aug. 21, 1955; children—Robert Eric, Elizabeth Anne. Pvt. practice dentistry, Hollywood, Fla., 1958—. Pres., Rothfield Enterprises, Inc., 1967—. Mem. exec. bd. Am. Jewish Com., Miami, 1966-67, 70-72, Jewish Family and Children's Service, Miami, 1967-68. Served to capt., Dental Corps, AUS, 1956-58. Mem. Am., Fla. dental assns., East Coast Dist., North Dade, Greater Hollywood dental socs., Alpha Epsilon Pi, Alpha Omega. Mason (32 deg.). Clubs: Mens - Greater Miami Philharmonic Society; Jockey (Miami). Home: 2080 NE 197 Terrace North Miami Beach FL 33162 Office: 6099 Hollywood Blvd Hollywood FL 33024

ROTHMAN, SAM, govt. ofcl.; b. N.Y.C., Feb. 1, 1920; s. Jacob and Sarah (Moveretz) R.; B.S., L.I. U., 1943; M.A., Am. U., 1954, Ph.D., 1959; m. Florence Rosen, Dec. 11, 1944; children—Arlene Linda, Sandra Ruth. Chemist, Nat. Bur. Standards, Washington, 1946-55; research and devel. adminstr. Navy Dept., Washington, 1955—. Adj. prof. Am. U. Served with USAAF, 1943-46. Mem. Am. Chem. Soc., A.A.A.S. Home: 613 Hyde Rd Silver Spring MD 20902 Office: Crystal Plaza 6 Arlington VA

ROTHROCK, JOHN A., JR, county judge; b., 1924; B.S., Northwestern U.; LL.B., George Washington U. Admitted to Va. bar, 1954; now judge Fairfax County, Va. Address: County Courthouse Fairfax VA 22030*

ROTHSCHILD, DAVID, II, textile co. exec.; b. Columbus, Ga., Jan. 10, 1921; s. Irwin Bernard and Aleen Moore (Samuels) R.; B.S. in Commerce, U. Va., 1941; J.D., Yale, 1947; m. Barbara Galeski, Dec. 16, 1949; children—Aleen, David III, Walter Galeski, John Lowenberg. Admitted to Ga. bar, 1948; practice in Columbus, 1948; v.p. sales David Rothschild Co., High Point, N.C., 1949-55, exec. v.p., Columbus, 1956—; dir. 1st Nat. Bank, Columbus; v.p. Eagle Broadcasting Co., Sta. WYEA-TV, Columbus, 1969—; pres. David Realty Co., Columbus, 1962—. Mem. exec. com. Columbus Mus. Arts and Crafts, 1970—. Bd. dirs. Musuogee County Sch. Dist., United Givers. Served to capt. AUS, World War II; ETO. Decorated Bronze Star medal. Mem. Ga. Sch. Bd. Assn. (dir. 3d dist. 1970—), State Bar Ga. Jewish religion. Mason (Shriner), Rotarian. Clubs: Green Island Country, Harmony (Columbus). Home: 2134 Springdale Dr Columbus GA 31906 Office: 500 11th St Columbus GA 31902

ROTHSCHILD, EDWARD A., lawyer; b. Chgo., Mar. 8, 1926; s. Emanuel A. and Mina (Straus) R.; B.S., U. Louisville, 1949; LL.B., Jefferson Sch. Law, 1952; m. Frances Hoffman, Sept. 23, 1954; children—Diane, Peter, Nancy, Edward A. II. Admitted to Ky. bar, 1952; mem. firm Washer, Kaplan, Rothschild & Aberson, Louisville, 1962—; sec. Western Dry Wall Corp., Louisville, 1969—, Ad Mailing Service, Inc.; dir. Staples Advt., Inc., Southland Electric Co.; prof. fed. estate and gift tax law U. Louisville, part-time 1971-72. Bd. dirs. Jewish Hosp. Assn.; pres. Jewish Vocational Service, Louisville, 1970-71; trustee March of Dimes. Served with USNR, 1944-46; CBI, PTO. C.P.A., Ky. Mem. Louisville, Ky., Am. bar assns., Ky. Soc. C.P.A.'s. Jewish religion (past dir. temple). Rotarian (pres.). Clubs: Hi Twelve, Standard Country (Louisville). Home: 2218 Wynnewood Circle Louisville KY 40222 Office: ME Taylor Bldg Louisville KY 40202

ROTHSCHILD, LOUIS, JR., journalist; b. Washington, Feb. 16, 1930; s. Louis and Dorothy (Cohen) R.; B.S., M.S. Medill Sch. Journalism Northwestern U.; m. Sonia Steinberg, June 23, 1963; children— Karen Lynn, Alan Louis. With UPI, Washington, 1952-55, F-D-C Reports, Inc., Washington, 1955-59, Food Chem. News Washington, 1959—. Mem. Inst. Food Technologists, Ind. Newsletters Assn., Sigma Delta Chi. Club: National Press (Washington). Home: 11609 Milbern Dr Rockville MD 20854 Office: Food Chem News Warner Bldg Washington DC 20004

ROTHSCHILD, LOUIS SAMUEL, bus. exec.; b. Leavenworth, Kan., Mar. 29, 1900; s. Louis Philip and Nora (Westheimer) R.; Ph.B., Yale, 1920; m. Emily Bettman, Oct. 7, 1929. With Rothschild & Sons, Inc., Kansas City, Mo. and Oklahoma City, 1920-56, sec., 1931-34, v.p., 1934-42, pres., 1942-55; chmn. bd. Inland Waterways Corp., 1953-59; chmn. Fed. Maritime Bd., maritime adminstr., U.S. Dept. Commerce, 1953-55, under sec. of commerce for transp., 1955-58; pres. dir. Transport Equities Corp., 1958-61, 65—; pres., dir. Intermediate Credit Corp., 1962-65; pres., dir. Standard R.E. Improvement Co., 1965—; dir. 1st Nat. Employee Benefit Fund, Mech. Enterprises, Inc. U.S. delegate NATO Planning Bd. for Ocean Shipping, 1953. Chmn. Air Coordinating Com., 1955-58; mem. commn. govt. security, 1955-56; U.S. del. to ILO conf., 1958. Mem. city planning common., Kansas City, Mo., 1937-53, chmn., 1946-53; dir. Community Studies, Inc.; chmn. Menorah Found. for Med. Research; dir. Midwest Research Inst., Kansas City, Mo.; trustee William Allen White Found. Served with USN, 1918-19. Home: 4000 Massachusetts Av Washington DC Office: 1629 K St NW Washington DC

ROTROFF, ROBERT WILLIAM, banker; b. Tipton, Ind., Apr. 8, 1922; s. Louis Melvin and Mildred (Pangborn) R.; student Ball State U., 1940-42, Tex. A. and M. U., 1942-43; m. Bettie Eileen Maxwell, Apr. 23, 1943; 1 son, Stephen Robert. Mgr. Franklin Security Co., Muncie, Ind., 1945-51; asst. credit mgr. Cleve. Trust Co., 1951-56; asst. cashier Irwin Union Bank & Trust Co., Columbus, Ind., 1956-60; sr. v.p. Alexandria Nat. Bank (Va.), 1960—; dir. Helms Concrete Pipe Co., Sunset Devel. Co. (both Alexandria). Bd. dirs. Alexandria Hosp. Served with USAAF, 1942-45. Mem. Robert Morris Assos., Alexandria C. of C. (pres. 1967). Republican. Methodist. Rotarian. Mailing Address: 1211 Villomoy Blvd Alexandria VA 22307 Office: 330 N Washington St Alexandria VA 22313

ROUBEY, LESTER WALTER, clergyman, educator; b. Balt., Feb. 11, 1915; s. Abraham and Sara (Cordish) R.; A.M., Johns Hopkins, 1936, Ph.D., 1938; M.H.L. and Rabbi, Hebrew Union Coll., 1947, D.D. (hon.), 1972; m. Charlotte Helen Stern, June 1, 1947; 1 son, Robert Arthur Stern. Rabbi, 1947; rabbi, Lancaster, Pa., 1947-53, Reading Pa., 1954-64, East Orange, N.J., 1964-66, Baton Rouge, 1966; adj. prof. religion Franklin and Marshall Coll., Lancaster, 1951-53; asso. prof. Romance langs. Kutztown (Pa.) State Coll., 1961-64; lectr. Romance langs. La. State U., Baton Rouge, 1966-70, asso. prof., 1970—. Mem. civic com., Lancaster, 1950-53; mem. adv. bd. Baton Rouge Gen. Hosp., 1967—; mem. religious com. reading round table Nat. Conf. Christians and Jews; chmn. reading com. Am. Jewish Tercentenary, 1954-55; bd. dirs. A.R.C., 1968—. Mem. Central Conf. Am. Rabbis, Hebrew Union Coll.-Jewish Inst. Religion Alumni Assn. (trustee 1953-56), Am. Assn. Tchrs. French, Am. Assn. Tchrs. Italian, Am. Assn. U. Profs., Modern Lang. Assn., Am. Council Teaching Fgn. Langs., South Central Modern Lang. Assn. (chmn. Italian sect. 1969), Phi Sigma Iota. Mason (32 deg. Shriner), Rotarian. Club: Baton Rouge Country Producer, conductor series of TV worship programs, Lancaster, 1951-53. Home: 3212 McConnell Dr Baton Rouge LA 70809 Office: 3354 Kleinert Av Baton Rouge LA 70806 also Dept Fgn Langs La State U Baton Rouge LA 70803

ROUGEOU, CLYDE LEE, univ. pres.; b. Lecompte, La., Sept. 22, 1915; s. Benjamin Moise and Rhoda (Warner) R.; B.S., U. Southwestern La., 1936; M.S., Tex. A. and M. U., 1937; Ph.D., U. Minn., 1949; m. Ruth Houston, Aug. 20, 1940; children—Patricia Eileen (Mrs. J.W. Plauche), Marie Louise (Mrs. George Bennett), Benjamin Charles, Clyde Lee, Ruth Ann (Mrs. Richard Hargett), Randolph Warner, Carol Jeanne, Elizabeth Antoinette, Nancy Jo. Instr. dairy husbandry U. Southwestern La., Lafayette, 1937-41, asst. prof., 1943-44, prof. and head dept. dairy husbandry, 1944-65, v.p. in charge edn. center, 1965-66, pres., 1966—. Dir. Home Savs. & Loan Assn., Lafayette, La. Gulf Coast Oil Expn., Lafayette. Bd. dirs. La. Council on Econ. Edn., finance chmn., 1967-70; 3d v.p. Bayou council Girl Scouts U.S.A.; mem. Council for Devel. French in La., 1968—. Trustee Gulf South Research Inst., Baton Rouge, 1966—, mem. council, 1966—; bd. dirs. Our Lady of Lourdes Hosp., Lafayette, 1967—. Named Man of Year in La. Agr., Progressive Farmer's mag., 1965; Outstanding Alumnus in Agr., U. Southwestern La., 1966; Man of year, La. Cattlemen's Assn., 1967; Sportsman of Year, Lafayette Civitan Club, 1970; King Cotton XVII La. Cotton Festival Assn., 1970. Mem. Greater Lafayette C. of C. (dir. 1966-69), Am. Jersey Cattle Club (dir. 1958-61, pres. 1961-64), Deep South Writers and Artists Conf., Blue Key, Phi Kappa Phi, Kappa Delta Pi, Alpha Zeta, Omicron Delta Epsilon, Theta Xi. Democrat. Methodist (steward 1966—). Mason (Shriner), Rotarian. Address: Drawer 1008 U Southwestern La Lafayette LA 70501

ROUGHTON, RICHARD WELLS, motel exec.; b. Perry, Ga., July 4, 1924; s. Rawlings Howard and Eunice (Wells) R.; grad. high sch.; m. Alice Jewel Tucker, Jan. 10, 1954. Owner, R.W. Roughton Constrn. Co., Perry, 1952-64; prin., owner Capri Motel and Restaurant, Perry, 1966—. Mem. Bd. Appeals City Perry, 1966—. Served with Mcht. Marine, 1943-48, with AUS, 1948-51; Korea.

Mem. C. of C. (charter), V.F.W. Club: Perry Country. Home: 1209 Cater Circle Perry GA 31069 Office: Capri Motel Perry GA 31069

ROUNTREE, AUBREY EUGENE, vending co. exec.; b. Dunbarton, S.C., July 21, 1938; s. Aubrey B. and Minnie (McElveen) R.; B.S., U. S.C., 1961; m. Emily Ida Sprawls, July 13, 1957; children—Dana Ruth, Julie Anne, Gina Claire, Emily Maria, Amy Carol. Mgr., Price Waterhouse & Co., Charlotte, N.C., 1961-67; pres., dir. Food Service, Inc., Columbia, S.C., 1967—. Tchr. accounting Richland Tech. Edn.Center, 1969—. C.P.A., N.C. Mem. Am. Inst. C.P.A.'s, Nat. Assn. Accountants. Baptist. Club: Gamecock (Columbia). Home: 286 Sandhurst Rd Columbia SC 29210 Office: 1238 Arrowwood Rd Columbia SC 29210

ROUNTREE, GORDON ELLIOTT, lawyer; b. Houston, May 14, 1938; s. William F. and Elsie (Huegel) R.; B.A., Washington and Lee U., 1960; LL.B., La. State U., 1966; m. Laurice Lee Wickersham, Dec. 30, 1960; children—Julia Elise, Laura Ashley, Gordon E. Admitted to La. bar; partner firm Cook, Clark, Egan, Yancey & King, Shreveport, La., 1966—; dir. Rountree Olds-Cadillac Co., Inc., Rountree Realty, Inc. (both Shreveport). Mem. Bd. 9, SSS, 1968-70. Bd. dirs. Shreveport Legal Services Corp., Caddo Found. for Exceptional Children, Caddo Bossier Council Alcoholism; trustee Southfield Sch., Shreveport. Served with AUS, 1961-63; Germany. Mem. Ark.-La.-Tex. Tax Inst. (dir.), Am., La., Shreveport (sec.-treas. 1970-71, pres. young lawyers sect.) bar assns., Order Coif, Phi Kappa Phi, Phi Delta Phi, Omicron Delta Kappa. Club: Shreveport Country. Mng. editor La. Law Rev., 1965-66. Home: 4464 Richmond St Shreveport LA 71106 Office: Commercial National Bank Bldg Texas and Edwards Shreveport LA 71102

ROUNTREE, THOMAS JEFFERSON, educator, author; b. Pinckard, Ala., July 22, 1927; s. Nathan Harmon and Hortense (Warren) R.; B.A., Troy State U., 1950; M.A., U. Ala., 1952; Ph.D., Tulane U., 1962; m. Virginia Earle Ward, Aug. 12, 1967. Instr. English, Troy (Ala.) State U., summer 1953, 54, asst. prof., summer 1957; instr. English, East Tex. State U., Commerce, 1956, asst. prof., 1960-61; asst. prof. English, Southeastern La. Coll., Hammond, 1958-60; instr. English, U. Ala., University, 1961-62, asst. prof., 1962-65, asso. prof., 1965-71, dir. creative writing program, 1963-71; prof., chmn. dept. English U. South Ala., 1971—. Guest lectr. creative writing S.D. Fine Arts Conf., Yankton, 1962, 63. Served with USNR, 1945-46, AUS, 1954-56. Recipient Prewitt Semmes, Jr. creative writing awards, 1952, 53, 1st prize Short Story award Birmingham Festival of Arts, 1963; Carnegie scholar, 1953-54. Mem. Modern Lang. Assn. Am., South Atlantic Modern Lang. Assn., Ala. Coll. English Tchrs. Assn., So. Literary Festival, Wordsworth Circle, Rydal Mt. Summer Sch. Assn., Episcopalian. Author: This Mighty Sum of Things: Wordsworth's Theme of Benevolent Necessity, 1965; study guides on The Last of the Mohicans (Cooper), 1965, Emma (Austen), 1967, also articles, short stories, poems. Editor: Critics on Melville, 1972; Critics on Hawthorne, 1972. Address: Box U-342 U South Ala Mobile AL 36688

ROUS, JOHN HENRY, news photographer; b. Meridian, Miss., Oct. 2, 1912; s. George Layfield and Clara (Springfield) R.; student Pleasant Hill Acad., Tenn., 1929, 30; m. Constance Evelyn Hicks, Sept. 4, 1937. Photographer, Washington Times, 1934-38, Washington Times-Herald, 1939, 40, 41; chief div. photography, domestic br. O.W.I., 1942-44; photographer A.P., 1944—. Recipient gold medal award 10th Ann. World Photography Exhbn., 1966. Mem. White House News Photographers Assn. (treas. 1952-56, pres. 1958-59, chmn. exec. com.). Mason. Club: National Press (Washington). Home: 3201 Russell Rd Alexandria VA 22305 Office: 1300 Connecticut Av NW Washington DC 20036

ROUSE, HUBERT BLAIR, educator; b. Orange, Va., Oct. 31, 1912; s. Edgar Hubert and Elizabeth (Button) R.; B.A., Randolph-Macon Coll., 1933; M.A., U. Va., 1938; Ph.D. (fellow), U. Ill., 1942; m. Fanchon Remund, May 30, 1942; children—James Blair, Janet Elizabeth (Mrs. Mayer D. Schwartz). Tchr. English and Latin, Marshall (Va.) High Sch., 1932-36; tchr. English Harrisonburg (Va.) High Sch., 1936-40; instr. English, Ohio State U., Columbus, 1946-49; asst. prof. English Emory U., Atlanta, 1949-55; asso. prof., head English dept. Mt. Union Coll., Alliance, O., 1955-57; asso. prof. U. Ark., Fayetteville, 1957-61, prof., 1961—. Instr. summer session U. Cal. at Berkeley, 1946, Pa. State U., 1948. Served to lt. comdr. USNR, 1942-46. Recipient Faculty Achievement award for research U. Ark., 1967. Mem. Modern Lang. Assn. Am., South Central Modern Lang. Assn., Modern Humanities Research Assn., Am. Assn. U. Profs., Coll. English Assn., P.E.N., Phi Beta Kappa. Methodist. Author: Letters of Ellen Glasgow, 1958; Ellen Glasgow, 1962. Editor: Style. Contbr. revs. to profl. publs. Home: 941 Crest Dr Fayetteville AR 72701

ROUSE, MILFORD OWEN, physician; b. Jacksonville, Tex., Aug. 10, 1902; s. William Thomas and Sallie (Milford) R.; A.B., Baylor U., 1922, M.A., 1923, M.D., 1927, LL.D., 1967; m. Leaureame McDavid, 1927; 1 dau., Mrs. Curtis L. Sawyer. Intern, Sta. Hosp., Ft. Sam Houston, 1927-28; clin. prof. medicine Southwestern Med. Sch., U. Tex., 1943—; mem. staff Baylor U. Med. Center, Med. Arts Hosp. Pres. Dallas Health and Sci. Mus., 1969-70, Greater Dallas Community Nutrition Council, 1970-71; gen. chmn. community health focus project pub. health com. Dallas C. of C., 1969-70. pres. A.M.A.-Edn. and Research Found., 1968-69. Served as 1st lt. M.C., U.S. Army Res., 1927-28. Recipient Ho Din award Southwestern Med. Found., 1945; 1st Health award Dallas Hosp. Council, 1947. Diplomate Am. Bd. Internal Medicine, Am. Bd. Gastroenterology. Fellow A.C.P., Am. Coll. Nutrition; mem. Am. Gastroent. Assn., A.M.A. (speaker ho. of dels. 1963-66, pres. 1967-68; mem. council on foods and nutrition 1972—), So. Med. Assn. (pres. 1958-59; Distinguished Service award 1965), Am. Therapeutic Soc., Tex. Med. Assn. (pres. 1956-57, Distinguished Service award 1964). Baptist. (deacon, dir. Bapt. Standard 1959-68; mem. Sunday sch. bd. So. Bapt. Conv. 1972—). Mason. Optomist. Home and office: 8326 Garland Rd Dallas TX 75218

ROUSE, PARKE SHEPHERD, found. exec.; b. Smithfield, Va., July 20, 1915; s. Parke Shepherd and Pauline (Dashiell) R.; A.B., Washington and Lee U., 1937; m. Elizabeth Marshall Gayle, Oct. 3, 1946; children—Elizabeth Marshall, Sarah Dashiell, Parke Shepherd III. Reporter, Newport News (Va.) Times-Herald, 1937-40; polit. writer Richmond (Va.) Times-Dispatch, 1930-42, editorial writer, 1946-48, Sunday editor, 1948-50; dir. publs. Colonial Williamsburg (Va.), 1950-54; exec. dir. Jamestown (Va.) Found., 1954—. Acting exec. dir. Va. Independence Bicentennial Commn., 1970—; pres. Williamsburg Community Council, 1960-61. Bd. dirs. Jamestown Found. Inc.; trustee Jamestown Corp. Served with USNR, 1942-46. Research grantee Old Dominion, 1966, Am. Philosoph. Found., 1968. Mem. Williamsburg C. of C. (pres. 1965-66), Phi Beta Kappa, Omicron Delta Kappa, Sigma Delta Chi. Democrat. Episcopalian (sr. warden 1959-61). Author: James Blair of Virginia, 1971; Below the James Lies Dixie, 1968; Planters and Pioneers, 1968; Tidewater Virginia in Color, 1968; Virginia, The English Heritage in America, 1966; Roll, Chesapeake, Roll, 1972. Home: 14 Bayberry Lane Williamsburg VA 23185 Office: Jamestown Festival Park Jamestown VA 23185

ROUSE, RAYMOND VICTOR, profl. soccer team coach; b. Swansea, Wales, Mar. 16, 1936. With English League for Crystal Place, 1956-62, Oxford United, 1963-64, Leyton Orient, 1965-66; with Atlanta Chiefs, 1967—, asst. coach, dir. youth devel., 1969-70, head coach, gen. mgr., 1970—. Named to Welsh Nat. Team, 1960, 61. Office: Atlanta Chiefs Atlanta Stadium Atlanta GA 30312*

ROUSELLE, CHARLES RODNEY, social worker; b. Wilmington, Del., Jan. 7, 1935; s. Maurice and Lydia (Camper) R.; student Central State Coll., 1952-55; B.A., Morgan State Coll., 1957; M.S.W., Howard U., 1960; m. Yvonne Edwards, Aug. 30, 1958; children—Vida Lynn, Avis Renee. Social worker Montgomery County, Md., 1959-61, D.C. Pub. Welfare, 1961-64; chief social services Christ Child Settlement House, 1964-66; chief psychiat. social worker D.C. Dept. Vocational Rehab., 1966-67; dir. Offender Rehab. Services, D.C. Legal Aid Agy., Washington, 1967-69; asso. supt. for community services Youth Div. D.C. Dept. Corrections, 1969-71; chief offender rehab. div. Pub. Defender Service, Washington 1971—. Mem. profl. adv. bd. Shaw Residential Treatment Facilities, 1969—; mem. Crime and Delinquency Council Health and Welfare Council, 1967—, Lamond-Riggs Civic Assn., 1961—. Bd. dirs. D.C. Corrections Visitors Services Center; bd. dirs. pretrial justice program Am. Friends Service Com. Mem. Nat. Assn. Social Work, Howard U. Alumni Assn., Kappa Alpha Psi. Home: 5262 Chillum Pl NE Washington DC 20011

ROUSH, HARRY, dentist; b. Phila., Oct. 1, 1915; s. Louis and Rose (Likoff) R.; B.S., Duke U., 1936; D.D.S., 1940; m. Ann Herman, July 4, 1947; children—Alan Loni, Lois Beth. Pvt. practice dentistry, Arlington, Va., 1940—. Mem. Comprehensive Health Planning Council No. Va., 1970—; adv. council No. Va. Community Coll., 1966-69. Served with USNR, 1942-46. Mem. Arlington (pres. 1956), No. Va. (pres. 1969) dental socs., Alpha Omega (v.p. 1942). Mem. Jewish religion. Lion (pres. N.W. Arlington 1962). Home: 6308 Waterway Dr Falls Church VA 22044 Office: 3801 N Fairfax Dr Arlington VA 22203

ROUSSEL, HERBERT JOSEPH, JR., engring. co. exec.; b. New Orleans, July 13, 1931; s. Herbert Joseph and Dorothy (Moll) R.; B.C.E., Tulane U., 1961, M.C.E., 1964, postgrad., 1964—; m. Joyce Ellen Freeling, Aug. 4, 1956; children—Herbert Joseph III, Karen Elizabeth. Engr., Shell Oil Co., Norco, La., 1961-62, J. Ray McDermott & Co., New Orleans, 1962-64, Avondale Shipyards Inc., New Orleans, 1964, Boeing Co., New Orleans, 1964-65; asso. N.P. Jeffrey, New Orleans, 1965-68; pres. Roussel Engring., Inc., Metairie, La., 1968—; vis. lectr. civil engring. dept. Tulane U., 1964—. Served with AUS, 1952-54. Recipient La. Hwy. Engr. Assn. award, 1961; W.F. Thompkin's award, 1961, Alumni award, 1969 (both Tulane U.). Mem. Am. Concrete Inst., Am. Soc. C.E., Soc. Tulane Engrs., La. Engring. Soc., Nat. Soc. Profl. Engrs., Am. Soc. for Testing and Materials, Am. Welding Soc., Sigma Xi, Tau Beta Pi, Alpha Sigma Lambda. Home: 1901 Cleary Av Metairie LA 70001 Office: 3814 Veterans Blvd Metairie LA 70002

ROUTH, DONALD EUGENE, electronics engr.; b. Mountain View, Mo., Aug. 14, 1936; s. Alvis Clarence and Thelma Jane (Blew) R.; B.S. in Elec. Engring., Washington U., St. Louis, 1960; postgrad. Auburn U., 1966, U. Ala. at Huntsville, 1968-69; m. Wilma Marie Quick, June 10, 1956; children—Marcy, Katherine, Linda. Systems and Liaison engr. McDonnell Aircraft Co., St. Louis, 1958-63; sect. chief Astronics Lab., NASA Marshall Space Flight Center, Hunstville, Ala., 1969—. Registered profl. engr., Ala. Mem. Ala. Soc. Profl. Engrs., MARS Assn. Marshall Space Flight Center (pres. 1965), Marshall Space Flight Center Exchange Club (sec. 1970-72). Baptist. Home: 9001 Willow Hills Dr Huntsville AL 35802 Office: S&E-ASTR-R Marshall Space Flight Center Huntsville AL 35812

ROUTH, PORTER (WROE), ch. exec.; b. Lockhart, Tex., July 14, 1911; s. Eugene Coke and Mary M. (Wroe) R.; A.B., Okla. Baptist U., 1934, LL.D., 1951; postgrad. So. Baptist Theol. Sem., 1937, U. Mo., 1938, George Peabody Coll., 1946-47; m. Ruth Elizabeth Purtle, June 7, 1936; children—Eugene Charles, Elizabeth Ann, Dorothy Kate, Mary Susan, Lelia Ruth. Dir. publicity and instr. polit. sci. Okla. Bapt. U., 1935, dir. univ. press, 1936-37, instr. journalism, editorial staff Shawnee News, 1938-40; asso. sec. Okla. Bapt. Sunday Sch. and Tng. Union Dept., Oklahoma City, 1940-41, sec. Okla. Bapt. Brotherhood and Promotion Dept., 1942-43; sec. dept. survey, statis. and information Bapt. Sunday Sch. Bd., Nashville, 1945-51; exec. sec. of exec. com. So. Bapt. Conv. 1951—; mem. exec. com. Bapt. World Alliance, 1955—, mem. adminstrv. com., 1956—; treas. Conv. Found. Mem. Nat. council Boy Scouts Am.; mem. com. on medicine and religion A.M.A. Mem. So. Bapt. Hist. Soc., Am. Bible Soc. (dir.). Author: My World Too, 1948; Meet the Presidents, 1952; 77,000 Churches, 1964. Editor: Okla. Bapt. Messenger, 1943-45; Quar. Rev., 1945-52. Home: 3426 Hampton Av Nashville TN 37215 Office: 460 James Robertson Pkwy Nashville TN 37219

ROVELSTAD, GORDON HENRY, scientist; b. Elgin, Ill., May 19, 1921; s. Henry Randolph and Margot Helen (Greenhill) R.; student St. Olaf Coll., 1939-41; D.D.S., Northwestern U., 1944, M.S., 1948, Ph.D., 1960; D.Sc., Georgetown U., 1971; m. Barbara Jean Johnson, Apr. 8, 1945; children—Craig Gordon, Martha Kay, Andrew Todd. Instr., Northwestern U. Dental Sch., Chgo., 1944-45, 1946-48, asst. prof., 1949-53; commd. lt. Dental Corps USN, 1944, advanced through grades to capt., 1959; dental research officer USN Dental Research Facility, Bainbridge, Md., 1954-58; dir. research and scis. dept. Naval Dental Sch., Bethesda, Md., 1960-65; officer-in-charge Naval Dental Research Inst., Great Lakes, Ill., 1965-69; head dental research br., dental research program coordinator Bur. Medicine and Surgery, dental research adviser Office Naval Research, Washington, 1969—; chief dental service Children's Meml. Hosp., Chgo., 1949-53. Mem. dental study sect. Nat. Inst. Dental Research, 1961-65, mem. dental research program projects com., 1969-71; mem. dental caries research program adv. com. NIH, 1971-73; cons. dental research council Am. Dental Assn., 1971-72. Mem. boys work com. YMCA, Elgin, Ill., 1952-53. Diplomate Am. Bd. Pedodontics. Fellow Am. Coll. Dentists, Am. Acad. Pedodontics, A.A.A.S.; mem. Internat. Assn. Dental Research (pres. 1971-72), Am. Coll. Dentists (chmn. research com. 1969-70), Am. Acad. Pedodontics (trustee 1955-59), Am. Bd. Pedodontics (pres. 1961), A.A.A.S. (councilor at large 1969-73), Am. Dental Assn. (chmn. research sect. 1968), Sigma Xi, Omicron Kappa Upsilon. Lutheran (trustee 1970-73). Rotarian. Home: 11909 Falkirk St Potomac MD 20854 Office: Dental Div Bur Medicine and Surgery Dept Navy Washington DC 20390

ROVIRA, EDWIN JOSEPH, JR., accountant; b. New Orleans, Oct. 5, 1929; s. Edwin Joseph and Bernadette (Webre) R.; B.B.A., Tulane U., 1950; m. Anne Marie Zeringue, May 23, 1953; children—Kyle Anne, Dwayne Edwin, Keith Joseph. Jr. accountant E.J. Rovira, Sr., C.P.A., New Orleans 1950-53; sr. accountant Malcolm M. Dienes & Co., New Orleans, 1953-54; pvt. practice pub. accounting, Metairie, La., 1956—; treas., dir. Masonry Products Sales, Inc., New Orleans, 1966—. Bd. dirs. Christian Bros. Found., East Jefferson Hosp. Found. Served with USCGR, 1954-56. C.P.A., La. Mem. Am. Inst. C.P.A.'s. La. Soc. C.P.A.'s, Metairie Club Gardens Assn. (dir., pres.). Democrat. Roman Catholic. Club: Metairie Country. Home: 402 Vincent Av Metairie LA 70005 Office: 3212 16th St Metairie LA 70002

ROWAN, CARL THOMAS, journalist; b. Ravenscroft, Tenn., Aug. 11, 1925; s. Thomas David and Johnnie (Bradford) R.; student Tenn. State U., 1942-43, Washburn U., 1943-44; A.B., Oberlin Coll., 1947, D.Litt., 1962; M.A., U. Minn., 1948; D.Litt., Simpson Coll., 1957, Hamline U., 1958; L.H.D., Washburn U., 1964, St. Olaf Coll., 1966, Knoxville Coll., 1966; LL.D., Howard U., 1964, Alfred U., 1964, Temple U., 1964, Atlanta U., 1965, Allegheny Coll., 1966, Colby Coll., 1968; D.P.A., Morgan State Coll., 1964; m. Vivien L. Murphy, Aug. 2, 1950; children—Barbara, Carl, Goeffrey. Reporter, Mpls.-Tribune, 1948-61; dep. asst. to sec. state, Washington, 1961-63; ambassador to Finland, 1963- 64; dir. USIA, 1964-65; syndicated columnist, TV commentator Post-Newsweek Broadcasting Co., Washington, 1965—; dir. D.C. Nat. Bank. Mem. com. of 100 legal def. fund N.A.A.C.P., 1964—, chmn. adv. com. Nat. Com. Against Discrimination in Housing, 1967. Served with USNR, 1943-46. Recipient numerous awards, including Sidney Hillman Found. award, 1952, Am. Teamwork award Nat. Urban League, 1955, Distinguished Achievement award Regents of U. Minn., 1961, Golden Ruler award Phila. Fellowship Commn., 1961, Communications award in Human Relations, Anti-Defamation League of B'nai B'rith, 1964, Distinguished Service award Capital Press Club, 1964, Nat. Brotherhood award Nat. Conf. Christians & Jews, 1964; Elijah P. Lovejoy award, 1968. Mem. Sigma Delta Chi. Author: South of Freedom, 1953; The Pitiful and the Proud, 1956; Go South to Sorrow, 1957; Wait Till Next Year, 1960. Home: 3116 Fessenden St NW Washington DC 20008 Office: 1101 17th St NW Washington DC 20036

ROWE, BONNIE GORDON, music co. exec.; b. Buford, Ga., May 3, 1922; s. Bonnie Gordon and Alma (Poole) R.; student Ga. Evening Coll., 1939-41, U. Wichita, 1948-49, Ga. State Coll., 1949-52; m. Mary Wilburta Shidler: 1 dau., Sharon Lynn; m. 2d, Gloria Lucille Fairfax, Feb. 17, 1962; 1 dau., Susan Rebecca. Traffic mgr. Bonanza Air Lines, Las Vegas, 1946-48; music tchr. 1948-52; owner Rowe Accordion Distbg. Co., Rowe Accordion Center, Atlanta, 1952-56, Atlanta Music Pub. Co., 1956—, B. Rowe Music Co., Atlanta, 1957—. Served to lt. col. USAAF, World War II; ETO. Decorated Air medals with three oak leaf clusters. Mem. Southeastern Accordion Assn. (past pres.), Nat. Assn. Music Mchts., Atlanta Fedn. Musicians, Travelers Protective Assn., Atlanta C. of C. Res. Officers Assn., Internat. Platform Assn., Gamma Delta Phi. Elk. Club: Dobbins AFB Officers. Composer: Accordionique, 1953, Vivolet, 1956, More and More and More, 1964, Dedication, 1964, All I Really See Is You, 1965, I Love Only You, 1965, Predudio Reminisci, 1969. Home: 5085 Erin Dr Atlanta GA 30331 Office: Greenbrier Pkwy SW Atlanta GA 30331

ROWE, CHARLES EUGENE, textile mfg. exec.; b. Heathsville, Va., June 13, 1911; s. Carroll J. and Evelyn (Hall) R.; B.S., Va. Polytech. Inst., 1933; advanced mgmt. program Harvard Grad. Sch. Bus. Adminstrn., 1950; m. Mary Lewis Johnston, Mar. 20, 1937; children—Charles Eugene, Nancy Hull. Accounting clk. Continental Oil Co., Richmond, Va., 1933-34; with Burlington Industries, Greensboro, N.C., 1935-53, controller, 1945-47, treas. 1947-53; controller D.H. Baldwin Co., 1953-55; treas. Dan River Inc., 1955-66, v.p., 1966—, also dir., chief financial officer; dir. Iselin-Jefferson Financial Co., N.Y.C., First Nat. Bank, Danville, Va. Bd. visitors, rector Va. Poly. Inst., dir. Ednl. Found., 1950-53, 64; trustee Averett Coll., Stillman Coll. Mem. Financial Execs. Inst., Nat. Assn. Accountants, Va. Poly. Inst. Alumni Assn. (pres. 1962-64, dir.), Harvard Bus. Sch. Alumni. Presbyn. Kiwanian. Clubs: Greenville Valley Country; Poinsett. Home: 425 Mohawk Dr Greenville SC 29609 Office: PO Box 6126 Greenville SC 29606

ROWE, HAROLD CLIFTON, assn. exec.; b. Springfield, Mass., Feb. 28, 1925; s. Harold Clifton and Henrietta (Trunkfield) R.; B.S., Am. Internat. Coll., 1947; postgrad. Springfield Coll., 1947-48, Yale, 1949-55, Mich. State U. Inst. Organizational Mgmt., 1956; m. Evelyn M. Valerie, Feb. 5, 1957; children—Chrisse Ann, Harold Clifton III, Suzanne, Gail, Russell. Research dir. Springfield Taxpayers Assn., 1950-52; exec. sec. Brookville (Pa.) C. of C., 1952-54; exec. v.p. Middletown (Conn.) C. of C., 1954-58; sec. commodity div. Nat. Assn. Waste Material Dealers, N.Y.C., 1958-60; sec. membership relations Printing Industries Met. N.Y., N.Y.C.; exec. dir. Environmental Mgmt. Assn., Clearwater, Fla., 1962—. Mem. S.A.R., Am., Fla. (v.p. 1971-72) socs. assn. execs., Sigma Alpha Phi. Home: 2429 Fiarbanks Dr Clearwater FL 33516 Office: 1710 Drew St Clearwater FL 33515

ROWE, JAMES MELVIN, journalist; b. Nagasaki, Japan, Dec. 17, 1910 (parents Am. Citizens); s. John Hansford and Margaret (Cobb) R.; student Baylor U., Centenary Coll., U. Tex., 1930-34; m. Florence Arline Womack, Apr. 10, 1950; children—James Melvin (dec.), John Hansford. With country weekly newspapers, Quitman, Tex. and Aransas Pass, Tex., 1937-40; reporter, polit. writer Corpus Christi (Tex.) Caller-Times, 1940-54, editorial writer, 1954-60, chief editorial writer, 1960—, Served to maj. AUS, 1941-46. Decorated Bronze Star medal. Democrat. Baptist. Home: Route 1 Box 990 Ingleside TX 78408 Office: PO Box 9136 Corpus Christi TX 78408

ROWE, KWANG WOOK, dentist; b. Seoul, Korea, Feb. 5, 1922; s. Chung-il and Sun-il (Lee) R.; D.D.S., Seoul Nat. U., 1943; certificate in periodontics N.Y.U., 1956; D.M.D., U. Ala., 1959; m. Hyosuk Lee, Feb. 5, 1955; children—Lynn, Susan, Hahn, Won. Came to U.S., 1953, naturalized, 1965. Asst. prof. Seoul Nat. U., 1946-50; lectr. Ewha Coll., 1952-53; practice dentistry, Balt., 1959-60, Pocomoke City, Md., 1960-63, Camp Springs, Md., 1963—. Chmn. Com. In U.S. For Peaceful Unification Korea, 1972. Bd. dirs. Korean Student Scholarship Fund, Korean Com. for Fair Election. Fellow Guggenheim Dental Clinic, 1954-55; recipient Merit award Am. Soc. Children's Dentistry, 1959. Mem. Internat. Acad. Orthodontics, Am. Dental Assn., Korean Soc. Met. Washington (pres. 1969-70). Home: 12213 Holly Banks Dr Oxon Hill MD 20022 Office: 5209 Brinkley Rd Washington DC 20031

ROWE, LOUIS PAUL, dentist; b. Good Luck, Ky., Nov. 14, 1939; s. Paul Bedford and Vera Lillian (Ford) R.; D.M.D., U. Louisville, 1964; m. Dianna Winifred Boylan, Sept. 21, 1960; children—Louis Paul, Kirk A., Kelly S. Practice dentistry, Louisville, 1964-65, Erlanger, Ky., 1968—. Served with Dental Corps, AUS, 1966-67. Decorated Army Commendation medal. Mem. Am. Dental Assn., Gideons Internat. (pres. No. Ky. 1970—, zone leader Ky. 1970—), Phi Kappa Tau, Psi Omega. Baptist (deacon 1964). Home: 328 Stevenson St Erlanger KY 41018 Office: 24 Commonwealth Av Erlanger KY 41018

ROWE, MAURICE B., state ofcl.; m. Joyce M.; children—Caroline, Maurice B. IV. Commr., Va. Dept. Agr. and Commerce. Home: 4121 Southhaven Rd Richmond VA 23235 Office: 203 N Governor St Richmond VA 23219

ROWE, OEHMIG DANIEL, dentist; b. Chattanooga, Oct. 16, 1923; s. Daniel L. and Annie (Bowman) R.; B.S., Appalachian State U., 1950; D.D.S., U. N.C., 1957; m. Erma Colleen Houck, Sept. 16, 1955;

children— Vickie, Marilyn, Diane, Daniel, James. Tchr., Oak Hill High Sch., Morganton, N.C., 1949-53; gen. practice dentistry, Marion, N.C., 1957—. Mem. bd. commrs. McDowell County, N.C., 1964—; mem. McDowell County Bd. Health, 1969-70. Bd. dirs. Marion Gen. Hosp. Served with AUS, 1943-45. Mem. N.C. Dental Soc., N.C. Spurgon Dental Soc. (v.p. 1956-57), Xi Psi Phi. Democrat. Baptist. Lion, Moose. Club: Marion Lake (N.C.). Home: 215 Cresent Dr Marion NC 28752 Office: Drawer 10 Marion NC 28752

ROWE, WALLACE P., physician, govt. ofcl.; b. Balt., Feb. 20, 1926; student Coll. William and Mary, 1943-44, summer 1945; M.D., Johns Hopkins U., 1948; m. 2 children. Student asst. N.Y. State Tb Sanarotium, Ray Brook, 1947; intern N.C. Baptist Hosp., Winston-Salem, 1948-49; research fellow Bowman Gray Sch. Medicine, Wake Forest Coll., 1949; virologist Naval Med. Research Inst., Bethesda, Md., 1949-52; commd. sr. asst. surgeon USPHS, 1952, advanced through grades to med. dir., 1960; investigator Nat. Inst. Allergy and Infectious Diseases, NIH, Washington, 1952—, chief oncolytic and oncogenic virus unit virus sect., 1957-68, chief Lab. Viral Diseases, 1968—. Served with USNR, 1945; to lt., M.C., 1949-52. Office: Lab Viral Diseases Nat Inst Allergy and Invectious Dis NIH Washington DC 20014*

ROWELL, JOHN THOMAS, psychologist; b. Lloyd, Fla., Mar. 21, 1920; s. Irvin Caleb and Ester Estelle (Rouden) R.; R.N., McLean Hosp. Sch. Nursing, 1942; A.B., U. Mich., 1949; Ph.D., Fla. State U., 1958; m. Mabel Zelma Mason, Aug. 15, 1942; children—James Roger, Douglas Hugh, Martin Allen. Chief psychologist Milledgeville (Ga.) State Hosp., 1951-57; human factors scientist RAND Corp., Santa Monica, Cal., 1957; mgr. anti-submarine warfare programs System Devel. Corp., Falls Church, Va., 1958-69, pres. N.C. Leadership Inst., Inc., 1969-72; v.p. Essex Corp., 1972—; pres. John Rowell Assos., 1972—. Served with AUS, 1943-46. Mem. Am., Southeastern psychol. assns., Human Factors Soc., A.A.A.S. Author: National Document Handling Systems for Science and Technology, 1967. Home: 2903 Greenbrook Dr Greensboro NC 27408 Office: Exec Sq 2720 N Church St Greensboro NC 27405

ROWEN, HOBART, journalist; b. Burlington, Vt., July 31, 1918; s. Moses G. and Sarah (Rosenberg) R.; B.S. in Social Sci., Coll. City N.Y., 1938; m. Alice B. Stadler, Aug. 5, 1941; children—Judith Diane, James Everett, Daniel Jared. Reporter, N.Y. Jour. Commerce, N.Y.C., 1938-41, Washington corr., 1941-42; with information div. WPB, Washington, 1942-44; corr. Washington bur. Newsweek mag., 1944-65; Bus. Trends editor, 1957-65; bus.-financial editor Washington Post, 1966—. Councilman, Town of Somerset, Md. 1957—. Bd. dirs. Nat. Council Aging. Recipient spl. achievement award Loeb. mag. 1961—; Mem. Sigma Delta Chi (Distinguished Service award for mag. writing 1961), Tau Delta Phi. Democrat. Jewish religion. Club: Nat. Press, Federal City (Washington.) Contbr. articles and columns to various mags. and newspapers, including Harpers, New Republic. Author: The Free Enterprisers-Kennedy, Johnson and the Business Establishment, 1964. Home: 5701 Warwick Pl Chevy Chase MD 20015 Office: 1515 L St Washington DC 20006

ROWLAND, ARTHUR RAY, librarian; b. Hampton, Ga., Jan. 6, 1930; s. Arthur and Jennie (Goodman) R.; A.B., Mercer U., 1951; M. Librarianship, Emory U., 1952; m. Jane Thomas, July 1, 1955; children—Dell Ruth, Anna Jane. Circulation asst. Ga. State Coll. Library, Atlanta, 1952, circulation librarian, 1952-53; librarian Armstrong Coll., Savannah, Ga., 1954-56; head circulation dept. Auburn (Ala.) U. Library, 1956-58; librarian, asso. prof. library sci. Jacksonville (Fla.) U., 1958-61, Augusta (Ga.) Coll., Ga., 1961—; lectr. library edn. U. Ga., 1962-66. Trustee Historic Augusta, Inc., 1969—. Served with USNR, 1948-49. Mem. Am., Southeastern, Ga. (v.p. 1965-67, 71—), Central Savannah River Area (pres. 1964-65), Duval County (v.p. 1960-61) library assns., Ga., Richmond County (curator 1964—, dir. 1965-67, pres. 1967-70), Ga. Bapt. hist. socs., Nat. Trust for Historic Preservation, Am. Assn. State and Local History, Kappa Phi Kappa. Baptist. Author: Bibliography of the Writings of Georgia History, 1966; A Guide to the Study of Augusta and Richmond County, Georgia, 1967. Editor: Reference Services, 1964; Historial Markers of Richmond County, Georgia, 1966, rev. edit., 1971; The Catalog and Cataloging, 1969; Richmond County History, 1969—. Contbr. articles to profl. jours. Home: 1339 Winter St Augusta GA 30904 Office: 2500 Walton Way Augusta GA 30904

ROWLAND, DAVID JACK, coll. pres.; b. Columbus, O., June 17, 1921; s. David Henry and Ethel (Ryan) R.; B.S., Ohio U., 1949; M.A., U. Ala., 1951; L.H.D., Athens Coll., 1963; LL.D., Jacksonville U., 1969; grad U.S. Army Command and Staff Coll., 1971; m. Mary Ellen Stinson, Apr. 8, 1944; children—David Allen, Ryan Stinson, Sue Ellen. Prin. Mineral Springs Jr. High Sch., Birmingham, Ala., 1950-51; asst. prin. McAdory High Sch., Bessemer, Ala., 1951-52; prin. Warrior (Ala.) High Sch., 1952-56; pres. Walker Coll., Jasper, Ala., 1956—. Dir. First Nat. Bank of Jasper. Vice pres. Walker County Mental Health Assn., 1958-60; chmn. Mountain dist. Boy Scouts Am., 1960-63, pres. Black Warrior council; asso. bd. mem. Meth. Children's Home. Mem. North Ala. Meth. Conf. Bd. Edn., mem. commn. on Christian vocations; dist. lay leader; jurisditional del. Meth. Ch. Mem. adv. bd. Ednl.-TV; Ala. adv. bd. Am. Coll. Testing Program; mem. bd. Ala. Space Museum. Dir. Birmingham Community Chest. Served to capt. AUS, 1942-46; col. Res. Recipient Jr. C. of C. Distinguished Citizens award, 1957, Walker County and Jasper Young Man of Yr., 1957; Silver Beaver award Boy Scouts Am. Mem. Ala. Edn. Assn. (pres. div. higher edn.), Ala. Assn. Coll. Adminstrs. (v.p.), Jasper C. of C. (pres.), Reserve Officers Assn., Am. Legion, Kappa Phi Kappa, Alpha Phi Omega (pres.'s sectional rep.). Phi Delta Kappa. Methodist, (dist. lay leader). Mason. (Shriner), Rotarian (pres.). Club: Relay House. Home: 1005 Valley Rd Jasper AL 35501

ROWLAND, MARSHALL WILLIAM, broadcasting exec.; b. Brunswick, Ga., Jan. 23, 1931; s. John A. and Chloe (Trippe) R.; ed. pub. schs.; m. Carol Casey, May 16, 1955; children—Marshall William, Richard Hal, Brian, Stephen. Owner, pres. radio stas. WQIK, also WQIK-FM; Chevrolet dealer. Home: Amelia Rd Fernandina Beach FL 32034 Office: Box 6400 Jacksonville FL 32205

ROWLES, BARRY M., former pres. Theodore Hamm Brewing Co. now pres. Ky. Fried Chicken Corp., Louisville. Address: Box 13331 Louisville KY 40213

ROWLETT, RAYMOND, hosp. adminstr.; b. Calvin, Ky., Mar. 1, 1929; s. Dexter Marvin and Millie (Brooks) R.; student Nat. Sch. Bus., 1949-50; Lincoln Meml. U., 1957-58; m. Laura Jean Pursifull, Nov. 17, 1951; 1 son, Brooks Ashley. Stock, salesman Scotts Dept. Store, Pineville, Ky., 1947-49; br. office mgr. Pinnacle Motors, Pineville, Ky., 1953-56; accounts receivable clerk Middlesboro (Ky.) Meml. Hosp., 1956-58; bus.-admissions supr. McDowell (Ky.) Meml. Hosp., 1958-63; asst. patient accounts mgr. U. Ky. Med. Center, Lexington, 1963-65; adminstrv. asst. McDowell Appalachian Regional Hosp., 1965-66; adminstrv. asst. Williamson (W.Va.) Appalachian Regional Hosp., 1966-67, asst. adminstr., 1967—; acting adminstr. Whitesburg (Ky.) Appalachian Regional Hosp., 1969-70. Served with AUS, 1951-53. Baptist (Sunday sch. supt. 1959-61). Home: 14R 1st St South Williamson KY 25661 Office: 2000 Central Av South Williamson KY 25661

ROWLEY, GEORGE ARTHUR, JR., ednl. adminstr.; b. Ringwood, Okla., Apr. 18, 1927; s. George Arthur and Beulah Mae (Wimberly) R.; A.B., Northwestern State Coll., 1949; M.A., Phillips U., 1953; Ed.D., Okla. State U., 1967; m. Alice Fern Doll, Dec. 21, 1946; children—Jerry Warren, Kenny Dean, Robert Wayne, Valli Jo. Prin., Freedom (Okla.) High Sch., 1949-51; supt., Crawford, Okla., 1951-56, Coyle, Okla., 1956-62; dir. Oklahoma City Schs. Food Service Div., 1962-63; supt. Perkins (Okla.) Pub. Schs., 1963-66, Blackwell (Okla.) Schs., 1966—. Mem. Okla. Commn. on Ednl. Adminstrn., 1971-74. Chmn. ednl. div. United Fund, 1967-69; v.p. Bi-State Mental Health Found., 1969-70. Bd. dirs. Kay County Juvenile Com. Served with USNR, 1945-46. Recipient Grant NSF, 1957; named Boss of the Year Jr. C. of C., 1971. Mem. Am., Okla. (pres. 1971-72) assns. sch. adminstrs., Okla. Edn. Assn., Blackwell C. of C. (dir. 1970-72), Phi Kappa Phi, Phi Delta Kappa. Democrat. Presbyn. (elder 1971-72). Rotarian. Home: 307 Fairview St Blackwell OK 74631 Office: 934 S 1st St Blackwell Ok 74631

ROWLEY, JAMES J., dir. U.S. Secret Service; b. Bronx, N.Y., Oct. 14, 1908; s. James and Bridget (McTigue) R.; student St. John's Coll., 1929-31; LL.B., St. John's U., 1935, LL.M., 1936; m. Mabel Rita Cluen, Apr. 15, 1940; children—Claudia, Linda, Donna. Credit investigator Bank of U.S., N.Y.C., 1926-30; investigator, liaison between banking div. and legal dept., on liquidation work N.Y. State Banking Dept., 1930-36; spl. agt. FBI, 1937-38; agt. U.S. Secret Service, 1938—, asst. supervising agt. White House detail, 1945-46, supervising agt., 1946-61, dir. U.S. Secret Service, 1961—. Recipient Career Service award Nat. Civil Service League, 1963, Mr. Sam award Touchdown Club, Washington, 1968, Exceptional Service award Treasury Dept., 1968, President's award for distinguished fed. civilian service, 1968. Mem. Soc. Former FBI Agts., Internat. Assn. Chiefs Police. Home: 3501 Rittenhouse St NW Washington DC 20015 Office: 1800 G St NW Washington DC 20226

ROWSOME, FRANK H(OWARD), JR., writer, govt. ofcl.; b. Dedham, Mass., Mar. 12, 1914; s. Frank H. and Caroline M. (O'Grady) R.; A.B., Harvard, 1935; m. Phala A. Hale, Apr. 1, 1935; 1 son, Frank Howard III. Free-lance writer, 1935-39; asso. editor Med. Econs., Rutherford, N.J., 1940-41, mng. editor, 1942-43; asso. editor Popular Sci. Monthly, N.Y.C., 1943-48, asst. mng. editor, 1948-57, mng. editor, 1957-62; dir. tech. publs. NASA, 1962—. Author: Trolley-Car Treasury, 1956; They Laughed When I Sat Down, 1959; The Verse by the Side of the Road, 1965. Home: 3021 Dent Pl NW Washington DC 20007 Office: NASA Washington DC 20546

ROY, RALPH GALLEGLY, farmer; b. Oxford, Miss., Sept. 8, 1938; s. Clifton Stewart and Mable (Gallegly) R.; student N.W. Jr. Coll., 1958-59, U. Miss., 1961; m. Amy Byrd, Apr. 7, 1961; children—Suzanne, Kimberly, Lisa. Engaged in retail grocery bus., 1962-64; farmer, Abbeville, Miss., 1964—. Mem. Miss. Nat. Guard, 1951-57; active Civil Def. Election commr., 1967-71. Trustee College Hill Acad. Named Farmer of Year Oxford Jr. C. of C., 1969. Mem. Farm Bur. (dir. 1968-70), N.E. Power Assn. (dir. 1965-71), Lafayette County Farmers Assn. (treas. 1969-71), C. of C., Oxford Jr. C. of C., Sigma Pi. Democrat. Baptist. Mason. Home: Abbeville MS 38601

ROYAL, DARRELL K., univ. athletic dir., football coach; b. Hollis, Okla., July 6, 1924; s. Burley Ray and Katy Elizabeth (Harmon) R.; B.S. in Bus., U. Okla., 1950; m. Edith Marie Thomason, July 26, 1944; children—Marian (Mrs. Abraham Kazen III), Mack, David. Asst. football coach N.C. State U., Raleigh, 1950, Tulsa U., 1951, Miss. State Coll., Starkville, 1952; head football coach Edmonton Eskimos, Canadian Profl. League, 1953, Miss. State Coll., 1954-55, U. Wash., Seattle, 1956; head football coach U. Tex., Austin, 1957—, athletic dir., 1962—, prof., 1963—, dir. intercollegiate athletics, 1962—. Bd. dirs. Pan-Am. Sch., Kingsville, Tex., Stillman Coll. Served with USAAF, 1943-45. Named Football Writers' Coach of year, 1961, 63, Am. Football Coaches Assn. Coach of Year, 1963, 70, Tex. Sports Writers' Coach of Year, 1961, 63, 69, 70, Southwesterner of Year, 1961, 62, 63, 69, 70, Mr. South Tex., 1972. Mem. Delta Upsilon. Presbyn. Author: Darrell Royal Talks Football, 1963. Home: 1200 Belmont Pkwy Austin TX 78703

ROYALS, JAMES LEE, physician; b. Meridian, Miss., June 3, 1915; s. James Lee and Minnie Maude (Guyton) R.; B.A., U. Miss., 1936; M.D., Tulane U., 1940; m. Mary Alice Brookshire, Jan. 15, 1946; children—James Lee III, Charles Brookshire. Intern Brook Gen. Hosp., San Antonio, 1940-41, U. Pa. Grad. Sch. Medicine, 1946-47; resident St. Margaret Meml. Hosp., Pitts., 1947-49; practice medicine specializing in obstetrics and gynecology, Jackson, Miss., 1950—; clin. prof. U. Miss. Sch. Medicine. Served to lt. col., M.C., AUS, 1941-46. Decorated Bronze Star. Diplomate Am. Bd. Obstetrics and Gynecology. Fellow A.C.S., Am. Coll. Obstetrics and Gynecology; mem. Am., Miss. (pres. 1969-70) med. assns., Central Med. Soc., Southeastern (past pres.), Miss. (past pres.) obstet. and gynecol. socs., Jackson Gynecoligic Soc. Home: 3645 Cavalier Dr Jackson MS 39211 Office: 918 N State St Jackson MS 39201

ROYCO, EMIL, architect; b. St. Louis, Oct. 20, 1908; s. George and Susanna (Stancik) Rojko; B.Arch., Washington U., St. Louis, 1934; m. Emilia Branska, Apr. 26, 1938; 1 dau., Emiline (Mrs. Marvin Charles Ott). Instr. math. and mech. drawing Jefferson Jr. Coll., St. Louis, 1934-35; chief draftsman Gale E. Henderson, architect, St. Louis, 1935-42; project architect Mauran, Russel, Crowell & Mullgargdt, architects, St. Louis, 1944-50; chief architecture div. Leo A. Daly Co., architect-engr., St. Louis, 1950-56; asso. Helmuth, Obata & Kassabaum, 1956-61; jr. partner Vlastimil Koubek, architect, Washington, 1961-62; asst. dir. Washington office Hudgins, Thompson, Ball, architect-engrs., 1966—. Mem. A.I.A., Czechoslovak Soc. Arts and Scis. (nat. treas. 1966—), Czechoslovak Nat. Council (chpt. pres. 1970—). Mason (32 deg.). Home: 6616 Tulip Hill Terrace Washington DC 20016 Office: Nat Press Bldg Washington DC 20004

ROYCROFT, HOWARD FRANCIS, lawyer; b. Balt., Sept. 9, 1930; s. Howard F. and Bessie (Weaver) R.; B.A., U. Md., 1953; LL.B., Georgetown U., 1958; m. Barbara Lee Seal, Mar. 20, 1954; children—Suzanne Carol, Nancy Lee. Admitted to D.C. bar, 1958, since practiced in Washington; mem. firm Hogan & Hartson, 1958, now partner, mem. exec. com., 1970—. Asst. chief operations Waynewood Recreation Assn., Alexandria, Va., 1965-66, pres., dir., 1969-70, swim team mgr., 1967-68. Served to 1st lt. USMC, 1953-55. Mem. Am., Va. State, Fed. Communications bar assns., Bar Assn. D.C., Nat. Broadcasters Club, Barristers, Nat. Acad. TV Arts and Scis., Bryce Mountain Assn. (dir.), Kappa Alpha, Beta Kappa. Republican. Methodist. Home: 8703 Eaglebrook Ct Alexandria VA 22308 Office: 815 Connecticut Av Washington DC 20006

ROYO, REINALDO ANTONIO, JR., broadcasting exec.; b. Rio Piedras, P.R., Jan. 9, 1939; s. Reinaldo M. and Josefina (Quilichini) R.; B.B.A. magna cum laude, U. P.R., 1961; M.B.A., U. Miami, 1965; m. Nora Zayas, Nov. 23, 1967; 1 dau., Diana Marie. Gen. mgr. Ponce TC Corp. (P.R.), Sta. WRIK-TV, 1965-68; v.p., gen. mgr. El Mundo Broadcasting Corp., WKAQ Radio, San Juan, P.R., 1968—. Prof. econs., money and banking Cath. U. P.R., Ponce, 1966. Consular agt. of France in P.R. Home: 605 Torrealta Calla Mejico Hato Rey PR 00914 Office: Roosevelt Av Hato Rey PR 00936

ROYSTER, GEORGE ERWIN, life ins. co. exec.; b. Statesville, N.C., July 10, 1928; s. Ira Gay and Catherine Margaret (Poesy) R.; B.A., U. Tenn., 1955; m. Joy Angeline Inman, Nov. 23, 1968; 1 dau., Joy Angeline. Asst. v.p. Integon Corp., Winston-Salem, N.C., 1955-68; v.p. Liberty Life Ins. Co., Greenville, S.C., 1968—; pres., dir. LIBCO, Inc., Greenville, 1970; sr. v.p. marketing Am. Found. Life Ins. Co., Little Rock, 1971—. Pres., bd. dirs. Durham County March Dimes, 1962. Mem. Nat. Assn. Securities Dealers, Nat. Assn. Life Underwriters, Sigma Alpha Epsilon. Episcopalian (lay reader 1962). Clubs: Twin City (Winston-Salem); Greenville Country, Poinset (Greenville); Little Rock, Racquet (Little Rock, Ark.). Home: 8 Huntington Rd Little Rock AR 72207 Office: 4th and Ringo Sts Little Rock AR 72203

ROYSTER, VERMONT CONNECTICUT, journalist, educator; b. Raleigh, N.C., April 30, 1914; s. Wilbur High and Olivette (Broadway) R.; grad. Webb Sch., Bellbuckle, Tenn., 1931; A.B., U. N.C., 1935, LL.D., 1959; Litt.D., Temple U., 1964; L.H.D., Elon Coll., 1971; m. Frances Claypoole, June 5, 1937; children—Frances Claypoole, Sara Eleanor. Reporter, N.Y.C. News Bur., 1936; reporter Wall Street Jour., 1936, Washington corr., 1935-41, 1945-46, chief Washington corr., 1946-48; editorial writer and columnist, 1946-48; asso. editor, Wall Street Jour., 1948-51, sr. asso. editor, 1951-58, editor, 1958-71, contbg. editor, columnist, 1971—; sr. v.p., dir. Dow Jones & Co., Inc., 1965-71, dir., 1970—; prof. journalism and pub. affairs U. N.C., 1971—; comentator CBS radio and TV, 1972—; dir. Dow Jones-Irwin, Inc., 1968-71, Wachovia Bank & Trust Co., N.A., 1971—. Mem. adv. com. Pulitzer prizes Columbia, 1968—; bd. dirs. Newspaper Fund, Inc. Commd. ensign USNR, 1940, active duty from 1941; served 48 months in Atlantic, Caribbean, Pacific, until 1945; exec. officer USS LaPrade; comdg. officer USS Jack Miller, USS PC-1262; inactive duty lt. comdr. Awarded Pulitzer prize for editorial writing, 1953, medal for distinguished service in journalism by Sigma Delta Chi, 1958; William Allen White award U. Kan., 1971. Mem. Am. Soc. Newspaper Editors (president from 1965-66), Nat. Conf. Editorial Writers (chairman 1957), Phi Beta Kappa Assos., Phi Beta Kappa. Episcopalian. Clubs: University (N.Y.C.); Nat. Press (Washington). Author: (with others) Main Street and Beyond, 1959; Journey Through the Soviet Union, 1962; A Pride of Prejudices, 1967. Contbr. numerous articles on financial and econ. subjects to periodicals. Appears on pub. affairs programs on TV and radio. Home: 903 Arrowhead Rd Chapel Hill NC 27514

ROZZELL, FORREST, assn. exec.; b. Gore, Okla., Aug. 18, 1908; B.A., Coll. of Ozarks, hon. degree, 1969; M.S. in Sch. Adminstrn., U. Ark.; LL.B., Ark. Law Sch.; m. Agnes Carroll; children—Allen, Carol (Mrs. James Cheek), Joyce (Mrs. Ronald Harper), Betty. Tchr. pub. schs., 1931-40; dir. field service Ark. Edn. Assn., Little Rock, 1940-54, exec. sec., 1954—. Ednl. adviser to numerous state govt. agys., bds., commns.; N.E.A. del. Assembly World Confedn. Orgns. of Teaching Profession, 1959, 64; del. White House Conf. on Edn., 1955. Mem. Ark. Ho. of Reps., 1939-44; del. Nat. Democratic Conv., 1952, 56. Named Outstanding Alumnus of Year, Coll. of Ozarks, 1949. Mem. N.E.A. (ednl. policies commn., spl. legislative rep. 1942-43, chmn. legislative commn., 1950-51, cons. 1951—), Ark. Edn. Assn. (v.p. dept. classroom tchrs. 1939-40), Phi Delta Kappa, Kappa Delta Pi. Mem. Christian Ch. (Sunday sch. tchr., bd. mem.). Office: 1500 W 4th St Little Rock AR 72201*

RUANO, ARGIMIRO LAIGLESIA, educator; b. Salamanca, Spain, Oct. 3, 1924; s. Sebastian Luengo Ruano and Maria Luisa (Laiglesia); grad. U. Salamanca, 1948, Louvain U., 1954; Ph.D., Santo Domingo U., 1956, U. Navarra, 1966; m. Christiane Fischer Ackert, Aug. 14, 1966; children—Sebastian, Maria Teresa. Monk, 1940-47; ordained priest Roman Catholic Ch., 1948; priest, Avila, Spain, 1949-53, Madrid, 1954, Santo Domingo, Dominican Republic, 1956-58, Havana, Cuba, 1958-59, Mexico City, 1959-62, P.R., 1962-65; prof. Instituto de Cultura Religiosa Superior Avila, 1949-54; prof. med. deontology Santo Domingo U., 1957-58; prof. logics and psychology State U. Mex., Mexico City, 1961-62; prof. mental health and ethics Cath. U. P.R., Ponce, 1962; prof. humanities, Spanish studies, P.R. U., Mayaguez, 1963—. Chaplain Marion Hosp., Santo Domingo, 1957-58; counselor films censure Archbishop of Santo Domingo, 1957-58; Seki-Sano assessor Bellas Artes Palace, Mexico City, 1959. Served as 1st lt. Dominican Air Force, 1956-57. Mem. Order Rosicrucians. Author: Filosofia de la Mistica, 1953; La Mistica de Occidente, 1956; Logica y Mistica, 1970; San Juan de la Cruz Clasico, 1971, others. Translator autobiog. manuscripts including: St. Therese of Lisieux, 1962. Home: 96 Alhambra St Residencial Sultana Mayaguez PR 00708 Office: Dept Humanities U PR Mayaguez PR 00708

RUBEN, ANN GERTRUDE MOLIVER (MRS. GERSHON RUBEN), educator; b. Pitts., Jan. 9, 1925; d. Max and Fannie (Landy) Moliver; B.S. in Elementary Edn., U. Pitts., 1961, M.Ed. in Counselor Edn., 1965, Ph.D. in Higher Edn., 1969; m. Gershon Ruben, June 26, 1943; children—Stephen B., Richard Lee, David Allan. Tchr. various schs., Pitts., 1961-64; sch.-community agt. Pitts. (Pa.) Pub. Sch. System, 1964-66; ednl. cons. dept. psychiatry U. Pitts.; now asso. prof. Grad. Sch. Edn. Barry Coll., Miami Shores, Fla. Cons. adminstrs. and tchr. Carlynton Sch. Dist., Carnegie, 1969—; mental health cons. policemen-in-training Pitts. Police Acad., 1969—; ednl. cons. tchrs. Sch. for Pitts., 1969—. Recipient Outstanding Service award VA Hosp., Pitts., 1955. Mem. Am. Orthopsychiatric Assn., Am. Personnel and Guidance Assn., Ladies Hosp. Aid Soc., B'nai B'rith Women's Council (v.p. 1951-53), Hadassah Women, Pioneer Women, Brandeis U. Women's Orgn., Children's Aid Soc. Jewish religion. Author: We've Got to Get in Order to Give. Home: 9974 SW 88th St Miami FL 33156 Office: Barry Coll Miami Shores FL

RUBEN, LEONARD, artist, educator, advt. agy. exec.; b. St. Paul, June 3, 1921; s. Theodore and Elizabeth (Hauchman) R.; B.F.A., Pratt Inst., 1952; M.A. in Fine Arts, Columbia, 1961; Ph.D., N.Y.U., 1970; m. Sue L. Winchester, Dec. 23, 1970. Art dir. Young & Rubicam, Inc., N.Y.C., 1955-60; head art group North Advt., N.Y.C., 1960-62; instr. Columbia U., 1962-63; v.p. asso. creative dir. J.M. Mathes, Inc., N.Y.C., 1966-68; creative dir. Lake Spiro Shurman, Memphis, 1968-69; pres. Len Ruben & Friends Advt., 1969—; asst. prof. art N.E. La. U., Monroe, 1969-71, U. Tex., Austin, 1971—. Served to 1st lt. AUS, 1940-46. Recipient numerous awards from Am. TV Commls. Festival, N.Y. Art Dirs., Am. Inst. Graphic Arts, Graphex 70, Art Dirs. and Designers Assn. of New Orleans, Memphis Advt. Club, Memphis Art Dirs. Club, Mid-South Art Dirs. Show, Am. Advt. Fedn., N.Y. Advt. Club, Am. TV and Radio Commls. Festival. Address: 4000 Pete's Path Austin TX 78731

RUBENSTEIN, MARVIN DAVID, food co. exec.; b. Dallas, June 30, 1924; s. Sidney and Bertha (Siegel) R.; B.B.A., U. Tex., 1948; m. Rita Levinson, Mar. 28, 1948; children—Judy, Barry, Patricia. With Rubenstein Foods, Inc., Dallas, 1948—, pres., 1965—. Served with AUS, 1943-46. Mem. Nat. Fishery Inst., Tau Delta Phi. Jewish religion. Mem. B'nai B'rith. Club: Columbian Country (Carollton).

Home: 5915 Meadowcrest St Dallas TX 75230 Office: 1111 Hall St Dallas TX 75201

RUBENSTEIN, MORRIS BERNARD, air force officer; b. Eastover, S.C., Apr. 8, 1928; s. Joseph and Sara (Franklin) R.; B.S., The Citadel, 1949; m. Ravenel Marie Jeffcoat, Nov. 19, 1948; children—Loretta Karen, Alan Bruce, Deborah Gail. Commd. lt. USAF, 1949, advanced through grades to col., 1969; supply officer, Randolph AFB and Goodfellow AFB, Tex., 1949-50, base civil engr., Andersen AFB, Guam, 1950-52, McConnell AFB, Kan., 1952-56, chief engr. Inland Petroleum System, San Pablo, Spain, 1956-60, base civil engr., Shaw AFB, S.C., 1960-62, chief of mgmt., Langley AFB, Va., 1962-63, dep. chief project control, Wiesbaden, Germany, 1963-64, dep. dir. resource planning, 1964-65, dir. generator maintenance, 1965-66, chief plans and exercise div., civil engring., Langley AFB, Va., 1966-68, base civil engr., Udorn Royal Thai AFB, Thailand, 1968-69, dir. engring. and resource planning, Langley AFB, 1969—. Decorated Bronze Star medal. Registered profl. engr., Kan. Mem. Soc. Am. Mil. Engrs. Mason. Contbr. articles to profl. jours. Patentee in field. Home: 349 Gunston Hall Ct Hampton VA 23369 Office: Hq TAC DEPL Langley AFB VA 23365

RUBIN, ALVIN BENJAMIN, judge; b. Alexandria, La., Mar. 13, 1920; s. Simon and Frances (Prussack) R.; B.S. in Bus. Adminstrn., La. State U., 1941, LL.B. 1942; m. Janice Ginsberg, Feb. 19, 1946; children— Michael H., David S. Admitted to La. bar, 1942; practiced in Baton Rouge, 1946-66; partner firm Sanders, Miller, Downing, Rubin & Kean, 1946-66; U.S. dist. Judge Eastern Dist. La., New Orleans, 1966—. Vis. lectr. law La. State U. Law Sch., 1946—; lectr. taxation Tulane U. Tax Inst., Ga. Tax Inst., La. State U. Mineral Law Inst.; arbitrator Fed. Mediation and Conciliation Service, 1950-66. Chmn. Baton Rouge Zoning Study Com.; mem. La. Legislative Administrv. Procedure Com. Sec. Baton Rouge United Givers Fund, 1954-67; past bd. dirs. Baton Rouge chpt. Girl Scouts U.S.A., Mental Health Guidance Center, Community Chest, Community Services Council, Nat. Assn. Crippled Children and Adults; past adv. bd. local Salvation Army, YWCA, Blundon Orphanage. Served to capt. AUS, 1942-46; ETO. Recipient Golden Deeds award for civic service, 1964, Brotherhood award, 1968. Mem. Am. (chmn. estate and gift tax com. 1964, chmn. sect. bar activities 1963, lawyer referral), La. (chmn. sect. trust estates, probate and immovable property law 1961, chmn. labor law sect. 1957, jr. bar sect. 1955) bar assns., Nat. Acad. Arbitrators, Am. Arbitration Assn., La. Law Inst., Order of Coif, Phi Delta Phi, Omicron Delta Kappa. Mason (32 deg.). Author: (with McMahon) Louisiana Pleadings and Judicial Forms Annotated; (with Janice G. Rubin) Louisiana Trust Handbook. Home: 225 Walnut St New Orleans LA 70118 Office: 400 Royal St New Orleans LA 70130

RUBIN, PAUL HAROLD, educator; b. Boston, Aug. 9, 1942; s. Joseph and Freda (Goldhagen) R.; B.A. with honors, U. Cin., 1963, M.A., 1964; M.S. (Krannert fellow), Purdue U., 1968, Ph.D., 1970; m. Marcia Ann Claybon, June 14, 1964; children—Joseph Saul, Rachel Beth. Instr. Purdue U., West Lafayette, Ind., 1964-67; economist, Small Bus. Adminstrn., Washington, 1966; asst. prof. econs. U. Ga., Athens, 1968—. Chmn. Employment Com. Athens Council Human Relations, 1967-71. Mem. Am., So. econs. assns., Am. Assn. U. Profs. (treas. U. Ga. chpt. 1971-72). Home: 260 Pine Forest Dr Athens GA 30601

RUBIN, ROBERT HILLIARD, fraternal orgn. exec.; b. N.Y.C., Oct. 24, 1935; s. Henry Hilliard and Ella Mae (Waite) R.; B.S., U. Ariz., 1957, M.Ed., 1968; m. Susan Smith, Sept. 4, 1965; 1 son, Mark Daniel. Tchr., Flowing Wells Pub. Schs., Tucson, 1960-64; exec. sec. Nat. Office Kappa Kappa Psi and Tau Beta Sigma, Stillwater, Okla., 1964—. Vis. prof. Okla. State U., 1970-71. Served with AUS, 1957-60. Recipient Centennial Gold medal Nat. Collegiate Athletic Assn., 1969. Mem. Am. Bandmasters Assn., N.E.A., Coll. Band Dirs. Nat. Assn., Music Educators Nat. Conf., Anti-Defamation League, N.Am. Band Dirs. Coordinating Council, Women Band Dirs. Nat. Assn., Orders and Medals Soc. Am. Stillwater C. of C., Sousa Meml. Inc., Phi Mu Alpha, Alpha Kappa Psi, Tau Beta Sigma, Kappa Kappa Psi, Alpha Epsilon Pi. Mem. B'nai B'rith, Rotarian. Home: 2419 N Jefferson St Stillwater OK 74074 Office: 122 Seretean Center Okla State U Stillwater OK 74074

RUBINO, RICHARD GENE, ednl. adminstr.; b. Haverhill, Mass., Aug. 4, 1932; s. Henry Peter and Dolly (Luksis) R.; B.A., So. Ill. U., 1960, postgrad., 1960-61; m. Donna Jean Brenstrom, June 15, 1957; children—Jon Michael, Mark David. Field advt. mgr. Procter & Gamble Co., Cin., 1952-57; research chief Gen. Planning & Resource Cons., Inc., St. Louis, 1961-62 asst. chief planning Vt. Devel. Dept., Montpelier, 1962-63, dir. Vt. Central Planning Office, 1963-67; dep. dir. U. N.C. Inst. on State Programming for '70s, Chapel Hill, 1967—. Chmn., New Eng.-N.Y. State Planning Dirs., 1964-65; chmn. planning com. Interstate Commn. on Lake Champlain Basin, 1964; mem. exec. com. Vt. Rural Areas Devel., 1963-67; mem. faith and order com. Vt. Council Chs., 1965-67; mem. project adv. com. New Eng. Econ. Research Council, Boston, 1965-67; mem. Conservation Law Found., 1967—. Served with AUS, 1954-56. Mem. Am. Inst. Planners (chmn. nat. com. state planning 1966—), Am. Soc. Planning Ofcls., Community Planning Assn. Can. Mem. United Ch. Christ (deacon). Elk. Contbr. articles to profl. jours. Work in state, regional planning, zoning, scenery preservation. Home: 1502 Lamont Ct Chapel Hill NC 27514 Office: Northwestern Mutual Life Bldg Chapel Hill NC 27514

RUBINOWITZ, ARTHUREA BROWN (MRS. STANLEY HENRY RUBINOWITZ), supt. schs.; b. nr. Mobile, Ala.; d. Arthur Isom and Beatrice (Knight) Brown; student Livingston (Ala.) Coll., 1934-36, Hardin-Simmons U., 1941-42; B.A., Am. U., 1958, M.A., 1960, Ed.D., 1966; m. Stanley Henry Rubinowitz, Aug. 6, 1943; children—Arthur Lee, Ben Brown. Tchr. schs., Ala., Tex., Va., Germany, 1935-60; prin. Fairfax (Va.) Pub. Schs., 1961-68; asst. adminstr., dir. instrn. K-12 Fairfax County Pub. Schs., 1968-70, area supt., 1970—; professorial lectr. Am. U., 1964—, U. Va., 1967—. Cons. Title III Edn. Center. Mem. Nat., Va., Fairfax County (personnel policy and salary coms.) edn. assns., Nat. Council on Measurement Edn., Assn. Supervision and Curriculum Devel., Nat., Va., Fairfax County (pres. 1967-68), elementary prins. assns., Am. Edn. Research Assn. (participant 1967 pre-session), Assn. for Childhood Edn. Internat., Dept. Elementary Sch. Prins., Delta Kappa Gamma, Alpha Delta Kappa. Author articles in field. Home: 6115 Clearbrook Dr Springfield VA 22150 Office: 6402 Franconia Rd Springfield VA 22150

RUBLY, GRANT RUSSELL, mining engr.; b. Cleve., June 7, 1906; s. Carl John and Louise F. (Sump) R.; B.S., Case Inst. Tech., 1928, E.M., 1939; m. Lucille Alyce Pickering, Oct. 5, 1929; children—John Charles, Grant Allen, Elizabeth Anne (Mrs. Charles E. Sills), Carl Andrew, Sharon Eloise (Mrs. William D. Tilley). Mine engr. Miami Copper Co. (Ariz.), 1928-37, chief mine engr., 1937-44; resident engr. Magma Copper Co., Superior, Ariz., 1944-45, San Manuel Copper Corp., Superior, 1945-47; check and right of way engr. Ore. Hwy. Commn., Salem, 1947-48; mining supr. Magnet Cove Barium Corp., Malvern, Ark., 1948-50; engr. Def. Minerals Adminstrn., U.S. Bur. Mines, Campus U. Ariz., Tucson, 1950-51; asst. chief mine engr. Reynolds Mining Corp., Bauxite, Ark., 1951-56, jr. staff engr., 1956-58, sr. staff asst., 1958—. Fellow A.A.A.S.; mem. Am. Inst. Mining, Metall. and Petroleum Engrs., Sigma Xi, Phi Kappa Tau, Theta Tau. Methodist. Mason (32 deg., K.T.). Contbr. articles to profl. jours. Home: PO Box 154 Malvern AR 72104 Office: Reynolds Mining Corp Bauxite AR 72011

RUBOTTOM, ROY RICHARD, JR., univ. pres.; b. Brownwood, Tex., Feb. 13, 1912; s. Roy Richard and Jennie Eleanor (Watkins) R.; B.S., So. Meth. U., 1932, M.A., 1933; grad. study U. Tex.; LL.D., Southwestern Coll., Winfield, Tex., 1968; m. Billy Ruth Young, Dec. 23, 1938; children—Eleanor Ann, Frank, John. Traveling sec. Lambda Chi Alpha frat., 1933-35; bus. positions, 1935-37; asst. dean of student life U. Tex., 1937-41; v.p. State Nat. Bank, Corsicana, Tex., 1946-47; apptd. fgn. service officer, 1947; sec. of embassy and consul, Bogota, Colombia 1947-49; officer-in-charge Mexican affairs State Dept., 1950; dep. dir. Middle Am. Affairs, 1951, dir., 1952-53; 1st sec. embassy, Madrid, 1953, counselor of embassy, 1954; dir. U.S. Operations Mission, Madrid, 1954-56; acting asst. sec. of state for Inter-Am. Affairs, 1956; asst. sec. of state, 1957-60; became U.S. ambassador to Argentina, 1960; State Dept. adviser Naval War Coll., Newport, R.I., 1962-64; v.p., So. Meth. U., Dallas, 1964-71, also prof. govt.; pres. U. Americas, Puebla, Pue., Mexico, 1971—. Served with USN, 1941-46, disch. to res. as comdr. Mem. Sigma Delta Chi, Lambda Chi Alpha. Methodist. Rotarian. Home: Apartado 507 Puebla Pue Mexico

RUBY (GLENN) RUSSELL, lawyer; b. Albany, Mo., Nov. 19, 1911; s. Gordon Romeo and Minnie (Hazelrigg) R.; student Palmer Coll. 1929-31; B.J., U. Mo., 1933; LL.B., Tulsa U., 1939; m. Elizabeth Bradford Popkin, Feb. 11, 1939 (dec. Aug. 1967); children—Michael Gordon, Adrienne Elizabeth, Glenn Russell; m. 2d, Dorothea King, June 1972. Admitted to Okla. bar, 1939; practiced in Muskogee, Okla. 1940—; spl. agt. FBI, 1942-47; mem. Okla. Ho. of Reps., 1954-66, exec. com. legislative council. Mem. Muskogee City Council, 1968-72, vice-mayor, 1969-72. Bd. dirs. Muskogee Community Concert Assn., Family Guidance Center, Kate Frank Manor. Mem. Am., Okla., Muskogee (pres. 1967) bar assns., Assn. Fed. Attys., Soc. Former Agts. FBI, S.A.R. Democrat. Episcopalian. Clubs: Muskogee Country, Wauhillau Outing, University (Tulsa). Mason (Shriner, Jester). Home: 4500 Girard Muskogee OK 74401 Office: Comml Bank Bldg Muskogee OK 74401

RUCH, JAMES BERNHARDT, govt. ofcl.; b. Santa Fe, June 9, 1935; s. Monroe Kuntz and Carolyn (Asplund) R.; B.A., Colo. Coll., 1956; m. Sandra Christine Barrett, June 11, 1956; children—Julis Christine, Laura Alexia, Sara Carolyn. Editor, Western Outdoor News, Newport Beach, Cal., 1959-62; pub. information officer Cal. Dept. Fish and Game, Sacramento, 1962-66; asst. to Cal. dir. Bur. Land Mgmt., U.S. Dept. Interior, Sacramento, 1966-70; southwestern field rep. Nat. Wildlife Fedn., Carmichael, Cal., 1970-71; spl. asst. to asst. sec. interior for fish, wildlife and parks, Washington, 1971—; free lance writer, 1960—; pub. relations cons., 1962—; partner Barrett-Ruch Ranch Enterprises, Ojai, Cal., 1960—. Mem. Cal. Adv. Com. Conservation Edn., 1970-71, Colo. Plateau Environmental Adv. Council, 1970-71; mem. conservation com. Golden Empire council Boy Scouts Am., 1962-68. Bd. dirs. Edwin S. Capps Meml. Wildlife Found. Served to lt. (j.g.) USNR, 1956-59. Recipient award of merit Cal. Conservation Council, 1965, Superior Performance award Dept. Interior, 1968, 69. Mem. Outdoor Writers Assn. Am., Pub. Relations Soc. Am. Author: (with others) California Fish and Wildlife Plan, 1965, California Desert, 1969. Home: 4807 Dorset Av Chevy Chase MD 20015 Office: US Dept Interior Interior Bldg Washington DC 20240

RUCKDESCHEL, FREDERIC BRILL, economist; b. Phila., Mar. 7, 1937; s. John Kessler and Anna Elizabeth (Brill) R.; A.B., Earlham Coll., 1959; M.A., Princeton, 1962; Ph.D., U. Pa., 1971; m. Kristin Shackford, Aug. 10, 1963; children—David Brill, Jonathan. Economist, Bd. Govs. Fed. Res. System, Washington, 1963—. Dir. River Park Mutual Homes, Inc., 1970—. Mem. Washington Soc. Investment Analysts. Home: 1328 4th St SW Washington DC 20024 Office: Fed Res Bd Washington DC 20551

RUCKEL, CHARLES WALTER, JR., banker; b. Pensacola, Fla., Jan. 1, 1927; s. Charles Walter and Marion (Plew) R.; student Davidson (N.C.) Coll., 1944-45, N. Ga. Coll., Dahlonega, 1945; diploma, Soule Bus. Coll., New Orleans, 1948; m. Gilda Juliet Meaut, Feb. 9, 1946; children— Charles Walter III, James Plew, Gregory Meaut; m. 2d, Wava Dyer, July 7, 1964; children—Marion Louise, Sharon Joyce; stepchildren—Stephen W., Martin L. Tille. With Valparaiso Bank &Trust Co. (Fla.), 1948—, dir., asst. v.p., 1950-51, pres., chmn. bd., 1951-64, chmn. bd., 1964—; pres., dir. Ruckel Properties, Inc., 1955—; dir. Gulf Power Co., Pensacola, F.W. Means & Co., Chgo. Pres. exec. bd. Gulf Coast council Boy Scouts Am., 1961-62; pres. Okaloosa County Community Chest, 1965-66; lt. col. Civil Air Patrol, Fla. Wing, 1960—. Bd. dirs. Okaloosa Island Authority, 1967-71. Served with USAAF, 1944-47. Named Man of Yr., Niceville-Valparaiso Rotary Club, 1957, 70. Mem. Fla. Bankers Assn., Krewe of Bowlegs. Republican. Rotarian. Clubs: Fort Walton Yacht (Ft. Walton Beach, Fla.); Eglin Golf, Rocky Bayou Country (Niceville). Home: Route 1 Box 176-R Niceville FL 32578 Office: 23 S John Sims Pkwy Valparaiso FL 32580

RUCKER, HAROLD JAMES, lawyer; b. Paducah, Ky., Dec. 8, 1921; s. Morton Val Dean and Birdie (Flora) R.; A.B., U. Ky., 1947, J.D., 1949; m. Helen McCauley, Apr. 29, 1946; children—Carol Jane, Morton Val Dean, Douglas McCauley, Helen Lynne Louise. Admitted to Ky. bar, 1949, Tex. bar, 1950; mem. staff land dept. Shell Oil Co., Midland, Tex., 1949-50; practiced in Midland, 1950—; mem. firm. Perkins, German, Mims & Bell, 1951-54, Perkins & Bezoni, 1955-56, Rucker & Rassman, 1958-60; dir. Brantly Drilling Co., Inc., Huckabay Chevrolet, Inc., West Tex. Enterprises, Inc., Chancellor Chair Co., Chaparral Cars, Inc. (all Midland); Black Bear Oil & Gas Corp. (W.Va.), Brantly Internat., Rio de Janeiro, Brazil. Past pres., mem. bd. Am. Cancer Soc., Midland, 1960-61; mem. Midland YMCA, 1961-68, pres., dir. bd., 1962-68, chmn. endowment com., 1964-65, chmn. Century Club, 1965-66, pres., bd. dirs. S.W. Area Council, 1962-66, mem. program com., chmn. workshop area council meeting, Dallas, 1963; past dir. Midland County Child Welfare Unit, 1957-58; pres., bd. dirs. Midland Diagnostic Cancer Clinic, 1961-62; pres. bd. trustees Trinity Sch., Midland; trustee St. Andrew's (Tenn.) Sch., Sch. Bd. of Diocese of N.W. Tex. (Episcopal). Served to 1st lt. AUS, 1942-46. Named Boss of Year, Legal Secs. Assn., Midland, 1963. Mem. Am., Midland County, Ky. bar assns., State Bar Tex., Am. Judicature Soc., Phi Alpha Delta, Sigma Chi. Episcopalian (vestryman). Kiwanian (pres., dir. 1955-57). Clubs: Racquet, Torrero (Midland). Office: First Nat Bank Bldg Midland TX 79701

RUCKER, JERALD JUAN, educator; b. Lexington, Ky., Nov. 5, 1931; s. Smith B. and Anna Lee (Rose) R.; B.B.A., U. Cin., 1957; M.S (scholar), U. Ill., 1963; m. Sylvia Mary Bratfish, Aug. 31, 1957; 1 dau., Leslie Lynne. Asst. prof. marketing U. Ga., Athens, 1960—, dir. news and publicity Coll. Bus. Adminstrn., 1963-69, asst. chmn. marketing dept., 1968—. Cons., researcher chambers commerce Glass Mfrs. Inst., Central Savannah Planning and Devel. Commn., various cos. Served with USNR, 1951-55. Mem. Am., So. marketing assns., Am. Acad. Advt., U. Ga., U. Cin., U. Ill. alumni assns., Am. Assn. U. Profs., Alpha Kappa Psi, Pi Sigma Epsilon, Beta Gamma Sigma (chpt. pres. 1969-70). Methodist (publicity com. 1971). Author retail trade reports. Home: 214 Marion Dr Athens GA 30601

RUCKER, NORMAN HENRY, physician; b. Washburn, Tenn., Feb. 26, 1918; s. John Thomas and Doris (Clark) R.; M.D., U. Tenn., 1940; postgrad. Columbia, 1949; m. Katharan Gladys Bradley, 1944; children—Patricia (Mrs. Jack Walker), Ann (Mrs. Jesse Lynn), John, Bradley. Intern, Knoxville Gen. Hosp., 1940-41; resident Manhattan St., Columbia Presbyn. Hosp., 1945-48; practice medicine specializing in psychoanalysis, New Orleans, 1949—; mem. staff Charity Hosp.; asst. prof. psychiatry Tulane U., 1949-51; clin. prof. psychiatry La. State U. 1967—; tng. and supervision analyst New Orleans Psychoanalytic Inst., 1954—; cons. Childrens Bur., VA Hosp. Sec., Green Acres Civic Assn. Bd. dirs. Family Service Soc. Served to maj. AUS, 1942-45. Mem. A.M.A., Am. Psychiat. Assn., Am. Psychoanalytic Assn., Phi Rho Sigma. Democrat. Baptist. Home: 316 Green Acres Rd Metairie LA 70003 Office: 1328 Aline St New Orleans LA 70115

RUCKER, VERNON BRUCE, city ofcl.; b. Coleman, Tex., Mar. 30, 1917; s. Henry Franklin and Ola Lee (Berry) R.; grad. high sch.; m. Bernice Sherman, Aug. 22, 1937; children—Frances Elaine (Mrs. Sidney P. Aleander), Marilyn Bernice, Ed Barcuch. With Killeen (Tex.) Fire Dept., 1941—, fire chief, 1951—. Instr. A. and M. U. Fire Sch., 1952-72; mem. State Pension Bd., 1963-68; adv. bd. Firemen's Tng. Sch., 1963-72. City councilman, Killeen, 1947-51. Served with USNR, 1945-46. Named Killeen Man of Year, V.F.W., 1961. Mem. Internat. Assn. Fire Chiefs (1st v.p. S.W. div. 1971—), State Firemens and Fire Marshals Assn. (pres. 1961-62), Am. Legion (chaplain 1947-49), C. of C. Mason (32 deg., Shriner), Kiwanian. Home: 1015 Carrie Circle Killeen TX 76541 Office: 114 West Av D Killeen TX 76541

RUDD, BILLY JACK, dentist; b. Ballinger, Tex., Apr. 21, 1937; s. John William and Billie (Eads) R.; B.A., So. Meth. U., 1960; postgrad. U. Tex. Sch. Dentistry, 1960-62; D.D.S., U. Mo., Kansas City, 1965; m. Lucy Katherine Campbell, Aug. 28, 1960; children—Frank William, Katherine Ann. Pvt. practice gen. dentistry, Lubbock, Tex., 1965—. Bd. dirs. Presbyn. Med. Center, 1966-70, treas., 1968-69, chmn., 1970; bd. dirs. Lubbock City County Dental Clinic, 1966-67, Tex. Found. for Dental Health and Edn., 1970—. Full scholarship athletic trainer So. Meth. U., 1955-59. Mem. Am. Soc. Preventive Dentistry, Am. Acad. Gen. Dentistry, Am. Soc. Dentistry for Children (Sr. award), Am., South Plains (pres. 1972-73), Tex. dental assns., Delta Sigma Delta, Sigma Alpha Epsilon. Presbyn. (deacon). Home: 3813 63d Dr Lubbock TX 79413 Office: 3716 21st St Lubbock TX 79410

RUDD, GEORGE ELLIS, physician; b. Birmingham, Ala., Apr. 10, 1928; s. George W. and Bessie (Ellis) R.; B.S., U. Ala., 1950; M.D., 1955; m. Patricia Sprague, Oct. 18, 1958; children—Ellis, Julia, Rebecca. Intern, Caraway Methodist Hosp., Birmingham, 1955-56, now staff mem.; gen. practice medicine, Pinson, Ala., 1956—; mem. staff East End Meml. Hosp., Birmingham, also mem. exec. com. 1971—. Mem. adv. bd. Roebuck br. City Nat. Bank, Birmingham, 1970—. Vice pres. P.T.A., Pinson, 1967-68; chmn. Community Com. for Locating Jr. Coll. in Jefferson County, 1965—; mem. Com. for New Pinson Valley High Sch., 1970-71; mem. adv. com. health service Jefferson State Jr. Coll., Birmingham, 1966—; physician, adviser State Tng. Sch. for Girls, Birmingham, 1968—. Bd. dirs. Community Service Council, Birmingham, 1969—. Served to lt. (j.g.), M.C., USNR, 1956-59. Named Man of Year, Eastern Area Birmingham C. of C., 1969. Mem. A.M.A., Med. Assn. Ala., Jefferson County Med. Soc. (trustee, pres.-elect 1971-72), Am. (past pres.), Ala. (dir.) acads. gen. practice. Methodist (chmn. com. on stewardship and finance). Clubs: Civitan (Pinson); The Club, Metropolitan Dinner of Greater Birmingham, Pioneer-Diner's, Cumberland Lake Country (Birmingham). Home: 1019 Oak St Pinson AL 35126 Office: N Main St Pinson AL 35126

RUDDOCK, ANDREW EMERSON, govt. ofcl.; b. West Lebanon, Pa., Nov. 11, 1918; s. Andrew J. and L. Louise (Lytle) R.; A.A., Blackburn Coll., Carlinville, Ill., 1939; LL.B., Nat. U., 1942, LL.M., 1943; m. Margaret Swindell; children—Ann Louise (Mrs. Thomas Gray), Carole Sue. With U.S. Civil Service Commn., Washington, 1939—, chief retirement div., 1953-59, dir. Bur. Retirement, Ins. and Occupational Health, 1959—; admitted to D.C. bar, 1942. Served with USAAF, 1944-45. Recipient Distinguished Service award Civil Service Commn., 1961. Home: 1411 Pathfinder Lane McLean VA 22101 Office: Civil Service Commn Washington DC 20415

RUDE, JOE CHRISTOPHER, physician; b. Granite, Okla., Oct. 27, 1905; s. Joe Christopher and Ella Nancy (Lowder) R.; B.A., U. Okla., 1926, B.S., 1928, M.D., 1930; m. Eleanor Wallenfels, May 5, 1934; children—Eleanor Jo, Franklin J., Elizabeth Carolyn, Joe Christopher III. Intern, Parkland Hosp., Dallas, 1930-31; asst. resident radiology U. Mich., 1933-34; resident radiology N.Y. Hosp. and Cornell Med. Center, 1935-38; Littauer Fellow in radiology Harvard, 1938-39; also asst. roentgenologist C.P. Huntington Meml. Hosp., Boston, 1938-39; instr. radiology U. Tex., Galveston, 1940, chief dept., prof. radiology, 1949-53; instr. Duke, 1941-42; radiologist Brackenridge Hosp., Austin, Tex., 1953—; cons. radiology Bergstrom AFB; nat. cons. to Office Surgeon Gen., 1955-58, Austin State Hosp., 1953—; hon. cons. 2d Air Force Strategic Air Command. Mem. Teletherapy Evaluation Bd., Oak Ridge, 1950-53. In res., AUS, 1930—, now col., M.C. Diplomate Am. Bd. Radiology. and Nuclear Medicine. Fellow Am. Coll. Radiology; mem. Aerospace Med. Assn., Radiol. Soc. N.Am., A.M.A., Tex., Travis County med. socs. Home: 4005 Balcones Dr PO Box 5125 Austin TX 78703 Office: 15th St and East Av Austin TX 78767

RUDER, PHILLIP SAUL, musician, educator; b. Chgo., Sept. 21, 1939; s. Leo and Isabell (Bronson) R.; B.A. summa cum laude, Hartt Coll. Music, U. Hartford, 1964, M.A., 1965; m. Ruth Louise Adler, Aug. 5, 1967; 1 son, Eric David. Debut recital Carnegie Hall N.Y.C., 1964; concertmaster New Orleans Philharmonic, 1965-67, Dallas Symphony, 1969—, Santa Fe (N.M.) Opera Orch., 1969—; artist-in-residence N.C. Sch. Arts, 1967-69; mem. Casals Festival Orch., 1968-70; participant Festival of Two Worlds, Spoleto, Italy, 1964, Slzburg Festival, Austria, 1965. Mem. Dallas Chamber Music Soc. (program com. 1969-71). Home: 6441 Joyce Way Dallas TX 75225 Office: Dallas Symphony Orch Dallas TX 75205

RUDIN, STANLEY ARTHUR, psychologist; b. Charleston, W.Va., Jan. 16, 1929; s. Samuel and Lillian (Cohen) R.; B.A., W.Va. U., 1950; Ph.D., U. Ill., 1955; m. Eleanor May White, Oct. 8, 1955; 1 son, Dorian N.A. Instr. W.Va. U., Morgantown, 1955-57; asst. prof. psychology Skidmore Coll., Saratoga Springs, 1957-58; research scientist USAF, Lackland AFB, Tex., 1958-60; asst. prof. Ga. Inst. Tech., Atlanta, 1960-62; Dalhousie U., Halifax, N.S., Can., 1962-64; staff psychologist VA Hosp., Lexington, Ky., 1964-65; chief research psychologist Rollman Psychiat. Inst., Cin., 1965-68; asso. prof. U. Cin., 1965-68, York U., Toronto, Ont., Can., 1968-70; chief personality and clin. unit psychology sect. Nat. Inst. Mental Health Clin. Research Center, Lexington, 1970—. Cons. psychologist Lockheed-Ga., Marietta, summer 1963, DeHaviland of Can.,

Toronto, 1968-70. Mem. Am., Midwestern psychol. assns., A.A.A.S. Home: 3523 Tates Creek Rd Apt 108 Lexington KY 40502 Office: Nat Inst Mental Health Clin Research Center Lexington KY 40507

RUDNICK, VAUGHN JOSEPH, judge; b. Chgo., May 15, 1932; s. Joseph Anthony and Dorothy (Blaha) R.; A.A., North Park Jr. Coll., 1952; B.A., Augustana Coll., 1954; J.D., U. Miami, 1959; postgrad. Nat. Coll. State Trial Judges, 1968; m. Bonita Mary Haflett, Apr. 8, 1961; children—Douglas Michael, Keith Joseph. Admitted to Fla. bar, 1959; practiced firm J. Leo Chapman, West Palm Beach, 1959-67; judge Criminal Ct. of Record, Palm Beach County, West Palm Beach, 1967—. Adviser to law enforcement planning counsel office Gov.'s Task Force on Narcotics, Dangerous Drugs and Alcohol Abuse, 1969—. Judge ad litem Municipal Ct., West Palm Beach 1961-66. Served with AUS, 1954-56. Mem. Am., Palm Beach County bar assns., Fla. Bar. Episcopalian. Lion (pres. 1967-68). Office: Palm Beach County Courthouse West Palm Beach FL 33401

RUEPPEL, MERRILL CLEMENT, mus. adminstr.; b. Haddonfield, N.J., May 7, 1925; s. George H. and Nellie (Lester) R.; B.A., Beloit Coll., 1949; M.A., U. Wis., 1951, Ph.D., 1955; m. Joan Marie Storberg, Sept. 15, 1956; children—Philip Cameron, Sarah Githens. Research asst. Mpls. Inst. Arts, 1956-57, asst. to dir., 1957-59, asst. dir., 1959-61; asst. dir. City Art Mus., St. Louis, 1961-64; dir. Dallas Mus. Fine Arts, 1964—. Asso. prof. dept. art and archeology Washington U., St. Louis, 1963; cons. mus. curatorial tng. program Ford Found., 1963—. Served with AUS, 1943-46. Mem. Assn. Art Mus. Dirs. (sec.-treas. 1967), Am. Assn. Museums, Archaeol. Inst. Am. Club: City (Dallas). Contbr. articles to mus. jours. Home: 9225 Guernsey Lane Dallas TX 75220 Office: Dallas Mus Fine Arts Fair Park Dallas TX 75226

RUESTER, RAYMOND JOHN, newspaper editor; b. East St. Louis, Ill., July 5, 1929; s. Herbert L. and Julia Victoria (Campo) R.; student U. Ga., 1952-53, Fla. State U., 1953-54, U. Cin., 1955; m. Janis Juanita Corbett, June 20, 1950; children—Rene Jon, Lenny Vic, Christopher Lee. TV-radio announcer WDBO-TV, WKIS, Orlando, Fla., 1954, 58; radio sports dir., TV weatherman WDBO Radio-TV, Orlando, 1959-61; dir. news and spl. events WFTV, Orlando, 1961-69, v.p., 1965-69; polit. editor Daytona Beach (Fla.) News Jour., 1969—, asso. editor, 1971—. Bd. counselors Bethune-Cookman Coll., Daytona Beach, 1970-71. Served with USMC, 1948-51. Mem. Fla. Assn. Broadcasters, UPI Fla. Broadcasters Assn. (pres. 1962-68), Radio-TV News Dirs. Assn. Home: 210 Jennie Jewel Dr Orlando FL 32806 Office: PO Box 431 Daytona Beach FL 32015

RUETER, HARRY ROY, mech. engr.; b. Cleve., June 1, 1929; s. Roy and Florence H. (Eckerman) R.; B.Mech. Engring., Cleve. State U., 1953; postgrad. N.C. State U., 1961, Wake Forest Coll., 1964. With Griscom Russell Co., Massillon, O., 1953-60; planning engr. Nike X project engring. dept. Western Electric Co., Burlington and Winston Salem, N.C., 1960-66; sr. mech. engr. facility design sect. Field Research Center, Melpar, Inc., Falls Church, Va., 1966-67; systems engr. ocean engring. br. U.S. Dept. Navy, Arlington, Va., 1967—; project engr. for U.S. Navy's Prototype Deep Diving System. Instr. hydraulic and pneumatic system design Western Electric Co., 1964-66. Prodn. adviser Jr. Achiever Assn., Massillon, O., 1958-59; speaker civic groups on Nike Zeus project, 1962-65. Recipient Attendance award Western Electric Co., 1965. Registered profl. engr., N.C., Va. Mem. Nat., N.C., Va. socs. profl. engrs., Am. Soc. M.E., Assn. Sr. Engrs. NavShips of Navy. Home: 3211 Allen St Falls Church VA 22042 Office: Nat Center Bldg 3 Arlington VA 22202

RUFF, RAYMOND, broadcasting exec. Pres., gen. mgr. KELI, Tulsa. Office: PO Box 3685 Tulsa OK 74152*

RUFFIN, JAMES STERLING, JR., physician; b. Covington, Tenn., Feb. 24, 1911; s. James Sterling and Mary Caroline (Feezor) R.; M.D., U. Tenn., 1936 ; m. Kathryn Witherington, Aug. 20, 1940; children—James Sterling III, Patsy Ann (Mrs. Ronald G. Pairamore). Intern, John Gaston Hosp., Memphis, 1936-37, asst. resident medicine, 1937-38; resident physician U. Tenn. Hosp., Knoxville, 1938-41; gen. practice medicine, Covington, 1946—; chief staff Tipton County Meml. Hosp. Vice pres. Tipton County Fed. Savs. & Loan Assn.; dir. Union Savs. Bank. Mem. Tifton County Quarterly Ct., 1956—; mem. Covington Planning Commn., 1957—, chmn., 1965—; historian Tipton County, 1966—; mem. Covington Sch. Bd., 1948-66. Served from 1st lt. to lt. col., M.C., AUS, 1941-46. Mem. Am. Acad. Family Practice, A.M.A., Am. Legion, Mid-South (v.p. 1971), Tenn. med. assns., Tipton County Med. Soc. (pres. 1967—), Kappa Sigma, Theta Kappa Psi. Presbyn. (elder 1969—). Mason (Shriner), Lion. Home: 328 E Liberty Av Covington TN 38019

RUFFIN, JULIAN MEADE, physician; b. Norfolk, Va., Aug. 26, 1900; s. Edmund Sumter and Cordelia Willing (Byrd) R.; A.B., U. Va., 1921, A.M., 1922, M.D., 1926; m. Lucy Landon Noland, June 22, 1929; children— Lucy Landon (Mrs. Henry H. Sprague), Jane Byrd (Mrs. Robert Ayerst), Judith Meade (Mrs. David G. Simpson). Intern Bellevue Hosp., N.Y.C., 1926-28; instr. medicine George Washington U., 1928-30; asst. prof. medicine Duke Sch. Medicine, 1930-37, asso. prof., 1937-49, prof. medicine, 1949-70, prof. emeritus, 1970—, dir. med. clinic, 1930-65; area cons. internal medicine and gastroenterology VA; mem. subsplty. bd. gastroenterology Am. Bd. Internal Medicine; mem. study sect. medicine NIH. Recipient Seale Harris award So. Med. Assn., 1969. Master A.C.P.; mem. Assn. Am. Physicians, Am. Gastroent. Assn. (pres.; Julius Friedenwald medal 1968), Am. Clin. and Climatol. Assn., Am. Soc. Clin. Investigation, Phi Beta Kappa, Sigma Xi, Alpha Omega Alpha. Democrat. Episcopalian. Author articles. Home: 816 Anderson St Durham NC 27706 Office: Duke Hosp and Croasdaile Clinic Durham NC 27705

RUIZ-FORNELLS, ENRIQUE, educator; b. Madrid, Spain, Dec. 6, 1925; s. Camilo and Teresa (Silverde) R.-F.; M.A., Madrid Ofcl. Sch. Journalism, 1951; M.A., U. Madrid, 1952, Ph.D., 1958; m. Cynthia Young, Mar. 21, 1959. Came to U.S., 1961. Lectr. Spanish, McGill U., Montreal, Que., Can., 1957-61; asst. prof. U. S.C., Columbia, 1961-63; asso. prof. Romance langs. U. Ala., University, 1963-66, prof., 1966—. U. Madrid rep. in U.S., 1967—; vis. prof. Washington U., St. Louis, 1967-68; part-time vis. prof. Miss. State U., 1968—. Mem. Am. Assn. Tchrs. Spanish and Portuguese (pres. Ala. chpt. 1967, exec. council 1970-72, scholarship com. 1971—), Modern Lang. Assn. Am., Am. Assn. U. Profs., Oficina de Informacion y Vigilancia del Espanol, Asociacion Cultural Iberoamericana, Asociacion Cultural Hispano-Norteamericana, Asociacion Internacional de Hispanistas, Sigma Delta Pi. Author: (with Robina E. Henry) Joaquin Calvo Sotelo's La muralla, 1962; Estudiantes espanoles en los Estados Unidos: Diez anos de intercambio, 1956; Doctoral Dissertations in Hispanic Languages and Literature, 1876-1966: (with James R. Chatham) The United States, Canada and Puerto Rico, 1970; A Concordance to Gustavo Adolfo Becquer's Poetry, 1970. Asst. editor Mundo Hispanico, 1954-55, Cuadernos Hispanoamericanos, 1958-59, Ediciones Cultura Hispanica, 1958-59, editor Revista de Estudios Hispanicos, 1967—. Contbr. numerous articles and revs. to profl. publs. Home: 222 The Highlands Tuscaloosa AL 35401 Office: PO Box 4931 University AL 35486

RULFO, JUAN, author; b. Sayula, Jalisco, Mexico, 1918; student U. Guadalajara, U. Mexico City, (fellow) Centro Mexicano de Escritores. Author: (short stories) El Llano en Llamas, 1953 (translated into English as The Burning Plain and Other Stories); (novel) Pedro Paramo, Address: care Centro Mexicano de Escritores Valle Arizpe 18 Mexico DF 12 Mexico*

RUMAGGI, LOUIS JACOB, ret. army ofcl., cons.; b. Memphis, Dec. 3, 1900; s. Louis and Garnet (Huntsbarger) R.; student Miami U., Oxford, O., 1917-18; B.S., U.S. Mil. Acad., 1922; B.S. in Civil Engring., U. Cal. at Berkeley, 1927; m. Miriam Louise Tuggle, Mar. 30, 1950; 1 dau., Louise Herron (Mrs. Alan Lyndal Reed). Commd. 2d lt. C.E., U.S. Army 1922, advanced through grades to maj. gen., 1953; acting chief engr. Army Forces, S.W. Pacific, 1945-46; engr. 8th U.S. Army, Korea, 1952-53; dep. chief engrs. U.S. Army, 1954-55; chief staff 6th U.S. Army, 1955-57; div. engr. North Central div., Corps Engrs., 1957-59; asso. Tex. Instruments, Inc., 1959-62. Decorated Legion of Merit with oak leaf cluster, D.S.M.; Ulchi medal (Korea). Fellow Am. Soc. C.E.; mem. Mil. Order World Wars, S.A.R., Newcomen Soc. N.Am. Mason (Shriner). Home: 8639 Edgemere Rd Dallas TX 75225

RUMBAUGH, RONALD R., exec. v.p. Am. C. of C. Execs. Address: 1522 K St NW Washington DC 20005

RUMLEY, JAMES DEWEY, JR., clergyman; b. Burlington, N.C., Dec. 1, 1920; s. James Dewey and Octavia Eula (Wilson) R.; A.B., Elon Coll., 1941; B.D., Lancaster Theol. Sem., 1958; m. Charlotte Grovelin Bridewell, June 6, 1958; children—James Dewey III, Caroline Elizabeth. Ordained to ministry United Ch. Christ, 1958; minister Lincoln Charge United Ch. Christ, Maiden, N.C., 1958-65, South Norfolk United Ch. Christ, Chesapeake, Va., 1965-66, St. Mark's United Ch. Christ, Cressona, Pa., 1966-72, Holiday (Fla.) United Ch. Christ, 1972—. Conf. rep. to dept. evangelism Pa. Council Chs., 1967-68; sec. commn. on evangelism Pa. S.E. Conf. United Ch. Christ, 1967-69; chmn. com. on evangelism Schuylkill Assn. Pa. S.E. Conf., 1967-69, moderator, 1969-71; pres. Schuylkill Assn. Ministerium Pa. S.E. Conf., United Ch. Christ, 1968-70; del. to Gen. Synod United Ch. Christ, 1971-73. Mem. Blue Mt. chpt. Am. Field Service, 1967-70. Mem. Lancaster Sem. Alumni Assn. Home: 1703 Forest Hills Dr Holiday FL 33589 Office: 1303 Pine Bough Lane Holiday FL 33589

RUMSFELD, DONALD, govt. ofcl.; b. Evanston, Ill., July 9, 1932; s. George Donald and Jeanette (Husted) R.; A.B., Princeton, 1954; m. Joyce Pierson, Dec. 27, 1954; children—Valerie Jeanne, Marcy Kay. Adminstrv. asst. to Congressman Dennison, 1958; registered rep. A.G. Co., Chgo., 1960-62; mem. 88th-90th Congresses, 13th Dist. Ill.; dir. Office Econ. Opportunities, 1969-71; counsellor to the Pres., 1971—. Mem. Council for Urban Affairs, 1969—. Served with USNR, 1954-57. Republican. Home: 2530 Crawford Evanston IL 60202 Office: White House 1600 Pennsylvania Av Washington DC 20500

RUNDLES, RALPH WAYNE, educator, physician; b. Urbana, Ill., Sept. 10, 1911; s. Don Cameron and Edith Grace (Hollopeter) R.; A.B., DePauw U., 1933; Ph.D., Cornell U., 1937; M.D., Duke, 1940; m. Mary Alice Cunningham, June 9, 1936 (div.); children—Susanna (Mrs. John Dunn), Charlotte, Ward Frederick; m. 2d, Marguerite S. Grafton, Nov. 28, 1968. Successively intern, asst. resident, resident medicine Univ. Hosp., Ann Arbor, Mich., 1940-43; instr. medicine, research asso. Simpson Meml. Inst., U. Mich., 1943-45; mem. faculty dept. medicine Duke Sch. Medicine, 1945—, prof. medicine, 1957—, head hematology and chemotherapy labs., 1947—; spl. research neuroanatomy, diabetes, blood diseases, cancer chemotherapy, gout. Chmn. S.E. Cancer Chemotherapy Coop. Study Group, 1956-66. Mem. Am. (pres. 1966-67), Internat. socs. hematology, Am., Durham-Orange County med. assns., Am. Fedn. Clin. Research, Assn. Am. Physicians, Am. Assn. Cancer Research, Phi Kappa Phi, Alpha Omega Alpha. Author papers in field. Home: 132 Pinecrest Rd Durham NC 27706

RUNGE, DELYLE PAUL, librarian; b. Madison, Wis., Feb. 3, 1918; s. Charles Delial and Josephine (Niebuhr) R.; B.A., U. Wis., 1940; B.S. in L.S., 1943; m. Ethelyn Fay Green, Sept. 26, 1943; children—Richard Rene, Willa Dee, Robert Roy. Dir. pub. relations, coordinator reference services, Grand Rapids (Mich.) Pub. Library, 1946-53; library dir. St. Petersburg (Fla.) Pub. Library, 1953—; library bldg. cons., 1964—. Mem. Fla. Library Adv. Com., 1971—. Served with AUS, 1943-46; ETO; mem. Res. Mem. Fla. Library Assn. (treas. 1955-57, chmn. pub. libraries sect. 1964-65, v.p. 1967-68, pres. 1968-69, exec. bd. 1969-72). Kiwanian. Home: 4520 Cortez Way S St Petersburg FL 33712 Office: 3745 9th Av N St Petersburg FL 33713

RUNKLE, ROBERT SCOTT, med. device research and devel. co. exec.; b. Washington, Mar. 9, 1936; s. Lloyd Manor and Louise (Armstrong) R.; B.S., Ga. Inst. Tech., 1960; m. Marion Elisabeth Grater, Mar. 26, 1960; children—Beth Armstrong, Brynn Allison. Project engr. research facilities planning br. Div. Research Services, NIH, Bethesda, Md., 1962-64, vice-chmn. Biohazards segment Nat. Cancer Inst., 1964-67; research contracts mgr. Becton, Dickinson & Co., Rutherford, N.J., 1967-69, adminstrv. mgr. research center, Raleigh, N.C., 1969—. Cons. Am. Inst. for Biol. Scis. Mem. adv. council com. Manpower staff Wake Opportunities Inc., 1971—. Mem. edn. com. Young Democratic Club of Wake County, 1971—. Served to lt. comdr. USPHS, 1962-67. Mem. Raleigh C. of C. (nat. legislation com. 1971—), Am. Pub. Health Assn., Am. Assn. for Lab. Animal Sci., Soc. Research Adminstrs., Am. Assn. Contamination Control (editor Jour. 1970—), Ga. Tech. Nat. Alumni Assn. Democrat. Episcopalian (chmn. racial and urban affairs div. program task force, 1970). Home: 344 Buncombe St Raleigh NC 27609 Office: PO Box 11276 Raleigh NC 27604

RUNKLE, WILLIAM AUBURN, physician; b. Greer, Va. Jan 3, 1900; s. Algernon Milton Eldred and Carrie (Gibson) R.; M.D., U. Va., 1925; m. Louise Dane, Jan 8, 1934; 1 son, William Auburn. Intern U. Va. Hosp., Charlottesville, 1924-25; house officer Worcester City Hosp., 1925-27; asst. resident radiology New Haven Hosp., 1927-28, resident, 1928-29; asst. in radiology Yale Sch. Medicine, 1927-29; practice medicine, specializing in radiology, Memphis, 1929-62; asst. roentgenologist Baptist Meml. Hosp., Memphis, 1929-30; roentgenologist Rudner Clinic, Memphis, 1930-62, staff radiologist VA MTG Hosp., Memphis, 1963-65; radiologist Cannon Meml. Hosp., Banner Elk, N.C., 1965—. Served from maj. to lt. col., M.C., AUS, 1942-46; ETO. Diplomate Am. Bd. Radiology. Fellow Am. Coll. Radiology; mem. Am., So. med. assns., Gen. Soc., N.C., Avery County med. socs., Am. Legion, 40 and 8, Radiol. Soc. N.Am., Memphis Roentgen Soc. (pres. 1953-54). Democrat. Methodist. Kiwanian. Home: Box 157 Banner Elk NC 28604 Office: Cannon Meml Hosp Banner Elk NC 28604

RUNNELS, POLLARD RHODE, III, dentist; b. Terrell, Tex., Mar. 9, 1943; s. Pollard Rhode and Nelle (Boggess) R.; B.A., U. Tex., 1965, D.D.S., 1969; m. Martha Joan Thomas, June 17, 1967; children—Angela Michele, Kelly Elizabeth. Pvt. practice dentistry, Terrell, 1969—. Pres., Kaufman County unit Am. Cancer Soc., 1970—; campaign chmn. Greater Terrell United Fund, 1971. Mem. 4th Dist. Dental Soc., Tex., Am. dental assns., Terrell C. of C. (dir.), Psi Omega (chief inquisitor 1966-67). Mem. Christian Ch. (sec. bd. 1970-71). Rotarian. Club: Oak Grove Country. Home: 806 Griffith St Terrell TX 75160 Office: 300 N Catherine St Terrell TX 75160

RUPE, JESSE CLIPPER, ret. research psychologist; b. Bethany, Mo., Jan. 5, 1906; s. Thomas N. and Alice (Hoylman) R.; B.A., Doane Coll., 1929; M.S., Purdue U., 1946, Ph.D., 1950; m. L. Pauline Smith, Oct. 19, 1935 (div. Dec. 1941); 1 dau., Barbara L. (Mrs. Keith Harrod); m. 2d, Inez F. White, July 29, 1950; 1 son, Jarrold Craig. Instr., Carnegie Inst. Tech., Pitts., 1946-48, Purdue U., Lafayette, Ind., 1948-50; research psychologist Air Force Personnel and Tng. Research Center, Lackland AFB, Tex., 1950-57, Lockheed Missile & Space Co., Sunnyvale, Cal., 1957-59, Human Resources Research Office, Alexandria, Va., 1959-64, N.Am. Rockwell, Washington, 1964-68, U.S. Army Behavior and Systems Research Lab., Arlington, Va., 1968-71; ret. Served with USAAF, 1943-45. Fellow Am. Psychol. Assn.; mem. Sigma Xi. Contbr. articles to publs. Home: 5301 Yvette Av El Paso TX 79924

RUPERT, CLAUD S(TANLEY), biophysicist, educator; b. Porterville, Cal., Feb. 24, 1919; B.S., Cal. Inst. Tech., 1941; Ph.D. in Physics, Johns Hopkins U., 1951; m. 1954; 2 children. Engr. trainee, sr. detail draftsman Lockheed Aircraft Corp., 1941-42; jr. instr. physics Johns Hopkins U., Balt., 1946-50, research asst., 1950-52, Am. Cancer Soc. fellow in biophysics, 1952-54, asst. prof., 1954-57, research asso. Sch. Hygiene and Pub. Health, 1957-58, asst. prof., 1958-62, asso. prof., 1962-65; prof. biology S.W. Center Advanced Studies, Dallas, 1965—. USPHS sr. research fellow, 1958-65; lab. guest Inst. Microbiology, Copenhagen, Denmark, 1961-62. Served to lt. comdr. USNR, 1942-46. Recipient Finsen medal Internat. Commn. on Photobiology, 1964. Mem. A.A.A.S., Biophys. Soc. Research on microbial reprodn. of infection and transformation of bacteria by nucleid acids, photochemistry, photobiology, Ph enzyme in virus and bacteria. Home: 3505 Gillon St Dallas TX 75205*

RUPP, ADOLPH FREDERICK, basketball coach; b. Halstead, Kan., Sept. 2, 1901; s. Henry and Anna (Lichti) R.; A.B., Kan. U., 1923; M.A., Columbia, 1930; m. Esther SMith, Aug. 29, 1931; 1 son, Adolph Frederick. Head basketball coach U. Ky., Lexington, 1930—. Dir. Central Dist. Warehousing Corp., Lexington. Mem. Nat. Basketball Rules Com., 1961—. Chmn., Shrine Crippled Childrens Hosp., 1942—. Named Southeastern Conf. Coach of Yr., 1963-66, 68-72, Nat. Coach of Yr., U.P.I., A.P., 1951, 59, 66. Mem. Ky. Hereford Assn. (pres. 1953-69), Nat. Assn. Basketball Coaches (dir. 1961—, pres. 1970-71), Delta Sigma Pi, Omicron Delta Kappa. Mason. Author: Championship Basketball, 1948, 56; Adolph Rupp's Basketball Guidebook. Home: 175 Eastover Dr Lexington KY 40502

RUSH, FRANK WILFORD, JR., business exec.; b. Selma, Ala., Oct. 31, 1938; s. Frank W. and Leila (Hillman) R.; student Jones County Jr. Coll., 1956-58; B.S., Miss. State U., 1964; m. Mary Frances Brown, Aug. 1, 1964; children—Misty Rose, Randy Wilford. With Arthur Anderson & Co., New Orleans and Memphis, 1964-69, sr. accountant, Memphis, 1967-69; treas. Bagwell-Neal div. Macke Co., Baton Rouge, 1969-70; controllor Schulte & Dieckhoff (USA), Inc., Charlotte, N.C., 1970—. Served with AUS, 1959-62. C.P.A., Miss., Tenn., La. Mem. Am. Inst. C.P.A.'s. Office: PO Box 10751 Charlotte NC 28201

RUSH, HOWARD JERALD, finance co. exec.; b. Georgetown, La., Sept. 14, 1927; s. Luther Bennette and Alma (Edwards) R.; grad. high sch.; m. Doris Clark, Mar. 4, 1950; children—Howard Jerald, Kenneth Ray, Kathryn Ann, Kelly Jane. Owner, Rush Furniture Co., Oakdale, Alexandria, Glenmora and Oberlin, La., 1948—; pres. Rush Finance Co., Oakdale, Glenmora Finance Co., Gt. Central Life Ins. Co., Oakdale, 1965—, Rush Funeral Homes, Oakdale, Pineville and Pine Prairie, La., 1966—, Resthaven Cemetery, Oakdale, 1968—; dir. Allen State Bank, Oakdale, L'Angelus Funeral Home, Ville Platte. Baptist (deacon 1957—). Home: Hwy 165 N Oakdale LA 74163 Office: 217 6th Av Oakdale LA 74463

RUSH, MADELON REINE FRANCIS (MRS. ALAN SYDNEY RUSH), clubwoman; b. Long Branch, N.J.; d. Charles Asa and Helen (Lylburn) Francis; B.S. cum laude, Syracuse U., 1927; m. Alan Sydney Rush, Aug. 14, 1929 (dec. Apr. 1946); children—Alan Francis, William Asa. Legal sec. Applegate, Stevens, Foster, Leonard & Reusille, lawyers, Red Bank, N.J., 1928-29; parish sec. Holy Trinity Episcopal Ch., West Palm Beach, Fla., 1947-57; dir. pub. relations Hotel George Washington, 1961-62; asst. sec. Hotel Pa., 1962-63; asst. parish sec. Ch. Bethesda-by-Sea, Palm Beach, Fla., 1958-60. Div. rec. sec. Fla. Assn. U. Women, 1960-64; div. sec. Fla. Secs. Assn., 1962-63; pres. Palm Beach County br. Am. Assn. U. Women, 1965-67. Bd. dirs. Community Services Council, West Palm Beach, 1951-52; sec. Palm Beach County Library Adv. Bd. Mem. Phi Kappa Phi, Gamma Epsilon Pi, Zeta Tau Alpha. Home: 812 Flamingo Dr West Palm Beach FL 33401

RUSH, NIXON ORWIN, librarian; b. Sapulpa, Okla., Aug. 18, 1907; s. Nixon Irdell and Fary (Woodward) R.; A.B., Friends U., Wichita, Kan., 1931; B.S., Columbia, 1932, M.S., 1945; m. Dorothy Louise Painter, June 14, 1933; children—Barbara, Donald, Bradford, Susan. Asst., Columbia U. Library, 1931-32, N.Y. Pub. Library, 1932-36; librarian, asst. prof. bibliography Colby Coll., Waterville, Me., 1936-45; librarian, asso. prof. bibliography Clark U. 1945-47; exec. sec. Assn. Coll. and Reference Libraries, Chgo., 1947-49, treas. 1946-47; dir. U. Wyo. Library, 1949-55, prof. library sci., 1955-58; dir. of libraries, prof. Fla. State U., 1958— Fulbright grantee for research in Gt. Britian, 1952-53. Mem. Am. (chmn. Am. Library History Round Table). Me. (pres. 1938-41), Mountain Plains (pres. 1955-56) library assns., Bibliog. Soc. Am. Phi Delta Kappa. Republican. Mem. Soc. of Friends. Kiwanian. Author: A Bibliography of the Published Writings of Rufus M. Jones, 1944; History of College Libraries in Maine, 1946; Mercer's Banditti of the Plains, 1961; Frederic Remington and Owen Wister: The Story of a Friendship, 1961; Spain's Final Triumph Over Great Britain in the Gulf of Mexico, 1966. Editor: Rufus Jones' Selected Stories of Native Maine Humor, 1945; Letters of G. Stanley Hall to Jonas Gilman Clark, 1948; Maine Library Assn. Bull., 1943-45; The Virginian, 1958; List of Books for High School Libraries, 1958. Contbr. to profl. and gen. periodicals. Home: 427 Vinnedge Ride Tallahassee FL 32303

RUSH, ORVILLE FINDLEY, lawyer, bus. exec.; b. Florence, S.C., July 18, 1909; s. Frank A. and Nora Leota (Roberts) R.; A.B., U. Ala., 1930; LL.B., U. Miss., 1933, J.D., 1968; grad. law sch., Georgetown U., 1933-34; LL.D., Olivet Coll., 1965, Atlanta Law Sch., 1967; m. Mary Wren, Aug. 21, 1941; children—Orville, Findley, Franklin Archibald, Robert Lindsey, Mary Penelope, Patricia, Pamela, Kingsley P. Editor-in-chief Bessemer (Ala.) Advertiser, 1926, also reporter Birmingham Age-Herald, 1925-26; corr. A.P. U.P. and several daily newspapers, also mags., 1926-30; men. editorial staff St. Louis Times, and publicity dir., Hotel Jefferson, St. Louis, 1930; admitted to Miss. bar, 1933; atty. PWA, Washington and Montgomery, Ala., 1933-35; personal rep., counsel Gov. Bibb Graves of Ala., 1935-38; spl. rep. State of Ala. in Washington, and dir. state planning bd., dir. state indsl. bd., 1935-38; rep., counsel several prominent fgn. and domestic corps., Washington, 1938— under own name; operator farms in Ala., Va., Md., 1940—; also citrus grove in Fla.; chmn. bd. Hicks Corp., Asheville, N.C., 1962—, Lynn Corp., Boston, 1962—, Channel Wing Corp., Enid, Okla., 1970-71; v.p. Hart & Burns, Inc.; dir. Fugazy Traveling, Inc., N.Y.C., Enerton Corp., Garfield, N.J., Heidelberg, Germany; Stewart Iron Works Co., H.K. Ferguson Co.; pres., dir. Spl. Indsl. Radio Services Assn., Inc., Washington. Mem. Washington Bd. Trade. Exec. com. Washington Conv. and Visitors Bur. Local bd. govs. Greenville (S.C.) unit and Phila. unit Shriners Hosp. for Crippled Children; chmn. bd. Shriners Hosp. for Crippled Children for N.Am; trustee George Washington U., 1969—, Boy's Club of Washington; personal rep. of gov. Ala. and ofcl. rep state of Ala. in Washington, 1956—; lt. col. Ala. Air Militia; men. Order of Ky. Cols. Mem. exec. com. Democratic Nat. Com. Jefferson-Jackson Day Dinners, 1949-51; mem. adv. com. Dem. Nat. Com., 1954; del. Dem. Nat. Conv. 1936, Young Dem. Conv. 1936. Named Man of Year Dixie Mag., 1967. Mem. Fedn. Ry. Progress, A.A.A.S., Washington Grand Opera, Birmingham C. of C., U. Ala. Alumni Assn. (pres. Washington and Eastern div., 1947-49), Columbia Hist. Soc., Miss. State Bar, Def. Orientation Conf. Assn., Am. Bar Assn., Am. Ordnance Assn., Assn. Governing Bds. Univs. and Colls., U. Ala. Nat. Alumni Assn. (v.p. at large). Nat. Sojourners, Heroes of 76, Ala. State Soc. (pres. Washington), Phi Sigma Kappa (Internat. Man of Year 1970). Methodist. Mason (33 deg., Shriner), Demolay Legion of Honor; Jester; imperial potentate and chmn. bd. dirs. Shrine of N.Am.; chmn. Shrine conv. Washington 1967), Rotarian. Clubs: Arlington-Fairfax (past pres.; Arlington, Va.); Touchdown, Alabama (pres.) (Washington); Cornell (N.Y.C.); U. Ala. Alumni (pres.) (Washington). Asso. editor: Ala. Law Jour., 1928-29. Contbr. numerous stories to mags. and newspapers. Home: 7300 Georgetown Pike McLean VA 22101 Office: Washington Bldg Washington DC 20005

RUSH, RICHARD HENRY, financier, economist; b. N.Y.C., Mar. 6, 1915; s. Henry F. and Bessie (Vreeland) R.; A.B. summa cum laude, Dartmouth, 1937, M.C.S., 1938; M.B.A. with highest distinction, Harvard, 1941, D.C.S. (Littauer fellow), 1942; m. Julia Halloran, Aug. 15, 1956; 1 dau. by previous marriage, Sally Haywood. Statistician, Tide Water Asso. Oil Co., 1938-40; asst. to chief div. regional economy U.S. Dept. Commerce, 1942-43; spl. asst. to pres. All Am. Aviation, 1943-45; chief aviation U.S. Bur. Fgn. and Domestic Commerce, Washington, 1945-46; exec. head Supermarket Inst., Boston, 1947-48; Washington rep. of J. Paul Getty, financier, mfr., Tulsa, 1951-52; partner Rush and Halloran, financiers, insurers, Washington, 1952-57; pres. Richard H. Rush Enterprises, Washington, 1958—; prof., dir. finance program Am. U., 1967-70; pres., chmn. bd. N.Am. Acceptance Corp., Washington, 1956-59; dir. aircraft div. DPA. 1951. NSRB, 1948-51; columnist Wall Street Transcript, 1971—. Trustee, chmn. finance com. also mus. com. Finch Coll., 1968-72. Mem. Am. Marketing Assn. (chmn. aviation com.), Am. Econ. Assn., Am. Assn. U. Profs., Internat. Platform Assn., Phi Beta Kappa, Omicron Delta Kappa, Phi Kappa Phi. Episcopalian. Club: Harvard (N.Y.C.). Author: Opportunities for Establishing New Business in Aviation, 1947; Trade Barriers in the Food Industry, 1943; Art as an Investment, 1961; A Strategy of Investing for Higher Return, 1962; The Techniques of Becoming Wealthy, 1963; Antiques As An Investment, 1968; The Wrecking Operation: Phase One, 1972. Contbg. editor Wall Street Reports, 1971—, Delegates World Bull., 1971—. Contbr. articles in Aviation Maintenance, 1947; Air Transport, 1944-47; Broadcasting, 1942; Domestic Commerce, 1942, 46; Flying Age, 1946; Jour. Marketing, 1943; Railway Age, 1944; Shipping Management, 1945; Soaring, 1945, 46; Traffic World, 1942. Contbr. articles to profl. jours. Lectr. on investments, art, and antiques. Address: 2039 New Hampshire Av NW Washington dc 20009 also 434 North St Greenwich CT 06830 also Villa Palladio Piombino Dese Italy

RUSHING, BARNIE ELMER, JR., retail co. exec.; b. Plainview, Tex., Oct. 27, 1916; s. Barnie Elmer and Zelma A. (Flake) R.; student Tex. Technol. Coll., 1933-35, U.S. Coast Guard Acad., 1944; m. Dorothy Ann York, Feb. 11, 1939; 1 son, Robert York. With Hemphill-Wells Co., Lubbock, Tex., 1934—, v.p., sec., 1952—. Pres., United Fund, Lubbock, 1959-60, Better Bus. Bur., Lubbock, 1958-59. Bd. dirs. Tex. Found. Mental Health and Mental Retardation, 1970—, Tex. Tech. Med. Found., 1970, Tex. Tech. U. Found., 1970—; vice chmn. bd. dirs., Textile Research Found., Tex. Technol. U., 1969-70; chmn. bd. mgrs. Lubbock County Hosp. Dist., 1969—; mem. Tex. Bd. Mental Health and Mental Retardation, 1970—; trustee Spencer A. Wells Found., 1958—, Hemphill-Wells Found., 1963—. Served with USCG, 1941-45. Recipient Distinguished Salesman's award for community service, 1965. Mem. Kappa Sigma, Delta Sigma Pi. Mem. Christian Ch. (chmn. ofcl. bd. 1954, chmn. bd. elders 1956). Mason (Shriner), Kiwanian. Clubs: Lubbock Country, Lubbock. Home: 4510 W 17th St Lubbock TX 79416 Office: PO Box 981 1212 Av J Lubbock TX 79408

RUSHING, JOE BOB, coll. chancellor; b. Zephry, Tex., May 23, 1921; s. Cordie M. and Vallie (Parson) R.; B.A., Howard Payne Coll., 1946; M.A., East Tex. State Coll., 1949; Ph.D., U. Tex., 1952; postdoctoral study U. Mich., 1959; m. Elaine Whitis, Dec. 21, 1946;children—Anita Sherron, Cynthia Ann, Robert Scott. Tchr. sci., adminstr. Levelland (Tex.) High Sch., Mt. Pleasant (Tex.) High Sch., 1946-50; teaching fellow, U. Tex., 1950-52; dir. adult edn. Wharton Jr. Coll., 1952-54; dean grad. div. Howard Payne Coll., 1954-58, adminstrv. v.p., 1956-60; pres. Jr. Coll. of Broward County. Ft. Lauderdale, Fla., 1960-65; pres. Tarrant County Jr. Coll. Dist., Ft. Worth, 1965-69, chancellor, 1969—. Served with AUS, 1942-46; maj. USAF Res., 1951—. Mem. Pi Sigma Alpha, Phi Delta Kappa, Kappa Delta Pi. Baptist. Home: Ft Worth Nat Bank Bldg Fort Worth TX 76101

RUSHLOW, PHILIP LEO, indsl.-fashion exec.; b. Covington, Ky., Feb. 2, 1929; s. Leo B. and Elinor (Slater) R.; B.A., Wayne State U., 1945; M.A., Mich. State U., 1949; m. Bonnie L. Miller, June 25, 1945; children—Philip Lee, David R. Regional mgr. B.F. Goodrich Co., Detroit, 1949-56; pres. Lansing Gen. Tire Co. (Mich.), 1956-59, Azure Internat. Corp., Lansing, 1959-64; pres. Fashion Industries, Inc., Miami, Fla., 1964-69, also chief exec. officer; chief exec. officer Motivational Marketing Systems, Inc., Miami, Richelieu Assos., Inc., Wig Lady, Inc.; dir. Mona Lisa Co., N.Y.C., Venture Internat. Corp., Ft. Lauderdale, Fla., LaRonde Fashion Products, Inc., Miami; v.p., dir. H.B. & R. Advt. Cons., Miami. Cons., Nat. Fashion Assn. Contbr. articles to profl. jours. Home: 2823 NE 26th Pl Fort Lauderdale FL 33306 Office: 2555 E Sunrise Blvd Fort Lauderdale FL 33304

RUSHTON, WILLIAM JAMES, life ins. exec.; b. Birmingham, Ala., July 10, 1900; s. James Franklin and Willis (Roberts) R.; B.S., Washington & Lee U., Lexington, Va., 1921; H.H.D., Southwestern at Memphis, 1959; m. Elizabeth Perry, November 24, 1926; children—William James, III, James. Asst. mgr. Birmingham Ice & Cold Storage Co., 1922-27, v.p., 1927-32, pres. 1932-38, v. chmn. bd., sec., 1938-57; pres. Protective Life Ins. Co., 1937-67, chmn. bd. dirs., 1967—; mem. adv. bd. Investment Co. of Am.; chmn. bd. Franklin Coal Mining Co., 1927-42; dir. First Nat. Bank of Birmingham, Alabama Power Co., Gulf, Mobile & Ohio R.R. Co. Served to col., U.S. Army, World War II. Chief, Birmingham Ordnance Dist., U.S. Army, 1946-61. Vice chmn., trustee, So. Research Inst. Pres. Birmingham Boy Scout Council, 1927-30 (dir. 1925-55); mem. nat. citizens com. United Community Campaigns Am., 1961; dir. Birmingham Community Chest, 1937— (pres., 1954), Birmingham Mus. Art; trustee Children's Hosp., Agnes Scott Coll., Decatur, Ga., 1935-45. Mem. Am. Ordnance Assn. (v.p.), Nat. Assn. Ice Indus (dir. 1928—; pres. 1936-37); Nat. Assn. Refrigerated Warehouses (pres. 1933-35; mem. Nat. Code Authority), Am. Warehousemen's Assn. (pres. 1935-36), Life Ins. Assn. of Am. (dir. 1955-61), Health Ins. Assn. Am. (dir. 1964—), Am. Life Conv. (Ala. v.p.), Beta Gamma Sigma, Beta Theta Pi, Omicron Delta Kappa, Delta Sigma Rho. Presbyn. (mem. bd. annuities and relief Presbyn. Ch. in U.S. 1959—). Mason (32 deg., Shriner). Dec. Legion of Merit. Clubs: Rotary (pres. 1952-53), Mountain Brook, Country, Downtown, The Club (Birmingham). Home: 2848 Balmoral Rd Birmingham AL 35223 Office: Protective Life Ins Co Birmingham AL 35203

RUSKIN, DAN BERNARD, bus. exec.; b. Bklyn., Oct. 5, 1899; s. Harris L. and Anna (Oginz) R.; grad. Eron Coll., 1920; m. Mollie Kaplan, July 12, 1922; children—Charlyne (Mrs. James Meyer), Lloyd L., Andrea (Mrs. Robert C. Magoon). Co-owner Pub. Nat. Investors, 1961— sec.-treas. O and R Co., 1945—; v.p. Rusoro Corp., 1955—; pres. P & P Holding Corp., 1960— (all Greater Miami, Fla.); dir. Community Nat. Bank & Trust Co., Bal Harbour, Fla. Campaign chmn. Greater Miami Jewish Fedn., 1950, pres., 1951-52, hon. pres., 1952; mem. citizens bd. U. Miami, 1959—. Trustee Mt. Sinai Hosp.; 1946-, v.p., 1952-; trustee Temple Israel Greater Miami. Served with USCGR, 1944-45. Mason (Shriner), Elk. Home: 10245 Collins Av Bal Harbour FL 33154 Office: 1 Lincoln Rd Miami Beach FL 33139

RUSSELL, ALLAN WILSON, social worker; b. Hempstead, L.I., N.Y., Oct. 3, 1931; s. Frank Wilson and Pearl (Horsefield) R.; B.S., Fla. State U., 1959, M.S.W., 1959; m. Marcia Lorena McPherson, Nov. 23, 1950 (div.); children—Sharron Lanette, Carol Celeste, Jenean Suzanne, Wendy Gayle; m. 2d, Doris Dunn Young, May 13, 1972. Formerly with social service dept. Fla. State Hosp. at Chattahoochee, Dade County (Fla.) Child Guidance Clinic; mem. social service dept. Jackson Meml. Hosp. Psychiat. Inst., Miami, Fla., 1959-61, also instr. U. Miami Sch. Mental Medicine; exec. dir., chief social worker Dougherty County Mental Health Clinic, Albany, Ga., 1961—. Lectr. hypnosis Family Inst., New Orleans; psychiat. social work cons. Phoebe Putney Meml. Hosp., Naval Air Sta., Albany, Ga. Bd. dirs. Community Orgn. Drug Abuse Control. Squadron information officer Civil Air Patrol, 1967—. Served with USN, 1949-53. Mem. Nat. Acad. Certified Social Workers, Am. Acad. Health Adminstrn., Ga. Pub. Health Assn., Ga. Community Mental Health Program Dirs. Assn. (past pres.), Royal Soc. Health (London), Nat. Assn. Social Workers, Southeastern (treas.), Atlanta (sec.-treas.) group psychotherapy socs., Canadian Inst. Hypnosis, Internat. Soc. for Profl. Hypnosis. Club: Exchange. Home: 1106 Peachtree Terrace Albany GA 31705 Office: 2031 Newton Rd PO Box 127 Albany GA 31702

RUSSELL, BENJAMIN, realtor; b. Alexander City, Ala., Jan. 18, 1938; s. Robert Alston and Adelia (McConnell) R.; student Mercer U., 1957-59, U. Ala., 1959-60; m. Luanne Radney, Apr. 8, 1961; 1 dau., Adelia McConnell. Pres. Russell Lands, Inc., Alexander City, Ala., 1970—, also dir.; dir. Russell Mills, Inc., 1960—. Leader Explorer Tuckabatchee council Boy Scouts Am., 1962-65, instl. rep., 1969; vol. fireman, Alexander City, 1962-67; pres. Alexander City Girl's Camp Assn., 1969-71, Lake Martin Recreation Assn., 1970—; chmn. Indsl. Park Bd., Alexander City, 1971-72; exec. dir. Windcreek Park, 1969-71; chmn. Alexander City Airport Com., 1968. Mem. Ala. Commn. Consumer Health and Edn. Bd., adv. bd. Ala. Health Environmental Quality. Bd. dirs., v.p. Benjamin Roberta Charitable Found.; trustee Lyman Ward Acad. Served with Air Nat. Guard, 1959-65. Mem. C. of C. (2d v.p. 1971, dir. 1967-71), Tallapoosa Hist. Assn., Sigma Nu. Baptist. Elk, Kiwanian. Club: Internat. Underwater Explorers (Freeport, grand Bahama). Home: 203 Ridgeway Dr Alexander City AL 35010 Office: PO Drawer 272 Alexander City AL 35010

RUSSELL, BERNARD CURRY, librarian, educator; b. Palmetto, Fla., Nov. 19, 1914; s. Absalom McKinney Curry and Ethel Harris (Durst) R.; A.B., Asbury Coll., 1936; B.D., Emory U., 1940; Ph.D., Drew U., 1951; postgrad. Mansfield Coll., Oxford, Eng., 1966; m. Frances Virginia Tucker, June 7, 1942; children—Rosa Linda (Mrs. Steven Lee Talbert), Edwin L., Samuel S., Frances Adele. Ordained to ministry Methodist Ch., 1939; pastor, LaBelle, Fla., 1939-41, East Setauket, N.Y., 1941-44, Greensboro, Fla., 1944-46; prof. religion and philosophy Emory and Henry Coll., 1946-53, Lambuth Coll., Jackson, Tenn., 1953-55; prof. religion and philosophy Pfeiffer Coll., Misenheimer, N.C., 1955—, dir. library, 1966—. Mem. Am. Acad. Religion, N.C. Tchrs. Religion, N.C., Southeastern library assns. Methodist. Home: PO Box 36 New London NC 28127 Office: Pfeiffer Coll Misenheimer NC 28109

RUSSELL, CARL HAIRSTON, mortician, city ofcl.; b. Winston-Salem, N.C., Sept. 18, 1910; s. Charles G. and Mary R. (Hairston) R.; B.S., Johnson C. Smith U., 1933; postgrad. U. Minn., 1938-39; m. Florrie M. Sitgraves, Oct. 3, 1937; children—Charlene G., Carolyn A., Carl Hairston, Christopher, Constance, Camille R., Cynthia F., Cedric L., Carmen D. Tchr.-prin. elementary high sch., Rural Hall, N.C., 1933-34; owner, mgr. Russell Funeral Home, Winston- Salem, 1939—. Alderman, Winston-Salem, 1961—, mayor pro-tem, 1967—; mem. Winston-Salem Citizens Coalition. Mem. Civil Def. Adv. Council, Art Council. Bd. dirs. Expt. in Self Reliance; trustee Kittrell (N.C.) Coll. Mem. Nat., N.C. funeral dirs. assns., N.A.A.C.P., Winston-Salem C. of C., Urban League, Omega Psi Phi. Mem. A.M.E. Ch. (trustee). Mason (32 deg., Shriner). Home: 2200 23d St NE Winston Salem NC 27105 Office: 822 N Ridge Av Winston Salem NC 27101

RUSSELL, CHARLES STEVENS, SR., judge; b. Richmond, Va., Feb. 23, 1926; s. Charles H. and Nita M. (Stevens) R.; B.A., U. Va., 1946, LL.B., 1948; m. Carolyn Elizabeth Abrams, Mar. 18, 1951; children—Charles Stevens, David Tyler. Admitted to Va. bar, 1949; practiced in Arlington and Fairfax Counties, Va., 1951-67; mem. firm Jesse, Phillips, Klinge & Kendrick (name later changed to Phillips, Kendrick, Gearheart & Aylor). Arlington, 1951-57, partner, 1957-67; judge 35th Circuit, Va., 1967—. Dir. Mt. Vernon Nat. Life Ins. Co., Arlington. Counsel, Va. Hwy. Commn., 1957-67. Mem. Arlington County Commn. Precinct Revision, 1962-64, Commn. on Youth Arlington County, 1965-67. Served to lt. comdr. USNR, 1943-46, 49-51. Mem. Am., Va. (exec. com., council 1960-67, ethics com. 1965-67), Arlington County (v.p. 1959-60) bar assns., Raven Soc., Jefferson Soc., Sigma Nu Phi, Sigma Phi Epsilon, Omicron Delta Kappa. Episcopalian (vestryman). Home: 4618 N Dittmar Rd Arlington VA 22207 Office: Arlington County Ct House Arlington VA 22201

RUSSELL, DAN M., JR., U.S. dist. judge; b. Magee, Miss., Mar. 15, 1913; s. Dan M. and Beulah (Watkins) R.; B.A., U. Miss., 1935, LL.B., 1937; m. Dorothy Tudury, Dec. 27, 1942 children—Ronald Truett, Dorothy Dale, Richard Brian. Admitted to Miss. bar, 1937; practiced in Gulfport and Bay St. Louis, Miss.; U.S. judge So. Dist. Miss., Biloxi, 1965—. Dir. So. Savs. & Loan Assn., Gulfport. Chmn. Hancock (Miss.) Civic Action Assn., 1964—. Democratic presdl. elector, 1964; chmn. Hancock County Election Commn., 1959-64. Served to lt. comdr. USNR, 1941-45. Mem. Miss. Hancock County (v.p. 1964-65) bar assns., Hancock County C. of C. (pres. 1946), Scribblers, Tau Kappa Alpha. Rotarian (pres. Bay St. Louis 1946). Home: 321 Main St Bay St Louis MS 39520 Office: US Courthouse Biloxi MS 39533

RUSSELL, DAVID EMERSON, cons. mech. engr.; b. Jacksonville, Fla., Dec. 20, 1922; s. David Herbert and Wilhelmina (Ash) R.; B.Mech. Engring., U. Fla., 1948. Mech. engr. United Fruit Co., N.Y.C., 1948-50, U.S. Army Corps Engrs., Jacksonville, 1950-54; v.p. Beiswenger Hoch and Assos., Inc., Jacksonville, 1954-57; owner, operator David E. Russell and Assos., cons. engrs., Jacksonville, 1957—. Chmn. Jacksonville Water Quality Control Bd., 1969-72. Served to 2d lt. AUS, 1943-46. Registered profl. engr., Fla., Ga. Mem. Am. Soc. M.E. (chmn. N.E. Fla. 1967-68). Nat. Soc. Profl. Engrs., Am. Soc. Heating. Refrigerating and Air Conditioning Engrs., Fla. Engring. Soc. Episcopalian. Clubs: Seminole; University (Jacksonville). Home: 1606 King St Jacksonville FL 32204 Office: 110 Riverside Av Jacksonville FL 32202

RUSSELL, DAVID LEE, dentist, educator; b. Frederick, Okla., Nov. 22, 1936; s. Joe Alvin and Alta (Grissom) R.; student U. Okla., 1955-56; B.S., Abilene Christian Coll., 1959; D.M.D., U. Ala., 1962, M.S. in Clin. Dentistry, 1967; m. Jane Brock Abell, June 28, 1969; 1 son, David Lee. Asst. prof. dentistry (pedodontics) U. Ala. Sch. Dentistry, Birmingham, 1967-70, asso. prof. dentistry, 1970—, chmn. dept. pedodontics, 1968—; mem. staff Children's Hosp., Birmingham, 1968—, chief dental services, 1968—; dir. dental clinic Center for Devel. and Learning Disorders, 1968—. Served to capt. Dental Corps, USAF, 1962-64; MTO. NIH trainee fellow, 1960. Mem. Am. Dental Assn., Am. Acad. Pedodontics, Am. Soc. Dentistry for Children, Am. Assn. Dental Schs., Southeastern Soc. Pedodontics, Sigma Xi, Omicron Kappa Upsilon, Psi Omega. Mem. Ch. of Christ. Home: 600 Devon Dr Birmingham AL 35209

RUSSELL, DONALD STUART, U.S. circuit judge; b. Lafayette Springs, Miss., Feb. 22, 1906; s. Jesse and Lula (Russell) R.; A.B., U. S.C., 1925, LL.B., 1928, LL.D.; postgrad. U. Mich., 1929; LL.D., Wofford Coll., Lander Coll., The Citadel, U. So. Cal., Clemson U., C.W. Post, L.I.; m. Virginia Utsey, June 15, 1929; children—Donald, Mildred, Scott, John. Admitted to S.C. bar, 1928, practiced in Spartanburg, 1930-42; asso. firm Nicholls, Wyche & Byrnes, Nicholls, Wyche & Russell, and Nicholls & Russell, 1930-38; pvt. practice, 1938-42; mem. Price Adjustment Bd., War Dept., Washington, 1942; asst. to dir. econ. stablzn., 1942, asst. to dir. war moblzn., 1943; dep. dir. Office War Mobzn. Reconversion, 1945; asst. sec. state, 1945-47; pres. U. S.C., 1951-57; pvt. law practice, 1957-63; gov. State of S.C., 1963-65; apptd. to U.S. Senate from S.C., 1965; U.S. dist. judge S.C., 1967-71; U.S. circuit judge 4th Jud. Circuit, 1971—. Mem. Wriston Com. Fgn. Service, 1954. Trustee Emory U., Converse Coll., Spartanburg Jr. Coll., Benedict Coll.; bd. dirs. Christ Sch. Served as maj. AUS, 1944; ETO. Mem. Am. Legion, Phi Beta Kappa. Methodist. Home: 716 Otis Blvd Spartanburg SC 29302 Office: Fed Bldg 205 Magnolia St Spartanburg SC 29301

RUSSELL, EMMETT, JR., ins. co. exec.; b. Wartrace, Tenn., Feb. 11, 1905; s. Emmett and Bertha (Townes) R.; B.A., Vanderbilt U., 1928; m. Lutie Price, Oct. 30, 1932 children—Lutie Lane (Mrs. W. R. Newsom III), Emmett III. With Life & Casualty Ins. Co. Tenn., Nashville, 1929—, v.p., 1952-68, sr. v.p. 1968—. Chmn. Nashville Davison County chpt. A.R.C., 1956. Mem. So. Round Table Life Ins. Advertisers (chmn.), Nat. Life Advertisers Assn. (exec. com.), Am. Bus. Club (past pres.) Inst. Home Office Underwriters (founder, past charter pres.), Eta Sigma Phi, Lambda Chi Alpha. Methodist. Clubs: State Exchange (past pres.); Hillwood Country (a founder); Nashville City (founder). Home: 2428 Abbott Martin Rd Nashville TN 37215 Office: Life and Casualty Tower Nashville TN 37219

RUSSELL, ERNEST, JR., govt. ofcl.; b. Massillon, O., Feb. 16, 1936; s. Ernest and Alzater (Carter) R.; student Western Res. U., 1951-53; B.A., U. Kan., 1958; certificate Fisk U. Inst. Human Relations, 1962; m. Signe Hippert, Nov. 24, 1967; children—Robert Sheldon, Koren Heather. Employment interviewer Kan. Employment Service, Topeka, 1959-60; ednl. dir. Kan. Commn. on Civil Rights, Topeka, 1960-62; exec. dir. Des Moines Commn. on Human Rights, 1962-65; dir. Bur. Employment and Tng., Charlotte, 1965-66; VISTA tng. officer, Washington, 1966-67; sr. VISTA program analyst, regional office Office Econ. Opportunity, San Francisco, 1967-69, VISTA adminstr., regional office, N.Y.C., 1969-70, dep. asst. dir. VISTA, Washington, 1970-71; asso. dir. for adminstrn. Office of Adminstr., Office Econ. Opportunity, Washington, 1971—. Cons. race relations. Recipient award Nat. Assn. Equal Housing Opportunity, 1962, Nat. Assn. Colored Women's Clubs, 1963, N.A.A.C.P., 1964, award for meritorious service Settlement House, Des Moines, 1965, Outstanding Performance award Office Econ. Opportunity, 1970, 71. Mem. Nat. Assn. Inter Group Ofcls., Pub. Personnel Assn. Home: 3061 Porter St NW Washington DC 20008 Office: Office Econ Opportunity 1200 19th St NW Washington DC 20506

RUSSELL, JAMES RICHARD, editor; b. Wingo, Ky., Apr. 21, 1933; s. Voris Boaz and Cleo Patra (Holloway) R.; A.B., Ind. U., 1961; postgrad. U. Ky., 1963-64; m. Diana Ruth Bryant, Aug. 11, 1956; children—James Nathan, Cassandra Ruth. Copy editor Evening Republican, Columbus, Ind., 1961; asst. publs. editor Cooperative Extension Service U. Ky., Lexington, 1962-68, chmn. pub. information, 1968-71; farm editor Louisville (Ky.) Courier Jour., 1971—. Served with USNR, 1952-56. Named Ky. col. Mem. Ky. Hist. Assn., Ky. Farm Press and Radio Assn., Newspaper Farm Editors Am. Home: 820 Marengo Dr Middletown KY 40243 Office: 525 W Broadway Louisville KY 40202

RUSSELL, JERRY LEWIS, advt., pub. relations exec.; b. Little Rock, July 21, 1933; s. Jerry Lewis and Frances (Lieb) R.; B.A. in Journalism, U. Ark., 1958; m. Alice Anne Cason, Feb. 14, 1969; children—(by previous marriage)—Jerry L. III, Susan Frances; Leigh Anne, Andrew J. III. Pub. relations dir. Little Rock C. of C., 1958; editor, pub. The Visitor, Little Rock, 1959-60; sec.-mgr. Ark. Press Assn., Little Rock, 1960-61; account exec. Brandon Agy., Little Rock, 1961-65; founder Guide Advt. (now part of River City Enterprises), also River City Pubs., Little Rock 1965-70, 72—; dir. pub. relations services S.M. Brooks Agy., Little Rock, 1970-72. Pres., Pulaski County Young Democrats Club, 1963; mem. Pulaski County Dem. Com., 1966-67. Served with AUS, 1953-56. Mem. Little Rock Advt. Club (pres. 1967-68, sec. 1963-65, 69-71), Pub. Relations Soc. Am. (dir. Ark. chpt.), Rackensack Folklore Soc., Little Big Horn Assos., Ark., Pulaski County hist. socs., Am. Assn. Local and State History, Civil War Round Table Ark. (charter pres. 1964-65), Civil War Round Table Assos. (exec. dir.), Circus Fans Assn. Am., Circus Hist. Soc., Westerners International. Club: Optimist of Heights (sec.-treas. 1960-72 Little Rock). Home: 9 Lefever Lane Little Rock AR 72207 Office: 7624 Cantrell Rd Little Rock AR 72207

RUSSELL, JOHN J., bishop; b. Balt., Dec. 1, 1897; s. John W. and Mary V. (Joyce) R.; student St. Charles Coll., A.B., St. Mary's Sem., 1919, A.M., 1920; S.T.D., U. Rome, 1923. Ordained priest Roman

Catholic Ch., 1923; pastor St. Ursulas Ch., Balt., 1937-46. St. Patrick's Ch., Washington, 1946-48, Ch. of Nativity, 1948-50; domestic prelate, 1945; consecrated bishop, Charleston, S.C., 1950; bishop, Richmond, Va., 1958—. Dir. Catholic Big Bros., 1927-46, Jr. Holy Name Socs., Catholic Evidence Guild, Archdiocesan Catholic Charities. Home: 800 Cathedral Pl Richmond VA 23220

RUSSELL, LAO (MRS. WALTER RUSSELL), educator; b. nr. Tring, Eng.; d. Alfred William and Florence (Hills) Cook; naturalized, 1947; ed. pvt. tutors; m. Walter Russell, July 29, 1948. Founder, Walter Russell Found. (now known as U. Sci. and Philosophy), Waynesboro, Va., 1948, pres., 1948-57, dir., 1957—; founded Shrine of Beauty known as Swannanoa Palace and Sculpture Gardens, 1948. Founder Man-Woman Equalization League, 1955, Age of Character Clubs, 1966. Author: Scientific Answer to Human Relations, 1948; God Will Work With You But Not For You, 1955; Love-A Scientific and Living Philosophy of Love and Sex, 1966; (with Walter Russell) Home Study Course in Universal Law, Natural Science and Living Philosophy, 1950, Atomic Suicide, 1957; World Crisis-Its Explanation and Solution, 1958, The One-World Purpose, 1960, An Eternal Message of Light and Love, 1964. Executed statue (with husband) The Christ of the Blue Ridge. Address: Univ Science and Philosophy Swannanoa Waynesboro VA 22980

RUSSELL, LEWIS FRANKLIN, judge; b. Dallas, Apr. 19, 1915; s. John L. and Rebecca (Jones) R.; B.A., So. Methodist U., 1935, LL.B., 1941; postgrad. Columbia Law Sch., 1941; m. Katherine Higginbotham, July 20, 1940; children—Carol, Lewis Franklin, Lee H., Katherine. Admitted to Tex. bar, 1941; atty. U.S. Bd. Tax Appeals, 1942; spl. agt. FBI, 1942-47; practiced in Dallas, 1947-58; judge Juvenile Ct., Dallas County, 1959—. Chmn. Juvenile Bd. Dallas County; lectr. S.W. Legal Found. Bd. dirs. East Dallas YMCA. Mem. Nat. Council Juvenile Ct. Judges (v.p.), Nat. Council Crime and Delinquincy (adv. council judges), Tex. Council Adminstrn. of Justice, State Bar Tex., Am., Dallas bar assns. Baptist (chmn. bd. trustees). Mason (Shriner), Lion (dir., pres. 1969-70). Home: 6758 Avalon St Dallas TX 75214 Office: Ct House Dallas TX 75202

RUSSELL, ORPHA REA BRANNON, accountant, journalist; b. Porter, Ark., Oct. 23, 1908; d. Floyd Taylor and Susie Mae (Tabor) Brannon; student Walton Sch. Commerce, 1926-29, U. Okla., summers 1939, 45, 53, 57, 58, U. Tulsa, 1940-57; m. Millard Fillmore Russell, Sept. 21, 1929 (div. Mar. 1945); children—Loanne Joe (Mrs. Bill M. Burney), Betty Rea (Mrs. Charles E. Schaub). Accounting clk. White Truck Co., 1923-26, Ind. Oil & Gas Co., 1926-29; free-lance tng. inventory crew, 1929-40; accounting clk. Bethlehem Supply Co., 1940-47; chief accountant Refinery Engring. Co., Tulsa, 1947-60, sec.-treas., 1969-70; ind. accountant, Tulsa, 1960—. Life mem. Five Civilized Tribes Mus., Nat. Hall of Fame for Am. Indians. Recipient Outstanding Employee of Year award Refinery Engring. Co., 1952. Mem. Am. Soc. Women Accountants, Nat. Fedn. Bus. and Profl. Womens Clubs, Tulsa Bus. and Profl. Womens Club (treas., past pres.), Okla. Fedn. Bus. and Profl. Womens Club (past pub. relations chmn.), Inter-Club Council Tulsa Bus. and Profl. Womens Clubs (pub. relations chmn.), Tulsa Fedn. Womens Clubs (past auditor), Okla. (life, dir. 1971-73), Tulsa County (dir. 1971-73) hist. socs., Thomas Gilcrease Inst. Am. History and Art, Smithsonian Instn. (asso.), Nat. League Am. Pen women (nat. registrar 1960-62, nat. biennial chmn. 1964-66, Okla. pres. 1962-64, Tulsa pres. 1958-60, 66-68, Okla. v.p. 1970-72, treas. Tulsa 1970-74, nat. treas. 1972—), Nat. Hist. Soc. (founding asso.). Editor: The Bedouin, 1961—; Headband & Feather, 1968-69. Contbr. articles to profl. publs. Address: 8920 E Oklahoma Pl Tulsa OK 74115

RUSSELL, PHEBE GALE (MRS. FRANK M. RUSSELL), broadcasting, TV exec.; b. N.Y.C., Dec. 23, 1910; d. George H. and Marian (Hyde) Gale; grad. high sch.; m. Frank M. Russell, Sept. 25, 1940; children—Gale, Morgan N. Publicity dir. NBC, Washington, 1929-39; v.p. radio sta. WICO, Salisbury, Md., 1958-62; pres. Ellensburg (Wash.) TV Corp., 1961-68, PGR Enterprises, 1962—; owner TV Cable Cos., Appalachia, Norton, and Big Stone Gap, Va., 1962-71. Mem. women's bd. George Washington U. Hosp. Mem. D.A.R., Mayflower Soc. Huguenot Soc., Internat. Platform Assn., Nepal Soc. U.S., D.C. Women's Golf Assn., Daus. of Cincinnati. Clubs: Congressional Country (Washington); Kenwood Garden (pres. 1962-64). Address: 5101 River Rd Apt 918 Washington DC 20016

RUSSELL, RICHARD ROBERT, physician; b. Dallas, Nov. 19, 1931; s. William Byron and Mattie Bennie (Russell); B.S., So. Meth. U., 1953; M.D., U. Tex., 1956; m. Bertha Joy Liles, Nov. 29, 1957; children—Gina Lori, Lisa Michelle, Brian Keith. Intern, U.S. Naval Hosp., San Diego, 1956-57; practice medicine, specializing in family practice, Mesquite, Tex., 1960—; mem. staff Mesquite Meml. Hosp., chief staff, 1964-66, 72—, also mem. bd. dirs. Dir. Mesquite State Bank, Aloe Vera Am., Inc. Mem. bd. edn. Mesquite (Tex.) Ind. Sch. Dist., 1971—. Trustee, sec. bd. Christian Coll. S.W. Served with USNR, 1956-60. Diplomate Am. Bd. Family Practice. Mem. Am. Acad. Family Physicians (pres. Dallas chpt. 1970-71). Mem. Ch. of Christ (deacon 1970—). Home: 410 Riggs Circle Mesquite TX 75149 Office: 200 W Kearney St Mesquite TX 75149

RUSSELL, ROBERT BAXTER, constrn. co. exec.; b. Rock Hill, S.C., Sept. 22, 1919; s. Robert B. and Edna (Banks) R.; B.S., The Citadel, 1941; postgrad. Pa. State Coll., 1941.; m. Cecile Arnold Martin, June 9, 1946; children—Robert Baxter, Lynn Arnold, Nancy Martin. Chief engr., project mgr. V.P. Loftis Co., Charlotte N.C. and Charleston, S.C., 1941-49; pres. Ruscon Constrn. Co., Charleston, 1949-71, chmn. bd., chief exec. officer, 1971—; pres. Constrn. Equipment Corp., Charleston, 1955—. Constrn. Equipment Sales, Inc., Charleston, 1963—; chmn. bd. R-C Steel Bldg. Co., Inc. Charleston, 1964—; pres. Superior Services Co., Inc., 1967—; partner Robert B. Russell & Assos., Charleston, 1960—; dir. Empire Home Loans, Inc., Knight and Miller Oil Co., Investors Heritage Life Ins. Co. of South. Former mem. S.C. Commn. on Higher Edn., 1965—; asso. mem. Citadel Edn. Found. Trustee Clemson Coll. Archtl. Found.; bd. dirs. Charlestown Devel. Bd., R.B. Russell Found., Charleston; Mem. Navy League (past pres.), S.C., Charleston Trident, U.S. chambers commerce, Asso. Gen. Contractors Am. (Carolinas past pres.), Am. Soc. C.E., Nat. Soc. Profl. Engrs., Soc. Am. Mil. Engrs., Hibernian Soc. Rotarian, Elk. Clubs: Carolina Yacht, Charleston Country, Snee Farms (Charleston); Palmetto (Columbia, S.C.); Poinsett (Greenville, S.C.); Old Baldy (Saratoga, Wyo.); City (Charlotte, N.C.). Home: 120 S Battery Charleston SC 29401 Office: 149-151 E Bay St Charleston SC 29401

RUSSELL, RUTH, mem. Democratic Nat. Com.; b. Gallatin, Tenn., Feb. 28,, 1908; d. Frank Bernard and Nancy (Jackson) Seay; student Gallatin Pvt. Inst., 1925-27; m. Oscar Alexander Russell, June 4, 1927. Ct. reporter, Summer Trousdale, Wilson and Macon counties, Tenn., 1928-58; dep. clk. Chancery Ct., Summer County, 1946-59; mem. Tenn. Dem. Exec. Com., 1946-59, chmn., 1956-59; mem. Dem. Nat. Com., 1957—. Dir. First Mortgage Co., Gallatin, Tenn. Registration chmn. Summer County chpt. A.R.C. Named bus. woman of yr. Gallatin Bus. and Profl. Women's Club, 1956. Mem. Tenn. Clks. Assn. (chmn. Middle Tenn. div. 1958-59), Gallatin Bus. and Profl. Women's Club (past pres., chmn. career advancement). Mem. Order Eastern Star (past matron). Home: Gallatin TN 37066 Office: Ct House Gallatin TN 37066

RUSSELL, SPRUELL ALTON, JR., san. engr.; b. Wharton, Tex., Oct. 24, 1939; s. Pruell Alton and Harriet (Kowalski) R.; B.S. in Civil Engring., U. Tex., 1962, M.S. in Environmental Health Engring., 1964; m. Jeanette Jones, July 11, 1970. Project engr., adminstrv. officer firm S.A. Russell & Assos., Inc., Rosenberg, Tex., 1966-71; san. engr. U.S. Environmental Protection Agy., Dallas, 1971—. Chmn. Rosenberg City Planning Commn., 1969—, Richmond State Sch. Swimming Pool Project, Rosenberg, 1970—. Served to 1st lt. AUS, 1964-66. USPHS water resources fellow, 1962-64. Registered profl. engr., Tex. Mem. C. of C. (chmn. pub. works com.), Jr. C. of C. (interclub dir.), Tex. Soc. Profl. Engrs., Am. Soc. C.E., Water Pollution Control Fedn., Tau Beta Pi, Chi Epsilon. Episcoplalian. Rotarian. Home: 6435 Shady Brook Dallas TX 75206 Office: 1402 Elm St Dallas TX 75202

RUSSELL, WILLARD LORANE, lawyer; b. Hallettsville, Tex., Aug. 14, 1898; s. Henry Hamilton and Annie (Hemphill) R.; B.S., U. Tex., 1924; A.M., Baylor U., 1930; LL.B., South Tex. Sch. Law, 1933; LL.D., Tex. Wesleyan Coll., 1959, Howard Payne Coll., 1965; m. Stella Wolters, Dec. 24, 1928. Supt. pub. schs., Hallettsville, 1925-29; instr. Baylor U., 1930; admitted to Tex. bar, 1933, since practiced in Houston; chmn. bd. Shiner Oil Mill & Mfg. Co. (Tex.); v.p., dir. So. Warehouse Corp.; owner, operator farm and ranch enterprises. Founder, donor Russell Found., religious, edn., charitable trust, 1948. Trustee, mem. exec. com. U. St. Thomas, Houston; trustee Baylor U., Waco, Tex., Baylor Med. Coll., Houston; bd. dirs. Houston St. and Newsboys Club, Lincoln Ednl. Found., N.Y.; mem. exec. com. Christian Rural Overseas Council. Mem. State Bar Tex., Am., Houston bar assns., Ind. Rice Growers Assn. Baptist, Mason (Shriner), Odd Fellow, Rotarian. Clubs: Farm and Ranch, Torch (Houston); Knife and Fork (dir.). Author: Peace and Power Within, 1951; Invincible Forces, 1959; Belief and Respect, 1961; Belief and Human Worth, 1967. Contbr. to mags. Home: 3412 S Parkwood Dr Houston TX 77021 Office: 4101 San Jacinto St Houston TX 77004

RUSSELL, WILLIAM EDWARD, accountant, data processing exec.; b. Greensboro, N.C., July 12, 1934; s. Harry Edward and Annie (Smith) R.; student U. Miami, 1956-60. Asst. prodn. supr. Service Bur. Corp., Miami, Fla., 1957-60; mgr. systems, programming Miami Data Processing Center, Inc., 1960-65, gen. mgr., 1965-66; instr. Miami Dade Jr. Coll., 1965-67; v.p., sec., dir., co-founder Electronic Bookkeeping Service, Inc., Miami, 1966-70; v.p., dir. Hurricane Air Service, Inc., Coral Gables, Fla., 1967-70; sec.-treas., dir. Fla. Drapery Specialists, Inc., Miami, 1967-70. Served with USNR, 1953-55. Baptist. Home and office: 3098 NW 93rd St Miami FL 33147

RUSSELL, WILLIAM LAWSON, geneticist; b. Newhaven, Eng., Aug. 19, 1910; s. Robert Lawson and Ellen Frances (Frost) R.; B.A., Oxford (Eng.) U., 1932; Ph.D. (fellow), U. Chgo., 1937; m. Elizabeth B. Shull, Aug. 29, 1936; children—Richard L., John S., James J., Ellen M.; m. 2d, Liane R. Brauch. Sept. 23, 1947; children—David L., Evelyn R. Came to U.S., 1932. Sherman Pratt fellow Amherst Coll., 1932-33; asst. U. Chgo., 1934-36; research asso. Roscoe B. Jackson Meml. Lab., Bar Harbor, Me., 1937-47; prin. geneticist Oak Ridge Nat. Lab., 1947—, chief mammalian genetics sect., 1953-68, sci. dir. sect., 1969—, spl. work genetic effects radiation in mice. Mem. U.S. delegation Geneva confs. Peaceful Uses Atomic Energy. 1955, 58, 71; mem. com. genetic effects atomic radiation Nat. Acad. Scis., 1955—; mem. adv. com. Fed. Radiation Council, 1964—; adviser U.S. delegation UN Sci. Com. on Effects Atomic Radiation, 1962—; mem. bd. Nat. Council Radiation Protection and Measurements, 1965—. Mem. Genetics Soc. Am. (pres. 1965), Radiation Research Soc. (asso. editor 1958-59), Am. Soc. Human Genetics, Am. Soc. Zoologists, Assn. Southeastern Biologists. Oak Ridge Camera Club (pres.), Tenn. Citizens for Wilderness Planning (dir. 1969-70, pres. 1971—), Tenn. Scenic Rivers Assn. (dir.), Wilderness Soc., Nat. Audubon Soc., Sierra Club. Mem. editorial bd. Mutation Research. Home: 130 Tabor Rd Oak Ridge TN 37830 Office: Biology Div PO Box Y Oak Ridge TN 37830

RUSSELL-REDMAN, JAMES SAMUEL, geophysicist; b. Romsey, Hampshire, Eng., May 24, 1925; s. William Samuel and Louisa Agnes (Smart) Redman; student Wolsey Hall, Oxford, 1944-47; B.Sc., London (Eng.) U., 1952; m. Josephine Pamela Kathleen Daniell, Apr. 3, 1950 children— William James Ean, Katherine Mary Louise. Geologist, Brit. Petroleum Co., Eng. and Aden Protectorate, 1952-54; geophysicist Geoprosco, Ltd., Spain, 1954, 60, Kenya and Tanzania, 1955-56, Libya, 1957, Iran, 1957-58, London, 1958-60, Pakistan, 1961; tchr., geophys. cons., Eng., 1962-65; supr. gravimetric operations Petty Geophys. Engring. Co., Australia, 1965-66, San Antonio, 1966-68; mgr. geophys. applications Computer Systems Corp., Dallas, 1968-70; mgr. marine geophys. data processing Exploration Surveys Inc., Dallas, 1970—. Served with Royal Engrs., 1943-47. Fellow Geol. Soc. London; mem. Instn. Mining and Metallurgy, Soc. Exploration Geophysicists, European Assn. Exploration Geophysicists, Am. Mensa. Club: Dallas Sports Car. Home: 1301 N Waterview Dr Richardson TX 75080 Office: 6400 N Central Expressway Dallas TX 75206

RUSSO, DANIEL MARK, economist; b. Bronx, N.Y., Oct. 30, 1935; s. Pasquale and Amelia (Ragone) R.; B.A., Rutgers U., 1961, postgrad., 1962—; m. Rosalie J. Dooley, June 14, 1959; children—Rosalie M., Patrick D. Asst. credit mgr. Sears Roebuck & Co., York, Pa., 1961-62; NSF research asst. office sci. and tech. research Rutgers U., New Brunswick, N.J., 1962-63, research asst. Rutgers Research Council, 1963-64, NASA pre-doctoral research fellow Bur. Econ. Research, 1964-67; cons. Shell Chem. Co., Princeton, N.J., 1966-67; asst. prof. econs. East Tenn. State U., Johnson City, 1967—, now also dir. Bur. Econ. Research. Served with AUS, 1955-57. Mem. Am., So. econ. assns., Regional Sci. Assn., Nat. Tax Assn., Tenn. Edn. Assn., Internat. Platform Assn. Home: 1917 Clearwood Dr Johnson City TN 37601

RUSSUM, JAMES WOODFORD, bank exec.; b. Dora, Ala., June 23, 1908; s. James Milton and Eva Victoria (Roberts) R.; student Jacksonville U., 1926, Wheeler Bus. Coll., 1927-28, U. Ala., 1941-67; m. Virginia Letura Clowdus, Aug. 9, 1934; 1 dau., Henrisue (Mrs. Alton Finn Thompson, Jr.). With State Nat. Bank Ala., Oneonta, 1938—, sr. v.p., 1971—. Mem. State Banking Bd., 1962-67. Mem. Oneonta City Council, 1941-54, mayor, 1954-60. Bd. dirs. Blont Meml. Hosp. Served with USNR, World War II. Mem. Am. Legion. Baptist. Mason; mem. Order Eastern Star. Club: Civitan (Oneonta). Home: Box 235 Oneonta AL 35121 Office: Box 100 Oneonta AL 35121

RUST, EDWIN COOPER, ednl. adminstr.; b. Hammonton, Cal., Dec. 5, 1910; s. Edwin Stiltz and Clara Louise (Cooper) R.; student Deep Springs Coll., 1929-32, Cornell, 1932-34; B.F.A., Yale, 1936. Asso. prof., head art dept. Coll. William and Mary, Williamsburg, Va., 1936-43; nat. art dir. A.R.C., Washington, 1943-46; sculptor, N.Y.C., 1946-49; dir. Memphis Acad. Arts, 1949—. Mem. Nat. Accessions Com., Art in the Embassies Program, 1965, Nat. Reading Council, 1970-71; chmn. visual arts adv. panel Tenn. Arts Commn., 1970-72. Sculpture works exhibited at U. Tenn., U. Miss., Memphis State U., Bapt. Meml. Hosp., Memphis Pub. Library, others. Home: 3725 Waynoka Av Memphis TN 38111 Office: Overton Park Memphis TN 38112

RUST, GORDON DICKINSON, architect; b. Washington, Oct. 15, 1918; s. Robert Nelson and Joshan (Brown) R.; B.S., Va. Poly. Inst., 1942; m. Lilian Paige Martin, Jan. 2, 1943; children—Josephine (Mrs. Alton Noble Palmer, Jr.), Caroline (Mrs. John Chisman Hanes, Jr.), Gordon Dickinson, James Smith, Laurence Martin. Pvt. archtl. practice, Alexandria, Va., 1948—. Mem. Archtl. Bd. Rev., Alexandria, 1953-62, 70—, Alexandria Bldg. Code Com., 1965-70, Alexandria Urban Renewal Archtl. Panel, 1970—. Served with AUS, 1943-46. Fellow Constrn. Surveyors Inst., Internat. Inst. Arts and Letters, Am. Registered Architects (mem. adv. com. 1957); mem. A.I.A., Nat. Trust for Historic Preservation. Club: Alexandria Businessmen's. Home: Little Persimmon Box 43 Rural Route 1 Round Hill VA 22141 Office: Little Persimmon Box 43 Round Hill VA 22141

RUST, ROD, football coach; b. Webster City, Ia., Aug. 2, 1923; s. Orville W. and Betty (Eno) R.; B.S. in Phys. Edn., Ia. State U., 1950; M.A. in Polit. Sci., State U. Ia., 1956; m. Marianne Lester, Dec. 22, 1951; children—Jeffrey L., Gregory Alan. Tchr., coach pub. schs., Webster City, Ia., 1950-51, Toledo, Ia., 1953-54, Belle Plaine, Ia., 1954-56, Knoxville, Ia., 1956-59, Ottumwa, Ia., 1959-60; asst. football coach U. N.M., 1960-63, Stanford, 1963-66; head coach N. Tex. State U., 1967—. Served with AUS, 1951-53. Mem. Am. Football Coaches Assn. Office: Athletic Dept N Tex State U Denton TX 76203

RUSTAD, ELMER LEWIS, govt. ofcl.; b. Wakonda, S.D., Aug. 11, 1908; s. John and Hannah (Forsethlien) R.; B.A. cum laude, Sioux Falls Coll., 1929; M.A., U. Minn., 1938; postgrad. U. So. Cal., 1939; m. Berniece E. Hillery, Aug. 8, 1932; children—Patricia (Mrs. Walter J. Herrmann, Jr.), Robert L. Coach, prin., supt. Egan (S.D.) Consol. Schs., 1929-34; guidance dir., prin. Jr. High Schs., Aberdeen, S.D., 1934-41; state dir. U.S. Savs. Bonds div., S.D., 1941-52, asst. nat. dir., nat. sales mgr. U.S. Savs. Bonds div. U.S. Dept. of Treasury, Washington, 1952-69, nat. dir. U.S. Savs. Bond div., 1969-72. Served as lt. comdr., USNR, 1943-46. Mem. Am. Legion. YMCA. Baptist. Lion, Elk. Home: 2019 Lorraine Av McLean VA 22101 Office: 1111 20th St NW Washington DC 20036

RUTENBERG, ARTHUR, constrn. co. exec.; b. Chgo., June 12, 1927; s. Reuben and Mary (Quadow) R.; B.S. in Chem. Engring., Northwestern U., 1949; m. Bernice Berman, Feb. 24, 1947; children—Barry, Sharon, Jan. Partner, Tri-R Furniture & Appliance, Chgo., 1948-53; owner, pres. Rutenberg Homes, Inc., Clearwater, Fla., 1953-69, chmn. bd., 1970—; pres. U.S. Home & Devel. Corp., 1969-70; chmn. bd. Omega Properties, Inc., 1970—, Rutenberg Corp., 1970—. Mem. Pinellas County Com. of 100, 1967—. Served with USNR, 1945-46. Democrat. Jewish religion. Home: 18 S Pine Circle Clearwater FL 33516 Office: 2905 West Bay Dr Belleair Bluffs FL 33540

RUTH, EARL BAKER, congressman; b. Spencer, N.C., Feb. 7, 1916; s. Earl Monroe and Marion (Baker) R.; A.B., U. N.C., 1938, M.A., 1942, Ph.D., 1955; m. Jane Wiley, Dec. 27, 1938 children—Billie Jane (Mrs. Franklin Foil), Earl Wiley, Marian Ann (Mrs. Joe Reber), Jacqueline Dell (Mrs. Clay Burleson). Tchr., coach Chapel Hill (N.C.) High Sch., 1938-39, Piedmont Jr. High Sch., Charlotte, N.C., 1939-40; with shipping dept. McCrary Mills, Asheboro, N.C., 1940-41; asst. supt. N.C. State Parks, 1941; grad. asst. phys. edn. U. N.C., 1941-42; dir. recreation, King Mountain, N.C., 1945-46; football coach, baseball and basketball coach, athletic dir., chmn. dept. phys. edn., dean students Catawba Coll., Salisbury, N.C., 1946-68; mem. 91st-92d congresses from 8th Dist. N.C. Mem. city council, Salisbury, also mayor pro tem, 1967-68. Active local Boy Scouts Am. Bd. dirs. Salisbury YMCA. Served as lt. USNR, 1942-45. Mem. Am. Legion, V.F.W., Nat. Sportscasters and Sportswriters (past pres. awards program). Republican. Presbyn. (elder). Elk. Club: Civitan. Home: 2601 Woodley Pl Washington DC 20008 Office: 129 Cannon House Office Bldg Washington DC 20515

RUTH, IRA THOMAS, constrn. co. exec.; b. Beechwood, Ky., May 7, 1915; s. Thomas and Margaret (Lynn) R.; m. Evalena Wells, June 10, 1939; children—L.T., Judy Ann, David Lynn, Darby Allen, Judy (Mrs. Carroll Glenn Oldfield). Vice pres., treas. East Ky. Paving Corp., Grayson, 1956—; v.p. Big Sand Ready Mix Co., Grayson, 1963—, Ken More Stone, Inc., Georgetown, Ky., 1969—; mgr. hwy. constrn. Ky. Read Oiling Inc., Georgetown, 1971—; dir. First Nat. Bank, Grayson. Mem. Spl. Indsl. Assn. (nat. sec. treas. 1954-55). Mason. Club: El Hasa (Ashland, Ky.). Home: 1800 Barwick Dr Lexington KY 40505 Office: 511 Gand Av Georgetown KY 40324

RUTH, WILLIAM EDWARD, elec. machinery mfg. co. exec.; b. Leitchfield, Ky., Oct. 21, 1930; s. Willie Edward and Sarah Frances (McClure) R.; B.S. in Commerce, U. Louisville, 1962; m. Lillian Loretta Wyatt, Oct. 17, 1953; children—Rebecca Leigh, Edward Keith, Stacy Garnet. Indsl. engr. Gen. Electric Co., Louisville, 1955-64; mgr. indsl. engring. Thomas Industries, Sparta, Tenn., 1964-65; v.p. mfg. Revco Inc., Williston, S.C., 1965—. Pres., Kelly Edwards Middle Sch. P.T.O., Williston, 1970—; mem. Bi-Racial Com., Barnwell County Sch. Dist. No. 29 1951-54. Baptist (deacon). Lion. Home: 204 Clemson St Williston SC 29853 Office: PO Box 68 Williston SC 29853

RUTHERFORD, CHARLES HENRY, JR., lawyer; b. Nashville Tenn., Nov. 15, 1906; s. Charles H. and Ella Clyde (Wheeler) R.; B.A., Vanderbilt U., 1930, J.D., 1931; m. Alice Maude Martin, Aug. 8, 1962; children—Charles H. III, Miriam Austin, Robert Wheeler, Anne C., Linda C. Admitted to Tenn. bar, 1930, practiced Nashville, 1931—. Mem. Am. Arbitration Assn., Delta Theta Phi. Presbyn. Democrat. Mason (Shriner), Kiwanian. Club: Nashville Torch. Contbr. articles in field to profl. jours. Home: 5870 E Ashland Dr Nashville TN 37215 Office: Nashville Tr Bldg Nashville TN 37201

RUTHERFORD, GORDON HENRY, univ. adminstr.; b. Elkins, W.Va., Aug. 5, 1936; s. Henry Ames and Marjorie Leona (Bennett) R.; B.Arch., Pa. State U., 1959; m. Annella Lundberg, July 18, 1959; children—Gordon B., Carolyn C., Mary A., Stephen H. Cons. architect State of N.C., Raleigh, 1963-70; dir. facilities planning U. N.C., Chapel Hill, 1970—. Served with C.E.C., USNR, 1959-63. Mem. A.I.A., Triangle. Democrat. Episcopalian. Home: 3113 Glenridge Dr Raleigh NC 27604 Office: U NC Chapel Hill NC 27514

RUTLEDGE, ARTHUR BRISTOW, ch. ofcl.; b. San Antonio, Apr. 30, 1911; s. Abram Burl and Sarah (Graham) R.; B.A., Baylor U., 1936, LL.D., 1967; Th.M., So. Baptist theol. Sem., 1939; Th.D., Southwestern Bapt. Theol. Sem., 1944; D.D., East Tex. Bapt. Coll., 1956;; m. Vesta Mae Sharber, June 8, 1936; children—Arthur Burt (dec.), David Wayne, Frances Elaine (Mrs. Clifford M. Ables III). Pastor rural chs. Tex., Ky., Ind., 1930-42; pastor Central Bapt. Ch., San Antonio, 1942-45; First Bapt. Ch., Marshall, Tex., 1945-57; sec. stewardship, direct missions Bapt. Gen. Conv. of Tex., 1957-59; dir. div. missions Home Mission Bd. So. Bapt. Conv., Atlanta, 1959-64, exec. sec.-treas., 1965—. Vis. prof. missions So. Bapt. Theol. Sem., 1964. Mem. Alpha Chi. Author: Homes that Last, 1952, Mission to America, 1969. Contbr. articles to religious publs. Home: 215

Piedmont Av NE Apt 1401 Atlanta GA 30312 Office: 1350 Spring St NW Atlanta GA 30309

RUTLEDGE, NEAL PERSON, lawyer; b. St. Louis, Feb. 23, 1927; s. Wiley Blount and Annabel (Person) R.; student Harverford Coll., 1944-45; B.A., Harvard, 1947; LL.B., Yale, 1950; m. Catherine LeFevre, June 22, 1948; children—Peter Hollis, Wiley Seymour, Phillip Layne, Sarah LeFevre, Neal Andrew. Admitted to D.C. bar, 1951, N.M. bar, 1953, Fla. bar, 1953; law clk. Judge Charles Fahy, U.S. Ct. Appeals, Washington, 1950-51, Justice Hugo L. Black, U.S. Supreme Ct., 1951-52; atty. U.S. AEC, Los Alamos, 1952-53; practiced in Washington, 1953—, also Miami, Fla., 1953—; mem. firm Neal P. Rutledge, Miami; office counsel Wald, Harkrader & Rockefeller, Washington. Lectr. law U. Miami, 1954; dir. Econ. Opportunity Legal Services Program, Dade County, Fla., 1966. Pres., dir. United Cerebral Palsy Fla., 1958, dir., 1965—; chmn. Dade County Council Community Relations, 1958, chmn. edn. com., 1964. Atty. Democratic exec. com. of Dade County, 1964. Served with USMC, 1945. Recipient award United Cerebral Palsy Fla., 1958, commendation League Women Voters of Fla., 1965, citation Fla. Mediation and Conciliation Service, 1966. Fellow Acad. Fla. Trial Lawyers; mem. Am., Dade County bar assns., Fla. Bar, N.M. Bar, Am. Trial Lawyers Assn. Clubs: Harvard, Yale (Miami). Home: 6130 SW 79th St South Miami FL 33143 Office: Flagler Fed Bldg Miami FL 33132

RUTLEDGE, RALPH JENNINGS, JR., dentist; b. San Antonio, July 30, 1937; s. Ralph Jennings and Nonie Virginia (Ewing) R.; A.B., W.Va. U., 1959; D.D.S., 1963; m. Sally Ann Jordan, July 7, 1956; 1 son, Mark. Pvt. practice dentistry, Colonial Heights, Va., 1966—. Mem. Bd. Health Planning Com., 1971—. Bd. dirs. Colonial Heights-Chesterfield Cancer Soc. Served with Dental Corps, AUS, 1963-66. Mem. Acad. Gen. Dentistry, Am., Va. dental assns., Southside Va. Dental Soc., Am. Legion, Delta Sigma Delta. Methodist (bd. mem. 1968-70). Mason (32 deg., Shriner), Kiwanian (pres. Colonial Heights 1971-72). Home: 204 Fairmont Dr Colonial Heights VA 23834 Office: 3401 Boulevard St Colonial Heights VA 23834

RYAN, CLARENCE FLETCHER, digital systems engr.; b. Eola, Tex., Apr. 23, 1927; s. Clarence F. and Lillian (Killam) R.; student San Angelo Jr. Coll., 1946-48, Internat. Corr. Schs., 1949-52; E.E., Odessa Jr. Coll., 1956; student Nat. Radio Inst., 1957-59; m. Patricia Sue Dantin, Apr. 28, 1966; children—Michael Ray, Steven Curtis, Carla D'awn, Kimberly Ranae. Engr. research and devel. Rotary Engring. Co., Midland, Tex., 1949-59, Ray Geophys. Co. Mandrel Industries, Inc., Houston, 1959-67; v.p., system engr. Geophys. Data Processing Center, Inc., Houston, 1967—. Cons. digital data systems and numerical controls. Served with USNR, 1944-46. Mem. Soc. Exploration Geophysicists, A.A.A.S., Smithsonian Assn. Mason. Home: 4218 Knotty Oaks Trail Houston TX 77045 Office: 5322 Elm St Houston TX 77036

RYAN, DEVOY ALONZO, univ. ofcl.; b. Shaberg, Ark., Oct. 28, 1916; s. Charles W. and Fannie (Moore) R.; B.S., S.W. Mo. State Coll., 1943; M.Ed., U. Mo., 1949, Ed.D., 1953; m. Leota Mae Swearingen, Dec. 31, 1937; children—Madge Jeanette Paroz, Allen Devoy. Elementary tchr., Jasper County, Mo., 1940-42; secondary sch. tchr., Mo., 1942-49; supt. schs., Sheldon, Mo., 1949-51, Jasper, Mo., 1951-52; asst. to supt., Riverview Gardens, St. Louis County, Mo., 1953-56; prof. E. Tex. State U., Commerce, 1956-59, U. N.M., Albuquerque, 1959-67; chmn. dept. ednl. adminstrn. and supervision Memphis State U., 1967-70, asso. dean Coll. Edn., 1969—. Served as lt. (j.g.) USNR, 1943-46. Mem. N.E.A., Am. Assn. Sch. Adminstrs., Assn. Higher Edn. Home: 6737 Hickory Crest Cove Memphis TN 38138

RYAN, JOHN K., clergyman, author; b. Caledonia, Minn., Oct. 29, 1897; s. Thomas F. and Mary (Kelly) R.; B.A., Holy Cross Coll., 1920; S.T.B., Urban U., Rome, Italy, 1922; student St. Paul Sem., 1923-24; Ph.D., Catholic U. Am., 1933. Ordained priest Roman Cath. Ch., 1924; apptd. domestic prelate with title of Right Rev. Monsignore, by Pope Pius XII, 1947; instr. philosophy St. Mary's Coll. and Coll. St. Teresa, Winona, Minn., 1924-30; mem. faculty Sch. Philosophy Cath. U. Am., 1931-56, dean Sch. Philosophy, 1956-67, also prof.; mem. staff Trinity Coll., 1932-45; religious cons. U.S. Army, 1956; editorial bd. New Cath. Ency., 1960—; founder, editor Studies in Philosophy and the History of Philosophy, 1961—. Served with U.S. Army, 1918. Recipient Benemerenti medal, Papal, 1961. Editorial adviser Ency. Americana, 1945—. Author or co-author numerous books, latest publs.: The Reputation of St. Thomas Aquinas Among English Protestant Thinkers of the 17th Century, 1948; St. Frances de Sales' Introduction to the Devout Life (translator, editor), 1950; The Most Reverend Francis M. Kelly, D.D., A Memoir and a Tribute, 1951; Philosophical Essays in Honor of the Very Reverend Ignatius Smith, O.P., 1952; A Quest of Thoughts, 1952; Holy Trinity Book of Prayers, 1953; Basic Principles and Problems of Philosophy, rev. edit., 1954; Quodlibetal Questions, 1955; Confessions of St. Augustine (translator, editor), 1960; Twentieth-Century Thinkers, 1965; Studies in Philosophy and the History of Philosophy, 6 vols. Address: Catholic Univ of America Washington DC 20017 also 3133 Connecticut Av NW Washington DC 20008

RYAN, KATHLEEN, clergywoman; b. Rocky Ford, Colo., July 7, 1937; d. Millard Emerson and Hazel Lucille (Ritchie) Ryan; B.A., U. No. Colo., 1958; M.Div., Ch. Div. Sch. of Pacific, 1969. Tchr. spl. edn. Denver Pub. Schs., 1959-61; tchr. spl. edn. U.S. Air Force Dependent Schs., Japan, France; tchr. spl. edn. Santa Fe Pub. Schs., 1964-66; Christian edn. cons. St. Philip's in Hills Episcopal Ch., Tucson, 1969—, deacon, 1970—. First woman ordained deacon Episcopal Ch., 1970. Home: 6180 E Pima St Tucson AZ 85712 Office: PO Box 4948 Tucson AZ 85717

RYAN, ROBERT JOHN, SR., accountant, govt. ofcl.; b. Champaign, Ill., May 18, 1920; s. Edward Travis and Rose (McAdams) R.; B.S., U. Ill., 1942; m. Mary Leona Conn, Sept. 21, 1943; children—Robert John, Ruth Ann (Mrs. Byron B. Barnes). Sr. accountant Haskins & Sells, C.P.A.'s, Chgo., 1945-46, 49-54, San Francisco, 1954-55; asst. comptroller W. Lewis & Co. Dept. Store, Champaign, Ill., 1946-49; chief accountant Fibreboard Paper Products Corp., San Francisco, 1955-57; supervisory accountant U.S. Gen. Accounting Office, San Francisco, 1957-60, def. div., Washington, 1960-69, asst. dir. financial mgmt. staff div. financial and gen. mgmt. studies, Washington, 1969—. Served with USNR, 1942-45. C.P.A., Ill., Cal. Mem. Am. Inst. C.P.A.'s, Am. Accounting Assn., Fed. Govt. Accountants Assn. Home: 8249 Branch Rd Annandale VA 22003 Office: Room 5476 441 G St NW Washington DC 20548

RYAN, ROBERT MILFORD, city ofcl.; b. Columbus, Neb., Feb. 5, 1928; s. Milford D. and Julia (Juhnkee) R.; B.S., Colo. State U., 1954; m. Susan J. Smith, Mar. 20, 1952; children—Peggy Ann, Robert P., Jennifer Ann, Katy Ann. Bridge design engr. U.S. Bur. Reclamation, Denver, 1955-58; structural engr. Martin Co., Littleton, Colo., 1958-60; dir. pub. works City of Littleton, 1960-66; dir. pub. service City of Pensacola, Fla., 1966—. Bd. dirs. Pensacola Hist. Restoration Soc. Registered profl. engr., Fla., Colo. Mem. Am. Pub. Works Assn., Inst. Traffic Engrs., Fla. Engring. Soc. Lutheran. Kiwanian. Home: 839 Fairfax Dr Pensacola FL 32503 Office: 331 S Jefferson St Pensacola FL 32502

RYAN, WALTER FRANCIS, economist; b. Walla Walla, Wash., Sept. 13, 1908; s. Francis M. and Anna G. (Brogan) R.; A.B., Whitman Coll., 1930; M.A., Tufts Coll., 1932; Ph.D., Cornell U., 1937; m. Myra Emerson, June 26, 1936; children—Patricia (Mrs. David A. Davis), Katherine (Mrs. George F. Kabus). Asst. dir. Office Statis. Standards, Bur. of Budget, Washington, 1942-57, dep. dir., 1959-68; prin. statis. adviser Philippines, UN Tech. Assistance Adminstrn., 1957-59; asso. dir. Bur. of Census, Washington, 1968—. Fellow Am. Statis. Assn.; mem. Am. Econ. Assn., Inter-Am. Statis. Inst., Phi Beta Kappa. Home: 3550 Chiswick Ct Silver Spring MD 20906 Office: Census Bur Washington DC 20233

RYAN, WILLIAM HENRY, architect; b. Oklahoma City, Oct. 18, 1924; student U. Okla., 1947-51. Draftsman, Bailey & Bozalis, 1949-53, Leon B. Senter, 1952-53, William H. Wolaver, 1953-54; prin. William Henry Ryan, architect, Tulsa, 1954-55, Wolaver & Ryan, architects, Tulsa 1955-59, Ryan Assos., architects & developers, Tulsa, 1959—. Served with USNR, 1946-51. Registered architect, Okla. Mem. A.I.A. Mason (32 deg.) Work includes comml., indsl., religious, ednl., pub., mil., residential structures; also city planning, landscape and interior design. Home: 3421 E 21st St Tulsa OK 74114

RYDELL, SIDNEY, stock broker; b. N.Y.C., Nov. 6, 1904; s. Abraham M. and Bertha (Rubin) R.; student N.Y.U., 1927-28; m. Evelyn Cohn, Mar. 18, 1928; children—Mark, Judith Wagner, Allen M. With Fenner & Beane, N.Y.C., 1923-27, Harriss, Irby & Vose, N.Y.C., 1927-31, Stern, Lauer & Co., N.Y.C., 1931-54, Model, Roland & Co., Inc., N.Y.C., 1954-67; partner Kohlmeyer & Co., mems. N.Y. Stock Exchange, Miami Beach, Fla., 1967—; dir. Starrett Housing Corp. Chmn. exec. com. Shield Inst. for Retarded Children. Clubs: Elmwood Country (White Plains, N.Y.); Lone Star Boat (N.Y.C.); Kings Bay Yacht and Country (Miami). Home: 5600 Collins Av Miami Beach FL 33140 also 1025 Fifth Av New York City NY 10028 Office 5401 Collins Av Miami Beach FL 33140

RYDER, CLAIRE FRANCES, pub. health physician; b. Boston, July 23, 1920; d. Richard Young and Mary Stella (Girrior) McIntyre; A.B. cum laude, Radcliffe Coll., 1940; M.D. magna cum laude, Tufts U., 1944; M.P.H. cum laude, Harvard, 1952; D.Med. Sc (hon.), Womens Med. Coll. Pa., 1961; m. Brooks Ryder, Dec. 23, 1943 (div. 1956); m. 2d, Andrew J. Warhola, Apr. 15, 1961. Intern, teaching and research resident Boston City Hosp., 1944-47; epidemiologist, pub. health physician Mass. Dept. Pub. Health, 1947-53; lectr. gerontology Harvard Sch. Pub. Health, 1953-57; commd. surgeon USPHS, 1957, med. dir., 1960; chief long term illness program, div. chronic diseases, USPHS, 1961-62, asso. chief care services, div. chronic diseases, 1962-65, chief home health and related services br., div. med. care adminstrn., 1965-68, spl. asst. for continuum care div. health resources, 1968-69, chief tng. and studies br. div. health planning, 1969-71, chief home health br. div. Health Resources, Health Services and Mental Health Adminstrn., 1972—. Mem. Am. Med. Womens Assn. (rec. sec. 1957-58, pres. 1960-61), A.M.A., Med. Soc. D.C., Womens Med. Soc. D.C., Am. Pub. Health Assn., Phi Beta Kappa, Alpha Omega Alpha, Delta Omega. Contbr. articles in field. Home: 7613 Elba Rd Alexandria VA 22306 Office: Parklawn Bldg 5600 Fishers Lane Rockville MD 20852

RYDMAN, EDWARD J., psychologist, marriage counselor; b. Toledo, Aug. 3, 1916; s. Edward Joseph and Nell (Vail) R.; B.S., Ohio State U., 1938, M.A., 1954, Ph.D., 1965; postgrad. Columbia, 1942-43; m. Jean Storey, Dec. 29, 1939; children—Edward Jay, Nancy Lynn (Mrs. Richard G. Ellis), Suzanne Claire (Mrs. Clark M. Straw), Joan Christine. With YMCA, Cin., 1938-41, Bklyn. and Queens, N.Y., 1941-44, Miami, Fla., 1944-46; minister to youth First Community Ch., Columbus, O., 1946-54; exec. dir. Planned Parenthood of Columbus, also pvt. practice marriage conseling, 1955-59; exec. dir. Planned Parenthood of Dallas, pvt. practice marriage counseling, 1959-67; exec. dir. Am. Assn. Marriage Counselors, Inc., pvt. practice, Dallas, 1967-72; pvt. practice marriage counseling, 1972—. Tchr. marriage and family life edn. Denison U., 1958-59, So. Meth. U., 1966-67, Perkins Sch. Theology, 1968-69; lectr. Meth. Hosp. Sch. Nursing, Dallas, Tex. Womens U. Sch. Nursing; cons. profl. staff Dallas YMCA, USAF Family Life, 1968. Pres., Dallas Council for Family Life Edn.; v.p. Bd. Edn. Grandview Heights, O. Bd. dirs. Ohio-W.Va. area YMCA, Community Action program Office Econ. Opportunity, Dallas, Urban Generation Found. Fellow Am. Assn. Marriage Counselors, Am. Orthopsychiat. Assn.; mem. Am. Psychol. Assn., Am. Sociology Assn., A.A.A.S., Groves Conf. on Marriage and Family, Nat. Council on Family Relations (dir.), Am. Camping Assn. (pres. Central Ohio sect.). Home: 12651 Croydon Circle Dallas TX 75230

RYLANDER, VERSHAL VERNON, petroleum co. exec.; b. Junction, Tex., Oct. 30, 1913; s. Charles Washington and Ethel (Callcott) R.; B.B.A., U. Tex., 1939; m. Willene Hendrix, June 16, 1940; children—Ronald Charles, Sharolyn (Mrs. James E. Mobley), Kip Harrell, Rodney (dec.). With Champlin Petroleum Co., Enid, Okla., 1941—, treas., asst. sec. treasury dept., 1968—; asst. treas. natural resources div. U.P. R.R. Co., 1970-71. Active Enid Community Chest, YMCA. Trustee, treas. Lemen Missionary Found. Mem. Petroleum Accountants Soc. (pres. 1963-64), Am. Petroleum Inst., Enid C. of C., Methodist (treas. 1965—). Lion. Club: Oakwood Country (Enid). Home: 1526 S Johnson St Enid OK 73701 Office: 318 W Cherokee St Enid OK 73701

RYON, THOMAS S(HIPLEY), tobacco co. exec.; b. Washington, May 29, 1917; s. Norman Eugene and Mary (Shipley) R.; A.B., Duke, 1938; m. Ruth Elizabeth Green, Apr. 12, 1940; children—Thomas Shipley, David Osmond. Travel and study in Europe and Africa, 1938; real estate and income tax specialist, Washington, 1939; mgr. A.C. Monk Enterprises, 1940-43; accountant A.C. Monk & Co., Inc., Farmville, N.C., 1943-45, asst. sec., 1945-54, sec., 1954—, v.p., 1971—; sec., dir. Eastern Tobacco Co.; sr. v.p., dir. First Fed. Savs. & Loan Pitt County, 1972—. Pres. Farmville Tobacco Bd. Trade, 1966-68. Chmn. Farmville com. Boy Scouts Am., 1957-63; dir. Farmville Little League, Farmville Community Chest, Farmville United Fund; vice chmn. Farmville Sch. Bd., 1957, chmn. 1958-63. Mem. N.C. World Trade Assn. (dir.), Farmville C. of C. (dir.). Democrat. Episcopalian. Clubs: Wilson Coin; Farmville Coin, Farmville Country (past sec.-treas.). Home: 1007 Fountain Hwy Farmville NC 27828 Office: West Marlboro Rd Farmville NC 27828

SAAD, AHMED ZAKL, spl. counselor to King of Saudi Arabia; b. Belbeis, Egypt, Feb. 21, 1900; s. Joseph and Farida (Ibrahim) S.; LL.B., U. Cairo, 1922; J.D., U. Paris, 1928; m. Hoda Ruffet, Jan. 1940. Asst. atty. gen. of Egypt, 1922-29; Egyptian consul, Genoa, Italy, 1929-31, Hamburg, Germany, 1931-33, Liverpool, Eng., 1933-37, Dublin, Ireland, 1933-37; charge d'affaires, Bagdad, Iraq, 1937-38; 1st sec. Egyptian Embassy, London, 1938; dir. dept. for alien affairs, Cairo, 1939-44; postmaster gen., 1944; under-sec. of state in ministry of finance Egyptian govt., 1945-51; gov. Nat. Bank of Egypt, 1951-52, 55-57; exec. dir. IMF, 1946—, gov. 1946-52, 58—; gov. Internat. Bank for Reconstrn. and Devel., 1946-52, 1955—, chmn. bd. govs., 1955, 62; spl. counselor H.M. King Saud of Saudi Arabia. Home: 4201 Cathedral Av NW Washington DC 20016 Office: 19th and H Sts NW Washington DC 20431

SAARINEN, ARTHUR WILLIAM, JR., civil engr.; b. West Palm Beach, Fla., Dec. 9, 1927; s. Arthur William and Elsie (Gillespie) S.; student Ga. Inst. Tech., 1944-45; B.C.E., U. Fla., 1950; m. Mary Jane Emig, June 30, 1950; children—Mary Louise, Linda Jane. With Fla. Bd. of Health, 1950, Broward County Bd. County Commrs., 1951; staff engr. J.H. Philpott, engrs., 1953-54, v.p., 1954-67, pres, 1967—, Philpott, Ross & Saarinen, Inc., Fort Lauderdale, Fla. Cons. to Govt. of Bahama Islands for water supply, 1966—. Vice pres. Fla. Atlantic U. Found. Mem. exec. council South Fla. council Boy Scouts Am.; hon. trustee Broward Community Coll. Served with AUS, 1946-47. Diplomate Am. Acad. Environmental Engrs. Fellow Am. Soc. C.E.; mem. Cons. Engrs. Council Fla. (pres. 1962-63), Am. Water Works Assn., Water Pollution Control Fedn., Sigma Chi. Methodist. Clubs: Fort Lauderdale Rotary (pres. 1964-65), University Fla. Alumni (dist. v.p. 1966). Home: 5920 Almond Terrace Plantation FL 33313 Office: 2001 NW 62d St Fort Lauderdale FL 33309

SABES, WILLIAM RUBEN, educator; b. St. Paul, Jan. 18, 1931; s. Henry Leonard and Frieda (Mark) S.; B.S., U. Minn., 1959, D.D.S., 1959, M.S., 1961; m. Evelyn Bellman, Oct. 28, 1951; children—Sherlyne, Caryn, Michael. Teaching asst. U. Minn., 1959-61; asst. prof. Temple U., 1961-63; asst. prof., chmn. sect. histology and pathology U. Detroit, 1963-65, asst. prof., chmn. dept. histology, pathology and diagnosis, 1965-66, asso. prof., chmn. dept., 1966-68; asso. prof. oral pathology U. Ky., Lexington, 1968—, chmn. dept., 1971—. Cons. oral pathology VA Hosp., Phila., 1961-63, VA Hosp., Allen Park, Mich., 1965-68; asso. dentist A. B. Chandler Hosp. Med. Center, Lexington, 1968—. Adviser Young Judea Youth Group, Lexington, 1968-69. Served with USAF, 1951-53. Recipient award Am. Acad. Dental Medicine, 1959. Diplomate Am. Bd. Oral Pathology, 1969. Fellow Am. Acad. Oral Pathology; mem. A.A.A.S., Am. Assn. U. Profs., Internat. Assn. Dental Research, Am. Dental Assn., Am. Soc. Forensic Odontology, Eastern Soc. Tchrs. Oral Pathology (exec. sec. 1968-71), Mich. Soc. Pathologist, Sigma Xi, Alpha Omega, Omicron Kappa Upsilon. Mem. B'nai B'rith. Contbr. articles to profl. jours. Home: 3086 Montavesta Rd Lexington KY 40502

SABGHIR, AARON SEYMOUR, economist; b. Bklyn., Apr. 21, 1921; s. Jacob and Mollie (Vernoff) S.; B.S., City Coll. N.Y., 1941; postgrad. Columbia U., 1941-42, Am. U., 1946-48; m. Beatrice Janet Simmons, Aug. 30, 1942; children—Naomi (Mrs. Allen R. Zeiger), David, Judith, Jonathan. With Fed. Govt. Career Service, 1942—, successively economist in OPA, chief sampling techniques Bus. Census, U.S. Bur. Census, dir. survey review div. OPS, dir. quality control bus. census U.S. Bur. Census, 1942-55, chief economist bldg. materials and constrn. div. U.S. Dept. Commerce, 1955-68, dir. constrn. and bldg. materials div., 1968—. Dir., bd. dirs. Group Health Assn., Inc., Washington, 1963-65. Mem. Am. Statis. Assn., Soc. Govt Economists. Editor Construction Rev., monthly dept. of commerce publ., 1959-68, 70—. Home: 723 Lowander Lane Silver Spring MD 20901 Office: 14th and Constitution Av Washington DC 20230

SABISTON, DAVID COSTON, JR., educator, surgeon; b. Onslow County, N.C., Oct. 4, 1924; s. David Coston and Marie (Jackson) S.; B.S., U. N.C., 1943; M.D., Johns Hopkins, 1947; m. Agnes Barden, Sept. 24, 1955; children—Anne Barden, Agnes Foy, Sarah Coston. Successively intern, asst. resident, chief resident surgery Johns Hopkins Hosp., 1947-53; successively asst. prof., asso. prof., prof. surgery Johns Hopkins Med. Sch., 1955-64, Howard Hughes investigator, 1955-60; Fulbright research scholar U. Oxford (Eng.), 1960; research asso. Hosp. Sick Children, U. London (Eng.), 1961; prof. surgery, chmn. dept. Duke Med. Sch., 1964—. Served to capt. M.C., AUS, 1953-55. Recipient Career research award NIH, 1962-64. Fellow A.C.S.; mem. Soc. Univ. Surgeons, Am., So. surg. assns., Am. Assn. Thoracic Surgery, Soc. Clin. Surgery, Internat. Soc. Cardiovascular Surgery, Soc. Vascular Surgery, Halsted Soc., Surg. Biology Club II, Soc. Thoracic Surgery, Soc. Surgery Alimentary Tract, Soc. Thoracic Surgeons Great Britain and Ireland, Co-editor: Davis-Christopher Textbook of Surgery. Editorial bd. Annals Surgery, Jour. Cardiovascular and Thoracic Surgery, Circulation, Lewis-Walters Practice Surgery. Home: 1528 Pinecrest Rd Durham NC 27706

SACHS, SIDNEY STANLEY, lawyer; b. Washington, Dec. 25, 1916; s. William Michael and Rebecca (Krupsaw) S.; B.A., Am. U., 1937; LL.B., Georgetown U., 1941; m. Betty Kossow, Nov. 20, 1941; children—Ellen Rodin, Susan Goldman, Jane, John. Admitted to D.C. bar, 1942, Md. bar, 1949, also U.S. Supreme Ct.; law clk. to judge U.S. Emergency Ct. Appeals, 1943-45; asst. U.S. atty. D.C., 1945-49; pvt. practice law, Washington, 1949—; instr. Washington Coll. Law, Am. U., 1947-52; mem. bd. Inst. Criminal Law and Procedure, Georgetown U., 1955—. Mem. Jud. Conf. for D.C., 1958—, sec., dir.Capitol Inst. Tech., 1965—. Bd. dirs. D.C. Assn. Mental Health, 1964-66; trustee Pub. Defender Service, 1965—. Bd. dirs. Citizens Communication Center. 1967. Mem. Am. (state del. 1972—), Fed. bar assns., Bar Assn. D.C. (pres. research found. 1959, pres. assn. 1966-67), Am. Civil Liberties Union. Democrat. Jewish religion. Clubs: Federal City, Burning Tree. Home: 2717 Daniel Rd Chevy Chase MD 20015 Office: 1620 Eye St NW Washington DC 20006

SACHSE, VICTOR A., lawyer; b. Baton Rouge, Sept. 21, 1903; s. Victor A. and Frannye (Bloomenstiel) S.; LL.B., La. State U.; m. Janice Rubenstein, Jan. 2, 1929; children—Victor A. III, Harry R. Admitted to La. bar, 1925; practice law, Baton Rouge; mem. firm Breazeale, Schse & Wilson; 1st asst. gen. counsel, gen. counsel Surplus Property Adminstrn., 1945-46. Dir. Fidelity Nat. Bank. Chmn. City-Parish Plan Commn., 1947-48; parish atty., East Baton Rouge, 1949-50. Chmn. Air Force Adv. Com. Prisoners War, 1964. Exec. com. Council for Better La., Found. for Better La.; dir. La. State U. Found.; trustee La. Arts and Sci. Center, 1964-67. Served to lt. col., Judge Adv. Gen. Dept., AUS, 1942-45. Decorated Legion of Merit. Fellow Am. Coll. Trial Lawyers; mem. Am., La. (bd. govs. 1957-58), Baton Rouge (pres. 1941-42) bar assns., Am., La. (council) law insts., Mil. Order World Wars, Am. Legion, Am. Jewish Com. (mem.-at-large ho. dels.), Order Coif, Phi Delta Phi. Mason (master 1936). Home: 370 S Lakeshore Dr Baton Rouge LA 70808 Office: Fidelity Bank Bldg Baton Rouge LA 70801

SACKETT, PAUL EDMUNDS, banker; b. Lynchburg, Va., Aug. 29, 1907; s. Henry Mosley and Mina (Otey) S.; B.A., U. Va., 1929, LL.B., 1931; m. Elizabeth Graves, Nov. 4, 1933; children—Paul E., William Graves. Admitted to Va. bar, 1930; practiced in N.Y.C., 1931-32; mem. firms Carter, Ledyard & Milburn, attys., N.Y.C., 1931-32, Williams & Sackett, attys., Lynchburg, Va., 1932-38; sec.-treas. The Lynchburg Trust & Savs. Bank, 1938-48, v.p., 1948-54, pres., 1954-55; sr. v.p., trust officer First Nat. Trust & Savs. Bank (name now changed to United Va. Bank/First Nat.), 1955-61, pres., 1955-61, pres., 1961—, also dir.; chmn. exec. com., dir. United Va. Bankshares, Inc.; dir. Ala.-Tenn. Natural Gas Co., First Colony Life Ins. Co., Lynchburg Gas Co., Montague-Betts Co., Inc., WLVA Inc.; v.p. Va. Hot Springs Inc. Mem. adv. council Lynchburg Coll., 1965—; mem. adv. com. Randolph-Macon Woman's Coll., 1964—. Bd. dirs.

Lynchburg Gen.-Marshall Lodge Hosps., Inc. Mem. Va. State Bar Assn., Lynchburg C. of C. (treas. 1950-70). Home: 2003 Link Rd Lynchburg VA 24503 Office: 1010 Main St Lynchburg VA 24504

SACKRIN, SEYMOUR MELVYN, govt. ofcl.; b. Bklyn., June 22, 1915; s. Meyer and Mary (Cohen) S.; B.A. cum laude, Bklyn. Coll., 1936, M.A., 1939; postgrad. Grad. Sch. U.S. Dept. Agr., 1954-56; m. Angelica Robles, Jan. 2, 1947; children—Joel Arthur, Beverly Carol. Instr., Bklyn. Coll., 1937-38; tchr. N.Y.C. Bd. Edn., 1939-41; statistician U.S. Dept. Agr., Madison, Wis., 1942, analytical statistician, Washington, 1954-68; bus. economist OPA, Washington, 1943-45; internat. economist U.S. Dept. Commerce, Washington, 1946-51; price economist OPS, Washington, 1951-53; internat. economist U.S. Tariff Commn., Washington, 1968—. Recipient U.S. Dept. Agr. certificate of merit, 1965. Mem. Am. Econ. Assn., Am. Agrl. Econs. Assn. Author: (with A.G. Conover) Tobacco Smoking in the United States in Relation to Income, 1957. Home: 816 Talbert Lane Hyattsville MD 20783 Office: US Tariff Commn Washington DC 20436

SACONAS, EDWARD SHERMAN, real estate developer, banker; b. Elkhart, Ind., May 7, 1939; s. George and Louise (Tamburine) S.; B.A. summa cum laude, St. Mary's U., San Antonio, 1960; LL.D. cum laude, U. Houston, 1965 Pres., Bayou Vista Land Corp., Hitchcock, Tex., 1963—; dir. Mainland Bank, Texas City, Tex., 1966—, vice chmn., 1969—; dir. Citizens Nat. Bank, Beaumont, Tex., Vidor State Bank; chmn. E. Tex. State Bank, Buna. Mem. Galveston County Seawall Adv. Com., 1968—. Served to lt. AUS. Mem. Hitchcock C. of C. Home: 638 Warsaw Dr Hitchcock TX 77573 Office: PO Box 8 Hitchcock TX 77563

SADDORIS, JAMES ALBERT, dentist; b. Decatur, Ill., Sept. 17, 1928; s. Marvin and Eula (Foster) S.; B.A., U. Okla., 1950, M.Ed., 1951; D.D.S., Baylor U., 1958; m. Wanda Spencer, Jan 27, 1951. Practice dentistry, Cleveland, Okla., 1958-64, Tulsa, 1964—. Vice-pres. Cleveland (Okla.) Sch. Bd., 1963-64. Served with AUS, 1952, USAF, 1952-54. Mem. Okla. State Dental Assn. (pres. 1973-74), Tulsa County Dental Soc. (pres. 1969-70), Oil Capitol Dental Study Club, Oil Capitol C. of C., Omicron Kappa Upsilon. Rotarian. Club: Oaks Country, Cedar Ridge Country (Tulsa). Home: 6062 E 55th St Tulsa OK 74135 Office: 5416 S Yale St Tulsa OK 74135

SADIK, MARVIN SHERWOOD, govt. ofcl.; b. Springfield, Mass., June 27, 1932; s. Harry Benjamin and Florence (Askinas) S.; A.B., Harvard, 1954, A.M., 1961. Curator, Mus. Art, Bowdoin Coll., 1961-64, dir., 1964-67; dir. Mus. Art, U. Conn., 1967-69; dir. Nat. Portrait Gallery, Smithsonian Instn., Washington, 1969—. Author: Colonial and Federal Portraits, 1966; Exhibition Catalogues; The Drawings of Hyman Bloom, 1968; The Paintings of Charles Hawthorne, 1969. Home: 429 N St SW Washington DC 20024 Office: 8th and F St NW Washington DC 20560

SADLER, GUY ALBERT, architect; b. Norfolk, Va., Sept. 6, 1933; s. Robert Dewey and Dorothy Lovisa (Diggs) S.; B.Arch., Va. Poly. Inst., 1960; m. Orpha Ann Quesenberry, Apr. 22, 1961; 1 dau., Pamela. Intern archtl. firms, Washington, 1960-64; architect, Beery & Rio, architects, Annandale, Va., 1964-67; self-employed as architect and land planner, Falls Church, Va., 1967—. Served with USAF, 1951-55. Mem. A.I.A. Methodist. Prin. archtl. works include Adeson Residence, Village Square Townhouse Project, Wheystone Court Townhouse Project, Franconia Village Townhouse Project, Fairfax County, Va., United Methodist Ch., Fredericktown, O. Home: 2920 Marshall St Falls Church VA 22042 Office: 803 W Broad St Falls Church VA 22046

SADLER, HOWARD C., lawyer; b. Port Arthur, Tex., July 19, 1924; s. Robert H. and Mary (Branch) S.; student Baylor U., 1943-44, U. Tex., 1947-48; J.D., U. Tex., 1951; m. Michele G. Delbeck, July 6, 1946; children—Robert Jerry, Patricia Beverly. Was admitted to the Texas State bar, 1951; mem. firm Sadler & Sadler, Port Arthur, Tex., 1952—. Former trustee Port Arthur Coll. Active A.R.C. Pres. adv. council St. Mary's Hosp., also counsel, bd. dirs. Served with AUS, 1943-47, 51-52; lt. col. Res.; ret. Decorated Belgium Fourrageres (Belgium); Bronze Star medal, Combat Infantryman's Badge (U.S.). Mem. Am., Jefferson County (pres. 1965-66), Port Arthur bar assns., Tex. Trial Lawyers Assn. (dir. 1963-65), State Bar Tex., Am. Trial Lawyers Assn., Res. Officers Assn., Soc. Hosp. Attys. Elk. Club: Port Arthur Town. Home: 4500 Evergreen Dr Port Arthur TX 77640 Office: Box 3466 Sadler Bldg 2300 Memorial Blvd Port Arthur TX 77642

SAEGERT, CLARENCE EMIL, advt. co. exec.; b. Seguin, Tex., July 10, 1919; s. Joe F. and Clara (Haenel) S.; student Tex. Luth. Coll., 1935-36; B.S., ampla cum laude, U. Tex., 1941; m. Evelyn Gartman, July 18, 1939; children—Joel Gartman, Jerry Charles, Claire Louise. Pres., Tex. Mailing & Printing Co., Austin, 1955—, Clarence E. Saegert Pub. Co., Austin, 1963—, H.E. Enterprises, Austin, 1969—; v.p. Decision Dynamics, Inc., Austin, 1963—. Vice pres. Austin Symphony Soc., 1970-72; pres. Austin U.S.O., 1971-72; vice-commodore Austin Aqua Festival, 1968-70; mem. exec. com. Austin Better Bus. Bur. Bd. dirs. Nat. Conf. Christians and Jews, Austin, 1968-70. Served to lt. USNR, 1943-46; PTO. Mem. Austin Advt. Club (pres. 1959-60), Austin C. of C. (v.p., dir., chmn. Austin postal com.). Lutheran (chmn. membership services com. Internat. Laymen's League 1964-66, supt. Bible classes 1968—, dir. Ann. Visitation and Stewardship Effort 1969—). Home: 3300 Kim Lane Austin TX 78705 Office: 703 W 7th St Austin TX 78701

SAFAR, MILO RUDOLPH, dentist; b. Chgo., Nov. 30, 1924; s. Rudolph and Marie (Komarek) S.; student Roosevelt U., 1946-48; B.S., U. Ill., 1950, D.D.S., 1952; m. Janice Lee Williams, Dec. 26, 1949; children—Marcia Ellen, Laurie Ann. Intern, Fitzsimons Army Hosp., Denver, 1952-53; commd. 2d lt. U.S. Army, 1952, advanced through grades to lt. col., 1966; chief clinician Sand Hill (Ga.) Dental Clinic, 1970-71; ret., 1971; asso. prof., dir. dental hygiene program Columbus Coll., 1971—. Decorated Bronze Star medal. Mem. Am. Dental Assn., Western Dist. Dental Soc. Ga., Assn. U.S. Army, Nat. Rifle Assn. Home: 1310 Trenton Ct Columbus GA 31907 Office: Columbus Coll Columbus GA 31907

SAFER, JOEL JARRETT, dentist; b. Baton Rouge, Mar. 13, 1940; s. Mike S. and Nina L. (Jarrett) S.; B.S., La. State U., 1962; D.D.S., Loyola U. South, 1966; m. Joy Lee Hodges, Aug. 15, 1964; children—Heidi Elizabeth, Joel Jarrett II. Practice dentistry, Baton Rouge, 1968—; pres. Capitol Steel, Inc., 1969-70, Safer Corp., 1970—. Mem. Baton Rouge Area Com. on Dental Care for Underpriviledged, 1968-72; mem. staff Baton Rouge Gen., Our Lady of Lake hosps. Chmn. dental div. United Givers Fund Campaign, 1972-73. Served with Dental Corps AUS, 1966-68. Mem. Am. Dental Assn., Acad. Gen. Dentistry, 6th Dist., East Baton Rouge. Parish dental socs., Republican. Club: Roundtable. Home: 6185 Esplanade St Baton Rouge LA 70806 Office: 900 S Acadian St Baton Rouge LA 70806

SAFFELS, GEORGE AARON, educator; b. nr. Ala., Oct. 10, 1923; s. George Anderson and Sarah Jane (Chandler) S.; B.S., Jacksonville State U., 1949; M.A., U. Ala., 1952, postgrad., 1971-72; m. Anna Wayne Brothers, Dec. 21, 1946; children—Michael Aaron, Elizabeth Anne. Prin., Ivalee Elementary Sch., Attalla, Ala., 1949—. Served with USAAF, 1943-45. Mem. Ala., Etowah County edn. assns., Ala. Dept. Elementary Sch. Prins., Etowah County Prins. Assn. (past pres.), Kappa Delta Pi, Kappa Phi Kappa. Democrat. Baptist (chmn. bd. deacons). Mason. Home: Route 1 Box 358 Attalla AL 35954 Office: Route 2 Attalla AL 35954

SAFFIR, HERBERT SEYMOUR, cons. civil engr.; b. N.Y.C., Mar. 29, 1917; s. A. L. and Gertrude (Samuels) S.; B.S. in Civil Engring. cum laude, Ga. Inst. Tech., 1940; m. Sarah Young, May 9, 1941; children— Richard Young, Barbara Joan. Civil engr. TVA, Chattanooga, 1940, NACA, Langley Field, Va., 1940-41; structural engr. Ebasco Services, N.Y.C., 1941-43, York & Sawyer & Fred Severud, N.Y.C., 1945; engr. Waddell & Hardesty, Cons. Engrs., N.Y.C., 1945-47; asst. county engr. Dade County, Miami, Fla., 1947-59; cons. engr. Herbert S. Saffir, Coral Gables, Fla., 1959—. Adj. lectr. civil engring. Coll. Engring., U. Miami, 1964—; cons. Govt. Bahamas on bldg. codes; cons. on engring. in housing to UN. Served with AUS, 1943-44. Recipient Outstanding Service award Fla. Profl. Engrs., 1954. Registered profl. engr., Fla., N.Y., Tex., P.R., Miss. Fellow Am. Soc. C.E. (sect. past pres.), Fla. Engring. Soc.; mem. Soc. Am. Mil. Engrs., Am. Concrete Inst., Am. Soc. for Testing Materials, Colegio de Ingenieros P.R., Nat. Panel Arbitrators, Am. Arbitration Assn., C. of C. Miami, Tau Beta Pi. Author: Housing Construction in Hurricane Prone Areas, 1971. Contbr. articles to profl. jours. Home: 4818 Alhambra Circle Coral Gables FL 33146 Office: 123 Madeira Av Coral Gables FL 33134

SAFIRE, WILLIAM, govt. ofcl., author; b. N.Y.C., Dec. 17, 1929; s. Oliver C. and Ida (Panish) S.; student Syracuse U., 1947-49; m. Helene Belmar Julius, Dec. 16, 1962; children—Mark Lindsey, Annabel Victoria. Reporter, N.Y. Herald Tribune Syndicate, 1949-51; corr. WNBC-WNBT, Europe and Middle East, 1951; radio-TV producer NBC, N.Y.C., 1954-55; v.p. Tex McCrary, Inc., 1955-60; pres. Safire Pub. Relations, Inc., 1960-68; spl. asst. to Pres. Nixon, 1969—. Chief spl. projects Nixon-Lodge campaign, 1960; dep. mgr. Javits campaign, 1962; spl. asst. to Richard Nixon, 1966-68. Trustee Brotherhood-in-Action, Boys Athletic League, N.Y.C. Served with AUS, 1952-54. Mem. Pub. Relations Soc. Am., Newcomen Soc. Republican. Club: Overseas Press Am. (N.Y.C.). Author: The Relations Explosion, 1963; (with Marshall Leob) Plunging into Politics, 1964; The New Language of Politics, 1968. Address: The White House Washington DC 20500

SAGE, RUSSELL RICHARD, lawyer; b. Omaha, Aug. 27, 1931; s. James Russell and Claire (Frank) S.; B.S. in Law, U. Minn., 1953, LL.B., 1955; m. Arleta Marie Jons, Feb. 10, 1952; children—Robert Richard, James Russell, Vickie Ann. Admitted to Minn. bar, 1955, D.C. bar, 1962, Va. bar, 1968; atty. ICC, Washington, 1957-62; practice law, Washington, 1962—; mem. firm Turney, Major and Sage, 1963-67, Major, Sage & King, 1968—. Served with AUS, 1955-57. Mem. D.C., Minn., Va. bar assns., Assn. ICC Practitioners, Motor Carrier Lawyers Assn. Democrat. Presbyn. Home: 4807 Manion St Annandale VA 22003 Office: Tavern Square Alexandria VA 22314

SAGEBIEL, RALPH FREDERICK, dentist; b. Brenham, Tex., Sept. 20, 1917; s. Edward Alfred and Louise (Trimpler) S.; A.A., Tex. Luth. Coll., 1937; D.D.S., U. Tex., 1942; m. Mary Martha Billnitzer, Aug. 24, 1941; children—James Edward, Rosemary (Mrs. Mark Carl Fetter), Ralph Frederick. Practice gen. dentistry, Yorktown, Tex., 1942-43, Seguin, Tex., 1946—; mem. staff Gonzales Warm Spring Elks Crippled Childrens hosps., Ottine, Tex., Guadalupe Valley Hosp., Seguin. Active Boy Scouts Am., 1954-60. Bd. dirs. Girl Scouts U.S.A., Seguin; bd. regents Tex. Luth. Coll., Seguin. Served to capt. USNR, 1943-46. Fellow Tex. Dental Assn. (mem. Ho. of Dels. 1959, 71, 72); mem. Am., Guadalupe Valley (past pres.) dental assns., Seguin C. of C., Tex. Luth. Coll., Seguin High Sch. booster clubs., Am. Legion. Lutheran (Sunday sch. supt.-sponsor Luther League, Youth program, dir. Seguin Youth Center). Lion. Home: Route 2 Box 236 Seguin TX 78155 Office: 402 E Mountain St Seguin TX 78155

SAIN, CHARLES HASKELL, cons. engr.; b. New Market, Ala., Jan. 23, 1923; s. Will Oris and Clayta (Speck) S.; student Lincoln Meml. U., 1940-42; B. Civil Engring magna cum laude, U. Fla., 1949; m. Marie Myers, Aug. 8, 1942; children—Charles Randolph, Elizabeth Lester, Ann Marie. Project mgr. Moss-Thornton Co., Inc., Texarkana, Tex., 1949-52, chief engr., Leeds, Ala., 1952-54, v.p. 1954-60; gen. mgr. Vecellio & Grogan, Inc. Beckley, W.Va., 1960-64; v.p. A.E. Burgess Co., Inc., Birmingham, Ala., 1964-67; exec. v.p. Peyton & Sain Co., Inc., 1967—; v.p., dir. Ranger Fuel Corp., Beckley, Golf Center, Inc., Birmingham; owner Charles H. Sain & Assos. Expert witness on constrn. problems. Named Ky. col. Registered profl. engr., W.Va., Ky., Ala., Ark., Tex., Ga., Miss., Tenn., Fla. Mem. W.Va. Soc. Profl. Engrs. Am. Soc. C.E. (mem. maintenance com.), Am. Rd. Builders Assn., Asso. Gen. Contractors Am., Soc. Am. Mil. Engrs., Kappa Alpha, Sigma Tau, Tau Beta Pi, Gamma Lambda Sigma. Independent. Mason. Clubs: The Club; Green Valley Country. Contbg. author: Civil Engineering Handbook, 1966. Contbr. articles profl. jours. Home: 1320 Badham Dr Birmingham AL 35216 Office: 2233 Highland Av Birmingham AL 35205

SAINE, LEONARD WATSON, contractor; b. Acworth, Ga., July 1, 1894; s. James Paty and Elizabeth (Watson) S.; student civil engring. Ga. Sch. Tech., 1911-14; student law U. Mich., 1915; LL.B., Atlanta Law Sch., 1916; m. Mary Ruth Hudson, Apr. 17, 1918; 1 dau., Mary Elizabeth (Mrs. Robert Reynolds). Engr., constrn. supt. J.B. McCrary Co., Atlanta, 1917-27, salesman, sales mgr., dir. Central Foundry Co., N.Y.C., 1927-33, sales engr. Walworth Co., N.Y.C., 1935-40; pres., dir. Saine Co., Inc., gen. contractors, 1942—, owner Leonard W. Saine Registered Dealers, municipal and utility supply co., Orlando. Served with C.E. Corps, USN, 1918-19. Registered profl. engr. Mem. Nat. Soc. Profl. Engrs., Fla. Engring Soc., Beta Theta Pi. Mason. Home: 1555 W Fairbanks Av Winter Park FL 32789 Office: 314 Piedmont St Orlando FL

ST. CLAIR, HAL KAY, elec. engr.; b. Los Angeles, Oct. 11, 1925; s. Millard T. and Ruth (McGrew) St. C.; student U. So. Cal., 1943-44; B.S., U. Cal., Berkeley, 1946, M.S., 1948; m. Jane Creely, June 24, 1949; children—Gregory, Russell, Elizabeth. Research engr. Marchant Calculators, Emeryville, Cal., 1948-52; project engr. RCA, Camden, N.J., 1953-54; program mgr. IBM, San Jose, Cal., 1954-69, tech. staff, Boca Raton, Fla., 1969-72, mgr. input/output devel., 1972—; instr. U. Cal. Extension Div., 1951-52. Tech. adv. U.S. Nat. Com. Internat. Electrotechnical Comm, 1967-69. Mem. Republican Central Com. of Cal., 1962-66. Served to lt. (j.g.) USNR, 1943-46. Mem. I.E.E.E., Phi Beta Kappa, Sigma Xi, Tau Beta Pi, Eta Kappa Nu. Home: 2101 Banyan Rd Boca Raton FL 33432 Office: 2000 NW 51st St Boca Raton FL 33432

ST. CLAIR, MARTHA LOUISE, educator; b. Greenville, Tex.; d. Ellis and Pearl (Kilman) St. Clair; B.A., Howard Payne Coll., 1946, postgrad., 1964; M.R.E., Southwestern Bapt. Theol. Sem., Fort Worth, 1948; postgrad. Okla. State U., 1963. Student-youth dir. Paris (Tex.) Jr. Coll. and Paris 1st Bapt. Ch., 1948-50; dir. Bapt. student activities E. Central Coll., Ada, Okla., 1950-54; dir. youth activities 1st Bapt. Ch., Waco, Tex., 1953-56; dir. student activities and promotion, asst. prof. psychology Howard Payne Coll., Brownwood, Tex., 1956-65; program dir., coordinator sororities S.W. Tex. State Coll., San Marcos, 1965—. Tchr. psychology Upward Bound program, 1967. Mem. Bus. and Profl. Women's Club, Am. Assn. U. Women, Tex. Assn. Women Deans and Counselors, Assn. Coll. Unions Internat., Internat. Platform Assn., Delta Kappa Gamma. Baptist. Clubs: Altruse, Faculty Women's. Contbr. articles to profl. jours. Home: 128 Nichols Dr San Marcos TX 78666

ST. CLAIR, NORBERT, librarian; b. Budapest, Hungary, July 27, 1924; s. Janos Szentklaray and Amalia (Roder) S.; B.M.S. Royal Hungarian Mil. Acad., 1944; B.A., U. Budapest, 1950; M.L.S., Western Mich. U., 1965; m. Suzanne Forsyth, July 28, 1969. Came to U.S., 1957, naturalized, 1963. Cataloger, Boston Pub. Library, 1963-66; cataloger Mass. Inst. Tech., Cambridge, 1966-68; asso. Librarian Fla. Technol. U., Orlando, 1968—. Served as 2d lt. Hungarian Army, 1944-45. Am., Fla. library assns., Alumni Assn. Western Mich. U. Home: 310 Robin Hill Dr Altamonte Springs FL 32701

ST CYR, CAROL RUTH, educator; b. Meriden, Conn., Dec. 25, 1924; d. Donald J. and Margaret (Horan) St. Cyr; B.S., Willimantic State Coll., 1946; M.A., Trinity Coll., 1949; Ph.D., U. Mich., 1955. Elementary tchr., Meriden, 1946-53; research asst. U. Mich., Ann Arbor, 1953-55; vis. prof. U. N.C., summer 1955; asst. prof. George Washington U. Sch. Edn., Washington, 1955-60, asso. prof., 1960-64, prof., 1964—. Ednl. cons. Mem. Am. Assn. U. Women, Am. Assn. U. Profs., Nat. Aerospace Edn. Assn. (bd. dirs. 1967—, pres. 1972—), Assn. for Supervision and Curriculum Devel., A.A.A.S., Pi Lambda Theta. Home: 1701 N Kent St Arlington VA 22209 Office: Sch of Edn George Washington U Washington DC 20006

ST.JOHN, JOHN, food co. exec.; b. Battle Creek, Mich., Aug. 8, 1921; s. Raymond Martin and Hazel (Eastman) St. J.; B.A., Mich. State U., 1943; m. Lorraine Margaret McCarthy, Feb. 27, 1943; 1 dau., Shannon Elaine. With Minute Maid Co., and predecessors, 1949—, financial v.p., 1963-65, pres. 1965—; v.p., dir. Granada Groves Corp.; dir. Minute Maid Groves Corp., Fla. Orange Marketers, Inc. Gay H. Pdyor Co., College Park Nat. Bank. Trustee Orlando Jr. Coll., Loch Haven Art Center, Orlando. Served with USAAF, 1943-46. Episcopalian. Clubs: Winter Park (Fla.) Racquet; University, Country (Orlando). Home: 910 Pace Av Maitland FL 32751 Office: 1200 W Colonial Dr Orlando FL 32802

ST. JOHN, VERNON LAFAYETTE, ednl. cons.; b. Somerville, Ala., Sept. 25, 1905; s. William Joseph and Emma Perry (Jones) St. J.; B.S., U. Ala., 1928, M.A., 1948; m. Virginia Thomas, June 5, 1930. Tchr., coach Marion County Bd. Edn., Hackleburg, Ala., 1928-29, Moulton, Ala., 1930-35, Curry High Sch., Jasper, Ala., 1929-30; prin. Town Creek (Ala.) Elementary and High Sch., 1935-45; supt. Opp (Ala.) City Schs., 1945-71; ednl. cons. Am. Educators Ins. Co., Birmingham, Ala., 1971—. Mem. U.S.S. Battleship Commn., 1963—; active Boy Scouts Am.; mem. exec. com United Fund; pres. Mental Health Assn. Covington County, Ala., 1960-62; mem. Ala. Baptist Exec. Com., 1969—, chmn., 1972—; mem. Ala. Bapt. Adminstrn. Com., 1969—. Recipient Silver Beaver award Boy Scouts Am., 1963. Mem. N.E.A. (life), Ala. Edn. Assn. (pres. 1968-69), Am. Assn. Sch. Adminstrs., Am. Assn. Secondary Sch. Prins., Am. Assn. Elementary Sch. Prins., Phi Delta Kappa. Mason, Rotarian (pres. Opp 1956-57). Address: Woodhaven Dr Opp AL 36467

ST. PETER, ALPHONSE FRANCIS, gas co. exec.; b. St. Johnsbury, Vt., Nov. 18, 1914; s. A.L. and Francella (Downing) St. P.; B.S., Marquette U., 1951; M.B.A., U. Wis., 1954; m. Margaret E. Whitney, Oct. 6, 1944; children—James W., Frances H. Staff asst. employee relations Mobil Oil Co., Milw., 1939-56; personnel mgr. Kyle Products Plant of Line Material Indsl., Milw., 1956-59; indsl. relations mgr. Delhi-Taylor Oil Corp., Dallas, 1959-63; dir. adminstrv. services So. Union Gas Co., Dallas, 1963-69, v.p. adminstrv. services, 1969—. Instr. Marquette U., 1955-57. Bd. dirs. Dallas Mental Health Assn. Served with USAAF, 1942-46. Mem. Am. Soc. Personnel Adminstrn., Am. Mgmt. Assn., Am., So. gas assns., Dallas Personnel Assn. (past pres.). Presbyn. (elder). Kiwanian (past pres., past lt. gov., dist. chmn.). Home: 5225 Preston Haven Dr Dallas TX 75229 Office: Fidelity Union Tower Dallas TX 75201

SAKELL, ACHILLES NICHOLAS, pub. affairs adviser; b. Greece, Jan. 27, 1906; s. Nicholas and Matenia (Economides) Sakellarides; Diplome, Nat. Sch. Langs. and Commerce, Istanbul, Turkey, 1923; M.Sc., Lehigh U., 1936; M.A., Princeton, 1939; Ph.D. in Polit. Sci. and Internat. Law, 1941; m. Alexandra Calbos, Feb. 28, 1945; 1 dau., Matenia. Came to U.S., 1923, naturalized, 1938. Chief near Eastern sect. news bur., OWI, 1941-43, rep. to UNRRA Conf., Atlantic City, N.J., 1943, chief fgn. lang. press and radio dir., 1944-45; sec., mem. bd. Allied Mission to Observe Greek Elections, 1946; editor report on Greece, FAO, 1947; lectr. internat. law George Washington U., 1948-50; vis. lectr. internat. law Nat. War Coll. and Fgn. Service Inst., Dept. State, 1953-54; chief fgn. langs. publs. br. Dept. State, 1950-53, fgn. affairs information officer, 1955, dir. Pub. Services div., 1969—; lectr. internat. law Fgn. Service Inst. Dept. State. Decorated Grand Keeper of Records, Patriarch Greek Orthodox Ch. Mem. Am. Soc. Internat. Law, Am. Polit. Sci. Assn., Am. Acad. Polit. and Social Scis., Pan-Macedonian Assn. Am., Inst. Homeric Studies (hon.), Fgn. Corrs. Greece, Acad. Balkan Studies. Mem. Greek Orthodox Ch. Clubs: Nat. Press. Princeton (Washington). Author: Careers in the Foreign Service; Our Southern Partners; You and the United Nations; Communist Infiltration in Latin America. Contbr. articles to State Dept. publs. Home: 300 Woodland Terrace Alexandria VA 22302 Office: Dept State Washington DC 20520

SALATICH, BLAISE PETER, orthopedic surgeon; b. New Orleans, Jan. 8, 1912; s. Rinaldo J. and Lawrence Marie (Songy) S.; D.D.S., Loyola U. of South, 1933; M.B., La. State U., 1939, M.D., 1939; m. Phalbia Rebecca Hanly, June 29, 1943; children—Laurence Marie, Blaise Peter III. Intern Charity Hosp., New Orleans, 1939-40, resident, house surgeon, 1941-42, sr. orthopedic surgeon, 1947-54; practice medicine, specializing in orthopedic surgery, New Orleans, 1947—; vis. surgeon Hotel Dieu Hosp., 1947—. Served with USAAF, 1942-46. Decorated Bronze Star medal. Mem. Am., So., World med. assns., Orleans Parish, La. med. socs., British Med. Council, Omicron Kappa Epsilon. Club: Southern Yacht. Home: 24 Warbler St Lake Vista New Orleans LA 70124 also 801 E Scenic Dr Pass Christian MS Office: Maison Blanche Bldg New Orleans LA 70112

SALATICH, JOHN SMYTH, physician; b. New Orleans, Nov. 28, 1926; s. Peter B. and Gladys (Malter) S.; B.S. cum laude, Loyola U., New Orleans, 1946; M.D., La. State U., 1950; m. Patricia L. Mattison, Sept. 26, 1959; children—John Smyth, Elizabeth, Allison, Stephanie. Intern Charity Hosp., New Orleans, 1950-51, resident, 1951-54, dir. emergency rooms and satellite clinics; practice medicine, specializing in cardiology and internal medicine, New Orleans, 1954—; dir. EKG dept. Southeastern La. Hosp., Mardeville, La., Plaguemines Parish

Hosp., Port Sulphur, La., St. Joseph's Hosp., Thibodaux, La.; asst. prof. clin. medicine La. State U.; mem. staff Touro Infirmary; chmn. dept. medicine Hotel Dieu. Bd. dirs. La. Regional Med. Program, 1972. Adv. bd. Bank La. Served to capt. M.C., AUS, 1954-56; Korea. Decorated Medallion of Greek Army. Diplomate Am. Bd. Internal Medicine. Fellow Am. Coll. Chest Physicians, A.C.P.; mem. Am., La. (dir.) heart assns., New Orleans Acad. Internal Medicine, La. Thoracic Soc., La. Soc. Internal Medicine, A.M.A., La., Orleans Parish med. socs., Theta Beta, Alpha Sigma Nu, Delta Epsilon Sigma. Clubs: New Orleans Country. Contbr. to profl. jours. Home: 433 Country Club Dr New Orleans LA 70112 Office: Maison Blanche Bldg New Orleans LA 70112

SALAZAR, RUBEN, journalist; b. Chihuahua, Mexico, Mar. 3, 1928 (came to U.S. 1929, naturalized 1949); s. Salvador and Luz (Chavez) S.; B.A., U. Tex. at El Paso, 1954; m. Sally Robare, May 12, 1958; children—Lisa Marie, Stephanie Ann, John Kenneth. With El Paso Herald-Post, 1952-54, Santa Rosa Press Democrat, 1954-56, San Francisco News, 1957-59, Los Angeles Times, 1959—, assigned Vietnam, 1965-66, bur. chief, Mexico City, 1966—. Served with AUS, 1950-52. Home: Galileo 219 Mexico City Mexico Office: Paseo de la Reforma 122 Mexico City Mexico

SALE, JAMES PROWANT, govt. ofcl.; b. Stillwater, Okla., Oct. 21, 1921; s. William Claude and Lucy (Prowant) S.; B.S., Okla. State U., 1943; postgrad. Harvard, 1943, Mass. Inst. Tech., 1951; m. Betty Tourtellotte, Sept. 15, 1943; children—Claudia B. (Mrs. Bruce Kieley), James P., Elizabeth Louise, Penny Sue. Chief soils and found. div. U.S. Army Engrs., Ohio River Div. Labs., Cin., 1946-56; chief airfield pavement investigations Mil. Constrn. Directorate, Office of Chief-of-Engrs., Washington, 1956-61, spl. engr. asst. to dir. topography and mil. engrs., 1962-69; chief soils div. U.S. Army Engrs. Waterways Expt. Sta., Vicksburg, Miss., 1969—. Lectr., Cin. U. 1952-53. Served from 2d lt. to capt. C.E., AUS, 1943-46. Registered profl. engr., Okla. Mem. Am. Soc. C.E., Nat. Acad. Sci., Sigma Tau, Chi Epsilon, Blue Key, Sigma Chi. Home: 9 Lake Circle Dr Lake Park Estate Route 1 Vicksburg MS 39180 Office: Soils Div US Army Engr Waterways Expt Sta Vicksburg MS 39180

SALEM, JOE THOMAS, mcht., civic worker; b. Kafarakab, Lebanon, Mar. 25, 1904; s. Salem Abraham Malouf and Sahdah (Bahos) S.; student pub. schs. Lebanon, 1910-12, Utah and Tex., 1912-16; m. Nettie Elizabeth Harkey, Sept. 3, 1928; children—Robert J., Bettie Mae (Mrs. J. Korioth). Came to U.S., 1912, naturalized, 1930. Mcht., Tex., 1917-54; pres. S. Plains council Boy Scouts Am., 1954-56; bd. dirs. A.R.C., Lamb County, Tex., 1945-53; ofcl. bd. First Meth. Ch., Sudan, Tex., 1932-63, 65; bd. dirs. Tex. Council Chs., 1953-67, chmn. dept. Ch. World Service, Tex. Council Chs., 1958-61; adv. bd. Salvation Army, Lamb County, Tex., 1956-60; lay leader Meth. N.W. Tex. Conf., 1959-63; trustee Meth. Hosp., Lubbock, 1954-60, 62-72; chmn. Tex. CROP-Ch. World Service Bd., 1964-65; del. Meth. Jurisdictional Confs., 1948, 52, 56, 60, 64, 68, 72, Meth. Gen. Confs., 1956, 60, 64, 66, World Meth. Confs., 1956; mem. Meth. Mexico Mission, 1961, S. Am. Evangelistic Mission, 1964, Orient and Philippines Evangelistic Mission, 1968; founder, pres. Lotws, Sudan, 1963-67; mem. Nat. council Boy Scouts Am., 1966-69. Recipient Silver Beaver award Boy Scouts Am., 1947; Outstanding Community Service citation Sudan C. of C., 1960, Exceptional Service citation Tex. Council Chs., 1961. Mem. Sudan C. of C. (past pres.), W. Tex. C. of C. (dir. 1936). Mason (Shriner); mem. Order Eastern Star, Odd Fellow, Rotarian. Chmn. Sudan Fall Festival with theme the UN and World Peace, 1952-57; mem. Meth. group touring USSR and Europe, 1958; participant UN Sem. and 10th anniversary observance, 1955. Home: Box 218 Sudan TX 79371

SALEM, JOHN PETER, JR., drug co. exec.; b. Port Arthur, Tex., Dec. 18, 1929; s. John Peter and Gertrude (Hartman) S.; student Lamar Tech. U., 1948-51; m. Alice Fay Brantley, Feb. 14, 1953; children—Thomas Lee, Ricky Lynn, Susan May, Wayne Brantley, Kay Elizabeth. Bus. mgr. Salem Wholesale Drug Co., Port Arthur, 1945—. Bd. dirs. A.R.C. Served with AUS, 1951-53. Republican. Presbyn. (elder 1970). Mason (32 deg., Shriner). Home: 3220 Lay Av Groves TX 77619 Office: 3148 Gulfway Dr Port Arthur TX 77640

SALINAS MARTINEZ, ARTURO, lawyer; b. Monterrey, Mexico, Aug. 25, 1924; Bachiller, U. Nuevo Leon, 1941; Licenciado en Ciencias Juridicas, 1947; Docteur en Droit, U. Paris, 1949; diploma in comparative law Inter-Am. Law Inst., N.Y. U., 1950; Docteur Honoris Causa, U. Bordeaux, France, 1963. Admitted to Mexico bar, 1947; prof. corp. law U. Nuevo Leon, 1951-63, dean Law Sch. 1961-63, dir. Inst. Comparative Law, 1961-63; prof. corp., comml., tax law and finance, Inst. Tecnologico de Monterrey, 1951-61, 66-70; dean Law Sch., U. de Monterrey, 1970—. Lectr. Nat. U. Mexico, 1959, Inst. Comparative Law, Nat. U. Mexico, 1960, Sch. Law St. Mary's U., San Antonio Tex., 1962. Mem. Colegio de Abogados de Nuevo Leon, Inter-Am. Bar Assn. Author: Participating Certificates, 1947. Contbr. articles on law to profl. jours. Office: Edificio Chapa Monterrey Nuevo Leon Mexico*

SALINGER, PIERRE EMIL GEORGE, corp. exec., author; b. San Francisco, June 14, 1925; s. Herbert and Jehanne (Bietry) S.; B.S., U. San Francisco, 1947; m. Nancy Brook Joy, June 28, 1957 (div.); children—Marc, Suzanne, Stephen; m. 2d, Nicole Helene Gilmann, June 18, 1965; 1 son, Gregory. Reporter, night city editor San Francisco Chronicle, 1946-55; guest lectr. journalism Mills Coll., 1950-55; West Coast editor, contbg. editor Collier's mag., 1955-56; investigator select com. to investigate improper activities in labor or mgmt. field U.S. Senate, 1957-59; press sec. to U.S. Senator Kennedy, 1959-60, to Pres. Kennedy, 1961-63, to Pres. Johnson, 1963-64; U.S. Senate from Cal., 1964; v.p. Nat. Gen. Corp., 1965; pres. Fox Overseas Corp., 1965—; v.p. internat. affairs Continental Airlines, Inc. and Continental Air Services, Inc. subsidiary, 1965-68; pres. Gramco Devel. Corp., 1968—. Press officer Cal. Stevenson for Pres. campaign, 1952, Richard Graves for Gov. Cal. campaign, 1954. Served with USNR, World War II. Decorated Navy and Marine Corps medal. Club: Nat. Press (Washington). Author: With Kennedy, 1966; On Instuctions of My Government, 1971. Home: 14 Avenue du Square Paris 16 France Office: Norfolk House Frederick St PO Box 4883 Nassau Bahamas

SALLAWAY, GEORGE HENRY, religious assn. ofcl.; b. Bronxville, N.Y., May 31, 1930; s. George Henry and Louise Agatha (Giblin) S.; B.A., St. Thomas Sem., 1951; S.T.B., Pontifical Gregorian U., Rome, Italy, 1953, S.T.L., 1955. Ordained priest Roman Catholic Ch., 1954; pastor Diocese Amarillo, Tex., 1960-69; asso. exec. dir. Tex. Conf. Chs., Austin, 1969—; adminstr. S.W. Tng. Labs., 1969—. Adminstr., Tex. Consultation on Religion and Edn., 1971; cons. Tex. Cath. Conf., 1963—. Bd. dirs. S.W. Career Devel. Center, Arlington. Observer for bishops com. on ecumenism and other interreligious affairs Commn. Regional and Local Ecumenism, Nat. Council Chs. Christ, 1971. Mem. John Henry Newman Hon. Soc. Author: Follow Me: Be Human, 1966. Home: 1122 Colorado St Austin TX 78701 Office: 2704 Rio Grande 9 Austin TX 78705

SALLET, RICHARD, educator, author; b. Strasburg, Germany, Feb. 17, 1900; s. Daniel Gottfried and Martha (Galling) S.; student Columbia, 1927; A.B., Harvard, 1928; M.A., Ph.D., U. Konigsberg (Germany), 1930; postgrad. Northwestern U., 1930-32; m. Ilse Toppenthal, June 16, 1969; children (by previous marriages)—Maja (Mrs. H. Josef Thywissen), Herbert W., Dirse W., Gottfried (dec.), Michael. Editor, Dakota Free Press, New Ulm, Minn., 1921-26; lectr. polit. sci. Northwestern U., Evanston, Ill., 1931-33, Coll. Polit. Sci., Berlin, Germany, 1933-34; served to counselor of legation German Fgn. Service, Berlin, Washington, Lisbon, 1934-45; exec. sec. Inter-Univs. Commn., U. Gottingen (Germany), 1945-47; fgn. affairs cons. League of Refugees, Bonn, Germany, 1953-55; vis. prof. polit. sci. Alma (Mich.) Coll., 1960-63; prof. polit. sci., head dept. Livingstone Coll., Salisbury, N.C., 1963—, head social scis. div., 1964—. Lectr., U. Hamburg (Germany), summer 1932, Halle U. (Germany), summer 1932, Gottingen U., 1969. Served to lt. German Army, 1915-20. Life mem. Acad. Polit. Sci., Am. Acad. Polit. and Social Sci., Archaeol. Inst. Am., Minn. Hist. Soc., Brown County Hist. Soc.; charter mem. King of Prussia (Pa.) Hist. Soc.; mem. Internat., Am. polit. sci. assns., Am. Soc. Internat. Law, Anglo-German Soc. (Bonn), Soc. of Friends of Kant (Gottingen). Club: Harvard (N.Y.C., Charlotte, N.C.). Author: Russian-German Settlements in the U.S., 1931; Map of Russian-German Settlements in the U.S., 1939; The Diplomatic Service, Its History and Organization in France, Great Britain and the U.S., 1953; Diplomaticheskaya Sluzhba, 1956; The U.S.A., Country, People, Institutions, 1956; On Francis Lieber and His Contribution to the Law of Nations of Today, 1963. Initiated League of Nations Nansen Office, Geneva, a rescue operation for Mennonite refugees in Manchuria, 1931; helped to re-open West German univs. and restore acad. life, 1945-47. Home: 318 S Ellis St Salisbury NC 28144 also Calle Joaquin Arroyo 4 Madrid 16 Spain

SALLEY, CRAIG HOMER, architect; b. Balt., Sept. 28, 1938; s. Hilliard Homer and Mabel Viola (Cutsale) S.; student Orlando Jr. Coll., 1956-58; B.Arch., U. Fla., 1965; m. Geraldine Elizabeth Willis, Feb. 21, 1958; children—Brent Craig, Shawn Todd. Partner, Arthur Lee Campbell and Craig H. Salley Asso. Architects, Gainesville, Fla., 1967-70; partner Campbell, Salley & Asso. Architects, Inc., Gainesville, Fla., 1970-71; supervising architect dist. 3-A Fla. Div. Hotels and Restaurants, 1970—. Mem. Gainesville Jr. C. of C., Gainesville C. of C., Fla. Assn. Architects, A.I.A. (v.p. 1969-70). Kiwanian (v.p. 1971—, editor Bull. 1971—). Club: Gainesville Torch (charter). Important works include Life Sci.-Psychology Bldg., U. Fla., 1966-69, Hawthorne (Fla.) Jr.-Sr. High Sch., 1968-70. Home: 2530 NW 10th Av Gainesville FL 32601 Office: 218 SE 1st St Gainesville FL 32601

SALOOM, KALISTE JOSEPH, JR., judge; b. Lafayette, La., May 15, 1918; s. Kaliste and Asma (Boustany) S.; B.A. with high distinction, Southwestern La. Inst., 1939; J.D., Tulane U., 1942; m. Yvonne Adele Nassar, Oct. 19, 1958; children—Kaliste Joseph III, Douglas Leanne, Gregory John. Admitted La. bar, 1942; pvt. practice, 1942—; city atty. Lafayette, 1948-52, city judge, 1953—. Mem. judicial council La. Supreme Court. Chmn. La. Parish Draft Bd., 1950-71; mem. La. Youth Commn., 1958—, chmn., 1970—; mem. com. cts., codes and laws La. Hwy. Safety Commn.; mem. La. Pub. Affairs Research Council. Bd. dirs. S.W. La. Mardi Gras Assn., United Democrates La., 1957-59; trustee Am. Lebanon-Syrian Asso. Charities, 1957-65. Del. White House Conf. on Children and Youth, 1960; invitee 1st Nat. Conf. on Bail and Criminal Justice, Dept. Justice, Washington, 1963; chmn. com. on traffic law revision Jud. Council of La. Supreme Ct. Dir. La. Gulf Coast Oil Expn.; exec. bd. Evangeline area council Boy Scouts Am.; mem. bd. dirs. United Givers Fund; founder Lafayette Area Safety Council, 1961; mem. bd. Lafayette Mental Health Assn.; bd. dirs. Lafayetts Diocese Cath. Youth Orgn. Chief U.S. del. World Congress Christian Bros. Sch. Alumni, Spain, 1964, Can., 1967. Served as spl. agt. CIC, U.S. Army, 1942-45. Recipient Alumni award; U. Southwestern La., 1939, grant-in-aid, Esso Safety Found., Traffic Safety Conf., 1958, award traffic safety program, Am. Bar Assn., 1958, 59, 61, 63, 64; Lafayette Civic Cup award, 1965; named Man of Year, Salvation Army, 1966. Fellow Law-Science Acad. Am.; mem. Am. (lectr. traffic ct. advance seminars, mem. asso. and adv. com., recipient Outstanding Traffic Ct. judge award 1969), Lafayette (pres. 1955-56) bar assns., Am. Judicature Soc., Nat., La. (pres. 1963-64) councils juvenile court judges N.Am. (bd. govs. 1969—), La. City judges assns. (past pres.), La. Law Inst. (adv. com.), Am. Legion (judge adv. La. 1953-56), La. Conf. Social Welfare (dir. 1961), Blue Key, Nat. Inst. Municipal Law Officers, S.W. La. Univ. Alumni Assn. (pres. 1959—), Nat. Council on Crime and Delinquency; Nat. Council Municipal Judges, La. Hist. Soc., Order Coif, Kappa Sigma, Pi Gamma Mu, Pi Kappa Delta, Alpha Phi Omega, Phi Alpha Theta, Phi Kappa Phi. Clubs: Knife and Fork (dir.), Lafayette Town House (dir.), Rotary. Author: Traffic Court Judge's Check List, 1965. Home: 502 Marguerite Blvd Lafayette LA 70501 Office: 211 W Main St Lafayette LA 70501

SALTMAN, ROY GILBERT, computer scientist, govt. ofcl.; b. N.Y.C., July 15, 1932; s. Ralph H. and Josephine (Stern) S.; M.S., Mass. Inst. Tech., 1955; Profl. Engr., Columbia, 1962; m. Lenore Edelman, May 31, 1959; children—David, Eve, Steven. Research asst. Mass. Inst. Tech. Servomechanisms Lab., 1954-55; engr., research sect. head Sperry Gyro Co., Great Neck, N.Y., 1955-64; adv. systems analyst IBM Corp., Bethesda, Md., N.Y.C., 1964-69; sect. chief Nat. Bur. Standards, Washington, 1969—; exec. sec. Com. on Automation Opportunities in Service Areas, Fed. Council for Sci. and Tech. Bd. dirs. Montgomery County Citizens Planning Assn., 1969. Mem. I.E.E.E., Assn. Computing Machinery. Jewish religion. Home: 7701 Geranium St Bethesda MD 20034 Office: Tech Bldg Bur Standards Washington DC 20234

SALTZMAN, HERMAN, lawyer; b. New Haven, Jan. 29, 1916; s. Joseph N. and Frances (Levin) S.; A.B., U. Fla., 1940; J.D., John B. Stetson U., 1950; m. Irene P. Cameron, Mar. 21, 1946; children—Martin Howard (dec.), Arlene Norma. Enlisted USAAF, 1941, commd., 1942, advanced through grades to lt. col., 1962; served PTO and CBI, 1943-45, Germany and Morocco, 1953-56; former mem. staff judge adv. Moody AFB, Ga.; staff judge adv., Kadena AFB, Okinawa, 1962-63; chief mil. justice div. Amarillo Tech. Tng. Center, Texas, 1963-66; ret., 1966; practice law, Jacksonville, Fla., 1966—. Fellow Internat. Biog. Assn.; mem. Am., Jacksonville bar assns., Trial Lawyers Assn., Fla. Bar, Am. Judicature Soc., Judge Adv. Assn. Mason (Shriner). Home: 2701 Ocean Dr S Jacksonville Beach FL 32250 Office: Saltzman Bldg Jacksonville FL 32202

SALWIN, LESTER NATHAN, lawyer, govt. ofcl.; b. Kansas City, Mo., Nov. 18, 1911; s. Earl R. and Minnie (Wolf) S.; student Jr. Coll. Kansas City, 1927-29; A.B. cum laude, U. Ill., 1931, LL.B. cum laude, 1933; m. Lillian Levinson, Jan. 13, 1932; 1 dau., Marjorie Beth. Admitted to Ill. bar, 1933, Mo. bar; practiced in Chgo., 1933-39; adjudicator Social Security Adminstrn., Washington, 1940-42; with OPA, 1942-43; asst. to gen. counsel Smaller War Plants Corp., 1943-44; court review, research and opinion div. OPA, 1944-45; alien property custodian Office of Gen. Counsel, 1945-46; chief trade laws and spl. asst. for legal affairs Econ. and Sci. sect., SCAP, 1945-52; chief Japan mission U.S. Dept. Justice, Am. Embassy, Tokyo, Japan, 1952-60; with legislative div. U.S. Civil Adminstrn. of Ryuku Islands, 1960-61; spl. asst. Legal Investment div. Office Gen. Counsel, Small Bus. Adminstrn., 1961—; spl. counsel on adminstrv. procedures Nelsen Commn., 1971—. Mem. Atlantic Council of U.S. Mem. Fed., Mo., Ill. bar assns., Acad. Polit. Sci., Acad. Polit. and Social Scis., Nat. Lawyers Club, Phi Beta Kappa, Order of Coif. Author articles in field. Home: 3812 N Nelson St Arlington VA 22207 Office: Imperial Bldg 1441 L St NW Washington DC 20005

SALYER, KERMIT WAKEFIELD, editor, pub.; b. nr. Castlewood, Va., May 29, 1914; s. Robert Erkie and Auda M. (Isaacs) S.; B.A., Emory and Henry Coll., 1936; Radio-writing Workshop, N.Y.U., 1947; advt. course Internat. Corr. Schs.; m. Betty Frances Farmer, June 24, 1954; children—Diane Katherine, Kermit Wakefield, Robert Kyle. Served as seaman, U.S. Mcht. Marine, 1936-42, officer, 1942-44, chief officer, 1944-52; mng. editor of Mast Mag., 1947; asst. editor of Motorship, 1948; editor Yearbooks Pub. Co., 1949; editor, pub. Franklin News-Post, 1952—, Franklin Gazette, Rocky Mount, 1958-67, Salem Times-Register, 1958-60; pres. Post Pub. Corp., Radio Franklin, Inc. Mem. Rocky Mount Retail Merchants Assn. (founder, past pres.). Episcopalian. Home: 2223 Grandin Rd SW Roanoke VA 24015 Office: Post Publishing Corp 129 Church St Rocky Mount VA 24151

SAMFORD, FRANK PARK, ins. co. exec.; b. Troy, Ala., Nov. 1, 1893; s. William Hodges and Kate (Park) S.; student State Normal Coll., Troy; B.S., Ala. Poly. Inst., 1914; LL.D., Samford U., Auburn U., 1963, U. Ala., 1969; m. Hattie Mae Noland, Dec. 23, 1919; children—Frank Park, Ann (Mrs. Sam E. Upchurch). Deputy ins. commr. of Ala., 1915-19; Ala. mgr. Lumbermans Mut. Casualty Co., 1919-21; sec. Liberty Nat. Life Ins. Co., 1921-32, v.p., 1932-34, pres., 1934-60, chmn. bd., 1960—; dir. Malone Freight Line, Birmingham Trust Nat. Bank, Brown-Service Mfg. Co. Mem. bd. Life Ins. Sales Research Bur., 1931-34. Bd. dirs., mem. exec. com. Birmingham C. of C., 1937; pres. Indsl. Insurer's Conf., 1938-40; pres. Birmingham Community Chest, 1940-42; bd. dirs. Jefferson County Community Chest, Ala. Heart Assn.; pres. Jefferson Tb Sanitorium Soc., 1942-44; bd. dirs. Asso. Industries Ala., Inst. Life Ins., 1944; state v.p. Am. Life Conv.; pres. Ala. State C. of C., 1946-49; past U.S. C. of C. Pres. bd. trustees Samford U.; trustee Ala. Poly. Inst., So. Research Inst. Mem. Alumni Assn. Ala. Poly Inst. (pres. 1943-44), Ala. Acad. Honor (hon. mem.), Alpha Tau Omega, Omicron Delta Kappa. Democrat. Baptist. Mason (Shriner). Clubs: Rotary (pres. 1936-37; dist. gov. 1940-41), Birmingham, Birmingham Country, Mountain Brook Country. Home: 2700 Mount Brook Pkwy Birmingham AL 35213 Office: PO Box 2612 Birmingham AL 35202

SAMFORD, FRANK PARK, JR., life ins. co. exec.; b. Montgomery, Ala., Jan. 29, 1921; s. Frank Park and Hattie Mae (Noland) S.; student Auburn U., 1937-38; B.A., Yale, 1942; LL.B., U. Ala., 1947; m. Virginia Carolyn Suydam, May 27, 1942; children—Frank Park III, Laura Alice, John Singleton Pitts, Mae Virginia. With Liberty Nat. Life Ins. Co., Birmingham, Ala., 1947—, v.p., 1955-60, pres., 1960—, also dir.; dir. Hackney Corp., South Central Bell Telephone Co., Ala. Gt. So. R.R., Golden Flake, Inc. Pres. Jefferson County Community Chest, 1965. Bd. dirs. United Community Funds and Councils of Am.; bd. govs. Indian Springs Sch., Helena, Ala.; mem. exec. com. Am. Life Conv., Life Ins. Conf.; trustee U. Montevallo (Ala.), Independent Coll. Funds of Am. Served to lt. USNR, 1942-45. Mem. Assn. Chartered Life Underwriters, Am. Coll. Life Underwriters, Alpha Tau Omega, Phi Delta Phi, Berzelius. Presbyn. Rotarian. Clubs: Birmingham Country, Mountain Brook Country. Home: 3530 Redmont Rd Birmingham AL 35213 Office: PO Box 2612 Birmingham AL 35202

SAMFORD, THOMAS DRAKE, III, lawyer; b. Opelika, Ala., Mar. 4, 1934; s. Thomas Drake and Aileen (Maxwell) S., Jr.; A.B. magna cum laude, Princeton, 1955; LL.B., U. Ala., 1961; m. Jacqueline Screws, June 7, 1955; children—Thomas Drake IV, Jacquelyn, Robert Maxwell, Richard Drake. Admitted to Ala. bar, 1961, since practiced in Opelika; partner firm Samford & Samford, 1961—. Judge, Recorders Ct., Opelika, 1961—; owner, mng. partner realty, broadcasting, timber and farming operations; lectr., contbr. continuing legal edn. program Ala. State Bar, 1963—. Dir. Diversified Products Corp. Chmn., Opelika Downtown Action Com., 1967—; atty. Auburn U., 1967—, Ala. Wildlife Research Found., 1965—, Auburn Research Found., 1967—, Ala. 4-H Clubs, 1961—. Dir. bd. trustees Opelika Community Chest, 1965-68, pres., 1966-67; bd. dirs. U. Ala. Law Sch. Found., Jr. Achievement Chattahoochee-Lee. Served from 2d lt. to capt. USMCR, 1955-58. Recipient John G. Buchanan prize in politics Princeton, 1955, Farrah Order of Jurisprudence U. Ala., 1958, named one of Outstanding Young men of Ala., Jr. C. of C., 1967. Mem. Opelika C. of C. (pres. 1967), Am., Lee Co. (pres. 1965) bar assns., Ala. State Bar, U. Ala. Nat. Alumni Assn. (pres. 1966-67), Phi Beta Kappa, Alpha Tau Omega, Phi Delta Phi, Omicron Delta Kappa. Presbyn. (chmn. bd. deacons 1965-66). Kiwanian (dir. 1966-67, pres. 1969-70). Editor-in-chief Ala. Law Rev., 1960-61. Home: 805 Ridgewood St Opelika AL 36801 Office: Samford Bldg Av A Opelika AL 36801

SAMLI, A. COSKUN, educator; b. Istanbul, Turkey, July 21, 1931; s. Suleyman Seref and Ayse (Tuncer) S.; came to U.S., 1954; B.A., Istanbul Acad. Comml. Scis., 1953, M.A., 1953; M.B.A., U. Detroit, 1956; Ph.D., Mich. State U., 1962; m. Marcqueta Hill, June 18, 1959; 1son, Evan Kaya. Asst. prof. bus. adminstrn. Sacramento State Coll., 1961-65; asso. prof. marketing, asst. dir. bus. research bur. So. Ill. U., Carbondale, 1965-66; asso. prof. marketing, asst. dir. research inst. bus. and econ. U. So. Cal., Los Angeles, 1966-68; prof. bus. adminstrn. Va. Poly. Inst. and State U., Blacksburg, 1968—. Dir. Sacramento Consumers Coop., 1963-65, Nu-Mac Inc., Marion, Ill., 1965-66. Ford Found. fellow, 1963-64; Internat. Bus. Workshop fellow, 1966. Mem. Am., Western, So. econ. assn., Am., So. marketing assns., Gerontological Soc., Beta Gamma Sigma, Alpha Kappa Psi. Contbr. to profl. jours. Home: 1106 Kam Dr Blacksburg VA 24061

SAMMON, PATRICK FRANCES, city ofcl.; b. N.Y.C., Feb. 15, 1926; s. Patrick F. and Cecelia (O'Reilly) S.; grad. high sch.; m. Dorothy Laverne Sheffield, Jan. 20, 1945; children—Dorothy Jan, Patrick Thomas, Stacey Teresa. Control tower supr., link instr. So. Airways, Bainbridge, Ga., 1951-61; owner, operator Pat Sammon Ins. & Realty Agy., Colquitt, Ga., 1949—; commr., chmn. Housing Authority, of Colquitt 1957-60, exec. dir., 1960—; mem. Miller County-City of Colquitt Planning Commn., Airport Authority, 1968—. Adviser, Miller County Hosp., Colquitt, 1967—; dir. Civil Def. Colquitt-Miller County, 1961-66, Miller County Redevel. Corp., 1965—, Office Econ. Opportunity, 1966—. Served with USAAF, 1944-45. Mem. Am. Legion (past comdr.). Mason, Lion. Home: Oak Dr Colquitt GA 31737 Office: 102 1st St Colquitt GA 31737

SAMMONS, WILLIAM COLON, banker; b. Uvalda, Ga., Sept. 15, 1940; s. Claude Colon and Mildred (Gibbs) S.; A.A., Brewton Parker Coll., 1960; B.S., Ga. So. Coll., 1965; m. Linda C. Carter, Aug. 21, 1964; children— William, Brent, Brian. Tchr. Jeff Davis High Sch., Hazlehurst, Ga., 1965-66; bus. mgr. Brewton Parker Coll., 1966-71; exec. v.p. Mt. Vernon (Ga.) Bank, 1971—, dir., 1971—. Baptist (tchr. Sunday sch. 1967—). Lion (v.p. 1971—). Home: Route 1 Ailey GA 30410 Office: Mt Vernon Bank Mt Vernon GA 30445

SAMOL, HARRY HOWARD, entomologist; b. Erie, Pa., Oct. 15, 1942; s. John A. and Theresa (Hoppa) S.; B.S. in Agr., U. Fla., 1964; M.S. in Entomology, U. Fla., 1968; m. Carol Ann Troy, June 6, 1964; children—Anthony, Michael. Tchr. vocational agr. Fort Meade (Fla.)

High Sch., 1965; entomologist Fla. Sugar Cane League, Inc., Clewiston, 1967—. Mem. Entomol. Soc. Am., Fla. Entomol. Soc., Am., Internat. socs. sugar cane technologists. Lion. Home: PO Box 327 Clewiston FL 33440 Office: PO Box 1148 Clewiston FL 33440

SAMS, FULLER, broadcasting exec. Pres. WQXL, Columbia, S.C. Office: 3300 Main St Columbia SC 29211*

SAMS, JAMES HAGOOD, III, air force officer, civil engr.; b. Greenville, S.C., July 15, 1933; s. James Hagood and Elizabeth (Dargan) S.; B.C.E., Clemson U., 1954; M.S., U. Ill., 1955; postgrad. U. Colo., 1959-70, Ga. Inst. Tech., 1967-68; m. Dorothy Ann Cox, Jan. 31, 1955; children—Cynthia Ann, Candace Dargan, Timothy Hagood. Asso. aircraft engr. Lockheed Aircraft Corp., Marietta, Ga., 1954; research asst. civil engring. dept. U. Ill. at Urbana, 1954-55; engring. div. Boeing Airplane Co., Melborne, Fla., 1957-58; design specialist Martin-Marietta Corp., Denver, 1958-64; scientist Lockheed-Ga. Co., Marietta, 1964-71; commd. officer U.S. Air Force, 1954, now maj., civil engr. N.G. bur., Washington, 1971—. Cons. asso. Tanner, Thomas, D'Alli, Heartz & Assos., Melborne Beach, Fla., 1958. Served to 1st lt. USAF, 1955-57. Registered profl. engr., Ga., Colo.; recipient certificate Nat. Council Engring. Examiners. Mem. Am. Soc. C.E., Air Civil Engrs. Assn., N.G. Assn. U.S., Sigma Xi, Tau Beta Pi, Phi Kappa Phi, Phi Eta Sigma. Episcopalian. Contbr. articles to profl. jours. Home: 8811 Stockton Pkwy Alexandria VA 22308 Office: Air Civil Engring Div NG Bur Pentagon Washington DC 20310

SAMSON, DONALD ROBERT, elec. equipment co. exec.; b. Great Falls, Mont., Feb. 17, 1921; s. Earl George and Alexia Ann (MacKenzie) S.; B.S. in Elec. Engring., Mont. State Coll., 1947; m. Bette June White, July 6, 1943; children—Margaret Ann (Mrs. Chappel M. Cory III), Joseph E., Robert P., Charles M. With Gen. Electric Co., Pittsfield, Mass., 1947-65, mgr. advt. and sales promotion, 1954-59, mgr. export sales, 1959-65; mgr. utility merchandizing Allis Chalmers, West Allis, Wis., 1965-68, mgr. marketing power circuit breakers, 1968-69; pres. So. States, Inc., Hampton, Ga., 1969—, Dominion Cutout Ltd., Toronto, Ont., Can., 1970—. Served with CIC, AUS, 1942-46. Registered profl. engr., N.Y. Mem. A.I.M. (presidents council), I.E.E.E. Home: 1799 Castleway Lane NE Atlanta GA 30345 Office: Georgia Av Hampton GA 30228

SAMUELS, LEO SOLOMON, motel propr.; b. Chgo., June 26, 1900; s. Albert and Mary (Caplan) S.; Ph.B., U. Chgo., 1921; m. Helen Talpis, June 5, 1925; 1 son, Richard L. Admitted to Ill. bar, 1921; practice Chgo., 1921-60; sr. mem. Samuels, Samuels & Goodstein, 1935-41, Samuels & Samuels, 1941-60; owner, mgr. Islander Motel, Islamorada, Fla., 1960—; dir. 333 Bldg., Arlee Corp., Chgo. Served with U.S. Navy, 1918-20. Mem. Chgo., Am. bar assns., Am. Judicature Soc., Fla. Upper Keys C. of C. Jewish religion. Rotarian; mem. B'nai B'rith. Address: PO Box 766 Islamorada FL 33036

SANABRIA, ARTURO ENRIQUE, physician; b. San German, P.R., Dec. 12, 1921; s. Nicolas and Ines (Cotis) S.; B.A., Inter-Am. U., 1946; M.D., Jefferson Med. Coll., 1952; m. Ana Teresa Rivera, Dec. 21, 1962; children—Ivelisse, John E.; (by previous marriage)—Vivian, Arturo Enrique. Intern, Arecibo (P.R.) Dist. Hosp., 1952-53; med. dir. Ciales Hosp., 1953-63; practice gen. medicine, Ciales, P.R., 1963—. Med. cons. Selective Service, Ciales, 1969—. Mem. local com. Popular Democratic party, 1960—. Mem. P.R. Med. Assn. Home: Jaguas County Ciales PR 00638 Office: 10 Palmer St Ciales PR 00638

SANBORN, DAN, ins. and travel exec.; b. Kankakee, Ill., May 9, 1904; s. Wallis R. and Ada (Carmony) S.; student Colgate U., Kenyon Coll., 1922-25; m. Eleanor Harding, July 16, 1932; children—Sue (Mrs. Colbert Glenn Jr.), Mary Ann (Mrs. Hal Perry), Sara, William. Former pres. Lehigh Stone Co., Kankakee; founder Sanborn's Mexican Tourist Travel & Ins. Orgn.; pres. Sanborn & Co., Sanborn Land & Devel. Corp., Sanborn, Inc.; owner Sanborn's travel and ins. agys. Mem. Tex. Tourist Devel. Bd. Mem. Alpha Delta Phi. Episcopalian. Mason, Elk, Rotarian. Home: 600 Wichita St McAllen TX 78501 Office: Box 1210 McAllen TX 78501

SANBORN, HERBERT JAMES, museum ofcl.; b. Worcester, Mass., Oct. 28, 1907; s. Herbert C. and Grace A. (Thayer) S.; Pulitzer Traveling fellow, Nat. Acad. Design, 1926-29; student Columbia U. Tchrs. Coll., 1930-31, U. Chgo., 1934-35; m. Kathrine Kincaid Blood, June 20, 1934; 1 son, Herbert James. Instr. graphic arts, U. Ia., Iowa City, 1932-33; dir. Davenport Municipal Art Gallery, Davenport Ia., 1934-35, Museum Oglebay Inst. Wheeling, W.Va. 1936-43; exhibits officer Library Congress, Washington, 1946—; works exhibited throughout US., 1946—; represented in permanent collections Library Congress, Nat. Collection Fine Arts, Hunterdon County Art Center, Clinton, N.J. Served with USNR, 1943-46. Mem. Print Club Phila., Am. Inst. Graphic Artists, Washington Soc. Printmakers, Hunterdon County Art Assn. Contbr. articles profl. jours. Home: 3541 Forest Dr Alexandria VA 22302 Office: Library Congress 1st and Constitution Av Washington DC 20540

SANBORN, WAYNE GAYNOR, city ofcl.; b. Bridgton, Me., July 20, 1936; s. Charles Benjamin and Bertha (Kimball) S.; B.A., U. Me., 1958; M.B.A., U. Pa., 1960; m. Dixie M. Naugler, July 12, 1958; children— Rhonda Beth, Randolf Wayne, Russell Allen Charles, Renee Lynn. Asst. city mgr., finance dir., Titusville, Fla., 1960-61; city mgr., Arcadia, Fla., 1961-67, Deland, Fla., 1967—. Bd. dirs. Deland Devel. Corp., 1967-69, Deland Commn. 100, 1967—. Mem. Internat., Fla. (bd. dirs.) city mgrs. assns. Kiwanian (bd. dirs. 1969-70), Elk. Home: 1040 E University Av Deland FL 32720 Office: 120 S Florida Av Deland FL 32720

SANCHEZ, RAMIRO, banker; b. Nuevo Laredo, Mexico, Sept. 25, 1910; s. Celso Castro and Manuela (Aguirre) S.; brought to U.S., 1912, naturalized, 1938; Dipl. Comml. Banking, Stonier Grad. Sch., Rutgers U., 1954; m. Verena Guerra, Oct. 5, 1930; children— Sylvia (Mrs. Rogelio Salinas), Elva (Mrs. Servando Ramos), Delia (Mrs. Israel Gonzales), Martha (Mrs. Augustine Galvan), Ramiro Sanchez. Exec. v.p. Laredo Nat. Bank (Tex.), 1963-68, pres., 1968—. Chmn., Regional Export Expansion Council, Dept. Commerce, 1961—; chmn. Small Bus. Adminstrn., San Antonio, 1965—. Chmn. fund drive A.R.C., 1950—; 1st v.p. Easter Seal Soc. Tex. Treas. City of Laredo, 1970—. Bd. dirs., sec. Boys Club, 1958—. Mem. Laredo C. of C. (past pres.), Nat. Fedn. Ind. Bus. (county chmn.), Winter Garden Bankers Assn. (past pres.). Roman Catholic. Lion. Clubs: French, Knife and Fork (pres.), Order Alhambra (Laredo). Home: 1302 Mier St Laredo TX 78040 Office: 700 San Bernardo Laredo TX 78040

SANCHEZ-VILELLA, ROBERTO, govt. ofcl.; b. Mayaguez, Puerto Rico, Feb. 19, 1913; s. Luis. Sanchez-Frasqueri and Angela Vilella Velez; B.S. in Civil Engring., Ohio State U., 1934, LL.D. (hon.), 1965; m. Conchita Dapena Quinones, July 19, 1936; children—Vilma Josefina, Evelyn Guadalupe; m. 2d, Jeanette Ramos Buonomo; children—Roberto Jose, Olga Elizabeth. Civil engr. insular and fed. govts., 1934-41; asst. commr. interior, P.R., 1941-42; dir. P.R. Transp. Authority, 1942-45; mayor San Juan, P.R., 1945-46; spl. asst. to pres. Senate, P.R., 1946-47; exec. sec. P.R., 1949-51; commr. interior P.R., 1951-52, sec. of state, 1952-64, sec. pub. works, 1952-59; gov. Commonwealth of P.R., 1965-69. Pres. People Party. Recipient Medal of the Americas, Chamber of Commerce of Latin America, 1965. Mem. Am. Soc. Pub. Adminstrn., Colegio de Ingenieros de P.R., Tau Beta Pi. Address: 156 Franklin D Roosevelt Av Hatorey PR 00919

SANDEFUR, DAVID EDWARD, social worker; b. Temple, Tex., Sept. 6, 1937; s. David Lovell and Doris (Cunningham) S.; B.A., Southwestern U., Tex., 1960; M.S. in Social Work, U. Tex., 1962; m. Helen Ruth Matous, June 14, 1958; children—Randall Bruce, Ronald Brian. Supply pastor Salado (Tex.) Meth. Ch., 1958-60; counselor Family Service Bur., Houston, 1962-64; med. psychiat. social worker Gatesville (Tex.) State Schs. for Boys, 1964, dir. reception, classification and chief social service, 1964-72; dir. child care and tng. Tex. Youth Council, Austin, 1972—. Mem. organizational com. Clayton Homes Project, Houston, 1963-64. Dist. sec. United Fund, Houston, 1962, 63. Named Jaycee of Month, 1965. Mem. Acad. Certified Social Workers, Nat. Council on Crime and Delinquency, Tex. Juvenile Officers Assn. (2d v.p. 1967-68, pres. 1968-69), Tex. Inst. on Children and Youth (chmn. bd. 1969—). Democrat. Methodist. Optimist (charter pres. local chpt. 1968-69). Home: 1823 Terry Lane Georgetown TX 78626 Office: Sam Houston State Office Bldg Austin TX 78701

SANDEFUR, JAMES DANIEL, optometrist; b. Alexandria, La., Dec. 9, 1941; s. Marshall Nugent and Grace (Christian) S.; student La. Poly. Inst., 1959, 62, La. State U., 1960-61, 63; D.Optometry, So. Coll. Optometry, 1965; m. Lana Ruth Mynatt, June 15, 1968. Asso. in optometry, Ruston, La., 1965-66; individual practice optometry, Farmerville, La., 1966-67; asso. in optometry with Schnitt, Voss & Lewis, Shreveport, La., 1967-68; individual practice optometry, Oakdale, La., 1968—. Vision cons. spl. classes Oakdale Elementary Sch., 1968. Asst. chmn. Attakapas council Allen Parish Boy Scouts Am., 1968, chmn. Explorer Scouts, 1968, dist. chmn. council, 1971—, exec. bd., 1971—. Fellow Am. Acad. Optometry; mem. Am. Optometric Assn., Optometric Extension Program, La. State Assn. Optometrists (dir.), Central La. Optometric Soc., La. Acad. Optometry, La. (regional v.p. 1968), Oakdale (Jaycee of Year 1968-69, dir., v.p. 1969) jr. chambers commerce, So. Coll. Optometry, Gold Key (charter mem.), Kappa Alpha, Omega Delta. Methodist. (mem. adminstrv. bd.). Rotarian. Home: Davis Rd Oakdale LA 71463 Office: 5th Av Center Oakdale LA 71463

SANDEFUR, WAYNE T., educator; b. Evansville, Ind., May 12, 1914; s. William H. and Ida (Kempf) S.; B.S., Purdue U., 1936; M.S. in Edn., Ind. U., 1947, D. Health and Safety Edn., 1952; m. Sarah Margie Rhodes, Nov. 15, 1942; children—Sarah Ann (Mrs. Donald Roach), Rebecca Susan, Mary Virginia. Tchr., athletic coach F.J. Reitz High Sch., Evansville, Ind., 1936-46; dir. phys. edn. and athletics Biloxi (Miss.) pub. schs., 1947-48, prin. Biloxi Sr. High Sch., 1948-50; asst. supt. Biloxi schs., 1950-53; faculty U. Fla., 1953—, prof., chmn. dept. profl. curriculum, Coll. Phys. Edn. and Health, 1959—. Served to maj. AUS, World War II; PTO; col. Res. 1968—. Decorated Silver Star with oak leaf cluster, Purple Heart with oak leaf cluster, Bronze Star medal. Mem. N.E.A., Am. (conv. mgr. so. dist. 1954, editor newsletter 1956-57), Fla. (editor newsletter 1958-62) assns. health, phys. edn. and recreation, Delta Chi. Roman Catholic. Author: (with others) curriculum guides health edn., Pinellas County, Fla. Contbr. preparation ednl. bulls. Fla., Miss. depts. edn.; contbr. articles profl. jours. Home: 1418 NW 16th St Gainesville FL 32601

SANDERFORD, HOMER FRANKLIN, ins. co. exec.; b. Belton, Tex., Sept. 18, 1893; s. Warren Franklin and Margaret Parham (Smith) S.; student Baylor U., 1914-17; m. Margie Dorcas Austin, Feb. 15, 1921; 1 son, Homer Franklin (dec.). Tchr. rural pub. schs., Bell County, Tex., 1912-13; sr. partner Sanderford's Booterie, Wichita Falls, 1919-31; life ins. gen. agt. Liberty Life Ins. Co., Topeka and Ft. Worth, 1932-33, sr. ins. examiner State of Tex., Austin, 1933-40; 1st supervising examiner Tex. Ins. Dept., Austin, 1940-44; v.p., treas., dir. Am. Life Ins. Co., 1958—; now exec. v.p., dir. Am. Indemnity Co., Galveston, Am. Fire & Indemnity Co., 1953, Tex. Gen. Indemnity Co., 1948—; dir., mem. exec. and trust com. 1st Hutchings-Sealy Nat. Bank; exec. v.p., dir. Am. Finance Co., 1963-66; v.p., dir. 1936 Devel. Corp., 1963-66. Dir. United Fund, Galveston, 1950-60; past mem. Galveston Planning Bd. Trustee Sealy and Smith Found. for John Sealy Hosp.; v.p., dir. Letitia Rosenberg Home for Women. Served as 2d lt. F.A. and Artillery Aerial Observer, Air Corps, 1917-19. Mem. C. of C. Methodist (chmn. bd. trustees). Clubs: Galveston Country (dir.); Kiwanis (pres. Wichita Falls, Tex. 1929; dir.). Home: 5028 Crockett St Galveston TX 77550 Office: 2115 Winnie St Galveston TX 77552

SANDERFORD, JOHN ROY, banker; b. Belton, Tex., Oct. 3, 1895; s. Waren Franklin and Margurate (Smith) S.; student Baylor U., 1915-16; m. Thetis Clay Campbell, Nov. 15, 1921; children—Susan (Mrs. J.D. Bragg), Thetis (Mrs. Edward O. Gardner), John R. (dec.). Co-founder, sec.-mgr. Tex. Aero Co., Temple, 1927-32; founder, mgr. S.W. Transit Co., Belton, Tex., 1942-58, KTON radio, Belton, 1961-66; dir. Peoples Nat. Bank of Belton, 1941—. Mem. Tex. Senate, 1932-37; mayor Belton, 1961-62. Bd. dirs. Tex. Good Roads Assn. Served as fighter pilot Flying Service, Signal Corps, 1917-19. Mem. Tex. Motor Transp. Assn. (past pres.), E. Tex. C. of C. (pres. 1961), Belton C. of C., Am. Legion. Baptist. Rotarian, Mason. Home: 201 E 13th St Belton TX 76513 Office: 108 N Main St Belton TX 76513

SANDERFORD, T. E., transp. co. exec.; b. Belton, Tex., July 30, 1893; s. John Rice and Emily Viola (Lacy) S.; B.A., Baylor U., 1916; postgrad., U. Tex., 1917; m. Nellie Ruth Munford, Aug. 4, 1933; children—Sarah Jane (Mrs. Clark Potter), Thomas E. Contractor, 1933; With Southwestern Transit Co., Inc., Belton, Tex., 1942—, pres.; dir. First Nat. Bank Killeen. Instr. journalism Mary Hardin Baylor Coll., Belton, 1929-33. Pres., Ex-Students Assn. Baylor U., 1952-54; mem. Central Tex. Adv. Council, Ft. Hood, Tex., 1966—; mem. Baylor U. Council Instnl. Devel., 1967. Mayor, Belton, Tex., 1925-33; county judge, Belton, 1933-38. Mem. adv. bd. Scott & White Meml. Hosp., Temple, Tex., Scott, Sherwood & Brindley Found.; trustee Mary Hardin Baylor Coll., 1969—. Served with AUS, 1918-19. Recipient Mary Hardin Baylor Community Coll. award. Mem. Am. Legion, Nat. Def. Transp. Assn., Assn. U.S. Army, Belton C. of C. Baptist. Mason (Shriner, K.T.). Home: 1011 N Main St Belton TX 76513 Office: 126 N Main St Belton TX 76513

SANDERLIN, JOHN BOSWELL, aluminum co. exec.; b. Georgetown, Ky., July 2, 1926; s. Jonathan Riddick and Sarah (Boswell) S.; B.S., U. Va., 1950; M.B.A., Harvard, 1952; m. Ann Tefft Hutchinson, June 23, 1951; children—John Kimbrough, George Hutchinson. Mgmt. trainee Citizens Fidelity Bank and Trust Co., Louisville, 1952-54; asst. controller Morton Frozen Foods, Louisville, 1954-56; with Anaconda Aluminum Co., Louisville, 1957—, v.p. finance, 1967—, dir., 1970—; v.p. Anaconda Jamaica Inc., 1970—; mem. exec. com. Alumina Partners Jamaica; dir. Farms Jamaica. Mem. adv. bd. Louisville YWCA. Served with USNR, 1944-46. Mem. Financial Execs. Inst. (bd. dirs. Louisville 1962-69). Clubs: Harvard Business of Kentucky (pres. 1964-65); Pendennis, Harmony Landing Country, Filson (Louisville); Harvard (N.Y.C.). Home: 178 Arrowhead Rd Louisville KY 40207 Office: 1251 S 4th St Louisville KY 40203

SANDERS, AARON PERRY, educator; b. Phoenix, Jan. 12, 1924; s. DeWitt and Ruth (Perry) S.; B.S., Tex. Western Coll., 1950; M.S. (AEC fellow), U. Rochester, 1952; Ph.D., U. N.C., 1964; m. Betty Mae Gelein, Aug. 11, 1944 (div.); children—Merle Anne, Julie Ruth, James DeWitt. Asso. health physicist Brookhaven Nat. Lab., Upton L.I., N.Y., 1951-53; instr. physics, radiol. safety officer N.C. State Coll., 1953; instr. radiology Duke Med. Center, Durham, N.C., 1953-56, dir. radioisotope lab., 1953-65, asso. radiology, 1956-57, asst. prof., 1957-64, asso. prof., 1964-65, asso. prof., dir. div. radiobiology, 1965-71, prof., dir. div. radiobiology, 1971—, also asst. prof. physiology. Cons., N.C. Bd. Health, 1961—. Served with USNR, 1942-45. Fulbright lectr. health physics, Argentina, 1958-59. Diplomate Am. Bd. Health Physics. Mem. A.A.A.S., Am. Phys. Soc., Soc. Exptl. Biology and Medicine, Health Physics Soc., Soc. Nuclear Medicine, Biophys. Soc., Radiation Research Soc., Undersea Med. Soc. Sigma Xi, Sigma Pi Sigma. Contbr. articles to profl. jours. Address: Box 3164 Duke U Med Center Durham NC 27710

SANDERS, ALLEN, banker; b. Lawton, Okla., Apr. 16, 1932; s. Quincy A. and Mildred (Graves) S.; A.B. cum laude, Harvard, 1954, M.B.A., 1956; m. Dorothy Ann Mould, Sept. 4, 1954; children—Julia, Christopher. With First Nat. Bank, Dallas, 1956—, asst. v.p., 1961-63, v.p., 1963-67, sr. v.p., 1967—; pres. First Dallas Capital Corp.; dir. Hutson Corp., Macatee Capital Corp., Baldwin-Harris, Inc. Instr. Am. Inst. Banking, Southwestern Grad. Sch. Banking. Group chmn. Dallas County United Fund, 1969-70. Democratic precinct chmn., 1964-66. Methodist (chmn. adminstrv. bd.). Club: Harvard Business School (past pres. Dallas-Ft. Worth). Home: 13517 Far Hills Lane Dallas TX 75240 Office: 1401 Elm St Dallas TX 75222

SANDERS, ALLISON, newspaper columnist; b. Washington, Sept. 3, 1902; s. John Wiley and Lela (Allison) S.; student Tex. A. and M. U., 1921-24; m. Thelma Ann McCarty, June 18, 1924; children—Gay (Mrs. Gay Bugbee), Allison. Reporter, Houston Press, 1931-33; reporter, city editor Houston Chronicle, 1945-54, feature editor, 1954-56, columnist, 1956—. Mem. Am. Newspaper Guild (1st pres. Houston chpt.). Club: Press (past pres.) (Houston). Home: 3771 Rice Blvd Houston TX 77005 Office: Houston Chronicle 512 Travis St Houston TX 77001

SANDERS, CHARLES ROLAND, JR., textile mills exec.; b. St. Matthews, S.C., Dec. 23, 1926; s. Charles Roland and Annie (Keller) S.; A.B. in Journalism, U. S.C., 1946; m. Frances Earle Halford, Oct. 12, 1956; children—Annie Frances, Charles Roland III, James Gordon Halford. Wire editor, govtl. affairs editor, Columbia Newspapers, Inc. (S.C.), 1946-59, city editor, 1959-62, mng. editor, 1962-65; dir. corporate pub. relations, govtl. affairs Greenwood Mills (S.C.), 1965—. Mem. S.C. Pardon, Probation and Parole Bd., 1968—. Mem. Pub. Relations Soc. Am. Presbyn. Home: 129 N Cedar Dr Greenwood SC 29646 Office: Box 1017 Greenwood Bldg Greenwood SC 29646

SANDERS, DANIEL WERT, sch. adminstr.; b. Lewisburg, Tenn., Mar. 26, 1910; s. Ewell C. and Sarah (Stallings) S.; student David Lipscomb Coll., 1929-30; B.S., Middle Tenn. U., 1936; M.A., George Peabody Coll., 1946; m. Willa Frances Journey, May 12, 1934; 1 dau., Joan Ruth. Tchr. pub. schs., Chapel Hill, Tenn., 1930-35; jr. high sch. prin., Mooresville, Tenn., 1935-37; prin. Star (N.C.) High Sch., 1938-45; prin. Hugh Morison High Sch., Raleigh, N.C., 1945-54; prin. Garner (N.C.) High Sch., 1954-67; with Fed. Aid Program, New Careers, Raleigh, 1967; prin. Franklin (Tenn.) High Sch., 1968—. Mem. Phi Kappa Phi, Phi Delta Kappa. Mem. Christian Ch. Rotarian. Club: Raleigh Executive (v.p. 1951-52). Home: Gen Hood Dr Battlewood Estates Franklin TN 37064

SANDERS, DONALD HOWARD, educator; b. East St. Louis, Ill., Oct. 13, 1932; s. Vernon Joyce and Minnie (Smith) S.; B.B.A., Tex. A. and M. U., 1959, M.B.A., 1961; Ph.D., U. Ark., 1965; m. Joyce Ann Hyatt, June 22, 1952; children—Gary Donald, Linda Joyce, Ronald Craig. Asst. prof. U. Tex. at Arlington, 1963-65; prof. mgmt. Memphis State U., 1965-66; prof. mgmt. Tex. Christian U., 1966—; manuscript cons. McGraw-Hill Book Co., N.Y.C.; chmn. computers and data processing Examination Com. Coll. Entrance Exam. Bd. Served with USAF, 1952-56. Mem. Acad. Mgmt., Am. Inst. Decision Scis., Southwest Social Sci. Assn. Author: Introducing Computers to Small Business, 1966; Computers in Business, 1968; Computers and Management, 1970; Computers in Society, 1973. Home: 4009 Sarita Dr Ft Worth TX 76109 Office: Neeley Sch Bus Tex Christian U Ft Worth TX 76129

SANDERS, HARLAND DAVID, food franchising chain exec.; b. Henryville, Ind., Sept. 9, 1890; m. Claudia Ledington, Nov. 17, 1948. Ambassador of good will Ky. Fried Chicken Corp. Recipient Horatio Alger award, 1965. Home: PO Box 270 Shelbyville KY 40065 Office: PO Box 13331 Louisville KY 40213

SANDERS, HAROLD GLEN, clergyman; b. Aurora, Mo., Aug. 2, 1907; s. Charles T. and Margaret Ellen (Wheeler) S.; A.A., S.W. Bapt. Coll., 1930; A.B., William Jewell Coll., 1932; postgrad. U. Mo., 1932-33; Th.M., So. Bapt. Theol. Sem., 1937, Th.D., 1941; D.D., John B. Stetson U., 1961; grad. Am. Mgmt. course, Ch. Exec. Devel. Conf.; m. Mary Lou Myers, Apr. 30, 1936 (dec. Oct. 1950); children—Margaret Ellen, Harold Glen; m. 2d, June Celeste Holloway, Aug. 1, 1952; children—Susan, Ronald. Pastor Pleasant Home Baptist Ch., Spruce, Mo., 1932-35, Bapt. Ch., Christianburg, Ky. and New Liberty Bapt. Ch., Ind., 1936-39, Riverview Bapt. Ch., Cox's Creek, Ky., 1939-41, Norwood Bapt. Ch., Birmingham Ala., 1941-43; pastor First Bapt. Ch., Tallahassee, 1946-61; exec. sec.-treas. Ky. Bapt. Conv., Middletown, Ky., 1961-72. Exec. bd. Fla. Bapt. Conv., 1947-54, pres., 1953-54; chmn. trustees Bapt. Retirement Centers, 1958-61; chmn. stewardship commn. So. Bapt. Conv., 1960-62; pres. United Christian Action, 1958-60. Served as Chaplain USNR, 1943-46; PTO. Recipient citation for achievement William Jewell Coll., 1952; Life Service award S.W. Bapt. Coll., 1962. Mem. Tallahassee, Louisville chambers commerce, So. Bapt. Chaplains Assn. (pres.), Mil. Chaplains Assn. (area v.p.), V.F.W. (nat. chaplain 1956-57), Am. Legion, Order Ky. Cols. Contbr. to various religious periodicals. Home: 5404 Pawnee Trail Louisville KY 40207 Office: Ky Baptist Bldg Middletown KY 40243

SANDERS, HARVEY GIBERT, JR., lawyer; b. McCormick, S.C., Nov. 19, 1936; s. Harvey G. and Sue Lee (Keown) S.; B.S. in Bus. Adminstrn., U. S.C., 1957, LL.B., 1960; m. Barbara Ann Langley, June 10, 1956; children— Suzanne Kaye, Harvey G. III, Barry Langley. Admitted to S.C. bar, 1960; asso. Leatherwood, Walker, Todd & Mann, Greenville, 1960-65, partner, 1966—. Instr., Palmer Bus. Coll., Columbia, S.C., 1958-60; dir. A/G Investment Co., Inc., Greenville, S.C. Aabco Industries, Inc., Gaffney, S.C., Diran Corp., Greenvillle, S.C. Pres., U. S.C. Law Fedn., 1959; parliamentarian August Rd. Sch. P.T.A., 1964-65; mem. Mayor;s All Am. City com., 1965; Mayor's adv. com. on Certified Workable Housing Program, 1970—; mem. adv. com. Community Service and Continuing Edn. Seminars, 1967; mem. Greenville County Commn. on Alcoholism, 1968-71. Mem. Am., S.C. (exec. com. Young Lawyers sect. 1965-66),

Greenville Co. bar assns., Cornerstone Investment Club (pres. 1964-65), Greenville Young Lawyers Club (v.p. 1965), Greenville Jr. C. of C. (pres. 1966-67, named Outstanding Local Pres. 1966-67), Greater Greenville C. of C. (adv. com., chmn. bus. ethics com. housing com., dir. 1967, v.p. 1972), Greenville Literacy Assn. (pres. 1969-70), Order of Wig and Robe, Greenville Art Museum (dir. 1968), U.S.C. Alumni Assn. (circuit v.p. 1971-72), Phi Alpha Delta. Baptist (Sunday sch. tchr. 1960—, deacon). Clubs: Greenville-Pickens Gamecock (pres. 1965-66); Greenville Touchdown, Greenville Country. Home: 1414 Parkins Mill Rd Greenville SC 29607 Office: 217 E Coffee St Greenville SC 29602

SANDERS, HORACE GLENN, hosp. adminstr.; b. Trafford, Ala., Aug. 9, 1929; s. Hatton Lewis and Mary Kate (Floyd) S.; B.S. in Accounting, U. Ala., 1950; m. Mary Jane Thompson, Aug. 25, 1950; children—H. Glenn, Stephen, William S. With Ernst & Ernst, Birmingham, Ala., 1950-55, sr. accountant, 1953-55, cons. mgmt. services div., 1956-59, Mobile, Ala., 1959-64, Huntsville, Ala., 1964-68; asst. sec., controller Fidelity Service Ins. Co., Birmingham, 1955-56; pres., treas., adminstr. Sanders Mgmt., Inc., Russellville, Ala., 1968—; adminstr. North Ala. Hosp., Russellville, 1968—. Served with AUS, 1951. C.P.A., Ala. Mem. Ala. Soc. C.P.A.'s, Am. Inst. C.P.A.'s, Nat. Assn. Accountants (pres. North Ala. chpt. 1968-69; nat. dir. 1970—), Fedn. Am. Hosps. (dir. 1971—), Ala. Hosp. Assn. (com. chmn. 1971), North Ala. Hosp. Council (pres. 1971). Presbyn. (elder 1970—, commr. gen. assembly 1971—). Clubs: Twin Pines Country (Russellville); Civitan (dist. chmn. Ala.-West Fla. dist. 1963-64; pres. 313th Russellville 1971—). Office: PO Box 1089 Jackson Hwy Bypass Russellville AL 35653 Home: 515 Summit Dr Russellville AL 35653

SANDERS, JACK HILTON, banker; b. McComb, Miss., Mar. 15, 1921; s. Thomas and Mary (Mixon) S.; student Millsaps Coll., 1945-47, 50-52; m. Erna Moore, Dec. 23, 1942; children—Mary Ella, Rebecca Moore. Radio announcer, writer WSKB, McComb, 1939-40, WSLI, Jackson, 1946-52; gen. mgr. WSKB, McComb, 1952-54; with Herbert S. Benjamin Assos., advt. agy., Baton Rouge, La., 1954-57; advt. mgr. Goudchaux's, Baton Rouge, 1957-66; v.p. Capital Bank and Trust Co., Baton Rouge, 1966-70; v.p. Am. Bank & Trust Co., Baton Rouge, 1970—. Lectr. 1st ann. advt. workshop La. State U., 1966. Advt. publicity chmn. Parish Savs. Bond Program, 1966-67; active various fund drs.; pres. Robert E. Lee High Sch. Dad's Club, 1967. Bd. dirs. Baton Rouge Symphony, 1966—, pres., 1969—; bd. dirs. La. Arts and Sci. Center, 1969, 70, 71; bd. dirs. Internat. Hospitality Found. Served to capt. AUS, 1940-46; ETO. Mem. C. of C. (chmn. civic affairs com. 1967), Baton Rouge chpt. Pub. Relations Soc. Am. (past pres., chmn. mid south dist., 1969), Baton Rouge Advt. Club (past pres.). Home: 5845 S Pollard Pkwy Baton Rouge LA 70808 Office: Plank Rd at Choctaw Baton Rouge LA 70802

SANDERS, JAMES LINDELL, aerospace exec.; b. Meridian, Miss., Feb. 10, 1927; s. James Eugene and Margaret (McElroy) S.; B.A., Auburn U., 1948; M.E., Yale, 1951; m. Elizabeth Ellen Kirk, Dec. 25, 1946; children— Elizabeth Irene, Linda Ellen, Lesa Jane. Atlas propulsion pros. engr. Ramo-Wooldridge, 1957; engring. specialist Chance Vought, 1958-60; asst. to dir. Future Projects Office, MSFC-NASA, 1962, br. chief, 1969—; preliminary design of missiles systems and space vehicles systems Dept. mgr. Brown Engring., Huntsville, Ala., 1965-69. Served with USAAF, 1945-46. Registered profl. engr., Ala. Mem. Am. Astronautical Soc., Tau Beta Pi, Phi Kappa Phi, Gamma Alpha, Scabbard and Blade. Home: 705 Watts Dr SE Huntsville AL 35801 Office: Redstone Arsenal AL 35812

SANDERS, JASON CHASE, physician; b. Krum, Tex., Feb. 16, 1918; s. Jason Poland and Myrtie (Chase) S.; B.S., La. State U., 1939, M.D., 1943; m. Dimple June Fovery, Mar. 21, 1943; children—Thomas Jason, Mary, Joan. Intern, Doctors Hosp., Fairfield Hosp., 1943; resident Shreveport (La.) Charity Hosp., 1943-44; practice medicine, specializing in gen. medicine, Shreveport, 1947—; pres. staff Doctors Hosp., 1961; med. dir. Trans World Life Ins. Co., 1960—. Served with AUS, 1944-46; ETO. Diplomate Am. Bd. Family Practice. Mem. A.M.A., Am., La. (pres. 1956-59) acads. gen. practice, So., Shreveport med. socs. Baptist. Mason (Shriner). Clubs: Optimist (pres. 1960), Toastmasters (pres. 1959)(Shreveport). Home: 857 River Rd Shreveport LA 71104 Office: 106 E Kings Hwy Shreveport LA 71104

SANDERS, JOE WILLIAM, state justice; b. Pleasant Hill, La., May 31, 1915; s. Oliver Lud and Ozie (Allen) S.; B.A., La. State U., 1935, LL.B., 1938; m. Marie Sistrunk, Oct. 26, 1940. Admitted to La. bar, 1938; pvt. practice, Many, 1938-42, Baton Rouge, 1946-54; judge Family Ct. Parish E. Baton Rouge, 1954-60; asso. justice Supreme Ct. La., 1960—. Chmn. E. Baton Rouge Parish Juvenile Commn., 1951-54; chmn. Blue Ridge Tng. Inst. So. Juvenile Ct. Judges, 1957, mem. adv. council judges Nat. Council Crime and Delinquency, 1955—. Mem. La. Ho. of Reps. from Sabine Parish, 1940-44; del. La. Democratic Conv., 1940, Nat. Dem. Conv., 1952. Bd. dirs. Baton Rouge, YMCA 1952-55, 58-61. Served to capt. AUS, 1942-46. Mem. Am., La. bar assns., Am. Judicature Soc., Nat. Council Juvenile Ct. Judges, Am. Legion, Amvets (past post comdr.), V.F.W., Order of Coif, Am., La. law insts., Phi Kappa Phi, Omicron Delta Kappa, Gamma Eta Gamma, Pi Sigma Alpha, Pi Gamma Mu, Theta Xi. Mason; mem. Woodmen of World. Home: 209 Lover's Lane Dr Baton Rouge LA 70806 Office: Supreme Ct Bldg 301 Loyola Av New Orleans LA 70112

SANDERS, LYLES WILLIAM, oil equipment co. exec.; b. Landrum, S.C., July 31, 1926; s. David Eston and Eva Louise (Jones) S.; B.S., Clemson U., 1950; postgrad. in Indsl. Mgmt., U. Ga., 1964; m. Mary Edith Carter, Sept. 4, 1954; 1 son, Thomas. Asst. chief engr. P & N Ry. Co., Charlotte, N.C., 1950-53; div. engr. Am. Oil Co., Charlotte, 1954-59, asst. regional engr., Atlanta, 1959-69; v.p. Gate City Oil Equipment Co., Atlanta, 1969—, also dir. Served with USAAF, 1943-45. Mem. Petroleum Engrs. Assn. (past pres.), S.E. Region Antique Automobile Club Am. Mason (32 deg.). Home: 2564 Clairmont Rd NE Atlanta GA 30329 Office: 1500 Marietta St NW Atlanta GA 30318

SANDERS, MELVIN HILL, indsl. engr.; b. Atlanta, Sept. 9, 1928; s. Shelby Lockard and Ada (Hill) S.; student Troy State U., 1948-50; B.S., Auburn U., 1952; m. Mary Lloyd Kelly, Feb. 26, 1954; children—Cheryl Elaine, Cathy Lynn, Ginger Marie. Asst. engr. wage incentives Western Electric Co., Burlington, N.C., 1952-56, indsl. engr., 1956-63, sr. indsl. engr. work measurement program, 1963-68, sr. planning engr. Safeguard Anti-Ballistic Missile project, 1968—, instr. ednl. TV courses, 1968—. Precinct judge, Graham, N.C., 1968. Served with USNR, 1946-47. Registered profl. engr., N.C. Mem. Nat. Soc. Profl. Engrs., Profl. Engrs. N.C., Am. Inst. Indsl. Engrs. (pres. Raleigh chpt. 1966-67, dir. 1968, chmn. standing com. 1962-69, membership chmn. region 31968-70), Burlington-Graham Engrs. Club, Delta Sigma Phi. Presbyn. Club: Piedmont Crescent Country. Home: 618 Johnson Av Graham NC 27253 Office: 204 Graham-Hopedale Rd Burlington NC 27215

SANDERS, MICHAEL I., lawyer; b. Bklyn., Dec. 23, 1938; s. Aaron and Minna (Odesky) S.; B.S. summa cum laude, N.Y.U., 1960, LL.B., 1964; LL.M., Georgetown U., 1967; m. Judith Seltzer, June 21, 1969. Admitted to N.Y. bar, 1964; accountant Beck & Field, N.Y.C., 1960-61, Anchin, Block & Anchin, 1961-64; trial atty. refund litigation sect. of tax div. U.S. Dept. Justice, Washington, 1964-68; atty.-adviser to asst. sec. treasury for tax policy, Washington, 1968-70; tax atty. Ginsburg, Feldman & Bress, Washington, 1970—. Served with AUS, 1960. Recipient Arthur A. Rosenkampf award N.Y.U., 1957, Am. Jurisprudence prize fed. tax practice and procedure N.Y.U. Sch. Law, 1964; Samuel Rubin scholar, 1960-61, alumni scholar, 1961-64. C.P.A., N.Y. Mem. Am. Inst. Pub. Accountants, N.Y. State Soc. C.P.A.'s (Outstanding Grad. award 1960), Beta Gamma Sigma, Beta Alpha Psi, Phi Delta Phi. Home: 9 Lakenheath Ct Potomac MD 20854 Office: 1700 Pennsylvania Av Washington DC 20028

SANDERS, MURRAY JONATHAN, physician; b. Chelsea, Mass., Apr. 11, 1910; s. Louis and Rose (Gould) S.; B.Sc., Tufts Coll., 1931; student (scholar) Heidelberg (Germany) U., 1929; M.D., U. Chgo., 1936; m. Margaret Weatherly, Dec. 19, 1959; children—Frank Weatherly Hersey, Murray Jonathan. Asst. Office of Coroner, Chgo., 1936; asst. in pathology U. Chgo. Rush Med. Coll., 1936; rotating intern Evanston (Ill.) Gen. Hosp., 1936-38; Oliver Rea Scholar Columbia Coll. Phys. and Surg., N.Y.C., 1938-40, instr. bacteriology, 1940-41, asst. prof., 1941-45, asso. prof., 1945-47; prof. bacteriology U. Miami, Coral Gables, Fla., 1948-52; research prof., dir. dept. microbiology U. Miami, South Miami, Fla., 1952-60; med. dir., v.p. Pan Am. Pharms., Inc., Ft. Lauderdale, Fla., 1960; cons. pathology City of N.Y. Dept. Hosps., Harlem Hosp., 1947—; dir. research Variety Children's Hosp., Miami, 1952-53; cons. Nat. Children's Cardiac Hosp., Miami, 1950—, Blood Plasma Corp. Japan, Osaka, 1950—; hon. med. staff, cons. Guam Meml. Hosp., Agana, 1950—; chmn. dept. biol. scis. Fla. Atlantic U., 1962-65; med. dir., v.p. Gray Industries, Inc., also Gray Research Found., Inc.; founder, med. dir. Sanders Med. Research Found., Delray Beach, Fla. Nobel prize nominee in medicine, 1966; mem. Outstanding Citizen Assn., Miami. Served from maj. to lt. col. M.C., AUS, 1940-46. Decorated Legion of Merit, D.S.M.; recipient commendation for med. intelligence service Gen. Eisenhower, 1946. Fellow A.A.A.S., N.Y. Acad. Scis. (life), Royal Soc. Health; mem. Am. Assn. Pathologists and Bacteriologists, Soc. Exptl. Biology and Medicine, Am., Fla., pub. health assns., Am. Fedn. Clin. Research, Soc. Am. Bacteriologists, Tissue Culture Assn., So. Med. Assn., N.Y. Acad. Medicine, Fla. Acad. Scis., Sociedad Cubana de Salubridad Publica (corr.), Ret. Officers Assn., Sigma Xi. Club: Cosmos (Washington). Contbr. numerous articles and chpts. to profl. publs. Editor Jour. Indsl. Medicine. Originator 1st 2d, 3d symposia on Applied Virology, co-editor proc., editor proc., 1966, 68, 70. Home: 3009 Spanish Trail Delray Beach FL 33444 Office: 3009 Spanish Trail Delray Beach FL 33444 also 2 E Atlantic Av Delray Beach FL 33444

SANDERS, PAUL DELEON, editor; b. West, Miss., Oct. 28, 1901; s. John DeLeon and Zemuly (Weeks) S.; B.Sc., Miss. State Coll., 1922; M.Sc., U. Md., 1924, D.Sc., 1947; M.A., Harvard (sabbatical leave from U. of Md.), 1930; work completed for Ph.D., Am. U., Washington; D.Agr., Salem Coll., W.Va., 1953; LL.D., Med. Coll. Va., 1958; m. Thema Franke, Nov. 29, 1934. Jr. entomologist U.S. Dept. Agr., 1922; grad. asst. U. Md., 1922-24, extension entomologist, 1924-28, asso. entomologist (state, station and extension), 1929-31; extension entomologist U.S. Dept. Agr., 1931-34; editor So. Planter, 1934-44, editor, exec. v.p., 1944-68; exec. dir. Keep Va. Beautiful, Inc., Richmond, 1969—; dir. Bank of Va.; dir. C.&P. Telephone Co. of Va., Fuel Oils, Inc., Atlantic Rural Expn.; mem. Gov.'s Council on Va. Economy, chmn. com. on population, 1948-49. Bd. visitors Va. Poly. Inst. Served as 2d lt. Inf., O.R.C., World War I. Recipient Nat. Safety Council award, 1945-54; Nat. 4-H Club award, 1947, 54; Distinguished Service award Va. Poly. Inst., 1952; Hon. Am. Farmer Degree, 1952; Gold Seal award Nat. Council State Garden Clubs, 1955; Conservation award Am. Forestry Ann., 1956; named Man of Year in Forestry, 1971. Master, Va. State Grange, 1946-50, Va. Farm Bur. Fedn. Mem. Am. Assn. Econ. Entomologists, Entomol. Soc. Am., Am. Forestry Assn. (hon. v.p.), Washington Entomol. Soc., Am. Agrl. Editors Assn. (pres. 1947-49), Va. Social Sci. Assn., Nat. Planning Assn. (mem. agrl. com.). Theta Chi, Epsilon Sigma Phi. Clubs: Torch (dir. Internat. Assn.), Harvard (Va.); Commonwealth, Democrat, Country of Va., Bull and Bear. Home: 316 Clovelly Rd Richmond VA 23221 Office: 205 W Franklin St Richmond VA 23220

SANDERS, RALPH WAID, orgn. exec.; b. Ft. Smith, Ark., Feb. 15, 1937; s. Floyd Hall and Ruth (Cooper) S.; A.A., Ft. Smith Jr. Coll., 1957; B.A., U. Tulsa, 1959; m. Roberta Hood, Apr. 2, 1960; children— Ralph Terrell, Mary Anne, Timothy Waid. Freelance writer, photographer, 1955-56; journalist KOTV News, Tulsa, 1957-60; dir. pub. relations U.S. Jr. C. of C., Tulsa, 1960-63; exec. v.p. World Neighbors, Oklahoma City, 1963—. Mem. Pub. Relations Soc. Am., Am. Mgmt. Assn., Internat. Platform Assn., Sigma Delta Chi. Home: 10821 Greystone St Oklahoma City OK 73120 Office: 5116 N Portland St Oklahoma City OK 73112

SANDERS, ROBERT VESTER, hosp. adminstr.; b. Birmingham, Ala., Jan. 13, 1927; s. Robert Vester and Lula M. (White) S.; B.S. in Accounting, Samford U., Birmingham, 1949; m. Bettye J. Means, Dec. 27, 1952; children—Rob, Mike, Barre, Joan. Bus. mgr. Norwood Clinic, Birmingham, 1949-56; bus. mgr. Carraway Meyer Rehab. Center, 1953-55; asst. div. accountant Union Supply div. U.S. Steel Co., 1956-57; adminstr. Hill Crest Hosp., Birmingham, 1963—; adj. asst. prof., preceptor Sch. Community and Allied Health Resources, U. Ala. at Birmingham. Chmn. bd. dirs. Community Hosp., Ensley, Birmingham; mem. bd., mem. exec. com., project rev. com., health facility tech. adv. com. Community Health Planning Commn., chmn.; mem. paramed. adv. com. Jefferson State Jr. Coll.; chmn. Mental Health Tech. Com.; mem. Citizens Adv. Com. to Jefferson County Bd. Health; pres. Birmingham Regional Hosp. Council. Pres. Hill Crest Found.; trustee Indsl. Health Council. Served with AUS, 1945-46. Mem. Am. Coll. Hosp. Adminstrs., Am. Acad. Med. Adminstrs., Assn. Mental Health Adminstrs., Ala. Hosp. Assn. Baptist (deacon). Lion, Mason. Office: PO Box 2896 Birmingham AL 35212 Home: 2640 Dolly Ridge Rd Birmingham AL 35243

SANDERS, STANLEY GORDON, educator; b. Burlington, Ia., May 6, 1923; s. Andrew Gordon and Betty Juliana (Braasch) S.; student Burlington Jr. Coll., 1940, U. N.D., 1943-44; B.A., Ia. Wesleyan Coll., 1946-47; postgrad. Drake U., 1947; M.A., U. N. Colo., 1951; Ph.D., U. Ia., 1966; postgrad., Peabody Coll., 1952; m. Marjorie Louise Agans, May 27, 1947; children—Kirby D., Bonnie J., Barbara J. Tchr. pub. schs., Ia., 1947-51; prin. Villisea (Ia.) High Sch., 1951-53; supt. Poweshiek County (Ia.) Schs., 1953-59; research asst. Ia. Center for Research in Ednl. Adminstrn., Iowa City, 1959-60; asst. prof. ednl. adminstrn. U. Houston, 1960-67, asso. prof., 1967—. Dir. research Gulf Sch. Research Devel. Assn., 1960-65. Served with AUS, 1943-46. Mem. N.E.A. (life), Am. Assn. Sch. Adminstrs., Nat. Orgn. on Legal Problems Edn., Phi Delta Kappa. Contbr. articles to profl. jours. Home: 6003 Effingham Dr Houston TX 77035

SANDERS, WADE M., govt. ofcl.; b. Dodson, La., Mar. 27, 1920; s. William Huffman and Maggie (Gaar) S.; B.S., La. Poly. Inst., 1949; student Clemson Coll., 1948; post-grad. U. Ala., 1966-67, U. Okla., 1967; m. Amanda Jane McColloch, Dec. 1, 1956; children— Linda (Mrs. Joe Tidwell), Wanda Jean, Wade M., T. Huffman, Mary Margaret. Chief clk. C.E. U.S. Army, Dunnelion, Fla., 1941-42, engr., Tullahoma, Tenn., 1952-56; sr. clk., Savannah, Ga., 1946; engr. S.E. Huey & Co., Monroe, La., 1949-50, Gulf Oil Corp., New Orleans, 1951, Arnold Engr. Devel. Center, USAF, Tullahoma, 1957; city engr., Monroe, La., 1958; staff engr. U.S. Army Missile Command, Redstone Arsenal, Ala., 1958-68, U.S. Army Safeguard System Command, Huntsville, Ala., 1968—. Served with A.C., AUS, 1942-46. Registered profl. engr., Ala., La., Tenn. Mem. Soc. Logistics Engrs., Soc. 40 et 8, Am. Legion. La. Engring. Soc. Lion. Home: 2333 Gallatin St Huntsville AL 35801 Office: US Army Sentinel Command Box 1500 Huntsville AL 35807

SANDERS, WILLIAM E., coadjutor bishop Protestant Episcopal Ch., Knoxville, Tenn. Address: Knoxville Bank Bldg Knoxville TN 37902*

SANDERS, WILLIAM KING, gas co. exec.; b. Poteau, Okla., Apr. 28, 1905; s. Wiley L. and Martha (Miller) S.; m. Bertha B. Capper, Dec. 2, 1933; 1 son, Charles King. With Panhandle Eastern Pipe Line Co., Kansas City, Mo.; 1928-50, pres., chief exec. officer, 1965-68, chmn. bd., chief exec. officer, 1968-71, dir., cons., 1971—; dir. Trunkline Gas Co., Houston, 1950—, pres., 1957—; dir. Kaiser Steel Corp., Oakland, Cal., So. Nat. Bank, Houston. Home: 5442 Tupper Lake Houston TX 77027 Office: 3000 Bissonnet St Houston TX 77005

SANDERS, WILLIE FRED, city ofcl.; b. Rome, Miss., Feb. 12, 1928; s. Amel R. and Julia (Lieunberger) S.; B.B.S., Tulane U., 1966; m. Gerda E. Schulze, Dec. 3, 1955; children—George D., William M. Inventory control accountant Coleman E. Adler & Sons, New Orleans, 1958-60; accountant I, City of New Orleans, 1960-62, accountant II, 1962-68, adminstrv. analyst II, 1968-71; dir. fiscal and services div. New Orleans Police Dept., 1971—. Served with USAF, 1949-52. Home: 8921 Dinkins St New Orleans LA 70127 Office: 715 S Broad St New Orleans LA 70119

SANDIDGE, FORREST BRENT, state ofcl.; b. Lynchburg, Va., June 8, 1926; s. Harry Hill and Nellie Trevellian (Bristow) S.; B.A., Lynchburg Coll., 1950; M.Ed., U. Va., 1955; m. Jeanne Gasque, May 9, 1959; children—Elizabeth Adams, Martha Damon. With Agusta County (Va.) Pub. Schs., 1950-55, prin., 1953-55; prin. Staunton City (Va.) Pub. Schs., 1955-57, dir. instrn. 1960-64; gen. supr. Warren-Rappahannock Counties (Va.) Pub. Schs., 1957-60; supt. Culpeper County (Va.) Pub. Schs., 1964-68; dir. div. spl. services Va. Dept. Edn., Richmond, 1968—. Mem. Stonewall Jackson area council Boy Scouts Am., 1962-64. Served with AUS, 1944-46; ETO. Decorated Purple Heart. Mem. Va. Assn. for Supervision and Curriculum Devel., Va. Edn. Assn. (pres. 1963-65), Nat. Assn. for Supervision and Curriculum Devel., Phi Delta Kappa. Episcopalian (mem. vestry 1963-64, 67-68). Rotarian. Club: Ruritan (local pres. 1954-55). Home: 1016 Pepper Av Richmond VA 23226 Office: Dir Div Special Service State Dept Edn Richmond VA 23216

SANDIFER, DANIEL PADGETT, architect; b. Shreveport, La., Mar. 1, 1927; s. William Davis and Dell (Batchelor) S.; student La. State U., 1944-48, Centenary Coll., 1950-52; B.Arch., Tulane U., 1956; m. Patricia Ann Dickson, Feb. 1, 1949; children—Richard Dale, Patricia Suzanne, Jett Ellen. Draftsman, Wm. B. Wiener, Architect, Shreveport, La., 1950, 52, 55, 56-57, Nield-Somdal, Architect, Shreveport, La., 1953; partner, architect Wilson and Sandifer, Architects, Shreveport, La., 1958—. Profl. football player Nat. Football League, 1948-53. Chmn. Shreveport Met. Planning Commn., 1965—. Mem. Caddo Parish Democratic Com., 1966—. Bd. dirs. YMCA Shreveport, 1968; Nat. chmn. La. State U. Alumni Fund, 1971. Mem. A.I.A. (chpt. v.p. 1967-68, pres. 68-69), La. Architect Assn., Tau Sigma Delta. Baptist (deacon). Elk. Clubs: Petroleum, Cotillion, Pierremont Oaks Tennis (past v.p.). Home: 174 Richard St Shreveport LA 71105 Office: 622 Comml-Nat Bank Bldg Shreveport LA 71101

SANDIFER, SAMUEL HOPE, educator; b. Walterboro, S.C., May 27, 1916; s. Myron Guy and Cornelia (Hope) S.; B.S., The Citadel, 1937; M.D., Med. Coll. S.C., 1941; m. Thelma Jones Hanold, May 23, 1970; children—Frederick Hanold, Sandra (Mrs. George W. Murphy), Betsy (Mrs. Martin H. Reiff). Intern, Brooke Gen. Hosp., San Antonio, 1941-42; resident internal medicine Coll. of Va., Richmond, 1947-49, cardiology Fitzsimons Gen. Hosp., Denver, 1954-55; commd. 2d lt. U.S. Army, 1942, advanced through grades to col., 1965; ret., 1965; surgeon The Citadel, 1965-68; asso. prof. medicine and preventive medicine Med. U. S.C., Charleston, 1968—. Project dir. S.C. Community Pesticide Study, 1969—. Diplomate Am. Bd. Internal Medicine. Fellow A.C.P., Am. Coll. Cardiology, Am. Coll. Preventive Medicine; mem. Am., So., S.C. med. assns., Assn. Mil. Surgeons. Episcopalian (vestryman 1970). Kiwanian. Home: 153 Tradd St Charleston SC 29401

SANDITEN, EDGAR RICHARD, tire co. exec.; b. Okmulgee, Okla., Feb. 1, 1920; s. Herman and Anna (Sanditen) S.; student Western Mil. Acad., 1934-37; B.S. in Bus., Okla. U., 1941; m. Isabel Raffkind, Jan. 26, 1945; children—Linda Caryl, Judith Marie (Mrs. Singer), Ellen Jane, Michael Jay. With Okla. Tire & Supply Co., Tulsa, 1941—, exec. v.p., 1970—; dir. Merc. Nat. Bank, Tulsa, Western Diversified Industries. Chmn. United Jewish Appeal, Tulsa, 1960; mem. adv. bds. U. Okla. Alumni, 1962—, Y.M.C.A., Tulsa, 1966—; chmn. Tulsa Charity Horse Show, 1969-71; Bd. dirs. Tulsa Opera, 1967—, Civic Ballet, 1960-68 Tulsa Econ. Devel. Commn., St. John's Hosp. Served with USAAF, 1943-46; CBI. Decorated Purple Heart; recipient Alumni Devel. Fund citation U. Okla., 1968. Mem. Tulsa Jr. C. of C. (bd. dirs., mem. material conservation com. 1940-43; honor award 1943), Quarter Century Club Automotive Industry. Jewish religion (pres. temple 1969-71). Clubs: Summit, Meadowbrook Country (Tulsa). Home: 2140 E 30th St Tulsa OK 74114 Office: PO Box 885 Tulsa OK 74102

SANDLIN, FRED C., city ofcl.; b. Lockney, Tex., Jan. 28, 1917; s. Hardy L. and Cynthia (McMillan) S.; B.S. in Civil Engring., Tex. A. and M. Coll., 1940; m. Shirley Shipley, Apr. 25, 1943; children—John Hardy, Ann. Engr.-in-tng. Tex. Hwy. Dept., Beaumont, 1940-41; engr. L.V. Norris, Cons. Engrs., Beaumont, 1946-52; city engr. Bryan, Tex., 1954-58, city mgr., 1958—. Served from 2d lt. to maj. C.E., AUS, 1941-45, 52-53. Registered profl. engr., Tex. Mem. Tex. Soc. Profl. Engrs. (pres. 1957, Engr. of Year, Brazos chpt. 1958). Methodist (chmn. ofcl. bd.). Lion. Home: 401 Helena St Bryan TX 77801 Office: 300 S Washington St Bryan TX 77801

SANDLIN, GEORGE WILSON, real estate broker, mortgage banker; b. Glen Rose, Tex., May 13, 1912; s. Walter Algie and Margaret (Parks) S.; ed. pub. schs., also Schreiner Inst.; m. Ruth Ina Zollinger, Sept. 17, 1941; children—George Walter Raoul, Carole Ruth, Sarah Louise, Margaret Ina. Field rep. HOLC, San Antonio, 1934-36; pres. Sandlin Mortgage Corp., Austin, Tex., also owner Sandlin & Co., 1936—; chmn. bd. Internat. Creations, Inc.; ind. fee appraiser. Chmn. Tex. Real Estate Commn., 1949-55. Mem. Austin City Planning Commn., 1947-52, chmn., 1951-52. Chmn. Tex. Democratic Exec. Com., 1952-56. Pres., chmn. bd. Tex. Found., 1955—. Served as lt. comdr. USNR, World War II; PTO. Mem. Tex. Real Estate Assn. (past dir.), Austin Real Estate Bd. (past pres.). Inst. Real Estate Mgmt., Inst. Real Estate Brokers, Mortgage Bankers

Assn., Home Builders Assn., Am. Legion, V.F.W. (citizenship award 1957). Episcopalian. Clubs: Headliners, Austin Country. Home: 2113 Highgrove Terrace Austin TX 78703 Office: 308 W 15th St Austin TX 78701

SANDLIN, GLENN DOUGLAS, astrophysicist; b. Bokoshe, Okla., Mar. 27, 1940; s. Horace D. and Syble L. (Brooks) S.; B.S. in Physics and Math. with honors, U. Ark., 1962; M.S. in Astronomy, U. Mich., 1964, postgrad., 1964-66; m. Jeanne M. Besner. Observatory research asst. dept. Astronomy, U. Mich., 1962-63, tech. photographer, 1963-65, instr. astronomy, 1965-66; solar astrophysicist Naval Research Lab., Washington, 1966—. Recipient NRL Ann. Publs. award, 1971; Thomas A. Edison Meml. fellow, 1968-70. Mem. A.A.A.S., Am. Astron. Soc., Astron. Soc. of the Pacific, Pi Mu Epsilon, Sigma Pi Sigma. Research and publs. in astronomy, astrophysics, physics. Home: 204 Jefferson St Alexandria VA 22314 Office: Naval Research Lab Code 7142-S Washington DC 20390

SANDOVAL, HILARY JOSEPH, JR., govt. ofcl.; b. El Paso, Tex., Jan. 29, 1930; s. Hilary Joseph and Theodora (Aguirre) S.; B.A., U. Ariz.; m. Dolores B. Morales, Aug. 11, 1951; children—Mary Dolores, Irene Roberta, Hilary Joseph III, George Edward, Anthony F. Pres. Sandoval News Service, Inc., 1953-69; adminstr. Small Business Adminstrn., 1969—. Area coordinator Internat. Exec. Service Corps, 1967; mem. Lubbock (Tex.) adv. council Small Bus. Adminstrn. Chmn. exec. com. El Paso County Republican Com., 1962; asst. chmn. Republican Com. Tex., 1966. Served with AUS, 1951-53; capt. Res. Mem. El Paso Sales and Marketing Execs. Internat., Mid-Am. Periodicals Distbrs. Assn., Bur. Ind. Pubs. and Distbrs. (co-chmn.), League United Am. Citizens (pres. council 8), El Paso C. of C. Rotarian (bd. dirs. El Paso). Home: 9917 Fenway St El Paso TX 79925 Office: 1441 L St NW Washington DC 20416

SANDOZ, GEORGE ELLIS, JR., polit. scientist; b. New Orleans, Feb. 10, 1931; s. George Ellis and Ruby (Odom) S.; B.A., La. State U., 1951, M.A., 1953; Dr. oec. publ., U. Munich (W. Germany), 1965; student U. N.C., summer 1950, Georgetown U., 1952-53, U. Heidelberg, 1956-58; m. Therese Alverne Hubley, May 31, 1957; children—Ellis III, Lisa, Erica, Jonathan. Instr., asst. prof., asso. prof. polit. sci. and philosophy La. Polytech. Inst., Ruston, 1959-67, prof., 1967-68, dir. Center for Comparative Internat. Studies, 1966-68, prof., head dept. polit sci. E. Tex. State U., 1968—. Cons. La. Pilot Project Internat. Edn., 1966-68, Mem. exec. council S.W. Alliance for Latin Am., 1966-68. Served with USMC, 1953-56. Recipient Fulbright Scholar, 1964; Fulbright Achievement Certificate, 1965; H. B. Earhart fellow, 1964. Fellow Germanistic Soc. Am.; mem. Am., So., SW (mem. exec. council) polit. sci. assns., Internat. Studies Assn., Am. Soc. for Polit. and Legal Philosophy. Author: Political Acocalypse: A Study of Dostoevsky's Grand Inquisitor, 1971. Contbr. articles in field to profl. jours. Home: PO Box 4315 E T Sta Commerce TX 75428

SANDRIDGE, WILLIAM PENDLETON, lawyer; b. Roanoke, Va., July 25, 1904; s. William Pendleton and Ida Lee (Watkins) S.; B.S., U. Va., 1925, LL.B., 1928; m. Kathryn Mosby, June 3, 1931; children—William Pendleton, Kate Mosby (Mrs. C. Duncan Cater, Jr.). Admitted to Va. and N.C. bar, 1928; with law dept. C.&O. Ry., 1929-30; pvt. practice, Winston-Salem, 1930—; mem. firm Womble, Carlyle, Sandridge & Rice, 1937—; lectr. labor relations law Wake Forest Coll. Law Sch., 1961. Councilor N.C. State Bar. Mem. Am. Bar Assn., Am. Judicature Soc., Am. Coll. Trial Lawyers, Phi Beta Kappa, Raven Soc., Omicron Delta Kappa, Delta Sigma Rho, Phi Delta Phi. Home: 1857 Virginia Rd Winston-Salem NC 27104 Office: Wachovia Bank Bldg Winston-Salem NC 27101

SANDS, ORILAS LESLIE, city ofcl.; b. Pine Grove, W.Va., Mar. 14, 1908; s. Leslie O. and Rosamond (Kimball) S.; B.S. in Bus. Adminstrn., U. Fla., 1930; m. Leona Henderson, May 15, 1932; children—Lawrence O., Ralph O. Dep. hotel commr. State of Fla., 1937-40; dir. aviation City of Orlando (Fla.), 1940-54; chief of aviation Commonwealth P.R., 1954-60; dir. aviation City of New Orleans, 1960—. Mem. Airport Operators Council Internat. (bd. dirs., mem. exec. com. 1969—, pres. 1971—). Democrat. Mason. Home: 684 Pine Lane Kenner LA 70062 Office: Airport Terminal Bldg PO Box 20007 New Orleans LA 70141

SANDVED, KURT GEORGE, govt. ofcl.; b. Ogna, Norway, May 18, 1929 (came to U.S., 1958, naturalized 1961); s. Kristoffer and Mathea (Boe) S.; Ex. Artium, Stavanger Coll. (Norway), 1947; m. Ana Louisa Gonzalez, Nov. 10, 1957; 1 dau., Karin Maria. Research analyst Arctic Inst. N.Am., Washington, 1958-62; information officer Office Antarctic Programs NSF, Washington, 1962-65, asst. program dir. internat. cooperation, 1965-68, dir. polar information service Office Polar Programs, 1969-72, exec. asst. nat. and internat. programs, 1972—. Served with Norwegian Army, 1948-49. Recipient Antarctic medal. Mem. A.A.A.S., Am. Geophys. Union, Am. Geol. Soc. Editor Antarctic Jour. U.S., 1966-72. Contbr. articles to profl. jours. Home: 304 Brewster Ct Silver Spring MD 20901 Office: 1800 G St NW Washington DC 20550

SANDZA, JOSEPH GERARD, chemist; b. N.Y.C., Feb. 4, 1917; s. Francis and Rose (Campana) S.; B.S., Poly. Inst. Bklyn., 1937; M.S., Fordham U., 1940, Ph.D., 1942; m. Rositalia Torres-Braschi, Jan. 29, 1942 children—Joseph G., Raymond C., Richard W., Walter F., Peter A. Rockefeller Found. research asso. Northwestern U., 1942-44; head dept. penicillin process improvement Lederle Labs., Pearl River, N.Y., 1942-47; sr. devel. chemist Hoffman-LaRoche, Nutley, N.J., 1948; asst. dir. eastern research center Stauffer Chem. Co., Chauncey, N.Y., 1949-63; cons. Econ. Devel. Adminstrn., Commonwealth of P.R., San Juan, 1963-68; pres. Caribbean Tech. Assos. and Caribee Labs., Inc. (San Juan), 1968—. Prof. chemistry, chmn. div. sci. and tech. World U., San Juan, P.R., 1965—. Mem. Am. Chem. Soc., Am. Inst. Chem. Engrs., Colegio de Quimicos de P.R., Chemists Club, Sigma Xi, Phi Lambda Upsilon. Home: 192 Pajuil St Rio Piedras PR 00926 Office: PO Box 2242 San Juan PR 00936

SANFORD, J(AMES) KENNETH, univ. ofcl.; b. Clyde, N.C., Jan. 23, 1932; s. James Edward and Bernice (Crawford) S.; A.A., Mars Hill Coll., 1952; A.B., U. N.C., 1954, M.A., 1958; m. Alice Pearl Reavis, Sept. 22, 1957; children—Timothy Edward, Scott Vernon. Pub. relations officer United Appeal of Asheville and Buncombe County, Asheville, N.C., 1954; reporter, 2d copy editor Winston-Salem Jour. and Sentinel, 1957-59, asst. state editor, 1959-61, news editor, 1961-63, editorial writer, 1963-64; dir. information U. N.C., Charlotte, 1964—. Served with AUS, 1954-56. Mem. Charlotte Pub. Relations Soc. (treas. 1971, sec. 1972), Coll. News Seminar of Carolinas (chmn. 1967), Charlotte C. of C. (pub. relations com. 1971), Kappa Tau Alpha. Baptist (chmn. bd. asso. deacons 1967). Home: 5436 Kerry Lane Charlotte NC 28215

SANFORD, JAY PHILIP, physician; b. Madison, Wis., May 27, 1928; s. Joseph Arthur and Arlyn (Carlson) S.; M.D., U. Mich., 1952; m. Lorraine Burklund, Apr. 7, 1950; children—Jeb, Nancy, Sarah, Philip, Catherine. Intern Peter Bent Brigham Hosp., Boston, 1952-53; research fellow Harvard Med. Sch., Boston, 1953-54; resident Duke U. Hosp., Durham, N.C., 1956-57; practice medicine, specializing in internal medicine, Dallas, 1957—; mem. staff Parkland Meml. Hosp., St. Paul Hosp., Presbyn. Hosp. (all Dallas), John Peter Smith Hosp., Ft. Worth. Mem. faculty U. Tex. Southwestern Med. Sch. at Dallas, 1957—, prof. internal medicine, 1965—; chief microbiology lab. Parkland Meml. Hosp., 1957—, pres. med. staff, 1968-69; cons. Dallas VA Hosp., Wilford Hall USAF Hosp., Brooke Gen. Hosp., Ft. Sam Houston. Mem. adv. council Dallas Health & Sci. Mus., 1968—; mem. Gov.'s Commn. Phys. Fitness, 1971—. Bd. dirs. Dallas County chpt. 1965—, med. adviser, 1966—. Served with M.C., AUS, 1954-56. Recipient Certificate of Award, Div. Health Moblzn., USPHS, 1963, 64, Pfizer award for civil def., 1965, Presdl. citation for health moblzn. planning, 1970. Fellow Am. Acad. Microbiology, A.C.P.; mem. Assn. Am. Physicians, Nat. Inst. Allergy and Infectious Diseases (chmn. tng. grant com. 1971), Am. Fedn. Clin. Research (pres. 1968-69), A.A.A.S., Am. Soc. Microbiology, Am. Rheumatism Assn., Central Soc. Clin. Research, Soc. Exptl. Biology and Medicine, Am. Soc. Clin. Investigation, Am. Thoracic Soc., Infectious Disease Assn. Am., Sigma Xi. Contbr. papers to profl. jours. Home: 3516 St John's Dr Dallas TX 75205 Office: 5323 Harry Hines Blvd Dallas TX 75235

SANFORD, WALTER ERWING, JR., ret. govt. ofcl.; b. Washington, May 18, 1923; s. Walter Erwing and Cora E.(Morris) S.; B.S., Southeastern U., 1943, M.C.S., 1947; diploma Fgn. Service Inst., 1954, 62; M.F.A. Cath. U. of Am., 1955; m. Mary Ellen Newkirk, Mar. 13, 1970; 1 son, Walter Erwing III. Sr. insp. Potomac River Command, USN, 1941-48; with Dept. Labor, Washington, 1949-71, labor adviser, 1961-71. Mem. firm Sanford Assos., Alexandria, Va., 1956-67, pres., 1967—. Real estate broker, 1956—; notary public, D.C., 1967-71; sec. For-San Export Import, Ltd., 1968—. Pres., P.T.A., Alexandria, 1959-60; mem. Va. Gov.'s Com. Employment of Handicapped; mem. Va. War Meml. Commn., 1950—, Alexandria Civil Def. Adv. Com., 1954-64, Va. Vets. Reemployment Adv. Com.; dir. Alexandria Coop. Sch., 1962-65; instnl. rep. Boy Scouts, 1960-61, scoutmaster, 1964-69; parole adviser D.C. Parole Bd., 1966-70; dir. Sheltered Enterprises of Alexandria, Inc., 1968-72. Served with USAAF, World War II. Recipient Distinguished Achievement award USAF, 1959, commendation for Fed.-State program devel., Dept. of Labor 1955; certificate from Alexandria City Council, 1963; Americanism plaque Marine Corps League, 1968. Mem. Accountants Soc. Va., Inc. (life, pres. 1948-49), D.A.V. (comdr. Va. 1949-50), Internat. Assn. Machinists (1941—), Brotherhood Ry. and Airline Clks., S.A.R., Am. Legion (post comdr. 1968-70), Chi Sigma Mu. Home: 608 Woodland Terrace Alexandria VA 22302

SANG, HERB ALLEN, ednl. adminstr.; b. Van Buren, Mo., Nov. 11, 1929; s. Charles Ersken and Omah Alla (Towler) S.; B.S., U. Mo., 1952, M.Ed., 1953; m. Alice Jean Coleman, Aug. 3, 1952; children—Julie Anne, Allen Coleman. Sec., asst. treas. Burstein-Applebee Co., Kansas City, Mo., 1957-64; asst. supt. schs., Kansas City, Mo., 1964-70; asso. supt. schs. Duval County Sch. Dist., Jacksonville, Fla., 1970—. Mgmt. cons., instr. salesmanship and accounting Met. Jr. Coll., 1958-70, Kansas City Retail Mchts. Assn., 1964-66. Trustee Southwest Baptist Coll., Bolivar, Mo. Mem. Club Presidents Round Table Kansas City, Am. Assn. Sch. Adminstrs., Assn. for Ednl. Data Systems, N.E.A., Mo. State Tchrs. Assn., Sch. Masters Club. Baptist. Club: Sertoma (Kansas City, Mo.). Home: 3742 Colony Cove Trail Jacksonville FL 32202

SANSBURY, LEMONT THEODORE, banker, mayor; b. Timmonsville, S.C., Oct. 26, 1905; s. James Baxter and Minnie (Anderson) S.; B.S., Furman U., 1926; M.A., U. S.C., 1934; m. Kathleen Lindler, Aug. 2, 1929. Supr., Volusia County Bd. Edn., 1926-43, 47-65; dir. Halifax Nat. Bank, Port Orange, Fla., 1965—; mayor, Port Orange, 1970—. Served to lt. USNR, 1944-47; lt. Res. (ret.). Decorated Purple Heart. Lion. Club: Crisco Hunting. Home: 201 Halifax Dr Port Orange FL 32019 Office: 209 Dunlawton Av Port Orange FL 32019

SANTAMARIA, RALPH MARIO, physicist; b. Hopelawn, N.J., Oct. 1, 1928; s. Philip and Mary (Bortone) S.; B.S., U. N.M., 1951; M.S., U. Ill., 1952; m. Audrey Ann Hopkins, Sept. 6, 1953. Naval architect design div. Norfolk Naval Shipyard, Portsmouth, Va., 1952-56; Structural research engr., underwater explosions research div., 1956-59; physicist, weapon effects br., Naval Ship Research and Devel. Center (formerly David Taylor Model Basin), Washington, 1959-66; operations research analyst, 1966—. Served with AUS, 1954-56. Registered structural engr., Va. Mem. Am. Soc. C.E., Am. Concrete Inst., Nat. Soc. Profl. Engrs. Roman Catholic. Home: 3124 Christine Dr Beltsville MD 20705 Office: Naval Ship Research Devel Center Bethesda MD 20034

SANTAMARINA, LUIS G., orthodontist; b. Havana, Cuba, Sept. 29, 1922; s. Fernando G. and Maria Luisa (Marino) S.; B.S., Colegio de Belen, 1940; D.D.S., U. Havana, 1944; Proficiency Orthodontics, Columbia, 1946; D.M.D., U. P.R., 1963; m. Silvia Onetti, Feb. 3, 1952; children—Silvia, Mary Lou, Luis, Maria Teresa, Miguel. Came to U.S., 1960, naturalized, 1968. Practice dentistry specializing in orthodontics, Havana, 1946-60, Hato Rey, P.R., 1964-66, Caparra Heights, P.R., 1966-71, Miami, 1969—. Organizer orthodontic dept. Cuban Army, 1952; research asst. U. P.R. San Juan, 1961, asst. prof. orthodontia, 1964. Mem. Am. Dental Assn., Am. Assn. Orthodontia, So. Orthodontic Soc., Columbia Alumni Assn., Royal Soc. Health (Eng.), Assn. de Dentistas Cubanos (Miami), Colegio de Cirujanos Dentistas (P.R.), Greater Miami Acad. Orthodontists. Roman Catholic. Club: Big Five (Miami). Home: 185 Palm Island Miami FL 33139 Office: 131 Madeira Av Coral Gables FL 33134

SANTANA-BECERRA, CARLOS, asso. justice Supreme Ct. P.R. Address: Supreme Ct Av Ponce de Leon Parada 8 San Juan PR 00936*

SANTIAGO-MELENDEZ, ARTURO, dentist, educator; b. Orocovis, P.R., Aug. 15, 1929; s. Olimpio Santiago and Juana Melendez; B.A., U. P.R., 1952, B.S., 1953, D.M.D., 1961, postgrad., 1961-64; m. Norma I. Rubero, May 18, 1957; children—Arturo, Gerardo. Tchr., Orocovis High Sch., 1952-54; instr. U. P.R., 1956-57, asst. prof. Sch. Dentistry, 1964-68, asso. prof., 1968—, lectr. chronic diseases Sch. Medicine, 1966—; attending prosthodontist Oncologic, Univ. hosps., Rio Piedras, P.R.; cons. prosthodontics VA Hosp., Rio Piedras. Served with AUS, 1954-55. Mem. Am. Acad. Maxillofacial Prosthetics, Am. (sec. student clinicians 1967-69), P.R. (chmn. table clinics com. 1966-70) dental assns., Colegio Cirujanos Dentistas de P.R. (treas. 1966, 67), U. P.R. Alumni, U. P.R. Sch. Dentistry Alumni, Xi Psi Phi (dep. supreme pres. 1964-68). Home: B-8 52 Torrimar Bayamon PR 00619 Office: UPR Sch Dentistry San Juan PR 00905

SANTIAGO MELENDEZ, MIGUEL, dir. P.R. Urban Renewal Adminstrn. Office: Av Dr Barbosa 606 Edificio Juan Cordero Davila Hato Rey PR 00919*

SANTIAGO-ORTIZ, PEDRO N., physician; b. Comerio, P.R., Aug. 10, 1919; s. Jose Antonio and Hipolita (Ortiz) S.; B.S., U. P.R., 1942; M.D., Hahnemann Med. Coll., 1946; m. Marta Berrios, Jan. 10, 1948; children— Pedro Horacio, Luis Francisco, Jorge Oscar, Martita, Jose Fernando. Med. dir. Barranquitas (P.R.) Municipal Hosp., 1947-48; mem. med. staff Colon Hosp., Canal Zone, 1948-49; mem. med. staff Gorgas Hosp., Canal Zone, 1949-50; mem. med. staff Rodriguez Gen. Hosp., San Juan, 1950; practice gen. medicine, Barranquitas, 1950—; cons. in field. Med. adviser Barranquitas Selective Service, 1950-72. Mem. Barranquitas Ednl. and Recreative Center, 1950-72. Served to capt. M.C., AUS, 1948-50. Mem. P.R. Med. Assn., Phi Eta Mu. Roman Catholic. Independent Party. Rotarian. Home and office: Ext Calle Barcelo Barranquitas PR 00618

SANTIAGO VAZQUEZ, ANTONIO, minister pub. works P.R. Address: care Dept Pub Works Av Ponce de Leon Parada 22 1/2 San Juan PR 00908*

SANZ, ROBERT BOISSON, author, educator; b. Madrid, Spain, June 7, 1913; s. William R. and Lucila (Rodriquez) Boisson-Sanz; Alcala de Henares, Royal Conservatory Madrid, 1932; A.B., U. Madrid, 1933; m. Elaine Terry Boughner, Sept. 30, 1939; children—Elaine B. (Mrs, Frank Engels), Robert L. Came to U.S., 1937, naturalized, 1944. Founder, pres. Sanz Sch. Langs., Washington, 1939—; owner Sanz Publs. Recipient Air Force A award for excellent performance, 1960. Clubs: Congressional Country, International (Washington). Author: Metodo Sanz, 1939; Spanish for All, 1945; English With Sanz, 1949; German With Sanz, 1950; French With Sanz, 1950; Russian With Sanz, 1951; Italian With Sanz, 1955; Portuguese With Sanz, 1950; Spanish With Sanz, 1972. Home: 1 Goldsboro Ct Bethesda MD 20034 Office: 1404 New York Av NW Washington DC 20005

SAPERO, JAMES JOSEPH, physician, tropical medicine cons.; b. Denver, Apr. 24, 1906; s. Kalmen Charles and Irene (Yokum) S.; A.B., Stanford U., 1928, M.D., 1932; postgrad. U.S. Naval Med. Sch., 1945. Commd. lt. j.g., M.C., U.S. Navy, 1931, advanced through grades to rear adm., 1955; dir. Naval Med. Research Inst., Cairo, Egypt, 1949-52; chief preventive medicine div. USN Bur. Medicine, Washington, 1953-55; tropical medicine cons. Miami, Fla., 1955—. Decorated D.S.M. (U.S.); Order El-Maref (Egypt); recipient Gorgas medal and award for distinguished service, 1944. Diplomate Am. Bd. Preventive Medicine. Fellow A.C.P.; mem. Am. Soc. Tropical Medicine (v.p.), Phi Kappa Psi, Nu Sigma Nu. Contbr. articles to profl. jours. Address: 1122 NW 102d St Miami FL 33150

SAPIENZA, JOHN THOMAS, lawyer; b. South Orange, N.J., Feb. 26, 1913; s. James C. and Rosalie (Giaimo) S.; A.B., Harvard, 1934, LL.B., 1937; m. Virginia H. Gignoux, Feb. 12, 1972; children (by previous marriage)—John Thomas, James K. Admitted to N.Y. bar, 1938, D.C. bar, 1943; law clk., Judge A. Hand. N.Y.C., 1937-38; Justice Stanley Reed, Washington, 1938-39; asso. firm Wright, Gordon, Zachry and Parlin, N.Y.C., 1939-41; asso. firm Covington & Burling, Washington, 1941-48, partner, 1949—. Served to lt. comdr. USNR, 1943-46. Mem. Am., Fed., D.C. bar assns., Am. Law Inst., Confrerie des Chevaliers du Tastevin, Phi Beta Kappa. Clubs: Burning Tree, Metropolitan, Internat. (Washington). Home: Watergate East 2510 Virginia Av NW Washington DC 20037 Office: 888 16th St NW Washington DC 20006

SAPIR, EDDIE, city ofcl.; b. Harrisburg, Pa., Feb. 12, 1937; s. Abe John and Paula (Fialkow) S.; B.S., U. Ala., 1958; postgrad. Loyola U. Law Sch., 1959-62. Mem. La. Ho. of Reps., 1966-67; councilman City of New Orleans, 1967—. Served to 1st. lt. AUS, 1962-64. Home: 3328 Louisiana Av Pkwy New Orleans LA 70125 Office: City Hall New Orleans LA 70112

SAPP, ARMISTEAD WRIGHT, JR., lawyer; b. Greensboro, N.C., Feb. 28, 1929; s. Armistead Wright and Dorothy (Greenlaw) S.; student N.Y.U., 1948-50, 1952-64; LL.B., U. N.C., 1957; m. Ada Jane Moore, Mar. 21, 1959; children—Armistead Wright, III, Henry King, William Moore. Admitted to N.C. bar, 1957; partner Sapp & Sapp, Greensboro, N.C., 1957—. Served with USNR, 1950-52. Mem. Internat., Am., N.C., Greensboro Dist. bar assns., Am. Trial Lawyers Assn., Am. Soc. Juvenile Ct. Judges. Am. Soc. Internat. Law, Am. Acad. Polit. and Social Sci., Am. Judicature Soc., C. of C. Presbyn. Lion (bd.). Home: 2417 Berkley Pl Greensboro NC 27403 Office: 219 W Washington St Greensboro NC 27401

SAPP, EDWARD O'NEILL, elec. mfg. co. exec.; b. Louisville, May 6, 1928; s. Raymond Paul and Beulah Lee (Pierce) S.; student Xavier U., Cin., 1946-48; B.A. in Math., U. Louisville, 1956; m. Patricia Delores Albert, Aug. 2, 1950; children—Edward O'Neill, Cheryl Anne, Stephanie Lynne. Sales corr. Tube Turns Inc., Louisville, 1952-55; mfg. engr., systems analyst Gen. Electric Co., Louisville, 1955-66, quality control mgr., 1968—; indsl. engring. mgr., materials mgr. Cabot Piping Systems, Louisville, 1966-68. Served with USNR, 1948-52. Named Ky. col. Registered profl. engr., Ky. Mem. Kentuckiana Football Ofcls. Assn., Ky. and Ind. High Sch. Athletic Assn. Roman Catholic. Moose, K.C. Home: 2806 Dell Brooke Av Louisville KY 40220 Office: Appliance Park Louisville KY 40225

SAPP, ELLIOTT HENRY, food processing co. exec.; b. Brunswick, Ga., Apr. 17, 1929; s. J.Q. and Nell (Edwards) S.; student U. Fla., 1950-53, Massey Bus. Coll., 1953-57; m. Jacqueline Doss Bell, June 30, 1962; children—Andrew, Russell. Plant mgr. Horne Enterprises, Bayard, Fla., 1953-61; with Fine Products, Co., Inc., Augusta, Ga., 1961—, mgr. prodn. control, 1968-69, v.p. mfg., 1969—. Served with USNR, 1946-50. Pres., Indsl Mgmt. Central Savannah River Area, 1968-69. Home: 2150 Kingsley Ct Augusta GA 30906 Office: 827 Telfair St Augusta GA 30903

SAPP, GEORGE THOMAS, wholesale co. exec.; b. Mays' Lick, Ky., Dec. 30, 1920; s. Charley and Della (Bierlin) S.; grad. high sch.; m. Velma Lee Huges, July 10, 1943 (dec. Aug., 1965); children—Brenda (Mrs. Herman Frodge), Robert L. Salesman Gilbert Grocery Co., Maysville, Ky., 1942-50; mgr. E.A. Robinson Co., Maysville, 1950—; dir. security Bank and Trust Co., Maysville. Chmn. Maysville Municipal Housing Authority, 1962—. Served with USMCR, 1942-46. Mem. Christian Ch. (deacon). Mason, Rotarian. Home: 124 W 3d St Maysville KY 41056 Office: 128-130 W 3d St Maysville KY 41056

SAPP, PHYLLIS WOODRUFF (MRS. J.D. SAPP), author, lectr.; b. Oklahoma City, Oct. 21, 1908; d. John A. and Maude (Laws) Woodruff; student Oklahoma City U., 1926-27; B.A., Okla. U., 1930; m. J.D. Sapp, June 5, 1930; children— Kathryn (Mrs. Karl Malthaner), John Davis, Phillip Woodruff. Organizer, dir. Oklahoma City's first children's theatre, 1930-35; dir. Okla. City Theatre Guild, 1940-42; jr. high sch. tchr. drama Oklahoma City pub. schs., 1946-49; part-time instr. J.D. Sapp Sch. Real Estate. Recipient 4,000 first prize Zondervan's Christian Fiction Contest, 1957. Mem. Internat. Platform Assn., Nat. League Am. Pen Women (br. v.p. 1963-65, pres. local br. 1968-70, nat. 4th v.p. 1970-72, chmn. nat. letters bd. 1972—), Mortar Bd., Alpha Phi, (Distinguished Alumnus award honor 1972), Pi Kappa Delta. Baptist. Author: Accidental Hero (3-act play), 1949; The Ice Cutter, 1948; Whisper Out of the Dust, 1951; For Such a Time, 1954; The Long Bridge, 1957; God of All the Earth, 1960; Gifts from God, 1962; Small Giant, 1957; Life at Its Best, 1963; Living for Jesus, 1961; Working Together in Our Church, 1963; Lighthouse on the Corner, 1964; Creative Teaching in the Church Sch., 1967; 59 Programs for Pre-Teens, 1969; (juvenile) Who Am I, 1972; (juvenile) Jeff the Baptist, 1973. Contbr. to Sunday sch.

quarterlies So. Bapt. Sunday Sch. Bd. Address: 7100 S Kentucky St Oklahoma City OK 73159

SAPPINGTON, RICHARD FRANCIS, JR., physician; b. Washington, Dec. 23, 1933; s. Richard Francis and Grace (Grove) S.; B.S., Georgetown Coll., 1956, M.D., 1960; m. Nancy Lee Smith, Aug. 20, 1966; children—Richard Francis III, Robert Grove, Virginia Patricia. Intern, U.S. Naval Hosp., Chelsea, Mass., 1961; resident VA Hosp., Washington, 1963-66; pvt. practice pulmonary medicine, 1966—; dir. Pulmonary Lab. No. Va., Alexandria, 1968—; faculty Georgetown Med. Sch., 1970—; mem. staff Alexandria Pub. Health Tb Control and Emphysema Clinic, 1966—; faculty Met. Washington Regional Med. Program, 1968—. Bd. dirs. Potomac Tb and Respiratory Disease Assn. Served with USNR, 1960-63. Mem. A.C.P., Am. Thoracic Soc., Am. Rehab. Assn., Va. Med. Soc., A.M.A. Club: Army Navy Country. Mailing Address: 5665 Rayburn St Alexandria VA 22311 Office: 101 S Whiting St Alexandria VA 22304

SAPUTO, ALBERT JOSEPH, architect; b. New Orleans, Feb. 26, 1924; s. Sam and Marianne (Cusimano) S.; student U. Hawaii 1944; B.Arch., Tulane U., 1949; m. Elizabeth Gulotta, July 1, 1944; children— Catherine Lee (Mrs. Elbert Goodier). Partner firm Saputo & Rowe, New Orleans, 1949—. Dir. So. Savs. Assn., New Orleans. Chmn. New Orleans City Planning Commn., 1969-71, also mem., 1963—. Served with USAAF, 1942-46; PTO. Mem. A.I.A., La. Architects Assn., Am. Soc. Planning Ofcls. Kiwanian, K.C.. Home: 606 Aymard Ct New Orleans LA 70124 Office: 501 N Jeff Davis Pkwy New Orleans LA 70119

SARSYCKI, JOSEPH HERBERT, civil engr.; b. Ft. Smith, Ark., Feb. 1, 1911; s. Frank S. and Alma Mae (Brehm) S.; student Internat. Corr. Schs., 1939; m. Dora E. Pierce, Jan. 4, 1936 (dec. July 1962) children— Frank H., Robert G., Joe D., Patricia A. (Mrs. James Garner); m. 2d, Leona Mae Hock, Jan. 11, 1964. Civil engr. charge field and constrn. engring. Dept. Pub. Works, City of Oklahoma City, 1947—. Registered profl. engr., Okla. Fellow Am. Soc. C.E.; mem. Soc. Am. Mil. Engrs., Nat., Okla. socs. profl. engrs., Am. Pub. Works Assn. Democrat. Roman Catholic. Home: 2521 NW 38th St Oklahoma City OK 73112 Office: 200 N Walker St Oklahoma City OK 73102

SARTAIN, AARON QUINN, educator; b. Gibtown, Tex., Sept. 5, 1905; s. Lee Russell and Iva Jane (Heasley) S.; A.B., So. Meth. U., 1928; MA., 1930; Ph.D., U. Chgo., 1939; m. Thelma Wylie, June 12, 1930; children—Richard Wylie, Margaret Gwen, Barbara Susan. Prin. high sch., Hobbs, N.M., 1931-32; with So. Meth. U., Dallas, 1932—, from instr. to asso. prof. psychology, 1932-46, prof., 1946—, chmn. dept., 1946-52, chmn. dept. personnel adminstrn., 1947-59, prof. indsl. relations, 1959-68, prof. indsl. relations and psychology, 1968-71, emeritus, 1971—, dir. grad. studies dept. mgmt., 1959-63, dean Sch. Bus. Adminstrn., 1963-68. Mem. Am., S.W. psychol. assns., A.A.A.S., Phi Beta Kappa, Sigma Xi, Beta Gamma Sigma. Methodist. Author: (with W.W. Finlay and W.M. Tate) Human Behavior in Industry, 1954; (with others) Psychology: Understanding Human Behavior, 3d edit., 1967; (with Alton W. Baker) The Supervisor and His Job, 1965. Home: 3924 University Blvd Dallas TX 75205

SASHOFF, STEPHAN P(ENCHEFF), educator; b. Drenovo, Bulgaria, Sept. 22, 1901; s. Pencho and Meta (Detcheva) S.; came to U.S., 1921, naturalized 1930; student Nat. Boys Gimnasium, Gabrovo, Bulgaria, 1915-20; B.S. in E.E., Purdue U., 1925; M.S., U. Pitts., 1929, pre-doctorate student, 1929-31; m. Zilla Bodie, Sept. 2, 1937 (dec. 1953); m. 2d, Elizabeth McCollum, Dec. 24, 1961. Research engr. Westinghouse Electric, Pitts., 1925-31; television research engr. RCA, Camden, N.J., 1931-32; asst. prof. elec. engring. U. Fla., Gainesville, 1932-37, grad. prof. elec. engring. 1951—. Served as comdr. USNR, 1941-46. Received commendation from Sec. of Navy, 1945. Registered profl. engr., Fla. Mem. Am. Phys. Soc., Soc. Profl. Elec. Engrs., A.A.A.S., I.E.E.E., Fla. Acad. Sci. Sigma Xi, Sigma Tau. Democrat. Orthodox. Contbr. articles on electron tubes and circuits to profl. jours. Holder of patents and patent disclosures on electron tubes and circuits. Home: Rural Route 1 Box 303 Melrose FL 32666 Office: Elec Engring Dept U Fla Gainesville FL 32601

SASLAW, MILTON SIBLEY, physician; b. Bklyn., May 1, 1911; s. Isidor and Esther (Wallach) S.; B.S., Washington Sq. Coll., N.Y.U., 1931; M.D., N.Y.U. and Bellevue Hosp. Med. Coll., 1934; M.P.H., U. Cal. at Los Angeles, 1967; m. Adeline Sokoloff, Apr. 28, 1937; children—Shari Lenore (Mrs. Esbitt), Gerald Evan. Intern North Hudson Hosp., Weehawken, N.J., 1934-35; pvt. practice internal medicine and cardiology, 1937-40, 46-51; dir. med. research Nat. Children's Cardiac Hosp., Miami, Fla., 1951-64; dir. research and epidemiology Dade County Dept. Pub. Health, Miami, 1965-67, asst. county health dir., 1967-69, dir., 1969—; research asso. prof. dept. microbiology, 1959, 60, clin. asso. prof. dept. preventive medicine Sch. Medicine, U. Miami, 1960-69, prof., 1970—; sr. research scientist Grad. Sch. U. Miami, 1965; mem. dental program project com. Nat. Inst. Dental Research, 1965-69; cons. Dept. Health P.R.; spl. cons. USPHS. Pres. Heart Assn. Greater Miami, 1953-54; pres. Fla. Heart Assn., 1957-58; fellow council on Epidemiology, Am. Heart Assn., 1965; mem. Fla. Textbook Com. on Sci., 1964-66; chmn. health div., dir. Welfare Planning Council, 1960-61; dir. Fla. Found. Future Scientists, Nat. Assn. Gifted Children; chmn. platform com. Fla. Cooperating Council on Children and Youth. Served as lt. col. M.C., AUS, World War II. Recipient citations Employ Physically Handicapped Miami C. of C., 1954, Nat. Employ The Physically Handicapped, Pres.'s Com., 1954. Fellow Am. Coll. Chest Physicians, Am. Coll. Cardiology (gov. Fla.), Am. Pub. Health Assn., Royal Soc. Health; mem. Dade County Med. Assn. (mem. pub. health adv. com.), Internat. Assn. for Dental Research Am. Soc. Microbiology. Author numerous sci publs. Home: 90 Edgewater Dr Coral Gables FL 33133 Office: Dade County Dept Pub Health 1350 NW 14th St Miami FL 33125

SASS, REED, banker; b. Marietta, Okla., Mar. 24, 1908; s. Nathan and Lalla (Reed) S.; student Tex. Christian U., Ft. Worth, 1927-28, U. Mo., 1928-29, Jefferson Sch. Law, 1932; LL.B., North Tex. Sch. Law, 1934; m. Kathryn LaVerne Beck, Feb. 14, 1942; children—Sharon Leigh (Mrs. William L. Feather), Shelley Kay. With Ft. Worth Nat. Bank, 1926—, successively messenger boy, clk., teller, various positions trust, advt. bus. devel. depts., asst. cashier, asst. v.p., 1926-51, v.p., dir. pub. relations and research dept., 1952—; lectr. Sch. of Banking of South, La. State U.; lectr., thesis cons., examiner Stonier Grad. Sch. Banking, Rutgers U., S.W. Grad. Sch. Banking, So. Meth. U. Admitted to Tex. bar, 1935. Sec.-treas. Ft. Worth Clearing House Assn., 1958. Dir. Ft. Worth council Camp Fire Girls, 1956-59; trustee Tex. Boys Choir, 1960—; exec. com. United Fund Tarrant County, 1961-62. Served from 2d to maj. USAAF, 1942-46. Mem. Bank Marketing Assn. (pres. 1959-60, mem. long range planning com.), Ft. Worth and Tarrant County Bar Assn., Am. Inst. Banking, Am. Bankers Assn. (chmn. pub. relations com. 1964-67), Ft. Worth C. of C. (bd. dirs. 1962-63), Downtown Ft. Worth Assn. (director 1957-61). Mem. Christian Ch. Club: Steeplechase. Contbr. articles banking publs. Home: 2717 Colonial Pkwy Fort Worth TX 76109 Office: PO Box 2050 Fort Worth TX 76101

SASSER, DOROTHY PILLEY (MRS. JOHN T. SASSER), educator; b. Pantego, N.C., Aug. 15, 1926; d. Leonard R. and Mattie (Winfield) Pilley; B.S. in Secretarial Adminstrn., Woman's Coll. U. N.C., 1947; postgrad. U. Tenn., 1952; m. John T. Sasser, Dec. 30, 1951 children—Sandra, Sabrina. Co-owner, dir. Myrtle Beach (S.C.) Bus. Coll., 1952; owner Quality Mimeograph Shop, Fayetteville, N.C., 1953—; tchr. pub. schs., Clarkton, N.C., 1953-57; tchr. Hallsboro (N.C.) Sch., 1957-59, Elizabethtown (N.C.) Sch., 1959, Alexander Graham Jr. High Sch., Fayetteville, N.C., 1960; chmn. bus. edn. dept. Terry Sanford Sr. High Sch., Fayetteville, 1961—. Mem. Nat., N.C. edn. assns., Bus. and Profl. Woman (corr. sec. 1958), Delta Kappa Gamma. Democrat. Presbyn. Clubs: Evening Garden (sec. 1957-58), Executives, Merrymakers (Elizabethtown). Home: 906 Emeline Av Fayetteville NC 28303 Office: Fort Bragg Rd Fayetteville NC 28303

SASSER, DOUGLAS REID, coll. adminstr.; b. Ga.; grad. Young Harris Coll., Columbia; postgrad. Emory U.; H.H.D., Ky. Wesleyan Coll., 1969; m. Trelle Joyner; children—Julia Frances, Jennifer Lynn, Douglas Reid. Staff mem., dept. English, Ky. Wesleyan Coll., successively asst. to pres., dean students, v.p.; pres. Young Harris (Ga.) Coll.; pres., also prof. English Pfeiffer Coll., Misenheimer, N.C., 1971—. Chmn. regional bd. dirs. Appalachian Adult Basic Edn. Commn.; mem. exec. com. Coll. Coordinating Council, Western N.C. United Methodist Conf. Bd. dirs. Piedmont U. Center. Served with USNR, Korean war. Mem. Council Pvt. Colls. and Univs., Am. Assn. Jr. Colls., Albemarle-Stanly County C. of C., Phi Theta Kappa (hon. nat.), Alpha Kappa Psi, Phi Delta Sigma, Sigma Nu. Methodist. Rotarian. Clubs: Stanly County Country, Charlotte City. Office: Pfeiffer Coll Misenheimer NC 28109

SASSER, JOHN THOMAS, sch. adminstr.; b. Wilson, N.C., Apr. 6, 1923; s. James Tonkin and Bettie (Howell) S.; A.A., Mars Hill Coll., 1942; B.A., Wake Forest Coll., 1944, M.A., 1948; postgrad. U. N.C., 1950-51; m. Dorothy Pilley, Dec. 30, 1951; children—Sandra, Sabrina. Researcher Library of Congress, 1944; prin. Topsail Pub. Sch., Hampstead, N.C., 1944-47, Leaksville-Spray High Sch., Leaksville, N.C., 1947-51; pres. Myrtle Beach Bus. Coll., 1951-53; prin. Whiteville High Sch., Whiteville, N.C., 1953-59, Elizabethtown (N.C.) pub. schs., 1959-60, Terry Sanford Sr. High Sch., Fayetteville, 1960—. Mem. Nat. Assn. Secondary Sch. Prins., N.C. Prins. Assn., Nat. (life), N.C. (pres. Whiteville unit 1954-55) edn. assns., Horace Mann League Am. Presbyn. Rotarian (pres. 1957-58). Home: 906 Emeline Av Fayetteville NC 28303 Office: Fort Bragg Rd Fayetteville NC 28303

SASSER, LAURENCE HENRY, supt. schs.; b. Highlandville, Mo., Dec. 4, 1908; s. Thomas Aden and Lela Ann (McCarty) S.; B.S., Okla. State U., 1931, M.S., 1940; m. Alice Mae Hodge, Sept. 30, 1933; children—Ben, Joe. Prin., supt. Sickles Schs., Lookeba, Okla., 1931-37; prin. Davenport (Okla.) Schs., 1937-42; supt. Wellston (Okla.) Schs., 1942-51; supt. Hinton (Okla.) Schs., 1951-54; supt. Deer Creek Schs., Edmond, Okla., 1954-66; supt. Calumet (Okla.) Schs., 1966—. Mem. N.E.A., Okla. Edn. Assn. (del.), Lincoln County Tchrs. Assn. (pres.), Nat., Okla. assns. sch. adminstrs. Baptist. Mason, Kiwanian, Lion. Address: Box 10 Calumet OK 73014

SASSER, TERRY J., ins. and real estate co. exec.; b. Austin, Tex., Dec. 2, 1941; s. Sterling Joseph and Margret (Bryan) S., Sr.; student Concordia Luth. Coll., 1963; grad. Nat. Assn. Mut. Agts. Sch., Oberlin Coll., 1963; m. Jannet Eloise Arbogust, Aug. 30, 1968; 1son, Jarrett Lamar. With Sterling Sasser & Sons, Austin, 1963—, partner, 1965—; partner Sterling Investments Ltd., 1968—; gen. partner Maniposia Investments Ltd., Comml. Investors Ltd.; partner Sasser Properties. Pres. Austin Aqua Festival, 1972; commodore Austin Aqua Festival, 1971; chmn. bus. div. Cancer drive, Travis County, Tex., 1966. Precinct chmn. Democratic party, 1966-67. Mem. Ins. Adv. Bd., Nat., Tex. assns. realtors, Nat. Assn. Mut. Ins. Agts., Sales and Marketing Execs. Internat. (blue ribbon com. 1969), Sales and Marketing Execs. Austin (pres. 1969-70). Contbr. articles to profl. jours. Home: 4528 Balcones Dr Austin TX 78753 Office: 719 W 6th St Austin TX 78701

SATO, MOTOAKI, geologist; b. Tokyo, Japan, Oct. 11, 1929; s. Iwazo and Kyoko (Ito) S.; B.S., U. Tokyo, 1953, M.S., 1955; Ph.D., U. Minn., 1959; m. Ellen Bartlett Levinson, Feb. 11, 1961; children—Emily Coates, Alice Haire, Thomas Bartlett. Came to U.S., 1963. Postdoctoral fellow Harvard U., Cambridge, Mass., 1958-61; asso. prof. geology Thermal Springs Research Inst., Okayama U., Tottori, Japan, 1961-63; research geologist U.S. Geol. Survey, Washington, 1963—, now project leader. Cons. Japanese Atomic Fuel Corp., Tokyo, 1962-63. Fullbright Smith-Mundt scholar, 1955-57. Mem. Soc. Econ. Geologists, Geochem. Soc., Geochem. Soc. Japan, Am. Geophys. Union, Geol. Soc. Washington. Club: Cosmos (Washington). Contbr. articles to profl. jours. Home: 407 S Fairfax St Alexandria VA 22314 Office: US Geol Survey 18th and E Sts Washington DC 20242

SATTERFIELD, DAVID EDWARD, III, lawyer, congressman; b. Richmond, Va., Dec. 2, 1920; s. David Edward Jr. and Blanche (Kidd) S.; student U. Richmond, 1939-42; LL.B., U. Va., 1948; m. Anne Elizabeth Powell, Dec. 27, 1943; children—David Edward IV, John B. Admitted to Va. bar; asso. firm Denny Valentine & Davenport, Richmond, 1948-50, Satterfield, Haw, Anderson, Parkerson & Beazley, Richmond, 1953-70; asst. U.S. atty. Eastern Dist. Va., 1950-53; mem. 89th to 92d Congresses from 3d Va. dist. Mem. Richmond City Council, 1954-56; mem. Va. Ho. of Dels., 1960-64. Served with USNR, 1942-45. Decorated Air Medal with three gold stars, Purple Heart. Mem. Va., Richmond bar assns., Phi Gamma Delta, Phi Alpha Delta. Democrat. Episcopalian. Mason (32 deg. Shriner), Kiwanian. Home: 511 St Christophers Rd Richmond VA 23226 Office: Fed Bldg Richmond VA 23240 also House Office Bldg Washington DC 20525

SATTERFIELD, JAMES MCSWAIN, govt. ofcl., aerospace engr.; b. Salisbury, N.C., Oct. 14, 1928; s. McSwain and Julia (Chatfield) S.; B.E.E., N.C. State U., 1949, M.E.E., 1963; m. Jacqueline Marie Creef, June 28, 1952; children—James McSwain, Georgielee Creef. Transmission engr. Carolina Tel. & Tel. Co., Tarboro, N.C., 1949-51; asso. engr. Indsl. Research Labs., Balt., 1953-55; engr. Hastings-Raydist, Inc., Hampton, Va., 1955-59; aerospace technologist NASA, 1959—, asst. div. chief, Flight support div. Manned Spacecraft Center, Houston, 1971—. Space communications lectr. Dept. Def. Space Medicine Sch., Patrick AFB, Fla., 1961-62. Served to 1st lt. USAF, 1951-53. Recipient Am. Spirit Honor medal USAF, 1951; Superior Achievement award NASA, 1969, Apollo 7 Operations Team award, 1968, Outstanding Performance award, 1969; Apollo 15 TV Team award, 1971. Registered profl. engr., Tex. Mem. Sigma Phi Epsilon, Tau Beta Pi, Eta Kappa Nu., Phi Kappa Phi (hon.). Contbr. articles to profl. lit. Home: 15531 Baybrook Dr Houston TX 77058 Office: Manned Spacecraft Center Houston TX 77058

SATTERWHITE, JERRY LAMAR, social worker; b. Salisbury, N.C., Feb. 9, 1937; s. Clyde B. and Kathleen (Hicks) S.; A.B., Catawba Coll., 1959; M.S.W., U. Tenn., 1965; m. Marjorie Jean Singer, Dec. 24, 1961; children— Ashley, Alison, Amy. Child welfare worker Rowan County Dept. Pub. Welfare, Salisbury, 1965-66, supr., 1966-67; social worker VA Outpatient Clinic, Winston-Salem, N.C., 1967-69, Oteen (N.C.) VA Hosp., 1969—. Mem. adv. bd. Asheville Hotline. Served with AUS, 1959-60, 61-62. Mem. Nat. Assn. Social Workers (chmn. Central area, exec. com. western N.C. chpt.), N.C. Workers in Mental Health. Lion. Home: 122 Idlewood Dr Asheville NC 28806 Office: Oteen VA Hosp Oteen NC 28805

SATTERWHITE, RAYMOND DAVIS, physician; b. Dallas, Apr. 27, 1926; s. Raymond Roy and Ida (Davis) S.; B.S. in Pharmacy, U. Tex., 1949, M.D., 1957; m. Doris Jean Thompson, Mar. 6, 1946; children—James Randal, Gilbert Ray, Gaye Ann, Ginger Kayl. Intern, USPHS Hosp., Balt., 1957-58, asst. surgeon, Fort Worth, 1958-59; practice gen. medicine, Fort Worth, 1959—; mem. staff All Saints, Harris, Cooks, St. Joseph hosps., all Fort Worth. Served with USNR, 1942-45, USPHS, 1957-59. Recipient Scholarship award Phi Beta Pi, 1957, Mosby scholarship award, 1957. Diplomate Am. Bd. Family Practice. Mem. Tarrent County, Tex., Am. med. assns., Am. Adac. Family Practice (pres. 1969), Am. Council Med. Staffs (regional bd. dirs.), Fort Worth C. of C. (health com.), Alpha Omega Alpha, Phi Beta Pi. Patentee obstetrics device. Home: 4244 Dunwick Ct Fort Worth TX 76109 Office: 5182 Ollie St Fort Worth TX 76119

SATTERWHITE, THOMAS BRANSCOMB, lawyer, farmer; b. Lexington, Ky., Oct 22, 1910; s. Thomas B. and Nanettte Stuart (Smith) S.; A.B., Swarthmore Coll., 1933; M.A., U. Ky., 1935, LL.B.; m. Barbara Jane Bennett, Oct. 28, 1944; children—Thomas B. III, Ann Bennett. Owner, operator Greenway Farm, Woodford County, Ky., 1946—; pres. Ball and Co., Lexington, 1957-61; dir. Sovereign Industries Inc., WLEX-TV, Inc. Prof. econs. Transylvania Coll. Trustee Shakertown at Pleasant Hill, Inc.; bd. visitors Guilford Coll. Served as lt. USNR, World War II. Mem. Ky. Hist. Soc., Am. Judicature Soc., Am., Ky., Fayette County bar assns., Audubon Soc., Cumberland Falls Preservation Assn. (sec.). Episcopalian, Club: Filson; Idle Hour Country (Lexington, Ky.); Wausaukee (Wis.); Iroquois Hunt, Chevy Chase (Washington). Address: Greenway Farm Versailles KY 40383

SATZ, PAUL, research psychologist; b. Ware, Mass., Sept. 12, 1932; s. Leo and Milly (Hurst) S.; student Boston U., 1953-54; B.A., U. Miami, 1957, M.S., 1959; Ph.D., U. Ky., 1963; post-doctoral, U. Fla., 1963-64; m. Gladys E. McLeod, Sept. 5, 1957; children—George Scott, Mark Gregory, Julie Gavina. Prof. psychology and clin. psychology, dir. Neuropsychology Lab. U. Fla., Gainesville, 1967—, asso. prof., 1967-71, asst. prof., 1964-67. Cons. VA. Mem. Internat. Neuropsychology Soc. (sec., program chmn.), Am. Psychol. Assn., Acad. Aphasia, Psychonomic Soc. Author: Specific Reading Disability: Advances in Theory and Method, 1970; The Disabled Learner: Early Detection and Intervention, 1972. Contbr. numerous research articles profl. jours. Home: 3916 NW 21st Terrace Gainesville FL 32601

SAUCIER, WALTER JOSEPH, educator; b. Moncla, La., Oct. 5, 1921; s. Louis E. and Sidonie (Moncla) S.; B.S., U. Southwestern La., 1942; S.M., U. Chgo., 1947, Ph.D., 1951; m. Helen A. Nobles, May 8, 1943; children—Walter Joseph, Susanne C., Diane H., Janine M., Gerard T., Laurence E., Loraine A. Asst., instr. meteorology U. Chgo., 1946-52; asst. prof. Tex. A. and M. U., 1952-54, asso. prof., 1954-58, prof. meteorology, 1958-60; prof. meteorology U. Okla., 1960-69, chmn. dept., 1965-68, dir. atmospheric research lab., 1960-68; prof. meteorology N.C. State U. at Raleigh, 1969—. Cons. World Book Ency., USAF, U.S. Army, Nat. Oceanic and Atmospheric Adminstrn.; trustee University Corp. Atmospheric Research, Boulder, Colo., 1967-69. Served to capt. USAAF, 1942-46; col. Res. Fellow A.A.A.S.; mem. Am. Meteorol. Soc. (bd. certified cons. meteorologists 1970—), Am. Geophys. Union, Sigma Xi. Author: Principles of Meteorological Analysis, 1955. Research in atmospheric circulation systems. Home: 2000 Hillock Dr Raleigh NC 27612

SAUER, LESTER MARTIN, banker; b. Michigan City, Ind., Sept. 24, 1920; s. O. Adelbert and Beata (Thieme) S.; B.S., U. Richmond, 1941; certificate in Prodn. Engring., Pa. State Coll., 1942; m. Elsie E. Ellington, Apr. 19, 1947; children—Richard, Mark, Martha. With First & Mchts. Nat. Bank, Richmond, Va., 1942—, asst. cashier, 1955-61, asst. v.p., 1961-66, v.p., 1966-71, sr. v.p., 1971—; mem. faculty Va.-Md. Sch. Bank Mgmt., Charlottesville, 1967—. Pres. Civic Assn., 1966; treas. Luther Meml. Sch., 1966—; pres. Chamberlayne Laburnum Athletic Assn., 1968; dist. dir. Boy Scouts Am., 1968. Bd. dirs. Bethlehem Lutheran Found. Mem. Am. Statis. Assn., Nat. Financial Analysts Fedn. (v.p.), Inst. Chartered Financial Analysts, Am. Assn. Bus. Economists, Am. Inst. Banking (past pres. Richmond), Richmond Financial Analysts (past pres.). Lutheran. Home: 308 Burnwick Rd Richmond VA 23227 Office: 827 E Main St Richmond VA 23217

SAUL, BERT, civil engr.; b. Atlanta, Feb. 24, 1933; s. Herbert and Ida (Bock) S.; student Ga. Inst. Tech., 1950-53, U. Ga., 1953-54; B.S. in C.E., U. Miami, 1957; m. Madelyn Weiman, Sept. 4, 1955; children—Howard, Brenda. Structural engr. Jules P. Channing, Miami, Fla., 1957-59, Charles Payne & Assos., Miami, 1959-62, Bertram S. Warshaw, Miami, 1963-67; owner Bert Saul Cons. Engr., Inc., Coral Gables, Fla., 1968—; pres. Fibre Pile, Inc., Precon, Inc. Registered profl. engr., Fla., Ga. Mem. Am. Soc. C.E., Am. Concrete Inst., Nat. Soc. Profl. Engrs., Fla. Engring. Soc., Bus. League (pres. 1969-70), Tau Epsilon Phi. Jewish religion (dir. congregation 1968-71, treas. 1971-72, v.p. 1972-73). Home: 7665 SW 144th St Miami FL 33158 Office: 9655 S Dixie Hwy Miami FL 33156

SAUNDERS, CHARLES BASKERVILLE, JR., govt. ofcl.; b. Boston, Dec. 26, 1928; s. Charles Baskerville and Lucy (Carmichael) S.; grad. St. Marks Sch., 1946; A.B., Princeton, 1950; m. Margaret MacIntire Shafer, Sept. 9, 1950: children—Charles Baskerville III, George Carlton, Margaret Keyser, Lucy Carmichael, John Rolfe. Engaged as news reporter and polit. columnist Ogdensburg (N.Y.) Jour., 1950-51; edn. reporter Hartford (Conn.) Times, 1951-53; asst. dir. pub. relations Trinity Coll., Hartford, 1953-55; asst. dir. pub. information Princeton, 1955-57; legislative asst. Sen. H. Alexander Smith, 85th Congress, 1957-58; asst. to asst. sec. for legislation U.S. Dept. Health, Edn. and Welfare, 1958-59, adminstrv. asst. to sec., 1959-61, dep. asst. sec. for legislation U.S. Dept. Health, Edn. and Welfare, 1969-71, dep. commr. for external relations U.S. Office of Edn., 1971—; asst. to pres. The Brookings Instn., 1961-69. Mem. Montgomery County Bd. Edn., 1966-70. Trustee Montgomery Coll., 1969-70. Republican. Presbyn. Club: University Cottage. Author: The Brookings Institution: A Fifty-Year History, 1966; Upgrading The American Police: Education and Training for Better Law Enforcement, 1970. Home: 7622 Winterberry Pl Bethesda MD 20034 Office: 400 Maryland Av SW Washington DC 20003

SAUNDERS, EDWARD RIPLEY, JR., sci. adminstr.; b. Washington, Sept. 30, 1924; s Edward Ripley and Pearle (Murray) S.; student U. Pitts., 1942-43, Mich. State Coll., 1943-44, U. Mich., 1944; B.S., U. Md., 1948; m. Hazel Bernice Perry, Sept. 5, 1947; children—Dawn Carol, Edward Ripley III, Timothy Glenn, Thomas Gregory, Todd Robin. Electronic sci. Nat. Bur. Standards, Washington, 1948-55; dir. nuclear weapons test operations FCDA,

Battle Creek, Mich., 1955-60; dep. dir. chem., biol. and radiol. def. OCDM, Battle Creek, 1960-61; chief tech. analysis div. Office Emergency Preparedness, Exec. Office of Pres., Washington, 1961-64, prin. adviser for research, 1964-67, exec. asst. and spl. asst. for research, nat. resource analysis center, 1967-68; dep. dir. Nat. Resource Analysis Center, 1967-71, dep. asst. dir., 1971—. Pres. Lone Oak Recreational Assn. Vice pres. Office Emergency Planning Fed. Credit Union. Served with AUS, 1943-46. Recipient Arthur S. Flemming award as One of Ten Outstanding Young Men in Fed. Service, 1957. Mem. I.E.E.E., Health Physics Soc., Commd. Officers Assn., A.A.A.S., Pi Kappa Alpha. Methodist (dir.). Mason. Clubs: Ruritan (pres. 1968), Lions (pres. 1970-71). Patentee in field. Home: The Plains VA 22171 Office: Exec Office Bldg Washington DC 20504

SAUNDERS, HAROLD HENRY, govt. ofcl.; b. Phila., Dec. 27, 1930; s. Harold Manuel and Marian (Weihenmayer) S.; A.B. magna cum laude, Princeton, 1952; Ph.D., Yale, 1956; m. Barbara Ann McGarrigle, May 4, 1963; children—Catherine Elizabeth, Mark Harril. Asst. to dean of freshmen Yale, 1955-56; lectr. U.S. history Coll. Gen. Studies, George Washington U., 1959-61, 63-65; with Nat. Security Council, White House, Washington, 1961—, sr. staff mem., 1967—. Served to 1st lt. USAF, 1956-59. Mem. Am. Hist. Assn., Phi Beta Kappa. Presbyn. Home: 2119 Great Falls St Falls Church VA 22043 Office: Exec Office Bldg 17th and Pennsylvania Av Washington DC 20506

SAUNDERS, HARRIS, JR., truck leasing co. exec.; b. Birmingham, Ala., Jan. 26, 1925; s. Harris and Zoe (Black) S.; B.S., Ga. Inst. Tech., 1945; m. Jean Rowan, Aug. 9, 1949; children—Sarah Jo (Mrs. Robert Keith Tice), Cynthia Rowan, Susan Jean, Nancy Zoe, Rebecca Harris and Mary Elizabeth (twins). Vice pres., br. mgr. Saunders System Corp., Houston, 1947-57; exec. v.p. Saunders Leasing System, Inc., Birmingham, 1957-58, pres., 1959—, also treas., chief exec. officer, dir.; dir. Ames Bag & Packaging Corp. Sec. chair pvt. enterprise Samford U. Bd. dirs. Anti-Tb. Assn. Served as ensign USNR, World War II. Mem. Soc. Automotive Engrs., Pvt. Truck Council Am., Car and Truck Rental and Leasing Assn., Ala. Trucking Assn. (dir.), Newcomen Soc., Young Pres. Orgn., Am. Mgmt. Assn. Methodist. Rotarian. Clubs: Birmingham Country, Downtown, Relay House, The Club, Metropolitan Dinner (Birmingham). Home: 3148 Guilford Rd Mountain Brook Birmingham AL 35223 Office: 201 Office Park Dr Birmingham AL 35223

SAUNDERS, JOSEPH BENJAMIN, JR., petroleum exec.; b. Hillsboro, Tex., July 25, 1901; s. Joseph Benjamin and Irene Imogene (McQuatters) S.; grad. Chillicothe (Mo.) Bus. Coll., 1923; m. Gladys LaVerne Edmondson, Oct. 9, 1926 (dec. Apr. 17, 1966); children—Eleanor Suzanne (Mrs. L.M. Inkley, Jr.), Joseph Benjamin III; m. 2d, Georgia J. Comegys, Mar. 30, 1968. Various positions oil industry, 1923-37; partner Triangle Refineries, 1937-46; pres. Triangle Refineries, Inc., Houston, 1946-62, chmn. bd., 1963-72, dir., 1946—; pres., dir. Withers & Wellford Oil Co., Memphis, until 1950; v.p., dir. Transcentral Oil Corp., Chgo., to 1952; v.p., dir., also chmn. Triangle Pipeline Co., Shreveport, La., until 1954; v.p. Tex. Eastern Transmission Corp., 1954-58; chmn. bd., dir. Triangle Realty Co., Houston; v.p., dir. Moran Shoe Co., Carlyle, Ill., 1962-66; sr. v.p., dir. Kerr-McGee Corp., Oklahoma City, 1957-65; exec. v.p. Kerr-McGee Corp., Oklahoma City, 1965-68, vice chmn. bd., 1968-72, also dir.; v.p., dir. Atlas Processing Co., Shreveport, La., 1946-66; dir. Liberty Nat. Bank, Oklahoma City, First State Bank & Trust Co., S.W. Title & Trust Co., Oklahoma City, Cato Oil & Grease, Moss-Am., Inc.; chmn. bd., dir. petroleum products terminals in Atlanta, Birmingham, Chattanooga, LaGrange, Mo., Louisville, Mobile, Ala., Nashville, St. Louis, Niceville, Fla., 1948-66; dir. J.R. Butler & Co., Houston, So. States Towing Co., St. Louis. Exec. com. bd. trustees Oklahoma City U.; mem. exec. com., bd. dirs. Oklahoma City Beautiful, Inc.; mem. pres.'s Bd. Okla. Christian Coll.; mem. Presbyn. Med. Center Okla., Inc.; bd. dirs. Oklahoma City Symphony Soc., United Fund Greater Oklahoma City; trustee, chmn. exec. com., treas. Nat. Cowboy Hall of Fame; trustee Oklahoma City Community Found. Mem. Oklahoma City C. of C. (bd. dirs.), Nat. Petroleum Refiners Assn., Am. Peroleum Inst., Independent Petroleum Assn. Am., Internat. Supreme Council Order of DeMolay (hon.). Presbyn. (trustee). Mason (Shriner, K.T., DeMolay Legion Honor). Clubs: River Oaks Country, Lakeside Country, Coronado, Houston, Internat., Cork (Houston); Petroleum, Oklahoma City Golf and Country, Beacon, Chandelle, Tower (Oklahoma City); Petroleum (Dallas; New Orleans); St. Louis, Athletic (St. Louis); Chicago, Chicago Oil Men's; Shreveport; Sleepy Hollow Country (Scarsborough, N.Y.); Seigniory (Que., Can.). Home: River Oaks Apts 3435 Westheimer Rd Houston TX 77027

SAUNDERS, JOSEPH FRANCIS, chemist, govt. ofcl.; b. Mt. Pleasant, Pa., Apr. 2, 1927; B.S., Duquesne U., 1950; M.S., Georgetown U., 1955, Ph.D., 1960; m. Pauline Claire Dugan, Nov. 23, 1950; children—Joseph Francis, William Paul. Asst. to head medicine and dentistry br. Office Naval Research, 1952-57, sci. project officer, 1957-59, asst. head, 1959-60, head medicine and dentistry br., 1960-64; biosatellite program scientist, asst. chief of environmental biology, Office of Space Sci. and Applications, NASA Hdqrs., Washington, 1964-66, chief environmental biology, biosatellite program scientist Office Space Sci. and Applications, 1966-70, chief biology programs Office of Life Scis., Office Manned Space Flight, 1971—; organized research program on transplantation of tissues and cryobiology, program for research on indefinite preservation of whole blood at ultra-low temperatures. Instr. hematology and lab. techniques Bus. Tng. Coll. of Pitts.; guest scientist Naval Med. Research Inst., 1958-60. Served with USNR, 1945-46, 51-52. Recipient Arthur S. Flemming award in sci., 1962. Fellow Am. Inst. Chemists; mem. Am. Chem. Soc., Internat. Inst. for Refrigeration, Soc. Cryobiology, Sigma Xi, Alpha Chi Sigma. Author numerous tech. reports. Editor: Bioregenerative Systems, 1968, The Experiments of Biosatellite II, 1971; co-editor Depressed Metabolism, 1969; editor, narrator movies on biosatellites. Home: 8131 Greeley Blvd Springfield VA 22152 Office: Office Life Scis OMSF NASA Hdqrs Washington DC 20546

SAUNDERS, RALPH L., newspaper bus. exec.; b. Roanoke, Va., Apr. 16, 1933; s. Hammett L. and Lena (Pasley); B.S. in Bus. Adminstrn., Va. Poly. Inst., 1959-3m. Barbara Sanders, Sept. 13, 1958; children—Kevin, Scott, Karen, Steve. Asst. controller Washington Star, 1961-65; bus. mgr. Nashville (Tenn.) Tennessean, 1965—, treas., 1967—. Served with AUS, 1953-55. C.P.A., Tenn. Mem. Am. Inst. C.P.A.'s, Tenn. Soc. C.P.A.'s. Kiwanian (dir.). Home: 219 La Vista Dr Nashville TN 37215 Office: 1100 Broadway St Nashville TN 37203

SAVAGE, TOY DIXON, JR., lawyer; b. Norfolk, Va., Oct. 12, 1921; B.A., U. Va., 1942, LL.B., 1948; m. Hunter Hankins, Oct. 19, 1946; children—Tracy Gatewood, Toy Dixon, III. Admitted to Va. bar, 1948; partner firm Willcox, Savage, Lawrence, Dickson & Spindle, Norfolk. Dir. Va. Nat. Bank. Lectr. N.Y. U., U. Va., W. and M. Fed. Tax Insts. Commr. Norfolk area Med. Center Authority, 1964-66; chmn. Norfolk Med. Center Commn., 1963-64; mem. Hampton Rds. Area Com., chmn., 1963-64; mem. Hos of Dels. of Gen. Assembly of Va., 1954-63; chmn. 2d dist. Democratic Com., 1960-64; mem. Va. Dem. State Central Com., 1960-64. Trustee Norfolk Gen. Hosp. (pres. 1966-68), Old Dominion U. Found. (v.p. 1962—); bd. dirs. United Community Fund. Mem. Am. (sect. on taxation), Va. (pres. 1969-70) bar assns., Va. State Bar (chmn. sect. bus. law 1959-60), Phi Kappa Sigma, Alpha Kappa Psi, Phi Delta Phi, Order of Coif. Baptist (trustee ch.). Clubs: Virginia (pres. 1966-68); Princess Anne Country; Norfolk Yacht and Country; Commonwealth; Cedar Point Country; Norfolk German. Contbr. articles to various legal and tax periodicals. Home: 1349 W Princess Anne Rd Norfolk VA 23507 Office: Va Nat Bank Bldg Norfolk VA 23510

SAVAGE, WILLIAM WOODROW, educator; b. Onley, Va., Jan. 9, 1914; s. Frank Howard and Florence Elmira (Twyford) S.; A.B., Coll. William and Mary, 1937; M.A., U. Chgo., 1946, Ph.D., 1955; student U. Va., summer 1951; m. Margaret Jane Clarke; children—Earl R., William W. Research editor, div. rural research Fed. Emergency Relief Adminstrn., Richmond, Va., 1935-36; div. mgr. Montgomery Ward & Co., Newport News, Va., 1937-38; statis. worker WPA, Richmond, 1938-39; counselor Va. Consultation Service, Richmond, 1939-42, acting dir., 1942-45; asst. state supr. guidance and consultation services Va. Dept. Edn., 1946-47; dean Longwood Coll., Farmville, Va., 1947-52; project coordinator, asso. dir. Midwest Adminstrn. Center, U. Chgo., 1952-56; dean Sch. Edn., U. S.C., 1956-65, prof. edn., 1965—. Mem. visitation and appraisal com. Nat. Council Accreditation Tchr. Edn., 1964-67. Mem. Am. Assn. Sch. Adminstrs. (mem. com. advancement sch. adminstrn., 1955-56), Am. Assn. U. Profs., Phi Delta Kappa. Methodist (ofcl. bd.). Club: Executives (Columbia). Co-author: Readings in American Education, 1963. Author: Interpersonal and Group Relations in Educational Administration, 1968. Editor: Work and Training, monthly Va. Bd. Edn., 1941-47, Administrator's Notebook, monthly Midwest Adminstrn. Center, 1954-56, U. S.C. Edn. Report, 1957—; adv. com. Sch. Rev., 1954-56. Contbr. articles various jours. Home: 6316 Eastshore Rd Columbia SC 29206

SAVERANCE, CLIFTON R., supt. schs.; b. Bethune, S.C., Sept. 16, 1913; s. Junius Edwin and Beulah I. (Carter) S.; B.S., Clemson U., 1938; M.Ed., U. S.C., 1955; m. Martha Augusta Godbold, June 16, 1939; children—Clifton R., Robert Edwin. Tchr., Williamsburg County Schs., Hemingway, S.C., 1938-42; tchr. Lamar (S.C.) Schs., 1946-50, prin., 1953-57; supt. Hemingway Area Schs., 1957-68, Lamar (S.C.) Schs., 1968—. Served to maj., inf. AUS, 1942-46; PTO; 1950-52. Mem. S.C., Am. assns. sch. adminstrs., S.C., Darlington County, Williamsburg County edn. assns., Am. Legion, Alpha Tau Alpha. Prsbyn. Mason. Club: Civitan (Lamar). Home: Box 603 Lamar SC 29069

SAVIT, CARL HERTZ, geophysicist; b. N.Y.C., July 19, 1922; B.S. with honors, Cal. Inst. Tech., 1942, M.S., 1943, postgrad. also teaching fellow in advanced math. 1943-44, 46-48; m. 1946; three children. Statis. cons. Long Range Meteorology Project USAF, 1943-45; asso. prof. math. San Fernando Valley (Cal.) State Coll., 1959-60; chief mathematician Western Geophys. Co., Litton Industries, Inc., 1948-60, dir. systems research, 1960-65, v.p. systems research devel. 1965-70; asst. for earth, sea, air scis. to Pres.'s Sci. Adv.; chmn. Interagy. Com. for Atmospheric Scis., 1970-71; mem. panel On-Site Inspection Unidentified Seismec Events, Disposition of Oil Leasing in the Santa Barbara Channel, Offshore Pollution, U.S. Initiatives in Transp., 1971, com. on Seismology Nat. Acad. Scis.-NRC, 1971—; dir. Nat. Ocean Industries Assn. Served as 2nd lt., USAAF, 1944-46. Fellow Geol. Soc. Am.; mem. Assn. Earth Sci. Editors, European Assn. Exploration Geophysicists, Associacion Mexicana de Geofisicos de Exploracion, Marine Tech. Soc., Am. Petroleum Inst., Soc. Exploration Geophysicists (named Classic Author of Geophysics 1960, editor jour. 1968-69, del. to U.S.S.R. 1971, pres. 1971-72), Cosmos Club, Sigma Xi. Address: 13626 Tosca Lane Houston TX 77024*

SAWYER, COLONEL CHARLESTON, lawyer; b. Indpls., May 28, 1906; s. Herbert Charleston and Elma (Reid) S.; m. Dorothy Marguerite Lash, Aug. 13, 1932. Admitted to Ind. bar, 1933; partner Aikman & Sawyer, Newport, Ind., 1933-35; practicing lawyer, 1935-37; spl. atty. Dept. Financial Instrns., Ind. 1936-37; sr. atty., prin. atty. NLRB, 1937-44; asso. with firm Pruitt, Desvernine & Coursen, N.Y.C., 1944-48; asso. counsel Consol. Vultee Aircraft Corp., San Diego, 1944-55; asso. counsel Gen. Dynamics Corp., 1955-64, asso. chief counsel Spl. Corporate Counsel, 1964—; v.p. Airfleets, Incs., 1951-54. Home: 2301 Ridgmar Plaza Fort Worth TX 76116 Office: Gen Dynamics Fort Worth TX 76101

SAWYER, FLOYD DANIEL, coll. adminstr.; b. Durham, N.C., Jan. 17, 1929; s. Charles Franklin and Blanche Anne (Wright) S.; B.A., Duke, 1959; postgrad. U. Ky., 1967-70; m. Marion Florence Buttry, June 11, 1950; children—Floyd Daniel, Sharon Kay, Timothy Douglas. Chief accountant Duke, 1959-67; v.p. bus., treas. N.C. Wesleyan Coll., Rocky Mount, 1967—. Active Travel Council. Bd. dirs. United Fund. Served with C.E., AUS, 1952-54. Decorated Army Commendation medal. Mem. Nat. Auditors Coll. and Univ., Coll. and Univ. Personnel Assn., Nat. Assn. Coll. and U. Bus. Officers, So. Assn. Coll. and Univ. Bus. Officers, Ednl. and Instl. Inst., C. of C. (mem. edn. com. 1969-71), Nat. Assn. Ednl. Buyers. Methodist (finance chmn. 1970-71). Kiwanian (dir. 1969-72). Home: 1200 West Haven Blvd Rocky Mount NC 27801

SAWYER, VERNON DONALD, city ofcl.; b. McGehee, Ark., Dec. 24, 1937; s. Jasper Vernon and Margaret (Hampton) S.; B.S. in Math., Ark. A. and M. Coll., 1959; m. Ellen Rose Ollar, Jan. 27, 1959; 1 dau., Mary Ellen. Tchr., coach Pine Bluff (Ark.) Pub. Sch., 1959-60; mathematician White Sands (N.M.) Missile Range, 1960-61; partner J.V. & Bon Sawyer, Contractors, McGehee, Ark., 1961-66; exec. dir. McGehee Housing Authority, 1966—; with Mut. Ins. Agy., 1970—. Mem. Ark. A. and M. Alumni Assn. (dir. 1965-67), Nat. Assn. Housing and Renewal Ofcls., McGehee Jr. C. of C. (pres. 1963), Ark. Jr. C. of C. (v.p. 1964). Methodist. Lion (sec. 1968, 3d v.p. 1969). Home: 1600 N 3d St McGehee AR 71654 Office: PO Box 801 McGehee AR 71654

SAWYER, WARREN ALLEN, librarian; b. Bay Shore, N.Y., June 22, 1937; s. George John and Thelma (Caldwell) S.; B.S., Hampden-Sydney Coll., 1959; M.S. in Library Sci., U. N.C., 1961; m. Judith Alvord Littlepage, Jan. 25, 1958; children—Anne Louise, Angus Caldwell. Librarian Augusta Mil. Acad., Fort Defiance, Va., 1964-66, Coll. Charleston (S.C.), 1966-68; dir. libraries Med. U. S.C., 1968—, and Coll. Charleston, 1970—. Served with AUS, 1962-64. Mem. Am., Med., S.C., Southeastern library assns., Am. Assn. U. Profs. Home: 27 Gadsden St Charleston SC 29401 Office: 80 Barre St Charleston SC 29401

SAWYERS, JOHN LAZELLE, physician; b. Centerville, Ia., July 26, 1925; s. Francis Lazelle and Almira (Baker) S.; A.B., U. Rochester, 1946; M.D., Johns Hopkins U., 1949; m. Julia Edwards, May 25, 1957; children—Charles Lazelle, Al Baker, Julia Edwards. House officer surgery Johns Hopkins Hosp., Balt., 1949-50; asst. resident, resident in surgery Vanderbilt U. Hosp., Nashville, 1953-58; pvt. practice surgery, Nashville, 1958—; surgeon Edwards-Eve Clinic, 1958-60; chief surg. service Nashville Gen. Hosp., 1960—; prof. surgery Vanderbilt U. Dir. Davidson County unit Am. Cancer Soc. Served from lt. (j.g.) to lt., M.C., USNR, 1950-52. Diplomate Am. Bd. Surgery, Am. Bd. Thoracic Surgery. Fellow A.C.S.; mem. Am. Surg. Assn. Home: 403 Ellendale Dr Nashville TN 37205 Office: Gen Hosp Nashville TN 37210

SAXON, JAMES BRUNSON, elec. engr.; b. Birmingham, Ala., Apr. 9, 1934; s. George Reuben and Beatrice (Brunson) S.; B. in Mech. Engring., Auburn U., 1957, B. Elec. Engring., 1965; m. Grady Sue Leftin, Aug. 27, 1955; children—Kathryn Sue, James Grady. Engr., Fla. Power & Light Co., Ft. Lauderdale, 1957-63; with Anderson Electric Corp., Leeds, Ala., 1965—, engring. adminstr., 1969-71, chief engr., 1972—. Registered profl. engr., Ala., Fla. Mem. Am. Soc. M.E. (chmn. 1970-71), Phi Kappa Phi, Eta Kappa Nu, Tau Beta Pi, Phi Kappa Tau. Patentee in elec. power connectors. Home: 948 Ridgewood Circle Birmingham AL 35235 Office: Anderson Electric Corp Leeds AL 35094

SAYAD, WILLIAM Y(OHANNAN), physician, surgeon; b. Rizaieh, Iran. Jan. 1, 1896; s. Dr. Yohannan and Sheerin Malick (Yonan) S.; B.S., Davidson Coll., 1917, Sc.D., 1949; M.D., Yale, 1921; m. Judith Morris, Oct. 21, 1931; children—Judith, William Y., Patricia Ann. Came to United States, 1913, naturalized, 1918. Intern Vassar Hosp., 1921-23; resident physician N.Y. Eye and Ear Infirmary, 1923-26; attending surgeon Good Samaritan Hosp., St. Mary's Hosp., Palm Beach, Fla., 1926—; pvt. practice surgery eye, ear, nose and throat, Palm Beach, 1926—; mem. adv. bd. Iran Found., Fla. Council for Blind; chmn. med. adv. com. Fla. Soc. Prevention Blindness. Fellow Internat.; mem. Palm Beach County (past pres.), So., Fla. med. socs., A.M.A., Fla. Soc. Opthalmology and Otolaryngology, Yale U. Med. Sch. Alumni Assn., Alpha Kappa Kappa, Omicron Delta Kappa. Mason. Clubs: Everglades, Bath and Tennis (Palm Beach); University (N.Y.C.). Contbr. profl. jours. Home: 330 Cocoanut Row Palm Beach FL 33480

SAYE, JAMES ANGUS, JR., advt. agcy. exec.; b. Montezuma, Ga., Apr. 4, 1929; s. James A. and Muriel (Heard) S.; B.A., Emory U., 1951; B.A., U. Ga., 1954; m. Geraldyne A. Whitfield, Apr. 18, 1956; children—James A. III, Timothy D. Advt. asst. Atlanta Gas Light Co., 1954-55; account exec. McCann-Erickson, Inc., Houston, 1955-60, Rives-Dyke & Co., Houston, 1960-61, Robinson-Gerrard, Inc., Houston, 1961-66; pres., founder Star Advt. Agy., Houston, 1966—. Publicity chmn. Harris County delegation Tex. Democratic Conv., 1962; precinct chmn. Republican party, Goldwater for Pres., 1964. Served to lt. (j.g.), USNR, 1951-53. Recipient 1st award Pub. Utilities Advt. Assn., 1955, 2d Pl. award ad compaign Wessendorff, Nelms, 1964, honor certificate award Freedoms Found., 1972. Mem. Am. Legion, S.C.V. (adj. 1969-70), Order of Stars and Bars (comdr. Tex. chpt. 1972), Houston Advt. Club (Best Indsl. Ad award 1958), Alpha Delta Sigma, Sigma Chi Alumni Assn. Republican. Baptist. Club: (Houston). Home: 4838 Kingfisher St Houston TX 77035 Office: 3501 W Alabama St Houston TX 77027

SAYLER, HENRY BENTON, state senator; b. Savannah, Ga., Jan. 16, 1921; s. Henry B. and Jessie (Dixon) S.; B.S., U.S. Mil. Acad., 1943; m. Wyline Chapman, Mar. 22, 1947; children—Lee, Alan, Robin, Van. Pres. Security Planning Fla., Inc., St. Petersburg, 1955—; mem. Fla. Senate, 1966—. Dir. Bank of Seminole, Founders Life Assurance Co., R.W. Page Corp. Bd. dirs. YMCA, St. Petersburg. Served to lt. col., USAF, 1943-55. Decorated D.F.C., Air Medal with six clusters. Republican. Kiwanian. Home: 280 Rafael Blvd St Petersburg FL 33704 Office: 333 31st St N St Petersburg FL 33713

SAYLOR, BILL, cartoonist Houston Post. Address: 2410 Polk St Houston TX 77001*

SAYRE, EDWIN MUREL, profl. orgn. exec.; b. Silver City, N.M., Dec. 19, 1915; s. Arthur Nuell and Edna (Yarbro) S.; grad. U.S. Army Command and Gen. Staff Coll., 1950, Armed Forces Staff Coll., 1954, Army War Coll., 1961; m. Betty Jane Mavrico, Sept. 7, 1946. Commd. 2d lt. U.S. Army, 1941, advanced through grades to col., 1950; comdr. 1st bn. 17th Inf., 7th Inf. Div., Korea, 1951-52; chief operations Far East Command, Tokyo, Japan, 1952-54; operational planner Armed Forces Staff Coll., Norfolk, Va., 1955-58; operational planner, mem. staff Gen. Westmoreland, Vietnam, 1964-65; operational planner Joint Chiefs Staff, Pentagon, Washington, 1965-68; ret., 1968; mgr. Breckenridge (Tex.) C. of C., 1968—. Sec. Breckenridge Indsl. Found., 1968—. Decorated D.S.C., Silver Star, Legion of Merit with oak leaf cluster, Bronze Star with 3 oak leaf clusters, Air medal, Purple Heart with 2 oak leaf clusters Mem. V.F.W., Am. Legion. Presbyn (elder). Rotarian, Mason. Home: Route 1 Box 225 Breckenridge TX 76024 Office: 112 W Walker St Breckenridge TX 76024

SAYRE, JOHN LESLIE, clergyman, educator; b. Hannibal, Mo., Mar. 28, 1924; s. John Leslie and Clara (Haden) S.; student U. Okla., 1942-43; A.B., Phillips U., 1947; B.D. cum laude, Yale, 1950; M.L.S., U. Tex. at Austin, 1963; postgrad. Union Theol. Sem., 1955; Ph.D. candidate, U. Tex. at Austin, 1972; m. Herwanna Lee Harrouff, June 18, 1948; children—Barbara Ann, John Richard, Alan Douglas, Melody Lyn. Ordained to ministry Christian Ch. (Disciples of Christ) 1946; asso. minister Christian chs., Enid, Okla., 1945-47, minister, Stillwater, Okla., 1950-57, Austin, Tex., 1957-62; instr. Phillips U., 1954-55, asso. prof. theol. bibliography, 1962—, sem. librarian, 1962-71, dir. univ. libraries, 1971—; instr. Okla. State U., 1950-57; sometimes lectr. Mem. Am. Theol. Library Assn., Am., Okla., S.W. library assns., Beta Phi Mu, Theta Phi, Phi Kappa Phi. Democrat. Author: A History of Disciples Student Work, 1950; A Manual of Forms for Term Papers and Theses, 1966; An Index to Festschriften in Religion, 1971; An Illustrated Guide to the Anglo-American Cataloging Rules, 1971; Tools for Theologica Research, 1972. Home: 2416 E Elm St Enid OK 73701

SAYRE, MALCOLM MAYNARD, surgeon; b. Mason City, W.Va., June 13, 1928; s. Robert Fawcett and Orilla Mae (Ruckman) S., Jr.; student Emory Jr. Coll., 1946-47; B.S., U. Ga., 1955; M.D., Med. Coll. Ga., 1959; m. Mary Frances Searcy, Feb. 11, 1949; children—Tammy Renee, Michael Kevin. Rotating intern Orange Meml. Hosp., Orlando, Fla., 1959-60; mem. med. staff, asst. chief surgery Palmetto Med. Clinic and Hosp., Wauchula, Fla., 1960-67, asst. adminstr., 1960-67, adminstr., 1967—, chief surgery, 1967—. Vice pres. Profl. Properties, Inc., Wauchula, 1960-67, pres., 1967—; surgeon Seaboard-Coastline R.R., 1965—. Bd. dirs. Fedn. Am. Hosps.; trustee, chmn. legislative com. Fla. League of Hosps. Served with USNR, 1947-50, AUS, 1950-62. Recipient certificate merit Explorer Scouts Am. Mem. Am. Acad. Gen. Practice, DeSoto-Hardee-Glades County Med. Soc. (pres. 1969), Am. Soc. Abdominal Surgeons, Am. Profl. Practice Assn., A.M.A., Fla. Med. Assn., Am. Mus. Natural History, Nat. Geog. Soc., Defenders of Wildlife, Hardee County Farm Bur., Sarasota Amateur Radio Assn., Phi Chi. Baptist (choir mem. 1948—). Elk. Home: Altman Rd PO Box 428 Wauchula FL 33873 Office: Palmetto Med Clinic and Hosp Wauchula FL 33873

SCALES, CLARENCE RAY, lawyer; b. Morton, Miss., Aug. 23, 1922; s. Felix A. and Zola (Dubose) S.; LL.B., U. Miss., 1949; m. Lura Evelyn Lee, Aug. 20, 1948; children—Clarence Ray, Linda Evelyn, Philip Lee. Admitted to Miss. bar, 1949; gen. practice law, Jackson, 1949—, sr. mem. firm Scales & Scales, 1956—. Served with AUS, 1942-46. Mem. Am., Hinds County bar assns., Miss. State Bar. Home: 1220 Druid Hills Dr Jackson MS 39206 Office: Deposit Guaranty Bank Bldg Jackson MS 39201

SCALES, JAMES RALPH, univ. pres.; b. Jay, Okla., May 27, 1919; s. John Grover and Kate (Whitley) S.; A.B., Okla. Baptist U., 1939; M.A., U. Okla., 1941, Ph.D., 1949; postgrad. U. Chgo., 1945-47, U. London, 1958; m. Elizabeth Ann Randel, August 4, 1944; children—Laura (dec.), Ann Catherine. Reporter, Miami (Okla.) News Record, 1934-35, Shawnee (Okla.) News-Star, 1935-36; instr. Okla. Baptist U., Shawnee, 1940-42, asst. prof., 1946-47, asso. prof., 1947-51, prof. history, govt., 1951-61, v.p., 1950-53, exec. v.p., 1953-61, pres., 1961-65; dean arts and scis. Okla. State U., Stillwater, 1965-67; pres. Wake Forest U., Winston-Salem, N.C., 1967—. Dir. Integon Corp., Home Fed. Savs. & Loan Assn. Mem. Pres.'s Com. Edn. Beyond High Sch., 1957, Okla. Commn. Tchr. Edn. and Certification, 1955-61. Exec. com. Last Frontier council Boy Scouts Am., 1960-67; exec. com. Shawnee United Fund, 1955-65; pres. Shawnee Community Concert Assn., 1950-54. Mem. Okla. delegation Democratic Nat. Conv., 1956. Bd. dirs. Pottawatomie County chpt. A.R.C.; trustee Presbyn. Hosp., Oklahoma City. Mem. Am. Hist. Assn., Am. Polit. Sci. Assn., Am. Assn. U. Profs., N.E.A., So. Assn. Bapt. Colls. (pres. 1969-70), N.C. Assn. Ind. Colls. (pres. 1969-71), Winston-Salem C. of C. (dir.), Phi Beta Kappa, Phi Eta Sigma, Pi Kappa Delta, Kappa Delta Pi. Baptist (deacon). Rotarian. Address: President's Home Wake Forest U Winston-Salem NC 27109

SCALES, RAY GUEST, advt.-pub. relations co. exec.; b. Ada, Okla., Apr. 14, 1925; s. John Anthony and Lillie (Guest) S.; student Phillips U., 1941-42, Tex. Christian U., 1942-43, 46-47; B.A., Okla. U., 1948; m. Katy Dickson, Feb. 25, 1950. Reporter, Shawnee (Okla.) News-Star, 1948-49; city editor Garden City (Kan.) Daily Telegram, 1949-50; pub. relations dir. WKY and WKY TV, Oklahoma City, 1950-53, Humphrey-Williamson-Gibson, Oklahoma City, 1956-59, Ackerman Assos., Oklahoma City, 1959-62; pub. TeleViewer mag., 1953-56; pres. Ray Scales Assos., Inc., Oklahoma City, 1962—, exec. v.p. Okla. Oil Marketers Assn., 1965—. Pres., Oklahoma City Jr. Symphony Soc., 1958; publicity chmn., mem. bd. Okla. County March of Dimes, 1962-65; pres. Oklahoma City Festival of Arts, 1965-67. Served to lt. (j.g.) USNR, 1943-46. Mem. Okla. Pub. Relations Assn. (pres. 1965-67), Pub. Relations Soc. Am. (chpt. pres. 1971, sec., treas. 1969). Home: 314 NE 61st St Oklahoma City OK 73105 Office: 3313 Classen Blvd Oklahoma City OK 73118

SCALI, JOHN ALFRED, Presdl. cons.; b. Canton, O., Apr. 27, 1918; s. Paul M. and Lucy (Leone) S.; B.S. in Journalism, Boston U., 1942; m. Helen Lauinger Glock, Aug. 30, 1946; children—Donna Claire, Paula, Carla. Reporter, Boston Herald, 1942, Boston bur. U.P., 1942-43; with A.P., 1944-61, war corr., ETO, 1944, then diplomatic corr., and with Washington Bur., 1945-61; diplomatic corr. ABC TV and Radio, Wash., 1961-71; cons. to Pres. of U.S., Washington, 1971—. Recipient Journalism award U. So. Cal., 1964, spl. award Washington chpt. Nat. Acad. Arts and Scis., 1964, Man of year award in journalism Boston U., 1965, spl. award Overseas Press Club, 1965; John Scali award created by Washington chpt. A.F.T.R.A., 1964. Mem. A.F.T.R.A., Sigma Delta Chi. Clubs: Nat. Press, Internat. (Washington); Kenwood (Md.) Golf and Country. Home: 2400 Pennsylvania Av NW Washington DC 20016

SCANLAN, ALFRED L., lawyer; b. Elizabeth, N.J., Mar. 13, 1920; A.B., Columbia, 1941; LL.B., George Washington U., 1946, LL.M., 1947; m. Jean E. Aaron; 5 children. Admitted to D.C. bar, 1946, Ind. bar, 1949, U.S. Supreme Ct. bar, 1954, Md. bar, 1955; asst. prof. law Notre Dame Law Sch., 1947-50, now partner firm Sheat Gardner, Washington. Mem. arbitration panel Ind. Pub. Employees Disputes Act, 1949-50; asst. counsel munitions bd. Dept. Def., 1950-52; chmn. adminstrv. law sect. D.C. bar, 1967-68; spl. adviser V.I. Constl. Conv., 1965-66; mem. Md. Constl. Conv. Commn., 1965-67; del., chmn. com. rules, credentials and conv. budget Md. Constl. Conv., 1967-68; bd. trustees for Pub. Defender Md., 1967. Mem. Bar Assn. D.C. (bd. dirs. 1964-66, 68-69), Am., Md. bar assns., Am. Law Inst., Order Coif, Phi Delta Phi. Editor: Natural Law Inst. Proc., 1948. Address: Walker Bldg 734 15th St NW Washington DC 20005

SCARBOROUGH, CLAUDE MOOD, JR., lawyer; b. Columbia, S.C., Dec. 7, 1929; s. Claude M. and Gelene (Stallworth) S.; student U. of South, 1947-49; A.B., U.S.C., 1951, LL.B., 1952; m. Sarah Carpenter, June 30, 1955; children—Sarah Catherine, Elizabeth Ann, Claude M. III, Gelene Bivins. Admitted to S.C. bar, 1952, U.S. Ct. Appeals, 1957; asso. firm Nelson, Mullins & Grier, Columbia, S.C., 1955-61, partner Nelson, Mullins, Grier & Scarborough, 1961—. Spl. hearing officer U.S. Dept. Justice, 1962-68. Trustee Legal Aid Soc. Richland Co., 1960-67, pres. 1960-64. Served to 1st lt. AUS, 1952-55. Mem. Internat. Assn. Ins. Counsel, Am., S.C. (treas. 1968-72, exec. com. 1972—) Richland County bar assns., Am. Judicature Soc., Phi Delta Phi. Episcopalian. (lay reader, vestryman) Clubs: Palmetto, Forest Lake Country. Home: 1514 Tanglewood Rd Columbia SC 29205 Office: 1321 Bull St Columbia SC 29201

SCARBOROUGH, HOMER MCCRARY, JR., lawyer; b. Macon, Ga., July 20, 1941; s. Homer McCrary and Vivian (Keeling) S.; J.D., U. Ga., 1966. Admitted to Ga. bar, 1966, since practiced in Macon; mem. Ga. Ho. of Reps., 1968—. Mem. Bibb County Democratic Exec. Com., 1970—. Mem. State Bar Ga., Phi Alpha Delta. Methodist. Moose, Eagle, Elk. Home: 3342 Pio Nono Circle Macon GA 31206 Office: Am Fed Bldg Macon GA 31201

SCARBOROUGH, ROBERT BOWMAN, state senator, life ins. co. exec.; b. Charleston, S.C., June 28, 1928; s. Yance Wilcox and Lillie (Thomas) S.; A.B., The Citadel, 1950; m. Elizabeth Adelia Martin, Jan. 10, 1953; children—Robert Bowman, Wallace B. Agt., Cosmopolitan Life Ins. Co., Charleston, S.C., 1950-53, spl. agt., 1954; sec. Atlanta Coast Life Ins. Co., Charleston, 1954-57, sec.-treas., 1957—; mem. S.C. Ho. of Reps., 1962-68, state senator, 1968—. Chmn. Charleston County chpt. A.R.C., 1958-59, chmn. S. Atlanta Blood Adv. Com., 1960-63, chmn. Home Service Com., 1960-62, mem. Nat. Blood Procurement Study Panel, 1961, mem. S.E. area Adv. Council, 1962-65; bd. govs. Am. Nat. Red Cross, 1966-69; active Charleston United Fund, 1954—, chmn. W. Ashley bus. group, 1956, chmn. higher edn. div., 1971; Cancer Crusade chmn. Charleston Cancer Soc., 1952, bd. dirs., 1956-59; mem. Pres.'s Traffic Safety Com., 1956; mem. S.C. State Safety Com., 1963—. Bd. dirs. Salvation Army, Charleston. Recipient Distinguished Service award Charleston Jr. C. of C., 1962; named Man of Yr., Charleston Exchange Club, 1955, 58, 59. Mem. Sumter Guards, Assn. Citadel Men (dir. 1958-59, pres. 1968), Charleston Navy League (pres. 1963-64), Hibernian Soc., Charleston C. of C. (v.p. 1962, 64), S.C. Assn. Life Ins. (bd. dirs. 1962-64). Episcopalian (chmn. ch. warden assn. 1962). Mason (32 deg., Shriner). Clubs: Charleston Country, Carolina Yacht, Exchange (pres. Charleston 1957, sec. S.C. 1958, pres. 1960, nat. bd. dirs. 1962-65, nat. pres. 1969). Home: 26 Broughton Rd Charleston SC 29407 Office: 149 Wentworth St Charleston SC 29401

SCARBOROUGH, WALTER WILLIAM, architect; b. Houston, Apr. 21, 1936; s. Walter Welborn and Florine (Davis) S.; student Rice Inst., 1954-55, U. Houston, 1957-58; studied under Frank Lloyd Wright, 1956; B.S. in Architecture, U. Tex., 1962; m. Marion Harriet Bergensen, Mar. 21, 1970; children—Julie, Walt, Jack. Designer, William Robert King, Architect & Engr., Austin, Tex., 1960-65; practice architecture, Houston, 1965—. Mem. A.I.A., Tau Sigma Delta. Office: 7011 Southwest Freeway Houston TX 77036 Home: 711 Bayridge Rd Morgans Point TX 77571

SCARTH, PETER, ednl. cons.; b. Buffalo, Apr. 8, 1932; s. Harry and Priscilla (Wolfe) S.; B.A., U. N.H., 1955, M.Ed., 1960; Ed.D., Boston U., 1966. Tchr. sociology Laconia (N.H.) High Sch., 1958-59; asst. sch. psychologist Portsmouth (N.H.) Sch. Dept., 1960-61, sch. psychologist, 1962-64; dir. guidance Supervisory Union No. 55, Plaistow, N.H., 1961-62; cons. psychologist Tamworth (N.H.) Pub. Sch., 1962-65; instr. U. N.H., Durham, 1963-64; progranalyst Action for Boston Community Devel., 1965; exec. asso. Upward Bound project Ednl. Projects, Inc., Washington, 1965-66, dir. migrant and seasonal farm worker project, 1966-68, v.p. for program, 1967-68; pres. Ednl. Systems Corp., Washington, 1968—, Exec. Systems Corp., Washington, 1968-71, Am. Vocational Research Corp., 1971-72, Fibercraft, Inc., 1957-60. Chmn. sch. drop-out study Seacoast Regional Guidance Council, 1963-65; mem. ad-hoc com. role and function jr. and community colls. U.S. Senate, 1969; co-chmn. com. on Negro in higher edn., 1968. Bd. dirs. Portsmouth Mental Health Clinic, 1962-64. Served with USAF, 1955-57. Mem. Am. Psychol. Assn., Am. Soc. Adlerian Psychology, N.E.A., Am. Personnel and Guidance Assn. (program chmn. New Eng. conv. 1964). Author: Individual Psychology: Its Implications for School Psychology, 1966; Bibliography for Migrant Education Programs, 1967; also articles. Home: 4555 MacArthur Blvd NW Washington DC 20007 Office: 806 Connecticut Av NW Washington DC 20525

SCHAAF, ROBERT WARREN, librarian, govt. ofcl.; b. Rochester, N.Y., June 6, 1926; s. Warren William and Gula Almeda (Reeves) S.; B.A., Hamilton Coll., 1950; M.A., Sch. Advanced Internat. Studies, Johns Hopkins, 1952; m. Mary Angeline Drennan, Aug. 20, 1955; 1 son, Thomas Gerard. With Library of Congress, Washington, 1952—, asst. head internat. orgns. sect., 1956-65, head, 1966-70, head union catalog and internat. orgns. references sect., 1970—. Sec., Springfield Village Homeowners Assn., Springfield, Va., 1969-70, mem. Archtl. Control Com., 1971—. Served with AUS, 1944-46. Mem. A.L.A., (sec. law and polit. sci. subsect. 1964-67), D.C. Library Assn. Democrat. Roman Catholic. Club: Springfield Swimming and Racquet (Springfield). Home: 7247 Reservoir Rd Springfield VA 22150 Office: Library of Congress 10 1st St SE Washington DC 20540

SCHACHNER, STEPHEN HAROLD, physician; b. N.Y.C., May 30, 1937; s. Arthur M. and Lillian (Pollack) S.; M.D., Creighton U., 1961; m. Dianne Fellman, June 7, 1961; children—Seth, Jill. Intern, L.I. Jewish Hosp., New Hyde Park, N.Y., 1961-62; resident internal medicine Mount Zion Hosp. and Med. Center, San Francisco, 1962-63, VA Hosp., Bronx, N.Y., 1963-64; NIH fellow in endocrinology and metabolism Ohio State U. Hosps., 1964-65; asst. clin. prof. medicine George Washington U. Med. Sch., 1968—; pvt. practice medicine specializing in endocrinology, Falls Church, Va., 1968—; chief sect. endocrinology Fairfax Hosp., Falls Church, 1970—. Served with AUS, 1966-68. Diplomate Am. Bd. Internal Medicine, Nat. Bd. Med. Examiners. Fellow A.C.P.; mem. A.M.A., Am., D.C. diabetes assns. Home: 8707 Chippendale Ct Annandale VA 22003 Office: 7 Corners Med Bldg Falls Church VA 22044

SCHACHTEL, HYMAN JUDAH, rabbi; b. London, Eng., May 24, 1907; s. Bernard and Janie (Spector) S.; came to U.S., 1914, naturalized, 1921; B.A., U. Cin., 1928; B.H. Rabbi, Hebrew Union Coll., 1931; student Columbia Tchrs. Coll., 1933-37; Ed. D., U. Houston, 1948; D.D., Hebrew Union Coll., 1958; D.H.L., Southwestern U., 1955; m. Barbara H. Levin, Oct. 15, 1941; children—Bernard, Ann Mollie. Ordained rabbi, 1931; rabbi West End Synagogue, N.Y.C. 1931-43; chief rabbi Temple Beth Israel, Houston, 1943—; tchr. philosophy U. Houston, 1950-55. Pres. Tex. Kallah Rabbis, 1962, Houston Rabbinical Assn., 1960; mem. exec. bd. Central Conf. Am. Rabbis, 1965-67, v.p., sec.-treas. Southwest region, 1966—; chaplain Variety Club, Houston, 1955—, Houston Fire Dept., 1964—; v.p. N.Y. Bd. Rabbis, 1942-43. Pres. Harris County Mental Health Assn., 1960; bd. dirs. Houston Symphony Soc., 1955—, San Jacinto council Girl Scouts U.S.A., 1962—, Houston Heart Assn., 1964—, Houston Crime Commn., 1962-65; mem. nat. planning bd., trustee United Fund Harris County, 1965—; bd. overseers Hebrew Union Coll.-Jewish Inst. Religion, 1961-65. Recipient Coronat medal St. Edward's U., Aústin, Tex., 1963. Mem. Phi Delta Kappa, Phi Epsilon Pi (hon.). Kiwanian. Author: Real Enjoyment of Living, 1954; The Life You Want to Live, 1956; The Shadowed Valley, 1964; Aspects of Jewish Homiletics, 1964. Home: 2527 Glenhaven St Houston TX 77025 Office: 5600 N Brateswood Houston TX 77035

SCHAD, THEODORE MACNEEVE, govt. ofcl.; b. Balt., Aug. 25, 1918; s. William Henry and Emma Margaret (Scheldt) S.; B.E., Johns Hopkins, 1939, postgrad. in hydrology, postgrad. hydrology, 1939-40; m. Kathleen White, Nov. 5, 1944; children—Mary Jane, Rebecca Christina. Civilian engr. C.E., U.S. Army, 1939-40, 42-46; engr. U.S. Bur. Reclamation, 1940-42, 46-54; budget examiner U.S. Bur. Budget, 1954-58; sr. specialist Legis. Reference Service, Library of Congress, Washington, 1958-68, dep. dir., 1967-68; staff dir. Select Com. on Nat. Water Resources, U.S. Senate, Washington, 1959-61; exec. dir. Nat. Water Commn., Arlington, Va., 1969—. Treas., Nat. Speleological Found., 1964-69; v.p., bd. dirs. Vets Coop. Housing Assn., 1960—. Recipient Superior Accomplishment award Interior Dept., 1950. Mem. Am. Soc. C.E. (pres. nat. Capitol sect. 1967-68), Nat. Speleological Soc., Am. Acad. Environmental Engrs., Am. Water Works Assn. (hon.), Am. Geophys. Union, Soc. Am. Mil. Engrs., Internat. Assn. Nav. Congresses (permanent commn. 1963-70), Tau Beta Pi, Pi Delta Epsilon. Clubs: Potomac Appalachian Trail (council 1954-55); Colo. Mountain; Cosmos (Washington); Seattle Mountaineers. Contbr. numerous articles to tech. jours. Home: 4138 26th Rd N Arlington VA 22207 Office: 800 N Quincy St Arlington VA 22203

SCHAEFER, JOE EDWARD, precast concrete co. exec.; b. Cisco, Tex., June 27, 1933; s. Rudolph and Lola (Lennon) S.; grad. Cisco Jr. Coll., 1952; student U. Tex., 1952-53, B.S. in Archtl. Engring. 1960; student McMurray Coll., 1955-56; m. Mary K. Smith, Dec. 11, 1965; children—James E., Rita M. Archtl. engr. E.I. DuPont de Nemours & Co., Inc., Wilmington, Del., 1960-61; archtl. engr. Freese, Nichols & Endress, Ft. Worth, 1961-67; sales engr. Tex. Industries Inc., Arlington, 1967-69, prodn. mgr., 1969—. Mem. Bldg. Code Bd. of Adjustment and Appeal, Arlington, 1970—. Bd. dirs. MoSai Inst. Served with AUS, 1953-55. Mem. Constrn. Specification Inst. (v.p. 1964-65, pres. 1966-68), Am. Soc. C.E., Tex. Soc. Profl. Engrs. Club: Arlington Sportsman's (sec. 1962-66, pres. 1968-69, 72). Home: 2110 Laura Lane Arlington TX 76010 Office: PO Box 400 Arlington TX 76010

SCHAEFFER, N(ORMAN) M(ORRIS), research and devel. co. exec.; b. Camden, Ark., Nov. 1, 1927; s. Sam and Lena (Sabludowsky) S.; B.S., La. State U., 1947, M.S., 1949; Ph. D., U. Tex., 1953; m. Cecille Marion Levinson, Aug. 14, 1949; children—Marc Alan, Jeannette Ann, Susan Rae. Research scientist def. research lab. U. Tex., Austin, 1950-53; chief nuclear research Gen. Dynamics, Ft. Worth, 1953-63; pres., founder Radiation Research Assos., Inc., Ft. Worth, 1963—. Mem. Am. Phys. Soc., Am. Nuclear Soc. (charter mem. shielding div.). Research in nuclear radiation transport. Office: 3550 Hulen St Ft Worth TX 76107

SCHAEFFER, WENDELL GORDON, educator; b. Waverly, Ill., Nov. 5, 1917; s. Samuel Carlyle and Minnie Pearl (Morton) S.; student Oceanside (Cal.) Jr. Coll., 1935-36; A.A., Bakersfield (Cal.) Jr. Coll., 1937; B.S., U. So. Cal., 1939; M.A., U. Cal., Berkeley, 1946, Ph.D., 1949; m. Luella Pauline Elmes, Nov. 24, 1939; children—Thomas Leslie, Wendy Elizabeth. Investigator, Retail Credit Co., San Francisco, 1939-42; asst. prof. history, polit. sci. U. Fla., 1948-50; publs. dir., hdqrs. supr., chief of party, resident rep. in Burma Pub. Adminstrn. Service, Chgo., 1950-59; asso. prof. pub. affairs, prof. pub., internat. affairs, asst. dean U. Pitts., 1960-63, asso. dean, 1963-66, dean faculties in Ecuador, 1963-66; chmn. dept. govt., also Herman Brown prof. Tex. Christian U., 1969—; pres. Govtl. Affairs Inst., Washington, 1966-69, chmn. bd., 1968-70; cons. AID, 1969-70, UN, 1971-72. Served to 2d lt. USAAF, World War II. Mem. Am. Polit. Sci. Assn., Am. Soc. Pub. Adminstrn., Phi Beta Kappa. Presbyn. Author: (with Donald Worcester) The Growth and Culture of Latin America, 1956, rev. edit., 1970-71; Modernizing Government Revenue Administration, 1961. Home: 3900 Annels Court Fort Worth TX 76109 Office: Tex Christian U Fort Worth TX 76129

SCHAFER, FREDERICK, lawyer; b. Washington, May 21, 1901; s. Frederick and Susan (Barnes) S.; B.S. in Civil Engring., George Washington U., 1925, LL.M., 1951; LL.B., Georgetown U., 1928; m. Isabel Haydn, Sept. 4, 1928; 1 dau., Ann (Mrs. Brooks Dodge). Admitted to D.C. bar, 1928, since practiced Washington; asso. atty. Donovan, Leisure, Newton & Lumbard, 1929-38; lawyer patent div. legal dept. E.I. du Pont de Nemours & Co., 1939-67, mgr. Washington office, 1958-66, Washington patent counsel, 1966-67; cons. asso. atty. McLean, Morton & Boustead, Washington, 1967-70. Served from lt. to lt. comdr., USN, 1943-46, now capt. USNR, ret. Mem. Am., D.C. bar assns., Am. Patent Law Assn., Am. Legion. Clubs: National Press, Army and Navy, Columbia Country, Kenwood Golf and Country. Home: 2912 New Mexico Av NW Washington DC 20016

SCHAFER, GEORGE E., physician, air force officer; b. Cin., 1922; M.D., U. Cin., 1946. Intern, St. Joseph Hosp., Ft. Wayne, Ind., 1946-47; commd. in U.S. Army, 1947, advanced through grades to brig. gen.; trainee Sch. Aviation Medicine, Randolph AFB, Tex., 1947; trainee in preventive medicine and pub. health Nat. Naval Med. Center, Bethesda, Me., 1956; hosp. comdr. 7330th Air Force Hosp., Furstenfeldbruck, Germany, USAF Hosp., Davis-Monthan AFB, Ariz., Air War Coll., Maxwell AFB, Ala., 1962; vice comdr. aerospace med. div. Brooks AFB, Tex., 1965-67, now comdr., also dep. comdr. Mil. Airlift Command; comdr. Sch. Aerospace Medicine, 1967-69; surgeon 7th Air Force, Vietnam, from 1969. Diplomate Am. Bd. Preventive Medicine. Mem. A.M.A., Aerospace Med. Assn., Am. Coll. Preventive Medicine, Assn. Air Force Flight Surgeons. Office: Brooks AFB San Antonio TX 78235*

SCHANDLER, AARON MANEY, food store exec.; b. Asheville, N.C., July 10, 1913; s. David Sigmund and Sarah (Salem) S.; B.A., Asheville-Biltmore Coll., 1932; certificate of registered grocer Nat. Grocers Inst., 1940; m. Shirley Lee Senner, Jan. 1, 1942; children—Roberta Faun (Mrs. Joshua Grossman), Trudy Anne, Linda Jeanne (Mrs. Fred Newman). With Schandler's Pickle Barrell, Asheville, N.C., 1940—, pres., 1948—. Vice pres., dir. Mut. Distbg. Co., Asheville, 1955—. Served from pvt. to lt. col., AUS, 1940-46; ETO; Res. ret. Decorated 3 Battle Stars. Mem. Res. Officers Assn. (pres. West N.C. chpt. 1967), Asheville Jr. C. of C., Gold Nuggett Stock Investment Club (pres. 1966-67). Jewish Religion (bd. dirs. 1964—). Mem. DeMolay Chevalier (mem. ct. 1935—, scribe 1936-40). Home: 285 Macon Av Asheville NC 28807 Office: 50 Broadway Asheville NC 28807

SCHANGER, WILLIAM THOMAS, journalist; b. N.Y.C., Feb. 21, 1919; s. Jacob Jay and Sylvia (Reh) S.; A.A.S. Coll. City N.Y., 1954, N.Y. U., 1942; m. Edith Apfelroth, Feb. 11, 1954 (dec. Nov. 1959). Promotions dir., asst. advt. dir. Ever Ready Label Corp., N.Y.C. also Belleville, N.J., 1949-58; writer-editor Mil. Med. Supply Agy., Bklyn., 1958-59; information specialist N.Y. Naval Shipyard, 1959-61; editor Statis. Summary U.S. Dept. Agr., Washington, 1964-71, contbg. writer Agrl. Situation, 1970—, information specialist, 1962—. Mem. Fed. Editors Assn. Patente-designer Plastolier Reversible Plastic Tables. Home: 5597 Seminary Rd Falls Church VA 22041 Office: South Bldg US Dept Agr Washington DC 20250

SCHARDT, ALOIS WOLFGANG, govt. ofcl.; b. Dresden, Germany, Sept. 15, 1923; s. Alois Jacob and Mary Sophia (Dietrich) S.; student Loyola U., 1941-42; B.S., Cal. Inst. Tech., 1944, Ph.D. magna cum laude, 1951; m. Carla L. Curtis, Apr. 18, 1953; children—James Alois, Bruce Curtis, Mary Martha, Thomas Dorn, Elizabeth Ann. Came to U.S., 1939, naturalized, 1944. Asso. physicist Brookhaven Nat. Lab., Upton, N.Y., 1950-54; staff physicist, Los Alamos Sci. Lab., N.M., 1954-61; chief High Altitude Test Detection, ARPA, Office of Sec. Def., Washington, 1961-63, dep. dir. Nuclear Test Detection, 1963; chief particles and fields NASA Hdq., Washington, 1963-70, dep. dir. physics and astronomy, 1970—. Served with AUS, 1944-46. Mem. Am. Phys. Soc., Am. Geophys. Union, Am. Astron. Soc., Fed. Exec. Inst., A.A.A.S., Sigma Xi, Tau Beta Phi. Roman Catholic. Research in nuclear reactions and radio activity. Contbr. articles in field to profl. jours. Home: 926 Woburn Court McLean VA 22101 Office: 400 Maryland Av Washington DC 20546

SCHARLAU, CHARLES EDWARD, gas co. exec.; b. Chgo., Apr. 24, 1927; s. Charles Edward and Esther (Powell) S.; J.D., U. Ark., 1951; m. Clydene Yi Sloop, Aug. 17, 1960; children—Charles Edward IV, Martha Iva, Caryn Lyn, Robin Rai, Greg Scott. Admitted to Ark. bar, 1951; gen. atty. Ark. Western Gas Co., Fayetteville, 1951-59, asst. sec.-asst. treas., 1959-66, v.p., 1966-67, exec. v.p., 1967-68, pres., 1968—. Mem. State Council on Econ. Edn., 1970-72; mem. State Econ. Expansion Study Commn., 1969—; mem. U. Ark. Devel. Council, 1969-72; mem. adv. council U. Ark. Bus. Sch., 1970-71. Served with USMCR, 1945-46. Mem. So. Gas Assn., Ark. Bar Assn. (officer mineral law sect. 1967-68), Ark. State (dir. 1970-71), Fayetteville (pres. 1967-68) chambers commerce, U. Ark. Alumni Assn. Methodist (bd. stewards 1970-71). Home: 410 Oliver St Fayetteville AR 72701 Office: 28 E Center St Fayetteville AR 72701

SCHATZ, CLARENCE FRANCIS, JR., dentist; b. Washington, Oct. 29, 1924; s. Clarence Francis and Goldie Aileen (Alley) S.; student Eastern Ky. State U., 1943, George Washington U., 1946-47; D.D.S., Georgetown U., 1951; m. Nancy Mae Price, Aug. 20, 1966. Pvt. practice dentistry, Washington, 1951—. Asst. prof. Georgetown U. Sch. Dentistry, 1951-60. Served with AUS, 1943-46; ETO. Mem. Acad. Gen. Dentistry, Am. Dental Assn., So. Md., D.C. dental socs., Sigma Chi, Psi Omega, Omicron Kappa Upsilon. Republican. Presbyn. Kiwanian. Clubs: Kenwood Golf and Country (Bethesda, Md.); Corinthian Yacht (trustee Washington). Home: 530 N St SW Washington DC 20024 Office: 4704 Wisconsin Av NW Washington DC 20016

SCHATZMAN, JOHN RING, constrn. co. exec.; b. St. Louis, Apr. 13, 1941; s. Thomas Francis and Jane (Ring) S.; B.A. in Journalism, N.M. State U., 1963; m. Dorothy McNamee Ainsa, June 5, 1963; children—Mary Evelyn, Laurie Jane, John Ring. Jr. partner Image Homes, Inc., and Bonded Homes, Inc., El Paso, Tex., 1965-69; pres. Serenada Homes, Inc., El Paso, 1969—; pres., owner Blue Dolphin Swim Club, El Paso, 1965—; pres., partner H & S Gen. Contractors, El Paso, 1971—. Vice pres. East Valley Y Mens' Club, 1971; mem. Tex. Spl. Adv. Council on Housing. Bd. dirs. East Valley YMCA. Mem. El Paso Assn. Builders (pres.), El Paso Bd. Realtors, Blue Key, Sigma Alpha Epsilon. Roman Catholic. Office: 3711 Admiral El Paso TX 79925

SCHAUBEL, HOWARD JAMES, surgeon; b. Grand Rapids, Mich., May 20, 1916; s. Charles Theodore and Jennie (Slager) S.; Asso. Sci., Grand Rapids Jr. Coll., 1936; A.B., Hope Coll., 1938; M.D., U. Mich., 1942; certificate orthopedics Duke, 1946; m. Marjorie Faye Moody, June 19, 1943; children—Candice (Mrs. James M. Edwards), Janis (Mrs. Robert C. Timmons), Wendy, Gayla Sue. Intern, Duke Hosp., Durham, N.C., 1942-43; resident N.C. Orthopedic Hosp., Gastonia, 1943-44, Duke Hosp., 1944-46; sr. orthopedic surgeon Butterworth, St. Mary's, Ferguson, Sunshine hosps., Grand Rapids, 1951—, Mary Free Bed Vocational Instn., Grand Rapids, 1951—; chief clin. surgeon Saladin Shrine Crippled Children's Unit, Grand Rapids, 1950—; cons. Holland (Mich.) Municipal, North Ottawa Community, Zeeland Community, Pennock, Ionia Meml., Greenville Meml., Kelsey hosps.; corporate practice orthopedic surgery, Key West and Marathon, Fla., 1970—; sr. orthopedic surgeon Lower Keys Community Hosp., Key West, Fisherman's Hosp., Marathon, 1970—; instr. orthopedic surgery Duke, Lower Keys C. of C., 1969—. Bd. dirs. Camp Blodgett, Grand Rapids, v.p., 1972. Served to maj. M.C., AUS, 1954. Diplomate Am. Bd. Orthopedic Surgery. Fellow Internat. Coll. Surgeons; mem. Eastern, Fla., Piedmont orthopaedic socs., Blue Key, Phi Rho Sigma. Mason (Shriner, Jester). Clubs: Spring Lake Country (Mich.); Key West Country. Contbr. articles to med. jours. Home: Whispering Pines Big Pine Key FL 33043 also 10843 Lake Shore Dr West Olive MI 49460 Office: 124 E Fulton St Grand Rapids MI 49502 also 638 United St Key West FL 33040

SCHEB, JOHN MALCOLM, lawyer; b. Orlando, Fla., Apr. 25, 1926; s. Francis J. and Mary (Ruppert) S.; J.D., U. Fla., 1950; m. Mary Burns, Apr. 5, 1953; children—Dianne, John M. II, Robert Paul. Admitted to Fla. bar, 1950; practiced in Sarasota, Fla., 1950—; mem. firm Wood, Scheb, Whitesell, Drymon & Warren, 1969—. Asso. municipal judge, Sarasota, Fla., 1957-59, city atty., 1959-70. Served with USAAF, 1944-46. Mem. Sarasota County Bar Assn. (pres. 1966), Phi Alpha Delta, Lambda Chi Alpha. Kiwanian (pres. 1963). Home: 1700 Cunliff Lane Sarasota FL 33579 Office: 2187 Siesta Dr PO Box 15425 Sarasota FL 33579

SCHEELE, CARL HARRY, govt. ofcl.; b. Cleve., June 19, 1928; s. Carl August and Frances Jane (Standring) S.; grad. Cleve. Inst. Art, 1952; B.F.A., U. Ill., 1954; M.A. in History, Western Res. U., 1957; m. Joanne Bales Brewer, June 21, 1954; children—Martha Anne, August Kurt. Comml. artist, Cleve., 1946-48; tchr., pub. schs., Cleve., 1957-59; asst. curator div. postal history Smithsonian Instn., Washington, 1959-63, asso. curator, 1963-70, curator in charge div., 1970-71, chmn. dept. applied arts, 1969-71; dir. Nat. Mus. History & Tech., Washington, 1971—. Served with AUS, 1954-56. Mem. Am. Hist. Soc., Postal History Soc. Ams., Am. Philatelic Congress, Am. Acad. Philately, Am. Philatelic Soc., Soc. Philatelic Ams., Am. Air Mail Soc. Author: A Short History of the Mail Service, 1970; Neither Snow Nor Rain..., 1970; also numerous articles. Home: 3541 Ordway NW Washington DC 20016 Office: 12th & Constitution Av Washington DC 20560

SCHEER, LEO S., condr., music educator; b. Jersey City, Oct. 2, 1909; s. Jonas Maurice and Amelia (Luft) S.; student San Diego State Coll., 1936-37, Inst. Mus. Art, 1929-30; grad. with honors U.S. Naval Sch. Music, 1931; pvt. study with Pierre Monteux, Arnold Schoenberg, Naoum Blinder; m. Ruth Helen Jenner, Nov. 18, 1934; children—Antoinette Ruth (Mrs. Harry Robert Stowe), David Leon, Rosalind Jenner (Mrs. Godfrey David Carvan John). Tchr. instrumental music San Diego County schs., 1935-45; condr. Fed. Symphony, San Diego, 1938-41; asso. condr. San Diego Symphony, 1940-43; founder, condr. San Diego Youth Symphony, 1944-52; asso. condr. San Diego Civil Light Opera Co., 1944-50; condr. Eagle Rock Civic Symphony, Los Angeles, 1951-52; faculty Los Angeles Conservatory, 1947-52; music dir. Uniao Cultural Brasil-Estados Unidos, Sao Paulo, Brazil, 1953-55; asst. condr. Kansas City Philharmonic, 1955-56; music ednl. dir. Jenkins Music Co., Kansas City, 1956-60; founder, condr. Kansas City Youth Orch., 1958-60; condr. Abilene Philharmonic, 1960-65; condr., artist in residence Hardin-Simmons U., Abilene, Tex., 1963-65; music dir., condr. Lexington (Ky.) Philharmonic, 1965-71; asst. prof. music U. Ky., Lexington, 1965-71. Served with USN, 1931-35. Recipient nat. award for composition Composer's Press, 1944; citizen's award for youth symphony work, San Diego, 1952. Mem. Am. Fedn. Musicians, Nat. Assn. Am. Composers and Condrs., Nat. Soc. Arts and Letters (hon.), Rotary Internat., Phi Mu Alpha. Christian Scientist. Author: Scheer Violin Method, 3 vols., 1945. Composer: Lament for English horn and piano, 1944. Home: 136 N Peterson Av Louisville KY 40206 Office: Starks Bldg Louisville KY 40202

SCHEINBERG, PERITZ, physician; b. Miami, Fla., Dec. 21, 1920; s. Mendel S. and Esther (Asch) S.; A.B., Emory U., 1941, M.D., 1944; m. Chantal D'Adesky; children—Philip Asch, Richard David. Intern, Grady Meml. Hosp., Atlanta, 1944-45, resident, 1946-47; resident Duke, 1947-48; practice medicine, specializing in neurology, Miami, Fla.; instr. Duke U. Med. Sch., 1949-50; asst. prof., dept. physiology U. Miami Med. Sch., 1950-53, asso. prof. neurology, 1955-60, prof., chmn. dept. neurology, 1962—. Served to lt. M.C., USNR, 1945-46; served as lt. M.C., USNR, 1953-55. Diplomate Am. Bd. Internal Medicine, Am. Bd. Neurology. Fellow A.C.P., Am. Acad. Neurology. Home: 3329 Flamingo Dr Miami Beach FL 33140 Office: Dept Neurology U Miami Med Sch Miami FL 33152

SCHELEEN, JOSEPH CARL, pub. co. exec.; b. Newark, Aug. 12, 1904; s. Carl Algot and Mathilda (Anderson) S.; B.S. in Journalism, Butler U., 1928; m. Alice DeVol Phillips, Nov. 28, 1931; 1 dau., Sarah (Mrs. Linton E. Kilmon, Jr.). Reporter, Shelbyville (Ind.) Republican, 1928-30, city editor, 1931-36, 1938-40; asst. mgr. Indpls. Better Bus. Bur., 1937; reporter Traffic World, Washington, 1940-48, chief news bur., 1948-51, mng. editor, 1952-53, editorial dir., 1954-55; editor, 1956—; v.p. Traffic Service Corp, Traffic World, 1957—. Mem. adv. com. transp. studies Am. U., Washington, 1955—. Mem. Am. Soc. Traffic and Transp., Delta Nu Alpha, Delta Tau Delta, Sigma Delta Chi. Clubs: Nat. Press., University, Nat. Aviation (Washington). Presbyn. Home: 3211 Old Dominion Blvd Alexandria VA 22305 Office: Washington Bldg Washington DC 20005

SCHELHORN, FREDERICK BERNARD, pulp and paper co. exec.; b. Phila., Aug. 10, 1918; s. Frederick G. and Dora A. (Heil) S.; B.S. in Chem. Engring., U. Pa., 1939; M.S., Inst. Paper Chemistry, 1941, Ph.D., 1943; postgrad. Harvard, 1958; m. Amalia Griebenow, May 15, 1943; children—Mary Anne, Frederick Paul, Peter John, Jean Ellen, Amalia Jane. Gen. supt. paper div. Brown Co., Berlin, N.H., 1943-44, 46-53; tech. supt. Nat. Container Corp., Valdosta, Ga., 1953-54, v.p. mfg., Jacksonville, Fla., 1954-56; v.p. research and engring. Owens-Ill., Inc., Toledo, 1956-63; with Tenn. River Pulp & Paper Co., Counce, 1963—, pres., 1967—. Bd. dirs. Hardin County Library, Hardin County United Fund. Vice pres. Pulp and Paper Found. N.C. State U., Raleigh, 1969-71, pres., 1971—. Served to lt. (j.g.) USNR, 1944-46. Mem. Am. (trustee), So. (pres. 1969-70) Forest insts., So. Pulpwood Conservation Assn. (v.p. 1968-69), Tenn. Mfrs. Assn. (bd. govs.), T.A.P.P.I., Paper Industry Mfg. Assn. Episcopalian. Mason (32 deg.). Club: Athletic (Memphis). Patentee method for making heavy gauge plastic sheets, 1967. Home: 1104 Cedar St Savannah TN 38372 Office: PO Box 33 Counce TN 38326

SCHELLSTEDE, ELOISE JEANNETTE, artist; b. Tulsa, Sept. 11, 1918; d. Delmer Robert and Carrol (Rouse) Rees; B.A., Tulsa U., 1939; m. John E. Schellstede, Nov. 30, 1940; children—John Robert, Richard Lee. Co-owner D.R. Rees & Co. Ins. Agy., Tulsa, 1939—; instr. art, 1939—; exhibited numerous one-man shows including YMCA, various chs., clubs, 1963—; exhibited group shows including Mayo Hotel, Oliver Bldg., Gilcrease Mus. (Tulsa), Coll. Union, Tahlequah, Okla., Shangri-la Lodge on Grand Lake, Afton, Okla., Kerr Mus., Poteau, Okla.; owner Gallery of Fine Art, Tulsa, 1970—; mem. Gilcrease Mus.; Philbrook Art Center; represented in Kerr Mus., in permanent collections. Mem. Green Country Art Assn. (founder), D.A.R., Okla. Heritage Assn., Tulsa County Hist. Soc., Kappa Delta. Presbyn. Club: Soroptimist. Home: 6254 S Utica St Tulsa OK 74135 Office: 1307 S Main St Tulsa OK 74119

SCHEMAN, L. RONALD, internat. finance co. exec.; b. Bklyn., Aug. 9, 1931; s. Mac and Eleanor (Minkowitz) S.; B.A., with distinction cum laude (Rufus Choate scholar), Dartmouth, 1953; J.D., Yale, 1956; m. Ethel Goldman, June 5, 1955; children—Ann, Corinne, Jennifer, Daniel. Admitted to N.Y. bar, 1956; practiced law, Hartford, Conn., 1957, N.Y.C., 1958-59; Inter-Am. Cultural Conv. fellow, Brazil, 1960-61; atty. dept. legal affairs OAS, Washington, 1961-64, planning officer, 1968-70; secretariat Inter-Am. Commn. on Human Rights, 1961-64; exec. dir. Pan Am. Devel. Found., 1964-68; pres. Porter Internat. Co., Washington, 1970—; exec. v.p., dir. Intercomp, S.A., 1971—. Asst. treas. Inter-Am. Bar Found., 1967—. Trustee Pan Am. Devel. Found., v.p., 1968—; bd. dirs. Nat. Child Research Center, Tools for Freedom Found., 1965, Inter-Am. Literacy Found. Recipient Order Bernardo O'Higgins, Govt. Chile, 1967. Mem. Soc. for Internat. Devel., Inter Am. Bar Assn., Washington Fgn. Law Soc. (bd. govs. 1964-67, pres.), Am. Fgn. Law Assn. (v.p. 1971), Phi Beta Kappa. Author: Foundations of Freedom, 1966. Contbr. articles to profl. jours. Home: 3322 Newark St NW Washington DC 20008 Office: 1776 K St NW Washington DC 20006

SCHENCK, ARTHUR CARL, constrn. co. exec.; b. Phila., July 31, 1910; s. Rev. Dr. A. Clarence and Hattie Olive (Ritter) S.; B.S., U. Ala., 1934; m. Eloise Elena Williams, July 6, 1934; children—Nancy Elizabeth (Mrs. Robert Edward Smith), Jean Gray (Mrs. Richard George Rice). Field and resident engr. Stone & Webster Engring. Corp., 1934, 1936-42; engr. Stone & Webster Engring. Corp., 1934, 1936-42; insp. U.S. C.E., Phila., 1935-36; v.p. Carpenter Constrn. Co., Inc., Norfolk, Va., 1942-63; prin., A. Carl Schenck & Assos., constrn. mgmt. & engring. cons., 1963—. Mem. Bd. Review Real Estate Assessments; mem. Va. Airports Authority. Mem. Engring. Com. Devel. Council, U. Ala., 1958-62. Exec. council Tidewater chpt. Boy Scouts Am. Chmn. DePaul lay adv. bd.; mem. Citizens Adv. Com. Norfolk, 1965-68; mem. adv. council Norfolk Area Med. Center Authority. Mem. Va. Soc. Profl. Engrs., Asso. Gen. Contractors Am. (pres. Va. br. 1962), Builders and Contractors Exchange (past dir.), Am. Arbitration Assn., Tau Beta Pi, Theta Tau, Chi Beta Phi. Lutheran Clubs: Engineers (Hampton Roads); Kiwanis (pres. 1966), Virginia (Norfolk); Cedar Point Country, Harbor. Home: 5601 Huntington Pl Norfolk VA 23509 Office: PO Box 7097 Norfolk VA 23509

SCHENCK, HERBERT HOLTZCLAW, corp. exec., engr.; b. Chattanooga, June 11, 1911; s. Charles Herbert and Virginia Pauline (Dicks) S.; B.S., U. Tenn., 1935; m. Norma McLeod, 1946; 1 son, Anthony Norman. Elec. engr. Tenn. Elec. Power Co., 1934-39; communications engr. So. Bell Tel. Co., Atlanta, 1939-45; radio engr. Internat. Tel. & Tel. Corp., N.Y.C. and Havana, 1945-47; v.p., gen. mgr., dir. Radio Corp. of Cuba, 1947-49; v.p., gen. plant mgr. Cuban Tel. Co., 1949-50; mng. dir., dir. Cia. Radio Internacional do Brasil, Rio de Janeiro, 1950-57; v.p., dir. Standard Electrica, 1953-57; dir. Cia. Telefonica Nacional, 1955-57; v.p., dir. engring. Page Communications Engrs., Inc. (subsidiary Northrop Corp.), Washington, 1958-60; exec. v.p., gen. mgr. U.S. Underseas Cable Corp. 1960-70, pres., 1970—. Served with Signal Corps, AUS, 1941-46; with G.H.Q., S.W. Pacific Area in Australia, New Guinea, P.I., Japan. Decorated Legion of Merit, Philippine Liberation medal. Registered profl. engr., Md. Sr. mem. I.E.E.E.; mem. Armed Forces Communications and Electronics Assn., Am. C. of C. of Rio de Janeiro (past dir. and sec.), U.S. Naval Inst. Clubs: George Town, Internat. (Washington). Editor, pub. Underseas Cable World, 1966-70. Home: 4935 Crescent St Chevy Chase MD 20016 Office: 5454 Wisconsin Av Washington DC 20015

SCHENKER, TILLIE ABRAMSON, librarian; b. Baton Rouge, Nov. 12, 1910; d. Abraham and Matilde (Mendelsohn) Abramson; B.S., La. State U., 1930, B.S. in L.A., 1934; m. Michael Max Schenker, Mar. 31, 1940 (dec. 1953). Field worker circulation dept. La. State Library, 1934-39; asst. librarian E. Baton Rouge Parish Library, 1939-46, librarian, 1947—. Bd. dirs. Community Services Council, 1957-63, Baton Rouge Area Tb Assn., 1960—, Baton Rouge Guidance Center, 1962-63, Family Counseling Service, 1957-60, Mem. Am., La. (pres. 1962-63), Southwestern library assns., La. Adult Edn. Assn. Jewish religion (bd. dirs. synagogue 1953-65). Club: Baton Rouge Library. Home: 220 Steele Blvd Baton Rouge LA 70806 Office: 700 Laurel St Baton Rouge LA 70802

SCHEPPEGRELL, CERIL SOLON, dentist; b. New Orleans, July 29, 1911; s. George Henry and Lily Louise (Wuertz) S.; student Tulane U., 1931, 32, La. State U., 1932-33; D.D.S., Loyola U. of the South, 1939; m. Virginia Mary Kepper, Jan. 27, 1940; children—John Ceril, Elizabeth Mary, June Marie, George William, Virginia Mary, Ann (Mrs. Earl Joseph Parr), Stewart James. Intern, U.S. Marine Hosp., New Orleans, 1939-40; served as lt. comdr. USPHS, 1940-47; pvt. practice dentistry, New Orleans, 1947—. Instr. crown and bridgework Loyola Dental Sch., 1946-47. Mem. Cath. Alumni Soc. Loyola U. (pres. 1951-61). Clubs: Paul Morphy Chess (mem. bd. govs.), Exchange (pres. 1960-61) (New Orleans); Green Acres Country (Metairie, La.). Home: 2008 Colony Rd Metairie LA 70003 Office: Hibernia Bank Bldg New Orleans LA 70112

SCHEPS, CLARENCE, univ. adminstr.; b. Houston, Jan. 16, 1915; s. Benjamin and Libby (Solman) S.; B.A., Rice Inst., 1935; M.S., Columbia, 1936; Ph.D., La. State U., 1943; m. Mary E. Brown, Aug. 28, 1939; children—Philip, Edward. Instr. accounting La. State U., 1936-41; supr. finance La. Dept. Edn., 1941-46; comptroller U. Miss., 1946-47; exec. asst. to pres. Tulane U., 1947-48, comptroller, 1948-57, v.p., comptroller, 1957-66, exec. v.p., 1966—. Dir. Internat. City Bank New Orleans. Gen. chmn. United Fund Campaign Greater New Orleans, 1958; chmn. New Orleans A.R.C., 1966-68; mem. bd., exec. council Internat. House, New Orleans; pres. Southeastern La. Girl Scout Council, 1962-65. Mem. Orleans Parish Sch. Bd., 1950-56, pres., 1952-55. Mem. Nat. Assn. Coll. and Univ. Bus. Officers (pres. 1965-67), Nat. Fedn. Coll. and Univ. Bus. Officer Assns. (exec. com. 1959, dir. 1952-68), Controller's Inst., So. Assn. Coll. and Univ. Bus. Officers (pres. 1959-60, Sec. 1961-65). Author: Accounting for Colleges and Universities, 1949, rev. edit., 1971. Home: 6321 Freret St New Orleans LA 70118

SCHERER, CLARENCE HENRY, city ofcl.; b. Timber Lake, S.D., Apr. 21, 1926; s. Clement and Anna (Kamperschroer) S.; B.S., St. John's U. (Collegeville, Minn.), 1950; M.S., Trinity U., 1953; m. Eoline G. Jordan, Dec. 2, 1947; children—Andrew, Bonnie (Mrs. Harrel Alcorn), Mary, Susan, David, Theresa. Chemist, City San Antonio, 1950; dir. research Tex. State Health Dept., Donna, Tex., 1951-52; research scientist U. Tex., Austin, 1953; supt. water supply treatment and reclamation City Amarillo, Tex., 1954—. Owner, cons. water and wastewater Chemlab. Service of Amarillo, 1960—. Vice chmn. environmental com. Panhandle Regional Planning Commn., 1970—; mem. water quality monitoring com. Canadian River Water Authority, 1969—; mem. Tex. Bd. Water and Waste Water Certification, 1972—. Served with Paratroops, AUS, 1945-47. Mem. Tex. Water Utilities Assn. (past v.p. various coms.), Water Pollution Control Fedn. (George B. Gascoigne award 1953, 71, William D. Hatfield award 1970), Am. Water Works Assn., Am. Pub. Works Assn. Republican. Roman Catholic. K.C. Author: (with others) Manual for Sewage Plant Operators, 1964; (with others) Manual for Wastewater Operations. Home: 7202 Applewood St Amarillo TX 79108 Office: PO Box 1971 Amarillo TX 79105

SCHERER, LESTER EUGENE, county govt ofcl.; b. St. Augustine, Fla., Dec. 16, 1937; s. Alvin Whitney and Meta (Price) S.; B.S. in Agr., U. Fla., 1961, M.S., 1963; m. Anne Mason, June 9, 1962; children—Gregory, Scott, Clay. Research asst. U. Fla., Gainsville, 1960-61; research asst. U.S. Dept. Agr., Gainesville, 1961-63; asst. dir. Palm Beach County Mosquito Control Bd., Stuart, Fla., 1963-68; dir. Martin County Mosquito Control, Stuart, 1968—. Tchr. adult edn. courses Martin County, 1969—. Pres. Civitan Club, Stuart, 1970—. Recipient Distinguished Service award Jr. C. of C., 1970. Mem. Am., Fla. Entomol. socs., Am. Mosquito Control Assn., Hyacinth Control Soc., Audubon Soc. Martin County. Home: 1024 E 5th St Stuart FL 33494 Office: 2280 S Dixie Hwy Stuart FL 33494

SCHERER, PAUL CLARENCE, lawyer; b. Evansville, Ind., Mar. 5, 1926; s. Paul Carl and Mildred (Rowe) S.; B.B.A., U. Tex., 1949, LL.B., 1949; m. LaNoe Fenner, July 28, 1949; children—Michael, Leta, Jane. Admitted to Tex. bar, 1948; asso. firm Peareson & Peareson, Richmond, 1949-51; partner firm Peareson, Scherer, Roberts & Slone, Richmond, Tex., 1952—. Dir. Sugar Land State Bank (Tex.), Gulf Coast Savs. & Loans Assn., Richmond. Atty., City of Richmond, 1949—. Trustee Lamar Consol. Sch. Dist., 1955—. Served with AAC, 1944-45. Mem. Am., Tex., Fort Bend County bar assns., Phi Delta Phi., Am. Legion. Methodist (trustee). Rotarian. Home: 915 Foster St Richmond TX 77469 Office: 210 3d St Richmond TX 77469

SCHERMBECK, CLARENCE EDWARD, govt. ofcl.; b. Leavenworth, Kan., Apr. 22, 1922; s. Edward Fredrick and Helen (White) S.; student Kan. State Coll., 1940-41; B.A., Tex. Christian U., 1948, M.A., 1951; m. Venicia Guajardo, May 20, 1967; children—Barbara Gwynn, James Edward. Tchr. social sci. Crane (Tex.) Pub. Schs., 1951-52; research asst. Kan. Legislative Council, 1952-53; research asso. Inst. Pub. Affairs, U. Tex., 1955-57; with Urban Renewal Adminstrn, Dept. Housing and Urban Devel., Ft. Worth, 1957—, area coordinator Colo., Kan., Okla., Region V, 1967-70, program mgr. Oklahoma City area office, 1970—. Served with USAAF, 1942-45. Mem. Am. Polit. Sci. Assn., Common Cuase, Pi Sigma Alpha. Author: Parking Traffic and Transportation in Texas Cities, 1956; Urban Renewal for Texas, 1957. Contbr. articles profl. jours. Home: 5952 NW 71st St Oklahoma City OK 73132 Office: 301 N Hudson Oklahoma City OK 73102

SCHERPEREEL, RICHARD CHARLES, educator; b. Mishawaka, Ind., Dec. 1, 1931; s. Charles Alfonse and Alice Maria (Van Wynsberghe) S.; B.F.A., U. Notre Dame, 1955, M.F.A., 1962; M.Ed., McMurry Coll., 1959; Ed.D., George Peabody Coll for Tchrs., 1966; m. Sara Marie Brogan, Aug. 30, 1958; children—Charles Damian, Sean Richard. Tchr. art Irving (Tex.) Ind. Sch. Dist., 1959, Elkhart (Ind.) Schs., 1960-62; chmn. art dept. Bloomsburg (Pa.) State Coll., 1964-67, Tex. A. and I. U., Kingsville, Tex., 1968—. Exhibited in one-man show Art Mus. S. Tex., 1970 (Found. Purchase prize). Served with USAF, 1955-58. Mem. Coll. Art Assn., Nat., Tex. art edn. assns., Art Mus. S. Tex., S. Tex. Art League, Tex. Fine Arts Assn. Rotarian. Home: 1213 Santa Gertrudis Kingsville TX 78363

SCHERTZ, WALTER ARTHUR, city ofcl.; b. Schertz, Tex., Feb. 17, 1920; s. Walter Joseph and Alma Ida (Wuest) S.; student Draughons Bus. Coll., 1936-40; real estate certificate St. Mary's U., 1965; m. Lula Mae Gottschall, June 2, 1953. Water supt., part owner Schertz Water Works, Inc., 1941-63; Councilman City of Schertz, 1958-63; water supt., 1963-65; exec. dir. Urban Renewal Agy., Schertz, 1965—; chmn. bd. Randolph Field Nat. Bank, Universal City, Tex. Sec., Tex. Urban Renewal Assn., 1970-71, Green Valley Devel. Co., Inc., 1964—, Lone Oak Home Builders, Inc., 1968—. Served with USAAF, 1941-46. Mem. V.F.W., C. of C. (dir.). Methodist. Lion. Home: PO Box 386 321 Main St Schertz TX 78154 Office: 507 Main St Schertz TX 78154

SCHEVING, LAWRENCE EINAR, educator; b. Hensel, N.D., Oct. 20, 1920; s. Einar L. and Mary (Brown) S.; B.S. in Biology, DePaul U., 1949, M.S. in Zoology, 1950; Ph.D., Loyola U., Chgo., 1957; m. Virginia M. Krumdick, Aug. 6, 1949; children—Lawrence, Mary, John, Gennifer, Patricia (dec.). Mem. faculty Lewis Coll., Lockport, Ill., 1950-57, successively instr., asst. prof., asso. prof. and head dept. biol. sci. 1950-57; prof. anatomy Chgo. Med. Sch., 1957-67, La. State U. Med. Sch., New Orleans, 1967-70; prof. anatomy U. Ark. Med. Sch., Little Rock, 1970—. Served to capt. AUS, 1940-45. Decorated Bronze Star medal; recipient Research award, Chgo. Med. Sch. Bd. Dirs., 1962; named Prof. Year, Student Council Chgo. Med. Sch., 1964; recipient Golden Apple award student body U. Ark. Med. Sch., 1972. Mem. Am. Soc. Anatomists, Am. Soc. Zoologists, Internat. Soc. Electro-Myographic Kinesiologists, Internat. Soc. Chronobiology (sec.-treas.), So. Assn. Anatomists (councillor), Sigma Xi. Contbr. chpts. to books, articles in field of chronobiology and other biol. areas to profl. jours. Editorial bd. Chronobiology. Home: 1 Redcoat Lane Little Rock AR 72207

SCHEWEL, ELLIOT SIDNEY, furniture retail chain exec.; b. Lynchburg, Va., June 20, 1924; s. Abraham Moses and Anna (Temko) S.; B.S. in Econs., Washington and Lee U., 1948; m. Rosel H. Hoffberger, June 12, 1949; children—Stephen, Michael, Susan. With Schewel Furniture Co., Lynchburg, 1948—, v.p., 1960—; founding dir. Jefferson Nat. Bank; pres. Elro Investment Co., 1965; v.p. Mchts. Realty Corp., 1971—, Gen. Investment Co., 1967—; sec. Abbe Devel. Co., 1962— (all Lynchburg). Chmn., A.R.C., Lynchburg, 1954, United Negro Coll. Fund, 1964-66; vice chmn. Va.

AntipDefamation League, 1958-61; mem. United Jewish Appeal Young Leadership Cabinet, 1964-67; mem. pres.'s adv. council Lynchburg Coll., 1967—, chmn. Lynchburg Coll. Assos., 1968—; pres. Lynchburg Area Devel. Corp., 1970—. Mem. Lychburg City Council, 1965-69. Trustee Randolph Macon Women's Coll., Lynchburg. Recipient Outstanding Young Man Year award Lynchburg Jr. C. of C., 1952; Distinguished Service award Phi Epsilon Pi, 1955. Served with USAAF, 1943-46. Mem. Isaiah 58:12 Corp. (founder, dir.). Jewish religion. Mason; mem. B'nai B'rith. Clubs: Boonsboro Country, Oakwood Country. Home: 4316 Gorman Dr Lynchburg VA 24503 Office: 1031 Main St Lynchburg VA 24504

SCHEXNAYDER, MAURICE, bishop; b. Wallace, La., Aug. 13, 1895; s. Adam and Jeanne Marie (Dutreix) S.; student Chenet Inst., 1909-12, St. Joseph Sem., 1916-19; B.A., St. Mary's Sem., 1920, M.A., 1921; S.T.B., North Am. Coll., Rome, Italy, 1921, S.T.L., 1924. Ordained priest Roman Cath. Ch., 1925; asst. pastor St. John Evangelist, Plaquemine, La., 1925-29; chaplain La. State U., 1929-46; pastor St. Francis de Sales Ch., Houma, La., 1946-51, St. Michael's Ch., Crowley, La., 1951-56; made domestic prelate by Pope Pius XII, May 1947; titular bishop of Tuscamia, aux. to bishop of Lafayette, La., 1951-56; consecrated bishop, Lafayette, 1956—; Episcopal Moderator Newman Clubs in U.S., 1953-60. Mem. La. Hist. Soc., Inst. Francais of Washington, Omicron Delta Kappa, Theta Kappa Phi. K.C. (state chaplain 1932-44). Address: Bishop's House Lafayette LA 70501

SCHICK, FRANK LEOPOLD, librarian; b. Vienna, Austria, Feb. 4, 1918 (came to U.S. 1938, naturalized 1943); s. Egon and Anna (Lapper) S.; B.A., Wayne State U., 1946; B.L.S., M.A., U. Chgo., 1948; M.L.S., U. Mich., 1955, Ph.D., 1957; m. Renee Silberfeld, Aug. 9, 1938; children—Thomas Egon, James Benjamin, Ellen Diane. Jr. asst. librarian Wayne State U., Detroit, 1948-54, asst. librarian, 1955-58; lectr. U. Mich., 1951-54, 55-58; asst. to dean Columbia U., N.Y.C., 1954-55; coordinator adult edn. and library statistics, asst. dir. library services br. U.S. Office Edn., Washington, 1958-66, chief library surveys br. Nat. Center for Ednl. Statistics, 1971—; dir., prof. Sch. Library and Information Sci., U. Wis. at Milw., 1966-71; vis. prof. U. N.C., 1962, 64. Rapporteur, UNESCO Conf. on Pub. Statistics, Paris, 1964, pres. UNESCO Conf. on Library Statistics, Paris, 1970; pres. Internat. Library Statistics Conf., The Hague, Netherlands, 1966, Prague, Czechoslovakia, 1971. Guest lectr. West German library schs., 1967; cons. Israel libraries, 1968; chmn. library statistics com., tech. com. 46, Internat. Orgn. for Standardization, Berlin, 1964—. Served with AUS, 1943-45. Mem. A.L.A. (chmn. library edn. legislation com., statistics coordinating com.; mem. council), Internat. Fedn. Library Assns. (chmn. library a statistics and standard com. 1972—), Spl. Libraries Assn. (chmn. documentation group Washington chpt.), Am. Nat. Standards Inst. (chmn. library statistics subcom.). Author: The Paperbound Book in America, 1958. Editor: Trends in Am. Book Publishing, 1958; The Future of Library Service, 1959; North Am. Library Edn. Directory and Statistics, 1966-68, 69-71; Survey of Spl. Libraries Serving the Fed. Govt., 1968; Directory of Health Scis. Libraries U.S., 1969; Bowker Ann., 1969, 70, 71, 72. Contbr. over 100 articles to profl. jours. Home: 2809 Blazer Ct Silver Spring MD 20906 Office: 400 Maryland Av SW Washington DC 20202

SCHIFF, FRANK WILLIAM, economist; b. Greifswald, Germany, July 15, 1921; s. Fritz and Hildegarde (Caro) S.; came to U.S., 1936, naturalized, 1944; A.B., Columbia, 1942, postgrad., 1946-49 Instr. econs. Columbia, 1946-51; with Fed. Res. Bank N.Y., 1951-64; sr. staff economist Pres.'s Council Econ. Advisers, 1964-68; dep. undersec. monetary affairs U.S. Treasury, 1968-69; v.p., chief economist Com. for Econ. Devel., Washington, 1969—. Adviser, Nat. Bank Vietnam, 1955, 57; chief finance div. U.S. AID Mission, Saigon, 1955. Chmn., Downtown Economists Luncheon Group, N.Y.C., 1961-63. Served with AUS, 1943-45; ETO. Decorated Bronze Star. Mem. Council Fgn. Relations, Am. Econ. Assn.; Phi Beta Kappa. Home: 1330 New Hampshire Av NW Washington DC 20036 Office: 1000 Connecticut Av NW Washington DC 20036

SCHIFFER, GEORGE PHILIP, JR., steel mfg. co. exec.; b. Covington, Ky., Oct. 17, 1930; s. George Philip and Nancy Durant (Smith) S.; B.Indsl. Mgmt., U. Cin., 1963; M.B.A., Xavier U., 1970. Estimator, Cin. Cleaning & Finishing Machinery Co., Sharonville, O., 1955-56; designer Acme Newport Steel Co. (now Interlake Inc.), Newport, Ky., 1957-64, mech. engr. Interlake, Inc., 1965-69, environmental control engr., 1970—. Scoutmaster, Dan Beard council Boy Scouts Am., 1964—, explorer adviser, 1971—. Served with Signal Corps, AUS, 1953-55. Registered profl. engr., Ky. Mem. Nat., Ky., No. Ky. socs. profl. engrs. Presbyn. (elder, ch. sch. supt. 1960—, vocational guidance coordinator). Mason (32 deg.). Home: 833 St James Av Covington KY 41011 Office: 9th & Lowell Sts Newport KY 41071

SCHIFFERLI, HARRY ALLAN, dentist; b. Fredonia, N.Y., Mar. 3, 1938; s. Harry J. and Agnes (Williams) S.; B.S. in Geology, Alfred U., 1960; D.M.D., U. Louisville, 1965; postgrad. oral surgery Stuttgart (Germany) U., 1965-67; m. Ann D. Gayle, June 24, 1961; children—Catherine G., John Allan. Dental cons. S.C. Dental Health Dept., Aiken, 1968—; practice dentistry, Aiken, 1970—. Cons. Aiken County Sch. Dist., 1968—. Mem. Sertoma, 1971—; mem. adv. council Boy Scouts Am., 1956—, Am. Cancer Soc., 1969—. Served to capt. Dental Corps, AUS, 1965-68. Mem. Am. Dental Soc., Am. Soc. Dentistry Children, Quintessence Internat., Delta Sigma Delta. Club: Big Horn Hunt (Allendale, S.C.). Home: 870 Azalea St Aiken SC 29801 Office: 117 Trafalgar Lane Aiken SC 29801

SCHILLING, EDWIN CARLYLE, JR., lawyer; b. Greensburg, La., Sept. 25, 1921; s. Edwin Carlyle and Myrtle (Holland) S.; LL.B., La. State U., 1948; m. Ann LeTard, Feb. 7, 1942; 1 son, Edwin Carlyle III. Admitted to La. bar, 1948, since practiced in Amite; individual practice law, 1948-62; mem. law firm Schilling & Simpson, 1963—. Dir. Hammond Bldg. & Loan Assn. (La.); dir., chmn. bd. Advanced Edn., Inc., Baton Rouge. Trustee La. Coll., Pineville. Served with AUS, 1943-46. Mem. Am., La., Twenty First Jud. Dist. bar assns., Amite C. of C. (past pres.). Baptist (deacon). Rotarian (past pres.). Home: 305 Cedar St Amite LA 70422 Office: 109 N Bay St Amite LA 70422

SCHILLING, RALPH FRANKLIN, coll. pres.; b. Morris, Okla., July 5, 1921; s. R.F. and Mattie E. (Crume) S.; Ed.D., Tex. Tech. Coll., 1957; M. Ed., Okla. U., 1950; B.A., Oklahoma City U., 1948; m. Mary Katherine Brooks, Jan. 19, 1942; 1 son, Ralph Franklin. Instr., asst. coach Oklahoma City U., 1947-50; high sch. prin., Crosbyton, Tex., 1950-52, Littlefield, Tex., 1952-54; supt. schs., Littlefield, 1954-60; pres. Pan Am. Coll., Edinburg, Tex., 1960—. Chmn. adv. bd. Littlefield Salvation Army, 1959. Named Littlefield Man of Year, 1958. Mem. N.E.A. (life), Tex. P.T.A. (life), Am. Assn. Sch. Adminstrs., Tex. Tchrs. Assn., Tex. Adminstrs. Assn. Methodist (past chmn. stewards). Rotarian (pres. Littlefield 1959-60). Home: Box 232 Edinburg TX 78503

SCHIMMEL, JOSEPH, govt. ofcl.; b. Balt., Apr. 7, 1899; s. David and Muriel (Appel) S.; student Balt. City Coll., 1912-16, Johns Hopkins, nights, 1917-18, Carnegie Inst. Tech., 1923, George Washington U. Law Sch., 1927-34; m. Libby Winik, Jan. 11, 1925; 1 dau., Ruth Sonia (Mrs. Robert Loevinger). Analytical chemist Mut. Chem. Co. Am., Balt., 1917-19; examiner U.S. Patent Office, 1924-47; patent atty., 1947-57, dep. solicitor, 1957-66, solicitor, 1966-69; dir. Patent Office Cirdit Union, 1943-69, v.p., 1958-63, pres., 1965-68; lectr. U.S. Patent Office Acad., 1958-69. Recipient Gold medal award for exceptional service Dept. Commerce, 1959; certificate of award U.S. Patent Office, 1959-65. Mem. Am., Fed. bar assns. Jewish religion (pres. congregation 1961-64). Home: 8019 Eastern Av Silver Spring MD 20910 Office: US Patent Office Crystal Pl Arlingon VA 22202

SCHIMPELER, CHARLES CARTER, planning and constrn. exec.; b. Louisville, Aug. 5, 1939; s. Charles Henry and Helen (Bartley) S.; B.S. in Civil Engring., U. Ky., 1960, M.S., 1962; Ph.D., Purdue U., 1967. Lectr. math. Bellarmine Coll., Louisville, 1963-65; urban planning engr. Louisville Met. Comprehensive Transp. and Devel. Program, 1964-65; tech. dir., 1966-68, dir., 1968-69; dir. planning and programming Louisville and Jefferson County Air Bd., 1969-72; prin. Schimpeler-Corradino, engrs. and planning consultants, 1968—; adj. asso. prof. U. Louisville, 1969—. Mem. Am. Soc. C.E., Nat. Acad. Scis., Nat. Acad. Engring. (hwy. research bd.), Am. Inst. Planners, Inst. Traffic Engrs., Regional Scis. Assn., Am. Soc. Planning Ofcls., Operations Research Soc. Am., Inst. Mgmt. Scis., Econometric Soc., Am. Acad. Polit. and Social Sci. Roman Catholic. Optimist. Contbr. to profl. jours. Home: 331 Central Av Pewee Valley KY 40056 Office: PO Box 21176 Standiford Field Louisville KY 40221

SCHINDLER, ALBERT ISADORE, physicist; b. Pitts., June 24, 1927; s. Jonas and Esther (Nass) S.; B.S., Carnegie Inst. Tech., 1947, M.S., 1948, D.Sc., 1950; m. Phyllis Irene Liberman, June 17, 1951; children—Janet Mae, Jerald Scott, Ellen Susan. Research physicist Carnegie Inst. Tech., Pitts., 1950-51; physicist U.S. Naval Research Lab., Washington, 1951-60, head metal physics br., metallurgy div., 1961—. Recipient E. O. Hulburt award, 1956. Fellow Am. Phys. Soc.; mem. Washington Acad. Scis., Washington Philos. Soc., Research Soc. Am. (br. pres. 1965-66, mem. nat. bd. govs. 1968—). Contbr. numerous articles in field to profl. jours. Patentee in field. Home: 1012 Crest Park Dr Silver Spring MD 20903 Office: Code 6330 US Naval Research Lab Washington DC 20390

SCHINHAN, JAN PHILIP, educator; b. Vienna, Austria, Oct. 17, 1887; s. Adolph and Hermine Uiblein (Stein) S.; student of Prof. Joseph Renner, Jr., Regensburg, Bavaria, 1906-08; A.B., U. Cal., 1931, A.M., 1933; postgrad. (Dean's scholar), Columbia, 1934-35; Ph.D., Vienna, 1937; student Munich Acad. Music, 1908-10; m. Camilla J. von Egloffstein, July 12, 1915; 1 son, Philip Camill; m. 2d, Elizabeth Logan. Condr. opera co., Germany, 1911-13, U.S., 1913-15; pvt. teaching, 1913-25; head organ dept. Conservatory of Music, San Francisco, 1925-33, under direction Ernest Bloch; organ soloist for San Francisco Symphony, 1930-33; appearances under Alf. Hertz, Bernard Molinari; guest organist Palace of Legion of Honor, 1924-33; research U. Vienna, 1933-34, summers 1935, 37; asst. prof. music U. N.C., 1935, asso. prof., 1942-46, prof. music, 1946-58, prof. emeritus, 1958—, dir. Inst. Folk Music. Vice pres., trustee N.C. State Symphony. Bd. dirs. N.C. Fedn. Music Clubs; chmn. com. judges for 000 Benjamin award; nat. archivist, chmn. folk music and research, bd. mem., life mem. Nat. Fedn. Music Clubs. 1st recipient commn. for orchestral composition by N.C. Symphony; tree planted in his honor nr. Hebrew U. Med. Center, Jerusalem; named Sr. Man of Year, Jr. C. of C.; recipient state citation for distinguished service N.C. Fedn. Music Clubs, 1968, 1st award of Brown-Hudson Folklore, 1970; Presdl. citation Nat. Fed. Music Clubs. Mem. Am., Nat. musicol. socs., Internat. Soc. Ethnology and Folklore, Am. Folklore Soc., Internat. Platform Assn., Golden Fleece (U. N.C.), Phi Mu Alpha. Club: Bohemian (Cal.). Author: Spanish Foklore from Tampa, Fla., 1939; the music of the Papago and Yurok, 1972. Editor part of Frank C. Brown Collection of North Carolina Folklore, Vol IV, Music of the Ballads, 1957, Vol V, Music of the Folk Songs, 1962. Composer 80 songs, several anthems. Home: 608 W 22d St Kannapolis NC 28081

SCHINNERER, VICTOR OSCAR, ins. co. exec.; b. Wyncote, Pa., Feb. 13, 1906; s. Frederick D. and Sarah (Field) S.; A.B., Pa. State U., 1928; m. Muriel Reid Johnson, Sept. 8, 1934; children—Sally (Mrs. Thomas D. Fant), William Reid, Sandra (Mrs. John J. Younger), Underwriter, spl. agt., ins. analyst Aetna Casualty & Surety Co., Phila., 1928-37, supt. of agts., Washington, 1937-38; formed own firm in 1938, which inc. in 1947 as Victor O. Schinnerer & Co., Inc., (became div. Marsh & McLennon Inc.), now chmn.; sr. v.p., Marsh & McLennon, Inc., 1970—, dir. Nat. Sav. & Trust Co., Washington. Bd. assos. Gettysburg Coll., 1965—. Dir. Met. Washington Bd. of Trade, 1954-67, pres., 1958-59, mem. sr. council, 1959—; chmn. Washington Conv. and Visitors Bur., 1962-65, mem. exec. com., 1965—; adv. council Boy Scouts Am., 1963—; pres. D.C. Soc. for Crippled Children, 1962-64; bd. dirs. Washington Heart Assn., 1960-61. Mem. D.C. (past pres.), Nat. (past dir.) assns. ins. agts., Am. Mgmt. Assn., Nat. Assn. Life Underwriters, Newcomen Soc. (mem. Washington com.), Better Bus. Bur., Phi Kappa Psi. Clubs: University: Kiwanis (Washington); Columbia Country, Seaview Country; Ocean Reef Yacht, Key Largo Anglers. Home: 9020 Brickyard Rd Potomac MD 20854 Office: Schinnerer Bldg 5028 Wisconsin Av NW Washington DC 20016

SCHLANT, ROBERT CARL, physician, educator; b. El Paso, Tex., Apr. 16, 1929; B.A., Vanderbilt U., 1948, M.D., 1951. Intern, Peter Bent Brigham Hosp., Boston, 1951-52, jr. asst. resident in medicine, 1952-53, sr. asst. resident, 1955-56, asst. in medicine, 1956-58; research fellow in medicine Harvard Med. Sch., 1956-58; asst. prof. medicine Emory U. Sch. Medicine, 1958-62, asso. prof., 1962-66, prof., 1967—. Fellow Am. Coll. Cardiology (gov. Ga.), A.C.P., Council on Clin. Cardiology Am. Heart Assn.; mem. Am. Assn. U. Cardiologists, Am. Fedn. Clin. Research, So. Soc. for Clin. Investigation (mem. subsplty. bd. cardiovascular disease). Home: 3340 E Wood Valley Rd NW Atlanta GA 30327 Office: 69 Butler St SE Atlanta GA 30303

SCHLATTNER, HENRY WIGGE, cons. structural engr.; b. Nashville, Nov. 12, 1929; s. William Hayes and Rose (Wigge) S.; student Vanderbilt U., 1947-51; B.S., U. Tex., 1961; m. Frances Elizabeth Perkerson, May 9, 1953; children—Henry Wigge, Karen Ann, William Richard. Structural engr. C.E. Stringer, Las Vegas, Nev., 1961-62, James B. McDaniel, Las Vegas, 1962-63, Miller & Turner, Las Vegas, 1963-64, Aillet, Fenner, Jolly & McClelland, Inc., Shreveport, La., 1964-66, Reynolds & Ikels & Co., Cons. Engrs., San Antonio, 1966-69; cons. engr., pres. Schlattner & Chetter, Inc., San Antonio, 1969—. Served with USAF, 1951-55. Registered profl. engr., Tex. Mem. Nat., Tex. (chpt. v.p. 1969-70) socs. profl. engrs., Tau Beta Pi, Chi Epsilon, Phi Kappa Psi. Roman Catholic. Elk. Club: Sertoma (exec. bd. 1969-70; pres. 1972). Modifier, painter 5 new seals State of Tex. Home: 10706 Cedar Elm Dr San Antonio TX 78230 Office: 7077 San Pedro Av San Antonio TX 78216

SCHLEGEL, DOROTHY MILDRED BADDERS (MRS. MARVIN W. SCHLEGEL), educator; b. Harford County, Md., July 18, 1910; d. John Joseph and Lucy Alice (Davis) Badders; B.A., Dickinson Coll., 1932; M.A., Coll. William and Mary, 1948; Ph.D., U. N.C., 1954; postgrad. U. Vienna, 1954, Sorbonne, 1955, U. Frankfort, 1954-55, 62; m. Marvin W. Schlegel, Apr. 9, 1941. Tchr. English, Hannah Penn Jr. High Sch., York, Pa., 1932-34; tchr. English, French, Latin, William Penn Sr. High Sch., York, 1934-47; instr. English, St. Helena Extension, Coll. William and Mary, 1948; asst. prof. English and comparative lit. Longwood Coll., Farmville, Va., 1953-57, asso. prof., 1957-63, prof., 1963-66, chmn. freshman English, 1964-66; prof. English, Norfolk State Coll., 1966—. Mem. Internat. Comparative Lit. Assn., Freies Deutches Hochstift, Modern Lang. Assn., South Atlantic Modern Lang. Assn., Coll. English Assn. N.C.-Va. Coll. English Assn., Nat. Council Tchrs. English, Va. Assn. Tchrs. English, Am. Assn. U. Profs., Va. Council on Human Relations, Cabell Soc. (pres. 1969—), Soc. 18th Century Studies, D.A.R., Mayflower Soc., Phi Beta Kappa, Sigma Alpha Iota. Episcopalian. Author: Shaftesbury and the French Deists, 1956; Writing from Research, 1964; also articles. Home: 476 Linkhorn Dr Virginia Beach VA 23451 Office: Norfolk State Coll Norfolk VA 23504

SCHLESINGER, EUGENE RICHARD, economist; b. N.Y.C., Mar. 19, 1925; s. Julius and Rhea (Rogen) S.; A.B., Harvard, 1947, A.M., 1948, Ph.D., 1950; m. Louise Fleur Myers, June 19, 1948 (div. June 1967); children— Louis, Thomas, Kenneth, Kathryn. Economist Fed. Res. Bank N.Y., 1948-52, World Bank, 1952-54; mng. partner Eugene Schlesinger & Co., 1954-59; asst. prof. N.Y. U., 1954-60, asso. prof., 1960-64; chief economist U.S.-P.R. Commn. on Status of P.R., 1964-66; lectr. Econ. Devel. Inst., Internat. Bank of Reconstrn. and Devel., Washington, 1966—. Cons. U.S. Dept. Commerce, Econ. Commn. Latin Am., Fiscal div. UN, Joint Tax program Latin Am. Served to lt. (j.g.) USNR, 1943-46. Recipient Ford Faculty Research fellowship, 1960-61. Mem. Am. Econ. Assn., Am. Finance Assn., Nat. Tax Assn., Soc. Internat. Devel., Phi Beta Kappa. Author: Multiple Exchange Rates and Economic Development, 1952; (with J.H. Adler and E. Olsen) Public Finance and Economic Development, 1952; (with J.H. Adler and E. Van Weslerberg) The Pattern of United States Import Trade, 1952. Home: 2301 E St NW Washington DC 20037 Office: 1818 H St NW Washington DC 20433

SCHLESINGER, JAMES RODNEY, govt. ofcl.; b. N.Y.C., Feb. 15, 1929; s. Julius and Rhea (Rogen) S.; A.B. summa cum laude, Harvard, 1950, A.M., 1952, Ph.D., 1956; m. Rachel Mellinger, June 19, 1954; children—Cora K., Charles L., Ann R., William F., Emily, Thomas S., Clara, James R. Asst. prof., then asso. prof. U. Va., 1955-63; sr. staff mem. RAND Corp., 1963-67, dir. strategic studies, 1967-69; asst. dir. Bur. of Budget, 1969-71; chmn. U.S. AEC, 1971—; cons. in field. Mem. bd. assos. Fgn. Policy Research Inst., U. Pa., 1962-63. Recipient Frederick Sheldon prize fellowship Harvard, 1950-51. Mem. Am. Econ. Assn., Phi Beta Kappa. Republican. Lutheran. Author: The Political Economy of National Security, 1960; Organizational Structures and Planning, 1967. Co-author: Issues in Defense Economics. Asso. editor Jour. Finance, 1964-65. Home: 3601 N 26th St Arlington VA 22207 Office: 1717 H St NW Washington DC 20545

SCHLOSSER, JOSEPH LEO, architect; b. Phila., Aug. 22, 1925; s. John and Teresa Mary (Stuhl) S.; B.S., Ga. Inst. Tech., 1953, B.Arch., 1954; m. Delia Gray Brown, June 14, 1947; children—Teresa, Joe, Jane Marie, Joann. Draftsman, designer Laurence S. Miller, Brunswick, Ga., 1954-61; v.p., architect Miller, Schlosser & Miller, Brunswick, 1961-67; pres., architect Schlosser & Miller, Inc., Brunswick, 1967-72; individual practice, 1972—; dir. Sea Circus, Inc., Jekyll Island, Ga. Owner, Ponderosa Motels, Inc., Brunswick. Pres., Glynn County Heart Assn., 1968—; mem. Glynn County Bldg. Code Appeals Bd., 1966—; sec. Brunswick Housing Standards Appeal Bd., 1968—. Served with USNR, 1943-46. Roman Catholic (chmn. sch. bd. 1964-68). Kiwanian. Illustration of architl. work Brunswick Mall pub. in Chain Store Age, 1970. Home: 1027 Lanier Blvd Brunswick GA 31520 Office: Office Park Bldg Brunswick GA 31520

SCHMAUS, FRANCIS THEODORE, librarian; b. Lancaster, Pa., Nov. 2, 1919; s. Harold Eugene and Eleanor (Uhlir) S.; A.B., U. Colo., 1950; M.A. in English, U. Denver, 1951, M.A. in L.S., 1953; postgrad. U. Tex., 1954-59; m. Joan Barditzky, Feb. 13, 1955; Faculty, U. Denver, 1950-54; with reference dept. U. Tex. at Austin, 1954-59, engring. librarian, 1959—. Served with AUS, 1941-45. Mason. Author: A Library Reference Manual for Engineering Student, 1963. Home: 4515 Rosedale Av Austin TX 78756

SCHMERTMANN, HAROLD, govt. ofcl.; b. N.Y.C., Mar. 28, 1935; s. John and Margaret (Carstens) S.; B.A., Fla. State U., 1961, M.S. in Geography, 1962; m. Gloria Jean Bowen, Dec. 22, 1962; children—Gregory, Kerry. Community planner Fla. Devel. Commn., Tallahassee, 1963-66; city planner St. Petersburg, 1966-67; dir. planning and recreation div. Fla. Devel. Commn., 1967-69, planning mgr. Fla. Dept. Community Affairs, 1969-71, chief, bur. community devel., 1971—. Served with USAF, 1953-57. Home: 1529 E Indian Head Dr Tallahassee FL 32301 Office: 2711 Apalachee Pkwy Tallahassee FL 32301

SCHMIDT, ARTHUR EARL, physician; b. St. Louis, Jan. 1, 1923; s. Arthur Earl and Elsa (Kallmeyer) S.; M.D., Washington U., St. Louis, 1946; m. Norma Jean Saggau, July 6, 1947; children—Robert Eric, Christine Ann, Arthur Earl III, Cindy Lou. Intern, Presbyn. Hosp., Chgo., 1946-47, resident, 1951-53; resident St. Louis County Hosp., Clayton, Mo., 1950-51; fellow in cardiology U. Okla. Hosp., 1953-54; chief med. service Central State Hosp., Norman, Okla., 1954-56; practice medicine specializing in internal medicine and cardiology, Oklahoma City, 1956—; mem. staff Univ., Baptist, Deaconess, St. Anthony, Mercy, VA hosps. (all Oklahoma City); instr. dept. medicine U. Okla. Med. Sch., 1954-63, asst. clin. prof. medicine, 1963-70, asso. clin. prof. medicine, 1970—. Active Okla. Heritage Found., Okla. Mus. Art, Red Ridge, Okla. Art Center. Served to capt., M.C., AUS, 1943-46, 47-50. Mem. A.M.A., A.C.P., Am. Coll. Cardiology, Am. Coll. Chest Physicians, Am. Heart Assn., Okla. Thoracic Soc., Am., Okla. (pres. 1963) socs. internal medicine, Okla., Oklahoma County med. assns. Mason. Club: Quail Creek Golf and Country (Oklahoma City). Home: 2416 NW 55th Terrace Oklahoma City OK 73112 Office: 3141 NW Expressway Oklahoma City OK 73112

SCHMIDT, CHARLES LYNN, securities co. exec.; b. Temple, Tex., June 2, 1936; s. Adolph Otto and Jessie (Young) S.; B.B.A., U. Houston, 1957; m. Patricia Ann Toms, Oct. 25, 1958; 1 dau., Heather Elizabeth. Advt. asst. Procter & Gamble Co., Cin., 1958-61; systems analyst Gt. Am. Res. Ins. Co., Dallas, 1961-71, equity funds adminstr., 1971—; registered prin., sec. GARCO Equity Sales, Inc., Dallas, 1969—, also dir. Instr., Found for Adminstrv. Research, Colorado Springs, Colo., 1966-69. Adviser, Jr. Achievement, Dallas, 1962-64. Served to 2d lt. Adj. Gens. Corps, AUS, 1957-58. Fellow Life Office Mgmt. Assn. Inst.; mem. Am. Soc. C.L.U.'s, Jr. C. of C. (Jaycee of Month 1968), Univ. Hills Homeowners Assn. Republican. Presbyn. (ruling elder). Author: Let's Communicate, 1970. Home: 213 E Rochelle Blvd Irving TX 75062 Office: 2020 Live Oak St Dallas TX 75201

SCHMIDT, FREDERICK HENRY, govt. ofcl.; b. Deer Park, O., Nov. 30, 1910; s. Henry B. and Cora (Arnsperger) S.; B.S., Wooster (O.) Coll., 1932; LL.B., Salmon P. Chase Law Sch., Cin., 1940; m. Olwen A. Jones, Aug. 28, 1941; 1 son, Terry A. Investigator State of

Ohio, 1935-40; admitted to Fla. bar, 1940, Ohio bar, 1946, Md. bar, 1953; spl. agt. F.B.I., 1940-53; dir. security Dept. Health, Edn. and Welfare, Washington, 1953—. Mem. Soc. Former Spl. Agts. FBI, Inc. Presbyn (elder). Home: 106 Devon Ct Silver Spring MD 20910 Office: Dept Health Edn and Welfare Washington DC 20201

SCHMIDT, HAROLD EUGENE, civil engr., land co. exec.; b. Cedar Rapids, Ia., Oct. 12, 1925; s. Alfons W. and Lillie (Schlegel) S.; B.S., U. Ia., 1949; M.S., Mass. Inst. Tech., 1953; m. Lucy Hermann, Apr. 13, 1957; children—Harold, Sandra. Research, devel. engr. Chgo. Pump Co., 1949-51; engr. A.B. Kononoff, Engrs., Miami, Fla., 1956-58; with Gen. Devel. Corp., Miami, 1958—, v.p. utilities, 1966-67, corporate officer, asst. v.p., 1967—. Served to capt. Med. Service Corps, USAF, 1951-56. Mem. Am. Water Works Assn., Water Pollution Control Fedn., Sigma Xi, Chi Epsilon. Home: 641 W 53d St Hialeah FL 33012 Office: 1111 S Bayshore Dr Miami FL 33131

SCHMIDT, WILLIAM EUGENE, dentist; b. Phillip, S.D., June 14, 1938; s. Carl George and Ethel (Weich) S.; B.A., Adelphi Coll., 1959; D.D.S., N.Y. U., 1963; m. Elizabeth Marie Fesenmeyer, July 4, 1963; children— Kevin Eugene, Colleen Marie, Catherine Ann, Carol Lynn, William Joseph. Intern, G. Pierce Wood Meml., Arcadia, Fla., 1963-64; individual practice dentistry, Winter Haven, Fla., 1964—. Neighborhood commr. Boy Scouts Am., Winter Haven, 1966—; active United Fund. Pres., Young Ams. for Freedom, 1966, treas., 1967; v.p. Young Republicans, Winter Haven, 1967. Named Community Leader of Am., News Pub. Co., 1969. Mem. Am., Fla., West Coast (editor 1972), Polk County dental assns., Acad. Gen. Dentistry, Am. Acad. Periodontology, Royal Soc. Promotion of Health, Fla. Outdoor Writers Assn., Outdoor Writers Assn. Am., Xi Psi Phi. Roman Catholic. Clubs: Sertoma (v.p. 1966-67), Toastmasters (treas. 1969, v.p. 1970, pres. 1971); Winter Haven Bass (v.p. 1971, pres. 1972). Author column The Great Outdoors, Winter Haven Herald and Lake Wales (Fla.) Highlander. Home: Route 3 Box 324D Winter Haven FL 33880 Office: 737 Cypress Gardens Rd Winter Haven FL 33880

SCHMIED, RONALD DENNIS, engr., planner; b. Chgo., Aug. 13, 1930; s. Helmuth Walter and Ethel (Ross) S.; B.S., U. Ill., 1954; m. Joan Eileen Lorentzen, Dec. 28, 1955; children—Diana Lee, Lori Ann, Susanne Loren, Joanna Rachel. Civil engr. H. Balke Engrs., Cin., 1954-57; with Harland Bartholomew & Assos., Planners, Engrs., Architects, Memphis, 1957-71, planning dir., 1965-71, asso. partner, 1961-71; v.p. William S. Pollard Cons., Planners, Engrs., Memphis, 1971—. Instr. chemistry St. Bernard's Sch. Nursing, Chgo., 1951; instr. engring. tech., Memphis State U., 1966. Cons. rep. Miss.-Ark.-Tenn. Council Govts., 1967-68; mem. Germantown Design Review Commn. Served with AUS, 1951. Registered profl. engr., Ill., Tenn., Ohio, Ala. Mem. Am. Inst. Planners, Am. Soc. Planning Ofcls., Nat. Acad. Sci., Nat. Soc. Profl. Engrs., Am. Soc. C.E., Am. Soc. Photogrammetry. Club: Germantown Civic. Home: 7605 Ashworth Rd Germantown TN 38138 Office: 100 North Main Bldg Memphis TN 38103

SCHMITT, GILBERT EUGENE, utility exec.; b. Seguin, Tex., Aug. 27, 1906; s. Lorenz and Mathilde (Glaeser) S.; B.S. in Elec. Engring., U. Tex., 1928; m. Maudine Hampton, Dec. 25, 1930; 1 dau., Patricia Nadine (Mrs. Henry A. Bunting III). Engr. substa. design and constrn. Central Power & Light Co., Corpus Christi, Tex., 1928-32, resident engr., 1929, gen. engr. design and constrn. changes, 1933-38; transmission supt. operations, engring. cons. Lower Colorado River Authority, Austin, Tex., 1939-40, chief engr., 1941-43, asst. gen. mgr., chief engr., 1944—. Fellow I.E.E.E. (past v.p.); mem. Tex. Soc. Profl. Engrs. (past pres.), Austin C. of C. (past v.p.), Ramshorn Club, Eta Kappa Nu. Mem. Ch. of Christ. Kiwanian. Home: 2804 Greenlee Dr Austin TX 78703 Office: PO Box 220 Austin TX 78767

SCHMITT, HARRISON HAGAN, geologist, astronaut; b. Santa Rita, N.M., July 3, 1935; s. Harrison A. and Ethel (Hagan) S.; B.S., Cal. Inst. Tech., 1957; postgrad. (Fulbright fellow) U. Olso, Norway, 1957-58; Ph.D. (NSF post doctoral fellow), Harvard, 1964. Geologist, U.S. Geol. Survey, 1964-65; astronaut NASA, Houston, 1965—; lunar module pilot Apollo 17, 1972. Address: Manned Spacecraft Center NASA Houston TX 77058

SCHMITT, VINCENT JEROME, realtor; b. N.Y.C., Nov. 29, 1911; s. John F. and Florence R. (Cumiskey) S.; student U. Mich., 1930; m. Margaret C. Reilley, Apr. 22, 1939; children—John, Richard, Alicia. Draftsman, John McMillan Co., N.Y.C., 1934-35; with Pan Am. Refining Corp., Texas City, 1935-47; owner V. J. Schmitt & Co., Texas City, Tex., 1947—; pres. Meml. Properties, Inc., 1967—; dir. Mainland Bank, Texas City. Chmn. Texas City Planning Commn., 1966—. Named Tex. Realtor of the Year, 1961. Mem. Nat. Assn. Real Estate Bds. (dir. 1954, 66-68, 69-71, trustee ins. trust real estate group 1972—), Tex. Assn. Realtors (pres. 1953-54, chmn. legislative taxation com. 1961, chmn. edn. com. 1967, chmn. mag. com. 1964-66), Texas City Real Estate Bd. (pres. 1957, 61), Texas City-LaMarque Assn. Ins. Agts. (pres. 1956-57). Texas City (dir. 1962-64), Texas City-LaMarque (dir. 1968-70) chambers commerce. Roman Catholic. K.C. Home: 1121 Mainland Dr Texas City TX 77590 Office: 524 9th St Texas City TX 77590

SCHMITZ, TERRY R., accountant; b. Colt, Ark., Aug. 22, 1936; s. Garland L. and Sue (Gilbert) S.; B.B.A., Memphis State U., 1962; children—Lee, John, Morgan. Staff accountant Harris, Kerr, Forster & Co., Memphis, 1962-63, Minor & Moore, C.P.A.'s, Memphis, 1963-65; audit supr. James Talcott, Inc., Atlanta, 1965-66, Ernst & Ernst, Jackson, Miss., 1966-70; individual practice accounting, Jackson, 1970—. Served with USAF, 1954-58. C.P.A., Tenn., Miss. Mem. Am. Soc. C.P.A.'s, Nat. Assn. Accountants, Miss. Art Assn., Memphis Jr. C. of C., Am. Legion, Delta Sigma Pi (life). Home and Office: 1152 Robinson Rd Jackson MS 39209

SCHNEIDAU, KARL, petroleum co. exec.; b. New Orleans, June 11, 1921; s. Karl and Marjorie (Herrmann) S.; student Tulane U., U. Houston; m. Freda Mae McDaniel, Mar. 1, 1951; children—Kathryn Reyes, Kristina, Cynthia Kay, Karl Byron. Vice pres., chief geologist Austral Oil Co., Inc., Houston, 1951—; partner Leisk, Cole & Wintrop Co., Houston, 1960—, Leisco, Ltd., Houston, 1964—. Served with USAAF, 1943-46. Mem. Houston Geol. Soc., Soc. Tulane Engrs. Club: Houston. Home: 12210 Old Oaks St Houston TX 77024 Office: Humble Bldg 800 Bell Houston TX 77002

SCHNEIDER, CALVIN DWAINE, supt. sch.; b. Custer, Okla., Nov. 7, 1931; s. Thomas Raymond and Emma (Hamburger) S.; B.S. in Edn., Southwestern State Cobl., Weatherford, Okla., 1953; M.S. in Ednl. Adminstrn., Okla. U., 1959, profl. diploma ednl. adminstrn., 1971; m. Wanda Fay Motley, Aug. 18, 1956; children—Vickie Ann, Thomas Dwaine, Valinda Kay, Vinita Fay. Tchr., Bradley High Sch., 1955-58; tchr., adminstr., Custer (Okla.) High Sch., 1959-68; supt. Thomas (Okla.) High Sch., 1968—. Farming mgr. R. Schneider Trusts, Custer, 1965—, trustee, 1965—. Served with AUS, 1953-55. Mem. Thomas C. of C. (dir. 1970—), N.E.A., Okla. (mem. 1st del. assembly 1969—), Custer County edn. assns., Okla. Assn. Sch. Adminstrs., Am. Assn. Sch. Adminstrs. Methodist (dist. lay leader Okla. Conf. 1970—). Home: 406 E Roh St Thomas OK 73669 Office: 920 N Main St Thomas High School Thomas OK 73669

SCHNEIDER, CHARLES HAROLD, newspaperman; b. Miller, Miss., Jan. 17, 1912; s. William and Jennie (Schwam) S.; grad. high sch.; m. Katherine Kasaftes, July 24, 1932; 1 dau., Tina M. (Mrs. George L. Powell). Successively office boy, librarian, cub reporter, photographer, staff photographer, feature writer Memphis Press-Scimitar, 1929-34, editor, 1962—; gen. assignment reporter Cleve. Press, 1934-35, drama critic, entertainment editor, 1935-37, dir. pub. service, 1937-48; nat. promotion editor, also dir. nat. spelling bee, Scripps-Howard Newspapers, 1948-57; editor San Francisco News, 1957-59, San Francisco News-Call Bull., 1959-62. Mem. Am. Soc. Newspaper Editors, Am. Soc. Sunday and Feature Editors, Sigma Delta Chi. Rotarian. Clubs: Cercle de L'Union (San Francisco); Nat. Press (Washington). Home: 230 Belvedere Blvd Memphis TN 38101 Office: 495 Union Av Memphis TN 38103

SCHNEIDER, DANIEL JACOB, educator; b. Madison, Wis., Mar. 24, 1932; s. Henry and Amelia Christine (Winger) S.; M.D., U. Cal. at Los Angeles, 1958; M.P.H., U. Cal. at Berkeley, 1967; m. Kum Sun Kim, Sept. 16, 1961; children—Gyeong Ok, Andre Daniel. Intern Gorgas Hosp., Balboa Heights, C. Z., 1958-59; dir. med. research, transp. research command U.S. Army, Fort Eustis, Va., and Phoenix, 1961-62; asst. dir., then dir. pub. health Trust Ter. Pacific Islands, hdqrs. Saipan, 1963-65; prin. sci. cons. Lockheed Missiles and Space Corp., Sunnyvale, Cal., 1967-69; cons. pub. health manpower planning, South Vietnam, 1967-68; asso. prof. Sch. Pub. Health U. Tex., Houston, 1968—. Chmn. Social Operations Research Corp., Houston, 1970—, Omnicomm Internat., Houston, 1965-71. Am. Assn. Gen. Practice fellow chest diseases Highland Hosp., Oakland, Cal., 1962-63. Mem. Korean-Am. Fellowship Assn. (chmn. pub. relations, 1971—), U.S.-Mexico Border Pub. Health Assn. (gov., 1970-71). Rotarian. Home: 5006 Beechnut St Houston TX 77035

SCHNEIDER, DONALD JACOB, hotel exec.; b. Columbus. O., Apr. 24, 1924; s. Herbert Uhlrich and Gladys (Davis) S.; student Jones Bus. Coll., 1953-54, U. Fla., 1954-55; m. Ruth Louise Higginbotham, Sept. 3, 1949; children—Donald Jacob, Patricia Michele, Nancy Ann. Asst. sales mgr. Culligan Soft Water Co., Jacksonville Beach, Fla., 1947-49; with Ponte Vedra Club, Ponte Vedra Beach, Fla., 1949—, asst. mgr. reservations, 1963-66, v.p., mgr., 1966—; dir. Ponte Vedra Corp., Pres., P.T.A. Ponte Vedra-Palm Valley High Sch., 1971; mem. exec. com. Shawnee council Boy Scouts Am., 1962—; mem. adv. com. hotel curriculum Fla. Jr. Coll., 1970—; coach-player Jacksonville Beach Dolphins basketball team, 1953-58, baseball teams, 1963-65. Served with inf. AUS, 1943-46; ETO. Decorated Bronze Star medal (2); Croix de Guerre (France). Mem. Fla. Hotel and Motel Assn. (bd. dirs.), Ponte Vedra Men's Golf Assn. Republican. Baptist. Club: Quarterback (Jacksonville Beach). Home: 194 San Juan Dr Ponte Vedra Beach FL 32082 Office: Ponte Vedra Blvd Ponte Vedra Beach FL 32082

SCHNEIDER, ERNEST HENRY, lawyer; b. nr. Rosenberg, Tex., Oct. 7, 1924; s. Henry Fred and Bertha (Moench) S.; B.B.A., U. Houston, 1949; LL.B., S. Tex. Coll. 1953; m. Eugenia Smith, July 23, 1949; children— Gayle, Clarke, Bedelle, Laurie, Sherye, Brett. Admitted to Tex. bar, 1953; practiced in Houston, 1953—; partner firm Butler, Binion, Rice, Cook & Knapp, 1963—. Served with USNR, 1942-46. Mem. State Bar Tex., Am., Houston bar assns. Democrat. Conglist. Club: Meyerland. Home: 5310 Darnell St Houston TX 77035 Office: Esperson Bldg Houston TX 77002

SCHNEIDER, LOUIS, educator; b. Vienna, Austria, Mar. 22, 1915; s. Gustave and Frieda (Salz) S.; came to U.S., 1921, naturalized, 1927; B.A., Coll. City N.Y., 1935; M.A., Columbia, 1938, Ph.D., 1947; m. 2d, Josephine A. Sundine, Jan. 3, 1956; 1 dau., Valerie S.; children by previous marriage—David S., Dana A. Tutor sociology Bklyn. Coll., 1937-43; labor economist WPB, 1943-45; economist OPA, 1945-47; asst. prof. sociology Colgate U., 1947-49; asso. prof. sociology Purdue U., 1949-54, prof., 1954-59; prof. sociology U. Ill. at Urbana, 1960-67, head dept., 1960-64; prof. sociology U. Tex., Austin, 1967—; vis. prof. Dartmouth, 1959-60. Fellow Center Advanced Study Behavorial Scis., 1954-55. Fellow Am. Sociol. Assn.; mem. Ohio Valley Sociol. Soc. (pres. 1959-60), Phi Beta Kappa. Author: Freudian Psychology and Veblen's Social Theory, 1948; (with Ogle and Wiley) Power, Order and the Economy, 1954; (with S.N. Dornbusch) Popular Religion, 1958; also articles profl. jours. Asso. editor Am. Sociol. Rev., 1958-61. Editor: Problems of Economics and Sociology (by Carl Menger), 1963; The Scottish Moralists on Human Nature and Society, 1967; editor, contbr. Religion, Culture and Society, 1964. Home: 4210 Prickly Pear Av Austin TX 78731

SCHNEIDER, PER KAY, cons. engr.; b. Lubbock, Tex., May 13, 1941; s. Valerie and Dorothy (Brown) S.; student Pan Am. Coll., 1958-60; B.S., U. Tex., 1962; postgrad. St. Mary's U., 1967-68; m. Margaret Doris Doneis, Aug. 31, 1962; children—Charles Vincent, Janet Leigh. Project engr. Bryant-Curington, Inc., Cons. Engrs., Austin, Tex., 1962-65, Frank G. Bryant & Assos., Inc., Austin, 1965-66; office mgr., project engr. Frank G. Bryant & Assos., Inc., San Antonio, 1966-69; partner David E. Williams Engring. Co., San Antonio, 1969-70; partner, exec. v.p. Williams & Schneider, Inc., Cons. Engrs., San Antonio, 1970—. Scoutmaster, Boy Scouts Am., 1958-64. Mem. Nat. Soc. Profl. Engrs., Am. Soc. C.E. (asso.). Home: 454 Sprucewood St San Antonio TX 78216 Office: 1800 Plaza Bldg West San Antonio TX 78217

SCHNEIDER, RAYMOND THEODORE, chem. engr.; b. Cin., July 17, 1929; s. Joseph A. and Eleanor (Schaefer) S.; Chem.E., U. Cin., 1952; m. Mary Jovita Diersen, July 5, 1958; children—Rita M., Ruth A., Joseph R., Mary M., Carol M. Chem. engr. U.S. AEC, Fernald, O., 1952-54; process engr. Vulcan-Cin. Inc., 1956-62; project engr. Formica Corp., Cin., 1962-63; sr. process engr. Chem. & Indsl. Corp., Cin., 1963-65; sr. devel. engr. Wellman-Lord Inc., Lakeland, Fla., 1965-69; individual practice as cons. chem. engr., Lakeland, 1970-72; pres. Schneider Engring., Inc., Lakeland, Fla., 1972—. Bd. dirs. St. Joseph Sch., Lakeland, 1969—, pres. parents' club, 1969-70. Served with AUS, 1954-56. Registered profl. engr., Fla., Ohio. Mem. Nat. Soc. Profl. Engrs., Fla. Engring. Soc., Cons. Engrs. Fla., Am. Inst. Chem. Engrs., Am. Chem. Soc. Rotarian, K.C. Research in nitric acid manufacture, sulfur dioxide recovery. Home: 1338 Robinhood Lane N Lakeland FL 33803 Office: Box 2765 Lakeland FL 33803

SCHNEIDER, RICHARD ELMER, oil co. explorationist; b. Cleve., Aug. 15, 1930; s. Elden E. and Thelma (LeBeau) S.; B.S. in Geology, Western Res. U., 1952; m. Barbara Irie, June 9, 1951; 1 son, Richard Stanley. Geophysicist, Petty Geophys. Engring. Co., San Antonio, 1952-56; with Continental Oil Co., 1956—, now sr. staff geophysicist exploration-geophysics, Ponca City, Okla. Cons., Mexican Sulphur Co., 1966-69. Chmn., United Fund, Ponca City, 1968, bd. dirs., 1967—; bd. dirs. A.R.C., Ponca City, 1968—, Ponca City YMCA, 1969—. Recipient awards including Able Toastmaster award, 1969; Distinguished Toastmaster award (1st Oklahoman), 1971; Key Man award, 1972. Mem. Soc. Exploration Geophysicists, Internat. Platform Assn., Pi Kappa Alpha, Kappa Kappa Psi. Presbyn. Elk. Club: Toastmasters International (local pres. 1965, state gov. 1969, 70, dir. 1972). Home: 2115 Garden St Ponca City OK 74601 Office: Conoco-Geophysics Box 1267 Ponca City OK 74601

SCHNEIDER, WILBERT MARION, coll. pres.; b. Loyal, Okla., Apr. 15, 1918; s. C.C. and Sarah (Voth) S.; B.A., Union Coll., 1940; M.B.A., U. Okla., 1944; Ph.D., U. So. Cal., 1951; m. Ardith Chase, Nov. 13, 1941; children—Douglas, Shirley, Janet, Sara. Accountant White Meml. Hosp., 1941-42; head dept. bus. adminstrn. Southwestern Jr. Coll., 1942-45, Walla Walla Coll., 1945-53; head dept. bus. adminstrn. Emmanuel Missionary Coll., 1953-55, acad. dean, 1955-58; treas. Loma Linda Food Co., 1958-60; acad. dean So. Missionary Coll., Collegedale, Tenn., 1960-63, pres., 1967—; acad. dean Pacific Union Coll., Angwin, Cal., 1963-67. Dir. Temperance Ins. Exchange. Mem. Am. Econ. Assn., Am. Accounting Assn., Omicron Delta Gamma. Author: History of American Bankers Association, 1956. Home: PO Box 444 Collegedale TN 37315

SCHNEIDER, WILLIAM CHARLES, govt. ofcl.; b. N.Y.C., Dec. 24, 1923; s. Charles J. and Margaret (Stoeffler) S.; B.S., Mass. Inst. Tech., 1949; M.S., U. Va., 1952; postgrad. Catholic U., 1960-65; m. Rose Ann Vasco, Oct. 6, 1964; children—Catherine M., Jeanne M., Robert J., Robert S. Research scientist NACA Langley Research Center, Hampton, Va., 1949-55; asst. br. head Air-to-Air Missiles Bur. Air, Washington, 1955-60; dir. space vehicles USN Bur. Weapons, Washington, 1960-61; dir. space systems Internat. Tel & Tel., Nutley, N.J., 1961-63; dep. dir. Gemini program Office Manned Space Flight NASA Hdqrs., Washington, 1963-65, Mission dir. Gemini program, 1965-66, dir. Apollo applications missions, 1966-67, dep. dir. for missions Apollo program, 1967-68, dir. SKYLAB program, 1968—. Served with USNR, 1942-46. Recipient Exceptional Service medal, also Distinguished Service medal NASA; named Man of Year, Montgomery County, Md., 1970. Mem. Am. Inst. Aeros. and Astronautics. Home: 11801 Clintwood Pl Silver Spring MD 20902 Office: NASA Hdqrs Code ML Washington DC 20546

SCHNELLBACHER, EMIL ST. ELMO, govt. ofcl.; b. Quincy, Ill., Dec. 18, 1901; s. Charles Christian and Anna (Beach) S.; A.B., U. Ill., 1923; LL.B., Georgetown U., 1926; m. Mary Elizabeth Holt, Feb. 4, 1926; children—Emil, Margaret Ann, Charles William. Purchasing agt. United Foundry Co., Quincy, 1917-19; asst. librarian Ill. Natural History Survey, Urbana, 1921; real estate listing, Urbana, 1922-23; bus. asst. Bur. Fgn. and Domestic Commerce, Washington, 1924-26, asst. chief comml. intelligence div., 1926-40, chief, 1940-42, chief div. commerce and econ. information, 1942-45. dir. intelligence and services div. Office Internat. Trade, 1946-50, asst. dir., 1950-53, dir. office intelligence and services Bus. Fgn. Commerce, 1953-56, dir. office trade promotion, 1956—, asst. dir. Bur. Internat. Bus. Operations, 1961-63, asst. dir. Bur. Internat. Commerce, 1963—. Mem. ECA Commerce Mission to Europe, 1949, co-chmn. U.S. del. Regional Conf. Trade Promotions, UN Econ. Commn. Asia and Far East, 1951. dep. chmn. U.S. delegation Caribbean Conf. Trade Promotion, 1954. chmn. U.S. Trade Mission, India, 1955, Union of South Africa, 1957; U.S. del. 2d meeting Trade Com. ECAFE, Tokyo, 1956; cons. to fgn. trade Dept. Commerce. Recipient gold medal Dept. Commerce, 1950; Man of Year award World Trade Writers Assn., 1956. Mem. Corda Fratres, Assn. Cosmopolitan Clubs, Scabbard and Blade, Phi Alpha Delta, Delta Phi Epsilon (nat. pres. 1964-68). Roman Catholic. Author: Credit and Payment Terms, 1931; Sources of Foreign Credit Information, 1931; Export and Import Practice (with F.R. Eldridge), 1938; Government and Foreign Trade, 1954. Contbr. articles bus. publs. Home: 4540 Warren St NW Washington DC 20016 Office: Dept Commerce Washington DC 20230

SCHNITZER, MARTIN COLBY, educator; b. Wilmette, Ill., Aug. 20, 1925; s. Leon Wendell and Homera (Portman) S.; grad. Phillips Exeter Acad., 1944; student U. of the South, 1944-46; B.A., U. Ala., 1949, M.B.A., 1951; Ph.D., U. Fla., 1960; m. Joan Brown, June 30, 1951; children—Melanie, Meredith, Marcy. Asst. prof. U. Ark., 1955-58; asst. prof. U. Fla., 1958-60; asst. prof. Va. Polytech. Inst., 1960-64, prof. bus. dept., also editor Va. Social Sci. Jour. 1964—. Mem. econ. adv. bd. U.S. Dept. of Commerce; mem. Va. Gov.'s Small Bus. Adv. Council; mem. Pres.'s Pub. Welfare Task Force. Served with U.S. Mcht. Marine, 1945. Ky. Col. Mem. Am., So. econ. assns. Episcopalian. Rotarian. Author: The Economy of Sweden; Comparative Economic Systems; Reading in Public Finance and Public Policy; East and West Germany: A Comparative Economic Analysis; Regional Unemployment and the Relocation of Workers. Home: 1 Rainbow Ridge Dr Blacksburg VA 24060

SCHNOES, ROBERT FREDERICK, business exec.; b. Mt. Lebanon, Pa., Apr. 4, 1926; s. Sebastian J. and Henrietta C. (Schertler) S.; grad. U. Pitts., 1949; m. Dolores K. Hewston, Aug. 13, 1949; children— Carolyn S., Christine P., Nancy E., Judith A. Sales, Midwest territory Autographic Register Co., Hoboken, N.J., 1949-50; quality control dept. Fisher Body div. Gen. Motors Corp., Pitts., 1950-51; with Bettis Atomic Power div. Westinghouse Electric Corp., Pitts., 1951-68, buyer, supervisory buyer, asst. purchasing agt., to asst. to surface ship project mgr., 1951-59, dir. material and facilities Am. Standard, Mil. Products div., Norwood, Mass., 1959-62, exec. v.p. Hamill Mfg. Co., Monroeville, Pa., 1962-63, gen. mgr. aero research instrument dept. Am.-Standard, Chgo., 1963-65, pres. controls div., 1965-68; pres. Dresser Industrial Valve & Instrument div. Dresser Industries, Inc., Stratford, Conn., 1968-70, pres. Indsl. Spltys. group, Stratford, 1970-71; v.p. operations Office of Pres., Dresser Industries, Dallas, 1971—. Served with USNR, 1944-46. Mem. Engring. Soc. Detroit. Club: Dallas. Home: 5131 Tanbark Rd Dallas TX 75229 Office: Republic Nat Bank Bldg Dallas TX 75221

SCHNOOR, RICHARD HARRY, govt. ofcl.; b. N.Y.C., Mar. 14, 1931; s. Harry Henry and Eleanor E. (Speer) S.; student St. Louis U., 1949-50; B. Indsl. Engring., N.Y. U., 1953, M. Indsl. Engring., 1958; m. Mary Jane McAllister, June 13, 1953. Indsl. engr. Aluminum Co. Am., Bridgeport, Conn., 1956-57; sr. indsl. engr. Atomics Internat. div. N. Am. Rockwell Corp., Canoga Park, Cal., 1958-61; prof. indsl. engring. A.F. Inst. Tech., Dayton, O., 1961-64; dep. chief Mgmt. Systems Office, chmn. NASA Exchange Council, J.F. Kennedy Space Center, NASA, Kennedy Space Center, Fla., 1964—. Instr. mgmt. courses Brevard Jr. Coll., Cocoa, Fla., 1965-67. Dist. comdr. U.S. Power Squadrons, 1972—; comdr. Cape Canaveral Power Squadron, 1966-67. Served to lt. USAF, 1954-56, maj. Res. Registered profl. engr., Mass. Mem. Am. Inst. Indsl. Engrs. (chpt. pres. 1963-64). Home: 1010 N Fiske Blvd Cocoa FL 32922 Office: John F Kennedy Space Center NASA Mgmt Systems Office Kennedy Space Center FL 32899

SCHNUR, SIDNEY, physician; b. Bklyn., June 23, 1910; s. Joseph and Sadie (Broadman) S.; B.S., Coll. City N.Y., 1930, M.S., 1931; M.D., N.Y.U., 1935; m. Wilma Adalene Boyce, Mar. 12, 1944; 1 stepson, Joseph H. Parnell III. Intern, Morrisania City Hosp., N.Y.C., 1935-37; resident internal medicine Kings County Hosp., N.Y.C., 1937-38; resident pathology Jefferson Davis Hosp., Houston, 1938-39, asso. physician, 1940—, chief dept. electrocardiology, 1945-50, chief cardiac clinic, 1945-51, chief 4th div. medicine, 1958-60; practice medicine, specializing in cardiology and internal medicine, Houston, 1939—; attending specialist cardiology VA Regional Office and Hosp., 1946—; asso. physician Meth. Hosp.,

1946-53, attending physician, 1954-64, cons. staff, 1966—; chief medicine, electrocardiology St. Joseph Hosp., 1954—, pres. med. staff, 1962-65; electrocardiology Med. Arts Hosp., 1958-60, chief medicine, 1963, pres. staff, 1962-63; attending physician Ben Taub Hosp., 1964—; cons. internal medicine USPHS, 1946-50, St. Luke's Hosp., 1954—; cons. cardiologist, electrocardiologist So. Pacific Hosp., 1954-61; cons. cardiologist San Jacinto Meml. Hosp., Baytown, Tex., 1954-58, Polly Ryon Meml. Hosp., Richmond, 1957-59; clin. asst. prof. medicine Postgrad. Sch. Medicine, Grad. Sch. Biomed. Scis., U. Tex., 1950-52, clin. asso. prof., 1952-57, clin. prof., 1957—, coordinator cardiology courses, 1953—, chmn. affiliated hosp.'s com. internal medicine residency, 1955-61; clin. asst. prof. medicine Coll. Medicine, Baylor U., 1946-51, clin. asso. prof., 1951-62, clin. prof., 1962—, mem. faculty affairs com., 1957-58, acad. council, 1965—. Trustee Houston Mus. Natural Sci., 1965—, exec. com., 1969—. Served to lt. col., M.C., USAAF, 1940-45. Decorated Bronze Star medal. Diplomate in cardiovascular disease Am. Bd. Internal Medicine. Fellow A.C.P., Am. Coll. Chest Physicians, Am. Coll. Cardiology; mem. A.M.A., So., Tex. med. assns., Harris County Med. Soc. (chmn. grievance com. 1959, chmn. bd. censors 1962; mem. exec. bd. 1962; pres. 1972), Houston Soc. Internal Medicine (past chmn. cardiology sect.; pres.), A.A.A.S., Am. Fedn. Clin. Research, Am. (past Tex. del.), Tex. (dir. 1957-59, mem. exec. com., chmn. sci. program com. 1957—; pres. 1971), Houston (dir., mem. exec. com. 1950—, pres. 1960) heart assns., Houston C. of C. (past chmn. indsl. health conf.), Tex. Acad. Internal Medicine (past gov.). Editorial cons. Heart Bull., 1951—; contbg. editor Med. Record and Annals, 1952-62; editorial bd. Cardiology Digest, 1966—. Contbr. articles to profl. jours. Home: 2139 Sunset Blvd Houston TX 77005 Office: St Joseph Profl Bldg Houston TX 77002

SCHOEL, JOSEPH DAWSON, civil engr.; b. Birmingham, Ala., July 6, 1926; s. Walter and Annie Mary (Dawson) S.; student U. Ala., 1946-50, 52-60; m. Dorothy Elise Walters, Aug. 22, 1970; 1 dau., Melissa Leigh. Engr., land surveyor Walter Schoel Engring. Co., Inc., Birmingham, 1950-61, partner, 1961-69, sec.-treas., 1969-72, v.p., treas., 1972—. Served with A.C., USNR, 1944-46. Mem. Ala. Soc. Profl. Land Surveyors. Methodist. Home: 1329 Willoughby Rd Birmingham AL 35216 Office: Jefferson Fed Bldg Birmingham AL 35203

SCHOEL, WALTER, JR., cons. engring. firm exec.; b. Birmingham, Ala., Jan. 23, 1924; s. Walter and Annie Mary (Dawson) S.; student Ga. Inst. Tech., 1943-44; B.S. in Civil Engring., U. Ala., 1957; m. Martha Erline Watson, Dec. 11, 1948; children—Martha Watson, Walter III. With Walter Schoel Engring. Co., Birmingham, 1945—, partner, 1960-68, pres., 1968—; city engr. Vestavia Hills, Ala., 1964—. Served with USMCR, 1943-45. Mem. Am. Soc. C.E., Consulting Engrs. Council Ala., Phi Gamma Delta. Baptist. Clubs: The Club (Birmingham); Vestavia Country. Home: 1341 Moutain Laurel Circle Birmingham AL 35216 Office: Jefferson Fed Bldg 213 N 21st St Birmingham AL 35203

SCHOEN, KENNETH BERNARD, investment banker; b. Louisville, Feb. 2, 1921; s. William Joseph and Virginia (Key) S.; B.A. U. Notre Dame, 1943; postgrad. N.Y. Inst. Finance, 1946; m. Gloria Catignani, Oct. 14, 1944 children—Michael Joseph, Patrick Edward. Vice pres. gen. partner J.C. Bradford & Co., Nashville, 1945-71; regional cons. A.G. Edwards & Sons, Inc., 1971—; financial v.p., sec., treas. Aurora Publishers, Inc. Bd. dirs., treas. Cath. Youth Orgn., 1953-70; pres. Nashville Area Council Alcoholism, 1966-68, Project Equality, 1966-70; mem. exec. com. Nashville U.S.O., 1950-69; mem. Nat. Cath. Community Service, 1967—; v.p., dir. Travelers Aid Soc., 1964-71; chmn. Tenn. Alcoholic Beverage Study Commn., 1965-67; state mem. John F. Kennedy Meml. Library Com., 1964-67. Trustee Aquinas Jr. Coll., 1966—, Samaritans Anonymous, 1960-68; chmn. bd. St. Thomas Hosp. Sch. Nursing, 1960-68; mem. bd. Davidson County YMCA. Served with USCGR, 1943-45. Apptd. Knight of St. Gregory, Pope Paul VI, 1966. Mem. Nat. Nashville (pres. 1955) assns. security dealers, Nat. Council Cath. Men. Roman Catholic. Elk, K.C. (4 deg.). Clubs: Serra (past v.p. internat.), Richland Country, City, Westside Aquatic (pres. 1952-53). Home: 2303 Golf Club Lane Nashville TN 37215 2303 Golf Club Lane Nashville TN 37215 Office: 170 4th Av N Nashville TN 37219

SCHOENBERGER, PODINE CONRAD POPE, editor; b. Baton Rouge; d. George Christian and Podine (Pope) Schoenberger; B.A., La. U.; postgrad. U. Ark., Columbia. Sci. editor Times-Picayune, New Orleans. Mem. Am. Women's Vol. Services, 1941-45. Recipient awards for best stories, articles, etc. La. Press Women, annually 1955-64, 68-71, Nat. Fedn. Press Women, 1956, 62, 63, 70, 71 Press Club of New Orleans, annually 1959-62, 63, 66, 67-71, Am. Cancer Soc., 1964-67, United Cerebral Palsy Assn., 1967, La. Heart Assn., 1966-71, La. chpt. Nat. Found March Dimes, 1966, Com. on Alcoholism for Greater New Orleans, 1964, Orleans Parish Med. Soc., 1967, La.-Miss. Asso. Press Assn., 1965-67; S.E. regional award Arthritis Found., 1966, honorable mention, 1970, Journalism award Am. Soc. Abdominal Surgeons, 1971 other awards. Mem. Am. Assn. U. Women, Nat. League Am. Pen Women, Nat. Assn. Sci. Writers, La. Press Club of New Orleans (bd. dirs. 1960-62, 55, awards com. 1959-64, v.p. 1965), Am., New Orleans dental assns., Delta Delta Delta. Club: Orleans (hon.). Home: 622 Audubon St New Orleans LA 70118 Office: 615 North St New Orleans LA 70130

SCHOENBORN, ROBERT MORTON, constrn. co. exec.; b. Rocky Hill, Conn., July 30, 1910; s. Maxwell Robert and Marie (Morton) S.; B.S. in Chem. Engring., U. Fla., 1932; m. Margaret Epps, Apr. 19, 1935 (div. Oct. 1969); children—Robert Joel, Carlton Morton, Judith (Mrs. Charles Fleming Jr.); m. 2d, Annalisa Oosting, Nov. 5, 1969. With W.L. Cobb Constrn. Co., Tampa, Fla., 1934—, asst. sec., 1955—, chief engr., 1966—, also dir.; dir. Pinellas Industries, Inc., St. Petersburg, Fla. Pres., East Seminole Civic Club, 1945-50, Fla. Sheriff's Boys Ranch, contbr. U. So. Fla. Found., 1967—. Mem. U. Fla. Alumni Club Tampa. Republican. Methodist (chmn. bd. stewards 1956-58). Lion. Club: University Florida Century (Gainesville, Fla.). Home: 2612 Pearce Dr Apt 310 Clearwater FL 33516 Office: 5002 E Hills Av Tampa FL 33610

SCHOENIG, ARTHUR FERDINAND, JR., civil engr.; b. Boerne, Tex., May 26, 1926; s. Arthur Ferdinand and Alma Marie (Rittiman) S.; B.S. in Elec. Engring., U. Okla., 1946; postgrad. St. Mary's U. San Antonio, 1948-49; m. Jean Mary Overland, Feb. 12, 1953; 1 stepdau., Priscilla Alden; children—Dorothy Eleanor, Tammis, Arthur Ferdinand III. Representative for comml. dept. City Pub. Service Bd., San Antonio, 1953-54; design engr. Tex. Automatic Sprinkler Corp., San Antonio, 1954-55; gen. engr. U.S. Army Dept., Ft. Sam Houston, San Antonio, 1955-59; mech. engr. 3700th Civil Engring. Group, Lackland AFB, Tex., 1959-64; civil engr. const. div., dep. chief staff for civil engring., USAF Hdqrs. Air Tng. Command, at Columbus, Craig, Moody and Lackland AFB's 1964-72; asst. chief OPS and Maintenance Div. OCS/CE, USAF, ATC, 1972—. Served to lt., USNR, 1943-53. Mem. Nat., Tex. socs. profl. engrs., Soc. Am. Mil. Engrs., Res. Officers Am. (past pres. San Antonio chpt.), Naval Res. Assn. (past chpt. pres.), Navy League (past pres. Alamo council), Eta Kappa Nu. Contbr. articles to profl. jours. Home: 815 Ridgemont Av San Antonio TX 78209 Office: Hdqrs Air Tng Command USAF Bldg 905 Randolph AFB TX 78148

SCHOFIELD, CHARLES STIKELEATHER, hotel exec.; b. Florence, S.C., Dec. 21, 1916; s. Robert Pace and Ivey (Stikeleather) S.; grad. high sch.; m. Elizabeth Person Cooke, July 20, 1940; children—Charles Marshall, James Thomas. Vice pres., sec.-treas. Schofield Hardware Co., Inc., Florence, 1933-66; pres., chmn. bd. Carolina Enterprise, Inc., Florence, 1951—. Mem. Wofford Coll. Parents Adv. Council. Served with AUS, 1943-45; PTO. Mem. Am. Legion, V.F.W. Republican. Methodist. Club: Florence Country. Home: 1431 Madison Av Florence SC 29501 Office: PO Box 672 Florence SC 29501

SCHOFIELD, LEMUEL BRADDOCK, II, TV broadcasting exec.; b. Gouverneur, N.Y., Jan. 13, 1935; s. Joseph A. and Mary (Lewis) S.; B.A., U. Pa., 1956; LL.B., U. Pa. Coll. Law, 1959; m. Shirley M. Peck, Oct. 24, 1959; children—Braddock, Jennifer. Admitted to N.Y. State bar, 1959; asst. dist. atty. N.Y. County, 1959-63; sales adminstr. NBC, N.Y.C., 1964-65; gen. counsel Overmyer Communication Co., N.Y.C., 1966-68; gen. counsel, sec. Corinthian Broadcasters Corp., N.Y.C., 1968-71; program dir. KOTV, Tulsa, 1971—. Home: 3950 S Delaware Av Tulsa OK 74105 Office: 302 S Frankfort St Tulsa OK 74120

SCHOGGEN, PHIL, educator; b. Tulsa, Aug. 28, 1923; s. Walter B. and Emma (Alexander) S.; A.B., Park Coll., 1946; M.A., U. Kan., 1951; Ph.D., 1954; m. Maxine F. Spoor, June 28, 1944; children—Leida Beth, Christopher Phil, Ann Louise, Susan Diane. Research asso. Wayne State U., 1954-55; research asso., lectr. U. Kan., 1955-57; asst. prof. to asso. prof. U. Ore., 1957-66; prof., chmn. dept. psychology George Peabody Coll., Nashville, 1966—; psychol. cons. VA. Served to lt. comdr. USNR, 1943-46, 50-51. Fellow Am. Psychol. Assn.; mem. A.A.A.S., Soc. for Research Child Devel., Sigma Xi. Home: 6729 Curreywood Dr Nashville TN 37205

SCHOLES, CHARLES MARCEL, aviation co. exec.; b. League City, Tex., Aug. 26, 1903; s. Robert Hamilton and Geneva (Dibrell) S.; LL.B., Houston Law Sch., 1936; m. Dora Frances Petmecky, Dec. 22, 1945. With Humble Oil & Refining Co., Houston, 1920—, pilot, 1940-42, chief pilot, 1942-45, mgr. aviation dept., 1945—. Mem. Nat. Pilots Assn., Air Force Assn., Airplane Owners and Pilots Assn., Tex. Aero. Assn., Tex. Pvt. Flyers, Quiet Birdman. Methodist. Mason. Home: 7500 Dawn Hill Circle Austin TX 78746 Office: Humble Bldg Houston TX 77001

SCHOLTES, ROBERT MARTIN, educator, civil engr.; b. Biloxi, Miss., May 28, 1928; s. Leo Martin and Marguerite (Stroeker) S.; B.S., Miss., State U., 1951, M.S., 1956; Ph.D., Ga. Inst. Tech., 1964; m. Hilda L. Beck, Jan. 1, 1954; children—Sharon Rae, Cynthia Joan, Sandra Ann, Robert Beck. Mem. faculty Miss. State U., 1951—, prof. civil engring., 1963—, head dept., 1966—; cons. engr., 1956—. Registered profl. engr., Miss. Mem. Nat., Miss. socs. profl. engrs., Am. Soc. Engring. Edn., Am. Soc. C.E., Sigma Xi, Phi Kappa Phi, Chi Epsilon, Tau Beta Pi. Presbyn. Club: Starkville Exchange (pres. 1967-68). Home: 108 Briarwood Dr Starkville MS 39759 Office: Drawer CE State College MS 39762

SCHOON, OWEN HARRY, labor union ofcl.; b. Gary, Ind., June 26, 1914; s. Jacob J. and Catherine (Koedyker) S.; grad. high sch.; m. Margaret L. Hollopeter, Dec. 25, 1936; children—Allan R., Garry O., Marilyn J., Paul R. Clk., U.S. Post Office, 1938—; financial sec. local 266 Nat. Fedn. Postal Clks., 1940-42, nat. state rep. Ind., 1946-56, nat. v.p., 1956-62; sec.-treas. Ind. Fedn. Postal Clks., 1942-46; nat. sec.-treas. United Fedn. Postal Clks., Washington, 1962—; gen. sec.-treas. Am. Postal Workers Union AFL-CIO, Washington, 1971—. Mason. Home: 10209 Dickens Ct Bethesda MD 20014 Office: 817 14th St NW Washington DC 20005

SCHOONOVER, ROBERT ANDREW, journalist; b. Knoxville, Pa., Mar. 13, 1922; s. Lewis Andrew and Anna (Prentice) S.; student Bob Jones U., 1949-52; B.S., Temple U., 1956; M.A., Am. U., 1962; m. Lillian B. Schoonover, June 2, 1953. Sports editor Coatesville (Pa.) Record, 1956-57; reporter Corning (N.Y.) Leader, 1957-61; editor Fla. Health Notes, Jacksonville, 1962—. Mem. Cummer Gallery Art, Village Art Group (pres., 1967). Bd. dirs. Jacksonville chpt. Am. Epilepsy Found. Mem. Fla. Pub. Health Assn., Sigma Delta Chi. Methodist. Home: 7695 Rolling Hills Dr Jacksonville FL 32205 Office: 1217 Pearl St Jacksonville FL 32202

SCHOPLER, ERIC, psychologist, educator; b. Furth, Germany, Feb. 8, 1927 (came to U.S. 1938, naturalized 1943); s. Ernest H. and Erna (Oppenheimer) S.; A.B., U. Chgo., 1949, M.A. (USPHS fellow), 1955, Ph.D. (Nat. Inst. Mental Health fellow), 1964; children (by previous marriage)—Susan, Robert, Thomas; m. 2d, Margaret D. Lansing, Apr. 8, 1972. Family counselor Family Service of Rochester, N.Y., 1955-58; acting chief psychiat. social worker Bradley Hosp., Providence, 1958-60; research asso. Treatment and Research Center for Childhood Schizophrenia, Chgo., 1960-64; asso. prof. psychology, dir. research devel. Child Psychiatry div. Sch. Medicine U. N.C. at Chapel Hill, 1964—; dir. Childhood Psychosis Project. Served with AUS, 1945-47. Fellow Am. Orthopsychiatric Assn.; mem. Am. Psychol. Assn., A.A.A.S., Soc. Research Child Devel., Sigma Xi. Home: 43 Oakwood Dr Chapel Hill NC 27514

SCHOTT, JOE LAWRENCE, publisher; b. Castroville, Tex., Oct. 4, 1933; s. Joe F. and Lucille (Tschirhart) S.; B.J., U. Tex., Austin, 1955; m. Barbarajo Woerner, June 17, 1956; children—Robert Joseph, Kathryn Anne. Reporter, San Antonio Light, 1955-63, picture editor, 1963-68, asst. city editor, 1968-70, city editor, 1970—; co-founder Medina Valley and County News Bull., Castroville, 1958, pub., 1958—. City councilman, Castroville, 1958-59. Served with AUS, 1956-58. Mem. Nat. Newspaper Assn., San Antonio Press Club, Tex. Press Assn., Castroville C. of C. (past mgr.), Sigma Delta Chi. Home: Karm St Castroville TX 78009 Office: Castroville TX 78009

SCHRAG, DONALD EUGENE, clin. psychologist; b. Kingman, Kan., Jan. 20, 1935; s. Marvin D. and Frieda (Graber) S.; B.A., Bethel Coll., 1956; M.Ed., Wichita State U., 1962; Ph.D., La. State U., 1966; m. Carol Lee Krehbiel, Aug. 26, 1956; children—Jon Douglas, Susan Lynn, Mark Alan. Acting chief psychologist Hammond (La.) State Sch., 1967; asst. prof. psychology U. Ala., Tuscaloosa, 1967; staff psychologist student health service, 1967, individual practice clin. psychology, Tuscaloosa, Ala., 1967—; cons. Muscle Shoals Mental Health Center, Florence, Ala., 1967—. Mem. Am., Southeastern, Ala. psychol. assns., Phi Kappa Phi. Presbyn. Research in field. Home: 52 Woodridge St Tuscaloosa AL 35401

SCHRAMM, TEXAS EDWARD, profl. football exec.; b. Los Angeles, June 2, 1920; s. Texas Ernest and Elsa J. (Steinwender) S.; B.A. in Journalism, U. Tex., 1947; m. Martha Anne Snowden, Apr. 15, 1942; children—Mardee Anne, Christi Lee, Kandy Gayle. Sports editor Austin (Tex.) Statesman, 1946-47; publicity dir., gen. mgr. Los Angeles Rams Football Club, 1947-57; asst. dir. sports CBS, 1957-60; v.p., gen. mgr. Dallas Cowboys Football Club, Inc., 1960-66, pres., gen. mgr. 1966—; pres. Tex. Stadium Corp., Dallas Cowboys Enterprises, Inc., Cebe Corp.; dir. Park Cities Bank & Trust Co. Served to capt. USAAF, 1941-45. Home: 9355 Sunny Brook Lane Dallas TX 75220 Office: 6116 N Central Expressway Dallas TX 75206

SCHREIBER, EDWARD, city ofcl.; b. N.Y.C., Nov. 12, 1905; s. Max and Sarah (Kartin) S.; student pub. schs.; m. Sue Gold, Nov. 27, 1928; children—Melvyn Hirsh, Stanley Murray. Partner Schreiber & Miller Furniture Co., Galveston, Tex., 1933—. Chmn. Police, Firemen's Civil Service Bd., 1947-59, United Fund campaign, 1954. Chmn. commn. Galveston Charter, 1960; mayor Galveston, 1961-62, 63-71, mem. city council, 1962-63; pres. Houston-Galveston Area Council. Bd. govs. Shrine Crippled Children's Hosp., Burn Inst. Named Outstanding Citizen Galveston Jr. C. of C., 1955; Outstanding Credit Man of Year for U.S. and Can., Nat. Retail Credit Assn., 1956; Outstanding Retail Furniture Dealer Tex., Tex. Furniture Dealers, 1957; Boss of Year, Retail Credit Execs., 1964; East Texan of Month, Sept. 1971. Mem. Galveston Mchts. Assn. (pres. 1955-56), Retail Mchts. Assn. Tex. (pres. 1950-51), Retail (pres. 1944-45), Galveston (pres. 1943-44) furniture assns., Retail Credit Execs. Tex. (pres. 1948-49), Navy League (adv. com.), Tex. Municipal League (region pres. 1965-66; mem. revenue and taxation com.), Galveston County Mayors' and Councilmen's Assn. (past pres.), Galveston C. of C. (pres. 1958). Jewish religion (congregation pres. 1935-36). Mason (Shriner), Eagle. Clubs: Kiwanis (pres. 1941-42, past dist. lt. gov.), Traffic, Propeller, Country, Galveston County Knife and Fork (past pres.). Home: 38 Cedar Lawn St Galveston TX 77550 Office: 2318 Market St Galveston TX 77550

SCHREIBER, JOSEPH PHILIP, retail sales co. exec.; b. Madison, Wis., Mar. 3, 1917; s. Cecil E. and Harriet Leone (Spoor) S.; B.A., U. Wis., 1940; m. Ruth Helen Lassen, Mar. 9, 1957; 1 son, Barry Alan. Staff auditor Arthur Andersen & Co., Chgo., 1940-42; comptroller, T.C. Esser Co., Milw., 1946-60; v.p., treas., dir. Advance Distbrs. Inc., Advance Publishers, Inc., Adon, Inc., Mid-Fla. Collection Service, Inc., all Orlando, Fla., 1960—. Treas. Polit. Action Assn., Central Fla., 1965-66. Served to lt. Supply Corps, USNR, 1943-46; PTO. Mem. Nat. Assn. Accountants. Presbyn. Elk. Clubs: Central Florida Executives, Orlando AFB Officers. Home: 2123 Chippewa Trail Maitland FL 32751 Office: 2826 Edgewater Dr Orlando FL 32804

SCHREINER, GEORGE E., physician, educator; b. Buffalo, Apr. 26, 1922; s. George F. and Eleanor (Krieg) S.; B.A. magna cum laude, Canisius Coll., 1943; M.D. cum laude, Georgetown U., 1946; m. Joanne Baker, Apr. 4, 1949; children—George F., Mary Elaine, Meredith Ann, William Porter, Sara Baker, Peter K., Joanne Elizabeth. Intern, Boston City Hosp., 1946-47; asst. in physiology N.Y. U. Sch. Medicine, 1947-48, fellow in medicine, 1947-49, instr. in physiology, 1948-50; fellow in medicine, clin. asst., vis. physician N.Y. U. Bellevue Med. Center, 1949-50; sr. resident in medicine VA Hosp., Washington, 1950-51; clin. instr. medicine Georgetown U. Sch. Medicine, Washington, 1951-52, instr. medicine, dir. renal clinic, 1952-55, asst. prof. medicine, dir. renal clinic, 1955-58, asso. prof. medicine, dir. renal and electrolyte div., 1958-61; prof. medicine, dir. renal and electrolyte div. Georgetown U. Hosp. and Sch. Medicine, Washington, 1961—; dir. clin. study unit Georgetown U. Hosp., 1961-72; cons. Walter Reed Army Med. Center, Washington, VA Hosp., Washington, Nat. Naval Med. Center, Bethesda, Md., NIH, Bethesda, Washington. Spl. adviser Nat. Zool. Park, Smithsonian Inst., 1967; mem. com. on code of ethics for clin. investigation, 1964. Served to capt. M.C., AUS, 1951-52. Fellow A.C.P., A.A.A.S.; mem. Assn. Am. Physicians, Am. Fedn. Clin. Research (pres. 1962-63), Am. Soc. Clin. Investigation, Washington (pres. 1969-70), Am. (exec. com. renal sect. 1961) heart assns., Soc. for Exptl. Biology, Am. Soc. for Artificial Internal Organs past pres., (mem. council 1956—), Harvey Soc., A.M.A. (chmn. nephrology panel 1963), Internat. Soc. Nephrology (sec. gen III Internat. Congress Nephrology 1964-66, v.p. 1969—), Council on Drugs (com. on adverse reactions 1963), Nat. Drug Research Bd. (chmn. com. on establishment Armed Forces Inst. Pathology Registry 1963), So. Soc. for Clin. Research (chmn. nominating com. 1962), Nat. Kidney Found. (pres. Washington chpt. 1969-71), Med. Arts Soc. (sec.-treas. 1958), So. Salt, Water and Kidney Club, Nat. Drug Research Bd., D.C. (mem. editorial bd. 1957) Med. Soc., Sigma Xi, Alpha Omega Alpha. Editor-in-chief Nephron, 1963-72, Transactions Am. Soc. for Artificial Internal Organs, 1955—; mem. editorial bd. Am. Jour. Medicine, 1960-70, Med. Annals D.C., 1957—, Kidney Internat., 1972; cons. editor Biomed. Measurements, 1968, Modern Medicine, 1969. Author: (with J.F. Maher) Uremia: Biochemistry, Pathogenesis and Treatment, 1961; Acute Renal Failure and Diseases of the Kidney, 1967; (with J.F. Maher) Dialysis of Acute Poisoning; Ethics of Chronic Dialysis; Symposium on Asymptomatic Bacteriuria. Contbr. articles to profl. jours. Home: Tallwood St Great Falls VA 22066 Office: 3800 Reservoir Rd NW Washington DC 20007

SCHREINER, RAYMOND LESLIE, JR., state ofcl.; b. Washington, Nov. 7, 1921; s. Raymond Leslie and Helen (Hardy) S.; student U. Md., 1940-41; m. Alice May Gartrell, May 30, 1942; children—Leslie (Mrs. William Bolster), Alice (Mrs. J. Wayne Beachy), Raymond Leslie, Barbara. Announcer, WPID, Petersburg, Va., 1941-42, WHNC, Henderson, N.C. 1946, WBTM, Danville, Va., 1946-50, WHTN, Huntington, W.Va., 1950; program dir. WRNL, Richmond, Va., 1950-62; mgr. WBCI, Williamsburg, Va., 1962-64; news dir. WXEX-TV, Petersburg-Richmond, 1964-66; dir. information Va. Dept. Agr. and Commerce, Richmond, 1966—. Served with AUS, 1943-46. Mem. So. Assn. Information Officers State Depts. Agr. (pres. 1971—), Nat. Assn. Farm Broadcasters (asso.), Richmond Pub. Relations Soc., Sigma Delta Chi. Home: 2537 E Tremont Ct Richmond VA 23225 Office: 203 N Governor St Richmond VA 23219

SCHROEDER, DOROTHY JEAN STEWART (MRS. WILLIAM G. SCHROEDER, JR.), educator; b. Waco, Tex., Oct. 1, 1915; d. Hugh L. and Ruth (Stiff) Stewart; student U. Tex., 1932-34; B.A., Baylor U., 1936; M.Ed., Howard Payne Coll., 1956; postgrad. Trinity U., 1958, 61, Sam Houston State Mexican Field Sch., 1964, 65; m. William G. Schroeder, Jr., Oct. 28, 1939; children—William G. III, Jean Ann (Mrs. Roger H. Clark), Bonnie. Tchr., Winters (Tex.) High Sch., 1936-38; instr. Howard Payne Coll., Brownwood, Tex., 1946-48, asso. prof. sociology, 1956—. Sec.-treas., Brownwood Crystal Ice Co., 1968. Sec., Brown County Hosp. Authority, 1965—, Pub. Facilities Com., 1958-62; dir. Am. Shrines Travelling Sem., 1968. Democracy in Action chmn. Howard Payne Coll., 1964—. Mem. Am. Assn. U. Women, D.A.R., Nat. Council Family Relations, Kappa Delta Pi, Alpha Lambda Delta, Delta Chi Rho. Club: Dollie Robnett Faculty (pres. 1967). Home: 1715 Vincent St Brownwood TX 76801

SCHROEDER, FRANK, JR., govt. ofcl.; b. Bartlesville, Okla., Sept. 8, 1927; s. Frank and Clara (Coperton) S.; B.S., U. Ill., 1949, M.S., 1951; m. Patricia Julia Bothwell, Aug. 31, 1949; children—Karl, Katherine. Physicist, sect. chief, br. mgr. atomic energy div. Phillips Petroleum Co., Idaho Falls, Ida., 1951-68; dep. dir. div. reactor licensing U.S. A.E.C., Washington, 1968-72, asst. dep. for tech. rev. Directorate Licensing, 1972—. Served with USNR, 1945-46. Fellow Am. Nuclear Soc. (dir. 1968-71, mem. exec. com. 1968-71). Home: 802 S Belgrade Rd Silver Spring MD 20902 Office: US Atomic Energy Commission Washington DC 20545

SCHROEDER, GEORGE CHESTER, JR., elec. engr.; b. New Orleans, Oct. 28, 1922; s. George Chester and Dagmar Mathilda (Erickson) S.; student Loyola U. of South Sch. Music, 1941-42; B.S., Tulane U., 1949; m. Carolyn Cutler, June 28, 1945; children—George

Chester III, Robert Leonard. Design engr., asso. Louis N. Goodman & Assos., cons. elec. engrs., New Orleans, 1949-55; pres. Schroeder & Assos., cons. elec. engrs., New Orleans, 1955—. Served to maj. USAF, 1942-45; ETO. Decorated Air medal with 2 oak leaf clusters; recipient Lighting awards Illuminating Engring. Soc., 1954, 55, 58, 59, 62, 64, 65, Goddard award, 1966, Guth awards, 1966, 69. Mem. I.E.E.E., Illuminating Engring. Soc., Soc. Tulane Engrs., Cons. Engrs. Council. Lutheran. Home: 6945 Catina St New Orleans LA 70124 Office: 148 W Harrison Av New Orleans LA 70124

SCHROEDER, HERMAN MARCEL, lawyer; b. New Orleans, July 16, 1922; s. Herman A. and Marie (Cauhape) S.; LL.B., Loyola U., 1953; m. Ann Fleming, Nov. 16, 1963. Admitted to La. bar, 1953; partner firm Schroeder, Kuntz & Miranne, and predecessor firm, New Orleans, 1953—. Served to 2d lt. USAAF, World War II. Decorated Air Medal. Mem. La. Trial Lawyers Assn. Democrat. Roman Catholic. Lion. Home: 6127 Perlita St New Orleans LA 70112 Office: Richards Bldg New Orleans LA 70112

SCHROEDER, LAWRENCE ALEXANDER, dept. store exec.; b. La Grange, Tex., Oct. 16, 1921; s. Alexander A. and Charlotte (Brandes) S.; B.B.A., U. Houston, 1949, M.B.A., 1952; certified consumer credit exec., 1963; m. Geraldine Neal, Mar. 19, 1943; 1 son, Ronald Neal. Asst. mgr. Western Newspaper Union, Houston, 1941-42, 46-53; auditor Dennis Pitcock, C.P.A., Houston, 1953; exec. asst. Comet Rice Mills, Houston, 1953-54; collection mgr. Sears, Roebuck & Co., Houston, 1954-57; mgr. credit sales, corporate sec. Oshman's Sporting Goods, Inc., Houston, 1957—; corp. sec. Power Pak Co., Inc., Houston, 1962-68. Chmn., Oshman's div. United Fund, 1968-72; chmn. spl. gifts sect. Pres.'s Fund, U. Houston, 1970; chmn. Retail Credit Sch., Houston, 1964, also lectr., 1961-64. Served with USAAF, 1942-45. Mem. Oshman's Employees Club (pres. 1968), Houston Retail Credit Assn. (pres. 1963), Active Corps Execs., S.W. Basketball Ofcls. Assn., U. Houston Alumni Fedn., Sigma Chi Epsilon. Democrat. Baptist. Home: 18301 Upper Bay Rd 224C Nassau Bay TX 77058 Office: PO Box 18234 2302 Maxwell Lane Houston TX 77023

SCHROEDER, ROBERT VIRGIL, dentist; b. Owasso, Okla., July 30, 1926; s. Edwin Jacob and Kathryn (Voth) S.; student Tabor Coll., 1947-48; B.A., Baylor U., 1950, M.A., 1952, D.D.S., 1962; postgrad. U. Tex., 1955-56; m. Carolyn Marie Koller, June 30, 1951; children—Janet Carol, Judith Kay. Customer service coorinator Tex. Instruments Co., Dallas, 1957-58; practice dentistry, Dallas, 1962—; clin. instr. Baylor U. Coll. Dentistry, Dallas, 1962-65. Mem. organizing com. Criswell Bible Inst., Dallas, 1970-71. Served with CIC, AUS, 1945-46, as pilot, USAF, 1951-55. Mem. Dallas County Dental Soc., Tex., Am. dental assns., Kappa Delta Pi. Baptist (deacon). Home: 3961 Cobblestone Dr Dallas TX 75229 Office: 8617 NW Plaza Dr Dallas TX 75225

SCHROEDER, STEPHEN EDWIN, utilities exec.; b. Yorktown, Tex., Aug. 16, 1932; s. Edwin Otto and Ella (Kruse) S.; A.A., Tex. Luth. Coll., 1951; m. Billie Juanell Hutchins, June 14, 1953; children—Stephen Michael, Susan Michelle, Sondra Meliss. Apprentice lineman Central Power & Light Co., Kenedy, Tex., 1953-59, serviceman, Runge, Kenedy, Tex., 1959-62, mgr. Goliad, Berclair, Tex., 1962-69, mgr., Cotulla, Dilley and Millett, Tex., 1969—, conf. leader, 1960-62. Chmn. fund drive Boy Scouts Am., 1964; chmn. nominating com., bd. dirs. Coastal Bend Respiratory Assn., 1969. Bd. dirs. Goliad County Fair Assn. Served with AUS, 1954-56. Recipient pres.'s plaque for outstanding mgr. in marketing program Guadalupe Dist. Central Power & Light Co., 1967, S.Tex. C. of C. plaque for outstanding service, 1967. Mem. Goliad County (dir., past pres.), S. Tex. (dir.), Cotulla (pres. 1970-71) chambers commerce. Lutheran (lay reader). Lion. Home: 1008 Carizzo St Cotulla TX 78014 Office: 113 Center St Cotulla TX 78014

SCHROEDER, WILLIAM JENNINGS, JR., data processing cons.; b. New Orleans, Mar. 19, 1930; s. William Jennings and Mary (Bujacic) S.; B.B.A., Loyola U. of South, 1951; M.B.A., Tulane U., 1953; m. Julie Hall, Feb. 14, 1956 (dec.); children—William Timothy, Teresa Colette, Tracy Ann; m. 2d, Beverly Rein, July 31, 1970; 1 son, Alan Conrad. Asst. dept. head tabulating and statis. Esso Standard Oil Co., New Orleans, 1955-59; staff asst. to gen. mgr. New Orleans Retailers Credit Bur., Inc., 1959; sr. systems engr. IBM Corp., New Orleans, 1959—; sec.-treas. Coldway Truck Line, Inc. C.P.A., La. Mem. Nat. Assn. Accountants (past pres. New Orleans chpt.), Am. Inst. C.P.A.'s. Home: 6451 Center St New Orleans LA 70124 Office: 2026 St Charles Av New Orleans LA 70153

SCHROETTER, HILDA BLOXTON NOEL (MRS. SAMUEL T. SCHROETTER, JR.) author, educator; b. Lynchburg, Va., Oct. 11, 1917; d. Jesse Cleveland and Hilda (Bloxton) Noel; A.B., Randolph-Macon Woman's Coll., 1938; M.A., U. Va., 1946; m. Samuel T. Schroetter, Jr., June 27, 1944. High sch. tchr., 1938-45; reporter Herald Courier, 1946-47, 50-52; historian Va. World War II History Commn., 1947-50; copy chief WINA Radio, Charlottesville, 1952-54; editor U. Va. Record, 1954-66; mem. faculty Va. Commonwealth U., Richmond. Mem. exec. bd. Women of St. James's Episcopal Ch., chpt. devotional chmn. 1969-70; ch. rep. to Ch. Women United, 1969-70. Mem. Poetry Soc. Va., Woman's Com. Richmond Symphony. Democrat. Club: Va. Writer's. Author: Flowers From St. Francis, 1967; Prayers From the Bible, 1967; Great Thoughts from Knox, 1968; Great Thoughts from Luther, 1968; Great Thoughts From Wesley, 1968; Great Thoughts of Freedom, 1968; Bethune Center Nursery School, 1948. Reviewer book sect. Richmond (Va.) Times-Dispatch, 1949—. Home: 100 W Franklin St Richmond VA 23220

SCHRYVER, KENNEY, hotel exec.; b. Chgo., June 21, 1938; s. Maynard Wesley and Catherine (Kenney) S.; student U. Fla., 1957-61; m. Alida Van Steeden, Mar. 19, 1966; children—Belinda, Christopher, Peter, Jeffrey, Gregory. Sales mgr. Dodge Forsythe Co., St. Petersburg, Fla., 1961-63; owner, prin. Adesigns Advt. Co., Naples, Fla., 1963-67; pub. Naples Pub. Co., 1967-69; pres. Cove Inn Hotel, Naples, 1969—, Waterview Realty, Inc., Naples, 1970—. Chmn. student div. Fla. March Dimes, 1953. Recipient various awards Mead Library Great Ideas, 1964-66; several other advt. awards, 1961-63. Mem. Jr. C. of C., Collier County Hotel and Motel Assn. (pres.). Republican. Roman Catholic. Home: 206 Ridge Dr Naples FL 33940 Office: 1191 8th St S Naples FL 33940

SCHUBERT, RICHARD FRANCIS, govt. ofcl.; b. Trenton, N.J., Nov. 2, 1936; s. Yaro and Frances Mary (Hustak) S.; B.A., Eastern Nazarene Coll., 1958; LL.B. cum laude, Yale, 1961; m. Sarah Jane Lockington, Aug. 24, 1958; children—Robyn, David. Admitted to Pa. bar, U.S. Supreme Ct.; arbitration atty. Bethlehem Steel Co., Bethlehem, Pa., 1961-66, asst. mgr. labor relations, 1966-70; exec. asst. to under sec. Labor, Washington, 1970, exec. asst. to sec. Labor, 1970, solicitor of labor, 1971—. Active Boy Scouts Am., Easton, Pa., 1967-70. Bd. trustees Eastern Nazarene Coll., Quincy, Mass. Mem. Pa., Northampton County bar assns., Am. Arbitration Assn., Am. Iron and Steel Inst., Eastern Nazarene Alumni Assn. (pres. 1969-71), Phi Alpha Delta. Mem. Ch. of the Nazarene. Home: 6734 Melrose Dr McLean VA 22101 Office: 14th and Constitution Av Washington DC 20210

SCHUDER, RAYMOND FRANCIS, lawyer; b. Wickford, R.I., Dec. 27, 1926; s. Rollie Milton and Selma (Ball) S.; A.B., Emory U., 1949, J.D., 1951; m. Betty Jo Williams, Apr. 14, 1948; children—Gregg Williams, Glen Arva. Admitted to Ga. bar, 1951; adminstrv. asst. tax div. trust dept., Trust Co., Ga., Atlanta, 1951-54; asso. firm Wheeler, Robinson & Thurmond, Gainesville, Ga., 1954-59; pvt. law practice, Gainesville, 1959—. Dir. Lanier Securities, Inc., Peek Bros. Importers, Inc. City recorder municipal ct. judge, Gainesville, 1956-60. Bd. dirs. Charles Thompson Estes Found., Inc., Gainesville. Served to cpl. USMCR, 1944-46. Mem. Am., Gainesville-Northeastern (pres. 1969-70) bar assns., State Bar Ga. (gov. 1966-70), Am. Legion, U.S. Power Squadron (Lake Lanier), V.F.W., Phi Alpha Delta. Methodist. Clubs: Chattahoochee Country, Elks. Home: 2224 Riverside Dr NE Gainesville GA 30501 Office: First Nat Bank Bldg Gainesville GA 30501

SCHUELER, WILLIAM D., broadcasting exec. Pres. KTOK, Oklahoma City. Office: 1800 W Main St Oklahoma City OK 73101*

SCHUESSLER, MORGAN MCQUEEN, textile exec.; b. Roanoke, Ala., Aug. 7, 1935; s. John Morgan and Lila (Murfee) S.; B.I.E., Ga. Inst. Tech., 1957; postgrad. U. Cal. at Los Angeles, 1957-58; M.B.A., Harvard, 1964; m. Nan Enloe, June 1, 1957 children—John Morgan II, Nan Swann, Sam Enloe, Morgan McQueen. Market Analyst West Point Mfg. Co., N.Y.C., 1964-65; product mgr. West Point Pepperell, N.Y.C., 1965-67, div. controller, N.Y.C., 1966-68, v.p. corp. devel., West Point, Ga., 1968-70, v.p. operations Alamac Knitting div., 1970-72; corporate v.p. operations Gable Industries, Atlanta, 1972—. Served to 1st lt. USAF, 1957-60. Methodist. Home: 172 Maribeau Sq Cross Creek Atlanta GA 30327 Office: 700 Candler Bldg Atlanta GA

SCHUL, NORMAN WILLARD, coll. dean; b. nr. New Burlington O., Mar. 3, 1935; s. Willard LeRoy and Katherine (Keyser) S.; B.S., Miami U., Oxford, O., 1956, M.A., 1957; Ph.D., Syracuse U., 1962; m. Marianne Virginia Moffett, Aug. 23, 1958; children—Karl Norman, Kenneth Moffett. Mem. faculty U. N.C., Charlotte, 1967—, asst. prof. geography, Greensboro, 1961-67, chmn. dept. geography, geology, asso. prof. geography, 1967-69, chmn. div. social and behavioral scis., prof. geography, 1969-70, dean Coll. Social and Behavioral Scis., Charlotte, 1970—. Dir. Inst. Urban Studies, U. N.C., Charlotte, 1970—. Mem. Assn. Am. Geographers, Nat. Council Geog. Edn., Assn. Asian Studies, Am. Soc. Planning Ofcls., Am. Assn. U. Profs., Pi Kappa Alpha. Presbyn. Contbr. articles to profl. jours. Home: 3531 Donovan Pl Charlotte NC 28215

SCHULDT, WALTER JOHN, psychologist, educator; b. Sheboygan, Wis., Dec. 9, 1932; s. Walter J. and Irene (Rickmeier) S.; B.S., U. Wis., 1959; M.A., Mich. State U., 1962, Ph.D., 1964; m. Doris Ann Schuh, Aug. 16, 1958; children—Andrea Jean, Eric John. Teaching asst. U. Wis. at Milw., 1958-59; psychol. trainee VA Hosp., Dearborn, Mich., 1959-60; psychol. trainee VA Hosp., Battle Creek, Mich., 1960-61; intern Child Guidance Clinic, Lansing, Mich., 1961-62; grad. teaching asst. Mich. State U., 1962-63, asst. instr., 1963-64; asst. prof. U. Ark., Fayetteville, 1964-69, dir. Psychol. Clinic, 1967—, asso. prof., 1969—. Served with USAF, 1952-56. Mem. Am., Ark. psychol. assns., Am. Assn. U. Profs. Home: 1523 Hotz Dr Fayetteville AR 72701

SCHULER, CHARLES FRANKLIN, banker; b. Columbus, O., Mar. 4, 1922; s. Virgil Edwin and Ruth Lue (Eckelberry) S.; student Ohio State U., 1940-44, Franklin U., 1948; m. Bertha Neeld, Jan. 3, 1945; children— Charles Franklin, Melanie L. With trust dept. City Nat. Bank, Columbus, O., 1946-54; trust officer Union Nat. Bank, Pitts., 1954-65; v.p., trust officer First Bank & Trust Co., Boca Raton, Fla., 1965—. Served with USNR, 1942-45. Elk. Kiwanian. Home: 1041 NW 6th St Boca Raton FL 33432 Office: 150 E Palmetto Park Rd Boca Raton FL 33432

SCHULER, THEODORE ANTHONY, civil engr.; b. Louisville, July 1, 1934; s. Henry R. and Virginia (Meisner) S.; B.C.E., U. Lousiville, 1957; m. Joel Beverly Bader, June 22, 1957; children—Marc, Elizabeth. Design, constrn. engr. Brighton Engring. Co., Frankfort, Ky., 1960-65; design engr. Hensley-Schmidt Inc., Chattanooga, 1965-68, asso. mem., 1969—. Served to lt. (j.g.) USNR, 1957-60. Registered profl. engr., Ky., Tenn.; registered land surveyor, Ky. Mem. Nat., Tenn. socs. profl. engrs., Am. Soc. C.E. Home: 1300 James Blvd Signal Mountain TN 37377 Office: Am Nat Bank Bldg Chattanooga TN 37402

SCHULERT, ARTHUR ROBERT, biochemist, educator; b. Gladwin, Mich., Feb. 26, 1922; s. Oscar Edward and Ruth (Sanford) S.; B.S., Wheaton Coll., 1943; M.A., Princeton, 1947; Ph.D., U. Mich., 1951; m. Ruth Barbara Darling, June 17, 1949; children—Barbara, Mark, Jean, Philip, Andrew, Peter, Timothy. Research asso. Lamont Geochem. Lab., Columbia U., 1955-61; acting dir., 1958-59; head biochemistry dept. U.S. Naval Med. Research Unit No. 3, Cairo, Egypt, 1961-66; asst. prof. biochemistry Vanderbilt U., Nashville Tenn., 1961-64, asso. prof., 1964—. Pres. Environmental Sci. & Engring. Corp., 1970—. Pres. Darling Found., 1968—. Fellow Am. Assn. Clin. Chemists, Am. Inst. Chemists; mem. Am. Chem. Soc., A.A.A.S., Health Physics Soc., Soc. Nuclear Medicine, N.Y. Acad. Sci., Am. Inst. Nutrition, Soc. Toxicology. Contbr. articles in field to profl. jours. Home: Route 1 Mount Juliet TN 37122

SCHULKE, FLIP PHELPS GRAEME, photojournalist; b. St. Paul, June 24, 1930; s. Walter Edward and Elizabeth (Kalman) S.; B.A., Macalester Coll., 1953; m. Marlene Phyllis Wallner, Aug. 7, 1950 (div.); children— Robin, Paul Lisa, Maria; m. 2d, Pauline Kay Gillham. Univ. Photographer U. Miami, Fla., 1953-57; staff photographer Black Star Pub. Co., N.Y.C., 1957—; contract photographer Life mag., N.Y.C., 1965-69; owner Flip Schulke Enterprises, Inc., N.Y.C. Served with AUS, 1950-51. Recipient Underwater-Photographer of the Year award, 1967. Mem. Nat. Press Photographers Assn., Am. Soc. Mag. Photographers, Acad. Underwater Photographers. Home: 8305 SW 72d Av Miami FL 33143 also 12 Enderley House Sylvan Rd Upper Norwood London SE 19 England Office: 450 Park Av S New York City NY 10016

SCHULMAN, ABBOTT JAY, educator, psychologist; b. Providence, Dec. 7, 1938; s. Irwin Malcolm and Helen (Seegal) S.; B.A., Duke, 1958; M.A., East Carolina Coll., 1960; Ph.D., Fla. State U., 1965; m. Helaine Bette Samuelowitz, Aug. 8, 1965. Intern clin. psychology U. Fla. Teaching Hosp. and Clinics, Gainesville, 1964-65; post-doctoral fellow clin. child psychology Devereux Found., Devon. Pa., 1965-66; asst. prof. psychology Moorhead (Minn.) State Coll., 1966-68; asst. prof. div. clin. psychology, coordinator group psychotherapy tng., dept. psychiatry Med. Coll. Va., Richmond, 1968—, acting chmn., 1971—. Individual practice as psychologist, Richmond, 1968—; cons. psychologist to U. Va. Student Counselling Center, Charlottesville, 1968-70. Mem. Clay County Mental Health Com., Moorhead, 1967-68, Clay County Youth Council, 1967-68; chmn. Mental Health Survey Com., Clay County, 1967-68. Mem. Am., Southeastern, Va., Richmond psychol. assns., Am., Mid-Atlantic group psychotherapy assns. Home: 10301 Apache Rd Richmond VA 23235 Office: 1200 E Broad St Richmond VA 23219

SCHULTE, JOHN KEMP, pub. relations firm exec.; b. Chgo., May 18, 1932; s. John Kemp and Margaret (Roberts) S.; B.A., U. Miami, 1954; m. Judith Anne Roe, May 30, 1959; children—Kathy Ann, Lynn Margaret. Pub. relations dir. Miami (Fla.) Stadium, 1952-54, Orange Bowl Festival, Miami, 1956-60; v.p., sec., stockholder firm Newman/Schulte/Reece, Inc., Miami, 1961—; dir. Mfrs. Nat. Bank, Hialeah, Fla.; pres. Am. Corporate Counselors, Inc., Miami, 1961—. Mem. Miami Citizens Adv. Com., 1965-68. Bd. dirs. Grove House Art Center, Miami. Served to lt. Signal Corps, AUS, 1954-56. Mem. Am. Pub. Relations Assn. (Silver Anvil citation 1959), Pub. Relations Soc. Am., Sigma Delta Chi (pres. Greater Miami chpt. 1966). Club: Ocean Reef (Key Largo, Fla.). Home: 3571 N Prospect Dr Miami FL 33133 Office: 5810 Biscayne Blvd Miami FL 33137

SCHULTE, WILLIAM CHARLES, oral surgeon, air force officer; b. Vandalia, Ill., Mar. 2, 1921; s. Charles Reinhart and Virginia L. (Farmer) S.; B.S., U. Ill., 1944, D.D.S., 1946; M.Sc.D., U. Kansas City, 1960; m. Adona Anne Plymen, Dec. 12, 1949. Resident oral surgery Kansas City Gen. Hosp., 1958-60; commd. 1st lt. USAF, 1946, advanced through grades to col., 1967; chief dental service USAF Hosp., Chateauroux, France, 1951-54; head dept. clin. dentistry Sch. Aviation Medicine, Gunter Br., Montgomery, Ala., 1954-57; chief dental service, Swindon, Eng., 1960-64; chief oral surgery service, dir. dental edn. Med. Center, Wright-Patterson AFB, O., 1964-69; chief oral surgery dept. Clark AFB, Philippines, 1969-71; ret., 1971; individual practice, Hot Springs, Ark., 1971—. Diplomate Am. Bd. Oral Surgery. Fellow Internat. Soc. Oral Surgery, Am. Coll. Dentists; mem. Am. Dental Assn., Am. Soc. Oral Surgeons, Ark. Dental Soc., Alpha Tau Omega, Delta Sigma Delta. Home: 318 Robinwood Dr Hot Springs AR 71901 Office: Med Arts Bldg Hot Springs AR 71901

SCHULTZ, BENJAMIN, rabbi; b. Bklyn., Mar. 12, 1906; s. Joseph and Rose (Minskey) S.; B.A., U. Rochester, 1929; M.H.L., Jewish Inst. Religion, 1931; m. Charlotte Elkind, June 6, 1944. Rabbi, 1931; asso. rabbi Temple Ahavath Sholom, Bklyn., 1931-35, rabbi Temple Emanuel, Yonkers, N.Y., 1935-47; nat. exec. dir. Am. Jewish League against Communism, N.Y.C., 1948-60; rabbi Temple Beth Tefilloh, Brunswick, Ga., 1960-62, Temple Beth Israel, Clarksdale, Miss., 1962—. Chmn. N.Y. joint com. against communism, N.Y.C., 1952-60. Recipient Gold medal of Good Citizenship, SAR, 1955. Mem. Coahoma County Ministerial Assn. (pres. 1964—), Central Conf. Am. Rabbis. Mem. B'nai B'rith. Rotarian. Profl. lectr. on Europe and communism in Miss. Home: 1124 Rose Circle Clarksdale MS 38614 Office: 401 Catalpa St Clarksdale MS 38614

SCHULTZ, DONALD GILBERT, ednl. adminstr.; b. Oak Park, Ill., Aug. 30, 1929; s. Edward William and Frieda (Wentland) S.; Mus.B., Northwestern U., 1951, M.M., 1956; Ed.D., U. Ga., 1967; m. Donna Jean Korrell, Oct. 24, 1953; children—Patricia, Susan, Robert. French hornist Atlanta Symphony Orch., 1954-60; band dir. Atlanta Pub. Schs., 1954-60; band dir. Briarcliff High Sch., DeKalb County, Ga., 1960-62; asst. prin. Chamblee High Sch., 1962-65; prin. Towers High Sch., Decatur, Ga., 1966—. Served with AUS, 1951-54. Mem. Nat. Assn. Secondary Sch. Prins., Ga., DeKalb assns. educators, Music Educators Assn. (dist. pres. 1960-64), DeKalb Adminstrs. Club (v.p. 1969-70). Lutheran (pres. 1968-72). Home: 4544 Allgood Springs Dr Stone Mountain GA 30083 Office: 3919 Brookcrest Circle Decatur GA 30032

SCHULTZ, EVERETT HOYLE, JR., physician; b. Winston-Salem, N.C., Sept. 13, 1927; s. Everett Hoyle and Etta (Transou) S.; student U. N.C., 1944-45, 1946-48; M.D., Bowman Gray Sch. Medicine, 1952; m. Nancy Mary Jansson, June 24, 1955; children—Susan Carol, Frank Everett, Janet Loesch, Sally Louise. Intern, U. Okla. Hosp., 1952-53; resident N.C. Meml. Hosp., 1955-57, Univ. Okla. Hosp., 1954-55; practiced medicine in Cambridge, Mass., 1957-58; asst. in radiology Mass. Inst. Tech., Cambridge, 1957-58; asst. prof. radiology U. Fla., Gainesville, 1958-61; asso. prof. radiology U. N.C., Chapel Hill, 1961-67; chief radiology St. Anthony's Hosp., St. Petersburg, Fla., 1967—; cons. radiology Watts Hosp., Durham, N.C., 1961-67. Served with USNR, 1945-46. Fellow Am. Coll. Radiology; mem. So. Radiol. Conf. (chmn. 1966), A.A.A.S., A.M.A., Alpha Omega Alpha. Editorial cons. Yearbook of Cancer, 1963—. Home: 1005 Eden Isle Dr St Petersburg FL 33704 Office: St Anthony's Hosp St Petersburg FL 33705

SCHULTZ, FREDERICK THOMAS, JR., supt. schs.; b. Hardinsburg, Ky., Nov. 12, 1922; s. Frederick Thomas and Louise Fisher (Lewis) S.; student Murray State U., 1940-43, B.S., 1946, M.A., 1948; student Tufts U., 1943; postgrad. Peabody Coll., summers 1962, 63, 65; m. Martha Jo Crass, Nov. 20, 1945; 1 dau., Selwyn Louise. Sci. tchr. Murray (Ky.) High Sch., 1948-57, prin., 1957-62; supt. schs. Murray pub. schs., 1962—. Vice chmn. Murray-Calloway County United Fund, 1967; chmn. Ky. Dept. Edn. study com. on extended sch. year, 1971—. Served with USNR, 1943-46; PTO. Mem. Am. Assn. Sch. Adminstrs., N.E.A., Ky. Assn. Sch. Adminstrs., Ky., Murray edn. assns., First Dist. Ky. Edn. Assn., Sigma Pi Sigma. Baptist. Club: Oaks Country (Murray). Home: 802 Olive St Murray KY 42071

SCHULTZ, JULIUS, biochemist; b. Rochester, N.Y., May 7, 1914; s. Benjamin and Ann (Duran) S.; student Cornell, 1932-34; B.S., U. Mich., 1936, Ph.D., 1940; postdoctoral studies U. Pa. Sch. Medicine, 1939-46; m. Betty Jane Splane, Oct. 14, 1942. Asst. prof. biochemistry Temple U. Sch. Medicine, 1951-57; asso. prof. Hahnemann Med. Sch., 1957-62, prof., 1962; dir. Papanicolaou Cancer Research Inst. Miami, Fla., 1968—; adj. prof. U. Miami Med. Sch. Fellow A.A.A.S.; mem. Am. (sec. div. biochemistry), English biochem. socs., Am. Chem. Soc. (sec. div. biochemistry), Am. Assn. Cancer Research, Recticulo-Endothialal Soc., Am. Soc. Biol. Chemists, Nat. Acad. Sci. (com. enzymes). Home: 240 W San Marino Dr Miami Beach FL 33139 Office: 1155 NW 14th St Miami FL 33136

SCHULTZE, HENRY CHRISTIAN, sci. adminstr., bus. exec.; b. Charleston, S.C., Mar. 14, 1915; s. Charles F. and Ethel (Reid) S.; B.S., Coll. Charleston, 1937; Ph.D., U. N.C., 1941; m. Julia Rachel Hunter, Sept. 25, 1940; children—Margaret, Rachel. With research and devel. dept., chems. div. Union Carbide Corp., South Charleston, W. Va., 1941-64, asst. to dir., 1957-58, staff asso., 1958-64, tech. service mgr. Cardinal Chem. Corp., Columbia, S.C., 1964-65; dir. devel. research center S.C. State Devel. Bd., Columbia, 1965-68, mgr. tech. programs, 1968-69; v.p., mgr. eastern operations Chem-Nuclear Services, Inc., Columbia, 1969—. Cons. in field. Mem. Am. Chem. Soc., Am. Nuclear Soc., Sigma Xi. Patentee in field. Home: 3760 Greenleaf Rd Columbia SC 29206 Office: PO Box 6336 3101 Carlisle St Columbia SC 29205

SCHULZ, HARRY JOHN, lawyer; b. Falls City, Tex., Mar. 27, 1913; s. John G. and Catherine (Sheehy) S.; student St. Mary's U., 1930-32; LL.B., U. Tex., 1935; m. Virginia Swett, Dec. 21, 1938; children—Mary Virginia (Mrs. Jack Johnson), Harriet Ann, Harry J., Betty, Peggy. Admitted to Tex. bar, 1935; individual practice law, Three Rivers, Tex., 1935—; county atty. Live Oak County, Tex., 1936-40; city atty. Three Rivers, Tex., 1945—. Pres., dir. Schulz Live Stock Co., Three Rivers, 1942-49, Spur S. Farm, Inc., Three Rivers, 1965—; dir. 1st State Bank, Three Rivers. Dir. Nueces River Authority. 1964—. Mem. state exec. com. Democratic party,

1964-66. Trustee Three Rivers Ind. Sch. Dist., 1956—, pres., 1966—; bd. dirs. Coastal Bend Council of Govts., Corpus Christi, Tex. Mem. Am. Bar Assn., Tex. Bar Found., Tex. State Bar, Three Rivers C. of C. Roman Catholic (Papal Knight, Order of St. Gregory). K.C. Rotarian. Home: 101 Hazel St Three Rivers TX 78071 Office: 623 Harborth St Three Rivers TX 78071

SCHULZ, MICHAEL ANTHONY, JR., civil engr., contractor; b. New Orleans, Dec. 17, 1934; s. Michael Anthony and Hilda (Monnin) S.; B.Sc., La. State U., 1959; m. Ann Miller Hawkins, Aug. 15, 1958; 1 dau., Terri Lynn. Engr., estimator Crawford Corp., Baton Rouge, 1956-57; plant mgr. Tidewood Corp., Baton Rouge, 1957-58; eng., estimator La. Concrete Products, Baton Rouge, 1959-61; dept. head Wilson P. Abraham Constrn. Co., Baton Rouge, 1961-64; constrn. mgr. Odis F. Haymon, Baton Rouge, 1964-67; sec., treas. The Bedford Corp., Baton Rouge, 1967—. Served to 2d lt. with AUS, 1958. Mem. Am. Soc. C.E., La. Engring. Soc., Soc. Am. Mil. Engrs., Alpha Tau Omega. Epsicopalian. Designed and constructed Chateau Carre' Apts., New Orleans; Francis Apts., Baton Rouge; Colony House Apts., Baton Rouge. Home: 864 Albert Hart Dr Baton Rouge LA 70808 Office: 871 W Garfield St Baton Rouge LA 70802

SCHULZ, ROBERT L(UDWIG), spl. asst. to Pres. U.S.; b. N.Y.C., Sept. 17, 1907; s. Carl and Alice (Zallveis) S.; m. Dorothy E. Cost, Oct. 28, 1943; children—Karen Elizabeth, (Mrs. Richard L. Weber), Carl Frederick, Carol Roberta. Indsl. traffic mgr., Chgo., 1938-42; transp. cons. War Dept., 1942; commd. capt. Transp. Corps, U.S. Army, 1942, advanced through ranks to brig. gen., 1962; aide-de-camp Gen. Dwight D. Eisenhower, 1947-52; mil. aide Pres. U.S., 1953-61; exec. asst. to ex-pres. Dwight D. Eisenhower, 1961-69; spl. asst. to Pres. Nixon for liaison with former presidents, Washington, 1969—. Decorated Legion Merit. Mem. Am. Soc. Traffic and Transp., Traffic Club Chgo. Club: Dacor (Washington). Home: 5521 Bradley Blvd Alexandria VA 22311 Office: The White House Washington DC 20500

SCHULZE, ELAINE MARY PATIN (MRS. HERMAN L. SCHULZE), social worker; b. Breaux Bridge, La.; d. John J. and Birdie (Dupuis) Patin; B.A., Southwestern La. Inst., 1939; certificate in social work La. State U., 1940; M.S., Simmons Coll., 1947; m. Herman J. Schulze, Apr. 30, 1949 (dec. 1971); children— Elaine, Herman, Gretchen, Diane, Richard, Rudolph. Welfare visitor St. Landry Dept. Pub. Welfare, Opelousas, La., 1941-42; caseworker Area Hosp. Service, A.R.C., Atlanta, 1942-46, asst. field dir. sta. hosps., 1946, asst. dir. hosp. service, 1947-48; med. social cons. La. State Dept. Health, New Orleans 1948-49; clin. social worker Tulane U. Cardiac Work Evaluation Unit, New Orleans, 1960-62; chief social worker Delgado Vocational Rehabilitation Center, New Orleans, 1962-69; dir. social service dept. Touro Infirmary, New Orleans, 1969-71; med. social worker La. State Welfare Med. Center and Rehab. Inst., New Orleans, 1971—. Mem. Acad. Certified Social Workers, Nat. Assn. Social Workers, Nat. Rehabilitation Assn., Am. Hosp. Assn. Social Work Dirs. Home: 7830 Freret St New Orleans LA 70118 Office: 1542 Tulane Av New Orleans LA 70112

SCHULZE, JOHN PAUL, physician; b. Cotulla, Tex., Nov. 21, 1929; s. John William and Mable (Oakes) S.; B.S., Southwestern U., 1951; M.D., U. Tex., 1955; m. Sylvia Anne Harris, Aug. 21, 1951; children— Cynthia Ann, Paula Lea, John Edward, Deborah Lynn. Intern, Meth. Hosp., Dallas, 1955-56; gen. practice medicine and surgery, Corpus Christi, Tex., 1959—; mem. staff Doctors, Meml., Spohn, Physicians and Surgeons hosps., Corpus Christi. Served to capt. USAF, 1956-58. Mem. Am., Tex. assns. gen. practice, A.M.A., Tex. Med. Assn., Phi Chi. Methodist. Home: 625 Louisiana Blvd Corpus Christi TX 78404 Office: 3166 Reid Dr Corpus Christi TX 78404

SCHUMACHER, SNEAD, cons. engr.; b. Walhalla, S.C., Mar. 8, 1924; s. George D. and Clara (Snead) S.; A.S.T.P., Tex. A. and M. U., 1944; B.S., Clemson Coll., 1947; m. Jimmie Crofford, Apr. 27, 1945; 1 dau., Susan. Constrn. engr., contractor, S.C., Ga., 1947-58; tchr. schs., Walhalla, also Seneca, S.C., 1958-65; civil engr., owner Schumacher Engring. Service & Land Surveyor, Walhalla, S.C., 1958—; mem. S.C. State Senate, 1967—. Mem. S.C. Ho. of Reps., 1965-66; mayor pro tempore, Walhalla, S.C., 1964, city councilman, 1959-60, 62-64; mem. Oconee County Planning Bd., 1956-65, dir., 1958; chmn. Oconee County Christmas Seal Campaign, 1964-65. Bd. dirs. Oconee Meml. Hosp., 1967—; mem. civil engring. and constrn. mgmt. adv. com. Tri-County Tech. Edn. Center, 1969—. Served with AUS, 1942-45. Registered profl. engr., S.C., Ga. Mem. Sons Confederate Veterans, V.F.W. Lutheran. Mason (Shriner), Lion (pres. 1954). Club: Sertoma. Home: 502 N Broad St Walhalla SC 29691 Office: 500 N Broad St Walhalla SC 29691

SCHUON, KARL ALBERT, author, editor; b. Allentown, Pa., Nov. 26, 1913; s. Harold Benjamin and Bessie M. (Weiler) S.; grad. pub. schs., Allentown, Pa.; m. Lucia Elizabeth Nelli, Oct. 6, 1950; children—Marshall, Joseph, Lucia, Marie. Editor, Leatherneck (USMC mag.), Washington, 1945—, now editor-in-chief. Served with USMCR, World War II. Mem. Marine Corps League, Marine Corps Combat Corr. Assn. Democrat. Mem. Evangelical Ch. Club: Manor. Author: Marines and What They Do, 1962, John H. Glenn: Astronaut, 1962, Home of the Commandants, 1966. Editor: The Leathernecks, 1963, Biographical Dictionary of the U.S. Marine Corps., 1963. Service-Women and What They Do, 1964, Biographical Dictionary of the U.S. Navy, 1965, Bowling, 1966, The First Book of Acting, 1966. Home: 3846 Gallows Rd Annandale VA 22003 Office: Box 1918 Quantico VA 22134

SCHURMAN, GEORGE RANKIN, oilman, realtor; b. Medford, Mass., Jan. 3, 1932; s. Benjamin Colin and Grace (Rankin) S.; B.S., Centenary Coll., Shreveport, La., 1957; m. Aline Spence, Apr. 25, 1952; children—George Rankin, Lisa Gaye, Stephen Wayne, Lori Louise, Bonnie Susan. Geologist, Skelly Oil Co., Shreveport, 1957-63; ind. oil operator, realtor, Shreveport, 1963—; cons. petroleum landman, 1963—. Pres., Y's Men's Club Shreveport. Served with USAF, 1950-54. Mem. Petroleum Club Shreveport, Assn. Petroleum Landmen, Sigma Gamma Epsilon. Democrat. Methodist (dist. dir. lay speaking). Club: Shreveport Country. Home: 6231 S Inwood Rd Shreveport LA 71109 Office: Petroleum Tower Shreveport LA 71101

SCHUSTER, FRANKLIN PHILLIP, JR., physician; b. El Paso, Tex., Aug. 1, 1927; s. Franklin Philip and Hallie (Morton) S.; B.A., Leland Stanford Jr. U., 1948; M.D., U. Tex. at Galveston, 1953; m. Bettie Banks Manning, June 26, 1953 (div.); children—Franklin Phillip III, Jeffrey David, Jonathan Banks, Paul Featherstone; m. 2d, Sarah E. Fletcher, May 17, 1972. Intern, S. P. Gen. Hosp., San Francisco, 1953-54; resident John Sealy Hosp., Galveston, Tex., 1954-55, 57-59; mem. faculty U. Tex. Med. Br., Galveston, 1958-59; practice medicine specializing in psychiatry, El Paso, Tex., 1959—; mem. staffs Providence Meml., Hotel Dieu, R.E. Thomas Gen., Sun Towers, Southwestern Gen., St. Josephs hosps.; research psychiatrict Yough Devel. Project, 1958-59; chief outpatient psychiatry Thomason Hosp., El Paso, 1963-68; med. dir. Child Treatment Center, El Paso, 1965-68. Mem. adv. com. Tex. Comprehensive Health Planning Counsel, 1969—. Mem. Gov's. com. State-Wide Mental Health Planning, 1962-64; trustee Mental Health-Mental Retardation, 1965-69, 70—. Served to capt., with M.C., AUS, 1955-57. Fellow Am. Psychiat. Assn.; mem. Tex. Mental Health Assn. (exec. com. 1964—, v.p. 1969—), Am. Orthopsychiat. Assn., A.M.A. Author: (with others) Multiple Impact Therapy with Families, 1964; Family Therapy for the Scape goat child. Office: 312 University Towers El Paso TX 79902

SCHWAB, JOHN JOSEPH, physician, educator; b. Cumberland, Md., 1923; M.D., U. Louisville, 1946; M.Sc. in Cardio-Renal Physiology, U. Ill. Intern, Phila. Gen. Hosp., 1947-48; fellow in medicine U. Ill., 1948-49; asst. resident and resident in medicine Louisville Gen. Hosp., 1949-50; fellow in psychosomatic medicine Duke U. Hosp., 1950-51; resident in psychiatry U. Fla., Gainesville, 1959-61, chief psychiatrist cons. service, 1961-64, instr. psychiatry, 1961-64, asst. prof., 1964-65, asso. prof. psychiatry and medicine, 1965-67, prof., 1967—, chmn. history and philosophy of medicine, 1965—, chief investigator mental health research, 1969—. Career tchr. Nat. Inst. Mental Health, 1962-64. Served to capt., M.C., AUS, 1949-54. Diplomate Am. Bd. Psychiatry and Neurology. Mem. A.M.A., Am. Psychiat. Assn., Acad. Psychosomatic Med. (pres.-elect). Home: 4500 Clear Lake Dr Gainesville FL 32601*

SCHWALENBERG, FRANK ALOYSIUS, ins. co. exec.; b. Newport News, Va., Sept. 14, 1922; s. Frank A. and Clare (Glover) S.; student Newport News Apprentice Sch., 1940-44; m. Mattie Louise Lowe, Apr. 11, 1944; children— Mary Jo (Mrs. Kenneth L. Dawson), Frank C. Apprentice, Newport News Shipbldg. & Dry Dock Co., 1940-44; model maker NASA, Langley AFB, Va., 1944-45; field underwriter Home Life Ins. Co. N.Y., Newport News, 1955—. Chmn. bus. solicitation Peninsula Heart Fund, City of Hampton, Va., 1967-68; mem. Va. Gov.'s Commn. to study health costs. Served with USAAF, 1944-46. Named Man of Year, Peninsula Life Underwriters Assn., 1967; recipient Nat. Sales Achievement award, 1966-70. Mem. Million Dollar Round Table, Nat. (Nat. Quality award 1956-70), Va. (pres. 1969-70), Peninsula (pres. 1965-66) assns. life underwriters, Peninsula Football Ofcls. Assn. (pres. 1960-61). Clubs: Sertoma (pres. 1968-69) (Hampton); Peninsula Sports (pres. 1971). Home: 232 Dominion Dr Newport News VA 23602 Office: PO Box 541 2600 Washington Av Newport News VA 23607

SCHWANTES, WILLIAM LELAND, coll. exec.; b. Birmingham, Ala., Dec. 14, 1917; s. Walter Julius and Abbie (Jannett) S.; student Birmingham Bus. Sch., 1940, Auburn Extension Coll., 1941-42; m. Lovoro Carnathan, Aug. 28, 1940; children—Judy (Mrs. David Quackenbush), Leland, Neal. Storekeeper, Birmingham So. R.R., 1936-46; bus. adminstr. First Bapt. Ch., Oklahoma City, 1946-48, First Bapt. Ch., Austin, Tex., 1948-58, Myers Park Bapt. Ch., Charlotte, N.C., 1958-68; treas.-bus. mgr. Montreat-Anderson Coll., Mountain Retreat Assn., Montreat, N.C., 1969—. Mem. Nat. Assn. Ch. Bus. Adminstrs. (pres. 1958-59, chpt. pres. 1971). Presbyn. (deacon 1969—). Home: Lookout Rd Montreat NC 28757 Office: PO Box 38 Montreat NC 28757

SCHWARTZ, AARON ROBERT, lawyer, state senator; b. Galveston, Tex., July 17, 1926; s. Joe and Clara (Bulbe) S.; student Tex. A. and M. Coll., 1944-47; LL.B., U. Tex., 1951; m. Marilyn Cohn, July 14, 1951; children—Robert Allen, Richard Austin, John Reed, Thomas Lee. Admitted to Tex. bar, 1951; practiced in Galveston, 1951—; asst. county atty., Galveston, 1951-53; mem. Tex. Ho. of Reps., 1954-58; mem. Tex. Senate, 1959—, pres. pro tem., 1965-66. Vice pres. Harbor Broadcasting Co., Galveston. Chmn. southwestern regional bd. Anti Defamation League of B'nai B'rith, 1961-65, mem. nat. commn. of league, 1966. Served with USNR, 1944-46. Recipient awards State of Tex., N.G. Assn. Tex., Tex. Municipal Police Assn., Tex. Council of Retarded Children, Anti Defamation League of B'nai B'rith; Friend of Journalism award Sigma Delta Chi, 1967. Home: 10 S Shore Dr Galveston TX 77550 Office: Cotton Exchange Bldg Galveston TX 77550

SCHWARTZ, BENJAMIN L., mathematician; b. Pitts., Jan. 11, 1926; s. Benjamin L. and Sarah (Rubinstein) S.; B.S., Carnegie Inst. Tech., 1946, M.S., 1947; Ph.D., Stanford, 1965; student Brown U., 1947-50; m. Joan H. Koslan, Sept. 9, 1956; children—Justin, Beryl, Mila. Asst. prof. math. Duquesne U., Pitts., 1950-53; asst. div. chief Battelle Meml. Inst., Columbus, O., 1953-58; mgr. systems analysis Monterey (Cal.) Lab., 1958-65; mem. tech. staff Inst. for Defense Analyses, Arlington, Va., 1965-67; subdept. head Mitre Corp., Arlington, Va., 1967-70; cons. in field, 1970—. Vis. asso. prof. U.S. Naval Postgrad. Sch., Monterey, Cal., 1963-65; vis. lectr. George Washington U., Washington, 1966—; adj. prof. Am. U., 1970—; cons. Matson Navigation Co., San Francisco, 1964-65, Ampex Corp., Redwood City, Cal., 1964-65; Smithsonian Instn., Washington, 1969—. Served with USNR, 1942. Fellow A.A.A.S.; mem. Am. Math. Soc., Math. Assn. Am., Operations Research Soc. Am., Assn. for Computing Machinery. Asso. editor: Mathematics mag. Contbr. articles to profl. jours. Home: 7013 Duncraig Ct McLean VA 22101

SCHWARTZ, LEON M., govt. ofcl.; b. Balt., Apr. 26, 1928; s. Paul H. and Pauline (Shulman) S.; A.B. in Econs. (Alumni scholar), Johns Hopkins, 1950; m. Joan Schinker, July 16, 1953; children—Howard, Richard. Asst. treas. Carpel, Inc., Balt., 1953-60; chief program rev. Goddard Space Flight Center, NASA, Greenbelt, Md., 1960-67; asst. commr. for adminstrn. Office Edn., Dept. Health, Edn. and Welfare, Washington, 1967-71, asso. dir. for adminstrn. NIH, Washington, 1972—; dep. asst. dir. for program mgmt. NSF, Washington, 1971. Served with AUS, 1950-52. Recipient Superior Service award Dept. Health, Edn. and Welfare. C.P.A., Md. Home: 12105 Hitching Post Lane Rockville MD 20852 Office: Nat Sci Found Washington DC 20550

SCHWARTZ, LOUIS, JR., financial services co. exec.; b. Chgo., June 21, 1934; s. Louis and Mary Elizabeth (Dunn) S.; B.S., Georgetown Sch. Fgn. Service, 1956; M.A., Loyola U., 1960; postgrad., Georgetown U., 1960, 64, 65, Am. U., 1968; m. Patricia Ann Scanland, Aug. 8, 1963; children—Christopher, Michael, Jennifer. Indsl. engr., Cin., Chgo., 1956, 58-59; instr. Mundelein Coll., Chgo., 1959; officer U.S. Fgn. Service, Germany, Indonesia, 1960-65; mem. White House staff, 1965-67; mgmt. cons., 1967-68; mem. staff NSC, 1968-69; exec. UniCapital Corp., Atlanta, 1969—. Served to 1st lt., AUS, 1956-58. Cardinal Stritch scholar, 1952—. Roman Catholic. Home: 4385 Stonington Circle Atlanta GA 30341 Office: First Nat Bank Tower Atlanta GA 30303

SCHWARTZ, LOUIS ALBERT, lawyer; b. New Orleans, Apr. 4, 1901; s. George and Anna (Cirino) S.; student Soule Coll., 1917; LL.D., Loyola U., 1925; m. Gladys Brennan, July 29, 1933; children—Louis A., Diane Marie (Mrs. Donald Szabo), John G. Admitted to La. bar, 1925; practiced in New Orleans, 1925—; Norman Breckwoldt & Schwartz, 1925-30; gen. mgr. New Orleans Traffic and Transp. Bur., 1945—. Gen. chmn. S.W. Shippers Adv. Bd., 1955, S.E. Shippers Adv. Bd., 1957. Mem. Nat. Indsl. Traffic League (exec. com. 1969—), Am. Soc. Traffic and Transp. (pres. La. chpt. 1967, Traffic Club New Orleans (treas. 1969), Nat. Shippers Adv. Bds. (pres. 1959). Home: 3220 Nashville Av New Orleans LA 70125 Office: Trade Mart Tower New Orleans LA 70130

SCHWARTZ, PAUL PAISACH, mech. engr.; b. Vitznitz, Rumania, Nov. 24, 1920 (came to U.S. 1928, naturalized 1928); s. Benzion and Betty (Zwiebach) S.; student Coll. City N.Y., 1938-41; B.S., U. Tex., 1948; m. Margot Rosenthal, Apr. 3, 1944; children—Richard Lloyd, Faye Lynn. With C.E., 1948—, chief mech. sect., Fort Worth, 1959-68, asst. chief design br., 1968-72, chief design br., 1972—. Served to 1st lt. USAAF, 1941-45. Recipient Sustained Superior Performance award C.E., 1960, Outstanding Performance award, 1953. Registered profl. engr., Tex. Mem. Am. Soc. M.E. (chmn. 1958), Tex. Soc. Prof. Engrs. (pres. 1967-68), Am. Soc. Heating, Refrigerating and Air Conditioning Engrs. Jewish religion (v.p. congregation). Home: 3724 Wosley Dr Fort Worth TX 76133 Office: PO Box 17300 Fort Worth TX 76102

SCHWARTZ, PAUL R(AYMOND), real estate exec.; b. Memphis, Oct. 27, 1905; s. Elias and Nellie Elsie (Fite) S.; student pub. and pvt. schs.; m. Dorothy Lavona Aylor, July 14, 1928; 1 dau., Dorothy Joe (Mrs. William A. Langhofer). With Chgo. Mill & Lumber Co., 1929-65, successively office mgr., Blytheville, Ark., charge accounting and lumber prodn. activities, Tallulah, La., plant mgr., Rockmart, Ga., plant mgr. charge lumbering operations, South Fork, Colo., asst. to pres., Chgo., mgmt. and development work, crude oil div., 1958-60, mgr. oil and gas div., 1958-63, mgr. La. div., 1963-65, chmn. Killens Ferry Gasoline Plant, 1959-62; with Paul R. Schwartz and Assos., 1965-67; realtor, Memphis, 1967—. Dir. Civil Def., Madison Parish, La., 1964-66. Democrat. Presbyn. Mason (32 deg., Shriner), Elk, Rotarian. Club: Country, Petroleum, Shreveport. Home: 811 Bayou Dr Tallulah LA 71282 Office: 1535 Monroe Av Memphis TN 38104

SCHWARTZ, PETER ASTON, headmaster; b. Wynnewood, Pa., Dec. 13, 1912; s. David Louis and Georgianna Fuller (Ghormley) S.; B.A., Princeton, 1936; m. Alice Crosby Sinclair, Dec. 18, 1937; children—Carol (Mrs. Carl H. Haag), Peter Aston, Donald S. Headmaster Allendale Sch., Rochester, N.Y., 1948-53, Pembroke Country Day Sch., Kansas City, Mo., 1953-63; founding headmaster Fort Worth Country Day Sch., 1963—. Trustee Selwyn Sch., Denton, Tex., 1965—, Marine Mil. Acad., Harlingen, Tex. Served to lt. (j.g.) USNR, 1943-46. Mem. Country Day Sch. Headmasters' Assn., Ind. Schs. Assn. (pres., 1972-73). Rotarian. Club: Princeton (N.Y.C.). Home: Route 1 Box 48 Aledo TX 76008 Office: 4200 Country Day Lane Fort Worth TX 76116

SCHWARTZ, RAYMOND LAURENCE, educator; b. N.Y.C., Aug. 16, 1913; s. Frank and Amelia (Shoen) S.; A.B., Cornell U., 1934, M.D., 1937; m. Ruth Ellen Smith, May 21, 1943; children—Raymond, Richard, Ruth, Roberta, Regina, Roger, Rosalyn, Reita. Intern Bellevue Hosp., N.Y.C., 1937-38, resident, 1938-41; med. officer Glenndale Sanatorium, Washington, 1941-43; chief medicine Arlington (Va.) Hosp., 1947-57, chief of staff, 1957-62; clin. prof. medicine Georgetown U. Sch. Medicine, 1948—. Served to maj. M.C., AUS, 1943-46. Fellow A.C.P., Am. Coll. Chest Physicians; mem. Alpha Omega Alpha. Kiwanian. Home: 3231 Juniper Lane Falls Church VA 22044 Office: 1029 N Stuart St Arlington VA 22201

SCHWARTZ, RICHARD, assn. exec.; b. N.Y.C., Aug. 6, 1929; s. Samuel and Ida (Shapiro) S.; A.B., Princeton, 1951; LL.B., Yale, 1956; m. Sally-Jane Heit, June 20, 1954; children—Dianne Rachel, Lori Ann, Pamela Caryl. Admitted to N.Y., Fla. bars, 1957, U.S. Supreme Ct., D.C. bars, 1960; Honor law grad. program atty. Office Gen. Counsel, U.S. AEC, Washington, 1956-59; atty. adv. Chief Judge William Brennan, U.S. Tax Ct., Washington, 1959-61; asst. to pres. Dynalectron Corp., Washington, 1961-64; mem. firm Dawson, McLeod & Stivers, pub. relations and advt., Washington, 1964-65; prin. founder, pres. Boat Owners Assn. U.S., Washington, 1965—. Served to 1st lt. AUS, 1951-53. Mem. Am. Bar Assn., Am. Soc. Assn. Execs. Clubs: Princeton, Yale Law School, Hexagon. Home: 3706 Huntington St NW Washington DC 20015 Office: 1028 Connecticut Av NW Washington DC 20036

SCHWARZ, FELIX CONRAD, artist, writer; b. N.Y.C., Apr. 13, 1906; s. Osias L. and Anna (Reifler) S.; First Honors, Corcoran Sch. Art, 1923-26; A.B., George Washington U., 1927, A.M., 1930; Ph.D., Columbia; m. Myrtle Cooper, 1940. Prof. art Mary Washington Coll. (Va.), 1930-34, State Tchrs. Coll. of Minn., 1934-39; research fellow Columbia U., 1939-41, Coll. William and Mary S.S., 1941; feature writer Washington News 1930-32; dir. adult classes in creative writing Community Center, 1932-34; prof. and dir. Sch. Art. Phillaps U., 1944-48; vis. prof. art, Northwestern State Coll., La.; prof., chmn. dept. fine arts Wesleyan Coll., Macon, Ga., 1957-61; prof. art Pembrooke (N.C.) State Coll., 1961—; prof. fine art Livingston (Ala.) U., 1966-71; vis. prof. Monticello Coll., Alton, Ill., 1963-65, Parsons Coll., summer 1964, Wis. State U., Superior, 1965-66. Exhibited paintings throughout country's leading galleries and museums since 1923. Lectr. and painting demonstrator. Fellow Internat. Inst. of Arts and Letters; mem. Soc. Free Lance Writers (pres. 1928-34), Minn. Coll. Art Tchrs. (pres. 1935-39), Okla. Edn. Assn. (chmn. art sect. 1946-47), Enid Artists League (pres.), Nat. Art Edn. Assn., Western Arts Assn., Am. Assn. U. Profs. Contbr. numerous articles to scholarly and popular periodicals. Editor: Advanced Sch. Digest. Columbia, 1939-41. Home: 1500 North Dakota Av NE St Petersburg FL 33703

SCHWARZ, HUGH WALTER, business exec.; b. N.Y.C., Aug. 16, 1918; s. Walter Max and Hazel (Frensdorf) S.; B.S., Dartmouth, 1940; M.S., Mass. Inst. Tech., 1942; m. Mary L. Conners, Dec. 18, 1943; children— Pamela, Nancy, Jeffrey. Process engr. Nat. Research Corp., Cambridge, Mass., 1943-48; v.p. Minute Maid Co. div. Coca-Cola Co., Orlando, Fla., 1949-67, v.p., dir. corporate planning parent co., 1968—; pres. Minute Maid Groves Corp. Mem. Sigma Xi, Phi Beta Kappa. Office: PO Drawer 1734 Atlanta GA 30301

SCHWARZ, JOSEPH EDMUND, educator, artist; b. Hartford, Conn., May 13, 1929; s. Jules and Doris (Sklarinsky) S.; B.F.A., Ohio Wesleyan U., 1950; M.F.A., U. Ill., 1952; Ph.D., Ohio State U., 1957; m. Jean Bunker Chalmers, Jan. 21, 1953; children—David, Dina, Jonathan, Adam; m. 2d, Sarah Rollins, Nov. 21, 1971. Teaching asst. U. Ill., 1950-52; instr. Ohio State U., 1952-57; faculty U. Ga., 1957-67, asso. prof., 1962-67; prof. art, dir. grad. studies Va. Commonwealth U., Sch. of Arts, Richmond, 1968—. Exhibited one-man shows including U. Tenn., 1961, Ga. State Gallery, 1963, Peabody Coll. Gallery, 1966, Augusta Mus., 1967, Ala. State Gallery, 1967; exhibited in group shows Butler Art Inst., 1949, 55, Southeastern Ann. Exhbn. Painting, 1957, 59, 60, 61, 66, 67, Chrysler Show, 1958, Whitney Mus., 1958, Hunter Gallery, 1960, 61, 62, 67; represented in permanent collections. Sarah H. Moss fellow for advanced study, 1964-65. Recipient prizes for art. Mem. Delta Phi Delta, Phi Kappa Phi. Home: 1126 West Av Richmond VA 23220

SCHWARZE, ESTELLA GERALDINE, social work adminstr.; b. New Orleans; d. William J. and Mary (Reynolds) Schwarze; B.S.Social Sci., Loyola U., New Orleans, 1957, grad. student, 1958-59, 61-62; M.S.W., Tulane U., 1962. With Asso. Cath. Charities, 1946-59; exec. dir. Assn. for Retarded Children, 1956-57; with social service dept. Charity Hosp. of La., New Orleans, 1958—, supr., 1965—. Field work instr. Atlanta U. Grad. Sch. Social Work, 1967—. Cons. social work. Treme Neighborhood Improvement Assn. Founder, charter mem. Irish Channel Action Found., New Orleans, 1964; organizer Parent's Inst., New Orleans, 1962; organizer, originator Projects Aquarius; del. White House Conf. on Children and Youth, 1970, White House Conf. on Aging, 1971; lectr. community medicine La. State U., Tulane U. Mem. adv. bd., cons. health consumer edn. program New Orleans Urban League. Mem. Nat. Assn. Social Workers, (Social Worker of Yr. award S.E. La. chpt. 1965), Am. Pub. Health Assn., Mercy Acad. Alumnae (pres. 1956-58), League Women Voters. Democrat. Home: 915 Jefferson Av New Orleans LA 70115 Office: Social Service Dept Charity Hosp of La 1542 Tulane Av New Orleans LA 70130

SCHWARZSCHILD, RICHARD ISAAC, banker; b. Richmond, Va., July 29, 1912; s. William Harry and Rosa Lee (Held) S.; B.S., U. Pa., 1934; m. Betty Berne, Oct. 26, 1935; children—Ellen Louise (Mrs. Jack M. Kreuter), J. William, Richard J. Training Corps Chase Manhattan Bank, N.Y.C., 1934-35; credit supr. C.I.T. Corp., N.Y.C., 1935-37; with Central Nat. Bank, Richmond, Va., 1937—, sr. v.p., 1967; treas. Schwarzschild Bros., Inc., Richmond, 1957—; dir. Broad-Grace Arcade Corp. Treas. Schwarzschild Found., 1956—. Mem. Richmond Sch. Bd., 1970—. Bd. dirs. Lakeside Park, Richmond Jewish Community Council. Mem. Richmond C. of C. (dir. 1954-55). Clubs: Jefferson-Lakeside Country (dir. 1970—), Bull and Bear (Richmond). Home: 5110 Cary St Rd Richmond VA 23226 Office: 219 E Broad St Richmond VA 23261

SCHWARZSCHILD, WILLIAM HARRY, JR., banker; b. Richmond, Va., Sept. 19, 1903; s. William Harry and Rosalie (Held) S.; A.B., U. Va., 1923; M.B.A., Harvard, 1925; m. Kathryn Emsheimer, Sept. 6, 1945; children—Kathrin, William Harry. With J. & W. Seligman & Co., 1926-30, v.p. Central Nat. Bank, 1931-41, exec. v.p., 1945-49, pres., chief exec. officer, 1949-71, chmn. bd., 1967—, also dir.; dir., mem. exec. com. Richmond Hotels; pres., chmn. bd., dir. Central Nat. Corp.; dir. Lawyers Title Ins. Corp., Richmond Corp. Chmn. Va. Bd. of Vocational Rehab.; bd. dirs. Richmond chpt. A.R.C., also chmn. gen. fund drive, Henrico, Richmond, and Chesterfield, 1952; mem. Va. Comprehensive Health Planning Council. Bd. dirs. Richmond Meml. Hosp. Served as lt. comdr. USN, 1942-45, exec. officer U.S.S. Bremen. Mem. Assn. Res. City Bankers, Richmond C. of C. (pres. 1955-57), Am. Inst. of Banking, Phi Beta Kappa. Clubs: Indian Creek Yacht & Country, Jefferson Lakeside, Va. Yacht, Fishing Bay Yacht. Home: 210 Overlook Rd Route 13 Richmond VA 23229 Office: 219 E Broad St Richmond VA 23219

SCHWEICKART, RUSSELL L., astronaut; b. Neptune, N.J., Oct. 25, 1935; s. George L. Schweickart; B.S. in Aero. Engring., Mass. Inst. Tech., 1956, M.S. in Aeros. and Astronautics, 1963; m. Clare Grantham Whitfield; children—Vicki Louise, Elin Ashley, Russell Brown and Randolph Barton (twins), Diana Croom. Was research scientist Mass. Inst. Tech. Exptl. Astronomy Lab.; now astronaut NASA Manned Spacecraft Center, Houston; lunar module pilot on Apollo 9, 1969. Served as pilot USAF, 1956-60, 61, Capt., Mass. Air N.G. Mem. Soc. Exptl. Test Pilots. Office: NASA Manned Spacecraft Center Houston TX 77058

SCHWEIKERT, JOHN FREDRICH, automobile parts co. exec.; b. Phila., July 8, 1912; s. William P. and Clotilde (Suro) S.; B.S. in Commerce, Temple U., 1934; m. Jean McCulloch Young, Sept. 19, 1936; children—John Fredrich, Donald Young. Accountant, George K. Watson & Co., Phila., 1935-47; treas., dir. Quaker City Motor Parts Co., Phila., 1947-65; treas. Colyear Motor Sales Co., Los Angeles, 1965-67, Genuine Parts Co., Atlanta, 1967—. C.P.A., N.J., Pa., Cal. Mem. Am., Pa. insts. C.P.A.'s, Cal., Ga. socs. C.P.A.'s. Home: 750 Weatherly Lane NW Atlanta GA 30328 Office: 299 Piedmont Av NE Atlanta GA 30308

SCHWEITZER, FRANK JACOB, III, hosp. adminstr.; b. Louisville, Feb. 26, 1924; s. Frank Jacob and Nellie (McCullom) S.; student U. Louisville, 1942, Meadows-Draughon Bus. Coll., 1947, Texarkana Coll., 1968-69; m. Plesine Barker, Mar. 13, 1945; children—Betty Jean (Mrs. Robert M. Toups), Marianne, John Franklin. Profl. detailman E.R. Squibb & Sons, Ky., 1948; resident adminstrn. T.J. Samson Community Hosp., Glasgow, Ky., 1948-49; adminstr. Lafayette County Meml. Hosp., Lewisville, Ark., 1949—. Pres., S.W. Ark. Hosp. Dist., 1953. Mem. Ark.'s Hosp. Adv. Council, 1972—. Served with Hosp. Corps, USNR, 1943-46. Mem. Am., Ark. hosps. assns., Am. Coll. Hosp. Adminstrs., Am. Med. Technologists. Home: 311 W 11th St Lewisville AR 71845 Office: 1105 Chestnut St Lewisville AR 71845

SCHWEITZER, GERTRUDE, artist; b. N.Y.C. One-woman shows Montclair (N.J.) Art Mus., Washington Water Color Club, Cayuga Mus. History and Art, Auburn, N.Y., Potsdam Gallery Art, Currier Gallery of Art, Manchester, N.H., Bevier Gallery, Rochester (N.Y.) Inst. Tech., Erie (Pa.) Pub. Mus., Cortland Library, N.Y.C., Norton Gallery and Sch. Art, West Palm Beach, Fla., Galerie Charpentier, Paris, France (1st Am. one-man show), Hanover Gallery, London, Eng., Worth Av. Gallery, Palm Beach, Fla., Galleria Al Cavallino, Venice, Italy, Galleria Il Naviglio, Milan, Italy, Galleria L'Obelisco, Rome, Italy, High Mus., Atlanta, Witte Meml. Mus., San Antonio, Phila. Art Alliance, Hokin Gallery, Palm Beach, Fla. many others; exhibited in Washington, Chgo., Phila., Denver, Sarasota, Fla., N.Y.C., Los Angeles, Bklyn., Minn., Ill., Santa Fe, Newark, Providence, Muncie, Ind., San Francisco, Menina, Sicily; represented in permanent collections Bklyn. Mus., Toledo Mus., Haekley Art Gallery (Muskegon, Mich.), Davenport (Ia.) Municipal Gallery, Canajoharie (N.Y.) Library and Art Gallery, Norton Gallery and Sch. of Art, W. Palm Beach, Witte Meml. Mus. San Antonio, Mus. Modern Art, Paris, Albi Mus. (1st Am. rep.), France, Rochester (N.Y.) Meml. Art Gallery, Met. Mus. Art, N.Y.C., Whitney Am. Art, N.Y.C., Walker Art Mus. Bowdoin Coll., Brunswick, Me., Atlanta Art Assn. Galleries, Montclair (N.J.) Art Mus., Chgo. Art Inst., others; also numerous pvt. collections, U.S., Eng., France. Served as chmn. arts and skills corps, N.Y. chpt. A.R.C., Ft. Jay Regional Hosp., Governor's Island, N.Y., World War II. Recipient Am. Water Color Soc. medal; Am. Artists Profl. League medal for water color, State of N.J., Pauline Wick award (oil); Philadelphia Water Color prize, Pa. Acad. of Fine Arts; First prize Norton Gallery of Art, West Palm Beach, Fla.; First prize Soc. Four Arts; Watercolor award, Grand National Exhbn., Miami, Fla.; 1st prize, best woman painter N.J. State Exhbn.; N.Y. State award Am. Artists Profl. League, Nat. Arts Club; First prize Am. Artists Profl. League, Seton Hall U.; First Grumbacher Purchase award Audubon 17th Am. Exhbn., N.Y.C.; Grumbacher award for watercolor Audubon 27th Ann Exhbn., N.Y.C.; Alumni medal Pratt Inst., others. Mem. Nat. Acad., Am. Water Color Soc., Fla. Artists Gourp, Audubon Soc., N.J. Water Color and Sculpture Soc. Home: Colts Neck NJ 07722 also Palm Beach FL 33480

SCHWEITZER, PAUL ROBERT, govt. ofcl.; b. Budapest, Hungary, Sept. 17, 1930; s. Ivan and Wanda (Rusz) S.; B.A., Sir George Williams U. (Can.) 1959; M.A., McGill U. (Can.) 1961; m. Agnes Fischer, May 15, 1955; children—John, Alexandra. Came to U.S., 1959, naturalized, 1964. Exec. trainee Canadian Bank Commerce, Montreal, Que., Can., 1957-59; economist Canadian Dept. Labor, Ottawa, Ont., Can., 1959. cons. in econs., Washington, 1960-62; economist Nat. Planning Assn., Washington, 1962-64; economist Fed. Res. System Bd. Govs., Washington, 1964—. Lectr. Howard U., 1962-70. Mem. Am. Econ. Assn. Home: 4309 Van Ness St NW Washington DC 20016 Office: 600 New Hampshire Av Washington DC 20551

SCHWEITZER, PIERRE-PAUL, monetary fund ofcl.; b. Strasbourg, France, May 29, 1912; s. Paul and Emma (Munch) S.; grad. univs. Strasbourg and Paris, also Ecole Libre des Sciences Politiques; LL.D., Harvard, Yale, 1966, New York U., Leeds (Eng.) U., 1968, U. Wales, 1972, George Washington U., 1972; m. Catherine Hatt, Aug. 7, 1941; children—Louis, Juliette. Ofcl., French Treasury, 1936-47; alternate exec. dir. for France, Internat. Monetary Fund, 1947-48; sec. gen. Interministerial Com. European Econ. Coop., 1948-49; financial attache embassy, Washington, 1949-53; dir. treasury Ministry Finance, 1953-60; dep. gov. Bank of France, 1960-63; mng. dir. IMF, 1963—, also chmn. exec. bd., inspecteur general des finances. Decorated comdr. Legion of Honour, Croix de Guerre, Medaille de la Resistance. Mem. Am. Philos. Soc. Home: 1717 Foxhall Rd NW Washington DC 20007 Office: Internat Monetary Fund 19th and H Sts NW Washington DC 20431

SCHWEITZER, RAYMOND D., city ofcl.; b. Dodge City, Kan., Jan. 16, 1936; s. Howard R. and Mildred (Montgomery) S.; A.A., Dodge City Jr. Coll., 1961; A.B., Fort Hayes Kan. State Coll., 1963; postgrad. U. Kan., 1964; m. Jean Barker, May 30, 1966; stepsons—Steve Barker, Gary Barker. Adminstrv. intern City Dayton, O., 1964-65; dir. finance City Gladstone, Mo., 1965; asst. city mgr. Oshkosh, Wis., 1965; asst. city mgr. City Oak Ridge, 1965-68; city mgr. Alcoa, Tenn., 1968—. Mem. Tenn. delegation Nat. League Cities, 1970—. Served with USNR, 1955-59. Sears Roebuck Found. grantee, 1971. Mem. Internat. City Mgmt. Assn., Pub. Personnel Assn., Tenn. City Mgr. Assn., Nat., Tenn. municipal leagues. Kiwanian (Service citation Oak Ridge 1966). Home: 1617 Springbrook Rd Alcoa TN 37701 Office: Municipal Bldg Alcoa TN 37701

SCHWING, CHARLES EDWARD, architect; b. Plaquemine, La., Nov. 21, 1929; s. Calvin Kendrick and Mary Howard (Slack) S.; B.S., Ga. Inst. Tech., 1953, B.Architecture, 1954; 3e Assessit de'Architecture, Ecole Des Beaux-Arts; student, La. State U., 1947-51; m. Cynthia Benjamin, June 14, 1952. (div. 1967); children—Calvin Kendrick III, Therra Cynthia; m. 2d, Geraldine Fleniken Hofmann, Dec. 27, 1969; 1 stepson, Steven Blake. Field insp. Bodman, Murrell and Smith, Baton Rouge, 1954-55; asso. architect Post & Harelson, Baton Rouge, 1955-59; partner Hughes and Schwing, Baton Rouge, 1959-61; owner Charles E. Schwing, Baton Rouge, 1961-69, Charles E. Schwing & Assos., Baton Rouge, 1969—; dir. Schwing Inc. Mem. A.I.A. (sec. Baton Rouge chpt. 1960-61), La. Architect Assn. (sec.-treas. 1971, v.p. 1972), C. of C., La. State U. Alumni Fedn., Ga. Tech. Alumni Club, Sigma Alpha Epsilon. Episcopalian. Elk. Clubs: Baton Rouge Country, City. Home: Route 2 Box 380 Baton Rouge LA 70816 Office: 721 Government St Baton Rouge LA 70802

SCISM, MACK, theater exec.; b. Anadarko, Okla., July 26, 1926; s. Delos M. and Grace (Hux) S.; B.S., U. Okla., 1947. Tchr. math. and English, Capitol Hill High Sch., Oklahoma City, 1947-49; founding mem. Mummers Theatre, Inc., Oklahoma City, 1949, producer, dir., 1949—. Bd. dirs., mem. exec. com. Theatre Communications Group, 1961-68. Served with USNR, 1943-45. Ford Found. grantee, 1958. Home: 1130 N E 11th St Oklahoma City OK 73117 Office: 400 W Sheridan Oklahoma City OK 73106

SCIUCHETTI, LEO ANTON, found. exec.; b. Harrison, Ida., Apr. 7, 1913; s. Giacomo and Theresa (Tam) S.; B.S. in Pharmacy, Ida. State U., 1940; M.S. in Pharmacy, Wash. State U., 1942; Ph.D. in Pharmacognosy (Am. Found. Pharm. Edn. fellow), U. Wash., 1957; m. Emma J. Scheer, July 6, 1943; children—Caryl Therese (Mrs. Dennis Thomas), Larry Leo. Instr. pharm. chemistry Creighton U., 1942-43; prof. pharmacy Louisville Coll. Pharmacy, 1943-46; asst. prof. pharmacy Ore. State U., 1946-48, asso. prof., head pharmacognosy, 1948-59, prof., chmn. pharmacognosy, 1959-66; asso. program dir. undergrad. student program NSF, Washington, 1966—. Chmn. first aid Benton County (Ore.) A.R.C., 1948-52. Fellow A.A.A.S.; mem. Ore. Pharm. Assn. (trustee 1963-66), Am. Soc. Pharmacognosy (exec. com. 1965-68), Acad. Pharm. Sci., Am. Pharm. Assn., Assn. Schs. Allied Health Professions, N.Y. Acad. Scis., Sigma Xi, Phi Kappa Phi, Kappa Psi (nat. officer 1963-67), Rho Chi, Phi Sigma. Editor Garden Gate mag., 1952-53. Contbr. articles to profl. jours. Research in growth regulators and medicinal plants, alkaloid biogenesis, phytochem. screening of medicinal plants. Home: 7701 Lee Hwy Falls Church VA 22042 Office: NSF 1800 G St NW Washington DC 20550

SCOFIELD, JOHN, editor; b. Washington, Sept. 17, 1914; s. Kendrick and Violetta (Sprigg) S.; ed. pub. schs., Washington; m. Audrey Kendrick, Mar. 22, 1948; children—Sally, Kendrick. Editorial asst., news editor, asso. editor Am. Rifleman mag., 1935-42, mng. editor, 1946-51; mem. editorial staff Nat. Geog. mag., 1954-58, asst. editor, 1959-65, sr. asst. editor, 1966—; numerous articles and photographs have appeared in magazine. Served to capt. AUS, 1942-46, 51-52. Recipient 1st pl. portrait category Pictures of Year contest, 1963, 3d pl. picture story category, 1963, 2d pl. mag. news category, 1964. Home: 7110 Broxburn Dr Bethesda MD 20034 Office: Nat Geog Soc Washington DC 20036

SCOGGIN, ROBERT LEE, judge; b. nr. Rome, Ga., Jan. 13, 1923; s. William Gordon and Ruth (Salmon) S.; B.S., Berry Coll., 1944; LL.B., John Marshall U., 1966; m. Sara Marie Terrell, Jan. 13, 1946; children—Bobye Marie, Robin Lee, Marian Kay, William Samuel. Admitted to Ga. bar, 1947; mem. Ga. Ho. of Reps., 1949-62, speaker pro tem, 1961-62; judge Superior Ct., Rome, Ga., 1962—. Served with USNR, 1944-46. Mem. Am. Legion. Baptist. Mason, Elk. Club: Civitan. Home: 312 E 3d St Rome GA 30161 Office: Courthouse Rome GA 30161

SCOGGINS, ALVIN EARON (JOSH), JR., ednl. adminstr.; b. Rome, Ga., Apr. 28, 1938; s. Alvin Earon and Hazel (Williams) S.; A.B., West Ga. Coll., 1960; M.Ed., U. Ga., 1965, Ed.D., 1970; m. Sandra Kay Hulgan, June 6, 1969. Guidance counselor, football coach, tchr. Chattooga County Bd. Edn., 1961-62, 1963-65, prin., 1966-67; tchr. Rome City (Ga.) Schs., 1962-63; prin. Wilkes County Sch. Bd., Washington, Ga., 1970—. Mem. Nat., Ga., Wilkes County assns. educators. Home: Route 1 Box 84B Washington GA 30673 Office: Washington Central Jr High Sch Washington GA 30673

SCOTT, ALAN, educator; b. Marietta, O., Nov. 21, 1912; s. Isadore and Rebecca Glasser (Shiffman) S.; B.J., U. Mo., 1934, A.B., 1934, M.A. in Journalism, 1938; Ed.D., U. Tex., 1955; m. Sylvia Ruth Shuman, Mar. 27, 1940; children—Anthony Roger, Lizbeth Ann (Mrs. Scott Schleif). With A.P., 1933-35, OWI, San Francisco and N.Y.C., 1942-45; faculty U. Cal. at Berkeley, 1941-42, Mich. State U., 1945-49; faculty U. Tex., 1949—, prof. journalism, 1964—. Exec. dir. Tex. Pub. Relations Assn., 1954-69; Tex. rep. Dudley-Anderson-Yutzy, 1955—. Pub. relations counsel Mayor's Council on Child Devel., 1969—, City of Austin Aqua Festival, 1965—, Travis County Med. Soc., 1970—; coordinator pub. relations 10th Internat. Cancer Congress, Houston, 1970. Bd. dirs. Tex. div. Am. Cancer Soc. Pub. Relations Soc. Am. fellow, 1965. Mem. Pub. Relations Soc. Am., Assn. for Edn. in Journalism, Tex. Pub. Relations Assn., Kappa Alpha, Sigma Delta Chi, Alpha Delta Sigma, Phi Delta Kappa. Author: Contemporary Public Relations, 1955. Editor, Travis County Medical Soc. Jour., 1970—. Home: 7920 Rockwood Lane Austin TX 78758

SCOTT, ANDREW MACKAY, educator; b. Pasadena, Cal., Nov. 27, 1922; s. Andrew MacKay and Ruth (Jarvis) S.; A.B., Dartmouth Coll., 1946; M.A., Harvard, 1949, M.P.A., 1949, Ph.D., 1950; m. Anne Byrd Firor, June 2, 1947; children—Rebecca Jarvis, David MacKay, Donald MacKay. Intelligence officer CIA, Washington, 1949-51; fgn. affairs officer Mutual Security Agy., 1951-54; asst. prof. Dartmouth Coll., Hanover, N.H., 1953-54; asst. prof. internat. politics and Am. fgn. policy Haverford (Pa.) Coll., 1954-58; asso. prof. U. N.C., Chapel Hill, 1958-65, prof., 1965—. Served with USNR, 1943-45. Fulbright fellow Bologna, Italy, 1960-61. Mem. Am. Polit. Sci. Assn. Author: The Anatomy of Communism, 1951; Political Though in America, 1959; (with Earle Wallace) Politics: USA, 1969 (3d edit.); (with Raymond Dawson) Readings in the Making of American Foreign Policy, 1965; The Revolution in Statecraft: Informal Penetration, 1965; (with William A. Lucas and Trudi M. Lucas) Simulation and National Development, 1966; (with Margaret Hunt) Congress and Lobbies: Image and Reality, 1966; The Functioning of the International Political System, 1967; Competition in American Politics: An Economic Model, 1970; (with others) Insurgency, 1970. Home: 1028 Highland Woods St Chapel Hill NC 27514

SCOTT, BENJAMIN BERNARD, mech. engr.; b. Bellevue, Pa., Feb. 3, 1908; s. Benjamin Bernard and Adele (Heine) S.; B.S., Carnegie Inst. Tech., 1933; m. Phyllis Brown Mathiasen, Oct. 26, 1946; children—Phyllis Lynn, Benjamin Bernard III. Mem. staff coal research labs., faculty Carnegie Inst. Tech., 1933-37; various engring. and mgmt. positions Gen. Electric Co., Pitts., Schenectady, Louisville, 1937-65; cons. elec. mech. engr., Louisville, 1966—; mech. engr. U.S. Naval Ordnance, Louisville, 1966—. Served with Signal Corps, C.E., AUS, 1941-46; lt. col. Ret. Res. Recipient Coffin award Gen. Electric Co., 1951, Mgrs. awards, 1940, 49, 55; named Ky. col. Registered profl. engr., Ky. Mem. Nat., Ky. socs. profl. engrs., I.E.E.E., Soc. Plastics Engrs., Ret. Officers Assn., Fraternal Order Police (asso.), Am. Legion, Theta Chi. Mason (Shriner). Clubs: General Electric Elfun, OX-5, South Side Hunting and Fishing. Patentee in field. Address: 2318 Village Dr Louisville KY 40205

SCOTT, BERNICE SCHNEIDER, educator; b. N.Y.C.; d. Julius and Anna Schneider; B.A., Hunter Coll., 1942; M.Ed., U. Pitts., 1958; Ed.D., Columbia, 1967; postgrad. U. Fla., 1967, U. London, 1960; m. children— Stephen Allen, Fredric Joseph, Penny Jane. Tchr. Oakmont (Pa.) Pub. Schs., 1957-58; tchr. English, pub. schs., Pitts., 1958-62, guidance counselor, 1962-65; asst. prof. edn. Jacksonville U., Fla., 1966; dir. research and program evaluation Duval County Schs., Jacksonville, Fla., 1966-70, dir. planning and design, 1970—; adj. prof. edn. Fla. A. and M. U., Tallahassee, 1968—; adj. prof. edn. Nova U., Ft. Lauderdale, Fla., 1971—. Cons., State Depts. Edn., Miss., S.C., Fla. Recipient award for excellence in edn., Jacksonville, 1970. Mem. Am., Fla. ednl. research assns., Am. Personnel and Guidance Assn., Assn. Supervision and Curriculum Devel., Kappa Delta Pi, Pi Lambda Theta. Home: 2325 Costa Verde Blvd Jacksonville Beach FL 32250

SCOTT, BRUCE MILTON, gen. contractor; b. Hardin, Mont., Apr. 23, 1935; s. Frank Max and Sarah (Burnley) S.; B.S., Va. Poly. Inst.; m. Mary Trent, June 12, 1959; children—Julia King, Frank Jeffery, Susan Hamilton, John Burnley. Pres. B. Scott Constrn., Inc., 1960-63; sales mgr. Cooper-Trent div. Keuffel & Esser Co., Arlington, Va., 1963-68; owner Bruce Scott Constrn., Inc., Falls Church, Va., 1968—. Vice pres. Fairfax County Vocational Found. Served with AUS, 1959-60. Mem. No. Va. Builders Assn. (1st v.p.), Annandale (Va.) Jr. C. of C. (past pres., keyman). Episcopalian (warden). Mason. Home: 4604 N 37th St Arlington VA 22207 Office: 450 W Broad St Falls Church VA 22046

SCOTT, CARL MCDONALD, JR., state govt. ofcl.; b. Folkston, Ga., Apr. 20, 1922; s. Carl McDonald and Margaret (Robinson) S.; B.A., Emory U., 1950; postgrad. U. Ga., 1950-51; m. Carolyn Lloyd Schoen, June 28, 1952; children—Carl M., Carol Lynn. Communicable diseases investigator Ga. Dept. Pub. Health, Waycross, 1951-56; asst. dir. Ga. Dept. Entomology, Atlanta, 1956-58; asst. dir. div. entomology Ga. Dept. Agr., 1958-63, dir., 1963—. Chmn. Ga. Structural Pest Control Commn., 1965-67, vice chmn., 1967—; chmn. Imported Fire Ant Research Workers, 1963—. Vice chmn. So. plant bd. Leafmore-Creek Park Civic Club, 1957—. Served with USNR, 1942-46. Mem. Ga., Southeastern, Am. entomol. socs., Ga. Beekeepers Assn., Greater Atlanta Structural Pest Control Assn., Ga. Pest Control Assn., Ga. Nurserymen's Assn., Am. Camellia Soc. Club: Leafmore-Creek Park Social (Decatur). Home: 1400 Knollwood Terrace Decatur GA 30033 Office: Capitol Sq Atlanta GA 30334

SCOTT, (FLORRIE) CAROLYNNE BLACKWELL (MRS. KARL LEGRANT SCOTT), editor; b. Birmingham, Ala., Feb. 10, 1937; d. Walter Craig and Florrie (Webb) Blackwell; A.B., Samford U., 1958; m. Karl Legrant Scott, Apr. 18, 1964. Asso. editor Shades Valley Sun, 1958; tchr. Hewitt-Trussville High Sch., 1959-60; reporter women's dept. Birmingham News, 1960-64; fashion editor Birmingham Post-Herald, 1964; asst. editor So. Veterinarian, Birmingham, Ala., 1964, mng. editor, 1965—; editor Blue Cross Wise, Blue Cross-Blue Shield Ala., 1969-70. Publicity dir. Birmingham Centennial, 1971-72. Recipient 1st prize in fiction Scope Lit. Competition, Birmingham Festival Arts, 1967; 2d prize Hackney Lit. Competition, Birmingham, 1969, 71; 1st prize Ala. Regional Photog. Competition, 1969. Mem. Birmingham Assn. Indsl. Editors, Ala. Conservancy, Ala. Hist. Assn., Nat. Trust Historic Preservation, St. Clair Hist. Soc. (pres. 1972-73), Zeta Tau Alpha. Episcopalian (v.p. women of ch. 1965-66). Contbg. author: Alabama Prize Stories, 1970. Editorial staff Overture, Birmingham Symphony Orch. mag., 1966. Address: Route 1 Box 241 Springville AL 35146

SCOTT, CHARLES RAY, judge; b. Adel, Ia., Jan. 13, 1904; s. Walter E. and Elma (Harrington) S.; LL.B., Valparasio U., 1924; m. Exie Smith, June 17, 1933 (dec. Nov. 1942); children—Barbara Exie (Mrs. O. Lamar Majure, Jr.), William Harrington, Charlene Stephanie; m. 2d, Grace Kathryn Stephens, Mar. 21, 1947. Admitted to Ind. bar, 1925, Fla. bar, 1926; asso. and partner Fleming, Hamilton, Diver & Jones, and Fleming, Jones, Scott & Botts, 1926-55; sr. mem. Fleming, Scott & Botts, 1955-57, Scott & Cox, 1957-60; circuit judge, 4th jud. circuit ct., 1960-66; U.S. dist. judge Middle Dist. Fla., 1966—. Mem. Fla. Bd. Law Examiners, 1954-55. Fellow Am. Coll. Trial Lawyers; mem. Fla. Bar (gov. 1958-61), S.A.R. Presbyn. (elder). Mason (Shriner, Jester). Clubs: Ponte Vedra, San Jose Country. Home: 739 Alhambra Dr N Jacksonville FL 32207 Office: Duval County Courthouse Jacksonville FL 32202

SCOTT, CHARLEY, educator; b. Meridian, Miss., June 10, 1923; s. James Jack and Alice (Adams) S.; B.S., Miss. State U., 1944; M.S., Ga. Inst. Tech., 1950; Ph.D., Purdue U., 1953; postgrad. U. Mich., 1962-63; m. Uldine McDonald, Apr. 5, 1947; children—David Keith,

Joseph Leigh. Instr., Miss. State U., 1946-47, asst. prof., 1949-51, asso. prof., 1953-56; thermodynamicist Materials Research Center, Miss. State U., State College, 1961-63, prof. mech. engring., 1956-63; asst. dean, grad. sch. U. Ala., Tuscaloosa, 1963-68, asso. dean, 1968-72, dean, 1972—, prof. mech. engring., 1963-66, 69—, coordinator Grad. Sch. of Library Service, 1970-71; dir. instrn., Huntsville, 1963-66; dir. acad. affairs U. Ala. at Huntsville, 1966-68; prof. mech. engring., 1966-69, dir. div. engring., 1966-68; dir. div. grad. programs, 1968-69; instr. W.Va. U., Morgantown, 1947-48, Meridian Jr. Coll., Miss., 1947; asst. engr. Manhattan Project, Oak Ridge, Tenn., 1944-46; research engr. Army Ballistic Missile Agy., Huntsville, Ala., 1957, 58. Mem. planning com. Tenn. Valley Edn. Center, 1967. Bd. dirs. Community Council of Huntsville and Madison County, 1965-69; mem. Burritt Meml. Park and Mus. Com., Huntsville, 1964-69. Served with AUS, 1945-46. Fellow Am. Soc. M.E.; mem. Am. Soc. Engring. Edn., Sigma Xi, Tau Beta Pi, Phi Kappa Phi, Omicron Delta Kappa, Pi Tau Sigma, Sigma Pi Sigma. Rotarian. Home: PO Box 1336 University AL 35486 Office: PO Box W University AL 35486

SCOTT, CORNELIUS A., publisher; b. Edwards, Miss., Feb. 8, 1908; s. William Alexander and Emmeline (Southall) S.; student Morehouse Coll., Atlanta, 1930-31, U. Kan., 1931; m. Ruth D. Perry, Jan. 27, 1940; children—Jocelyn, Portia. Asst. gen. mgr. Atlanta Daily World, 1928-34, then gen. mgr., now publisher; dir. Mut. Fed. Savs. & Loan Assn. of Atlanta. Mem. Met. Atlanta Rapid Transit Study Commn.; mem. Fulton County Welfare Bd. Bd. mgrs. Butler Street YMCA. Recipient citation Lincoln U., 1957. Mem. Nat. Newspaper Publs. Assn. Republican. Methodist. Home: 1317 Hunter Rd NW Atlanta GA 30314 Office: 210 Auburn Av NE Atlanta GA 30303

SCOTT, DAVID R., astronaut; b. San Antonio, June 6, 1932; s. Rom. W. Scott; student U. Mich., D.Sc. (hon.), 1971; B.S., U.S. Mil. Acad., 1954; M.S. in Aeros. and Astronautics, Engr. Aeros. and Astronautics, Mass. Inst. Tech., 1962; grad. Air Force Aerospace Research Pilot Sch., Edwards AFB, Cal., 1963; m. Ann Lurton Ott; children—Tracy Lee, William Douglas. Joined USAF, 1954, advanced through ranks to col.; now astronaut NASA Manned Spacecraft Center, Houston; Gemini VIII, Mar. 1966, Apollo 9, 1969, Apollo 15, 1971. Mem. Sigma Xi, Tau Beta Pi, Sigma Gamma Tau, Sigma Chi. Office: NASA Manned Spacecraft Center Houston TX 77001

SCOTT, DONALD GRIGGS, univ. adminstr.; b. Boston, Apr. 29, 1921; s. Donald Griggs Scott; grad. Worcester Acad.; A.B. in Biology, Bowdoin Coll.; M.S. in Zoology-Physiology, U. Miami (Fla.); Ph.D. in Adminstrn. of Higher Edn., Fla. State U. Edn. coordinator, State of Fla.; v.p. also acad. dean Bryan Coll., Dayton, Tenn.; v.p. Compro, mgmt. cons. firm for higher edn., Chgo.; now pres. U. Plano (Tex.). Cons. to Council for Advancement of Small Colls. Served with USAF, World War II. Mem. Am Assn. Higher Edn., Phi Delta Kappa. Office: U Plano Plano TX 75740*

SCOTT, ELLIS LAVERNE, educator; b. Casey, Ia., June 11, 1915; s. Alexander Catell and Cora (Tilman) S.; B.S. in Edn. summa cum laude, Ohio State U., 1947, Ph.D., 1953; m. Florence Louise Green, Sept. 7, 1950; children—Susan Eileen, Katherine Ellen, Robert Tilman. Teaching asst., research asso. Ohio State U., 1946-53; asst. prof. U. N.M., 1953-56; asso. social scientist Rand Corp., 1957; human factors scientist System Devel. Corp., 1957-64; prof. mgmt. U. Ga., Athens, 1964—. Pres., Center for Study of Automation and Soc., 1969—; chmn. com. on social implications of automation Internat. Fedn. of Automatic Control, 1972—; chmn. automation com. Am. Automatic Control Council, 1970—; mem. sci. and mgmt. adv. com. U.S. Army Computer Systems Command, 1972—. Served with AUS, 1942-46. Mem. Am. Sociol. Assn., Soc. Mgmt. Information Systems, Assn. Computing Machinery. Co-editor: Automation and Society, 1969; EDP Systems for Public Management, 1968. Home: 124 Colonial Dr Athens GA 30601

SCOTT, GEORGE ARMISTEAD, JR., banker; b. Fredericksburg, Va., Feb. 1, 1915; s. George A. and Nellie (Boatwright) S.; student Hampden-Sydney Coll., 1932-33; certificate Am. Inst. Banking, 1950; m. Lucy Mae Copley, Nov. 4, 1938; 1 dau., Nancy Lee. With Nat. Bank Fredericksburg (Va.), 1933—, v.p., 1952-69, sr. v.p., 1970—, dir., 1945—. Served with N.G. Mem. Va. Bankers Assn. (past mem. com. fed. legislation), Kenmore Assn. (treas. 1956-58, trustee). Kiwanian. Home: 1222 Brent St Fredericksburg VA 22401 Office: 900 Princess Anne St Fredericksburg VA 22401

SCOTT, GEORGE GALLMANN, trucking co. exec.; b. Hattiesburg, Miss., July 8, 1928; s. John Havers and Rebecca Evelyn (Gallmann) S.; B.S., Millsaps Coll., 1949; m. Patsy T. Womack, June 27, 1953; 1 son, George Gallmann. Clk., Spanish Trail Transport, Mobile, Ala., 1949-50, asst. auditor, 1953-55; bookkeeper Met. Engraving & Electrotype Co., Richmond, Va., 1952-53; chief clk Central Truck Lines of Tampa, Fla., Mobile, 1955-56; gen. auditor M.R.&R. Trucking Co., Crestview, Fla., 1956-66, sec.-treas., 1967—. Mem. data processing adv. com. Okaloosa-Walton Jr. Coll., Niceville, Fla., 1965-66. Served with AUS, 1950-52. Mem. Am. Trucking Assn. (nat. accounting and finance council 1956—), Greater Crestview C. of C., Pi Kappa Alpha. Methodist (chmn. ofcl. bd. 1971-72). Kiwanian.‡

SCOTT, GEORGE V., pres. Lawyers Title Insurance Co. Office: Lawyers Title Ins Co 3800 Cutshaw Av Richmond VA 23230*

SCOTT, HELEN ELIZABETH DIETZ (MRS. GEORGE F. SCOTT), statistician; b. Pine Hill, N.Y., June 30, 1915; d. Albert E. and Helen (Toth) Dietz; student Northwestern U., 1933, Harvard, 1934-37, U. Pa., 1938-39, George Washington U., 1961, Am. U., 1962; m. George F. Scott, June 26, 1937; children— Nancy D., Donald E., Ronald E. Adv. commn. Council Nat. Def. head of summary date dept. WPT, 1940-46; statistician U.S. Congress, 1954; with statis. techniques lab. electronic data processing computer programing Internal Revenue Service, 1955-57; survey-analytical statistician USPHS, Dept. Health, Edn. and Welfare, 1957; biostatistician Army Office Surgeon Gen., 1958-59; security statistician Office of Sec., Dept. of Interior, 1959-60; chief survey statistics VA Central Lab., Armed Forces Inst. Pathology, Walter Reed Army Med. Center, 1960-64; child matron Masonic and Eastern Star Home, 1962-63 (all Washington); research statistician, computer programmer, campus cons. U. So. Fla., 1963-70; cons. Fla. Research Bur., 1970—. Tax specialist, cons. McCar Accounting Co., St. Petersburg, Fla., 1963, J.M. Fields, 1963—; lectr. A.M.A., Am. Pub. Health Assn., 1960-64; cons. Fla. Research Bur. Mem. Am. Statis. Assn., Royal Soc. Health (London), Nat., Am., D.C. pub. health assns., Internat. Platform Assn., Assn. for Instnl. Research. Club: Professional Women's. Author: This and This or This, 1960, rev. 1962; Bias Statistic Distortion, 1961, rev. 1963. Home: 5242 Fowler Av Tampa FL 33617

SCOTT, HENRY WILLIAM, JR., surgeon, educator; b. Graham, N.C., Aug. 22, 1916; s. Henry William and Claire (Turner) S.; A.B., U. N.C., 1937; M.D., Harvard, 1941; m. Mary Louisa Vanamee, Oct. 17, 1942; children—Henry William III, Mary Elizabeth, Virginia Wright, Patricia Vanamee. Intern Peter Bent Brigham Hosp., Boston, 1941-42, Children's Hosp., Boston 1941-42; resident surgeon Children's Hosp., 1943-44; Harvey Cushing fellow neurosurgery Harvard, 1945-46; resident surgeon Johns Hopkins Hosp., 1946-47; practice medicine specializing in surgery, Balt., 1947-52, Nashville, 1952—; surgeon-in-chief Vanderbilt U. Hosp., 1952—; instr. Johns Hopkins U. Sch. Medicine, 1946-48, asst. prof., 1948-50, asso. prof., 1950-52; prof. surgery, chmn. dept. Vanderbilt U. Sch. Medicine, Nashville, 1952—. Chmn. surgery study sect. B, USPHS, 1965-70. Diplomate Am. Bd. Surgery (mem. bd. 1956-62, vice chmn. 1961-62). Fellow A.C.S. (bd. govs. 1963-67, treas. 1967—); mem. Am. (treas. 1958-65), So., Pan Pacific (v.p. 1966-69) surg. assns., Soc. U. Surgeons (pres. 1960-61), Halsted Soc. (pres. 1968-70), Soc. Clin. Surgery (pres. 1970-72), Soc. Surgery Alimentary Tract (pres. 1970-71), Soc. Vascular Surgery, Internat. Soc. Surgery (sec. N.Am. chpt. 1967—), Internat. Cardiovascular Soc., Phi Beta Kappa, Phi Delta Theta, Alpha Omega Alpha. Club: Belle Meade Country. Home: 1050 Tyne Blvd Nashville TN 37215 Office: Vanderbilt U Hosp Nashville TN 37203

SCOTT, HUGH J., supt. schs.; b. Detroit, Nov. 14, 1933; s. Layton Leston and Hazel (Freeman) S.; B.S. in Edn., Wayne U., 1956; M.Ed., Wayne State U., 1960, Edn. Specialist, 1964; Ed.D., Mich. State U., 1966; m. Florence Edwards, Oct. 8, 1961; children—MarvaLisa (stepdau.), Hugh. Tchr. pub. schs., Detroit, 1956-65, asst. to dep. supt., 1967-68, regional asst. supt., 1968-70; supt. schs., Washington, 1970—. Instr. social studies Mich. State U., East Lansing, 1966-69; instr. sociology Wayne State U., Detroit, 1969-70. Bd. visitors faculty ednl. studies State U. N.Y. at Buffalo. Served with AUS, 1956-58. Recipient Distinguished Alumni award Mich. State U. Coll. Edn., 1970. Mem. N.A.A.C.P., Soc. Black Ednl. Adminstrs. (vice chmn. 1968-70), Phi Delta Kappa. Home: 5426 27th St NW Washington DC 20024 Office: Presidential Bldg 415 12th St NW Washington DC 20004

SCOTT, IRENE FEAGIN, U.S. judge; b. Union Springs, Ala., Oct. 6, 1912; d. Arthur H. and Irene (Peach) Feagin; A.B., U. Ala., 1932; LL.B., 1936; LL.M., Cath. U. Am., 1939; m. Thomas Jefferson Scott, Dec. 27, 1939; children—Thomas Jefferson, Irene. Law librarian U. Ala. Law Sch., 1932-34; admitted to Ala. bar, 1936; atty. Office Chief Counsel, Internal Revenue Service, 1937-50, mem. excess profits tax council, 1950-52; spl. asst. to head appeals div. Office Chief Counsel, 1952-59, staff asst. to chief counsel, 1959-60; judge U.S. Tax Ct., 1960—. Mem. Ala. Bar, D.C. (hon.), Am., Fed. bar assns., Am. Judicature Soc., Kappa Delta, Kappa Beta Pi. Methodist. Club: Nat. Lawyers. Home: 4815 25th Rd N Arlington VA 22207 Office: US Tax Ct Box 70 Washington DC 20044

SCOTT, ISAAC ALEXANDER, JR., lawyer; b. Trenton, N.J., Aug. 23, 1934; s. Isaac Alexander and Sherwin (Gilbert) S.; B.A., Harvard, 1956; LL.B., U. Ark., 1959; m. Margaret Elaine Hoffman, Aug. 24, 1957; children— Melissa Elaine, Caitlin Munday, Bronwen Amanda. Admitted to Ark. bar, 1959; practiced in Little Rock, 1960—; clk. fed. dist. judge Eastern Dist. Ark., 1960-61; asso. Chowning, Mitchell, Hamilton & Burrow, 1961-65; asso. Wright, Lindsey & Jennings, 1965-66, partner, 1967—. Pres., Chamber Music Soc. Bd. dirs. Urban League Greater Little Rock; incorporator, bd. dirs. Legal Aid Bur. Pulaski County, 1967-69. Served with AUS, 1959-60, 61-62. Mem. Pulaski County Bar Assn. (sec. 1964-65). Home: 621 N Pine St Little Rock AR 72205 Office: Worthen Bank Bldg Little Rock AR 72201

SCOTT, JACK JEFFERS, banker; b. nr. Elizabethtown, Ky., July 27, 1922; s. Walter Lee and Ruth (Fontaine) S.; B.S. with distinction, U. Ky., 1948; postgrad. Evansville Coll., 1958-60, U. Wis., 1961-62; m. Minnie Alice Bondurant, Mar. 16, 1941; children—Alice (Mrs. Lyle Robey), Rachel (Mrs. William James), John Jeffers, William Lee, Ann Bondurant. Tchr., Breckinridge County Schs., Irvington, Ky., 1948-49; dist. supr. Farmers Home Adminstrn., Marion, Ky., 1950-57; trust officer Ohio Valley Nat. Bank Henderson, Ky., 1958-62; v.p., corr. Merc. Trust Co., St. Louis, 1963-64; pres. Citizens Bank, Elizabethtown, 1964—. Mem. Critendon County Bd. Edn., 1955-56. Pres. bd. dirs. Crittendon County Library, 1954-57. Served with USNR, 1942-45. Mem. Elizabethtown (pres. 1969-70), Ky. chambers commerce, Lincoln Trail Farm Analysis Group (pres. 1966-69), Ky. Soc. Farm Mgrs. and Rural Appraisers (pres. 1969). Methodist (lay leader). Mason, Rotarian, Kiwanian. Home: 200 Logan Av Elizabethtown KY 42701 Office: 425 W Dixie Av Elizabethtown KY 42701

SCOTT, JAMES HENRY, JR., supr. schs.; b. Osawatomie, Kan., June 9, 1927; s. James Henry and Ethel (Sublett) S.; A.B., Va. Union U., 1951, B.D., 1954; student U. Va., 1961, 1964; M.S., Va. State Coll., 1965; m. Karen Clarissa Weaver, Aug. 21, 1954; children—James Henry III, Sonja Renee, Anthony Pierre. Ordained minister, Baptist Ch., 1947; prin. D. Webster Davis Elem. Sch., Staunton, Va., 1954-59, Augusta County Training Sch., Staunton, Va., 1959-61, Central Augusta High Sch., Staunton, Va., 1961-66, Cedar Green Elem. Sch., Staunton, Va., 1961-66, Oak Grove Elem. Sch., Staunton, Va., 1965-66; gen. supr. Augusta County Pub. Schs., Staunton, Va., 1966—; pastor Ebenezer Baptist Ch., Staunton, Va., 1952-67; pastor Mt. Zion Baptist Ch., Christians, Va., 1959—; mem. faculty Eastern Mennonite Coll., summer 1970, Blue Ridge Community Ch., eves. 1970. Vice-pres. Staunton Community Action Inc.; governing bd. Manpower Devel. Bd.; v.p. Staunton chpt. Am. Cancer Soc. Trustee Berean Valley Baptist Assn.; chmn. bd. dirs. Staunton Area Assn. for Retarded Children. Served with USAAF, 1945-46. Mem. Nat., Va. edn. assns., Staunton Area Ministerial Assn., Valley Supervisors Assn., N.A.A.C.P. (pres. Staunton br. 1968-72), Kappa Alpha Psi, Alpha Kappa Mu, Kappa Gamma Chi. Baptist. Home: 547 Calvert St Staunton VA 24401 Office: Box 1268 Staunton VA 24401

SCOTT, JOHN WALKER, orgn. exec.; b. Okadale, Pa., Dec. 8, 1917; s. Frank Walker and Nellie (DeVassie) S.; ed. pub. schs.; m. Dorothy McCandless, Aug. 25, 1939; children—James W., Thomas W., David M. Farmer, Butler County, Pa., 1934-62; master Pa. Grange, 1962-68; gatekeeper Nat. Grange, 1963-65, sec., 1965-68, nat. master, 1968—. Dir. Farmers & Traders Life Ins. Co., Nat. Grange Mut. Ins. Co. Pres. Agrl. Extension Assn., 1957-59; mem. Gov. Pa. Com. Preservation Agrl. Land, 1967, Gov. Pa. Priority Needs, 1968; mem. Pa. Adv. Com. Agrl. Research, 1965-69; exec. com. Agrl. Adv. Council, Pa. State U., 1964—; mem. Pa. Council Farm Orgns., 1963-69, Pa. Rural Area Devel. Bd., 1962-69; mem. World Food Crisis Com., Am. Freedom from Hunger Found., Rural Safety Council, Nat. Livestock and Meat Bd. Pres. Slippery Rock Area Sch. Bd., 1955-62, Butler County Sch. Bd., 1958-62, Pa. Adv. Council Bd. Edn., 1963-69; mem. steering com. Gov. Pa. Conf. Natural Beauty, 1965-69, Pres.'s. Commn. Employment Handicapped, 1969—, CARE, 1968—. Bd. dirs. Nat. Safety Council, 1969—; adv. com. Pa. Vocational and Tech. Schs., 1964-69; dir. Found. Am. Agr., 1969—. Named Butler County Man of Year in Agr., 1960; recipient Agr. award of merit New Holland Machine Co., 1966; hon. degree Slippery Rock chpt. Future Farmers Am., 1952; Agrl. Service award Pa. Potato Growers Assn., 1969. Mem. Pa. C. of C. Home: 5213 Terrace Rd Mechanicsburg PA 17055 Office: 1616 H St NW Washington DC 20006

SCOTT, LAMAR E., bank dir.; b. Dardanelle, Ark., Mar. 22, 1917; s. James Edward and Laura Oceola (Crow) S.; A.A., Ark. Poly. Coll., 1937; m. Nanette Herrick, Oct. 1, 1939; children—Jon Michael, Gary Keith, Diane Elizabeth. Bookkeeper Nat. Bank Tulsa, 1937-42; accountant Carter Oil Co., 1942, Scott's Office Supply, Bartlesville, Okla., 1963—; organizer, 1st v.p., dir. Plaza Nat. Bank, Bartlesville, Okla., 1963—; realtor, developer, 1957—. Commr., City Bartlesville, 1956-57. Mem. Pres.'s adv. council Bartlesville Wesleyan Coll., 1971-72. Served with USNR, 1942-45. Mem. Bartlesville Bus. Men's Assn. (pres., 1956-57), Bartlesville Bd. Realtors (pres., 1962), Bartlesville, Okla., Nat. bds. realtors. Republican. Methodist. Lion, Elk. Home: 2224 Venus Ct Bartlesville OK 74003 Office: 320 S Delaware St Bartlesville OK 74003

SCOTT, LAWRENCE VERNON, educator; b. Anthony, Kan., Jan. 28, 1917; s. Lawrence Garfield and Mable Grace (Madden) S.; B.A., Phillips U., 1940; M.S., U. Okla., 1947; Sc.D., Johns Hopkins, 1950; m. Elizabeth Buchanan Rowe, Jan. 28, 1945; children—James Robert, Jean Elizabeth, Lawrence Rowe. Asst. prof. bacteriology U. Okla. Sch. Medicine, Oklahoma City, 1950-53, asso. prof., 1953-58, prof. microbiology, 1958—, chmn. dept., 1961—; cons. St. Anthony Hosp., Oklahoma City, 1957—, VA Hosp., Oklahoma City, 1953—. Served to lt. USNR, 1942-46. Fellow Am. Acad. Microbiology; mem. A.A.A.S., Am. Soc. Microbiology (pres. Missouri Valley bd.), S.W. Soc. Exptl. Biology and Medicine, S.W. Cancer Research Soc., N.Y., Okla. (pres.) acads. scis. Research in viral diseases of man. Home: 4125 NW 61st Terrace Oklahoma City OK 73112

SCOTT, LEGRAND THURMAN, JR., physician; b. Florence, S.C., Jan. 23, 1937; s. Legrand Thurman and Janie Belle (Jones) S.; B.S., Wofford Coll., 1959; M.D., U. S.C., 1963; m. Ashby Moncure Dunn, Aug. 30, 1960; children—Marie Dunn, Jane Ashby. Intern Spartanburg (S.C.) Gen. Hosp., 1963-64; gen. practice medicine, Rockingham, N.C., 1966—; mem. staff Richmond Meml. Hosp., Rockingham, mem. exec. com., 1970—. Served with AUS, 1964-66; Viet Nam. Mem. C. of C. (dir. 1968-71), Am. Acad. Gen. Practice, N.C. State Med. Soc., Richmond County Med. Soc., A.M.A., Kappa Sigma. Home: 2004 Brookbank St Rockingham NC 28379 Office: 307 Leak St Rockingham NC 28379

SCOTT, MARGARET ANN, social worker; b. Waco, Tex., Aug. 20, 1929; d. Curtis Kelton and Adele (Pritchett) Scott; B.S. in Home Econs., Tex. Christian U., 1950; M.S. in Social Work, U. Tex., Austin, 1960. With Tex. Dept. Pub. Welfare, Fort Worth, 1951—, regional dir. child welfare div., 1965-69, program dir. social services, 1969—. Sec. Southwest Regional Conf., Child Welfare League Am., 1970; mem. adv. com. child care program Tarrant County Jr. Coll., 1968-72; mem. profl. adv. com. homemaker program Family Service Assn., 1968-71; del. Nat. Conf. Day Care Services, Washington, 1965, Invitational Centennial Conf. U. Ill. on Regulations of Child-Care Facilities, Chgo., 1967; mem. Cath. Charities Commn. of Diocese Ft. Worth, 1970-71; mem. nat. day care licensing task force Office Child Devel., Dept. Health, Edn. and Welfare. Mem. Acad. Certified Social Workers, Am. Pub. Welfare Assn., Nat. Assn. Social Workers (charter mem.), Tex. Assn. Edn. Young Children Inc. (bd. mem.), Nat., Fort Worth assns. edn. young children, So. Assn. Children Under Six, Tex. Christian U. Women Execs., Alpha Chi. Democrat. Roman Catholic. Home: 2307 W Magnolia Av Fort Worth TX 76110 Office: 308 E 4th St Fort Worth TX 76102

SCOTT, MARGARETE, broadcasting exec. Operations mgr. stas. WJAX, WJAX-FM, Jacksonville, Fla. Office: 1 Broadcast Pl P O Box 1740 Jacksonville FL 32201

SCOTT, NED VAUGHAN, JR., chem. co. exec.; b. Houston, Sept. 28, 1929; s. Ned V. and Sue (Haley) S.; B.S. in Petroleum Engring., U. Tex., 1952; m. Carol Norwood, Sept. 6, 1969. Engr., Standard Oil Co., Houston, 1955-57, Houston Natural Gas Co., 1958-60; pres. Filter Media Co., Houston, 1960—, also dir. Served with USNR, 1952-55. Registered profl. engr., Tex. Mem. Vermiculite Assn. (dir.), Perlite Inst. (dir.), Filtration Soc., Kappa Sigma. Presbyn. Club: Houston Racquet. Home: 12522 Overcup Dr Houston TX 77024 Office: 1616 W Loop S Houston TX 77027

SCOTT, NORMA LINN (MRS. JOHN MITCHELL SCOTT), ret. educator, club woman; b. Wharton, Tex., Oct. 13, 1894; d. John Edward and Elizabeth Frances (Bolton) Linn; student Hollins Coll., 1913-14; B.S. in Edn., U. Tex., 1943, M.A., 1949; m. John Mitchell Scott, July 22, 1914; children—John Linn, Norma Elizabeth (Mrs. John R. Johnson), Lawrence Evans, Virginia Randolph (Mrs. N. B. Dismukes), Patricia Ruth (Mrs. Louis Meade Burton). Tchr. history, govt. and English in high schs. of Tex., 1918-65; with McCallum High Sch. Austin, until 1965, now retired; asst. dept. govt. U. Tex., 1946-49; prin. Mullin (Tex.) High Sch., 1925-33, Buffalo (Tex.) High Sch., 1945-47; Leon County chmn. Jr. Red Cross, 1943-47; chmn. Buffalo (tex.) chpt. A.R.C., 1945-46; v.p. YWCA, Austin, 1968-70, pres., 1970-72; active Infantile Paralysis, War Bond, United Fund, Community Chest drives; mem. Travis County and Austin Community Council. Recipient Kellog Found. scholarship U. Tex., 1944. Mem. Am. Assn. U. Women (br. parliamentarian 1960—; pres. Austin 1962-64). Austin Classroom Tchrs. Assn. (pres. 1958-60), Heritage Soc. Austin, Tex. Geneal. Soc., U.D.C. (state pres. 1968-70, 70-72, chmn. Norma Linn Scott scholarship 1961-72), Tex. Tchrs. Assn. (pres. English sect. dist. X 1956—, mem. ho. dels. 1956—), Austin Ret. Tchrs. Assn. Delta Kappa Gamma (pres. local chpt.), Alpha Epsilon, Gamma Psi. Baptist. Clubs: Forty Acres (U. Tex.); Austin Women's Home: 3001 Beverly Rd Austin TX 78703

SCOTT, RALPH ASA, JR., govt. ofcl.; b. Sterling, Ill., July 23, 1930; s. Ralph Asa and Hazel Irene (Llewellyn) S.; B.S., U. Ill., 1952; M.S. (NSF fellow, AEC fellow), U. Okla., 1954; Ph.D. (NSF fellow, AEC fellow, Tex. Acad. Sci. fellow), Tex. A. and M., 1957; m. Kathryn Louise Hartman, Nov. 27, 1959; children—Susan Irene, Craig Philip. Radiochemist, Okla. Research Inst., 1952-53; research plant breeder W. Atlee Burpee Seed Co., Cal., 1954-55; prin. research chemist and dir. waste eval. program Internat. Minerals & Chem. Corp., Fla., 1957-58; research plant physiologist Olin Mathieson Chem. Corp., N.Y., 1958; plant physiologist cotton research center, Crops Res. Div. Agr. Research Service, U.S. Dept. Agr., Phoenix, 1958-61, sr. research plant physiologist Boll Weevil Research Lab., State Coll., Miss., 1961-62; chief chemist U.S. Dept. Defense, U.S. Air Force, N.M., 1962-64; sr. chemist Adv. Test Tech., Joint Chiefs Staff, Desert Test Center, Ft. Douglas, Utah, 1965-66, chief div. chem. Dept. Pub. Health, Washington, 1966-67; dir. aquatic plant control program, Office Chief of Engrs., U.S. Army, Dept. of Def., Washington, 1967-69; chief chem. scientist Office Sec. Def., Dept. of Def. Explosives Safety Bd., Washington, 1969—; cons., 1958—; spl. cons. to Sec. of State, 1969—. Recipient numerous awards. Fellow Am. Inst. Chemists; mem. Am. Chem. Soc., Sigma Xi, Lambda Tau, Phi Sigma. Home: 2819 Elsmore St Fairfax VA 22030 Office: Office Sec Def Explosives Safety Bd Dept Def Washington DC 20314

SCOTT, RICHARD PHILIPPE, librarian; b. Tokyo, Japan, Apr. 6, 1932; s. Ralph Walker and Rose (Ferraris) S.; A.A., Md. State Coll., 1954; B.A. in History, U. Md., 1956; M.S. in L.S., Cath. U. Am., 1958. Asst. librarian Nat. War Coll., Ft. McNair, Washington, 1958-59; asst. librarian NSF, Washington, 1959-62, cataloging librarian, 1962—. Recipient certificate of commendation NSF, 1964. Mem. A.L.A., Spl. Libraries Assn., Am. Soc. for Information Sci., A.A.A.S., Nat. Hist. Soc. (charter), Nat. Philatelic Soc., NSF Employees' Assn. (v.p. for coop. activities 1970-71), Soc. Philatelic Ams., World of Wine Soc.

Home: 860 S Greenbrier St Arlington VA 22204 Office: 1800 G St NW Washington DC 20550

SCOTT, ROBERT CLAUDE, JR., edn. center adminstr.; b. Anderson, S.C., Feb. 16, 1923; s. Robert Claude and Lucy Freeman (Toney) S.; B.A., Furman U., 1949; M.A., George Peabody Coll., 1962; m. Louise Helen Tinsley, Oct. 5, 1946; children—Ronald Charles, Susan Lee. Tchr., coach Anderson County Sch. Dist 4, Pendleton, S.C., 1949-59; adminstrv. asst. Lauren County Sch. Dist., Laurens, S.C., 1959-66; asso. dir. Florence-Darlington Tech. Edn. Center, Florence, S.C., 1966-67, dir. PeeDee Edn., 1967—. Ind. cons. in edn., 1965—. Served with AUS, 1943-46. Decorated Purple Heart, Bronze Star with oak leaf cluster. Mem. Am. Assn. for Sch. Adminstrs., Assn. Suprs. and Curriculum Devel., Nat. Soc. for Study Edn., S.C. Personnel and Guidance Assn., Phi Delta Kappa, Kappa Alpha. Kiwanian. Home: 1430 Fairfax Rd Tarleton W Florence SC 29501 Office: PO Box 829 142-B S Dargan St Florence SC 29501

SCOTT, ROBERT LEROY, business exec.; b. Fredericktown, Mo., Jan. 21, 1924; s. Kenner Girard and Cora M. (Whitchurch) S.; B.S., S.E. Mo. State Coll., 1949; M.P.H., U. N.C., 1962; m. Ruby Hesford Plaskett, May 31, 1947; children—Rebecca Jane, William Kenner, Jon Mark, Robert Bruce, James Donald, Brian Patrick. Pub. health sanitarian Mississippi County Health Dept., Charleston, Mo., 1949-55; state field cons., adminstrv. asst. to dir. Mo. Heart Assn., Columbia, 1955-57; state exec. dir. Mo. Assn. Mental Health, Columbia, 1957-58; health educator, adminstrv. asst. to dir. Jefferson County Health Dept., Hillsboro, Mo., 1958-61; asst. exec. dir. N.C. div. Am. Cancer Soc., Raleigh, 1962-64; exec. dir. Union County Indsl. Devel. Commn., Monroe, N.C., 1964—; chmn. bd. Am. Indsl. & Comml. Services Ltd., Internat. Textiles, Ltd., Precision Metal & Supply Co. Pres., Monroe City High Sch. P.T.A., 1968-69. Served with USNR, 1942-46. Mem. Columbia Jr. C. of C., N.C. Indsl. Developers Assn. (bd. dirs.), So. Indsl. Devel. Council, U.S. Pub. Health Res. Commn., Pi Mu Omicron (pres. 1947-48). Democrat. Methodist. Rotarian (sec. 1968-69), Lion. Clubs: Rolling Hills Country, Silhouette Dance (Monroe). Home: 1213 Woodland Dr Monroe NC 28110 Office: 608 Sutherland Av Box 853 Monroe NC 28110

SCOTT, ROBERT WALTER, gov. N.C., farmer; b. Haw River, N.C., June 13, 1929; s. William Kerr and Mary E. (White) S.; student Duke, 1947-49; B.S. in Animal Industry, N.C. State Coll., 1952; m. Jessie Rae Osborne, Sept. 1, 1951; children—Mary Ella and Margaret Rose (twins), Susan Rae, W. Kerr, Janet Louise. Mgr. dairy farm on Haw River; lt. gov. State of N.C., Raleigh, 1964-68; gov. of N.C., 1968—. N.C. chmn. United Forces for Edn., 1963; former chmn. N.C. Bd. Conservation, Devel. Parks Com., N.C. Consumers Com. for Low Cost Power; former mem. N.C. Seashore Commn.; chmn. So. Regional Edn. Bd., 1970-71; mem. exec. com. Nat. Govs. Conf., 1970-71; mem. Steering com. Ednl. Commn. States, 1970-71, chmn., 1971-72; chmn. subcom. on revenue sharing Nat. Govs. Conf., 1971. Former precinct chmn., county vice-chmn., state solicitorial dist. exec. committeeman Democratic party; nat. chmn. Rural Ams. for Johnson-Humphrey; chmn. Dem. Govs. Caucus, 1970-71; vice chmn. Dem. Party Nat. Com., 1971. Served with AUS, 1953-55. Named Outstanding Young Farmer Alamance County. Mem. Soc. Farm Mgrs. and Rural Appraisers (past pres. N.C.), U.S. Poultry and Egg Producers Assn. (past pres.), N.C. Grange (master 1961-63, with wife voted one of five outstanding Young Grange Couples in nation 1959), V.F.W., Phi Kappa Phi, Blue Key, Alpha Zeta. Presbyn. (ruling elder). Home: Executive Mansion Raleigh NC 27601 Office: Capitol Bldg Raleigh NC 27601

SCOTT, ROGER MCDONALD, city ofcl.; b. Winston-Salem, N.C., Sept. 26, 1936; s. Robert Pfohl and Doris (Ziglar) S.; B.A., Mars Hill Coll., 1956; postgrad. U. Va., 1957-59; B.S., Va. Poly. Inst., 1962; m. Beverly Kay Thompson, Feb. 25, 1956; children—Angela Elizabeth, Claren Yvette. Hwy. design draftsman Hayes, Seay, Mattern & Mattern, Roanoke, Va., 1956-59; asst. planning engr., City of Roanoke, Va., 1959-61; asst. to city mgr., City of Albany, Ga., 1962-65; asst. city mgr., City of Virginia Beach, Va., 1965-68, city mgr., 1968—. Mem. Va. Met. Areas Transp. Study Commn., 1968-69; trustee Tidewater Va. Devel. Council, 1968—. Mem. Internat. City Mgmt. Assn., Carolina June Germans, Va. State C. of C., Va. Beach Jr. C. of C. (dir. 1967). Presbyn. Clubs: Sertoma (Albany, Ga.). Home: 4504 Par Dr Virginia Beach VA 23462 Office: City Hall Virginia Beach VA 23456

SCOTT, ROLAND BOYD, pediatrician; b. Houston, Apr. 18, 1909; s. Ernest John and Cordie (Clark) B.; B.S., Howard U., 1931, M.D., 1934; m. Rosetta Weaver, June 24, 1935; children—Roland Boyd, Venice Rosetta, Estelle Irene. Intern Kansas City (Mo.) Gen. Hosp., 1934-35; resident pediatrics Provident Hosp., Chgo., 1935-36; resident, fellow Inst. Allergy Roosevelt Hosp., N.Y.C., 1950-51; Gen. Edn. Bd. fellow pediatrics U. Chgo., Children's Meml. Hosp., Chgo., Chgo. Municipal Hosp. Contagious Diseases, Chgo., 1936-39; chief pediatrician Freedmen's Hosp., 1947—; attending pediatrician D.C. Gen. Hosp., 1949—, chief pediatric allergy clinic, 1956—; staff Children's Hosp., 1955—, Providence Hosp., 1955—; cons. allergy Children's Convalescent Hosp. (all Washington); cons. pediatrics clin. NIH, Bethesda, Md., 1953—; asst. prof. pediatrics Howard U., Washington, 1939-47, asso. prof., 1947-52, prof., 1952—; professorial lectr. in child devel. George Washington U. Sch. Medicine; vis. lectr. hosps. Rio de Janiero, Sao Paulo, Brasilia (all Brazil), 1967. Mem. com. on clinic programs mentally retarded children, U.S. Children's Bur., Washington, 1964—; cons. Washington Head Start, 1967, active Washington United Cerebral Palsy, D.C., other civic orgns. Bd. dirs. D.C. Health Found., past. bd. dirs. Nat. Med. Fellowships. Diplomate Nat. Bd. Med. Examiners; certified pediatric allergy Am. Bd. Pediatrics. Mem. Nat. Med. Assn. (chmn. pediatrics sect. 1952-54, distinguished service award 1966), A.M.A., Am. Acad. Allergy (v.p. 1966-67), D.C. Allergy Soc. (pres. 1967-68), Pub. Health Adv. Council, Am. Assn. Sex Educators and Counselors, D.C., So. med. socs., Am. Acad. Pediatrics, Am. Pediatric Soc., Soc. Pediatric Research, Am. Fedn. Clin. Research, Am. Coll. Allergists, Internat. Congress Pediatrics, Assn. Med. Sch. Pediatric Dept. Chmn., A.A.A.S., numerous other med., profl., alumni socs., Sigma Xi, Phi Beta Kappa, Kappa Pi, Alpha Omega Alpha, Beta Kappa Chi. Editorial bd. Clinical Pediatrics, 1967—; cons. editor Med. Aspects of Human Sexuality, 1967—. Research, publs. on growth, development, pediatric allergy and sickle cell anemia in infants and children.‡

SCOTT, RONALD FAIRBANKS, state planner; b. South Milwaukee, Wis., May 18, 1915; s. Ronald MacDonald and Viola (Zimmerman) S.; B.S. in Civil Engring., U. Mich., 1938; student Layton Sch. Art, Milw., 1936-37; m. Raiford Cooper, Sept. 10, 1945; children—Lauren Carol, Marian Lee, Beverly Cooper, Perry Alan. Planning engr. City of Superior (Wis.), 1938-42; regional dir. Tenn. Planning Com., Johnson City, 1945-49; dir. planning City of Greensboro (N.C.), 1949-66; regional planning cons. N.C., 1966-69; N.C. state planning officer, 1969—; vis. lectr. city planning Inst. of Govt., U.N.C., Chapel Hill, 1955—. Registered profl. engr., Wis., N.C. Mem. Am. Inst. Planners (pres. S.E. chpt. 1963-64), Am. Soc. C.E., Am. Congress on Surveying and Mapping, Am. Soc. Planning Ofcls., N.C. Soc. Engrs., Tau Beta Pi. Unitarian- Universalist. Club: Torch (pres. Greensboro 1962-63). Home: 2108 Dunnhill Dr Raleigh NC 27608 Office: 116 W Jones St Raleigh NC 27603

SCOTT, SAMUEL DEVOND, JR., motor co. exec.; b. Boardman, N.C., Mar. 15, 1913; s. Samuel Devond and Janie E. (Powell) S.; student U.N.C., 1930-32; m. Agnes Inez Martin, Oct. 3, 1937; children—Samuel Devond, Christopher M., Anne (Mrs. J. H. Miles). Partner, Scotty Theatre, Fair Bluff, N.C., 1937-54; pres. Motor Parts & Equipment Co., Inc., Dillon S.C. and Lancaster, S.C., 1948-52; sec.-treas. Scott Motor Co., Inc., Fair Bluff, N.C., 1936—; partner, Scott Enterprises, Fair Bluff, 1936—; sec.-treas. Scotts, Inc., Whiteville, N.C., 1959—, Dillon, S.C., 1964—; pres. Service Parts Co., Inc., Whiteville and Chadbourn, N.C., 1964—; pres. Fair Bluff Devel. Corp.; dir. First Union Nat. Bank, Fair Bluff. Town commr., Fair Bluff, 1968—. Democrat. Methodist (mem. bd. stewards). Rotarian. Home: Gapway Rd Fair Bluff NC 28499 Office: 100-106 W Main St Fair Bluff NC 28439

SCOTT, TASSO HAROLD, lawyer; b. Natoma, Kan., Jan. 25, 1905; s. Paul Dawson and Sadie Velzetta (Kroh) S.; A.B., U. Colo., 1931; M.S. in Fgn. Service, Georgetown U., 1933; J.D., George Washington U., 1940; m. Kathryn M. Terhune, Dec. 5, 1942; children—Watson T., Thomas Harold, Douglas Bennett. Various positions, Colo; asst. in Senate Folding Room, U.S. Senate; Sgt. U.S. Capitol Police; card searcher card div. Library Congress; asst. Sec., legislative adviser U.S. Senator Adams of Colo., 1934-41; admitted to D.C. bar, 1940, also U.S. Supreme Ct.; atty. FTC. 1941-60, legal adviser charge radio, TV and periodical advt., 1957-58; asso. commr. Indian Claims Commn., 1960-68; mem. law firm Rhyne & Rhyne, Washington, 1969—. Mem. Bar Assn. D.C., Inter-Am., Fed., Am. bar assns., Colo. State Soc. (past pres.), Am. Judicature Soc., World Peace Through Law Center, St. Andrews Soc., Phi Kappa Tau. Methodist. Mason (Shriner). Clubs: National Lawyers (Washington); Kenwood (Chevy Chase, Md.). Author articles, reports in field. Home: 9615 Hillside Dr Kensington MD 20795 Office: Hill Bldg 839 17th St NW Washington DC 20006

SCOTT, TOM, coll. athletic dir.; b. Pittsburg, Kan., Jan. 6, 1908; s. Joseph James and Bertha (Brand) S.; B.S., Kan. State Tchrs. Coll., 1930; M.A., Ia. U., 1937; Ed.D., Columbia, 1955; m. Bessie Edith House, June 1, 1935; children—Thomas Walter, Kristi Jo. Instr., coach Halstead, Moundridge high schs., Kan., 1930-35; athletic dir., basketball coach Concordia Coll., Moorhead, Minn., 1935-38, Central Mo. State Coll., Warrensburg, 1938-41, 45-46; basketball coach U. N.C., 1946-52; basketball coach, sales engr. Phillips Petroleum Co., Bartlesville, Okla., 1952-54; athletic dir. Davidson Coll., 1955—. Chmn. Nat. Collegiate Athletic Assn. Basketball Tournament Com., 1966; pres. So. Conf. Athletic Dirs., 1970-73. Served to lt. comdr. USNR, 1942-45. Mem. Nat. Assn. Collegiate Dirs. Athletics (exec. com. 1966-69), Am. Assn. U. Profs., Basketball Coaches Assn., Golf Coaches Assn. Home: 422 Woodland St Davidson NC 28036

SCOTT, TOM BURKETT, JR., savs. and loan assn. exec.; b. Pasadena, Cal., Oct. 16, 1922; s. Tom Burkett and Lola (Emery) S.; student Millsaps Coll., 1940-42; LL.B., U. Miss., 1948; m. Laura Elizabeth Hewes, May 28, 1946; children—Sharon Scott, Deborah, Tom Burkett III, Charles Christopher IV. Admitted to Miss. bar, 1948; asst. to clk. Miss. Ho. of Reps., 1948; partner firm Scott, Barbour & Scott, Jackson, Miss., 1949—; pres. First Fed. Savs. and Loan Assn., Jackson, 1962—; dir. Deposit Guaranty Nat. Bank, Standard Life Ins. Co. Bd. dirs. Jackson YMCA, 1965—, Jackson Symphony Orch. Assn., 1966—, Jackson Music Assn., 1966—. Served to capt. USAAF, 1943-46. Decorated Air medal with 3 oak leaf clusters. Mem. U.S. Savs. and Loan League (dir., mem. exec. com., pres. 1968—), Jackson C. of C. (bd. dirs. 1964—, pres. 1966), Am., Miss. bar assns., Kappa Alpha. Episcopalian (vestryman). Kiwanian (pres. 1965). Clubs: Jackson Country, Capital City, River Hills (Jackson). Home: 2505 Eastover Dr Jackson MS 39211 Office: 525 E Capitol St Jackson MS 39201

SCOTT, TOM WILLIAM, JR., hotel exec.; b. San Antonio, Feb. 5, 1941; s. Tom William and Marian (Davis) S.; student U. Tex., 1958-60; B.S. in Bus. Adminstrn., U. Denver, 1963; m. Maryellen Hurd, June 15, 1963; 1son, Michael Randolph. Resident mgr. Del E. Webbs Ocean House, San Diego, 1964; conv. service mgr. Del E. Webbs Town House, Phoenix, 1965; v.p., gen. mgr. Hilton Head Inn/Sea Pines Plantation Co., Hilton Head Island, S.C., 1970—. Pres. Hilton Head Island precinct Republican exec. com., 1970—. Mem. S.C. Innkeepers Assn. (dir.-at-large), Jr. C. of C. (named Outstanding Region 15 Pres., 1971), Beta Theta Pi. Methodist (trustee). Rotarian. Home: 9 Twin Pines Rd Hilton Head Island SC 29928 Office: Hilton Head Inn Forest Beach Dr Hilton Head Island SC 29928

SCOTT, VICTOR BILLY, cons. livestock nutrition; b. Dodson, La., July 3, 1931; s. Victor Robert and Lurline (Waters) S.; student La. Poly. Inst., 1948-52, 56, 59, B.S., La. State U., 1960, M.S., 1965, Ph.D., 1970; m. Robbie Lee Hale, Aug. 6, 1955; children— Stephen Robert, Debra Lurline, Judith Diane, Rosemary. With Bodman-Murrell-Smith, architects, Baton Rouge, 1959-60; pilot So. Airways, Inc., 1960-63; faculty La. State U., Baton Rouge, 1963-70, asso. prof. nutrition, 1965-70, research asso., 1963-70; pres. La. Livestock Feeding & Cons. Corp., Baton Route, 1971—. Cons. livestock nutrition, physiology, prodn. and feedlot mgmt. Comdg. officer Anti-Submarine Fighter Squadron 70 at Naval Air Sta., New Orleans, 1969-71. Scoutmaster, Boy Scouts Am., Baton Rouge, 1967—. Served with USNR, 1952-58. Recipient Eagle Scout award Boy Scouts Am., 1944, Order of Arrow, 1945. Mem. Am. Soc. Animal Sci., Am. Soc. Agrl. Consultants. Methodist. Home: 9623 Perkins Rd Baton Rouge LA 70810

SCOTT, WALTER COKE, sugar co. exec., lawyer; b. Norfolk, Va., July 20, 1919; s. Walter Coke and Rosemary (White) S.; B.S., Hampden-Sydney Coll., 1939; LL.B., U. Va., 1948; m. Virginia Kemper Millard, May 14, 1949; children—Mary Lyman, Roberta Coke, Alexander McRae, Buford Coke. Admitted to Va. bar, 1947, Ga. bar, 1954; atty. U.S. Dept. Justice, Jacksonville, Fla., 1948; commerce atty. S.A.L. Ry., Norfolk, 1948-54; commerce counsel, gen. solicitor Central of Ga. Ry., Savannah, 1954-60, v.p., 1960-62, now dir.; partner law firm Hitch, Miller & Beckmann, Savannah, 1956-60; sr. v.p., sec. Savannah Foods & Industries, Inc. (formerly) Sugar Refining Corp., 1962—, also dir.; v.p., sec., dir. Everglades Sugar Refinery, Inc., Clewiston, Fla.; sec., mem. exec. com., dir. The Jim Dandy Co., Birmingham, Ala., 1968—. Western Grain Co., Birmingham, 1968—; dir. Stevens Shipping & Terminal Co., Savannah. Pres., chmn. exec. com. Historic Savannah Found., 1963-64; bd. dirs. United Community Services, 1965-68, pres., 1967; gen. chmn. United Community Appeal, 1966; trustee, chmn. finance com. Telfair Acad. Arts and Scis., 1964-66; trustee, vice chmn. Savannah Country Day Sch. Mem. U.S. C. of C., Va. State Bar, ICC Practitioners Assn., Ga., Savannah bar assns., Kappa Sigma, Omicron Delta Kappa, Phi Alpha Delta, Chi Beta Phi, Pi Delta Epsilon. Episcopalian. Rotarian. Clubs: Savannah Golf, Oglethorpe. Home: 56 E 54th St Savannah GA 31405 Office: Savannah Bank Bldg Savannah GA 31401

SCOTT, WALTER LOUIS, JR., educator; b. Germantown, Pa., July 8, 1936; s. Walter Louis and Mary (White) S.; student Loyola U. South, 1954-56, Tulane U., 1956-57; B.S., Southeastern La. U., 1958; M.S., La. State U., 1960; Ph.D., (U. fellow) Tex. A. & M. U., 1964; m. Shirley Ann Wilson, Jan. 24, 1959 (div. Mar. 1970); children—Glenda Shann, Mary Minturn; m. 2d, Diane E. Sperling, Nov. 1971. Med. technologist, profl. sales rep. Schering Pharm. Corp., New Orleans, 1960-61; asst. prof. biol. scis. Southeastern La. U., Hammond, 1964-69; asso. prof., chmn. dept. med. tech. Ga. State U., Atlanta, 1969—; research participant Oak Ridge (Tenn.) Inst. Nuclear Studies, summer 1965. Instr. civil def., La. office Civil Defense, Tangipahoa Parish, 1965-67. Served with USNR, 1954—, now lt. comdr. Mem. La. Soc. Electron. Microscopy, La. Tchrs. Assn., A.A.A.S., Am., Ga. socs. med. technologists, Sigma Xi, Tau Kappa Epsilon, Phi Kappa Phi, Lambda Tau. Contbr. articles to profl. jours. Office: PO Box 700 33 Gilmer St SE Atlanta GA 30303

SCOTT, WILLARD PHILIP, lawyer; b. Columbus, O., Jan. 8, 1909; s. Wirt Stanley and Mabel Lynne (Rond) S.; A.B. with honors, Ohio State U., 1930; LL.B (Deans Scholar), Columbia, 1933; m. Lucille Westrom, June 27, 1936; children—Robert W., David W., Anne L. Admitted to N.Y. bar, 1934, D.C. bar, 1934, Okla. bar, 1969; partner Oliver &Donnally, N.Y.C., 1938-66; dir. Am. Potash & Chem. Corp., 1951-70; v.p., 1955-68, vice chmn. bd. dirs., 1968—; v.p., gen. counsel Kerr-McGee Corp., 1968-70; counsel for bondholders com. in various railroad reorganizations, 1936-54; gen. counsel Savs. Bank Assn. N.Y. Mem. bd. of appeals, 1957-68, mayor, Scarsdale, 1955-57, trustee, 1951-55, police commr., 1953-55, acting mayor, 1953-55. Fellow Am. Bar Found., Southwestern Legal Found.; mem. Internat. Bar Assn. (patron, editor Bus. Lawyer, 1958-59), Am. (chmn. sect. corp. banking and bus. law 1960-61, chmn. com. corp. laws 1964-70); N.Y., Okla., D.C. bar assns., Am. Law Inst., Assn. Bar City N.Y., Phi Beta Kappa, Phi Kappa Sigma, Phi Delta Phi, Phi Alpha Theta, Pi Sigma Alpha. Republican. Presbyn. Clubs: Union League, Madison Square Garden (N.Y.C.); Metropolitan (Washington); Oklahoma City Golf and Country, Whitehall, Beacon (Oklahoma City); Scarsdale Golf. Arthor: various articles on corporate law. Home: 1812 Drury Lane Oklahoma City OK 73116 Office: Room 812 Kerr-McGee Bldg Oklahoma City OK 73102

SCOTT, WILLIAM KELLY, banker; b. McKenzie, Tenn., Sept. 5, 1932; s. Robert Milton and Ethel (Boaz) S.; B.B.A., U. Miss., 1954; postgrad. Northwestern U., 1960, Rutgers U., 1965; m. Billie Helene Bell, July 20, 1957; children—William Kelly, Betsy Bell. With Nat. Bank Commerce, Norfolk, Va., 1957-63, asst. v.p., 1960-61, v.p. nat. accounts and corr. banks, 1961-63; marketing dir. Va. Nat. Bank, Norfolk, 1963-68, sr. v.p., 1968—. Served with USNR, 1954-57. Mem. Am. Bankers Assn., Va. Bankers Assn. (chmn. banking edn. and pub. relations com. 1964), Bank Marketing Assn. (mem. long-range planning com. 1970). Methodist (lay leader). Clubs: Norfolk Yacht and Country, Harbor (Norfolk). Home: 1036 Cambridge Crescent Norfolk VA 23508 Office: One Commercial Pl Norfolk VA 23510

SCOTT, WILLIAM LLOYD, congressman; b. Williamsburg, Va., July 1, 1915; s. William David and Nora Bell (Ingram) S.; LL.B., Nat. U., 1938, LL.M., 1939; m. Ruth Inez Huffman, Feb. 5, 1940; children—Gail Ann (Mrs. Charles H. Eldred), William Lloyd, Paul Alvin. Admitted to Va. bar; trial atty. Dept. Justice, 1942-60; spl. asst. to solicitor, Dept. Interior, 1960-61; pvt. practice law, Fairfax, Va., 1961-66; mem. 90th to 92d Congresses 8th dist. Va. Mem. Va. Republican Central Com., 1964-68. Served with AUS, World War II. Mem. Am., Va., Fairfax County bar assns., Am. Legion, 40 and 8, Sigma Nu Phi (past chancellor). Methodist. Lion, Mason (Shriner). Home: 3930 W Ox Rd Fairfax County VA 22030 Office: Langworth House Office Bldg Washington DC 20515

SCOTT, WILLIAM MARTIN, banker; b. Norway, June 24, 1897; s. Harry W. and Asta (Olsen) S.; brought to U.S., 1907, naturalized, 1919; student Grad. Sch. Banking, Rutgers U., 1937-40; m. Borghild Olsen, May 20, 1922; children—William R., Bernard E., John P., Barbara (Mrs. Robert H. Stegemann). With Nat. City Bank, N.Y.C., until 1951; pres. Pa. Exchange Bank of N.Y., N.Y.C., 1951-56; pres. First State Bank & Trust Co., Eustis, Fla., 1956-67, chmn. bd., 1967—. Home: 424 Orange Av Eustis FL 32726 Office: Drawer A Grove and Magnolia Sts Eustis FL 32726

SCOTT, WILLIAM ROBERT, earth scientist; b. Des Moines, July 14, 1924; s. Donald and Zula (Goodyear) S.; student Ia. State Coll., 1942-43, U. Wis., 1943-44; B.S., Tulane U., 1950; m. Dorys Palermo, Dec. 31, 1955; children—William James, Delbia Maye. Party chief, fgn. geophys. crew Explorations Surveys, Inc., Dallas, 1950-54; cons. geophysicist Adminstrn. Nat. de Combustibles, Alcohol Y Portland, Montevideo, Uruguay, 1954-56; geophys. interpreter Geophys. Services, Inc., Dallas, 1956-61; exec. v.p. Photogravity Co., Inc., Houston, 1961—; v.p. Allied Consultants Inc., Houston, 1969—, also dir. Mem. Latin Am. evaluation team AID, 1965. Served with USAAF, 1943-46. Mem. Soc. Exploration Geophysicists, Geophys. Soc. Houston, Soc. Tulane Engrs. Registered profl. engr., La. Home: 3736 Arnold St Houston TX 77005 Office: 6440 Hillcroft St Houston TX 77036

SCOTT, WILLIAM WARREN, physician; b. Little Rock, Mar. 7, 1924; s. Ottis Al and Ruth (Matthews) S.; N.D., U. Ark., 1946; m. Helene Jayne Barre, June 29, 1945; children—Karen, Warren Eric, Timothy. Intern U.S. Naval Hosp., Corpus Christi, Tex.; practice gen. medicine, Pocahantas, Ark.; chief staff Randolph County Meml. Hosp., Pocahantas. Dir. Pocahontas Fed. Savs. & Loan. Founding mem. Pocahontas Planning Commn., 1964—; chapter mem. Randolph United Fund. Mem. City Council Pocahontas, 1969—. Served with USNR, 1943-49. Mem. Ark. Med. Soc., N.E. Ark. Regional Med. Program (charter mem.), Randolph County Med. Soc., C. of C. (pres.). Rotarian, K.C. Club: Arkansas Cadeus (Little Rock). Home: 1917 Randolph St Pocahontas AR 72455 Office: 213 W Broadway St Pocahontas AR 72455

SCOTT, WILLODENE ALEXANDER (MRS. RAY DONALD SCOTT), librarian; b. Ethridge, Tenn., Sept. 4, 1922; d. Jesse Cary and Maud (Goff) Alexander; B.A., George Peabody Coll. for Tchrs., 1946, B.S. in Library Sci., 1947, M.A., 1949, postgrad, 1963—; m. Ray Donald Scott, Nov. 27, 1959; 1 dau., Pamela Dean. Librarian Sylvan Park Elementary Sch., Nashville, 1947-51, Waverly Belmont Jr. High Sch., Nashville, 1951-54, Howard High Sch., Nashville, 1954-62, Peabody Demonstration Sch., Nashville, 1962-63, McCann Elementary Sch., Nashville, 1963-66; supr. instructional materials, library div. Metro Nashville-Davidson County Schs., Nashville, 1966—. Lectr. Peabody Coll. Library Sch., Nashville, summers, 1950-66, 71—, U. Tenn., Nashville Center, 1970—. Mem. A.L.A., Southeastern (mem. scholarship com. 1968-70), Tenn. Library Assns. (membership chmn. 1955, 64). library assns., Tenn. (pres. library Sect. 1954), Met. Nashville edn. assns., N.E.A., Woman's Nat. Book Assn. (charter mem.), D.A.R. (Buffalo River chpt. organizing treas. 1967-69). Baptist. Mem. Order Eastern Star. Club: Nashville Library (pres. 1952-53). Home: 525 Clematis Dr Nashville TN 37205

SCOTT, WINSTON MACKINLEY, ret. fgn. service officer; b. Jemison, Ala., Mar. 30, 1909; s. Morgan Winston and Betty Gothard (MacKinley) S.; student Livingston Coll.; B.S., U. Ala., 1931, M.A., 1933; Ph.D., U. Mich., 1939; m. Maev Paula Murray, Feb. 15, 1950 (dec. 1962); 1 son, Michael MacKinley; m. 2d, Janet Graham, Dec. 20, 1962; stepchildren—Gregory, John, George, Paul L., Suzanne.

Semi-profl., profl. baseball player, 1927-39; tchr. mathematics, Ala., 1927-30; instr. applied mathematics U. Ala., 1931-33; instr., asst. prof. mathematics, 1933-41; spl. agt. FBI, 1941-44; fgn. service officer, 1946-69; assigned London, 1946-50, Washington, 1950-56, Mexico City, 1956-69; 1st sec., spl. asst. to Ambassador, Mexico City, 1956-69; cons. actuary, Mexico City, 1969—. Served to lt. comdr. USNR, 1944-46. Decorated Bronze Star. Mem. Am. Society (Mexico City), Am. Legion, A.A.A.S., Am. Mathematics Soc., Pi Mu Epsilon, Theta Zi. Roman Catholic. Clubs: Cosmos (Washington); University, Chaultepec Golf, Churubusco Country (Mexico City); Belle Haven Country (Alexandria, Va.); Bella Vista Golf. Contbr. articles profl. jours. Home: Mexico City Mexico Office: Reforma 403-401 Mexico City 5 Mexico

SCOVIL, JAMES ARGERSINGER, architect; b. Johnstown, N.Y., July 12, 1916; s. Raymond Sylvester and Isabelle Judson (Argersinger) S.; B.Arch., Rensselaer Poly. Inst., 1938; m. Elizabeth Lynch Hume, Nov. 11, 1939; children—James Argersinger, Elizabeth (Mrs. John W. Carlo), Margaret, John. Interior designer Rodgers Assos., N.Y.C., 1939-40; draftsman, Randolph Evans, architect, N.Y.C., 1940-41, Am. Houses, Inc., N.Y.C., 1942-44; architect Cy Williams, Inc., Port Washington, N.Y., 1946-51; asso. architect Leif Valand & Assos., architects, Raleigh, N.C., 1951-64; partner, McGee, Scovil & Assos., architects, Raleigh, N.C., 1964—. Served with AUS, 1944-46. Mem. A.I.A. Presbyn. Club: Carolina Country (Raleigh, N.C.). Home: 2900 Fairview Rd Raleigh NC 27608 Office: 3803 Computer Dr Raleigh NC 27609

SCREVEN, J. O., lawyer, bus. exec.; b. Birmingham, Ala. Aug. 11, 1925; s. J. O. and Cecile (Allen) S.; B.S., U. Ala., 1947, LL.B., 1950; LL.M., N.Y.U., 1951; m. Gaynor Anderson, Sept. 15, 1948; children—J. O. III, E.F., J.S. Admitted to Ala. bar; practiced in Birmingham; asso. firm White, Bradley, Arant, All & Rose, 1951-56; gen. atty., sec. Vulcan Materials Co., 1957—. Trustee Birmingham U. Sch. Served with AUS, 1944-46. Mem. U. Ala. Alumni Assn. (past pres. Jefferson County), Phi Delta Theta. Club: Birmingham County. Home: 3568 Riverbend Rd Birmingham AL 35243 Office: PO Box 7497 Birmingham AL 35223

SCRIVNER, FRANK HERMAN, civil engr.; b. Fort Worth, Oct. 12, 1908; s. Arthur James and Helen (Saunders) S.; B.S., U.S. Naval Acad., 1931; m. Bonnie Conlee, Dec. 23, 1938 (dec. Feb. 1966); 1 dau., Suzanne. Research engr. Tex. Hwy. Dept., Austin, 1946-55, Nat. Acad. Scis., Ottawa, Ill., 1956-61, Tex. Transp. Inst., College Station, 1961—; project dir. S.J. Buchanan Assos., London, Eng., 1955-56. Served to lt. comdr. USNR, 1941-46. Mem. Nat. Acad. Scis. (chmn. rigid pavement design com. hwy. research bd. 63-70), Am. Soc. C.E., Sigma Xi. Home: 1929 Wayside Dr Bryan TX 77801 Office: Tex Transp Inst Tex A and M U College Station TX 77843

SCRIVNER, JOE BILL, supt. schs.; b. Wister, Okla., Sept. 15, 1922; s. Fred and Judson (Cheek) S.; B.S., McMurry Coll., 1948; M.A., Hardin-Simmons U., 1953; postgrad. Sul Ross Coll., 1956; m. Eleanor Green, Aug. 15, 1944; children—Joe B., James Thomas. Prin., head athletic coach high sch., Mertzon, Tex., 1948-50; head coach, athletic coach, Rankin, Tex., 1950-54, jr. high sch. prin., 1954-55, became supt. schools, 1955; supt. schs., Goliad, Tex., until 1961, Dumas, Tex., 1961-69, Taylor, Tex., 1969—. Chmn. Rankin Youth Council, 1952-55; adv. council Southwestern Edn. Developmental Labs. Served from pvt. to sgt. USAF, 1941-45. Mem. N.E.A. (area chmn.), Tex. Coaching Assn. (v.p. 1954), Tex. Sch. Adminstrs. Assn. (exec. com.; chmn. dist. 6 1956), Am. Assn. Sch. Adminstrs., Tex. Tchrs. Assn. (dist. chmn. legistlative com.), Univ. Interscholastic League (dist. chmn.), Tex. P.T.A. Scholarship Soc. (chmn.), Panhandle Leaders Assn., (v.p.). Methodist. Rotarian (dir.), Lion (dir.). Home: 1705 Lexington St Taylor TX 76574

SCRUGGS, C. G., editor; b. McGregor, Tex., Nov. 4, 1923; s. John Fleming and Adeline (Hering) S.; B.S., Tex. A. and M. U., 1947; m. Miriam June Wigley, July 5, 1947; children—John Mark, Miriam Jan. Asso. editor Progressive Farmer, Dallas, 1947-61, editor, 1962—, v.p., 1964—, exec. editor, 1972; pres. Tex. Comml. Agr. Council, 1953-54; sec. 1960—. Mem. Govs. Com. for Agr., 1950; Tex. Animal Health Council, 1955-61; chmn. So. Brucellosis Com., 1956; pres. Tex. Rural Safety Com., 1957-59; mem. farm conf. Nat. Safety Council, 1958—; chmn. Nat. Brucellosis Com., 1958-59; del. World Food Congress, 1963; mem. coordinating bd. Tex. Coll. and U. System, 1965-69; bd. regents Tex. Tech. U., 1971—. Chmn. Joint Senate-House Interim Com. Natural Fibers Tex. Legislature. Pres., S.W. Animal Health Research Found., 1961-63, trustee, 1961—; bd. govs. Nat. Agrl. Hall of Fame. Served to lt. col. U.S. Army Res. ret. Recipient Southwestern Cattle Raisers award, 1962; Am. Seed Trade Assn. award, 1963; Reuben Brigham award Am. Assn. Agrl. Coll. Editors, 1965; Distinguished Service award Tex. Farm Bur., 1966; Journalistic Achievement award Nat. Plant Food Assn,, 1967. Mem. Am. Agrl. Editors Assn. (pres. 1963), Tex. Agrl. Workers Assn., Tex. Assn. Future Farmers Am. (pres. 1940-41), Dallas Agrl. Club (pres. 1951), Nat. Livestock Confedn. Mexico (hon.), Alpha Zeta, Sigma Delta Chi. Office: Box 2581 Birmingham AL 35202

SCRUGGS, EDWARD NEAL, judge; b. Tuscaloosa, Ala., Jan. 29, 1923; s. Claud D. and Dolly (NeSmith) S.; B.S., U. Ala., 1943, LL.B., 1948; grad. Nat. Coll. State Judiciary, 1971; m. Rebekah Jones, July 2, 1942; children—Edward N., Nancy Ann. Admitted to Ala. bar, 1949; practiced in Guntersville, Ala., 1949-59; circuit judge 27th Jud. Circuit Ala., Guntersville, 1959—. County solicitor, Marshall County, Ala., 1950; county chmn. Marshall County Rural Devel. Assn., 1958-59. Served to capt. AUS, 1943-46. Mem. Marshall County Bar Assn. (past pres.), Ala. Circuit Judges Assn., Kappa Alpha, Phi Delta Phi, Farrah Order Jurisprudence. Methodist. Home: PO Box 543 Guntersville AL 35976 Office: P O Box 543 Guntersville AL 35976

SCRUGGS, ELIZABETH BURGESS (MRS. AMOS LEE SCRUGGS), educator; b. Kingstree, S.C., Dec. 2, 1917; d. Robert James and Lula (McConnell) Burgess; B.A., U.S.C., 1955, M.A., 1960; m. Amos Lee Scruggs, May 8, 1938. Bookkeeper Exchange Bank of Kingstree (S.C.), 1936-42; with OPA, 1942-45; sec. to supt. of schs. and bus. mgr. Kingstree Rea Schs., 1945-55; bus. edn. tchr., guidance counselor Kingstree (S.C.) High Sch., 1955-60, counselor, 1967—; dir. guidance services Williamsburg County Schs., 1960-67. Mem. Coll. Entrance Exam. Bd., 1972—; instr. U.S.C. Sec. County Mental Health Assn., 1965-67; mem. Kingstree (S.C.) Zoning Commn. and Bd. of Adjustment, 1954-59. Mem. Am. Personnel and Guidance Assn. (br. sec. 1965-67), S.C. Bus. Educators Assn. (pres. 1960-61), Williamsburg County (Distinguished Citizen award 1971, mem. adv. council So. region.) S.C. edn. assns., League Women Voters, Delta Kappa Gamma (pres. 1968-70). Baptist (chmn. ch. nominating com.). Home: 1104 2d Av Kingstree SC 29556

SCRUGGS, RICHARD TURNER, aluminum co. exec.; b. Birmingham, Ala., Apr. 4, 1915; s. Josiah Hubert and Willye (Turner) S.; student Birmingham So. Coll., 1933-34, U. Ala., 1934-36; m. Marilyn Perkins Bade, Sept. 7, 1938; children—Marilyn Craig (Mrs. Charles L. Tucker), Margaret Sarah (Mrs. Jarrel Estes), Richard Turner, John Hubert. Salesman, So. Culvert Co., Birmingham, Ala., 1936-38, v.p., 1938-42; asst. chief aircraft insp. Bechtel-McCone Corp., Birmingham, 1942-46; co-founder Vulcan Metal Products, Inc., Birmingham, 1946, pres., 1956—; pres. Scruggs Investment Co., Inc.; v.p. Ala. Metal Co., Muscle Shoals. Mem. adv. bd. Salvation Army. Mem. steering com. Lee Assos. Washington and Lee U., Lexington, Va. Recipient Silver Circle award Alpha Tau Omega, 1959. Mem. Screen Mfrs. Assn. (pres.), C. of C. (dir.), S.A.R., Sales Exec. Club, Newcomen Soc. Methodist (steward). Clubs: Rotary, Birmingham Country, Downtown, The Club. Home: 3524 Victoria Rd Birmingham AL 35223 Office: PO Box 6788 Birmingham AL 35210

SCULLY, FRANCIS JOSEPH, physician; b. Bottineau, N.D., June 28, 1891; s. John Joseph and Anne (Gardner) S.; A.B., U. Wis., 1912; M.D., Rush Med. Coll., 1915; m. Bea Estelle Wolfe, Oct. 29, 1919. Intern, Cook County Hosp., Chgo., 1915-17; gen. practice medicine, Hot Springs, Ark., 1918—; mem. staff St. Joseph's Hosp., Hot Springs. Served to 1st lt. U.S. Army, 1917-18. Fellow A.C.P.; mem. Am. Bd. Internal Medicine Am. Bot. Soc., Am. Rheumatism Assn., Phi Rho Sigma, Chi Phi. Mason (33 deg., Shriner, K.T.), Rotarian (pres. 1943). Author: History of Grand Encampment Knights Templar U.S.A., 1952; History of Hot Springs, Arkansas and Hot Springs National Park, 1966. Home: 16 Conway Blvd Hot Springs AR 71901

SEABRON, WILLIAM MANSON, govt. ofcl.; b. Chgo., Mar. 23, 1908; s. William H. and Charlotte (McIntyre) S.; B.A., U. Ia., 1940; student U. Mich., 1951-52; m. Nevada Thornton, Mar. 12, 1936; children—Carolyn Ann. Deborah Alice, Stephen McIntyre. Indsl. sec. Mpls. Urban League, 1944-50 adminstrv. asst. to dir. Detroit Urban League, 1950-56; dep. dir. Mich. Fair Employment Practices Commn., 1956-62; asst. to dir. personnel Dept. Agr., 1962-65; asst. to sec. agr., 1965—. Mem. S.S.S., Detroit, 1955-62. Mem. Frontiers Clubs Am., Alpha Phi Alpha. Mason (32 deg., Shriner). Home: 1703 Taylor St NW Washington DC 20011 Office: Dept of Agriculture 14th and Independence Av SW Washington DC 20250

SEAGLE, WILLIAM, editor, author, lawyer; b. N.Y.C., Jan. 14, 1898; s. Jacob and Yetta (Schapiro) S.; B.A., Coll. City N.Y., 1920; J.D., Columbia, 1922; m. Miriam Goldberg, Feb. 17, 1928; children—Ronah (Mrs. Richard T. Brodkin), Jonathan Judah. Practice of law, 1922-24; mag. writer, 1924-28; asst. editor Ency. Social Scis., 1928-34; sr. atty. Petroleum Bd., Washington, 1934-35; trial examiner NLRB, 1937-40; pvt. practice of law, N.Y.C., 1940-41; asst. solicitor U.S., Dept. Interior, Sept. 15, 1941-Feb. 10, 1943; asst. chief Indian div. Office of Solicitor, U.S. Dept. Interior, 1943-54, atty.-adviser, mem. bd. contract appeals, 1954-60; trial examiner NLRB, 1960-69. Mem. Mystery Writers Am. Author: To the Pure—A Study of Obscenity and the Censor (with Morris L. Ernst), 1928; Cato, or the Future of Censorship, 1930; There Ought to Be a Law, 1933; The Quest for Law, 1941; Men of Law; From Hammurabi to Holmes, 1947; Law: The Science of Inefficiency, 1952; Acquitted of Murder, 1958. Home: 2727 29th St Washington DC 20008 Office: 1231 25th St NW Washington DC 20570

SEAGLER, HOMER CLAUDE, govt. ofcl.; b. Macon, Ga., Dec. 14, 1935; s. William Joe and Annie Ola (McGee) S.; student Middle Ga. Coll., 1953-55, Auburn U., 1955-56, Mercer U., 1956; m. Rita DuBose, June 18, 1955; children—Deborah, Wanda, Homer Neal, Kimberly Ann. Owner, operator Crawford County Newspaper, Knoxville, Ga., 1957-61; owner, pres. H. C. Seagler Ins. Agy., Knoxville, Ga., 1958—; Tax commr., Crawford County, Ga., 1957—; sec. bd. County Commrs., 1958—; dir. Central Ga. Council, Boy Scouts Am., 1959—. Methodist. Mason, Woodmen, Kiwanian. Home: PO Box 147 Roberta GA 31078 Office: Courthouse Knoxville GA 31050

SEALE, ALLEN THOMAS FRANKLIN, oil co. exec.; b. Alvarado, Tex., June 28, 1907; s. T. L. and Pearl (Milwee) S.; student North Tex. Jr. A. and M. Coll., 1926-29; B.S., Tex. A. and M. Coll., 1940; m. Gladys Taliaferro, Dec. 25, 1932. With Tex. Hwy. Dept., 1929-41; with Kerr-McGee Corp., Oklahoma City, 1945—, chief engr., 1945-54, v.p. operations, 1956-67, sr. v.p., 1967—, also dir.; pres., dir. Franjo, Inc., Kermac Nuclear Fuels Inc.; v.p., dir. Kerr-McGee Bldg. Corp., Downtown Airpark, Kerr-McGee Iranian Oil Co.; v.p. Am. Potash & Chem. Corp., Triangle Refineries, Inc.; dir. Transocean Drilling Co., Ltd., Capitol Hill State Bank & Trust Co., Transworld Drilling Co., Kermac Drilling Co. of Venezuela, C.A., Kermac Contractors, Inc., Kerr-McGee Pipeline Corp., Transshore Drilling Co. Ltd. Bd. dirs. Oklahoma City A.R.C. Served from capt. to lt. col. C.E., AUS, 1941-45. Recipient citation for exceptionally meritorious servce Office Chief Engrs., ASF. Mem. Am. Soc. C.E., Am. Petroleum Inst., Ind. Petroleum Assn. Am., Petroleum Club Oklahoma City (past pres.). Home: 1601 Wilshire Blvd Oklahoma City OK 73116 Office: Kerr-McGee Bldg Oklahoma City OK 73102

SEALE, JOHN THOMAS, lawyer; b. El Dorado, Ark., Jan. 6, 1934; s. Percy and Edna Ruth (Martin) S.; student Phillips U., 1951-52; B.S., La. Poly. Inst., 1959; J.D., Tulane U., 1961; m. Mary Frances Bradshaw, Jan. 2, 1954; children—John Bradshaw, Jay Wesley. Admitted to La. bar, 1961; with land dept. Cal. Oil Co., New Orleans, 1961-64; asso. Lancaster & Baxter, Tallulah, La., 1964; partner Lancaster, Baxter & Seale, Tallulah, 1965—. Asst. dist. atty. 6th Jud. Dist. of La., 1968—. Chmn., Madison Parish Welfare Adv. Bd., 1967—. Mem. Tallulah and Madison Parish Democratic Exec. Coms., 1966—. Trustee Madison Parish Library. Served with USNR, 1952-56. Mem. Madison Parish C. of C. (dir. 1965-68, 70—, pres. 1965-66), Am., La., 6th Jud. Dist (pres. 1966-67) bar assns., Am. Legion (commdr. 1967-69), Phi Delta Phi, Omicron Delta Kappa, Kappa Delta Phi. Home: 209 Virginia St Tallulah LA 71282 Office: PO Box 70 Tallulah LA 71282

SEALE, RICHARD, banker; b. Eunice, La., Jan. 21, 1931; s. Lemuel George and Alma (Fontenot) S.; B.S., Tex. A. and M. U., 1957; m. Julia Ann Stagg, Jan. 26, 1957; children—Richard Mannie, Martha Amanda, Susan Marie. Agrl. rep. First Nat. Bank Edna (Tex.), 1957-59, v.p., 1959-65; v.p., sr. loan officer First Nat. Bank Angleton (Tex.), 1965-66; exec. v.p. First Nat. Bank Crowley (La.), 1966-68, pres., 1968—, also dir. Mem. adv. council Small Bus. Adminstrn., La., 1969—. Bd. dirs. Greater Crowley Indsl. Devel. Corp. Served with USNR, 1951-53. Mem. Southwestern Clearing House Assn. (pres. 1969—), Greater Crowley C. of C. (ambassador 1969—), Acadia Parish Cattlemen's Assn. Rotarian. Club: Crowley Town (dir.). Home: 529 W 14th St Crowley LA 70526 Office: PO Box 267 Crowley LA 70526

SEALE, ROY Q(UINCY), educator; b. Dallas, Jan 9, 1898; s. William Quincy and Josie (McGlothlin) S.; B.A., So. Meth. U., 1919; M.A., Columbia, 1920; Ph.D., Stanford, 1935; m. Georgie Hudspeth, Dec. 30, 1923; 1 son, George Quincy. Asst. engr. Southwestern Bell Telephone Co., 1920-21, engr., 1921-22; instr. math. dept. So. Meth. U., 1922-24, asst. prof., 1924-31, summer 1933, 34-35, asso. prof. math. 1942-44, prof., 1944-63, emeritus prof., 1963—; now engaged in math. research, mech. invention; asst. in instrn. Stanford, 1931-34; prof. math. and physics, head dept. Del Mar Coll., Corpus Christi, Tex., 1935-42. Mem. Am. Math. Soc., Math. Assn. Am., Am. Assn. U. Profs., A.A.A.S., Tex. Acad. Scis., Alpha Sigma Lambda, Kappa Mu Epsilon, Sigma Alpha Epsilon. Methodist. Mason. Club: Dallas Athletic. Author: Aerial Navigation Sheets, 1941. Inventor oil well testing equipment and airplane engine control devices. Home: 3609 University Blvd Dallas TX 75205

SEALE, THOMAS FREDERICK, ednl. adminstr.; b. Electra, Tex., Dec. 25, 1919; s. James Edgar and Beulah Mae (Hilburn) S.; B.Mus. (fellow in brass), Houston Conservatory Music, 1940; M.Mus., N.Tex. State U., 1941; postgrad., Vanderbilt U., 1946-47; m. Betty Lou Davis, July 14, 1947; children—Dana Lynn, Marsha Kay, James Paul. Trombonist, Houston Symphony Orch., 1936-41; instr. instrumental music Goose Creek Consol. Ind. Sch., Baytown, Tex., 1936-41, supr. pub. sch. music, art, and crafts, 1947—; instr. brass instruments Houston Conservatory Music, 1937-41; instr. music edn. Lee Coll. Baytown, Tex., 1939-41, 49-52. Cons. visual perception. Mem. Baytown Welfare League Bd., 1952-64, pres., 1955-64; active Baytown Community Chest, 1954-55. Served with AUS, 1942-46. Mem. N.E.A., Baytown Edn. Assn., Tex. Tchrs. Assn., Tex. Music Edn. Assn. (pres. suprs.' div. 1958-59), Music Educators Nat. Conf., Am., Tex. choral dirs. assns., Tex. Assn. Sch. Adminstrs. Episcopalian (sr. warden 1953). Elk, Kiwanian. Contbr. articles to profl. jours. Home: 2008 Woodlawn Baytown TX 77520 Office: PO box 30 Baytown TX 77520

SEALS, WOODROW, U.S. dist. judge; b. Bogalusa, La., Dec. 23, 1917; s. Charles Bradley and Ruby (Hughey) S.; LL.B., U. Tex., 1949; m. Sarah Elizabeth Newman, June 1, 1942; 1 son, Bradley Newman. Admitted to Tex. bar, 1949; U.S. atty. So. Dist. Tex., 1961-66; now U.S. dist. judge. Served to lt. col. USAF Res. ret. Home: 1510 Lehman St Houston TX 77018 Office: US Courthouse Houston TX 77002

SEALY, DESMOND HOLLINSWORTH, govt. ofcl.; b. Trinidad, W.I., Feb. 24, 1924; s. Joseph Nathaniel and Estelle Jestina (Spencer) S.; came to U.S., 1952, naturalized, 1958; B.A. in Econs., Bklyn. Coll., 1959; M.A., U. Chgo., 1960; diploma Dale Carnegie Inst., 1966; m. Beverly Joan Rice, Nov. 25, 1961; children—Desa Joan, Denise Jacquelyn. Econ. analyst Com. for Econ. and Cultural Devel., Chgo., 1962-64; asso. dir. Washington bur. Nat. Urban League, Inc., 1964-66; dir. equal opportunity Bur. Work Programs, Manpower Adminstrn., Labor Dept., Washington, 1966-67, chief div. program and budget planning Manpower Adminstrn., 1967-68, chief div. spl. programs, 1968-69, spl. asst. to dir. Office Tng. and Employment Opportunities, Manpower Adminstrn., 1969—. Panelist White House Conf. Equal Opportunity, 1965, Conf. Tech. Assistance, U.S. Equal Employment Opportunity Commn., 1965; mem. membership and budget com. Nat. Capital Area Health and Welfare Council, 1971. Nat. Urban League fellow, 1965. Mem. Am. Acad. Polit. and Social Sci., Am. Econ. Assn., Washington Urban League. Home: 1880 Columbia Rd NW Washington DC 20009 Office: 1741 Rhode Island Av NW Washington DC 20036

SEAMANS, ROBERT CHANNING, JR., sec. of the Air Force; b. Salem, Mass., Oct. 30, 1918; s. Robert Channing and Pauline (Bosson) S.; B.S., Harvard, 1939; M.S., Mass. Inst. Tech., 1942, Sc.D., 1951; grad. exec. program bus. adminstrn., Columbia, 1959; D.Sc. (hon.), Rollins Coll., 1962, Dr. Engring. (hon.), Norwich U., 1970; m. Eugenia Merrill, June 13, 1942; children—Katherine Arlaund (Mrs. Louis Padulo), Robert Channing III, Joseph, May (Mrs. Eugene Baldwin III), Daniel. Instr. aero. engring. Mass. Inst. Tech., 1941-55, successively staff engr. instrumentation lab., asst. prof. project leader instrumentation lab., asso. prof., chief engr. project Meteor, 1950-55, dir. flight control lab., 1953-55; mgr. airborne systems lab., chief systems engr. airborne systems dept. RCA, 1955-58, chief engr. missile electronics and controls div., 1958-60; asso. adminstr. NASA, 1960-65, dep. adminstr., 1965-68; vis. prof. aero. and astronautics, Jerome Clarke Hunsaker prof. Mass. Inst. Tech., 1968-69; U.S. sec. of air force, 1969—. Mem. USAF Sci. Adv. Bd., 1957-62, asso. adviser, 1963-67. Mem. bd. overseers Harvard; trustee Nat. Geog. Soc. Recipient Naval Ordnance Devel. award, 1945; Godfrey L. Cabot Aviation award Aero Club New Eng., 1965; Distinguished Service medal NASA, 1965, 69; Robert H. Goddard Meml. trophy, 1968. Fellow I.E.E.E.; mem. Internat. Nat. Acad. Astronautics, Nat. Acad. Engring., Am. Soc. Pub. Adminstrs., Am. Inst. Aeros. and Astronautics (pres. 1968; Lawrence Speery award 1951; hon. fellow 1969), Am. Astronautical Soc., A.A.A.S., Am. Acad. Arts and Scis., Am. Ord. Assn., Sigma Xi. Home: 3921 Idaho Av NW Washington DC 20008 Office: The Pentagon Washington DC 20330

SEARCY, ANNA ASHBURN PIDCOCK (MRS. FLOYD HARTSFIELD SEARCY), banker; b. Moultrie, Ga.; d. Frank Ramsey and Willie (Ashburn) Pidcock; A.B., Shorter Coll., 1929; m. Floyd Hartsfield Searcy, June 29, 1934; children—Floyd Hartsfield, Ashburn Pidcock, William Harris (dec.), William Nelson, John Frank (dec.). With Citizens Bank, Cairo, Ga., 1962—, v.p., 1962—, also dir. Salesman World Book Ency., 1960-65. Bd. dirs. Thomasville (Ga.) YMCA, 1955-64; tchr. adult ladies Sunday Sch. First Baptist Ch., Thomasville, 1946—; Sunbeams dir. Woman's Missionary Union, 1967-71, pres. 1961-64; pres. Womans Missionary Soc., 1961-62, Bible study leader, 1966-70, chaplain, 1968-69, vice regent, 1969-70. Mem. D.A.R. (regent Thomasville chpt. 1971-73). Club: Briarcliff Garden. Home: Cubana Thomasville GA 31792 Office: 128 S Broad St Cairo GA 31728

SEARCY, CLAYTIE ODESSA ROSS (MRS. DETROIT SEARCY), found. exec.; b. Pittsburg, Tex., Sept. 28, 1916; d. Clifton and Mary (Neil) Ross; B.S., Bishop Coll., 1955; M.A., U. Tex., 1956; postgrad. So. Meth. U., 1964-65, E. Tex. State U., 1965; m. Detroit Searcy, June 11, 1934; 1 foster son, Anderson Hugh. Adminstrv. asst. boys work dept. Moorland br. YMCA, 1945-48; tchr. art Dallas Ind. Sch. Dist., 1956-60; instr. art Bishop Coll. Extension Sch., Dallas, 1956-58, instr. edn. Bishop Coll., 1961-66, freshman counselor, 1961-63; founder Searcy Youth Found., Dallas, 1966, dir., 1966—, also pres. Del., Fifth World Youth Conf., Toronto, Ont., Can., 1958; vol., sponsor Dallas Soc. Negro Blind, 1947-50; chmn. re-location fund raising campaign women's div. Bishop Coll., 1956-61; mem. Gov.'s Com. on Human Relations. Recipient Woman of Year award Iota Phi Lambda, Dallas, 1947; Membership Leader award Negro C. of C., Dallas, 1954; Service award Bishop Coll. Women's Council, 1965; Ch. Service award Good St. Bapt. Ch., Dallas, 1965; Citizenship award KNOK, 1965; Hats-Off award Dallas Council Republican Women, 1967; Trail Blazier award South Dallas Bus. and Profl. Assn., 1971. Mem. N.E.A., Am. Assn. U. Profs., N.A.A.C.P., Internat. Platform Assn., Bishop Coll. Alumni Assn. (nat. pres.), Nat. Council Negro Women, Alpha Kappa Alpha, Alpha Kappa Mu. Home: 2642 Plaza Blvd Dallas TX 75241 Office: 6042 Highland Hills Dr Dallas TX 75241

SEARS, ERNEST EUGENE, JR., assn. exec.; b. Birmingham, Ala., Dec. 6, 1923; s. Ernest Eugene and Orie Mae (Howard) S.; B.A., U. Ky., 1952, postgrad., 1952; m. Mary Ann Hoyer, Aug. 22, 1964; 1 son, Charles Ernest. Mng. editor Somerset (Ky.) Commonwealth, 1952-53; reporter Muncie (Ind.) Evening Press, 1953-57; pub. relations dir. Portland Cement Assn., Ky. Dist., 1957-66; pub. relations dir. Ky. C. of C., Louisville, also editor, gen. mgr. Ky. Bus. Mag., 1966—. Free-lance writer; pub. relations cons. Served with USNR, 1943-47; PTO. Mem. Ky. Hwy. Users Conf. (exec. committeeman), Am., Ky. assns. C. of C. execs., Ky. Press Assn. Mason. Contbr. articles to trade publs. Home: 4424 Westport Rd Louisville KY 40207 Office: 300 W York St Louisville KY 40203

SEARS, JAMES H., constrn. co. exec.; b. McKinney, Tex., May 30, 1923; s. Louis Alonzo and Minnie Viola (Reneau) S.; B.S. in Civil Engring., Tex. U., 1951; m. Marilyn Sue Miller, Mar. 23, 1961; 1dau., Cynthia Ann. Mgr. Central Tex. territory Austin Bridge Co., Dallas, 1953-69; v.p. Southwestern Contracting Co., Dallas, 1969- . Served with USAAF, 1943-46. Registered profl. engr., Tex. Home: 1110 Hadrian Ct Irving TX 75062 Office: 305 Stemmons Tower S Dallas TX 75207

SEARS, JOHN PATRICK, govt. ofcl.; b. Syracuse, N.Y., July 3, 1940; s. James Louis and Helen Mary (Fitzgerald) S.; B.S., Notre Dame U., 1960; LL.B., J.D., Georgetown U., 1963; m. Carol Jean Osborne, Aug. 25, 1962; children—James Louis, Ellen Margaret, Amy Elizabeth. Admitted to N.Y. bar, 1963; clk. N.Y. Ct. Appeals, 1962-65; asso. firm Nixon, Mudge, Rose, Guthrie, Alexander & Mitchell, 1965-66; mem. staff Richard M. Nixon, 1966-69; dep. counsel to Pres. Nixon, 1969—. Home: 8001 Chaute Pl Falls Church VA 22042 Office: The White House Washington DC 20500

SEARS, MARCIA JANIS MOCKETT (MRS. RALPH W. SEARS), newspaper editor; b. Lincoln, Neb., Aug. 24, 1927; d. Edwin O. and Perdita (Jameson) Mockett; A.B., U. Neb., 1948; postgrad. U. So. Cal., summers 1949-51; m. Ralph W. Sears, June 19, 1948; children—Steven, Sara Joan, Randall Jane. Tchr., Montevallo (Ala.) High Sch., 1949-50; founder, dir. Meadowlark Nursery Sch., Montevallo, Ala., 1954-61; instr. Spanish, U. Montevallo, 1959-65; v.p. Shelby County Advt. Corp., Calera, Ala., 1959—; v.p., editor Shelby County Reporter, Inc., Columbiana, Ala., 1967—. Chmn. Montevallo Community Chest, 1957-59; pub. relations chmn. Cahaba council Girl Scouts U.S.A., 1965-67. Bd. dirs. Montevallo Library, 1963—, chmn. bd., 1966—. Mem. Ala. Press Assn., Am. Assn. U. Women, Bus. and Profl. Womens Club, Mortar Bd., Theta Sigma Phi, Psi Chi. Democrat. Presbyn. Home: 596 Ashville Circle N Montevallo AL 35115 Office: PO Box 947 Columbiana AL 35051

SEARS, RALPH WESTGATE, coll. ofcl.; b. Grand Island, Neb., Oct. 8, 1922; s. Mark P. and Alma (Westgate) S.; B.S., U. Neb., 1948; postgrad. U. So. Cal., 1949-51; m. Marcia Mockett, June 19, 1948; children— Steven Ralph, Sara Joan, Randall Jane. Staff announcer KOLN Radio, Lincoln, Neb., 1947-48; dir. radio, asst. prof. speech Ala. Coll., Montevallo, 1948-51; mem. staff Radio KUSC, Los Angeles, summers 1949-51; mem. staff Radio WUOA, Tuscaloosa, Ala., 1951; dir. pub. relations U. Montevallo, 1952—. Pres. Shelby County Advt. Corp., 1959—; owner Radio WBYE, Calera, Ala., 1959—; pub., owner Sheby County Reporter, weekly Columbiana, Ala., 1967—, Childersburg (Ala.) Star, 1972—. City councilman, Montevallo, 1956—; sec. Shelby Indsl. Devel. Bd., 1956-57. Served with AUS, 1943-45. Mem. Pub. Relations Council Ala. (pres. 1961-62), Ala. Coll. Pub. Relations Soc. (pres. 1958), Am. Coll. Pub. Relations Assn. (dist. dir. 1966-67, dist. chmn.), Assn. Ala. Coll. Adminstrs., pres. (1967-68), C. of C. (pres. 1960-61), Execs. Club Birmingham, Sigma Phi Epsilon, Sigma Gamma Epsilon, Alpha Epsilon Rho. Presbyn. (elder). Clubs: Rotary (pres. 1956-57), University Montevallo Faculty (pres. 1951-52), University Montevallo Golf (pres. 1956-57); Birmingham Press. Home: 22 Asheville Circle Montevallo AL 35115

SEARS, ZENAS, broadcasting exec. Program dir. WAOK, Atlanta. Office: 110 Edgewood Av NE Atlanta GA 30303*

SEASE, TILLMAN R., head football coach Howard U. Address: Athletic Dept Howard Univ Washington DC 20001*

SEATON, ALBERTA JONES (MRS. EARLE E. SEATON), educator; b. Houston, Dec. 31, 1924; d. Charles A. and Elizabeth (Polk) Jones; B.S., Howard U., 1946, M.S., 1947; Sc.D., Universite Libre de Bruxelles, Brussels, Belgium, 1949; m. Earle E. Seaton, Dec. 24, 1947; children—Elizabeth Wamboi, Dudley Charles. Instr. zoology Howard U., Washington, 1947; mem. faculty, chmn. biology dept. Wiley Coll., Marshall, Tex., 1950-51; demonstrator Makerere Coll., Kampala, Uganda, 1952; asst. prof. Spelman Coll., Atlanta, 1953-54; asso. prof. Tex. So. U., 1954-60, prof. biology, dir. freshman studies, 1960—; postdoctoral fellow Cal. Inst. Tech., 1959-60. Dir., NSF Sci. Inst., Tex. So. U., Houston, 1958 (summer); NSF faculty fellow U. Brussels, 1965-66. Pres., Daus. of the King, Episcopal Ch., 1962-63, dir. Jr. Daus. of the King, 1963-64; pres. Jack and Jill Am., Houston, 1967-69. Mem. Am. Assn. U. Profs. (sec., treas. state conf. Tex.), Nat. Assn. Biology Tchrs., Am. Assn. U. Women, Am. Soc. Zoologists, Tex. Acad. Sci. Club: Radcliffe (Houston). Author: Manual of Vertebrate Embryology, 1971. Contbr. articles in field to profl. jours. Home: 3711 Eagle St Houston TX 77004

SEATON, EARL ALVA, JR., publisher, editor; b. Swifton, Ark., Sept. 28, 1919; s. Earl Alva and Nora M. (Clark) S.; A.A., Little Rock U., 1947; B.S. in M.E. with honors, U. Ark., 1949; m. Reba Pickard, Dec. 26, 1941; children—Rebecca June, Lynn Earl. Engr., Cities Service Oil Co., Shreveport, La., 1949-54; editor Oil and Gas Equipment, Tulsa, 1954-67, pub., editor Oil, Gas & Petrochem Equipment (name changed 1969), 1967—. Served with USNR, 1941-45. Registered profl. engr., Okla. Mem. Am. Soc. M.E. Unitarian. Home: 4913 E 26th Pl Tulsa OK 74114 Office: PO Box 1260 Tulsa OK 74101

SEATON, STUART LUMAN, physicist; b. Kirkwood, Mo., Nov. 16, 1906; s. George Lewis and Sara (Wall) S.; student U. Md., George Washington U., 1930-42; B.S., U. Alaska, 1942, D.Sc. (hon.), 1949; postgrad. George Washington U., 1946-47; m. Nancy Lillian Withnall, Nov. 24, 1937; children—Faye Seaton Brooks, Gail (Mrs. Richard Nobles), Kathleen (Mrs. Stephen Cottrell), Margaret. Elec. design draftsman Potomac Electric Power Co., Washington, 1922-29; physicist Carnegie Instn. Washington, 1929-46, Watson Labs., USAF, Red Bank, N.J., 1946-48; dir. Geophys. Inst., U. Alaska, College, Alaska, 1948-50; physicist Ordnance Engring. Corp., Rockville, Md., 1952-55; tech. asst. to chief, instrument research div. NASA, Langley Research Center, Hampton, Va., 1962-72; mem. faculty George Washington U., Hampton, 1968—. Pres., chmn. bd. Geo-Sci. Inc., Washington Grove, Md., 1951-54, dir., 1954-56; pvt. cons. practice, 1950-52, 55-62. Mem. Arctic Glossary Bd. Cons., 1950-52. Registered profl. engr., Alaska. Fellow N.Y. Acad. Scis., Physical Soc. (Eng.). Republican. Episcopalian. Club: Saint George's Dinghey and Sports (Bermuda). Contbr. articles in field profl. jours. and books. Home: 460 Windmill Point Hampton VA 23364 Office: George Washington U 2019 Cunningham Dr Hampton VA 23366

SEAVER, DONALD MACDONALD, univ. ofcl.; b. Johnson City, Tenn., Mar. 16, 1929; s. Wiley Rex and Barbara Jeanette (Fulton) S.; student Richmond U., 1946-47, Appalachian State Tchrs. Coll., 1947-48; A.B. in Journalism, U. N.C., 1957; m. Nancy Rebecca Lee, Sept. 19, 1959; children—Donald Macdonald, Sandra Lee, Debra Jean. Med. writer Charlotte (N.C.) Observer, 1957-63; news dir. Duke U. Med. Center, Durham, N.C., 1964-66, asst. dir. news service Duke U., 1966-70, news dir., 1970—. Dir. N.C. Mental Health Assn., 1960-66, recipient newspaper award, 1960. Bd. dirs. Durham County Golden Age Soc., (v.p. 1970—), Coordinating Council for Sr. Citizens, Durham County. Recipient Med. Press award N.C. Med. Soc., 1960, 61, Green Eyeshade award Sigma Delta Chi, 1960, Albert Lasker Journalism award, 1960. Hist. writer USAF, 1950-54. Mem. Phi Beta Kappa, Theta Chi. Home: 2948 Welcome Dr Durham NC 27705

SEAVER, E. ROBERT, govt. ofcl.; b. Beloit, Kan., July 24, 1915; s. Samuel Ross and Ethel (Bush) S.; J.D., U. Mo. at Kansas City, 1940; postgrad. U.S. Naval Acad., 1942, Pa. State U., 1942; m. Emily Hope McCoy, June 10, 1943; children—Elizabeth Ross (Mrs. Douglas Curtler), Carolyn (Mrs. Ian O'Flaherty), Susan (Mrs. John Kasberger), John Ellington. Admitted to Mo. bar, 1940, Va. bar, 1950; individual practice law, Kansas City, Mo., 1945-49; asst. city counsellor, Kansas City, 1945-49; successively asst. dep. atty. gen., gen. counsel Fed. Maritime Commn. and Maritime Commn., atty.-in-charge N.Y. Admiralty office Justice Dept., 1949-63; fed. hearing examiner CAB, and Fed. Maritime Commn., Washington, 1963-70; clk. Supreme Ct. U.S., 1970—. Served to capt. USNR, 1941-45. Mem. Am. Law Inst., Fed. Bar Assn., Phi Alpha Delta. Contbr. articles profl. jours. Home: 1117 Balls Hill Rd McLean VA 22101 Office: 1 1st St NE Washington DC 20543

SEAWRIGHT, MARGARET ELIZABETH ALSOBROOK (MRS. ROBERT M. SEAWRIGHT), psychiat. social worker; b. Rock Springs, Ga., Aug. 3, 1911; d. Daniel C. and Goma (Forrester) Alsobrook; B.S., U. Chattanooga, 1931; M.S., U. Tenn., 1959; m. Robert M. Seawright, July 24, 1936 (dec. Feb. 1956); 1 son, Robert D. With Miss. Bd. of Health, Jackson, 1959—, mental health cons., 1966—. Mem. Nat. Assn. Social Workers, Miss. Assn. Social Workers, Miss. Conf. Social Welfare, Miss. Pub. Health Assn. Home: 4081 Redwing Av Jackson MS 39216 Office: PO Box 1700 Jackson MS 39205

SEAY, WILLIAM H., ins. co. exec.; b., 1919; B.B.A., U. Tex., 1941; m. Partner, Henry, Seay & Black, 1948-57; v.p. Universal Life & Accident Ins. Co., 1958-61, pres., 1961—; exec. v.p. Southwestern Life Ins. Co., 1968-69, pres., 1969—, also dir.; dir. Guardian Savs. & Loan Assn., Dallas, Southwestern Investors Inc., Tex. Life Conv., Dallas. Served to capt. AUS, 1942-46. Office: PO Box 2699 Dallas TX 75221*

SEAY, WILLIAM JACKSON, educator; b. Birmingham, Ala., Apr. 5, 1930; s. William Berkley and Gladys (Long) S.; B.A. in Indsl. Design, Ala. Poly. Inst., 1956; m. Virginia Andress, Dec. 23, 1951; children— Laura Lee, Brian Brooks. With Atlanta Paper Co. (Ga.), 1956, Robert K. Price Co., Fayetteville, 1957; mem. faculty Ga. Inst. Tech., Atlanta, 1958—, asso. prof. archtl. and indsl. design, 1970—, chmn. dept. design, 1971—, adminstr. plastics short courses dept. continuing edn., 1963—. Dir. Atlanta Dynamics Corp. Indsl. design cons., cons. to 3d Army Tng. Aids Centers, 1965—. Served with AUS, 1951-53. NSF grantee, 1967-68; recipient Patriotic Civilian Service award. Mem. Soc. Plastics Engrs. (So. region edn. chmn. 1967—, pres. 1968, outstanding service award 1968, chmn. vinyl conf. 1969), World Future Soc. (dir. 1971), Am. Soc. Indsl. Designers, So. Indsl. Designers (sec. 1967), Auburn Art Guild, Lambda Chi Alpha (v.p. 1955), Tau Sigma Delta. Unitarian-Universalist. Club: Bickers. Home: 330 Woodward Way NW Atlanta GA 30305

SEBASTIAN, REX ARDEN, mfg. co. exec.; b. Robinson, Ill., Sept. 16, 1929; s. Dean and Rhea (Gideon) S.; B.S., Purdue U., 1951; M.B.A., Ind. U., 1952; m. Dorothy Lynne Bryson, Sept. 1, 1951; children—Steven Bryson, Annie Laurie, David Rex, Lisa Gay, Amy Lynne. Prodn. foreman Proctor & Gamble, Cin., 1952; various positions Cummins Engine Co., Inc., Columbus, Ind., 1955-60, mng. dir., Shotts, Lanarkshire, Scotland, 1960-63, v.p. internat., Columbus, 1963-64, London, Eng., 1964-66; v.p. internat. operations Dresser Industries, Inc., Dallas, 1966-71, v.p. operations office of pres., 1971—. Served to lt. Supply Corps, USNR, 1952-55. Mem. Dallas C. of C., Am. Mgmt. Assn., Machinery and Allied Products Inst., Nat. Fgn. Trade Council, Nat. Indsl. Conf. Bd., Sigma Phi Epsilon. Republican. Presbyn. Home: 4526 Dorset Rd Dallas TX 75229 Office: Republic Bank Bldg P O Box 718 Dallas TX 75221

SEBEL, HARRY LEE, JR., kennels co. exec.; b. Chgo., May 2, 1931; s. Harry Lee and Margaret (Klein) S.; B.A., Ind. U., 1951; M.S., Northwestern U., 1953; M.A., U. Pitts., 1954; m. May Pearlstone Loeb, May 10, 1956 (div.); children—Lee William, Lauren Claire. Trainee Carson Pirie Scott & Co., Chgo., 1954-56; mgr. Saks Fifth Av., Chgo., 1956-58; buyer Finchley, Chgo., 1958-60; account exec. E.F. Hutton & Co., Dallas, 1960-65, Eastman Dillon, Dallas, 1965-66, Kidder Peabody, Dallas, 1966-69; v.p. Walston & Co., Dallas, 1969-71; v.p., resident mgr. Kohlmeyer & Co., Dallas, 1971-72; pres. Kennel Kare, Inc., Dallas, 1972—. Served with AUS, 1954-56. Mason (Shriner). Clubs: Tex. Kennel, Brookhaven Country, (Dallas). Home: 10715 Sandpiper Lane Dallas TX 75230 Office: 14300 Noel Rd Dallas TX 75240

SEBO, STEVE, univ. ofcl.; B.S., M.A. Dir. intercollegiate athletics U. Va., Charlottesville. Address: Athletic Dept U Va Charlottesville VA 22903*

SEBOR, MILOS MARIE, geographer, planner; b. Zbiroh, Czechoslovakia, Sept, 3, 1911; s. Vojtech and Marie (Kopriva) S.; Iur. Dr., Charles U., Prague, 1936; M.A. McGill U. (Can.), 1955; postgrad. La. State U., 1957-58; Ph.D., Polish U., London, 1964; m. Bozena Rutrle, Sept. 3, 1936; 1 dau., Yana de Nepomuk. Came to U.S. 1956, naturalized 1962. With Czechoslovak State Security, 1935-48; head research div., del. to Interpol, Paris, 1946-48; geographer Lutetia Press, Paris, 1948-53; with Canadian Dept. Mines, 1955-56; faculty Spring Hill (Ala.) Coll., 1956-57; asso. prof. geography Tenn. Technol. U., Cookeville, 1958-67; prof. geology Weber State Coll., 1967-68; prof. geography grad. sch. Eastern Ky. U., Richmond, 1968—, dir. planning programs. Sr. planner, Tenn. State Planning Commn., 1962-67; vis. prof. geography U. Miami, 1965; field work on coastal forms and related urban pattern, N.W. Europe, 1966, planning tropical urban communities, Grenada, W.I., summer 1969; research and planning specialist Ky. Program Devel. Office, 1970—. Served to 1st capt. Czechoslovak Gendarmery, 1942-45. Recipient medal Czechoslovak Resistance, 1946. Mem. Assn. Am. Geographers, Am. Inst. Planners, Am. Assn. U. Profs., Czechoslovak Soc. Arts and Scis., Am. Austrian Soc., Geol. Soc. Am., Utah Geol. Assn., Am. Legion (Ky. planner-in-charge 1969). Co-author of new regional div. State of Tenn. into planning regions, 1962-67. Home: Route 7 Stateland Richmond KY 40475

SEDAM, GLENN JAY, publisher; b. Monongahela, Pa., Aug. 19, 1916; s. Earl Jay and Ica (Baltzell) S.; student Duquesne Sch. Advt. and Journalism, Pitts., 1940-41; m. Dorothy Harriet Gillingham, May 23, 1936; children—Glenn Jay, Tommy Alan, Linda Kay (Mrs. Tom A. McCulloch), Cythia Louise (Mrs. Ted A. Ganczak). Advt. salesman, mgr. Monongahela Daily Republican, 1936-39; advt. salesman McKeesport (Pa.) Daily News, 1939-41, Pitts. Press, 1941-44; advt. dir. Wilmington (N.C.) Post, 1944-45, Clarksburg (W.Va.) Exponent-Telegram, 1945-53; advt. dir., bus mgr. Gadsden (Ala.) Times, 1953-58; pub. Bay City (Tex.) Daily Tribune, 1958—; v.p. So. Newspapers, Inc., Ala., 1957-58. Pres., Matagorda Retarded Children's Council, Bay City, 1960-63; Mem. Tex. Christian U. Adv. Bd., 1965—, Com. 100, 1968—. Bd. dirs. Tex. United Fund. Recipient Citizen award Gadsden, 1956-57; nominated Fair award as outstanding layman Bay City Ministerial Alliance, 1960. Mem. Etowah County Hist. Soc. (pres. 1956-58), Tex. Press Assn. (v.p.), Bay City C. of C. (dir.), Sigma Delta Chi. Mem. Disciples of Christ Ch., (pres. Ala. Christian Men's Fellowship 1955-58, v.p., nat. fellowship 1956-57, pres. 1957-58, pres. Tex. fellowship 1965-66). Home: 2113 Hillcrest Dr Bay City TX 77414 Office: 3013 7th St Bay City TX 77414

SEDBERRY, MARGARET CELESTE MOORE (MRS. MILES E. SEDBERRY), physician; b. Carthage, Tex., Jan. 31, 1925; d. James B. and Maggie (Miller) Moore; B.S., La. State U., 1945; M.D., U. Tex., 1950; m. Miles E. Sedberry, Mar. 9, 1952; children—Lory Lyn, Kirk Miles, Intern Parkland Hosp., Dallas, 1950-51; resident psychiatry U. Tex. Med. Br., Galveston, 1951-54; clin. dir. Austin (Tex.) State Hosp., 1954—. Mem. A.M.A., Tex. Med. Assn., Travis County Med. Soc., Austin Soc. Pub. Adminstrn., Am. Med. Womens Assn., Am., Dist. Br. psychiat. assns., Titus Harris Soc. Home: 3909 Balcones Dr Austin TX 78731 Office: Austin State Hosp Austin TX 78751

SEDKI, NEBIL BASHIR, structural engr.; b. Baghdad, Iraq, June 20, 1940 (came to U.S. 1963); s. Bashir and Mary (Jebran) S.; B.Sc. magna cum laude, Al-Hikma U. Baghdad, 1961; M.S. in Civil Engring., Ga. Inst. Tech., 1964. Engr. trainee Brown & Root Sudamericana Ltd., 1961; v.p. William E. Edwards Structural Engrs., Inc., Atlanta, 1964—; pres. P.E. Corp., 1966—. Served as lt. Iraqi Army, 1962-63. Registered profl. engr., Ga., Fla., N.C., Ky. Mem. Am. Soc. C.E., Am. Concrete Inst., Prestressed Concrete Inst., Cons. Engrs. Council Ga., Ga. Tech. Alumni Assn. Club: Executives Assn. (Atlanta). Home: 207 Springdale Dr NE Atlanta GA 30305 Office: 26 Peachtree Pl NW Atlanta GA 30309

SEDWICK, ROBERT CURTIS, educator; b. Pitts., June 27, 1926; s. Hyram Jobe and Annabelle (Silver) S.; B.S., Coast Guard Acad., 1949; M.Engring. Adminstrn., George Washington U., 1960, D.B.A., 1964; m. Elizabeth Angeline King, June 3, 1949; children—Robert Curtis, Elizabeth Ann. Staff engr. Emerson Research Lab., Silver Spring, Md., 1956-57; plant mgr. Polytronics, Inc., Rockville, Md., 1957-58; chief engring. adminstrn. Allis-Chalmers Nuclear Power Dept., Washington, 1958-62; sr. contracts negotiator and adminstr. Johns Hopkins Applied Physics Lab., Silver Spring, Md., 1962-65; dir. Tidewater Center, George Washington U., Hampton, Va., 1965—, prof. bus. adminstrn., 1965—. Dir. Adminstrv. Research Assos., Hampton, Va. Bd. dirs., treas. Heritage council Girl Scouts Am. Served to lt. USCG, 1949-56. Mem. Am. Econ. Assn., Am. Mgmt. Assn., Soc. Naval Architects and Marine Engrs., U.S. Naval Inst. Presbyn. (deacon, elder). Dir. research, pub. Mortgage Market Survey, Williamsburg, Va., 1966, Econ. Survey, Hampton Waterfront, 1967. Contbr. articles to profl. jours. Home: 505 Carters Grove Ct Hampton VA 23363

SEE, MARION JACK, lawyer; b. Saltpeter, W. Va., Sept. 15, 1904; s. Charles Frederick and Elizabeth (Goff) S.; student Cumberland Coll., 1926; A.A., U. Ky., 1929, A.B., 1929; m. Dorothy Elizabeth Heston, Dec. 26, 1933; children—Marion Jack, Charles Frederick III. Admitted to Ky. bar, 1937; editor Lawrence County Recorder, Louisa, Ky., 1926-27; instr. Staunton (Va.) Mil. Acad., 1927-28, Louisa High Sch., 1931-40; prin. Louisa Consol. Sch., 1931-40; partner firm C.F. See, Jr. (merger See & See) 1940—; atty. Lawrence County, 1940-42, Louisa City, 1942-44, 46-52, 63; asst. atty. gen. revenue and tax Govt. of Guam, 1957-59; atty. gen. Trust Ter. Pacific Islands, 1959-61; spl. judge Circuit Ct., Eastern Ky. dists., 1956-62. Mem. Am., Ky., Lawrence County (sec.) bar assns. Baptist. Mason; mem. Order Eastern Star, Rotarian (pres. 1941). Club: Nat. Lawyers. Home: 607 Lock Av Louisa KY 41230 Office: Recorder Bldg Louisa KY 41230

SEE, RICHARD, govt. ofcl.; b. Hackensack, N.J., Dec. 3, 1923; s. Albert Bentley and Elizabeth (Muns) S.; B.A., Harvard, 1949; postgrad. U. of Oslo (Norway), 1949; M.A., U. Cal., 1950, postgrad., 1950-52; m. Chia Chih Yuan, 1958; children—Yu Ku Ku (stepson), Eileen, Aimee, Erik, Alex, Anna. Profl. asst. NSF, Washington, 1958-62, asst. program dir. mech. transl., 1962-64, program dir. information systems Office Sci. Information Service, 1964-66, program dir. research and studies, 1966-67; chief research and devel. br. Nat. Library Medicine, Bethesda, Md., 1967-70; head data processing dept. U.S. Naval Med. Research Unit 2, Taipei, Taiwan, 1970—. Translator Chinese lang. Served with USAAF, 1943-45. Mem. Am. Math. Soc., Linguistic Soc. Am., Assn. Computing Machinery, Am. Soc. Information Sci., Assn. Computational Linguistics, Pierian Sodality of 1808, Pi Mu Epsilon. Home: 2609 Nicholson St West Hyattsville MD 20782 Office: Naval Med Research Unit 2 Box 14 APO San Francisco CA 96263

SEEBER, ROBERT LYNN, govt. ofcl.; b. Clinton, Tenn., Sept. 7, 1926; s. Thomas Lawrence and Leola Vera (Disney) S.; B.S. in Indsl. Mgmt., U. Tenn., 1949, J.D., 1951; m. Julia Ann Jennings, Dec. 28, 1946. Admitted to Tenn. bar, 1951; atty. div. law TVA, Knoxville, 1952-67, dir. div. reservoir properties, 1967, solicitor div. law, 1967-69, asst. gen. mgr., 1969-70, gen. mgr., 1970—. Served with AUS, 1946-48. Mem. Tenn. Bar Assn. Rotarian. Home: Route 1 Lowes Ferry Rd Louisville TN 37777 Office: TVA 508 Union Av Knoxville TN 37902

SEELIG, JOHN EARL, coll. adminstr.; b. Fredericksburg, Tex., Dec. 11, 1924; s. Charles M. and Katy (Leyendecker) S.; B.S., Hardin-Simmons U., 1946, Dr. Humanities, 1969; M.Religious Edn., Southwestern Baptist Theol. Sem., Fort Worth, 1949; m. Virginia Garrett, Oct. 16, 1947; children—Stephen Clyde, Timothy Garrett. Minister edn. Evans Av. Bapt. Ch., Fort Worth, 1947-49, Birchman Av. Bapt. Ch., Fort Worth, 1950-51, Highland Bapt. Ch., 1951-52. dir. edn. and promotion Dallas Bapt. Assn., 1952-56; minister Travis Av. Bapt. Ch., Fort Worth, 1956-60; asso. tng. union sec. Bapt. Gen. Conv. Tex., 1956-58; asst. to pres. Southwestern Bapt. Theol. Sem., Fort Worth, 1960—. Mem. pub. relations adv. com. Bapt. Gen. Conv. of Tex., then chmn. Mem. citizens adv. bd. The Mary Hardin-Baylor Coll.; loan exec. United Fund. Mem. Pub. Relations Soc. Am., Am. Coll. Pub. Relations Assn. (trustee; mem. nat. publs. com. 1969), Religious Pub. Relations Council (past pres.), Tex. Bapt. Pub. Relations Assn. (past pres.), Bapt. Pub. Relations Assn. (pres. 1969), Fort Worth C. of C. (edn., pub. relations com.), Southwestern Bapt. Theol. Sem. Alumni Assn. (sec. treas. 1960). Baptist (deacon). Lion. Clubs: Ridglea Country, Meadowbrook Wranglers, The Fort Worth Breakfast (Fort Worth); Saddle and Sirloin of Kansas City (Mo.). Home: 4441 Stanley Av Fort Worth TX 76115 Office: Box 22000-3e Fort Worth TX 76122

SEELIG, JOSEPH ROBERT, dentist; b. New Orleans, Feb. 22, 1906; s. Phillippe Wolf and Dora Bertha (Lazarus) S.; D.D.S., Tulane U., 1927; m. Babette Claire Klotz, July 30, 1939; children—Donald Philip, Kenneth Roy. Mem. staff, Charity Hosp., 1928-30, Child Welfare Dental Clinic, 1929-32; practice dentistry, New Orleans, 1927—; chief dental services Touro Infirmary, New Orleans, 1958-62. Mem. La. Com. on Aging, 1957—; chmn. dental div. United Fund, 1935. Mem. So. Acad. Periodontology, Southeastern Acad. Prosthodontia, Internat. Fedn. Dentists, Tulane Dental Alumni Assn. (pres. 1968-69), New Orleans Dental Conf. (mem. con. 1962), Am. Acad. Geriatric Dentistry; life mem. Am., La., New Orleans (pres. 1962) dental assns. Mason (Shriner, Jester). Clubs: New Orleans

Athletic, Hi-Twelve (New Orleans). Home: 4133 Vincennes Pl New Orleans LA 70125 Office: Pere Marquette Bldg New Orleans LA 70112

SEERLEY, ROBERT WAYNE, educator; b. Indpls., Oct. 6, 1930; s. Don Anderson and Mary Helen (Surber) S.; B.S., Purdue U., 1952; M.S., Mich. State U., 1957, Ph.D., 1960; m. Norma Inez Reeve, Aug. 19, 1951; children—Don Allen, Ronald Wayne. Extension animal scientist Purdue U., Lafayette, Ind., 1952-54; asst. prof. animal sci. S.D. State U., Brookings, 1960-63, asso. prof., 1963-67; asso. prof. animal sci. U. Ga., Athens, 1967—. Cons. to AID, South Korea, 1965, U.S. Feed Grain Council, South Korea, Taiwan, 1968, AID Cassava Project, 1970-72. Served with USMCR, 1954-56. Mem. Am. Inst. Nutrition, Am. Assn. Scientists, Am. Soc. Animal Sci., Sigma Xi, Alpha Zeta, Gamma Sigma Delta, Alpha Gamma Rho. Rotarian. Contbr. articles to profl. jours. Home: 291 Cedar Creek Dr Athens GA 30601

SEES, JAMES EDWIN, electronics and microwave engr., radio astronomer, educator; b. Adair County, Mo., Mar. 23, 1913; s. Irvie and Etta (Miller) S.; B.S. in Physics and Math., N.E. Mo. State Tchrs. Coll., 1933-37; M.S., U. Okla., 1939; postgrad. Cath. U. Am., 1950—; m. Maybelle Evans, Sept. 15, 1940; 1 son, Robert Alan. Chief computer seismograph div. Stanolind Oil & Gas Co., 1940-42; sect. head, radio astronomy br. Naval Research Lab., Washington, 1942-58; asso. prof. elec. engring. U. S.C., 1958—. Mem. A.A.A.S., Am. Phys. Soc., Sci. Research Soc. Am., Am. Soc. Engring. Edn., Am. Geophys. Union, Sigma Xi, Sigma Pi Sigma. Home: 1517 Alpine Dr West Columbia SC 29206 Office: Univ SC Columbia SC 29206

SEGAL, LEON, research chemist; b. Memphis, Tenn., Jan. 28, 1918; s. Maurice and Anna (Paseltiner) S.; B.S., Miss. State Coll., 1940; M.S., La. State U., 1942; Ph.D., Tulane U., 1954; m. Doris Couvillion, Apr. 18, 1970; children by previous marriage—Evelyn Ann (Mrs. Lane T. deBardeleben), Sera Rae (Mrs. Clifford B. Alsberg). With So. Regional Research Lab., U.S. Dept. Agr., New Orleans, 1942—, successively jr. chemist, 1942-46, asst. chemist, 1946-48, asso. chemist, 1948-53, prin. chemist, 1953, group supr., 1952-58, sr. research chemist, 1958-65, prin. research chemist, 1965—. Acting asso. prof. chemistry Tulane U., 1957. Served from ensign to lt. (j.g.) with USNR, 1943-46; Res. ret. Mem. Research Soc. Am., Am. Inst. Chemists, Am. Chem. Soc. (sect. chmn. 1965), Fiber Soc., Am. Assn. Textile Chemists and Colorists, Sigma Xi, Sigma Alpha Mu, Phi Lambda Upsilon, Alpha Chi Sigma, Kappa Mu Epsilon, Phi Eta Sigma. Patentee in field. Home: 3224 45th St Metairie LA 70001 Office: 1100 Robert E Lee Blvd New Orleans LA 70179

SEGAL, MORLEY, educator; b. San Francisco, Dec. 7, 1933; s. Max R. and Edna Ludwig S.; A.B., San Francisco State Coll., 1957, M.A., 1959; Ph.D., Claremont Grad. Sch., 1965; m. Joyce Holly, Aug. 10, 1954; children—Arline Holly, Eric Max, Adam Blair. Intern elections and reapportionment com. Cal. Legislature, 1963; asst. prof. Cal. State Coll., Hayward, 1963-66; mem. faculty Am. U., Washington, 1967—, asso. prof. polit. sci., 1967-70; prof. Am. govt. and pub. adminstrn., 1970—; faculty fellow Washington Center Met. Studies, 1969-70. Cons. Internat. City Mgrs.' Assn., Washington Center Met. Studies. Chmn. So. Alameda County Citizens for Fair Housing, 1963. Spl. asst. to Sen. Thomas Kuchel, 1966, Rep. James Schever, 1966—. Served with AUS, 1954-56. Recipient Congl. fellowship Am. Polit. Sci. Assn., 1960. Mem. Am. Polit Sci. Assn. Home: 23 Cedar St Alexandria VA 22301 Office: Nebraska and Massachusetts Av Washington DC 20006

SEGAL, PAUL MANUEL, municipal govt. ofcl.; b. Jersey City, Jan. 12, 1920; s. David A. and Anna (Feller) S.; B.B.A., Coll. City N.Y., 1948; M.Pub. Adminstrn., N.Y.U., 1949; certificate urban and met. planning Am. U., 1958; m. Shirley R. Klauber, Apr. 4, 1954; children—Charles Lawrence, Brad Marshall. Transp. economist Bur. Pub. Rds., Washington, 1949-58; planning dir. Cecil County, Md., 1959-61; Norwalk, Conn., 1961-65, Plainfield, N.J., 1965-66, Sarasota, Fla., 1966—. Cons. and lectr. in field. Pres., Sarasota County Health Planning Council, 1969; v.p. West Central Fla. Comprehensive Health Planning Council, 1969-71; sec. Sarasota Planning Bd., 1966—. Served with AUS, 1943-45. Mem. Am. Inst. Planners, Am. Soc. Planners, Fla. Planning and Zoning Assn. (v.p. 1969-70), Nat. Assn. Housing and Redevel. Ofcls. Contbr. articles to profl. jours. Home: 722 Siesta Key Circle Sarasota FL 33581 Office: City Hall PO 1058 Sarasota FL 33578

SEGAL, SAMUEL JEROME, physician; b. Atlanta, July 16, 1933; s. Morris Isadore and Sara (Kurtz) S.; student Emory U., 1951-54; M.D., Med. Coll. S.C., 1958; m. Yetta Berkman (div.); children—Rebecca, David, Sharon, Michele. Intern, Med. Coll. Hosps., Charleston, S.C., 1959; gen. practice medicine, St. Petersburg, Fla., 1963—; mem. staffs Palms of Pasadena Hosp., St. Petersburg (Fla.) Gen. Hosp.; guest lectr. psychology dept. U. South Fla., 1970-71; med. dir., chief investigator P.A.R. Methedone Maintenance Clinic, 1971. Mem. Adv. Council on Drug Abuse, 1971; mem. Citizens Council on Crime Inc., 1970—; pres. Facts Inc., telephone counseling service, 1971—. Served with AUS, 1960-62. Mem. Am., Pinellas County, So. med. assns., Parents Awareness and Responsibility (pres. 1969—). Jewish religion (dir. 1966—). Home: 473 79th St S St Petersburg FL 33707 Office: 8073 38th Av N St Petersburg FL 33710

SEGALL, LEE, broadcasting exec.; b. Dallas, July 18, 1905; s. Simon and Jennie (Sachs) S.; student U. Tex., 1923; m. Mildred Dolores Metzger, Feb. 28, 1929. Mgr. Metzger Dairies, Houston, 1929—; owner Segall & Goodwin Advt. Agy., Houston, 1939—; pres. KIXL and KIXL-FM Radio, Dallas, 1957—; producer-writer various network shows N.Y., 1945—. Creator, owner Dr. I.Q., 1935—, also creator TV version. Cons. to radio, TV stas.; advt. cons. in bus. Radio cons. Eighth service command, War Bond dir., Dallas, 1947—. Dir. Dallas Symphony Orch. Active on civic & pub. service coms.; charter corporate mem. Boys Club Dallas. Tex. rep. broadcasting, voting mem. Am. Heart Assn.; mem. found. com. Tex. Heart Assn. Named Outstanding Broadcaster of 1961, Assn. Broadcasting Execs. Tex. Author: The Wonderful Think-It-Overs; Teasers for Your Think-Tank. Home and office: 3525 Turtle Creek Blvd Dallas TX 75219

SEGARS, CHARLES ARTHUR, SR., bus. exec.; b. Sumter, S.C., Dec. 23, 1935; s. Raymie Virgene and Louise (Snow) S.; B.S., Clemson U., 1958; m. Addie Louise Wise, Feb. 16, 1962; children—Charles Arthur, William Camp, Sarah Louise, George Wise, Burrell Raymie. Farm mgr. R.V. Segars Co., Oswego, S.C., 1963—; dir. Segars-Willis Storage Warehouses, Inc., Eastern Storage, Inc., Ag-Roto, Inc. Chmn. Lee County Planning Bd., 1970-72; chmn. Lee County Resource and Devel. Bd., 1969-72; committeeman Agrl. Stblzn. Conservation Service, 1970-72. Served to lt. USNR, 1958-62. Recipient Dist. award Cotton Yield Contest, S.C. Crop Improvement Assn., 1965. Mem. Sumter Agr. Soc. Methodist (mem. adminstrv. bd. 1971-72). Clubs: Sunset Country, Les Trente Dance (Sumter, S.C.). Home: 709 Henderson St Sumter SC 29150 Office: Hwy 441 Oswego SC 29121

SEGARS, KELLY SCOTT, physician, banker; b. Red Bay, Ala., Mar. 11, 1930; s. Dock Scott and Ora Esther (Sims) S.; B.S. in Pharmacy with honors, Auburn U., 1952; M.D. with honors, U. Miss., 1959; m. Martha Ann Thompson, Oct. 3, 1952; children—Kelly Scott, Mark Thompson, Leigh Ann. Intern, USPHS, Norfold, Va., 1959-60; practice medicine, Iuka, Miss., 1960—; pres. Tri-State Savs. and Loan, Iuka, 1963-64; founder, pres. 1st Nat. Bank Iuka, 1964—; chief, med. staff Tishomingo County Hosp., 1968, responsible for constrn. coronary care unit; pres. Horizon Broadcasting, radio stas. WVOM, WTIB, 1970—; dir. various ins., real estate, cattle and farming operations. Chmn. constrn. com. Iuka Airport, 1966-67; chmn. constrn. com. Iuka Municipal Library, 1970; mem. exec. council Yocona area Boy Scouts Am., 1971-. Served to 1st lt. AUS, 1953-55. Col. staff Gov. John Bell Williams. Mem. A.M.A., So., Miss. med. assns., Am., Miss. bankers' assns., Flying Physicians Assn., Internat. Flying Bankers Assn. Methodist (ofcl. bd.). Home: Route 1 Box 165 Iuka MI 38852 Office: 1413 W Quitman St Iuka MI 38852

SEGLER, FRANKLIN MORGAN, educator; b. Ardmore, Okla., Apr. 11, 1907; s. Samuel Matthew and Ada (Gabriel) S.; A.B., Okla. Bapt. U., 1930; Th.M., Southwestern Bapt. Sem., 1938, Th.D., 1945; postdoctorate Union Theol. Sem., N.Y.C., 1953, Boston U., 1957-58; m. Fannie Mae McCord, June 11, 1935; children—Dana Franklin, Samuel Louis, Sylvia (Mrs. Kyle Rost). Ordained to ministry Baptist Ch., 1934; asso. minister First Bapt. Ch., Duncan, Okla., 1931-32, Capital Hill Bapt. Ch., Oklahoma City, 1933-34, First Bapt. Ch., Ardmore, Okla., 1935, Polytechnic Bapt. Ch., Fort Worth, 1936-67; pastor Carlisle Bapt. Ch., Henderson, Tex., 1938-40, First Bapt. Ch., Garland, Tex., 1940-45, Emmanuel Bapt. Ch., Alexandria, La., 1945-51; mem. faculty dept. pastoral ministry Southwestern Bapt. Sem., Fort Worth, 1951—. Trustee La. Bapt. Hosp., Alexandria, 1948-51. Sealantic Study fellow, 1957-58. Mem. Am. Acad. Religion, Assn. Clin. Pastoral Educators. Author: A Theology of Church and Ministry, 1960; The Christian Layman, 1964; Christian Worship, Its Theology and Practice, 1965; The Broadman Minister's Manual, 1968; Your Emotions and Your Faith, 1970; A Pailful of Stars, 1972. Home: 30 Cliffside Dr Fort Worth TX 76134 Office: Box 22098 Fort Worth TX 76122

SEGREST, ROSS ALTON, electric coop. ofcl.; b. Hamlin, Tex., Jan. 20, 1910; s. William Noah and Sarah (McBrayer) S.; B.A. summa cum laude, Baylor U., 1931; m. Hazel Lenore Tiner, Sept. 7, 1946; children—Sara Linda, Melissa Caroline. Sr. accountant A. C. Upleger & Co., C.P.A.'s, Waco, 1931-36, partner, 1936-42; auditor, adminstrv. asst. Brown Ship-bldg. Co., Houston, 1942-45; comptroller Nat. Instrument Corp., Houston, 1945-49; asst. gen. mgr., comptroller Brazos Electric Power Coop., Inc., Waco, 1950-72, now gen. mgr.; dir. Lake Air Nat. Bank; sec.-treas. Southwestern Energy Corp.; treas. Tex. Municipal Power Pool, Inc.; mem. exec. com. Electric Reliability Council of Tex. Tchr. accounting night sch. Baylor U., Waco, 1951-52. Mem. citizens adv. com. to Juvenile Judge, Econ. Opportunities Advancement Corp., Greater Waco United Fund, Waco Civic Theatre. Bd. dirs. A.R.C., Am. Cancer Soc., others. C.P.A., Tex. Mem. Am. Inst. C.P.A.'s, Tex. Soc. C.P.A.'s (past pres. Central Tex. chpt., soc. dir.), Tex. Electric Coop.'s (past pres.), Mid-West Power (past pres.) accounting assns. Democrat. Baptist. Mason (Shriner). Club: Woodland West Country (past pres., bd. dirs.). Contbr. articles to profl. publs. Home: 4511 Pine Av Waco TX 76710 Office: 2404 LaSalle Av Waco TX 76706

SEGUINE, VIRGINIA MARGERY, librarian; b. Chgo., Feb. 20, 1932; d. Melvin Manee and Frances (Waffle) Seguine; B.A., Bryan Coll., 1954; postgrad. U. Tenn., 1956-57; M.A., Western Mich. U., 1965. Instr., Tenn. State Sch. for Deaf, Knoxville, 1957-58, Ind. State Sch. for Deaf, Indpls., 1958-59, Pennfield Schs., Battle Creek, Mich., 1959-62, Appalachian Bible Inst., Bradley, W.Va., 1962-64; librarian Bryan Coll., Dayton, Tenn., 1964—. Soprano soloist local coll. prodns. Mem. Christian Librarians' Fellowship, A.L.A., Tenn. Library Assn., Christian Bus. and Profl. Women (com. chmn. 1959-62), Delta Kappa Gamma (chpt. pres. 1968—, state 1st v.p. 1971—). Presbyn. (ch. pianist 1964—, Sunday sch. tchr. 1964—). Address: Bryan Coll Dayton TN 37321

SEGURA, MICHAEL GERALD, mental health center adminstr.; b. Abbeville, La., Mar. 30, 1936; s. William A. and Doris (Gooch) S.; B.A., U. Southwestern La., 1958; M.S.W., La. State U., 1960; m. Loretta Guidroz, Nov. 28, 1957; children—Clement, Mark, John, Anne. Exec. dir. Terrebonne Guidance Center, Houma, La., 1960-63, regional coordinator Region VIII, 1963-67, regional mental health adminstr., 1967—. Cons. Lafourche-Terrebonne Council on Alcoholism, 1969—; chmn. Juvenile Detention Center Adv. com., 1969—; coordinator Regional Planning Council for Alcohol Abuse, 1972—. Recipient Profl. of the Year award La. Assn. Mental Health, 1969. Fellow La. Assn. Clin. Social Workers; mem. Acad. Certified Social Workers, Terrebonne Deanery Council, Regional Health Planning Council. Roman Catholic. Home: 310 Foster Av Houma LA 70360 Office: 500 Legion Av Houma LA 70360

SEGURA, PEARL MARY, librarian, educator; b. Lafayette, La., June 12, 1909; d. Joseph Sidney and Celestine (Gutierrez) Segura; B.A., U. Southwestern La., 1930, postgrad. summer 1932, 42-43, 46-48, 51-52; B.S. in L.S., La. State U., 1941; postgrad. summers, Tulane U., 1931, Columbia, 1939, U. Ill., 1948, U. Houston, 1954. Tchr., librarian Indian Bayou (La.) High Sch., 1930-31; tchr. Maurice (La.) High Sch., 1931-33, tchr., librarian, 1933-41; asst. circulation librarian Stephens Meml. Library U. Southwestern La., Lafayette, 1941-44, acting reference librarian, 1944-46, reference librarian, 1946-62, librarian Jefferson Caffery La. room Dupre Library, 1962—, asso. prof. library sci., 1953—. Mem. Am., Southwestern, La. library assns., Spl. Libraries Assn., Am. Assn. State and Local History, Assn. Coll. and Reference Libraries, Am. Assn. U. Women, Nat. Trust for Historic Preservation, La., Attakapas hist. assns., La. Geneal. and Hist. Soc., La. Folklore Soc., La. Tchrs. Assn,, Met. Opera Guild. Lafayette Community Concerts Assn., Lafayette Little Theatre, Lafayette Art Assn., Am. Camellia Soc., La. State U., U. Southwestern La. alumni assns., D.A.R. (1st chpt. vice regent 1968-71, state chmn. U.S.A. bicentennial com. 1967-71, chpt. chmn. 1969—), U.D.C., Cath. Daus. Am., St. Ann's Guild, Am. Iris Soc., S.W. La. Poetry Soc., France Amerique de la Louisiane Acadienne (sec. 1964—), Phi Kappa Phi (pub. relations officer), Beta Phi Mu, Delta Kappa Gamma (pres. chpt. 1947-49), Kappa Kappa Iota (state handbook chmn. 1960-61, pres. Lambda conclave 1957-60). Democrat. Roman Catholic. Author: Acadians in Fact and Fiction: AClassified Bibiliography, 1955. Contbr. articles to profl. jours. Home: 140 S Magnolia St Lafayette LA 70501

SEHRT, CLEM HENRY, lawyer, banker; b. New Orleans, Aug. 19, 1909; s. William Jacob and Catherine (Sulfstede) S.; LL.B., Loyola U. of South, 1932; m. Norris Lola Tricon, June 6, 1934; children—Gretchen Sonja, Clem Tricon. Admitted to La. bar, 1932; mem. firm Sehrt, Boyle, Wheeler & Butler, and predecessor law firm, New Orleans, 1948—; gen. counsel Louisiana Banking Dept., 1948-52; dir. Nat. Am. Bank, New Orleans, 1958—, pres., 1963—. Mem. La. State Bank Commn., 1969—. Pres. La. Democratic Assn., 1948-50; pres., chmn. Regular Dem. Orgn., 1950-56. Mem. C. of C. New Orleans Area, Am., La., New Orleans bar assns., Am. Judicature Soc., Young Men's Bus. Club, So. Athletic Assn. Ofcls. Clubs: New Orleans Athletic (past dir., mem. governing com.), Internat. House (New Orleans). Home: 5870 Canal Blvd New Orleans LA 70124 Office: 200 Carondelet St New Orleans LA 70130

SEIBELS, GEORGE, mayor; b. Cal., July 15, 1913; s. George Goldthwaite and Aileen (Pettit) S.; B.S., U. Va.; m. Norma Graham, 1949; children—George Goldthwaite III, Laura. Councilman, Birmingham, 1963-67, Ala., mayor, 1967—. Served to lt. USNR, World War II. Mem. Birmingham Jr. C. of C. Home: 1324 Swallow Lane Birmingham AL 35213 Office: City Hall Bldg Birmingham AL 35203

SEIBERT, SISTER MARY ANGELICE, educator; b. Louisville, Jan. 16, 1922; d. William Karl and Cathedrine A. (Schmidt) Seibert; B.S. summa cum laude, Ursuline Coll., 1947; M.S., Institutum Divi Thomae, 1950, Ph.D., 1952; Damon Runyon post doctoral fellow St. Louis U., 1953-54. Tchr. Cath. elementary schs., Louisville, 1942-47; instr. chemistry and biology Ursuline Coll., Louisville, 1950, chmn. div. natural scis., 1952-65, dir. coll. relations and devel., 1960-62, acting pres., 1964-65, pres., 1965-68; Fulbright-Hays vis. lectr. U. Coll., Galway, Ireland, 1968-69; vis. prof. biochemistry Smith Coll., 1969-70; prof. chemistry, coordinator div. allied med. scis. Jefferson Community Coll., Louisville, 1970—. Mem. Ky. Acad. Sci., Am. Chem. Soc., Ky. Sci. Tchrs. Assn., A.A.A.S., Ky. Chemistry Tchrs. Assn., Albertus Magnus Guild, Nat. Cath. Edn. Assn. (mem. exec. com.), Sigma Xi. Address: 3105 Lexington Rd Louisville KY 40206

SEIDENBERG, JACOB, labor arbitrator; b. N.Y.C., Oct. 25, 1914; s. Abraham Michael and Sophie (Levin) S.; B.S., Temple U., 1937; LL.B., U. Pa., 1940; Ph.D., Cornell U., 1951; m. Mercet W. Murphy, Nov. 2, 1955; children—John Prentice, Susan Sophie. Admitted to Pa. bar, 1941; atty. War Dept., Phila., 1941, War Labor Bd., Phila., 1943-46, WSB, 1951; exec. dir. Pres.'s Com. Contract Compliance, Washington, 1958-60; individual practice labor arbitrator, 1946—; chmn. Fed. Services Impasse Panel, 1970—; instr. Haverford Coll., 1947-48; professorial lectr. Am. U., 1951; cons. Sec. Labor, 1969-70. Mem. Fed. Bar Assn., Nat. Acad. Arbitrators. Author: Negroes in Work Group, 1950; Labor Injunction in New York City, 1951; Evolution of Current Pay Practices in Over-the-Road Freight Industry, 1962. Address: 6318 Cavalier Corridor Falls Church VA 22044

SEIDENSTRICKER, LEONARD FREDERICK, agr. co. exec.; b. DeValls Bluff, Ark., Nov. 28, 1917; s. Arthur Frederick and Rosa Katherine (Kreiselmeier) S.; student pub. schs., 1923-31; m. Dorothy LaVerne Hemme, Aug. 12, 1956; children—Robert Hemme, Karen LaVerne. Mgr. rice and soybean farm, De Valls Bluff, 1937—; dir. Riceland Foods Inc., (formerly Ark. Grain Corp.) Stuttgart, Hazen Grain Drying Co. (Ark.). Leader 4-H Club, 1962—. Mem. bd. Prairie County Farm Bur., 1956-72; mem. Prairie County Devel. Bd., 1960-68, East Ark. Devel. Bd., 1968-70, Hazen Pub. Sch. Bd., 1970—; treas. Pairie County Republican party, 19——. Bd. dirs. Prairie County 4-H Found., 1970-72. Named Ark. Farm Family of Year, Ark. press, Ark. Power Light, 1960; recipient Master Farmer award Progressive Farmer, 1969, Ark. 4-H Alumni award, 1954, Soil Conservation award Goodyear and Soil Conservation Dist., 1969; named Ark. 4-H Champion Boy, 1934. Lutheran (elder). Home: DeValls Bluff AR 72041 Office: 120 N Grand Av Stuttgart AR 72160

SEIFERT, DAVID WALTER, JR., dentist; b. Weldon, N.C., Oct. 9, 1919; s. David Walter and Florence Fairlamb (Rowe) S.; student N.C. State U., 1938; A.B., U. N.C., 1942; D.D.S., Emory U., 1945; m. Flora McDonald, Dec. 1, 1945; children—Flora Stewart (Mrs. Robert Turnage Stewart), Ann Stedman, Caroline Battle. Practice dentistry, Raleigh, N.C., 1947—; dir. Coca-Cola Bottling Works, Manchester, N.H., Coca-Cola Bottling Works of Dover, Del., Inc., Coca-Cola Bottling Works of Salem, N.H., Inc.; dir., sec. Coca-Cola Bottling Works of Henderson, N.C., 1970—; dental cons. N.C. Indsl. Com., 1970—; chmn. Local Bd. for Piloting, 1971; dental chief of staff Rex Hosp., Raleigh, 1958-60. Served with AUS, 1943-44, USNR, 1945-47. Mem. Raleigh Power Squadron, U.S. Power Squadron. Mem. N.C. (mem. ho. of dels. 1970-71), 4th Dist. (pres. 1971—), Raleigh (pres. 1956-57) dental socs., Kappa Alpha, Delta Sigma Delta. Democrat. Episcopalian. (pres. Layman League 1953-54). Clubs: Carolina Country, Sphynx, Raleigh Toastmasters (pres. 1950-51). Patentee Hypodermic syringe. Home: 3708 Shadybrook Dr Raleigh NC Office: 2016 Cameron St Raleigh NC 27605

SEIFERT, LEE ROE, banker; b. Mobile, Ala., Feb. 13, 1917; s. William Ross and Esther (McAuley) S.; student Spring Hill Coll., 1934-36; m. Dorothy Marie Goodman, July 16, 1942; children—Lee R., Gail (Mrs. Matthew J. Dick), William R. With First Nat. Bank of Mobile, 1937—, v.p., 1955-68, sr. v.p., 1968—; dir. Modern Diversified Industries Inc., Valdosta, Ga. Mem. consulting com. on forestry research Auburn U., 1963—; mem. regional export council Dept. Commerce, 1963—, Nat. Export Expansion Council, 1969—. Bd. dirs. Mobile Port Traffic Bur. Served to 2d lt., AAC, 1942-45. Mem. Internat. Trade Club (pres.), Ala. World Trade Assn. (v.p.), Bankers Assn. Fgn. Trade (past sec.). Nat. Def. Transp. Assn., Mobile Traffic and Transp. Club, Miss. Valley World Trade Assn., Mobile Area C. of C. Episcopalian. Clubs: Internat. House (New Orleans); Propeller of U.S., Mobile Country, Touchdown, Bienville, Three Mystic Socs. (Mobile). Home: 606 E Chelsea Dr Mobile AL 36608 Office: 31 N Royal St PO Box 1467 Mobile AL 36621

SEIGEL, ROBERT KEARNEY, motor lodge exec.; b. Bayonne, N.J., Mar. 16, 1942; s. Max and Margaret (Kearney) S.; student Seton Hall U., 1960-62, Fairleigh Dickinson U., 1962-63; m. Carol Wotanowski, Apr. 20, 1962; children—Scot K., Douglas K., Rodd K. Vice pres., dir. Max Seigel Realty Corp., Clifton, N.J., 1964-68; pres., dir. Continental Inns of Am., Savannah, Ga., 1968—; dir. Savannah Assos., Inc., Hilltop Motor Inn, Inc., Heart Charleston, C.I.A. Motor Lodge, Inc., Interstate Restaurant Supply Corp., Rodd Motel Corp., Savannah Motel, Inc., Scott-Douglas Corp. Clubs: Greater Metropolitan Dinners, Chatham (Savannah); University (Jacksonville, Fla.); Savannah Inn and Country; Shee Farms (Charleston, S.C.); Palmetto Dunes Country (Hilton Head, S.C.); Turf Valley Country (Balt.); XIX (London, Eng.). Home: Route 2 Box 356 Savannah GA 31404 Office: 3710 Ogeechee Rd Savannah GA 31405

SEIGENTHALER, JOHN LAWRENCE, newspaper editor; b. Nashville, July 17, 1927; s. John and Mary (Brew) S.; student Peabody Coll.; Nieman fellow, Harvard; m. Dolores Watson, Jan. 3, 1955; 1 son, John Michael. Staff corr. Nashville Tennessean, 1949-60, editor, 1962—, also pub.; adminstrv. asst. to atty. gen. U.S., 1961; dir. Tennessean Newspapers, Inc. Mem. U.S. Adv. Commn. Information. Bd. dirs. So. Edn. Reporting Service. Mem. Am. Soc. Newspaper Editors, Sigma Delta Chi. Home: Vaughn Rd Nashville TN 37221 Office: 1100 Broadway St Nashville TN 37203

SEILER, KARL, III, economist; b. Phila., Aug. 21, 1921; s. Karl Jr. and Marguerite (Auer) S.; B.S. in Econs., U. Pa., 1948; M.B.A., Temple U., 1957; m. Mary Louise Ashcraft, Oct. 2, 1948; 1 dau., Mary Beth. Chief economist def. div. RCA, Moorestown, N.J., 1955-64; mem. research staff Inst. for Def. Analyses, Washington, 1964-66; sr. economist Comsat. Corp., Washington, 1967; supr. operations research Lockheed Electronics Corp., Plainfield, N.J., 1968; bus.

systems cons. Bell Telephone Labs., New Brunswick, N.J., 1969—; adj. prof. Temple U., Phila., 1970; lectr., 1957-59; cons. USAAF Rand Corp., 1963; U.S. del. to 5th Internat. Conf. on Operations Research, Venice, Italy, 1969. Dir., Edn. Inst. Computer Command & Control Co., Phila., 1969. Served with USNR, 1943-46. Mem. Operations Research Soc. Am., Econometric Soc., Delta Kappa Epsilon, (dir. Delta Kappa chpt. 1956-59), Alpha Delta Sigma. Author: Introduction to Systems Cost-Effectiveness, 1969. Patentee in field. Contbr. papers to Operations Research Jour., German Operations Research Jour., others. Home: 1229 Old Stable Rd McLean VA 22101

SEINSHELMER, J(OSEPH) F(ELLMAN), JR., ins. exec.; b. Galveston, Tex., Aug. 25, 1913; s. J. F. and Irma (Kraus) S.; grad. Mercersburg Acad., 1932; B.B.A., Tulane U., 1936; m. Jessie Lee Gould, July 19, 1938; children—Joseph Fellman III, Virginia Lee, Robert Louis. Salesman, Seinsheimer Ins. Agy., 1936-41; with Am. Indemnity Group, 1941—, successively agy. mgr., asst. sec., sec., v.p., 1941-51, pres. dir., 1951—; pres., dir. Am. Indemnity Co., Am. Fire & Indemnity Co., Am. Computing Co., Tex. Gen. Indemnity Co., Am. Finance Co., Galveston, U.S. Securities Corp.; dir. Galveston Corp., Cotton Concentration Co., 2217 Bldg., Inc., Tex. Fibreglass Products, Inc., U.S. Nat. Bank, Galveston Engring. Tech. Inc. Clubs: Artillery, Galveston. Home: 4809 Woodrow St Galveston TX 77550 Office: 2115 Winnie St Galveston TX 77550

SEITH, ROBERT THEODORE, paper mill exec.; b. Racine, Wis., Aug. 12, 1926; s. Theodore Lewis and Ruth (Cleaver) S.; B.S. in Chem. Engring., Purdue U., 1949; m. Ruth Marilyn Sievert, Oct. 12, 1946; children—Michael Robert, Deborah Lynn, Elizabeth Jane. With Mosinee Paper Mills Co. (Wis.), 1949-69, successively research chemist, dir. product devel., sales mgr., 1957-61, v.p. marketing, 1961-69, exec. v.p. Celluponic System, Inc., 1962-69; v.p. marketing paper div. Gulf States Paper Corp., 1969—; dir. Bag West Paper Co., 1965-69, also dir. Shuld Mfg. Co. Active Children's Service Soc. Wis., Wis. Assn. for Mental Health. Co-chmn. Marathon County Republican Com., 1953. Served with AUS, 1944-46. Mem. Def. Supply Assn. (dir., past pres. Midwest), Salesmens Assn. Paper Industry (v.p. Wis. div. 1962-63 nat, pres. 1966—) Am. Paper Inst. (bd. govs.), Am. Legion, Bleached Converting Assn. (dir.), Kraft Paper Assn. (exec. com. 1960, mem. research and devel. com.), Am. Legion, Sigma Alpha Epsilon. Lutheran, Mason, Lion (pres. 1953-54). Author various articles profl. jours. Patentee in field. Home: 808 Indian Hills Dr Tuscaloosa AL 35401 Office: Holt Rd Tuscaloosa AL 35401

SEIWELL, PORTER WILLIAM, educator; b. St. Clair, Pa., Aug. 18, 1912; s. Homer Bartlet and Anna (Gicking) S.; A.B., Catawba Coll., 1935; B.D., Theol. Sem. of Evang. and Reformed Ch. at Lancaster (Pa.), 1938; D.D., Elon Coll., 1971;; m. Maria Elizabeth Long, June 21, 1939; children—Martha (Mrs. James C. Dayvault), Richard Joslin. Ordained to ministry Evang. and Reformed Ch., 1938; pastor Minersville-St. Cair Charge, Minersville, Pa., 1938-42, Grace Ch., Shippensburg, Pa., 1942-54, Ch. of the Redeemer Littlestown, Pa., 1954-57, First United Ch. Christ, Salisbury, N.C., 1957-60; campus pastor Catawba Coll., 1960—, asso. prof. religion, 1965—. Mem. Nat. Assn. Coll. and U. Chaplains, Am. Acad. Religion, Nat. Religious Edn. Assn. Home: 149 Lilly Av Salisbury NC 28144 Office: The Chapel Catawba Coll Salisbury NC 28144

SELBY, DONALD JOSEPH, educator; b. Kansas City, Mo., Feb. 7, 1915; s. Benjamin Wood and Evelyn May (Wharton) S.; A.B., William Jewell Coll., 1946; B.D., Andover Newton Theol. Sch., 1949; Ph.D., Boston U., 1954; m. Clarice Allene Beggs, June 10, 1939; children—Robert Wallace, Donald Lee. Ordained to ministry Congl. Ch., 1948; pastor, Pilgrim Congl. Ch., 1948-56; instr. Boston U. Sch. Theology, 1955-56; asso. prof. dept. religion Catawba Coll., Salisbury, N.C., 1956-61, prof., 1961—, chmn. dept., 1966—. Vis. prof. N.T., Hood Theol. Sem., 1957—. Mem. Soc. Bibl. Lit. and Exegesis, Am. Acad. Religion, Am. Schs. Oriental Research. Author: Toward the Understanding of St. Paul, 1962; Introduction to the New Testament, 1971. Home: 204 Maupin Av Salisbury NC 28144

SELBY, JOHN HORACE, surgeon; b. Springfield, Mass., Nov. 11, 1919; s. Howard Williams and Ethel (Wagg) S.; A.B., Dartmouth Coll., 1941; M.D., Boston U., 1944; postgrad. U. Pa., 1948; children (by previous marriage) John H., Susan, Sherrill, Lucinda; m. 2d, Carolyn Symes, Feb. 14, 1970. Intern Mary Hitchcock Meml. Hosp., Hanover, N.H., 1944-45; resident New Eng. Deaconess Hosp., 1945-46, Mass. Meml. Hosp., 1949-50, Boston City Hosp., 1950-51 (all Boston), practice medicine, specializing in thoracic surgery, Lubbock, Tex., 1952—; chief surgery Meth. Hosp., Lubbock; courtesy staff St. Mary's, W. Tex. hosps., Lubbock, Mercy Hosp., Slaton, Tex.; asso. clin. prof. Surgery Tex. Tech. Med. Sch.; trustee, med. dir. All Am. Security Life Ins. Co. Bd. dirs. Tex. Tb Assn., pres., 1967-68; bd. dirs. Lubbock Community Planning Council, 1954-56; chmn. adv. bd. Salvation Army, 1956-57; bd. dirs. Inst. for Internat. Research and Devel. Diplomate Am. Bd. Thoracic Surgery, Am. Bd. Surgery. Fellow A.C.S., Am. Coll. Chest Physicians, Internat. Coll. Surgeons; mem. So. Thoracic Surgery Assn., S.W. Surg. Conf., Am. Thoracic Soc., Tex. Trudeau Soc. (pres. 1959-60), Lubbock-Crosby County Med. Soc., Panhandle S-Plains Med. Soc., Tex. Med. Assn., A.M.A., Am. Cancer Soc. (dir. Tex. div.), S. Plains Heart Assn. (pres. 1957), Lubbock County Tb Assn. (pres. 1959-60). Home: Altura Towers 1617 27th St Lubbock TX 79405 Office: Med-Profl Bldg 3801 19th St Lubbock TX 79410

SELDEN, HARVEY FITZGERALD, dentist; b. Richmond, Va., Aug. 24, 1941; s. Edward Booker and Frances Ann (Madison) S.; B.S. in Math. cum laude, Hampden Sydney Coll., 1959; postgrad. (A.D. Williams Scholar 1967), Med. Coll. Va., 1967; m. Sharon Page Hollins, Aug. 13, 1943; children—Elizabeth Paige, Stephen Fitzgerald. Pvt. practice dentistry, Mechanicsville, Va., 1969—. Served to lt. Dental Corps, USNR, 1967-69. Mem. Am., Va., Richmond dental assns., Mechanicsville Jr. C. of C. (com. dir. 1970, dir. 1970-71), Bus. Mens Assn., Theta Chi, Psi Omega, Chi Beta Phi. Mem. Ch. of Christ. Rotarian (treas. 1970-71). Clubs: Ruritan (Mechanicsville); Confederate Hills Country Highland Springs, Va.). Home: 5721 Clark Circle Mechanicsville VA 23111 Office: 1020 Edgeworth Rd Mechanicsville VA 23111

SELDEN, RAY LEONARD, lawyer; b. Sinclairville, N.Y., Apr. 2, 1894; s. John Harris and Lora (Blackney) S.; LL.B., Hamilton Coll., 1920, J.D., 1930; m. Jeannette Ridgway, Apr. 11, 1914 (dec. 1965); children— Lois (Mrs. Al Brown), John Harris; m. 2d, Rhoda Fay, Sept. 24, 1967. Admitted to Fla. bar, 1920, Ga. bar, 1930, Ind. bar, 1930, U.S. Supreme Ct. bar; practiced in Daytona Beach, Fla., 1920—; mem. firms Selden, Hodgen & Couchman, 1929-36, Selden, Blackney & Williams, Inc., Daytona Beach, Fla., 1945—; pres., atty. Double R Dixie Ranch, Williston, Fla., 1957—, v.p., gen. counsel Fla. Mut. Fire & Marine Ins. Co., 1930—, Fidelity & Surety Co. Fla., Inc., Daytona Beach, 1945—. Dir., v.p. Dick E. Hotchkin Co., Inc., Daytona Beach. Chmn., Fla. Safety Council, Tampa. Chmn., Fla. Congl. Democratic Exec. Com., 1932-40; v.p. Fla. Electoral Coll., 1944-45. Mem. Am., Volusia County bar assns., Fla. Bar (recipient 50-year plaque), Internat. Soc. Tax Consultants, Saddle Horse Assn., Selden Soc. Eng., Epsilon Delta Chi. Democrat. Episcopalian. Elk, Odd Fellow, Moose. Clubs: Optimist (sec. 1952, pres. 1953), Exchange (sec. 1941) (Daytona Beach), University. Home: 800 Main St Daytona Beach FL 32018 Office: Selden Bldg Daytona Beach FL 32018

SELF, GLENDON DANNA, indsl. engr.; b. Waveland, Ark., Jan. 1, 1938; s. Charlie William and Alma (Vinesette) S.; Asso. Sci., Ark. Tech., 1956; B.S., U. Ark., 1958, M.S., 1959; Ph.D., Okla. State U., 1963; m. Sharon Darlene Glenn, June 4, 1960. Statis. quality control engr. Sandia Corp., Albuquerque, 1959-63; project analyst Gen. Dynamics, Ft. Worth, 1963-65; asst. prof. Tex. A. and M. U., College Station, 1965-66, 66-68, asso. prof., 1968-69; research specialist Boeing Co., Renton, Wash., 1966; tech. staff mem. Center for Naval Analyses, Arlington, Va., 1968; mgr. operations research Electronic Data Systems, Dallas, 1969-71, v.p. Dallas, 1971—; adj. prof. math. Tex. Christian U., 1964-65. Cons. in field. Mem. Operations Research Soc. Am., Inst. Mgmt. Sci., Am. Statis. Assn., Am. Soc. for Engring. Edn., Sigma Xi, Tau Beta Pi, Alpha Pi Mu. Baptist. Contbr. articles to profl. jours. Home: 6002 Village Glen Dr Dallas TX 75206 Office: 1300 Exchange Park Dallas TX 75235

SELF, JACKSON HOUSTON, dentist; b. Brownwood, Tex., Jan. 22, 1937; s. Houston B. and Juanita (Pentecost) S.; student McMurry Coll., 1955-59; D.D.S., U. Mo., 1964; m. Margie Louellen Burns, July 7, 1962; children—Mark Houston, Susan Melinda, Matthew Holt. Pvt. practice gen. dentistry, San Angelo, Tex., 1966—. Mem. Bd. of City Devel.; rep. to San Angelo Council of Chs., 1969—. Bd. dirs. Concho Valley Home for Girls, San Angelo; trustee Tom Green County Sch. Bd., 1970-72. Served to capt. USAF, 1964-66. Mem. Am., Tex. dental assns., Am. Soc. Preventive Dentistry, Am., Tex. acads. gen. dentistry, San Angelo Dist. Dental Soc., Psi Omega. Democrat. Methodist. Mason, Lion. Home: 3018 Woodland Circle San Angelo TX 76901 Office: 1897 Pecos St San Angelo TX 76901

SELF, MARGARET CABELL, author; b. Cin., Feb. 12, 1902; d. Hartwell and Margaret Polk (Logan) Cabell; student Chatham Hall, 1915-17, N.Y. Sch. Applied Design for Women, 1917-19; m. Sydney Baldwin Self, June 11, 1921; children—Sydney Baldwin, Shirley (Mrs. John O. Brotherhood Jr.), Hartwell C., Virginia (Mrs. Harris Bucklin). Portrait artist, 1923-38; author specialty, tech., children's and travel books related to horses, also lectr. relating to subjects; cons. Ecole Equiestre do San Miguel; musician mem. Chamber Orch. of San Miguel. Founder, commandant New Canaan Mounted Troop, Jr. Cavalry Am. Mem. No Friends of Music, Author: Teaching the Young to Ride, 1935; Horses, Their Selection, Care and Handling, 1943; Those Smith Kids, 1945; The Horseman's Encyclopedia, 1945; Ponies on Parade, 1945; Chitter Chat Stories, 1946; A Treasury of Horse Stories, 1946; Riding Simplified, 1948; Horseman's Companion, 1949; Horsemastership, 1953; Irish Adventure, 1954; Pictorial History of the Royal Canadian Mounted Police, 1958; The American Horse Show, 1958; Riding and Hunting Simplified, 1959; Jumping Simplified, 1959; Riding with Mariles, 1960; The How and Why of Horses, 1961; Horses of the World, 1961; Complete Book of Horses and Ponies; Riding Step by Step; The Happy Year; Horses of Today; The Shaggy Little Burro of San Miguel, 1965; The Horseman's Almanac, 1966; Henrietta, 1966; At the Horseshow with Margaret Cabell Self, 1966; In Ireland with Margaret Cabell Self, 1967; The Morgan Horse in Pictures, 1967; Come Away, 1968; The Quarter Horse in Pictures, 1969; The Young Rider and His First Pony, 1969; Sky Rocket, the Story of a Little Bay Horse, 1970; How to buy the right Horse, 1971; The Hunter in Pictures, 1972. Home: Block Island RI also San Miguel de Allende GTO Mexico

SELF, WILLIAM COLUMBUS, supt. schs.; b. Newton, N.C., Jan. 6, 1920; s. R.L. and Macie (Grigg) S.; A.B., Catawba Coll., 1941; M.A. in Sch. Adminstrn., U. N.C., 1948, Ed.D., 1955; m. Hilda Huggins; 1 dau., Leslie. Tchr. math. Reynolds High Sch., Winston-Salem, N.C., 1946-48; asst. prin. Forest Park Elementary Sch., Winston-Salem, 1948-53; prin. Ardmore Elementary Sch., Winston-Salem, 1953-55; dir. secondary edn. Winston-Salem City Schs., 1955-57, asst. supt., 1957-62; asso. supt. Charlotte (N.C.)-Mecklenburg Schs., 1962-67, supt., 1967—. Served with AUS, 1941-46. Recipient Liberty Bell award 26th Jud. Dist. Bar, 1971. Mem. Am. Assn. Sch. Adminstrs., N.E.A., So. Assn. Colls. and Schs. (exec. council commn. on colls.), N.C. Assn. Educators (Ednl. Leadership award Charlotte-Mecklenburg unit 1971), Phi Delta Kappa. Presbyn. Rotarian. Home: 5834 Kirkpatrick Rd Charlotte NC 28211 Office: 701 E 2d St PO Box 149 Charlotte NC 28201

SELFRIDGE, RALPH GORDON, educator; b. London, Eng., July 30, 1927; s. Harry Gordon and Charlotte Elsie (Dennis) S.; B.S., Mass. Inst. Tech., 1947; M.A., Cornell U., 1949; Ph.D., U. Ore., 1953; m. Iris Dunn, Aug. 5; 1965. Mathematician, Naval Ordnance Test Sta., China Lake, Cal., 1951-59; asso. prof. math., also dir. computing center, Miami U., Oxford, O., 1959-61; prof., dept. math. U. Fla., Gainesville, 1961—, dir. computing center, 1965—. Home: 4117 NW 36th Terrace Gainesville FL 32601

SELIGMAN, LEONARD JOSEPH, apparel mfg. co. exec.; b. Balt., Nov. 4, 1914; s. Nathan and Sara (Markell) S.; student Emory U., 1933-34, Atlanta Bus. U., 1935, Ga. Tech., 1938, Tulane U., 1943; m. Irene Gartner, Nov. 4, 1951. Mgr., Empire Theater, Atlanta, 1936-41; with N. Seligman & Co., Atlanta, 1945-51; co-founder Lad'n Dad Slacks, Alpharetta, Ga., 1951-56; with Bressler Bros., Inc., Atlanta, 1956—, 1st v.p., treas., 1961—; sec. Lee Mfg. Co., Newnan, Ga., 1962—. Instn. rep. Boy Scouts Am., 1958-60. Trustee Profit Sharing Fund, 1968—. Served with USAAF, 1941-45; ETO. Mem. Tau Epsilon Phi (past pres.), Ta Epsilon. Jewish religion. Club: Progressive (treas. 1967, dir. 1965-67) (Atlanta). Home: 29 Ivy Square Atlanta GA 30342 Office: PO Box 4204 Atlanta GA 30302

SELIGMAN, MOISE BENJAMIN, JR., paper co. exec.; b. Jacksonville, Tenn., Oct. 8, 1918; s. Moise B. and Lucille (Flynn) S.; B.A., Ouachita Bapt. U., 1941; postgrad. Army Command and Gen. Staff Coll., 1943; m. Mary Elizabeth Strong, Apr. 5, 1942; children—Susan (Mrs. Daniel Fuller), Moise Benjamin III, Mary Elizabeth. Pres., Ark. Paper Co., Little Rock, 1965—; v.p. Consol. Marketing Inc., Shreveport, La., 1969—, also dir.; v.p. Alco-Columbia Paper Co., New Orleans, 1967—; mem. adv. council Nekoosa-Edwards Paper Co., 1968—; v.p. Elms Realty Co. Mem. Little Rock Tollway Authority, 1968—. Bd. dirs. Met. YMCA, Little Rock. Served to lt. col., AUS, 1941-45. Mem. Res. Officers Assn. (Ark. pres. 1953), Little Rock C. of C. (dir. 1963-70, sec.-treas. 1969). Baptist. Kiwanian (local pres. 1967). Club: Pleasant Valley Country. Home: 1900 Beechwood Av Little Rock AR 72207 Office: 2000 E Roosevelt Rd Little Rock AR 72206

SELKIRK, GEORGE ALEXANDER, profl. baseball exec.; b. Huntsville, Ont., Can., Jan. 4, 1908; s. William and Margaret (Dykes) S.; ed. pub. schs.; m. Norma Fox, June 22, 1931; 1 dau., Betty Louise (Mrs. William G. Hine). Played in outfield N.Y. Yankees (succeeding Babe Ruth), 1934-45; appeared two All-Star Games, also 21 games World Series; minor league mgr., Newark, 1946; minor league mgr. and troubleshooter N.Y. Yankees, 1947-48; minor league mgr., Binghamton, N.Y., 1949-50, Kansas City Blues, 1951-52, Toledo, 1953-55, Wichita, Kan., 1956; field coordinator Kansas City Major League Club, 1957-61; field coordinator Balt. Orioles, 1961-62; gen. mgr. Washington Senators Baseball Club, 1962—. Served as aerial gunnery officer A.C., USNR, 1942-45. Mason (32 deg., Shriner). Home: 8484 16th St Silver Spring MD 20918 Office: DC Stadium 22d and E Capital St Washington DC 20003

SELLERS, FRED COURT, accountant; b. Ft. Worth, Jan. 19, 1924; s. James Henry and Etta (Court) S.; student U. Houston, 1940-43; m. Ray Vina Aucoin, Oct. 24, 1942; children—Fred Court, Sharon Ann. Sr. accountant United Gas Corp., Houston, 1941-59; self-employed, Houston, 1959—; sec.-treas. Merc. Investment Corp., 1965-72. Chmn. Houston C.P.A.'s Speakers Bur. 1969-71. Pres. Harris County Youth Scholarship Found. Served with USAAF, 1943-46. Recipient Key Man award Jr. C. of C., 1948. Mem. Am. Inst. C.P.A.'s, Tex. Soc. C.P.A.'s. Baptist (deacon). Clubs: Optimist (v.p., dir. 1959-65), Rotary. Home: 11601 Green Oaks St Houston TX 77024 Office: 3915 Essex Lane Houston TX 77027

SELLERS, GENE MARION HERRICK (MRS. MATTHEW BACON SELLERS), civic worker; b. Salt Lake City, Nov. 10, 1922; d. Harold Lewis and Marion (Wheelon) Herrick; student Traphagen Sch. Fashion, 1941-42; m. Matthew Bacon Sellers, June 1, 1946; children—Wendy (Mrs. Henry Medford Howell), Tracy. Bd. mem. Friends of Fort Lauderdale Mus. Arts, 1969. Committeewoman Broward County Republican Exec. Com., 1967—. Club: Coral Ridge Yacht (Ft. Lauderdale). Home: 3030 NE 40th Ct Fort Lauderdale FL 33308

SELLERS, JACK LEROY, telephone co. exec.; b. Blackwell, Okla., Feb. 18, 1933; s. Charley and Lela Jewell (Wood) S.; B.S., Okla. State U., 1956; m. Maureen Vere Matthews, June 2, 1956; children—Kevin Lamont, Dana Matthew, Michael Kent, Melinda Michelle. Instr. electronics Okla. State U., 1956; with Southwestern Bell Telephone Co., 1956—, staff asst., Oklahoma City, 1956, 1958-59, wire chief, Henryetta, Okla., 1959, plant foreman, Ponca City, Okla., 1960, wire chief, Enid, Okla., 1961-62, dist. engr., Bartlesville, Okla., 1962-63, supervising repair foreman, Tulsa, 1963-64, dist. plant supt., Bartlesville, Okla., 1965-68, personnel devel. supr., Oklahoma City, 1969, mgmt. devel. supr., Oklahoma City, 1969—. Pack chmn. Cub Scouts Am., Bartlesville, 1968; active Boy Scouts Am., 1970—; dir., sec. Bartlesville Fed. Little League Baseball, 1966-68. Served to 1st lt. Signal Corps, AUS, 1956-58. Mem. Bartlesville Engring. Club (dir. 1965-68), Okla. Soc. Profl. Engrs. (chpt. com. chmn. 1965-68), Beta Theta Pi. Mem. Disciples Christ Ch. (deacon 1965-68, elder 1971-72). Club: Toastmaster (v.p. 1966-67). Home: 3129 Brookhollow Rd Oklahoma City OK 73120 Office: 707 N Robinson St Oklahoma City OK 73102

SELLS, HARRY GEORGE, lawyer; b. Bellaire, O., Sept. 25, 1922; s. Harold W. and Leeta (Spengler) S.; student Wheeling Coll. Commerce, 1941-42; A.B., U. Pitts., 1949; J.D., George Washington U., 1953; m. Dorothy M. Sells, Sept. 6, 1946; children—Deborah M., David M. (dec.). Admitted to D.C. bar, 1954; law clk. Dow, Lohnes & Albertson, Washington, 1950-54, asso., then jr. partner, 1954-58, partner, 1958-63; partner Sells & Gregory, Counsellors at Law, Washington, 1964—. Officer, dir. Prince William Broadcasting Corp., Manassas, Va., 1957—, Stalcup Furniture Co., Falls Church, Va., 1959—; WQVA, Inc., Quantico, Va., 1961—, WISZ, Inc., Glen Burnie, Md., 1964—; trustee Boston Celtics basketball team. Justice of peace Dranesville Magisterial Dist., Fairfax, Va., 1956-60. Served with USAAF, 1942-45. Mem. Va. State, D.C. bars, Am., D.C., Fed. Communications bar assns., Falls Church C. of C., Nat., Va., Md., Ohio assns. broadcasters, Chesterbrook Citizens Assn. (past pres.), Delta Theta Phi. Methodist (ofcl. bd. 1954—, trustee). Home: 1453 Laburnum St McLean VA 22101 Office: 2000 L St NW Washington DC 20036

SELLS, JAMES WILLIAM, ret. clergyman; b. Atchison, Kan., June 27, 1897; s. James LeGrande and Clara (Hull) S.; A.B., Millsaps Coll., 1929; LL.D., LaGrange Coll., 1955; D.D., Emory U., 1964; m. Vera Maude Britt, Jan. 13, 1921; 1 dau., Shirley Jeanne (Mrs. J. Robert Adams) (dec.). Ordained to ministry Meth. Ch., 1916; ordained deacon Miss. Annual Conf., 1927, elder, 1929; supply pastor Taylorsville (Miss.) Meth Ch., 1920-21, Georgetown (Miss.) Meth. Ch., 1921-23; supply pastor Meth. Ch., Pascagoula, Miss., 1925, pastor, 1925-29; pastor Meth. chs., Summit, Miss., 1929-30, Ocean Springs, Miss., 1930-32, Forest, Miss., 1932-36, Hattiesburg, Miss., 1936-40, Crystal Springs, Miss., 1940-44; field sec. Whitworth-Millsaps Coll., 1930; exec. sec. Seashore Meth. Assembly, Biloxi, Miss., 1930-32; producer Meth. series The Protestant Hour, Atlanta, 1945-72, Southeastern Jurisdictional Council, 1945-72; dir. Joint Radio Com., 1945-72; pres. Spiritual Life Publishers, Inc., Atlanta, 1966—, Communicative Arts, Inc., 1970—; rural ch. editor Progressive Farmer, 1944-67, exec. dir. Inst. Communicative Arts, Inc., 1960-69, pres., 1969—; vis. prof. Candler Sch. Theol., Emory U., 1964. Bd. dirs. Protestant Radio and Tv Center, Atlanta, Hinton Rural Life Center, Hayesville, N.C., Paine Coll., Augusta, Ga.; pres. Spiritual Life Research Found. Served with USN, 1917-19. Recipient Rural Minister of the Year award, 1965. Mem. Nat. Meth. Rural Life Conf. (sec. 1947), Miss. Rural Life Council (sec. 1944-45). Author: How God Can Change Your Life; Effective Communication—the Person to Person Process. Home: 457 Burlington Rd NE Atlanta GA 30307 Office: 1380 Oxford Rd NE Atlanta GA 30307

SELMAN, WILLIAM LAURIE, clergyman; b. Sylvania, Ga., May 20, 1918; s. Roland Wooton and Augusta (Burch) S.; A.B., U. Chattanooga, 1947; B.D., Southwestern Bapt. Theol. Sem., 1949; m. Marjorie Shedd Brown, Apr. 13, 1941; children—Marjorie Demcie (Mrs. C. John Re), Augusta Anne, William Laurie. Ordained to ministry Bapt. Ch., 1947; minister First Bapt. Ch., Ringgold, Ga., 1949-51, Northside Dr. Ch., Atlanta, 1951-57, Celeenese Bapt. Ch., Rome, Ga., 1951-59, First Bapt. Ch., Ft. Oglethrope, Ga., 1959-63, First Bapt. Ch., Cuthbert, Ga., 1963-71, West Bainbridge Bapt. Ch., 1971—; headmaster The Oaks Acad., Bainbridge, Ga., 1971—. Mem. exec. com. Ga. Bapt. Conv., 1949—; pres. Bethel Assn. Minister's Conf., 1965, 68, Rome Ministers Assn., 1959, Catoosa Ministers, 1949; instr. speech Andrew Coll., Cuthbert, 1964-68. Chmn., Ga. Bapt. Hosp. Fund Assn., 1948. Served with AUS, 1942-45; ETO. Home: 801 Griffin St Bainbridge GA 31717

SELOVER, JOHN CHARLES, r.r. exec.; b. Pueblo, Colo., Feb. 13, 1911; s. Alpheus Olin and Mary (Robertson) S.; B.A., U. Kan., 1932; m. Mary Elizabeth Livingston, Nov. 4, 1939; children—Paul Nicholas, Stephanie Lynne (Mrs. Maurice Wilson), Timothy Lee, Andrea Marie (Mrs. Darrel Aldrich), Robin Livingston. With M.P. R.R., 1936—, asst. to v.p. traffic, St. Louis, 1962-63, traffic mgr. Western region, Kansas City, Mo., 1963-68, v.p. Tex. dist., Dallas, 1968—; pres., dir. Mchts. Cold Storage Co., Eagle Ford Land & Indsl. Co.; dir. Abilene & So. Ry., Ft. Worth Belt Ry. Co., Gt. S.W. R.R., Inc., Tex.-N.M. Ry. Co., Weatherford-Mineral Wells & Northwestern Ry. Mem. Transp. Club Dallas. Democrat. Presbyn. Clubs: Dallas City, Dallas Athletic. Home: 5533 Meletio Lane Dallas TX 75230 Office: Fidelity Union Tower Dallas TX 75201

SELPH, WILLIAM FRANKLIN, JR., lawyer; b. Laurel, Miss., May 23, 1929; s. William Franklin and Oris (Clegg) S.; B.B.A., U. Miss., 1950, J.D., 1954; m. Ella N. White, Dec. 15, 1950; children—Deborah, William Franklin III. Admitted to Miss. bar, 1954, with land div. Shell Oil Co., New Orleans and Baton Rouge,

1954-57; mgr. adminstrv. div., The Atlantic Refining Co. (U.S., Can.), Dallas, 1957-62; practiced in Jackson 1962—; mem. firm Binder, Bush & Selph, 1962-69, Youngblood & Selph, 1969—. Hon. col. Gov.'s staff, Paul B. Johnson, 1964-68, John Bell Williams, 1968-72. Served to capt. Inf., AUS, 1950-52; ETO. Mem. Am., Miss., Hinds County bar assns., Am. Judicature Soc., Jackson C. of C., Am. Assn. Petroleum Landmen, V.F.W., Phi Delta Phi, Omicron Delta Kappa, Pi Kappa Alpha. Episcopalian (vestryman). Home: 5420 Runnymede Rd Jackson MS 39211 Office: Capitol Towers PO Box 1567 Jackson MS 39205

SEMTNER, ROY HERMAN, lawyer; b. Oklahoma City, Apr. 13, 1924; s. Otto William and Jennie Bob (Fullbright) S.; A.B., St. Benedicts Coll., 1946; J.D., U. Okla., 1948; m. Patricia Ann Schooling, Dec. 27, 1946; children—Karl Bernard, Christopher Benedict, Nicholas Otto, Roy Herman, Thomas Russell. Admitted to Okla. bar, 1948; pvt. practice law, Oklahoma City, 1948—; asst. county atty., Oklahoma County, 1949-53; municipal judge, Oklahoma City, 1956-58, asst. municipal counselor, 1958-61, municipal counselor, 1961—. Trustee Oklahoma City Municipal Improvement Authority. Dir. Oklahoma City chpt. Nat. Conf. Christians and Jews. Mem. Holy Child Sch. Adv. Bd., St. Vincents Home Adv. Bd. Mem. Okla. (mem. com. legal internship 1968—, mem. com. real property 1969-70), Am., (council local govt. sect. 1965—, com. on liaison with Nat. Inst. Law Officers 1965-71, Oklahoma City meeting, chmn. 1972, editor Newsletter 1968—, adv. bd. to editor The Urban Lawyer 1969—), Oklahoma County (dir. 1968-71) bar assns., Okla. Municipal League (mem. com. legislation 1968—), Bar ICC, Cath. Lawyers Soc. (v.p. 1960), Oklahoma City Soc. Title Attys. (pres. 1971), Oklahoma City Title Attys. Assn. (pres. 1972), Okla. Assn. County Attys. (pres., 1952), Okla. Assn. Municipal Attys. (pres. 1963-64), Nat. Inst. Municipal Law Officers (regional v.p. 1966—, state chmn. 1965-66, chmn. annexation com. 1966—), Oklahoma City (pres. 1960, dir. 1961), Nat. (dir. 1960) alumni St. Benedicts Coll., Oklahoma Diocesan Confraternity Christian Doctrine (v.p. 1959, pres., dir. 1960), C. of C., Tyro Players, Phi Delta Phi. Roman Catholic. K.C. (4 deg., grand knight 1953-55, state sec. 1953-59; state adv. 1959-61, state dep. 1961-63), Lion. Clubs: Gibbons Dinner (pres. 1957), Serra (vice pres. 1959) (Oklahoma City). Home: 828 NW 34th St Oklahoma City OK 73118 Office: Municipal Bldg Oklahoma City OK 73102

SENCER, DAVID JUDSON, physician; b. Grand Rapids, Mich., Nov. 10, 1924; s. Martin J. and Helen (Furniss) S.; student Wesleyan U., Middletown, Conn., 1942-44; M.D., U. Mich., 1951; M.P.H., Harvard, 1958; m. Jane P. Blood, Aug. 25, 1951; children—Susan, Ann, Stephen. Intern Univ. Hosp., Ann Arbor, Mich., 1951-52, resident, 1952-54; med. officer USPHS, 1955-60, asst. chief, 1960-62, dep. chief, 1962-66, dir. Center for Disease Control, Atlanta, 1966—; prof. Emory U. Sch. Medicine; vis. lectr. Harvard Sch. Pub. Health; cons. WHO. Served with USNR, 1944-46; to asst. surgeon gen. USPHS, 1955—. Recipient Meritorious Service award USPHS, 1968. Diplomate Am. Bd. Preventive Medicine. Fellow Am. Pub. Health Assn.; mem. A.M.A., Am. Tropical Medicine Soc., Am. Thoracic Soc. Home: 892 Clifton Rd Atlanta GA 30307 Office: 1600 Clifton Rd Atlanta GA 30333

SENDER, HENRY HERMAN, bldg. corp. exec.; b. Saar, France, Jan. 13, 1925 (came to U.S. 1938, naturalized 1943); s. Arthur and Lilly (Salomon) S.; B.C.E., Vanderbilt U., 1949; m. Pauline Cohen, June 7, 1947; children—Lauren Elyse, Randall Gary. Chief engr. R.E. Dunn Co., 1949-51, partner, 1951-55; with Bloomfield Bldg. Industry, 1955-64, exec. v.p., 1960-64; chief exec. officer Nat. Bldg. Corp., Nashville, 1964—, chmn. bd., 1964—; dir. Vernon Corp., Huntsville, Ala. Dir. Indsl. Commn. City of Albuquerque, 1965-67. Col. aide de Camp to Gov. Jack M. Campbell, 1965—. Served to capt., C.I.C., 1943-46. Decorated Purple Heart, Bronze Star medal. Registered profl. engr. Mem. Am. Soc. C.E., Zionists Am. (pres. 1967-69). Jewish religion (pres. West End synagogue). Mason (32 deg., Shriner), Elk. Home: 4302 Lillywood Rd Nashville TN 37205 Office: Pkwy Tower Nashville TN 37219

SENNING, CHARLES EUGENE, banker; b. Spur, Tex., July 28, 1922; s. Clem Alifare and Adelaide (Finch) S.; B.S., Tex. Tech. U., 1944, M.S., 1945; postgrad. Grad. Sch. Banking, So. Meth. U., 1968-70; m. Marilyn Gay, July 27, 1949; children—Charles Bain, Thomas Mark. Co-owner Charles Lee Co., Austin, Tex., 1948-52; co-owner Compere & Senning, Abilene, Tex., 1953-62; mgr. United Improvement & Investing Corp., N.Y.C. and Houston, Tex., 1962-65; v.p., mgr. real estate dir. Tex. Commerce Bank, Houston, 1966-72; exec. v.p. Guaranty Mortgage, Inc., Jackson, Miss., 1972—. Chmn. Abilene Tax Equalization Bd., 1961. Mem. Soc. Real Estate Appraisers (dir. Houston chpt. 1970-72, pres. W. Tex. chpt. 1962-63), Houston C. of C., Soc. Master Brokers Tex. (past pres.), Nat. Assn. Mortgage Bankers. Episcopalian. Mason. Author: Houston Industrial Development: A Pattern for the Future, 1970. Home: 12606 Rip Van Winkle St Houston TX 77024 Office: Deposit Guaranty Bldg Jackson MS 39201

SENOUR, CHARLES, ret. cons. civil engr.; b. St. Louis, Apr. 30, 1892; s. Harry Koch and Mary (Clase) S.; B.S. in Civil Engring., Washington U., 1915; m. Alice E. Richmond, June 10, 1916; 1 son, John Charles. With U.S. Corps Engrs., Miss. River Commn., 1915-50, surveyor, St. Louis and Vicksburg, Miss., 1915-17, jr. engr., 1917-23, asst. engr., 1923-26, asso. engr., 1926-29, engr., 1929-30, sr. engr., 1930-36, prin. engr., 1936-41, head engr., 1941-45, chief civilian engr., asst. to pres. Miss. River Commn., div. engr. Lower Miss. Valley div. Corps Engrs., 1945-50; pvt. practice as cons. civil engr., Texarkana, Tex., 1950-53, N.Y.C., 1953-55, Coral Gables and Miami, Fla., 1955-69. Fellow Am. Soc. C.E.; mem. Sigma Nu. Christian Scientist. Home: 6400 SW 123d Terrace Miami FL 33156

SENTENEY, CHESTER THOMAS, farmer; b. Weiner, Ark., Sept. 9, 1913; s. Thomas Jasper and Mary (Schisler) S.; grad. pub. high sch.; m. Belva Huber, Mar. 28, 1937; children—Daisy (Mrs. Paul Joseph Matthews), Martha. Farmer, Weiner, 1936—; charter mem. bd. Ark. Rice Growers Coop., Weiner, 1948-72, pres., 1967-72. Chmn. Weiner Dist. 2 Sch. Bd., 1949-64. Trustee Memphis Christian Coll. Mem. Christian Ch. (elder, chmn. bd.). Mason (32 deg.). Home: PO Box 266 Weiner AR 72479

SENTER, JAMES D., JR., lawyer; b. Humboldt, Tenn., Apr. 28, 1905; LL.B., Vanderbilt U., 1928. Admitted to Tenn. bar, 1928, since practiced in Humboldt; city atty., 1950-55, 57-60, 62-63; mem. Adv. Commn. on Rules of Civil Procedure; spl. justice Tenn. Supreme Ct., 1968. Served to lt. comdr. USNR, 1942-45. Mem. Am., Tenn. (mem. central council 1948-49, 54-56; v.p. 1957-58, 67-68; pres. 1969-70), West Tenn. (v.p. 1957-58), Gibson County (pres. 1949, 63-64) bar assns. Office: Main Street Corp Bldg Humboldt TN 38343*

SENTER, WILLIAM DONALD, ins., real estate exec.; b. Aspermont, Tex., May 11, 1930; s. Earl E. and Elizabeth (Jordan) S.; B.B.A., Tex. Tech. Coll., 1951; grad. Realtors Inst.; m. Lila Ellexson, May 27, 1950; children—Bill Scott, Steven Earl, Sydney Ann. Salesman South Plains Drug, Inc., Lubbock and Midland, Tex., 1951-53; area mgr. A. H. Robins Co., Midland, 1953-56; partner Wicker-Senter Ins. & Real Estate, Abilene, 1956-62; owner Senter & Senter, Ins. and Real Estate, 1962—; pres. Abilene Leasing Corp., Wicsen, Inc., W.E.B., Inc.; treas. Tom Sports Co.; v.p. Chaparral Homes, Inc. Mem. gov.'s legislative study com. on multiple use and pollution of all waters in Tex., 1965-67. Named Outstanding Young Man of Abilene, 1962. Mem. Assn. Ins. Agts., Abilene Assn. Ins. Agts. (pres.), Abilene Bd. Realtors (pres.), Nat. Inst. Real Estate Brokers, Abilene C. of C. Democrat. Mem. Christian Ch. Mason (32 deg., Shriner, K.T.). Clubs: Abilene Country, Exchange (Abilene, Tex.). Home: 2918 Ventura Abilene TX 79605 Office: 2901 S 1st St Abilene TX 79605

SEOANE, RHODA LOW, artist, author; b. Bklyn.; d. William Gilman and Rhoda (Howe) Low; grad. Chapin Sch., N.Y.C., 1923; m. Consuelo Andrew Seoane, Feb. 12, 1952. Artist; works exhibited Argent Gallery, N.Y.C., 1946—, Lynn Kottler Gallery, N.Y.C., 1967, Arts Club Washington, 1969—. Mem. Colonial Dames Am. Clubs: York (N.Y.C.); Army and Navy (Washington). Author: The Whole Armor, 1965; Uttermost East and The Longest War, 1969. Home: Topton NC 28781

SEPMEYER, MERLIN WILLIAM, sign maintenance co. exec.; b. Edwardsville, Ill., Sept. 22, 1925; s. William Conrad and Louise (Lubbert) S.; student St. Louis U., 1947-48; A.B., Valparaiso U., 1950; m. Betty Jane Grogitsky, Aug. 28, 1948; children—Kristen Louise, Mary Ann. Various mgmt. positions Ford Motor Co., Dearborn, Mich. 1950-67; v.p., asst. sec., asst. to pres. Cummings & Co., Nashville, 1967—. Mem. adv. bd. Salvation Army, 1959-63; mem. businessmen's adv. bd. Middle Tenn. State U., 1969—; mem. adv. council Nat. Women's Exec. Soc., 1971—. Served with USCGR, 1943-46; PTO, ETO. Mem. C. of C., Nat. Elec. Sign Assn. (dir.). Lutheran (v.p. Tenn. dist. Layman's League 1970-71, pres. 3 chs. 1951, 67, 70). Home: 817 Highland Park Ct Nashville TN 37205 Office: 200 12th Av S Nashville TN 37203

SERANT, JOYCE IDELL BIRKELBACH, ins. co. exec.; b. Brenham, Tex.; d. Harry A. and Ruby (Nagel) Birkelbach; student Southwestern U., 1946-47, U. Houston, 1947-48; B.A., U. Tex., 1950; m. William Boris Serant, Dec. 5, 1953 (div. Mar. 1958); 1 son, Michael W. Sec.-treas., dir. Old Nat. Ins. Co., 1950-62; office mgr. Gulf Coast Home Builders, Inc., 1962-64; v.p., sec., dir. Lamar Livestock Ins. Co., 1964-66; v.p., sec., dir. San Jacinto Life Ins. Co., 1966— (all Houston); dir. Tex. Pet Cemeteries, Inc., San Jacinto Funeral Services, Inc., So. States Investment Corp. (all Houston). Mem. Alpha Delta Pi. Home: 2051 Winrock St Houston TX 77027 Office: PO Box 66196 Houston TX 77006

SEROTTA, ELLIOTT CECIL, accountant; b. Savannah, Ga., July 1, 1912; s. Abram J. and Dora (Lewis) S.; student Jr. Coll. Augusta, Ga. 1929; B.S. in Commerce magna cum laude, U. Ga., 1931; m. Eve Dorothy Robinson, Feb. 18, 1940; children—Betty Jayne, Abram Jacob. Adminstrv. positions Augusta Arsenal, 1935-46; pvt. practice accounting, 1946-52; partner firm Bell and Serotta, C.P.A.'s, Augusta, 1952-55; owner accounting firm, Augusta, 1955-71; pres. Serotta, Madlocks & Serotta, C.P.A.'s, 1971—; asst. sec. Stapleton Garment Inc., asst. sec., dir. Richmond Shippers, Inc., Augusta, Benson Mfg. Co.; dir. Kamo Mfg. Co. Inc., Marks Realty Co., Sales Agts., Inc. Co-founder, dir. Southeastern Research Found. Lectr. on various subjects, 1952—; lectr. Minority Bus. Enterprises, 1970; moderator, participant radio-TV C.P.A. Internal Revenue Service Income Tax Information Programs, 1953-60. Head adviser Aleph Zadik Aleph, 1934-52, adviser emeritus, 1952—, So. regional dept., 1937-42; organizer troop 18 Boy Scouts Am., 1940, committeeman, 1940, treas., troop committeeman, 1959. Bd. dirs. YMHA Augusta, 1937-42, 57; trustee Maxwell J. and Naomi P. Estroff Found., Belle S. Marks Found., Libby Fink Found., Hannah Simowitz Found. Recipient commendation certificate for 10 years service Army Service Forces, 1945. C.P.A., Ga. Mem. Am. Inst. C.P.A.'s (pub. relations com. 1954-56), Ga. Soc. C.P.A.'s (pres. Augusta chpt. 1952-54, regional v.p. bd. trustees 1952-54, trustee at large 1956-58 chmn. pub. relations com., 1953-55, chmn. history and archives com. 1959-64, chmn. profl. and trade group cooperation com., mem. bull. com., mem. com. assistance to minority bus. Enterprises 1970-71), Augusta C. of C. (chmn. adminstrv. com. 1958), Beta Gamma Sigma, Beta Alpha Psi, Phi Kappa Phi. Jewish religion (financial sec. 1950-53). Mason (32 deg., chmn. pub. relations com. 1963—), Elk; mem. B'nai B'rith (pres. Augusta 1937; chmn. youth orgn. com. Augusta, vice chmn. So. region adult div.). Clubs: Toastmaster (pres. Augusta 1951), Optimist chmn. publicity com., vice-chmn. youth appreciation com. 1963-64) (Augusta). Reviewer, Auditing Handbook, 1971. Home: 3101 Ramsgate Rd Augusta GA 30904 Office: 500 Bldg Augusta GA 30902

SERRANO, ALBERTO CARLOS, physician, educator; b. Buenos Aires, Argentina, Apr. 7, 1931 (came to U.S. 1957, naturalized 1962); s. Alberto P. and Regina (Robredo) S.; B.A., Colegio Mariano Mereno, 1948; M.D., U. Buenos Aires, 1956; m. Maria Nidya Pages, June 15, 1957; children—Marcos Alberto, Henry John, Claudia Ingrid, Christopher William. Resident psychiatry U. Tex. Med. Br., Galveston, 1957-60, resident child psychiatry, 1962-64, research psychiatrist, 1959-62, asst. prof. div. child psychiatry, 1964-66; dir. Community Guidance Center, Bexar County, Tex., 1966—; clin. asso. prof. U. Tex. Med. Sch., San Antonio, 1966—, dir. child psychiatry, 1969—. Served with Argentine Army, 1954. Diplomate in psychiatry and child psychiatry Am. Bd. Psychiatry and Neurology. Mem. A.M.A., Am. Psychiat. Assn., Am., Southwestern (pres. 1969-71) group psychotherapy assns., Soc. Adolescent Psychiatry, Tex. Child Psychiatry Soc. (soc.-treas. 1969-70), Author: (with R. MacGregor et al) Multiple Impact Therapy with Families, 1964. Home: 927 Fabulous St San Antonio TX 78213 Office: 2135 Babcock St San Antonio TX 78229

SERRANO, ERNEST E., physician; b. Tampa, Fla., Oct. 29, 1913; s. Ernest C. and Matilde (Gomez) S.; A.B., U. Ala., 1933; M.D., Washington U., St. Louis, 1938; m. Mary B. Burgess, Nov. 21, 1938; children— Ernest E., Paul. Intern St. Louis County Hosp., 1938-39; resident St. Joseph's Hosp., Parkersburg, W.Va., 1940; practice medicine, specializing in family medicine, Hollywood, Fla., 1946—; sr. staff mem. Meml. Hosp., Hollywood, Hollywood Drs. Hosp., Broward-Holy Cross Hosp., Fort Lauderdale. Mem. Tb Soc., 1946—, Am. Heart Assn., 1948—. Served with USNR, 1939-46. Decorated Atlantic Star. Mem. Am., Broward County (pres.), Fla. med. assns., Phi Chi. Democrat. Roman Catholic. K.C. Home: 1230 Jackson St Hollywood FL 33020 Office: 1643 Hollywood Blvd Hollywood FL 33020

SERVIES, JAMES ALBERT, librarian; b. Lafayette, Ind., Sept. 2, 1925; s. Byron Beatty and Mildred Margaret (Boonstra) S.; Ph.B., U. Chgo., 1946, M.A., 1949; m. Ruth Janet Oostmeyer, Sept. 27, 1945; children—Janet Lynn, Jeanne Ann. James Albert, John Edward. Asst. to circulation librarian U. Miami, Coral Gables, Fla., 1949-53; reference and circulation librarian Coll. William and Mary, 1953-57, librarian, 1957-66; dir. libraries U. West Fla., Pensacola, 1966—. Served with AUS, 1945-46. Mem. Southeastern, Va. library assns., Va. Hist. Soc., Phi Gamma Delta. Democrat. Methodist. Editor: The Three Charters of the Virginia Company of London, with seven related documents, 1606-1621, 1957, co-editor: The Poems of Charles Hansford, 1961. Compiler: A Bibliography of John Marshall, 1956; (with E. G. Swem and J. M. Jennings) A Selected Bibliography of Virginia, 1607-1699, 1957. Home: 60 Rockwood Rd Pensacola FL 32504

SESSIONS, CLIFF, journalist; b. Bolton, Miss., Sept. 26, 1931; s. Valentine Hunter and Daisy (Farr) S.; B.S., U. So. Miss., 1955; m. Shirley Edwards, Dec. 31, 1952; children—Carol, Steven. Successively announcer, news reporter, program mgr. radio sta. WFOR, Hattiesburg, Miss., 1952-57; staff reporter, then mgr. Jackson (Miss.) bur., U.P.I., 1957-64; staff reporter, Washington bur. U.P.I., 1964-66; with Dept. Justice, 1966-69, dir. pub. information, spl. asst. to atty. gen., 1967-69; mng. editor Nat. Jour., Washington, 1969—. Served with AUS, 1951-52. Mem. Sigma Delta Chi. Home: 7702 Granada Dr Bethesda MD 20034 Office: 1730 M St NW Washington DC 20036

SESSIONS, GEORGE PURD, physician; b. Dawson, Ga., July 9, 1931; s. George Purdee and Jessie (Ferguson) S.; student Ga. Southwestern Coll., 1948-50, U. Ga., 1950-51; M.D., Med. Coll. Ga., 1955; m. Martha Ann Hernandez, June 30, 1960; children—William Dean, Neal Bradley, Annette Elaine. Intern, Macon (Ga.) Hosp., 1955-56; resident Charity Hosp., New Orleans, 1958-60; instr. dept. anesthesia Emory U., Atlanta, Ga., 1960-61; chief dept. anesthesiology DeKalb Gen. Hosp., Decatur, Ga., 1961—, Scottish Rite Hosp. for Children, Decatur, 1965—; pres. DeKalb Anesthesia Assos., P.A., 1970—. Served with USPHS, 1956-58. Diplomate Am. Bd. Anesthesiology. Mem. A.M.A., DeKalb County, Ga., So. med. assns., Am., Ga. socs. anesthesiologists, Theta Kappa Psi. Home: 1658 Mason Mill Rd NE Atlanta GA 30329 Office: PO Box 33306 Decatur GA 30033

SESSIONS, JOHN MORRIS, banker; b. Balt., Mar. 8, 1911; s. John M. and Irene (Hellman) S.; ed. U. Va., Columbia; m. Ellen Guard, Apr. 7, 1945; children—Michael A., Patrick E. Loan Officer Bank of Silver Springs (Md.), 1945-49, Nat. Met. Bank, Washington, 1949-51; exec. v.p., dir. First Nat. Bank of Miami (Fla.), 1950—; chmn. bd. Coral Way Nat. Bank, First City Bank, Tampa; dir. 1st Nat. Bank Miami Springs (Fla.), First Fgn. Investment Corp. Miami. Served as capt. USAAF, World War II. Decorated D.F.C., Air medal (U.S.), Legion of Honor (France). Mem. Miami C. of C. Democrat. Episcopalian. Clubs: Riviera Country, Miami (Miami). Home: 1230 Mendavia Av Coral Gables FL 33146 Office: 100 Biscayne Blvds Miami FL 33131

SESSIONS, MARK WILLIAM, supt. schs.; b. Babcock, Ga., Feb. 14, 1907; s. James Henry and Geta (Johnson) S.; A.B., Mercer U., 1938; M.Ed., U. Ga., 1942; specialist in edn., 1964; m. Jane Lucile Pope, July 29, 1939; children—Cindy (Mrs. Robert Roser), Herman. Prin., Terrell High Sch., Dawson, Ga., 1947-54, Jonesboro (Ga.) High Sch., 1954-56, Waynesboro (Ga.) High Sch., 1956-63, Waynesboro (Ga.) Elementary Sch., 1963-68; supt. Burke County, (Ga.) Schs., Waynesboro, 1969—. Mem. Burke County Bd. Health, 1969-72. Mem. N.E.A., Ga. Assn. Sch. Adminstrs. (pres. 1964-65). Ga. Assn. Educators, Ga. Assn. Sch. Supts., Kappa Delta Pi. Methodist (mem. adminstrv. bd). Rotarian. Home: 517 Sunset Dr Waynesboro GA 30830 Office: 840 Academy Av Waynesboro GA 30830

SESSUMS, THOMAS TERRELL, lawyer; b. Daytona Beach, Fla., June 11, 1930; s. Thomas L. and Dorothy (Cornwall) S.; B.A., U. Fla., 1952, LL.B., 1958; m. Neva Ann Steeves, Aug. 16, 1958; children—Thomas T., Richard H., Sandra Lynn. Admitted to Fla. bar, 1958; asso. Hardee & Ott, Tampa, 1958-60; partner Albritton, Sessums & Grandoff, Tampa, 1961—. Mem. Fla. Ho. of Reps., 1963—, speaker pro tem, 1968-70. Served to capt. USAF, 1954-56. Mem. Greater Tampa C. of C. (com. 100), Am. Bar Assn., Fla. Bar. Clubs: Davis Island Yacht, University, Kiwanis. Home: 1113 Dunbar Av Tampa FL 33609 Office: 1st Fed Bldg Tampa FL 33602

SETO, YEB JO, elec. engr., educator; b. China, July 31, 1930; s. Jo Ting and Shee (Chang) S.; came to U.S., 1951, naturalized, 1962; B.S., U. Ida., 1957; M.S., U. Wash., 1960; Ph.D., U. Tex., 1964; m. Jane Mei-Chun Wong, Feb. 14, 1958; children—Samuel K., Susanna L. Research engr. Boeing Airplane Co., Renton, Wash., 1957-60; instr. U. Houston (Tex.), 1960-61, asst. prof., 1964-66; instr. U. Tex., Austin, 1961-63; prof. elec. engring. Tulane U., New Orleans, 1966—, dir. electrosci. and biophysics research group, 1969—. Pres., dir. Applied Research Corp., New Orleans, 1967-71, Sealong, Inc., New Orleans, 1971—. Served with AUS, 1953-55. Recipient NASA-Am. Soc. Engring. Edn. fellowship, 1964, 65. Mem. I.E.E.E., Profl. group on Antenna, Propagation (sect. chmn. 1967—), Sigma Xi, Tau Beta Pi, Eta Kappa Nu. Contbr. sci. articles to profl. jours. Home: 4824 Purdue Dr Metairie LA 70003 Office: Tulane U New Orleans LA 70118

SETSER, WINFRED AUGUSTUS, JR., banker; b. Tulsa, Mar. 13, 1929; s. Winfred Augustus and Katherine (Owens) S.; B.S., U. Tulsa, 1955; postgrad. So. Meth. U., 1965; m. Joanne Marie Gilger, June 28, 1952; 1 dau., Sandra JoAlyce. Mgr. civic and govt. affairs Tulsa C. of C., 1956-59; dir. pub. relations Tex. Nat. Bank Houston, 1959-64; v.p., mgr. marketing Bank of S.W. Houston, 1964-68; sr. v.p., dir. marketing 4th Nat. Bank Tulsa, 1968—, Instr., Am. Inst. Banking, 1964-66. Treas., dir. Houston Internat. Fair, 1965-66; chmn. Econ. Devel. Commn. Tulsa, 1969—; treas. Tulsa-Rogers County Port Authority, 1971—. Bd. dirs. Downtown Tulsa Unltd.; bd. dirs., chmn. Tulsa Jr. Coll. Found., 1971—. Served with USAF, 1950-54. Recipient Silver Anvil award Pub. Relations Soc. Am., 1961. Mem. Bank Pub. Relations and Marketing Assn. (western U.S, chmn. 1969—), Tulsa C. of C., Ark. Basin Devel. Assn., U. Tulsa Alumni Assn. (pres. 1970-71), Pi Kappa Alpha. Kiwanian. Clubs: Summit, Propeller, Sales Executives of Tulsa; Cedar Ridge Country. Home: 67-7 S 71st E Av Tulsa OK 74133 Office: 515 S Boulder St Tulsa OK 74119

SEVERY, MERLE EUGEN, editor; b. Los Angeles, Aug. 3, 1922; s. William Carlson and Enid (Severy) Smith; A.B., Columbia, 1942, M.A., 1948, postgrad., 1949-52; m. Teresa Bookholz, 1942 (div. 1951); 1 son, Alan Wayne; m. 2d, Patricia Aman, 1951; children—Randall Carlson, Karen Linwood, Melissa Adams, Leslie Burnett. Asso. editor, trade book div. Prentice-Hall, Inc.; spl. projects editor Doubleday and Co.; sr. editor A.A. Wyn, Inc., 1950-53; mem. editorial staff Nat. Geog. Soc., 1954—, chief Nat. Geog. book service, 1957—. Served with AUS, 1942-46; ETO. Recipient awards Dog Writers' Assn. Am., 1959, Freedoms Found., 1962, Chgo. Book Clinic, 1963, 64, Art Dirs. Club Met. Washington, 1963, 67, 68, 69, 70. Mem. Am. Hist. Assn., Mediaeval Soc. Am., Renaissance Soc. Am., Haukluyt Soc., Am. Inst. Graphic Arts Club. Nat. Press (Washington). Co-author: Danger is My Destiny, 1955. Editor: Indians of the Americas, 1955; The World in Your Garden, 1957; The National Geographic Book of Dogs, 1958; America's Wonderlands, 1959; Wild Animals of North America, 1960; America's Historylands, 1962; Men, Ships, and the Sea, 1962; Great Adventures with National Geographic, 1963; Song and Garden Birds of North America, 1964; Water, Prey, and Game Birds of North America, 1965; This England, 1966; Everyday Life in Bible Times, 1967; Greece and Rome: Builders of Our World, 1968; The Age of Chivalry, 1969; The Renaissance: Maker of Modern Man, 1970; Vacationland USA, 1970; (with others) American College Dictionary, 1947. Contbr. articles to Nat. Geog. Home: 8814 Chalon Dr Bethesda MD 20034

SEVIER, FRANCIS ALOYSIUS CHARLES, lawyer, mathematician; b. Phila., Sept. 16, 1924; s. Francis A. and Carmelia (D'Angelo) S.; student LaSalle Coll., 1942-44; B.S., U. Pa., 1947, M.S., 1947, Ed.D., 1955; postgrad, U. Buffalo, 1952-53, Rutgers U., 1957; J.D., Temple U., 1961, LL.M., 1966; postgrad. U. Miami, 1965; m. Natalie F. Magill, Nov. 16, 1957. Instr. math. Pa. State U., 1947-51; aerodynamicist Bell Aircraft Corp., Buffalo, 1951-53; systems engr. Glenn L. Martin Co., Little River, Md., 1953; asst. prof., chmn. dept. math. Rutgers U. Coll. of S.Jersey, 1953-57; asso. prof. math. Glassboro (N.J.) State Coll., 1957-58; applied math., mgr. digital computation RCA, Moorestown, N.J., 1958-63; admitted to Fla. bar, 1962, D.C. bar, U.S. Supreme Ct. bar; practiced in Miami, 1963—; trial lawyer, sr. partner Stephens, Magill, Thornton & Sevier; dir. Applied Math. Program at RCA, Villanova U., 1961-63; vis. prof. math. West Chester (Pa.) State Coll., 1961-63, Dade County Jr. Coll., Miami, 1963-68; vis. lectr. applied math. Wayne State U., 1956; lectr. actuarial math. Pa. Mut. Life Ins. Co., Phila., 1957-59; lectr. law Dade County Jr. Coll., 1965, U. Miami Sch. Medicine, 1969; cons. Burroughs Corp., 1956-58, Raytheon Corp., 1956-57, Westinghouse Air Arm, 1955. Served with A.C., USNR, 1942-44. Recipient Sara Shull award in legal writing, 1961. Mem. Am., Fla., Dade County bar assns., Am., Fla. trial lawyers assns., Am. Arbitration Assn., Operations Research Soc. Am., Am. Assn. U. Profs., Am. Math, Assn., U. Pa., Temple U. alumni assns., Def. Research Inst., Nat. Intercollegiate Soccer Ofcls. Assn., Phi Beta Kappa, Kappa Phi Kappa. Contbr. articles profl. jours. Home: 9400 SW 62d Ct Miami FL 33156 Office: Biscayne Bldg Miami FL 33130

SEVIER, JAMES, ceramic tile co. exec.; b. Asheville, N.C., Jan 29, 1918; s. Joseph Thomas and Caroline (Rollins) S.; B.S. in Ceramic Engring., N.C. State U., 1941; m. Ilma Claire LaBar, Dec. 11, 1941; children—Christy Noelle (Mrs. Richard Francis Whitfield), James Rollins, Frank LaBar, John Kibler Buchanan. Plant mgr. W.S. George Pottery Co., Cannonsburg, Pa., 1946-48; exec. v.p. So. Potteries, Inc., Erwin, Tenn., 1948-57; v.p. Stylon Corp., Florence, Ala., 1957-68; pres. Mosaic Tile Co., Florence, 1968-70; v.p. DCA Devel. Corp., Florence, 1970—. Served to lt. comdr. USNR, 1941-45. Fellow Am. Ceramic Soc.; mem. Nat. Inst. Ceramic Engrs. Kiwanian, Rotarian. Home: 1842 Hermitage Dr Florence AL 35630 Office: 833 Rickwood Rd Florence AL 35630

SEVISON, ELWOOD (WOODY) FRANKLIN, city govt. ofcl.; b. Eysburg, Pa., Nov. 30, 1925; s. Sherman David and Grace (Boop) S.; student Lamar Coll., 1957; m. Mary Lee Yeakel, May 5, 1946; children—Linda (Mrs. Jim Thibodeaux), Bonnie (Mrs. Dale Cuthbertson), Candance, Elwood Franklin. Mem. fire dept., Port Arthur, Tex., 1948-50; adviser fire and safety crew, instr. safety dept. Tex. U.S. Chem. Co., Port Meches, 1950-57; safety supr. Firestone Petro Chem. Co., Orange, Tex., 1957-58; safety engr. Hydro-Carbon Research Co., Athens, Greece, 1958-60; fire marshall, Groves, Tex., 1960-66; fire chief Tex. A. and M. U., College Station, 1966-70, City of College Station, Tex., 1970—. Officer Tex. Arson Conf., 1960—; v.p. Jefferson County chpt. March Dimes, 1963-66; bd. dirs., coordinator disaster and rescue Civil Def., Jefferson County, 1960-66, bd. dirs., Brazos County, 1967—; instr. Rescue Sch., Brazos County, 1967—. Served with USNR, 1944-46. Recipient Community Service awards Groves, Tex., 1958, Am. Legion, 1970, Kiwanis Club, 1970. Mem. Tex. Jr. C. of C. (v.p. 1962), Nat. Gun and Safety Program (chmn. 1957). Methodist. Mason, Optimist (charter mem., treas. 1971-72). Home: Apt 203 700 Dominik Dr College Station TX 77840 Office: PO Box 9960 100 Gilchrist St College Station TX 77840

SEWELL, GRANVILLE CLARK, assn. exec.; b. Lexington, Ky., Oct. 7, 1898; s. James Witt and Elizabeth (Kidd) S.; student Vanderbilt U., 1916-18, Tulane, 1919-20; m. Everall Burdon, June 20, 1925; children— Marianne (Mrs. Warwick Aiken, Jr.), Granville H., John Burdon. Copy chief Chambers Advt. Agy., New Orleans, 1922-33; mgr. Walker Saussy Advt. Agy., New Orleans, 1933-44; pres., owner Sewell Advt. Agy., New Orleans, 1945-65; mgr. Picayune (Miss.) C. of C., 1965—. Instr. advt. copywriting Tulane U., New Orleans, nights, 1950-53. Chmn. budget com. New Orleans Community Chest, 1955; mgr. Picayune United Fund, 1971-72. Served with U.S. Army 1918. Mem. New Orleans Assn. Advt. Agys. (founder 1960, pres. 1960-63). Episcopalian. Mason, Rotarian. Clubs: Orleans Camera, Delta Camera. Home: 1229 Stemwood Dr Picayune MS 39466 Office: Chamber of Commerce 201 Hwy 11 N Picayune MS 39466

SEWELL, HARVEY WELDON, physician; b. Wills Point, Tex., Nov. 10, 1916; s. Julian T. and Ola (Norman) S.; student U. Tex. at Austin, 1933-35; M.D., Baylor U., 1939; m. Charlene Spoonts, Apr. 2, 1942; children— Betty, Anne (Mrs. Clay Johnson), Robert. Intern Parkland Hosp., Dallas, 1939-40, resident surgery, 1940-41; practice medicine, specializing in gen. practice, Belton, Tex., 1941—; health officer Bell County, 1950—. Co-owner Salado (Tex.) Galleries, 1970—. Mem. Belton Sch. Bd., 1961-64. Methodist (steward). Lion (pres.). Home: 402 E 14th St Belton TX 76513 Office: 205 N Pearl St Belton TX 76513

SEWELL, HARVEY WILSON, JR., banker; b. Houston, Aug. 23, 1934; s. Harvey Wilson and Georgia Frances (George) S.; B.S., U. Houston, 1961; m. L. Joan McClain, Sept. 18, 1965; 1 dau., Amy Elizabeth. Loan service officer Med. Center Nat. Bank, Houston, 1961-64; asst. v.p. mortgage loan dept. Western Nat. Bank, Amarillo, Tex., 1964-66; v.p. Republic Nat. Bank, Houston, 1966—; dir. tool technologists, Inc. Mem. Houston C. of C. Republican. Club: Neighborhood Civic (Houston). Home: 12458 Barryknoll St Houston TX 77024 Office: 5200 N Shepherd St Houston TX 77018

SEWELL, WARREN PALMER, clothing mfg. exec.; b. Graham, Ala., Oct. 29, 1888; s. Willis Columbus and Willie (Gay) S.; student pub. schs., Graham; m. Ava Lee Fowler, June 19, 1912; children—Frances Sewell (Mrs. Lamar R. Plunkett), Charlotte (Mrs. Jack W. Worley), Warren Palmer. Formerly traveling salesman for John E. Hurst, Balt.; pres. Warren Sewell Clothing Co., Bremen, Ga., 1947—; v.p. Comml. and Exchange Bank, Bremen, 1945—; pres. Monroe Mfg. Co. (La.), 1944—; chmn. bd. Hubbard Pants Co., Higgins Slacks, Lineville, Ala.; dir. Comml. Bank, Bowdon, Ga., Bank of Canton (Ga.). Mem. Cotton Producers Assn. Inc. Atlanta (pres.). Baptist. Home: Fairview Av Bremen GA 30110 Office: Warren Sewell Clothing Co Bremen GA 30110

SEWELL, WILLIAM LAMAR, clergyman; b. Birmingham, Ala., Sept. 9, 1912; s. William Lunsford and Elizabeth (Watkins) S.; student Clarke Meml. Coll., 1933-35; B.A., Miss. Coll., 1937; Th.M., New Orleans Bapt. Theol. Sem., 1941, Th.D., 1944; m. Willie Maude Reeves, Oct. 11, 1931; children—Evelyn Joyce (Mrs. Charles Raymond Muller), Carol Ann (Mrs. Millard A. Beason, Jr.). Ordained to ministry Baptist Ch., 1934; pastor Prentiss (Miss.) Ch., 1944-48, First Ch., Bossier City, La., 1948-59; asso. exec. sec. La. Bapt. Conv., 1959—, pres., 1952-54, chmn. exec. com., exec. bd., 1956-57. Trustee Acadia Bapt. Acad., So. Bapt. Theol. Sem., La. Bapt. Exec. Bd., Clarke Meml. Coll. Lion. Home: 103 Hill Top Pineville LA 71360 Office: 1250 MacArthur Dr Alexandria LA 71301

SEXTON, CLAUDE LEE, dentist; b. Lillington, N.C., Aug. 29, 1899; s. William and Laura (Johnson) S.; student Emory U. Dental Sch., 1920-24; m. Kathryn Melvin, June 29, 1927; 1 dau., Kathryn Elizabeth (Mrs. Dennis Williams). Practice dentistry, Florence, S.C., 1925—; owner, partner Sexton-Shealy Dental Clinic, 1925—. Active with underpriviliged children and patients at Tb San., also chmn. bd. Mem. Tenn. Breeders Assn. Cows and Horses, Xi Psi Phi. Methodist (chmn. bd. 1963-64, chmn. bd. Christians 1959-63). Mason (Shriner), Elk, Moose, Kiwanian (lt. gov. 1951-52, pres. Florence chpt. 1942-43). Home: 1403 W Palmetto St Florence SC 29501 Office: 377 W Palmetto St Florence SC 29501

SEXTON, IRWIN, librarian; b. Lafayette, Ind., Nov. 7, 1921; s. Orville C. and May Della (Hayth) S.; B.S. in Trade and Indsl. Edn., Purdue U., 1949; M.S. in L.S., Western Res. U., 1952; m. Kathryn Segee, Nov. 24, 1950; 1 son, David. Dir. St. Joseph (Mo.) Pub. Library, 1955-57, Oklahoma City Libraries, 1958-60, San Antonio Pub. Library, 1961—. Pres., St. Joseph Mental Health Assn., 1957. Served with USAAF, 1942-46. Mem. Am., Tex. library assns. Clubs: Rotary (dir. St. Joseph 1957); San Antonio Torch. Author: Industrial Techniques for the School Shop, 1955. Home: 603 Cobble Dr San Antonio TX 78216 Office: 203 S St Marys St San Antonio TX 78205

SEXTON, JAMES EDWARD, dentist; b. Knoxville, Tenn., Mar. 2, 1936; s. Charles Orin and Pauline (Wade) S.; D.D.S., U. Tenn., 1962; m. Patricia Anne Dillon, Nov. 24, 1961; children—James Edward II, Gregory Scott, Stephen Barrett. Individual practice dentistry, Memphis, 1964—. Asst. dist. commr. Boy Scouts Am., Memphis, 1966-68. Vice chmn. bd. mgmt. Davis YMCA. Served with USAF, 1962-64; maj. Tenn. Air N.G., 1967—. Mem. Am., Tenn. dental assns., Acad. Gen. Dentistry, Memphis Dental Soc., Memphis Dental Legion, Am. Soc. Dentistry for Children, Gideons Internat., Whitehaven Dental Study Club (pres. 1970), Phi Sigma Kappa, Delta Sigma Delta. Republican. Baptist (deacon). Mason. Home: 4021 Mary Lee Dr Memphis TN 38116 Office: 4299 Elvis Presley Blvd Memphis TN 38116

SEXTON, OSWELL STANTON, sch. adminstr.; b. Oneida, Tenn., Mar. 21, 1908; s. Caswell and Rachel R. (Cecil) S.; B.S., Tenn. Technol. U., 1937; M.S., U. Tenn., 1951; m. Rema Jeffers, Aug. 17, 1929; children—O. Sibley, Curtis, Donna Kay (Mrs. Robert L. Tallent), Ray Owen, Dwight David, Ella Rachel. Tchr., prin., elementary schs. Scott County, Tenn., 1927-37; coach Robins (Tenn.) High Sch., 1937, prin., 1937-46; edn. supr. Scott County (Tenn.) Schs., 1946; prin. Huntsville (Tenn.) High Sch., 1946-55, Madisonville (Tenn.) High Sch., 1955-64, Cohutta (Ga.) Elementary Sch., 1964—; instr. Hercules Powder Co., Chattanooga, 1942. Chmn. war fund A.R.C., Scott County, 1943-44; dir. Sabin-Polio Clinic; dir. Monroe County Heart Assn.; chmn. ednl. dept. United Appeal Fund Drive, Whitfield County, 1968. Mem. town council Town Cohutta, Ga., 1969—. Life mem. N.E.A.; hon. life mem. Tenn. Edn. Assn.; mem. Internat. Platform Assn., Ga. Edn. Assn., Ga. Elementary Principals Assn., Nat. Assn. Secondary Sch. Prins., Monroe County Ednl. Assn. (pres. 1959-60), Whitfield County Adminstrs. Ednl. Assn. (pres. 1968), Phi Delta Kappa. Baptist (deacon). Mason; mem. Order Eastern Star. Clubs: Lions (pres. Madisonville 1960); Ruritan (dir.) (Cohutta, Ga.). Home: PO Box 38 Cohutta GA 30710

SEXTON, VINCENT LEGRAND, JR., judge; b. Pocahontas, Va., Mar. 21, 1902; s. Vincent LeGrand and Leola (Alderson) S.; student Coll. William and Mary, 1922-25; m. Mildred Morris, Apr. 12, 1932; children—Vincent LeGrand III, William Morris. Admitted to Va. bar, 1925; practiced law, Bluefield, Va., 1925-46; town atty. Bluefield, 1942-45; trial justice Tazewell County (Va.), 1942-45; judge 22d Jud. Circuit Va., Tazewell, 1946—. Dir. Bluefield Office Bldg. Co., 1946—. Mem. Pi Kappa Alpha, Omicron Delta Kappa. Democrat. Presbyn. (elder). Rotarian. Home: S College Dr Bluefield VA 24605 Office: County Court House Tazewell VA 24651

SEYDEL, JOHN RUTHERFORD, chem. co. exec.; b. Jersey City, May 16, 1918; s. Paul Bernard and Mildred (Woolley) S.; student in chem. engring. Ga. Inst. Tech., 1935-37; m. Jane Reynolds, Dec. 30, 1937; children—Elizabeth (Mrs. John Lewis Morgan), Scott O'Sullivan, Susan (Mrs. Susan Cofer), Mildred Woolley. With Eagle & Phenix Cotton Mills, Columbus, Ga., 1937; with Penn Mut. Life Ins. Co., Atlanta, 1937-38; with Seydel-Woolley & Co., Atlanta, 1938—, v.p., div. sales mgr., 1951-61, exec. v.p., 1961, pres., 1962—; v.p., dir., mem. exec. com. Mar Gold Margarine Corp., 1948-58; dir. Pot-O-Gold Dairy Stores, Atlanta, AZ Products, Inc., Lakeland, Fla. Active fund drives United Appeal. Trustee Seydel-Wooley Found.; chmn. bd. trustees Vasser Woolley Found.; trustee Seydel-Woolley Pension Trust. Mem. Textile Research Inst., Sigma Chi. Episcopalian. Rotarian. Clubs: Piedmont Driving, Commerce (Atlanta). Home: 1027 Peachtree Battle Av NW Atlanta GA 30327 Office: 762 Marietta Blvd NW Atlanta GA 30318

SEYDELL, MILDRED (MRS. MAX SEYDEL), writer, lectr., traveler; b. Atlanta; d. Vasser and Elizabeth Cobb (Rutherford) Woolley; ed. Washington Sem., Atlanta, The Lucy Cobb Inst., Athens, Ga., and Sorbonne, Paris; m. Paul Bernard Seydel (dec.); children—Paul Vasser, John Rutherford; m. 2d, Max Seydel. Columnist Charleston (W.Va.) Gazette, 1921; rep. Hearst Crime Commn., in Europe, 1926, collecting data for series of articles and interviews; traveled in Belgium and Ireland, 1927, in Balkan States, Hungary, Turkey and Greece, 1929, Sweden, Germany and France, 1931; contributed Talks with Celebrities; made spl. study of liquor regulation in Sweden; traveled through Africa from Capetown to Cairo and into Palestine, 1934; made spl. study of history of diamonds and gold in S. Africa and native customs of Belgian Congo, investigation of activity of Jews in Palestine; adventure in friendship to South Sea Islands, New Zealand and Australia, 1937; Internat. News Service rep. in Germany and Czechoslovakia, 1938, Finland, 1939; corr. U.S. papers; adventures in Europe, 1955, Eng., Wales, 1956; pres. Mildred Seydell Pub. Co. Belgian dir. World Poetry Day. Mem. Ga. Mothers Com.; v.p. Meml. Day Com. Mem. Tape Talk Internat. (pres.), Nat, League Am. Pen Women, Ga. Press Assn., Internat. Periodic Press (dir. poetry Belgian sect.), Assn. Des Journalistes Periodiyues Belges et Etrangers (hon.), Friends of Emory U. Library (hon.), Beta Sigma Phi (hon.). Clubs: Peony Garden (hon.); American Women's (Brussels). Author: Secret Fathers, 1930; Chins Up, 1939; Come Along to Belgium, 1969. Editor: Poetry Profile of Belgium, 1960. Publisher: Silent Singing (poems); Essays Wise and Otherwise. Mem. adv. bd. Sunshine Mag., Fellowship in Prayer mag. Home: 3183 Argonne Dr NW Atlanta GA 30305

SEYFFERT, WILLIS ADOLPH, JR., physician; b. Joplin, Mo., Sept. 9, 1934; s. Willis Adolph and Wanda (Poulson) S.; B.A., Tex. Western Coll., 1955; M.D., U. Tex. Southwestern Med. Sch., 1959; m. Judith Marie Spencer, Dec. 12, 1959; children—Willis Adolph III, Frederick Poulson. Intern, VA Hosp., Dallas, 1959-60, resident, 1960-61; resident Parkland Meml. Hosp., Dallas, 1964-65; research fellow metabolic diseases dept. internal medicine Southwestern Med. Sch., 1965-66; pvt. practice medicine, specializing in internal medicine and endocrinology, El Paso, Tex., 1966—; cons. internal medicine Thomason Gen. Hosp., El Paso; chief of staff Providence Meml. Hosp., El Paso, 1970. Treas., councilman Yucca council Cub Scouts pack 2 Boy Scouts Am., 1969—. Served to capt. AUS, 1962-64. Diplomate Am. Bd. Internal Medicine. Fellow A.C.P.; mem. El Paso County Med. Soc. (sec. 1971-72), Matrix Soc., A.M.A., Am. Heart Assn., Am. Soc. Internal Medicine, So. Med. Assn., El Paso County Med. Soc. Rotarian. Home: 3707 Laguna Ct El Paso TX 79902 Office: Coronado Towers 6006 N Mesa El Paso TX 79912

SEYMOUR, RAYMOND BENEDICT, educator, cons., chem. engr.; b. Boston, July 26, 1912; s. Walter A. and Marie E. (Doherty) S.; B.S., U. N.H., 1933, M.S., 1935; Ph.D., State U. Ia., 1937; postdoctoral Rensselaer Poly. Inst., 1963, U. Utah, 1964; m. Frances B. Horan, Sept. 16, 1936; children—David Ray, Susan (Mrs. Howard Smith), Peter, Phillip Alan. Instr. chemistry U. N.H., 1933-35, U. Ia., 1935-37; research chemist Goodyear Tire & Rubber Co., Akron, O., 1937-39; chief chemist Atlas Mineral Products div. Electric Storage Battery Co., Mertztown, Pa., 1939-41, exec. v.p., gen. mgr., tech. dir., 1949-54, pres., dir., 1954-55; research group leader Monsanto Co., Dayton, O., 1941-45; dir. research, U. Chattanooga, 1945-48; dir. research Johnson & Johnson, New Brunswick, N.J., 1948-49; pres., tech. dir. Loven Chemical of Cal., 1955-58; pres. Corrosion Resistant Products, Inc., 1956-57; pres., chmn. bd. Alcylite Plastics & Chem. Corp., 1958-60. Prof. chemistry, chmn. sci. div. Sul Ross State U., 1959-64; asso. chmn. chemistry dept. U. Houston. 1964-66, coordinator polymer chemistry, 1964—, asso. prof. chemistry, 1964-69, prof., 1969—, asso. dir. research, 1966-68. Cons. edn. AID, U.S. Dept. State, E. Pakistan, 1968. Dir. NSF Inst., 1965. Registered profl. engr., Tex., Ohio. Recipient Western Plastics award, 1960. Fellow A.A.A.S., Am. Inst. Chemists, Tex. Acad. Sci.; mem. Am. Inst. Chem. Engrs., Am. Chem. Soc. (Southeastern Tex. Ann. award 1972), Soc. Plastics Industry, Nat. Assn. Corrosion Engrs., Am. Soc. Oceanography, Am. Assn. U. Profs., Soc. Plastic Engrs., Houston Soc. Scientists and Engrs., Sigma Xi, Alpha Chi Sigma, Gamma Sigma Epsilon. Rotarian. Club: Golfcrest Country (Houston). Author: National Paint Dictionary, 3d edit., 1948; Plastics for Corrosion Resistant Applications; 1955; Hot Organic Coatings, 1959; Introduction to Polymer Chemistry, 1971; General Organic Chemistry, 1971; Experimental Organic Chemistry, 1971; Ann. Plastic Review 1948—; also articles. Patentee in field. Mem. exec. reserves Dept. Def. Home: 4830 Rockwood Dr Houston TX 77004

SHACKELFORD, HARRY CARL, ednl. adminstr.; b. Durham, Ark., Oct. 18, 1905; s. Mondrel Ellington and Sarah Elizabeth (Hobbs) S.; B.S., John Brown Coll., 1929; B.A., Northeastern State Coll., 1950; M.Ed., Phillips U., 1955; m. Reta Pritchard, Feb. 25, 1944; 1 son, James. Tchr. pub. schs., Kan., Okla., 1929-39; supt. schs. Delaware County (Okla.), 1941-44, Laverne, Okla., 1947—. Mem. Okla. Bd. Edn., 1963—. Mem. Okla. Ho. of Reps., 1939-41. Mem. N.W. Okla. Tchrs. Assn. (pres.), Laverne C. of C. Mason, Lion. Home: Box 632 Laverne OK 73848 Office: Box 40 Laverne OK 73848

SHACKELFORD, HERSHEL CARTWRIGHT, bank dir.; b. Gloucester County, Va., Feb. 3, 1910; s. John Matthew and Alice Senora (Hogge) S.; student Norfolk Bus. Coll., 1929-30; m. Minnie Katherine Hogge, May 5, 1934; children—Hershel Cartwright, Nancy (Mrs. James Arthur Jones III). With Bank Gloucester (Va.), 1931-44, dir., 1936—; pres. H.C. Schackelford & Sons, Inc., Goucester Point, 1944—; dir. United Realty Corp., Hayes, Va. Mem. Va. Oil Men's Assn., Va. Petroleum Jobbers Assn., Ruritan Club Abingdon. Democrat. Baptist (trustee, deacon). Mason, Rotarian. Home: Gloucester Point VA 23062 Office: Bank Gloucester Gloucester VA 23061

SHACKELFORD, LENORE GOLDEN (MRS. HERBERT D. SHACKELFORD), guidance counselor; b. Quitman, Ga., Apr. 17, 1929; d. A. Z. and Corine (Golden); B.S., Savannah State Coll., 1950; M.Ed., Fla. A. and M. U., 1959; postgrad. Tenn. A. and I. U., summer 1966, Extension U. Ga., 1969; m. Herbert D. Shackelford, Dec. 24, 1954; children—Herbert D.; 1 step-son Phillip D. Tchr., Morven Rosenwald Elementary and High Sch., Morven, Ga., 1950-54, New Empress Elementary Sch., Quitman, Ga., 1955-59; tchr., counselor Washington St. High Sch., Quitman, Ga., 1959-63, guidance counselor Brook County Jr. High Sch., Quitman, 1963—, cons. home econs. com., 1968-70. Mem. Tri-County Mental Health Program, 1967-68; vice chmn. Brooks County Community Action Com.; mem. adv. bd. Day Care Center; mem. Interagy Mental Health Com. Sec., Tri-County Savings Club, 1962-70. Named hon. counselor U.S. Naval Acad., Annapolis, Md., 1972. Mem. Ga. Tchrs. and Edn. Assn. (dept. asst. sec. 1967-68), Am., Ga. personnel and guidance assns., Am. Sch. Counselor Assn., Baptist (trustee, clerk 1969-70). Mem. Order Eastern Star. Home: 801 S Walker St Quitman GA 31643

SHACKELFORD, LYNE MONCURE, banker; b. Orange, Va., May 22, 1914; s. Virginius Randolph and Peachy Gascoigne (Lyne) S.; grad. Woodberry Forest Sch., 1932; student U.S. Mil. Acad., 1932-34, Hampden-Sydney Coll., 1935; B.S., U. Va., 1938; m. Elizabeth Burrow, Oct. 2, 1948; 1 son, Lyne Moncure. With Nat. Bank & Trust Co., Orange, Va., 1952—, cashier, 1961-70, v.p., 1962—. Trustee Stuart Hall, Inc., Staunton, Va., 1960—. Served to maj. AUS, 1941-46. Decorated Bronze Star (U.S.); Croix de Guerre with palm (Belgium); Medaille de la Reconnaissance (France); Cross of Merit (Poland); knight Order Crown of Italy (Italy); Medal of Merit (Czechoslovakia). Rotarian. Home: 151 Landon Lane Orange VA 22960 Office: 185 Madison Rd Orange VA 22960

SHACKFORD, ROLAND HERBERT, fgn. corr.; b. Westbrook, Me., Mar. 13, 1908; s. Marvin L. and Edith M. (Bodkin) S.; B.S., Antioch Coll., 1931; m. Augusta McMurray, Jan. 31, 1936; children—Kristin (Mrs. Frederic B. Ruckdeschel), John S., James L. Corr. with United Press, N.Y.C., 1935-37, Washington, 1937-43, diplomatic corr., 1943-48, gen. European news mgr., London, Eng., 1948-52; European corr. Scripps-Howard Newspapers, 1952-54, diplomatic corr., Washington, 1954-66, Asian corr., Hong Kong, 1967-68, diplomatic corr., D.C., 1968—. Author twice weekly column, Report on Red China, 1964-68. Recipient Journalism award Nat. Headliners Club, 1946, Lawrence S. Mayers Peace award, 1955, and William the Silent award for journalism, 1960. Clubs: National Press, Overseas Writers (Washington); Foreign Correspondents (Hong Kong). Author: The Truth About Soviet Lies, 1962. Home: 530 N St SW Washington DC 20024 Office: 1013 13th St Washington DC 20005

SHACKLEFORD, JAMES RUFUS, III, computer center exec.; b. Nashville, June 26, 1937; s. James R. and Robbie (Allison) S.; B.Engring., Vanderbilt U., 1960; M. Engring., U. Fla., 1964; m. Margaret Wade Lauderdale, June 18, 1960; children—Margaret Ashley, James Rufus IV, Mary Brenda. Field engr. Chgo. Bridge & Iron Co., Birmingham, Ala., 1960-61; structural engr. Ellers & Reaves, Cons. Engrs., Memphis, 1964-65; systems engr. IBM, Nashville, 1965-69; mgr. IBM Basic Systems Center, Nashville, 1969-70, systems engring. mgr., 1970—. Served to 1st lt. AUS, 1961-63. Registered profl. engr., Tenn. Mem. Data Processing Mgmt. Assn., Assn. for Computing Machinery, U.S. Chess Fedn., U.S. Lawn Tennis Assn., Mensa. Home: 2156 Chickering Lane Nashville TN 37215 Office: 450 James Robertson Pkwy Nashville TN 37219

SHACKLETON, POLLY (MRS. ROBERT W. SHACKLETON), city ofcl.; b. Brookline, Mass., June 19, 1910; d. Adolph and Marion Ehrlich; student Simmons Sch. Social Work, Boston U., Mass. Inst.

Tech., New Sch. Social Research; m. Robert W. Shackleton, July 1, 1946. Editor reference books Am. Fedn. Arts, Who's Who in Am. Art, Am. Art Ann., 1939-41; information specialist, picture editor OWI, Dept. State, Dept. Army, 1942-48; editor bi-weekly newsletter, pub. relations activities as mem. hdqrs. staff A.I.A., Washington, 1950-66. Bd. dirs. Family and Child Services of Washington; sec. Soc. for A More Beautiful Nat. Capital, Inc. Democratic nat. committee-woman from D.C., 1961-67, del. Dem. Nat. Cov., 1956, 60, 64, mem. platform com., 1956, 64; mem. D.C. Dem. Central Com., 1954-67; mem. D.C. City Council, 1967—; mem. Woman's Nat. Dem. Club. Mem. A.I.A. (hon.). Home: 3232 Reservoir Rd NW Washington DC 20007 Office: City Hall Washington DC 20013

SHADE, CAMILLE STIVERS, librarian; b. Lake Charles, La., Apr. 23, 1905; d. Edward C. and Hettie (Gardner) Stivers; A.B., So. U. 1928; B.L.S., Hampton Inst., 1929; A.M., Columbia, 1947; m. Robert Lee Shade, Dec. 25, 1926; 1 dau., Roberta (Mrs. Bertrand Oliver Tyson). Head librarian So. U. and A. and M. Coll., 1929—, prof., 1964—. Bd. dirs. Family Counseling Service, Blundon Home, Girl Scouts Am.; bd. dirs., chmn. program com. Baton Rouge Area YMCA. Mem. A.L.A. Home: 2466 Harding Blvd Baton Rouge LA 70807

SHAFER, ELIZABETH GLOVER (MRS. GEORGE SCOTT SHAFER), educator; b. Boston; d. John Loring and Louise (Strange) Glover; B.A., Fla. State U., 1960, M.S., 1961, Ph.D., 1968; m. George Scott Shafer, 1936 (dec. Aug. 1957); children—Deane (Mrs. Robert W. Colby), Scott Dunbar. Tchr., Brevard Jr. Coll., Cocoa, Fla., 1961-62; dean students Monticello Coll., Godfrey, Ill., 1962-63; asst. dean women for freshmen Madison Coll., Harrisonburg, Va., 1963-69, coordinator masters degree program, 1969—. Mem. Am. Assn. U. Women, So. Assn. Counselor Edn. and Supervision, Nat. Assn. Women Deans and Counselors, Am. Personnel and Guidance Assn., Pilot Internat. (charter mem. Harrisonburg br.), Delta Kappa Gamma, Kappa Delta. Home: 183 Colonial Dr Harrisonburg VA 22801

SHAFTON, ELAINE H. LEVINE (MRS. KIRVIN K. SHAFTON), food brokerage exec.; b. Chgo., Sept. 5, 1910; d. Samuel and Esther (Goldstreich) Levine; student Northwestern U., 1928-30; m. Edward Berger, Mar. 20, 1930 (div. Dec. 1938); m. 2d, Kirvin K. Shafton, Jan. 20, 1940 (dec. Oct. 1963); children— Perry M., Carol Jane (Mrs. Arne Rock). Exec. sec. Mr. Borin, Borin-Art Products, Chgo., 1930-40; with Shafton Co., Miami, Fla., 1945—. chmn. bd., 1965—, sec.-treas., 1965—; sec. Shafton Co., Tampa Fla., 1967—. Mem. Nat. Food Brokers Assn., Fla. Restaurant Assn., Cedars of Lebanon Hosp. Auxiliary. Jewish religion. Mem. Hadassah. Home: 2451 Brickell Av Miami FL 33129 Office: 5900 NW 35th Av Miami FL 33142

SHAHEEN, JOHN, broadcasting exec. Pres. WSMB, New Orleans. Office: 901 Canal St New Orleans LA 70112*

SHAHUN, LEON, JR., wholesale tobacco co. exec.; b. Memphis, Dec. 12, 1926; s. Leon and Carolena (Strassner) S.; B.A., Va. Mil. Inst., 1949; postgrad. Memphis State U., 1962-65; m. Suzanne G. Beyer, Nov. 22, 1951; children—Leslie, Meryl, Constance, Gregory. With Leon &Leon Cigar Co., Memphis, 1949-69, partner, gen. mgr., 1950-69; chmn. bd., chief exec. officer Samelson-Leon Co., Inc., Memphis, 1969—. Bd. dirs. Liberty Bowl Festival Assn. Served with inf. AUS, 1945-46. Decorated Bronze Star medal. Mem. Nat. Assn. Tobacco Distbrs. (dir. 1960—). Club: Ridgeway Country (Memphis). Home: 5273 Southwood Dr Memphis TN 38117 Office: 160 Cumberland St Memphis TN 38112

SHALOWITZ, ERWIN EMMANUEL, civil engr.; b. Washington, Feb. 13, 1924; s. Aaron Louis and Pearl (Myer) S.; student U. Pa., U. Notre Dame, 1944-45; B.C.E., George Washington U., 1947, postgrad. 1948-49; grad. soil mechanics Cath. U., 1951; M.A. in Pub. Adminstrn. (fellow U.S. Civil Service Commn.), Am. U., 1954; m. Elaine Mildred Langerman, June 29, 1952; children—Ann Janet, Aliza Beth, Jonathan Avram. Engr., Klemitt Engring. Co., N.Y.C., 1947; with cons. firm Whitman, Requardt & Assos., Balt., 1947-48; chief structural research engr., head def. research sect., project officer and tech. adviser for atomic tests Bur. Yards and Docks, Dept. Navy, Washington, 1948-59; supervisory gen. engr. spl. asst. for protective constrn. programs, project mgr. for bldg. systems, chief research br., chief mgmt. information Pub. Bldgs. Service, Gen. Services Adminstrn., Washington, 1959—. Chmn. fed. exec. tng. program U.S. Civil Service Commn., 1950; fallout shelter analyst Dept. Def. Served to engring. officer USNR, 1944-46. Registered profl. engr., Washington. Recipient Gen. Services Adminstrn. Commendable Service award, 1968. Fellow Am. Soc. C.E.; mem. Soc. Advancement Mgmt., Soc. Am. Mil. Engrs., Sigma Tau, Pi Sigma Alpha. Jewish religion (tchr. dept. religions). Contbr. articles to profl. jours. Home: 5603 Huntington Pky Bethesda MD 20014 Office: 19th and F Sts NW Washington DC 20405

SHAMBLIN, JOHN KENNETH, clergyman; b. Ozark, Ark., Feb. 11, 1917; s. Aaron Leonard and Leila Mae (Green) S.; B.A., U. Ark., 1937; B.D., So. Methodist U., 1940; D.D., Hendrix Coll., 1954; postgrad. Boston U., 1946; m. Virginia Maude Late, Dec. 25, 1937; children—John Kenneth, Lynda. Ordained to ministry Meth. Ch., 1933; minister Meth. Chs., Winslow, Ark., 1933-37, Nevada, Tex., 1939, Lamar, Ark., 1939-40, Atkins, Ark., 1940-43, West Memphis, Ark., 1943-47; dist. supt. Searcy Dist. No. Ark. Conf., 1947-48, Pulaski Heights, Little Rock, 1948-61, St. Luke's, Houston, 1961—; mem. bd. missions Houston-West Dist. Meth. Ch.; del. Gen. Conf. Meth. Ch., 1964, del. Jurisdictional Conf., 1964; del. World Meth. Conf., London, Eng., 1966; television minister KPRC-TV; radio minister Spires of the Spirit. Chmn. Bd. Edn. Tex. Conf., 1964. Pres. Nat. Meth. Conf. on Christian Edn.; trustee Meth. Hosp., Houston, Lon Morris Coll., Jacksonville, Tex., Homes for Older People, Lakeview Meth. Assembly, Palestine, Tex., United Fund Harris County; mem. exec. bd. Goodwill Industries. Clubs: Downtown Rotary, River Oaks Country. Author: Life Comes As Choice, 1967. Home: 2300 Timber Lane Houston TX 77027 Office: 3471 Westheimer Rd Houston TX 77027

SHAMBURGER (ALICE) PAGE, author; b. Aberdeen, N.C.; d. Frank Dudley and Alice (Page) Shamburger; grad. St. Mary's Sch. and Jr. Coll., 1945, Marjorie Webster Coll., 1947. Roving editor Am. Aviation Mag., 1949-51; script writer Radio Sta. WHUC, 1951-53; Eastern editor Cross Country News, 1954-67, contbg. editor Air Progress, 1966—; mem. Woman's Adv. Com. on Aviation, 1964-68; mem. aviation div. N.C. Emergency Transp. Task Force, 1966-67, cons. N.C. Vet. Research Found. Sec. Mid-South Horse Show Assn.; asst. sec. Moore County Hounds. Recipient commendations N.C. Gov., 1967-68, USAF Tactical Command, 1966; Doris Mullen Meml. Scholarship for helicopter tng., 1969, Lady Hay Drummond-Hay award, 1971. Mem. Aviation/Space Writers Assn., 99s-Internat. Orgn. Licensed Woman Pilots, Aircraft Owners and Pilots Assn,, Nat. Aero. Assn., Carolina Aero Club, Nat. Pilots Assn., Air Force Hist. Found., Air Force Assn., Am. Aviation Hist. Soc., Wingfoot Lighter-than-air Soc., Antique Airplane Assn., Exptl. Aircraft Assn., Southeastern Aviation Trades Assn., 99's (gov. S.E. sect. and mem. exec. bd. 1969-70, 71, curator mus. 1969—), Univ. Aviation Assn. (dir.), Nat. Intercoll. Flying Assn. (adv. bd.), Whirly-Girl 142. Democrat. Methodist. Club: South Carolina Breakfast. Author: Tracks Across The Sky, 1964; Classic Monoplanes, 1966; co-author: Command the Horizon, 1968; World War I Aces and Planes, 1968; Summon the Stars (named best non-fiction aviation book 1970 Aviation Space Writers Assn.), 1970; The Curtiss Hawks, 1972. Contbr. articles profl. publs. Address: 500 Carolina St Aberdeen NC 28315

SHANAHAN, JOHN HARROLD, JR., city planner; b. Rockville Centre, N.Y., Dec. 29, 1941; s. John Harrold and Evelyn Odell (Wood) S.; B.A. (Gibraltar scholar), U. St. Thomas, 1966; M.Arch., Tex. A. and M. U., 1968, M. in Urban and Regional Planning (Community Service fellow), 1970; m. Carol Jeanette Bradshaw, Oct. 7, 1967; children—Erin Elizabeth, Susan Claire, Daniel Patrick. Asst. dir. dept. urban planning Tex. A. and M. U., College Station, 1967-69; model cities coordinator Office Gov. Tex., Austin, 1969-71; ltd. partner Lifson, Wilson, Ferguson & Winick, mgmt. cons., Houston, 1971—. Lectr. grad. program community planning U. Tex. at Austin, 1970-71; mem. State Adv. Com. Urban Edn., 1970-71, state adv. council Dept. Housing and Urban Devel., 1969-71; mem. Mayor's Adv. Com. on Housing, Houston, 1966-67. Served with USNR, 1962-64. Recipient Econ. award Wall St. Jour., 1966; Outstanding Service award Am. Inst. Planners, 1970. Mem. Am. Inst. Planners (chmn. edn. com. 1969—), Am. Soc. Planning Ofcls., Am., So. econ. assns., Omicron Delta Dpsilon. Roman Catholic. Club: Houston. Home: 4031 Tartan Lane Houston TX 77025 Office: Suite 212 3223 Smith St TX 77006

SHANEYFELT, LYNDAL LEROY, document and photog. analyst; b. Dalton, Neb., June 16, 1915; s. Joseph LeRoy and Erma (May) S.; B.C.S., Southeastern U., 1950; m. Shirley Nadene Fearn, June 16, 1940; 1 son, Terry LeRoy. Photographer, Hastings (Neb.) Daily Tribune, 1936-40; photographer FBI, Washington, 1940-51, spl. agt., 1951-52, spl. agt., document examiner, photog. specialist, 1952—. Served with AUS, 1945. One of prins. in planning and carrying out re-enactment of assassination of Pres. John F. Kennedy for Warren Commn., 1964; examined photog. evidence related to assassination. Mem. Am. Acad. Forensic Scis. Home: 6125 Vernon Terrace Alexandria VA 22307

SHANEYFELT, SHIRLEY NADENE FEARN, artist; b. Hastings, Neb.; d. Oris C. and Calla (Wary) Fearn; student Hastings Coll.; pvt. study with Andrea Di Zerega, Laura Douglas, Joseph Pielage, Yolande Mayhall; m. Lyndal L. Shaneyfelt, June 16, 1940; 1 son, Terry Leroy. One-man shows at Lee Galleries, Alexandria, Va., 1961, FBI, Washington, 1965—, Heron House Gallery, Reston, Va., 1966, Galleries, Art League No. Va., 1967, others; exhibited in group-shows at Smithsonian Instn., Washington, 1952, 57, Georgetown U., Washington, 1963, Old Towne Gallery, Alexandria, 1965, Washington Gallery Art, 1965, U. Va., Charlottesville, 1965, Hadassah Invitational Shows, Gadsby's Tavern, Alexandria, Va., 1967, 68, 69, Alexandria br. Pen Women Group Show, Gallery on Mall, 1969, Gilliam Show, Alexandria Art League, 1972, others; represented in permanent collections Gen. Testing Labs., Alexandria, Crestwood Elementary Sch., Springfield, Va., Atlantic Research Corp., Alexandria; also pvt. collections; tchr., dir. Shane Painters, 1962-72. Recipient 1st prize Springfield Contemporary Show, 1956; 4th prize No. Va. Art League, 1959, 2d, 3d prizes, 1959; 1st prize (2), 2d prize Women's Club of Va., 1959; 1st prize Art League Marshall Show, 1961; 1st prize Art League, 1963, 3d prize, 1963; 3d prize Picasso Show, Hecht's Washington, 1963; 1st prize Galleries, Art League, 1967; hon. mention Corcoran Art Sch. Spring Show, George Washington U., 1972. Mem. Nat. League Am. Pen Women (1st v.p., 1964-65), Art League No. Va. (2d v.p. 1962-63; gallery hanging chmn. 1967), Am. Art League. Clubs: Women's Belle-Haven (art chmn. Alexandria 1963-65). Address: 6125 Vernon Terrace Alexandria VA 22307

SHANHOLTZ, MACK IRVIN, physician, state ofcl.; b. Cold Stream, W.Va., Dec. 11, 1905; s. Taylor B. and Ollie (Riley) S.; B.S., U. Va., 1930, M.D., 1934; M.P.H., Johns Hopkins, 1938; m. Elizabeth Baldwin, May 25, 1938; children—Susan Riley (Mrs. Thomas S. Tredway), John Taylor. Intern, U. Va. Hosp., Charlottesville, 1934-35; resident W.Va. Tb Sanatorium, Beckley; 1935-36; health officer Washington County, Va., 1936-38; dir. Commonwealth Fund demonstration Seminole County Health Dept., Wewoka, Okla., 1938-46; dir. preventive services Okla. Health Dept., 1946-51; commr. health State of Va., Richmond, 1951—; lectr. preventive medicine Med. Coll. Va., 1951—. Bd. dirs. Va. Tb Assn., 1951—, Va. Heart Assn., 1958—, Keep Va. Beautiful, 1963—; pres. Conf. State and Provincial Health Authorities N.Am., 1964-65; chmn. Va. Regional Med. Program, 1965-71; 1st v.p. Va. Council Health and Med. Care, 1961—; mem. Selective Service Adv. Com. Va., 1951—; med. adv. com. Va. League Planned Parenthood, 1961—; adv. council U. N.C. Sch. Pub. Health, 1958—; adv. com. USPHS Quarantine Activities, 1965-66; mem. Pres.'s Air Quality Adv. Bd., 1968-71; mem. alumni adv. com. U. Va. Sch. Medicine. Recipient Award Honor, Va. Council Health and Med. Care, 1969; Louise Obici Meml. Hosp. award, 1970. Diplomate Am. Bd. Preventive Medicine and Pub. Health. Fellow Am. Pub. Health Assn., Am. Coll. Preventive Medicine; mem. A.M.A., Va. Med. Soc. (mem. governing council), Assn. State and Territorial Hosp. and Med. Facilities Survey and Constrn. Authorities (pres. 1964), Assn. State and Territorial Health Officers (pres. 1960-61), Va. State Dental Assn. (hon.), Nat. Assn. Sanitarians (hon.), Richmond Acad. Medicine, Alpha Omega Alpha. Mem. Disciples of Christ Ch. Rotarian (past pres.). Home: 5912 Upham Dr Richmond VA 23227 Office: 109 Governor St Richmond VA 23219

SHANHOLTZ, VERNON ODELL, educator; b. Romney, W.Va., Apr. 22, 1935; s. Jacob Taylor and Ruth (Ryan) Rudolph; student Potomac State Coll., 1953-55; B.S., W.Va. U., 1958, M.S., 1963; Ph.D., Va. Poly. Inst. and State U., 1970; m. Mary Ellen McGuire, Apr. 17, 1965; children—Diane Carole, Darlena Dawn. Agrl. engr. U.S. Dept. Agr., Moorefield, W.Va., 1958, agrl. engr., Coshocton, O., 1960-61, research hydraulic engr., Blacksburg, Va., 1963-65, Beltsville, Md., 1965-66; research instr. Va. Poly. Inst. and State U., Blacksburg, 1966-70, asst. prof., 1970—. Served with AUS, 1958-60. Va. Water Resource Reseach Center grantee, 1965-70. Mem. Am. Geophys. Union, Am. Soc. Agrl. Engring., Soil Conservation Soc. Am., Tau Beta Bi, Gamma Sigma Delta, Sigma Phi Omega. Lutheran. Moose. Developed simulation model for moisture accounting in conventional tillage and no tillage corn systems. Home: 300 Dogwood St Christiansburg VA 24073 Office: Seitz Hall Va Poly Inst and State U Blacksburg VA 24061

SHANK, RUSSELL, librarian; b. Spokane, Sept. 2, 1925; s. Harry and Sadie (Hytowitz) S.; B.S., U. Wash., 1946, B.A. in L.S., 1949; M.B.A., U. Wis., 1952; D.L.S., Columbia, 1966; m. Doris Louise Hempfer, Nov. 9, 1951; children—Susan Marie, Peter Michael, Judith Louise. Reference librarian U. Wash., 1949; asst. engring. librarian U. Wis., 1949-52; chief in-service tng. and personnel Milw. Pub. Library, 1952; engring.-phys. scis. librarian Columbia, 1953-59; asst. univ. librarian U. Cal. at Berkeley, 1959-64; sr. lectr. Columbia Sch. Library Service, 1964-66, asso. prof., 1967; dir. libraries Smithsonian Instn., 1967—; vis. asst. prof. U. Wash., summer 1956; officer of instrn. Columbia Sch. Library Service, 1954-59; lectr. U. Cal. at Berkeley, 1959-64. Dir. sci. library project N.Y. Met. Reference and Research Library Agy., 1966-68. Served with USNR, 1943-46. Recipient Distinguished Alumnus award U. Wash. Sch. Librarianship, 1968. Mem. A.L.A. (chmn. personnel adminstrn. sect. 1965-66, pres. information sci. and automation div. 1968-69, mem. council 1961-65), Assn. Coll. and Research Libraries (pres. 1972-73), Spl. Libraries Assn. (chmn. engring. div. 1968-69), Am. Soc. Information Sci., A.A.A.S. Author: Regional Access to Scientific and Technical Information, 1966; also articles. Home: 1054 Dalebrook Dr Alexandria VA 22308 Office: Smithsonian Instn Washington DC 20560

SHANKLE, ROBERT JACK, educator, dentist; b. Walker County, Ga., Sept. 17, 1923; s. Robert Davis and Ada (Goodson) S.; student North Ga. Coll., 1941-43, U. Ga., 1943, Washington U., 1944; D.D.S., Emory U., 1948; m. Nancy Lee Bruckman; children—Robert Davis II, Jane Lewis. Instr., Emory U. Sch. Dentistry, 1949-51; asso. prof. U. N.C., 1951-61, prof., 1961-66, prof., dept. chmn., 1966—; cons. Womack Army Hosp., dir. admissions; cons. Ft. Knox, Ky., Ft. Benning, Ga. Dir. admissions U. N.C. Sch. Dentistry. Served with AUS, 1943-44, capt. USAF, 1955-57. Diplomate Am. Bd. Endodontists. Fellow Am. Assn. Endodontists, Am. Coll. Dentists, Internat. Coll. Dentists; mem. Omicron Kappa Upsilon (pres. supreme chpt.), Alpha Epsilon Delta. Republican. Episcopalian. Author (with Brauer and Richardson) The Dental Assistant, 1964; (with others) The Art and Science of Operative Dentistry, 1968. Home: 1306 Mason Farm Rd Chapel Hill NC 27514

SHANKLIN, ROBERT LEE, chemist; b. Terre Haute, Ind., June 16, 1926; s. Vernon A. and Olive Paulette (Mann) S.; B.S., Ind. State U., 1950; m. Patricia Anne Burrell, May 23, 1947; 1 son, Robert Lee Shanklin II. Lab. supr. E.I. duPont de Nemours, Dana, Ind., 1951-57, Wilmington, Del., 1957-58, New Johnsonville, Tenn., 1958-64; chief chemist Mosites Rubber Co., Fort Worth, Tex., 1964—. Served with USNR, 1944-46. Mason. Developer non-burning elastomers used in space exploration. Home: 3716 Orchard St Fort Worth TX 76119 Office: 2720 Tillar St Fort Worth TX 76107

SHANNON, DAVID ALLEN, univ. ofcl., historian; b. Terre Haute, Ind., Nov. 30, 1920; s. John Raymond and Esther (Allen) S.; B.S., Ind. State Coll., 1941; M.S., U. Wis., 1946, Ph.D., 1951; LL.D., Ind. State U., 1972; m. Jane Short, Aug. 31, 1940; children—Molly (Mrs. Harry Osborne), Sarah (Mrs. Gary Olson). Instr. history Carnegie Inst. Tech., 1948-51; asst. prof., then asso. prof. Columbia Tchrs. Coll., 1951-57; mem. faculty U. Wis., 1957-65; prof. history, 1960-65; prof., chmn. dept. history U. Md., 1965-68; prof., chmn. dept. history Rutgers U., 1968-69; prof. history, dean faculty arts and scis. U. Va., Charlottesville, 1969-71, v.p., provost, 1971—; tchr. U. Cal. at Berkeley, spring 1956, 57, U. Stockholm (Sweden), fall 1959, U. Lund (Sweden), spring 1960, U. Aix-Marseille (France), 1962-63. Served with USAAF, 1943-45. Mem. Orgn. Am. Historians (past exec. com.), Am., So. hist. assns. Author: The Socialist Party in America: A History, 1955; The Decline of American Communism, 1959; Twentieth Century America, 1963; Between the Wars, 1965. Co-author: A History of Teachers College, Columbia University, 1954. Editor: The Great Depression, 1960; Beatrice Webb's American Diary, 1898, 1963; Progressivism and Postwar Reaction, 1966. Home: Pavilion V West Lawn Charlottesville VA 22903

SHANNON, DONALD SUTHERLIN, educator; b. Tacoma Park, Md., Dec. 28, 1935; s. Raymond Corbett and Elnora Pettit (Sutherlin) S.; B.A., Duke, 1957; M.B.A., U. Chgo., 1964; Ph.D., U. N.C., 1972; m. Virginia Ann Lloyd, June 24, 1961; children—Stacey Eileen, Gail Allison, Mem. auditing staff Price Waterhouse & Co., N.Y.C., 1957-61; sr. accountant Price Waterhouse, Chgo., 1964-65; instr. Duke U., Durham, N.C., 1964-69; asst. prof. bus. adminstrn. U. Ky., Lexington, 1969—. Served with AUS, 1958-59, 61-62. Mem. Am. Accounting Assn., Am. Inst. C.P.A.'s, Ill. Soc. C.P.A.'s, So. Econ. Assns., Am. Finance Assn., Beta Gamma Sigma. Club: University Chicago. Home: 775 Cindy Blair Way Lexington KY 40503

SHANNON, EDGAR FINLEY, JR., univ. pres.; b. Lexington, Va., June 4, 1918; s. Edgar Finley and Eleanor (Duncan) S.; A.B., Washington and Lee U., 1939, Litt.D., 1959; A.M., Duke, 1941; A.M., Harvard, 1947; Rhodes scholar Merton Coll., Oxford, 1947-50, D. Phil., Oxford (Eng.) U., 1949; LL.D., Southwestern-at-Memphis, 1960, Duke U., Centre Coll., 1968, Hampden-Sydney Coll., 1971; H.H.D., Wake Forest Coll., 1964; L.H.D., Jefferson Med. U., 1966, Bridgewater Coll., 1970; m. Eleanor H. Bosworth, Feb. 11, 1956; children—Eleanor, Elizabeth, Lois, Susan, Virginia. Grad. asst. in English, Duke, 1939-40, 41; asso. prof. naval sci. and tactics Harvard, 1946; instr. English Harvard, 1950-52, asst. prof. English, 1952-56; Guggenheim fellow, 1953-54; Fulbright research fellow to Eng., 1953-54; asso. prof. English, U. Va., 1956-59, prof. English, pres. univ., 1959—. Pres. Council So. Univs., 1962-64, State Univs. Assn., 1963-64; exec. com. Assn. State Univs. and Land Grants Colls., 1963-67; pres. Nat. Assn. State Univs. and Land Grant Colls., 1965-66, chmn exec. com., 1966-67; bd. govs. Nat. Com. Accrediting, 1961-67; mem. state and dist. selection coms. Rhodes Scholarship; bd. visitors U.S. Naval Acad., 1962-64; U.S. Air Force Acad., 1965-67, So. Regional Edn. Bd., 1963-71; bd. adminstrn. Va. Inst. Marine Sci., 1963-71; trustee Mariners' Museum, 1966—; bd. dirs. Am. Council on Edn., 1967-70, vice chmn., 1972; trustee Darlington Sch., Rome, Ga., council Harvard Grad. Soc. for Advanced Study and Research, 1965-71; bd. consultants Nat. War Coll., 1969-71; pres. Assn. Va. Colls., 1969-70. Served from midshipman to lt. comdr. USNR, 1941-46, PTO; capt. res. Decorated Bronze Star medal. Mem. Modern Lang. Assn. Am., Soc. of Cin., Signet Soc., Raven Soc., Phi Beta Kappa (senator-at-large, united chpts. 1967—), Omicron Delta Kappa. Presbyn. Author: Tennyson and the Reviewers, 1952; also articles and revs., primarily on 19th century English lit. in various jours. Home: Carrs Hill Charlottesville VA 22903

SHANNON, GEORGE MCDANIEL, physician; b. Itta Bena, Miss., Dec. 15, 1917; s. Hervey Linwood and Marie (Beavans) S.; student Sunflower Jr. Coll., 1939-40; B.S., Miss. State Coll., 1947; postgrad. U. Miss., 1948; M.D., U. Tenn., 1951; m. Bessie Guillory, Nov. 15, 1942; children—Doris (Mrs. J.D. Dumas), Anna Marie, George, Sheila, Juliette, Sylvia, John, Robert. Intern, St. Joseph Hosp., Memphis, 1951-52; practice medicine, specializing in gen. practice, Flora, Miss., 1952-54, Eunice, La., 1954-57, West Monroe, La., 1957—; mem. staff Glenwood Hosp., West Monroe, La., St. Francis Hosp., Monroe. Served to lt. (j.g.) USNR, 1942-45. Decorated Air medal. Mem. St. Landry Paris (v.p., 1956), Ouachita Parish, La. med. socs., A.M.A., Sigma Chi, Alpha Epsilon Delta. Home: 202 Parkwood Dr West Monroe LA 71291 Office: 302 N 3d St West Monroe LA 71291

SHANNON, HARPER, clergyman; b. Birmingham, Ala., July 7, 1931; s. John Roy and Ruby (Harper) S.; B.A., Samford U., 1952, D.D., 1968; B.D., So. Bapt. Theol. Sem., 1957; m. Elsie Lou Batemon, June 5, 1953; children—Kenneth Norman, Martha Grace. Ordained to ministry Bapt. Ch., 1949; pastor Harmony Bapt. Ch., Birmingham, 1949-54, First Bapt. Ch., Ghent, Ky., 1956-57; evangelist, 1957-59; pastor Eastern Hills Bapt. Ch., Montgomery, Ala., 1959-62, First Bapt. Ch., Dothan, Ala., 1962—. Teaching fellow So. Bapt. Sem., Louisville, 1957; tchr. Howard Coll. Extension div. Samford U., 1961.

Mem. So. Bapt. Conv. (dir. home mission bd. 1964-71; 2d v.p. 1970), Ala. Bapt. Exec. Bd. (adminstrv. com. 1962-68). Dothan Ministerial Assn. (pres. 1964-65). Dothan C. of C. (youth and edn. com. 1967-69), Trident. Kiwanian. Author: Beliefs That Are Basic, 1969; Riches in Romans, 1969; Trumpets in the Morning, 1970. Home: 105 S Denton St Dothan AL 36301 Office: PO Box 874 Dothan AL 36301

SHANNON, JACK THOMAS, lumber co. exec.; b. Memphis, Feb. 25, 1924; s. James Egbert and Anna May (Strube) S.; student Vanderbilt U., 1942, Memphis State U., 1946-47; m. Amelia Russell, June 15, 1950; children— Jack Thomas, Carroll, Richard L. With Shannon Bros. Lumber Co., Memphis, 1947-—, pres., 1970-—; v.p. Shannon Bros. Enterprises, Memphis, 1965-—; dir. Union Planters Nat. Bank, Memphis. Pres. Memphis Cotton Carnival Assn., 1967; commr. Auditorium and Conv. Center, Memphis; mem. adv. com. Shelby County Sheriff Dept., 1968-—. Bd. dirs. Hutchison Sch. for Girls, Memphis. Served with USAAF, 1942-46. Mem. Beta Theta Pi. Republican. Episcopalian. Clubs: Memphis Country, Memphis Hunt and Polo. Home: 45 S Norwall St Memphis TN 38117 Office: PO Box 6108 1684 Florida St Memphis TN 38106

SHANNON, JAMES WILLIAMS, animal scientist; b. Meridian, Miss., Feb. 23, 1935; s. George W. and Lattie (Speak) S.; B.S., Miss. State U., 1958, M.S., 1971, postgrad., 1971-—; m. Ella Eloise McClinton, June 9, 1963; children—James Williams, Samuel Patrick. Mgr. Shamrock Acres Polled Hereford Farm, Meridian, 1958-60; asso. county agt. Miss. Ext. Service, Clarke County, Miss., 1960-69; research asst. animal sci. dept. Miss. State U., 1969-71; livestock specialist Miss. Coop. Extension Service, State College, Miss., 1971-—. Mem. Quitman Vol. Fire Dept., 1964-69. Mem. Am. Soc. Animal Sci., Miss. State Alumni Assn., Alpha Zeta. Baptist (sec. Sunday sch. class 1970-71). Clubs: Block and Bridle. Research sychronization of estrus in gilts with use of aimax and gonadotrophins; reproduction efficiency in gilts due to confinement stress. Home: Box 3788 State College MI 39762 Office: Box 5425 State College MI 39762

SHANNON, JOHN SANFORD, ry. exec.; b. Tampa, Fla., Feb. 8, 1931; s. George Thomas and Ruth (Garrett) S.; A.B., Roanoke Coll., 1952; LL.B., U. Va., 1955; m. Elizabeth Howe, Sept. 22, 1962; children—Scott Howe, Elizabeth Garrett, Sandra Denison. Admitted to Va. bar, 1955; asso. mem. firm Hunton, Williams, Gay, Powell & Gibson, Richmond, Va., 1955-56; with Norfolk & Western Ry. Co., Roanoke, Va., 1956-—, gen. counsel, 1968-69, v.p. law, 1969-—; dir. Wheeling & Lake Erie Ry. Co., Cleve., Trailer Train Co., Chgo. Bd. dirs. Legal Aid Soc. Roanoke Valley, 1969, Help, Inc., Roanoke, 1970-—. Mem., Am., Va., Roanoke bar assns., Roanoke C. of C., Order Coif, Sigma Chi, Omicron Delta Kappa, Phi Delta Phi. Episcopalian. Clubs: Roanoke Country, Shenandoah (Roanoke); Metropolitan (Washington). Home: 706 Cassell Lane SW Roanoke VA 24014 Office: 8 N Jefferson St Roanoke VA 24011

SHANNON, MARGARET RUTLEDGE, newspaper reporter; b. New Albany, Miss., July 4, 1917; d. James Biggs and Fannie (Rutledge) Shannon; B.J., U. Mo., 1939. With Neshoba Democrat, Philadelphia, Miss., 1939-40, Suffolk (Va.) News-Herald, 1941, Tupelo (Miss.) Jour., 1942-43; Atlanta Jour., 1944-67; with Atlanta Jour. and Constn. Mag., 1968-—. Recipient Headliners, Sigma Delta Chi, Edn. Writers Assn. awards, 1951; Reid fellow, 1952. Presbyn. Office: 72 Marietta St NW Atlanta GA 30302

SHANNON, MARY COLEEN, social worker; b. Port Arthur, Tex., Oct. 17, 1940; d. George Charles and Fern (Jefferson) Shannon; B.A., Tex. Christian U., 1962; M.S.W., Tulane U., 1965. Social worker Homestead Child Placement Agy., Ft. Worth, 1962-63; case aid Family Service Assn., Ft. Worth, 1964, caseworker, 1965-68, dir. profl. services, 1968-69; field instr. U. Tex. at Arlington, 1969-71, asst. prof. Grad. Sch. Social Work, 1971-—. Field instr. U. Tex., Austin, 1968-69, cons. Volunteers of Am., YWCA, Pub. Health Dept., Sister of St. Mary of Namur, Jr. League Ft. Worth, St. Joseph Hosp. Bd. dirs. YWCA, 1970-—. Mem. Family Service Assn. Am., Nat. Assn. Social Workers, Acad. Certified Social Workers, Tau Beta Sigma, Quill and Scroll. Episcopalian. Home: 4725 Madella St Fort Worth TX 76117 Office: Univ Tex Arlington TX 76010

SHAO, STEPHEN PINYEE, educator; b. I-hing, Kiangsu, China, Jan. 24, 1924; s. Chu Tang and Shawyuen (Wang) S.; B.S., Nat. Hunan U. China, 1946; M.A., Baylor U., 1949; Ph.D., U. Tex., 1956; m. Betty Lucille Outen, June 18, 1953; children—Stephen Pinyee, Dale Hilton, Lawrence Peter, Alan Terence. Came to U.S., 1948, naturalized, 1956. Chief accountant Bd. for Tex. State Hosps. and Spl. Schs., 1952-54; prof., head bus. adminstrn. dept. Bluefield (Va.) Coll., 1954-56; lectr. Univs. Taiwan (Formosa), Hong Kong, summer 1961; sr. statistics and mgmt. cons. U.S. Naval Supply Center, Norfolk, Va., 1962-68; prof. mgmt. and statistics Coll. William and Mary, Norfolk, 1956-62; prof., chmn. dept. quantitative scis. in bus. econs. Old Dominion U., Norfolk, 1962-—. Mem. Am. Econ. Assn., Am. Accounting Assn., Am. Statis. Assn., So. Mgmt. Assn., Alpha Kappa Psi. Author: Mathematics of Finance, 1962; Statistics for Business and Economics, 1st edit., 1967, 2d edit., 1972; Mathematics for Management and Finance, 1969. Home: 5161 Lake Shore Rd Virginia Beach VA 23455 Office: Sch Bus Old Dominion U Norfolk VA 23508

SHAPERO, SANFORD MARVIN, assn. exec.; b. Cin., Mar. 4, 1929; s. David Theodore and Leah Freda (Adler) S.; B.A., U. Dayton, 1950; B. in Hebrew Lit., Hebrew Union Coll., Cin., 1952, M. in Hebrew Lit., 1954, D. H.L., 1959; m. Harriet Plotkin, Apr. 22, 1956; children— Andrea, Seth, Jonathan, Adam. Rabbi, 1955; Rabbi, Temple Emanuel, Beverly Hills, Cal., 1964-68, Park Av. Temple, Bridgeport, Conn., 1959-64, Temple B'nai Israel, Elmira, N.Y., 1956-59; exec. v.p. Alliance Med. Industries, Stratford, Conn., 1967-69; v.p. N. Am. Biologicals, North Miami, Fla., 1969-71; dir. S.E. region Union Am. Hebrew Congregations, Miami, 1971-—. Lectr. Columbia, N.Y.C., 1964-65, Tchrs. Colls. Oiso, Japan, 1956. Mem. N.Y. Gov's Commn. on Youth, 1956-57. Bd. dirs. U. Bridgport (Conn.), 1963-68, Hebrew Union Coll., Cin., 1950-55. Served with USNR, 1955-57. Mem. New England Clergy (pres. 1964). Rotarian. Author: Stories for Children, 1962; Reform Judaism, 1964; Creative Services and Cantatas, 1963-68; others. Contbr. articles, reviews to prof. jours. Home: 19030 NE 21st Av North Miami Beach FL 33162 Office: Suite 519 101 E Flagler St Miami FL 33131

SHAPIRO, HARVEY, economist, govt. ofcl.; b. N.Y.C., Jan. 31, 1932; s. Irving and Frieda (Butler) S.; B.A., Coll. City N.Y., 1953; M.A., U. Wis., 1954, Ph.D., 1961; m. Juliette Plotkin, June 26, 1960; children—Maria, Karen. Instr. dept. econs. Ia. State U., Ames, 1959-60; fiscal economist Econ. Research Service, U.S. Dept. Agr., Washington, 1960-65; fiscal economist Bur. of the Budget, Washington, 1965-67, Office Tax Analysis, Treasury Dept., Washington, 1967-—; instr. money and banking U.S. Dept. Agr. Grad. Sch., 1962-—. Served with AUS, 1954-56. Mem. Am. Econ. Assn., Nat. Tax Assn. Contbr. articles to profl. publs. Home: 1332 4th St SW Washington DC 20024 Office: Office Tax Analysis Treasury Dept Washington DC 20224

SHAPIRO, HERBERT SAUL, lawyer; b. N.Y.C., Mar. 17, 1911; s. Pincus and Estelle (Bennett) S.; student Lycee du Puy, LePuy, France, 1930-31; B.A. with honors, Columbia Coll., 1931; LL.B., Columbia U., 1934; m. Ruth Brown, Jan. 27, 1946. Admitted to N.Y. bar, 1934, Fla. bar, 1946; asso. House, Grossman, Vorhaus & Hemley, N.Y.C., 1934-35, Rosenberg, Goldmark & Colin, N.Y.C., 1935-37; pvt. practice, N.Y.C., 1937-46; partner Berick, Shapiro & Fried, Miami, Fla., 1946-55, Shapiro, Fried, Weil & Scheer, 1955-—. Asst. county solicitor Dade County, Fla., 1949-53; prosecuting atty. City North Bay Village (Fla.), 1955-62, city judge, 1967-70. Chmn. Fla. wills and bequests com. Am. Friends of Hebrew U.; hon. founder Technion Soc. Hon. trustee Hope Sch. for Retarded; bd. dirs. Histadrut Found., Asthmatic Children's Found., N. Miami Beach, Fla.; v.p., bd. dirs. Hebrew Acad., Miami Beach. Served to 1st lt. with USAAF, 1942-45. Decorated Bronze Star medal. Mem. Miami Beach Bar Assn. (pres., 1958), United Synagogues Am. (sec. 1965). Jewish religion (pres. temple). Mason (32 deg.), Elk. Home: 4816 Lakeview Dr Miami Beach FL 33140 Office: 407 Lincoln Rd Miami Beach FL 33139

SHAPIRO, LEONARD, former air force officer, govt. ofcl.; b. Rochester, N.Y., Feb. 1, 1917; s. Sam and Rose (Tomkin) S.; B.A., U. Ill., 1939; M.A., Georgetown U., 1948, Ph.D., 1949; m. Judith Torruella, Aug. 16, 1947; 1 son, John L. Commd. 2d lt., advanced through grades to col. USAF, 1951, chief operations Missile Test Center, 1959-61, Congo, 1961-62, tech. tng., Amarillo, Tex., 1962-65, ret.; dir. Internat. Studies, Northrup Corp., Beverly Hills, Cal., 1965-69; asst. adminstr. Econ. Devel. Adminstrn., Govt. P.R., 1970-—, International corr. El Dia, Ponce, P.R. Mem. Cal. Citizens Committee, Nat. Council on Crime and Delinquency. Active Boy Scouts. Bd. govs. Georgetown U. Decorated Legion of Merit D.F.C., Air medal with 13 oak leaf clusters. Fellow Am. Inst. Aeros. and Astronautics. Roman Catholic. Club: Wings (N.Y.C.). Author Soviet Treaty Series, 2 vols., 1949, 52. Home: 860 Ashford Av Apt 9 A Santuree PR 00907 Office: Econ Devel Adminstrn GPO Box 2350 San Juan PR 00907

SHAPIRO, MYRON (MIKE) FREDERICK, communications co. exec.; b. Mpls., Dec. 16, 1918; s. Leo and Miriam (Levin) S.; student Duluth Jr. Coll., 1937-38, U. Minn., 1939; m. Conway Helen King, Oct. 24, 1942; 1 dau., Lynne Carole (Mrs. Duke Covert). Mgr. KTXL-Radio, San Angelo, Tex., KECK-Radio, Odessa, Tex., 1945-52; sales rep. WFAA-TV, Dallas, 1952-53; comml. mgr. KDUB, Lubbock, Tex., 1953-54; account exec. Avery Knodel, Chgo., 1954-55; v.p., mng. dir. Griffin Telecasting Properties, Tulsa and Little Rock, 1956-58; mgr. WFAA-TV, 1958-60, gen. mgr., 1960-—; v.p. A.H. Belo Corp. (owners WFAA), Dallas, 1970-—, also dir.; pres. KFDM-TV, Beaumont, Tex., 1969-—. Chmn. Dallas March of Dimes, 1970-71; mem. devel. bd. Jacksonville Lon Morris Coll., Jacksonville, Tex., 1971-—, mem. adv. bd. Communications Sch., U. Tex. at Austin, 1969-—. Bd. dirs. Family Guidance Center, 1967-69, Am. Cancer Soc., 1965-—. Served with A.C., AUS, 1941-45. Recipient Outstanding Broadcaster award Assn. Broadcast Execs. Tex., 1962. Mem. Nat. Assn. Broadcasters (chmn. bd. dirs. TV 1965-66), ABC-TV Affiliates Assn. (chmn. bd. govs. 1961-63), Assn. Broadcast Execs. Tex. (pres. 1959-60), Dallas Ad Club (bd. dirs. 1968-69), Dallas Ad League (bd. dirs. 1968-69), Better Bus. Bur. (bd. dirs. 1965-—), Salesmanship Club. Initiated weekly TV show pub. service Let Me Speak To The Manager, 1961-—. Home: 6911 Waggoner Pl Dallas TX 75230 Office: WFAA AM-FM-TV Communications Center Dallas TX 75202

SHAPIRO, ROBERT ALLEN, educator; b. Long Branch, N.J., Aug. 14, 1930; s. Louis and Kathryn (Marten) S.; B.S., Okla. State U., 1953, M.S., 1964, Ph.D., 1964; m. Stella Jane Darlow, June 14, 1953; children— David Allen, John Edward, Steven Darlow. Div. prodn. engr. Shell Oil Co., 1953-61; prof. indsl. engring. U. Okla., Norman, 1964-72, dir. indsl. engring., 1966-72, asst. to pres., 1967-68, asso. v.p. for adminstrn. and finance, 1972-—. Cons. Gen. Electric Co., P.O. Dept., Dept. Def., Tenneco Oil Co., USPHS. Registered profl. engr., Okla. Mem. Am. Inst. Indsl. Engrs., Soc. Petroleum Engrs. (Distinguished lectr. 1969-70), Am. Soc. Engring. Edn., Sigma Tau, Alpha Pi Mu, Phi Kappa Tau. Presbyn. (trustee 1966-—). Home: 1821 Peter Pan St Norman OK 73069 Office: 660 Parrington Oval Univ Okla Norman OK 73069

SHAPLEY, FERN RUSK, museum curator; b. Mahomet, Ill., Sept. 20, 1890; d. William Humphrey and Anna Lucinda (Renner) Rusk; A.B., U. Mo., 1913. A.M. 1914, Ph.D. (resident fellow), 1916, A.F.D., 1959; m. John Shapley, Sept. 19, 1918; children—Dora (Mrs. Uco van Wijk), Ellen (Mrs. James Fish). Fellow archaeology Bryn Mawr Coll., 1914-15; European Fellowship grant, 1915; asst. in art and archaeology U. Mo., 1916-17. asst. prof. art. summer 1925; research asst. Nat. Gallery, Washington, 1943-47, curator paintings, 1947-56, asst. chief curator, 1956-60; curator paintings Samuel H. Kress Found., 1960-—. Mem. Phi Beta Kappa. Author: George Caleb Bingbam. The Missouri Artist, 1947; European Paintings from the Gulbenkian Collection, 1950; Paintings from the Samuel H. Kress Collection: Italian Schools, vol. 1, 1966, vol. 2, 1968, vol. 3, 1972. Co-author: Comparisons in Art. 1957. Contbr. profl. jours. Office: Nat Gallery of Art Washington DC 20565

SHAPLEY, WILLIS HARLOW, govt. ofcl.; b. Pasadena, Cal., Mar. 2, 1917; s. Harlow and Martha (Betz) S.; student Harvard, 1934-36; A.B., U. Chgo., 1938; m. Virginia Curry Bishop, June 12, 1940; children—Sarah Stowell, Deborah. Research asst. polit. sci. U. Chgo., 1938-42; with Bur. of Budget, Exec. Office of Pres., 1942-65, dep. chief mil. div., 1961-65, asst. to dir., 1965; asso. dep. adminstr. NASA, 1965-—. Recipient Rockefeller Pub. Service award, 1956; Exceptional Service award Bur. of Budget, 1963; D.S.M., NASA, 1969; Career Service award Civil Service League, 1971. Mem. Phi Beta Kappa. Club: Cosmos (Washington). Home: 3040 P St NW Washington DC 20007 Office: 400 Maryland Av SW Washington DC 20546

SHARE, LEONARD, physiologist; b. Detroit, Oct. 14, 1927; s. Jacob and Mildred (Tobachnick) S.; A.B., Bklyn. Coll., 1947; A.M., Oberlin Coll., 1948; Ph.D., Yale, 1951; m. Carol R. Robey, Aug. 28, 1949; children—Michael E., Donald S., Frederick C. USPHS postdoctoral fellow Western Res. U., 1951-52, instr. physiology, 1952-54, sr. instr., 1954-57, asst. prof., 1957-63, asso. prof., 1963-68; prof. physiology Case Western Res. U., 1968-69; prof., chmn. dept. physiology and biophysics U. Tenn., 1969-—; researcher Inst. Biol. Chemistry of U. Copenhagen (Denmark), 1962-63; mem. gen. medicine Bstudy sect. NIH, 1965-69; cons. VA Hosp., Memphis. Mem. Am. Physiol. Soc., Endocrine Soc., Memphis Heart Assn., A.A.A.S., Internat. Soc. Neuroendocrinology, Sigma Xi. Contbr. articles to profl. jours. Home: 340 Shady Woods Cove Memphis TN 38117

SHARKEY, ROBERT POINDEXTER, educator; b. Atlanta, Sept. 7, 1926; s. Henry James and Verla (Poindexter) S.; A.B., Princeton, 1948; Ph.D., Johns Hopkins, 1958; m. Virginia Williams, Feb. 19, 1949 (div.); 1 dau., Rebecca Blair. Asst. dir. admissions Johns Hopkins, 1953-56, asst. to pres. 1960-61; asst. prof. economics U. S.C., 1957-59; asst. prof. history Princeton, 1962-63; asso. prof. econ. history George Washington U., Washington, 1963-65, prof., 1966-—. Fulbright prof. U. Cologne (Germany), 1961-62, Johns Hopkins Bologna (Italy) Center, 1966-67. Served with USNR, 1945-46. Mem. Am. Hist. Assn., Orgn. Am. Historians, Econ. History Assn. Clubs: Johns Hopkins (Balt.); Princeton (N.J.) Terrace; Cosmos (Washington). Author: Money, Class, and Party: An Economic Study of Civil War Reconstruction, 1959.Home: 2921 Olive St NW Washington DC 20007

SHARMA, PRAKASH CHANDRA, sociologist; b. Aligarh, Uttar Pradesh, India, July 20, 1938; s. Bhu Datta and Misra (Devi) S.; B.S., Balwant Rajput Coll. U. Agra (India), 1960, M.S., 1962; M.S., U. Guelph (Ont., Can.), 1967; Ph.D., U. Ga., 1970; m. Yogesh Kumari, June 29, 1961; children—Udit P., Neal. Came to U.S., 1967. Asst. prof. U. Agra, 1962-63; asst. prof. Uttar Pradesh Agrl. U., Pantnagar, India, 1963-64; research asst. U. Man., Winnepeg, Can., 1964-65; research asst. U. Guelph (Can.), 1965-67; research asst., instr. U. Ga., Athens, 1967-70; asst. prof., acting chmn. sociology dept. U.S. Ala., Mobile, 1970-72; asso. prof. Florence (Ala.) State U., 1972-—. Mem. adv. bd. Indian; Jour. Soc. Research, 1972-—. U.S. Ala. research grantee, 1970-71. Mem. Am. Sociol. Assn., Population Assn. Am., Rural Sociol. Soc., Ala. Acad. Sci., So. Sociol. Soc., Internat. Assn. Agrl. Economists, Indian Agrl. Econs. Soc., Ala.-Miss. Sociol. Assn., Assn. So. Agrl. Workers, Mobile YMCA, Alpha Kappa Delta, Delta Tau Kappa, Gamma Sigma Delta. Clubs: Cosmopolitan (Mobile). Rev. editor Internat. Rev. Sociology, 1971-—. Contbr. articles and revs. to Nat. and internat. jours. Home: Bhavigarth Aligarth Uttar Pradesh India Office: Dept of Sociology Florence State Univ Florence AL 35630

SHARMAN, GEORGE ALBERT, dentist; b. Houston, July 13, 1917; s. George Robert and Cora Jane (Duke) S.; student U. Houston, 1935; D.D.S., Tex. Dental Coll., 1940; postgrad. Am. Sch. Applied Hypnotherapy, Hypnoanesthesia, 1952; m. Margie Eloise Worsham, June 22, 1940; 1 son, Robert Wayne. Practice dentistry, Houston, 1940-—. Served to capt. USAAF, 1942-46. Mem. Houston Dist., Tex., Am. dental assns., Psi Omega. Home and Office: 2110 Airline Dr Houston TX 77009

SHARMAN, JAMES EDWARD, educator; b. Roanoke, Ala., Mar. 14, 1920; s. Edward Bartow and Pollie E. (Taylor) S.; B.S., Howard Coll., 1943; M.S., George Peabody Coll., 1949; Ed.D., U. Ala., 1968; m. Frances Marie Duke, Apr. 23, 1944; children—Cathy, Mike, Carol, Sue, Don. Instr., Howard Coll., Birmingham, Ala., 1942-43; asst. prin., athletic dir. D.A.R. Sch., Grant, Ala., 1946-51; asst. prin., athletic dir. George Peabody Coll., Nashville, 1951-52; chmn. div. health, phys. edn. and recreation, athletic dir. Samford U., Birmingham, 1952-69; dir. health, phys. edn., athletic dir. U. Ala., Birmingham, 1969-—. Cons., dir. numerous camps and recreational facilities. Served to lt. USNR, 1943-46. Recipient Ala. State Assn. for Health, Phys. Edn. and Recreation Honor award, 1968. Mem. Am. Sch. Health Assn., Coll. Men's Phys. Edn. Assn., Am. Assn. Health, Phys. Edn. and Recreation, Kappa Phi Kappa, Omicron Delta Kappa. Republican. Author: History of the Alabama State Association for Health, Physical Education and Recreation, 1965; History of Health and Physical Education in Alabama Schools, 1968. Contbr. articles to profl. publs. Home: 1720 Vestaview Lane Birmingham AL 35216

SHARP, ERNEST LEONARD, social worker; b. Porterville, Miss., Mar. 25, 1926; s. George Bernard and Linnie (Danner) S.; A.A., E. Miss. Jr. Coll., 1948; B.S., Miss. State U., 1950; M.S.W., Tulane U., 1962; m. Birdie Ethel Parker, June 10, 1948; children—Leonard Ray, Sandra Elaine. Field instr. Pontotoc (Miss.) High Sch., 1950-52; tchr. Porterville High Sch., 1952-53; computer Western Geophys. Co. Am., Los Angeles, 1953-54; supr. Miss. Dept. Pub. Welfare, 1954-61; caseworker, supr. Jefferson County Child Welfare unit Tex. Dept. Pub. Welfare, 1962-63; dir., child welfare supr. Lubbock City-County Child Welfare unit Tex. Dept. Pub. Welfare, 1963-71; chief social services, asst. supt. Crockett (Tex.) State Sch. for Girls, 1971-—. Field instr. Worden Sch. Social Service, Our Lady of the Lake Coll., San Antonio, 1967-71. Served with USNR, 1944-46; PTO. Mem. Nat. Assn. Social Workers (chpt. registrar, past treas.), Acad. Certified Social Workers, Am. Pub. Welfare Assn., Council on Social Work Edn., Tex. United Community Services (past chpt. treas.), Tex. Social Welfare Assn. (past v.p.), Tex. Corrections Assn., Child Welfare League Am., Alpha Tau Alpha. Methodist. Lion. Home: PO Box 689 Crockett TX 75835 Office: Crockett State Sch for Girls PO Box 411 Crockett TX 75835

SHARP, LEOLA E., educator; b. Prairie Grove Ark., Mar. 11, 1911; d. John Arthur and Ada Leola (Combs) Sharp; B.S., U. Ark., 1939, M.S., 1948; postgrad. George Peabody Coll., summer 1941, U. Colo., U. Okla. State, Southwestern Mo. State Coll., U. Okla., Northeastern State Coll. Tchr. pub. schs., Washington County, Ark., 1928-35, Prairie Grove (Ark.) Elementary Sch., 1936-38, Marion (Ark.) High Sch., 1939-43, secondary schs., Muskogee, Okla., 1946-48; instr. math. Alice Robertson Jr. High Sch., Muskogee, 1948-63, sch. counselor, testing supr., 1963-71; instr. math. Haskell (Okla.) High Sch., 1971-—. Mem. Muskogee Mayor's Council on Youth, 1968-—. Mem. sch. math. study group for secondary sch. Math. text NSF, summer 1960. Served with WAVES, 1943-45. Mem. Muskogee Assn. Classroom Tchrs. (past pres.), Nat., Okla., Muskogee (past pres.) edn. assns., N.E.A., Am. Okla. personnel and guidance assns., Am. Assn. U. Women, Am. Legion, Internat. Platform Assn., Smithsonian Assos, Nat. Hist. Soc. Democrat. Methodist. Clubs: Knife and Fork, Wesleyan Service Guild (pres. 1949-51, 63). Home: 2215 Hayes St Muskogee OK 74401 Office: Haskell High Sch Haskell OK 74436

SHARP, PAUL FREDERICK, univ. pres.; b. Kirksville, Mo., Jan 19, 1918; s. Frederick J. and L. Blanche (Phares) S.; A.B., Phillips U., 1939; Ph.D., U. Minn., 1947; LL.D. (hon.), Tex. Christian U., 1961; L.H.D. Buena Vista Coll., 1967; Litt. D., Limestone Coll., 1971; m. Rosella Ann Anderson, June 19, 1939; children—William, Kathryn, Paul Trevor. Instr. U. Minn., 1942, 46-47, vis. lectr., 1948; asso. prof. Am. history, chmn. Am. Instns. program U. Wis., 1954-57, vis. lectr., 1953; vis. lectr. San Francisco State Coll., 1950, U. Ore. 1955; Fulbright lectr. Am. Instns., univs. Melborne and Sydney, Australia, 1952; pres. Hiram Coll., 1957-64; chancellor U. N.C., Chappel Hill, 1964-66; pres. Drake U., Des Moines 1966-71, U. Okla., 1971-—. Served from ensign to lt. (s.g.), USNR, 1943-46; naval liaison officer Royal Australian Navy, 1944-45. Research grants Minn. Hist. Soc., 1947, 48, Social Sci. Research Council, 1949, 51; Ia. State Coll. Alumni Fund award, 1952; Fulbright award to Australia, 1952; Ford Faculty fellow, 1954; recipient award of merit Am. Assn. State and Local History, 1955; Silver Spur award Western Writers Am., 1955; Guggenheim fellow, 1957. Mem. Phi Beta Kappa, Phi Kappa Phi, Pi Gamma Mu, Phi Alpha Theta. Mem. Disciples of Christ Church. Author of Agrarian Revolt in Western Canada, 1948; Old Orchard Farm; Story of an Iowa Boyhood, 1952; Whoop-Up Country; Canadian American West, 1955. Editor: Documents of Freedom, 1957. Cons. author: Heritage of Midwest, 1958; regional editor Montana mag., editorial cons. Americana Press, 1955-—. Contbr. articles profl. jours. Home: 1200 S Pickard St Norman OK 73069

SHARP, RUTH COLLINS (MRS. CHARLES S. SHARP), civic worker; b. Dallas; d. Carr P. and Ruth (Woodall) Collins; B.A., So. Meth. U., 1948; m. Charles S. Sharp, June 21, 1947; children—Sally, Stanton, Susan. Pres. Jr. League, 1961-62, ofcl. hostess Internat. Conf. in Dallas, 1961; pres. Vis. Nurse Assn., 1956-58; pres. Dallas Day Nursery Assn., 1964-66. Sec. bd. dirs. YMCA, 1961-62; bd. dirs. KERA Ednl. TV, Grand Jury Assn.; trustee So. Meth. U. Recipient

Zonta award as Dallas Woman of Year, 1965, Golden Plate award Am. Acad. Achievement for Community Service, 1965; Woman of Achievement award So. Meth. U., 1966; Arete award for community service, 1969. Methodist. Club: Dallas Woman's (pres. 1967-69). Home: 5227 Meaders Lane Dallas TX 75229

SHARP, SUSIE MARSHALL, state judge; b. Rocky Mount, N.C., July 7, 1907; d. James Merritt and Annie (Blackwell) Sharp; LL.B., U. N.C., 1929; LL.D., Woman's Coll. U. N.C., 1950, Queen's Coll., 1962, Elon Coll., 1963, Catawba Coll., 1970, U. N.C., 1970; L.H.D., Pfeiffer Coll., 1960; LL.D., Wake Forest Coll., 1965 Admitted to N.C. bar, 1928; gen. practice firm Sharp & Sharp, Reidsville, 1929-49; city atty., Reidsville, 1939-49; spl. judge Superior Ct. N.C., 1949-61; asso. justice Supreme Ct. N.C., 1962—. Mem. Am., N.C. bar assns., Am. Law Inst., Order of Coif, Phi Beta Kappa, Order Valkyries, Delta Kappa Gamma. Democrat. Methodist. Clubs: Altrusa; Sorptomist. Home: 629 Lindsey St Reidsville NC 27320 Office: Supreme Ct Justice Bldg Raleigh NC 27611

SHARP, WILLIAM HERSHEL, fire chief; b. Glasgow, Ky., Mar. 7, 1918; s. Basil Oma and Maud (Bradshaw) S.; student Delehanty Inst., N.Y.C., 1950-51, N. Tex. U., 1965, U. Md., 1964; m. Mildred Eileen Owens, Dec. 24, 1936; 1 son, William Wayne. With Dallas Fire Dept., 1941-61, bn. chief, 1955-61; chief Garland (Tex.) Fire Dept., 1961-66; chief Lubbock (Tex.) Fire Dept., 1966—. Mem. adv. bd. firemens tng. sch. Tex. A. and M. U., 1970—; sec. Tex. Commn. on Fire Protection Personnel Standards and Edn., 1970—. Mem. exec. bd. Metro Lubbock March Dimes, 1970, South Plains council Boy Scouts Am., 1968—. Bd. dirs. A.R.C., 1967-70. Served with USNR, 1942-45. Named Fire Prevention Man of Year, Dallas, 1960. Raeford scholar, 1965. Mem. Internat. Assn. Fire Chiefs, Tex. Fire Chiefs Assn. (pres. 1962), N. Tex. Fire Chiefs Assn. (pres. 1964), Dallas County Fire Chiefs Assn. (pres. 1963). Baptist. Mason (Shriner). Home: 4716 48th St Lubbock TX 79413 Office: PO Box 2000 Lubbock TX 79457

SHARP, WILLIAM NEWTON, assn. exec.; b. Birmingham, Ala., Aug. 10, 1911; s. W.N. and Bonnie (Heaton) S.; B.S. in Elec. Engring., Auburn U., 1934; m. Margaret Young, Sept. 6, 1939; children—William Newton., Bebe (Mrs. W. H. Holland), Caroleta (Mrs. J. L. Jackson). Cartographic engr. Soil Conservation Service, Ala., 1934-42; mgr. Opelika (Ala.) C. of C., 1966—. Sec.-treas. Opelika Indsl. Devel. Bd., 1960-71; sec. Opelika Interclub Council, 1955-71. Served with AUS, 1942-45. Decorated Bronze Star. Mem. C. of of C. Execs. Assn. Ala. (pres. 1950), So. C. of C. Execs. Assn., So. Indsl. Devel. Bd. (dir. 1954). Methodist. Home: 1507 Rocky Brook Rd Opelika AL 36801 Office: PO Box 2366 Opelika AL 36801

SHARPE, JOHN ALLEN, JR., newspaper editor; b. Lumberton, N.C., Oct. 20, 1912; s. John Allen and Daisy (Courtney) S.; A.B., Duke, 1932; m. Helen Allen Seawell, Jan. 1, 1950; children—John Allen III, Clifford Seawell, Hal Courtney. Newspaper reporter Robesonian, Lumberton, 1932-39, asso. editor, 1940-43, 46-48, editor, 1948—; pres. Robeson Broadcasting Co. Served with USAAF, 1943-46. Mem. N.C. Press Assn. (v.p. 1967-68). Methodist. Home: 1015 Riverside Blvd Lumberton NC 28358 Office: 121 W 5th St Lumberton NC 28358

SHARPE, JOHN LAWRENCE, III, editor; b. Columbia, S.C., Oct. 25, 1939; s. John Lawrence and Mardenia (Hatchell) S.; A.B., Wofford Coll., 1961; B.D., Duke U., 1965, Ph.D., 1969; student St. Mary's Coll. (Scotland), 1965-66; student Frederick-Alexander Universitat (Germany), 1966; m. Josey Anne De Witt, Aug. 19, 1961; 1 son, John Christopher. Curator rare books William R. Perkins Library, Duke U., Durham, N.C., 1967—, editor Library Notes, 1967—, lectr. dept. art Duke U., 1970—; field dir. Patmos Monastery Library Project for Inst. Antiquity and Christianity, Claremont, Cal., 1971—. Mem. A.L.A., Soc. Bibl. Lit., Am. Acad. Religion, Bibliog. Soc. Va., Pi Kappa Alpha. Editor: Essays for the Dedication of Perkins Library; Marginal Notes. Home: 815 Camden Av Durham NC 27701 Office: Perkins Library Duke U Durham NC 27706

SHARPE, MILES, editor and communications specialist; b. Buffalo, Ala., Aug. 28, 1917; s. M. H. and Eloree Sharpe; M.Agr., U. Fla., 1948; Ph.D., Pa. State U., 1951; m. Gladys Crews, June 11, 1942; 1 son, Miles Hervey. Faculty Pa. State U., 1949-51; faculty U. Fla., Gainesville, 1953—, editor, chmn. editorial dept. Inst. Food and Agrl. Scis. Home: 1615 NW 7th Av Gainesville FL 32601

SHARPE, THOMAS GILBERT, JR., lawyer; b. San Antonio, Dec. 26, 1935; s. T. Gilbert and Dorothy (Stovall) S.; B.A., U. Tex., 1960, LL.B., 1963; m. Shirley Ritter, Aug. 27, 1960; children—John Carlyle, Thomas Steele, James Gilbert. Admitted to Tex. bar, 1963, Colo. bar, 1972, U.S. Supreme Ct. bar; practiced in Brownsville, 1963—; partner firm Hardy & Sharpe, 1963—. Served with 17th inf. regiment, AUS, 1955-57; Korea. Named Outstanding Young Man Brownsville, 1969. Mem. Am. Trial Lawyers Assn. (nat. safety committeeman), Am., Cameron County (pres. 1971-72) bar assns., State Bar Tex. (named Gen. Practitioner Yr. 1972), Nat. Assn. Def. Lawyers in Criminal Cases, Cal. Trial Lawyers Assn., Law-Sci. Acad. Am. (gold medal award 1969; chancellor 1972), Tex. Criminal Def. Lawyers Assn. (dir. 1971—), Phi Alpha Delta. Clubs: Valley Inn and Country (pres. 1969), Kiwanis (pres. 1969). Home: 2020 Palm Blvd Brownsville TX 78520 Office: 1010 E Washington St Brownsville TX 78520

SHARPE, TOM H., utility co. exec.; b. Nacogdoches, Tex., June 19, 1921; s. Hamilton H. and Mary P. (Hearn) S.; B.S., Stephen F. Austin State Coll., 1942; m. Martha Ann Pickens, May 22, 1948; children—Tom H., Dan Albert, Stephen, Michael. Sports editor Tyler (Tex.) Courier-Times, 1946-49; mng. editor Lufkin (Tex.) Daily News, 1949; oil news reporter Rinehart Oil News Service, Tyler, 1950; pres., gen. mgr. Reliance Gas Co., Athens and Kaufman, Tex., 1950—. Owner, Athens Furniture Co., 1966—. dir. 1st Nat. Bank, Athens. Served to lt. (s.g.), USNR, World War II; PTO. Mem. Athens C. of C. (pres. 1962). Methodist. Rotarian. (pres. 1958-59). Home: 1009 Mill Run Rd Athens TX 75751 Office: 220 N Prairieville St Athens TX 75751

SHARPE, WILLIAM GRAY, III, ret. ins. agy. exec., lawyer; b. Elm City, N.C., Aug. 4, 1905; s. William Gray and Fannie (Peacock) S.; A.B., Duke, 1926; postgrad. grad. Pell Law Sch., 1933; m. Naomi Cannaday, May 21, 1930; children—Frances Louvenia (Mrs. Charles Franklin Ritch II), William Gray IV. Teller, Toisnot Banking Co., Elm City, 1927-31; admitted to N.C. bar, 1933; asst. cashier Br. Banking & Trust Co., Elm City, 1931-33, cashier, 1933-54; owner Sharpe Ins. Agy., Elm City, 1954-70; pres. Elm City Devel. Corp., 1963-67, v.p., 1967—. Active various community drives. Mem. Bd. Edn. Elm City, 1948-66. Mem. Lambda Chi Alpha. Methodist (chmn. ofcl. bd. 1966-67). Rotarian. Elk. Home: PO Box 465 Elm City NC 27822 Office: 121 1/2 E Main St Elm City NC 27822

SHARPLEY, JOHN MILES, lab. exec.; b. Norfolk, Va., Jan. 28, 1918; s. John Edward and Annie Carter (Miles) S.; B.A., Hampden-Sydney Coll., 1941; M.S., U. Richmond, 1949; Ph.D., U. London (Eng.) 1951; m. Virginia Leah Tarpin, July 16, 1941. Chief microbiologist Froehling and Robertson Inc., Richmond, Va., 1945-47; dir. microbiol. research, Buckman Labs., Inc., Memphis, 1950-60; pres. Sharpley Labs. Inc., Fredericksburg, Va., 1960—; prof. dept. biology, Va. Commonwealth U., 1965—. Vis. lectr. Am. Inst. for Biol. Scis. Served to lt. col., USAF, 1941-45. Decorated Purple Heart medal. Fellow Am. Inst. Chemists, A.A.A.S.; mem. Soc. Indsl. Microbiology (dir. 1949-52), Am. Chem. Soc., Soc. Am. Bacteriologists, Soc. for Gen. Microbiology. Author: Applied Petroleum Microbiology, 1960, Elementary Hydrocarbon Microbiology, 1964. Contbr. articles to profl. publs. Home: Belle Plains Belle Plains Rd Fredericksburg VA 22401 Office: Box 846 Fredericksburg VA 22401

SHATTUCK, JOHN ARTHUR, dentist; b. Lockport, N.Y., June 20, 1935; s. Ralph Lavery and Helen Louise (Arthur) S.; student Lafayette Coll., 1953-56; D.D.S., U. Pa., 1960; m. Isabel Alison Govan, Sept. 1, 1957; children—Heather Lang, Jeffrey Alan. Intern U.S. Naval Hosp., Great Lakes, Ill., 1960-61; practice dentistry, Herndon, Va., 1964-66, Reston, Va., 1966—. Mem. faculty Med. Sch., Georgetown U., Washington, 1967-71. Served with USNR, 1960-64. Mem. Am. Dental Assn., No. Va., Va. dental socs., Nat. Rifle Assn., Nat. Wildlife Fedn., Mu Upsilon Sigma, Alpha Chi Rho, Xi Psi Phi. Episcopalian (exec. council Va. dicoese 1967, 68). Club: Londoun Hunt (Leesburg, Va.). Home: Route 1 Box 86 Leesburg VA 22075 Office: 1712 Clubhouse Rd Reston VA 22070 also Dulles Internat Med Center Sully Rd Sterling VA 22070

SHAVER, JOHN EDWARD, JR., accountant, educator; b. Ruston, La., Jan. 20, 1938; s. John Edward and Mary (Brewer) S.; B.S., La. Poly. Inst., 1960, M.B.A., 1967; m. Virginia Claire Skains, Apr. 25, 1958; 1 dau., Kimberly Marie. Jr. accountant Interstate Oil Pipe Line Co., Shreveport, La., 1960-61; accountant Placid Oil Co., Shreveport, 1961-64; staff accountant Savage, Moore & Miles, C.P.A.'s, Monroe, La., 1964-65, Holladay & Pierce, C.P.A.'s, Ruston, 1965-67; asst. prof. accounting La. Tech. U., Ruston, 1967—; partner Pierce & Shaver, C.P.A.'s, Ruston, 1968-70. Active various fund drives. Served with USNR, 1955-63. C.P.A., La. Mem. Am. Inst. C.P.A.'s, Soc. La. C.P.A.'s, Am. Accounting Assn., Beta Gamma Sigma, Delta Sigma Pi, Beta Alpha Psi (sec. chpt. 1959-60), Omicron Delta Epsilon. Baptist. Home: 602 Glendale Dr Ruston LA 71270

SHAW, AGNES, educator; b. Gulfport, Miss., Feb. 3, 1914; d. Hobart Doane and Olive (Brown) Shaw; M.E., Belhaven Coll., 1937; B.S., U. Miss., 1954, M.Ed., 1964. Tchr., Belzoni (Miss.) High Sch., 1937-42; recreational dir. U.S.O. Jacksonville, N.C., 1942-46, guidance counselor West Monroe (La.) High Sch., 1946—; dir. Camp Gulf Park, Gulfport, Miss., 1936—. Exec. sec. La. Assn. Student Councils, 1966-72. Mem. La. (pres. 1970-71), N.E. La. Area (pres. 1962, 70) guidance assns. Am., La. personnel and guidance assns., La. Tchrs. Assn., Nat. Assn. Student Councils Exec. Secs. Presbyn. Home: 4801 Bon Air Dr Monroe LA 71201

SHAW, CLINTON ROBERT, economist, govt. ofcl.; b. Springfield, Mass., Oct. 2, 1932; s. Arthur Merrill and Enid (Eves) S.; A.B., U. Mass., 1959; J.D., George Washington U., 1964; m. Georga Fisher Collins, Mar. 30, 1956; 1son, Clinton Robert. Economist, U.S. Tariff Commn. Washington, 1959—. Served from 2d lt. to capt. USAF, 1952-56. Mem. Am. Econ. Assn., Delta Theta Phi. Contbr. tech. reports U.S. Tariff Commn. Home: 3106 N Taylor St Arlington VA 22207 Office: US Tariff Commn Washington DC 20436

SHAW, GEORGE VINCENT, JR., data processing co. exec.; b. Rochester, N.Y., Sept. 6, 1928; s. George Vincent and Katherine Louise (McGreal) S.; B.A., Yale, 1950; m. Eva Darlene Blue, Nov. 30, 1957; children— Cynthia, Sally, George Vincent III, Jennifer. Asst. controller Allied Stores Corp., Dey Bros. & Co., 1951-56; controller, v.p. Maverick Clarke, San Antonio, 1956-62; accountant Haskings & Sells, Houston, 1962-63; partner Holmes & Raquet, San Antonio, 1963-68; v.p. Holmes & Shaw, Inc., San Antonio, 1968—; dir. S. States Oil & Gas Co. C.P.A., Tex. Mem. Am. Inst. C.P.A.'s. Roman Catholic (finance chmn. 1968, 71). Clubs: San Antonio, Northern Hills Country (San Antonio). Home: 9003 Valley View Lane San Antonio TX 78217 Office: Milam Bldg San Antonio TX 78205

SHAW, HENRY MARCHAND, mfg. co. exec.; b. Oxford, N.C., Sept. 14, 1900; s. Henry Marchand and Bessie (Buxton) S.; B. in Engring., N.C. State U., 1922; m. Blanche Martin, May 21, 1927; children—Henry Marchand, Ann (Mrs. George Henry Cornelson). Asst. treas. Robert G. Lassiter Co., Raleigh, N.C., 1922-28; treas. Raleigh Granite Co., 1928-39, So. Aggregates Co., Raleigh, 1930-39; with N.C. Products, Inc., Raleigh, 1939-72, pres., 1945-72, dir., 1939—; dir. Superior Stone Co., Raleigh, Univ. Motel, Chapel Hill, N.C., Pines Restaurant, Chepel Hill, Triangle Motel, Raleigh; mem. city bd. N.C. Nat. Bank, Raleigh. Partner, College Inn, Raleigh, 1960-72. Trustee Meredith Coll., Raleigh, 1970-72. Mem. N.C. Masonry Assn. (pres. 1945-46), Southeastern (pres. 1960-61, bd. dirs. 1965-69), Am. conrete pipe assns., Phi Kappa Phi, Tau Beta Pi. Baptist. Home: 2419 Anderson Dr Raleigh NC 27608 Office: PO Box 27077 Raliegh NC 27611

SHAW, HENRY OVERSTREET, transp. exec.; b. Adel, Ga., Oct. 21, 1893; s. Archibald Hiram and Elizabeth (Overstreet) S.; intensive course U.S. Naval Acad., 1918; m. Vivian Izona Riggs, June 19, 1920 (dec. May 1967); 1 dau., Sylvia Byron (Mrs. David Nicholas Blount); m. 2d, Mary H. Gardner, Apr. 28, 1971. With Ga. Lumber & Supply Co. and Shaws, Inc., Miami, Fla., 1914-29, v.p., treas., 1923-29; with Shaw Bros. Oil Co. and predecessor cos., Miami, Fla., 1916—, chmn. bd. dirs., exec. officer, 1950-61; land developer, 1916—; partner Shaw Bros. Docks and Shaw Bros. Shipping Co., 1943—; pres. Shaw Bros. Shipping Co., 1955—, Shaw Marine Co., Shaw Gold Coast Co.; owner Shaw Fgn. Trade Warehouse; dir. Fla. Nat. Bank & Trust Co. of Miami, Fla. First Nat. Bank of Opa Locka. Chmn. Dade County chpt., A.R.C. war fund drive, 1942, dir. county chpt., 1942-43, vice chmn., 1943; dir. Dade County Community Chest, 1950-51. Pres. South Atlantic and Fla. Ports Conf., 1945-47; chmn. Miami Rate and Traffic Bd., 1927-33, Port and Harbor Bd., 1937-38, 1939; mem. Am. and Fla. petroleum industries coms., 1931—; mem. Gov. spl. com. on freight rates (Fla.), 1940-45. Mem. Citizens bd. U. Miami, 1946—, pres., 1950. Served as ensign Supply Corps, USNRF, 1918-19; mem. Civilian aide com. of comdg. gen. AAF, 1942. Mem. Miami C. of C. (dir. 1944-49, pres. 1944-46), Greater Miami Traffic Assn., Internat. Platform Assn. Mason (K.T., Shriner), Elk, Rotarian (pres. Miami club 1934-35). Home: 881 Ocean Dr Key Biscayne FL 33149 Office: 501 NE 1st Av Miami FL 33132

SHAW, JOHN WILLIAM, petroleum co. exec.; b. Vinton, La., Feb. 3, 1923; s. John William and Gracie (Perry) S.; student Southwestern La. Inst., 1939-40, U. Hawaii, 1945, Internat. Corr. Schs., 1946-52, Lamar U., 1954-60, 71; m. Ida Clare Helms, Feb. 27, 1943 (div. Dec. 1967); children—Charlton (Mrs. David Schochler), Penny, Donna Lane; m. 2d, Velma Louise Hargrove, June 13, 1969. Credit, ins. inspector Retail Credit Corp., Beaumont, Tex., 1946; loan mgr. Univ. C.I.T. Corp., Beaumont, 1947; with Sun Oil Co., Nederland, Tex., 1948—, supt., 1958-66, mgr., 1966—; dir. Nederland State Bank; partner Refuse Disposal Service, Inc., Nederland, 1961-66, Real Estate Devel. Co., Vinton, La., 1954—; pres. Real Estate Devel. Co., Nederland, 1972—; self-employed archtl. designer, Beaumont, 1950—. Founding pres. Home Health Services, Lake Charles, La., 1969—; bd. advisers vocational edn. Nederland Sch. Dist., 1969-70; mem. artifacts com. Spindletop Oilfield Mus., 1970—; mem. Sabine-Neches Chiefs Relief Assn., 1964—, Jefferson County Air Pollution Abatement Com., 1964-71, Clean Air - Clean Water, Inc., Beaumont, 1969—; active fund drives numerous orgns., 1952—; chmn. Neches River Oil Spill Abatement Orgn. Trustee Spindletop Oilfield Mus. Served with USNR, 1943-46; PTO. Decorated Fleet Admiral's Citation. Mem. Packaging Inst., Am. Soc. Lubricating Engrs., Soc. Automotive Engrs., Nederland C. of C. (dir. 1971—). Democrat. Methodist. Mason (32 deg., Shriner, Jester), Rotarian. Club: Bus. and Profl. Mens (past pres.) (Beaumont). Home: 695 18th St Beaumont TX 77706 Office: PO Box 758 Nederland TX 77627

SHAW, MARGERY WAYNE SCHLAMP (MRS. CHARLES RAYMOND SHAW), physician, educator; b. Evansville, Ind., Feb. 15, 1923; d. Arthur George and Louise (Meyer) Schlamp; student Hanover Coll., 1940-41; A.B. magna cum laude, U. Ala., 1945; M.A., Columbia, 1946; postgrad. Cornell U., 1947-48; M.D., U. Mich., 1957; m. Charles Raymond Shaw, May 31, 1942; 1 dau., Barbara Rae (Mrs. Frederic L. Ferri). Intern, St. Joseph Mercy Hosp., Ann Arbor, Mich., 1957-58; practice medicine, specializing in human genetics, Ann Arbor, Mich., 1958-67, Houston, 1967—; instr. dept. human genetics Med. Sch. U. Mich., 1958-61, asst. prof., 1961-66, asso. prof., 1966-67; asso. prof. dept. biology Grad. Sch. Biomedical Scis. U. Tex., Houston, 1967-69, prof., 1969—; dir. Med. Genetics Center, Houston, 1971—; mem. genetics study sect. NIH, Bethesda, Md., 1966-70, mem. genetics tng. com. 1970—, chromosome studies astronauts NASA, 1970-71. First aid instr. A.R.C., 1962-67; unit chmn. United Fund, 1966. Recipient Billings Silver medal A.M.A., 1966; Achievement award Am. Assn. U. Women, 1970-71. Mem. Am. Soc. Human Genetics (past sec., dir.), Genetics Soc. Am. (sec. 1971-73), Tissue Culture Assn. (trustee 1970—), Environmental Mutagen Soc. (dir. 1972-74), Phi Beta Kappa, Alpha Omega Alpha. Asso. editor: Am. Jour. Human Genetics, 1962-68; editorial bd. In Vitro. Cons. editor: Cytogenetics, 1962—. Contbr. articles to profl. jours. Home: Apt 1307 1600 Holcombe Blvd Houston TX 77025 Office: MD Anderson Hosp and Tumor Inst Houston TX 77025

SHAW, PHILIP SIDDEL, state ofcl.; b. Montpelier, Vt., Jan. 17, 1915; s. William and Bertha (Clark) S.; A.B., Duke, 1937; M.A., U. Fla., 1944; postgrad. Fla. State U., 1959-60; m. Lois Cleveland, Mar. 26, 1936; children—Philip S., William A. Asst. auditor to auditor Fla. Auditing Dept., Tallahassee, 1942-54; comptroller Bd. County Commrs., Pinellas Co. (Fla.), 1955-60; asst. div. dir. finance Fla. Dept. Edn., Tallahassee, 1964-65, comptroller, 1965—. Sci. tchr., prin. Fla. pub. schs., 1938-42; cons. handbook devel. sect. U.S. Office Edn., 1964—, mem. com. revision of forms, grant and loan mgmt. br., 1965-66; mem. Nat. Com. on Financial Accounting for Pub. Schs., 1965—; cons. Ednl. Information Systems, P.R., 1967; mem. tech. adv. com. Ala. Dept. Edn., 1970—. Mem. Assn. Ednl. Data Systems (dir., treas. 1964—), Southeastern Edn. Lab. (chmn. data systems group 1966-67). Co-author: Principles of Public School Accounting. Home: 1221 Brandt Dr Tallahassee FL 32303 Office: 100 Knott Bldg Tallahassee FL 32304

SHAW, PHILIP WALKER, city ofcl.; b. Gulfport, Miss., Apr. 13, 1918; s. Hobart Doane and Louise Olive (Brown) S.; B.S., Miss. State U., 1940; M.S., Harvard, 1946; m. Marion Joyce Bendler, Aug. 10, 1946; children—Philip Walker, Anna (Mrs. Richard Erdman), Joyce. San. engr. Miss. State Bd. Health, 1940; prof. Miss. State U., 1946-47; cons. civil engr., Gulfport, 1947-69; mayor City of Gulfport, Miss., 1969—. Mem. intergovtl. relations com. Nat. League Cities, 1971. Trustee-at-large Kidney Found. State Miss. Served to lt., C.E., AUS, 1941-45, 51-52. Decorated Silver Star, Bronze Star medal. Mem. Miss. State Municipal Assn. (mem. exec. com. 1969—), Miss. Coast Municipal Assn. (pres. 1970-71), Miss. State Bd. Registration Profl. Engrs., V.F.W., Am. Legion, Theta Xi. Democrat. Presbyn. (elder 1964-70). Mason (32 deg., Shriner), Elk, K.P., Moose, Rotarian. Home: 4113 Washington Av Gulfport MS 39501 Office: 2309 15th St Gulfport MS 39501

SHAW, ROBERT, music condr.; b. Red Bluff, Cal., Apr. 30, 1916; s. Shirley Richard and Nelle Mae (Lawson) S.; A.B., Pomona Coll., 1938, Mus.D. (hon.), 1953; Mus.D. (hon), Coll. Wooster, 1951, St. Lawrence U., 1955, Mich. State U., 1960, Cleve. Inst. Music, 1966, Western Res. U., 1966, Emory U., 1967, Fla. State U., 1968; D.F.A. (hon.), U. Alaska, 1963; L.H.D., Kenyon Coll., 1963; m. Maxine Farley, Oct. 15, 1939; children—Johanna, Peter Thain, John Thaddeus. Dir. Fred Waring Glee Clubs, 1938-45; choral dir. Aquacades, 1942-43, Carmen Jones, 1943, Seven Lively Arts, 1944, My Darlin Aida, 1953; guest condr. CBS Symphony series, 1944-45, ABC Symphony series, 1945, NBC Symphony, 1946, N.Y.C. Symphony, 1946, Boston Symphony Orch., 1958, N.Y. Philharmonic, 1970, Nat. Symphony Orch., 1959, Chgo. Symphony Orch., 1960, Houston Symphony, 1970, Dallas Symphony, 1969, Minn. Orch., 1972, Richmond (Va.) Symphony, 1971; dir. choral music Berkshire Music Center, 1946-49; dir. choral activities Juillard School Music, 1946-49; condr. San Diego Summer Symphony, 1953-58; asso. condr. Cleve. Symphony Orch., 1956-67; music dir., condr. Atlanta Symphony Orch., 1967—; artistic dir. Alaska Festival of Music, 1956—; dir. Meadow Brook Sch. Music, 1965-67, Blossom Festival Sch., Cleve. Orch.-Kent (O.) State U., 1968—. Founder, dir. Robert Shaw Chorale, which has made ann. tours of U.S., 1948—, Middle East and Europe, 1956, USSR, 1962, S.Am., 1964. Recipient Nat. Assn. Am. Composers and Condrs. award for outstanding Am. born condr., 1943; Guggenheim fellow, 1944, founder-dir. The Collegiate Chorale, 1941. Mem. Ga. Art Commn., 1967—.‡

SHAW, ROBERT JENNINGS, chmn. Ga. Republican Com.; b. Bronwood, Ga., Aug. 21, 1929; s. Robert Edward and Vesta (Jennings) S.; student Ga. Inst. Tech., 1947, U. Ga. at Atlanta, 1948-50; m. Mary Elaine Smith, Dec. 25, 1950; children—Maria Elena, Melanie Dawn, Susan June, Bobbie Elizabeth Ann. Gen. agt., Pan-Am. Life Ins. Co., 1961—. Pres., Bolton Civic Assn. 1966—. Vice chmn. finance com. Fulton County (Ga.) Rep. com., 1963, chmn. speakers' bur., 1964, ho. dist. chmn. also campaign mgr. for candidate for Ga. state representative, 1965, first vice chmn. also chmn. candidate com., 1966, chmn., 1968—, chmn. exec. com., 1970—, chmn., Rep. Central Com., 1970—; mem. exec. com. Fifth Congl. Dist. Rep. Com., 1965—; mem. Ga. State Rep. Centennial Com., 1966, first vice chmn., 1970—; first vice chmn. Ga. Rep. Com., 1970-71, chmn., 1971—; first vice chmn. Ga. Rep. Exec. Com., 1970—. Bd. dirs. Atlanta Hosp. Served as staff sgt. USAF, 1950-51; PTO. Mem. Atlanta Assn. Life Underwriters, Gen. Agts. and Mgrs. Assn. of Atlanta, South Cobb Jaycees (hon. life), Phi Sigma Epsilon (hon.) Baptist (music dir.). Home: 295 Glen Lake Dr NW Atlanta GA 30327 Office: 1819 Peachtree St NE Atlanta GA 30309*

SHAW, SARAH WIMBERLY (MRS. OLIVER N. SHAW), civic worker; b. nr. Perry, Ga.; d. Ezekiel Henry and Alice (de Haven) Wimberly; spl. student Oglethorpe U., 1946, Emory U., Agnes Scott Coll., U. Ga.; student Queen's Coll., Charlotte, N.C., 1965-67, Sorbonne, U. Paris, 1951; m. G. Grady Poole (dec.); 1 dau., Saralyn (Mrs. George John Hadgopoulos); m. 2d, Oliver N. Shaw, June 27, 1960. Asst. exec. placement dir. Retail Credit Co., Atlanta; dir. spl. services, pub. relations Davison's affiliate R. H. Macy of N.Y.C., also exec. tng. dir., Atlanta, prior 1953; nat. exec. sales adviser equipment service Girl Scouts U.S.A., N.Y.C., 1955-58; lectr. Am. Indian; lectr.

Delhom Gallery, Inst. Ceramic Research, Mint Mus. Art, Charlotte, N.C. Pres. Atlanta City Mission Bd., 1935; v.p. women's aux. Charlotte Mint Mus. Art, 1961-67, chmn. women's aux. membership com., 1971-72; chmn. women's div. United Arts Fund Council, Charlotte; life mem. chmn. personnel and world fellowship coms., YWCA; judge Nat. Flower Show; participant Charlotte TV panels, 1965-67; mem. Charlotte Opera Assn., 1961—. Bds. dirs. Charlotte, Atlanta YWCA'S, Charlotte Symphoney Orch. Assn. Mem. D.A.R. (regent jr. chpt., Habersham), Nat. League Am. Pen Women (lectr), Latin-Am. Club (hon. 1949—), Phi Mu (dist. dir. 1964-65). Presbyn. (life mem. women's soc. Atlanta) Clubs: Young Matrons' Circle Tallulah Falls Sch. (past pres.), Druid Hills Garden (past pres.), Ga. Garden (past sec.) (all Atlanta), Charlotte (N.C.) Country, Charlotte City. Contbr. book reviews. Address: 227 Hempstead Pl Charlotte NC 28207

SHAW, THOMAS NEVILLE FAWCETT, sch. adminstr.; b. N.Y.C., June 19, 1925; s. William Fawcett and Margaret (Nicholson) S.; A.B. cum laude Princeton, 1949; M.A., Columbia, 1956; m. Peggy Wolfe, Sept. 2, 1950; children— Anne Gibson, Peter Wolfe. Ordained priest Protestant Episcopal Ch., 1966; tchr. English and history, dir. studies Wooster Sch., Danbury, Conn., 1949-61, dir. Wooster Summer Sch. Reading Skills, 1957-61; dir. Camp Pequot, Ivoryton, Conn., 1951-56; headmaster Trinity Episcopal Sch., New Orleans, 1961—. Trustee St. Martin's Episcopal Sch., New Orleans. Served with AUS, 1943-46. Mem. Nat. Assn. Episcopal Schs. (pres. 1971-73), La. Episcopal Sch. Assn. (pres. 1969-71), Ind. Schs. Assn. of Southwest (mem. standards and research com. 1966-70). Author: A Manual for Reading, 1955. Home: 1305 Jackson Av New Orleans LA 70130 Office: 2111 Chestnut St New Orleans LA 70130

SHAW, THOMAS SHULER, educator; b. Loveland, Colo., Oct. 25, 1906; s. Thomas Irving and Carie Elbertie (Shuler) S.; student Colo. State U., 1925-28; B.A., George Washington U., 1930, postgrad., 1930-32; B.S. in L.S., Columbia, 1946; m. Mary Elizabeth Miller, Feb. 23, 1952. With Library of Congress, Washington, 1930-62, asst. in charge pub. reference sect., 1944-53, head sect., 1953-62; vis. prof. bibliography, reference and govt. publs. Sch. Library Sci., La. State U., 1962-64, prof., 1964—. Prof. bibliography and reference Sch. Library Service, U. Cal. at Los Angeles, summer 1961; prof. govt. publs. and book selection Grad. Sch. Library Sci., U. Ill., summer 1962; lectr. reference and bibliography Dept. Library Sci., Catholic U. Am., 1947-49, U. Cal. at Berkeley, 1949-50, U. So. Cal., summer 1952. Cons. govt. publs. collection Joint U. Libraries, Nashville, 1971. Mem. A.L.A. (v.p. reference service div. 1959-60, Mudge citation 1968), La. Library Assn., Assn. Coll. and Research Libraries (treas. 1949-52), Assn. Am. Library Schs., Southwestern Library Assn., Kappa Sigma. Author: Index to Profile Sketches in New Yorker Magazine, 1946, rev., 1971. Editor Bull. La. Library Assn., 1964-65. Home: 835 Delgado Dr Baton Rouge LA 70808 Office: Sch Library Sci La State U Baton Rouge LA 70803

SHAW, WILLIAM FREDERICK, statistician; b. Bklyn., Feb. 24, 1920; s. Charles Peter and Josephine Veronica (Seusing) S.; B.B.A., U. Miami, 1949; M.A., George Washington U., 1953; m. Josephine Cannington Kerbey, Jan. 18, 1947; children—William Frederick, Teresa Anne. With Research and Statistics div. FHA, Washington, 1950—, chief statistician, 1969—. Served with F.A., AUS, 1943-45. Decorated Bronze Star medal for heroism. Mem. Am. Statis. Assn., Am. Econ. Assn., Alpha Kappa Psi. Home: 6527 Byrnes Dr McLean VA 22101 Office: 7th and D Sts SW Washington DC 20411

SHAW, WILLIAM HARLAN, educator; b. Tulia, Tex., Apr. 3, 1922; s. Willie Sample and Delia (Harlan) S.; B.A., Hardin-Simmons U., 1943, M.A., 1949; Ph.D., La. State U., 1955; m. Majorie Lee McQuade, Nov. 1, 1945; children—Delia Belle, Morgan Roe. Grad. asst. La. State U., Baton Rouge, 1948-49, 53-54; instr. Hardin-Simmons, Abilene, Tex., 1949-50, asst. prof., 1955-56, Ill. State U., Normal, 1950-53; asst, prof. Washington U., St. Louis, 1956-61; asst. prof. Fla. State U., Tallahassee, 1961-67, asso. prof., 1967-68; asso. prof., coordinator grad. studies dept. drama La. State U., New Orleans, 1968-72, prof., 1972—. Costume dir. Asolo Theater Festival, State Theater of Fla., 1962-68. Served with USNR, 1943-46. Presbyn. (deacon). Home: 7450 Fieldston Rd New Orleans LA 70126

SHAW, WILLIAM WESLEY, educator; b. Phila., Oct. 19, 1910; s. William Henry and Mary (Burt) S.; B.A., Dickinson Coll., 1932; M.A., Princeton, 1934, Ph.D., 1935; m. Mary Elizabeth Cole, June 8, 1938; children—Judith C. (Mrs. Steven A. Davidow), William Wesley, Regina E. (Mrs. Gerard P. van As). Tech. asst. N.J. State Civil Service Dept., Trenton, N.J., 1936-38; dir. personnel San Diego County, Cal., 1938-41; asso. dir. Municipal Service Bur., N.Y. State Civil Service Commn., Albany, N.Y., 1941-42; dir. personnel City New Orleans, 1942-71; prof. polit. sci. Tulane U., New Orleans, 1947—, dir. Urban Studies Center, 1971—. Bd. dirs. United Fund Greater New Orleans, 1967—. Mem. Pub. Personnel Assn. (pres. 1957,58), Am. Polit. Sci. Assn., Am. Soc. Pub. Adminstrs. Home: 1721 Robert St New Orleans LA 70115

SHAWCROFT, BRIAN, architect; b. Nottingham, Eng., Feb. 24, 1929; s. Herbert Thomas and Annie (Tatman) S.; grad. Southwest Essex Tech. Coll. and Sch. of Art, 1953; M.Arch., Mass. Inst. Tech., 1959-60; m. Anne Marie Rogers, Sept. 13, 1968. Came to U.S., 1959, naturalized, 1965. Architect, Slater, Uren & Pike, Architects, London, Eng., 1954-56, Page & Steele, Architects, Toronto, Ont., Can., 1956-59; partner MacMillan, MacMillan, Shawcroft & Thames, Raleigh, N.C., 1968-70; partner Environmental Planning Assos., Raleigh, 1971—. Asso. prof. architecture Sch. Design N.C. State U., Raleigh, 1960-68; Cons. architect Holloway-Reeves Architects, Raleigh, 1964—. Mem. State Capitol Planning Commn., Raleigh, 1963-65, Heritage Sq. Planning Commn., Raleigh, 1963-65. Served with Ednl. Corps, Royal Army, 1947-49. Mem. A.I.A. (N.C. chpt. award of merit 1962, 68, House and Home House for Better Living award of merit 1962), Royal Inst. Brit. Architects (asso.). Home: 210 Ashe Av Raleigh NC 27605 Office: 333 Fayetteville St Raleigh NC 27601

SHAWE, ARTHUR THACKERAY, contractor; b. Balt., June 13, 1927; s. Percy Theodore and Lita (Brannan) S.; B.S. in M.E., Ga. Inst. Tech., 1951, M.S. in M.E., 1953; m. Julia Cecelia McDonough, July 4, 1948; children—Anne Theresa, Mark Thackeray, Thomas Theodore. Test engr. Balt. Consol. Electric Light & Power Co., 1951-52; v.p. Erickson's, Inc., Savannah, Ga., 1953—, So. Engrs. & Contractors, Savannah, Ga., 1953—. Served with USNR, 1945-47. Registered profl. engr., Ga. Mem. Am. Soc. Heating, Refrigerating and Air Conditioning Engrs. (bd. govs. 1965—), Pi Tau Sigma. Home: 521 E 45th St Savannah GA 31405 Office: 1711 Prine St Savannah GA 31405

SHAY, VIOLET AMELIA BROWN (MRS. JOHN HENRY SHAY, JR.), artist, poet, writer; b. New Orleans; d. Thomas Beggs and Ethel (Schultz) Brown; grad. bus. coll., New Orleans, 1929; student Famous Writers Sch.; m. John Henry Shay, Jr., June 15, 1940. Free lance writer, 1940—; poetry published in anthologies including Avalon, Am. Sonnets and Lyrics, others; prose pub. in mags. including Coronet, Canadian Home Jour., Seventenn, Pathfinder, The Pen Woman, Town Jour.; juvenile stories in publs. including Stories for Children, Council Fires, Trailblazer; editor little mags., 1945-50; ceramics exhibited Pirate's Alley Art Show, New Orleans, 1950-51. Recipient awards for writing Nat. League Am. Pen Women, La. Press Women; hon. mention ceramics Pirate's Alley Art Show, 1950; award Deep South Writers Conf., 1968. Mem. Avalon World Arts Acad. (La.) (pres. 1952-54), Nat. Hist. Soc. (founding asso.), Composers, Authors and Artists Assn. Am., Nat. Poetry Day Com. (state chmn. 1949-56), Nat. League Am. Pen Women (br. pres. 1951-53), Avalon World Arts Acad., United Amateur Press Assn. Am. (past chief lit. dir.), Wendell Willkie Found. Contbg. author: Louisiana Vignettes, 1967. Address: 1231 Congress St New Orleans LA 70117

SHEAHAN, FRANCES CATHERINE RILING (MRS. ROBERT FRANCIS SHEAHAN), civic worker; b. Burlington, Ia.; d. Frank Joseph and Alice Jane (Bauch) Riling; B.A., St. Mary-of-the-Woods Coll., 1928; m. Robert Francis Sheahan, Sept. 10, 1930 (dec. Feb. 1959); children—Robert Riling, John Patrick, Margaret Jane (Mrs. Patrick Henry O'Neill), Michael Francis, Mary Frances (Mrs. Aubrey Van Buren Spear, Jr.). Chmn. bd., treas. Shamrock Farms, Inc., Gladstone, Ill., 1963-69. Bd. dirs. St. Peter's Home for Children of Memphis, 1967—, Goldsmith's Civic Garden Center, 1960-67; Pres. Bond of Faith Circle Kings Daus., 1967. Mem. Mpls. League Cath. Women (past sec., past bd. mem.). Club: Town and Country Garden (pres.). Home: 2926 Tishomingo Lane Memphis TN 38111

SHEAKS, BARCLAY, artist; b. East Chicago, Ind., Oct. 22, 1928; s. Earl L. and Jeanie (Rice) S.; B.F.A., Va. Commonwealth U., 1949; m. Edna Mae Daniel; 1 son, Owen James. Art tchr., 1949—; head art dept. Va. Wesleyan Coll., Norfolk, 1970—; artist-in-residence Humanities Center, Richmond, Va., 1971—; art cons. for Hunt Mfg. Co., Inc. Phila., 1968—; lectr. Va. Mus. Exhibited in one-man shows at Va. Mus., 1969, Columbia (S.C.) Mus., 1971, Mobile (Ala.) Mus., 1968; exhibited in group shows Nat. Acad., Corcoran Gallery, Norfolk, Va. mus., Butler Inst. Am. Art, others; represented in permanent collections Va. Mus., Columbia Mus., Butler Inst. Am. Art, Youngstown, O. Mem. Va. Mus., Norfolk Mus., Peninsula Arts Assn., Tidewater Artists, La. Watercolor Assn. Author: Painting in Acrylics From Start to Finish, 1972. Home: 51 Hopkins St Newport News VA 23601

SHEAR, DAPHFINE LUNDY (MRS. WARREN SHEAR), mem. Democratic Nat. Com.; b. Davis, Okla., May 15, 1919; d. Benjamin Franklin and Eula Mae (Boyles) Lundy; student So. Meth. U., 1938; m. Warren Shear, Aug. 29, 1940; children—Ken Sue (Mrs. John Stephen Doerfel), Lynn (Mrs. Thomas Balint), Sloane, David. Dir. Milford Oil & Gas Ltd. (Eng.), Argosy GmbH (Germany), Milford Danske (Denmark). Chmn. 6th Congl. Dist. Dem. Com., 1962-64; mem. Dem. Nat. Com. for Okla., 1964—; Okla. rep. platform com. Dem. Nat. Conv., 1964, 68. Episcopalian. Address: Box 14440 Oklahoma City OK 73114

SHEARIN, FORREST GREENE, assn. ofcl.; b. nr. Weldon, N.C., Mar. 13, 1903; s. John Wesley and Eugenia (Kilpatrick) S.; student pub. schs., Weldon; m. Virgie Elizabeth Grizzard, Dec. 23, 1923; children— Beatrice Eugenia, Forrest Greene. Mem. N.C. Jr. Order United Am. Mechanics, 1924—, sec., gen. mgr. state council ins. dept., 1940—, state mgr. ins. dept., nat. council, 1949—, controller, bd. trustees N.C. Jr, O.U.A. M. Children's Home, nat. council bd. trustees Children's Home, mem. ritual com. nat. council, 1955-59, chmn. Good of the Order com. nat, council, 1957; nat. vice councilor Jr. O.U.A.M., 1961-63, nat. councilor, 1963-65, mem. nat. council bd. control com. on investments and program, 1967—, mem. exec. bd. nat. council bd. of officers, nat. council treas., 1972—; owner, sec. treas. Colonial Frozen Foods, Inc.; owner Forrest G. Shearin, finance bus., gen. real estate bus.; owner, operator Forrest G. Shearin, Ins. Agy.; pres. Investment Enterprises, Inc., 1961—, also dir., sec., treas. Scotland Neck Devel. Corp. Chmn., mem. Halifax Devel. Commn., 1965—; chmn. Region L Council of Govts., 1965-69, chmn., 1969—. Sec.-treas. Scotland Neck Bus. Bur., 1959—; mem. City Council, Scotland Neck, 1946—, finance officer, 1949—. Bd. trustees, finance com. Chowan Coll., Murfreesboro, 1947-50; trustee Bapt. Orphanages N.C., 1951-55; chmn. bd. trustees Our Community Hosp., Scotland Neck, 1955-58, chmn., acting adminstr., 1961-64; served as mem. Health Com. Lower Halifax County; mem. Bicentennial Com. Halifax County, 1958. Mem. N. Roanoke Bapt. Assn. (treas. 1958-63, chmn. constn. and by-laws com. 1956; gen. bd. state conv. 1957-60; chmn. social service com.; exec. com.); mem. exec. and budget com. State Bapt. Conv. N.C.; mem. corp. bd. Bapt. Home for Aging. Democrat. Baptist (deacon, trustee). Home: W 17th St Scotland Neck NC 27874 Office: N Main St Scotland Neck NC 27874

SHEARMAN, WILLIAM HUGH, publisher; b. Oak Park, Ill., Feb. 21, 1921; s. Thomas Broadus and Flora (Inglis) S.; student Wabash Coll., 1939-41; B.S., McNeese Coll., 1965; m. Ada Brand, Jan. 3, 1945; children—William Hugh, John Thomas, Nancy (Mrs. Walter Theriot, Jr.), Walker Ward, Stacy Lynn, Douglas Randolph. Bus. mgr. Lake Charles (La.) Am. Press, 1946-56, pub., 1959—; bus. mgr. Mansfield (O.) Jour., 1956-59; dir. Hobbs (N.M.) Daily News Sun, Trinidad Chronicle News, Gulf Nat. Bank, Lake Charles. Pres. A.R.C., 1955; campaign chmn. United Appeal Fund, 1960-61; active YMCA. Bd. dirs. Lake Charles Meml. Hosp. Served to 1st lt. USMCR, 1942-46. Named Man of Year Lake Charles Assn. Commerce, 1966. Mem. Lake Charles Assn. Commerce (dir. 1964-70), Phi Gamma Delta. Democrat. Episcopalian (vestryman 1963-67). Clubs: Pioneer, Country (Lake Charles, La.); Boston (New Orleans). Home: 109 Pithon St Lake Charles LA 70601 Office: 710 Bilbo St Box 2893 Lake Charles LA 70601

SHEEHAN, SISTER HELEN, librarian; b. Manchester, N.H., July 25, 1904; d. John A. and Georgia M. (Beebe) Sheehan; A.B., Trinity Coll., 1924; B.S. in L.S., Simmons Coll., 1926. Mem. Sisters of Notre Dame de Namur; journalism staff Manchester (N.H.) Mirror, 1924-25; tchr. New Eng. High Sch., 1931-34; br. librarian Manchester (N.H.) City Library, 1926-30; librarian Cathedral Library, 1930-31, Trinity Coll., 1934-72. Chmn. 1965 Workshop Coll. Libraries, Phila. Mem. Am., Cath. (exec. bd. 1959-65, 67—, pres. 1969-71) library assns. Author: History Manchester City Library, 1929; The Small College Library, 1962. Chmn. editorial bd. Choice, 1966-70; editorial bd. Library Coll. Jour., 1967-71. Address: Trinity Coll Washington DC 20017

SHEEHAN, JAMES GORDON, business cons., educator; b. Falmouth, Ky., June 7, 1918; s. John Andrew and Lauretta (Kelly) S.; student U. Ky., 1937-38; B.S., Xavier U., 1941; M.A., U. Cin., 1952; Ph.D., Ohio State U., 1955; m. Patricia Ann Thomson, Sept. 10, 1945; children— Mary Michele, James Michael, John Gregory, Daniel Rourke, Thomas Gordon, Jeanne Andrea, Anne Marie, Maureen Lauretta, Susan Patricia. Sr. partner Asso. Bus. Consultants, Cin., 1957—; prof. marketing U. Cin., 1954-61. Past chmn. Campbell County (Ky.) Indsl. Devel. Commn. Served from 2d lt. to lt. col., Q.M.C., AUS, 1941-51. Recipient ann. award for contbn. to marketing sci. Southwestern Ohio chpt. Am. Marketing Assn., 1958. Mem. Am. Econs. Assn., Soc. Advancement Mgmt., Am. Marketing Assn. (past chpt. pres.), Cin. Sales Execs. Council (past v.p., dir.), Campbell County Com. of 500 (past v.p.). Roman Catholic. Author: Uses and Marketability of Urban Renewal Land for Industrial and Commercial Purposes, 1957; The Impact of Planned Shopping Centers on the Metropolitan Cincinnati Market 1959; A Reappraisal of the Shopping Center Movement, 1961; Planning for the Future of Commerce and Revitalization of Business Districts in East Central Florida, 1965. Home: 500 NE 102d St Miami Shores FL 33151 Office: Carew Tower Cincinnati OH 45202

SHEEHAN, JAMES HARLEY, lawyer, accountant; b. Macon, Ga., May 4, 1931; s. James B. and Frances (Harley) S.; B.S. with honors, U. Fla., 1961; J.D. with high honors, Fla. State U., 1971; m. Caroline Martha Smith, Nov. 22, 1952; children—James Gregory, Kelly Elizabeth. Agt., Internal Revenue Service, Jacksonville, Fla., 1961-65; tax mgr. Milligan & Burke, C.P.A.'s, Jacksonville, 1965-68; lectr. fed. income taxation Fla. State U., Tallahassee, 1968-71; partner Arthur Young & Co., Jacksonville, 1971—; admitted to Fla. bar. Mem. exec. com. N.E. Fla. Estate Planning Council, 1968-69; active Community Chest, United Fund. Served with USNR, 1949-53. C.P.A., Fla. Mem. Fla. (Jacksonville chpt. award for excellence 1967, state taxation com.) Am. insts. C.P.A.'s, Fla. Bar, Am. Bar Assn., Delta Theta Phi. Beta Alpha Psi, Alpha Kappa Psi. Methodist. Contbr. articles to profl. jours. Home: 8342 Calento St Jacksonville FL 32211

SHEEHAN, WILLIAM HAROLD, lawyer; b. Childress, Tex., Mar. 6, 1928; s. Gerald and Mazzie (Lewis) S.; LL.B., Baylor U., 1951; m. Mary Louise Mayers, May 30, 1948; children—Mary Margaret, Kathleen J., John P., Jack Hale. Admitted to Tex. bar, 1950; pvt. practice, Friona, Tex., 1950-65; partner Dubuque & Meredith, Dumas, Tex., 1966—; county atty. Parmes Co. (Tex.), 1955-57; dist. atty. 154th Jud. Dist., 1957-61. Chmn. March of Dimes, Friona, 1954-55, Community Chest, Friona, 1960-61; pres. Dumas Concert Assn., 1966—; pres. Dumas YMCA, 1969-70. Served with AUS, 1946-47, 52-54. Mem. Dumas C. of C. (pres. 1968-69), Am., Dumas, 69th Dist, bar assns., State Bar Tex. (council mem., chmn. gen. practice sect.). Baptist (deacon). Lion. Home: 601 Bennett Dr Dumas TX 79029 Office: 105 W 7th St Dumas TX 79029

SHEEHAN, WILLIAM JOHN, librarian; b. Syracuse, N.Y., Jan. 1, 1937; s. William Jeremiah and Margaret Mary (Horrigan) S.; B.A., U. Toronto, 1960; S.T.B., U. St. Michael's Coll., 1965; M.S. in L.S., Case Western Res. U., 1968. Joined Congregation of Priests of St. Basil, 1955, ordained priest Roman Catholic Ch., 1966; tchr. Aquinas Inst., Rochester, N.Y., 1960-62; tchr. Catholic Central High Sch., Detroit, 1962-63; asst. librarian St. Basil's Sem., Toronto, Ont., Can., 1963-67; asst. librarian U. St. Thomas, Houston, 1968-69, dir. libraries, 1969—. Mem. A.L.A., Catholic Library Assn. (chmn. coll. and univ. sect. Bishop Byrne unit 1969—). Address: 3812 Montrose Blvd Houston TX 77006

SHEEHY, MARIE ANN PAVELKA (MRS. VINCENT THOMAS SHEEHY), govt. ofcl.; b. Kyjov, Czechoslovakia, Apr. 1, 1920; d. Joseph Louis and Marie (Navratil) Pavelka; came to U.S., 1924, naturalized, 1930;; student Bryant and Stratton Bus. Coll., Chgo., 1938; m. Vincent Thomas Sheehy, May 13, 1941; 1 dau., Marie W. (Mrs. Thomas M. Lisi). Sec., Ingersoll-Rand Machinery Co., Chgo., 1939-40; sec. Internat. Boundary Commn. U.S. and Can., Dept. State, Washington, 1940—, adminstrv. asst., 1956-63, adminstrv. officer 1963—. Asst. financial drives Trinity Coll. Alumni, Washington, 1968. Roman Catholic. Home: 2205 Beechwood Rd Lewisdale-Adelphi MD 20783 Office: GAO Bldg 441 G St NW Washington DC 20548

SHEETS, NAN, artist; b. Albany, Ill.; d. George Duffield and Orvilla (Booth) Quick; Ph.G., Valparaiso U., 1905; postgrad. Utah U., 1908-09, Broadmoor Art. Acad., 1921-24; m. Fred C. Sheets, June 28, 1909. Art column Daily Oklahoman Sun Edn., Oklahoma City, 1934-62; dir. Oklahoma Art Center, Oklahoma City, 1935-65, tr. ret., 1965, trustee; exhibited one-man shows Okla. Art Center, 1950, Ft. Worth Arts Center, 1929, Mus. Art, Okla. U., 1930; Philbrook Art Center, Tulsa, 1949, 1952, Witte Meml. Mus., San Antonio, 1929, Mus. Fine Arts, Houston, 1929; exhibited group shows State Fair of Okla., 1927, Tulsa U., 1932, Philbrook Art Center, 1952, Okla. Art Center, 1967. Named to Okla. Hall of Fame, 1953; named Woman of Year in Radio and TV, Okla. Sooner chpt. Am. Women in Radio and TV, 1959; named Outstanding Citizen Greater Oklahoma City, 1962. Fellow Royal Soc. Arts (Eng.); mem. Okla. Art League (hon.), U. Okla. Alumni Assn. (hon.), Ill. Acad. Fine Arts (hon. life), Beta Sigma Phi (hon.), Delta Kappa Gamma (hon.), Kappa Pi (hon.). Club: Altrusa (hon). Address: 401 NW 18th St Oklahoma City OK 73103

SHEFFEY, JOHN PRESTON, govt. ofcl.; b. Marion, Va., Apr. 21, 1919; s. John Preston and Virginia (Harrington) S.; student Marion Coll., 1935-37; B.S., U.S. Mil. Acad., 1942; M.A., George Washington U., 1962; m. Shirley Vera Jennings, Dec. 19, 1948; children—Katherine Jean, Shirley Theresa. Commd. 2d lt. U.S. Army, 1942, advanced through grades to col., 1962; instr. U.S. Mil. Acad., 1945-48; gen. staff officer and armor unit comdr., 1954-58; adviser to Army of South Vietnam, 1959-60; gen. staff officer Dept. Army, 1961-65; ret., 1965; exec. sec. Atlantic-Pacific Interoceanic Canal Study Commn., Washington, 1965-66, exec. dir., 1967-70; spl. adviser Dept. of State, 1971—. Bd. dirs. Colombian Prep. Sch. Found. Decorated Bronze Star medal, Legion of Merit; recipient Civilian awards for outstanding achievement Combined Fund Drive, 1966, 67, 68. Mem. Assn. Grads. U.S. Mil. Acad. (past trustee), Ret. Officers Assn. Republican. Presbyn. Home: 1313 Kingston Av Alexandria VA 22302 Office: Dept of State Washington DC 20520

SHEFFIELD, CHARLES WILLIAM, county ofcl.; b. Ridley Park, Pa., Feb. 21, 1934; s. Walker and Marion (Hicks) S.; B.C.E., U. Fla., 1957; M.S. in San. Engring., U. Cin., 1966; m. Barbara Jean Greis, Feb. 8, 1958; children—Michelle, Jonathen, Kerry, Tamey. Design engr. Michaels Engring. Co., Orlando, Fla., 1959-60; dir. san. engring. dept. Orange County Health Dept., Orlando, Fla., 1960-65; pollution control officer Orange County Pollution Control Dept., Orlando, 1966—. Chmn., Gov's. Lake Apopka Tech. Com., 1966-69; mem. Gov's. Aquatic Research and Devel. Com., 1966-70. Served to lt. (j.g.) USPHS, 1957-59. Recipient Govt. Conservation award 1969. Registered profl. engr., Fla. Mem. Nat. Soc. Profl. Engrs., Am. Soc. C.E., Fla. Engring. Soc. (past chmn. engrs. in govt. sect., mem. exec. com.), Fla. Pollution Control Assn. (indsl. waste com. 1972—), Conservation 70 (tech. com. 1969), C. of C. (conservation-environmental com. 1966—). Contbr. articles to profl. jours. Home: 3509 Edland St Orlando FL 32806 Office: 2008 E Michigan Av Orlando FL 32806

SHEFTEL, HARRY BERNARD, govt. ofcl.; b. Clinton, Mass., July 9, 1906; s. Morris and Molly (Siff) S.; A.B., Clark U., 1927; M.A., Am. U., 1944; m. Alice Naistat, Sept. 21, 1935; children—Janice S. (Mrs. Ira L. Flotkin), Rosalyn L. (Mrs. Alan I. Stiefel). Chief analysis sect. Bur. Labor Statistics, Washington, 1935-41; asst. chief constrn. research div. WPB, 1941-45; dir. econ. research Fed. Works Adminstrn., 1945-50; bus. economist Def. Prodn. Adminstrn., 1950-52; program analyst Dept. Def., 1952-55; asso. clearance officer, Office of Mgmt. and Budget, Exec. Office of Pres., Washington, 1956—. Pres. Coolidge High Sch. Home and Sch. Assn. Mem. Nat. Press Club, Am. Econ. Assn., Am. Statis. Assn., Toastmasters, Tau Kappa Alpha. Home: 5813 3d Pl NW Washington DC 20011 Office: New Exec Office Bldg Washington DC 20503

SHEILD, FRANCIS WARREN, dentist; b. Newport News, Va., Aug. 15, 1935; s. George Henry and Katherine Warren (Houston) S.; A.B., Va. Mil. Inst., 1957; D.D.S., Med. Coll. Va., 1961; m. Margaret Phelps Dixon Posey, Aug. 20, 1960; children—Katherine Elizabeth, George Cabell. Dentist, Hampton, Va., 1963—. Co-owner Rhododendron Nursery, Newport News, 1970—. Mem. adv. bd. Am. Cancer Soc., 1963-66, Thomas Nelson Community Coll., Hampton, 1965—, also budgetary and finance chmn. Served with AUS, 1957-63. Mem. exec. bd. Hampton Rds Cotillion, 1966—; charter mem. Hampton Rds. Assembly, 1952—. Mem. Am., Va., Peninsula dental assns., Fedn. Dentaire Internat., Am. Rhododendron Soc., Hampton Horticulture Soc., So. Appalachian Bot. Club. Episcopalian. Clubs: Hampton Roads German, Lafayette Gun, Hampton Yacht. Author: A Star To Guide You, 1968. Patentee, mfr. navigational computer. Home: 118 Woodland Dr Newport News VA 23606 Office: 1610 Aberdeen Rd Hampton VA 23366

SHELBOURNE, ROY MAHLON, judge; b. Bardwell, Ky., Nov. 12, 1890; s. Moreau Thomas and Jenny Lind (Dennis) S.; ed. pub. Schs., Bardwell; A.B., Union Univ., Jackson, Tenn., 1912; LL.B., Cumberland U., 1913; LL.D., Catherine Spalding Coll., Louisville, 1964; m. Edith Richardson, Oct. 8, 1914; children—Mahlon R., Jane, Nancy. Admitted to Ky. bar, 1913; practice of law at Bardwell (with father) under firm name of Shelbourne & Shelbourne, until father's death, 1927; county atty. Carlisle Co., 1918-26; pres. Bardwell Deposit Bank, 1926-36; became partner in law firm Wheeler & Shelbourne, Paducah, Ky., practiced there to Feb. 1946; U.S. dist. judge Western Dist. of Ky., 1946-64, sr. U.S. dist. judge, 1964—. Mem. Ky. Hwy. Commn., 1930-32. Pres. Four Rivers council Boy Scouts of Am., 1939-41; Silver Beaver Award. Mem. Ky. Bd. Bar Examiners, 1940-46; mem. McCracken County Bar Assn. (pres. 1941). Kappa Sigma. Democrat. Christian Ch. Rotarian (pres. Paducah chapter, 1938-39). Home: 715 Waterford Rd Louisville KY 40207 Office: Fed Bldg Louisville KY 40202

SHELBURNE, C. DANIEL, banker; b. Green Bay, Va., Mar. 31, 1915; s. Thomas Pettus and Mabel (Daniel) S.; B.S., Hampden-Sydney Coll., 1936; M.B.A., U. Pa., 1939-40; postgrad. Stonier Grad. Sch. Banking, Rutgers U., 1946-49; m. Edith McDanel, Dec. 27, 1941; children—John Daniel, Edward McDanel, Thomas Maynard. Bank examiner Fed. Res. Bank, Richmond, Va., 1945-48, sr. bank examiner, 1949-50; with Wachovia Bank & Trust Co., N.A., Winston-Salem, N.C. and Raleigh, N.C., 1950—, v.p. in charge loan adminstrn. dept., 1955-69, sr. v.p. in charge loan adminstrn. dept., 1969—. Instr., Sch. Consumer Banking, U. Va., 1961—. Active United Fund; past pres. adv. bd. Wake County Salvation Army, Boy Scouts Am.; past pres. Mental Health Bd. Wake County, Raleigh. Served with Supply Corps, USNR, 1941-45; lt. comdr., ret. Recipient Silver Beaver award Boy Scouts Am., 1969. Mem. C. of C., Robert Morris Assos. (past pres. Carolinas-Va. chpt.), Sigma Chi. Episcopalian. Clubs: Carolina Country, Executives (Raleigh). Home: 2551 Wake Dr Raleigh NC 27608 Office: POBox 1951 Raleigh NC 27602

SHELBY, CHARLES EDWIN, geneticist; b. Salem, Ky., July 19, 1925; s. Richard Romeo and Amy (Gibbs) S.; B.S., U. Ky., 1948, M.S., 1949; Ph.D., Ia. State U., 1952; m. Dorothy Ellen Scott, Sept. 11, 1955; children—Mary Christine, Dorothy Ellen, Susan Marie, Richard Romeo. Research geneticist U.S. Range Livestock Expt. Sta., Miles City, Mont., 1952-55; research geneticist Beef Cattle Breeding research Agrl. Research Service U.S. Dept. Agr., Denver, 1955-59; investigations leader, dir. regional Swine Breeding Lab. U.S. Dept. Agr. Agrl. Research Service, Ames, Ia., 1959-70, mem. grad. faculty Ia. State U., 1966-70, asso. prof., 1965-70; liaison officer U.S. Dept. Agr. Ky. State Coll., 1970—. Served with USNR, 1944-46. Mem. Am. Genetic Assn., Am. Meat Sci. Assn., Am. Soc. Animal Sci., Genetic Soc. Am., Biometric Soc., Am. Inst. Biol. Sci., A.A.A.S., Am. Assn. U. Profs., Sigma Xi, Alpha Gamma Rho. Mem. Christian Ch. Contbr. articles to sci. jours. Home: 431 Tatato Trail Frankfort KY 40601 Office: Ky State U Frankfort KY 40601

SHELBY, MCDALTON, hwy. research engr.; b. Austin, Tex., July 5, 1910; s. Lemeul Evart and Mabel (Wright) S.; B.S. in Elec. Engring., U. Tex., 1931; m. Frances Jeanette Campbell, Apr. 8, 1934; children—Donald M., Robert N., Lilas Janice (Mrs. Sam E. Kinch, Jr.), Judith Ann (Mrs. J. Q. Edwards, Jr.). With Tex. Hwy. Dept., Austin, 1931-65, successively asst. engr., 1931-41, resident engr., Brownwood, Tex., 1941-47, structural found. design engr., Bridge div., Austin, 1947-54, research engr., 1954-65; hwy. research engr. Tex. Transp. Inst., Tex. A. and M. U., College Station, 1965—. Fellow Am. Soc. C.E. (pres. Austin br. 1963); mem. Nat. Soc. Profl. Engrs. (pres. Travis chpt. 1957), Am. Soc. Testing and Materials, Nat. Acad. Sci. (mem. dept. design Hwy. Research Bd., and chmn, gen. design div.), Internat. Platform Assn., Sigma Xi. Methodist. Rotarian. Home: 2103 Vinewood Bryan TX 77801 Office: Hwy Research Bldg Tex Transp Inst Tex A and M Univ College Station TX 77843

SHELDEN, FRANK CLIFTON, JR., constrn. co. exec.; b. Houston, Jan. 15, 1928; s. Frank Clifton and Elviera (Heim) S.; B.S. with distinction in Mech. Engring., Rice U., 1948; m. Millicent Brown, Apr. 5, 1952; children—Frank Clifton III, Sam McClintock, Maura Millicent. Engr. trainee J.T. Thorpe, Inc., Los Angeles, 1948-49, office engr., Houston, 1949-54; v.p., dir. J.T. Thorpe Co., Houston, 1954-57, pres., dir., 1957—; pres., dir. Thorpe Realty Co., 1963-69, J.T. Thorpe (Can.) Ltd., Edmonton, Alta., 1964—, Thorpe Insulation Co., Corpus Christi, Tex., 1965—; dir. South Park Nat. Bank, Houston. Registered profl. engr., Tex., La. Mem. Nat., Tex. socs. profl. engrs., Young Pres.'s Orgn., Tau Beta Pi. Club: Houston Racquet. Home: 1202 Riverbend Dr Houston TX 77042 Office: 6833 Kirbyville St Houston TX 77033

SHELDON, ANSON HOISINGTON, polit. worker, bus. exec., farmer; b. Nehawka, Neb., June 5, 1905; s. George Lawson and Rose (Higgins) S.; student pub. schs.; m. Beatrice Everett, Feb. 5, 1939; children—Patricia Ann (Mrs. Harry Strauss), Anson Holsington, Lawson Everett. Various positions to service sta. mgr. Standard Oil Co. of Ky., 1921-22; dealer Internat. Harvester Co., 1924-26, road engr., sales southeastern U.S., 1926-29; sales Allis Chalmers Mfg. Co., Memphis br., 1930-36; distbr. Miss. and Ark., Massey Harris Co., 1938-39; dirt contractor and heavy equipment rentals, 1945-50; mfrs. agt. Baker Plow Co., 1957-67; factory rep. Howard Rotavator Co., 1961-68; Miss. state real estate broker, 1968—; chmn. bd. Machinery, Inc., 1968—; distbr. Grove Mfg. Co., 1962-66; farmer, 1923—. Commr. Washington County Soil Conservation Dist., 1947—. Mem. legislative com. Delta Council Water Resources Com., 1964-65. Mem. Miss. state exec. com. Republican Party, 1944-64, state chmn., 1948-52, vice chmn., 1952-60; del Rep. Nat. Conv., 1956, 60. Mem. Miss. Soil Conservation Commrs. Episcopalian. Elk. Address: Avon MS 38723

SHELDON, BEATRICE EVERETT (MRS. ANSON H. SHELDON), polit. worker; b. Gunn, Miss., May 16, 1915; d. John Broadus and Pency Ann (Wooley) Everett; R.N., Dr. Willis Walley Sch. Nursing, Jackson, Miss., 1937; m. Anson H. Sheldon, Feb. 5, 1939; children—Patricia Ann (Mrs. Harry C. Strauss), Anson H., Lawson. Nurse, Kings Daus. Hosp., Canton, Miss., 1937, Greenville, Miss., 1937, Helena (Ark.) Hosp., 1938-39; sec.-treas. Machinery, Inc., 1966—. Mem. county com. Miss. Republican Party, 1944-60; alternate del. to Rep. State Conv., 1948, 52, 56, 60. Trustee South Washington County Hosp. Mem. Miss. Registered Nurse Assn., Miss. Fedn. Women's Clubs. Episcopalian. Home: Keystone Plantation Avon MS 38723

SHELDON, CHARLES STUART, II, govt. ofcl.; b. Shanghai, China, May 18, 1917 (parents Am. citizens); s. Sidney Roby and Eunice (Fife) S.; B.A. magna cum laude, U. Wash., 1936, M.A., 1938; A.M., Harvard, 1939, Ph.D., 1942; m. Margaret Jean Reed, Mar. 21, 1942; children—Margaret (Mrs. David L. Mallino), Pamela (Mrs. Robert K. Morris), Nancy Jean. Asst. prof. transp. econs. U. Wash., 1940-55; chief Pacific sect. cargo requirements War Shipping Adminstrn., 1942-43; chief fgn. and domestic commerce, research and programs Econ. and Sci. Sect., Gen. Hdqrs., Supreme Comdr. Allied Powers, Tokyo,Japan, 1948-49; sr. specialist transp. Legislative Reference Service, Library Congress, 1955-58; tech. dir. House Com. on Sci. and Astronautics, 1959-61; sr. staff Space Council, White House, Washington, 1961-66; chief sci. policy research div. Library of Congress, Washington, 1966—. Cons. Sabena Belgian World Airlines, 1953-55; commentator on Soviet space program NBC and CBS TV, 1965—. Mem. planning commn., Puget Sound, Wash., 1940-42, chmn. road commn., 1942-43; mem. Municipal League, Seattle, 1946-50. Served to capt. USNR, 1943-46, 50-52. Recipient Commendation U.S. Congress House Com. on Sci. and Astronautics, 1961. Fellow Am. Astronautical Soc., British Interplanetary Soc., Am. Inst. Aeronautics and Astronautics (distinguished traveling lectr. 1968-72); mem. Am. Econ. Assn., Pan Xenia (internat. sec. 1937-42), Internat. Acad. Astronautics (corr.), Phi Beta Kappa. Presbyn. Author: Soviet Economic Growth, 1957; Review of the Soviet Space Program, 1967; The Soviet Space Program, 1971. Home: 3507 N Piedmont St Arlington VA 22207 Office: Congl Research Service Library Congress Washington DC 20540

SHELDON, ROGER ALPHA, printing and pub. co. exec.; b. Baton Rouge, May 12, 1922; s. William Hannaman and Arta (Sims) S.; B.A., La. State U., 1942, postgrad., 1946; m. Suzanne R. Eaton, Jan. 30, 1972; children by previous marriage—Mark, Elizabeth (Mrs. Alan Danneman), Bonnie, Paul, David, Patricia. Dep. information officer Houston regional office WAA, 1946-47; account exec. George Kirksey & Assos., Houston, 1947-49; pub. relations counsel Tex. div., Am. Cancer Soc., Houston, 1949-51; editor-writer Merkle Press, Inc., Washington, 1951-61, v.p., editorial dir., 1962-71, v.p. spl. projects, 1971—; information officer Pres.'s Commn. on Status of Women, Washington, 1962. Troop committeeman Nat. Capitol Area council Boy Scouts Am., 1968—; community relations chmn. Allied Civic Group, Montgomery County, Md., 1955-56. Democratic precinct chmn., Montgomery County, 1968-70. Served with USAAF, World War II. Decorated Air medal; recipient Service certificate Boy Scouts Am., 1960. Mem. Washington Newspaper Guild (mem. bd. 1959-60), Internat. Platform Assn. Unitarian. Home: 3828 Calvert St NW Washington DC 20007 Office: 810 Rhode Island Av NE Washington DC 20018

SHELEY, CLAYTON DANIEL, sch. adminstr.; b. Halcyon Dale, Ga., Dec. 1, 1918; s. Clayton D. and Rosalie (Evans) S.; B.S., Ga. So. Coll., 1939; M.A., George Peabody Coll., 1947; Ed.D., U. Ga., 1961; m. Lois Durrence, Dec. 20, 1940. Tchr. pub. schs., Richmond County, 1939-43, 46; prin. Westside High Sch., Augusta, Ga., 1971—. Chmn. edn. div. United Fund of Augusta, 1967—, chmn. community planning com. Bd. dirs. Civic Music Assn. Served with AUS, 1943-46; PTO. Decorated Purple Heart, Bronze Star medal. Mem. N.E.A. (life), Am. Legion (recipient medal for excellence in edn. 1963), Phi Delta Kappa, Nat. Congress Parents and Teachers (life, hon. founder). Methodist (tchr.). Club: Exchange (sec.-treas. 1966—. Home: 3238 Ramsgate Rd Augusta GA 30904 Office: 1002 Stelling Rd Augusta GA 30907

SHELL, GEORGE RICHARD EDWIN, ednl. adminstr.; b. Phoebus, Va., Oct. 20, 1908; s. John Montgomery and Catherine Virginia (McAlwee) S.; B.S in E.E., Va. Mil. Inst., 1931; grad. Marine Corps Officer's Basic Sch., 1931-32; LL.D., Washington and Lee U., Theil Coll.; m. Alice Reid Cushing, July 22, 1933; children—Elizabeth Reid (Mrs. R. A. Allen, USN), Beverly Cushing, George Richard. Commd. 2d lt U.S. Marine Corps, 1931, advanced through grades to brig. gen., 1956; mil. asst. to comdr. Alaskan Sector, 1940-42; comdr. arty. btn. 2d Marine Div., Guadalcanal, Tarawa, Saipan islands, 1942-43; wounded in action, hospitalized, 1944-46; staff Naval War Coll., 1946-49; mem. joint staff, staff asst. for nat. security matters Joint Chiefs of Staff, 1949-51; dep. chief policy sect. SHAPE, Paris, 1951-52, chief staff Marine Corps Sch., Quanitoc, Va., 1952-53; mem. Marine Corps Advanced Research Group, 1953-54; chief staff Fleet Marine Force, Atlantic Fleet, 1954-56; comdr. 1st Marine Air-Ground Brigade, Kaneoke, Hawaii, 1956-57; chief E. coast recruit tng., Parris Island, S.C., 1957-58; dep. chief staff research and devel. Hdqrs. USMC, 1958-59; comdg. gen. Marine Corps Recruit Depot, Parris Island, 1959-60; retired, 1960; supt. Va. Mil. Inst., 1960—. Home: 412 VMI Parade Lexington VA 24450 Office: Supt's Office Va Mil Inst Lexington VA 24450

SHELL, NELL ELISE SMITH (MRS. VERNON MCTYEIRE SHELL), genealogist; b. Eufaula, Ala.; d. William Furlow and Mary Adell (Wilson) Smith; grad. Winthrop Coll., 1915; m. Vernon McTyeire Shell, Dec. 23, 1915; 1 son, Vernon McTyeire. Tchr. pub. sch., Spartanburg County, S.C., 1915; conducted pvt. sch., Fort Oglethorpe, Ga., 1921-25; x-ray technician, Brownsville, Tex., 1930-34; profl. genealogist, hist. researcher, Arden, N.C., 1960—. Mem. D.A.R. (chpt. historian 1962-65), Nat. League Am. Pen Women (recording sec. 1966-67), Nat. Soc. Colonial Dames 17th Century of N.C. (chpt. v.p. 1965-66, curator 1967-69). Daus. Am. Colonists (2d vice regent 1964-67), Magna Charta Dames, Order of Garter, Hughenot Soc. S.C., Dames Ct. of Honor, Order of Crown, Ams. Royal Descent, Plantagenet Soc., U.D.C. Episcopalian. Clubs: Literary Book, Fortnightly Literary (2d v.p. 1966-67). Home: 14 Appian Way Royal Pines Arden NC 28704

SHELL, TERRY LEE, judge; b. Franklin, Ark., Apr. 2, 1922; s. Elmer G. and Roxie E. Shell; B.S. in Edn., Ark. State Coll., 1945; postgrad. U. Tex. Law Sch., 1946-47; J.D., U. Ark., 1949; m. Sara Jo McCutcheon, July 8, 1945; children—Suzanne, Jeanne Carol. Admitted to Ark. bar, 1949; practiced in Jonesboro, Ark.; mem. Ark. Ho. of Reps., 1953-54; pros. atty. 2d Jud. Circuit Ark., 1954-61; chancellor, probate judge 12th Chancery Circuit Ark., Jonesboro, 1961—; pres. Ark. Jud. Council, 1971-72. Served with inf. AUS, 1943-45. Mem. Ark. State Pros. Atty. Assn. (pres. 1960). Am. Legion. Baptist. Kiwanian, Elk. Home: 1315 S Main St Jonesboro AR 72401 Office: PO Box 1426 Jonesboro AR 72401

SHELTON, DAVID HOWARD, univ. dean; b. Winona, Miss., Nov. 30, 1928; s. Tuttle M. and Kate (Moss) S.; B.A., Millsaps Coll., 1951; M.A., Ohio State U., 1952, Ph.D., 1958; m. Margaret Murff, Feb. 4, 1951; children—David Keith, Sarah Katherine, Susan Esther. Asst. prof. U. Del., Newark, 1958-63, asso. prof., 1963-65; prof. econs. U. N.C. at Greensboro, 1965—, dean Sch. Bus. and Econs., 1970—. Chmn., N.C. Council on Econ. Edn., 1969—. Served with USN, 1946-48. Mem. Acad. of Mgmt., Am. Econ. Assn., Beta Gamma Sigma, Omicron Delta Kappa, Kappa Sigma. Home: 3609 Dogwood Dr Greensboro NC 27403

SHELTON, JAMES MAURICE, educator; b. Collinwood, Tenn., July 27, 1924; s. Arch M. and Beulah Ethel (Pigg) S.; B.S., U. Tenn., 1948; M.S., Tex. A. and M. U., 1953, Ph.D., 1957; m. Lucy Vise, Aug. 28, 1950; children—Larry H., Michael V., Donald M., Stephen Andrew. Instr., U. Tenn., 1948-50; instr. Tex. A. and M. U., College Station, 1950-53, prof. animal sci., 1957—; asso. prof. Am. U. Beirut (Lebanon), 1954-56. Served with USNR, 1943-46. Mem. Am. Soc. Animal Sci., Am. Genetic Assn., Soc. for Study Reprodn., Research Soc. Am. (pres. Central Tex. br. 1969-70), Sigma Xi. Republican. Lion. Home: 2939 Cumberland St San Angelo TX 76901 Office: RFD 1 Box 950 San Angelo TX 76901

SHELTON, JOHN BANNER, broadcasting exec.; b. Mayodan, N.C., July 5, 1916; s. Walter Roscoe and Minetti (Fulton) S.; A.A., Mars Hill Coll., 1939; m. Mary Helen Carter, Nov. 15, 1941. Order clk. Gam Dandy, Inc., Madison, N.C., 1939-40, asst. supt., 1940-48; founder pres., dir. Mayo Broadcasting Corp., Madison, 1948—. Chmn., Republican Party 5th Dist. N.C., 1958—. Trustee Morehead Meml. Hosp. Mem. Rockingham County Fine Arts Festival Assn. (membership chmn. 1958-60, pres. 1960-62), Mars Hill Bus. Club Alumni Assn. (pres. 1939-40, 63-64), A.I.M. (fellow pres.'s council). Baptist. Clubs: Rotary; Deep Springs Country (Madison, N.C.). Home: RR 1 Stoneville NC 27048 Office: PO Box 311 Madison NC 27025

SHELTON, OPIE LEE, assn. exec.; b. Mt. Airy, N.C., Feb. 28, 1915; s. William Paul and Ada (Lowe) S.; student U. N.C., 1937; m. Mollie Irene Murph, Sept. 29, 1940; children—Mollie, Sally. Mgr. chambers commerce, Orangeburg, S.C., 1940-41, Meridian, Miss., 1946-48, Spartanburg, S.C., 1949-51, Baton Rouge, La., 1951-60; exec. v.p. Atlanta C. of C., 1960-70; exec. v.p. Asheville (N.C.) C. of C., 1971—. Served with USAAF, 1941-45. Recipient Freedoms Found. awards, 1949, 59. Mem. Am. C. of C. Execs. Episcopalian. Author articles on orgn. activity. Home: 6 Lucky Lane Asheville NC 28804 Office: Chamber of Commerce Bldg 51 Haywood St Asheville NC 28802

SHENTON, LEONARD ROY, statistician, educator; b. Staffordshire, Eng., Feb. 4, 1909; s. John William and Sarah (Adams) S.; student Manchester U., 1927-32; B.S., Edinburgh U., 1932, Ph.D., 1940, D.Sc., 1959; m. Margaret Elaine Jackson, Aug. 23, 1935. Mathematician, lectr., reader Manchester U., 1948-60; prof. Va. Poly. Inst., 1961-62; research statistician Nat. Lab., Oak Ridge, 1963; prof. Computer Center, U. Ga., Athens, 1965—; statis. cons., 1963—. Served with RAF, 1939-45. Mem. Am., Manchester statis. socs., Edinburgh Math. Soc., Math. Assn. Contbr. articles profl. jours. Home: 210 Pine Valley Dr Athens GA 30601

SHEPARD, ALAN BARTLETT, JR., astronaut; b. Derry, N.H., Nov. 18, 1923; s. Alan Bartlett and Renza (Emerson) S.; grad. Pinkerton Acad., Derry, N.H., 1940; student Admiral Farragut Acad., 1940; B.S., U.S. Naval Acad., 1944; grad. Naval War Coll., 1958; m. Louise Brewer, Mar. 3, 1945; children—Juliana, Laura. Commd. ensign U.S. Navy, 1944, advanced through grades to rear adm., 1971; designated naval aviator, 1947; assigned destroyer U.S.S. Cogswell, Pacific, World War II, Fighter Squadron 42, 1947-49, aircraft carriers in Mediterranean, 1947-49; with U.S. Navy Test Pilot Sch., 1950-53, 55-57; took part in high altitude tests, experiments in test and devel. in-flight refueling system, carrier suitability trials of F2H3 Banshee, also trials angled carrier deck; operations officer Fight Squadron 193, Moffett Field, Cal., and in carrier U.S.S. Oriskany, Western Pacific, 1953-55; test pilot for F3H Demon, 1956, F8U Crusader, 1956, F4D Skyray, 1955, F11F Tigercat, 1956; project test pilot F5D Skylancer, 1956; instr. Naval Test Pilot Sch., 1957; aircraft readiness officer staff Comdr.-in-Chief Atlantic Fleet, 1958-59; joined Project Mercury man in space program, NASA, 1959; first American in space May 5, 1961; chief of astronaut office, 1965—, comdr. Apollo 14 Lunar Landing Mission, until 1971; del. to UN 1971. Decorated D.S.M, D.F.C.; recipient NASA Distinguished Service Medal; recipient Langley medal Smithsonian Instn., 1964. Fellow Soc. Exptl. Test Pilots; mem. Order Daedalians, Soc. Colonial Wars. Lion, Kiwanian, Rotarian. Address: Manned Spacecraft Center NASA Houston TX 77058

SHEPARD, CHARLES C., physician; b. Ord. Neb., Dec. 18, 1914; B.S., Northwestern U., 1936, M.S., 1938, M.B., 1940, M.D., 1941. Commd. med. officer USPHS, 1941; with NIH, 1942-48, 49-50, Biochem Inst., Uppsala, Sweden, 1948-49, Rocky Mountain Lab., 1950-53; chief leprosy and rickettsial disease unit virology sect. Center for Disease Control, Atlanta, 1954—. Vis. prof. U. Ala., 1956-60; mem. Rickettsial Disease Commn., Armed Forces Epidemiol. Bd., 1959—; chmn. leprosy panel Japan-U.S. Coop. Med. Sci. Program, 1965—. Recipient Kimble Methodology award and Gergos medal, 1963; World Leprosy Day award, 1970. Mem. A.A.A.S., Am. Soc. Microbiology, Soc. Exptl. Biology, Am. Assn. Immunology. Research in infectious diseases, especially rickettsiae and leprosy; bacterial anatomy; fluorescent antibody. Office: Center for Disease Control Atlanta GA 30333*

SHEPARD, HAROLD HENRY, agr. cons.; b. Templeton, Mass., Mar. 8, 1898; s. John Baker and Mabel Hale (Smith) S.; B.S., U. Mass., 1924, Ph.D., 1931; M.S., U. Md., 1927; m. Eleanor Chalmers Geiger, Sept. 5, 1924. With Dept. Agr., Washington, 1926-31, 46-68, entomologist, 1946-50, staff specialist agrl. chems., 1950-68; asst. prof. entomology U. Minn., St. Paul, 1931-43; pesticides specialist War Food Adminstrn., Washington, 1943-45. asso. prof. insect toxicology, Cornell U., Ithaca, N.Y., 1945-46; cons. Beech Nut Packing Co., Canajoharie, N.Y., 1934-46, Agr. Dept., Washington, 1968—, AID, 1970—; lectr. U. Md., College Park, nights, 1947-63; cons. editor Farm Chemicals, Willoughby, O., 1969—. Recipient Superior Service award Agr. Dept., 1960. Fellow A.A.A.S.; mem. Entomol. Soc. Am., Entomol. Soc. Washington (pres. 1962), Washington Acad. Scis. (mgr. 1962-64), Insecticide Soc. Washington, Sigma Xi, Phi Kappa Phi. Clubs: Cosmos, Torch (Washington). Author: Chemistry and Toxicology of Insecticides, 1939; (with Ralph Macy) Butterflies, 1941; Applied Entomology, 1955; Methods of Testing Chemicals on Insects, Vol. I, 1958, II, 1960. Home and Office 2701 S June St Alrington VA 22202

SHEPARD, HENRY BURGARD, constrn. exec.; b. New Orleans, May 9, 1916; s. Theodore Howell and Helen (Burgard) S.; B.S. in Civil Engring., Tulane U., 1937; m. Janet Johnstone, June 10, 1938; children—Helen W. (Mrs. Norman D. Stockwell), Cheryl A., Leslie L., Henry. Vice pres. R. P. Farnsworth & Co., New Orleans, 1937-57; pres. H.B. Shepard & Co., 1957-65; exec. v.p. George Farnsworth Constrn. Corp., New Orleans, 1965-67, dir., 1965-67; pres. Shepco, Inc., New Orleans, 1968—; mgr. heavy constrn. div. T. L. James & Co., Inc., Kenner, La., 1969—. Presbyn. (elder). Home: 5018 Bancroft Dr New Orleans LA 70122 Office: PO Box 51986 New Orleans LA 70151

SHEPARD, KATHARINE, art mus. curator; b. Bristol, Conn.; d. Charles Norman and Marguerite (Dunbar) Shepard; B.A., Bryn Mawr Coll., 1928, M.A., 1929, Ph.D., 1936; student Am. Sch. Classical Studies, Athens, Greece, 1930-31 Pvt. tutoring, research, N.Y.C.,

1936-41; mus. aide Nat. Gallery Art, Washington, 1941-43, asst. registrar, 1943-55, asst. curator graphic arts, 1955—; lectr. grad. sch. dept. art Catholic U. Am., 1960-69. Mem. Am. Assn. Museums, Archaeol. Inst. Am. (sec. Washington chpt.), Print Council Am. Episcopalian. Home: 1260 21st St NW Washington DC 20036 Office: Nat Gallery of Art Washington DC 20565

SHEPARDSON, DAVID LEONARD, banker; b. Birmingham, Ala., Dec. 16, 1938; s. Vene Phillip and Ione (VonDroskie) S.; B.A., Randolph-Macon Coll., 1961; m. Melinda Luck, Jan. 6, 1962; children—Linda Montague, David Leonard. With Bank Va., Richmond, 1961—, v.p., 1968-70, sr. v.p., 1970—. Mem. Am. Cancer Soc., 1968-69, Big Brot's. Richmond, 1968-70; campagin chmn. March Dimes, 1970-71; pres. Richmond Community Service Center, 1971—. Mem. Richmond City Council, 1969-70; mem. Richmond Human Relations Commn., 1969—. Bd. dirs. Multiple Sclerosis, 1968-70, Region 19 Community Coll., Richmond, 1969-70, Atlantic Rural Exposition, 1971—; trustee Markets Diversified, Richmond, 1968—. Recipient Mem. Richmond Jr. C. of C. (Distinguished Service award 1970), Central Richmond Assn., Phi Kappa Sigma. Methodist. Rotarian. Home: 29 Maxwell Rd Richmond VA 23226 Office: 800 E Main St Richmond VA 23219

SHEPHERD, CHARLES WESLEY, hosp. adminstr.; b. nr. Theadville, Miss., Apr. 25, 1934; s. Hamilton W. and Lois (Rolison) S.; student Gradwohl Sch. Lab. Technique, 1953; A.A., Meridian Jr. Coll., 1957; student U. So. Miss., 1957-58; LL.B., Jackson Sch. Law, 1961; certificate, U. Ala. in Birmingham, 1972; m. Lora Gossard, July 16, 1955; children—Charles Wesley, Susanne, Sherri. Admitted to Miss. bar, 1961; lab. asst. St. Luke's Hosp., St. Louis, 1952-53; med. technologist Watkins Meml. Hosp., Quitman, Miss., 1953-55, hosp. adminstr., 1955-58, 1967—; med. technologist St. Dominics Hosp., Jackson, Miss., 1959-61; gen. ins. agt., Meridian and Quitman, Miss., 1961-67. Chmn., Clarke County Home Health Adv. Com., 1969-70; pres. Clarke County Wildlife Conservation League, 1955-56; sec., treas., dir. Miss. Wildlife Fedn., 1961-63; chmn. Clarke County Heart Assn., 1957-58; active Clarke County Red Cross, Clarke County March of Dimes; sec., treas., dir. Clarke County Planning Commn., 1966-69. Recipient Miss. Wildlife/Sears-Roebuck Found. State Game and Fish Conservation award, 1963; Outstanding Alumni award U. So. Miss., 1966-67; Distinguished Achievement award Am. Med. Technologists, 1956. Mem. Am., Miss. (chmn. council emergency service 1969-70) hosp. assns., East Miss. (pres. 1965-66), Miss. assns. ins. agts., Quitman Jr. C. of C., Nat. Wildlife Fedn. Methodist (commn. chmn. 1962—, lay speaker 1962—). Lion (Outstanding Pres. award Quitman 1965, pres. 1964-65), Mason (master 1965—). Club: Quitman Country. Home: PO Box 93 Quitman MS 39355 Office: 120 E Water St Quitman MS 39355

SHEPHERD, CORNELIOUS ALSTON, JR., educator; b. Birmingham, Ala., Mar. 30, 1923; s. Cornelious Alston and Reba (Webb) S.; B.S., Howard Coll., 1948; J.D., Samford U., 1966; m. Betty Sue Garner, July 11, 1950; children—Susanne Elizabeth, Jacqueline Yvonne. Home office rep. Old Republic Life Ins. Co., Chgo., 1948-49; owner C.A. Shepherd Constrn. Co. Inc., Birmingham, 1949-62; adminstr. Judson Coll., Marian, Ala., 1966-70; admissions and devel. counselor Samford U., Birmingham, 1971—. Served to 1st lt. USAAF. Decorated D.F.C., Air medal. Mem. Bapt. Pub. Relations Assn., Newcomen Soc., Pi Kappa Alpha, Tau Kappa Alpha, Pi Gamma Mu, Alpha Kappa Psi, Sigma Delta Kappa, Omicron Delta Kappa. Mason (Shriner), Lion, Rotarian. Clubs: Monday Morning Quarterback, Zamora Country. Baptist (deacon). Home: 909 Southridge Dr Birmingham AL 35216

SHEPHERD, KATE BERRY, social worker; b. Woodville, Miss., June 26, 1910; d. Arthur Morson and Louise (Hider) Shepherd; A.A., All Saints' Episcopal Jr. Coll., 1930; student U. Miss., 1930-31; B.A., Peabody Coll., 1948; A.M., U. Chgo., 1951. Sec. to dean, bookkeeper, tchr. comml. subjects All Saints' Episcopal Sch., Vicksburg, Miss., 1935-40; clk.-stenographer Office Undersec. War, Washington, 1940-42; recreation worker Red Cross Hosp., Fiji Islands, India, Burma, 1942-45; child welfare worker, Jackson, Miss., 1949-50, supr., 1951-53; supr. child welfare suprs. and tng. Miss. Dept. Pub. Welfare, Jackson, 1953-58, dir. tng., 1958-60; dir. tng. State of N.C., Raleigh, 1960-64; asso. prof. Sch. Social Welfare, La. State U., Baton Rouge, 1964-70, field work faculty rep., 1964-70; head undergrad. dept. social work U. Miss., University, 1970—. Bd. dirs. Crestview Home for Unmarried Mothers, Jackson, 1958-60, Blundon Home for Children, Baton Rouge, 1965-70, Miss. Conf. on Social Welfare, North Miss. Retardation Center, 1972—. Recipient Mary E. Boretz Nat. award Child Welfare League Am., 1957; Grace Abbott fellow, 1950. Mem. Miss. State Conf. Pub. Welfare (past pres.), Nat. Assn. Social Workers (mem. nat. commn. social work edn.), Am. Assn. U. Women, Internat. Conf. Social Work, Am. Pub. Welfare Assn., Am. Assn. Social Workers (acad. mem.), Child Welfare League Am. (mem. program planning com. S.E. Regional Conf.), Delta Delta Delta, Pi Gamma Mu. Episcopalian (vestryman). Club: Altrusa. Home: Box 502 University MS 38677

SHEPHERD, RICHARD BUTLER HOOKE, civil engr.; b. Pond, Miss., Feb. 10, 1905; s. Arthur Merson and Louise Maria (Hider) S.; student Cornell U., 1922-23, Miss. State U., 1924, U. Mo., 1925-27, U. Tenn., 1945. Insp. Corps Engrs., Vicksburg, Miss., 1928-31, Memphis, 1931-32, civil engr., Memphis, 1932-47; geod. engr. 29th Engring. Ba. Base Topo, Manila, P.I., 1948-54; cartographer U.S. Army Map Service, Far E., Tokyo, Japan, 1954-60; ret. 1960; vol. ednl. therapy VA Hosp., Memhis, 1961-63, 69—; registered rep. White & Co., Memphis, 1964-69. Extension instr. U. Tenn., 1942-46, U. Ark., 1944. Fellow Am. Soc. C.E., Am. Congress on Surveying and Mapping (life); mem. Memphis Engrs. Club, A.I.M., Soc. Am. Mil. Engrs., Cornell Soc. Engrs., Pi Tau Sigma. Episcopalian. Clubs: Memphis University; Tokyo Lawn Tennis, Memphis Civitan. Home: 1380 Lamar Av Memphis TN 38104

SHEPHERD, ROBERT ASHLAND, lawyer; b. Huntsville, Tex., July 7, 1894; s. James L. and Julia (Josey) S.; grad. Sam Houston State U., 1914; student U. Tex. at Austin, 1916-17; m. Opal Powell, July 8, 1922; children—Robert Ashland, William Leftwich. Admitted to Tex. bar, 1921; with James L. Shepherd, Cisco, Tex., 1921; with Vinson, Elkins, Searls & Smith, Houston, 1921-70, partner, 1929—, mng. partner, 1951-59. Vice pres., dir. Duval Corp., 1947-70; chmn. bd., dir. Heights State Bank, Houston. Trustee Tex. Med. Center, Meth. Hosp., Houston, Tex. Meth. Found., Lon Morris Coll., Jacksonville, Tex. Served as 2d lt., F.A. and aviation, U.S. Army, World War I. Mem. Am., Tex., Houston bar assns., S.A.R., Sons Republic Tex. Democrat. Methodist (trustee). Mason (Shriner, K.T.). Home: 2136 Inwood Dr Houston TX 77019 Office: First City Nat Bank Bldg Houston TX 77002

SHEPHERD, ROBERT ASHLAND, JR., lawyer; b. Mexia, Tex., Nov. 6, 1923; s. Robert Ashland and Opal (Powell) S.; LL.B., U. Tex., 1948; m. Estelle Streetman Lindsey, July 28, 1945; children—Marion Lindsey, Robert A. III, David Powell. Admitted to Tex. bar, 1948, since practiced in Houston; mem. firm Vinson, Elkins, Searls, Connally & Smith, 1948—, partner- 1959-67; pres. Austral Oil Co., Houston, 1967-69. Trustee Meth. Hosp. Served with AUS, 1943-45; ETO. Decorated Purple Heart. Mem. Am. Judicature Soc., Am., Houston bar assns., state Bar of Tex., Phi Delta Phi, Kappa Sigma. Presbyn. Clubs: River Oaks Country, Houston Country, Ramada, Texas Corinthian Yacht; Links (N.Y.C.). Home: 3414 Overbrook Lane Houston TX 77027 Office: Cullen Center Bank Bldg Houston TX 77002

SHEPHERD, ROBERT LENWARD, TV exec.; b. Atlanta, Aug. 21, 1933; s. Earl Lenward and Linda (Grubbs) S.; A.B., U. Ala., 1959; m. Beverly Joyce Crowell, Oct. 1, 1960; children—Nancy Lynn, Scott Lenward and Susan Leigh (twins). Dir., announcer U. Ala. Broadcasting Services, Tuscaloosa, 1958; producer, dir. WEDU-TV, Tampa, Fla., 1959; prodn. mgr. St. Petersburg, Fla., 1959-63; program prodn. mgr. WDCN-TV, Nashville, Tenn., 1963-65; gen. mgr., 1965—; exec. v.p. Nashville Pub. TV Council, Inc., 1971—. Dir. summer lab workshops in ednl. TV, Belmont Coll., Nashville, 1966-67; coordinator Vanderbilt U. M.A. in Teaching Seminars, Nashville, 1966—. Bd. dirs. Middle Tenn. Radio and TV Council, 1965-67; bd. dirs., pub. edn. dir. Pinellas County Unit, Am. Cancer Soc., St. Petersburg, Fla., 1962-63. Served with CIC, AUS, 1955-57; PTO. Mem. Internat. Platform Assn., Nat. Assn. Ednl. Broadcasters, Pi Kappa Phi (pres. 1958, treas. 1957). Recipient George Washington Honor Medal awards Freedoms Found., Valley Forge, 1964, 66. Home: 713 Georgetown Dr Nashville TN 37205 Office: Box 12555 15th and Compton Avs Nashville TN 37212

SHEPPARD, JAMES DANIEL, banker; b. Houston, Feb. 29, 1928; s. George B. and Priscilla (Spaulding) S.; grad. Hill Sch., 1946; A.B., Princeton, 1950; grad. Stonier Grad. Sch. Banking, 1967; m. Frances Boggs, Mar. 14, 1962. With S.C. Nat. Bank, Greenville, 1954—, mgr. comml. credit dept., 1961—, v.p., 1967—. Served with USNR, 1950-53. Mem. Robert Morris Assos. Home: 209 W Mountain View Av Greenville SC 29609 Office: PO Drawer 969 Greenville SC 29602

SHEPPARD, JOE ALLEN, sch. adminstr.; b. Birmingham, Ala., Jan. 31, 1925; s. Claude Allen and Eleanor Mathews (Ingram) S.; B.S., Miss. State U., 1950; m. Beulah Elizabeth Skelton, June 7, 1946; children—Anne Marie and Jo Ann (twins). Profl. baseball pitcher, Tampa, Fla., 1951-54; funeral dir. Brown Service Funeral Home, Birmingham, 1951-56; athletic dir., Leeds, Ala., 1954-68; prin. Leeds Elementary Sch., 1956—. Policeman, Leeds, 1955-64. Served with USNR, 1943-46; ETO. Decorated Silver Star. Mem. Am. Legion, Submarine Vets. World War II, Jefferson County Elementary Prins. Assn. (v.p., treas.). Methodist. Clubs: Terry Walker Country (mgr. swimming pool), Civitan (Leeds); Professional Baseball Players of Am. (Tampa). Home: 519 N 23d St Leeds AL 35094 Office: 2d Av 30th Leeds AL 35094

SHEPPERD, JOHN BEN, lawyer; b. Gladewater, Tex., Oct. 19, 1915; s. Alfred Fulton and Berthal (Phillips) S.; LL.B., U. Tex., 1941; LL.D., N. Tex. State Coll., 1951, Chapman Christian Coll., Los Angeles, 1953, Southwestern U., 1955; m. Mamie Strieber, Oct. 6, 1938; children—Alfred Lewis, John Ben, Marianne and Suzanne (twins). Admitted to Tex. bar, 1941, mem. Kenley, Sharp, Shepperd and Ritter, Longview, Tex., 1941—; Tex. sec. state, 1950-52; atty. gen. of Tex., 1952-56; gen. counsel Rodman-Noel oil interests, Odessa, 1957—. Mem. Bd. Edn. Tex., 1949-50; sec. Tex. Economy Commn., 1950-51; pres. Sabine River Watershed Assn., 1949-52; mem. Tex. Indsl. Commn., Tex. Civil War Centennial Commn.; v.p. Tex. Tourist Council, 1961. Pres. Tex. Jr. C. of C., 1941, U.S. Jr. C. of C., 1947; nat. council rep. E. Tex. area Boy Scouts Am., 1948-51; pres. Tex. Hist. Survey Com., 1963—. Mem. Nat. Assn. Attys. Gen. (pres. 1956). Democrat. Mem. Christian Ch. Author: The President's Guide to Club and Organization Management and Meetings. Home: 3107 Windsor Dr Odessa TX 79760 Office: PO Box 3908 Odessa TX 79760

SHERIDAN, JACK WALRATH, editor, author; b. Los Angeles, May 6, 1916; s. Daniel Hugh and Vesta (Crook) S.; student San Mateo Jr. Coll., 1934-35. Copywriter J. Walter Thompson Co., San Francisco, 1939-41; freight accounting office W.P. R.R. Co., San Francisco, 1948-50; free lance columnist, novelist, 1950-55. 55—; fine arts editor Avalanche Jour., Lubbock, Tex., 1955—. Bd. dirs. Lubbock Symphony Orch. Served with USAAF, 1942-45. Recipient George Foster Peabody award for pub. service in radio, Sta. KFYO, 1956. Mem. Authors League Am., Sigma Delta Chi. Club: Press and Union League (San Francisco). Author: They Never Had it so Good, 1946; Mischief Done, 1947; Mamie Brandon, 1950; Girl from Town, 1953; Fire in the Flesh, 1960; Down the Road a Piece, 1962; Hint of Thunder, 1964; Circle of Friends, 1965; The Scornful Madonna, 1965; (play) Touch of Irony, 1965; many others. Home: 1809 17th St Lubbock TX 79401 Office: Avalanche-Jour Lubbock TX 79408

SHERMAN, CARL BENJAMIN, utility exec.; b. Rusk, Cherokee County, Tex., Dec. 13, 1915; s. Clifford Carl and Birdie Louise (Babers) S.; J.D., Baylor, 1938; m. Mary Virginia Lorigan, Nov. 16, 1940; children—Steven David, Jonathan Scott, Kirk Babers. Admitted to Tex. bar, 1938; practice in Rusk, Tex., 1938-39; with FBI, 1939-51; with Houston Lighting & Power Co., 1951—, v.p. 1952-67, exec. v.p. 1967-70, pres., 1970—, dir., 1960—, v.p., asst. to pres., 1963—. Mem. indsl. relations com. Edison Electric Inst. Mem. exec. bd. Sam Houston council Boy Scouts Am.; gen. campaign chmn. United Fund Houston-Harris County, 1960. Bd. dirs. Better Bus. Bur. Houston, United Fund Houston-Harris County, Jr. Achievement Houston, Houston Livestock and Rodeo Assn.; bd. regents S. Tex. Coll., Houston, U. Houston Found. Mem. Houston C. of C. (dir., v.p.), Newcomen Soc. N. Am. Mason. Clubs: Quarterdeck (Galveston, Tex.); Headliners (Austin, Tex.); Houston, Lakeside Country, Internat. (Houston). Home: 10223 Pierman Dr Houston TX 77035 Office: 611 Walker Av Houston TX 77002

SHERMAN, EARL THOMAS, dentist; b. Poughkeepsie, N.Y., Jan. 16, 1938; s. Earl F. and Catherine (Chrimmey) S.; B.S., Spring Hill Coll., 1959; D.D.S., Va. Dental Sch., 1963; m. Ellen Gillio, Sept. 7, 1963. Pub. health dentist Orange County Health Dept., Orlando, Fla., 1965-66; practice dentistry, Orlando, 1966—; mem. staff Orange Meml., Mercy, Holiday hosps. Served to capt. Dental Corps, AUS, 1963-65. Mem. Am., Central Dist., Orange County dental socs., South Orange Jr. C. of C., Tri Beta, Delta Sigma Delta. Elk, K.C. (4 deg.). Club: Tohopekaliga Yacht (dir. Kississimme). Home: 7724 Skyview Dr Orlando FL 32806 Office: 22 Lake Beauty Dr Orlando FL 32802

SHERMAN, GERALD HOWARD, lawyer; b. N.Y.C., Aug. 29, 1932; s. Abraham and Jean (Rose) S.; B.B.A., Coll. City N.Y., 1953; LL.B., Harvard, 1958; m. Lola Barbara Kay, Mar. 19, 1961; children—Jonathan, Ann. Admitted to N.Y. bar, 1959; D.C. bar, 1960; practiced in Washington, 1958—; mem. firm Cooper & Silverstein, 1958-61, partner Silverstein & Mullens, 1961—. Mem. adv. bd. tax mgmt., 1960—. Mem. Am. Bar Assn., Bar Assn. D.C. Home: 11112 Whisperwood Lane Rockville MD 20852 Office: 1776 K St NW Washington DC 20006

SHERMAN, HAROLD MORROW, author, lectr.; b. Traverse City, Mich., July 13, 1898; s. Thomas Henry and Alcinda E. (Morrow) S.; student U. Mich., 1918-19; m. Martha Frances Bain, Sept. 26, 1920; children—Mary Alcinda (Mrs. Bernard J. Kobiella), Marcia Anne (Mrs. Wendell R. Smith). Reporter, Marion (Ind.) Chronicle, 1921-24, free lance writer, N.Y.C., 1924-35; author Your Key to Happiness radio program CBS, 1935-36, The Adventures of Mark Twain produced by Warner Brothers, 1942; founder, pres., dir. ESP Research Assos. Found., Little Rock, 1964—; investigator, experimenter, authority on extra-sensory perception; co-developer Blanchard Springs Caverns, Stone County, Ark. Mem. Authors League Am. (life), Dramatists Guild. Lion. Author: How to Make ESP Work for You, 1964; How to Solve Mysteries of Your Mind and Soul, 1965; The New TNT—Miraculous Power Within You, 1966; Wonder Healers of the Philippines, 1967; Your Mysterious Powers of ESP, 1969; How to Foresee and Control Your Future, 1970; How to Take Yourself Apart and Put Yourself Together Again, 1971, (with Ambrose and Olga Worrall) Your Power to Heal, 1972; (with Sir Hubert Wilkins) Thoughts Through Space; numerous others. Record albums include: How to Develop ESP, 1964; Advanced Techniques of ESP, 1964; How to Foretell Your Future 1964. Experiments in long distance telepathy with Arctic explorer Sir Hubert Wilkins. Home: Kahoka Route Mountain View AR 72560 Office: ESP Research Assos Union Nat Plaza Bldg Little Rock AR 72201

SHERMAN, KATHERINE LEOTA MARSHALL (MRS. ROBERT WALTER SHERMAN), hosp. adminstr.; b. St. Catherine, Ont., Can., Oct 6, 1916; d. Roscoe Gow and Grace Mae (Dixon) Marshall; student pub. schs.; m. Robert Walter Sherman, June 21, 1942; children— Marshall Robert, John Allen. Gen. duty nurse Albany (N.Y.) Hosp., 1939-42; first aid nurse Dispensary, Army Quartermaster Depot, Schenectady, 1942-43; adminstr. S. Lake Meml. Hosp., Clermont, Fla., 1949—. Mem. tech. adv. com. Lake-Sumter Jr. Coll., 1966-68. Mem. Am. Coll. Hosp. Adminstrs., Fla. Hosp. Assn. (council profl. services 1967-68), East Central Fla. Hosp. Council (pres. 1969-70). Presbyn. Club: Pilot (pres. 1970—). Home: Killarney FL 32740 Office: 847 8th St Clermont FL 32711

SHERMAN, WILBUR BROWN, oil co. exec.; b. Turner, Kan., Nov. 4, 1911; s. S. Franklin and Inez (Byers) S.; A.B., U. Cal. Los Angeles, 1939; m. Virginia LaRue Tucker, Nov. 28, 1936; children—Dorothy Virginia, Richard Allyn, Elizabeth Ann. Geophys. computer Am. Petroleum Corp., Los Angeles, 1940-41; field geologist Superior Oil Co., 1941-42; v.p., dir. engring. and geol. cons. De Goyer & McNaughton, Dallas, 1948-58; pres. Panoil Co., 1958-70, chmn. bd., 1971; dir. Premier Consol. Oil fields, Ltd., London, Eng., 1959-72. Petroleum cons., 1971—. Served from 1st lt. to lt. col., USAF, 1942-47. Registered profl. engr., Tex. Mem. Am. Inst. Mining and Metallurgy, A.A.A.S., Am. Assn. Petroleum Geologists, Am. Geophys. Union, Am. Meterol. Soc., Dallas Geol. Soc. Republican. Methodist. Clubs: Dallas Country, Preston Trail Golf, Petroleum; Athletic (N.Y.). Contbr. profl. mags. Home: 3716 Caruth Blvd Dallas TX 75225 Office: 4224 Republic Nat Bank Tower Dallas TX 75201

SHERMAN, WILLIAM EURASTI, lawyer; b. Tampa, Fla., Apr. 28, 1927; s. William Eurasti and Maryetta (Abbott) S.; B.A., U. Fla., 1950, J.D., 1953; m. Frances Jeannette Rogers, Feb. 1, 1950; children—William Eurasti III, Valerie Ann. Admitted to Fla. bar, 1953; spl. asst. to Atty. Gen. Fla., Tallahassee, 1953; asso. Francis P. Whitehair, DeLand, Fla., 1954-57; practiced in DeLand, 1958—; mem. firm Hall, Sweeney & Godbee, 1958-59, Hull, Landis, Graham &French, 1961-66, Landis, Graham, French, Husfeld and Sherman, 1966-69, Landis, Graham, French, Husfeld, Sherman & Ford, PA., 1969—. Mem. Volusia County Charter Study Commn., 1969-71. Bd. dirs. Internat. Music Festivals, Inc., 1969-71, Montreat (N.C.)-Anderson Coll., 1961-71, Mountain Retreat Assn., 1961-71. Served with Signal Corps, AUS, World War II. Mem. Fla. Bar (gov. 1970—), Am., Volusia County (pres. 1969-70) bar assns., DeLand C. of C. (v.p. 1970-71), Phi Delta Phi, Pi Kappa Alpha, Alpha Delta Sigma. Democrat. Presbyn. (elder). Rotarian. Clubs: Lake Beresford Yacht (commodore 1966). Home: 800 N Frankfort St DeLand FL 32720 Office: 110 W Indiana Av DeLand FL 32720 also 412 N Wild Olive Daytona FL 32018

SHEROUSE, KENNETH BERTRAM, JR., lawyer; b. Detroit, Mar. 8, 1925; s. Kenneth Bertram and Jeanne (Martin) S.; A.B. cum laude, U. Miami, 1949, LL.B. cum laude, 1950; Sterling Doctoral fellow Yale, 1950-51; m. Eve Thomas, Sept. 1, 1950; children—Thomas McDougal, Kate Ellen, Scott Carlyle. Marine engr. 1943-46; instr. U. Miami Sch. Law, 1950-51; admitted to Fla. bar, 1949; atty. U.S. Dept. Justice, Washington, D.C., 1951-53; exec. dir. The Fla. Bar, 1954-57; pvt. practice law, Miami, 1957—. Sec.-treas. Internat. Bar Found. Bd. dirs. U. Miami Law Sch. Alumni Assn. Served as officer U.S. Maritime Service, World War II. Mem. Inter-Am., Am., D.C., Fla., Dade County bar assns., Fedn. Ins. Counsel, Am. Judicature Soc., Iron Arrow, Omicron Delta Kappa, Phi Kappa Phi. Clubs: Coral Reef Yacht, Miami Beach Rod and Reel. Ed. in chief Fla. Bar Jour., 1954-57, U. Miami Law Review, 1958-59; mem. editorial com. Fedn. Ins. Counsel Quarterly, 1961-62. Address: 28 W Flagler St Miami FL 33130

SHERRER, WAYMAN GRAY, lawyer; b. Birmingham, La., Nov. 15, 1927; s. Claude Wayman and Rosalee (Garner) S.; A.B., Samford U., 1952; LL.B., U. Ala., 1956; m. Betty Lou Rodgers, Aug. 13, 1960; children— Elizabeth Ann, William Jefferson. Spl. agt. FBI, Los Angeles, 1956-58, Washington, 1958-62; admitted to Ala. bar, 1956; practice law, Oneonta, Ala., 1962-69; U.S. atty. No. Dist. Ala., Birmingham, 1969—. Solicitor, Blount County, Ala., 1965-69. Atty., Republican Party, Blount County, Ala., 1962-69; del. Rep. Nat. Conv., 1968; mem. Ala. Rep. Exec. Com., 1962-69. Served with USMCR, 1946-48. Mem. Ala., Blount County (pres. 1966-67) bar assns., Soc. Former FBI Agts. (chmn. 1966-67), Omicron Delta Kappa, Pi Gamma Mu, Sigma Nu, Alpha Kappa Psi. Rotarian (pres. Oneonta 1966-67). Methodist (lay leader 1971—). Home: 107 Redbud Rd Oneonta AL 35121 Office: Room 276 Federal Courthouse Birmingham AL 35203

SHERRILL, JAMES FENTON, mfg. co. exec.; b. Columbus, Miss., Dec. 19, 1924; s. Leon T. and Bertha E. (Geer) S.; student engring. U. Ala., 1946-54; LL.B., LaSalle Extension U., 1966; m. Hazel Joyce Kilgore, July 30, 1949; children—James Fenton, William Lynn, Julia LuAnn. Prodn. and material control mgr. Butler Mfg. Co., Birmingham, Ala., 1951-62; prodn. specialist Chrysler Corp., Huntsville, Ala., 1962-69; div. plant mgr. Thomas Industries, Inc., Johnson City, Tenn., 1969-70; v.p. mfg. Mor-Flo Industries, Inc., Johnson City and Cleve., 1970—; also dir.; gen. mgr. Tenn. Tank Co., Johnson City. Served with USNR, 1943-46, 50-51. Mem. Am. Prodn. and Inventory Control Soc., Civitan Internat. (program dir. 1960-62), Exchange Club (dir. 1968-69). Baptist. Club: Johnsity City Country. Home: 1900 Sinking Creek Rd Johnson City TN 37601 Office: PO Box 788 Johnson City TN 37601

SHERRILL, LUBY THADDEUS, JR., dentist; b. High Point, N.C., Sept. 11, 1925; s. Luby Thaddeus and Nell Frances (Pearce) S.; B.S., U. N.C., 1956, D.D.S., 1960, M.P.H., 1965; m. Paulette J.A. Vaillant, Dec. 22, 1948; children—Alan Glen, Martine Louise. Practice dentistry, Shelby, N.C., 1960-61; staff dentist N.C. Bd. Health, 1961-64; dental dir. Mecklenburg County Dept. Pub. Health, 1965—. Cons. dental health edn. Head Start, 1965—, Proctor & Gamble Co., 1966—; instr. Central Piedmont Community Coll., Charlotte, N.C. 1966—. Served with USAF, (1943-54). Mem. N.C. Pub. Health Assn. (v.p. 1970), Am. Dental Assn., Am. Pub. Health Assn., Am.

Assn. Pub. Health Dentists, Am. Assn. Preventive Dentistry, N.C. Dental Soc., Phi Beta Kappa. Home: 5242 Addison Dr Charlotte NC 28211 Office: 1200 Blythe Blvd Charlotte NC 28203

SHERRILL, ROBERT GLENN, editor; b. Frogtown, Ga., Dec. 24, 1925; s. Henry Clifton and Susan Olive (McGinley) S.; B.A., Pepperdine Coll., 1949; M.A., U. Tex., 1956; M.A., U. Minn., 1960; m. Mary Elizabeth Bergeson, May 5, 1950. Reporter Ariz. Times, Phoenix, 1948-49, Standard Times, San Angelo, Tex., 1951, Am.-Statesman, Austin, Tex., 1954-55, Nashville Tennessean, 1957-58; instr. English, U. Tex. Austin, 1955-56, Tex. A. and M., Bryan, 1956-57, U. Mo., Columbia, 1958-59; asso. editor Tex. Observer, Austin, 1960-63; polit. writer Miami Herald, 1964-65; Washington editor, The Nation, 1965—. Contbr. polit. articles Sunday N.Y. Times, Playboy, Pageant, other mags. Served with U.S. Mcht. Marine, 1942-46. So. Rockefeller fellow, 1957; recipient ann. award Soc. Mag. Writers, 1967, Edit. Ann. award Playboy, 1970. Author: The Accidental President, 1967; Gothic Politics in the Deep South, 1968; The Drugstore Liberal, 1968; Military Justice Is to Justice as Military Music Is to Music, 1970; Why They Call It Politics, 1972. Address: 617 North Carolina Av SE Washington DC 20003

SHERROD, KY, sch. adminstr.; b. Swenson, Tex., Sept. 3, 1929; s. Lester Algie and Claudie Belle (Hall) S.; B.S., W. Tex. State U., 1951, M.E., 1952; m. Frances Bussard, Aug. 23, 1952; children— Randall, Brent, Mark. Coach, tchr. Channing (Tex.) High Sch., 1952-53, prin., 1953-56; supt. schs. Channing Ind. Sch. Dist., 1956—. Mem. Am. Assn. Sch. Adminstrs., Tex., Panhandle sch. leaders assns., Tex. State, Dallam-Hartley (past pres.) tchrs. assns. Mason, Lion (past pres.). Home: PO Box A Channing TX 79018

SHERROD, ROBERT LEE, writer; b. Thomas County, Ga., Feb. 8, 1909; s. Joseph Arnold and Victoria Ellen (Evers) S.; A.B., U. Ga., 1929; m. Elizabeth Hudson, Oct. 8, 1936 (dec. Dec. 1958); children—John, Robert Lee; m. 2d, Margaret Carson Ruff, May 5, 1961 (div. 1972); m. 3d, Mary Gay Labrot Leonhardt, Aug. 26, 1972. Reporter Atlanta Constitution, Palm Beach (Fla.) Daily News, others, 1929-35; with Time and Life mags. as Washington corr., asso. editor, war and Far East corr., 1935-52; Far East corr. Sat. Eve. Post, 1952-55, mng. editor, 1955-62, editor, 1962, and editor-at-large, 1963-64; v.p., editorial coordinator Curtis Pub. Co., 1965-66; writing on fgn. affairs and history, 1966—; contract writer Life mag., N.Y.C., 1966-68. Mem. Pres.'s Com. to Employ Handicapped. Commended by U.S. Navy Dept., Battle of Attu, May 1943, Battle of Tarawa, Nov. 1943; recipient Headliners Club award, for war reporting, 1944; Benjamin Franklin award U. Ill., 1954; Overseas Press Club certificate, 1955. Mem. Mil. Order of Carabao. Episcopalian. Clubs: Federal City, National Press (Washington); Overseas Press (trustee Corr. Fund), Century, Dutch Treat, Coffee House (N.Y.C.). Author: Tarawa, the Story of a Battle, 1944; On to Westward, 1945; History of Marine Corps Aviation in World War II, 1952; also of text for Life's Picture History of World War II, 1950 and Kobunsha's Picture History of the Pacific War (in Japanese), 1952. Home: 4000 Massachusetts Av NW Washington DC 20016

SHERROD (BLACKIE) WILLIAM FORREST, sports columnist, editor; b. Belton, Tex., Nov. 9, 1920; s. Marvin F. and Leola (Forrest) S.; student Baylor U., 1937-38; B.A. in Journalism, Howard Payne Coll., 1941; m. Marilyn Paschal, Mar. 28, 1947. Mem. staff Temple (Tex.) Daily Telegram, 1946, Ft. Worth Press, 1946-58; with Dallas Times Herald, 1958—, now exec. sports editor; dir. Dallas Times Herald Printing Co. Served with Air Corps, USNR, 1942-46. Decorated Air medal (2), Navy Commendation medal; named Nat. Headliner Sports Columnist of Year, 1962. Mem. Football Writers Assn. Am. (pres. 1963-64). Author: (with Darrell Royal) Darrell Royal Talks Football, 1963; (with Freddie Steinmark) I Play to Win, 1971. Home: 7139 Wildgrove Av Dallas TX 75214 Office: Times Herald Herald Sq Dallas TX 75202

SHERVINGTON, WALTER W., psychiatrist; M.D., U. Md., 1963. Intern, South Balt. Gen. Hosp., 1963-64; resident U. Md., Balt., 1964-65, Sheppard and Enoch Pratt Hosp., Towson, Md.; surgeon USPHS, 1967-69; staff psychiatrist Med. Center Fed. Prisoners, Springfield, Mo.; staff psychiatrist also chief med. officer, Fed. Correctional Inst., Milan, Mich.; adj. staff psychiatrist Mt. Zion Hosp., San Francisco; now chief psychiat. tng., div. manpower and tng., Nat. Inst. Mental Health, Washington. Asst. prof., dept. psychiatry, lectr. Sch. Law, cons. dept. psychology, U. Mich.; cons. also bd. dirs. Baker Place, psychiat. halfway house. Mem. Citizens' Adv. Council Washtenaw (Mich.) County Juvenile Ct.; commr. Joint Commn. Church in Human Affairs. Mem. Am. Psychiat. Assn., Black Psychiatrists Am. Psychiat. Assn., Md. Psychiat. Soc., Am. Acad. Psychiatry and Law, Nat. Med. Assn., John Hale Med. Soc., Am. Coll. Psychiatrists. Episcopalian. Contbr. to prof. jours. Address: 700 New Hampshire Av NW Washington DC 20037*

SHETLER, STANWYN GERALD, botanist; b. Johnstown, Pa., Oct. 11, 1933; s. Sanford Grant and Florence (Young) S.; student Eastern Mennonite Coll., 1951-53; B.S. with distinction, Cornell U., 1955, M.S., 1958; postgrad. U. Mich., 1958-62; m. Elaine Marie Retberg, Feb. 2, 1963. Staff, asst. curator Smithsonian Instn., Washington, 1962-63, asso. curator Phanerogams, 1963—, sci. administr. botany, 1969—. Mem. A.A.A.S., Am. Inst. Biol. Scis. (sec. flora N.Am. program 1966-71, dir. 1972—), Arctic Inst. N.Am., Biol. Soc. Washington (council 1969-70), Bot. Soc. Am., Internat. Soc. Plant Taxonomy, Am. Soc. Plant Taxonomists, Audubon Naturalist Soc. Washington (program chmn. natural history forum 1968-70; dir. 1971—), also other profl. socs. Author: The Komarov Botanical Institute: 250 Years Of Russian Research, 1967; also papers. Home: 4142 Suitland Rd Washington DC 20023 Office: Dept Botany Smithsonian Instn Washington DC 20560

SHEVIN, ROBERT LEWIS, state ofcl.; b. Miami, Fla., Sept. 19, 1934; s. Aaron Shevin and Pauline (Bott) S.; B.A., U. Fla., 1955; LL.B., magna cum laude, U. Miami, 1957; m. Myrna Bressack, Jan. 27, 1957; children—Laura Dawn, Hilary Beth. Atty. firm Shevin, Goodman & Holtzman, 1957—; mem. Fla. Senate 43d Dist., after 1967; now atty. gen. State of Fla. Mem. Fla. Com. Law Enforcement and Adminstrn. Justice; del. Pres. Conf. Law Enforcement; chmn. Miami Econ. Adv. Bd., Fair Share Com. Roads and Representation and Cts. Budget Com.; mem. Govt. Research Council and Indsl. Devel. Bd. dirs., Nat. Multiple Sclerosis Soc., South Fla. Epilepsy Found., Youth Employment Ser. Dade County, Miami Youth Symphony; bldg. chmn. United Fund Drive; regional bd. Anti-Defamation League B'nai B'rith, Jewish Family and Children's Ser. Served with AUS. Recipient Allen Morris award freshman mem. Fla. Legislature, 1965. Democrat. Jewish religion (dir. synagogue). Office: Office Atty Gen State Capitol Bldg Tallahassee FL 32304

SHEWMAKE, CHARLIE BURREL, constrn. co. exec.; b. Coffeeville, Ala., May 10, 1916; s. T. J. and M. C. (Clanton) S.; m. Janie M. McKenzie, Sept. 17, 1939. Pres., Algernon Blair, Inc., Montgomery, Ala., 1960—; chmn. bd. Algernon Blair Indsl. Contractors, Inc. Active YMCA, Landmarks Found. Mem. Men Montgomery. Home: 2006 Myrtlewood Dr Montgomery AL 36104 Office: Bell Bldg Montgomery AL 36111

SHIELDS, CHARLES L., advt. agy. exec.; b. Lombard, Ill., Apr. 3, 1926; s. Charles Emerson and Janet Lucile (Kepner) S.; student U. Ga., 1946-47; m. Mildred Reynolds, Dec. 22, 1951; children—Patricia Ann, Charles Jonathan, Richard Scott. Script writer Pearltone Studio Prodns., Des Moines, 1945; copywriter, announcer radio sta. WMJM, Cordele, Ga., 1946; copywriter radio sta. KCBC, Des Moines, 1947, radio sta. KRNT, Des Moines, 1948-50; writer Gen. Pictures Prodns., Des Moines, 1947-48; free lance radio copy Lessing Advt. Co., Des Moines, 1950; radio, TV copy specialist Bozell & Jacobs, Inc., Omaha, 1952, Burke Dowling Adams, Inc., Atlanta, N.Y.C., 1952-53; radio, TV copy dir. Kirland, White & Schell, Atlanta, 1953-55; copy dir. Liller, Neal, Battle & Lindsey, Atlanta, 1955-59; pres. Chuck Shields Advt., Inc., Atlanta, 1960-69, Clearwater, Fla., 1969—. Co-chmn. advt. Atlanta United Appeal, 1963. Advt. cons. Ga. Congressman Charles L. Weltner, 1962, 64, 66; advt. dir. Fulton County Democratic exec. com., Atlanta, 1964. Home: 1203 Bay Dr Belleair Beach FL 33535 Office: 2617 Jewel Rd Belleair Bluffs FL 33540

SHIELDS, DAVID WILLIAM, JR., lawyer; b. Rensselaer, Ind., Jan. 12, 1899; s. David William and Emma (Gay) S.; student Sch. Law, Vanderbilt U., 1921-22; m. Arlie Cox, May 8, 1930; children—David William III (dec.), John Alfred, James Edward, Sam Jarrett. Tchr. county schs., 1922-25; county supt. schs., 1927-32; admitted to Tenn. bar; pvt. practice law, Manchester, 1932-62, 65—; county judge, Coffee County, 1951-65. Dir. Coffee County Fair Assn., 1933-53; mem. Coffee County Bd. Edn., 1939-40; chmn. County Hwy. Com., 1947-51; chmn. Coffee County Hosp. Commn., 1954-62, Citizens Welfare Council. Mem. Tenn. Ho. of Reps., 1941-43. Mem. Am. Bar Assn., Bar Assn. Tenn., Am. Legion. Mason, Odd Fellow, K.P. Home: Route 4 Manchester TN 37355 Office: Peoples Bank Bldg Manchester TN 37355

SHIELDS, GEORGE THOMAS, lawyer; b. Crowder, Miss., Aug. 29, 1940; s. James Riley and Amy (Enlowe) S.; student Miss. State U., 1958-60, La. State U., 1960-61; B.S. summa cum laude, Delta State Coll., 1962; J.D., Vanderbilt U., 1969; m. Marilyn Ann May, June 3, 1960; children—Jeffrey Thomas, Laura Ann. C.P.A. tax dept. Price Waterhouse & Co., Nashville, 1962-66; instr. accounting Vanderbilt U., 1967-69; admitted to Tenn. bar, 1969; atty. Gullett, Steele, Sanford & Robinson, Nashville, 1969-71; partner firm Williams & Shields, Madison, Tenn., 1971—. Cons. accountant Jamison Bedding, Inc., 1968. C.P.A., Tenn. Mem. Am., Tenn., Nashville bar assns., Tenn. Soc. C.P.A., Am. Inst. C.P.A.'s, Toastmasters Internat., Phi Alpha Delta. Methodist (mem. adminstrv. bd. 1967—). Home: 2037 Castleman Dr Nashville TN 37215 Office: 310 Gallatin Rd S Madison TN 37115

SHIELDS, JOHN EDGAR, editor; b. Camden, N.J., May 8, 1924; s. Emmett Paxton and Marion Amy (Kilheffer) S.; B.A., U. Md., 1950; m. Louisa Conaway Room, Mar. 24, 1951; children—David Sanford, Richard Paxton, Diane Karen. Producer, dir. CBS, Washington, 1946-49; sec. Ambassador William C. Bullitt, 1950; with CIA, 1950-52; exec. Asia Found., various Far Eastern countries, 1952-55; fgn. corr., author, editor various media, 1952-62; asso. editor Congl. Digest, Washington, 1962-68, editor, 1968—; dir. corps. in aircraft mining, food processing fields. Served with USNR, 1942-45. Mem. S.A.R., Mensa, Phi Kappa Phi, Sigma Alpha Epsilon. Methodist. Clubs: Overseas Press (Tokyo, Hong Kong). Author books on local history, genealogy, including A History of the Shields Family, 1968; East Tennessee Migrations: Factors and Families, 1969; The Scotch-Irish in Augusta County, Virginia, 1971. Home: 19128 Roman Way Gaithersburg MD 20760 Office: 3231 P St NW Washington DC 20007

SHIELS, EUGENE FRANCIS, bus. exec.; b. Dallas, Aug. 11, 1920; s. Robert T. and Eunice (Crabb) S.; B.S. in Elec. Engring., Tex. A. and M. U., 1941; m. Doris Stone, Oct. 16, 1955; children—Laura Anne, Emily Catherine, Howard Eugene, Robert Gordon. With Gen. Electric Co., Schenectady, 1941-42, Dresser Industries, Dallas, 1946-66; exec. v.p., also dir. Zapata Corp., Houston, 1966—; chmn. bd. Zapata Off-Shore Co. Served to maj., F.A., AUS, 1941-46; PTO. Mem. Am. Assn. Oilwell Drilling Contractors (dir.), Petroleum Club of Houston. Clubs: Lakeside Country; Northwood (Dallas). Home: 11219 Tynewood Dr Houston TX 77024 Office: 1701 Houston Club Bldg Houston TX 77002

SHIELS, JAMES HENRY, JR., advt. and indsl. art. co. exec.; b. Dallas, Feb. 19, 1930; s. James Henry and Mary (Robbins) S.; B.A., So. Methodist U., 1957; m. Gay Nell Steelmen, June 28, 1957; 1 son, James Henry, III. Staff artist, sales rep., 1956-58; owner, art dir. Henry Shiels Indsl. and Advt. Art Studio, Dallas, 1958—. Vice pres., vice chmn. bd. Mary Shiels Hosp., 1966—. Served to 1st lt. USAF, 1952-56, capt. USAF Res., 1960—. Mem. Nat. Soc. Art Dirs., Dallas-Ft. Worth Art Dirs. Club, Dallas-Ft. Worth Soc. Visual Communications (dir.). Presbyn. Home: 2905 Purdue Dallas TX 75225 Office: Dallas Athletic Club Bldg Dallas TX 75201

SHINDLER, THOMAS OSBORNE, orthopedic surgeon; b. Hempstead, Tex., Dec. 11, 1919; s. J.T. and Louise (Osborne) S.; B.A., U. Tex., 1941, M.D., 1943; m. Betty Randal, Dec. 29, 1950; children—Byron, John. Intern, Hosp. P.E. Ch., Phila., 1943-44; research fellow U. Tex. Med. Br., Galveston, 1947-48, resident, 1948-50; resident Arabia Temple Crippled Childrens Hosp., Houston, 1950-51; pvt. practice medicine specializing in orthopedic surgery, Houston, 1951—; sr. attending Hermann Hosp.; lectr. U. Tex. Postgrad. Sch. Medicine; instr. Baylor U. Coll. Medicine; orthopedic surgeon Houston Oiler Profl. Football Team, 1960-70. Adviser Liberty Mut. Ins. Co. Served to capt. AUS, 1944-46. Decorated Bronze Star medal; recipient Gold medal for research Am. Acad. Orthopedic Surgeons, 1949. Mem. Am. Acad. Orthopedic Surgery, A.C.S., A.M.A., Assn. Bone and Joint Surgery, Clin. Orthopedic Soc., Houston Surg. Soc. (past v.p.), Houston Orthopedic Soc. (past pres.), Internat. Soc. Orthopedic Surgery and Traumatology, Singleton Surg. Soc. (pres.), Profl. Football Physicians Soc. (past pres.). Episcopalian. Clubs: River Oaks Country, Petroleum. Contbr. articles to profl. jours. Home: 3609 Meadow Lake St Houston TX 77027 Office: Hermann Profl Bldg Houston TX 77025

SHINE, HENRY MARTIN, JR., govt. ofcl., lawyer; b. Lincoln, Me., June 7, 1921; s. Henry Martin and Mary Ann (Carter) S.; A.B., Harvard, 1947; LL.B. cum laude, U. Notre Dame, 1951; grad. fellow oil and gas law So. Meth. U. Sch. of Law, 1951-52; m. Marguerite Anne Timlin, Sept. 30, 1961; children—Mari Marguerite, Christana Jeanne. Admitted to Tex. bar, 1953, DC. bar, 1961; dir. publs. Southwestern Legal Found., Dallas, also adminstrv. editor Oil and Gas Reporter, 1952-53; asst. to commnr. 2d Hoover Commn., Washington, 1953-55; fgn. atty. Dresser Industries, Dallas, 1955-57, Washington rep., 1957-58; asst. staff dir. U.S. Commn. on Civil Rights, Washington, 1958-60; exec. dir., counsel U.S. Sci. Exhibit, Seattle World's Fair, Dept. Commerce, 1960-61; legislative dir. Nat. Assn. Home Builders, 1961-67; dir. Cal. Dept. Profl. and Vocational Standards, 1967-69; asst. to Sec., dir. Congl. liaison Dept. of Interior, 1969; exec. dir. Pres.'s Council on Youth Opportunity, Washington, 1969-71; dir. govt. and industry relations Pres.'s Commn. on Financial Structure and Regulations, 1971-72. Served with USN, 1942-46; PTO.; lt. comdr., USNR. Mem. Am., Fed. bar assns., Naval Res. Assn., Naval Res. Lawyers Assn., Nat. Lawyers Club. Club: Metropolitan (Washington). Contbr. articles legal publs. Home: Metropolitan Cub 1700 H St NW Washington DC 20006 Office: Pres's Commn on Financial Structure and Regulation Washington DC 20036

SHINN, EUNICE ADELINE, librarian; b. Russellville, Ark., Apr. 7, 1907; d. Nathaniel Duncan and Betty (Thompson) Shinn; student Ark. Polytech. coll., 1927-29; B.S.E., State Coll. Ark., 1945; student U. Ark., summer 1947; B.S. in L.S., La. State U., 1954. Tchr. elementary sch., Ark., 1929-47; librarian high sch., Ark., 1947-62; reference librarian Ark. Library Commn., 1962-65, library cons., 1965—. Sec., P.T.A., 1947. Mem. Women's Nat. Book Assn., Ark. Library Assn. (sch. div. sec. 1949, sec., 1963), Am. Assn. U. Women (sec. 1955), A.L.A., Delta Kappa Gamma. Methodist (tchr., v.p. Wesleyan Service guild). Home: 205 Country Club Rd North Little Rock AR 72116 Office: 506 1/2 Center St Little Rock AR 72201

SHIPLEY, CARL L(AYTON), lawyer, govt. ofcl.; b. Spokane, Wash., Dec. 16, 1919; s. Edmund D. and Inez (Beale) S.; B.S., Georgetown U., 1942; LL.B., Harvard, 1948; m. Nancy Jo Kane, Sept. 8, 1948; children—Zachary Kane, Joshua Beale. Admitted to Mass. bar, D.C. bar, 1948, pvt. practice Washington, 1948—; spl. asst. to atty. gen. U.S., 1953-56; spl. hearing officer U.S. Dept. Justice, 1955-56; adj. prof. Am. U., 1952-62. Pres. Nat. Realty 1966—; pres. Williams County Broadcasting System, Inc. Mem. Union Renewal Council D.C. Govt., 1956-58. Chmn. Nat. Symphony Orch. Sustaining Fund, 1954-58. Chmn. D.C. Republican Com., 1958-68; mem. Rep. Nat. Com., 1968—. Bd. dirs. Oceanographic Fund. Home: 3740 Fordham Rd NW Washington DC 20016 Office: Nat Press Bldg Washington DC 20004

SHIPLEY, MORRIS, airline exec.; b. Bklyn., Dec. 26, 1911; s. Frederic B. and Estelle (Van Trump) S.; student Princeton U., 1929-30; m. Anne Wilson Burke, 1944; 4 sons, 5 daus. With Am. Airlines, 1939-62; with Delta Air Lines, Atlanta, 1962—, dir. civic affairs, 1962-67, asst. v.p. civic affairs, 1967-69, v.p. govt. affairs, Washington, 1969—. Office: 1629 K St NW Washington DC 20006

SHIPMAN, HAROLD R., civil engr.; b. Rock Rapids, Ia., Feb. 20, 1911; s. Elvin Laforester and Leora (Macdonald) S.; B.S., U. Minn., 1937, M.S., 1948; m. Lois M. Brown, Aug. 22, 1938; children—Bruce Macdonald, Richard Pierce. Asst. engr. Minn. Dept. Health, 1937-40, dist. engr., Mankato, 1942-44, dir. div. hotels, resorts and restaurants, 1946-50; asst. engr. FSA, Minn., 1940-42; san. engr. adviser UN Civil Assistance Command, Korea, 1950-51; san. engr. adviser to Turkish Govt., WHO, 1951-54, san. engr. adviser to Govt. of Egypt, 1954-58; chief engr. Pan Am. Health Orgn., 1958-62; chief water supply div. World Bank, Washington, 1962—. Chmn. UN's Interagy. Subcom. on Water Resources, 1971. Trustee Environmental Engring. Intersoc. Bd. Served from capt. to lt. col., San. Corps, AUS, 1944-46. Recipient Govtl. citation Egypt, 1958. Registered profl. engr., Minn. Diplomate Am. Acad. Environmental Engrs. Fellow Am. Soc. C.E., Am. Pub. Health Assn.; mem. Nat. Soc. Profl. Engrs., Am. Water Works Assn., Interam. Assn. San. Engrs., Internat. Water Supply Assn., Am. Photogrammetry Soc. Contbr. articles to profl. jours. Home: 7108 Edgevale St Chevy Chase MD 20015 Office: 1818 H St Washington DC 20433

SHIPP, BERT NICOLO, television news dir.; b. Artesia, N.M., Nov. 26, 1929; s. Bert N. and Anna Mae (Bruce) S.; student Abilene Christian Coll., 1952-55, So. Meth. U., 1955-56; m. Shirley Ann Upham, Aug. 29, 1953; children—Bruce Edward, Brett Ramsey, Stefanie Ann. Reporter, Abilene (Tex.) Reporter, 1955, Dallas Times Herald, 1956-57; editor Garland (Tex.) Times Reporter, 1958; nresman WBAP-TV, Ft. Worth, Tex., 1959-60; asst. news dir. WFAA-TV, Dallas, 1961-65, news dir., 1965—. Adviser to pub. relations bd. North Tex Tb and Respiratory Assn.; committeeman Cub Scouts Circle 10 council Boy Scouts Am., 1968—. Mem. Radio-TV News Dirs. Assn., Press Club Dallas (pres.), Sigma Delta Chi. Mem. Ch. of Christ (trustee). Home: 4902 Abbott Av Dallas TX 75205 Office: Communications Center Dallas TX 75202

SHIPP, HENRY LEE, lawyer; b. nr. Douglasville, Tex., Dec. 16, 1924; s. Henry Lee and Mary H. (Henderson) S.; A.A., Kilgore Coll., 1944; J.D., U. Notre Dame DuLac, 1948; m. Joan Barbara Vatter, Dec. 29, 1954; 1 son, Michael Lee. Admitted to Tex. bar, 1948; since practiced in Dallas; partner Shipp & Crooks, 1964—; dir., sec., gen. counsel Frymire Engring. Co. Mem. Am., Tex., Dallas bar assns. Club: Dallas Athletic. Home: 4224 Stanford St Dallas TX 75225 Office: Republic Nat Bank Tower Dallas TX 75201

SHIPPEY, ORRLINE ELLIS (MRS. WOODROW W. SHIPPEY), librarian; b. Italy, Tex.; d. Forest Pierce and Mary Ella (Orr) Ellis; B.A., Trinity U., 1936; B.L.S., Tex. Woman's U., 1938; postgrad. George Peabody Coll., summer 1941; m. Woodrow W. Shippey, Oct. 21, 1945. Librarian pub. schs., Jefferson, Tex., 1936-39, White Oak Pub. Schs., Longview, Tex., 1939-58; cataloger Engring. Library, Tex. A. and M. Coll., College Station, summer 1942; dir. Nicholson Meml. Pub. Library, Longview, 1958—. Mem. Am. Assn. U. Women, A.L.A., Tex. Library Assn. (chmn sch. div. 1944-45, chmn. children's div. 1950-51, dist. chmn. 1968). Methodist. Contbr. articles profl. jours. Home: PO Box 1311 Longview TX 75603 Office: 400 S Green St Longview TX 75601

SHIRA, CHARLES N., athletic dir., head football coach Miss. State U. Address: Athletic Dept Miss State U State College MS 39762*

SHIRCLIFF, ROBERT THOMAS, bottling co. exec.; b. Vincennes, Ind., May 20, 1928; s. Thomas Maxwell and Martha (Somes) S.; B.S., Ind. U., 1950; m. Carol Reed, May 9, 1953; children—Laura Reed, Elizabeth Somes. Vice pres., gen. mgr. Pepsi-Cola Bottling Co., Bloomington, Ind., 1950-55, v.p., treas., Charleston, W. Va., 1955-63; pres. Pepsi-Cola Allied Bottlers, Inc., Jacksonville, Fla., 1963—; dir. General Cinema Corp., Boston, 1968—, Normandy Atlantic Bank. Chmn. bd. Duval County chpt. A.R.C., 1972—, YMCA, United Fund; pres. Speech and Hearing Clinic, Jacksonville, 1972. Mem. Nat. Pepsi-Cola Bottlers Assn. (dir., pres. 1971), Jacksonville C. of C. (v.p.), Sigma Alpha Epsilon. Clubs: River, Seminole, Timuquana Country, University (Jacksonville); Rotary (dir., pres. 1969-70). Home: 4918 Prince Edward Rd Jacksonville FL 32210 Office: 155 S Edgewood St Jacksonville FL 32205

SHIREY, VIOLET HENSON (MRS. WILLIAM W. SHIREY), educator; b. Albuquerque, May 12, 1923; d. Alva St. Clair and Eva (Daniels) Henson; student Albuquerque Bus. Coll., 1940; B.S., East Tex. State U., 1955, M.Ed., 1956, postgrad., 1965, 66, 67; m. William Shirey, Nov. 22, 1944; 1 dau., Linda Sue (Mrs. Atilano V. Perez). Sec., legal, ins., Civil Service positions, 1940-47; chief clk. Vocational Sch., Quitman, Tex., 1947-56; elementary tchr. Austin (Tex.) pub. schs., 1956-61; asso. prof. Jarvis Christian Coll., Hawkins, Tex., 1961-67; supr. student tchrs., vocational occupational instr. Bee County Coll., Beeville, Tex., 1967-70, chmn. bus. div., 1970—. Mem. telephone com. Democratic Women, 1962. Mem. Am. Assn. U. Profs., Tex. Soc. Coll. Profs. Edn., Am. Soc. for Curriculum Devel., Nat., Tex., Mountain Plains bus. edn. assns., Tex. Jr. Coll. Tchrs. Assn., Alpha Delta Kappa (publicity chmn. 1961, finance chmn. 1963), Pi Omega

Pi, Alpha Chi, Delta Kappa Gamma. Contbr. articles to profl. jours. Home: 748 Pine Rockport TX 78382 Office: Bee County Coll Beeville TX 78102

SHIRK, GEORGE HENRY, lawyer; b. Oklahoma City, May 1, 1913; s. John H. and Carrie (Hinderer) S.; A.B., U. Okla., 1935, LL.B., 1936. Admitted to Okla. bar, 1936, since practiced in Oklahoma City; spl. justice Supreme Ct. Okla., 1963; mayor Oklahoma City, 1964-67. Pres., Oklahoma City Safety Council, 1959-63; mem. Okla. Civil War Centennial Commn., 1961-65. Bd. dirs., exec. com. United Fund Oklahoma City, 1961—. Served to Col. Gen. Staff Corps, AUS, 1944-45. Decorated Bronze Star medal, Legion of Merit (U.S.); Legion of Honor (France). Mem. Gt. Plains (adv. bd. 1962—), Okla. (pres. 1959—), hist. socs., Phi Delta Theta, Phi Delta Phi. Lutheran. Mason (Jester). Author: Oklahoma Place Names, 1965. Home: 5201 Vernon Rd Oklahoma City OK 73111 Office: Colcord Bldg Oklahoma City OK 73102

SHIRK, MILDRED ROCKWELL (MRS. FRANK CHARLES SHIRK), librarian; b. Inverness, Md., Apr. 2, 1918; d. Charles Berman and Mildred (Bennett) Rockwell; B.S., Mary Washington Coll. of U. Va., 1939; B.L.S., Drexel Inst. Tech., 1940; m. Frank Charles Shirk, Apr. 30, 1942; children—David Frederick, Linda (Mrs. Wood). Library asst. Morristown (N.J.) Pub. Library, 1940-42; head librarian Caldwell (N.J.) Pub. Library, 1942-44; librarian pub. elementary sch., Blacksburg, Va., 1950-59; reference librarian Va. Poly. Inst. Library, Blacksburg, 1959-61; regional dir. Montgomery-Radford Regional Library, Radford, Va., 1961-70; library dir. Radford Pub. Library, 1970—; library dir. New River Valley Community Coll., Radford, 1967-69. Mem. Blacksburg Jr. Woman's Club, 1945-53, pres., 1953; co-founder, v.p. Blacksburg Intermediate Woman's Club, 1952-55; mem. Town and Country Garden Club, Blacksburg, 1950—, sec., 1954-55; chmn. cancer crusade Blacksburg, 1953. Mem. Va., Southeastern library assns., Zeta Tau Alpha. Home: 111 Country Club Dr Blacksburg VA 24060 Office: Recreation Bldg Radford VA 24141

SHISKIN, JULIUS, govt. ofcl.; b. N.Y.C., Oct. 13, 1912; s. Abraham and Bella (Bender) S.; A.B., Rutgers U., 1934, M.A., 1936; postgrad. Columbia U., 1936-37; m. Frances Levine, Nov. 21, 1937; children—Laura, Carol. Instr. econs. and statistics Rutgers U., 1934-38; research asst. Nat. Bur. Econ. Research, N.Y.C., 1938-42; head economist WPB, Washington, 1942-45; chief econ. statistician Bur. Census, Washington, 1945-68, asst. dir., 1968-69; asst. dir. statis. policy Bur. Budget, 1969-70; chief statistician Office Mgmt. and Budget, Washington, 1969—. U.S. rep. Statis. Commn. UN, 1969—. Cons. Council Econ. Advisers, 1957-60. Orgn. for Econ. Coop. and Devel., 1960, UN, 1962, IMF, 1964. Recipient Rockefeller Pub. Service award, 1956; award Nat. Assn. Bus. Economists, 1971. Fellow Am. Statis. Assn., A.A.A.S.; mem. Internat. Statis. Inst., Am. Econ. Assn. Author: Electronic Computers and Business Indicators, 1957; Signals of Recession and Recovery, 1961; (with Geoffrey H. Moore) Indicators of Business Expansions and Contractions, 1967; also articles. Home: 8920 Whitney St Silver Spring MD 20901 Office: Office of Mgmt and Budget Washington DC 20503

SHNEIDEROV, ANATOL JAMES, cosmophysicist; b. Ekaterinburg, Russia, July 29, 1894; s. James G. and Alexandra (Petukhov) S.; C.E., Petrograd Mil. Engring. Sch., 1917, Mag. Mil. Eng., 1918; B.Elec. Engring., George Washington U., 1944; M.A., Tchrs. Coll., Columbia, 1948; postgrad. Johns Hopkins U., 1945-46, Cath. U. Am., 1944-45, 55-58; m. Siren O. Martirosiantz, Sept. 30, 1930 (dec. Dec. 1958); 1 dau., Svetozara Anatol'evna (Mrs. Maxim D. Persidsky). Came to U.S., 1941, naturalized 1950. Owner, Izida Assns., Harbin-Shanghai, China, 1924-41; mng. dir. Shneider Process Co., Ltd., Hong-Kong, Shanghai, Washington, 1941-45; chmn., pres. Polycultural Instn. Am., Washington, 1945—, prof. Russian lang. and culture, 1950—; geophysicist U.S. Geol. Survey, 1958-62; fellow European Center for Research on Gravitation, Rome, Italy, 1961, del. to U.S., 1962, prof., 1964; engr., geophysicist arctic bibliography project Arctic Inst. N. Am., Washington, 1962—. World lectr., 1964-65. Mem. Am. Geophys. Union, Am. Phys. Soc., Philos. Soc. Washington, Fedn. Am. Scientists, A.A.A.S., Am. Ordnance Assn., Arctic Inst. N.Am., Am. Inst. Aeros. and Astronautics. Author: The Dreams I Dreamt & the Life I Lived, 1927; The Little Blue Book of Shanghai, 1932; editor: Dynamics and Mobilism of an Expanding Earth. Research, publications on radional field theory; pioneer in earth's expansion theory; author of expulsion planetery theory. Home: 1673 Columbia Rd NW Washington DC 20009 Office: care Arctic Inst N Am 406 E Capital St Washington DC 20003

SHOBERT, KENDALL JOE, pub. relations exec.; b. Washington, Okla., Nov. 3, 1935; s. Joe and Hazel E. (Wilbanks) S.; student Okla. U., 1954-58, 60-61. Author radio and TV scripts WNAD, Okla. U., Norman, 1957-58, 60-61, KUVY, radio sta. U. Okla., 1960-61; supr. KOMA radio, Moore, Okla., 1961-62, KWTV-TV, Oklahoma City, 1960, TV prodn. exec. and writer, 1960-61; TV prodn. specialist, dir. instrn. TV prodn. unit USAAMS, Fort Sill, Okla., 1966-68; writer Eagle-Lion Prodns., Hollywood, Cal., 1968-69; free-lance writer, 1969—. Served with AUS, 1958-60, 62-65. Mem. Writer's Guild Am., Nat. Assn. Ednl. Broadcasters, Interagy. Bd. U.S. Civil Service Examiners. Author TV play: The Off-Breed, NBC Matinee Theatre, 1956; movie scripts: Impact Zone, The Warring Kind—How I came to Kill My Uncle During My Summer Vacation; Something Like Spying, 1968; novel: My Son, The Tramp. Home: 1116 W Eufaula St Norman OK 73069

SHOCKEY, ROBERT DREXEL, agrl. co. exec.; b. Rosefork, Ky., Aug. 19, 1933; s. Alex Raymond and Marie (Huff) S.; grad. Wolf County High Sch., 1954; m. Wanda Pearl Dunn, Sept. 17, 1955; children—Leigh Ann, Leslie Kay. Clerical worker McCalls, Dayton, O., and Aetna Paper Co., Dayton, 1955-58; foreman Oxford Paper Co., West Carrollton, O., 1958-59; salesman Niagara Chem. div. F.M.C. Corp., Middleport, N.Y., 1960-62; salesman Tobacco States Chem. Co., Lexington, Ky., 1963-64; salesman The Ansul Co., Marinette, Wis., 1965-67, nat. sales mgr., Memphis, 1967-72, marketing mgr. Agrl. Chems. div., 1972—. Served with AUS, 1951-53. Decorated Purple Heart. Republican. Mason. Home: 1531 Briar Cove Memphis TN 38116 Office: 3385 Airways Blvd Memphis TN 38116

SHOEMAKE, ROBERT ELLIS, ednl. adminstr.; b. Ovett, Miss., Feb. 12, 1909; s. Henry James and Christine (Hutto) S.; B.S., Miss. So. Coll., 1938; M.A., 1950; m. Helen Hinton, Oct. 8, 1932; children—Juanine (Mrs. Jerry Lowery), Jack, Elaine, Edith. Instr. math. Perry County (Miss.) Schs., 1930-34; supt. Beaumont (Miss.) High Sch., 1934-40; county supt. edn., Perry County, Miss., 1940-48; adminstr., supr. Jr. Coll., 1948-49; supt. Forrest County Agrl. High Sch., Brooklyn, Miss., 1949—, prin. Trade and Tech. High Sch., 1949—. Chmn. pub. relations Boy Scouts Am., 1958; past co-chmn. Dist White House Conf.; past del. State Conv. White House Conf. Mem. Nat., Miss. edn. assns., Forrest County Tchrs. Assn. (past pres.), Miss. State Sch. Adminstrs. (past pres.), Miss. So. Alumni Assn. (pres. 1959-60), C. of C., Indsl. Bd. Forrest County, Am. Assn. Sch. Adminstrs. Red, Red Rose, Gamma Gamma, Phi Delta Kappa. Mason; mem. Order Eastern Star, Lion, Kiwanian. Club: Beta (mem. exec. council). Home: Forrest County Agrl High Sch Brooklyn MS 39425

SHOEMAKER, DON(ALD) (CLEAVENGER), editor; b. Montreal, Que., Can., Dec. 6, 1912; s. Richard Samuel and Alberta (Stone) S. (Am. citizens); A.B., U. N.C., 1934; LL.D., Hollywood Coll.; m. Lyal Reynolds, Oct. 30, 1937 (dec. July 1968); 1 dau., Elizabeth; m. 2d, Suzanne Elaine Statler, Aug. 2, 1969; 1 dau., Charlotte. Telegraph editor Greensboro (N.C.) Record, 1934-37, Asheville (N.C.) Times, 1937-41; asso. editor Asheville Citizen, 1941-47, editor, 1947-55; exec. dir. So. Edn. Reporting Service, 1955-58; editor, editorial page Miami Herald, 1958-62, editor, 1962—, also dir. Chmn. N.C. Conf. Editorial Writers, 1951-52; lectr. in field. Sec. Fla. World's Fair Authority, 1964; mem. Gov.'s Bicentennial Commn., mem. Fla. Ednl. Facilities Adv. Commn.; journalism fellowship program and commn. higher edn. for adults So. Regional Edn. Bd.; mem. information chmn. Orange Bowl Com.; pres. Area Wide Health Facilities Planning Council. Chmn. Community Mental Health Services Fund, 1970, Miami Philharmonic Soc. Bd. dirs. Race Relations Information Center; trustee U. Miami, Mus. of Sci. Recipient award merit Asheville Sch. Mem. Fla. Council of 100 (vice chmn. 1969-72), Miami Beach Com. 100, Am., Fla. socs. newspaper editors, Order Golden Fleece (U. N.C.), Pi Kappa Alpha, Sigma Delta Chi. Democrat. Episcopalian. Clubs: Two Hundred (founder mem.; pres.), Palm Bay, Jockey, International, Bath, Miami, Standard (Miami). Editor: Henry George: Citizen of the World (by Anna George de Mille), 1950; Middle East Journey; The Case of the Lively Ghost, 1957; With All Deliberate Speed, 1957. Contbr. mags. Home: 617 Sabal Palm Rd Bay Point Miami FL 33137 Office: Miami Herald Miami FL 33131

SHOEMAKER, DONALD HOWARD, educator; b. LaPorte, Ind., Sept. 19, 1926; s. Harry Cecil and Wanda (Rosenbaum) S.; student Rose Poly. Inst., 1944-45; B.S., Ind. U., 1950, M.S., 1953, Ed.D., 1964; m. Evelyn Helen Gembala, June 18, 1949; children—Gregory, Pamela. Sci. tchr., prin. Ind. pub. schs., 1950-57; lectr., program supr. Ind. U., Bloomington, 1957-62; dir. regional bur. teaching materials U. Va., Charlottsville, 1962— asst. prof. to prof. edn., 1962-70, prof. edn., 1970—; cons. audio-visual communications pub. schs. Va. Served with USAAF, 1945-46. Mem. N.E.A., Assn. Ednl. Communications and Tech. (bd. dirs. 1969-71, Outstanding Media Educator of Yr. award Va. chpt. 1970-71), Va. Edn. Assn. (pres. dept. teaching materials 1963-64), Nat. Assn. Ednl. Broadcasters, Phi Delta Kappa (faculty advisor 1967-71; Distinguished Service award 1972). Home: 2511 Smithfield Rd Charlottesville VA 22901

SHOEMAKER, LEONARD WILEY, cons. engr.; b. Long Beach, Cal., Nov. 11, 1937; s. Leonard Miller and Josephine (Berry) S.; B.S., Tex. A. and M. Coll., 1961; m. Bobby Jean Foster, June 1, 1958; 1 dau., Sharon Dawn. Civil engr. U.S. Forest Service, Lufkin, Tex., 1961-64, supervisory civil engr., Cleve., 1964-66; asso., v.p. Dannenbaum Engring. Corp., Houston, 1966-69; prin. R.G. Miller Engrs., Houston, 1969-70; pres. Leonard W. Shoemaker & Assos., Inc., Houston, 1970—. Mem. Nat., Tex. (pres. Sam Houston chpt. 1970-71, Outstanding Young Engr. 1969) socs. profl. engrs., Am. Soc. C.E., Harris County Heritage Soc. Presbyn. (elder, deacon). Club: Optimist (v.p. 1969-70). Home: 127 Plantation St Houston TX 77024 Office: 9235 Katy Freeway Houston TX 77024

SHOEMAKER, RALPH JOSEPH, library cons., author; b. East Lansdowne, Pa., July 13, 1906; s. Frank W. and Harriet (Mathews) S.; m. Elsie M. DeGraff, Dec. 9, 1951. Asst. librarian Phila. Pub. Ledger, 1920-34; asso. librarian Phila. Evening Ledger, 1934-42; chief librarian Courier-Jour. and Louisville Times, 1947-62; now library cons. and author. Vice chmn. of Phila. Library Council, 1933-34. Served from pvt. to capt., AUS, 1942-46. Named Ky. col., 1963. Mem. Ky. Library Assn. (pres. 1955-56), Spl. Libraries Assn. (chmn. newspaper div. 1935-36), Louisville Library Club (pres. 1950-51). Author: Memorial Tribute to Joseph F. Kwapil, 1934; The Presidents Words, vols. 1-7, 1954-61; Subject Classifications for Clipping and Picture Files, 1958; Newspaper Library Filing Systems, 1962; East Lansdowne: Early Facts and Fond Recollections, 1969; In the Classics series, 1970. Contbr. articles and book revs. to mags., newspapers. Address: 5136 28th Av N St Petersburg FL 33710

SHOEMAKER, WILLIAM MILLARD, r.r. exec.; b. Lake Cormorant, Miss., July 6, 1909; s. William Millard and Floy (Buford) S.; B.S.C., U. Miss., 1931-35; m. Alice Denman, Feb. 18, 1939; children—William Millard, Susan, Richard. Various positions I.C. R.R., 1936-51; gen. traffic mgr. Meridian & Bigbee R.R., Meridian, Miss., 1952-56, exec. v.p., gen. mgr., 1956—, dir., mem. exec. com., 1957—; dir. Citizens Nat. Bank. Mem. adv. bd. Choctaw Area council Boy Scouts Am., 1957—, v.p., 1960—; mem. exec. com. Research and Devel. Council, 1972. Trustee Instns. Higher Learning Miss.; bd. dirs. Miss. Econ. Council. Named Boss of Year, Meridian chpt. Nat. Assn. Secs., 1962; Ky. col.; hon. lt. col. Ala. Mem. Am. Short Line Assn. (legislative com. 1962-67, dir. 1972), Birmingham Traffic and Transp. Club, Meridian C. of C. (dir.), Pi Kappa Alpha. Baptist. Rotarian. Clubs: Downtown, Northwood Country (Meridian); Club (Birmingham). Home: 3131 29th Av Meridian MS 39301 Office: 119 22d Av S Meridian MS 39301

SHOFFNER, CLARENCE LORENZO, dentist; b. Greensboro, N.C., Dec. 13, 1921; s. Ira Benjamin and Lelia Bernice (Harriston) S.; B.S., A. and T. U., Greensboro, 1942; D.D.S., Howard U., 1951; postgrad. U. Pa., 1946-47; m. Carrie Tena Carter, Nov. 13, 1943; children—Selia Lorene, Annah Yvonne. With div. oral hygiene N.C. Dept. Health, Raliegh, 1951-52; practice gen. dentistry, Weldon, N.C., 1952—. Pres., Hillcrest Realty Subdiv., Roanoke Rapids, N.C. Mem. N.C. Human Relations Commn., 1970—, Halifax County Selective Service Bd., 1969—. Bd. dirs. Weldon Bus. Bur., Rheasville Vol. Fire Dept.; trustee Halifax Tech. Inst. Served with USAAF, 1942-45. Mem. Acad. Gen. Dentistry, Am. Dental Assn., N.C., Old North State dental socs., Eastern Carolina Med., Dental and Pharm. Soc., Rocky Mount Acad. Medicine, Roanoke Rapids C. of C., Basilius Omega Psi Phi. Democrat. Roman Catholic Mason (32 deg.). Club: Meadowbrook Country (life). Home: PO Box 266 Weldon NC 27890 Office: 100 Elm St Weldon NC 27890

SHOFNER, GEORGE EDWIN, JR., govt. ofcl., structural engr.; b. Memphis, Aug. 7, 1930; s. George Edwin and Aimee (Myers) S.; B.S. in Civil Engring., U. Tenn., 1952; m. Mildred Marie Gibson, Sept. 12, 1952; 1 dau., Mildred Gibson. Structural engr. Ford Motor Co., Nashville, 1959-60; chief structural-civil br. facilities office Marshall Space Flight Center, NASA, Huntsville, Ala., 1960—. Cons. engr. fallout shelter analysis, 1967—. Scoutmaster, Tenn. Valley council Boy Scouts Am., 1953-58, commr., 1967—. Served to lt. SAC, USAF, 1953-55. Registered profl. engr., Ala., Tenn. Mem. Am. Soc. C.E., Ala. Soc. Profl. Engrs. (Engr. of Year 1967-68 Huntsville chpt., Outstanding Service award 1968, chpt. pres. 1971-72; nat. dir. 1972—). Home: 914 Fagan Springs Dr Huntsville AL 35801 Office: Marshall Space Flight Center AL 35812

SHOLAR, NORMAN PERCIVAL, dentist; b. Bessemer City, N.C., Mar. 19, 1916; s. Merrimon Isham and Annie (Wootten) S.; student Wake Forest Coll., 1936-37; D.D.S., Emory U., 1942; m. Louisa Williams Templeton, July 18, 1944; children—Norman, Lynda, John, Thomas, Clay. Practice gen. dentistry, Mooresville, N.C., 1946—. Dir. Carolina First Nat. Bank, Lincolnton, N.C. Mem. adv. bd. N.C. Zool. Authority. Trustee Mitchell Coll., Statesville, N.C., 1957-60. Served to lt. comdr. USNR, 1942-46. Recipient medal for 1st breeding Port Lincoln parrot in N. Am., Avicultural Soc. Am., 1962. Mem. 2d Dist., N.C., Am. dental socs. Presbyn. (elder). Kiwanian. Home: Box 180 741 Pinewood Circle Mooresville NC 28115 Office: Box 180 212 S Academy St Mooresville NC 28115

SHOLIS, VICTOR A., broadcasting exec. Pres. WHAS, Louisville. Office: 520 W Chestnut St Louisville KY 40202*

SHOMLER, RUSSELL PAUL, accountant; b. Melcher, Ia., Jan. 30, 1917; s. Glenn William and Annie (Greaser) S.; B.B.A. cum laude, U. Wis., 1947; m. Pauline April Lathrop; children—Ruth Karen, John Lathrop. With Haskins & Sells, C.P.A.'s, 1947—, partner, 1957—, charge Atlanta, 1963—; instr. extension div. U. Cal. at Los Angeles, 1953-57; arbitrator for Am. Arbitration Assn., Los Angeles, 1958-62; instr. USAF Tech. Tng. Command. Bd. dirs. Met. Atlanta Community Chest, 1965—. C.P.A., Cal., N.Y., Ga., La., Tenn., N.C. Mem. Am. Inst. C.P.A.'s, Cal. (v.p. Los Angeles 1961-62), Ga. (v.p. Atlanta 1966-67, pres. 1968-69), socs. C.P.A.'s. Home: 815 N Island Dr NW Atlanta GA 30327 Office: C & S Nat Bank Bldg Atlanta GA 30303

SHOOLBRED, AUGUSTUS WAITE, JR., civil engr.; b. Columbia, S.C., Dec. 29, 1926; s. Augustus Waite and Margaret (Fowler) S.; B.S., Clemson U., 1949; m. Mary Ann Elliott, Apr. 29, 1950; children—William Augustus, Margaret Louise, Mary Ann. Insp., S.C. Hwy. Dept., 1949-50; design engr. Harwood Beebe Co., Spartanburg, S.C., 1950-60, chief engr., sec., dir., 1960-63, v.p., 1963—; exec. v.p., dir. Spartan Assos., Inc.; v.p., dir. Lyles, Bissett, Carlisle & Wolff. Served with C.E., AUS, 1945-47. Recipient certificate of meritorious service S.C. Soc. Profl. Engrs., 1966, 69. Mem. Nat., S.C. (dir., past chpt. pres.) socs. profl. engrs., Am. Water Works Assn. Episcopalian. Clubs: Sertoma, Lan Yair Country (Spartanburg). Home: 205 Emory Rd Spartanburg SC 29302 Office: PO Box 2646 2000 E Main St Spartanburg SC 29302

SHOR, SAMUEL WENDELL WILLISTON, naval engr.; b. N.Y.C., June 25, 1920; s. George Gershon and Dorothy (Williston) S.; student Harvard, 1937-39; B.S., U.S. Naval Acad., 1942; naval engr., Mass. Inst. Tech., 1949; M.S. in Math., N.Y. U., 1963; m. Joan Bopp, June 21, 1958; children—Peter Williston, Molly Hathaway. Commd. ensign U.S. Navy, 1942, advanced through grades to capt., 1962; served in cruisers Chicago, St. Louis, and Quincy, Pacific and Atlantic, 1942-46; assigned San Francisco Naval Shipyard, 1949-52; AEC rep. for nuclear matters in U.S.S. Nautilus and U.S.S. Seawolf, also for Shippingport (Pa.) Atomic Power Sta., 1953-58; design supt., prodn. engring. officer N.Y. Naval Shipyard, 1958-63; dir. sonar systems office Naval Ship Systems Command, 1963-67, exec. dir. plans, 1967-69, dep. comdr. engring., 1969-71, project mgr. Temp/Rewson, 1971—. Mem. Soc. Naval Architects and Marine Engrs., Soc. Naval Engrs., Am. Math. Soc., Am. Phys. Soc., Sigma Xi. Unitarian. Author tech. papers. Home: 6614 32d St NW Washington DC 20015 Office: Naval Ship Systems Command Washington DC 20360

SHORE, CLOVER VIRGINIA PETERS (MRS. DAVID PRESTON SHORE), artist; b. Durango, Tex., Aug. 1, 1906; d. William Allen and Virginia (McCreary) Peters; student Toby Bus. Coll.; m. David Preston Shore, Dec. 29, 1927; children—Shirley Clover (Mrs. Lloyd Smith Parker), David Preston II. Art tchr. Fort Worth pub. high schs., 1944-46; asst. prof. art Tex. Christian U., Fort Worth, 1945-48; mem. faculty Arlington State Coll., 1957, 60, 61, 62; chmn. art Ft. Worth Christian Coll., 1968—. Exhibited one-man shows Collin' Art Gallery, Fort Worth, 1958, Hellum's Gallery, Fort Worth, 1953, 57, Denton (Tex.) Gallery, 1959, Studio Gallery, Waco, Tex., 1960; exhibited in group shows including Tex. Fedn. Womens Clubs, Austin, Abilene (Tex.) Mus. Art, Fort Worth Art Center, Dallas Mus. Art, Jackson (Miss.) Mus. Art, Birmingham (Ala.) Mus. Art, Smithsonian Instn. Annex Gallery, Washington, Butler Art Inst., Youngstown, O., Del Gado Mus. Art, New Orleans, Tex. Fine Arts Assn. Exhbn., Austin; traveling exhbns. Tex. Fine Arts Assn. Austin, 1960-61, 62-63, Nat. League Am. Pen Women Cultural Exchange Art Exhibit, 1966; represented in permanent collections. Recipient First Place in Graphics, Abilene (Tex.) Mus. Art, 1952, Blanche McVeigh award Fort Worth Art Center, 1964. Mem. Fort Worth Art Assn., Nat. League Am. Pen Women (pres. br. 1964-66, 68-70, Tex. pres. 1968-70). Tex. State Tchrs. Assn. (life), Delta Zeta (State council pres. dist. 4, 1968, Fort Worth alumnae pres. 1966-68), Kappa Pi. Club: Fort Worth Womans. Home: 2200 Glenco Terrace Fort Worth TX 76110

SHORE, SHERMAN, journalist; b. Yadkinville, N.C., Aug. 28, 1909; s. Sexton Denny and Minnie (Haire) S.; A.B., U. N.C., 1932; m. Patricia Patterson, Apr. 12, 1947 (div. Sept. 1970); 1 son, Mark Jeffrey. Reporter, feature writer Greensboro (N.C.) Daily News, 1932-38; with Winston-Salem (N.C.) Jour. and Sentinel, 1939-70, successively writer, city editor, Sunday feature editor, lit. critic, 1939-70; city editor Forsyth Weekly News, 1970; editor Pilot Piper, Pilot Mountain, N.C., 1970—. Instr. Army Command Gen. Staff Coll., 1961-64. Dir. Warden Services Br. Civil Defense Orgn., Forsyth County, N.C., 1957—. Served with AUS, 1942-45; col. Res. ret. Mem. Am. Assn. Sunday and Feature Editors, Delta Upsilon. Democrat. Methodist. Author lit. column, The Shoreline. Home: 204 Wake Dr Winston-Salem NC 27106

SHORT, HERMAN B., police ofcl.; b. Gauley Mills, W.Va., May 22, 1918; s. Enos Herman and Freda Mae (Black) S.; grad. Am. Detective Sch. and Am. Finger Print System N.Y., 1939; m. Nettie Lucille Kesterson, Aug. 3, 1949; 1 son, Robert Enos. Mem. Houston Police Dept., 1945—, insp., 1963-64, chief police, 1964—; engaged as real estate broker, Houston, 1966—. Bd. dirs. Houston Farm and Ranch Club, 1965-67, Houston Livestock Show and Rodeo, 1965-67. Served with USCGR, 1942-45. Mem. Houston Police Officers Assn., Tex. Police Assn., Internat. Assn. Chiefs Police, Tex. Municipal Police Officers Assn. Baptist. Home: 9106 Almeda Genoa Rd Houston TX 77034 Office: 61 Reisner St Houston TX 77002

SHORT, JAMES DAVID, mfg. co. pres.; b. Abington, Pa., Mar. 1, 1942; s. William Howard and Rita Mary (Kauffman) S.; B.S., So. Meth. U., 1964, M.S. in Engring., 1967; m. Suzanne Potter, Nov. 23, 1963; children—Kristina Kay, Suzanne Pauline, Joanna Nicol. Student engr. Collins Radio Co., Dallas, 1960-64; engr. Microwave Physica Corp., Garland, Tex., 1964-66; staff engr. Collins Radio Co., Dallas, 1966-67; pres., dir. Electro/Data, Inc., Garland, 1967—; v.p., dir. Care Electronics, Inc. Huntsville, 1971—. Mem. I.E.E.E., Assn. Old Crows, Phi Gamma Delta. Republican. Home: 11915 Brookmeadow Dr Dallas TX 75218 Office: 1621 Jupiter Rd Garland TX 75042

SHORT, MILLICENT SCUDDER (MRS. ROBERT B. SHORT, JR.), journalist; b. Honolulu, June 24, 1929; d. Irvine C. and Hazel (Jones) Scudder; B.A. in Journalism, La. State U., 1951, M.A., 1953; postgrad. U. Ga., 1954, Catherine Spalding Coll., Louisville, 1964-65; m. Robert B. Short, Jr., July 31, 1961; children—Steven, Susan, Cynthia. Editorial asst. La. State U. Agrl. Extension Service, Baton

Rouge, 1953, editor La. State U. Ann., 1951; free-lance feature writer Baton Rouge Morning Advocate Sunday Mag., 1950-51; editorial work La. Dairyman, Baton Rouge, 1953; proofreader Agrl. Extension Service publs., Pritzen Printing Co., Baton Rouge, 1953; circulation and editorial asst. La. Farm Bur. News, Baton Rouge, 1953-54; dir. radio continuity WAFB Radio and TV, Baton Rouge, 1953-54; TV copywriter and coordinator Alvin Meyer Advt., Baton Rouge, 1954; adminstrv. asst. for pub. relations Ft. Benning (Ga.) Children's Schs., 1954; instr. Columbus Coll., U. Ga., 1954-55; chief of circulation Infantry Mag., Ft. Benning, 1955, information specialist Infantry Sch., 1955-58, 60-61; information officer IV Army Corps, Birmingham, Ala., 1958-60; dir. pub. relations Louisville chpt. A.R.C., also tech. information cons. to 20 other chpts. Ky. and Ind. counties, 1964-65; editor Armor Sch., Ft. Knox, Ky., 1966-68; instr. journalism, adviser to sch. newspaper and ann. Jackson (Tenn.) State Coll., 1968-71. Editor Graymoor News, Louisville, 1966-67. Publicity chmn. Community Chest, Ft. Benning, 1955-58, 60. Mem. Armed Forces Writers League (charter mem.), Daus. U.S. Army (publicity chmn. Ft. Benning 1954-61), Chi Omega, Theta Sigma Phi, Pi Alpha Mu, Phi Kappa Phi, Pi Gamma Mu, Phi Lambda Pi, Alpha Lambda Delta, Mu Sigma Rho. Episcopalian. Home: 6314 Shadow Wood Ct Prospect KY 40059

SHORT, ROBERT E., baseball exec. Pres., Tex. Rangers baseball club. Address: Arlington Stadium PO Box 1111 1500 Copeland Rd Arlington TX 76010*

SHORT, ROY HUNTER, clergyman, bishop; b. Louisville, Oct. 19, 1902; s. Jesse Peters and Minnie (Badders) S.; A.B., U. Louisville, 1924; B.D., Louisville Presbyn. Sem., 1927, Th.M., 1929; D.D., Ky. Wesleyan Coll., Winchester, 1939; LL.D., Fla. So. U., 1949; Litt.D., Tenn. Wesleyan, 1957; D.D., Emory U., 1958; Dr. Canon Law, Emory and Henry Coll., 1959; m. Louise Clay Baird, Sept. 1, 1926; children—Hunter Baird, Murray Malcolm, Riley Phillips. Ordained to ministry Meth. Ch., 1921; pastor, Mount Holy Ch., 1922-26, Oakdale Ch., 1926-28, Marcus Lindsey Ch., 1928-30 (all Louisville), Greenville (Ky.) Ch., 1930-35; dist. supt. Elizabethtown (Ky.) Dist., 1935-37; dist. supt. Louisville Dist., 1937-41; pastor St. Pauls Ch., Louisville, 1941-44; editor The Upper Room, religious quarterly, 1944-48, elected bishop, 1948; resident bishop Fla. Area, 1948-52; resident bishop Nashville Area, Meth. Ch., 1952-64; resident bishop Louisville Area, 1964—; sec. of United Meth. Ch. Mem. Theta Phi. Author: Your Church and You (membership Meth. boys and girls), 1942; Evangelistic Preaching: Evangelism Through the Local Church, 1956. Home: 512 Brandon Rd Louisville KY 40207

SHORT, SINCLAIR GREG, oral surgeon; b. Chgo., May 26, 1942; s. Clair V. and Cynthia Ann (Gragg) S.; B.S. in Zoology, Okla. State U., 1964, postgrad., 1964-65; D.D.S., U. Tenn., 1968. Dental intern St. Francis Hosp., Honolulu, 1968-69; commd. capt. U.S. Army, 1969; dental officer Camp Long, Korea, 1969-70, Ft. McPherson, Ga., 1970-72; resident in oral surgery U. Minn., Mpls., 1972—. Recipient Internat. Coll. Dentists award, 1968. Mem. Am. Dental Assn., Am. Acad. Dental Medicine, Odontological Soc., Pi Kappa Alpha, Delta Sigma Delta, Omicron Kappa Upsilon. Home: 3351 Spanish Trail No 313 B Delray Beach FL 33444 Office: U Minn Minneapolis MN 55444

SHORT, WILLIAM GILBERT, educator, author; b. Des Moines, N.M., June 26, 1928; s. William Thomas and Geneva (House) S.; B.A., U. Tex., 1951; M.Ed., Trinity U., 1952; Lic., U. Madrid (Spain), Ph.D., 1968; diploma Colgate U., 1965; postgrad. U. Heidelberg, Germany, 1955, U. N.Y. at Albany, 1971-72; Dr. Polit. Sci. (hon.), El Salvador-Academiade Bejar, 1972; m. Maria Pilar Molina Martin, Nov. 29, 1956; m. 2d, Rosa Maria Ceruera Valencia, Nov. 29, 1969. Expediter, interpreter U.S. Mission to Spain, 1956-58; with U.S. Civil Service, 1958-63, edn. officer U.S. Forces in Eng., 1958-59, edn. officer, San Antonio, 1959-63; lang. tchr. San Antonio Coll., 1960-64; dir. Inter-Am. Inst., Freeport, N.Y., 1964-72; coordinator modern fgn. lang. edn., supr. Spanish edn. State U. N.Y., Albany, 1969—. Fgn. lang. specialist Central High Sch. Dist. 3, Merrick, L.I.; dir. 1st Yucatan Inter-Am. Studies Program for U.S. High Sch. Students; asso. dir. Instituto Inter-Americano de Yucatan. Mem. med. adv. bd. Care-Medico, San Antonio, 1964-69. Served with AUS, 1946-47, USAF, 1951-54. Recipient John F. Kennedy award, 1962; Alliance for Progress award, 1962; Presdl. citation, 1962; Vice presdl. citation, 1962; Bolsa de Estudios, Inst. de Cultura Hispanica, 1963, others; decorated La Order de Bejar. Mem. N.Y. Fedn. Lang. Tchrs., Am. Assn. Tchrs. Spanish and Portuguese, N.A.A.C.P., Indian Rights Assn., Am. Assn. U. Profs., Internat. Platform Assn. Author: La Politica educativa de los Estados Unidos entre los indios Navajo, 1968; El Hombre Folsom, 1970; El Pueblo Navajo, 1969; Junior Year in Spain, 1971, others. Contbr. articles to jours., also monographs. Home: 722 Weizmann Blvd San Antonio TX 78213 Office: 135 Western Av Albany NY 12203

SHORTALL, JOHN WILLIAM, physicist; b. Chgo., Apr. 18, 1926; s. John William and Marie (Wolford) S.; B.S., Northwestern U., 1950; postgrad. U. Cal. at Los Angeles, 1950-52; m. Claire Parker Bowley, Aug. 11, 1962; 1 stepson, William T.; children—Star V., Thomas C. Physicist, Los Alamos Sci. Lab., 1950-52, Livermore Research Lab., 1952-54, Lockheed Aircraft Corp., 1954-55, Hdqrs. Command, USAF, Washington, 1955-62; sci. adviser USAF Europe Hdqrs., Wiesbaden, Germany, 1956-59; European rep. Fund for Peaceful Atomic Devel., Rome, Italy, 1962-65; rep. Gen. Electric Research Lab., Hong Kong, China, 1965-67; cons. Gen. Electric Tempo Center Advanced Studies, Washington, 1967-70; with Internat. Indsl. Consultants, Caribbean Marine Ltd., 1970—. Hon. mem. Nuclear Pub. Relations Contact Group, Rome, 1962. Active Boy Scouts Am., 1962—. Served as ensign U.S. Maritime Service, 1944-47. Mem. A.A.A.S., Am., Italian phys. socs., Am. Nuclear Soc., Atomic Indsl. Forum. Author: (with Claire Shortall) Artichokes Apartments and Aristocats, Live in Italy and Like It, 1967. Editor: Atomic Handbook Volume One Europe, 1965. Contbr. numerous articles to profl. jours. Home: 10822 92d Av N Seminole FL 33542

SHORTER, EDWARD SWIFT, artist, museum dir. emeritus; b. Columbus, Ga., July 2, 1902; s. Dr. James Hargraves and Elizabeth (Swift) S.; A.B., Mercer U., 1924; student Corcoran Sch. Art, 1924-28, Boston Museum Sch., 1925. Fontainevieau (France), with Andre Lhote (Paris), Wayman Adams, Hugh Breckenridge; m. Mildred Watts, Oct. 3, 1953. Mem. staff Corcoran Sch. Art, 1930; exec. dir., also instr. art Columbus Mus. Arts and Crafts, 1952-70; past lectr. U. Ga. Extension; represented in museums in cities throughout U.S., including: Atlanta, Montgomery, Macon, Columbus, Savannah (all Ga.), N.Y.C., Washington, New Orleans, Waco (Tex.), Ft. Hays (Kan.). Trustee Boys' Club, Shorter Coll., Symphony Orch., Coweta Meml. Assn., Columbus, Ga., Ga. Mus. Art (Athens), Atlanta Art Assn.; Ga. Hist. and Fine Arts Commn.; bd. dirs. Atlanta Art Inst., Columbus Symphony, Brookstone Sch. Corcoran Art scholar, Paris, 1931, Algenon Sydney Sullivan award, Mercer U.; recipient Gari Melchers medal Artists Fellowship Inc. Mem. Assn. Ga. Artists (pres.), S.E. Art Mus. Dirs. Assn. (dir.), Assn. Am. Mus. Dirs., Am. Fedn. Arts, Ga. Hist. Soc., Artists Equity Assn., Am. Artists Profl. League, Nat. Art Club, 3 Arts League (mem. bd.), Nat. Audubon Soc., Sigma Alpha Epsilon. Baptist. Clubs: Green Island Country, Bid Eddy, Candun; Salamagundi (N.Y.C.). Home: Folly Hill River Rd Columbus GA 31904 Office: 1251 Wynnton Rd Columbus GA 31906

SHORTER, HAZEL KATHRYN APPLEGET, ednl. administr.; b. Hightstown, N.J., Oct. 18, 1901; d. David Baird and Ella (Messler) Appleget; grad. in bus. edn. N.J. State Tchrs. Coll., 1921; student Columbia, 1927-28, Am. U., 1947-48; m. Fred Wendall Shorter (div. Sept. 1943). Tchr. bus. edn. depts. pub. schs. N.J., 1921-29; clk. War Dept., Picatinny Arsenal, N.J., 1930-40, chief clk. Ravenna (O.) Ordnance Plant, 1940-41, chief clk. Scioto Fuze and Booster Plant, Marion, O., 1941-42, adminstrv. officer Office Chief Ordnance, Detroit, 1942-45; head mgmt. div. Bur. Ships, Navy Dept., Washington, 1946-48; mgmt. analyst and spl. asst. ICA, Washington, 1948-57, exec. officer Office Econ. Coordinator, Korea, 1954-56; acting Nr. East loan officer Devel. Loan Fund, Washington, 1957-60; sec. Allentown (N.J.) Bd. Edn., 1960-61; cons. AID, 1962—. Treas., Children's Hosp., Korea, 1954-56. Mem. N.J. Assn. Pub. Sch. Bus. Ofcls. Mem. Order Eastern Star. Home: 250 S Boca Ciega Point Blvd St Petersburg FL 33708

SHOSTECK, ROBERT, mus. curator; b. Newark, Apr. 25, 1910; s. Saul and Bessie (Rubin) S.; A.B., George Washington U., 1937, M.A., 1953; m. Dora Rabinovitz, May 9, 1936 (dec. May 1969); children—Herschel, Sara Williams; m. 2d, Ruth Dub, Dec. 1970. Dir. research B'nai B'rith Vocation Service, 1945-59; asst. chief placement Nat. Roster Sci. and Specialized Personnel, 1940-45; curator B'nai B'rith Exhibit Hall, Washington, 1959—. Mem. Am. Jewish Hist. Soc., Am. Assn. Museums, Am. Assn. State and Local History, Jewish Hist. Soc. Greater Washington (pres. 1960-62), Audubon Soc. Author: Careers in Retail Business Ownership, 1946; Small Town Jewry Tell Their Story, 1953; College Finder, 1959; College Guide for Jewish Youth, 1959; Potomac Trail Book, 1968; Weekender's Guide, 1969; Dr. John de Sequeyra—The Portugese—Jewish Physician of Colonial Williamsburg, 1971. Home: 5100 Alta Vista Rd Bethesda MD 20014 Office: 1640 Rhode Island Av NW Washington DC 20035

SHOUSE, KENNETH MITCHELL, communications co. exec.; b. Okmulgee, Okla., Apr. 22, 1925; s. James Mitchell and Delana (Green) S.; B.S. in Elec. Engring., U. Okla., 1949, M.S. in Elec. Engring., 1954; m. Pluma LaFaune Davis, Mar. 9, 1952; children—Patricia Anne, Kenneth Guy, Karen Ernestine. Instr., U. Okla., 1949-50; engr. S.W. Bell Telephone Co., Oklahoma City, 1950-55, gen. staff, St. Louis, 1956, sr. engr. Bell Telephone Labs., N.J., 1956-58, sr. engr. gen. staff, St. Louis, 1958-59, test center foreman, supervising installation foreman, St. Louis, 1959-61, dist. plant supt., plant supr., Oklahoma City, 1961-64, div. plant supt., 1964—. Pres., Stonegate P.T.A., Oklahoma City, 1967-68. Served to 2d lt. USAAF, 1943-46, to capt. USAF, 1951-52. Registered profl. engr., Okla. Mem. I.E.E.E., Oklahoma City Engrs. Club, Tau Beta Pi, Eta Kappa Nu. Baptist. Club: Exchange of Oklahoma City (past pres.).‡

SHOWS, CLARENCE OLIVER, dentist; b. nr. Brantley, Ala., Oct. 17, 1920; s. John Oliver and Cora (Nichols) S.; student Wis. State Coll., 1946-47; D.D.S., Northwestern U., 1951; m. Rachel LaRene Price, July 24, 1943; children—Toni Cherie (Mrs. August F. Dennig), Kristin Clare, Bradley Scott, Gregory Norman, Jeffery Ryan. Pvt. practice dentistry, Valparaiso, Fla., 1951-53, Pensacola, 1953—. Mem. Pensacola Art Assn.; past pres. Escambia County Unit Am. Cancer Soc., now bd. dirs. Fla. unit; mem. Eagle Scout Bd. Rev., Escambia County. Served with USCG, 1939-46. Fellow Am. Acad. Gen. Dentistry (pres.-elect Fla. unit); mem. Internat. Orthodontic Assn., Gulf Breeze C. of C. (past pres.), Fla. Soc. Dentistry for Children (past pres.), Acad. Gen. Dentistry, Am. Assn. Dentists, Am. Dental Assn., Am. Soc. Preventive Dentistry, Fedr. Pehtaire Internat., Am. Inst. Oral Biology, Am. Assn. Clin. Hypnosis, Northwestern U. Alumni Assn., Navy League, Psi Omega. Democrat. Presbyn. Mason (Shriner), Elks. Clubs: Pensacola, Exchange. Home: 516 Navy Cove Blvd Gulf Breeze FL 32561 Office: 3090 Navy Blvd Pensacola FL 32505

SHRADER, EDWARD FRANKLYN, educator; b. Martinsburg, W.Va., Dec. 24, 1917; s. Edward Franklin and Mary (Blake) S.; B.A., Randolph Macon Coll., 1940; S.T.B., Westminster Sem., 1943; M.A., George Washington U., 1962, D.Ed., 1966; A.P.C., Hunter Coll. City Coll. N.Y., 1963; m. Elaine Loretta Shinners, Aug. 23, 1958; children—Heather Ann, Thurston Drew, Mimi Victoria. Ordained to ministry Meth. Ch., 1943; minister Camp Hill Ch., Harpers Ferry, W.Va., 1946-50, St. Mathews Episcopal Ch., Wheeling, W.Va., 1955-56; sales rep. Interwoven Stocking Co., New Brunswick, N.J., 1951-56; tchr. Storer Coll., Harpers Ferry, Brooklyn Park, Annapolis, Md., Golden Ring Sch., Baltimore County, Md., Loudoun County, Va., 1956-59; counselor High Point Sr. High Sch., Beltsville, Md., 1959-67; prof. counselor edn. Coll. Edn., Fla. Atlantic U., Boca Raton, 1967—. Committeeman Boy Scouts Am., Martinsburg, W.Va., 1943-46, Harpers Ferry, 1946-50; county com. mem. March Dimes, Loudoun County, Va.; zone chmn. Harpers Ferry P.T.A., 1946-47, 56-62; program chmn. bridge dedication ceremonies, Harpers Ferry, 1949. Served with USNR, 1944-46, 50-51. Mem. Nat. Honor Soc., N.E.A., Acad. Tchrs. Occupations, Am. Personnel and Guidance Assn., Md., Prince George's County tchrs. assns., Am. Assn. U. Profs., Omicron Delta Kappa, Tau Kappa Alpha, Phi Delta Theta, Phi Delta Kappa. Author: Readings in Counseling: Process, Practice and Projections, 1970. Home: 2210 NE 48th Ct Lighthouse Point Fl 33064 Office: Fla Atlantic U Boca Raton FL 33432

SHREEVES, EVELYN ROBERTSON (MRS. CHARLES SHREEVES), librarian; b. Portsmouth, Va., Dec. 13, 1911; d. Joseph Henry and Zanaida (Liggan) Robertson; B.A., Coll. William and Mary, 1934; m. Charles Bidgner Shreeves, July 10, 1937; children—Margaret (Mrs. A. Garland Moseley), Charles Edward. Librarian, Waynesboro (Va.) High Sch., 1934-36, Petersburg High Sch., 1936-37, County Warwick (Va.), 1951-52, City Warwick, 1952-58, City Newport News, 1958-69; librarian sch. bd. City Newport News, 1969—; tchr., pvt. sch. Newport News, 1943-45. Mem. Am. Assn. U. Women, Va. Library Assn., N.E.A., Kappa Delta Pi, Delta Kappa Gamma. Home: 24 Holly Dr Newport News VA 23601

SHREVES, MELVIN LANKFORD, JR., coll. exec.; b. Nassawadox, Va., May 30, 1942; s. Melvin Lankford and Virginia (Odam) S.; B.A., Elon Coll., 1966; m. Peggy Hill, May 27, 1966; children—Michael David, Christopher Michael. Dir. pub. relations Hargrave Mil. Acad., Chatham, Va., 1966; instr. English-journalism Dan River High Sch., Ringgold, Va., 1966-69; mgr. bus., advt. Star-Tribune, Chatham, 1969-71; dir. news bur. Elon Coll., 1971—. Cub master Chatham Cub Scouts, 1969-70; pres. Hargrave Alumni Assn., 1969-71. Named Outstanding Sertoman, 1967. Mem. Sigma Mu Sigma. Presbyn. Home: Box 801 Gibsonville NC 27249 Office: Box 2208 Elon College NC 27244

SHRIVER, EDGAR LOUIS, psychologist, scientist; b. Canton, O., Apr. 1, 1927; s. Elmer George and Clara (Kellogg) S.; B.A., Washington and Jefferson Coll., 1950; M.A., U. Rochester, 1951; Ph.D., U. Pitts., 1953; m. Beatrice Melrowin, 1951 (div. 1961); 1 son, John Adam; m. 2d, Sara Baker Eden, Aug. 15, 1961; children—Katherine, Craig Edgar, Paul Kellogg. Research psychologist Am. Inst. for Research, Pitts., 1951-52; sr. staff scientist Human Resources Research Office, Washington, 1953-68; v.p., dir. Matrix Corp., Alexandria, Va.; pres. Tech. Tng. Corp., Washington, 1961—; chmn. bd. Broadview Research Corp., 1957-58, Meipar Corp., 1961—, Human Scis. Research Inc. Served with USNR, 1945-46. Fellow Am. Psychol. Assn.; mem. A.A.A.S., Eastern, D.C. psychol. assns., Phi Kappa Sigma. Presbyn. Clubs: Tantallon Country, Tricorn. Home: 100 Prince St Alexandria VA 22314 Office: 7245 Arlington Blvd Falls Church VA 22042

SHRIVER, THOMAS A., judge; b. Wartrace, Tenn., Feb. 4, 1895; s. Thomas A. and Elizabeth (Holt) S.; student U. of Va., 1915-16; grad. Govt. Sch. Marine Engring., 1917-18; LL.B., Cumberland U., 1920; J.D., Cumberland Law Sch. of Sanford U., 1969; m. Attie G. Humphreys, Aug. 6, 1926; children—Thomas H., Richard V., Don Albert. Tchr., prin. high sch., Bedford County, Tenn., 3 yrs.; law practice, 1920-40, partner Shriver and Shriver; apptd. Chancery Ct., Tenn., 1940, elected 1942-50, 50-55; judge Tenn. Ct. Appeals, 1955—, presiding judge, 1962—. Pres. Nashville Fgn. Relations Com. Mem. S.A.R. (pres. chpt.; pres. Tenn.). English Speaking Union (pres. chpt.), Tenn. Hist. Soc. Democrat. Methodist. Clubs: Exchange, Freolac, Shakespeare. Author articles; Published Opinions. Home: 1709 Bonner Av Nashville TN 37215 Office: Supreme Ct Bldg Nashville TN 37219

SHRODER, MORRIS, govt. ofcl.; b. Buffalo, June 3, 1918; s. Max and Fannie (Mildwoff) S.; B.S., Cornell U., 1939; LL.B., Georgetown U., 1955; m. Florence L. Davis, Mar. 28, 1953; children—Mark Davis, Susan Joy, and David Lewis. Tng. officer VA, Buffalo, 1946-50; analytical statistician VA, Washington, 1950-54; chief resources analysis br., directorate of plans, supplies and operations Office of Surgeon Gen., Dept. Army, 1954-63; statistician Pub. Housing Adminstrn., 1963-65, dep. asst. commr. for program planning, 1965-68; dir. program devel. div. Housing Assistance Adminstrn., Dept. Housing and Urban Devel., 1968-70, dir. publicly financed housing div., 1970—; dir. Navy Fed. Credit Union, 1959, asst. treas., 1960, treas., 1961-63, chmn. supervisory com., 1957-59. Served from pvt. to sgt. AUS, 1942-46. Mem. Am., Fed. bar assns. Home: 407 Deerfield Av Silver Spring MD Office: 451 17th St SW Washington DC 20410

SHROPSHIRE, WILLIAM TUCKER, coll. adminstr.; b. Douglasville, Ga., Nov. 22, 1923; s. Jim Henry and Eddie (Dobbs) S.; A.B., Morehouse Coll., 1947; M.B.A., St. Edwards U., 1972; student U. Neb., 1953, U. Tex., 1963, 1970-71; m. Verona Baxter, Aug. 23, 1949; children— Willa, Rodney, Eric. Budget asst., chief accountant Savannah State Coll., 1947-54; comptroller Albany State Coll., 1954-61; bus. mgr. Huston-Tillotson Coll., 1961—; cons. So. Assn. Colls. and Schs. Bd. dirs. Austin Human Opportunities Corp. Served with USNR, 1943-46. Ford Found. Advanced Study grantee, 1970—. Mem. Nat. Assn. Coll. and U. Bus. Officers, Nat. Accountants Assn. (dir. Austin chpt. 1971-72), Nat. Assn. Ednl. Buyers, Phi Beta Lambda, Kappa Alpha Psi. Mem. African Methodist Episcopal Ch. Lion. Home: 1705 E 11th St Austin TX 78702 Office: Huston-Tillotson Coll Austin TX 78702

SHRUM, ROBERT MARSHALL, architect; b. Jeanette, Pa., Sept. 29, 1921; s. Lawrence Emmett and Mary Margaret (Gongaware) S.; student Seton Hill Coll., 1946-47; B.Arch., Carnegie Inst. Tech., 1952; m. Shirley Ann Larimer, Sept. 10, 1948; children—Deborah Ann, Beverly Louise, Karen Lynn, Robin Denise. Architect, Sorber & Hodne, Greensburg, Pa., 1952-55, Bennett Assos., Morgantown, W.Va., 1955-57, Edwin T. Reeder Assos., Miami, Fla., 1957-58, S. L. Shephard & Assos., Miami, 1958-60, Rader & Assos., Miami, 1960-61; pvt. practice architecture, North Miami, Fla., 1961—. Mem. North Miami Archtl. Rev. Bd., 1970—. Bd. dirs. North Dade YMCA, 1967-70. Served with AUS, 1941-46; PTO. Decorated Purple Heart. Certified Nat. Council Archtl. Registration Bds. Mem. A.I.A. (Fla. Assn.), Am. Defenders Bataan and Corregidor (Fla. chpt.). Lutheran. Home: 14535 NE 5th Ct North Miami FL 33161 Office: 1001 NE 125th St North Miami FL 33161

SHRUM, SAMUEL HOPKINS, constrn. co. exec.; b. Dayton, Va., June 19, 1912; s. George Edgar and Annie (Rolston) S.; B.S., Va. Poly. Inst., 1933; postgrad. Westminster Choir Coll., 1938; m. Evelyn L. Vaughan, June 14, 1941; children—Edgar Vaughan, Marilyn Ann. Partner George E. Shrum & Son, masonry contractors, 1933-42; prodn. engr. Newport News Shipbuilding and Drydock Co., 1942-45; exec. v.p., gen. mgr. treas., dir. Nielsen Constrn. Co., Harrisonburg, Va., 1945-61, pres., 1961—; pres., dir. Century Realty Co., 1954-58; exec. v.p., dir. Alexandria Prestressed, Inc., 1961; became exec. v.p., gen. mgr., bd. dirs. Shen Valley, Inc., 1964, pres., 1967-71; sec.-treas., gen. mgr., dir. Valley Developers, Inc., 1964-67; dir. Exploraciones Columbianas, S.A.; bd. dirs., chmn. capitol stock com., chmn. bldg. com. Rockingham National Bank; mem. Shenandoah Valley, Inc., Rockingham Devel. Corp. Trustee, asst. treas. Sunnyside Presbyn. Home, 1952, pres., 1966-71; trustee, v.p. Massanetta Springs Bible Conf., 1953-58; chmn. campus Christian life com. Westminster Fellowship, 1958—; mem. Lexington Presbytery's Com. on nominations, 1962—; mem. steering com., publicity chmn. Bridgewater Coll. Crusade for Excellence, 1960—; mem. local steering com. Internat. Christian Laymen's-Mayor Prayer Breakfast, Harrisonburg, 1964—; commr. to gen. assembly Presbyn. Ch. U.S.; mem. Lexington Presbytery's Commn. on Homes for Ret. Ministers, 1965—; mem. Synod of Va. bd. trustees Presbyn. Nursing Homes, Inc., 1965—; chmn. Va. Synod Coordinating Com. on Homes for Aging, 1969—; mem. steering com. financial campaign Rockingham Meml. Hosp., Harrisonburg, 1965—; mem. state adv. council for vocational edn. Commonwealth Va., 1971—. Mem. Harrisonburg-Rockingham C. of C., Va. C. of C., Engrs. Soc., Nat. Small Bus. Men's Assn., Nat. Labor-Mgmt. Found., Asso. Gen. Contractors (bd. dirs. Va. br. 1965—, chmn. Plan Bulldozer 1965—, pres. 1969-70; mem. nat. com. on emergency planning 1964—), Internat. Platform Assn. Presbyn. (elder). Mason, Rotarian (dir. 1965—, pres. Harrisonburg 1967-68). Home: 710 New York Av Harrisonburg VA 22801 Office: 56 W Johnson St Harrisonburg VA 22801

SHUFORD, ABNER POPE, mfg. co. exec.; b. Norfolk, Va., July 11, 1940; s. Harley Ferguson and Nancy (Pope) S.; B.S., U. N.C., 1962; m. Peggy Baker, Aug. 2, 1962; children—Jim, Stephenson, Dorothy. With Shuford Mills, Inc., Hickory, N.C., 1962—, asst. div. mgr., 1965-68, div. mgr., 1968—, also dir.; dir. Century Furniture Co., Century Chair Co., N.C. Nat. Bank, Hickory. Pres., United Fund, 1969—; vice chmn. Hickory Recreation Commn., 1970-71. Bd. dirs. A.R.C., 1969-72, Salvation Army 1969-72, N.C. United Community Services, 1969-72. Mem. Inst. Textile Tech., C. of C. (v.p., 1969, 71). Rotarian (pres. Hickory club 1970), Moose. Home: 565 11th Av Circle Hickory NC 28601 Office: Drawer 2228 Hickory NC 28601

SHUFORD, FORREST HERMAN, II, state ofcl.; b. Gastonia, N.C., Nov. 3, 1923; s. Forrest H. and May (Renfrow) S.; student Wake Forest Coll., 1941-43; LL.B., Duke-Wake Forest Law Sch., 1946; m. Grace McD. Ray, Sept. 7, 1946; children—Forrest Herman III, May Janice. Admitted to N.C. bar; staff atty. N.C. Atty. Gen.'s Office, Raleigh, 1946-49; atty., adviser, solicitor's office U.S. Dept. Labor, Washington, 1949-53; dep. commr. N.C. Indsl. Commn., 1953-62, commr., 1962—. Mem. N.C. State Bar, N.C. Bar Assn. Presbyn. Rotarian. Home: 1212 Bancroft Dr Raleigh NC 27609 Office: NC Indsl Commn Raleigh NC 27601

SHULA, DON FRANCIS, profl. football coach; b. Grand River, O., Jan. 4, 1930; s. Dan and Mary (Miller) S.; B.S., John Carroll U., Cleve., 1951; M.A., Western Res. U., 1953; m. Dorothy Bartish, July 19, 1958; children—David, Donna, Sharon, Anne, Michael. Profl. football player, Cleve. Browns, 1951-52, Balt. Colts, 1953-56, Washington Redskins, 1957; asst. coach U. Va., 1958, U. Ky., 1959, Detroit Lions, 1960-62; head coach Balt. Colts, 1963-70; head coach, v.p., part owner Miami Dolphins, 1970—. Served with Ohio N.G., 1952. Recipient Coach of Yr. award, 1964, 67, 68, 70, 71. Roman Catholic. Address: 330 Biscayne Blvd Miami FL 33152

SHULL, WARREN EUGENE, journalist; b. Upland, Ind., June 18, 1910; s. William Edward and Guernsey Glyceria (Bowen) S.; B.S., Okla. State U., 1950; m. Doris Marie Geiser, Dec. 1, 1938; children—William Eugene, Susan Marie. Exec. sec. Nat. Assn. Student Councils, Sapulpa, Okla., 1932-36; reporter Sapulpa Daily Herald, 1935-41; editor Sapulpa Democrat News, 1941-42; asst. advt. mgr. Sapulpa Herald, 1942-43, city editor, 1946-47; student journalism lab. instr. Okla. State U., Stillwater, 1947-48; asst. editor Okla. State U. Alumni Mag., 1949-55, editor, head dept. Alumni publns., 1955—. Served with AUS, 1943-45. Mem. V.F.W., Am. Alumni Council (mem. alumni publs. adv. com. 1964-66), Nat. Assn. Student Councils (1st nat. pres., founder), Sigma Delta Chi. Democrat. Methodist. Club: Stillwater Writers (past pres). Home: 233 S West St Stillwater OK 74074

SHULMAN, ARNOLD, lawyer; b. Phila., Apr. 12, 1914; s. Edward Nathaniel and Anna (Leshner) S.; student Emory U., 1931; J.D., U. Ga., 1936; m. Mary Frances Johnson, Nov. 26, 1943; children—Diane (Mrs. Elliot Lifshey), Warren Scott, Amy Lynn. Admitted to Ga. bar, 1937; mem. firm Shulman, Alembik & Rosenbluth, Atlanta, 1970—. Tchr. Atlanta Law Sch., 1964—. Chmn. DeKalb County (Ga.) Sch. Study Commn., 1962-64, DeKalb County Sch. Salary Commn., 1960-62; mem. Fulton County-Atlanta Ct. Study Commn., 1961—. Served to capt. AUS, 1941-46. Mem. Am., Atlanta bar assns., Ga. State Bar. Club: Lawyers (Atlanta). Author: (with Wiley H. Davis) Georgia Practice and Procedure, 1948, 3d edit., 1968. Contbr. articles to legal jours. Home: 1420 Stephens Dr NE Atlanta GA 30329 Office: 1218 Fulton St Nat Bank Bldg Atlanta GA 30303

SHULMAN, EDWARD M., govt. ofcl.; b. Atlanta, May 10, 1907; s. Max and Fanny (Singer) S.; J.D., Ohio State U., 1930; m. Rosalind Ziskind, Sept. 23, 1934; 1 son, Richard. Admitted to Ohio bar, 1930, D.C. bar, 1968, U.S. Supreme Ct. bar, 1934; practiced in Dayton, O., 1930-34; atty. Office of Solicitor, U.S. Dept. of Agr., 1934-42; chief, commodity purchases, loans and distbn. div., 1942-43, chief commodity credit corp. div., Office of Solicitor, War Food Adminstrn. and U.S. Dept. of Arg., 1943-45; asso. solicitor in charge legal work Commodity Credit Corp., Fed. Crop Ins. Corp., Sch. Lunch Program, Agrl. Conservation Program, Farm Marketing Quota Program, U.S. Dept. of Agr., 1945-51; dep. gen. counsel, U.S. Dept. Agr., dep. gen. counsel, C.C.C. and Fed. Crop Ins. Corp., 1951-68, gen. counsel, 1968—. Mem. gen. adminstrn. bd. Graduate Sch., United State Dept. Agr., 1968—; mem. Adminstrv. Conf. U.S., 1971. Recipient Superior Service award U.S. Dept. Agr., 1958, Distinguished Service award, 1971. Mem. Fed., Am. bar assns., Pi Delta Epsilon, Sigma Alpha Mu. Home: 6621 32d St Washington DC 10015 Office: US Dept of Agriculture Washington DC 20505

SHULTS, OTTO A., accountant; b. Wayland, N.Y., Feb. 6, 1898; s. Conrad D. and Elizabeth (Pirrung) S.; student Rochester Bus. Inst., 1916, Pace Inst. Accountancy, 1917-19; C.P.A., U. State N.Y., 1929; m. Alma Jessie Roseberry, May 11, 1920 (dec. June 1969); m. 2d, Mabel A. Eaton, Dec. 8, 1971. With Wilson, Shults & Co. and predecessors, C.P.A.'s, 1919-60, exec. dir., 1925-60; partner Peat, Marwick, Mitchell & Co., C.P.A.'s, 1961-64, merger 1961, cons., 1964—; dir. Crossman Arms Co., Inc., Central Trust Co. of Rochester (N.Y.), Wm. J. Schmitt, Inc., Genesee Brewing Co., Inc. chmn. bd. emeritus, trustees Nazareth Coll.; trustee emeritus St. John Fisher Coll.; trustee, dir. Columbus Civic Center. Mem. Rochester Mus. Assn. (life), Rochester Meml. Art Gallery, Am. Inst. C.P.A.'s, Am. Ordnance Assn. (life), N.Y. State Soc. C.P.A.'s, Nat. Assn Accountants, Rochester C. of C., Acad. Polit. Sci. N.Y. (life mem.). K. C. (4 1/2), Order Alhambra, Elk. Clubs: Automobile (dir.), City, Locust (hon.), Oak Hill Country, Rochester, Genesee Valley, Country (Rochester, N.Y.); Westchester Country (Rye, N.Y.); N.Y. Athletic (N.Y.C.); Union League (Chgo.); Coral Ridge Yacht, Coral Ridge Country (Ft. Lauderdale). Home: 2601 NE 37th Dr Fort Lauderdale FL 33308 Summer 1400 East Av Rochester NY 14610 Midtown Tower PO Box 9458 Rochester NY 14604

SHULTZ, GEORGE PRATT, govt. ofcl.; b. N.Y.C., Dec. 13, 1920; s. Birl E. and Margaret Lennox (Pratt) S.; B.A., Princeton, 1942; Ph.D. in Indsl. Econs. (fellow Social Sci. Research Council 1947-48), Mass. Inst. Tech., 1949; m. Helena M. O'Brien, Feb. 16, 1946; children—Margaret Ann, Alexander George. Mem. faculty Mass. Inst. Tech., 1946-57, asso. prof. indsl. relations, 1955-57; prof. indsl. relations Grad. Sch. Bus., U. Chgo., 1957-69, dean sch., 1962-69; sec. of labor, 1969-70; dir. Office of Mgmt. and Budget, Washington, 1970—. Dir. Borg-Warner Corp., Stein, Roe & Farnham Stock Fund, Inc., Gen. Am. Transp. Corp., Stein, Roe & Farnham Balanced Fund, Inc. Chmn. task force to review U.S. Employment Service programs; sr. staff economist President's Council Econ. Advisers, 1955-56; cons. Office Sec., Dept. Labor, 1959-60, mem. steering com. study collective bargaining in basic steel industry, 1960; staff dir. nat. labor policy study Com. Econ. Devel., 1961; cons. President's Adv. Com. Labor-Mgmt. Policy, 1961-62; mem. Gov. Ill. Com. Unemployment, 1961-69; co-chmn. Automation Fund Com., 1962-69; mem. various arbitration panels, 1960—. Bd. dirs. Nat. Opinion Research Center, Chgo., 1962-69. Served to capt. USMCR, 1942-45. Mem. Am. Econ. Assn., Indsl. Relations Assn., Nat. Acad. Arbitrators. Author: (with T. A. Whisler) Management Organization and the Computer, 1960; (with Arnold R. Weber) Strategies for the Displaced Worker, 1966; also articles, chpts. in books, reports. Home: 273 S Fort Scott Dr Arlington VA 22202 Office: Exec Office of the President Washington DC 20503

SHULTZ, HARRY STOVER, banker; b. Staunton, Va., Aug. 28, 1905; s. Walter Thornton and Bertha (Hoover) S.; student U. Va., 1926-27; m. Frances L. Crafton, June 18, 1955. Dist. rep. Comml. Credit Corp., Washington, Roanoke, Va., 1932-39; operations and sales rep. auto div. Bank of Va., 1939-47; dist. rep. auto financing Commonwealth Discount Corp., 1947-60; v.p. in charge dealer finance div. Fidelity Nat. Bank, Lynchburg, Va., 1960—. Served with AUS, 1941-44. Presbyn. Clubs: Lynchburg Sports; Bull and Bear (charter mem.) (Richmond, Va.). Home: 1505 Club Terrace Lynchburg VA 24503 Office: 901 Main St Lynchburg VA 24505

SHUPERT, GEORGE THOMAS, broadcasting exec.; b. Alpena, Mich., July 24, 1904; s. Harry L. and Grace (Bostwick) S.; A.B. in Lit., U. Mich., 1926; m. Evlyn LaLonde, Feb. 21, 1928; children—George Thomas, Sally Jean (Mrs. James Shepard), Joanne (Mrs. David Johnsen). Investment banker, Detroit, 1926-38; founder George T. Shupert & Co., 1936, gen. partner until 1938; dir. sales comml. film div. Paramount Pictures Corp., 1940-42, TV dept., 1942-51; v.p., dir. comml. TV operations Paramount TV Prodns., Inc., 1946-51; v.p. Peerless TV Prodns., Inc., 1951-52; v.p., gen. mgr. United Artists TV Corp., 1952-53; v.p. film syndication ABC, 1953-54; pres. ABC Films, Inc., 1954-59; v.p. charge TV, MGM, Inc., 1959-61; v.p. 20th Century Fox TV Corp., 1961-64; pres. Sunrise Broadcasting Corp., Ft. Lauderdale, 1964—. Mem. Am. TV Soc. (past pres., dir.; spl. award 1941-42), Radio and TV Execs. Soc. (past pres.; hon. life mem.), Television Pioneers Soc., Acad. TV Arts and Scis. Clubs: N.Y. Athletic, Yacht, Univ. Mich., Lambs (N.Y.C.). Home: 333 Sunset Dr Ft Lauderdale FL 33301 Office: Sunrise Broadcasting Corp Oakland Park Blvd Ft Lauderdale FL 33306

SHURBET, MACK, banker; b. nr. Floydada, Tex., Feb. 25, 1939; s. Marvin Henry and Mildred Juanita (Welborn) W.; B.S. in Agr., Tex. Technol. U., 1961 children—Melissa Lou, Melanie Sue, Misty Lee. With Hale County State Bank, Plainview, Tex., 1963—, sr. v.p., 1967-69, exec. v.p., 1969—, dir., 1970—. Vice pres. Plainview Livestock Show, 1970, pres., 1971, bd. dirs., 1966—. Bd. dirs. Hale County chpt. Am. Cancer Soc. Mason (32 deg.), Elk, Kiwanian (v.p. 1971, dir. 1965—). Home: 603 Kirchwood Dr Plainview TX 79072 Office: Box 970 Plainview TX 79072 mailing address: Box 970 Plainview TX 79072

SHURLEY, JAY TALMADGE, physician; b. Sonora, Tex., Dec. 20, 1917; s. Ira Lawrence and Jewell (Choate) S.; student San Angelo Coll., 1934-36; B.A., U. Tex., 1940; M.D., U. Tex. Med. Br., 1942; m. Emily Webb Alexander, Jan. 4, 1964; children—Ronald G., Tom Henry, Guy Gibbs, Philip Sherwood, John Dodd. Intern, Ind. U. Med. Center, Indpls., 1943; resident Inst. for Mental Hygiene, Pa. Hosp., Phila., 1944-47; pvt. practice medicine specializing in psychiatry, Phila., 1947-51, Austin, Tex., 1951-53, San Antonio, 1953-54, Chevy Chase, Md., 1955-57; acting chief adult psychiatry br. Nat. Insts. Mental Health, NIH, Bethesda, Md., 1955-57; chief psychiatry service, 1957-61; sr. med. investigator VA, also dir. behavioral sci. labs. VA Hosp., Oklahoma City, 1961—; prof. psychiatry U. Okla., 1957-61, career research prof. psychiatry, 1961—; adj. prof. human ecology Okla. U., 1971—. Chmn. panel on biology and med. scis., mem. com. on polar research Nat. Acad. Sci.-NRC, 1970—. Served to capt. M.C., AUS, 1952-54. Diplomate in psychiatry Am. Bd. Psychiatry and Neurology. Fellow Am. Psychiat. Assn., Am. Coll. Psychiatrists, Royal Coll. Psychiatry, A.A.A.S.; mem. A.M.A., Soc. for Psycho Physiol. Research, Assn. for Psychophysiol. Study of Sleep. Contbr. articles to sci. publs. Home: 900 NW 41st St Oklahoma City OK 73118 Office: VA Hosp Oklahoma City OK 73104

SHWAB, HUGH MCNEILLY, JR., banker; b. Nashville, June 4, 1909; s. Hugh McNeilly and Martha (Mann) S.; A.B., Yale, 1932; grad. Am. Inst. Banking; m. Lois K. Wolfe, Jan. 4, 1936; children—Hugh McNeilly III, Thomas W., Martha Lois. With 1st Nat. Bank of Louisville, 1933—, vice chmn., 1969-70, chmn. bd., chief exec. officer, 1970—, also dir.; dir. Ky. Trust Co., Louisville, 1st Ky. Co., Louisville, Fed. Res. Bank Louisville, Commonwealth Life Ins. Co., Louisville. Co-chmn. Community Chest Fund Drive, 1947; chmn. fund drive A.R.C., 1958; pres. Louisville and Jefferson County Children's Home, 1950-52. Trustee Bishop Dudley Meml. Found.; bd. dirs. Home of Innocents, 1963-69, Salvation Army, 1959-72. Served with USAF, 1942-46. Mem. Louisville C. of C. Episcopalian. Rotarian. Clubs: River Valley, Wynn Stay, Louisville Country, Ducks Unlimited. Home: 10 River Hill Rd Louisville KY 40201 Office: 216 S 5th St Louisville KY 40202

SIBLEY, D. JACOBI, JR., physician; b. Bertram, Tex., Mar. 5, 1913; s. D. Jacobi and Effie (Potts) S.; jr. coll. diploma, N.M. Mil. Inst., 1931; B.A., U. Tex., 1933, M.D., 1937; m. Jane Horton Dunn, Mar. 1, 1950; children—Dunn Jacobi III, Mahala Victoria, Hiram Andrew. Intern, asst. resident, resident in medicine St. Joseph's Hosp., Balt., 1937-40; gen. practice resident City-County Hosp., El Paso, 1949; gen. practice med., surg., Ft. Stockton, 1949-61; postgrad. student U. Tex. Post Grad. Sch. Medicine, Tex. Med. Center, Houston, 1961-62; with Clayton Biochem. Inst., U. Tex., Austin, 1962-66, as research scientist, med. asso., research scientist drug-plastic research and toxicology U. Tex., 1966-71, dir. med. research, drugs Plastic Research and Toxicology Lab. Tex. state chmn. Am. Med. Edn. Found., 1957-60; mem. state exec. com. Tex. div. Am. Cancer Soc., 1960-61; mem. ways and means com. for preservation Indian pictographs Amistad Recreation Area. Charter pres. Ft. Stockton Hist. Soc., 1952-55; trustee Annie Riggs Meml. Mus., Ft. Stockton; bd. dirs. Laguna Gloria Art Mus., 1964-66, Tex. State Hist. Found. Served from 2d lt. to lt. col. AUS, 1940-48; PTO. Decorated Bronze Star medal. Fellow Southwestern Surg. Congress; mem. So. Med. Assn., Travis County Med. Soc., Tex. Ind. Producers and Royalty Owners Assn., Assn. Am. Physicians and Surgeons, English-Speaking Union (program chmn. 1965-66, pres. Austin br. 1967-68), A.M.A., Tex. Med. Assn., Austin Ballot Soc. (v.p. 1967-68), Internat. Platform Assn., Alpha Omega Alpha, Alpha Epsilon Delta. Episcopalian (lay reader). Clubs: Westwood Country, Headliners. Home: 2210 Windsor Rd Austin TX 78703 Office: Balcones Research Center U Tex Austin TX 78756

SIBLEY, JAMES ASHLEY, JR., educator; b. Shreveport, La., Oct. 21, 1916; s. James Ashley and Lucian Katherine (Hammond) S.; B.A., Centenary Coll., 1940, postgrad., 1941-53; M.Ed., La. State U., 1963; m. Anna May Switzer, Feb. 1, 1963. Asst. mgr. Sibley's Hardware and Variety Stores, 1935-41; farmer, Shreveport, 1941-45; tchr. sci., phys. edn. supr. Lab. Sch., Centenary Coll., Shreveport, 1941-42; tchr. pub. schs., Shreveport, 1942-44, Baton Rouge, 1958-71; dir. VITAL Career Information Center, Dept. Edn., Baton Rouge, 1971—; coordinator cultural resources Unit Project for humanities East Baton Rouge Parish Sch. Bd.; personnel technician, examiner La. Civil Service Dept., Baton Rouge, 1944-48; employment counselor, test technician La. Employment Service, Shreveport, 1948-57; ednl. cons. Gulf S. Research Inst.; coordinator La. Arts and Sci. Center Planning Project, E. Baton Rouge Parish Schs. Mem. econ. council East Baton Rouge Parish Sch. Bd., 1963-64; exec. asst. region 7, La. Jr. Acad. Scis., 1963-64; adviser Nat. Conf. on Employment Am. Indian. Past mem. bd. dirs. Found. for Hist. La. Co-founder, sponsor Jr. Archeol. Soc., Inc., Meml. Mus. and Library Fund. Recipient Merit award for outstanding service to pub. La. chpt. Internat. Assn. Personnel in Employment Security, 1952. Mem. Assn. Childhood Edn. Internat. (cons. elementary sci. and social studies sect. 1963-64), Nat. Social Studies Council (pres. East Baton Rouge Parish chpt. 1964-65), Am. Acad. Polit. and Social Sci., Am. Personnel and Guidance Assn., La. Personnel and Guidance Assn. (exec. com., bd. 1972-73), Nat. Vocational Guidance Assn., (del.), La. Guidance Assn., Nat. Sci. Tchrs. Assn., Archeol. Inst. Am., Soc. for Am. Archeology, La. Acad. Scis., N.E.A., Nat. Congress Parents and Tchrs., La., La. Sci. tchrs. assns., Am. Assn. Museums, La. Vocational Guidance Assn. (pres. 1971-73), Nat. Assn. for Humanities Edn., Am. Anthrop. Assn., East Baton Rouge Classroom Tchrs. Assn., La., No. La. (charter, past pres.) hist. assns., Ark., Ala., Fla., Okla., La. (past dir.), Tex. archeol. socs., Phi Delta Kappa, Psi Chi (charter mem. L.S.U. chpt.). Episcopalian (past treas. and vestryman). Author: Louisiana's Ancients of Man, 1967; The Junior Archeological Society, 1967; Geology of Baton Rouge and Surrounding S.E. La. Area, 1972, others. Editor: Cultural Heritage of East Baton Rouge Parish, 1969; The Development and Use of Behavioral Objectives, 1970. Contbr. articles to profl. publs. Home: 2007 Cloverdale Av Baton Rouge LA 70808 Office: PO Box 2950 Baton Rouge LA 70806

SIBLEY, WILLIAM ARTHUR, physicist; b. Fort Worth, Nov. 22, 1932; s. William Franklin and Sada (Rasor) S.; B.S., U. Okla., 1956, M.S., 1958, Ph.D., 1960; m. Joyce Elaine Gregory, Dec. 21, 1957; children—William Timothy, Lauren Shawn, Stephen Marshall. Research physicist Inst. Metal-physics, Tech. U. Aachen (Germany), 1960-61, solid state div. Oak Ridge (Tenn.) Nat. Lab., 1961-70; prof., chmn. dept. physics Okla. State U., Stillwater, 1970—. Served to lt. AUS, 1951-53. Fellow Am. Phys. Soc.; mem. Sigma Xi. Baptist. Home: 4911 Country Club Dr Stillwater OK 74074

SIBLEY, WILLIAM LANGLEY, surgeon; b. Birmingham, Ala., July 7, 1906; s. Barney Dunbar and Carrie (Harris) S.; M.D., U. Va., 1930; M.S., U. Minn., 1937; m. Ara Rosamond Anthony, Feb. 12, 1930; 1 son, William Langley. Intern Charity Hosp., New Orleans, 1931-32, Lewis Gale Hosp., Roanoke, Va., 1932-33; fellow surgery Mayo Found., 1934-37; resident surgeon St. Mary's Hosp., Mayo Clinic, 1937-38; practicing physician, surgeon, Roanoke, Va., 1938—; chief surgery Community Hosp., Roanoke Valley, 1969-70; pres. Lewis-Gale Clinic; staff, chief surg. service and pres. bd. dirs. of hosp. Lewis-Gale Hosp.; cons. surgeon VA Hosp.; staff Roanoke Meml. Hosp.; Jefferson Hosp. Chmn. Va. Trauma Com.; bd. dirs. Lewis-Gale Hosp., Inc., Community Hosp., Hosp. Div. Civil Def.; bd. govs. Hosp. Corp. Am., 1972. Served as capt. to lt. col., U.S. Army, 1942-46. Diplomate Am. Bd. Surgery. Fellow A.C.S.; mem. A.M.A., Southeastern Surg. Congress, Roanoke Acad. Medicine, So. (life), Southwestern Va., Va. med. socs., Va. Surg. Soc., Priestly Surg. Soc., Mil. Order World Wars (comdr. 1949-50), Raven, Sigma Phi Omega, Phi Gamma Delta, Iota Sigma, Nu Sigma Nu. Roman Catholic. K.C. Lion. Club: Roanoke Country. Contbr. articles med. jours. Home: 2242 Mt Vernon Rd SW Roanoke VA 24015 Office: Lewis-Gale Clinic Salem VA 24153

SIDLINGER, BRUCE CHESTER, mfg. co. exec.; b. Cedar Rapids, Ia., Dec. 10, 1927; s. Paul E. and Ruth (Wilson) S.; student U. Ia., 1948, U. Ill., 1949-51; m. Joanne Leonard, May 16, 1956; 1 son, Bruce Douglas. Pres., Sidlinger Products Co., Inc., Garland, Tex., 1948—; profl. trampolinist, 1951-67; appeared at Radio City Music Hall, 1955, Gary Moore Show, 1957, Paul Winchell Show, 1957. Served with AUS, 1946-48. Mem. Theta Xi. Patentee in field. Home: 2810 Country Club Rd Garland TX 75041 Office: 208-214 International Rd Garland TX 75040

SIEGEL, CHARLES HOLLADAY, carpet and flooring co. exec.; b. Balt., Dec. 13, 1941; s. Rudolph Augustus and Marion (Kasten) S.; B.A., Yale, 1963, LL.B., 1966; m. Mary Ann Garvin, Sept. 3, 1967; children—Emily Hughes, Charles Halladay. Carpet mgr., dir. R.A. Siegel Co., Atlanta, 1969—. Zone chmn. United Appeal, 1970; participant Leadership Atlanta, 1971-72; vol. probation officer Fulton County, 1971—. Served to 1st lt. USAF, 1966-69. Mem. Ga. Bar Assn., Yale Alumni Assn. (alumni bd. 1971). Episcopalian (vestryman). Clubs: Yale Ga. (pres. 1971-73), Piedmont Driving (Atlanta). Home: 2311 Dellwood Dr NW Atlanta GA 30305 Office: 1175 Chattahoochee Av NW Atlanta GA 30325

SIEGEL, GERALD WILLIAM, newspaper co. exec.; b. Waterloo, Ia., Sept. 21, 1917; s. Samuel and Rebecca (Wartey) S.; A.B. magna cum laude, U. Ia., 1941; LL.B., Yale, 1947; m. Helene L. Jacober, Aug. 22, 1948; children—Robin Elizabeth, Robert Arthur. Exec. asst. to chmn. U.S. Securities and Exchange Commn., 1947-53; chief counsel U.S. Senate Democratic Policy Com., Washington, 1953-58; lectr. Harvard Bus. Sch., 1958-61; v.p., counsel Washington Post Co., 1961—, dir., 1961-71; v.p., council Washington Post, 1971—. Trustee, Fed. City Council; bd. dirs. Nat. Conf. Christians and Jews; bd. dirs. Met. Washington Urban Coalition. Childrens Hosp. Mem. Fed. Bar Assn., Yale Law Sch. Assn., Phi Beta Kappa. Democrat. Home: 4921 30th Pl NW Washington DC 20008 Office: 1515 L St NW Washington DC 20005

SIEGEL, JOSEPH HERMAN, psychologist; b. Tyler, Tex., Dec. 31, 1924; s. Maurice and Annie (Eisenberg) S.; B.S. in Biology, So. Meth. U., 1948, M.A. in Psychology, 1949; Ph.D. in Psychology, U. Okla., 1954; m. Eve Perlstein, Aug. 19, 1945; children—Jeffrey, Drew, Brett. Staff psychologist Dallas Child Guidance Clinic, 1949-50; psychologist Tex. Dept. Pub. Welfare, Dallas, 1949-50; asst. psychologist Central State Hosp., Norman, Okla., 1950-52; instr. U. Okla., 1952-53, instnl. counselor, 1953-54; cons. psychologist Family Consultation Service, Tuckahoe, N.Y., 1954-56; clin. psychologist Dallas Soc. Crippled Children, 1956-57; clin. dir. Children's Devel. Center, Dallas, 1956-62; cons. psychologist Angels, Inc., 1963—; chmn. profl. adv. com. Dallas Council Retarded Children; pvt. practice of clin. psychology, Dallas, 1956—. Lectr. psychology So. Meth. U., 1956, 62. Bd. dirs. Planned Parenthood of Dallas; adviser Trustees Lena Callier Trust Fund. Served with AUS, 1943-46. Certified psychologist Tex. Bd. Examiners of Psychologists. Mem. Am., S.W., Tex., Dallas (pres. 1961-62) psychol. assns., Am. Assn. on Mental Deficiency, Nat. Rehab. Assn., Am. Acad. Psychotherapists, Am. Group Psychotherapy Assn., Rorschach Inst., Dallas Soc. Clin. Psychologists, Am., N.Y. acads. sci. Home: 11330 Hillcrest Rd Dallas TX 75230 Office: 3519 Cedar Springs St Dallas TX 75219

SIEGFRIED, RAY H., ins. co. exec.; b. Pitts., July 28, 1894; s. Christian A. and Mary (McCue) S.; student pub. schs.; m. Ruth McBride, Nov. 26, 1914; 1 son, Robert M. Various positions Ill. Pipe Co., Ind., Ill., 1907-11; with Tex. Pipeline Co., Tulsa, 1911-18; supt. prodn. and pipeline Pierce Oil Corp., Tulsa, Ft. Worth, 1918-20; dir. R.H. Siegfried Co., Tulsa, 1920—; pres. R.H. Siegfried, Inc., Tulsa, 1950—. Knight of Malta; K.C. Home: 2629 S Trenton Tulsa OK 74114 Office: Box 3308 Tulsa OK 74101 mailing address: Box 3308 Tulsa OK 74101

SIEGLER, HOWARD MATTHEW, physician; b. N.Y.C., May 26, 1932; s. Samuel Lewis and Shirley Kendall (Matthews) S.; B.A., Hofstra U., 1951; postgrad. Yale, 1949, St. Andrews U., 1958; M.D., N.Y. Med. Coll., 1965; m. Toinette Andrau, Dec. 1, 1953; children—Samuel Lewis II, Karel Lynn, Jacqueline Andrau, Todd Bradford. Intern, N.Y.U. Med. Center, N.Y.C., 1965-66, New Rochelle (N.Y.) Hosp., 1966-67; asst. to dean U. Tex. Med. Sch., Dallas, 1967-68; sr. fellow dept. phys. medicine Baylor Coll. Medicine, 1968-69; gen. practice medicine, Houston, 1970—; clin. fellow in obstetrics and gynecology St. Lukes Episcopal Hosp., Houston, 1971—. Co-chmn. Muscular Dystrophy Soc., 1966-67; active Assn. to Help Retarded Children, Protestant Charities N.Y. Mem. Am. Fertility Soc., Royal Soc. Health, Am. Geriatrics Soc., A.A.A.S., N.Y. Acad. Sci. (life), Am. Diabetes Assn., Am. Social Health Assn., Am. Soc. Bariatrics, Christian Med. Soc., Am. Med. Soc. Alcoholism, Phi Chi. Episcopalian. Home: 1 Longfellow Lane Houston TX 77005 Office: Hermann Profl Bldg Suite 1020 6410 Fannin St Houston TX 77025

SIENER, LEO COLUMBUS, clergyman, social worker; b. Chattanooga, June 15, 1923; s. Leo Columbus and Bernadette (Murphy) S.; A.B., St. Mary U. (Balt.), 1943; S.T.B., St. Mary Pontifical U., 1945; S.T.L. magna cum laude, St. Mary U., 1948; M.A.,

Catholic U. of Am., 1957; M.S., U. Tenn., 1961. Ordained priest Roman Catholic Ch., 1949; dir. social sci. dept. Father Ryan Sch., Nashville, 1949-60; state dir. Cath. Charities of Tenn., Nashville, 1953-—; sec. Roman Cath. Bishop of Nashville, Cath. Charities and Civic Concerns, Nashville, 1966-—; elevated to rank Honory Prelate, 1968. Mem. state bd. dirs. Tenn. Mental Assn., 1964-70; state dir. Tenn. Human Relation Council, 1966-70, vice chmn., 1968-—; sec.-treas. Cath. Charities of Tenn., 1962-—, Diocesan Properties, Inc., 1968, St. Mary Villa, Inc., 1966; vice chmn. Model Cities of Met. Nashville. Served with USAF, 1963-66. Mem. Commn. on Families and Children, Nat. Conf. Cath. Charities, Acad. Certified Social Workers, Tenn. Conf. on Social Welfare (pres. 1968-69), U. Tenn. Sch. Social Work Alumni Assn. (v.p. 1966-67). Home: 3001 Belmont Blvd Nashville TN 37212 Office: 421 Charlotte Av Nashville TN 37217

SIFFORD, CHARLES DARRELL, journalist; b. Moberly, Mo., Sept. 19, 1931; s. Charles Dewey and Hazel Odell (Bland) S.; B.J., U. Mo., 1953; m. Verna Mae Angerer, Apr. 18, 1954; children—Jay, Grant. News reporter Columbia Missourian, 1952-53; sports editor Post-Tribune, Jefferson City, Mo., 1955-56, city editor, 1956-61, mng. editor, 1961-62; night city editor Courier-Journal, Louisville, 1962-66; mng. editor Charlotte (N.C.) News, 1966-71, exec. editor, 1971-—. Served as cpl., C.E., AUS, 1953-55. Mem. Mo. Sportswriters Assn. (v.p. 1956), Sigma Delta Chi. Lutheran. Clubs: Pine Lake Country; Hunting Creek Country. Author articles sports periodicals, also short stories. Home: 3742 Larkston Dr Charlotte NC 28211 Office: Box 360 Charlotte NC 28201

SIFFORD, DEWEY HURSCHEL, educator; b. La Grange, Ark., Sept. 9, 1930; s. John Avril and Irene (Stacy) S.; B.S., Ark. State U., 1952; Ph.D., Okla. U., 1962; m. Margaret Teresa Unzner, Aug. 16, 1958; children— Mark, John, Susan, Charles, Mary. Asst. prof. chemistry Ark. State U., State University, 1961-63, asso. prof., 1963-65, prof. chemistry, 1965-—, acting chmn. div. phys. scis., 1968-69, chmn. div., 1970-—. Served with AUS, 1952-54. Mem. A.A.A.S., Am. Chem. Soc., Ark. Acad. Sci., Am. Inst. Chemists, Sigma Xi, Tau Kappa Epsilon, Alpha Chi Sigma, Phi Lambda Upsilon. Mason. Home: 1109 Thrush St Jonesboro AR 72401 Office: Box CC State University AR 72467

SIFONTES, ORVAL EMILIO, architect; b. Arecibo, P.R., May 22, 1932; s. Jose E. and Josefa (Fontan) S.; student U. P.R., 1951-53; B.Arch., Tulane U., 1957; m. Gladys Louise Smith, 1956; children—Carmen, Roxanne, Vanessa, Maria Dolores, Orval E., Maria del Pilar. Asso. in charge of design, firm Pedro A. Miranda, San Juan, P.R., 1958-62; partner Sarriera Sifontes Assos., San Juan, 1963-66; prin. firm Orval E. Sifontes, Hato Rey, P.R., 1967-—. Mem. A.I.A., P.R. Coll. Engrs., Architests and Surveyors, Inter-Am. Planning Soc. Home: 372 Edie Cracia St Hato Rey PR 00918 Office: 531-A Sergio Cuevas St Hato Rey PR 00918

SIGEL, M(OLA) MICHAEL, educator; b. Nieswiez, Poland, June 24, 1920 (came to U.S. 1937; naturalized 1941); s. Zundel and Helen (Lubecka) S.; B.A., U. Tex., 1941; Ph.D., Ohio State U., 1944; m. Mary Elizabeth Wynne, Dec. 22, 1941; children—Suzanne Lee (Mrs. Robert Hood Barth, Jr.), Vicki Adelaide Breina, Rachel Delelaw Sarah, Valerie Harriet Louise, David Edward Burl. Officer in charge bacteriology Army Service Command Lab., 1943-46; asso. virology U. Pa., 1946-50, asst. prof. virology, 1950-53; in charge virus diagnostic lab., Children's Hosp., Phila., 1946-53; chief reference diagnosis and research unit USPHS, Montgomery, Ala., 1953-55; spl. cons. WHO, Europe, 1956; asso. prof. U. Miami, Fla., 1955-58, prof. microbiology, sch. medicine, 1958-—. Dir. Virus Labs., Variety Children's Research Found., 1955-60, research dir., chmn. research staff, 1960-70; research asso. Lerner Marine Lab., Bimini, Bahamas, 1963-—; mem. editorial staff Translation Project Fedn. Am. Socs. Exptl. Biology, 1963-67; mem. research council U. Miami, 1964-—; hon. prof. U. W.I., 1960-—. Served to col. AUS. Diplomate Am. Bd. Microbiology. Fellow A.A.A.S., N.Y. Acad. Scis.; mem. Am. Soc. Microbiology (vice chmn. nat. meeting 1969; pres. So. Fla. br. 1969-70; councillor 1971-72), Soc. Exptl. Biology and Medicine, Soc. Pediatric Research, Am. Assn. Immunologists, Soc. Gen. Microbiology, Reticuloendothelial Soc., Oceanography, Am. Soc. Cell Biology, Am. Assn. Cancer Research, Tissue Culture Assn. (program chmn. 1969-70), Phi Beta Kappa, Sigma Xi. Author: (with A.R. Beasley) Viruses, Cells and Hosts, 1962. Editor: Lymphogranuloma Venereum, 1962; Differentiation and Defense Mechanisms in Lower Organisms In Vitro, 1968; asso. editor Cancer Research, 1969-—; editor (with R.A. Good) Tolerance, Autoimmunity and Aging, 1972. Contbr. articles to profl. jours. Home: 7980 SW 58th St Miami FL 33143

SIGHOLTZ, ROBERT HARRIS, univ. athletic dir.; b. Phila., Nov. 4, 1923; s. Samuel and Lenore Catherine (Griffith) S.; B.A., U. Md., 1964; M.S.T., Am. U., 1966; Ed.D., George Washington U., 1971; m. Roberta Catherine Wynne, Mar. 7, 1942; children—Robert Harris, Cathy Roberta, Susan Ann. Served from pvt. to col., U.S. Army; served in Korea; comdr. parachute unit, Vietnam, now ret.; asst. athletic dir. Georgetown U., Washington, 1968-69, athletic dir., 1969-—. Mem. U.S. Olympic Com.; pres. internat. approved basketball ofcls. Bd. dirs. Nat. Football Found. Decorated Silver Star with two oak leaf clusters, Bronze Star with two oak leaf clusters, D.F.C., Legion of Merit with two oak leaf clusters. Mem. Phi Delta Kappa. Home: 8356 Queen Elizabeth St Annandale VA 22003 Office: Athletic Dept Georgetown University Washington DC 20007

SIGLER, ORVIS UTOPIA, JR., coll. ofcl.; b. Springfield, Mo., June 22, 1922; s. Orvis Utopia and Betty (Inman) S.; student Drury Coll., 1940-42; B.S. in Edn., S.W. Mo. State Coll., 1948; postgrad. U. Mo., 1954; m. Doris Simmons, Mar. 12, 1944 (dec. Aug. 1969); children—Susan Erica (Mrs. Don Updegraff), Sally Elizabeth (Mrs. Richard Bruer), Steven Orvis; m. 2d, Joanne Sherrod Whittington, June 1970; stepchildren—Betty Anne, Cynthia Elizabeth. Basketball coach St. Agnes High Sch., Springfield, 1947-48, West Plains (Mo.) High Sch., 1948-52, S.W. Mo. State Coll., Springfield, 1952-53, Mo. Valley Coll., Marshall, 1953-54, U.S. Mil. Acad., West Point, N.Y., 1954-58; athletic dir. Centenary Coll., Shreveport, La., 1958-—. Bd. dirs. Shreveport Sports Found. Served to lt. (j.g.) AC, USNR, 1942-46; PTO. Decorated Air medal (3). Mem. Nat. Basketball Coaches Assn., Nat. Assn. Collegiate Dirs. of Athletics, Shreveport C. of C. (athletic affairs com., 1961-—), Am. Legion. Mem. Christian Ch. (deacon). Home: 474 Pennsylvania St Shreveport LA 71105

SIGUR, FREDERICK JOSEPH, real estate corp. exec.; b. New Orleans, Apr. 8, 1917; s. Sidney Charles and Ida (Prevost) S.; student Loyola U., 1947-48; m. Marguerite Bradbury, June 29, 1941; children— Frederick J., Carolyn Ann, Kenneth M., David J., Daniel P. Condr., N.O. Pub. Service, Inc., New Orleans, 1936-40; custom guard U.S. Govt., New Orleans, 1941-42; tool and die maker Consol. Vultee Aircraft Corp., New Orleans, 1942-45; salesman Dutel Real Estate, New Orleans, 1945-48; broker Frederick J. Sigur Realty Co., Arabi, La., 1948-—; pres. Carolyn Homes, Inc., Arabi, 1952-55, Ridgeland Terrace, Inc., Arabi, 1954-66, Carolyn Park, Inc., 1955-—, Boulevard Homes, Inc., Arabi, 1955-—, Mid-South Land Corp., Arabi, 1962-—, Delta Dredging Corp., Chalmette, La., 1962-—, Arabi Properties, Inc., 1962-—, Carolyn Devel. Corp., New Orleans, 1964-—, Fred J. Sigur & Sons, Inc., Chalmette, 1964-—; treas. Southeast Properties, Inc., New Orleans, 1962-—; v.p. Normand Co., New Orleans, 1959-—, Fazzio Excavating Corp., New Orleans, 1966-—, Chalmette Marina, Inc., 1969-—; v.p. dir. St. Bernard Bank & Trust Co., 1964-—; dir. La. So. Rwy. Co. Mem. St. Bernard Port Authority, 1962-—; dir. New Orleans Area Health Planning Council, 1969; chmn. St. Bernard Easter Seal Soc., 1969. Bd. dirs. A.R.C., St. Bernard Parish. Recipient Outstanding Citizen award C. of C., 1965, Man of Year award St. Bernard Parish Bus. and Profl. Women's Orgn., 1970. Mem. C. of C. (dir. met. area com. 1967-—), St. Bernard Hist. Soc. K.C., Kiwanian. Club: Braithwaite (La.) Golf. Home: 2301 Paris Rd Chalmette LA 70043 Office: 100 Rowley Blvd Arabi LA 70032

SIKES, L. B. T., supt. schs.; b. Leonard, Tex., Sept. 10, 1915; s. Richard Green and Hattie (Tefteller) S.; B.S., Tex. A. and M. U., 1938; M.S., East Tex. State U., 1945; m. Geraldine Thrasher, Feb. 24, 1939; children—David, Richard, Betsy. Tchr., coach Rosebud Schs., 1938-40; high sch. prin. Ozona (Tex.) Pub. Schs., 1940-48; supt. Crockett County schs., Ozona, 1953-—; supt. Wortham Ind. Sch. Dist., 1948-51; supt. Calvert Ind. Sch. Dist., 1951-53. Mem. N.E.A., Am., Tex. assns. sch. adminstrs., Tex. Tchrs. Assn. (pres. Dist. XI). Mason, Lion. Home: 1303 Av C Ozona TX 76943 Office: 797 Av D Ozona TX 76943

SIKES, MELVIN PATTERSON, educator; b. Charleston, Mo., Dec. 24, 1917; s. Dorothy Edward and Kimmie (Patterson) S.; B.A., N.C. Coll., 1938; M.A., U. Chgo., 1948, Ph.D., 1950; m. Zeta Bledsoe, Oct. 17, 1953; children—Cheryl Lynn, Bertha Kimeta. Prof., dean Bishop Coll., 1952-55, Wiley Coll., 1955-60; supr. Gt. Southwest Life, 1955-60; clin. psychologist VA Hosp., 1960-68; asst. regional dir. Dept. Justice, 1968-69; prof. psychology, U. Tex., Austin, 1969-—. Pvt. practice psychology, part-time, 1950-69; dir. Houston Co-op. Crime Prevention Program, 1967-68; dir. Program for Treatment of Alcoholism, VA Hosp., Houston, 1960-68. Mem. Austin Human Relations Commn.; chmn. 1st Nat. Congress Black Profls. in Higher Edn. Served to 2d. lt. USAF, 1943-46. Recipient Meritorious Service award VA, 1968. Mem. Am., Tex., Houston, Southwestern psychol. assns., N.Y. Acad. Scis., N.E.A., Nat. Council Alcoholism, Houston Council Human Relations. Home: 8703 Point West Dr Austin TX 78736

SIKES, ROBERT L. F., congressman; b. Isabella, Ga., June 3, 1906; s. Benjamin Franklin and Clara Ophelia (Ford) S.; B.S., U. Ga., 1927; M.S., U. Fla., 1929; LL.D., Stetson U., 1969, U. W. Fla., 1970; L.H.D., St. Leo Coll., 1969; Hon. Doctorate, U. Inca Garcilaso de la Vega (Peru), 1970; m. Inez Tyner; children—Mrs. Edward F. Wicke, Robert Keyes. Agrl. and indsl. research, 1928-32; pub. Oklaloosa News-Journal, Crestview, Fla., and other newspapers, 1933-40. Mem. State legislature, 1936-40; chmn. County Dem. Com., 1934; mem. 77th to 92nd Congresses from 1st Fla. Dist. Chmn. Fla. delegation Dem. Nat. Conv., 1956-60. Del. Pan Am. Rds. Conf., Venezuela, 1954, Interparliamentary Conf., Warsaw, 1959; dir., v.p. Nat. Rive's and Harbors Congress, 1959-67; del. to Sixth World Forestry Congress, Madrid, 1966. Bd. visitors USAF Acad. Served to maj. gen. AUS, World War II; ETO. Decorated Legion of Merit; recipient Nat. Affairs Leadership award, 1951, Nat. Leadership award Am. Gun Dealers Assn., 1959, Distinguished Service award Res. Officers Assn. U.S., 1958, 66, Gov.'s Conservation Award, 1960, Guatemalan Order Merit, 1961, Young Dem. Clubs Fla. award, 1961, Am. Legion Distinguished Service award, 1962, Navy Times Good Neighbor award, 1962; Fla. Council of 100 Distinguished Service award, 1962, Humanitarian award Children's Asthma Research Ins., 1963, Outstanding Service award Fla. Nat. Guard, 1963, George Washington Meml. award, 1966, Good Govt. award Pensacola Realty Bd., 1966, Defender of Free Enterprise award Life Underwriters, 1966, Hon. State Farmer award Fla. Assn. Future Farmers Am., 1967, alumni award Alpha Gamma Rho, 1968, Fla. Public Service award U.P.I., 1968, Distinguished Service award Water Resources Congress, 1972, Gen. Louis E. Brereton award Fla. Air Force Assn., 1972, numerous others; hon. faculty chair in govt. Okaloosa-Walton Jr. Coll. named in his honor. Mem. Mil. Order World War, Am. Legion, V.F.W., Nat. Assn. Suprs. (hon.), Nat. Rivers and Harbors Congress (nat. v.p. 1959-70, nat. dir. 1959-70), Fla. Hist. Soc. (dir., v.p.), Res. Officers Assn. (Hall of Fame 1963, minute man hall of fame 1964, man of year 1967), Fleet Res. Assn. (hon. life mem.), Navy League (hon. life mem.), Naval Aviation Mus. Assn. (trustee), Am. Soc. Arms Collectors, Am. Fedn. Govt. Employees, United Fedn. Postal Clks. (hon.), Nat. Rifle Assn. (life), 40 and 8, Nat. Sojourners, Nat. Assn. Master Mechanics and Foreman Assn. (hon.), S.C.V., Blue Key, Phi Kappa Phi, Sigma Delta Chi, Alpha Zeta, Phi Sigma, Alpha Gamma Rho. Methodist. Mason (33 deg., Shriner, K.T., Grotto; grand orator Fla. lodge 1968-69), K.P., Elk, Moose; mem. Order of Ahepa (hon. mem.). Clubs: Kiwanis (lt. gov. 1940), Lions (hon.), Rotary (hon.), Civitan (hon.), Toastmasters Internat. Home: Crestview FL 32536 Address: Rayburn House Office Bldg Washington DC 20515

SIKORA, EUGENE STANLEY, profl. engr.; b. Duquesne, Pa., July 21, 1924; s. Adam Joseph and Helen (Pietrowska) S.; student Okla. Bapt. U., 1943-44; B.S. in Indsl. Engring., U. Pitts., 1949; C.E., Carnegie Inst. Tech., 1951; m. Corinne Mary Coliane, Sept. 7, 1946; children—Karyn Ann, Leslie Ann. Bridge design engr. Gannett, Fleming, Corddry & Carpenter, Pitts., 1949-50; structural designer Rust Engring. Co., Pitts., 1950-51, chief field engr., 1951-52, asst. project engr.; project engr. Frank E. Murphy & Assos., Bartow, Fla., 1952-55; v.p. Wellman-Lord Engring. Co., Lakeland, Fla., 1955-61; pres. Gulf Design Co., Lakeland, 1961-—; v.p. Badger Co. Inc., Cambridge, Mass., 1968-—; dir. Southeastern Chem. Corp., Lakeland, 1962-—, Nat. Office Bldgs. Corp., Lakeland, 1962-—, Largo Vista, Inc., Lakeland, 1962-—, Bus. Computers, Inc., Dallas, Continental Chem. Processors, Inc., N.Y.C. Served with USAAF, 1943-45. Mem. Nat. Soc. Profl. Engrs., Am. Inst. Mining, Metall. and Petroleum Engrs., Am. Mgmt. Assn., Am. Inst. Chem. Engrs., Am. Inst. Indsl. Engrs., Fla. Engring. Soc. Democrat. Roman Catholic. Rotarian. Home: 1400Seville Pl Lakeland FL 33803 Office: US Hwy 98 S and Reynolds Rd Lakeland FL

SIKORSKI, LUDWIK STANISLAW, musician-composer; b. New Haven, Jan. 16, 1911; s. Antoni and Anna (Solecka) S.; B.Mus., Yale, 1936, M.Mus., 1946, postgrad. summers 1968, 69; pupil Hugo Kortschak, 1947-49; m. Alys Missirian, Feb. 8, 1936; 1 dau., Pravda (Mrs. Bruce Carruth). First violinist New Haven and Conn. Symphony Orchestras, 1936-50; composer, arranger, condr. symphony orchs., ensembles in concert and on radio; chmn. music U. Conn., 1947-50; chmn. music dept. Emory and Henry Coll., Emory, Va., 1950-—; music chmn. Va. Highlands Festival, 1951-—, also festival trustee; condr. Highlands Chamber Orch., 1955-—. Mem. bd. Va. State Orch., 1965. Served as non-commd. officer Signal Corps, Spl. Services, AUS, 1943-45. Recipient Ditson award for symphonic composition, 1936; Woods Chandler award for chamber work; certificate of merit Yale U. Sch. Music Alumni Assn., 1969. Mem. Nat. Assn. Am. Composers and Condrs., Am. Acad. Polit. and Social Scis., Am. Fedn. Composers and Arrangers (A.F.M.), Blue Key. Methodist. Kiwanian. Compositions include: Christmas Oratorio, 1964; Easter Cantata, 1966; Suite for Orch. for 200th anniversary of Appomattox, Va., 1966. Address: Emory and Henry Coll Emory VA 24327

SILBERG, MARGARET INEZ LUNSFORD, educator, soprano; b. Paris, Tex.; d. Robert Jenkins and Margaret Inez (Mitchell Scott; student Longy Sch. Music, Boston, 1932-33, Chgo. Musical Coll., 1934-36; B.M., Kansas City Conservatory, 1938, M.M., 1940; studnet U. Kan., 1937-38, San Francisco Conservatory, summer 1943; m. Dr. William F. Lunsford, Dec. 20, 1929 (dec. July, 1939); 1 son, William Thomas; m. 2d Max M. Silberg, Mar. 10, 1943. Soloist, soprano, various symphonies, Ark., Mo., Mass., 1930-38; with Van Duzee Singers, Kansas City Conservatory, 1937-39; choir soloist, various churches, Mo., Mass., 1932-39; choir dir., Okla., 1940-62; soloist, choir dir., opera dir. Oklahoma City U., 1962-—; voice tchr. Kansas City Conservatory, 1939-40, Okla. State U., 1940-45; voice tchr. Oklahoma City U., 1945-—, dir. Opera Theatre, prof. voice, chmn. voice dept., 1962-—; vocal coach Oklahoma City Lyric Theatre, summer 1962. Rep., Nat. Opera Assn., N.Y.C., 1971, Central Opera Service Nat. Conv., Tulsa, 1971. Mem. women's com. Oklahoma City Symphony, 1956-—; mem. YWCA; worker Lyric Theater, 1962-—; Symphony Drive worker, 1950-—; worker Civic Music Assn., 1956-—; mem. Great Artists and Connoisseur Concerts, 1957-—; state rep. Tulsa Opera Assn.; bd. mem. Inspiration Point Fine Arts Colony, Eureka Springs, Ark.; mem. Gov.'s Spl. Adv. Com. Arts and Humanities Council Okla.; adjudicator coll. students Nat. Competition, Nat. Assn. Tchrs. Singing Nat. Conv., St. Louis 1971-72. Named Woman of Yr. in Arts, Theta Sigma Phi, 1970, Outstanding Mem. of Yr. in Music, Alpha Phi, 1969. Mem. Ladies Music Club (bd. dirs., v.p.), McDowell Club Allied Arts (bd. dirs.), Art League, Okla. Music Tchrs. Assn. (dir.), Music Tchrs. Nat. Assn., Nat. Assn. Tchrs. Singing (dir. state pres. 1970; mem. program com. nat. conv. 1970), Am. Assn. U. Profs., Okla. Fedn. Music (dir.; opera chmn. 1957-64), Sigma Alpha Iota (pres. 1950-52, dir., Sword of Honor); bd. dirs. nat. found. 1971-—), Pi Kappa Lambda, Alpha Phi (dir.). Home: 2517 Warwick Dr Oklahoma City OK 73116

SILBERMAN, LAURENCE HIRSCH, govt. ofcl.; b. York, Pa., Oct. 12, 1935; s. William and Anna (Hirsch) S.; B.A., Dartmouth, 1957; LL.B., Harvard, 1961; m. Rosalie Gaull, Jan. 5, 1957; children—Robert, Katherine, Anne. Asso. firm Moore, Torkildson & Rice, Quinn & Moore, 1961-64; partner Moore, Silberman & Schulze, Honolulu, 1964-67; atty. NLRB, Washington, 1967-69; solicitor labor, Labor Dept., 1969-70, under sec. labor 1970-—. Served with AUS. Mem. Am. Bar Assn., Bar Assn. Hawaii. Address: 12436 Over Ridge Rd Potomac MD 20854

SILER, EUGENE EDWARD, JR., lawyer; b. Williamsburg, Ky., Oct. 19, 1936; s. Eugene Edward and Lowell (Jones) S.; B.A. cum laude, Vanderbilt U., 1958; LL.B., U. Va., 1963; LL.M. (E. Barrett Prettyman fellow), Georgetown U., 1964; m. Christy Dyanne Minnich, Oct. 18, 1969. Admitted to Ky. bar, 1963, Va. bar, D.C. bar; legal intern, Washington, 1963-64; practice in Williamburg, 1964-65; county atty. Whitley County, Williamsburg, 1965-70; U.S. atty., Lexington, Ky., 1970-—. Sec., dir. Whitely Republican, Inc., 1968-70; co-chmn. Rep. campaign 5th Congl. Dist., 1966; pres. 5th Congl. Dist. Lincoln Club, 1969-70. Trustee, Cumberland Coll., Williamsburg, 1965-—. Recipient Freedom's Found. medal, 1968. Mem. Ky., Va., Fed. bar assns., Bar Assn. D.C., Gideons. Baptist. Optimist. Home: 820 Walnut St Williamsburg KY 40769 Office: Federal Bldg Lexington KY 50501

SILER, RICHARD KEITH, meteorologist; b. Coffeyville, Kan., Jan. 23, 1928; s. Richard Emberson and Bernice (Hanes) S.; A.A., Bakersfield (Cal.) Coll., 1949; A.B., U. Cal. at Los Angeles, 1951; m. Patricia Ann Morrow, Aug. 4, 1949; children—Richard K., Kathleen A., Mark M. Profl. meteorologist Nat. Weather Service, Las Vegas, 1951-56, Honolulu, 1956-64, Washington, 1964-65, Cape Kennedy, Fla., 1965-67, Houston, 1967-—. Served with USAAF, 1946-47. Mem. Am. Meteorol. Soc., Aircraft Owners and Pilots Assn. Democrat. Methodist. Contbr. articles to profl. jours. Home: 4114 Shady Springs Dr Seabrook TX 77586 Office: NASA-Manned Spacecraft Center Spaceflight Meteorology Bldg 30 Houston TX 77058

SILLIMAN, JULIAN WINTHROP, san. engr.; b. Palestine, Tex., Aug. 15, 1909; s. John Calvin and Bertha (Umstead) S.; A.B., Stanford, 1930, engr., 1932; m. Anne Marie Tucker, Sept. 27, 1936; children—Jay Robert, Nancy Theodore. Surveyor, resident engr., designer Cal. Div. Hwys., 1932-40; commd. lt. C.E., U.S. Navy, 1940, advanced through grades to capt., 1953; engr. constrn. of fld. base, 1941-42; with U.S. See Bee program, 1943-47; assigned to Spain, 1954-56; ret., 1960; chief engr. Mills Petticord & Mills., Washington, 1960-64; project engr. George Washington U. Hosp., Washington, 1964-66; chief engr. Airways Engring., Washington, 1966-70; asst., now dir. Dept. San. Sewers, Tampa, Fla., 1970-—. Fellow Am. Soc. C.E.; mem. Water Pollution Control Fedn., Tau Beta Pi. Registered profl. engr. Fla., N.Y., Cal., Va. Home: 2413 S Dundee St Tampa FL 33609 Office: Dept Sanitary Sewers Tampa FL 33602

SILVER, SAMUEL, govt. ofcl.; b. Wilmington, Del., Nov. 10, 1914; s. Abraham and Sophia (Levin) S.; A.B., Am. U., 1935; LL.B., U. Pa., 1939; m. Edith Newman, July 2, 1944; 1 son, Ira H. Admitted to D.C. bar, 1940; labor relations specialist War Dept., 1942-46, procurement specialist, 1946-48; labor economist Office Sec. Def., 1948-53, dep. dir. indsl. relations Dept. Def., 1953-58, dir. indsl. relations, 1958-61, indsl. relations adviser Office Asst. Sec. Def. for Installations and Logistics, 1961-71; Equal Employment Opportunity officer Dept. of Def., Washington, 1971-—. Home: 8808 Spring Valley Rd Chevy Chase MD 20015 Office: Brookmont MD 20025

SILVERGLEID, DAVID, labor union ofcl.; b. N.Y.C., Jan 16, 1909; s. Samuel and Ida (Raff) S.; student Coll. City N.Y., 1925-28; LL.B., Bklyn. Law Sch., 1931; m. Dorothy Hoffman, Sept. 2, 1933; children— Michael, Arthur Jay. Admitted to N.Y. bar, 1932; practice in N.Y. State, 1932-59; pres. Bklyn. Postal Union, 1944-59; sec.-treas. Nat. Postal Union, 1959-68, pres. 1968-—. Home: 1220 East West Hwy Silver Spring MD 20910 Office: 425 13th St NW Washington DC 20004

SILVERMAN, ABNER DAVID, govt. housing ofcl.; b. N.Y.C., Jan. 8, 1909; s. Abraham Samuel and Kate (Goodman) S.; student Townsend Harris Hall, N.Y.C., 1923-26; student Coll. City N.Y., 1926-29; LL.B., N.Y. U., 1931, LL.M., 1934; m. Eleanor Frankel, June 8, 1934; 1 dau., Kate. Admitted to N.Y. State bar, 1934; engaged in pvt. real estate brokerage and property mgmt., N.Y.C., 1928-38; with U.S. Housing Authority and Fed. Public Housing Authority, Washington, 1938-43, dep. asst. commr. for project mgmt., 1943-46; dir. of mgmt. Am. Community Builders, Inc., Chgo., 1947-48; asst. commr. for operations, Pub. Housing Adminstrn., Washington, 1948-69; gen. dep. housing assistance adminstr. Dept. Housing and Urban Devel., Washington, 1969-—. Cons. and expert examiner in field of housing mgmt. Buffalo Municipal Civil Service Commn., 1941, N.Y.C. Municipal Civil Service Commn., 1940; lectr. in housing mgmt. N.Y. U., Am. U., 1941-—. Served with U.S. Army Engrs., World War II. Recipient Rockefeller Pub. Service award, 1959. Mem. Nat. Assn. Housing Ofcls., Nat. Housing Conf., Am. Pub. Health Assn. (chmn. subcom. on occupancy standards of com. on hygiene of housing), Am. Soc. for Pub. Adminstrn., Washington Housing Assn., Citizens Council for Communty Planning, (bd. dirs. Washington 1947), Theta Sigma Lambda, Tau Delta Phi. Contributor of numerous articles in national real estate mags. Home: 9908 Parkwood Dr Bethesda MD Office: Longfellow Bldg Washington DC 20025

SILVERMAN, JACQUES BERNARD, cons. engr.; b. Los Angeles, Aug. 29, 1899; s. Michael Gabriel and Miriam (Silverman) Solomon; E.E., U. Cin., 1923; m. Helen Josephine Hughes, Dec. 15, 1929; 1 dau., Viola Miriam (Mrs. James Donald Clayton). Engr., Cin., Newport & Covington Ry. Co., Covington, Ky., 1932-37; layout engr. elec. projects Louisville Gas and Elec. Co., 1937-46; chief elec. engr. Chanaberry Engring. Co., Inc., Louisville, 1946-52; individual practice as cons. engr., Louisville, 1952-—. Mem. Bd. Elec. Control, City Louisville and Jefferson County, 1955-60. Served with U.S. Army, 1918. Mem. Internat. Assn. Elec. Insps., Ky. Soc. Profl. Engrs. Methodist (mem. ofcl. bd. 1948-51). Mason Responsible for outdoor lighting of Baha-i House of Worship, Wilmette, Ill., 1952. Home and office: 428 Southern Heights West Louisville KY 40214

SILVEY, LARRY PAUL, editor; b. Indpls., Sept. 25, 1938; s. Paul Wachtell and Mabel Lydia (Bartelt) S.; B.A. in Journalism, Okla. State U., 1962; m. Mary Margaret O'Neill, July 13, 1963; children—Scott, Susanne, Stephan, Shannon. Reporter, asst. mng. editor Altus (Okla.) Times Democrat, 1965-67; mgr. communications, editor Tulsa Mag., Met. Tulsa C. of C., 1967-—. Served to 1st lt., C.I.C., AUS, 1962-65. Recipient Media award Nat. Conf. Christians and Jews, 1968. Mem. Am. Assn. Commerce Publs. (treas., dir. 1971-—), Okla. Cath. Diocese Bd. Communications (dir. 1970-—), Arts Commn. Tulsa (dir. 1971-72), Arts Dirs. Club Tulsa (dir.). Club: Tulsa Press (dir. 1972-73). Editor The Great Waterway, commemorative edit. in conjunction with opening of McClellan-Kerr Ark. River Waterway, 1971. Home: 5136 E 27th Pl Tulsa OK 74114 Office: 616 S Boston Av Tulsa OK 74119

SILVEY, THOMAS JESSE, supt. schs.; b. Roston, Ark., June 21, 1912; s. Jesse B. and Viola S. (Bailey) S.; B.S., U. Ark., 1937, M. Ednl. Adminstrn., 1963; m. Bobbie Nell Martin, June 5, 1938; 1 dau., Fredrica Nell. High sch. tchr., basketball coach, Patmos, Ark., 1933-35; adminstrv. officer Agr. Adj. Adminstrs. Office, Faulkner County, Ark., 1937; asst. county agt. Washington County, supr. U. Ark. Agr. Srs. majoring in agrl. extension, 1938, county agrl. agt., 1939-42; tchr. vets. on farm tng., 1945-51; high sch. prin., 1952-53; supt. Bodcaw Schs., 1953-64; supt. Calico Rock (Ark.) Schs., 1964-—; operator farm, 1945-64. Co-organizer, pres. U. Ark. Boys 4-H House, 1936, v.p. Agr. Day Assn. U. Ark., 1937; chmn. Joint State Adv. Council on Sch. Health, 1959-61; dist. commr., mem. exec. com. Boy Scouts Am., 1958-63; mem. Calico Rock City Planning Commn., 1969. Bd. dirs. White River Planning and Devel. Dist. Served with USNR, 1942-45. Recipient State Community Devel. Leadership award, 1968. Mem. N.E.A., Ark. Edn. Assn., Supts. Assn., Am., Ark. sch. adminstrs. assns., Ark. Sch. Bds. Assn., Assn. Sch. Curriculum Devel., Am. Legion (past post comdr.), 40 and 8, S.W. Ark. Schoolmasters Club, S.W. Ark. Poultry Producers Assn. (past pres.), U.S. Poultry and Egg Producers Assn. (past nat. v.p.), Izard County Tchrs. Assn. (pres.), Calico Rock C. of C. (past pres.). Baptist (deacon). Lion. Home: Karla St Calico Rock AR 72519 Office: College St Calico Rock AR 72519

SILVIOUS, OWEN FRANKLIN, music pub., record mfg., mail order co. exec.; b. Luray, Va., Jan. 15, 1939; s. Omey F. and Effie (Jewell) S.; student pub. schs.; m. Nancy A. Gochenour, Aug. 12, 1961 (div.); children—Owen F. II, Eugene F. Pres., Luray Industries, Inc. (Va.), 1966-—, Luray Music Co., 1966-—, Frankie Record Co., Luray, 1966-—. Songwriter, Broadcast Music, Inc., N.Y.C. and Nashville, 1967-—; mng. dir. World Real Estate Investment Fund Ltd., Bahamas, 1971-—, Diamonds Investment Fund Ltd., Bahamas, 1971-—. Served with AUS, 1956-65. Mem. Nat. Songwriters Guild. Home: Luray VA 22835 Office: PO Box 62 Luray VA 22835

SIMCAK, ANDREW, JR., clergyman; b. Garfield, N.J., Aug. 15, 1930; s. Andrew and Justina (Pollack) S.; student Concordia Collegiate Inst., 1944-50, Valparaiso U., summer 1953; B.D., Concordia Sem., St. Louis, 1955; m. Jacqueline Jennie Cardaro, June 5, 1955; children—Timothy Andrew, Sharon Ann, Deborah Marie, Christine Ruth. Ordained to ministry Lutheran Ch., 1955; pastor Grace Luth. Ch., Sequin, Tex., 1955-58, St. Matthew Luth. Ch., San Antonio, 1958-61, St. John Luth. Ch., Corpus Christi, Tex., 1961-69, St. Michael Luth. Ch., Houston, 1969-—. Pastoral adviser Lone Star dist. Luth. Laymen's League, 1971-—; chmn. Tex. dist. Pastor's-Tchrs. Conf., 1971-—, Tex. dist. Commn. on Fraternal Orgns., 1965-—; mem. ad hoc com. to study pastoral approach to lodge problem Mo. Synod Luth. Ch., 1969-71. Home: 4315 Brookfield St Houston TX 77045 Office: 4740 W Orem St Houston TX 77045

SIMMEN, EDWARD ROBERT, educator; b. Galveston, Tex., Nov. 27, 1933; s. Frank Emil and Homoiselle (Tolex) S.; B.A., U. Tex., 1955, M.A., 1959; Ph.D., Tex. Christian U., 1966. Instr. English, Frederick Coll., Portsmouth, Va., 1959-60, Tyler (Tex.) Jr. Coll., 1960-63; asso. prof. English, Pan Am. State U. Tex., Edinburg, 1966-—. Served to lt. USNR, 1955-57. Mem. South Central Modern Lang. Assn., Rio Grande Valley Council Tchrs. English (dir.), Delta Tau Delta. Editor The Chicano: From Caricature to Self-Portrait, 1971; Pain and Promise: The Chicano Today, 1972. Contbr. articles to profl. jours. Home: b Route 1 Box 179 McAllen TX 78501 Office: Pan Am U Edinburg TX 78539

SIMMERMAN, JOHN ROBINSON, auditor; b. Max Meadows, Va., July 17, 1925; s. Thomas Edward and Miriam (Robinson) S.; B.B.A., with Honors, Va. Poly. Inst., 1950 Account clk. Coop. Fertilizer Service of Norfolk, Va., 1950-51, collection officer, 1951-53; agt.-auditor Internal Revenue Service, Norfolk, Va., 1953-56; comptroller Green-Gifford Motor Corp., Norfolk, 1956-62; audit field rev. Chrysler Motors Corp., Detroit, 1962-65, auditor marketing and investments dept., Centerline, Mich., 1965-—. Active Norfolk Y's Men, 1959-61. Served with USNR, 1943-46. C.P.A., Va. Mem. Am. Inst. C.P.A.'s, Va., Tidewater socs. C.P.A.'s, Alpha Kappa Psi, Phi Kappa Phi. Mem. Lynch Anchorage. Presbyn. (treas. Sunday Sch. 1959-60). Home: 911 Spotswood Av Norfolk VA 23517 Office: PO Box 70 Centerline MI 48015

SIMMONS, ALBERT WENDALL, accountant; b. Foshee, Ala., Oct. 21, 1920; s. Albert William and Bessie (Hammac) S.; A.B., Birmingham So. Coll., 1943; postgrad. Northwestern U., 1945-46; m. Martha George McLaughlin, Aug. 2, 1947; children—Sandra Sue (Mrs. Estes), Scott Thomas Wendall. Staff accountant Ernst & Ernst, Birmingham, Ala., 1946-54, mgr. tax dept., 1954-61, partner, 1961-—. Instr. accounting Northwestern U., 1945-46, U. Ala., 1947-56. Bd. dirs., v.p. Goodwill Industries. C.P.A., Ala. Mem. Am. Inst. C.P.A.'s (mem. com. on fed. taxation), Ala. Soc. C.P.A.'s, Asso. Industries Ala., Birmingham C. of C., Ala. C. of C., Omicron Delta Kappa, Beta Alpha Psi. Methodist. Kiwanian. Home: 3117 Ryecroft Rd Birmingham AL 35223 Office: First Nat Bldg Birmingham AL 35203

SIMMONS, BARRY DAVID, dentist; b. Atlanta, Jan. 7, 1937; s. Perry and Vivian Hannah (Folkman) S.; D.D.S., Emory U., 1963. Practice of dentistry, Athens, Ga., 1963-—. Active in vol. dental program in underdeveloped countries. Served with AUS, 1956-59. Named Young Man of the Year, Athens, 1971, One of 10 Outstanding Young Men, 1971, Ga.'s Outstanding Young Men, 1971, all U.S. Jaycees. Mem. Am., Ga. dental assns., Eastern Dist. Dental Soc., Canadian-Am. Med. Dental Assn., Delta Sigma Delta. Jewish religion. Mem. B'nai B'rith. Home and office: 847 S Milledge Av Athens GA 30601

SIMMONS (JOSEPH) EDGAR, educator, poet; b. Natchez, Miss., May 28, 1921; s. Joseph Edgar and Dorothy (Clark) S.; student Copiah-Lincoln Jr. Coll., 1939-41; B.S., M.A., Columbia U.; postgrad. U. Paris (France), 1953-54; m. Kathleen Ellen Florence Vera Floyd, Jan.2, 1954; children—Joseph Edgar III, Edward Floyd. Instr. English, DePauw U., 1948-50; columnist Irish Press, Dublin, 1954-55; editorial writer New Orleans Times Picayune, 1956; asst. prof. English, Coll. William and Mary, 1955-57; mng. editor Natchez Times, 1958-59; lectr. So. Ill. U., 1962-63; asst. prof. English Miss. Coll., Clinton, 1963-66; dir. creative writing English dept. U. Tex. at El Paso, 1966-—. Served with USAAF, 1942-44, AUS, 1944-45. Recipient Bellamann Lit. award for poetry Bellamann Lit. Found. 1964. Mem. Am. Soc. for Aesthetics, Modern Lang. Assn. Methodist. Author: Pocahontas and Other Poems, 1957; Driving to Biloxi (award Tex. Inst. Letters, Writers Roundup award Austin Profl. chpt. Theta Sigma Phi), 1968; contbg. author: New Southern Writing, 1965; New Directions 20; The Honey and the Gall, 1967; Red Clay Reader, 1967; Poems Southwest, 1968; Decade of Poems Southern Poetry Review, 1969; Doors into Poetry, 1970; New York Times Book of Poems, 1970. Contbr. poems to publs. including Yale Rev., New Republic, Nation, Prairie Schooner, Chgo. Rev., Harper's mag., Mass. Rev., N.Y. Times, other periodicals and books, also book reviews to St. Louis Post-Dispatch, Kansas City Star. Home: 3116 Piedmont El Paso TX 79902

SIMMONS, FREDERICK MARTIN, architect; b. Paris, Tex., Jan. 21, 1915; s. John Fred and Rosa (Mauney) S.; student N.C. State U., 1934-35, Warren Sch. Aeronautics, 1936, Aero Industries Tech. Inst., 1937, The Citadel, 1940-44; m. Eunice May Sharpe, Dec. 17, 1937; children—Fredrika Carol, Suzanne Sharpe. Draftsman SP2-8, U.S. Naval Base, Charleston, S.C., 1938-56, V.W. Breeze, Architect, Shelby, N.C., 1946-49; architect Fred M. Simmons, Shelby, N.C., 1949-53, 56-—, J.N. Pease & Co., Charlotte, 1953-56; pres. Cleveland Aircraft Co., 1970-—. Comml. pilot, 1944-—; instr. CAA Flight & Ground Sch., 1948-—; chief engring. and pub. works Cleve County Dept. Civil Def., 1959-—; mem. fine arts com. N.C. Luth. Synod, 1967-—; dir. county fire vol. dept., 1961-70. Democratic candidate N.C. Ho. Reps., 1964. Mem. A.I.A., Nat. Geog. Soc., Antique Airplane Assn. Found. Lutheran. Comdr. first Coast Guard Aux. Air Squadron organized Charleston, S.C., 1946; designed first air conditioned sch. in N.C. with fallout protection for 1200 students. Home: Route 5 Box 129 Shelby NC 28150 Office: 924 E Dixon Blvd Shelby NC 28150

SIMMONS, HOWARD HELMUTH, educator; b. N.Y.C., June 26, 1915; s. Frederick Herbert and Martha Marie (Winkler) Simon; certificate in commerce U. San Francisco, 1941; A.B., George Washington U., 1949; M.B.A., Stanford, 1951; postgrad. Am. U., 1966-69, N.Y.U., 1954-56; m. Ruth Ellen Barnett, Dec. 27, 1941; children—Marla (Mrs. Bruce Betzel), Howard Keith. Commd. 2d lt. U.S. Army, 1937, advanced through grades to col., 1958; comptroller Seventh Army, 1953-54; mem. joint programs office Joint Chiefs Staff, 1959-61; pres. Finance Corps Bd., 1963-64; dir. accounting Comptroller of the Army, 1965-66; chmn. social sci. dept. No. Va. Community Coll., Annandale, 1966, dean student services, 1967-71, prof. bus. mgmt., 1971-—. Adj. prof. Southeastern U., 1964-66, chmn. dept. financial adminstrn., 1965-66. Pres. Anglo-Am. Schs., Athens, Greece, 1952-53. Decorated Legion of Merit with oak leaf cluster; recipient Outstanding award Fed. Govt. Accountants Assn., 1965. Mem. Am. Soc. Mil. Comptrollers (v.p. 1965-66), Am. Econ. Assn., Am. Accounting Assn., North Ridge Citizens Assn., Alpha Phi Omega. Democrat. Lutheran. Home: 3202 Old Dominion Blvd Alexandria VA 22305 Office: 8333 Little River Turnpike Annandale VA 22003

SIMMONS, JAMES BENJAMIN, lawyer; b. Whiteville, Tenn., Aug. 11, 1908; s. James Thomas and Mary Elizabeth (Sammons) S.; LL.B., Cumberland U., 1927; J.D., George Washington U., 1938, LL.M., M.P.L., 1939; m. Dorothy Payne, Feb. 26, 1943; children—Mary Sue, Jo Ann, Nancy Marie, Kathie Lorraine. Admitted to D.C. bar, 1939, Va. bar, 1945, Md. bar, 1948; practiced in D.C., 1949-—; now partner Ward & Simmons; officer, dir., White Hall Manor, Inc., 1948-—. Mem. Am., D.C., Md., Va. bar assns., Am. Judicature Soc., Internat. Platform Assn., Am. Acad. Polit. and Social Sci., Phi Beta Gamma (chief justice of the Washington alumni chpt. 1956-57). Office: 850 Sligo Av Silver Spring MD 20910

SIMMONS, JOHN WALTON, govt. ofcl.; b. Orange, Tex., Jan. 17, 1911; s. Walton Byron and Lucile (Ball) S.; B.S. in Chem. Engring., Tex. A. and M. Coll., 1931; m. Daisy B. Simmons; 1 son, Barre W. Chem. engr. The Tex. Co., 1931-47, on Bahrein Island, Persian Gulf, 1938-41; dir. Orange Indsl. Devel. Commn., exec. v.p. Orange C. of C. 1947-56; exec. v.p., gen. mgr. Sabine River Authority of Tex. (state agy.), Orange, 1956-—. Spl. cons. to Gov. Tex. on Water affairs, 1970-—. Dir. Tex. Water Conservation Assn., 1949-—, pres., 1962-69; pres., dir. Sabine River Authority of Tex., 1949-56; mem. Gov.'s Water Com., 1953-54, 57; v.p. Nat. Rivers and Harbors Congress, Washington, 1954-68, nat. dir. 1968-71; dir. Water Resources Congress, 1971-—; mem. exec. com., 1972-—; mem. U.S. nat. commn. Internat. Commn. on Irrigation and Drainage. Served from 2d lt. to lt. col., USAAF, 1942-46; PTO, 1945; dep. air chem. officer Hdqrs. AAF, Washington, 1946. Recipient Outstanding Citizen award Greater Orange Area C. of C., 1967, Conservation Service award U.S. Dept. Interior, 1967; TWCA Ann. Conv. Dedication award 1970; Water Conservation Individual award Ft. Worth C. of C., 1970. Mem. Am. Chem. Soc., Tex. Soc. Profl. Engrs., Am. Water Works Assn., Nat. Water Resources Assn. (nat. dir. 1969-—, treas. 1972), Municipal Finance Officers Assn. Club: Sportsmens of Texas. Home: 1955 Camelot Dr Apt 7 Orange TX 77630 Office: PO Box 579 Orange TX 77630

SIMMONS, MABEL CLARKE, journalist; b. Tuscumbia, Mo., Sept. 5, 1899; d. Charles H. and Mattie (Clark) Clarke; B.J., U. Mo., 1923; m. George Evans Simmons, June 25, 1921; children—George Clarke, Kirksey. Reporter, Nashville Tennessean, 1922-24; free lance writer, 1925-52; literary editor New Orleans Times Picayune, 1954-—, also travel editor. Home: 2439 Nashville Av New Orleans LA 70115 Office: Times-Picayune 3800 Howard Av New Orleans LA 70140

SIMMONS, RICHARD GLENN, city mgr.; b. Kissimmee, Fla., Aug. 6, 1928; s. Henry T. and R. L. (Fletcher) S.; B.S., U. Fla., 1950, M.A., 1951; m. Kay Upson, July 2, 1955; children—Sandra, Susan. City mgr., Melbourne, Fla., 1954-55, 67-69, Haines City, Fla., 1956-59, Winter Park, Fla., 1959-67, West Palm Beach, Fla., 1969-—; intern, Kissimmee, Fla., 1950, Phoenix, 1952-53. Past pres. Central Fla. Council for Hard of Hearing Children. Bd. dirs. United Fund of Palm Beach County. Served from 1st lt. to capt. USAF, 1955-57. Recipient Distinguished Service award Jr. C. of C., 1964, awards of merit City of Winter Park, 1967, Melbourne, 1969. Mem. Internat., Fla. (past pres., dir.) city mgrs. assns., West Palm Beach C. of C., Fla. Chi Phi Assn. (bd. mem.). Methodist (chmn. adminstrv. bd.). Kiwanian (past pres., dir.). Home: 356 Potter Rd West Palm Beach FL 33405 Office: City Mgr's Office City Hall West Palm Beach FL 33402

SIMMONS, ROBERT FRANCIS, educator; b. Quincy, Mass., May 14, 1925; s. Timothy Francis and Jacqueline (Eaton) S.; B.A., U. So. Cal., 1949, M.A., 1950, Ph.D. in Psychology, 1954; m. Patricia June Enderson, Oct. 10, 1950; children—Sandra, Erin, Steven, Kelly, Darcy. Research psychologist Psychol.Services, Inc., Los Angeles, 1949-54; research statistician Douglas Aircraft Corp., Los Angeles, 1954-55; psychologist Rand Corp., Santa Monica, Cal., 1955-57; head lang. processes research Systems Devel. Corp., Santa Monica, 1957-68; prof. computer sci. U. Tex., Austin, 1968-—. Lectr. psychology U. So. Cal., Los Angeles, 1965; prof. linguistics U. Cal. at Los Angeles, 1966. Served with USNR, 1942-46. Mem. Am. Psychol. Assn., Assn. Computer Machines. Contbr. articles on computer processing natural langs. to profl. jours. Home: 1408 Ridgecrest St Austin TX 78746 Office: U Tex Dept Computer Scis Austin TX 78712

SIMMONS, ROY LEONARD, mfg. co. exec.; b. Henderson, Tenn., Aug. 31, 1923; s. Roy Leonard and Katie Lee (Privett) S.; student Union U., Jackson, Tenn., 1946; B.S., U. Tenn., 1949, M.S., 1950; postgrad. Sch. Mgmt. Inst. Emory U., 1968; m. Nanci Ellis, July 12, 1958; children—Kent Freeman, Elizabeth Lee. With Lockheed Ga. Co., Marietta, 1951-—, pub. relations coordinator, 1958-68, mgr. community affairs and customer relations, 1968-—; dir. Smyrna Bank, Smyrna Investment Co. Pres. Kennestone Hosp. Guild, 1971-72; chmn. various community charity drives. Chmn. trustees Fellowship Christian Athletes, 1971-72. Recipient Honor Key, Civitan Internat., 1968, Community Service award C. of C., 1970, U.S. Savs. Bond award U.S. Treasury, 1970; named Lockheed Mgmt. Club Man of Year, 1954, Citizen of Year Smyrna, 1967, Civitan of Year, 1964. Mem. Pub. Relations Soc. Am. (accredited), Cobb County (pres. 1967), Smyrna (pres. 1965) chambers commerce, Civitan Internat. (internat. v.p. 1960-62, internat. trustee 1963-64). Sigma Alpha Epsilon. Baptist. Club: Cherokee Town and Country (Atlanta). Home: 104 Skyline Trail Smyrna GA 30080 Office: South Cobb Dr Marietta GA 30060

SIMMONS, SAMUEL JOHN, JR., govt. ofcl.; b. Phila., Sept. 3, 1909; s. Samuel John and Lillian (Simmers) S.; grad. Lehigh U., 1933; m. Evelyn Marie Anderson, Jan. 16, 1943; children—Susan A., Joyce A., Anne L. With Aluminum Co. Am., Pitts., 1934-69, gen. mgr. sales devel. div., 1959-61, v.p. industry sales, 1961-69, v.p. product sales, 1963-67, v.p., asst. gen. sales manager, 1967-69; asst. sec. equal opportunity Dept. Housing and Urban Devel., Washington, 1969-—; dir. Alcoa Bldg. Products, Inc. Mem. Delta Upsilon. Clubs: Duquesne (Pitts.); Oakmont (Pa.) Country; Seaview Country (Absecon, N.J.); University. Home: 111 Forest Dr Pittsburgh PA 15238 Office: Dept Housing and Urban Devel Washington DC 20410

SIMMONS, SAMUEL WILLIAM, govt. ofcl.; b. Benton County, Miss., June 5, 1907; s. Britt L. and Ida E. (Pegram) S.; B.Sc. with honors, Miss. State U., 1931; A.M., George Washington U., 1934; Ph.D., Ia. State U., 1938; m. Lois Grantham, Aug. 5, 1928; children—Samuel William, Grant P. With U.S. Dept. Agr., Bur. Entomology, 1931-44; with USPHS, 1944-71, dir. Carter Meml. Lab., 1944-47, chief tech. devel. br., 1947-53, chief technology br. communicable disease center 1953-66; chief pesticides program Nat. Communicable Disease Center Atlanta, 1966-68; dir. div. pesticide community studies FDA, 1968-71; dir. div. pesticide community studies Environmental Protection Agy., Washington, 1971-—. Vis. lectr. tropical pub. health Harvard, 1952-67; asso. preventive medicine and community health Emory U., 1957-—. USPHS rep. Fed. Com. on Pest Control. Recipient Alumni Achievement award George Washington U., 1946, Alumni Centennial Citation award Ia. State U., 1958, Distinguished Service medal USPHS, 1965, William Crawford Gorgas medal Assn. Mil. Surgeons U.S., 1968. Hon. cons. Army Med. Library, 1940-53. Adv. bd. Inst. Agrl. Medicine, U. Ia. Sch. Medicine, U.S.-Japan Com. on Sci. Cooperation. Diplomate Am. Bd. Microbiology. Fellow Am. Soc. Tropical Medicine and Hygiene (councilor 1953), Chem. Specialties Mfrs. Assns. (interdepartmental com. pest control, subcom. vector control inter-agy. com. water resources, chmn. 1964-66), U.S.-Mexico Border Health Assn., WHO (chmn. com. on pesticides 1951, 56, 57), A.M.A., (com. on insecticides 1950-59, com. on toxicology 1960), Research Soc. Am., Entomol. Soc. Am., Nat. Malaria Soc. (sec.-treas. 1951), Nat. Environmental Health Assn., Agrl. Research Inst., Horological Socs., Am. Mosquito Control Assn., Armed Forces Pest Control Bd., Nat. Research Council, Sigma Xi, Phi Kappa Phi, Gamma Sigma Delta, Los Hidalgos. Contbr. articles profl. jours. Editor and co-author, The Insecticide DDT and Its Significance, vol. II. Contbr. to Human and Veterinary Medicine, 1959. Home: 2050 Blackfox Dr NE Atlanta GA 30345 Office: 4770 Buford Hwy Chamblee GA 30341

SIMMONS, STACY EARL, architect; b. Jackson, Miss., July 26, 1938; s. Andrew Henry and Ercell Lucille (Putnam) S.; B.Arch., Auburn U., 1961; m. Sara Jo Shields, Dec. 19, 1957; 1 dau., Rache Michelle. Draftsman, Painter, Weeks & McCarty, Knoxville, Tenn., 1961-63; architect Freeman-White Assos., Charlotte, N.C., 1964-70; architect, interior designer, pres. Omnia Design, Inc., Charlotte, 1970-—. Recipient South Atlantic Regiona Design award A.I.A., 1966, South Atlantic Regional Design award, 1970. Mem. A.I.A. (dir. Charlotte sect.), Am. Inst. Interior Designers, Guild Religious Architecture, Phi Kappa Tau, Phi Mu Alpha. Democrat. Presbyn. Designer, Hamlet (N.C.) Sch. Nursing, 1965, Omnia Design Offices, Charlotte, 1968; Farmville (N.C) United Methodist Ch., 1971. Office: PO Box 1843 Charlotte NC 28201 PO Box 1843 Charlotte NC 28201 Home: 9331 Providence Rd Matthews NC 28105

SIMMONS, THOMAS JEFFERSON, editor; b. Dallas, Aug. 13, 1914; s. John Middleton and Ada May (Lindop) S.; student Jefferson Sch. Law, 1932-33; m. Jean Adelaide Webb, Nov. 11, 1939; 1 dau., Susan Adelaide. Reporter Dallas Jour., 1931-34; reporter, editor Dallas Morning News, 1934-—; journalism instr. So. Meth. U., 1947-62. Served with AUS, 1944-46. Mem. Sigma Delta Chi. Christian Scientist. Clubs: Kiwanian (past pres.), Press of Dallas (past pres.).Home: 3601 Shenandoah Dallas TX 75205 Office: Communications Center Dallas TX 75222

SIMMONS, WILLIAM ISAAC, dentist; b. Waco, Tex., Feb. 14, 1924; s. Jared Claude and Blanche (Schwarz) S.; D.D.S., Loyola U., New Orleans, 1946; certificate in orthodontics, U. Pa., 1950; m. Evelyn Kottle, June 11, 1967; children—Jared Claude, Walter Neil, Gina Denise. Tchr., U. Tex. Dental Sch., 1951; pvt. practice dentistry, specializing in orthodontics, Shreveport, La., 1951-—. Served with USAF, 1946-48. Mem. Am. Dental Assn. (v.p. 4th Dist.), Am. Orthodontic Soc., Royal Soc. Health. Jewish religion. Mason. Clubs: Pieremont Oaks Tennis, Petroleum (Shreveport); Barksdale Air Force Officers. Office: 2042 Line Av Shreveport LA 71104 also 3019 Old Minden Rd Bossier City LA 71010

SIMMONS, WILLIAM LEWIS, dentist; b. Greer, S.C., Jan. 31, 1934; s. Newton Hughy and Marion Pauline (Culbreth) S.; B.S., U. S.C., 1960; D.D.S., U. Tenn., 1964; m. Billie Hope Golden, June 24, 1955; children— Mark Golden, Warren Lewis. Practice dentistry, Bennettsville, S.C., 1964-67, Anderson, S.C., 1967-—; mem. staff Anderson Meml. Hosp. 1967-—. Pres. Whitehall P.T.A., 1970-72, pres. dist. 5, 1971-72; chmn. Cancer Bd., 1970—. Bd. dirs. YMCA. Served with USAF, 1952-57. Mem. Am., S.C., Anderson (sec. council 1969—), Piedmont dental assns., S.C. Dentists Anesthesiology Assn., Royal Soc. Health (Eng.), Alpha Omicron. Home: 513 Timber Lane Anderson SC 29201 Office: 1109 N Fant St Anderson SC 29201

SIMMONS, WILLIAM PHELPS, JR., lawyer; b. Jacksonville, Fla., July 1, 1910; s. William Phelps and Lillie (Pepper) S.; A.B., U. Fla., 1934, LL.B., 1934; m. Clara Mae Noble, June 22, 1935 (dec. Feb. 1967); 1 son, William Noble; m. 2d, Evaline R. Underwood, Feb. 24, 1968. Admitted to Fla. bar 1934; asst. counsel Fla. R.R. Comm., Tallahassee 1936-41; practiced in Miami, Fla., 1945—; mem. firm Shutts and Bowen, 1949—. Mem. Fla. Jud. Council, 1958-62. Trustee U. Fla. Found., 1953—. Served to lt. col. AUS, 1941-45; brig. gen. ret. Fla. Army N.G. Mem. Am. (ho. of dels. 1969—), Dade County (pres. 1957-58) bar assns., Fla. Bar (pres. 1967-68), Miami-Dade County C. of C. (pres. 1961-62), Chi Phi, Phi Alpha Delta. Democrat. Mem. Disciples of Christ Ch. (elder). Elk. Club: Miami Exchange (pres. 1955). Home: 5051 SW 85th St Miami FL 33143 Office: First Nat Bank Bldg Miami Fla 33131

SIMMS, BEVERLY SINGLETON, lawyer; b. Barnwell, S.C., Aug. 15, 1910; s. Charles Carroll and Fanny (Maher) S.; LL.B., Nat. U., 1931; J.D., George Washington U. Admitted to D.C. bar, 1931, since practiced in Washington; atty. Railroad Retirement Bd., 1934-38; hearing examiner ICC, 1938-51; pvt. practice, 1951—; asso. Wrape & Hernly, 1951-58; mem. firm Rhodes, Simms, & Boss and predecessor, 1958—. Served to capt. with AUS, 1942-46; ETO. Mem. Motor Carrier Lawyers Assn. (pres. 1967-68), Am., Fed. bar assns., Bar Assn. of D.C., Judge Advs. Assn., Am. Judicature Soc., Am. Legion, Mil. Order Purple Heart, Sigma Delta Kappa. Clubs: Kenwood Golf and Country, Army and Navy. Home: 3903 Morrison St NW Washington DC 20015 Office: 1100 17th St NW Washington 20036

SIMMS, HARRY WILLIAM, banker; b. Chgo., Feb. 21, 1928; s. Harry William and Rosamond Lorena (DeLee) S.; student U. Chgo., 1947-48; B.A., U. Ill., 1951, J.D., 1952; postgrad. Rutgers U. Grad. Sch. Banking, 1960-62; m. Jane Lu Cook, June 27, 1953; children—Michael A., Kenneth W., Robert S., Elizabeth A., John E. Admitted to Ill. bar, 1952; with Tex. Commerce Bank, Houston, 1952—, mgr. trust dept., 1966—, exec. v.p., 1971—. Bd. dirs. Houston Symphony, 1970, Neighborhood Day Care Assn., 1969-70. Served with AUS, 1946-47. Mem. Houston Corp. Fiduciary Assn. (pres., 1965-66), Phi Alpha Delta. Club: Houston. Home: 342 Tamerlaine St Houston TX 77024 Office: PO Box 2558 Houston TX 77001

SIMMS, LEROY ALANSON, editor, publisher; b. Emelle, Ala., Sept. 17, 1905; s. John Thomas and Minnie Epes (Thomas) S.; student U. Ill., 1924-25; m. Flora Virginia Hammill, June 30, 1926 (dec. Oct. 1966); 1 dau., Lucie Grey (Mrs. Charles Clifford Grubbs); m. 2d, Martha H. Richardson, May 17, 1969. Reporter Birmingham (Ala.) News, 1925; reporter, asst. city editor Tampa (Fla.) Morning Tribune, 1925-26; city editor Birmingham Post, 1927-29, mng. editor, 1930-31; copy editor Newspaper Enterprise Assn. Service, Inc., Cleve., 1931-32; day editor Asso. Press, Birmingham, 1933-38, corr., 1939-58; mng. editor Birmingham News, 1959-61; editor Huntsville (Ala.) Times, 1961—, v.p., dir., 1963—, pub., 1964—. Bd. dirs. United Givers Fund; bd. dirs. Huntsville Indsl. Expansion Com., pres. 1970. Mem. Ala. Asso. Press Assn. (sec. 1939-58, pres. 1965-66), Birmingham Press Club (past v.p., past dir.), Ala. Press, Assn. (dir. 1964-65), Am., So. newspaper pubs. assns., Am. Soc. Newspaper Editors, Sigma Delta Chi (pres. Ala. profl. chpt.; chmn. Ala. 1960), Theta Chi. Clubs: Rotary, Huntsville Country, Willowbrook Country. Home: 1 Cruse Alley SE Huntsville AL 35801 Office: Huntsville Times Meml Pkwy Huntsville AL 35807

SIMMS, STEWART BROADUS, clergyman; b. Raleigh, N.C., Apr. 9, 1921; s. Robert Nirwana and Virginia Adelaide (Egerton) S.; B.A., Wake Forest Coll., 1942; B.D., S.W. Bapt. Theol. Sem., Fort Worth, 1947; m. Mary Ann Canaday, Jan. 2, 1943; children—Stewart Broadus, Robert Franklin, Carol Ann. Ordained to ministry Bapt. Ch., 1940; pastor Bailey (N.C.) Ch., 1939-40. Calvary Ch., Raleigh, N.C., 1940-42, First Ch., Grandview, Tex., 1943-45. Ridglea Ch., Fort Worth, 1945-48. Meml. Ch., Williamston, N.C., 1948-51, Woodland Heights Ch., Richmond, Va., 1951-61, 1st Ch., Greer, S.C., 1961—. Moderator Roanoke Bapt. Assn., 1950-51; exec. com. Richmond Bapt. Assn., 1954-61; pres. Richmond Bapt. Pastors Conf., 1960; v.p. Bapt. Gen. Assn., Va. 1961; mem. Va. Bapt. Gen. Bd.; mem. Bapt. Extension Bd. Va., 1959-61; exec. com. So. Bapt. Conv., 1967—, parliamentarian, 1970, 1st v.p., 1971, pres., 1972, chmn., 1972. Mem. Greer Bi-Racial Com. Trustee S.C. Bapt. Hosps., 1963-67, 69—; bd. dirs. Greer Relief Agy. Clubs: Rotary (Grandview, Tex.); Kiwanis (Fort Worth and Williamston, Tex., Greer, S.C.). Home: 308 W Poinsett St Greer SC 29651 Office: First Bapt Ch PO Box 531 Greer SC 29651

SIMON, BERNARD, assn. exec.; b. West New York, N.J., May 7, 1920; s. Max and Mary (Kell) S.; B.S. in Journalism, N.Y. U., 1941; m. Dorothy Ligeti, May 24, 1942; children—Gary Leonard, Linda Fran, David Judah. Reporter Religious News Service, N.Y.C., 1946-47; asso. dir. pub. relations anti-defamation league B'nai B'rith, N.Y.C., 1947-55, dir. pub. relations B'nai B'rith, 1955—; editor The Nat. Jewish Monthly mag., Washington, 1970—. Served with AUS, 1942-46. Mem. Pub. Relations Soc. Am., Am. Jewish Pub. Relations Soc. Jewish religion. Mem. B'nai B'rith. Club: National Press (Washington). Home: 2405 Colston Dr Silver Springs MD 20910 Office: 1640 Rhode Island Av NW Washington DC 20036

SIMON, DOROTHEA JONES (MRS. GEORGE MANNING SIMON), Christian Sci. practitioner; b. Rayville, La.; d. Clarude Charles and Ada (Ellis) Jones; certificate home econs. St. Mary's Sch., Raleigh, N.C., 1924; m. George Manning Simon, Jan. 2, 1927; 1 son, George Manning. Joined Christian Sci. Sc.; Christian Sci. practitioner, Baton Rouge, 1947—. Mem. Com. Arsenal Museum, 1960; mem. Baton Rouge Found. Hist. La., Inc. (life). Chmn. bldg. trustees Christian Sci. Orgn., La. State U., 1961—. Mem., Young Women's Christian Orgn. (life), Colonial Dames of Am. (life), D.A.R., Delta Delta Delta. Club: Woman's. Home: 2995 Reymond Av Baton Rouge LA 70808

SIMON, GEORGE ALEXANDER, realtor; b. Antwerp, Belgium, Feb. 17, 1921 (came to U.S. 1940, naturalized 1942); s. Alfred and Hilde (Weinberg) S.; student U. Lauzanne, Switzerland, 1937-39; m. Charlotte Boshnack, Sept. 15, 1946; children—Kathi Michelle, Andrew Gerald. Pres., George A. Simon-Realtors, Miami, Fla., 1948—, Ridge Land Corp., Simco Devel. Corp.; dir. Bahamas Internat. Trust Co., Ltd., U.S. Mgmt. Corp., First Internat. Realty Securities Fund. Site chmn. Operation Miami for Underprivileged Children, 1968; real estate team capt. United Fund, 1966-68. Trustee Cedars of Lebanon Hosp. Served to maj. CIC, AUS, 1942-46; ETO. Decorated Bronze Star medal with cluster, Purple Heart with cluster; Belgian Fourragere. Mem. Fla. Assn. Realtors (dir., com. chmn.), Diamond Pin Club of Fla. Assn. Realtors (past pres.), Nat. Inst. Real Estate Brokers (past state chmn.), Internat. Real Estate Fedn., Nat. Real Estate Fliers Assn. (past pres.), Am. Soc. Appraisers, Nat. Assn. Real Estate Bds. (dir.), Nat. Inst. Farm and Land Brokers (past pres.), Miami Bd. Realtors (pres. 1961), Miami-Dade County (past pres. internat. affairs council) chambers commerce, C. of C. of Ams. (past pres.), Res. Officers Assn. (past v.p.), Omega Tau Rho. Home: 1624 Micanopy Av Miami FL 33133 Office: 100 S Orange Av Orlando FL 32801

SIMON, H(UEY) PAUL, lawyer; b. Lafayette, La., Oct. 19, 1923; s. Jules and Ida (Rogers) S.; B.S., U. Southwestern La., 1943; J.D., Tulane U., 1947; m. Carolyn Perkins, Aug. 6, 1949; 1 son, John Clark. Admitted to La. bar, 1947, since practiced New Orleans; asst. prof. advanced accounting U. Southwestern La., 1944-45; prin. in C.P.A. firm Haskins & Sells, New Orleans, 1945-57; partner Deutsch, Kerrigan & Stiles, New Orleans, 1957—. C.P.A., La., Miss. Mem. Am. Judicature Soc., Internat. (com. on securities issues and trading 1970—), Inter-Am., Am. (mem. com. ct. procedure 1958—), La., New Orleans bar assns., Am. Inst. C.P.A.'s, New Orleans Assn. Notaries, Soc. La. C.P.A.'s, C. of C. (mem. council), Tulane Tax Inst. (program com 1960—), Am. Accounting Assn., Nat. Assn. Accountants, Am. Assn. Atty.-C.P.A.'s, Tulane Alumni Assn., Phi Delta Phi (past pres. New Orleans chpt.), Sigma Pi Alpha. Clubs: Young Men's Business (legislation com.), Lamplighter, Press, Toastmasters, New Orleans Country, Petroleum (New Orleans); International House; Paul Morphy Chess. Author: Changes Effected by the Louisiana Trust Code, 1965; Gifts to Minors And the Parent's Obligation of Support, 1968. Asso. editor La. C.P.A., 1956-60; mem. bd. editors Tulane Law Rev., 1945-46. Home: 6075 Canal Blvd New Orleans LA 70124 Office: 1 Shell Sq Suite 4700 New Orleans LA 70139

SIMON, JOSEPH WESLEY, JR., assn. exec.; b. New Orleans, Aug. 12, 1907; s. Joseph W. and Jeanne (Jaubert) S.; B.A., Tulane U., 1928; m. Dorothy L. Gaiennie, Nov. 4, 1950; children—Diane, Barbara. With Gulf Oil Corp., New Orleans, 1930-63; became dir. governmental affairs and pub. relations New Orleans C. of C., 1963, now exec. v.p.; dir. Flambeau Pub. Co., New Orleans. Mem. exec com. Met. Crime Commn. Bd. dirs. New Orleans chpt. A.R.C.; bd. dirs., past pres. Met. Safety Council, New Orleans Jazz and Heritage Found. Mem. New Orleans C. of C. (pres. 1962), Oceanography Soc., Cath. Internat. House, Phi Kappa Sigma. Kiwanian (pres. 1958). Home: 2516 Pine St New Orleans LA 70125 Office: 301 Camp St New Orleans LA 70130

SIMON, KENNETH ALAN, govt. ofcl.; b. Mt. Jewett, Pa., Feb. 28, 1916; s. George Preston and Bertha Irene (Rathburn) S.; B.S., Lock Haven State Coll., 1950; M.Ed., Pa. State Coll., 1953; Ed.D., Pa. State U., 1959 div.; children—Kenneth A., Carol (Mrs. William Norfolk). Prin., Lafayette Twp. Sch. Dist., McKean County, Pa., 1951-55; research and statis. program specialist Pa. Dept. Pub. Instrn., Harrisburg, 1955-59; chief Reference, Estimates and Projections br. Nat. Center for Edn. Statistics, U.S. Office Edn., Washington, 1959—. Cons., Ministry Edn., Jamaican Govt., 1965; part-time lectr. Am. U., 1964, U. Md., 1965. Served with USMCR, 1943-45; PTO. Recipient Superior Service award Dept. Health, Edn. and Welfare, 1970. Mem. N.E.A. (life). Club: Capitol Yacht (Washington). Contbr. articles to profl. lit. Home: 1301 Delaware Av SW Washington DC 20024 Office: 400 Maryland Av SW Washington DC 20202

SIMON, LORENA COTTS (MRS. SAMUEL C. SIMON), music tchr.; b. Sherman, Tex., Jan. 16, 1897; d. George Godfrey and Willie (Jones) Cotts; student Am. Conservatory, summer 1938; Julliard Music Sch., summer 1939; diploma Sherwood Music Sch., 1941; D. Lit. Leadership, Internat. Acad. Leadership, Philippine Islands, 1967; Mus. D., St. Olav's Acad., Sweden, 1969; L.H.D., Nother Pontifical Acad.; m. Samuel C. Simon, Nov. 6, 1918 (dec.). Tchr. violin, piano, theory and harmony, Port Arthur, Tex., 1919—. Organizer, dir. Schubert's Violin Choir, Port Arthur, 1919-55. Judge Internat. Poetry Peace Award Contest, 1965. Works of poetry in Internat. Poetry Archives, Manchester Central Library, Eng., 1965. Named Poet Laureate of Tex. 1961; Poet Laureate of Magnolia Dist., 1962-64; Poet Laureate of Port Arthur, 1962—; recipient gold plaque Tex. Fedn. Women's Club, 1962, spl. award 1st place in poetry and music Tex. heritage dept., 1963, spl. award in music and fine arts and outstanding service awards, 1965; 1st place in poetry, 1966; Medal of Honor and Diploma of Merit, Centro Studi Scambi Internat., Rome, Italy, 1965, Silver, Gold medals of merit, 1967, diploma of merit, 1966, 67; Hon. Poet Laureate-Musician, United Poets Laureate Internat., 1966, Karte of award, 1968, Hon. Internat. Catholic Poet Laureate, 1968; Contemporary Internat. Poet Hall of Fame, 1968; honored by Tex. Senate and Ho. of Reps., 1967. Mem. Internat. Platform Assn., Nat., Tex. press womens assns., Nat. Council Cath. Women, Nat. Guild Piano Tchrs. (charter mem.; adjudicator), Am. Coll. Musicians (adjudicator), Am. Poetry League, Poets Soc. Tex. (counselor 1967—, critic judge), Am. Poets Fellowship Soc. Corp., U.S., UN Assn.-U.S.A., Alpha Delta Kappa. Clubs: Writers' (pres. 1963-64), Symphony. Author: The Golden Key, 1958; From My Heart (1st place award Ann. Poetry Writers Contest of Tex. Press Women's Assn. 1961), 1959; Children's Story Hour (1st place award Nat. Fedn. Press Women's Ann. Writers' Contest 1962), 1960; In Music Land, 1965; That Blessed Night, 1966. Songs pub. include Live Expectantly, 1962, In Search for Growth, 1963, Freedom's Light, 1963, What Can I Do for Jesus, 1963. Donor funds for constrn. of churches in Africa. Address: 411 Fifth Av Port Arthur TX 77640

SIMON, ROY MICHAEL, architect; b. Delray Beach, Fla., Oct. 24, 1930; s. Alexander A. and Linda (Zaine) S.; B.S., Ga. Inst. Tech., 1952, B.Arch., 1953; m. Mary Elizabeth Wilder, July 29, 1961; children—Roy Michael, Laura Lee, John Christopher. Apprentice Kenneth Jacobson, architect, Delray Beach, Fla., 1949-58, asso., 1958-59; individual practice architecture, Delray Beach, 1959—. Mem. Recreation Adv. Bd., 1957-59; sec. Bd. Adjustments, 1959, 61, 63, chmn., 1960, 62, 64, 66; mem. Delray Beach (Fla.) Planning and Zoning Commn. Bd. dirs. Community Chest, 1959-68. Served to capt., USAF, 1954-56. Named one of 5 outstanding young men of year Delray Beach, 1962; Mem. Jr. C. of C. (pres. 1959-60; state dir. 1960-61, 1963-64, Jaycee of Year, 1961, 63, recipient Distinguished Service award 1962, 65); C. of C. (dir. 1959—; pres. 1964-65, 68-69), Ga. Tech. Alumni Assn. (pres. 1961-62), A.I.A. (pres. Spanish River sec. 1971), Fla. Assn. Architects, Fla. Assn. Am. Inst. Architects (mem. exec. com. Palm Beach chpt. 1967—, sec. 1971—; Architect Community Service award 1971), Sigma Phi Epsilon. Episcopalian (vestry 1960-64). Lion (dir. 1957-67; pres. 1965-66). Home: 1616 N Swinton Av Delray Beach FL 33444 Office: 94 NE 5th Av Delray Beach 33444

SIMON, WILLIAM LEONARD, film writer; b. Washington, Dec. 3, 1930; s. Isaac B. and Marjorie (Felstiner) S.; B.E.E., Cornell U., 1954; m. Arynne Lucy Abeles, Sept. 18, 1966; 1 dau., Victoria Marie; 1 stepson, Sheldon M. Bermont. Writer documentary and indsl. films TV programs, 1958-64; pres. William L. Simon Film Scripts, Inc., Washington, 1964—. Cons. films, TV Dem. Central Com., 1966-67; lectr. George Washington U., 1968-70. Pres. Foggy Bottom Citizens Assn., 1963-65, mem. exec. bd., 1965-69; v.p. Shakespeare Summer Festival, 1966-67, trustee, 1965-70. Served to lt. with USNR, 1954-58. Recipient 3 Golden Eagle awards Cine Film Festival, numerous other awards. Mem. Nat. Acad. TV Arts and Scis. (gov. D.C. chpt.), Am. Film Inst., Univ. Film Assn., Industry Film Producers' Assn., Eta Kappa Nu (chpt. pres. 1953-54), Tau Beta Pi. Writer numerous produced works for motion pictures and TV. Home: 2407 1/2 Eye St NW Washington DC 20037

SIMONS, ARTHUR HENRY, advt. co. exec.; b. N.Y.C., Feb. 26, 1924; s. Eustace H. and Vera (Goldsmith) S.; student Ore. State Coll., 1943-44, Columbia, 1945; m. Ellen C. Frederickson, Apr. 2, 1950; children—David F., Victoria A., Kathleen E., Arthur Henry, Jr. With pub. relations office Edward L. Bernays, N.Y.C., 1945-46; active advt. and merchandising, Miami, Fla., 1951—; co-founder Miller, Bacon, Avrutis & Simons, Inc., advt. and pub. relations, Miami, 1955-67, pres. Advt. & Marketing Assos., Inc., 1967—. Cons., Fla. Internat. U. Served with AUS, World War II. Mem. Am. Assn. Polit. Cons. Clubs: Advt. of Miami, Key Biscayne (Fla.) Yacht. Home: 269 Cranwood Dr Key Biscayne FL 33149 Office: 1260 Biscayne Blvd Miami FL 33132

SIMONS, CHARLES EARL, JR., U.S. judge; b. Johnston, S.C., Aug. 17, 1916; s. Charles Earl and Frances (Rhoden) S.; A.B., U. S.C., 1937, LL.B. cum laude, 1939; m. Jean Knapp, Oct. 18, 1941; children—Charles Earl III, Paul Knapp, Richard Brewster, Jean Brewster. Admitted to S.C. bar, 1939; mem. firm Lybrand, Simons & Rich, Aiken, S.C., 1939-64, U.S. dist. judge District S.C., 1964—. Mem. S.C. Constl. Revision Com., 1948; mem. Bd. Discipline and Grievance S.C. Bar, 1958-61. Adv. bd. Aiken County (S.C.) Retarded Children's Assn., 1962; bd. dirs. United Fund for Aiken County (S.C.). Mem. S.C. Ho. of Reps. 1942, 47-48, 61-64, mem. ways and means com., 1947-48, 61-64. Served with USNR, World War II. Recipient Algernon Sidney Sullivan award, 1937, 64. Mem. S.C. (exec. com.), Am. bar assns., Am. Law Inst., Aiken C. of C. (past v.p.), Am. Legion, V.F.W., U. S.C. Alumni Assn. (past pres.), U. S.C. Devel. and Adv. Council. Baptist (bd. deacons, past chmn. finance com.). Lion. Club: Aiken Bus. Men's. Home: 910 Valley Green Dr SW Aiken SC 29801 Office: US Courthouse Aiken SC 29801

SIMONS, CHARLES J., airline co. exec., 1918; B.S., Fordham U., 1938; m. With Lehigh Coal & Navigation Co., 1938-40; with Eastern Air Lines Inc., 1940—, v.p., chief financial officer, 1968-69, sr. v.p., chief financial officer, 1969-71, exec. v.p. finance and adminstrn., 1971—, also dir.; treas., dir. Eastern Aviation Services, Inc.; pres., chief exec. officer, dir. Dorado Beach Devel., Inc., Dorado Beach Estates, Inc., Dorado Beach Hotel Corp; treas., dir. Eastern Airlines P.R., Inc.; treas. Pkwy. Indsl. Center, Inc.; v.p., dir. Terminal Sales Co.; dir. SoGen Internat. Fund, Inc., S.E. 1st Nat. Bank of Miami Springs, Nat. Distributive Services, Rockresorts, Inc., Bank of Commerce, N.Y. Home: 631 Arvida Pkwy Coral Gables FL 33156 Office: Miami Internat Airport Miami FL 33148

SIMONS, HOWARD, journalist; b. Albany, N.Y., June 3, 1929; s. Rubin and Mae (Chesler) S.; B.A., Union Coll., 1951; M.S., Columbia, 1952; Nieman fellow Harvard, 1958-59; m. Florence Katz, Nov. 11, 1956; children—Anna, Isabel, Julie, Rebecca. Reporter, editor Sci. Service, Washington, 1954-59; free-lance writer, 1959-61; reporter Washington Post, 1961-66, asst. mng. editor, 1966-69, dep. mng. editor, 1969-71, mng. editor, 1971—. Am. columnist New Scientist, London, Eng., 1963-67. Cons. Nat. Acad. Scis. Office of Information, 1959-61. Served with AUS, 1952-54. Mem. Overseas Writers, Council on Fgn. Relations. Club: Federal City (Washington). Contbr. articles to Harper's, Saturday Review, Saturday Evening Post, others. Home: 906 N Overlook Dr Alexandria VA 22305 Office: 1515 L St NW Washington DC 20005

SIMONTON, WILLIAM CHRISTOPHER, editor; b. Covington, Tenn., Nov. 10, 1928; s. William C. and Emma (Long) S.; B.A., Centre Coll., 1950; m. Elizabeth Jane Butler, Aug. 18, 1949; children—Gail M., Kevin W. News editor Covington Leader, 1950-57, mng. editor, 1957-65, editor, 1965—. Football ofcl. Tenn. Secondary Sch., 1950—; mem. Covington Bd. Edn., 1957-71, chmn., 1961-69. Bd. dirs. Tenn. Sch. Bds. Assn., 1969-71; bd. dirs. Civington Indsl. Devel. Commn., chmn. 1970—. Mem. Tenn. Press Service (dir.), Am. Newspaper Reps. (dir. 1962-66), Tenn. Press Assn. (pres. 1967-68), Big Ten Ofcls. Assn. (pres. 1966-67), Covington C. of C. (pres. 1965, indsl. chmn. 1965—), Sigma Delta Chi, Sigma Alpha Epsilon. Home: 1 King Circle Covington TN 38019 Office: 2001 Hwy 51 S Covington TN 38019

SIMPSON, BRYAN, judge; b. Kissimmee, Fla., May 30, 1903; s. Arthur Allen and Mary Elizabeth (Bryan) S.; LL.B., U. Fla., 1926; LL.D., John B. Stetson U., 1958; m. Sarah George Hall Hixon, Feb. 15, 1941; 1 son, Bryan; stepchildren—John H. Hixon, George C. Hixon, Joseph M. Hixon; m. 2d, Sally Thompson Jones, Mar. 1, 1968; stepchildren—Eve Dunbar Jones, Isaac F. Jones III. Admitted to Fla. bar, 1926; practiced in Jacksonville, 1926-39; asst. state atty. 4th Fla. Circuit, 1933-37; judge Criminal Court of Record, Duval County, Fla., 1939-46; circuit judge 4th Fla. Circuit, 1946-50; U.S. dist. judge So. Dist. Fla., 1950-62, chief judge, 1961-62; chief judge Middle Dist. Fla., 1962-66; U.S. circuit judge Fifth Circuit, 1966—. Served as 1st lt. AUS, 1943-45; ETO. Trustee emeritus The Bolles Sch., Jacksonville; trustee Cummer Gallery of Art, 1960—; emeritus mem. state bd. Children's Home Soc. Fla. Recipient citation U. Fla. Centennial, 1953. Mem. Am. Jacksonville bar assns., Fla. Bar, Phi Delta Phi, Kappa Alpha. Democrat. Episcopalian. Rotarian. Clubs: Ponte Vedra, Fla. Yacht, Timuquana Country (Jacksonville); Pinnacle (Augusta, Ga.); Fort Worth (hon.); Lawyers Club (hon.) (Washington). Home: 4157 Ortega Blvd Jacksonville FL 32210 Office: US Post Office and Court Bldg Jacksonville FL 32201.

SIMPSON, CHARLES REAGAN, U.S. judge; b. Danville, Ill., June 16, 1921; s. Frank and Mamie (Moreland) S.; B.A. with highest honors, U. Ill., 1944, J.D. with high honors, 1945; LL.M., Harvard, 1950; m. Ruth V. Thomason, June 5, 1948. Admitted to Ill. bar, 1945; pvt. practice Champaign, Ill., 1946-49; atty. OPS, 1951-52; with legislation and regulations div. Office Chief Counsel, Internal Revenue Service, 1952-65, dir. office, 1964-65; judge U.S. Tax Ct., 1965—. Teaching fellow Harvard Law Sch., 1950-51. Chmn., Champaign County chpt. Nat. Found. Infantile Paralysis, 1947-49. Mem. Ill. Gen. Assembly from 24th Dist., 1947-50. Recipient Justice Tom C. Clark award Fed. Bar Assn., 1964. Mem. Am. Bar Assn., Am. Law Inst., Am. Judicature Soc., Phi Beta Kappa, Order of Coif, Phi Kappa Phi. Democrat. Home: 2500 Virginia Av NW Washington DC 20037 Office: US Tax Court Washington DC 20044

SIMPSON, GEORGE LEE, JR., univ. chancellor; b. Concord, N.C., Oct. 27, 1921; s. George Lee and Willie (Hudson) S.; B.A., U. N.C., 1941, M.A., 1944, Ph.D., 1951, LL.D., 1969; m. Louise Miller Hartsell, Dec. 4, 1942; children—George Lee III, Joe H. Asso. prof. sociology U. N.C., 1952-56, prof., 1956-63; exec. dir. Research Triange Com. N.C., 1956-58, chmn. exec. com., 1958-62, cons., 1958-62; cons. N.C. Gov. Luther Hodges, 1958-60; cons. N.C. Gov. Terry Sanford, 1961-62; asst. adminstr. pub. affairs NASA, Washington, 1962-63, asst. adminstr. for tech. utilization and policy planning, 1963-64, asst. adminstr. policy planning, 1964-65, asst. dep. adminstr., 1964-65; chancellor Bd. Regents Univ. System of Ga., Atlanta, 1965. Mem. Ga. Edn. Authority, 1965—; mem. bd. control So. Regional Edn. Bd., 1965—, mem. exec. com., 1969, 70; mem. Ga. Edn. Coordinating Com., 1965—; mem. Ga. Sci. and Tech. Commn., 1966—; mem. NSF's Adv. Com. for Instnl. Relations, 1969-70. Mem. Ga. Study Commn. on Law Enforcement Officer Standards and Edn.,

1968—; mem. Ga. Planning Assn., 1968-70; mem. Gov.'s Interagy. Council on Human Relations, 1968-70; mem. Ga. State Manpower Planning Council, 1971—; mem. Met. Atlanta Commn. on Crime and Juvenile Delinquency, Inc., 1966-70, vice-chmn., 1967-68, chmn., 1968-69. Trustee Richard B. Russell Found. Served with USN, 1942-45. Named Ga. Key Citizen, 1968-69. Guggenheim fellow, 1954-55. Author: The Cokers of Carolina, 1955. Home: 2875 Habersham Rd NW Atlanta GA 30305 Office: 244 Washington St SW Atlanta GA 30334

SIMPSON, GRELLET COLLINS, univ. pres.; b. Norfolk, Va., Apr. 20, 1909; s. John C. and Mabyn (Branch) S.; A.B., Randolph-Macon Coll., 1930, LL.D. (hon.) 1959; A.M., U. Va., 1936, Ph.D., 1949; Litt.D. (hon.), Flagler Coll., 1972; m. Dorothy Cottrell, June 28, 1939. Instr. English Randolph-Macon Acad., 1930-31; instr. Randolph-Macon Coll., 1931-36, asst. prof. 1936-38, asso. prof., 1938-43, prof., 1943-44, 1946-55, dean of faculty, 1952-55; pres., chancellor Mary Washington Coll., U. Va., Fredricksburg, 1956—; chmn. U. Center in Va., 1969-71. Chmn. U.S. India Women's Coll. Exchange Program. Am. Consortium, 1968-72. Field supr. ARC for So. Italy. Service to Allied Personnel Families, 1944-46. Mem. Raven Soc., Assn. of Va. Colls. (pres. 1959), Phi Beta Kappa, Omicron Delta Kappa, Phi Delta Theta. Methodist. Home: Brompton Mary Washington Coll Fredericksburg VA 22401

SIMPSON, LEWIS PEARSON, educator; b. Jacksboro, Tex., July 18, 1916; s. John Pearson and Grace (Sidebottom) S.; B.A., U. Tex., 1938, M.A., 1939, Ph.D., 1948; m. Mary Elizabeth Ellis, July 14, 1941; 1 son, Lewis David. Instr. U. Tex., 1941-42, 44-48; civilian instr. U.S. Navy Flight Sch., 1942-44; asst. prof. La. State U., 1948-53, asso. prof., 1953-60, prof., 1960-64, prof. and co-editor Southern Rev., Baton Rouge, 1964-71, William A. Read prof. English lit., 1971—; Lamar Meml. lectr. So. lit. Mercer U., 1973. John Simon Guggenheim Meml. Found. fellow, 1954-55; La. State U. Found. Distinguished Faculty fellow, 1971-72. Mem. Am. Assn. U. Profs., Modern Lang. Assn., Am. Studies Assn., Soc. for Study So. Lit. (exec. council 1968-70), Orgn. Am. Historians, So. Hist. Assn., South Central Modern Lang. Assn., Thoreau Soc., Emerson Soc. Author: The Federalist Literary Mind, 1962; Profile of Robert Frost, 1971; The Poetry of Community, 1972. Editor: Library of Southern Civilization; adv. editor, Southern Writers Series, Arlington Quar.; co-editor The So. Rev., 1971—. Editorial bd. Am. Lit., George Washington Cable. Contbr. articles in field to profl. jours. Home: 965 Aberdeen Av Baton Rouge LA 70808

SIMPSON, MAURICE HENRY, govt. ofcl.; b. Camden, N.J., Apr. 24, 1913; s. Harry Bowers and Elizabeth (King) S.; B.S., Drexel Inst. Tech., 1953, postgrad., 1953-55, M.S., 1966; m. Doris May Gardner, May 1, 1943; children—Maureen Doris (Mrs. Herman Boehm), Lucinda May, Barry Henry. Mech. engr. York Corp., Phila., Allentown, Pa., 1941-42, 46-50; mech. engr. Carrier Corp., Phila., 1950-51; civilian mech. engr. U.S. Army, Phila., 1951-67, system engr., mgr. Combat Devel. Command, Ft. Belvoir, Va., 1967—. Webelos master Nat. Capitol council Boy Scouts Am., 1968-69. Served with AUS, 1942-46. Mem. Inst. Environmental Scis. (sec. edn. com.), Nat. Soc. Profl. Engrs., Research Soc. Am., A.A.A.S., Am. Acad. Polit. and Social Sci. Presbyn. (deacon). Contbr. articles to profl. jours. Home: 8128 Bard St Lorton VA 22079 Office: US Army Combat Devel Command Fort Belvoir VA 22060

SIMPSON, RICHARD LEE, sociologist, educator; b. Washington, Feb. 2, 1929; s. Donald Dake and Lottie (Lee) S.; A.B., U. N.C., 1950, Ph.D., 1956; M.A., Cornell U., 1952; m. Ida Ann Harper, July 10, 1955; children—Robert Donald, Frank Daniel. Instr. sociology Pa. State U., University Park, 1956-57; asst. prof. sociology Northwestern U., Evanston, Ill., 1957-58; asst. prof. sociology U. N.C. at Chapel Hill, 1958-61, asso. prof., 1961-65, prof., 1965—. Cons. editor sociology Charles E. Merrill Pub. Co., Columbus, O., 1967-72. Mem. bd. U. N.C. Press, 1962—. Mem. Am., So. (1st v.p. 1968-69, pres. 1971-72) sociol. assns., Soc. for Study of Social Problems. Author: Attendants in American Mental Hospitals, 1961. Editor Social Forces, 1969-72; co-editor, contbr. Social Organization and Behavior, 1964—, Institutions and Social Exchange, 1971—. Home: 604 Brookview Rd Chapel Hill NC 27514

SIMPSON, ROBERT HOMER, meteorologist; b. Corpus Christi, Tex., Nov. 19, 1912; s. Clyde Robert and Annie Laurie (Rainey) S.; B.S., Southwestern U., 1932; D.Sc., 1963; M.S., Emory U., 1935; Ph.D., U. Chgo., 1962; m. Joanne Gerould, Jan. 6, 1965. Tchr., Tex. Pub. Schs., 1935-40; with U.S. Weather Bur., 1940—, dep. dir. research div., 1960-62, asso. dir. Weather Bur., Washington, 1963-67, dir. Nat. Hurricane Center, Miami, Fla., 1967—. Mem. Am. Meteorol. Soc., A.A.A.S., Am. Geophys. Union, Sigma Xi. Contbr. articles profl. jours. Home: 9380 Gallardo St Coral Gables FL 33156 Office: PO Box 8286 Coral Gables FL 33124

SIMPSON, ROBERT TENNENT, judge; b. Florence, Ala., Sept. 2, 1893; s. Robert Tennent and Nellie (Moody) S.; grad. Florence (Ala.) Normal Coll., 1912; A.B., U. Ala., 1915, LL.B., 1917; m. Emily Ford, Oct. 15, 1917 (dec.); children—Robert Tennent IV, William Ford; m. 2d, Sally Sewell Bodiford, Dec. 28, 1958 (dec.); m. 3d, Ann Moses Parham, July 3, 1968. Tchr., Colbert County, Ala., 1911; labor helper in shops So. Ry., Sheffield, Ala., 1912-13; timekeeper Hales Bar Dam, Guild, Tenn., 1913; admitted to Ala. bar, 1917; practiced law with father, as Simpson & Simpson, Florence, 1919-29; solicitor 11th Jud. Circuit of Ala., 1929-40; judge Ct. of Appeals of Ala., 1940-44; asso. justice Supreme Ct. of Ala., 1944—. Served as capt. 327 Inf., 82d Div., A.E.F. U.S. Army, World War I; participated in engagements at Lucey, Marbache, St. Mihiel, Meuse-Argonne, 1918. Decorated Brigade Citation, Silver Star. Mem. Am., Ala. State bar assns., Ala. State Jr. C. of C. (past pres.), Am. Legion, 40 and 8, D.A.V., V.F.W., Mil. Order World Wars, Sons Confederate Vets. (past camp comdr.), S.A.R. (past state pres.), Phi Beta Kappa, Sigma Alpha Epsilon, Sigma Delta Kappa. Presbyn. Elk. Clubs: Unity, Beauvoir, Montgomery Country, Knife and Fork (Montgomery). Home: 35 W Ogden Rd Montgomery AL 36105 Office: Jud Bldg Montgomery AL 36101

SIMPSON, WALTER ROBERT, JR., clergyman; b. Marrero, La., Jan. 29, 1926; s. Walter Robert and Isabel July (Brisolara) S.; B.A., Simpson Coll., 1954; B.D., Eden Theol. Sem., 1958; m. Doris Elsie Mehrtens, June 5, 1957; children—Sheryl Lynn, Walter Robert III, Diane Elzine. Ordained to ministry United Ch. of Christ, 1958; pastor Round Groves United Ch. of Christ, 1958-59, Zion United Ch. of Christ, Clifton, Tex., 1959-66, St. John and Trinity United Ch. of Christ, Kyle, Tex., 1966-69, St. Paul United Ch. of Christ, Schulenburg, Tex., 1969—. Moderator Brazos Assn. United Ch. of Christ, 1970—; mem. bd. South Central Conf. United Ch. of Christ, 1971—. Scoutmaster Live Oak council Boy Scouts Am., 1969-71; mem. Schulenburg Vol. Fire Dept. Bd. dirs. Campus Christian Community S.W. Tex. State U., 1967-69; bd. dirs., pres. bd. Back Stage Inc. Served with USN, 1946-48; PTO. Colo. State U. grantee Great Plains Town and Country Pastor's Leadership Sch. Home: Box 186 Schulenburg TX 78956 Office: 712 Summit St Schulenburg TX 78956

SIMPSON, WILLIAM CORNELIUS, educator; b. Ohatchee, Ala., Feb. 25, 1925; s. E. Cresswell and Elsie (Hodges) S.; A.B., Mercer U., 1947; M.S., U. Ky., 1950; Ph.D., U. Va., 1955; m. Susan L. Bell, May 27, 1945; children—Sally, Amy, Ellen, Lucy. Prof., Ga. Inst. Tech., 1955-65; prof. physics, dean Morehead (Ky.) State U., 1965—. Served with USNR, 1943-46, 51-53. Mem. A.A.A.S., Am. Assn. Physics Tchrs., Blue Key, Sigma Xi, Sigma Pi Sigma, Kappa Sigma. Home: 1341 Knapp Av Morehead KY 40351

SIMPSON, WILLIAM HARVEY, ins. co. exec.; b. Montreal, Que., Can., Jan. 28, 1938; s. William and Myrtle Irene (Kosmack) S.; student George Washington U., 1955-65; m. Paula Sue Scott, July 27, 1968; children—William Scott, Susanne Paulette. Underwriter Acacia Mut. Life Ins. Co., Washington, 1957-61; adminstrv. v.p. Am. Capital Life Ins. Co., Washington, 1961-64; underwriter Variable Annuity Life Ins. Co., Washington, 1964-65; v.p. brokerage sales Fidelity Bankers Life Ins. Co., Richmond, Va., 1965-72; pres. Life Ins. Services, Inc., Charlotte, N.C., 1972—. Served with USAF, 1961-62; Berlin. C.L.U. Fellow life Office Mgmt. Assn.; mem. Richmond, Va. (lobbyist Va. legislative com. 1969-71), life underwriters assns., Jr. C. of C. Richmond. Home: 9701 Evansway Lane Richmond VA 23235 Office: Life Ins Services Inc 1420 E 7th St Suite 203 Charlotte NC 28204

SIMS, BENNETT, Episcopal bishop. Address: 2744 Peachtree St NW Atlanta GA 30305*

SIMS, ELMER RICHARD, JR., oil exploration engr.; b. Cardenas, Cuba, June 30, 1912; s. Elmer Richard and Margaret (Dobbs) S.; B.S., U. Tex., 1938; m. Ola Irene Trollope, July 13, 1950; children—Nene, Paige. Geophysicist, Humble Oil Co., East Indies, 1939-41; dist. geophysicist Carter Oil Co., 1946-48; pres. Mountain States Exploration Drilling, 1948-51; regional engr. Teledyne Exploration, Houston, 1951-71; electronics engr. Globe Universal Sci., Midland, Tex., 1971—. Served to lt. col. AUS, 1942-46. Decorated Legion of Merit, Bronze Star medal with oak leaf cluster. Mem. Permian Basin Geophys. Soc., Soc. Exploration Geophysicists. Pioneered use of surface tools, weight drop and gas gun methods of oil exploration. Home: 820 Twin Hills Dr El Paso TX 79912 Office: 4805 Andrews Hwy Midland TX 79701

SIMS, ERNEST THEODORE, JR., scientist, educator; b. Atlanta, Aug. 29, 1932; s. Ernest Theodore and Louise (Miller) S.; B.S.A., U. Ga., 1954; M.Sc., Ohio State U., 1959, Ph.D., 1962; m. Margaret Elizabeth Richter, Dec. 28, 1963; children—Ernest Theodore III, John Christopher Richter. Pomologist, Sims Fruit Farms, Conyers, Ga., 1956-57; grad. research asst. Ohio State U., 1957-62; asst. prof. horticulture Clemson (S.C.) U., 1962-67, asso. prof. horticulture, postharvest physiologist, 1967-72, prof., 1972—, mem. grad. faculty, 1968—, faculty senate, 1969-71. Troop committeeman Boy Scouts Am., 1967-69. Served with AUS, 1954-56. Mem. Assn. Southeastern Biologists, Res. Officers Assn. U.S., Am. Soc. Hort. Sci., Am. Soc. Plant Physiologists, Internat. Soc. Hort. Sci., Sigma Xi, Phi Kappa Phi, Alpha Zeta, Gamma Sigma Delta. Presbyn. Lion. Contbr. articles to profl. jours. Home: 117 Poole Lane Clemson SC 29631

SIMS, FINIS EZRA, govt. ofcl.; b. Rutherford, Tenn., July 17, 1904; s. James Bailey and Minnie (McBride) S.; B.S., Memphis State U., 1929; M.A., George Peabody Coll., 1939; m. Lockye Marie McLean, June 14, 1930; 1 son, Billy Charles (dec.). High sch. prin. Springhill High Sch., Trenton, Tenn., 1929-36, Medina, Tenn., 1936-41, Middleton, Tenn., 1941-43; county supr. Farm Security Adminstrn., Lawrence County, Lawrenceburg, Tenn., 1943-44; postmaster Medina, Tenn., 1945—. Democrat. Methodist. Mason, Lion (zone chmn. Internat. 1961-62; dep. dist. gov. 1962-63, del. internat. conv. 1969). Home: 305 W Church Av Medina TN 38355 Office: 108 N Main St Medina TN 38355

SIMS, JAMES NATHAN, petroleum co. exec.; b. Orange, Tex., Jan. 16, 1918; s. James Nathan and Nora (Baker) S.; B.S., U. Houston, 1940; m. Nelda Fagan, Oct. 24, 1947; children—Gail, Howard. Petroleum geologist Phillips Petroleum Co., Houston, 1941-56, exploration geologist, 1945-48, sr. exploration geologist, 1948-56; partner Acorn Oil Co., Houston, 1956-64; owner, prin. Acorn Oil and Gas Co., Houston, 1964—. Mem. Houston Geol. Soc., Am. Assn. Petroleum Geologists, Soc. Ind. Profl. Earth Scientists, Houston Assn. Petroleum Landmen. Methodist. Home: 4 Valley Forge St Houston TX 77024 Office: 935 San Jacinto Bldg 911 Walker St Houston TX 77002

SIMS, JOHN MALLORY, JR., civil-structural engr., constrn. co. exec.; b. Pensacola, Fla., Jan. 6, 1923; s. John Mallory and Rebekah Elizabeth (Groskoph) S.; B.S. in Civil Engring., The Citadel, 1949; M.S., U. Fla., 1950; m. Virginia Luke, Nov. 18, 1944; children—Marilyn (Mrs. Ben Larry Maxey), Janet Fay, John Mallory III. Project mgr. Robert S. Kerr Lock & Dam, Sallisaw, Okla., 1965-68, Perini, Morrison-Knudsen & Leavell, 1965-68; asst. chief engr. Michael Baker, Jr., Inc., Cons. Engr., Jackson, Miss., 1968-69; chmn. Biddy & Sims, Inc., Cons. Engrs. (name changed to Coastal States Cons. 1971), Jackson, 1969—; owner Allied Builders System, Jackson, 1969-70. Served with C.E., AUS, 1943-46. Registered profl. engr., Miss., Fla., Ga., Que., Nfld. Fellow Am. Soc. C.E.; mem. U.S. Com. Internat. Commn. Large Dams. Home: Route 1 Box 657 Cantonment FL 32533 Office: 812 W Amito St Jackson MS 39206

SIMS, ROBERT BRADFORD, banker; b. Athens, Ala., Mar. 8, 1918; s. Raz Fulton and Martha Beatrice (Garner) S.; student Auburn U., 1939-41; m. Virginia Lee Vinson, Aug. 8, 1943; children—Martha Virginia (Mrs. James Thomas Odom), Mary Barbara. Asst. cashier First Nat. Bank, Auburn, Ala., 1939-41, cashier, 1943-48, v.p., 1953—; sr. v.p. Rhodes Furniture Co., Opelika, Ala., 1948-53. Chmn. water bd., City of Auburn. Ala., 1968—. Served with USAAF, 1941-42. Mem. Bank Adminstrn. Inst. (pres. 1964), Am. Legion (pres. 1965). Methodist (treas. 1967—). Mason, Lion. Club: Civitan (pres. 1967-68) (Auburn). Home: 539 Heard Av Auburn AL 36830 Office: PO Box 2149 Auburn AL 36830

SIMS, WILLIAM CAMDEN, truck rental co. exec.; b. Elizabeth, W.Va., May 19, 1929; s. Camden Arthur and Jessie (Jobes) S.; B.S., Marshall U., 1951; m. Doris Cornett, Jan. 27, 1951; children—Gregory Scott, Lisa Clare. Salesman, Gen. Mills Co., Miami, Fla., 1955-57; mgmt. trainee Ryder Truck Rental, Inc., Miami, 1957-58, br. mgr.-dist. mgr., Augusta, Ga., 1958-65, regional mgr., Atlanta, 1965-68, v.p. rental and western area, 1968—. Served with USAF, 1951-55. Mem. Ryder Millinn Dollar Roundtable. Home: 100 Edgewater Dr Apt 345 Coral Gables FL 33133 Office: PO Box 816 Miami FL 33133

SIMS, WILLIAM EDWARD, univ. pres.; b. Chickasha, Okla., Mar. 28, 1921; A.B., Lincoln U., 1949; M.A., Colo. State Coll., 1952, Ed.D., 1963; m. Muriel Crowell, June 27, 1945; 1 dau., Dana Rae. Tchr., Tulsa Pub. Schs., 1948-53; asso. prof. music, chmn. dept. Langston (Okla.) U., 1963-65, dean acad. affairs, 1965-69, pres., 1970—. Served with USNR, 1942-46. Mem. Soc. for Advancement of Mgmt., Kappa Delta Pi, Phi Delta Kappa, Kappa Alpha Psi. Home: P O Box 907 Langston OK 73050

SINCLAIR, JOHN L., broadcasting exec. Pres. WANT, Richmond, Va. Office: Broad-Grace Arcade Bldg Richmond VA 23219*

SINCOX, FRANCIS JOHN, JR., physician; b. Saginaw, Mich., May 11, 1932; s. Francis John and Erna (Hefke) S.; B.A., Emory U., 1954, M.D., 1958; m. Frances Barker, June 21, 1958; children—Douglas John, Kathleen Barker. Intern U.S. Naval Hosp., St. Albans, N.Y., 1958-59; practice medicine McGill Clinic, Kings Mountain, N.C., 1963—; mem. staff Kings Mountain Hosp. FAA med. examiner, 1963—. Mem. Kings Mountain Police Res., 1969—. Bd. dirs. A.R.C., 1964-65. Served with USNR, 1959-63. Diplomate Am. Bd. Family Practice. Mem. Am. Acad. Gen. Practice, Practice, Cleveland County Med. Soc. v.p., 1966-67), Kings Mountain C. of C. (dir., 1970—), A.M.A., N.C. Med. Soc. Presbyn. (deacon). Mason (32 deg.), Kiwanian. Home: 404 Edgemont Dr Kings Mountain NC 28086 Office: PO Box 392 Kings Mountain NC 28086

SINGER, PATSY RUTH DUNN (MRS. EDWIN SINGER), civic leader; b. Corpus Christi, Tex., Sept. 13, 1922; d. Burton and Buena (Hill) Dunn; student U. Tex., Del Mar Coll., U. Corpus Christi, U. of Pacific; m. Ben Harrison Gibson, June 25, 1943 (dec. Dec. 25, 1944); 1 dau., Jennifer (Mrs. J. Dickson Merkle); m. 2d, Edwin Singer, Aug. 1, 1946; children— Kenneth Edwin (killed in action), Lauret Lynn (Mrs. Bruce Bridgford). Co-owner (with E. Singer) Paisano Ranch, Three Rivers, Tex., 1968—. Campaign coordinator fund raising campaign Art Mus. S. Tex., Corpus Christi, 1967—; pres. Corpus Christi Symphony Soc., 1957-58; v.p. Corpus Christi Art Found., 1967-69, v.p. bd. govs., 1972-73; v.p. Municipal Arts Commn., 1969-70; mem. Tex. Commn. on Arts and Humanities, 1969—; mem. internat. council Mus. Modern Art, 1971—. Mem. Jr. League Corpus Christi, Pi Beta Phi. Home: 3642 Aransas St Corpus Christi TX 78411 Office: PO Box 29 Corpus Christi TX 78403

SINGER, STUART ALAN GORDON, chem. engr.; b. Toronto, Ont., Can., May 19, 1922; s. Joseph George and Hazel Ellen (Marshall) S.; B.A.Sc., U. Toronto, 1943, M.A.Sc., 1945, Ph.D., 1947; m. Rosalie Jacqueline Holling, June 12, 1948; children—Gayle Joanne, Sherry Leigh. Came to U.S., 1947, naturalized, 1956. Devel. engr. Research Enterprizes, Ltd., 1943-44, asst., Toronto, 1944-46, instr. chem. engring., indsl. chemistry, 1947; research engr. rayon dept. E.I. duPont de Nemours & Co., Buffalo, 1947-50, tech. investigator film dept., Wilmington, Del., 1950-52, tech. supt., Columbia, Tenn., 1952-55, Buffalo, 1955-59, dir. Film Research & Devel. Lab., Richmond, Va., 1959-69, research mgr., 1969—. Mem. Am. Inst. Chem. Engrs. Episcopalian (vestryman). Home: 3206 Stratford Rd Richmond VA 23225 Office: PO Box 27222 Richmond VA 26261

SINGLETARY, JOHN N., ins. co. exec.; b. Henderson, Tex., Nov. 9, 1917; s. John N. and Lillian P. (Beam) S.; B.A., U. Okla., 1938, LL.B., 1941; m. Virginia Southwell, Oct. 17, 1942; children—Anita Jo, John N. III. Admitted to Okla. bar, 1941; practiced in Oklahoma City, 1941-42, 45-51; co-founder Globe Life & Accident Ins. Co. Oklahoma City, 1951—, chmn. bd., pres., 1951—; dir. Globe Color Press, 1st Nat. Bank & Trust Co. Oklahoma City, other indsl. firms; pres. Carport, Inc., Hudson Hotel, Globe Realty Devel. Corp.; chmn. bd. Am. Life & Accident Ins. Co., Fort Worth. Served to capt. USAAF, 1942-45. Mem. Oklahoma City C. of C. (dir., 1966-72), Optimists (pres., 1948-49), Alpha Tau Omega. Home: 1704 Bedford Dr Oklahoma City OK 73116 Office: 311 W Sheridan St Oklahoma City OK 73102

SINGLETARY (EADDY) MCLEOD, lawyer; b. Bishopville, S.C., June 12, 1919; s. Robert Howell and Ila (McLeod) S.; A.B., U. S.C., 1940, LL.B., 1947; m. Virginia Ann Buckner, Dec. 27, 1955; 1 dau., Joan T. (Mrs. Daniel M. Fraley, Jr.). Admitted to S.C. bar, 1947, since practiced in Columbia; partner firm McLeod & Singletary, 1947-72, McNair, Konduros, Corley, Singletary & Dibble, 1972—. Mem. S.C. Aero. Commn.; gov.'s appointee on election law study com. Bd. visitors Coker Coll. Served with AUS, 1942-46; col. Judge Adv. Gen. Corps. Mem. Am., S.C., Richland County (pres.) bar assns., S.C. Trial Lawyers Assn., Kappa Sigma, Blue Key. Presbyn. Home: 408 Edisto Av Columbia SC 29202 Office: Barringer Bldg Columbia SC 29201

SINGLETARY, OTIS ARNOLD, JR., univ. pres.; b. Gulfport, Miss., Oct. 31, 1921; s. Otis Arnold and May Charlotte (Walker) S.; B.A., Millsaps Coll., 1947; M.A., La. State U., 1949, Ph.D., 1954; m. Gloria Walton, June 6, 1944; children—Bonnie, Scot, Kendall Ann. Mem. faculty U. Tex., 1954-61, prof. history, 1960-61, asso. dean arts and scis., 1956-59, asst. to pres., 1960-61; chancellor U. N.C. at Greensboro, 1961-66; v.p. Am. Council on Edn., Washington, 1966-68; dir. Job Corps, Office Econ. Opportunity, Washington, 1964-65; exec. vice chancellor acad. affairs U. Tex. System, 1968-69; pres. U. Ky., Lexington, 1969—. Bd. dirs. Am. Assn. Higher Edn., 1969—, Ednl. Change Inc., 1968—, Inst. Services to Edn., 1969—, So. Regional Edn. Bd., 1970—. Regional chmn. Woodrow Wilson Nat. Fellowship Found., 1959-61; chmn. N.C. Rhodes Scholarship Com., 1964-66, chmn. Ky. com., 1970-72. Served with USNR, 1943-46, 51-54; comdr. Res. Recipient Scarborough Teaching Excellence award U. Tex., 1958, Students Assn. Teaching Excellence award, 1958, 59; Grantee Carnegie Corp., 1961. Mem. Am., So. hist. assns., Am. Mil. Inst. (Moncado Book Fund award 1954), Phi Beta Kappa, Phi Alpha Theta, Pi Kappa Alpha. Democrat. Methodist. Author: Negro Militia and the Reconstruction, 1957; The Mexican War, 1960; American Universities and Colleges, 1968. Office: U Ky Lexington KY 40506

SINGLETON, EUSTACE BYRON, lawyer; b. Lufkin, Tex., Oct. 3, 1909; s. James Madison and Carolyn Elizabeth (Haygood) S.; A.B., U. Tex., 1933, J.D., 1933; m. Elsie Adeline Bell, May 16, 1936; children—Eustace Byron II, Savannah Adeline. Admitted to Tex. bar, 1933, U.S. Supreme Ct. bar, 1941, U.S. Ct. Claims bar, 1952, U.S. Ct. Customs and Patent Appeals bar, 1956, also others; mem. firm Underwood, Strickland & Singleton, Amarillo, Tex., 1933-38, Monning & Singleton, Amarillo, 1939-49, Singleton & Trulove, Amarillo, 1950-60; practiced in Amarillo, 1961—; atty. corp. counsel City of Amarillo, 1941-48; part-time referee in bankruptcy U.S. conciliation commn., 1933-40. Pres. Venture-Assos. Mgmt. Corp. Exec. committeeman Young Dems. of Tex., 1935-46; finance committeeman Amarillo Dem. Com., 1936-40. Chmn. Amarillo chpt. A.R.C.; dep. dir. War Savs. Staff, Austin, Tex., 1939-43; nat. committeeman War Finance Com., Dallas, 1943-46. Bd. dirs. Edna Gladney Home; bd. govs. Arthritis and Rheumatism Found. Mem. Am., Fed., Amarillo bar assns., State Bar Tex., Am. Judicature Soc. Home: 2405 Lipscomb St Amarillo TX 79109 Office: Am Nat Bank Bldg Amarillo TX 79101

SINGLETON, HELEN MARIE MCKINNEY (MRS. ARTHUR GLEN SINGLETON), county ofcl.; b. Ballinger, Tex., Dec. 8, 1914; d. Curtis B. and Annie Frances (Harmon) McKinney; grad. Draughon's Bus. Coll., 1934; m. Arthur Glen Singleton, June 22, 1936; 1 son, Curtis Fred. With First Nat. Bank, Edinburg, Tex., 1935; 1st asst. county auditor Hidalgo County, Edinburg, 1942; treas. Hidalgo County, Edinburg, 1947—. Hostess to Conf. County Treas's. State Tex., 1964. Active mem. Edinburg Hosp. Aux. Recipient Gold Medallion of Mexico, 1963; named Outstanding County Treas. of Tex., 1971-72. Mem. County Treas.'s Assn. Tex. (pres. 1964; **dir.**

1964), Nat. Assn. County Treas. and Finance Officers (sec., treas. 1966, 3d. v.p. 1967—). Presbyn. (chmn. bus. and profl. women's circle 1969). Club: Zonta (pres. 1963). Home: PO Box 564 810 S 8th St Edinburg TX 78539 Office: Court House Edinburg TX 78539

SINGLETON, JOHN VIRGIL, JR., U.S. dist. judge; b. Kaufman, Tex., Mar. 20, 1918; s. John Virgil and Jennie (Shelton) S.; B.A., U. Tex. Law Sch., 1942; m. Jane Guilford Tully, Apr. 18, 1953. Admitted to Tex. bar, 1942; mem. firm Fulbright, Crooker & Jaworski, 1953-57; partner firm Betes, Riggs & Singleton, 1953-57, Bell & Singleton, 1957-61, Barrow, Bland, Rehmet & Singleton, 1962-66; U.S. dist. judge So. Dist. Tex., 1966—. Pres. Houston Jr. Bar Assn., 1952-53; co-chmn. 5th Circuit dist. judges div. Jud. Conf., 1969, chmn., 1970. Dir. Central Nat. Bank, Houston, 1964-66. Mem. Tex. Depository Bd., 1963-66. Co-chmn. Harris County Lyndon B. Johnson for Pres. Com., 1960-61; del.-at-large Democratic Nat. Conv., 1956, 60, 64; regional coordinator Dem. Party Lyndon B. Johnson-Hubert Humphrey Campaign for Pres., 1964. Served to lt. USNR, 1942-46. Mem. Am., Houston (v.p. 1956-57, editor Houston Lawyer 1954-55) bar assns., Tex. State Bar (chmn. grievance com. for Harris County 1963-66, bd. dirs. 1966), U. Tex. Ex-Students Assn. (life pres. Houston 1961-62; rep.-at-large exec. council), Cowboys, Delta Tau Delta (pres. 1940-41), Phi Alpha Delta. Episcopalian. Rotarian. Club: Lakeside Country (past bd. dirs.) (Houston). Home: 221 Sage Rd Houston TX 77027 Office: 515 Rusk St Houston TX 77002

SINGLETON, RUDOLPH GRANTLEY, JR., lawyer; b. Lexington, Ky., May 24, 1930; s. Rudolph Grantley and Eula (Peterson) S.; student Mars Hill Coll., 1948-50; A.B., Wake Forest U., 1952, J.D., 1954; m. Jennette Johnston, Sept. 20, 1958; children—Sarah Scott, Rudolph Grantley III. Admitted to N.C. State bar, 1954; pvt. practice law, Fayetteville, 1954-56; asst. solicitor Cumberland County Superior Ct., 1955-56; partner Nance, Collier, Singleton, Kirkman & Herndon, Fayetteville, 1958—; city atty. Fayetteville, N.C. Chmn. So. dist. Boy Scouts Am., 1963-64; pres. Cumberland County Heart Assn., 1966-67. Chmn. pub. relations com. City Fayetteville, 1968-69. Pres. Cumberland County Young Dem. Club, 1958-59; precinct chmn. Dem. party, 1966-68; mem. county Dem. Exec. Com., 1966-68. Served with AUS, 1956-57. Mem. N.C., Am. bar assns., Am. Arbitration Assn. (panel, 1971—), Fayetteville C. of C. (dir. 1967—, pres. 1970), Sigma Phi Epsilon, Phi Alpha Delta. Democrat. Baptist. Clubs: Exchange of N.C. (dist. gov. 1963-64), Exchange of Fayetteville (pres. 1962-63), Highland Country (dir. 1972—). Home: 1 Skye Pl Fayetteville NC 28303 Office: PO Drawer 1210 First Union Nat Bank Bldg Fayetteville NC 28301

SINKFORD, STANLEY MCCLELLAN, pediatric cardiologist; b. Kimball, W. Va., May 9, 1929; s. Stanley M. and Marjorie (Adams) S.; B.S., Howard U., 1951, M.D., 1956; m. Jeanne Craig, Dec. 8, 1951; children—Dianne Sylvia, Janet Lynn, Stanley McClellan III. Resident, U. Chgo., 1960-64; asst. prof. pediatrics Coll. Medicine, Howard U., 1964-69, asso. prof., 1969—; cardiologist D.C. Gen. Hosp.; dir. pediatric cardiac clinic Freedmen's Hosp., Washington, 1965—. Served with USAAF, 1956-60. Mem. A.M.A., Am. Bd. Pediatrics, Alpha Omega Alpha. Contbr. articles to profl. jours. Home: 1765 Verbena St Washington DC 20012 Office: 2833 Georgia Av Washington DC 20001

SINKO, LOUIS, govt. ofcl.; b. Chgo., Jan. 23, 1928; s. Louis and Ethel (Horvath) S.; B.S., Ill. Inst. Tech., 1949; m. Elaine E. Butler, July 30, 1960 (div. Nov. 1969); children—Louis IV, Gellert. Jr. engr. Riechel & Drews, Inc., Chgo., 1950; engr. C.E. U.S. Army, Chgo., 1952-57, Army Ballistic Missile Agy., 1957-59; sr. engr. Missile and Space Systems Div., United Aircraft Corp., East Hartford, Conn., 1959-60; supr. Marshall Space Flight Center, Ala., 1960—. Served with AUS, 1950-52. Registered profl. engr., Ala., Ill. Mem. Nat. Council State Bds. Engring. Examiners, Nat. Rifle Assn. (life). Home: P O Box 1074 Huntsville AL 35807 Office: Marshall Space Flight Center AL 35812

SINTZ, EDWARD FRANCIS, library adminstr.; b. New Trenton, Ind., Feb. 6, 1924; s. John and Edith (Rudicil) S.; B.A., U. Kan., 1950; M.A. in L.S., U. Denver, 1954; M.S. in Pub. Adminstrn., U. Mo., 1965; m. Donna Norris, Apr. 12, 1952; children—Ann Kriston, Lesley Elisabeth, Julie Melinda. Various positions Kansas City (Mo.) Pub. Library, 1954-64, asst. librarian, 1964-66; asst. librarian St. Louis Pub. Library, 1966-67, asso. librarian, 1967-68; dir. Miami-Dade Pub. Library System, 1968—; instr. library sci. Washington U., St. Louis, 1966-67. Served with USAAF, 1942-45. Mem. Am., Fla. library assns. Editor: Mo. Library Assn. Quar., 1956-58. Home: 5730 SW 56th Terrace Miami FL 33143 Office: 1 Biscayne Blvd Miami FL 33132

SIPIORA, LEONARD P., museum dir.; b. Lawrence, Mass., Sept. 1, 1934; s. Walter and Agnes (Kolodziej) S.; A.B. cum laude, U. Mich., 1955, M.A., 1956; m. Sandra Joyce Coon; children—Alexandra W., Erika. Faculty State U. Ia., 1956-60, U. Tex. at El Paso, 1961-67. Sec., treas. El Paso Council for Internat. Visitors, 1968-71; pres. El Paso Arts Council, 1969-71. Trustee, El Paso Mus. of Art, Community Concert Assn., El Paso Symphony. Mem. Hist. Soc. El Paso, Nat. Soc. Soc. Arts and Letters (1st v.p. El Paso chpt.), Symphony Assn., Tex. Mus. Conf. (dir.), Mountain-Plains Mus. Conf. (membership chmn.), Am. Assn. Museums, Am. Fedn. Arts, Internat. Platform Assn., Kappa Pi. Republican. Lutheran. Home: 1012 E Blanchard El Paso TX 79902 Office: 1211 Montana El Paso TX 79902

SIQUEIROS, DAVID ALFARO, painter; b. Mexico City, Mexico, 1896; student Escuela Nacional de Bellas Artes, also schs. in Spain, France, Italy, 1917-22. Officer, Carranza's Army, 1910-16; mil. attache, Paris, 1917; editor Vida Americana, Spain; sec.-gen. Sindicato de Pentores, also editor house organ El Machte; organizer (with Amado de la Cueva) Alianza de Obreros Pintores, Guadalajara, 1925; founder Federacion Minera de Jalesco; rep. various Mexican workers' orgns. to Russia, 1928, del. workers' meetings in S.A., 1929; polit. exile, 1931; prof. Chouinard Sch. Art, Los Angeles, 1932-33; developed method for use air brushes to apply paint to outdoor murals; del. Congress Mexican Artists to Congress Revolutionary Artists, N.Y.C., 1936; established art sch., N.Y.C., 1936; prin. works include Fresco Chouinard Sch. Art, Plapa Art Center, Los Angeles, Mus. Modern Art, N.Y.C., Museo de Sao Paulo, Museo de Rio De Janeiro; murals in Bellas Artes, Hosp. de la Raza, Centro Medico, Museo de Historia, Castillo de Chapultepec, Escuela Nacional Preparatoria, U. Guadalajara (all Mex.), also in Argentina, Chile, Cuba. Served with Spanish Republican Army, 1937. Contbr. articles on art Mexican, European, South American periodicals. Address: care Revista de Mexico 3 Uruguay Mexico City DF Mexico

SIQUEIROS, JOSE LUIS, lawyer; b. Chihuahua, Mexico, June 7, 1924; student Inst. Cientifico y Literario de Chihuahua, Nat. U. Mexico, Harvard. Admitted to Mexico bar, 1947; prof., pvt. internat. law Nat. U. Mexico, 1952-54, 63-69; now practice law in Mexico City; mem. firm Hidalgo Barrera Siqueiros & Torres Landa. Legal adviser Fgn. Office, 1971. Lt. gov. State of Chihuahua, 1956-62. Mem. Barra Mexicana (v.p. 1966-71). Author: Las Reclamaciones Internacionales, 1947, Las Sociedades Extranjeras en Mexico, 1953, Panorama del Derecho Internacional Privado, 1967-71; (with S.A. Bayitch) Conflict of Laws: Mexico and The United States, 1968. Editor: Law Review. Office: Hidalgo Barrera Siqueiros & Torres Landa Torre Latino AmericanaMexico City Mexico*

SIRICA, JOHN J., U.S. judge, b. 1904; LL.B., Georgetown U., 1926; m. Lucile M. Camalier, Feb. 26, 1952; children—John J., Patricia Ann, Eileen Marie. Former mem. firm Hogan & Hartson, Washington; now chief judge U.S. Dist Ct. for D.C.; adj. prof. law Georgetown U. Law Center. Mem. Am. Bar Assn., Bar Assn. D.C. (hon.), Phi Alpha Delta. Clubs: Congressional Country, Nat. Lawyers, Lido Civic. Home: 5069 Overlook Rd NW Washington DC 20016 Office: US Ct House Washington DC 20001

SIS, RAYMOND FRANCIS, veterinarian; b. Munden, Kan., July 22, 1931; s. Frank J. and Edvie (Shimanek) S.; B.S., Kan. State U., 1953, D.V.M., 1957; M.S., Ia. State U., 1962, Ph.D., 1965; m. Janice L. Murphy, Aug. 31, 1953; children—Susan, Valerie, Mark, Michael, Amy. Clinician, Blue Cross Animal Hosp., Albuquerque, 1957; grad. asst. small animal surgery Ia. State U., Ames, 1961-62, instr. anatomy, 1962-64, asst. prof. small animal surgery, 1964-65; asso. prof. anatomy Tex. A. and M. U., College Station, 1965-68, prof., head dept. anatomy, 1968—. Bd. dirs. United Fund, Ames, 1963-65. Served with USAF, 1957-61. Mem. Am., Tex. vet. med. assns., Am. Animal Hosp. Assn., Am. Assn. Lab. Animal Sci., Am., World assns. vet. anatomists, Am. Assn. Vet. Clinicians, Brazos Valley Vet. Med. Assn. (pres. 1971), Sigma Xi, Phi Zeta (exec. councilman 1969), Alpha Zeta, Blue Key, Phi Kappa Phi, Alpha Gamma Rho (adv. 1962-65, pres. 1953). K.C. (trustee 1969, pres. 1968). Home: 2519 Willow Bend Bryan TX 77801 Office: Tex A and M U College Station TX 77843

SISCO, JOSEPH JOHN, govt. ofcl.; b. Chgo., Oct. 31, 1919; s. John and Angela S.; student Morton Jr. Coll., 1937-39; B.A., Knox Coll., 1941; M.A., U. Chgo., 1947, Ph.D., 1950; m. Jean Churchill Head, Mar. 26, 1946; children—Carol, Jane. Dir Office UN Polit. Affairs, N.Y.C., 1960-64; dep. asst. sec. for internat. orgn. affairs, Washington, 1964, asst. sec. state for internat. orgn. affairs, 1965-68, asst. sec. state for Near Eastern and South Asian affairs, 1969—. Lectr., Fgn. Ser. Inst., State Dept. Bd. dirs. Airlie Found., Warrenton, Va. Served with AUS, 1941-45. Recipient Nat. Civil Service award, 1966; Superior Service award State Dept., 1960. Mem. Am. Polit. Sci. Assn., Soc. Internat. Law, Tau Kappa Epsilon, Phi Beta Kappa. Home: 5344 Falmouth Rd Washington DC 20016 Office: 21st and Virginia Washington DC 20520

SISCO, NONA KATHERINE, adminstrv. asst.; b. Newbern, Tenn., Jan. 15, 1916; d. Henry and Addie (Richardson) Sisco; student Freed-Hardeman Coll., 1934-35; B.S. in Music, Memphis State U., 1938, postgrad. in bus. adminstrn., 1958, L.S., 1959-62; postgrad. Interlochen Nat. Music Camp, 1953; studied violin with J. Cortesi, J. Henkel, J. Haber, J. Fuchs, Joy Wiener. Instr. violin Freed-Hardeman Coll., Henderson, Tenn., 1934-35; instr. violin, Memphis, 1935—; clk.-stenographer 2d Army Hdqrs., 1940-42; sec. to chief psychiatry service, chief radiology service Kennedy VA Hosp., Memphis, 1942-55; sec. to chief finance sect. U.S. Army Engrs., Memphis, 1955-56; sec. personnel dir. regional P.O. Dept., Memphis, 1956-58; adminstrv. asst. to dean Harding Grad. Sch. Religion, 1958-62; adminstrv. asst. to dean hosp. affairs U. Tenn., to chief of staff City of Memphis Hosps., 1962—. Pres., Silver Savers Store, 1965—; violinist Memphis Symphony Orch., 1936-42, 52—; mem. Memphis Opera Theatre Orch., 1961—; mem. Jackson (Tenn.) Symphony Orch., 1963—, Ark. Symphony Orch., 1964—; mem. various univ. orchs. Mem. Am. String Tchrs. Assn., Internat. Soc. Music Educators (del. U.S. meeting 1966), Music Educators Nat. Conf., Pi Rho Zeta (chpt. pres.). Mem. Ch. of Christ (mem. med. center group 1964—). Club: Beethoven. Home: 40 S Holmes St Memphis TN 38111 Office: 860 Madison Av Memphis TN 38103

SISK, HENRY LYBRAN, educator; b. Los Angeles, June 22, 1914; s. Joseph L. and Henrietta (Berry) S.; A.B., Ariz. State U., 1935; M.A., U. Ariz., 1937; Ph.D., Cornell U., 1939; m. Hazel Swain Halladay, Apr. 6, 1946; 1 son, Duncan L. Cons., Stevenson Jordan & Harrison, Inc., Chgo., 1947-49; dir. indsl. relations Milprint, Inc., Milw., 1949-52; supt. orgn. devel. Continental Can Co., Chgo., 1952-56; asst. to v.p. Dresser Co., Dallas, 1956-59; prof. bus. adminstrn. N. Tex. State U., Denton, 1960—. Labor arbitrator, also cons.; mem. Fed. Mediation Conciliation Service, Nat. Mediation Bd. Served to capt. AUS, 1942-46. Author: Principles of Management: A Systems Approach to The Management Process, 1969. Home: 2803 Foxcroft Circle Denton TX 76201

SISK, JOHN KELLY, communications exec.; b. Cookeville, Tenn., Mar. 3, 1913; s. Thurman Kelly and Martha Jane (Sewell) S.; B.S., U. Ala., 1934; m. Isbell Lane, Sept. 30, 1936; children—John Kelly, Isbell Lane (Mrs. Lawton Irick, Jr.). Pres., chief exec. officer Multimedia Inc., 1968—; pres. pub. Greenville News-Piedmont Co. (S.C.); pres. Advertiser Co., Montgomery, Ala.; chmn. exec. com. Asheville Citizen-Times Printing Co. (N.C.), Multimedia Broadcasting Co., Greenville; dir. S.C. Nat. Bank, Liberty Life Ins. Co., A.P. Past mem. bd. dirs. YMCA; past chmn. Greenville County Planning and Devel. Bd.; past chmn. Greenville County chpt. A.R.C. Trustee Converse Coll., Duke Endowment; adv. trustee Furman U.; past chmn. bd. trustees Greenville Gen. Hosp. C.P.A. N.Y., S.C. Mem. Downtown Greenville Assn. (dir. 1957), Am., So. (chmn. bd. 1964) newspaper pubs. assns., S.C. Press Assn. (pres. 1962), Greater Greenville C. of C. (pres. 1953), Phi Gamma Delta. Methodist. Clubs: Nat. Press; Poinsett, Greenville Country, Green Valley Country, Cotillion (Greenville); Baltimore (N.C.) Forest Country; Mountain City (Asheville, N.C.). Home: 104 Parkins Lake Rd Greenville SC 29607 Office: 305 S Main St Greenville SC 29602

SISK, JOHN ROBERT, physician; b. Trenton, Tenn., May 16, 1923; s. John Richard and Lizzie (Davis) S.; student Memphis State U., 1941-42; 46-47; M.D., U. Tenn., 1950; m. Betty Louise Benroth, June 20, 1952; children—Susan Ellen, John Leslie, Sarah Elizabeth. Intern, Lima (O.) Meml. Hosp., 1950-51; resident U. Tenn. Meml. and Research Hosp., Knoxville, 1961-65; practice medicine, specializing in gen. surgery, Harriman, Tenn., 1952—; mem. active staff Harriman Gen. Hosp.; mem. courtesy staffs U. Tenn. Hosp., Chamberlain Meml. Hosp., Rockwood, Tenn. Fellow A.C.S.; mem. A.M.A., Tenn., Roane-Anderson med. socs. Home: 401 Devonia St Harriman TN 37748

SISK, LONE LEONIDAS, educator; b. Newport, Tenn., Sept. 2, 1900; s. Robert Taylor and Zollie (Scott) S.; A.B., Garson-Newman Coll., 1922; B.S., East Tenn. State U., 1929; M.A., George Peabody Coll., 1952; m. Carrie Alberta Garrett, June 11, 1925; children—Lone Leonidas, Alfreda Kathleen, Zenobia Ann. Tchr., coach Biltmore (N.C.) High Sch., 1922-23, Harriman High Sch., 1923-24; prin., coach Everette (Tenn.) High Sch., 1924-26; physics tchr. Science Hill High Sch., Johnson City, Tenn., 1926-43; vocational advisor VA, 1946-48; prof. chemistry Milligan Coll. (Tenn.), 1948—. Chmn., Area Sci. Learning; v.p. Vol. State Athletic Conf. Served to maj. USAAF, 1943-46. Fellow Am. Inst. Chemists; mem. Am. Chem. Soc., Carter County C. of C., Johnson City Edn. Assn., A.A.A.S., Am. Assn. U. Profs., Tenn. Acad. Sci., Assn. Am. Med. Coll., Phi Delta Kappa. Author: Calcium Assimilation and Retention, 1956. Home: Mountain View Dr Johnson City TN 37601 Office: Milligan Coll Milligan College TN 37682

SISK, MELVIN O., orgn. exec.; b. Bowie, Tex., Nov. 11, 1915; s. John Walter and Dora (Campbell) S.; B.A., Tex. Tech. Coll., 1937; m. Mary Ernestine Davis, Sept. 27, 1947; children—John Timothy, James Anthony, Joseph Michael, Rebecca Darlene, David McDaniel. Exec. v.p. Levelland (Tex.) C. of C., 1940-41; with Graham (Tex.) C. of C., 1941-42, Wichita Falls (Tex.) C. of C., 1946-48; Sherman (Tex.) C. of C., 1948-53, Tyler (Tex.) C. of C., 1953-56; exec. v.p. San Antonio (Tex.) C. of C., 1956—. Served with USAAF, 1942-46. Mem. Tex. C. of C. Mgrs. Assn. (past pres.), So. Assn. of C. of C. Execs. (dir.). Presbyn. Rotarian. Home: 202 E Commerce St San Antonio TX 78206 Office: 153 Navarro St San Antonio TX 78205

SISKIN, MILTON, dentist; b. Cleveland, Tenn., May 14, 1921; s. Max and Gertrude (Jacobson) S.; B.A., U. Tenn., 1942, D.D.S., 1945; m. LaVerne Lazarov, June 20, 1948; children—Milton, Gregory. Intern Walter G. Zoller Meml. Dental Clinic, Billings Hosp., Chgo., 1946-47, resident, 1947; instr. Coll. Dentistry, U. Tenn., 1947-51, asst. prof., 1951-58, asso. prof., 1958-64, prof., 1964—, chief div. oral medicine and surgery, head dept. oral medicine, 1955-58, lectr., dept. gen. anatomy and embryology Orthodontics; Grad. Sch. cons., VA Hosp., Lamar, 1951-57, VA Hosp., Kennedy br., Memphis, 1953—, John Gaston Hosp., Memphis, 1953—, central office VA, 1965—, Dental Adv. Service, Little People of Am., Harvard Sch. Dental Medicine, Indian Health Service; endodontic cons. Tenn. State Bd. Examiners, 1967—; others; cons. endodontics test constrn. com. Nat. Bd. Dental Examiners, 1972—. Rep. Regional Library Adv. Com. Served as lt. (j.g.) USNR, 1947. Recipient Thomas P. Hinman medallion, 1966; Tenn. Dental Assn. fellow, 1967. Diplomate Am. Bd. Oral Medicine, Am. Bd. Endodontics (com. on constn. and by-laws 1971—). Fellow A.A.A.S., Internat., Am. colls. dentists, Am. Acad. Oral Pathology, Am. Assn. Endodontics (dir. registry periapical lesion, chmn. edn. com. 1969-70, com. constn. and by-laws 1971—); mem. Am. Acad. Oral Roentgenology, Am. Acad. Dental Medicine (edn. com. 1962—, pres. tri-state sect. 1962, 63), Am. Assn. Dental Editors, Inst. Dental Medicine, Am. Inst. Oral Sci. (exec. com.), Am. Soc. Dentistry Children, N.Y. Acad. Scis., So. Endodontics Study Group, Am. Med. Writers' Assn., Am. Soc. Clin. Hypnosis, Am. Dental Assn. (cons. council on dental edn. 1967—, cons. council on hosp. dental service 1968—, council on fed. dental service 1971—, del. 13th and 14th Internat. Dental Congress), Fedn. Dentaire Internationale, Am. Cancer Soc. (local unit dir. 1958-62, 64-68, 70, exec. com. 1971—, elected to Hall Fame Memphis and Shelby County unit 1966, hon. dir. 1963-64, profl. edn. com. Tenn. div. 1971—, dir. 1971—), Zeta Beta Tau, Alpha Omega, Omicron Kappa Upsilon. Club: Executives (Memphis.), Century, President's. Editorial staff Jour. Tenn. Dental Assn., 1951-55; guest editor Am. Profl. Pharmacists, 1962; asst. editor Jour. Dental Medicine, 1963—; cons. editor, contbr. Dental Clinics of N.Am.; editorial bd. Am. Assn. Endodontists, 1964; editor Proc. Conf. on Biology Human Dental Pulp, 1970-72. Contbr. articles profl. jours. and books. Home: 5209 Walnut Grove Rd Memphis TN 38117 Office: U Tenn Coll Dentistry 847 Monroe Av Memphis TN 38103

SISLER, FREDRICK DAVID, oceanographer; b. Washington, June 24, 1916; s. Clarence Eugene and Mildred (Brown) S.; B.S., U. Md., 1938, M.S., 1940; Ph.D., Scripps Inst. Oceanography, 1949; m. Mary Cissel, Mar. 7, 1941; children—Rosemary, Carolyn, Frederick. Research asso. Scripps Inst. Oceanography, LaJolla, Cal., 1946-51; cons. scientist U.S. Govt., Washington, 1951-56; oceanographer USN Mine Def. Lab., Panama City, Fla., 1956-59; head spl. studies unit Geol. Survey, Washington, 1959-63; sr. scientist water pollution control Dept. Interior, Washington, 1963—. Served to capt. with chem. corps, AUS, 1942-46. Mem. Am. Soc. Microbiology, A.A.A.S., Am. Soc. Limnology and Oceanography. Inventor biochem. fuel cell, 1961, automatic fuel connector kits for outboards. Research organic matter in meteorites, chem. stability of the atmosphere, ocean pollution. Home: 5005 Wapakoneta Rd Washington DC 20016 Office: Dept Interior 18th and C St NW Washington DC 20240

SISTRUNK, JAMES DUDLEY, clergyman, librarian; b. Jayess, Miss., Aug. 13, 1919; s. James Cannon and Amelia Frances (Smith) S.; student La. State U., 1945-46, Clarke Meml. Coll., 1951-52; B.A., Baylor U., 1954, postgrad., 1954; B.D., Southwestern Bapt. Theol. Sem., 1957; B.S. in L.S., N. Tex. State U., 1959; postgrad. U. N.C., 1960; m. Helen Anna Wilson, Dec. 19, 1942; children—James Dudley, Richard Stanley. With Interstate Oil Pipe Line Co., Natchez, Miss., 1946-51; ordained to ministry Bapt. Ch., 1952; pastor Belfalls (Tex.) Bapt. Ch., 1952-54, Fairview Bapt. Ch., Valley Mills, Tex., 1955-57; circulation librarian Southwestern Bapt. Theol. Sem., 1957-59; adminstrv. librarian Southeastern Bapt. Theol. Sem., 1959-64; librarian, prof. Campbell Coll., Blues Creek, N.C., 1964—. Bd. dirs. Wake Forest Pub. Library, 1961-64. Served with 82d Airdrome Squadron, USAAF, 1942-45. Mem. Am., Southeastern, N.C. (membership com. 1963-64) library assns., Am. Theol. Library Assn. (membership com. 1963-64), Assn. Eastern N.C. Colls. (chmn. commn. on library affairs), Alpha Lambda Sigma. Lion (dir.). Author: History of Carrie Rich Memorial Library, 1887-1966. Address: Box 415 Buies Creek NC 27506

SISTRUNK, WALTER EVERETT, educator; b. Montbrook, Fla., Apr. 6, 1920; s. Odis Carlos and Ruby Letillie (Howard) S.; A.A., Central Fla. Jr. Coll., 1960; B.A. in Edn. with honors, 1962, M.Ed., 1963, Ed.D., 1966; m. Marian Godwin, Feb. 6, 1943; children—Mary Kathryn, Michael E., David F., Carlos L., Walter Eugene, Brenda Gail. Farmer, mcht., 1945-55; asst. circulation mgr. Fla. Times Union, 1955-58; credit mgr. Marion Hardware Co., Ocala, Fla., 1958-62; head dept. social studies Bradford High Sch., Starke, Fla., 1962-65; dir. continuing edn. Brunswick Coll. (Ga.), 1965-66; asst. prof. elementary and secondary edn., dir. student tchrs. Miss. State U., 1966-68, asst. prof. ednl. adminstrn., dir. learning labs., 1968-72, prof. ednl. adminstrn., 1972—. Cons., 1971-72, Choctaw Indian Schs., and many pub. sch. dists. Chmn. Com. for Acad. Affairs, 1967—. Trustee Wood Jr. Coll. So. Edn. fellow, 1963-66; Fla. Tchr. scholar, 1959-62; named Bradford County Tchr. of Year, Fla. Edn. Assn., 1965. Mem. Am. Assn. Sch. Adminstrs., Miss. Edn. Assn., Miss. Assn. for Supervision and Curriculum Devel., Southeastern Region Assn. Tchr. Educators (1st v.p. 1971-72), Assn. Tchr. Educators, Kappa Delta Pi, Phi Kappa Phi, Phi Delta Kappa. Democrat. Methodist. Mason, Rotarian. Author: (with Robert C. Maxson) A Practical Approach to Social Studies, 1972; ATheoretical Framework for Instructional Practice, 1971. Home: 1103 Robin Hood Rd Starkville MS 39759 Office: Drawer LH State College MS 39762

SITES, JOHN EDWARD, educator; b. Dayton, O., June 27, 1938; s. John Wilber and Peggy (Hunter) S.; B.A. in Edn., U. Fla., 1960; J.D., U. Miami, 1966; M.A., Appalachian State U., 1970; m. Joan Marie Paris, Sept. 24, 1965; 1 son, Jack Clinton. Classroom tchr. social studies Dade County (Fla.) Pub. Schs., 1960-63, inst. TV tchr. history, 1963-65, asst. prin. for adminstrn., 1965-66; research asst. Bradley, Johnson, Nelson & Young, Attys., Fla., 1966-67; prof. social scis. Brenau Coll., Gainesville, Ga., 1967-68, dean coll., prof. social scis., 1968—. Cons. Gainesville Model Cities, 1968—, U. Miami Endowment Com., 1969—, Ga. Council on Edn., 1968—. Recipient Outstanding Educator award Brenau Coll., 1971. Mem. Am., Ga. sociol. assnsn., So. Sociol. Soc., Ga. Conf. on Social Welfare (dir.), Acad. Deans So. States, Am. Conf. Acad. Deans, Am. Assn. for Higher Edn., A.A.A.S., Pi Kappa Alpha, Delta Theta Phi, Phi Delta

Kappa, Phi Alpha Theta. Author: (with others) Teacher's Guide to Basic Education, 1961; Teacher's Guide to World Geography, 1964; Teacher's Guide to ITV American History, 1965. Home: 916 Chattahoochee Dr NE Gainesville GA 30501

SITES, JOHN WILBUR, horticulturist, univ. dean.; b. Syracuse, N.Y., July 11, 1912; s. John Milton and Kathryn McKee (Hillery) S.; B.S., Ohio State U., 1935, M.S., 1940, Ph.D., 1950; m. Peggy Hunter, July 11, 1936; children—John Edward, Sharon Eleanor (Mrs. Joseph Pesek III), Kathryn Hunter (Mrs. Robert T. Shewey). Jr. horticulturist Dept. Agr., Zanesville, O., 1935-36, asst. horticulturist, 1936-42; asso. horticulturist U. Fla. Agrl. Expt. Stas., Lake Alfred, 1942-45, horticulturist, 1946-55, Gainesville, 1955-67, asst. dir., 1955-57, head fruit crops dept., 1957-60, asso. dir., 1960-67, dir., dean for research, 1967—. Pres., Winter Haven Pops (Fla.) Orch. Assn., 1954. Recipient Agrl. award for meritorious service Charles H. DuPont Found., 1970. Mem. Am. Soc. Hort. Sci. (Gourley award for pomol. research 1951), Fla. Hort. Soc. (Krome Meml. Inst. award 1962), Soil and Plant Soc. Fla., Nat. Research Inst., Sigma Xi, Alpha Gamma Rho, Gamma Sigma Delta, Pi Alpha Xi. Episcopalian (vestryman 1968—). Kiwanian (pres. Winter Haven 1950). Club: University of Fla. Faculty (pres. 1963-64). Home: 1819 SW 35th Av Gainesville FL 32601

SITTERSON, JOSEPH CARLYLE, univ. chancellor; b. Kinston, N.C., Jan. 17, 1911; s. Simon Carlyle and Gladys (Mitchell) S.; A.B., U. of N.C., 1931, A.M., 1932, Ph.D. (fellow in history, 1933-34), 1937; Litt.D., U. Chattanooga, 1967; m. Nancy Dixon Howard, Sept. 9, 1944; children—Joseph Carlyle, Mary, Curtis. Instr. Ga. Mil. Acad., 1932-33; dir. N.C. Hall of History, Raleigh, 1934-35; instr. U. of N.C., 1935-39, asst. prof., 1939-44, asso. prof., 1944-47, prof. history, 1947—, dean Coll. Arts and Scis., 1955-65, dean gen. coll., 1961-65, Kenan prof., 1961—, vice chancellor univ., 1965-66, chancellor, 1966—; lectr. summer schs. Coll. William and Mary, 1939; N.C. Coll., Durham, 1947; Policy analyst W.P.B., 1944-46. Served with AUS, 1942. Social Science Research council fellow, 1931-32; Julius Rosenwald fellowship, 1940-41. Mem. Am. Conf. Academic Deans (chmn. 1964-65), Am. Hist. Assn., So. Hist. Assn. (sec.-treas. 1948-51; exec. council 1952-55), Mississippi Valley Hist. Assn., Hist. Soc. of N.C., Phi Beta Kappa. Democrat. Episcopalian. Author: Secession Movement in N.C., 1939; American Society and the Changing World, (with C. H. Pegg and others), 1942; Industrial Mobilization for War (with J. W. Fesler and others), 1947; Sugar Country, 1953; Studies in Southern History, 1957. Editor: Edmund Ruffin's Essay on Calcerous Manures, 1961. Contbr. to hist. revs. Mem. bd. editors jour. of Southern History. Home: 217 Hillcrest Circle Chapel Hill NC 27514

SITTON, CLAUDE FOX, newspaper editor; b. Emory, Ga., Dec. 4, 1925; s. Claude B. and Pauline (Fox) S.; A.B., Emory U., 1949; m. Eva McLaurin Whetstone, June 5, 1953; children—Lauren Lea, Clinton, Suzanna, McLaurin. Reporter, Internat. News Service, 1949-50; with U.P., 1950-55, writer-editor N.Y.C., 1952-55; information officer USIA, 1955-57; mem. staff N.Y. Times, 1957-68, nat. news dir., 1964-68; editorial dir. The News and Observer Pub. Co., Raleigh, N.C., 1968-71, v.p., 1971—, editor The News and Observer, 1970—. Served USNR, 1943-46. Mem. Am. Soc. Newspaper Editors, Nat. Conf. Editorial Writers, Sigma Delta Chi. Presbyn. Club: Watauga. Home: 3104 Monticello Dr Raleigh NC 27612 Office: News and Observer 215 S McDowell St Raleigh NC 27601

SITWELL, PHRONSIE IRENE MARSH (MRS. HERBERT CECIL FITZROY), SITWELL), poet, feature writer, educator; b. nr. Lynchburg, Va., Apr. 1, 1907; d. Peter Addison and Constance (Fisher) Marsh; student Lynchburg Coll., 1924-26; B.S., Mary Washington Coll., Fredericksburg, 1927; M.A., Columbia, 1932; summer study U. Va., 1925, 71, Inst. on World Affairs, Geneva, Switzerland, 1935, N.Y.U., 1940-41, U. Pa., 1957; postgrad. Va. Poly. Inst., 1966-67, U. Va., 1970-71; m. Erik Solling Monberg, Apr. 25, 1943 (div. 1947); 1 son, Edmund Marsh; m. 2d, Herbert Cecil FitzRoy Sitwell, May 14, 1961 (dec. Aug. 1965). Tchr. Salem (Va.) High Sch., 1927-28, E. C. Glass High Sch., Lynchburg, 1928-30, Oyster Bay, N.Y., 1930-34, Washington, 1934-44, 50-62; adminstrv. asst. TVA, 1933; gen. supr. edn. Wythe County Schs., Wytheville, Va., 1945-46; instr. Phillips Coll., Lynchburg, 1946-47; ednl. adviser Sullins Coll., Bristol, Va., 1947-49; social studies chmn. Capitol Page Sch., 1949-50; Ofcl. visitor 3d Internat. Congress on Comparative Law, The Hague, Netherlands, 1937; mem. Columbia Writers' Conf., 1966. Del. Va. Dem. Conv., 1970; mem. Dem. Com. of Bedford County. Recipient fellowship to Nat. Music Camp, Interlochen, Mich., to write scripts for NBC broadcast, 1940, fellowship to N.Y.U., 1941, U. Pa., summer 1957. Mem. Am. Acad. Polit. Sci., Modern Lang. Assn., Soc. Archtl. Historians, Poetry Soc. Va., Nat. Trust Historic Preservation, League Am. Pen Women (v.p. charge creative activities D.C. br. 1939-41), Arts Club Washington, U.D.C., Internat. Platform Speakers Assn., Poetry Soc. Bedford (co-founder, pres. 1961-62, 70-71), English Speaking Union, Va., Lynchburg, Bedford hist. socs., Pi Gamma Mu, Episcopalian. Clubs: Specs, Writers of Va., Woman's (pres. Oyster Bay, N.Y. 1932-34). Contbr. poems Maelstrom, VPI, 1966, others; also articles. Home: Three Otters Estate RFD 2 Bedford VA 24523 also 1435 Holly St NW Washington DC 20012 also 1021 Federal St Lynchburg VA 24504

SIVLEY, ROBERT BENTON, psychologist; b. Chattanooga, Feb. 2, 1934; s. Grover Benton and Alma (Boyd) S.; B.A., David Lipscomb Coll., 1955; M.A., George Peabody Coll., 1956, Ph.D., 1960; m. Barbara Outten, Apr. 23, 1960; children—Bobby, John, William. Chief psychologist Central State Hosp., Nashville, 1960-61; psychologist VA Hosp., Murfreesboro, Tenn., 1961-67; exec. dir. Pennyroyal Regional Mental Health Center, Hopkinsville, Ky., 1967—; vis. lectr. U. Ky., Hopkinsville Community Coll.; cons. Western State Hosp., Outwood State Hosp. and Sch. Mem. Human Relations Commn., 1969—. Mem. Am., Southeastern, Ky. psychol. assns. Rotarian. Home: 131 S Sunset Circle Hopkinsville KY 42240 Office: 735 North Dr Hopkinsville KY 42240

SIZEMORE, MARGARET DAVIDSON, coll. dean; b. Birmingham, Ala.; d. Julius Weston and Ruth (Lee) Davidson; A.B., Samford U., 1928, M.A., 1930; normal degree U. Paris, 1929; postgrad. Western Res. U., U. Ala., Sorbonne, Paris; m. James Middleton Sizemore, June 19, 1937; children—James Middleton, Ruth Lee. Asso. prof. modern langs. Howard Coll., 1947-58, dean of women, 1950—. Chmn. speakers' bur. Birmingham Civic Opera Bd., 1959-60; mem. adv. bd. Birmingham Mus. Art; mem. woman's com. Birmingham Symphony; bd. dirs. Ala. Pops' Orch.; chmn. Birmingham Festival of Arts, 1960-61, hon. chmn., 1962, sec., 1962-63; bd. visitors Monterrey Tech. (Mex.); mem. Dept. Def. Adv. Com. Women in Service; bd. dirs. Lighthouse Lectrs.; pres. Freedom Ednl. Found.; dir. Am. Scholars Library Ala. Lives; mem. Gov.'s Com. Status Women; pres. Women's Com. 100 Greater Birmingham, 1968-70; mem. Ala. Constn. Revisions Commn., 1969—, Tannehill Mine and Foundry Commn., Ala. Commn. Ethics and Morals, 1971—, Jefferson County Hist. Commn., Bi-Centennial Commn. Ala., Gov.'s Com. Employment Handicapped, 1971; co-chmn. all cultural events Birmingham Centennial, 1971-72. Recipient citation Ami de France, City Paris, 1951, Scroll from Archbishop of Canterbury, England, 1951, ofcl. guest City of Birmingham, England, 1953, Woman of Achievement in Edn., 1956, Birmingham Woman of the Year 1962; recipient Freedoms Found. Valley Forge award 1963; Vigilant Patriot award 1963; Ala. Merit Mother, 1964; award for civic service Birmingham Jaycees, 1965; Service to Mankind award Sertoma Clubs, 1971; named Alumna-of-Yr., Samford U., 1971. Fellow Royal Soc. Arts (London); mem. Nat. Assn. Women Deans (membership chmn. Ala.), Nat. League Am. Penwomen (pres. Birmingham 1966-68), Antiquarian Soc. (pres. 1960-61), Nat. Soc. Arts and Letters, Ala., Birmingham hist. socs., English-Speaking Union, Presidents and Deans Am. Colls., Brit. Am. Soc. Am., Ala. Assn. of Women Deans (sec. 1951-53), Ala. Guidance Assn. (pres. 1955-57), Am. Assn. U. Women, Antiquarian Soc. (pres. 1960-61), Ala. Writers Conclave (pres. 1962-63), Daus. Colonial Wars, Daus. Barons of Runnemede, D.A.R., Daus. Am. Colonists (state regent 1964-67). Arlington Hist. Assn. (pres. 1970—), Soc. Lees Va., U.D.C., Internat. Platform Assn., Forney Hist. Soc. (v.p. 1969-70, trustee), Alpha Delta Pi. Clubs: Bibliophiles, New Era Concordia, Faculty Wives (hon.); Altrusa (pres. Birmingham 1955-56), Metropolitan Dinner (dir.); Overseas (pres.), Scottish Clan (Chattan). Co-author: The Amazing Marriage of Marie Eustis and Josef Hofmann, 1965; also author hist. sketches. Home: 3084 Sterling Rd Birmingham AL 35213

SIZEMORE, ORAL GLEN, educator; b. Macomb, Okla., Nov. 19, 1927; s. Cecil Bailey and Madge (Cook) S.; A.B., E. Central State Coll., Ada, Okla., 1949; M.S., Ind. U., 1950; Ed.D., Okla. State U., 1961; m. Margaret Ann Smith, Feb. 6, 1959; children—Elizabeth Ann, David Fulton, Christopher Glen. Tchr. math. Broken Arrow (Okla.) Jr. High Sch., 1952-54; grad. asst. Kellogg Found. grant Okla. State U., 1954-55; dir. audio-visual dept. Northeastern State Coll., Tahlequah, Okla., 1956-63, prof. psychology, 1963—. Served with C.E., AUS, 1945-47. Recipient NSF grant State U. Ia., summer 1962. Mem. Okla. Edn. Assn. (past dept. pres.), Am. Psychol. Assn., Phi Delta Kappa. Lion. Home: 1012 Mike St Tahlequah OK 74464

SKAGGS, AUSTIN RICHARD, dentist; b. Louisville, Mar. 25, 1920; s. Raymond Walter and Viola Mae (Schmeltz) S.; B.S., U. Lousville, 1949, D.M.D., 1953; m. Marjorie Juanita Cook, June 19, 1945; children—Linda Lea (Mrs. Fred Edward Marshall III), Donna Sue. Practice dentistry, Louisville, 1953—; pvt. practice Jefferson County Bd. of Health, 1954-60. Program chmn. Republican. Club, Louisville, 1966. Served with USNR, 1941-45. Mem. Am., Ky. dental assns., Louisville Dental Soc., Delta Sigma Delta (life). Presbyn. (deacon 1959). Mason, Kiwanian (chmn. program com. 1965). Home: 18 Rio Vista Dr Louisville KY 40207 Office: 120 Village Sq Louisville KY 40243

SKAGGS, HORACE GRANT, dentist; b. Sublett, Ky., Sept. 11, 1912; s. Doctor Randolph and Sallie Mandy (Lemaster) S.; student U. Ky., 1932-33, postgrad., 1935-39; D.M.D., U. Louisville, 1939; m. Mildred Louise Mansfield, Sept. 2, 1933; children—William Randolph, Horace Grant. Pvt. practice dentistry, Paintsville and Lynch, Ky., 1939-41, Ashland, Ky., 1945—; mem. staff Kings Daus. Hosp., Ashland. Mem. YMCA, 1953—. Bd. dirs. Tb Assn. Mem. Ky. Dental Assn., Eastern Dist. Dental Soc. (pres. 1956), Am. Dental assn., S.A.R., Psi Omega. Baptist. Mason (32 deg.), Rotarian, Toastmaster (past pres.). Home: 2638 Virginia Av Ashland KY 41101 Office: 307-8 2d Nat Bank Bldg Ashland KY 41101

SKAGGS, JERRY RAY, agrl. exec.; b. Gorman, Tex., Oct. 9, 1934; s. Archie E. and Georgia (Sanders) S.; Asso. Sci., Tarleton State Coll., 1955; B.S., Tex. Tech. Coll., 1957; m. Virginia Nelson, May 23, 1959; children—Susan Beth, Sharon Rene. Area sales rep. Van Waters & Rogers, Inc., Dallas and Lubbock, Tex., 1959-63; sales mgr. Shur-Gro Liquid Feed, Hereford, Tex., 1963-71, pres., gen. mgr., 1971—, dir., v.p. Shur-Gro Industries, Inc., Clovis, N.M. Served with AUS, 1957-59. Mem. Am. Soc. Animal Sci. Baptist. Home: 248 Centre St Hereford TX 79045 Office: Box 1150 Hereford TX 79045

SKEEN, CLYDE, airplane co. exec.; b. Kusa, Okla., Jan. 31, 1917; s. Clyde and Matilda (McCoy) S.; B.A., Kan. State Coll., 1940; student mgmt., Harvard Bus. Sch., 1945; LL.D., Okla. Christian Coll., 1969; m. Helen M. Fowler, Aug. 30, 1941; children—William C., James R., Shelly. Chief accountant Wichita division Boeing Airplane Co., 1945-49, asst. sec. and treas., divisional controller Wichita div., 1949-52, asst. controller hdqrs. office, 1952-53, controller hdqrs. office, 1953-58, asst. gen. mgr. systems mgmt. office, 1958-59, vice pres. program mgmt., 1959-60; exec. v.p., gen. mgr. Ling-Temco Electronics, Inc., Temco Electronics & Missiles Co., 1960-61; exec. v.p. Ling-Temco-Vought, Inc., 1961-64, pres., chmn. bd., 1964-70; spl. exec., 1970-71; chmn. exec. com. Omega-Alpha, Inc., 1971—, also dir.; chmn. bd., dir. Crescent Gen. Corp., Beverly Hills, Cal., Illustrated World Ency., Inc., Woodbury, N.Y.; dir. Tex. Bank & Trust Co., Gen. Automotive Parts Co. (both Dallas), others. Trustee Nat. Security Indsl. Assn. Mem. Aero-Space Industries, Financial Execs. Inst., Am. Rocket Soc., Tax Execs. Inst. Home: 7140 Spring Valley Rd Dallas TX 75240

SKELTON, BILLY JONES, newspaper editor; b. Eupora, Miss., Oct. 4, 1922; s. Alonzo and Essie (Jones) S.; B.A., Miss. Coll., 1943; m. Marion Wagner Waller, Aug. 23, 1947; children—Robert Waller, Dana, Deborah. Reporter, Clarksdale (Miss.) Daily Register, 1946-47, Comml. Appeal, Memphis, 1950-51; Sunday Mag. editor Clarion-Ledger, Jackson, Miss., 1947-50, reporter, 1965—; city editor Clarksdale Press-Register, 1951-65, columnist, Jus' Strummin', 1957—. Served with USNR, 1943-46. Mem. Sigma Delta Chi. Baptist. Contbr. articles to popular mags. Home: 1010 Tanglewood Dr Clinton MS 39056 Office: 311 E Pearl St Jackson MS 39201

SKELTON, BYRON GEORGE, judge; b. Florence, 1905; s. Clarence Edgar and Avis (Bowmer) S.; student Baylor U., 1923-24; A.B., U. Tex., 1927, M.A., 1928, LL.B., 1931; m. Ruth Alice Thomas, Nov. 28, 1931; children—Sue, Sandra. Admitted to Tex. bar, 1931, Circuit Ct. Appeals, 1937, U.S. Supreme Ct., 1946, FCC, 1950, Tax Ct., U.S., 1952, U.S. Treasury Dept., 1952, ICC, 1953; practice of law, Temple, Tex., 1931-66; partner Saulsbury & Skelton, 1934-42, Saulsbury, Skelton, Everton, Bowmer & Courtney, 1944-55, Skelton, Bowmer & Courtney, 1955-66; judge U.S. Court of Claims, Washington, 1966—. County atty. Bell County, Tex., 1934-38; spl. asst. U.S. ambassador to Argentina, 1942-45; city atty., Temple, 1944-60. Mem. Democratic Nat. Com., 1956-64, del. Dem. Nat. Conv., 1948, 56, 60, 64, Tex. Dem. Conv., 1946, 48, 50, 52, 54, 56, 60, 64, vice chmn., 1948, 58; chmn. Dem. Adv. Council Tex., 1955-57. Pres., Temple Indsl. Found., 1966. Apptd. Ky. Col. and Adm. in Tex. Navy, 1959. Mem. State Bar Tex., Am., Bell-Lampasas and Mills Counties (past pres.) bar assns., Am. Law Inst., Am. Judicature Soc., C. of C. (past pres., dir.), Ex-Students' Assn. U. Tex. (past pres., mem. exec. council), Phi Beta Kappa, Pi Sigma Alpha, Sigma Delta Pi, Delta Theta Phi (hon.). Democrat. Methodist (steward). Mason (Shriner; past worshipful master), Kiwanian (past pres.). Home: Salado TX 76571 also 2500 Virginia Av NW Washington DC 20037 Office: 717 Madison Pl NW Washington DC 20005

SKELTON, DOROTHY GENEVA SIMMONS (MRS. JOHN WILLIAM SKELTON), educator; b. Woodland, Cal.; d. Jack Elijah and Helen Anna (Siebe) Simmons; B.A., U. Cal., 1940, M.A., 1943; m. John William Skelton, July 16, 1941. Sr. research analyst War Dept., Gen. Staff, M.I. Div. G-2, Washington, 1944-45; vol. researcher, monuments, fine arts and archives sect. Restitution Br., Office Mil. Govt. for Hesse, Wiesbaden, Germany, 1947-48; vol. art tchr. German children in Bad Nauheim, Germany, 1947-48; art educator, lectr. Dayton (O.) Art Inst., 1955; art educator Lincoln Sch., Dayton, 1956-60; art edn. instr. U. Va. Sch. Gen. Studies, Charlottesville, 1962—; researcher in genealogy; exhibited in group shows, Cal., Colo., Ohio, Washington and Va. Represented in permanent collections Madison Hall, Charlottesville, Madison Center, Madison, Va. Mem. Nat. League Am. Pen Women, Am. Assn. Museums, Coll. Art Assn. Am., Nat. Soc. Arts and Letters, Inst. for Study of Art in Edn., Dayton Soc. Painters and Sculptors, Va. Mus. Fine Arts, Cal. Alumni Assn., Air Force Officers Wives Club. Republican. Methodist. Clubs: Army Navy Country; Lake of the Woods (Va.) Golf and Country. Address: Lotos Lakes Brightwood VA 22715

SKELTON, ROBERT BEATTIE, educator; b. Auburn, Mich., Apr. 23, 1913; s. Glen Beattie and Irene (Richardson) S.; student Bay City Jr. Coll., 1934-35; A.B., Eastern Mich. U., 1937; M.A. (Univ. scholar 1937-38), U. Mich., 1938, Ph.D. (Horace H. Rackham spl. fellow 1949-50, Am. Council Learned Socs. grantee Linguistics Inst. 1950), 1950; Roosevelt fellow, U. Brazil, 1942-43, Chilean Govt. fellow, U. Chile, 1943; m. Mary Carmack, June 2, 1940; children—Susan, Robert Thomas, Rebecca and Melissa (twins). Mem. faculty Auburn U., 1939—, prof., 1954—, research prof. comparative linguistics, 1967—, head dept. fgn. langs., 1954-57. Served ensign to lt., USNR, 1943-46. Mem. Nat. Geog. Soc., Modern Lang. Assn., Am. Assn. Tchrs. French, Am. Assn. Tchrs. German, Am. Assn. Tchrs. Spanish and Portuguese, Linguistic Soc. Am., Inst. Internat. Edn. (asso.), Nat. Assn. Standard Med. Vocabulary, Free Soc. Assn., Internat. Platform Assn., Am. Mus. Natural History (asso.), Acad. Tamil Culture (asso.). Contbr. articles, monographs profl. jours. Home: 426 Scott St Auburn AL

SKILES, FRANCES MARGARET STEWARDSON (MRS. SAMMIE EARL SKILES), banker; b. Shields, Tex., Apr. 8, 1927; d. Hardy E. and Birdie J. (Barton) Stewardson; student Weatherford Jr. Coll., Tex. Bus. Coll., Weatherford, 1945-46, Am. Inst. Banking, 1950-51; m. Sammie Earl Skiles, July 2, 1944; 1 son, Harold Stewardson. Bookkeeper, teller Santa Anna (Tex.) Nat. Bank, 1942-44; sec. Tex. Power & Light Co., Weatherford, 1945-46; asst. tax collector Parker County, Weatherford, 1947-48; bookkeeper, proof operator, teller, asst. cashier Mchts. & Farmers State Bank, Weatherford, 1949—. Organizer, pres. Parker County Young Homemakers, 1962; treas. Campbell Meml. Hosp. Aux., 1965—; co-chmn. Am. Cancer Soc., Parker County, 1965. Named Outstanding Clubwoman, Pioneer dist. Tex. Fedn. Women's Clubs, 1963. Mem. Tex. Fedn. Women's Clubs (chmn. Tex. Heritage dept., chmn. conservation dept.; dist. pres. 1970-72), Area V. Assn. Young Homemakers Tex., Future Farmers Am. (Weatherford chpt.), Nat. Assn. Bank Women, Weatherford C. of C., Epsilon Sigma Alpha. Baptist Clubs: Weatherford Lady Lions (past pres.), Twentieth Century (v.p. homd sci. dept., past pres.). Home: PO Box 156 1224 S Brazos St Weatherford TX 76086 Office: PO Box 760 102 N Main St Weatherford TX 76086

SKINNER, FRANK DOUGLAS, editor; b. Shreveport, La., May 13, 1926; s. Douglas N. and Charlotte (Rohrbough) S.; B.A. in Journalism, U. Okla., 1947; m. Anna Jean Gray, Dec. 12, 1953; children—Douglas Gray, Mary Craig. News editor, Anadarko (Okla.) Daily News, 1948-53; asst. news editor Mich. State U., 1953-56; univ. news editor, 1956-62; pub. information officer Chatham Coll., 1963-66; editor Higher Edn. and Nat. Affairs, Am. Council on Edn., Washington, 1966—. Recipient feature writing, make-up awards Okla. Press Assn., 1949, 1951, Edn. News award Am. Coll. Pub. Relations Assn., 1960. Mem. Edn. Writers Assn. Contbr. to profl. jours. Home: 6319 Utah Av NW Washington DC 20015 Office: 1 Dupont Circle Washington DC 20036

SKINNER, HENRY T(HOMAS), biologist; b. East Sutton, Eng., Sept. 24, 1907; s. William and Gertrude (Pitman) S.; student Wisley Sch., Royal Hort. Soc., 1923-26; B.Sc., Cornell U., 1936, M.S., 1938, Ph.D., U. Pa., 1952; m. Anna Mildred Wood, Nov. 10, 1951; 1 dau., Susan Pitman. Came to U.S., 1927, naturalized, 1943. Student asst. Arnold Arboretum, Harvard, 1927-29; instr. horticulture Cornell U., 1931-40; curator Morris Arboretum, U. Pa., 1940-43, 45-52; dir. Nat. Arboretum, Washington, 1952—. Chmn. U.S. Dept. Agr. survey team on establishment Hawaiian Tropical Bot. Garden, 1962. Served with USAAF, 1943-45. Recipient Jackson Dawson medal Mass. Hort. Soc., 1943. Am. Home Achievement medal, 1961, Arthur Hoyt Scott Hort. award, 1963, Gold medal Am. Rhododendron Soc., 1965; Coleman award Am. Assn. Nurserymen, 1968; Superior Service award U.S. Dept. Agr., 1970; Silver Seal medal Nat. Council State Garden Clubs, 1970; Gold medal Nat. Garden Club Am., 1971; grantee Am. Philos. Soc., for population studies in native azaleas Eastern N.Am., 1951. Mem. Am. Assn. Botanic Gardens and Arboreta (pres. 1947), Am. Hort. Council (v.p., commn. chmn. 1958-60), Internat. Soc. Hort. Sci. (council, 1966—), Am. Hort. Soc. (pres. 1962-63), Bot. Soc. Am., Sigma Xi, Phi Kappa Phi, Pi Alpha Xi; hon. mem. Mass. Hort. Soc., Women's Nat. Farm and Garden Assn. Editor: Garden Plants in Color, 1959. Home: 2817 Bosworth Lane Bowie MD 20715 Office: US Nat Arboretum Washington DC 20002

SKINNER, HUBERT C(LAYTON), educator; b. Tulsa, Oct. 3, 1929; s. Orlo C. and Onamae (Hood) S.; B.S. in Geology, U. Okla., 1951, M.S., 1953, Ph.D., 1954; m. Judith Ann Miller, Dec. 27, 1958; children—Susan, Sharon, Kathryn. Museum technician U. Okla., 1951-52, grad. asst., 1952-53, teaching asst., summer 1953, instr. geology, 1953-54, summer 1954; supr. Paleontol. Lab. La. div. Texaco, Inc., 1954-57; asst. prof. Tulane U., 1954-57, asso. prof., 1957-62, prof., 1962—, editor Tulane Studies in Geology and Paleontology, 1962—; vis. prof. U. Okla., summer 1965. Served with USAFR, 1951-58. Fellow Geol. Soc. Am.; mem. Paleontol. Soc., Paleontol. Assn. Great Britain, Am. Assn. Petroleum Geologists, Soc. Econ. Paleontologists and Mineralogists, Sigma Xi, Sigma Gamma Epsilon (nat. pres. 1965-70), Phi Sigma. Research, numerous pubs. sci., tech. jours. Home: 3737 Napoleon Av New Orleans LA 70125

SKINNER, JACK DITTO, oil producer; b. Tulsa, Aug. 25, 1924; s. Burnice Jack and Mable Inez (Ditto) S.; student Kilgore Jr. Coll., 1946-47, U. Houston, 1954-55, U. Miss. Extension, 1956-58; m. Mary McCune Causey, Oct. 5, 1961; children—Kathryne, Ann, Jack Ditto, Michael, Jeffery. Chief clk., regional non-tech. super. Atlantic Refining Co., Tex., N.M. and Gulf Coast, 1948-55; gen. supt. land and prodn. Vaughey & Vaughey, Jackson, Miss., 1955-71; ind. oil producer and lease broker, Jackson, 1971—. Served as lt. USNR, World War II. Mem. Miss. Landmens Assn., Miss. Geol. Soc., Miss. Thoroughbred Breeders and Owners Assn. (v.p.), Jackson Petroleum Club: Home and office: 1817 Northwood Circle Jackson MS 39213

SKINNER, MARY LOU HEATON, govt. ofcl.; b. Dalhart, Tex., Dec. 22, 1909; d. Roy Henry and Hazel (Conger) Heaton; B.S. in Edn., U. N.D., 1935; M.P.H. in Health Edn., U. Cal. at Berkeley, 1948; m. Howard Edward Skinner, Jan. 9, 1944 (div. Oct. 1948). Dietetic intern Grasslands Hosp., 1935-36; dietitian charge therapeutic diets N.Y. Infirmary for Women and Children, 1936-37;

health edn. sec. Yonkers (N.Y.) Tb and Health Assn., 1937-38; exec. sec. Newburgh (N.Y.) Tb and Health Assn., 1938-41; field advisor on local work N.Y. State Com. on Tb and Pub. Health, 1941-44; substitute tchr. Tulare County Schs., Cal., 1944-45; cons. Cal. Tb and Health Assn., 1945-46; asso. in pub. health U. Cal. Sch. Pub. Health at Berkeley, 1947-49; health educator div. dental pub. health USPHS, 1949-52, health edn. cons. regions I and II, N.Y.C., 1953-55, Indian health behavior study, 1955-59, health edn. cons. region IV, Atlanta, 1959—. Adv. com. to Nat. Tng. Labs., N.E.A.; adv. com. Atlanta-Regional Lab. Community Leadership Devel., 1966-67. Fellow Am. Pub. Health Assn. (chmn. health edn. sect. So. br. 1966-67, sect. chmn. program com. 1967), Soc. Pub. Health Educators (treas., 1953-55, eligibility com. 1959-61); mem. Adult Edn. Assn. U.S.A., Soc. for Psychol. Study Social Issues, Commd. Officers Assn. USPHS (v.p. 1970, sec. 1969, pres. Atlanta br. 1971), Internat. Union for Health Edn. of Pub., Delta Omega, Pi Lambda Theta, Nu Delta Pi, Pi Beta Phi. Contbr. articles to profl. jours. Office: Dept Health Education and Welfare USPHS 50th 7th St NE Atlanta GA 30323

SKINNER, ROY GENE, basketball coach; b. Paducah, Ky., Apr. 17, 1930; s. Marion Henry and Ruby (Tapp) S.; diploma Paducah Jr. Coll., 1950; A.B., Presbyn. Coll., 1952; M.A., George Peabody Coll., 1958; m. Betty Jo Ledford, June 3, 1952; children—Kim Henry, Brad Steven, Chris, Joe Brant, Tapp Blaine, Dea. Dir., Found. Boys' Club, Portsmouth, Va., 1953; tchr., coach Cradock High Sch., Portsmouth, 1954-56, Paducah Jr. Coll., 1957; asst. coach Vanderbilt U., Nashville, 1957-61, head basketball coach, 1961—. Lectr., coach under U.S. State Dept. specialist grant, Taipei, Taiwan, 1963. Named Coach of Year, Nashville Banner, 1963, Young Man of Year, Jr. C. of C., 1963, S.E. Conf. Coach of Year, 1965, 1967. Mem. Nat. Collegiate Athletic Assn., Basketball Assn. Republic China (hon.). Mem. Christian Ch. Contbr. articles to sports publs. Office: Vanderbilt U Nashville TN 37203

SKIPPER, C(HARLES) W., editor; b. Houston, Oct. 13, 1914; s. Charles W. and Bessie (Davis) S.; student U. Houston; m. Kathryn Rhodes, Oct. 5, 1940; children—Kay, Karen. With accounting dept. Hughes Tool Co., 1936-42; asst. mgr. Houston Candy Co., 1946-48; became reporter Houston Post, 1948, night city editor, 1961, then asst. city editor, asst. Sunday editor, city editor, 1965-70, travel and Sunday supplement editor, 1970—. Served with AUS, 1942-46. Home: 8315 Concho Lane Houston TX 77036 Office 4747 Southwest Freeway Houston TX 77001

SKIPPER, HOWARD EARLE, biochemist; b. Avon Park, Fla., Nov. 21, 1915; B.S., U. Fla., 1938, M.S., 1939, Ph.D. in Nutrition, Biochemistry, 1941; m. 1941; two children. Head biochemistry div., So. Research Inst., 1946-48, asst. dir., 1948-63; v.p. also dir. Kettering-Meyer Labs, 1964—; prof. exptl. pathology Med. Center, U. Ala., 1955—. Mem. adv. com. isotopes, AEC, 1953-56; pharmacological and exptl. therapeutical study sect. USPHS, 1954-56; pharmacol.-biochem. panel Cancer Chemotherapy Nat. Service Center, 1956-59, drug evaluation panel, 1958-59, also chmn. cancer chemotherapy rev. bd. NIH, 1958-60; nat. adviser Cancer Council, 1958-60, 64—, dissemination, field testing com., U.S. Army Chem. Corps., 1961-63, also bd. sci. cons. Nat. Cancer Inst., 1961-64; sci. adv. com., Sloan-Kettering Inst. Cancer Research. Trustee, C.F. Kettering Found. Served with CWS, AUS, 1941-46. Mem. Chem. Soc., Soc. Biol. Chem., Assn. Cancer Research. Address: 703 Euclid Av Birmingham AL 35213*

SKLAR, ALEXANDER, bus. cons.; b. N.Y.C., May 18, 1915; s. David and Bessie (Wolf) S.; student Cooper Union, N.Y.C., 1932-35; m. Hilda Rae Gevarter, Oct. 27, 1940; 1 dau., Carolyn Mae (Mrs. Louis M. Taff). Chief design engr. Aerovox Corp., New Bedford, Mass., 1933-39; mgr. mfg., engring. Indsl. Condenser Corp., Chgo., 1939-44; owner Capacitron, Inc., 1944-48; v.p. mfg. Jefferson Electric Co., Bellwood, Ill., 1948-65; v.p., gen. mgr. electro-mech. div. Essex Wire Corp., Detroit, 1965-67; v.p. operations Circle F. Industries, 1968; adviser, dir. various corp., 1969—; adj. prof. mgmt. Fla. Atlantic U., Boca Raton, 1970—; lectr. profl. mgmt. U. Cal., Los Angeles, Harvard Grad. Sch. Bus. Adminstrn., U. Ill. Coll. Dentistry. Chmn., Century Club Community Fund, 1961; mng. com. Oak Park Community Lectures, 1963-66. Vice pres., bd. dirs. Nat. Conf. Christians and Jews. Address: 4100 Galt Ocean Dr Fort Lauderdale FL 33308

SKLAR, CHARLES BURROWES, lawyer; b. Keyport, N.J., Dec. 19, 1934; s. Harry S. and Georgia (Hyer) S.; B.S. magna cum laude, La. State U., 1956, LL.B., 1959; m. Deanna Lewis, Feb. 24, 1968; children—Maurice H., Gloria. Admitted to La. bar, 1959; tax accountant Bourgeois Russell & Co., C.P.A.'s, New Orleans, 1958-60; atty. Regional Counsel's Office, Internal Revenue Service, Dallas, New Orleans, 1960-64, supr. tax dept. Peat, Marwick, Mitchell & Co., New Orleans, 1964-65; atty. tax ct., Greensboro, N.C., Atlanta, 1965-70; atty. Watson, Blanche, Wilson & Posner, Baton Rouge, 1971—. Mem. Am., La. State, East Baton Rouge bar assns., Am. Inst. C.P.A.'s, La. Soc. C.P.A.'s, Am. Assn. Atty.-C.P.A.'s. Home: 12030 Chester Dr Baton Rouge LA 70810 Office: 505 North Blvd Baton Rouge LA 70821

SKOBBA, JOSEPH STANLEY, psychiatrist, educator; b. Nanticoke, Pa., Oct. 24, 1904; s. Stanley Martin and Josephine (Chrobak) S.; B.S., Ind. U., M.D., 1930; m. Hope Toman, Aug. 15, 1940 (dec. 1967); 1 dau., Ann (Mrs. Harold T. Barrett, Jr.). Gen. practice medicine Fort Wayne, Ind., 1931-32; asst. physician Fort Wayne State Sch., 1932-36, Central State Hosp., Indpls.; med. supt. Muscatatuck State Sch., Butterville, Ind., 1940-41; pvt. practice psychiatry, Atlanta, 1946-68; dir. Ga. Inst. Mental Health, 1969-71; asst. in psychiatry Ind. U. Sch. Medicine, 1937-39, asso., 1939-41; asso. in psychiatry Emory U. Sch. Medicine, 1942-48, asst., 1948-50, asst. clin. prof., 1950-56, asso. prof., 1956-58, clin. prof., acting chmn. dept., 1956-58, prof. psychiatry 1968—; cons. staff Piedmont Hosp., St. Joseph's Infirmary. Peachtree-Parkwood Hosp., Met. Atlanta Psychiat. Center; cons. staff Emory U. Hosp., Grady Meml. Hosp.; cons. physician to 3d Army. Mem. Med. Adv. Com. to Selective Service, Med. Assn. Ga. Served with mil., 1941-46. Fellow Am. Psychiat. Assn. (life), Am. Coll. Psychiatrists, A.A.A.S., So. Psychiat. Assn. (pres. 1965); mem. Soc. Cons. to Armed Forces. Address: Woodruff Bldg Emory U Atlanta GA 30322

SKRABANEK, ROBERT LEONARD, sociologist, educator; b. Snook, Tex., Nov. 18, 1918; s. John T. and Frances (Bravenec) S.; B.S., Tex. A. and M. U., 1942, M.S., 1946; Ph.D., La. State U., 1949; m. Kathryn A. Kohler, Dec. 1, 1943; children—John, Marian. Grad. asst. Tex. A. and M. U., 1946-47; research asst. and instr. La. State U., 1947-49; asst. prof. sociology to prof. sociology Tex. A. and M. U., College Station, 1949—, chmn. sociology div., 1963-70, head dept. sociology and anthropology, 1970—; vis. prof. So. Meth. U., 1961, Iliff Sch. Theology, 1964; cons. U.S. AID in Colombia and Ecuador, 1962, Ford Found. in Dominican Republic, 1963. Mem. bd. dirs. Brazos County Counselling Service, 1965—, Tex. Social Welfare Assn., 1967. Served to lt. USNR, 1942-46; PTO. Mem. Am., Southwestern (past pres.) sociol. assns., Population Assn. Am., Southwestern Social Sci. Assn., Tex. Acad. Sci., Rural Sociol. Soc., Phi Kappa Phi, Sigma Xi, Alpha Kappa Delta, Gamma Sigma Delta. Contbr. articles in field to profl. jours. Home: 307 Gilchrist Av College Station TX 77840

SKRIP, RICHARD JOSEPH, architect; b. Detroit, Feb. 18, 1937; s. Joseph and Jean (Widawski) Skrzypkowski; B.Arch., U. Fla., 1959; m. Cynthia Waller, Aug. 27, 1960; children—Stephen Bradley, Richard Randolph, Scott Royal. Draftsman, Connell Assos., Miami, 1955, Rader Assos., Miami, Fla., 1956—, Gen. Devel. Corp., Miami, Fla., archtl. dept. Vensel and Savage, 1960-63; architect, Tripp and Skrip, architect, and planners, Miami, 1963—. Served to capt. AUS, 1959-67. Recipient nat. archtl. awards. Mem. A.I.A., Fla. Assn. Architects, Viscayans, Kappa Sigma. Kiwanian. Club: Coral Gables Country; University. Works include St. Lucie Country Club and Conv. Center, Ponce de Leon Bldg., Mayan Towers North, Myakka Country Club. Home: 477 Marquesa Dr Coral Gables FL 33156 Office: 2973 Coral Way Miami FL 33134

SKYE, WILLIAM EMILE, lawyer; b. Alexandria, La., Feb. 26, 1921; s. Emile and Ethel (Hemphill) S.; student Tulane U., 1937-38, La. Coll., 1938-39; B.A., U. Wis., 1942; J.D., La. State U., 1950; m. Sue Bennye Gilham, Apr. 9, 1970; 1 dau., Julie Roberta. Admitted to La. bar, 1950; since practiced in Alexandria, 1950—. Mem. Rapides Parish Sch. Bd., 1966-72. Served with USMC, 1942-45. Mem. Am., La., Alexandria (pres. 1965-66) bar assns., Am. Legion, Am. Judicature Soc., Order Coif., V.F.W. Democrat. Mason (Shriner). Home: 2702 Elliott St Alexandria LA 71301 Office: 608 Murray St Alexandria LA 71201

SLADE, ROY, artist, ednl. adminstr.; b. Cardiff, U.K., July 14, 1933; s. David Trevor and Millicent (Stone) S.; N.D.D., Cardiff Coll. Art, 1954; A.T.D., U. Wales, 1954; m. Rona Jones, July 20, 1957. Came to U.S., 1967. Tchr. art and crafts Heolgam High Sch., Wales, 1956-60; lectr. art Clarendon Coll., Nottingham, Eng., 1960-64; sr. lectr. fine art Leeds Coll. Art, Eng., 1964-67; prof. painting Corcoran Sch. Art, Washington, 1967-68, asso. dean, 1969-70, dean, 1970—; sr. lectr. Leeds Coll. Art, Eng., 1968-69; exhibited one-man shows Howard Roberts Gallery, Cardiff, Wales, 1958, New Art Center, London, Eng., 1960, U. Birmingham, 1964, 69, Herbert Art Gallery and Museum, Coventry, 1964, Va. State Art League, 1967, Museum of Arts and Crafts, Columbus, Ga., 1968, Jefferson Place Gallery, Washington, 1968, 70, Park Square Gallery, Leeds, 1969, St. Mary's Coll. (Md.), 1971, Guelph U. (Can.), 1971; exhibited group shows U.K., N.Y.C., Can.; represented in permanent collections Arts Council Great Britain, Contemporary Art Soc., Nuffield Found., Ministry of Works, Eng., British Embassy, Washington, British Overseas Airways Corp., U. Birmingham, Wakefield City Art Gallery, Clarendon Coll., Cadbury Bros. Ltd., Eng., Lord Ogmore, Local Education Authorities; vis. Boston Museum of Fine Arts, 1970. Served with Brit. Army, 1954-56. Fulbright scholar, 1967-68. Club: George Washington University. Home: 2327 Ashmead Pl Washington DC 20009 Office: 17th St and New York Av Washington DC 20006

SLAGLE, CLIFFORD VAN, aeronat. engr.; b. Taylor, Tex., June 18, 1924; s. Van Price and Parrie (Webb) S.; B.S., A. and M. Coll. Tex., 1949; m. Henrietta Gertrude Keyes, Jan. 23, 1957; children—James Earl, Susan Kay, Barbara Anne. Jr. engr. Boeing Airplane Co., Seattle, 1949-51; became project engr. Temco Aero systems, Greenville, Tex., 1951; now project engr. LTV Electrosystems Inc., Greenville. Mem. steering com. Dallas Council for Fgn. Visitors, 1966-70; mem. Dallas County Democratic Exec. Com., 1968—. Served with AUS, 1942-45. Registered profl. engr., Tex. Mem. Am. Inst. Aero. and Astronautics, Nat., Tex. socs. profl. engrs. Methodist (adminstrv. bd.). Club: George B. Bealey Dads (pres. 1966-67). Home: 14400 Noel Rd Dallas TX 75240 Office: Box 1056 Greenville TX 75401

SLAGLE, WILLIAM F., JR., dentist; b. Alpina, Ark., Feb. 3, 1929; s. William F. and Jannie Lou (Watts) S.; B.S., Central State U., 1950; D.D.S., U. Mo., 1957; m. Shannon N. Penrod, July 15, 1971; 1 dau. (by previous marriage), Jan Elaine. Clin. instr. operative dentistry U. Mo. at Kansas City, 1957-58; practice dentistry, Oklahoma City, 1958-72; asso. prof., also coordinator occlusion U. Tenn. Coll. Dentistry, Memphis, 1972—; asst. prof. oral surgery U. Okla. Sch. Medicine, 1962-72. Founder Okla. Dental Polit. Action Com., 1968, cons., 1968-72; mem. Gov's. Council on Vocational Edn., 1965-72; cons. Okla. Cerebral Palsey Center, 1960-72; pres. Registered Dentists State Okla., 1970-72. Trustee Okla. Dental Found., 1960-65. Served with USAF, 1951-52. Named Man of the Year in Dentistry, Okla. State Dental Assn., 1967-68. Mem. Am. Dental Assn., Am. Assn. Dental Examiners, Am. Assn. Dental Anesthesiology, Okla. State Dental Assn. (chmn. council on legislation 1969-70). Episcopalian (jr. warden 1967-68). Clubs: Northwest Cosmopolitan (dir. 1965-67) (Oklahoma City). Home: 2675 Central Terrace Memphis TN 38111 Office: U Tenn Coll Dentistry 847 Monroe Av Memphis TN 38103

SLAIMAN, DONALD S., union ofcl.; b. N.Y.C., Mar. 18, 1919; s. Philip and Betty (Simon) S.; B.S.S., City Coll. N.Y., 1939; student U. Mich., 1939-40; M.A., U. Buffalo, 1953; student Univ. Coll., Cardiff, Wales, 1953-56; m. Marjorie Lawler, Sept. 10, 1946; children—Curtis Frederick, Gary David, Donald Craig, Tracey Jean. With Bell Aircraft Corp., 1940-43, 46-49; crane chaser turret-lathe operator 1950-53; mem. UAW-AFL-CIO, 1940—; dir. Jewish Labor Com. and Mich. Labor Com. for Human Rights, Detroit, 1957-59; asst. dir. dept. civil rights AFL-CIO, 1959-64, dir., 1964—. Served with AUS, 1943-45; ETO. Mem. Nat. Citizens Com. Community Relations (exec. com.), N.A.A.C.P., Nat. Assn. Intergroup Relations Ofcls., Nat. Com. Against Discrimination in Housing (bd. dirs.), League Indsl. Democracy (bd. dirs.), Workers Def. League (bd. dirs.), Washington Urban League (bd. dirs.), A. Philip Randolph Inst., Neighbors, Inc., Washington. Home: 6503 8th St NW Washington DC 20012 Office: 815 16th St NW Washington DC 20006

SLAPPEY, MARY MCGOWAN, journalist; b. Kittrell, N.C., Nov. 22, 1914; d. Walter Gordon and Mary Jouvette (McGowan) Slappey; student Am. U., 1938-39; A.B. in Polit. Sci., George Washington U., 1947; student Corcoran Sch. Art, 1950-57. Tchr. in charge Nat. Bus. Sch., Washington, 1952-59; asst. to editor nat. publs. Nat. Council Catholic Men, Washington, 1959-66; exec. editor Nat. Newman Apostolate, U.S. Cath. Conf., 1966-69; free-lance reporter, writer, Washington, 1969—. Served with WAVES, 1942-46. Mem. Fed. Poets Washington (rec. sec.), Internat. Platform Assn., Am. Artists Profl. League, Nat. Writers Club, Columbian Women George Washington U., Pi Gamma Mu. Author: Firelosophy & Inspiration, 1932, Crossroads of Eternity, 1947; editor Cath. Traveler, 1967. Home: 4500 Chesapeake St N W Washington DC 20016

SLATE, HERMAN IVAN, surgeon; b. Meadows, N.C., Dec. 26, 1902; s. Francis Augustin and Josephine (Smith) S.; B.S., Columbia Union Coll., 1932; M.D., Loma Linda U., 1934; m. Esther Grace Heiser, Sept. 1, 1940; children—Grace Alfreda, Glenda Jane. Rotating intern Md. Gen. Hosp., Balt., 1933-34; asst. resident in pathology Balt. City Hosps., 1934; asst. resident North Hudson Hosp., Weehawken, N.J., 1934-35; resident Martins Ferry Hosp., O., 1935, Southside Community Hosp., Farmville, Va., 1938; chief resident, surg. resident St. Francis Hosp., Charleston, W.Va., 1939-40; resident in thoracic surgery Biggs Meml. Hosp., Ithaca, N.Y., 1940-41; sr. surg. resident Confederate Meml. Med. Center, Shreveport, La., 1942-43; gen. med. practice, Cadiz, O., 1936-37; surg. practice Alexandria and Arlington, 1943—; chief of surgery Hadley Meml. Hosp., Washington, 1952-68, attending surgeon, 1952—, chief of staff, 1961; surgeon, McCluer Tumor Clinic, Alexandria, Va., 1946—; cons. surgeon Leland Meml. Hosp., Riverdale, Md., Tidewater Meml. Hosp.; attending surgeon Alexandria Hosp. (Va.), 1948—, Fairfax Hosp. (Va.), 1961—; lectr. surgery Sch. Nursing, Alexandria Hosp., 1950—. Diplomate Am. Bd. of Surgery. Fellow A.C.S., Southeastern Surg. Congress, Internat. Coll. Surgeons; mem. Hawthorne Surg. Soc. U. Pa., Soc. Surgeons Loma Linda U., No. Va. Acad. Surgery, Am. Soc. Abdominal Surgeons, Am., Va., Alexandria med. assns. Republican. Mem. Seventh-day Adventist Ch. Home: 1012 S 26th St Arlington VA 22202 Office: 815 Prince St Alexandria VA 22313

SLATER, OLIVER EUGENE, bishop; b. Sibley, La., Sept. 10, 1906; s. Oliver Thornwell and Mattie (Kennon) S.; A.B., So. Meth. U., 1930, B.D., 1932; D.D. (hon.), McMurry Coll., Abilene, Tex., 1951; L.H.D., Southwestern Coll., Winfield, Kan., 1961; LL.D., Baker U., 1962, So. Meth. U., 1964; m. Eva B. Richardson, Nov. 25, 1931; children—Susan (Mrs. H. Kipling Edenborough), Stewart Eugene. Ordained to ministry Methodist Ch., 1932; pastor in Rochelle, Tex., 1932-33, Menard, Tex., 1933-36, Ozona, Tex., 1936-42, San Antonio, 1942-44, Houston, 1944-50, Polk St. Ch., Amarillo, Tex., 1950-60; consecrated bishop, 1960; bishop of Kan. Area Meth. Ch., 1960-64, of San Antonio-N.W. Tex. area, 1964-68; bishop San Antonio area, 1968—. Mem. Interbd. Commn. for Enlistment Ch. Occupations, 1968-72. Mem. jurisdictorial confs., Meth. Ch., 1948, 56, 60, gen. confs., 1956, 60, pres. gen. bd. edn., 1964-72. Mem. Bd. Edn., 1960-72; pres. Council of Bishops, 1972—. Mem. Commn. on History and Archives, 1972—. Mem. bd. Global Ministries, 1972—; trustee So. Meth. U., Southwestern U. Home: 4022 Fawnridge Dr San Antonio TX 78229 Office: 535 Bandera PO Box 28509 San Antonio TX 78228

SLATER, RICHARD DEAN, ednl. adminstr.; b. Peoria, Ill., Dec. 4, 1929; s. Howard Smith and Florence (Hrinrich); B.S., Bradley U., 1951, M.A., 1952; Ed.D., U. Houston, 1961; postgrad. Harvard, 1964; m. Phyllis Jean Cassens, May 30, 1952; children—Karen, Russell, Judith and Kenneth. Elementary tchr. Houston (Tex.) Ind. Sch. Dist., 1955-59, secondary sch. counselor, 1959-60, sch. psychologist, 1960-61, asst. dir. psychol. services, 1961-62, dir. psychol. services, acting asst. supt. spl. services, 1962-63, asst. supt. spl. services, 1963-68, asso. dep. supt. div. of curriculum, ednl. research and program devel., 1968-70; dir. pupil appraisal and psychol. services Region IV, Ednl. Service Center, 1970—. Mem. Nat. Assn. Adminstrs. Pupil Personnel Services Adminstrn. (charter mem.), Tex. State Tchrs. Assn. (life), Am., Tex. (pres.-elect div. sch. psychology) psychol. assns., Council Exceptional Children, Houston Council Edn., Houston Assn. Sch. Adminstrs. (pres. 1966-67), Phi Delta Kappa. Lutheran. Home: 7426 Redding Rd Houston TX 77036 Office: 202 N Loop W Houston TX 77018

SLATER, TERRENCE LYONS, lawyer; b. Syracuse, N.Y., Dec. 20, 1928; s. Joseph Harold and Marie (Argus) S.; B.A., Georgetown U., 1951, LL.B., 1954; m. Joan Salomone, Oct. 8, 1960; children—Katherine Marie, Maureen Anne. Admitted to D.C. bar, 1954; atty. Fed. Communications Commn., Washington, 1956-66; atty. Internat. Tel. & Tel. Corp., Washington, 1966—. Served with AUS, 1954-56. Mem. Fed., Am. bar assns., Fed. Communications Bar Assn., Eta Sigma Phi. Home: 6320 N 24th St Arlington VA 22207 Office: 1707 L St NW Washington DC 20036

SLAUGHTER, ELMER CUNNINGHAM, mfg. exec.; b. Houston, Sept. 12, 1920; s. Elmer Carlton and Margaret (Cunningham) S.; student N. Tex. State U., 1936-37; E.E., U. Cin., 1942; m. Jeannette Kearney, June 27, 1942; children—Jean (Mrs. M. Johnson), Susan (Mrs. H. Sachs), Dorothy (Mrs. R. Barnes), Edward, Mary, John, Richard, Michael, Doris, Rebecca, Nancy, Janet. Established test lab. Lear, Inc., Piqua, O., 1942-45, chief design engr., 1945-46, chief engr., Grand Rapids, Mich., 1946-47; chief engr. Piqua Machine & Mfg. Co., 1948-54; pres. E-M Corp., Fletcher, O., 1947-48, Slaughter Co., Ardmore, Okla., 1954—. Cons., Lear, Inc., Grand Rapids, Mich., 1947-48, Polo Pump Co., Ill., 1947-49, Safa Alarm Co., Orrville, O., 1948-50; chmn. Mayor's Indsl. Adv. Com., 1971—. Commr., Piqua Boys Baseball Assn., 1958-61; chmn. Ardmore Edn. Council, 1970—; pres. bd. dirs. Ardmore Sheltered Workshop, 1970—. Mem. I.E.E.E., A.A.A.S., Ardmore C. of C. (v.p., dir. 1972—), Tau Beta Pi, Eta Kappa Nu, Sigma Xi. Office: Moore and Hailey Sts Ardmore OK 73401

SLAUGHTER, FREEMAN CLUFF, dentist; b. Estes, Miss., Dec. 30, 1926; s. William Cluff and Vay (Fox) S.; student Wake Forest Coll., 1944; student Emory U., 1946-47, D.D.S., 1951; m. Genevieve Anne Parks, July 30, 1948; children—Mary Anne, Thomas Freeman, James Hugh. Practice gen. dentistry, Kannapolis, N.C., 1951—. Mem. N.C. Bd. Dental Examiners, 1966—, pres., 1968-69, sec.-treas., 1971—; chief dental staff Cabarrus Meml. Hosp., Concord, N.C., 1965-66; mem. N.C. Adv. Com. for Edn. Dental Aux. Personnel-N.C. State Bd. Edn., 1967-70. Pres. Kannapolis chpt. N.C. Symphony Soc., 1961, trustee, 1962-68; active Boy Scouts Am. Served with USNR, 1944-46; ETO, MTO. Fellow Am. Coll. Dentists; mem. Am. Legion, Kannapolis Jr. C. of C. (v.p. 1952), Toastmasters Internat. (pres. Kannapolis 1963-64), Am. Dental Assn., Am. Assn. Dental Examiners, So. Conf. Dental Deans and Examiners (v.p. 1969), N.C. Dental Soc., N.C. Dental Soc. Anesthesiology (pres. 1964), Southeastern Acad. Prosthodontics, So. Acad. Oral Surgery, Am. Soc. Dentistry for Children (pres. N.C. unit 1957), Internat. Assn. for Dental Research, Cabarrus County Dental Soc. (pres. 1953-54, 63-64, 69). Mason (Shriner). Club: Kannapolis Music (pres. 1962-63). Home: 506 Dawn St Kannapolis NC 28081 Office: Professional Bldg Kannapolis NC 28081 Mailing address: Professional Bldg Kannapolis NC 28081

SLAUGHTER, JOHN WILLIAM, JR., securities co. exec.; b. Columbus, Miss., Dec. 29, 1925; s. John William and Josie Galloway (Howell) S.; A.B., Princeton, 1947; m. Eleanor Smith, Aug. 27, 1947; 1 dau., Patricia. Asst. mgr. Gilmer Hotel, Columbus, 1949-53; asst. controller Miss. div. Am. Bosch, Columbus, 1954-67; v.p. Chandler Securities Corp., Columbus, 1968—; dir. Am. Bus. & Indsl. Devel. Corp., Forest, Miss., Mark Designs Internat., Columbus; gen. agt. Dixie Nat. Life Ins., Jackson, Miss., 1967—. Treas. Prarie council Girl Scouts U.S., 1970—; mem. citizen adv. com. to City of Columbus, 1969—. Mem. City Planning Commn., 1971—, City Bd. Zoning Adjustment, 1971—; sec.-treas. Lowndes County Republican party, 1960—. Served with USAAF, 1944-46; PTO. Mem. Nat. Assn. Securities Dealers, Hist. Soc. (v.p. 1971), S.A.R., C. of C., V.F.W. Elk, Kiwanian. Clubs: Metropolitan Dinner, Country, Elm. Home: 905 N 8th Av Columbus MS 39701 Office: PO Box 413 Columbus MS 39701

SLAWSON, BOBBY JOE, pub. co. exec.; b. Jacksonville, Tex., Apr. 19, 1939; s. Harvey E. and Eva (Hammonds) S.; student Baylor U., 1958-59; A.A., Lon Morris Coll., 1960; B.B.A., Sam Houston State U., 1962; M.B.A., So. Meth. U., 1971; m. Harriet N. Whigham, Sept. 1, 1961; children—Steven Edward, Susan Eleanor. Mgr. gen. accounting, budgeting and cost accounting Tex. Instruments, Dallas, 1965-71; controller Taylor Pub. Co., Dallas, 1971—. Served to lt. USAF, 1965-68. C.P.A., Tex. Mem. Am. Inst. C.P.A.'s, Tex. Soc.

C.P.A.'s. Home: 1106 Park East Dr Garland TX 75041 Office: PO Box 597 Dallas TX 75221

SLAYTON, DONALD KENT, astronaut; b. Sparta Wis., Mar. 1, 1924; s. Charles Sherman and Victoria Adelia (Larson) S.; B.Aero. Engring., U. Minn., 1949; Sc.D. (hon.), Carthage Coll., 1960; D. of Engring. (hon.), Mich. Technol. Inst.; m. Marjory Lunney, May 15, 1955; 1son Kent Sherman. Served to capt., USAAF, 1942-46; engr. Boeing Aircraft Co., 1949-51; commd. capt. USAF, 1951, advanced to maj., 1959, resigned, 1963; fighter pilot, maintenance officer, Germany, 1952-55; fighter test pilot Edwards AFB, Cal., 1955-59; joined Project Mercury, manned space flight, NASA, 1959, chief astronaut, 1962-63, asst. dir. flight crew operations, 1963-66, dir. flight crew operations, 1966—. Asso. fellow Soc. Exptl. Test Pilots; fellow Am. Astronautical Soc.; mem. Order of Daedalians, Exptl. Aircraft Assn., Am. Fighter Aces, Nat. Rifle Assn. Home: Box 637 Friendswood TX 77546 Office: Manned Spacecraft Center NASA Houston TX 77002

SLEIGHT, DOROTHY MARIE BARDEN, psychologist; b. Benton, N.Y., July 24, 1920; d. Frank E. and Vera (Seymour) Barden; B.S. in Edn., State U. N.Y., Geneseo, 1942; M.S. in Edn., Purdue U., 1947; m. Robert B. Sleight, May 7, 1944; 1 son, Robert Barry. Tchr. elem. pub. schs., Painted Post, N.Y., 1940-42; civil service librarian U.S. Naval Tng. Sta., Sampson, N.Y., 1943-44; br. children's librarian Enoch Pratt Free Library, Balt., 1949; librarian McDonogh (Md.) Sch., 1949-51; v.p. Century Research Corp., Arlington, Va., 1957—; sch. psychologist Washington Pub. Schs., 1963-66; asst. prof. dept. psychology Marymount Coll., Va. Named Woman of Year Arlington Inter-Service Club Council, 1966; recipient Distinguished Alumna award State U. N.Y. at Geneseo. Mem. Nat. Jr. Coll. Faculty Assn., Arlington Com. 100, Am. Psychol. Assn., A.A.A.S. Clubs: Soroptimist of Arlington, Purdue of Washington. Home: 3717 N 27th St Arlington VA 22207 Office: 4113 Lee Hwy Arlington VA 22207

SLEIGHT, ROBERT BENTON, psychologist; b. Hemlock, N.Y., Sept. 16, 1922; s. Edson F. and Marian (Hoppough) S.; B.Ed., U. State N.Y. Tchrs. Coll., Geneseo, 1946; M.S., Purdue U., 1947, Ph.D., 1949; m. Dorothy M. Barden, May 7, 1944; 1 son, Robert Barry. Research fellow Purdue U., 1946-48; asst. prof., research psychologist Johns Hopkins, 1948-51; research scientist and cons. Naval Research Lab., 1952; pres., chmn. bd. Century Research Corp., 1952—. Mem. Citizens zoning adv. com. D.C., 1955-57; mem. Arlington County Sch. Bd. Curriculum Council; pres. Riverwood Citizens Assn. Bd. dirs. Arlington Com. 100. Served as naval aviator USNR, 1943-45. Fellow Am. Psychol. Assn., A.A.A.S., Human Factors Soc.; mem. Am. Inst. Aeros. and Astronautics, Eastern, D.C. psychol. assns., Am. Ordnance Assn., Arlington C. of C., Internat. Assn. Applied Psychology, Sigma Xi. Contbr. articles to textbooks and profl. jours. Home: 3717 N 27th St Arlington VA 22207 Office: 4113 Lee Hwy Arlington VA 22207

SLEPICKA, IRVIN MILES, JR., bus. cons.; b. Evanston, Ill., Oct. 3, 1924; s. Irvin M. and Mabelle (Johnston) S.; M.E., Stevens Inst. Tech., 1945; M.S., U. Ill., 1948; m. Lorraine June Pihl, Oct. 3, 1949; children—Bradford Miles, Mark Joktan. Instr., U. Ill., 1947-48; with Crane Co. Sales & Service Engr., 1948-51, Honeywell, Inc., 1953-64; central field sales mgr. Robertshaw Controls Co., 1964-68; partner NASCO, Houston, 1968—; pres. Generation Devel. Corp., Houston, 1969-70; v.p., dir. Adv. Internat. Marketers, Inc., 1969-70; pres. Profl. Bus. Planners, Houston, 1970—; dir. Dorn Corp. Mem. marketing devel. faculty U. Houston, 1967—. Bd. dirs. Houston Council Navy League. Chmn., Navy Sea Cadet Com., 1965—, regional dir. program, 1971. Served with USNR. Recipient Service award U.S. Navy League, 1969. Registered profl. engr., Tex. Mem. Houston C. of C., Res. Officers Assn. (v.p. 1968-71), Nat., Tex. socs. profl. engrs., Naval Res. Assn., Instrument Soc. Am., Am. Marketing Assn., Am. Heating, Ventilating and Air Conditioning Engrs., Theta Xi, Sigma Iota Epsilon, Pi Sigma Epsilon. Lutheran. Club: Republic Victory (Houston). Home: 10023 Candlewood Lane Houston TX 77042 Office: 6601 Hillcroft Av Houston TX 77036

SLEVIN, JOSEPH RAYMOND, journalist; b. N.Y.C., Nov. 27, 1918; s. Theodore and Katherine (Bluh) S.; B.A., Yale, 1939, postgrad., 1939-40; postgrad. U. Neb., 1940-41; M.A., U. Ill., 1942; m. Katherine Day, Dec. 8, 1943; children—Ann Day, Michael Scott, Jonathan Day, Peter Day. Staff editor Kiplinger Mag., 1946-47; Washington corr. Jour. Commerce, 1947-55; nat. econs. editor N.Y. Herald Tribune, 1955-66; editor, pub. Washington Bond Report, 1962—; syndicated columnist Newsday, Washington, 1966-71, Phila. Inquirer, Washington, 1971—. Commentator Voice Am., 1960-62. Served to lt. USNR, 1942-45. Mem. Am. Polit. Sci. Assn., Overseas Writers, White House Corr. Assn., State Dept. Corr. Assn., Nat. Press Club. Clubs: Federal City, Exchequer, Yale (Washington). Home: 16 E Melrose St Chevy Chase MD 20015 Office: Nat Press Bldg Washington DC 20004

SLOAN, EARL LEROY, civil engr.; b. Boise City, Okla., Apr. 25, 1909; s. Dudley C. and Neva (Powell) S.; B.S. in Civil Engring., Kan. State Coll., 1929; M.S., Mass. Inst. Tech., 1930; m. Geneva Landrum, Apr. 2, 1933. Engr. constrn. pub. bldgs. Underhill Constrn. Co., Wichita, Kan., 1930-32; engr. rd., bridge constrn. Okla. Hwy. Dept., 1933-35, design engr. bridges, 1935-39; with Phillips Petroleum Co., Bartlesville, Okla., 1939—, project engr., 1958—; with Petrochim N.V., Antwerp, Belgium, 1966-70; on loan to Alyeska Pipeline Service Co., Houston, 1970—. Mem. Nat., Okla. socs. profl. engrs. Baptist (deacon). Club: Hillcrest Country (Bartlesville). Home: 1401 Hampden Rd Bartlesville OK 74003 Office: Phillips Petroleum Co Bartlesville OK 74003

SLOAN, EUGENE HOLLOWAY, educator; b. Lebanon, Tenn., Sept. 14, 1907; s. Henry Churchill and Effie (Holloway) S.; A.B., Cumberland U., 1927, LL.B., 1928, J.D., Samford U., 1969; M.A., Peabody Coll., 1939; m. Lillian Rachel White, June 12, 1929; children—Gene H., Joseph White, William Henry, Lilli Anne Twining. Editor, Lebanon (Tenn.) Democrat, 1926-28; prin. Gladeville (Tenn.) High Sch., 1928-31; tchr., coach Lebanon (Tenn.) High Sch., 1931-36, prin., 1938-45; city supt. schs., Lebanon, 1937-38; state editor Nashville (Tenn.) Banner, 1945; pub. relations dir. Tenn. Dept. Edn., 1945-46; tchr., dir. pub. relations Middle Tenn. State U., 1946—, prof. bus. law, 1946—. Admitted to Tenn. bar, 1928. Mem. Am. Bus. Law Assn., Pi Omega Pi, Sigma Delta Kappa, Pi Mu Sigma, Alpha Kappa Psi. Mem. Ch. of Christ. Democrat. Mason. Club: Lions. Author: Personages in American History, 1939; With Second Army in Tennessee, 1956; co-author: Business Law, 1962, Modern Journalism, 1963, History at Wilson County, 1965 articles pub. in profl. jours., mags., newspapers. Home: 728 Greenland Dr Murfreesboro TN 37130

SLOAN, JAMES MINOR, JR., fire chief; b. Cordele, Ga., July 28, 1922; s. James Minor and Clara Belle (Black) S.; grad. high sch.; m. Beatrice Mae Skinner, May 3,1942; children—Robert Kenneth, Edward Donald. With Fire Dept., West Palm Beach, Fla., 1946—, dep. chief, 1956-62, chief, 1962—. Mem. Youth Baseball Assn., 1959-66, v.p., 1961-63, league dir., 1961-63. Served with USNR, 1942-45. Mem. Internat. Assn. Fire Chiefs, Fla. Fire Chiefs Assn., Palm Beach County Fire Chiefs Assn., Nat. Fire Protection Assn., Internat. Assn. Fire Fighters. Home: 911 30th Ct West Palm Beach FL 33407 Office: 222 N Dixie St West Palm Beach FL 33401

SLOAN, JAMES PARK, educator; b. Clinton, S.C., Oct. 2, 1916; s. Eugene Blakely and Janie Pressly (Lindsay) S.; B.A., Erskine Coll., 1937; M.A., Tulane U., 1938; m. Alice Catherine Gaines, June 26, 1941; children—James Park, Edwin Gaines. Tchr. econs., govt., sociology, English, Ga. Mil. Acad., College Park, 1938-39; tchr. history, govt. Clinton (S.C.) High Sch., 1939-41; asst. to chmn. S.C. Def. Council, Clinton, 1941-42; paymaster Joanna Mills Co. (S.C.), 1942, personnel dir., 1946-58, dir. indsl. relations, 1958-64; editor co. monthly mag. The Joanna Way, 1950-64; asst. prof. polit. sci. Coll. of Charleston (S.C.), 1964-67; asst. prof. polit. sci., asst. dir. acad. affairs Spartanburg regional campus U. S.C. 1967—. Mem. adv. council S.C. Employment Security Commn., 1955—; mem. planning bd. S.C. Accident Prevention Conf., 1954-57; mem. edn. task force Model Cities Program, City of Spartanburg, 1971—; mem. long-range planning com. City of Spartanburg, 1970—. Vice chmn. Laurens County S.C. Heart Assn., 1953-64; mem. Laurens County Tri-Centennial Com., 1970; vice chmn. Laurens County Am. Cancer Soc., 1956-64, exec. dir. Joanna Community Chest, 1950-64; mem. standing com. on communications Asso. Reformed Presbyn. Synod, 1970—; mem. Laurens County Bd. Election Commrs., 1970—. Mem. S.C. Ho. of Reps., 1940-42; mem. Clinton City Council, 1954-60, mayor pro tem, 1958-60; del. Nat. Dem. Conv., 1956; del. S.C. Dem. Conv., 1942, 46, 48, 52, 54, 56, 60; mem. Laurens County Dem. Exec. Com., 1950-60, chmn., 1948-50; county chmn. S. Carolinians for Ind. Electors, 1956; del. to S.C. Republican Conv., 1968, 70, 72; chmn. Laurens County Rep. Conv., 1972. Trustee Erskine Coll., 1949-53, Joanna Found., 1955-66; bd. dirs. Clinton-Newberry Natural Gas Authority, 1954-60. Served from apprentice seaman to lt. USNR, 1942-46; ETO, PTO. Recipient George Washington Honor medal Freedoms Found., 1963. Mem. South Caroliniana Soc., Am. Assn. Indsl. Editors (dir. 1950, 58-60, pres. 1960-61), So., S.C. polit. sci. assns., Laurens County Hist. Soc. (charter). Mem. Asso. Ref. Presbyn. Ch. (ruling elder, 1947-70, life ruling elder 1971, supt. Sunday sch. 1939-60, now tchr. men's class). Club: Piedmont (Spartanburg, S.C.). Author articles trade jours., religious publs. Home: 103 Maple St Clinton SC 29325 Office: Univ South Carolina Spartanburg SC 29303

SLOAN, JOHN, merchant; b. Nashville, June 28, 1904; s. Paul Lowe and Anne (Joy) S.; grad. Wallace U. Sch., 1921; B.A., Vanderbilt U., 1925; m. Margaret Howe, Feb. 7, 1935; children—John, George A. II, Thomas Howe, Paul Lowe, III. With Cain-Sloan Co., Nashville, 1925—, successively salesman, dept. mgr., v.p., pres., 1937-70, chmn., 1970—; dir. First Am. Nat. Bank, Forrest Life Ins. Co. Magistrate 15th dist. Williamson County (Tenn.), 1948—. Trustee Vanderbilt U.; pres. bd. trustees Montgomery Bell Acad. Mem. Vanderbilt Alumni Assn. (pres. 1941-45), Kappa Alpha. Rotarian. Clubs: Coffee House, Hillsboro Hounds, Belle Meade Country, Cumberland (Nashville). Home: Maple Grove Farm Route 1 Brentwood TN 37027 Office: Cain-Sloan Co Nashville TN 37027

SLOAN, MARY KATHLEEN LEWIS (MRS. EUGENE BLAKELY SLOAN), author; b. Winnsboro, S.C.; d. Thomas Walter and Mary Ellen (Street) Lewis; student U. S.C., 1936-38; postgrad.; A.B., Furman U., 1940; m. Eugene Blakely Sloan, Aug. 4, 1951 (dec. Apr. 1969); children—Mary Lindsay, Laura Lewis. Free-lance photo-journalist, 1942—; editor Oliver Beacon, and pub. relations dept. Oliver Gen. Hosp., Augusta, Ga., 1943-47; editorial staff News and Herald, Winnsboro, 1951; mng. editor S.C. Meth. Adv., Columbia, 1956-63; editor U. S.C. Press, 1965-68, advt., promotion dir., 1967-68; travel writer S.C. Dept. Parks, Recreation and Tourism, 1968-69; pres. Lewis-Sloan Pub. Co. Cons. writing, book and related publishing. Mem. Richland County Tricentennial Commn. Recipient spl. award for periodical lit. S.C. Fedn. Women's Cubs, 1970. Mem. South Caroliniana Soc., Historic Columbia Found., S.C., Fairfield County hist. socs., Nat. Trust for Historic Preservation, Outdoor Photographers League. Presbyn. Contbr. articles to profl. jours. Co-editor: A Documentary Profile of the Palmetto State, 1971. Home: 215 S Harden St Columbia SC 29205

SLOAN, NORMAN, basketball coach N.C. State U., Raleigh. Office: Athletic Dept NC State U Raleigh NC 27607*

SLOAN, RUTH CATHERINE (MRS. ARTHUR W. SLOAN), pub. co. exec.; b. Akron, O.; d. William Austin and Jennie Lillis (Martin) McNeil; student U. Cin., 1917-18, Miami U., 1918-19; B.A., Akron U., 1930; postgrad. U. Mich., summer 1930, Oxford U., summer 1932; M.A., Western Res. U., 1935, Ph.D., 1939; m. Arthur William Sloan, Sept. 17, 1927. Personnel work B.F. Goodrich Co., 1920-28; instr. Akron U., 1930-34; acting labor and cultural attache Am. Embassy, Cairo, Egypt, 1944-46; chief African div. U.S. Information Agy., Dept. State, 1946-54; exec. dir., pres. Ruth Sloan Asso., pub. and pub. relations Africa and Nr. East, 1954—. Decorated chevalier Order of Crown of Belgium. Fellow African Studies Assn.; mem. Middle East Inst., Royal African Soc., African Bur., Woman Geographers Assn., Phi Sigma Alpha, Phi Delta Gamma. Author: African Education, 1953; Resources and Needs for Training of Africans, 1956; African News (monthly newsletter), 1953-56. Pub.: The Coptic Church, Christianity in Egypt, 1955; The Press of Africa, 1956; The Educated African, 1962. Home: 2500 Virginia Av NW Washington DC 20037 Office: 2500 Virginia Av NW Washington DC 20037

SLOAN, WYMAN P., JR., physician; b. McDonough, Ga., Dec. 17, 1919; s. Wyman P. and Helen (Harris) S.; B.A., Emory U., 1940, M.A., 1941; M.D., Tulane U. Sch. Medicine, 1944; M.S., U. Minn., 1950; m. Jeanne Stenly, Nov. 22, 1948; children—Stephen, Wyman III, Scott, Anne, Carl, Helen. Intern, Charity Hosp., New Orleans, 1944-45; fellow in medicine Mayo Found., 1946-49, first asst., 1949-50; gen. practice internal medicine Atlanta, 1950—; asso. clin. prof. medicine Emory U., 1962—; asso. chief of medicine Ga. Bapt. Hosp., 1964—. Served with USNR, 1945-46, 63-65. Fellow A.C.P.; mem. Am. Soc. Internat. Medicine, Am., So. med. assns., Phi Chi, Sigma Pi. Home: 3430 Old Plantation Rd Atlanta GA 30305 Office: 340 Boulevard NE Atlanta GA 30313

SLOCUM, ALVAH WALTHALL, rancher; b. Cresson, Tex., Nov. 21, 1902; s. Ferdinand and Alvaretta (Middleton) S.; student Weatherford Coll., 1922, Met. Coll., 1924; m. Ruth Bruce, June 19, 1923; children—Wayne, Alve Jean (Mrs. Graham Hinkley Cole, Jr.), Dub. Chmn. bd. Slocum Ranch, Inc., Cresson, 1969—; pres. Johnson County Electric Coop., Cleburne, Tex., 1964—, dir., 1948—; dir. First Nat. Bank, Weatherford, Tex.; co-owner Slocum Cattle Co., Cresson, 1940—. Mem. Am. Nat. Cattlemens Assn. Denver. Baptist (deacon 1935—). Mason (32 deg., Shriner). Home: Rural Delivery PO Drawer 8 Cresson TX 76035

SLOCUM, EUGENE FLOYD, mech. engr.; b. Trumansburg, N.Y., May 14, 1926; s. Clyde Lawrence and Mildred (Cronk) S.; grad. Radio and Radar Sch., Memphis, 1945; student Cornell U., 1948-51; B.Sc. in Engring., U. Los Angeles, 1970; M.B.A., F.R.I., 1972; m. Bobbie Ellen Peeples, Dec. 23, 1945; children—Kristi Ellen, Linda Jean, Betty Louise. Sr. mech. engr. Radiation Inc., Melbourne, Fla., 1956-60; mech. service dept. head I.C.F., Inc., Melbourne, 1960-62; project engr. Bendix, Hawaii, 1962-63; pres., dir. Autotronics, Inc., Melbourne, 1963-64; instrumentation engr. Rust Engring. Co., Birmingham, Ala., 1964-65; project engr. Advanced Research & Devel. Co., Orlando, Fla., 1965-66; supr. systems checking Hayes Internat., Titusville, Fla., 1966-67; mech. engr. anti submarine warfare systems Magnavox, Ft. Wayne, Ind., 1967; systems engr. Dow Chem. Co., Titusville, Fla., 1967-69; electro-mech. engr. Bell Telephone Labs., Greensboro, N.C., 1969—; mech. engr. Tropospheric Scatter Tele-Communications System, DCA, Boynton Beach, Fla., 1971-72. Mem. bd. So. Tier Timing Assn., 1953-54; chmn. bd., pres. Auto Sports, Inc., 1962-63. Served with AC, USNR, 1944-46. Recipient Apollo VIII award Kennedy Space Center, 1969, Apollo VIII Astronaut Medallion award Dow Chem., 1969. Registered profl. engr., Fla. Mem. Nat. Soc. Profl. Engrs. (sr.), Fla. Engring. Soc., Cornell Soc. Engrs., Fla. Assn. Engrs. Industry, Am. Soc. M.E., Cornell Alumni Assn., Nat. Mgmt. Assn. Club: Cornell (East Fla.). Address: 2506 Country Club Rd Melbourne FL 32901

SLONE, DENNEY WOOD, lawyer; b. Mascotte, Fla., Mar. 6, 1907; s. R.W. and Roalia P. (Carter) S.; student U. Fla., Troy State Tchrs. Coll., Valdosta State Coll., 1950-51; LL.B., Atlanta Law Sch., 1946; m. Voncile Fleming, Nov. 5, 1941; children—William L., Albert E. Tchr. pub. schs., 1925-26; clk. U.S. P.O., 1940-42, admitted to Ga. bar, 1946; gen. practice law, Atlanta, 1946-47, Lakeland, Ga., 1947—; Lanier County atty., 1952-56, 65—; councilman City of Lakeland, Ga., 1965-68; atty. City of Lakeland, 1969—. Served with USCGR, 1942-45. Mem. Ga. Municipal Assn., Ga. Assn. County Commrs., 8th Congl. Dist. Ga. County Officers Assn. (exec. com. 1965), Internat. Platform Assn., Am. Legion, Sigma Delta Kappa. State Bar Ga. Democrat. Baptist. Lion. Home: 443 Pecan St Lakeland GA 31635 Office: 105 N Center St Lakeland GA 31635

SLOTT, IRVING, research exec.; b. Jacksonville, Fla., Nov. 2, 1922; s. Joseph Harry and Celia (Gottlieb) S.; B.S., U. Fla., 1947; B.I.E., N.Y.U., 1956; M.B.A., Rollins Coll., 1966; m. Lois Mark, Mar. 8, 1951; children—Michael, Marla Jean, Joseph, William. Indsl. engring. mgr. Electronic Instruments Co., N.Y.C., 1953-57; mgr. mgmt. engring. Martin Marietta Corp., Orlando, Fla., 1957-67; mgr. operations research Franklin Inst., Phila., 1967-69; dep. dir. Nat. Inst. Law Enforcement & Criminal Justice, U.S. Dept. of Justice, Washington, 1969—; lectr. Crummer Sch., Rollins Coll., 1966-67. Pres. Central Fla. Jewish Community Council, 1966-67. Served with AUS, 1943-47. Republican. Jewish religion. Home: 9812 Marquette Dr Bethesda MD 20034 Office: Nat Inst Law Enforcement US Dept of Justice Washington DC 20530

SLUSHER, RALPH CHARLES, physician; b. Terre Haute, Ind., Aug. 18, 1932; s. Covilla Charlie and Edrie Lee (Hylton) S.; B.S., Va. Poly. Inst., 1953; M.D. (Florence Smith med. scholar), Med. Coll. Va., 1957; grad. Command and Staff Coll., 1968, Indsl. Coll. Armed Forces, 1970; m. Nancy Anne Spangler, Dec. 20, 1953; children—Ralph Mark, Misty Jill, Ralph Kendall. Intern Norfolk Gen. Hosp., 1957-58; practice family medicine, Altavista, Va., 1958—; mem. staff Lynchburg Gen. Hosp., Va. Bapt. Hosp., Lynchburg; med. adviser Altavista Life Saving Crew, Blood Mobile; organizer dir. polio and rubella clinics. Pres. Altavista elementary P.T.A., 1967-68; active Piedmont Area council Boy Scouts Am., 1965—, scoutmaster, 1968—, area instr. leader tng., 1968—. Recipient Exceptional Physician award A.M.A., 1970, Order Merit award Boy Scouts Am., 1970, Scouter's Key, 1970, Scouter's Tng. award, 1967; A.D. Williams fellow, 1954-55. Diplomate Am. Bd. Family Practice. Mem. Res. Officers Assn., Lynchburg Acad. Medicine, Jr. C. of C., Med. Soc. Va., Alumni Assn. Med. Coll. Va., A.M.A., So. Med. Assn., Va., Am. acads. family practice, Alumni Assn. Va. Poly. Inst., Phi Kappa Phi, Phi Lambda Epsilon, Phi Sigma. Club: Investment (pres. 1966). Home: 1828 Sunset Dr Altavista VA 24517 Office: 507 7th St Altavista VA 24517

SMALL, ALBERT H., economist; b. N.Y.C., Dec. 2, 1919; s. William and Rebecca (Jaffa) S.; A.B. magna cum laude, Bklyn. Coll., 1941; A.M., Am. U., 1948, Ph.D., 1971; m. Sylvia Schertzer, Aug. 16, 1942; 1 son, Jeff. With OPA, 1941-46, Dept. Commerce, 1946-56, Gen. Services Adminstrn., 1956-60, Dept. State, 1960-65, Tariff Commn., 1965-68; spl. asst. program coordination Dept. Commerce Office Internat. Trade Promotion, Washington, 1968-71; asst. dir. operations Price Commn., Exec. Office Pres., Washington, 1971—; market research cons.; lectr. market research and internat. bus. Am. U. Mem. U.S. Delegations to GATT, 1962, 63, 64, 66. Mem. Am. Econ. Assn., Am. Mgmt. Assn., Am. Marketing Assn., Nat. Assn. Bus. Economists. Club: International (Washington). Home: 7119 Braeburn Pl Bethesda MD 20034 Office: Exec Office Pres Washington DC 20005

SMALL, KENNETH FREDERICK, broadcasting exec.; b. Camden, N.J., Apr. 5, 1909; s. Harry A.C. and Ethel (Hollingshead) S.; student Cornell U., 1926-28, Pa. Acad. Fine Arts, 1928-30; m. Elizabeth C. Adams, Jan. 14, 1932; children—Elizabeth C. (Mrs. Gordon D. Price), Kenneth H. Exec. v.p. Newman, Lynde & Assos., Inc., Jacksonville and Miami, Fla., 1945-52; asst. gen. mgr. radio sta. WPDQ, Jacksonville, also sec. Jacksonville Broadcasting Corp., 1952-56; mng. dir. radio stas. WRUF, WRUF-FM, U. Fla., 1956—, asst. prof. coll. Journalism and Communications. Pres. Civic Round Table, Jacksonville, 1949-52. Mem. Fla. Assn. Broadcasters (exec. sec. 1962—), Jacksonville Advt. Club (past pres.). Democrat. Rotarian (bd. dirs.). Clubs: Propeller (Jacksonville); Torch (Gainesville, Fla.). Home: 1936 NE 7th St Gainesville FL 32601

SMALL, LONNIE DALTON, coll. exec.; b. Fair Bluff, N.C., May 20, 1915; s. Maxcey Dalton and Lillian (Davis) S.; student Kings Coll., 1934-35, Wake Forest Coll., 1934, U. Ky., summers 1955, 56, 57, LaSalle U., 1938, N.C. State Coll., 1945-50; m. Elgie Lee May, Dec. 7, 1937; children—John, Calvin, Janet Lee. Asst. to bus. mgr. N.C. State Coll., 1945-50; bus. mgr. Campbell Coll., Buies Creek, N.C., 1951—, chief finance officer, 1951—, treas., 1951—, sec. bd. trustees, 1952—. Mem. So. Assn. Coll. Bus. Officers, Alpha Phi Omega. Mason. Home: PO Box 97 Buies Creek NC 27506

SMALL, MELVIN D., physician, educator; b. Somerville, Mass., May 22, 1925; s. Sidney J. and Ida (Gelbsman) S.; student Boston U., 1942, U. Colo., 1942-43, Ga. Tchrs. Coll., 1943, U. N.H., 1943, State U. Ia., 1943-44, Boston Coll., 1950; A.B., U. Wis., 1950; postgrad. U. Vt., 1950-51, U. Lausanne, 1954-56, Harvard, 1957-58; M.D., Duke U., 1959; m. Judith Nogee, Dec. 23, 1962; children—Michael Dorian, Michele. Fellowship in gastrointestinal research Mass. Meml. F. Ingelfinger, 1951-53, Boston City Hosp. N. Zamchek, 1953-59; research asst. Boston U. Sch. Medicine, 1956-57; intern Georgetown U. Hosp., 1959-60, resident in medicine, 1960-61, chief gastrointestinal research, 1961-64; chief gastroenterology service Georgetown div. D.C. Gen. Hosp., 1964-69; instr. Georgetown U., 1961-67, clin. asst. prof. medicine, 1967; bd. dirs. Jefferson Meml. Hosp., 1965—. Witness, U.S. Senate Small Bus. Subcom. on Drug Pricing; chmn. Internat. Faculty for Postgrad. Med. Edn. Served with AUS, 1943-45. Mem. Am. Physiol. Soc., Am. Inst. Nutrition, A.A.A.S., A.M.A., Am. Coll. Gastroenterology, A.C.P., Am. Gastroent. Assn., Am. Fedn. for Clin. Research, Am. Soc. Internal Medicine. Contbr. articles in field to profl. jours. Home: 2914 N 27th

St Arlington VA 22207 Office: 2946 Sleepy Hollow Rd Falls Church VA 22044

SMALL, RANDOL LEPHON, pub. sch. adminstr.; b. Nichols, S.C., Mar. 25, 1930; s. Teasley and Golie (Hinson) S.; student North Greenville Coll., 1953-54; B.A. cum laude, Carson Newman Coll., 1956; M.A., Appalachian State U., 1965, postgrad., 1965-66; m. Carolyn McElveen, June 30, 1962; 1 dau., Caroline McElveen. Dep. clk. U.S. Dist. Ct., Eastern Dist. S.C., Charleston, 1956-57; instr. Porter Mil. Acad., Charleston, 1957-60; dep. clk. ct. Horry County Ct. Common Pleas, Conway, S.C., 1961-63; chief sales rep. for S.C., Robertson Chem. Corp., Norfolk, Va., 1963-64; area supt. Bethune (S.C.) pub. schs., 1966-70, adminstrv. prin., 1970—. Served with AUS, 1951-53. Mem. N.E.A. (life), Kershaw County, S.C. edn. assns., Am., S.C. assns. sch. adminstrs., Nat., S.C. assns. secondary sch. prins., Nat., S.C. assns. elementary sch. prins., S.C. Assn. Supervision and Curriculum Devel., S.C. State High Sch. League (sec. treas. Conf. III, class A schs.), Blue Key, Phi Delta Kappa. Baptist (deacon). Home: Norwood St Bethune SC 29009 Office: PO Box 217 Bethune SC 29009

SMALL, ROBERT SCOTT, textile co. exec.; b. Charleston, S.C., July 18, 1915; s. Robert Scott and Louise (Johnson) S.; B.S., Coll. Charleston, 1936; LL.D., Clemson U., 1964; m. Sallie Tyler, June 17, 1938; children—Scottie (Mrs. Robert C. Johnson), Robert Scott, Charles Inness, Elizabeth Johnson, Oscar Johnson. With S.C. Nat. Bank, Pickens, 1936-38, asst. mgr., Greenville, 1938-41, cashier, trust officer, 1941-47; pres., treas. Ottaray Textiles &Haynsworth Mills, Anderson, S.C., 1947-51; v.p., dir. Woodside Mills, Greenville, 1951-58, pres., treas., dir., 1958-65; pres., chief operations officer Dan River Mills, Inc., Greenville, 1965-68, pres., chief exec. officer, 1968—, also dir.; dir. Iselin-Jefferson Co., Liberty Life Ins. Co., Piedmont Natural Gas, Featherknit Fabrics, Textile Hall Corp., Carolinas Capital Corp., S.C. Nat. Bank, So. Bell Tel. & Tel. Co., Atlanta. Mem. mgmt.-labor textile adv. com. Dept. Commerce. Campaign chmn. United Fund, 1957; mem. spl. gifts com. Nat. Conf. Christians and Jews; finance chmn. Episcopal Ch. Home for Children, York; chmn. bd. trustees Greenville Gen. Hosp., Coll. Charleston; bd. assos. Converse Coll.; adv. bd. Furman U. Mem. S.C. C. of C., S.C. Textile Mfrs. Assn. (pres. 1963), Am. Textile Mfrs. Inst. (dir. 1961-62). Clubs: Green Valley Country (pres. 1962), Poinsett, Cotillion (v.p. 1964), Greenville Country. Home: 420 E Parkins Mill Rd Greenville SC 29606 Office: Dan River Inc Danville VA 24541

SMALL, WALTER LOWRY, naval officer; b. Elizabeth City, N.C., Oct. 16, 1916; s. Walter Lowry and Elizabeth Buxton (White) S.; grad. Woodberry Forest Sch., 1934; B.S., U.S. Naval Acad. 1938; grad. Armed Forces Staff Coll., 1953; Naval Acad., 1938; grad. Armed Forces Staff Coll., 1953; Naval War Coll., 1958; m. Jane Van Rensselaer Harris, June 12, 1940; children—Elizabeth C., Jane C. Commd. ensign U.S. Navy, advanced through grades to rear adm.; patrols in submarines, World War II; aide to chief naval operations Fleet Adm. Nimitz; comdg. officer submarines and destroyer; dir. sci. and engring. U.S. Naval Acad.; dir. strategic plans div. office Chief Naval Operations; dir. naval war games; comdr. Middle East Force, Submarine Force Pacific Fleet; chmn., U.S. rep. Allied Mil. Study Group on Atlantic Nuclear Force; now chmn., U.S. Navy mem. Joint Mexican U.S. Def. Commn. Decorated Silver Star (2), Legion of Merit (20), Navy Commendation medal (2). Mem. U.S. Naval Acad. Alumni Assn. (past nat. dir., past v.p. Coronado-San Diego, past pres. Annapolis chpt.). Naval Hist. Found., U.S. Naval Inst. Home: 204 Colonial Av Elizabeth City NC 27909 Office: Donata Bldg 1525 N Lynn St Arlington VA 22209

SMALLHORST, DAVID FRANCIS, city ofcl.; b. St. Louis, Oct. 2, 1911; s. David E. and Frances S. (Smith) S.; B.S. in C.E., U. Tex., 1936; m. Blanche Lundquist, Dec. 18, 1937 (dec. Oct. 1965). With Tex. State Dept. Health, 1936-66, dir. water pollution control div., 1948-66, exec. sec. Water Pollution Control Bd., 1961-66; staff engr. water and wastewater dept., City of Austin, Tex., 1966—. Trustee V. M. Ehlers Meml. Fund, Inc. Served to maj., San. Corps, AUS, 1942-46. Registered profl. engr., Tex. Diplomate Am. Acad. Environmental Engrs. Mem. Water Pollution Control Fedn. (life), Am. Soc. C.E., Am. Water Works Assn., Nat. Soc. Profl. Engrs., Tex. Pub. Health Assn. (life), Tex. Water and Sewage Assn. (life), Tau Beta Pi, Chi Epsilon. Home: 4811 Caswell Av Austin TX 78751 Office: PO Box 1088 Austin TX 78767

SMART, GEORGE MCCOLLUM, architect; b. Newberry, S.C., Jan. 18, 1931; s. Coyle Bedford and Gladys Verl (McCollum) S.; B.A., Randolph-Macon Coll., 1952; A.B., N.C. State U., 1959; postgrad. Duke Div. Sch.; m. Ann Marie Seltman, Mar. 2, 1961; 1 son, George McCollum. Draftsman, Haskins & Rice, architects, Raleigh, N.C., 1955-56; designer, Holloway-Reeves, architects, Raleigh, 1958-59, Walter C. Burgess, architect, Raleigh, 1959; asso. architect, Haskins & Rice, architects, 1959-62, John Erwin Ramsay, architects and assos., Salisbury, N.C., 1962-63; partner, Burgess & Smart, architects, Raleigh, 1963-64; owner, George M. Smart, architect, Raleigh, 1964-67; pres., Smart & Woodall, architects, Raleigh, 1967-69, Smart-Woodall, Isley, Inc., Raleigh, 1969-70, Smart, Woodall, Isley & Herring, Inc., Raleigh, 1971—; partner Hall-Smart, Woodall Apts., Woodall-Smart, Craige Mountain Apts.; treas. Fed. Projects, Inc. Mem. Gov.'s State Govt. Reorgn. Com., 1970; mem. Raleigh Housing Authority, 1971; coach, Little League Baseball, Raleigh, N.C., 1960-62; v.p., treas. Va. Conf. Meth. Young, 1949-50; boys work sec. YMCA, Raleigh, N.C., 1953-54; crafts dir. Camp Sea Gull, Arapahoc, N.C., 1953-54; active Boy Scouts Am.; pres.-elect Raleigh Little Theatre, 1972. Del. N.C. Democratic conv., 1960-72. Served with AUS, 1956-58. Recipient Certificate of Recognition for excellence in rural ch. design Meth. Bishop's Archtl. Com., 1963. Mem. A.I.A. (chmn. honor awards N.C. chpt. 1965-67), Raleigh Council Architects (pres. 1967), Raleigh C. of C., Lambda Chi Alpha. Episcopalian. Home: 2439 W Lake Dr Raleigh NC 27609 Office: 113 N Boylan Av Raleigh NC 27603

SMATHERS, ROBERT HENRY, drugstore chain exec.; b. Charlotte, N.C., Jan. 5, 1936; s. Robert Hoyle and Katharine (Lewis) S.; A.B., Duke, 1958; m. Margaret Jane Brown, Dec. 20, 1958; 1 son, Robert Hoyle. Accountant, Dombhart & Holden, C.P.A.'s, Charlotte, 1958-60; v.p., treas. Eckerd Drugs, Inc., Charlotte, 1960—. C.P.A., N.C. Mem. Am. Inst. C.P.A.'s, Duke U. Alumni Assn. (treas. Charlotte assn. 1969-72), Sigma Chi. Methodist. Home: 6736 Burlwood Rd Charlotte NC 28211 Office: 1111 Hawthorne Lane Charlotte NC 28205

SMELLEY, CAROL BARCLAY LINDSAY (MRS. FRANCIS AARON SMELLEY), govt. ofcl.; b. Atlanta, Oct. 17, 1922; d. John Samuel and Florence Gertrude (Hand) Lindsay; student U. Ala., 1952; m. Francis Aaron Smelley, June 30, 1948; children—Dorothy Ann Echols (Mrs. Richard Raymond), Susan Grace. With Dept. Health, Edn. and Welfare, Social Security Adminstrn., Tuscaloosa, Ala., 1946—, claims rep., 1947-55, field rep., 1955—. Neighborhood chmn. Tombigbee council Girl Scouts U.S.A., 1959-62. Mem. Tuscaloosa County Preservation Soc. (trustee 1969—, recording sec. 1970), Birmingham Geneal. Soc. Methodist. Clubs: Altrusa (dir. 1968—, 1st v.p. 1970-71, pres. 1971-72), Tuscaloosa (Ala.) Country; Woodland Hills Garden (pres. 1965-66) (Tuscaloosa), Woodland Hills Swim (Tuscaloosa). Home: 171 Woodland Hills Tuscaloosa AL 35409 Office: 1118 Greensboro Av Tuscaloosa AL 35401

SMELLEY, F(RANCIS) AARON, banker; b. Tuscaloosa, Ala., July 4, 1919; s. Francis M. and Fannie (Busby) S.; B.S., U. Ala., 1947; postgrad. Alexander Hamilton Inst., 1965-67, Sch. Banking, U. Wis., 1971; m. Carol Lindsay, June 30, 1948; children—Dorothy Echols (Mrs. Richard Raymond), Susan. With Social Security Bd., Washington, 1941; storekeeper Northington Gen. Hosp., Tuscaloosa, 1943-44; accountant Ala. Binder & Chem. Co., Tuscaloosa, 1947-49, asst. comptroller, 1949-51, asst. treas., 1951-59, comptroller, 1959-60, treas., 1960-66; comptroller City Nat. Bank Tuscaloosa, 1966—. Active various community drives. Served with AUS, 1942. Mem. Am. Inst. Banking (treas. Tuscaloosa chpt. 1967), Bank Adminstrn. Inst., Tuscaloosa Preservation Soc., Commerce Exec. Soc., U. Ala. Alumni Assn., Am. Legion. Methodist (treas.). Clubs: Tuscaloosa Country, Kiwanis (dir. 1966), Toastmaster (pres. 1962). Home: 171 Woodland Hills Tuscaloosa AL 35401 Office: PO Box 2509 Tuscaloosa AL 35401

SMELTZER, JOHN FROST, educator; b. Shamokin, Pa., Jan. 23, 1909; s. Frost Edwin and Emma (Williamson) S.; B.S., Franklin and Marshall Coll., 1931; B.D., Lancaster Theol. Sem., 1934; postgrad. (grantee), Harvard Div. Sch., 1938-39, U. Pitts., 1939-40; M.A., Middle Tenn. State U., 1967; m. Thelma Kathryn Lytle, Nov. 29, 1934; children—Paul N., John P., James F. Ordained to ministry Evang. and Ref. Ch., 1934; pastor Evang. and Ref. Ch., Pa., Md., 1934-42, Denver, Pa., 1946-51; asst. prof. psychology Cleveland (Tenn.) State Coll., 1967—; psychol. testing and evaluation Headstart, 1969-70. Dist. commnr. Boy Scouts Am., 1969-71. Served as chaplain USAAF, 1941-46, ETO; from lt. col. to col. USAF, 1951-67. Decorated Bronze Star medal. Mem. Hist. Soc. Pa., Tenn. Ednl. Assn., Sigma Pi. Democrat. Mem. United Ch. of Christ. Mason, Lion. Home: 3602 Belmont Circle Cleveland TN 37311 Office: PO Box 1205 Cleveland State Coll Cleveland TN 37311

SMETANA, JOSEPH LAWRENCE, orgn. exec.; b. Temple, Tex., Mar. 8, 1930; s. Joseph Edward and Alice Annie (Gerngross) S.; student Temple Jr. Coll., 1949-50, U. Tex., 1951-52; B.S. in Vocational Agr., Sam Houston State U., 1953 Insp. Tex. Dept. Agr., 1953-54, bus. mgr. seed div., asst. to chief seed div., 1954-60; safety dir. Tex. Farm Bur., Waco, 1960—. Mem. safety-loss control com. Southwestern Ins. Information Service. Recipient Citizenship award Am. Farm Bur., 1962; Dist. Service award Tex. Safety Assn., 1963; TV film award Nat. Safety Council, 1966. Mem. Falls County Farm Bur., Nat. Inst. for Farm Safety, Am. Soc. for Safety Engring. (asso.), Pub. Relations Soc. Am., Farm-Ranch-Tex. Safety Assn. (v.p. 1968—), Tex. Farm and Ranch Safety Council (pres. 1969-70). Roman Catholic. K.C., Elk. Home: Route 2 Box 95 Lott TX 76656 Office: Box 489 Waco TX 76703

SMIDDY, JOSEPH CHARLES, food co. exec.; b. Jellico, Tenn., Feb. 16, 1926; s. Sillus David and Emma Elizabeth (West) S.; m. Wilma Jean Marion, Nov. 16, 1946; children—Gloria (Mrs. Robert Clinton Price), Robert Milton, Nancy Carolyn. Co-owner, mgr. S.D. Smiddy & Son Grocery, Jellico, 1946-48; salesman Remfro Wholesale Grocery, Williamsburg, Ky., 1948-52; salesman J. Allen Smith & Co., Knoxville, 1952-53, sr. salesman, 1953-54, ty. mgr., 1954-55, dist. mgr., 1955-60; co-owner Mymatt-Smiddy Brokerage Co., Knoxville, 1960-62; merchandising mgr. J. Allen Smith Co., Knoxville, 1962-66; sales mgr. Gt. Western Foods Co., Knoxville, 1966—. Served with USMCR, 1944-46; PTO. Baptist. Mason (32 deg.), Lion. Home: 4028 Longwood Dr Knoxville TN 37918 Office: 108 Depot St NE Knoxville TN 37917

SMILEY, EMMETT LYNFIELD, dentist; b. nr. Montgomery, Ala., June 14, 1922; s. George Washington and Hattie (Dabney) S.; B.S., Prairie View U., 1944; D.D.S., Meharry Med. Coll., 1950; m. Mary Jo Carter, Aug. 14, 1953; children—Lynn, Karen, Kim, George Wesley. Pvt. practice dentistry, Montgomery, 1950—. Active YMCA, 1950—; Urban League, 1969—. Served with M.C., AUS, 1942-45. Mem. Am. Bridge Assn. (life), Am. Contract Bridge Assn., Montgomery C. of C., Nat., Ala. dental assns., Capital City Med. Soc., Alpha Phi Alpha, Sigma Phi. Baptist. Elk. Clubs: Clique, Century. Home: 2402 W Edgemont Av Montgomery AL 36108 Office: 1031 Oak St Montgomery AL 36108

SMILEY, GARY RAY, educator, dentist; b. Spartanburg, S.C., Sept. 13, 1936; s. Harry and Rose (Hecklin) S.; B.S. in Dentistry, U. N.C., 1958, D.D.S., 1961, M.Sc. in Orthodontics, 1965; m. Sandra Lee Margolis, July 3, 1960; children—Steven Jay, Karen Beth, Suzanne Cheryl. Asst. prof. orthodontics U. N.C. at Chapel Hill, 1965-67, asso. prof., 1967-71, prof., 1971—, asst. dean research, 1971—, dir. orthodontic grad. research, 1967—. Orthodontic cons. N.C. Bd. Health, 1966—. Served to capt. USAF, 1961-63. USPHS grantee, 1967—. Mem. Am. Assn. Orthodontists, So. Soc. Orthodontists, Am. Cleft Palate Assn., Internat. Assn. Dental Research, A.A.A.S., Am. Dental Assn., Teratology Soc., Am. Cleft Palate Assn. (sec. 1971—), Phi Beta Kappa, Omicron Kappa Upsilon, Sigma Xi. Research and publs. on normal and abnormal growth and devel. of craniofacial complex especially formation of secondary palate. Home: 1704 Fountain Ridge Rd Chapel Hill NC 27514

SMILEY, GERALD THOMAS, space products co. exec.; b. Bristol, Que., Can., Sept. 23, 1925; s. Harold Ephriam and Charlotte Elizabeth (Russell) S.; B.E.E., Clarkson Coll. Tech., 1950; m. Sarah Elizabeth Meeker, Sept. 6, 1948; children—David, Linda, Steven, Patrick. Engr. heavy mil. elec. dept. Gen. Electric Co., 1951-55, program mgr., 1955-59, mgr. systems engring. defense systems div., 1959-62, program mgr. Apollo systems dept., Daytona Beach, Fla., 1962-63, mgr. Kennedy operations, Cape Canaveral, Fla., 1963-68, gen. mgr. Apollo and ground systems dept., Daytona Beach, 1968—. Chmn. World Affairs Forum, Daytona Beach, 1970; mem. Civic League Halifax Area, 1968—. Bd. dirs., dep. campaign chmn. United Fund Brevard County, 1966-67. Served with USNR, 1943-46. Recipient Pub. Service award NASA, 1969. Mem. Am. Inst. Aeros. and Astronautics (membership chmn. 1967), Air Force Assn., I.E.E.E., Am. Ordance Assn., Nat. Space Club, Eta Kappa Nu. Rotarian. Home: 230 Landmark Circle Ormond Beach FL 32074 Office: PO Box 2500 Daytona Beach FL 32015

SMILEY, JOSEPH ROYALL, univ. pres.; b. Dallas, Mar. 17, 1910; s. S. Lehman and Mabel (Royall) S.; A.B., So. Meth. U., 1931, A.M., 1932, LL.D., 1964; Ph.D., Columbia, 1947; LL.D., U. Denver, 1966; m. Mary Fincher, May 25, 1935; children—Stephen, Mary. Instr. Ark. A. & M. Coll., Magnolia, 1934-35; instr., asst. prof., asso. prof., North Tex. State Coll., Denton, 1935-38, 40-43, 46-47; lectr. Columbia, 1938-40; asst. prof. U. Ill., 1947-49, asst. dean grad. coll., 1949-50, asso. dean, 1950-51, prof. French, 1951-58, head dept., 1952-54, dean coll. liberal arts and scis., 1954-58; pres. Tex. Western Coll., U. of Tex., 1958-60; v.p., provost U. Tex., Austin, 1960-61, pres., 1961-63; pres. U. Colo., Boulder, 1963-69, U. Tex., El Paso, 1969—. Dir. El Paso Electric Co. Mem. bd. advisers Mountain States Telephone Commr. Western Interstate Commn. on Higher Edn., 1963-67, exec. com., 1965-67; chmn. U.S. Adv. Commn. on Internat. Ednl. and Cultural Affairs, 1966-69; mem. Govt. Adv. Com. Internat. Book Programs, 1966-68; chmn. Boulder Housing Authority, 1966-68; mem. adv. com. for instl. relations NSF, 1967-69. Dir. Midwest Research Inst.; bd. Asso. Rocky Mountain Univs., 1963, sec.-treas., 1965-66, vice chmn., 1966-67. Fulbright research fellow, France, 1953-54; mem. President's Commn. on White House Fellows. Mem. bd. visitors Air U., 1968-70. Served as lt. USNR, 1943-46. Decorated chevalier Legion of Honor (France). Mem. Phi Kappa Phi, Kappa Alpha, Phi Beta Kappa. Episcopalian. Author: Diderot's Relations with Grimm, 1950. Contbr. profl. jours. Address: 711 Cincinnati Av El Paso TX 79902

SMILEY, ROBERT LEE, entomologist; b. Birmingham, Ala., June 14, 1929; s. James and Cherry (Fuller) S.; B.S., Ala. A. and M. U., 1959; postgrad. Ohio State U., 1962-67, U. Md., 1971—; m. Cleeretta L. Henderson, Sept. 21, 1955; children—Consuela, Robert, Lisa, Joan. Agrl. research technician U.S. Agr. Dept., Washington, 1961-67, research entomologist, 1967—. Scoutmaster, Boy Scouts Am., 1962-63, committeeman, 1963-64. Served with AUS, 1951-53. Alpha Kappa Mu scholar, 1968; named hon. citizen Minn., 1968. Mem. Entomol. Soc. Am., Entomol. Soc. Washington (custodian 1963-68), A.A.A.S., Acarology Assn. Baptist. Contbr. articles to profl. jours. Home: 1444 Primrose Rd NW Washington DC 20012 Office: Agr Research Sta US Agr Dept Washington DC 20250

SMILEY, WENDELL WAYNE, librarian; b. Bryson City, N.C., June 15, 1908; s. Arthur Lee and Sallie (Stevenson) S.; Grad. Mars Hill Coll., 1926; A.B., U. N.C., 1928, B.L.S., 1933; M.S., U. Ill., 1939; m. Elva Ruth Parkinson, Nov. 23, 1932; children—Ralph Parkinson, Wendell Wayne, Sara Elva, Scott Landrum, John Stevenson. Tchr. pub. schs., N.C., 1926-27, 28-29; staff U. N.C. Library, 1929-39; librarian Ga. Tchrs. Coll., 1939-42, Mercer U., 1942-43, East Carolina U., 1943-67, dir. library services, also prof. library scis., 1967—; instr. library sci. U. Ill., summer 1942. Licensed radio engr. FCC. Mem. Am., Southeastern, N.C. (v.p. 1947-49), Ga. (v.p. 1940-41, pres. 1941-43) library assns., N.C. Edn. Assn., A.A.A.S. Democrat. Baptist. Rotarian. Editor: N.C. Press Views The Ku Klux Klan. Home: Hillcrest Greenville NC 27834

SMITH, ALBERT HENRY, JR., metallurgist; b. Anniston, Ala., Mar. 10, 1928; s. Albert Henry and Eunice (Kitchens) S.; student Auburn U., 1948-49; B.S., Jacksonville State U., 1951; m. Sara Anne Geier, Sept. 7, 1950; children—David Albert, Sheila Ann. Chemist, Ala. Pipe Co., Anniston, Ala., 1950-53; research chemist Monsanto Chem. Co., Anniston, Ala., 1953; metallurgist, chief metallurgist, asst. plant mgr. Ala. Pipe Co., Anniston, Ala., 1954-67; tech. and quality control dir. SPARM, Woodward Iron Co., Anniston, Ala., 1967-71; mgr. quality control and metallurgy Woodward Soil Pipe group Woodward Co., Anniston, 1971—. Troop committeeman Boy Scouts of Am., 1967—. Served with AUS, 1946-48. Mem. Am. Soc. for Testing and Materials, Am. Standards Assn., Am. Foundrymens Soc. (chpt. chmn. 1968-69), Cast Iron Pipe Research Assn., Cast Iron Soil Pipe Inst. Baptist. Home: 29 Timothy Trace Anniston AL 36201 Office: PO Box 309 Anniston AL 36201

SMITH, ALFRED GLAZE, JR., economist, educator; b. Urbana, Ill., Dec. 28, 1913; s. Alfred Glaze and Lucy Catharine (Prutsman) S.; A.B., Columbia, 1934, A.M., 1939, Ph.D., 1954; m. Katharine Cushing Brown, May 9, 1936; children—Alfred Glaze III, LeRoy Fairchild. With personal div. S.H. Kress & Co., 1936-38; instr. econs. U. S.C., 1938-42, asst. prof., 1942-47, asso. prof., 1947-54, prof., 1954—, head dept. econs., 1958-70; discussant First Ann. Conf. Econ. Devel. South, 1960; Fulbright prof., Bologna, Italy, 1963-64. Owner, operator farm, Lexington County, S.C. Served as officer USNR, 1943-46; comdr. Res. Mem. Am., So. econ. assns., Econ. History Assn. Club: Torch (pres.). Author: Economic Readjustment of an Old Cotton State: South Carolina, 1820-1860, 1958. Home: 1816 Enoree Av Columbia SC 29205

SMITH, AMELIA HALL, musician; b. Oklahoma City; d. Charles Jordan and Marie Helen (Ferris) Hall; grad. Drew Sem. for Young Women, Carmel, N.Y., 1930; summer student Woman's Coll., Greensboro, N.C., Julliard Sch. Music, N.Y.C.; certificate Am. Guild of Organists, 1954; student operatic seminar Manhattan Sch. Music, 1970; m. Willard Cardwell, Nov. 18, 1936 (div. Nov. 1954); children—Marie Lorraine (Mrs. James Albert Harrill, Jr.), Christine Amelia (Mrs. Ray D. Dodge); m. 2d, Harry Logan Smith, Jr., Aug. 19, 1956. Profl. accompanist, 1925—; soprano soloist, 1934—, appeared with Piedmont Festival Orch., 1943-49, Jacksonville (Fla.) Symphony Orch., 1957, others; appeared as Marie, Bartered Bride, 1941; founder, leading soprano Music Theatre Repertory Group, 1947-52; founder, dir. Opera Workshop, Jacksonville U. Coll. Music, 1956-61; founder mng. dir. Opera Repertory Group (TV and touring opera co.), 1961—, also pres.; music columnist N.C. and Fla. newspapers; pianist Jacksonville Symphony Orch., 1963-67; music faculty Edward Waters Coll., Jacksonville, 1967-68; organist, choirmaster 1st Meth. Ch., 1954-59, Grace Chapel Parish, 1959-67, Presbyn. Ch. Southside Estates, 1968-72, San Jose Episcopal Ch., 1972—. Active Arts Festival of Jacksonville Council Arts, 1958—, music chmn., 1958-59; dean. Am. Guild Organists, Jacksonville, 1958-61, chmn. Southeastern regional conv., 1963. Mem. Music Tchr. Assn. Jacksonville, Am. Guild of Organists, Jacksonville Council Arts, Nat. Assn. Tchrs. Singing, Nat. Assn. Am. Composers and Condrs., Jacksonville Opera Guild (founder), Central Opera Service, Am. Guild Mus. Artists, Musicians Assn. Jacksonville. Episcopalian (mem. music commn. Diocese of Fla. 1966-67). Club: Altrusa (pres. 1967-68, com. 1963-64) (Jacksonville). Music columnist The Trend, Jacksonville, 1969—; corr. Mus. Am. Home: 4227 Peachtree Circle E Jacksonville FL 32207 Office: 7423 San Jose Blvd Jacksonville FL 32217

SMITH, ANGIE FRANK, JR., lawyer; b. Detroit, Tex., Nov. 3, 1915; s. A. Frank and Bess Patience (Crutchfield) S.; B.A., Rice U., 1937; LL.B., U.Tex., 1940; m. Mary Hannah, June 15, 1939; children—Tweed, Karen, A. Frank III, Alison, Leslie Ann. Partner Vinson, Elkins, Searis, Connally & Smith and predecessor; dir. Cullen Center Bank & Trust. Quintana Petroleum Corp., Austral Oil Co., Crutcher Resources Corp. Mem. bd. publs. United Meth. Ch. Trustee Meth. Hosp., Houston, Southwestern U., San Jacinto, Mus. Histroy Assn., Cullen Found., bd. dirs. Houston Symphony Soc. Served with USNR, 1942-45. Mem. Sons Republic Tex., Knight San Jacinto, Am., Tex., Houston bar assns., Houston C. of C. (dir.), Order of Coif, Phi Delta Phi, Phi Delta Theta. Methodist. Clubs: River Oaks Country; Broadmoor Golf, Garden of Gods (Colorado Springs). Home: 3420 Piping Rock Lane Houston TX 77027 Office: First City Nat Bank Bldg Houston TX 77002

SMITH, ASHBY GORDON, union ofcl.; b. Danville, Ky., Mar. 29, 1905; s. John Thomas and Elizabeth (Griffin) S.; student Butler U., 1925-27; Ph.B., U. Chgo., 1930, J.D., 1932; m. P. Melba Dixon, June 14, 1930; 1 son, Ashby Gordon. Joined U.S. Postal Service, 1928; mem. Nat. Alliance Postal Employees, 1940—, editor mag., Voice, 1940-61, nat. v.p., 1959-61, nat. pres., 1961—; columnist Chgo. Bee, 1939-42. Mem. Pres.'s Com. on 50th Anniversary Dept. Labor, 1962—. Mem. exec. bd. Leadership Conf. Civil Rights, 1961-63; pres. Park Manor Neighbors, Chgo., 1957-60, Citizens Housing, Chgo., 1960-61. Home: 1909 19th St NW Washington DC 20009 Office: 1644 11th St NW Washington DC 20001

SMITH, AUBURN PINKNEY, coll. athletic dir., educator; b. Louann, Ark., Dec. 13, 1913; s. Andrew Pinkney and Anna (Neeley) S.; B.A., Hendrix Coll., 1938; M.S., George Peabody U., 1953; postgrad. U. Ark., 1964-65 Tchr., coach Morrilton High Sch., 1938-41, Camden High Sch., 1941-42, 1946-47; instr., coach So. State Coll., Magnolia, Ark., 1947-54, head coach, athletic dir., asst. prof., 1954-69, athletic dir., asso. prof. phys. edn., 1969—, dir. financial aids, 1972—. Pres. Ark. Athletic Dirs. Intercollegiate Conf., 1972. Served with USAAF, 1942-46. Decorated Bronze Star medal. Mem. Magnolia C. of C., Am. Legion, V.F.W., Ark. Edn. Assn., N.E.A., A.A.H.P.E.R., Ark. Coaches Assn., Nat. Assn. Intercollegiate Coaches Assn., Nat. Assn. Intercollegiate Athletics (chmn. exec. com. 1967—). Methodist (chmn. ofcl. bd. 1961-62). Kiwanian, Rotarian. Home: 1305 Lacari St Magnolia AR 71753

SMITH, B. FRANK, JR., pharm. service rep.; b. Sturgis, Miss., Aug. 26, 1916; s. B. Frank and Florence (Kornegay) S.; B.S., U. Tenn., 1949, postgrad., 1949-50; m. Emily Edith Berryhill, Nov. 28, 1946. U.S. dep. collector Internal Revenue Dept., Memphis, 1944-45; territory sales W. A. Shaeffer Pen Co., Ga., S.C., 1950-52; profl. pharm. service rep. Stuart Pharms., Tenn., Ga., N.C., Ky., 1952-66, Treasure Island, Fla., 1966-72; terr. mgr. Stuart Pharm. div. ICI America Inc., 1972—. Unit leader Shrine Crippled Children, 1964-65; adviser Easter Seal Soc., 1962-63; asst. chmn. com. Elk Crippled Children Rehab., 1968—. Served with AUS, 1940-44. Mem. Pharm. Reps. Assn. (dir.), Tampa Bay Pharm. Reps. Assn. Republican. Lutheran. Mason (32 deg., Shriner), Elk. Clubs: Seminole Country, Bath. Home: 10215 3d St E Treasure Island FL 33706

SMITH, BARNETT FRISSELL, biologist, educator; b. Montgomery, Ala., Jan. 17, 1909; s. Thomas J. and Alice (Johnson) S.; B.S., Morehouse Coll., 1932; M.S., Atlanta U., 1934; Ph.D., U. Wis., 1944; m. Grace Burley Boggs, Aug. 22, 1962; children—Barnett Frissell, Olivia Boggs. Tchr. biology, gen. sci. city schs., Atlanta, 1935-36; asso. prof. biology Ala. State Coll., 1937-45; prof. biology Spelman Coll., Atlanta, 1945—. Ford Found. fellow, 1954-55; La. State U. fellow, Central Am., summer 1966. Contbr. articles to sci. jours. Home: 1198 Fountain Dr SW Atlanta GA 30314

SMITH, BENJAMIN FRANKLIN, council ofcl.; b. Holcomb, Miss., Dec. 22, 1917; s. Ben F. and Allene (DeShazo) S.; B.S., Delta State Tchrs. Coll., 1939; grad. student George Peabody U.; m. Mary Alyce Bounds, Aug. 31, 1941; children—James Winfred, Lelia Elaine. Instr. biol. sci., Arcola (Miss.) Sch., 1939-41, Jackson City Sch., 1941-42; tng. officer V.A., 1946-47; asst. mgr. Delta Council, 1947-49, secretary, mgr., 1949-57, exec. v.p., 1957—. Mgmt. rep. Labor Mgmt. Manpower Com. Region IV, 1957-64; mem. Nat. Cotton Adv. Com. Served as capt. AUS, 1942-46. Recipient Man of Year award Progressive Farmer, 1962; Spl. Service award U. S. Weather Bur., 1964; Outstanding Alumni award Delta State Coll., 1964; Golden Anniversary Fed. Land Bank award, 1967; Silver Beaver Boy Scouts Am. Mem. Miss., Nat., So. assns. C. of C. execs., Delta State Alumni Assn. Methodist. Club: Lions. Author articles in tech. jours. Contbr. Delta Looks Forward, 1949; Flood Control in the Mississippi Valley, 1952. Editor: Delta Council News. Home: Leland MS 38756 Office: Stoneville MS 38776

SMITH, BENJAMIN JULIAN, bishop; b. Barnesville, Ga., Dec. 27, 1899; s. Rev. John Benjamin and Martha Angeline (Thomas) S.; A.B., Howard U., 1924; B.D., Garrett Theol. Sem., 1927; student Northwestern U.; D.D., Lane Coll., 1944; m. Hermion V. Jackson, Mar. 3, 1928; children—Roy Morgan, Carol Susan, Benjamin Julian. Ordained to ministry Christian Methodist Episcopal Ch.; asst. pastor Israel Met. Ch., Washington, 1922-24; pastor New Hope Ch., Evanston, Ill., 1924-28; dir. religious edn. 8th Episcopal Dist., acting pastor Williams Instl. Ch., N.Y.C., 1928-29; pastor Jubilee Temple, Chgo., 1929-30, Jamison Temple, Kansas City, Mo., 1930-35; gen. sec. bd. religious edn. C.M.E. Ch., 1935-54, bishop, 1954-69, also pres. bd. Christian edn.; presiding bishop 1st Episcopal dist. Christian Methodist Episcopal Ch., 1969—; v.p. Interdenominational Theol. Center, Atlanta. Mem. nat. council Boy Scouts Am. Pres. bd. trustees Lane Coll., Jackson, Tenn.; trustee Miss. Indsl. Coll.; bd. dirs. Fund for Theol. Edn. Mem. Nat. Council Chs. Christ U.S. (past v.p.), World Council Christian Edn. and Sunday Sch. Assn. (v.p.), World Council Chs. (exec. com. U.S. conf., bd. mgrs.), N.A.A.C.P., Phi Beta Sigma. Writer in field. Office: 564 E Frank Av Memphis TN 38106

SMITH, BENJAMIN SHAW, JR., petroleum co. exec.; b. Mexia, Tex., Jan. 23, 1917; s. Benjamin Shaw and Natalie (Machon) S.; student Rice U., 1934-35, Met. Bus. Sch., 1935-36; m. C. Ruth McDonald, Dec. 30, 1942; children—Benjamin Shaw III, C. Rebecca. Dir. indsl. relations Lion Oil Co., El Dorado, Ark., 1937-55; dir. personnel research Monsanto Co., St. Louis, 1955-58; gen. mgr. adminstrv. services Murphy Oil Corp., El Dorado, 1958-69, v.p., 1969—; dir. Nat. Bank Commerce, El Dorado. Chmn. El Dorado Airport Commn., 1962—; gen. chmn. United Campaign, 1967. Bd. dirs. Greater El Dorado Com. Mem. Am. Petroleum Inst., Am. Mgmt. Assn., El Dorado C. of C. Methodist. Rotarian. Home: 101 Fairway Lane El Dorado AR 71730 Office: Murphy Bldg El Dorado AR 71730

SMITH, BILLIE ANITA FOUTCH (MRS. VINCENT SMITH, JR.), educator; b. Smithville, Tenn., July 18, 1928; d. William Repsie and Martha L. (Keith) Foutch; student Florence State Tchrs. Coll., 1945, 49, Athens Coll., 1945-46, U. Ala., 1947; B.S., Eastern Mich. U., Ypsilanti, 1954, M.A., 1958, Specialist in Arts, 1967; m. Hilliard M. Terry, Feb. 18, 1946 (dec. May 1955); m. 2d, Vincent Bryant Smith, Jr., Aug. 9, 1958; 1 son, Vincent Bryant III. Tchr. Lawrence County Pub. Schs., Moulton, Ala., 1947-50; bookkeeper-checker Atlantic and Pacific Tea Co., Ypsilanti, Mich., 1950-53; elementary tchr. Willow Run Pub. Sch., Ypsilanti, 1954-61; elementary prin., Henry J. Kaiser Sch., Ypsilanti, 1961-68; classroom tchr., elementary prin., instr. Mich. Bapt. Inst., 1968; prin. Medlock Elementary Sch., Decatur, Ga., 1968—; guest lectr. Eastern Mich. U., 1966—. State dir. Young Woman's Aux. Bapt. State Conv. Mich., 1959-62, mem. exec. bd., 1961-65, 67—, mem. exec. com., 1962-65; dir. Vacation Bible Sch. Huron Valley Assn., Ypsilanti, 1957-61, Greater Detroit Assn., Detroit, 1962—. Mem. Nat., Mich. edn. assns., Nat., Mich. (pres. 1970), DeKalb (sec. 1969), Ga. (chmn. resolutions com. 1972) assns. elementary sch. prins., P.T.A., DeKalb Adminstrs. Club (pres. 1972), Delta Kappa Gamma (Beta chpt.; mem. research com. 1967-68, corr. sec. 1968—). Baptist (pianist 1964-66; dir. edn. Ypsilanti, 1956-61, dir. edn. Plymouth, Mich., 1965-68). Home: 3816 Norman Rd Clarkston GA 30021 Office: 2418 Wood Trail Lane Decatur GA 30033

SMITH, BUDD ELMON, coll. pres.; b. Benson, N.C., Feb. 9, 1910; s. James L. and Hettie (Lee) S.; A.B., U. N.C., 1931, M.A., 1934, Ph.D., 1942; postgrad. Duke U., 1950-51; LL.D., Wake Forest Coll., 1961; m. Ethel Lillie Knott, Dec. 27, 1943; children—James Fielding, William Budd. Prof. biology Coker Coll., 1934-35, 39-46; plant breeder Coker's Pedigreed Seed Co., Hartsville, S.C., 1935-39; prof. biology Wake Forest Coll., 1946-51; supt. schs. Oxford, N.C., 1951-53; pres. Wingate Coll., 1953—. Dir. Wingate State Bank. Mem. Nat. Accrediting Commn. Higher Edn.; chmn. Christmas Seals; chmn. N.C. Transfer Studies. Trustee Union Meml. Hosp.; mem. indsl. commn. Union County, 1954-57; pres. Union Co. Indsl. Devel. Commn., 1960-61. Served petty officer 2d class to lt. USNR, 1942-45. Named Man of Year, Union County, 1961. Mem. A.A.A.S., Am. Assn. Sch. Adminstrs., Bot. Soc. Am., Am. (dir.), So. (pres.), N.C. (pres., organizer) assns. jr. colls., N.C. Assn. Ind. Colls. and Univs. (exec. com.), So. Assn. Schs. and Colls. (chmn. standards com.), Nat. Council Ind. Two-Yr. Colls. (exec. com.), N.C. Acad. Sci., Southeastern Assn. Biologists, Union-Monroe C. of C. (pres. 1972), Phi Beta Kappa, Sigma Xi, Beta Beta Beta, Omicron Delta Kappa, Alpha Sigma Phi, Alpha Epsilon Delta. Democrat. Baptist (deacon, lay leader). Clubs: Lions, Rotary. Home: Northwood Wingate NC 28174

SMITH, CALVIN MILES, dentist; b. Atlanta, Dec. 11, 1924; s. Harvey Miles and Stella Idaray (Bryant) S.; B.S., Morehouse Coll., 1948; D.D.S., Howard U., 1953; m. Margaret Odessa Nixon, Sept. 22, 1949; children—Calvin Miles, Stephen La Coste, Lynn Lavada, Kim Clarice. Tchr. gen. scis. Ballard High Sch., 1948-49; practice dentistry, Atlanta, 1953—; dental cons. Atlanta Residential Man-Power Tng. Center, 1969—. Panel chmn. Atlanta Community Chest, 1966-67; pres. N.A.A.C.P., Atlanta, 1963, 64, treas., 1962, 65-66, life mem., 1970—; mem. Atlanta Com. Cooperative Action, 1961—, Mayor's Com. for Hotel and Restaurant Desegregation, 1961; mem. exec. com. Atlanta Model Cities Program, 1967—, Atlanta Youth Council, 1968—. Vice pres. Fulton County Democratic Club, 1963-71. Chmn. bd. Atlanta Home for Convalescing and Aged, 1953—. Served with USMCR, 1944-46; PTO. Named Atlanta Citizen of Year, 1964; recipient Achievment award Guardsmen, 1964. Mem. Am., Ga. (pres. 1964, 65), N. Ga. (pres., 1963-64) No. Dist. dental assns., Omega Psi Phi. Baptist. Mason (32 deg., Shriner). Club: Graduate Bridge. Contbr. articles to newspapers, periodicals. Home: 469 Haldane Dr SW Atlanta GA 30311 Office: 2380 Sewell Rd SW Atlanta GA 30311

SMITH, CHARLES EDWARD, physician; b. Omaha, Nov. 16, 1917; s. Maurice I. and Rebecca (Ratner) S.; student U. Md., 1934-37; A.B., George Washington U., 1939, M.D., 1941; postgrad. Columbia, 1950-51; m. Phyllis Stein Lange, June 12, 1941; children—Timothea Ann (Mrs. Jurgen-Harald Zimmermann), Jonathan Charles. Intern, USPHS Hosp., Balt., 1941-42; staff psychiatrist VA Hosp., Northport, N.Y., 1945-49; chief med. officer, psychiatrist Fed. Correction Inst., Ashland, Ky., 1949-50; resident USPHS Hosp., S.I., N.Y., 1950-51; chief Psychiat. Service Med. Center for Fed. Prisoners, Springfield, Mo., 1951-55; asst. med. dir. Fed. Bur. Prisons, Washington, 1956-62, med. dir., 1962-66; chief of service West Side div. St. Elizabeth Hosp., Washington, 1966-67; asso. prof. psychiatry U. N.C. Sch. Medicine, Chapel Hill, 1967—; sr. psychiat. cons. N.C. Dept. Corrections, 1967—. Mem. profl. council Nat. Council on Crime and Delinquency, 1965—, mem. adult corrections panel, adv. council N.C. Council, 1968—. Served as capt. M.C., AUS, 1943-46. Fellow Am. Psychiat. Assn., A.A.A.S.; mem. A.M.A. Democrat. Conglist. Mason (Shriner), Kiwanian. Contbr. numerous articles to profl. jours. Home: S Lakeshore Dr and Rolling Rd Chapel Hill NC 27514 Office: Dept Psychiatry U NC Sch Medicine Chapel Hill NC 27514

SMITH, CHARLES G., JR., editor; b. Shreveport, La., Feb. 27, 1925; s. Charles G. and Annie (Browning) S.; B.A., Miss. Coll., 1949, M.A., 1952; postgrad. U. So. Miss., 1953, La. State U.; m. Sara C. Smith, Nov. 27, 1957. Instr. Journalism Central High Sch., Jackson, Miss., 1952-62; staff writer, contbg. mem. Clarion-Ledger, Jackson, Miss., 1957-65, city editor, 1965—. Served with AUS, 1943-46. Mem. Miss. Journalism Assn. (past pres.), Sigma Delta Chi (chpt. past. pres.), C. of C. Episcopalian. Miss. Wing staff mem. Civil Air Patrol, 1957—. Office: 311 E Pearl St PO Box 40 Jackson MS 39205

SMITH, CHARLES H., JR., pub. co. exec. Pres., publisher Roy N. Lotspeich Pub. Co. Inc., Knoxville. Office: 210 W Church Av Knoxville TN 37901*

SMITH, CHARLES JAMES, III, bottling co. exec.; b. Savannah, Ga., Oct. 7, 1926; s. Charles James and Katrina (Lowe) S.; A.B., Tenn. A. and I. State U., 1947; M.A., U. Ia., 1948; postgrad. Fla. A. and M. U., 1956-63, U. Minn., 1961; m. Norma Jean Halloway, June 7, 1954; children—Donna Marie, Charles James IV. Dir. publs. and publicity Savannah State Coll., 1948-50; dir. pub. relations, asst. prof. journalism Fla. A. and M. U., 1952-63; dir. spl. markets activities Royal Crown Cola Co., Columbus, Ga., 1963—. Recipient Alumni citation Tenn. State U., 1962, Meritorious Achievement award Fla. A. and M. U., 1965. Mem. Nat. Assn. Market Developers (pres. 1970-71), Am. Marketing Assn., Pub. Relations Soc. Am., Sigma Delta Chi, Phi Delta Chi. Home: 1357 Juniper St NW Washington DC 20012 Office: PO Box 1440 Columbus GA 31902

SMITH, CHARLES LEAVELL, JR., city engr.; b. Pensacola, Fla., Mar. 4, 1914; s. Charles Leavell and Marie (McGill) S.; B.S. in Elec. Engring., Ga. Inst. Tech., 1935; m. Sara Lewis, Sept. 7, 1940; children—Sara Lewis (Mrs. Michael J. Grode), Charlotte Jon. Asst. sales engr. Westinghouse Elec. Corp., 1935-38; engr. Wright & Logez, Cedartown, Ga., 1938-41, Smith-Bittenbring, Inc., Cedartown, 1945-50; supt. light, water and sewage dept. City of Griffin (Ga.), 1950—. Served to comdr. USNR, 1941-45. Mem. I.E.E.E., Tau Beta Pi, Sigma Alpha Epsilon, Phi Kappa Phi, Phi Eta Sigma, Omicron Delta Kappa. Democrat. Episcopalian. Elk. Club: Exchange (pres. Griffin 1957, dist. gov. 1958-59). Contbr. article to profl. publ. Home: 652 Brook Circle Griffin GA 30223 Office: Light and Water Dept Griffin GA 30223

SMITH, CHARLES LLOYD, county agt.; b. Morganton, Ga., Jan. 7, 1921; s. Andrew Daniel and Lola G. (Panter) S.; B.S., U. Ga., 1951; m. Christine Cobb, Feb. 20, 1945; 1 son, Roy Wilson. Farm vet. instr., Blue Ridge, Ga., 1951-52; county agt. Agrl. Extension Service, U. Ga., Ellijay, 1952—; sec.-treas. Gilmer Enterpises, Inc. Served with AUS, 1942-45. Decorated Purple Heart. Methodist (chmn. adminstrv. bd. 1970-71). Mason, Lion. Home: 20 Logan St Ellijay GA 30540 Office: 48 Dodge St Ellijay GA 30540

SMITH, CHARLES MIAH, physician; b. Bogalusa, La., Aug. 24, 1930; s. C. Miah and Viola (Jenkins) S.; B.S., La. State U., 1951, M.D., 1955. Intern, Confederate Meml. Hosp., Shreveport, La.; resident Lafayette Charity Hosp.; practice medicine specializing in gen. and indsl. medicine, Sulphur, La., 1959—; mem. staff various hosps. Served as flight surgeon USAF, 1956-58. Mem. A.M.A., Am. Acad. Gen. Practice, So., La. med. socs. Baptist. Rotarian. Home: 702 Ruth St Sulphur LA 70663 Office: 211 Pine St Sulphur LA 70663

SMITH, CHARLES ULLMAN, educator; b. Birmingham, Ala., Oct. 16, 1923; s. William Pernell and Ella Marzetta (Johnson) S.; B.S., Tuskegee Inst., 1944; M.A., Fisk U., 1946; Ph.D., Wash. State U., 1950; postgrad. U. Conn., 1958; m. Marolyn Camille Warner, Aug. 21, 1951; 1 dau., Shauna Yvonne. Faculty Fla. A. and M. U., Tallahassee, 1950—, prof., chmn. sociology dept., 1951—; adj. prof. sociology Fla. State U., 1964—. Pres., Tallahassee Council Human Relations, 1960-62; mem. Gov.'s Interagy. Law Enforcement Planning Council, 1969—, Fla. Commn. on Human Relations, 1969—; Fla. del. White House Conf. on Children, 1970, White House Conf. on Aging, 1971. Mem. exec. com. Leon County Democratic Party, 1966—. Trustee Fla. Council on Aging. Grantee, coordinator sever coll. study on student unrest Russell Sage Found., 1967—. Recipient Silver medallion Mental Health Assn. Fla., 1968, Gold medallion, 1971. Mem. Am., So. (v.p. 1967-68, mem. exec. com. 1969—) sociol. socs., Assn. Social and Behavioral Scientists (exec. com. 1969—), Am. Assn. U. Profs., N.E.A., Fla. Edn. Assn., Fla. (bd. dirs.), Leon County (bd. dirs.) assns. mental health, Alpha Phi Alpha. Presbyn. Editor: Diamond Anniversary Essays, 1962. Adv. editor Social Forces; editorial bd Agewise. Contbr. articles to books and profl. jours. Home: 2611 Pottsdamer St Tallahassee FL 32304

SMITH, CHLOETHIEL WOODARD, architect; b. Peoria, Ill., Feb., 2, 1910; d. Olliver Ernest and Coy Blanche (Johnson) W.; B.Arch. with honors, U. Ore., 1932; M.Arch., Washington U., 1933; m. Bromley Keables Smith, Apr. 5, 1940; children—Bromley Keables, Susanne Woodard. Various drafting positions, Portland, Ore., Seattle, 1929-32, drafting and design, N.Y.C., 1933-36; chief research and planning FHA, Washington, 1936-39; asso., pvt. practice architecture, Washington, 1939-40; city planning exhibit, drafting, Montreal, Can., 1940-41; prof. architecture U. San Andres, cons. Servicio Cooperativo de Salud Publica, La Paz, Bolivia, 1942-45; prin. Chloethiel Woodard Smith & Assos., Washington, 1945—; prin. works include Am. Embassy Chancery and Residence, Asuncion, Paraguay, Chestnut Lodge, Rockville, Md., Capitol Park apt. and town houses, Washington, bookstore Harcourt, Brace & World, Inc., N.Y.C., master plan for Washington Channel Waterfront, E St. Expressway, Washington, numerous pvt. residences, also urban renewal plans. Jury mem. house awards A.I.A., Nat. Assn. Home Builders; design review panel Boston Redevel. Agy.; participated exhibits City for Living, Montreal, Canada, 1940, German Building Exposition, Hanover, 1951; mem. architects adv. com. Nat. Capital Downtown Com. Inc.; mem. President's Adv. Council on Pennsylvania Av., 1963. Trustee Fred L. Lavanburg Found. Recipient Award of Merit, A.I.A., 1960; 1st honor award, award of merit FHA, 1963; John Simon Guggenheim Meml. Found. fellow, 1944. Fellow A.I.A. (chmn. 1965 Pan-Am. Congress com.); mem. Am. Inst. Planners Com. of 100 on Fed. City, Washington Bldg. Congress, Washington Planning and Housing Assn., Columbia Hist. Soc., Met. Washington Bd. Trade, Am. Fedn. Arts, Soc. Archtl. Historians, Alpha Omicron Pi. Home: 2328 Massachusetts Av NW Washington DC 20008 also Monterey Blue Ridge Summit PA Office: 1056 Thomas Jefferson St NW Washington DC 20007

SMITH, CLIFFORD WELDON, banker; b. Greensboro, Ga., Apr. 3, 1918; s. Clifford Alexander and Olive (Cawthon) S.; grad. high sch.; m. Marjorie Taylor, Apr. 6, 1941; children—Clifford Weldon, Laurence D., Cecily (Mrs. John R. Callaway). With Bank Greensboro (Ga.), 1937—, v.p., 1965-66, exec. v.p., 1966—. Pres. Greensboro Indsl. Corp., 1948-71; dir. Greensboro Investment Corp. Mayor, Greensboro, 1968—. Served with AUS, 1943-46; ETO. Methodist. Mason, Lion. Home: Appalachee Av Greensboro GA 30642 Office: Greensboro Bank Greensboro GA 30642

SMITH, CLINTON GROVE, polit. party ofcl.; b. Balt., Sept. 22, 1924; s. Frederick Lee and Betty (Grove) Hardesty; A.B. cum laude, Princeton, 1948; m. Frances Scott Fitzgerald, July 28, 1967; children—Paul Martin, Jacqueline Cardon. Mgr., Grid-L-Redi Processing Co., Washington, 1950-51; dir. Reddi-Wip Md., Inc., Washington, 1949-50; account exec. Young & Rubicam, Inc., N.Y.C., 1951-56; v.p. J. Walter Thompson Co., Ltd., Montreal, Que., Can., 1956-58; dir. J. Walter Thompson Co. S.A., Antwerp, Belgium, 1958-63; internat. marketing cons., Washington, 1963-65; exec. dir. Nat. Marketing Adv. Com., U.S. Dept. of Commerce, Washington, 1965-71, with Office of Domestic Bus. Policy, 1971-72; mem. McGovern Nat. Finance Com., 1972. Served with AUS, 1943-46. Mem. Am. Marketing Assn. (chpt. 2d v.p. 1966-67). Democrat. Episcopalian. Clubs: Colonial (Princeton, N.J.); 1925 FSt (Washington). Home: 3235 R St NW Washington DC 20007 Office: McGovern for President Com 1910 K St NW Washington DC 20006

SMITH, CRAIG MCCULLOH, financial exec.; b. Plainfield, N.J., Aug. 27, 1929; s. Mark Allison and Dorothy (McCulloh) S.; B.S., U. Va., 1955, postgrad., 1955-56; m. Carolyn Sue Fullerton, June 16, 1954; children—Allison Lucy, Craig McCulloh. Financial analyst Carborundum Co., Niagara Falls, N.Y., 1956-59; sr. adminstr. Ark. Indsl. Devel. Commn., State Capitol, Little Rock, 1959-63; adminstrv. asst. to Winthrop Rockefeller, Little Rock, 1963—; pres., dir. Petit Jean Air Service, Inc., Petit Jean Attractions, Inc.; v.p., dir. Ark. Travelers Baseball Assn.; dir., mem. exec. com. Hamlin Products, Inc. Mem. Citizens Adv. Commn. to Gov. Ark., 1967—, Fabricated Metals Task Force Study Group, 1967—. Pres., bd. dirs. Rockwin Fund; bd. dirs. Winthrop Rockefeller Fund, Health and Welfare Council Pulaski County. Served with AUS, 1952-54. Mem. Nat. Assn. Accountants, S.A.R. (v.p. Ark.), Chi Psi. Republican. Presbyn. (deacon). Rotarian. Clubs: North Hills Country, Top of Rock, Little Rock (Little Rock). Author: (with William R. Legg) Economic History of Arkansas, 1962. Home: 2909 N Pierce St Little Rock AR 72207 Office: Tower Bldg 4th and Center Sts Little Rock AR 72201

SMITH, CYRIL LEE, judge; b. Munford, Ala., Nov. 22, 1918; s. Lee and Minnie Sue (Gauldin) S.; B.S. in Law, U. Ala., 1955, LL.B., 1957; m. Nell Bridges, May 28, 1959; children—Cyril Lee, Joe Alfred. Enforcement agt. Ala. Alcoholic Beverages Commn. Bd., 1942-55; investigator Ala. Dept. Indsl. Relations, 1955-57; admitted to Ala. bar, 1957; individual practice law, Gadsden, Ala., 1957-59; partner firm Barnes & Smith, Gadsden, 1959-63; county judge Etowah County, 1963—. Active various civic and charitable orgns. Served with USAAF, 1943-46; PTO. Mem. Nat., Ala. juvenile judge councils, Ala. Bar Assn., Am. Legion, Sigma Delta Kappa (grand exec. pres. 1966-67, nat. grand pres., 1967-68). Democrat. Baptist (deacon). Kiwanian, Elk. Home: 210 Cordell St Gadsden AL 35901 Office: 800 Forrest Av Gadsden AL 35901

SMITH, DAVID V., educator, forester; b. Lumpkin, Ga., July 12, 1921; s. David V. and Nelle (Siddall) S.; B.S.F., U. Ga., 1946; M.F., Duke U., 1950, postgrad. 1950-52; Ph.D., Coll. Forestry at Syracuse, 1968; m. Mary Frances Evans, June 8, 1947; children—Susan C., Mary Katherine. Jr. forest technician S.C. Commn Forestry, Walterboro, S.C., 1947, sr. forest technician, 1948, asst. forester, 1949; grad teaching asst. Duke U., 1950-51, instr., 1952, vis. asst. prof. summer 1953; asst. prof. forestry Va. Poly. Inst., Blacksburg, 1952-57, asso. prof., 1957-70; prof. forest engring. Stephen F. Austin State U., Nacogdoches, 1970—. Forest cons. cities Pulaski and Martinsville, Va.; Norfolk and Western Rys., Roanoke, Va., Barnes Lumber Co., Charlottesville, Va., Appalichian Power Co., Roanoke, Lester Brothers Lumber Co., Martinsville, Freeport Sulphur Co., N.Y.C., Allied Chem. Co., Morristown, N.J. Served to 1st lt. with AC, AUS, 1942-45; ETO. Mem. Am. Soc. Photogrammetry, Am. Congress on Surveying and Mapping, Photogrammetric Soc. (London), Soc. Photo-optical Instrumentation Engrs., Soc. Am. Foresters (chmn. chpt. 1958), Sigma Xi, Alpha Gamma Rho, Phi Sigma Xi. Methodist. Home: 2101 Creek View Bend Nacogdoches TX 75961

SMITH, DAVID WALTER, JR., dentist; b. Roanoke, Va., July 13, 1936; s. David Walter and Sara (Ready) S.; student Clemson U., 1956, U. S.C., 1956-59, Emory U., 1960-64; m. Frances Byrd Smith, June 17, 1961; children—Ann Ready, Sara Fitzmaurice, Frances Graybeale. Practice gen. dentistry, Camden, S.C., 1966—; mem. staff Kershaw County Meml. Hosp., Camden. Served to lt. USNR, 1964-66. Mem. C. of C. (chmn. Nat. Children's Dental Health Week Kershaw County 1966-69), Am. Dental Assn., PeeDee Dist.,

Richland County dental socs., Nat. Bd. Dental Examiners, Sigma Chi. Episcopalian (vestryman). Kiwanian. Home: 805 Kirkwood Circle Camden SC 29020 Office: 2602 N Broad St Camden SC 29020

SMITH, DAYTON E., aircraft repair co. exec.; b. Portland, Ore., Sept. 15, 1926; s. Dayton E. and Jean (Werle) S.; B.B.A., U. Miami, 1949; m. Joan I. Frey, Aug. 16, 1946; children—Kathy (Mrs. Robert Ferencik, Jr.), Diane M., Regina I., Dayton E. III. Accountant, Haskins & Sells (formerly Purvis, Pentland, Keller & Co.), Miami, Fla., 1949-51; treas., sec., dir. Aerodex Inc., Miami, 1951—; sec.-treas. API Corp. subsidiary, 1958—. Served with USNR, 1944-46. Home: 7360 SW 131st St Miami FL 33156 Office: PO Box 123 Miami FL 33148

SMITH, DEAN, basketball coach U. N.C. Office: Athletic Dept U NC Chapel Hill NC 27514*

SMITH, DEL PARKS, newspaper exec.; b. Belleville, W. Va., July 1, 1916; s. Grant and Nancy (Parks) S.; A.B., U. Ala., 1939; m. Julia Mallory, June 3, 1962; step children—Frank Mallory Bowler, Judy Bowler (Mrs. Millard Preston Hall, Jr.), Ellen Bowler. Sports editor E. Liverpool (O.) Rev. 1940-41; staff Constn., Atlanta, 1941-51; news editor Valley Morning Star, Harlingen, Tex., 1951-53; make-up editor Gazette, St. Joseph, Mo., 1954-59; mng. editor The News, Lynchburg, Va., 1959—. Mem. Asso. Press Mng. Editors Assn., Va. Press Assn., Newcomen Soc., Lynchburg C. of C. Home: 1515 Somerset Dr Lynchburg VA 24504 Office: 857 Church St Lynchburg VA 24505

SMITH, DEWITT, JR. (DICK), newspaper pub.; b. Phila., Oct. 18, 1927; s. DeWitt and Lessie (Brown) S.; student E. Miss. Jr. Coll., 1944-45; m. Wanda Tinsley Smith, Oct. 8, 1948; children—Dixie Gaye, Tommy Norris. Sports writer, sports editor The Meridian (Miss.) Star, 1945-58; editor, pub. Sumter County Journal, York, Ala., 1958—; pres. Dixie Bus. Forms Co.; pres. Dallas Pub. Co., Selma, Ala.; v.p. West Ala. Printing Co., Selma. Chmn. city parks-recreation commn. of Meridian, Miss., 1953-58; founder first Parks-Recreation Dept., Meridian, 1953; mem. York City Planning Commn., 1962—; chmn. York Indsl. Devel. Bd. Bd. dirs. Ala. Sheriffs Boys Ranch. Served as apprentice seaman, USNR, 1942-46; capt., USAAF, 1951-52. Mem. Southeastern Sportswriters Assn. (pres. 1950), Big Eight Writers Assn. (pres. 1950), C. of C. (pres.). Recipient D. P. Dear award for service to youth, Meridian, 1956. Mem. Nat. Editorial Assn., Ala. Press Assn. Presbyn. (deacon). Mason (Shriner), Lion (York past pres.; dep. dist. gov., Man of Year, York 1965). Club: Sumter Country (past pres.). Home: 424 Derby Dr York AL 36925 Office: 200 Main St York AL 36925

SMITH, DOCK GARNER, JR., lawyer; b. Clayton, N.C., May 20, 1935; s. Dock Garner and Helen (Rains) S.; B.S., E. Carolina U., 1957; LL.B., U. N.C., 1960; m. Peggy Faye Smith, 1957; children—Dock Garner III, Douglas G., Sandra Kay, Daniel G. Admitted to N.C. bar, 1960; individual practice in Robbins, N.C., 1961—. Pres. Robbins Improvement Co., Inc. Pres. Robbins Mchts. Assn., 1963-64. Pres. Moore County Young Democrats, 1964-66. Sec., dir. Northmoore Student Loan Found., Inc.; mem. Gov.'s N.C. Task Force on Adjudication. Mem. N.C., Moore County bar assns., Jr. C. of C. (pres. 1963-64). Methodist. Elk. Clubs: Montgomery County Country; Riverside Golf and Country, Pinehurst, Inc. Home: 310 Frye St Robbins NC 27325 Office: 118 E Salisbury St Robbins NC 27325

SMITH, DONALD LAMAR, lawyer, ins. exec.; b. Charlotte, N.C., Jan. 3, 1936; s. J. Lamar and Dorothy (Campbell) S.; B.S., Ga. Inst. Tech., 1958; LL.B., U. Fla., 1963; m. Frances Matthews, June 16, 1959; children—Donald Lamar, Sandlin Matthews, Ivy Hendrix II. Admitted to Fla. bar, 1964; mem. firm Jennings, Watts, Clarke & Hamilton, 1963-65; individual law practice, 1965—; sec. Carolina Casualty Ins. Co., 1965—; pres., chmn. bd. Blvd. Investment Co., 1966—; sec. Ivy H. Smith Co., 1970 (all Jacksonville, Fla.). Served to capt. USAF, 1958-61. Mem. Am., Jacksonville bar assns., Fla. Bar, Phi Delta Theta, Phi Delta Phi. Clubs: Ponte Vedra, San Jose Country, Hidden Hills Country, University, Ye Mystic Revelers. Home: 1069 Arbor Lane Jacksonville FL 32207 Office: Barnett Bank Bldg Jacksonville FL 32202

SMITH, DONALD STEELE, II, hosp. adminstr., educator; b. St. Paul, Dec. 15, 1929; s. Donald Steele and Gertrude (Reinhardt) S.; A.B., Dartmouth, 1951; M.H.A., U. Minn., 1953; m. Virginia Hannah Swain. Adminstrv. asst. Mary Hitchcock Meml. Hosp., Hanover, N.H., 1953; adminstrv. asst. nat. co-ordinator Med. Edn. for Nat. Defense program, Washington, 1956-59; adminstrv. asst. Duke Hosp., Durham, N.C., 1959—; coordinator grad. program hosp. adminstrn. Duke, 1959—, instr., 1959-61, asst. prof., 1961—, coordinator Center for Hosp. Continuing Edn., 1964—; adj. asst. prof. pub. health adminstrn. U. N.C., Chapel Hill, 1967—. Served to lt Med. Service Corps, AUS, 1953-56. Mem. Am. Coll. Hosp. Adminstrs., Am., N.C. hosp. assns., Am. Pub. Health Assn., Am. Sociol. Assn., Am. Mgmt. Assn., Theta Chi. Conglist. Home: 4167 Deepwood Circle Durham NC 27707 Office: Duke Univ Med Center Durham NC 27706

SMITH, DONALD VINCENT, publisher; b. Fitzgerald, Ga., Dec. 16, 1933; s. Sewell Lamar and Ruby (Smith) S.; student U. Miami, 1958-59. Founded Olivant Press, Atlanta, 1952; chief editor Olivant Quarterly (now Weid; The Sensibility Revue), 1952—; cons. literary pubs. Bd. dirs. Miami-Dade, Fla. Poetry Center. Served with AUS, 1954-57. Author: Five Sonnets, 1967; Tiredlove Poems, 1968; New Poems, 1968; Odyssey, 1969; Vacationing in Contemporary Greece, 1970. Address: Drawer 1409 Homestead FL 33030

SMITH, DOUGLAS CLARK, architect, city planner; b. Hastings, Neb., Nov. 8, 1932; s. Howard Agnew and Georgia (North) S.; B.Arch. with honors, U. Kan., 1959; m. Joan Marsh, Jan. 21, 1957; children—Vincent Lloyd, Aaron Douglas. Prin. planner Urban Renewal Agy. of Kansas City (Kan.), 1959-61; asst. dir. land clearance for Redevel. and Housing Authorities, Independence, Mo., 1961-63; city planner Hare & Hare, Kansas City, Mo., 1963-65; chief urban renewal planner, sect. chief Howard, Needles, Tammen & Bergendoff, Kansas City, Mo., 1965—, mgr. Washington Office, 1966—; staff Hwy. Users Fedn. for Safety and Mobility, 1969—, now planner-in-charge Mo., O., N.Y., Pa., W.Va. Cons. architect, city planner, 1959—; lectr. U. Kan., U. Mo. at Kansas City, Cottey Coll., Nevada, Mo., U. Ill., U. Wis., Hood Coll., Frederick, Md., U. Miss., Va. Poly. Inst.; mem. panel judges Highway and its Environment competition U.S. Dept. Transp., 1972. Mem. inner city com. Episcopal Diocese of West Mo., 1964-67; mem. Reston (Va.) Archtl. Bd. Rev., 1972. Served with AUS, 1953-55. Registered architect, Kan., Mo. Mem. A.I.A. (mem. urban planning and design com.), Am. Inst. Planners, Am. Acad. Polit. and Social Sci., Nat. Parks Assn., Am. Forestry Assn., Internat. City Mgmt. Assn. (cooperating mem.), Nat. Assn. Housing and Redevel. Ofcls., Sierra Club, Nat. Wildlife Fedn., Smithsonian Assos., Va. Wilderness Com., Scarab, Tau Beta Pi, Tau Sigma Delta, Sigma Phi Epsilon. Episcopalian (vestryman 1965-67). Prin. works include: Argentine Heights Urban Renewal Project, Kansas City, Kan., 1960-61, Northwest Pkwy. Urban Renewal Project, Independence, Mo., 1962-63, Zanesville (O.) Community Renewal Plan, 1965, Nor-Center 2 Urban Renewal Project, Norwood, O., 1965-68, Bluffs Center I Urban Renewal Project, Council Bluffs, Ia., 1966-67, Norwood (O.) Comprehensive Plan, 1967-69, Augusta County (Va.) Comprehensive Plan, 1969. Contbr. articles to profl. jours. Home: 12120 Quorn Lane Reston VA 22091 Office: 1776 Massachusetts Av NW Washington DC 20036

SMITH, DOYLE RABUN, dentist; b. Farmerville, La., Dec. 20, 1925; s. Doyle and Mearle (Rabun) S.; student La. Inst. Tech., 1942-44; D.D.S., Loyola U., New Orleans, 1947; m. Billie Childress, May 25, 1946; children—Doyle Rabun, Thomas C., J. Curtis, Melanie A., Charles E. Practice dentistry Monroe, La., 1947-70, Farmerville, La., 1970—. Pres., Conservatives, Inc., 1951—, D. Rabun Smith Builders Supply Co., 1969. Served with USNR, 1944-46, 50-52. Mem. Internat. Coll. Dentistry, Ark.-La.-Tex. Dental Congress (past pres.), Am., La. (bd. govs.), 5th Dist. (past pres.) dental assns., Kappa Sigma, Delta Sigma. Presbyn. (elder). Lion. Home: Lake D'Arbonne Farmerville LA 71241 Office: 201 E Jackson St Farmerville LA 71241

SMITH, DUDLEY, trade assn. exec., sugar cons., author; b. Campbellsville, Ky., Dec. 6, 1904; s. Herbert G. and Addie (Feather) S.; B.S., U. Ky., 1931; postgrad. U.S. Dept. Agr. Grad. Sch., 1931-35; m. Verta Enid Templeton, June 9, 1935; children—Mary Lou (Mrs. John William Harrell Brown), Dudley Templeton, Elizabeth Verta. Specialist tobacco marketing U. Ky., 1929-31, Fed. Farm Bd., 1931-32; with U.S. Dept. Agr., 1933-36; with Washington Office Assn. Sugar Producers P.R., 1936—, v.p., 1941—; tobacco and livestock farmer, Mitchellville, Md., 1941-68; cons. sugar and tobacco U.S. and fgn. countries, 1940—. Chmn., Md. Tobacco Authority, 1960-66; mem. Gov.'s Commns. on Utilization Water Resources, Feasibility of State Dept. Agr.; mem. Task Group on Sugar, Pres.'s Bi-Partisan Commn. on Increased Indsl. Use Agrl. Products; chmn. Sugar Research and Marketing Adv. Com., 1951-58; chmn. Chairmen All Agrl. Research Service Adv. Coms., 1954; bd. dirs. Md. Tobacco Co-op., 1956-67; lay com. Prince George (Md.) Jr. Coll., 1962-69; exec. bd. Tobacco Growers Information Com., 1962-67. Recipient award for outstanding service to agr. Prince George's C. of C., 1962. Mem. Internat., P.R., Queensland sugar technologists assns., Md. Agrl. Soc., Md. Farm Bur. (past county pres., dir. Md.), Sugar Club, Alpha Gamma Rho, Alpha Zeta. Democrat. Methodist. Mason. Club: University. Editor, Sugary Azucar Yearbook, 1971—. Contbr. articles on sugar and tobacco to trade publs. Home: 3001 Veazey Terrace NW Washington DC 20008 Office: 3005 Van Ness St NW Washington DC 20008

SMITH, DWIGHT HAZELTON, physician; b. Saluda, S.C., Dec. 13, 1921; s. George William and Naomi (Burnett) S.; B.S., Furman U., 1943; M.D., Med. U. S.C., 1946; m. Miriam King, Sept. 27, 1942; children—Preston, Brende, Judith, Dwight Hazelton, King. Intern, Med. Coll. Va. Hosp., 1946-47; practice medicine specializing in family practice, Williamston, S.C., 1950—; owner Williamston Hosp., 1950—; med. examiner FBI, 1948; FAA, 1960; team physician Palmetto High Sch., Williamston 1950—. Chmn. bd. dirs. Saluda Valley Fed. Savs. & Loan Assn., Williamston, 1964—; dir. So. Bank & Trust Co., Greenville, S.C. Pres., Anderson County Property Owners Assn. 1971; mem. Anderson County (S.C.) Bd. Edn., 1966-70. Served to lt (j.g.) USNR, 1943-46, 57-59. Diplomate Am. Assn. Family Practice. Mem. Am., So. med. assns., Am. Acad. Gen. Practice, Greenville County Med. Soc. Methodist (chmn. ofcl. bd. 1965-66). Home: 219 Hamilton St Williamston SC 29697 Office: PO Box 246 Williamston SC 29697

SMITH, EDDIE GLENN, JR., dentist, med. found. exec.; b. Palatka, Fla., Nov. 13, 1926; s. Eddie Glenn and Mamie (Jenkins) S.; B.S., Howard U., 1952, D.D.S., 1959; m. Callie Glasby, June 20, 1954; children—Katressia M., Katherine J. Intern, Crownsville (Md.) State Hosp., 1959-60; gen. practice dentistry, Washington; 1960—; dental dir. Community Group Health Found., Washington, 1968-70, dir. health services, 1970, project dir., 1971—. Asst. prof. dept. community dentistry Howard U. Coll. Dentistry, 1969—; pres. Nat. Dental Assn., 1972—; cons. Am. Dental Assn., Nat. Urban Coalition, Washington; cons. to sec. Dept. Health, Edn. and Welfare, 1968-72. Tech. adviser Washington Model Cities Program, 1969-70; parliamentarian Citizens for Better Health Care, 1971; 1st vice-chmn. bd. mgmt. YMCA, Washington, 1971. Bd. dirs. Health and Welfare Council, D.C., 1972; bd. regents Nat. Library Medicine, 1972—. Adv. bd. dirs. Nat. Med. Assn. Found. Served with USAAF, 1945-47. Recipient Meritorious award Howard U. Coll. Dentistry, 1969; Zone v.p. award Nat. Dental Assn., 1967, Dentist of Year award, 1969; Pub. Service award Washington Urban League, 1971. Mem. N.A.A.C.P., Fedn. Civic Assns., Robert T. Freeman Dental Soc. (award 1970, pres. 1968-71, editor Newsletter 1965-67), D.C. Dental Soc. (chmn. speaker's bur. 1968-69), Howard U. Dental Alumni Assn. (nat. pres. 1967-69), Omega Psi Phi. Baptist (trustee). Home: 7815 Orchid St NW Washington DC 20012 Office: Community Group Health Found 3308 14th St NW Washington DC 20010

SMITH, EDMUND CHRISTIAN, mfg. co. exec.; b. Clarksville, Tenn., Mar. 16, 1910; s. Frederick Norman and Corinne (Northington) S.; B.A., Vanderbilt, 1931, LL.B., 1934; m. Nelle McMahan, June 7, 1938; children—Barbara (Mrs. Doyle J. Smith, Jr.), Edmund Christian. Admitted to Tenn. bar, 1934; with Conwood Corp. (formerly Am. Snuff Co.), Memphis, 1934—, v.p., 1956-64, sec., 1964—, also dir. Mem. Memphis and Shelby County Bar Assn., Am. Soc. Corp. Secs., Delta Tau Delta, Phi Delta Phi. Baptist. Rotarian. Club: Memphis Country. Home: 4262 Tuckahoe Rd Memphis TN 38117 Office: 701 N Main St Memphis TN 38101

SMITH, EDWARD ARMSTRONG, supt. schs.; b. Farmville, Va., Aug. 23, 1907; s. Cary Marshall and Etta (Agee) S.; B.S., Coll. William and Mary, 1929, M.A., 1936; m. Lucile Burke, June 9, 1930; 1 dau., Susan Lynn (Mrs. Melville Garland Wright III). Prin., John Randolph High Sch., Farmville, 1930-44, Cumberland (Va.) High Sch., 1944-61; div. supt. schs., Cumberland County, Va., 1961—; dir. First Nat. Bank, Farmville. Mem. adv. com. State Supt. Schs., 1968-71, pres. supts. Southside and Central Va., 1968-71. Bd. dirs. Southside Hosp. Corp., 1972—, pres., 1965-69. Mem. Alpha Kappa Psi, Omicron Delta Kappa. Rotarian (pres. 1939). Club: Ruritan (pres. 1946) (Cumberland). Home: 902 High St Farmville VA 23901 Office: Supt Schs Cumberland VA 23040

SMITH, EDWARD DEVEREUX, banker; b. Birmingham, Ala., Mar. 9, 1912; s. Edward D. and Florida Whiting (Graves) S.; A.B., Emory U., 1932; LL.B., Harvard, 1935; m. Laura Baxter Maddox, Apr. 7, 1938; children— Laura Maddox (Mrs. William B. Spearman), Florida Graves (Mrs. W.D. Ellis, Jr.). Admitted Ga. bar, 1935, since practiced in Atlanta; partner firm Smith, Klipatrick, Cody, Rogers & McClatchey, Atlanta, 1942-54; pres. First Nat. Bank of Atlanta, 1954—, chmn. bd., 1969—, also chief exec., dir.; dir. So. Bell Tel. & Tel. Co., Eastern Air Lines, Retail Credit Co., Ga. Power Co., The Kroger Co. PTO. Gen. chmn. Greater Atlanta Community Chest, 1951-52; pres. Met. Atlanta Community Services, Inc., 1953-54; bd. govs. Am. Nat. Red Cross, 1962-68. Trustee Conf. Bd., 1959-68, now sr. mem.; trustee Emory U., Logistics Mgmt. Inst. Served as lt. USNR, 1943-45. Mem. Am., Ga., Atlanta bar assns., Assn. Res. City Bankers, C. of C. (past pres.), Internat. Monetary Conf. (past pres.), Chi Phi. Clubs: Lawyers (past pres.), Capital City (past pres.), Piedmont Driving (past pres.), Rotary (past pres.); Peachtree Golf; University (N.Y.); Commerce (dir.); Augusta National Golf. Home: 3540 Woodhaven Rd NW Atlanta GA 30305 Office: First Nat Bank PO Box 4148 Atlanta GA 30302

SMITH, ELIZABETH WIESS (MRS. LLOYD H. SMITH), civic worker; b. Beaumont, Tex., Jan. 29, 1916; d. Harry Carothers and Olga (Keith) Wiess; student Miss Porter's Sch., Miss Helen Stout's Schs.; m. Lloyd Hilton Smith, on May 25, 1940; children—Sandra K. (Mrs. Smith Gerry), Sharon L. (Mrs. David William Keller), Sydney C. Trustee Ballet Found., 1950-70, Southampton Hosp., 1958-70, Houston Mus. Fine Arts, 1951—, Houston Ballet Found., 1957—, Vis. Nurse Assn., 1947-52, Michael E. DeBakey Med. Found., 1970—, art assos. St. Thomas U., 1963—; bd. dirs. Inst. for Antiquities and Christianity of Claremont grad. sch., 1970—. Mem. Am. Fedn. Art, Southampton Hist. Soc. Clubs: Houston Garden, Assembly, Bayou, Ramada Allegro (Houston); River (N.Y.C.); Southampton Garden; Curzon House (London, Eng.). Home: 2 Longfellow Lane Houston TX 77005

SMITH, ETHEL LILLIE KNOTT (MRS. BUDD ELMON SMITH), librarian; b. nr. Oxford, N.C., July 21, 1915; d. Fielding and Lillie (Overton) Knott; student Queens Coll., 1933-34; A.B., Meredith Coll., 1937; B.L.S., U. N.C., 1942; M.A., Appalachian State Tchrs. Coll., 1955; postgrad. U. Chgo.; m. Budd Elmon Smith, Dec. 28, 1943; children—James Fielding, William Budd. Tchr., Guilford (N.C.) Coll. High Sch., 1937-38, Roanoke Rapids (N.C.) High Sch., 1938-42; librarian Gastonia (N.C.) High Sch., 1942-43, U.S. Army, Camp Butler, N.C., 1943-44, Cornell Library Assn. Library, 1944-45; instr. Wake Forest Coll., 1946-51; librarian Oxford City Schs., 1952-53; instr. Wingate (N.C.) Coll., 1953-55, librarian, 1955—. Exec. sec. N.C. Nat. Library Week, 1963. Sec., Wingate P.T.A., 1957-58, Woman's Missionary Union, 1958-60, Union County Planning Bd., 1964—; mem. com. Self-Study Baptist Colls. N.C., 1964-65. Mem. Am. Assn. U. Women (pres. N.C. 1970-72), Am., Southeastern, N.C. (past chmn. jr. coll. sect., chmn. coll. and univ. sect.) library assns., Nat. Council Tchrs. English, Modern Lang. Assn., Delta Kappa Gamma. Democrat. Baptist. Clubs: Woman's Garden. Asso. editor: The Junior College Library Collection. Contbr. articles to profl. jours. Home: Northwood Wingate NC 28174 Office: 301 Elm St Wingate NC 28174

SMITH, EUCLID, educator; b. Caldwell, Tex.; d. George Lewis and Josie (Simpson) S.; B.S., Tex. State Coll. Women, 1923; M.A., Columbia, 1925; Ph.D., Tex. Woman's U., 1953; postgrad. U. Mo., 1944-45, U. Wis., 1948, Tex. A. and M. Coll., 1950, Cornell U. 1951. Head home econs. dept. San Marcos (Tex.) Acad., 1923-24; dir. home econs. Kidd-Key Coll., 1925-27; acting head home econs. Bradley U., Peoria, Ill., 1928; dir. home econs. Phoenix Coll., 1928-44; asso. prof. U. Akron, 1945-48; asso. prof. Stockton Coll. and Coll. of Pacific, Stockton, Cal., 1948-52; research asso. prof. Nelda Childers Stark Nutrition Clinic, Tex. Woman's U., 1953-54; dir. home econs. Pan Am. Coll., Edinburg, Tex., 1954—. Adv. bd. Who's Who Am. Women. Recipient Pan Am. Coll. Research grant, 1959-60, 63-64. Mem. Am., Tex, home econs. assns., Am. (ho. of dels. 1946-48), Tex. (exec. bd. 1963—, chmn. scholarship com. 1963—), Rio Grande Valley (pres. 1962-63) dietetic assns., A.A.A.S., Tex. Nutrition Council, Am. Pub. Health Assn., Tex. Acad. Sci., Nat. Geog. Soc., Am. Assn. U. Women (v.p. chpt. 1955-56). Maternal and Infant Health Adminstrs. Assn., S. Tex. Assn. Mental Retarded (Council home econs.), S. Tex. Rehab. Soc., Am. Mus. Natural History, Tex. State Geneal. Soc., Internat. Platform Assn., Edinburg Bus. and Profl. Women's Club (charter mem.; v.p. 1957-60), Alpha Mu Gamma, Iota Sigma Pi (chpt. treas. 1952-54), Delta Kappa Gamma (chmn. program and community activities 1961-62). Club: Zonta (bd. dirs. 1957-59, Internat. relationships chmn. 1957-58, Amelia Earhart chmn. 1958-59). Co-author: Adventure in Friendship in Europe. Contbr. articles profl. jours. Research in field of nutrition. Address: 503 W Burke St Caldwell TX 77836

SMITH, FRANCIS PALMER, architect; b. Cin., Mar. 27, 1886; s. Henry Howard and Eva Belle (Kendall) S.; B.S. in Architecture, U. Pa., 1907; m. Ella Sorin, June 15, 1910 (died 1930); children—Margaret Ella (Mrs. Henry Rauh Kingdon), Francis Palmer, Jr. (dec.), Robert, Henry Howard. Draughtsman, Cin. and Columbus, 1907-08; travel and study in Europe, 1909; prof. architecture Georgia Sch. of Tech., Atlanta, 1909-22; mem. firm Pringle & Smith, architects; designer 1st Nat. Bank, Wm. Smith, Atlanta, 1922-34; pvt. practice, 1934—; now partner firm Francis P. Smith & Henry H. Oliver Bldg., Doctors Bldg., Rhodes Haverty Bldg., Whitehead Bldg., Cox Carlton Hotel, Atlanta, Lynch Bldg., Jacksonville, Venetian Hotel, Miami, (Pringle & Smith), Druid Hills Presbyterian Ch., annex to Trust Co. of Ga. Bldg., Cathedral of St. Philip (Ayers & Godwin Assos.), Atlanta Comml. Bank & Trust Co., Ocala, Fla., Decatur br. First Nat. Bank, Atlanta, Ga., also numerous churches, residences, comml. works in the South and S.E. Recipient Brooke Silver medal U. of Pa., Walter Cope Meml. Prize. Served from capt. to maj. C.E., AUS, 1942-46; asst. to dist. engr., Atlanta, exec. and engring. officer with Post Engr., Troop Supply officer, Post. Engr., and Custodial officer, Camp Tyson, Tenn. Fellow A.I.A. (past pres. Ga. chpt.), Stained Glass Assn. of Am. (asso. mem.), Sigma Xi, Phi Kappa Phi. Episcopalian. Translator and publisher of Voillet-le-Duc's Mediaeval Stained Glass. Home: 1135 Lullwater Rd Atlanta GA 30307 Office: Whitehead Bldg Atlanta GA 30303

SMITH, FRANK ELLIS, writer, former govt. ofcl.; b. Sidon, Miss., Feb. 21, 1918; s. Frank and Sadie Kathleen (Ellis) S.; student Sunflower Jr. Coll., Moorhead, Miss., 1934-36; A.B., U. Miss., 1941; student Am. U., Washington, 1946; m. Helen Ashley McPhaul, Dec. 15, 1945; children—Frederick Cecil, Kathleen Ashley. Mng. editor, Greenwood Morning Star, 1946-47. Elected Miss. state senator, 1947; mem. 82d to 87th Congresses, 3d Miss. Dist.; dir. TVA, 1962—. Served with AUS, 1942-46; with 243d F.A. Bn., U.S. Third Army, ETO, 1944-45. Decorated Bronze Star. Mem. Beta Theta Pi. Democrat. Methodist. Author: The Yazoo; Congressman from Mississippi, 1964; Look Away From Dixie, 1965; The Politics of Conservation, 1966; (with Audrey Warren) Mississippians All, 1968; Land Between the Lakes, 1971. Editor: Conservation in the United States: A Documentary History, 1971. Home: 204 Suburban Rd Knoxville TN 37119

SMITH, FRANK MAXWELL, fire chief; b. Fryeburg, La., Sept. 15, 1915; s. Alpheus and Julia Etta (Green) S.; student numerous fire dept. courses La. State U. Extension, 1961-70; m. Mildred Virginia Jones, June 14, 1941; children—Frank Kenneth, James Edwin, Sandra Beth. With Bossier (La.) City Fire Dept., 1937—, chief, 1950—. Served with USNR, 1942-45. Mem. Internat. Assn. Fire Chiefs (dir. 1962-67; pres. S.W. div. 1961), La. Firemen's Assn. (pres. 1960). Lion. Home: 1125 Waller St Bossier City LA 71010 Office: 700 Barksdale Blvd Bossier City LA 71010

SMITH, FRANK PRINCE, lawyer, banker; b. Albion, Okla., Jan. 19, 1931; s. Thomas H.P. and Hazel (Looper) S.; B.S., Okla. State U., 1958; LL.B., Okla. U., 1958; postgrad. U. Tex. at Arlington, 1972—; m. Audrey L. McQuigg, June 4, 1959; 1 dau., Janet. Admitted to Okla. bar, 1958; practiced in Ponca City, Okla., 1958-59; trust examiner Fed. Res. Bank of Kansas City (Mo.), Kansas City Life Ins. Co., 1963-65; v.p., trust officer N.M. Bank & Trust Co., Hobbs, 1965-67; v.p., trust officer Arlington (Tex.) Bank & Trust Co., 1967-72. Past mem. adv. bd., treas. Salvation Army, Hobbs, now mem. adv. bd., Arlington, Tex. Served with USAF, 1951-54. Mem. Okla., Am. bar assns., Delta Theta Phi. Republican. Methodist (past steward). Home: 232 Westview Terrace Arlington TX 76013

SMITH, FREDERICK ALLEN, elec. engr.; b. Tavares, Fla., Jan. 1, 1929; s. George Earle and Pearl Emily (Ayers) S.; grad. Capitol Radio Engring. Inst., 1950; student Lake Coll. of Commerce, 1953; m. Alma Charlotte Etheredge, Jan. 24, 1951; children—Deborah Anne, Frederick Allen, Ronald Earle. Staff engr. Radio Sta. WRNO, Orangeburg, S.C., 1950; field engr. Philco Corp., Phila., 1951-54; electronics engr. U.S. Navy, Charleston, S.C., 1954-57, supr. radar engring. br., 1957-61, supr. radar and communications engring. br., 1961-64, head aero. engring. div., 1964-65; owner, dir. Allen Wired Music Co., Charleston, 1954-59; cons. Frederick A. Smith, cons. engr., 1961—; owner Burgla-Matic Alarm Co., 1970—, Ashley Marina Co., 1970—. Expert engr. FCC, 1966—; mem. adv. bd. S.C. Tech. Edn. Center. Trustee James Island Pvt. Sch. Found., Charleston, S.C. Served with USNR, 1946-48. Registered profl. engr. S.C. Mem. I.E.E.E. (sect. treas. 1963-64, pres. 1964-65), Nat. Soc. Profl. Engrs., Constrn. Specification Inst., U.S. Power Squadron. Mason (32 deg.), Elk. Club: Exchange (pres. 1960, v.p. 1959). Home: 863 Robert E Lee Blvd Charleston SC 29412 Office: Ashley House Charleston SC 29401

SMITH, GEORGE ADRIAN, state ofcl.; b. Amory, Miss., Mar. 17, 1934; s. George Albert and Biddie (Allgood) S.; student Clarke Meml. Coll., 1957-59; B.A., U. So. Miss., 1960-62; m. Sarah Lois Turner, Dec. 21, 1955; children—Shelia, Brenda Lee, Stuart W. Asst. cashier Peoples Bank of Union (Miss.), 1956-64; exec. dir. Miss. Regional Housing Authority No. 5, Newton, 1964—. Served with USNR, 1952-56. Mem. Jaycees. Baptist. Mason. Clubs: Lions, Newton Flying (v.p. 1964—). Home: 108 Parker St Newton MS 39345 Office: PO Box 197 Newton MS 39345

SMITH, GEORGE L., II, lawyer, state legislator; b. Stillmore, Ga., Nov. 27, 1912; student U. Ga. Admitted to Ga. bar, 1932; mem. firm Williams, Smith & Shepherd, Swainsboro, Ga.; solicitor Swainsboro City Ct., 1937-44; mem. Ga. Ho. of Reps., 1945—, speaker pro tem, 1947-54, speaker, 1959-62, 67—. Mem. Ga. (past gov.), Emanuel County bar assns., Nat. Conf. State Legislative Leaders. Address: Mitchell Bldg Swainsboro GA 30401 also State Capitol Bldg Atlanta GA 30334

SMITH, GEORGE PATRICK, II, lawyer; b. Wabash, Ind., Sept. 1, 1939; s. George Patrick and Marie Louise (Barrett) S.; B.S. (Wade Meml. scholar), Ind. U., 1961, J.D. with honors, 1964; certificate Academie De Droit International, De La Haye, Palais De La Paix, The Netherlands, summer 1965. Krannert teaching fellow law Ind. U., Bloomington, 1964-65; admitted to Ind. bar, 1965, D.C. bar, 1966, U.S. Supreme Ct. bar, 1968; gen. ltd. practice law, 1965—; spl. counsel Environmental Protection Agy., Washington, 1971—. Instr. law U. Mich., Ann Arbor, 1965-66; legal adviser fgn. claims settlement commn. State Dept., Washington, 1966; asst. prof., asst. dean Law Sch. State U. N.Y. at Buffalo, 1967-69; vis. prof. law George Washington U. Law Center, summer 1968; asso. prof. law U. Ark., Fayetteville, 1969-71; adj. prof. Georgetown Law Center, Washington, 1971—; cons. Ark. Planning Commn., 1970-71. Ombudsman, U. Ark., 1969-70; spl. counsel environmental control legislation Gov. Ark., 1970-71; mem. Ark. Waterway Study Commn., 1970-71; chmn. Commn. on Environmental Control, State Arts and Sci. Com. Ark., 1970-71; life mem. Ind. U. Found., 1962—; mem. NRC-Nat. Acad. Scis.; active Smith Meml. Law Collection, Wabash County Library (Ind.), 1963—. Mem. Am. (chmn. Young Lawyers sect. environmental quality 1971—), Ind. bar assns., Fed. Bar Council, Soc. Legal History, Am. Soc. Internat. Law, Nat. Lawyers Club, Am. Judicature Soc., Environmental Def. Fund, Selden Soc., Nat. Planning Assn., U. Prof.'s for Acad. Order, Ozark Soc., Nat. Cathedral Soc., Ind. Soc. Washington, Sigma Alpha Epsilon, Phi Alpha Delta, Alpha Kappa Psi, Order of Omega. Episcopalian. Club: Capitol Hill. Contbr. articles to profl. jours. Home: 1400 S Joyce St Arlington VA 22202 Office: Office Gen Counsel Environmental Protection Agy 4th and M Sts Washington DC 20460

SMITH, GEORGE ROSE, state supreme ct. justice; b. Little Rock, July 26, 1911; s. Hay Watson and Jessie Alice (Rose) S.; student Washington and Lee U., 1928-31; LL.B., U. Ark., 1933; m. Peg Newton, Dec. 3, 1938; 1 dau., Laurinda Hempstead. Admitted to Ark. bar, 1933, practiced in Little Rock, 1933-49; mem. firm Rose, Dobyns, Meek &House; asso. justice Supreme Ct. Ark., 1949—. Mem. Ark. Supreme Ct. Com. on Jury Instructions. Served from 2d lt. to maj. A.C., AUS, 1942-46. Mem. Ark. Bar Assn., Inst. Jud. Adminstrn., Sigma Alpha Epsilon, Phi Delta Phi. Author: Arkansas Annotations to Restatement of Trusts, 1938; Arkansas Mining and Mineral Law, 1942. Home: 2 Cantrell Rd Little Rock AR 72207 Office: Justice Bldg Little Rock AR 72201

SMITH, GEORGE SEVERN, lawyer; b. Van Wert, O., Jan. 31, 1901; s. Harvey C. and Nella (Severn) S.; LL.B., Nat. U., 1928; m. Thelma Gertrude Horst, Jan. 12, 1935; 1 son, George Severn. Admitted to D.C. bar, 1931; chief license div. Fed. Radio Commn., 1929-32; asso. with Paul M. Segal, 1932-41; partner Segal, Smith & Hennessey, attys., Washington, 1942-57, Smith, Hennessey & McDonald, Washington, 1958-62; legal adviser to commr. FCC, 1962-66, chief braodcast bur., 1966-70; cons. Marmet & Webster, Washington, 1971—. Del. Fed. Communications Bar Assn. to house of dels. Am. Bar Assn., 1958-59. Served with Med. Dept., U.S. Army, 1918-19. Mem. Am. Bar Assn., Fed. Communications Bar Assn. (Washington pres. 1957), Bar Assn. D.C. Republican. Methodist. Home: Chesapeake Ranch Club Box 102R Lusby MD 20657 Office: 1822 Jefferson Pl NW Washington DC 20036

SMITH, GERALD LYNN, educator, researcher; b. Seminole, Okla., Feb. 3, 1934; s. Paul Clifford and Florence Edith (Wallen) S.; B.S. in Elec. Engring., B.S. in Mech. Engring., U. Okla., 1957, M.S. in Elec. Engring., 1959, Ph.D., 1965; m. Shirley Joyce Smith, June 6, 1965. Asso. research engr. Cities Service Research Co., Tulsa, 1957-58; design engr. Douglas Aircraft Co., 1959-60; instr. elec. engring. U. Okla., Norman, 1960-63; dept. head elec. engring. U. Tulsa, 1964—. Served with USNR, 1958-63. Registered profl. engr., Okla., Tex. Mem. Am. Soc. M.E., Am. Inst. Mining, Metall. and Petroleum Engrs., I.E.E.E. (regional vice dir., chmn. Tulsa chpt.), Am. Soc. Engring. Edn., A.A.A.S., Nat., Okla. socs. profl. engrs., Sigma Xi, Tau Beta Pi, Sigma Tau, Pi Tau Sigma, Eta Kappa Nu, Sigma Pi Sigma, Pi Mu Epsilon. Home: 4336 S Allegheny St Tulsa OK 74135

SMITH, HAROLD HENKEL, lawyer; b. South Branch, W.Va., Jan. 28, 1918; s. C. Victor and Anna (Henkel) S.; B.S., W.Va. U., 1939; LL.B., Harvard, 1950; m. Eileen Lucille Jarrell, Oct. 10, 1942; children— Sharon Eileen, Harold Henkel, Charles Gregory, Richard Alan. Admitted to W.Va. bar, 1950, N.C. bar, 1963; asst. county agrl. agt. W.Va. Agrl. Extension Service, 1939; spl. agt. N.Y. Life Ins. Co., 1946-47; asso. atty. Scherer, Bowers & File, Beckley, W.Va., 1950-54; pvt. practice Beckley, 1955-62; partner firm Hartsell, Hartsell & Mills, Concord, N.C., 1963-65; atty. legal dept. Cannon Mills Co., dir. Amazon Cotton Mills Co. Served from 2d lt. to lt. col. U.S. Army, 1939-46. Decorated Silver Star, Bronze Star, Purple Heart, Combat Inf. badge. Mem. Am., N.C., Cabarrus County, (pres. 1972), W.Va. bar assns., Am. Legion, Internat. Platform Assn., Am. Judicature Soc., Mil. Order World Wars (pres. Charlotte, N.C. chpt. 1972), World Peace Through Law Center, Ret. Officers Assn. (pres. Piedmont chpt. 1965). Republican. Elk. Home: 142 Union St S Concord NC 28025 Office: Cabarrus Bank Bldg Concord NC 28025

SMITH, HEDRICK LAURENCE, journalist; b. Kilmacolm, Scotland, July 9, 1933 (parents Am. citizens); s. Sterling L. and Phebe (Hedrick) S.; grad. Choate Sch., 1951; B.A., Williams Coll., 1955; postgrad. (Fulbright scholar) Balliol Coll., Oxford, Eng., 1955-56; m. Ann Bickford, June 29, 1957; children—Laurel Ann, Jennifer Laurence, Sterling Scott. With U.P.I., Memphis, Nashville, Atlanta, 1959-62; with N.Y. Times, 1962—, temporary corr. in Vietman, 1963-64, Middle East corr., Cairo, U.A.R., 1964-66, diplomatic news corr., Washington, 1962-64, 66—. Served with USAF, 1956-59. Nieman fellow Harvard, 1969-70. Mem. Phi Beta Kappa, Alpha Delta Phi. Home: 3409 Patterson St NW Washington DC 20015 Office: 1920 L St NW Washington DC 20036

SMITH, HENRY JEFFERSON, horticulturist; b. Bradenton, Fla., Mar. 28, 1922; s. Oscar and Bessie (Thomason) S.; B.S., M.S.A., U. Fla., 1949; m. Sara Louise Bays, May 16, 1953; children—Jeff, Sally Elizabeth. Instr., asst. greenhouse mgr. Miss. State U., Starkville, 1949, landscape specialist, 1950-66; landscape editor So. Living Mag., Birmingham, Ala., 1966-70; landscape horticulturist N.C. State U., Raleigh, 1970—. Cons. landscape of pvt. homes, pub. bldgs., Ala., Miss., Fla., Tex., N.C., 1950—. Served with AUS, 1953-56. Mem. Am. Soc. for Hort. Sci., Garden Writers Assn. Am., Am. Hort. Soc., Nat. Council Instrs. in Landscape Architecture (asso.), Epsilon Sigma Phi, Sigma Delta Chi. Baptist (deacon). Club: Civitan. Home: 2901 Augusta Ct Raleigh NC 27607

SMITH, HENRY JOSEPH, astronomer; b. Boston, Jan. 10, 1928; s. Robert Paul and Bertha (Fonseca) S.; B.S., Harvard 1950, M.A., 1951, Ph.D., 1955; m. Elske von Panhys, Sept. 10, 1950; children—Geoffrey, Kenneth. Supt. Harvard U. Boyden Sta., S. Africa, 1952-54; astronomer-in-charge Harvard Coll. Obs. Field Sta., Sunspot, N.M., 1955-59; physicist Sacramento Peak Obs., Sunspot, 1959-62; supervisory physicist Central Radio Propagation Labs., Nat. Bur. Standards, Boulder, Colo., 1962-63; chief solar physics, physics and astronomy programs Office Space Sci. and Applications, NASA Hdqrs., Washington, 1963-66, dep. dir. physics and astronomy programs, 1966-68, dep. asso. adminstr. space sci., 1968—. Served with USAF, 1946-47. Mem. Am. Geophys. Union, Am. Astronom. Soc., Internat. Astron. Union, Royal Astron. Soc. Office: 400 Maryland Av SW Washington DC 20546

SMITH, HERBERT JONES, banker; b. Bowling Green, Ky., Oct. 29, 1918; s. Roland W. and Mary J. (Jones) S.; B.S., Bowling Green Bus. U., 1940; m. Norine Sharp, Nov. 14, 1942; children—Herbert Jones, Jennifer (Mrs. Christian Van Arsdel), Thomas J., Nancy, Sarah, Frederick, Elizabeth. Traveling auditor Ill. Central R.R., Chgo., 1940-42; sec.-treas. Burford Tobacco Co., Bowling Green, 1945-61; pres. Dibrell-Burford, Inc., Bowling Green, 1961-66; pres. Am. Nat. Bank & Trust Co., Bowling Green, 1966—; dir. Louisville br. Fed. Reserve Bank St. Louis. Acting regent, trustee Ogden Coll. Found., Bowling Green, 1952—. Served with USNR, 1942-45. Mem. C. of C. (pres. 1970-71). Rotarian. Home: 1839 Nashville Rd Bowling Green KY 42101 Office: PO Box 718 Bowling Green KY 42101

SMITH, HERSCHEL LEROY, JR., physicist; b. Oklahoma City, Apr. 18, 1921; s. Herschel LeRoy and Wilhelmina (Erickson) S.; A.A., Oklahoma City Jr. Coll., 1940; B.S. in Engring. Physics, Okla. U., 1943; postgrad. U. Md., intermittently 1946-52; m. Ina Modena Fowler, Jan. 23, 1943; children—Herschel Larry, Alan Wayne, James David. Instr. lab. physcis U. Okla., 1942-43; physicist armor materials U.S. Naval Research Lab., Washington, 1943-46, physicist fracture mechanics area, 1946—, head fracture study sect., 1958—. Pres., chmn. bd. Potomac Heights Mut. Home Owners Assn., Inc., 1953-54. Served as ensign USNR, 1945; now lt. comdr. Res. Recipient Am. Soc. Testing Materials award, 1960. Mem. Am. Phys. Soc., Am. Inst. Aeros. and Astronautics, Research Soc. Am., Am. Soc. Testing and Materials, Sigma Pi Sigma. Baptist (chmn. deacons 1960-67). Club: Toastmasters (pres. 1964-65). Contbr. articles to tech. publs. Patentee micro-tensile machine. Home: 3804 Hemlock Pl SE Temple Hills Park MD 20031 Office: 4555 Overlook Av SW Washington DC 20390

SMITH, HERSHEL FRANCIS, stock broker; b. Birmingham, Ala., Mar. 31, 1933; s. Hershel Francis and Alta Odessa (Arnold) S.; student Ga. State Coll. Bus. Adminstrn., 1955-56 1 dau., Sarah Frances. Registered rep. Johnson, Lane Space Corp., Atlanta, 1951-62; v.p. Pierce, Wulbern, Murphey Corp., Jacksonville, Fla., 1962-70; v.p. First Equity Corp. Fla., Jacksonville, 1970—. Mem. Jacksonville Financial Analysts Soc. Mason. Clubs: Atlanta Athletic; Ponte Vedra (Fla.); University (Jacksonville). Home: 1560 Lancaster Terrace Jacksonville FL 32204 Office: Gulf Life Tower Jacksonville FL 32207

SMITH, HOWARD KINGSBURY, news commentator; b. Ferriday, La., May 12, 1914; B.A., Tulane U., 1936, LL.D., 1955; L.H.D., Alfred U., 1959, Thiel Coll., 1961, U. Md., 1970; LL.D., Roosevelt U., Centenary Coll., 1971; D.Litt., St. Norbert's Coll.; m. Benedicte Traberg, Mar. 1942; children—Jack, Catherine. Studied Nazism, Berlin, 1936; reviewer fgn. dispatches New Orleans Item-Tribune; Rhodes scholar Merton Coll., Oxford, Eng., 1937, revisited Germany, Russia, Holland and Austria; fgn. corr. in London, United Press, 1939; Berlin corr. CBS, Switzerland, 1941, war corr. 9th Army, 1944, covered Nuremberg trials, 1944, chief European corr., European dir., London, Eng., 1946-57, corr. Washington bur., 1957-61, chief corr., gen. mgr., 1961-62; news analyst ABC, Washington, 1962—. Recipient Overseas Press award for best radio reporting from abroad, 1951-54; DuPont award, 1955, 63; Sigma Delta Chi award for radio journalism, 1957, George Polk Meml. award documentary The Population Explosion, 1960, co-recipient George Peabody award, 1960; Emmy award TV Acad. Arts and Scis., 1960; Sylvania award, 1959; Radio-TV Daily award as commentator of yr., 1960; Am. Jewish Congress award, 1962; Overseas Press award, best radio interpretation fgn. affairs, 1961; Radio-TV News Dirs. Assn. Paul White Meml. award, 1962. Author: Last Train from Berlin, 1942; The State of Europe, 1949; Washington, D.C., 1967. Office: 6450 Brooks Lane Washington DC 20016

SMITH, HOWARD MCQUEEN, librarian; b. Charlotte, N.C., July 25, 1919; s. Daniel Holt and Pearl Elizabeth (Truitt) S.; B.A., U. Va., 1941; A.B. in L.S., U. Mich., 1946, M. Pub. Adminstrn., 1947; m. Elaine Betty Wiefel, June 27, 1949; children—Carol Leslie, Steven Holt. Reference asst. Enoch Pratt Free Library, Balt., 1947-49; coordinator library activities Richmond (Va.) Area Univ. Center, 1949-50; exec. asst. to dir. Enoch Pratt Free Library, 1950-53, head films dept., 1953-55; personnel officer Free Library Phila., 1955-59; city librarian Richmond Pub. Library, 1959—. Bd. dirs. Richmond Symphony. Served to lt. USNR, 1942-46. Mem. A.L.A. Rotarian. Home: 4120 Hillcrest Rd Richmond VA 23225 Office: Richmond Pub Library Richmond VA 23219

SMITH, IVAN HERBERT, lawyer; b. Downs, Kan., Jan. 9, 1921; s. Zeb Herbert and Carrie Lorena (Williams) S.; B.A., Hastings Coll., 1947; postgrad. U. Mich. Law Sch., 1947-48; J.D., U. Ark., 1950; m. Wanda Dale Leatherman, June 4, 1943 (div. June 1968); children—Diana Dale, Debra Dawn; m. 2d, Middie True (Poteete) Moore, Jan. 30, 1970. Admitted to Ark. bar, 1950; practiced in Little Rock, 1950, 51; departmental atty. Ark. Dept. Pub. Welfare, Little Rock, 1952-63, state information officer under reciprocal support act, 1953—, program coordinator, dir. legal services, 1962—. Vice pres. Ark. Conf. on Social Welfare, 1956, treas., 1958-64; area cons. Ark. Plan for Mental Health, 1963—; emergency welfare coordinator State of Ark., 1962—; chmn. exec. com. Nat. Reciprocal Support Conf., 1957, mem. exec. com., 1957—; dist. committeeman Boy Scouts Am., 1957-59; Ark. dep. compact adminstr. Interstate Compact on Juveniles. Served to lt. col. AUS, 1942-46; now col. Res. Decorated Bronze Star. Mem. Ark., Pulaski County bar assns., Am. Jurisprudence Assn., Am. Legion, Am. Pub. Welfare Assn., Res. Officers Assn. Democrat. Methodist (ofcl. bd.). Mason (Shriner); mem. Order Eastern Star. Author: Manual of Procedure on Reciprocal Support Act, 1961; Manual on Statute Draft, 1950. Home: 500 S Summit Little Rock AR 72202 Office: Employment Security-Welfare Bldg Little Rock AR 72201

SMITH, IVAN HURON, architect; b. Danville, Ind., Jan. 25, 1907; s. Calvin Wesley and Irma (Huron) S.; studnet Ga. Tech., 1926; B.S. in Arch., U. Fla., 1929; m. Susan Butler, Aug. 18, 1972; 1 dau., Norma (Mrs. Benton). Prin., Ivan H. Smith, Jacksonville, Fla., 1936-41; partner Reynolds, Smith & Hills, Jacksonville, Tampa, Orlando, Merritt Island and Hollywood, Fla., 1941—, chmn. bd., exec. v.p., 1971—; partner Lewis & Eaton, Partnership, Jackson, Miss., 1969; dir. So. Indsl. Bank, Jacksonville, Fla. Dealers & Growers Bank, Jacksonville. Chmn., Jacksonville Constrn. Trades Qualification Bd., 1971. Mem. Duval County Govt. Study Commn., 1966-67; sec. Jacksonville Bldg. Code Adv. Bd., 1951-68. Bd. dirs. Duval County-Jacksonville Safety Countil, Jacksonville U. Council. Served with USNR, 1943-45: CBI. Fellow A.I.A. (pres. Fla. N. chpt. 1952, Jacksonville chpt. 1956); mem. Fla. Assn. Architects (chmn. profl. practice commn. 1965-67, Pullera award for Outstanding Service to Profession 1965), Jacksonville C. of C. (bd. govs. 1957-59), Newcomen Soc., Beta Theta Pi, Phi Kappa Phi, Sigma Tau. Rotarian. Clubs: Gargoyle (U. Fla.); River, Ponte Vedra, St. Johns Dinner, San Jose Country (Jacksonville). Architect Fla. Field Stadium U. Fla., 1953; Duval County Ct. House, 1958; Jacksonville City Hall, Student Center Jacksonville U., 1960. Home: 10460 Sylvan Lane W Jacksonville FL 32217 Office: 4019 Boulevard Center Dr Jacksonville FL 32201

SMITH, JACK CARROLL, C. of C. exec.; b. Meridian, Miss., Mar. 22, 1923; s. Elmo and Dora (Connor) S.; B.B.A., U. Ga., 1948; m. Melissa Moultrie Smith, July 30, 1948; children—Carroll, Jack Carroll, Claire. Staff supr. personnel Newport News Shipbuilding & Dry Dock Co., 1948-60; exec. v.p. Roanoke Valley C. of C., Roanoke, Va., 1960—. Chmn. Indsl. Devel. Authority, City of Roanoke; sec. Greater Roanoke Valley Devel. Found.; sec.-treas. Miss Virginia Pageant, Inc., 1964—, also exec. dir. Mem. World Trade Conf. Com., Gov.'s Travel Adv. Com., Bicentennial Commn.; mem. indsl. devel. com., chmn. travel devel. com. Va. State Chamber. Bd. dirs. Nat. Assn. Miss America State Pageants, Va. Thanksgiving Festival, Roanoke Symphony Soc., served with AUS, 1943-45. Club: Roanoke Valley Booster (pres.). Home: 201 Parkcrest Rd SW Roanoke VA 24014 Office: PO Box 20 Roanoke VA 24001

SMITH, JACK CUTTS, mfg. co. exec.; b. Moultrie, Ga., May 30, 1923; s. Charles Owen and Esther (Cutts) S.; student McCallie Sch., 1940-41; B.B.A., Emory U., 1944; m. Rhett Jenkins, July 2, 1948; children—Jack Cutts, Owen Arthur, Erin Rhett, Jebb McArthur, Roger Jenkins. Partner, C.O. Smith Guano Co., Moultrie, 1944-63, pres., 1963-65; partner C.O. Smith Warehouse Co., 1944-63; pres. Smith Chem. Corp., 1965-67, Smithfield Land Co., 1962—, Ga.-Atlantic Co., 1967—, C.O. Smith Guano, 1967—. Bd. dirs. Colquitt County Cancer Soc., 1956-61; v.p., dir. Moultrie YMCA, 1949-61, pres., 1968-69, now bd. dirs.; bd. dirs. Colquitt Music Assn., pres. United Givers Colquitt County, 1957; dir. 5th dist. Ga. Nat. Polio Found., 1952-53. Trustee Tift Coll., 1957—, chmn. bd. trustees, 1961-63; trustee Ga. Conservancy. Mem. Ind. Plant Food Mfrs. Assn. Ga. (pres. 1962-64, dir.), Ga. Cotton Warehouse Compress Assn. (dir. 1958-60), Ga. Ednl. Plant Food Soc. (dir. 1961-63), Ga. Hist. Soc., Ga. Cotton Ginners Assn. (dir. 1965), Moultrie Jr. C. of C. (dir; 1948-50), C. of C. (dir. 1950-60), Young Pres.' Orgn., McCallie Sch. Alumni Assn. (dir. 1965-67), Soc. Colonial Wars in Ga., Kappa Alpha, Alpha Kappa Psi. Baptist (deacon). Home: 1310 Thomasville Rd Moultrie GA 31768 Office: 201 13th Av SW ..Ioultrie GA 31768

SMITH, JACK DARLING, machinery co. exec.; b. Madison, Fla., Jan. 25, 1920; s. Amos Charles and Ida Mae (Gissendaner) S.; student South Ga. Coll., 1948-50; A.B., Valdosta State Coll., 1952, B.S., 1952; B.D., Emory U., 1955, M.Div., 1972; LL.B., Blackstone Sch. Law, 1970, J.D., 1971; m. Jane Frances Kappel, Dec. 13, 1970; children by previous marriage—Lyndell Darling, Joan Renice (Mrs. Kenneth Cole), Walton Earle. Vice pres., gen. mgr. Nat. Pub. Relations, Inc., Thomasville, Ga., 1946-48; ordained to ministry Meth. Ch., 1952; pastor, Ludowici, Ga., 1948-52, Stockbridge, Ga., 1952-55, Wadley (Ga.) 1st Ch., 1955-60, Sylvania, Ga., 1960-64, Dublin, Ga., 1964-68; v.p. pub. relations Fulghum Industries, Inc., Wadley, 1968—, also dir. County chmn. Gov. Carter's campaign, 1970. Trustee Ga. Magnolia Manor, Americus, 1965—; trustee Epworth-by-the-Sea. Served with USAAF, 1940-45. Mem. Ga. gov.'s staff, 1966-68, 68-70; named Adm. Ga. Navy, 1971—. Democrat. Mason, Lion, Rotarian. Pub., Dixie Logger, Lumberman Mag., 1969—. Home: Box 703 Wadley GA 30477 Office: Box 487 Wadley GA 30477

SMITH, JAMES BURT, JR., hosp. found. adminstr.; b. Galveston, Tex., July 13, 1937; s. James Burt and Mamie (Teutsch) S.; student Tarleton State Coll., 1954-56; B.B.A., N. Tex. State Coll., 1958; m. Nancy Fay Strickland, June 21, 1958; 1 dau., Jenny Beatrice. Plant mgr. Tex. Milling Co., Clifton, 1961-66; hosp. adminstr. Goodall-Witcher Hosp. Found., Clifton, 1966—. Mem. Clifton City Council, 1963—; v.p. Heart of Tex. Council Govts., Waco, 19—. C.P.A., Tex. Mem. Tex. Soc. C.P.A.'s, Tex. Hosp. Assn. Mason, Lion. Home: 415 Northern Av R Clifton TX 76634 Office: 503 W 5th St Clifton TX 76634

SMITH, JAMES EDWARD, ednl. adminstr.; b. Norman, Ark., Jan. 23, 1909; s. Alexandera Chapman and Daisy (Phillips) S.; student Magnolia A. and M. (now So. State Coll.), 1928-32; B.S. in Edn., Ark. State Tchrs. Coll. (now State Coll. Ark.), 1934; M.A., George Peabody Coll. Tchrs., 1942; diploma advanced standing U. Ark., 1965; m. Lois Pet Joplin, 1937; 1 dau., Claudette (Mrs. Tom R. Ford). Tchr. math., sci., coach Polk County (Ark.) Schs., 1932-37; supt. schs. Okolona, Ark., 1937-45, Prescott, Ark., 1945—. Mem. Ark. Edn. Assn., N.E.A., Ark Activities Assn. (exec. com.), Prescott, Nevada County chambers commerce. Methodist. Rotarian., Mason. Home: 228 Rosston Rd Prescott AR 71857 Office: 762 Martin St Prescott AR 71857

SMITH, JAMES HADLEY, data control co. exec.; b. Mount Airy, N.C., Aug. 17, 1928; s. James Raymond and Annie Jamie (Hadley) S.; grad. Woodberry Forest Sch., 1946; A.B., Duke, 1950; m. Emily Elizabeth Blum, Feb. 24, 1951; children—Emily Elizabeth, Helen Blum. Office mgr. Nat. Furniture Co., Mount Airy, 1952-60; pres. Skyline Motors, Inc., Mount Airy, 1960—; dir. Electronics Data Controls Corp., Winston-Salem, N.C., 1963-70, chmn. bd., 1970—. Chmn., Mount Airy United Fund, 1958-59. Served with AUS, 1950-52. Methodist. Mason, Elk. Club: Mount Airy Country. Home: 216 Howard St Mount Airy NC 27030 Office: PO Box 430 Mount Airy NC 27030

SMITH, JAMES LEONARD, pub. co. exec.; b. Jacksonville, Fla., Sept. 26, 1916; s. Charles Eugene and Mary Ella (Doyle) S.; student LaSalle Inst., Chgo., 1946-50; m. Johanna Aje Wesseling, June 16, 1945; children—James Leonard, Michael Lee, Janna Lynne. With Fla. Pub. Co., Jacksonville, 1938—, gen. accountant, 1946-48, sec.-treas., 1948—, also dir.; dir. St. Augustine Record, Inc. (Fla.). Bd. dirs. Fla. Pub. Charities; sec., bd. dirs. Duval County Taxpayers Assn., 1964-68. Served with F.A., AUS, 1942-44. Mem. Newspaper Controllers and Finance Officers Assn., Financial Execs. Inst. Democrat. Roman Catholic. Clubs: San Jose Country, University. Home: 3848 Via de la Reina Jacksonville FL 32217 Office: 1 Riverside Av Jacksonville FL 32201

SMITH, JAMES LONNIE, lawyer; b. Hattiesburg, Miss., Sept. 26, 1936; s. Lonnie and Velma (Waldrop) S.; B.A., U. Miss., 1958, LL.B., 1960. Admitted to Miss. bar, 1960; asso. Bobby J. Garraway, Lumberton, Muss., 1960-61; gen practice Poplarville, Miss., 1962; with Magnolia Title Co., Picayune, Miss., 1963-65; partner firm Williams & Smith, Picayune, Miss., 1965—. Mem. Miss. Ho. of Reps., 1968—. Bd. dirs. Poplarville (Miss.) Pub. Library. Mem. C. of C., Phi Delta Phi. Baptist. Mason. Rotarian. Home: 205 N Hickory St Popularville MS 39470 Office: 109 N Main St Picayune MS 39466

SMITH, JAMES REGINALD, physician, savs. and loan exec.; b. Aurora, Ill., Apr. 25, 1918; s. Ferdinand Nathaniel and Carrie Bell (Patterson) S.; B.S., Northwestern U., 1941; M.D., Meharry Med. Coll., 1944; postgrad. U. Pa., 1958; m. Bettye Sue Holmes, Dec. 27, 1945; children—Jinx C., Kurt, James Reginald. Pvt. practice medicine, Lynchburg, Va., 1946, Washington, N.C., 1947-48, Orlando, Fla., 1948—; founder, dir., pres. chmn. bd. Washington Shores Fed. Savs. & Loan Assn., 1964—. Pres., Washington Shores Assn. for Recreation, Inc., Washington Shores Citizens Com. Served with AUS, 1941-44. Mem. Kappa Alpha Psi. Mason. Address: 640 W South St Orlando FL 32805

SMITH, JAMES WILLIAM, clothing co. exec.; b. London, Laurel, Ky., Sept. 15, 1934; s. Huey Albert and Della Mae (Turner) S.; student Sue Bennett Coll., 1954-55; m. Shirley Ruth Patton, June 22, 1955; children—James Wandin, LaDonna Lynn. Asst. mgr. Daniels Dept. Store, London, 1955-59; mgr.-buyer Hackney Bros. & Co., London, 1959-67; owner, mgr. His & Hers Shoppe, London, 1967—, Winchester, Ky., Danville, Ky., 1970—; owner-founder His & Hers Shoppe of Londontown, Inc.; pres. James W. Smith Cos., Inc. Pres., Full Gospel Businessmens Assn., Gideon Internat. Local Campzone leader, London-Laurel Devel. Assn. Trustee Barbourville Orphanage. Named Hon. Citizen Hazard, Ky., 1966. Mem. Full Gospel Bus. Men's Fellowship Internat. (pres., dir.). Rotarian. Home: Route 6 Box 194B London KY 40741 Office: 206 S Main St Box 521 London KY 40741

SMITH, JEAN CHANDLER, librarian; b. Phila., Apr. 13, 1918; d. Chandler White and Philena P. (Cheetham) Smith; A.B., Bryn Mawr Coll., 1939; M.S., Yale, 1953. Circulation librarian, reference librarian D.C. Pub. Library, Washington, 1939-43; translator U.S. Office Censorship, Panama Canal Zone, 1943-44; librarian Kaneohe (T.H.) Naval Air Sta., 1944-46; reference asst., asst. reference librarian, research asst. Yale U. Library, New Haven, 1947-58; reference librarian biol. scis., acting chief acquisitions sect. NIH, Library, Bethesda, 1959-63; chief reference services dept. library Dept. Interior, Washington, 1963-65; asst. dir. libraries Smithsonian Instn., Washington, 1965-68, spl. asst. to dir. libraries for biol. sci. programs, 1968-72, asst. dir. libraries for bur. services, 1972—. Guest investigator Osborn Meml. Lab., Yale, 1953-57. Mem. Am. Soc. Information Sci., Spl. Libraries Assn. (treas. D.C. chpt. 1966-69, 2d v.p. D.C. chpt. 1969—, nat. sec., treas. natural resources div. 1969—), Conn. Acad. Arts and Scis., Am. Soc. Limnology and Oceanography, Bibliog. Soc. Am. Home: 3601 Connecticut Av NW Washington DC 20008 Office: Smithsonian Instn Washington DC 20560

SMITH, JERRY MILLARD, financial exec.; b. Oklahoma City, Aug. 20, 1931; s. M. W. and Lucille (Tipton) S.; B.S., Kan. U., 1954, M.Pub. Adminstrn., 1960; m. Erma Lee Lutz, Jan. 26, 1951; children—Stephanie, Sara. Asst. city mgr., city planner, Lawrence, Kan., 1958-60; city mgr., Parsons, Kan., 1960-62, Pittsburg, Kan., 1963-68, Norman, Okla., 1968-72; exec. v.p. Western Home Service Corp., Norman, 1972—. Instr. Sch. Engring. U. Kan., 1955-58. Served with USMCR, 1953-54. Mem. Internat. City Mgrs. Assn., Scarab, Pi Sigma Alpha. Rotarian. Office: 105 E Comanche St Norman OK 73069 Home: 441 Thorton St Norman OK 73069

SMITH, JESSIE CARNEY, librarian; b. Greensboro, N.C., Sept. 24, 1930; d. James Ampler and Vesona Bigelow Carney; B.S., N.C. A. and T. State U., 1950; student Cornell U., fall 1951; M.A., Mich State U., 1956; A.M., George Peabody Coll. Tchrs., 1957; Ph.D., U. Ill., 1964; m. Frederick Douglas Smith, Dec. 22, 1950; 1 son, Frederick Douglas. Head cataloger, instr. library sci. Tenn. A. and I. State U., 1957-60; teaching asst. U. Ill., 1961-63; coordinator library service, asst. prof. Tenn. A. and L. State U., 1963-65; univ. librarian, prof. Fisk U., 1965—; asso. prof., cons. Sch. Library Media Ala. A. and M. U., part-time 1971—; lectr. Peabody Library Sch. George Peabody Coll. for Tchrs., 1969—; cons. So. Assn. Colls. and Schs., 1968—. Bd. dirs. Bethlehem Center, Nashville, 1965-68. Mem. Am. (Black caucus), Southeastern, Tenn., Med. library assns., Beta Phi Mu, Pi Gamma Mu, Alpha Kappa Alpha. Democrat. Methodist. Home: 1813 25th Av N Nashville TN 37208

SMITH, JOEL PERRY, physician; b. Richland, Ga., Aug. 15, 1912; s. Joel Olin and Mary (Perry) S.; O.D., So. Coll. Optometry, 1937; O.D., Emory U., 1942; B.S., LaGrange Coll., 1944; M.D., U. Ga. 1947; m. June Goforth, June 5, 1933; children—Joel Perry II, Michael Gordon, Ellen Janet, Lynda Jean. Owner, LaGrange Optical & Jewelry Co. (Ga.), 1934-44; intern Norfolk (Va.) Gen. Hosp., 1947-48; resident surgery Crawford W. Long Hosp., Atlanta, 1948-49; pvt. practice medicine specializing in ophthalmology and otolaryngology Atlanta, 1949—; staff mem. Ga. Bapt., Grady, Crawford W. Long, Henrietta Egleston hosps., Atlanta; clin. instr. otolaryngology Emory U. Med. Sch., 1956—; founder, med. dir. Drs. Meml. Hosp., Atlanta, 1969—. Dir. Electronic Equipment Co. Atlanta. Sec., dir. Ga. Found. Otolarnygology; mem. Deafness Research Found., N.Y.C. Served as capt. AUS, 1953-55. Fellow Soc. Mil. Ophthalmology; mem. A.M.A., So., Ga. med. assns., Alpha Kappa Kappa. Democrat. Methodist. Mason (32 deg., Shriner), Lion. Club: Atlanta Athletic. Contbr. article to profl. jours. Home: 1618 Lady Marion Lane NE Atlanta GA 30309 Office: 573 W Peachtree St NW Atlanta GA 30308

SMITH, JOHN DAVID, III, constrn. exec.; b. Winston-Salem, N.C., Apr. 16, 1938; s. John and Opal Roland (Lawson) S.; grad. Hargrave Mil. Acad., 1956; B.S., N.C. State Coll., 1960; m. Patricia Sears, Oct. 22, 1961; children—Patricia Lynn, April Leigh. With John Smith & Sons, Inc., Eden, N.C., 1961—, v.p., 1963-69, sec.-treas., 1969—; sec. MacSmith Corp., Roselawn Meml. Gardens, Inc.; sec.-treas. Daljon Corp. Pres., Eden Boys Club Am., 1969; dir. Eden Rescue Squad, 1969; mem. Rockingham County Airport Authority, 1968—. Served as lt. AUS, 1960-61. Registered profl. engr., N.C. Mem. Eden C. of C., Eden Mchts. Assn. (dir.). Mason. Home: Route 1 Box 5A Eden NC 27288 Office: PO Box 589 Eden NC 27288

SMITH, JOHN EDMOND, civil engr.; b. Plainview, Ark., Dec. 6, 1928; s. Clayton Richard and Fannie (Tippy) S.; B.S., U. Ark., 1950; m. Jo Ann Truax, Oct. 17, 1954; children—Robert Edmond, Teresa Lynn. Jr. engr. Lion Oil Co., El Dorado, Ark., 1952-53; engr. Mo. Pacific R.R. Co., St. Louis, Little Rock, 1953-57, Garver & Garver Cons. Engrs., Little Rock, 1967-68; civil engr. USAF, Little Rock AFB, 1958-62, Barksdale AFB, La., 1962-70, Carswell AFB, Tex., 1970—. Active Boy Scouts Am. Served to 1st lt. AUS, 1950-52. Registered profl. engr., Ark., La. Methodist (ofcl. bd. 1963—, chmn. finance commn. 1965-67, chmn. ofcl. bd., trustee 1968, 71, layleader 1969). Home: 4917 Harrell St Fort Worth TX 76118 Office: De Carswell AFB TX 76127

SMITH, JOHN GETTYS, devel. co. exec.; b. York, S.C., Nov. 24, 1932; s. Clyde B. and Ora (Gettys) S.; A.B., U. S.C., 1956; m. Nelle Elliott McCants, June 25, 1955; children—John Gettys, Spencer McCants, Ora Elliott. Tchr., York High Sch., 1956-57; with York County Health Dept., 1957-59; York bur. chief Rock Hill (S.C.) Evening Herald, 1959-61; salesman Smith Furniture, York, 1961-63; dir. pub. relations Sea Pines Plantation Co., 1963-64, v.p. pub. relations, community devel. Sea Pines Co., Hilton Head Island, S.C., 1964—, also dir.; v.p. Sea Pines Investment Co., 1969—; pres. Harbour Ventrues, Inc., Caliboque Properties Inc. Coordinator, Internat. Inst. Advancement Creative Arts, 1967-70; founder York Mus. Assn. 1956, York County Meml. Mus., 1958; dir. ann. tour York homes; mem. York County Hist. Commn., 1960-63; chmn. Western York County Crippled Children's Soc., 1959-63; adv. mem. S.C. Confederate Centennial Commn., 1961-65; exec. com. Savannah Symphony Sec., 1969—; mem. Beaufort County Bd. Edn., 1967-69; pres. Carolina Low Country Hist. Found.; v.p. Sea Pines Acad., Sea Pines Ednl. Found.; chmn. Gov.'s Conf. on Travel and Tourism, 1971-72, CBS Tournament Tennis Champions, 1971, CBS Tennis Classic, 1971, P.G.A. Sea Pines Heritage Golf Classic, 1969—. Served with AUS, 1954-56. Mem. Historic Beaufort Found. (fund raising com. 1971—), York County (charter) hist. socs., Artists' Guild York, Chester, Lancaster Counties S.C. (exec. com.), S.C. (adv. com. for tourist promotion 1959-61), Hilton Head Island (v.p. 1964-66, pres. 1967), Beaufort County (tourist promotion com. 1966) chambers commerce, S.C. Travel Council, Hugenot Soc., Hilton Head Island Homebuilders' Assn. (sec.-treas. 1965-66), Sigma Nu, Kappa Pi. Episcopalian (vestryman). Clubs: Chatham, Oglethorpe (Savannah, Ga.); Plantation (Hilton Head Island); Pinacle (Augusta). Author: A Family of York, 1967. Contbr. articles to mags., newspapers. Home: Sea Pines Plantation 48 Beach Lagoon Hilton Head Island SC 29928 Office: Sea Pines Co Hilton Head Island SC 29928

SMITH, JOHN JOSEPH, lawyer; b. Pitts., Nov. 14, 1911; s. John Joseph and Alta Ethel (McGrady) S.; A.B., Birmingham So. Coll., 1931; A.M., U. Va., 1932; LL.B., U. Ala., 1937; m. Ruth Lee Snavely, July 11, 1942; children—John Joseph, Robert William. Instr., U. Ala., 1934-37; admitted to Ala. bar, 1937, bar Supreme Ct. U.S.; asso. Murphy, Hanna & Woodall, 1937; asst. prof. U. Va., 1937-39; atty. Office Solicitor Labor, U.S. Dept. Labor, 1939-42; enforcement atty. rent div. OPA, 1942-43; legal counsel aircraft div. Bechtel-McCone Corp., Birmingham, 1943-46; pvt. practice law, Birmingham, 1946—. Mem. gov.'s staff, 1963-71. Active Community Chest, YMCA, Better Bus. Bur.; committeeman Boy Scouts Am.; founder, commr. Homewood Joy Open Baseball League, 1958-72, chmn. bd., 1972—; chmn. Homewood Citizens Action Com. Against Annexation. Recipient Nat. Pop Warner award for service to youth, 1961. Mem. Am., Ala., Birmingham bar assns., Farrah Order Jurisprudence (founder, nat. pres. 1969-71), Am. Econ. Assn., U. Va., U. Ala. alumni assns., Homewood C. of C., Pi Gamma Mu, Tau Kappa Alpha, Delta Sigma Phi. Methodist (founder, dist. dir. young adult fellowship classes). Mason (Shriner). Club: The Club. Author: Selected Principles of the Law of Contracts, Sales and Negotiable Instruments, 1938. Home: 1506 Primrose Pl Birmingham AL 35209 Office: First Nat Bldg Birmingham AL 35203

SMITH, JOHN LEWIS, JR., U.S. dist. judge; b. Washington, Sept. 20, 1912; s. John Lewis and Claribel (Cassin) S.; grad. Lawrenceville Sch., 1931; A.B. cum laude, Princeton, 1935; LL.B., Georgetown U., 1938, LL.M., 1939; m. Madeline Cotter, Oct. 3, 1940 (dec. 1967); children—John Lewis III, Madeline (Mrs. Lawrence G. Lynn), Joseph Cotter, Janet Ambler, Barbara Cassin. Admitted to D.C. bar, 1938, U.S. Supreme Ct. bar; asst. U.S. atty. D.C., 1940-46; pvt. practice, Washington, 1946-56; mem. D.C. Pub. Utilities Commn., 1956-57; asso. judge D.C. Ct. Gen. Sessions, 1957-59, chief judge, 1959-66; U.S. dist. judge D.C. Dist., 1966—. Chmn. profl. group Am Cancer Soc. campaign, 1949-50; pres. Kalorama Citizens Assn., 1953-54; mem. Nat. Capital U.S.O., 1966—. Chmn., Republican Vets. Com. for D.C., 1952, Vets. Com. for Eisenhower-Nixon Inaugural, 1953, 57; pres. Rep. Club D.C., 1955-56. Trustee Boys Club Washington; bd. dirs. D.C. chpt. A.R.C., Washington Heart Assn., 1967—. Served to col. AUS, World War II. Recipient 1st scholarship prizes Georgetown U. Law Sch., 1936, 37, Princeton Class award, 1959. Georgetown U. Alumni Achievement award. 1960. Mem. Am., D.C. bar assns., Barristers, Am. Judicature Soc. Roman Catholic. Clubs: National Lawyers (founder), Princeton, Vinson, Lawyers (Washington); Chevy Chase (Md.). Home: 2424 Tracy Pl NW Washington DC 20008 Office: US Dist Ct Washington DC 20001

SMITH, JOHN MALCOLM (MAC), lawyer; b. Marion, Ark., July 20, 1911; s. Dolph and Annabele (Nance) S.; student U. Ark., 1929-32, LL.B., 1934; m. Gladys Wright, Apr. 18, 1942. Admitted to Ark. bar, 1934; pvt. practice, Marion, 1934-41, West Memphis, Ark., 1942; partner Rieves & Smith, Marion, 1946-49, West Memphis, 1949-62, pvt. practice, 1963—. Spl. justice Supreme Ct. Ark., 1955; dir. 1st Nat. Bank; mem. exec. com., dir., sr. v.p., gen. counsel Cooper Communities, Inc. (formerly Cherokee Village Devel. Co., Inc.), Belle Vista, Ark.; spl. legal counsel agr. com. U.S. Ho. of Reps., 1961; chief exec. officer Mchts. & Planters Bank, 1950-52, dir., 1942-52; mem. Ark. Ho. of Reps., 1939-42. Bd. dirs. West Memphis Boys Club, Meth. Found. Ark. Served from capt. to lt. col. AUS, 1942-46. Mem. Am., Ark. bar assns., Law-Sci. Acad. Am., Am. Judicature Soc., Am. Legion, V.F.W., Judge Advs. Assn., Blue Key, Sigma Alpha Epsilon. Methodist (trustee). Clubs: Meadowbrook Country (West Memphis); Summit (Memphis); National Lawyers (Washington). Home: 415 Cooper St West Memphis AR 72301 Office: PO Box 830 West Memphis AR 72301

SMITH, JOHN MARLIN, ednl. adminstr.; b. Gainesville, Ga., Jan. 23, 1939; s. Alvin and Willa (Smith) S.; B.S., North Ga. Coll., 1963; Ednl. Adminstrn., U. Ga., 1967, Specialist Ednl. Adminstr. Degree, 1967; m. Evelyn Hurley, Mar. 16, 1958; children—Johnie Belinda, Rickey Marlin. Tchr. pub. schs. Gainesville, Ga., 1958-63; prin. pub. schs. Dahlonega, Ga., 1963-69, supt., 1969—. Chmn. steering com. 9th Dist. Ednl. Services Center, Cleveland, Ga., 1970—. Mem. Lumpkin County Edn. Assn. (pres. 1967-68), 9th Congl. Dist. Supt.'s Orgn. (pres.), N.E.A., Ga. Assn. Educators, Ga. Assn. Sch. Supts., Dahlonega-Lumpkin County C. of C. (past dir.), Kappa Delta Pi. Democrat. Baptist. Club: Lins (Dahlonega). Home: Rte 2 Dahlonega GA 30533 Office: PO Box 277 Dahlonega GA 30533

SMITH, JOHN MICHAEL, lawyer, state ofcl.; b. Ft. Bragg, N.C., May 27, 1936; s. Michael Gibson and Marion (Deason) S.; student The Citadel, 1954-56; LL.B., U. S.C., 1963; m. Sarah Elizabeth Brant, Feb. 27, 1967. Admitted to S.C. bar, 1963; asso. firm Brown, Jefferies & Mazursky, Barnwell, S.C., 1963-71; pvt. practice law, Barnwell, 1971—. Exec. dir. S.C. Regional Housing Authority, 1966—. Mem. Am., S.C. bar assns. Democrat. Episcopalian. Lion. Club: Ellenton Agriculture. Home: 2023 Main St Barnwell SC 29812 Office: PO Box 805 Barnwell SC 29812

SMITH, JOHN OWEN, bishop; b. Johnston, S.C., Sept. 21, 1902; s. Walter Hill and Annie (Long) S.; A.B., Wofford Coll., 1922, D.D. (hon.), 1947; B.D., Yale, 1925; m. Mildred Brown, Dec. 27, 1924; children—Mildred Adela (Mrs. John G. Lepingwell), Betty Jean (Mrs. William G. Katzenmeyer). Ordained to ministry Methodist Ch., 1925; pastor in S.C., 1925-49, Central Meth. Ch., Spartanburg, S.C., 1949-54; supt. Spartanburg Dist., 1954-60; consecrated bishop, 1960; bishop of Ga., Atlanta, 1960—. Del. gen. and jurisdictional confs. Meth. Ch., 1948—; accredited visitor World Council Ch., Amsterdam, 1948, voting del., Evanston, Ill., 1954; mem. World Meth. Council, 1954—; mem. gen. bd. edn. Meth. Ch., 1952—; sec. Southeastern Jurisdictional Council, 1956-60. Mem. Phi Beta Kappa, Theta Phi, Delta Sigma Phi, Book and Bond (Yale). Home: 3724 Wieuca Rd NW Atlanta GA 30342 Office: 63 Auburn Av NE Atlanta GA 30303

SMITH, JOHN RANDALL, interior designer; b. Jacksonville, Fla., Oct. 27, 1941; s. John Albert and Fanney Elizabeth (West) S.; student Fla. State U., 1960-62, Edison Jr. Coll., evenings 1967; B.F.A., Ringling Sch. Art, 1967; m. Jane Leonard, Mar. 29, 1964; children—Randall Bryan, John Clayton. Designer, Holland Salley Interior Designs, Inc., Naples, Fla., 1966-72; interior designer Killearn Properties Inc., Tallahassee, 1972—. Mem. publs. bd. Collier Democrat, Naples, 1971—; co-chmn. Com. to Elect Askew-Adams, 1971; vice chmn. Gov. Askew Adv. Com. Collier County, 1970. Mem. Am. Inst. Interior Designers, Jr. C. of C., Gulf Coast Investment Club Naples, Alpha Tau Omega. Democrat. Baptist. Home: 1801 Myrick Rd Tallahassee FL 32303

SMITH, JOHN SYLVESTER, coll. pres.; b. Phila., Aug. 18, 1914; student Muhlenberg Coll., 1932; B.S., Temple U. Tchrs. Coll., 1937; S.T.B. with honors, 1938; M.A., Drew U., 1940. Ph.D., 1948; postdoctoral study, Columbia; m. Margaret Viola Giebel, January 7, 1939; children—Roy Harold (dec.), Barbara Lynn (Mrs. John Morgan). Ordained to ministry Methodist Ch., 1938; pastor, Bklyn., 1943-46; protestant chaplain Bklyn. State Hosp., later N.Y.N.G., 1943-46; asst. to pres. Washington Coll. Chestertown. Md. 1946-51; with Ia. Wesleyan Coll., 1951-53, head dept. philosophy and religion, chmn. div. humanities, then dean of coll.; head dept. philosophy and religion, adminstrv. adviser to pres. Bethune-Cookman Coll., Daytona Beach, Fla., 1953, dean, 1953-54, dean and registrar. 1954-58; dean Dillard U. New Orleans, 1958-59; v.p. univ. dean Ill. Wesleyan U., 1959-62; chmn. div. humanities Findlay Coll., 1962-66; acad. dean, v.p. Lake City (Fla.) Jr. Coll. and Forest Ranger Sch., 1966-67; pres. Fla. Keys Coll., Key West, 1967—. Mem. Lambda Chi Alpha. Presbyn. Home: 2 Allamanda Terrace Key West FL 33040

SMITH, JOHN WALTER, r.r. exec.; b. Balt., July 20, 1900; s. James Goldfinch and Christina (Reifschneider) S.; B.S., C.E., U. Md., 1921; m. May Elizabeth Appel, Sept. 4, 1926; children—Anne (Mrs.John Westcott Stewart), John Walter. Engring. insp. constrn. work S.A.L. Ry. Co., 1924, maintenance of way dept., 1925, div. engr., 1932, operating and engring. dept., 1936-44, asst. chief engr., asst. gen. supt., 1944-46; asst. to pres. S.A.L. R.R. Co., 1946-50, v.p. adminstrative, 1950-52, pres., dir., 1952-67; chmn. bd., dir., mem. exec. com. succeeding co. Seaboard Coast Line R.R. Co., 1967-71, now only dir.; chmn. bd., dir., mem. exec. com. Taveres & Gulf R.R. Co.; pres., dir. Ga., Fla. & Ala. R.R. Co., Southeastern Investment Co.; chmn. bd., dir. Gainesville Midland R.R. Co.; chmn. exec. bd. Clinchfield R.R. Co.; dir., mem. exec. com. Louisville & Nashville R.R. Co., Jacksonville Terminal Co. (Fla.); dir. Tampa & Gulf Coast R.R. Co., Tampa Union Sta. Co., Richmond, Fredericksburg & Potomac R.R. Co., Richmond-Washington Co., Richmond Terminal Ry. Co., State Planters Bank of Commerce & Trusts. Trustee Richmond Meml. Hosp. Mem. Am. Ry. Engring. Assn., Nat. Def. Transp. Assn. Episcopalian. Clubs: University, Traffic, Links (N.Y.C.); Princess Anne Country (Virginia Beach, Va.); Forum, Country of Virginia, Commonwealth (Richmond, Va.); Oglethorpe (Savannah, Ga.); Burning Tree (Bethesda, Md.); Deerwood (Jacksonville, Fal.); Pinehurst (N.C.) Country; University (Tampa, Fal.); Metropolitan (Washington). Home: 8916 Tresco Rd Richmond VA 23229 Office: 3600 W Broad St Richmond VA 23230 also Seaboard Coastline Bldg Jacksonville FL 32202

SMITH, JOHN WAYNE, librarian; b. Barberton, O., Sept. 26, 1936; s. Dorsie B. and Edna Francis (Cheadle) S.; B.B.A., Tex. Western Coll., 1964; M.A., U. Denver, 1965. Head circulation dept. Tex. Western Coll., 1965-67; asst. dir. libraries El Paso (Tex.) Pub. Library, 1967, dir. libraries, 1967—. Tech. adviser Mayor's Program, Community Renewal Program, Dept. Housing and Urban Devel., 1970; cons. for Research Assos. Bd. dirs. El Paso Arts Council; mem. adv. com. Parents Without Partners. Served with USNR, 1956-60. Mem. Tex. Municipal Librarians Assn. (pres.), Tex. (chmn. pub. library div.), Southwestern (1st chmn.) library assns., Asociacion Mexicana de Bibliotecarios, Arabian Horse Assn., Border Arabian Horse Assn. Club: El Paso Riding and Driving (treas.). Contbr. to Ency. Americana, 1971. Home: 4037 Emory St El Paso TX 79912 Office: 501 N Oregon St El Paso TX 79901

SMITH, J(OSEPH) COWIN, ins. exec.; b. Corbridge, Northumberland, Eng., Nov. 25, 1901; s. Joseph Melrose and Catherine Jane (Cowin) S.; ed. various schs. in Eng.; m. Myrtle Rives Ramey, Aug. 14, 1930; 1 dau., Elizabeth (Betty) Rives. Came to U.S., 1920, naturalized, 1925. Asso. with Woolcott & Woolcott, solicitors and barristers, Liverpool, Eng., 1915-16; Rose Bros., Ltd., accountant Northern Mfg. Co. Gainsborough, 1916; accountant Cooperative Wholesale Soc., Gainsborough, 1917-20; accountant Life Ins. Co. of Va., Richmond, 1920-37, asst. sec., 1937-43, asst. v.p., 1943-48, v.p., 1948—, sec., 1958—. Asst. sec. Richmond Meml. Hosp., 1949—. Mem. Life Ins. Agy. Mgmt. Assn., Life Ins. Assn. Am., C. of C., Am. Soc. Corporate Secs. Episcopalian. Mason (32deg., Shriner). Club: Virginia Boat. Home: 1608 Bellevue Av Richmond VA 23227 Office: Capitol and Tenth Sts Richmond VA 23209

SMITH, JOSEPH VERTREES, grocery co. exec.; b. Electra, Tex., Aug. 6, 1914; s. Dozier J. and Mabel (Vertrees) S.; B.S., East Central State Coll., Ada, Okla., 1936; m. Bobbie Lee Henshaw, Aug. 13, 1936; children—Richard V., Randall H., Gerald L., Marian E. Pres., chief exec. officer, dir. J.V. Smith Sales Co. (merged with Scrivner-Boogaart, Inc. 1967), Oklahoma City, 1935-67, now pres. Scrivner-Boogaart, Inc. Served with USNR, 1942-44. Mem. Nat. Assn. Wholesale Grocers Am., Super Market Inst., Oklahoma City C. of C., Newcomen Soc. N.Am. Democrat. Presbyn. (elder 1964-66, trustee 1968—). Lion. Clubs: Oklahoma City Golf and Country, Aviation (Oklahoma City). Home: 1610 Randel Rd Oklahoma City OK 73116 Office: PO Box 26146 Oklahoma City OK 73126

SMITH, KEN MCFARLANE, lawyer; b. Kokomo, Ind., Feb. 12, 1927; s. James McFarlane and Pearl (Johnston) S.; B.S., Ind. U., 1948, LL.B., 1950, J.D., 1967; m. Mildred Alice Howell, Aug. 16, 1953; children— Timothy McFarlane, James Michael. Admitted to Ind. bar, 1950, Va. bar, 1954; practiced in Arlington, Va., 1954—; asst. pub. defender State Ind., 1950; law clk. U.S. Civil Service, 1953; pvt. practice, 1954—; asst. commonwealth atty. Arlington County, 1955-59, substitute judge, 1961-66, 67—, asst. commr. accounts, 1960—; tchr. bus. law U. Va. Extension, 1957; mem. Va. Adv. Legislative Council Study on Consol. Local Govts., 1959; mem. Nat. Traffic Ct. Conf. for Judges Northwestern U., 1963; mem. Va. Adv. Legislative Council Study Group on Commrs. of Fiduciaries and Accounts, 1963—. Sec.-treas., Universal Bldg. Co., Inc.; chmn. bd. Bank Arlington. Chmn., Ct. of Honor Arlington council Boy Scouts Am., 1955-59, area explorer chmn., 1971-72; chmn. March of Dimes, 1959; vice chmn. YMCA, 1959-61; chmn. Heart Assn., 1962. Pres., Arlington (Va.) Young Democrats, 1958-29, chmn. 10th dist., 1959-60; exec. v.p. Va. Young Democrats, 1960-61, dist. v.p., 1962-63, counsel, 1964-65. Pres. Inter-Service Club Council Arlington, 1965; bd. dirs. Alcoholics Rehab., Inc., 1965—; chmn. adv. bd. Salvation Army, 1963-67; mem. adv. bd. Mental Hygiene Center, 1963-66, Council Ind. Colls. Va., 1971—; adv. com. Arlington Sch. Bd., 1972—. Served with Signal Corps, AUS, 1950-52. Recipient Distinguished Service award Jr. C. of C., 1962; named Kiwanis Man of Year, 1964, 71; named Man of Yr., Inter Service Club Arlington, 1971. Mem. Am., Va., Arlington bar assns., Arlington Outdoor Edn. Assn. (dir. 1972—), Phi Kappa Psi, Phi Delta Phi. Baptist (moderator 1971—). Home: 4056 N 27th Rd Arlington VA 22207 Office: 2007 N 15th St Arlington VA 22216

SMITH, KENNETH JUDSON, JR., chemist; b. Raleigh, N.C., Sept. 4, 1930; s. Kenneth Judson and Irene (Strickland) S.; A.B., E. Carolina Coll., 1957; M.A., Duke, 1959, Ph.D., 1961; m. Dorothy Margaret Ratcliffe, Mar. 6, 1953; children—Patricia Lynne, Pamela Jean. Research chemist Chemstrand Research Center, Durham, N.C., 1961-65, sr. research chemist, 1965-68; asst. prof. polymer research Syracuse (N.Y.) State U. Coll. Forestry, 1968-70, asso. prof., 1970—, asst. dir. Polymer Research Center, dir. Organic Materials Sci. Program, 1971—. Served with USMCR, 1951-54. Mem. A.A.A.S. Contrbr. articles to profl. jours. Home: 215 Dexter Av Liverpool NY 13088 Office: State U Coll Forestry Syracuse NY 13210

SMITH, KIRBY HART, JR., hosp. adminstr.; b. Kinston, N.C., Jan. 16, 1938; s. Kirby Hart and Clara Adeliade (Baldree) S.; B.A., U. N.C., 1960; M.H.A., Med. Coll. Va., 1963; m. Caroline Winder Ashford, June 10, 1961; children—Kirby, Caroline. Staff asso. Rowan Meml. Hosp., Salisbury, N.C., 1964-66; dir. Onslow Meml. Hosp., Jacksonville, N.C., 1966—. Treas., dir. T.P. Ashford Oil Co., Inc., New Bern, N.C., 1970—. Mem. adv. com. licensed practical nurses Coastal Carolina Community Coll., 1967—. Bd. dirs. Onslow County chpt. A.R.C., 1968—, treas., 1970—. Mem. Am., N.C. (trustee, exec. com.) hosp. assns., Am. Coll. Hosp. Adminstrs. (nominee). Episcopalian. Home: 317 Forest Grove Av Jacksonville NC 28540 Office: P O Box 129 Jacksonville NC 28540

SMITH, LAWRENCE EVERETT, educator; b. Rossburg, O., Aug. 20, 1920; s. Emerson E. and Ida (Hittle) S.; B.A., U. Louisville, 1943; postgrad. Cornell, 1946; M.A., U. Mich., 1952; Ed.D. (grad. fellow 1954-56), U. Fla., 1956; m. Timothy C. Riggs, Nov. 11, 1944; children—Kay Frances (Mrs. Keith W. Leonard), Wayne Errol. Prin. Marlow (Ga.) High Sch., 1945-54; asst. dir. Bur. Ednl. Research, U. Ala., University, 1956-59; asso. prof. Glasboro (N.J.) State Coll., 1959-61, 62-65; vis. asso. prof. U. Fla., 1961-62; prof. Inst. Ednl. Research, Fla. Atlantic U., Boca Raton, 1965—, dir., 1965—. Exec. sec. 1st dist. Ga. High Sch. Assn., 1952-54; cons. Ala. Legislative Commn., 1958-59; research dir. Curriculum Devel. Council So. N.J., 1963-65; mem. adv. council Southeastern Ednl. Lab., Atlanta, 1966—. Served with USMCR, 1943-45. Mem. Am., Fla. ednl. research assns., Am. Assn. Sch. Adminstrs., Am. Assn. U. Profs., N.E.A., Fla. Edn. Assn., Franklin Inst. Sci. and Mechanic Arts, Phi Delta Kappa, Kappa Delta Pi, Phi Kappa Phi. Mem. Ch. of Nazarene. Producer instructional TV series on ednl. supervision Fla. Atlantic U., 1966—. Home: 899 SW 9th Terrace Boca Raton FL 33432

SMITH, LAWRENCE NORFLEET, banker; b. Roanoke, Va., June 1, 1937; s. Norfleet A. and Margaretta (Brady) S.; B.S., Hampden-Sydney Coll., 1959; postgrad. U. Richmond, 1960, Stonier Grad. Sch. Banking, Rutgers U., 1968; m. Sally Birdsong, Apr. 15, 1961; children—Lawrence N., Harvard B., Susan N. Salesman, F.W. Craigie & Co., Richmond, 1959-61; investment banker, mgr. municipal bond dept. Mason & Co., Inc. (now Legg-Mason), Newport News, Va., 1961-64; with United Va. Bank/Seaboard Nat., Suffolk, Va., 1964-70, v.p., 1968-70, exec. v.p., Norfolk, Va., 1971—, sec. bd. dirs., 1967—; dir. Empire Machinery & Supply 09& Supply Suffolk/Nansemond Cons. Study Commn., 1970—; mem. Suffolk Zoning Bd. Appeals, 1969—. Bd. dirs. Cypress Devel. Corp., Suffolk, Suffolk Recreational and Charitable Assn. Mem. Va. Bankers Assn. (dir. Group I), C. of C., Tri-County, Regional Emergency (exec. mgr.) clearing house assns. Episcopalian (asst. treas.). Rotarian. Clubs: Suffolk Sports, German (Suffolk), Cedar Point Country (Crittenden, Va.). Home: 826 Riverview Dr Suffolk VA 23434 Office: Box 3127 Norfolk VA 23434

SMITH, LELAND JAMES, archtl. engr.; b. Fairbury, Neb., Apr. 3, 1925; s. Otis Lawrence and Bertha (Mathy) S.; student Fairbury Coll., 1946-48; B.S. in Archtl. Engring., U. Neb., 1952; m. Beverly Jean Kirchmeyer, Apr. 8, 1961; children—Leanne Marie, Kristin Leigh. Salesman, Fairbury Pump & Supply (Neb.), 1951-52; with Continental Oil Co., Ponca City, Okla., 1952—, archtl. design engr., 1961-70, tng. supr. refinery personnel, 1970—. Area chmn. fund raising dr. YMCA, Ponca City, 1966-67. Bd. dirs. Ponca City chpt. A.R.C., 1969—, Ponca City unit United Fund, 1972—. Served with USAAF, 1943-46. Registered profl. engr., Okla. Mem. Am. Petroleum Inst. (vice chmn. midcontinent dist. 4 tng. com. 1970—), Am. Soc. Tng. and Devel., Am. Legion (chmn. bldg. corp. 1966-70). Democrat. Roman Catholic (chmn. parish council 1970-71). K.C. Home: 701 E Madison Av Ponca City OK 74601 Office: 1000 S Pine St Ponca City OK 74601

SMITH, LEMUEL AUGUSTUS, JR., justice; b. Holly Springs, Miss., Aug. 30, 1904; s. Lemuel Augustus and Louise (Robertson) S.; LL.B., U. Miss., 1926; m. Chesley Thorne, Dec. 2, 1931; children—Caffey (Mrs. E.E. (Litkenhous), Lemuel Augustus. Admitted to Miss. bar, 1926, practiced in Holly Springs, 1926-65; dir. First State Bank Holly Springs. County pros. atty., 1935-50; atty. Marshall County Bd. Suprs., 1948-65; asso. justice Supreme Ct. of Miss., 1965—. Spl. chancellor 3d Chancery Ct. Dist. Miss., 1958-59. Pres. bd. trustees Holly Springs Municipal Separate Sch. Dist., 1946-57. Mem. Miss. Ho. of Reps., 1929, 32, 33, 36. Served as lt. comdr. USNR, 1942-45. Mem. Am., Miss. (past complaint commr.), Marshall County (pres. 1957) bar assns., Kappa Alpha. Episcopalian (former vestryman). Home: 631 Chulahoma Av Holly Springs MS 38635 Office: New Capitol Bldg Jackson MS 39205

SMITH, LEROY FLEMING, JR., physician; b. Savannah, Ga., Oct. 7, 1935; s. Leroy Fleming and Helen (Tuten) S.; A.B., King Coll., 1956; M.D., Med. Coll. Ga., 1960; m. Elizabeth Hilsman, July 18, 1959; children— Leslie, Powell, Edward. Intern, Harrisburg (Pa.) Hosp., 1960-61; resident Cleve. Clinic Found., 1963-67; pvt. practice medicine specializing in hematology, med. oncology, Alexandria, Va., 1967—; asst. clin. prof. medicine Georgetown U. Med. Sch., 1970—. Pres. bd. trustees Alexandria Community Health Center, 1970—. Served with USAF, 1961-63. Diplomate Am. Bd. Medicine. Mem. A.C.P. Home: 1105 Vassar Rd Alexandria VA 22314 Office: 4801 Kenmore Av Alexandria VA 22304

SMITH, LEROY VICTOR, football coach; b. Lexington, Ky., Aug 4, 1938; s. Henry Clay and Mary (Byrd) S.; B.S., Jackson (Miss.) State Coll. 1958; M.S., U. Ky., 1963; m. Mary Levi, Mar. 14, 1958; children—Darryl Victor, Angela Maria, Danee LaVon. Surp., Lexington (Ky.) Recreation Dept., summers 1956-63; with Miss. Valley State Coll., 1958-59; head football coach Randolph High Sch., Pass Christian, Miss., 1959-63; with Meigs High Sch., Nashville, 1963-64; head football coach Tuskegee Inst., 1964—. Cons. community edn. program, Tuskegee, 1966. Mem. Am. Football Coaches Assn., Kappa Alpha Psi. Alpha Kappa Mu. Democrat. Episcopalian. Author articles. Home: Pine Hurst Apts Tuskegee Institute AL 36088

SMITH, LEVIE DAVID, JR., realtor; b. Lakeland, Fla., Oct. 19, 1924; s. Levie David and Grace (Ross) S.; B.S., Fla. So. Coll., 1947; student U. Miami, 1943-44; m. Annie Laurie Hogan, Aug. 29, 1948; children—Nancy Carol, Levie David III, Judith Ann. Appraiser, Smith & Smith, Realtors, Lakeland, Fla., 1948-50, 52—, now with Smith & Son, Appraisers, Lakeland. Served as ensign USNR, 1943-46, as lt., 1950-52. Mem. Am. Inst. Real Estate Appraisers (v.p. Fla. chpt. 1961, pres. 1962), Soc. Residential Appraisers (pres. W. Coast chpt. 1957), Am. Right-of-Way Assn., Lakeland Bd. Realtors (pres. 1958), Fla. Assn. Realtors (v.p. 10th dist. 1968, pres. 1970). Democrat. Presbyn. Rotarian. Home: 515 Laurel Lane Lakeland FL 33803 Office: 215 1/2 E Lemon St Lakeland FL 33802

SMITH, LLOYD HILTON, ind. oil and gas producer; b. Pitts., July 9, 1905; s. Roland Hilton and Jane (Lloyd) S.; Ph.B., Yale, 1929; m. Jane Clay Zevely, Sept. 7, 1931; 1 dau., Camilla; m. 2d, Elizabeth Keith Wiess, May 25, 1940; children—Sandra Keith, Sharon Lloyd, Sidney Carothers. Statistician Biggs Mohrman & Co., N.Y.C., 1932; mgr. N.Y. office Laird & Co., 1933-34; v.p. Argus Research Corp., 1934-35; pres., dir. Paraffine Oil Corp., 1949—; dir. Curtiss-Wright Corp., First City Nat. Bank of Houston, Nat. Rev. Inc., Falcom Seaboard Corp., Kinetics Internat. Corp; chmn. Horner & Smith, Inc. Bd. dirs. Houston Symphony Soc., Houston Soc. for Prevention Cruelty to Animals, Houston Mus. Natural Sci.; trustee Pine Manor Jr. Coll., Chestnut Hill, Mass. Republican. Clubs: Bayou, Houston, Ramada, Plaza, University, Tejas (Houston); Racquet and Tennis, Brook, River (N.Y.C.); Nat. Golf Links of America, Southampton, Beach, Meadow (Southhampton, N.Y.), Dallas. Home: 2 Longfellow Lane Houston TX 77005 Office: 3210 One Shell Plaza Houston TX 77002

SMITH, LORNE ALEXANDER, petroleum co. exec.; b. Winnipeg, Man., Can., Dec. 29, 1916; s. Arthur and Margaret Ann (Mathews) Sm; B.S., U. Man., 1938; m. Renee Claudia Cavanna, Feb. 20, 1943; children—Janet Frances, Lorne Albert, Margaret Ann. Field geologist Imperial Oil Co., Can., 1940, geol. party chief Ecuador, 1940-46, div. geologist, Peru, 1946-51, field mgr., asst. gen. mgr., 1951-57, gen. mgr., Colombia, 1957-61, dep. producing coor., N.Y.C., 1961-62, gen. mgr., Peru, 1962-64, producing coordinator, N.Y.C., 1964-68; exec. v.p. Esso Interamerica, Inc., Coral Gables, Fla., 1968—. Mem. Am. Assn. Petroleum Geologists, Am. Inst. Petroleum Engrs. Clubs: University (N.Y.C.); Key Biscayne (Fla.) Yacht. Home: 870 Harbor Dr Key Biscayne Miami FL 33149 Office: 396 Alhambra Circle Coral Gables FL 323134

SMITH, LUTHER, coll. adminstr.; b. Bessemer, Ala., Oct. 14, 1927; s. Luther and Julia (Dawson) S.; B.S., Auburn (Ala.) U., 1949; M.A., U. Ia., 1951; B.D., So. Bapt. Theol. Sem., 1957; Ph.D., Fla. State U., 1967; m. Norma Jean Scarbrough, Aug. 24, 1954; children— Lugenia, Linda. Editor, Auburn Alumnews, Auburn U., 1948-51; exec. sec. Ga. Found. for Ind. Colls., 1957-59; dir. devel. and pub. relations Furman U., Greenville, S. C., 1959-61; asst. to pres. U. Richmond (Va.), 1961-65; adminstrv. staff officer Western Ky. U., Bowling Green, 1967-68; dir. spl. projects George Peabody Coll. for Tchrs., Nashville, 1968—. Served with USMCR, 1945-46, 52-54. Mem. Am. Assn. for Higher Edn., Am. Assn. Sch. Adminstrs., Sigma Delta Chi, Phi Delta Kappa, Lambda Chi Alpha. Home: Pattilloch Route 1 Cedar Hill TN 37032 Office: Box 161 George Peabody Coll for Tchrs Nashville TN 37203

SMITH, LUTHER ELGIN, JR., realtor, ins. broker; b. Chattanooga, Dec. 22, 1925; s. Luther Elgin and Anna (Clonts) S.; grad. high sch.; m. Jean Cofield, Oct. 2, 1949; 1 dau., Susan Carol. Mgr., Acme Blind & Floor Co., Chattanooga, 1950-58; owner Elgin Smith Co., Chattanooga, 1958—; pres. Town and Country Developers, Inc. Pres., Gideons, 1963-66; mem. Tenn. Real Estate Commn., 1972—. Vice-chmn. bd. trustees, mem. exec. com. Tenn. Temple Coll.; bd. dirs. East Ridge YMCA. Served with USNR, 1944-46. Named Realtor of Yr., Tenn. Assn. Real Estate Bds., 1968. Mem. Chattanooga Bd. Realtors (pres. 1966-67), (dir.; nat. state chmn. 1963-64, mem. com. on bd. jurisdictions, profl. standards com., state assn. com.), Tenn. (pres. 1967) assns. real estate bds., Nat. Inst. Real Estate Brokers (state chmn. 1963-64), Greater Chattanooga C. of C. (v.p. 1972). Baptist (sec. to bd. deacons). Club: Chattanooga Optimist (Man of Year 1965, pres. 1964-65, Tenn. chmn. boys work activities 1965, gov. Tenn. dist. 1968-69, Distinguished Gov.'s award 1969). Home: 4401 Mayfair Av Chattanooga TN 37411 Office: 2401 E Main St Chattanooga TN 37404

SMITH, MALCOLM DUNKIN, farmer; b. Montgomery, Ala., Nov. 2, 1939; s. Albert Fay and Evelyn (Dunkin) S.; student Auburn U., 1957-59, Belhaven Coll., 1960-61; m. Jane Drinkard, Aug. 6, 1966. With McQueen Smith Farms, Prattville, Ala., 1965—, farm mgr., 2d v.p., 1970—. Supr. Autanga County com. Agr. Stblzn. Conservation Service, 1972—. Mem. city council, Prattville, Ala., 1971—. Bd. dirs. Montgomery Area Mental Health Bd. Served with U.S.N.G., 1962-70. Mem. Autauga County Hog Producers Assn. (pres. 1969-71), Ala. Cattleman's Assn., Presbyn. (chmn. bd. deacons 1968-69). Home: 1257 Huie St Prattville AL 36067 Office: Route 6 Box 277 Prattville AL 36067

SMITH, MARVIN MCLEOD, elec. engr.; b. Walhalla, S.C., Nov. 24, 1911; s. Dresden Anderson and Julia Elizabeth (McLeod) S.; B.S. in Elec. Engring., Clemson U., 1932; m. Ann LeGarde Printup, July 20, 1941; 1 son, Marvin McLeod. Design engr. Duke Power Co., Charlotte, N.C., 1947—. Served to capt. AUS, 1940-42; ETO. Registered profl. engr., N.C. Mem. I.E.E.E. (sr.), Illuminating Engring. Soc., Tau Beta Pi. Home: 3141 Windsor Dr Charlotte NC 28209 Office: PO Box 2178 Charlotte NC 28201

SMITH, MCGREGOR, utilities exec.; b. Cooksville, Tenn., June 5, 1899; s. Rutledge and Graeme (McGregor) S.; B.S. in C.E., U. of Tenn., 1921; student Vanderbilt U., Nashville, 1926-27; m. Elizabeth Wilson, Nov. 12, 1924; children—McGregor, Wilson. Asst. engr. Tenn. R.R. & Pub. Utilities Commn., 1921-22, engr., 1922-26; mgr. South New Orleans Light & Traction Co., 1926-27; v.p. and gen. mgr. La. Power & Light Co., Algiers, La., 1928-36, pres. and gen. mgr., 1936-39; v.p. and gen. mgr. Fla. Power & Light Co., 1939, pres., 1939-54, chmn. bd., 1954—, chmn. exec. com. Mem. Phi Gamma Delta. Presbyn. Mason. Clubs: Coral Gables Country; Riviera; Surf; New York Athletic. Home: 1132 South Greenway Dr 33134 Coral Gables FL 33834 Office: Fla Power & Light Co 4200 W Flager St Miami FL 33134

SMITH, MELTON VERN, psychologist; b. Tahoka, Tex., Nov. 14, 1928; s. R. Lambert and Zelma (Huckleberry) S.; B.S., N. Tex. State Coll., 1948; M.Ed., U. Tex., 1951, M.A., 1957, Ph.D., 1958, J.D., 1960; m. Shila Anne McComb, July 30, 1955; children—David Lambert, Jennifer Lynn. Tchr., student counselor Pilot Point Ind. Sch. Dist., 1948; tchr. Carey Pub. Sch., 1948-49, Austin Pub. Sch., 1949-54; asst. prof. edn. psychology U. Tenn., 1959-60; asst. prof. U. Mo., 1960-63, asso. prof., 1963-64; psychologist Rohrer, Hibler & Replogle, Houston, 1964-70, partner, 1971—; admitted to Tex. bar, 1961; practiced in Houston, part-time 1965—; farmer, Savoy, Tex., 1967—; rancher, Bells, Tex., 1969-72. Served with USAF, 1954-56. Mem. Am., Tex., Houston psychol. assns., Am., Tex., Dallas, Houston bar assns., Am. Assn. U. Profs., Phi Alpha Delta, Phi Delta Kappa. Presbyn. Clubs: Plaza, Inns of Court (Houston). Author: Self Representations of American and Korean Youth, 1958. Home: 326 Chapel Bell Houston TX 77024 Office: SW Tower 707 McKinney Houston TX 77002

SMITH, MELVIN DONALD, supt. schs.; b. Elbert, Tex., Aug. 22, 1926; s. Perry and Fannie Josephine (Herblin) S.; student Weatherford Jr. Coll., 1947-48; B.S., Tex. Wesleyan Coll., 1950; M.E., Tex. Christian U., 1953; postgrad. North Tex. State U., 1968-72; m. Martha Ann Turner, Feb. 1, 1947; children—Tommy, Craig, Sue Ann. Prin. jr. high sch. Granbury (Tex.) Ind. Sch. Dist., 1950-53, prin. sr. high sch., 1954-55; prin. high sch. Jacksboro (Tex.) Ind. Sch. Dist., 1955-64, supt. schs., 1964-71; supts. schs. Cleburne (Tex.) Ind. Sch. Dist., 1971—. Served with USAAF, 1944-46. Named Outstanding Citizen Jacksboro C. of C., 1970. Kettering Found. fellow, summer 1969. Mem. Tex. Tchrs. Assn., Tex., North Tex. (past chmn.), Nat. sch. adminstrs. Assns., Jacksbooro C. of C. (pres. 1962), So. Assn. Schs. and Colls., C. of C. (dir.). Mem. Christian Ch. (elder). Lion. Home: 1208 Glenhaven St Cleburne TX 76031 Office: 103 S Walnut St Cleburne TX 76031

SMITH, MILTON SHUMWAY, educator; b. Cranston, R. I., Sept 2, 1912; s. Lowndes Alexander and Florence May (Duck) S.; B.A., Wesleyan U., 1933; M.A., Harvard, 1934; Ph.D., Fordham U., 1955; postgrad. Yale, 1934-37, U. Wash., 1962; m. Marie Catherine Herr, Aug. 12, 1960. Sec. to coroner Middlesex County, Middletown, Conn., 1933-37; research asst. Yale, 1938-41; instr. English, U. Hartford, 1946-47, asst. prof., 1947-51; research asso. U. Sheffield, (Eng.), 1954-56; asso. prof. English Southeastern La. Coll., 1956-61; prof., chmn. dept. English, humanities Yankton (S.D.) Coll., 1961-63; prof., chmn. English dept. Houston Baptist Coll., 1963-67; prof. lit., coordinator humanities Va. Western Community Coll., Roanoke, 1967—; prof. English Mitchell Coll., New London, Conn., 1961-65 (summers). Served with USNR, 1943-45; ETO. Mem. Houston Council Tchrs. Eng. (sec. 1965-66), Am. Studies Assn. (sec., treas., Tex., 1965-67), Am. Assn. U. Profs., Coll. English Assn., Modern Lang. Assn., N.E.A., Modern Humanities Research Assn., Nat. Geog. Soc., Nat. Parks Assn., Nat. Wildlife Fedn., Am. Forestry Assn., Wilderness Soc., Nat. Trust for Historic Preservation, Coll. Conf. Tchrs. English, Renaissance Soc. Am., U.S. Power Squadron, Newcomen Soc. N. Am., Lambda Iota Tau (internat. treas. 1961-63), Delta Upsilon. Mason, Rotarian (dir. community service, Houston, 1964-67, dist. scholarship com. R.I. Dist. 589, 1966-67). Author: Ancient Sea Charts, 1941; Modern Sea Charts, 1941; The Starboard Tradition, 1942; A Checklist of the Correspondence of Edmund Burke, 1955; Emerson's Idealism in the Hot War of Ideologies, 1958; Hayward's Historiography in the Tacitean Tradition, 1961. Home: 1929 Greenwood Rd SW Roanoke VA 24015

SMITH, MORRIS RUDOLPH, ednl. adminstr.; b. Lockhart, Tex., May 11, 1905; s. Joseph Edgar and Julia (Osteen) S.; B.S., S.W. Tex. U., 1932; M.Ed., U. Tex., 1939; m. Carleta Elizabeth Tunnell, Sept. 1, 1931; children—Jack Morris, Elizabeth Ann, Richard K. Tchr., coach Lytle, Tex., pub. schs., 1931-35; prin. Macdona (Tex.) Sch., Tex., 1935-37, Pharr, Tex., 1937-43; area supr. Tex. Bd. Vocational Edn., Austin, 1946-47; county coordinator, Pharr, 1948-52; elementary prin. Clover Sch., San Juan, Tex., 1952-55; supt. Hidalgo County schs., Edinburg, Tex., 1955—. Pres. Valley Retarded Sch. Bd., 1955-56. Served to capt. USAAF, 1943-46. Mem. N.E.A. (dist. membership chmn.), Nat. Assn. Sch. Adminstrs. Mason, Kiwanian. Home: 217 E Jones St Pharr TX 78577 Office: Courthouse Bldg Edinburg TX 78539

SMITH, NORMAN, wood flooring co. exec.; b. Phila., Aug. 25, 1905; s. Charles Haskell and Rose (Knazz) S.; student pub. schs.; m. Carmen Lucille Sandstrom, June 4, 1957; children—Reesa Karen (Mrs. Gerald Lavitt), Charles Joel. Field mgr. middle Atlantic states P. Lorrillard Co., tobacco, 1927-40; spl. rep. charge war rationing program Liquor Distilling Industry, Pacific Coast, 1941-44; pres. Columbia Liquors, Los Angeles, 1944-49; v.p. Swedish Foods, nat. marketing scandinavian products, N.Y.C., 1949-52; pres. Norjac Trading Corp., Phila., 1952-58; v.p. New Deal Lifetime Homes, Phila., 1958-62; v.p. Wilson Oak Flooring, Sykes Flooring Co., Inc., Warren, Ark., 1962—. Mem. Nat. Council Research in Alcoholism, 1945-48; pres. Phila. Little Symphony Assn., 1954-56; pres. Colonial Phila. Hist. Soc., 1965-71. One of founders Progressive Party, 1948, nat. treas. 1948-49. Recipient Silver plaque Sec. Treasury Vinson, 1945; honored Nat. Jewish Com., 1948; honored Colonial Phila. Hist. Soc., 1972. Mem. Hist. Soc. Pa., Freedoms Found., A.L.A. Home: 1374 Avenida Ashford SB Santurce PR 00907 Office: Sykes Flooring Co Inc PO Box 420 Warren AR 71671

SMITH, NORMAN CUTLER, geologist, co. exec., cons.; b. Paterson, N.J., Mar. 18, 1915; s. Archibald Nicholas and Ruth (Cutler) S.; student Pennington Sch., 1930-33, Drew U., 1933-34; A.B. cum laude, Washington and Lee U., 1937; postgrad. Harvard, 1940-42, Okla. U., 1947; m. Dorothy Phyllis Barnes, June 12, 1942; children—Roxanne Lorraine (Mrs. Charles Annen), Lee Cutler. Field geologist Standard Oil Co. Venezuela, 1938-40; teaching fellow Harvard Grad. Sch. Geology, 1941-42; geologist Humble Oil & Refining Co., 1946-49; cons. geologist and photo-geol. specialist,

1949-62; exec. dir. Am. Assn. Petroleum Geologists, 1963-72; pres. World Resources Corp., 1972—, Operations Central, Inc., 1972—. Founder, 1st pres. Council Sci. Socs., Dallas-Ft. Worth Area, 1958, chmn. bd., 1960. Trustee Tulsa Sci. Center. Served to lt. USNR, 1942-46; PTO. Fellow Geol. Soc. Am., A.A.A.S.; mem. Am., Tulsa socs. assn. execs. (pres. 1968), Dallas (hon., pres. 1958-59, exec. com. 1960), Tulsa geol. socs., Soc. Petroleum Engrs., Am. Assn. Petroleum Geologists, Soc. Exptl. Geophysicists, Council Engring. and Sci. Soc. Contbr. articles to profl. jours., chpts. to books. Home: 2781 E 28th St Tulsa OK 74114 Office: 6111 E Skelly Dr Tulsa OK 74135

SMITH, NORMAN W., social worker; b. Norman, Okla., Dec. 2, 1933; s. Marion Jefferson and Ruth (Catlett) S.; B.A., U. Okla., 1958, M.S.W., 1965; m. Retha Dean Pugh, May 25, 1952; children—Terry Wade, Shelley Dawn, Regina Norine. Social work asst. Pauls Valley (Okla.) State Sch. for Mentally Retarded, 1962-65, social worker, 1965-66, supr. social services, 1966-70, adminstrv. asst. to instn. supt., 1970—. Mem. Okla. Bd. Registered Social Workers. Mem. Nat. Assn. Social Workers, Am. Assn. Mental Deficiency (Okla. state reporter Region V), Acad. Certified Social Workers. Baptist. Elk. Home: Box 609 Pauls Valley OK 73075

SMITH, ORMA RINEHART, judge; b. Booneville, Miss., Sept. 25, 1904; s. Jefferson Davis and Lena (Rinehart) S.; LL.B., U. Miss., 1927; m. Margaret Elizabeth Fernandez, June 17, 1930; 1 son, Orma Rinehart. Admitted to Miss. bar, 1927; practice in Corinth, 1928-68; mem. firm Smith & Smith, 1959-68; U.S. dist. judge No. Dist., 1968—. Fellow Miss. Bar Found.; mem. Am., Alcorn County bar assns., Miss. State Bar (past pres.), U. Miss. Alumni Assn. (pres. 1961-62), Alpha Tau Omega. Baptist. Mason (33 deg., Shriner, K.T.), Rotarian. Home: 812 Gloster St Corinth MS 38834

SMITH, OSCAR DALLAS, JR., circuit ct. judge; b. Columbus, Ga., July 21, 1920; s. Oscar D. and Marie (Bertling) S.; student Ga. Southwestern Coll., 1938-40, U. Va., 1946-47; m. Jane Latane Bryan, Jan. 10, 1948; 1son, Oscar Dallas III. Admitted to Ga. bar, 1947, practiced in Columbus, 1947-62; judge City Ct. Columbus, 1962-69; 3d judge Superior Ct. of Chattahoochee Circuit (Ga.), 1970—. Served with USAF, 1941-45. Decorated D.F.C., Air Medal with 2 oak leaf clusters. Mem. Am. Bar Assn., Am. Judicature Soc., State Bar of Ga., Mil. Order of World Wars, Assn. of the U.S. Army. Presbyn. (elder). Clubs: Columbus Lawyers, Columbus Executive. Office: Govt Center Columbus GA 31901

SMITH, OTHO EUGENE, apparel co. exec.; b. Fries, Va., July 10, 1925; s. Reginald Olney and Agnes May (Byrd) S.; B.S. in Naval Sci., Ga. Inst. Tech., 1945, B. in Indsl. Engring., 1948; m. Dorothy Trentadue, June 27, 1959; children—Dorlisa Michelle, Eric Eugene. Indsl. engr. Genesco, Inc., Various locations, 1947-53, 56-57, cons. engr., Eastern U.S., Nashville, 1953-56, 57-58, shoe plant mgr., N.Y.C., 1958-61, cons. mgmt. engr., various locations, 1961-67, mgr. quality engring., internat. operations, Nashville, 1967-69, dir. materials, product quality internat. operations, Nashville, 1969-70, planning cons., 1970—. Co-chmn. Davidson County House to House campaign Republican party for Eisenhower-Nixon, 1952. Served to lt. (s.g.) USNR, 1943-46. Registered profl. engr., Tenn. Mem. Nashville C. of C., U.S. Jr. C. of C., Am. Inst. Indsl. Engrs., Am. Soc. Quality Control, Am. Soc. Testing and Materials, Tenn. (publicity chmn. 1967-68), Nat. soc. profl. engrs., Ga. Tech. Alumni Club Nashville, Ga. Tech. Nat. Alumni Assn. Methodist. (trustee, vice chmn. adminstrv. bd., chmn. finance com.). Clubs: Bluegrass Country (Hendersonville, Tenn.). Home: 389 Greene Harbor Rd Old Hickory TN 37138 Office: 111 7th Av N Nashville TN 37202

SMITH, PATRICK CHESLEY, state govt. ofcl.; b. Easley, S.C., Mar. 25, 1914; s. Roy R. and Fay (Sellers) S.; B.S. in Commerce, U. S.C., 1936; m. Nell Bewley Keith, June 15, 1940; children—William Chesley, James Keith, Luta Catherine (Mrs. William L. Watson, III). With S.C. State Govt., Columbia, 1936—, supr. schoolbook commn., 1936-43, dir. finance Dept. Edn., 1943-51, asst. dir. Edn. Finance Commn., 1951-60, asst. state auditor, 1960-66, state auditor, 1966—. Presbyn. Rotarian. Home: 2609 Stratford Rd Columbia SC 29204 Office: Wade Hampton Bldg Columbia SC 29211

SMITH, PAUL ALBERT, corp. cons.; b. Morning Sun, Ia., Jan. 9, 1901; s. Jonas W. and Estella (McLellan) S.; B.S., U. Mich., 1924; D.Sc., U. Alaska, 1972; m. Sylvia Juanita Ralston, July 9, 1923; children—Paul A., Kathryn Caroline (Mrs. Robert Gifford). Instr. survey and geodesy U. Mich., 1923-24; chief aero. chart br., asst. to dir. U.S. Coast and Geodetic Survey and field surveys, U.S., Alaska, Philippines, 1924-45; alternate U.S. rep. Council Internat. Civil Aviation Orgn., U.S. Dept. State, Montreal, Que., Can., 1946-48, rep., 1948-53, 1st v.p. council, 1950; cons. to asst. sec. def. research and devel., spl. asst. to dir. Advanced Research Projects Agy., Dept. Def., 1953-59; engr. Rand Corp., Washington, 1959-66, cons., 1966—; mem. USAF Sci. Adv. Bd., 1958-69, chmn. geophysics panel, 1959-64; mem. USAF Range Tech. Adv. Group, 1965-68. Mem. adv. com. U. Alaska, 1962—; cons. U. Mich., 1960-65; mem. various Nat. Acad. Scis.-NRC coms., 1963—, chmn. com. on N.Am. Datum, Nat. Acad. Scis.-Nat. Acad. Engring., 1968-69. Trustee Bur. Social Sci. Research. Served from ensign to rear adm. U.S. Coast and Geodetic Survey, 1924-53. Recipient Exceptional Service award Dept. Commerce, 1953; Exceptional Service decoration USAF, 1964, 69; Sesquicentennial award U. Mich., 1967. Fellow Geol. Soc. Am., Am. Inst. Aeros. and Astronautics (asso.), Am. Soc. C.E., A.A.A.S., Am. Geog. Soc., Washington Acad. Sci. (Engring. award 1939); mem. Arctic Inst. N.Am., Inst. Nav., Sigma Xi, Tau Beta Pi. Clubs: Cosmos (Washington). Home: 4714 26th St N Arlington VA 22207 Office: 2100 M St NW Washington DC 20037

SMITH, PAUL EDMUND, JR., educator; b. Northampton, Mass., Feb. 6, 1927; s. Paul Edmund and Mary Jane (Murphy) S.; B.A., U. Mass., 1948; postgrad. Harvard, 1948-49; M.A., Boston U., 1957; B.D., Columbia Theol. Sem., 1957, M.Div., 1971; postgrad. U. N.C., 1967-68. Instr. Latin and French, Chester (Vt.) High Sch., 1949-53, Loris (S.C.) High Sch., 1953-54; lectr. U. Ga., Albany, 1957-59; instr. Latin Rocky Mount (Va.) High Sch., 1959-61; asst. prof. religion Ferrum (Va.) Coll., 1961-68; vis. lectr. history John Tyler Community Coll., Chester, Va., 1968-69; asst. prof. philosophy and religion Richard Bland Coll., Petersburg, Va., 1968-71, asst. prof., chmn. dept., 1971—. Mem. Am. Hist. Assn. Democrat. Presbyn. Home: Lakewood Estates 3774 Westwood Dr Petersburg VA 23803

SMITH, PETER GARTHWAITE, natural gas co. exec., lawyer; b. South Orange, N.J., July 22, 1923; s. Karl Garthwaite and Fannie A. (Jones) S.; A.B., Princeton, 1948; LL.B., Yale, 1951; m. Anne Allerton Ward, Dec. 23, 1950; children—Allerton G., Thomas G., Amy G., Abigail G. Admitted to N.Y. bar, 1951; practiced in N.Y.C., 1951-54; atty. So. Natural Gas Co., Birmingham, Ala., 1955-58, asst. sec., atty., 1958-62, sec., atty., 1962-65, sec., gen. counsel, 1966-67, v.p., sec., gen. counsel, 1967-71, exec. v.p., 1971—, dir., 1969—; v.p., sec., dir. Mesopotamian Petroleum Corp., 1964-68; dir. Offshore Co., So. Natural Resources, Inc., So. Ocean Exploration Co. So. Prodn. & Refining Co.; mem. mgmt. com. Boise So. Co., Sea Robin Pipeline Co. Vice pres., bd. dirs. Birmingham Jr. Programs, 1959-61; pres. bd. trustees Ala. Found. for Hearing and Speech, 1967-69; trustee Birmingham council Camp Fire Girls. Served with USAAF, 1943-46. Mem. Am. Bar Assn., Independent Natural Gas Assn., Phi Delta Phi. Episcopalian. Clubs: Relay House, Princeton of N.Y., Mountain Brook. Home: 3710 Montrose Rd Mountain Brook AL 35213 Office: Watts Bldg Birmingham AL 35202

SMITH, PHILIP ALAN, clergyman; b. Belmont, Mass., Apr. 2, 1920; s. Herbert L. and Elizabeth (MacDonald) S.; A.B., Harvard, 1942; B.D., Va. Theol. Sem., 1949; m. Barbara Ann Taylor, June 12, 1949; children—Sarah Elizabeth, Ann Warren, Jeremy Taylor. Ordained to ministry P.E. Ch., 1949; curate All Saints Ch., Atlanta, 1949-52; rector Christ Ch., Exeter, N.H., 1952-59; asst. prof. pastoral theology Va. Theol. Sem., Alexandria, 1959-62, chaplain, 1962-70, asso. dean for student affairs, 1968-70; suffragan bishop Va., 1970—. Bd. govs. St. Stephen's Sch., Alexandria; trustee Diocese of Va. Ch. Schs. Served to capt. AUS, 1942-46. Decorated Bronze Star. Home: 920 Vicar Lane Alexandria VA 22302 Office: 4800 Fillmore Av Alexandria VA 22311

SMITH, PRESTON, gov. Texas; b. Williamson County, Tex., Mar. 8, 1912; s. Charles Kirby and Effie Mae (Strickland) S.; B.B.A., Tex. Tech. Coll., 1934; m. Ima Mae Smith, June 20, 1935; children—Preston Michael, Jan Lauren. Owner motion picture theatres in Tex., 1936—; mem. Tex. Ho. of Reps., 1944-50, Tex. Senate, 1957-63; lt. gov. Tex., 1963-69, gov., 1969—. Active local United Fund, A.R.C., Salvation Army. Mem. Lubbock C. of C. Democrat. Kiwanian. Home: Gov's Mansion Austin TX 78701 Office: 105 College St Lubbock TX 79401 also Capitol Station Austin TX 78711

SMITH, RANKIN MCEACHERN, football exec., ins. co. exec.; b. Atlanta, Oct. 29, 1925; ed. Emory U., U. Ga. With Life Ins. Co. Ga., 1957—, sr. v.p., 1968—; chmn. bd. Atlanta Falcons football team. Trustee U. Ga. Found., Reinhardt Coll.; bd. dirs. Ga. Heart Assn. Mem. Atlanta C. of C. (dir.), Atlanta Assn. Life Underwriters, Chi Phi. Methodist. Mason (Shriner). Home: 3470 Tuxedo Rd NW Atlanta GA 30305 Office: 521 Capital Av SW Atlanta GA 30312

SMITH, RAY S., speaker Ark. Ho. of Reps. Office: State Legislature Little Rock AR 72201*

SMITH, RAYFORD HAROLD, dentist; b. Scottsboro, Ala., Apr. 21, 1922; s. John Arvel and Frances (Guffey) S.; D.D.S., U. Mo., 1953; m. Irene Mary Kay, Nov. 4, 1944; children—Joyce (Mrs. Harold Russell Knight), Rayford Harold. Practice gen. dentistry, Sapulpa, Okla., 1953—; mem. staff Bartlett Meml. Hosp., Sapulpa. Served to capt. USAAF, 1941-46. Mem. Okla., Am. dental assns., Am. Soc. Dentistry for Children, Acad. Gen. Dentistry, C. of C., Jr. C. of C. (v.p. 1956), Xi Psi Phi, Alpha Chi. Baptist. Kiwanian. Home: 929 Luker Lane Sapulpa OK 74066 Office: 17 S Poplar St Sapulpa OK 74066

SMITH, RAYMOND ALFRED, furniture mfg. co. exec.; b. Mount Airy, N.C., July 4, 1924; s. James Raymond and Annie James (Hadley) S.; grad. Woodberry Forest Sch., 1942; B.A. in Bus. Adminstrn., Duke, 1945; m. Love Banner Diffee, June 10, 1950; children—James Raymond II, Michael David. Dir., sec.-treas. Nat. Furniture Co., Inc., Mount Airy, N.C., 1953-72, v.p., 1972—; dir. Northwestern Bank, Mount Airy. Mem. Mount Airy urban Redevel. Commn., 1959-63; treas. Mount Airy-Surry Count Airport Authority, 1963—; chmn. adv. bd. Surry Community Coll. Nursing Sch., 1969-70; pres. No. Surry Hosp. Found., 1969. Bd. dirs. Mount Airy Youth Found., Reeves YMCA. Named Young Man of Year, Jr. C. of C., 1955. Mem. So. Furniture Mfrs. Assn. (dir. 1961—). Methodist (steward 1955—, bldg. fund chmn. 1960—). Rotarian. Club: Mount Airy Country (dir. 1948-65). Home: 1309 Crescent Dr Mount Airy NC 27030 Office: 215 Factory St Mount Airy NC 27030

SMITH, RICHARD ELDON, hotel exec.; b. Arlington, Mo., 29, 1922; s. Walter 29 922; s. Walter Cash and Arlie Ruth (Gregory) S.; student U. Ill., 1943-44, So. Ill. U., 1944-46; B.S., Mo. State Coll., 1948; postgrad. U. Colo., 1962-63, U. Denver, 1963; m. Maralyn Louise Shackelford, July 27, 1962; children—Shelly Margaret, Sean Gregory. Instr. bus. edn. Morgan Park Mil. Acad., Chgo., 1948-52; hotel mgr. Am. Hotel Corp., N.Y.C., 1952-58; instr., acting coordinator bus. edn. pub. schs. Denver, 1958-64; innkeeper Holiday Inns, Inc., Los Angeles, 1964-66, asso. dir. personnel, 1966-68, dir. personnel, 1968-69, v.p. personnel, Memphis, 1969—. Instr. calculating machines U. Denver, 1961. Bd. dirs. corps. divs. campaigns Shelby United Neighbors, Memphis. Pres., Com. on Hiring Handicapped, Washington, 1971. Mem. Memphis Employers Merit Employment Assn., Nat. Alliance Bus. Men, Memphis Personnel Assn., Am. Soc. Personnel Adminstrs., Conf. Personnel Officers (sec.-treas. 1970-71, pres. 1971-72), Am. Hotel Assn. (planning com. 1969-71), Nu Epsilon Alpha. Episcopalian. Mason. Home: 2292 Lynnfield Rd Memphis TN 38138 Office: 3742 Lamar Av Memphis TN 38118

SMITH, RICHARD THOMAS, educator; b. Oklahoma City, Apr. 15, 1924; s. Harvey Taylor and Rachel (Grant) S.; student U. Tex., 1941-44; M.D., Tulane U., 1950; m. Jean Whisenant, Aug. 7, 1946; children—Mary Schell, Richard Thomas, Joseph Ryan, John Taylor, Claudia Jane. Intern pediatrics U. Minn. Hosps., 1950-51; resident pediatrics U. Minn., 1951-52, Helen Hay Whitney research fellow, 1952-55, asst. prof. pediatrics, 1955-57; research fellow NRC, 1952-53; sr. investigator Nat. Arthritis and Rheumatism Found., 1955-60; asso. prof. pediatrics U. Tex., Southwestern Med. Sch., 1957-58; prof. pediatrics, chmn. dept. U. Fla., 1958-67; chief pediatrics U. Fla. Teaching Hosp. and Clinics; prof., chmn. dept. pathology U. Fla. Hosps., 1967—, also chief pathology; cons. to surgeon gen. USPHS. Served as lt. (j.g.) USNR, 1944-46. Recipient TOYM award U.S. Jr. C. of C. 1958; E. M. Johnson Research prize, 1963. Mem. So. Soc. Clin. Research, Soc. Pediatric Research, Am. Soc. Clin. Investigation Central Soc. Clin. Research, Am. Assn. Immunologists Soc. Exptl. Biology and Medicine, A.A.A.S., Am. Fedn. Clin. Research, Am. Pediatric Soc., Sigma Xi, Alpha Omega Alpha. Contbr. research, clin. papers to sci. periodicals. Home: 1704 SW 8th Dr Gainesville FL 32601

SMITH, ROBERT CORNELIUS, petroleum co. exec.; b. Hammond, Ind., Sept. 10, 1925; s. John Decatur and Grace (Kirtley) S.; student U. Tex., 1942-43; B.B.A., Tulane U., 1947, LL.B., 1948; m. Jeannette Vaughn Renegar, Dec. 23, 1944; children—Kirtley, Douglas, Vaughn, Calvin. Admitted to La. bar, 1948; with firm Milling, Godchaux, Saal & Milling, New Orleans, 1948-50; chief atty. criminal div. New Orleans Legal Aid Bur., 1951-53; atty. Amoco Prodn. Co., New Orleans, 1953—. Part-time instr. bus. law Tulane U., 1951-53. Vice pres. New Orleans Civic Council, 1967-69; pres. New Orleans Com. Pub. Edn., 1960-64; exec. com. New Orleans area Boy Scouts Am., 1969, council commr., 1971-72, mgr. nat. council, 1971-72; mem. Nat. Com. Support Pub. Schs., 1966—; mem. bd. Orleans Parish Schs., 1966—; pres. bd. New Orleans Pub. Schs., 1969-70. Bd. dirs. Assn. Retarded Children, 1967—, pres., 1972; bd. dirs. La. Sch. Bd. Assn. Served with USNR, 1943-46. Recipient Outstanding Scouter award Boy Scouts Am., 1966, Silver Beaver award 1972. Mem. La., New Orleans bar assns. Democrat. Baptist (deacon 1951—, chmn. bd. trustees 1963-65). Home: 1217 Webster St New Orleans LA 70118 Office: PO Box 50879 New Orleans LA 70150

SMITH, ROBERT F., state ofcl.; b. Limestone, Tenn., June 17, 1920; s. John C. and Nell (Shields) S.; student U. Tenn., East Tenn. State U.; m. Jean Cox; children—Carolyn, Patricia, Ann. Owner, operator Bob Smith Constrn. Co., Greeneville, Tenn., until 1970; former owner Keebler-Smith Hardware Co., Limestone; former comml., indsl. and residential real estate developer, automobile and farm supply co. exec.; dir. 1st Nat. Bank of Greeneville; commr. Tenn. Dept. Hwys., Nashville, 1971-72, Tenn. Dept. Transp., Nashville, 1972—. Dir., Johnson City Power Bd. Bd. dirs. Johnson City Meml Hosp., Washington County, Tenn. Served with AUS, World War II. Mem. Greeneville C. of C. (past pres., dir.), Ruritan (pres. 1961). Methodist. Mason (Shriner). Office: Room 817 State Highway Bldg Nashville TN 37219*

SMITH, ROBERT FENTON, dentist; b. Canton, O., Mar. 19, 1928; s. French Nestor and Martha (Matheney) S.; B.S., Tex. A. and T. U., 1960; D.D.S., Baylor U., 1954; m. Wilma Jayne Thrall, Jan. 30, 1949; children—Leslie Karen, Jana Denise, Elizabeth Anne. Gen. practice dentistry, Harlingen, Tex., 1956-58, Austin, Tex., 1958—; mem. Austin staff Brackenridge Hosp.; founder East Austin Indigent Children Dental Clinic, 1964. Mem. human opportunities com. Austin Community Council, 1965. Served with USNR, 1954-56. Mem. Tex. Acad. Gen. Dentistry, Am., Tex. dental assns., Austin Dist. Dental Soc. (pres. 1968). Methodist (mem. ch. bd.). Kiwanian. Home: 3413 Shinoak St Austin TX 78731 Office: 508 W 13th St Austin Tx 78701

SMITH, ROBERT JACKSON BATES, JR., govt. ofcl.; b. Augusta, Ga., Nov. 9, 1941; s. Robert Jackson Bates and Mary (Willis) S.; B.B.S., U. Ga., 1963, LL.B., 1965; m. Kittie Potter Graham, Aug. 11, 1962; children— Robert Jackson Bates III, Samuel T.G., Mary Willis. Admitted to Ga. bar, 1965; partner firm Yow, Lee & Smith, Augusta, 1966-67; partner Allgood & Childs, Augusta, 1968-69; U.S. atty. So. Dist. Ga., 1969—. Part time instr. law Augusta Coll., 1966-69. Legal counsel, mem. exec. com. Richmond County (Ga.), 1967-69. Bd. dirs. Augusta Easter Seal Soc., 1965-69, 1st v.p. 1967-68. Named Outstanding Young Man of Richmond County, Jr. C. of C., 1969-70. Mem. Am., Augusta, Fed. bar assns., Augusta Trial Lawyers Assn., Phi Alpha Delta. Home: 1138 Glenn Av Augusta GA 30904 Office: PO Box 1703 Augusta GA 30903

SMITH, ROBERT SELLERS, lawyer; b. Samson, Ala., July 31, 1931; s. Abb Jackson and Rose (Sellers) S.; B.S., U. Va., 1953; LL.B., 1958; m. June Claire West, Feb. 2, 1963; children—Robert Sellers, David West, Rosemary True. Admitted to Ala. bar, 1959; asst. counsel spl. com. to investigate campaign expenditures U.S. Ho. of Reps., 1960; counsel U.S. Senate Labor and Pub. Welfare Com., 1961-63; gen. practice, Huntsville, Ala., 1963—; partner Smith & Huckaby. Instr. econs., Am. econ. history U. Ala., 1963-64. Mem. industry adv. com., select com. on small bus. U.S. Senate; pres. Legal Aid Soc. Madison County. Served with USN, 1953-57. Mem. Am., Ala. bar assns., Assn. Huntsville Area Cos. Episcopalian. Elk, Kiwanian. Author: Alabama Legal Forms Annotated; Modern Office Forms for Lawyers. Home: 1007 Cleermont Dr Huntsville AL 35801 Office: State Nat Bank Bldg Huntsville AL 35801

SMITH, ROBERT SULLINS, physician; b. Del Rio, Tenn., May 28, 1929; s. Robert Taylor and Ollie Lillie (Moore) S.; B.S., Randolph-Macon Coll., 1951; M.D., Med.Coll. Va., 1956; m. Nancy Virginia Kibler, Aug. 26, 1950; children—Carol, Michelle, Robert Sullins, Janet. Intern, Mercy Hosp., Springfield, O., 1956-57; gen. practice medicine Dinwiddie, Va., 1958-69; Va. med. examiner, med. examiner FAA, Dinwiddie, 1958-69, State Va., Dinwiddie County, Dinwiddie, 1958—; mem. staff Petersbury (Va.) Hosp., Mem. Va. Com. Study Abortion, 1969-70, Physician Shortage, 1970-71. Vice pres. Dinwiddie Citizens Orgn. for Better Edn. and Other Improvements, 1963-64. Bd. dirs. Ruritan Civic and Recreation Assn., John Tyler Community Coll., Chester, Va. Served to capt. M.C., USAF, 1957-58. Named Most Outstanding Sr. Citizen Dinwiddie County, 4 Ruritan clubs Dinwiddie County, 1964. Diplomate Am. Bd. Family Practice. Mem. Randolph Macon Alumni Assn., A.M.A., 4th Dist., Va. med. socs., Va. (sec. 1970—), Tri City Area (pres. 1968-71), Am. acads. gen. practice, Acad. Family Practice, Va., Am. med. polit. action coms., Med. Coll. Va. Alumni Assn., Am. Coll. Emergency Physicians, Va. Council Health and Med. Care, Omicron Delta Kappa, Chi Beta Phi, Beta Beta Beta, Alpha Sigma Chi, Lamba Chi Alpha, Theta Kappa Psi. Methodist. Mason. Club: Walter Hines Page. Address: Route 1 Box 16 Dinwiddie VA 23841

SMITH, ROGER CROWELL, psychologist; b. Pitts., May 28, 1937 Arthur Crowell and Mabel (Fields) S.; A.B., U. Ky., 1960, M.S., 1963, Ph.D., 1967; m. Alice Ann Champion, July 14, 1962. Research asst. dept. psychology U. Ky., Lexington, 1960-64, intern clin. psychology, 1964-65, teaching asst., 1965-66; instr. U. Tex., El Paso, 1967-68; chief clin. psychology, learning processes research psychology lab. Civil Aero. Inst., FAA, Oklahoma City, 1968—. Cons. Family Service, El Paso, 1967-70, Child Treatment Center, El Paso, 1967-68, adolescent clinic Children's Meml. Hosp., Oklahoma City, 1970—, com. psychiat. evaluation pilots Flying Physicians Assn., 1969—; adj. asso. prof. med. psychology U. Okla. Sch. Medicine, Oklahoma City, 1968—, adj. asso. prof. child psychology, 1970—, adj. asso. prof. psychology, Norman, 1972—. Served with AUS, 1966-68. Recipient Certificate Achievement; USPHS fellow, 1960-64. Mem. Am., Midwestern, Southwestern, Western, Okla. (editor Newsletter 1972—) psychol. assns., A.A.A.S., Aerospace Med. Assn., Psychonomic Soc., Assn. Aviation Psychologists, N.Y. Acad. Scis., U. Ky. Alumni Assn. (dir.), Okla. State Bd. Examiners Psychologists (vice chmn.), Sigma Xi. Contbr. articles to profl. jours. Home: 1217 N Glade Av Oklahoma City OK 73127 Office: AAC-118 CAMI-FAA PO Box 25082 Oklahoma City OK 73125

SMITH, ROLAND, clergyman; b. Decatur, Ga., Feb. 26, 1902; s. Anderson and Mattie (Beauman) S.; A.B., Morehouse Coll., 1929, D.D., 1967; D.D., Selma U., 1944; D.D. (hon), Allen U., 1952, Morris Brown Coll., 1958; LL.D., Ark. Bapt. Coll., 1958; A.M., Atlanta U., 1961; m. Mary Shepard. Ordained to ministry Bapt. Ch., 1924; pastor Met. Ch., Columbus, Ga., 1929-31, First Ch., Tuscaloosa, Ala., 1931-36, Macon, Ga., 1936-37, First Bapt. Ch., Little Rock, 1947-66; statistician Nat. Bapt. Conv. U.S.A., 1932-54; sec. Nat. Bapt. Tng. Bd., So. Bapt. Tng. Bd., 1954-57; sec. Negro work Home Mission Bd., 1942-49. Bd. dirs. Nat. Bapt. Conv. U.S.A. Chmn. bd., exec. officer Citizens Bldg. Corp. Atlanta; dir. Citizens Trust Co., S.E. Fidelity Fire Ins. Co., Atlanta. Recipient Human Relations award Phi Beta Sigma, 1950, Golden Leaf award Ga. State U., Atlanta, 1971. Mem. Fed. Council Chs. of Christ in Am. (exec. com.), World Bapt. Alliance Relief Commn., Joint Commn. Pub. Affairs for Bapts. Am., Little Rock Ministerial Assn. (pres. 1956), Kappa Alpha Psi, Sigma Rho. Mason. Editor: Ga. Bapt. Home: 1337 Thurgood St SW Atlanta GA 30314

SMITH, RUSSELL CALVIN, city ofcl.; b. Haines City, Fla., Feb. 26, 1925; s. George Rosse and Grace (Kelly) S.; B.S. in C.E., U. Fla., 1950; M.S. in Mgmt., Rollins Coll., 1971; m. Frances E. McGehee, Sept. 4, 1949; children—Stephen Kelly, Holly Elizabeth. Constrn. engr. Bur. Reclamation, Grand Coulee, Wash., 1950-51; asst. city engr. City Daytona Beach, Fla., 1953-55, city engr., 1955-63, dir. pub. works, 1963-68, dir. pub. services, 1968-71, city mgr., 1971—. Served to 1st lt. USAF, 1942-46, 1951-52. Decorated D.F.C., Air medal with two oak leaf clusters. Registered profl. engr., Fla. Mem. Am. Pub. Works Assn. (chpt. pres. 1970), U. Fla. Alumni (pres. 1969), Internat. City Mgmt. Assn., Jr. C. of C. (first v.p. 1960), Fla. Engring. Soc. Presbyn. Rotarian. Club: Daytona Beach Quarterback. Home: 536 S Seneca Blvd Daytona Beach FL 32014 Office: 209 Orange Av Daytona Beach FL 32014

SMITH, RUSSELL KIETH, govt. ofcl.; b. Fullerton, Neb., Jan. 27, 1917; s. Charles James and Anna Marie (Murray) S.; B.S., Colo. State U., 1932; m. Margie Marie Reed, May 1, 1954; children—Keith, Kurt, Kevin, Kathleen. Forest entomologist U.S. Forest Service, Denver, 1933-37, dist. forest ranger, Custer, S.D., 1937-42, forest supr., Neb. Nat. Forest, Lincoln, 1947-52, br. chief, forest entomologist div. forest pest control, Washington, 1955-58, fgn. relations, Afghanistan br., Washington, 1953-54, chief div. forest pest control S.E. area, 1966-69, asst. area dir. environmental protection and improvement, Southeast area, Atlanta, 1969—. Served with AUS, 1942-46. Recipient Superior Service award Dept. Agr., 1966. Mem. Entomol. Soc. Am. Home: 2372 Brookhurst Dr Chamblee GA 30341 Office: 1720 Peachtree Rd NW Atlanta GA 30309

SMITH, SAM, gas co. exec.; b. Hazel Green, Ky., Feb. 11, 1927; s. Sam J. and Nannie (Rose) S.; student U. Tex., El Paso, 1947-48; LL.B., U. Ky., 1951; m. Kenadean Mabel Wright, Oct. 19, 1946; children—Sandra Lynette, Brenda Carol, Samuel Vance, Laura Jeanette. Admitted to Ky. bar, 1951; with El Paso Natural Gas Co. (Tex.), 1952—, dir. exploration, 1966—. Mem. mgmt. com. Geonuclear Nobel Paso and co. rep. to Atomic Indsl. Forum, Inc., 1967—. Served with AUS, 1945-46. Mem. Am. Assn. Petroleum Landmen, Ind. Producers Assn. Am., Rocky Mountain, N.M. oil and gas assns., Ky. Bar Assn., Phi Delta Phi. Home: 1200 Cincinnati St El Paso TX 79902 Office: 304 Texas St El Paso TX 79999

SMITH, SAM MAYER, childrens home adminstr.; b. Saluda, S.C., Oct. 24, 1907; s. Robert Louis and Happie (Berry) S.; A.B., Furman U., 1930, H.H.D., 1958; postgrad. N.Y. Sch. Social Work, 1932; m. Ann Wilkerson, Apr. 2, 1936; children—June (Mrs. Henry Summerall, Jr.), Jeanie (Mrs. C.G. Mitchell), Mary Linca (Mrs. James M. Holt, Jr.). Field rep. Connie Maxwell Children's Home, Greenwood, S.C., 1930-36, asso. supt., 1937-46, supt., treas., 1946—. Chmn., Juvenile and Family Ct., Greenwood, 1956-62; mem. adv. bd. Child Welfare League Am., N.Y.C., 1962-67. Named Man of Year, Greenwood Rotary, 1968, Greenville Lions, 1969. Mem. Child Care Assn. So. Bapts. (pres.), Southeastern Child Care Assn. (pres.), S.C. Bapt. Conv. (pres.), S.C. Conf. Social Work (pres.), Nat. Assn. Social Workers. Rotarian (pres. Greenwood club, dist. gov.). Home: Timberlake Greenwood SC 29646 Office: Connie Maxwell Childrens Home Greenwood SC 29646

SMITH, SAMUEL BOYD, educator; b. Adams, Tenn., Oct. 23, 1929; s. Carl S. and Annie (Tolleson) S.; student Milligan Coll., 1947-48, U. Tenn., 1948-49, Syracuse U., 1951-52; B.S., Peabody Coll., 1956; M.A., Vanderbilt U., 1960, Ph.D., 1962; m. Martha Sue Fitzsimmons, Dec. 23, 1956; children—David Fitzsimmons, Mark Tolleson, Stephen Boyd. Asst. prof. history U. South Fla., 1961-64; state librarian and archivist, chmn. Tenn. Hist. Commn., 1964-69; asso. prof. History, U. Tenn., Knoxville, 1969-72, prof., 1972—; lectr. history Peabody Coll., 1965-66. Served with USAF 1951-54. Mem. Am. Hist. Assn., Orgn. Am. Historians Tenn. Hist. Socs., So. Hist. Assn. Democrat. Methodist. Editor Andrew Jackson Papers. Home: 1801 Kingsbury Dr Knoxville TN 37919

SMITH, SAMUEL ELBERT, JR., dentist; b. Fordoche, La., Oct. 14, 1922; s. Samuel Elbert and Andrea (Vedross) S.; student La. State U., 1939-40, La. Poly. U., 1941, Southwestern La. Inst., 1941-43, U. Chgo., 1943-44; D.D.S., Emory U., 1948; postgrad. U. So. Cal., 1952, U. Ind., 1966; m. Mary Martin Brown, May 3, 1941; children—Lauree Faith, Samuel Kemper; m. 2d, Eva Mae Jackson, July 22, 1972. Practice gen. dentistry, Shreveport, La., 1948-51, 54—; mem. staff Confederate Meml. Med. Center, Pines Sanitarium, Highland, Willis-Knighten Meml. hosps. Dir. dental asst. tng. program La. Dept. Edn., temporary chmn. 4th Dist., State La., 1958; instr. pilot sch. Vocational Sch., Shreveport, 1948—. Speaker Americanism forum P.T.A., 1955—; mem. John Birch Soc., 1967-69. Bd. dirs. YMCA, Shreveport. Served with inf. AUS, 1942-44, Dental Corps, USNR, 1951-53; PTO. Mem. Am., La. dental assns., 4th Dist. Dental Soc., Internat. Acad. Orthodontics, Am. Legion, Gideons Internat., Delta Sigma Delta. Democrat. Baptist. Clubs: East Ridge Country, Shreveport Parks and Recreation. Home: 3825 Pines Rd Shreveport LA 71108 Office: 3834 Southern Av Shreveport LA 71106

SMITH, SAMUEL IRBY, dentist; b. in Whiteville, N.C., July 18, 1937; s. Statford Samuel and Dolphine (Irby) S.; A.B., U. N.C., 1961; D.D.S., 1965; m. Elizabeth Ann Thomason, June 7, 1957; 1 dau., Julie Ann. Practice dentistry, Roanoke Rapids, N.C., 1966—. Mem. Am., N.C. dental socs., Am. Profl. Practice Assn., Am. Analgesia Soc., Acad. Gen. Dentistry, Holland (sec.), H.E.N. study clubs, N.C. Wildlife Fedn., N.C. Assn. Professions, Ducks Unltd., Southeastern Analgesia Soc. (charter). Clubs: Occaneechee 2 (Halifax); Chockeyotte Country (Roanoke Rapids). Home: 129 Valley Dr Roanoke Rapids NC 27870 Office: 1048 E 10th St Roanoke Rapids NC 27870

SMITH, SHEARN, judge; b. Port Arthur, Tex., Oct. 27, 1927; s. John Barkley and Beulah (Oldham) S.; J.D., U. Houston, 1951; m. Annell Schaefer, Apr. 11, 1954; children—Ronald, Donald, Cheryl, Shearn. Admitted to Tex. bar, 1951; practiced in Houston, 1951-68; judge 61st Dist. Ct., Harris County, Tex., 1968—. Bd. dirs. Ben Taub County Hosp. Served with A.C., USNR, 1946-48. Mem. State Bar Tex., Houston Bar Assn., Trial Lawyers Assn. (past pres.). Lutheran. Mason. Home: 315 Rainier Dr Houston TX 77024 Office: Civil Courts Bldg Houston TX 77002

SMITH, SIDNEY M., securities co. exec.; b. Anniston, Ala., Dec. 25, 1904; s. Columbus and Sallie (March) S.; B.S., in M.E., Ga. Sch. Tech., 1927; m. Adele Metzler, June 6, 1939; children—Wendy (Mrs. Charles Sheron), Cathie. Vice pres. Clement A. Evans & Co., Inc. investment bankers, Atlanta, 1933-60; v.p., Robinson-Humphrey Co., Inc., Atlanta, 1960—; also dir.; asso. mem. N.Y. Stock Exchange, 1952—; pres., dir. Traffic Equipment Co., Atlanta, 1941—, Interstate Bond Co., Chgo., 1968—. Trustee Levi Nat. Meml. Hosp., Hot Springs, Ark. Mem. Commerce Club. Mem. B'nai B'rith. Club: Standard Town and Country. Home: 3680 Tuxedo Rd NW Atlanta GA 30305 Office: 2 Peachtree St NE Atlanta GA 30303

SMITH, SIDNEY OSLIN, JR., judge; b. Gainesville, Ga., Dec. 30, 1923; s. Sidney O. and Isabelle (Charters) S.; student Middlesex Sch., 1938-41; A.B. cum laude, Harvard, 1947; LL.B. summa cum laude, U. Ga., 1949; m. Patricia Irwin Horkan, Aug. 4, 1944; children—Charters, Ellen, Sidney Oslin III. Admitted to Ga. bar, 1948; mem. firm Sloan & Telford, Gainesville, 1949-51; partner Telford, Wayne & Smith, Gainesville, 1951-62; asst. solitor gen. Northeastern circuit, Ga., 1951-61; judge Superior Ct., 1962-65; U.S. judge No. Dist. Ga., 1965—, chief judge 1968—. Mem. Ga. Bd. Bar Examiners, 1961-62. Chmn., Gainesville Bd. Edn., 1959-62. Trustee Gainesville Art Assn. Served to capt C.E., AUS, 1943-46; ETO. Mem. Am., Ga., Gainesville bar assns., Phi Beta Kappa, Phi Delta Theta, Phi Delta Phi, Phi Kappa Phi. Democrat. Episcopalian (vestryman, sr. warden 1962). Rotarian. Clubs: Hasty Pudding, Owl, Chattahoochee Country (Gainesville); Atlanta Athletic, Capital City. Home: 2541 Club Dr NW Gainesville GA 30501 Office: Fed Bldg Gainesville GA 30501

SMITH, STARR, pub. relations firm exec.; b. Kosciusko, Miss., Aug. 24, 1917; s. Floyd Rowan and Myrtle (Davis) S.; B.A., U. Ala., 1952, M.A., 1953; m. Virginia R. Seifert, July 15, 1942; 1 dau., Sandra Starr (Mrs. Scott Miller). Polit. writer Press-Register, Mobile, Ala., 1947-49; corr. Newsweek mag., Mobile, Atlanta, 1949-50, NBC, Chgo., N.Y.C., Washington, 1953-54; dir. pub. relations Portland Cement Assn., Montgomery, 1955-60; owner, prin. Starr Smith Pub. Relations, Montgomery, Ala., 1960—. Instr. creative writing U. Ala., Montgomery, 1957—; asso. editor South mag., 1967-70; lectr., writer, producer-moderator TV, 1961—. Candidate Democratic party 2d Dist. Ala., U.S. Congress, 1962. Mem. adv. bd. St. Margaret's Hosp., Montgomery, 1971—. Served with USAAF, 1941-47; ETO. Decorated Air Force Commendation medal with one oak leaf cluster. Mem. Nat. Press Club, Pub. Relations Soc. Am., Air Force Assns, Res. Officers Assn., V.F.W., Am. Legion, Sigma Delta Chi. Democrat. Clubs: Montgomery Country; The Club (Birmingham). Home: 2103 Campbell Rd Montgomery AL 36111

SMITH, THOMAS BAKER, JR., architect; b. New Orleans, Nov. 7, 1929; s. Thomas Baker and Odelia (Wright) S.; high sch diploma, Marion, Inst., Ala., 1949; B.Arch., Auburn U., 1959; m. Frances Kirk Jones, Mar. 14, 1959. Pvt. archtl. practice, numerous residential, comml. and instl. bldgs., New Orleans, 1960—. Cons. architect Eastside and Westside brs. Bank of Terre bonne & Trust Co., Houma, La., Am. Bank & Trust Co., Houma, Fed. Land Bank New Orleans. Served with USAF, 1953-57; maj. Res. Mem. Mem. A.I.A., La. Assn. Architects, C. of C. Episcopalian (vestry, jr. warden). Home: 5353 Perrier St New Orleans LA 70115 Office: 5350 Perrier St New Orleans LA 70115

SMITH, THOMAS PIERCE, JR., accountant; b. Orlando, Fla., July 30, 1926; s. Thomas Pierce and Ethel (Payne) S.; B.S. in Bus. Adminstrn., Fla. State U., 1949; m. Mary Mildred Bowman, Feb. 23, 1958. Mem. staff M.A. Montenegro & Co., Tampa, Fla., 1950-70, partner firm, 1961-70; prin. firm Arthur Young & Co., Tampa, 1970—. Treas., Tampa Area Mental Health Bd. Bd. dirs. Guidance Center Hillsborough County, Fla. Kiwanis Found. Served with USNR, 1944-46. C.P.A., Fla. Mem. Am., Fla. insts. C.P.A.'s, Delta Tau Delta. Kiwanian (sec. Temple Terrace, Fla. 1961-65, pres. 1966; lt. gov. Fla. dist. 1970-71). Home: 7123 Woodfield Dr Tampa FL 33617 Office: PO Box 789 Tampa FL 33601

SMITH, THURMAN G., ednl. adminstr.; b. Poughkeepsie, Ark., Feb. 2, 1920; s. Allen G. and Ada (Freeman) S.; B.S. in Edn., Ark. Coll., 1948; M.Ed., U. Ark., 1955, Diploma Advanced Study, 1965; m. Etta U. John, Feb. 24, 1947; children—Charles, Thurman, Ann, John. Prin. Cave City (Ark.) Sch. Dist., 1952-56; supt. Vandale (Ark.) Sch. Dist., 1956-57; adminstrv. asst. Springdale (Ark.) Sch. Dist., 1957-63, supt., 1963—. Served with USCGR, 1942-45. Mem. Am. Assn. Sch. Adminstrs., N.E.A., Ark. Edn. Assn., Northwest Ark. Schoolmasters Club, Ark. Sch. Adminstrs. Assn., C. of C., Rotarian. Home: PO Box 385 307 Sanders St Springdale AR 72764 Office: 202 W Emma St Springdale AR 72764

SMITH, TOM E., oil co. exec.; b. Burlington, Tex., Dec. 18, 1908; s. Vinny L. and Carrie A. (Barnes) S.; B.S., So. Meth. U., 1929; M.D., Baylor U., 1933; m. Marianna McKamy, June 2, 1937; children—McKamy, Tom, Marianna (Mrs. Jerry Powell), Sally (Mrs. Dan Wolfe). Intern, Baylor U. Hosp., Dallas, 1933-34; resident St. Mark's Hosp., London, Eng., 1934-35; practice medicine specializing in proctology, Dallas, 1935-64, Tyler, Tex., 1965-69; mem. staff various hosps.; ret. from medicine, 1969; sr. v.p. Harding Oil Co., Dallas, 1962—, dir. corporate planning and research, 1971—. Asso. prof. proctology Baylor U., 1935-42. Dir. Middle Sabine River Authority, 1971—. Served to lt. col. AUS, 1942-46. Fellow A.C.S., Am. Proctologic Soc.; mem. Tyler C. of C. (v.p. bd. dirs. 1968-71), Alpha Omega Alpha, Lambda Chi Alpha, Phi Chi. Rotarian (dist. gov. 1959-60); Mason (Shriner, Jester). Clubs: Willowbrook Country, Petroleum (Tyler); Northwood Country, Chaparral (Dallas). Home: River Hills Ranch Box 4447 Tyler TX 75701 Office: 4317 Oak Lawn St Dallas TX 75219

SMITH, TOMMY VERNON, state govt. ofcl.; b. Austin, Tex., Jan. 29, 1938; s. Chester V. and Agnes (Eck) S.; B.E.E., U. Tex., 1961; m. Sharon Lynn Andrewartha, Sept. 27, 1958; children—Steven Randall, Cynthia Lynn. Maintenance engr. Dover Elevator Co., Austin, 1958-65; chief dep. Tex. Bur. Labor Statistics, Austin, 1966-67, adminstrv. head, 1967, acting commr., 1967-69, commr., 1969—. Mem. N.G., 1955-58. Mem. Elevator Constrn. Union (rec. sec., bus. rep. 1958-65). Home: 7704 Gault St Austin TX 78757 Office: PO Box T Capitol Sta Austin TX 78711

SMITH, TROY A., civil engr.; b. Sylvatus, Va., July 4, 1922; s. Wade Hampton and Augusta Mabel (Lindsey) S.; B.C.E., U. Va., 1948; M.S. in Engring., U. Mich., 1952, Ph.D. in Engring. Mechanics, 1970. Structural engr. C.E., U.S. Army, 1948-59; chief structural engr. Brown Engring Co., Inc., Huntsville, Ala., 1959-60; structural research engr., then aerospace engr. U.S. Army Missile Command, Redstone Arsenal, Ala., 1960—. Served with USNR, 1942-46. Registered profl. engr., Va., Ala. Mem. Soc. Am. Mil. Engrs., Sigma Xi (asso.). Elk. Contbr. tech. articles to profl. jours. Home: 2406 Bonita Dr SW Huntsville AL 35801 Office: Directorate of Research Devel Engring and Missile Systems Lab US Army Missile Command Redstone Arsenal AL 35809

SMITH, TRUMAN WALLACE, nursing center exec.; b. Hollis, Okla., Mar. 24, 1933; s. Lee Franklin and Mamie Vera (Prock) S.; student Okla. U., 1951-52; B.S., Southwestern State Coll., 1955; m. E. Jane Smith, Oct. 20, 1952; children—Joe Bruce, Danna Lynn, Lee Franklin II. Pres., chmn. bd. Pioneer Nursing Centers, Inc., Frederick, Okla., 1964—; dir. Parker Sq. State Bank, Wichita Falls, Tex. Mem. Distinguished Athletes Assn., Nat. Assn. Intercollegiate Athletics. Lion. Club: Quarterback (pres. 1971-72) (Frederick). Home: 520 N 18th St Frederick OK 73542 Office: 108 S 10th St Frederick OK 73542

SMITH, VANETTA VAN GEEM (MRS. JOSEPH CLINTON SMITH, JR.), govt. ofcl.; b. Eastland, Tex.; d. John Stuart and Levie (Roper) Van Geem; student Tex. State Coll. for Women, 1946-47, Am. U., 1948, 49, 57-59, 61-62; m. Joseph Clinton Smith, Jr., June 23, 1951; children—Joseph Clinton III, David Van Geem, Stevan Robert. Lab. technician's aide FBI, Washington, 1944-46; mgr. Tarr System, Inc., Washington, Kansas City, Mo., 1948, 49; clerical asst. Dept. State, 1950-56, supr. adjudication, 1956-58; chief processing br. Passport Office, Dept. State, Washington, 1958-61, asst. chief domestic adjudication br., Passport Office, 1961-66, staff asst. to div. chief, 1966-69, chief passport telephone information sect., 1969-71, staff asst. to div. chief, 1971—. Mem. Soc. for Personnel Adminstrn., Pi Sigma Alpha. Home: 5607 Westgate Lane Lanham MD 20801 Office: Passport Office 1425 K St NW Washington DC 20524

SMITH, VIRGIL, musician; b. Bridgeton, Ind., Dec. 13, 1902; s. Charles F. and Alta (Humphrey) S.; Mus. B., Am. Conservatory Music, Chgo., 1929, Mus. M., 1942; pvt. studies piano with Egon Petri, 1944; m. Alice Stephenson, Dec. 29, 1933; 1 dau., Anita Louise. Head piano dept. Memphis Conservatory Music, 1929-33; tchr. piano and theory Memphis Coll. Music, 1933-35; dir. music Coker Coll., Hartsville, S.C., 1935-72; pianist, condr. in concerts and recitals; dir. choir First Bapt. Ch., Hartsville, 1963-64; dir. choir 1st Presbyn. Ch., Hartsville, 1972—. Chmn. adv. bd. Hartsville Arts Council. Mem. Hartsville Community Concerts Assn. (v.p.), Corr. Chess League Am., Am. Assn. U. Profs. (chpt. pres. 1961-63), Nat. Fedn. Music Clubs, Music Tchrs. Nat. Assn., S.C. Music Tchrs. Assn. (pres. 1968-70), U.S. Chess Fedn. Rotarian. Home: 510 Richardson Circle East Hartsville SC 29550

SMITH, WALTER GOLD, mech. engr.; b. Palmyra, Va., July 19, 1919; s. Wilmer Irwin and Luster (Gold) S.; B.S., Duke, 1941; m. Kathryn Felton, July 20, 1943; 1 son, Walter Gregory. Design engr. Westinghouse Electric Co., Balt., 1946-47; v.p. foundry Walter James Corp., Durham, N.C., 1947-49; engr. Arrow Plumbing & Heating Co., Durham, 1949-53; mem. faculty Duke, 1953-54; cons. engr., Durham, N.C., 1954—. Served to lt. comdr. USNR, 1941-45. Registered profl. engr., N.C., Va., S.C., Fla. Mem. Nat., N.C. socs. profl. engrs., N.C. Soc. Engrs., Durham Engrs. Club. Clubs: Durham City (past dir.), Durham Wildlife, Sertoma. Home: 507 Brookwood Dr Durham NC 27707 Office: NC Bank Bldg PO Box 2165 Durham NC 27702

SMITH, WALTER TILFORD, shipbldg. co. exec.; b. Norfolk, Va., Oct. 9, 1907; s. Walter Edmond and Laura Alice (Griffin) S.; B.S. in Civil Engring., N.C. State Coll., 1929; grad. Coll. Indsl. Armed Forces, 1952, Advanced Mgmt. Program Harvard, 1955; m. Elizabeth Harriet Parrish, Aug. 20, 1933; 1 son, Walter Tilford. With Newport News Shipbldg. & Dry Dock Co. (Va.), 1929—, asst. to pres., 1962-63, v.p. charge prodn., 1963-64, exec. v.p., 1964-66, sr. v.p., 1966—, asst. to pres., 1969—; dir. Central Nat. Bank, Richmond, Va. Vice pres., dir., mem. exec. finance com. Shipbuilders Council Am. Met. chmn. for Nat. Alliance Businessmen, 1969—; vice chmn. Newport News chpt. A.R.C. Trustee Patrick Henry Hosp., Newport News, Penisula United Fund. Recipient Distinguished Engring. Alumnus award N.C. State U., 1966. Mem. Soc. Naval Architects and Marine Engrs., Am. Soc. Naval Engrs., Navy League U.S. (pres. Hampton Roads council 1972—), Nat. Def. Transp. Assn. (v.p.), N.A.M. (nat. def. com.), Va. C. of C. (chmn. nat. affairs com. 1970—), N.C. State Coll. Alumni Assn. (bd. dir.), Newcomen Soc., Engr.'s Club N.Y.C., Scabbard and Blade, Theta Tau, Phi Kappa Phi. Episcopalian. Lion. Clubs: Propeller U.S. (past pres. Newport News, past nat. v.p.), James River Country (dir., past pres. Newport News). Home: 129 James River Dr Newport News VA 23601 Office: Newport News Shipbldg & Dry Dock Co Newport News VA 23601

SMITH, WARREN HUNTINGTON, architect; b. Spokane Wash., Jan. 23, 1925; s. Earl Robert and Esther (Hines) S.; student Wash. State U., Pullman, 1942-43; B.Arch., U. Ore., 1949; M.Arch., Mass. Inst. Tech., 1950; m. Margaret Isabel Griffiths, June 17, 1949; children— Christopher Earl, Theodore Jesse. Architect, Bindon & Wright, architects, Seattle, 1950-55; project architect Arabian-Am. Oil Co., The Hague, Netherlands, 1955-57; chief architect Bechtel Assos., N.Y.C., 1957-60; mgr. bldg. product devel. U.S. Plywood Corp., N.Y.C., 1960-62; cons. architect Wellman-Lord Engring., Inc., Lakeland, Fla., 1962-64; prin. Warren H. Smith & Assos., Lakeland, 1964; now sr. partner Smith & Swilley, Architects, Lakeland. Chmn., City Lakeland Bd. Standards and Appeals; mem. pub. adv. panel on archtl. services Gen. Services Adminstrn.; mem. Polk County Citizen's Adv. Com. for Econ. Devel. Assistance. Bd. dirs., pres. Lakeland YMCA. Served with USAAF, 1943-45; ETO. Decorated Purple Heart; recipient Award for Excellence in Indsl. Design, Factory Mag., 1961. Mem. A.I.A. (corporate mem., pres. Polk County sect.), Nat. Soc. Interior Designers, Delta Upsilon. Episcopalian. Kiwanian. Clubs: Fla. Sailing Assn. (St. Petersburg); Imperial University (Lakeland), Lakeland Yacht. Prin. works include: Fla. Technol. U., Orlando Imperial U. Club, Lakeland, Sci. and Tech. Bldg. U. South Fla., Tampa. Home: 2725 Oakland Dr Lakeland FL 33803 Office: 2401 Florida Av Lakeland FL 33803

SMITH, WAYNE OSMER, dentist; b. Elyria, O., Nov. 15, 1926; s. Charles Gerald and Marjorie Elizabeth (Osmer) S.; student Princeton, 1946, Ohio U., 1947; B.S., Western Res. U., 1955, D.D.S., 1959; m. Yvonne Peairs, Sept. 5, 1952; children—Courtney, Bradord, Whitney, Kent. Endodontist, Jacksonville, Fla., 1959-61, West Palm Beach, Fla., 1961—. Pres., owner Ohio Battery Warehouse, Cleve., 1970—, Cumberland Batteries Inc. (Md.), 1968—; dir. endodentic sect. research group Palm Beach Jr. Coll., 1965—. Served as test pilot USNR, 1952-54. Diplomate Assn. Am. Endodontists (dir.). Mem. Am., Fla. dental socs., Psi Omega. Rotarian. Republican. Patentee fixed removal safety cover for outdoor swimming pool. Home: 222 Monterey Rd Palm Beach FL 33480 Office: Citizens Bldg West Palm Beach FL 33401

SMITH, WENDELL EUGENE, hardware wholesale co. exec.; b. Albuquerque, Nov. 4, 1909; s. Frank Joseph and Ollie (McDonald) S.; student W. Tex. State Coll., 1935; m. Esther Doris Evans, Sept. 29, 1928; 1 son, Wendell Eugene. With Morrow-Thomas Hardware Co., Amarillo, Tex., 1928-50, exec. v.p., 1942-50, gen. mgr., 1945-50; pres., chmn. bd. Okla. Hardware Co., Oklahoma City, 1951—, also dir.; chmn. bd. Nash Hardware Co., Fort Worth, 1962—, also dir. Mem. Oklahoma City Bond Adv. Com., Oklahoma City Symphony. Recipient Outstanding Achievement in Hardware Wholesaling award Canadian Wholesale Hardware Assn., 1959. Mem. Nat., So. wholesale hardware assns., Nat. Tax Equality Assn. (dir.), Oklahoma City C. of C., Frontiers of Sci. Republican. Mason (Shriner), Rotarian. Clubs: Petroleum, Sirloin, Touchdown. Home: 3400 Partridge Rd Oklahoma City OK 73120 Office: 31 E California St Oklahoma City OK 73125

SMITH, WENDELL ROWE, elec. engr.; b. Brownfield, Tex., Feb. 14, 1919; s. Fred Clarence and Mattie (Rowe) S.; student So. Meth. U., 1936-37; B.S., Tex. Tech. Coll., 1942; m. Montez Marie Hudson, May 29, 1968; children (by previous marriage)—Patricia Ann (Mrs. Richard L. Renko), Barbara Lea (Mrs. John E. Melde III), Wendell Kaye (Mrs. Jimmie Vaughan), Nancy Virginia (Mrs. Kim McGregor); stepchildren—Randall L. Howard, Jeri Sue Howard. Engr., Curtis Wright Corp., Louisville, 1943; tchr. Tex. Technol. Coll., Lubbock, 1944; computer Petty Geophys. Co., San Antonio, 1944; engr. Southwestern Pub. Service Co., Plainview, Tex., 1946-48, engr. Plains div., 1948—. Mem. Civil Def. Com., Plainview, 1964—, chmn., 1969—. Served with USNR, 1944-45; PTO. Registered profl. engr., Tex. Mem. I.E.E.E. (chpt. chmn. 1963-64), Hi Plains Geol. Soc. (pres. 1971—). Methodist. Mason (dist. dep. 1963); mem. Order Eastern Star. Home: 1200 Travis St Plainview TX 79072 Office: 304 W 6th St Plainview TX 79072

SMITH, WILLARD JOAL, wood processing co. exec.; b. Zanesville, O., Sept. 16, 1887; s. Joal Kirk and Laura (Hibbs) S.; student Ohio State U., 1966-67; m. Mayme Kinsall, Sept. 17, 1917 (dec.). Pres. W.J. Smith Wood Preserving Co., Denison, Tex., 1929—; chmn. bd. Citizens Nat. Bank, 1945—, Citizens Investment Co., Denison, 1951—; v.p. Fed. Bldg. & Loan Co., Denison, 1950—. Chmn.

Denison Zoning Bd., 1962—. Bd. dirs. Cedar Lawn Cemetary, Denison. Mem. Denison C. of C. (past pres.). Mason. Clubs: Rod and Gun (past pres.) (Denison); Tanglewood Country. Home: 1401 Woodard St Denison TX 75020 Office: Box 703 1700 Morton St Denison TX 75020

SMITH, WILLIAM ARTHUR, supt. schs.; b. Converse, S.C., June 26, 1908; s. Charles W. and Annie (Jones) S.; B.A., Furman U., 1929; Ed.M., Duke, 1940; postgrad. Tchrs. Coll. Columbia U., 1953; m. Ollie Sanders, Nov. 28, 1934; 1 son, Arthur O. Tchr. Hartsville High Sch., 1934-45, prin., 1945-50; supt. Bennettsville City Schs., 1950-55, Conway Area Schs., 1955-61, Florence County Sch. Dist. 3, Lake City, S.C., 1961—. Dir. S.C. Edn. Investors Corp., Columbia, S.C. Mem. S.C. Edn. Assn. (pres. 1963-64), S.C. Sch. Supts. Assn. (pres. 1958-59), Am. Assn. Sch. Adminstrs. Baptist (deacon, chmn. bd. 1965-66). Rotarian (dir.) Home: 205 Palmetto St Lake City SC 29560

SMITH, WILLIAM BREVARD, banker; b. Woodbury, Tenn., June 10, 1918; s. George Stanton and Linda (Brevard) S.; certificate Am. Inst. Banking; grad. Sch. Banking La. State U., 1959; m. Dorothy Dell, Oct. 12, 1940 (dec. 1969); children—William Michael, Steve Alexander. With various trucking firms including McBroom Truck Co., Tenn. Motor Lines, Nashville, Tenn. Carolina Transp., Nashville, 1937-50; with Bank Commerce, Woodbury, 1950—, cashier, v.p., 1955-66, pres., 1967—; also dir. Chmn. Heart Fund, 19—, March of Dimes. Trustee bd. devel. Middle Tenn. State U., Murfreesboro, 1970—. Mem. Ch. of Christ. Lion. Home: 316 Murfreesboro Rd Woodbury TN 37190 Office: 200 Public Sq Woodbury TN 37190

SMITH, WILLIAM EDWIN, city ofcl.; b. Sanger, Tex., Apr. 21, 1910; s. Joseph Ellis and Mary Theresa (Stover) S.; student Tex. Christian U., 1939-41; m. Helon Marie Pirtle, Dec. 29, 1936; children—Sherry (Mrs. Max L. Rightmar), William Edwin. Comml. constrn. bus., 1941-46; ind. fee appraiser, 1946-55; tax accessor-collector Hurst-Euless-Bedford Ind. Sch. Dist., 1955-65; bus. mgr., assessor-collector taxes Wilmer-Hutchins Ind. Sch. Dist., 1965-67; finance officer City Texarkana, Tex., 1968—. Tchr. finance and real estate taxation Texarkana Jr. Coll., 1969—; cons. finance and advolorem taxes, local govts. central and E. Tex. Mem. C. of C. (pres. 1955-65), Nat., Tex. assns. assessing officers, Am. Soc. Appraisers (sec.-treas. 1970-71), Municipal Finance Officers. Lion. Home: 1901 Richmond Rd Texarkana TX 75501 Office: PO Box 1967 Texarkana TX 75501

SMITH, WILLIAM FRANCIS, educator; b. McDonogh, Md., June 21, 1905; s. William Ballard and Emmette (Brooks) S.; A.B., Washington and Lee U., 1926; M.A., Tulane U., 1930; postgrad. Universidad Central de Madrid, 1929, U. N.C., summer 1932; Ph.D., U. Tex., 1940; m. Ruth Alice Sheilds, Aug. 18, 1931; children—Margaret Lyle (Mrs. James William Keating). Instr., Tulane U., New Orleans, 1926-43, asst. prof., 1943-46, asso. prof., 1946-65, prof., 1965-71, prof. emeritus, 1971—; acting head Spanish dept. Coll. Arts and Scis., 1943-46, 50-51, 59-60, acting chmn. dept. Spanish in Grad. Sch., 1959-60. Ford Found. fellow, 1951-52. Mem. Modern Lang. Assn., Am. Assn. Tchrs. Spanish and Portuguese (past com. chmn.), S.C. Modern Lang. Assn. (past pres., mem. exec. com.), Phi Sigma Iota (past nat. treas.), Delta Sigma Pi, Pi Kappa Phi. Presbyn. (elder). Contbr. articles to profl. jours. Home: 1119 Jefferson Av New Orleans LA 70115 Office: Tulane U New Orleans LA 70118

SMITH, WILLIAM GRISWOLD, constrn. co. exec.; b. Durham, N.C., Mar. 18, 1921; s. Frank Patillo and Mary Bryan (Griswold) S.; B.S., U. N.C., 1947; m. Jane Armstrong Robinson, June 28, 1947; children—Maura (Mrs. Philip Roe), Penelope, Mary Bryan. Chmn. bd. First So. Co., finance co., Greensboro, N.C., 1951-65; pres. Key Co., constrn., housing subdivs., mfr. mobile homes, Greensboro, 1952—; dir. Educators Investment Co. of Kan., Inc., Emporia. Bd. dirs. Bus. Found. N.C., N.C. Outward Bound Sch.; trustee U. N.C. Served to capt. USAAF, 1942-46. Decorated Air medal. Mem. Nat. Assn. Real Estate Bd., Inst. Real Estate Mgmt., Greensboro C. of C. Episcopalian. Clubs: Greensboro Country; Country of N.C. (Pinehurst); University (N.Y.C.). Home: 210 Irving Place Greensboro NC 27408 Office: 1020 E Wendover Av Greensboro NC 27405

SMITH, WILLIAM HOWARD, physician; b. Woodward, Okla., Jan. 15, 1925; s. Charles Bernard and Catherine (Campbell) S.; B.S., Northwestern State Coll., 1944; M.D., Okla. U., 1947; m. Joy Stafford, Nov. 21, 1946 (div. 1960); children—Su Su, Kelly, Joel; m. 2d, Joy Mock, June 13, 1971; 1 adopted dau., Karla Kay. Intern, Kansas City Gen. Hosp., 1947-48; practice medicine, Lindsay, Okla., 1948-51, 53-62, medicine and surgery, Pasadena, Tex., 1962— mem. staff Pasadena Bayshore, Pasadena Gen., Bapt. Meml. hosps., Houston; med. dir. Southmore Hosp. Mem. Lindsay Pub. Sch. Bd., 1953-54. Served as capt. M.C., AUS, 1951-53. Diplomate Am. Bd. Family Practice. Fellow Am. Acad. Family Practice; mem. Am., Tex., Indsl. med. assns., Harris County Med. Soc., Assn. Mil. Surgeons, Assn. Ry. Surgeons, Houston Acad. Medicine. Home: 2312 Lillian St Pasadena TX 77502 Office: 906 E Southmore Pasadena TX 77502

SMITH, WILLIAM OGDEN, physicist; b. Ithaca, N.Y., Aug. 19, 1898; s. John Hays and Johanna (Leidner) S.; B.S., U. Pitts, 1921, postgrad., 1921-25; postgrad. U. Cal. at Berkeley, 1925-26, Cal. Inst. Tech., 1926-27, 32-33; m. Ruby Virginia Dempster (dec. Jan. 1953); 1 son, William Moore. Instr. U. Pitts., 1921-25; fellow Mellon Inst. Indsl. Research, Pitts., 1927-29; physicist Gulf Research &Devel. Co., Pitts., 1929-32; physicist U.S. Dept. Agr., Washington, 1934-42; mem. staff radiation lab. Mass. Inst. Tech., 1942-46; physicist U.S. Geol. Survey, Washington, 1946-69; pvt. practice, 1969—. Project chief Lake Mead sedimentation survey, 1947-50, Chgo. bedrock survey, 1950-51, Passamaquoddy bedrock survey, 1951-52, Chesapeake Bay studies, 1952-53; adviser geol. studies Channel Tunnel study. Fellow Geol. Soc. Am.; mem. N.Y. Acad. Sci., Am. Geophys. Union, Philos. Soc. Washington, Geol. Soc. Washington. Presbyn. Contbr. articles in physics, soils, geophysics, hydrology to profl. publs. Home: 8508 Springvale Rd Silver Spring MD 20910

SMITH, WILLIAM PERNELL, educator; b. Birmingham, Ala., Oct. 2, 1919; s. William Pernell and E. Marzetta (Johnson) S.; B.S., Tuskegee Inst., 1939; M.Ed., Rutgers U., 1947, Ed.D., 1959; m. Dorothy Horton, Jan. 16, 1944; children—Barbara J., William Pernell III, Eric B. Instr. Tuskegee (Ala.) Inst., 1947-51; clk. VA, Constrn. Cos., Newark, N.J., 1951-52; asst. prof. Ala. State Coll., Montgomery, Ala., 1952-55, asso prof. edn., 1956-60; asso. prof. edn. Tuskegee Inst., 1960-69; prof. edn., chmn. div. tchr. edn. and psychology Ala. State U., Montgomery, 1969-71, area coordinator guidance and psychology, 1971—. Vis. lectr. Rutgers U., New Brunswick, N.J., 1957-58; regional rep. Stanford Research Inst., 1968—. Vice pres. Com. for Greater Tuskegee, 1969-70, pres. 1970-71. Served with AUS, 1942-46. Mem. Ala. Edn. Assn., Am. Personnel and Guidance Assn., Nat. Vocational Guidance Assn., Student Personnel Assn. for Tchrs in Edn., Assn. for Measurement and Evaluation in Guidance, N.E.A. (life), Phi Delta Kappa, Kappa Delta Pi. Cons. in guidance and psychology Office of Econ. Opportunity and other fed. projects, 1964—. Address: 2502 Howard Rd Tuskegee Institute AL 36088 Office: Div Tchr Edn and Psychology Ala State U Montgomery AL 36104

SMITH, WILLIAM REECE, JR., lawyer; b. Athens, Tenn., Sept. 19, 1925; s. William Reece and Gladys (Moody) S.; B.S., U. S.C., 1946; LL.B., U. Fla., 1949; Rhodes scholar Oxford U., 1949-52; m. Marlene Medina, Aug. 8, 1963; 1 son, William Reece III. Admitted to Fla. bar, 1949; mem. firm Carlton, Fields, Ward, Emmanuel, Smith & Cutler, and predecessor firm, Tampa, 1965—; city atty., Tampa, 1963—; asst. prof. law U. Fla., 1952-53; part-time lectr. law Stetson U., 1953. Past pres. Tampa chpt. United Cerebral Palsey, Tampa Philharmonic Assn.; pres. Fla. Gulf Coast Symphony, Inc., 1967—; trustee Charlotte Bartlett Meml. Scholarship. Served to ensign USNR, 1945-46. Named Outstanding Young Man of Tampa, 1961; recipient Good Govt. award Fla. Jr. C. of C., 1965. Fellow Am. Law Inst., Internat. Acad. Trial Lawyers, Am. Bar Found.; mem. Am. (chmn. jr. bar conf. 1960-61; mem. ho. of dels. 1962—, asst. sec. 1963-67, sec. 1967—), Hilsborough County (pres. 1963) bar assns., Fla. Bar (dir. jr. bar sect.). Baptist. Home: 61 Davis Blvd Tampa FL 33606 Office: Box 3239 Tampa FL 33601

SMITH, WILLIAM SPENCER, JR., tobacco co. exec.; b. Blackstone, Va., Dec. 23, 1918; s. William Spencer and Nancy (Williamson) S.; student Rutgers U. Grad. Sch. Sales Mgmt., 1965-66; m. Dorothy Clements, Jan 30, 1942; children—Katherine Lavassuer, Nancy Clements, William Spencer III. With R.J. Reynolds Tobacco Co., 1939-42, 46—, asst. div. mgr., 1952-53, sales staff, Winston-Salem N.C., 1953-58, asst. sales mgr., 1958-59, sales mgr., 1959-61, v.p., 1961-66, exec. v.p., 1966-70, pres., chief exec. officer, 1970—, also dir.; dir. Hanes Corp., Reynolds Industries, Carolina & Northwestern Ry. Co., Wachovia Bank & Trust Co. Trustee Old Salem; bd. dirs. Winston-Salem chpt. A.R.C. Served with AUS, 1942-46. Named Tobacco Man of Year, So. Tobacco and Candy Assn., 1966; named to Nat. Assn. Tobacco Distbrs. Hall of Fame, 1972. Mem. Am. Soc. Corporate Execs., Honorable Order Ky. Cols. Democrat. Methodist. Rotarian. Clubs: Old Town, Bermuda Run Golf and Country (Winston-Salem); Lone Palm Golf (Lakeland, Fla). Home: 349 N Pine Valley Rd Winston-Salem NC 27104 Office: Corner 4th and Main Sts Winston-Salem NC 27102

SMITH, WILLIE TESREAU, JR., lawyer; b. Sumter, S.C., Jan. 17, 1920; s. Willie T. and Mary (Moore) S.; student Benedict Coll., 1937-40; A.B., Johnson C. Smith U., 1947; LL.B., S.C. State Coll., 1954; m. Anna Marie Clark, June 9, 1955; 1 son, Willie T. III. Admitted to S.C. bar, 1954; began gen. practice, Greenville, 1954; now sr. asst. atty. Legal Services Agy. Greenville County, Inc. Mem. adv. bd. Greenville Tech. Edn. Center Adult Edn. Program, S.C. Regional Med. Program; mem. Greenville County Redevel. Authority. Bd. dirs. Greenville County Housing Found., Nat. Alliance Bus. Men, Greenville Family and Childrens Service, Southeastern Biophys. and Anthrop. Found. Served with AUS, 1942-45, USAF, 1949-52. Mem. Am., S.C., Greenville County bar assns., Southeastern Lawyers Assn., Am. Legion, Greater Greenville C. of C. (chmn. community relations com., dir.), N.A.A.C.P., Omega Psi Phi, Presbyn. Mason (Shriner). Home: 601 Jacob Rd Greenville SC 29605 Office: 135 S Main St Greenville SC 29601

SMITHBURG, DONALD WINSTON, educator, ednl. adminstr.; b. Seattle, May 9, 1916; s. John E. and Anna (Olsen) S.; A.B., U. Washington, 1937; postgrad. U. Minn., 1940-42; Ph.D., Harvard, 1951; m. Mary Harper McAnlis, Feb. 10, 1942; children—Donald Rowan, Laura Harper. Teaching asst. U. Minn., 1940-42; procedures analyst OWI, 1942-43, OPA; 1943-45; Social Sci. Research Council fellow Harvard, 1945-46; faculty Ill. Inst. Tech., 1946-66, prof., 1960-66; prof. polit. sci. U. Ala., Huntsville, 1967-68, dir. div. social and behavioral scis., 1969—. Host tv series Am. Scene, WMAQ, 1961-64; cons. Army Missile Command, 1967—. Democrat. Rotarian. Club: Armour Faculty. Author: (with H.A. Simon, V.A. Thompson) Public Administration, 1950. Home: 2303 Annanddale Dr SE Huntsville AL 35801

SMITHER, CHARLES GABRIEL, ins. exec., state senator; b. New Orleans, Nov. 28, 1914; s. James William and Louise (Person) S.; B.A., Tulane U., 1936; m. Charlotte Mary Hardie, Oct. 17, 1939; children—Charles Hardie, Louise Person (Mrs. Denis H. McDonald), Charlotte Sanders. Spl. agt. Union Central Life Ins. Co., New Orleans, 1936-40, mgr., 1967-71, spl. agt., 1971—; partner James W. Smither & Sons, gen. agts., New Orleans, 1940-67; v.p., dir. Ferd, Marks-Smither & Co., Ltd., ins. agts. and brokers, New Orleans, 1969—; chmn. bd. Kalvar Corp., New Orleans, 1959-64, 67—; dir. Jefferson Cold Storage, Inc., Asso. Cold Storage, Inc., So. Microfilm Corp., Metro-Kalvar, Inc., Date Processing Center, Inc.; mem. La. Senate, 1968—. Campaign chmn. Community Chest, 1952-53. Chmn. New Orleans Pub. Library Bd., 1946-61; mem. Sewerage and Water Bd., 1949-51; mem. La. Ho. of Reps., 1962-68. Bd. dirs. Internat. House, 1948-51; bd. adminstrs. Tulane U. Ednl. Fund, 1967—; pres. bd. Motairie Park Country Day Sch., 1955-57, Crippled Children's Hosp., 1959-60. Served to maj. AUS, 1942-45; ETO. Decorated Silver Star, Bronze Star, Purple Heart; Croix de Guerre (France). C.L.U. Mem. Nat. Assn. Life Underwriters, Am. Soc. Chartered Life Underwriters. Democrat. Episcopalian (trustee Diocese of La. 1960-70). Clubs: Boston; New Orleans Country, Stratford (New Orleans). Home: 440 Audubon St New Orleans LA 70118 Office: 1600 Canal St New Orleans LA 70112

SMITHEY, ROBERT ARTHUR, educator; b. Norfolk, Va., Dec. 18, 1925; s. Philip Jefferson and Lovie Gertrude (Jordan) S.; A.B., DePauw U., 1950; A.M., U. Wis., 1953, Ph.D. (IBM fellow, Vilas fellow, Ford fellow, Univ. fellow), 1971; postgrad. Cornell U., summer 1954; A.M., Harvard, 1963. Instr. English, Tuskegee Inst., summer 1953; asst. prof. Prairie View A. and M. Coll., 1953-54; instr. U. Md. Overseas Program, Tachikawa, Japan, 1955-58; asst. prof. So. U., 1958-60, Talladega Coll., 1960-62; asso. prof. U. Mo., Kansas City, 1968-70; vis. prof. U. Houston, 1970-71, asst. prof. English, 1971—. Mem. bd. examiners coll. level exams. Ednl. Testing Service, Princeton, N.J., 1971—. Nat. pres. Youth Conf. N.A.A.C.P., 1944-45. Served with AUS, 1945-46; with USAF, 1955-58. Mem. Nat. Council Tchrs. English (dir.), Conf. on Coll. Composition and Communication (exec. com. 1964-68), Phi Beta Kappa, Sigma Gamma Mu. Democrat. Episcopalian. Author: Faulkner and the Status Quo, 1965; Coleridgean Elements in Browning's The Ring and The Book, 1970. Home: 1617 Fannin St Houston TX 77002

SMOKE, WILLIAM GLADDEN, JR., cotton oil co. exec.; b. St. Matthews, S.C., Aug. 28, 1938; s. William Gladden and Aurelia (Antley) S.; B.S., Clemson U., 1960; m. Sheila M. Hampton, Aug. 22, 1970. Project engr. indsl. gas and cryogenics sect. Army Research and Devel. Lab., Ft. Belvoir, Va., 1960-62, fuel cell sect. electric power br., 1962-65; asst. gen. mgr. Victor Cotton Oil Co., Gaffney, S.C., 1965-67, partner, gen. mgr., 1967—; pres. Humphries Gin Corp., 1967-71; owner Smoke Chem. Co., 1965—, W.G. Smoke Oil Co.; partner Cooksey Oil Co.; mgr. State Commodity Warehouse, 1965—. Dist. adv. bd. Small Bus. Adminstrn. Explorer scout adviser Boy Scouts Am., 1967-69; capt. profl. div. Cherokee County Community Chest, 1969. Mem. S.C. Republican Exec. Com. Bd. dirs. Cherokee County Boys Club, 1970-72; bd. visitors S.C. Meth. Homes, 1971—. Served to 2d lt. AUS, 1960-61. Mem. Gaffney Jr. C. of C. (1st v.p. 1969, Distinguished Service award 1970, Young Man of Yr. award 1970), Am. Inst. Chem. Engrs., Western S.C. Chem. Engrs. Club, Gaffrey C. of C. (dir. 1971-73), Cherokee Historic Preservation Soc. Methodist (ofcl. bd. 1968—). Kiwanian (pres. Gaffney 1970-71). Home: 312 E Frederick St Gaffney SC 29340 Office: 314 E Frederick St Gaffney SC 29340

SMOLKIN, STEPHEN WILLIAM, univ. ofcl.; b. San Antonio, Aug. 30, 1941; s. Harry A. and Carolyn (Ghetzler) S.; B.B.A., U. Tex., 1964; m. Sandra von Werssowetz, Jan. 27, 1964; 1 dau., Sheryl Wynne. Computer systems analyst W.R. Smolkin & Assos., Inc., New Orleans, 1964-65, data processing dir., 1966-67, v.p., 1968-69; admistrv. systems mgr. Tulane U., faculty Univ. Coll., New Orleans, 1970—. Bd. advisers Mobile Home Communities, Inc., Denver, 1968-69. Mem. Am. Mgmt. Assn., Assn. for Systems Mgmt., Sigma Alpha Mu. Home: 302 Bella Dr Metairie LA 70005 Office: Computer Lab Tulane U New Orleans LA 70118

SMOOT, JOE ASHLEY, osteo. physician; b. Laverne, Okla., Apr. 10, 1916; s. Edward M. and Mary Etta (Browning) S.; A.B., Phillips U., 1936; D.O., Kansas City Coll. Osteopathy and Surgery, 1941; m. Kathryn Mae McArron, Dec. 24, 1940; children—Susan Kay (Mrs. Daniel G. Staudt), Paula Jeanne (Mrs. James W. Ogg), Sammye Jo (Mrs. David E. Sullivan), Ashley Anne (Mrs. William M. Hurlbutt). Intern, Lakeside Hosp., Kansas City, Mo., 1941-42, resident, 1942-43; gen. practice osteo. medicine, surgery, Tulsa, 1943—; chief of staff Okla. Osteo. Hosp., Tulsa, 1962, 63. State chmn. Osteo. Medicare and Med. Rev. Bd., 1968—; pres. SGH Bldg. Corp., Tulsa, 1962—; dir. Nat. Equity Life Ins. Co. Bd. mem., mem. exec. com. Okla. Christian Home, Edmond, 1954-62. Mem. Am., Okla. (pres. 1967-68, legislative com. 1970—) osteo. assns., Tulsa Dist. Osteo. Soc. (pres. 1951), Am. Osteo. Acad. Orthopedics (asso). Mem. Christian Ch. (elder). Clubs: Optimist (bd. mem. 1945—), Tulsa (pres. 1951- 52). Home: 2838 S Florence Av Tulsa OK 74114 Office: 1936 S Harvard Av Tulsa OK 74112

SMOTHERMAN, KENNETH LEE, hotel exec.; b. Magnolia, Ark., Apr. 24, 1939; s. Joseph Alvis and Mary Margaret (Nebgen) S.; B.S., U. Southwestern La., 1963; m. Rita Camille Brasseux, June 1, 1960; children—Kenneth Lee, Kay Lee. Mgr., co-owner Traveldodges, Lafayette and Baton Rouge, 1963-69; owner, mgr. Fleur de Lis Motel, Alexandria, La., 1970—; owner Skylight Terrace Motel, Marshall, Tex. Coach, Little League team, 1969—; den father Cub Scouts, 1970-71. Bd. dirs. Civitan Club, Alexandria. Mem. La., Alexandria, Baton Rouge (v.p., 1969) motel assns., Alexandria C. of C. Home: 2810 Mary Mack Dr Marshall TX 75670 Office: 502 E End Blvd S Hwy 59 Marshall TX 75670

SMYER, SIDNEY WILLIAM, JR., realtor; b. Birmingham, June 4, 1928; s. Sidney William and Frances Macy (Moore) S.; B.S., U. Ala., 1949, LL.B., 1951; m. Ingrid Fougner Lassen, Sept. 22, 1950; children—Sidney William III, Ingrid Frances, Harald L. Admitted to Ala. bar, 1951; mem. firm Smyer, White, Reid & Acker, Birmingham, 1951-57; v.p. Birmingham Realty Co., 1957-67, pres., 1967—, also dir.; pres., dir. Dolcito Quarry Co., Birmingham, 1967—, Montevallo Limestone Co., Birmingham, 1969—. Mem. Ala. Democratic Exec. Com., 1958-64, del. Nat. Conv., 1956. Bd. dirs. Birmingham Opera Assn., 1970—, Birmingham Symphony Assn., 1967, Spastic Aid Ala., 1960-67, Camp Fire Girls Birmingham, 1967—, Birmingham Festival of Arts, 1965—. Mem. C. of C. (bd. dirs., 1966-69), Birmingham Bd. Realtors (dir. 1966-69), Asso. Industries Ala. (dir. 1968—). Republican. Methodist. Rotarian. Club: Birmingham Country. Home: 3804 Knollwood Lane Birmingham AL 35243 Office: 2118 1st Av N Birmingham AL 35203

SMYLIE, THOMAS MELVILLE, mfg. co. exec.; b. Brookhaven, Miss., Oct. 31, 1916; s. Thomas Melville and Dora (Hubbard) S.; B.S., Miss. State U., 1939; postgrad. La. State U., 1947; Harvard, 1956; m. Patricia Clare O'Brien, Apr. 19, 1941; children—D'Arcy Clare, John Hubbard. Wtih Ethyl Corp., Baton Rouge, N.Y.C., 1940—, pres., chief exec. officer William L. Bonnell Co., 1965-66, corporate v.p., dir. 1966—, chmn., chief exec. officer Capitol Products, 1969—; dir. Bromet Co., Magnolia, Ala. Mem. Lead Industries Assn. (v.p., dir.), Am. Petroleum Inst., Am. Inst. Chem. Engrs. (past sect. chmn.), Blue Key, Kappa Alpha, Tau Beta Pi. Clubs: Baton Rouge Country; Canadian, Metropolitan (N.Y.C.). Home: 5937 Goodwood Av Baton Rouge LA 70806 Office: Ethyl Tower 451 Florida St Baton Rouge LA 70821

SMYLIE, VERNON GUY, JR., pub. relations cons., author; b. Houston, Aug. 10, 1920; s. Vernon Guy and Alice (Marshall) S.; A.B in Govt. and Journalism, Tex. Christian U., 1941; grad. Pub. Relations Inst., 1959; m. Arlene Frances Simon, Nov. 14, 1949; children— Eric, Alisa Ann, Regina. Reporter, Houston Press, 1942, investigative writer, 1948-50; investigative writer Albuquerque Tribune, 1945-46, El Paso (Tex.) Herald-Post, 1946-48; capitol corr. Scripps-Howard Newspapers, Austin, Tex., 1950, Santa Fe, 1951; Tex. dir. pub. relations Aluminum Co. Am., Port Lavaca, Tex., 1951-53; pub. relations cons., Corpus Christi, Tex. 1953—. Pres., Montclair P.T.A., 1958-59, Corpus Christi Fine Arts Colony, 1961, Nueces County Hist. Soc., 1967-69; chmn. Nueces County chpt. March of Dimes, 1959. Served with USAAF, 1942-45. Recipient A.P. Community Service citation, 1947. Episcopalian. Club: Corpus Christi Knife and Fork (pres. 1970-71). Author: Padre Island Report, 1960; Thirteenth Grade, 1961; Taming of the Texas Coast, 1963; The Secrets of Padre Island, 1964; The Moon Belongs to Houston, 1966; Edward C. Lasater, Texas Trail Blazer, 1968; A Noose for Chipita, 1970. Home: 425 University Dr Corpus Christi TX 78412 Office: Six Hundred Bldg Corpus Christi TX 78403

SMYTH, GEORGE FRANK, furnitute co. exec.; b. Henderson, Ala., July 30, 1917; s. George W. and Kate Scott (Ellison) S.; student Troy State U., 1938, U. Wis., 1942; m. Emma Elizabeth Woodson, July 2, 1941; 1 son, Frank Woodson. Salesman, S.D. Winn Tobacco Co., Montgomery, Ala., 1938-40, Nat. Biscuit Co., 1940-42; partner, mgr. Baldwin Furniture Stores, Foley, Robertsdale, Bay Minette, Ala., 1946—; dir. Riviera Utilities, Farmers & Mchts. Bank, Baldwin Mut. Ins. Co. (all Foley). Chmn., South Baldwin Emergency Relief Fund, 1965—; mem. City Council, 1972. Bd. dirs. South Baldwin United Fund. Served to capt. AUS, 1942-46. Mem. South Baldwin C. of C. (dir.), Ala. Retail Furniture Assn. Methodist. Mason (Shriner), Rotarian. Club: Gulf Shores Golf. Home: PO Box 788 Foley AL 36535 Office: 317 W Satsuma Foley AL 36535

SMYTHE, JULES WALKER, dentist; b. Gale City, Va., Sept. 2, 1924; s. Clarence Alexander and Effa M. (Johnson) S.; B.S., Emory and Henry Coll., 1947; D.D.S. magna cum laude, U. Tenn., 1951; m. Andrea Cory Adams, July 30, 1971; children—Jules Walker, Preston. Practice dentistry Smythe Dental Clinic, Bristol, Tenn., 1951—. Joint owner Holston Plaza Real Estate Devel. Mem. Sullivan County Bd. Health. Served with AUS, 1943-46. Recipient 1st Place award dental exhibits Tenn. Dental Meeting, 1962. Mem. Am. Acad. Oral Medicine, Pierre Fauchard Acad., 1st Dental Dist. Tenn. (pres.), Omicron Kappa Upsilon. Contbr. articles to profl. jours. Home: 700 Vance St Bristol TN 37620 Office: 800 Hill St Bristol TN 37620

SNAPP, HARRY FRANKLIN, educator, historian; b. Bryan, Tex., Oct. 15, 1930; s. H.F. and Ethel (Manning) S.; B.A., Baylor U., 1952, M.A., 1953; Ph.D., Tulane U., 1963; m. Elizabeth Mitchell, June 1, 1956. Instr., U. Coll. Tulane U., 1960-62; asst. prof. history Wofford

Coll., 1963-64; asst. prof. history N. Tex. State U., Denton, 1964-69, asso. prof., 1969—. Mem. Friends Winchester Cathedral, Am. Com. for Irish Studies. Recipient N. Tex. State U. Faculty Research award, 1966, 67. Mem. Am. Assn. U. Profs. (pres. N. Tex. chpt. 1968-69, pres. Southwestern regional conf. 1971-72), So. Conf. on Brit. Studies (sec.-treas.), Am. So. hist. assns., Hist. Assn. (London), Northamptonshire Record Soc., Butler Soc. (Ireland), Econ. History Soc., Ch. Hist. Soc., Tex. Assn. Coll. Tchrs., Tulane U. Alumni Assn., Alpha Chi. Episcopalian. Editor: Brit. Studies Mercury, 1970—. Contbr. to profl. jours. Home: PO Box 1427 Denton TX 76201

SNAUFER, LARRY LYNN, bank exec.; b. Springfield, O., Oct. 7, 1939; s. Roger J. and Mary Ann (DeLay) S.; B.S., U. Cin., 1962; M.B.A., Lamar U., 1970; m. Karen Mae Spriggs, Aug. 11, 1962; children—Mark Jeffrey, Kimberly Jolene, Kendra Michele. Coop student Internat. Harvester Co., Springfield, 1957-62; asst. v.p. in charge of data processing, First Security Nat. Bank, Beaumont, Tex., 1965-68, v.p., 1968-72, sr. v.p., 1972—; v.p., sec. First Security Nat. Corp., 1972—. Instr. math. Allan Hancock Jr. Coll., Santa Maria, Cal., 1963-65; instr. Bank Adminstrv. Inst., 1969-71. Served with USAF, 1962-65. Mem. Data Processing Mgmt. Assn. (pres. chpt. 1968-69), 1965-70), Am. Banking Assn. (nat. automation com. 1970—), Young Men's Bus. League, C. of C., Pi Kappa Alpha. Methodist. Kiwanian. Clubs: Pinewood Country, Business and Professional Men's, Knife and Fork (Beaumont). Home: 1755 Bandera Dr Beaumont TX 77706 Office: 505 Orleans St Beaumont TX 77706

SNAVELY, GUY EVERETT, coll. chancellor; b. Antietam, Md., Oct. 26, 1881; s. Charles Granville and Emma (Rohrer) S.; A.B., Johns Hopkins, 1901, Ph.D., 1908; Alliance Francaise, Paris, summer 1905; LL.D., Emory U., 1925, Stetson U., 1936, Washington Coll., 1937, Allegheny Coll., 1938, MacMurray Coll., 1942, Marietta Coll., 1945, U. Pitts., 1946, Alfred U., 1948, U. Chattanooga, 1949, Mt. Mary Coll., Valparaiso U., Tex. Christian U., 1950, U. Detroit, Ripon Coll., 1952, Barry Coll., 1957, Lafayette Coll., 1959; Ed.D., Whitman Coll., 1945; D.C.L., Birmingham-So. Coll., 1938; L.H.D., Boston U., 1937, Albion Coll., 1946, Cornell Coll., 1953; Litt.D., Fla. So. Coll., 1930, Cumberland U., 1932; m. Ada Rittenhouse, Sept. 27, 1905 (dec. 1948); children—Guy Everett, Brant Rittenhouse, Charles Albert; m. 2d, Louise Hutcheson, 1950 (dec. 1963); m. 3d, Madelyn T. Hale, July 17, 1964. Instr., Md. Nautical Acad., Easton, 1901-02; vice prin. Milton Acad., Balt., 1902-05; faculty Allegheny Coll., 1906-19, prof. Romance langs., lit., 1910-19, registrar, 1908-19, on leave of absence as dir. so. div. A.R.C., Atlanta, 1917-19; asst. to gen. mgr. A.R.C., Washington, 1919; dean Converse Coll., Spartanburg, S.C., 1919-21; pres. Birmingham (Ala.) So. Coll., 1921-38, 55-57, chancellor, 1957—; interim pres. Lafayette Coll., 1957-58, Athens Coll., 1966. Hon scholar in edn. Tchrs. Coll. Columbia, vis. prof. Romance langs. N.Y. U., 1914-15. Exec. dir. Assn. Am. Colls., 1937-54; mem. Jefferson County Civil Service Bd.; mem. Birmingham Housing Commn.; chmn. State NRA Bd. for Ala.; v.p. Nat. Service Fund; chmn. Nat. Com. Colls. and Civilian Def.; lt. col. Ala. N.G. on staff of gov., 1923-26. Pres. Birmingham S.S. Assn., 1922-24; vice chmn. Internat. Sunday Sch. Exec. Com. Trustee Miles Coll., Hood Coll., Am. U. Mem. Modern Lang. Assn. Am., Nat. Adv. Com. on Edn., Ala. Coll. Assn. (pres 1926-27), So. Assn. Colls. and Secondary Schs. (sec., treas. 1926-37), Assn. Am. Colls. (pres., 1929-30), Am. Council on Edn. (exec. com. 6 years, vice chmn. 1937-38), Assn. Urban Univs. (pres. 1936-37); chmn. scholarship dept. Presser Found.; trustee, exec. com Nat. Conf. Christians and Jews; v.p. Citizens Nat. Com.; chmn. Ala. YMCA State Com., 1931-33, Joint Meth. Hymnal Com.; del. So. Meth. Gen. Conf., 1934, 38. Mem. Phi Beta Kappa, Phi Beta Kappa Alumni in N.Y. (pres.), Phi Beta Kappa Alumni of D.C. (pres.), Nat. Phi Beta Kappa Com. on Assns. (chmn.). Kappa Phi Kappa (nat. pres., 1927-31), Phi Gamma Delta, Omicron Delta Kappa (nat. pres., 1935-37), Phi Sigma Iota, Pi Tau Chi (nat. pres.). Methodist. Officer d'Academie, 1941; Officer French Legion of Honor, 1947; corr. mem. Royal Spanish Am. Acad., Cadiz, Spain; pres. Alliance francaise of U.S. and Canada. Clubs: Rotary; Cosmos (Washington). Author: Choose and Use Your College, History of Southern College Assn.; The Church and The Four Year College; A Search for Excellence: Memoirs of a College Administrator. Editor: Alarcon's El Capitan Veneno, 1917; Valdez, Jose (with R. C. Ward), 1919. Contbr. phil. and ednl. jours. Address: Birmingham-So Coll Birmingham AL 35204

SNAVELY, GUY EVERETT, JR., orgn. exec.; b. Baldwin, Md., June 30, 1906; s. Guy E. and Ada (Rittenhouse) S.; A.B., Birmingham-So. Coll., 1927; L.H.D., Athens Coll., 1950; m. Helen McNeill, June 3, 1930; children— Sherry Louise, Dan McNeill. Bus. mgr. Ala. Inst. for Deaf and Blind, 1933-38; exec. sec., trustee Pickett & Hatcher Edni. Fund, Inc., Columbus, Ga., 1938-62, exec. v.p., 1962—. Mem. adv. com. Higher Edn. Act 1965, U.S. Office Edn., 1965-69, mem. adv. com. Nat. Vocational Student Loan Ins. Act 1965, 1965-69; mem. membership com., coll. scholarship service Coll. Entrance Exam. Bd., 1966-68. Treas., Ga. Ala. council Boy Scouts Am., 1955-63, treas. Chattahoochie council, 1964—; adv. bd. Columbus Citadel, Salvation Army; dir. Family Service Bur., 1939-41, 54-58; counselor Miss Ga. Scholarship Fund, 1947-53; dir. Nat. Conf. Christians and Jews, 1950-53; dir. Columbus Appeals Rev. Bd., 1951-53; chmn. Ga. com. Am. Assn. for UN, 1952-56; pres. Columbus Community Chest, 1948-50; pres. Muscogee Mental Health Assn., 1953, v.p., 1958, 1962-65. Bd. dirs. of Jr. Achievement, Columbus Sch. Speech; trustee Ga. Found. Ind. Colls. Served as maj. F.A., AUS, 1942-46; ETO, 1944-45. Decorated Bronze Star. Mem. Columbus C. of C. (chmn. edn. com. 1948-49), Mil. Order World Wars (chpt. adj. 1961-62, comdr. 1965-66), Assn. U.S. Army, Brimingham-So. Coll. Alumni Assn. (past pres.), So. Assn. Student Financial Aid Adminstrs. (sec.-treas. 1963-70), Omicron Delta Kappa, Alpha Tau Omega. Presbyn. (vice chmn. com. on homes and ednl. instns. Synod Ga. 1962-66, mem. com. on campus Christian life 1965-66, elder). Kiwanian (sec. Ga. dist. 1950). Club: Big Eddy. Home: 2619 Habersham Av Columbus GA 31906 Office: 1800 Buena Vista Rd Columbus GA 31906

SNEAD, EDWIN BRAZELTON, crushed stone co. exec.; b. Waco, Tex., Oct. 3, 1904; s. Edwin Reynolds and Mary (Brazelton) S.; B.S., in C.E., Tex. A. and M. U., 1925; m. Anna Louise deSteiguer, Aug. 2, 1926; children—Edwin D., Mary Lou (Mrs. Whitman Frazer), William B. Constrn. engr. P.O.'B. Montgomery, Dallas, 1925-32; owner E.B. Snead Constrn. Co., Austin, Tex., 1932-52; with Tex. Crushed Stone Co., Austin, 1947—, pres., chmn. bd., 1960—; dir. Rwy. Indsl. Equipment Co., Austin, Citizens State Bank, Georgetown, Tex. Regional v.p. Nat. Limestone Inst., Washington, 1960—. Mason. Clubs: Petroleum (Houston); Chapparral (Dallas); Westwood Country (Austin). Home: 5105 Ridge Oak Dr Austin TX 78731 Office: Route 1 Georgetown TX 78626

SNEAD, HAROLD FLEMING, state judge; b. Richmond, Va., June 16, 1903; s. Edloe Gathright and Ada (Riddell) S.; B.A., U. Richmond, 1925, LL.B., 1929, LL.D., 1958; m. Elizabeth Somerville Call, Apr. 2, 1937; 1dau., Elizabeth Call (Mrs. David C. Dorset). Admitted to Va. bar, 1929; practiced in Richmond, 1929-48; trial justice Henrico County, 1935-48; judge Circuit Ct. Henrico County, Circuit Ct. Richmond, 1948-57; asso. justice Va. Supreme Ct. Appeals, 1957—, now chief justice. Dir. Franklin Fed. Savs. & Loan Assn., Richmond. Bd. dirs. Christian Children's Fund, Richmond; trustee U. Richmond. Mem. Phi Beta Kappa, Omicron Delta Kappa, Kappa Sigma, Delta Theta Phi. Democrat. Baptist. Home: 9301 River Rd Richmond VA 23229 Office: Supreme Ct Bldg Richmond VA 23219

SNEED, HENRY LEE, JR., sch. adminstr.; b. Troy, Ala., Apr. 11, 1914; s. Henry Lee and Delia (Osborne) S.; B.A., Erskine Coll., 1936; M.A., U. S.C., 1943; postgrad. Kent State U., 1969; m. Addie Meador, Dec. 21, 1937; children—Henry Lee, William Daniel. Teaching prin., coach, Clover, S.C., 1938-42; supt. Piedmont (S.C.) Pub. Schs., 1942-44, 46-49; prin. Chester (S.C.) High Sch., 1949-51; supt. Chester Area Schs., 1951-60, Bennettsville (S.C.) Schs., 1960-61, Florence (S.C.) Sch. Dist. 1961—. Guest instr. Francis Marion Coll., Florence, 1971—. Mem. S.C. Adv. Com. Title III, 1969—, S.C. Vocational Adv. Commn., 1971—; mem. numerous evaluation coms., 1948—. Bd. dirs. YMCA. Served with USNR, 1944-46. Mem. S.C. Assn. Sch. Adminstrs., Am., S.C. assns. sch. supts., N.E.A., S.C. Edn. Assn., Florence C. of C. (dir., Leadership, Service award 1971), S.C. High Sch. League (past pres.). Presbyn. (elder). Rotarian. Home: 1101 Melrose Av Florence SC 29501 Office: 109 W Pine St Florence SC 29501

SNEED, JOSEPH ELLISON, JR., banker; b. Decatur, Ala., Oct. 18, 1932; s. Joseph Ellison and Ruth (Chunn) S.; B.S., U. Ala., 1958; m. Barbara Shaw, Aug. 11, 1956; children—Shaw Arthur, Joseph Ellison III, Fredrick Lawson Chunn, Benjamin Lawrence. With The Mchts. Nat. Bank, Mobile, Ala., 1957-62; with The Bank of Ozark (Ala.), 1962—, asst. v.p., 1964-67, v.p., 1967-69, exec. v.p., 1969-72, pres., chief exec. officer, 1972—, also dir.; farmer, Ozark, 1971—. Pres. Dale County Heart Assn., 1966—. Served with AUS, 1953-55. Mem. Am., Ind. Ala. bankers assns., C. of C. Rotarian. Club: Ozark Country. Home: 311 Bufaula St Ozark AL 36360 Office: Reynolds St Ozark AL 36360

SNEED, RONALD ERNEST, engr.; b. Oxford, N.C., Nov. 23, 1936; s. Henry Ernest and Jewel (Hughes) S.; B.S., N.C. State U., 1959, Ph.D., 1971; m. Shelba Jean Walters, June 8, 1958; children—Kathy Geneva, Jennie Leigh. Sales trainee John Deere Co., Monroe, Ga., 1959-60; extension agrl. engr. N.C. State U., Raleigh, 1960-69, 70—; grad. fellow U.S. Army C.E., Wilmington, N.C., 1969-70. Served with AUS, 1960. Mem. Am. Soc. Agrl. Engrs., N.C. Irrigation Soc., Soil Sci. Soc. N.C., Res. Officers Assn., Sigma Xi, Alpha Zeta, Epsilon Sigma Phi. Baptist (deacon 1971—, chmn. bldg. and grounds com. 1971-72). Home: 3405 Malibu Dr Raleigh NC 27603 Office: PO Box 5906 NC State U Raleigh NC 27607

SNEED, SEBRON MORRIS, banker; b. Shreveport, La., July 23, 1933; s. Hugh McArthur and Matteile (Frazier) S.; B.S., La. Poly. Tech., 1955; student Sch. Banking, La. State U., 1962-65; m. Louise Murchison, Aug. 14, 1955; children—Sebron Stanton, Sarah Dillon, James MacArthur, Henry Dillon. Asst. v.p., sec. National Bank, Alexandria, La., 1959-64; exec. v.p. American Bank, Monroe, La., 1964—; dir. Am. Bank and Trust Co., Monroe, La., Monroe Computer Services, Monroe. Bd. dirs. United Givers Fund, Northeast La. State Scholarship Found., La. Poly. Alumni Found. Served with USAF, 1955-59. Mem. Monroe C. of C. (dir., pres.). Rotarian. Home: 1114 Riverside Dr Monroe LA 71201 Office: PO Box 7232 Monroe LA 71201

SNELGROVE, CLARENCE P(REDEW), univ. librarian; b. Gilbert, S.C., Dec. 13, 1908; s. Carey A. and Bessie (Keisler) S.; A.B., U. S.C., 1932; B.L.S., Peabody Library Sch., 1935; m. Louise Youmans, June 9, 1936; children—James Lewis, Susan Louise. Librarian, Leesburg (Fla.) High Sch., 1935, Tenn. Poly. Inst., Cookeville, 1936—. Served as lt. USNR, 1944-46; ETO, MTO. Mem. Tenn. Library Assn., Tenn. Edn. Assn., Tenn. Folklore Soc. (pres. 1968-69, contbr. to Bull.), Am. Legion, Kappa Delta Pi, Sigma Upsilon. Democrat. Presbyn. Rotarian. Contbr. to Ency. Am. Home: 655 Valley Forge Rd Cookeville TN 38501

SNELL, DAVID, journalist; b. Minden, La., Mar. 28, 1921; s. John Barnard and Ada Jack (Carver) S.; student La. State U., 1939-43. children by previous marriage—Barry, Jan Whitfield; m. 2d, Dixie Baye Oliver, Sept. 1, 1956; children—Steven Mark, Sandra Robin. Reporter, Minden Herald & Webster Rev., 1936-37, Atlanta Constn., 1943-44; rewrite man U.P., N.Y.C. bur., 1946-47; reporter N.Y. Sun, 1947-50; radio and TV commentator WOR-Mutual, 1950-52; reporter feature writer N.Y. World Telegram & Sun, 1950-55; mem. staff Life mag., 1955-69, corr. Europe, Africa and Middle East, Paris, France, 1957-61, London, Eng., 1961-62, asso. editor, 1962-63, sr. editor, 1963-69, author column Dateline America; writer under contract to Life mag., 1969-71, Time-Life Books, 1972—; pres. Internat. Writers, Ltd., 1971—; dir. Internat. Spl. projects consultants, Inc. Served with AUS, 1945-46. Recipient George Polk Meml. award, 1952, Sportsmanship Brotherhood award, 1954, Citizenship award Am. Legion, 1938, Sci. award Bausch & Lomb, Inc., 1938; cited by Inst. Edn. by Radio-TV, Ohio State U., 1951. Mem. A.A.A.S., Press Club of Houston, Sigma Nu. Methodist. Artist in oil, also cartoonist pub. nat. mags. Contbr. articles to Life, Smithsonian, Signature, Today's Health, other nat. mags. Office: 440 Pinehaven Houston TX 77024 also care Paul R Reynolds Inc 599 Fifth Av New York City NY 10017

SNELL, HAMPTON KENT, educator, trans. cons.; b. Harvey, Ill., Mar. 10, 1904; s. Sanford S. and Myla (Cooke) S.; B.A., U. Wis., 1925, M.A., 1928; Ph.D., Yale, 1941; m. Margaret E. Frye, June 9, 1928; 1 son, Hampton K. (dec.). Economist, statistician Am. Elec. Ry. Assn., 1929, Am. Tel. & Tel. Co., 1929-30; asst. asso. prof. econ. Mont. State U., 1930-36; asso. prof. trans. U. So. Cal., 1936-42; vis. asso. prof. Stanford U., 1938; chief R.R. Unit, OCR, WPB., Washington, 1942; head program specialist Office Def. Transp., 1942-44; cons. Resources Protection Bd., 1942-45; asst. dir. research Ind. Coll. of Armed Forces, 1944-45; asst. to v.p. research. Assn. Am. R.R.'s, 1945-47; prof. Sch. Fgn. Service, Georgetown U., 1946-47; prof. transp. U. Tex., Austin, 1947—; vis. prof. U. Fla., 1949; transp. cons. 2d Hoover Commn., 1954; cons. Barge Lines of U.S., 1957-58, UN cons. Govt. Egypt, Cairo, 1959; Internat. Coop Adminstrn. cons. Republic of Indonesia, Djakarta, 1961, AID, Ministry of Planning, Brazil, 1964-65; cons. to assns. r.r., truck, bus, barge and airlines, municipalities, shippers and industry, also U.S. Dept. Commerce, Fed. Maritime Commn., U.S. Dept. Transp., Congl. coms.; mem. Nat. Def. Exec. Res., Office Emergency Transp., 1964—; sec., editor S.W. Shippers Adv. Bd., 1970—. Mem. Am. Soc. Traffic and Transp., Nat. Def. Transp. Assn., Am. Econ. Assn., Tex. Ind. Traffic League, Nat. Small Shipments Traffic Conf. (v.p.), Southwest Shippers Motor Carrier Conf. (chmn. 1960-61), Transp. Research Forum, Delta Nu Alpha, Delta Phi Epsilon, Delta Sigma Pi. Author: Air Transportation, Inland Waterway Transportation. Contbr. articles, monographs in field. Home: 3409 Mountain Top Circle Austin TX 78731 Office: Bus-Econ Office Bldg U Tex Austin TX 78712

SNELL, JOHN NEWTON, JR., dist. judge; b. Latexo, Tex., July 30, 1912; s. John N. and Linnie (Garrett) S.; LL.B., Houston Sch. Law, 1934; m. Jean James, June 1, 1935; children—James Allen, John Newton III. Admitted to Tex. bar, 1935, since practiced law in Houston; asst. dist. atty., 1942-45; judge County Ct. at Law No. 2, 1948-54; judge 152d Dist. Ct., Harris County, Tex., 1954—. Mem. State Bar Tex., Houston Bar Assn. Democrat. Baptist. Mason (32 deg., Shriner). Home: 4611 Dunsmere St Houston TX 77018 Office: Civil Cts Bldg Houston TX 77002

SNELL, LAWRENCE WORDSWORTH, JR., lumber and land devel. co. exec.; b. N.Y.C., June 5, 1929; s. Lawrence Wordsworth and Dorothy (Draper) S.; grad. Hill Sch., 1946; B.A., U. Cal. at Berkeley, 1951; M.B.A., N.Y. U., 1958; m. Sheila Brigit Frazer, Feb. 10, 1967; children—Kathleen Margaret, Prescott Richard Donaldson. Asst. indsl. relations Armco Steel, Middletown, O., 1956-57; personnel mgr. Western Electric Co., Kearny, N.J., 1957-59; orgn. planner Johnson & Johnson, New Brunswick, N.J., 1959-62; compensation mgr. W.Va. Pulp & Paper Co., N.Y.C., 1962-68; pres. Westvaco Devel. Corp., Summerville, S.C., 1968—; dir. 1st Nat. Bank S.C. Mem. N.J. Gen. Assembly, 1958-62. Charleston (S.C.) chmn. Nat. Alliance Businessmen. Exec. com. bd. dirs. Blue Shield S.C. Served as 1st lt. inf. AUS, 1946-47, from capt. to lt. col., inf., 1951-56. Decorated Silver Star, Bronze Star, Legion of Merit. Mem. Res. Officers Assn., Am. Land Devel. Assn. (chmn. pub. affairs com.), Nat. Assn. Home Builders (nat. leisure home com.), Am. Legion, V.F.W. Episcopalian. Clubs: Army and Navy, Church, S.E.C. (N.Y.C.). Home: 220 Sumter Av Summerville SC 29483 Office: 404 N Pine St Summerville SC 29483

SNELLGROVE, JAMES ROYCE, ret. supt. schs.; b. nr. Ozark, Ala., Nov. 22, 1910; s. Charle Lee and Henretta (Kyser) S.; B.S., Troy U., 1936; M.S., Auburn U., 1943; m. Myra Watson, May 28, 1933; 1 son, Robert Royce. Tchr., Coffee County Schs., 1933-35, prin., 1935-41; prin. Hayneville High Sch., Lowndes County, 1941-48; supt. Enterprise (Ala.) City Schs., 1948-72. Pres. Enterprise Investors Cooperation, 1950. Named Man of Year Enterprise, 1953. Mem. Ala. Edn. Assn. (dist. pres.), S. Ala. Supts. Orgn. (pres.). Baptist. Rotarian. Home: 706 W Lee St Enterprise AL 36330

SNETHEN, ROLLIN KENNETH, city ofcl.; b. Pontiac, Ill., Oct. 19, 1908; B.S. in Ry. Elec. Engring., U. Ill., 1930; postgrad. Command and Staff Coll. Army, 1956-62; m. Lucille Hortense Myer, Oct. 1, 1929; children—James Alan, Marilyn Suzanne (Mrs. Ralph Earnest Clark), Barbara Dolores (Mrs. Robert David Leonard), Carol Louise (Mrs. Richard Willis Reed). Jr. engr. Ill. Hwy. Dept., Ottawa, 1936-40; engr. Hasie & Green, Engrs., Lubbock, Tex., 1947; city engr., mgr. City Plainview, Tex., 1948-56; mgr. City Colorado City, Tex., 1956-60, City of Corsicana, Tex., 1960-69, Sapulpa, Okla., 1969—. Mem. Okla. Planning Congress. Bd. dirs. Okla. Municipal League, United Fund, Central Okla. Devel. Dist. Served to lt. col. AUS, 1940-47. Registered profl. engr., Tex., Okla., Colo. Mem. Internat., Tex., N. Tex. (pres. 1964), Okla. city mgrs. assns., U.S. Mil. Engrs. Soc., Tex. Water Conservation Assn., Corsicana (dir., chmn. water resources 1967), Sapulpa (dir.) chambers commerce, Nat., Okla. socs. profl. engrs. Baptist. Research on chilled car wheels. Home: 11 N Moccasin Pl Sapulpa OK 74066 Office: PO Box 1130 Sapulpa OK 74066

SNIDER, OSCAR, dentist; b. Caneyville, Ky., Feb. 3, 1911; s. Harvy B. and Judy (Bratcher) S.; student Western Ky. U., 1929-31; D.D.S., U. Louisville, 1934; postgrad. oral surgery Northwestern U., 1937; m. Dorthy Larned, Dec. 28, 1940; 1 son, Harvy Larned. Practice gen. dentistry Greenville, Ky., 1934-38, Russelville, Ky., 1938-42, 46—; mem. staff Logan County Hosp., Russellville, 1946-61. Served to lt. col. Dental Corps, AUS, 1942-46; ETO. Named Ky. col. Mem. Am., Ky., Pennyrile dental assns. Democrat. Episcopalian (mem. Bishop's com. 1956-64). Mason, Rotarian. Home: Rte 5 Russellville KY 42276 Office: PO Box 87 Russellville KY 42276

SNIDER, ROBERT LARRY, electronics co. exec.; b. Muskogee, Okla., Aug. 10, 1932; s. George Robert and Kathryn (Smiser) S.; student Phillips U., 1950-51, Tex. A. and M. Coll., 1952; B.S. in Indsl. Engring., U. Houston, 1955, postgrad., 1956; postgrad. Pomona Coll., 1960; m. Gerlene Rose Tipton, Nov. 26, 1953; children—Melody Kathryn, Rebecca Lee. Instr., Coll. Engring., U. Houston, 1955-56; sr. indsl. Sheffield Steel Corp., Houston, 1955-59, Kaiser Steel Co., Fontana, Cal., 1959-60; cons. Arthur Young & Co., Los Angeles, 1960-61; mgmt. analyst Iranian Oil Exploration & Producing Co., Masjidi-Suliman, Iran, 1961-62; cons., 1962-64, asso., 1964-65, v.p. operating methods div. Booz, Allen & Hamilton, Inc., Dallas, 1965-67, v.p., mng. officer internat. prodn. and inventory control div., 1967-69; prin., gen. cons. practice Peat Marwick Mitchell, Houston, 1969-71; exec. v.p., dir. Sterling Electronics Co., Houston, 1971-72, pres., chief operating officer, dir., 1972—. Served with C.E. AUS, 1956. Recipient Outstanding Mil. Engr. award Soc. Mil. Engrs., 1955. Sr. mem. Am. Inst. Indsl. Engrs.; mem. Soc. Advancement Mgmt., Am. Mgmt. Assn. (mem. pres.'s assn.), Phi Theta Kappa, Phi Kappa Phi. Home: 530 Ramble Wood Rd Houston TX 77024 Office: 4211 Southwest Freeway Sterling Electronics Bldg Houston TX 77002

SNIDER, TED LOWELL, radio sta. exec.; b. Rockwood, Tex., Dec. 16, 1928; s. Andy Jasper and Julia (Hull) S.; B.A., Baylor U., 1949, M.A., 1950; certificate U. Cal., Los Angeles, NBC-TV Inst., 1950; m. Jane Julian, Dec. 6, 1950; children—Cathron Julaine, Ted Lowell. Mgr. KOAT-TV, Albuquerque, 1953-55, KXOC, Chico, Cal., 1955-57; program dir. WTCN-TV, Mpls., 1957-59; mgr. KBST, Big Spring, Tex., 1959-61, KPAY, Chico, Cal., 1961-66; v.p., gen. mgr. KARK AM/FM, Little Rock, 1966—. Mem. City Council, Chico, Cal., 1965-66. Pres. adv. bd. Salvation Army, Chico, Cal., 1964; pres.-elect Butte County (Cal.) chpt. Am. Cancer Soc., 1964; pres., bd. dirs. Chico (Cal.) YMCA, 1962. Served with USMCR, 1951-52. Recipient Community Service award Chico Rotary Club, 1963; named Broadcaster of Distinction, Baylor U., 1969. Republican. Baptist (mem. exec. bd. So. Bapt. gen. conv. Cal. 1962-64). Rotarian. Home: 1104 Biscayne Dr Little Rock AR 72207 Office: 1001 Spring St Little Rock AR 72203

SNIDER, WADE THOMAS, land surveyor; b. Denton, N.C., July 11, 1940; s. Arthur Roosevelt and Nettie Josephine (Davis) S.; student Wingate Coll., 1958-60; m. Nancy Hendren, Aug. 3, 1963; children—Warren Thomas, Melody Rose, Amiee Annette. Supr. surveying dept. Moore Gardner & Assos., Asheboro, N.C., 1962-67; partner individual land surveying practice, Lexington, N.C., 1968-70; prin. Wade T. Snider Surveying Services, Lexington, 1970—. Served with AUS, 1964. Mem. N.C. Soc. Surveyors. Baptist (deacon 1964-71; chmn. 1967-70). Home and office 134 Eastside Dr Lexington NC 27292

SNIDER, WILLIAM DAVIS, newspaper editor; b. Salisbury, N.C., June 7, 1920; s. William Marvin and Mildred (Davis) S.; A.B., U. N.C., 1941; m. Florence Lide, June 12, 1948; children—Jane Telfair, Mary Alice Cordon, Florence Lide, Mildred Davis. Reporter, Salisbury Evening Post, 1941-42, 46-48; pvt. sec. N.C. gov. R. Gregg Cherry 1948, adminstrv. asst. to gov. W. Kerr Scott, 1949; adminstrv. asst. N.C. Hwy. Commn., 1950-52, asso. editor Greensboro (N.C.) Daily News, 1951-65, editor, 1965—; editor Greensboro Record, 1966—. Lectr. journalism U. N.C., 1963-64. Pres., Nat. Conf. Editorial Writers, 1969, editor Masthead, 1961-63. Mem. N.C. Constn. Commn., 1957-59; chmn. N.C. Awards Commn., 1963—. Chmn. bd. trustees Greensboro Pub. Library. Served to 2d lt. Signal Corps, AUS, 1942-46; CBI. Mem. Am. Soc. Newspaper Editors, N.C. Editorial Writers (pres.), Sigma Nu. Democrat. Presbyn. Club: Greensboro Country. Home: 1405 Briarcliff Rd Greensboro NC 27408 Office: 220 N Davie St Greensboro NC 27420

SNODGRASS, WILLIAM R., state ofcl.; b. Sparta, Tenn., Sept. 15, 1922; s. Robert J. and Nannie (Lee) S.; grad. David Lipscomb Coll., 1942; student U. Pa., 1942-43; B.S. in Bus. Administrn., U. Tenn., 1947, postgrad. in accounting; m. Faye Birdwell Bailey, Dec. 28, 1968; children—Emily Faye, Sarah Elizabeth, William R. Research asst. bur. bus. research U. Tenn., 1947-51; cons. municipal accounting and finance municipal tech. adv. service, 1951-53; dir. budget, dir. local finance, 1953-55, comptroller Tenn. Gen. Assembly, 1955—. Mem. Tenn. Commn. Inter-govtl. Coop. Served in mil., 1943-46. Mem. Am. Legion, Nat. Assn. State Auditors, Comptrollers and Treas., Nat. Assn. Tax Adminstrs., Council State Govs. Mem. Ch. of Christ. Office: Office of Comptroller State Capitol Nashville TN 37219

SNOOK, JOHN LLOYD, bus. exec.; b. Troy, O., Nov. 25, 1896; s. Clarence Guy and Anna B. (Counts) S.; Ph.B., Kenyon Coll., 1919; m. Alice V. Winger, June 21, 1923 (dec. Dec. 1967); children—John Lloyd, Elizabeth Anne, Julia Winger, Alice Winger; m. 2d, Mary C. Gayler, Jan. 1972. Sec., treas., plant mgr. Kitchen Aid Mfg. Co., Springfield, O., 1919-24; prof. indsl. research Antioch Coll., Yellow Springs, O., 1924-30; pres., gen. mgr. J. L. Snook Co. (formerly Antioch Shoe Project, Inc.), 1930-60. Cons., SCORE, 1966—. Chmn., Scioto County chpt. A.R.C., 1946-59, Greater Lakeland (Fla.) chpt., 1965-69; mem. nat. nominating com., 1948-49, Eastern area adv. council, 1950-52, vice chmn. mems. and funds Ohio, 1953-55, mem. nat. bd. govs., 1957-61, mem. Fla. conf. com., 1965-68; dir. YMCA, 1957-62, pres. Clay Twp. br., 1960-62, dir. Lakeland Family YMCA, 1968—; chmn. Scioto County Community Chest, 1950; dir. Scioto County Crippled Children's Soc., 1948-60, pres., 1950-56; Ohio Soc. Crippled Children, 1949-55, pres. 1951-52; dir. Nat. Soc. Crippled Children, 1951-52; pres. Scioto County Council Social Agys., 1953-55; chmn. Com. for Ministry to Def. Community in Scioto Valley, 1952-56; mem. Portsmouth Town Hall Forum Com., 1942-60, chmn., 1955-59; exec. com. Ohio Citizens Council for Health and Welfare, 1954-59; dir. United Cerebral Palsy of Polk County, Fla., 1962—, v.p., 1964—; bd. dirs. United Fund of Greater Lakeland, 1964—, exec. com., 1970—; chmn. adv. bd. Salvation Army, 1969-71; dir. Creative and Performing Arts Council Lakeland; pres. Lakeland Concert Assn; chmn. Polk County Manpower Devel. and Tng. Adv. Com., 1971—. Past sr. warden Episcopal Ch., mme. bishop and chpt. Diocese of So. Ohio, 1956-59, del. ho. of deps., 1955, chmn. dept. stewardship and every mem. canvas Diocese S. Fla. 1964-70; pres. Portsmouth Assn. Chs., 1949-50; adminstrv. com. Ohio Council Chs., 1954-61, trustee Found., 1961-62; mem. Lakeland Com. on Creative and Performing Arts, 1972—, Fla. Ancillary Manpower Planning Bd., 1972—. Mem. Portsmouth City Charter Revision Com., 1951-52. Served as ensign AC, USN, 1918-19; lt. comdr. USNR, 1944-46. Recipient citation for outstanding performance Navy Dept., 1945. Mem. Nat. Mgmt. Assn. (charter), Delta Kappa Epsilon. Episcopalian (vestryman, jr. warden 1966—, exec. bd. Diocese S. Fla. 1966-69). Mason, Rotarian (past pres., past dist. gov.). Home: 1342 Edgewater Beach Dr Lakeland FL 33801

SNOOK, JOHN MCCLURE, telephone co. exec.; b. Toledo, May 31, 1917; s. Ward H. and Grace (McClure) S.; student Ohio State U., 1936-43. Instr. history, fine arts and scis. Ohio State U., Columbus; exec. v.p. Gulf Telephone Co., Foley, Ala., 1955-70, pres., 1970—. Chmn., Baldwin Sesquicentennial, 1969; mem. hon. staff Gov. Ala., 1967—. Hon. a.d.c. lt. col. Ala.; hon. Ala. state trooper; recipient Citizen of Year award Gulf Shores, 1956-57. Mem. Nat. Rifle Assn. (life), Am. Ordnance Assn., South Baldwin C. of C., Delaware County, Baldwin County hist. assns., Ohio State Alumni Assn., Ala. Ind. Telephone Assn., Telephone Pioneers, Ind. Pioneers. Kiwanian, Lion. Office: Box 670 Foley AL 36535

SNOW, BREWSTER, union ofcl. Sec.-treas. Va. AFL-CIO. Office: 102 N Belvidere St Richmond VA 23220*

SNOW, JOEL ALAN, physicist; b. Brockton, Mass., Apr. 1, 1937; s. George Herbert and Mary Wilson (Sproul) S.; B.S., U. N.C., 1958; M.A., Washington U., St. Louis, 1963, Ph.D., 1967; m. Laetitia Mary Harrer, June 27, 1959; children—Jonathan, Nicholas. Instr. physics and electronics U.S. Naval Power Sch., Conn., 1958-61; instr. physics Washington U., summer 1962; asst. program dir. theoretical physics NSF, Washington, summer 1966, asso. program dir. theoretical physics, 1967-68, head Office Interdisciplinary Research, 1969-70, dep. asst. dir. for sci. and tech., 1971—; research asso. physics U. Ill., 1967-68. Served to lt. USNR, 1958-61. Fellow A.A.A.S.; mem. Am. Phys. Soc., Am. Assn. Physics Tchrs., Philos. Soc. Washington, Com. for Environmental Information (sci. div.), World Future Soc., Phi Beta Kappa, Sigma Xi. Home: 6619 Byrnes Dr McLean VA 22101 Office: Nat Sci Found 1800 G St NW Washington DC 20550

SNOW, THOMAS WAYNE, JR., state ofcl.; b. Old Hickory, Tenn., Jan. 10, 1936; s. Thomas Wayne and Johnnie Pearl-(Huffine) S.; A.B., U. Ga., 1958, LL.B., 1960. Admitted to Ga. bar, 1959; practice in Rossville, 1960—; city atty. Ft. Oglethorpe, Ga., 1964—, Chickamauga, Ga.; atty. Chickamauga Sch. Bd.; mem. Ga. Ho. of Reps., 1962—, chmn. ho. judiciary com., 1969—. Ga. del. Nat. Legislative Leadership Conf., Washington, 1966, Atlanta, 1969. Mem. 7th Dist. Legislative Assn. (past pres.), Rossville Jr. C. of C. (past pres.), Rossville Boosters, Hon. Future Farmers Am., Am. Judicature Soc., Ga. Bar Assn., Lookout Mountain Judicial Bar Assn., U. Ga. Alumni Assn. (pres. Walker County chpt.). Democrat. Methodist (lay leader, Sunday sch. tchr.). Elk. Club: Exchange (Rossville). Home: Route 2 Chickamauga GA 30707 Office: 308 Spring Rossville GA 30741

SNOWDEN, JACK BENTLEY, dentist; b. Paris, Tex., Mar. 24, 1928; s. Leonard Alley and Minnibel (Bentley) S.; B.A., Tex. Tech. Coll., 1949; D.D.S., Baylor U., 1957; m. Elizabeth Jean Seward, Apr. 8, 1955; children—John Seward, Mary Anne, Allen Bentley. Practice dentistry, Arlington, Tex., 1957—; asst. clin. prof. periodontics Baylor Coll. Dentistry, 1957—. Bd. dirs. YMCA, 1965-67. Served with M.C., AUS, 1950-52. Fellow Am. Coll. Dentists, Acad. Gen. Dentistry; mem. Am., Tex. dental assns., Southwestern Soc. Dental Medicine (pres. 1968-69), Fort Worth Dist. Dental Soc. (sec.-treas. 1971-72; pres. elect 1972-73), Fort Worth (pres. 1971), Tex. (v.p. 1972-73) acads. gen. dentistry, Arlington Dental Study Club (pres. 1969-70), C. of C. (dir. 1965-66), Omicron Kappa Upsilon. Presbyn. (ruling elder 1961—; gen. supt. Sunday Schs. 1965-68). Mason (Shriner). Clubs: Sportsman, Civitan (pres. 1963-64) (Arlington). Home: 4104 Curry Rd Arlington TX 76016 Office: 801 E Border St Suite A Arlington TX 76010

SNUGGS, HERSCHELL FRANCIS, county mgr.; b. Badin, N.C., June 18, 1919; s. Walter Artis and Lettie (Russell) S.; B.A. in Pub. Adminstrn., U. N.C., 1950; m. Christine Tyson Hellen, June 21, 1947; children—Frances Christine, Charles Russell. City mgr. Highland Park, Ill., 1951-54, Penn Twp., Pa., 1954-55, Lake Worth, Fla., 1955-57, Thomasville, Ga., 1957-63, Colonial Heights, Va., 1963-66, Mooresville, N.C., 1966-70; county mgr. Stanly County, Albemarle, N.C., 1970—. Dir. Entertainment Found., Youth Center, 1958—, treas., 1960-61; dir. Salvation Army. Served with inf. AUS, 1941-45, PTO. Mem. Internat., Ga. (pres.) city mgrs. assns., Am. Soc. Pub. Adminstrn., C. of C. (dir. 1958—), Ga. Municipal Assn. (dir. 1958—), P.T.A. (v.p. 1967), Band Boosters (pres. 1968). Baptist. Kiwanian (pres. 1963, 66). Home: Box 128 Crestview Dr Albemarle NC 28001 Office: County Courthouse Albemarle NC 28001

SNYDER, CHARLES FREDERICK, restaurant exec.; b. Reading, Pa., July 23, 1932; s. Walter Earl and Edith Marie (Howerter) S.; student Middlebury Coll., 1950-54; m. Rosemary Kathryn Jackson, Mar. 26, 1966; children— Julie Beth, Eric Jon, Peter Kurt, Michael Jay. Unit mgr. Marriott Corp., Washington, 1959-62; gen. mgr. Kansas City Stockyards Co., Washington, 1962-66; v.p. research Bonanza Internat., Inc., Dallas, 1966—. Research grantee Tex. A. & M. Research Found., 1970-72. Mem. Nat. Restaurant Assn., Inst. Food Technologists. Republican. Lutheran. Home: 3815 Calculus Rd Dallas TX 75234 Office: 811 S Central Expressway Richardson TX 75080

SNYDER, DICK PHILIP, accountant; b. Covington, Okla., Aug. 11, 1936; s. William Bryan and Edith (Kirk) S.; B.S., Okla. State U., 1958, M.S., 1960. Staff accountant Haskins & Sells, Tulsa, 1960-61, 62-63; asst. treas. U.S. Liquidgas, Inc., Tulsa, 1963-66; sr. accountant Peat, Marwick, Mitchell & Co., Tulsa, 1966-72; asst. controller Williams Energy Co., Tulsa, 1972—. Vice pres. Stillwater Delta Tau Delta Housing Corp. Served with USAF, 1961-62. C.P.A., Okla. Mem. Am. Inst. C.P.A.'s, Okla. Soc. C.P.A.'s, Beta Alpha Psi, Delta Tau Delta, Alpha Kappa Psi, Alpha Kappa Psi Alumni. Mem. Christian Ch. Home: 1623 S Utica Av Tulsa OK 74104 Office: Nat Bank of Tulsa Bldg Tulsa OK 74103

SNYDER, DONALD RAY, drug co. exec.; b. Richmond, Ky., July 24, 1933; s. Harlan and Virginia (Ross) S.; B.A., Eastern Ky. U., 1961, M.A., 1962. Div. Sept. 1969; children—Donna Sue, Elizabeth Carol, Gary Eugene; m. Madia Fern Carroll, Nov. 26, 1969. Bank examiner U.S. Treas. Dept., Washington, 1962-65; sec., treas. Begley Drug Co., Richmond, 1965—, also dir., dir. subsidiary cos. Served with USNR, 1953-57. Mem. Nat. Commerce Soc., S.A.R., Epsilon Pi Epsilon. Democrat. Baptist. Mason (K.T.), Elk, Rotarian. Home: 112 Paula Dr Hillcrest Richmond KY 40475 Office: PO Box 1000 Richmond KY 40475

SNYDER, EDWINA HUNTER, educator; b. Coushatta, La., Apr. 4, 1932; d. Edison Everett and Cora Lee (Jones) Hunter; B.A., La. Coll., 1952; M.R.E., Southwestern Bapt. Theol. Sem., 1955; M.A., Northwestern U., 1958, Ph.D. (Univ. scholar), 1965; m. James Robert Snyder, June 2, 1960; 1 dau., Wendy Jo. Youth dir. Parkview Bapt. Ch., Shreveport, La., 1952-53; youth dir. Univ. Bapt. Ch., Fort Worth, 1954-55; ednl. dir. First Bapt. Ch., Galax, Va., 1955-57; speech instr. Bapt. Missionary Tng. Sch., Chgo., 1957-58; faculty speech dept. Georgetown (Ky.) Coll., 1958—, prof., 1971—, chmn. dept., 1964-67. Trustee Visitation Montessori Sch. Georgetown, chmn. faculty and acad. coms., 1970-71, v.p. bd. trustees, 1971-72, pres. bd. trustees, 1972-73. Georgetown Coll. research and writing grantee, 1969. Mem. Am. Assn. U. Profs., Am., So. speech communication assns., Ky. Assn. Communication Arts (pres. 1971-72), Pi Kappa Delta, Alpha Chi, Alpha Lambda Delta. Democrat. Baptist (deacon 1969—). Contbr. papers to profl. convs. Organizer Wordmasters, speech performing ensemble touring U.S., abroad, 1958—. Home: 1113 Choctaw St Georgetown KY 40324

SNYDER, FALLON, printing exec.; b. Dallas, July 28, 1925; s. Bryan and Margurite (Shumate) S.; student Tex. A. and M. U., 1942, Ga. Inst. Tech., 1943; B.B.A., So. Meth. U., 1948; m. Shirlee Doris Stovall, July 17, 1947; children—Anna Victoria, Nancy Margaret, Cartier Fallon, Stuart Webster. With Johnston Printing Co., Dallas, 1947—, v.p., sales mgr., 1956-66, pres., 1966—. Served with USMCR, 1943-46. Decorated Purple Heart; named Most Valuable Mem., Dallas Advt. League, 1957. Mem. Dallas Mgmt. Assn., Advt. Club Dallas (pres. 1964), Kappa Sigma. Episcopalian. Home: 10949 Candlelight St Dallas TX 75229 Office: 2700 N Haskell St Dallas TX 75206

SNYDER, HARRY GLENN, coll. adminstr.; b. Festus, Mo., Sept. 29, 1911; s. Charles Tibbels and Kate (Herbert) S.; D.D.S., Washington U., St. Louis, 1934; certificate prosthesis N.Y. U., 1952; m. Jeanette Maness, Oct. 5, 1940; children—Jerry Glenn, Thomas Alan. Gen. practice dentistry, St. Louis, 1934-42; commd. 2d lt. U.S. Army, 1942, advanced through grades to col., 1959; dental surgeon C.E., Vogelweh, Germany, 1956-59, Western Area command, Germany, 1956-59, Ft. Meyer, Va., 1959-60, Ft. Belvoir Army Engr. Center, Va., 1960-66; ret., 1966; dir. dental programs Central Piedmont Community Coll., Charlotte, N.C., 1966—. Field dir. St. Louis council Boy Scouts Am., 1934-36; pres. Kaisersalutern, Germany, 1958-59, Little League, Ft. Belvoir, 1964-65, P.T.A., East High Sch. Booster Club, Charlotte, 1971-72. Decorated Legion of Merit. Mem. N.C., 2d Dist. dental assns., Charlotte Dental Soc., Am. Assn. Dental Schs., Ret. Officers Assn., Washington U. Dental Alumni. Mason; mem. Order Eastern Star. Clubs: Loyal Order Boar, Heroes, Sojourners. Home: 461 Lyttleton Dr Charlotte NC 28211

SNYDER, JOSEPH FREMONT, dentist; b. Deland, Fla., Dec. 5, 1931; s. Joseph Fremont and Mildred Humphrey (Barnes) S.; A.A., U. Fla., 1957; D.D.S., Med. Coll. Va., 1961; m. Alynn Cordell, Dec. 17, 1955; children—Joseph Fremont III, Suzanne Alynn. Practice of dentistry, Daytona Beach, Fla., 1961—. Commr. South Penisula Zoning Comm., 1968—. Trustee Museum of Arts and Sciences, pres., 1966—. Served with AUS, 1949-53. Mem. Am., Fla. dental assns., Am. Soc. Preventive Dentistry, Acad. Gen. Dentistry, Fla. Acad. Dental Practice Adminstrn. Presbyn (elder 1968—). Home: 2424 S Peninsula Av Daytona Beach FL 32018 Office: 159 Broadway Daytona Beach FL 32018

SNYDER, LENARD DAVID, engring. exec.; b. Bristow, Okla., Dec. 27, 1920; s. Earl P. and Julia E. (Ladd) S.; B.S., Okla. State U., 1943; m. Beatrice Mae Strom, Jan. 17, 1943; children—Donna B., David R. Design engr. George E. Failing Supply Co., Enid, Okla., 1946-51; mech. engr. Continental Oil Co., Ponca City, 1952-53; chief engr. Drilling Accessory & Mfg. Co., Dallas, 1953-55; chief engr., product mgr. oil field drill div. Joy Mfg. Co., 1955-58; with Dodge Mfg. Corp. div. Reliance Electric Co., Dallas, 1958—, dist. mgr., 1965-71, area mgr., 1971—. Served to capt. AUS, 1943-46, 51-52. Registered profl. engr., Okla., Tex. Mem. Am. Soc. M.E. Patentee drilling equipment. Home: 8944 Lockhaven Dr Dallas TX 75238

SNYDER, MARION GENE, congressman; b. Louisville, Jan. 26, 1928; s. M. G. and Lois (Berg) S.; J.D., U. Louisville, 1950, LL.B. cum laude, Jefferson Sch. Law, Louisville, 1950; m. Louise Hodges, Mar. 23, 1951; 1 son, Mark. Admitted to Ky. bar, 1950, D.C. bar, 1970; real estate broker, 1948—; practiced in Louisville, 1950—; engaged in residential constrn. bus., 1958-67, in farming, 1957-67; city atty. Jeffersontown, 1953-57; magistrate 1st dist. Jefferson County, 1957-61; mem. 88th Congress, 3d Dist. Ky.; mem. 90th-92d Congresses from 4th Dist. Ky. Vice pres. Ky. Magistrates and Commnrs., 1958. Pres., Jeffersontown Civic Center, 1953-54, legal adviser Jeffersontown Community Council, 1951-52. Pres., Lincoln Republican Club Ky., 1960-61, 1st Magisterial Dist. Rep. Club, 1955-57; mem. South End Rep. Club. Mem. Ky., D.C. bar assns., Louisville C. of C., Ky. Farm Bur., Nat. Inst. Real Estate Brokers, Flying Realtors Assn. Club: Optimists (pres. Jeffersontown 1957-58). Home: 2308 Blankerbaker Lane Jeffersontown KY 40299 Office: 140 Chenoweth Lane Louisville KY 40207 also Cannon Bldg Washington DC

SNYDER, ROBERT MURRAY, oceanographic engr.; b. Penn Yan, N.Y., Feb. 19, 1932; s. Theodore Adelbert and Stella (Stow) S.; B.S. in Physics, Rensselaer Poly. Inst., 1959; m. Beatrice Stelle Miller, May 5, 1969; children—Kenneth Edward Baxter, David Robertson Baxter. Research asst. Woods Hole (Mass.) Oceanographic Instn., 1959-60, 63-63; mohole staff engr. Nat. Acad. Sci., Washington, Houston, Los Angeles, 1960-61; project engr. Ocean Sci. & Engring., Washington, 1963-69; dir. technol. research Oceanography Mariculture Industries, Riviera Beach, Fla., 1969-70; pres. Snyder Oceanography Services, 1970—, Offshore Mooring Services, Inc. Mem. Oceanography Council, Palm Beach County Devel. Commn., 1968—. Served with USCG, 1951-54. Mem. Marine Tech. Soc. (chpt. vice chmn. 1967-68), Nat. Security Indsl. Assn., Sigma Xi. Co-author: Handbook of Ocean and Underwater Engineering, 1969. Contbr. articles to profl. jours. Home: 169 Beacon Lane Jupiter FL 33458 Office: 169 Beacon Lane Jupiter FL 33458

SOBRINO, JOSEPHINE, educator; b. San Antonio, Aug. 1, 1915; d. Fausto and Maria (Gutierrez de la Vega) Sobrino; A.B., Incarnate World Coll., 1936; diploma (U.S. State Dept. grantee), U. Mexico, 1945; M.A., U. Tex., 1946; Ed.D., U. Houston, 1960; postgrad. U. Valladolid, 1953, (Instituto Spanish cultural grantee) U. Madrid, 1954. Chmn. dept. modern langs. Tex. Southmost Coll., Brownsville, 1942-59; chmn. dept. Spanish, U. Houston, 1959—. Cons., Spanish for Modern Lang. Assn., 1963-65, Tex. Edn. Agy., 1960-63; del. conv. Internat. Fedn. U. Woman, Paris, 1956. Mem. bd. Brownsville Library Assn., 1954-59, Charro Days, Inc., Brownsville, 1949-59, Mercy Hosp. Nursing Sch., Brownsville, 1955-59. Nat. Conf. Christians and Jews grantee, 1954. Recipient Magnificate Medal award Mundelein Coll., Chgo., 1962; Spanish Consulate Gen. award, 1962; Matrix award Theta Sigma Phi, 1965; Faculty Research grantee U. Houston, 1968. Mem. Internat. Fedn. Cath. Alumnae (state sec. 1940), Am. Assn. U. Women (Brownsville pres. 1954-56, state conv. chmn. 1958), Tex. Fgn. Lang. Assn. (pres. 1954-56, 66-68), Houston Council Tchrs. Fgn. Langs. (pres. 1962-63), Alliance Francaise (mem. bd. Houston 1964—). Author: Influence of Continuing Cultural Patterns Reflected by Pertinent Folklore of Selected Indian Tribes on the Education in Mexico, 1960; The Bilingual Child, 1961; (with others) Espanol: La Teoria y la Practica, 1971, Repaso de Espanol: Lo esencial, 1972. Contbr. articles to profl. jours. Home: 5326 Darnell St Houston TX 77035

SOCOLOFSKY, MARION DAVID, educator; b. Marion, Kan., Sept. 23, 1931; s. A. L. and Mary (Reneau) S.; B.S., Kan. State U., 1953; M.A., U. Tex., 1955, Ph.D., 1961; m. Esther M. Green, June 28, 1953; children— Kathleen Marie, Mary Sue. Faculty La. State U., Baton Rouge, 1961—, asso. prof. microbiology, 1964—, chmn. dept., 1966—, prof., 1968—. Served to capt. USAF, 1953-58. Mem. A.A.A.S., Am. Soc. Microbiology, Soc. Gen. Microbiology, Electron Microscope Soc. Am., Sigma Xi, Phi Kappa Phi. Home: 8236 Menlo St Baton Rouge LA 70808

SODOLSKI, JOHN, assn. exec.; b. Menasha, Wis., Apr. 11, 1931; s. Leo Vincent and Laone (Pinkowsky) S.; B.S. in Polit. Sci., U. Wis., 1953; m. Carol Jeannette Eppard. With Stanford Paper Sales Corp., Washington, 1957-59, Atlantic Research Corp., Alexandria, Va., 1959-62; dir. indsl. electronics div. Electronic Industries Assn., Washington, 1962-69, v.p. communications indsl. electronics div., 1969—. Served to 1st lt. USMCR, 1953-55. Mem. Washington Opera Soc., Sigma Chi. Club: National Press (Washington). Home: 1310 Swan Harbour Rd Washington DC 20022 Office: 2001 I St NW Washington DC 20006

SOENNEKER, HENRY JOSEPH, clergyman; b. Melrose, Minn., May 27, 1907; s. Henry and Mary (Wessel) S.; B.A., Josephinum Coll. and Sem., Worthington O., 1930; J.C.L., Cath. U. Am., 1950. Ordained priest Roman Catholic Ch., 1934; asst. parish of St. Anthony, St. Cloud, Minn., 1934-40, also tchr. Cathedral High Sch., St. Cloud and chaplain VA Hosp.; chaplain Sisters of St. Francis, Little Falls, Minn., 1940-48; spiritual dir. St. John's Major Sem., Collegeville, Minn., 1950-61; bishop Diocese of Owensboro (Ky.), 1961—. Home: 1535 Frederica St Owensboro KY 42301 Office: PO Box 773 Owensboro KY 42301

SOHLER, KATHERINE BEATRICE BERRIDGE, pub. health educator; b. Cambridge, Mass., May 31, 1919; d. William Arthur and Ruth (Reid) Berridge; B.A., Radcliffe Coll., 1941; M.A., Yale, 1943, Ph.D., 1950, M.P.H., 1961, Dr. P.H., 1966; m. Theodore Paul Sohler, May 31, 1941 (div. June 1953); children—Edith, Theodore Berridge. Research asst. Yale, 1942-47, Sterling fellow, 1947-48, research asst. 1956-60, post-doctoral fellow, 1960-61, 63-66, research asso. dept. epidemiology and pub. health, 1966-67; study dir. Community Health Information Center, Mendocino State Hosp., Talmage, Cal., 1967-69; asst. prof. biostatistics and epidemiology Sch. Health, U. Okla., Oklahoma City, 1969-71, asso. prof., 1971—; dir. field office Dutchess County Evaluation Studies, Hudson River State Hosp., Poughkeepsie, N.Y., 1961-63; research asso. Columbia, 1961-63. Fellow Am. Pub. Health Assn.; Mem. Am. Statis. Assn., A.A.A.S., Am. Assn. U. Profs., Am. Acad. Polit. and Social Sci., Soc. Epidemiologic Research, Audubon Soc., Phi Beta Kappa. Unitarian. Clubs: Sierra; Appalachian Mountain. Home: 324 NW 86th St Oklahoma City OK 73114 Office: 800 NE 13 Oklahoma City OK 73104

SOJKA, NICKOLAS JOSEPH, educator; b. Page, Neb., June 15, 1934; s. Walter and Anna (Boguz) S.; B.S., Kans. State U., 1958 D.V.M., 1958; M.S., U. Va., 1969; m. Eleanor June Cox, Apr. 23, 1960; children— Nickolas Joseph, Thomas John. Gen. vet. practice, Storm Lake, Ia., 1960; plant supt. agrl. marketing service U.S. Dept. Agr., Phila., 1961-62; asso. in vet. medicine Duke, 1962-65; asso. prof. surgery Sch. Medicine U. Va., Charlottesville, 1966—. Com. chmn. cub scouts Stonewall Jackson council Boy Scouts Am., 1970-72. Served to maj. AUS, 1958-60. Mem. Va. Acad. Sci. (sec. med. sect. 1970-71), Am. Assn. Lab. Animal Sci. (program chmn. 1967, 69), Am., Va., N.C., Blue Ridge vet. med. assns., Am. Soc. Animal Sci., Va. Acad. Sci., A.A.A.S., Alpha Zeta, Gamma Sigma Delta. Home: 305 Eastbrook Dr Charlottesville VA 22901 Office: Sch Medicine U Va Charlottesville VA 22901

SOKOLOFF, BORIS THEODORE, med. scientist, author; b. St. Petersburg, Russia, Nov. 12, 1889; s. Theodore and Maria (Verchovtzev) S.; Ph.D. U. St. Petersburg, 1913; M.D., 2d Med. Sch., Petrograd, Russia, 1917; Sc.D., U. Charles, 1916; m. Alice Hunt, June 3, 1912; children—Boris Theodore, Kiril. Came to U.S., 1929, naturalized, 1933. Head exptl. medicine Nat. Inst. Sci., 1918-20; fellow U. Brussels (Belgium), 1923-24, Pasteur Inst., Paris, France, 1925-26, U. Prague (Czechoslavakia), 1927; with Rockefeller Inst. Med. Research, N.Y.C., 1929-30; with Cancer Inst., Columbia, 1930-31, research fellow physiology and chemistry Columbia, 1935-42; research fellow dept. pathology Med. Sch. Washington U., St. Louis, 1931-35; dir. So. Bio-Research Inst., Fla. So. Coll., Lakeland, 1947—. Served to capt. M.C., Russian Army, 1917-18. Decorated St. Vladimir Order. Mem. Royal Soc. Medicine, Royal Soc. Arts and Letters, Am. Assn. Cancer Research, Am. Chem. Soc.,

N.Y. Acad. Scis., Am. Soc. Biol. Editors, A.A.A.S. Author: The Achievement of Happiness, 1936; Napoleon, Medical Biography, 1937; The Story of Penicillin, 1945; Science and the Purpose of Life, 1950; August Comte, Biography, 1961; Careinoid and Serotonin, 1968; The Permissive Society, 1972. Mng. editor: Jour. Growth, 1963—. Home: 825 Vistabula St Lakeland FL 33801 Office: So Bio-Research Inst Fla So Coll Lakeland FL 33802

SOKOLOSKY, DOMINIC MITCHELL, pharmacist; b. McAlester, Okla., Jan. 12, 1932; s. Dominic and Michilina (Nosock) S; B.S., Southwestern State Coll., 1955; m. Phyllis Jewell Wright, Jan. 21, 1956; children—Dee, Noble, Ann, Sue. Owner, operator Soc's Drug, Owasso, Okla., 1956-72; owner Plaza Drug, Sand Springs, Okla., 1971-72; pres. Owasso Investment Co., 1971; pres. Owasso Finance Corp., 1971-72; sec. W.S. & W. Devel. Co., Owasso, 1967-72; dir. First Bank of Owasso. Treas. Rural Water Dist., 1970-71, chmn., 1972; mem. Planning Comm. Bd., Rogers County, 1971—. Mem. Am., Okla. pharm. assns., C. of C. (pres. 1961-62), Club: Quarterback (Owasso). Home: PO Box 8 Owasso OK 74055 Office: 120 S Main St Owasso OK 74055

SOKOLOWSKI, EDWARD HIPOLIT, civil engr.; b. Bklyn., Mar. 24, 1927; s. Hipolit and Josephine (Sokolski) S.; m. Maureen Baldock, Apr. 25, 1953. Jr. civil engr. Vogt, Ivers, Seaman & Assos., Cin., 1950-51, Giffels & Vallet, Detroit, 1951-52, civil engr., project engr. Vogt, Ivers & Assos., 1952-59; chief engr. San Antonio office, 1959-69; rep. exec. com. Internat. Aerial Mapping Co., San Antonio, 1959-63, gen. mgr., 1963-70, v.p., 1966-70, pres., 1970—. Athletic commr. YMCA, Cin., 1951-53. Served with USN, 1944-46. Registered profl. engr., Tex., W.Va., O., Mich., Wash., Ia., N.M. Mem. Am., Tex. socs. civil engrs., Soc. Am. Mil. Engrs., Inst. Traffic Engrs., Armed Forces Communications and Electronics Assn., Am. Congress Surveying and Mapping, Am. Soc. Photogrammetry. Rotarian. Home: 7426 Robin Rest Dr San Antonio TX 78209 Office: 127 Internat Dr San Antonio TX 78213

SOKOLSKI, ALAN, govt. ofcl.; b. N.Y.C., Jan. 5, 1931; s. Irving and Pearl (Herzig) S.; B.M.E., Cornell U., 1953; M.B.A., Columbia, 1959, Ph.D. (Eastman Kodak Bus. fellow, Carnegie Travel fellow), 1962; m. Carol Stitt, July 27, 1956; children—Lynn, Lauren. Project engr., contract adminstr. Foster Wheeler Corp., N.Y.C., 1957-59; economist, bd. govs. Fed. Res. System, 1962-63; asst. program economist, acting program officer for capital devel. U.S. AID, Lagos, Nigeria, 1963-65; sr. economist, dep. dir. Office Econ. Research and Analysis, Dept. State, 1965-70; econ. research officer CIA, Washington, 1970—; lectr. Fgn. Service Inst., 1965-68; professorial lectr. Cath. U. Am., 1967-69. Served as 1st lt. USAF, 1954-56. Fellow African Studies Assn.; mem. Am. Econ. Assn., Sierra Club. Author: The Establishment of Manufacturing in Nigeria, 1965. Home: 915 Hyde Rd Silver Spring MD 20902 Office: CIA Washington DC 20505

SOLER-CLOQUELL, ENRIQUE RAFAEL, architect; b. Arecibo, P.R., Mar. 24, 1927; s. Enrique Rafael and Ana Elisa (Cloquell) S.; B.Arch., U. Fla., 1950; m. Doris Armstrong, Oct. 2, 1955; children—Sylvia, Enrique Alberto. Architect, Toro-Ferrer, Architects, San Juan, P.R., 1950-61; partner architect Horacio Diaz-Enrique Soler, San Juan, 1961-69; chmn. P.R. Planning Bd., Santurce, 1969—. Vice pres. P.R. Hwy. Authority, 1969—; mem. P.R. Pub. Bldg. Authority, 1969—; mem. Environmental Quality Bd., 1970—; mem. Gov.'s Adv. Council, 1969—; mem. Gov.'s Financial Com., 1969—; mem. P.R. Mining Commn., 1969—. Served with AUS, 1951-53. Recipient Urbe Mag. Design award, 1965. Mem. P.R. Inst. Engrs., Architects and Surveyors (v.p. 1966-68), A.I.A., P.R. Inst. Architects, U.S. Housing Conf., Gargoyle. Clubs: Bankers, Caribe Hilton Swimming and Tennis (San Juan); Casino de Puerto Rico. Home: 2163 McLeary Av Santurce PR 00913 Office: Box 9447 Santurce PR 00908

SOLES, WILLIAM ROGER, ins. co. exec.; b. Whiteville, N.C., Sept. 16, 1920; s. John William and Margaret (Watts) S.; B.S. in Commerce, U. N.C., 1947, postgrad. exec. program, 1956; m. Majelle Marrene Morris, Sept. 20, 1956; children—William Roger, Majelle Janette. Security analyst Jefferson Standard Life, Greensboro, N.C., 1947-51, asst. mgr. securities dept., 1951-56. 2d v.p., asso. mgr. securities, 1956-59, mgr. securities, 1959-62, v.p., mgr. securities, 1962-64, asst. to pres., 1964-66, exec. v.p., 1966-67, pres., 1967—, also dir.; pres., dir. Jefferson-Pilot Corp.; dir. So. Fire & Casualty Co., J-P Investments, Inc., Piedmont Natural Gas Co., Pilot Life Ins. Co., Jefferson Standard Broadcasting, Jefferson-Carolina Corp., Jefferson-Pilot Fire & Casualty Co., Jefferson-Pilot Title Ins. Co. Bd. dirs. N.C. Citizens Assn.; trustee Wesley Long Community Hosp., High Point Coll. Served with USAAF, 1941-45. C.L.U. Methodist (steward, past chmn. bd.). Rotarian. Club: Greensboro Country (past pres.). Home: 604 Kimberly Dr Greensboro NC 27408 Office: PO Box 21008 Greensboro NC 27420

SOLIEN, WILLIAM ALDON, banker; b. Stoughton, Wis., June 14, 1921; s. William O. and Anna J. (Johnson) S.; B.A., U. Wis., 1945, LL.D., 1947; m. Elayne L. Johnson, May 31, 1942; children—Mark A., Ann Louise. Admitted to Wis. bar, 1947, Fla. bar, 1966; with Lighthouse Point Bank, Pompano Beach, Fla., 1963—, pres., 1966—, dir., 1964—. Served with AUS, 1942-45. Mem. Lighthouse Point Library Assn. (founding dir. 1964), Phi Delta Phi. Son of Norway. Club: Lighthouse Point Yacht and Tennis. Home: Lighthouse Point FL 33064 Office: Box 579 Pompano Beach FL 33061

SOLKA, JACK, urban planner, architect; b. Mexico City, Mex., May 20, 1935; s. Isaac and Rose (Neumann) S.; B. Arch., Tex. A. and M. U., 1958; M.S., Columbia, 1962; m. Davie Lou Ettelman, Feb. 28, 1960; children—Michael Benjamin, Steven Morris, Gary Leonard. Came to U.S., 1945, naturalized, 1952. Instr. architecture Columbia 1963; with Morris Ketchum & Assos., N.Y.C., 1964, Hans &Bennett Assos., Corpus Christi, Tex., 1964-66; partner Martin & Solka, Corpus Christi, Tex., 1967-68, Bennett, Martin & Solka, Corpus Christi, Tex., 1967-68, Bennett, Martin, & Solka, 1969—. Housing cons., 1969—. Co-ordinator Tex. Gov.'s Conf. on Community and Urban Affairs, 1969; exec. dir. Community Devel. Corp., Corpus Christi, 1967-69; chmn. Municipal Arts Commn., 1968-69; leader Boy Scouts Am., 1967-69. Bd. dirs. Tex. A. and M. Hillel Found. Served with AUS, 1958-59. Mem. A.I.A. (pres. chpt. 1971), Tex. Soc. Architects (dir. 1972—), Nat. Assn. Nonprofit Housing Orgns. (dir. 1969). Rotarian. Home: 501 Bermuda St Corpus Christi TX 78411 Office: 4659 Everhart Rd Corpus Christi TX 78411

SOLLEE, ARTHUR NEYLE, civil engr.; b. Tifton, Ga., May 23, 1900; s. William C.B. and Elizabeth (Walsh) S.; B.C.E., U. Fla., 1922, C.E., 1926; m. Edna Marie Reiter, Jan. 9, 1937; children—Arthur Neyle, Annette T. (Mrs. Girard T. Lew), William L., Richard P., Katherine M. Resident engr. George B. Hills Co., Jacksonville, Fla., 1922-27; harbor engr. Port Everglades, Broward County Port Authority, Fla., 1928-30; with Duval County, Fla., 1931-56, asst. county engr., 1931-38, county engr., 1939-56; exec. dir. Jacksonville Transp. Authority, 1956—. Mem. Jacksonville City Planning Adv. Bd., 1939—. Bd. dirs. Cath. Charities Bur. Served with AUS, 1918. Mem. Fla. Engring. Soc., Nat. Soc. Profl. Engrs., Soc. Am. Mil. Engrs., Jacksonville Engring. Professions Club. Home: 10135 Scott Mill Rd Jacksonville FL 32217 Office: 1022 Prudential Dr Jacksonville FL 33207

SOLLERS-RIEDEL, HELEN, entomologist; b. Balt., Sept. 29, 1911; d. William Alexander and Helen (Day) Sollers; B.S., James Ormond Wilson Tchrs. Coll., 1934; m. F. A. Riedel, May 11, 1962 (dec.). With U.S. Bur Entomology and Plant Quarantine, Washington, 1937-53, sci. aide div. insect pest survey, 1937-42, jr. entomologist div. insects affecting man and animals, 1942-47, asst. entomologist, 1947-53; entomologist Plant Protection div. Agrl. Research Service, U.S. Dept. Agr., Washington, 1953-71; prin. investigator, mosquito lit. research specialist NIH-Entomol. Soc. Am. Grant, Washington, 1971—. Hon. fellow Indian Soc. for Malaria and Other Communicable Diseases; fellow Royal Soc. Tropical Medicine and Hygiene (London); mem. Insecticide Soc. Washington, Entomol. Soc. Am., Entomol. Soc. Washington (pres. 1969), Entomol. Soc. Can., Am. Soc. Tropical Medicine and Hygiene, Tropical Medicine Soc. Washington (dir. exec. com. 1961-64), Am. Mosquito Control Assn. (dir. S.E. Central region 1962-64), Am. Soc. Parasitologists, Australian Entomol. Soc., Entomol. Soc. Egypt, Ga. Entomol. Soc., Fla. Anti-Mosquito Assn. Club: Plant Pest Control (pres. 1960-61). Asso. editor Mosquito News. Contbr. articles to profl. jours. Home: 1218 Floral St NW Washington DC 20012 Office: PO Box 19009 Washington DC 20036

SOLMSON, HARRY BERLIN, pharm. co. exec.; b. Oklahoma City, Mar. 31, 1911; s. Harry Berlin and Gertrude (Myar) S.; B.A., U. Wis., 1932; J.D., U. Chgo., 1934; m. Harriet Sternberger, Apr. 5, 1938; children— Harry Berlin III, William S., Robert. Admitted to Ark. bar, 1933; with firm Robinson, House & Moses, Little Rock, 1934-39; with Plough, Inc., Memphis, 1939—, adminstrv. v.p., 1948-50, exec. v.p., 1950-72, pres., 1972—, v.p., dir. Schering-Plough Corp., 1972—. also dir. Mem. bd. regents Christian Bros. Coll. Memphis; trustee Memphis State U. Found., B'nai B'rith Hosp.; bd. dirs. Jr. Achievement, Cancer Soc., Memphis Indsl. Council, Mem. Tenn. Mfg. Assn., Proprietary Assn. Washington. Served to capt. USAAF, 1942-46. Home: 475 N Highland Memphis TN 38122 Office: 3022 Jackson Av Memphis TN 38112

SOLOMON, ERWIN SEYMOUR, lawyer; b. Belle Harbor, N.Y., Feb. 5, 1918; s. Samuel Sidney and Rose (Bisgyer) S.; B.A., Emory and Henry Coll., 1942; postgrad. Johns Hopkins, 1946-47; LL.B., U. Va., 1950; m. Joyce Marie Hiner, July 9, 1949; children—Michael, Deborah Joyce, Eve Starr, Hope Sidney. Admitted to Va. bar, 1949; pvt. practice law, Hot Springs, Va., 1950—; dist. atty. County Bath, Va., 1962—. Dir. Mason-Dixon Realty Co., Inc., Gripstop, Inc. Mem. Va. State Crime Commn., 1965—. Vice chmn. Bath County Democratic Com., 1960. Served with USAAF, 1942-46. Mem. Am. Bar Assn., Va. State Bar, Am. Legion. Lion (pres. 1963). Author: (with E. Abbott) Instructions to Jury for Virginia, West Virginia, 3 vols., 1964; (with Arthur Phelps) Divorce and Alimony, 1965. Home: Box R Hot Springs VA 24445 Office: Main St Hot Springs VA 24445

SOLOMON, FREDERIC, lawyer, banker; b. Ft. Valley, Ga., Aug. 1, 1911; s. Aaron Moses and Mayme (Wice) S.; B.S. summa cum laude, U. Ga., 1933, J.D. with honors, 1933; certificate banking Rutgers U., 1941; m. Anita Ostrin, July 4, 1954; children—Andrew Mark, Laurie Ann. Admitted to Ga. bar, 1933, U.S. Supreme Ct. bar, 1938, D.C. bar, 1949; practice law, Atlanta, 1933-34; with legal div. bd. govs. Fed. Res. System, Washington, 1934-42, 45-59, dir. div. supervision and regulation, 1959—; asst. gen. counsel to bd. govs. Fed. Res. System and Fed. Open Market Com., 1948-59. Adviser, Bur. Budget, 1947; lectr. U. Wis., Madison, 1960—. Served from 1st lt. to maj. USMCR, 1942-45; col. Res. (ret.). Recipient Ross Essay award Am. Bar Assn., 1948, Honor medal Freedoms Found., 1950. Mem. Am., Fed. bar assns., U. Ga. Alumni Assn. (v.p. 1963), Am. Econ. Assn., Sphinx, Phi Beta Kappa, Phi Kappa Phi. Jewish religion (bd. mgrs. congregation). Club: Woodmont Country. Contbg. Author; Bankers' Handbook, 1966; contbr. articles in field. Home: 7517 Holiday Terrace Bethesda MD 20034 Office: Fed Res Bldg 20th St and Constitution Av Washington DC 20551

SOLOMON, MARTIN B., JR., univ. adminstr.; b. Chgo., Aug. 8, 1933; s. Martin B. and Beatrice A. (Neufeld) S.; B.S., U. Ky., 1955, M.B.A., 1960, Ph.D., 1967. Asst. dir. U. Ky. Computing Center, Lexington, 1960-67, dir., 1967—, asso. prof. bus. adminstrn., 1967—, chmn. coordinating com. Systems Planning Project, 1968—, chmn. adv. computing com., 1968-70. Mem. Higher Edn. Information Mgmt. Systems, So. Regional Edn. Bd., 1968—; vis. scientist Assn. Computing Machinery and NSF, 1969; editorial adviser Jour. Econ. Studies, Glasgow. Served with USAF, 1955-57. Mem. Am. Econ. Assn., Assn. Computing Machinery, Am. Mgmt. Assn., Am. Statis. Assn., Inst. Mgmt. Sci., Beta Gamma Sigma. Author: Investment Decisions in Small Business, 1963; (with N. G. Lovan) Annotated Bibliography of Films in Automation, Data Processing and Computer Science, 1967; (with M.A. Kennedy) Ten Statement Fortran, 1970, Eight Statement PL/C. Contbr. chpts. to Management: Cases and Concepts, 1969, Essentials of Management, 1965. Contbr. articles to profl. jours. Home: 709 Cumberland Rd Lexington KY 40503 Office: U Ky Computing Center Lexington KY 40506

SOLOMON, ROBERT, govt. ofcl.; b. N.Y.C., May 2, 1921; s. Sol and Betty (Brownstone) S.; B.A., U. Mich., 1942; M.A., Harvard, 1947, Ph.D., 1952; m. Fern R. Rice, Sept. 11, 1946; children—Carol Ann, Barbara B., Anne E. With Fed. Res. Bd., Fed. Res. System, 1947—, sr. staff economist council econ. advisers, 1963-64, adviser to bd., 1965—, dir. div. internat. finance, 1966—. Adj. prof. Am. U., 1962-67. Served with USAAF, 1942-45; Decorated Air medal D.F.C. (U.S.); officier Ordre Nationale du Merite (France); recipient Rockefeller Pub. Service award, 1971. Mem. Am. Econ. Assn., Am. Finance Assn. Club: Cosmos (Washington). Home: 8502 W Howell Rd Bethesda MD 20034 Office: 20th and Constitution Av Washington DC 20551

SOLTERO, SAL SALVADOR, architect; b. Mayaguez, P.R., Oct. 11, 1937; s. Salvador and Maria (Cuebas) S.; B.Arch., Syracuse U., 1961; m. Ary Fernandez, Jan. 2, 1961; children—Arysol, Raluan. Designer firm Diaz & Assos., Ponce, P.R., 1960; student architect firm Sargent, Webster, Crenshaw, Syracuse, N.Y., 1961; architect firm Luciano Grossi Bianqui, Genova, Italy, 1962, firm Henry Klumb, & Assos., San Juan, P.R., 1962-63; prin. Sal Salvador Soltero's Assos., San Juan, 1964—. Pres. Punta Salinas Corp., San Juan, 1965—; v.p. LIMM Enterprizes, San Juan, 1971—; cons. P.R. Planning Bd., 1969, also bd. dirs., 1967-69; asso. mem. Colegio de Ingenieros Arquitectos y Agrumensores de P.R., 1966. Mem. Popular Democratic Central Council, 1970. Recipient 1st prize Cyanamid Internat. Corp., 1964-65. Mem. Sociedad de Planificacion (v.p.), Am. Soc. Planning Ofcls., A.I.A., Urban Land Inst., Inst. Architects P.R., Coll. Engineers, Architects, Surveyors of P.R., P.R. C. of C. Lion. Club: Casino de P. R. (San Juan). Originator Exclusive Bus Lines Mass Transit System, San Juan, 1971. Home: 11 Carrion Ct San Juan PR 00911 Office: 212 Ponce de Leon St San Juan PR 00907

SOLYMOSY, SIGMOND, botanist, educator; b. Hungary; B.S. in Agrl. Engring., Polytechnic U., Zurich, Switzerland; Ph.D. in Natural Scis., Budapest (Hungary) U. Dir., Hatzendorf Bot. Garden, Austria; mgr. Cornelius Nurseries, Inc., Houston; mem. faculty U. Southwestern La., Lafayette, 1959—, now prof. hort. research. Condr. plant collection expdn. to Mexico, Venezuela. Mem. Am., La. hort. socs., La. Soc. for Hort. Research (editor Newsletter). Contbr. articles to profl. jours. Office: Dept of Horticulture University of Southwestern La Lafayette LA 70501*

SOLZBACHER, WILLIAM ALOYSIUS, linguist, govt. ofcl.; b. Honnef, Germany, Feb. 1, 1907; s. Carl and Josepha (Schmitz) S.; student U. Bonn, 1926-28; Ph.D., U. Cologne, 1931; m. Regina Reiff, July 27, 1931; children—Josephine (Mrs. Patrick Evetts Kennon), Irene (Sister Irene Marie), Regina (Mrs. Richard O. Rouse), Eve (Mrs. Richard D. Cuthbert). Came to U.S., 1941, naturalized, 1947. Interpreter, organizer internat. confs., 1925-39; founder, editor La Juna Batalanto (internat. youth mag. in Esperanto), 1926-34; faculty Am. Peoples Coll. in Europe, Oetz, Tyrol, 1932-37; lecture tours, Europe, 1925-40, U.S., 1933; exiled by Nazis, as free lance writer, journalist, lectr. in Luxembourg and Belgium, 1933-40; escaped from Nazi occupied Belgium and France, 1940; asso. editor Cath. Intercontinental Press, N.Y.C., 1942-50, treas., 1947-48, v.p., 1948-49; asst. prof. history and polit. sci. Coll. Mt. St. Vincent, 1950-51; fgn. lang. editor, chief program schedule sect. Voice of Am., Dept. of State, 1951-53; ednl. dir. study tours ASSIST, 1953-54; chief monitoring staff Voice of Am., 1954-67, policy application officer, 1967—, dir. worldwide Esperanto broadcasts, 1960-61. Led internat. delegation presenting Esperanto petition to UN, 1950; attended World Esperanto congresses, 1953-72; del. 3d conf. U.S. Nat. Commn. UNESCO, 1952, World Congresses Sociology, Liege, Belgium, 1953, Amsterdam, 1956, Stresa, 1959, Washington 1962, Varna, Bulgaria, 1970. Fellow Am. Sociol. Assn.; mem. Esperanto Assn. N.Am. (past pres.) Internat. Commn. Esperanto and Sociology (chmn.), Esperanto Acad., Am. Assn. for Advancement Slavic Studies, Speakers Research Com. for UN, Polynesian Soc., A.A.A.S., Modern Lang. Assn., Soc. for Sci. Study Religion, Linguistic Soc. Am., Am. Hist. Assn., Am. Acad. Polit. and Social Sci. Author: Walther Rathenau als Sozialphilosoph, 1932; Devant Hitler et Mussolini, 1933; Pie XI contre les Idoles, 1939; Rome en de Afgoden van Onzen Tijd, 1940; (with George Alan Connor, Doris T. Connor) Esperanto: The World Interlanguage, 1948; Say It In Esperanto, 1948; 56, 66. Contbr. to encys. Home: 6030 Broad St Washington DC 20016 Office: 330 Independence Av Washington DC 20547

SONDERLING, EGMONT, broadcasting exec. Pres. WDIA, Memphis. Office: PO Box 12045 Memphis TN 38112*

SONGSTER, GERARD FRANCIS, elec. engr.; b. Darby, Pa., Aug. 29, 1927; s. John J. and Florence (Schaeff) S.; B.S., Drexel Inst. Tech., 1951; M.S., U. Pa., 1956, Ph.D., 1962; m. Elizabeth R. Uhl, Apr. 11, 1953; children—Sheila, Claudia. Elec. engr. Philco Corp., Phila., 1951-52; staff engr. Moore Sch. Elec. Engring., U. Pa., 1952-56; asso. prof. elec. engring. Drexel Inst. Tech., 1956-63, acting dir. biomed. engring., 1963; sr. scientist Melpar, Inc., Falls Church, Va., 1963-64; elec. engr. U.S. Naval Research Lab., Washington, 1964-65; NIH spl. fellow Mass. Inst. Tech., Cambridge, 1965-67; biomed. engr. NASA Electronic Research Center, Cambridge, 1967-70; prof., chmn. dept. elec. engring. Old Dominion U. Sch. Engring., Norfolk, 1970—. Dir. Life Sci. Engring. Corp., Waltham, Mass. Served with USNR, 1945-46. Mem. I.E.E.E., A.A.A.S., Sci. Research Soc. Am. Home: Sch Engring Old Dominion U Norfolk VA 23508

SONNER, JOHN LOUIS, II, physician; b. Knoxville, Tenn., June 23, 1937; s. John Boyd and Evelyn Ruth (Burkhart) S.; B.A., U. Tenn., 1962; M.D., U. Tenn., 1962; m. Jewel Dean Clark, July 22, 1964; children—John Boyd, II, Robert Louis, Andrew Clark. Intern, U. Tenn. Meml. Research Center and Hosp., Knoxville, 1962-63; gen. practice medicine, Buena Vista, Ga., 1964-65, Sevierville, Tenn., 1965—; chief staff Sevier County Hosp., Sevierville, 1971—. Served to capt. M.C., AUS, 1963-65. Diplomate Am. Bd. Family Practice. Mem. Sevier County Med. Soc. (pres. 1969, sec., treas. 1970), Tenn. Med. Assn., A.M.A., Am. Coll. Emergency Physicians. Home: Route 4 Sevierville TN 37862 Office: Burchfiel Med Bldg Sevierville TN 37862

SONNINO, MARIO ANTHONY, govt. ofcl.; b. Rome, Italy, May 1, 1915; s. Umberto and Letitia (Amati) S.; grad. Royal Tech. Inst., 1934; C.Sc.D., U. Rome, 1938; M.A., George Washington U., 1946; Ph.D., Am. U., 1949, M.B.A., 1955; postgrad. N.Y. U., 1940-42, Am. U., 1955-65; m. Frances Cosimano, June 3, 1945; children—Daniel Frank, Anthony Stephen. Came to U.S., 1940, naturalized, 1942. Treas., Motor Corp. Aircraft Co., 1939-40; pub. accountant, 1940-42; v.p., treas. S.W. Airlines, 1953; air transport examiner CAB, Washington, 1943-53, chief econ. research, 1954-60, supervisory economist and chief comml. rates, 1960-69, spl. asst. for research and planning, 1970-71; rate adviser Postal Rate Commn., Washington, 1971—. Professorial lectr. bus. econs. and mgmt. Am. U., 1949—, mem. dissertation com., 1950—, admissions com., 1960-66; lectr. Prince Georges Coll., 1960—, mem. coll. senate exec. com. 1965-68. Mem. Suitland Citizens Council, 1955-60; active Prince Georges County chpt. A.R.C., 1955—. Recipient Distinguished Service award CAB, 1968, Superior Performance awards, 1948, 51, 54, 64. Mem. Am. Econ. Assn., Nat. Planning Assn., Am. Soc. Traffic and Transp., Am. Transp. Assn., Soc. Advancement of Mgmt., NRC, Alpha Kappa Psi, Delta Nu Alpha. Home: 2023 Jameson St Washington DC 20031 Office: 2000 L St NW Washington DC 20268

SOPKIN, RONALD BARTON, apparel mfg. co. exec.; b. Chgo., Feb. 17, 1922; s. Alvin A. and Sadie (Hall) S.; student Nichols Coll., 1940-41; m. Doris Lenore Wald, Apr. 6, 1946; children—Nancy (Mrs. James R. Pettit), Gail, Bonnie. With Wentworth Mfg. Co., Lake City, S.C., 1945—, pres., 1964—; dir. Peoples Bank S.C., Florence, Sparkle Mill, Olanta, S.C., 1969-70. Commr., Florence City/County Airport, 1970—. Bd. dirs. Florence Little Theater, 1962—, chmn. bd. trustees, 1967—. Served with USAAF, 1942-45. Home: 510 Ridgewood Dr Florence SC 29501 Office: Blanding St Lake City SC 29560

SORELLE, ANDREW CURRIE, JR., engr.; b. Rosenberg, Tex., May 18, 1920; s. Andrew Currie and Nita Ray (SoRelle) SoR.; B.S., Tex. A. and M. U., 1942; m. Maxine Chambers, Mar. 22, 1943; children—Virginia Lee, Andrew Currie III. Ind. oil operator and producer, 1945-57; investments, 1957—. Bd. dirs. Star of Hope Mission, Houston, Com. of Fourteen. Served from 2d lt. to maj. USAAF, 1942-45. Decorated Silver Star, D.F.C., Air medal with 17 oak leaf clusters. Mem. Am. Inst. Mining, Metall. and Petroleum Engrs., Full Gospel Bus. Men's Fellowship Internat. (dir.), Clubs: Petroleum, Lakeside Country, Houston. Home: 10220 Memorial Dr Houston TX 77024 Office: 1818 W Capitol Av Houston TX 77007

SORENSON, HELMER ELLSWORTH, coll. dean; b. Elk Mound, Wis., Sept. 17, 1910; s. Gabriel E. and Betsy (Munson) S.; B. Ed., Eau Claire State Coll., 1935; Ph.M., U. Wis., 1939, Ph.D., 1948; m. Ida F. Friddle, Sept. 19, 1946; children—Joe C., Russell G., Janet, Lee A. Tchr. pub. schs., Wis., 1939-42; asst. prof. edn. Ia. State Tchrs. Coll., 1948-49; asso. prof. Okla. State U., Stillwater, 1949-52, prof. edn., 1953—, vice dean Coll. Edn., 1955-64, dean, 1964—. Served to lt. USNR, 1942-46. Mem. N.E.A., Okla. Edn. Assn., Am., Okla. assns. sch. adminstrs., Nat. Soc. for Study Edn., Stillwater C. of C. Rotarian. Methodist. Home: 1706 N Glenwood Circle Stillwater OK 74074

SORGE, WILLIAM ADOLPH, geophys. engr.; b. Hastings, Okla., Mar. 2, 1914; s. Adolph I. and Josie (Nelson) S.; B.S., U. Okla., 1937; M.S., U. Tulsa, 1954; Ph.D., Okla. State U., 1960; m. Sadie Harlan, June 28, 1952; children—Celia Elaine, Gregory Manley. Seismic party chief Internat. Petroleum Co., Guayaquil, Ecuador, 1943-46; seismic party chief Carter Oil Co., Tulsa, 1946-51, research engr., 1951-58; sr. research engr. Jersey Prodn. Research Co., 1958-65; lectr. dept. math. U. Tulsa, 1965—. Registered profl. engr., Okla., Tex. Mem. I.E.E.E., Geophys. Soc. Houston, Soc. Exploration Geophysicist, Soc. Indsl. Applied Math. Home: 8213 E 32d St Tulsa OK 74145

SORKNESS, ROBERT ELDREN, cons.; b. Watertown, S.D., Nov. 16, 1913; s. Oscar and Dora (Dahl) S.; B.S. in Elec. Engring., U. Tex., 1951; M.E., U. Cal. at Los Angeles, 1963; m. Lucille R. Rahe, Nov. 27, 1940. Dept. chief, base depot Randolph Field, Tex., 1942-47; instrumentation engr. Arnold Research and Devel. Center, Tullahoma, Tenn., 1951-52; adminstr. engring. Norair div., Northrop Corp., Hawthorne, Cal., 1952-71, engring. supr., 1956-60; now cons. Served with USAAF, 1936-42. Registered profl. engr., Tex., Cal. Mem. Am. Radio Relay League, I.E.E.E. (sr.), Am. Mgmt. Assn. Lutheran. Author: (with W.C. Hansen) Supervisory Training, 1943; (with others) A Theory of Planning for Research and Development, 1963. Address: 519 Beverly Lane New Braunfels TX 78130

SORRELL, DARRELL FRANCIS, bank exec.; b. High Point, N.C., Nov. 21, 1933; s. Owen Preston and Grace Louise (Pierce) S.; B.A. in Accounting, Duke, 1956; postgrad. Carolina Sch. Banking, 1968, Stonier Grad. Sch. Banking, Rutgers U., 1970-71; m. Jane Kathryn Greene, July 7, 1956; children—David Preston, Kathryn Ann, Douglas Baxter. Jr. accountant Arthur Andersen & Co., N.Y.C., 1956-57; asst. dist. mgr. Carnation Co., Charlotte, N.C., 1960-65; pres. Spartan Sports, Monroe, N.C., 1965-66; with N.C. Nat. Bank, Charlotte, 1966-70, v.p. Morganton, 1970—. Mem. adv. council Sch. Bus. Applachian State U., 19—. Served with USMC, 1957-60. Methodist (mem. adminstv. bd. 1971). Club: Grandfather Golf and Country (Linville, N.C.). Home: 207 Riverside Dr Morganton NC 28655 Office: 104 S Sterling St Morganton NC 28655

SORRELLS, BOBBY GENE, pub. co. exec.; b. Hartford, Ala., Oct. 18, 1937; s. F. L. and Ruby (White) S.; B.A., Auburn U., 1961; postgrad. Columbia U., 1965; m. Theresa Dancy, Mar. 22, 1956; children—Robert, Jeffrey, Sandra. Cost Accountant St. Marys Kraft Corp. (Ga.), 1961-62; asst. comptroller Ledger-Enquirer Co., Columbus, 1962-66; comptroller R.W. Page Corp., Columbus, 1966—. Served with USNR, 1956-58. Mem. Inst. Newspaper Controllers (membership com. 1971—). Republican. Baptist (supt. young people 1971-72). Lion. Home: 2504 Brookwood Circle Phenix City AL 36867 Office: 17 W 12th St Columbus GA 31901

SORRELLS, JOHN HARVEY, newspaper editor; b. Oklahoma City, Jan 14, 1923; s. John Harvey and Ruth (Arnett) S.; B.S. in Bus. Adminstrn., Washington and Lee U., 1948; m. Mary Morris Blakely, Jan. 4, 1944; children—John Harvey III, Mary Morris, Nancy Gordon. Research dir. Knoxville (Tenn.) News-Sentinel, 1948-50, gen. advt. salesman, 1950-55; gen. advt. salesman Memphis Pub. Co., 1955-58; spl. sects. editor Comml. Appeal, Memphis, 1958-60, gen. assignment reporter, 1960-61, night city editor, also asst. city editor, 1961-63, promotions editor, 1963—. Mem. pub. affairs com. Memphis chpt. A.R.C., 1964—; sec.-treas. Am. Legion-Comml. Appeal Christmas Basket Fund, 1963—. Bd. dirs. Boys Town. Served with AUS, 1942-46; ETO; col. Res. Decorated Bronze Star medal with V, Purple Heart with oak leaf cluster, Combat Infantry badge. Mem. C. of C., Mil. Order World Wars, Am. Legion, Internat. Newspaper Promotion Assn., Sigma Delta Chi, Phi Kappa Psi. Presbyn. (elder). Home: 4209 Waymar Dr Memphis TN 38117 Office: 495 Union St Memphis TN 38101

SORRELS, DONALD RAY, hosp. adminstr.; b. Jackson, Miss., Nov. 10, 1929; s. Sidney E. and Myrtle (Nettles) S.; A.A., Whitworth Coll., 1959; m. Doris Edna Cook, Apr. 16, 1954; children—James Phillip, Marie Kathleen, Thomas Matthew. Adminstr. asst. Daus. Hosp., Brookhaven, Miss., 1957-66; adminstr. Hardy Wilson Meml. Hosp., Hazlehurst, Miss., 1966—. Chmn. health com. Copiah County Devel. Corp., 1967—; pres. Southwest Miss. Hosp. Council, 1970. Sec., Hazlehurst Sch. Bd., 1971—. Bd. dirs. Hazlehurst Youth Center, Central Miss. Health Planning Council. Served with Hosp. Corps, USNR, 1948-57. Mem. C. of C. (pres. 1971). Woodman of World (state v.p. 1967-68, nat. fraternal com. 1968, nat. rep. 1969—). Methodist (vice chmn. bd. 1968—. Home: 774 Georgetown St Hazlehurst MS 39083 Office: Magnolia St Hazlehurst MS 39083

SORRELS, WILLIAM WRIGHT, newspaper editor; b. Cordova, Tenn., July 28, 1924; s. Chelsea Howard and Mary (Wright) S.; student Miss. State U., 1946-47; B.J., U. Mo., 1949; M.A., Memphis State U., 1969; m. Carolyn Ramsey, June 28, 1954; children—Deborah, John Clarke, Reporter, editor West Point (Miss.) Daily Times Leader, 1949-53; reporter Honolulu Star-Bull., 1953-54; reporter, asst. city editor Comml. Appeal, Memphis, 1954-61, asst. mng. editor, 1962-68, mng. editor, 1968—; mng. editor Evening Ind., St. Petersburg, Fla., 1961-62. Owner, Indian Mound Farm, Starkville, Miss.; instr. journalism Memphis State U. Bd. dirs. Mile-O-Dimes. Served with USNR, 1943-46. Mem. Sigma Delta Chi (pres. Mid-South chpt. 1965-66), Kappa Alpha Tau. Presbyn. Kiwanian. Club: Summit. Author: Memphis' Greatest Debate, 1970. Home: 1453 Finley St Memphis TN 38116 Office: 495 Union St Memphis TN 38101

SOTERIADES, MICHAEL COSMAS, educator; b. Istanbul, Turkey, Mar. 25, 1923; s. Cosmas and Evouli (Tsaoussoglou) S.; student Athens Coll., Athens, Greece, 1933-41; Diploma Engr., Nat. Tech. U. Athens, 1948, Dr. Engring., 1952; Sc.D., Mass. Inst. Tech., 1954; m. Rose Marie Rentroia, Aug. 5, 1962. Asso. engr. A. Woolf Assos., Boston, 1954-55; Greek Govt. in charge of Aseismic Design and Specifications for rebuilding City of Volos, Greece, 1955-56; chief engr. Capitol Engring. Corp., Boston, 1956-58; v.p. engring. Doxiadis Assos., Inc., Washington, 1958-61, dir., treas., 1959-61; prof. Cath. U. Am., 1961—; dir. treas. Technol. Products, Inc., 1967—; cons. Nat. Acad. Scis., Dept. Commerce, Dept. Navy, 1961—. Served to 2d lt. Greek Army, 1948-52. Fellow Am. Soc. C.E.; mem. Tech. Chamber of Greece, Sigma Xi, Tau Beta Pi. Author: Aseismic Construction—Design, Erection, 1956. Home: 3380 Stephenson Plaza NW Washington DC 20015 Office: Cath U Washington DC 20017

SOULE, GEORGE, coll. pres.; b. New Orleans, Nov. 24, 1896; s. Albert Lee and Anna Sophronia (Cooper) S.; student Isadore Newman Sch., Georgia Mil. Acad., Soule Coll., La. State U.; m. Mary Brooks Ragland, Feb. 21, 1922; children—George, Evan R., Mary Brooks. Clk. and asst. instr. Soule Coll., 1919, successively tchr., asst. treas., treas. (1926), sec. and mgr. in charge adminstrn., 1929—, partner firm A. L., E. E. and George Soule, owners of Soule Coll., Inc., 1936-48, pres., 1948—; past v.p. Am. Empire Ins. Co.; dir. Union Savs. & Loan Assn.; dir., past v.p. Bur. Govtl. Research New Orleans. Past pres. New Orleans chpt. Nat. Officers Mgmt. Assn.; past bd. dirs. Magnolia Sch. for Exceptional Children, pres., 1945, 46; chmn. campaign execs. com., United Community and War Chest, 1945; past pres. New Orleans Community Chest; chmn. New Orleans Ednl. Found; past vice chmn. City Planning and Zoning Commn. New Orleans; organizer, exec. officer New Orleans regiment U.S. Coast Guard Vol. Port Security Force, World War II. Campaign vice chmn. United Fund, 1952. La. elector at large on George Wallace Presdl. ticket, 1968. Served to 2d lt. F.A., U.S. Army, 1917-18. Recipient Americanism award Am. Legion, 1960. Mem. New Orleans C. of C., Young Men's Bus. Club. Discussions Unltd. (hon. life), Soc. War 1812 (historian La.). Episcopalian (sr. warden; pres. St. Thomas). Clubs: Gyro of New Orleans (past pres., past dist. gov.), New Orleans Executive of La. (pres. 2 terms), Boston, Pendennis (past pres.) (New Orleans). Home: 4825 Carondelet St New Orleans LA 70115 Office: 1410 Jackson Av New Orleans LA 70130 also PO Box 53306 New Orleans LA 70153

SOUTHER, ROY HOBART, water pollution research cons.; b. nr. Elkin, N.C., July 25, 1897; s. William A. and Fannie (Norman) S.; B.S. in Chem. Engring. and Chemistry, U. N.C., 1920, postgrad. 1941-42, 44, 56. With Cone Mills Corp., Greensboro, N.C., 1920-59, research dir., 1944-59; sci. and engring. research cons. in water conservation, Greensboro, 1960—. Mem. adv. bd. Inst. Textile Tech., Charlottesville, Va., 1948-51, Textile Research Inst., Princeton, N.J., 1957-60; chmn. chem. processing industries task group Nat. Tech. Task Com. on Indsl. Waste, USPHS, 1960—. Afounder, sec.-treas. Greensboro Evening Coll., 1947-53; mem. adv. bd. Greensboro div. Guilford Coll., 1947—, recipient Coll. Adminstrn. award, 1960; mem. N.C. adv. com. on sci., engring. and specialized personnel SSS, 1957—. Precinct chmn. Democratic party Guilford County, N.C., 1940-52. Mem. Am. Assn. Textile Chemists and Colorists (sec. nat. com. on stream sanitation tech. 1964—), Water Pollution Control Fedn. (Indsl. Waste medal award 1959), Am. Chem. Soc., Am. Soc. Quality Control, N.C. Acad. Sci., Greensboro C. of C., U. N.C. Alumni Assn. (pres. Greensboro chpt. 1949-50), Textile Quality Control Assn. (founding mem.), Civitan Internat., Toastmasters (N.C. Community Service award 1971), Phi Beta Kappa, Alpha Chi Sigma. Presbyn. Mason. Club: Greensboro Writers. Contbr. articles on research in water conservation, pollution abatement, statis. quality control and textile processing to profl. jours., chpts. to books. Developer indsl. waste-water control system used by various industries, municipalities. Home: 3116 Summit Av Greensboro NC 27405 Office: 501 W Washington St Greensboro NC 27401

SOUTHERLAND, HENRY DELEON, JR., steel co. exec.; b. Birmingham, Ala., Sept. 8, 1911; s. Henry deLeon and Edwina (Hamilton Williams) S.; B.S., U. Ga., 1934; M.S., U. Tenn., 1941; LL.B., Columbia, 1948; m. Louise Harris Wilson, Jan. 22, 1955. Admitted to Ala. bar, 1949; with U.S. Steel Corp., 1948—, mgr. So. lands and timber, Fairfield, Ala., 1968—. Mem. Mountain Brook Planning Commn., 1957—. Served to lt. col. AUS, World War II. Fellow Am. Soc. C.E.; mem. Am., Ala., Birmingham bar assns. Soc. War of 1812 (Ala. pres. 1968-69), Soc. of Cin., S.R. (Ala. pres. 1964-66, gen. v.p. 1967—), Soc. Colonial Wars, Tau Beta Pi, Phi Kappa Phi, Sigma Alpha Epsilon. Episcopalian. Mason (past master). Club: Birmingham Country. Home: 47 Greenway Rd Mountain Brook AL 35213 Office: PO Box 599 Fairfield AL 35064

SOUTHEY, DAVID LUDGATE, architect; b. Bridgeport, Conn., Aug. 17, 1911; s. Ernest Guy and Lena Frances (Dean) S.; B.Arch., U. Pa., 1936; m. Ann Kathleen Robertson, June 20, 1945. Partner E.G. Southey, Bridgeport, 1936-41; prin. David L. Southey, Bridgeport, 1947-52; architect, bur. medicine and surgery Dept. Navy, Washington, 1951—. Served to lt. comdr. USNR, 1943-46. Recipient Meritorious Civilian Service award Navy Dept., 1965, Superior Civilian Service award, 1968, Outstanding Performance awards, 1964, 65, 66, 67, 70. Mem. A.I.A., Conn. Soc. Architecs, Archtl. Assn. London, Am. Hosp. Assn., Ret. Officers Assn., Res. Officers Assn. U.S., Alpha Tau Omega. Club: Brooklawn Country (Fairfield, Conn.). Home: 2801 Quebec St NW Washington DC 20008 Office: Bur Medicine and Surgery Navy Dept 23d and E Sts NW Washington DC 20390

SOUTHWELL, SAMUEL BEALL, educator; b. Lockhart, Tex., Jan. 15, 1922; s. George Thomas and Lucile (Beall) S.; B.J., U. Tex., 1946, M.A., 1949, Ph.D., 1956; D. Honoris Causa, Universidad Autonoma de Guadalajara, 1965; m. Mary Jane Bamford, Dec. 16, 1944; children—Michael Beall, Teresa Bamford. Mem. faculty Tex. A. and M. U., 1947-59; ednl. exchange officer Am. embassy, Mexico, 1959-60; U.S. consul, Guadalajara, 1961-65; asso. prof. English, U. Houston 1965-70, prof., 1970—, asst. to v.p., dean of faculties, 1967-69, chmn. dept. English, 1969—. Served to lt. (j.g.) USNR, 1944-45. Mem. Modern Lang. Assn., S. Central Modern Lang. Assn., Coll. English Assn. Roman Catholic. Author: If All the Rebels Die, 1966. Home: 10703 Ashcroft St Houston TX 77035

SOVDE, ROGER LINTON, newspaper exec.; b. Archie Henry and Esther (Zelke) S.; student Minn. Sch. Bus., 1954; m. Joy Dorothy Eberspacher, Apr. 30, 1955; children—David Arthur, Jon Hugh, Steven Craig, Susan Carol. Vice pres. Richardson-Sovde Co., Inc., Mpls., 1954-62; salesman Twin City Lino, Inc., Mpls., 1962; asst. to pub. Mankato Free Press (Minn.), 1962-67; gen. mgr. Evening Herald, Rock Hill, S.C., 1967—, asst. pub., 1970—; sec. Herald Pub. Co., Rock Hill; dir. Pat-Print, Inc. Mem. adv. com. Mankato Bd. Edn., 1965; mem. All Am. Cities Com., Rock Hill, 1967. Editor city newspaper Republican Party, Bloomington, Minn., 1961, city vice chmn., 1962. Chmn. Rock Hill Better Bus. Bur. Com, 1969. Bd. dirs. York County unit Am. Cancer Soc., 1972—; mem. adv. com. Community Pre-release Center, Rock Hill, 1972—. Served with USNR, 1951-54. Mem. Rock Hill C. of C. (chmn. retail task force com. 1970). Home: 2386 Ferncliff Rock Hill SC 29730 Office: 132 W Main St Rock Hill SC 29730

SOWA, EVA INGERSOLL LONG (MRS. WALTER D. SOWA), social worker; b. Birmingham, Ala., Sept. 4, 1910; d. John Hamner and Fannie (Ingersoll) Long; B.A., U. Pitts., 1930, M.A., 1933; M.S. in Social Service Adminstrn., 1941; m. Walter D. Sowa, Apr. 4, 1942; children—Peter William, Thomas Michael. Tchr., Bentleyville (Pa.) High Sch., 1930-32; social worker Allegheny County (Pa.) Emergency Relief Bd., Pitts., 1934-36, Mothers' Assistance, Old Age Pension, Blind Pension, Pitts., 1936-38, Travelers Aid Soc., Pitts., 1938-40; probation officer Allegheny County Juvenile Ct. Pitts., 1940-43; case worker Childrens Aid Soc., Birmingham, 1960-67; supr. Travelers Aid Soc., Birmingham, 1967—. Active P.T.A. Mem. Nat. Assn. Social Workers, Acad. Certified Social Workers, Sigma Kappa Phi, Pi Lambda Theta. Club: Social Workers. Home: 2121 16th Av S Birmingham AL 35205 Office: 3600 8th Av S Birmingham AL 35222

SOWA, WALTER D., educator, lawyer; b. McKeesport, Pa., Jan. 17, 1907; s. Peter and Anna (Jankowska) S.; A.B., U. Pitts., 1928, Litt.M., 1940; J.D., Duquesne U., 1933; m. Eva Ingersoll Long, Apr. 4, 1942; children—Peter William, Thomas Michael. Tchr. elementary sch., Alliquippa, Pa., 1928-30, high sch., Pa., 1930-42; probation officer Juvenile Ct., Allegheny County, Pa., 1940-41; joined U.S. Army, 1942, advanced through grades to lt. col., 1962; acad. coordinator Baylor U., 1943-44, Tex. A. and M. Coll., 1944-46; judge adv. Korea Base Command, 1946-48; at Pa. State Coll., 1948-50; asst. judge adv. X Corps, Korea, 1950-51; sec. gen. staff X Corps, 1951-52; chief contracting div. Hdqrs. 3d Army, 1952-56; legal assistance adviser, 1956-60; trial observer-lawyer, 1960-62, ret., 1962; prof. criminal law Cumberland Law Sch. Howard Coll., Birmingham, Ala., 1963—; prof. criminal law and evidence Samford U., Birmingham, 1963—. Decorated Bronze Star. Mem. Am., Ga., Ala. bar assns., Pa. Edn. Assn. Methodist. Mason. Home: 2121 16th Av S Birmingham AL 35205

SOWDER, WILSON THOMAS, state health ofcl.; b. Callaway, Va., 1910; M.D., U. Va., 1932; M.P.H., Johns Hopkins, 1933. Intern, U. Ia. Hosps., 1932-33; asst. resident physician St. Luke Hosp., San Francisco, 1933-34; practice medicine specializing in preventive medicine and pub. health; mem. staff USPHS Hosps., 1934-38; state health officer Fla. Div. Health (formerly Fla. Bd. Health), Jacksonville, 1945-61, 63-69, dir. div. Dept. Health and Rehab. Services, 1969—; chief officer aging USPHS, 1961-62. Diplomate Am. Bd. Preventive Medicine and Rehab. Fellow Am. Pub. Health Assn.; mem. A.M.A. Office: PO Box 210 Jacksonville FL 32201

SOWELL, JAMES RALPH, JR., pub. relations counselor, printing co. exec., lawyer, state legislator; b. Canton, Miss., July 3, 1940; s. James Ralph and Hazel (Darby) S.; B.A., Millsaps Coll., Coll., 1962; postgrad. Miss. Coll., 1962-64; LL.B., Jackson Sch. Law, 1969; m. Gloria Winstead, July 10, 1966. Account exec. L.E. Davis & Assos., advt. and pub. relations, 1962-63; owner Capital City Advt. and Pub. Relations, 1963-64; instr. journalism pub. relations dir., chmn. dept. journalism Hinds Jr. Coll., 1964-69; pres. Franklin Printers, Inc., Jackson, Miss., 1969—; mem. Miss. Ho. of Reps., 1968-72; owner Pub. Relations Counselors. Bd. dirs. Community Hosp., Hinds County Mental Health Assn., Civic Arts Council, Keep Jackson Beautiful, Miss. Easter Seal Soc., Central Dist. Miss. Multiple Sclerosis Assn. Named Outstanding Young Man of Jackson, 1967, Outstanding Young Man of Miss., 1967. Mem. Jackson Jr. C. of C. (Outstanding Jaycee 1964, past pres.), Miss. Jr. C. of C. (pres. 1970-71), Miss. Jr. Coll. Pub. Relations Assn. (past. pres.), Omicron Delta Kappa, Alpha Psi Omega, Kappa Alpha. Baptist. Editor: Miss. Barber's News, 1964—; Miss. Jaycee Image, 1967, 69. Home: 5221 Wayneland Dr Jackson MS 39211 Office: PO Box 3162 Jackson MS 39207

SOWELL, KATYE MARIE OLIVER (MRS. JESSE CLARENCE SOWELL), educator; b. Winston-Salem, N.C., Apr. 6, 1934; d. William Manton and Katye (Price) Oliver, Sr.; B.A., Flora Macdonald Coll., 1956; M.S., U. S.C., 1958; postgrad. U. So. Miss., 1961-62; Ph.D., Fla. State U., 1965; m. Jesse Clarence Sowell, Sept. 7, 1957(dec. Feb. 1961); 1 son, David Clarence. Instr., Flora Macdonald Coll., Red Springs, N.C., 1958; asst. prof. Elon (N.C.) Coll., 1958-60; instr. U.So. Miss., Hattiesburg, 1960-63, Fla. State U., Tallahassee, 1965; faculty E. Carolina U., Greenville, N.C., 1965—, asso. prof. math., 1967-72, prof., 1972— supr. student teaching math., 1966—, dir. NSF Inst. for Secondary Tchrs. Math., 1968-69, NSF Inst. for Jr. High Sch. Tchrs. Math., 1970-71, 72—. Lectr., cons. Mem. Math. Assn. Am., Am. Math. Soc., Nat. Council Tchrs. Math., N.C. Council Tchrs. Math. (pres. Eastern region 1971—), Am. Assn. U. Profs., N.C. Assn. Educators, Pi Mu Epsilon. Democrat. Presbyn. Home: 103 Garrett St Greenville NC 27834

SOWER, FRANK WILLIAM, retail trade co. exec., city ofcl.; b. Frankfort, Ky., Dec. 10, 1910; s. John Rodman and Rose Elma (Edwards) S.; B.S., Northwestern U., 1933; m. Minnie Lynn Evans, Aug. 22, 1937; children—Frank William, Lynn (Mrs. Michael E. Bufkin), John. Owner Sower Hardware, Frankfort, 1937-59, Sower Office Equipment, Frankfort, 1940—; mayor of Frankfort, 1968-72; dir. Farmers Bank & Capital Trust Co. of Frankfort. Mem. Capital Planning and Zoning Commn., 1950-59. Mem. adv. bd. Kings Daus. Hosp. Served to lt. USNR, 1944-46. Mem. Ky. Retail Hardward Assn. (pres. 1957), Capital City Softball Assn. (pres. 1952), Ky. Hist. Soc. (pres. 1966-68), S.A.R., Ky. Civil War Round Table, Am. Legion, V.F.W., C. of C. (pres. 1947), Sigma Nu. Democrat. Roman Catholic (mission committeeman 1961-62). Rotarian (pres. 1958). Home: 112 Wilkinson St Frankfort KY 40601 Office: 217 St Clair St Frankfort KY 40601

SOWERS, GEORGE VERNON, dentist; b. Weldon, Tex., Feb. 27, 1919; s. Jessie Blanton and Fannie (Matson) S.; B.A., Sam Houston State U., 1946; D.D.S., U. Tex., 1950; m. Jean Lavon McDaniel, Aug. 20, 1949; children—Suzanne Ruth, George Vernon, Howard McDaniel. Mgr., owner truck farm, Huntsville, Tex., 1935-40; instr. chemistry Sam Houston State U., 1940-42; gen. practice dentistry, Tomball, Tex., 1952—; cons. Leon Meml. Clinic; dental adviser Tomball Hosp. and Med. Center, 1958-68; cons. Harris County Health Dept., 1967-71; landscaper. Chmn. Tomball Ind. Sch. Dist. Bd. Edn., 1959-65. Served with AUS, 1942-46, as capt. Dental Corps, USAF, 1950-52. Recipient Fuchard Medal of Honor, 1953. Mem. Am., Tex. dental assns., Houston Dist. Dental Soc., Tomball C. of C., Psi Omega. Lion (dir. 1953-56), Rotarian (dir. 1958-68). Home: 308 Holderrieth St Tomball TX 77375 Office: 307 W Main St Tomball TX 77375

SOWERS, ROY GERODD, JR., state ofcl.; b. Sanford, N.C., Sept. 9, 1928; s. Roy Gerodd and Evelyn (Bazemore) S.; B.S., Wake Forest U., 1949; m. Joyce Howell, Oct. 16, 1949; children—Roy Gerodd III, Joyce Lynn. Adjustor 1st Citizens Bank & Trust, 1949-52; owner real estate firm, 1956-62; asst. to pres. Roberts Co., 1962-67; now dir. N.C. Dept. Conservation and Devel. Chmn., N.C. Gov.'s Adv. Com. on Econs. and Environment. Mem. N.C. Rural Electrification Authority, 1964; mem. Sanford Bd. Aldermen, 1961-67; a.d.c. Gov. of N.C., 1961-65; mem. N.C. Democratic exec. com., 1961-69; del. Dem. Nat. Conv., 1964. Bd. visitors Wake Forest U. Served to lt. col. AUS. Mem. Am. Legion, Kappa Sigma. Methodist. Mason (Shriner), Elk, Moose. Home: 816 Gulf St E Sanford NC 27330 Office: Adminstrn Bldg Jones St Raleigh NC 27611

SOWERS, WADE ANDREW, dentist; b. nr. Lexington, N.C., Apr. 29, 1899; s. Luther Columbus and Fannie Florence (Long) S.; B.A., Wake Forest Coll., 1921; M.A., Lincoln Meml. U., 1923; D.D.S., Med. Coll. Va., 1924; m. Lena Maye Beck, Aug. 26, 1924; 1 son, Wade Philip. Asst. prin., then prin. Liberty-Piedmont Inst., 1921-24; prin. Arcadia High sch., 1925, Mineral Springs High Sch., Forsyth County, N.C., 1925-27; practice dentistry, Lexington, 1921—. Pres., trustee Daniel Boone Meml. Park, 1957. Mem. Pierre Fauchard Acad., Acad. Internat. Medicine and Dentistry, N.C., Davidson County dental socs., Am. Dental Assn., Davidson County Hist. Soc., Second Dist. Dental Soc. (pres. 1952). Mason. Home: Route 5 Lexington NC 27292 Office: Courthouse Sq Lexington NC 27292

SPAIN, AUGUST O., educator; b. Austin, Tex., Oct. 15, 1907; s. Oran Roberts and Nana Linnea (Headstrom) S.; A.B., U. of Tex., 1929, A.M., 1931; Ph.D. (Cowles fellow 1931-34), Yale, 1937 1 dau. by past marriage, Janet; m. 2d, Matilde Garvia, 1957. Tchr., Tex. U., 1930-31; Colgate U., 1934-36, Hendrix College, 1936-38; asso. prof. govt., 1946-50, 69—, chmn. dept. Tex. Christian U., 1950-69, chmn. Inst. World Affairs, 1952; exchange lectr. U. San Andres (Bolivia), 1957; lectr. Inst. Internat. Relations St. Marys U. Consumer credit, finance, Ft. Worth, 1938-42. Mem. Mayors Com. on UN, 1955. Mem. com. on charter revision Ft. Worth Town Hall, 1963-64; mem. citizens' com. on law enforcement N. Central Tex. Council of Govts., 1967-68; pres. S.W. Council Latin Am. Studies, 1967-68. Served from lt (j.g.) to lt. comdr. USN, 1942-46; mem. USNR. Fellow in bus.

Found. Econ. Edn., 1954. Mem. Southwestern Social Sci. Assn. (chmn. govt. sect. 1950-51, 53-54), Am., So. polit. sci. assns., Asociacion Boliviana de Ciencias Economicas, UN Assn., Freedom House. Phi Beta Kappa (pres. Ft. Worth assn. 1966-67), Pi Sigma Alpha, Delta Tau Delta, Sigma Delta Pi, Alpha Sigma Lambda. Mem. Disciples of Christ Ch. Mason. Contbr. to edn. jours. Author: The Political Theory of John C. Calhoun, 1951; co-author: Urban Politics in the Southwest, 1967; also author, editor monographs. Asso. editor S.W. Social Sci. Quarterly, 1961-65. Home: 2320 Edwin St Fort Worth TX 76110

SPALDING, BILLUPS PHINIZY, educator; b. Atlanta, Sept. 29, 1930; s. Hughes and Bolling (Phinizy) S.; A.B., U. Ga., 1953, M.A., 1957; Ph.D., U. N.C., 1963; m. Margaret Anne Roscoe, Aug. 18, 1969; 1 son, Billups Phinizy. Asst. prof. history Coll. Charleston, S.C., 1963-66; asso. prof. U. Ga., Athens, 1966—. Chmn., Ferdinand Phinizy Lectureship Com. Bd. sponsors Atlanta Symphony Orch. trustee Athens-Clarke Heritage Found.; bd. dirs. U. Ga. Found. Served with USNR, 1953-55. Mem. S.C., Ga. (curator 1968—), Athens (pres. 1970) hist. socs., Ga. Conservancy, Nat. Trust, Am. Assn. U. Profs., Gridiron Secret Soc., Nine O'Clocks, So. Hist. Assn., Kappa Alpha. Democrat. Clubs: Le Petite Francais (London); Piedmont Driving (Atlanta); Athens. Home: 573 Hill St Athens GA 30601

SPALDING, HENRY A., mining engr.; b. Ky., Mar. 20, 1899; s. J.D. and Alice (Estes) S.; studied under personal tutors; m. Gertrude Petrey, Feb. 8, 1923; children—Jack P. (dec.), Richard D. Gen., widely diversified engring. practice; inventor metall. processes; pres. H.A. Spalding, Inc.; mgr., part owner Old Va. Land Co. Recipient Outstanding Citizen award Hazard Civic Club, 1958. Registered profl. engr. Mem. Am. Soc. C.E., Am. Inst. Mining Metall. and Petroleum Engrs., Ky., Soc. Profl. Engrs. (pres. 1949-50, hon.), Ky. Acad. Sci., Appalachian Geol. Soc., Ky. Hist. Soc., Nat. Rifle Assn. (exec. com., dir.). Club: Filson. Co-author: Engineers Vest Pocket Book. Contbr. articles to profl. jours. Home: Broadway Hazard KY 41701 Office: Baker Bldg Hazard Ky also 1928 Connecticut Av NW Washington DC 20009

SPALDING, HUGH C., supt. schs.; b. Raywick, Ky., Aug. 13, 1912; s. Thomas Elder and Elizabeth (Mattingly) S.; A.B., Western Ky. State Coll., 1935; M.A., U. Ky., 1949; m. Bernadette Hill, June 12, 1942; children—Sarah, Elizabeth, Catherine, Rose, Hugh. Tchr. schs., Marion County, Lebanon, Ky., 1931-36, supr., 1936-38; supt. Marion County Schs., Lebanon, 1938—. Served with AUS, 1942-46. Mem. Nat., Ky. edn. assns., Am. Legion. Roman Catholic. K.C. Home: 335 Spalding Av Lebanon KY 40033 Office: 344 Spalding Av Lebanon KY 40033

SPALDING, JACK JOHNSON, newspaperman; b. Atlanta, Feb. 7, 1913; s. Hughes and Billing Stovall (Phinizy) S.; grad. Georgetown Prep. Sch., 1932; student Georgetown U., 1933-34; A.B., U. Ga., 1936; m. Anne Wakefield Gowen, June 25, 1955; children—Charles Gowen, Elizabeth Hughes, John Phinizy, James Wakefield, Mary Anne Latimer. Timekeeper, United Fruit Co., Puerto Barrios, Guatemala, 1936-37; with Atlanta Constn., 1938-40; reporter Atlanta, N.Y.C. burs. U.P.I., 1941-42; account exec. Merrill Lynch. Pierce, Fenner & Beane, Atlanta, 1947-48, Clement A. Evans & Co., Atlanta, 1949-50; staff Atlanta Jour. 1951—, editor, 1956—. Bd. dirs. Travelers Aid Soc. Atlanta; bd. sponsors High Mus. Art. Served from ensign to lt. USNR, 1942-46. Mem. Am. Soc. Newspaper Editors, Am. Legion, Ga., Atlanta (trustee) hist. socs., Chi Phi, Sigma Delta Chi. Roman Catholic. Clubs: Piedmont Driving, Nine O'Clocks (Atlanta). Home: 6905 Riverside Dr NW Atlanta GA 30328 Office: Box 4689 72 Marietta St NW Atlanta Ga 30302

SPALDING, JOHN FRANKLIN, physicist; b. Aug. 4, 1926; s. John F. and Anne (Harvey) S.; B.S., Mich. State U., 1951; student U. Chgo., 1946-49; postgrad. U. Cal., 1953-55; m. Jean Jackson, May 29, 1952; children—Katherine, Nancy, Nicholas, Kenneth. Jr. optician Lick Obs., Mt. Hamilton, Cal., 1951-53; engr. Gen. Electric Co., gen. engring. lab., Schenectady, 1955-64; physicist Perkin-Elmer Co., Wilton, Conn., 1964-67; optical physicist Range Measurements Lab., Eastern Test Range USAF, Patrick AFB, Fla., 1968—, chmn. com. optical drawing standards, 1971. Instr. Mohawk Valley Tech. Inst., evenings and adult edn., 1956-57; G.E. Co., adult edn. courses, 1959-64. Served with inf. AUS, 1944-46. Recipient Outstanding Performance award U.S. Air Force, 1971. Fellow A.A.A.S.; mem. Soc. Photog. Instrumentation Engrs., Am. Astron. Soc., Sigma Pi Sigma, Alpha Delta Phi. Presbyn. (deacon 1970). Pioneer in application image orthicons to astronomy, 1962. Home: PO Box 303 Melbourne Beach FL 32951 Office: Range Measurement Lab Patrick AFB FL 32925

SPALDING, LESTER HELM, lawyer; b. Lebanon, Ky., June 16, 1920; s. Bennie Grant and Hazel (Helm) S.; A.B., Western Ky. State Coll., 1941; J.D., U. Louisville, 1948; m. Nell Terry, Sept. 12, 1942; children—Larry Helm, Susan Terry, Steven Lynn. Tchr., Phillipsburg (Ky.) Graded Sch., 1941-42; admitted to Ky. bar, 1948; practiced in Lebanon, 1948-51, 53—; atty. Marion County Bd. Edn., 1957—; city atty., Lebanon, 1956-58; commonwealth's atty. 11th jud. dist., Marion, Washington, Green, Taylor counties, 1958—; pres. Masonic Temple Co., 1957—; dir. Marion Nat. Bank Bd. dirs. Marion County Pub. Library. Mem. Lincoln Trail Crime Commn., 1969—. Served to 1st lt. USAAF, 1942-46; from capt. to maj., 1951-53; now maj. USAF Res. Mem. Ky. (pres. 1972—), Marion County, Lebanon bar assns., Am. Legion (comdr. 1954-55), V.F.W. (dept. staff judge adv. 1955-58), Ky. Hist. Soc., Phi Alpha Delta, Omicron Delta Kappa. Methodist (steward, mem. finance com.; dist. lay speaker). Kiwanian (v.p. 1956). Home: Park Heights Lebanon KY 40033 Office: 7 Court Sq Lebanon KY 40033

SPALDING, RICHARD LEROY, hosp. adminstr.; b. LaGrange, Mo., Apr. 18, 1936; s. Edward William and Thelma (Keith) S.; student Culver-Stockton Coll., 1955, Hardin-Simmons U., 1964, Columbia 1965; m. Beulah Kaye Barrigar, June 3, 1956; children—Kathleen J., Richard L., John E. Announcer, account exec. WCAZ Radio, Carthage, Ill., 1954-58; exec. v.p. Circle-S, Inc., Eastland, Tex., 1959-61; adminstr. Eastland Meml. Hosp., 1961-62; adminstrv. asst. Hendrick Meml. Hosp., Abilene, Tex., 1962-66; exec. dir. Meml. Hosp., Denison, Tex., 1966—. Pres., North Grayson unit Am. Cancer Soc., 1968-69, Denison Concert Assn., 1969-70; chmn. community relations Profile for Ednl. Progress Denison Pub. Schs., 1968-69; chmn. Texoma Area Health Services Planning Council, 1969—. Recipient Winner-Speak Up Jr. C. of C. award, 1963. Mem. Tex. Hosp. Assn. (chmn. council pub. edn. 1969—, chmn. Blacklands div. 1969-70). Baptist. Mason. Home: 931 W Bond St Denison TX 75020 Office: 1000 Memorial Dr Denison TX 75020

SPALTEN, ROBERT GEORGE, dentist; b. San Antonio, Apr. 2, 1929; s. Edward Henry and Hilda Ann (Mueller) S.; student St. Mary's U., 1946-49, U. Tex., 1949-50; D.D.S., St. Louis U., 1954; m. Jacqueline Barbara Jacobson, Nov. 29, 1954; children—Robert George, Steven Joseph, Jill Marie, John Edwin. Pvt. dental practice, San Antonio, 1956—; lectr. Bd. dirs. Ursline Acad., 1966-71. Served with USAF, 1954-56. Mem. Am., Tex. dental assns., San Antonio Dist. Dental Soc. (dir. 1966-68), Southwestern Dental Assembly, Austin and San Antonio Dental Study Club. K.C., Kiwanian (dir. 1966-68). Contbr. articles profl. jours. Home: 111 Wyndale St San Antonio TX 78209 Office: Milam Bldg San Antonio TX 78205

SPANDORF, LILY GABRIELLA, artist; b. Austria; d. Leon and Regina (Bornstein) S.; grad. Acad. of Arts, Vienna. One-man shows, London, Foyles Art Gallery, 1956, Sassari, 1957, Cagliari, Rome, London, 1958, Rome, London, 1959, Bodley Gallery, N.Y., Collectors Gallery, Washington, 1960, Alexandria Pub. Library, The Art's Club, 1961, Lee Gallery, Alexandria, Pan-American, London, 1962; English-Speaking Union, 1963, Washington County Mus. Fine Arts, Hagerstown, Md., 1963, Margaret Dickey Gallery, Washington, 1964, Agra Gallery Washington, 1964-67, 70, 72, Agra Gallery Palm Beach (Fla.), 1972; exhibited in group shows Met. Art, Smithsonian Instn., Washington Water Colour Soc., Norfolk Mus., Va., others; represented in permanent collections Library of Congress, Smithsonian Instn., Municipal Mus., Rome, The White House, Washington County Mus. Fine Arts, Mrs. Aristotle Onassis, Princess Margaret and Lord Snowdon, and others. Designed U.S. postage stamp for Christmas, 1963. Mem. Press Club Washington, Artists Equity Assn., Am. Arts League, Watercolour Soc. Contbg. artist to Washington newspapers and Christian Sci. Monitor. Address: 1603 19th St NW Washington DC 20009

SPANGENBERG, THEODORE SANDERS, state ofcl.; b. Miami, Fla., Sept. 22, 1924; s. Carl Henry and Lily May (Pettyjohn) S.; B.C.E., U. Fla., 1951; m. Marion Averett Hawthrone, June 5, 1950; children—Mary Sandra, Theodore S., Mayrene Caryl, Marion Diane, Erin Lee. Engring. insp., engring. trainee, maintenance engr., asst. engr. Fla Rd. Dept., Chipley, 1951-61, dist. maintenance engr., 1962—. Dist. commr. Boy Scouts Am., 1965-67, asst. dist. commr., 1968—. Served with AUS, 1944-46. Decorated Purple Heart. Registered profl. engr., surveyor, Fla. Fellow Fla. Engring. Soc.; mem. Nat. Soc. Profl. Engrs., Am. Civil Engring. Soc., Fla. Soc. Profl. Land Surveyors. Baptist (deacon). Home: PO Box 446 Chipley FL 32428 Office: PO Box 607 Chipley FL 32428

SPANGLER, DORN ODELL, supt. schs.; b. Mayberry, Va., Jan. 17, 1912; s. Frank Wallace and Lottie (Mahala) S.; student Presbyn. Jr. Coll., 1929-31; A.B., Westminster Coll., 1934; M.Ed., Duke, 1943; postgrad. Appalachian State U., 1948-50; m. Gaynelle Reynolds, Feb. 20, 1937; children—Phyllis, Sylvia (Mrs. Charles Hawkins), Larry, Terry. Tchr. schs., Patrick County, Va., 1936-41, prin., 1942-50, supr., 1950-65, supt., 1965—; prin. Carroll County, Va., 1941-42; Pres., Patrick County Farmers Mut. Ins. Co., 1952—. Mem. adv. bd. Danville Community Coll., 1965—, Patrick Henry Community Coll., 1965—; chmn. Franklin-Patrick Regional Library Bd., 1965—; scoutmaster Blue Ridge council Boy Scouts Am., 1946-50. Mem. Patrick County Devel. Corp., 1960—. Served with USNR, 1943. Mem. Va. Assn. Sch. Adminstrs., Va. Edn. Assn. Presbyn. Rotarian. Club: Ruritan (Meadows of Dan). Home: Dan VA 24120 Office: Stuart VA 24171

SPANGLER, WILLIAM BRUCE, civil engr.; b. Good Hope, Ill., Aug. 20, 1902; s. Jacob Anton and Nellie (York) S.; student Ia. State U., 1922-24; m. Olive Independence Bellus, Apr. 22, 1925; 1 son, Robert Bruce. Resident engr. Ia. Hwy. Commn., 1928-42; project engr. U.S. Army Research & Devel. Lab., Ft. Belvoir, Va., 1942-43, chief landing mat sect., 1943-54; chief landing mat sect. U.S. Army Waterways Expt. Sta., Vicksburg, Miss., 1954-56; chief metallurgy-radiation br. U.S. Army Mobility Equipment Research and Devel. Center, Ft. Belvoir, 1956-68, mem. design coupling tech. working group, 1963-68; cons. portable surfacing materials U.S. Waterways Expt. Sta., Vicksburg, 1956-58. Fellow Am. Soc. C.E.; mem. Am. Soc. Metals, Soc. Am. Mil. Engrs. Methodist. Mason. Mem. Order Eastern Star. Patentee interlocking structural units; structural assemblies composed of anti-creeping interchangeable interlocking units; portable structural assembly and interlocking units for constructing the same; connector structure for sectional material. Home: 6011 Mayfair Lane Alexandria VA 22310 Office: 6011 Mayfair Lane Alexandria VA 22310

SPANIOL, JOSEPH F., JR., govt. ofcl. Asst. dir. Adminstrv. Office of the U.S. Cts., Washington. Mem. Fed. (pres. local chpt. 1967-68), Am. bar assns., Am. Judicature Soc. Am. Law Inst. Editor: Fed. Bar Jour., 1968-71. Office: Lafayette Bldg Washington DC 20544*

SPANN, JAMES HENRY, ret. supt. schs.; b. Elloree, S.C., Dec. 12, 1916; s. James Henry and Lessie Christine (Welch) S.; B.S. in Edn., U. S.C., 1937, M.A., 1941; postgrad. George Peabody Coll., 1948, U. S.C., 1969-70; m. Elinor Gibbes Brand, Jan. 31, 1942; children—James Henry, Frank Brand, Robert McFaddin. Tchr. St. John's High Sch., 1937-40; tchr. Marion (S.C.) High Sch., 1946; prin. Myrtle Beach (S.C.) Elementary Sch., 1940-42, 46-50, supt. schs., 1950-58; asst. supt. schs. Greenwood (S.C.) County Sch. Dist. 50, 1958-69, supt. schs., 1969-72; ret.; tchr. math. Brunswick (Ga.) High Sch., 1972-73. Instr. extension classes and summer session Sch. Edn. U. S.C., 1949. Pres. Greenwood YMCA, 1962. Bd. dirs. Greenwood Heart Assn., Greenwood Community Chest, Greenwood Mentally Retarded Children's Assn. Served to lt. USNR, 1942-46. Decorated Air Medal. Mem. N.E.A., Assn. Am. Sch. Adminstrs., S.C., Greenwood County edn. assns., S.C. Dept. Audio Visual Instrn. (pres. 1967-69), Greenwood C. of C. (dir. 1970-72). Lion, Rotarian. Home: 792 Beachview Dr Jekyll Island GA 31520

SPANN, PHILIP NORMAN, architect; b. Dothan, Ala., May 11, 1936; s. Norman Dantzler and Lois (Dean) S.; B.Arch., Auburn U., 1959; m. Joyia Wilson, Aug. 23, 1956; children—Juliene, Philip Norman IV. Br. office mgr. Biggers & Neal, Architects, Dothan, 1959-68; partner firm Biggers-Neal-Spann & Hall, Architects, Dothan, 1968; partner firm Spann and Hall, Architects, Dothan, 1968—; partner Chateau Estates; treas. Creative Camera Inc. Mem. Dothan Planning Bd., 1961-67; chmn. Dothan Bd. Adjustment & Appeal, 1971—. Mem. Dothan-Houston County C. of C., Ala. Archaeol. Soc. (dir. 1967—), A.I.A., Kappa Sigma. Methodist. Club: Dothan Country. Home: 407 Santolina St Dothan AL 36301 Office: 220 Plaza 2 Dothan AL 36301

SPANN, ROBERT SIDNEY, utilities exec.; b. Greenville, S.C., Dec. 31, 1934; s. Olin Hart and Sara (Davis) S.; B.S., U. S.C., 1958; grad. N.Y. Inst. Photography, 1955; m. Barbara W. Edwards, Aug. 25, 1956; children—Robert Trent, Kathleen W., Brian C., A. Ivey. Sales rep. IBM Corp., Greenville, 1960-1963; sales rep. Winchester Arms Co., Fla., 1964-66; asst. to gen. mgr. Tampa Electric Co., Ruskin, Fla., 1966—; freelance photographer, writer. Chmn. boys work Columbia Even. Optimist Club, 1958-60; dir. dist. edn. Greenville Sales and Marketing Execs. Assn., 1960-61; founding dir. Brandon Area Recreational Youth Ednl. Assn., 1966-69. Pres., dir. S.C. Trapshooting Assn., 1963-64; v.p., dir. S.C. Sports Car Club, 1962-63; dir. Greenville Gun Club, 1963-64; chmn. pub. relations, dir. Brandon Sertoma Club, 1965-68; chmn. pub. relations Downtown Greenville Sertoma Club, 1963-64. Served with USAF, 1955-61. Winner various trap shooting championships, 1961-64, skeet shooting championships, 1961-64, sports car 1st places, 1960-64; recipient award of honor Brandon Sertoma Club, 1968. Mem. Greater Ruskin C. of C. (pres., dir., named Man of Yr., 1971), Nat. Soc. Pershing Rifles. Home: 105 4th Av SW Ruskin FL 33570 Office: PO Box 907 Ruskin FL 33570

SPANN, RONALD DEVOYE, dentist; b. Little Rock, Oct. 25, 1942; s. Clyde DeVoye and Lera Lorece (James) S.; student State Coll. of Ark., 1960-63; D.D.S., U. Tenn., 1966; m Nancy Smith, June 16, 1964; children—Shannon Paige, Ashli Tara. Dentist Memphis Pub. Health Dept., 1966; pvt. practice dentistry, Arkadelphia, Ark., 1968—; con. Riverwood Nursing Home, 1968—. Served as capt. USAF, 1966-68. Mem. Ark. Football Ofcls. Assn., Am., Ark. Dental assns., C. of C., Ark. Alumni Assn., Sigma Tau Gamma (dir. 1970-71). Baptist. Rotatian, Kiwanian. Club: Arkadelphia Country (pres. 1971-72, dir.). Home: 121 Leewood Dr Arkadelphia AR 71923 Office: 908 Main St Arkadelphia AR 71923

SPARKMAN, JOHN, U.S. senator; b. Morgan County, Ala., Dec. 20, 1899; s. Whitten J. and Julia Mitchell (Kent) S.; A.B., U. Ala., 1921, LL.B., 1923, A.M., 1924, LL.D., 1958; LL.D., Auburn U., Spring Hill Coll., Seoul Nat. U. (Korea); m. Ivo Hall, June 2, 1923; 1 dau., Julia (Mrs. Tazewell Shepard, Jr.). Admitted to Ala. bar, 1925; YMCA sec. U. Ala., 1923-25; instr. Huntsville Coll., 1925-28; practicing atty., Huntsville, Ala., 1925-37; U.S. commr., 1930-31; mem. 75th to 79th Congresses (1937-47), 8th Ala. Dist.; elected to U.S. Senate, Nov. 1946 to fill unexpired term late Senator John H. Bankhead, reelected for full terms, 1954, 60, 66. U.S. del. UN, 1950-51, Japanese Peace Treaty Conf., 1951, signed for U.S.A. Democratic nominee U.S. vice pres., 1952. Trustee Athens Coll., Am. U. Served S.A.T.C., 1918; col. U.S. Res. Corps. Mem. Am. Legion (past comdr.), Huntsville C. of C. (pres. 1935-36), Phi Beta Kappa, Pi Kappa Alpha, Phi Alpha Delta. Democrat. Methodist (dist. lay leader). Woodman, Kiwanian (ex-dist. gov.), Mason; mem. Eastern Star. Home: Huntsville AL 35801 also 4928 Indian Lane NW Washington DC 20016

SPARKMAN, ORVAL PRICE, hosp. adminstr.; b. nr. Hartselle, Ala., July 30, 1924; s. Clarence L. and Lillie (Legg) S.; B.S., Florence State U., 1954, Prin., Oak Rdige Sch., 1947-50; asst. prin. F.E. Burleson Elementary Sch., Hartselle, 1954-56; bus. mgr. Hartselle Hosp., Inc., 1958, owner-adminstr., 1961-69, adminstr., 1969—. Fellow Am. Acad. Med. Adminstrs.; mem. Fedn. Am. Hosps. (dir.), Am., Ala. hosp. assns., Am. Radiography Technologists, Nat. Assn. Hosp. Purchasing Agts., Florence State U. Alumni Assn., Ala. League Nursing. Methodist. K.P., Elk. Home: Lakeview Dr Hartselle AL 35640 Office: Hartselle Hosp Inc Hartselle AL 35640

SPARKS, CHARLES PAUL, indsl. psychologist; b. nr. Louisa, Ky., Oct. 9, 1915; s. Charles Clarence and Fannie (France) S.; B.S., Ohio State U., 1936, M.A., 1938; postgrad. Tulane U., 1949-51; m. Jean Case, Nov. 19, 1941; children—Paul E., Steven D. Psychologist pub. schs., Mansfield, O., 1937-40; dir. psychol. services Indpls. Pub. Schs., 1940-42; unit head personnel research Adj. Gen. Office, U.S. Army, 1946-48; project dir. Richardson, Bellows, Henry & Co., 1948-50, regional dir., 1951-54, v.p., 1955-62, pres., 1963; personnel research coordinator Humble Oil & Refinig Co., Houston, 1964—; adj. prof. U. Houston, 1970—. Served to capt., AUS, 1942-46. Fellow Am. Psychol. Assn. Author: (with D.H. Fryer, E.R. Henry) Outline of General Psychology, 1951. Home: 7715 Dashwood Dr Houston Tx 77036 Office: 800 Bell St Houston TX 77001

SPARKS, MEREDITH PLEASANT, chemist, patent atty.; b. Palestine, Ill., Dec. 9, 1905; d. John L. and Laura (Bicknell) Pleasant; A.B. with distinction, Ind. U., 1927, A.M., 1928; Ph.D., U. Ill., 1936; LL.B., J.D., Rutgers U., 1958; m. William J. Sparks, Dec. 31, 1930; children—Ruth Katherine, Charles, John. Editorial work Du Pont Co., Niagara Falls, N.Y., 1929-34; research on cosmetics Northam Warren Co., N.Y.C., 1939; chemist, chem. patents Am. Cyanamid Co., Bound Brook, N.J., 1941-46. Admitted to Fla. bar, 1958. Mem. Assn. Ind. U. Chemists (pres. 1950-51), Internat., Am. bar assns., Am., N.J. patent law assns., Internat. Patent and Trademark Assn., Am. Chem. Soc. (woman's com. for nat. meetings in N.Y.C.), Nat. Assn. Women Lawyers, Phi Beta Kappa, Sigma Xi, Sigma Delta Epsilon, Iota Sigma Pi. Club: Westfield (N.J.) College Woman's (treas. 1951-53). Contbr. article to Ber deut. Chem. Ges., 1929, chem. jour. Patentee in field. Home: 5129 Granda Blvd Coral Gables FL 33146 Office: 169 E Flagler St Miami FL 33131

SPARKS, SHERMAN PAUL, osteo. physician, surgeon; b. Toledo, Ill., Jan. 23, 1909; s. Ernest Melvin and Nancy Jane (Keller) S.; B.S., U. Ill., 1932, M.S., 1938; D.O., Kirksville Coll. Ostepathy and Surgery, 1945; m Joyce Marie Patterson, Jan. 23, 1965; children—by previous marriage—James Earl, Randal Paul, Robert Dale, Paul David. Intern Sparks Hosp., Dallas, 1945; practice osteo. medicine specializing in surgery, Rockwall, Tex., 1946—. Tchr. High Sch. Mt. Olive, Ill., 1932-42. Civil Def. coordinator, Rockwall County, 1950—; pres. P.T.A., Rockwall, 1958-59, Band Boosters, 1960-61, Rockwall Centennial Celebration, 1954; Republican chmn. Rockwall County, 1964—. Mem. Am., Tex. (v.p. 1954), Rockwall (pres. 1955-56), Dist. 5 osteo. assns., Am. Coll. Gen. Practitioners. Mason (Shriner). Inventor photo-electric turbidimeter for quick quantitative counting bacteria. Home: 406 W Rusk St Rockwall TX 75087 Office: 106 N 2d St Rockwall TX 75087

SPARKS, THOMAS EVERETT, lawyer; b. Crossett, Ark., Aug. 15, 1911; s. Albert Theodore and Clara (Morton) S.; A.B., Hendrix Coll., 1932; LL.B., Washington and Lee U., 1935; m. Julia Benton, June 29, 1940; children—Thomas Everett, Julianna (Mrs. Joseph T. Dickey), Helen Benton. Admitted to Ark. bar, 1935, since practiced in Fordyce; mem. Ark. Ho. of Reps., 1967—. Pres., Benton Realty Co., Inc., Benton Hardware Co., Inc., Benton Casket Mfg. Co., Inc., Benton Furniture Co., Inc.,; owner Morton Abstract Co. Pres., Dallas County Indsl. Devel. Corp. Served to lt. USNR, 1943-46. Mem. Am., Ark. bar assns., Ark. Trial Lawyers Assn., Fordyce C. of C. (past pres.). Democrat. Methodist. Rotarian. Home: RFD 2 Fordyce AR 71742 Office: PO Box 784 Fordyce AR 71742

SPARLING, JOSEPH JAMES, educator; b. Umatilla, Fla., Dec. 19, 1935; s. Joseph Paul and Elizabeth (Hamrick) S.; B.S., Fla. State U., 1957, M.S., 1958; Ph.D., U. Mich., 1968; m. Marilyn Claire Bull, June 22, 1963; 1 dau., Kimberly. Tchr., Fla., Cal., Mich., 1958-63; curriculum cons. community schs., Grand Blanc, Mich., 1963-64, prin., 1964-65; asso. dir. Frank Porter Graham Child Devel. Center, U. N.C., Chapel Hill, 1967—, asst. prof. edn., 1969—. Mem. Am. Ednl. Research Assn., Assn. Supervision Curriculum Devel., A.A.A.S. Author: (with J.J. Gallagher) Research Directions for the 70's in Child Development, 1971. Contbr. articles to profl. jours. Home: Bayberry Dr Chapel Hill NC 27514

SPAUGH, HERBERT, bishop, newspaper columnist; b. Winston-Salem, N.C.; A.B., LL.D., Moravian Coll.; B.D. Moravian Theol. Sem.; M.A., D.D., Davidson Coll.; m. Ida Brown Efird; children—Earle, Herbert, Mrs. Robert Farmer, Jr. Furniture mfr., Winston-Salem; ordained to ministry Moravian Ch., pastor Little Ch. on Lane, Charlotte, N.C., 1924-66; columnist Charlotte News, 1933—. Bishop, past mem. various exec. bds. Moravian Ch. Am.; bd. govs., past v.p. Moravian Ch. Am. South, mem. finance bd. Past chmn. Consol. Sch. Bd. Charlotte and Mecklenburg County; chaplain Charlotte Police Dept.; past pres. Charlotte-Mecklenburg Ministerial Assn., Mecklenburg A.R.C.; organizer Charlotte Pub. Sch. Music System; mem. N.C. Sch. Bd. Assn., N.C. Council Chs., Charlotte Alcohol Edn. Com., Groves Conf. Marriage and Home, Charlotte

Mental Hygiene Soc., Charlotte Family Life Council. Moravian Ch. Archives Bd. Trustee Moravian Coll., Bethlehem (Pa.), Salem (N.C.) Coll. Mil. service World War I. Recipient Silver Beaver award Boy Scouts Am.; Rotary citizenship award. Mem. Am. Legion (hon. life chaplain), Order of St. Luke the Physician. Clubs: Executives, City (Charlotte); Civitan (citizenship award, past chaplain Carolina dist., past chaplain internat.). Author: The Pathway to Contentment; Everyday Counsel for Everyday Living; The Pathway to a Happy Marriage; The Boy, the Man, the Bishop; Psalms for Everyday Living. Contbr. articles to numerous mags. Home: 130 N Canterbury Rd Charlotte NC 28211 Office: 528 Moravian Lane Myers Park Charlotte NC 28207

SPAULDING, AARON LOWERY, govt. ofcl.; b. Durham, N.C., Mar. 16, 1943; s. Asa Timothy and Elna (Bridgeforth) S.; student N.C. Central U., 1960-64, U. Pa., 1966-68, Naval Officers Candidate Sch., 1969, Naval Supply Corps Sch., 1969-70. Financial and systems analyst RCA, N.Y. and N.J., 1964-66, budget analyst, N.Y., summer 1967; co-founder, treas., dir. Re-Con Services, Inc., Phila., 1968-69; instr. progress mgmt. and econ. devel., 1968-69; commd. ensign USN, 1969; with Naval Command Systems Support Activity, Washington, 1970-72; comptroller John F. Kennedy Center for Performing Arts, 1972-—. Cons. to Manpower and Edn. Task Force, Phila. Urban Coalition, 1969, Human Resources Center U. Pa., 1969. Mem. Wharton MBA Assn. (pres. 1968). Home: 1608 Lincoln St Durham NC 27701 Office: John F Kennedy Center for Performing Arts Washington DC 20566

SPAULDING, ASA TIMOTHY, JR., exec. mgmt. cons.; b. Durham, N.C., Sept. 21, 1934; s. Asa Timothy and Elna (Bridgeforth) S.; A.B., Morehouse Coll., 1956; M.B.A., N.C. Central U., 1965; m. Shirley B. Atwell, Sept. 6, 1958; children—Pamela Frances, Asa Timothy III. With controller's dept. N.Y. Life Ins. Co., N.Y.C., 1956-57; sr. systems analyst U.S. Trust Co., N.Y.C., 1959-60; methods rep. Electronic Data Processing div. RCA, N.Y.C., 1960-61; asst. planning dir., later asst. v.p. systems and policy services N.C. Mut. Life Ins. Co., Durham, 1961-69; pres., chief exec. officer Information Services Corp., Durham, 1968-—; chief exec. officer Asa Spaulding and Assos. Mem. Durham Council on Human Relations, N.C. Task Force on Planned Variations; pres. Emorywoods Community Assn., 1971. Chmn. bd. dirs. Found. for Econ. and Environmental Devel., 1968-—. Served with AUS, 1957-59. Recipient Distinguished Service award Durham Jr. C. of C., 1964. Mem. Assn. for Systems Mgmt. (dir. 1965-67, Nat. Distinguished Service award 1971), Data Processing Mgmt. Assn., Durham C. of C. (chmn. manpower devel. com. 1970), Durham Bus. and Profl. Chain, Omega Psi Phi. Democrat. Baptist. Mason. Clubs: Durham Striders Track, Durham Sports. Contbr. articles on systems and data processing to profl. publs. Home: 1110 Jerome Rd Durham NC 27707 Office: 811 W Main St PO Box 1010 Durham NC 27702*

SPAULDING, GEORGE WARREN, mgmt. cons.; b. Haron Lake, Minn., Oct. 5, 1895; s. Willis E. and Etta B. (Higgins) S.; student Colo. State Tchrs. Coll., 1927, S.D. State Coll., 1933; m. Octa G. Lucy, Dec. 4, 1944; children—Thelma Warrene (Mrs. Denzel R. Gibbens), Evon Jean (Mrs. Simon O. Hood, Jr.). With Bur. Indian Affairs, 1924-58; head dept. Vocational Edn. Flandreau (S.D.) Indian Sch., 1924-34, Haskell Inst., Lawrence, Kan., 1934-38, supt. 1938-41; supr. Indian Edn. Washington, 1941-44; supt. Cheyenne River Agy., S.D., 1944-49; area dir. Aberden, S.C., 1949-51; dir. Div. Program Planning, Washington, 1951-54; gen. supt. Navajo Agy., Window Rock, Ariz., 1954-58; ret., 1958; mgmt., orgn. cons. Navajo Tribe, Window Rock, Ariz., 1959; dir. public services div. Navajo Tribe, 1960; engaged as mgmt. cons., Midwest City, Okla., 1963-—. Recipient Distinguished Service award and gold medal Dept. of Interior, 1959. Mem. N.E.A., Internat. for Community Devel., Am. Vocational Assn., C. of C. Episcopalian. Lion, Rotarian, Kiwanian. Patentee hydraulic blockmachine. Home: 536 E Harmon Dr Midwest City OK 73110

SPEAKES, LARRY MELVIN, journalist; b. Cleveland, Miss., Sept. 13, 1939; s. Harry Earl and Ethlyn Frances (Fincher) S.; student U. Miss., 1957-61; m. Laura Christine Crawford, Nov. 3, 1968; children—Sondra LaNell, Barry Scott, Jeremy Stephen. News editor Oxford (Miss.) Eagle, 1961-62; news editor Bolivar Comml., Cleveland, 1962-63, mng. editor, 1964-66; dep. dir. Bolivar County Civil Def., Cleveland, 1963-64; gen. mgr. Progress Publishers, Leland, Miss., 1966-68, editor Leland Progress, Hollandale Herald, Bolivar County Democrat, Sunflower County News; mem. staff U.S. Senate, Press Sec. Sen. J. O. Eastland, Washington, 1968-—. Active Girl Scouts Am., Boy Scouts Am. Recipient Gen. Excellence award Miss. Press Assn., 1968; named Reporter of Year The Mississippian, U. Miss., 1958; Lambda Sigma award, 1960. Mem. Kappa Sigma, Lambda Sigma, Omicron Delta Kappa, Sigma Delta Chi. Methodist. Clubs: Senate Press Secretaries, Senate Staff (Washington). Home: 1000 6th St SW Washington DC 20024 Office: 1st and Constitution Av NE Washington DC 20510

SPEAKS, WICKLIFFE DAVIS, dentist; b. Monroe, La., June 27, 1901; s. William Alexander and Varina Lavertte (Davis) S.; student U. Chgo., 1921-22, Loyola U., Chgo., 1924-26; B.S., Northwestern U., 1928, D.D.S., 1929; m. Nelda Allen Mann, Aug. 19, 1946; 1 dau., Lynda Varina. Comml. press telegrapher Western Union Press Service, Shreveport, La., 1917-19, Chgo., 1921-28; faculty Northwestern U. Dental Sch., 1929-37; pvt. practice dentistry, Evanston, Ill., 1937-42; dir. Miss. out-patient dental program, chief dental services VA Hosp. Center, Jackson, 1946-—. Served to capt. Dental Corps, USNR, 1943-46; PTO. Mem. Am., Miss. dental assns., Am. Legion, D.A.V., Xi Psi Phi, Theta Nu Epsilon, Trowel. Democrat. Presbyn. (deacon). Mason, Elk. Club: Confederate Heights Country. Home: 4120 Council Circle Jackson MS 39206 Office: 1500 E Woodrow Wilson St Jackson MS 39206

SPEAR, ADOLPH FLATAUER, financial exec.; b. Apalachicola, Fla., Apr. 29, 1917; s. Emory M. and Tessie (Flatauer) S.; A.B., Oglethorpe U., 1939; postgrad. Harvard, 1943; m. Edith Jane Knight, Mar. 5, 1949; children—Barbara, LLoyd, Robert, James, Kenneth. Auditor, Ernst &Ernst, C.P.A.'s, Atlanta, 1939-43, 1945-46; with Am. Standard, N.Y.C., 1947-52; sec., treas., dir. Gen. Plywood Corp., Louisville, 1953-62, Consider H. Willett, Inc., Louisville, 1963; pres., dir. Adolph F. Spear & Co., Inc., Louisville, 1964-—; mgr. finances Indsl. Services Am., Inc., Louisville, 1969-70; chmn. Casa Madero, Inc., 1971-—; dir. Internat. Resources Corp., Recreation and Leisure Time Devel. Corp., Investment Planning, Inc. Chmn., United Cerebral Palsy Fund drive, 1959. Served from ensign to lt. USNR, 1943-45; PTO. C.P.A., Ga., Ky. Mem. Order Confederate Cols. Ky. (gen. 1956-—), Order Ky. Cols., Am. Inst. C.P.A.'s, Tax Execs. Inst. (v.p. 1960-61), So. Inst. Mgmt. (founding mem.), Financial Execs. Inst. Kiwanian (chmn. underprivileged childrens com. 1961-62). Clubs: Admirals, Pendennis (Louisville). Home: 1723 Devondale Dr Louisville KY 40222 Office: PO Box 7164 Louisville KY 40207

SPEARMAN, CRAWFORD HENRY, JR., lawyer; b. Edmond, Okla., Apr. 27, 1930; s. Crawford H. and Freda M. (Stewart) S.; B.A., Central State Coll., 1952, LL.D., 1970; LL.B., U. Okla., 1955; m. Shirley Ann Landon, Feb. 10, 1959; children—Mark, Tina, John, Paul. Admitted to Okla. bar, 1955, since practiced in Edmond. Asso. in govt. Central State Coll., 1957-60. Mem. Okla. Ho. Reps., 1965-—. Mem. Am., Okla. bar assns. Research on constl. convention. Home: 333 Memory Lane Edmond OK 73034 Office: 19 E First St Edmond OK 73034

SPEARS, ADRIAN A(NTHONY), judge; b. Darlington, S.C., July 8, 1910; s. J. Monroe and Mary Agnes (Moore) S.; student The Citadel, 1927, U. N.C., 1928; LL.B., U. S.C., 1934; m. Elizabeth Wylie, June 10, 1937; children—Sara (Mrs. Tor Hultgreen), Claude, Thomas, Carolyn Blakely, James Adrian. Admitted to S.C. bar, 1934, Tex. bar, 1937; in pvt. practice law, Darlington, S.C., 1934-36, San Antonio, 1937-61; U.S. dist. judge, 1961-62, chief judge, 1962-—. Spl. dist. judge, 1951; faculty Seminar for Newly Apptd. Judges. Chmn. bd. adjustment City Alamo Heights, 1947-49; chmn. ofcl. Charter Revision Com., 1949; mem. com. on adminstrn. criminal law Jud. Conf. U.S., 1969-—. Del., Democratic Nat. Conv., 1952, 56, 60; mem. Tex. Dem. Exec. Com., 1950-52. Bd. dirs. Fed. Jud. Center. Recipient Rosewood Gavel award St. Mary's U. Law Sch., 1971. Mem. Am., San Antonio (pres. 1959-60) bar assns., State Bar Tex., State Bar S.C. (del. 5th circuit jud. conf. 1955-58), Pi Kappa Phi, Phi Delta Phi, Omicron Delta Kappa. Methodist. Mason (33 deg., K.T., Shriner), Rotarian. Club: Monday Morning Quarterback (pres. 1961). Home: 2167 NE Loop 410 San Antonio TX 78216 Office: PO Box 798 San Antonio TX 78293

SPEARS, GRAYSON ELDRIDGE, carpet mill exec.; b. Spearsville, La., Dec. 20, 1928; s. Grayson Lee and Lillian (Rockett) S.; student Northwestern State Coll., 1948, Centenary Coll., 1949, So. Meth. U., 1963-—; m. Geraldine Carter; children—Linda, Don, Mark, Duane, Dawn. Mgr., Hemenway Furniture Co., Vivian, La., 1953-58, Jay's Furniture Co., Dangerfield, Tex., 1958-63; v.p., gen. mgr. Colonial South Life Ins. Co., Ruston, La., 1963-65; v.p., gen. mgr. Cherokee Carpet Mills, Inc., Lewisville, Ark., 1965-—; co-organizer Marlin Mills, Inc. (Tex.), 1965-—, v.p. mfg., 1970-71; organizer Spears Carpet Mills, Inc., 1971-—; also dir. state mgr. Imperial Securities Co., Little Rock, 1965. Served with AUS, 1946-47. Mem. Ch. of Christ. Rotarian. Home: 404 E 17th St Hope AR 71801 Office: Hwy 29 N N Indsl Park Hope AR 71801

SPEARS, JAMES WM., lawyer, educator; b. Jasper, Ark., July 21, 1934; s. James Franklin and Constance (Cooper) S.; student Ark. Poly. Coll., 1952-54; B.S. in Indsl. Engring., U. Ark., 1958, J.D., 1964. With Guy A. Moore's Ozark Abstract Co., Jasper, Ark., 1958-60; admitted to Ark. bar, 1964; partner, Walker, Villinies & Spears, Harrison, Ark., 1965; asst. prof. law, U. Ark., Fayetteville div., 1965, Little Rock div., 1966-69, asso. prof., 1969-—. Mem. research staff 7th Ark. Constl. Conv. Mem. Ark. Bar Assn., Nat. Rifle Assn., Pi Kappa Alpha, Phi Alpha Delta. Democrat. Jewish religion. Mason, Elk. Home: 800 N Van Buren St Little Rock AR 72205 Office: 300 Broadway Little Rock AR 72201

SPEARS, JOHN HERMAN, lawyer; b. Imboden, Ark., Oct. 10, 1901; s. Ben and Kate (Odom) S.; student U. Ark., 1927-28, Memphis State Coll., 1928-29; m. Willie Sue Robertson, Jan. 4, 1930. Admitted to Ark. bar, 1935, since practiced in West Memphis; dep. pros. atty. Crittenden County, Ark., 1940-44; city atty. West Memphis, 1945-52. Dir., atty. West Memphis Fed. Savs. & Loan Assn., Bank of West Memphis. Mayor, Turrell, Ark., 1938-39. Chmn., Local Draft Bd., 1946-71. Trustee So. Bapt. Coll., Walnut Ridge, Ark., Bapt. Meml. Hosp., Memphis. Mem. Crittenden County Bar Assn. (past pres.). Baptist (trustee, Sunday sch. tchr.). Club: West Memphis Country. Home: 217 Roosevelt St West Memphis AR 72301 Office: 500 E Broadway West Memphis AR 72301

SPEARS, JOSEPH CARROLL, assn. exec.; b. nr. Greeneville, Tenn., Apr. 18, 1929; s. W. Lee and Mildred I. (Smith) S.; student Tusculum Coll., 1946-47; B.S., U. Tenn., 1951;; m. Ruby L. Scott, Aug. 14, 1948; children—Scott L., Lisa L. Exec. dir. Boaz (Ala.) C. of C., 1959-60; asst. mgr. Gadsden (Ala.) C. of C., 1961-62; exec. v.p. Lancaster County (S.C.) C. of C., 1962-65; exec. v.p. Bristol (Tenn.-Va.) C. of C., 1966-68; exec. v.p. Athens (Tenn.) Area C. of C., 1969-—; non-credit salesmanship instr. East Tenn. State U., 1968; v.p. Roger Q. Williams Tours, Inc., Knoxville, Tenn., 1969-—. Chmn. Mayor's Adv. Com., Athens, 1970-—; v.p. Lower Hiwassee River Watershed Devel. Assn., 1971; chmn. Health and Ednl. Facilities Bd., City of Athens, 1971-—. Served with inf., U.S. Army, 1952-54. Named Key Man Jr. C. of C., 1965. Mem. So., Tenn., East Tenn. indsl. devel. councils, Am., Tenn. C. of C. execs. Methodist. Mason (Shriner), Elk. Home: 916 Towanda Trail Athens TN 37303 Office: 213 Washington St Athens TN 37303

SPEARS, MACK JUSTIN, univ. dean; b. Wilson, La., May 1, 1912; s. Charley and Mary (Wheelock) S.; A.B., Dillard U., 1942; M.A., Xavier U., 1949; Ed.D. (Univ. fellow), Harvard, 1954; m. Olga Veronica Abadie, Nov. 8, 1939; 1 dau., Olga Veronica (Mrs. Bruce C. Mason). Tchr. elementary sch., jr. high sch. Orleans Parish Sch. Bd., New Orleans, 1933-48, asst. prin., 1948-49, elementary sch. prin., 1949-53, secondary sch. prin., 1954-67; prof. edn. Dillard U., New Orleans, 1967-—, dean student affairs, 1968-—. Vis. prof. edn. So. U., 1958-68; guest lectr., guest cons. Nat. Assn. Secondary Sch. Prins., 1960-—; guest cons. U.S. Office Edn., 1963-64. Co-gen. chmn. United Negro Coll. Fund, New Orleans, 1961, 62; mem. Human Relations Com. of New Orleans, 1968-—; mem. v.p. Orleans Parish Sch. Bd., 1966-—, pres., 1971-72. Bd. dirs. Total Community Action. Recipient Distinguished Alumni award Dillard U., 1967. Mem. N.E.A., Nat. Assn. Secondary Sch. Prins., Nat. Assn. U. Profs., Assn. for Supervision and Curriculum Devel., Nat. Assn. Sch. Personnel Adminstrs., Phi Delta Kappa. Conglist. (pres. 1960-—). Contbr. articles to edn. jours. Home: 1951 Law St New Orleans LA 70119

SPECK, DONALD HOUSTON, ch. ofcl.; b. Grand Prarie, Tex., Jan. 25, 1927; s. Henry Bascomb and Cora (Leonard) S.; B.Arch., U. Tex., 1954; student Dallas Art Inst., 1948-49, El Centro Coll., 1967; postgrad. U. Birmingham (Eng.), 1969; m. Phyllis Arlene Danhof, July 31, 1949; children—Don Houston, Jon Philip, Cheryl Lyn, Carol Ann. Prin. firm Donald H. Speck, Dallas, 1959-67; ofcl. Presbyn. Ch., Atlanta, 1967-—, coordinator gen. assembly ministries, 1970-71, asso. exec. sec. Bd. Nat. Ministries, Atlanta, 1971-—. Mem. exec. com. Div. Christian Life and Mission, Nat. Council Chs., 1970-—; pres. Nat. Conf. Religious Architecture, 1970-—. Bd. dirs. v.p. Interfaith Research Center Architecture, N.Y.C. Served with USNR, 1945-46. Mem. A.I.A., Ga. Guild for Religious Architecture. Presbyn. Contbr. articles to profl. jours. Home: 3356 Lynnray Dr Doraville GA 30040 Office: 341 Ponce de Leon Av Atlanta GA 30308

SPECK, JOHN KING, lawyer; b. Crawford, Tex., Aug. 4, 1904; s. James Malachi and Mary (King) S.; student Okla. State U., 1921-22; B.S., U. Okla., 1928; LL.B., Oklahoma City U., 1941; m. Lavon Evelyn Gildersleeve, July 14, 1929; children—James Stanley, Carolyn Kay (Mrs. Bob Schronrenberg), Bonnie Jean (Mrs. John F. Schroer, Jr.). Mdse. mgr. Central States Power & Light Co., Stillwater, Okla., 1928-31; commd. agt. Continental Oil Co., Stillwater, 1930-33; owner John K. Speck, Accountant, Stillwater, 1931-35; auditor income tax div. Okla. Tax Commn., Oklahoma City, 1935-37; dir. income tax div. Kan. State Tax Commn., Topeka, 1937-40; admitted to Okla. bar, 1939; practiced in Oklahoma City, 1940-—; mem. firm Speck, Fleig, Hewett & Philbin, 1955-—. Instr., Oklahoma City U., 1940-41. Past pres. Oklahoma City Estate Planning Council, Oklahoma City Tax Lawyers Group; pres. Okla. Christian Found.; men's com. Japan Internat. Christian U. Found. Trustee Okla. Med. Research Found., Phillips U., Okla. Ind. Coll. Found., Morse Found., Okla. Eye Found.; trustee, pres. Okla. Halfway House. Mem. Am., Okla., Oklahoma County bar assns., Okla. Inst. on Taxation (founder, past pres.), Oklahoma City C. of C., Okla. Poetry Soc., Oklahoma City Econ. Club, Christian Men's Fellowship (past state pres., nat. adv. bd.). Republican. Mem. Christian Ch. (elder). Mason (Shriner, Jester), Lion. Clubs: Men's Dinner, Sooner Dinner, Chandelle, Petroleum, Quail Creek Golf and Country, Fortune (past pres.), Twin Hills Golf and Country (past treas., dir.). Contbr. articles to profl. jours. Home: 1609 Glenbrook Terrace Oklahoma City OK 73116 Office: Liberty Bank Bldg Oklahoma City OK 73102

SPECK, LOUISE BARRETT (MRS. FRANK STANIFORD SPECK), human biologist; b. Phila., May 22, 1916; d. Johns Hopkins and Florence V. (Clay) Barrett; B.A., U. Pa., 1938; M.A., U. Denver, 1950; Ph.D., U. Colo., 1955; m. Frank Staniford Speck, June 10, 1940; children—Staniford Clay, Richard Pell. Instr., U. Denver, 1950-51; research fellow U. Colo. Med. Sch., 1953-55, instr., 1955-62; research physiologist Clin. Neuropharmacology Research Center, Nat. Inst. Mental Health, Washington, 1962-66, adminstr. psychopharm. research br., 1966-68; with U.S. Army, Alexandria, Va., 1968-—. Vol., Wash. Internat. Center. Mem. Am. Pub. Health Assn., Am. Soc. Cybernetics, Am. Physiol. Assn., Am. Chem. Soc., A.A.A.S., Central Assn. Electroencephalographers, Soc. Psychophysiol. Research, N.Y. Acad. Sci., I.E.E.E., Sigma Xi. Home: 105 Franklin St Alexandria VA 22314 Office: USA CDCINCS Fort Belvoir VA 22060

SPEECE, HERBERT ELVIN, educator; b. Meadowlands, Minn., Oct. 29, 1914; s. Ray M. and Grace (Lytle) S.; A.B., York Coll., 1938; M.A., Tex. Christian U., 1943; M.S., N.C. State U., 1951; Ph.D., U. N.C., 1956; m. Ruth E. Lowrance, July 28, 1945; children—Ray Elvin, Deborah Grace. Tchr. sci. Tivy High Sch., Kerrville, Tex., 1946-47; instr. physics Trinity U., San Antonio, summer 1947; instr. math. N.C. State U., Raleigh, 1947-56, asst. prof., asso. prof. math., 1956-62, prof. math. and sci. edn., 1962-—, chmn. dept. math. and sci. edn., 1952-—; dir. NSF Acad. Insts., NSF Acad. Earth Sci. Project, NSF Implementation Center for Engring. Concepts Curriculum Project, 1970-—. Chmn. in-service com. Edn. Council State Bd. Edn., 1962-—. Served with USAAF, 1942-45. Mem. A.A.A.S., Math. Assn. Am., Nat. Sci. Tchrs. Assn., Nat. Council Tchrs. Math., N.C. Acad. Sci. (pres. 1970-71), Phi Kappa Phi, Kappa Phi Kappa, Pi Mu Epsilon. Methodist. Mason. Home: 3408 Wade Av Raleigh NC 27607

SPEEL, HENRY CHARLES, chemist; b. Phila., Nov. 21, 1908; s. John Field and Clara (McClatchey) S.; A.B., Harvard, 1930, spl. student, 1931-33; m. Mary Ella Urquhart, Sept. 1, 1934; 1 dau., Gwen (Mrs. Gerald P. Kaplan). Chem. engr. Atlas Powder Co., 1934-45; new comml. products research Gen. Mills, Inc., 1945-46; tech. rep. Alrose Chem. Co., 1947-48, Gen. Aniline & Film Corp., 1948-50; dir. devel. Wyandotte Chem. Corp., 1951-52; cons. Speel & Asso., 1952-—, pres., 1952-60; v.p. Schwarz, Speel & Assos., 1959-60; marketing research adviser Universal Oil Products Co., Des Plaines, Ill., 1960-63; became staff specialist chems. products and process evaluation staff, Office Adminstr., Agrl. Research Service, U.S. Dept. Agr., Washington, 1963, now indsl. analyst program devel. staff. Fellow Am. Inst. Chemists (life); mem. Am. Chem. Soc., Am. Oil Chemists Soc. (nat. chmn. joint com. with Am. Soc. Testing and Materials on analysis soaps and detergents 1961-68), Am. Soc. Testing and Materials (councillor Middle Atlantic dist.), Comml. Chem. Devel. Assn., Midwest Chem. Marketing Assn. (founder, chmn. group 1963-64), Soc. Cosmetic Chemists, Chem. Market Research Assn., Am. Assn. Textile Chemists and Colorists (sec. Western New Eng. sect. 1959-60). Presbyn. (treas. New Eng. synod council Presbyn. Men 1955-58). Clubs: Chesapeake; Harvard Varsity; Chemists (N.Y.C.). Editor: 2 edits. Textile Chems. and Auxs., 1952, 57, Japanese edit., 1962. Contbr. to tech. publs. Patentee in field. Home: 821 S Lee St Alexandria VA 22314 Office: ARS OA PDS US Dept Agr Washington DC 20250

SPEIDEL, JOE, III, broadcasting exec. Pres. WTMP, Tampa, Fla. Office: Washington Blvd PO Box 1101 Tampa FL 32301*

SPEIR, WILSON E., state ofcl.; b. Gilmer, Tex., Aug. 28, 1917; s. John William and Epsie Jane (Ellison) S.; B.S., E. Tex. State U., 1940; m. Ann Marie Allen, Aug. 10, 1940; children—Larry Michael, Elwyn Duane, John Marcus. Tchr. pub. sch., prin. Harmony High Sch., Upshur County, Tex., until 1941; with Tex. Dept. Pub. Safety, Austin, 1941-—, advanced through ranks to asst. dir., now dir. Mem. Tex. Commn. on Law Enforcement Officer Standards and Edn., Bd. Pvt. Investigators, Gov.'s Criminal Justice Council. Served to capt. USAAF, 1942-45; ETO. Mem. Tex. Police Assn. (past pres.). Baptist. Mason, Rotarian. Home: 6623 Argentia Rd Austin TX 78751 Office: Box 4087 Austin TX 78751

SPEKTER, LOUIS, physician, govt. ofcl.; b. Russia, July 8, 1908; s. Samuel and Luba (Yoslefsky) S. came to U.S., 1910, naturalized, 1928; B.S., Trinity Coll., Hartford, Conn., 1929; M.D., U. Rochester, 1933; M.P.H., Harvard, 1942; m. Edythe G. Schneider, Apr. 24, 1944; children—Beth M., Susan Z., Amy L. Intern, Duke Hosp., Durham, N.C., 1933-34; resident in pediatrics Doernbecker Meml. Hosp. for Children; Portland, Ore., 1934-35, Duke Hosp., 1935-36; practice medicine specializing in pediatrics, Hartford, Conn., 1937-38; chief crippled children sect. Conn. Dept. Health, 1938-54, maternal and child health sect., 1954-64; instr. pediatrics Duke Hosp. 1935-36; clin. instr. pediatrics Yale, 1955-64; asso. dir. health services div. Children's Bur., U.S. Dept. Health, Edn. and Welfare, Washington, 1964-65, dir. health services div. Maternal and Child Health Service, Health Services and Mental Health Adminstrn., USPHS, 1965-—. Fellow Am. Acad. Pediatrics; mem. A.M.A., Am. Pub. Health Assn., Alpha Omega Alpha. Author: The Pediatric Years, 1955. Home: 4915 Albemarle St NW Washington DC 20006 Office: Parklawn Bldg 5600 Fishers Lane Rockville MD 20852

SPELL, DANIEL MELVIN, JR., aerospace co. engring. exec.; b. Brunswick, Ga., Nov. 13, 1931; s. Daniel Melvin and Grace (Reed) S.; B.Indsl. Engring., Ga. Inst. Tech., 1959; postgrad. U.S. Fla., 1968-—; m. Anne Marie Petri, Aug. 22, 1953; children—Dawn Marie, Daniel Melvin III, Regina Anne, Richard Scott. Indsl. engr. Westinghouse Electric Corp., Fairmont, W.Va., 1959-62; with Honeywell, Inc., St. Petersburg, Fla., 1962-—, chief indsl. engr., 1967-—. Cons. mgmt., engring. Committeeman, Boy Scouts Am., Dunedin, Fla., 1969-—; mgr., v.p. Little League, Dunedin, 1963-67. Served with USAF, 1950-54. Registered profl. engr., Fla. Mem. Nat. Soc. Profl. Engrs., Fla. Engring. Soc., Am. Inst. Indsl. Engrs. Democrat. Baptist. Club: Toastmasters International. Home: 66 Lexington Dr Dunedin FL 33528 Office: 13350 US Hwy 19 St Petersburg FL 33733

SPENCE, FLOYD DAVIDSON, congressman; b. Columbia, S.C., Apr. 9, 1928; s. James Wilson and Addie (Lucas) S.; A.B., U.S.C., 1952, J.D., 1956; grad. nat. security seminar Indsl. Coll. Armed Forces; m. Lula Hancock Drake, Dec. 22, 1952; children—David, Zack, Banjamin Caldwell. Admitted to S.C. bar, 1956; partner from Callison and Spence, West Columbia, S.C., 1956—; mem. S.C. Ho.

Reps., 1956-62; mem. S.C. Senate, 1966-70, minority leader, 1966-70, chmn. joint com. investigate communist activities, 1969; mem. 92d Congress from S.C.; mem. Armed Services Com. Past chmn. Ridge dist. Central S.C. council Boy Scouts Am., 1965-66, exec. bd., 1963—; chmn. Lexington County Mental Health Assn., 1959; mem. exec. com. Columbia Bd. dirs. Mid-Carolina Mental Health Assn., 1970. Served with USNR. Mem. Am. Legion, (mem. counter-subversive activities com. 1966, 67), V.F.W., Res. Officers Assn., Navy League, Columbia Carillon (dir. 1966-70), West Columbia-Cayce, Lexington, S.C. chambers commerce. Lutheran. Contbr. articles on communism to profl. jours.; lectr. in field. Home: Box 815 Lexington SC 29072 Office: Box 11378 Columbia SC 29211

SPENCE, JAMES ROBERT, banker; b. Lillington, N.C., Sept. 25, 1927; s. George Broughton and Lillie (Patterson) S.; LL.B., U. N.C., 1953;; m. Marilyn S. Younce, Jan. 10, 1953; children—Helyn S., James Robert, Louise Y. Admitted to N.C. bar, 1953; v.p. High Point (N.C.) Bank & Trust Co., 1967-71; pres. Southeast Nat. Bank of Orlando (Fla.), 1971—; vis. lectr. banking High Point Coll., 1969-70. Chmn. High Point (N.C.) Democratic Party, 1968-69. Served with USNR, 1945-47. Mem. N.C. State Bar. Kiwanian. Author: The Making of a Governor, 1968. Home: 1394 Stewart St Winter Park FL 32789 Office: PO Box 80 Orlando FL 32801

SPENCE, JOHN MCCLURKIN, architect; b. Charlotte, N.C., July 10, 1909; s. Cleveland A. and Dolores (Powell) S.; B.Arch., George Washington U., 1936; m. Myrta Dutton Williams, Feb. 4, 1939; children—Karl D., Susan (Mrs. William Martin Biggs). Individual practice architecture, Washington, 1946-50; chief mil. housing architect, residential planning cons. U.S. Dept. Navy, Washington, 1950—. Served with USNR, 1942-46. Registered architect, D.C., Va., Md. Mem. A.I.A. Club: Congressional 3221 Oliver St NW Washington DC 20015

SPENCE, JOHN SELBY, clergyman, educator; b. Balt., May 1, 1909; s. John S. and Katherine G. (Hartman) S.; student Loyola Coll., Balt., 1927-29; St. Mary's Sem., 1929-30; S.T.B., Propaganda and Gregorian Univs., Rome (Italy), 1930, S.T.L., 1934. Ordained priest Roman Cath. Ch., 1933, papal chamberlain, 1948, domestic prelate, 1955; curate Sacred Heart Shrine, Washington, 1934-40, St. Anthony's Ch., 1940-42, St. Matthew's Cath., 1942-51; pastor St. John Baptist de La Salle Ch., Chillium, Md., 1951-58; pastor Shrine of the Sacred Heart, Washington, 1958—; named aux. to archbishop of Wash., 1964, now bishop, Washington; judge matrimonial curia, 1936—; dir. Women's Retreat League, Washington Archdiocese, 1934-44, dir. edn., 1948-64. Home: Shrine of Sacred Heart 16th and Park Rd NW Washington DC 20010 Office: 1721 Rhode Island Av NW Washington DC 20036

SPENCER, CHESTER EDWARD, JR., orthodontist; b. Bastrop, La., May 23, 1934; s. Chester Edward and Emma Lou (Carpenter) S.; B.S. in Mech. Engring., Okla. State U., 1957; D.D.S., Baylor U., 1967, M.S., 1969; m. Wanda June Melton, Nov. 21, 1953; 1 dau., Stephanie Lou. Prodn. engr. Humble Oil & Refining Co., Magnolia, Ark., Grand Isle, La., 1957-63; practice dentistry, specializing in orthodontics, Grand Prairie, Tex., 1969—. Pres. Grand Prairie br. Am. Cancer Soc., 1969-70. Served to capt. AUS, 1961-62. Recipient award Tex. Acad. Gen. Dentistry, 1967, Dental Gold Medal award Baylor U., 1967. Mem. Am. Assn. Orthodontics (S.W. Soc.), Tex. Dental Assn., Baylor Orthodontics Alumni Assn., Odontological Honor Soc. Psi Omega, Omicron Kappa Upsilon. Lion. Home: 1313 Roman Rd Grand Prarie TX 75050 Office: 738 Dalworth St Grand Prarie TX 75050

SPENCER, DONALD FORD, electronics engr.; b. Bellevue, Ky., Apr. 16, 1924; s. Merle Wilson and Mildred (Ford) S.; B.S., U. Cin., 1951; m. Phyllis Esther Parry, Dec. 30, 1950; children—Barton Parry, Sherra Ford, Wendra Whitman. Electronic engr. USN Bur. Ships and Naval Research Lab., Washington, 1951-56; head air-to-surface missile guidance unit USN Bur. Aeros., 1956-59; chief avionics and guidance div. Office Communications and Electronics, Office Dir. Def. Research and Engring., 1959-70; electronics indsl. specialist Office Asst. Sec. Def., 1970—. Served with USNR, 1943-46. Registered profl. engr., D.C. Asso. fellow Am. Inst. Aeros. and Astronautics; mem. I.E.E.E. (sr.), Inst. of Nav. (chmn. Washington sect., mem. nat. council), Nat. Aerospace Electronics Conf. (v.p.). Presbyn. Mason. Clubs: Mt. Vernon Yacht (dir.); Annapolis Yacht. Home: 4311 Ferry Landing Rd Alexandria VA 22309 Office: The Pentagon Washington DC 20301

SPENCER, EMORY MAURICE, lawyer, oil operator; b. Redwater, Tex., Mar. 13, 1905; s. Cuthbert and Thursey (McBeth) S.; A.B., Rice Inst., 1926; postgrad. U. Tex. Law Sch., 1931-33; m. Mildred Farrow, Sept. 17, 1943; children—Sandra Carol, James Darrell (adopted), Mary, Alicia. Geophysicist, Sun Oil Co., S.W. U.S., 1927-34; admitted to Tex. bar, 1936, since practiced in Rockport; city atty., 1943-45; county judge Aransas County, 1948-49; county atty., 1939-43, 45-48; oil operator, 1948—; dir. Portland State Bank (Tex.). Mem. Coastal Bend Regional Council Govts. Chmn., Ark. County Democratic Exec. Com., 1955-58. Mem. State Bar Tex., Tex. Bar Found., Delta Tau Delta. Episcopalian. Home: Majorca Rockport TX 78382 Office: PO Drawer 1207 Rockport TX 78382

SPENCER, FERN E. SMITH (MRS. LUCIAN W. SPENCER), civic worker; b. Wheeler, Tex., May 13, 1920; d. Bonner and Laura (Lamberth) Smith; student Amarillo Jr. Coll.; m. Lucian Witten Spencer, May 20, 1949; children—Patricia Ann (Mrs. W.C. McElhannon), Laura Beth (Mrs. Robert D. Hill, Jr.), Lucian W. Bd. dirs. Moore County Concert Assn., Girl Scout council; mem. bd. Dallas Civic Ballet; vol. worker Presbyn. Hosp., mem. San Antonio Little Theatre, Dallas Symphony Orch. League. Named Woman of Year, Beta Sigma Phi, 1962. Mem. Christian Ch. (deaconess.). Clubs: Woodlawn Garden; Dumas Garden, 1932 Study; Tanglewood Hills Country. Home: 1119 Western Blvd Arlington TX 76013

SPENCER, FRANK EDWARD, JR., air force officer; b. Lynchburg, Va., Aug. 31, 1929; s. Frank E. and Eldridge (Williams) S.; student Augusta Mil. Acad., 1949; B.S., Va. Mil. Inst., 1953; m. Ida Page Watts, July 11, 1953; children—Sandra, David, Thomas, Mary, Jane. Commd. 2d lt. USAF, 1953, advanced through grades to lt. col., 1970; civil engr. various locations, 1954—, project engr. programs mgmt. div. Hdqrs. USAF, Pentagon, Washington, 1967-71; base civil engr. Shaw AFB, S.C., 1971—. Recipient Meritorious Service medal U.S. Air Force, 1970. Registered profl. engr., Vt., Colo. Mason. Home: 216 Magnolia St Shaw AFB SC 29152

SPENCER, GLENN WINFIELD, civil engr.; b. Redwater, Tex., Jan. 14, 1927; s. Gaskel R. and Mary Edna (Robertson) S.; student La. State U., 1944-45; B.S. in Civil Engring., U. Houston, 1958; m. LuNan Lakey, July 23, 1955; children—Catherine, Carolyn, Susanne. Design engr. City Houston, 1956-59; design engr., planner indsl. park, resident engr. r.r. constrn. S.P. Co., Houston, 1959-64; design engr. Dow Chem. Co., Houston, 1964-65; prin. civil engr. facilities Manned Spacecraft Center, NASA, Houston, 1965—. Bd. dirs. Nassau Bay Civic Assn. Served with USAAF, 1945-46. Recipient Sustained Superior Performance award Manned Spacecraft Center, NASA, 1968. Mem. Am. Soc. C.E. (committeeman Houston br.), Nat., Tex. socs. profl. engrs., Engrs. Council Houston, Tau Beta Pi. Baptist (deacon). Home: 18623 Capetown Dr Houston TX 77058 Office: Manned Spacecraft Center Nasa Rd 1 Houston TX 77058

SPENCER, MARY MILLER, civic worker, club woman; b. Comanche, Tex., May 25, 1924; d. Aaron Gaynor and Alma (Grissom) Miller; B.S., N. Tex. State U., 1943; 1 dau., Mara Lynn. Cafeteria dir. Mercedes (Tex.) Pub. Schs., 1943-46; home economist coordinator All-Orange Dessert Contest, Fla. Citrus Commn., Lakeland, 1959-62, 64; children's services worker Fla. Div. Family Services, Lakeland, 1969-70, social worker, 1970—. Tchr. purchasing sch. lunch dept. Fla. Dept. Edn., 1960. Clothing judge Polk County (Fla.) Youth Fair, 1951-68, Polk County Federated Women's Clubs, 1964-66; pres. Dixieland Elementary Sch. P.T.A., 1955-57, Polk County Council P.T.A.'s, 1958-60; dist. 7. Fla. Congress Parents and Tchrs., 1961-63; chmn. pub. edn. com. Polk County unit Am. Cancer Soc., 1959-60, bd. dirs., 1962—; charter mem., bd. dirs. Lakeland YMCA; sec. Greater Lakeland Community Nursing Council, 1965-69; trustee, vice chmn. Polk County Eye Clinic, 1962-64, pres., 1964—; bd. dirs. Polk County Scholarship and Loan Fund, Inc.; mem. exec. com. West Polk County (Fla.) Community Welfare Council, 1960-62, 65-68; mem. budget and audit com. Greater Lakeland United Fund, 1960-62; mem. adv. bd. Polk County Juvenile and Domestic Relations Ct., 1960-69,; mem. exec. com. Sun Coast Health Council, 1968—, vol., disaster res. social worker A.R.C., 1970—; mem. Fla. Health and Welfare Council, 1970—, Polk County Mental Health Assn., 1970—. Sec. bd. dirs. Fla. West Coast Ednl. Television, 1960—. Mem. Fla. Congress Parents and Tchrs. (hon. life, pub. relations chmn. 1962-66.), Fla. Pub. Health Assn., Alumni Assn. N. Tex. State U. Democrat. Methodist. Mem. Order Eastern Star. Home: 535 W Beacon Rd Lakeland FL 33803 Office: PO Box 2161 Lakeland FL 33803

SPENCER, PLATT ROGERS, accountant; b. Port Orange, Fla., Mar. 27, 1935; s. Platt R. and Marion (Stover) S.; B.S., Fla. State U., 1957; m. Rosemary Yarr, Dec. 25, 1962. Staff accountant Allen & Allen, C.P.A., 1957-60; state auditor Fla., 1961-63; partner John W. Hosford & Co., C.P.A.'s, Tallahassee, 1964—. Mem. cons. com. Clara Lewis Scholarship Trust for Girls, Fla. State U., 1967—. C.P.A., Fla. Mem. Am., Fla. Insts. C.P.A.'s. Mem. Christian Scientist Ch. Mason. Home: 733 Arkansas St Tallahasse FL 32302 Office: 219 S Calhoun St Tallahassee FL 32301

SPENCER, ROMULUS SANDERSON, JR., retail trade exec.; b. Engelhard, N.C., Dec. 1, 1940; s. Romulus Sanderson and Elizabeth Leigh (Baum) S.; student U. N.C., 1959-60; B.S., East Carolina U., 1963; m. Judy Elizabeth Broughton, June 20, 1964; 1 son, Romulus Sanderson III. Tchr. East Hyde High Sch., 1963-64, Mattamuskeet Sch., Swan Quarter, N.C., 1964-72, coach, 1966-72, mgr. R.S. Spencer Furniture Store, Inc., Engelhard, 1964-71, v.p. 1971—; v.p. R.S. Spencer Gen. Store, Inc., Engelhard, 1971—; dir. East Carolina Bank. Recipient Hyde County Outstanding Young Educator award Mattamuskeet Jaycees, 1969. Mem. N.C. Assn. Educators, Hyde County Edn. Assn. (pres. 1965-66), Hyde County Hist. Assn. Democrat. Baptist (sec. bd. deacons 1969—). Address: Engelhard NC 27824

SPENCER, SHERWOOD, lawyer; b. Ashland, Ky., Jan. 23, 1913; s. Holmes A. and Mary (Baker) S.; B.B.A., U. Fla., 1933, J.D., 1936; m. Jean Rowe, Dec. 15, 1939; children—William Sherwood, Carol Ann. Admitted to Fla. bar, 1936, U.S. Supreme Ct. bar, 1963; pvt. practice law, Hollywood, Fla., 1939—; city atty. Hollywood, 1949-53. Dir. gen. counsel Hollywood Fed. Savs. & Loan Assn.; dir., gen. counsel Southeast Bank Hollywood Hills, Southeast Bank of Miramar. Mem. grievance com. 15th Jud. Circuit, 1950-55; mem. com. of 100. Mem. Broward County (pres. 1949), Fla. (bd. govs. 1953-63, dir. real property sect. 1971—), Am. (standing com. unauthorized practice of law) bar assns., Fla. Title Assn. (chmn. title examiners' div. 1950-51). Rotarian. Clubs: Yacht (vice commodore 1948), Lauderdale Yacht. Home: 1600 Rodman St Hollywood FL 33021 Office: Hollywood Fed Bldg Hollywood FL 33022

SPENCER, THOMAS M., coll. pres.; b. Nolan County, Tex., Nov. 30, 1916; s. Thomas Monroe and Dell (Whitley) S.; B.S., Sam Houston State Tchrs. Coll., 1935, M.A., 1939; Ed.D., U. Houston, 1947; m. Rachel Bradham, Nov. 26, 1936; children—Betty (Mrs. W. M. Von-Maszewski), Thomas M., Anna Lou (Mrs. Robert Bragg), Willie Jo (Mrs. Gerald Mace). High sch. prin., Holland, Tex., 1935-37; supt. Thrall (Tex.) Ind. Sch. Dist., 1937-41, Llano (Tex.) Ind. Sch. Dist., 1941-42; dep. supt. pub. instrn. State of Tex., 1942-43; supt. Cypress Fairbanks-(Tex.) Ind. Sch. Dist., 1943-47; pres. Blinn Coll., Brenham, 1947-57, South Plains Coll., Levelland, 1957-61; pres. San Jacinto Coll., Pasadena, 1961—. Mem. Tex. Adv. Bd. for Nurses Tng., 1951-57; mem. adv. com. to Tex. Commn. on Higher Edn., 1965—; mem. liaison com. Tex. Coordinating Commn. Higher Edn., 1965—; mem. steering com. Tex. Conf. on Edn.; mem. Tex. Council on Aerospace Edn. Chpt. chmn. Washington County A.R.C., 1950—; dist. chmn. Boy Scouts Am., 1956—. Bd. dirs. House Speaker's Com. of 100. Mem. Am. Assn. Jr. Colls. (mem. legislative com. 1947—), Tex. Pub. Jr. Coll. Assn. (pres. 1949—), Pasadena C. of C. (past pres.), Woodmen of World, Kappa Delta Pi, Pi Kappa Delta. Mem. Christian Ch. (past chmn. ofcl. bd.). Lion, Rotarian. Home: 706 Cherokee Dr Pasadena TX 77502 Office: 8060 Spencer Hwy Pasadena TX 77505

SPENCER, WILLA BELLE, educator; b. Chickasha, Okla, July 22, 1913; d. Jefferson Lee and Jessie (Condron) Carter; B.S., Okla. Coll. for Women, 1935; M.S., Okla. State U., 1939; m. Lee Bowen Spencer, Aug. 19, 1939; children—Lee Bowen, Mary Ann, Sarah Margaret. Tchr. Konawa (Okla.) High Sch., 1935-36; instr., asst. prof., asso. prof., dir. women's phys. edn. Okla. Bapt. U., 1936-63; asst. prof. phys. edn. State Coll. Ark., 1963—. Dir. Community Swimming Program, Shawnee, Okla., 1953-63. Bd. dirs. Pottawatomie County chpt. A.R.C., 1950-63, Campfire Girls, U.S.A., Shawnee, Okla., 1958-63. Mem. Am. Assn. U. Women (past pres. Shawnee br.), Okla. Soc. Mayflower Descs. (state elder), Am., Ark., Okla. (state chmn. coll. sect. 1961-62) assns. health, phys. edn. and recreation, Delta Kappa Gamma. Home: 2002 Prince St Conway AR 72032

SPENCER, WILLIAM MICAJAH, JR., lawyer; b. Gallion, Ala., June 29, 1890; s. William Micajah and Bertha Gracey (Steele) S.; B.S., Marion Inst., 1908, U. Ala., 1910; LL.B., Harvard, 1913; m. Margaret Woodward Evins, June 23, 1915 (dec. June 1966); children—Margaret (Mrs. Edgar G. Givhan, Jr.), William Micajah III, Bertha (Mrs. Adrian Alton Ringland, Jr.). Admitted to Ala. bar, 1913, since practiced in Birmingham. Staff, Birmingham Ordnance Dist., World War II; dir. Woodward Iron Co. (Ala.), Robertson Banking Co., Black Warrior Electric Membership Corp., Demopolis, Ala., Owen-Richards Co., Inc., Metalplate & Coatings, Inc. (both Birmingham). Chmn. mus. bd. Birmingham Mus. Art; bd. regents Ala. Mus. Natural History; dir. Ala. State Fair Authority; trustee Children's Hosp. of Birmingham; bd. dirs., chmn. arboretum com. Birmingham Bot. Soc. Served to 1st lt. AUS, World War I; ret. as lt. col. O.R.C., 1935. Named Man of Yr., Birmingham, 1968. Mem. Warrior-Tombigbee Devel. Assn. (dir.), Am. Ordnance Assn., Am., Ala., Birmingham bar assns., Newcomen Soc. N.Am., Delta Kappa Epsilon, Theta Nu Epsilon. Episcopalian (registrar Ala. Diocese). Clubs: Country, Mountain Brook, Redstone, Downtown, The Club, Rotary (Birmingham). Home: 14 Ridge Dr Birmingham AL 35213 Office: Suite 2000 First National-So Natural Bldg Birmingham AL 35203

SPENCER, WILLIAM MICAJAH, III, engring co. exec.; b. Birmingham, Ala. Dec. 10, 1920; s. William M. and Margaret Woodward (Evins) S.; B.S., U. of South, 1941; postgrad. Harvard, 1947; m. Evalina Sommerville Brown, Sept. 28, 1946; children—Murray Brown, Margaret Anne. With Owen-Richards Co., Inc., Birmingham, 1947-71, treas., 1950-52, v.p., treas., 1952-53, pres., 1953-71; pres. Bearings & Transmissions Supply Co., 1952-59, Bearings & Transmissions Supply Co. of Fla., 1959-71; pres. BATS of Miss., 1964-71, BATS of La., 1965-71, Owen-Richards Co. of Ga., 1963-71; pres. Gen. Engring Co., Inc., Jacksonville, Fla., 1967-71; pres. Motion Industries, Inc. (consol. above cos. 1971), Birmingham, 1971—. Dir. First Nat. Bank of Birmingham, Allied Life Ins. Co., Goodall-Brown Dry Goods Co., Altec Inc., Altec Mfg. Co., Inc., (all Birmingham), Mead Corp., Dayton, O. Pres. Birmingham Festival of Arts, 1964. Bd. dirs. Community Chest, Baptist Hosps. Found., Indian Springs Sch. Found. Served to capt. USMC, 1941-46. Decorated Bronze Star medal. Mem. Birmingham C. of C. (pres. 1963), Young Presidents Orgn., Chief Execs. Forum, World Bus. Council, Phi Beta Kappa, Omicron Delta Kappa, Phi Delta Theta, Blue Key. Clubs: Mountain Brook Country (pres. 1959), Downtown. Home: 3035 Cherokee Rd Birmingham AL 35223 Office: 824 31st St N Birmingham AL 35203

SPERBER, PERRY ARTHUR, physician; b. Providence, Oct. 11, 1907; s. Hugo and Hattie (Mann) S.; B.A., Brown U., 1928; M.D., N.Y. U., 1932; m. Muriel Hope Reed, Sept. 28, 1939; children—Gayle Patricia (Mrs. Thomas Eugene Freeman), Perry Reed. Intern, N.Y.C. Hosp., 1932-33, resident, 1933-34; resident Correction Hosp., N.Y.C., 1934-35; practice medicine specializing in dermatology, allergy, Providence, 1937-50, Daytona Beach, Fla., 1951—; former mem. staff R.I., Jane Brown hosps., Providence, mem. staff Halifax Dist., Ormond Beach Meml. hosps., Daytona Beach. Curator, Daytona Beach Sea Zoo, 1951-61. Chmn. patrons com. Am. Heart Assn., Daytona Beach, 1967. Fellow Am. Assn. Clin. Immunology and Allergy (pres. Southeastern region 1971-72), A.A.A.S., Am. Med. Writers Assn., Am. Geriatrics Soc., Am. Acad. Allergy; mem. A.M.A., Fla., So. med. assn., Am. Acad. Dermatology, Assn. Mil. Dermatologists, Assn. Cosmetic Plastic Surgeons, Soc. Contemporary Medicine and Surgery. Baptist (deacon). Kiwanian (past pres., lt. gov.-elect 5th div. Fla. 1972—). Author: Treatment of the Aging Skin and Dermal Defects, 1965; Sex and the Dinosaur, 1970; Drugs, Demons, Doctors and Disease, 1972. Contbr. articles to profl. jours. Address: 536 S Ridgewood Av Daytona Beach FL 32014

SPERELAKIS, NICK, educator; b. Joliet, Ill., Mar. 3, 1930; s. James and Arestea (Kayadakis) S.; B.S., U. ill., 1951, M.S., 1955, Ph.D., 1957; m. Dolores Martinis, Jan. 28, 1960; children—Nicholas, Mark Demetri, Christine Marie, Sophia Ann, Thomas Andreas and Anthony James (twins). Instr. physiology Western Res. U., Cleve., 1957-59; asst. prof. physiology, 1959-66, asso. prof., 1966; prof. physiology U. Va. Med. Sch., Charlottesville, 1966—. Served with Project Hope in Peru, 1962. Served with USMC, 1951-53. Mem. Am. Physiol. Soc., Biophys. Soc., Am. Soc. Zoologists, Am. Assn. U. Profs., A.A.A.S., I.E.E.E., Soc. Neuroscis., Soc. Gen. Physiologists, Cardiac Muscle Soc., Sigma Xi, Phi Kappa Phi. Greek Orthodox Ch. Asso. editor Scientific Jour. Contbr. articles in field to profl. jours. Home: 1615 Cedar Hill Rd Charlottesville VA 22901

SPERLING, GODFREY, JR., journalist; b. Long Beach, Cal., Sept. 25, 1915; s. Godfrey and Ida (Bailey) S.; B.S., U. Ill., 1937; LL.B., U. Okla., 1940; m. Betty Louise Feldmann, June 22, 1942; children—Mary, John Godfrey. Admitted to Ill. bar, 1940; practice in Urbana, Ill., also reporter Champaign-Urbana News-Gazette, 1940-41; mem. staff Christian Sci. Monitor, 1946—, Midwest bur. chief, 1957-62, N.Y. bur. chief, 1962-65, news mgr., asst. chief Washington bur., 1965—; lectr. nat. affairs, 1955—. Served to maj. USAAF, 1941-46; col. Res. Mem. Okla., Ill., Mass. bar assns., Congl. Press Corr. Assn., White House Press Corr. Assn., Sigma Delta Chi. Christian Scientist. Club: Nat. Press, Overseas Writers, Sperling Roundtable (host) (Washington). Home: 7706 Chatham Rd Chevy Chase MD 20015 Office: Nat Press Bldg Washington DC 20004

SPERO, SHERWIN LEE, social worker; b. Toledo, Nov. 20, 1925; s. Herbert I. and Evelyn (Yuro) S.; B.S., Ohio State U., 1952; M.S.W., U. Louisville, 1956; m. Shirley Berg, June 23, 1949; children—Stephen L., Robert B., Jeffrey D. Supr., Jefferson County (Ky.) Juvenile Ct., 1956-58; caseworker Jewish Social Service Agy., Louisville, 1958-62; exec. dir. Council for Retarded Children, Louisville, 1962-64; program dir. Jewish Community Center, Louisville, 1964-66; community planner Health and Welfare Council, Louisville, 1966-68; dir. Social Service Unit, Comprehensive Health Care Center, Louisville, 1968—. Bd. dirs. Community Coordinated Child Care Program, 1969—. Served with USNR, 1943-46. Mem. Nat. Assn. Social Workers (past chpt. treas., del. Assembly, chpt. pres. 1971-72). Jewish religion (trustee). Home: 3304 Willow Way Louisville KY 40218 Office: 323 E Chestnut St Louisville KY 40202

SPERONIS, STEPHEN LOUIS, educator; b. Lowell, Mass., Dec. 1, 1920; s. Louis Stephen and Katherine (Theodorou) S.; B.A., Boston U., 1947, M.A., 1948; Ph.D., U. Mich., 1956; m. Constance Anne Hatges, June 25, 1950. Teaching fellow U. Mich., 1950-54; prof. U. Tampa, Fla., 1956-59, dean eve. div., 1959-61, v.p. for devel., 1961-68, spl. asst. to pres., 1969—, prof. contemporary Am. history, Russian, Middle East, Far East, polit. sci. Resident news analyst WFLA-TV and radio, Tampa, 1958; NBC news staff Radio Free Europe, 1958. Middle East editor, mem. Am. Security Council. Am. Served with AUS, 1942-45. Mem. Merchants Assn. Tampa (dir.), Sales and Marketing Execs. of Tampa, Phi Alpha Theta, Phi Kappa Phi, V.F.W., Am. Legion, Reserve Officers Assn., Lambda Chi Alpha. Mason (32 deg.), Rotarian. Home: 5012 San Miguel St Tampa FL 33609

SPERRY, JOSEPH AUSTIN, II, assn. adminstr.; b. Woodbury, N.J., Jan. 14, 1899; s. Washington Elliot Langley and Sarah (Ridgely) S.; student Washington Coll. Accounting, 1919-21; m. Myrtle Onice Palmer, Sept. 4, 1920; children—Helen (Mrs. R.R. Zimmerman), Myrtle, Joseph Austin III, Dorothy (Mrs. R.V. Legere). With Bur. Internal Revenue, 1919-22; accountant, West Palm Beach, Fla., 1922-36, Fla. Auditing Dept., 1936-39, Bradenton and Tampa, Fla., 1939-41; asst. sec. Superior Fertilizer Co., Tampa, 1941-45; accountant, Sulphur Springs, Fla., 1946—, Dade City Fla., 1951—; mgr. sec. North Tampa C. of C., 1965—. C.P.A., Fla. Home: 6106 Branch Av Tampa FL 33604 Office: PO Box 8247 Tampa FL 33604

SPICKARD, WILLIAM ANDERSON, JR., physician, educator; b. Englewood, N.J., Aug. 17, 1931; s. William A. and Elizabeth (Creighton) S.; B.A. cum laude, Vanderbilt U., 1953, M.D. 1957; m. Susan Micher, Mar. 28, 1959; children—Susan, Anderson, David. Intern Vanderbilt Hosp., 1957-58, asst. resident, 1958-59, Hugh Morgan chief med. resident, 1962-63; asst. resident Johns Hopkins Hosp., 1959-60; instr. medicine George Hunter Lab., Vanderbilt Med. Sch., Nashville, 1963-64, asso. prof. dept. medicine, 1969—; asst. clin. prof. dept. medicine Meharry Med. Sch.; practice medicine specializing in internal medicine, Nashville, 1964—; med. dir. Vanderbilt U. Clinic, Nashville, 1969—; mem. staffs Vanderbilt Hosp., St. Thomas Hosp., Hubbard Hosp., Nashville. Served with USPHS, 1960-62. Diplomate Am. Bd. Internal Medicine. Fellow A.C.P.; mem. A.M.A., Nashville Acad. Medicine, Tenn. Med. Assn. Home: 2435 Bear Rd Nashville TN 37215 Office: Vanderbilt U Clinic Nashville TN 37232

SPICOLA, GUY WILLIAM, lawyer, state legislator; b. Tampa, Fla., Feb. 27, 1938; s. Joseph G. and Alma (Norona) S.; B.A., U. Fla., 1960, LL.B., 1962; m. Bonnie Sharon Wallace, Aug. 19, 1961; children—Brandon Sean, Betsy Sue. Admitted to Fla. bar, 1962; atty. finance and taxation coms. Fla. Ho. of Reps., 1963, mem., 1967—, majority whip, 1969—, chmn. subcom. on natural resources and agr., environmental pollution control com.; atty. City of Temple Terrace (Fla.), 1963-66. Pres., bd. dirs. Young Democrats Hillsborough County, 1965-66; alternate del. Dem. Nat. Conv., 1968. Mem. Am., Tampa-Hillsborough County bar assns., Fla. Bar, Am., Bay Area trial lawyers assns., Acad. Fla. Trial Lawyers, Am. Judicature Soc., Tampa, Tampa Jr chambers commerce, Circle K., Phi Delta Phi, Alpha Tau Omega. Roman Catholic. Club: Merrymakers. Address: 725 E Kennedy Blvd Tampa FL 33602*

SPIEWAK, IRVING, nuclear engr.; b. Bklyn., Jan. 5, 1928; s. Meyer and Ethel (Teichteil) S.; B. Chem. E., Cooper Union, 1947; M.S., Mass. Inst. Tech., 1948; m. Mary Bryan, July 19, 1953; children—Alan Richard, Jonathan Andrew, Leah. With Oak Ridge Nat. Lab., 1949—, dep. dir. nuclear desalination program, 1965—. Pres. Oak Ridge Playhouse, 1957; concertmaster Oak Ridge Symphony, 1953; mem. Anderson County (Tenn.) Sch. Bd., 1967—. Mem. Am. Inst. Chem. Engrs., Am. Nuclear Soc. Jewish religion (pres. congregation, 1965-68). Mem. B'nai B'rith. Home: Route 3 Box 138 Clinton TN 37716 Office: Oak Ridge Nat Lab PO Box Y Oak Ridge TN 37830

SPILDE, LULU MARY CASLEY (MRS. OTIS SPILDE), educator; b. Flandreau, S.D.; d. Hugh and Elizabeth (Lane) Casley; B.S., S.D. State U., 1914; M.A., U. S.D., 1925; Ed.D., N.Y. U. 1942; m. Otis Spilde, June 8, 1921. Prin pub. schs., Bryant, S.D., 1914-21, Vienna, S.D., 1921-23; dean women, dir. tchr. tng. U. S.D. at Springfield, 1925-39, Fordham U., N.Y.C., 1944-46; prof. edn., dir. tchr. tng. St. John's U., Jamaica, N.Y., 1946-65; prof. edn. Niagara U., Niagara Falls, 1966-68, Ft. Lauderdale (Fla.) U., 1968—. Lectr., dir. testing and guidance, dir. extension centers; cons. state dept., Pierre, S.D.; active sch. surveys Nassau County, N.Y., 1961-62, Pres. So. dist. P.T.A., S.D., 1937-39, Am. Legion Aux., Vienna, S.D., 1923-25; supreme nat. dir. edn. Cath. Daus. Am., 1940-65. Mem. Am. Assn. U. Women, Am. Assn. U. Profs., N.E.A., Nat. Cath. Edn. Assn. Author: Audio-Visual Aids in Education, 1958, Observation and Student Teaching, 1961, Techniques of Oral Book Reviews, 1963. Contbr. articles to profl. mags. Home: 1201 SE 2d St Fort Lauderdale FL 33301

SPILHAUS, ATHEISTAN, meterologist and oceanographer; b. Cape Town, Union of S. Africa, Nov. 25, 1911; s. Karl Antonio and Nellie (Muir) S.; B.Sc., U. Cape Town, 1931, D.Sc., 1948; S.M., Mass. Inst. Tech., 1933; D.Sc., Coe Coll., 1961, Hahnemann Med. Coll., 1968, U.R.I., 1968, Phila. Coll. of Pharmacy and Sci., 1969, Hamilton Coll., 1970, Southeastern Mass. U., 1970, Durham (Eng.) U., 1970, U. S.C., 1971, Southwestern at Memphis, 1972; LL.D., Nova U., 1970; m. Gail Griffin, 1964; children by previous marriage—Athelstan F., Mary Muir, Eleanor, Margaret Ann, Karl Henry. Came to U.S., 1931, naturalized, 1946. Research asst. Mass. Inst. Tech., 1934-35; asst. dir. tech. services Union of S. Africa Def. Forces, Pretoria, 1935-36: research asst. Woods Hole Oceanographic Instn., Woods Hole, Mass., and Cambridge, Mass., 1936-37, investigator in phys. oceanography, 1938, phys. oceanographer, 1940—; asst. prof. meterology N.Y. U., 1937, asso. prof., 1937-42, prof., 1942, dir. research, 1946; meteorol. adviser to Union S. Africa Govt., 1947; dean Inst. Tech. U. Minn., 1949-66, prof. physics, 1966-67; pres. Franklin Inst., Phila., 1967-69; Woodrow Wilson fellow Internat. Center for Scholars Smithsonian Instn., Washington, 1972—. Science Service, Inc.; trustee Aerospace Corp., Los Angeles; U.S. commr. Seattle World's Fair, 1961-62; chmn. nat. fisheries center and aquarium adv. bd. U.S. Dept. Interior. Mem. adv. coms. for armed forces; mem. nat. com. Internat. Geophys. year; mem. com. on oceanography, com. on polar research Nat. Acad. Scis.; mem. exec. bd. UNESCO, 1955-58. Trustee Woods Hole Oceanographic Instn., St. Paul Inst.; mem. Nat. Sci. Bd., 1966-72. Served from capt. to lt. col. USAAF, 1943-46. Decorated Legion of Merit, Exception Civilian Service award Dept. Army. Fellow Royal Meterol. Soc., Am. Inst. Aeros. and Astronautics; mem. Am. Soc. Limnology and Oceanography, Am. Soc. Engring. Edn., Minn. Soc. Profl. of Engrs., Am. Meteorol. Soc., Royal Soc. So. Africa, A.A.A.S. (pres. elect 1969, pres. 1970, chmn. bd. 1971), Am. Philos. Soc., Am. Geophys. Union, Tau Beta Pi, Sigma Xi, Iota Alpha. Episcopalian. Clubs: Raquet (Phila.); Cosmos (Washington). Inventor of Rathythermograph., 1938. Contbr. Jour. of Marine Research. Jour. of Meterology; author: Workbook of Meteorology: Weathercraft: Meteorological Instruments; Satellite of the Sun, Our New Age, Turn to the Sea, The Ocean Laboratory. Home: 3245 Cleveland Av NW Washington DC 20008 Office: Internat Center for Scholars Smithsonian Instn 1000 Jefferson Dr Washington DC 20560

SPILLMAN, FRANCIS JOSEPH, restaurant exec.; b. Ashland, Kan., Apr. 10, 1937; s. Lewis Joseph and Frances (Dome) S.; student St. Joseph Mil. Acad., 1961-63; m. Norma Jean Halsey, Aug. 10, 1957; children—Tammie, Timothy, Chris, Joe, Jean Ann. Insp. Boeing Aircraft Co., Wichita, Kan., 1956-57; dist. mgr. Am. Nat. Ins. Co., Wichita, 1957-59; with Pizza Inn, Inc., Dallas, 1959—, pres., 1962—. Democrat. Roman Catholic. K.C. Home: 1571 Bar Harbor Dr Dallas TX 75232 Office: 2930 Stemmons Freeway Dallas TX 75247

SPILLMAN, JOHN HARRY, dentist; b. Jackson, Miss., Jan 15, 1923; s. Louis Cromwell and Lula (Melvin) S.; student Millsaps Coll., 1941-42; D.D.S., Emory U., 1950; m. Nancy Elizabeth Fairley, Mar. 2, 1957; children—John Harry, Catherine Fairley, Thomas Archie. Individual practice dentistry, Winston-Salem, N.C., 1950—. Mem. Winston-Salem Bd. Health, 1968—; mem. adv. com. Winston-Salem Animal Shelter, 1970—; commnr. Community Devel. Program, 1971—, Bd. dirs. N.C. Dental Found. Served to lt. col. USAF, World War II. Mem. N.C. Assn. Professions (dir.), Am. Coll. Dentists, Forsyth County Dental Soc. (pres. 1958; pres. 2d dist. 1968). Episcopalian. Rotarian. Clubs: Twin City, Old Town. Home: 2860 Holyoke Pl Winston-Salem NC 27106 Office: 140 Lockland Av Winston-Salem NC 27103

SPILMAN, LOUIS, editor; b. Crawfordsville, Ind., Jan. 7, 1899; s. Theodore Bruce and Susan Dale (Boughner) S.; student Wabash Coll.; m. Emily Jane Moon, Sept. 15, 1920; children—Susan (Mrs. V.F. Reynolds), Mary Emily (Mrs. E.O. Davisson), William, Louis, Robert, Martha (Mrs. Paul R. Clark). City editor Marion (Ind.) Chronicle, 1920-24; editor-mgr. Lyman Publ. Corp. div. Fed. Bus. Publ., N.Y.C., 1924-29; pres., editor, pub. News-Virginian, Waynesboro, Va., 1929-64, chmn. bd., 1964—; daily columnist, 1934—; sec., dir. Waynesboro Hotel Corp., 1937-41; corr. U.S. Atomic Bomb Tests, Bikini, 1946; chmn. bd. Glasgow (Ky.) Daily Times, 1957—; Mem. Meth. Com. Overseas Relief, 1952-64, mem. pub. relations and Meth. Information com., 1964-68; chmn. Gov.'s Study Commn. on Vocational Rehab., 1967-69; mem. U.S. Dept. Commerce Trade Mission to Germany, 1962. Chmn., Waynesboro Flood Control Commn., 1972—. Bd. dirs. Germanna Found. Served as sgt. U.S. inf., 1916-17, 2d lt. USAAC, 1917-18. Mem. Va. Press Assn. (pres. 1933-35), Va. UN Assn. (dir.), So. Newspaper Pub. Assn., Va. Farm Bur., Am. Legion, Phi Gamma Delta, Sigma Delta Chi. Democrat. Mason (Shriner), Rotarian. Author: So This Is South America, 1962. Home: 700 Locust Av PO Box 747 Waynesboro VA 22980 Office: 544 W Main St PO Drawer 1027 Waynesboro VA 22980

SPILMAN, WILLIAM BRUCE, newspaper exec.; b. N.Y.C., July 28, 1927; s. Louis and Emily (Moon) S.; A.B., Wabash Coll., 1950; m. Patricia Elaine Black, Feb. 3, 1951; children—Rebecca Elaine, Elizabeth Jane, Barbara Ellen, William Black. With Waynesboro Pub. Co. (Va.), 1937—, rural editor, 1952, sports editor, 1953-54, mech. supt., 1955-58, bus. mgr., 1958-63, pres. corp., 1963—. Chmn. fund drive A.R.C., Waynesboro, E. Augusta County, 1953; presdl. appointee Ann. Assay Commn., Phila., 1967; treas. Waynesboro YMCA, 1971—. Served with USMCR, 1944-46, to 2d lt., 1950-51. Mem. Va. Press Assn. (pres. 1968-69), Waynesboro C. of C., Waynesboro Retail Mchts. Assn. (pres. 1971-72), Nat. Rifle Assn., Am., Va. numis. assns., Am. Legion, Marine Corps Res. Officers Assn., Aircraft Owners and Pilots Assn., Token and Medal Soc. (nat. pres. 1966-68), Sigma Delta Chi, Phi Gamma Delta, Pi Delta Epsilon. Democrat. Methodist. Mason (Shriner), Rotarian. Club: U.S. Auto (life mem.). Home: 1837 Cherokee Rd Waynesboro VA 22980 Office: 544 W Main St Waynesboro VA 22980

SPINK, JOSEPH CLAUDE, JR., banker; b. Jacksonville, Fla., Nov. 4, 1923; s. Joseph Claude and F.I. (Gullette) S.; standard certificate Am. Inst. Banking, 1956; grad. Sch. Banking, U. Wis., 1958; student Jacksonville U., 1959; m. Florence Gertrude Connors, Nov. 31, 1942; children—Joseph Claude II, Exter Lee, Timothy Matthew, Barbara Grace. With Jacksonville br. Fed. Res. Bank of Atlanta, 1945-61, dept. mgr., 1957-61; v.p., cashier First Bank & Trust Co. of Jacksonville, 1961-64, pres., 1964-67; pres. St. Johns River Bank, Jacksonville, 1967—. Mem. Jacksonville Expressway Authority, 1968—; active Com. of 100, Downtown Council. Regional treas., Senator Chiles campaign, 1970; treas. for Mayor Tanzler campaign, 1971. Served with AUS, 1943-45. Mem. Am. Inst. Banking (Jacksonville chpt. pres. 1958-59), Nat. Assn. Bank Audit and Control (dir. 1964—), Jacksonville Area C. of C., Gator Bowl Assn. Democrat. Clubs: University (bd. govs. 1968—), Deerwood, Quarterback (Jacksonville). Home: 5350 Rivers Edge Apts Jacksonville FL 32211 Office: PO Box 2340 St Johns River Bank Jacksonville FL 32203

SPITZER, CARY REDFORD, instrumentation engr.; b. New Hope, Va., July 31, 1937; s. Clyde Burke and Marion Jeanette (Redford) S.; B.S., Va. Poly. Inst., 1958; M.S. in Adminstrn., George Washington U., 1970; m. Carrie Laura Ruth Logan, June 18, 1960; 1 son Stiegel Logan. Instrumentation engr. NASA, Hampton, Va., 1962-69, molecular analysis expts. mgr. Project Viking, 1969-70, phys. and magnetic properties investigations mgr., 1970—. Served with USAF, 1959-62. Mem. I.E.E.E. (sr.), sect. chmn. 1968-69), Aerospace and Electronic Systems Group (v.p. tech. operations, 1969—), Pi Delta Epsilon, Rho Tau Sigma. Methodist (lay leader 1966-67, chmn. adminstrv. bd. 1972—). Patentee in field. Home: Route 1 Box 227B Williamsburg VA 23185 Office: Langley Sta MS 159 Hampton VA 23365

SPITZER, CHARLES EDGAR, JR., metals co. exec.; b. Lynchburg, Va., May 11, 1924; s. Charles Edgar and Ora (Monroe) S.; B.S. in Archtl. Engring., Va. Poly. Inst., 1949; m. Jean Lucille Hess, July 20, 1946; children—Charles E., J. Garry, B. Scott, Cynthia Jean. Engr., draftsman Va. Metal Products, Orange, Va. 1949-50; with So. Iron Works, Inc., Springfield, Va., 1950—, exec. v.p., 1963-64, pres., 1964—. Bd. dirs. Alexandria (Va.) Hosp. Corp., 1966-69. Served to 1st lt. C.E., AUS, 1943-46; PTO. Mem. Va.-Carolinas Structural Steel Fabricators Assn. (pres. 1969), Tau Beta Pi, Tau Sigma Delta. Methodist. Club: Belle Haven (Alexandria, Va.). Home: 1606 Mason Hill Dr Alexandria VA 22307 Office: 6600 Electronic Dr Springfield VA 22150

SPIVAK, LAWRENCE E(DMUND), TV-radio producer; b. N.Y.C.; s. William B. and Sonya (Bershad) S.; A.B., Harvard; LL.D., Wilberforce U.; D.Litt., Suffolk U.; L.H.D., Tampa U.; m. Charlotte Beir Ring; children—Judith (Mrs. Wm. Lee Frost) (dec.), Jonathan. Bus. mgr. Antiques Mag., 1921-30; asst. to the pub. Hunting and Fishing, Nat. Sportsman mags., 1930-33; bus. mgr. Am. Mercury, 1934-39, pub. 1939-44, editor, pub., 1944-50; founder, pub. Ellery Queen's Mystery Mag., The Mag. of Fantasy and Science Fiction, Mercury Mystery Books, Bestseller Mysteries, Jonathan Press Books, until 1954. Producer-founder TV program Meet the Press, radio, 1945—, TV, 1947—. Recipient two Peabody awards. Home: Sheraton Park Hotel Washington DC 20008 Office: 2660 Woodley Rd NW Washington DC 20008

SPIVEY, CARL BASCOM, supt. schs.; b. Pensacola, Fla., Apr. 13, 1927; s. Bascom C. and Anna Nancy (Crews) S.; A.B., Asbury Coll., 1951; M.A., U. Ky., 1955; specialist in phys. sci. teaching Washington U., St. Louis, 1960; certificate in adminstrn., U. Ky., 1970; m. Jo Ann Naylor, May 30, 1951; children—Denise Dale, Shelley Jay, Aletha Gay. With Fayette County Pub. Schs., Lexington, Ky., 1955—, tchr. physics, 1955-61, dir. pupil transp. dept., 1961-69, asso. supt., 1969—. NSF fellow Murray State U., 1958-59, Washington U., 1959-60. Mem. Am. Assn. Sch. Adminstrs. (nat. adv. com. 1969—), Am. Assn. Physics Tchrs., Ky. Assn. sch. Adminstrs., Phi Delta Kappa. Home: 3136 Trinity Rd Lexington KY 40503 Office: 400 Lafayette Pkwy Lexington KY 40503

SPIVEY, HERMAN RAY, lumber mfg. co. exec.; b. Nashville, May 2, 1923; s. Herman Roscoe and Minnie (Barnes) S.; student U. Tenn., 1941-43; B.S. in Elec. Engring., U. S.C., 1944; m. Mary M. Sumner, Sept. 20, 1953; children—Elizabeth Sumner, Mary Sandra, Herman Ray. Engr., TVA, Chattanooga, 1946-49; treas. Cumberland Lumber & Mfg. Co., McMinnville, Tenn., 1949-52, pres., 1952—; partner Roane Broadcasting Co., Rockwood, Tenn., 1957-60; v.p. WMSR Broadcasting Co., Inc., Manchester, Tenn., 1965—; dir. Crestline Finance Corp., Jackson, Tenn.; comml. tree farmer, 1961—. Served with USNR, 1943-46. Mem. Nat. Oak Flooring Mfg. Assn. (dir. 1970—), Am. Legion. Democrat. Baptist. Office: 0202 Red Rd McMinnville TN 37110

SPIVEY, JAMES SHERWOOD, exporter; b. Lufkin, Tex., Mar. 2, 1915; s. Madden Calender and Lillie (Hennington) S.; B.S., Tex. A. and M. U., 1937; m. Marilyn Patterson, Nov. 4, 1939; children—Susan, Peter. Mgr., Terrell (Tex.) C. of C., 1939-42; pres., chief exec. officer James S. Spivey, Inc., Washington, 1946—; dir. Haranel Internat. Pty., Ltd., Melbourne, Australia. Pres., Spivey Internat., Inc., Washington, 1950—. Served to lt. col. AUS, 1942-46. Decorated Silver Star, Purple Heart, Bronze Star medal with oak leaf cluster (U.S.); Croix de Guerre (France). Mem. Ind. Telephone Pioneer Assn., Washington Bd. Trade, 90th Div. Assn. Presbyn. (elder). Rotarian (pres. Washington). Clubs: Congressional Country (Washington). Home: 10828 Alloway Dr Potomac MD 20854 Office: 3817 Livingston St NW Washington DC 20015

SPIVEY, JOHN B., lawyer; b. Adrian, Ga., Jan. 29, 1897; s. Levi and Katharine (Drew) S.; student pub. schs., Adrian, Ga.; m. Florrie Dean Ricks, Apr. 12, 1918; children—Julia Christine (Mrs. Walter Hodges Rountree), Ruby Kathryn (Mrs. Ernest Alexander Grindler). Admitted to Ga. bar, 1915; practiced in Swainsboro, 1919—; mem. firm Spivey and Carlton, 1919—; judge Superior Ct., Middle Judicial Circuit, 1966. Pres., 1st Fed. Savings & Loan Assn., Swainsboro, 1965—, Spivey State Bank, Swainsboro, 1965—; chmn. bd. Swainsboro Gas Co., 1950—. City councilman, Swainsboro, 1925, mayor pro-tem, 1925-30; mem. Ga. Ho. of Reps., 1930-36; pres. Ga. State Senate, 1937-41. Served with inf. U.S. Army, 1918. Mem. Am., Ga., Middle Jud. bar assns. Methodist (trustee). Rotarian. Home: 326 W Main St Swainsboro GA 30401 Office: 102 N Main St Swainsboro GA 30401

SPONG, WILLIAM BELSER, JR., lawyer, U.S. senator; b. Portsmouth, Va., Sept. 29, 1920; s. William Belser and Emily (Nichols) S.; student Hampden-Sydney Coll., 1937-40, LL.D., 1968; LL.B., U. Va., 1947; postgrad. U. Edinburgh (Scotland), 1947-48; m. Virginia Wise Gallford, June 3, 1950; children—Martha Kingman, Thomas Nichols. Admitted to Va. bar, 1947; practiced law, Portsmouth, 1949—; mem. Va. Ho. Dels., 1954-55, Va. Senate, 1955-66; U.S. senator from Va., 1966—, mem. coms. on fgn. relations, commerce. Lectr. law Coll. William and Mary, 1948-49. Chmn., Va. Commn. Pub. Edn., 1958-62. Trustee Portsmouth Gen. Hosp.; bd. dirs. Portsmouth Hist. Found. Served with USAAF, 1942-45. Mem. Va. (pres. elect 1965-66), Portsmouth-Norfolk County (pres. 1951) bar assns., Order of Coif, Phi Alpha Delta, Omicron Delta Kappa, Pi Kappa Alpha. Democrat. Home: 316 North St Portsmouth VA 23704 Office: Senate Office Bldg Washington DC 20510

SPOONER, ROBERT, city ofcl.; b. Bainbridge, Ga., Oct. 23, 1911; s. Oscar Ruffard and Rosie (Littlefield) S.; student FBI Nat. Acad., 1946, Keeler Inst., 1948; m. Anna Sue Gainey, Dec. 15, 1940; children—Robert Edward, Jane Ann (Mrs. Cabaly). With Police dept., City of Plant City, Fla., 1938-41, 50—, chief of police, 1950—; mem. staff Sheriff's office, Hillsborough County, Fla., 1941-50. Bd. dirs., Little League Baseball, 1955-58, Boy Scouts Am., 1949-55; chmn. Baseball Commn., 1952-60. Adv. bd. St. Leo Coll., 1970-71, Hillsborough Community Coll., 1970-71. Served with USNR, 1943-46. Recipient 16 Safety awards for traffic safety, City of Plant City, Fla., 1951-70. Mem. FBI Nat. Acad. Assos. of Fla., Fla. Police Chiefs Assn., Fla. Peace Officers Assn., Tampa Bay Area Chief's Assn., 40 and 8, Internat. Assn. Police Chiefs. Democrat. Presbyn. Elk, Lion (pres. 1967-68). Home: 706 W Saunders St Plant City FL 33566 Office: 206 S Evers St Plant City FL 33566

SPORL, CYPRIAN ANDREW, ins. co. exec.; b. New Orleans, Oct. 19, 1905; s. Cyprian Andrew and Adrienne Jeanne (deLappe) S.; LL.B., U. Notre Dame, 1928; m. Dorothy Gibbons, Dec. 14, 1961. Partner of C. A. Sporl, New Orleans, 1928-29; with C. A. Sporl & Co., Inc., New Orleans, 1930—, v.p., 1930-36, pres., 1936-66, chmn. bd., chief exec. officer, 1966—, dir., 1970—; chmn. bd., chief exec. officer Frank B. Hall & Co. La. C.A. Sporl div., 1972—; dir. Frank B. Hall & Co., Inc., N.Y.C., Delta Steamship Lines, Inc., New Orleans. Served with USCGR, 1941-45. Mem. Internat. House, Am., La. bar assns., Am. Judicature Soc., Assn. Average Adjusters U.S. Clubs: Plimsoll, Country, Pickwick, Southern Yacht, New Orleans Athletic, Stratford, Lamplighters', Propeller (New Orleans). Home: 1004 Falcon Rd Metairie LA 70005 Office: 1001 Lykes Center 300 Poydras St New Orleans LA 70130

SPOTO, ANGELO PETER, JR., physician; b. Tampa, Fla., Mar. 25, 1933; s. Angelo Peter and Zillah Marie (Renfroe) S.; student U. Fla., 1950-53, Fla. So. Coll., 1953; B.S., Duke, 1956, M.D., 1957; m. Carolyn Jeanette Barbee, Aug. 30, 1958; children—Keith Peter, Elizabeth Anne, Jacqueline Marie. Intern Duke Hosp., Durham, N.C., 1957-58, med.-allergy fellow, 1958-59; resident internal medicine USAF Hosp., Lackland AFB, Tex., 1960-62, allergy resident Walter Reed Army Med. Center, Washington, 1962-63; physician Watson Clinic, Lakeland, Fla., 1966—, partner, 1968—; mem. staff Lakeland Gen. Hosp. Bd. dirs. Lakeland Family YMCA. Served to maj. USAF, 1959-66. Recipient Triangle award YMCA, 1971. Fellow Am. Acad. Allergy, Am. Assn. Certified Allergists (bd. govs. 1970—); mem. Polk County, Fla., So. med. Assns., A.M.A., Fla., Southeastern allergy assns., Fla., Am. socs. internal medicine. Presbyn. (elder). Research in sickle cell anemia, antihistamine drugs, respiratory failure drug therapy. Contbr. articles to profl. jours. Home: 2515 Hollingsworth Hill Lakeland FL 33803 Office: Watson Clinic 1600 Lakeland Hills Blvd Lakeland FL 33802

SPOTTSWOOD, STEPHEN GILL, bishop; b. Boston, July 18, 1897; s. Abraham Lincoln and Mary Elizabeth (Gray) S.; B.A., Albright Coll., 1917; Th.B., Gordon Div. Sch., 1919; postgrad. Yale, 1923-24; D.D. (hon.), Livingstone Coll., 1939; m. Viola Estelle Booker, June 10, 1919 (dec. 1953); children—Virginia Ruth (Mrs. Simon), Stephen Paul, Constance Booker (Mrs Miller), Viola Stephanie (Mrs. Cabaniss), Alleyne Hankerson (Mrs. Hall); m. Mattie Johnson Elliott, Dec. 15, 1969. Ordained to ministry A.M.E. Zion Ch., 1920; pastor, West Newton and Lowell, Mass., 1918-20, Portland, Me., 1920-22, New Haven, 1922-25, Winston-Salem, N.C., 1925-28, Indpls., 1928-32, Buffalo, 1932-36, Washington, 1936-52; elected bishop, 1952; presiding bishop W. Tenn. and Miss., S. Miss., N. Ark., Okla., Tex. and Colo. confs., 1952-56, Allegheny, Ohio, Mich. and Ind. confs., 1956-68, Guyana, Mich., New Eng., Phila. and Balt., V.I. confs., 1968-72. Chmn. Bd. Transp., Commn. Chaplains, Commn. Housing and Community Devel., A.M.E. Zion Ch., vice chmn. Connectional Budget Bd., Connectional Trustees, Bd. Audit; exec. com. World Meth. Council; mem. Nat. Council Chs.; past pres. Ohio Council Chs., 1968-70. Frequent speaker civil rights; mem. N.A.A.C.P., 1919—, pres. D.C. br, 1947-52, nat. bd. dirs., 1954—, chmn. bd., 1961—. Trustee Livingstone Coll. Home: 1931 16th St NW Washington DC 20009

SPRABERRY, RUFUS BENJAMIN, clergyman; b. Anniston, Ala., Oct. 7, 1929; s. Rufus B. and Della (Phillips) S.; B.A., East Tex. Bapt. Coll., 1953; B.D., Southwestern Bapt. Theol. Sem., 1956; D.D., Jackson Coll., 1963; m. Doris Wells, Aug. 14, 1959; children—Kimberly Lynn, Stephen B., Rebecca Elizabeth. Ordained to ministry Bapt. Ch., 1950; Bapt. student dir. Tex. A. and M. U., 1958-59; Bapt. student dir. Sam Houston State Coll., 1959-61, asso. prof. Bible, 1959-61; pastor First Bapt. Chs., Lampasas, Tex., 1961-65, Mineral Wells, Tex., 1965—. Mem. exec. bd. Bapt. Gen. Conv. Tex., 1963-71, v.p. conv., 1964-65; mem. exec. com. So. Bapt. Conv., 1968—. Trustee Hardin-Simmons U., Abilene, Tex. Served with USAF, 1948-50; with AUS, 1956-58. Mem. N.G. Assn. U.S., N.G. Assn. Tex. Mason, Kiwanian. Home: 317 NW 4th Av Mineral Wells TX 76067 Office: 501 SE 1st St Mineral Wells TX 76067

SPRABERY, ARCHIE PATRICK, physician; b. Tupelo, Miss., Dec. 18, 1942; s. Archie Trevelin and Anne Rae (Burch) S.; student U. Miss., 1960-63, M.D., 1967; m. Carol Ann Forister, May 29, 1967; 1

son, Scott Ellis. Intern Miss. Bapt. Hosp., Jackson, 1967-68; pvt. practice medicine, specializing in family practice, Fulton, Miss., 1968—; chief staff Itawamba County Hosp., Fulton. Mem. Itawamba County Jr. C. of C., A.M.A., Miss. Med. Assn., Alpha Epsilon Delta. Republican. Baptist. Address: PO Box 280 Fulton MS 38843

SPRADLEY, JULIAN ROY, food broker, relator; b. Hawkinsville, Ga., Aug. 2, 1907; s. Mack Duron and Lula (Smith) S.; student Dale Carnegie Schs., 1941-42; m. Sybil Ruth Soar, July 5, 1937; children—Margaret Lavinia (Mrs. Anthony F. Mielczarski, Jr.), Julian Roy. With Hoskins & Green, Inc., food brokers, Miami, Qla., 1935-37; chmn. bd., sec. Spradley, Riley & Slaughter, Inc., Miami, 1937—; realtor Keyes Co., Miami. Mem. Miami Civic Music Assn., 1954—. Mem. exec. com. Miami Bapt. Assn. Served with U.S. Army, 1928-31. Recipient Exceptionally Meritorious Service awards Miami Food Brokers Assn., 1968, Nat. Food Brokers Assn., 1961-62. Mem. Nat. (regional dir.), Miami (pres.) food brokers assns. Bapt. (deacon). Mason. Home: 9811 NW 1st Av Miami Shores FL 33150 Office: 3550 NW 60th St Miami FL 33142

SPRAGENS, THOMAS EUGENE, banker; b. Ellisburg, Ky., July 12, 1897; s. William Arthur and Frances (Reynierson) S.; B.S., Georgetown Coll., 1917; m. Edna Grace Clark, Feb. 26, 1924; children—William Clark, Thomas Eugene, Ruth (Mrs. Russel Fred Gilbert). Tchr., Richmond (Ky.) High Sch., 1923-24; bookkeeper Farmers Nat. Bank, Lebanon, Ky., 1924-30, teller, 1930-36, asst. cashier, 1936-42, cashier 1942-59, pres. 1959-65, chmn. bd. 1965—. Sponsor, fund raiser Boy Scouts Am., 1966-69. Trustee W. C. McChord Estate, 1957-68. Mem. Am. Bankers Assn. (v.p. 1948-51), Ky. Bankers Assn. (pres. group six 1958), Alpha Lambda (pres. 1916-17), Pi Kappa Alpha. Baptist. Home: 236 S Proctor Knott Av Lebanon KY 40033 Office: 136 W Main St Lebanon KY 40033

SPRAGUE, DAVID CARTER, dept. store exec.; b. Lawton, Okla., July 28, 1929; s. Robert S. and Zelpha (Carter) S.; B.A., Abilene Christian Coll., 1950; postgrad. Tex. Christian U., 1952-53; m. Wilma Jean Neal, July 23, 1950; children—Angela, Robert. Partner, mgr. Sprague's Furniture Mart, Lawton, Okla., 1955-60; v.p. Trade Mart Dept. Stores, Oklahoma City, 1961-65, pres., 1970—, also dir.; exec. v.p. IHC, Inc., Oklahoma City, 1966-70, dir., 1967-70. Dir. Nat. Playtime Villages, Inc., Oklahoma City, chmn., dir. First Bank Atoka, Okla. Bd. dirs. Okla. State Mental Health Assn., 1964-65. Served to 1st lt. AUS, 1953-55. Home: 1820 Drury Lane Oklahoma City OK 73116 Office: 5901 North May St Oklahoma City OK 73112

SPRAGUE, HAROLD EDWIN, civil engr.; b. Hillsdale, Mich., Sept. 17, 1906; s. Frank Kline and Grace M. (Brown) S.; B.S., Mich. State U., 1930; m. Georgia Wilma Gan, June 6, 1931; 1 son, Harold Edwin II. Commd. 2nd lt., U.S. Army, 1929, advanced through grades to col.; chief operations 409th Brigade, Korea, 1952-53; chief, Japan Constrn. Agy., U.S. Army, Tokyo, 1954-55; dist. engr. C.E., Pitts., 1955-58; chief Army Constrn., Washington, 1958-60; exec. Beach Erosion Bd., C.E., Washington, 1960-61; resigned, 1961; mem. Canal Commn., Winter Haven, Fla., 1962-70. Mem. Polk County (Fla.) Citizens Adv. Council on Aging, 1966-67. Pres. bd. dirs. Polk County Mental Health Center, Bartow, Fla., 1966—. Decorated Bronze Star. Registered prof. engr., Washington. Fellow Am. Soc. C.E.; mem. Am. Soc. Mil. Engrs., Am. Legion, Winter Haven C. of C. (anti-pollution com. 1970), Pi Kappa Phi, Scabbard and Blade. Methodist. Mason (Shriner), Elk, Kiwanian (pres. 1966). Home: 1335 S Lake Roy Dr Winter Haven FL 33880

SPRAGUE, JAMES TRUMAN, civil engr.; b. Des Moines, Aug. 31, 1906; s. James A. and Maud (Davis) S.; B.S., Ia. State U., 1930; m. Mildred L. Bishop, June 11, 1929; 1 dau., Dixiana (Mrs. William F. Hanks). Engr., materials insp. Mo. Hwy. Dept., 1930-33; jr. engr. Kan. Hwy. Dept., 1936-41; constrn. engr. Def. Constrn., 1941-43; city engr. City Miami (Okla.), 1946—. Instr. san. engring. Sch. Mil. Govt., Princeton, N.J., 1945-46. Served with USNR, 1943-46. Recipient Hatfield award Water and Pollution Control Fedn., 1962. Registered profl. engr., Okla. Home: 40 F NW St Miami OK 74354 Office: 129 5th Av NW Miami OK 74354

SPRAGUE, ROBERT SUMMERS, mcht.; b. Cache, Okla., June 28, 1904; s. Roger Alger and Luella (Wycoff) S.; student LaSalle Extension U., 1926; m. Zelpha Chestine Carter, Sept. 1, 1923; children—Mary (Mrs. John McNayr), David, Robert Paul, Martha (Mrs. Edwin Mitchell). Accountant, Payne-McGee Grocery Co., 1922-24; owner, operator Sprague's Food Mart, 1924-50, Sprague's Furniture Mart, 1950-60; co-owner Trade Mart Dept. Store, Inc., 1960-70; sec. Eastern Indsl. Sites, Inc., 1960—, Indsl. Sites, Inc., 1965—; v.p., chmn. bd. Geronimo Property, Inc., 1964—; pres. Westgate Devel. Co., Inc. 1961-70 (all Lawton, Okla.); co-owner Ark. Seawey Indsl. Complex, Ozark. Mem. adv. bd. Abilene Christian Coll., 1954-72, lectr., 1962; lectr. Pepperdine Coll., Los Angeles, 1963-64. Bd. dirs. Columbia Christian Coll., Portland, Ore. Mem. Lawton C. of C. (past v.p.), Lawton Grocery Assn. (past pres.), Lawton Retail Mchts. Assn. (past pres.), Internat. Platform Assn. Mem. Ch. of Christ (past elder). Democrat. Author: Grass Money, 1970; Ghosts of Palo Duro Canyon, 1972. Contbr. articles to ch. pubs. Home: 1 N 35th St Lawton OK 73501 Office: 425 S 11th St Lawton OK 73501

SPRAGUE, WILLIAM GEORGE, oral pathologist; b. Cleve., Apr. 15, 1923; s. George William and Ella Virginia (Stubbs) S.; student Ohio U., 1941-43; B.S., Western Res. U., 1945, D.D.S., 1947; m. Harriet Ida Rice, June 19, 1948; children—Barbara (Mrs. David Allen Miller), Patricia Alice, Nancy Lyn. Intern, Cleve. State Hosp., 1947-48; resident Western Res. U. Inst. Pathology, 1948-52; commd. 1st lt. USAF, 1952, advanced through grades to col., 1964; staff oral pathologist USAF Sch. Aviation Medicine, 1952-54; chief dental and oral pathology div. Armed Forces Inst. Pathology, Washington, 1954-57, chief oral pathology div., 1965-69; chief oral pathology USAF Hosp., Lackland AFB, 1957-65; dir. dental services Ramey AFB, P.R., 1969-72, Hdqrs. AFSC-SGD, Washington, 1972—. Instr. operative dentistry Western Res. U., 1947-48, instr. pathology, 1948-52; asso. clin. prof. pathology U. Tex., 1957-65, Med. Coll. Va., 1965-69; nat. mil. cons. USAF, 1969—. Pres., Bd. Edn., Ramey AFB Sch. Systems, 1971-72. Decorated USAF Commendation medal. Fellow A.A.A.S., Am. Acad. Oral Pathology, Am. Coll. Dentists; mem. Am. Dental Assn., Am. Soc. Clin. Pathologists, Am. Acad. Oral Pathologists (past pres.), Omicron Kappa Upsilon. Mason. Contbr. chpt. to Oral Pathology, 1964. Contbr. articles profl. jours. Home: 1112-1 Columbus Circle Andrews AFB Washington DC 20331 Office: Hdqrs AFSC-SGD Washington DC 20331

SPRAGUE, WILLIAM WALLACE, JR., food co. exec.; b. Savannah, Ga., Nov. 11, 1926; s. William Wallace and Mary (Crowther) S.; B.S., Yale, 1950; m. Elizabeth Louise Carr, Oct. 3, 1953; children—Lauren and Courtney (twins), William Wallace III, Elizabeth. With Savannah Sugar Refining Corp. (name changed to Savannah Foods & Industries, Inc., 1970), 1952—, sales mgr. indsl. products, 1959, asst. sec., 1959-60, sec., 1961-62, v.p., 1962-72, pres., chief exec. officer, 1972—, also dir.; v.p. Everglades Sugar Refinery, Clewiston, Fla., Jim Dandy Co., Birmingham, Ala., Adeline Sugar Factory Co., Ltd., Jeaneretta, La.; dir. Citizens & So. Nat. Bank, Atlanta, Stevens Shipping Co., Savannah, Atlantic Towing Co., Savannah. Asso. chmn. div. United Community Appeal, 1970-72. Bd. dirs. Savannah Port Authority. Served with USNR, 1945-46. Mem. Savannah Area C. of C., Carolina Plantation Soc. Clubs: Oglethorpe, Century, Cotillion (Savannah). Home: 24 E 50th St Savannah GA 31405 Office: PO Box 339 Savannah GA 31402

SPRAKER, HAROLD STEPHEN, educator; b. Cedar Bluff, Va., May 13, 1929; s. Stephen Marco and Cynthia (Cook) S.; B.S., Roanoke Coll., 1950; M.Ed., U. Va., 1955, D.Advanced Grad. Study, 1959, D.Ed., 1960; postgrad. Peabody Coll., 1956; m. Betty Jean Conley, Oct. 2, 1954; children—John S., Mark Conley. Tchr. math. Falls Church (Va.) High Sch., 1950-51, Richlands (Va.) High Sch., 1953-57; asst. prin. Richlands High Sch., 1955-57; apprentice coordinator Tazewell and Buchanan Counties, Va., 1953-57; research asso. U. Va., Charlottesville, 1958-60, instr. extension, 1959-60; asst. prof., asso. prof. math. Middle Tenn. State U., Murfreesboro, 1960-65, prof., 1965—, chmn. dept. math., 1967—, dir. NSF Inst., 1966-67, NSF Math. Inst. Mem. vis. scientist program Tenn., 1964—. Served with AUS, 1951-53. Mem. Math. Assn. Am., Am. Math. Soc., Nat. Council Tchrs. Math., Tenn. Math. Tchrs. Assn., N.E.A., Tenn. Edn. Assn., Pi Mu Epsilon. Lutheran (council). Home: Route 6 Murfreesboro TN 37130

SPRATT, JOHN M., lawyer; b. Ft. Mill, S.C., Apr. 21, 1907; s. Thomas Benjamin and Eleanor (Harris) S.; A.B., Presbyn. Coll., 1928; LL.B., Yale, 1931; m. Jane Bratton, Mar. 24, 1934; children—Mrs. Hugh L. McColl, Jr., John M. Admitted to S.C. bar, 1931; pvt. practice law, York, S.C., 1931—; pres. Bank of Ft. Mill; dir. Bank of York, 1st Fed. Savs. & Loan Assn. Bd. visitors Clemson U., Presbyn. Coll. Served as capt. AUS, World War II. Mem. S.C. Bar Assn. (pres. 1970). Home: 233 Kings Mountain St York SC 29745 Office: 26 W Liberty St York SC 29745

SPRAY, PAUL ELLSWORTH, surgeon; b. Wilkinsburg, Pa., Apr. 9, 1921; s. Lester Ellsworth and Gertrude (Hull) S.; B.S., U. Pitts., 1942; M.D., George Washington U., 1944; M.S. in Orthopedic Surgery, U. Minn., 1950; m. Louise Conover, Nov. 18, 1943; children—David Conover, Thomas Laton, Mary Lynn. Intern, Stapleton U.S. Marine Hosp., S.I., N.Y., 1944-45; resident Mayo Found., Rochester, Minn., 1945-46, 48-50; pvt. practice medicine specializing in orthopedic surgery, Oak Ridge, 1950—; staff Oak Ridge Hosp., cons. med. div. Oak Ridge Inst. Nuclear Studies, Cumberland Clinic, Chamberlain Meml. Hosp., LaFollette (Tenn.) Community Hosp.; courtesy staff E. Tenn. Bapt., U. Tenn. hosps. Mem. bd. orthopedics overseas div. Medico-Care, 1961—, sec. bd., 1971—, chmn. Nigeria Orthopedic Project, 1965-70; cons. regional med. program stroke rehab. project Daniel Arthur Rehab. Center, Oak Ridge, 1971—; mem. area adv. group Knoxville Area Regional Med. Program, 1970—; mem. Anderson County Health Council, 1968—; mem. medico adv. bd. CARE, 1969—; A.M.A. vol. physician, Viet Nam, 1967. Bd. dirs. Council So. Mountains, 1961-68, sec., 1965-66. Served as capt. AUS, 1946-48. Diplomate Am. Bd. Orthopedic Surgeons. Fellow A.C.S.; mem. A.M.A., Roane-Anderson County Med. Soc. (past pres.), Tenn. Orthopedic Soc., Knoxville Surg. Soc., Knoxville Orthopedic Club, Am. Acad. Orthopedic Surgeons, Am. Fracture Assn., Am., So. med. assns. Internat. Coll. Tropical Medicine, UN Assn. (past pres. Tenn.). Mem. Soc. of Friends. Lion (Humanitarian Service award dist. 12N 1968). Home: 507 Delaware Av Oak Ridge TN 37830 Office: Doctors Bldg Oak Ridge TN 37830

SPREHE, PAUL FRANCIS, mech. engr.; b. Oklahoma City, Aug. 8, 1930; s. Francis L. and Stella (McGuire) S.; B.S., U. Okla., 1952; m. Beverly Jordan, Feb. 3, 1951; children—Mary, Paul Francis, David, Elizabeth, Jennifer, Nancy, Jane, Timothy. Chief design engr. Sorey, Hill & Surey, architects, engrs., 1955-59; established Soter & Sprehe Engrs., Inc., Oklahoma City, 1959, pres., 1959—; partner Louer-Sprehe, architects, engrs., planners, 1971—. Mem. Oklahoma City Bldg. Code Commn., 1967—. Served to lt. USNR, 1952-55; now lt. comdr. Res. Mem. Am. Soc. Heating, Refrigerating and Air Conditioning Engrs., Cons. Engrs. Council, Nat. Assn. Laymen (dir.). Club: Serra (local pres. 1966-67). Founder Community of John XXIII, 1966. Home: 3158 Thornridge St Oklahoma City OK 73120 Office: 3535 NW 58th St Oklahoma City OK 73112

SPRINGER, LESTER DAVIS, JR., psychiat. social worker; b. Memphis, Aug. 5, 1930; s. Lester Davis and Merle (Farris) S.; B.A., Henderson State Coll., 1952; M.S.W., Tulane U., 1956; m. Sara Limerick, Sept. 6, 1959; children—Lester D., III, William F. Clin. 1956-57, Augusta, Ga., 1957-61; exec. dir. mental health div. Macon-Bibb Health Dept., Macon, Ga., 1961-71, dist. chief mental health N. Central Health Dist., 1971—. Cons. social work psychiat. service Macon Hosp., 1962—, College Street Hosp., 1968—. Served with AUS, 1952-54; served with Army Res., 1957. Mem. Nat. Assn. Social Workers, Macon Bibb Mental Health Assn. (mem. exec. bd. 1963-67), Acad. Certified Social Workers. Home: 1991 Neville Way Macon GA 31206 Office: 770 Hemlock St Macon Ga 31201

SPRINGFIELD, MYRNA ESTHER COLGLAZIER (MRS. JOHN FRANK SPRINGFIELD), club woman, exec.; b. McPherson, Kan.; d. David Dawson and Mary Esther (Pratz) Colglazier; student Jr. Coll., Hutchinson, Kan., 1917; grad. secretarial course Salt City Coll., 1920; studied voice under Mrs. Marguerite Pound Tyler, Lester Brenzier; m. John Frank Springfield, Dec. 18, 1924 (dec. Mar. 1955). Tchr. pub. schs., Lewis, Kan., 1918; sec. to pres. and gen. mgr. United Water, Gas & Electric Co., Hutchinson, Kan., 1921-24; sec.-treas. Austin Transit Co. (Tex.), 1928-45. Sec., Hutchinson Music Club, 1922-23, corr. mem., 1925—; chmn. community music Kan. Fedn. Music Clubs, 1923-24; music chmn. Kan. conf. D.A.R., 1924, regent Thankful Hubbard chpt., 1958-60, chaplain chpt., 1966-68, rec. sec. chpt., 1968-70, gen. chmn. Tex. conf., 1960, mem. exec. bd., 1970-72, registrar chpt., 1970-72, pres. chpt. regents club Tex. soc., 1963-64, Tex. curator, 1960-64, bd. dirs., 1960-64, del. Continental Congress, 1957-72, gen. co-chmn. Tex. soc., 1968; charter mem. Embassy chpt. Tex. Soc. Colonial Dames XVII Century, 1941, pres., 1961-63, chaplain chpt., 1967-69, Tex. chaplain, bd. dirs., 1963-65, 2d v.p., 1965-67; mem. U.S. Daus. 1812; treas., mem. Pathfinders Club, 1966—; Tex. historian Daus. Am. Colonists, 1965-67, charter mem. Treaty Oak chpt., chpt. regent, 1967-69, chpt. registrar, 1969-71, mem. exec. bd., 1969-71, 2d v.p. state soc., 1969-71; past mem. Altrusa Club; mem. Sovereign Colonial Soc. Ams. Royal Descent, Colonial Order Crown, Magna Charta Dames, Forty Acres Club, Knife and Fork Club, Driskill Club, mem. Tex. Fedn. Woman's Clubs, Violet Crown Garden Club; charter mem. Austin Geneal Soc., 1960, bd. dirs., 1960—; mem. Heritage Soc. Austin; treas. Austin Woman's Club, 1958-60, 63-64, bd. dirs., 1958-60, 62-64, 72—, finance com. chmn., 1962-63, 64-65, mem. policy com., 1962-63, weekly luncheon chmn., 1966-68, chmn. by-laws revision com., 1971-73, chmn. nominating com., 1972—; World Conv. Disciples of Christ, Toronto, Ont., Can., 1955, Edinburgh, Scotland, 1960; soloist First Christian Ch., Hutchinson, Kan., 1922-25, Central Christian Ch., Austin, Tex., 1925-44; treas. Christian Woman's Fellowship, University Christian Ch., Austin, 1956-57, ch. service chmn., 1962-64. Home: 2110 Rio Grande St Austin TX 78705

SPROULL, ROBERT CHRISTLEY, dentist, army officer; b. New Cumberland, W.Va., Nov. 5, 1920; s. Bert Christley and Emma (Allen) S.; D.D.S., U. Pitts., 1950; postgrad. U. So. Cal., 1956-57; m. Mary M. Moran, June 3, 1949; children—Robert M., Elizabeth A., William A., Brian E. Enlisted man U.S. Army, 1942-46; commd. officer U.S. Army, 1950, advanced through grades to col., 1967; dep. 8th Army dental surgeon, Korea, 1953-54; chief fixed prosthodontic service William Beaumont Gen. Hosp., El Paso, Tex., 1966—, chief hosp. dental clinic, 1970-72. Cons. fixed prosthodontics U.S. Army, Europe, 1961-65, Continental U.S., 1966-72; asst. to Dr. Berndmark Heukemes, archaeologist, Heidelberg, Germany, 1961-65. Decorated Bronze Star medal. Diplomate Am. Bd. Prosthodontics. Fellow Am. Coll. Dentists, Am. Coll. Prosthodontists (chmn. edn. and advancement com. 1971-73); mem. Am. Acad. History Dentistry (chmn. membership com. 1970-72), Am. Dental Assn., Colour Group (Gt. Britain). Club: Prospectors (pres. 1972) (El Paso). Research on color matching in dentistry, laser and holography. Home: 2405 Gairloch St El Paso TX 79925 Office: Box 640 El Paso TX 79920

SPROUSE, ERNEST GILBERT, social worker; b. nr. Staunton, Va., June 9, 1935; s. Ernest and Virginia (Buchanan) S.; B.A., King Coll., 1961; postgrad. Va. Commonwealth U., 1966; m. Linda Carol McGlamary, Feb. 1, 1965; children—Robin Michelle, Tamara Lin. Child welfare worker Bristol (Va.) Dept. Pub. Welfare, 1961-65, sr. social worker, 1966, supt., 1966—. Supr. undergrad. students East Tenn. State U., Johnson City, 1967-71; dir., treas. Bristol Speech and Hearing Center, Bristol, 1968-71. Served with AUS, 1956-58. Mem. Tenn.-Va. Council Social Agys. (treas. 1969-71), Child Devel. Center (mem. adv. com. 1967—, chmn. 1969-71), Va. Council Social Welfare (bd. dirs. 1969—). Baptist (bd. dirs. 1971—). Club: Optimist (pres. 1970-71, Optimist of Yr. 1970, bd. dirs. Bristol). Home: 1627 Pineview St Bristol VA 24201 Office: 36 Moore St Bristol VA 24201

SPURLOCK, JACK MARION, engring. research cons.; b. Tampa, Fla., Aug. 16, 1930; s. Joseph Marion and Gertrude (Saffold) S.; B.Chem. Engr., U. Fla., 1952; M.S., Ga. Inst. Tech., 1958, Ph.D., 1961; m. Phyllis Lowene Ridgway, June 30, 1952; children—Barbara Lynn, Scott Edward, Paul Andrew, Teresa Anne. Quality control engr. Auto-Lite Battery Co., East Point, Ga., 1954-55; research asso., asst. prof. Ga. Inst. Tech., Atlanta, 1955-62; mgr. aeroscis. research dept. Martin Co., Orlando, Fla., 1962-64; dir. engring. research dept. Atlantic Research Corp., Alexandria, Va., 1964-69; exec. v.p. Health and Safety Research Inst., Springfield, Va., 1969—; engring cons. Theodore Jonas and Assos., Washington, 1971—. Mem., chmn. SAE Com. on Spacecraft Environmental Control and Life Support Systems, 1965—. Served to lt. USAF, 1952-54. Fellow Am. Inst. Chemists; asso. fellow Am. Inst. Aero. and Astronautics; mem. Am. Inst. Chem. Engrs., Aerospace Med. Assn., Am. Chem. Soc., A.A.A.S. Presbyn. (elder). Author: (with Thomas W. Jackson) Research and Development Management, 1966. Home: 6144 Roxbury Av Springfield VA 22152 Office: Suite 903 1625 Eye St NW Washington DC 20006

SPURLOCK, JEANNE, educator, physician; b. Sandusky, O., 1921; M.D., Howard U., 1947. Intern, Provident Hosp., Chgo., 1947-49; resident psychiatry Cook County (Ill.) Psychopathic Hosp., 1948-50; fellow Inst. Juvenile Research, Chgo., 1950-51; dir. child Psychiatry clinic, Michael Reese Hosp., clin. asst. prof. psychiatry U. Ill. Med. Sch. (both Chgo.), 1953-59; head psychiatry dept. Meharry Med. Coll., Nashville, 1968—. Recipient Strecker award Inst. Pa. Hosp., 1971. Diplomate Am. Bd. Psychiatry and Neurology. Mem. A.M.A., Am. Psychiat. Assn. Office: Meharry Med Coll Nashville TN 37208

SPURR, STEPHEN HOPKINS, univ. pres.; b. Washington, Feb. 14, 1918; s. Josiah Edward and Sophie Clara (Burchard) S.; B.S. with highest honors, U. Fla., 1938, D.Sc. (hon.), 1971; M.F. cum laude, Yale, 1940, Ph.D. (Oberleander Trust fellow), 1950; m. Patricia Chapman Orton, Aug. 18, 1945; children—Daniel Orton, Jean Burchard. Instr., asst. prof., acting dir. Harvard Forest, Harvard, 1940-50; asso. prof. U. Minn., 1952; prof. U. Mich., Ann Arbor, 1952-71, asst. to v.p. acad. affairs, dean Sch. Natural Resources, 1962-65; dean Horace H. Rackham Sch. Grad. Studies, 1964-71, v.p., dean univ., 1969; prof. botany and pub. affairs, pres. U. Tex., Austin, 1971—. Chmn., Grad. Rec. Exam. Bd., Council Grad. Schs., 1969-71; mem. Commn. on Non Traditional Study, 1971. Dir. Huron Valley Nat. Bank. Trustee Carnegie Found. for Advancement of Teaching. Sci. faculty fellow NSF, 1957-58; Fulbright research scholar, New Zealand and Australia, 1960; vis. scholar Center for Advanced Studies Behavioral Scis., 1966-67. Fellow Soc. Am. Foresters (mem. council, founding chmn. div. forest mgmt.); mem. New Zealand Inst. Foresters (hon.), Ecol. Soc. Am., Conf. Biol. Editors (exec. com.), Lake States Forest Tree Improvement Com. (chmn.), Orgn. for Tropical Studies (pres. 1967-68), Mich. Acad. Sci., Arts and Letters (pres. 1968-69). Unitarian. Author: Aerial Photographs in Forestry, 1948; Forest Inventory, 1952; Photogrammetry and Photo-Interpretation, 1960; Forest Ecology, 1962; Academic Degree Structures, 1970. Founding editor Forest Sci., 1955-60. Inventor photogrammetric devices. Home: 2101 Meadowbrook Dr Austin TX 78703

SPURRIER, MARGARET NORVELL (MRS. KEITH MCCAULEY SPURRIER), Republican nat. committeewoman; b. Nashville, Apr. 7, 1919; d. Richard and Margaret (Parker) Norvell; ed. Wellesley Coll., Vanderbilt U.; m. Keith McCauley Spurrier, June 26, 1940; children—Lucia Parker (Mrs. William Lee Drier), Irene LeJau (Mrs. John Alan Pendergrast). Co-chmn. Shelby County (Tenn.) Republican party, 1962-66; mem. Tenn. Rep. Exec. Com., 1966-70, Rep. nat. committeewoman, 1968—. Mem. Tenn. Commn. Status of Women. Bd. dirs. Shelby United Neighbors, Tenn. Bot. Gardens and Fine Arts Center. Mem. Nat. Fedn. Rep. Women, Memphis Symphony League, Memphis Jr. League, Nat. Congress Parents and Tchrs., Kappa Alpha Theta, Chi Delta Phi. Episcopalian. Address: 89 Goodwyn St Memphis TN 38111

SQUIRE, PETER WEAVER, physician; b. Fairmont, W.Va., Mar. 25, 1926; s. Edward Allen and Sara Lewis (Waters) S.; B.S., Hampden Sydney Coll., 1948; M.D., Med. Coll. Va., 1952; m. Nancy Hall Barker, Apr. 12, 1953; children—Harry Edward, William Byron, Peter Weaver, Robert Hall. Intern Stuart Circle Hosp., Richmond, Va., 1952-54; pvt. practice medicine, specializing in family practice, Emporia, Va., 1954—; mem. staff Roanoke Rapids (N.C.) Hosp., Greensville Meml. Hosp., Emporia. Dir. Citizens Nat. Bank, Emporia. Mem. Old Dominion Area council Boy Scouts Am., 1956-68. Served to lt. (j.g.) USNR, 1943-46. Diplomate Am. Bd. Family Practice. Mem. Med. Soc. Va., A.M.A., Am., Va. acads. gen. practice, Theta Chi, Omicron Delta Kappa, Phi Chi. Presbyn. (deacon 1964-71). Rotarian. Home: 428 Laurel St Emporia VA 23847 Office: 219 Weaver Av Emporia VA 23847

SQUIRES, DAVID DENTON, realtor; b. Bristol, Va., Aug. 11, 1906; s. William Henry Tappey and Anna (Hull) S.; B.S., Hampden-Sydney Coll., 1927; m. Sara Lee Cross, Oct. 24, 1931; children—Sara Lee (Mrs. Richard Culver Erickson), Emily Hull. With Standard Oil Co. (N.J.), 1927-37, advt. dept., Norfolk, Va., 1927-30, N.Y.C., 1931, Washington, 1932, sales dept., Hagerstown, Md., 1934-36, asst. dist. mgr. sales dept., Washington, 1936-37; owner retail petroleum products bus., Alexandria, Va,, 1937-51; realtor Squires & Co., Alexandria, 1951—; dir. Alexandria 1st Fed. Savs. & Loan Assn,, Alexandria Nat. Bank. Trustee Hampden-Sydney Coll., chmn. trustees, 1968-69; trustee Union Theol. Sem., Presbyn. Home,

Lynchburg, Va.; bd. govs. St. Christophers Episcopal Sch. Mem. Theta Chi, Omicron Delta Kappa, Chi Beta Phi. Presbyn. Home: 921 N Quaker Lane Alexandria VA 22302 Office: 618 N Washington St Alexandria VA 22313

SQUIRES, MAUDEST EVADNE KELLY (MRS. JAMES ALBERT SQUIRES), educator; b. Georgetown, S.C., Dec. 18, 1907; d. Peter Carlise and Catherine A. (Green) Kelly; B.S., S.C. State Coll., 1941, M.S., 1953; m. James Alvin Squires, Apr. 5, 1927; children—Kathryn Frances (Mrs. Thomas H. White), Mae Yvonne (Mrs. Tracy Walton, Jr.). Tchr. elementary schs., Shelby, N.C., 1929-35; tchr., supr. intermediate grades Whittemore High Sch., Conway, S.C., 1935-41; prin. Felton Tng. Sch., S.C. State Coll., 1942-44, tchr., trainer, 1944-51; supr. schs. Georgetown County, Georgetown, S.C., 1951-57; prin. Choppee Sch., 1957—; cons. sch. systems, 1952—. Organizer, exec. sec. Baruch Playground Orgn., Georgetown, 1951-53; exec. com. Georgetown County Improvement Orgn., 1963—, mem. Georgetown Municipal Bd. Health, 1967—. Trustee Georgetown County Meml. Library. Mem. Nat. Assn. Negro Bus. and Profl. Women's Clubs (organizer, pres. 1960-61), N.E.A., Nat. Assn. Secondary Sch. Prins., Nat. Assn. Elementary Sch. Prins., Internat. Reading Assn., S.C. Edn. Assn., So. Assn. Colls. and Schs., Georgetwon County Tchrs. Assn., Delta Sigma Theta. Contbr. articles profl. jours. Home: 213 Orange St Georgetown SC 29440

SQUIRRU, RAFAEL, author, cultural promoter, art critic; b. Buenos Aires, Argentina, Mar. 23, 1925; s. Carlos Maria and Celina (Gonzalez) S.; B.L., U. Edinburgh (Scotland), 1948; D.Humanities (hon.), U. Neuquen (Argentina), 1967; m. Mary Dodd, Mar. 21, 1948; children—Augusta, Eloisa. Dir. Museum Modern Art, Buenos Aires, 1955-62; dir. cultural relations Argentine Ministry Fgn. Affairs, 1962-63; dir. fep. cultural affairs. OAS, 1963—. Decorated grand ofcl. Nat. Order Cruzeiro de Sul (Brazil). Author: Poetry, 1957-66; Philosophy of Abstract Art, 1960; Challenge of the New Man, 1964. Home: 3115 44th St Washington DC 20016 Office: Panamerican Union Washington DC 20013

SQUYRES, BERRY NEWAL, physician; b. Haskell, Tex., May 1, 1924; s. Riley Newal and Lillian (Smith) S.; B.A., Tex. Tech. Coll., 1944; M.D., U. Tex., 1950; m. Una Christene Maxwell, Mar. 7, 1945; children— Berry Newal, Leah, Leslie, Matthew Steven. Engr. Phillips Petroleum Co., 1944-46; intern Kings Daus. Hosp., Temple, Tex., 1950-51; practice medicine, specializing in family practice, Bowie, Tex., 1953-60, Denver City, Tex., 1960—; mem. staff Bowie Clinic-Hosp., 1953-60, Yoakum County Hosp., 1960—. Served with USAF, 1951-53. Named Citizen of the Year, Bowie C. of C., 1956, Denver City C. of C., 1962. Diplomate Am. Bd. Family Practice. Mem. Am., Tex. acads. family practice, A.M.A., Tex. Med. Assn., Dawson, Terry, Lynn, Gaines, Yoakum County Med. Soc. Home: 1401 N Av E Denver City TX 79323 Office: 412 N Av F Denver City TX 79323

STAAB, WILLIAM CARL, banker; b. Springfield, Ill., Feb. 12, 1927; s. Carl Herman and Helen Katherine (Metzger) S.; A.B., Springfield Jr. Coll., 1948; B.S. in Commerce, St. Louis U., 1949, J.D., 1954; m. Nancy Mae Wright, July 28, 1956; children—William Carl., Jannifer, Patrick. Accountant, Union Electric Co., St. Louis, 1949-55; admitted to Mo. bar, 1954, Ill. bar, 1955; mem. firm Sullivan, Staab & Joyce, St. Louis, 1955-56; with Merc. Trust Co., St. Louis, 1956-61; with Ouachita Nat. Bank, Monroe, La., 1961—, trust officer, 1961—, v.p., 1961—. Active A.R.C., Boy Scouts Am., United Givers Fund, Monroe Area Guidance Center, Alexandria Diocese Cath. Charities Bd. Chmn. adv. bd. St. Joseph's Home for Aged; mem. adv. bd. St. Frederick High Sch. Served with USNR, 1945-46. Mem. Ill. Bar Assn., Mo. Bar. Roman Catholic (pres. adv. council). K.C. Clubs: Lotus, Bayou Desiard Country (Monroe). Home: 3800 Loop Rd Monroe LA 71201 Office: PO Box 1412 Monroe LA 71201

STACEY, JOHN MARKELL, med. center dir.; b. Ilion, N.Y., Jan. 23, 1918; s. Alfred Edwin, Jr., and Hazel (King) S.; B.A., Wesleyan U., 1939; m. Charlotte Florence Smith, June 26, 1945; children—Pamela, John Markell, Ned Martin. Exec. asst. St. Luke's Hosp., N.Y.C., 1939-42; med. adminstr. Standard Oil Co. (N.J.), N.Y.C., 1946-51; cons. Booz, Allen & Hamilton, N.Y.C., 1951-53; dir. U. Va. Hosp., Charlottesville, 1953-64; dir. U. Va. Med. Center, 1964—; lectr. U. Va. Med. Sch., 1953—. Dir. Va. Hosp. Service Assn., 1954-72; pres. Va. Council Health and Med. Care, 1965-67; cons. Govt. of Aruba. Served from 1st lt. to maj. AUS, 1942-46. Fellow Am. Coll. Hosp. Adminstrs., Royal Soc. Health; mem. Va. Hosp. Assn. (pres. from 1964-65), Am. Hosp. Assn. (del. at large 1965-68), Assn. Am. Med. Colls., Psi Upsilon. Presbyn. Rotarian. Clubs: Torch, Farmington Country. Home: 1889 Westview Rd Charlottesville VA 22901

STACEY, TRUMAN, editor; b. Port Arthur, Tex., Dec. 8, 1916; s. James H. and Billie (Davis) S.; Ph.B., U. Detroit, 1946, M.A., 1951; postgrad. Cath. U. Am., 1951, George Washington U., 1951; m. Dorothy Mary Piboin, May 25, 1963; step-children—Patricia, Cheryl. Reporter, Beaumont (Tex.) Enterprise, 1937-42, Okla. City Daily Oklahoman, 1943-44, Detroit Free Press, 1944-45, Washington Times-Herald, 1950-51; pub. relations dir. U. Detroit, 1945-49; sports editor, Lake Charles (La.) Am. Press., 1951-60, editor, 1961—. Organizer, co-chmn. Lake Charles chpt. Nat. Conf. Christians and Jews; mem. Nat. Com. Cath. Scouting; lay chmn. Com. Cath. Scouting Diocese of Lafayette; pres. S.W. La. chpt. Council Devel. French in La. Bd. dirs. La. Council for Music and Performing Arts. Served to sgt. AUS, 1942-43. Recipient Civic Service award Greater Lake Charles C. of C., 1971; Distinguished Service award K.C., 1972; decorated knight Order St. Gregory, knight comdr. Order of Fleur de Lis. Mem. Am. Soc. Newspaper editors, Nat. Conf. Editorial Writers, Asso. Press Mng. Editors Assn. Democrat. Roman Catholic. K.C. Club: Serra (pres. 1971-72). Home: 814 W McNeese St Lake Charles LA 70601 Office: 710 Bilbo St Lake Charles LA 70601

STACKHOUSE, ROY DAVID, real estate investor; b. Chico, Cal., Nov. 21, 1914; s. Roy G. and Martha (Barnett) S.; m. Ruby Lee Jones, Nov. 8, 1935; children—Roy David, Deborah Lee. Engaged in gen. constrn., mortgage financing, 1936—; pres., gen. mgr. Stackhouse Corp., Titusville, Fla., 1960—. Mem. Com. of 100, Titusville, 1964—; pres. North Brevard Devel. Commn., Titusville, 1969—. Served with USNR, 1944-45. Named Man of Year C. of C., 1965. Mem. C. of C. (v.p.). Methodist (trustee). Kiwanian. Home: 48 Fairglen St Titusville FL 32780 Office: Magnolia Office Bldg S Hopkins Av Suite 1C1 Titusville FL 32780

STACY, THOMAS DONNIE, engr.; b. Houston, Jan. 13, 1934; s. Thomas Dillard and Bonnie (Batts) S.; B.S., Louisiana Tech., 1957, M.S., 1962; PhD., Miss. State U., 1966; m. Wanda Geraldine Taylor, Aug. 20, 1954; children—Chris Alan, Kathy Illean, David Wayne, Shari Lynn. Petroleum engr. Pan American Petroleum Corp., Duncan, Okla., 1957-58, Oklahoma City, 1962-63; asst. prof. Coll. Engring. Miss. State U., 1963—; dist. engr. Amoco Prodn. Co., 1970—. Served to 1st lt. USAF, 1958-61. Mem. A.A.A.S., Am. Inst. M.E., Am. Petroleum Inst., Canadian Inst. M.E., Omicron Delta Kappa, Phi Kappa Phi, Tau Beta Pi, Sigma Gamma Epsilon, Pi Epsilon Tau. Home: 1222 Woodchurch St Route 16 Houston TX 77016 Office: PO Box 3092 Houston TX 77001

STADLER, JOHN BUCHAN, realtor, mortgage banker; b. Cleve., Oct. 25, 1907; s. John Louis and Angeline (Hauserman) S.; B.S. in Bus. Adminstrn., U. Fla., 1930; m. Lucille P. Rose, Aug. 11, 1938; children— Angeline (Mrs. William Fox Eckbert, Jr.), Linda Marleen (Mrs. Howard Richard Bates), John William. Asst. sec., dir. First Fed. Savs. & Loan Assn., Miami, Fla., 1933—; realtor John B. Stadler, Coral Gables, Fla., 1943—. Mem. Fla. Blue Key, Kappa Sigma, Alpha Kappa Psi. Home: 3272 Riviera Dr Coral Gables FL 33134 Office: 375 Miracle Mile Coral Gables FL 33134

STAFFORD, DON LAFAYETTE, wholesale paper co. exec.; b. Taylorsville, N.C., July 30, 1922; s. Perry F. and Lottie (Fox) S.; A.B., Lenoir Rhyne Coll., 1948; postgrad. U. N.C., 1949-50; m. Vivienne Poteat, June 19, 1949; children—Gary Randolph, Perry Edward, Donna Adele. Tchr., also coach Catawba County Sch. System Newton, N.C., 1948-51, Coll. Park Sch., Hickory, N.C., 1952-54; salesman Gen. Paper Co., Hickory, N.C., 1954-58, mgr. part owner, 1958-69; pres. Tarheel Paper Co., 1969—. Dir. Nat. Lefty-Righty Golf Tournament, 1964-67. Served with USNR, 1942-45. Mem. Hickory C. of C. Methodist (ofcl. bd. 1967-71). Clubs: Hickory Civitan; Catawba Country (dir. 1967-70), Blowing Rock Country. Home: 1150 11th St Circle NW Hickory NC 28601 Office: 1210 2d Av SW Hickory NC 28601

STAFFORD, DONALD BENNETT, educator; b. Forsyth County, N.C., Oct. 30, 1938; s. Samuel Bennett and Lillie Pearl (Teague) S.; B.S.C.E., N.C. State U., 1961, M.S. (Engring Found. fellow), 1963, Ph.D., 1968; m. Marilyn Ann Kimball, June 9, 1962; 1 son, Shannon Dale. Instr. civil engring. N.C. State U., Raleigh, 1963-68; asst. prof. Clemson (S.C.) U., 1968-71, asso. prof. civil engring., 1971—. Cons. part-time Miller, Warden-Western Cons. Engrs., Raleigh and Lincoln, Neb., 1964-66, S.C. Appalachian Regional Planning and Devel. Commn., Greenville, S.C., 1969—. Recipient NSF sponsored Geometronics Inst., Purdue U., 1966; NASA Summer Faculty fellow Manned Spacecraft Center, Houston, summer 1970. Mem. Am. Soc. C.E., Hwy. Research Bd., Am. Soc. Photogrammetry, Am. Soc. Engring. Edn., Inst. Traffic Engrs., Sigma Xi, Chi Epsilon, Tau Beta Pi, Phi Kappa Phi. Home: S Woodbury Rd Bayshore Box 279 Route 2 Seneca SC 29678 Office: Dept Civil Engring Clemson U Clemson SC 29631

STAFFORD, ROY ELMER, geneticist; b. Republic, Kan., Dec. 28, 1930; s. Clarence E. and Clara G. (McClure) S.; B.S., Kan. State U., 1953; M.S. in Plant Genetics, U. Minn., 1962, Ph.D., 1964; m. Marlene Ann Reed, June 14, 1959; children—Rebecca Ann, John David, Matthew Reed, Stephen Earl, Philip Roy. Research asst. U. Minn., 1959-65; plant breeder Am. Crystal Sugar Co., Rocky Ford, Colo., 1965-68; research geneticist U.S. Dept. Agr., Lubbock, Tex., 1968—. Mem. Am. Soc. Agronomy, Crop Sci. Soc. Am., Am. Soc. Sugar Beet Technologists, Sigma Xi, Phi Kappa Phi, Alpha Zeta, Gamma Sigma Delta. Contbr. articles to profl. jours. Home: 3901 Bismarck St Vernon TX 76384 Office: Tex A and M U Route 3 Vernon TX 76384

STAFFORD, THOMAS PATTEN, astronaut; b. Weatherford, Okla., Sept. 17, 1930; B.S., U.S. Naval Acad., 1952; student USAF Exptl. Flight Test Sch., 1958-59; m. Faye Laverne Shoemaker; children—Dionne, Karin. Commd. 2d lt. USAF, 1952, advanced through grades to brig. gen.; chief performance br. Aerospace Research Pilot Sch., Edwards AFB, Cal., with Manned Spacecraft Center NASA, Houston, 1962—, now chief U.S. astronauts; pilot Gemini VI, command pilot Gemini IX, comdr. Apollo X; dept. dir. flight crew operations. Co-author: Pilot's Handbook for Performance Flight Testing, Aerodynamics Handbook for Performance Flight Testing. Address: Manned Spacecraft Center NASA (CA Houston TX 77058

STAGG, FREDERICK RAYMOND, steel co. exec.; b. Irondequoit, N.Y., Feb. 14, 1918; s. Philip Walter and Edith (Burkin) S.; Secretarial Diploma, Rochester Sch. of Commerce, 1938; Structural Engring. degree, Internat. Correspondence Schs., 1947; m. Phyllis Marie Chandley, May 12, 1946; children—Susan (Mrs. Robert Boyd Pamplin), Frederick Raymond. Small sales, drafting dept. Asheville Steel Co. (N.C.), 1945-53, head draftsman, 1953-59, engr. sales mgr. 1959-63, v.p. prodn., 1964—, also dir. Bd. dirs. Y.M.C.A., 1964. Served with M.C., AUS, 1941-45. Mem. Engrs. Soc. (pres. 1963), Welding Soc. (pres. 1969). Conglist. (deacon 1950—, chmn. 1969). Kiwanian (pres. 1963). Home: 69 Edwin Pl Asheville NC 28801 Office: Box 691 Meadow Rd Asheville NC 28802

STAGG, TOM, lawyer; b. Shreveport, La., Jan. 19, 1923; s. Thomas Eaton and Beulah (Meyer) S.; B.A., La. State U., 1943; LL.B., 1949; m. Margaret Mary O'Brien, Aug. 21, 1946; children—Julie, Margaret Mary. Admitted to La. bar, 1949; with firm Hargrove, Shreveport, 1949-53; pvt. practice, Shreveport, 1953-58; sr. partner firm Stagg, Cady & Beard, Shreveport, 1958—. Pres. Abe Meyer Corp., 1960—, Stagg Investments, Inc., 1964—; mng. partner Pierremont Mall Shopping Center, 1963—; v.p. King Hardware Co., 1955—. Active Republican party, 1950—, del. convs., 1956, 60, 64, 68, 72, mem. Nat. Com. for La., 1964-68, mem. exec. com., 1964-68; Rep. candidate for atty. gen. La., 1972. Chmn., Gov.'s Tidelands Adv. Council, 1969-70, Shreveport Airport Authority, 1970—; mem. Gov.'s Adv. Com. on Offshore Revenues, 1972—. Pres., Shreveport, Jr. C. of C., 1955-56; v.p. La. C. of C., 1956-57. Served to capt. inf. AUS, 1943-46; ETO. Decorated Bronze Star, Purple Heart with oak leaf cluster. Mem. Am., La. bar assns., Photog. Soc. Am., La. Forestry Assn., La. Wildlife Fedn., La. State U. Found., Wilderness Soc. Club: Sierra (vice chmn. Ark.-La.-Tex. group). Office: 808 Beck Bldg Shreveport LA 71101

STAGGERS, RUCKER LEWIS, physician; b. Birmingham, Ala., Aug. 30, 1930; s. William Llewellyn and Frances (Howe) S.; B.S., Auburn U., 1953; M.D., Med. Coll. Ala., 1957; m. Nettie Simpson Mayo, June 6, 1951; children—Sara Howe, William Rucker, Caroline Mayo, Robert Jackson. Intern Univ. Hosp., Birmingham, 1957-58; resident Carraway Meth. Hosp., Birmingham, 1958-59; gen. practice medicine, Benton, Ala., 1959-63, Eutaw, Ala., 1963—; mem. staff New Vaughan Meml. Hosp., Selma, Ala.; courtesy staff Greene County Hosp., Eutaw. Pres. Warrior Pvt. Sch. Found., 1967-70, bd. dirs., 1967—; bd. dirs. Ala. Soc. Crippled Children, 1959-69, county chmn., 1959—. Served with AUS, 1948-49. Mem. Alpha Omega Alpha, Pi Kappa Alpha, Nu Sigma Nu, Alpha Epsilon Delta. Presbyn. (ruling elder 1960—). Lion (pres. 1968-69). Home: 508 Wilson St Eutaw AL 35462 Office: 202 Pickens St Eutaw AL 35462

STAGNER, DELMER LEROY, lawyer; b. Perry, Okla., Jan. 30, 1920; s. William Floyd and Bessie (Thedford) S.; LL.B., U. Okla., 1949; m. Frances Doreen Newton, Dec. 1, 1945; children—Gayle Louise (Mrs. Steve Alan Troutman), Donna Kay (Mrs. R. Dale Travis). Admitted to Okla. bar, 1949; practice law, Oklahoma City, 1949—; partner Stagner & Alpern, 1952-57, Stagner, Alpern, Powers & Tapp, 1957-63, Halley, Spradling, Stagner & Alpern, Oklahoma City, 1967—. Mem. faculty domestic relations Coll. Law, U. Okla., 1955-56. Active Ecumenical Inst. Okla., 1967—. Served with Q.M. Corps, AUS, 1942-45. Mem. Am., Okla. bar assns., Am. Civil Liberties Union, Phi Delta Phi. Democrat. Mem. Disciples of Christ Ch. Home: 4809 NW 32d St Oklahoma City OK 73122 Office: 657 Skirvin Tower Oklahoma City OK 73102

STAHL, BEN, artist, writer; b. Chgo., Sept. 7, 1910; s. Ben F. and Grace (Meyer) S.; student pub. schs.; m. Ella M. Lehocky, Dec. 19, 1940; children—Ben F., Gail, Regina, David. Illustrator Sat. Eve. Post, other nat. mags., 1933—; mem. founding faculty Famous Artists Schools (now Famous Schs. Internat.), Westport, Conn., 1949—; mem. Fla. Art Commn.; bd. advisers Am. Art. Found.; v.p. Sarasota Mus. of the Cross (creator all paintings and drawings exhibited); exhibitor Nat. Acad. Design, Art Inst. Chgo., Audubon Museum, others; one-man shows Soc. Ill., N.Y.C., 1945, Stevens Gross Galleries, Chgo., 1950, Scarab Club, Detroit, 1951, Sarasota Art Assn., 1950, Cellar Gallery, Chgo., 1971, U. Brigeport, 1971, Parker Playhouse, Ft. Lauderdale, 1971, Top Flight Gallery, Sarasota, 1971, Darro Gallery, Wilmette, Ill., 1971, others; painted and exhibited the 14 stas. of the cross for Cath. Bible and Catholic Press, Chgo., 1955; illustrated 2 volumes Bible, also ltd. edit. of Gone With the Wind, 1960. Recipient numerous nat. awards, including Saltus gold medal Nat. Acad. Design, 1949, Sequoyah Book Award (for Blackbeard's Ghost), Okla. Library Assn., 1969. Mem. Soc. Illustrators, Artists and Writers, Westport Artists (co-founder, 1st pres.), Sarasota Art Assn. (v.p. 1953), Internat. Platform Assn. Club: Players (N.Y.C.). Author, illustrator: Blackbeard's Ghost, 1965 (Walt Disney film, released 1968); The Secret of Red Skull, 1971. Home: 4214 Higel Av Sarasota FL 33577

STAHL, O(SCAR) GLENN, educator, govt. ofcl.; b. Evansville, Ind., Apr. 30, 1910; s. Oscar and Mayme (Wittmer) S.; A.B., U. Evansville, 1931; M.A., U. Wis., 1933, Ph.D., N.Y.U., 1936; m. Marie Jane Rueter, June 26, 1934; children—Elaine Marie, Alan G. Instr. govt. N.Y.U., 1933-35; personnel officer TVA, 1935-41; with Fed. Security Agy., 1941-51, director personnel, 1948-51; with U.S. Civil Service Commn., 1951-69, dir. bur. policies and standards, 1955-69; adj. prof. pub. adminstrn. Am. U., 1949-69; part-time prof. U. Tenn., 1939, Dept. Agr. Grad. Sch., 1941-49; vis. lectr. various univs.; lectr. Salzburg Seminar in Am. Studies, 1965. Tech. assistance adviser to Venezuela, UN, 1958-59, 72; U.S. rep. UN Conference, Ethiopia, 1964; Ford Found. cons. to India, 1968, 69, 71, to Nepal, 1969; U.S. rapporteur Internat. Congress Adminstrv. Scis., Dublin, 1968; U.S. rep. UN Seminar, Tashkent, USSR, 1969; U.S. AID cons., Pakistan, 1969, 71; adviser Pub. Adminstrn. Service and Govtl. Affairs Inst., 1972—. Mem. Arlington County (Va.) Sch. Bd., 1948-50; pres. Arlington Com. to Preserve Pub. Schs., 1958—. Trustee Group Health Assn., 1958-61. Recipient Distinguished Service award Civil Service Commn., 1960, Stockberger award Soc. Personnel Adminstrn., 1962; Career Service award Nat. Civil Service League, 1967. Mem. Am. Acad. Polit. and Social Sci., Am. Polit. Sci. Assn., Am. Soc. Pub. Adminstrn. (editorial bd. 1955-58), Internat. Inst. Adminstrv. Sci., Pub. Personnel Assn. (exec. council 1951-54, pres. 1965-66, Washington rep. 1971-72, hon. life mem.), Soc. Personnel Adminstrn. Presbyn. Author: Training Career Public Servants for the City of New York, 1936; Public Personnel Administration, 6th edit., 1971; The Personnel Job of Government Managers, 1971; also articles. Editor Personnel Administration, 1945-55. Address: 3600 N Piedmont St Arlington VA 22207

STAHL, RAY EMERSON, coll. adminstrn. exec.; b. Latrobe, Pa., Mar. 24, 1917; s. Curtis E. and Josephine (King) S.; A.B., Bethany Coll., 1938; B.D., Butler U., 1943; Ed.M., U. Pitts. 1946; postgrad. St. Vincent Coll., 1939. Pitts. Sch. Accountancy, 1939-40, U. Ky., 1955; M.A., Ohio State U., 1969; m. Faith Worrell, Aug. 25, 1941; children—Ellen Josephine (Mrs. Lawrence Carpenter), Ray Emerson. Ordained to ministry Disciples of Christ Ch., 1941; minister Brentwood Christian Ch., Pitts., 1943-46, First Christian Ch., Erwin, Tenn., 1946-50; exec. sec. in charge bus. adminstrn., pub. relations Milligan Coll., Tenn., 1950-68; dir. pub. relations E. Tenn. State U., Johnson City, 1968—. Bd. dirs. Reece Mus., Johnson City Symphony Orch. Mem. Council for Advancement Small Colls. (chmn. pub. relations 1957-61), Johnson City C. of C. (dir.), Kappa Alpha, Theta Phi, Kappa Tau Alpha. Republican. Mem. Christian Ch. Kiwanian. Club: Johnson City Country. Author: How to Finance the Local Church, 1953. Contbr. articles to profl. jours. Home: 108 Park Ct Johnson City TN 37601

STAHLMAN, JAMES GEDDES, publisher; b. Nashville, Feb. 28, 1893; s. Edward Claiborne and Mary (Geddes) S.; grad. Webb Sch., Bell Buckle, Tenn., 1912; A.B., Vanderbilt U., 1916; postgrad. U. Chgo., 1916; LL.D., Atlanta Law Sch., 1939; m. Mildred Thornton, Jan. 20, 1917; children—Ann Geddes (Mrs. George R. Hill), Mildred Stahlman; m. 2d, Effye Chumley, Jan. 10, 1939 (dec.); m. 3d, Gladys P. Breckenridge, June 1, 1953. Pres., pub. Nashville Banner, 1930—; chmn. bd. Newspaper Printing Corp., 1937—. Mem. nat. council Boy Scouts Am. Trustee Vanderbilt U., Cordell Hull Found., MacArthur Meml. Found., Hermitage, Home Andrew Jackson. Served as pvt. U.S. Army, World War I; capt. USNR, World War II. Recipient Am. award Americas Found., 1956, Freedoms Found. Washington medal, 1961, 65, 4th Estate award Am. Legion, 1970. Mem. Inter-Am. Press Assn. (pres. 1955-56), Am. (pres. 1937-39), So. (pres. 1932-33, chmn. bd. 1933-34) newspaper pubs. assns., Am. Soc. Newspaper Editors, Phi Beta Kappa, Sigma Chi, Sigma Delta Chi, Omicron Delta Kappa, Sigma Upsilon. Presbyn. Mason (33 deg., K.T., Shriner, past potentate). Clubs: Belle Meade Country, Hillsboro Hounds, Cumberland; Army-Navy, Army Navy Country, Nat. Press (Washington); Metropolitan, University, Dutch Treat (N.Y.C.); Circumnavigators. Home: 815 Tyne Blvd Nashville TN 37215

STAHLMAN, MILDRED THORTON, physician; b. Nashville, July 31, 1922; d. James G. and Mildred (Thornton) Stahlman; B.A., Vanderbilt U., 1943, M.D., 1946. Intern, Lakeside Hosp., Cleve., 1946-47, Boston Children's Hosp., 1947-48; mem. faculty dept. pediatrics Vanderbilt Med. Sch., 1951—, asso. prof. pediatrics, 1965—. Mem. Am. Pediatric Soc., Soc. Pediatric Research, So. Soc. Pediatric Research (1st pres.), So. Soc. Clin. Investigation, Am. Fedn. Clin. Research, Am. Physiol. Soc. (human embrology and devel. study sect. 1964-68), Sigma Xi, Phi Beta Kappa, Alpha Omega Alpha. Home: Beech Creek Rd Brentwood TN 37027 Office: Vanderbilt Hosp Nashville TN 37203

STAHMER, HAROLD MARTIN, educator; b. Bklyn., Aug. 7, 1929; s. Harold Martin and Ann (Truntz) S.; B.A., Dartmouth Coll., 1951; student Benedictine Abbey of Maria Laach, 1951-52; B.D., Union Theol. Sem., 1955; Ph.D., Cambridge U., 1959; m. Jean Craig Smith, Sept. 22, 1956; children—Sarah Anne, Jennifer Betsy, Hannah Mary. Instr. religion Barnard Coll., 1957-60, acting chmn. dept., 1958-60, asst. prof., 1961-62, asso. prof., 1962-67, prof., 1967-69, chmn. religion dept., 1962-68, dir. undergrad. program in religion, 1966-67; dir. Harvard-Yale-Columbia Intensive Summer Studies Program, 1967-69; prof. religion and philosophy, asso. dean Coll. Arts and Scis. U. Fla., 1969—. Recipient E. Harris Harbison Distinguished Teaching prize, 1968; Rockland County B'nai B'rith Community Service award, 1966. Mem. Am. Assn. U. Profs., Am. Council Learned Socs., Soc. for Sci. Study of Religion, Am. Acad. Religion, Soc. for Religion in Higher Edn., Am. Civil Liberties Union. Author: Speak That I May See Thee, 1968. Editor Religion and Contemporary Society, 1963. Home: 101 NW 44th St Gainesville FL 32601 Office: 102 Anderson Hall Gainesville FL 32601

STAINTON, FRANK ROSS, JR., oil co. ofcl.; b. New Orleans, Apr. 20, 1926; s. Frank Ross and Katie Emma (Bush) S.; student U. N.C., 1944; B.A., Tulane U., 1949; m. Joan Ellen Price, June 2, 1956; children—Frank Ross, Kenneth Charles. State editor Times-Picayune, New Orleans, 1949-54; editor, rep. pub. relations Shell Oil Co., New Orleans, 1954-67, sr. writer, N.Y.C., 1967-68, mgr. pub. relations, Denver, 1968-69, Atlanta, 1969—. Chmn. pub. relations com. Fla. Petroleum Council. Served with USNR, 1943-46. Mem. Pub. Relations Soc. Am. Mason (32 deg.). Club: Atlanta Press. Home: 3563 Cantrell Rd NE Atlanta GA 30319 Office: Shell Oil Co Peachtree Center Bldg Atlanta GA 30303

STAIR, FRED ROGERS, JR., sem. pres.; b. Knoxville, Tenn., Mar. 7, 1918; s. Fred Rogers and Christyne (Miller) S.; B.S., Davidson Coll., 1939, D.D., 1960; B.D., Union Theol. Sem., Va., 1947, Th.M., 1948; student U. Edinburgh, 1945; LL.D., Davis and Elkins Coll., 1969; m. Martha Osborne, Dec. 19, 1942; children—Mary Miller (Mrs. R. Whitfield Bass), Thomas Osborne. Ordained to ministry Presbyn. Ch., 1943; asst. to pres. Union Theol. Sem., Va., 1948-53; pastor in Hickory, N.C., 1953-59, Atlanta, 1959-67; pres. Union Theol. Sem., Va., 1967—. Served with inf. AUS, 1942-46. Moses D. Hoge fellow, 1948. Mem. Phi Beta Kappa, Phi Gamma Delta, Omicron Delta Kappa. Club: Richmond Forum. Home: 1216 Rennie Av Richmond VA 23227

STALDER, JOHN LUTHER, banker; b. Anadarko, Okla., Apr. 6, 1908; s. John Edward and Lillie Mae (Coburn) S.; m. Ethel M. Stalder, 1930 (dec. 1964); children—Johnetta, Betty, Bill; m. Mary Phelps, Sept. 26, 1970. With First Nat. Bank, Anadarko, Okla., 1924-41; v.p., cashier, dir. Anadarko Bank & Trust Co., Anadarko, Okla., 1943—. Treas., dir. Indian City U.S.A., 1955. Treas., Tb. Assn., County Heart Fund, March of Dimes. Mem. C. of C. (bd. dirs. 1955-60). Mason, Kiwanian. Home: Route 3 Box 667 Anadarko OK 73005 Office: 101 W Broadway Anadarko OK 73005

STALEY, THOMAS F., educator, univ. dean; b. Pitts., Aug. 13, 1935; B.A., B.S., Regis Coll., 1957; M.A., U. Tulsa, 1958; Ph.D. (fellow), U. Pitts., 1962; m. 1960; 4 children. Asst. prof. English, Rollins Coll., 1961-62; vis. prof. U. Pitts., summers 1962, 67; Fulbright resident prof., Trieste, Italy, 1966-67; asso. prof. English, U. Tulsa, 1968-70, pres., 1970—, dean Grad. Sch., 1969—. Co-chmn. Internat. James Joyce Symposium, Dublin, 1967, chmn., 1969; Danforth asso. Am. Council Learned Socs. grantee, 1969. Mem. South Central Modern Lang. Assn. (chmn. comparative lit. sect. 1965-66). Author: Approaches to Ulysses, 1970; also chpts. in books. Editor: James Joyce Today, 1966; Dubliners: A Critical Handbook, 1969; co-editor U. Tulsa Monograph Series; mem. bd. editors 20th Century Lit. Research on James Joyce, comparative lit., modern European and Brit. fiction. Office: Office of Dean Graduate School University of Tulsa Tulsa OK 74104*

STALKER, WILLIAM WEIDMANN, educator; b. New Albany, Ind., Oct. 25, 1912; s. William H. and Lorena (Widemann) S.; A.B., DePauw U., 1933; M.A., Ind. U., 1942; M.S., U. Louisville, 1945; postgrad. Harvard, 1949-50; m. Varena Gilpin, Jan. 31, 1953; children—Marc Gilpin, Eve Marie. Instr. biology and chemistry New Albany Sr. High Sch., 1938-43; asso. in occupational health dept. pub. health and preventive medicine U. Louisville, 1946-57; dir. div. occupational health Ky. Health Dept., 1944-54; cons. to spl. air pollution study Louisville and USPHS-Jefferson County, 1954-58; mng. dir. Occupational Health Inst. Ky., 1954-58; resident dir. Nashville Community Air Pollution Study, USPHS, Cin., 1958-62, prin. investigator Ala. Air Pollution Study, 1962-64; clin. asst. prof. occupational health Med. Coll. Ala., 1963-64; dir. Jefferson County Air Pollution Program, 1965-66; asso. prof. occupational health dept. pub. health and epidemiology U. Ala. Med. Coll., Birmingham, 1965—. Mem. chem. measurements panel Nat. Bur. Standards, 1971—. Diplomate Am. Bd. Indsl. Hygiene. Mem. Am. Indsl. Hygiene Assn., Air Pollution Control Assn., Sigma Xi. Contbr. articles to profl. jours. Home: 3923 Shannon Lane Mountain Brook AL 35213 Office: 1921 9th Av S Birmingham AL 35205

STALLARD, HARLEY TRIGG, supt. schs.; b. Wise, Va., May 12, 1917; s. Jerry Trigg and Flora Belle (Taylor) S.; student Miligan Coll., 1934-35, 36-37; B.S., Radford Coll., 1947; M.S., Va. Poly. Inst., 1951; m. Bunnie Frances Robinette, May 8, 1941; children—Harley, Robert, Anita (Mrs. Gary Dorton), Michael, Larry, Nancy, Addie. Elementary head tchr. Wise County Sch. Bd. (Va.), 1937-43, 45-49, tchr. high sch., 1949-51, bd. clk., 1951-53, prin. elementary schs., 1953-54, prin. high schs., 1954-61, elementary supr., 1961-63, dir. instrn., 1963-71, div. supt., 1971—. Mem. Wise County com. Democratic party, 1954. Served with AUS, 1943-45. Mem. Va. (pres. Dist. 0 1951, dir. 1951), Wise County (sec. 1947-51) edn. assns., S.W. Suprs. (pres. 1966-67). Baptist (tchr. men's bible class 1954—, Sunday sch. supt. 1960-62, chmn. bd. deacons 1967-70). Moose, Lion (charter pres. Wise 1953-54) (dep. dist. gov. 1958-59, 62-63). Home: Box 418 Big Stone Gap VA 24219 Office: PO Box 1217 Wise VA 24293

STALLINGS, FRANK HALL, educator; b. Smith's Grove, Ky., Feb. 8, 1909; s. William Marion and Lina Thomas (Hall) S.; student Ky. Wesleyan Coll., 1926-27, U. Ky., 1927-28; A.B., U. Louisville, 1931, M.A., 1937; Ed.D., U. Ky., 1959; m. Evalyn Mae Strange, Jan. 30, 1932; children—William Marion II, Linda Lee (Mrs. Gregory P. Grantham). Tchr. pub. schs., Clark County, Ky., 1928-29, Louisville, 1942-58; lectr. U. Louisville, 1951-58, mem. faculty, 1958—, prof. edn., head dept., 1961-68, chmn. unit for adminstrn. and supervision, 1968—. Cons. 2d annual conf. schs. in transition U.S. Comm. Civil Rights, 1960; ofcl. del. White House Conf. Children and Youth, 1960; adv. mem. Ky. Council Pub. Higher Edn., 1966—. Mem. Mallon Com. Met. Govt. Louisville and Jefferson County, 1956-58; chmn. Peoples Com. for Annexation, 1948-51. Mem. Ky. Dept. Elementary Sch. Prins. (pres. 1956), Ky. Assn. Colls., Elementary and Secondary Schs. (pres. 1965—), N.E.A., Kappa Delta Pi, Phi Delta Kappa. Democrat. Baptist. Author: Let's Take a Field Trip, 1955; A Study of the Effects of Integration on Scholastic Achievement in the Louisville Public Schools, 1958: Development of Alternative Models for the Preparation of Elementary School Guidance Personnel (with others), 1967. Home: 3717 Norbourne Blvd Louisville KY 40207

STALLINGS, GENE CLIFTON, univ. football coach; b. Paris, Tex., Mar. 2, 1935; s. Eugene C. and Neil (Moye) S.; B.S., Tex. A. and M. U., 1958; m. Ruth Ann Jack, Dec. 1, 1956; children—Anna Lee, Laura Nell, John Mark, Jacklyn Ruth. Asst. football coach U. Ala., 1958-64; head football coach, dir. athletics Tex. A. and M. U., 1964—. Dir. Bank of A&M, College Station, Tex., Rolling Internat., Inc., Dallas. Spalding sports cons. Mem. Sam Houston council Boy Scouts Am. Mem. Nat. Assn. Collegiate Dirs. Athletics, Am. Football Coaches Assn., Fellowship Christian Athletes. Mem. Ch. of Christ. Author articles. Home: 830 N Rosemary Bryan TX 77840 Office: Athletic Dept Tex A and M Univ College Station TX 77843

STALLINGS, JAMES CAMERON, educator, chemist; b. Denton, Tex., Jan. 16, 1919; s. Arthur Bunyan and Mona (Coker) S.; B.S., North Tex. State U., 1942, M.S., 1943; Ph.D. (Gen. Aniline fellow 1948-49), U. Tex., 1950; m. Otelia Olga Limmer, Dec. 18, 1949; children—Stephanie Ann, Deborah. Chemist Wilson Labs., Denton, Tex., 1942-43; prof. chemistry dept. Sam Houston State U., Huntsville, Tex., 1949-57, prof., dir. chemistry dept., 1959—; sr. research chemist Celanese Chem. Co., Corpus Christi, Tex., 1957-59. Served to comdr. USNR, 1943-46; PTO. Fellow Am. Inst. Chemists; mem. Am. Chem. Soc., Phi Lambda Upsilon. Lutheran. Home: 1912 18th St Huntsville TX 77340

STALLINGS, JAMES HENRY, govt. ofcl.; b. Bryan, Tex., Sept. 20, 1892; s. William Daniel and Emma Elizabeth (Josey) S.; B.S., Tex. A. and M. U., 1914; M.S. (Research fellow) Ia. State U., 1917, Ph.D., 1926; m. Pearl Louise Drummond, Aug. 1, 1923; children—George Drummond, James Henry. Asst. prof. Ia. State U., 1919-20; head soils dept. Tex. A. and M. U., 1920-26; agronomist Penny-Gynn Inst., 1926-28, Nat. Fertilizer Assn., 1929-33; regional dir. Soil Conservation Service, U.S. Dept. Agr., 1934-37, organizer, dir. flood control program, Washington, 1937-42; dir. fertilizer program War Food Adminstrn., Washington, 1942-44; prin. research specialist Soil Conservation Service, 1945-59; soil sci. editor Biol. Abstracts, 1952—, Webster's Internat. Dictionary. Mem. N.Y. Acad. Scis., Soil Sci. Soc. Am., Agronomy Assn., Internat. Platform Assn., Sigma Xi. Author: Soil Conservation, 1957; Soil Use and Improvement, 1957. Contbr. articles to profl. jours. Address: 5146 Nebraska Av NW Washington DC 20008

STALLINGS, NELL ALLEN, educator; b. Louisburg, N.C., July 15, 1915; d. George B. Haywood and Christiana (Lacy) Stallings; B.S., U.N.C., 1936, M.A., 1942. Tchr. sr. high sch., High Point, N.C., 1936-42; Lenoir Rhyne Coll., Hickory, N.C., 1942-43; faculty E. Carolina U., Greenville, N.C., 1943—, prof. phys. edn., 1963—. Staff mem. Nat. Aquatic Sch., 1958—. Water safety chmn. Pitt County chpt. A.R.C., 1962—. Recipient Honor award N.C. Assn. for Health, Phys. Edn. and Recreation, 1968. Fellow Am. Assn. Health, Phys. Edn. and Recreation; mem. N.E.A., Am. Assn. U. Women (pres. 1953-54), Nat., So. assns. phys. edn. for coll. women, N.C. Edn. Assn., N.C. Assn. Health, Phys. Edn. and Recreation (pres. 1954-55). Home: 2411 Umstead Av Greenville NC 27834

STALLONES, REUEL ARTHUR, physician, educator; b. N. Little Rock, Ark., Oct. 10, 1923; s. Wilner Leroy and Jet (Wilson) S.; student Visalia Jr. Coll., 1941-42, Ripon Coll., 1943-44, U. Mich., 1944-45; M.D., Western Reserve U., 1949; M.P.H., U. Cal. at Berkeley, 1952; m. Joyce Graves, Aug. 14, 1945; children—Jorel, Lorann, Jared Reuel, Intern, Letterman Hosp., San Francisco, 1949-50; lectr. U. Cal. at Berkeley, 1956-59, asso. prof. epidemiology, 1959-64, prof., 1964-68; dean sch. pub. health U. Tex. at Houston, 1968—. Served with AUS, 1943-46, 49-56. Home: 33 Patti Lynn St Houston TX 77024

STALNAKER, LEO, JR., educator; b. Tampa, Fla., Oct. 18, 1923; s. Leo and Judson (Vest) S.; student U. Tampa, 1941-42, Coll. William and Mary 1943-44; B.A., U. S. Fla., 1962; m. June Esther Kuebler, Oct. 5, 1946; children—Lance K., Jeffrey Clay. Staff writer, Tampa Times, 1946-49, city editor, 1950-55, asso. state editor Tampa Tribune, 1955-57, night city editor, 1957-65, city editor, 1965-66, asst. mng. editor, 1966-70; asst. prof. mass communications U. S. Fla., 1970—. Served with AUS, 1943-46. Decorated Purple Heart, 3 battle stars; ETO, combat medal. Mem. Sigma Delta Chi. Lutheran. Home: 1907 Heather Av Tampa FL 33612

STALTER, SAMUEL EVERETT, meat packing co. exec.; b. La Junta, Colo., Oct. 1, 1911; s. Samuel S. and Hulda (Thutt) S.; ed. pub. schs.; m. Helen Bridge, Dec. 24, 1933; 1 dau., Mary Virginia (Mrs. P. H. Taylor). With Great Atlantic and Pacific Tea Co., 1928-47, 49-52, asst. dir. meat operations central Western div., 1950-52; meat program dir. Fleming Co., Topeka, 1947-48; propr. Just Right Meats, Inc., Duluth, Minn., 1952-55; with Klarer of Ky., Inc., Louisville, 1955—, exec. v.p., 1963-65, pres., 1965-70; pres. Bardstown Farms, Inc., (Ky.), 1971—. Mem. Bardstown C. of C., Am. Meat Inst., Optomist Internat. Republican. Presbyn. (elder). Mason (Shriner). Clubs: Big Spring, Pendenis (Louisville). Home: 104 West Wind Trail Bardstown KY 40004 Office: 31 E Nazareth Rd Bardstown KY 40004

STAMPER, JOE ALLEN, lawyer; b. Okemah, Okla., Jan. 30, 1914; s. Horace Allen and Ann (Stephens) S.; B.A., U. Okla., 1933, LL.B., 1935; m. Johnnie Lee Bell, June 4, 1936; 1 dau., Jane Allen (Mrs. Ernest F. Godlove). Admitted to Okla. bar, 1935; practiced in Antlers, Okla., 1935-36, 46—; atty. Pushmataha County, 1936-39; mem. Okla. indsl. commn., 1939-40; spl. justice Okla. Supreme Ct., 1948. Pres., Antlers Sch. Bd., 1956-67, Pushmataha Found., 1957—. Mgr., Okla. Democratic party, 1946; chmn. dist., 1946-50; alternate del. Dem. Nat. Conv., 1951. Served from 2d lt. to col. AUS, 1935-46, ETO. Decorated Bronze Star. Mem. Am., Okla. (bd. govs.) bar assns., S.A.R., Pi Kappa Alpha. Baptist (deacon). Mason (32 deg., Shriner), Lion. Club: Whitehall (Oklahoma City). Home: 1000 NE 2d St Antlers OK 74523 Office: PO Box 100 Antlers OK 74523

STAMPS, HERMAN FRANKLIN, dentist; b. Washington, Jan. 20, 1924; s. Herman Franklin and Alice Beatrice (Bowman) S.; B.S., Howard U., 1945, D.D.S., 1948; M.Sc., U. Mich., 1953; m. Pauline Duvall, Oct. 2, 1948; children—Eric, Alisa. Gen. practice dentistry, Washington, 1948—. Mem. faculty Howard U., Washington, 1948—, dir. clinics, 1967-70, prof. Coll. Dentistry, 1969—; coordinator facilities, systems and planning, 1970—; cons. Montgomery County Jr. Colls., 1966, Washington Bd. Edn., 1963-65, Manpower Bd. Labor Dept., 1964-67. Chmn. supervisory com. Armstrong Neighborhood Fed. Credit Union, 1964-66; Bd. dirs. Washington Urban League, 1958—, chmn. membership drive, 1960-61, bd. dirs. COIN, 1962-65. Served with AUS, 1942-44. Diplomate Am. Bd. Endodontics. Mem. Robert T. Freeman Dental Soc. (pres. 1959-61), Nat., Am. dental assns., Washington Dental Soc., Am. Dental Assn., Am. Soc. History Dentistry (charter), Am. Assn. Endodontics, Omicron Kappa Upsilon. Author: Modern Prescription Writing, 1954. Home: 7541 16th St NW Washington DC 20012 Office: 2328 Georgia Av NW Washington DC 20001

STANALAND, WILLIAM WHIT, JR., accountant; b. Benson Junction, Fla., Mar. 15, 1930; s. William Whit and Goldie (Merritt) S.; B.S. in Bus. Adminstrn., U. Fla., 1957, postgrad., 1959; postgrad. Rollins Coll., 1964; m. Norma Lee Ober, June 24, 1961; children—Sherry D., William Whit III, Terence B., Dana Lee; m. 2d, Sandra L. Swann, Dec. 1, 1972. Jr. accountant Pepsi Cola Bottling Co., 1957-58; accountant Wells, Laney, Earlich & Baer, 1958-59, A.J. Mixner, C.P.A., 1961-63; controller Halco Products, Inc., 1959-61; C.P.A., Orlando, Fla., 1963—. Served with USMC, 1948-52. C.P.A., Fla., Ga. Mem. Am., Fla. insts. C.P.A.'s. Kiwanian, Toastmaster. Home: 3111 Knollwood Circle Orlando FL 32804 Office: 5400 Diplomat Circle Orlando FL 32810

STANBERY, CECIL HENLEY, dentist; b. nr. Chattanooga, Tenn., Apr. 12, 1929; s. William Cecil and Etta Moyers (Henley) S.; B.A., U. Tenn., 1952, B.S., 1954, D.D.S., 1958; m. Johnnie Anette Richardson, June 15, 1957; children—William Cecil II, John Samuel. Faculty, U. Chattanooga, 1953-54; practice dentistry, Cleveland, Tenn., 1958—. Instr. geography Cleveland State Community Coll., 1968. Dental missionary, Bolivia, 1969. Vice pres. Bradley County Capitol Club, 1971—; Bradley County campaign mgr. for Richard Nixon, 1968. Mem. Am., Tenn. dental assns., Third Dist. Dental Soc., Pierre Fauchard, S.A.R., Sigma Nu, Delta Sigma Delta. Rotarian, Elk. Home: North Lee Hwy Cleveland TN 37311 Office: 423 Central Av NW Cleveland TN 37311

STANDER, ROBERT ANGUS, chem. co. exec.; b. Balt., July 7, 1928; s. Henricus Johannes and Florence Mary (Creelman) S.; student Cornell U., 1946-47; A.B. in Physics, Colby Coll., 1950; m. Maurine Masal Maust, June 4, 1951; children—Mary (Mrs. John G. Landry), Linda, Robert Angus, Timothy. Trainee physicist Texaco, Inc., 1950-51; with Chem. Service, Inc., 1955-62, br. mgr., Baton Rouge, 1956-58, gen. mgr., Lafayette, La., 1958-62; founder, Chem. Applicators of Lafayette, Inc., 1963, chmn. bd., pres., gen. mgr., 1963—; dir. Burlastan. Served with USAF, 1952-55; Korea. Mem. Nat. Assn. Corrosion Engrs. (chpt. pres. 1960-61), Nat. Assn. Power Engrs. (custodian 1970—), Natural Gas Processors Assn., Am. Petroleum Inst., Nat. Pilots Assn., Aircraft Owners and Pilots Assn., Air Force Assn., Am. Legion. Republican. Presbyn. Inventor chem. and mechanic procedures. Home: 313 Thibodeaux Dr Lafayette LA 70501 Office: PO Box 45 Duson LA 70529

STANDEVEN, JAMES WYLIE, hosp. supt.; b. Hancock, Ia., Jan. 25, 1916; s. John Frank and Elsie (Wylie) S.; B.S., State U. Ia., 1940, M.D., 1940; m. Jean E. Beckwith, Apr. 30, 1960; children—John, Steven. Intern Neb. Methodist Hosp., Omaha; gen. practice medicine, Oakland, Ia., 1946-57; with VA, 1957—, dir. VA Hosp., Montgomery, Ala., 1968—. Mem. Gov. Ala. Com. Employment Handicapped. Councilman, Oakland, Ia., 1950-54. Bd. dirs. local A.R.C. Served to capt. USAAF, 1941-45. Mem. Am. Coll. Hosp. Adminstrs., A.M.A. Aerospace Med Assn., Fed. Execs. Assn., Alpha Omega Alpha, Alpha Kappa Kappa. Rotarian. Home: 215 Perry Hill Rd Montgomery AL 36109

STANFILL, WILLIAM JAMES, constrn. co. exec.; b. nr. Franklin, Tenn., Sept. 16, 1925; s. William Thomas and Katie (Hill) S.; student Austin Peay State Coll., 1949-50, U. Tenn., 1964; m. Mildred Hooten, Apr. 10, 1954; children—Cynthia Lynne, Melinda Jo. Payroll clk. Nicholson Co., Inc., N.Y.C., 1947-48, field office mgr., 1951-56; field office mgr. Seth E. Giem & Assos., Memphis, 1948-51; cost accountant Va.-Carolina Chem. Co., Mt. Pleasant, Tenn., 1956-57; field office mgr. O'Brien & Padgett, Memphis, 1957-58; chief accountant Oman Constrn. Co., Inc., Nashville, 1958-64, asst. sec.-treas., 1964-69, comptroller, 1969—. Served with AUS, 1944-46. C.P.A., Tenn. Mem. Am. Inst. C.P.A.'s., Tenn. Soc. C.P.A.'s. Mem. Ch. of Christ. Home: 895 Rodney Dr Nashville TN 37205 Office: PO Box 146 Nashville TN 37202

STANFORD, CHARLES WHITSON, JR., mus. exec.; b. Durham, N.C., Sept. 13, 1924; s. Charles Whitson and Mary (McIver) S.; A.B., U. N.C., 1947; postgrad. Columbia, 1948-49, Princeton, 1949-53. Curatorial asst. Colonial Williamsburg, Inc., 1955-56; curator edn. N.C. Mus. Art, Raleigh, 1958-70, dir., 1970—. Mem. Gov.'s Bldg. Commn. Head, State Agy., 1970—; dir., v.p. Redfields, Inc., Chapel Hill; lectr. art history on TV, radio. Vice chmn. Exec. Mansion Fine Arts Commn. Bd. dirs. Mary Duke Biddle Gallery for Blind, N.C. Mus. Art, Raleigh, N.C. Symphony Soc. (exec. com.), N.C. Art Soc. (exec. com.), Historic Hillsborough Commn.; dir. adv. bd. N.C. Ednl. TV, div. humanities N.C. Dept. Pub. Instrn.; bd. dirs. Reynolds House, Winston-Salem. Recipient N.C. award (Gold medal) in fine arts, 1969. Mem. N.C. Mus. Council (past dir.), Coll. Arts Assn., N.C. Art Soc., Assn. Art Mus. Dirs. Clubs: Princeton (N.Y.); Nassau (Princeton, N.J.). Democrat. Author: Masterpieces in the North Carolina Museum of Art, 1966, 2d edit., 1972; Selections from British and American Painting, 1967. Contbr. articles to profl. periodicals. Home: Redfields Route 1 Box 79 Chapel Hill NC 27514 Office: Dirs Office NC Mus Art Raleigh NC 27601

STANFORD, DONALD ELWIN, educator; b. Amherst, Mass., Feb. 7, 1913; s. Ernest Elwood and Alice Lyndon (Carrol) S.; A.B., Stanford, 1933, Ph.D., 1953; M.A., Harvard, 1935; m. Maryanna Peterson, Aug. 14, 1953. Instr. English, Colo. State Coll., 1935-37, Dartmouth, 1937-41, U. Neb., 1941-42; instr. La. State U., Baton Rouge, 1948-49, asst. prof., 1953-55, asso. prof., 1955-62, prof. English, 1962—, editor Humanities Series, La. State U. Press, 1962-67, editor So. Rev., 1963—. Guggenheim fellow, 1958-59. Mem. Modern Lang. Assn., Melville Soc., P.E.N. Author: The New England Earth (poems), 1941; The Traveler (poems), 1955; Edward Taylor, 1965. Editor: The Poems of Edward Taylor, 1960. Home: 776 Delgado Dr Baton Rouge LA 70808

STANFORD, GEORGE ALONZO, fgn. service officer; b. Crystal, Mich., Feb. 2, 1917; s. George Perry and Florence Evelyn (Wright) S.; student Central State Tchrs. Coll., Mt. Pleasant, Mich., 1934-36; B.A., Albion Coll., 1939; summer postgrad. U. Mich., 1939, U. Wyo., 1940, U. Tex., 1941; M.A., U. Ia., 1941; postgrad. U. Mich., 1941-42; m. Alice Louise Hyslop, Sept. 9, 1942; children—Alice Gail, Theodore Dale. Teaching asst. Spanish, U. Ia., 1939-41; teaching fellow Spanish and Portuguese, U. Mich., 1941-42; joined U.S. Fgn. Service, 1942; cultural relations asst., Santiago, Chile, 1942-45; tchr. English, U. Chile, 1943-44; asst. cultural officer, Rio de Janeiro, 1945-47; vice consul, 3d sec., Havana, 1947-49; vice consul, 2d sec., Helsinki, 1949-53; consul, 2d sec., chief. econ. sect., Reykjavik, 1953-55; fgn. affairs specialist State Dept.,1955-58; student NATO Def. Colls., Paris, France, 1958-59; 2d sec., consul, chief polit. sect., Stockholm, 1959-61; comml. officer Dept. Commerce, 1961-63; consul, dep. dir. U.S. Trade Center, Frankfurt, Germany, 1963-65; consul, 1st sec., asst. comml. attache Am. embassy, Mexico City, Mexico, 1965-69; 1st sec., comml. attache Am. embassy, Caracas, Venezuela, 1969-71; comml. counselor Am. Consulate Gen., Rio de Janeiro, Brazil, 1971—. Mem. Am. Fgn. Service Assn. Rotarian. Office: Am Consulate Gen Rio de Janeiro Brazil

STANFORD, ROY ELLINGTON, JR., dentist; b. Winston-Salem, N.C., Mar. 21, 1932; s. Roy Ellington and Mary Brenda (Ireland) S.; student U. Richmond, 1952-54; D.D.S., Med. Coll. of Va., 1958. Gen. practice dentistry, Fairfax, Va., 1959-66, McLean, Va., 1967—; lectr. dental occlusion. Mem. No. Va. Gnathological Research Group (pres. 1966-68), Am. Dental Assn., Am. Soc. Preventive Dentistry, McLean Bus. and Profl. Assn. (v.p. 1971), Highlands Civic Assn., McLean Knights of the Round Table, Psi Omega. Republican. Presbyn. Lion. Club: Congressional Country (Bethesda, Md.). Home: 607 S 23rd St Arlington VA 22202 Office: 6829 Tennyson Dr McLean VA 22101

STANGER, RUSSELL, orch. condr.; b. Boston; grad. New Eng. Conservatory Music; student Tanglewood. Condr. Cecelia Soc. Boston, 1953; organizer Boston Little Orch., 1958; asst. condr. N.Y. Philharmonic, 1960; Mpls. Symphony Orch. (name now Minn. Orch.), 1964-66; music dir. Norfolk (Va.) Symphony Orch., 1966—. Guest condr. leading Am. and European orchs., including Phila. Orch., N.Y. Philharmonic, CBC Symphony, Buffalo Philharmonic, Oslo Philharmonic, Royal Philharmonic, Orchestre Symphonique des Reims. Composer: Buffons (A Merry Overture), 1964; Childhood Images, 1968; Rock Opus (for Symphony Orch. and Optional Rock Group), 1970. Office: 700 Board of Trade Bldg Norfolk VA 23510*

STANISLAUS, DOROTHY JEANNE HERRINGTON (MRS. DOYLE STANISLAUS), polit. party ofcl.; b. Tulsa, Sept. 8, 1925; d. Van Dolph and Sibyl (Schuler) Herrington; grad. Stephens Coll., 1943; student Okla. U., 1944-45; m. Doyle Stanislaus, June 2, 1945. Vice-chmn. Okla. Republican party, 1965-69; del. nat. conv., mem. nat. platform com., 1964; mem. Rep. Nat. Com., 1968—. Mem. Delta Delta Delta. Home: 1381 E 26th St Tulsa OK 74114

STANLEY, CARL MEADOWS, lumber co. exec.; b. Spencer, Tenn., May 27, 1935; s. John Kendrick and Mary R. (Bennett) S.; B.S., Tenn. Tech. U., 1955; m. Reita Chandler, Sept. 17, 1954; children—Shannon Stanley, Mary Ann. Staff auditor Ernst & Ernst, McMinnville, Tenn., 1960-63; exec. v.p. Burroughs-Ross-Colville Co., McMinnville, 1963—; dir. Whitson Land Co., McMinnville, 1st Nat. Bank, McMinnville. Pres. United Givers Fund, 1967-69. Govs. campaign mgr. Dem. Party, 1964. Served with AUS, 1957-59. Named Outstanding Young Man of Year, Jaycees, 1968. Mem. Jr. C. of C. (pres. 1962). Mem. Ch. of Christ. Rotarian. Home: 318 Post Rd McMinnville TN 37110 Office: 301 Depot St McMinnville TN 37110

STANLEY, CURTIS E., educator; b. Valdosta, Ga., Mar. 26, 1917; s. Odis and Emma (Byron) S.; A.B., Johnson C. Smith U., 1939; M.A., Fisk U., 1949; postgrad. U. Pitts., 1951-54, N.Y. U., 1959, 65; LL.D., Daniel Payne Coll., 1972; m. Louise Murray, Feb. 3, 1943. Dist. mgr. Afro Am. Life Ins. Co., 1946-47; prin. Darwin High Sch., Cookeville, Tenn., 1948-52, Washington High Sch., Blakely, Ga., 1952-60; freshman dean Ala. State U., Montgomery, 1960-63, asso. prof. edn., 1953—. Dir. Am. Cancer Soc., 1954-56, Ala. State U. Credit Union, 1961-69. Served to 1st lt. AUS, 1942-46; PTO. Mem. Ga. Tchrs. and Ednl. Assn., Am. Assn. U. Profs., N.E.A., Assn. for Supervision and Curriculum Devel., Ala. Edn. Assn., Omega Psi Phi. Mem. A.M.E. Ch. (steward 1960—). Elk, Mason (32 deg., Shriner). Home: 2952 Vandy Dr Montgomery AL 36110

STANLEY, DAVID TAYLOR, researcher; b. East Orange, N.J., Aug. 18, 1916; s. Edward Otis and Mary (Taylor) S.; A.B., Princeton, 1937; M.A., Am. U., 1961; m. Helen H. Swan, Apr. 19, 1941; children—David H., Margaret (Mrs. K. Peter Henrickson), Mary Elizabeth. Personnel officer FCA, 1938-42, VA, 1946-48, Dept. Def., 1948-53; mgmt. analyst AEC, 1953-56, Pub. Health Service, 1956-58; dir. mgmt. policy Dept. Health Edn. and Welfare, 1958-61; sr. fellow Brookings Instn., Washington, 1961—. Served with USAAF, 1942-45. Named Layman of Year, Greater Washington Assn. Unitarian Universalist Chs., 1968. Mem. Am. Polit. Sci. Assn., Am. Soc. Pub. Adminstrn., Soc. Personnel Adminstrn., Pub. Personnel Assn. Unitarian (chmn. commn. appraisal 1961). Author: Professional Personnel for the City New York, 1963; The Higher Civil Service, 1964; Changing Administrations, 1965; Men Who Govern, 1967; Bankruptcy: Problem, Process, Reform, 1971; Managing Local Government Under Union Pressure, 1972. Home: 1720 Brookside Lane Vienna VA 22180 Office: 1775 Massachusetts Av NW Washington DC 20036

STANLEY, DOROTHY EVELYN, educator, artist, author, lectr.; b. Nuremberg, Germany, Sept. 18, 1909; d. William H. Sellings and Lucie (Danziger) Peiser; came to U.S., 1937, naturalized, 1943; B.A., Maidenhead Coll., London, 1928; M.A., Hunter Coll., 1951; postgrad. Columbia, 1946-47, U. Heidelberg, U. Munich, U. Paris, 1930-34; m. Jan. 31, 1932; children—Brigitte Strauss (Mrs. Peter A. Saunders), Frank Strauss. Head proofroom George Grady Press, N.Y.C., 1939-42; asst. head monitoring sect. Overseas Radio div. U.S. State Dept., N.Y.C., 1942-45; tchr. French, English, Lycee Francais, N.Y.C., 1945-46; tchr. French, Latin, Acad. Sacred Heart, N.Y.C., 1946-49; tchr. French, German, Acad. Lang., N.Y.C., 1949-52; translator, interpreter 1st Nat. City Bank N.Y., 1952-59; asst. prof. modern langs. Old Dominion U., Norfolk, Va., 1960—. Exhibitor art galleries N.Y.C., 1954-59, Va., 1960—; lectr. creative living, 1959—; translator local orgns., bus., 1940. Recipient Grand Nat. Finalist award Am. Artists Profl. League, 1956, 57. Mem. Tidewater Artists Assn., Am. Assn. U. Women, Alliance Francaise, Norfolk Mus. Lutheran. Author: Die Kunterbunte Spielkiste, 1929, Das Lustige Kinderbuch, 1931, They Call It Courage, 1968. Home: 1349 Buckingham Av Norfolk VA 23508

STANLEY, DUFFY BROCK, architect; b. Midland, Tex., Feb. 14, 1923; s. Benjamin M. and Mary (White) S.; student Tex. A. and M. U., 1941-43, B.Arch., 1948; m. Irene Marie Muller, July 31, 1948; children— Sheila, Lars, Brock, Sonya, Sharon. Draftsman-designer J.J. Black, Architect, Midland, 1948-51; job capt. Carroll & Daeuble, Architects, El Paso, Tex., 1951-57; prin. Duffy B. Stanley, Architects, El Paso, 1957—. Mem. El Paso Zoning Bd. Adjustment, 1959-69, chmn., 1970; mem. Open Space Com. El Paso, 1970-71; vice chmn. Citizens Environmental Council, 1971. Served to capt. AUS, 1943-46. Decorated Bronze Star, Silver Star. Presbyn. Mason. Author: Open Space in the El Paso Region, 1970. Home: 3120 Wheeling St El Paso TX 79930 Office: Bassett Tower El Paso TX 79901

STANLEY, EARL R., lawyer; b. Windham, O., Mar. 8, 1921; s. Harry Grimm and Grace (Waller) S.; B.S., Kent State U., 1943; J.D. with honors, George Washington U., 1949, LL.M., 1950; m. Alberta R. Royal, Jan. 29, 1945; children—Ann Royal, Margaret Alison. Admitted to D.C. bar, 1949; atty. adviser FCC, Washington, 1949-53; asso. firm Dow, Lohnes & Albertson, Washington, 1953-54; partner, 1954—. Served with USNR, 1943-46; PTO. Mem. Am., Fed., FCC, D.C. bar assns., George Washington Law Assn., S.A.R. Delta Theta Phi (nat. chancellor). Mason (Shriner). Contbr. articles to profl. jours. Home: 11005 Stanmore Dr Potomac MD 20854 Office: 1225 Connecticut Av NW Washington DC 20036

STANLEY, EDWIN M(ONROE), dist. judge; b. Forsyth County, N.C., Mar. 9, 1909; s. John Brantson and Nettie Louise (Atkins) S.; LL.B., Wake Forest Coll., 1931, LL.D., 1964; m. To Lottie Belle Myers, June 30, 1933; children—Susanne and Robert Myers (twins). Admitted to N.C. bar, 1930, practiced in Greensboro, 1931-54; judge Greensboro Juvenile Ct., 1951-54; U.S. atty. Middle Dist. N.C., 1954-57, U.S. dist. judge, 1957—, chief judge, 1961—. Mem. com. on trial practice and technique Jud. Conf. U.S., 1965-68, com. on ct. adminstrn., 1969—; mem. Adv. Com. on Innovation and Devels. Fed. Jud. Center, 1968—. Trustee Wake Forest U., bd. visitors Sch. Law, 1964—, chmn., 1968—. Mem. Am., N.C., Greensboro bar assns., Gen. Alumni Assn. Wake Forest Coll. (pres. 1953). Baptist (deacon). Club: Civitan (past pres.). Home: 107 E Greenway South Greensboro NC 27402

STANLEY, ELIOT HUNGERFORD, found. exec.; b. Baton Rouge, Jan. 4, 1942; s. Allan John and Ruth (Moore) S.; B.A. cum laude, Harvard, 1963; J.D., George Washington U., 1972; m. Nancy Elizabeth Schmid, Aug. 27, 1966. Asst. to dir. Oklahoma City Urban Renewal Authority, 1963-64; legislative asst. for urban affairs U.S. Senator Fred R. Harris, 1964-65; spl. asst. for legislation Office Sec., U.S. Dept. Housing and Urban Devel., 1965-66; adminstrv. asst. Hon. B.S. Farnum, Mich., 1966-67; adminstrv. asst. U.S. rep. Chet Holifield of Cal., Washington, 1967-69; asso. dir. Citizens Adv. Center, Washington, 1971—. Mem. Seminar on Nat. Security and Budget Priorities, Brookings Instn., Washington, 1969-70. Mem. advance staff 1968 Democratic presdl. nominee Hubert H. Humphrey, 1970 staff R. Sargent Shriver. Mem. bd. Housing Opportunities Made Equal, Oklahoma City, 1963-64. Mem. Am. Polit. Sci. Assn. Unitarian. Home: 2818 Connecticut Av NW Washington DC 20008 Office: Assns Bldg 1145 19th St NW Washington DC 20036

STANLEY, GORDON LAMBERT, JR., textile co. exec.; b. Danvers, Mass., Feb. 8, 1938; s. Gordon L. and Clara M. (McFarland) S.; B.S., Presbyn. Coll., 1960; m. Mary Nancy Youngblood, June 27, 1959; children—Gordon Lambert III, Jeffrey Craig. Supt., Deering-Milliken, Union, S.C., 1960-68; plant mgr. Beaunit Textiles, Clinton, N.C., 1968—. Mem. Tuscarora Council Exec. Bd., 1968—. Mem. C. of C. (com. chmn. 1970), Jr. C. of C. (treas. 1963-64). Mason, Elk, Rotarian, Lion. Home: 600 Allen St Clinton NC 28328 Office: PO Box 1069 Clinton NC 28328

STANLEY, JAMES GORDON, engring. marketing mgr.; b. Birmingham, Ala., Feb. 13, 1925; s. Joseph Gordon and Amy I. (Crocker) S.; B.S., U. Ala., 1949; m. children—Cynthia Ruth, Pamela Anne, Gordon Bruce, James Alan, Joseph Christopher; m. 2d, Patricia Ann Peuvion, 1969. Instr. Miss. State U. Extension, Jackson, 1956; tech. rep. S.E., Price Brothers Co., Dayton, 1957-59; project mgr., dept. mgr. Brown Engring. Co., Kennedy Space Center, Fla. and Huntsville, Ala., 1959-64; dir. engring., reliability Bendix Launch Support Div., 1964-67; mgr. reliability, systems engr. Dow Chem. Co., Kennedy Space Center, 1967-71, mgr. engring. marketing, Houston, 1971—. Served to lt. (j.g.) USNR), 1943-66. Mem. Cocoa Beach C. of C., Phi Gamma Delta. Democrat. Baptist. Home: 2334 Greyburn Lane Houston TX 77055 Office: 3636 Richmond Av Houston TX 77027

STANLEY, JOE ANDREW, san. engr.; b. Ft. Worth, Sept. 30, 1915; s. Joseph Andrew and Florence (Lewis) S.; student Sul Ross Coll., 1933-35; grad. Tex. Technol. Coll., 1939; postgrad. Vanderbilt U., 1940; m. Mildred Dutton Knox, July 28, 1940; children—Carole Ann, Joseph A. III. Jr. engr. Tex. Hwy. Dept., Pecos, Odessa, 1937-40; jr. engr., dist. san. engr. Tex. Dept. Health, Lubbock, 1940-46; san. engr. City of Lubbock, 1946-47; owner-mgr. Hygeia Bottled Water Co., Lubbock, 1947—; owner Hygeia Sprinkler & Equipment Co., Lubbock, 1949—. Chmn., City County Bd. Health, Lubbock, 1951-54; mem., chmn. Municipal Utilities Bd., 1959-65; chmn. City-County Health Bd., Lubbock, 1966-68; chmn. Citizens Adv. Com., 1966-69. Del., Tex. State Democratic Conv., 1954; mem., sec. bd. mgrs. Lubbock County Hosp. Dist., 1968—. Bd. dirs., sec.-treas. bd. Lubbock Boys Clubs, 1968—; pres. bd. dirs. YMCA, 1957. Served with USPHS, 1954-56. Named One of 5 Outstanding Young Men, Tex. Jr. C. of C., 1946; Engr. of Year, 1970. Mem. Nat., Tex. socs. profl. engrs., Am. (pres. 1966, sec.-treas. 1967), Tex. (pres. 1963, 65) bottled water assns., Tex. Turf Irrigation Assn. (pres. 1967), Am. Water Works Assn., Sales and Marketing Execs. Internat., Phi Kappa Psi. Baptist. Rotarian, Mason. Clubs: Lubbock, Lubbock Country. Patentee water purification equipment. Home: 28 Country Pl Lubbock TX 79407 Office: 405 Av U Lubbock TX 79401

STANLEY, LILA GAIL, polit. scientist; b. Marietta, Ga., Mar. 23, 1941; d. James Miller and Louise (Land) Stanley; A.B., Randolph-Macon Woman's Coll., 1963; M.A., Emory U., 1964; postgrad. Am. U., 1967-68. Instr. polit. sci. W. Ga. Coll., Carrollton, 1964-66; tchr. Am. history dept. Foxcroft Sch., Middleburg, Va., 1966-67; staff asst., caseworker Congressman John J. Flynt, Jr., Washington, 1967—. Mem. Am., So. polit. sci. assns., D.A.R., Phi Sigma Alpha, Zeta Tau Alpha. Democrat. Methodist. Home: 2450 Virginia Av NW Washington DC 20037 also 297 Freyer Dr Marietta GA 30060 Office: Rayburn House Office Bldg Washington DC 20515

STANLEY, ROBERT ALTON, educator; b. Steiner, Tex., May 3, 1917; s. Lawrence B. and Margie K. (Adcock) S.; B.S., N. Tex. State U., 1946; M.A., Sul Ross State Coll., 1949; m. Anna Marie Seljos, Dec. 23, 1938; children—Lee Burnett, Randall Leighton, Warren Llewellyn. Tchr. pub. schs. Tex., 1937-42; prin. high sch. Granfills Gap, Tex., 1946-51, Brewer High Sch., Fort Worth, 1951-58; supt. Granbury Ind. Sch. (Tex.), 1958-71; tchr. Cleburn (Tex.) Ind. Sch. Dist., 1971—. Served with C.E., AUS, 1942-46; PTO. Mem. Tex. Tchrs. Assn., Tex. Assn. Sch. Adminstrs., N.E.A., Am. Iris Soc., Am. Assn. Sch. Adminstrs. Home: 1210 Hemphill Cleburne TX 76031 Office: 810 E Willingham Cleburne TX 76031

STANLEY, THOMAS GRANVILLE, dentist; b. Maryville, Tenn., Dec. 12, 1906; s. Oliver Thomas and Ida Jane (Seaton) S.; student Maryville Coll., 1925-28; D.D.S., U. Tenn., 1932; m. Barbara Spear Chisholm, Aug. 9, 1937; children—David Granville, John Oliver, Thomas Chisholm, Stephen Daniel, Muriel Anne. Intern, Forsyth Infirmary for Children, Boston, 1932-33; pvt. practice dentistry, Maryville, 1933—; mem. staff Blount Meml. Hosp. Pres., Maryville High Sch. P.T.A., 1956-57; active Boy Scouts Am.; mem. Maryville City Sch. Bd., 1955-71. Served to maj. AUS, 1942-46. Mem. Am. Dental Assn., Second Dist. Dental Soc., Xi Psi Phi. Republican. Methodist (lay witness worker 1967—). Mason. Home: 1501 Robin Rd Maryville TN 37801 Office: 301 Gamble Bldg Maryville TN 37801

STANLEY, THOMAS HIRAM, beverage co. exec.; b. Wayne County, Miss., Dec. 1, 1895; s. George S. and Albany (Gatlin) S.; student Miss. So. Coll., 1912-15; A.B., Miss. Coll., 1926; m. Bonnie Martin, Sept. 29, 1917. Sch. tchr., supt. schs., Miss., 1915-29; in soft drink bus., Alexandria, La., 1929-30; with Royal Crown Cola Co., Columbus, Ga., 1930—, v.p., 1940-55, dir., 1945—, chmn. exec. com., 1955, chmn. bd., 1965-60; pres. Am. Fed. Savs. & Loan Assn.; mem. adv. bd. First Nat. Bank. Pres., United Givers; pres. bd. Bapt. Village; pres. Muscogee County Bd. Edn.; chmn. bd. regents U. Systems of Ga. Trustee Mercer U., Tift Coll., So. Bapt. Theol. Sem. Mem. Omega Delta Kappa. Baptist (deacon). Kiwanian. Club: Gridiron of Ga. (Athens). Home: 2501 Lookout Dr Columbus GA 31906

STANLEY, WILLIAM DANIEL, educator; b. Bladenboro, N.C., June 13, 1937; s. John D. and Sallie (Dowless) S.; B.S., U. S.C., 1960; M.S., N.C. State U., 1962, Ph.D., 1963; m. Mary Louise Nichols, Aug. 26, 1962; 1 dau., Karen Louise. Devel. engr. Elecro-Mech. Research, Inc., Sarasota, Fla., 1963; asst. prof. Clemson (S.C.) U., 1964-66; asso. prof. elec. engring. Old Dominion U., Norfolk, Va., 1966-72, prof., 1972—, dir. grad. program elec. engring., 1969-70, chmn. dept. engring. tech., 1970—. Cons. NASA, Hampton, 1967-69. Mem. Am. Soc. Engring. Edn., I.E.E.E. (subsect. program chmn. 1966), Phi Beta Kappa, Sigma Xi, Phi Kappa Phi, Tau Beta Pi, Eta Kappa Nu, Pi Mu Epsilon. Author: Transform Circuit Analysis for Engineering and Technology, 1968. Home: 1315 Milton St Norfolk VA 23505

STANONIS, FRANCIS LEE, geologist; b. Louisville, July 9, 1931; s. Frank and Lelia (Lehman) S.; B.S., U. Ky., 1951, M.S., 1956; Ph.D., Pa. State U., 1958; m. Gia Denton Nicholson, July 7, 1956; children—Frank L., Virginia N. Owner, Frank L. Stanonis Oil Co., Henderson, Ky., 1964—; pres. Enviro-Sci. Corp., Evansville, Ind., 1970—. Asso. prof. geology and geography Ind. State U., Evansville, 1969—. Served with inf. AUS, 1951-53. Mem. Am. Inst. Profl. Geologists, Am. Inst. Mining and Metal. Engrs., Geol. Soc. Am., Geol. Soc. Ky., Geol. Soc. Ill., A.A.A.S., Sigma Zeta, Alpha Chi Sigma. Home: 142 N Arlington St Henderson KY 42420

STANS, MAURICE HUBERT, sec. of commerce; b. Shakopee, Minn., Mar. 22, 1908; s. J. Hubert and Mathilda (Nyssen) S.; student Northwestern, 1925-28, Columbia, 1928-30; LL.D., Ill. Wesleyan U., 1954, Northwestern U., 1960, DePaul U., 1960; D.P.A., Parsons Coll., 1960; LL.D., Grove City Coll., St. Anselm's Coll., 1969, U. San Diego, Gustavus Adolphus, Pomona Coll., 1970; m. Kathleen Carmody, Sept. 7, 1933; children—Steven, Maureen, Theodore, Terrell. Joined Alexander Grant & Co., C.P.A.'s, Chgo., 1928, exec. partner, 1940-55; treas., dir. Moore Corp., stove mfrs., Joliet, Ill., 1938-45, chmn. bd. 1942-45; dir., mem. exec. com. James Talcott, Inc., N.Y.C., 1941-55; financial cons. to postmaster gen. U.S., 1953-55; dep. postmaster gen. U.S., 1955-57; dep. dir. Bur. Budget, 1957-58, dir., 1958-61; pres. Western Bancorp., Los Angeles, vice chmn., dir. United Cal. Bank, 1961-62; syndicated columnist, 1961-62; sr. partner William R. Staats & Co., 1963-64; pres. William R. Staats Co., Inc., 1964-65, Glore Forgan, William R. Staats, Inc., N.Y.C., 1965-69; sec. commerce, 1969—. Founder, pres., dir. Stans Found. Chgo. Trustee Tax Found. Recipient Gt. Living Am. award U.S. C. of C., 1961; named to Accounting Hall Fame, 1960. C.P.A., N.Y., Ohio, Ill., Wis., Minn., Ind., Cal., Va. Mem. Am. Inst. C.P.A.'s (pres. 1954-55, Ann. award 1954), Ill., N.Y., Cal., Hawaii socs. C.P.A.'s, Nat. Assn. Accountants, Am. Accounting Assn. (nat. Alpha Kappa Psi award 1952, Ann. award 1952), Am. Soc. Pub. Adminstrn., Fed. Govt. Accountants Assn., D.C. Inst. C.P.A.'s, Nat. Assn. Postmasters, Am. Soc. for Pub. Adminstrn., Iron Moulders and Foundry Workers Union (hon.). Clubs: Economic, Union League, Adventurers (Chgo.); California (Los Angeles): Shikar-Safari, East African Professional Hunters (hon.), Explorers (N.Y.C.); Safari, Capitol Hill (Washington); Recess, Metropolitan (past gov.) (N.Y.C.). Home: 2500 Virginia Av NW Washington DC 20037 Office: Dept Commerce Washington DC 20230

STANSBURY, WILLIAM P., b. Middleport, O.; student Ohio State U., Ohio U.; Ph.G., U. Denver; m. Helen Halterman S., Nov. 3, 1940; children—C. William, Jacqueline Sue. Vice pres., gen. mgr. Eckerd Drugs of Fla., Clearwater, 1952-67, ret. as exec. v.p., 1968; now operating Four S Farms, saddlebred horses and hybrid cattle, Hernando, Fla. and Burgin, Ky.; dir. Farmers Nat. Life Ins. Co., St. Petersburg, Fla., Dr. Chateliers Plant Food Co.; prin. owner, pres. W.P. Stansbury & Assos., Inc., Hernando; chmn. bd. Oakwood Inc., Hernando. Served from pvt. to capt. Med. Adminstrn. Corps., AUS, 1942-46. Address: PO Box 207 Hernando FL 32642

STANTON, ROBERT LOWELL, physician; b. Des Moines, Feb. 18, 1924; s. Judson Horatio and Ozella (Hull) S.; B.S., U. Miami, 1948; M.D., Temple U., 1953; m. Betty Mae Tyrell Phillips, Sept. 15, 1945; children— Michael Phillips, Peter Wares, Scott Hull. Intern Temple U. Hosp., Phila., 1953-54; resident Dade County Hosp., Miami, Fla., 1954-55, resident internal medicine, VA Hosp., Miami, 1955-56; practice medicine, specializing in family practice, Miami, 1957—; mem. sr. attending med. staff, mem. med. bd. Variety Children's Hosp., Miami; mem. staff Baptist Hosp., Miami. Served with USNR, 1942-45. Decorated Silver Star. Mem. A.M.A., Dade County, Fla. med. assns., So. Med. Group (founder), Am. Acad. Gen. Practice, Beta Beta Beta, Alpha Epsilon Delta, Phi Chi. Unitarian (pres. congregation). Club: Kings Bay Yacht (Miami). Home: 9430 SW 53d St Miami FL 33165 Office: 9090 SW 87th Ct Miami FL 33156

STAPH, HORACE EUGENE, research lubrication engr.; b. Petrolia, Tex., Jan 8, 1921; s. Eugene William and Alice (Dammer) S.; B.S., Rice Inst., 1943; M.S., U. Tex., 1951; Ph.D., U. Minn., 1959; m. Rachel Evelyn Ruth, June 29, 1950; children—Catherine, Dana, Eric. Design draftsman Douglas Aircraft Co., Long Beach, Cal., 1943-45; instr. U. Tex., Austin, 1946-51, asst. prof., 1951-60; lectr. U. Minn., Mpls., 1953-55; sr. research engr. S.W. Research Inst., San Antonio, 1960—. Cubmaster, Boy Scouts of Am., 1966-69. Served with AUS, 1945-46. Mem. Am. Soc. M.E., Am. Soc. Lubrication Engrs., Sigma Xi, Tau Beta Pi, Pi Tau Sigma. Lutheran. Home: 6526 Redbird Lane San Antonio TX 78228 Office: 8500 Culebra Rd San Antonio TX 78228

STAPLES, EUGENE LEO, hosp. adminstr.; b. Walker, Minn., Aug. 26, 1926; s. Frank August and Elizabeth Josephine (Leibl) S.; B.A., U. Minn., 1950, M.H.A., 1952; m. Noreen Janice Henry, June 23, 1951; 1 dau., Barbara Elizabeth. Resident in hosp. adminstrn. U. Minn., 1951-52; adminstrv. asst. U. Minn. Hosp., Mpls., 1952-53, asst. to dir., 1953-55, asst. dir., also asst. prof., 1955-60; dir. W.Va. U. Hosps., Morgantown, 1960—. Bd. dirs. Morgantown Hosp. Service, 1966—; mem. adv. bd. W.Va. Health Dept., 1968—; mem. NIH Council on Edn. for Health Professions, 1966-72, NIH site teams, 1969—; cons. NIH, 1972—; mem. W.Va. Regional Med. Program adv. group, 1968, W.Va. Adv. Council for Comprehensive Health Care, 1969-70. Active United Fund, Am. Cancer Soc. Mem. W.Va. Gov.'s Adv. Commn. on Salaries, 1966-67. Bd. dirs. W.Va. Hosp. Research and Edn. Found., pres., 1962—. Served with USNR, 1944-46. Fellow Am. Coll. Hosp. Adminstrs. (regent 1972); mem. Am. (Blue Cross council; del. at large 1963-66), W.va. (dir. 1962—, pres. 1969-71) hosp. assns., Ohio Valley Hosp. Council (pres. 1965-66), Southeastern Hosp. Conf. (dir. 1971-72), Blue Cross Assn. (Medicare provider appeals com.). Home: 665 Bellaire Dr Morgantown WV 26505 Office: West Virginia U Hosp Morgantown WV 26506

STAPLES, WILLIAM RUSSELL, oral-maxillo-facial surgeon; b. Rumford, Me., Nov. 28, 1922; s. Russell James and Mildred Bernice (Westcott) S.; D.M.D., Tufts U., 1946; postgrad. Naval Dental Sch., 1950-52, Georgetown U., 1951-52, Temple U., 1955-56; m. Alice Elizabeth Maynard, July 27, 1946; children—Jane Elizabeth (Mrs. George Thomas Gantt), David William. Enlisted U.S. Navy, 1942, commd. ensign, 1943, advanced through grades to capt., 1962, ret. 1966; faculty Emory U., 1966-67; practice oral-maxillo facial surgery, Jacksonville, Fla., 1967—. Mem. Am., Fla. dental assns., Southeastern Soc. of Oral Surgeons, Am. Dental Soc. of Anesthesiology, Am., Fla. socs. oral surgeons. Mason. Club: Hidden Hills Country (Jacksonville). Contbr. articles to profl. jours. Home: 4005 Cove St Johns Rd Jacksonville FL 32211 Office: 3434 Atlantic Blvd Jacksonville FL 32207

STAPP, WILLIE LEE BROOME (MRS. CARL HERBERT STAPP), accountant; b. Snyder, Okla., Mar. 4, 1913; d. William Benjamin and Kate (Ross) Broome; grad. Draughon's Bus. U., 1935; student Okla. State U. Extension Div., 1936-37; m. Carl Herbert Stapp, Nov. 23, 1938; children—Bruce Michael, Patricia Kay (Mrs. Bert Walker, Jr.), Roger Leon. Sec., Rev. H. C. Ownbey, Bible Bapt. Ch., Oklahoma City, 1935-36; with Okla. Edn. Assn., Norman, 1935-36; office sec. Okla. Congress of Parents and Tchrs., Norman, 1936-44, asso. exec. sec., 1957-59, exec. sec., 1959-69; asst. editor, bus. mgr. Okla. Parent-Tchr., Norman, 1936-44, mng. editor, 1963-69; real estate saleslady Carl H. Stapp Co., Oklahoma City, 1948-56; accountant athletic dept. U. Okla., 1969—. Mem. Okla. Congress Parents and Tchrs. (life), Okla. Edn. Assn. (asso.). Baptist. Mem. Order Eastern Star. Home: 200 W Symmes St Norman OK 73069 Office: 180 W Brooks St Norman OK 73069

STARK, CARL ELLROY, physician; b. Poughkeepsie, N.Y., Sept. 28, 1921; s. Howard Cyrus and Hilda Mary (Roe) S.; B.S., U. Va., 1948, M.D., 1952; m. Katharine Grason Reynolds, June 14, 1947; children— Katharine Blair, Hilda Roe. Chemist Naval Research Lab.,

Washington, 1942; biochem. pollution cons. Am. Viscose, Front Royal, Va., 1948; intern Reading (Pa.) Hosp., 1952, resident, 1952-53; gen. practice medicine, Wytheville, Va., 1953—; mem. staff Chatwood Meml. Hosp., Wytheville Hosp., Pulaski (Va.) Hosp. Bd. dirs. Chitwood Meml. Hosp. Corp., pres., 1968; bd. dirs. Mt. Rogers Devel. Corp., Marion, Va., 1967-68; med. examiner State of Va., 1964—. Chmn. Wythe-Bland Water and Sewer Authority, 1967—; chmn. Mt. Rogers Regional Planning Commn., 1968-71; 2d. v.p. Great Lakes to Fla. Hwy. Assn., 1968-71; 1st v.p. Va. Municipal League, 1971-72; mem. adv. com. emergency med. service Commonwealth Va., 1968-71, mem. govs. adv. com. state and local affairs, 1970-71; mayor Town of Wytheville, 1962—. Bd. dirs. Upward-Bound Va. Poly. Inst., Mountain Community Action Program. Served with AUS, 1943-46. Decorated Corix De Guerre (Belgium). Mem. State Soc. S.A.R. (pres. 1971-72), Southwestern Va. Med. Soc. (pres. 1967-68), Va. State Med. Soc. (dir.), Wythe Baseball Assn. (exec. mem. 1968-71), Med. Soc. Va. (pres. 1972—), Va. Farm Bur., V.F.W., Iron Boot Soc., Soiree Soc., Phi Chi, Sigma Alpha Epsilon. Episcopalian (lay reader, vestryman 1952, exec. com. 1968-71). Mason, Lion; mem. Order Eastern Star (worthy patron 1966, 70). Home: 805 W Fulton St Wytheville VA 24382 Office: Main St Wytheville VA 24382

STARK, JOHN REGAN, govt. ofcl.; b. S.I., N.Y., Jan. 18, 1918; s. Raymond Sylvester and Mary Catherine (Regan) S.; B.A., Cornell U., 1938; M.A., N.Y. U., 1941; J.D., George Washington U., 1952; m. Edna Fay Kolberk, Dec. 28, 1940; children—Suzanne (Mrs. Richard Krause), Brian. Economist, U.S. Bur. Budget, Washington, 1946-56; admitted to Va. bar and D.C. bar; asst. dir. price div. Bur. Labor Statistics, Washington, 1956-57; individual practice law, Washington and McLean, Va., 1958-61; clk., economist Joint Econ. Com. U.S. Congress, Washington, 1961-64; gen. counsel Banking and Currency Com., U.S. Ho. of Reps., Washington, 1964-65; exec. dir. Joint Econ. Com., U.S. Congress, Washington, 1967—; prof. law George Washington U., Washington, 1965—. Served to lt. (j.g.) USCGR, 1942-46. Mem. Am., Fed. bar assns., Am. Soc. Pub. Adminstrn. Democrat. Unitarian. Author: (with Phillip B. Yeager) Your Inalienable Rights, 1959. Co-author syndicated column Law in the News, 1954-60. Contbr. articles to mags. and profl. jours. Home: 4815 Grantham Av Chevy Chase MD 20015 Office: New Senate Office Bldg Washington DC 20510

STARKS, FRANKLIN FERGUSON, JR., bldg. operations co. exec.; b. Louisville, Feb. 17, 1924; s. Franklin Ferguson and Mary Gunn (Powell) S.; grad. Woodberry Forest Sch., 1942; B.S., Yale, 1948; m. Noell Marvin, Dec. 8, 1951; children—Seashols Noell, Franklin Ferguson III, Henry Powell. With Starks Bldg. Co., Louisville, 1948—, sec., 1949-53, v.p., 1953-57, pres., 1957—. Dir. First Nat. Bank of Louisville, Ky. Trust Co., Louisville Investment Co. Bd. dirs., YMCA, 1966-71, Boy Scouts Am., 1962-69; pres. dirs. Child Guidance Clinic, 1950-71. Served with 11th Airborne div. Signal Corps, AUS, 1943-46; PTO. Mem. So. Conf. Bldg. Owners and Mgrs. (pres. 1957-58), Louisville Assn. Bldg. Owners and Mgrs., Louisville C. of C. (dir. 1971—), Louisville Central Area (dir. 1957-71). Rotarian. Clubs: Louisville Country, Pendennis (Louisville). Home: 512 Club Lane Louisville KY 40207 Office: 823 Starks Bldg Louisville KY 40202

STARKS, RALPH JAMES, research engr.; b. Gentry, Ark., July 2, 1923; s. David and Viola Ethyl (Boaz) S.; A.A., Joplin Jr. Coll., 1950; B.S. in Physics, Kan. State Coll., 1952, M.S. in Math., 1953, postgrad. in Solid State Physics, 1961-63; m. Mary Louisa McDaniel, Sept. 5, 1947; 1 son, Ralph James. Research engr. exploratory research sect. Joplin research dept. Eagle-Picher Industries, 1952-56, sr. research engr. Miami Research Labs. (Okla.), 1956-70, dir. research, 1970—. Served with USAAC, 1942-45; ETO Decorated Air medal with two oak leaf clusters. Mem. Am. Soc. for Testing and Materials, Am. Soc. for Quality Control, Am. Nuclear Soc., V.F.W. Mem. Christian Ch. (elder 1970—). Mason (32 deg., Shriner). Contbr. articles to profl. jours. Home: 2602 Illinois St Joplin MO 64801 Office: 200 Ninth Av N E Miami OK 74354Mailing address: PO Box 1090 Miami OK 74354

STARLING, JAMES HOLT, educator, biologist; b. Troy, Ala., June 28, 1912; s. James Jefferson and Minnie (Radford) S.; B.A., U. Ala., 1933, M.A.; 1937; Ph.D., Duke, 1942; student British Museum Natural History, summer 1953, Oak Ridge Inst. Nuclear Studies, summer 1961; m. Mary Nell Lewis, Nov. 14, 1936; 1 son, John Lewis. Sci. tchr. Troy High Sch., 1934-39; grad. asst. zoology Duke, 1939-42; mem. faculty Washington and Lee U., 1942—, prof. biology, 1951—, cordinator pre-med. studies, 1964—; vis. prof., cons. NSF Insts., summers 1955-65. Pres. Rockbridge Tb Assn., 1948-50; bd. dir. Va. Tb Assn., 1948-50. Served to capt. AUS, 1943-46. Mem. Va. Acad. Sci., A.A.A.S., Southeastern Biologists Assn., Sigma Xi, Alpha Epsilon Delta, Sigma Alpha Epsilon. Presbyn. (deacon, elder). Author research publs. Home: 207 Paxton Rd Lexington VA 24450

STARLING, THOMAS MADISON, educator; b. nr. Ridgeway, Va., Aug. 12, 1923; s. Leonard Anderson and Florine (Anderson) S.; B.S., Va. Poly. Inst., 1944; M.S., Ia. State U., 1947, Ph.D., 1955; m. Evelyn Cleo Barker, July 15, 1961; children—Sarah Beckwith, Linda Marie. Asst. prof. Va. Poly. Inst., Blacksburg, 1944-46, asso. prof., 1948-61, prof. agronomy, 1961-70, asso. dean grad. sch., 1970-71, prof. agronomy, 1971—. Mem. Am. Soc. Agronomy, Crop Sci. Soc. Am., A.A.A.S., Sigma Xi, Phi Kappa Phi, Alpha Zeta, Gamma Sigma Delta. Methodist. Lion (pres. 1961-62). Home: 618 Woodland Dr Blacksburg VA 24060

STARNES, BETTY TOWNSLEY HUGHEN (MRS. JAMES L. STARNES), lectr.; b. Wilson, Okla., Nov. 21, 1925; d. Roy and Maude (Rice) Hughen; B.S., Oklahoma City U., 1946; m. James L. Starnes; children—Courteney, Leslie, Bonnie, Mark, John, Teresa, Randy. Instr. biology lab. Oklahoma City U., 1946; tng. supr. retailing Maison Blanche, New Orleans, 1948; lectr. various profl., bus. orgns., social clubs, chs., schs. throughout U.S., 1949—; styling cons., lectr. Am. Airlines Stewardess Coll., 1958-60; lectr., styling cons., staff asst. Delta Airlines, 1960—. Chmn. bd. Meth. Children's Home. Mem. Order Flying Orchid, Cardinal Key, Internat. Platform Assn., Phi Gamma Mu, Beta Beta Beta. Address: 573 Papermill Rd Chattahoochee Plantation Marietta GA 30060

STARNES, JULIA BAYLIS, librarian; b. Columbia; d. Robert Jabus and Birdie (Warren) Baylis; student Whitworth Coll., Brookhaven, Miss.; degree in law library adminstrn., Columbia Univ., New York, N.Y., 1944 unmarried. Chief dep. sheriff's office, Marion County, Miss., 1932-36; claims examiner Miss. Unemployment Compensation Commn., Jackson, 1936-39,; librarian State of Miss., 1940—. Mem. Miss. State Bar (hon.). Am. Legion Aux. Democrat. Mem. Methodist Ch. Club: Mississippi Official Woman's Jackson. Home: Edwards Hotel Jackson MS Office: Mississippi State Law Library Jackson MS 39205

STARNES, RICHARD, newspaperman; b. Washington, July 4, 1922; s. John Irby and Eveline (Belt) S.; m. Nancy Ely, Mar. 15, 1947. With Scripps-Howard newspapers, 1938—, successively copy boy, reporter, asst. city editor, news editor, asst. mng. editor Washington Daily News, also corres. Scripps-Howard Newspaper Alliance, 1949-53, mng. editor N.Y. World-Telegram and Sun, 1953-60; daily syndicate columnist, 1960—. Clubs: Dutch Treat (N.Y.C.); Manhasset Bay Yacht (Port Washington, N.Y.); Nat. Press (Washington). Author: Requiem In Utopia, 1968; The Flypaper War, 1969. Office: 1013 13th St NW Washington DC 20005

STARNES, ROY GLENN, educator; b. Clyde, N.C., Mar. 8, 1914; s. John F. and Verna (Gillespie) S.; A.B., U. N.C., 1940; M.M.Ed., U. Mich., 1950. Music tchr. Angier (N.C.) Pub. Schs., 1940-41; choral music tchr. Burlington (N.C.) City Schs., 1946-49; choral music tchr. Balt. City Schs., 1950-51; choral dir., gen. music tchr. Durham (N.C.) High Sch., dir. vocal music edn. Durham City Schs., 1951—. Pres., Durham Civic Choral Soc.; pres. Durham chpt. N.C. Symphony Soc., 1962-64. Served with AUS, 1941-46. Mem. N.C. Music Educators Assn. (pres. 1958-61, chmn. ednl. affairs com. choral sect. 1970—) Music Educators Nat. Conf., N.E.A., N.C. Edn. Assn., Allied Arts of Durham, Am. Choral Dirs. Assn. Democrat. Methodist (choir dir. 1966-71). Home: 1008 Virgie St Durham NC 27705 Office: N Duke St Durham NC 27701

STARNES, WILLIAM HERBERT, JR., chemist; b. Knoxville, Tenn., Dec. 2, 1934; s. William Herbert and Edna (Osborne) S.; student Union Coll., 1950-52; B.S. with honors, Va. Poly. Inst., 1955; postgrad. Duke, 1955-56; Ph.D., Ga. Inst. Tech., 1960. Research chemist Humble Oil & Refining Co., Baytown, Tex., 1960-62, sr. research chemist, 1962-64; research specialist Esso Research & Engring. Co., Baytown, 1964-67, research asso., 1967-71; research fellow dept. chemistry U. Tex. at Austin, 1971—. Vis. scientist Tex. Acad. Sci., 1964-67. NSF fellow, 1958-60; recipient Monie A. Ferst Doctoral Research award, 1960, Profl. Progress award Soc. Profl. Chemists and Engrs., 1968. Mem. Am. Chem. Soc. (dir. Southeastern Tex. sect. 1970), A.A.A.S., Sigma Xi, Phi Kappa Phi, Phi Lambda Upsilon (pres. chpt. 1954-55). Methodist. Contbr. articles to profl. jours. Patentee in field. Home: No 112 1007 S Congress St Austin TX 78704

STARR, DAVID WRIGHT, educator; b. Anna, Tex., Dec. 8, 1912; s. Walter Benjamin and Edna Earle (Wright) S.; B.A., So. Meth. U., 1933; M.A., U. Ill., 1937, Ph.D., 1940; m. Elsie Ritchey, Nov. 23, 1961; children—(by previous marriage) David Wright, Sally (Mrs. Glenn Howard Tucker). Tchr., principal Sadler (Tex.) High Sch., 1933-34; tchr. Denison (Tex.) High Sch., 1934-37; asst. in math. U. Ill., Champaign-Urbana, 1938-40, fellow, 1937-38; instr. math. and aviation So. Meth. U., Dallas, 1940-43, coordinator aviation, 1941—, asst. prof. math., 1943-46, assoc. prof., 1946-48, prof., 1948—, chmn. dept. math., 1963—; coordinator CAA War Tng. Program, 1941-44. Fellow Tex. Acad. Scis.; mem. Am. Math. Soc., Math. Assn. Am. (chmn. Tex. sect. 1951-52), Nat. Council Tchrs. Math., Blue Key, Phi Beta Kappa, Kappa Mu Epsilon, Pi Mu Epsilon, Sigma Alpha Epsilon. Methodist. Mason, Lion. Contbr. articles to profl. jours. Home: 3503 Normandy St Dallas TX 75205

STARR, DOROTHY CLARA SIMPSON (MRS. RICHARD FRANCIS STRONG STARR), civic worker; b. Chgo., June 23, 1906; d. Elmer Ellsworth and Clara (Seacrist) Simpson; Ph.B. U. Chgo., 1929; m. Richard Francis Strong Starr, June 7, 1930; 1 son, Nicholas. Commr., No. Va. Regional Planning and Econ. Devel. Commn., 1956-64, chmn. commn., 1961-63; mem. Alexandria (Va.) Civil War Centennial Com., 1960-64, Urban Renewal Com., Alexandria, 1958, Nat. Capital Regional Planning Council, 1963-64; Gov.'s comm. Alexandria Hist. Restoration and Preservation Commn., 1964-71. Bd. govs. Archeol. Inst. Am., Washington, 1958-61, No. Va. Conservation Council, 1967-70. Recipient Citizenship Achievement award Civitan Club, 1958; certificate of recognition League Women Voters, 1963; Award of Distinction, U.S. Civil War Centennial Commn., 1964; Appreciation for Service certificates Nat. Capitol Regional Planning Council, 1964, No. Va. Regional Planning and Econ. Devel. Commn., 1964, City Alexandria, 1964; Dorothy C.S. Starr Library, Civil War research facility at Fort Ward dedicated by City Alexandria, 1971. Instrumental in pub. acquisition and preservation Ft. Marcy, Va., Ft. Ward, Va., and devel. City Park and Civil War Mus. complex, Alexandria. Home: PO Box 172 Upperville VA 22176

STARR, HOWARD ALLEN, educator; b. Waco, Tex., Apr. 7, 1938; s. Clarence J. and Ouida (Bowman) S.; B.A., U. Dallas, 1960; M.A., So. Meth. U., 1963; Ph.D., E. Tex. State U., 1969; m. Julie King Eliis, Aug. 1970. Tchr. biology Richardson (Tex.) High Sch., 1960-65, counselor, 1962-65; became admissions counselor Austin Coll., 1965, now asso. prof. psychology, chmn. dept. psychology and sociology, coordinator ednl. adv. system, 1970—, coordinator individual devel. program, 1972, coordinator mentor tng., 1972. Mem. Am., Tex. (pub. relations com.) personnel and guidance assns., Nat. Assn. Biology Tchrs., A.A.A.S., Tex. Tchrs. Assn., Am. (asso.), S. Western, Tex. (asso.) psychol. assns., Phi Delta Kappa, Kappa Delta Pi. Mem. Disciples of Christ Ch. Home: 1802 Skyline Dr Sherman TX 75090 Office: Austin Coll Dept Psychology Box 1595 Sherman TX 75090

STARR, STEVE DAWSON, photographer; b. Albuquerque, Sept. 6, 1944; s. Richard Vernon and Carol (Harley) S.; student Antioch Coll., 1962-63, Bethel Coll., 1963-64; B.A., San Jose State Coll., 1967; m. Marilynne Sue Anderson, Aug. 6, 1965; 1 son, Stephen Richard. Photographer San Jose (Cal.) Mercury-News, 1966-67; photographer, picture editor A.P., Recipient Pulitzer prize spot news photography, 1970, Nat. Headliners award, 1970, George Polk Meml. award, 1970, Pictures of the Year hon. mention, 1970. Mem. Nat. Press Photographers Assn., Sigma Delta Chi. Home: 2400 Northwest North River Dr Miami FL 33125 Office: 2125 Biscayne Bldg Miami FL 33137

STARR, WILLIAM JOSEPH, violinist, educator; b. Concordia, Kan., May 23, 1923; s. Robert Ellis and Katherine (Kelly) S.; B.Mus., Eastman Sch. Music, 1944, M.Mus., 1947; postgrad. DePaul U., 1948-49; m. Constance Koebelin, June 21, 1947; children—Kathleen, Teresa, Gregory, Timothy, Judith, William, Michael, David. Prin. violinist Denver Symphony, 1947-48; with fine arts dept. U. Tenn., 1949—, successively instr. 1949-51, asst. prof. 1951-56, asso. prof. 1956-62, prof., 1962—; program annotator Univ. FM Sta., 1961—; concertmaster Knoxville Symphony Orch., 1949—; guest instr. Talent Edn. Inst., Matsumoto, Japan, 1968-69, Asociacion Venezolana de Conciertos, Caracas, summer 1970. Bd. dirs. Knoxville Symphony Soc., 1951—, Newman Found., U. Tenn., 1958-60, Knoxville Montessori Assn., Talent Edn., U.S.A. Served to lt. (j.g.) USNR, 1944-46. Mem. Music Tchrs. Nat. Assn., Am. String Tchrs. Assn., C. of C., Phi Mu Alpha Sinfonia, Pi Kappa Lambda. Roman Catholic. K.C. Author: Scored for Listening, 1959; Perceiving Music, 1962; Music Scores Omnibus, 1962; Basic Piano Technique for Classroom Teachers, 1970. Home: 7225 Wellswood Lane Knoxville TN 37919

STASAVICH, BECKY ANN, ednl. adminstr.; b. Hickory, N.C., June 5, 1940; d. Clarence and Helen (Warlick) Stasavich; A.B. in English and history, Catawba Coll., 1961; M.A. in Edn. E. Carolina U., 1967. Tchr. English various high schs., Albemarle, N.C., 1961-66, Greenville, 1966-67; asso. dean students, instr. psychology Pfeiffer Coll., Misenheimer, N.C., 1967-72; asso. dean students Lenoir Rhyne Coll., Hickory, N.C., 1972—. Mem. Nat. N.C. (program com. chmn. 1970-71, mem. nominating com.) assns. women deans and counselors, Am. Personnel and Guidance Assn., Am. Coll. Personnel Assn., So. Coll. Personnel Assn., Alpha Delta Kappa (v.p. Xi chpt. 1972—). Democrat. Presbyn. Club: Pfeiffer Woman's (pres. 1969-71). Home: 47 Colonial House 818 2d Pl NE Hickory NC 28601

STASAVICH, CLARENCE, athletic dir.; b. Georgetown, Ill., Feb. 9, 1913; s. Walter and Alexandra (Vencka) S.; B.S., Lenoir Rhyne Coll., 1935; M.A., U. N.C., 1946; m. Helen Rebecca Warlick, Aug. 11, 1935; children—Rebecca Ann, Mary Helen, Walter Lewis. Coach football, basketball, baseball Campbell Coll., 1935-38; coach football, basketball, tennis Lenoir Rhyne Coll., 1938-42, dir. health, phys. edn., athletic dir., 1946-62; football coach, asso. prof. East Carolina Coll., Greenville, N.C., 1962—, athletic dir., 1963—. Served to lt. USNR, 1942-46. Named Football Coach of Year, Nat. Assn. Intercollegiate Athletics, 1959; Coll. Coach of Year, Am. Football Coaches Assn., 1964; named to Helms Hall of Fame, 1960. Mem. Am. Football Coaches Assn. (rules com.), Mu Sigma Epsilon. Democrat. Presbyn. (elder). Moose. Home: 205 Lewis St Greenville NC 27835

STATEN, GEORGE COWDEN, JR., architect; b. El Paso, Tex., July 2, 1931; s. George Cowden and Ruth (Cummings) S.; student U. Tex. at El Paso, 1949; B.A. (Jesse Jones scholar), Rice U., 1953, B.Arch., 1954; m. Shirley Gore, Oct. 11, 1958; children—Gregory Gore, James Burleson. Designer, Percy W. McGhee, Architect, El Paso, Tex., 1947-53; draftsman Dunaway and Jones Architects, Houston, 1953-54; designer, draftsman Carroll, Daeuble & Assos., Architects, El Paso, 1957-58; prin. George Staten, Jr., Architect, 1959-62; partner Middleton and Staten, Architects, 1962-68; partner Kuykendall, McCombs, Middleton & Staten, Architects, El Paso, Tex., 1969-70; prin. George Staten & Assos., Architects and Planners, 1970—. Mem. Zoning Bd. Adjustment, El Paso, 1959-70; co-chmn. Citizens Adv. Council, El Paso, 1955-56; bd. dirs. El Paso County Assn. for Blind, 1960-72, Am. Cancer Soc., El Paso, 1969-72. Served with USN, 1954-57; PTO. Recipient Walsh 2d prize Rice U., 1953, A.I.A. runner up award Henry Adams Fund, 1954. Mem. Navy League El Paso, Naval Reserve Assn., El Paso C. of C., A.I.A. (chpt. pres. 1969), Constrn. Specifications Inst. (pres. 1963-64), Tex. Soc. Architects (dir. 1972—), Sigma Alpha Epsilon. Kiwanian (dir. 1965). Home: 237 Viking Dr El Paso TX 79912 Office: Suite 225 Koger Bldg 444 Executive Center Blvd El Paso TX 79902

STATON, JON TOM, sch. adminstr.; b. Hollis, Okla., Jan. 7, 1933; s. William Francis and Sarah (Clark) S.; B.S., Okla. Bapt. U., 1956; Ed.M., U. Okla., 1959, Ed.D., 1962; m. Carolyn Brown, Sept. 28, 1954; children—Kelsey, Kevin, Sarah. Tchr. Caney High Sch., Caney, Kan., 1956-57, Roswell (N.M.) High Sch., 1957-60; Kellogg fellow U. Okla., 1960-61, dir. gen services, 1961-62; supt. schs., Mountain Grove, Mo., 1963-67, Muskogee, Okla., 1967—; vis. prof. sch. adminstrn, Drury Grad. Sch. Edn., 1965—. Bd. dirs. Okla. chpt. Soc. Crippled Children. Served with AUS, 1954-56. Mem. Am. Assn. Sch. Adminstrs. (life), Okla. Bapt. U. Alumni Athletic Assn. (pres.), N.E.A., Assn. Student Teaching, Am. Childhood Edn., Phi Delta Kappa. Rotarian. Home: 4301 W Broadway Muskogee OK 74401

STATON, WILLIAM WAYNE, state senator; b. Olive Branch, N.C., Oct. 11, 1916; s. Oscar M. and Addie Mae (Young) S.; B.S., Wake Forest Coll., 1938, J.D., 1941; grad. student U. N.C., 1946; m. Ellen Douglas Boone, June 28, 1947; children—William Wayne, Allyn Moore. Admitted to N.C. bar, 1941; practice in Sanford, 1946—; mem. firm Pittman, Staton & Betts, 1946—; county atty. Lee County, 1956-60; city atty., Sanford, 1963-66; now atty. Central Carolina Tech. Inst.; mem. N.C. senate, 1969—. Pres. Young Democratic Clubs N.C., 1952; asst. campaign mgr. Frank P. Graham for U.S. Senate, 1952; personal campaign mgr. Gov. Terry Sanford in elections, 1960; del. Nat. Dem. Conv.,Com., 1960-64; mem. Dem. Nat. Com. from N.C., 1962-66; member Ho. of Reps, N.C., 1966-68. Mem. N.C. Commn. Improved Cts., 1958, N.C. Vets. Commn., 1957-60; mem. N.C. Commn. for Rules of Civil Procedure, 1967-68; pres. Lee County United Fund; mem. N.C. Jud. Council, 1969—, N.C. Capitol Planning Commn., 1971—. Mem. exec. bd. Occoneechee council Boy Scouts Am., 1956—; trustee Wake Forest Coll., 1955—. Served to capt. F.A., AUS, 1942-46, ETO; col. N,C. N.G. Decorated Purple Heart, Bronze Star medal. Mem. Am., N.C., Lee County bar assns., Am. Legion (past judge advocate N.C.), Sanford C. of C. (past pres.), Omicron Delta Kappa. Baptist (past bd. deacons). Club: Sanford Executive (past pres.). Home: 636 Palmer Dr Sanford NC 27330 Office: 205 Courtland Dr Sanford NC 27330

STAUBER, LESLIE EDWIN, mfg. exec.; b. Rural Hall, N.C., Mar. 28, 1903; s. William Edwin and Lillian (Felts) S.; A.B., U. N.C., 1925; m. Jessie Louise Brown, May 10, 1930; children—Leslie Edwin, Barbara June (Mrs. Fred Mexwell Fultz). Owner, Rural Telephone Co., 1927-28; partner Rural Hall Veneer Co., 1928-53, owner, 1954—, mfr. wood veneers, 1928—, plywood, 1936—. Organizing mem., sec.-treas. Rural Hall San. Dist., 1938-50; charter mem. Rural Hall Fire Dept., 1938-50; justice of peace, 1932-34. Charter rep. from Moravian Ch. on com. Rural Hall Meml. Park. Club: Civic (pres. 1947). Home: Corner Broad and Wall Sts Rural Hall NC 27045 Office: 1st St Rural Hall NC 27045

STAVISKY, SAMUEL ELLIOT, pub. relations cons.; b. Chelsea, Mass., Dec. 6, 1914; s. Jacob Zedel and Jennie (Cohen) S.; B.S. in Journalism, Boston U., 1936; m. Bernice Ruth Seigle, Dec. 31, 1946; children— Robin, Judith. Reporter, editor, columnist Boston Am., Rochester (N.Y.) Jour., Washington Herald, Washington Post, 1933-54; pres. Samuel E. Stavisky & Asso., Inc., pub. relations, Washington, 1954—. Cons. Cuban Sugar Industry, U.S. Cuban Sugar Council, Banco Nacional de Cuba, 1954-60. Internat. Coffee Agreement, 1961-63, U.S. Cane Sugar Refiners Assn., Pan Am. Coffee Bur., 1963—, Colombian Center, N.Y.C., 1965-66; cons. govt. agys. and industry Mexico, Brazil, Colombia, Portugal, U.K.; exec. dir. World Coffee Information Center, Washington, 1965—. Served USMCR, 1942-45; PTO. Mem. Pub. Relations Soc. Am. Clubs: International, National Press, Broadcasters (Washington). Contbr. numerous articles to popular mags. Home: 7021 Oak Forest Lane Bethesda MD 20034 Office: 1100 17th St NW Washington DC 20036

STAYMAN, HAROLD WILLIAM, JR, civic orgn. exec.; b. Tamaqua, Pa., Mar. 27, 1933; s. Harold William and Elinor Mae (Wagner) S.; student U. Md., 1952-54, 56; m. Veronica Van Allen, Nov. 23, 1967; children—Veronica, Valerie Elizabeth. Nat. Yellow Page rep. So. Bell Telephone Co., Miami, Fla., 1957-65; from dir. pub. relations to exec. dir. Republican State Exec. Com., Fort Lauderdale, Fla., 1966-67; exec. dir. Fla. Turnpike Authority, Ft. Lauderdale, 1967-69, Fla. Council of 100, Tampa, 1970—; sec. dep. profl. and occupational regulation State of Fla., Tallahassee, 1969-70. Mem., dist. coordinator Fla. Gov.'s Com. for Employment of Handicapped, 1970—; founder, dir., vice chmn. Ams. for Constl. Action, 1965-68. Nat. committeeman Fla. Fedn. Young Republicans, 1965-66; 1st v.p. Dade County Young Rep. Club, 1965-66; founder, editor-in-chief Fla. Rep. Challenger (newspaper), 1966-67. Bd. dirs., treas. Fla.-Colombia Alliance. Served with AUS, 1953-57. Named One of Outstanding Young Men in Am., U.S. Jr. C. of C., 1969, Fla. Young Rep. of Year, Dade County Young Rep. Club, 1965. Mem. Fla. Pub. Relations Assn., Fla. Indsl. Devel. Council, Fla. Agrl. Bus. Inst., Fla. Soc. Assn. Execs., Confrerie de la Chaine des Rotisseurs. Clubs: Killearn Country

(Tallahassee); Executive (Orlando, Fla.). Home: 66 Adalia Av Tampa FL 33606 Office: 1211 N Westshore Blvd Suite 105 Tampa FL 33607

STEADMAN, GORDON WILLIAM, dentist; b. Toronto, Ont., Can., Apr. 11, 1923; s. Henry and Helena Mary (Paisley) S.; B.A., Columbia Union Coll., 1948; D.D.S., Emory U., 1956; m. Marie Romedy, Mar. 8, 1942; children—Nancy Sue, Kathy Marie, Gordon William. Tchr. sci. Duval County Sch. Bd., Jacksonville, Fla., 1948-52; gen. practice dentistry Jacksonville, 1956—. Pres. Duval County Dental Research Clinic, 1963. Charter chmn. Mayor's Health Adv. Bd., 1968; adviser Fla. Sch. Health Com., 1964-71. Served with AAC, 1942-44. Mem. Fla. Dental Soc. (alternate del., 1958; del. 1972), Emory U. Alumni Assn. (pres., 1962), Jacksonville Dental Soc. (pres., 1964), N.E. Dist. Dental Soc. (1st v.p.), Am. Dental Assn., Am. Dental Soc. Children, Jacksonville Area C. of C. (sec., 1971), Delta Sigma Delta. Lion (pres. 1968). Club: Seminole. Home: 1403 Azalea Dr Jacksonville FL 32205 Office: 2549 Park St Jacksonville FL 32204

STEAKLEY, ZOLLIE COFFER, JR, justice Supreme Ct. Tex.; b. Rotan, Tex., Aug. 29, 1908; s. Zollie Coffer and Frances Elizabeth (McGlasson) S.; B.A., Hardin-Simmons U., 1929, LL.D., 1959; J.D., U. Tex., 1932; LL.D., U. Corpus Christi, 1958; m. Ruth Butler, June 3, 1939. Admitted to Tex. bar, 1932; engaged in pvt. practice law, 1932-39, 46-57; asst. atty. gen. Tex., 1939-42; sec. state Tex., 1957-60; asso. justice Supreme Ct. Tex., Austin, 1961—. Served with Usnr, 1942-46. Mem. Am. Bar Assn., State Bar Tex., Philos. Soc. Tex. Democrat. Home: 3302 Mt Bonnell Dr Austin TX 78731 Office: Supreme Ct Bldg Austin TX 78711

STEARMAN, LEWIS ARTHUR, newspaper exec.; b. Alexandria, Va., Feb. 8, 1924; s. Joseph and Esther (Rose) S.; student pub. schs.; m. Mildred Ruth Myers, Oct. 8, 1950; children—David Warren, Douglas Alan, Joseph Michael. Mem. exec. staff Alexandria Gazette, 1940—, gen. mgr., 1952—, bus. editor, 1955, v.p., treas., 1966—, also dir.; dir. Park & Shop, Inc., Alexandria. Corp. mem. Alexandria Hosp. Corp., 1965—; mem. Friendship Fire Co. (life), 1953—. Bd. dirs. Am. Cancer Soc., Alexandria Boys Club (v.p.), Alexandria A.R.C., Mental Hygiene Adv. Bd., Alexandria Civic Orch., Salvation Army (pres. 1961-63). Pres., Alexandria Community Mental Health Center, 1968-69, Sr. Citizens Employment Service Alexandria, 1970-71; divisional v.p. Alexandria Bd. Trade, 1968-69. Recipient Outstanding Merit award in promoting better community relations Maurice D. Rosenberg Lodge B'nai B'rith, 1953; Outstanding Merit award Salvation Army Alexandria, 1959; Pub. Service award U.S. P.O., 1967; Community Service award Boys Clubs Am., 1971, others; named Man of Year, Salvation Army, 1965, 67. Mem. Retail Mchts. Assn. (sec.-treas., 1960-61), Alexandria (v.p. 1966-67), Fairfax County chambers commerce, Inst. Newspaper Controllers and Finance Officers (tech. adv. bd.), So. Newspaper Assn., Va. Press Assn., Nat. Press Club, Nat. Editorial Assn. Mem. B'nai B'rith (Outstanding Community Service award 1968, trustee lodge). Club: Optimist (Alexandria). Home: 6421 Bluebill Lane Alexandria VA 22307 Office: 717 North St Asaph St Alexandria VA 22313

STEBBINS, ROBERT HARNDEN, geologist; b. Boston, Nov. 14, 1924; s. George Hobart and Edna (Harnden) S.; B.S., Mass. Inst. Tech., 1950; M.A., Columbia, 1957; m. Elinor Fairchild, Sept. 8, 1950; children— Lorna, Paul, Rodger, John, Elin. Staff geologist State of Wash., Olympia, 1950-51; chief geologist Pend Oreille Mines & Metals, Metelin Falls, 1951-53; party chief U.S. Steel Co., B.C. and S.E. Alaska, 1954, exploration geologist Western U.S., S.E. Alaska, B.C., 1955-59; gen. mgr. Hunting Geophys. Services, N.Y.C., 1959-63; pres. Stebbins Mineral Survey, Old Greenwich, Conn., 1963-66; v.p. exploration Golf Resources & Chem. Corp., Houston, 1967—; dir. Bunker Hill, Kellogg, Ida.; pres., dir. GeoSensors, Dallas, Vanguard Exploration, Houston, Vangulf Exploration, Houston. Served with AC, AUS, 1942-46. Fellow Geol. Soc. Am., Geol. Soc. Can.; mem. A.A.A.S., Am. Inst. Mining Metall. and Petroleum Engrs., Geochem. Soc., Soc. Exploration Geophysicists, Soc. Econ. Geologists, Assn. Exploration Geochemists, Canadian Inst. Mining & Metallurgy, Canadian Mining and Metall. Soc. Clubs: Houston; Mining (N.Y.C.); Plaza, Memorial Drive Country (Houston); Rocky Point (Old Greenwich, Conn.); Southwest Mining (Tucson, Ariz.). Home: 216 Merrie Way Houston TX 77024 Office: 2125 Tenneco Bldg Houston TX 77002

STEED, TOM, congressman; b. farm nr. Rising Star, Tex., Mar. 2, 1904; m. Hazel Bennett, Feb. 26, 1923; 2 sons (Roger, officer USMCR dec. China, May 1947). Connected with Okla. daily newspapers, 20 yrs.; mng. editor Shawnee News & Star, 4 yrs. Mem. 81st to 92d Congresses, 4th Okla. Dist. Served from pvt. to 2d lt. A.A.A., AUS, 1942-44, with OWI, 1944-45; CBI. Home: 1904 N Pennsylvania Shawnee OK 74801 Office: Rayburn House Office Bldg Washington DC 20515

STEEL, CHARLES EUGENE, chem. co. exec.; b. Anson, Tex., July 8, 1934; s. Herman T. and Gladys (Propst) S.; B.S., Tex. Tech. U., 1957; m. Anne Akers, Aug. 25, 1954; children—Gary Lee, Frances Anne, Julie Marie. Chemist, Celanese Chem. Co., Pampa, Tex., 1957-60, supr. personnel 1960-62, labor relations rep. Celanese Fibers Co., Cumberland, Md., 1962-63, labor relations supr., Pearisburg, Va., 1963-65, indsl. relations mgr., 1965-69, dir. adminstrn. Celanese Chem. Co. Tech. Center, Corpus Christi, Tex., 1969-70; plant mgr. Celanese Chem. Co., Pampa, 1970—. Mem. Ind. Sch. Bd., Pampa, Tex., 1967-68; exec. bd., v.p. Coastal Bend United Fund, 1970-71. Recipient Adult Order of the Arrow award, Boy Scouts Am., 1971. Mem. C. of C. (dir. 1966-68). Methodist (chmn. council on ministries 1970-71). Home: 1900 Grape St Pampa TX 79065 Office: Box 937 Pampa TX 70965

STEEL, MARSHALL T., coll. pres.; b. Ft. Smith, Ark., Jan. 2, 1906; s. E. R. and Kate (Tyler) S.; B.A. with honors, Hendrix Coll., Conway, Ark., 1927, D.D. (hon.), 1939; B.D., Union Theol. Sem., N.Y.C., 1931; LL.D. (hon.), So. Methodist U., 1948; m. Ouita Burroughs, Sept. 4, 1930; children—William E., Sarah (Mrs. Norwood O. Hill), Robert T. Ordained to ministry Meth. Ch., 1928; pastor in Ark., 1927-36, Highland Park Meth. Ch., Dallas, 1936-57; pres. Hendrix Coll., 1958-69; speaker Meth. Men's Hour, nationwide radio broadcast, 1952-58. Dir. Ark. Power & Light Co. Address: Route 6 Box 728 Hot Springs AR 71901

STEELE, BERNADINE BROWN (MRS. JOHN L. STEELE), educator; b. nr. Central City, Ky., Mar. 1, 1912; d. Charles and Bernice (Millard) Brown; B.S., Western State U., 1949, M.A., 1957; postgard Peabody Coll., 1959, U. Hawaii, 1961; m. John L. Steele, Sept. 26, 1931. Tchr. elementary sch., Muhlenberg County, Ky., 1937-43; supr. Lanham Act Nursery Schs., Fayetteville, N.C., 1943-45; elementary tchr. Central City Ind. Schs., 1946-62, counselor, supr., 1962—. Mem. Mid-western Regional Mental Health-Mental Retardation Bd., 1967—; life mem. P.T.A. Mem. N.E.A. (life, mem. adv. council 1966-67), Ky. edn. Assn. (life, pres. 1966-67), Bus. and Profl. Womens Club, Central City C. of C., Delta Kappa Gamma (state chmn. 1967-68). Home: 312 W 2d St Central City KY 42330 Office: W Main St Central City KY 42330

STEELE, CLARENCE ATKINSON, hwy. engr.; b. Brailey, O., Apr. 19, 1906; s. James R. Laird and DeEtta (Atkinson) S.; B.S. in Civil Engring., Purdue U., 1929; M.Philosophy, U. Wis., 1933; m. Elizabeth Marie Garrison, May 25, 1935; children—James J., Richard G., Thomas A., William J. With Wabash R.R., 1925-26, 27-28, 29, 31; surveyor Ind. Hwy. Commn., 1930; with U.S. Bur. Pub. Rds., 1933-70, dep. chief, econs. and requirements div. Office Research and Devel., Washington, 1962-70; spl. asst. to chief transp. econs. dir. and to dir. program and policy planning Fed. Hwy. Adminstrn., Washington, 1971—. Mem. dept. econs., finance and adminstrn. Hwy. Research Bd., 1957-70, mem. adv. com. conf. on transp. and community values, 1968—. Mem. adv. council No. Va. Center, U. Va., 1949-59, chmn., 1954-59; mem. Overlee Community Assn. Methodist. Mason. Contbr. articles to profl. publs. Home: 5901 18th St N Arlington VA 22205 also RFD St David's Church VA 22652 Office: Fed Hwy Adminstrn Washington DC 20591

STEELE, GARLAND FREDRICK, JR., govt. ofcl.; b. Columbus, Ga., Oct. 27, 1929; s. Garland Fredrick and Elizabeth Richardson (Jenkins) S.; student No. Ga. Coll., 1947, Ga. Sch. Tech., 1953; m. Elizabeth Sherwood, Sept. 9, 1949; children—Robert, Wayne, Brian, Carol. Survey rodman, constrn. insp., instrumentman, chief of survey Ga. Hwy. Dept., 1947-49; project engr. City of Atlanta, 1949-54; research engr. Nat. Surety Corp., 1954-56; asst. supt. engring. So. Group Ins. Cos., 1956-58; v.p., mgr. Newton Ins. Agy., 1958-62; pres., chmn. bd. Triangle Underwriters, Inc., Durham, N.C., 1962-69; fed. co-chmn. Coastal Plains Regional Commn., Washington, 1969—. Chmn. Durham County Republican com., 1962-66; Rep. nominee for congressman from 5th N.C. dist., 1966, 4th N.C. dist., 1968. Mem. Ga. Engring. Soc., Am. Soc. Mil. Engrs. Methodist. Home: 7834 Kent Rd Alexandria VA 22308 Office: 2000 L St NW Suite 414 Washington DC 20036

STEELE, HENRY MAXWELL, educator; b. Greenville, S.C., Mar. 30, 1922; s. John May and Minnie Ardella (Russell) S.; student Furman U., 1939-41; B.A., U. N.C., 1946; student Vanderbilt U., 1943-44; postgrad. Academie Julienne, Paris, France, 1951, Sorbonne U., 1952-54; Litt.D., Belmont Abbey Coll., 1970; m. Diana Whittinghill, Dec. 31, 1960; children—Oliver Whittinghill, Kevin Russell. Lectr. dept. English, U. N.C., Chapel Hill, 1956-58, writer in residence, 1966; asso. prof. English, dir. creative writing 1967—; prof. English, 1972—; lectr. U. Cal. at San Francisco, 1962-64; mem. staff Writer's Community, Squaw Valley, 1970—. Served with USAAF, 1943-46. Recipient Harper Pub. Co. Novel Prize, 1950, Mayflower Soc. award, 1950, O'Henry Prize Story award Doubleday Pub. Co., 1955, 69. Nat. Found. Arts and Humanities grantee, 1967, 70; named Distinguished Alumnus, Furman U., 1971. Author: Debby, 1950; Where She Brushed Her Hair, 1968; The Cat and The Coffee Drinkers, 1969; Am. Literary Anthology No. 3, 1970. Adv. editor The Paris Review, 1952—. Home: Mason Farm Rd Chapel Hill NC 27514

STEELE, JACK, journalist; b. North Manchester, Ind., Sept. 15, 1914; s. Roscoe and Dessie (Wonderly) S.; A.B., Middlebury (Vt.) Coll., 1936; M.S. in Journalism, Columbia, 1937; m. Barbara Louise Lyons, Sept. 30, 1939; children—Jeffrey L., Peter C. Reporter, N.Y. Herald Tribune, 1937-53; chief polit. writer Scripps-Howard Newspaper Alliance, 1953—. Recipient Raymond Clapper award, 1949, Sigma Delta Chi award, 1949. Heywood Broun award, 1951, Ernie Pyle award, 1963. Clubs: Nat. Press Gridiron (Washington). Presbyn. Home: 5824 Osceola Rd Washington DC 20016 Office: 1013 13th St NW Washington DC 20005

STEELE, JAMES COLUMBUS, JR., machinery mfg. co. exec.; b. Statesville, N.C., July 10, 1913; s. Henry Oscar and Annie (Parker) S.; grad. U. N.C., 1935; m. Grace Shelton Carpenter, May 4, 1940; children—James Columbus III, Henry Forest, John Shelton, Thomas Parker. With J.C. Steele & Sons, Inc., Statesville, 1935—, now chmn. bd.; dir. Pine Hall Brick & Pipe Co., Inc., Winston-Salem, N.C.; dir. Pub. Service Co. of N.C., Gastonia, Northwestern Bank, Statesville. Past chmn., Statesville Planning and Zoning Bd.; chmn. Statesville Redevelopment Commn., 1966—. Bd. dirs. N.C. Engring. Found. Served to lt. USNR, World War II; PTO. Fellow Am. Ceramic Soc.; mem. Kappa Sigma. Presbyn. (elder). Rotarian (past pres.). Clubs: Statesville Country; Blowing Rock (N.C.) Country (past pres.). Home: 429 Summit Av Statesville NC 28677 Office: 710 S Mulberry St Statesville NC 28677

STEELE, JOHNNIE HUGH, ins. exec.; b. Covington, Ga., Nov. 3, 1925; s. Johnnie James and Ada (Kitchens) S.; student Emory at Oxford Coll., 1946-47; m. Dorothy Virginia Lassiter, Aug. 10, 1947; children—Johnnie Hugh, Margaret Susan. Teller, Bank of Covington (Ga.), 1947-58; owner Steele Ins. Agy., Covington, 1958-66; partner Steele-Prescott Ins. Agy., Covington, 1966—; chmn. bd. First Nat. Bank of Newton County, Covington, 1963—. Tax receiver Newton County (Ga.), 1960-64. Mem. bd. visitors Emory U., Atlanta, 1969—; trustee Piedmont Acad., Monticello, Ga., 1971—. Served with AUS, 1945-46. Named Agt. of Year, Ga. Mutual Ins. Assn., 1969. Mem. Ga. Assn. Mutual Ins. Agts. (dir.), Am. Legion, Newton County C. of C. (pres. 1969). Baptist (deacon). Mason, Rotarian (pres. 1967-68), Elk. Home: 3135 Ellen Ct Covington GA 30209 Office: 1132 Floyd St NE Covington GA 30209

STEELE, JOSEPH RODGERS, coast guard officer; b. Birmingham, Ala., Jan. 20, 1920; s. George Curtis and Anne (Rodgers) S.; student Birmingham-So. Coll., 1936-39; B.A., U. Ala., 1940; B.S. in Engring., U.S. Coast Guard Acad., 1943; postgrad. U. Ill., 1949-50; M.S. in Aero. Engring., U.S. Air Force Inst. Tech., 1952;; m. Jeanne Marie Drake Smith, Apr. 15, 1967; 1 son, Joseph Rodgers. Commd. ensign, U.S. Coast Guard, 1943, advanced through grades to rear adm., 1971; chief engring. div. 17th Coast Guard Dist., Juneau, Alaska, 1967-69; chief operations div. 2d Coast Guard Dist., St. Louis, 1970-71; chief, office of personnel U.S. Coast Guard Hdqrs., Washington, 1971—. Mem. Soc. Am. Mil. Engrs., Operations Research Soc. U.S., Pi Kappa Alpha. Presbyn. Clubs: Army-Navy (Washington); Army-Navy Country (Arlington, Va.). Home: 6357 Crosswoods Dr Falls Church VA 22044 Office: Coast Guard Hdqrs 400 7th St SW Washington DC 20590

STEELE, MARION ARCHIBALD, cons. engr.; b. Nashville, Sept. 9, 1938; s. Marion A. and Mary (Daniel) S.; student Vanderbilt U., 1957-58; Ga. Inst. Tech., 1958; B.S.C.E. Va. Mil. Inst., 1961; postgrad. W. Va. U., 1964-65; m. Brenda Elizabeth Gantt, Nov. 9, 1963; children—Mary Margaret, Marion Archibold Jackson. Office engr. Ingersoll-Rand Co., Richmond, Va., N.Y.C., 1960-1961-62; engr. mgr. Morgantown (W. Va.) San. Bd., 1965-66; design engr. Wiley & Wilson, cons. engrs.-architects-planners, Lynchburg, Va., 1966-71, project mgr., 1966-67, mgr. Manassa, Va., 1967-69, asst. dir. constrn. adminstrn., Lynchburg office, 1969-70, head civil engring. dept., Lynchburg, 1970-71; mgr. offices Stottler Stagg and Assos., Brevard Engring. Co., Winter Haven and St. Petersburg, Fla., 1971-72; sales engr. Taulman Co., Charlotte, N.C., 1972—. Mem. Va. Adv. Legislative Council, 1968-70. Served to capt. AUS, 1962-64. Recipient Army Commendation Medal, V-Corps Certificate Achievement. Registered profl. engr., W. Va., Va., N.C. Mem. Nat., Va. (sec., treas. Lynchburg 1967-68, dir. 1969) socs. profl. engrs., Fla., Va. (v.p. 1971), W.Va. Water pollution control assns. Home: 10709 Forest Dr Matthews NC 28105 Office: 201 S Tryon St Box 2447 Charlotte NC 28201

STEELE (HENRY) MAX(WELL), author, educator; b. Greenville, S.C., Mar. 30, 1922; s. John M. and Minnie (Russell) S.; student Furman U., 1939-41, Vanderbilt U., 1943; B.A., U. N.C., 1946; postgrad. Academie Julienne, Paris, France, 1951-52, Sorbonne, U. Paris, 1952-55; m. Diana Whittinghill, Dec. 31, 1960; children—Oliver Whittinghill, Keven Russell. Lectr. creative writing U. N.C., Chapel Hill, 1956-58, writer-in-residence, 1966—, lectr., 1967-68, asso. prof., dir. creative writing program, 1968—; lectr. creative writing U. Cal. Extension, 1963-64. Served with USAAF, 1942-46. Nat. Endowment for Arts grantee, 1967. Author: Debby, 1960 (reissued as The Goblins Must Go Barefoot, 1966) (Harper prize novel 1960, Harper's Eugene F. Saxton Meml. Trust award, Mayflower Cup for best book by a North Carolinian); Where She Brushed Her Hair, and Other Short Stories, 1968; (juvenile) The Cat and the Coffee Drinkers, 1969. Adv. editor Paris Rev., 1952—. Contbr. short stories to Atlantic, Harper's, New Yorker, Colliers, Cosmopolitan, Esquire, Mademoiselle, Quar. Rev. Lit., also other lit. jours. Office: Dept of English University of NC Chapel Hill NC 27514*

STEELE, RICHARD KENNETH, photog. equipment co. exec.; b. Geneva, N.Y., May 26, 1940; s. Lewis Crawford and Florence (Guest) S.; B.S. in Optical Engring., U. Rochester, 1963; m. Georgia Ann Yaw, May 4, 1963; children—Richard, Elizabeth, Robert. Engr. aeronutronics div. Philco-Ford, Newport Beach, Cal., 1963-64; optical design engr. Perkin-Elmer, Costa Mesa, Cal., 1964-65; chief optical engr. applied optics and mechanics div. Electro-Optical Systems, Arcadia, Cal., 1965-66; founder pres. Optek Inc., Costa Mesa, 1967—, Optek div. mgr. SEACO Computer-Display, Inc., Garland, Tex., 1971—, dir. SEACO Computer-Display Inc. Cons., Bausch & Lomb, Rochester, N.Y., 1968—, Poly-Optics, Santa Ana, Cal., 1967—. Mem. Optical Soc. Am., Soc. Photo. Scientists and Engrs., Soc. of Photo-Optical Instrumentation Engrs. Home: 7117 Briar Cove Dr Dallas TX 75240 Office: 2714 National Circle Garland TX 75041

STEEN, HUGH FLEMING, gas co. exec.; b. Eula, Tex., Mar. 28, 1911; s. Preston C. and Maude C. (Fleming) S.; student La. State U., 1931-32; m. Mary Marshall, Aug. 10, 1937; children—Stephen M., Stanley H. With El Paso Natural Gas Co., 1932—, v.p., mgr. pipeline operations, 1957-65, pres., 1965—, also dir.; dir. El Paso Natural Gas Products Co., Farah Mfg. Co., Fed. Res. Bank Dallas. Mem. Am. (dir.), So., Pacific Coast (pres. 1972, dir.) gas assns. Home: 1009 Broadmoor El Paso TX 79912 Office: PO Box 1492 El Paso TX 79999

STEEN, SIDNEY JAMES, newspaper editor; b. Orongo, Mo., Apr. 29, 1908; s. Frank and Edna (Rickman) S.; student Okmulgee (Okla.) Jr. Coll., 1926-27; m. Flora Frayer, Mar. 5, 1931; children—Sylvia, Sidney James. Sports editor Okmulgee (Okla.) Times, 1926-28, 29; reporter Ark. Gazette, Little Rock, 1928-29; asst. sports editor Tulsa Tribune, 1929-32, police reporter, asst. sports editor, 1934-37; asst. sports editor Tulsa World, 1937-43, telegraph editor, 1943-48, city editor, 1948-53, mng. editor, 1953-60, exec. editor, 1960—. Adv. bd. Tulsa St. John's Hosp. Episcopalian. Lion. Clubs: Press (past pres.), Downtown, Tulsa (Tulsa); Oaks Country. Home: 1547 E 35th Pl Tulsa OK 74105 Office: 315 S Boulder St Tulsa OK 74102

STEEN, WILSON DAVID, educator; b. Hugo, Okla., July 21, 1923; s. Wilson D. and Maude (Ellis) S.; B.S., U. Okla., 1949, Ph.D., 1964; M.S., Columbia Sch. Pub. Health, 1952; m. Beatrice Joyce Kilburne, June 20, 1948; children—Wilson David, Kathy Joyce. With Kiowa County Health Dept., 1949-51 Okla. State Dept. Health, 1952, Okla. Adv. Health Council, 1953-54, Am. Cancer Soc., 1955; faculty U. Okla., Oklahoma City, 1956—, prof. health adminstrn., preventive medicine Sch. Medicine, asso. dean Sch. Health, 1967—, cons. dept. health studies Coll. Continuing Edn., 1965—. Chief office edn. and tng. Okla. Dept. Health, 1963—; sr. scientist USPHS, 1956—. Treas., Okla. Tb and Respiratory Diseases Assn., 1966—; pres. Okla. Health Scis. Facilities, 1966—. Served with USAAF, 1942-46. Fellow Am. Pub. Health Assn.; mem. Okla. Pub. Health Assn. (pres. 1958), Tchrs. of Preventive Medicine. Methodist. Editor: Okla. Jour. Pub. Health, 1958. Home: 2618 Chateau Dr Norman OK 73069 Office: 800 NE 13th St Oklahoma City OK 73104

STEENSMA, RICHARD, advt. exec.; b. Paterson, N.J., Dec. 18, 1915; s. Peter and Agnes (Hoogstra) S.; B.S. in Elec. Engring., Newark Coll. of Engring., 1937; M.S., N.Y.U., 1951; m. Geraldine Jacqueline Jaarsma, Dec. 24, 1940; children—Nancy J. (Mrs. John E. Fennema), Kathleen E. (Mrs. Howard J. Doornbos), Kenneth Richard. Supr. prodn. coordination sect. Wright Aero. Corp., Paterson, N.J., 1939-43, asst. project engr., 1943-46; indsl. engr. Richardson Scale Co., Clifton, N.J., 1946-48, adv. sales promotion mgr., 1948-55, v.p., account exec. W. L. Towne Co., Inc., N.Y.C., 1955-62; pres. Richard/Steensma Advt./Marketing, Saddle River, N.J., 1962-70, Signal Mountain, Tenn., 1971—. Active Bergen County Health and Welfare Council. Past pres. Eastern com. Bethany Christian Home. Past bd. mgrs., v.p., Florence Christian Home. Mem. Tau Beta Pi. Mem. Christian Ref. Ch. Patentee of turbine flameout detector. Address: 822 Murrell Rd Signal Mountain TN 37377

STEERE, BRUCE MIDDLETON, truck line exec.; b. Evanston, Ill., Dec. 29, 1918; s. Kenneth David and Grace (Duffield) S.; B.A., Yale, 1942; indsl. adminstrn., Harvard Bus. Sch., 1943; m. Anne MacCuen Bullivant, July 5, 1968; children—Lucy Duffield, Grace McLaurin, Mrs. Douglas E. Kliever, Richard M. H. Harper III, Patricia B. Harper, Stuard L. Harper. Indsl. engr. Chance Vought Aircraft, Bridgeport, Conn., 1943-45; pres. Steere Tank Lines, Dallas, 1945—. Pres., dir. So. Ins. Co., Dallas, 1952—; dir. Republic Ins. Co., Vanguard Ins. Co., Allied Finance Co., Indsl. Life Ins. Co., (all Dallas). Mem. Tex. Tank Truck Carriers Assn. (past pres.), Tex. Motor Transp. Assn. (past pres.), Nat. Tank Truck Carriers Assn. (dir.), Beta Theta Pi. Democrat. Mem. Christian Ch. Clubs: Brook Hollow Golf (Dallas); Koon Kreek (Athens, Tex.) N.Y. Yacht (N.Y.C.); Stone Horse Yacht (Harwich Port, Mass.); Athletic, Gun (both Dallas). Home: 4412 N Versailles St Dallas TX 75209 Office: 2808 Fairmount St Dallas TX 75201

STEFFEN, STEVE, interior designer; b. Chgo., Mar. 8, 1918; s. Louis Joseph and Emilia Josephine (von Dvorak) S.; student Northwestern U., 1936-37, U. Turin (Italy), 1946-47, Parsons Sch. of Design, 1948-50, N.Y. U., 1948-50. Interior designer Marshall Field & Co., Chgo., 1950-54, Richard Plumer Co., Miami, 1954-64, Beresford Interiors, 1964-67; partner, designer Steve Steffen Assos., 1968—; instr. interior design Miami Dade Jr. Coll., 1969. Served with USCGR, 1941-43. Mem. Am. Inst. Interior Designers (pres. Fla. dist. chpt. 1960). Address: 5901 SW 50th St Miami FL 33155

STEFFEN, THEODORE NICHOLAS, surgeon; b. Hammond, Ind., Mar. 28, 1929; s. Dewey Theodore and Ethel (Bartley) S.; B.A., Yale, 1950; M.D., U. Va., 1954; M.S., State U. Ia., 1961. Intern, Virginia Mason Hosp., Seattle, 1954-55; resident otolaryngology State U. Ia., 1958-61; NIH spl. trainee Los Angeles Found. Otology, 1961-62, gen. dir., 1965-67; asso. Otol. Med. Group, Los Angeles, 1961-62; asst. prof. otolaryngology U. Fla., 1962-65; individual practice otology,

Louisville, 1967—. Served to capt. M.C., AUS, 1955-58. Diplomate Am. Bd. Otolaryngology. Fellow Am. Acad. Otology, A.C.S., Am. Otol., Rhinol. and Laryngol. Soc.; mem. Nu Sigma Nu. Club: Hampton (Va.) Yacht. Author tng. films on ear surgery. Contbr. articles to profl. jours. Home: 800 S 4th St Louisville KY 40203 Office: 1169 Eastern Pkwy Louisville KY 40217

STEGALL, DAVID LAWRENCE, dentist; b. Ft. Worth, Aug. 6, 1942; s. Eugene Thomas and Marion (Goodman) S.; student Tex. Christian U., 1960-61, Tex. Wesleyan of Ft. Worth, 1961-63; D.D.S., Baylor U., 1967; m. Sandra Camille Powers, May 26, 1967; children—Britton Lawrence, Kathryn Camille. Practice dentistry, Ft. Worth, 1967-68, Dallas, 1968—; instr. gnathology. Active, Dallas Civil Opera Co. and Guild, Dallas Mus. of Fine Arts. Recipient Horace Beachum award for denture prosthesis Baylor U. Coll. Dentistry, 1967. Mem. Am., Tex. dental assns., Dallas County Dental Soc., Peter K. Thomas Gnathological Study Group (pres. 1968—), Dr. Charles Stuart's Gnathological Soc. (pres. 1967—). Episcopalian. Home: 5322 Montrose St Dallas TX 75209 Office: 8226 Douglas St Dallas TX 75225

STEGER, HUGH LYNN, lawyer; b. San Angelo, Tex., July 3, 1915; s. Allen Homer and Alva Delilah (Perkins) S.; B.B.A., U. Tex., Austin, 1938, LL.B., 1939; m. Maxine Wilson, June 7, 1941; children—Carol Ann (Mrs. Robert Lawrence Adams), John Allen. Admitted to Tex. bar, 1939; practice in San Antonio, 1939-40, Rankin, 1940-41, Dallas, 1946—; spl. agt. FBI, Washington, Indpls., N.Y.C., 1941-46; partner firm Storey, Sanders, Sherrill & Armstrong, 1946-52, Storey, Armstrong & Steger, 1952—. Chmn. bd. Camp Grady Spruce, Town North YMCA; v.p. Met. YMCA Dallas. Mem. Am., Tex., Dallas (pres.) bar assns. Methodist. Clubs: Dallas, Chaparral (Dallas). Home: 11340 E Ricks Circle Dallas TX 75230 Office: Republic Bank Tower Dallas TX 75201

STEGER, JOHN E., assn. exec. Exec. v.p. Birmingham Area C. of C. Office: 1914 6th Av N Birmingham AL 35203*

STEHL, EDWARD, III, lawyer; b. Pitts., June 28, 1921; s. Edward and Catherine (Aten) S.; A.B., George Washington U., 1948, LL.B., 1950, J.D., 1951; children—Dunlaney Hunter, John Ashley, Carol Blanton, Catherine Lee. Admitted to Va. bar, 1951; practiced in Bowling Green, 1951—; partner Blanton, Mason & Stehl, 1951-55; partner Mason & Stehl, 1955-58; judge Caroline County Ct., 1958-69; pvt. practice law, 1958—. Chmn. bd. dirs. Caroline Pines, Inc., Lake Land'or, Inc. Chmn. Caroline County Cancer Drive, 1952-53; chmn. fund drive Boy Scouts Am., 1955-56; chmn. Heart Fund Drive, 1957-58; chmn. Mary Washington Hosp. Drive, 1956-57. Bd. dirs. Caroline County Devel. Corp. Served with C.E., AUS, 1942-45. Mem. Order of Coif, Delta Theta Phi. Democrat. Methodist. Office: 115 Court House Lane Bowling Green VA 22427

STEHLING, JACK ARTHUR, architect; b. Fredericksburg, Tex., Mar. 2, 1930; s. Arthur Emil and Beatrice (Deen) S.; Degree in Piano, Lamont Sch. Music, 1948; B.A. in English and History, U. Tex., 1952, B.Arch., 1956; postgrad. U. Tex. Law Sch., 1951-53; m. Jane Bridge, Nov. 8, 1952 (div.); children—Michael, George, Phillip, Tara. Mem. staff Kuehne, Brooks & Barr, 1952-56, Tex. State Bldg. Commn., 1957-59, Southwestern Architects & Engrs., 1959-60; supervising architect Am. embassy U.S. Dept. State, Mexico City, Mexico, 1960-63; partner Kelin Partnership Architect/Engrs., 1968-70; architect Jack A. Stehling, Houston, 1970—. Recipient Resort Center of Year Project award Instns. Mag., 1965. Mem. A.I.A., Pre-Stressed Concrete Inst. Rotarian. Prin. works include Inn of the Hills, Kerrville, Tex., 1965, St. Johns Episcopal Ch., New Braunsfels, Tex., 1967, Panorama Country Club, 1970. Home: Yorktown Townhouses 2610 Yorktown St Houston TX 77027 Office: East Tower Exec Plaza 4615 Southwest Freeway Houston TX 77027

STEIN, BERNARD REUBIN, program analyst; b. Boston, Aug. 5, 1927; s. Harry and Miriam (Orent) S.; B.S., Northeastern U., 1949; M.S., U. Tenn. 1950; postgrad. Catholic U. Am., 1952-54; Dr. Rer. Nat., U. Gottingen (Germany), 1957; m. Eleonora Elena Scarpa, May 22, 1957; children—Costanza, David, Raffael. Post-doctoral fellow U. Ottawa, 1957-58; phys. chemist U.S. Army Research Office, 1958-60; chief chemistry br. U.S. Army Research and Devel. Group, 1960-63; phys. chemist U.S. Army Research Office, 1964-65; program analyst NSF, Washington, 1965—. Served with AUS, 1945-47. Mem. Am. Chem. Soc., A.A.A.S., Sigma Xi. Home: 6727 Rosewood St Annandale VA 22003 Office: 1800 G St NW Washington DC 20550

STEIN, CHARLES HOWARD, recreation co. exec.; b. N.Y.C., Dec. 13, 1927; s. Gilbert and Fritzie (Lieberman) S.; student U. Miami, 1945-46, N.Y.U., 1946-47; m. Rusty Senft, Nov. 27, 1953; children—Bradley, Clifford, Candice. Pres., prin. shareholder Orange State Processing Corp., 1951-56; gen. mgr. citrus div. Kraft Foods Co., Lakeland, Fla., 1956-65; pres. Kitchens of Sara Lee, dir., v.p. Consol. Food Corp., Deerfield, Ill., 1965-67; pres., chmn. bd. Hardwicke Cos., Inc., N.Y.C., 1968—; chmn. bd. Leisure Time Co. Mem. Fla. Council of 100, 1965—. Mem. Young Presidents Orgn. Home: 5345 Pinetree Dr Miami Beach FL 33140 Office: 767 Fifth Av Suite 2715 New York City NY 10022

STEIN, FRANCIS B., oil co. exec.; b. Warwick, N.Y., Sept. 6, 1914; s. Bruno and Emma (Bousquet) S.; B.S., La. State U., 1937; postgrad. Northwestern U., 1959; m. Velma Mae Browning, Sept. 10, 1938; children—Patty Louise, Michael Rotolo, Nancy Jean, Phillip Pond. With Tidewater Oil Co., 1938-50, Callery & Hurt, 1950-52; with Tenn. Gas Transmission Co., 1952-61; co-owner Nellcor Oil Co., Houston, 1961—; cons. oil and gas, 1961—. Mem. Am. Assn. Petroleum Geologists. Home: 10034 Bordley St Houston TX 77042 Office: Chamber of Commerce Bldg Houston TX 77002

STEIN, GILBERT TAYLOR, constrn. co. exec.; b. Chattanooga, Feb. 20, 1928; s. John Gilbert and Evelyn Douglass (Taylor) S.; B.S., U. Tenn., 1950; m. Virginia June Harris, Oct. 4, 1952; children—Virginia Evelyn, Frank Douglas, John Taylor. Partner, Porzelius & Stein, cons. engrs., Chattanooga, 1955-71; partner Stein Constrn. Co., 1950—; v.p. Chattanooga Indsl. Devel. Corp., 1960—. Founder, mem. Scenic Cities Beautiful Commn., Chattanooga, 1962—. Bd. dirs. Hamilton County Sch. Bd., 1967—, Mental Health Assn., Chattanooga Psychiat. Clinic. Served to lt. (j.g.) USNR, 1954-56. Registered profl. engr., Tenn. Mem. Asso. Gen. Contractors Am., Nat. Soc. Profl. Engrs., Am. Soc. C.E., Chattanooga C. of C. (exec. com., bd. dirs.), Phi Kappa Phi, Chi Epsilon, Tau Beta Pi, Kappa Sigma. Republican. Episcopalian (supt. Sunday sch.). Clubs: Mountain City, Civitan, Chattanooga Yacht; Lookout Mountain Fairyland. Home: 281 Stephenson Av Lookout Mountain TN 37350 Office: 3611 Amnicola Hwy Chattanooga TN 37406

STEIN, JAKE, discount corp. exec.; b. Greenwood, Miss., Mar 16, 1911; s. Sam and Fannie (Arenzon) S.; student U. Ala., 1931-32; m. Freda C. Grundfest, May 31, 1935; 1 son, Jay. Partner, Sam Stein Co., Greenwood, Miss., 1933-68; pres. Stein Marts, Inc., Greenville, 1968—; dir. First Nat. Bank, Jackson, Miss. Mem. Greenville City Council, 1941-43; pres. Greenville Baseball Assn., 1940-43, Greenville Community Fund, 1952-53, Greenville Park Commn., 1955-59. Bd. dirs. Hebrew Union, Greenville, 1935-62, pres., 1944-46. Served to 1st lt. AUS, 1943-46. Mem. C. of C. (pres. 1950-51). Kiwanian. Home: Wilzen Park Greenville MS 38701 Office: PO Box 1298 Greenville MS 38701

STEINBACH, KARL HEINRICH, physicist; b. Bonn, Germany, Feb. 19, 1928; s. Franz and Mathilde (Braunshausen) S.; D.Engring., U. Munich, 1953; m. Dobrila Bojanovic, Dec. 28, 1955; children—Bernard Zdravko, Carlo Franz, Boris John. Came to U.S., 1959, naturalized, 1965. Physicist, Pintsch Electro Co., Konstanz, Germany, 1953-57; chief electronics lab. Telefunken Co., Munich, also Konstanz, 1957-59; chief microwave, electronics unit U.S. Army Research and Devel. Lab., Ft. Belvior, Va., 1959-65, chief research, design br., barrier, intrusion detection div., 1965-67, chief research div., intrusion detection and sensor lab. U.S. Army Mobility Equipment Research and Devel. Center, 1967—. Recipient award for outstanding achievement Army Sci. Conf., West Point, 1962; research and devel. award Dept. Army, 1969. Mem. I.E.E.E. Roman Catholic. Patentee in field. Home: 9115 Coronado Terrace Fairfax VA 22030 Office: US Army MERDC Fort Belvoir VA 22060

STEINDL, FRANK GEORGE, educator; b. Chgo., Aug. 26, 1935; s. Frank and Anna (Bumeder) S.; B.A., DePaul U., 1957; A.M., U. Ill., 1958; Ph.D., U. Ia., 1963; m. Joyce Becker, Aug. 26, 1961; children—David F., Andrew M., Peter E., Matthew T. Instr. econs. St. Benedict's Coll., Atchison, Kan., 1958-59; faculty Okla. State U., Stillwater, 1962—, asso. prof. econs., 1965-70, prof., 1970—. Vis. economist Fed. Res. Bank Cleve., 1966-67. Mem. Am. Assn. U. Profs., Am., Midwest, Southwestern econ. assns., Econometric Soc., Beta Gamma Sigma, Omicron Delta Epsilon. Contbr. articles to profl. jours. Home: 902 Osage Dr Stillwater OK 74074

STEINER, LEO KEITH, JR., former banker; b. Birmingham, Ala., Mar. 3, 1903; s. Leo Keith and Dian (Holzer) S.; grad. Culver (Ind.) Mil. Acad., 1920; B.S. in Econs., Wharton Sch. U. Pa., 1924; m. Sylvia Forman, Oct. 15, 1924 (div.); children—Leo Keith III, Dorothy Forman (Mrs. Jacob W. Schott). Exec. v.p. Steiner Bros. Bank, 1940-62; pres. Guardian Realty Co., Birmingham, 1942-62; dir. Old Republic Life Ins. Co., Chgo. Served as maj. USAAF, 1942-44. Clubs: Xanadu Yacht and Tennis (Freeport, Grand Bahama Island); Jockey (Miami, Fla.). Home: Jockey Club 11111 Biscayne Blvd North Miami FL 33161

STEINER, LEONARD EDWARD, physician; b. Milw., July 13, 1930; s. Theodore and Selma (Broder) S.; B.S., U. Wis., 1952, M.D., 1956; m. Phyllis Ann Goldman, June 12, 1960; children—Steven, Tami, Theodore. Intern, Mt. Sinai Hosp., Milw., 1956-57; resident anesthesiology Charity Hosp. of La., New Orleans, 1957-59; med. dir. respiratory therapy Cedars of Lebanon Hosp., Miami, Fla., 1967—, chief dept. anesthesiology, 1971—; med. dir. Respiratory Care Center, Inc., Miami Beach, 1971—; clin. asst. prof. anesthesiology U. Miami Med. Sch., 1965—. Served with USNR, 1959-61. Diplomate Am. Bd. Anesthesiology. Mem. Greater Miami Soc. Anesthesiologists (pres. 1967-68). Home: 63 S Prospect Dr Coral Gables FL 33133 Office: 1150 NW 14th St Miami FL 33136

STEINFELD, SAMUEL SIMONS, judge; b. Louisville, Feb. 16, 1906; s. Emile and Florence (Simons) S.; LL.B., U. Louisville, 1928; m. Flora Loebenberg, July 24, 1929; children—Helene S. (Mrs. Howard B. Grossman), James F. Admitted to Ky. bar, 1928; asso. Gifford & Steinfeld, 1928-33; partner Steinfeld & Steinfeld, Louisville, 1933—; judge Ky. Ct. Appeals, Frankfort. Vice pres., dir. Llewellyn St. Matthews Laundry; pres., dir. Lorenza Realty Co.; sec., dir. Coin Laundromat, Inc., Modern Loan Co., Financial Investment Corp., Mid-Land Warehouse Co.; dir. Sympson Bros. Coal Co. Civic sec. Jewish Community Center Louisville, 1956, v.p., 1957, trustee, 1951—. Pres. Louisville Young Men's Republican Club, 1939; alternate del. Rep. Nat. Conv., 1940, 56; mem. Jefferson County Rep. Exec. Com. Mem. Ky., Louisville (legal chmn. jud. and rules com. 1950-57) bar assns., Comml. Law League Am. Jewish religion. Clubs: L (U. Louisville); Adath Israel Men's (past pres.), Lincoln. Home: 1856 Princeton Dr Louisville KY 40205 Office: Ky Court of Appeals New Capitol Bldg Frankfort KY 40601

STEINFINK, HUGO, educator; b. Vienna, Austria, May 22, 1924; s. Mendel and Malwina (Fiderer) S.; B.S. Coll. City N.Y., 1947; M.S., Columbia U., 1948; Ph.D., Bklyn. Poly. Inst., 1954; m. Cele Intrator, Mar. 21, 1948; children—Dan E. Susan D. Research chemist Shell Devel. Co., Houston, 1948-51, 53-60; prof. chem. engring. U. Tex., 1960—. Served with AUS, 1944-46. Fellow Am. Mineralogica Soc.; mem. Am. Chem. Soc., Am. Crystallographic Soc., Phi Beta Kappa, Sigma Xi, Phi Lambda Epsilon. Contbr. articles in field to profl. jours. Home: 3811 Walnut Clay Austin TX 78731 Office: U Tex Austin TX 78712

STEINHAUS, JOHN EDWARD, physician, educator; b. Omaha, Feb. 23, 1917; s. Emil F. and Pearl (Haynie) S.; B.A., U. Neb., 1940, M.A., 1941; M.D., U. Wis., 1945, Ph.D., 1950; m. Mila Jean Pinkerton, Feb. 21, 1943; children—Katherine (Mrs. Wayne Shrake), Carolyn, Barbara, William, Elizabeth. Intern Cin. Gen. Hosp., 1945-46; resident Univ. Hosp., Milw., 1953-55; asso. prof. pharmacology, Sch. Medicine, U. Wis., 1951-53, asst. prof. anesthesiology, 1954-58; prof. and chmn. dept. anesthesiology, Emory U. Sch. Medicine, Atlanta, 1959—; chief anesthesiology Grady Meml. Hosp., Atlanta, 1959—; dir. Ga. Assn. Pastoral Care. Served to capt., M.C., AUS, 1946-48. Diplomate Am. Bd. Anesthesiology. Mem. A.M.A. (sec. anesthesiology council 1971), Am. Soc. Anesthesiologists (pres. 1970), Assn. Univ. Anesthetists (pres. 1971), Am. Soc. Pharmacology and Exptl. Therapeutics, Am. Coll. Anesthesiologists (1964-69), Internat. Anesthesia Research Soc., Sigma Xi. Home: 836 Castle Falls Dr NE Atlanta GA 30329 Office: 69 Rutler St SE Atlanta GA 30303

STEINICHEN, JOHN, architect; b. Stone Mountain, Ga., Apr. 29, 1907; s. John and Ada (Wallace) S.; apprentice in sculpture under Herman Steinichen, 1922-26; student Ga. Inst. Tech., 1945; m. Laura Octavia Johnson, Aug. 5, 1929; children—John III, Joyce Kay (Mrs. Glenn E. Wiltsey). Designer, sculptor, 1926-31; freelance artist, sculptor, musician, 1931-41; with Firestone Aircraft Plant, Atlanta, 1942-45; architect with various archtl. firm, Atlanta, 1945-50; asso. architect Finch, Alexander, Barnes, Rothschild & Paschal and predecessar firms, Atlanta, 1950—. Sculptures and paintings exhibited in group shows, Atlanta, Washington, N.Y.C., others, 1931—; represented in pvt. collections. Mem. Am. Fedn. Musicians, A.I.A., Soc. Mil. Engrs., Allied Artists Am. (asso.), Rockdale C. of C. Presbyn. Home: PO Box 59 Route 3 Conyers GA 30207 Office: 44 Broad St Atlanta GA 30303

STEINLE, JOHN HENRY, JR., bus. cons., ret. govt. ofcl.; b. Austin, Tex., Jan. 3, 1910; s. John Henry and Paula (Meyer) S.; student A. and M. Coll. Tex., 1926-27; B.B.A., U. Tex., 1931; m. Henrietta Wattinger, Sept. 3, 1931; children—John Henry III, Jack Louis. Asst. dir. research and accounting State Dept. Edn., Austin, 1928-37; became dir. machine accounting Tex. Employment Commn., 1937, past dir. automated data processing; pres. Eagle Prodn. Co.; treas., dir. Austin Concrete Works, Inc. Mem. Travis County Grand Jury, 1961. Faculty cons. in ADP, Mich. State U., 1967. Mem. All Vets. Day Com. Austin and Travis County. Served from lt. (j.g.) to lt., USNR, 1943-45; now lt. comdr. Res. ret. Licensed pub. accountant, Tex. Mem. Tex. Pub. Employees Assn. (past chpt. pres.), Am. Soc. Pub. Adminstrn., Navy League U.S. (dir. Austin), Am. Statis. Assn., Univac Users Assn., Res. Officers Assn. U.S. (v.p. Navy sect. Tex. 1955-56, past pres. Austin chpt.), Tex., Travis County grand jury assns. Theta Xi. Episcopalian (vestryman). Kiwanian. Clubs: Armed Forces, Forty Acres. Home: 2506 Harris Blvd Austin TX 78703 Office: PO Box 1731 Austin TX 78767

STEINLE, LEON FRANCIS, lawyer; b. Jourdanton, Tex., Mar. 22, 1918; s. Alfred Ney and Cedalia Frances (Wurzbach) S.; student St. Mary's U., 1935-37; LL.B., U. Tex., 1940; m. Virginia Franklin, June 5, 1937; children—Angela (Mrs. T.L. Hairston III), Leon Franklin. Admitted to Tex. bar, 1940; with Martin Abstract Co., Jourdanton, 1940-41, land dept. Humble Oil & Refining Co., Corpus Christi, Tex., 1941-43; practice law, Jourdanton, 1946—; dir. Jourdanton State Bank, Atascosa Savs. Assn., Jourdanton. Pres., Jourdanton Vol. Fire Dept., 1948-50; pres. Atascosa Hosp. Assn., 1968—. Served from ensign to lt. USNR, 1943-46; ETO. Mem. Jourdanton C. of C. (pres. 1958-59), Atascosa County Bar Assn. (pres. 1960—). Roman Catholic (pres. parish council 1969—). K.C. Home: 814 Zanderson Av Jourdanton TX 78026 Office: 101 Main St Jourdanton TX 78026

STEINSCHULTE, THILO, architect; b. Berlin, Germany, July 4, 1926; s. Josef and Nora (Cleff) S.; B.A. (scholar), Tech. U. Munich (Germany), 1950; M.A. (scholar), 1953; postgrad. (exchange scholar urban planning), U. Wash., 1950-51; m. Izora Elisabeth Rikard, Nov. 24, 1954; 1 dau., Nora E. Came to U.S., 1953. Architect Bain & Overturf, Seattle, 1953-54; partner Barron, Heinberg & Brocato, architects and engrs., Alexandria, La., 1954—. Various exhbns. paintings arts shows La., 1968—. Pres. Rapides Symphony Orchestra, Alexandria, La., 1971; v.p. Central La. Art Assn., 1971. Trustee Wesley Found. La. State U., Alexandria, 1971; bd. dirs. Central La. Community Theatre, Alexandria, 1969-70. Served with German Armed Forces, 1943-45. Mem. A.I.A. (pres. Central La. chpt. 1968), La. Architects Assn. (v.p., 1970-71), Am. Inst. Archeology. Methodist (trustee, chmn. bd. trustees 1969-70). Rotarian. (v.p. 1971-72). Clubs: Alexandria Investment, Alexandria Aquatic. Home: 3107 Pershing St Alexandria LA 71301 Office: 1015 Wisteria St Alexandria LA 71301

STENBACK, WAYNE ALBERT, researcher, educator; b. Brush, Colo., June 12, 1929; s. Christian and Mabel (Christensen) S.; B.S., U. Colo., 1955; M.S. with honors, U. Denver, 1957; Ph.D., U. Mo., 1962; m. Lillian Marie Cacciatore, June 6, 1954; 1 son, Peter Kara. Baylor Coll. Medicine, Houston, 1962—, instr., 1962-66, asst. prof. electron microscopy, 1966—. Research on oncogenic viruses. Mem. Am. Soc. Microbiology, Electron Microscopy Soc. Am., A.A.A.S., Am. Assn. Cancer Research, Sigma Xi, Alpha Epsilon Delta, Phi Sigma, Mu Beta Kappa. Home: 5518 Lymbar Dr Houston TX 77035

STENBERG, ROBERT THEODORE, physician; b. Austin, Tex., Feb. 23, 1923; s. Theodore Thorson and Elizabeth (Noble) S.; B.A. with honors, U. Tex., 1943, M.D., 1946; m. Johnnie Mae Gable, Nov. 19, 1953; 1 son, Gary Morris. Intern, Kansas City (Mo.) Gen. Hosp., 1946-47; resident psychiatry U. Mich., 1949-50; staff psychiatrist Ft. Custer (Mich.) VA Hosp., 1950; asst. chief psychiatry and neurology service VA Hosp., Ft. Benjamin Harrison, Ind., 1950-51; staff psychiatrist Richmond (Ind.) State Hosp., 1951; supt. Spencer (W.Va.) State Hosp., 1951-52; psychiatrist VA Regional Office Mental Hygiene Clinic, Huntington, W.Va., 1952; staff psychiatrist, dir. Harris County unit Austin State Hosp., 1953-60, 62—, resident, 1960-62. Psychiatry, neurology cons. Brown Schs. for Exceptional Children, 1962-67. Served to capt. M.C., USAF, 1947-49. Fellow Am. Psychiat. Assn.; mem. Tex. Neuropsychiat. Assn., Austin Psychiat. Soc., Am., Tex. med. assns., Travis County Med. Soc., Acad. for Religion and Mental Health, Am. Group Therapy Assn., N.Y. Acad. Sci., A.A.A.S., Phi Beta Kappa, Alpha Epsilon Delta, Alpha Kappa Kappa. Home: 1512 Wayford Dr Austin TX 78758 Office: Box 96 4110 Guadalupe St Austin TX 78751

STENNIS, JOHN CORNELIUS, U.S. senator; b. Kemper County, Miss., Aug. 3, 1901; s. Hampton H. and Cornelia (Adams) S.; B.S., Miss. State Coll., 1923; LL.B., U. Va., 1928; Ph.D. (hon.), Millsaps Coll., U. Wyo.; LL.D., Miss. Coll.; m. Coy Hines, Dec. 24, 1929; children—John Hampton, Margaret Jane. Pvt. practice law, DeKalb, Miss.; mem. Miss. Ho. of Reps., 1928-32; dist. pros. atty., 1931-35; apptd. circuit judge, 1937, elected to same office, 1938, 42, 46; mem. U.S. Senate, 1947—, chmn. Senate Armed Services, Ethics coms., mem. Appropriations, Space coms. Mem. Am. Bar Assn., Phi Beta Kappa, Alpha Chi Rho, Phi Alpha Delta. Presbyn. Mason, Lion. Home: DeKalb MS 39328 Office: US Senate Washington DC 20510

STEPHAN, DAVID GEORGE, govt. ofcl.; b. Columbus, O., Feb. 8, 1930; s. Paul Raymond and Bess (Long) S.; B.Ch.E., Ohio State U., 1952, M.Sc., 1952, Ph.D., 1955; m. Dorothy Spetnagel, June 10, 1951; children—Douglas, Donn, Dean. Technologist, AEC Feed Materials Prodn. Center, Fernald, O., 1955; chief air pollution control research USPHS, Cin., 1956-60, dep. chief Advanced Waste Treatment Reasearch Program, 1961-64, dep. chief br. basic and applied scis., 1965-66; dir. research Fed. Water Pollution Control Adminstrn., Dept. of Interior, Arlington, Va., 1966-68, asst. commr. for research and devel. Fed. Water Quality Adminstrn., 1968-71; dir. research program mgmt. Environmental Protection Agy., Washington, 1971—. Served with USPHS, 1955-64. Mem. Am. Inst. Chem. Engrs., Am. Chem. Soc., Water Pollution Control Fedn., Am. Pub. Works Assn., A.A.A.S., Internat. Assn. for Water Pollution Research, Fed. Water Quality Assn., Ohio State U. Assn., Sigma Xi. Phi Lambda Upsilon, Tau Beta Pi, Texnikoi. Mem. Ch. of Christ (deacon). Home: 9127 Christopher St Fairfax VA 22030 Office: US Environmental Protection Agy Washington DC 20460

STEPHENS, BOBBY GENE, chemist; b. Glendale, S.C., Mar. 8, 1935; s. Dewey and Bertha (Mott) S.; B.S., Wofford Coll., 1957; M.S., Clemson U., 1961, Ph.D., 1964; m. Sandra Elizabeth White, June 27, 1957; children—Barbara, Edward, Robert, Adam. Textile chemist Reeves Bros., Inc., Fairforest, S.C., 1957-58; asst. prof. chemistry Wofford Coll., 1963-67, asso. prof., 1967-72, dean Coll., 1972—; research chemist Dept. Health, Edn. and Welfare, Cin., 1964. Chmn. Spartanburg (S.C.) Environmental Pollution Tech. Adv. Bd., 1968—; v.p. Spartanburg County Pollution Control Authority, 1971—. Served to 1st lt. AUS, 1958-60. Mem. Am. Chem. Soc., S.C. Acad. Sci. (recipient Jefferson award 1969), Am. Soc. Testing and Materials (mem. com. sampling and analysis atmospheres). Methodist. Home: 129 Bellwood Lane Spartanburg SC 29302

STEPHENS, CHARLES ANTHON, physician; b. Camden, Tex., Oct. 13, 1925; s. Buford Dured and Carrie (Collins) Stephens; B.A., U. Tex., 1950, M.D., 1954; m. Nancy Raisch, June 25, 1954; children—Deborah, Claudia, Charles Anthon II, Barbara, Jerry. Intern, Univ. Hosp., Little Rock, 1954-55; resident U. Tex. Med. Br., Galveston, 1955-58; practice medicine specializing in obstetrics-gynecology, Odessa, Tex., 1958—; mem. staff Med. Center Hosp., chief of staff 1962. Dir. Odessa Community Chest and United Fund, 1959-60; bd. Ector County Assn. Retarded Children. Served with USNR, 1943-46. Diplomate Am. Bd. Obstetrics and Gynecology. Fellow Am. Coll. Obstetrics-Gynecology; mem. Am.,

Tex. med. assns., Andrews, Ector County Med. Soc., Willard R. Cooke Obstetrics-Gynecology Soc., Pi Kappa Alpha, Phi Chi. Home: 3204 Blossom Lane Odessa TX 79760 Office: 808 Tower Dr Odessa TX 79760

STEPHENS, EDGAR JACOB, JR., lawyer, state legislator; b. New Albany, Miss., May 26, 1916; s. Edgar Jacob and Annabel (Wiseman) S.; student Erskine Coll., 1934-35; B.A., U. Miss., 1938, J.D., 1940. Admitted to Miss. bar, 1940; practiced in New Albany, 1941—; real estate broker, 1962—; pros. atty. Union County, New Albany, 1945-51; mem. Miss. Ho. of Reps., 1952—. Trustee, Pub. Employees' Retirement System; mem. Miss. Commn. Budget and Accounting, Miss. Medicaid Commn. Served USNR, 1942-45. Mem. Miss. State Bar, Am. Legion, Phi Delta Phi, Sigma Chi. Democrat. Presbyn. Home: Glenwood New Albany MS 38652 Office: PO Box 330 New Albany MS 38652

STEPHENS, ELTON BRYSON, diversified co. exec.; b. Clio, Ala., Aug. 4, 1911; s. James Nelson and Clara (Stuckey) S.; A.B., Birmingham So. Coll., 1932; LL.B., U. Ala., 1936; student Advanced Mgmt. Program, Harvard, 1960; m. Alys Varian Robinson, Nov. 28, 1935; children—James Thomas, Jane Elton (Mrs. Donald Comer, III), Elton Bryson, Dell Carter (Mrs. F. Dixon Brooke Jr.). Founder, chmn. bd. EBSCO Industries, Inc., 1943, divs. including Mil. Service Co., Periodical Sales, Read N Gifts, Vulcan Service, EBSCO Subscription Services, EBSCO Advt. Agy., Ednl. Products, Vulcan Industries, EBSCO Media, Vulcan-Burkhardt, Vulcan Binder and Cover, EBSCO Lettering and Drapery Services, also subsidiaries; dir. Bank for Savs. and Trust, 1960-63. Pres. Birmingham Downtown Improvement Assn., 1959-61. Bd. dirs. Operation New Birmingham, 1955-71, Jefferson County (Ala.) Freeway and Expressways Com., 1956-71, Father Red Maintain Expressway, Meth. Hosp.; trustee, mem. exec. com. Elton B. Stephens Scholarship fund, Elton B. Stephens Loan fund Birmingham So. Coll. Mem. Birmingham C. of C. (past dir.), Birmingham Sales Execs. Club (hon.), Newcomen Soc. N.Am., Alpha Tau Omega, Omicron Delta Kappa, Phi Alpha Delta. Methodists (trustee, chmn. bd. stewards). Rotarian (dir.). Clubs: Mountain Brook Country, Downtown, The Club, Vestavia Country, Relay House (Birmingham); Santa Rosa (Fla.) Golf. Home: 3200 Fernway Rd Birmingham AL 35223 Office: 1st Av N at 13th St Birmingham AL 35203

STEPHENS, ELVIS CLAY, educator; b. Childress, Tex., Jan. 9, 1934; s. Leslie and Dell (Farrow) S.; B.B.A., N. Tex. State U., 1958, M.B.A., 1959; D.B.A., Ind. U., 1966; m. Loleta Joyce Perkins, Feb. 4, 1956; children—Daryl Lynn, Jennifer Sue. With field advt. dept. Procter & Gamble Co., Cin., 1951-53; instr. Austin Coll., 1959-61; asst. prof. N. Tex. State U. Sch. Bus., Denton, 1963-69, asso. prof., 1969-71, prof., 1971—, chmn. dept., 1969—. Served to 1st lt. AUS, 1953-56. Mem. Indsl. Relations Research Assn. (chpt. sec.-treas. 1966-68), Am. Soc. for Personnel Adminstrn. (chpt. pres. 1969), Dallas Personnel Assn., Am. Soc. for Tng. and Devel. (pres. chpt. 1972), Beta Gamma Sigma. Methodist. Home: 2321 Kayewood Dr Denton TX 76201

STEPHENS, FRANCIS LEE, food store corp. exec.; b. Nacogdoches, Tex., Mar. 5, 1938; s. Edward C. and Edith (Gray) S.; student Stephen F. Austin State Coll., 1955-56, Syracuse U., 1956-57, San Antonio Coll., 1959-60; B.A. in Econs., U. Tex., 1962; m. Pollyanna Allison, Sept. 21, 1958; children—Susan Camille, Elizabeth Dawn. With Town & Country Food Stores, Inc., 1960—, v.p., 1964—, partner, 1965—, also dir. Dir. 1st Nat. Bank. Pres. county chpt. Am. Cancer Soc., 1969-71, state bd. dirs., 1971-72; bd. mem. Fort Concho Mus., San Angelo, Tex., 1968-71; mem. city commn., San Angelo, 1972-73. Bd. dirs. Tex. Jr. C. of C. Hosp. Found., 1968-69. Trustee MH-MR Center Greater W. Tex., 1970-71; trustee Tex. Law Enforcement and Youth Devel. Found., 1970-71, pres., 1972. Served with USAF, 1956-60. Recipient awards including Sparkplug of Year award Tex. Jr. C. of C., 1967; named One of Five Outstanding Young Texans, Tex. Jaycees, 1971. Mem. U.S. (nat. dir. 1968-69), Tex. (v.p. 1968-69), San Angelo (pres. 1967-68) jr. chambers commerce, Tex. Retail Grocers Assn. (dir. 1971-72), San Angelo C. of C. (v.p. 1971, dir. 1969-71), W. Tex. C. of C. (dist. v.p. 1970-72), Angelo State U. Ram Club (pres. 1971-72). Presbyn. (bd. deacons, tchr. Sunday Sch.). Home: 2919 Hemlock St San Angelo TX 76901 Office: 2021 Austin St San Angelo TX 76901

STEPHENS, FRED ALLAN, mfg. co. exec.; b. Birmingham, Ala., June 14, 1936; s. Fred Carter and Eleanor (Sizemore) S.; B.S. in Chemistry, Birmingham So. Coll., 1958; m. Meryl Hill, May 30, 1969; children— Michelle, Ladd. Asst. by-product foreman U.S. Pipe & Foundry Co., Birmingham, 1958-60, sales rep., chem. div., 1961-69; instrument engr., indsl. div. Honeywell, Inc., Birmingham, 1969—. Served with AUS, 1959, 61-62. Mem. Am. Chem. Soc., Instrument Soc. Am., Am. Water Works Assn., Birmingham Golf Assn. (v.p. 1972), Alpha Tau Omega. Clubs: Civitan (v.p. 1960-61), Chace Lake Country (pres. 1972) (Birmingham). Home: 3300 Monte D'Oro Dr Birmingham AL 35216 Office: 730 S 37th St Birmingham AL 35222

STEPHENS, GEORGE BENJAMIN DAVIS, physician; b. Norfolk, Va., Oct. 12, 1904; s. William George and Louise (Norfleet) S.; B.S., Howard U., 1930, M.D., 1935; m. Dolores Shirley Carr, Aug. 16, 1967. Intern, Freedmen's Hosp., Washington, 1935-36; practice medicine, specializing in gen. practice, Newport News, Va., 1936—; mem. staff Whittaker Meml. Hosp., Newport News; mem. infirmary staff Hampton (Va.) Inst. Patentee spl. ashtray. Home and office: 1250 27th St Newport News VA 23607

STEPHENS, HARLEY HAGGARD, supt. schs.; b. LaFollette, Tenn., Sept. 11, 1918; s. Sherman Oscar and Ledie (Haggard) S.; B.S. with honors, East Tenn. State U., 1947; M.S., U. Tenn., 1953, Ed.D., 1965; m. Verla S. Shoun, Apr. 14, 1940; children—Ralph, Rhonda. Tchr., prin. schs., Campbell County, Jacksonboro, Tenn., 1938-41; prin. supr. pub. schs., Athens, Tenn., 1947-60; supr., supt. Alcoa (Tenn.) Bd. Edn., 1969—. Mem. faculty, Wesleyan Coll., Athens, evenings, 1955-60. Served to maj. AUS, 1944-46, 50-52. Rotarian (pres. 1955-60). Home: 1771 Springbrook St Alcoa TN 37701 Office: Municipal Blvd Alcoa TN 37701

STEPHENS, JAMES CLAYTON, lawyer, judge; b. nr. Dublin, Ga., July 19, 1941; s. James Clayton and Nita (Luke) S.; A.B., Mercer U., 1963; LL.B., Walter F. George Sch. Law, 1965; m. Helena Lee Reeves, July 24, 1969. Admitted to Ga. bar, 1965; gen. practice law, Soperton, Ga., 1965—; judge Ct. Ordinary, Treutlen County, Ga., 1967—; solicitor-pro-tem, State Ct. Treutlen, 1969—; city atty., Soperton, Ga., 1969—. Chmn. Treutlen County A.R.C., 1966—. Mem. bd. dirs. Heart Ga. Planning and Devel. Commn., 1967-69. Served with AUS, 1965. Recipient Outstanding Citizen award Heart of Ga. Planning and Devel. Commn., 1968. Mem. Am. Judicature Soc., Lambda Chi Alpha, Phi Delta Phi. Lion (sec., treas. 1966—). Clubs: Treutlen Boosters (v.p. 1968), Treutlen County Sportsmen's (pres. 1969). Home: 114 New St Soperton GA 30457 Office: Treutlen County Courthouse Soperton GA 30457

STEPHENS, JOHN AMOS, physician; b. Monticello, Ga., June 10, 1914; s. Amos Mack and Lucille (Shell) S.; grad. Ga. Mil. Acad., 1930; student Emory U., 1930-34; A.B., U. Tenn., 1936; M.D., George Washington U., 1942; m. Eva Curtis Williamson, June 5, 1943; 1 dau., Dorothy Arnett (Mrs. Burton Kennedy Barrs II). Intern, Grady Hosp., Atlanta, 1942-43; practice medicine, Laurel, Md., 1946-50, Waycross, Ga., 1950-52; resident internal medicine Riverside Hosp., Jacksonville, Fla., 1952-54; pvt. practice specializing in internal medicine, Jacksonville, 1954-69; emergency room Bapt. Meml. Hosp., 1969-70; med. dir. Gulf Life Ins. Co., Jacksonville, 1970—; med. officer U.S. P.O., Jacksonville, 1970—. Courtesy staff Bapt. Meml., Methodist, St. Vincent's, St. Luke's hosps., Duval Med. Center. Trustee Bapt. Home for Children. Served to capt. USAAF, M.C., AUS, 1943-46. Mem. A.C.P. (life), Am. Soc. Internal Medicine, Assn. Life Ins. Med. Dirs. Am., Fla. Med. Assn., A.M.A., Duval County Med. Soc. (chmn. com. on medicine and religion, 1965-66), Sigma Nu, Phi Chi. Baptist (deacon). Clubs: South Jacksonville Civitan, San Jose Country; Pontevedra, University. Home: 4382 San Jose Lane Jacksonville FL 32207 Office: Gulf Life Tower Jacksonville FL 32207 also Health Unit West Bay Annex Jacksonville FL 32203

STEPHENS, JOHN KIRKER, educator; b. Chgo., July 10, 1941; s. Rothwell and Margaret (Clark) S.; B.A. with high honors, Swarthmore Coll., 1962; M.A., U. Ill., 1963, Ph.D., 1967; postdoctoral research fellow, Yale U., 1971-72; m. Dorothy Claire Faust, June 9, 1961; children—Fern Margaret, Owen Kirker Clifford. Mathematician, U.S. Naval Missile Center, Pt. Mugu, Cal., summers 1965, 66; asst. prof. econs. U. Okla., Norman, 1967-71, asso. prof., 1971—. Cons. economist Bur. for Bus. and Econ. Research, 1968-71. Cons. Okla. Gov.'s Adv. Com. on Taxation, 1968-70. Fellow NSF Cooperative. Recipient Nat. Merit Scholarship. Mem. Am., Western econ. assns., Econometric Soc., Math. Assn. of Am., Am. Assn. U. Profs., Phi Beta Kappa, Sigma Xi, Omicron Delta Epsilon, Pi Mu Epsilon, Beta Gamma Sigma, Tau Alpha Omicron. Republican. Episcopalian. Contbr. articles to profl. jours. Home: 1206 Classen Blvd Norman OK 73069

STEPHENS, PAUL MADISON, constrn. co. exec.; b. Rocky Mount, N.C., Dec. 21, 1936; s. Paul Madison and Ruby Leighn (Coggins) S.; B.S., N.C. State U., 1960; m. Patricia Ann Lewis, Feb. 1, 1959; children—Paul Madison III, Kathryn Elma, Samuel Garland, Patricia Lewis. Partner speculative home bldg., Rocky Mount, 1960; civil engr. city Winston-Salem, N.C., 1960-64; mgr. engring. Hanes Corp., Winston-Salem, 1964-70; mgr. Butler Bldg. div. R.B. Deal Constrn. Co., Winston-Salem, 1970—. Precinct worker Republican party, 1968—. Bd. dirs. Winston-Salem Nat. Little League, N.W. Midget Football League. Served with USMCR, 1955. Registered profl. engr., N.C. Mem. Nat., N.C. socs. profl. engrs., Jr. C. of C. Elk. Home: 526 Walter Ct Winston-Salem NC 27103 Office: PO Box 5453 Winston-Salem NC 27103

STEPHENS, ROBERT F., county judge, b. 1927; grad. Ind. U.; LL.B., U. Ky. Admitted to Ky. bar, 1951; now judge, Fayette County. Office: Fayette County Court House Lexington KY 41007*

STEPHENS, ROBERT GRIER, JR., U.S. congressman; b. Atlanta, Aug. 14, 1913; s. Robert Grier and Martha Lucy (Evans) S.; A.B., U. Ga., 1935, M.A., 1937, LL.B. cum laude, 1941; exchange student U. Hamburg (Germany), 1935-36; m. Grace Winston, July 20, 1938; children—Grace Winston (Mrs. D.R. Bianchi), Robert Grier III, Mary Winston, Lawton Evans. Mem. staff dept. history and polit. sci. U. Ga., 1936-41, 46; admitted to Ga. bar, 1941; practice in Athens, 1946-60; city atty. Athens, 1947-50; mem. Ga. Senate, 1951-53, Ga. Ho. of Reps., 1953-59; mem. 87th-93d congresses, 10th Dist. Ga. Gen. counsel Ga. Press Assn., 1959-61. Mem. Ga. Democratic Exec. Com. Bd. dirs. Athens YMCA. Served with AUS, 1941-46; legal staff Nuremberg Trial, 1945; lt. col. Res. Mem. Am. Legion, V.F.W., Athens C. of C. (dir.), Phi Beta Kappa, Phi Kappa Phi, Omicron Delta Kappa, Kappa Alpha. Presbyn. (elder). Kiwanian (lt. gov.), Elk. Home: 435 Woodward Way Athens GA 30601 Office: House Office Bldg Washington DC 20515

STEPHENS, ROBERT KENNETH, accountant; b. Newbern, Tenn., Nov. 23, 1914; s. Thomas David and Mary Louise (Denton) S.; B.S. in Commerce, U. Tenn., 1937; postgrad. accounting LaSalle Extension U., 1939-42; m. Lillian Magdalene Leigh, July 2, 1938; children—Linda Louise (Mrs. Steven Hodges Brasfield), Mary Catherine (Mrs. Donald Estes). Tchr., Miller-Hawykins Bus. Coll., Memphis, 1937-38; dean, tchr. Tupelo (Miss.) Bus. Coll., 1938-39; auditor U.S. Dept. Agr., Little Rock, 1940-42, Jackson, Miss., 1942-46; pvt. practice pub. accounting, Jackson, 1946—; sec.-treas. Underwood Glass Co., New Orleans, 1956—. C.P.A., Miss., Tenn. Mem. Am. Inst. C.P.A.'s, Miss. Soc. C.P.A.'s, Miss. Econ. Council, Jackson C. of C. Baptist (sec., clk.). Club: Jackson Country. Home: 3939 Hawthorn Dr Jackson MS 39206 Office: 2715 N State St Jackson MS 39216

STEPHENS, ROBERT OREN, educator; b. Corpus Christi, Tex., Oct. 2, 1928; s. Joseph Key and Mary Emma (Robertson) S.; student Del Mar Coll., 1945-47; B.A., Tex. Coll. Arts and Industries, 1949; M.A., U. Tex., 1951, Ph.D., 1958; m. Carey Virginia Jones, Sept. 8, 1956; children—Nancy Leigh, Melissa Ann, Robert Allan. Tchr. English, Shiner (Tex.) High Sch., 1949-50; spl. instr. English, U. Tex., 1957-58, 58-61; asst. prof. English, U. N.C. at Greensboro, 1961-66, asso. prof., 1966-68, prof., 1968—. Served to lt. USNR, 1951-55. Mem. Am. Studies Assn., Am. Assn. U. Profs., Modern Lang. Assn., South Atlantic Modern Lang. Assn. Presbyn. (elder 1965). Author: Hemingway's Nonfiction: The Public Voice, 1968. Contbr. articles to profl. jours. Home: 1706 Sylvan Rd Greensboro NC 27403

STEPHENS, STEVE, pub. relations, advt. co. exec.; b. Newport, Ark., Apr. 22, 1930; s. Owen and Allie Mae (Rozzell) S.; student U. Little Rock, 1948; B.S. in Bus. Adminstrn., U. Ark., 1951; postgrad. U. Miss., 1954-55; L.H.D., Southwestern Coll., Oklahoma City; m. Ellen Beede, Apr. 21, 1957; children—Stanton, Steele. With CBS-TV, Little Rock, 1957-65; spl. asst. to U.S. Senator John L. McClellan, Washington, 1965-68; corporate v.p. pub. relations and advt. Nat. Investors Life Ins. Co., Little Rock, 1968-69; pres., chmn bd. Stephens Internat., Ltd., Little Rock, 1969—; chmn. bd., chief exec. officer Stephens & Goodwin Investments, Inc.; dir. Bolivian Internat. Devel., Sociedad Anomina. State adviser Nat. Found., 1960-64; mem. exec. com. Radio Free Europe, 1961-62; state chmn. Arthritis Found., 1969; state adviser Youth Leadership Council, 1961-65; chmn. Little Rock City Beautiful Commn., 1961-62; mem. Pulaski County Health and Welfare Council, 1961-62; del. Inter-Am. Partners Alliance for Progress Conf., Lima, Peru, Partners of Ams. Hemispheric Conf., San Jose, Costa Rica, 1968; chmn. publicity United Fund campaign, 1968, bd. dirs., 1969-71; publicity chmn., dist. vice chmn. Pioneer dist. Boy Scouts Am., 1969-70; state chmn. March Dimes, 1972; state chmn. Internat. Youth for Understanding; mem. internat. adv. council Direct Relief Found. Named Bolivian Counsel for Ark., Bolivian Pres., 1969. Served with USMC, 1951-54. Recipient Service to Humanity award Little Rock Jaycees. Mem. Pub. Relations Soc. Am., Ark. Advt. Fedn., Internat. Assn. Polit. Consultants, Little Rock C. of C., Brit. Inst. Pub. Relations (overseas asso.), Sales and Marketing Execs. Pub. Relations Soc. Am. Mason (Shriner, 32 deg.). Clubs: Little Rock, Racquet, Capitol, Pleasant Valley Country; Bahama Sound Beach. Home: 2823 Painted Valley Dr Little Rock AR 72207 Office: Tower Bldg Little Rock AR 72201

STEPHENS, WILLIAM DAVID, chemist; b. Paris, Tenn., Nov. 11, 1932; s. Claude Elmer and Lillian (Cole) S.; B.S., Western Ky. State U., 1954; Ph.D., Vanderbilt U., 1959; m. Marilyn Jean Miller, Sept. 11, 1954; children—William Daniel, Steve-Anna, Jennifer Lynn. Chief organic chem. sect. Thiokol Chem. Co., Redstone Arsenal, Huntsville, Ala., 1959-63, supr. synthetic chemistry and propellant research group, 1966—; head basic materials research lab. Goodyear Tire & Rubber Co., Akron, O., 1963-66. Asso. prof. chemistry U. Ala., Huntsville, 1966—. Mem. Am. Chem. Soc. (sect. mem. bd. dirs.). Home: 8912 Willow Hills Dr Huntsville AL 35802 Office: Thiokol Chem Corp Redstone Arsenal Huntsville AL 35807

STEPHENS, WILLIAM THEODORE, lawyer; b. Balt., Mar. 31, 1922; s. William A. and Mildred (Griffin) S.; student Balt. City Coll., 1939-41, U. Md., 1946-47; A.B., J.D., George Washington U., 1950, postgrad., 1951; m. Arlene Alice Lesti, June 2, 1958; children—William Theodore, Renee Adena. Admitted to D.C. bar, 1951; mem. firm J.L. Green, Washington, 1950-51, J.M. Cooper, Washington, 1952-54; own law firm William T. Stephens, Washington, 1955—. Dir. Exotech, Inc., Gaithersburg, Md., Andromeda, Inc., Kensington, Md., SDA Corp., Landover, Md., Nationwide Trailer Rental System, Inc., Wichita, Kan., Hamilton Bank & Trust Co., Bailey's Cross Roads, Va. Mem. exec. com. Nat. Com. on Uniform Traffic Laws and Ordinances. Trustee Ophthalmic Research Found., Washington, Fairfax-Brewster Sch., Falls Church, Va., Am. Bikeways Found., Washington. Served to 1st lt. AUS, 1941-46. Mem. Bar Assn. D.C. (com. on taxation 1959-68), Am. (sec. taxation 1959—, sec. corps., banking and bus. law 1960—), Md., Va. bar assns., XVI Corps Assn. (pres. 1967), Kappa Alpha (Ct. of Honor), Delta Theta Phi. Clubs: Commonwealth (Cal.), University, National Aviation, Capitol Hill (Washington); Racquet International, Jockey (Miami, Fla.). Home: 6636 Tansey Dr Falls Church VA 22042 also 881 Ocean Dr Key Biscayne FL 33149 Office: 1000 Vermont Av Washington DC 20005

STEPHENS, WILTON ROBERT, utility co. exec.; b. Prattsville, Ark., Sept. 14, 1907; s. Albert J. and Ethel (Pumphrey) S.; hon. doctorate Monticello A. & M. Coll.; LL.D., U. Ark.; m. Anna Bess Chisum, Aug. 6, 1956; children—Elizabeth Ann, Pamela Diane. Propr., Ark.-Okla. Gas Corp., Fort Smith, Ark., 1946, Stephens Prodn. Ft. Smith; with Ark. La. Gas Co., Little Rock, 1956—, pres., chmn. bd., 1956—; pres., dir. Arkla Exploration, Ark. Cement Corp., Arkla Industries, Arkla Chem. Chmn., Pulaski County March of Dimes, 1950; dir. Salvation Army Bldg. Fund, 1966. Chmn. bd. dirs. Ark. State Hosp.; bd. dirs. Ark. Livestock Commn. Served with AUS, 1930-32. Home: 2 Palisades St Little Rock AR 72207 also Prattsville AR 72150 Office: 400 E Capitol St Little Rock AR 72202

STEPHENSON, ALEXANDER BASIL, banker; b. Jacksonville, Fla., Oct. 9, 1925; s. John Edmond and Marie (Lohse) S.; student The Citadel, 1943; B.S. in Banking and Finance, U. Fla., 1949; m. Barbara Wickham, June 18, 1948; children—Robert, James, William. Loan officer Atlantic Nat. Bank, Jacksonville, 1950-52; 1st v.p., dir. Springfield Atlantic Bank, Jacksonville, 1952—. Served with USNR, World War II; PTO. Clubs: Jacksonville Marine Assn., St. John's River Yacht, North Florida Cruising. Home: 5525 Lakewood Circle E Jacksonville FL 32207 Office: W Bay Sta Jacksonville FL 32206

STEPHENSON, ALLEN DECOSTA, JR., assn. exec.; b. Raleigh, N.C., May 6, 1927; s. Allen D. and Georgia (Smith) S.; student N.C. State Coll., 1946-47; B.B.A., Wake Forest Coll., 1950; m. Betty Jean Herrington, Oct. 8, 1960; children—Lisa Marie, Sandra Jean. Asst. mgr. Rocky Mount C. of C. (N.C.), 1954-55; mgr. Carrollton C. of C. (Ga.), 1955-59; dir. indsl. relations Asso. Industries Ga., Atlanta, 1959-61; exec. dir. Athens Area C. of C. (Ga.), 1961—. Sec.-treas., dir. N.E.Ga. Area Planning and Devel. Assn., 1962—; exec. dir. Athens-Clarke County Indsl. Devel. Authority. Served with USNR, 1945-46. Mem. Am., So., Ga. (pres. 1967) chamber commerce execs. assns., Ga. Indsl. Developers Assn. (pres. 1972). Baptist (asso. deacon) Rotarian. Home: 201 Woodward Way Athens GA 30601 Office: PO Box 948 Athens GA 30601

STEPHENSON, CHARLES MILLARD, govt. ofcl.; b. Kite, Ga., Oct. 23, 1910; s. Jubilee S. and Annie (Hatcher) S.; B.B.A. cum laude, Emory U., 1930; M.A., U. Ky., 1932, postgrad., 1932-34; m. Laura Norwood Roberson, May 1, 1936; children—Ann Marie (Mrs. Bruce Lynn Welch), Peter Martin, Hilary (Mrs. Alvin Joyner Sanders), Laura Paine, Elizabeth. Research accountant Ky. Tax Reduction Assn., Louisville, 1933; state supr. municipal and county finance study Civil Works Adminstrn., Ky., 1933-34; adminstrv. asst. Bur. Bus. Research, U. Ky., Lexington, 1934; economist TVA, Knoxville, Tenn., 1934-68, chief govt. research staff, div. nav. devel. and regional studies, 1968—. Mem. Nat. Tax Assn. (mem. intergovt. fiscal relations com.), Am. Soc. for Pub. Adminstrn., Delta Sigma Pi, Beta Gamma Sigma. Democrat. Unitarian-Universalist. Author: Industrial Sites: A Community Problem, 1961. Home: 1803 Westchester Dr Knoxville TN 37918 Office: Arnstein Bldg Knoxville TN 37902

STEPHENSON, FRED DOUGLAS, psychiat. social worker; b. Pontiac, Mich., Sept. 21, 1939; s. Leonard Earl and Myrland (Coleman) S.; A.B., U. Mich., 1961; postgrad. U. Cal., 1962; A.M., U. Chgo., 1965; Diploma, Gestalt Inst. Cleve., 1972; m. Kay S. Donald, June 3, 1962; children—Shawn, Anne. Pub. health program asso. Tb and Health Assn., Santa Ana, Cal., 1961-63; psychiat. social worker Chgo. State Hosp., 1964, Tinley Park (Ill.) State Hosp., 1965-67; chief psychiat. social worker Community Mental Health Services, Gainesville, Fla., 1967-69; pvt. practice in individual marriage and family psychotherapy, Gainesville, 1969—; instr. psychiatry U. Fla. at Gainesville, 1969—. Mem. Nat. Assn. Social Workers (sec.-treas. treas. N.E. Fla. chpt. 1968-69), Am. Assn. Marriage and Family Counselors (clin. mem.), Acad. Certified Social Workers. Home: Route 5 Box 464 Gainesville FL 32601

STEPHENSON, JAMES LUCAS, JR., banker; b. Dallas, Apr. 17, 1937; s. James Lucas and Dorothy (Wyatt) S.; B.B.A., So. Meth. U., 1960; m. Nancy Jane Ray, Nov. 11, 1961; children—James Lucas III, Lucy Ann. With First Nat. Bank, Dallas, 1961—, asst. cashier nat. accounts div., 1963-67, asst. v.p., 1967-68, v.p. investment div., 1968—. Mem. Govs. Special Com. of Finance, 1970-71. Served to capt. AUS, 1965-67. Mem. Tex. Urban League. Home: 4305 Versailles St Dallas TX 75205 Office: PO Box 6031 Dallas TX 75222

STEPHENSON, JIMMYE MITCHELL, educator; b. Oklahoma City, June 18, 1928; d. Harold Gentry and Vera (Mitchell) Stephenson; B.A., John Brown U., 1950; B.S.N., Tulane U., 1953; diploma Mather Sch. Nursing, 1953; M.N., Emory U., 1960; Specialist in Coll. Teaching degree Murray State U., 1971. Staff nurse So. Bapt. Hosp., New Orleans, 1953; asst. instr. Northwestern St. Coll. la., Natchitoches, 1954-59, asst. prof., 1959-61; chmn. dept. nursing N.E. Miss. Jr. Coll., Booneville, 1962-69; asst. prof. nursing Berea (Ky.) Coll., 1963-69, student acad. adviser student nurse recruitment programs, 1963-69, adviser Berea Coll. Assn. Student Nurses, 1964-69; asso. prof. dept. nursing Murray (Ky.) State U., 1969—. Adviser 2d dist. Student Nurses Assn. Ky., 1963-67. Mem. Am., Ky. nurses assns., Nat., Ky. leagues for nursing. Democrat. Baptist. Home: Route 5 Box 2111 Murray KY 42071

STEPHENSON, MALVINA, syndicated columnist, radio reporter; b. Paris, Tex.; d. Robert E. and Allie (King) Stephenson; A.B. in Govt. History, Southeast State Coll., 1932; M.S. in Journalism, U. Okla., 1936. Feature writer, reporter Tulsa World, 1936-39, columnist, 1940-51, 63-—; with Stephenson News Bur., 1940-51, 63-—; radio reporter ABC, Washington, 1945-49; editorial and research asst. to Senator R.S. Kerr, 1951-63; syndicated columnist Washington Offbeat, Knight Newspapers, Inc., 1969-—; with Universal Press Syndicate, Washington, 1970-—. Mem. Delta Delta Delta. Clubs: Washington Press, Am. Newspaper. Co-editor: Land, Wood and Water (author Sen. Robert S. Kerr), 1960. Home: 330 A St SE Washington DC 20003

STEPHENSON, PHIL, finance co. exec.; b. Gaffney, S.C., Oct. 24, 1912; s. George L. and Osie (Simmons) S.; student Mars Hill Jr. Coll., 1932-33, U. S.C., 1933-37; m. Edna Louise Mottern, Aug. 12, 1937 (div. 1964); children—Phil, Robert, Kathy. Vice pres. Dixie Glove Mfg. Co., Gaffney, 1937-39; Ford dealer, Gaffney, 1939-—; organized Stephenson Finance Co., Inc., 1947, now operating 62 brs. in South; organizer Superior Automobile Ins. Co., Florence, S.C., 1952, Superior Life Ins. Co., 1954; organizer, chmn. bd. Westchester Nat. Bank of Dade County, Miami, Fla., 1964, Peoples Bank of S.C., Florence, 1965; organizer, dir. Midway Nat. Bank, Miami, Fla.; dir. NCNB Corp., Charlotte, N.C. Bd. dirs. S.C. Found. Ind. Colls., Inc., So. States Indsl. Council, Nothville, Tenn.; trustee Limestone Coll., Gaffney; mem. devel. adv. council U. S.C. Mem. Am. Indsl. Bankers Assn. (dir. at large). Episcopalian. Clubs: City (Charlotte), Poinsetta (Greenville, S.C.); Racquet, Palm Bay, Jockey (Miami, Fla.); Florence Country. Home: 950 Park Av Florence SC 29501 Office: 518 S Irby St Florence SC 29501

STEPHENSON, RICHARD MURRELL, clergyman; b. nr. Ivor, Va., Dec. 1, 1921; s. Edgar Vick and Eleanor (Daughtrey) S.; B.A., Hampden-Sydney Coll., 1943; Th.M., So. Bapt. Theol. Sem., 1946; D.D., U. Richmond, Va., 1966; m. Noralee Mellor, Feb. 1, 1949; children—Vivian, Lee, Richard. Ordained to ministry Bapt. Ch., 1944; pastor First Bapt. Ch., Ft. Myers, Fla., 1946-50; pastor Columbia Bapt. Ch., Falls Church, Va., 1950-67; exec. sec. Bapt. Gen. Assn. Va., Richmond, 1968-—; dir. So. Bapt. Found., Nashville. Trustee So. Bapt. Theol. Sem., Louisville, Hon. chaplain Army, 1965. Mem. Omicron Delta Kappa, Eta Sigma Phi. Kiwanian. Home: 8951 Bellefonte Rd Richmond VA 23229 Office: PO Box 8568 Richmond VA 23226

STEPHENSON, ROBERT EDWARD, librarian; b. Katonah, N.Y., June 22, 1923; s. John and Etta Lillian (Adams) S.; A.B., Hamilton Coll., 1948; M.S. in L.S., Columbia, 1950; m. Mary White Thompson, June 17, 1961; children—Thomas Robert, Barbara Ann. With Va. Poly. Inst. and State U. (formerly Va. Poly. Inst.), Blacksburg, 1949-—, documents librarian, acting asso. librarian tech. services, 1961-62, asso. librarian tech. services, 1962-71, architecture librarian, 1972-—. Vice pres. Blacksburg Regional Art Assn., 1970-71, pres., 1971-—; mem. Blacksburg Council on Human Relations, 1959-63; mem. Blacksburg Ministerial Assn., 1955-—. Served with USAAF, 1943-46. Mem. A.L.A., Va. (2d v.p. 1966-67), Southeastern library assns., Potomac Tech. Processing Librarians (exec. com. 1964-65), Am. Assn. U. Profs. (membership com. chpt. 1965-66). Christian Scientist. Clubs: Va. Polytechnic Institute University, Blacksburg Country (Blacksburg). Home: 1206 Highland Circle SE Blacksburg VA 24060

STEPHENSON, ROBERT LLOYD, archeologist; b. Portland, Ore., Feb. 18, 1919; s. George Albert and Myrtle (Smith) S.; B.A., U. Ore., 1940, M.A., 1942; Ph.D., U. Mich., 1956; m. Georgie Ellen Boydstun, Jan. 5, 1946. Supr. archeol. lab. U. Tex., 1940-41; excavation dir. Washington and Jefferson Coll., N.M., 1941; archeologist Smithsonian Instn., 1946-51, Mo. Basin River Project, Lincoln, Neb., 1952-63, River Basin Surveys dir., 1963-66; archeol. survey coordinator U. Nev., 1966-68; dir. Inst. Archeology and Anthropology U. S.C., Columbia, 1968-—; asso. prof. U. Neb., 1961-63. Served to 1st lt. USMCR, 1942-46. Fellow A.A.A.S., Soc. Applied Anthropology, Am. Anthrop. Assn.; mem. Soc. Am. Archeology, Sigma Xi. Editor: Plains Anthropologist, 1960-63; asst. editor Am. Antiquity, 1960-63. Contbr. articles profl. jours. Home: 5831 Satchel Ford Rd Columbia SC 29206

STEPHENSON, WILLIAM HAYWOOD, state ofcl.; b. Johnson County, Willow Springs, N.C., Nov. 26, 1927; s. William P. and Lois (Partin) S.; student Hoyles Bus. Sch., 1947-48; m. Della F. Coates, Mar. 10, 1949; children—William Timothy, John Phillip. Wtih U.S. Mcht. Marines, 1945-46; with N.C. Indsl. Commn., Raleigh, 1948-—, exec. sec., 1960-70, dep. commr., 1970, commr., 1970-—. Chmn. Wake County (N.C.) Bd. Elections, 1964-70. Mem. N.C. Shorthand Reporters Assn. (organizer, sec. 1957), Woodmen of World. Democrat. Methodist (v.p. Meth. Men 1967-—, asst. supt. Sunday sch. 1967-—). Clubs: Colonial (Garner pres. 1967-—), Elks. Home: 1207 Poplar Av Garner NC 27529 Office: Albemarle Bldg Raleigh NC 27611

STEPP, JAMES MARVIN, educator; b. Old Fort, N.C., July 26, 1913; s. John Marvin and Florence (Pendergrass) S.; B.A., Berea Coll., 1937; M.A., U. Va., 1938, Ph.D., 1940; m. Vivian Olivia Pittman, June 21, 1942; children—James Marvin, John E., Kenneth S., Benjamin T. Mem. faculty Clemson (S.C.) U., 1940-—, Alumni prof. agrl. econs., 1966-—; agrl. economist, div. land econs., Bur. Agrl. Econs., U.S. Dept. Agr., Atlanta, 1944. Econs. cons. Nat. Security Resources Bd., 1952, S.C. State Devel. Bd., 1962, Marine Resources Com. of Coastal Plains Regional Com., 1968, S.C. Water Resources Com., 1967-—. Mem. Am., So. (v.p. 1954-55) econ. assns., Am., So. agrl. econ. assns., A.A.A.S., S.C. Acad. Sci. Methodist. Club: Torch. Editor (with James C. Hite) Coastal Zone Resource Management, 1971. Contbr. to publs. in field. Home: 252 Riggs Dr Clemson SC 29631

STERLING, W. DAWSON, life ins. exec.; b. Waco, Tex., Dec. 29, 1922; s. Marion and Ruth (Esser) S.; student Baylor U., 1939-40; B.B.A. with highest honors, U. Tex., 1947; LL.B., So. Meth. U., 1953; student exec. program Columbia, 1958; m. Lynn; children—Clare, Evelyn. With Southwestern Life Ins. Co., Dallas, 1947-69, v.p., sec., 1958-62, pres., 1962-69; pres. Am. Gen. Life Ins. Co., Houston, Am. Gen. Life Isn. Co. of Del., Houston; dir. Patriot Life Ins. Co. N.Y.; v.p., dir. Am. Gen. Ins. Co., Houston, 1969-—; dir. No. Ins. Co. N.Y., Assurance Co. Am. Admitted to Tex. bar, 1953. Mem. exec. com. Am. Life Conv., 1966-69; dir. Internat. Ins. Seminars, Tex. Life Conv., 1962-64. Mem. Dallas Citizens Council, 1962-69; gen. chmn. Dallas United Fund campaign, 1967; pres., dir. Dallas Assembly, 1962-63. Served to 1st lt., pilot USAAF, World War II. Fellow Life Office Mgmt. Assn. (pres. 1967-68); mem. Dallas C. of C. (v.p.; dir. 1962-65), State Bar Tex., Order Woolsack, Beta Gamma Sigma, Rotarian. Address: PO Box 1931 Houston TX 77001

STERLING, WALTER GAGE, mfg. co. exec.; b. Anahuac, Tex., May 20, 1901; s. Ross Shaw and Maude (Gage) S.; LL.B., U. Tex., 1925; m. Ruth Dermody, Jan. 30, 1941. With Royalty Properties, Houston, 1927-—, v.p., 1946-—; pres. Sterling Oil & Refinery 1935-50, Richmond Mfg. Co., 1951-—; with Richmond Sales, 1952-—; dir. Citizens Nat. Bank & Trust Co., Baytown; trustee Mortgage & Trust Investors. Trustee Hermann Hosp. Estate, 1950-—, pres. bd. trustees, 1965-—; bd. dirs. Tex. Med. Center. Served to capt. USAAF, 1941-44. Mem. S.A.R. (pres. gen. 1968-69), Delta Kappa Epsilon. Home: 5701 Jackson St Houston TX 77004 Office: PO Box 2891 Houston TX 77001

STERN, ALFRED, philosopher, educator; b. Baden bei Wien, Austria, July 19, 1899; came to U.S. 1944, naturalized, 1949; s. Julius and Rose (Kohn) S.; Bachelor, Piaristepgymnasium, Vienna, 1919; Ph.D. with honors, U. Vienna, 1923; m. Gloria Maria Pagan y Ferrer, Nov. 15, 1946. Lectr., Sorbonne, Paris, 1934-39; prof. philosophy Inst. Higher Studies of Belgium, Brussels, 1935-40, Cal. Inst. Tech., Pasadena, 1947-68, U. Puerto Rico, Mayaguez, 1968-—. Adv. Folia Humanistica, Barcelona, Spain, Atenea, Mayaguez. Served to lt., Austrian Army, 1917-18; French Army, 1940. Decorated knight Legion of Honor (France); officer Order of Leopold II (Belgium); officer of Academic Palms (France). Mem. Am. Philos. Assn. (pres. Pacific div. 1964-64, Alliance Francaise (v.p. Los Angeles, 1962-68). Author: Philosophical Foundations of Truth, Reality and Value, 1932; Philosophy of Values, 1936; Philosophy of Politics, 1943; Philosophy of Laughter and Tears, 1949; Philosophy of History and the Problem of Values, 1962; Sartre—His Philosophy and Existential Psychoanalysis, 1967; The Search for Meaning, 1971. Home: 270 Luna St San Juan PR 00901 Office: U PR Mayaguez PR 00708

STERN, HAROLD P., art museum dir.; B.A., U. Mich., 1943, M.A., 1948, Ph.D., 1959. Asso. dir. Freer Gallery Art, Smithsonian Instn., Washington, until 1971, dir., 1971-—. Hon. lectr. Japanese art U. Mich. Author: Masterpieces of Korean Art, 1957; Hokusai: Paintings and Drawings in the Freer Gallery of Art, 1960; Master Prints of Japan Ukiyo-e Hanga, 1969; Freer Gallery of Art: Japan, 1971; Rimpa: Masterworks of the Japanese Decorative School, 1971. Research on Chinese art, Japanese painting, ceramics and decorative arts. Office: Freer Gallery Art Washington DC 20560*

STERN, PHILIP MAURICE, author; b. N.Y.C., May 24, 1926; s. Edgar Bloom and Edith (Rosenwald) S.; A.B. magna cum laude, Harvard, 1947; m. Helen Phillips Burroughs Sedgwick, Aug. 30, 1957; children—Henry D., Michael P., Helen P., David M., Eve. Reporter and editorial writer New Orleans Item, 1948; legislative asst. to U.S. Rep. Henry M. Jackson, 1949-50, U.S. Senator Paul Douglas, 1951-52; personal asst. Wilson W. Wyatt, campaign mgr. to Adlai E. Stevenson, 1952; dir. research Democratic Nat. Com., also sr. editor Dem. Digest, 1953-56; editor No. Virginia Sun, Arlington, 1957-60, editor and pub., 1960; dep. asst. sec. state for public affairs, 1961-62; mag. writer, 1962-—. Mem. Health and Welfare Council Greater Washington Area, 1960; chmn. Va. United Givers Fund, 1960, chmn. Arlington, 1959; dir. Council Founds. and Fair Campaign Practices Com. Pres. Stern Family Fund, Philip M. Stern Family Fund. Rockefeller fellow, 1948-49. Mem. Phi Beta Kappa. Club: Federal City. Author: The Great Treasury Raid; The Oppenheimer Case: Security on Trial; (with Helen B. Stern) Oh, Say Can You See: A Bifocal Tour of Washington; (with George de Vincent) The Shame of a Nation; Home: 2301 S St NW Washington DC 20008 Office: 200 L St NW Washington DC 20036

STERN, S. WALTER, JR., food products co. exec.; b. Chgo., Aug. 1, 1914; s. S. Walter and Josephine Ella (Mayer) S.; A.B., Harvard, 1935, M.B.A., 1937; m. Simonne Trey, Sept. 18, 1945; children—Catherine L., Carole Anne. With Lehman Bros., investment adv. service, N.Y.C., 1937-38; with Whitney Nat. Bank of New Orleans, 1938-59, v.p., 1955-59; v.p. J. Aron & Co., Inc., New Orleans, 1959-—; dir. William B. Reily & Co., Inc., Mermentau Mineral & Land Co. Treas. Bur. Govtl. Research, 1966-—. Pres. United Fund Greater New Orleans Area, 1966, New Orleans Area Health Planning Council, 1969. Bd. dirs. Touro Infirmary, New Orleans, 1955-—, Community Chest, 1970-—, La. State Health Planning Council, 1970-—; pres. bd. trustees Metairie Park Country Day Sch., 1961-63. Served with AUS, 1941-46. Mem. Asso. Harvard Alumni (dir. 1967-70). Club: New Orleans Country. Home: 2856 Camp St New Orleans LA 70115 Office: PO Box 30340 New Orleans LA 70190

STERNBERG, DANIEL ARLE, musician, condr., coll. dean; b. Lwow, Poland, Mar. 29, 1913; s. Philipp and Eva (Makowska) S.; baccalaureate, Realgymnasium, Vienna, 1931; student U. Vienna, 1931-35; diploma of condr., Vienna State Acad. Music, 1935; composition study with Karl Weigl, 1931-35; conducting with Fritz Stiedry, 1935-36; m. Felicitas Gobineau, July 29, 1936. Came to U.S., 1939, naturalized, 1946. Lectr. Vienna Volkshochschule, 1933-34; condr. Vienna Vets. Orchestra, 1934-35; asst. condr. Leningrad Philharmonic and Grand Opera, 1935-36; guest condr. Leningrad and Moscow radio orchestras, 1936, Dallas Symphony Orch., 1952, 65; music dir. Tiflis State Symphony Orch., Russia, 1936-37; head piano dept. Hockaday Inst. Music, Dallas, 1940-42; dean sch. music Baylor U., Waco, Tex., 1942-—; mus. dir., condr. Waco Symphony Orch., 1963-—; concert accompanist; lectr. mus. subjects. Awarded Abrams Meml. award for orchestral composition by Dallas Symphony Orchestra, 1948. Mem. Am. Assn. U. Profs., Music Tchrs. Nat. Assn. (pres. Southwestern div.), Sinfonia, Phi Mu Alpha, Omicron Delta Kappa. Author articles mags. Home: 3108 Robin Rd Waco TX 76708

STERNBERG, HANS JOACHIM, dept. store exec.; b. Aurich, Germany, July 4, 1935; s. Erich and Lea (Knurr) S.; A.B. magna cum laude, Princeton, 1957; m. Donna Gail Weintraub, Feb. 19, 1967; children—Erich, Julie Ellen, Deborah Ann. Came to U.S., 1937, naturalized, 1943. With Goudchaux's, Inc., Baton Rouge, 1960-—, exec. v.p., sec.-treas., 1963-—; partner Insa Sternberg & Bros., Baton Rouge, 1960-—; pres. 1550 Realty Co.; v.p. Erich Sternberg Realty Co., Inc.; dir. WLCS Radio Sta. Mem. adv. council marketing dept. La. State U., 1971-—; pres. Baton Rouge Jewish Welfare Fedn., 1971-72; mem. young leadership cabinet United Jewish Appeal, 1970-—. Bd. dirs. La. Heart Assn., 1970-71, La. Capital Area Health Planning Council, 1970-71, Baton Rouge Art Gallery, 1967-—. Served to lt. (j.g.) USNR, 1957-59. Jewish religion (treas. temple 1971-72, sec. Men's club 1969). Clubs: City, Bocage Racquet, Toastmasters, Round Table (Baton Rouge). Home: 2375 Kleinert Av Baton Rouge LA 70806 Office: PO Drawer 3478 Baton Rouge LA 70821

STERNE, AUGUSTUS HERRINGTON, banker; b. Montgomery, Ala., Feb. 28, 1913; s. Adolph H. and Sue (Brown) S.; A.B., U. Ga., 1934; postgrad. Emory U., 1934-35; m. Helen Hill Hopkins, Apr. 29, 1938; children—Helen Hopkins (Mrs. James S. Anderson), William A., Carroll P., Augusta Hill, Nancy Evans. Reporter, Retail Credit Co., Atlanta, 1935-36; with Trust Co. of Ga., Atlanta, 1936-—, asst. v.p., 1946-47, v.p., 1947-57, sr. v.p., 1957-64, pres., 1964-—, dir., 1963-—; dir. Trust Co. of Ga. Assos., Munich Am. Reassurance Co., J.O. King, Inc., Atlantic Steel Co., Oxford Industries, Inc., So. Natural Gas Co. Trustee, chmn. U. Ga. Found.; trustee Agnes Scott Coll.; mem. gov. bd. United Way Am. Served with USMC, 1942-45. Mem. Sigma Alpha Epsilon, Phi Delta Phi. Episcopalian. Clubs: Peachtree Golf, Piedmont Driving, Capital City, Nine O'Clocks, Augusta National Golf, Commerce (pres., dir.). Home: 2655 Rivers Rd NW Atlanta GA 30305 Office: PO Drawer 4418 Atlanta GA 30302

STERNER, JOHN, med. instrument mfr.; b. London, Eng., Oct. 26, 1912; s. Lawrence E. and Bleema (Levy) S.; came to U.S., 1915; B.S., Mass. Inst. Tech., 1933, D.Sc., 1950; m. Delphine T. Leary, Feb. 4, 1956; stepchildren—Patricia E. Leary, Pamela A. Leary. Vice pres., dir. Baird Atomic, Inc., Cambridge, Mass., 1939-54; dir. flight test operations Space Tech. Labs., TRW, Inc., Patrick Air Force Base, Fla., 1955-59; exec. v.p., dir. Cordis Corp., Miami, Fla., 1960-—. Served to lt. col. ordnance, AUS, 1942-45. Mem. Am. Phys. Soc., Optical Soc. Am., Am. Mgmt. Assn. Home: 8930 SW 52d Av Miami FL 33156 Office: 125 NE 40th St Miami FL 33137

STERNER, MICHAEL EDMUND, govt. ofcl.; b. N.Y.C., Dec. 26, 1928; s. Harold Walther and Leonie (Knoedler) S.; A.B., Harvard, 1951; m. Courtenay Read, Mar. 30, 1957; children—Lucian, Marcelin. Govt. relations rep. Arabian-Am. Oil Co., Dhahran, Saudi Arabia, joined Fgn. Ser., 1956; vice consul, Aden, 1957-58; polit. officer, Cairo, 1960-64; disk officer Near Eastern Affairs, State Dept., 1964-71, country dir. United Arab Republic Affairs, 1971-—. Served with AUS, 1954-56. Home: 2712 36th St Washington DC 20007 Office: NEA/UAR State Dept Washington DC 20520

STERRETT, SAMUEL BLACK, judge; b. Washington, Dec. 17, 1922; s. Henry Hatch Dent and Helen (Black) S.; student St. Albans Sch., 1933-41; grad. U.S. Mcht. Marine Acad., 1945 B.A., Amherst Coll., 1947; LL.B., U. Va., 1950; LL.M. in Taxation, N.Y.U., 1959; m. Jeane McBride, Aug. 27, 1949; children—Samuel Black, Robin Dent, Douglas McBride. With U.S. Mcht. Marine, 1943-46; admitted to D.C. bar, 1951, Va. bar, 1950; with law firm Alvord & Alvord, Washington, 1950-56; trial atty. Office Regional Counsel, Internal Revenue Service, N.Y.C., 1956-60; with firm Sullivan, Shea & Kenney, Washington, 1960-68; judge U.S. Tax Ct., Washington, 1968-—. Bd. mgrs. Chevy Chase Village, 1970-—. Democratic party candidate Md. Ho. of Dels., 1962. First v.p., bd. trustees Washington Hosp. Center, 1969-—. Served with AUS, 1943. Mem. Am., Fed. Va. bar assns., Bar Assn. D.C., Beta Theta Pi. Episcopalian. Clubs: Chevy Chase, Metropolitan Washington. Home: 8 Magnolia Pkwy Chevy Chase MD 20015 Office: United States Tax Court Box 70 Washington DC 20044

STEUBING, GAYLAND CLARENCE, physician; b. Rosenberg, Tex., Aug. 21, 1939; s. Herman Ondo and Louise (Anderson) S.; B.S., Sam Houston State U., 1961; M.D., U. Tex. Med. Sch., 1963; m. Sharley Louise Early, May 28, 1939; children—Shelley, Stephanie, Stacey. Intern Meml. Baptist Hosp., Houston, 1963-64; pvt. practice medicine, Houston, 1963-—; partner Gready Clinic, Houston, 1963-—. Mem. Am., Tex., So. med. assns., Am., Tex. assns. family practitioners. Baptist. Home: 1528 Kirby St Houston TX 77019 Office: 810 Caroline St Houston TX 77002

STEVEN, WILLIAM PICKFORD, editor; b. Eau Claire, Wis., Sept. 10, 1908; s. James David Ritchie and Merle Sears (Pickford) S.; Ph.B., U. Wis., 1933; m. Lucile Shoemaker, July 7, 1934; children—Margaret (Mrs. F.J. Benicy), Sara (Mrs. W.S. Stout), Lucinda (Mrs. R.C. Duncan), James David Ritchie. Mng. editor Tulsa Tribune, 1936-44; mng. editor Mpls. Tribune, 1944-50; exec. editor Mpls. Star & Tribune, 1950-60; editor Houston Chronicle, 1960-65; v.p. Chgo. Daily News/Sun Times, 1965-—; v.p., dir. Eau Claire Book & Stationary Co. Asst. dir. Office of Censorship, 1941-43. Mem. Asso. Press Mng. Editors (past pres.), Am. Soc. Newspapers Editors (past dir.). Clubs: Tavern (Chgo.); Coffee House (N.Y.C.); Bird Key Yacht (Sarasota). Home: 536 Blue Jay Pl Sarasota FL 33577 Office: 401 N Wabash Chicago IL 60611

STEVENS, A(DOLPH) EDWARD, assn. exec.; b. Glasgow, Scotland, May 19, 1899; s. Joseph John and Anna Josephine (Brewer) S.; came to U.S., 1909, naturalized, 1925; student DeLaSalle Inst., 1913-16; LL.B., DePaul U., 1922; m. Tynie Blazer, Mar. 3, 1935. Admitted to Ill. bar, 1922; practiced in Chgo., 1922-28; owner Eagle Music & Radio, Chgo., 1929-39, Eagle Radio & TV, Miami, Fla., 1939-70; exec. dir. Fla. Electronic Service Assn., 1971-—. Sec., treas. Central Brevard Christian Businessmen's Com., 1972-—. Mem. Television and Electronic Service Assn. Miami (recipient Merit award 1957, treas. 1950-59, pres. 1959-61), Profl. Television Assn. Inc. (hon.), Nat. Alliance Television and Electronic Service Assns. (gov. S. Atlantic, dir., gov. Fla. 1963-64; v.p. Eastern div. 1962-63), Fla. Electronic Service Assn. (charter and hon. life mem., pres. 1963-65, 1st ann. award plaque 1965, exec. dir. 1971-—), S. Fla. Indsl. Editors Assn. (treas. 1963-66), Better Bus. Bur. S. Fla. (dir. 1965-68), Brevard Electronic Service Assn. (hon. life), Christian Businessmen's Com. Central Brevard (sec.-treas. 1972-—). Editor: TESA Miami News, 1960-64, FESA News, 1964-65, Fla. Electronic Technician, 1969-70. Address: 3730 Leslie Dr Rockwell Estates Merritt Island FL 32952

STEVENS, ALBERT DONALD, banker; b. Jackson, Miss., Dec. 6, 1919; s. Albert and Margaret (Finn) S.; student U. Ky., 1936-40; LL.D., U. Louisville, 1951; m. Amanda Jane Hines, May 13, 1944; children—Margaret Jane (Mrs. Philip Herndon), Albert Donald. With Loan Guaranty, U.S. VA., Louisville, 1945-48; with So. Trust Co., Louisville, 1949-50; v.p. Louisville Trust Co. (Ky.)., 1952-—. Served with USAF, 1943-45, 50-52. Decorated Air medal with 2 oak leaf clusters. Mem. Ky., Louisville bankers assns., Nat. Assn. Real Estate Bds. sect. v.p.). Club: Riven Road Country (Louisville). Home: 606 Club Lane Louisville KY 40207 Office: 200 S 5th St Louisville KY 40202

STEVENS, DAVID BRUCE, orthopaedic surgeon; b. Louisville, July 11, 1929; s. Albert Clyde and Sue A. (Schan) S.; A.B., DePauw U., 1951; M.D., Northwestern U., 1955; m. Sarah Ann Symon, Sept. 1, 1952; children—Scott D., Patricia Sue. Intern, U. Mich., 1955-56, asst. resident in surgery, 1956-57; resident orthopaedics U. Mich., 1957-60; practice medicine, specializing in orthopaedic surgery, Lexington, Ky., 1960-— mem. staffs Good Samaritan, St. Joseph's, Central Baptist, Shriner's, Cardinal Hill hosps.; asst. clin. prof. surgery U. Ky. Sch. Medicine, Lexington, 1962-—; dir. Wallace's Bookstores, Inc., Lexington, 1965-—. Cons., Bur. Hearings and Appeals, Social Security Adminstrn., 1967-—; surgeon, pres. Ky. Commn. Handicapped Children, 1961-—. Mem. Ky. Central Com. Republican party, 1965-67. Bd. dirs. Opportunity Workshop of Lexington. Mem. A.M.A. (del. 1971-—), Ky. Med. Assn. (trustee), Orthopaedic Soc. (pres. 1965), Fayette County Med. Soc. (pres. 1968), Phi Beta Kappa, Alpha Omega Alpha, Sigma Nu. Rotatian. Club: Idle Hour Country (Lexington). Home: 346 Jesselin Dr Lexington KY 40503 Office: 333 Waller Av Lexington KY 40504

STEVENS, DON LORENZO, JR., naval architect; b. New Rochelle, N.Y., May 1, 1928; s. Don Lorenzo and Emily (Crandon) S.; B.C.E., U. Va., 1951; M. Engring., U. Cal. at Berkeley, 1960; m. Barbara Louise Thayer, June 16, 1951; children—Richard Alan, David Owen, Douglas Moore, Kathryn Diane. Naval architect preliminary design br. Bur. Ships, U.S. Navy, Washington, 1951-60, head structural and hydrofoil sect., 1960-66, project dir. ship concept design div., Naval Ship Engring. Center, 1966-70, dir. planning and coordination Undersea Long-Range Missile Submarine Design Project Office, Hyattsville, Md., 1970-—. Troop leader Boy Scouts Am., 1966-—. Bd. dirs. Claremont Citizens Assn., 1957-59. Registered profl. engr., Va. Mem. Soc. Naval Architects, Am. Soc. Naval Engrs. (mem. flagship sect. council 1969-—), Royal Instn. Naval Architects, Assn. Sr. Engrs. (exec. bd. 1961-62, 68-70), Instituto Panamericano Engenharia Naval, Trigon, Delta Upsilon.

Episcopalian. Home: 1212 S Forest Dr Arlington VA 22204 Office: Naval Ship Engring Center Hyattsville MD 20782

STEVENS, EDWARD JAMES, govt. ofcl.; b. Buffalo, June 13, 1911; s. Herbert E. and Eva (Clark) S.; B.A., U. Mich., 1934, M.B.A., 1937; m. Nancy Fletcher, Feb. 5, 1947. Various positions War Dept., Gen. Motors, Detroit Edison Co., 1937-44; Washington rep. Automobile Mfrs. Assn., 1944-56; cons. per diem com. Dept. Def., 1956-59; regional rep. Office Emergency Planning, Exec. Office Pres., 1959-64; program asst. NIH, 1964; program officer Office Edn., 1965, staff asst. Office Field Coordination, Dept. Health, Edn. and Welfare, 1965-71, editor weekly publ. Office Pub. Affairs, 1971—. Mem. Fed. Editors Assn., Govt. Information Orgn., Delta Sigma Pi. Elk. Clubs: University of Michigan (Washington); Punta Gorda Isles Yacht and Beach. Home: 5816 Hanover Av Springfield VA 22150 Office: HEW-North Bldg Washington DC 20201

STEVENS, ELBERT MERVIN, finance and ins. exec.; b. Harper, Tex., Apr. 14, 1902; s. Joseph Martin and Eva (Delavan) S.; student pub. schs., San Antonio; m. Thelma Riley, Oct. 31, 1928. Pres., chmn. bd. Gt. Western Loan & Trust Co., San Antonio, 1947—. Gt. Western Life Ins. Co., 1947—, Gt. Western Mut. Ins. Co., 1947—, Gt. Western Underwriters, 1956—, Gt. Western Leasing Co., 1960—, Gt. Western Finance Co., 1958—. Trustee S.W. Research Inst. San Antonio; bd. govs. Tex. Rural Communities, Dallas; bd. dirs. Keystone Sch., San Antonio Boys Clubs, Livestock Expn. Mem. Tex. Finance Conf. (past pres.), Am. Automobile Assn. (past nat. v.p.), C. of C. (past dir.), Tex. Farm Bur., Exotic Wildlife Assn. (pres.), Am. Indsl. Bankers Assn. (dir.), San Antonio Council Pres., Jr. C. of C. (past pres.), St. Hubertus Soc. Mason (K.T., Shriner), Clubs: Breakfast (past pres.), Alamo Motor (past pres.), Lions, San Antonio Gun. Office: 1000 N Alamo St San Antonio TX 78215

STEVENS, FRANCIS BOWDEN, writer, columnist; b. Norwich, N.Y., Apr. 6, 1905; A.B., Union Coll., 1926; student U. Berlin, 1926-27, U. Geneva, 1927, U., Besancon, summer 1927; LL.D. (hon.), Union Coll., 1951 1 son, Nicholas B. Clk., Am. consulate gen., later vice consul, Prague, 1931-32; vice consul, Warsaw, 1933; vice consul, lang. officer, Paris, 1934; 3d sec., Riga, 1935, Pretoria, 1936; assigned Dept. State, 1939; 2d sec., vice consul, Moscow, 1942; asst. chief Div. Eastern European Affairs, Dept. State, 1945-47, chief 1947-48; chief Spl. Research Div., Office U.S. High Commr. for Germany, Frankfurt-on-Main, 1949-52; spl. asst. to dir. Office Eastern European Affairs, Dept. State, 1952-55, dir., 1955-56; dep. chief Mission, Tehran, 1956-57; ret., 1957; staff mem. Pres.' Com. on Internat. Information Activities, 1953; sr. editor U.S. Joint Pubs. Research Service, 1957-58; tour dir. for Soviet delegations visiting U.S., 1958-59; mem. nat. staff U.S. News & World Report, 1959—. Home: 1722 19th St NW Washington DC 20009 Office: 2300 N St NW Washington DC 20037

STEVENS, H. MORRIS, state ofcl.; b. Omaha, Tex., Oct. 19, 1913; s. Harvey Bun and Nona (Boyet) S.; student Burleson Coll., 1930, Tyler Jr. Coll., 1931, Tex. U., 1931-32, Tex. Western U., 1934; m. Gwendolyn Schieffer, Dec. 27, 1941; children—Nancy Jeanette (Mrs. Thomas Hrin, Jr.), Mildred Nona (Mrs. Richard K. Rogers), Harvey Morris, Michael Richard. With Tex. Treasury Dept., Austin, 1936—, chief clk., 1946—. Mem. Tex. Pub. Employees Assn. (dir., 1st v.p. 1946-51), Nat. Assn. Unclaimed Property Adminstrs. (treas.). Home: 3901 Brookview Rd Austin TX 78722 Office: State Finance Bldg Austin TX 78711

STEVENS, JOHN FRANKLIN, textile co. exec.; b. Erwin, N.C., Aug. 2, 1939; s. Thomas Byron and Susie Elizabeth (Earnshaw) S.; B.S. (Shapiro scholar, Owens Corning scholar), N.C. State Coll., 1961; m. Ann Tone Clark, June 16, 1962; children—John Franklin, Julie Elizabeth. Salesman, Deering Milliken, Inc., N.Y.C., 1961-64; salesman Renfro Hosiery Mills Co., Inc., Mount Airy, N.C., 1964-66, dir. mfg., 1966—, v.p., 1967—. Bd. dirs. Y.M.C.A., 1966-70, pres. 1969; active Salvation Army. Mem. Sigma Nu. Episcopalian (sec. 1968). Rotarian (pres. 1971-72). Home: 122 Club View Dr Mt Airy NC 27030 Office: PO Box 908 Mt Airy NC 27030

STEVENS, JOSEPH BLACKBURN, physician; b. Kimball, W.Va., Jan. 2, 1911; s. Wilkin Blackburn and Rosetta Barlow (Davidson) S.; B.S., Davidson Coll., 1932; M.D., Duke, 1936; m. Mary Barrett, June 5, 1935 (dec. Apr. 1959); 1 dau., Betsy (Mrs. Ronald Kemp Murrelle); m. 2d, Margaret Johnson Hammer, May 15, 1960. Intern, Duke Hosp., 1936-37, asst. resident, 1937-39, resident neurology 1939-40; practice medicine, specializing in internal medicine, Greensboro, N.C., 1940-42, 45—; mem. staff Moses H. Cone Meml. Hosp., Wesley Long Community Hosp.; instr. medicine Duke, 1940-50; instr. neurology Bowman-Gray, 1945-50; prof. clin. medicine U. N.C., Chapel Hill, 1968; trustee N.C. Blue Cross-Blue Shield, 1967-75. Trustee Moses H. Cone Meml. Hosp., 1949-52. Served to lt. col., M.C., AUS, 1942-45. Fellow A.C.P. (gov. N.C. 1968-74); mem. Am. Acad. Neurology, Am. (nat. committeeman 1967-69), N.C. (pres. 1966) socs. internal medicine, A.M.A., Beta Theta Pi, Alpha Omega Alpha. Republican. Episcopalian. Home: 102 Irving Park Ct Greensboro NC 27408 Office: 1017 Profl Village Greensboro NC 27401

STEVENS, JOSEPH TRAVIS, engrosser and manuscript illuminator; b. Marietta, Okla., July 18, 1922; s. Homer Shelby and Clemmie (Starritt) S.; B.A. in Edn., E. Central State Coll., Ada, Okla., 1951; postgrad. Centenary Coll., Shreveport, La., 1958; m. Anne Pajonas, Sept. 3, 1945; children—Victor Shelby, Joseph Frederick, Lilly Anne. Field dir. A.R.C., St. Louis, 1951-52; dir. exploration and producing supr. drafting and graphic arts Mobil Oil Corp., Shreveport, La., 1953-69; dir. exploration and producing drafting and graphic arts Placid Oil Co., Dallas, 1969—. Lectr. on art of manuscript illuminating before audiences, radio, television, 1960—; represented in permanent collection Riverside Gallery, Shreveport; exhibited art shows State Mus., Shreveport, Okla. Art Center, Oklahoma City; engrosser for Ind. Order Foresters. Served with AUS, 1940-45. Mem. Nat. Soc. Arts and Letters (pres. Shreveport chpt. 1962), Gamma Theta Upsilon Republican. Episcopalian. Research on medieval illuminated manuscripts; contbr. to newspapers; prin. art works include illuminated Ode to Joy (Beethoven's 9th Symphony), Apostles Creed, St. Andrew's, Roswell, N.M., other scrolls in pvt. collections. Home: 4326 Cinnabar Dallas TX 75227 Office: 1st Nat Bank Dallas TX 75202

STEVENS, MELVILLE MACEO, labor ofcl.; b. St. Croix, V.I., Sept. 16, 1905; s. Alfred and Ruth (Peterson) S.; B.S., Hampton Inst., 1938; LL.B., Temple U., 1952; m. Josephine Phillips, Dec. 23, 1968. Farm supr. Farm Security Adminstrn., U.S. Dept. Labor, V.I., 1938-46; examiner NLRB, Region 2, N.Y., 1959-65; commr. of labor Govt. of V.I., St. Croix, 1965—. State chmn. Coop. Area Manpower Planning System, V.I., 1967; mem. V.I. Apprenticeship and Tng. Council, 1965. Mem. V.I. Bar Assn., Nat. Assn. Labor Relations Agys. (pres.), Internat. Assn. Govt. Labor Ofcls., Kappa Alpha Psi. Contbr. articles to profl. jours. Home: 29 Peters Farm Christiansted St Croix VI 00820 Office: 27 Company St Christiansted St Croix VI 00820

STEVENS, PRESTON STANDISH, JR., architect; b. Atlanta, May 25, 1930; s. Preston Standish and Hermione Ross (Walker) S.; B.S., Ga. Inst. Tech., 1952, B. Arch., 1953; m. Marian Stannard Hutter, Nov. 1, 1958; children—Marian Christain, Preston Standish III, Rebecca Blair. With Stevens & Wilkinson, Inc., architects-engrs.-planners, Atlanta, 1957—, v.p., 1969—; v.p. Stevens Properties. Mem. Atlanta-Fulton County Joint Planning Bd., 1967—; pres. Architects Found. Ga., 1971. Trustee Ga. Conservancy, Fernbank Sci. Center. Served to 1st lt. AUS, 1953-55. Mem. A.I.A. (pres. North Ga. chpt. 1971, Ivan Allen award 1970), Chi Phi. Episcopalian. Home: 185 River North Dr NW Atlanta GA 30328 Office: 100 Peachtree St NW Atlanta GA 30303

STEVENS, ROGER L., theatrical producer; b. Detroit, Mar. 12, 1910; s. Stanley and Florence (Jackson) S.; student Choate sch., 1928, U. Mich., 1928-30, D.H.L., 1964; H.H.D. (hon.), Wayne State U., 1960; D.H.L., Tulane U., 1960; LL.D. Amherst Coll., 1968; hon. degrees U. Mich., 1964, Skidmore, 1969, Boston U., 1970; m. Christine Gesell, Jan. 1, 1938; 1 dau., Christabel. Producing partner in over 100 Broadway shows in last ten years; including West Side Story, Cat on a Hot Tin Roof, Bus Stop, Tea and Sympathy, Mary, Mary, etc. Former real estate broker specializing in hotels and investment properties, 1934-60. Spl. asst. to the President on the arts, 1964-68; chmn. Nat. Council on the Arts, 1965-69; chmn. Nat. Endowment for the Arts, 1965-69; pres. Nat. Opera Inst.; chmn. Am. Film Inst. Chmn. adv. com. Nat. Book Awards, Chmn. finance com. Democratic Party, 1956. Chmn. bd. trustees John F. Kennedy Center Performing Arts; trustee Am. Shakespeare Theater and Acad.; bd. dirs. Met. Opera Assn. Fellow Royal Soc. Arts; mem. ANTA (treas. 1951-65), Phi Gamma Delta. Clubs: Bohemian (San Francisco); Racquet and Tennis, Century Assn., Pilgrims (N.Y.C.); 1925 F St. (Washington). Adv. com. Partisan Rev. Home: 1686 34th St NW Washington DC 20007 Office: John F Kennedy Center for Performing Arts 726 Jackson Pl NW Washington DC 20566

STEVENS, ROGER TEMPLETON, research engr.; b. Syracuse, N.Y., Jan. 11, 1927; s. Raymond Alfred and Mabel (Templeton) S.; B.A., Union Coll., Schenectady, 1949; M.A., Boston U., 1959; LL.B., Blackstone Sch. Law, 1966; m. Mildred Lorraine Hasbrouck, June 12, 1948; children—Margaret Ann, David Keith. Sr. engr. Spencer-Kennedy Labs., Boston, 1955-56, Avco Mfg. Co., Boston, 1956-57, Electronics Systems, Inc., Boston, 1957-60; staff asst. to chief engr. and supr. video and display sect. Sanders Assos., Nashua, N.H., 1960-65; mem. tech. staff advising USAF on Command & Control Systems, Mitre Corp., Bedford, Mass., 1965-67; sr. research engr. Dikewood Corp., Albuquerque, 1967-70; mem. tech. staff, sub-dept. head Mitre Corp., McLean, Va., 1970—. Mem. I.E.E.E. (sr. mem., sec. 1963-64, vice chmn. N.H. sect. 1964-65). Mason. Contbr. articles to profl. jours. Home: 1701 Fox Run Ct Vienna VA 22180 Office: Mitre Corp Westgate Research Park McLean VA 22101

STEVENS, ROY ARTHUR, county mgr.; b. Benson, N.C., Aug. 30, 1924; s. Arthur Festus and Lalon (Strickland) S.; grad. Worth Bus. Coll., Fayetteville, N.C., 1942, Southeastern Inst. for Orgn., 1958, Bus. Mgmt. Inst., Jacksonville, N.C., 1959; m. Nora Alma Wood, June 21, 1947; children—Roy Arthur, Gloria Delilah. Clk., A.E. Rankin Co., Inc., Fayetteville, 1942-43, bookkeeper, 1946-49; chief clk., office mgr. Becker County Sand & Gravel Co., Cheraw, S.C., 1949-55; owner, operator Stevens Bookkeeping Service, 1955; asst. mgr. C. of C., Fayetteville, 1956; mgr. Jacksonville C. of C., 1957-64; dir. Resources Devel. Commn. for Brunswick County, Southport, 1965-69; mgr. Onslow County, 1969-71; dir. Carteret County Econ. Devel. Council, Morehead City N.C., 1971—. Mem. exec. bd., past pres. Ocean Hiway Assn.; past pres., bd. dirs. Travel Council N.C.; former dir. N.C. Indsl. Developers Assn. Served with USAAF, 1943-46. Named Tarheel of Week, 1964. Baptist. Home: West Car Meadows Morehead City NC 28557 Office: 917 Arendell St Morehead City NC 28557

STEVENS, ROY W., food co. exec.; b. Ottumwa, Ia., Oct. 28, 1924; s. Manley O. and Ruth (Worrell) S.; B.Sc., State U. Ia., 1948; m. Donna R. Borman, June 7, 1952; children—Katharine A., Thomas W., John M. Marketing rep. Coca-Cola Co., Chgo., Mpls. 1948-54; with Gen. Foods Corp., Chgo., 1954-67, nat. sales mgr. Birds Eye, 1964-67; exec. v.p. Riviana Foods Inc., Houston, 1967—. Bd. dirs. Houston Met. YMCA, 1969-71, Alley theatre, Goodwill Industries, Houston. Served as ensign USNR, 1943-46. Mem. Sigma Alpha Epsilon. Episcopalian. Club: Houston Country. Home: 6010 Deerwood Houston TX 77027 Office: PO Box 2636/2727 Allen Pkwy Houston TX 77001

STEVENS, THOMAS, state legislator; b. Dade City, Fla., May 20, 1931; student U. Fla., 1949-50, Leo Jr. Coll., 1961, U. South Fla.; div.; children—Thomas, Warren, Mary Lou, Nancy, Laura. Ins. agt. State Farm Ins. Co.; mem. Fla. Ho. of Reps., 1962—, chmn. transp. com. Mem. Fla. N.G. Mem. Assembly of God Ch. Mason. Address: 405 E Church Av Dade City FL 33525*

STEVENS, WILLIAM DALE, computer tech. adv.; b. Topeka, Nov. 8, 1929; s. Floyd Wayne and Flossie (Northup) S.; B.S. in Chem. Engring., Kan. State U., 1952; m. Mary Charlotte Anderson, Sept. 18, 1954; children—John Stewart, Charles David. Chemist, Sunray Oil Co., Duncan, Okla., 1954-56; process engr. DX Sunray Oil Co., Duncan, 1956-58, computer econs. engr., Tulsa, 1958-61; process engr. Skelly Oil Co., Tulsa, 1961-62, supr. process econ. engring., 1962-67, tech. asst. to computer dept. mgr., 1967—. Project mgr. SHARE, 1967-69, div. mgr., 1969-71; project mgr. GUIDE, 1967-71. Served with AUS, 1952-54. Registered profl. engr., Okla. Mem. Inst. Mgmt. Scis. (pres. southwestern chpt. 1967-68), Am. Inst. Chem. Engrs., Mensa (Tulsa test adminstr.), INTERTEL (asst. internat. gen. sec. 1970—, chmn. membership com. 1971—; pres. chpt. 1969-70), Assn. for Computing Machinery, Tulsa Computing Soc. Republican. Episcopalian (lay reader; sch. supt.). Home: 218 S 102d East Av Tulsa OK 74128 Office: 15th St at Boulder Av Tulsa OK 74102

STEVENSON, CHESTER JOHN, elec. utility co. exec; b. Scranton, Pa., Jan. 17, 1924; s. John George and Sophia (Zychal) Sobonski; student Wharton Sch. Bus., U. Pa., 1947-49, marketing Internat. Corr. Schs., 1956; certificate in Elec. Engring., U. Ky., 1957; m. Helen Ruth Schweitzer, Nov. 3, 1951; children—Cathy, Wayne, Paul, Nancy. Field mgr. Fuller Brush Co., Lexington, Ky., 1954-55; comml. service adviser Ky. Utilities Co., Lexington, 1955-59, local mgr., Georgetown, Ky., 1959-60, Flemingsburg, Ky., 1960-66, div. mgr. bus. devel., Lexington, 1966—. Mem. beautification com. Ky. Dept. Natural Resources, 1964-71. Assembly rep. Lexington United Community Fund, 1966-69. Served with AUS, 1943-45; ETO. Decorated Purple Heart, Soldier's Medal; recipient Five Star awards, Sons Am. Legion, 1940; named Man of Year, Jr. C. of C. Scott County (Ky.), 1959, Man of Year, Fleming County (Ky.), 1963. Mem. Ky. (co-chmn. community devel. 1966—), Fleming County (pres. 1963), Fayette County chambers commerce, Internat. Platform Assn. Republican. Lutheran (supt. Sunday sch. 1967-69, deacon 1969—). Mason, Lion (pres. 1972—, v.p. 1969). Home: 1029 Whitehall Pl Lexington KY 40507 Office: 120 S Limestone St Lexington Ky 40502

STEVENSON, ELDON, JR., ins. co. exec; b. Nashville; s. Eldon and Minnie (Gleaves) S.; B.S., Vanderbilt U.; m. Sarah Shannon. With Nat. Life and Accident Ins. Co. beginning as agt., successively br. office cashier, insp., supr. and dist. mgr.; later transferred to home office and made asst. mgr. ordinary dept., later mgr. and then v.p. charge ordinary, dir. of co., 1925—, exec. v.p., 1938, pres., 1953-63, vice chmn., 1963-65, hon. vice chmn., 1965-70, cons., 1970—; vice chmn. bd. dirs. WSM-WSM-TV; emeritus dir. Standard Brands, Inc.; past chmn. Combination Cos. Past chmn. bd. Life Ins. Sales Research Bur., Hartford, Conn.; mem. bd. Life Insurers Conf., Richmond, Va., also pres., 1954-55. Trustee, vice chmn., past chmn. finance com. Vanderbilt U. Enlisted USN, World War I; commd. ensign; instr. U.S. Naval Acad.; officer in U.S.S. George Washington. Mem. Vanderbilt Alumni Assn. (past dir.; exec. com.; nat. pres.), Phi Delta Theta. Mason. Clubs: Link's, Brook (N.Y. C.); Cumberland, Belle Meade Golf and Country (Nashville); Linville (N.C.) Golf; Augusta (Ga.) National Golf; Mountain Lake Colony, Lake Wales (Fla.) Home: 4406 Tyne Blvd Nashville TN 37215 Office: Nat Life Center Nashville TN 37203

STEVENSON, EVERETT EARL, educator; b. Buffalo, Jan. 14, 1923; s. George E. and Fanny E. (Renning) S.; B.S., State U. Coll. Buffalo, 1944; M.Ed., U. Houston, 1952; Ph.D., Ohio State U., 1961; m. Cloy Virginia Edwards, Jan. 7, 1945; children—George Edwards, Cloy Virginia, Barbara Sue. Master University Sch., Shaker Heights, O., 1946-47; instr. Ins. Co. N.Am., Phila., 1948-51; commd. 2d lt. USAAF, 1944, advanced through grades to lt. col., 1969; asso. prof. math, USAF Acad., 1956-59, 61-67; faculty Indsl. Coll. Armed Forces, 1967-68; with Task Force Alpha in S.E. Asia, 1968-69; prof. math., asso. chmn. dept. Memphis State U., 1969—. Served with USAAF, 1944-45. Decorated Bronze Star medal, Joint Services Commendation medal, AF Commendation medal. Mem. Am. Math. Soc., Nat. Council Tchrs. Math., Math. Assn. Am. Methodist (ofcl, bd. 1948-67). Mason (Shriner comdr. 1965-66). Home: 4792 Cole Rd Memphis TN 38117

STEVENSON, FRANK GEORGE, JR., securities dealer; b. Americus, Ga., Apr. 21, 1932; s. Frank George and Dorothy (Baugh) S.; B.B.A., U. Ga., 1954; m. Joan Wilson Askew, Sept. 7, 1957; children—Mary Kathryn, Karen, John Askew. With Robinson-Humphrey Co., Inc., Atlanta, 1963—, now v.p. sales; exec. v.p., treas., dir. Hawick Fund, Inc., Atlanta, 1968—; dir. Castleberry's Food Co., Augusta, Ga. Precinct chmn. Fulton County Republican Com., 1971-72. Served with USAF, 1954-56. Mem. Nat. Assn. Security Dealers. Clubs: Peachtree Golf, Peachtree Racket, Piedmont Driving, Commerce (Atlanta). Home: 901 Hawick Dr NW Atlanta GA 30327 Office: 2 Peachtree St Atlanta GA 30303

STEVENSON, FRANK MOODY, real estate exec.; b. Birmingham, Ala., Aug. 11, 1920; s. Horace Adlai and Maude (Moody) S.; A.B., Birmingham So. Coll., 1941; m. Evelyn McClain Lewis, July 31, 1943; children—Frank Moody, Edward Lewis. Sec., dir. Westside Lumber Co., Huntsville, Ala., 1961-62; sr. real estate appraiser FHA, Birmingham, 1949-59; partner Thomas & Stevenson Constrn. Co., Huntsville, 1959-69; real estate appraiser F.M. Stevenson, Huntsville, 1959-69; pres. Frank & Stevenson Realty Co., Inc., Huntsville, 1966—; v.p., dir. Huntsville Asso., Inc., 1966—; sec.-treas., dir. Stak Devel. Co., Inc., 1962—, Stakbilt Homes, Inc., 1963—. Mem. Huntsville Indsl. Expansion Com., 1967—. Mem. Nat. Soc. Real Estate Appraisers, Am. Soc. Real Estate Appraisers, Birmingham-So. Coll. Alumni Assn. (dir. 1970—), Nat. Assn. Real Estate Bds., Huntsville, C. of C., Kappa Alpha. Presbyn. Home: 2903 Drexel Dr SE Huntsville AL 35801 Office: 915-C Franklin St SE Huntsville AL 35801

STEVENSON, HENRY EDWIN, govt. ofcl., editor; b. Moorhead, Minn., May 25, 1916; s. Henry Ebeneezer and Nina Lillian (Edminster) S.; B.S., Moorhead State Coll., 1939; postgrad. U. Chgo., 1946-49; m. Almira Abbot, Oct. 15, 1949; children—Henry Edminster, Abbot. Reporter, Moorhead Daily News, 1936-38; reporter Fargo (N.D.) Forum, 1938-39; tchr. pub. schs., Burtrum, Minn., 1940-42; tchr. Sidwell Friends Sch., Washington, 1949-51; edn. specialist Navy Tng. Publs. Center, Washington, 1951-54; supervisory editor Naval Photog. Interpretation Center, Washington, 1954-62; asst. for res. officer tng. Bur. Naval Weapons, Washington, 1962-63; program mgr. various tng. manuals Bur. Naval Personnel, Washington, 1963—. Served from 2d lt. to 1st lt., USMCR, 1942-45, from 1st lt. to lt. col. Res., 1945-67. Mem. Marine Corps Res. Officers Assn., Gamma Theta Upsilon, Beta Theta Pi. Author: (with others) The Marine Corps Reserve - A History, 1966. Editor: The Reserve Weaponeer, 1962-63; Naval Tng. Bull., 1963—. Home: 5512 30th St NW Washington DC 20015 Office: Naval Tng Support Command Washington DC 20370

STEVENSON, IAN, psychiatrist; b. Montreal, Que., Can., Oct. 31, 1918; s. John and Ruth (Preston) S.; student U. St. Andrews, Scotland, 1937-39; B.S., McGill U., 1940, M.D., 1943; m. Octavia Reynolds, Sept. 13, 1947. Came to U.S., 1945, naturalized, 1949. Intern, asst. resident Royal Victoria Hosp., Montreal, 1944-45; intern, resident St. Joseph's Hosp., Phoenix, 1945-46; fellow internal medicine Alton Ochsner Med. Found., New Orleans, 1946-47; Commonwealth fellow medicine Cornell U. Med. Coll., 1947-49; asst. prof. psychiatry La. State U. Sch. Medicine, 1949-52, asso. prof., 1952-57; prof. psychiatry, chmn. dept. psychiatry and neurology U. Va. Sch. Medicine, 1957-67, Carlson prof. psychiatry, 1967—. Diplomate Am. Bd. Psychiatry and Neurology. Fellow Am. Psychiat. Assn.; mem. A.M.A., Med. Soc. Va., Am. Psychosomatic Soc., A.A.A.S. Am. Soc. for Psychical Research. Author: The Diagnostic Interview, 2d edit., 1971; Twenty Cases Suggestive of Reincarnation, 1966; The Psychiatric Examination, 1969; Telepathic Impressions, 1970. Home: Wintergreen Old Lynchburg Rd Charlottesville VA 22903

STEVENSON, JAMES PRESTON FANT, clergyman; b. Hartselle, Ala., Oct. 5, 1919; s. James Preston and Claribel (Fant) S.; grad. Fort Smith Jr. Coll., 1939; A.B. (Kneeland theol. award), Coll. of Ozarks, 1941, D.D., 1950; B.D., Columbia Theol. Sem., 1944, M.Div., 1971; m. Kathryn McGee, Jan. 3, 1942; children—Victoria Fant (Mrs. Phillip Land II), Sarah Kay. Ordained to ministry Presbyn. Ch., 1944; pastor First Presbyn. Ch., Uniontown, Ala., 1944-46, Canal St. Presbyn. Ch., New Orleans, 1946-50, First Presbyn. Ch., Clarksdale, Miss., 1952-68, Central Presbyn. Ch., Bristol, Va., 1968—. Vice pres. New Orleans Ministerial Assn., 1949; pres. Coahoma County Ministerial Assn., Clarksdale, 1958; mem. edn. study com. Presbyn. Ch. in U.S., chmn. standing com. woman's work, 1958, chmn. permanent com. of minister and his work in gen. assembly, 1964—; chmn. com. on minister and work Presbyn. Ch. State of Miss.; chaplain Miss. Ho. of Reps., 1959; chaplain of day Ho. of Reps., Washington, 1969. Camp chaplain Boy Scouts Am.; chaplain City of Coahoma County, City of Bristol, Va., Appalachian Crime Clinic; clergy rep. Coahoma County Parents League; youth counselor Youth Court, Coahoma County; dir. religious affairs Va. Civil Def. Bd. dirs. Columbia Theol. Sem., Decatur, Ga. A.R.C.; bd. dirs., mem. exec. com. Va. Highlands Community Coll., Bristol Meml. Hosp.; chmn. bd. dirs. Coahoma County Nursing Sch. Served as capt., chaplain, USAF, 1950-52, Korea. Recipient Alumnus of Year award Coll. of Ozarks, 1949. Mason (chaplain New Orleans shrine 1948—). Mem. Coahoma County Bristol chambers commerce, S.A.R., Alumni of

Columbia Theol. Sem. (v.p. 1955-57). Co-author: The Manual for Ordination and Installation of Ministers, 1963. Home: 504 Lawrence Av Bristol VA 24201

STEVENSON, JOHN MARSHALL R., educator, editor; b. Little Rock, June 6, 1930; s. Arthur Leonard and Isabel Lawson (Broy) S.; grad. Rust Coll. Prep. Sch., 1946; B.A., Ark. A. and M. and Normal Coll., 1952; M.A., U. Ark., 1956, Ed.D., 1965; postgrad. Cornell U., Ph.D., State U. Ia.; m. Culey Mae Vick, Aug. 25, 1956; children—John Marshall R., Sybil Giovanna, Heidi Alexandra, Afrique Isabel. Instr. English, N.C. Agrl. and Tech. State U., Greensboro, 1955-58, prof. English, 1962-68, prof. speech and theatre arts, head dept. speech communication, 1968-—; instr. communication skills U. Ia., Iowa City, 1958-59; asso. prof. English, Ark. A. and M. and Normal Coll., Pine Bluff, 1959-61; research asst. U. Ark., Fayetteville, 1961-62; founder, editor, pub. Carolina Peacemaker, weekly newspaper, Greensboro; dir., pres., chmn. Carolina Newspaper, Inc., Greensboro. Bd. dirs. N.C. Children's Home Soc. Served with USNR, 1949-50, 52-54. Mem. Nat. Assn. Dramatic and Speech Arts (pres. 1965-67), N.C. Speech and Drama Assn., Am. Ednl. Theater Assn., Speech Communication Assn., Am. Assn. U. Profs., N.C. Press Assn., N.A.A.C.P. (chmn. labor and industry com. Greensboro br. Phi Delta Kappa. Alpha Psi Omega, Sigma Delta Chi, Omega Psi Phi. Democrat. Jewish religion. Mem. B'nai B'rith. Producer-dir. coll. ednl. theater prodns. Home: 1910 Carlton Av Greensboro NC 27406

STEVENSON, JOHN MOTE, paper co. exec.; b. Cin., May 17, 1930; s. Frank E. and Neva (Mote) S.; A.B., Harvard, 1952, M.B.A., 1954; m. Roxanna Louise Harrington, June 25, 1954; children—Frank, John, Amy, Sarah, David. With Champion Internat. Corp. and subsidiary cos., 1954-—, v.p., Southwestern div. mgr. DairyPak, Paper Converting div., Fort Worth, 1966-—; dir. Continental Nat. Bank Fort Worth. Pres., Retarded Children Services Assn. Tarrant County, 1966-67; mem. Mayor's Com. for Streams and Valleys. Bd. dirs. Fort Worth Park and Recreation Dept., 1969-—; trustee Fort Worth Country Day Sch., 1971-—; bd. dirs., past pres. Child Study Center, Ft. Worth; mem. exec. council Longhorn council Boy Scouts Am.; v.p. United Fund of Tarrant County; mem. bd. Ft. Worth Symphony Orch. Assn. Mem. Sales and Marketing Execs. Fort Worth (v.p. 1969-—, dir.). Republican. Presbyn. (elder). Clubs: Hasty Pudding Harvard, Harvard Business School (Dallas Fort Worth), Fort Worth; Chaparral, Rivercrest Golf, Ridglea Golf, Webhannet Golf. Home: 1207 Hillcrest St Fort Worth TX 76107 Office: 1901 Windsor Pl Fort Worth TX 76110

STEVENSON, LIONEL, author; b. Edinburgh Scotland, July 16, 1902; s. Henry and Mabel Rose (Cary) S.; B.A., U. B.C., 1922; M.A., U. Toronto, 1923; Ph.D., U. Cal., 1925; B. Litt., U. Oxford, 1935; F.R.S.L.; m. Lillian Sprague Jones, Apr. 10, 1954; 1 dau. Instr. U. Cal., 1925-30; prof. English and head dept., Ariz. State Coll., Tempe, 1930-37; asst. prof. English, U. So. Cal., 1937-41, asso. prof., 1941-44, prof., 1944-55, head dept., 1943-55; prof. English, Duke U., 1955-72, chmn. dept., 1964-67; prof. English, U. Houston, 1972-—; vis. prof. summers, U.B.C., 1930, 40, 54, N.Y.U., 1948, 62, U. Colo., 1950, U. Ill., 1952-53; vis. lectr. Oxford U., 1960; Berg vis. prof. N.Y.U., 1967-68. Mem. of Western Coll. Assn., v.p., 1946-47. Mem. Philol. Assn. Pacific Coast (pres. 1948-50), Coll. English Assn. (v.p. 1954), English Speaking Union (pres. Raleigh-Durham br. 1958-60). Clubs: Authors (London, Eng.); Arts and Letters (Toronto); Cal. Writers (pres. 1928-30); P.E.N. (del. to Internat. Congresses, Vienna, 1929, Edinburgh, 1934, Paris, 1937, Lausanne, 1951; pres. Los Angeles chpt. 1943-53), Canadian Authors Assn. Author: Appraisals of Canadian Literature, 1926; A Pool of Stars (poetry), 1926; Darwin Among the Poets, 1932; The Rose of the Sea (poetry), 1932; The Wild Irish Girl, 1936; Doctor Quicksilver, 1939; The Showman of Vanity Fair, 1947; English Literature of the Victorian Period (with J.D. Cooke), 1949; The Ordeal of George Meredith, 1953; The English Novel, a Panorama, 1960; The History of the English Novel, Yesterday and After, 1967; The Pre-Raphaelite Poets, 1972. Editor: Victorian Fiction: A Guide to Research, 1964. Contbr. to lit. jours. in U.S., Can., Eng. Home: 3106 Devon Rd Hope Valley Durham NC 27707

STEVENSON, MARY PASCO CONRAD (MRS. JAMES A. STEVENSON), librarian; b. Harrisonburg, Va., July 5, 1902; d. George Newton and Emily (Pasco) Conrad; student Oberlin Coll., 1922-23; A.B., Randolph-Macon Women's Coll., 1924; m. James A. Stevenson, Aug. 22, 1929; children—Emily P., James Conrad. Asst. librarian Chatham Square Br., N.Y.C. Pub. Library, 1926-27; asst. librarian Clemson (S.C.) Univ. Library, 1927-30, acting librarian, 1931, head catalog dept., 1933-38, 44-45, 49-68, spl. collections librarian, 1968, ret., 1968; writer, illustrator and researcher non-profit orgns., 1968-—; tchr. library sci., summers 1938-39. Bd. dirs. Found. for Historic Restoration in Pendleton Area, S.C. Mem. Soc. Am. Archivists, S.C. Hist. Soc., Nat. Trust for Historic Preservation, U.D.C., Nat. Geneal. Soc., Am. Assn. State and Local History. Home: 103 Hillcrest Av Clemson SC 29631

STEVENSON, ROBERT LOUIS, educator; b. Nashville, Dec. 16, 1939; s. Roy James and Thelma Bernice (Smith) S.; B.S., Tenn. A. and I. State U., 1961, M.S., 1962; postgrad. Ind. U., summers 1967, 68; m. Charlease Thomas, Dec. 29, 1964; children—Jan Elease, Robert Louis II. Instr. drama and speech S.C. State Coll., Orangeburg, 1962-64; asst. prof. drama and speech So. U., Baton Rouge, 1964-65; asst. prof. English and drama Savannah (Ga.) State Coll., 1965-—, dir. drama, 1965-—. Trustee Savannah Speech and Hearing Center. Mem. Nat. Assn. Speech and Dramatic Arts, Speech Assn. Am., Ga. Theatre Conf., Am. Assn. U. Profs., ANTA, Theta Alpha Phi. Democrat. Baptist. Home: 1626 Glen Ridge Dr Savannah GA 31401

STEWARD, CARL WARREN, citrus processing co. exec.; b. Cardington, O., Mar. 4, 1922; s. Harry Burton and Mary Elizabeth (Daily) S.; B.B.A., Ohio State U., 1943; postgrad. U. Cal. at Berkeley, 1946, Princeton, 1964, Rollins Coll., 1971-—; m. Ethel Grace Billingham, Oct. 23, 1946; children—Dorothy Lee, Carl Warren, William Charles. Mgr. accounting Farm Bur. Coop., Columbus, 1946-56; controller Mt. Vernon Bridge Co. (O.), 1956-60, Pa. Farm Bur., Harrisburg, 1960-65; controller, sec., treas. B. C. Cook & Sons, Inc., Haines City, Fla., 1965-—, asst. gen. mgr., 1971-—; sec., treas. Growers Processing Service, Inc., Highland City, Fla., 1968-—. Served with AUS, 1943-46. Decorated Bronze Star medal, Bronze Arrowhead. Mem. Nat. Assn. of Accountants (dir. 1961-—), pres. Mid-Fla. chpt. 1971-72), C. of C., Delta Sigma Pi. Mem. Christian Ch. (chmn. bd. 1963-65). Home: 1017 E Ledwith St Haines City FL 33844 Office: 413 N 12th St Haines City FL 33844

STEWART, ALBERT, JR., physician; b. Fayetteville, N.C., Sept. 23, 1920; s. Albert and Winnie Davis (Bruton) S.; student U. S.C., 1936-37; A.B., U. N.C., 1941; M.D., Washington U., 1944; m. Mary Inglesby DuBose, Oct. 5, 1951; children—Albert III, David DuBose, Paul Finley, Charles Inglesby, James Bruton. Intern Barnes Hosp., St. Louis, 1944-45; fellow medicine Washington U., St. Louis, 1946-47; ships surgeon Grace Line, N.Y.C., 1947; resident physician Meml. Hosp., Charlotte, N.C., 1948; fellow gastroenterology Lehey Clinic, Boston, 1949; practice medicine specializing in internal medicine, Fayetteville, N.C., 1950-—; attending physician Highsmith, Cape Fear Valley hosps.; cons. U.S. VA Hosp.; clin. asso. prof. medicine U. N.C. Sch. Medicine, 1968-—; mem. Cumberland County Hosp. Authority, 1968-69. Bd. dirs. Fayetteville Acad. Served with M.C., USNR, 1945-46, 52-54. Diplomate Am. Bd. Internal Medicine. Fellow A.C.P.; mem. A.M.A., N.C., Cumberland County med. socs., Am., N.C. socs. internal medicine. Episcopalian. Kiwanian. Club: Highland Country. Home: 1507 Morganton Rd Fayetteville NC 28305 Office: 114 Broadfoot Av Fayetteville NC 28305

STEWART, BURTON GLOYDEN, JR., banker; b. Clayton, N.C., Mar. 14, 1933; s. Burton Gloyden and Evelyn I. (Stallings) S.; B.A., Duke, 1955; grad. student Sch. Banking of South, La. State U., 1968-70; m. Patricia Taylor, June 16, 1956; children—Burton III, Herbert Taylor. Trainee, Allstate Ins. Co., Charlotte, 1957, agt., 1957, sales trainer, 1958-59, dist. sales mgr., Columbia, S.C., 1959-60, Greensboro, N.C., 1960-64, field sales mgr., Jackson, Miss., 1964, Charlotte, N.C., 1964, regional sales mgr., 1964-66; v.p. Branch Banking & Trust Co., Wilson, N.C., 1966-72, mgr. marketing dept., 1967-71, mgr. bus. devel. div., 1971-—, sr. v.p., 1972-—. Treas., Wilson Arts Council, 1969-71; active United Fund, N.C. Heart Assn. Served as lt. USNR, 1955-57. Mem. Sales and Marketing Execs. Club, N.C. Bankers Assn. (mem. marketing com. 1970), Bank Marketing Assn. Methodist (mem. adminstrv. bd. 1968-71). Rotarian. Home: 1134 Knollwood Dr Wilson NC 27893 Office: 223 W Nash St Wilson NC 27893

STEWART, CAROL RAY, gas co. exec.; b. Atlanta, Tex., Mar. 13, 1929; s. Joe Justice and Lula Mae (McConnell) S.; B.A., Tex. Tech. U., 1963; m. Coleta Ann New, May 24, 1952; children—Michael David, Glynn Wayne. Field supr. Parker Drilling Co., Hobbs, N.M., 1950-52, v.p., 1968-—; drilling supt. Western Natural Gas Co., Can., 1952-57; mgr. Parker Drilling Co. of Brazil, Belem do Para, 1958-60, Parco, Inc., Laz Vegas, 1964-69; dir., mem. exec. com. Alaska Airlines, Seattle. Active United Fund. Served with USNR, 1946-49. Mem. Am. Assn. Oilwell Drilling Contractors (dir. 1969-71), Am. Mgmt. Assn. Clubs: Tulsa, Southern Hills Country, Financial (Tulsa). Contbr. articles to profl. jours. Home: 2729 E 61st St Tulsa OK 74136 Office: Nat Bank of Tulsa Bldg Tulsa OK 74103

STEWART, DAVID KEITH, supt. schs.; b. Olathe, Kan., May 22, 1921; s. Bernard and Louverna Adele (Brown) S.; B.A., Central Mo. State Coll., Warrensburg, 1948; M.A., Tchrs. Coll., Columbia, 1950; postgrad. U. Ia., 1952-58, Cornell U., Ithaca, N.Y., summer 1968; Ed.D., N.Y. U., 1969; m. Nina Farmer, Aug. 15, 1942; children—Judith (Mrs. Charles L. Brader, Jr.), Diane Kathryn, Jeanne Elizabeth. Teaching prin. Plainville (Kan.) Elementary Sch., 1948-49; tchr. Greenwich (Conn.) pub. schs., 1949-50; prin. sch., Muncie, Kan., 1950-52; dir. elementary edn. Iowa City pub. schs., 1952-58; instr. State U. Ia., summers 1955-57; dir. elementary edn. Kenosha (Wis.) pub. schs., 1958-64; prin. Murray Av. Sch., Mamaroneck, N.Y., 1964-68; asst. supt. personnel Mamaroneck pub. schs., 1968-70; supt. McCracken County Pub. Schs., Paducah, Ky., 1970-—. Vis. prof. Carthage Coll., Kenosha, summers 1963-64; editor, host Chalk Dust, ednl. radio series, weekly, Iowa City, 1955-57. Served with USAAF, 1942-45; PTO. Contbr. articles to profl. jours. Home: 165 Randa Circle Reidland Route 4 Paducah KY 42001 Office: Route 6 Paducah KY 42001

STEWART, E.L., JR., govt. ofcl; b. Ft. Benning, Ga., June 7, 1928; s. Elam L. and Angie (Lateer) S.; A.B. DePauw U., 1950; m. Katharine Sherman, Apr. 7, 1951; 1 son, Matthew Sherman. Landman Humble Oil & Refinery Co., 1951-61; partner Sigma Oil and Gas Co., 1961; fed. co-chmn. Ozarks Regional Commn., Dept. Commerce, Washington, 1969-—. Precinct chmn. Republican Party, 1961, chmn. Pottawatomie (Okla.) County Com., 1963-65; chmn. Okla. State Rep. Com., 1965-69; v.p. DePauw U. Rep. Club. Served to capt. AUS. Mem. Am. Assn. Petroleum Landmen, Sigma Chi. Home: Muskogee OK 74401 Office: Commerce Bldg 14th and E Washington DC 20006

STEWART, EDGAR ALLAN, lawyer; b. Selma, Ala., Sept. 1, 1909; s. Edgar A. and Irma (Mallory) S.; B.A., U. of South, 1929; LL.B.,; m. Mamie V. Packer, Oct. 15, 1938; children—Edgar A. III (dec.), Martha M. Admitted to Ala. bar, 1932, since practiced in Selma; sr. partner, Reeves & Stewart 1947-—; spl. agt. F.B.I., 1942-45. Dir. Selma Nat. Bank. Trustee Selma Schs.; dir., pres. Selma Y.M.C.A., 1952-68. Mem. Am. Bar Assn., Internat. Assn. Ins. Counsel, Nat. Assn. R.R. Counsel, Am. Counsel Assn., Am. Judicature Soc., Phi Delta Theta, Phi Delta Phi. Contbr. articles to legal jours. Home: 124 Mallory Dr Selma AL 36701 Office: PO Box 457 Selma AL 36701

STEWART, EUGENE DONALD, newspaper exec.; b. Glamorgan, Va., Sept. 22, 1922; s. Charles P. and Carrie Dora (Denham) S.; student pub. schs.; m. Gladys Emmer Kinser, June 6, 1944; children—Donna Jean (Mrs. Robert Miller), Jentlea Emmer, Sara Jane, Eugene Donald, Robert Kinser. Shop foreman Wise Printing Co., Big Stone Gap, Va., 1952-58; supt. prodn. Manchester (Tenn.) Times, 1959; owner, editor, pub. Clinch Valley Times, St. Paul, Va., 1960-—; owner Stewart Pub. Co., St. Paul, 1960-—, pres., 1967-—. Pres., P.T.A., St. Paul, 1965-68; v.p. AWARE, Wise County, 1964-65, dir., 1963-65. Mem. St. Paul City Council, 1963-67, 69-—. Served with AUS, 1941-45. Mem. Nat., Va. press assns., V.F.W., Wise County (Va.) C. of C. (past officer), Am. Legion. Methodist (supt. Sunday sch. 1965-—). Lion (named Lion of Year St. Paul 1965), Moose. Home: 15 Wise St St Paul VA 24283 Office: Clinch Valley Times Broad St St Paul VA 24283

STEWART, FRANK, broadcasting exec. Vice pres., gen. mgr., sta. mgr. KTRH, Houston. Office: Rice Hotel Annex Houston TX 77052*

STEWART, G. KINSEY, psychologist; b. Des Moines, Sept. 9, 1925; s. Lloyd George and Gladys (Kinsey) S.; student Millsaps Coll., 1943-44, Franklin and Marshall Coll., 1944; B.A., Drake U., 1948; M.S., Tulane U., 1956, Ph.D., 1960;; m. Marguerite Stanley, July 7, 1945; children—Kathryn Lynn (Mrs. Mark Blasingame), Karen Lee (Mrs. Gordon Langseth), Maureen Kay. Psychologist, La. Dept. Hosps., Shreveport, 1950-53; field rep., asst. dir. La. Assn. for Mental Health, New Orleans, 1953-56; guidance officer Tulane U., New Orleans, 1956-60; asst. prof. La. State U., New Orleans, 1960-62; sr. psychologist Kennedy Child Study Center, Santa Monica, Cal., 1962-68; clin. psychologist, Gulfport, Miss., 1968-70; dir. Gulf Coast Mental Health Center, 1970-—. Bd. dirs. Juvenile Delinquency Commn. Santa Monica, Gulf Coast Assn. for Mental Health, Nat. Council Community Mental Health Centers, 1972-—. Harris County Drug Council. Served with USMCR, 1943-46. Mem. Am., La. (sec. 1961-62), Cal., Miss. psychol. assns., Am. Assn. U. Profs., Am. Assn. on Mental Defiency, Mental Health Assn. Staff Council, Sigma Xi. Home: Route 1 Box 328 Saucier MS 39574 Office: 1326 Broad Av Gulfport MS 39501

STEWART, GEORGE TAYLOR, III, life ins. co. exec.; b. N.Y.C., Dec. 29, 1924; s. Fargo Calvin and Bertha (Pelleton) S.; A.B., Wesleyan U., Middletown, Conn., 1947; m. Bonnie Elizabeth Myers, Sept. 14, 1946; children—Diane Barbara, Susan Gail. With Hartford Accident & Indemnity Co., N.Y.C., 1947-48; security analyst Geyer & Co., Ins., N.Y.C., 1948-54, Shelby Cullom Davus & Co., N.Y.C., 1954-56; v.p. Blyth & Co., Inc., N.Y.C., 1956-65; chmn. bd., pres. First Colony Life Ins. Co., Lynchburg, Va., 1965-—; former vice chmn. bd., chmn. exec. com. Channing Financial Corp., N.Y.C.; dir. Am. Empire Ins. Co., Watertown, N.Y.; pres., dir. Penn-Jeff Corp., Kansas City, Mo.; dir. United Va. Bank/First Nat., Carter Glass & Sons, Pubs., Inc. Trustee Lynchburg Coll. Served to ensign USNR, 1943-45; PTO. Mem. N.Y. Soc. Security Analysts. Presbyn. (elder). Clubs: California (Los Angeles); Twenty Nine, Metropolitan, Drug and Chemical (all N.Y.C.); James River, Boonsboro Country (both Lynchburg). Contbr. chpt. to Investing in American Industries, 1960. Home: 210 Charlotte St Lynchburg VA 24503 Office: 700 Main St Lynchburg VA 24505

STEWART, GUSTAVUS HOFFMEYER, power and light co. exec.; b. Florence, S.C., Oct. 23, 1913; s. Alexander Toland and Agnes Margaret (Hoffmeyer) S.; B.S., Clemson U., 1935; M.S., Va. Poly. Inst., 1938; m. Juanita Gladys Mitchell, Sept. 2, 1944; children—Patricia Diane (Mrs. Leaman Gerarde Norris), William Alexander, Julian Gustavus. Leader agr. engring. extension work Clemson U., 1936-56; mgr. S.C. area devel. Carolina Power & Light Co., Florence, 1956-—; treas. Greater Carolinas Corp., 1971; pres. Gem Cove Inc., 1966-—, Stewart Enterprises, 1963-—; sec., dir. Greater Carolinas Life Ins. Co., 1972-—; dir. Enterprise Devel. Co., Bristol, Tenn., 1972-—. Mem. Gov.'s Mgmt. and Review Commn., 1971; tchr. Florence Darlington Tech., 1963-66. Chmn., Florence County Resources Devel. Commn., 1963-—; chmn. legislative com. Gov's. Beautification and Community Improvement Bd., 1970-71; chmn. congl. dist. Student Tchr. Achievement Recognition Program, 1966-71; mem. S.C. Traffic Council, 1967-—; mem. U.S. Sec. of Commerce Regional Export Expansion Council, 1969-—; bd. visitors Coker Coll. Served from 2d lt. to col., AUS, World War II. Decorated Bronze Star; recipient Plaque for meritorious service 4-H, 1970, Community Leader of Am. award, 1969-71, Distinguished Service award, 1972; Distinguished Service award S.C. Assn. Future Farmers, 1972; Community Devel. award S.C. Jaycees, 1969-70. Registered profl. engr., S.C. Mem. Am. Soc. Agrl. Engrs. (chmn. S.E. sect. 1956), Res. Officers Assn. (pres. 1963), S.C. State C. of C. (dir. 1963-64), Southeastern Community Devel. Assn. (pres. 1969-70), V.F.W., Am. Legion, Alpha Zeta, Sigma Epsilon. Methodist. Elk, Rotarian. Clubs: Kilowatt, Country (Florence); Palmetto (Columbia, S.C.). Home: 809 W Palmetto St Florence SC 29501 Office: Darlington Hwy Florence SC 29501

STEWART, HARRIS BATES, JR., oceanographer, govt. ofcl.; b. Auburn, N.Y., Sept. 19, 1922; s. Harris B. and Mildred (Woodruff) S.; grad. Phillips Exeter Acad., 1941; A.B., Princeton, 1948; M.S., Scripps Instrn. Oceanography, U. Cal., 1952, Ph.D., 1956; m. Elise Bennett Cunningham, Feb. 21, 1959; 1 dau., Dorothy Cunningham. Hydrographic engr. U.S. Hydrographic Office expdn. to Persian Gulf, 1948-49; instr. Hotchkiss Sch., 1949-51; research asst. Scripps Instrn. Oceanography, 1951-56; diving geologist, project mgr. Geol. Diving Cons., Inc., San Diego, 1953-57; chief oceanographer U.S. Coast & Geodetic, Survey, 1957-65, dept. asst. dir., 1962-65; dir. Inst. Oceanography, Environmental Sci., Services Administration, U.S. Dept. Commerce, 1965-69, director Atlantic Oceanographic and Meteorol. Labs., 1969-—. Mem. Fla. Commn. Marine Sci. and Tech.; exec. com., earth scis. div. Nat. Acad. Scis.; chmn. adv. bd. Nat. Oceanographic Data Center; chmn. survey panel interagy. com. oceanography Fed. Council Sci. and Tech.; chmn. adv. com. underseas features U.S. Bd. Geog. Names; mem. sci. party No. Holiday Expdn., 1951, Capricorn Expdn., 1952-53; chief scientist Explorer Oceanographic Expdn. 1960, Pioneer Indian Ocean Expdn., 1964; mem. U.S. delegation Intergovtl. Oceanographic Commn., 1961, 62, 63, 64, 65; mem. Gov. Cal. Adv. Commn. Marine Resources. Served as pilot USAAF, 1942-46; PTO. Recipient Meritorious award Dept. Commerce, 1960, Exceptional Service award, 1965. Fellow A.A.A.S.; mem. Geol. Soc. Am., Am. Geophys. Union, Marine Tech. Soc. (bd. govs.), Marine Hist. Assn., Old Dartmouth Hist. Soc. Presbyn. Clubs: Cosmos (Washington); Explorers (N.Y.C.). Author: The Global Sea, 1963; Deep Challenge, 1966. Home: 737 N Greenway Dr Coral Gables FL 33134 Office: Atlantic Oceanographic and Meteorological Labs S Miami Av Miami FL 33130

STEWART, HENRY ALLEN, SR., lawyer; b. Aragon, Ga., Sept. 19,, 1910; s. F. M. and Willie Mae (Turner) S.; B.S., U. Ga., 1933, J.D. and M.A., 1934; m. Rebecca Henslee, Jan. 31, 1937: 1 son, Henry Allen. Admitted to Ga., bar, 1934; instr. history U. Ga., 1933-34; dep. commr. revenue, Ga., 1934-37; practice law, Cedartown, Ga., 1934-—; vice chmn., dir. Comml. Nat. Bank, Cedartown Loan & Finance Co., Colonial 5, 10 and 25 cent Stores, Inc., Cedartown; dir. Guaranty Title Ins. Co., Atlanta. Vice chmn. Ga. State Bd. Edn.; vice chmn. State Democratic Exec. Com. Mem. Polk County (pres.), Tallapoosa Circuit (pres.), Tallapoosa, Ga., Am. bar assns., C. of C., Sigma Delta Kappa, Alpha Kappa Psi. Elks. Mason (Shriner). Clubs: Cherokee County, Legion, Exchange (state pres.), Gridiron. Home: 728 N College St Cedartown GA 30125 Office: Stewart Building Cedartown GA 30125

STEWART, HOMER FRANCIS, lawyer; b. Little Rock, Ark., Mar. 26, 1915; s. Homer Clifford and Velma (Ruff) S.; student Ark. State Tchrs. Coll., 1935-37; B.B.A., U. Tenn., 1940, J.D., 1941; m. Nelle Yoest Dale, Dec. 22, 1940; children—Vivian Nannette, Clifford Francis, Andrew Dale, Jonathan Travis. Admitted to Tenn. bar, 1947, pvt. practice law, Nashville, 1947-56; partner firm Watkins, McGugin & Stewart, Nashville, 1956-70; pres. H. Francis Stewart, Nashville, 1970-—; sec., dir. Broadway Tire Co. Mem. devel. council U. Tenn., 1960-65. Served with USNR, 1943-46. Mem. Nashville, Tenn., Am., Fed. bar assns., Tenn. Def. Lawyers Assn., Assn. Ins. Counsel, Fedn. Ins. Counsel, U. Tenn. Alumni Assn. (pres. Davidson County chpt. 1957), Nashville C. of C. (chmn. edn. com. 1964-65). Presbyn. (deacon 1954-—). Mason (Shriner). Club: City in Nashville. Home: Wilsonia Dr Nashville TN 37205 Office: 14th Floor 3d Nat Bank Bldg Nashville TN 37219

STEWART, IRVIN, educator, pub. adminstr.; b. Fort Worth, Oct. 27, 1899; s. William Henry and Sara Aline (Howell) Stewart; student U. Okla., 1917-19; LL.B., U. Tex., 1920, A.B., A.M., 1922; Ph.D., Columbia, 1926; LL.D., Waynesburg Coll., 1946, West Va. Wesleyan U., 1948, W.Va. State Coll., 1948, Marshall Coll., 1953; Litt.D., Bethany Coll., 1954; m. Florence E. Dezendorf, July 31, 1926; 1 son, Richard Edwin. Instr. govt. U. Tex., 1922-25, adj. prof., 1925-26, asso. prof., 1928-29; asst. solicitor U.S. Dept. State, Washington, 1926-28; prof., head dept. govt. Am. Univ. Grad. Sch., Washington, 1929-30; tchr. summer sessions Duke Univ., Columbia, U. Cal. at Los Angeles; in charge elec. communications, treaty div. Dept. State, Washington, 1930-34; mem. Am. delegations to internat. radio confs., Washington, 1927, Copenhagen, 1931, Madrid, 1932, Mexico City, 1933, to PanAm. Comml. Conf., Washington, 1931, Internat. Telegraph Conf., Madrid, 1932; mem. FCC, Washington, chmn. telegraph div., July 11, 1934-June 30, 1937, vice chmn. of commn., Apr. 18, 1935-June 30, 1937; dir. Com. on Scientific Aids to Learning, 1937-46; exec. sec. Nat. Defense Research Com., 1940-45; exec. sec. OSRD, exec. sec. Com. on Med. Research (Office for Emergency Mgmt.), 1941-45; dep. dir., OSRD 1946; pres. W.Va., U., Morgantown, 1946-58, prof. govt., 1958-67; cons. Nat. Acad. Pub. Adminstrn., 1967-—; on leave as dir. telecommunications mgmt. Exec. Office Pres., 1962-63. Chmn. Pres.'s Communications Policy Bd., 1950; nat. com. Devel. of Scientists and Engrs. 1956, nat. adv. com. for Rural Defense 1956; chmn. **Am. del.**

Internat. Conf. on Orgn. and Adminstrn. Applied Research, 1956; mem. W.Va. Commn. on Constl. Revision, 1957-62. Mem. bd. edn. Am. Bapt. Conv. 1952-58. Recipient President's Medal for Merit, 1948; Humanities award W.Va. chpt. B'nai B'rith. Mem. Am. Assn. Land Colls. Colls. and State Univs. (pres. 1956), Am. Soc. Pub. Adminstrn., Am. Polit. Sci. Assn., Phi Beta Kappa, Phi Delta Phi, Pi Sigma Alpha. Mem. bars Tex. and U.S. Supreme Ct. Democrat. Baptist. Clubs: Century (N.Y. City); Cosmos (Washington). Author: Consular Privileges and Immunities, 1926; Organizing Scientific Research for War, 1948. Editor: Radio, 1929, Local broadcasts to schools, 1939. Home: 2939 Van Ness St NW Washington DC 20008

STEWART, JACOB THOMAS, educator; b. Dinwiddie, Va., Nov. 5, 1915; s. John Ambler and Ida (Chatman) S.; B.S., Hampton Inst., 1949; M.B.A., U. Cal. at Los Angeles, 1950; Ph.D., U. Tex., 1956; m. Ruth Caldwell, July 3, 1952; children—Karen Ruth, Robert Walter. Instr. Tex. So. U., 1950-54, asso. prof., 1954-56; prof., head dept. bus. Grambling (La.) Coll., 1956-59, prof., dean div. applied scis. and tech., 1959—; vis. prof. bus. adminstrn. La. Tech. Inst., Barksdale Center, 1967-68. Bd. dirs., treas. Grambling Fed. Credit Union, 1957—. Served with AUS, 1941-45. Mem. Sigma Iota Epsilon, Alpha Kappa Mu (regional bd. dirs. 1958-66), Alpha Phi Alpha (regional v.p. 1963-66). Episcopalian. Home: 305 Lincoln St Grambling LA 71245

STEWART, JAMES HENRY, JR., univ. adminstr.; b. Acton, Tex., Aug. 7, 1935; s. James Henry and Mary Elizabeth (Cleveland) S.; B.S., North Tex. State U., 1954, M. Ed., 1959, Ed.D. (scholar), 1970; m. Janet Colleen Sole, Nov. 26, 1958; children—Bryan, Wade. Classroom tchr. Snyder (Tex.) Pub. Schs., 1954-59, asst. prin., 1959-64; asst. to dean grad. sch. North Tex. State U., Denton, 1964-65, dir. devel., 1970-71, asst. to pres., 1971—; asst. supt. Masonic Home and Sch. of Tex., Ft. Worth, 1965-66, supt., 1966-68, supt. devel., 1968-70; prof. psychology Tarrant County Jr. Coll., Ft. Worth, 1970-71. Mem. Tex. Gov's. Com. on Human Relations, 1969-73. Bd. dirs. Tex. DeMolay Found., Davidson Family Found. Served to lt. AUS, 1957—. Mem. Am. Coll. Pub. Relations Assn., N.E.A., Am., Tex. assns. sch. adminstrs., Tex. Tchrs. Assn., Tex. Classroom Tchrs. Assn., Phi Delta Kappa, Kappa Delta Pi, Pi Sigma Alpha. Democrat. Methodist (mem. adminstrv. bd. 1970-71). Mason (Shriner). Home: 428 Northridge St Denton TX 76201

STEWART, JAMES MCGRANAHAN, dentist; b. West Palm Beach, Fla., Sept. 5, 1924; s. Ira Jay and Ruth Geraldine (McGranahan) S.; B.S., State U. Ia., 1945, D.D.S., 1947; m. Nancy Vassar Irwin, Mar. 31, 1964. Practice of dentistry specializing in oral surgery, West Palm Beach, 1953—; pres. Ruth M. Stewart Meml. Research Lab., Inc., West Palm Beach., 1959—, Stewart Research, Inc., West Palm Beach., 1966—; chief dental service Good Smamaritan Hosp., West Palm Beach, 1967—. Served with AUS, 1943-44, 51-53. NIH research grantee 1959, John A. Hartford Found. research grantee, 1961. Contbr. articles to profl. publs. Patentee in field. Home: 314 29th St West Palm Beach FL 33407 Office: 1717 N Flagler Dr West Palm Beach FL 33407

STEWART, JAMES RANDOLPH, state ofcl.; b. West Palm Beach, Fla., Sept. 22, 1923; s. Clifford B. and Ruby Mae (McKissick) S.; grad. U. Fla., 1952; m. Iris Camilla Parsons, Sept. 3, 1950; 1 son, James Randolph. Research asst. to city mgr., Daytona Beach, Fla., 1952; city mgr., Dania, Fla., 1953, Titusville, Fla., 1953-58, Clearwater, Fla., 1958-67; adminstr. of Pinellas County, 1967-71; dir. Gov.'s Council on Criminal Justice, Tallahassee, 1971—. Served to pharmacist 2d class, USNR, 1942-46. Mem. Internat., Fla. (past pres.) city mgrs. assns., Nat. Conf. State Planning Agy. Dirs. Home: 2210 Cline St Tallahassee FL 32303 Office: 307 E 7th Av Tallahassee FL 32303

STEWART, JAMES RAYMOND, JR., judge; b. Chgo., Feb. 15, 1933; s. James Raymond and Virginia (Supple) S.; B.S., U. Ill., 1954; LL.B., U. Miami, 1960; m. Jane M. Poole, June 23, 1954; children—Lynn C., John R., Nancy J. Admitted to Fla. bar, 1960, since practiced in Miami; asso. firm Dixon, Dejarnette, Bradford, Williams, McKay and Kimbrell, 1960; practiced West Palm Beach, Fla.; asso. firm Wood and Cobb, 1961-63, mem. firm Wood, Cobb, Robinson, Falcon and Letts, 1963-67; asst. atty., Palm Beach County, Fla., 1965-67; county judge Palm Beach County, 1967-69; circuit judge State of Fla., 1969—. Pres. Assn. Religious Orgns., 1968-69, bd. dirs., 1968—. Bd. dirs. Family Service Agy. Palm Beach County, 1963, Mental Health Assn., 1968-69, YMCA, 1969-71. Served to 1st lt. USMC, 1954-57. Methodist. Home: 6599 Katherine Rd West Palm Beach FL 33406 Office: Courthouse West Palm Beach FL 33401

STEWART, JOHN CRAIG, educator, author; b. Selma, Ala., Jan. 20, 1915; s. Horace H. and Mary (Craig) S; B.A., U. Ala., 1948, M.A., 1950; m. Lila Harper, Oct. 15, 1960; 1 son Bruce Craig. Instr. U. Ala., Tuscaloosa, 1950-55, asst. prof. English and creative writing, 1955-60; asst. prof. English and creative writing U. Ala. Extension Center Mobile, 1960-64; asst. prof. U. So. Ala., Mobile, 1964-66, asso prof. English and creative writing, 1967-71, prof., 1971—, acting chmn. dept. English, 1964-66. Cons. faculty Air U., Maxwell Field, Ala., 1951; dir. publs. div. Army Ballistic Missle Agy., Huntsville, Ala. summer 1960. Served to major USAAF, 1941-45. Mem. Am. Assn. U. Profs., Phi Delta Theta. Author: Through the First Gate, 1950; Muscogee Twilight, 1965; Know Alabama, 1957; Prose and Poetry for Enjoyment, 1955; short stories in popular mags., as Atlantic Monthly, Am. Mercury, Saturday Evening Post, True, Comment, many others.Home: Route 2 Box 328-C Theodore AL 36582 Office: U. So Ala Gaillard Dr Mobile AL 36608

STEWART, JOHN DAUGHERTY, pub. co. exec.; b. Indiana, Pa., Oct. 16, 1915; s. Ernest Taylor and Caroline (Daugherty) S.; A.B., Princeton U., 1937; postgrad. Harvard, 1938-39; m. Helen Gambrill, Sept. 23, 1940 (dec. Jan. 1964); children—Caroline Leigh (Mrs. Carl G. Estabrook, Jr.), Susan (Mrs. James G. Stockard, Jr.); m. 2d, Margret Pahl, Feb. 18, 1967. Instr. Sch. Pub. and Internat. Affairs, Princeton (N.J.) U., 1937-38; mem. editorial staff The Bur. Nat. Affairs, Inc., Washington, 1939—, v.p., 1947-64, pres., editor-in-chief, 1964—; dir. Tax Mgmt. Inc., Washington, Fisher-Stevens, Inc., Clifton, N.J.; adv. dir. Union Trust Co., Washington, 1969—. Mem. exec. res. Dept. Labor, Washington, 1958—; chmn. tripartite industry com. for minimum wage regulation Am. Samoa, V.I., P.R., Sec. Labor, 1957-60. Pres. Southeastern Econ. Devel. Found., 1970—, Multiple Sclerosis Assn. Washington, 1957—. Mem. Indsl. Relations Research Assn. (pres. 1953), White House Corrs. Assn. Clubs: River Bend Country, Nat. Press. Editor: The New Labor Law, 1947; The Landrum-Griffin Act, 1959. Home: 2869 Beechwood Circle Arlington VA 22207 Office: 1231 25th St NW Washington DC 20037

STEWART, JOHN ELLIOTT, investment counsel; b. Chgo., Dec. 1, 1912; s. Robert Wright and Maude (Elliott) S.; ed. Yale, 1935; m. Mary Terry Schlamp, May 9, 1936; children—James Jeremiah, Sara Royall, John Elliott. Salesman Colonial Beacon Oil Co., N.Y.C., 1935-36; pres. Stewart, Warren & Co., N.Y.C., 1937-40; comml. aviation pilot, flight instr., A & H Flying Service, Asheville, N.C., 1940-42; asst. supt. stas. operations and flight dispatch mgr. Pan Am. Airways, Inc., Atlantic div., N.Y.C., 1947-50; asso. Neergard, Miller & Co., N.Y.C., 1950-57, Coffin & Burr, Inc., N.Y.C., 1957-61, Laird, Bissell & Meeds, 1961-62; formed own investment counseling firm, Madison, 1962; dir. North Madison Representative Orgn., 1966-68, pres., 1967-68. Sec. Federated Assns., Greenwich, 1952-54; dir. Am. Coalition, Washington, 1957-60; chmn. U.S. Day Com. Greenwich, 1954; v.p. Madison Land Conservation Trust, 1966-67, pres., 1968—, dir., chmn. land acquistion com., 1968-71, justice of peace, 1964-71; mem. Conn. Power Facility Evaluation Com., 1971; mem. Conn. Am. Revolution Bicentennial Council, 1971—. Mem. Rep. Town Com. Madison, 1964-71; bd. dirs. Palm Beach Republican Club, 1972—. Served as lt. comdr. USNR, 1942-46. Mem. Greenwich C. of C. (past v.p., dir. 1956-60, chmn. legislative com., edn. com.), S.A.R. (bd. mgrs., sr. v.p. Conn. soc. 1962-64, pres. Conn. Soc. 1964-66, nat. trustee for Conn., 1965-67), C.A.R. (mem. bd. Conn. soc.; sr. pres. Lt. William Stewart Soc.). Republican. Clubs: Metropolitan (gov. 1958-62) (N.Y.C.); Racquet (Chgo.); Madison Beach, Madison Rotary (dir. v.p. 1966-67, pres. 1968—) (Madison); Biltmore (N.C.) Forest Country; Beach (Palm Beach, Fla.); International de Bridge (Madrid, Spain); Marbella (Spain). Home: La Casa Pequena 730 North County Rd Palm Beach FL 33408

STEWART, JOHN SYLVESTER, III, mfg. co. exec.; b. Houston, Nov. 11, 1920; s. John Sylvester and Cornelia Ennis (Cargill) S.; student Tex. A and M, 1937-41, U. Tex., 1938-40; m. Jane Farish Colhoun, Oct. 24, 1942; children—Jane Lucinda (Mrs. Harry Bradford Fleming III), John Sylvester IV, Charles Colhoun. Engr., Mission Mfg. Co., Houston, 1941-51, city sales, 1951-55, asst. domestic sales mgr., 1955-59, domestic sales mgr. 1959-62; asst. to pres. Wilson Industries Inc., Houston, 1962-64, v.p. sales, 1964—; dir. Wilson Marine Systems, Inc. Active United Fund, Pin Oaks Horse Show, Heart Fund. Served to 1st lt. AUS, 1943-46; PTO. Mem. C. of C. (dir. Am. Arab chpt. 1970-71), Am. Petroleum Inst., Soc. Petroleum Engrs., Am. Inst. Mining, Metall. and Petroleum Engrs., Ind. Petroleum Assn. Am., Tex. Ind. Producers and Royalty Owners Assn., Houston C. of C. Club: Houston. Home: 1753 Milford St Houston TX 77006 Office: 1301 Conti St Houston TX 77002

STEWART, JOHN WESLEY, supermarket exec.; b. Trent, Tex., Mar. 3, 1918; s. George Thomas and Zadie E. (Estep) S.; student pub. schs.; m. Bennie Fee Stone, Jan. 14, 1940; children—Johnnie Ray, Jimmie V., Ronald Wesley. Owner grocery story, Quemado, Tex., 1938-39, Borden & Ray Grocery, Asherton, Tex., 1939-48; owner Stewart's I.G.A. Store, Cotulla, Tex., 1941-42; rancher, Asherton, 1939-48; owner Stewart's I.G.A. Foodliner, Uvalde, Tex., 1948-66, Stewarts United Supermarket, Uvalde, 1967—; partner radio sta. KPSO, Falfurrias, Tex., 1955-65, radio sta. KSOX, Raymondville, Tex., 1959-65; rancher, Uvalde County, 1965—, Catarina, Tex., 1969—; dir. Uvalde Nat. Bank. Baptist (deacon). Mason, Lion (past pres.). Home: PO Box 1633 Uvalde TX 78801 Office: 600 E Main St Uvalde TX 78801

STEWART, JOHN WESLEY, JR., chmn. Com. New Orleans Jazz Mus. and Archives. Address: 6025 Freret St New Orleans LA 70118*

STEWART, JOSEPH GORDON, dentist; b. Anniston, Ala., Mar. 8, 1929; s. James Douglas and Mamie Louise (McClellan) S.; B.S., Birmingham So. Coll., 1952; D.M.D., U. Ala., 1954; m. Roxie Catherine Grace, Aug. 24, 1952; children—Labella, Roxanna, Joanna, Joseph Gordon. Practice pediatric dentistry, Montgomery, 1956—. Cons. Montgomery Children's Center, 1957—. Pres., Montgomery Community Action Com., 1967, Central Ala. Timberland Inc., 1970-71. Bd. dirs. Tukabatchee Area council Boy Scouts Am., pres. 1968-70; bd. dirs. Montgomery Children's Center, Ala. Dental Found., Ala. Heart Assn. Served to capt. Dental Corps, AUS, 1954-56. Named one of four outstanding young men of Ala., Ala. Jr. C. of C., 1964, Most Distinguished Alumnus, U. Ala. Sch. Dentistry, 1968; recipient Silver Beaver award Boy Scouts Am., 1964, Distinguished Service award Montgomery Jr. C. of C., 1964. Fellow Am. Coll. Dentists; mem. Am. (del. 1964-70), Ala. (trustee 1968-71, pres. 1970-71) dental assns., Ala. Dental Alumni Assn. (pres. 1961), Montgomery County Dental Soc. (pres. 1959), Am. Soc. Dentistry for Children (pres. 1962), Alpha Tau Omega, Psi Omega. Methodist (steward 1964-68). Home: 2052 Myrtlewood Dr Montgomery AL 36111 Office: 330 S Ripley St Montgomery AL 36104

STEWART, LINDA JOAN WILLIAMS (MRS. DOUGLAS STEWART), educator; b. Monterey Park, Cal., Oct. 17, 1938; d. Ralph F. and Maude (Spicer) Williams; B.A. in Edn., Northwestern State Coll., 1962, M.Ed., 1964; Ed.D., Okla. State U., 1970; m. Douglas Stewart, Dec. 22, 1962. Tchr. English, speech Medicine Lodge (Kan.) High Sch., 1963; tchr., counselor Harper (Kan.) High Sch., 1964-66; instr. speech Northwestern State Coll., Alva, Okla., 1968, acting chmn. speech dept., 1969-71, prof. speech, 1971—, also dir. drama prodns. Sponsor, Castle Players; mem. Nesatunga Arts and Humanities Council. Mem. Bus. and Profl. Guidance Assn., Alvah C. of C., Am. Ednl. Theatre Assn., Speech Assn. Am., N.E.A., Am. Assn. U. Women, Alpha Psi Omega (sponsor). Republican. Conglist. Mem. Order Eastern Star. Home: 1202 2d St Alva OK 73717

STEWART, LLOYD MAY, newspaper editor; b. Port Arthur, Tex., Jan. 15, 1924; d. Lloyd Martin and May (Cowart) Stewart; B.J., U. Tex., 1945. Reporter, Wichita Falls (Tex.) Record News, 1945, Marshall (Tex.) News Messenger, 1946-47; editor Cleburne (Tex.) Times-Rev., 1947-49; with Ft. Worth Star-Telegram, 1949—, soc. editor, 1950—, art editor, 1959-63, woman's editor, fashion editor, 1963—. Recipient 1st place award, women's news Tex. A.P. Mng. Editors Assn., 1966. Mem. Am. Assn. U. Women, Tex. Congress Parents and Tchrs., Theta Sigma Phi (chpt. pres. 1962-64, mem. nat. bd. 1964—, nat. pres. 1968-71). Episcopalian. Clubs: Zonta, Woman's, Woman's Shakespeare (Ft. Worth). Home: 710 N Main St Cleburne TX 76031 Office: 400 W 7th St Fort Worth TX 76101

STEWART, POTTER, asso. justice U.S. Supreme Ct; b. Jackson, Mich., Jan. 23, 1915; s. James Garfield and Harriet Loomis (Potter) S.; student Hotchkiss Sch.; B.A. cum laude, Yale, 1937, LL.B. cum laude, 1941, LL.D., 1959; fellow Cambridge U., Eng., 1937-38; m. Mary Ann Bertles, Apr. 25, 1943; children—Harriet Potter (Mrs. Richard Virkstis), Potter, David Bertles. Admitted to Ohio bar, 1941, N.Y., 1942; asso. Debevoise, Stevenson, Plimpton & Page, N.Y.C., 1941-42, 45-47; asso. Dinsmore, Shohl, Sawyer & Dinsmore, Cin., 1947-50, mem. firm, 1951-54; U.S. judge Ct. Appeals, 6th Circuit, 1954-58; asso. justice U.S. Supreme Ct., 1958—. Mem. com. White House Conf. on Edn., 1954-55. Mem. Cin. City Council, 1950-53, vice mayor, 1952-53. Served as lt. USNR, 1942-45. Mem. Am., Ohio, Cin. bar assns., Am. Law Inst., Yale Law Sch. Assn. (exec. com.), Order of Coif, Phi Beta Kappa, Delta Kappa Epsilon, Phi Delta Phi. Episcopalian. Clubs: Camargo, Commonwealth, Commercial, University (Cin.); Chevy Chase (Washington). Home: 5136 Palisade Lane Washington DC 20016 Office: Supreme Ct Bldg Washington DC 20543

STEWART, ROBERT, educator, composer; b. Buffalo, Mar. 6, 1918; s. William Murphy and Mary (Owens) S.; Mus.M., Am. Conservatory Music, Chgo., 1946; m. Sue Ellen Crumley, Aug. 7, 1949; children—Robert Murphy, Patrick Crumley. Tchr. theory and violin Am. Conservatory Music, 1939-53; tchr. theory, composition and edn. Ark. State Tchrs. Coll., 1953-54; prof. music and fine arts, dir. music Washington and Lee U., 1954-70, chmn. dept. music and drama, 1970—; free-lance profl. violinist, Chgo., 1940-53; concertmaster Roanoke (Va.) Symphony Orch., 1960-64. Served with USNR, 1941-45. MacDowell fellow, 1956. Mem. Am. Composers Alliance, Am. Music Center, Southeastern Composer's League (pres. 1968-70). Composer orch. and chamber music. Home: 108 Rebel Ridge Dr Lexington VA 24450

STEWART, ROBERT GORDON, mus. curator; b. Balt., Mar. 5, 1931; s. Kenneth Elsworth and Ruth (Chambers) S.; B.F.A., U. Pa., 1954. Architect, Ind. Nat. Hist. Park, Phila., 1954, Nat. Park Service, Phila., 1956-57; architect, curator Jefferson Barracks Hist. Park, St. Louis, 1958-61; dir. properties Nat. Trust for Historic Preservation, Washington, 1961-64; chief curator Nat. Portrait Gallery, Washington, 1964—. Vis. lectr. George Washington U., 1967-70. Served with AUS, 1954-56. Mem. Md. Dorchester County, Lewes hist. socs., Am. Assn. Mus., A.I.A. (asso.), Coll. Art Assn., Zeta Psi. Episcopalian. Author: Nucleus for a National Collection, 1965; Recent Acquisitions, 1966; A Nineteenth Century Gallery of Distinguished Americans, 1969; Henry Benbridge (1743-1812) American Portrait Painter, 1971. Home: 2351 49th St NW Washington DC 20007 Office: Smithsonian Institution Washington DC 20560

STEWART, ROBERT H., III, banker; b. Dallas, Dec. 3, 1925; s. Robert H. Stewart; B.B.A. in Banking, So. Meth. U., 1949; m. Cynthia Giesecke, 1949; children—Cynthia Caroline, Alice Partee. With Empire State Bank, Dallas, 1949-50; with First Nat. Bank, Dallas, 1951—, v.p., 1953-59, sr. v.p., pres., now chmn., chief exec.; dir. Dallas Hotel Co., Allied Finance Co., Republic Ins. Co., Southwestern Life Ins. Co., Gifford-Hill & Co., Inc. (all Dallas), Braniff Airways, Inc., Pepsi-Cola Co. Bd. dirs. Dallas Citizens Council. Served to 1st lt. inf. AUS, 1944-46, also Korea. Clubs: Brook Hollow Golf (dir.), Terpsichorean (dir.), Idlewild (dir.) (Dallas). Home: 4626 N Lindhurst St Dallas TX 75229 Office: First Nat Bank Box 6031 Dallas TX 75222

STEWART, ROBERT PERCY, JR., ins. co. exec.; b. Natchez, Miss., Nov. 12, 1922; s. Robert Percy and Virginia Lowry (Hodge) S.; B.F.A., U. Ga., 1943; student So. Meth. U., 1953-56, S. Tex. Coll. Law, 1956-57, U. Houston Law Sch., 1956-57; m. Betty Lou George, Aug. 12, 1950; children—Katherine Louise, Virginia Anne, Robert Percy, Owen Thomas. Asst. sales mgr. S.W. div. Kraft Foods Co.; Garland, Tex., 1947-53; partner George & Stewart, attys., Dallas, 1953—; pres. S.W. Title Ins. Co., Dallas, 1963—, also dir.; dir. N. Dallas Bank and Trust Co., AAA Dallas Auto Club. Served with inf., AUS, 1942-46. Decorated Bronze Star with 2 oak leaf clusters. Mem. Am. Bar Assn., Title Underwriters of Tex. (pres., 1965), Tex. Land Title Assn. (v.p. 1966, dir. 1971), Delta Theta Phi, Phi Delta Theta. Presbyn. Clubs: Chaparral, City, Top-of-the Cliff (Dallas). Home: 4348 Shenandoah Av Dallas TX 75205 Office: 701 Elm St Dallas TX 75202

STEWART, VINCENT EVANS, state ofcl.; b. N.Y.C., Feb. 11, 1913; B.S., U. Fla., 1934, Ph.D. in Chemistry, 1937; m. 1937; 3 children. Chief chemist Fla. Racing Commn., 1937-39; dir. food and drug lab. Fla. Dept. Agr., Tallahassee, 1939-45, 46-59, state chemist, 1959—; research chemist Winthrop Chem. Co., N.Y.C., 1945-46. Lectr., Fla. State U., 1946-47; mem. fed. foods standards com. FDA. Mem. Am. Chem. Soc., Assn. Ofcl. Analytical Chemists, Inst. Food Technologists. Research on synthesis of deritatives of heterocyclic nitrogen compounds, analysis of food and drugs, toxicology and microidentification of drugs. Office: Fla Dept Agriculture Mayo Bldg Tallahassee FL 32304*

STEWART, WALTER BINGHAM, educator; b. Evanston, Ill., Aug. 15, 1913; s. Walter Morgan and Elizabeth (Bingham) S.; student U. Ill., 1932-33, Northwestern U., 1939-40, U. Wis., 1961-63, Upper Ia. U., 1962-63; A.B., U. N.C., 1938; B.S., Radford Coll., 1964; postgrad. U. Fla., 1966-68; m. Janie Veda Sinclair, July 3, 1939; children—Sinclair, Donald. Account exec. Erwin, Wasey, Chgo., 1939-40; advt. mgr. The Parker Pen Co., Janesville, Wis., 1940-44; sales and advt. mgr. Louis Melind Co., Chgo., 1945-47; advt. mgr. Reynolds Pen Co., Chgo., 1947-50; advt. mgr. H.W. Gossard Co., Chgo., 1950-61; mgr. Travelmats-Press Pub. Co., Prairie du Chien, Wis., 1961-63; chmn. journalism dept. Radford Coll., 1965—; freelance newspaperman; advt. cons. to Western Auto Stores, Travel Bur. Fla.; radio broadcaster. Mem. Pi Delta Epsilon, Kappa Delta Pi, Phi Delta Kappa, Phi Gamma Delta. Author: Do You Pass the Model Test, 1957; Do You Dress Like a Model, 1958; Do You Have a Model Figure, 1959; Adventures in Travel, 1962. Home: 101 Dogwood Lane Radford VA 24141

STEWART, WILLIAM HUFFMAN, physician; b. Mpls., May 19, 1921; s. Chester A. and Dorothy S. (Huffman) S.; student U. Minn., 1939-41; M.D., La. State U., 1945; m. Glendora F. White, June 29, 1946; children—Martha Ann, Laura H. Resident physician pediatrics Charity Hosp. of New Orleans, 1948-50; practice pediatrics, Alexandria, La., 1950-51; officer USPHS, 1951—, epidemiologist Communicable Disease Center, 1951-53, chief heart disease control program, 1954-56, asst. dir. Nat. Heart Inst., 1956-57, asst. to surg. gen., 1957-58, chief div. pub. health methods, 1958-64, asst. to spl. asst., 1964-65, surgeon gen., 1965-69. Diplomate Am. Bd. Pediatrics. Mem. Am. Pub. Health Assn., A.M.A. Contbr. articles sci. jours. Home: 9108 Ewing Dr Bethesda MD 20034 Office: USPHS Washington DC 20203

STIBBS, JOHN HENRY, univ. dean; b. Chgo., Feb. 10, 1909; s. Henry Howard and Bertha (Hemingway) S.; Ph.D., U. Mich., 1942; m. Phyllis Miner, May 25, 1941; children—Virginia Helen, Henry Howard II, John Henry. Teaching fellow U. Mich., 1937-42; instr. U.S. Naval Acad., 1946; with Tulane U., 1946—, successively asst. prof. English, asst. dean Coll. Arts and Scis., 1946-49, prof. and dean of students, 1949—. Mem. exec. com. Assn. Naval R. O.T.C. Colls., 1967-70; acad. council Coll. Student Personnel Inst., 1966-70. Dir. Louise McGehee Sch. 1953-66. Served with USNR, 1942-46, now comdr. Mem. Nat. Assn. Student Personnel Adminstrs. (pres. 1954-55), Am. Personnel and Guidance Assn., Am. Coll. Health Assn., Am. Assn. U. Profs., Orleans Audubon Soc. (pres. 1951-69), Modern, South Central lang. assns., Renaissance Soc., S.R., Soc. War 1812, Delta Kappa Epsilon, Phi Kappa Phi, Omicron Delta Kappa. Clubs: Internat. House, Boston, South Louisiana Gun (dir.), Southern Yacht, New Orleans Lawn Tennis (New Orleans). Author short stories; contbr. to profl. jours. Home: 6901 Willow St New Orleans LA 70118

STICKLEY, ELMER EUGENE, educator; b. Brackenridge, Pa., Jan. 23, 1915; s. Eugene Franklin and Mary Ann (Crawford) S.; B.S., Carnegie Inst. Tech., 1937; M.S., U. Pitts., 1940; Ph.D., 1942; m. Olivia Horner, Dec. 27, 1939; 1 son, Spencer Eugene. Instr., Pa. Coll. for Women (now Chatham Coll.), part-time, 1938-42; fellow Mellon Inst., Pitts., 1942-43; research physicist Pitts. Plate Glass Co., 1943-51; med. physicist Brookhaven Nat. Lab., 1951-61; attending physicist Presbyn. Hosp., N.Y.C., 1961-66, radiation safety officer, 1961-66, tchr. physics of radiology, diagnostic X-ray physics, nuclear medicine physics, 1961-66; asso. prof. radiology Coll. Physicians and Surgeons, Columbia U., 1961-66; prof. physics Med. Coll. Va., Richmond, 1966—. Cons. in radiol. physics. Fellow Am. Coll. Radiology; mem. Am. Assn. Physicists in Medicine, Soc. Nuclear

Medicine, Health Physics Soc., Am. Inst. Physics, Va. Acad. Sci., Radiol. Soc. N.Am., Radiation Research Soc., Am. Radium Soc., Sigma Xi. Home: 2750 Stratford Rd Richmond VA 23225 Office: 1200 E Broad St Richmond VA 23219

STICKNEY, STONEWALL B., physician, state ofcl.; b. Selma, Ala., 1924; B.S., Tulane U., 1944, M.D., 1947. Intern U. Wis. Med. Sch., Madison, 1948, Am. Hosp., Paris, France, 1949; resident in psychiatry U. Colo. Med. Sch., Denver, 1950, U. Pitts. Med. Sch., 1953-55; teaching fellow Western Psychiat. Inst., Pitts., 1953-55; practice medicine specializing in psychiatry, 1955-68; tng. in psychoanalysis Pitts. Psychoanalytic Inst., 1956-65; dir. Ala. Dept. Mental Health, Montgomery, 1968—; clin. asso. prof. psychiatry U. Ala. Coll. Medicine, 1968—. Chief psychiat. cons. mental health program Allegheny County Schs., Pitts., 1965-66; dir. mental health service Pitts. Pub. Schs., 1965-68. Served to 1st lt. M.C., AUS, 1951-52. Diplomate Am. Bd. Psychiatry and Neurology. Mem. Phi Beta Kappa. Office: 502 Washington Av Montgomery AL 36104*

STIEGLER, THEODORE DONALD, mech. engr.; b. Balt., May 28, 1934; s. August and Helene (Giese) S.; B.S. in Mech. Engring., Duke, 1956; postgrad. U. Va., 1962-63; m. Beth Collins Sutton, July 6, 1957; children— Linda Catherine, Sally Collins. With E.I. duPont de Nemours & Co., Richmond, Va., 1958—, research engr., 1966—. Served to lt. (j.g.) USNR, 1956-58. Registered profl. engr., Va. Mem. Nat. Rifle Assn., Delta Tau Delta. Mem. United Ch. of Christ. Co-inventor film winding apparatus. Home: 1329 Pulliam St Richmond VA 23235 Office: PO Box 27222 Richmond VA 23261

STIFF, ASHBY GORDON, JR., educator; b. Balt., Oct. 18, 1930; s. Ashby Gordon and Mary Ellen (Waring) S.; A.B., Johns Hopkins, 1951; M.S., Fla. State U., 1957. Mgmt. trainee Sheraton Corp. Am., Balt., 1956; mgmt. trainee Hotel Corp. Am., Washington, 1957; asst. mgr. Many Glacier Hotel, Glacier Park Co., Glacier, Mont., summer 1958, gen. mgr., 1959-60; gen. mgr. Canyon Village Yellowstone Park Co., Yellowstone Park, Wyo., summers 1961, 64, gen. mgr. Lake Hotel, summer 1962; dir. food, housing Nat. Def. Edn. Act French Insts., Tallahassee, 1963; instr. Sch. Bus., Hotel Adminstrn. Fla. State U., Tallahassee, 1957-61, asst. prof., 1961-68, asso. prof., 1968—, dir. European study program, 1970—. Served with USAF, 1951-55. Named Ky. col. Mem. S.A.R. (past chpt. sec.-treas.), Soc. War 1812 in Md., Order First Families Va., Council Hotel, Restaurant and Instl. Edn. (mem. research com. 1968—, head research project new concepts comml. food edn. 1968, charter mem.), Soc. Hosts, League Hospitality Execs., Soc. Scullions (past pres.), Am. Assn. U. Profs., Navy League, Alpha Kappa Psi, Alpha Psi Omega, Lambda Chi Alpha. Elk. Club: Johns Hopkins (Balt). Publs. editor League Hospitality Execs., 1964—. Contbr. articles to profl. jours. Home: 1481 Marion Av Tallahassee FL 32303

STIFF, JOHN STERLING, city mgr.; b. McKinney, Tex., Feb. 14, 1921; s. James Harrison and Elva (Boone) S.; student Tex. A. and M. Coll., 1938-41; B.E., Yale, 1947; m. Harriet Rashig, May 21, 1946; children—Mark, Justin. Office engr. City of Big Spring, Tex., 1938-39, 41-42; city engr., Abilene, Tex., 1947-51, city mgr., Irving, Tex., 1953-57; gen. mgr. Hardee-Pipkin Constrn. Co., Irving, 1957-58; city mgr., Garland, Tex., 1958-63, Amarillo, Tex., 1963—. Mem. Tex. Gov.'s Com. on Intergovtl. Relations, 1970. Served with USNR, 1942-46, 51-52. Registered profl. engr., Tex. Mem. Internat. (v.p. 1968), Tex. (past pres.) city mgrs. assns., Internat. City Mgmt. Assn. (pres. 1970-71), Amarillo, Dallas (central hwy. com.) chambers commerce, Garland Home Builders Assn. Methodist (steward). Rotarian (past dir. Garland). Clubs: Amarillo A. and M., Amarillo Yale. Home: 7100 Dreyfuss Amarillo TX 79106 Office: PO Box 1971 Amarillo TX 79105

STIFF, ROBERT MARTIN, newspaper editor; b. Detroit, Aug. 25, 1931; s. Martin L. and Gladys (Mathews) S.; B.A., Ohio State U., 1953; m. Janet Carol Kaser, Oct. 10, 1953; children—David, Amy. Reporter, Painesville (O.) Telegraph, 1953-55, bur. chief, 1955-57, city editor, 1957-61; with St. Petersburg (Fla.) Times, 1961-67, sports editor, 1962, city editor, 1962-63, state editor, 1964-65, asst. mng. editor, 1965-67; editor St. Petersburg Evening Ind., 1967—; dir. Times Pub. Co. Mem. A.P. Assn. Fla. (v.p. 1969-70; pres. 1970-71), Am., Fla. (dir.) socs. newspaper editors, Sigma Delta Chi (v.p. 1969-70; pres. 1970-71). Home: 1491 87th Av N St Petersburg FL 33702 Office: 490 1st Av S St Petersburg FL 33701

STIGERS, ROBERT WINSTON, dentist; b. Shelbyville, Ky., July 7, 1925; s. Willie Edgar and Mary Francis (Young) S.; student Centre Coll., 1946-49; D.M.D., U. Louisville, 1959; m. Anne McWilliams, Sept. 16, 1951; children—Stephen, David, Lee Anne. Practice of dentistry, 1959-60; staff dentist VA Hosp., Lexington, Ky., 1960—, chief dental service, 1968—; part-time faculty Coll. Dentistry, U. Ky., 1968—. Pres., P.T.A., 1968-69. Served with USAAF, 1943-45. Mem. Christian Ch. Lion, Optimist. Club: Spindletop Hall (Lexington, Ky.). Home: 1620 Kensington Way Lexington KY 40504 Office: VA Hosp Lexington KY 40507

STIGLER, WILLIAM ARTHUR, museum dir.; b. Ruleville, Miss., July 15, 1910; s. William Arthur and Frances (Word) S.; LL.B., U. Miss., 1936; m. Jeanette Louise Amidon, July 1, 1938. Admitted to Miss. Bar, 1963; practiced in Tunica, 1936-39, spl. agt., supr. FBI, 1939-51; asst. dep. adminstr. Maritime Adminstrn., Washington, 1952-60; dir. Bur. Fgn. Regulation, Fed. Maritime Commn., Washington, 1960-65; exec. dir. Miss. Nursing Home Assn., Jackson, 1968-71; supt. Jefferson Davis Shrine and Museum, Biloxi, Miss., 1971—. Address: Box 200 W Beach Blvd Biloxi MS 39531 Office: 200 W Beach Blvd Biloxi MS 39531

STILES, RAEBURN BRACKETT, state ofcl.; b. Middlebury, Vt., Mar. 14, 1915; s. John E. and Caroline (Brackett) S.; A.B., Middlebury Coll., 1938; M.A., Peabody Coll., 1949; B.S., Vanderbilt U., 1958; m. Carolyn Louise Flascher, Dec. 19, 1941; 1 dau., Susan B. (Mrs. Richard B. Sibley). Tchr. math., coach Green (N.Y.) Central High Sch., 1938-41; tchr., recreation dir. Southfield Sch., Shreveport, La., 1941-42; asso. prof. applied math. Vanderbilt U., 1946-64; engr., dir. computer services div. Tenn. Dept. Hwys., Nashville, 1964-72; dir. regional computing State of Tenn., Nashville, 1972—; meteorologist U.S. Air N.G. Served with Air Corps, 1942-46; ETO: with USAF, 1951-53; to lt. col. Tenn. Air N.G., 1960-71. Registered profl. engr., Tenn. Mem. Am. Math. Assn., Am. Soc. Engring. Edn., Assn. Systems Mgmt., Nat. Soc. Profl. Engrs. Presbyn. (deacon, elder). Home: 3911 Trimble Rd Nashville TN 37215 Office: Andrew Jackson Bldg Nashville TN 37219

STILES, WARREN OAKLEY, cons. engr.; b. Alma, Mich., July 18, 1928; s. Charles Edward and Helen Lucile (Hayner) S.; student Eastern Mich. U., 1957; B.S.E. in Mech. Engring., Mich., 1960; m. Constance Ann Patrick, Sept. 11, 1952; 1 son, Jonathan. Engr., Cutler-Hammer, Milw., 1960-65, Koppers Co., Pitts., 1966; indsl. systems cons., Ypsilanti, Mich., 1966-68; with Aqua-Chem., Inc., Wrightsville Beach, N.C., 1968-71; cons. engr., Wrightsville Beach, 1971—. Pres., Aqua-Labs. of Wrightsville Beach, Inc., 1970—; v.p., dir. Arcon Devel. Corp., Wilmington, N.C., 1971—. Served with AUS, 1950-54. Mem. Nat. Assn. Professions, Profl. Engrs. N.C. (sec. Southeastern chpt.), Am. Soc. M.E., Am. Water Works Assn., Water Pollution Cpntrol Fedn., Assn. Iron and Steel Engrs., Pi Tau Sigma. Democrat. Club: Wilmington Engineers. Designer elec. motive system for stage wagon drives at New Met. Opera House, Lincoln Center for Performing Arts, N.Y. Home: 7000 Wrightsville Av Wrightsville Sound NC 28480 Office: PO Box 437 Wrightsville Beach NC 23480

STILL, CHARLES NEAL, physician; b. Richmond, Va., Apr. 15, 1929; s. Charles Wright and Ruth (Kemp) S.; B.S., Clemson U., 1949; M.S., Purdue U., 1951; M.D., Med. U. S.C., 1959; m. Dorothy Lee Varn, Dec. 27, 1958; children—Charles Herbert, Carl Nelson. Sara Alice. Lab. chemistry Clemson (S.C.) U., 1948-49; teaching fellow biochemistry Purdue U., Lafayette, Ind., 1949-51; instr. chemistry Clemson U., 1951-52, U.S. Mil. Acad., West Point, N.Y., 1953-55; intern U. Chgo. Clinics, 1959-60; resident Johns Hopkins Hosp. and Balt. City Hosp., 1960-63; postgrad. fellow Johns Hopkins, 1960-63; research fellow Harvard Med. Sch. and McLean Hosp. Research Lab., Belmont, Mass., 1963-65; chief neurology service William S. Hall Psychiat. Inst., Columbia, S.C., 1965—; vis. asst. clin. prof. neurology Med. U. S.C., 1967—; electroencephalographer S.C. Bapt. Hosp., Columbia, 1966—. Served to 1st lt. Q.M.C., AUS, 1952-55. Diplomate Am. Bd. Psychiatry and Neurology, Pan Am. Med. Assn. (mem. neurology council). Mem. Am. Acad. Neurology, A.M.A., Internat., Am. socs. for neurochemistry, S.C., So., med. assns., Johns Hopkins Med. and Surg. Assn., Sigma Xi. Baptist. Home: 2 Culpepper Circle Columbia SC 29209 Office: WS Hall Psychiat Inst Drawer 119 Columbia SC 29202

STILL, WILLIAM JAMES SANGSTER, pathologist, educator; b. Aberdeen, Scotland, Sept. 16, 1923; s. William and Jean (Sangster) S.; M.B. Ch.B., U. Aberdeen, 1951, M.D., 1960; m. Mary E.A. Duguid, Mar. 27, 1951; children—Mary J.E., William John Peter. Lectr. pathology U. London, 1956-60, sr. lectr., 1962-65; asst. prof. pathology Washington U., St. Louis, 1960-62; prof. pathology Med. Coll. Va., Richmond, 1965—. Served to lt. Royal Navy, 1941-46. Fellow Council on Arteriosclerosis, Am. Heart Assn.; mem. Coll. Pathologists Gt. Britain. Home: 4207 Kensington Av Richmond VA 23221

STILL, WILLIAM LEONARD, aerospace co. exec.; b. LaPanza, Cal., Sept. 16, 1919; s. Mently Frederick and Annabella (Ross) S.; B.S. in Aero. Engring., Air Force Inst. Tech., 1949, M.S. in Elec. Engring., 1954; m. Mary Cathryne Wilson, Aug. 17, 1945; children—William T., Robert J., Patricia A. Commd. 2d. lt. AC, U.S. Army, 1942, advanced through ranks to lt. col. USAF, 1962; research and devel. through the earth communications and ground communications and control minutemen missile, 1958-62; asst. to v.p. Deco Electronics div. Westinghouse, Leesburg, Va., 1962-67; chmn. bd., pres. Aerospace Indsl. Assos., Inc., Purcellville, Va., 1967—. Decorated Bronze Star. Mem. Am. Inst. Aeros. and Astronautics, Am. Ordnance Assn., Air Force Assn., Ret. Officers Assn. Patentee in field. Cons. editor Control Engring., 1962-67. Contbr. articles in field to profl. jours. Home: RFD 2 Box 73 Purcellville VA 22132 Office: PO Box 875 Purcellville VA 22132

STILLWELL, WALTER BROOKS, JR., dentist; b. Savannah, Ga., Dec. 27, 1919; s. Walter Brooks and Jane Caroline (Shuptrine) S.; student U. Md., 1938-39; D.D.S., Balt. Coll. Dental Surgery, 1943; m. Selpha Theresa Everson, Sept. 17, 1945; children—Walter Brooks, Caroline Marie, Serena Everson. Pvt. practice dentistry, Balt., 1946-49, Savannah, 1949—, specializing in pedodontia, 1955—; mng. partner Shuptrine Co., drug mfg. co., Savannah, 1961—; pres. Pedodontic Asso. of Savannah, 1970—. Active United Community Appeal, Boy Scouts Am., YMCA, Cancer Soc.; mem. Savannah Symphony Soc., Little Theatre of Savannah. Served to capt., Dental Corp, AUS, 1943-46. Fellow Am. Acad. Pedodontics, Am., Ga. dental assns., Internat. Coll. Dentists, Southeastern Soc. Pedodontics, Ga. Soc. Pediatric Dentistry, Savannah Dental Soc. (pres. 1955-56), Southeastern Dist. Dental Soc. (pres. 1964), Ga. Soc. Dentistry for Children (pres. 1969), Soc. Colonial Wars in Ga. Baptist (deacon 1952—). Clubs: Civitan, Savannah Yacht, Chatham, Cotillion. Home: 50 Richmond Dr Savannah GA 31406 Office: 211 E 31st St Savannah GA 31401

STILTZ, HARRY LANGLEY, housing cons. co. exec.; b. Hereford, Md., Aug. 7, 1920;. Emory Holton and Mamie (Langley) S.; student U. Chattanooga, 1948-49; B.S. in Elec. Engring., U. Tenn., 1951; m. Mary Alleen, June 9, 1965; 1 dau., Lea Ann. Project engr. E.I. du Pont de Nemours & Co., Inc., Chattanooga, asst. prof. U. Chattanooga, 1951-53; field test engr. TVA, Chattanooga, 1953-56; project engr. Lockheed Ga. Co., Marietta, 1956-58, group engr., 1959-62; group engr. Martin Co., Orlando, Fla., 1958-59; pres., chmn. bd. dirs. Aerosci. Electronics, Inc., Atlanta, 1962-66; founded Aerospace Telementry Sch., Atlanta, 1962, dir., 1962-68; pres. Stiltz Sales & Engring. Co., Atlanta, 1966-68; research engr. Ga. Inst. Tech., 1968-69; sr. partner Manufactured Housing Cons., Atlanta, 1969—; v.p., gen. mgr. W.P. Atkinson Industries, Inc., Shawnee, Okla., 1969-71; v.p., gen. mgr. TBR Homes, Inc., Pelham, Ga., 1972—. Bd. dirs. Orchid Bowl Assn., Chattanooga, 1947-48; neighborhood commr. Boy Scouts Am., Marietta, 1960-62. Served with USAAF, 1942-45. Recipient Gen. Electric Zero Defects award Aerosci. Electronics, Inc., 1966. Registered profl. engr., Tenn., Ga. Mem. I.E.E.E., Instrument Soc. Am., V.F.W., Eta Kappa Nu, Tau Beta Pi. Methodist. Author, editor: Aerospace Telemetry, vol. I, 1962, vol. II, 1966. Home: 500 Hillcrest Moultrie GA 31768 Office: Box 648 Pelham GA 31779

STIMBERT, ELDEN CARL, state ofcl.; b. Inland, Neb., Sept. 25, 1908; s. Carl Theobald and Clara Matilda (Schuck) S.; B.A., Neb. Wesleyan U., 1929; M.A., U. Neb., 1938; L.H.D., Southwestern U., 1965; m. Mildred Irene Crom, June 24, 1930; children—Phyllis Ann (Mrs. Ronald J. Patterson), Vaughn Elden. Tchr., coach, supt. schs., Johnson, Neb., 1929-31; supt. Nehawka (Neb.) Counsol. Sch., 1931-41, Lyons (Neb.) Sch., 1941-42; with Firestone Tire & Rubber Co., 1942-46; mem. staff Memphis pub. schs., 1946-71, asst., supt., 1955-57, supt., 1957-71; commr. edn. State of Tenn., 1971—. Bd. dirs. Memphis-Shelby County United Fund, Memphis-Shelby County Youth Guidance, Jr. Achievement Memphis, Mem. Nat., Tenn. (pres. adminstrv. sect. 1964-65, Western sect. 1962-63), Memphis edn. assns., Am., Tenn. (pres. 1963-64) assns. sch. adminstrs., Tenn. Assn. City and Spl. Sch. Dist. Supts. (pres. 1962-63), Century Club, Execs. Club Memphis (dir.), Phi Delta Kappa. Methodist. Lion (past pres. Memphis), Mason. Home: 4730 Lorece Av Memphis TN 38117 Office: 100 Cordell Hull Bldg Nashville TN 37219

STIMMEL, THOMAS STRIBLING, newspaperman; b. Vancouver, B.C., Can., Apr. 29, 1925; s. Samuel Robert and Roberta (Tener) S.; A.B., Bethany (W.Va.) Coll., 1949. Reporter, Times-Leader, Martins Ferry, O., 1950-53, A.P., Charleston, W.Va., 1953-56, Herald and News, Klamath Falls, Ore., 1958-60, Ore. Jour., Portland, 1960-64, Newhouse Nat. News service, Washington, 1964—. Served with AUS, 1944-46. Recipient First Pl. award wire news coverage W.Va. Press Assn., 1957. Mem. Phi Kappa Tau. Clubs: City (Portland); Nat. Press (Washington). Home: 638 Massachusetts Av NE Washington DC 20002 Office: 1750 Pennsylvania Av NW Washington DC 20006

STIMSON, DEPARX, cons. engr.; b. Florence, S.C., Dec. 13, 1908; s. Samuel Carl and Mary DeParx (Parks) S.; B.S., N.C. State U., 1930; B.S. in Mech. Engring., Auburn U., 1931; B.S. in Elec. Engring., Wofford U., 1932, M.S., 1933; m. Ethel Susan Williams, Oct. 3, 1939 (dec. May 1956); children—Samuel Edward, Richard Barrett; m. 2d, Emily Gail Sparks, Oct. 20, 1968; 1 dau., Maggi V. Tchr. S.C. Sch. for Deaf and Blind, Cedar Spring, 1931; instr. Wofford U., 1932; supervising prin. Francisco Dist. Pub. Schs., 1934-35; research engr., dir. tech. sales Bahnson Co., Winston-Salem, N.C., 1935-52; owner, chief engr. DeParx Stimson Engrs., cons. engrs., 1952—. Founder Cross and Crescent award Wake Forest U. Registered profl. engr. Mem. Am. Soc. Heating, Air-Conditioning and Refrigeration Engrs. (past pres.), Nat. Soc. Profl. Engrs., Winston-Salem Engrs. Club (past v.p.), N.C. Soc. Engrs., Profl. Engrs. N.C. (charter), Asso. Professions N.C., Lambda Chi Alpha. Baptist. Research on heat pump and refrigeration cycles, auto-incremental electrostatic precipitators; originator application of large incremental-centrifugal refrigeration for industry. Home: 121 Idlewilde Dr Winston-Salem NC 27106

STINCHCOMB, HAROLD RUSSELL, city ofcl.; b. Columbia Station, O., Dec. 28, 1925; s. Harry Clayton and Elsie Elletta (French) S.; student 1965-66, Fla. State Fire Coll. ann. seminars, 1955-71, Internat. Assn. of Fire Chief's Ann. Adminstrv. Seminar, 1966-70; m. Marjorie Martine Drake, Jan. 5, 1960; children—Marjorie, Susan, William. Soloist Orpheus Chorus, Cleve., 1945-51; second class fireman, City of Sarasota, Fla., 1954-55, 1st class fireman and dept. electrician, 1955-56, lt., 1956-58, battalion capt. 1958-66, fire chief, 1966—; cons. Exec. Dir. Internat. Fire Adminstrv. Inst., State U. N.Y., 1969—. Area safety dir. Boy Scouts Am., 1969-70; camp com. YMCA, 1966-68. Recipient Civic Service award Fraternal Order of Eagles, 1969. Mem. Fla. State Fire Chiefs' Assn. (v.p. 1971—), Internat. Assn. of Fire Chiefs, S.E. Fire Chiefs' Assn. (v.p. 1970-71). Methodist (adminstrv. bd. 1969-71). Home: 3136 Browning St Sarasota FL 33580 Office: 1445 4th St Sarasota FL 33577

STINE, DONALD MEDFORD, educator; b. Schenectady, Sept. 30, 1932; s. Medford Sheridan and Gladys Elizabeth (Regnier) S.; B.A. summa cum laude, State U. N.Y. at Albany, 1953; B.D., Princeton Theol. Sem., 1956, Th.D. magna cum laude, 1964; m. Esther Cornelius Swenson, July 21, 1972. Ordained to ministry Presbyn. Ch., 1956; teaching fellow in English Bible, Princeton Theol. Sem., 1956-57, instr., 1957-61, vis. lectr. in Bibl. studies, 1963-64; asst. prof. Bible and N. T. Greek Exegesis, N.Y. Theol. Sem., N.Y.C., 1961-63; prof. Bibl. lit. and Exegesis, N.Y. Theol. Sem., 1964-67; prof. religion, chmn. dept. philosophy and religion Maryville (Tenn.) Coll., 1967—. Active, Common Cause, Educators for Senator Albert Gore, 1970. Trustee Kabul (Afghanistan) Community Ch., 1963-67. Mem. Am. Assn. U. Profs. (pres. chpt. 1969-71), Soc. Bibl. Lit., Am. Schs. of Oriental Research. Democrat. Presbyn. Home: 203 Hummingbird Dr Maryville TN 37801 Office: Box 2841 Maryville Coll Maryville TN 37801

STINGILY, JAMES RAY, physician; b. Vicksburg, Miss., Nov. 6, 1928; s. Ernest Ray and Dixie Field (Collins) S.; B.B.A., U. Miss., 1953; postgrad. Miss. Coll., 1954-55; M.D., U. Miss., 1959; m. Margaret Jane Vance, June 2, 1956; children—Rebecca Susanne, Sharon Diane, James Ray. Intern, Miss. Baptist Hosp., 1959-60; practice medicine, partner, asso. Family Med. Clinic, Hazlehurst, Miss., 1960—; chief staff Hardy Wilson Meml. Hosp., 1965—. Sec., treas. ASC Realty Co. Inc., 1966—. Served with USN, 1946-49. Hon. col. on staff gov. Miss., 1972—. Mem. C. of C. (pres. 1967), Miss., County, Am. med. assns., Phi Chi. Baptist (chmn. deacons bd. 1970-72). Office: Family Med Clinic Hazlehurst MS 39083

STINSON, LLOYD GEORGE, financial exec.; b. Woodbine, Ky., Apr. 20, 1928; s. James A. and Ora (Sullivan) S.; student Eastern Ky. State Coll., 1948-52; m. Shirley Sue Thompson, Nov. 19, 1947; children— Michael O., Patricia M., Arland Mark. Mem. staff Lybrand, Ross Bros. & Montgomery, C.P.A.'s, Cin., 1952-56; controller Gruen Watch Co., Cin., 1956-58; corp. controller Direco-Wayne Corp., N.Y.C., 1958-67; financial v.p., treas., sec. Redman Industries, Inc., Dallas, 1967—; dir., sec. Universal Investment Corp., Dallas, 1967—; dir. New Funds, Inc., Dallas. Served with Signal Corps, AUS, 1946-47. C.P.A. Ohio. Mem. Am. Inst. C.P.A.'s, A.I.M. (pres.'s council), Ohio Soc. C.P.A.'s. Home: 11300 Strait Lane Dallas TX 75229 Office: 7800 Carpenter Fry Dallas TX 75247

STIPP, JOHN ROBERT, civil engr.; b. Toledo, Mar. 15, 1915; s. Nathan James and Edith Alice (Crays) S.; B.S., U. Ill., 1937; M.C.E., Cath. U. Am., 1970; m. Linda Ivanova, Dec. 16, 1942. Civil engr. Ill. Dept. Pub. Works and Bldgs., Springfield, 1937-38, 51-52, U.S. Geol. Survey, Champaign, 1939-42, 46-51, Los Angeles Dist. Corps Engrs., 1952-66, U.S. Bd. Engrs. for Rivers and Harbors, Washington, 1966—. Served to 1st lt. AUS, 1942-46. Registered profl. engr., Cal., Ill. Fellow Am. Soc. C.E.; mem. Nat. Soc. Profl. Engrs., Am. Geophys. Union, Am. Water Resources Assn., Nat. Assn. Parliamentarians. Democrat. Episcopalian. Patentee process for cold-working metal shapes. Home: 3800 26th St N Arlington VA 22207 Office: Bd Engrs for Rivers and Harbors Tempo C 2d and Q Sts SW Washington DC 20315

STIRLING, ALAN WILLIAM, electric co. exec.; b. London, Eng., Oct. 22, 1927; s. John and Edith Ellen (Smith) S.; B.S. in Spl. Physics, Univ. Coll., London, 1951; m Alice Ellen Edwards, Oct. 20, 1951; children— David, Jacqueline, Beverly. Came to U.S., 1963. Devel. engr. Lab. Standard Telephones and Cables, Internat. Tel. & Tel. Co., London, 1951-57; research engr. Standard Telecommunication Labs., Harlow, 1957-62; mgr. advanced capacitor devel. Gen. Electric Co., Irmo, S.C., 1963-68, mgr. engring. electronic capacitor dept., Columbia, S.C., 1969—. Served Royal Elec. and Mech. Engrs. 1946-48. Mem. Inst. Physics (asso.), Am. Phys. Soc. Patentee in field. Home: 3619 Deerfield Dr Columbia SC 29204 Office: 1388 Columbia SC 29202

STIRLING, EDWIN TILLMAN, lawyer; b. Washington, Nov. 5, 1927; s. William Calhoun and Margheritta (Tillman) S.; B.S., George Washington U., 1951, J.D., 1953; m. Genevieve Ruffner, Sept. 15, 1951; children— Catherine, Clark Tillman, Stephen Kondrup. Admitted to D.C. bar, 1954; U.S. Supreme Ct. bar, 1958, Md. bar, 1964; law clk. for U.S. Circuit Judge Wilbur K. Miller, 1953-54; asst. U.S. atty. for Washington, 1954-58; asso. firm Welch, Mott & Morgan, 1958-64; partner firm Reasoner, Davis, & Vinson, 1965—. Served with AUS, 1946-48. Mem. Am. Bar Assn., Soc. Cin., Bar Assn. D.C. Clubs: Chevy Chase, National Lawyers, George Washington Univ. Home: 7012 Beechwood Dr Chevy Chase MD 20015 Office: 800 17th St NW Washington DC 20006

STIRSMAN, WILLIAM ANDREW, state ofcl.; b. Greenville, Ky., Nov. 19, 1923; s. Hubert Altha and Lola Gladys (Adkins) S.; student Nashville Bus. Coll., 1946-47; m. Dorothy N. Settle, Nov. 3, 1944; children— William E., Jennifer (Mrs. Samuel Dean Sears). Lab. technician Gt. Lakes Steel Corp., Ecorse, Mich., 1942-43; sr. resident engr. Ky. Dept. Econ. Security, Madisonville, 1947-48, Ky. Dept. Hwys., 1948—. Chmn., Muhlenberg Water Dist., 1967—. Served with USNR, 1943-46. Mem. Assn. Ky. Hwy. Engrs. Baptist (deacon, chmn. brotherhood, treas., song dir.). Mason (Shriner). Home: Rural

Route 1 Box 375 Central City KY 42330 Office: PO Box 130 Madisonville KY 42431

STITT, LARRY BURGIE, investment co. exec.; b. Shattuck, Okla., July 20, 1922; s. Leslie Warren and Katherine Mae (Burgie) S.; B.B.A. with honors, U. Tex., 1943; m. LaRue McCanne, Aug. 23, 1943; 1 dau., Patricia RuNell (Mrs. David Coons). Individual practice C.P.A., Amarillo, Tex., 1948—; v.p. Phoenix Drilling Co., Spur Drilling Co., Inc., Amarillo, 1948-68; pres., Trion Investment Co., 1960—; v.p., treas., dir. A & C Industries, Inc., 1954—; dir. First State Bank of Amarillo, 1952-54. Class rep. Bus. Adminstrn. Adv. Council, U. Tex., 1967—. Served with USNR, 1943-46, 51-52. C.P.A., Tex. Mem. Am. Inst. Accountants, Tex. Soc. C.P.A.'s, Quiet Birdmen. Baptist. Lion (v.p. 1952). Home: 2204 Crockett St Amarillo TX 79109 Office: 804 Rusk St Amarillo TX 79106

STOBAUGH, ROY L., supt. schs.; b. Choctaw, Ark., July 15, 1917; s. Mark L. and Lillian (Huie) S.; student Ark. Tech. U., 1937-40; B.S., State Coll. Ark., 1945; M.Ed. Memphis State U., 1955; m. Wilma West, May 9, 1941; children—Suzanne (Mrs. Berkley Baker), Sara Jane (Mrs. Danny Flowers). Coach, Wilson (Ark.) High Sch., 1941-52; gen. mgr. Crain & Co., chain store, 1952-54; supt. schs., Turrell, Ark., 1954-59, Hughes, Ark., 1959—. Bd. dirs. Athletic Dist. 3, pres. 1947-49. Mem. Nat., Ark. (dir. 1955-58) edn. assns., Northeast Ark. Baseball Assn. (pres. 1960-61), P.T.A. (life), Am. Assn. Sch. Adminstrs. Methodist (bd. stewards (1945—; trustee 1970—). Home: Box 368 Hughes AR 72348

STOBS, JAMES ROBERT, constrn. co. exec.; b. Logan, Ia., Nov. 30, 1913; s. Matthew and Bonnie (Twiford) S.; B.F.A., U. Fla., 1937; m. Ruby Lee Wentworth, Mar. 5, 1939; children—James Robert II, Barbara Lee (Mrs. Fredrick Merrill Macy), Gayle Anne. Partner-founder Stobs Bros. Constrn. Co., Miami, Fla., 1937—; sec.-treas. Forming Services, Inc., Miami, 1965—; exhibited in group shows Tri-County Fair, Tampa, Fla., Soc. Four Arts, Palm Beach, Fla.; others; mem. Miami Art League Jury, 1972, Ann. Dade County Poincianna Art Exhbn., Jury, 1972. Mem. Miami Shores (Fla.) Planning Bd., 1950-53, Dade County Grand Jury Assn. Recipient Blue Ribbon, Tri-County Fair, Tampa, 1936, Cash prize Soc. Four Arts Exhbn., Palm Beach, 1937. Mem. Asso. Gen. Contractors (Safety award 1968-72, treas. nat. conv. 1952), Internat. Platform Assn., Delta Sigma Phi. Republican. Presbyn. (deacon 1961-63). Kiwanian. Club: Miami Shores Country. Home: 429 NE 101st St Miami Shores FL 33138 Office: 7010 NE 4th Ct Miami FL 33138

STOCKARD, RALPH REAVIS, educator; b. Burlington, N.C., July 23, 1939; s. Lee R. and Nellie Graham (Reavis) S.; B.S. in Elec. Engring., N.C. State U., 1962, postgrad. in Advanced Math., 1965-67; m. Hilda Gray Cantrell, Feb. 29, 1964; children—Susan, Ralph. Engr., Brown Engring. Co., Huntsville, Ala., 1962-64; engr. Research Triangle Inst., Durham, N.C., 1964-67; instr. Tech. Inst. Alamance, Burlington, 1967—. Exec. v.p. Graham (N.C.) High Sch. Sports Complex Authority, Inc., 1970—. Mem. Graham City Council, 1971—. Registered profl. engr., N.C. Mem. Graham Jr. C. of C. (Distinguished Service award 1972). Home: 307 E Harden St Graham NC 27253 Office: 411 Camp Rd Burlington NC 27215

STOCKER, EDWARD EUGENE, banker; b. Media, Pa., Dec. 17, 1917; s. George Patrick and Anna Katharine (Mengel) S.; B.S., U. Ark., 1938; J.D., Georgetown U., 1941; m. Margaret Elizabeth Jacoway, Oct. 1, 1948; children—Edward Eugene, Bronson Jacoway, Margaret Cooper. Admitted to D.C. bar, 1942, Ark. bar, 1947, Tex. bar, 1964; practice law, N.Y.C., 1946-47, Little Rock, 1947-50, 52-54; asst. trust officer First Nat. Bank, Dallas, 1954-56; exec. v.p., sr. trust officer Continental Nat. Bank, Fort Worth, Tex., 1956—. Mem. faculty Southwestern Grad. Sch. Banking, So. Meth. U., Dallas, 1959-60, 71. Mem. Tarrant County Community Council, 1971—. Trustee, Tarrant County Charitable Found. Trust, pres. 1968; bd. dirs. Child Study Center, pres. 1970; bd. dirs. Easter Seal Soc., Multiple Sclerosis Chpt.; bd. dirs. Tarrant County Heart Assn., chmn. 1963; bd. dirs. Retarded Childrens' Services; bd. dirs. Bell Hosp. Trust, chmn. 1970—; trustee W.I. Cook Meml. Hosp., 1971—. Panther Boys Club. Served to lt. comdr. USNR, 1942-46. Mem. Am., Tex., Fort Worth, Tarrant County bar assns., Sigma Nu, Alpha Kappa Psi, Delta Theta Phi, Pi Gamma Mu. Roman Catholic. Democrat. Rotarian. Clubs: River Crest Country, Fort Worth. Author: (with Paul C. Cook and Arch B. Gilbert) Manual for Preparation of Wills and Administration of Trusts in Texas, 1967. Home: 3517 Dorothy Lane S Fort Worth TX 76107 Office: Box 910 Fort Worth TX 76101

STOCKFORD, WILLIAM FREDRICK, mech. engr.; b. Windsor, Ont., Can., Sept. 8, 1927; s. Charles Joseph and Olive Edwina (Sanagan) Ouellette; came to U.S., 1942, naturalized, 1944; B.S. in Mech. Engring., Syracuse U., 1950; m. Anita Jessie Morris, Sept. 10, 1949; children— William Gordon, Robert Michael, Pamela Ann, Brian Morris, Charles Edward. With Porter Cable Machine Co., Syracuse, N.Y., 1950-51; tech. writer Techcraft, Inc., Syracuse, 1951-52; application engr., product sales mgr. Carrier Air Conditioning Co., Syracuse, 1953-62, instr. Engring. Sch., 1957; br. mgr. Climatic Corp., Greenville, S.C., 1962-67; chief engr. Gamewell Mech., Inc., Salisbury, N.C., 1967—. Condr. seminars for cons. engrs. and architects, 1964. Served with USNR, 1945-46. Registered profl. engr., N.C., S.C., Va., Ga. Mem. Nat. Soc. Profl. Engrs., Am. Soc. Heating, Refrigerating and Air Conditioning Engrs., Am. Legion. Republican. Episcopalian (sr. warden, vestry 1970—). Author: Load Estimating, Book 1, 1954-57. Patentee in field. Home: Route 2 Kings Forest Salisbury NC 28144 Office: PO Box 1430 Salisbury NC 28144

STOCKS, GIDEON JACKSON, JR., dentist; b. Leesburg, Ga., Apr. 25, 1922; s. Gideon Jackson and Annie Rabun (Crozier) S.; A.A., U. Fla., 1941; D.D.S., Northwestern U., 1944; m. Jane Johanson, Dec. 28, 1943; children—John T., Thomas M., Dale Elizabeth. Pvt. practice dentistry, Miami, 1946-52, 52—. Dir. Peoples Nialeah (Fla.) Nat. Bank; mem. adv. bd. Peoples First Nat. Bank, Miami Shores, Fla. Served to lt. USNR, 1944-46, 52. Mem. Fedn. Dentaire Internat., Pierre Fauchard Dental Acad., Fla., East Coast Dist. (v.p. 1971-72), Miami (pres. 1966-67) dental socs., Greater Miami Dental Study Group (pres. 1950-51), Omicron Kappa Upsilon. Democrat. Presbyn. Kiwanian. Clubs: Coral Reef Yacht (Miami); Miami Shores (Fla.) Country; Miami Yacht (commodore 1966-67). Home: 102 NE 108th St Miami Shores FL 33161 Office: 8340 NE 2d Av Miami FL 33138

STOCKS, JACK GILBERT, land surveyor; b. Nakina, N.C., July 17, 1934; s. Matthew Gaston and Oneta (FormyDuval) S.; A.A., Wilmington Coll., 1958; m. Delores Ann Inman, Oct. 23, 1956; children—Pamela Ann, Mark Allen. Land surveyor Corbett Package Co., Wilmington, N.C., 1958-65; individual practice land surveying, Wilmington, 1965—. Served with AUS, 1954-56. Mem. N.C. Soc. Surveyors, Nat. Assn. Home Builders. Home: 6 Holland Dr Castle Hayne NC 28429 Office: 304 C P & L Bldg Wilmington NC 28401

STOCKTON, CARL REX, educator; b. Monett, Mo., Oct. 13, 1935; s. Ira James and Edith (Turner) S.; B.S., Mo. State Coll., 1957; S.T.B., Boston U., 1960; D.Phil., Oxford (Eng.) U., 1970. Asso. chief party Internat. Voluntary Services, Vietnam, 1963-65, acting chief, 1965; asst. prof. history and religion, also acting chmn. social sci. div. McKendree Coll., Lebanon, Ill., 1967-70; prof. history, chmn. dept. Talladega (Ala.) Coll., 1970—. Bd. dirs. Internat. Voluntary Services, 1970-71. Recipient Medal of Merit 1st class (Govt. of Vietnam), 1967; named one of Outstanding Young Men Am., 1970; Nat. Found. for Humanities fellow Inst. Black Studies, U. Louisville, 1971. Mem. Am., So. hist. assns., Am. Soc. Ch. History, Wesley Hist. Soc. (Eng.), Am. Assn. Univ. Profs., Ch. Hist. Soc., N.A.A.C.P., Alpha Psi Omega, Phi Rho Chi, Alpha Chi. Democrat. Episcopalian. Club: Oxford-Cambridge (Eng.). Author: Origin and Development of Extra-Liturgical Worship in 18th Century Methodism, 1970. Editor: Kairos, 1960. Home: 509D W Battle St Talladega AL 35160

STOCKTON, RODNEY MAURICE, cosmetic co. exec.; b. St. Louis, Feb. 3, 1913; s. Rodney M. and Martha Julia (Harkins) S.; student Asbury Coll., 1930-33; m. Joan Denise Barnes, Feb. 15, 1963; 1 dau., Denise Twinkle. Indsl. sales engr. Sylvania Indsl. Corp., Chgo., 1937-41; chem. sales engr. L. Sonneborn & Sons, Chgo., 1941-47; pres., founder, chmn. bd. Aloe Creme Labs., Inc., Ft. Lauderdale, Fla., 1953—; chmn. bd., dir. L. E. R. Distbg. Corp. Fla., Ft. Lauderdale. Mem. council of 100 Ft. Lauderdale U.; mem. U.S. Pres.'s Com. on Employment Handicapped, Fla. Gov.'s Com. for Handicapped; life mem. Fla. Sheriffs Boys Ranch. Recipient Wisdom award of honor, 1970. Ky col. Mem. A.I.M. (fellow pres.'s council), Sales and Marketing Execs. Assn., Ft. Lauderdale Mail Users' Council, Cosmetics, Toiletries and Fragrance Assn., Aerospace Med. Assn., Fla. (dir. at large), Ft. Lauderdale chambers commerce. Home: 4120 NE 25th Av Fort Lauderdale FL 33308 Office: PO Box 9477 Fort Lauderdale FL 33310

STOCKWELL, BENJAMIN EUGENE, lawyer; b. Oklahoma City, Aug. 28, 1931; s. Benjamin Paul and Anna (Cunningham) S.; B.A., U. Okla., 1952, LL.B., 1956; m. Marjorie Ethel Ribble, Apr. 4, 1952; children—Margaret Lynn, David Alan. Admitted to Okla. bar, 1956; practiced in Oklahoma City, 1956-60, Norman, Okla., 1961—; mem. firm Benedum and Stockwell, 1961-62; now mem. firm, Stockwell and Pence; asst. prof. law, legal adviser to pres.'s office U. Okla., 1960-61. Chmn. Cleveland County Bd. Health, 1963-64. Bd. dirs. Cleveland County Cancer Soc. Served to 1st lt. AUS, 1952-54. Mem. Okla. State (mem. exec. council 1965—; chmn. spl. com. on implementation of judicial reform amendments 1967; v.p. 1969), Cleveland County (past pres.) bar assns., Okla. Inst. for Justice, Scabbard and Blade, Pi Kappa Alpha, Pi Gamma Mu. Episcopalian. Mason, Rotarian; mem. Order DeMolay. Home: 202 Westside Dr Norman OK 73069 Office: 119 E Main St Norman OK 73069

STODDARD, ROBERT LEE, lawyer, mayor; b. Owings, S.C., Dec. 10, 1918; s. Lander Boyd and Selina Parker (Roberts) S.; student Spartanburg Jr. Coll., 1939; B.S. in Agronomy, Clemson Coll., 1941; LL.B., U. S.C., 1947; m. Betty Frances Boyd, June 15, 1944; children— Betty Frances (Mrs. Wood), Robert Lee, Wesley Alexander, Allen McDavid, Ann Roberts, Louise Hicklin Boyd. Asst. foreman peach cannery S.C. Peach Growers Assn., 1941; jr. soil surveyor Soil Conservation Service, 1941-42; admitted to S.C. bar, 1947; jr. partner firm Moore, Stoddard, Sanders, Sanders & Cothran, and predecessor firm, Spartanburg, S.C., 1947—; mayor City of Spartanburg, 1962—. Mem. adv. bd. Clemson YMCA, Clemson Archtl. Found., 1956-62; mem. Gov.'s Com. Crime Prevention and Juvenile Delinquency. Trustee, Clemson Coll., 1956-62. Served to lt. USNR, 1941-45; PTO; lt. comdr. Res. Mem. Am., S.C., Spartanburg County bar assns., S.C. Municipal Assn. (pres.), Am. Judicature Soc., Greater Spartanburg C. of C. (dir. 1961-62), Am. Acad. Polit. and Social Sci., Internat. Platform Assn., Am. Legion, V.F.W., United Comml. Travelers. Presbyn. Kiwanian (pres. Spartanburg 1962). Club: Carolina Motor (dir.). Home: 601 Rutledge St Spartanburg SC 29302 Office: 207 Magnolia St Spartanburg SC 29301

STODDARD, THEODORE LOTHROP, anthropologist; b. Dennis, Mass., Nov. 15, 1926; s. Theodore Lothrop and Elizabeth (Bates) S.; A.B., Harvard, 1950, A.M., 1957; m. Jewel Stone Kraft, Mar. 15, 1962; children—Isaac Allerton, Frederick Lothrop, Andrew Freeman, Philip Kraft. Research fellow Peabody Found., Phillips Acad., Andover, Mass., 1954-57; research asso., instr. biomechanics lab. Tufts U., Medford, Mass., 1957-59; human factors engr. Gen. Electric Co., Washington, 1959-62; research scientist Am. Inst. for Research, Washington, 1962-64; dir. Inst. for Cross-Cultural Research, Washington, 1964—; cons. editor World Affairs, 1969—; editor Perspective, 1971—; sci. writer Voice of Am., 1960-69. Served with USNR, 1944-46. Fellow Am. Anthrop. Assn., A.A.A.S., Soc. for Applied Anthropology; mem. Anthrop. Soc. Washington, Soc. for Am. Archaeology, N.Y. Acad. Sci., A.F.T.R.A., Sigma Xi. Club: Harvard of Washington (exec. com. 1969-70, v.p. 1970—). Author: Area Handbook for Guyana, 1969; Area Handbook for the Indian Ocean Territories, 1971. Editor: Religion and Politics in Haiti, 1966; Indians of Brazil in the 20th Century, 1967; The Luo of Kenya, 1968. Home: 3500 Turner Lane Chevy Chase MD 20015 Office: 4000 Albemarle St NW Washington DC 20016

STOEVER, EDWARD CARL, JR., geologist, ednl. adminstr.; b. Milw., Mar. 13, 1926; s. Edward Carl and Klea M. (Brainerd) S.; B.S., Purdue U., 1948; M.S., U. Mich., 1950, Ph.D. (NSF grad. fellow), 1959; m. Norma Esther Johnson, Sept. 4, 1954; children—Catherine Ann, Gregory Edward Clark. Teaching fellow U. Mich., Ann Arbor, 1950-52, 54-55; research geologist Internat. Minerals & Chem. Corp., Lakeland, Fla. and Skokie, Ill., 1952-54; geologist Okla. Geol. Survey, Norman, 1956-57; mem. faculty U. Okla., Norman, 1956—, prof. geology, asso. dir. earth sci. curriculum project, 1969, asso. dir. undergrad. studies Sch. Geology and Geophysics, 1970—, dir. NSF Insts. Earth Sci., U. Okla., 1965-69, 70—; asso. program dir. summer study program NSF, Washington, 1969-70; exec. dir. State Earth Scis. Edn. Found. Com., 1972—. Dir. Okla. Geology Camp, Canon City, Colo., 1964-69; lectr. continuing edn. program Am. Assn. Petroleum Geologists, 1966-69. Served with USNR, 1944-46. Fellow Geol. Soc. Am.; mem. Am. Assn. Petroleum Geologists, A.A.A.S., Nat. Assn. Geology Tchrs. (sect. pres. 1962, 64, membership chmn. 1965-66), Sigma Xi. Home: 1706 Rowena Lane Norman OK 73069

STOKES, ARNOLD PAUL, educator; b. Bismarck, N.D., Jan. 24, 1932; s. Joel Edward and Elizabeth (Bauer) S.; student St. Martin's Coll., 1949-50, 1951-53; B.S., U. Notre Dame, 1955, Ph.D., 1959; postgrad. (NSF post-doctoral fellow), Johns Hopkins, 1960-61; m. Gaye Teresa Wims, Oct. 19, 1957; children—Michael, Jonathan, Thomas, Katherine, Christopher, Peter. Mathematician, Research Inst. Advanced Study, Balt., 1958-60; asst. prof. Cath. U., Washington, 1961-64, asso. prof., 1964-65; prof. Georgetown U., Washington, 1965—, chmn. math. dept., 1967-70. Cons. Goddard Space Flight Center, Green Belt, Md., 1962-68. Mem. Am. Math. Soc., Soc. Indsl. and Applied Maths. Home: 205 Primrose St Chevy Chase MD 20015 Office: Math Dept Georgetown U Washington DC 20007

STOKES, CARL NICHOLAS, constrn. co. exec.; b. Memphis, Jan. 26, 1907; s. John William and Edith Isabell (Burgess) S.; student Draughton's Bus. Coll., 1929-30; LL.B., U. Memphis, 1933; m. Laverne Judson, Aug. 21, 1930; children—Vicki Laverne (Mrs. Dennis Neff Koehn). Admitted to Tenn. bar, 1934; mem. firm Norvell & Monteverde, Memphis, 1934-38; with legal dept. Tenn. Unemployment Compensation Div., 1937-38; clk. City Ct. Memphis, 1938-42, Criminal Cts. Shelby County, 1946-50; judge City Ct. Memphis, 1950-52; mem. firm Shea & Pierotti, Memphis, 1952-62; v.p., gen. counsel Allen & O'Hara, Inc., Memphis, 1962. Adv. bd. Salvation Army; trustee Shrine Sch. for Handicapped Children. Served to capt., inf. AUS, 1942-46. Recipient award of merit Tenn. Bar Assn., 1958. Mem. Am., Tenn., Memphis and Shelby County bar assns., Am. Legion, Mil. Order World Wars, Navy League, Memphis Area C. of C. (chmn. welcome com. 1972-73). Mem. Christian Ch. Mason (33 deg., K.T., Shriner), Kiwanian (pres. 1971-72). Home: 2237 Massey Rd Memphis TN 38138 Office: 3385 Airways Blvd Memphis TN 38116

STOKES, COLIN, tobacco mfg. co. exec.; b. Winston-Salem, N.C., Apr. 4, 1914; s. Henry Straughan and Eloise (Brown) S.; grad. McCallie Sch., 1931; B.S., U. N.C., 1935; m. Mary Louise Siewers, Jan. 1, 1943; children—Louise Siewers (Mrs. Philip G. Kinken), Henry Straughan II, Daniel Shober. With R. J. Reynolds Tobacco Co., 1935—, asst. to supt. mfg., 1947-53, asst. supt. mfg., 1953-56, supt. mfg., 1956-59, dir., 1957—, v.p., 1959-61, exec. v.p., 1961-70, chmn. bd., 1970—; dir. R.J. Reynolds Industries, Inc., Winston-Salem Savs. & Loan Assn., Integon Corp., N.C. Nat. Bank. Bd. dirs. YMCA, 1946-52; campaign chmn. United Fund Forsyth County, 1957, dir., 1957-59; trustee N. Carolina Bapt. Hosps., 1958-61, 63-66, 68-71, chmn. trustees, 1960, 61, 69, 70, chmn. finance com., 1959; trustee Wake Forest U., 1971—, Salem Coll. and Acad., 1966—; dir. William and Kate B. Reynolds Meml. Park, 1958-64, Child Guidance Clinic, 1959-61. Served from pvt. to capt., inf. AUS, 1942-46. Mem. Winston-Salem C. of C. (dir. 1952-55, 68—), Zeta Psi. Baptist (deacon, finance com.). Kiwanian (pres. 1963, dir.). Home: 2701 Reynolds Dr Winston-Salem NC 27104 Office: RJ Reynolds Tobacco Co Winston-Salem NC 27102

STOKES, DAVID KERSHAW, JR., physician; b. Camden, S.C., Feb. 3, 1927; s. David Kershaw and Mary Belle (Smith) S.; B.S., Clemson U., 1948; M.S., U. Ga., 1952; Ph.D., Tex. A. and M. U., 1955; M.D., Med. U. S.C., 1957; m. Louise Wingo, June 9, 1950; children—Donna, David, Tina. Intern Spartanburg (S.C.) Gen. Hosp., 1958, dir. family practice residency, 1972—; practice medicine specializing in family practice, Inman, S.C., 1959—. Chmn. bd. trustees, Dist. 1Schs., Spartanburg County, S.C., 1966—. Served with AUS, 1945-47. Diplomate Am. Bd. Family Practice. Mem. Am., S.C. med. assns., Spartanburg County Med. Soc. (pres. 1972), Am. Assn. Physicians and Surgeons, Am. Heart Assn., So. Med. Assn. Home: 8 Canaday St Inman SC 29349 Office: 43 N Main St Inman SC 29349

STOKES, GRANVILLE WOOLMAN, univ. adminstr.; b. Anderson, Ind., Aug. 1, 1920; s. Albert F. and Catherine A. (Greenleaf) S.; B.S., Purdue U., 1949; M.S., U. Wis., 1951, Ph.D., 1953; m. Doris Crosson, Nov. 23, 1941; 1 son, Bradley Woolman. Asst. pathologist U. Ky., Lexington, 1953-56, asso. plant pathologist, 1956-61, prof. plant pathology and agronomy, 1961—, asso. dir. Agrl. Expt. Sta., 1966-69, dir. tobacco and health research program, 1967-69, asso. dean Coll. of Agr., 1969—. Served with USAAF, 1943-45. Mem. Am. Phytopathological Soc., Genetics Soc. Am., Am. Genetics Assn., Gamma Sigma Delta. Home: 721 Malabu Rd Lexington KY 40502

STOKES, JACK AVERY, physician; b. Lincoln County, Miss., Feb. 10, 1931; s. Ernest Gayle and Ida Mae (Grant) S.; student Miss. Coll., 1950; B.S., U. Miss., 1957, M.D., 1960; m. Sammie J. Wiseman, May 29, 1955; children—Mickey Eugene, Janet Michal. Intern, U. Miss. Med. Center, Jackson, 1960-61; gen. practice medicine, Pontotoc, Miss., 1961—; mem. staff Pontotoc Community Hosp., North Miss. Hosp., Tupelo. Chmn. Pontotoc County Home Health Care Program, 1970—; tchr. cardiopulmonary resuscitation, 1970—. Bd. Dirs. Pontotoc County Appalachian Devel. Served with USNR, 1950-54. Mem. A.M.A., Am. Geriatrics Soc., Am., Miss. heart assns., Nat., Miss. (pres. 1971-72) flying physicians assns., Aircraft Owners and Pilots Assn., Aviation Med. Examiner Assn.; Council on Med. Services, Miss. Med. Assn. (v.p. 1967-68), N.E. Miss. (pres. 1968-69, sec.-treas. 1971-73) (pres. 1967-68) med. socs., Pontotoc County Devel. Assn., Nu Sigma Nu. Baptist. Lion. Clubs: Flying, Pontotoc Country. Home: 1019 N Brooks St Pontotoc MS 38863 Office: 207 Holmes Rd Pontotoc MS 38863

STOKES, JAMES PORTER, clergyman; b. Greer, S.C., Mar. 14, 1926; s. Albert Broadus and Nannie Cora (Bright) S.; B.A., Furman U., 1946; B.D., So. Bapt. Theol. Sem., 1949; m. Marjorie Ussery, May 12, 1949; children—James Porter II, Mark Singleton, David Thomas, Marjorie Nanelle. Ordained to ministry Bapt. Ch., 1948; pastor Bethune (S.C.) Field of Chs., 1949-51, First Bapt. Ch., Blacksburg, 1951-56, Seneca (S.C.) Bapt. Ch., 1956—. Bd. dirs., tchr. Beaverdam Bapt. Sem. Extension Center, 1964—; chmn. com. on coms. S.C. Bapt. Conv., 1970, mem. gen. bd., 1956; mem. S.C. Bapt. spl. student study com. Furman U., 1967—. Trustee S.C. Bapt. Hosps., So. Bapt. Theol. Sem., Louisville; chmn. adminstrn. com. Easley (S.C.) Bapt. Hosp. Mem. Beaverdam Bapt. Assn. (moderator). Lion. Home: 114 E South 2d St Seneca SC 29678 Office: 201 S Fairplay St Seneca SC 29678

STOKES, JOHN MYERS, lawyer; b. Lufkin, Tex., Sept. 4, 1939; s. Caroll Myers and Evelyn (Brister) S.; A.B., Tex. Tech. Coll., 1961; J.D., George Washington U., 1964; m. Nancy Joan Baldwin, July 1, 1961; 1 son, John Myers. Law clk. Chief Judge Wilson Cowen, U.S. Ct. of Claims, Washington, 1964-66; admitted to D.C. bar, 1965, Tex. bar, 1969; practiced in Washington, 1966-68; legislative research dir. Republican Party of Tex., Austin, 1968, exec. dir., spl. counsel, 1968-70; officer grants mgmt. and budget control Office Child Devel., Dept. Health, Edn. and Welfare, Dallas, 1970, regional atty., 1970—. Vice chmn. Tex. Young Republican Fedn., 1961-62; pres., organizer Tex. Tech. Young Republican Club, 1960-61. Mem. Am., Fed., D.C. bar assns., State Bar Tex., George Washington Law Sch. Alumni Assn., Phi Delta Phi, Delta Tau Delta. Contbr. articles in field to profl. jours. Home: 2812 Crest Ridge Dallas TX 75228 Office: 1114 Commerce St Dallas TX 75702

STOKES, MARTIN LUTHER, physician; b. Frisco, Okla., Jan. 25, 1935; s. Thomas Jefferson and Clora Evelyn (Hill) S.; student St. Mary's U., 1959-60; B.S., East Central State Coll., Ada, Okla., 1963; M.D., Okla. U., 1968; m. Elinor Ann Venghaus, July 3, 1959; children—David Martin, Jeffrey Alan, Amy Carol. Intern, St. Anthony Hosp., Oklahoma City, 1968-69; practice medicine, specializing in family practice, Konawa, Okla., 1969—; mem. staff Seminole (Okla.) Municipal Hosp., sec., head infection com., 1970-71; mem. staff Valley View Hosp., Ada; med. cons. Redland Community Family Planning Action, 1970-71. Asst. county coroner, 1970-71; med. dir. Stroke Rehab. Program for Seven Counties-So. Okla. Served with USAF, 1955-58. Recipient award Am. Cancer Soc., 1959. Mem. A.M.A., Am. Acad. Gen. Practice, Smithsonian Inst., Okla. Acad. Family Practice (cancer com.), Seminole-Hughes County Med. Soc. (pres. 1971). Optomist. Home: 2130 E 11th St Ada OK 74820 Office: 527 W 3d St Konawa OK 74849

STOLAR, ROBERT, physician; b. Lithuania; s. Elias and Lana (Tobias) S.; brought to U.S., 1911, naturalized, 1916; A.B., George Washington U., 1931; M.D., Georgetown U., 1935; m. Frances Moore, Aug. 23, 1945. Intern, Gallinger Municipal Hosp., Washington, 1935-36; fellow Georgetown U., 1936-38; clin. asst. vis. dermatologist and syphilologist Bellevue Hosp., N.Y.C., 1938-40;

practice medicine, specializing in dermatology, Washington, 1940-41, 46—; clin. asso. prof. medicine Georgetown U. Med. Sch., 1947—; clin. prof. dermatology Howard U. Sch. Medicine, 1968—. Served with AUS, 1941-46; col. Res. (ret.). Mem. Balt.-Washington Dermatol. Soc. (pres. 1953-54), Internat. Soc. Tropical Dermatology (treas.-gen. 1964-70). Mason. Clubs: George Washington University, Cosmos (Washington). Office: Washington Medical Science Bldg 916 19th St NW Washington DC 20006

STOLEE, MICHAEL JOSEPH, educator; b. Mpls., Aug. 22, 1930; s. Gullik R. and Adeline (Thomason) S.; B.A., St. Olaf Coll., 1952; M.A., U. Minn., 1959, Ph.D., 1963; m. Marilyn K. Sandbo, June 6, 1952; children—Margaret Kay, Paul Andrew, Anne Marie. Tchr., Adams (Minn.) High Sch., 1952-54; prin. Welcome (Minn.) High Sch., 1954-56; supt. schs., Russell, Minn., 1956-59, Clarkfield, Minn., 1959-61; instr. U. Minn., 1961-63; asst. prof. edn. U. Miami, Coral Gables, Fla., 1963-65, prof. edn., 1966—, coordinator grad. studies Sch. Edn., 1968-70, asso. dean, 1969—; asst. prof. edn. U. Mass., 1965-66. Dir. Fla. Sch. Desegregation Cons. Center, 1966-69. Mem. N.E.A., Am. Assn. Sch. Adminstrs., Nat. Soc. for Study Edn., Nat. Assn. Secondary Sch. Prins. Phi Delta Kappa. Home: 6618 San Vicente Av Coral Gables FL 33146

STOLLEY, CHARLES ARTHUR, cons. engr.; b. Chgo., Feb. 4, 1923; s. Louis D. and Marion (Twigg) S.; student Central YMCA Coll., 1940-42; B.S., U. Ill., 1949; m. Ruth Elizabeth Krueger, Nov. 3, 1951; children—Kent Charles, Scott Louis. Mech. engr. Babcock & Wilcox Co., Chgo., 1949, Gerlitz Constrn. Co., Itasca, Ill., 1949-51, Racnar Benson, Inc., Chgo., 1951-55; project engr. Summer Sollitt Co., Chgo., 1955-65; asso. partner Engrs. Collaborative, Chgo., 1965-68; mech. engr. Alexander & Assos., Ft. Lauderdale, Fla., 1966-68; mech. engr., pres. Stolley & Assos., Ft. Lauderdale, 1969—. Served with AUS, 1943-46. Registered profl. engr. Fla., Ill., Ind., Mich., Ohio, Pa., Wis. Mem. Am. Soc. Heating, Refrigeration and Air Conditioning Engrs. U.S. Power Squadron, Pi Tau Sigma. Office: 1628 SE 10th Terrace Fort Lauderdale FL 33316

STONE, ALLAN DAVID, educator; b. Joliet, Ill., Jan. 9, 1937; s. William E. and Leona U. (Frich) S.; B.A., Beloit Coll, 1961; postgrad. George Washington U., 1956-57; M.A. (Woodrow Wilson fellow), U. Okla., 1964, postgrad., 1966-71; m. Peggy Jean Carter, Jan. 11, 1958; children—David A., Richard W. Asst. prof. econs. U. Tex., El Paso, 1963-65, Oklahoma City U., 1966—. Mem. Com. on Improvement, 1966-68. Served with AUS, 1956-58. Mem. Am. Econ. Assn., Phi Beta Kappa, Delta Sigma Pi, Omicron Delta Epsilon. Club: Faculty. Contbr. articles to profl. jours. Home: 4209 NW 12th St Oklahoma City OK 73107

STONE, BEN HARRY, lawyer, state ofcl.; b. Gulfport, Miss., Jan. 18, 1935; s. William Harry and Tressie (Lancaster) S.; B.B.A., Tulane U., 1957; LL.B., J.D., U. Miss., 1961; m. Nancy Jane Reed, Nov. 14, 1958; children—Nancy Jane, Virginia Louise, Kathleen Lancaster. With devel. dept. Tulane U., 1958-59; admittted to Miss. bar, 1961; practiced in Jackson, 1961-63; mem. firm Eaton, Cottrell, Galloway & Lang, Gulfport, 1963—; mem. Miss. Senate, 1968—. Teaching fellow U. Miss. Sch. Law. Chmn. Harrison County chpt. Am. Cancer Soc., 1965; bd. dirs. Salvation Army, Gulfport, 1965. Cath. Charities, Inc., 1968—. Bd. mem. Westminster Acad., Gulfport. Served with USAF, 1957-58. Mem. Am., Harrison County (pres. 1967) bar assns., Miss. State Bar, Miss. Jr. Bar Assn. (dir.), Miss. Econ. Council, Miss. Soc. Prevention Blindness, Miss. Research and Devel. Council (mem. exec. com. 1968—), Gulfport Area C. of C. (dir.), Jr. C. of C. (dir. 1969—), Miss. Council Devel. of Marine Resources (fed. coordinator 1969—), Sigma Alpha Epsilon, Phi Delta Phi. Presbyn. Home: 1320 E Beach Blvd Gulfport MS 39501 Office: 2300 14th St Gulfport MS 39501

STONE, EDWIN STANTON, JR., lawyer; b. Beaumont, Tex., Nov. 1, 1908; s. Edwin Stanton and Ruth Valeria (Cowart) S.; student U. Houston, 1947-48; LL.B., Houston Law Sch., 1939; m. Mary Jane Duncan, Feb. 6, 1965; children—Edwin Stanton III, Richard L. Admitted to Tex. bar, 1939; since practiced in Freeport, Tex.; mem. firm Stone, Davis & Stovall, and predecessor firm, Freeport, 1955—. County atty. Brazoria County (Tex.), 1943-44; chmn. Brazos River Harbor Nav. Dist., 1947-52; mem. Tex. Ho. Reps., 1953-56, chmn. revenue and taxation com., 1955-56; exec. asst. atty. gen. of Tex., 1963-65. Served with Intelligence Corps, AUS, 1944-45. Mem. Brazoria County Bar Assn. (pres. 1959), State Bar of Tex., Am. Legion. Democrat. Mem. Ch. of Christ. Mason. Home: 1215 Longfellow Dr Beaumont TX 77706 Office: 415 W 2d St Freeport TX 77541 also Sour Lake TX 77659

STONE, EUGENE EARLE, III, apparel co. exec.; b. Spartanburg, S.C., Aug. 14, 1907; s. Charles Rivers and Elizabeth Legare (Simmons) S.; student Ga. Inst. Tech., 1925-26; postgrad. U. S.C., 1926-29; m. Allene Lawton Wyman, Aug. 12, 1932; children—Charles Rivers, Eugene Earle, Mary Wyman (Mrs. Charles Elbert Fraser), Rosalie Legare (Mrs. Charles Hill Morris). Engr., Petroleum Heat & Power Co., Stamford, Conn., 1928; geologist Seaport Oil Co., Houston, 1929-30; apparel supt. St. John Mfg. Co., Greenville, SC., 1930-33; pres., owner Stone Mfg. Co., Greenville, 1933—; dir. Peoples Nat. Bank, Carolina Fed. Savs. & Loan Assn., So. Weaving Co. (all Greenville), Sec.-treas., adviser U.S. Dept. Commerce, Washington, 1964-66. Mem. S.C. Bd. Corrections 1962-68; mem. Gov's. Indsl. Devel. Com., 1958; chmn. long-range planning com. Camp Greenville div. YMCA, 1967—; mem. adv. council to bd. trustees Furman U., Greenville, 1962-64. Trustee Greenville Sch. Bd., 1949-51, Faith Meml. Chapel, 1951—; bd. dirs. Greenville County Found., 1956-59. Mem. Am. Apparel Mfrs. Assn. (dir. 1965-66), Am. Bus. Club, Greenville Exec. Sales Club (Distinguished Salesman's award 1969), Kappa Sigma, Beta Gamma Sigma, Delta sigma Pi. Rotarian. Clubs: Poinsett, Green Valley Country, Cotillion, Tarantella (Greenville). Patentee in automation of apparel mfg. field. Home: 1500 Poinsett Hwy Greenville SC 29608 Office: PO Box 3725 Park Pl Greenville SC 29608

STONE, HAZEL LUCY ROTH (MRS. NORREL L. STONE), purchasing exec.; b. Des Moines; d. William and Verne (Fessler) Roth; student U. Ia., 1937-39, Drake U., 1939-41, U. Kansas City Sch. Law, 1941-43; m. Norrel L. Stone, Jan. 8, 1954. Buyer regional office Montgomery Ward, 1941-43; citrus grower, Haines City, Fla., 1943-48; buyer Maas Bros., St. Petersburg, Fla., 1950—. Instr. marketing Jr. Coll., St. Petersburg, evenings 1950-55; prof. econs., English and reading comprehension, Am. Inst. Banking, St. Petersburg, evenings 1956—. Active various community fund drives; state adviser distributive edn., 1945-65, 69—. Charter mem. Republican Congl. Club. Named Outstanding Bus. and Profl. Woman of Year, 1956. Mem. Am. Inst. Banking (Service award Holiday Isle chpt. 1972), Internat. Platform Assn., Kappa Alpha Theta. Club: Bath. Contbg. author to textbooks. Home: 100 Brightwaters Blvd NE St Petersburg FL 33704 also Box 331 Highland Park FL 32401

STONE, HUBERT DEAN, journalist; b. Maryville, Tenn., Sept. 23, 1924; s. Archie Hubert and Annie (Cupp) S.; student Maryville Coll., 1942-43; B.A., U. Okla., 1949; m. Agnes Shirley, Sept. 12, 1953; 1 son, Neal Anson. Sunday editor Maryville-Alcoa Daily Times, 1949; mng. editor Maryville-Alcoa Times, 1949—; v.p. Maryville-Alcoa Newspapers, Inc., 1960—; pres. Stonecraft, 1954—. Mem. mayor's adv. com. City of Maryville. Bd. dirs. United Fund of Blount County, 1961-63, vice chmn. campaign, 1971—; bd. dirs. Nat. Hillbilly Homecoming Assn., Friendsville Acad., Alkiwan Crafts, Inc., Tee Bee Cee Corp., Inc., Maryville Utilities Bd.; trustee Smoky Mountain Passion Play Assn. Served from pvt. to staff sgt. AUS, 1943-45. Decorated Bronze Star; named Outstanding Sr. Man of Blount County, 1970. Mem. Profl. Photographers of Am., Tenn. Profl. Photographers Assn., Great Smoky Mountains Conservation Assn., Ft. Loudoun Assn., Tenn. Jaycees (editor 1954-55, life mem., sec.-treas. 1955-56), Jr. Chamber Internat. (senator) Maryville-Alcoa Jaycees (life mem., pres. 1953-54), Blount County (v.p. 1971), Townsend (dir. 1969-71) chambers commerce, Tenn. Asso. Press News Execs. Assn., Asso. Press Mng. Editors Assn., Am. Legion, V.F.W., Chilhowee Bapt. Assn. (chmn. history com.) U. Okla. Alumni Assn. (life mem., pres. E. Tenn. chpt. 1954-55), Sigma Delta Chi (life). Baptist (trustee, deacon, chmn. finance com.). Mason, Kiwanian (pres. 1969-70). Club: Green Meadow Country. Author articles in field. Home: 1510 Scenic Dr Maryville TN 37801 Office: 307 E Harper Av Maryville TN 37801

STONE, ISAAC G., govt. ofcl.; b. Boston, Aug. 30, 1902; s. Jacob and Esther (Linsky) S.; B.S. summa cum laude, Tufts Coll., 1925; LL.B., Washington Coll. Law, 1928, M.P.L., 1929; m. Lily Mickelson, May 20, 1935; 1 dau., Harriet Marsha. Admitted to D.C. bar, 1928; asst. patent examiner U.S. Patent Office, 1925-46, prin. examiner pharm. div., 1946-51, supervisory examiner, 1951-58, dir. patent research and exam. chem. group, 1958-62, acting examiner-in-chief, 1962-67, examiner-in-chief, 1967—. Mem. Patent Office Soc. Home: 7928 Orchid St NW Washington DC 20012 Office: US Patent Office Washington DC 20231

STONE, JOHN FLOYD, educator; b. York, Neb., Oct. 13, 1928; s. Harry F. and Anna (Klima) S.; student Neb. Wesleyan U., 1948-50; B.S., U. Neb., 1952; M.S., Ia. State U., 1955, Ph.D., 1957; m. Carol O. Youngson, Aug. 2, 1953; children—Mary, Margaret, David, Jana. Research asso. Ia. State U., Ames, 1955-57; asst. prof. Okla. State U., Stillwater, 1957-60, asso. prof., 1960-69, prof., dept. agronomy, 1969—. Served with USN, 1946-48. Mem. Am. Soc. Agronomy, Soil Sci. Soc. Am. (asso. editor 1968—), Am. Geophys. Union, Internat. Soil Sci. Soc., Sigma Xi. Office: Dept Agronomy Okla State U Stillwater OK 74074

STONE, (MARY) KATHARINE GANN (MRS. ERNEST STONE), educator; b. Sylacauga, Ala.; d. William C. and Mary (Twilley) Gann; B.S., Jacksonville State U., 1933; M.A., U. Ala., 1944, postgrad., 1960, 62; m. Ernest Stone, Aug. 18, 1934; 1 son, William Ernest. Prin., tchr., DeKalb County Schs., 1934-44; tchr. Jacksonville (Ala.) State U., 1944-46, dir. elementary lab. sch., 1948—. Condr. workshops for tchrs. Jefferson, Calhoun, Marshall, Butler, Cherokee counties; tchr. inst. numerous counties, cities; mem. Title III Adv. Council, State of Ala., 1968-72; mem. Gov.'s Com. on Adult Edn., 1968-72. Recipient Alumnus of Year award Jacksonville State U., 1961-62. Mem. Ala. Edn. Assn. (dist. pres. 1944-46), Edn. Profl. Standards Commn. (tchr. 1944-50), Am. Assn. U. Women (pres. 1950-52), N.E.A., Dept. Elementary Sch. Prins. (pres. dist. V 1971-72), Assn. Childhood Edn., Nat. Assn. Parliamentarians, Ala. Assn. Parliamentarians (historian 1963-65, sec. 1971-72), Nat. Council Tchrs. Math., Am. Assn. Sch. Adminstrs. Ala. Fedn. Women's Clubs (exec. bd. 1945-72), Delta Kappa Gamma (pres. chpt. 1940-44), Kappa Delta Pi, Alpha Xi Delta. Club: Progressive Study (pres. 1951-52). Home: President's Mansion 710 N Pelham Rd Jacksonville AL 36365

STONE, OLEN JERRY, ins. agy. exec.; b. Huntsville, Ark., July 22, 1916; s. Alison C. and Pearl (Ledbetter) S.; student Northeastern State Tchrs. Coll., 1933; grad. Chillicothe Bus. Coll., 1934-35, David Rankin Jr. Sch., 1938-39; student Mo. U., 1942; m. Alice E. Summerfield, Sept. 21, 1935; children—Carole Jean, David J. Sales engr, Mid-Valley Supply Co., St. Louis, 1935-58; ins. agt., real estate broker Fansher & Stone, Inc., 1959—, pres., 1967—; real estate broker, ins. agt. Fansher & Stone Real Estate Co., Okmulgee, Okla., 1959—, pres., 1967—; dir. Okmulgee Land Title Co., Citizens Nat. Bank, Okmulgee, Nat. Found. Life Ins. Co., Oklahoma City. Sec., treas. Okmulgee Realtors Bd., 1966-67, v.p., 1968-69, pres., 1970, 71; pres. Flordell Hills Improvement Assn., St. Louis, 1941. Bd. dirs. Salvation Army, Okmulgee, v.p. 1968-69, pres., 1970-71. Mem. Retail Mchts. Assn. (dir. 1962-68, pres. 1964). Baptist (deacon 1945-58, 1963-66, supt. Sunday sch. 1946-58, 63-64, 67-69). Lion (pres. 1964-66). Home: 1911 E 10th St Okmulgee OK 74447 Office: 215 E 8th St Okmulgee OK 74447

STONE, ROBERT HUGH, librarian; b. Lebanon, Tenn., Feb. 5, 1940; s. Marshall Leslie and Carrie Etta (Belcher) S.; student Cumberland Coll. Tenn., 1957-59; B.S., George Peabody Coll. Tchrs., 1961, M.A., 1962, M.L.S., 1967. Tchr. math. Cumberland Coll. Tenn., Lebanon, 1962-65; documentation specialist, Demonstration and Research Center for Early Edn., Peabody Coll. Nashville, 1967—; catalog librarian, Meharry Med. Coll., Nashville, 1969—. Mem. Am., Canadian, Cath., Southeastern, Med., Tenn., library assns., Nat. Council Tchrs. Math., Am. Assn. Physics Tchrs., Assn. Sci. Edn., So. Bapt. Music Conf. Baptist. Home: PO Box 542 813 Castle Heights Ave Lebanon TN 37087 Office: Meharry Med Coll Nashville TN 37208

STONE, ROBERT LEE, soft drink co. exec.; b. Sherman, Tex., Jan. 31, 1916; s. Lonnie Lee and Louise Catherine (Knox) S.; B.S., Tex. Technol. U., 1938; m. Edna Mae Wild, Aug. 27, 1938; 1 dau., Sharron Kaye (Mrs. Neal R. Walsh). Tchr. pub. schs., 1938-44; county agt. Lynn County, Tahoka, Tex., 1944-45; indsl. developer Tex. Electric Service Co., 1947-50; trainee Dr. Pepper Co., Dallas, 1950, zone mgr., 1950, sales promotion mgr., 1950-53, sales mgr. fountain div., 1953-55, asst. gen. sales mgr., 1955-57, mgr. fountain div., 1957-60, v.p. fountain, 1960-63, v.p. sales, 1963-70, v.p., gen. sales mgr., 1970—. Served to 2d lt. AUS, 1945-47. Mem. Sales and Marketing Execs. (pres. Dallas 1971-72). Methodist. Mason. Home: 6120 Preston Creek Dr Dallas TX 75240 Office: PO Box 5086 5523 E Mockingbird Lane Dallas TX 75222

STONE, ROBERT WILLIAM, pharm. co. exec.; b. Glasgow, Ky., Oct. 4, 1943; s. Robert and Alice Pauline (Bowles) S.; student Western Ky. U., 1960-62; B.S., U. Ky., 1965; m. Joyce Kaye Matthews, Aug. 15, 1964; children—Joseph Harlan, Robert Matthew. Pharm. intern Begley Drugs, Somerset, Ky., 1965-66; pharmacist Taylors Prescription Service, Inc., Glasgow, 1966-70; organizer Glasgow Prescription Center, Inc., 1970, pres., 1970—, chmn. bd., 1970—. Mem. Citizens Adv. Com. City of Glasgow, 1968-70. Named Outstanding Jaycee of Jr., Glasgow Jr. C. of C., 1967, 68. Mem. Am., Ky., 4th Dist (treas. 1967-68) pharm. assns., Glasgow Jr. C. of C. (pres. 1968-69, dir 1969-70). Methodist (dir. 1967-70). Kiwanian (treas. 1967-68). Home: 555 Lexington Dr Glasgow KY 42141 Office: Glasgow Prescription Center Inc W Public Square Glasgow KY 42141

STONE, ROY MAXWELL, record co. and publishing co. exec.; b. Live Oak, Fla., Jan. 9, 1916; s. William E. and Lola (Miller) S.; student U. Fla., 1938-39, South Tex. Law Sch., 1954-55; m. Lulu Pryor Cloud, Dec. 8, 1940; children—Maxwell Pryor, William Robert, Mary Alice. Religious songwriter J. H. Henson Music Co., Atlanta, 1950; with Baxter Music Co., Dallas, 1950-52, Stamps Quartet Music Co., Dallas, 1952-54, Country Music Band, 1934-39; owner R & M Record Shops, Inc., 1956- , Stoneway Record Co., Houston, 1964—, Roy M. Stone Pub. Co., 1964—, Stoneway Pub. Co., 1970—; pres. Wide World Records, 1969—. Mem. Country Music Assn. Baptist. Mason. Author, Composer: Our Hymns and Gospel Songs. Composer many songs including I Know That God is Real, Out of Order. Home: 10414 Shady Lane Houston TX 77016 Office: 2817 Laura Koppe Houston TX 77016

STONE, WALKER, newspaperman; b. Okemah, Okla., May 8, 1904; s. John Seborn and Stella (Bynum) S.; B.S., Okla. State U., 1926; postgrad. George Washington U., 1927-29; m. Donna Mae Smith, July 17, 1930; children—Sharon (Mrs. Michael Sean Kilpatrick), Sabra (Mrs. David Allen Smith). Writer, exec. Scripps-Howard newspapers in Washington, 1927—; editor Scripps-Howard Newspaper Alliance, 1943-52; editor in chief Scripps-Howard Newspapers, 1953-69. Pres., chmn. Scripps-Howard Found., 1969-71. Mem. Kappa Sigma. Clubs: National Press, Metropolitan. Home: Hawthorn Woodville VA 22749

STONE, WILLIAM ROY, city ofcl.; b. Longview, Tex., July 25, 1916; s. William Thomas and Clara Lee (Cagle) S.; ed. FBI Nat. Acad., 1957; m. Inez Faye Ferguson, Jan. 5, 1953; children—Patricia Faye, Pamela Kaye, William Roy. Route supr. Tex. Milk Products Co., Longview, 1936-42; chief of police, Longview, 1947—. Tchr. police adminstrn. Kilgore Coll., 1966-72, vis. instr. East Tex. Police Acad., 1966-72. Served with USAAF, 1942-46; PTO. Decorated Bronze Star medal. Mem. Tex. Police Assn. (pres. 1962-63), Tex. (pres. 1969-70), East Tex. (pres. 1965) police chief's assns., East Tex. Peace Officers Assn. (v.p. 1968-72). K.P. Home: 1605 Andrews St Longview TX 75601 Office: 100 E Cotton St Longview TX 75601

STONECIPHER, ELMER THOMAS, socio-econ. devel. co. exec.; b. LaCrosse, Ind., Feb. 6, 1920; s. Samuel Oliver and Mary Etta (McKim) S.; student Ind. U., 1938-40; B.A., Tulane U., 1949; M.A., George Washington U., 1964; postgrad. Naval War Coll., 1964; m. Rebecca Louise Lehner, Sept. 23, 1943; children—Susan, Charles, Sarah, Rebecca, Henry, Daniel. Commd. ensign USN, 1941, advanced through grades to capt., 1960, ret., 1965; dir. tech. tng. Dept. of Def. nuclear program, N.M., 1951-54, 57-60, dir. NATO Sch., Europe, 1960-63, mem. Joint Staff and Exec. Office Sec. Navy, 1964-65; civilian service Exec. Office of Pres., 1965-67; v.p. Avco Corp., socio-econ. devel., Washington, 1968—. Guest lectr. NATO Def. Coll., 1960-63. Active in youth oriented orgns. Decorated commendation medal. Recipient Freedom Found. medal, 1964. Mem. Am. Mgmt. Assn., Am. Soc. Tng. and Devel. Pa. German Soc., St. Andrew's Soc., S.A.R. (state dir. 1958-59), Fedn. German Am. Men's Clubs (dir. 1962-63). Methodist. Clubs: George Washington University, Army and Navy, Internat. (Washington). Home: 3118 Wynford Dr Fairfax VA 22030 Office: Avco Corp 1025 Connecticut Av NW Washington DC 20036

STONER, EDMUND CURTIS, JR., ret. telephone co. exec.; b. Riverside, Cal., Oct. 20, 1903; s. Edmund Curtis and Margaret (Copley) S.; student Lafayette Coll., 1921-22; B.S. in Elec. Engring., Yale, 1926; m. Margaret Dorman Hamilton, June 23, 1926 (dec. 1958); 1 dau., Margaret Hamilton (Mrs. John N. Schofield, Jr.); m. 2d, Mary J. Garcia, 1960. Chief engr. Internat. Tel. & Tel. Corp., Peru, Cuba and Spain, 1933-41; asst. v.p. Fed. Telephone & Radio, 1945-48; cons. engr. to minister of communications Govt. of Turkey, Ankara, 1948-51; chief engr. Gen. Telephone & Electronics Corp., Muskegon, Mich., 1954-58, chief engr., Tampa, Fla., 1958-65, engr. planning dir., 1965-68. Served to lt, col. USAAF, World War II (col. Res. ret.). Decorated Bronze Star; Mem. Ret. Officers Assn (pres. Tampa). I.E.E.E., Rochester, Tampa (mem. mil. affairs com.) chambers commerce, Order Brit. Empire (hon. officer mil. div.), Phi Kappa Psi. Presbyn. Clubs: University (Tampa, Fla.); Army-Navy (Washington); Order of Daedalians, Yale (N.Y.C.); Riverside (Conn.) Yacht. Author: Never for Me, 1968. Home: 310 S Burlingame Av Temple Terrace FL 33617

STOPHLET, DONALD VICTOR, univ. adminstr.; b. Oak Park, Ill., Nov. 12, 1918; s. Donald Stirling and Anne (Gilmer) S.; Ph.B., U. Wis., 1941, Ph.M., 1946; m. Janice Hutson, Apr. 22, 1962. Mng. dir. Central City Opera Assn., Central City and Denver, 1948-52; sec. of coll., dir. devel. Rockford (Ill.) Coll., 1952-58; dir. devel. programs U. Pitts., 1958-59; v.p. devel. Western Res. U., 1959-63; v.p. devel. affairs Miami (Fla.), 1963-67; v.p. for devel. Fla. Inst. Tech., 1967—. Served as pilot USAAF, 1943-46. Mem. Am. Coll. Pub. Relations Assn., Am. Alumni Council, Nat. Collegiate Players, Alpha Delta Phi. Rotarian. Home: 408 Driftwood Av Melbourne Beach FL

STORCK, AMBROSE HOWELL, surgeon; b. New Orleans, July 8, 1903; s. Jacob Ambrose and Minnie Edna (Howell) S.; B.S., Tulane U., 1923, M.D., 1925, M.S., 1934. Intern Charity Hosp. of La., New Orleans, 1925-27, house surgeon, 1927-31, vis. surgeon, 1932-40, sr. vis. surgeon, 1940—; practice medicine specializing in surgery, New Orleans, 1931—; instr. clin. surgery, Tulane U., 1931-39, asst. prof. clin. surgery, 1939-47, prof. clin. surgery, 1947-64, prof. surgery, 1964—; vis. surgeon Touro Infirmary, 1931—; sr. vis. surgeon So. Bapt. Hosp., 1939—. Cons. gen. surgery for VA, Tex. and La., 1946-54; surg. cons. 4th Army Station Hosp., New Orleans; mem. local unit La. Cultural Resources Commn.; mem. Charity Hosp. Tumor Registry Bd. Commd. maj., U.S. Army Med. Res., 1940, advanced through grades to Col., 1948; asst. cons. in surgery Office of The Surgeon Gen., March 14, 1942, later cons. in gen. surgery, E.T.O., and chief surg. service De Witt Gen. Hosp. Recipient Distinguished Service award American Cancer Soc., also research grants. Diplomate Am. Bd. Surgery. Fellow A.C.S. (gov. 1959-62); mem. Am., So. surg. assns., Surgeons Club, So. Surgeons Club, Soc. Univ. Surgeons, Soc. for Vascular Surgery, Soc. Med. Cons. to Armed Forces, A.M.A., Internat. Soc. Surgery, La. Surg. Assn. (pres. 1954), Southeastern Surg. Congress, Soc. Surgery Alimentary Tract (founder mem.), Am. Assn. Cancer Research, So. Med. Assn., La. State Med. Soc. (chmn. cancer commn.), A.A.A.S., New Orleans Acad. Scis., Assn. for Surgery of Trauma, La. Soc. S.A.R., Ednl. Council Orleans Parish Unit Am. Cancer Soc. (hon. dir. for New Orleans and La.), New Orleans Surg. Soc. (pres. 1958), Royal Soc. Medicine (Eng.), Nat. Trust Historic Preservation, Assn., Internat. House, La. Landmarks Soc. (dir.), Phi Delta Theta, Nu Sigma Nu. Democrat. Presbyn. Clubs: Boston, Louisana, Lake Shore, Pickwick. Author (book) Military Surgical Manual—Abdominal and Genito-Urinary Injuries; contbg. author, history U.S. Army Med. Dept. during World War II; Cancer of the Digestive Tract; also author med. articles in Annals of Surgery, Archives of Surgery, Gynecology and Obstetrics, New Orleans Med. and Surg. Jour. Co-editor Tulane Medicine. Editorial bd. Am. Surgeon. Home: 1458 Nashville Av New Orleans LA 70115 Office: 1430 Tulane Av New Orleans LA 70112

STORER, GEORGE BUTLER, radio, TV exec.; b. Champaign, Ill., Nov. 10, 1809; s. George Butler and Mabel (Mozier) S.; grad. Tome Sch. of Port Deposit, Md.; student, Cornell U., 1918-20; m. children—George Butler, James Perley, Peter, Robert Mozier; m. 3d, Dorothy M. Kiggins, July 16, 1960. Pres., gen. mgr. Standard Tube Co., Toledo, 1921-26, pres., gen. mgr., Detroit, 1928-43, chmn. bd. 1946-65; v.p.

steel and tubes div. Republic Steel Corp., Cleve., 1926-27; pres. Storer Broadcasting Co., 1927-61, now chmn.; chmn. N.E. Airlines, Inc. Asst. chmn. Broadcasters Victory Council, 1941-43. Served lt. comdr. to comdr., USNR, 1943-45. Trustee U. Miami, Coral Gables, Fla. Mem. Nat. Assn. Radio and TV Broadcasters (past dir.), Delta Kappa Epsilon. Republican. Clubs: Detroit, Detroit Athletic; Atlanta Athletic; Indian Creek Country (Miami Beach, Fla.); Cornell (Ithaca, N.Y.); Bloomfield Hills (Mich.) Country; La Gorce Country (Miami Beach, Fla.); Old Baldy (Sartoga, Wyo.); Lyford Cay (Nassau). Home: 26 Indian Creek Island Miami Beach FL 33154 also Storer Ranch Saratoga Wy (summer)Office: 1177 Kane Concourse Bay Harbor Island Miami Beach FL 33154 ALSO 118 E 57th St New York City NY 10022

STORER, JOHN JAMES, physician; b. Iowa, La., July 17, 1919; s. James Lawrence and Juanita Rae (McKinley) S.; B.S., U. So. La., 1940; M.D., La. State U., 1944; m. Cleta M. Tanquis, Apr. 11, 1945; children—Cleta Ann, John, Claire Rae, George, Ilene, Clarence, William, Kathleen. Teaching fellow Tex. A. and M. U., 1940; intern Mercy Hosp., New Orleans, 1944; gen. practice medicine, Kinder, La., 1946-71; chief staff Allen Parish Hosp., 1969-71; med. dir. Charity Hosp., Lake Charles, La., 1971—. Fellow Am. Acad. Family Physicians, Am. Geriatrics Soc., Royal Soc. Health; mem. A.M.A., Am. Quarter Horse Assn., Am. Legion, Woodmen of World, Allen Parish Farm Bur., La. State, Allen Parish med. socs., Phi Chi. Home: Kinder LA 70648 Office: Charity Hosp 1000 Walters St Lake Charles LA 70601

STORER, MORRIS BREWSTER, educator; b. Pitts., Nov. 14, 1904; s. Norman Wilson and Mary Elizabeth Wyman (Perry) S.; B.S., Dartmouth, 1926; M.A., U. Chgo., 1929; M.A., Harvard, 1932, Ph.D., 1937; m. Gretchen Geuder Schneider, Aug. 18, 1935; children—John Winthrop, Christopher Martin, Thomas Perry. Instr. philosophy U. Pitts., 1927-28, Lafayette Coll., 1929-30, Dartmouth Coll., 1932-35; social scientist U.S. Dept. Agr., 1936-46; dean instrn. Mt. Vernon Jr. Coll., 1946-47; prof. humanities U. Fla., Gainesville, 1947—. Served to capt. AUS, 1943-44. Mem. Am. Assn. U. Profs., Am. Fedn. Tchrs. (sec. local chpt. 1970-71), Am., Fla. philos. assns., Grange, Delta Upsilon. Unitarian (chmn. 1965-66). Club: Melrose (Fla.) Civic (pres. 1949-50). Home: 1503 NW 10th Av Gainesville FL 32601

STOREY, BEN CHARLES, physician; b. Washington, Ind., Aug. 3, 1933; s. Thomas G. and Mary (Russo) S.; student Wabash Coll., 1954; grad. Med. Sch. Ind., U., 1958; m. Mary Emma Farr, Sept. 2, 1955; children—Mark, Matthew, Todd, Troy, Monique. Intern Tampa (Fla.) Gen. Hosp., 1958-59; practice gen. medicine, Titusville, Fla., 1959—; mem. staff Jess Parrish Meml. Hosp., 1959—. Dir. Lantern Hills Devel. Corp., Fisher Constrn. Co., Superior Cabinet & Supply Co., Titusville Med. Facilities, Inc. Mem. Brevard Ednl. Com., 1971-72. Bd. dirs. Brevard Heart Loan Fund; bd. dirs., physician Pop Warner Hurricane League, Inc., Titusville. Recipient Distinguished Service award Titusville Jr. C. of C., 1969. Mem. Am., Fla., Canaveral (pres. 1968-70) heart assns., Fla. (chmn. pharmacy com. 1968-71), Brevard County (pres. 1968) med. assns., Phi Gamma Delta, Nu Sigma Nu. Moose. Home: Burkholm Rd Route 1 Box 386 Titusville FL 32780 Office: 500 N Washington Av Titusville FL 32780

STOREY, CLYDE HERBERT, glass co. exec.; b. Lynch, Ky., Sept. 28, 1934; s. Watson and Mildred Pearl (McIntire) S.; student Ga. Inst. Tech., 1952-53, U.S. Naval Acad., 1954-55; B.S. in Mining Engring., U. Ky., 1958; m. Betty Jo Groh, May 27, 1958; children—Rebecca Lillian, Lora Dawn, Rachel Ramona. Dir. indsl. engring. Princess Coals, Inc., 1959-61; with Corning Glass Works, Harrodsburg, Ky., 1961—, successively jr. glass technologist, foreman melting tank maintenance, shift melting foreman, sr. glass technologist, supr. optical properties, supr. glass tech., 1967—. Part-time land surveyer, 1963-66. Served with USNR, 1954-55. Registered profl. engr., Ky. Research in photochromic glass. Home: 774 Cane Run St Harrodsburg KY 40330 Office: 680 E Office St Harrodsburg KY 40330

STOREY, JOHN ELDRIDGE, ch. pension exec.; b. Galatia, N.C., May 9, 1936; s. Henry Clinton and Ruth (Sykes) S.; student Comml. Coll. Asheboro, 1956; m. Vera Jean Parks, Apr. 6, 1958; children—Stephen Allen, Starr Ellen. With First Nat. Bank, Asheboro, N.C., 1956-70, teller, loan adjuster, mgr. installment loan dept., 1956-61, asst. cashier, 1961-65, mgr. Midtown Office, 1963-68, asst. v.p., 1965-68, v.p., 1968-70; exec. dir. Wesleyan Pension Fund, 1970—. Conf. statistician N.C., Conf. Wesleyan Meth. Ch. of Am. Trustee Central Wesleyan Coll.; bd. dirs. Randolph County Tb Assn. Club: Optimist (pres., 1967, Optimist of Year 1967). Home: S Fayetteville St Extension Asheboro NC 27203

STOREY, ROBERT GERALD, lawyer; b. Greenville, Tex., Dec. 4, 1893; s. Frank Wilson and Mary Edith (Thomson) S.; student U. Tex., 1911-14; LL.D., Tex. Christian U., 1947, Laval U., 1953, Drake U., 1954; D.C.L., Chungang U., Korea, 1961; H.H.D., St. Paul's U., Japan, 1961; Dr. Humanities, U. Ryukyus, 1964; m. Frances Hazel Porter, July 26, 1917 (dec. 1962); children—Robert G. (dec.), Charles P. Admitted to Tex. bar, 1914; city atty., Troup, Tex., 1914-17; asst. atty. gen. Tex., 1921-23; spl. asst. dist. atty., Dallas, 1924; mem. firm Storey, Armstrong & Steger; chmn. bd. Lakewood State Bank; dir. Southwestern Bell Telephone Co.; dean law sch. So. Meth. U., 1947-59; pres. Southwestern Legal Found., 1947—. Served as U.S. exec. trial counsel to Justice Robert H. Jackson in Nuremberg trial of major war criminals, 1945-46; mem. New Hoover Commn. to reorganize exec. br. of govt., 1953-55; spl. rep. of State Dept. to conduct seminars among members of legal profession of friendly Free Nations, 1954-55; vice chmn. U.S. Civil Rights Commn., 1957-63; spl. counsel State Tex. Investigation Assassination of President Kennedy, 1963-64; mem., vice-chmn. U.S. Sea Level Canal Commn., 1965-70; mem. Pres.'s Law Enforcement Commn., 1965-66. Regent U. Tex., 1924-29; chmn. bd. fgn. scholarships Fulbright Bd., 1958-62. Pres. Dallas Park Bd., 1939-42. Served as 1st lt. U.S. Army, 1918-19; col., AUS, World War II. Decorated Legion of Merit, Bronze Star, Medal of Freedom (U.S.). Legion of Honor (France), Second Order of Merit, Japanese Government; recipient Linz civic leadership award, Dallas, 1955; Am. Bar Assn. gold medal, 1956. Mem. Internat. (mem. council 1950-56), Inter-Am. (pres. 1954-56), Am. (gov. 1949-54; chmn. sect. on legal edn. 1937-39; mem. ho. of dels.; pres. 1952-53), Tex. (pres. 1948-49), Dallas (pres. 1934) bar assns., Am. Legion (mem. nat. exec. com. 1920-21), Order of Coif, Phi Beta Kappa, Phi Alpha Delta; hon. mem. Candian, Peruvian, Mexican, Korean, Cuban and other nat. and state bar assns. Mem. Christian Ch. Mason (32 deg., Shriner), Kiwanian (pres. 1927; dist. gov. 1931). Club: Dallas Country. Home: 3525 Turtle Creek Dr Dallas TX 75219 Office: Republic Bank Bldg Dallas TX 75201

STOREY, WILLIAM MARION, bar assn. exec.; b. Savannah, Ga., Aug. 16, 1924; s. William Marion and Rubye (McDonald) S.; student Cornell Midshipmans Sch., 1943-44; A.B., U. N.C., 1947, LL.B., 1950; m. Lucille Ann Tucker, Apr. 19, 1952; children—James McDonald, Ann Tucker. Admitted to N.C. bar, 1950, practiced in Raleigh until 1955, gen. counsel N.C. Bd. Pharmacy, 1950-55; exec. sec.-treas. N.C. Bar Assn. and N.C. Bar Found., Raleigh, 1955-69, exec. v.p., treas., 1969—. Mem. N.C. adv. com. Practicing Law Inst., 1967—; mem. N.C. Penal System Study Commn., 1969—. Mem. U. N.C. adv. TV com., 1959—. Active Wake County Civil Def. Authority. Bd. dirs. N.C. Bar Found. Served to lt. USNR, 1942-46; lt. comdr. Res. Recipient Judge John Parker Meml. award for unusually outstanding and conspicuous service to cause of jurisprudence N.C. Bar Assn., 1971. Mem. Am., Wake County, N.C. (gov. 1955—) bar assns., Internat. Assn. Continuing Legal Edn. Adminstrs. (exec. com. 1970—), Am. Judicature Soc., Nat. Assn. Bar Execs., Am., N.C. State bars. Methodist (steward 1958—). Clubs: Raleigh Kiwanis (dir., sec. 1957-60, 63-65), Raleigh City, Carolina Country, Esquires. Home: 701 Yarmouth Rd Raleigh NC 27607 Office: North Carolina Bar Center 1025 Wade Av Raleigh NC 27605

STORM, FRED CAESAR, assn. exec.; b. Little Rock, Jan. 20, 1917; s. Guy Golden and Leulah Nettie (Edwards) S.; student Little Rock Jr. Coll., 1937; m. Geraldine Baird, June 18, 1942; 1 son, Stephen; m. 2d, Daphna Carolyn Lewis Goss, Oct. 2, 1959; 1 dau., Cecily; step-children—David, Steven, Martha. Chemist L. B. Forbes Labs., 1937-38; chem. engr. Van Trump Testing Lab., 1938-42; accountant Big Rock Stone & Material Co., 1946-67; mgr. North Little Rock (Ark.) C. of C. (dir. 1966-67). Mem., past pres. Bd. Edn. North Little Rock; pres. Ark. Sch. Bds. Assn.; pres.-elect So. Regional Sch. Bds. Assn. Mem. Ark. N.G. Assn. (past pres.), Ark. C. of C. Execs. Assn., Am. C. of C. Execs., So. Assn. C. of C. Execs. Methodist (trustee 1970—). Mason. Club: Little Rock Optimist (pres. 1965—). Home: 7 Laffite Circle North Little Rock AR 72116 Office: 601 Main St North Little Rock AR 72114

STORMONT, RICHARD MANSFIELD, hotel exec.; b. Chgo., Apr. 4, 1936; s. Daniel Lytle and E. Mildred (Milligan) S.; B.S., Cornell U., 1958; m. Virginia Louellen Walters, Nov. 21, 1959; children—Stacy Lee, Richard Mansfield, John Frederick. Food cost analyst, sales rep. Edgewater Beach Hotel. Cgho., 1957-58, asst. sales mgr. Marriott Motor Hotels, Inc., Washington, 1962-64; dir. sales Marriott Motor Hotel, Atlanta, 1964-68, resident mgr., 1969-71; gen. mgr. Marrott Motor Hotel, Dallas, 1971—. Campaign div. leader Salvation Army, 1969. Trustee Miss Atlanta Pageant. Served to lt. (j.g.) USNR, 1959-62. Recipient Distinguished Salesman of Year award Marriott, 1967. Mem. Sales and Marketing Execs. (exec. v.p. 1969-70, dir., pres. Atlanta chpt. 1970-71), Hotel Sales Mgmt. Assn. (past chpt. pres.), Pi Sigma Epsilon, Phi Kappa Psi. Home: 6563 Briarmeade Dr Dallas TX 75240 Office: 2101 Stemmons Hwy Dallas TX 75207

STORRS, ELEANOR E., asso. Gulf South Research Inst., New Iberia, La. Research in inducting armadillos with leprosy bacteria. Office: Gulf Research Inst New Iberia LA 70560*

STORRS, THOMAS IRWIN, banker; b. Nashville, Aug. 25, 1918; s. Robert Williamson and Addie Sue (Payne) S.; B.A., U. Va., 1940; M.A., Harvard, 1950, Ph.D., 1955; m. Kitty Stewart Bird, July 19, 1948; children—Thomas, Margaret. With Fed. Res. Bank, Richmond, Va., 1934-60, v.p. charge research, 1957-59, v.p. charge Charlotte br., 1959-60; exec. v.p. N.C. Nat. Bank, Greensboro, 1960-67, vice chmn. bd. dirs., 1967-69, pres., 1969—; pres. NCNB Corp., 1968—; dir. Texfi Industries, Inc., Greensboro, Black and Decker Mfg. Co. Chmn. bd. regents Stonier Grad. Sch. Banking. Served to lt. comdr. USNR, 1941-45, 51-52. Mem. N.C. Citizens Assn. (pres. 1971-72), Assn. Res. City Bankers, Robert Morris Assos., Raven Soc. Episcopalian. Clubs: Greensboro Country, Charlotte Country, Country of N.C., Charlotte City. Home: 330 Eastover Rd Charlotte NC 28207 Office: N C Nat Bank PO Box 120 Charlotte NC 28201

STORY, WILLIAM STEER, exec.; b. Winnipeg, Man., Can., June 6, 1921; s. William Morley and Marion (Plews) S.; B. Commerce, U. Man., 1948; M.B.A., U. Chgo., 1949; m. Myfanwy Evans, Dec. 27, 1952 (dec. 1970); children—William John Philiskirk, Marianne; m. 2d, Dianne Marie Ripp, June 29, 1971; 1 dau., Karla Marie. Came to U.S. 1947, naturalized, 1956. Asst. analyst U.S. Steel Corp., Pitts., 1949-50 asso. editor Am. Metal Market, N.Y.C., 1950-56; dir. pub. relations Inst. Scrap Iron & Steel, Inc., Washington, 1956-60, asst. exec. v.p., 1961-62, exec. v.p., 1962-71, v.p. marketing, gen. mgr. controlled interval scheduling, 1971; prin. William Story & Assos., 1972—. Served to lt. Canadian Army, 1942-45. Mem. Am. Mgmt. Assn., Am. Foundrymen's Soc., Assn. Iron and Steel Engrs., Am. Inst. Mining, Metall. and Petroleum Engrs., Spl. Service Force Assn., Am. Soc. Assn. Execs., Phi Delta Theta, Beta Gamma Sigma. Mem. United Ch. of Christ. Club: Nat. Press (Washington). Home: 6116 Maiden Lane Bethesda MD 20034 Office: 1729 H St NW Washington DC 20006

STOTHART, JAMES LONNIE, dentist; b. Greensboro, Ala., July 20, 1929; s. James Lonnie and Alice Creswell (Seed) S.; B.S., U. Ala., 1951, D.M.D., 1955; m. Gloria Burks McKeon, Sept. 11, 1954; children—Richard Burks, Alice Amanda. Gen. practice dentistry, Selma, Ala., 1957—; mem. staff New Vaughan Meml. Hosp., Selma Med. Center. Bd. dirs., sec. bd. Sturdivant Mus. Assn. Served from 1st lt. to capt. USAF, 1955-57. Mem. Am., Ala., Dallas County dental assns., U. Ala. Alumni Assn. (pres. Dallas County 1967), Psi Omega, Sigma Alpha Epsilon. Republican. Episcopalian. Club: Selma Country. Home: 2011 Church St Selma AL 36701 Office: PO Box 455 Selma AL 36701

STOUDEMIRE, STERLING A(UBREY), educator; b. Concord, N.C., Sept. 4, 1902; s. Palmer and Frances (Cranford) S.; A.B., U. N.C., 1923, M.A., 1924, Ph.D., 1930; m. Irene Slate, 1925 (dec. 1940); 1 dau., Marian S. (Mrs. James A. Hawlans); m. 2d, Mary Arthur Billups, 1946; 1 son, Sterling Cranford. Instr. Spanish U. N.C., 1924-30, asst. prof. Spanish, 1930-35; asso. prof. Spanish, 1935-41, prof. Spanish, 1941—, head dept. Romance langs., 1949-64. Served as lt. comdr. USNR, 1942-45. Mem. Modern Lang. Assn., S. Atlantic Modern Lang. Assn. (pres. 1962), Am. Assn. Tchrs. Spanish and Portguguese, Am. Name Soc., Phi Gamma Delta. Episcopalian. Author articles and book revs. on Spanish Romanticism; author and editor Spanish texts and anthologies. Translator: Oviedo's Natural History of the West Indies, 1959; Cuentos de Espana y de America, 1942; Christian Doctrine (Pedro de Cordoba), 1970; translator, editor Francisco Alvarez, English Colonies in America. Home: 712 Gimghoul Rd Chapel Hill NC 27514

STOUT, HUGH ALBERT, physician; b. Shattuck, Okla., June 17, 1909; s. Albert Franklin and Helen Caroline (Hayes) S.; B.A., U. Okla., 1933, B.S., 1936, M.D., 1937; M.S., U. Minn., 1946; m. Ruth Marie Baisch, Nov. 30, 1945; children—Bette Jo, Caroline Anne, Hugh Albert. Resident physician Mass. Gen. Hosp., 1937-39; fellow Mayo Clinic, 1941-46, cons., 1946-47; dir. labs., chief pathologist Mercy Hosp., Oklahoma City, 1948-68; practice medicine specializing internal medicine and pathology, Oklahoma City; mem. staff Univ., Mercy, Baptist, Clinton hosps.; asst. prof. U. Okla. Sch. Medicine, 1952. Founder Sch. Med. Tech., Mercy Hosp., 1950. Bd. dirs., chmn. bd. N.W. Nursing Center, Inc., 1965. Served to maj., M.C., USAAF, 1941-43; ETO. Named Outstanding Citizen in Medicine, Oklahoma City Jr. C. of C., 1962. Diplomate Am. Bd. Internal Medicine, Am. Bd. Pathology. Fellow A.C.P. (life), Coll. Am. Pathologists; mem. A.M.A., Okla. Med. Assn. (chmn. program com. 1960), Okla. Pathologists Assn. (pres. 1955), County Med. Soc., Phi Beta Kappa, Sigma Xi. Methodist (trustee 1969). Author: Secret of Human Drive, Pep and Energy, 1966. Contbr. articles to profl. jours. Discoverer external cardiac massage, 1957. Home: 13009 Oak Hollow Rd Oklahoma City OK 73120 Office: 1211 N Shartel St Oklahoma City OK 73103

STOUT, JOE FRANCIS, boot co. exec.; b. Granville, Tenn., Sept. 5, 1933; s. Clifford D. and Sally B. (Huff) S.; student pub. schs., Putnam County, Tenn.; m. Anita Sue Dye, Sept. 22, 1956; children—Jerry Morgan, Amy Renee. Machine operator Continental Aviation & Engring. Co., Detroit, 1951-56; exptl. hand former Mercury Metalcraft Co., Detroit, 1956-58; with Ga. Boot Co., Baxter, Tenn., 1958-64, now gen. mgr. Ga. div., Blairsville, Ga. Mem. com. Heart Fund, 1963. Bd. dirs. Am. Cancer Soc. Lt. col. on staff gov. Ga., 1968—. Mem. Ga. Sheriffs Assn. Mason; mem. Order Eastern Star. Clubs: North Ga. Sportsman, Quarterback (Blairsville). Home: Deep South Farm Rd Blairsville GA 30512 Office: Gainesville Hwy Blairsville GA 30512

STOUT, JOSEPH EARL, city ofcl.; b. Lake Charles, La., Apr. 27, 1927; s. Charles Earl and Mabel (Fargue) S.; student U. Tenn., 1960, La. State U., 1965, FBI Nat. Acad., 1967, Tex. A. and M. U., 1969; m. Dora Elaine Cole, Dec. 8, 1951; 1 dau., Martha Jane. Patrolman, Lake Charles (La.) Police Dept., 1948-49, sgt., 1949-53, detective sgt., 1953-56, capt., 1956-65, chief, 1965—. Vice chmn. adv. com. La. State U. Law Enforcement Tng., 1965—; mem. Commn. on Law Enforcement Standards and Edn., 1969; mem. La. Commn. Law Enforcement Adminstrn. of Criminal Justice, Com. on Law Enforcement, 1969-71; chmn. Red Carpet Com., 1968. Bd. dirs. S.W. Guidance Council. Recipient recognition certificate of merit Gov. La., 1971, certificate of merit La. State U., 1971, Tourism award Lake Charles Assn. Commerce, 1967, Law Enforcement award Optimist Internat., 1968. Mem. La. Assn. Chiefs Police (pres. 1967-68), La. Peace Officers Assn. (pres. 1970-71), Internat. Assn. Chiefs Police (chmn. membership com. 1966-68), Municipal Police Officers Assn., FBI Nat. Acad. Grads. (3d v.p. La. chpt. 1971-72), Greater Lake Charles C. of C. Methodist (dir. 1970-72). Rotarian. Club: Buccaneer (dir. 1971-72). Home: 2014 12th St Lake Charles LA 70601 Office: PO Box 1564 Lake Charles LA 70601

STOVALL, GUY FRANKLIN, JR., investment exec.; b. El Campo, Tex., Jan. 13, 1934; s. Guy Franklin and Edith I. (Perterka) S.; B.B.A., U. Houston, 1956; m. Kay Kuhn, Feb. 7, 1956; children—Guy Franklin III, Becky, Linda, David, Eric. Trader in oil, land, cattle, rice investments; dir. 1st Nat. Bank, El Campo, Tex., El Campo Citizen Publ., Inc. Trustee Gulf Coast Med. Found., former pres. and chmn. bd., now 1st v.p., chmn. exec. com.; trustee numerous trusts. Recipient Elk of year award, 1969-70. Mem. Petroleum Club. Methodist (trustee 1965-71). Elk (trustee). Club: Houston. Home: El Campo TX 77437 Office: 202 E Jackson St El Campo TX 77437

STOVALL, JAMES WATTS, clergyman; b. Mobile, Ala., Apr. 27, 1912; s. Albert Bee and Rosa Lee (McDowell) S.; student pub. schs.; m. Janet Elizabeth Myers, June 19, 1935 (dec. Aug. 1967); 1 dau., Mary Elizabeth. Blacksmith's helper Mobile County, Ala., 1930-38; asst. warehouseman Mobile County, 1938-43, warehouseman, 1943; minister Belforest Christian Ch., 1953-54, Robertsdale Christian Ch., 1955-66, 67—, Azalea Christian Ch., 1966-67. Lifetime blood donor A.R.C., 1957—. Recipient Town and Country Minister of Yr. award Ala. Christian Chs., 1963. Mason. Home: 300 Stocking Mobile AL 36604

STOVALL, REGINALD MORRIS, mayor; b. Tupelo, Okla., Aug. 1, 1916; s. William Dudley and Grace (Allen) S.; ed. Tex. Christian U., 1936; m. Amelia Zich, Sept. 9, 1939; children—Linda, Marsha, Peggy, Nancy (Mrs. S.R. Sanders). Pres., Panther City Office Supply Co., 1944—; v.p. Bell Reprodn. Co., 1950—; mayor, Fort Worth, 1969—. Mem. Fort Worth City Council, 1963-68. Episcopalian. Mason (Shriner). Home: 2428 Medford Ct E Fort Worth TX 76109 Office: Throckmorton St Fort Worth TX 76102*

STOVALL, THELMA L. (MRS. LONNIE RAYMOND STOVALL), state ofcl.; b. Munfordville, Ky., Apr. 1, 1919; d. Samuel Dewey and Addie Mae Hawkins; student LaSalle Extension U., U. Ky., Eastern State Coll.; m. Lonnie Raymond Stovall, Sept. 30, 1936. Mem. Ky. Ho. of Reps., sec. of state State of Ky., 1956-60, 64-68; treas. State of Ky., 1960-64, 68-72, sec. of state, 1972—. Active State Labor Movement; sec. Tobacco Workers Internat. Union; liaison officer Louisville Community Chest and labor unions; state chmn. Muscular Dsytrophy, 1957-70; v.p. Muscular Dystrophy Assn. Am., 1970-72, chmn. legislative com., 1972—; mem. Pres.'s Commn. on Status of Women, 1964-68. Nat. committeewoman Young Democratic Clubs Ky., 1952-56, pres., 1956-58. Bd. dirs. edn. dept. Ky. Fedn. Labor. Mem. Bus. and Profl. Women's Club. Democrat. Baptist. Moose; mem. Order Eastern Star. Club: Altrusa. Home: 104 Valley Rd Louisville KY 40204 Office: State Capitol Frankfort KY 40601

STOVER, CARL FREDERICK, cons.; b. Pasadena, Cal., Sept. 29, 1930; s. Carl Joseph and Marguerite (Muller) S.; B.A. magna cum laude, Stanford, 1951, M.A., 1954; m. Catherine Swanson, Sept. 3, 1954; children—Matthew Joseph, Mary Margaret, Claire Ellen. Instr. polit. sci. Stanford, 1953-55; fiscal mgmt. officer Office Sec. Dept. Agr., 1955-57; asso. dir. conf. program pub. affairs Brookings Instn., 1957-59, sr. staff mem. govtl. studies, 1960; fellow Center for Study Democratic Instns., Santa Barbara, Cal., 1960-62; asst. to chmn. bd. editors Ency. Brit., 1960-62; sr. polit. scientist Stanford Research Inst., 1962-64, dir. pub. affairs fellowship program Stanford, 1962-64; pres. Nat. Inst. Pub. Affairs, Washington, 1964-70; pvt. profl. cons., 1970—. Cons. to govt., 1953—. Treas., Nat. Com. U.S.-China Relations, 1966-71, pres., 1971-72, dir., 1966—; treas., dir. Coordinating Council Lit. Mags., 1966-68. Trustee Inst. Nations, 1962—, Nat. Inst. Pub. Affairs, 1967-71. Fellow A.A.A.S.; mem. Am. Soc. Pub. Adminstrn., Am. Polit. Sci. Assn., Am. Soc. for Cybernetics, Fedn. Am. Scientists, Soc. Internat. Devel., Nat. Acad. Pub. Adminstrn. (hon.), Phi Beta Kappa Assos., Phi Beta Kappa. Democrat. Presbyn. Author: The Government of Science, 1962; The Technological Order, 1963. Exec. editor Jour. Law and Edn., 1971—. Home: 1280 21st St NW Washington DC 20036

STOVER, CHARLES OSCAR, educator, band dir.; b. Coffeyville, Kan., Apr. 15, 1913; s. Charles Robert and Addie (Wood) S.; B.S., Kan. State Tchrs. Coll., 1940, M.S., 1946; postgrad. Mich. state U., 1949-53; m. Catherine Elizabeth Cooper, Aug. 23, 1936. Dir. vocal music, Roosevelt Jr. High Sch., Coffeyville, Kan., 1935-42; band dir. Kan. State Tchrs Coll., Pittsburg, 1942-47; supr. music, jr. coll. bd. dir. Coffeyville Pub. Schs., 1947-52; asst. dir. bands Mich. State U., 1953-60; asso. prof. Northwestern State Coll., Alva, Okla., 1960—, chmn. music dept., 1960—, band dir., 1960—. Band clinician, Slingerland Drum Co. Mem. Bd. Advisers, Niles, Ill., 1957-67; mem. adv. com. J.F. Kennedy Center for Performing Arts, 1970—. Served with AUS, 1943-46. Named Outstanding Tchr., Coffeyville Pub Schs., 1952, All Am. Bandmaster's Band, Chgo., 1956; named Tchr. of Year Northwestern State Coll., 1968-69. Mem. N.E.A., Okla. Edn. Assn., Music Educators Nat Conf., Okla. Music Educators Assn., Okla. Bandmaster's Assn., Coll. Bandmaster's Nat. Assn., Kappa Kappa Psi, Phi Beta Mu (state pres. 1971—), Phi Mu Alpha. Republican. Presbyn. (elder, choir dir.). Rotarian (pres. 1967—). Home: 716 Apache Dr Alva OK 73717

STOVER, LLOYD VERNON, educator; b. Belfast, Me., May 30, 1922; s. Walter Raymond and Neva Evelyn (Armstrong) S.; B.S., U. N.H., 1948; LL.B., U. Miami, 1951, J.D., 1964; m. Betty Jean Curry, May 21, 1955; children—Kim, Nan, Jil. Mgr. guided missile range operations Pan Am. Airlines, 1954-57; mgr. allied communications Europe Internat. Tel.; Tel., 1957-60; mgr. Titan site activation Martin Co., 1960-62; mgr. marine systems and technologies Gen. Electric Co., 1962-67; v.p. Oceans Gen., 1967-70, now dir., sr. research scientist U. Miami Inst. Atmospheric and Ocean Sci., 1967-70; pres. Ocean Marine Products, 1967-70; mgr. environmental systems Sanders & Thomas, Inc., 1970; prof. urban and environmental studies Fla. Internat. U., Miami, 1970—. Cons. Nat. Marine Sci. Commn., 1968-70, Ho. of Reps. Mcht. Marine and Fisheries Com., 1967-70, Senate Commerce Com., 1967-70; mem. Aspen Inst. Humanistic Studies, 1971; mem. Dade County Environmental Action Com., 1970-71; adviser Inter-Am. Inst. Ecology, 1970-71, Miami-Dade Jr. Coll., 1967-71. Served with USN 1940-46. Decorated Air Medal. Mem. Marine Tech. Soc. (chmn. Fla. chpt. 1967-70), Am. Trucking Assns. (asst. gen. council 1951-54), A.A.A.S., Fla., D.C. bars. Home: 9621 SW 62d Ct Miami FL 33156

STOVER, VERGIL G., transp. research exec.; b. Lake Park, Minn., June 7, 1933; s. Vergil D. and Edna (Larsen) S.; B.S., Ohio U., 1958; M.S., Purdue U., 1960, Ph.D., 1963; m. Mary Sue Punkar, Dec. 30, 1955; children—Kenneth, Terrance, Curt. Project engr. Ohio Dept. Hwys., Cleve., 1957-58; prin. investigator Joint Hwy. Research Project, instr. civil engring. Purdue U., Lafayette, Ind., 1958-63; asst. prof. U. S.C., Columbia, 1963-66; program mgr. transp. planning Tex. Transp. Inst., Tex. A. and M. U., College Station, Tex., 1966—, asst. prof., 1966-67, asso. prof., 1967-71, prof., 1971—. Project engr. Wilbur Smith & Assos., Columbia, S.C., 1963-65. Served with inf. AUS, 1951-53. Mem. Inst. Traffic Engrs., Am. Marketing Assn., Hwy. Research Bd., Am. Soc. Planning Ofcls., Sigma Xi. Home: 1017 Holt St College Station TX 77840 Office: Tex Transp Inst Tex A and M U College Station TX 77843

STOVER, WILLIAM REITZEL, educator; b. Waynesboro, Pa., June 8, 1906; s. Harry Edgar and Antoinette (Reitzel) S.; B.S., Temple U., 1938, Ed.M., 1940; Litt. D., Wagner Coll., 1953; m. Anna Mary Miller. June 5, 1928. Prin. Amon Heights and Jr. High Sch., Pennsauken, N.J., 1928-47, supt., 1947-55; supt. Central Regional High Sch. Dist., Bayville, N.J, 1955-58, Mainland Regional High Sch. Dist., Linwood, 1958-64. Ofcl. local congregation Luth. Ch., 1931—, ofcl. N.J. Synod, 1953-64; spl. steward Fla. Synod; instr. Christian edn., 1950—, del. Luth. Ch. Convs., 1952-64; mem. Luth. Laymen's Movement. Troop com. chmn. Boy Scouts Am., 1936-42, mem. bd. review 1941-42; pres. Condominium Assn. and area council, 1970-72; active various civic or charity drives. Bd. dirs. Wagner Coll., Mt. Airy Sem., Phila. Mem. N.E.A. (life), P.T.A. (life), N.J. Edn. Assn. (pres. 1951-53), Nat., N.J. assns. sch. adminstrs., Assn. Ret. Persons (local pres. 1966-68), Phi Delta Kappa. Lutheran. Mason (Shriner). Author: What You Need to Know about Condominiums, 1972. Home: 3272 Southfield Lane Sarasota FL 33580

STOWE, JAMES JUNIOR, advt. agy. exec.; b. Drumright, Okla., Mar. 5, 1921; s. James R. and Myrtle Louise (Pruitt) S.; student U. Md., 1955-60, Hills U., 1961-63; m. Mozel Aleen Staton, Nov. 30, 1940; children—James, Patricia, Pamela. Commd. officer U.S. Army, 1940, advanced through grades to maj., 1960; self-employed Sundries Store, 1960-61; accountant, auditor Ackerman Assos., Oklahoma City, 1963-65, sec.-treas., 1965—. Adviser, Call-A-Teen Summer Youth Employment Program, 1970—, Jr. Achievement Program, 1971—. Decorated Purple Heart with cluster, Silver Star, Bronze Star with cluster. Mem. Am. Accountants Assn. Mason. Home: 5912 Tiffany Circle Oklahoma City OK 73132 Office: 5708 Mosteller Dr Oklahoma City OK 73112

STOWE, ORVILLE HERSCHEL, ret. educator; b. Olney, Tex., Dec., 23, 1903; s. Bruce and Mattie (Rushing) S.; B.S., North Tex. State U., 1934; M.S., Tex. Christian U., 1939; LL.D., Tex. Wesleyan Coll., 1960; m. Willie Mae Watson, Aug. 23, 1933. Tchr. pub. schs., Olney, Tex., 1927-30, Iowa Park, Tex., 1930-31, Valley View (Iowa Park), Tex., 1931-34; tchr. Birdville Pub. Schs., Fort Worth, 1934-36, supt., 1936-42, county sch. supt. 1947-72. Served with USCGR, 1942-45. Mem. Tex. Assn. County Supts. (pres. 1954-55), Am., Tex. assns. sch. adminstrs., Tex. State Tchrs. Assn., Nat. County Supts. Assn., N.E.A. Kiwanian. Home: 5762 Rockhill Fort Worth TX 76112

STRACENER, WILLIAM GUY, clergyman, editor; b. Kipling, La., Dec. 8, 1905; s. William Neal and Olla (Van Brook) S.; student La. State U., 1924-26; D.D. (hon.), Stetson U., 1950; m. Alleyne Reed, July 22, 1928; children—Larry Allen, Gayle Reed. Ordained to ministry Bapt. Ch., 1932; sec. Logger's YMCA, Crossett, Ark., 1928-30, Thomasville, Ga., 1930-33; pastor Friendship Ch., Metcalfe Ga., Pavo (Ga.) Ch., 1932-34, 1st Ch., Arlington, Ga., 1934, Madison, Fla., 1934-38, Riverside Ch., Miami, Fla., 1938-44, E. Hill Ch., Pensacola, Fla., 1944-49; editor Fla. Bapt. Witness, Jacksonville, 1949-70. Pres. Fla. Bapt. Conv., 1970-71. Mem. So. Bapt. Press Assn. (pres. 1959-60). Home: 1348 Edgewood Av Jacksonville FL 32205

STRADER, HUNTER GORDON, JR., physician; b. Burlington, N.C., May 3, 1932; s. Hunter Gordon and Alline Elizabeth (Hay) S.; B.S., Davidson Coll., 1954; M.D., Duke, 1958; m. Helen Haynes, Dec. 18, 1955; children—Hunter Gregg, Richard Haynes, Pamela Lynn. Intern, Moses Cone Meml. Hosp., Greensboro, N.C., 1959-60; resident internal medicine Tulane Med. Service, New Orleans, 1960-61; gen. practice medicine, Lexington, N.C., 1962—; mem. staff Lexington (N.C.) Meml. Hosp., 1962, mem. exec. com., 1963-65. Med. cons. Pitts. Plate Glass, Lexington, 1969—, Henry Link Corp., Lexington, 1971—. Dir. Davidson County Little League. Served to capt. USAF, 1960-62. Mem. A.M.A., Am. Acad. Gen. Practice, So. Med. Assn., N.C. State, Davidson County med. socs., Phi Beta Kappa, Omicron Delta Kappa. Methodist. Kiwanian. Home: 208 Overbrook Dr Lexington NC 27292 Office: 2 Cherry St Lexington NC 27292

STRAIN, DAVID LEROY, bank exec.; b. Washington, Feb. 23, 1921; s. David Leroy and Ethel Lois (Ross) S.; LL.B., U.N.C., 1952; postgrad. Stonier Grad. Sch. Banking, 1958; m. Marian Frances Lance, May 7, 1955; children—Karen J., Susan M. Vice-pres. Nat. Bank Commerce (name now Va. Nat. Bank), Norfolk, Va., 1952-60; sr. v.p. Br. Bank & Trust Co., Wilson, N.C., 1960-62; pres. Charles F. Cates &Sons, Inc., 1962-64; exec. v.p. First Nat. Bank, Norfolk, Va., 1965-70, Peoples Nat. Bank, Greenville, S.C., 1970—; dir. Charles F. Cates & Sons, Inc., Faison, N.C., Asso. Distbrs., Charleston, S.C. Bd. dirs., pres. bd. Tidewater Community Coll., Chesapeake, Va. Served with USAAF, 1941-46. Mem. Newcomen Soc., Phi Delta Phi, Alpha Tau Omega. Baptist. Clubs: Greenville Country, Poinsett. Home: 9 Stonybrook Dr Greenville SC 29607 Office: PO Box 608 Greenville SC 29602

STRAIN, PAULA MARY, librarian; b. Brooke County, W. Va.; d. Paul Russell and Margaret (Evans) Strain; A.B, Bethany Coll., 1937; B.S., Carnegie Inst. Tech., 1938; postgrad. U. Pitts., 1940-41. Asst. librarian Westminster Coll., 1939-40; asst. librarian Carnegie-Ill. Steel Corp., Pitts., 1940-42; librarian, 1942-44; librarian U.S. Naval Photog. Interpretation Center, Washington, 1946-48, liaison and selection officer Library of Congress, 1948-57; sr. research analyst Library of Congress, 1957-60; tech. librarian Electronics Systems Center, IBM, Owego, N.Y., 1960-68; head librarian Booz Allen Applied Research, Inc., Bethesda, Md., 1968-70; mgr. library services MITRE Corp., McLean, Va., 1970—. Served with USNR, 1944-46. Bd. mgrs. Finger Lakes Trail Conf., 1962-68, editor, 1962-67, pres., 1967-68. Mem. Am. Assn. U. Women, Women's Nat. Book Assn., Appalachian Trail Conf., Spl. Libraries Assn. (editor geography and map div. 1962-65, chmn. 1968-69, pres. Upstate N.Y. chpt. 1967-68). Clubs: Potomac Appalachian Trail (pres. 1970-72) Washington); Adirondack Mountain. Author articles various periodicals and jours. Home: 8315 N Brook Bethesda MD 20014 Office: 1820 Dolley Madison Blvd McLean VA 22101

STRAIN, RICHARD EDGAR, physician, educator; b. Perry, Ia., Feb. 22, 1909; s. Robert S. and Katherine (McIntyre) S.; B.A., Maryville Coll., 1931; M.D., Vanderbilt U., 1935; m. Anne Price, Nov. 6, 1938; children—Mary Katherine (Mrs. A.L. King), Robert Sterling, and Richard Edgar Strain. Intern Stanford U. Hosp., San Francisco, 1935-36; asst. resident in surgery Stanford (Cal.) U. Hosps., 1936-37, fellow, asst. resident in neurosurgery Harvard Service, Boston City Hosp., 1946-48, Lahey Clinic, Boston, 1948-49; resident neurosurgery Harvard Service, Boston City Hosp., 1949; practice medicine, specializing in neurosurgery, Coral Gables, Fla., 1949—; med. missionary, Huchow, China, 1937-38, Miraj, India, 1939-42; asst. vis. surgeon Vanderbilt U. Med. Sch., Nashville, 1942-46; mem. Coll. Physicians and Surgeons, Man., Can., 1939; asst. prof. neurosurgery U. Miami, Coral Gables, 1952—, asso. prof., 1958; sr. neurosurgeon Jackson Meml. Hosp., Coral Gables, 1955; mem. staffs Doctors, Varsity Childrens hosps., Coral Gables, 1949, Baptist Hosp., Miami, Fla., 1960, South Miami Hosp., 1960; dir. neuro-physiol. research Eastern State Psychiat. Hosp., Knoxville, Tenn., 1968—; lectr. health edn. U. Tenn., Knoxville, 1968, asst. prof., 1969—. Bd. dirs. East Tenn. Council on Alcohol and Drug Abuse. Served with Chinese Nat. Army, 1938. Diplomate Am. Bd. Neurol. Surgery. Fellow A.C.S.; mem. Harvey Cushing Soc., Congress Neurol. Surgeons, So. Neurosurg. Soc., Southeastern Surg. Soc., Fla. Med. Soc (del. 1958-60), Coral Gables C. of C. (dir. 1959-62). Methodist. Rotarian (pres. 1959-60, dir., pres. Coral Gables 1960-61), Civitan (sec.-treas. Maryville). Contbr. numerous articles med. jours. Author: (with Mayshark, Kirk and Hornsby) Personal Health from the Ecological Perspective, 1972. Home: 1829 Westwood Dr E Maryville TN 37801

STRAKA, EDWARD ANTON, JR., dentist; b. Cicero, Ill., Nov. 3, 1930; s. Edward Anton and Alice Caroline (Nikola) S.; B. Gen. Edn., Morton Jr. Coll., 1950; postgrad. U. Ill., 1950-51; D.D.S., Northwestern U., 1955; m. Carleen Ann Ettinger, Aug. 8, 1953; children—Ann, Sally. Practice dentistry, Sarasota, Fla., 1957-68; pres. Edward A. Straka, D.D.S., Profl. Corp., 1968—. Dir. Marshall Motors Inc., M. M. Land Corp. Pres. Sertoma Speech and Hearing Clinic, 1966-72; mem. Local Govt. Study Commn., Sarasota Charter Commn., 1970-77; pres. Cardinal Mooney High Sch. Club, P.T.A., 1971-72; mem. adv. com. Sarasota County Sch. Bd., 1968-69; v.p. Commence, 1968; mem. finance com. L. D. Pankey Dental Found., 1968—. Bd. dirs. Sarasota Guidance Clinic, Health and Welfare Council. Served to capt., Dental Corps, AUS, 1955-57. Mem. Soc. Oral Physiology and Occlusion, Acad. Electro-Surgery and Dentistry, West Coast Dental Soc. (program chmn. 1970-71), South Gate (dir. 1963-64), Forest Lakes (dir. 1966-69) community assns., Family Motor Coach Assn. (dir. Fla. chpt. 1970-71). Club: Sertoma (pres. 1963-64) (Sarasota). Home: 2920 Pony Lane Sarasota FL 33580 Office: 1851 Arlington St Sarasota FL 33579

STRANAHAN, ROBERT PAUL, JR., lawyer; b. Louisville, Oct. 29, 1929; s. Robert Paul and Anna May (Payne) S.; A.B., Princeton, 1951; LL.B., Harvard, 1954; m. Louise Perry, May 12, 1956; children—Susan Dial, Robert Paul III, Carol Payne. Admitted to D.C. bar, 1954, Md. bar, 1964; practiced in Washington, 1957—; asso. firm Wilmer & Broun, 1957-62; partner, Wilmer, Cutler & Pickering, 1963—. Served to lst lt., USMCR, 1954-57. Mem. Am., Fed. bar assns., Bar Assn. D.C. Clubs: Princeton, Metropolitan (Washington); Chevy Chase (Md.). Home: 5316 Cardinal Ct Washington DC 20016 Office: Farragut Bldg 900 17th St NW Washington DC 20006

STRANSKY, JOHN JANOS, forester; b. Budapest, Hungary, Sept. 2, 1923; s. Janos and Ellionor (Milne) S.; student Poly. Inst., Hungary, 1941-45; B.F., Ludwig Maximilian U., Munich, Germany, 1947; M.F. (Bliss scholar, Fisher fellow), Harvard, 1954; m. Eva Gorgey, June 6, 1947; children—John H., Nicholas B. Came to U.S., 1950, naturalized, 1955. Research asst. Bussey Inst., Harvard, 1954-57; forester div. forest econs. research So. Forest Expt. Sta., U.S. Forest Service, 1957-58, research forester Wildlife Habitat and Silviculture Lab., 1958—, project leader, 1962—; instr. forest game mgmt. Stephan F. Austin State U. Sch. Forestry, Nacogdoches, Tex., 1967—. Mem. Soc. Am. Foresters (group chmn.), Wildlife Soc., Ecol. Soc. Am., Soil Sci. Soc., Internat. Soil Sci. Soc., Am. Soc. Agronomy, Am. Assn. U. Profs., Nat. Rifle Assn., Tex. Forestry Assn. (group chmn.). Contbr. articles to profl. jours. Home: 1533 Redbud St Nacogdoches TX 75961

STRASBURGER, LEROY, wholesale trade exec.; b. Columbia, S.C., Mar. 10, 1922; s. Lafayette and Augusta (Bruggeman) S.; student U. S.C., 1939-40, Mass. Inst. Tech., 1941; B.S., Columbia U., 1947; m. Edith Donaldson, Apr. 17, 1948; children—Carol, Richard, Frank. Marketing trainee Gen. Electric Co., 1947-48; asst. to marketing v.p., dist. sales mgr. Hotpoint Co., Chgo. and Cin., 1948-50; So. regional mgr. NESCO, Atlanta, 1950-52; partner, gen. mgr. L. Strasburger & Sons, wholesale trade, Columbia, S.C., 1952—; Pres. L. Strasburger's Inc., 1958—; chmn. distbr. panel Admiral Corp., 1970-71; adv. bd. Am. Bank and Trust Co. Pres., Columbia Music Festival, 1959-60; pres. Columbia Philharmonic Orch., 1967-68. Served with USMCR, 1942-46. Mem. Columbia C. of C. (dir. 1963-65, v.p. 1964-65). Presbyn. (chmn. bd. deascons 1963-64). Rotarian. Clubs: Palmetto, Spring Valley, Litchfield Columbia Executive (pres. 1966-67). Home: 1621 Adger Rd Columbia SC 29204 Office: 711 Bluff Rd Columbia SC 29201

STRATTON, HENRY DAVIS, lawyer; b. Pikeville, Ky., Aug 9, 1925; s. Pem Burton and Minnie M. (Davis) S.; student Asbury Coll., 1943, Pikeville Coll., 1946-47; LL.B., U. Louisville, 1950; m. Lois Jean Shipley, June 14, 1947; children—David Carey and Daniel Pemberton (twins), Teresa Louise. Admitted to Ky. bar, 1950; practice, Pikeville, Ky., 1950—; v.p., dir. Citizens Bank of Pikeville; pres., dir. Citizens Underwriter; v.p., dir. East Ky. Broadcasting Co.; dir. Campbell County Broadcasting Co., Lawrence County Broadcasting Co., Greater Ky. Broadcasting Co. Mem. Ky. Crime Commn., 1968—. Bd. dirs. Meth. Hosp. Ky., also gen. counsel; regent Eastern Ky. U., 1970—. Served with AUS, 1943-46. Mem. U.S. (dir.), Ky. (v.p.) jr. chambers commerce, Am., Ky. (mem. house dels. 1964-65, gov. 1966—) bar assns., Ky. Hist. Soc., Phi Alpha Delta, Omicron Delta Kappa. Methodist. Mason. Club: Filson; Greenmeadows. Home: 110 Cedar Dr Pikeville KY 41501 Office: 2d St Pikeville KY 41501

STRATTON, JAMES CURTIS, educator; b. Pueblo, Colo., Sept. 12, 1908; s. James P. and Georgia (Curtis) S.; B.A. cum laude, U. Colo., 1931; M.S. in Journalism, Northwestern U., 1940. Instr. English, journalism, publications adviser Pueblo Central High Sch., 1931-39; instr., asst. prof. English, journalism U. Wyo., Laramie, 1940-46; asst., asso. prof. journalism Okla. State U., Stillwater, 1946—, also dir. music ednl. radio sta. KOSU-FM; desk, exec. editor Laramie (Wyo.) Daily Bulletin (arrangement U. Wyo.), 1942-45; fine arts writer, editor Stillwater Daily News-Press, 1946—; broadcaster spl. recorded shows Radio KSPI, Stillwater, 1950—; music editor, program annotator Oklahoma City Symphony Orchestra, 1962—. Mem. Sigma Delta Chi, Pi Gamma Mu, Alpha Tau Omega, Kappa Tau Alpha, Omicron Delta Kappa. Lion. Home: 605B Bennett Stillwater OK 74074

STRAUB, CHARLES, JR., supt. schs.; b. London, Ky., Nov. 20, 1923; s. Charles and Lydia (Cornilus) S.; student Sue Bennet Jr. Coll., London, Ky., 1947-48; A.B., U. Ky., 1951, M.A., 1961, postgrad., 1967; m. Alpha Gill, July 22, 1947; children—Eddie, Tina (Mrs. Cracraft). Tchr. schs., Hancock County, Hawesville, Ky., 1951-53; tchr., coach Union County, Morganfield, Ky., 1953-57; tchr., coach Bourbon County, Paris, Ky., 1957-59; supt. schs. Mason County, Maysville, Ky., 1959—. Pres. Regional Ednl. Service Agy. Bd. dirs. Eastern Ky. Edn. Devel. Coop. Served with AUS, 1943-47. Mem. Am., Ky. (dir.) assns. sch. adminstrs., N.E.A., Ky., Eastern Ky. edn. assns., Phi Delta Kappa. Odd Fellow, Lion. Home: Box 643 Maysville KY 41056 Office: 33d W 3d Maysville KY 41056

STRAUS, R. PETER, broadcasting co. exec., govt. ofcl.; b. N.Y.C., Feb. 15, 1923; s. Nathan and Helen (Sachs) S.; B.A. cum laude, Yale, 1943; m. Ellen Louise Sulzberger, Feb. 6, 1950; children—Diane, Katherine, Jeanne, Eric. Chief sec., manpower div. U.S. Office Mil. Govt., Berlin, Germany, 1946-47; pub. relations exec. Edward L. Bernays, N.Y.C., 1946-48; dir. spl. features radio sta. WMCA, N.Y.C., 1948-50; exec. asst. to dir. gen. ILO, Geneva, Switzerland, 1950-55, dir. U.S. office, 1955-58; pres. Straus Broadcasting Group, 1958—; asst. adminstr. for Africa, AID, 1967—; spl. cons. USIA, 1966, Co-chmn. Interracial Council Bus. Opportunity, N.Y., 1966-67, Com. Constl. Issues, N.Y., 1966-67. Chmn. N.Y. State Democratic Campaign Com., 1964; N.Y. del. Nat. Dem. Convs., 1960, 64. Served to 1st lt. USAAF, 1943-45. Decorated Air medal with 5 oak leaf clusters; recipient award Harlem Lawyers Assn., 1964; New Sch. Social Research fellow, 1965—. Mem. Council Fgn. Relations, Internat. Radio and TV Soc., Young Pres. Orgn., N.Y. State Broadcasters Assn. (pres. 1964). Jewish religion. Mem. B'nai B'rith (exec. com.). Clubs: Federal City, Nat. Press, City Tavern (Washington); Century Country, Yale, Overseas Press (N.Y.C.). Home: 2915 Woodland Dr NW Washington DC 20008 Office: Dept of State Washington DC 20523

STRAUSS, CLIFFORD MARCUS, bank dir.; b. Memphis, Tenn., May 17, 1904; s. Fred and Carrie (Schuster) S.; grad. high sch.; m. Roselyn Lieber, Aug. 5, 1926; children—Jean (Mrs. Saul A. Mintz), Peggy S. (Mrs. James R. Greenbaum). Chmn. bd. Strauss Liquor Corp., Monroe, La., 1926-69, pres., Shreveport, La., 1946-69; pres. Gulf Inland Corp., Houston, 1931-69; chmn. bd. F. Strauss & Son, Inc., Tallulah, La., 1959-69, Strauss Distbrs., Little Rock, 1937-69, F. Strauss & Son, Inc., New Orleans, 1939-69; dir. Peoples Homestead & Savings Assn., Ouachita Nat. Bank. Pres. Wine and Spirits Found. La., 1952-53; developer, operator Eastgate, Northgate shopping centers, Monroe, 1964—. Pres. Ouachita Parish chpt. A.R.C., 1944-45; United Givers Fund, 1958-59; mem. Ration Bd., 1943-44; pres. Pub. Affairs Research 1967-68. Bd. dirs., chmn. bd. Carolyn Rose Strauss Rehab. Center, Monroe; bd. dirs. Council for Better La. Mem. Wine and Spirits Wholesalers Am. (chmn. bd. 1945-46), C. of C. (pres. 1950-51). Jewish religion (pres. 1960-61). Mason (32 deg., Shriner). Clubs: Lotus, Bayou Desiard Country. Home: 3706 Deborah Dr Monroe LA 71201 Office: PO Box 4828 Commerce Av Monroe LA 71201

STRAUSS, MARTIN, photo research and service co. exec.; b. Lelpzig, Germany, July 14, 1923; s. Leopold and Cessy (Gruenstein) S.; grad. The Technion, Haifa, Israel; m. Carolyn K. Futrovsky, May 13, 1956; children—Steven, Evalyn, Beth. Came to U.S., 1947, naturalized, 1953. Pres. Strauss Photo-Tech. Service Inc., Washington, Norfolk, Va.; v.p., dir. So. PTS, Inc., Charlotte, N.C., Jacksonville, St. Petersburg, Orlando, Miami, Fla., 1948—. Mem. exec. bd. Jewish Social Service Agy. Mem. Nat. Assn. Photo Equipment Technicians (pres.), Soc. Photog. Scientists and Engrs., Soc. Photo-Technologists, Soc. Motion Picture and TV Engrs., Master Photo Dealers and Finishers Assn. Jewish religion (dir. synagogue). Mason (33 deg.). Patentee in field. Home: 6005 Durbin Rd Bethesda MD 20034 Office: 1240 Mt Olivet Rd NE Washington DC 20002

STRAUSS, RICHARD CHARLES, real estate exec.; b. Dallas, Aug. 3, 1943; s. Robert S. and Helen (Jacobs) S.; student Parsons Coll., 1963-66; m. Daniele Bagon (div.); 1 dau., Tania. Asso., Henry S. Miller, 1967-68; partner Crawford-Strauss Properties, Dallas, 1968—; dir. Main St. Nat. Bank, Dallas. Mem. law enforcement com. Dallas Greater Community Relations Bd., 1971—. Chmn. Texans for Ben Barnes, Dallas Com., 1970. Served with Tex. Air N.G., 1965. Mem. Apt. Owners and Mgrs. Assn., Dallas Apt. Assn. (dir.), Home and Apt. Builders (state dir.), Nat. Apt. Assn., Asso. Gen. Contractors. Home: 5808 Prestonview Blvd Dallas TX 75247 Office: Crawford-Strauss Bldg 7141 Envoy Ct Dallas TX 75247

STRAUSS, ROBERT PHILIP, educator, govt. ofcl.; b. Cleve., May 11, 1942; s. Harry and Carrie (Axelrod) S.; B.A., U. Mich., 1966; Ph.D., U. Wis., 1970 ; m. Diane Carol Wheeler, Nov. 26, 1969. Fellow, Inst. for Research on Poverty, Madison, Wis., 1968-69; asst. prof. econs. U. N.C., Chapel Hill, 1969—; Brookings econ. policy fellow U.S. Treasury, Washington, 1970-71; spl. asst. to undersec. of treasury, Washington, 1971-72. Mem. Am. Econ. Assn., Econometric Soc., Nat. Tax Assn., Am. Statis. Soc. Home: 1310-1 Ephesus Ch Rd Chapel Hill NC 27514P Office: 3025 Main Treasury 15th and Pennsylvania Av NW Washington DC 20220

STRAYHORN, RALPH N., lawyer; b. Durham, N.C., Feb. 16, 1923; B.S., U. N.C., 1947, LL.B., 1950. Admitted to N.C. bar, Admitted to N.C. bar, 1950; mem. firm Newsom, Graham, Strayhorn, Hedrick & Murray, Durham. Mem. N.C. Ho. of Reps., 1959-60. Served to lt. comdr. USNR, 1943-46. Mem. Am., N.C. (gov. 1960-63, 66-69, pres.-elect 1970-71, pres. 1971-72), Durham County (sec. 1961) bar assns., N.C. State Bar, Phi Delta Phi. Address: Box 2088 Durham NC 27702*

STREAM, LAWRENCE, physician; b. Kansas City, Kan., Mar. 13, 1923; s. Lawrence Peter and Ruth Edith (Wiberg) S.; student U. Kan., 1941-43, Tex. A. and M. U., 1943-44, Baylor U., 1944; M.D., U. Okla., 1949; m. Millicent Anita Marrs, June 11, 1949; 1 son, Lawrence Wyatt. Intern St. Anthony Hosp., Oklahoma City, 1949-50; resident anesthesiology Univ. Hosp., Oklahoma City, 1952-54, mem. teaching staff, 1954-58; practice medicine specializing in anesthesiology, Oklahoma City, 1958—; mem. staff Mercy Hosp., Oklahoma City, Drs. Gen. Hosp., Oklahoma City, Univ. Hosp., Oklahoma City. Served with AUS, 1943-46, 51-52. Decorated Bronze Star medal. Diplomate Am. Bd. Anesthesiology. Mem. A.M.A., Am., Okla. (sec.-treas. 1956-58) socs. anesthesiologists, Okla. State, Okla. County med. socs., Phi Chi, Sigma Phi, Epsilon. Unitarian. Home:

6208 Post Oak Rd Oklahoma City OK 73105 Office: 1411 Classen St Oklahoma City OK 73106

STREET, EDWARD ROBERT, constrn. co. exec.; b. Charlotte, N.C., Nov. 15, 1938; s. Clarence Parke and Ruth Howerton (Wallace) S.; B.S., Davidson Coll., 1959; B.C.E. with highest honor, Ga. Inst. Tech., 1962; m. Jane Linda Brady, Dec. 19, 1959; children—Linda Brady, Margaret Atkinson, Edward Robert V. Engr. McDevitt & Street Co., Charlotte, 1962, project supt., 1963-64, project mgr., 1965-71, asst. sec., 1967-72, pres., 1972-—; asst. sec. C.P. Street Constrn. Co., Charlotte, 1967-72, pres., 1971-—; asst. sec. Parke Constrn. Co., Charlotte, 1967-72, v.p., 1970-72; dir. Charlotte br. Wachovia Bank & Trust Co. Mem. Chi Epsilon, Phi Kappa Phi. Presbyn. Clubs: Charlotte Country, Quail Hollow Country (Charlotte). Home: 4101 Foxcroft Rd Charlotte NC 28211 Office: PO Box 1847 Charlotte NC 28201

STREET, ROBERT DECATUR, ednl. adminstr.; b. Hickory, N.C., May 3, 1934; s. Monroe Garland and Amie Elizabeth (Britain) S.; B.B.A., Wake Forest Coll., 1960; M.Ed., U. N.C., 1967, postgrad. (Research fellow), 1967-—; m. Ann Marie Tillotson, June 12, 1960; children— Stephen Bradley, Sheila Kaye. Dept. mgr. Maas Bros. Dept. Store, St. Petersburg, Fla., 1961-62; tchr., Greensboro, Winston-Salem, Mocksville, N.C., 1963-68; dir. bus. affairs Richmond Tech. Inst., Hamlet, N.C., 1969-—. Served with USNR, 1952-56: ETO. Mem. N.E.A., Am. Vocational Assn., N.C. Assn. Community Coll. Bus. Ofcls., N.C. Assn. Educators. Mason. Club: Civitan (treas. 1970-71) (Rockingham, N.C.). Home: 208 E Temple Av Rockingham NC 28379 Office: PO Box 1189 Hamlet NC 28345

STREET, WALTER NEWBILL, JR., banker; b. Richmond, Va., Mar. 23, 1925; s. Walter Newbill and Laura (Wright) S.; student Hampden-Sydney Coll., 1942-44; B.S., Duke U., 1945; m. Jane Randall Furlong, Apr. 3, 1965; 1 son, Walter Newbill III. Buyer Universal Leaf Tobacco Co., Inc., Richmond, 1946-53; sr. v.p. United Va. Bank/State Planters, Richmond, 1953-68; pres. United Va. Bank/Citizens and Marine, Newport News, Va., 1968-—; dir. Trimmer Lumber Co., Inc., United Va. Bankshares, Inc., Brenco Inc., Smithfield Foods, Inc., Summit Container Corp. Bd. dirs. Riverside Hosp., Newport News, Va. Served with USNR, 1943-46. Mem. Kappa Alpha. Rotarian (dir. 1970-—). Clubs: Country of Virginia, Commonwealth (Richmond); James River Country, Huntington (NewPort News). Home: 7 Merry Lane Newport News VA 23606 Office: 2501 Washington Av Newport News VA 23607

STREIT, MAE HELEN GLASCOCK (MRS. JOHN SAM STREIT), editor; b. Hamilton, Ala., June 27, 1914; d. James Oscar and Lula (Owen) Glascock; grad. pub. schs.; m. John Sam Streit, Aug. 27, 1939 (dec. June 1953); 1 son, Samuel Allen. With Franklin County Times, Russellville, Ala., 1961-—, soc. editor, 1962-63, city editor, 1963-65, editor, 1965-—; corr. Birmingham (Ala.) Post-Herald newspaper, 1962-—. Bd. dirs. Franklin County chpt. A.R.C. Mem. Ch. of Christ. Clubs: Cultura Garden (pres. 1956-57). Home: 408 High St Russellville AL 35653 Office: 142 US 43 Bypass Hwy Russellville AL 35652

STRELAU, CONRAD ANDREW, computer co. exec.; b. Houston, Aug. 15, 1931; s. August Ernest and Florence Elizabeth (Wasson) S.; B.S., Tex. A. and M. U., 1953; m. Carol Catherine Walker, Aug. 3, 1951; children— Gary Dale, Shari Carol, Teri Suzanne, Cathy Marie. Customer engr. IBM Corp., Houston, 1953-58, field mgr., Houston, 1959-61, mgr. customer engring., Beaumont, Tex., 1962, San Antonio, 1963, mgr. personnel planning, White Plains, N.Y., 1964, asst. to pres. field engring. div., 1965-66, area mgr., San Francisco, 1967-68; v.p. field engring. Recognition Equipment, Inc., Dallas, 1969-70, sr. v.p. field operations, 1971, sr. v.p. operations, 1971-—. Presbyn. (deacon 1969). Home: 7206 Desco Dr Dallas TX 75225 Office: PO Box 22307 Dallas TX 75222

STRENCH, DONALD DAVIS, r.r. exec.; b. Ketchikan, Alaska, Mar. 14, 1921; s. William Gotfried and Mary (Minthorne) S.; student U. Hawaii, 1939-41; B.S., W.Va. U., 1944; student advanced mgmt. Northwestern U., 1961; grad. Advanced Mgmt. Program, Harvard, 1962; m. Mary Bibb Lamar, Jan. 14, 1956; children—Donald Davis, William Godfry, Bibb Lamar. With So. Ry. System, Atlanta, 1946-65, gen. mgr., 1962-65; exec. v.p. Atlanta's West Point, Western of Ala., Ga. R.R., Atlanta, 1965-66, pres., 1966-68; gen. mgr. Louisville & Nashville R.R., Louisville, 1968-69, v.p. operations, 1969-—; dir. Louisville Trust Bank, Terminal R.R. St. Louis, Ky. and Ind. Terminal Co. Served ast 1st lt. C.E., AUS, 1944-46. Republican. Episcopalian. Clubs: Hunting Creek Country (Louisville); Pendennis (Louisville). Home: 2910 Glen Hill Circle Louisville KY 40222 Office: 908 W Broadway Louisville KY 40202

STRETCH, DAVID ALBERT, corp. exec.; b. Trenton, N.J., Oct. 12, 1908; s. Albert T. and Ada M. (Rogers) S.; B.S., U.S. Naval Acad., 1930; LL.B., Harvard, 1933; m. Mary Schnitzius Osborn, Dec. 28, 1937. Admitted to Mass. bar, 1934, N.Y. bar, 1935, Tex. bar, 1967; asso. Gaston, Snow, Saltonstall & Hunt, Boston, 1933-34; asso. Simpson, Thacher & Bartlett, N.Y.C., 1934-47, mem. firm, 1947-55; exec. v.p. Atlas Corp., 1956-58, pres., dir., 1958-59, pres., chief exec. officer, 1960-65; dir. Northeast Airlines, Inc.; dir., chmn. exec. com. Tex. Industries, Inc., 1965-—; hon. dir. Ritter Pfaudler Corp. Chmn. Validation Bd. German Dollar Bonds U.S., 1953-65; chmn. Tribunal for Austrian Dollar Bonds, 1957. Vice pres. No. Tex. chpt. Arthritis Found., 1970-—, pres. Dallas Symphony Assn. 1968-71, chmn. bd., 1971-—. Trustee Naval Acad. Found., Pub. TV Found. No. Tex. Served with USNR, 1940-45, comdr. ret. Mem. Am., Dallas bar assns., Assn. Bar City N.Y., S.R., Naval Order U.S., Navy League. Clubs: Lotos, Recess (N.Y.C.); Storm King Golf (Cornwall N.Y.); Brook Hollow Golf (Dallas); National Aviation (Washington); LaQuinta (Cal.) Country. Home: 4819 Walnut Hill Lane Dallas TX 75229 Office: 8100 Carpenter Freeway Dallas TX 75247

STRICKLAND, ALLEN MCGILL (MRS. GEORGE M. STRICKLAND), artist; b. Washington; d. I. J. Nota and Frances M. (Maloy) McGill; student pvt. schs.; m. George Marion Strickland, Nov. 11, 1947. Salon in Paris Artistes Francais, 1924-—; one-man show at Daytona Beach (Fla.) Art League, 1956, Cinema Theatre Gallery, Daytona Beach, 1969; 2-man show Daytona Beach Art League, 1972; represented in pvt. collections in U.S. and France. Recipient numerous prizes Daytona Beach Art League, local br. League Am. Pen Women, 1950-—. Mem. Nat. League Am. Pen Women (pres. Daytona Beach br.), Fla. Fedn. Art, Daytona Beach Art League, St. Augustine Art Assn., Garden Club Am. (pres. Halifax County). Home: 487 John Anderson Hwy Ormond Beach FL 32074

STRICKLAND, GLEN HARROLL, accountant; b. Russellville, Ala., July 16, 1938; s. Dewey Gortez and Estelle (Greenhill) S.; B.S. in Math. and Accounting, Florence State U., 1956-60; m. Barbara Jane Epperson, May 21, 1958; children—Donna Jane, Cynthia Dianne. With McCarty, Dudley, Hopton-Jones, Sims & Freeman, C.P.A.'s. Birmingham, Ala., 1960-64; individual practice accounting Russellville, 1964-—, Haleyville, Ala., 1969-—. Instr. night sch. N.W. Ala. State Jr. Coll., Phil Campbell, Ala., 1964-—. Mem. adv. bd. trustees N.W. Ala. State Jr. Coll., 1968-—, also mem. scholarship com., 1968-—; mem. profl. adv. council Home Health Agy. Franklin County, 1968-—. Muscle Shoals (Ala.) Council Local Govts. comprehensive health planning com., 1970-—. Mem. City Council Russellville, 1968-—, chmn. pro-tem., 1968-—. C.P.A., Ala. Mem. Am. Inst. C.P.A.'s, Ala. Soc. C.P.A.'s (past vice chmn. North Ala. chpt.; mem. edn., continuity of practice coms.), Russellville Jr. C. of C. (dir. 1968-69). Russellville C. of C. Mem. Ch. Christ (deacon) Club: Twin Pines Country (dir., sec.). Home: Woodlands Hills Russellville AL 35653 Office: 510 St Clair St SE Russellville AL 35653

STRICKLAND, J.W., broadcasting exec. Gen. mgr. WJAX, Jacksonville, Fla. Office: 1 Broadcast Pl PO Box 1740 Jacksonville FL 32201*

STRICKLAND, MAURICE ALEXANDER, physician; b. Moultrie, Ga., Sept. 25, 1910; s. Matthew Lee and Mary (Nesbitt) S.; B.S., U. Ga., 1935; M.A., N.Y.U., 1936; Ph.D., 1939; M.D., Emory U., 1948; m. Irma Surovy, Mar. 5, 1938 (dec. Mar. 1970); children—Daniel Matthew, Maurice Henry, John Arthur. Grad. asst. econs. dept. N.Y.U., N.Y.C., 1937-39; instr. Coll. Engring., U. N.C. at Raleigh, 1939-40; asso. prof. Ga. Inst. Tech., Atlanta, 1940-43; intern U.S. Marine Hosp., Stapleton, N.Y., 1948-49; resident surgery Atlanta VA Hosp., 1949-50; asst. resident surgery Nassau Hosp., N.Y.C., 1951-52; sr. resident surgery Jefferson Hosp., Detroit, 1952-53; sr. resident surgery Buffalo VA Hosp., 1954-55; staff surgeon Bay Pines (Fla.) VA Hosp., 1955-56; staff surgeon Columbia (S.C.) VA Hosp., 1956-57; practice medicine specializing in surgery, Atlanta, 1957-60, Laredo, Tex., 1957-60; resident and matriculate in cancer and dermatology N.Y.U., Pastgrad. Hosp. and Bellevue Hosp., N.Y.C., 1960-62; practice medicine specializing in dermatology and cancer surgery, Bakersfield, Cal., 1963-64, Houston, 1965-—; staff mem. dermatology skin cancer surgery sect. Meml. Hosp. Houston, Meml. Bapt. Hosp. S.W., Bellaire Gen. Hosp., Sharptown Gen. Hosp., attending physician Houston Social Hygiene Clinic; staff mem. Ben Taub Gen. Hosp., Houston; instr. dermatology Baylor U. Med. Sch. Surgeon and commd. officer USPHS, Hosp., Tuba City, Ariz., 1953. Fellow A.C.S., Am. Geriatric Soc., Societas Internat. Dermat. Tropicae; mem. Am., So., Tex. med. assns., Harris County Med. Soc., Harris County Acad. Medicine, Acad. of Dermatology (asso.), Houston Dermatol. Sco., Pub. Health League, Bellaire C. of C., Beta Gamma Sigma, Delta Mu Delta. Rotarian. Home: 6801 Bellaire Blvd Houston TX 77036 Office: 6441 High Star Houston TX 77036

STRICKLAND, ROBERT LOUIS, retail co. exec.; b. Florence, S.C., Mar. 3, 1931; s. Franz M. and Hazel (Eaddy) S.; A.B., U. N.C., 1952; M.B.A. with distinction, Harvard, 1957; m. Elizabeth Ann Miller, Feb. 2, 1952; children—Cynthia Ann, Robert Edson. Advt. mgr. Lowe's Cos., Inc., North Wilkesboro, N.C., 1957-58, operations mgr., 1958-60, marketing mgr., 1960-61, dir. marketing, 1961-69, v.p. marketing, 1969-70, sr. v.p., 1970-—, mem. exec. com., dir., 1961-—; founder Sterling Advt., Ltd., 1966. Vice pres., mem. adminstrv. com. Lowe's Profit-Sharing Trust, 1961-—. Mem. N.C. Ho. of Reps., 1962-64; mem. Republican exec. com. N.C., 1963-—. Trustee, Sec. bd., Mem. personnel Com. Wilkes Community Coll., bd. dirs. Nat. Home Improvement Council. Served with USNR, 1952-55; lt. Res., 1955-62. Named Wilkes County Young Man of Yr., Wilkes Jr. C. of C., 1962, Retailer of Year, 1971; recipient Bronze Oscar of industry award, 1969, 70, 71, Silver Oscar of Industry award, 1970 (all Financial World), certificate of Distinction, Brand Names Found., 1970, Distinguished Merchant award, 1972. Mem. Newcomen Soc., Scabbard and Blade, Phi Beta Kappa, Pi Kappa Alpha. Presbyn. Elk, Kiwanian (sec. 1961-63). Club: Oakwoods Country (Wilkesboro); Roaring (N.C.) Gap Author: Lowe's, a Cybernetwork, 1969; Lowe's a Living Legend, 1970; Ten Years of Growth, 1971. Home: 226 N Stratford Rd Winston-Salem NC 27104 Office: Box 111 North Wilkesboro NC 28659

STRICKLAND, ROY ELKINS, JR., dentist; b. Louisville, Mar. 1, 1941; s. Roy Elkins and Billie Preditta (Whitfield) S.; student Clemson U., 1962; D.D.S., Med. Coll. Va., 1966; m. Rebecca Bowen, Aug. 15, 1964; 1dau., Dana Laine. Practice dentistry, Greenville, S.C., 1968-—. Served with USAF, 1966-68. Mem. Am. Dental Assn., U.S. Lawn Tennis Assn., Aircraft Owners and Pilots Assn., Greenville County (mem. membership com. 1970-71), Piedmont Dist. dental socs., Clemson U. Alumni Assn., Delta Kappa Alpha. Baptist. Clubs: Sertoma (receptionist 1970-—), Furman Racquet (Greenville, S.C.). Home: 6 Yancey Dr Greenville SC 29607 Office: 14 Rushmore Dr Greenville SC 29607

STRICKLAND, WILLIAM EDWARD, dairy exec.; b. Fayetteville, N.C., July 31, 1929; s. Edward Lee and Catherine (Johnson) S.; A.A., U. N.C., 1955; m. Harriet Gallup, Dec. 18, 1953; children—Harriet Allison, Susanne Lee, William Edward. With Sealtest Foods div. Kraftco Corp., 1954-—, dist. gen. mgr., Wilson, N.C., 1968-—. Bd. dirs. United Fund Wilson County (N.C.); bd. dirs., mem. exec. com. N.C. Dairy Found., 1968-—. Served to 1st lt. AUS, 1950-53. Decorated Bronze Star medal. Mem. So. Assn. Dairy Food Mfrs. (dir. N.C. chpt.), N.C. Dairy Products Assn., Sales and Marketing Execs. (pres. 1968-69), Fabulous Fishermen (pres. 1960-61). Rotarian (pres. 1969-70). Elk. Club: Wilson Country (dir.). Home: 1010 Ensworth Rd Wilson NC 27893 Office: 200 N Railroad St Wilson NC 27894

STRICKLER, WOODROW MANN, educator, univ. ofcl.; b. Columbia, Pa., Sept. 8, 1912; s. Simon Frey and Ethel (Mann) S.; B.S., Bucknell U., 1934; Ped.D., 1956; M.B.A., U. Pa., 1934-35; postgrad. Northwestern U., 1935-38; m. Florence Gertrude MacLeod, Dec. 21, 1938. Research asst. Ill. Commerce Commn., Chgo., 1935; asst. dept. bus. orgn. and indsl. mgmt. Northwestern U., 1937-38; cons. Lord and Thomas, advt., Chgo., 1937-38; pub. utility cons., Harrisburg, Pa., Chgo., Louisville, 1937-43; instr. econs. U. Louisville, 1938, asst. prof., 1939-42, asso. prof., 1942-54, prof., 1954-—, dir. dept. coop. edn., 1942-43, dir. summer sch., acting dean Coll. Arts and Scis., 1946, dir. div. adult edn., 1946-51, v.p., 1951-58, exec. v.p., 1958-68, pres., 1968-—, Mem. adv. com. econs. and bus. adminstrn. Bucknell U., 1960-—; dir. Center for Study Liberal Edn. for Adults, Chgo., 1951-56; v.p. So. U. Conf., 1962-63. Bd. dirs. Citizens Municipal Planning Council, Red Cross Hosp., Lions Eye Found. of Ky., Ky. Opera Assn., Louisville Orch., Ky. region Conf. Christians and Jews. Served as lt. USNR, 1943-46. Mem. So. Econ. Assn., N.E.A., Louisville C. of C. (dir.), Louisville Advt. Club. Louisville Better Bus. Bur. (dir.), Louisville Credit Men's Assn. (dir.), Newcomen Soc. N.Am., Omicron Delta Kappa, Delta Mu Delta, Kappa Delta Pi, Phi Kappa Phi, Delta Alpha Epsilon, Alpha Pi Omega, Sigma Alpha Epsilon. Lion (dir. Louisville). Contbr. articles to profl. publs. Home: 91 Valley Rd Louisville KY 40204

STRIEF, HARRY JOSEPH, JR., real estate exec.; b. Sioux City, Ia., Mar. 8, 1916; s. Harry Joseph and Mable Edna (Rabdau) S.; B.A. in Journalism, So. Meth. U., 1938; postgrad. Northwestern U., 1938-39; m. Doreen Elisa Mawson, Oct. 30, 1943; 1 son, Paul Arthur. Corr., U.P., Rio de Janeiro, Brazil, Buenos Aires, Argentina, 1939-41; with M.I., Office of Mil. Attache, Am. embassy, Buenos Aires and Washington, 1941-44; partner Sitco Lumber Co., Dallas, 1946-47; owner The Strief Co., Dallas, 1954-—; partner Strief Enterprises, Dallas, 1954-—; pres. Wichita Investment Co., Dallas, 1954-—; vice pres. Boston Realty Co., Dallas, 1954-68. Pres., Greenway Parks Home Owners Assn., 1956-57. Served with AUS, 1944-46. Mem. Nat. Assn. Real Estate Bds., Inst. Real Estate Mgmt., (pres. Dallas-Ft. Worth chpt. 1963-64), Internat. Council Shopping Centers, Nat. Inst. Real Estate Brokers, Tex. Real Estate Assn., Sertoma Internat. (pres. Dallas 1951-52; life), Internat. Trade Assn. Dallas (charter mem., pres. 1954), Dallas Real Estate Bd. (dir. 1958-59), Dallas C. of C. (dir. 1960-62). Clubs: Athletic, Country, Dallas, Chaparral, Petit, Trader Vics (Dallas). Home: 5515 Montrose Dallas TX 75209 Office: Republic Bank Tower Dallas TX 75201

STRINGER, ELLIS ARNOLD, librarian; b. Florien, La., Feb. 6, 1914; s. Silas Deane and Sarah Vilona (Arnold) S.; B.A., La. Coll., 1936; B.L.S., La. State U., 1941; B.D., New Orleans Bapt. Theol. Sem., 1950; m. Mary Lois Irby, Aug. 29, 1948; children—Mary (Mrs. William Pierce McKeithen), Letitia Rose. Ordained to ministry Bapt. Ch., 1948; pastor Bapt. Chs., Sandy Hook, Miss., 1948-50, Holden, La., 1950-52, Deerford, La., 1952-57, Sicily Island, La., 1957-59, Jonesville, La., 1960-—; adminstrv. librarian Catahoula Parish Libraries, 1959-—; tchr. Madisonville Jr. High Sch., St. Tammany Parish, La., 1938-40; prin. Tunica Jr. High Sch., West Feliciana Parish, 1941-42. Served with AUS, 1942-46. Mem. La. Library Assn., Pi Gamma Mu. Democrat. Home: 1302 N Park St Jonesville LA 71343 Office: PO Box 218 Harrisonburg LA 71340

STRINGER, JAY BUCKINGHAM, lawyer; b. Hopedale, O., Nov. 17, 1914; s. Jesse Hall and Mina (Buckingham) S.; A.B., Washington and Jefferson Coll., 1937; student Ohio State U., 1935-36; LL.B., John Marshall Law Sch., 1947; m. Dorothy Polders, May 18, 1946; children—John B., Mary Ann. Admitted to Ill. bar, 1947, Fla. bar, 1966, Tenn. bar, 1968; practiced law offices Wyatt Jacobs, Chgo., 1947-48, Jay B. Stringer, Mt. Vernon, Ill., 1948-68; partner Noone and Stringer, Chattanooga, 1968-—; gen. counsel Lincoln Heritage Life Ins. Co. Pub. defender, 1952-60; states atty., 1960-64; chmn. Jefferson County Republican Com., 1958-60. Served with inf. AUS, 1941-46. Decorated Purple Heart. Mem. Tenn., Ill., Hamilton County bar assns., Fla. Bar, Soc. Trial Lawyers, D.A.V. Elk, Moose. Club: Lookout Mountain Fairyland. Home: 116 Fleetwood Dr Lookout Mountain TN 37350 Office: 817 Broad St Chattanooga TN 37402

STRINGER, LEWIS ELDEAN, lawyer; b. Sayre, Okla., June 22, 1936; s. Rex Herman and Bessie (Morris) S.; B.A., Okla. State U., 1958; LL.B., Harvard, 1961; m. Carol Ann Woodson, Aug. 31, 1963; children—Craig Woodson, Laura DeAnn. Admitted to Okla. bar, 1961; asso. Crowe, Dunlevy, Thweatt, Swinford, Johnson & Burdick, Oklahoma City, 1961-68, partner, 1968-—. Mem. chmn.'s club Oklahoma County Democratic Party, 1969-—; chmn. task force on changes in forma party structure Oklahoma County Dem. Central Com., 1969-—. Served with AUS, 1961. Mem. Okla. State U. Alumni Assn. (pres. Oklahoma County 1964-66, dir. 1964-—, v.p. 1971-72, pres. 1972-—), Young Lawyers Conf. Oklahoma County (pres. 1965), Oklahoma County Bar Assn. (treas. 1967), Harvard Law Sch. Assn. (pres. Okla. 1969, 71, nat. v.p. 1971-—), Am., Okla., Oklahoma County bar assns., Okla. Assn. Def. Counsel, Nat. Guard Assn. U.S., Nat. Guard Assn. Okla. Methodist (adminstrv. bd. 1969-71, mem. finance commn. 1969-70). Home: 442 NW 18th St Oklahoma City OK 73103 Office: Liberty Tower Oklahoma City OK 73102

STRINGFELLOW, SAM PRICE, JR., newspaperman; b. Jefferson, Tex., Mar. 30, 1914; s. Sam Price and Mary Lea (Freeman) S.; A.A., E. Tex. Bapt. Coll., 1934; B.A., Baylor U., 1936; postgrad. N. Tex. State Tchrs. Coll., 1936, Syracue U., 1936; m. Judy Burbage Weidman, June 2, 1954; step-children—Julie (Mrs. J. Stewart Gent), Jon Howard Weidman. Reporter The Herald, Syracuse, N.Y., 1937; reporter Daily News, Galveston, Tex., 1937-39, state editor, 1939-41; courthouse reporter Times Herald, Dallas, 1941; reporter News Messenger, Marshall, 1945-50, city editor, 1950-51, co-mng. editor, 1951-55; news dir. radio station KMHT, 1955-64; corr. The Times, Shreveport, La., 1954-64, asst. city editor, 1964-68, city editor, 1968-70, night city editor, pub. relations rep., 1970-—; A.P. corr., Dallas, 1945-64, New Orleans, 1968-—. Served with AUS, 1941-45. Decorated Bronze Star medal. Mem. Am. Legion, Sigma Delta Chi. Methodist. Kiwanian (pres.). Clubs: Shreveport Press; Capitol Correspondents (Baton Rouge). Home: 3943 Balcom St Shreveport LA 71109 Office: Shreveport Times PO Box 222 Shreveport LA 71130

STRINGFIELD, HEZZ, JR., corp. and financial co. exec.; b. Heiskell, Tenn., Oct. 4, 1921; s. Hezz and Cecil Willie (Williams) S.; grad. bus. adminstrn. Draughon Coll., 1939; student finance and bus. U. Tenn.; m. Helen Louise Hinton, Mar. 20, 1939; children—Carolyn Mae Jolce (Mrs. James M. Corum), Don Wayne, Gail Louise (Mrs. Peter Eric Swersky), June. Finance and bus. adminstrn. exec. Clinton Engring. Works, E.I. duPont de Nemours & Co., 1943-44, Manhattan Dist. metall. project, U. Chgo., 1944-45, Monsanto Chem. Co., 1945-48, nuclear div. Union Carbide Corp., Oak Ridge Nat. Lab., 1948-—; ind. bldg. contractor, real estate developer, 1946-56; cons. gen. bus., real estate financing, 1946-—; mgmt. cons. mission to Middle East, Gen. Treaty Orgn., 1965; dir. Film Badge Fabricators, Inc. Bd. dirs. Found. Mgmt. Edn., Advanced Mgmt. Corp., Council Internat. Progress in mgmt., 1964-67, Found. Internat. Progress in Mgmt., 1964-67; mem. Adv. Council Univs. and Colls. Comdr. USCG Aux., 1962-63. Registered pub. accountant, Tenn. Fellow Soc. Advancement Mgmt. (Profl. Mgr. citation 1963; v.p. 1958-62; exec. v.p. 1962-63; pres. 1963-64; chmn. bd. 1964-65); mem. Am. Mgmt. Assn., Am. Inst. Accountants, Soc. for Advancement Mgmt. (top mgmt. adv. council 1972-—). Methodist. Contbr. articles to profl. jours. Home: 5000 Trent Lane Route 6 Concord TN 37720 Office: PO Box X Oak Ridge TN 37919

STROBEL, JOSEPH JULIUS, chem. engr., govt. ofcl.; b. Washington, Mar. 12, 1914; s. Luther W. and Martha A. (Nichols) S.; B.S. in Chem. Engring,, Va. Poly. Inst., 1935; m. Evelyn G. Fraley, Aug. 9, 1947; children—Russell A., Gene L. Chem. engr. Dow Chem. Co., Midland, Mich., 1936-42; chem. engr. C.W.S., Washington, 1946; chemist, chem. engr., sr. project engr. Naval Ordnance Lab., White Oak, Md., 1947-52; chem. engr. Office Saline Water, U.S. Dept. Interior, Washington, 1952-—, chief div. Processes devel., 1959-65, chief program analysis and coordinating staff, 1965-67, chief desalting feasibility and econs. studies staff, 1967-72, asso. dir., 1972-—. Served to maj. AUS, 1942-46; ETO. Registered profl. engr., D.C. Mem. Am. Chem. Soc., Am. Inst. Chem. Engrs., Soc. Plastics Engrs., Soc. Am. Magicians. Research on cellulose ethers, plastics applications, fresh water from salt water‡

STRODE, WILLIAM HALL, III, photojournalist; b. Louisville, Aug. 6, 1937; s. William Hall and Margaret (Diehls) S.; B.S., Western Ky. U., 1959; m. Elizabeth Ann Wheeler, Nov. 26, 1960; children—Alissa Michelle, Erin. News photographer Courier Jour. and Louisville Times, 1960-64, mag. photographer, 1964-67, asst. dir. photography, 1967-—; exhbns. include Fine Arts III, 1961, Profile in Poverty, Smithsonian Instn., 1966, J.B. Speed Art Mus., Louisville. Active local Boy Scouts Am. Served with AUS, 1959. Recipient Headliners best photojournalism award, 1965; citation of excellence for best mag. photog. reporting Overseas Press Club, 1967; Herald award Western Ky. U., 1967; named one of 10 outstanding young men Louisville Jr. C. of C., 1966. Mem. Nat. Press Photographers Assn. (Photographer of Yr. award 1966; nat. ednl. chmn. 1966-68, named picture editor of yr. 1968), Sigma Chi, Sigma Delta Chi, Kappa Alpha

Mu. Methodist. Home: 9411 Tiverton Ct Louisville KY 40222 Office: Courier Jour 6th and Broadway Louisville KY 40202

STROM, J.P., state ofcl. Chief, Law Enforcement div. State of S.C. Office: 1515 Elm Abode Terrace Columbia SC 29210*

STROMAN, JOSH HAMPTON, librarian; b. Ardmore, Okla., Oct. 11, 1938; s. Ewing Melvin and Velma Katharine (Foster) S.; B.A., Okla. State U., 1960; M.L.S., U. Okla., 1964. Jr. documents librarian Okla. State U., Stillwater, 1964-67, sr. documents librarian, 1967-72, head documents librarian, 1972—. Participant, Inst. on Govt. Publs., U.S. Office End., Emory U., 1969. Mem. A.L.A., Okla. Library Assn. (editor quar. jour. 1967-69). Home: 1002 E Virginia Stillwater OK 74074 Office: Okla State U Library Stillwater OK 74074

STRONG, ANNIE D. SINGFIELD (MRS LEONARD V. STRONG), social worker; b. Augusta, Ga.; d. Archie E. and Della (Ayers) Singfield; B.A. cum laude, Paine Coll., 1930; grad. Atlanta U. Sch. Social Work, 1940; m. Leonard V. Strong, Aug. 19, 1948. Tchr., Duplin County Tng. Sch., Faison, N.C., 1930-38; child welfare worker Five Points House, N.Y.C., 1940-42, Anson County Dept. Pub. Welfare, Wadesboro, N.C., 1942-46; social worker VA Hosp., Nat. Assn. Social Workers, Am. Acad. Certified Social Workers, Ala. Conf. Social Work. Home: PO Box 314 Tuskegee Institute AL 36088 Office: VA Hosp Tuskegee AL 36083

STRONG, FRANK RANSOM, educator; b. Lawrence, Kan., Apr. 4, 1908; s. Frank and Mary Evelyn (Ransom) S.; B.A., Yale, 1929, J.D., 1934; m. Gertrude Elizabeth Way, Aug. 31, 1929; children—John William, Mary Elizabeth (Mrs. Lawrence J. Brennan). Instr. econs. U. Del., 1929-31; instr., asst. prof. law U. Ia., 1934-37; asst. prof., asso. prof., prof. law Ohio State U., 1937-65, dean, 1952-65; prof. law U. N.C., Chapel Hill, 1965—, Cary C. Boshamer Distinguished prof., 1970—, vis. asso. prof. law Duke, 1940-41; J. DuPratt White prof. law Cornell U., 1963; faculty, orientation program in Am. law Princeton, 1966-67, seminar chmn., 1967; dir. law teaching clinics Assn. Am. Law Schs., 1968—. Mem. faculty Salzburg Seminar Am. Studies, 1959. Chmn. bd. trustees Ohio Legal Center Found., 1961-65. Recipient Distingusihed Service award Ohio State U., 1956, fellows award Ohio Bar Assn. Found., 1964. Mem. Assn. Am. Law Schs. (pres. 1960), Order of Coif (nat. sec.-treas. 1970—), Phi Beta Kappa. Independent. Home: 211 Markham Dr Chapel Hill NC 27514

STRONG, JACK PERRY, physician, educator; b. Birmingham, Ala., Apr. 27, 1928; s. Larkin B. and Mary Louise (Perry) S.; B.S., U. Ala., 1948; M.D., La. State U., 1951; m. Patricia Powers, Jan. 26, 1951; children—Mary Louise, Margaret Patricia, Martha Jane, Maury Elizabeth. Rotating intern Jefferson Hillman Hosp., Birmingham, Ala., 1951-52; asst. dept. pathology La. State U. Sch. Medicine, New Orleans, 1952-53, instr., 1955-57, asst. prof., 1957-60, asso. prof., 1960-64, prof. pathology, 1964—, chmn. dept. pathology, 1966—. Cons. Pathology Southwest Found. Research and Edn., 1954-55; sabbatical with Social Medicine Research unit Med. Research Council, London, Eng., 1962-63; assisting vis. pathologist Charity Hosp. La., New Orleans, 1952-53, 55-58, vis. pathologist, 1958-66, sr. vis. pathologist, pathologist-in-chief La. State U. div., 1966—; with pathology A study sect. USPHS, 1965-69, chmn., 1967-69. Mem. epidemiology and biometry adv. com. NIH, 1971—; mem. sci. adv. bd. cons. Armed Forces Inst. Pathology, 1971—. Vice pres. Jefferson Com. Better Schs., Metairie, La., 1964. Served to capt. USAF, 1953-55. Recipient Research Career Devel. award USPHS, 1962-64. Sr. research fellow USPHS, 1957-62. Diplomate Am. Bd. Pathology. Mem. Coll. Am. Pathologists, Am. Assn. Pathologists and Bacteriologists, Am. Soc. Exptl. Pathology, Internat. Acad. Pathology (mem. council 1968-71), Am. Soc. Clin. Pathologists, Am. Assn. Chmn. Med. Schs. Depts. Pathology (v.p. 1969, pres. 1970), Internat. Soc. Cardiology (mem. sect. epidemiology and prevention), La. (research com. 1960—, dir. 1967), Am. (fellow councils arteriosclerosis and epidemiology, mem. pathology research com. 1969—) heart assns., Phi Beta Kappa, Alpha Omega Alpha, Phi Kappa Phi, Sigma Chi. Methodist. Contbr. articles publs. Home: 4117 Cleveland Pl Metairie LA 70003 Office: 1542 Tulane Av New Orleans LA 70112

STRONG, MARLIN JEROME, physician, educator; b. Saginaw, Mich., Aug. 17, 1929; s. Marlin Bertram and Helen May (Tefft) S.; A.B., Calvin Coll., 1951; M.D., Boston U., 1956. Intern, U. Mich., 1956-57; resident anesthesiology Hosp. U. Pa., 1957-60; asst. anesthesiology U. Pa., 1960-63; instr. anesthesiology Baylor U. Coll. Medicine, Houston, 1963-64, asst. prof., 1964-68, asso. prof., 1968—; mem. staffs St. Luke's, Tex. Childrens, Meth., Ben Taub, Jefferson Davis hosps. (all Houston). Served to capt. M.C., AUS, 1960-62. Diplomate Am. Bd. Anesthesiology. Fellow Am. Soc. Pediatrics, Am. Soc. Anesthesiologists. Home: 3614 Montrose St Houston TX 77006 Office: Baylor Coll Medicine Houston TX 77025

STRONG, ROGER WILLIAM, violinist, educator; b. Cedar Rapids, Ia., Mar. 14, 1937; s. J.R. and Wilma (Back) S.; Mus.B., Oklahoma City U., 1960; M.Mus. Edn., U. So. Cal., 1963; D.Mus. Edn., U. Okla., 1968; m. Ruth Ann Taylor, Aug. 22, 1958; children—David William, Carol Kay. First violinist Oklahoma City Symphony, 1956-60, 68-69; instrumental music instr. Oklahoma City Schs., 1960; dist. tchr. string instrument activities Bethany (Okla.) Nazarene Coll., 1964-71; prof. violin and viola Central State U., Edmond, Okla., 1971—, also dir. Univ. Symphony Orch. Dir. music Westgate, Oklahoma City, 1961-62, Burbank First Ch. of Nazarene, 1963-64, trustee, 1963-64; founder Bethany Youth and String Orchs. Suzuki Inst. scholar Eastman Sch. Music, 1966. Mem. Am. String Tchrs. Assn., Music Educators Nat. Conf. Home: 3104 Grant St Bethany OK 73008 Office: Central State Univ Edmond OK 73034

STROTHER, DORA DOUGHERTY (MRS. LESTER J. STROTHER), aviation psychologist, pilot; b. St. Paul, Nov. 27, 1921; d. John Maynard and Esther Lucile (Wardle) Dougherty; A.A., Cottey Coll., Nevada, Mo., 1941; Ph.B., Northwestern U., 1949; M.S., U. Ill., 1953; Ph.D., N.Y. U., 1955; m. Lester J. Strother. Flight instr., ferry pilot airports in N.Y. and Ill., 1944-49; flight instr. Inst. Aviation, U. Ill., 1949-50, research pilot, research asso. Aviation Psychology Lab., 1950-54, 56-57; human engring. specialist Martin Co., Balt., 1957-58; human factors engr. Bell Helicopter Co. Ft. Worth, 1958-62, chief human factors group, 1962—; holder feminine world record altitude in rotorcraft, 1961-66, feminine world record point-to-point distance in rotorcraft, 1961-66; v.p., asst. treas. Tex. Met. Publs., Inc. Adv. council Tex. Aero. Comm., 1963-64; mem. gen. aviation safety com. Nat. Safety Council; judge Internat. Sci. Fair, Dallas, 1966; chmn. women's adv. com. on aviation FAA. Panel mem. Coll. Town Hall Programs, 1962. Chmn. bd. trustees Amelia Earhart Meml. Scholarship Fund of Ninety-Nines. Served as pilot WASP, USAAC, 1943-44; lt. col. Res. Recipient Achievement award N.Y.U., 1955, Amelia Earhart award Am. Women's Assn., 1957, Alumni award Cottey Coll., 1957, Recognition certificate Ft. Worth C. of C., 1961, Lady Hay Drummond-Hay trophy Women's Internat. Assn. Aeros., 1961, Aviation Woman of Year award Women's Nat. Aviation Assn., 1961; Achievement award, Am. Assn. U. Women, 1966, 67; merit award Northwestern U. Alumni Assn. Fellow Human Factors Soc. Am. (editorial bd. jour.), asso. fellow Am. Inst. Aeros. and Astronautics (tech. judge student papers 1961—, mem. tech. com. on life scis. and systems 1970—,; mem. Am., Southwestern, Tex., Tarrant County (pres.) psychol. assns., Assn. Aviation Psychologists (pres.), Am. Helicopter Soc., Assn. U.S. Army, Soc. Engring. Psychologists, Soaring Soc. Am., Tex. Soaring Assn., 99s (chmn. Ft. Worth), P.E.O., Whirley-Girls. Episcopalian. Mem. Order Eastern Star. Contbr. numerous articles, papers in field. Editor: Tex. Metro mag. Home: 3616 Landy Lane Fort Worth TX 76118 Office: Bell Helicopter Co Fort Worth TX 76101

STROTHER, HAZEL B., accountant; b. Akron, O., June 29, 1929; d. Lawrence McCauley and Josei (Friend) Beall; student West Va. Wesleyan Coll., 1947-49; A.A., George Washington U., 1951, A.B.; m. Samuel L. Strother, Oct. 23, 1953 (div. Feb. 1971). Sec., jr. accountant C. B. Stovall & Co., Washington, 1951-52; sec., ins. underwriter Washington Ins. Agy., Inc., 1952-57; accountant U.S. AEC, 1957-62; accountant, asst. chief, accounting and analysis br. Hdqrs. Marine Corps, Washington, 1962-66; staff accountant Hdqrs. NASA, Washington, 1966-68; staff accountant Hdqrs. Dept. Health, Edn. and Welfare, Washington, 1968—. Mem. Am. Accounting Assn., Fed. Govt. Accountants Assn. (nat. chmn. pub. relations com. 1972, 73), Internat. Platform Assn., George Washington U. Alumni Assn., W.Va. U. Alumni Assn., W. Va. State Soc., Alpha Beta Gamma. Democrat. Club: Braxton County (W.Va.) Young Democrats, George Washington University (charter mem.). Home: 3201 Landover St Alexandria VA 22305 Office: 300 Independence Av SW Washington DC 20201

STROTHER, LESTER JAMES, editor; b. Elizabeth, La., Mar. 9, 1924; s. Theodore H. and Ella (Laird) S.; B.J., U. Mo., 1950; m. Dora Jean Dougherty, Nov. 23, 1966; children—David Lester, Grant Douglas. Night editor El Dorado (Ark.) Daily News, 1950-51; news editor Lake Charles (La.) Am. Press, 1951-52; staff corr. U.P.I., Dallas, 1952-57; free lance writer, Dallas and Forth Worth, 1957-64; asst. city editor Ft. Worth Star Telegram, 1959-63; asso. dir. relations, asso. editor Ft. Wroth Mag., 1963-65; pres., chmn. bd. Tex. Met. Publs. Inc., 1965—, pub. Tex. Metro Mag., Arlington, Tex., 1965—; lectr. in field. Mem. Postal Commn., Arlington, 1968—; mem. communication adv. bd. U. Dallas, 1969—. Del. Tarrant County (Tex.) Democratic conv., 1968. Served with USNR, 1943-46. Mem. Ft. Worth (mem. Trinity River devel. com. 1971—), Dallas, Halton Richland Area (dir. 1968—), Grand Prairie, Arlington chambers commerce) Indsl. Editors Assn. (v.p. 1965-66), Dallas Sales and Marketing Exec., Mag. Pubs. Assn., Dallas Advt. League, Sigma Delta Chi, Sigma Phi Epsilon, Kappa Alpha Mu. Episcopalian (del. diocesan conv. 1971). Clubs: Fort Worth Advertising, Fort Worth Knife and Fork, Fort Worth Press; Dallas Press. Home: 3616 Landy Lane Fort Worth TX 76118 Office: PO Drawer 5566 Arlington TX 76011

STROUD, CHARLES DOUGLAS, dentist; b. Taylorsville, N.C., Sept. 25, 1941; s. John Bedford and Lillian Mae (McSwain) S.; student Lenoir Rhyne Coll., 1959-62; D.D.S., U. N.C., 1967; m. Beverly Marianne Smith, Sept. 2, 1963; children—Sharon Lynn, Mathew Bedford. Chemist, N.C. Dept. Agr., Raleigh, 1962-63; individual practice dentistry, Taylorsville, 1969—. Adviser to Regional Health Council, Morganton, N.C., 1969—. Dir., producer Miss Alexander County Pageant, 1971; chmn. Alexander County Christmas Parade, 1970. Bd. dirs. N.C. Easter Seal Soc. Served with USAF, 1967-69. Named Jaycee of Year Jr. C. of C., 1971. Mem. Appalachian Dental Acad. (sec.-treas.), Alexander County C. of C. (dir.), Taylorsville Jr. C. of C. (v.p. 1970-71). Home and Office: Box 755 Taylorsville NC 28681

STROUD, DAVID, JR., wholesale co. exec.; b. Kennett, Mo., July 2, 1913; s. David and Mary Maude (Striffler) S.; student S.E. Mo. State Coll., 1931-34; m. Mildred Ward Harrison, Jan. 14, 1939; 1 dau., Susan Elizabeth. Asst. purchasing agt. Mo. Utilities Co., Cape Girardeau, Mo., 1934-37; purchasing agt. Ark. Utilities Co., Helena, 1937-42; gen. mgr. A. S. Kelly Co., West Helena, Ark., 1946-47; comptroller, Lewis Supply Co., Inc., Helena, Ark., 1947-52; sec.-treas. Helena Wholesale, Inc. (Ark.), 1952—, financial v.p., 1968—, also dir., Chmn. West Helena Mayor's Adv. Council, 1966-68; West Helena Planning Commr., 1962—; ex-officio mem. Phillips County Planning Commn., 1964—, Area Planning Commn., 1966—; vice-chmn. West Helena Water Commn., 1964-71, chmn., 1971—, West Helena Sewer Commn., 1964-71, chmn., 1971—; v.p. West Helena Promotional Assn., 1971, vice chmn. Phillips County Port Authority 1971—. Bd. dirs., v.p. Mid-South Sight Service Inst., Memphis, 1962-70. Served to lt. (j.g.) USNR, 1942-46. Decorated Bronze Star medal; recipient Key to City West Helena, 1971, award Mid-South Sight Service Inst., 1971. Mem. Ark. Wholesale Grocers Assn. (com. chmn. 1962—). Republican. Methodist. Lion. Club: Ark. Razorback Booster. Home: 216 Richmond Hill West Helena AR 72390 Office: 201 York St Helena AR 72342

STROUD, HOWARD BURNETT, SR., ednl. adminstr.; b. Athens, Ga., Mar. 31, 1930; s. George Edward and Emma Mae (Flanigan) S.; B.S., Morehouse Coll., 1956; M.A., Atlanta U., 1968; m. Victoria Lee Baker, Oct. 10, 1960; 1 son, Howard Burnett. Classroom tchr. Union Inst., 1956, Burney Harris High Sch., 1956-65; guidance counselor, asst. prin., tchr. Lyons Jr. High Sch., Athens, 1965-67, prin., 1967—; sec. Frontline Corp., Fledgling Black Corp. Adult instr. Civil Def., 1960; pres. Harris br. YMCA, 1956—; mem. Athens-Clarke Charter Commn., 1968-69; lay v.p. Athens-Clarke County Cancer Soc., 1971—. Bd. dirs. Athens (Ga.) Regional Library. Served with AUS, 1951-53. Recipient Plaque for leadership YMCA, 1959. Certificate of Appreciation Am. Cancer Soc., 1970, Certificate of Appreciation V.F.W. 1961, 62. Mem. Nat. Assn. Secondary Sch. Prins., N.E.A., Ga. Clarke County edn. assns., Phi Delta Kappa, Kappa Alpha Psi. Baptist. Elk, Mason. Club: Optimist (v.p. 1971—) (Athens). Home: 175 Jones Dr Athens GA 30601 Office: 2190 Winterville Rd Athens GA 30601

STROUD, JAMES ERNEST, devel. co. exec., mayor; b. Weatherford, Okla., May 8, 1912; s. Jess W. W. and Samantha (Allbright) S.; student Southwestern State Coll., Weatherford, 1931; m. Nell Hume Stroud, Dec. 1, 1912; children—Richard, James Ernest, II, Timothy Hume, Sherelle S. (Mrs. Charles F. Culp), Gaynor (Mrs. L. Dean Tucker). Owner, N.M. Welding Supply Co., 1932-41; owner, pres. Tex-Air Gas Co., 1947-55, J. Ernest Stroud & Co., Amarillo, Tex., 1941—; pres. Stroud Devel. Co., Amarillo, 1960—; pres., owner Trades Fair Center Tex. Mayor, Amarillo, 1967—. Del. to Republican Nat. Conv., 1964, elector, 1968. Mem. C. of C. Club: Amarillo Country. Home: 1513 Bowie St Amarillo TX 79102 Office: 215 Buchanan St Amarillo TX 79105 also 503 Bank SW Bldg Amarillo TX 79105

STROUD, JAMES WILLIAM, state legislator; b. Denison, Tex., June 4, 1914; s. Lynn and Rose (Hickman) S.; m. Sara Frances White, Aug. 20, 1938 (div. Aug. 1954); children—James William, Robert Lynn, George Winton; m. Mary Ellon Birdwell, Oct. 7, 1960; children—Douglas Alan, Paul Jeffrey. Dep. to regional accountant Home Owner Loan Corp., Dallas, 1935-42; pres. Liberty Packing Co., 1940-50; regional ration banking officer, region mgr. dist. center OPA, 1942-47; regional dir. U.S. Census Bur., Dallas, 1948-64; mem. Tex. Ho. of Reps., 1964—, chmn. state electron code comn., 1968-70. Mem. regional coordinating com. Tex. Vocational Rehab.; mem. Dallas Council on Alcoholism. Mem. Phi Sigma. Home: 5507 McCommas St Dallas TX 75206 Office: Ho of Reps State Capitol Austin TX 75201

STROUD, ROBERT EDWARD, lawyer; b. Chester, S.C., July 24, 1934; s. Coy Franklin and Leila (Caldwell) S.; A.B., Washington and Lee U., 1956, LL.B., 1959; m. Katherine E. Clark, Apr. 8, 1961; children—Robert Gordon, Margaret Lathan. Admitted to Va. bar, 1959; asso. McGuire, Woods & Battle, Charlottesville, 1959-64, partner 1964—. Lectr. Grad. Sch. Bus. Adminstrn., U. Va., legal edn. insts., others. Pres. Charlottesville Housing Found., 1968—. Trustee Presbyn. Found. Served to 2d lt. with AUS, 1957. Mem. Am., Va. bar assns., Tax Inst. Am., Am. Judicature Soc., Phi Eta Sigma, Omicron Delta Kappa, Phi Delta Phi. Presbyn. (mem. gen. exec. bd. U.S.). Home: 104 Woodstock Dr Charlottesville VA 22901 Office: PO Box 1191 Charlottesville VA 22902

STROUD, WILLIAM JOSEPH, educator; b. Atkins, Ark., Mar. 26, 1937; s. Joe Bryan and Carrie Lee (Griffin) S.; B.A., Cal. Western U., 1959; B.D., Iliff Sch. Theology, 1964, Th.D., 1970; m. Judith Ann Beck, Dec. 30, 1956; children—Annette, Bruce. Tchr. San Miquel Sch., National City, Cal., 1959-60, Randell Sch., Denver, 1960-61, 63-64; instr. U. Denver, 1965-66; asst. prof. Wesleyan Coll., Macon, Ga., 1966-70; asst. prof. philosophy Salem (W.Va.) Coll., 1970—. Mem. Macon Council on Human Relations, 1967-70. Mem. Am. Civil Liberties Union (pres. Macon chpt. 1967-68), Am. Assn. U. Profs. (sec.-treas. Wesleyan Coll. chpt. 1968-69), C. S. Peirce Soc. Kiwanian. Contbr. articles to profl. jours. Home: 67 Pennsylvania Av Salem WV 26426

STROUPE, HENRY SMITH, univ. dean; b. Alexis, N.C., June 3, 1914; s. Stephen Morris and Auga (Lineberger) S.; student Mars Hill Jr. Coll., 1931-33; B.S., Wake Forest Coll., 1935, M.A., 1937; Ph.D., Duke, 1942; m. Mary Elizabeth Denham, June 2, 1942; children—Stephen Denham, David Henry. Faculty Wake Forest U., Winston-Salem, N.C., 1937—, asso. prof. history, 1949-54, prof., 1954—, chmn. dept. history, 1954-68, dir. evening classes, 1957-61, dir. div. grad. studies, 1961-67, dean grad. sch., 1967—. Vis. prof. history Duke, summer 1960. Mem. N.C. Civil War Centennial Commn., 1959-61. Served from ensign to lt. USNR, 1943-46. Mem. Am., So. hist. assns., N.C. Hist. Soc. (pres. 1965), N.C. Lit. and Hist. Assn. (past v.p.), Phi Beta Kappa, Omicron Delta Kappa. Democrat. Baptist. Author: The Religious Press in the South Atlantic States, 1802-1865: An Annotated Bibliography with Historical Introduction and Notes, 1956. Mem. editorial bd. N.C. Hist. Rev., 1963-69. Home: 2016 Faculty Dr Winston-Salem NC 27106

STROZIER, AUGUSTUS BUENAVISTA, III, dentist; b. Houston, Mar. 9, 1918; s. Augustus Buena Vista and Era (Weaver) S.; student U.S. Mil. Acad., 1936-37; U. Houston, 1937-39; D.D.S., Tex. Dental Coll., 1943; m. Helen Geers Willis, Mar. 30, 1943. Pvt. practice gen. dentistry, Houston, 1946—; pres., dir. Automotive Finance Corp., Houston, 1956—; pres., dir. Lone Star Trust Co., Houston, 1956-58; chmn. bd. dirs., 1958-59. Pres. Houston Property Owners Assn., 1948-49. Organizer, Democratic Party, S.E. Houston, 1948. Served to capt. D.C., AUS, 1943-46. Mem. Am. Dental Assn., Am. Acad. Gen. Dentistry., Tex., Houston dental socs., U. Houston Alumni Assn., U. Tex. Alumni Assn., Am. Legion, Zi Psi Phi. Club: Houston Morphy Chess (pres. 1950). Home: 5206 Braesheather St Houston TX 77035 Office: 7338 McHenry St Houston TX 77017

STRUBY, BERT, newspaper exec.; b. Macon, Ga., Jan. 19, 1917; s. Chester Albert and Julia (Riley) S.; A.B. magna cum laude, Mercer U., 1938; m. Jane Whitfield Spearman, May 24, 1947; children—Cynthia Jane, Neil Albert. Reporter, Macon Telegraph, 1938-40, state editor, 1940-41, asst. to publisher Macon Telegraph and Macon News, 1947-48, exec. editor Macon Telegraph, 1948-54, editor, 1954-58, gen. mgr. both papers, 1957—, exec. v.p. Macon Telegraph Pub. Co., 1958—, also dir. Chmn., Ga. Asso. Press, 1963-64; chmn. bd. So. Edn. Reporting Service, 1962-64. Chmn. Ga. citizens com. Nat. Council on Crime and Delinquency, 1961-65, mem. nat. bd. trustees, 1962-64; bd. Macon Housing Authority, 1952—, chmn. bd. commrs., 1961-64; mem. Ga. Bd. for Children and Youth, 1963—; mem. Gov.'s Youth Study Com., 1962; pres. Macon Big Bros. Assn., 1962, named Big Brother of Year, 1962, bd. dirs., 1959-65; mem. adv. bd. Bibb County Juvenile Ct., 1949-59; mem. steering com. Macon Council on World Affairs, 1954-62. Served to lt. comdr. USNR, 1941-46. Recipient certificate of Merit, Freedoms Found., 1950; citation Anti-Defamation League of B'nai B'rith, 1951; Mil. Service Cross, U.D.C., 1954; Silver Beaver award Boy Scouts Am., 1967. Mem. So. Newspaper Publs. Assn. (pres. 1966-67), Macon C. of C. (chmn. Downtown Council 1970-71, v.p. 1971-72), Mercer U Alumni Assn. (pres. 1956-57, mem. exec. com. 1960-65), Nat. Alliance Businessman (chmn. Macon Metro area 1971-72), Am. Legion. Baptist (deacon). Elk, Rotarian. Club: Idle Hour Country (Macon).Home: 1855 Waverland Dr Macon GA 31201 Office: 120 Broadway Macon GA 31201

STRUELENS, MICHEL MAURICE JOSEPH GEORGES, fgn. affairs cons.; b. Brussels, Belgium, Mar. 10, 1928 (came to U.S. 1960, naturalized 1966); B.A., Coll. St. Pierre, Brussels, 1944; M.A., Antwerp (Belgium) U., 1949; Ph.D., Am. U., Washington, 1968; m. Godelieve De Wilde, Aug. 2, 1949; children—Alain, Patricia, Brigitte, Bernard, Jean Paul. Insp. econ. affairs Congo Govt., Leopoldville, 1950-54, chief insp. econ. affairs, 1954-55, dep. commr. transp., 1955-57; dir. Information and Pub. Relations Office for Congo, Brussels, 1957-58, Congo Tourism Pavillion, Internat. World's Fair, Brussels, 1958-59; dir. gen. Belgian Congo and Ruanda Urundi Tourist Office, Congo, 1959; chmn. African Commn. Internat. Union Ofcl. Travel Orgns., Geneva, Switzerland, 1959-60; ofcl. Katanga rep. in U.S., N.Y.C., 1960-63; dir. gen. Internat. Inst. for African Affairs in Can., 1963-64; spl. asst. to prime minister Democratic Republic Congo, fgn. affairs minister, adviser to Congo UN delegation, adviser Congo embassy, Washington, N.Y.C., 1964-65; dir. Eurafrica, Consultants on Fgn. Affairs, Washington, 1966—. Prof. polit. sci., French, Am. U., 1968—, dir. Center Research and Documentation on European Community, 1971; adminstr. Congo Touring Clubs, Brussels, Leopoldville, 1959—. Recipient Internat. Union Ofcl. Travel Orgns. Poster award, Brussels, 1958; Etoile de Service en Argent, King of Belgium, 1956, chevalier de l'Ordre Royal du Lion, 1957. Mem. Phi Sigma Alpha. Rotarian. Club: Bukavu Royal Sports (founder Congo 1950; pres. 1951-54; hon. pres. 1957). Author: (with Inforcongo) Congo Belge et Ruanda-Urundi, 1958; (monograph) Le Canada a l'Heure de l'Afrique, 1964. Home: 1374 Woodside Dr McLean VA 22101 Office: 3510 Edmunds St NW Washington DC 20007

STRULL, NORMAN JAMES, oral surgeon; b. Louisville, July 2, 1937; s. Charles H. and Sarah B. (Baron) S.; D.M.D., U. Louisville, 1962; m. Nancy Dock, June 25, 1961; children—Gregory Evan, Dana Michelle, Vicki Lynn. Oral surgery intern U. Ala., Birmingham, 1962-63; resident in oral surgery U. Louisville Hosps., 1963-65; pvt. practice oral surgery, Louisville, 1965—; instr. U. Louisville Sch. Dentistry, 1965—. Mem. Am. (del. 1971—), Southeastern, Ky. (sec.-treas 1971—) socs. oral surgeons, Am., Ky. dental assns., Ky.

Med. Assn., Jefferson County Med. Soc. Home: 6210 Innes Trace Louisville KY 40207 Office: 4122 Shelbyville Rd Louisville KY 40207

STRUNK, FLONNIE SHOEMAKER (MRS DELMUS STRUNK), educator; b. Huntsville, Tenn.; d. George and Moda (Ellis) Shoemaker; B.S., Tenn. Poly. U., 1954; M.S., U. Tenn., 1956, Ed.D., 1967; m. Delmus Strunk, Dec. 23, 1935; children—Frankie June (Mrs. Arvis Blakley), Lonnie, Brenda (Mrs. Jim Bates), Kenneth Ray. Adminstrv. asst. to supt. Scott County Schs., Huntsville, 1950-54; tchr. Scott County Bd. Edn., 1954-58; faculty Cumberland Coll., Williamsburg, Ky., 1959-65, asso. prof., 1959-65; asso. prof. office adminstrn. dept. Western Ky. U., Bowling Green, 1966—. Mem. Am. Assn. U. Profs., Delta Phi Epsilon. Mem. Order Eastern Star. Home: 3001 Mohawk Dr Bowling Green KY 42101

STUART, ALBERT RHETT, clergyman; b. Washington, Jan. 20, 1906; s. Garden Clarkson and Florence (Beale) S.; A.B., U. Va., 1928; B.D., Va. Theol. Sem., 1931; D.D., Oglethorpe U., 1938, U. of South, 1955, Va. Theol. Sem., 1955; m. Isabella Alston, Sept. 25, 1945 (dec. 1964); children—Garden C., Isabella A. Ordained deacon, Episcopal Ch., 1931, ordained priest, 1931; rector Ch. of Resurrection, Greenwood, S.C., 1931-36, St. Michael's Ch., Charleston, S.C., 1936-47, dean Christ Ch. Cathedral, New Orleans, 1947-54; consecrated Bishop, State of Ga., 1954—. Mem. Nat. Council Episcopal Ch., 1939-43; dep. Gen. Conv., 1934, 40, 46, 49, 52; exec. council of Episcopal Ch. U.S.A., 1967—; pres. Fourth Province, Episcopal Ch., 1965-68. Served with Chaplain Corps, USNR, 1943-46; ETO. Mem. Raven Soc., Soc. Colonial Wars, Phi Beta Kappa, Omicron Delta Kappa, Phi Delta Theta. Democrat. Club: Ogerthorpe. Home: 438 Lincoln St Savannah GA 31401

STUART, BROOKS SWYGERT, county ofcl.; b. Coronaca, S.C., May 13, 1904; s. Robert Lee and Alice (Rice) S.; A.B., Wofford Coll., 1926; m. Lois Elizabeth Pettit, Oct. 14, 1933; s. Brooks Swygert, Alice Elizabeth. Bookkeeper, Nat. Loan & Exchange Bank, 1926-30, Central Union Bank, Greenwood, S.C., 1930-33; with County Bank, Greenwood, S.C., 1933-42, 46-69, sr. v.p., 1965-69, now dir.; treas. Greenwood County, 1969—; dir. Mut. Savs. & Loan Assn., Greenwood. Mem. Fed. Housing Authority, Greenwood, 1968—; chmn. Civil Def. Greenwood County, 1969—; commr. pub. works, Greenwood, 1963-65; mem. Commn. of Cokesbury Hist. and Recreational Commn.; chmn. bldg. com. Brewer Hosp., 1955. Mem. County Bd. Edn., 1947-48; mem. City Council, 1948-58. Bd. dirs., treas. A.R.C., 1955—; bd. dirs. YMCA, Community Chest; trustee, treas. Greenwood Meth. Home. Served with AUS, 1942-46. Mem. Am. Legion, Newcomen Soc. U.S., S.A.R. (pres. Cambridge chpt. 1966-68, state v.p. 1967-69), Greenwood C. of C. (dir. 1956-61), Sigma Alpha Epsilon. Methodist (chmn. bd. stewards 1956, 67). Kiwanian. Club: Greenwood Country (pres. 1951).Home: 407 Jennings Av Greenwood SC 29646 Office: County Courthouse Monument St Greenwood SC 29646

STUART, DAVID, pipe and plastic co. exec.; b. N.Y.C., Dec. 25, 1934; s. Hyman S.; B.S., Newark Coll. Engring., 1965; M.B.A., Rutgers U., 1967. Plant mgr. Allied Chem. Co., 1966-67; v.p., dir. Universal Pipe & Plastic, Inc., Palm Beach Gardens, Fla., 1967-71; founder, pres. World of Plastics Inc., Ft. Pierce, Fla., 1972—. Tchr., U.S. Power Squadron, 1970-71. Tax assessor, East Brunswick, N.J., 1963-66. Served with U.S. Mcht. Marine, 1953-57. Registered profl. engr., N.J. Mem. Am. Soc. M.E., Soc. Plastic Engrs. Home: 3206 Enterprise Rd Ft Pierce FL 33450 Office: World of Plastics Inc Ft Pierce FL 33450

STUART, EDWARD, JR., forest engr.; b. Boston, June 15, 1917; s. Edward and Helen (Fox) S.; B.S. in Forestry, U. Me., 1937; F.E. (hon.), Biltmore Forest Sch., Weisbaden, Germany, 1946; children—Edward, Diane and Bruce. Forester, Me. and Can., 1937, with U.S. Forest Service, in Mass., Colo., S.D., Wyo., 1938-42; cons. and practicing forester, Va., N.C., S.C., Md. W.Va., 1946-56; pres. chmn. bd. dirs. Eastern Forestry, Inc., Hampton, Va., 1956—; consulting and practicing forestry and real estate appraiser. Served from lt. to capt. AUS, 1942-46; mil govt. Forestry Office, Great Hesse, Germany, 1945-46. Decorated Commendation Medal Croix Militaire (Belgium). Mem. Nat. Assn. Cons. Foresters (pres. 1948-50; exec. council 1950-60, exec. sec. 1960—, editor The Consultant), Nat. Council Forestry Assn. Execs., Am. Soc. Appraisers, Am. Forestry Assn. (forest progress adv. council 1950-51), Soc. Am. Foresters (chmn. Rappahannock sect. 1960), Mil. Govt. Assn., Va. Forestry Council (sec.), Practicing Forestors Inst. (dir.), Gloucester, Mathews, Middlesex Realty Bd. (dir.), Nat. Assn. Real Estate Bds., Va. Real Estate Assn., S.A.R., Nat. Forest Products Assn. (mem. forestry adv. com.), Nat. Def. Exec. Res., Am. Legion. Author numerous tech. articles on forestry and appraising. Home: Stuart Landing Wake VA 23176 Office: Box 6 Wake VA 23176

STUART, HAL MARTIN, physician; b. Elkin, N.C., June 5, 1931; s. Luther Martin and Hallie Mae (Gilliam) S.; B.S. cum laude, Wake Forest Coll., 1953; M.D., Bowman Gray Sch. Medicine, 1956; m. Bonnie Jane Hall, Dec. 20, 1955; children—Amanda, Robinette. Intern, N.C. Bapt. Hosp., Winston-Salem, 1956-57; resident obstetrics-gynecology City Meml. Hosp., Winston-Salem, 1959-60; gen. practice medicine, Elkin, N.C., 1960—; mem. staff Hugh Chatham Meml. Hosp., Elkin; med. examiner, Surry County, 1971—. Dir. Yadkin Valley Bank & Trust Co., Elkin, N.C. Mem. N.C. Gov's. Com. to Bd. Air and Water Resources, 1970. Bd. dirs. Surry County Tb Assn. Served with USNR, 1957-59. Recipient Shepardson award Bowman Gray Sch. Medicine, 1956. Diplomate Am. Bd. Family Practice. Mem. A.M.A., Am. Acad. Gen. Practice, So. Med. Assn., N.C. State, Surry-Yadkin (v.p. 1970-71) med. socs., Alpha Omega Alpha. Methodist. Mason. Home: 306 Ivy Circle Elkin NC 28621 Office: 180-C Parkwood Dr Elkin NC 28621

STUART, HAROLD C(UTLIFF), lawyer, corp. exec.; b. Oklahoma City, July 4, 1912; s. Royal Cutliff and Alice (Bramlitt) S.; LL.B., U. Va., 1936; m. Joan Skeily, June 6, 1938; children—Randi (Mrs. Fred Wightman), Jon Rolf. Admitted to Okla. bar, 1936, D.C. bar, 1952; partner Doerner, Stuart, Saunders, Daniel & Langenkamp, Tulsa; judge Common Pleas Ct., 1941-42; asst. sec. of air force, 1949-51; pres., chmn. bd. Southwestern Sales Corp, (KVOO-radio, oil, real estate and investments); pres., dir., S.E. State Bank Tulsa, Skelly Oil Co., Tulsa, Assn. Maximum Service Telecasters, Inc., Fidelity Bank N.A., Greyhound Corp., First Nat. Bank & Trust Co. Tulsa, Phoenix, OKC Corp., Dallas, Armour & Co., Phoenix. Bd. dirs. Internat. Petroleum Expn., Aeorspace Education Found.; chmn. bd. Air Force Acad. Found.; trustee U. Tulsa, Baker U., St. John's Hosp., Tulsa; trustee, v.p. Lovelace Found., Albuquerque. Served from 1st lt. to col., USAAF, 1942-46. Decorated Bronze Star medal, Order of St. Olav (Comdr.), King Haakon 7th Victory Medal, Medal of Liberation (Norway) Croix de Guerre (Luxembourg). Mem. Am., Okla., D.C. bar assns., Air Force Assn. (dir.), C. of C., Delta Kappa Epsilon. Democrat. Clubs: Southern Hills Country, The Tulsa, Summit (Tulsa); Army-Navy, Burning Tree (Washington); Rolling Rock (Ligonier, Pa,). Home: 2930 S Yorktown Tulsa OK 74114 Office: 3701 S Peoria St PO Box 1349 Tulsa OK 74101

STUART, JESSE HILTON, author; b. W-Hollow, near Riverton, Ky., Aug. 8, 1907; s. Mitchell and Martha (Hilton) S.; A.B., Lincoln Memorial University, Harrogate, Tennessee, 1929, hon. D.H.L., 1950; student Vanderbilt U., 1931-32, Peabody Coll.; D.Litt., U. Ky., 1944; D.Litt., Marietta (O.) Coll., 1952; LL.D. Baylor U.; D.Litt. (hon.), Morris Harvey Coll.; 1959, Marshall U., 1962, No. Mich. U., 1964, Eastern Ky. State Coll., 1964; Dr. Pedagogy (hon.), Murray State University, 1968; m. Naomi Deane Norris, Oct. 14, 1939; 1 dau. Jessica Jane (Mrs. Julian Juergensmeyer). Taught school and lectured before colleges and universities since 1940; supt. city schs. Greenup, Ky., 1941-43; vis. lectr., prof. Am. Univ. Cairo, 1960-61; taught in Grad. Coll. Edn., U. Nev., summer 1958; writer in residence Eastern Ky. U. 1965-66; author short stories, poetry, articles. Specialist U.S. State Department United States Information Service, 1962-63. Am. representative Asian Writers' Conference, 1962. Member group to revise Kentucky State Constn. chmn. health, welfare and edn. com. Bd. dirs. Kentucky Heart Association, state chairman, 1964. Served as apprentice seaman USN, March 1944, commd. lt. (j.g.), Aug. 1944, stationed in Washington, D.C. Awarded Guggenheim fellowship for European travel, 1937; Jeanette Sewal Davis Poetry Prize, 1934; 5000 prize, Acad. of Arts and Sciences, 1941; 5000 prize Academy American Poets, 1961. Member of Poetry Society of America. Author: Man With a Bull-Tongue Plow (poems), published 1934; Head O'W-Hollow (stories) 1936; Beyond Dark Hills (autobiography), 1938; Trees of Heaven (novel), 1940; Mem of the Mountains (stories), 1941; Taps for Private Tussie (Thomas Jefferson Southern Award, 500; Book-of-the-Month, Dec. 1943); Mongrel Mettle (autobiography of adog), 1944; Album of Destiny (poems), 1944; Foretaste of Glory (novel), 1946; Tales From the Plum Grove Hills (Stories), 1946; The Thread That Runs So True, 1949 (N.E.A. selection as best book of 1949); Hie to the Hunters, 1950; Clearing in the Sky, 1950; Kentucky Is My Land (poems), 1952; The Good Spirit of Laurel Ridge, 1953; The Beatinest Boy, 1953; A Penny's Worth of Character; 1954; Red Mule (juvenile), 1954; The Year of My Rebirth, 1956; Plowshare in Heaven (collection of short stories), 1958; The Rightful Owner, 1960; God's Oddling, 1960; Andy Finds A Way, 1961; Hold April, 1962; A Jesse Stuart Reader, 1963; Save Every Lamb, 1964; Daughter of the Legend (novel), 1965; My Land Has A Voice, 1966; Ride with Huey the Engineer (junior book), 1966; Mr. Galhon's Novel, 1967; Come Gentle Spring, (story collection), 1969; To Teach to Love, published 1969. Author of short stories in anthologies: Best Short Stories, O. Henry Meml. Collection., Co-editor: Outlooks Through Literature (textbook). Contbr. Harpers, Atlantic Monthly, Esquire, Ladies' Home Journal. Poetry, etc. Republican. Methodist. Home: Greenup KY 41144

STUART, VIRGIL SAMUEL, city ofcl.; b. Atlanta, Dec. 29, 1907; s. James R. and LeNora (Holt) S.; student North Ga. Coll., 1925-27; m. Lillian Justice, July 4, 1931; children—Phyllis Ann, Virgil Samuel. Mcht., St. Augustine, Fla., 1928-33; police officer, St. Augustine, 1933, chief of police, City of St. Augustine, 1958—. Bd. dirs. St. Johns Assn. Mem. Fla. Peace Officers Assn. (sec., treas. 1945—, spl. legislative rep.), Internat. Assn. Chiefs Police, St. Augustine and St. Johns County C. of C. (dir.). Democrat. Methodist, Mason (Shriner, K.T.). Club: Shrine (pres. 1947) (St. Augustine). Home: 10 Hibiscus St Saint Augustine FL 32084 Office: PO Box 75 Saint Augustine FL 32084

STUBBLEFIELD, FRANK ALBERT, congressman; b. Murray, Ky., Apr. 5, 1907; s. Vernon C. and Virginia (Wilson) S.; student U. Ariz., 1927; B.S. in Commerce, U. Ky., 1932; m. Odessa Boaz, Feb. 4, 1934; children—Jennye Sue, Frankie Ann, Mary B. Retail druggist, Murray, Ky., 1935-58; mem. 86th-92d Congresses, 1st Dist. Ky. Mem. city council, Murray, Ky., 1939-43; mem. Ky. R.R. Commn., 1951-58. Served as lt. (j.g.) USNR, World War II. Mem. Murray C. of C. (dir.), Alpha Tau Omega. Democrat. Methodist. Elk, Rotarian. Home: 716 Poplar St Murray KY 42071 also 4619 Albemarle St Washington DC 20016 Office: House Office Bldg Washington DC 20525

STUBBS, ROBERT SHERWOOD, II, educator; b. St. Louis, Nov. 11, 1922; s. Sherwood Obear and Marie Clifton (deVaux) S.; student Johns Hopkins, 1939-41; A.B., U. Ala., 1942; J.D., George Washington U., 1952; m. Laura Ann Cobb, June 26, 1943; children—Robert Sherwood III, Anna Lucille. Commd. 2d lt. U.S. Marine Corps, 1943, advanced through grades to lt. col., 1959; ret., 1962; admitted to Ala. bar, 1952, D.C. bar, 1952, Hawaii bar, 1957, Ga. bar, 1968; instr. East Carolina Coll., 1959-62; asst. prof. law Emory U., Atlanta, 1963, asso. prof., 1964, prof., 1965—; spl. cons. Ga. State Bar Spl. Com. on Assistance to Indigent Criminal Defendants, 1964-67, Am. Bar Assn. standing com. on Legal Aid and Indigent Defendants, 1965-66; spl. cons. criminal justice com. State Bar Ga., 1967-68, mem., 1968-69; counsellor So. Regional Edn. Bd., 1967; mem. legal com. Ga. Com. on Crime and Delinquency, 1963-69, chmn. legal com., 1967-68; mem. Ga. Juvenile Ct. Law Study Com., 1967-71; cons. profl. adv. panel Ga. Council Crime and Delinquency, 1969—; cons. Ga. Dept. Family and Children Services, 1969, Ga. Dept. Edn., 1971-72; vice chmn. Criminal Justice Supervisory Bd., Atlanta Region Met. Planning Commn., 1971-72. Mem. Am., Ga. (mem. com. law schs. and practicing attys. 1971—), Decatur-DeKalb bar assns., Am. Trial Lawyers Assn., Am. Judicature Soc., Am. Assn. U. Profs., Nat. Council on Family Relations, Scribes, Tudor and Stuart Soc., Order of Coif, Kappa Alpha, Pi Delta Epsilon, Omicron Delta Kappa, Phi Delta Phi. Club: Atlanta Lawyers. Author: Marriage and Divorce in Georgia, 1964; Under the Gun, 1966; Georgia Law of Children, 1969; Criminal Practice and Procedure in Georgia in 1863, 1971. Contbr. articles to profl. jours. Home: 2630 Woodwardia Rd NE Atlanta GA 30345

STUCKEY, BYRON WELDON, computer co. exec.; b. Fort Worth, July 18, 1932; s. Herbert Floyd and Mollie Lee (Still) S.; B.B.A., U. Tex., 1964; J.D., So. Meth. U., 1968; m. Delores Ann Estes, June 6, 1951; children—Dave Weldon, Keith Alan. Sec. to corporate treas. Richardson Oils, Inc., Fort Worth, 1956-61; accountant, controller Campbell, Henderson & Co., Dallas, 1961-65; sec.-controller Moran Bros., Inc., Shaft Drillers, Inc., Wichita Falls, Tex., 1965-67; exec. v.p. Reach Corp., Dallas, 1967—. Served with USCG, 1952-56. Mem. Am. Judicature Soc., Am., Tex. bar assns., Dallas Forum, Delta Theta Phi. Baptist. Home: 3777 Weeburn Dr Dallas TX 75234 Office: 1712 Commerce St Dallas TX 75201

STUCKEY, JASPER L., geologist; b. Princeton, N.C., July 24, 1891; s. John Haywood and Betty Eliza (Bunn) S.; A.B., U. N.C., 1918, Am., 1920; student Grenoble U., 1919; Ph.D., Cornell U., 1924; D.Sc., N.C. State U., 1965; m. Anabel Stephenson, June 23, 1920 (dec.); m. 2nd, Gladys Brinkley, July 24, 1936; 1 son, William Jasper. Tchr. pub. sch., Johnston County, 1910-11; supt. Limestone Plant, N.C. Dept. Agr., Bridgeport, Tenn., 1917-18; asst. geologist, N.C. Geol. Survey, 1920, 21, 24 and summers 1922-23; instr. geology, U. N.C., 1921, Cornell U., 1922-24; state geologist, N.C. Dept. Conservation and Devel., 1925-26, acting dir., 1925; prof. geology, N.C. State Coll., 1926-55; mem. adminstrv. council Greater U. N.C., 1937-41; sr. geologist U.S. Army Engrs., 1930; became state geologist N.C. Dept. Conservation, 1940, head div. mineral resources, 1955, now retired; emergency co-ordinator of mines for N.C., 1941-43. Dir. N.C. State Coll. Minerals Research Lab., 1946-54, Served as cpl. Co. E., 323d Inf., A.E.F., 1918-19. Recipient Gov.'s Distinguished Citizens award, 1964. Fellow A.A.A.S., Mineral. Soc. Am., Geol. Soc. Am. (chmn. Southeastern sect. 1964-65), Am. Geog. Soc.; mem. N.C. Acad. Sci. (pres. 1940), Am. Ceramic Soc., Am. Inst. Mining, Metall. and Petroleum Engrs., Assn. Am. State Geologists (pres. 1958-59), Soc. Econ. Geologists, N.C. Soc. Engrs., Carolina Geol. Soc. (pres. 1947), Keramos (hon.), Sigma Gamma Epsilon, Phi Kappa Phi, Sigma Xi, Sigma Chi. Clubs: Engineers, Civitan, Torch (Raleigh, N.C.). Contbr. to bulls. and tech. jours. Home: 1911 Sunset Dr Raleigh NC 27608

STUCKEY, KENNETH FAIRCHILD, ednl. adminstr.; b. Columbia, S.C., Nov. 11, 1930; s. William Louis and Mable (Jackson) S.; B.A., U. N.C., 1953; postgrad. Boston U., 1961; M.Ed., U. S.C., 1971; postgrad. Middle Tenn. State U., 1971, U. S.C., 1972—; m. Josephine Elizabeth Watts, Jan. 3, 1960. French and English instr. Charlotte (N.C.) Country Day Sch., 1954-56; head lower sch. Aiken Prep. Sch., 1957-68; grad. asst. U. S.C., 1968-70; prin., headmaster Webb Sch., Bell Buckle, Tenn., 1970—. Founder, co-dir. Aiken (S.C.) Reading Clinic, 1961-68; resident dir. Camp Agawan-Kezar, Lovell, Me., 1962-63. Pres. honor council Aiken County dist. Boy Scouts Am., 1968. Mem. Phi Delta Kappa. Episcopalian (mem. mission council and liturgical com. 1971-72). Rotarian. Address: Webb Sch Bell Buckle TN 37020

STUCKEY, WALTER JACKSON, JR., physician; b. Fairfield, Ala., Mar. 6, 1927; s. Walter Jackson and Lena (Brackin) S.; B.S., U. Ala., 1947; M.D., Tulane U., 1951; m. Mildred Creel Roberts, Nov. 26, 1952; children—Walter Jackson III, John Hamlin, James Allen. Intern, Charity Hosp. La., New Orleans, 1951-52; resident in gen. practice Lafayette (La.) Charity Hosp., 1952; resident in internal medicine Tulane med. service Charity Hosp. La., VA Hosp. New Orleans, 1955-57; fellow, instr. dept. medicine Tulane U. Sch. Medicine, 1958-60, asst. prof., 1960-62, asso. prof., 1962-68, prof., 1968—, chief sect. hematology, 1963—, sr. vis. physician, 1968—; practice medicine specializing in hematology, New Orleans; cons. VA, USPHS, Meth., Mercy hosps., Hotel Dieu, New Orleans, Huey P. Long Charity Hosp., Pineville, La., VA Hosp., Alexandria, La., Lallie Kemp Charity Hosp., Independence, La. Served with USNR, 1952-54. Bd. dirs. Wesley Found. New Orleans, 1968-71, Cancer Assn. Greater New Orleans. Fellow A.C.P.; mem. A.A.A.S., Am. Assn. Cancer Edn., Am. Assn. Cancer Research, A.M.A., Am. Soc. Internal Medicine, La., Orleans Parish med. socs., New Orleans Acad. Internal Medicine, N.Y. Acad. Scis., La. Heart Assn. (undergrad. and postgrad. research coms. 1966—). Methodist. Home: 7325 Cameo St New Orleans LA 70124 Office: 1430 Tulane Av New Orleans LA 70112

STUCKEY, WILLIAMSON SYLVESTER, JR., congressman; b. Eastman, Ga., May 25, 1935; s. Williamson S. and Ethel (Mullis) S.; B.B.A., U. Ga., 1956, LL.B., 1959; m. Ethelyn McMillan, July 16, 1963; children—Williamson Sylvester III, Stuart Anne, Scott M., Stephanie, Jay-Gould. Former exec. v.p. Stuckey's Stores, Inc.; former pres. Stuckey Pecan Co., Stuckey Timberlands, Inc.; adviser to Stuckey div. Pet Milk Co.; mem. 90th-92d Congresses from 8th Ga. Dist., mem. House interstate and fgn. commerce com., finance and commerce subcom., D.C. com. Vice chmn. Central Ga. council Boy Scouts Am.; mem. Alumni Council. Bd. govs. Woodward Acad. Named Ga. Jaycee Man Yr., 1969. Mem. Nat. Young Presidents Orgn., Eastman Jr. C. of C. (past pres.), Gridiron, Sigma Alpha Epsilon, Phi Delta Phi. Democrat. Episcopalian. Mason, Elk, Rotarian. Home: College St Eastman GA 31023 Office: PO Box 310 Eastman GA 31023

STUDEBAKER, HERSEL SAMUEL, mfg. exec.; b. Ft. Wayne, Ind., Sept. 18, 1916; s. Harvey Charles and Nellie (Elliott) S.; B.S. magna cum laude, LeTourneau Coll., 1950; m. Eulah Louise Knighten, Feb. 4, 1939; children—Patsy Ann (Mrs. Harold Robert Hjort), Harvey Richard, Peggy Gail (Mrs. Larry W. Ebinger). Prodn. mgr. R.G. Le Tourneau Co., Inc., Longview, 1951-57; exec. v.p., gen. mgr. Strahan Mfg. Co., Inc., Tampa, Fla., 1957-68; pres. Studebaker So. Inc., Lake Wales, Fla., 1968—. Bd. dirs., mem. exec. bd. Warner So. Coll. Served with AUS, 1943-45. Mem. Lake Wales C. of C., Am. Soc. Tool Engrs., LaTourneau Coll. Alumni Assn. (past pres.), Am. Ordnance Assn., Gideon Internat. Mem. Ch. of God. Clubs: Optimist (past dir., chmn. bd. trustees), LeTourneau Management (past pres.). Home: Route 3 Box 805 Lake Wales FL 33853 Office: Studebaker So Inc Lake Wales FL 33853,

STULL, PHILIP BARTON, mfg. exec.; b. Chgo., Dec. 13, 1901; s. John Walter and Dorothy Evelyn (Case) S.; student Philips Acad., Andover, Mass., 1916-18, U. of Chgo., 1918-19, U. Pa., 1919-20; m. Florence Wilson Roper, June 6, 1923; children—Dorothy Wilson, Elizabeth Walmsley, Philip Barton; m. 2d, Katherine A. Dillard, July 16, 1948; children—Deborah, Stephanie, John Walter II. Asst. purchasing agt. Stamsocott Co., Hopewell, Va., 1920-23, sales mgr., 1923; v.p. Va. Cellulose Co., Hopewell, 1923-25, pres., 1925-28; gen. mgr. Va. Cellulose Div., Hercules Powder Co., 1928-37, gen. mgr. Paper Makers Chem. Div., Wilmington, Del., 1937-43, v.p., 1943-59, asst. to pres., 1959; pres, Am. Enka Corp., 1960-67, chmn., 1960—; chmn. bd. Akzona, Inc., 1970—; dir. Wachovia Bank and Trust Co., Winston-Salem, N.C. Prse., United Fund of Buncombe County and Asheville, N.C., 1965-66. Republican. Episcopalian, Clubs; Biltmore Forest Country (N.C.); Grandfather Country; Mountain City, Asheville City (Asheville). Home: 412 Vanderbilt Rd Biltmore NC 28803 Office: Akzona Inc Asheville NC 28802

STULL, RAYMOND EUGENE, govt. ofcl.; b. Tuscarawas, O., Aug. 15, 1922; s. John Gabriel and Grace (Frantz) S.; B.S. in Edn., Ohio State U., 1947; m. Margaret Kathleen Meese, Dec. 14, 1941; children— David, Karen, Mark, Kris, Kim, Jon. Tchr. high sch., Bowerston, O., 1947-49; reporter Daily Reporter, Dover, 1949-50, sports editor, 1950-52; sports editor Daily Jeffersonian, Cambridge, 1952-54; state-regional editor Internat. News Service, Columbus, 1954-58; pub. relations dir. Republican State Hdqrs., Columbus, 1961-65; asst. pub. relations dir. Rep. Nat. Com., 1965-69; dir. pub. information Small Bus. Adminstrn., Washington, 1969-71, dir. pub. affairs, 1971—. Free-lance writer, 1964—. Served with AUS, World War II. Republican. Mem. Moravian Ch. Home: 1632 Macon St McLean VA 22101 Office: 1441 L St NW Washington DC 20006

STULLER, HOWARD EDWARD, motor equipment co. exec.; b. Sterling, Kan., July 30, 1932; s. Claude Herman and Beulah Faye (Deatherage) S.; Asso. Engring., Coffeyville Coll., 1955; B.S. in Indsl. Engring., Tex. Tech. U., 1960; m. Barbara Joan Holland, June 7, 1950; children—Stephen Edward, Stephanie Ann. With drilling dept. Magnolia Petroleum Co., Seminole, Tex., 1950-52, Ohio Oil Co., Pawhuska, Okla., 1952-53; v.p. engring. Hancock Mfg. Co., Lubbock, Tex., 1955-66; v.p. engring. Hancock div. Clark Equipment Co., Lubbock, 1966—; dir. Road Constrn. and Machinery Co., Lubbock. Cubmaster, Arrowhead council Boy Scouts Am., 1962; mgr. Pony League, Lubbock, 1964-65, mgr. Colt League, 1966-67. Bd. dirs. charter mem. Babe Ruth League, Lubbock, Tex., 1969—; supr. bd. mem. South Plains Coll. Served with AUS, 1968-69. Mem. Am. Inst. Indsl. Engrs., Soc. Automotive Engrs., Am. Ordnance Assn., Assn. U.S. Army, Am. Inst. Mgmt., Lubbock C. of C. Club: Management (Lubbock). Patentee in field. Home: 4714 29th St Lubbock TX 79410 Office: Box 1859 Lubbock TX 79408

STULLKEN, DONALD EDWARD, aerospace operations exec.; b. Sullivan, Ill., Apr. 11, 1920; s. Edward H. and Mary (Shumacher) S.; B.A., DePauw U., 1941; M.S., Purdue U., 1942, Ph.D., 1950; D.Sc., DePauw U., 1967; m. Elizabeth Russell, Mar. 7, 1942; children—Russell E., William G., W. Kurt. Asst. prof. Purdue U., Lafayette, Ind., 1953-54; aviation physiologist Chief Naval Air Tng. Staff, U.S. Navy, Pensacola, Fla., 1954-62; chief flight control and recovery operations NASA, Manned Spacecraft Center, Houston, 1962—. Mem. Seabrook (Tex.) Vol. Fire Dept., 1962-70, pres., 1965; chmn. Clear Creek Swim League, 1966-67. Bd. dirs. Gulf Coast Sci. Found. Served with USNR, 1943-46, 50-53. Mem. A.A.A.S., Sigma Xi. Methodist. Home: 839 Timbercove Dr Seabrook TX 77586 Office: NASA Manned Spacecraft Center Houston TX 77058

STULTZ, BOBBY EVERETT, navy officer; b. Bristol, Va., Jan. 1, 1929; s. William Edwin and Loretta (Horne) S.; student Roanoke Coll., 1946-48; B.S. in Civil Engring., Va. Poly. Inst., 1951; m. Evelyn Sue Strickler, June 7, 1952; children—Jana Cheryl, Jon Christopher. Constrn. engr. E.I. du Pont de Nemours & Co., Inc., 1951-53; commd. ensign U.S. Navy, 1953, advanced through ranks to comdr., 1966; engring. officer Naval Sta., Argentia, Nfld., 1953-55; transp. and maintenance officer U.S. Naval Constrn. Battalion Center Port Hueneme, Cal., 1955-57; staff civil engr. Comdr. in Chief Atlantic Fleet, 1957-59; operations officer Amphibious Constrn. Br. 2, Norfolk, Va., 1959-61; sr. project mgr. Pub. Works Center, Pearl Harbor, 1961-64; asst. dir. facilities mgmt. gulf div. Naval Facilities Engring. Command, New Orleans, 1964-67; comdg. officer Mobile Constrn. Br. 121, Gulfport, Miss., 1967-69; staff civil engr. Hdqrs. USMC, Washington, 1969-71; asst. dir. Seabees Ashore/Self Help, Naval Facilities Engring. Command, Washington, 1971; asst. chief staff environmental quality Office Oceanographer Navy Dept., Washington, 1972—. Decorated Bronze Star medal (2), Navy Commendation medal, Cross of Gallantry with silver star (Vietnam). Registered profl. engr., Vt. Mem. Soc. Am. Mil. Engrs., Am. Soc. C.E., Pi Kappa Phi, Episcopalian. Home: 4824 Birch Lane Alexandria VA 22312 Office: Office Oceanographer Navy Dept Washington DC 20380

STUNTZ, HOMER CLYDE, physician; b. Lahore, Punjab, India, Feb. 25, 1923 (parents Am. citizens); s. Clyde Bronson and Florence Ada (Watters) S.; came to U.S., 1941; student Wesleyan U., 1941-43, Mich. State Coll., 1944, U. Tex., 1946-48; M.D., Southwestern Med. Sch., 1952; m. Billie Jean Williams, June 7, 1952; children—Beverly Ann, Jean Allison, Philip Williams. Intern, Baylor U. Hosp., Dallas, 1953; resident in surgery McKinney VA Hosp., 1954; gen. practice medicine, Orange, Tex., 1954—; chief staff Orange Meml. Hosp., 1959. Bd. dirs. Orange County Cancer Soc., Commn. on Alcoholism. Served to 2d lt. USAAF, 1943-46. Mem. A.M.A., So., Tex. med. assns., Orange County Med. Soc. (pres. 1958), C. of C., Conservative Union, Econ. found. Home: 2223 24th St Orange TX 77630 Office: 1214 16th St Orange TX 77630

STURGILL, EDGAR GORDON, dentist; b. Pikeville, Ky., Feb. 27, 1926; s. Edgar Kimble and Gracie (Brainard) S.; student Pikeville Jr. Coll., 1946-48; D.M.D., U. Louisville, 1954; m. Dorothy Lee Ward, June 6, 1948; 1 son, Marcus Gordon. Tchr., Floyd County Sch. System, Prestonburg, Ky., 1948-49; pvt. practice dentistry, Louisville, 1954-57, Hebron, Ky., 1958-59, Prestonsburg, Ky., 1961-63, Harold, Ky., 1963-65, Wheelwright, Ky., 1965—; with Ky. Dept. Health, 1959-61. Served with USNR, 1943-46; PTO. Mem. Am., Ky. dental Assns., Ky. Mountain Dental Soc. (pres. 1970-71), Am. Legion. Mason. Club: Pikeville Sportsman. Home: Route 3 Box 499 Pikeville KY 41501 Office: Box 457 Wheelwright KY 41669

STURM, DOROTHY, artist, educator; b. Memphis, Aug. 2, 1911; d. Frank Falls and Charlie Owen (Weddle) Sturm; student Art Students League, N.Y.C., 1930-33; student in biol. scis. and med. illustration Columbia, 1931-32. Illustrator in pathology Columbia Coll. Phys. and Surg., N.Y.C., 1932-34; TVA malarial research for Rockefeller Found. at U. Tenn. Med. Sch., Memphis, 1940-41, malarial research for War Emergency Council, 1942-43; instr. drawing and painting Memphis Acad. Arts, 1937-39, 42, asso. prof., 1966-70, prof. metal arts, 1970—; exclusive contract Betty Parsons Gallery, N.Y.C., 1952-70; hematology study Abbott Labs., 1968—. Saunders Pubs. grantee for blood morphology study, 1954-55. Author: (with Diggs and Bell) Morphology of Human Blood, 1956. Home: 3525 Oakley St Memphis TN 38111 Office: Memphis Academy of Arts Overton Park Memphis TN 38112

STURROCK, THOMAS TRACY, horticulturist, educator; b. Havana, Cuba, Dec. 9, 1921 (parents Am. citizens); s. David and Ruth (Earle) S. came to U.S., 1929; diploma Palm Beach Jr. Coll., 1941; B.S. with honors in Agr., U. Fla., 1943, M.S. in Agr., 1943, Ph.D., 1961; m. Betty Jeanne Norquist, June 30, 1948; children—Nancy Elizabeth, John David, Barbara Jeanne, Catherine Ann, Robert Charles. Grove maintenance Sturrock Tropical Fruit Nursery, West Palm Beach, Fla., 1946-56; insp. Fla. Plant Bd., West Palm Beach, 1956-57; tchr. biology Palm Beach High Sch., West Palm Beach, 1957-58; research asst. U. Fla., Gainesville, 1958-60; tchr. biology dept. Palm Beach Junior College, Lake Worh, Fla., 1960-64; asst. prof. biol. scis. Fla. Atlantic U., Boca Raton, 1964-68, asso. prof. botany, 1968—, asst. dean Coll. Sci., 1971—. Cubmaster, Boy Scouts Am., West Palm Beach, 1960-62, scoutmaster, 1946-54, dist. chmn., 1961-63; mem. exec. bd. Gulf Stream council, 1961—, v.p., 1969-70. Served to capt. USAAF, 1943-46; PTO; lt. col. Res. Recipient Silver Beaver award Boy Scouts Am., 1951. Mem. Am. Soc. for Hort. Scis., Fla. Hort. Soc., A.A.A.S., Fla. Acad. Scis., Internat. Soc. Hort. Sci., Fla. Mango Forum, Sigma Xi. Presbyn. (elder). Research on mangos. Home: 1010 Camellia Rd PO Box 6022 West Palm Beach FL 33405 Office: Fla Atlantic University Boca Raton FL 33432

STURTEVANT, WILLIAM CURTIS, anthropologist; b. Morristown, N.J., July 26, 1926; s. Alfred Henry and Phoebe (Reed) S.; B.A., U. Cal., Berkeley, 1949; Ph.D., Yale, 1955; m. Theda Maw, July 26, 1952; children—Kinthi D.M., Reed P.M., Alfred B.M. Instr. dept. anthropology, asst. curator anthropology Peabody Mus., Yale, 1954-56; ethnologist, gen. anthropologist Bur. Am. Ethnology, 1956-65, gen. anthropologist, curator Nat. Mus. Natural History, 1965—, mem. Center for Study of Man, Smithsonian Instn., Washington, 1968—. Fulbright lectr. U. Oxford, 1967-68. Served with USNR, 1945-46. Home: 7009 Florida St Chevy Chase MD 20015 Office: Smithsonian Instn Washington DC 20560

STYNE, ALEXANDER FREDERICK, cons. indsl. designer; b. Karisruhe, Germany, Nov. 15, 1913; s. Nathan and Recha (Straus) S.; student Munich (Germany) and Bern (Switzerland) univs., 1932-33; B.Arch., Brussels, Belgium, 1938; m. Mercedes Tarrida-Bertran; children—(by previous marriage) Joanna, Philip. Came to U.S., 1940, naturalized 1944. Mgr. display studio, instr. Reiman Sch., London, Eng., 1939; asst. to Joseph Aronson, designer and author, N.Y.C., 1940; pres. Styne & Ballard, Inc., N.Y.C., 1944-59; instr. N.Y. Sch. Interior Design, 1947-59; cons. indsl. designer, specializing in space planning, lighting, color styling, bldg. prodn. and furniture, North Miami, Fla., 1959—; instr. Miami Dade Jr. Coll., 1964-68; vis. lectr., critic, U. Miami, 1964—, co-chmn. advanced lighting course, 1971—; vis. prof. Sch. Architecture and Art, Auburn (Ala.) U., 1970, U. N.C. at Greensboro, 1971. Pres. Jr. Mus., Hempstead, N.Y., 1957-58. Served with C.E., AUS, 1942-43. Recipient 1st prize lighting competition Southeastern region, 1970. Mem. Am. Inst. Interior Designers (bd. govs. N.Y. chpt. 1956-59, v.p., 1958-59), Municipal Art Soc. N.Y. (com. interior design 1950-53), Indsl. Designers Soc. Am., Inter-Soc. Color Council (del., chmn. problem sub-com. on human response to color), Color Marketing Group, Illuminating Engring. Soc. (nat. allied arts com. 1964—, nat. com. on color 1972—), Internat. Commn. on Illumination (fundamentals of visual signalling com). Patentee in field. Contbr. articles profl. jours. Research and devel. project in marine lighting. Office: 15206 NE 8th Av Miami FL 33162

STYRON, CHARLES WOODROW, physician; b. New Bern, N.C., Nov. 6, 1913; s. Benjamin William and Annie (Howell) S.; B.S. in Chemistry, N.C. State Coll., 1934; M.D., Duke, 1938; m. Nell Devereux Joslin, Oct. 14, 1939; children—Charles Woodrow, Elizabeth Joslin. Intern Duke Hosp., Durham, N.C., 1938, Boston City Hosp., 1939-40; Elliott P. Joslin fellow medicine New Eng. Deaconess Hosp., 1940-42; pvt. practice medicine, Raleigh, N.C., 1946—; asst. prof. medicine Duke U. Med. Center, also N.C. State U. Served to lt. comdr. M.C., USNR, 1942-46. Decorated Bronze Star Medal, Silver Star, Purple Heart. Fellow A.C.P.; mem. Am. Diabetes Assn. (gov. N.C. 1953-59), Am., N.C. (bd. dirs.) heart assns., A.M.A., Am., N.C. (pres. 1957-58) socs. internal medicine, So. Med. Assn., Med. Soc. State N.C. (sec. 1962—, pres. 1971-72). Editorial bd. N.C. Med. Jour., 1960—. Contbr. articles to profl. jours. Home: 920 Williamson Dr Raleigh NC 27608 Office: 615 St Mary's St Raleigh NC 27605

SUAREZ, RALEIGH ANTHONY, historian, coll. dean; b. Plaquemine, La., Jan. 2, 1925; B.S., La. State U., 1948, M.A., 1949, Ph.D. in History, 1954; m. 1946. Asst. historian La. State U., 1951-54, instr., 1954-55; asso. prof. McNeese State U., Lake George, La., 1955-57, prof. 1957—, head dept. social scis., 1957-62, dean Sch. Humanities, 1962—. Adminstrv. asst. La. sec. of state, 1953-54; research cons. La. Archival Survey, 1954-55. Mem. La. Commn. Higher Edn., 1955-57, Mem. Am., So., La. (pres. 1966) hist. assns., Phi Kappa Phi. Contbr. hist. articles to profl. jours. Office: McNeese State Coll Sch Humanities Lake George LA 70601*

SUAU, FELIX VILELLA, physician. Diplomate Am. Bd. Surgery. Mem. P.R. Med. Assn. (pres.-elect). Address: Box 9387 Santurce PR 00908*

SUBER, SAMUEL ROBERT, JR., knit fabric co. exec.; b. Kings Mountain, N.C., Sept. 14, 1921; s. Samuel Robert and Artie (Parlier) S.; student N.C. Vocational Textile Sch., 1945-47; m. Rosalie Polk, May 20, 1943; children—Samuel Robert III, William Claude. Overseer, asst. supt. Holly Knit, Am. Efird Mills, 1948-53; asst. supt. Clover Spinning, 1953-54, supt., 1954-56; supt., gen. mgr. Aladdin Knit, 1956-66; pres., plant mgr. Kings Mountain Knit Fabrics Inc. (N.C.), 1966—, also dir.; v.p., dir. Dependable Knits, Mountaineer Knits, Wayside Fabrics Store; dir. 1st Citizens Bank & Trust Co., Kings Mountain. Served with inf. AUS, 1942-45; ETO. Decorated Purple Heart. Mem. Am. Legion, V.F.W. Lutheran (mem. ch. council 1961-65). Elk, Kiwanian. Club: Lake Montonia (pres., dir. 1969-70) (Kings Mountain). Home: 307 W Gold St Kings Mountain NC 28086 Office: Railroad Av and Oak St Kings Mountain NC 28086

SUBERMAN, JACK, educator; b. N.Y.C., June 18, 1920; s. Alex and Frieda (Caskill) S.; B.A., U. Fla., 1946, M.A., 1947; Ph.D., U. N.C., 1954; m. Marcella Kaufman, Jan. 30, 1942; 1 son, Rick Ian. Instr., U. N.C., 1949-50, 52-53; editorial chief Extension Course Inst., USAF, Montgomery, Ala., 1950-52; prof. English, N.C. State U., Raleigh, 1953-67, dir. summer sessions, 1959-67, dir. continuing edn. div., 1965-67; dean Coll. Humanities, Fla. Atlantic U., Boca Raton, Fla., 1967—. Served to capt. USAAF, 1942-45. Decorated Air medal with oak leaf cluster. Mem. Nat. Assn. Coll. and Univ. Summer Sessions (regional v.p. 1964-66), S. Atlantic Modern Lang. Assn., Assn. for Higher Edn., N.E.A. Author: Basic Composition, 1956, 2d edit., 1968; A Language Reader for Writers, 1966. Home: 700 NE 5th Av Boca Raton FL 33432

SUBLETT, CARL CECIL, educator; b. nr. Paintsville, Ky., Feb. 4, 1919; s. Tandy Taylor and Beulah (Fitzpatrick) S.; student Western Ky. State Coll., 1938-40, Univ. Study Center, Florence, Italy, 1945, U. Tenn., 1955-56; m. Helen Crawford Davis, Aug. 20, 1942; children—Carol Taylor (Mrs. Bert Edwin Witham), Eric Davis. Editorial artist Bristol (Va.) Newspaper Corp., 1949-52; asst. mgr. Bristol (Va.) Art Engravers, 1951-53; art dir. Charles S. Kane Co., Knoxville, Tenn., 1954-65; prof. art U. Tenn., 1966—. Exhibited Southeastern Ann., Atlanta, 1954-58, 60, Mid-South Exhbn., Memphis, 1956-58, Va. Intermont Coll., 1949-60, Provincetown Art Festival, 1958, Nashville Festival, 1958-60, Miss. Art Assn., 1958-59, Painters of New South, Birmingham, 1959, Butler Inst. Am. Art., 1959, Smithsonian Instn., 1960, others; work rep. in permanent collections E. Tenn. Coll., Knoxville Art Center, Stephens Coll., Columbia, Mo., Tenn. Botanical Gardens and Fine Arts Center, others. Served with AUS, 1943-45. Mem. Tenn. Coll. Art Assn., Mus. Modern Art, Birmingham Art Assn., Arts and Craft Soc., Dulin Gallery of Art, Knoxville Water Color Soc., Huntsville Art League. Methodist. Contbr. editorial art Kingsport Times. Home: 2104 Lake Av Knoxville TN 37916

SUBLETT, CHARLES WILLIAM, publishing co. exec.; b. Danville, Va., Jan. 1, 1906; s. Charles William and Martha Ethel (Smith) S.; LL.B., U. Va., 1927; m. Marian Lucille Pace, Jan. 8, 1950; children—Charles William, Martha Susan. Admitted to Fla. bar, 1928, Va. bar, 1931; mem. editorial staff Michie Law Pub. Co., Charlottesville, Va., 1927-28, 31-35, editor-in-chief, 1935-44, v.p., 1939—; practiced in West Palm Beach, Fla., 1928-31; pres. dir. Michie City Publs. Co., Charlottesville, 1943—; v.p., dir. Michie City Publs. Co., Los Angeles, 1958—. Mem. Gov's. Democratic Steering Com., 1961. Mem. Am., Va., Charlottesville, Albemarle bar assns., Jefferson Lit. Soc., Phi Alpha Delta. Democrat. Methodist. Mason. Clubs: Farmington Country, Falcon (Charlottesville). Home: 106 Minor Rd Charlottesville VA 22903 Office: 610 E Market St Charlottesville VA 22901

SUDIA, WILLIAM DANIEL, med. entomologist; b. Ambridge, Pa., Aug. 19, 1922; s. Frank T. and Patricia (Storoshka) S.; B.S. in Agr., U. Fla., 1949; M.Sc., Ohio State U., 1952, Ph.D., 1957; m. Margueritte Elizabeth Delony, Sept. 3, 1949; children—Shawn Davis, Shelly Anne. With Center for Disease Control. USPHS, Atlanta, 1951—, chief arbovirus ecology lab., 1967—. Served with AUS, 1942-46. Recipient Superior Performance award USPHS, Spl. Achievement award, 1972, Meritorious Service medal, 1972. Mem. Am. Mosquito Control Assn., Research Soc. Am., Am. Soc. Tropical Medicine and Hygiene. Inventor CDC battery operated light trap, lab. chill table. Author papers in field. Home: 1410 Willivee Dr Decatur GA 30033 Office: 1600 Clifton Rd Atlanta GA 30333

SUFFRIDGE, JAMES ARTHUR, labor union ofcl.; b. Knoxville, Tenn., Feb. 2, 1909; s. Chester A. and Angie (Dodson) S.; student extension courses, U. Cal.; m. Georgia Nutting, Nov. 18, 1928; children—Beverly M. (Mrs. Charles Osterling), Carole N. Mem. Retail Clks. Internat. Assn., 1934—, nat. pres., 1944-47, 55—, sec.-treas., 1947-55; mem. exec. council inter-Am. com., also econ. policy com. AFL-CIO, also 3d v.p. union label and service trades dept. and mem. exec. bd. indsl. union dept. Mem. WLB, Oakland, Cal., 1943-44; exec. com. I.F.C.C.T.E., Amsterdam. Lay mem. Nat. Council Chs. of Christ in U.S.A.; bd. dirs. Oakland YMCA, 1943-44. Republican. Mason. (Shriner). Home: 4000 25th Pl N Arlington VA Office: De Sales Bldg Washington DC 20006

SUGARMAN, GORDON R., bus. exec., lawyer, b. 1936; B.A., Harvard, 1958; LL.B., Yale, 1962; married. Admitted to Conn. bar, Ga. bar; with firm Haas, Holland, Freeman, Levison & Gibert, 1962-67, partner, 1964-67; sec. Nat. Service Industries, Inc., Atlanta, 1967-69, v.p. legal affairs, sec., 1969—.Office: 1180 Peachtree St NE Atlanta GA 30309*

SUGARMAN, MARVIN MEYER, dentist; b. Atlanta, Aug. 13, 1915; s. Samuel L. and Ida (Meyers) S.; D.D.S., Emory U., 1938; m. Rose Gilner, Mar. 5, 1939; children—Edward F., Brenda (Mrs. David Goldberg), Richard. Pvt. practice dentistry, Atlanta, 1938-50; pvt. practice dentistry specializing in periodontics, Atlanta, 1950—; asst. prof. periodontics Emory U., 1952—. Dir. Merc. Nat. Bank, Mgmt. Systems, Inc. Mem. Am. Coll. Dentists (sec.-treas. Ga. sect. 1970-72), So. Acad. Periodontology (pres. 1967), Ga. Dental Assn. (pres. 1969), Sigma Xi, Omicron Kappa Upsilon. Jewish religion. Club: Standard (Atlanta). Home: 3049 Nancy Creek Rd Atlanta GA 30327 Office: 384 Peachtree St Atlanta GA 30308

SUGG, HAROLD GRAY, newspaper editor; b. Greenville, N.C., Apr. 14, 1916; s. B. B. and Lillian (Gray) S.; B.S., Davidson Coll., 1937; m. Mary Jane Nesbitt, Feb. 12, 1944; children—Harold Gray, William N., Elizabeth E. City editor Stanly News and Press, Albermarle, N.C., 1938; polit. reporter, asso. editor The Virginian-Pilot, Norfolk, Va., 1939-57, asst. pub., 1957-65; sr. v.p., dir. Landmark Communications, Inc., Norfolk, 1965-71; editor editorial page Roanoke (Va.) Times, 1971—. Pres. Friends of Norfolk Pub. Library, 1955-61; bd. dirs. Norfolk Pub. Library, 1955-61; bd. dirs. Norfolk Pub. Library, 1962—. Served to capt. AUS, 1942-46. Mem. Phi Gamma Delta, Omicron Delta Kappa, Va. Club. Club: Norfolk Yacht and Country (Norfolk, Va.). Home: 1810 Greenwood Rd Roanoke VA 24015 Office: PO Box 2491 Roanoke VA 24010

SUGG, ROBERT WHITTINGTON, dentist; b. Durham, N.C., July 15, 1926; s. Avery Gordon and Cammie Elizabeth (Whittington) S.; A.B., Duke, 1949; D.D.S., U. N.C., 1955; m. Dorothy Maria Dezern, June 10, 1950; children— Deborah Anne, Patricia Louise, Robert W. Gen. practice dentistry, Durham, 1955—. Mem. N.C. State Bd. Dental Examiners, 1971—. Bd. dirs. Gov. Morehead Sch. Served with USNR, 1944-46. Mem. Am. Dental Assn., N.C. Dental Soc., Am. Assn. Dental Examiners, Am. Soc. Dentistry Children, Omicron Kappa Upsilon, Beta Theta Pi, Psi Omega. Home: 1402 Broad St Durham NC 27705 Office: 209 S Gregson St Durham NC 27701

SUGGS, EUGENE CUMMINGS, city mgr.; b. Hearne, Tex., Aug. 8, 1927; s. Melvin Eugene and Stella Alene (Bishop) S.; mgmt. and utility courses Tex. A. and M. U., 1964-66; m. Martha Louise Boggan, Jan. 25, 1947; children—Connie (Mrs. John W. Laster), Steven Eugene, Carla. With Utility Dept., City of Hearne, Tex., 1952-58, asst. utility supt., 1958-63, dir. pub. works, 1963-67, city mgr., 1967—. Chmn. trade devel. com., Hearne, 1970-71; com. chmn. Little League Baseball, 1953. Fire chief, City of Hearne, 1954. Served with USNR, 1944-46. Mem. Tex. City Mgrs. Assn., Brazos Colo. Utility Assn. (pres. 1965-66, 71—), Am. Water Works Assn., Brazos Electric Power and Interconnected Rural Electric Am. (municipal chmn. 1969), Indsl. Found. (dir. 1969-71). Mason, Lion (sec. 1960), Rotarian (v.p. 1971). Home: 907 Wheelock St Hearne TX 77859 Office: 210 Cedar St Hearne TX 77859

SUHOR, CHARLES AUGUST, ednl. adminstr.; b. New Orleans, June 3, 1935; s. Anthony Bernard and Marie Odette (Porte) S.; B.S., Loyola U., 1956; M.A., Cath. U., 1957; advanced certificate in edn. U. Ill., 1967; postgrad. Tulane U., 1962, (English-Speaking Union scholar) Oxford, 1965; m. Jessie Marie Miller, May 16, 1959; children—Michael, Gregory, Traci, Julie, Cathy and Beth (twins), Jean, Paul, David, Dianna. English tchr. New Orleans Pub. Schs., 1957-66, English supr., 1967—. Tchr., La. State U., New Orleans, 1963, Dillard U., 1964, 65. Served with AUS, 1958-59. Mem. Nat. (pres. New Orleans br. 1971-72), La. (high sch. rep. 1969-70) councils tchrs. English, La. Assn. Curriculum Devel. Democrat. Roman Catholic. Compiler anthologies. (With Frank D'Angelo and John Mayher) The Growing Edges of Secondary English, 1968, American Dream, 1972. Contbg. editor Media and Methods, 1969—, New Orleans Mag., 1967—. Contbr. articles to profl. jours. Home: 633 Exposition Blvd New Orleans LA 70118 Office: 731 St Charles Av New Orleans LA 70130

SUHRER, JAMES HARTMAN, physician; b. Jacksonville, Fla., Apr. 6, 1926; s. Julian George and Emma Marie (Nagel) S.; B.S., Emory U., 1948, M.D., 1951; m. Martha Jean Drane, Dec. 21, 1950; children—Janice, Denise, Elizabeth, James, Martha, George, Leslie, Stephen. Intern. Grady Meml. Hosp., Atlanta, 1951-52; gen. practice medicine, Aiken, S.C., 1952—; mem. staff Aiken Co. Hosp. Chmn. bloodmobile program A.R.C., 1954-56. Councilman, Aiken, S.C., 1966—. Served to 1st lt. AUS, 1944-46. Mem. A.M.A., S.C., Aiken County (past pres.) med. socs., Phi Beta Kappa, Theta Kappa Psi. Republican. Roman Catholic (lector). K.C. (4 deg.). Clubs: Fermata, Cotillion (Aiken). Home: 519 Coker Spring Av SW Aiken SC 29801 Office: 148 Waterloo St SW Aiken SC 29801

SUKI, WADI NAGIB, physician; b. Khartoum, Sudan, Oct. 26, 1934; s. Nagib Khalil and Fahima Hamdi (Hariz) S.; B.S., Am. U. Beirut, 1955, M.D. with distinction, 1959; m. Lailah Janet Stephan, May 6, 1967; children—Leila, Ramzy, Lenora, Wade. Came to U.S., 1959, naturalized, 1964. Fellow in exptl. medicine U. Tex. Southwestern Med. Sch., Dallas, 1959-61; resident in internal medicine Parkland Meml. Hosp., Dallas, 1961-63; fellow in nephrology U. Tex. Southwestern Med. Sch., 1963-65, instr., 1965-66, asst. prof. internatl medicine, 1966-68; asso. prof. medicine Baylor Coll. Medicine, Houston, 1968-71, prof., 1971—, chief renal sect., 1968—; practice medicine, specializing in internal medicine and kidney diseases, Dallas, 1965-68, Houston, 1968—; chief renal sect. Meth. Hosp., Houston; attending physician Ben Taub Gen. Hosp., Houston; cons. medicine VA Hosp., Houston. Chmn. med. adv. bd. Kidney Found. Houston and Greater Gulf Coast, 1969-71; chmn. nat. med. adv. council Nat. Kidney Found., 1971-72; mem. exec. com. council on kidney in cardiovascular disease Am. Heart Assn., 1971—. Recipient Research and Training Grants, NIH, USPHS, 1968—. Fellow A.C.P.; mem. Internat., Am. socs. nephrology, A.A.A.S., Am. Fedn. Clin. Research, Am. Physiol. Soc., Am., So. socs. clin. investigation, Alpha Omega Alpha. Mem. editorial bd. The Kidney, 1970—. Contbr. articles to profl. jours. Home: 4926 Glenmeadow St Houston TX 77035 Office: 6516 Bertner St Houston TX 77025

SULLIVAN, A(NNA) MANNEVILLETTE, metallurgist, govt. ofcl.; b. Washington, Aug. 18, 1913; d. Francis Paul and Vilette (Anderson) Sullivan; student Wellesley Coll., 1931-33; A.B., George Washington U., 1935; postgrad. Cath. U., 1935-36, M.S., U. Md., 1955. Asst.

metallurgist Carnegie Inst. Washington, 1942-45; metallurgist Nat. Bur. Standards, Washington, 1945-46, U.S. Naval Research Lab., Washington, 1947—. Mem. Research Soc. Am., Am. Soc. Metals, Am. Soc. Testing Materials, Alpha Delta Pi. Iota Sigma Pi. Club: Altrusa Internat. Research in fracture of metals with spl. reference to fracture mechanics. Home: 4000 Massachusetts Av NW Washington DC 20016 Office: US Naval Research Lab Washington DC 20390

SULLIVAN, CHARLES L., state ofcl.; b. New Orleans, Aug. 20, 1924; s. O.U. and Jennie (Lewis) S.; student Tulane U., 1946-47; LL.B., U. Miss., 1950; m. Mary Lester Rayner, Sept. 1949; children—Charles Lester, DAvid Hewitt, Mary Loten, John Marshall. Admitted to Miss. bar, 1950, since practiced in Clarksdale; sr. mem. firm Sullivan, Dunbar & Smith; municipal judge Clarksdale, 1953-55; dist. atty. 11th Jud. Dist., 1956-60; lt. gov. State of Miss., 1968—. Pres. N. Miss. Savs. & Loan Assn. Served with USAAF, 1942-46, USAF, 1951-52. Recipient Distinguished Civilian Service award, 1969; named Miss. Man of Year, 1959. Baptist. Mason (32 deg., Shriner), Lion. Home: 426 W 2d St Clarksdale MS 38614 Office: New Capitol Bldg Jackson MS 39205

SULLIVAN, DONALD RICHARD, city ofcl.; b. Lexington, Ky., Feb. 2, 1935; s. John Christopher and Laura Bell (Halsey) S.; student U. Ky., 1954-57; grad. Ky. State Fire Sch., 1963; m. Reba Marilyn Dill, Sept. 14, 1957; children—Martin Christopher, Dena Donalynn, Cynthia Ann. Firefighter, City of Lexington, Ky., 1960-63, lt., 1963-66, capt., 1966-69, maj., 1969—. Instr. Fire Sch. U. Ky. Extension Program, 1964—. Chmn. major retail bus. United Community Fund, 1970. Recipient Fireman of the Year award Lexington Bluegrass Breakfast Lions Club, 1969. Mem. Lexington Jr. C. of C. (Doug Sutherland award 1969; state dir. 1971-72), Greater Lexington Area C. of C. (dir. appointee 1969), Fraternal Order Firemen. Presbyn. Home: 1681 Margate Dr Lexington KY 40505 Office: 3d and Walnut Sts Lexington KY 40508

SULLIVAN, HELEN ESTELLE (STELLA SULLIVAN), artist; b. Houston, Oct. 11, 1924; d. Maurice Joseph and Anne (King) Sullivan; B.A., Rice U., 1945; student Mus. Sch. Art, 1949-50, Sch. Detroit Soc. Arts and Crafts, 1950-51; M.F.A., Cranbook Acad. Art, 1954. One-man shows in Columbus, O., Houston; exhibited in group shows in Houston; works represented in collections Contemporary Arts Mus., Houston; instr. Mus. Fine Arts Sch., Houston, 1961-70, U. Houston, 1962-66, Spring Br. Sch. Adult Edn., 1962-66; asst. prof. art Sam Houston State U., Huntsville, Tex., 1970-71; owner Stella Sullivan Sch. Art and Gallery, Houston, 1971—; vis. asst. prof. art U. Del., 1963; faculty Brazasport Art League, Freeport, Tex., 1961; Outdoor Painting Workshop, Sante Fe, summer 1970, Landscape Painting Workshop, Telluride, Colo., Summer 1971; co-founder, sec., treas. pres. Handmakers, Inc., Houston, 1957-60; asso. in formation of Galley 75, Conroe, Tex.; designer print room Rice U., 1966; executed murals and prints Flagship Hotel, Galveston, Tex.; executed prints Menger Hotel, San Antonio, Hotel Intercontinental, Manila, P.I., Fredonia Hotel, Nacogdoches, Tex.; represented by Laguna Gloria Mus. Art Kental, Austin, Tex. Recipient Shlumberger award Houston Artists 26th Ann., 1951, Fabric award Tex. Crafts 7th Ann., 1955. Roman Catholic. Club: Houston Yacht, (Houston). Home: 32 5353 Institute Lane Houston TX 77005 Office: 2409 Times Blvd Houston TX 77005

SULLIVAN, L. M., sch. adminstr.; b. Crescent, Okla., June 11, 1924; s. Roy Hampton and Lillis Martha (Prosser) S.; B.A., Northwestern State Coll., Alva, Okla., 1950; M.Ed., Phillips U., 1952; Ed.D., Okla. State U., 1968; m. Peggy Louise Rowley, Mar. 5, 1945; children—Michael, Steven. Adminstr. schs. in Okla., 1949—, sch. adminstr. Harrah pub. schs., 1968—. Mem. City-County Bd. Health, Oklahoma County, 1969—. Served with USAAF, 1942-45. Decorated D.F.C., Air Medal with five clusters. Mem. Nat. Acad. Sch. Execs., Am. Assn. Sch. Adminstrs. (tour Soviet Union 1971), Panhandle Edn. Assn. (pres. 1960-61). Democrat. Methodist (lay leader). Lion, Rotarian. Home: 119 Gold St Harrah OK 73045

SULLIVAN, LAWRENCE BROZAK, mech. engr.; b. Washington, Aug. 25, 1937; s. John Vincent and Alva (Herndon) S.; B.S. in Mech. Engring., Tex. A. and M. U., 1959, M.S., 1962; m. Sylvia Marie Frady, Sept. 6, 1958; children—Cynthia Marie, Lawrence Brozak. Research engr. Humble Oil & Refining Co., Houston, 1959-61; grad. research asst. Tex. Engring. Expt. Sta., College Station, 1961-62; fluid mechs. research engr. Gen. Electric, Schenectady, 1962-66; sr. engr. Texas Instruments Inc., Dallas, 1966—. Cons. electronic instrumentation mfr., 1967—. Registered profl. engr., Tex. Mem. Instrument Soc. Am., Tau Beta Pi, Phi Kappa Phi, Phi Eta Sigma. Republican. Roman Catholic. Home: 2908 Glencliff Pl Plano TX 75074 Office: PO Box 5621 Mail Sta 937 Dallas TX 75222

SULLIVAN, WILLIAM CLINTON, judge; b. Birmingham, Ala., Sept. 3, 1926; s. Archie H. and Louise (Montgomery) S.; LL.B., U. Ala., 1949; m. Helen Lob, Sept. 28, 1951. Admitted to Ala. bar, 1949; gen practice, Talladega, Ala., 1949-58; mayor, Lincoln, Ala., 1952-58; circuit judge Talladega County, 1958—. Mem. Ala. Pattern Jury Instructions Com. Served with USNR, 1944-46. Mem. Am., Talladega County (past pres.) bar assns., Ala. State Bar, Nat. Conf. State Trial Judges, Internat. Platform Assn., Chi Phi. Democrat. Methodist. Club: Talladega Country. Home: PO Box 235 Lincoln AL 35096 Office: Ct House Talladega AL 35160

SULLIVAN, WILLIAM LITSEY, lawyer, state senator; b. Harrodsburg, Ky., Nov. 1. 1921; s. Charles Blount and Anne (Litsey) S.; B.A., Centre Coll. of Ky., 1949; LL.B., U. Ky., 1948; m. Elizabeth Dor[illegible] Apr. 21, 1951; children—William Litsey, John Charles. Admitted to Ky. bar, 1948; with firm Dorsey and Sullivan, Henderson, Ky., 1956-70; commr. aeros. State of Ky. 1958-60; mem. Ky. Senate, 1954-57, 66—, majority leader, 1956, pres. pro tem, 1968-72. Served with USAAC, 1942-45; ETO. Named Outstanding Young Man of Ky., U.S. Jr. C. of C., 1956. Rotarian (pres. 1962). Home: 517 N Main St Henderson KY 42420 Office: 140 N Main St Henderson KY 42420

SULLIVAN, WILLIAM NICHOLAS, JR., govt. ofcl.; b. Lawrence, Mass., June 23, 1908; s. William Nicholas and Catherine (Lynch) S.; B.S.C., U. Mass., 1930, M.S.C., 1937. Jr. entomologist Entomology Research Div., Agrl. Research Service, Dept. of Agr., Beltsville, Md., 1931-37, entomologist, 1937-42, research entomologist, 1947—; cons. WHO. Served to maj. AUS, 1942-47. Recipient John Scott award City of Phila., 1945, Chem. Specialists Mfrs. Assn. Achievement award, 1954, Eric Rotheim award Fedn. European Aerosol Assn., 1970. Mem. A.A.A.S., Am. Inst. Biol. Scis., Entomol. Soc. Am., Washington Entomol. Soc., Insecticdal Soc. Washington, Sigma Xi. Co-Inventor insecticidal aerosol bomb, World War II. Home: 3601 Wisconsin Av NW Washington DC 20016 Office: Room 110 Bldg 307 ARC Beltsville MD 20705

SULT, ERROLL CLIFFORD, welding supply co. exec.; b. Crockett, Va., May 15, 1927; s. Walter Thomas and Laura Priscilla (Robinson) S.; student Naval Acad. Prep. Sch., 1946, Twin City Coll. Commerce, 1947; m. Elizabeth Thyra Jones, June 17, 1950; children—Deborah Joan, Erroll Clifford, Terry Lynn. Elec. tester Western Electric Co., Winston-Salem, N.C., 1947; with So. Oxygen Co., 1948-53, store mgr., 1952-53; asst. br. mgr., then br. mgr. Nat. Welders Supply Co., Inc., Florence, S.C., 1953-59, sales mgr., Charlotte, N.C., 1959-71, v.p. sales, 1971—; pres. Nat. Welders of Goldsboro (N.C.), 1962-67, Breathing Assos., 1971—. Served with USNR, 1945-46. Recipient S.M.E. Distinguished Sales award, 1971. Mem. Nat. Welding Supply Assn. (dir. 1970-71, zone v.p. 1971-72), Am. Welding Soc. (vice chmn. 1971-72, chmn. 1972-73), Charlotte C. of C. Mason. Home: Route 6 Box 652D 317 Pine Island Dr Charlotte NC 28208 Office: Box 8108 Charlotte NC 28208

SULZBY, JAMES FREDERICK, JR., realtor; b. Birmingham, Ala., Dec. 24, 1905; s. James Frederick and Annie (Dobbins) S.; student Howard Coll., Birmingham, 1925-26, A.B., Birmingham-So. Coll., 1928; grad. Am. Inst. Banking, 1934; Litt.D., Athens Coll., 1953; m. Martha Belle Hilton. Nov. 9, 1935; children—James Frederick III, Martha Hilton. Mem. staff trust dept. First Nat. Bank of Birmingham, 1929-43; partner Sulzby Realty Co., 1943—; v.p., dir. Fidelity Savs. & Loan Assn.; dir. Birmingham Real Estate Bd., 1953; pres. Norwood Gardens, Inc., 1948-49, sec.-treas. 1950, v.p., 1951. Trustee Birmingham Civic Symphony Assn.; mem. Jefferson County Personnel Bd. Bd. dirs. Birmingham Sunday Sch. Assn.; chmn. Planning Com., 1948-61; dir. Ala. Bapt. publ., 1945—; historian 75th anniversary celebration for Birmingham. 1946, also treas. deacon, mem. exec. com. Southside Baptist Ch.; pres. Ala. Baptist Young Peoples Union, 1932-33; chmn. Jefferson County Nat. Found. Infantile Paralysis, 1951-52. Bd. govs. Civic Theatre of Birmingham, 1946-48. Recipient Distinguished Service award Ala. Hist. Commn., 1972. Mem. Newcomen Soc. N.Am. (Ala. com.), Ala. Hist. Assn. (pres. 1947-49), Ala. Baptist (pres. 1947-49), Birmingham (sec. 1945-50, trustee) hist. socs., Avondale Civic Assn. (pres. 1946), Am. Planning and Civic Assn., Nat. Assn. Real Estate Bds. (dir. 1952-56), Ala. Real Estate Assn. (pres. 1952), Ala. Writers Conclave (pres. 1950), Birmingham Area Ednl. Television Assn. (treas., dir.), Ala. Acad. Sci. (pres. 1965-66), Birmingham C. of C. (chmn. edn. com. 1949-51), Birmingham So. Coll. Alumni Assn. (pres. 1960). Phi Beta Kappa, Delta Sigma Phi, Omicron Delta Kappa. Clubs: Mountain Brook Country; University (Tuscaloosa); The Club, Downtown. Author: Birmingham As It Was in Jackson County, 1944; Birmingham Sketches, 1945; Annals of the Southside Baptist Church. 1947; Historic Alabama Hotels and Resorts, 1960; Authur W. Smith: A Birmingham Pioneer, 1855-1944, 1961. Democrat. Baptist. Home: 3121 Carlisle Rd Birmingham AL 35213 Office: Massey Bldg Birmingham AL 35203

SULZER, ALEXANDER JACKSON, immunoparasitologist; b. Emmett, Ark., Feb. 13, 1922; s. Eugene A. and Edna J. (Weaver) S.; student Ia. Poly. Inst., 1940-41; B.A., Hardin-Simmons U., 1949; postgrad. Vanderbilt U., 1950-51; M.S., Emory U., 1960, Ph.D., 1962; m. Fay Catherine Ross, Oct. 3, 1942; children—Danny Lynn, Harry Eugene. Instr. biology Hardin-Simmons U., Abilene, Tex., 1949-50; AEC fellow Vanderbilt U., Nashville 1950-51; parasitologist U.S. Communicable Disease Center, Atlanta, 1951-59; NIH fellow Emory U., Atlanta, 1959-62; microbiologist U.S. Nat. Communicable Disease Center, Atlanta, 1962—. Served with AUS, 1942-43. Mem. Research Soc. Am., Am. Soc. Tropical Medicine and Hygiene, Am. Soc. Parasitologists. Home: 3711 Canadian Way Tucker GA 30084 Office: 1600 Clifton Rd Atlanta GA 30333

SUMMER, ALBIOUN F., lawyer, state ofcl.; b. Pelahatchie, Miss., Nov. 2, 1921; s. Sydney Lamar and Iva Lee (Hardy) S.; diploma Hinds Jr. Coll., 1942; student U. Miss. Law Sch., 1946-47; LL.B., Jackson Sch. Law, 1950; m. Mary Lois Campbell, June 1945; 1 son, Carl Bennison. Admitted to Miss. bar, 1950; atty. Town of Pelahatchie, 1950-51; mem. Miss. Bd. Vet. Affairs, 1957; exec. asst., legal adviser to gov. State of Miss., Jackson, 1958, chief asst., legal adviser, 1968-69; chancery judge 5th Dist. of Miss., 1958-61; atty. gen. State of Miss., 1969—. Mem. Beta Theta Pi, Phi Delta Theta. Office: State Capitol Jackson MS 39201*

SUMMERFORD, BEN LONG, artist, educator; b. Montgomery, Ala., Feb. 3, 1924; s. Ben Long and Ollie Jo (Gilchrist) S.; student Birmingham-Southern Coll., 1942-43; B.A., Am. U., 1948, M.A., 1954; student Ecole des Beaux Arts, Paris, 1949-50; m. Christene Morris, Jan. 30, 1951; children—Jeffrey, Rebecca, James. Fellow. Acad. Time, 1947, Fulbright fellow to France, 1949-50; staff art dept. Am. U., 1950—, chmn. dept., 1957-66, prof., 1960—; one-man exhbns. include: Balt. Mus. Art, Goucher Coll., Franz Bader Gallery, Washington, Jefferson Place Gallery, Washington; represented permanent collection Watkins Gallery, Phillips Gallery Art, Corcoran Gallery of Art (all Washington); numerous group shows of paintings. Served to ensign USNR, 1943-46. Home: 10216 Brown's Mill Rd Vienna VA 22180 Office: American University Washington DC 20016

SUMMERLIN, GLENN WOOD, JR., advt. exec.; b. Dallas, Ga., Apr. 1, 1934; s. Glenn Wood and Flora (Barrett) S.; student Ga. Inst. Tech., 1951-52; B.B.A., Ga. State U., 1956, M.B.A., 1967; m. Rebecca Anne Valley, Oct. 16, 1971; children—by previous marriage Glenn Wood III, Edward Lee. Prodn. mgr. Fred Worrill Advt., Atlanta, 1956-65; v.p. sales Grizzard Advt., Inc., Atlanta, 1965—. Trustee Ga. State U. Found. Named Outstanding Young Man in DeKalb County N. DeKalb Jr. C. of C., 1967; recipient C.S. Bolen award So. Council Indsl. Editors, 1967. Mem. Internat. Council Bus. Communicators, Asso. Mail advt. Agys., Ga. Assn. Bus. Communicators (pres. 1966-67), Mail Advt. Service Assn. (pres. N. Ga. chpt. 1959-60), Sales and Marketing Execs. (dir. Atlanta 1969-71), Am. Marketing Assn. (dir. Atlanta chpt. 1969—), Ga. Bus. and Indsl. Assn. (gov.), Atlanta Humane Soc. (dir. 1970—), Ga. State U. Alumni Assn. (pres. 1971-72), Lion. Ga State U. Grad. Bus. Club (v.p. 1969-70), Sigma Phi Epsilon. Home: 1133 Ragley Hall Rd NE Atlanta GA 30319 Office: 1144 Mailing Av SE Atlanta GA 30315

SUMMERS, FRANK WYNERTH, state justice; b. Abbeville, La., Sept. 5, 1914; s. Clay Ralph and Esther (LeBlanc) S.; B.A., U. S.W. La., 1938; LL.B., Tulane U., 1938; m. Beverly Miller, June 22, 1940; children—Frank Wynerth II, Preston Miller, Susan Priscilla, Clay James, William Charles, Beverly Marie. Admitted to La. bar, 1938; practice in Abbeville, 1938-41, 46-52, 55-60; dist. judge 15th Jud. Dist. Ct. La., 1952-54; asso. justice La. Supreme Ct., New Orleans. Campaign Vermilion Parish Chpt. A.R.C., 1947-48, past chmn. chpt. 1949; chmn. Vermilion dist. Boy Scouts Am., 1956, pres. Evangeline area council, 1958-60; chmn. Vermilion Parish U.S. Savs. Bonds. Served to lt. comdr. USNR, 1941-46. Mem. Am., La. bar assns., Am. Legion (past post comdr.), Order of Coif, Blue Key, Phi Delta Phi. Democrat. Roman Catholic. K.C. Clubs: Abbeville Country (past pres.); New Orleans Country. Home: 500 2d St Abbeville LA 70510 Office: Supreme Ct Bldg 301 Loyola Av New Orleans LA 70112

SUMMERS, JAMES WILLIAM, judge; b. Rusk, Tex., July 8, 1914; s. James Lee and Constance (Rock) S.; B.B.A., J.D., U. Tex., 1937; m. Inez Thompson Steed, Nov. 22, 1969; children—Julia Ann (Mrs. Charles E. Tucker), Raymond C. Steed. Admitted to U.S. Supreme Ct. bar., Tex. bar, 1937, practiced in Rusk, 1937-56; city atty., 1937-41; county atty. Cherokee County, 1941-42, 47-48, county judge, 1949-56; judge 2d Jud. Dist. Tex., Rusk, 1957—. Dir. First State Bank, Southwestern Title & Guaranty Co.; partner Summers Bros., land, cattle, timber. Dir. Civil Def., Cherokee County, 1949-56; mem. Cherokee County Heritage Assn.; mem. adv. council Criminal Justice Program, Stephen F. Austin U., vice chmn. Rusk Housing Corp. Bd. dirs. East Tex. area council Boy Scouts Am., Rusk Indsl. Found., Rusk United Way. Served as lt. USNR, 1942-46. Fellow Tex. Bar Found.; mem. Am. Judicature Soc., Am., East Tex., Cherokee County bar assns., State Bar Tex., Nat. Conf. State Trial Judges, County Judges and Commrs. Assn. Tex., Nat. Assn. County Ofcls., Am., Tex., East Tex. Aberdeen-Angus assns., U. Tex. Ex-Students Assn. (exec. council Austin, past pres. Cherokee County alumni club), Rusk C. of C. (chmn. govt. affairs com.), Tex. Farm Bur. Fedn., Cherokee County Hist. Soc. (dir.), Am. Legion, Beta Gamma Sigma, Phi Delta Phi, Phi Eta Sigma, Phi Delta Theta (v.p. East Tex. alumni). Methodist (ofcl. bd.), Mason (Shriner), Kiwanian (past pres.). Home: 200 W 5th St Rusk TX 75785 Office: Courthouse Rusk TX 75785

SUMMERS, JOSEPH KEITH, educator; b. Wilkes-Barre, Pa., Dec. 6, 1920; s. Samuel and Rose (Deutsch) S.; B.S., N.Y.U., 1951, M.B.A., 1960; m. Harriet Jacobs, Sept. 1, 1946; children—Laureen, Sheldon. Marketing dir. Am. Fluoride Corp., N.Y.C., 1955-56; prof. mgmt. U. P.R., San Juan, 1957—; adminstr. Clinica Antillas, Inc. P.R., 1958-62; adminstr. Presbyn. Hosp., Inc., 1962-69; dir., cons. Robert Scott Assos., Inc., N.Y.C.; cons. IBEC Realty, Inc. Vice pres., dir. Las Colinas, Inc.; asst. treas., dir. Internat. Life Ins. Co. P.R. Mem. Food Distbn. Com. for Gov. P.R., 1958-60; adviser, cons. Coop. Movement P.R., 1958-62. Bd. advisers Robinson Sch. Served with USAAF, 1942-45. Columnist, San Juan Star; feature writer San Juan Review. Contbr. articles to profl. jours. Home: 1223 Rafael Arcelay Rio Peidras PR 00924 Office: Box 249 San Juan PR 00902

SUMMERS, THOMAS EUGENE, entomologist; b. Seneia, Ga., June 7, 1919; s. Elijah Gary and Tinie (Cheek) S.; B.S.A., U. Ga., 1941; M.S., Ia. State Coll., 1947, Ph.D., 1950; m. Edith Hernandez, June 30, 1961; children—Thomas Morgan, Gary Robert, Ruth Anne, Elizabeth Christine. Plant pathologist Dept. Agr., State College, Miss. Belle Glade, Fla., 1950-65, entomologist sugarcane insects investigations Agrl. Research Sta., Canal Point, Fla., 1965—. Mem. grad. faculty U. Fla., 1966. Served with USAAF, 1941-46. Decorated Purple Heart, Air medal, D.F.C. Mem. Entomol. Soc. Am., A.A.A.S., Internat. Orgn. for Biol. Control, Fla. Entomol. Soc., V.F.W. Elk, Rotarian. Research on small grains diseases, diseases of stem and leaf fiber crops. Home: Lakeshore Dr Canal Point FL 33438 Office: PO Box 156 Canal Point FL 33438

SUMMERS, VICTOR LAWRENCE, ednl. adminstr.; b. St. Joseph, Mo., Apr. 29, 1928; s. Victor Lawrence and Viola Mae (Cline) S.; A.B., Rockhurst Coll., 1953; M.A., Am. U., 1966. Instr., Woodward Sch., Washington, 1956-57, U.S. Mil. Acad. Prep. Sch., Ft. Belvoir, Va., 1957-58; headmaster, Ascension Acad., Alexandria, Va., 1958—. Served with USN, 1946-49. Mem. Va. Assn. Secondary Sch. Prins., Va. Assn. Ind. Elementary Schs. (v.p. 1971-72), No. Va. Fine Arts Assn. (pres. 1966), Pi Sigma Alpha. Roman Catholic. Office: 4401 W Braddock Rd Alexandria VA 22304

SUMMERS, WILLIAM, broadcasting exec. Vice pres., gen. mgr. WLOU, Louisville. Office: 2549 S 3d St Louisville KY 40209*

SUMMERSELL, CHARLES GRAYSON, educator; b. Mobile, Ala., Feb. 25, 1908; s. Charles Fishweek and Sallie Rebecca (Grayson) S.; A.B., U. Ala., 1929, A.M., 1930; Ph.D., Vanderbilt, 1940; m. Frances Sharpley, Nov. 10, 1934. Instr. history U. Ala., University, 1935-40, asst. prof., 1940-46, asso. prof., 1946-47, prof., 1947—, head dept. history, 1954—. Radio commentator, Tuscaloosa and Selma, Ala., 1941-43. Commd. lt. (j.g.), USNR, 1942; active duty, 1943; served with U.S. Navy in PTO; lt. comdr.; comdr. Res., 1954; officer charge Naval Tng. School, Norfolk, Va., 1951-53; mem. steering com. organizing Tuscaloosa unit Organized Res. of Navy, 1947. Recipient Letter of Commendation USNR, 1945. Mem. So., Mississippi Valley, Ala. (pres. 1955-56) hist. assns., U.S. Naval Inst., Naval Hist. Found., S.A.R., (pres. Ala. 1957-58), Am. Assn. State and Local History (council 1965-71), Am. Hist. Assn., Phi Beta Kappa (pres. Ala. chpt. 1953-54), Phi Alpha Theta. Democrat. Club: University. Author: Historical Foundations of Mobile, 1949; Mobile History of a Seaport Town, 1949; Alabama History for Schools, 1957, rev., 1965, 70; (with Howard W. Odum and G.H. Yeuell) Alabama Past and Future, 1941, rev. edit. (with G.H. Yeuell and W.R. Higgs), 1950; (with Frances C. Roberts) Exploring Alabama, 1957, rev., 1961; (with Frances S. Summersell) Alabama History Filmstrips, 1961; (with F.S. Summersell and Rembert W. Patrick) Florida History Filmstrips, 1963; (with others) Texas History Filmstrips, 1965; The Cruise of the C.S.S. Sumter, 1965; Ohio History Filmstrips, 1967; (with others) California History Filmstrips, 1968, Illinois History Filmstrips, 1970. Mem. editorial adv. bd., Am. Neptune, 1946—; mem. editorial bd. Ala. Rev., 1964—. Contbr. articles and revs. to encys. and profl. jours. Home: 1411 Caplewood Dr Tuscaloosa AL 35401 Office: PO Box 1936 University AL 35486

SUMMERSELL, FRANCES S.(MRS. CHARLES GRAYSON SUMMERSELL), artist; b. Birmingham, Ala.; d. Arthur Croft and Thomas O. (Stone) Sharpley; student U. Montevallo, Peabody Coll.; m. Charles Grayson Summersell, Nov. 10, 1934. Comml. artist, Asso. Educators. Mem. Ft. Morgan Hist. Commn., 1959-63, vice chmn., 1960-63. Mem. Tuscaloosa County Hist. Preservation Soc. (dir.), D.A.R. (regent Tuscaloosa chpt. 1963-65), Magna Charter Dames (state vice regent 1963-65, state chaplain 1960-63), U. Women's Club (pres. 1957-58), Daus. Am. Colonists (organizing regent for Tuscaloosa, 1956-63, state v.p.), Nat. Trust for Historic Preservation, Estes Embroidery Circle, West Ala. Art Assn. Clubs: University, Tuscaloosa Study. Co-author: Alabama History Filmstrips, 1961; Florida History Filmstrips, 1963; Texas History Filmstrips, 1965; Ohio History Filmstrips, 1967; California History Filmstrips, 1968; Illinois History Filmstrips, 1970. Home: 1411 Caplewood Dr Tuscaloosa AL 35401

SUMMERSON, GEORGE WILLIAM, hotel exec.; b. Richmond, Va., Nov. 18, 1903; s. George Ralph and Eula Mead (Ford) S.; B.S., Washington and Lee U., 1927; m. Champe Grant, Dec. 24, 1932; children—Champe (Mrs. Don Hyatt), Sue (Mrs. Irvin Wells III), George William. Gen. auditor Robert E. Lee Hotel, Winston-Salem, N.C., 1929-35; mgr. Washington Duke Hotel, Durham, N.C., 1935-39; gen. mgr. Hotel Gen. Shelby, Hotel Bristol (Va.), 1939-56; pres., gen. mgr. Martha Washington Inn, Abingdon, Va., 1956—. Pres. Bristol Community Chest, 1950-51, Washington County United Fund, 1964-65; mem. state adv. com. Salvation Army, 1972—. Mayor, mem. City Council, Bristol, 1951-57; vice mayor, mem. Town Council, Abingdon, Va., 1968-70, 71-72, mayor, 1972—. Bd. visitors Sullins Coll., Bristol, Va.; bd. dirs., exec. com. Mt. Rogers Planning Commn., 1969-72. Recipient Bristol's Outstanding Citizen award V.F.W., 1953; City of Bristol Pub. Service Recognition award, 1954-56; Bristol Centennial Celebration award, 1956; Distinguished Service award Hotel-Motel Greeters, 1969, Va. Hotel-Motel Assn., 1971. Mem. Am. Hotel and Motel Assn. (trustee ednl. inst. 1958—, pres. inst. 1967-69), Am. (dir. 1949), Va. (pres. 1948), So. (pres. 1952) hotel assns., Hotel Greeters (chpt. pres. 1932), Bristol C. of C. (pres. 1952), Va. Travel Council (pres. 1950-51, outstanding service citation 1952), Abingdon C. of C. (pres. 1959-60), Va. State C. of C. (certificate appreciation 1961, v.p. 1969-71). Methodist (chmn. adminstrv. bd. 1966-69, lay leader 1970-72). Mason (Shriner), Kiwanian. Club: Glenrochie Country (pres. 1961) (Abingdon). Home:

150 W Main St Abingdon VA 24210 Office: Martha Washington Inn 150 W Main St Abingdon VA 24210

SUMMEY, BRETT TAYLOR, dentist; b. West Jefferson, N.C., Sept. 16, 1935; s. Ptolemy Durant and Jessie Dow (Jones) S.; A.B., U. N.C., 1957; D.D.S., U. Md., 1961; m. Gwendolyn Duncan Lemly, Sept. 12, 1958 (div. Sept. 1969); 1 dau., Lisa Dow. Practice dentistry, West Jefferson, 1961—; dir. Northwestern Bank, West Jefferson. Mem. Am. Dental Assn., N.C. Dental Soc. (life), Gorgas Odontological Soc., Jr. C. of C. (pres. 1966), Psi Omega. Baptist. Home: Box 28 West Jefferson NC 28694 Office: Box 28 West Jefferson NC 28694

SUMNER, LAURA VOELKEL (MRS. RAIFORD E. SUMNER), educator; b. Bklyn., Sept. 5, 1921; d. John Frederick and Laura (Bennett) Voelkel; A.B., Vassar Coll., 1942; M.A., Johns Hopkins, 1943, Ph.D., 1945; m. Raiford E. Sumner, Dec. 20, 1953; children—Laura Eve, Raiford Bennett, Robert Woodfin. Asst. prof. Latin and art history Wesleyan Coll., Macon, Ga., 1945-48, asso. prof., 1947-48; asst. prof., chmn. dept. classics U. Va., Mary Washington Coll., 1948-54, asso. prof. 1954-63, prof., 1963—, dir. summer session, 1968-71. Vis. prof. U. Wis., 1954-55; mem. staff U. Chgo. and Ind. U. excavation, Greece, 1963. Mem. Fredericksburg City Council, 1960—. Fellow Am., Royal numis. socs.; mem. Classical Assn. Va. (pres. 1958-60), C. of C. (dir. 1957-60), Am. Philological Assn., Archaeol. Inst. Am., Phi Beta Kappa. Episcopalian. Author: Sonnets, 1961; A Latin Coloring Book, 1963. Home: Box 1275 College Station Fredericksburg VA 22401

SUMNER, MARK REESE, theatre research adminstr.; b. Asheville, N.C., July 19, 1923; s. Clarence R. and Margaret C. (Worley) S.; B.S., U. N.C., 1948, M.A., 1955; postgrad. N.D. State U., Asheville-Biltmore Coll., Am. U.; m. Margaret deMerell, 1947 (div. 1958); children—Carl W., Douglas D., James W.; m. 2d, Glenn Allison Geddings, June 28, 1960; children—Laura Jean, Mark Reese, Kenneth W. Stage mgr. Md. Tobacco Festival Pageant, Harrington-Russell Festival Co., LaPlata, 1941; publicity dir. Carolina Playmakers, 1947-50; stage mgr. Pkwy. Playhouse, 1948-50; chmn. dept. drama and speech Mary Washingotn Coll., U. Va., 1951-63; dir. Inst. Outdoor Drama, U. N.C., Chapel Hill, 1964—. Bus. mgr., dir. Vagabond Players, Flat Rock Playhouse, State Theatre N.C., summers 1952-53; gen. mgr. Cape Cod Arena Theatre, Orleans, Mass., summer 1954; gen. mgr. Lighthouse Players, Inc., Ocean City, Md., summers 1957-60; gen. mgr. outdoor drama Home Is The Hunter, Harrodsburg, Ky., 1964; chmn. auditions Southeastern Theatre Conf., 1964-68, adminstrv. v.p., 1967, v.p., 1968, pres., 1969; project dir. Hammocks Beach Performing Arts Inst., 1969, Survey Outdoor Drama Techniques, Dept. Health, Edn. and Welfare, 1966; lectr. U. Va., Ga. So. Coll., U. Ga., Coll. William and Mary, U. N.C., Davidson Coll., Clatsop Coll., W.Tex. State U., Averett Coll. Mem. selection bd. Harry Davis Meml. Scholarship for Tchrs.; chmn. theatre adv. com. N.C. Arts Council; chmn. cultural affairs com. N.C. Travel Council; mem. adv. bd. Coll. Drama Festival Va. Bd. dirs. N.C. chpt. Nat. Repertory Theatre. Served with inf. AUS, 1943-46; ETO. Decorated Combat Inf. Badge, Bronze Star medal. Mem. Am. Ednl. Theatre Assn. (regional chmn.), ANTA, U.S. Inst. Theatre Tech., Nat. Council Govt. and Arts, Actors Equity Assn., S.C. Theatre Assn., N.C. Hist. Soc. Author: A Survey of Outdoor Drama Production Techniques, 1968; (plays) Rock Dust, 1947, Thunderhead, 1948. Notes from the First Playwrights Conference, 1964; An Ampitheatre for Epic Drama, 1965; Inst. of Outdoor Drama Newsletter, 1964—. Contbr. articles to profl. jours. Home: 2A Williams Chapel Hill NC 27514 Office: Inst Outdoor Drama U NC Chapel Hill NC 27514

SUMNER, MAURICE NEWTON, architect, engr.; b. Ganado, Tex., Jan. 17, 1929; s. Sylvan Joseph and Pauline (Newton) S.; B.Archtl. Engring., U. Houston, 1955, B.S. in Archtl. Engring., 1970, M.S. in C.E., 1970. Architect, engr. Robert W. Clemens & Assos., Bovay Engrs., McRan Co., Francis Niven, Davis & Sumner, R. George Cunningham, Johnson & Edwards, Jenkins & Hoff, 1950-65; pvt. practice architecture, Houston, 1965—. Served with AUS, 1953-55. Registered profl. engr., architect, Tex. Mem. Am. Soc. C.E., Am. Concrete Inst., Soc. Naval Architects and Marine Engrs. Contbr. articles to profl. jours. Patentee in field. Home: 4309 Yoakum St Houston TX 77006

SUMNER, RAIFORD E., educator; b. Asheville, N.C., Sept. 29, 1913; s. Lonnie and Eva (Eve) S.; B.A., U. Tenn., 1937; M.A., U. Miss., 1940; M.A., U. N.C., 1957; postgrad. Oxford U., 1953; m. Laura Bennett Voelkel, Dec. 20, 1953; children—Laura Eve, Raiford Bennett, Robert Woodfin. Area mgr. War Manpower Commn., 1941-46; prof. history Marion Inst., 1946-48; prof. polit. sci. Mary Washington Coll., U. Va., Fredericksburg, 1948—. Gen. chmn. Civil War Centennial Commn. Pres. adv. bd. Salvation Army; trustee United Givers Fund. Recipient State of Va. Merit award, 1962, City of Richmond (Va.) Certificate of Merit, 1963, City of Fredericksburg Certificates of Appreciation, 1963. Mem. Am. Acad. Polit. Sci., Am., So. polit. sci. assns., Am. Ordnance Soc. Democrat. Episcopalian. Rotarian. Club: Blowing Rock (N.C.) Country (dir.). Contbr. articles to profl. publs. Home: Box 1275 College Station Fredericksburg VA 22401

SUMRELL, GENE, research chemist; b. Apache, Ariz., Oct. 7, 1919; s. Joe B. and Dixie (Hughes) S.; B.A., Eastern N.M. U., Ph.D., U. Cal. at Berkeley, 1951. Asst. prof. chemistry Eastern N.M. U., 1951-53; sr. research chemist J. T. Baker Chem. Co., Phillipsburg, N.J., 1953-58; sr. organic chemist S.W. Research Inst., San Antonio, 1958-59; project leader Food Machinery & Chem. Corp., Balt., 1959-61; research sect. leader El Paso Natural Gas Products Co. (Tex.), 1961-64; project leader So. utilization research and devel. div. U.S. Dept. Agr., New Orleans, 1964-67, investigations head, 1967—. Served from pvt. to staff sgt., AUS, 1942-46. Mem. Am. Chem. Soc., A.A.A.S., N.Y. Acad. Scis., Am. Inst. Chemists, Am. Oil Chemists Soc., Am. Assn. Textile Chemists and Colorists, Research Soc. Am., Am. Assn. U. Profs., Sigma Xi, Phi Kappa Phi. Home: PO Box 24037 New Orleans LA 70124 Office: 1100 Robert E Lee Blvd New Orleans LA 70119

SUMWALT, ROBERT LLEWELLYN, JR., constrn. co. exec.; b. Columbia, S.C., Dec. 29, 1927; s. Robert Llewellyn and Caroline M. (Causey) S.; B.S. in Civil Engring., U. S.C., 1949; M.S. in Civil Engring., Mass. Inst. Tech., 1950; m. Mary Joyce Mills, Mar. 8, 1952; children— Elizabeth Ladson, Robert Llewellyn III. Area engr. E. I. duPont de Nemours & Co., Camden, S.C., 1950-52; constrn. engr. Columbia City Sch. System, 1952-58; exec. v.p., sec., dir. McCrory-Sumwalt Constrn. Co., Columbia, 1958—; dir. Palmetto Grading & Paving Co., Columbia. Pres. Richland County unit Am. Cancer Soc., 1956, Carolina Carillon Ball, 1963; sect. chmn. United Community Services, 1957. Bd. dirs. Am. Cancer Soc., S.C. chpt., 1957, Richland County unit A.R.C., 1955-56. Named Young Man of the Year, Columbia Jr. C. of C., 1958. Registered profl. engr., S.C. Mem. Asso. Gen. Contractors Am., Columbia Contractors Assn. (pres. 1969), S.C. Soc. Engrs., S.C. Soc. Profl. Engrs., Sigma Alpha Epsilon, Phi Beta Kappa, Omicron Delta Kappa, Tau Beta Pi. Presbyn. (chmn. bd. deacons 1968). Kiwanian (pres. 1962). Clubs: Forest Lake Country, Palmetto (Columbia). Home: 1420 Belmont Dr Columbia SC 29205 Office: 2632 Millwood Av Columbia SC 29202

SUN, HUAI CHIN, educator; b. Shantung, China, July 26, 1904; s. T.F. and Lee (Liu) S.; B.A., Peking Normal U., 1928; M.A., Colo. State Coll., 1945; postgrad. N.Y.U., Columbia, 1945-46; Ed.D., U. Colo., 1949; m. Chih Ming Liu, Jan. 10, 1934; children—Amie Ming Chiu (Mrs. Jon Ambrose), Diana. Dean of studies, tchr. English secondary schs., Shantung, 1928-34; prin. Hui-Min Exptl. Elementary Sch., 1934-35; prin. Shantung Ping-Yuan Normal Sch., 1935-37; prof. edn. Peking Normal U., 1948; prof., chmn. grad. dept. and div. edn., dean Bishop Coll., Dallas, 1952-63; vis. prof. Am. U., 1963-64, U. Md., 1964-65; prof. edn. Johnson C. Smith U., Charlotte, N.C., 1965-70, prof. edn., dir. grad. studies Hampton (Va.) Inst., 1970—. Summer vis. prof. U.Colo., 1947, 57, 59, N.M. Highlands U., 1952. U. N.M., 1960, Brigham Young U., 1961, 63, D.C. Tchrs. Coll., 1964, 65, U. Mont., 1968; Campus rep. Woodrow Wilson Found., 1957-60, Am. Assn. Colls. for Tchr. Edn., 1970—; cons. dept. ednl. service and sci. Research Assos., Inc., 1969-70; mem. adv. com. N.C. Commn. on Higher Edn. Facilities, 1969-70. Mem. staff Ministry Edn., Chungking, China, 1941-44. Sec., bd. dirs. Nat. Hupeh Secondary Sch., dir. social edn., bd. dirs. Nat. Hupeh War-Zone Tchrs. Corps. Mem. N.E.A., Assn. for Supervision and Curriculum and Devel., John Dewey Soc., Assn. for Higher Edn., Philosophy of Edn. Soc., South Atlantic Philosophy of Edn. Soc., Comparative Edn. Soc., Tex. Conf. on Tchr. Edn. (planning com. 1959-6o), Phi Delta Kappa, Kappa Delta Pi. Author: Advanced English Grammar, 1932; Introduction to Education, 1935. Contbr. articles to profl. jours. Home: 1356 Coral Pl Hampton VA 23369

SUNKEL, GEORGE FOREMAN, retail trade exec.; b. Paris, Ill., June 18, 1904; s. John William and Beatrice (Foreman) S.; student Austin Coll., 1922-23; m. Margaret Sue Smith, June 17, 1926; children—Marian (Mrs. Joseph L. Frank), Margaret (Mrs. Maxey Kyle Russell, Jr.). Partner, McCulloch Grocery Co., Clarksville, Tex., 1923-40; owner Piggly Wiggly Stores, Clarksville, Tex., 1940—; pres. Piggly Wiggly Operators Warehouse, Shreveport, La., 1965; chmn. bd. Piggly Wiggly Red River Co., Inc., Clarksville, Tex., 1957—; dir. Piggly Wiggly Operators Warehouse, Shop Rite Foods, Inc., Dallas. Alderman, Clarksville, Tex., 1935-40. Bd. dirs. Red River County Indsl. Found.; trustee Synod of Tex. Presbyn. Found. Mem. Nat. Piggly Wiggly Operators Assn. (pres. 1952), Clarksville C. of C. (pres. 1955). Presbyn. (ruling elder 1940). Mason (Shriner). Home: 1500 W Main St Clarksville TX 75426 Office: 800 W Main St Clarksville TX 75426

SURACI, CHARLES XAVIER, JR., govt. ofcl.; b. Washington, Feb. 10, 1933; s. Charles Xavier and June (Hunter) S.; student Pa. Mil. Coll., 1952-53, Columbia Union Coll., 1961-62; m. Florence Patricia DeMino, May 23, 1970. With Harry Diamond Lab, U.S. Army, Washington 1963—, material publs. asst., 1963-68, adminstrv. asst., head dispatcher for operations transp. officer, 1968—. Mem. youth com. Y.M.C.A., Silver Spring, Md., 1962-69, mem. bd. mgmt., 1967—. Served with USAF, 1953-57; Korea. Recipient certificate of commendation from Pres. Nixon, 1970. Mem. Civil Air Patrol (dep. comdr. Nat. Capitol Wing 1969—). Roman Catholic. Club: Andrews AFB Officers (Washington). Home: 12512 Village Sq Terrace Rockville MD 20852 Office: Conn Av and Van Ness St Washington DC 20438

SURBIS, ALBINA ANN YAKAITIS (MRS JOHN PETER SURBIS), educator; b. Harvey, Ill., Feb. 16, 1923; d. Felix and Anna (Gudaitis) Yakaitis; B.S., U. Chgo., 1945, M.S., 1949; Ph.D., U. Minn., 1955; m. John Peter Surbis, Apr. 8, 1967. Research fellow Detroit Inst. Cancer Research, 1956-58; research asso. dept. pathology U. Mich. Med. Sch., Ann Arbor, 1959-61; mem. faculty U. Miami (Fla.) Sch. Medicine, 1961—, asst. prof. biol. structure, 1961—. Mem. Am., So. assns. anatomists, Am. Soc. Hematologists, Fla. Acad. Sci., Sigma Xi. Home: 1905 NE 118th Rd North Miami FL 33161 Office: PO Box 875 Biscayne Annex Miami FL 33152

SURGINER, LESLIE, govt. ofcl.; b. nr. Brownfield, Tex., Jan 11, 1904; s. Isaac Carr and Lena (Snodgrass) S.; B.S., U. Tex., 1928; B.B.A., South Tex. Coll., 1940; m. Wilma Elizabeth Gound, July 18, 1928. Asst. cashier Floyd County Nat. Bank, Floydada, Tex., 1928-31, cashier, 1931; accountant Rio Grande Valley Vegetable Coop. Assn., Weslaco, Tex., 1931-32, sec.-treas., office mgr., 1932-34; accountant Fed. Land Bank, Houston, 1934-41; accountant FCA, Washington, 1941-44, chief accountant, 1944-47; asst. chief finance div. Rural Electrification Adminstrn., Dept. Agr., 1947-50, chief finance div., 1950-51, chief accounting and auditing div., 1951-52, controller, 1952-53; dep. regional dir. Kansas City (Mo.) region Army Audit Agy., 1953-55; accountant, accounting systems div. U.S. Gen. Accounting Office, Washington, 1955-56, head program and rev. staff, office of dir. Def. Accounting and Auditing div., 1956-57, asst. dir., 1957-59, asst. dir. in charge, 1959-61; controller Rural Electrification Adminstrn., 1961-66, dir. borrowers financial mgmt. div., 1966—. Conferee subcom. staff experts on accounting Nat. Assn. Regulatory Utility Commrs., 1964—; mem. Interagy. Regulatory Accountants Com., 1965—. Recipient Superior Service award U.S. Dept. Agr., 1969, Sec.'s Mgmt. Improvement award, 1970. C.P.A., Tex. Mem. Am. Inst. C.P.A.'s, Fed. Govt. Accountants Assn. (Distinguished Leadership award 1971), Acacia. Independent. Baptist (chmn. finance com. 1962, chmn. audit com. 1965-67, 70, chmn. bd. deacons 1969). Mason. Club: Washington Golf and Country. Home: 3800 N Oakland St Arlington VA 22207 Office: 14th St and Independence St SW Washington DC 20250

SURLES, CHARLIE WILLIAM, JR., dentist; b. Snow Hill, N.C., Oct. 20, 1934; s. Charlie William and Christine (Aswell) S.; student Campbell Coll., 1953-55; B.S., U. N.C., 1957, D.D.S., 1960; m. Patricia Jane Herman, Nov. 19, 1960; children—Charles Herman, John William, David Stewart. Instr. crown and bridge dept. U.N.C. Sch. Dentistry, Chapel Hill, 1960-61; pvt. practice dentistry, High Point, N.C., 1962—. Clin. instr. Dental Hygiene Sch. at Guilford Tech. Instn., part-time 1966; dir. Denland Corp., High Point, Invesco, Inc., High Point. Active various community drives bd. dirs. Salvation Army Boys Club, High Point. Served to capt. AUS, 1961-62. Recipient Spoke award High Point Jr. C. of C., 1963. Mem. Am., N.C. Guilford County, 3d Dist. (dental editor 1972) dental socs., Delta Sigma Delta. Methodist (v.p. asso. bd. stewards 1968-69, bd. stewards 1972—). Clubs: Emerywood Country, High Point Executives. Home: 1260 Westminster Dr High Point NC 27260 Office: 1124 E Lexington Av High Point NC 27262

SURLES, JESSE LENNOIL, accountant; b. Spotsylvania, Va., July 25, 1931; s. Jesse Thomas and Anna (Mastin) S.; student U. Va., 1951-52; B.C.S. with distinction, Strayer Coll. Accountancy, 1954; m. Betsy Anne Dickinson, Aug. 8, 1953; children—David Lynn, Linda Dianne, Stephen Edward. Office mgr. Monroe Motors, Inc., Fredricksburg, Va., 1954-55; staff accountant Baker, Rennolds, Thompson & Whitt, Fredericksburg, 1955-65, partner, Warrenton, Va., 1965-69; C.P.A. firm Jesse L. Suries, Warrenton, 1970-71; partner Surles & Vida, C.P.A.'s, Warrenton, 1971—. Chmn. performing arts Fauquier chpt. Va. Mus., 1967; mem. curriculum adv. com. Lord Fairfax Community Coll., 1969—. Served with USNR, 1948-51. Recipient Navy Battle Efficiency E award, 1950. Key Man, Jr. C. of C., 1961. Mem. Am. Inst. C.P.A.'s, Va. Soc. C.P.A.'s, Warrenton-Fauquier C. of C. (v.p., dir.), Va. Assn. Professions, Gideon Internat. Baptist (deacon 1959, treas. 1968—). Lion. Club: Fauquier County. Home: 25 Fox Trail Warrenton VA 22186 Office: PO Box 230 Warrenton VA 22186

SURLOCK, JAMES MARVIN, banker; b. Dallas, July 1, 1931; s. Franklin James and Gladys (Holliday) S.; B.B.A., U. Tex., 1954; postgrad. Southwestern Sch. Banking, So. Meth. U., 1965; m. Peggy Jan Beall, June 11, 1954; children—Susan Lynn, Karen Ann, Franklin James. Trust officer Republic Nat. Bank Dallas, 1956-63, Peoples Nat. Bank Tyler (Tex.), 1963—. Pres. East Tex. Symphony, 1967, Tyler YMCA, 1969, Tyler Estate Council, 1971, East Tex. Campfire Girls U.S., 1970. Bd. dirs. Smith County Youth Found., Smith County Heart Assn., Cancer Soc. Smith County, A.R.C., Child Welfare Bur. Smith County. Served to 1st lt. Adj. Gen. Corps, AUS, 1956. Named Outstanding Young Man Tyler, Tyler Jr. C. of C., 1967. Mem. Tyler Petroleum Club, Phi Gamma Delta. Episcopalian. Club: Willowbrook Country (Tyler). Home: 3827 Fry St Tyler TX 75501 Office: PO Box 2001 Tyler TX 75701

SURRAN, EDNA M. WALSH (MRS CARL ALGER SURRAN), writer, clubwoman; b. Chgo., Jan. 27, 1895; d. Francis Walter and Ida May (Wiley) Walsh; grad. N.J. State Tchrs. Coll., 1912; m. Carl Alger Surran, Sept. 26, 1916 (dec. June 5, 1971); 1 son, Carl Robert. Tchr., Atlantic City Pub. Sch., 1912-16, 18-19. Mem. hostess com. Miss Am. Pageant, 1935-53; chmn. fund raising Children's Seashore House; founder Edna M. Surran Award for Good Citizenship, 1942; mem. Rent Control Bd.; pres. Women's Aux. Atlantic County Med. Soc., 1935-36; chmn. Atlantic unit Am. Woman's Vol. Services, 1943-45, v.p. N.J., 1944, nat. bd. dirs., 1944; pres. Beta Delphian, 1929-45. Worker, Republican Party; mem. Volusia County Republican Club. Recipient awards for vol. services USAAF, City of Atlantic City, USO, A.R.C. Club: Atlantic City Woman's (charter mem., pres. 1956-57). Mem. Am. Mothers Assn., Am. Legion Aux., Internat. Platform Assn., Nat., Fla. audubon socs. clubs: Deland Women's, Deland Bridge, Deland Tourists. Home: 1050 Lindley Blvd DeLand FL 32720

SURRATT, JERRY LEE, coll. dean; b. Winston-Salem, N.C., Oct. 18, 1936; s. Robert Lee and Cleo Shirley (Phelps) S.; A.A., Wingate Coll., 1957, B.A., Wake Forest Coll., 1959; B.D., Southeastern Baptist Theol. Sem., 1962; Ph.D., Emory U., 1968; m. Alice Andrea Allen, June 16, 1963; children—Andrea Leigh, Emily Elizabeth. Instr. and acting chaplain, Salem Coll., Winston-Salem, 1965-67; prof. Wingate Coll. (N.C.), 1967—, acad. dean, 1968—. Chmn. joint com. on coll. transfer N.C. Bd. Higher Edn., 1970. Bd. dirs. Union County Mental Health Assn. Mem. Am. Acad. Religion, Am. Soc. Ch. History, Moravian Hist. Soc., N.C. Hist. and Lit. Soc., N.C. Assn. Jr. Colls. (v.p. 1971). Mason. Home: PO Box 487 Wingate NC 28174

SURVANT, WILLIAM GREGORY, educator; b. Owensboro, Ky., Aug. 26, 1907; s. Ellis and Lina Elizabeth (Gregory) S.; B.S., U. Ky., 1931, M.S., 1945; Ph.D., Ohio State U., 1951; m. Rubye Jean Bellamy, Nov. 27, 1936. Tchr. vocational agr. Whitesville High Sch., Daviess County, Ky., 1931-38; soil conservationist Soil Conservation Service, Morganfield, Ky., 1939-42; prof. agronomy U. Ky., Lexington, 1942—, acting asso. dean instrn. Coll. Agr., 1966-68, acting chmn. dept. forestry, 1969-70. Mem. Am. Soc. Agronomy, Soil Sci. Soc. Am., Soil Conservation Soc. Am. Home: 120 Tahoma Rd Lexington KY 40503

SUSMAN, MORTON LEE, lawyer; b. Detroit, Aug. 6, 1934; s. Harry and Alma (Koslow) S.; B.B.A., So. Methodist U., 1956, LL.B., 1958; m. Nina Meyers, May 1, 1958; 1 son, Mark Lee. Admitted to Tex. bar, 1958, Fed. bar, 1961; law clk. Wynne & Wynne, Dallas, 1958; asst. U.S. atty., Houston, 1961-65, 1st asst. U.S. atty., 1965-66, U.S. atty., 1966-69; mem. firm Susman & McKissick, Houston, 1969—. Past mem. bd. dirs. Houston Council Human Relations, Planned Parenthood Houston, S.W. Region Planned Parenthood; bd. dirs. Ct. Vol. Services, Houston, 1969—. Am. Jewish Com. Houston, S.W. Regional Council Am. Jewish Com. Mem. Tex. Bill of Rights Found., 1967—. Served to lt. with USNR, 1958-61. Recipient Younger Fed. Lawyer award Fed. Bar Assn., Washington, 1968. Mem. Am., Fed., Houston bar assns., State Bar Tex., Fed. Bus. Assn., Barristers, Sigma Alpha Mu (pres. 1954), Phi Eta Sigma, Phi Alpha Delta, Delta Sigma Pi. Jewish religion (trustee congregation 1968-72). Rotarian. Clubs: Racquet, Houston. Case note editor Southwestern Law Jour., 1957-58. Home: 11003 Landon Lane Houston TX 77024 Office: 2290 Two Shell Plaza Houston TX 77002

SUSSMAN, MARION BEATRICE BAUM (MRS IRVING SUSSMAN), ednl. adminstr.; b. Paterson, N.J.; d. Samuel and Adele (Gerstein) Baum; student U. Ala., 1940-42; B.Ed. cum laude, U. Miami, 1953, M.Ed., 1956, Ph.D., 1972; postgrad. U. N.C., 1969; m. Irving Sussman, Nov. 21, 1943; children—Nicki (Mrs. Steve Charles Horowitz), Roberta Joy. Sci. tchr. Kinloch Park Jr. High Sch., Miami, Fla., 1953-56, counselor, guidance chmn., test chmn., 1956-63, asst. prin. for guidance, 1969—; counselor, test chmn. S.W. Miami High Sch., 1963-68; grad. asst. U. Miami, Coral Gables, Fla., 1968-69; mem. staff Piedmont summer program Wake Forest U., Winston-Salem, N.C., 1972. Cons. on peer-group counseling. Active various community drives. Mem. N.E.A., Am., Fla., S. Fla., Dade County (pres. 1967-68) personnel and guidance assns., Fla. Edn. Assn., Dade County Sch. Adminstrs. Assn., Assn. on Humanistic Psychology. Mem. B'nai B'rith Women. Home: 8951 SW 60th Terrace Miami FL 33143

SUSTAD, JEANETTE ISABELLE, marine corps officer; b. Mpls., Sept. 9, 1922; d. Fred Inman and Ida (Olson) Sustad; B.A. in Sociology, U. Wash., 1943; postgrad. U. Minn., 1946-47. Commd. 2d lt. USMC, 1943, advanced through grades to col., 1968; airfield operations officer, 1943-45; inactive, 1946-48; recruit tng. staff Marine Corps Recruit Depot, Parris Island, S.C., 1949-50; adj. Marine Corps Base, Camp Pendleton, Cal., also comdg. officer Woman Marine Co., 1950-52; asst. head staff message control br. Hdqrs. U.S. European Command, Frankfurt, Germany and Camp des Loges, France, 1952-54; exec. officer Woman Recruit Tng. Battalion, Parris Island, 1954-57; head pub. relations br. 9th Marine Corp. Dist., Chgo., 1957-59; spl. projects officer G-1 Div., Hdqrs. USMC, 1959-62; operations officer Marine Corps Ednl. Center, Marine Corps Base, Quantico, Va., 1963-65; dep. dir. women marines Hdqrs. USMC, 1965-67; asst. G-1, Marine Corps Base, Camp Pendleton, 1968; dir. women marines, Washington, 1969—. Mem. Marine Corps Assn. (gov.), Women Marines Assns., Marine Corps Res. Officers Assn. Lutheran. Home: 2924 Viewpoint Rd Alexandria VA 22314 Office: HQMC (Code AW) Washington 20380

SUTER, LOUIS, JR., hotel exec.; b. N.Y.C., Mar. 17, 1901; s. Louis and Juliette (Madoule) S.; student N.Y. Coll. Music, 1914-17; B.C.S., N.Y.U., 1921; postgrad. Columbia; m. Eleanor May Patterson, June 26, 1937; children—Louis Edward, Claire Eleanor. Summer camp dir. Boy Scouts Am., Jersey City, 1917-21; rate case staff accountant N.Y. Telephone Co., 1921-28; dir. Am. Indian Pageant, World Scout Jamboree, Nat. Council Act Scout Exec., Mount Vernon, N.Y., 1929-30; C.P.A., Price Waterhouse, 1930-41; owner, Hotel Venezia Motor Inn, Venice, Fla., 1947—. Active Boy Scouts Am., Venice Community Service, P.T.A, Venice Art Assn., Little Theatre, Little League Baseball; chpt. chmn. A.R.C., 1960. Mayor, Venice, Fla., 1947-49; U.S. postmaster, Venice, Fla., 1950-51. Recipient Silver

Beaver award Boy Scouts Am., award A.R.C., Distinguished Community Service award Jersey City Rotary Club, 1916. Mem. Am. Hotel Assn. (dir. Fla. chpt. 1950-60), Venice Hotel and Motel Assn. Methodist (trustee 1960-70). Mason (32 deg., Shriner), Rotarian. Home: Hotel Venezia PO Box 765 Venice FL 33595 Office: PO Box 765 Venice FL 33595

SUTHERLAND, EARL WILBUR, JR., physician, educator; b. Burlingame, Kan., Nov. 19, 1915; B.S., Washburn Coll., 1937; M.D., Washington U., St. Louis, 1942; div.; 3 children. Intern, Barnes Hosp., St. Louis, 1942; asst. in pharmacology Washington U. Sch. Medicine, 1940-42, instr., 1945-46, biochemist, 1946-50, asst. prof., 1950-52, asso. prof., 1952-53; with OSRD, 1943-45; prof. pharmacology, dir. dept. Case Western Res. U. Sch. Medicine, Cleve., 1953-63; prof. physiology Vanderbilt U. Sch. Medicine, Nashville, 1963—. Mem. panel on metabolism sect. biochemistry com. on growth NRC, 1953-54; pharmacologist, exptl. therapeutist USPHS, 1954-58; mem. pharmacological tng. com. NIH, 1958-62, 63-65, mem. arthritis and metabolic disease program com., 1966—. Recipient Nobel prize in medicine and physiology for research in hormones, 1971. Mem. Nat. Acad. Sci., A.A.A.S., Soc. Biol. Chemists, Am. Chem. Soc., Soc. Pharmacology. Research on enzymatic and hormonal aspects of carbodhydrate metabolism, mechanism of action of hormones and drugs, intermediary carbohydrate metabolism, cyclic nucleotides. Office: Dept Physiology Vanderbilt University School of Medicine Nashville TN 37203*

SUTHERLAND, FRANK, editor; b. nr. Smyrna, Tenn., May 31, 1945; s. Ernest Franklin and Fontella (Moore) S.; B.A. in Philosophy, Vanderbilt U., 1970; m. Ann Katherine Sparkes, Dec. 28, 1967 (div.). Campus corr. Nashville Tennessean, 1963, gen. assignment reporter, 1954, youth page editor, 1965-66, reporter, 1966-69, edn. editor, 1969—. Mem. Sigma Delta Chi. Home: 3436 Love Circle Nashville TN 37212 Office: 1100 Broadway Nashville TN 37203

SUTHERLAND, JOHN ALFRED, petroleum co. exec.; b. Kansas City, Mo., Feb. 16, 1924; s. Jesse Dick and Grace (Slaughter) S.; student Kansas City Jr. Coll., 1941-43; B.S., U. Mo., 1948; m. Norma Elenore Doerner, June 25, 1949; children—Ellen Laura, Karen Lee. Jr. mech. engr. Stanolind Oil & Gas Co., Okla., Wyo., 1948-51; sr. engr. Sunray Oil Corp., La., Okla., 1951-55; v.p. Union Tex. Petroleum div. Allied Chem. Corp., Houston, 1955—; v.p., dir. Uno-Tex Petroleum Corp.; exec. v.p., dir. Refinadora Costarricense de Petroleo, S. Am., Costa Rica. Served with USNR, 1943-46. Registered profl. engr., Okla., La. Mem. Am. Petroleum Inst. (mem. gen. com. div. refining 1968-71), Nat. Gas Processors Assn. (dir. 1970-71), Tau Beta Pi. Patentee in field. Home: 415 Coachman Lane Houston TX 77024 Office: 3000 Richmond St Houston TX 77001

SUTHERLAND, JOHN PATRICK, journalist; b. Kansas City, Mo., June 12, 1920; s. Joseph Frederick and Hazel Marie (Hogan) S.; A.B., U. Mo., 1947, B.Jour., 1948; m. Virginia Claire Shockley, Oct. 19, 1942. Reporter, Spirit Lake (Ia.) Beacon, 1937; asst. editor Barrick Pub. Co., 1948-50; mem. Washington staff Wall Street Jour., 1951-52; White House corr. U.S. News and World Report, Washington, 1953—. Chmn. bd. trustees Merriman Smith Meml. Fund, Washington, until 1972. Served to lt. AUS, World War II; PTO. Mem. White House Corrs. Assn. (pres. 1971-72). Roman Catholic. Club: Nat. Press (Washington). Author: Men of Waterloo, 1966. Home: 3720 Gunston Rd Alexandria VA 22302 Office: US News and World Report 2300 N St NW Washington DC 20037*

SUTHERLAND, RAYMOND CARTER, educator; b. Horse Cave, Ky., Nov. 5, 1917; s. Raymond Carter and Ruth (Veluzat) S.; student Transylvania Coll., 1935-36; A.B., U. Ky., 1939, M.A., 1950, Ph.D., 1953; grad. Gen. Theol. Sem., 1942. Ordained to ministry Episcopal Ch., 1942; curate St. Luke's Ch., Anchorage, Ky., 1942-44; prof. U. Tenn., 1953-57, Ga. State U., Atlanta, 1957—; research grant U. Oxford, 1959. Served as chaplain, capt. AUS, 1944-47, PTO, ETO. Recipient research grant from Georgia State Coll. for work on medieval manuscripts. Mem. Am. Archaeol. Assn., Heraldry Soc. Eng., Medieval Acad. Am., Modern Lang. Assn., Oriental Ceramic Soc. (London), Heraldry Soc. (London). Am. Author: Medieval English Conceptions of Hell as Derived from Biblical, Patristic, and Native Germanic Sources, 1953; The Religious Background of Swift's A Tale of A Tub, 1958; Mechanics of Versification, 1963, 2d edit., 1964; The Celibate Beowulf, the Gospels and the Liturgy (Ga. State Coll. Monograph series), 1964. Contbr. articles profl. jours. Home: 50 Polo Dr NE Atlanta GA 30309

SUTHERLAND, THOMAS ALLEN, librarian; b. Owensboro, Ky., Oct. 24, 1940; s. Adron Cohen and Ruth Moina (Christian) Sutherland; B.A., Ky. Wesleyan Coll., 1964; M.L.S., U. Ky., 1965; m. Gayle Moss, Aug. 28, 1965; children—Ginna Ruth, Todd Allen. Library asst. Ky. Wesleyan Coll., 1963-64; regional dir. Ky. Dept. Libraries, Frankfort, 1965-68; dir. Paducah (Ky.) Pub. Library, 1968—. Instr., Sch. Library Sci., U. Ky., 1970—; mem. Ky. State Adv. Council on Libraries, 1971-73. Served with AUS, 1958-59, 61-62. Recipient trustees award Ky. Library Assn., 1970. Mem. Am., Ky. (exec. sec. 1971—; trustees award 1970), Southeastern library assns., Phi Delta Theta. Methodist. Rotarian. Book reviewer Library Jour., 1970—. Contbr. articles to profl. pubs. Home: 285 Sycamore Dr Paducah KY 42001 Office: 555 Washington St Paducah KY 42001

SUTTER, EDWARD HAROLD, banker; b. New Orleans, Dec. 2, 1912; s. Frederick W. and Gertrude (Staehle) S.; LL.B., Tulane U., 1935; m. Fairfax Foster, Sept. 5, 1963; children by former marriage—Julia Ann (Mrs. Fred B. Kramer Jr.), Ann Woodard (Mrs. James M. Langham). Admitted to La. bar, 1935; law practice, New Orleans, 1935-42; trust officer Fidelity Nat. Bank Baton Rouge, 1946-54, v.p., trust officer, 1954-62, sr. v.p., trust officer, dir., 1962-68; pres. Comml. Bank & Trust Co., Franklin, La.; pres. Young's Industries, Inc.; dir. Sterling Sugars, Inc. Bd. dirs. Stehlin Found. Cancer Research. Elk. Club: Baton Rouge Country; Belleview Country (Franklin). Home: Hwy 90 Franklin LA 70538

SUTTLE, WALTER CORRA, city ofcl.; b. Honey Grove, Tex., Aug. 26, 1904; s. Jefferson Davis and Elizabeth (Edwards) S.; grad. high sch.; m. Flora Marshall, Aug. 12, 1925 (dec. Aug. 1947); 1 son, Walter Marshall; m. Theta Wheeler, Jan. 8, 1955. With Scott's Grocery, Electra, Tex., 1919-24; city inspector, Electra, Tex., 1924-25; with Police Force, Electra, 1925-43, chief police, 1933-43; fire marshall, chief police, Vernon, Tex., 1943-52, chief police, Snyder, Tex., 1952-55; salesman Waples Platter Grocery Co., 1955-59; chief police, Vernon, 1959—. Maj. Tex. State Guard, 1960-71. Mem. exec. bd. on criminal justice Nortex Regional Planning Assn., 1970—; mem. ofcl. bd. Salvation Army, Vernon, Tex., 1959—; mem. Commn. of law Enforcement and Edn., 1965—. Mem. Tex. (mem. exec. bd.), Tex. Municipal, N. Tex. (pres. 1969—) police assns., Law Enforcement Officers Assn. Tex., C. of C. Baptist. Mason (32 deg., Shriner). Club: North Tex. Field and Stream (Wichita Falls); Greenbelt Sportman (Vernon); Vernon Boys. Home: 3230 Maiden St PO Box 391 Vernon TX 76384 Office: City Hall Vernon TX 76384

SUTTLES, WILLIAM MAURRELLE, clergyman, educator; b. Ben Hill, Ga., July 25, 1920; s. Wiley Maurrelle and Eddie Lou (Campbell) S.; B.C.S., Ga. State U., 1942; M.R.E., Emory U., 1953, M.Th., 1947; M. Div., Yale, 1946; Ed.D., Auburn U., 1958; D.D., Mercer U., 1972; m. Julia Lanette Lovern, Jan. 28, 1950. Ordained to ministry Baptist Ch., 1938; pastor Haralson (Ga.) Bapt. Ch., 1950—, Luthersville Bapt. Ch., 1951-62; faculty Ga. State U., Atlanta, 1942—, prof. speech, 1955—, exec. v.p., provost, 1969—, also prof. ednl. adminstrn. and higher edn., Dir. Bank of Fulton County (Ga.), Atlanta Fed. Savings and Loan Assn. Mem. Ga. Sci. and Tech. Commn., 1964—, Citizens Bond Study Commn., 1965—; past chmn. men's council Atlanta League Women Voters, 1963; past chmn. Walter H. and Marjorie M. Rich Scholarship Fund; mem. Christian Council Met. Atlanta. Mem. Com. 100 for Better Edn. in Atlanta; chmn. Joint Citizens Adv. com. to study Atlanta and Fulton County govts. Trustee Ga. State Coll. Athletic Assn., Ga. State U. Found., George M. Sparks Scholarship Fund, John and Mary Franklin Found., Tift Coll., Hillside Cottages; past bd. trustees Marion Howard Sch.; bd. dirs. Fulton County chpt. Am. Cancer Soc., Fulton-DeKalb chpt. March of Dimes. Served with USNR, 1944-46. Named Rural Minister of Year, State of Ga., 1959; Alumnus of Year, Ga. State U., 1964; Clergyman of Yr., Ga. region Nat. Conf. Christians and Jews, 1971; Faculty Mem. of Yr., Delta Zeta, 1964-65. Mem. Ga. State U. Alumni Assn. (trustee, pres.), Ga. Press Assn. (hon.), N.E.A., Ga. Assn. Educators, Atlanta C. of C., Am. Mgmt. Assn., Sigma Nu, Alpha Kappa Psi, Kappa Phi Kappa, Phi Delta Kappa, Kappa Delta Pi, Phi Eta Sigma, Sigma Pi Alpha, Phi Kappa Phi, Beta Gamma Sigma, Omicron Delta Kappa, Sigma Tau Delta. Mason (Shriner), Kiwanian (pres. 1966). Clubs: Commerce, Inquiry (Atlanta). Home: 2734 Piney Wood Dr East Point GA 30344

SUTTON, BERRIEN DANIEL, soft drink co. exec.; b. Axson, Ga., Jan. 24, 1926; s. B. Frank and Commie (Brooker) S.; B.B.A., U. Ga., 1948; m. Verda Lee Adams, June 6, 1953; 1 dau., Kathryn. From traveling auditor to St. Louis dist. mgr. Coca-Cola Co., 1948-62; from v.p. sales to pres., gen. mgr. Coca-Cola Bottling Co. St. Louis, 1962-66; pres. Asso. Coca-Cola Bottling Co., Inc., Daytona Beach, Fla., 1966—; mem. presidents adv. council Coca-Cola Co.; dir. First Atlantic Nat. Bank, Daytona Beach, Fla. Gen. campaign chmn., v.p., dir., mem. exec. com. United Fund E. Volusia County; mem. Civic League Halifax Area. Bd. counselors Bethune Cookman Coll. Served with USNR, 1944-46. Mem. Coca-Cola Bottlers Assn. (bd. govs.), Young Presidents Orgn. Methodist. Rotarian. Club: Oceanside Country (Ormond Beach). Home: 250 Landmark Circle Ormond Beach FL 32074 Office: 320 Orange Av Daytona Beach FL 32015

SUTTON, EDMONDE, editor; b. Mostaganam, Algeria (came to U.S. 1947, naturalized 1950); d. Jean Leopold and Lucienne Andree (Romeu) Duberos; M. Fgn. Langs., U. Algeria, 1942; m. Earl W. Sutton, Jr., Aug. 3, 1968. Sec. to pres. Delegations Financieres, Algeria, 1946; translator Marden Mfg. Co., 1953; with FMO Corp., Lakeland, Fla., 1954—; asst. to advt. mgr., 1954—, editor Fla. Div. Reporter, 1957—. Mem. Advt. Club Polk County (Fla.) (pres. 1967-69), Am. Advt. Fedn. (dir. 1965—); named Advt. Woman of Year 1970; Silver medal 1971). Home: 5314 Lisa Av Lakeland FL 33803 Office: PO Box 1708 Lakeland FL 33801

SUTTON, FREDERICK I., lawyer; b. Kinston, N.C., Sept. 7, 1886; s. Levi Mewborn and Cora Elizabeth (Grimsley) S.; A.B., U. N.C., 1908, law student summer 1910; student Harvard, summer 1907, LL.B., 1911; studied in Europe, 1911; m. Annie Gray Fry, Nov. 10, 1915; 1 son, Frederick Isler. Admitted to N.C. bar, 1910, began practice law, Kinston, 1912; city atty., Kinston; major, Kinston, 1913-19; mem. Sutton & Greene, Kinston, N.C., 1922—. Bd. dirs. A& NC R.R. Co., Carolina Tel. & Tel. Co. (exec. com., 1932—, now dir. emeritus), South Atlantic Bonded Warehouse Corp.; served as dir. 3 nat. and 1 state banks. Life mem. Nat. Conf. Commrs. Uniform State Laws. Served as chief Intelligence Bur., Kinston, mem. Home Guard, World War. Mem. N.C. Gen. Assembly, 1925-33, state senator, 1939-40, also chmn. judiciary com., chmn. com. on constl. amendments; presdl. elector, 1941; mem. Nat. Dem. Finance Com.; del. Dem. Nat. Conv., 1932. Sec.-treas. Carolina Municipal Assn.; v.p. N.C. Good Rds. Assn.; mem. Bd. Conservation and Devel., 1927-32; mem. Pan-Am. Congress; N.C. commr. uniform laws, 1939—. Trustee U. N.C., 1927-59, N.C. State Coll., 1931-59, Woman's Coll., U. N.C., Greensboro, 1931-59; bd. govs. Harvard Law Sch.; chmn. Lenoir County-City of Kinston Airport Com., 1947-50. Mem. Am., N.C. (pres. 1940-41, chmn. exec. com. 1938-39), 6th Dist. (pres. 1931) bar assns., Am. Judicature Soc., Am. Law Inst., 4th Circuit Fed. Jud. Conf., N.Y. C. of C., Acad. Polit. Sci., Newcomen Soc., Harvard Law Sch. Assn. (mem. bd. govs.), Gen. Alumni Assn., U. N.C. (pres.), Internat. Platform Assn., Harvard So. Club, Beale Law Club, Alpha Tau Omega, Pi Sigma; hon. mem. W. Va., Va., 11th Dist., 5th Dist. bar assns., Alumni Assn. N.C. State Coll. Mason (K.T., 32 deg., Shriner, acting Potentate and orator; jester, nobel dir. 1950-51). Clubs: Harvard (N.Y.); Monogram (U. N.C.); Doc Newton (N.C. State Coll.); Dunes (pres. 1939-40; bd. govs. 1940-41), Country (dir.), Harvard of N.C. (exec. com.), Sphinx (Raleigh, N.C.); Coral Bay, King Neptune's Ct. and Order of Shellbacks; Order Golden Dragon; Around the World. Home: Blandwood Harvey Circle Kinston NC 28501 also Morehead City NC 28557 Office: Sutton Bldg Kinston NC 28501 Died Jan. 1971

SUTTON, FREDERICK ISLER, JR., realtor; b. Greensboro, N.C., Sept. 13, 1916; s. Fred I. and Annie (Fry) S.; grad. Culver (Ind.) Mil. Acad., 1934; A.B., U. N.C., 1939, postgrad. Law Sch., 1939-41; grad. Realtor's Inst., 1956, postgrad. Grad. Sch., 1957; m. Helen Sykes Morrison, Mar. 18, 1941; children—Fred I. III, Frank Morrison. Propr., Fred I. Sutton, Jr., realtor, Kinston, N.C., 1946—; dir. Hotel Kinston; dean Realtors Inst., U. N.C., 1966, 67. Chmn. Kinston Parking Authority; v.p., dir. Ednl. Found., 1966; sec. Indsl. Devel. Com.; chmn. Kinston Water Resources Commn.; pres. United Fund, 1969-71. Served from ensign to lt. comdr., USNR, 1941-46. Mem. N.C. (v.p. 1957), Kinston (pres.) bds. realtors, N.C. Assn. Real Estate Bds. (dir.), Nat. (rep. N.C. Realtors State Assns. com. 1969, 70), N.C. (v.p. 1959, 61-63, chmn. edn. com. 1964, regional v.p. 1966) assns. realtors, Realtor's Inst. (trustee 1961-63, v.p. 1966), S.R., Kinston C. of C. (v.p. 1967, 69). Presbyn. (deacon). Mason (32 deg., Shriner), Kiwanian (pres. 1964). Home: 1101 N Queen St Kinston NC 28501 Office: Sutton Bldg Kinston NC 28501

SUTTON, GLENN W(ALLACE), cons.; b. Milan, Ind., July 25, 1904; s. Wallace and Goldie Helen (Tucker) S.; diploma Seymour (Ind.) Bus. Coll., 1922; B.S., Ind. U., 1926, A.M., 1927; Ph.D. Ohio State U., 1938; m. Rachel Sibley, Dec. 30, 1930; 1 son, William Wallace. Accountant wholesale grocery, elevator co., Seymour, 1922-23; research asst. Bur. Bus. Research, Ind. U., 1925-27; instr. econ. and editor Ida. Econ. Rev., U. Ida. 1927-29; prof. finance, chmn. finance div., dir. Bur. Bus. Research, U. Ga., 1929-46, dir. Savannah (Ga.) div. U. Ga., 1946-48, prof. finance chmn. finance div., 1948-54, chmn. grad. div. Coll. Bus. Adminstrn., 1950-54, dir. Vets Affairs Office, 1945-46; mem. U.S. Tariff Commn., Washington, 1954-72, vice chmn., 1966-67, acting chmn., 1967-69, chmn., 1969-72; cons. in field, 1972—. Dir. southeastern states, urban studies of consumer purchases and income Bur. Labor Statistics, U.S. Dept. Labor, Atlanta, 1936, dir. nat. tabulation office, Chgo., 1937, dir. southeastern states, survey of state, county and municipal employment and payrolls, Atlanta, 1939-40, nat. dir. survey, Phila., 1941; U.S. del. to GATT, 1956; mem. UN Econ. Com., 1955-59; participant 17th Ann. Globar Strategy Discussions, 1965; adviser to U.S. delegation Kennedy Round Tariff Negotiations, GATT, 1965. Served from lt. to comdr., USNR, 1942-45. Mem. A.I.M. (asso.), Am. Econ. Assn., Am. Legion, So. Econ. Assn., Am. Finance Assn., Am. Statis. Assn., Am. Assn. U. Profs., Naval Airmen Am., Res. Officers Assn. U.S., Naval Res. Assn., Omicron Delta Kappa, Beta Gamma Sigma, Alpha Kappa Psi, Phi Kappa Phi, Phi Eta Sigma, Phi Chi Theta. Methodist. Mason, Rotarian. Clubs: Gridiron, Tacomis; Cosmos (Washington). Contbr. papers to univ. bus. revs. also bulls. pub. by U.S. govt. Home: 649 Oglethorpe Av Athens GA 30601 Office: 208 Southern Mutual Bldg Athens GA 30601

SUTTON, HIRST, mgmt. cons., former govt. ofcl.; b. Atlanta, Dec. 8, 1911; s. Harper Hirst and Laura Estelle (Everett) S.; A.B., U. Mo., 1933; M.A. in Polit. Sci., So. Methodist U., 1941; m. Mary Ellen Fritz, Sept. 16, 1939; 1 son, Daniel Hirst. Asst. to city mgr., Dallas, 1934-35, Saginaw, Mich., 1936-39; procedures analyst WPA, 1935-36; with Pub. Adminstrn. Service, Chgo., 1939-42; exec. asst. to commnr. Fed. Pub. Housing Authority, 1942-43; with Bur. of Budget Exec. Office Pres., 1943-69, asst. chief Office Mgmt. and Orgn., 1950-58, chief labor and welfare div., 1958-65, chief gen. govt. div., 1965-67, asst. to dir., 1967-69; dir. budget and exec. mgmt. Govt. D.C., 1969-71; mgmt. cons., 1971—. Adviser on county orgn. Fairfax County (Va.) Fedn. Citizens Assns., 1955-57; pres. Falls Church (Va.) Citizens for Better City, 1971—. Mem. Am. Polit. Sci. Assn., Am. Soc. Pub. Adminstrn., Blue Key, Delta Sigma Phi, Alpha Kappa Psi, Pi Sigma Alpha, Phi Eta Sigma. Home: 206 Buxton Rd Falls Church VA 22046

SUTTON, PHILIP GARLAND, JR., marketing cons.; b. New Albany, Ind., May 8, 1936; s. Philip Garland and Ona (Tucker) S.; student Western Mich. U., 1954-56; B.S., Purdue U., 1958; postgrad. Northeastern U., 1962-63, Union Coll., 1964-65; m. Marsha Anne McCauley, June 10, 1961; children—Philip Garland III, David Maurice, Elizabeth Tucker. Tech. rep. Am. Cyanamid Co., Boston, 1958-63; market devel. specialist Gen. Electric Co., Waterford, N.Y., 1963-66, mgr. southwestern dist., Dallas, 1966-69, mgr. plastic additive project, Waterford, 1969-71, mgr. fluids sect., 1971-72; pres. Sutton Assos., marketing cons., Houston, 1972—. Served with USCGR, 1959-60. mem. Soc. Plastics Industries, Soc. Aerospace Materials and Process Engrs. Delta Chi. Unitarian. Lion. Home: 10711 Creektree Dr Houston TX 77040 Office: 9800 NW Freeway Houston TX 77018

SUTTON, WILLIAM WALLACE, biologist, educator; b. Monticello, Miss., Dec. 15, 1930; s. Talmon Lawrence and Bessie (Lewis) S.; B.A., Dillard U., 1953; M.S., Howard U., 1959, Ph.D., 1965; postgrad. U. Ore., summer 1960, U. Rochester, summer 1961; m. Leatrice Hubbard, Aug. 28, 1954; children—William Wallace, Jr., Averell Hubbard, Sheryl Lynn, Alan David, Allison Maria, Gavin Jerome. Med. technician D.C. Gen. Hosp., Washington, 1955-59; instr. biology Dillard U., New Orleans, 1959-65, asst. prof., 1965-66, asso. prof., 1966-69, prof. biology, acting chmn. div. natural scis., 1969-70, chmn. div. natural scis., 1970—. Vice chmn. Crescent Dist. com. Boy Scouts Am. Past pres. Pan Hellenic Council New Orleans; mem. adv. bd. Juvenile Ct. of New Orleans; bd. dirs. Urban League Greater New Orleans, New Orleans chpt. Nat. Conf. Christians and Jews, New Orleans Community Relations Council; mem. com. undergrad. research La. Heart Assn. Nat. Def. Edn. Act fellow, 1962-63; asso. Danforth Found. Mem. N.Y., La. acads. sci., Nat. Inst. Sci., A.A.A.S., Assn. Am. Med. Colls. (mem. com. med. edn. minority group students), Am. Inst. Biol. Sci., Am. Assn. U. Profs., Soc. Protozoologists, Sigma Xi, Omega Psi Phi, Beta Kappa Chi. Home: 1837 Pratt Dr New Orleans LA 70122 Office: 2601 Gentilly Blvd New Orleans LA 70122

SUYDAM, HENRY WEST, JR., journalist; b. Washington, May 24, 1926; s. Henry West and Anne (Gordon) S.; B.A., Princeton, 1951; m. Marjorie Gunhild Nardwon, May 26, 1949 (div. 1964); children—Helen Lisa, Henry, Anne; m. 2d, Jane Eustis Wheeler, Nov. 28, 1964. Spl. corr. Newark Star-Ledger, 1949-51, staff wirter, 1951; mem. mag. editorial staff Life mag., 1951—, chief corr. Chgo. bur., 1959-60, chief corr. Washington bur., 1960-64, chief So. and Latin Am. corr., 1964—. Served to lt. (j.g.) USNR, 1943-46. Mem. Aircraft Owners and Pilots Assn., White House Corrs. Assn. Club: Nat. Press (Washington). Home: 4001 La Playa Blvd Coconut Grove FL 33133 Office: Dupont Plaza Center Miami FL 33131

SVARLIEN, EARLE OSCAR, educator; b. Overhalla, Norway, Mar. 25, 1906 (came to U.S. 1926, naturalized 1934); s. Johan and Charlotte (Kolberg) S.; student Western Wash. Coll., 1933-36; B.A., U. Wash., 1937, M.A., 1939; Ph.D., U.N.C., 1942; m. Mattie Stinson, June 7, 1942; 1 son, John Earle. Social sci. analyst Library of Congress, Washington, 1942-46; asso. prof. polit. sci. U. Fla., 1946-55, prof., 1955—; cons. pub. internat. law Govtl. Affairs Inst., Washington, 1969—. Decorated Knight's Cross 1st class Royal Order St. Olav (Norway), 1966. Mem. Am. Assn. U. Profs., UN Assn. (pres. chpt. 1966), Am. Soc. Internat. Law (exec. council 1962-65), World Peace through Law Center, Consular Law Soc. Author: Introduction to Law of Nations, 1955; Eastern Greenland Case in Historical Perspective, 1964. Contbr. articles to profl. jours. Home: 4120 NW 39th Rd Gainesville FL 32601

SWAFFORD, HOYT VICKORY, lawyer; b. Pikeville, Tenn., May 3, 1912; s. R. James A. and Sarah Anna (Thurman) S.; student Tenn. Technol. U., 1931-35; J.D., Cumberland U., 1937; postgrad. Chattanooga Coll. Law, 1937-38; m. Anna Louise Barker, Nov. 23, 1938; 1 dau., Cheryl Ann (Mrs. Everett C. Brock III). Tchr. pub. schs., Bledsoe County, Tenn., 1932-35; admitted to Tenn. bar, 1937; mem. firm Trotter & Barger, Chattanooga, 1938-41; with claim dept. Md. Casualty Co., Balt., 1941-45; atty. VA, Nashville, 1945-47; with Pacific Employers Inst., Nashville, 1947-48; mem. firms Keyes, Redmond & Swafford, then Swafford & Looney, Crossville, Tenn., 1948—; sec.-treas., dir. Highland Fed. Savs. & Loan Assn., Crossville, Crossville Enterprises, Inc.; sec., dir. Loeffler Quarries, Crossville, Crossville Rubber Products, Inc.; dir. Tenn. Wholesalers, Crossville. Past pres. Cumberland County chpt. A.R.C. Served with AUS, 1943-44. Mem. Tenn., Cumberland County (pres. 4 terms) bar assns., Sigma Delta County (pres. 4 terms) bar assns., Sigma Delta Kappa. Methodist. (chmn. bd. stewards 1970-71). Kiwanian (pres. Crossville 1958), Mason (Shriner). Home: Oak Dr Crossville TN 38555 Office: PO Box 477 Crossville TN 38555

SWAFFORD, WILLIAM BRYSON, educator; b. Monterey, Tenn., Aug. 23, 1912; s. William Carlin and Pearl (Kidwell) S.; B.S., U. Tenn., 1948; M.S., U. Miss., 1955; M.A., Memphis State U., 1958; LL.B., So. U., 1962; m. Violet Jeannette Lain, Nov. 28, 1943; children—Barbara Lain (Mrs. Paul Jaffe), William Bryson, Patricia Ann (Mrs. Mark Grill). Instr., U. Tenn. Coll. Pharmacy, Memphis, 1945-55, asst. prof., 1955-61, asso. prof., head dept. pharm. adminstrn., 1961-63, prof., chmn. dept. pharmaceutics, 1963-71, asst. dean, 1971—. Cons. VA hosps., Memhis, Nashville; mem.research team Marion Labs. Indsl. Pharm. Research. Served to maj. AUS, 1941-46; ETO; col. Res. ret. Decorated Silver Star medal, Bronze Star medal, Purple Heart; French Fouragerre. Dilomate Am. Bd. Pharm. Dilomates. Fellow Am. Coll. Apothecaries; mem. Am., Tenn., Memphis, Shelby County pharm. assns., Mil. Order World Wars, Res. Officers Assn., Am. Assn. Colls. Pharmacy (chmn. conf. tchrs.), Delta Chi Delta, Phi Delta Kappa, Kappa Psi, Rho Chi. Author: Pharmacy and the Law, A Manual For Practicing Pharmacists, 1969; A Correspondence Course in

Pharmaceutical Law, 1969; A Correspondence Course Non-Prescription Drugs, 1971. Home: 1840 Poplar Estates Pkwy Germantown TN 38038 Office: 874 Union Av Memphis TN 38103

SWAIM, GUY WINFIELD, architect; b. Little Rock, Sept. 2, 1906; s. Guy Winfield and Annie Lillian (Cook) S.; B.Arch., Auburn (Ala.) U., 1932; m. Mildred Elizabeth Cox, Sept. 1, 1934; children—Sylvia (Mrs. Michael McWilliams), Cecilia (Mrs. Oliver Crary). Founder, Swaim, Allen, Wellborn & Assos., architect-engrs., Little Rock, 1933-—. Mem. Pulaski County Planning Bd., 1955-61, North Little Rock Planning Commn., 1956-60. Bd. dirs. Pulaski County chpt. A.R.C. Served as 2d lt., F.A., U.S. Army, 1931-38. Mem. A.I.A. (past pres. Ark. chpt.), North Little Rock C. of C. (dir., past pres.), Sigma Nu. Elk, Lion. Address: 215 Louisiana St Little Rock AR 72201

SWAIM, JOHNNY RAY, basketball coach; b. Jean, Tex., Sept. 9, 1929; s. Erin Ray and Dollie (Allen) S.; B.S. in Phys. Edn., Tex. Christian U., 1953, M.Ed., 1956; m. Joan Hewatt, Nov. 7, 1953; children— Michael Ray, Susan Elizabeth. Head basketball coach La Vega High Sch., Waco, Tex., 1955-56; asst. basketball coach Tex. Christian U., Ft. Worth, 1956-67, head basketball coach, 1967-—. Bd. dirs. Panther Boys' Club, Fort Worth. Served to 1st lt. USMCR, 1953-55. Named championship coach for team championship Southwestern Conf. Nat. Collegiate Athletic Assn., 1967-68, 70-71; named Southwestern Conf. Coach of Year, 1971, Nat. Collegiate Athletic Assn. Dist. VI Coach of Year, 1971. Mem. Tex. High Sch. Coaches Assn., Tex. Christian U. Ex-Lettermen's Assn. Mem. Christian Ch. Home: 3721 Fenton St Fort Worth TX 76133

SWAIN, DWIGHT VREELAND, educator; b. Rochester, Mich., Nov. 17, 1915; s. J. Edgar and Florence (Vreeland) S.; A.A., Jackson Jr. Coll., 1935; B.A., U. Mich., 1937; M.A., U. Okla., 1954; m. Joye Raechel Boulton, Feb. 12, 1969; 1 son, Thomas McCray. Newspaper and mag. editor, Mich., Pa., Cal., 1937-41; scriptwriter motion picture unit U. Okla., Norman, 1949-65, prof. journalism, 1952-—; v.p. BHS Prodns., Inc., 1961-71. Book critic Sunday Oklahoman, 1950-60; cons., mem. nat. adv. bd. Palmer Writers Sch., Mpls., 1966-—; judge film and novels Nat. Cowboy Hall of Fame and Western Heritage Center, Oklahoma City, 1960-—. Served with AUS, 1942-46. Mem. Sci. Fiction Writers Am., Univ. Film Prodns. Assn., Am. Med. Writers Assn., Am. Assn. U. Profs. Author: Tricks and Techniques of the Selling Writer, 1965. Producer, writer film Stark Fear, 1963. Contbr. articles to profl. jours. Home: 1304 McKinley Av Norman OK 73069

SWAIN, JAMES MAURICE, physician; b. San Jose, Costa Rica, June 19, 1924 (parents Am. citizens); s. James Obed and Nancy (Cox) S.; M.D., U. Tenn., 1947; m. Barbara Halsted, July 15, 1955; children— Thomas Lester, Michael Lee. Intern St. Joseph Hosp., Memphis, 1948-49; research asst. anatomy U. Tenn., 1948, instr. anatomy, 1950; fellow radiology Cleve. Clinic, 1950, 53-54; pvt. practice, Lake Charles, La., 1954-—; clin. instr. radiology La. State U., 1961; chief radiology Lake Charles Charity Hosp.; radiologist Lake Charles Meml. Hosp., Beauregard Meml. Bapt. Hosp. Served from pvt. to pfc, AUS, 1943-46; to capt. USAF, 1951-52. Diplomate Am. Bd. Radiology. Mem. Am. Coll. Radiology, Radiol. Soc. La., A.M.A., La. Med. Soc., So. Med. Assn., A.A.A.S., La.-Tex. Gulf Coast Radiol. Soc., Am. Musicological Assn. Editor newsletter Hist. Musical Instrument Soc. Home: 3929 Bayouwood Dr Lake Charles LA 70601 Office: 401 S Ryan St Lake Charles LA 70601

SWAIN, JAMES O(BED), educator; b. Greenfield, Ind., Dec. 31, 1896; s. Ashbell Willard and Laetitia (Lambert) S.; A.B., Ind. U., 1921, A.M., 1923; Ph.D., U. Ill., 1932; student U. Madrid, summer 1933, U. Chile, 1951-52; m. Nancy Jane Cox, June 19, 1923; children— James Maurice, Juan Robert. Mem. faculty Mich. State Coll., 1931-37, asst. prof. modern langs., 1935-37; prof. chmn. dept. Romance langs. U. Tenn. 1937-—; guest dir. summer langs. sch. Western Colo. Coll., 1937; guest lectr. Am. lit. U. Chile, summer session, 1952; guest lectr. U. Madrid, summer 1958, Maracaibo, Venezuela, 1959; exec. sec. Mountain Interstate Fgn. Lang. Conf., 1963-64; vis. prof. U. Ky., 1964-—, Maryville Coll., 1965, Roanoke Coll., 1966, Lee Coll., 1969-70. Served with C.E., U.S. Army, 1918-19. Mem. Modern Lang. Assn. Am. (sectional officer various times), Central, So. States, South Atlantic (pres. 1948-49) modern lang. assns., Am. Assn. Tchrs. Spanish (exec. com. 1949-52), Am. Assn. Tchrs. French, Am. Assn. Tchrs. Italian, Institute de Literature Iberoamericana, Sigma Delta Pi (nat. exec. sec. 1947-—). Methodist (deacon). Author: Rumbo a Mexico, 1942; Ruedo Antillano, 1946; Vicente Blasco Ibanez, Realistic Techniques, 1959; Juan Marin-Chilean, the Man and his Writings, 1971. Co-editor: Les Chemins de la Mer. Asso. editor Hispania, 1936-42; asst. bus. mgr. Modern Lang. Jour., 1938-51. Travel Europe, Latin Am., South Am. Contbr. to Compton's Pictured Ency., Latin Am. and Spanish Lit. Home: 414 Forest Park Blvd Carlton Towers Knoxville TN 37919

SWAIN, NANCY JANE COX(MRS. JAMES OBED SWAIN), educator; b. Elwood, Ind., Dec. 19, 1901; d. Alfred Thomas and Emma (Allen) Cox; A.B. with high distinction, Ind. U., 1923, postgrad., 1928; M.A., U. Tenn., 1951, postgrad., 1953; m. James Obed Swain, June 24, 1923; children—J. Maurice, J. Robert. Teaching missionary M.E. Ch., Costa Rica, 1923-28; instr. U. Tenn., Knoxville, 1943, 45, non-resident instr. corr. Extension Div., 1959-—; tchr. Oak Ridge High Sch., 1943-67, Hollins (Va.) Coll., 1967. Mem. Am. Assn. Tchrs. Spanish and Portuguese, East Tenn. Edn. Assn., South Atlantic Modern Lang. Assn., Phi Beta Kappa, Phi Kappa Phi, Sigma Delta Pi, Pi Delta Phi, Pi Lambda Theta. Republican. Methodist. Mem. P.E.O. Home: 414 Forest Park Blvd Knoxville TN 37919

SWAIN, ROBERT JAMES, JR., dentist; b. St. Petersburg, Fla., June 17, 1919; s. Robert James and Georgia Kate (Jackson) S.; student Fla. A. and M. U., 1937-40; D.D.S., Howard U., 1944; postgrad. U. Pa., 1947; m. Helen Scott, June 19, 1962; children—Lynnette, Tanya, Kimberly, Robert James III, Shana. Pvt. practice dentistry, St. Petersburg, 1947-—. Bd. dirs. City Hosps. Served from 1st lt. to capt., AUS, 1944-47. Mem. Nat. Dental Assn., Allied Med. Soc., Fla. Med., Dental and Pharm. Assn., U.S. Coast Guard Aux., Omega Psi Phi. Democrat. Baptist. Mason (32 deg., Shriner). Club: Ambassador (St. Petersburg). Home: 1408 Lakeview Av S St Petersburg FL 33705 Office: 1501 22d St S St Petersburg FL 33712

SWAIN, SAMUEL CURTIS, ins. agt., retail trade exec.; b. Sherman, Tex., Aug. 17, 1918; s. Samuel Curtis and Frances Marie (Hogan) S.; student So. Meth. U., 1938-39, Dallas Sch. Bus. Adminstrn., 1936-40; m. Jean Sanders, July 7, 1945; 1 dau., Jean Martha (Mrs. Ray Barrett Baldwin III). With Proctor & Gamble Co., Dallas, Houston and Lufkin, Tex., 1936-42; prin. Curtis Swain Ins., Lufkin, 1947-—; with Perry Bros., retail trade, 1947-—, chmn. bd., 1965-—; dir. First Bank & Trust Co., Tex. Foundries, Inc. Chmn., Angelina County Airport Bd., 1963-—. Served with USAAF, 1942-45 (prisoner of war Germany 1943-45). Decorated Air Medal, Purple Heart. Roman Catholic. Home: 712 Jefferson St Lufkin TX 75901 Office: 318 Perry Bldg Lufkin TX 75901

SWALIN, BENJAMIN FRANKLIN, orchestral dir.; b. Mpls., Mar. 30, 1901; s. Benjamin N. and Augusta (Johnson) S.; B.S., Columbia U., 1928, M.A., 1930; Ph.D., U. Vienna, 1932; diplomas, Inst. Mus. Art, N.Y.C., 1926, 28; fellow for study in Europe, Inst. Internat. Edn., 1930-32; diplomas, Hochschule fur Musik, Vienna, 1932; D.F.A. (hon.), U. N.C., 1971; m. Martha Maxine McMahon, Jan. 1, 1935. Violinist, Mpls. Symphony Orch., 1919-21; prof. violin and theory DePauw U., Greencastle, Ind., 1933-35; asso. prof. music U. N.C., 1935-46; dir. N.C. Symphony Orch., 1939-—. Recipient N.C. Gold Medallion award, 1966; Morrison award for performing arts N.C., 1968. Mem. Am. Musicol. Soc., MacDowell Colony, Nat. Fedn. Music Clubs, Delta Chi, Phi Mu Alpha Sinfonia. Clubs: Columbia University; Torch (Durham, N.C.). Author: The Violin Concerto: a Study in German Romanticism, 1941; contbr. articles music assn. jours. and books; composer of several orchestral works and compositions for violin and piano, chamber music and voice. Guest dir. in Guadalajara and Mexico City, Mexico. Home: Chapel Hill NC 27514

SWAN, CHARLES HAROLD, ins. cons.; b. Pitts., Aug. 25, 1910; s. Charles A. and Charlotte (Cochran) S.; J.D., Ohio No. U., 1930; student Case Sch. Applied Sci., 1930-32; m. Mary Jane Higley, Feb. 1, 1938 (dec. 1961); children—William H., Sally Anne (Mrs. H.B. Jackson,) C. Hal; m. 2d, Gladys Davis, Aug. 18, 1962. Home rep. Prudential Ins. Co., Newark, 1938-45; v.p. Marsh & McLennan, Inc., Pitts., 1945-66; ins. cons.; owner, operator Abbeyville Apts., Mt. Lebanon, 1966-70; underwriting mem. Lloyd's of London, 1970-—. Bd. dirs. Upper St. Clair Township Sch. Bd. Mem. Am. Bar Assn., Nat. Lawyers Club, Omega Xi, Sigma Phi Epsilon. Presbyn. (trustee, elder). Mason (Shriner). Clubs: Duquesne, St. Clair Country (pres.), Upper St. Clair Township Republican (dir.); Ponte Vedra. Home and office: Ponte Vedra Beach FL 32082

SWANN, HENRY FREDERIC, lawyer; b. Dandridge, Tenn., Oct. 24, 1903; s. James Edward and Miriam Josephine (Lyle) Swann; student U.N.C., 1922-23; LL.B., Tri State Coll., 1926; m. Nancy Irene All, Oct. 12, 1932; 1 son, Albert Henry. Admitted to Ind. bar, 1925, to Tenn. bar, 1928, U.S. Supreme Ct. bar, 1971; practiced in Dandridge, Tenn., 1928-—; dir. Jefferson County Bank, Dandridge. Mem. Republican exec. com., 1930-—; asst. atty. gen., 1942-58, Dist. Atty. Gen., 1958-—. Mem. Dist. Attys. Gen. Conf. (pres. 1968-69), Nat. Dist. Attys. Assn. (dir. 1968-69), Sigma Delta Kappa, Beta Phi Theta. Methodist. Club: Gatlinburg Country. Editor: Swann's Digest of Tenn. Criminal Law, 1970. Address: PO Box 275 Dandridge TN 37725

SWANN, THOMAS BURNETT, citrus grower; b. Dandridge, Tenn., May 13, 1897; s. Alfred Reuben and Sarah Frances (Burnett) S.; student Carson-Newman Coll., 1914-16, D.Bus. Adminstrn., 1965; A.B., U. Tenn., 1920; B.S., Wharton Sch. Finance and Commerce, U. Pa., 1923; LL.D., Fla. State U., 1962; m. Margaret Gaines, Oct. 31, 1922; children—Margaret (Mrs. John Langdon Norris), Thomas Burnett. Citrus grower, Fla., 1926-—; v.p., dir. Exchange Bancorporation, Tampa, Fla., 1970-—; dir. Superior Fertilizer & Chem. Co., Tampa; chmn. bd. Exchange Nat. Bank, Winter Haven, Fla. Hon. life chmn. bd. trustees Winter Haven Hosp. Served with Signal Corps, U.S. Army, 1918-19. Presbyn. Clubs: University, Palma Ceia Golf and Country (Tampa); Lake Region Yacht and Country (Winter Haven). Home: 2100 Lake Eloise Dr Winter Haven FL 33880 Office: P O Box 232 Winter Haven FL 33880

SWANSON, CHARLES HALLBERG, petroleum co., exec.; b. Luck, Wis., June 11, 1924; s. Charles and Annie (Hallberg) S.; B.C.S., Okla. Sch. Accountancy, 1948; m. Mertyce Christenson, Sept. 26, 1943; 1 dau., Toni (Mrs. George H. Meason III). Sales mgr. Anchor Petroleum Co., Tulsa, 1947-59; sr. v.p. Wanda Petroleum Co., Houston, 1959-71; owner, pres. Swanee Petroleum Co., Houston, 1971-—. Served with AUS, 1943-46. Decorated Bronze Star. Mem. Nat. Liquified Petroleum Gas Assn. (dir., exec. com. 1968-—). Mason. Home: 6314 Riverview St Houston TX 77027 Office: Swanee Petroleum Co Bank of Southwest Bldg Houston TX 77002

SWANSON, DEAN CHARLES, telephone co. exec.; b. Mpls., Apr. 26, 1932; s. Dean Leroy and Laurene Grace (Johnson) S.; B.S., U.S. Naval Acad., 1957; m. Helen Kay Stewart, June 9, 1957; children—Sabrina, Dean. Exec. v.p. Standard Telephone Co., Cornelia, Ga., 1963-—; dir. Teledata Corp.; sec.-treas. Multi-View TV, Inc. Chmn. Habersham County Indsl. Authority, 1970-—; mem. Cornelia Planning Commn., 1965-—; regional adviser Goals for Ga., 1971-—. Served to capt. USAF, 1957-63. Mem. U.S. Ind. Telephone Assn. (small bus. com. 1968-—), Ga. Telephone Assn. (pres. 1969-70), Ga. Mountain Assn. (pres. 1969-71), Cornelia C. of C. (pres. 1967), Ga. C. of C. (dir. indsl. devel. council 1968-—). Methodist. Rotarian. Club: Kingwood Country (Clayton, Ga.). Home: Box 43 Cornelia GA 30531 Office: Box 400 Cornelia GA 30531

SWANSON, EDWARD BRANT, govt. ofcl.; b. Sioux City, Ia., Mar. 10, 1922; s. Edward Elias and Emma (Brant) S.; student Morningside Coll., 1942-43; B.S. in C.E., State U. Ia., 1947; m. Jeanne Francis Swanson, June 2, 1945; children—Thomas Edward, Barbara Jean, Julie Ann, Patricia Lee. Civil engr. Soil Conservation Service, Sioux City, Ia., 1947-51. Black & Beatch Engring. Firm, Kansas City, Mo., 1951-52, Hdqrs. Central Air Def. Force USAF, Grandview, Mo., 1952-55; constrn. mgmt. engr. Hdqrs. Air Def. Command USAF, Colorado Springs, Colo., 1955-61; civil engr. Air Force Regional C.E., Portland, Ore., 1961-64, chief engr. Hdqrs. Alaskan Air Command, Anchorage, 1964-69; dep. dir. programs Hdqrs. Tactical Air Command, Langley AFB, 1969-—. Served with AC. USNR, 1943-44. Recipient outstanding award Hdqrs. Alaskan Air Command, 1968. Registered prof. engr., Kan. Mem. Nat. Soc. Profl. Engrs., Soc. Am. Mil. Engrs. (pres. Peninsula chpt.). Home: 5 Tiller Circle Hampton VA 23369 Office: HQTAC (DEP) Langley AFB VA 23365

SWANSON, ELLIS LESTER, architect; b. San Antonio, Feb. 12, 1927; s. William Lester and Minnie Maud (Smith) S.; student U. Houston, 1946-48; B. Arch., U. Tex., 1952; m. Betty Jean Armstrong, July 19, 1953; children—Eric Lyle, Elisa Lynn. Draftsman, Ned. A. Cole, Austin, Tex., 1952, Robert L. Vogler, Corpus Christi, Tex., 1952-53, Walter C. Bowman, Harlingen, Tex., 1954-57; partner Bowman Swanson Hiester, Harlingen, 1953-66, Swanson Heister Wilson Boland, architects and engrs., 1966-—; dir. BSH Service Corp., Harlingen. Pres., United Fund, Harlingen, 1969; Served with USNR, 1945-46, 50, 53-54. Mem. A.I.A. (chpt. pres. 1961). Episcopalian (sr. warden 1970). Clubs: Toastmasters (pres. 1960) (Harlingen). Lion (dist. gov. 1967). Prin. archtl. works include Mercedes High Sch., 1966, Harlingen Air Terminal, 1967, Harlingen Tourist Center, 1969, Harlingen C. of C. Office, 1969, LaJoya High Sch., 1971. Home: 1627 Sam Houston Dr Harlingen TX 78550 Office: 1220 W Harrison St Harlingen TX 78550

SWARTZ, WILLIAM PERRY, JR., diversified indsl. co. exec.; b. Seven Mile Ford, Va., Sept. 21, 1911; s. William Perry and Elya Blanche (Worrell) S.; E.E., Va. Poly. Inst., 1933; m. Suelle McKellar, Mar. 29, 1935; children—William Perry III, Elva Ann (Mrs. James H. Simmons), Charles Eugene, Suelle Marie. Owner, chmn. bd. William P. Swartz, Jr. & Co., Inc., Roanoke, Va., 1936-—; chmn. bd. Swartz Enterprises diversified industries, Roanoke, 1966-—; chmn. bd., pres. Gen. Automation Corp. United Va. Bank, 1963-66. Chmn. Roanoke Stadium Adv. Com., 1960-68; mem. Roanoke Bd. Health, 1965-69. Trustee Ferrum (Va.) Coll. Mem. Gideons, Pocket Testament League, YMCA, Ashram Movement, Faith at Work, Lay Witness Missions, Internat. Prayer Fellowship. Methodist. Author: The Key to the Kingdom, 1968; God is in Business, 1971. Home: 1341 Sewell Lane SW Roanoke VA 24015 also 3631 Royal Oak Dr Titusville FL 32780 Office: PO Box 22 420 W Church Av Roanoke VA 24001

SWAYZE, THOMAS RANDOLPH, realtor; b. New Orleans, Sept. 16, 1924; s. Nelson Ryan and Golda (Glass) S.; student Tulane U., 1941-43, 46-47; m. Martha Anne Taylor, Feb. 4, 1950; children—Thomas Randolph, N. Taylor, Robert L. Floor broker New Orleans Cotton Exchange, 1947-59; v.p. Hardie Meric Realtors, New Orleans, 1959; v.p. sales Gertrude Gardener Inc., New Orleans, 1960-62; owner firm Richards & Swayze Inc., New Orleans, 1962-70; v.p. Latter & Blum, Inc. Realtors, 1971-—. Served to 2d lt. USMCR, World Bar II, to capt. Korean Conflict. Decorated Air medal with gold star. Mem. New Orleans, Jefferson Parish real estate bds., Nat. Inst. Real Estate Brokers (pres. chpt.), Am. Inst. Real Estate Appraisers, Kappa Alpha. Club: Southern Yacht. Home: 1321 Nashville Av New Orleans LA 70115 Office: 7835 Maple St New Orleans LA 70118

SWEARINGEN, WAYNE ELWYN, oil co. exec.; b. Grant, Neb., Oct. 30, 1924; s. Laurrel Brooks and Edna Ruth (Frank) S.; student Okla. State U., 1942, Reed Coll., 1943-44, Amherst Coll., 1945; B.S., U. Okla., 1948; grad Advanced Mgmt. Program, Harvard, 1965; m. Dorothy Lorene Wilde, June 7, 1946; children—Scott, Lynn, Brett. Petroleum engr. Amoco Prodn. Co., Oklahoma City, 1948-54; mgmt. cons., Tulsa, 1954-61; v.p. Livingston Oil Co., Tulsa, 1961-66 (name now changed to LVO Corp.), pres. LVO Corp., 1966-71, chmn. bd., chief exec. officer, 1971-—. Served with USAAF, 1942-45. Mem. Am. Assn. Petroleum Geologists, Okla. Ind. Petroleum Assn. (pres. 1972), Ind. Petroleum Assn. Am. (v.p. 1969-—), Soc. Petroleum Engrs. (chmn. Mid.-Continent sect. 1963-64). Clubs: Petroleum (dir. 1968-71), Tulsa, Southern Hills Country (Tulsa). Home: 2526 E 31st St Tulsa OK 74105 Office: P O Box 2848 Tulsa OK 74101

SWECKER, CHARLES EMMETT, physician; b. Salem, Va., Feb. 20, 1925; s. James Allen and Alice Gladys (Given) S.; student Va. Poly. Inst., 1942-43; B.S., Roanoke Coll., 1949; M.D., Med. Coll. Va., 1954; m. Betty Jane Alexander, June 14, 1952; children—Charles Emmett, Suzanne, Melanie, Stephanie. Student physician Juvenile Detention Home, Richmond, Va., Va. State Penitentiary, 1951-54; intern DePaul Hosp., Norfolk, Va., 1954-55; practice medicine, specializing in family practice, Wise, Va., 1954-62, Roanoke, Va., 1962-—, owner, operator Poages Mill Med. Clinic, Roanoke, 1968-—; mem. staffs Roanoke Meml. Hosp., Community Hosp. of Roanoke Valley, Shenendoah Hosp., Roanoke, Lewis-Gale Hosp., Roanoke; med. examiner Wise County and City of Norton, 1962; med. cons. Armed Forces Exam. and Entrance Sta., Roanoke, 1963-68; compensation physician U.S. Govt. Employes, 1969-—, Eaton, Yale & Towne, Inc., 1967-—, McLean Trucking Co., Inc., 1970-—; exam. physician Roanoke County and City sch. bds., 1967-—; med. dir. Roanoke Meth. Home, 1964-—, Estate Life Ins. Co. of Am., 1970-—; med. examiner City of Roanoke, 1967-—; cons. Regional Medicare Office, 1971-—; pres., chmn. bd. Med. Services, Inc., 1967-—. Mem. town council, Wise, Va., 1961. Bd. dirs. P.T.A. Served with Air Corps, USNR, 1943-46. Decorated D.F.C., Air Medal with five Stars. Mem. Am., Va. Acads. gen. practice, Med. Soc. Va., Roanoke Acad. Medicine. Methodist (youth counselor 1957-71). Home: 1117 Oakwood Dr SW Roanoke VA 24015 Office: 2026 Brambleton Av SW Roanoke VA 24015

SWECKER, DONALD BRYAN, advt. and sales exec.; b. Huttonsville, W. Va., Mar. 19, 1920; s. Holt Samuel and Lucy (Kittle) S.; grad. Potomac State Coll. of W. Va. U., 1940; postgrad. Davis Elkins Coll., 1941; student 149th Life Ins. Agy. Mgmt. Sch., 1947; m. Charlotta Irene Deets, Oct. 4, 1943; children—Mark, Edith, Benjamin, Emily, Kim, Lisa, Jeffrey, Andrew. With Peoples Life Ins. Co., Washington, 1946-72, agt., 1946-50, asst. dist. mgr., 1950-55, field tng. supr., 1955-57, sales promotion mgr., 1957-66, asst. v.p. advt., 1966-70, 2d v.p. advt., 1970-72, editor co. mag. PLICO, 1958-72; 2d v.p. pub. relations Capital Holding Corp., Louisville, 1972-—. Moderator, instr. Communications Workshop, Coll. William and Mary, Williamsburg, Va., 1967. Pres. P.T.A., Elkins, W. Va., 1947. Served with AUS, 1941-45; PTO. Recipient Award of Merit, United Givers Fund, 1959. Mem. Life Ins. Advertisers Assn. (chmn. Eastern Round Table 1966; ednl. com. 1967; chmn. membership com. 1969; nat. sec., nat. exec. com. 1970), Financial Pub. Relations Council of Greater Washington, D.C. Life Underwriters, Assn., (program chmn. Mid-Atlantic Sales Congress 1966), Internat., Mid-Atlantic councils indsl. editors, Am. Wildlife Fedn., V.F.W., Phi Sigma Nu. Episcopalian (supt., vestryman 1962-66, 68-72, lay reader). Contbr. articles to profl. jours., poetry, non-fiction to Rotarian Mag., Poetic Voice Am., West Va. Review, newspapers, others. Home: 305 Marengo Dr Middletown KY 40243 Office: 674 S 4th St Louisville KY 40202

SWEENEY, JOSEPH FRANCIS, sch. adminstr.; b. Bklyn., Sept. 17, 1927; s. Joseph Francis and Ann (McDonough) S.; A.B., Spring Hill Coll., 1950; A.B. Woodstock Coll., 1951. Ordained in priest Roman Catholic Ch., 1957; tchr. St. Joseph's Prep., Phila., 1951-54; dir. admissions, Georgetown U. Undergrad. Sch., 1959-68; pres. Gonzaga Coll. High Sch., Washington, 1968-—. Workshop dir. Internat. Inst. Edn., Washington, 1963; mem. Counselling Com. Entrance Exam. Bd., 1962-65; chmn. Opportunity Project for Edn., 1967-70. Chmn. Sursum Corda Corp., 1968-—. Trustee Georgetown U. Address: 19 Eye St NW Washington DC 20001

SWEENEY, THOMAS PATRICK, dentist, army officer; b. Milw., Aug. 27, 1929; s. Walter Leo and Alice (Eigner) S.; student St. Benedicts Coll., 1947, U. Wis., 1950; D.D.S., Marquette U., 1955; m. Marie Gronseth, June 7, 1952; children—Patrick Sean, Colleen Erin. Commd. 1st lt. Dental Corps, U.S. Army, 1955, advanced through grades to lt. col., 1972; mem. prosthodontic staff U. Louisville Dental Sch., 1968-70; cons. prosthodontics 1st U.S. Army, 1968-70. Chmn., Baumholden Community Scholarship Assn., Germany, 1970-71; pres. Augsburg Am. Youth Activities, 1971-72. Diplomate Am. Bd. Prosthodontics. Fellow Am. Coll. Prosthodontists; mem. Am. Prosthodontic Soc., Phi Gamma Delta. Home: Canyon Lake TX 78130 Office: 769 Med Detachment Germany APO New York City NY 09178

SWEET, JOHN HOWARD, publisher; b. Emerson, Man., Can., Mar. 21, 1907; s. Henry Charles and Hannah (Mooney) S.; student U..Man., 1923-26; m. Lillian Flora Martin, Sept. 11, 1926; 1 son, John Allan; m. 2d, Anne Ethel Wallace, Oct. 4, 1940; children—Anthony Howard, Elizabeth Anne. Asst. circulation mgr. A.M.A., 1926-29; circulation mgr. Traffic World, 1929-37; v.p. Poor's Publishing Co., 1937-40, Dickie Raymond, Inc., 1940-42; circulation mgr. World Report, 1946-48; circulation dir. U.S. News and World Report, 1948-51, exec. v.p., pub., 1951-59, pres. and pub., 1959-—, also dir. Trustee James F. Mitchell Found. Mem. Conf. Bd. Served to lt. comdr. USNR, 1943-45. Presbyn. (trustee). Clubs: Princess Anne Country (Virginia Beach); Nat. Press, Internat., Army and Navy, Congressional Country, Metropolitan (Washington). Home: 2124 Bancroft Pl NW Washington DC 20008 Office: 2300 N St NW Washington C 20037

SWEIGERT, MILTON EDWARD, architect; b. Atlanta, Mar. 2, 1934; s. Ray Leslie and Edna (Powers) S.; B.S., Ga. Inst. Tech., 1956, B. Arch., 1959; m. Helen LaRue Horne, June 16, 1956; children—Vicki LaRue, Valerie Lea. Designer, L. Miles Sheffer, Architect, Atlanta, 1960; job capt. Cunningham & Forehand, Architects, Inc., Atlanta, 1961-65; project architect Lockwood Greene Engrs., Inc., Spartanburg, S.C., 1965-67, archtl. dept. head, Atlanta, 1967-68; v.p., chief architect Zachary W. Henderson & Assos., Atlanta, 1968-70; chief architect Sheetz & Bradfield, Architects, Inc., 1970—. Supporting mem. Arthritis Found., 1969—; sponsor Campus Crusade for Christ Internat., 1970—, Christian Children's Fund, 1965. Bd. dirs. Gamma Psi House Corp. Served with USNR, 1956-58. Mem. A.I.A., Constrn. Specifications Inst., Ga. Archtl. and Engring. Soc., Ga. Assn. Architects, Ga. Conservancy, Ga. Tech. Nat. Alumni Assn., Nat. Campers and Hikers Assn., Tau Sigma Delta, Delta Tau Delta. Republican. Mem. Christian and Missionary Alliance (deacon). Club: Dunwoody N Driving. Home: 4518 Kingsgate Dr NE Atlanta GA 30341 Office: 1132 W Peachtree St NE Atlanta GA 30309

SWENSSON, EARL SIMCOX, architect; b. Nashville, July 28, 1930; s. Earl Ebenezer and Viola La Zelle (Simcox) S.; B.S. in Bldg. Design with honors, Va. Poly. Inst., 1952, M.S. in Arch., 1953; M.S. in Arch., U. Ill., 1955; m. Suzanne Dickenson, June 6, 1953; children— Krista, Lin, Kurt. Designer Perkins Perkins & Will Architects, Chgo., 1956-60; jr. partner Donald E. Stoll, Architect, Nashville, 1960-61; pres. Earl Swensson Architects, Nashville, 1961—; adj. prof. grad. studies div. Va. Poly. Inst. Coll. Arch. at Blacksburg, 1971-72; pres. Better Environments, Inc., Nashville, 1969—; chmn. bd. Investment Property Services, Inc., Nashville. Mem. adv. bd. Salvation Army, Nashville, 1963-70; mem. Martha O'Brien Community Center, 1968—, vice chmn., 1971—. Mem. com. Met. Zoning Ordinance, 1967-69. Recipient design awards profl. orgns. Mem. A.I.A. (pres. middle Tenn. chpt. 1971—), Tenn. Soc. Architects (dir. 1967-71), Phi Kappa Phi, Tau Sigma Delta, Phi Delta Epsilon. Presbyn. (elder). Club: West Meade Swimming (Nashville). Prin. works include Tenn. Bapt. Conv. Hdqrs., Brentwood, 1969; campus master plan Union U., Jackson, Tenn., 1970, Nashville campus U. Tenn., 1971, Laurel (Del.) Dist. High Sch., 1972. Home: 6530 Curreywood St Nashville TN 37205 Office: 2104 Sunset Pl Nashville TN 37212

SWETMAN, GLENN ROBERT, educator, poet; b. Biloxi, Miss., May 20, 1936; s. Glenn Lyle and June (Read) S.; B.S., U. So. Miss., 1957, M.A., 1959; Ph.D., Tulane U., 1966; m. Margarita Ortiz, Feb. 8, 1964; children—Margarita June, Glenn Lyle Maximilian, Glenda Louise. Teaching fellow U. So. Miss., 1957-58, asst. prof., 1964-66; instr. Ark. State U., 1958-59, McNeese U., 1959-61; instr., teaching fellow Univ. Coll. Tulane U., 1961-64, spl. asst. dept. elec. engring., 1961; asso. prof. La. Inst. Tech., 1966-67; prof., head dept. langs. Nicholls State Coll., Thibodaux, La., 1967-69, head dept. English, 1969-71, prof., 1971—. Partner, Breeland Pl., Biloxi, Miss., 1960—; stringer corr. Shreveport (La.) Times, 1966—; cons. tech. writing Union Carbide Corp. Subdiv. coordinator Republican party, Hattiesburg, Miss., 1964. Served with AUS, 1957. Recipient Poetry awards KQUE Haiku contest, 1964, Coll. Arts contest, Los Angeles, 1966, Black Ship Festival, Yoqosuka, Japan, 1967; Green World Brief Forms award Green World Poetry Editors, 1965. Mem. Modern Lang. Assn., S. Central Modern Lang. Assn., Coll. Writers Soc. La. (pres. 1971-72), I.E.E.E., Am. Assn. Engring. Edn., La. Poetry Soc. (pres. 1971—), Internat. Boswellian Inst., Nat. Fedn. State Poetry Socs. (3d v.p., nat. membership chmn. 1972—), Phi Eta Sigma, Omicron Delta Kappa. Book reviewer Jackson (Miss.) State Times, 1961. Poems pub. in various publs. including Poet, Prairie Schooner, Trace, Ball State U. Forum, Film Quar.; (book of poems) The Tunnel of Love, 1972. Home: 638 Fairway Dr Thibodaux LA 70301

SWIFT, A(LBERT) ERVINE, bishop; b. Claremore, Okla., July 1, 1913; s. Dr. Albert Aaron and Margaret Anna (Clarkson) S.; student U. Tulsa, 1931-32; A.B., U. Okla., 1935; B.D., Episcopal Theol. Sch. 1938; S.T.D. (hon.), Gen. Theol. Sem. N.Y., 1953; S.T.D. (hon.), Ripon (Wis.) Coll., 1960; m. Elizabeth Ann Slusser, Sept. 9, 1940; children—Anne (Mrs. Jack Nietert), William. Ordained to ministry P. E. Church, deacon, 1938, priest 1939; instr. St. John's U., Shanghai, China, 1938-39; vicar Church of St. John the Evangelist, Hankow, China, 1939-41; curate St. David's Church, Balt., 1942-43; asst. sec. overseas dept. Nat. Council Episcopal Ch., N.Y.C., 1943-46, acting dir., 1947; rector Ch. of Holy Trinity, Manila, P.I., 1948-51 also instr. St. Andrew's Theol. Sem., acting dean 1950-51, elected bishop of P.R., Jan. 1951, consecrated, May 1951, resigned, 1965; asst. bishop. Pa., Phila., 1965-67; rector St. Gregory's Church, Boca Raton, Fla., 1967—; asst. bishop of South Fla., 1968—; Bishop-in-charge, V.I., 1951-63. Del. Gen. Conv. Episcopal Ch., 1946; examining chaplain, mem. council advice, sec. Convocation of P.E., 1950-51. Mem. boys work com. Y.M.C.A., P.I. 1951, also dir. Am. Assn.; mem. P.R. Insular council Boy Scouts. Mem. Phi Beta Kappa, Kappa Kappa Psi, Pi Kappa Phi. Address: St Gregory's Ch Box 942 Boca Raton FL 33432

SWIGERT, JOHN LEONARD, JR., astronaut; b. Denver, Aug. 30, 1931; s. John Leonard and Virginia (Seep) S.; B.S. in Mech. Engring., U. Colo., 1953; M.S. in Aero. Space Sci., Rensselaer Poly. Inst., 1965; postgrad. U. Cal. at Los Angeles, 1965-66; M.B.A., U. Hartford, 1967; D.Sc. (hon.), Am. Internat. Coll., 1970, Western Mich U., 1970; LL.D., Western State U., 1970. Served to capt. USAF, 1953-56; engring. test pilot Pratt & Whitney Aircraft, East Hartford, Conn., 1957-64, Space and Information Systems div. N.Am. Aviation, Downey, Cal., 1965-66; astronaut NASA, Manned Spacecraft Center, Houston, 1966—. Mem. Mass Air N.G., 1957-60, Conn. Air N.G., 1960-65. Recipient Presdl. medal for Freedom, 1970, U. Colo. Distinguished Alumnus award, 1970; City N.Y. gold medal, 1970; City Houston medal for Valor, 1970; City Chgo. gold medal, 1970. Asso. fellow Soc. Exptl. Tests Pilots, Am. Inst. Aeros. and Astronautics (Octave Chanute award 1966, Haley Astronautics award 1971), Am. Astronautical Soc. (Flight Achievement award 1971), Pi Tau Sigma, Sigma Tau, Phi Gamma Delta. Roman Catholic. Office: Manned Spacecraft Center Houston TX 77058

SWIHART, JOHN DONALD, JR., elec. engr.; b. Hobart, Okla., Aug. 3, 1936; s. John D. and Mary (Madden) S.; B.S. in Elec. Engring., U. Okla., 1959; postgrad. U. Fla., 1967, Tarrant County Jr. Coll., 1969, N. Tex. State U., 1970—; m. Mary Ann Nixon, Jan. 30, 1958; children—Susan LaRue, Timothy George, David Gerard, Mary Kathryn. Electronic engr. FAA, Oklahoma City, 1959-66, elec. engr. aircraft systems, Fort Worth, 1967—; electronic engr. Naval Tng. Device Center, Orlando, Fla., 1967. Asst. cubmaster, Webelos den leader, asst. scoutmaster Boy Scouts Am., 1967—; class rep. U. Okla. Alumni Devel. Fund. campaign, 1968. Served to lt. AUS, 1959. Registered profl. engr., Okla., Tex. Mem. I.E.E.E., Nat. Soc. Profl. Engrs., Toastmasters Internat., Tau Beta Pi, Eta Kappa Nu, Sigma Tau. Democrat. Roman Catholic. K.C. Home: 7313 Janetta Dr Fort Worth TX 76118 Office: FAA PO Box 1689 Fort Worth TX 76101

SWILLEY, ROSCOE HUBERT, city ofcl.; b. Tampa, Fla., May 7, 1919; s. William Hubert and Lilla Conellia (Massey) S.; student courses Northwestern U., 1955, U. La., 1962, and others; m. Olive Elizabeth Babbitt, Apr. 16, 1942; children—Patricia (Mrs. James Crotty), Alice Elizabeth. With Tampa Police Dept., 1946-66, sgt., 1953-66; with Largo (Fla.) Police Dept., 1966—, chief police, 1972—; Bonded dep. Pinellas Sheriff Dept., 1966—; mem. Govs. Council on Criminal Justice, 1971—; mem. Govs. Courts Task Force, 1971—. Served with AUS, 1940-46, PTO. Mem. Fla., Largo, Tampa Bay Area chiefs of police, Internat. Chiefs of Police, Fla. Peace Officers Assn. (pres. 1971-72), Fraternal Order Police, C. of C. Baptist (deacon 1969-71). Rotarian (treas. 1970—). Club: Tampa Police Pistol. Home: 1327 Pine St SW Largo FL 33540 Office: P O Box 296 305 1st Av SW Largo FL 33540

SWINDELL, PARK TRAMMELL, food co. exec.; b. Lakeland, Fla., Nov. 29, 1911; s. James Cicero and Bobbie Jane (Fletcher) S.; B.S., U. Fla., 1935; m. Mary Barco, Dec. 19, 1936; children—Mary Patricia (Mrs. James Gordon Siebert), James Baroo, Barbara Jane. With Fruit Treating Corp., Orlando, Fla., 1935-37; mgr. Lakeland Cold Storage Co. (Fla.), 1937-39; prodn. mgr. canning div. William P. McDonald Corp., Auburndale, Fla., 1939-46; mgr. canning div. Florence Citrus Growers Assn., Winter Haven, Fla., 1946-51; adminstrv. asst. Sargeant Citrus Products, Inc., Lakeland, 1951-54; plant mgr., v.p., adminstrv. asst. Golden Gift (name now changed to Universal Food Products, Inc.), 1954-64; independent cons., 1964-67; dir. spl. applications Carbonic Industries Corp., Orlando, 1965—, also dir. Mem. Fla. Canners Assn. (past dir.), Thyrsus, Chi Phi. Elk, Kiwanian. Home: 627 Av F NW Winter Haven FL 33880 Office: 1700 S Division Av Orlando FL 32802

SWINDLE, JOHN LORENZA, fire chief; b. Birmingham, Ala., Aug. 18, 1914; s. John Wesley and Lela (Smith) S.; grad. Phillips High Sch., Birmingham, 1933; attended Ala. Fire Coll., 1956-59; m. Margaret B. Guess, Nov. 4, 1938; 1 son, John Lorenza. With Birmingham Fire Dept., 1938—, lt., 1948-52, dep. chief, 1958-61, chief, 1961—. Active Cub Scouts, Birmingham Area Council Boy Scouts Am., 1948—. Mem. Southeastern Assn. Fire Chiefs (pres, 1967-68, sec. and treas. 1968-69), Met. Chiefs Com. Internat. Assn. Fire Chiefs. Clubs: Optimist (past pres.), Civitan. Home: 1012 22d St SW Birmingham AL 35211 Office: Fire Dept 1808 7th Av N Birmingham AL 35203

SWINFORD, MAC, judge; b. Cynthiana, Ky., Dec. 23, 1899; s. McCalla C. and Allie (McKee) S.; LL.B., U. Va., 1925, postgrad., 1924-25; LL.D., Chase Coll. Sch. Law, 1965; m. Benton Peterson, Nov. 17, 1927; children—Mary Jouett (Mrs. McKay Reed, Jr.), John McKee, Sarah Hanson (Mrs. Hall Kinney), Alice Jane (Mrs. Bruce Kolbe), Ann Gregg (Mrs. Delmer Dunn). Admitted to Ky. bar, 1922; practiced at Cynthiana, 1922-35; U.S. dist. atty. Eastern Dist. Ky., 1933-37; judge U.S. Dist. Ct. for Eastern and Western Dists. Ky., 1937—. Mem. Ky. Ho. of Reps., 1926-28. Mem. Am., Ky., Fed., Harrison County bar assns., Sigma Nu. Democrat. Presbyn. Author: Kentucky Lawyer. Home: 440 E Pike St Cynthiana KY 41031 Office: Fed Bldg Box 1489 Lexington KY 40501

SWING, ANN T. (MRS WILLIAM E. WILLIAMSON), physician; b. Millpoint, W.Va., June 9, 1910; d. Leonard G. and Mary (Matuzeck) Swing; A.B., U. W.Va., 1931, B.S., 1932; M.D., Med. Coll. Va., 1934, postgrad. (Immunology fellow), 1941-42; m. William E. Williamson, July 22, 1950. Intern, Med. Coll. Va., 1935-36; intern Willard Parker Hosp., N.Y.C., 1936-37, resident 1937-38; resident physician N.Y. Tng. Sch. for Girls, 1939-40, Farmville (Va.) State Tchrs. Coll., 1940-41; attending physician Bur. Maternal and Child Welfare, D.C. Pub. Health Dept., 1943-50; med. officer. Preventive Medicine div., Dept. Army Surgeon Gen., 1950-51; cons. pediatrician U.S. Army, Am. Hosp., France, 1952-54; med. officer U.S. Army Dispensary, Ft. Meyer, Va., 1955-67, chief pediatrics, 1967—. Mem. A.M.A., Am. Med. Women's Assn., Med. Women's Internat. Assn., Women's Med. Soc. D.C., Med. Soc. D.C., Bus. and Profl. Womens Club. Home: 1870 Wyoming Av NW Washington DC 20009 Office: Andrew Rader US Army Clinic Fort Myer VA 22211

SWING, RICHARD HILL, city ofcl.; b. Lexington, N.C., Jan. 30, 1928; s. Charlie Hill and Addie Idora (Hedrick) S.; student N.C. State U. Sch. Engring., 1945-46, 48-50; m. Patricia Neal Browne, Sept. 1, 1955; (div. July 1968) children—Richard Marshall, Jeffrey Neil. Engring. aide C.E., Anchorage, 1951-53; field engr. Erdman, Anthony & Hosley, cons. engrs., Rochester, N.Y., 1955-57; self-employed land surveyor, Asheboro, Thomasville, N.C., 1958-64; design engr. city of High Point, N.C., 1964—. Mem. Planning and Zoning Bd., Thomasville, 1962-64. Served with AUS, 1946-48. Registered profl. engr., N.C. Mem. Nat. Soc. Profl. Engrs., Am. Pub. Works Assn., Profl. Engrs. N.C. Mem. Ref. United Ch. Christ. Club: Civitan International (High Point). Home: 2415 Dallas Av High Point NC 27260 Office: 200 E Commerce High Point NC 27260

SWINK, WILLIAM J., oil co. ofcl.; b. Portia, Ark., Mar. 3, 1921; s. William I. and Willie (Allen) S.; student U. Ark., 1939-42; m. Mazie I. Eaton, Apr. 8, 1950; children—William Gregory, Douglas Alan, Karen Lynn. Salesman, Belford & Roe Oil Co., Imboden, Ark., 1939-42, asst. mgr., 1946-59, mgr., 1960—; tchr. Sloan Hendrix Acad., Imboden, 1941-42. Alderman, Imboden, 1949-51, 1957-62; chmn. City Water Commn., 1961-71, City Planning Commn., 1957-69. Served with USAAF, 1942-45; ETO. Mem. Nat. Oil Jobbers Council (dir.), Ark. Ind. Oil Marketers (pres.), Am. Legion (comdr. Imboden). Democrat. Mem. Ch. of Christ. Lion (1st v.p. Imboden). Home: 3d and Main Sts Imboden AR 72434 Office: Front and Walnut Sts Imboden AR 72434

SWOPE, MARY MARGARET RICHARDS (MRS. KING SWOPE), club woman; b. Morganfield, Ky.; d. Lewis R. and Margaret Blue (Cromwell) Richards; student Centre Coll., 1912-15, Pa. Coll. for Women, 1915-18; m. King Swope, Mar. 22, 1918 (dec. Apr. 1961); children—William Richards, King. Sec., Nat. Soc. Daus. Barons of Runnymede; nat. councillor Daus. Founders and Patriots Am., 1958-62; Ky. pres. Daus. Colonial Wars. 1959-62; pres. chpt. IX Colonial Dames Am., 1952-58. Mem. Nat. Soc. Arts and Letters (Ky. chapt.), Colonial Daus. 17th Century (nat. councillor 1967-70, pres.), Ky. Hist. Soc., Lexington Jr. League, Daus. Am. Colonists, D.A.R., Order of Crown (4th nat. v.p.), Ams. of Royal Descent, Magna Charta Dames, First Families Va., Ky. Burgess. Republican. Presbyn. Clubs: Lexington (Ky.) Country; Filson; Idle Hour Country. Home: 247 S Hanover Av Lexington KY 40502

SWORD, CHARLES DOUGLAS, dentist; b. Weeksbury, Ky., Nov. 3, 1942; s. John Mims and Nola Marie (Blevins) S.; D.M.D., U. Ky., 1968; m. Carol Sue Stanley, Sept. 14, 1963; children—Cara Denise, Charles Douglas, Candace Delona. Pvt. practice dentistry, Inez, Ky., 1968—. Vice pres. Saltwell Land Corp.; sec.-treas. Saltwell Constrn. Co. County chmn. Gov.'s Task Force for Exceptional Children, 1971—; mem. Martin County Bd. Health, 1968—, Big Sandy Area Comprehensive Health Planning Council, 1968—; pres. Martin County Mental Health-Mental Retardation Assn. Vice pres. County Young Democrats Club, 1970—. Bd. dirs. Martin County Devel. Assn., Mountain Mental Health. Mem. Am., Ky. dental assns., Ky. Mountain Dental Soc. (pres.), Ky. Soc. Dentistry for Children, U. Ky. Alumni Assn., Ky. Pub. Health Assn., Martin County Jr. C. of C. (dir.). Lion. Club: Century. Address: PO Box 456 Inez KY 41224

SWORDS, CLAUDE EVERETT, dentist; b. Terrell, Tex., Jan. 26, 1921; s. John Henry and Mattie Ethel (Logan) S.; student Tex. Mil. Coll., 1938-40; D.D.S., Baylor U., 1944; m. Marjorie Mae Swords, Nov. 11, 1945; children—James D., John H., Jerry A., Steve A., Sharee A. Individual practice dentistry, Dallas, 1946—. Active Circle 10 council Boy Scouts Am. Served with USN, 1944-46. Fellow Internat. Coll. Dentistry; mem. Southwest Acad. Restorative Dentistry (pres. 1969-70). Home: 823 Lockwood St Richardson TX 75080 Office: 1232 Med Arts Bldg Dallas TX 75201

SWORDS, HENRY LOGAN, physician; b. Terrell, Tex., May 12, 1918; s. John Henry and Mattie Ethel (Logan) S.; B.S., East Tex. State U., 1939; M.S., 1947; M.D., Southwestern Med. Sch., 1947; m. Ruth C. Riley, June 20, 1940; children—Henry Logan II, Sylvia Lorraine. Tchr., Ft. Worth (Tex.) Pub. Schs., 1939-41, prin., 1941-44; intern John Peter Smith Hosp., Ft. Worth, 1947-48; gen. practice medicine, Ft. Worth, 1948—; mem. staff St. Joseph's, Harris Meml., All Saints hosps., Ft. Worth; chief div. gen. practice St. Joseph Hosp., 1970-71. Served as cadet USAAF, 1942. Mem. Am., Tex. med. assns., Am., Tex. acads. gen. practice, Am. Geriatric Soc., Tarrant County Med. Soc. (v.p. 1967), Phi Beta Pi. Methodist (chmn. bd. 1957-58, pres. bd. trustees 1959-60). Rotarian (pres. N. Ft. Worth 1969-70). Home: 5808 Blue Ridge Dr Fort Worth TX 76112 Office: 301 W Central St Fort Worth TX 76106

SYKES, HARRY N., city ofcl.; b. Starkville, Miss., Apr. 1, 1927; s. P.K. and Marie (Hall) S.; B.S. in Phys. Edn., Ky. State Coll., 1952; postgrad. U. Ky., summer 1957, (Gen. Electric fellow in math.), Purdue U., summer 1958, (NSF grantee in math.), U. Minn., summer 1960; m. Geraldine Higgins, July 1, 1951; children— Harry Ernest, Melvin Kirk, Paula Arnette, Kevin Mark, Kermit Aubrey. With Harlem Globetrotters, 1952-54; tchr., basketball coach Lexington (Ky.) Pub. Sch. System, 1954-62; mgr. Holiday Bowling Lanes, 1962-64; life underwriter Commonwealth Life Ins. Co., 1964-69; dist. dir. Boy Scouts Am., 1969-70; in charge of bus. devel. 2d Nat. Bank & Trust Co., Lexington, 1970—. Mem. bd. mgrs. YMCA; mem. Ky. Crime Commn.; active Fayette Cancer Soc. Mem. Lexington City Commn., 1963—; candidate mayor Lexington, 1971. Trustee Blue Grass Regional Health Council. Mem. Nat. League Cities (dir.), Kappa Alpha Psi. Democrat. Baptist (trustee). Mason, Kiwanian. Home: 439 Bamberger Rd Lexington KY 40505 Office: 123 Cheapside St Lexington KY 40507

SYKES, L. BONSALL, dept. store owner, ex-state legislator; b. Haysi, Va., June 22, 1920; s. Avon B. and Alta P. (Hay) S.; student Hiwassee Coll., 1938-40, U. Pa., 1945, Clinch Valley Coll., 1956-57; m. Annette Stanley, June 27, 1942. Tchr., Dickenson County (Va.) Pub. Schs., 1940-42; dept. mgr. Clinchfield Coal Corp. Stores, Clincho, Va., 1942-43, Dante, 1946-47; owner dept. store, Clintwood, 1947—. Mem. Va. Ho. of Dels., 1962-65; asst. clk. Va. Senate, 1966, 72. Chief, Clintwood Vol. Fire Dept., 1957-58; chmn. Dickenson County Planning Comm.; treas. dir. Cumberland Plateau Econ. Devel. Dist.; mem. adv. com. Clinch Valley Coll.; adv. council Wise Appalachian Regional Hosp. Served with USNR, 1943-45; PTO. Mem. Clintwood Bus. and Profl. Assn. (past pres.), Breaks Interstate Park Assn. Democrat. Baptist (treas.). Mason (Shriner), Kiwanian (past pres. Clintwood); mem. Order Eastern Star. Clubs: Lonesome Pine Country; Hidden Valley Country (Clintwood). Address: PO Box 707 Clintwood VA 24228

SYLVESTER, BARBARA BOLEN (MRS. JOSEPH G. SYLVESTER), nat. Democratic committeewoman, civic worker; b. Florence, S.C., Mar. 8, 1929; d. Hugh Bernard and Ola Mae (Williamson) Thornton; student Mars Hill Coll., 1946, Western Carolina U., summers; m. Joseph Georg Sylvester, June 30, 1954; children—Pamela Mae, Elsa April. Sec., S.C. State Bd. Juvenile Corrections, 1969-71, chmn., 1971—; chmn. S.C. Dept. Youth Services, 1971—. S.C. Democratic exec. committeewoman, 1968—; chmn., Florence County White House Conf. on Children and Youth, 1970; chmn. 1st Step Kindergarten-Red Brick Sch., 1972—. Bd. dirs. S.C. Assn. Retarded Children, 1968-70; pres. Florence County Assn. for Retarded Children, 1969. Home: 510 Camellia Circle Florence SC 29501

SZABO, PAUL CHARLES, plastics co. exec.; b. Cleve., June 22, 1921; s. Paul and Anna (Hovan) S.; student John Huntington Poly., 1946-48; B.S., Fenn Coll., 1950; m. Alice Helene Kaczur, June 5, 1948; children—Terence, Georgiann, Brian, Alice Mary. Plant mgr. Tile-Rite Plastics Mfg. Co., 1948-55, Pyramid Products, Inc., 1955-60; gen. mgr. Asso. Plastics, Inc., 1960-63; group leader Dow Chem. Co., 1963-65; v.p. mfg. Better Plastics, Inc., 1965-67; head plastics div. Victor Metals Products Corp., Newport, Ark., 1967-69; v.p. Southeastern Plastics, Inc., Portsmouth, Va., from 1969—; now v.p.; mgr. R & K Plastics, Cleve. Republican central committeeman, 1961-64. Served to capt. USAF, 1942-45. Decorated Purple Heart, Air medal with three oak leaf clusters. Mem. Soc. Plastics Engrs. (treas. 1958-60), Cleve. Engr. Soc., Am. Legion. Home: 3733 Shannon Rd Portsmouth VA 23703

SZAZ, ZOLTAN MICHAEL, polit. scientist; b. Budapest, Hungary, Jan. 3, 1930 (came to U.S. 1950, naturalized 1955); s. Geza and Magda (Nagy) S.; student U. Munich (Germany), 1949-50; B.A. cum laude, St. John's U., Minn., 1951; M.A., Cath. U. Am., 1952, Ph.D., 1956; m. Jayne Anne Davis, Sept. 7, 1957;children—Claire Ann, Annamaria, Mary Carol, Christopher Michael. Washington corr. Radio Free Europe, 1953-55; editor Free World Forum, bi-monthly jour. fgn. affairs, 1958-61; instr., asst. prof. grad. history dept. St. John's U., 1960-64; lectr. history and govt. Seton Hall U., 1965-66, asso. prof. govt., 1966-68; exec. dir. Am. Inst. on Problems of European Unity, Washington, 1968—, adj. prof. Sch. Internat. Service, Am. U., 1970—; also asso. prof. polit. sci. Troy (Ala.) State U. Chmn., Internat. Relation Commn., D.C. Young Republicans, 1955-58; Young Rep. leader 11th Jud. Dist. State of N.Y., 1962-64; V.P. Everett McKinley Dirksen Forum, Washington, 1969-71. Mem. Am., Internat. polit. sci. assns., Am. Hungarian Fedn. (sec. internat. relations), Pi Gamma Mu. Author: Germany's Eastern Frontiers, 1960; Die deutsche Ostgrenze, 1961; Strategy and Tactics of the Hungarian Communist Party, 1918-45, 1972. Home: 3939 Livingston St NW Washington DC 20015 also 305 2d Av Troy AL 36081 Office: 3216 New Mexico Av NW Washington DC 20016 also Dept History and Social Sciences Troy State U Troy AL 36081

SZCZEPANSKI, ZDZISLAW CHARLES, govt. ofcl.; b. Krasiczyn, Poland, July 8, 1917; s. Stanislas and Jadwiga (Miser) S.; student Warsaw Polytechnic, 1935-41, Ecole des Beaux Arts of Paris, 1945-48, Town Planning Inst. Paris, 1948-50, Ecole des Beaux Arts of Que., 1955-56, Catholic U. Am., 1964; m. Anne Glowacki, Aug. 23, 1950; children—Wanda, Joanna. Came to U.S., 1958, naturalized, 1964. Bldg. contractor, Poland, 1940-44; architect, Paris, 1948-51, Montreal, 1951-53; Que., 1953-58, Buchart Assos., York, Pa., 1958-60; asso., architect-planner Satterle & Smith, Washington, 1962-66; dep. dir. grd. research and analysis Dept. Housing and Urban Devel., 1967—. Asso. prof. Catholic U. Am., 1962-66; partner APEC, 1966-67. Pres. Que. chpt. Community Planning Assn., 1958; exec. dir. Warsaw dist. Poland Boy Scouts, 1942-43. Bd. dirs. Holmes Run Acres Civic Assn. Served with Polish Army, 1938-39. Mem. Am. Soc. for Aesthetics, Washington Philos. Club: Am. Soc. Planning

Ofcls. Contbr. articles to profl. publs. Home: 3416 Executive Av Falls Church VA 22042 Office: 451 7th St SW Washington DC 20410

SZEGO, GEORGE CHARLES, chem. engr.; b. Budapest, Hungary, Aug. 10, 1919 (came to U.S. 1921, naturalized 1927); s. Paul S. and Helen (Ellek) S.; B.S., U. Denver, 1947; M.S., U. Wash., 1950, Ph.D., 1956; m. Marion E. Gowell, Oct. 1, 1938; children—Deirdre Alexandra, Luisa, Viviana, Thea, Rose, Isobel, Camilla. Engr., J.W. Green Co., Denver, 1946-47; teaching, research fellow U. Wash., Seattle, 1947-48; head dept. chem. engring. Seattle U., 1948-56, prof., 1951-56; owner, mgr. G.C. Szego & Assos., cons. engrs., Seattle, 1951-56; tech. mgr. Gen. Electric Co., Cin., 1956-59; mem. sr. tech. staff Space Tech. Labs. TRW, Los Angeles, 1959-61; mem. sr. staff, study dir. Inst. Def. Analyses, Washington, 1961-69; pres., chmn. InterTech. Corp., Barriers, Inc., Vivo Systems, Inc., Warrenton, Va., 1969—. Mem. sci. adv. group Mobility Equipment Command U.S. Army; mem. blue ribbon panel on Sheridan tank Sec. Def., 1969; breeder thoroughbred horses and Angus cattle. Bd. dirs. Communities Corp. Am. Served with AUS, 1943-46; ETO. Named Man of Year in Energy Conversion, 1966. Fellow Brit. Interplanetary Soc., Am. Inst. Aeros. and Astronautics (com. chmn.); mem. Am. Inst. Chem. Engrs. (past treas.; chmn. Puget Sound sect.; chmn. exec. com. Nat. Program), Intersoc. Energy Conversion Engring. Conf. (steering com. chmn.). Democrat. Patentee in field. Home: Oakwood Warrenton VA 22186

SZEKELEY, EDMOND B., biochemist, author. Founder family vacation spot Rancho La Puerta, Tecata, Mexico. Author: Golden Door Book of Beauty of Health, 1967. 9 Rancho La Puerta State Hwy 94 Tecata Mexico*

SZERYNG, HENRYK, violinist; b. Poland, 1921; studied with Carl Flesch, Berlin, Germany, Gabriel Bouillon, Paris Conservatoire, also with Nadia Boulanger. Public appearances, Warsaw, Bucharest, Vienna and Paris, 1933-39; Polish Army giving concerts 1940-45; world tours, 1952—; prof. a.h. Nat. Music Conservatory and Music Faculty, Mexico City. Decorated officer Order of Arts and Letters (France); comdr. Order of Lion (Finland); knight comdr. Order of Polonia Restituta (Poland) recipient Grand Prix du Disque, 1955, 57, 59, 60, 61, 67; Medal of City of Paris; others. Home: Arenida JM Marroqui 28 Mexico City Mexico Office: care Hurok 730 Fifth Av New York City NY 10019

SZUCH, SUE JENI ELIZABETH, advt. exec.; b. Toledo; d. John and Elizabeth (Bodak) Szuch; student Rollins Coll., 1951-53; A.B., U. Miami, Coral Gables, Fla., 1955. Artist, Harris & Co. Advt., Miami, Fla., 1957-60, Bishopric-Green-Fielden, Miami, Fla., 1960-66; art. dir. Design-Print, Miami, Fla., 1966-67; coordinator prodn. and traffic Advt. & Marketing, Inc., Miami, 1967—. Mem. Advt. Club Miami (nat. essay contest chmn. 1958, dir. 1960-62), Art Dirs. Club Miami (dir. 1961-67, awards chmn. 1966), Vizcayans, Opera Guild Miami, Gamma Alpha Chi. Republican. Clubs: Jamestown, Grove Sailing. Home: 3017 Blaine St Coconut Grove FL 33133 Office: 1200 Biscayne Blvd Miami FL 33132

TABB, HORACE ENGLISH, savings and loan exec.; b. Elizabethtown, Ky., Jan. 3, 1915; s. Edwin J. and Hattie (English) T; A.B., Duke, 1936; LL.B., U. Mich., 1939; m. Helen E. Nall, Nov. 15, 1941; children— Katherine T. (Mrs. James R. Lanz), Linda Sue. Admitted to Ky. bar, 1939, since practiced in Elizabethtown; with OPA, 1941-45; pres., atty., dir. 1st Fed. Savs. & Loan Assn., Elizabethtown, 1956—; pres. Ky. Bldg., Savs. & Loan League, 1966—. Co-owner Radio Stas. WIEL and WLBN, 1952—, Mid-Ky. Poster Co., Elizabethtown, 1959—. Bd. dirs. Southeastern Conf. U.S. Savs. and Loan League, 1966—, U.S. Savs. and Loan League, 1967—. Mem. Am. Judicature Soc., Ky., Hardin County bar assns., Ky. C. of C. (dir. 1970—), Sigma Nu. Clubs: Lions (past pres.), Rotary, Pendennis, Filson. Home: 1120 Oak St Elizabethtown KY 42701 Office: 202 W Dixie Av Elizabethtown KY 42701

TABB, JAMES HUGH, banker; b. Houston, Miss., Jan. 16, 1908; s. James Pounds and Katherine Blanche (Sanderson) T.; B.A., U. Miss., 1929; postgrad. Harvard, 1930-31; m. Eva Eudora Collins, Dec. 27, 1936; children—James Collins, Nancy (Mrs. Jack Ray Dendy). Establisher, J.H. Tabb & Co., Houston, Miss., 1936, pres., 1936—; pres. Houston State Bank 1939—; dir. Natchez Trace Electric Power Assn., Houston. Alderman, City of Houston, 1940-60. Trustee Miss. Meth. Found., Miss. Forestry Assn. Found. Recipient Silver Beaver award Boy Scouts Am., 1969. Mem. Ry. Tie Assn. (Man of Year award 1971, pres. 1955-56), Miss. Econ. Council, Miss. Mfrs. Assn., Pi Kappa Phi. Methodist (chmn. adminstrv. bd.). Mason. Club: Exchange (Houston). Home: 792 N Pontotoc St Houston MS 38851 Office: 105 W Washington St Houston MS 38851

TABB, JOHN DUANE, govt. ofcl.; b. Hayden, Colo., Aug. 24, 1936; s. Glenn Lee and Pauline (Purcell) T.; B.S. in Agrl. Engring., Colo. State U., 1959; m. Patricia Ann Turner, Nov. 24, 1963; children—Brenda Jean, Jeffrey Lynn. Dist. engr. Bur. Land Mgmt., Denver and Glenwood Springs, Colo., 1962-66, design and constrn. engr., Santa Fe, 1966-70, civil engr., Washington, 1970—. Served with AUS, 1960-62. Recipient Bausch & Lomb award, 1954, Superior Performance award Bur. Land Mgmt., 1967, 71. Mem. Am. Soc. Agrl. Engrs., Farm House. Home: 14608 Baugher Dr Centreville VA 22020 Office: Interior Bldg Bur Land Mgmt Washington DC 20240

TABOR, BRITTON DUNCAN, bank dir.; b. Checotah, Okla., Aug.29, 1914; s. Britton Hamilton and Bessie (Duncan) T.; B.A., U. of South, 1936; postgrad. Harvard U., summer 1936, Northwestern U., 1936-37, U. Va., 1940-41, U. N.M., 1948-49. Sr. credit man C.I.T. Corp., Chgo. also Dallas, 1937-39; tchg. fellowship U. Va., 1940-41; reporter, feature writer Muskogee (Okla.) Phoenix and Times-Democrat, 1942; mem. news and editorial staff Kingsport (Tenn) Times and News, 1946; news and editorial staff Knoxville (Tenn.) News Sentinel, 1946-47; press sec., legislative asst. to Congressman Ed Edmondson, Washington, 1955-60; free-lance writer, 1960—; dir. Peoples Nat. Bank, Checotah, Okla., 1961—. Fund drive chmn. North McIntosh County chmn. A.R.C., 1952; mem. Nat. Rivers and Harbors Congress, 1961. Served with AUS, 1942-45. Mem. S.A.R. (pres. Muskogee chpt. 1965), Am. Legion, Okla. Hist. Soc., Am. Mus. Natural History (asso.), Phi Beta Kappa, Omicron Delta Kappa, Pi Gamma Mu, Delta Tau Delta. Democrat. Episcopalian. Club: Nat. Press. Home: 631 W Lafayette Av Checotah OK 74426 Office: 631 W Lafayette Av Checotah OK 74426

TABORSKY, IVAN, educator; b. Prague, Czechoslovakia, July 11, 1915 (came to U.S. 1946; naturalized 1957); s. Edward and Oldra (Nekvasil) T.; Abitur, Acad. Comml. Sci., Prague, 1934; M.S., Czech Inst. Tech., Prague, 1939, Ph.D., 1946; m. Ema Liskova, Sept. 24, 1938; children—Ivanka, Dusan Edward, Nina Janet. Adminstrv. officer, Office of Mayor, Prague, 1934-45; 1st sec. Ministry Fgn. Affairs, Prague, 1945-46; sec. gen. Czechoslovak delegation to UN, N.Y.C., 1946-48, adminstrv. officer Secretariat of UN, 1948-49; exec. dir. Am. Fund Czechoslovak Refugees, N.Y.C., 1949-57, v.p., European dir., 1957-60; instr. govt. U. Tex. at Arlington, 1960-64, asst. prof., 1964-70, asso. prof., 1970—. Mem. Am. Polit. Sci. Assn., Soc. Arts and Scis. Home: 140 Varsity Circle Arlington TX 76013

TACHMINDJI, ALEXANDER JOHN, naval architect, marine engr.; b. Athens, Greece, Feb. 16, 1928 (came to U.S. 1950; naturalized 1958); s. John and Athena (Andreades) T.; B.Sc., Kings Coll. Durham (Eng.) U., 1949, B.Sc. (hons.); 1950; M.S., Mass. Inst. Tech., 1951; postgrad. U. Md., 1951-54; m. Diane Primeau, Dec. 4, 1965. Head research and propeller br. D.W. Taylor Model Basin, U.S. Navy Dept., Washington, 1951-59; with Inst. for Def. Analyses, Arlington, Va., 1959—, asst. dir. sci. and tech. div., 1963-67, dep. dir., 1967-69, dir. systems evaluation dir., 1969-72, dir. Tactical Tech. Office, Def. Advanced Research Projects Agy., 1972—; U.S. mem. Internat. Cavitation Com., 1955-59, also U.S. chmn. Am. Cavitation Com. Recipient U.S. Navy Meritorious Civilian award, 1955. Fellow Am. Inst. Aeros. and Astronautics, Royal Instn. Naval Architects; mem. Soc. Naval Architects and Marine Engrs. (chmn. panel hydroelasticity 1967—, mem. hydrodynamics com. 1967—), N.E. Inst. Engrs., A.A.A.S., N.Y. Acad. Sci., Sigma Xi. Club: Cosmos (Washington). Patentee ventilated propeller. Home: 4915 Sedgwick St Washington DC 20016 Office: Advanced Research Projects Agy Def Dept Pentagon Washington DC

TACHMINDJI, DIANE ELIZABETH PRIMEAU (MRS. ALEXANDER J. TACHMINDJI), civic worker, assn. exec.; b. Davenport, Ia., Dec. 3, 1936; d. Carl Donald and Fern (Elofson) Primeau; B.A., Marygrove Coll., 1962; m. Alexander J. Tachmindji, Dec. 4, 1965, U.S. congl. sec., 1957-59; legislative liaison Gen. Motors Corp., Washington, 1962-63; exec. sec. Inst. for Def. Analyses, Washington, 1963-64; asst. to dir. community relations service U.S. Conf. Mayors, Washington, 1964-65. Vol. canteen worker A.R.C., 1962-63; vol. Albert Deutsch Center, 1967-69, dir. vols., 1967-69, bd. dirs., sec., 1968-69, v.p., 1969-72; chmn. membership and vol. recruitment com. D.C. Mental Health Assn., 1968-69, mem. publicity com., 1969, mem. legislation and pub. policy com., 1970-71, bd. dirs., 1970-72, del. to health and welfare council, 1970-72, vice chmn. Mental Health Ball, 1971; rec. sec. Womens Com. Nat. Ballet, 1967-68, corr. sec., 1968-69, vice chmn., 1969-71, womens com. Nat. Symphony, 1967-68; bd. dirs. Washington Area Council on Alcoholism and Drug Abuse, 1972—, mem. Finance Com., 1972—; Mem. Nat. Ballet Soc. Home: 4915 Sedgwick St Washington DC 20016

TAEUBER, CONRAD, govt. ofcl.; b. Hosmer, S.D., June 15, 1906; s. Richard E. and Emmy (Mussgang) T.; A.B., U. Minn., 1927, M.A., 1929, Ph.D., 1931; postgrad. U. Heidelberg (Germany), 1929-30, U. Wis., 1929-30; m. Irene Barnes, July 26, 1929; children— Richard Conrad, Karl Ernst. Asst. prof. Mt. Holyoke Coll., 1929-33; asso. econ. analyst Fed. Emergency Relief Adminstrn., 1934-35; various positions to head agrl. economist Bur. Agrl. Economies, U.S. Dept. Agr., 1935-46; chief of statistics br. FAO of UN, 1946-51; asst. dir. charge demographic fields Bur. of Census, Washington, 1951-68, asso. dir., 1968—. Recipient Outstanding Achievement award U. Minn., 1951, Exceptional Service award Dept. Commerce, 1963. Fellow Am. Statis. Assn.; mem. A.A.A.S. (past v.p.), Am. Sociol. Assn. (past sec.), Population Assn. Am. (past pres.), Inter-Am. Statis. Inst. (pres.), Internat. Statis. Inst. Club: Cosmos (Washington). Author: (with C.E. Lively) Rural Migration in the United States, 1939; (with Irene B. Taeuber) The Changing Population of the United States, 1958; The People of the United States in the 20th Century, 1960. Contbr. articles profl. jours. Home: 4222 Sheridan St Hyattsville MD 20782 Office: Bur of the Census Washington DC 20233

TAFT, KINGSLEY ARTER, JR., forester; b. Cleve., Nov. 17, 1930; s. Kingsley Arter and Louise (Dakin) T.; A.B., Amherst Coll., 1953; B.S., U. Mich., 1957; M.S., N.C. State U., 1962, Ph.D., 1966; m. Eva Eileen Burkett, Mar. 4, 1955; children—Charisse Ann, Lynette Louise, Tiffany Norena. Forester, Nebo Oil Co., Minden, La., 1957-59; grad. asst. N.C. State U., Raleigh, 1959-63; forester geneticist TVA, Norris, 1963—. Served as pvt. 1st class AUS, 1953-55. Mem. Soc. Am. Foresters, A.A.A.S. Home: 55 Dogwood Rd Norris TN 37828 Office: Ridgeway Rd Norris TN 37828

TAFT, PAUL F., fiber glass co. exec.; b. Nashville, Oct. 10, 1933; s. James Maurice and Alois (Herndon) T.; B.S., Middle Tenn. State U., 1957; M.S., Vanderbilt U., 1958; m. Joyce Power, Jan. 31, 1958; children—Sheryl Dianne, James Warren. Research chemist Girdler Catalyst Co., Louisville, 1958-59, U.S. Tobacco Co., Nashville, 1959-65; tech. dir. Ferro Fiber Glass Co., Nashville, 1965—. Served with USMCR, 1951-54. Mem. Am. Chem. Soc., Soc. Plastic Engrs., Am. Assn. Quality Control. Home: 1310 McChesney Av Nashville TN 37216 Office: Fiber Glass Rd Nashville TN 37211

TAFT, RICHARD GEORGE, lawyer; b. Ann Arbor, Mich., Mar. 13, 1913; s. George J. and Wilhemina (Voigt) T.; B.S. in Bus., U. Okla., 1935, LL.B., 1940; m. Pauline Joyner, Sept. 17, 1942 (dec. 1944); 1 son, Richard George; m. 2d, Margaret Gessner Twyman, Sept. 10, 1946 (div. 1949); m. 3d, Louise Hutto Miller, Dec. 30, 1953 (div. Feb. 1960); m. 4th, Louise Holmberg Crawford, Dec. 30, 1960; 1 stepdau., Jamy Crawford (Mrs. Richard Judd). With FCA, 1935-37; admitted to Okla. bar, 1940; with firm Campbell, Randolph, Mahin & Mosteller, attys., 1940-41, Mosteller & McElroy, attys., 1946-48, Billups, Wood & Champlin, C.P.A.s, 1948-51; partner McAfee, Taft, Cates, Mark, Bond & Rucks attys., Oklahoma City, 1951—. Mem. Okla. State Bd. Corrections, 1967-72, pres., 1967-69; mem. Norman (Okla.) Planning Commn., 1966-69, Presbyn. Med. Center Found., 1961—, St. Anthony's Hosp. Found., 1965—. Trustee Oklahoma County Med. Soc. Community Found. Served to lt. col. USAAF, 1941-45. C.P.A., Okla. Mem. Am., Okla. bar assns., Am. Judicature Soc., Am. Inst. C.P.A.s, Phi Delta Phi, Phi Gamma Delta. Republican. Episcopalian. Home: 603 Okmulgee St Norman OK 73069 Office: 100 Park Av Oklahoma City OK 73102

TAGGART, PATRICK E., pres. Austin Am. and Statesman. Office: 308 Guadalupe St Austin TX 78767*

TAHIR, ASHIQ HUSSAIN, physician; b. Bahawal Pur, West Pakistan, Sept. 16, 1940; s. Zia Mohammad and Mumtaz (Begum) Khan; B.Sc., Govt. Coll., Lahore, West Pakistan, 1959; M.B.B.S., King Edward Med. Coll., Lahore, West Pakistan, 1964; m. Dixie Ann Webb, Apr. 17, 1970; 1dau., Lisa Shawn. Came to U.S., 1964, naturalized, 1970. Intern, Youngstown (O.) Hosp., 1964-65; resident surgery Lewis Gale Hosp., Roanoke, Va., 1965-66, St. Francis Hosp., Wichita, Kan., 1966-67; resident anesthesiology Charity Hosp., New Orleans, 1967-70, clin. instr. anesthesiologist, 1970—; clin. instr. dept. surgery Tulane U. Sch. Medicine, New Orleans, 1970—; cons. anesthesiologist Lallie Kemp Charity Hosp., Independence, La., 1970—. Recipient physicians recognition award A.M.A., 1969, numerous grants for research in anesthesiology. Fellow Royal Coll. Physicians (Can.), mem. Am. Soc. Anesthesiologists, Internat. Anesthesia Research Soc., Royal Soc. Health (Eng.) (hon.). Club: Roving and Mountaineering (sec. 1963-64). Contbr. articles to profl. pubs. Home: 4415 Stephen Girard St New Orleans LA 70126 Office: 1532 Tulane St New Orleans LA 70140

TAISHOFF, SOL JOSEPH, editor, pub.; b. Minsk, Russia, Oct. 8, 1904; s. Joseph and Rose (Order) T.; ed. pub. schs., Washington; m. Betty Tash, Mar. 6, 1927; children—Joanne (Mrs. Kenneth Cowan), Lawrence Bruce. Copy boy Washington bur. Asso. Press, 1920-21, successively dictation boy, telegraph operator, mem. news staff, 1922-26; reporter U.S. Daily (now U.S. News and World Report), Washington, 1926-31; radio editor Consol. Press (pen name Robert Mack), 1927-34; mng. editor, co-founder Broadcasting Pub., Inc., 1931-33, editor, 1933—; vice president, treas. Broadcasting mag., 1931-34, pres., editor, pub., 1944—; pres., editor, pub. Television mag., 1960—; v.p., dir. Tele-communications Reports, Inc., Food-Drug-Cosmetic Reports Inc.; pres. Jolar Corp.; past pres. Broadcast Pioneers. Mem. selection com. CBS Found., Inc.; bd. dirs. Washington Journalism Center. Recipient Distinguished Service in Journalism award U. Mo., 1953; Distinguished Service award Nat. Assn. Broadcasters, 1966. Mem. I.E.E.E. (sr. mem.), Sigma Delta Chi (past nat. pres.; journalism fellow 1964). Clubs: Nat. Press, Overseas Writers, Woodmont Country, Broadcasters. Advertising, Internat. (Washington). Home: 4201 Cathedral Av NW Washington DC 20016 Office: 1735 DeSales St Washington DC 20036

TAIT, COLUMBUS DOWNING, JR., psychoanalyst, educator; b. Valdosta, Ga., Sept. 3, 1923; s. Columbus Downing and Mary L. (Jacobs) T.; B.A., U. Va., 1943, M.D., 1947; m. Nancy Kirk Reep, Aug. 25, 1956; children—Carl Downing, Jennifer Bradshaw. Intern, Bellevue Hosp., N.Y.C., 1947-48; resident in psychiatry Compton (Cal.) Sanitarium, 1948-49, Rockland (N.Y.) State Hosp., 1950; AEC postdoctoral research fellow in med. scis. Duke, 1949, Yale, 1950; psychoanalytic student Columbia, N.Y.C., 1950, 53-57; practice medicine specializing in psychiatry and psychoanalysis, N.Y.C., 1953-64; instr. Psychoanalytic Clinic, Columbia, 1957-64; asso. prof. psychiatry Emory U. Sch. Medicine, Atlanta, 1964-67; prof. 1967—; dir. research Ga. Mental Health Inst., 1965-71; part-time practice psychoanalysis; Atlanta, cons. local juvenile cts. Research and cons. psychiatrist Washington Youth Council, 1954-61, Mblzn. for Youth, N.Y.C., 1962-64. Served to lt., M.C., USNR, 1951-53. Diplomate Am. Bd. Psychiatry and Neurology. Fellow Am. Psychiat. Assn. (com. on history of psychiatry 1969—); mem. Am., Internat. psychoanalytic assns., A.M.A., A.A.A.S., Ga., Atlanta med. socs., Phi Beta Kappa, Alpha Omega Alpha. Author: (with Hodges) Delinquents, Their Families, and the Community, 1962. Contbr. articles to profl. jours. Home: 820 Douglas Rd NE Atlanta GA 30342 Office: 1256 Briarcliff Rd NE Atlanta GA 30306

TALBERT, ANSEL EDWARD MCLAURINE, magazine editor; b. Washington, Jan. 6, 1912; s. Ansel D. and Lily (McLaurine) T.; grad. Landon Sch., Bethesda, Md., 1930; A.B., Columbia, 1934, Litt.B., 1935, M.S. (Henry Woodward Sackett fellow), 1935; spl. student McGill U.; m. Marlene Zimmer, 1951 (div. 1969). New York corr. at Sci. Service, 1935-36; with N.Y. Herald Tribune, 1936-58, spl. assignment, Europe, 1939, Far East, 1940, Korean war corr., also chief Tokyo bur., 1950-51, assigned Middle East, Japan, Korea, Alaska, Eng., France, 1951-53, Thule, Greenland, Ice Island T-3, North Pole, 1954, operation Deep Freeze, McMurdo Sound, Antarctica, also four flights over South Pole, 1956, Soviet Union, 1956, Scandinavia, Pakistan, Iran, 1957, mil. and aviation editor, 1954-58; exec. editor publs. and v. p. Flight Safety Found., 1959-67, writer column Defense and Aviation; mng. editor Air Transport World mag., 1967—; spl. broadcasts aerospace, and mil. devels. WQXR, 1960-61, WRUL-Worldwide Broadcasting System, 1962-63; dir. Fgn. News Service Syndicate, Inc., Tele Trip Inc. Trustee, past mem. adv. com. Harmon Internat. Aviation Trophies, past mem. Collier Trophy Com. Served from pvt. to lt. col., AUS, 1941-46. Decorated Chevalier Legion of Honor (France); Royal Jugoslav War Cross of St. Andrew; Medal of Merit of Santos Dumont (Brazil); recipient James J. Strebig trophy for outstanding writing on aviation, 1957; Gold medal from Adventurers Club, 1959. Mem. of Aviation Space Writers Assn. (past pres.), Am. Polar Soc., Arctic Inst. N.A., Elbeetian Legion, S.A.R., Am. Legion (past post comdr.), Woodmen of the World, Air Force Assn., Civil War Round Table, Columbia Univ. Alumni Assn., Am. Legion, Zeta Psi. Alumni. Clubs: Wings (past v.p.), Adventurers (past pres.), Dutch Treat (N.Y.C.); Overseas Press (mem. bd., past v.p.; trustee Found.), Nat. Press (Washington). Author: Famous Airports of the World, 1953. Co-author: How I Got That Story, 1967; Irreplaceable Randolph Churchill, 1969. Mem. editorial bd. Military Publishing Inst., 1958-65. Home: 2939 Van Ness St NW Washington DC 20008

TALBOT, ALFRED KENNETH, JR., educator; b. N.Y.C., Sept. 1, 1916; s. Alfred Kenneth and Sylvia Lucetta (Simpson) T.; B.S., Hampton Inst., 1940, M.A., 1949; postgrad. George Peabody Coll., 1955, N.Y. U., summers 1953, 54, 56, 59, U. Kan., 1965, Coll. William and Mary, 1970; m. Hazel Grace Green, Feb. 20, 1957. High sch. tchr., Accomack County, Va., 1941; elementary tchr., Newport News, Va., 1942-45; counselor intermediate boys Children's Center, N.Y. Dept. Welfare, 1945-46; critic tchr. Hampton Inst., 1946-47; prin. Carver Elementary Sch., Loudoun County, Va., 1947-55; asst. prin. Bruton Heights Sch., Williamsburg, Va., 1955-66; supr. elementary edn. Williamsburg Pub. Schs., 1966-68, dir. curriculum, 1968-70; asso. prof. sociology/edn. Salisbury (Md.) State Coll., 1971—. Dir. summer playgrounds Va. Pub. Schs., Newport News, 1942-44, Hampton, Va., 1945. Bd. dirs. Williamsburg Regional Library, Williamsburg Day Care Center. Recipient plaque Distinguished Service, Va. Congress Colored Parents and Tchrs., 1955-59; plaque Distinguished Service and Leadership, Va. Tchrs. Assn., 1962-64. Mem. Am. Assn. Sch. Adminstrs., N.E.A., Assn. Supervision and Curriculum Devel., Va. Edn. Assn., Va. Tchrs. Assn. (pres. 1962-64), Williamsburg Council on Human Relations. U.P. Ch. (dir. project for migrant workers 1961). Home: 1436 Government Rd Williamsburg VA 23185 Office: Salisbury State Coll Salisbury MD 21801

TALBOT, FRANK, III, textile co. exec., lawyer; b. Danville, Va., Mar. 26, 1929; s. Frank and Margaret (Jordan) T.; B.A., U. Va., 1951, LL.B., 1953; m. Mary Beverly Chewning, July 11, 1952; children—Beverly, Frank IV. Admitted to Va. bar, 1952; gen. practice law, Danville, 1956-66; with Dan River Mills, Inc., 1966—, v.p., gen. counsel, 1968—; dir. First Nat. Bank Danville. Vice chmn. Danville Sch. Bd., 1964—. Sec. Danville Democratic Com., 1962-63. Trustee U. Va. Student Aid Found., 1963-68; bd. dirs. United Fund Danville, 1959-63; bd. mgrs. U. Va. Alumni Assn., 1971—. Served with AUS, 1953-56. Decorated Commendation medal. Mem. Am., Va. (v.p. 1965-66, exec. com. 1967-70), Danville (pres. 1965-66) bar assns., Am. Judicature Soc., Newcomen Soc., Delta Psi, Phi Alpha Delta. Methodist. Clubs: Golf, German (Danville). Home: 420 Maple Lane Danville VA 24541 Office: 2291 Memorial Dr Danville VA 24541

TALBOT, LEE MERRIAM, ecologist; b. New Bedford, Mass., Aug. 2, 1930; s. Murrell Williams and Zenaida (Merriam) T.; student Deep Springs Coll., 1948-49; A.B., U. Cal. at Berkeley, 1953, M.A., 1963, Ph.D., 1963; m. Martha Walcott Hayne, May 16, 1959; 1 son, Lawrence Hayne. Staff ecologist Internat. Union for Conservation, Europe, Asia, Africa, 1954-56, dir. S.E. Asia Project, 1964-65; ecologist, dir. East African Ecol. Research Project, U.S. Nat. Acad. Scis., N.Y. Zool. Soc., Govts. of Kenya, Tanzania, 1959-63; wildlife adviser UN Spl. Fund, Africa, 1963-64; resident ecologist and Smithsonian field rep. for internat. affairs in ecology and conservation Smithsonian Instn., Washington, 1966-70; sr. scientist Council

Environmental Quality, Exec. Office of Pres., Washington, 1970—. Cons. U.S. Nat. Acad. Scis., UNESCO, UN Spl. Fund, Peace Corps, AID, Internat. Union for Conservation, Life Mag., fgn. govts.; dep. convener Internat. Biol. Program Conservation Sect. Trustee Population Reference Bur., Am. Com. for Internat. Wildlife Protection; mem. exec. bd. Internat. Union for Conservation. Served with USMCR, 1953-54. Recipient Outstanding Publ. award Wildlife Soc., 1963. Fellow A.A.A.S., N.Y. Zool. Soc.; mem. Wildlife Soc. (com. chmn.), Am. Soc. Mammalogists, Assn. for Tropical Biology (com. chmn.), Pacific Sci. Assn. (conservation chmn.) Soc. Range Mgmt. (dir.), Assn. Am. Geographers, Ecol. Soc. Am., Am. Com. for Internat. Wildlife Protection (chmn.), Zool. Soc. Korea, Fauna Soc. London, East Wildlife Soc., Order Golden Bear, Phi Kappa Sigma. Clubs: Explorers (N.Y.C.); Cosmos (Washington); Boone and Crockett, Sports Car of America. Author: books, monographs; (television documentary film) Man, Beast and the Land, 1968 (Cine Golden Eagle award 1969). Contbr. articles to profl. jours. Home: 6656 Chilton Ct McLean VA 22101 Office: Council Environmental Quality Exec Office President 722 Jackson Pl Washington DC 20006

TALBOTT, FRANK, JR., lawyer; b. Danville, Va., June 24, 1900; s. Frank and Ida W. (Lipscomb) T.; student Randolph-Macon Coll., 1917-18; A.B., U. of Va., 1921, B.L., 1924; m. Margaret C. Jordan, Dec. 11, 1926; children—Frank, III, Margie. Admitted Va. bar, 1923; gen. counsel, chmn. bd. dirs. Dan River Mills, Inc., 1952-66, chmn. exec. com., gen. counsel, 1966-68, chmn. exec. com. counsel, 1968—; dir. Am. Nat. Bank and Trust Co. Mem. Gov.'s Commn. Study State Govt., 1960. Bd. dirs. U. Va., 1949-60, rector, 1956-60, mem. alumni bd. trustees endowment fund; trustee Va. Mus. Fine Arts. Mem. Va. State Bar (council mem., pres. 1948-49), Va., Am. bar assns., Am. Judicature Soc., Am. Law Inst., Phi Beta Kappa, Phi Delta Phi, Phi Delta Theta. Clubs: Danville Golf, Commonwealth (Richmond); Farmington (Charlottesville). Home: 160 Linden Dr Danville VA 24541 Office: 2291 Memorial Dr Danville VA 24541

TALBURT, EVERETT E., state ofcl.; m. Bettye Clark, 1951; children—Jeanie Ann, Jennie Faith. Dir., Ark. Civil Def. Mem. Nat. Civil Def. Dirs. Assn. (regional v.p.), Jaycees (past pres.), Nat. Rifle Assn. Mason (32 deg., Shriner). Home: 7 Colonial Dr Conway AR 72032 Office: Ark Civil Def Agy PO Box 845 Conway AR 72032

TALIAFERRO, EDMUND PENDLETON, banker; b. Tampa, Fla., Sept. 1, 1928; s. E.P. and Sara Saunders (Hull) T.; student U. Fla., 1946-48, U. Tampa, 1948-49; grad. Sch. Banking of South, 1952; m. Jean L. Zeiner, Mar. 1, 1950; children—Jean Ellen, Edmund Pendleton, James Bryan, Dudley Saunders. With 1st Nat. Bank Tampa, Fla., 1950—, sr. v.p., 1964-66, exec. v.p., 1966, sr. exec. v.p., 1966-67, pres., 1967—, dir., 1962—; pres., dir. Union Security & Investment Co., Tampa First Financial Corp.; chmn. First Nat. Bank in Plant City; dir. 1st Nat. Bank Brooksville, 1st Nat. Bank Lakeland, 1st Nat. Bank Punta Gorda, Scotty's Home Builders supplies, Inc., Inter City Nat. Bank Bradenton. Mem. adv. bd. St. Joseph's Hosp., 1965—; treas. Hillsborough County unit Am. Cancer Soc.; commr. Fla. Devel. Commn., 1965-67; mem. Citizens Com. on Crime Prevention; mem. exec. adv. com. Tampa Sports Authority; active United Fund, Com. of 100, Fla. Council 100; chmn. 1970 Radio Free Europe Campaign, Fla.; mem. met. Tampa bus. adv. bd. Nat. Alliance Businessmen; bd. dirs. Fla. State Fair. Mem. Robert Morris Assos. (past pres. Southeastern chpt.), Greater Tampa C. of C. (bd. govs., exec. com.), Young Presidents Orgn., Ye Mystic Krewe of Gasparilla, Sigma Alpha Epsilon. Episcopalian. Club: Tampa Yacht and Country. Home: 4510 Bay to Bay Blvd Tampa FL 33609 Office: PO Box 1810 Tampa FL 33601

TALIAFERRO, LEWIS, lawyer, state senator; b. Kenton, Tenn., Oct. 25, 1921; s. James Lyndel and Ruby (Taylor) T.; B.S., Memphis State U., 1943; LL.B., U. Va., 1949; m. Bettye Frances Knox, Jan. 9, 1953; children—Elizabeth Wythe, Margaret Knox, Mary Lyndel. Admitted to Tenn. bar, 1949; practice law, Memphis, 1949—; partner Hoffman, Taliaferro, Hughes & Williams, 1963—; mem. Tenn. Senate, 1960—. Mem. adv. bd. Abilene Christian Coll., 1958—. Chmn. Shelby County Democratic Exec. Com., 1966—. Served to lt. USNR, 1943-46. Home: 6360 Heather Dr Memphis TN 38117 Office: N Main Bldg Memphis TN 38103

TALKINGTON, PERRY CLEMENT, physician; b. Waco, Tex., 1909; M.D., Baylor U., 1934. Intern, Hamot Hosp., Erie, Pa., 1934-35; resident in neurology and psychiatry Taunton (Mass.) State Hosp., 1935-37; resident in organic neurology Phila. Orthopedic Hosp. and Infirmary Nervous Diseases, 1937-38; chief psychiatrist Timberlawn Sanitarium, Dallas, 1949-68, cons. in psychiatry, 1968—; chief neurology and psychiat. service Baylor Hosp., Dallas, 1955-69; civilian cons. U.S. Surgeon Gen., 1946—; asst. clin. prof. neurology and psychiatry Baylor U., 1938-40, instr. clin. neurology and psychiatry, 1940-43; clin. asst. prof. neuropsychiatry Southwestern U., 1945-50, clin. asso. prof. neuropsychiatry, 1950-69, clin. prof. psychiatry, 1969—. Served as lt. col. M.C., AUS, 1941-45. Diplomate Am. Bd. Psychiatry and Neurology. Mem. A.M.A., Central Neuropsychiat. Assn., Am. Psychiat. Assn. (pres. elect 1972), So. Med. Assn., So. Psychiat. Assn., Am. Coll. Psychiatrists. Office: 4645 Samuell Blvd Dallas TX 75228*

TALLANT, HAROLD DONALD, clergyman; b. Chattanooga, Oct. 29, 1916; s. Rev. Joseph Bernard and Laura Jane (Green) T.; A.B., Carson-Newman Coll., 1938; Th.M., So. Bapt. Theol. Sem., 1941; D.D., Georgetown Coll., 1957; m. Rhoda Ellen Haun, May 14, 1939; children— Marilynn Sue (Mrs. Tallant Friel), Harold Donald. Music dir. Beechmont Bapt. Ch., Louisville, 1938; ordained to ministry, Bapt. Ch., 1939; asst. pastor Ninth and O Bapt. Ch. Louisville, 1938-41; asso. pastor First Bapt. Ch., Frankfort, Ky., 1941-42; pastor First Bapt. Ch., London, Ky., 1942-47, Madisonville, Ky., 1947-63, First Bapt. Ch., Daytona Beach, Fla., 1963-67; evangelist, cons. So. Bapt. Ch., 1967-68; pastor Farmdale Bapt. Ch., Louisville, 1968-70; evangelist Highview Bapt. Ch., Louisville, 1970—. Pres. tng. Ky. Bapt. Conv., 1947, 48, 49, vice chmn., bd. missions, 1953-54, 56-58, chmn. music com., 1952-54, hosp. commn., 1949-51, mem. exec. com., 1953-54, 57-58, 58-59, 59-60, chmn. exec. bd., 1959, 60, chmn. appropriations com., 1959, adminstrv. com., 1962, chmn. wage scale adminstr., 1961, 62; pres. Madisonville Ministerial Assn. 1960-63; trustee Fgn. Mission bd. So. Bapt. Conv., 1963; faculty Ridgecrest Bapt. Assembly of So. Bapt. Conv., 1947—, time and place com., 1954, trustee Sunday Sch. bd., 1954-62, teller, 1959, program, 1961, com. on coms. 1962—; moderator Little Bethel Baptist Assn., 1949-51, asst. moderator Gen. Assn. Ky. Bapts., 1956-57; exec. bd. Fla. Bapt. Conv., 1966—; moderator Halifax Bapt. Assn., 1965-66; dir. World Missions Conf., Long Run Bapt. Assn., 1969-71, mem. evangelism com., 1971-72. Mem. Social Service Adminstrn., Commonwealth of Ky., 1956-59; trustee Ky. Temperance League, 1955-63, Hopkins County chpt. A.R.C., 1959-65. Hopkins County Com. Retarded Children, 1960; instl. rep. Boy Scouts Am., 1949—. Trustee Georgetown Coll., 1948-64. Kiwanian (dir. Madisonville 1963; Distinguished Service award 1963, Legion of Honor award, Daytona Beach, Fla. 1968, dir. Louisville 1970). Home: 6204 Richiewayne Dr Louisville KY 40219 Office: 7711 Fegenbush Lane Louisville KY 40228

TALLEY, JAMES STATON, banker; b. Clarksburg, W.Va., Oct. 23, 1922; s. Nathan Maurice and Blanche Elizabeth (Staton) T.; student Benjamin Franklin U., 1940-41; B.A., George Washington U., 1949; m. Marilyn Jean Hunter, June 8, 1949; children—Anne-Elizabeth, Patricia, Michael, Jennifer. Various supervisory positions Gen. Motors Acceptance Corp., 1949-63, asst. sec., credit mgr., Washington, 1963-64; asst. v.p. First Va. Bankshares, indirect credit, Arlington, Va., 1964-69, v.p., 1969-71; v.p. First Va. Finance Plan, 1968-71, First Va. Bank, br. adminstrn., 1971—. Mem. Va. Bankers Installment Credit Com., 1968-69; moderator panels, credit confs., 1968-69; designer, instituted operations First Va. Finance Plan, 1967-69, developer loan adminstrn. program direct field, 1971. Served with USCGR, 1942-46. Mem. Kappa Sigma. Methodist (teller 1971-72). Home: 8929 Stark Rd Annandale VA 22003 Office: 2926 Columbia Pike St Arlington VA 22204

TALLEY, JERRY LEALAND, bank exec.; b. Kerens, Tex., Sept. 1, 1928; s. Milton E. and Gertrude Marie (Newsom) T.; A.A., Arlington State Coll., 1948; grad. Southwestern Grad. Sch. Banking, So. Meth. U., 1960; m. Rita Evelyn Pierce, July 17, 1950; children—Jan Ell, Jerri Kay. Radio announcer KGAF, Gainesville, Tex., 1948-50, program dir., 1952-54; farm dir. KFDX-TV, Wichita Falls, Tex., 1954-56; sales mgr. Gainesville Retail Establishment, 1956-58; asst. v.p. Grayson County State Bank, Sherman, Tex., 1958, v.p., dir., 1959, exec. v.p., 1960, pres., trust officer, 1964—; pres., chmn. Texoma Savs. Assn., Sherman, Tex., 1962-64, also dir.; dir. Day Mfg. Co., Medco, Inc., Constn. Village, Pylon Farms, DMC, Inc., Zona Leasing Corp.; adv. dir. Texoma Nat. Bank; dir., pres. Central S.W. Corp.; dir. v.p. Recovery Co.; pres. Gainesville Devel. Corp.; dir., treas. Grayson Computer Service. Mem. adv. com. S.W. Employees Incentive Plan, 1971—. Active Am. Cancer Soc., Sherman United Fund, Boy Scouts Am., Camp Fire Girls, Salvation Army, Texoma Expn. and Livestock Show; mem. devel. bd. Austin Coll., 1962-66; mem. Area and State Soil Conservation Selection Panel, 1962. Bd. dirs. Sherman Council on Drug Edn.; trustee Austin Coll., Sherman. Served with USAF, 1950-52. Named Outstanding Young Man of Sherman, Jr. C. of C., 1959; nominated Outstanding Young Texan, Jr. C. of C., 1961. Mem. Sherman C. of C. Am. Legion. Presbyn. (elder). Mason (32 degree, Shriner), Rotarian. Home: 1610 Lakewood St Sherman TX 75090 Office: 400 N Crockett St Sherman TX 75090

TALLEY, NEVA BENNETT (MRS. J. H. MORRIS), lawyer; b. Judsonia, Ark., Aug. 12, 1909; d. John W. and Erma (Rhew) Bennett; B.A., magna cum laude, Ouachita Coll., 1930; M.Ed., U. Tex., 1938, postgrad., 1939-41; m. Cecil C. Talley, Jan. 1, 1946 (dec. Oct. 1948); m. 2d, Joseph H. Morris, Mar. 22, 1952. Tchr. high sch., prin. White County, Ark., 1930-42; student asst. U. Tex., summers, 1937-41; ordnance insp. war service appointment U.S. Army Service Forces, 1942-45; law office apprentice, pvt. tutorship, North Little Rock, Ark., 1945-47; admitted to Ark. bar, 1947, pvt. practice in Little Rock. Chmn. Ark. Council of Children and Youth, 1952-54; pres. Nat. Women Lawyers Found., 1958-60; Recipient ann. award, Nat. Assn. Women Lawyers, 1962; Distinguished Service award Ark. Bar Assn., 1970. Fellow Am. Acad. of Matrimonial Lawyers (bd. govs. 1969—); mem. Nat. (life, council del. 1952—, pres. 1956-57, exec. council family law sect. 1958—), Little Rock (pres. 1950-51) assns. women lawyers, North Little Rock Bus. and Profl. Women's Club (pres. 1951-52), Am. Assn. U. Women (v.p. Little Rock br. 1955), Am. (council family law sect. 1958—, chmn. family law sect. 1969-70, mem. ho. dels. 1957-58, 70—), Ark. (chmn. family law reform com. 1960-61), Pulaski County bar assns., Am. Judicature Soc., Nat. Conf. Lawyers and Social Workers (mem. nat. exec. bd. 1962-67, 70—), Ark. Bar Assn. Found., Phi Alpha Delta (hon.), Delta Kappa Gamma. Author: Handbook of Family Law, 1973. Home: 101 N State St Little Rock AR 72201 Office: 722 W Markham St Little Rock AR 72201

TALLEY, WILLIAM GILES, JR., container mfg. co. exec.; b. Adel, Ga., Sept. 25, 1939; s. William Giles and Mary (McGlamry) T.; B.S. in Bus. Adminstrn., U. S.C., 1961; m. Jacqueline Vickery, Apr. 14, 1962; children—William Giles III, John Lindsey, Bronwyn Ashley. Mgmt. trainee Talley Veneer & Crate Co., Inc., Adel, 1961-62, plant mgr., salesman, Waynesboro, Ga., 1965-67; Talley's Box Co., Leesburg, Fla., 1962-65, plant mgr. 1967-69; partner, gen. mgr. Growers Container Corp. Inc., Leesburg, 1969—; dir. First Nat. Bank Leesburg. Bd. dirs. Leesburg Hosp. Assn. Served with USAAF, 1961. Mem. Leesburg C. of C. (dir.), Sigma Alpha Epsilon. Democrat. Methodist. Elk, Kiwanian. Home: Lake Griffin Leesburg FL 32748 Office: PO Box 817 Leesburg FL 32748

TALMADGE, HERMAN E(UGENE), U.S. senator; b. McRae, Ga., Aug. 9, 1913; s. Eugene and Mattie Thurmond (Peterson) T.; grad. Druid Hills Sch., Atlanta, 1931; LL.B., U. Ga., 1936; student Midshipman's Sch., Northwestern U., 1942; m. Leila Elizabeth Shingler, Dec. 24, 1941; children—Herman Eugene, Robert Shingler. Admitted to Ga. bar, 1936, practiced with father, Atlanta, 1936-41, 45-48; gov. Ga., 1948-55; gen. practice law, Atlanta, 1955-57; U.S. senator, 1957—. Served with USN, 1941-45; commd. ensign and advanced through grades to lt. comdr.; participated in invasion of Guadalcanal aboard U.S.S. Tryon; served as flag sec. to comdt. of Naval Forces at New Zealand, June 1943—Apr. 1944; exec. officer U.S.S. Dauphin, participated in engagements with Japanese Fleet and in Battle of Okinawa; entered Tokyo Bay, V-J Day. Mem. Navy League, Am. Legion, V.F.W., S.C.V., S.A.R., Am., Ga., Atlanta bar assns., Farm Bur., Sigma Nu, Sigma Delta Kappa, Sphinx. Democrat. Baptist. Mason (Shriner), Elk. Club: Touchdown (Athens, Ga.). Author: You and Segregation. Home: Lovejoy GA 30250 also 2801 New Mexico Av NW Washington DC 20007 Office: 275 W Peachtree St NE Atlanta GA 30303

TALTON, ALMANDA R. (MRS. FURMAN CARLTON ANDERSON), educator; b. Sterlington, La., Dec. 12, 1930; d. Henry Joseph and Katie (Moses) Talton; B.S., Grambling Coll., 1954; M.A., Columbia, 1958, profl. diploma, 1964; m. Furman Carlton Anderson, Aug. 23, 1966. Tchr., Grambling (La.) Coll. Nursery Sch., 1954-56, dir., tchr., 1956-63, tchr. Coll., 1964-66, coordinator head start staff tng. programs, 1966; head tchr., supervising tchr. Queens Coll. Early Childhood Edn. Center, Flushing, N.Y., 1963-64; regional tng. officer State of La.-Office Econ. Opportunity, Grambling, 1966-67; part-time tchr. Grambling Coll., part-time supr. kindergarten programs Lincoln Parish, cons. S. Central Regional Edn. Lab., Little Rock, 1967—. Cons. S.W. region Office Child Devel. Mem. La. Edn. Assn., Assn. for Childhood Edn. Internat., So. Assn. for Children Under Six, Nat. Assn. for Edn. Young Children, Am. Assn. U. Profs., Am. Home Econs. Assn., Day Care and Child Devel. Council Am., Alpha Kappa Alpha. Address: Box 314 Grambling LA 71245

TALTON, GORDON TYLER, dentist; b. Apopka, Fla., Dec. 25, 1915; s. William Goode and Julliett (Pollard) T.; B.S., Wake Forest Coll., 1940; D.D.S., Med. Coll. Va., 1943; m. Mildred Lyell James, Sept. 18, 1945; children—Catharine, Grace, Gordon, David, Bettye. Pvt. practice dentistry, Orlando, Fla., 1947—. Bd. dirs. Bapt. Terrace. Served with USNR, World War II. Mem. Am., Fla. dental assns., Central Dist. (pres. 1968-69), Orange County dental socs. Baptist. Lion. Home: 77 Interlaken Rd Orlando FL 32801 Office: 1017 E Robinson Av Orlando FL 32802

TAMAYO, RUFINO, painter; b. Oaxaca, Mexico, Aug. 26, 1899; s. Manuel Arellances and Florentina Tamayo; ed. Sch. Fine Arts, Mexico City; m. Olga Flores Rivas, Jan. 24, 1934. Head dept. ethnographic drawing Nat. Mus. Archaeology, 1921-26; tchr. drawing, painting Mexico City pub. schs., 1926; head dept. plastic arts Mexican Secretariat Edn., 1932; art instr. Dalton Sch., N.Y.C., 1938—, Bklyn. Mus. Art Sch., 1946; painter, one man shows Weyhe Gallery, N.Y.C., 1926, Art Center, N.Y.C., 1927, Nat. Theatre, Mexico City, 1929, John Levy Galleries, N.Y.C., 1931, Carolina Amor Gallery, Mexico City, 1935, Valentine Gallery, N.Y.C., 1939-47, Arts Club Chgo., 1945, Pierre Matisse Gallery, N.Y.C., 1948, Knoedler Gallery, N.Y.C., 1951—, Mus. Fine Arts, Houston, 1956, Palais des Beaux Arts, Brussels, 1950, Galeriedes Beaux Arts, Paris, 1950, and many others U.S., Europe, S.A. and Mexico; rep. permanent collections Mus. Modern Art, N.Y.C., Phillips Meml. Gallery, Washington, Art Inst. Chgo., N.Y. Pub. Library, Musee Nat. d'Art Moderne, Paris, and others in Europe, Mexico, U.S. Recipient 3d prize. Carnegie Internat., Pitts., 1952, 2d prize, 1955; recipient 1st prize. San Paulo (Brazil) Biennal, 1954. Decorated chevalier de la Legion d'Honneur (France). Hon. mem. Am. Acad. Arts and Letters. Home: Malintzin 20 Coyoacan Mexico

TAMBLYN, LEWIS RALPH, assn. exec.; b. St. Neot, Cornwall, Eng., June 16, 1923; s. Horace John and Henrietta Grace (Hancock) T.; came to U.S., 1924, naturalized 1946; student Muskegon Jr. Coll., 1946-48, Alma Coll., 1948; B.A., U. Mich., 1949, M.A., 1951, Ed.D., 1961; m. Audrey Florence Cornell, Dec. 22, 1946; children—Jane, Annette, Mary. Tchr., prin. Huron Valley Schs., Milford, Mich., 1953-55, prin., 1955-62; asst. dir. rural service N.E.A., Washington, 1962-68, coordinator rural service, 1968—. Vis. prof. Ohio U., 1962; cons. Office Commr. U.S. Office Edn., 1967-70, Bur. Research, 1968; mem. adv. com. Ednl. Resources Information Center/Clearinghouse on Rural Edn. and Small Schs., 1968. Served with RCAF, 1942-45. Mem. Am. Country Life Assn. (dir.), Council Nat. Orgns. Children and Youth (dir.), N.E.A., Am. Assn. Sch. Adminstrs., Phi Delta Kappa. Methodist. Mason. Author: Rural Education in the U.S., 1971; Research Abstracts in Rural Education, 1969. Home: 13122 Foxhall St Silver Spring MD 20906 Office: 1201 16th St NW Washington DC 20036

TAMM, EDWARD A(LLEN), U.S. circuit judge; b. St. Paul, Apr. 21, 1906; s. Edward Allen and Lucille Catherine (Buckley) T.; student Mt. St. Charles Coll., Helena, Mont., 1923-25, U. Mont., 1926-28; LL.B., Georgetown U., 1930, LL.D., 1965; J.S.D. (hon.), Suffolk U., 1971; m. Grace Monica Sullivan, Jan. 30, 1934; children—Edward Allen, Grace Escudero. Admitted to Minn. bar, U.S. Supreme Ct. bar; ofcl. FBI, 1930-48; judge, U.S. Dist. Ct. for D.C., 1948-65, U.S. Ct. Appeals for D.C. Circuit, 1965—. Trustee, St. Joseph Coll.; bd. dirs. Police Boys Club, Washington. Served as lt. comdr., USNR. Decorated comdr. Legion of Merit (Ecuador); Order of Balboa (Panama). Mem. Met. Bd. Trade, USCG Aux., Am., Fed. bar assns., Bar Assn. D.C., Am. Judicature Soc., Friendly Sons St. Patrick, Sons Union Vets., John Carroll Soc., La Confrerie des Chevaliers du Tastevin, Confrerie de la Chaine des Rotisseurs, Newcomen Soc., Am. Law Inst., Sigma Nu. Roman Catholic. Clubs: Columbia Country, Ocean City Light Tackle, Nat. Lawyers, Lawyers, Seaview Country. Home: 3353 Runnymeade Pl NW Washington DC 20015 Office: US Ct Appeals DC Circuit Washington DC 20001

TANENBAUM, HERBERT LOUIS, physician; b. Washington, Oct. 20, 1927; s. Samuel and Tessie (Silberman) T.; B.S. cum laude, Georgetown Coll., 1948, M.D. magna cum laude, 1952; m. Elaine Rhoda Bresler, July 27, 1958; children—Bruce, Michael, Robert, Steven, Mark. Intern, Boston City Hosp., 1952-53; resident Georgetown U. Hosp., 1953-54, Charity Hosp., New Orleans, 1954-55; clin. asso., investigator Nat. Heart Inst., Bethesda, Md., 1955-57; practice medicine, specializing in cardiology, Washington, 1958—; mem. staff Washington Hosp. Center; asst. clin. prof. medicine Georgetown Med. Sch., 1958—. Cons. Nat. Heart Inst., Bethesda, Md. Served with USPHS, 1955-57. Fellow A.C.P.; mem. Am. Coll. Cardiology, Am. Coll. Chest Physicians, Am. Heart Assn., Am. Fedn. for Clin. Research. Home: 9812 Belhaven Rd Bethesda MD 20034 Office: 4400 Connecticut Av Washington DC 20008

TANKERSLEY, JAMES INGRAM, food processing co. exec.; b. Knoxville, Tenn., Apr. 30, 1942; s. James O. and Ella (Ingram) T.; B.S. in Mech. Engring., U. Tenn., 1964; m. Edna Mae Weaver, July 25, 1960; children—Darla Ann, Kelle Leigh. Vice pres. mfg. Winter Garden Freezer Co., Inc., Bells, Tenn., 1966-72; pres. Tenn. Foods, Inc., Bells, 1969—. Dir. Agrl. Services Assn., Inc., Bells. Mem. City Planning Commn., Bells, 1969—, City Indsl. Devel. Bd., 1969—. Registered profl. engr., Tenn. Mem. Am. Soc. M.E., Phi Kappa Phi, Phi Eta Sigma, Tau Beta Pi. Methodist. Home: PO Box 299 Bells TN 38006 Office: PO Box 119 Bells TN 38006

TANKERSLEY, LADSON DELMUS, architect; b. Greenville, S.C., Aug. 31, 1932; s. Claude Delmus and Violet Pauline (Tucker) T.; B.S., Clemson U., 1955; m. Jacqueline Beth Hargrove, June 7, 1958; 1 son, John Scott. Vice pres. Tarleton-Tankersley Architects, Inc., Greenville, 1961-69, Tarleton-Tankersley Archtl. Group, Inc., 1969—. Mem. Greenville Archtl. Commn., 1964-67; vice chmn. Greenville County Bd. Zoning Appeals, 1970, chmn., 1971. Pres. Clemson Archtl. Found., 1971. Served to 1st lt. AUS, 1955-57. Mem. Greenville Council Architects (pres., 1963), A.I.A. (pres. S.C. 1968). Home: 5 Rockmont Rd Greenville SC 29607 Office: PO Box 5265-B Greenville SC 29606

TANKSLEY, JEPTHA CHARLES, judge; b. nr. Lula, Ga., Dec. 18, 1920; s. Adger Lee and Esther (Eller) T.; student North Ga. Coll., 1938-40; B.S., U.S. Mil. Acad., 1943; LL.B., Emory U., 1949; B.B.A., U. Ga., 1952; m. Frances McKay Rowan, May 13, 1948; children—Jeptha Reid, Charles Branch, Thomas Rowan. Admitted to Ga. bar, 1949, practice, Atlanta, 1949-52; asst. solicitor gen., Ga., 1952-56; judge Fulton Superior Ct., 1957—. Served from 2d lt. to capt., inf., AUS, 1947, ETO. Decorated Purple Heart, Silver Star. Mem. Am. Bar assn., State Bar Ga. (treas. 1964-70), Alpha Tau Omega, Phi Alpha Delta. Presbyn. Lion. Club: Lawyers. Home: 3440 Paces Forest Rd NW Atlanta GA 30327 Office: Court House Atlanta GA 30303

TANNENWALD, THEODORE, JR., judge; b. Valatie, N.Y., July 28, 1916; s. Theodore and Myra (Barnet) T.; A.B. summa cum laude, Brown U., 1936; LL.B. magna cum laude, Harvard, 1939; m. Selma Peterfreund, Aug. 3, 1940; children—Peter, Robert. Admitted to N.Y. bar, 1939, D.C., 1946; staff atty. Weil, Gotshal & Manges, N.Y.C., 1939-42, partner, 1947-65; judge U.S. Tax Ct., Washington, 1965—; lectr. George Washington U. Sch. Law, 1968—; prin. legal cons. Lend Lease Adminstrn., 1942; acting asst. chief, fgn. funds control div. Dept. State, 1942-43; spl. cons. Sec. War, 1943-45. Cons., Sec. Def., 1947-49; counsel to spl. asst. to Pres., 1950-51; asst. dir., chief of staff to dir. for mut. security Exec. Office Pres. 1951-53; spl. counsel to the Moreland Commn., 1955-58; N.Y. mem. Tri-State Tax Commn., 1958-59; mem. President's Task Force on Fgn. Aid and spl. asst. to sec. of state, 1961. Vice chmn. bd. govs. Hebrew Union Coll.-Jewish Inst. Religion; chmn. Washington operations com. Am. Jewish Com.; trustee U. State N.Y., 1958-59. Mem. Am., Fed., D.C. bar assns., Council Fgn. Relations, Assn. Bar City N.Y., Phi Beta Kappa, Sigma

Xi, Delta Sigma Rho. Home: 2916 Albemarle St NW Washington DC 20008 Office: US Tax Court Washington DC 20044

TANNER, JOHN PAUL, electronics co. exec.; b. Cleve., Sept. 22, 1927; s. William and Lucille (McKenney) T.; B.B.A., U. Miami, 1951, B.S., 1954; M.B.A., Rollins Coll., 1965; m. Mary Magdalen Johnson, Nov. 6, 1948; children—Timothy, Thomas, Christina, John, Roy, William, Joseph, Julia, Daniel, David, Mary Ellen. Engr., Chemstrand Corp., Pensacola, Fla., then sr. engr. Bendix Corp., South Bend, Ind., 1951-58; supr. prodn. engring. Radiation Inc., Melbourne, Fla., 1958-64; chief plans and programs LTV Aerospace Corp., Kennedy Space Center, Fla., 1964-67; dir. indsl. and prodn. engring. Electronic Communications Inc., St. Petersburg, Fla., 1967-—; pres. John P. Tanner & Assos., Cons. engrs., Orlando, Fla., 1969-—. Lectr. engring. tech. St. Petersburg Jr. Coll., 1968-70. Served to lt. USNR, 1951-53; Korea. Registered profl. engr., Fla., Ga. Mem. Am. Inst. Indsl. Engrs. (sr.). Democrat. Roman Catholic. Club: Rio Pinar Country (Orlando). Home: 1410 Pinar Dr Orlando FL 32807 Office: 1501 72d St N St Petersburg FL 33733

TANNER, LAWRENCE EDWARD, accountant; b. St. Louis, Apr. 7, 1940; s. Edward C. and Kathryn (Clifford) T.; B.B.A., So. Meth. U., 1963; m. Kathryn Ann Campbell, Aug. 31, 1963; children—Lawrence Edward, Michelle Marie, Kathryn Louise. Accountant, Ernst & Ernst, Houston, 1963-66; partner Fitts, Roberts & Co., Houston, 1966-—. Treas., Green Acres Civic Club, 1969-70, pres., 1970-—. C.P.A., Tex. Mem. Am. Inst. C.P.A.'s, Tex. Soc. C.P.A.'s, Houston Chpt. C.P.A.'s Lion (charter; sec.-treas. 1969-70, pres. 1970-71, dir. 1972-74). Home: 9011 Hazen St Houston TX 77036 Office: Sharpstown State Bank Bldg Houston TX 77036

TANNER, NATHAN HERBERT, JR., holding co. exec.; b. Radford, Va., May 30, 1922; s. Nathan Herbert and Bessie (Bond) T.; student Internat. Corr. Schs., 1940-41; m. Mary Grace Jones, Nov. 25, 1949; children—Stephen, David, Tommy. With Norfolk & Western Ry., Roanoke, Va., 1940-56, clerical position, 1946-56; with Roanoke Photo Finishing Co., Inc., 1956-65, sales mgr., mgr., v.p., 1961-65; v.p., gen. mgr. photo subsidiaries div. Swartz Enterprises, Roanoke, 1965-—, also dir. subsidiaries. Mem. Parents' Council Va. Mil. Inst., Lexington, 1970-—; mem. devel. council Ferrum (Va.) Coll., 1966-68. Bd. dirs. Va. Jr. Miss pageant. Served with USAAF, 1942-45; ETO. Mem. Roanoke Valley C. of C., Master Photo Dealers and Finishers Assn., Graphic Arts Assn. Va., Printing Industries Va. Assn., Nat. Assn. Broadcasters. Methodist (lay speaker). Club: United Commercial Travelers (Roanoke). Home: 3460 Grandin Rd Extension Roanoke VA 24018 Office: PO Box 22 Roanoke VA 24001

TANNER, PAUL FRANCIS, clergyman; b. Peoria, Ill., Jan. 15, 1905; s. Frank John and Laura (McGowan) T.; A.B., St. Francis (Wis.) Sem., 1930, A.M., 1931, S.T.B., 1931; student Marguette U., 1923-25, 33-36, Kenrick Sem. (St. Louis, Mo.), 1925-27. Ordained priest Roman Catholic Ch., 1931; sec. Cath. Action, also dir. Confraternity Chrisitan Doctrine, and dir. Cath. Youth activities Archdiocese Milw.; asst. dir. youth dept. 1940-42, dir., 1942-45, asst. gen. sec. N.C.W.C., 1945-58, gen. sec., 1958-68; bishop, St. Augustine, Fla., 1968-—. Apptd. Papal Chamberlain, 1948; domestic prelate, 1954; consecrated Titular Bishop Lamasba, 1965. Author: (with Dr. Edward Fitzpatrick) Methods of Teaching Religion in Elementary Schools, 1939. Editor Catholic Action, 1943-53. Home: 5051 Atlanta Blvd Jacksonville FL 32200 Office: Gulf Life Tower Jacksonville FL 32201

TANNER, RALPH M., coll. pres.; b. Jefferson County, Ala., Dec. 10, 1926; A.B., Birmingham-So. Coll., 1954, M.A. in History, 1957; Ph.D. in History, U. Ala., 1967; postgrad. Cumberland Sch. Law, Samford U., 1968-70; m. Judith Barry; 3 children. Head tchr. Jefferson County Pub. Schs., 1950-53; tchr. Warrior High Sch., 1953-56; prof. history and govt. Walker Jr. Coll., Jasper, Ala., 1956-60, dean coll., 1956-60; vis. asst. prof. history and polit. sci. Birmingham-So. Coll., 1960, asst. prof., 1960-67, asso. prof., 1967-72, dir. admissions, 1961-64, registrar, 1961-62, chmn. dept. history, 1970, dean coll., 1970-71, exec. v.p., chief exec. officer, 1971-72, pres., 1972-—. Head edn. div. Jefferson County Heart Appeal; mem. Ala. region exec. com. Nat. Conf. Christians and Jews. Bd. dirs. Birmingham Civic Ballet; mem. adv. com. Ala. Hist. Commn.; mem. commn. archives and history N. Ala. Conf. United Meth. Ch., chmn. commn., 1969-72. Mem. So. Hist. Assn., So. Polit. Sci. Assn., Ala. Hist. Assn. (mem. exec. com. 1969-—, chmn. program com. 1966-67, 70-71), Am. Assn. U. Profs., Ala. Assn. Collegiate Registrars and Admission Officers (pres., 1959-62), Ala. Assn. Coll. Adminstrs., Jefferson County Classroom Tchrs. Assn. (pres. 1952-54), So. Assn. Colls. and Schs. Evaluating Coms., Birmingham C. of C. (mem. com. on higher edn. 1972), Kappa Phi Kappa, Phi Alpha Theta, Pi Sigma Alpha, Omicron Delta Kappa. Contbr. numerous articles, book revs. to profl. jours. Address: Birmingham-Southern Coll Birmingham AL 35204

TANSEY, JOHN B., broadcasting exec. Exec. v.p., gen. mgr. WRVA, Richmond, Va. Office: 200 N 22d St PO Box 1516 Richmond VA 23212*

TANZER, LESTER, mag. editor; b. N.Y.C., Aug. 3, 1929; s. Charles and Clara (Ente) T.; A.B., Columbia, 1951, M.S., 1952; postgrad. George Washington U., 1965-—; m. Marlene June Luckton, June 29, 1949; children—Stephen, Jeffrey, Andrew, David. Reporter, Wall St. Jour., Washington, 1952-59; asso. editor Changing Times mag., Washington, 1959-64; asso. exec. editor U.S. News and World Report, Washington, 1964-—. Mem. Nat. Press Club, Am. Polit. Sci. Assn., Columbia Coll. Alumni Assn. Met. Washington (pres. 1962-64). Club: Nat. Press (Washington). Author: (with Stefan Ilok) The Brotherhood of Silence, 1962; Stretching Your Auto Dollar, 1964; Ten Champions, 1965. Editor: The Kennedy Circle, 1961. Home: 4859 N 30th St Arlington VA 22207 Office: 2300 N St Washington DC 20037

TANZLER, HANS G., JR., mayor; b. Charlotte, N.C., Mar. 11, 1927; s. Hans G. and Dorrette (Walker) T.; B.A., U. Fla., 1949, LL.B., 1951; m. Ann Jacqueline Lyerly, Sept. 18, 1948; 1 son, Hans G. III. Admitted to Fla. bar; with firm Tanzler and Maddox; now 1st county Solicitor; gen. counsel Fla. State Bd. Health, 1961-63; judge criminal ct., 1963-67; mayor Jacksonville, 1967-—. Served on Governor's Adv. Com. on Decent Lit.; chmn. speakers bur. March of Dimes; active Big Bros. Served with USNR, 1945-46. Mem. Jacksonville C. of C., Am., Fla., Jacksonville bar assns., Kappa Alpha. Mason (32 deg., Shriner), Moose. Presbyterian. Home: 1729 Woodmere Dr Jacksonville FL 32210 Office: 1401 City Hall Jacksonville FL 32202

TAORMINA, AUGUSTINE ANTHONY, architect; b. Bloomsburg, Pa., Dec. 24, 1936; s. Philip and Rose Katherine (Kurtz) T.; B.Arch., Pa. State U., 1959; postgrad. George Washington U., 1967-69. Project architect high rise office bldgs. V. Koubek, architect, Washington, 1963-68; gen. practice as architect, Washington, 1969; partner Battistone & Taormina, architects, 1969-70; project architect V. Koubek, architect, Washington, 1970-—. Served to lt. (j.g.) USNR, 1959-63. Mem. A.I.A. Home: 1581 Colonial Terrace Arlington VA 22209 Office: 1200 17th St NW Washington DC 20036

TAPP, WILLIAM ROY, JR., architect; b. Powder Springs, Ga., May 21, 1922; s. William Roy and Estelle Catherine (Leake) T.; B.S., Ga. Inst. Tech., 1943, B.Arch., 1948; m. Frances Briscoe Paine, June 20, 1953; children—Helen Preston. Designer, Joe E. Bright, architect, Valdosta, Ga., 1950-53; prin. W. R. Tapp, Jr., Architect & Assos., Marietta, Ga., 1953-—; dir. Cobb Fed. Savs. & Loan Assn. Mem. Cobb Recreation Authority, 1958-—; mem. Marietta Bd. Appeals. Served to lt. (j.g.) USNR, 1944-46. Mem. Cobb C. of C., A.I.A. (dir. Constrn. Specification Inst. 1972-73). Presbyn. (deacon). Club: Marietta Country Civitan (pres. 1969-70. Maj. works include Marietta 1st Nat. Bank, Cobb Fed. Savs. Bldg., Marietta Police Sta., Cobb YWCA, Lindley Jr. High Sch.; asso. architect Cobb County Pub. Bldg. complex, New Campus So. Tech. Inst. Home: 442 S Hillcrest Marietta GA 30060 Office: 22 Austin Av NE Marietta GA 30060

TARANTOLA, CHARLSIE LOVELL (MRS. MICHAEL NICHOLAS TARANTOLA), educator; b. Weatherford, Tex., Aug. 16, 1920; d. James Thomas and Pauline (Harris) Bradshaw; student George Washington U., U. Va., Am. U. Washington, North Tex. State Tchrs. Coll.; B.S., Smith Hughes, 1945; postgrad. Trenton State Tchrs. Coll., 1954-57; m. Michael Nicholas Tarantola, June 3, 1944; children—Michael Roy, John Terry. Tchr., Muenster (Tex.) Pub. Schs., 1941-43, Breckenridge (Tex.) Pub. Schs., 1945, Faruell (Tex.) Pub. Sch., 1947, Sasebo (Japan) Am. Sch., 1948-49; adult ednl. instr. TI— Div., Gelenhausen, Germany, 1954; elementary tchr. Gelenhausen Am. Sch., 1952-54, Pemberton (N.J.) Twp., 1954-57, Fort Myer (Va.) Elementary Sch., 1957-65; sci. tchr. Oakridge Elementary Sch., Arlington, Va., 1965-—. Mem. V.I.S.T.A., Nat. Va., Arlington edn. assns., Nat. Sci. Tchrs. Assn., Delta Kappa Gamma. Roman Catholic. Home: 515 N Longfellow St Arlington VA 22203

TARAVELLA, JOSEPH PHILIP, community devel. co. exec.; b. N.Y.C., Jan. 19, 1919; s. James and Margaret (Capuccio) T.; B.S., Fordham U., 1940; M.S., Columbia, 1940-41; m. Florence E. Wright, May 27, 1944; children—Joseph Philip, Mark James. Sales mgr. R. H. Macy Co., N.Y.C., 1940-41; exec. v.p., gen. mgr. Coral Ridge Properties, Inc. subsidiary Westinghouse Electric Corp., Ft. Lauderdale, Fla., 1945-66, pres., chmn. bd., 1960-—, also dir.; dir. Financial Life Ins. Co., Bank of Commerce, Bank of Fla., Bank of Coral Springs, Bankers Bank, Deane & Deane, Inc., Half Moon Bay, Cal., Curacao Properties, N.V. Mem. Fla. Environmental Land Mgmt. Bd.; mem. new communities council Urban Land Inst.; mem. Fla. Environmental Standards Com. Mem. exec. bd. S.E. Council Boy Scouts Am. Served to lt. USCGR, 1941-45. Mem. Urban Land Inst., Fla. C. of C. (dir.), Fla. Council 100, Fla. Land Sales Bd. Democrat. Roman Catholic. Clubs: Coral Springs (Fla.) Golf and Tennis; Coral Ridge Yacht, Coral Ridge Country (Ft. Lauderdale); Broken Woods Country. Home: 2641 Yacht Club Blvd Fort Lauderdale FL 33304 Office: 9500 W Sample Rd Coral Springs FL 33065

TARBOX, FREDERICK CHARLES, JR., computer co. exec.; b. Columbus, O., May 11, 1942; s. Frederick Chalmers and Grace (Guth) T.; B.S. in Mech. Engring., Case Inst. Tech., 1964; postgrad. Ohio State U., 1964-65, N.C. State U., 1967; m. Christina Kay, Nov. 28, 1964. Owner, Upper Arlington Lawn Service Co. (O.), 1951-60; mech. engr. Columbus & So. Ohio Electric Co., 1960-65; plant engr. Carolina Power & Light Co., Goldsboro, N.C., 1965-67; pres. Hydra Computer Corp., Raleigh, N.C., 1967-—. Fallout shelter analyst Office Civil Def., Columbus, O., 1965-—. Sponsor indsl. coop. tng. Enloe High Sch., Raleigh, 1969-—. Mem. Am. Soc. M.E., Alpha Phi Epsilon. Republican. Mem. United Ch. of Christ. Home: 300 Cedar Crest Dr Raleigh NC 27609 Office: PO Box 17883 Raleigh NC 27609

TARMAN, FRED E(ARLE), editor; b. Clearfield, Ia., Jan. 26, 1889; s. William B. and Ella F. (Bedell) T.; A.B., U. Okla., 1910; m. Billie E. Henkel, Jan. 1, 1918; children—Roger M. and Harriet (Mrs. R. F. Remmers) (twins). Reporter The Daily Oklahoman, Oklahoma City, 1910-11, sports editor, 1911-12, city editor, 1912-13, night editor, 1914-16; news editor Oklahoma City Times, 1916-17; asst. prof. journalism, U. Okla., 1917-20; asst. to pres. N. Am. Oil Co., 1920-22; editor The Norman Transcript, 1922-30, editor, publisher, 1930-68, now editor emeritus, cons. Mem. Norman Planning Commn., 1927-61. Bd. dirs. Frontiers of Sci. Found. of Okla.; trustee U. Okla. Found. Served in Army Intelligence, World War I, 1918. Elected to Okla. Hall of Fame, 1961; Distinguished Service citation, Univ. Okla., 1962. Mem. So. Newspaper Pubs. Assn., U. Okla. Alumni Assn. (past pres.), Okla. Press Assn. (treas. 1930-48, v.p. 1948-49, pres. 1949-50; Half Century Club 1958), Norman C. of C. (past pres.), Am. Legion, Phi Beta Kappa, Sigma Delta Chi, Phi Gamma Delta. Democrat. Episcopalian. Lion. Author: Away We Go; Cradles of Liberty. Dormitory at U. Okla. named Tarman Tower in his honor, 1965. Home: 630 Okmulgee St Norman OK 73069 Office: 215 E Comanche St Norman OK 73069

TARPLEY, JOHN WILLIAM, elec. engr.; b. Bonham, Tex., Nov. 8, 1919; s. William Everett and Cora (Bivans) T.; B.S., U. Tex., 1942; m. Alice Dora Morgan, Sept. 11, 1941 (div.); children—Bill, Joy Alice (Mrs. Carl H. Moneyhon). Asst. div. engr. Tex. Power & Light Co., McKinney, 1945-48; design engr., Austin, Tex., 1948-50; distbn. engr. Lubbock, Tex., 1950-52; elec. engr. for phys. plant U. Tex., 1952-58; cons. engr., Austin, 1958-—. Chmn. troop com. Boy Scouts Am., 1954-65. Served to lt. USNR, 1942-45. Mem. I.E.E.E. (sr.), Tex. Soc. Profl. Engrs. (sec.-treas. sect. 1968-70). Lion (sec. 1955-56), Kiwanian (dir. 1968-—). Club: Ramshorn (sec. 1958-59). Address: 1512 1/2 S Congress Austin TX 78704

TARR, CURTIS W., govt. ofcl.; A.B., Stanford, 1948, Ph.D., 1962; M.B.A., Harvard, 1950; L.H.D. (hon.), Ripon Coll., 1965, Grinnell Coll., 1969; m. Elizabeth Myers; children—Pamela, Cynthia. Research asst., instr. Harvard, 1950-52; v.p. Sierra Tractor & Equipment Co., 1952-58; asst. dir. summer session Stanford, 1961-62, asst. dean humanities and sci., dir. summer sch., 1962-63; pres. Lawrence U., 1963-69; asst. sec. Air Force for manpower and res. affairs, 1969-70; dir. Selective Service System, Washington, 1970-72; under-sec. of State for security assistance, Washington, 1972-—. Staff mem. 2d Hoover Commn., 1954-55. Candidate for U.S. Congress from Cal., 1958. Served with AUS, 1943-46. Home: 1504 Highwood Dr Arlington VA 22207

TARRAGO, LETICIA, graphic artist; b. Mexico, 1940; student Acad. Plastic Arts, Mexico; advanced studies in graphic arts with Guillermo Silva; also student Warsaw, Poland. Exhibited at U. P.R., Salon de la Plastica, Mexico City, Salon Debiutow, Warsaw, Poland, Mus. Modern Art, Tel Aviv, Israel, Welna Gallery, Mexico City. Recipient 1st prize Nat. Inst. Graphic Arts, Mexico, 1967. Address: care Welna Gallery Mexico City Mexico*

TARRANT, JOHN EDWARD, lawyer; b. Dyersburg, Tenn., Nov. 25, 1898; s. John Morgan and Penelope A. (Fumbanks) T.; B.S., U. Va., 1921; LL.B., Harvard, 1923; m. Mary Park Kaye, May 26, 1928; children—Mary Kaye (Mrs. Edwin Durham II), Eleanor (Mrs. Philip B. Newman III), Penelope (Mrs. Clay L. Morton). Admitted to Ky. bar, 1923; asso. Simpson, Thacher & Bartlett, N.Y.C., 1922, Bruce, Bullitt & Gordon, Louisville, 1923-26; partner Bruce & Bullitt, 1926-40, Ogden Tarrant, Galphin & Street, 1940-48, Bullitt, Dawson & Tarrant, 1948-70, Tarrant, Combs, Blackwell & Bullitt, 1970-—; gen. counsel Fed. Land Bank, Fed. Intermediate Credit Bank, Louisville, 1930; spl. judge Ct. Appeals, Ky., 1948; chmn. bd. Louisville Investment Co., 1958-—; dir. Churchill Downs Inc., Louisville Transit Co., Cybernetics & Systems, Inc.; dir. Citizens Fidelity Bank & Trust Co., 1957-69, adviser, 1969-71. Trustee U. Louisville, 1966-70, Norton Children's Hosps., YWCA, 1939-63; bd. dirs. Louisville Central Area Assn., 1966-—. Served O.T.C., Camp Fortress Monroe, Va., 1918. Fellow Am. Bar Found.; mem. N.C. Soc. Cincinnati, Ky. Soc. Colonial Wars, S.A.R., Am., Ky., Louisville bar assns., Am. Law Inst., Am. Judicature Soc., Phi Beta Kappa, Kappa Sigma. Republican. Episcopalian. Clubs: Pendennis, River Valley, Wynn Stay, Filson, Country (Louisville); Frankfort (Ky.) Country; Broad Street (N.Y.C.); Metropolitan (Washington); Union (N.Y.C.). Home: Beech Grove 3740 Upper River Rd Louisville KY 40207 Office: Kentucky Home Life Bldg Louisville KY 40202

TARVER, JACKSON WILLIAMS, newspaper exec.; b. Savannah, Ga., Mar. 2, 1917; s. Otis Merritt and DeLuth (Williams) T.; student U. Ga., 1936; A.B., Mercer U., 1938; LL.D., 1970; m. Margaret Birch Taylor, Mar. 24, 1940; children—Jack Williams, Margaret. Reporter Vidalia (Ga.) Advance, 1938; editor Toombs County (Ga.) Democrat, 1939-40, Macon (Ga.) News, 1940-43; asso. editor Atlanta Constn., 1943-49, asst. to pres. Atlanta Newspapers, Inc. (pub. Atlanta Jour., Atlanta Constn.), 1950-53, gen. mgr., 1953-58, v.p., 1956-58, pres., 1958-—, also dir.; pres., dir. Cox Enterprises, Inc.; chmn. Fed. Res. Bank of Atlanta, Theaters Service Co.; dir. Am. Motors, Metro Sunday Newspapers, A.P.; trustee C & S Real Estate Investment Trust. Mem. Ga. Bd. Edn., 1942-43. Trustee Mercer U. Reid Found. fellow to S.Am., 1949. Mem. So., Am. (chmn. bur. advt.) newspapers pubs. assns., Am. Soc. Newspaper Editors, Sigma Delta Chi, Sigma Alpha Epsilon. Clubs: Capital City, Piedmont Driving, Commerce (dir.), Stadium (Atlanta).Home: 459 Argonne Dr NW Atlanta GA 30305 Office: 10 Forsyth St Atlanta GA 30303

TARWATER, JAN DALTON, educator; b. Ft. Worth, Sept. 30, 1937; s. Roy L. and Margie (Dalton) T.; B.S., Tex. Tech. U., 1959; M.A., U. N.M., 1961, Ph.D., 1965; m. Nancy Pat Houston, Aug. 15, 1958; children—Jay D., Paul H., Patrick M. Asst. prof. math. Western Mich. U., Kalamazoo, 1965-67, North Tex. State U., Denton, 1967-68; asso. prof. math. Tex. Tech U., Lubbock, 1968-—, asso. chmn. dept., 1972-—. Mem. Am. Math. Soc., Sigma Xi, Phi Kappa Phi, Kappa Mu Epsilon, Phi Sigma Tau. Contbr. articles to profl. jours. Home: 3823 53d St Lubbock TX 79413

TARWATER, WILLIAM RAYMOND, ins. agt., state legislator; b. Duncan, Okla., Nov. 24, 1921; s. Olin Proctor and Ola (Carmichael) T.; student Okla. U., 1938-40; m. Jean Johnson, Apr. 4, 1943; children—William O., Judy A. Owner, Tarwater Ins. Agy., Duncan, 1948-—; mem. Okla. Ho. of Reps., 1966-—. Bd. dirs. Duncan Community Chest, 1950-53. Chmn. Stephens County (Okla.) Democratic central com., 1960-65. Mem. Am. Legion, Okla. State Golf Assn. (dir. 1959-—; pres. 1962). Elk, Rotarian. Home: 1001 N 9th St Duncan OK 73533 Office: 1301 W Main St Duncan OK 73533

TATE, ALBERT, JR., state supreme ct. justice; b. Opelousas, La., Sept. 23, 1920; s. Albert and Adelaide (Therry) T.; student La. State U., 1938-39, certificate, 1948; B.A., George Washington U., 1941; LL.B., Yale, 1947; m. Claire Jeanmard, Apr. 23, 1949; children—Albert III, Emma Adelaide, George J., Michael F., Charles E. Admitted to La. bar, 1948, practiced in Ville Platte, 1948-54; judge Ct. of Appeal, 1st Circuit of La., Baton Rouge, 1954-60; presiding judge Ct. Appeal, 3d Circuit, Lake Charles, 1960-70; asso. justice La. Supreme Ct., 1958, 70-—; prof. law La. State U., 1967-68. Mem. Jud. Council of State of La., 1960-70; mem. com. and council La. State Law Inst., 1954-59; faculty Inst. Jud. Adminstrn. N.Y.U., 1965-—, Appellate Judges Seminar, U. Ala., 1966, 70, U. Nev., 1967; chmn. La. Judiciary Commn., 1969-—; mem. adv. council Nat. Center for State Cts. Chmn. La. Commn. on Aging, 1956-59; pres. La. Cotton Festival, 1955-57; mem. Evangeline Area council Boy Scouts Am., 1948-—, dist. chmn., 1949-50. Served with AUS, 1942-45. Recipient Am. Trial Lawyers judiciary award, 1971. Mem. Am. (chmn. exec. com. appellate judges conf. 1966-—), La. bar assns., Am. Judicature Soc. (dir. 1969-—), La. Conf. Ct. of Appeal Judges (pres. 1967-70), Am. Legion, V.F.W., Order of Coif (hon.), Blue Key (hon.). Delta Kappa Epsilon. K.C., Woodmen of World, Rotarian. Author: Louisiana Civil Procedures, 1968; Treatises for Judges, 1971. Contbr. articles to profl. jours. Home: Box 409 Ville Platte LA 70586 also 2414 Octavia St New Orleans LA 70115Office: Supreme Court La 301 Loyola Av New Orleans LA 70112

TATE, ALLEN (JOHN ORLEY), critic, poet; b. Clarke County, Ky., Nov. 19, 1899; s. John Orley and Nellie (Varnell) T.; B.A., magna cum laude, Vanderbilt U., 1922; Litt.D., U. Louisville, 1948, Colgate U., 1956; U. Ky., 1960; M.A., Oxford, 1958; Litt.D., Carleton Coll., 1963; m. Caroline Gordon, novelist, Nov. 3, 1924; (div.); dau., Nancy Meriwether (Mrs. Percy Woods, Jr.); m. 2d, Isabella Gardner, Aug. 27, 1959 (div.); m. 3d, Helen Heinz, July 30, 1966. Free lance writer, 1924-—; Guggenheim Found. fellow 1928-30; lectr. English lit. Southwestern U., Memphis, 1934-36; prof. English, Woman's Coll., U. N.C., 1938-39; resident fellow in writing, creative arts program Princeton, 1939-42; incumbent chair of poetry Library of Congress, 1943-44; editor The Sewanee Review, 1944-46; editor poetry and belles lettres Henry Holt & Co., 1946-48; lectr. English, N.Y. U., 1947-51; prof. English U. Minn., 1951-66, Regents' prof. English, 1966-68; vis. prof. humanities U. Chgo 1949; Fulbright prof. U. Oxford, 1958-59; vis. prof. Vanderbilt U., 1967; sr. fellow Ind. Sch. Letters Recipient Midland Author's prize (Chgo.), 1933; Bollingen prize in Poetry, 1956; Brandeis U. Medal award for poetry, 1961; Medaglio D'Oro, Dante Soc. (Florence), 1962; 5,000 award Acad. Am. Poets, 1963. Mem. Am. Acad. Arts and Letters, Nat. Inst. Arts and Letters (pres. 1968-—), Am. Acad. Arts and Scis., Soc. Am. Historians, So. Hist. Assn., Phi Beta Kappa, Sigma Upsilon, Phi Delta Theta So. editor Hound and Horn, 1932-34, Democrat. Clubs: Princeton, Century Assn. (N.Y.C.); Authors (London). Author or co-author books since 1928; latest publs.: On the Limits of Poetry, 1948; The Hovering Fly, 1949; (with Caroline Gordon) The House of Fiction, 1950; The Forlorn Demon, 1953; The Man of Letters in the Modern World, 1955; Collected Essays, 1960; Poems, 1960; Essays of Four Decades, 1969; The Swimmers and Other Selected Poems, 1971; also articles and verse in various publs. Editor: Man and His Work (T.S. Eliot), 1966. Adv. editor Kenyon Rev., 1938-42. Regular mem. CBS radio program, Invitation to Learning, 1940-41. Address: Running Knob Hollow Rd Sewanee TN 37375

TATE, EARL RAY, ednl. adminstr.; b. Snyder, Tex., Feb. 18, 1932; s. Estil Clarence and Louise (Lipham) T.; B.S., Abilene Christian Coll., 1956, M.Ed., 1960; postgrad. Tex. A. and M. U., 1961; m. Keitha Gay Latham, July 4, 1958; children—Treva Renee, Trona Kay, Sheldon Ray. Prin., classroom tchr. Woodson (Tex.) High Sch., 1956-63, supt., 1963-67; supt. Paradise (Tex.) Sch., 1967-—. Served with USNR, 1951-52. Mem. Am., Tex. assns. sch. adminstrs., Tex. State Tchrs. Assn. (chmn. tri-county unit 1961-62), Tex. Small Schs. Assn. (v.p. 1971, pres. elect 1972). Mem. Ch. of Christ. Club: Nat. Beta (Tex. state councilman 1968-72). Address: PO Box 6578 Paradise TX 76073

TATE, GEORGE THOMAS, constrn. co. exec.; b. Forest City, N.C., Dec. 21, 1932; s. George D. and Marie (Hughes) T.; B.S. in Elec. Engring., Clemson Coll., 1955 children—George Thomas, Rebecca Susan. Student engr. Fla. Power & Light Co., Miami, 1959-62, dist. engr., Cocoa, Fla., 1962-65; div. mgr. Davis Elec. Constructors,

Albany, Ga., 1966; pres. Tate-Shelton, Inc., Lexington, Ky., 1966—, also dir.; pres., Elcon, Inc. Served to 1st lt. USAF, 1956-59. Registered profl. engr., Fla. Mem. I.E.E.E., Nat. Soc. Profl. Engrs. Presbyn. (deacon). Home: 1044-A Armstrong Mill Rd Lexington KY 40505 Office: 2224 Young Dr Lexington KY 40505

TATE, HORACE EDWARD, assn. exec.; b. Elberton, Ga., Oct. 6, 1922; s. Henry Lawrence and Mattie Beatrice (Harper) T.; B.S., Ft. Valley State Coll., 1943; Ed.D., U. Ky., 1961; m. Virginia Barnett, Dec. 23, 1949; children—Calvin Lee, Veloise Cecile, Horacena Edwean. Sci. tchr., prin., Union Point, Ga., 1943-45; prin. Greensboro (Ga.) High Sch., 1945-51, Fairmont High Sch., Griffin, Ga., 1951-57; asso. prof. Ft. Valley (Ga.) State Coll., 1959-61; exec. sec. Ga. Tchrs. Edn. Assn., Atlanta, 1961-70; asso. exec. sec. Ga. Assn. Educators, Atlanta, 1970—. Dir. Mut. Fed. Savs. & Loan Assn. Mem. Gov.'s Commn. to Improve Edn., 1962—; vice chmn. Ga. State Adv. Com. to Pres. Nixon's Cabinet Commn. on Edn., 1970—; mem. Atlanta Bd. Edn., 1965-69. Democratic candidate for mayor Atlanta, 1969; vice chmn. Ga. Dem. party, 1970—. Trustee Ga. Tchr. Retirement Bd. Mem. So. Edn. Found. Fellowship (nat. edn. policy comm. 1962-66), Ga. Assn. Educators, N.E.A. (dir.), Phi Delta Kappa. M.E. Ch. (steward 1961—, chmn. bd. trustee 1964—). Contbr. articles to profl. jours. Home: 621 Lilla Dr Atlanta GA 30310 Office: 201 Ashby St Atlanta GA 30314

TATE, JAMES OLIVER, psychologist, educator; b. Dallas, Apr. 29, 1929; s. Otho Stanley and Gertrude (Stevens) T.; student Abilene Christian Coll., 1949-51; B.B.A., So. Meth. U., 1952-53; Ed.D., North Tex. State U., 1961; m. Janet Elaine Gerleman, Nov. 29, 1957; children—James, Gregory, Carter, Blair. Supr. Bell Telephone Co., Dallas, 1956-58; asso. prof. psychology East Central State Coll., Ada, Okla., 1961-68; cons. Oklahoma City Neuropsychiat. Clinic, 1967—; clin. and counseling psychologist VA Hosp., Denver, 1968-69; mem. staff U. Okla., Norman, 1969—, now coordinator of evaluation, dir. adult guidance, evaluation and testing dept.; practice cons. psychologist, 1964—. Bd. dirs. Pontotoc County Mental Health Bd., 1962-65. Served with AUS, 1953-55. Named Tchr. of Year, East Central State Coll., 1962. Mem. Am. Psychol. Assn., Psi Chi, Sigma Tau Gamma. Home: 2517 Wildwood St Norman OK 73069 Office: 1700 Asp Av Norman OK 73069

TATE, LARRY VON, bank exec.; b. Longview, Tex., Jan. 14, 1935; s. Luster Von and Mable Dean (Ferguson) T.; B.A., Kilgore Jr. Coll., 1955; m. Joy Dean Freeman, Sept. 2, 1955; children—Mike, Melinda. Vice-pres. First Nat. Bank, Longview, 1954-67; pres. Am. Bank, Longview, 1969-70, Citizens State Bank, Kilgore, Tex., 1970—; dir. East Tex. Aviation, Longview, Citizen State Bank, Kilgore, Personal Finance Corp. Pres., Tex. Jr. C. of C. Found., 1963-70. Served with C.E., AUS, 1957-59. Named Jaycee of Year, Longview, 1960. Mem. U.S. (nat. dir. 1961-63), Tex. (pres. 1963-64), Longview (pres. 1961) chambers commerce. Rotarian. Home: 201 Wildwood St Kilgore TX 75662 Office: 306 Main St Kilgore TX 75662

TATE, PAUL CALVIN, lawyer; b. Mamou, La., July 11, 1922; s. Hosea and Lovina (Guillory) T.; LL.B., La. State U., 1950; m. Anna Soileau, Jan. 7, 1941; children—Sandy, Paul C.; m. 2d, Janice Farris Adam; children—Adam, Frank. Admitted to U.S. Supreme Ct. bar, La. bar, 1950, since practiced in Mamou, asst. dist. atty. 13th Jud. Dist., 1954-61; city atty., Mamou, 1950-61. Dir. Guaranty Bank of Mamou. Dist. dir. Boy Scouts Am., received Silver Beaver award, 1967; dir. Pub. Housing Adminstrn., 1952-54. Pres. Young Democrats of La., 1958-62. Pres. La. Folk Found. Served with Signal Corps, AUS, 1942-46. Fellow Am. Acad. Law and Sci.; mem. Am. Judicature Soc., Am., La. bar assns., La. Law Inst. Council, Nat., La. assns. claimants' compensation attys., Nat. Folk Festival Assn. (nat. adv. com.), Am. Legion (comdr. 1951; dist. comdr. 1961-62), Council for Devel. of French in La., Internat. Assn. French Speaking Parliamentarians (sec. La. chpt.), New Orleans Young Men's Bus. Club. Woodman of World (head consul of La. 1957-58), Rotarian (pres. 1950). Home: Route 2 Box 27 Mamou LA 70554 Office: 6th St at Chestnut St Mamou LA 70554

TATE, ROSCOE CHARLES, state ofcl.; b. nr. Dahlonega, Ga., Apr. 28, 1913; s. Emory and Lula (Dockery) T.; B.S. in Mech. Engring., Ga. Inst. Tech., 1942; m. Alberta Henderson, Oct. 31, 1942; children—James Roscoe, Albert Lee. With Ga. Highway Dept., 1938—, engaged in design urban hwys., until 1968, state utilities engr., in charge utilities div., Atlanta, 1968—. Served with USMC, 1933-37, to capt. USAAF, 1942-46. Registered profl. engr., Ga. Mem. Am. Soc. C.E., Am. Right of Way Assn. Methodist. Home: 4600 E Ponce De Leon Av Clarkston GA 30021 Office: 2 Capitol Sq Atlanta GA 30334

TATE, WILLIS MCDONALD, coll. chancellor; b. Denver, May 18, 1911; s. Robert Spence and Grace (Brown) T.; A.B., So. Meth. U., 1932, A.M., 1935; postgrad. U. Chgo., 1945, U. Tex., 1946-55; LL.D., Tex. Wesleyan Coll., 1951, Centenary Coll., 1954, U. Denver, 1957; L.H.D., Oklahoma City U., 1954; Sc.D., U. Tulsa, 1959; m. Joel Estes, Dec. 24, 1932; children—Willis McDonald, Joel Ann (Withers). Tchr. elementary sch. and prin. jr. high sch., Alamo Heights, San Antonio, 1932-43; exec. asst. to pastor First Meth. Ch., Houston, 1943-45; with So. Meth. U., 1945—, successively asst. dean students, dean, v.p., 1945-54, pres., 1954-71, chancellor, 1971—. Pres., Tex. Council Chs., 1960; pres. Nat. Assn. Schs. and Colls. of Methodist Ch., 1960; pres. Univ. Senate of Meth. Church, 1960; mem., past pres. Dallas Council World Affairs, Dallas Citizens Council. Recipient Meiklejohn award Am. Assn. U. Profs., 1965. Mem. Tex. Assn. Colls. (past pres.), Council Protestant Colls. and Univs. (past chmn. 1966), So. U. Conf. (pres. 1963), Philos. Soc. Tex. (v.p. 1971). Clubs: Petroleum, Cosmos. Author: (with A. Q. Sartain and W. W. Finlay) Human Behavior in Industry, 1954. Home: 3600 Marquette St Dallas TX 75225

TATUM, CLARENCE ALBERT, JR., utility exec.; b. Dallas, June 25, 1907; s. Clarence Albert and Annie Elizabeth (Wright) T.; B.A. in Physics, So. Meth. U., 1928; m. Caroline King, Dec. 16, 1936; children—Clarence Albert III, Henry King. Mem. staff comml. dept. Dallas Power & Light Co., 1928-39, comml. mgr., 1939-50, v.p., asst. to pres., 1950-53, pres., dir., gen. mgr., 1953-67, also dir.; pres., chief exec. officer, dir. Tex. Utilities Co., 1967-72, chmn. bd., chief exec. officer, 1972—; dir. Tex. Elec. Service Co., Tex. Power & Light Co., Fed. Res. Bank of Dallas. Trustee Com. Econ. Devel. Mem. exec. bd. and nat. council Circle Ten council Boy Scouts Am.; v.p. Callier Hearing and Speech Center; adv. mem. Dallas Citizen Council. Bd. dirs. State Fair of Tex., Dallas Theatre Center, Dallas Summer Musicals, Dallas Symphony Orch., Excellence in Edn. Found. Trustee So. Meth. U. and So. Meth. U. Found. for Sci. and Engring., Salk Inst., Southwestern Med. Found., Tex. Research Found. Mem. The Conf. Bd., Sigma Alpha Epsilon, Beta Gamma Sigma (hon.). Methodist. Clubs: City, Chaparral, Northwood, Salesmanship, Dallas Country, Petroleum (Dallas). Home: 10 Willow Wood Dallas TX 75205 Office: 1506 Commerce St Dallas TX 75201

TATUM, DONALD EDWARDS, ins. exec.; b. Clover, S.C., Jan. 1, 1924; s. William Otis and Elizabeth (Mayo) T.; student La. State U., 1940-42; C.L.U., Am. Coll. Life Underwriters, 1955, C.L.U. M., 1958; m. Sally J. Marsteller, Mar. 13, 1964; children—William Otis IV, Timothy B., Elizabeth E., Donald Edwards. With Conn. Gen. Life, Hartford, Conn., 1946-62, mgr., Pitts., 1956-62; v.p. Nat. Union Ins. Cos., 1962-67; pres., dir. South Coast Life Ins. Co., Houston, Gt. Nat. Life Ins. Co., Grenat Corp., 1967-70. U.S. Life Corp., N.Y.C., 1968-70; pres. dir. Peninsular Life Ins. Co., George Washington Life Ins. Co., 1970—; dir. Peninsular Fire Ins. Co., Peninsular Securities, Inc., Am. Annuity Life Ins. Co., Builders Life Ins. Co., Am. Automobile Dealers Assn., Jacksonville Nat. Bank. Active United Fund. Served to lt. USNR, 1943-46. C.L.U. Mem. Jacksonville Area C. of C. (gov.), Assn. Life Underwriters (chpt. dir. 1960-62), N. Am. Newcomen Soc., Life Ins. Trust Council, Pa. Ins. Fedn. (dir.). Presbyn. Clubs: Timuquana Country, San Jose Country, River, Ponte Vedra, Meninak, Houston. Contbr. to publs. Home: 2749 Forest Circle Jacksonville FL 32217 Office: Box 2667 Jacksonville FL 32203

TAUBKIN, IRVIN STEARNS, ret. pub. relations cons., newspaper exec.; b. N.Y.C., Nov.14, 1906; s. William and Fannie (Stern) T.; student U. Wis., 1923-24, N.Y.U., 1924-26; m. Vivian Richardson, Dec. 22, 1929 (dec. May 1963); m. 2d, Kiyoko Tsuboi, August 11, 1964. Reporter for Dallas Morning News, Tex. corr. N.Y. Times, 1928-34, copywriter, asst. promotion mgr., 1934-43; promotion dir. bur. advt. Am. Newspaper Pub. Assn., N.Y.C., 1945-47; with The N.Y. Times, 1947—, promotion mgr., 1947-59, gen. mgr. Internat. Ed., Paris, 1960-61, promotion dir., 1961-69, public relations dir., 1969—. Served with AUS, 1943-45. Mem. Internat. Newspaper Promotion Assn. (past pres.), Am. Newspaper Pubs. Assn. (past chmn. pub. relations com.), Pub. Relations Soc. Am. Clubs: Nat. Press, The Players. Home: Sarasota FL

TAUCH, WALDINE, sculptor; b. Schulenburg, Tex., Jan. 28, 1892; d. William and Elizabeth (Heiman) Tauch; ed. Brady (Tex.) High Sch.; pupil of Pompeo Coppini (Sculptor); hon. D.F.A., Howard Payne Coll., Brownswood, Tex., 1941. Asso. prof. fine art dept. Trinity U., San Antonio, 1943-45. Works include: Henderson Memorial, Richmond, Ky.; Soldiers, Sailors and Pioneer Monument, Bedford, Ind.; Le Seuer Smith Children, portrait fountain group, Pelham Manor, N.Y.; portrait bust Mrs. Eli Hertzberg, Tues. Mus. Club, San Antonio, San Antonio; bas-relief, Children's Reading Room, Jersey City Library; portrait relief George Washington, Washington Jr. High Sch., Mt. Vernon, N.Y., Texas Independence Monument, Gonzales, Tex.; portrait monument Mr. and Mrs. Isaac Van Zandt, Canton, Tex.; Heroic Moses Austin Monument, San Antonio; Gulf Breeze, Witte Meml. Mus., San Antonio; Innocence, ideal head, Woman's Club, San Antonio; meml. relief John Allen Walker, Howard Payne Coll., Brownwood, Tex.; Genius of Music, Anna Hertzberg Meml.; bust of Mirabeau Lamar, Alamo Library, San Antonio; heroic portrait statue group Buckner Ranch for Boys, Burnet, Tex.; Louis Kocurek children, garden group, San Antonio, Texas; life size figure of Pippa Passes, Baylor U.; heroic figure The Texas Ranger of Today, Dallas; portrait fountain group Louis Kocurek, Jr. children, San Antonio; portrait figure former mayor of Dallas; heroic figure of Gen. Douglas MacArthur, large heroic sized ideal figure representing higher edn. Trinity U., San Antonio, heroic bust of John Altgeld, bas-relief portrait of Dr. and Mrs. others. Charter mem. (sponsor) Coppini Acad. Fine Arts. Fellow Nat., Sculptor Soc.; mem. Nat. Soc. Arts and Letters, Artists and Craftsmen, San Antonio Art League. Methodist. Clubs: Tuesday Musical, Women's (San Antonio); Brady (Tex.) Tuesday. Address: 115 Melrose Pl San Antonio TX 78212

TAUNTON, VAN BUREN, bus. exec.; b. nr. Tallassee, Ala., Apr. 30, 1897; s. James Lee and Sara Elizabeth (Williams) T.; A.B., Birmingham So. Coll., 1928; postgrad. Auburn U., 1929-31; m. Sunshine Gaines, Feb. 9, 1935. Textile supr. West Point Mfg. Co., Lanett, Ala., 1917-22, textile exec., 1932-53; asst. supt. city schs. Lanett, 1928-32; ins. exec., spl. rep. Guaranty Savs. Life Ins. Co., Montgomery, Ala., 1953—; dir. Bank of Dadeville (Ala.), Home Fed. Savs. & Loan Assn. LaFayette, Ala. Pres., E. Tallapoosa Corp. Med. Center, Dadeville, 1960-65. Mem. Lanett Bd. Edn., 1936-53, chmn., 1945-53; mem. Dadeville City Gas Bd., 1958—; mem. Lanett Housing Authority, 1941-53, chmn., 1951-53; adminstr. E. Tallapoosa Hosp., 1965-68; lobbyist for hosp. in Dadeville, 1961; mem. Com. 100, Emory U., Atlanta, 1948-52. Mayor, Dadeville, 1960-64. Bd. dirs. Wesley Found., Auburn U., 1946—, vice chmn., 1957. Methodist (numerous offices including chmn. com. on camp assemblies N. Ala. Meth. Conf. 1965-67, 69-71). Mason, Kiwanian (lt. gov. 1949). Home: E South St PO Box 65 Dadeville AL 36853 Office: Bank Dadeville Dadeville AL 36853

TAVEL, ROBERT FREDERICK, dept. store exec.; b. Johnston City, Ill., June 7, 1943; s. James Robert and Vivian Lee (Brown) T.; student Alvin Jr. Coll., 1961-63; m. Lillie Faye Moffett; children—Phillip Jeffery, Sherry Michelle. Salesman, Brockman's Dept. Store, Angleton, Tex., 1963, shoe mgr., Lake Jackson, Tex., 1964, asst. mgr., Alvin, Tex., 1965, mgr., West Columbia, Tex., 1966-71, Deer Park, Tex., 1971—. Charter chmn. West Columbia Library Bd., 1968-71; chmn. West Columbia Beautification Assn., 1970; div. chmn. Brazoria County United Fund Communities, 1971; chmn. Sch. Dist. Drug Edn. Bd., 1970-71; mem. dist. com. Bay Area council Boy Scouts Am., 1969-70. Named West Columbia's Outstanding Young Man, Jr. C. of C., 1970; recipient First Outstanding Service award West Columbia City Council, 1971, citation Tex. Gov. Preston for service to Tex. Indsl. Commn., 1970. Mem. Tex., Am. library assns., Tex. Geneal. Assn., Tex. (pres. 1968), West Columbia chambers commerce. Baptist (Sunday Sch. supt. 1966-71). Mason, Rotarian (pres. 1970—). Home: 3456 Hickory St Deer Park TX 77536 Office: 1703 Center St Deer Park TX 77536

TAYLOR, ALBERT WILLIAM, cons.; b. Blair, Okla., Nov. 16, 1910; s. Robert Z. and Carrie R. (Wilson) T.; B.S., U. Okla., 1933; m. Leta Mae E. Rlizman, June 7, 1936; children—Susan G., William R. With Amerada Petroleum Corp., 1933-69, mgr. gas dept., 1956-60, exec. asst. 1960-61, v.p., 1961-68, sr. v.p., 1968-69, sr. v.p. Amerada div. Amerada Hess Corp., 1969-71; cons., Tulsa, 1971—. Mem. exec. bd. Indian Nations council Boy Scouts Am., mem. adv. bd. Salvation Army. Mem. Natural Gas Processors Assn. (past pres., dir.), Am. Inst. Mining, Metall. and Petroleum Engrs., Am. Petroleum Inst., Soc. Exploration Geophysicists. Republican. Methodist (steward). Clubs: Tulsa Country, Summit. Home: 4011 S Atlanta Pl Tulsa OK 74105 Office: Thompson Bldg Tulsa OK 74103

TAYLOR, ALONZO CLASON, cons. engr.; b. McKinney, Tex., Oct. 4, 1903; s. Alonzo Green and Sue (Border) T.; B.S., Tex. A. and M. U., 1924; m. Virginia Wood, May 29, 1932; 1 son, Lonn Wood. Insp. Miss. River Commn., Vicksburg, Miss., 1924-25; jr. engr. to asst. engr. U.S. Bur. Pub. Rds., Washington and Ft. Worth, 1925-29; insp. Tex. Hwy. Dept, Sherman, 1929-30; asst. engr. to hwy. engr. U.S. Bur. Pub. Rds., 1930-46, programming and planning engr., Manila, Philippines, 1946-49, supervising hwy. engr., Washington, 1949-51, div. engr., Manila, 1951-55, chief Office Fgn. Projects, Washington, 1955-56, regional engr., regional fed. hwy. adminstr., Ft. Worth, 1956-70; cons. engr. to Fed. Hwy. Adminstrn., Ft. Worth, 1971—. Recipient Adminstrs. award Fed. Hwy. Adminstrn., 1969, Pub. Works Man of Year award Kiwanis Internat. and Am. Pub. Works Assn., 1964; Award of Merit, Philippine Contractors Assn., 1955; decorated officer Legion of Honor (Philippines). Registered profl. engr., Pa., Tex. Fellow Am. Soc. C.E.; mem. Am. Rd. Builders Assn., Inst. Traffic Engrs., Soc. Am. Mil. Engrs., Nat. Soc. Profl. Engrs., Philippine Better Rds. Assn. (hon. life), Tau Beta Pi, Chi Epsilon. Club: Army and Navy (Manila). Home: 3961 Weyburn Dr Fort Worth TX 76109 Office: 819 Taylor St Fort Worth TX 76102

TAYLOR, BARBARA JO ANNE HARRIS (MRS. RICHARD POWELL TAYLOR), civic and polit. worker; b. Providence, Sept. 9, 1936; d. Ross Cameron and Anita (Coia) Harris; student Tex. Christian U., 1952, Salve Regina Coll., 1952-53, Our Lady of the Lake Coll. and Convent, 1953-54, St. Mary's U., summer 1954, Incarnate Word Coll., 1954-55, Georgetown U., 1956-60, 62-63, B.S.; m. Richard Powell Taylor, Dec. 19, 1959; 1 son, Douglas Howard. Adminstrv. asst. profl. devel. and welfare N.E.A., Washington, 1956-59; asst. to dr. Georgetown U. Washington, 1956-59; exec. asst. All Am. Conf. to Combat Communism, Washington, 1960. Mem. exec. bd. Salvation Army Aus., D.C., 1967—, chmn. membership com., 1969-70, mem. exec. com. of exec. bd., 1970—, treas., mem. finance com., 1970-71, v.p., 1971-72, historian, 1972—, editor Our Watchword Newsletter, 1968-69; mem. exec. bd. Welcome to Washington Internat., 1969—, bd. advisers, 1969—, dir. workshop, 1969—; exec. bd. Am. Opera Sch. Soc., Washington, 1970—, Episcopal Ch. Home for Aged Women's Aux., 1970—, Episcopal Center for Emotionally Disturbed Children Women's Aux., 1970—; exec. bd. St. David's Episcopal Ch. Aux., 1970—, v.p., 1970—, chmn. program com., 1970—; bd. dirs. treas. Spanish-Portuguese Study Group, 1970—. Mem. exec. bd. League Republican Women D.C., 1964-67, treas., 1964-67; mem. nat. council Womens Nat. Rep. Club, N.Y.C., 1969—, chmn. Washington-Md.-Va. legislative com., 1970—, co-chmn. ann. conf., 1971; mem. Nat. Fedn. Rep. Women, 1964—. Mem. Internat. Platform Assn., Spanish-Portuguese Study Group, D.A.R. (Chpt. nat. def. rep. 1972—). Clubs: International, Capitol Hill, Capital Speaker, Washington (mem. internat. com. 1971—); Congressional Country (Potomac, Md.). Home: 6007 Corewood Lane Sumner Washington DC 20016

TAYLOR, BILL EDWARD, dentist; b. Clinton, Okla., May 20, 1935; s. Raymond W. and Elsie L. (Behnke) T.; student U. Okla., 1953-57; D.D.S., U. Md., 1961; m. Eleanor Louise Stewart, Aug. 26, 1956; children— Louis Edward, Cynthia Elaine. Individual practice gen. dentistry, Enid, Okla., 1963—. Chmn., Enid Semi-pro Baseball, 1969-70; chmn. econ. devel. program Mayor's Goals Program, 1971-72. Trustee Okla. Dental Found. Served with USAF, 1961-63. Recipient Mosby award for Scholarship, Gold medal Thesis award, 1961. Mem. Am. Acad. Gold Foil Operators, Am., Okla., Garfield County dental assns. Methodist. Kiwanian. Club: Oakwood Country. Patentee Futures, 1971. Home: 1217 Indian Dr Enid OK 73701 Office: 617 S Quincy St Enid OK 73701

TAYLOR, BOB BYRON, cartoonist; b. Stockton, Cal., July 21, 1932; s. Orla J. and Bertha (Friesen) T.; A.A., Grant Tech. Jr. Coll.; B.A., Sacramento State Coll.; m. JoAnne B. Femling, Jan. 31, 1955; children—Kevin Scott, Cameron Matthew. Sports cartoonist Sacramento Union, 1950-54; editorial cartoonist Dallas Times Herald, 1958—. Served with USAF, 1954-58. Recipient several awards for boosting service morale Dept. Def., award Nat. Conf. Christians and Jews, 1964, Southwest Journalism Forum; Best Cartoon award Dallas Press Club, 1968; Grenville Clarke award, 1968. Home: 13843 Waterfall Pl Dallas TX 75240 Office: Herald Square Dallas TX 75221

TAYLOR, BOYD EUGENE, writer, newspaper exec.; b. Atlanta, July 31, 1901; s. Eugene Helm and Minnie (Jarrell) T.; B.S., Emory U., 1923; M.S., Sorbonne, 1926; M.A., U. Madrid, 1925; m. Cora Mina Moses, Feb. 22, 1922 (dec. 1927). Sci. writer Hearst Newspapers, 1919-40; tchr. Fulton High Sch., Atlanta, 1922-27; asst. night chief Atlanta bur. A.P., 1920; city editor Atlanta Constn., 1941-44; gen. mgr. Ind. Press, Atlanta, 1944—; pres. Southland, Inc., Stone Mountain Food Products, Inc., Community Newspapers, Inc. Pres. Separate Schs., Inc., Pvt. Sch. Found., Nat. Laymens Com. to Crush Communism in Chs.; cofounder Hartsfield Internat. Airport, 1925. Bd. dirs. Ga. Taxpayers Relief Assn., Genetics Research Library; trustee Historic House Mus. Corp. Served to 2d lt., Signal Corps, U.S. Army, World War I; to maj. USAAF, World War II. Recipient plaque Fulton County Tchrs. Assn., 1963. Life fellow Royal Soc. (London); mem. Am. Soc. Human Genetics, Genetics Soc. Am., Am. Genetic Assn., Population Assn. Am., Ga. Acad. Sci., Am. Inst. Biol. Scis., A.A.A.S., Brit. Assn. for Advancement Sci., Anglican Soc., Soc. For Study Evolution, Internat. Assn. for Advancement Eugenics and Ethnology, Am. Soc. Health Assn., Council For Basic Edn., Planned Parenthood Fedn. Am., Am. Acad. Polit. and Social Sci., Soc. for Preservation English Lang. and Lit. (founder), Nat. Wildlife Fedn., Nat. Rifle Assn. (life), Nat. Trust for Historic Preservation. Anglican Orthodox (co-founder, trustee). Club: Atlanta Billiard (pres.). Home: 327 St Paul Av SE Atlanta GA 30312 Office: PO Box 1 Atlanta GA 30301

TAYLOR, BURRELL GALE, oil co. exec.; b. Post, Tex., Oct. 8, 1925; s. Robert A. and Roxie (Capps) T.; B.S., Tex. Tech. U., 1949; m. Joy Mozelle Norwood, June 21, 1947; children—Vicki, Deborah, Mark, Craig. With Kerr-McGee Corp., 1949—, asst. to gen. mgr. uranium operations, Grants, N.M., 1961-62, gen. mgr. prodn. dept., 1962-69, v.p. oil and gas prodn. div., Oklahoma City, 1969—. Served with USNR, 1943-46. Mem. Oklahoma City C. of C., Am. Petroleum Inst., Soc. Petroleum Engrs. Home: 4924 NW 32d St Oklahoma City OK 73122 Office: Kerr-McGee Bldg Oklahoma City OK 73103

TAYLOR, C. J., JR., lawyer; b. Thrall, Tex., Feb. 3, 1923; s. C. J. and Esther (Jackson) T.; LL.B., U. Mo., 1952; m. Frances Lucille Moody, Nov. 21, 1947 (div.); children—Karen Lynn, Craig James; m. 2d, Dorothy Taylor, June 27, 1970. Admitted to Tex. bar, 1952; asst. city atty., Corpus Christi, Tex., 1954-57; first asst. city atty., Austin, Tex., 1957-62; asst. atty. gen. Tex., 1962; city atty., Irving Tex., 1963-65; city atty., Amarillo, Tex., 1965-70; partner law firm Clayton & Clayton, Amarillo, 1970—. Served with USNR, 1942-45. Mem. State Bar Tex., Amarillo Bar Assn. Home: 5705 Tawney St Amarillo TX 79106 Office: 2506 W 45th Av PO Box 7249 Amarillo TX 79109

TAYLOR, C.L., v.p., sec., treas. LTV Electro-systems, Inc. Address: PO Box 6030 Dallas TX 75222*

TAYLOR, CARROLL AUBREY, city mgr.; b. Snyder, Tex., Mar. 19, 1922; s. Sterling A. and Elizabeth (Payne) T.; student Tex. Tech. Coll., 1942, 46; m. Zanalee Jones, Oct. 23, 1943; children—Zee Lyn, Carol, Zana. Resident engr. H. N. Roberts & Assos., cons. engrs., 1947; city engr., Lamesa, Tex., 1948-49, city mgr., 1949—. Treas. Lamesa dist. Girl Scouts Am., chmn. property bd. trustees. Chmn. bd. health South Plains Health Unit, 1954-60; mem. gov.'s Hwy. Safety Commn., 1958-61. Served from 2d lt. to capt. USMC, 1942-46. Mem. Internat., Tex. (regional dir. 1961, pres. 1965-66) city mgrs. assns., Internat. Platform Assn., C. of C. Presbyn. (elder, clk. of sessions). Lion (dir. 1955, pres. 1962-63). Home: 812 N 15th St Lamesa TX 79331 Office: City Hall Lamesa TX 79331

TAYLOR, CECIL G(RADY), univ. ofcl.; b. Williamston, N.C., May 20, 1909; s. Henry Dawson and Laura Elizabeth (Peele) T.; A.B., U. N.C., 1929, A.M., 1930, Ph.D., 1935; student U. Paris (Am. Field Service fellow 1935-36), 1935-36; m. Ellen Eakin Albright, May 26, 1937; children—Vickie Albright, Ellen Albright, John Howell. Instr. romance langs. U. N.C., 1931-35; mem. faculty La. State U., 1936—, prof. romance langs., 1949—, dean Coll. Arts and Scis., 1949-65, chancellor, Baton Rouge campus, 1965—. Served as lt. (j.g.) and lt. USNR, 1943-46. Decorated Palmes Academiques (France). Mem. Modern Lang. Assn., South Atlantic, South Central modern lang. assns., Phi Beta Kappa, Omicron Delta Kappa, Phi Kappa Phi. Home: 2105 Kleinert Av Baton Rouge LA 70806

TAYLOR, CHARLES HART, state ofcl., real estate co. exec.; b. Brevard, N.C., Jan. 23, 1941; s. Robert G. and Loee (English) T.; B.A., Wake Forest U., 1963, J.D., 1966; M. Elizabeth Bryan Owen, Nov. 21, 1970. Mng. dir., gen. counsel Transylvania Tree Farms, Brevard, 1966—; Southeastern Real Estate and Discount Co., Brevard, 1966—., mem. N.C. Ho. of Reps., 1967—, house minority leader, 1968—. Dir. N.C. Consumers Council, 1971. Dir., Nat. Republican Legislators Conf., 1969—; mem. N.C. Rep. Central Com., 1968-71, exec. com., 1967-71. Bd. visitors Western Carolina U., Wake Forest U.; trustee Brevard Music Center, 1967—; mem. N.C. Bapt. Found., 1966—; bd. dirs. 4-H Devel. Fund, 1971. Recipient citation for Outstanding Service 4-H Club, 1969, Alumni award State 4-H Club, 1967, Outstanding Student award Phi Alpha Delta, 1966. Mem. Brevard C. of C. (dir.), 4-H Club State Honor Club, Phi Alpha Delta (mem. internat. bd.). Author: Timber Mortgage Loans, 1966, also articles. Home: Burrell Mountain Rd Brevard NC 28712 Office: PO Box 66 Brevard NC 28712

TAYLOR, CLARENCE EVERETT, librarian; b. Pratt, Mo., Oct. 30, 1914; s. General Franklin and Nora Susan (Lewis) T.; B.S. in Edn., Ohio State U., 1937; B.S. in L.S., Western Res. U., 1940, M.S. in L.S., 1956; m. Kathryn Elizabeth Mallett, Sept. 2, 1940; children—Karen Sue (Mrs. John F. Maxwell, Jr.), Ellen Elizabeth. Tchr., Green Rural High Sch., Laings, O., 1937-39; library asst. D.C. Pub. Library, 1940-41; cataloger Social Security Adminstrn., Washington, 1941, 45-46, Armed Forces Staff Coll. Library, Norfolk, Va., 1947, VA, Washington, 1948; gifts and exchange librarian Ohio State U., 1949; asso. librarian USAF Inst. Tech., Wright-Patterson AFB, O., 1950-53, librarian, 1954-55; asst. prof., asst. librarian Abilene (Tex.) Christian Coll., 1956-62, asso. prof., asst. librarian, 1963—. Served to 2d lt., Signal Corps, USAAF, 1942-45. Mem. Am., Tex. library assns., Beta Phi Mu. Home: 1001 Washington Blvd Abilene TX 79601

TAYLOR, CLAYBORNE DUDLEY, educator; b. Kokomo, Miss., July 15, 1938; s. Dudley Clayborne and Winnie (Holmes) T.; B.S., Miss. State U., 1961; M.S., N.M. State U., 1964, Ph.D., 1965; m. Mary Jean Blue, June 23, 1963; children—Clayborne Dudley, David Edward, Rebecca Lynn. Mem. tech. staff Sandia Lab., Albuquerque, 1965-67; asst. prof. physics Miss. State U., State Coll., 1967-69, asso. prof., 1969-70; prof. elec. engring. U. Miss., 1971—. Mem. Am. Phys. Soc., I.E.E.E., Miss. Acad. Scis., Sigma Xi, Phi Kappa Phi, Sigma Pi Sigma. Contbr. articles to profl. jours. Home: PO Box 184 300 College Hill Rd University MS 38677

TAYLOR, CLIFTON BRADLEY, dentist; b. Lebanon, Ky., Feb. 11, 1912; s. Robert Elmer and Grace Evelyn (Murphy) T.; student Mars Hill Coll., 1931-33; B.S., Wake Forest U., 1935; D.M.D., U. Louisville, 1940; m. Vera Elizabeth Chesolm, Aug. 3, 1939; children—Barbara (Mrs. George Bond Jr.), Grace (Mrs. Jim Tillotson), Martha, Virginia. Practice of dentistry, Hendersonville, N.C., 1940—; mem. staff Margaret Pardee Hosp. Commr. Town Laurel Park, 1950—. Vol. Hill Fire Dept. Bd. dirs. Henderson County YMCA, Henderson County Teen-Age Canteen. Served with dental corps., AUS, 1953-55. Mem. Am., N.C. dental assns., So., Henderson County, First Dist. dental socs., Internat. Acad. Dentistry, Am. Legion. Lion. Clubs: Cotillion, (Hendersonville). Hendersonville Country. Home: 128 Silver Pine Dr Hendersonville NC 28739 Office: 560 Fleming St Hendersonville NC 28739

TAYLOR, DALMAS ARNOLD, psychologist; b. Detroit, Sept. 9, 1933; s. Robert E. and Phanada (Price) T.; B.A., Western Res. U., 1959; M.S., Howard U., 1961; Ph.D., U. Del., 1965; m. Faye Jean Jefferies, May 20, 1961; children—Monique M., Carla E., Courtney. Lab. technician Atomic Energy Research Project, Western Res. U. Sch. Medicine, Cleve., 1956; research and teaching asst. dept. psychology Howard U., Washington, 1959-61; psychologist Nat. Inst. Neurol. Diseases and Blindness, NIH, Bethesda, Md., 1961-62; research fellow Center for Research Social Behavior, U. Del. at Newark, 1962-65; research psychologist Nat. Naval Med. Center, Naval Med. Research Inst., Bethesda, Md., 1965-69; asso. prof., chmn. dept. psychology Fed. City Coll., Washington, 1969-70; lectr. U. Md., College Park, 1965—, prof. psychology, 1970—; adj. prof. dept. psychology Am. U., Washington, 1968-69. Served with U.S. Army Surg. Research Unit, 1956-58. Recipient Postdoctoral fellowship Nat. Acad. Sci.-NRC, 1965-66. Mem. A.A.A.S., Am., Eastern psychol. assns., Soc. Psychol. Study Social Issues, Sigma Xi, Psi Chi. Contbr. articles to publs. Home: 4110 Whispering Lane Annandale VA 22003 Office: Dept Psychology U Md College Park MD 20742

TAYLOR, DAVID RAY, city ofcl.; b. Tarboro, N.C., Jan. 16, 1937; s. Russell and Margaret (Perry) T.; B.S. in Civil Engring., N.C. State U., 1959; m. Anne Hagwood, Aug. 11, 1958; children—Donna Annette, Mark David. Staff engr. City of Raleigh (N.C.), 1959-61, asst. to city mgr., 1961-65; town mgr. Town of Tarboro (N.C.), 1965—. Sec.-treas. Electri-Cities N.C., 1967—. Baptist. Rotarian. Home: 1902 Lewis St Tarboro NC 27886 Office: PO Box 278 Tarboro NC 27886

TAYLOR, DEAN MONTGOMERY, city ofcl.; b. Red Wing, Minn., Mar. 1, 1906; s. Clarence Tennyson and Rosemary (Season) T.; student Hamline U., 1924-26; B.Chem. Engring., U. Minn., 1930, M.S. in San. Engring., 1950; m. Mary Lovella Belden, Sept. 5, 1934; children—Barclay, Stephen, Candace. San. engr. Minn. Dept. Health, Mpls., 1930-51, USPHS, Cin., 1951-53, City Cin., 1953-57; supt. sewage disposal Met. Sewer Dist. Louisville, 1957—. Lectr., Sch. Pub. Health U. Minn., Mpls., 1936-51. Named Engr. of Distinction, Engrs. Joint Council, 1970. Registered profl. engr., Minn., Ohio, Ky. Diplomate Am. Acad. Environmental Engrs. Fellow Am. Soc. C.E.; mem. Water and Sewage Treatment Operators Assn. (pres. 1964), Ky.-Tenn. Assn. Water Pollution Control Fedn. (pres. 1965), Water Pollution Control Fedn. (Gascoigne medal 1958). Home: 4809 Miles Lane Louisville KY 40219 Office: 4522 Algonquin Pky Louisville KY 40211

TAYLOR, DYER JUSTICE, judge; b. Columbia, S.C., Sept. 25, 1922; s. Dyer John and Marymagdalene (Laws) T.; student Johns Hopkins, 1942, U.N.C., 1948; J.D., George Washington U., 1951; m. H. Patricia Owens, June 11, 1949; children—Kathleen Johanna, Janet Maria. Asso. firm Ballard & Beasley, Washington, 1951-55; with Justice Dept., Washington, 1955-57; asst. U.S. atty., D.C., 1957-58; jr. partner firm John Laskey, Washington, 1958-60; asst. solicitor Interior Dept., Washington, 1960-63; hearing examiner ICC, 1961-63; trial examiner FPC, 1963-70; asso. judge Superior Ct. of D.C., 1970—. Chmn. Municipal affairs Beverly Hills Citizens Assn., 1958. Served with USNR, 1943-45. Mem. Fed. Trial Examiners Conf., Nat. Conf. State Trial Judges, Am., Fed., D.C. bar assns. Home: 1946 Creek Crossing Rd Vienna VA 22190 Office: 613 G St NW Washington DC 20001

TAYLOR, EDDIE THOMAS, banker; b. Lubbock, Tex., Dec. 2, 1929; s. Jess H. and Lois (Eubank) McWherter; B.S., Tex. Technol. U., 1955; m. Martha Ann Chrisholm, Aug. 31, 1959; children—Carrie Sue, Stacy Ann. County supr. loan dept. Farmers Home Adminstrn., Plains, Tex., 1959-65; v.p. loan dept. Yoakum County State Bank, Denver City, Tex., 1965—. Served with AUS, 1951-53. Baptist. Mason (32 deg.), Lion. Home: 1315 N Av F Denver City TX 79323 Office: 221 Av B Denver City TX 79323

TAYLOR, EDNA HENDREN (MRS. SURSE S. TAYLOR), hosp. adminstr.; b. Delaware County, Okla., Feb. 27, 1897; d. James E. and Eliza J. (Pollan) Hendren; ed. Okla. Gen. Hosp., Tulsa, 1922; m. Surse S. Taylor, Aug. 31, 1944 (dec. Feb. 1965). Night supr. service Southwestern Bell Telephone Co., Vinita, Okla, 1917-18; hosp. adminstr. Vinita City Hosp., 1924-28; floor supr. nurses Enid (Okla.) State Hosp., 1931-32; dir. Craig County Dept. Pub. Welfare, Vinita, 1933-37; adminstr. Craig County Hosp., 1939-45, Hillcrest Gen. Hosp., Vinita, 1951-62, Taylor Meml. Hosp., Vinita, 1962—; rancher Taylor Ranch, 1967—. Mem. Okla. State Hosp. Assn., Okla. Cowbelles Assn., Vinita C. of C. Home: Route 1 Vinita OK 74301 Office: Taylor Meml Hosp Vinita OK 74301

TAYLOR, ELDON DONIVAN, govt. ofcl.; b. Holdenville, Okla., July 29, 1929; s. Rome B. and Alma (Collins) T.; student Murry State A. and M. Coll., 1948-49, George Washington U., 1949-50; B.S. cum laude, Am. U., 1959, M.A., 1966, postgrad., 1966-68; m. Hypatia Ethel Roberts, Feb. 7, 1953; 1 dau., Teresa Lynn. Research budget analyst, budgetary adminstrn. Office Naval Research Navy Dept., Washington, 1949-51, 55-56, chief research and devel. budget sect., research, devel. planning adminstrn., Bur. Ordnance, 1956-60; dir. program rev. and resources, mgmt. div. research, devel. planning, adminstrn., Office Space Scis., NASA, Washington, 1960—. Served with USAF, 1951-55. Recipient Commendation award for outstanding performance Dept. Navy, 1958, William A. Jump Meritorious award for achievement in pub. adminstrn., 1964. Mem. Am. Soc. Pub. Adminstrn. (past sec. com. research pub. adminstrn.), Pi Sigma Alpha, Phi Theta Kappa. Home: 7722 Jervis St Springfield VA 22151 Office: Fed Office Bldg 4th and Independence Av Washington DC 20003

TAYLOR, ELIZABETH DALE DABBS (MRS. JAMES L. TAYLOR), pharmacist, educator; b. Shannon, Miss., 1914; d. Rome Grafton and Jessie (Prude) Dabbs; student Blue Mountain (Miss.) Coll., 1933, postgrad., 1959, 65; student Millsaps Coll., 1936; B.S. in Pharmacy, U. Miss., 1937, B.A., 1938, M.S. in Pharm. Chemistry, 1955, postgrad., 1962, 66, 67, 70, Triple A Teaching Certificate, 1972; postgrad. Miss. State U., 1943, 60, 64-67, 70-71; m. James Leroy Taylor, Jan. 21, 1941; children—Elizabeth Dale, Jessie Roma. Pharmacist drugstores rural Miss., 1937-56; tchr. Shannon Consol. Sch., 1947-59; tchr. Tupelo (Miss.) pub. schs., 1959—, chmn. sci. dept., 1960; chmn. sci. dept. Milam Jr. High Sch., Tupelo, 1961-64, adviser Jr. Engring. Tech. Soc., 1962—; tchr. sci. N.E. Miss. TV Council Tupelo, 1964-71, cons. ednl. programs TV sta. WTWV, drug abuse, 1966, safety, 1967; sci. cons. Blue Mountain Coll., 1959, symposium George Marshall Space Flight Center, Huntsville, Ala., 1965; cons. Miss. Instructional Curriculum Lab., Jackson, 1968-69; sci. curriculum adv. tchr. Lee County Farm Bur., Tupelo, 1957-66. Leader Tupelo troops Girl Scouts Am., 1957-62, 55-63; instr. nursing, family health Shannon A.R.C., 1951; mem. Shannon Home Demonstration Club, Tupelo, 1950-61, P.T.A., Tupelo, 1959—, Lee United Neighbors, 1963—. Named Miss Shannon, 1932, Outstanding Jr. Engring. Tech. Adviser, Miss. State U. engring. extension service, 1963; recipient Miss. Merit Community Program award edn. Miss. Econ. Council, Tupelo, 1963, Pacemaker award Parade Mag., N.E.A., Tupelo, 1965. Mem. Miss. Acad. Sci., Tupelo Ednl. Assn., U. Miss. Alumni Assn., Miss. Sci. Tchrs. Assn., Miss. Pharm. Assn., Nat. Sci. Tchrs. Assn., Internat. Platform Assn., D.A.R. Baptist. Club: Shannon (Miss.) Women's (v.p. 1963, 68; pres. 1969). Contbr. articles to profl. jours. Office: Tupelo High Sch Varsity Dr Tupelo MS 38801 Sch Jefferson St Tupelo MI 38801

TAYLOR, ELLA LOUISE RICHARDS (MRS. HOWARTH E. TAYLOR), bus. exec.; b. Cumberland, Md., Apr. 2, 1925; d. William Carl and Emma (Wolfe) Richards; B.S., Wheaton Coll., 1947; Ph.D., U. Ill., 1952; m. Howarth E. Taylor, Sept. 27, 1952; children—David, Martha, Rebecca, Mary, Stephen, Ruth. Teaching asst. Wheaton (Ill.) Coll., 1944-47; chemist Celanese Corp. Am., Cumberland, 1947-48; teaching asst. U. Ill., 1948-52; tchr. Hickory Ridge (Ark.) High Sch., 1952-53; sec.-treas. Hickory Ridge Farm Supply Inc., 1962—, Hickory Ridge Rice Farms, Inc., 1961—,Taylor Seed Farms, Inc., 1958—, Taylor Seed Processing Plant, Inc., 1958—. Mem. Hickory Ridge P.T.A., 1959—, pres., 1962-64; leader 4-H CLUBS, Hickory Ridge, 1968—; mem. Cross County Miss Fluffy Rice Com., 1970—; mem. Cross County High Sch. Band Boosters, 1967—, v.p., 1972-73; mem. Cross County Health Com. Bd., 1972—. Recipient Ark. Farm Family of Year award, 1969. Mem. Sigma Xi, Sigma Pi Sigma, Sigma Delta Epsilon, Iota Sigma Pi. Baptist. Address: Hickory Ridge AR 72347

TAYLOR, ETHEL MAE HENDERSON (MRS. JOHN BENJAMIN TAYLOR), educator, broadcaster; b. nr. Laurens, S.C.; d. James William and Ella (Dendy) Henderson; B.A., Benedict Coll., 1946; summer study U. S.C., 1966; m. John Benjamin Taylor, Feb. 10, 1946; children—John B., Gwendolyn Bernice (Mrs. Robert Hall), James Howard, Ludwald Clifton, Audriene Denice, Deborah Elizabeth, Melonie Joyce, Cheryl Kaye. Sec., Hampton Printing Co., Columbia, S.C., 1949-52; tchr. Richland County Sch., Eastover, S.C., 1953-60, Columbia (S.C.) city schs., 1961—; part-time radio announcer radio sta. WOIC, Columbia, 1954—. Pub. relations dir. Fairwold Jr. High Sch., 1967—. Mem. Columbia Urban League, Nat., Richland Co. ednl. assns., Nat., S.C. councils tchrs. English, S.C. Tchr. Assn., Nat. Assn. TV and Radio Announcers. Baptist (organist). Home: 2221 Mance St Columbia SC 29203 Office: 830 Laurel St Columbia SC 29201

TAYLOR, EVERETTE LESTER, JR., physician; b. Scottsville, N.C., Jan. 23, 1925; s. Everette Lester and Malissa Cox (Hill) T.; student U. N.C., 1942, U. Ala., 1943, Washington and Jefferson Coll., 1943-44, Yale, 1944; A.B., Washington and Lee U., 1949; M.D., Duke, 1955; m. Carol Snow Anderson, Oct. 25, 1953; children—Mark Anderson, Mary Carol. Rotating intern Greenville (S.C.) Gen. Hosp., 1955; resident gen. practice Bluefield (W.Va.) sanitarium, 1956; gen. practice medicine, Sparta, N.C., 1957—; mem. staff Alleghany County Meml. Hosp. Cons., New River Mental Health Clinic, Boone, N.C., 1966—, Alleghany County Health Dept., Sparta, 1966—; med. examiner Alleghany County, 1970—; coroner Alleghany County, 1962-66, 70—. Served with C.E., AUS, 1943-46; CBI. Mem. A.M.A., Am. Acad. Family Practice, So. Med. Assn., N.C., Ashe-Alleghany (pres. 1971) med. socs., Phi Kappa Psi, Chi Phi, Alpha Epsilon Delta. Democrat. Presbyn. (deacon). Mason, Lion. Home: 305 Taylor St Sparta NC 28675 Office: 614 Doctors Bldg Sparta NC 28675

TAYLOR, FLONNIA CHAMBERS(MRS. RHEA A. TAYLOR), social worker; b. Williamsburg, Ky.; d. James Henry and Lassafaye (Hicks) Chambers; A.B. cum laude, Carson-Newman Coll., 1926; M.A., Ohio State U., 1933; M.A., U. Chgo., 1952; m. Rhea A. Taylor, June 26, 1930. Tchr. English and dramatics Bethel Coll., 1931-32, U. Ky., 1945, English, Georgetown Coll., 1955-56; social work cons. Ky. Child Welfare Div., Frankfort, 1937-42; area rep. A.R.C., Alexandria, Va., 1942-46; psychiat. social worker VA, Lexington, Ky., 1946-51; spl. supervisory and adminstrv. work A.R.C., Washington chpt., Family Service, Lansing, Mich., 1952-55; social worker Shriners Hosp., Lexington, Ky., 1955-57; exec. dir. United Cerebral Palsy of Bluegrass Agy., 1958—. Mem. Gov.'s Adv. Com. Child Welfare of Ky., 1960—, v.p., 1970; chmn. Gov.'s Adv. Com. Day Care, Ky., 1963—; mem. Nat. Adv. Com. on Social Service to Nat. United Cerebral Palsy Assn., 1959—; profl. cons. coms. on children and family Ky. White House Conf. Bd. dirs. Community Chest, Family Service, County Child Welfare, Florence Crittenden Home (pres.). Mem. Am. Assn. U. Women (pres. 1960-62), Ky. Welfare Assn. (pres. 1959-60), Central Ky. Philharmonic Orch. (sec. 1961-62, dir. 1961—), League Women Voters, Am. Assn. Social Workers, Nat. Assn. Social Workers, Acad. Certified Social Workers, State Mental Health Orgn., P.E.O. Clubs: Zonta, University of Kentucky Woman's. Home: Tayraf Hill Route 2 Harrodsburg Rd Lexington KY 40504 Office: 465 Springhill Dr Lexington KY 40503

TAYLOR, FOSTER JAY, coll. pres.; b. Gibsland, La., Aug. 9, 1923; s. Lawrence Foster and Marcia Aline (Jay) T.; student La. Poly. Inst., 1940-42; B.A., U. Cal. at Santa Barbara, 1948; M.A., Claremont (Cal.) Grad. Sch., 1949; Ph.D., Tulane U., 1952; m. Evelyn Marie Bast, Apr. 18, 1946; 1 son, Terry Jay. Asso. prof. history, dean men La. Coll., Pineville, 1952-56, prof., 1956-62, dean coll., 1960-62; pres. La. Poly. Inst., Ruston, 1962-70, La. Tech U., 1970—. Chmn. La. State Labor Mediation Bd. Served to lt. comdr., aviator USNR, 1942-46. Mem. Am., Miss. Valley, So. hist. assns., Phi Alpha Theta. Author: The United States and the Spanish Civil War, 1936-1939, 1956; Reluctant Rebel, The Secret Diary of Robert Patrick, 1861-1865, 1959. Home: Louisiana Tech Univ Ruston LA 71270

TAYLOR, FRANK A(UGUSTUS), museum exec.; b. Washington, Mar. 25, 1903; s. Augustus C. and Josephine M. (Kubel) T.; B.S. in Mech. Engring., Mass. Inst. Tech., 1928; LL.B., Georgetown U., 1934; m. Virginia I. McCaig, Aug. 28, 1937; 1 dau., Joan Josephine. With Smithsonian Instn. (U.S. Nat. Mus.), Washington, 1922—, head curator dept. engring. and industries, 1948-55, asst. dir. U.S. Nat. Mus., 1955-58, dir., 1962—, dir. Mus. History and Tech., 1958-64. Asso. dir. Am. Mcht. Marine survey WPB, 1936-37. Trustee Elec. Hist. Found. Served to capt. AUS, World War II. Recipient Nat. Civil Service League award, 1963. Mem. D.C. Bar Assn., Internat. Council Museums (chmn. com. museums and collections sci. and tech. 1962), Sigma Tau. Roman Catholic. Author descriptive catalog mech. engring. collections, Nat. Mus. Bull., 1939. Contbr. articles profl. jours. Editorial adv. bd. Am. Neptune. Home: 6605 32d St NW Washington DC 20015 Office: Smithsonian Instn Washington DC 20560

TAYLOR, FRANK HART, mech. engr.; b. San Antonio, Feb. 1, 1930; s. William H. D. and Alice (Hart) T.; student U. Md., 1947-49; B.Ch.E., Ga. Inst. Tech., 1958; m. Kay Lynette Riley, Jan. 26, 1957; children—Donna Marie, Lisa Lynn, Frank Mark. Wireline helper Otis Engring. Corp., Liberty, Tex., 1958-59, draftsman, Dallas, 1959-60, jr. design engr., 1960-61, design engr., 1961-67, project engr., 1967—. Served with USAF, 1952-57. Registered profl. engr., Tex. Mem. Tex. Soc. Profl. Engrs. Republican. Presbyn. (deacon). Author: (with others) Wireline Operations and Procedures, 1964. Patentee oil well tools. Home: 2024 Reagan St Carrollton TX 75006 Office: PO Box 34380 Dallas TX 75234

TAYLOR, GEORGE SAMPSON, supt. schs.; b. Maiden, N.C., Oct. 25, 1924; s. George Sampson and Lottie Mae (Sigmon) T.; student Mitchell Coll., 1948-50; B.S., Appalachian State U., 1955; M.Ed., U. N.C., 1961; m. Ella Stephanna Ervin, May 14, 1948; 1 dau., Donna. Tchr.-coach East Bend (N.C.) High Sch., 1950-52, Anderson High Sch., Burlington, N.C., 1953-55; prin., Prospect Hill (N.C.) Sch., 1955-61, Littlefield High Sch., Lumberton, N.C., 1961-67, Greene County Central High Sch., Snow Hill, N.C., 1967-69; supt., Greene County Schs., Snow Hill, 1969—. Bd. dirs. Greene County Health Dept., Greene Lamp, Inc. Served with USAAF, 1943-46. Mem. N.E.A., Am. Assn. Sch. Adminstrs., N.C. Assn. Educators. Democrat. Baptist. Moose, Rotarian. Home: PO Box 614 Snow Hill NC 27580 Office: PO Box 308 Snow Hill NC 28580

TAYLOR, GERALD HERMAN, hosp. adminstr.; b.Asheville, N.C., Jan. 8, 1937; s. Herman Melvin and Grace (Crook) T.; student U. Chattanooga, 1964; B.S., Mars Hill Coll., 1967; M.S., Samford U., 1968; m. Sandra Dianne Cole, May 28, 1967; children—Michael David, Kathy Jean. Tchr. mgmt. Vocational Tech. Sch., Asheville, 1966-67; dir. admitting U. Ala. Hosps. and Clinics, Birmingham, 1968; adminstr. Hancock Meml. Hosp., Sparta, Ga., 1968-69, Meml. Hosp., Adel, Ga., 1969—. Cons. N.E. Fla. Broadcasting, Inc. Served with USMCR, 1955-59. Elk, Lion. Home: 309 Bear Creek Rd Adel GA 31620 Office: N Parrish Av Adel GA 31620

TAYLOR, GERRY MAILAND, librarian; b. Eustis, Me., July 7, 1913; s. Everett Bowen and Amy Maria (Wilber) T.; student Farmington State Tchrs. Coll., 1930-32; B.A. cum laude, Baylor U., 1951, M.A. with honors, 1952; M.L.S., U. Tex., 1955; m. Myra Fairhead, Aug. 6, 1948. Grad. library asst. Baylor U., 1951-52; documents asst. U. Tex. Library, 1952-53; revisor Grad. Sch. Library Sci., U. Tex., 1953-54, sr. library clk. Law Sch. Library, 1954-55; asst. librarian Tex. Agrl. and Indsl. Coll., 1955-56; asso. librarian Sam Houston State U., 1956-66; head librarian Ark. State U., State University, 1966—. Library bldg. cons., City of Huntsville, Tex., 1965-66. Served with AUS, 1940-45; PTO. Mem. Am., N.E. Ark., Ark. (chmn. intellectual freedom com. 1967-68) library assns., Phi Delta Kappa, Psi Chi, Beta Phi Mu, Alpha Chi, Ark. Council on Library Edn., Ark. Sch. Masters Assn. Baptist. Mason (32 deg., Shriner). Home: Box 1017 State University AR 72467

TAYLOR, HAROLD RALPH, devel. exec.; b. Somerville, Mass., Nov. 2, 1918; s. Louise and Freda (Pearlson) T.; A.B., Harvard, 1939, M.P.A., 1947; M.A., La. State U., 1946; m. Henrietta Irene Medalia, Nov. 18, 1945; children—Allan, Robert, David. Exec. dir. New Haven Redevel. Agy., 1955-59; exec. v.p. Renewal and Devel. Co., N.Y.C., 1959-62; pres. H.R. Taylor Mgmt. Corp., N.Y.C., 1962-66; asst. sec. Dept. Housing and Urban Devel., 1966-69; exec. v.p. Mid-City Developers, Inc., 1969—. Spl. asst. to dir. Mass. Housing Bd., 1949-51; asst. dir. Somerville Housing Authority, 1951-55. Served with AUS, 1941-45. Mem. Nat. Assn. Housing and Redevel. Ofcls., Nat. Housing Conf. Home: 608 7th St SW Washington DC 20024 Office: 1133 15th St NW Washington DC 20005

TAYLOR, HENRY SPLAWN, author, educator; b. Lincoln, Va., June 21, 1942; s. Thomas Edward and Mary Marshall (Splawn) T.; B.A., U. Va., 1965; M.A., Hollins Coll., 1966; m. Frances Ferguson Carney, June 29, 1968; 1 son, Thomas Edward. Instr. Roanoke Coll., Salem, Va., 1966-68; asst. prof. U. Utah, Salt Lake City, 1968-71, dir. Writers' Conf., 1969—; asso. prof. lit. Am. U., Washington, 1971—. Recipient Poetry prize Acad. Am. Poets, 1962, 64, Utah State Inst. Fine Arts, 1969, 71. Author: (poetry) The Horse Show at Midnight, 1966; (poetry) Breakings, 1971. Founder, poetry editor Roanoke Rev., 1967-68; contbg. editor Hollins Critic, 1970—; asso. editor

Masterplots Ann., 1971—. Home: 6931 Hector Rd McLean VA 22101 Office: Dept Literature Am U Massachusetts and Nebraska Ave NW Washington DC 20016

TAYLOR, HERMAN, JR., agrl. co. exec.; b. Natchitoches, La., Oct. 31, 1932; s. Herman and Sadie (Cook) T.; student Northwestern St. U. La., 1951; B.S., La. State U., 1954; m. Evelyne Campbell, June 26, 1954; children—Herman, Mary Evelyne, Elizabeth Lynn. Pres., Taylor & Co., 1954—; C-T-C Land Corp., 1955—, H-T Stock Farms, Inc., 1954—, v.p. Delta South Oil Co., Inc., 1970—, Hickory Ridge Devel. Co., 1968—, Hickory Ridge Shopping Centers, 1971—, Cook-Taylor Land Corp.; People's Realty Co., 1969—, Broadmoor Shopping Cen. 1959-68; dir. People's Bank & Trust Co. (all Natchitoches). Nat. v.p., nat. trustee, mem. exec. com. Ducks Unlimited, 1969—; pres. Natchitoches Farm Bur., Natchitoches Wildlife Assn.; chmn. Natchitoches Cancer Soc., Agrl. Stblzn. and Conservation Service, Natchitoches, 1965—; vice chmn. La. Beef Promotion Commn., 1968, Natchitoches Water Bd. Dist. 1, 1961-72; v.p. Red River Valley Improvement Assn., 1961—; mem. La. Sovereignty Commn., 1960-64, La. com. Farmers Home Adminstrn., 1971—, Red River Nav. Commn., 1966—, Culver Ednl. Found., 1969—, La. State U. Found., 1964—, Northwestern State U. La. Found., 1969—, livestock adv. bd. La. State U., 1967—. Bd. dirs. Fed. Land Bank, Natchitoches County Fair, Ducks Unlimited (Can.). Recipient Gov. James H. Davis award outstanding future farmer, 1947-48; Gov. Earl K. Long award for livestock prodn., 1949, for outstanding farmer, 1950; State Farmer degree award Future Farmers Am., 1949, 1st prize La. pub. speaking contest La. Future Farmers, 1949, 50. Mem. La. Cotton Producers Assn., Nat. Cotton Council, Am. Brahman Breeders Assn., La. (past v.p.), Am. (finance com. 1962-63) cattlemen's assns., La. Farmer Elected Com. Assn. (v.p.), La. Brahmans Assns., La. Bankers Assn., Sigma Alpha Epsilon, Delta Zeta. Democrat. Methodist. Mason (32 degree, Shriner), Elk, Rotarian. Democrat. Methodist. Clubs: Culver (Ind.) Fathers Assn., Natchitoches Country. Home: Hickory Hill Natchitoches LA 71457 Office: PO Box 947 Natchitoches LA 71457

TAYLOR, HOWARD GREENWOOD, JR., motel co. exec.; b. Frederick, Md., Jan. 4, 1913; s. Howard Greenwood and Flora (Rippeon) T.; D.D.S., U. Md., 1934; m. Lorraine Virginia Watkins, Feb. 22, 1941; 1 dau., Tamara Olivia (Mrs. Richard Newman). Practice gen. dentistry, Frederick, 1934-42, Damascus, Md., 1946-69; pres. Ridge Ct., Inc., Largo, Fla., 1969—. Served to lt. comdr., Dental Corps, USNR, 1942-45. Mem. Am., Md. (past v.p.), Frederick (past pres.) dental assns., Gorgas Odontological Soc., Psi Omega, Omicron Kappa Upsilon. Lion. Home: 158 Ridge Rd NW Largo FL 33540 Office: Ridge Rd and 2d Av NW Largo FL 33540

TAYLOR, HOWARD JOSEPH, judge; b. New Orleans, Nov. 8, 1923; s. Robert Wesley and Esther (McGinn) T.; LL.B., Loyola U. New Orleans 1948; m. Carol Anna Fraering, Apr. 30, 1949; children—Howard J., Jr., Robert F., David P., Elizabeth A., Kenneth J. Admitted to La. bar, 1948, since practiced in New Orleans; with firm Taylor & Taylor, 1948—; asst. dist. atty. Orleans Parish, 1952-54; judge Traffic Ct. of New Orleans, 1954-60, dist. court Parish of Orleans, 1961-70, Ct. of Appeal, 4th Circuit La., 1970—. Pres. Francis Xavier Parish Bd. Edn., Metairie, La., 1967—; pres. Parish High Sch. of Religion, Metairie, 1962-63, 65-66. Served to 1st lt., USMCR, 1943-46; served to capt., USMCR, 1950-52. Decorated Purple Heart; named Outstanding Young Man of Year, New Orleans Jr. C. of C., 1954. Mem. Mil. Order of World Wars, Am. Legion, V.F.W., Am., La., New Orleans bar assns., Delta Theta Phi. K.C. Home: 116 Fairway Dr New Orleans LA 70124 Office: 421 Loyola Av New Orleans LA 70112

TAYLOR, HOWARD LEROY, ednl. adminstr.; b. Bruceton, Tenn., Jan. 24, 1924; s. Howard Green and Gladys (Bryant) T.; B.S., U. Tenn., 1950; M.A., Peabody Coll., 1951; m. Edwina Ruth Pierce, July 12, 1953; children—Howard Kimball, Randall Pierce, Janice Edwina. Sci. tchr., coach Rhea Central High Sch., Dayton, Tenn., 1951-58, prin., 1958-60; guidance counselor Soddy-Daisy Jr. High Sch., Daisy, Tenn., 1960-69; supt. schs., Rhea County, Tenn., 1969—. Committeeman Cherokee Area council Boy Scouts Am., 1958—; mem. adv. bd. Bryan Coll., 1971—. Served with AUS, 1943-46; ETO. Mem. N.E.A. (life), Am. Assn. Sch. Adminstrs., Tenn. Edn. Assn., U. Tenn. Alumni Assn., Sigma Epsilon Omicron. Republican. Methodist (mem. adminstrv. bd. 1954—). Rotarian. Club: Dayton Golf and Country. Home: PO Box 107 206 E 3d Av Dayton TN 37321 Office: Montague St Dayton TN 37321

TAYLOR, HOYT PATRICK, JR., state ofcl.; b. Wadesboro, N.C., Apr. 1, 1924; s. Hoyt Patrick and Inez (Wooten) T.; B.S., U. N.C., 1945, LL.B., 1948; m. Elizabeth Lockhart, Mar. 17, 1951; children—Elizabeth Ann, Hoyt Patrick III, Adam Lockhart. Admitted to N.C. bar; mem. N.C. Ho. of Reps., 1955-66, speaker, 1965-66; lt. gov. of N.C., 1969—. Served to 1st lt. USMCR, 1945-46, 51-52. Mem. Phi Gamma Delta, Delta Sigma Pi, Phi Delta Phi. Democrat. Methodist. Office: State Capitol Raleigh NC 27601*

TAYLOR, HUGH MOOR, judge; b. Tallahassee, Fla., Feb. 9, 1904; s. Walter Lloyd and Laura (Blake) T.; LL.B., Washington and Lee U., 1923; m. Martha R. Corry, Feb. 24, 1935; children—Mary T. (Mrs. W.R. Olive), Jefferson R. Admitted to Fla. bar, 1923; practice law, Quincy, Fla., 1923-45; judge Circuit Ct., Tallahassee, 1945—. Mem. Fla. Ho. of Reps., 1931; mem. Fla. Commn. on Constl. Govt., Fla. Constn. Adv. Commn., Fla. Constn. Revision Commn. Mem. Fla., Am. bar assns., Conf. State Trial Judges. Methodist. Club: Exchange. Home: 816 Forest Dr Quincy FL 32351 Office: County Court House Tallahassee FL 32302 also County Court House Quincy FL 32351

TAYLOR, IRVING HENRY, oil co. exec.; b. Detroit, Aug. 18, 1922; s. Irving Henry and Lavinia (Startzman) T.; student Swarthmore Coll., 1940-41; B.A., George Washington U., 1949; M.A., Columbia, 1951; m. Katherine Louise Needham, Feb. 6, 1943; 1 dau., Leslie Ann. Financial analyst Standard Oil Co. (N.J.), N.Y.C., 1952-55, mgr. Western Hemisphere and internat. finance div., 1966; financial adviser Internat. Petroleum Co., Ltd., Bogota, Colombia, 1956-57, treas., Lima, Peru, 1957-59, treas., Coral Gables, Fla., 1966—; asst. treas. Esso Internat., Inc., N.Y.C., 1959-63, mgr. fgn. sales, 1963-64, asst. gen. sales mgr., 1964-66; treas. Esso Inter-Am., Inc., 1966—. Bd. dirs. Dade County Jr. Achievement. Served with USAAF, 1942-46. Mem. Am. Econ. Assn., Artus, Coral Gables C. of C., Phi Beta Kappa, Pi Gamma Mu, Phi Sigma Kappa. Home: 12751 Old Cutler Rd Coral Gables FL 33156 Office: 396 Alhambra Circle Coral Gables FL 33134

TAYLOR, JAMES BRYANT, civil engr.; b. Lenoir, N.C., Oct. 27, 1943; s. Charles Bruce and Mabel Irene (Laney) T.; student N.C. State U., 1962-67; m. Mary Ann Heffner, June 6, 1965; 1 son, Andrew Bryant. Sr. designer atomic power div. Newport News Shipbuilding & Dry Dock Co. (Va.), 1967-69; mgr. pre-engineered homes div. Taylor Lumber Co., Lenoir, 1969-71; job supt. Lenoir Constrn. Co., 1971—. Tchr. constrn. apprentice program Caldwell Community Coll., Lenoir, evenings 1971—. Presbyn. Home: 104 Amhurst Park Lenoir NC 28645 Office: 1320 E Harper Av Lenoir NC 28645

TAYLOR, JAMES F., indsl. designer, 1939; B.S. in Mech. Engring., N.C. State U., 1962, B.S. in Product Design, 1967. Sr. designer Baermann Assos., Inc., Raleigh, N.C.; founder, pres., chmn. bd. Design Dimension, Inc., Raleigh. Recipient Student Merit award Indsl. Designer's Soc. Am., 1967, Ventures in Design award ALCOA. Address: 4217 Laurel Ridge Dr Raleigh NC 27609

TAYLOR, JAMES GODWIN, lawyer; b. Snow Hill, N.C., Feb. 16, 1934; s. Lowell Godwin and Nancy (Dawson) T.; B.S., Wake Forest Coll., 1955; LL.B., Duke, 1959; m. Martha Sue Moffitt, Nov. 12, 1966 (div. 1971). Admitted to N.C. bar, 1959, U.S. Ct. Mil. Appeals, 1962; intake officer Guilford County Domestic Relations Ct., Greensboro, N.C., 1959-60, asst. counsellor, clk., 1960; judge adv. USAF, Mather AFB, Cal., 1960-63, asst. staff judge adv., Sembach AFB, Germany 1963-64; practice law, Snow Hill, 1964; now counsel, research analyst com. on office atty. gen. Nat. Assn. Attys. Gen., Raleigh, N.C., 1969-70; spl. cons. Pres.'s com. Consumer Affairs, Washington, 1970-71; asst. pub. defender 12th Jud. Dist. N.C., 1970—. Lectr., Lenoir County Community Coll., Kinston, N.C., N.C. State U., 1970—. Vice chmn. young voters div. N.Y. County Citizens for Johnson, Humphrey, Kennedy, 1964; treas. Greene County Young Democrats, 1967—. Fund dr. chmn. Greene County A.R.C., 1965, Greene County Cancer Soc., 1967; town atty., Hookerton, N.C. Chmn. bd. Greene County Community Action Com.; bd. dirs. Greene Lamp, Inc., both under Office Econ. Opportunity, 1965-66. Mem. Am., N.C., bar assns. Baptist. Mason, Elk. Home: 2117 Forest Hills Dr Fayetteville NC 28303 Office: 120 Gillespie St Fayetteville NC 28301

TAYLOR, JAMES MARSHALL, assn. exec.; b. Port Arthur, Tex., May 28, 1936; s. Frank Marshall and Marie Delores (Schaffer) T.; B.B.S., Baylor U., 1959; m. Norma King, Nov. 18, 1967; 1 son, Dennis. Mgr., Cisco C. of C., 1960-61; asst. mgr. McAllen C. of C., 1961-62; asst. mgr. Orange C. of C., 1962-65; mgr. Waxahachie C. of C., 1965-70; indsl. mgr. Alice (Tex.) C. of C., 1970—. Sec. Alice Indsl. Found. Served with AUS, 1959-60. Mem. Tex. C. of C. Mgrs. (dir.), C. of C. Mgrs. and Secs. S.Tex. (sec.-treas.). Episcopalian. Rotarian, Kiwanian. Home: 1709 Olmos St Alice TX 78332 Office: 612 E Main St Alice TX 78332

TAYLOR, JAMES OLIVER, bank dir.; b. West Palm Beach, Fla., Sept. 7, 1927; s. Thomas DeWitt and Stella Cornelia (Kyzer) T.; student U. Fla., 1945, Stetson U., 1946-49; m. Lois Greenlund, June 6, 1950; children—Terrence, Timothy, Tina Marie. Owner Taylor's Grocery, Pierson, Fla., 1949-52; citrus and fern grower, Pierson, 1952—; dir. Fla. Bank at DeLand, 1968—. Justice of peace, Pierson, 1956—. Served with USNR, 1945-46. Mem. West Volusia C. of C. (dir. 1968-72). Lutheran. Lion. Home: PO Box 8 Pierson FL 32080 Office: Blake St Pierson FL 32080

TAYLOR, JAMES RODNEY, univ. adminstr.; b. Pensacola, Fla., Nov. 3, 1940; s. Herbert Jackson and Ruth (Stuart) T.; A.B., Samford U., 1962; B.D., Southeastern Bapt. Theol. Sem., 1965, Th.M., 1966; m. Catherine Patricia West, Dec. 26, 1960; children—Leigh Ann, Brian Rodney, Julie Patricia. Ordained to ministry So. Bapt. Ch., 1961; manuscript editor Bapt. Sunday Sch. Bd., Nashville, 1966-68; staff asst., field sec. Tenn. Med. Assn., Nashville, 1968-69; asso. dir. devel. Vanderbilt U., 1968-69; dir. devel. Va. Intermont Coll., Bristol, 1969-70; dir. devel. U. W.Fla., Pensacola, 1970—. Exec. sec. U. W. Fla. Found., 1970—. News sec. for congl. candidate, 1970—. Bd. dirs. Agape House, Inc., Pensacola Exchange. Mem. Pensacola C. of C., Fellowship Christian Athletes, Fla. High Sch. Activities Assn., Soc. Bibl. Lit., Am. Schs. Oriental Research. Republican. Editor: Young People's Life and Work Curriculum Materials, 1966-68. Contbr. to religious, hist. essays to various jours. Home: 5430 Primrose Dr Pensacola FL 32504

TAYLOR, JOHN ALLEN, geologist, engr.; b. Oklahoma City, Apr. 22, 1926; s. Ralph Staddan and Mary Ellen (Swift) T.; B.S., U. Okla., 1945, M.S., 1949; advt. bus. mgmt. Yale; m. Jo Ann Eaton, June 18, 1945; children—Jerry Alan, Douglas Lee, Kay Susan, Jacqueline Ann. Geologist, Shell Oil Co., LaJunta, Colo., 1946-47; instr. geology U. Okla., 1948-49; geologist Magnolia Petroleum Co., San Antonio, 1949-52, Houston, 1952, asst. exploitation geologist, Dallas, 1953-54, dist. geologist, Lake Charles, La., 1954-57, Mt. Vernon, Ill., 1957-59; dist. expln. supt. Mobil Oil Co., Oklahoma City, 1959-65; cons. geologist, petroleum engr., 1965—. Chmn. elect research com. Interstate Oil Compact Commn.; mem. task force for preparation efficiency study oil industry U.S. Sec. of Interior, 1964-65; founder Industry Adv. Council. Founder, U. Okla. Sch. Geology Found. Served to lt. (j.g.) USNR, 1943-46; PTO. Named Hon. Col., Gov. of Okla., 1962, Gov. of Ind., 1964. Mem. Mid Continent Oil and Gas Assn., Am. Assn. Petroleum Geologists (v.p. 1971-72), Am. Inst. Profl. Geologists (sec. pres. 1965-66, nat. exec. com. 1967), Soc. Petroleum Engrs., Soc. Expln. Geophysicists, U. Okla. Alumni Assn. (nat. pres. 1963-64, chmn. Oklahoma City alumni devel. fund 1965-66, dir. fund 1967), Geol. Soc. Am., S. La. (pres. 1956), Oklahoma City, Ardmore, Tulsa geol. socs., Oklahoma City C. of C. (dir. 1964-65, vice chmn. oil and gas com.), Oklahoma City Petroleum Club (dir. 1963-66, pres. 1966), Ind. Petroleum Assn. Am. (dir. 1972), Okla. Petroleum Assn. (v.p. 1969-71), Sigma Xi, Sigma Gamma Epsilon. Presbyn. (deacon, pres. men). Club: Oklahoma City Golf and Country. Contbr. articles to profl. jours. Home: 1607 Norwood Pl Oklahoma City OK 73120 Office: Liberty Tower Oklahoma City OK 73102

TAYLOR, JOHN EDWIN, JR., electronic mfr.; b. Charlottesville, Va., Dec. 16, 1934; s. John Edwin and Mildred (Garrett) T.; B.S., Randolph-Macon Coll., 1956; postgrad. law U. Va., 1956-57; m. Nancy Cecile Money, Aug. 17, 1957; children—John Edwin III, Cecil Garrett. Comptroller, Alderman's Studios, High Point, N.C., 1957-60; sec.-treas. Va. Panel Corp., Waynesboro, Va., 1960-64, pres., dir., 1964-71; v.p., gen. mgr. Airmark div. Sterling Electronics, Houston, 1971—. Mem. Data Processing Mgmt. Assn., I.E.E.E., Waynesboro C. of C., Phi Delta Theta. Methodist. Rotarian. Patentee in field. Office: Sterling Electronics Houston TX 77027

TAYLOR, JOSEPH RICHARD, educator, sculptor; b. Wilbur, Wash., Feb. 1, 1907; s. Moses Richard and Lula Adeline (Killman) T.; B.F.A., U. Wash., 1931, M.F.A., 1932; student Columbia, 1940; m. Elsie Rapier, Apr. 19, 1930. Faculty U. Okla., 1932—, prof. sculpture, 1941—. A. David Ross Boyd prof., 1963—; exhibitions include annual Northwest Art Exhbn., Seattle, 1931, 32, annual Midwest Art Exhibit, Kansas City, Mo., 1933, 35, 40, Pa. Acad., 1935, Corcoran Gallery, 1940, Metropolitan Mus., 1940, N.Y. World's Fair, 1939, also Chgo., Rochester, Oklahoma City, Tulsa, Lincoln (Neb.), Dallas, Ft. Worth, Houston, New Orleans and Albuquerque museums; monumental sculpture on Okla. U. campus at Norman, State Capital at Oklahoma City. Mem. Okla. Hall of Fame, Phi Beta Kappa, Delta Phi Delta. Home: 701 W Brooks St Norman OK 73069

TAYLOR, JOSEPH TALIAFERRO, III, physician; b. Charleston, S.C., July 24, 1937; s. Joseph Taliaferro and Eloise (Lanier) T.; B.S., Coll. Charleston, 1959; M.D. (fellow), Med. U. S.C., 1961; m. Susan Dwight Walker, July 11, 1959; children—Ellen Walker, Susan Sloan, Joseph Taliaferro. Intern, Med. U. S.C. Teaching Hosps., 1961-62; gen. practice medicine, Ridgeville, S.C., 1962-63, Summerville, S.C., 1963—; chief staff Dorchester County Hosp. Trustee, Summerville Acad., pres., 1968—. Served as capt. M.C., AUS, 1966-68. Decorated Bronze Star. Mem. Am., S.C. med. assns., Am. Acad. Family Practice, Dorchester County Med. Soc. (pres. 1969-71), Alpha Omega Alpha. Episcopalian (vestryman 1971—). Lion. Home: 108 Old Country Club Rd Summerville SC 29483 Office: 435 N Cedar St Summerville SC 29483

TAYLOR, JOSHUA CHARLES, educator, museum dir., art historian; b. Hillsboro, Ore., Aug. 22, 1917; s. James Edmond and Anna L.M. (Scott) T.; student Mus. Art Sch., Portland, Ore., 1935-39; B.A., Reed Coll., 1939, M.A., 1946; M.F.A., Princeton, 1949, Ph.D., 1956. Designer for theatre, 1936-41, for San Francisco Opera Ballet, 1936-37; tchr. theatre Reed Coll., 1939-41; tchr. history art Princeton, 1948-49; mem. faculty U. Chgo., 1949—, chmn. 1st yr. program humanities in coll., 1954-58, William Rainey Harper prof. humanities, also prof. history art. 1963—; dir. Nat. Collection Fine Arts, Smithsonian Instn., Washington, 1970—; lectr., U.S., on TV, 1953—; lectr. Inst. Interuniversitario, Argentina, 1962; spl. research 19th and 20th century painting and artistic theory Italy and U.S. Former mem. adv. com. 20th century art Art Inst. Chgo.; mem. faculty adv. com. Ency. Brit.; mem. adv. bd. Lillie P. Bliss Internat. Study Center Mus. Modern Art. Served to maj., inf., AUS, 1941-46; ETO. Mem. Coll. Art Assn. Am. (dir.), Am. Assn. Museum Dirs., Am. Assn. Museums, Royal Soc. Arts, Internat. Inst. Conservation Historic and Artistic Works, Phi Beta Kappa. Author: William Page, the American Titian, 1957; Learning to Look, 1957; Futurism, 1961; Graphic Works of Umberto Boccioni, 1961; Vedere prima di credere, 1970; also articles, revs. Home: 1250 31st St NW Washington DC 20007

TAYLOR, LEON MCCORD, ednl. adminstr.; b. Knoxville, Tenn., Dec. 15, 1916; s. William Henry and Era Irene (Kennedy) T.; B.A. cum laude, Trinity U., 1955; m. Annie Juanita Thompson, Feb. 1, 1941; children—James Allan, Thomas Stuart, Douglas Lee, Carolyn Sue, Joseph Michael, William Andrew. Bookkeeper, Consumer Ice & Coal Co., Port Arthur, Tex., 1935-37; announcer, continuity dir. sta. KFDM, Beaumont, Tex., 1937-41; dir. promotion KRNT Radio and Radio Theater, Des Moines, 1945-47; dir. pub. relations Trinity U., San Antonio, 1947—, v.p. univ. relations, 1969—, asso. prof. journalism, 1967—. Served with USAAF, 1941-45. Recipient Best Motion Picture Film award for higher ednl. instns. Am. Coll. Pub. Relations Assn., 1961. Mem. Pub. Relations Soc. Am. (chpt. pres. 1952), San Antonio C. of C., Sigma Delta Chi. Baptist. Home: 447 E Rosewood St San Antonio TX 78212

TAYLOR, LILLIAN ROSS MCCULLOCH (MRS. DAVID WYATT AIKEN TAYLOR), librarian; b. Elizabethtown, N.C., Mar. 29, 1928; d. Edgar F. and Jessie Lee (Sugg) McCulloch; A.B., Queens Coll., 1949; M.A., Presbyn. Sch. Christian Edn., Richmond, Va., 1951; M.A., Peabody Library Sch. of George Peabody Coll., 1963; Ednl. Specialist degree, 1970; m. David Wyatt Aiken Taylor, Aug. 25, 1951; children—Frances Bland, David W.A. Tchr. pub. schs., Richmond, Va., 1951-52, Harlingen, N.J., 1952-53; librarian Peabody Demonstration Sch. George Peabody Coll., Nashville, 1963-70, pres. faculty orgn., 1967-70; librarian Montgomery Bell Acad., Nashville, 1970—. Recipient Algernon Sydney Sullivan award, 1949. Mem. Am., Southeastern, Tenn. (edn. com.) library assns., Nashville Library Club (v.p. 1970—). Beta Phi Mu. Home: 4420 Milesdale Ct Nashville TN 37204 Office: 4005 Harding Rd Nashville TN 37205

TAYLOR, LOUIS HERMAN, educator; b. nr. Glasgow, Ky., Nov. 22, 1914; s. Philip Hershel and Lena Wallace (Tinsley) T.; A.B., Georgetown (Ky.) Coll., 1946; B.D., So. Bapt. Theol. Sem., 1951, Th.D., 1955; m. Lula Bicknell, Nov. 25, 1937; 1 dau., Linda Sue. Truck driver Hayes Grocery Co., Glasgow, 1931-36; salesman, Albany, Ky., 1936-40; salesman Waggener Grocery Co., Burkesville, Ky., 1940-43; prin. Woodford County (Ky.) Elementary Sch., 1946-48; ordained to ministry Bapt. Ch., 1943; pastor Bradfordsville (Ky.) Bapt. Ch., 1949-53, New Hope Bapt. Ch., 1953-55; prof. religion and philosophy Va. Intermont Coll., Bristol, Va., 1955—. Fellow archeology So. Bapt. Theol. Sem., 1954-55. Mem. Soc. Bibl. Lit. and Exegesis. Mason, Rotarian, Lion. Club: Civitan (Bristol). Author: The New Creation, 1958. Home: 12 Haverhill Rd Bristol VA 24201

TAYLOR, LUCILLE FARMER, govt. ofcl.; b. Richmond, Va.; d. Charles Elam and Agnes Susan (Fry) Farmer; certificate accounting, bus. administrn. Va. Mechanics Inst., 1942; m. Allen Lynwood Taylor, Nov. 3, 1928. Accountant, agt. U.S. Internal Revenue Service, Richmond, 1944-54, group supr. audit div., 1955-71, br. chief stblzn. div., 1971—. Mem. Am. Soc. Women Accountants (chpt. pres. 1954-56), Nat. Assn. Accountants (chpt. dir. 1963-65, sec. 1966-67, v.p. 1967-70; pres. 1970-71); Nat. Fedn. Fed. Employees (dir. 1947-49; v.p. 1950-51), Va. Soc. C.P.A.'s. Am. Women's Soc. C.P.A.'s Wesleyan Service Guild (pres. 1962-64; Richmond dist. chmn. 1968-70; Va. conf. sec. 1970-71, vice chmn. 1971—). Methodist (sec. bd. trustees 1959—; chmn. commn. finance and stewardship 1963-64; chmn. com. wills, legacies 1962-64). Club: Zonta (pres. 1963-64). Home: 5524 Westower Dr Richmond VA 23225 Office: 400 N 8th St Richmond VA 23225

TAYLOR, MARTHA SUE, educator; b. Asheville, N.C., Sept. 26, 1938; d. Richard F. and Elizabeth (Drummond) Taylor; B.S., Winthrop Coll., 1960; M.S., U. Tenn., 1963. Tchr. phys. edn. Greenwood (S.C.) Sch. Dist. No. 50, 1960-62; supr. elementary phys. edn. Knox County Sch. Dist., Knoxville, Tenn., 1962-63; instr. phys. edn. U. Tenn., Knoxville, 1963-65, Winthrop Coll., Rock Hill, S.C., 1965—. Head counselor, Camp Keystone, Brevard, N.C., 1967-69, head riding program, 1963-66. Mem. So. Assn. Phys. Edn. for Coll. Women (state newsletter reporter 1967-69), Nat. Assn. Phys. Edn. for Coll. Women, A.A.H.P.E.R., S.C. Assn. Coll. and Univ. Tchrs. Health, Phys. Edn. and Recreation (sec. 1970-71), Am. Camping Assn. (state treas. 1968-69), S.C. Assn. Health, Phys. Edn. and Recreation (v.p. recreation 1968, Phi Kappa Phi. Home: 15 Harrington Av Greenville SC 29607 Office: Winthrop College Rock Hill SC 29730

TAYLOR, MARVIN ELLIOTT, hosp. adminstr.; b. Greenville, S.C., Oct. 13, 1920; s. Robert Lafayette and Theodosia (McCall) T.; grad. George Washington U., 1950; m. Roberta Lou Owen, Nov. 26, 1954; children—Davis Hamilton, Jonathan Elliott, Gregory Franklin. Reporter, Greenville News, 1939-43; writer Dept. State, Washington, information officer U.S. embassy, Pusan, Korea, 1952-54; spl. asst. in edn. and cultural affairs officer U.S. embassy, Bonn, Germany, 1954-59; with USIA, Dept. State, Washington, 1959-62; consul U.S. embassy, Nairobi, Kenya, 1962-63; dir. pub. relations Greenville Hosp. System, 1963—. Chmn. pub. information Greenville County (S.C.) Found., 1968-72; mem. exec. com. S.C. Health and Sci. Fair, 1965—. Served with AUS, 1943-46; PTO. Mem. S.C. (pub. relations cons.), Am. (adv. com. pub. relations) hosp. assns., C. of C., Am. Soc. for Hosp. Pub. Relations, Advt. Club Greenville. Republican. Lutheran. Kiwanian. Home: 53 Woodvale Av Greenville SC 29605 Office: 100 Mallard St Greenville SC 29601

TAYLOR, MARVIN FRED, architect; b. Sesser, Ill., July 5, 1936; s. Clarence Oral and Geneverett Lea (Dorrough) T.; student U. Cin., 1954-56, Lee Coll., 1958; m. Loretta Sue Sanders, Aug. 15, 1959;

children— Mark Fred, Marlene Faye. Asso., Haglund & Venable Architects, Memphis, 1966-67; jr. partner Doggett/ Taylor Assos., 1967-68; design asso. George A. Thomason & Assos., 1968; individual practice architecture, planning, Memphis, 1968—. Mem. archtl. adv. com. Memphis-Shelby County, 1970—. Registered architect, 16 states, Nat. Council Archtl. Registration Bds. Mem. Memphis Jr. C. of C. (dir.), A.I.A., Tenn. Soc. Architects, Am. Soc. Registered Architects. Mem Ch. of God (mem. nat. archtl. bd. 1960-68, profl. advisor 1969—). Author: Plans for Churches, 1969, 71. Prin. works include women's Residence Hall Lee Coll., Cleveland, Tenn., U.S. Post Office Facility, Texarkana, Tex., Olive Branch, Miss., Starkville, Miss., Nursing Home, Forrest City, Ark., U.S. Post Office, Enterprise, Ala., Oak Forest Ch. of God, Memphis, Home for Children, Sevierville, Tenn. Home: 4640 Berta Rd Memphis TN 38109 Office: First Am Bank Bldg Memphis TN 38103

TAYLOR, MARY ANNE SMITH (MRS. RALPH EMERSON TAYLOR), civic worker; b. Port Gibson, Miss., Jan. 9, 1917; d. William Myles and Agnes (Pawlick) Smith; A.A., Copiah-Lincoln Jr. Coll., Miss., 1935; postgrad. Mich. State U., 1945; m. Ralph Emerson Taylor, July 15, 1934; 1 dau., Anne Lavin (Mrs. Christopher John Cannon). With Red Cross Motor Service, 1952-57; pres. Shoreacres Womens Club, 1958; v.p., program chmn. La Porte Bayshore Garden Club, 1959-60, pres., 1960-61, librarian, 1962-63, artistic com. chmn. and Flower Show chmn., 1963-64, publicity chmn., 1964-65; mem. Planning Commn., Shoreacres, 1960-64; chmn. Bd. Inspection, Shoreacres, 1962-64; councilman City of Shoreacres, Tex., 1964-68; mem. Gulf Coast Regional Planning Conf., 1966-68; mem. pub. relations com. Houston-Harris County Transp. Study, 1966—; geol. field asst., Western Australia, 1970-71. Recipient Five Year Service award Red Cross Motor Service, 1957. Mem. Houston Geol. Aux. (past com. chmn.), Womens Aux. Am. Inst. Mining and Metal. Engrs., Am. Civil Liberties Union, Tex. Conservation Council, Bay Area League Women Voters, Shoreline Art League. Democrat. Episcopalian. Clubs: Petroleum, Houston Yacht (past chmn. childrens sailing com.). Compiler, editor: Index to Geological Serials, 1965. Home: PO Drawer A LaPorte TX 77571

TAYLOR, MARY ANN HAMPTON (MRS. GERALD THOMAS TAYLOR), physician; b. Forest City, N.C., June 19, 1935; d. James Miles and Lavonia (Butler) Hampton; B.S. cum laude, Wake Forest Coll., 1956; M.D., 1960; m. Gerald Thomas Taylor, Dec. 20, 1962; children—Lisa Ann, Gregory Thomas, Mary Lynne. Intern Med. Coll. Va., Richmond, 1960-61; staff physician Wake Forest U. Student Health Service, Winston-Salem, N.C., 1961—, asst. dir., 1964—. Mem. A.M.A., N.C., Forsyth med. socs. Methodist. Club: Altrusa. Home: Green Meadows Route 8 Winston-Salem NC 27106 Office: Box 7386 Reynolds Sta Winston-Salem NC 27109

TAYLOR, MARY CURTIS SMITH (MRS. JOHN GORDON TAYLOR), musician; b. Shepherdsville, Ky., Jan. 9, 1937; d. Curtis Waldo and Hazel Dell (Trunnell) Smith; student U. Louisville, 1955; B.S. in Music, Murray State Coll., 1958, M.Ed., 1960; m. John Gordon Taylor, Aug. 16, 1958; children—John Gordon, Tiffany May, Whitney Adams. Soloist Louisville Orch., 1954, mem., 1963—; music educator, Benton, Ky., 1958-60, Jefferson County, 1960-64; concertmaster Louisville Civic Orch., 1963—; pvt. violin instrn.; mem. profl. strolling violinists; instr. music appreciation Alice Lloyd Coll., Pippa Passes, Ky. summer 1967; violinist Ky. Opera Assn., 1967—; 1st violinist Nashville Symphony, 1969—. Mem. Sigma Alpha Iota. Club: Murray (Ky.) Woman's. Home: 403 N 10th St Murray KY 42071

TAYLOR, MICHAEL ALAN, dentist; b. Tulsa, Jan. 26, 1940; s. William Franklin and Lovia Nina (Herrald) T.; student U. Okla., 1958-60; B.S., U. Tulsa, 1963; D.D.S., Baylor U., 1966; m. Gerri Helen Haines, Dec. 18, 1965; 1 dau., Teresa Michelle. Pvt. practice dentistry, Tulsa, 1966—. Mem. Am., Okla. (ho. of dels. 1971—) dental assns., Tulsa County Dental Soc., Tulsa County Endodontic Study Club, Phi Kappa Psi, Psi Omega. Club: Young Men's of Tulsa (v.p. 1970-71). Home: 2944 E 77th Pl Tulsa OK 74136 Office: 2865 E Skelly Dr Tulsa OK 74105

TAYLOR, OMER WILBERT, dentist; b. nr. Liberty, Ky., Aug. 6, 1914; s. James David and Minta Jane (Woodrum) T.; student U. Cin., 1934-38; D.D.S., U. Ind., 1950; m. Margaret Wilhelmina Johnson, Mar. 2, 1946; children—Susan Elaine, John Woodrum. With Am. Rolling Mill, Middletown, O., 1938-41; pvt. practice dentistry, Hendersonville, N.C., 1950—; mem. staff Pardee Meml. Hosp. Bd. dirs. Am. Cancer Soc. Served from pvt. to capt. AUS, World War II; ETO. Mem. Am. Dental Assn., N.C., Henderson County dental socs. Elk, Lion. Home: 111 Lake Dr Hendersonville NC 28739 Office: 558 Fleming St Hendersonville NC 28739

TAYLOR, ORACE CLEVELAND, ednl. adminstr.; b. Stanton, Tex., Jan. 4, 1932; s. L.O. and Dorothy I. (Anderson) T.; B.S., Tex. Wesleyan Coll., 1954, M.E., 1959; Ed.D., N. Tex. State U., 1971; m. Wilma R. Harper, June 5, 1953; 1 dau., Sherri D. Tchr., Odessa (Tex.) Pub. Sch., 1960-61, Little Lake (Cal.) Pub. Sch., 1961-62; high sch. prin. Shelby (Mich.) Pub. Sch., 1962-64; asst. supt. Oscoda (Mich.) Area Sch., 1964-65; supt. Grapevine (Tex.) Pub. Sch., 1965—. Served with AUS, 1954-56. Mem. N.E.A., Am., Tex. assns. sch. adminstrs., Tex. State Tchrs. Assn., C. of C. (dir.), Phi Delta Kappa. Rotarian. Home: 312 Azalea Dr Grapevine TX 76051 Office: 405 Austin St Grapevine TX 76051

TAYLOR, ORLANDO LEROY, educator; b. Chattanooga, Aug. 9, 1936; s. LeRoy and Carrie (Sanders) T.; B.S., Hampton Inst., 1957; postgrad. Denison U., 1966; M.A., Ind. U., 1960; Ph.D., U. Mich., 1966; m. Loretta Clements, June 6, 1957; children—Orlando LeRoy, Ingrid. Speech and hearing therapist Fort Wayne (Ind.) State Sch., 1957-58; dir. speech and hearing dept., 1960-62; clinician speech and hearing clinic Ind. U., Bloomington, 1958-59, asst. prof., dept. speech, 1965-69; instr. dept. speech U. Mich., 1965; cons. Center for Applied Linguistics, Washington, 1968-69, U.S. Office Edn., 1969; asso. dir. lang. in edn. program Center for Applied Linguistics, Washington, 1969-71. Adj. asso. prof. U. Pitts., 1969, vis. prof. Howard U., Washington, 1969-70; prof. communication scis. Federal City Coll., Washington, 1970—, also dir. Inst. Urban Lang. Research. Mem. Bloomington Fair Housing Com., 1966-68. Recipient scholarships Ind. Div. Mental Health, 1958-59, Ind. Dept. Health, 1958, John Hay Whitney Found., fellow 1962-63, Am. Speech and Hearing Assn., fellow 1963, USPHS fellow, 1963-65. Fellow Am. Speech and Hearing Assn.; mem. Am. Psychol. Assn., Linguistics Soc. Am., Am. Civil Liberties Union, N.A.A.C.P. (pres. Ind. U. chpt. 1959-60, Fort Wayne 1961-62), Fort Wayne Jr. C. of C., Am. Assn. U. Profs., Kappa Alpha Psi, Phi Kappa Phi, Psi Chi. Home: 11705 East West Hwy Silver Spring MD 20910 Office: 1717 Massachusetts Av NW Washington DC 20036

TAYLOR, PAUL PEAK, dentist, educator; b. Childress, Tex., May 11, 1921; s. Noah Peak and Lois (Vinson) T.; student W. Tex. State Coll., 1940; D.D.S., Baylor U., 1944, M.S., U. Mich., 1951; m. LaVerne Countryman, Aug. 11, 1945; children—Peri Ann, Scott Vinson. Pvt. practice pedodontics, Dallas, 1952-69; prof., chmn. grad. pedodontics, Baylor U. Coll. Dentistry, 1960-69, prof., chmn. pedodontic dept., 1969—; dir. dentistry Childrens Med. Center, Dallas, 1960—. Served to capt. AUS, 1951-53. Recipient Mott Found. fellowship. Diplomate Am. Bd. Pedodontists. Fellow Am. Coll. Dentists; mem. Am. Soc. Dentistry for Children (pres. Tex. unit 1946-47), S.W. Soc. Pedodontists, Am. Dallas County dental assns., Am. Acad. Pedodontics, Am. Assn. Sheriff Posses and Riding Clubs (regional v.p. 1969-70), Dallas Execs. Assn. (pres. 1970—). Mason (Shriner). Episcopalian. Contbr. articles to dental jours. Home: 2615 Briarcove Plano TX 75074 Office: 1935 Amelia St Dallas TX 75235

TAYLOR, PRENTISS, artist; b. Washington, Dec. 13, 1907; s. John Eastlack and Beatrice (Hottel) T.; student Art Students League; pupil Charles W. Hawthorne. Scenic artist, 1926—; lithograph, watercolor artist, 1931—; painter in oils, 1943—; art therapist, psychotherapy dept. St. Elizabeths Hosp., 1943-54, Washington; professorial lectr. Am. U.; art therapist Chestnut Lodge, Rockville, Md. Represented Library of Congress, Phillips Collection, N.Y. Mus. Modern Art, Wadsworth Atheneum (Hartord, Conn.), Addison Gallery (Andover, Mass.), Whitney Mus. Am. Art, Balt. Mus. Art, Seattle Art Mus., N.Y. Pub. Library, Boston Mus. Fine Arts, Phila. Mus., Valentine Mus. (Richmond), Va. Mus. Fine Arts, Yale U. Gallery, Gibbes Gallery, Charleston, S.C., Smithsonian Instn., Washington, Boston Pub. Library, several univs. Exhibited painting in U.S., 1946-49, Carnegie Inst., Corcoran Biennial, 1949-51; A.N.A. lectr. Founder, illustrator Winter Wheat Press; founder Golden Stair Press with Langston Hughes. Recipient Am. Artists Group lithograph prize, 1953; Cannon graphic prize N.A.D., 1954; purchase award lithography, nat. exhbn. DePauw U., 1959. Mem. Artists Guild Washington, Soc. Am. Graphic Artists, Soc. Washington Printmakers, Print Club of Albany, Boston Printmakers. Home: J-718 Arlington Towers Arlington VA 22209

TAYLOR, RALPH ORIEN, JR., developer, investor; b. Kansas City, Mo., Jan. 6, 1919; s. Ralph Orien and Genevieve (Sturgeon) T.; student U. Kansas City, 1936-38; B.S., U. Mo., 1940; m. Betty Boswell, Dec. 7, 1940 (dec. 1959); children—Bradley, Nancy. Partner Sturgeon & Taylor, 1940-42; owner Sturgeon & Taylor, Inc., Kansas City, Mo., 1942—, chmn. bd., 1959—; pres. Sturgeon & Taylor Investment Co., Inc., 1949—, chmn. bd., 1959—; pres. Sturgeon &Taylor Devel. Co., 1950—, chmn. bd., 1959—; pres. Sturgeon-Taylor Realty Co., Inc., 1955—; pres., chmn. bd. Park Estates, Inc., Tiger Constn. Co., Inc., Charm Homes, Inc., Bengal Homes, Inc., Westbrooke Hotels, Inc., Candelight Sq. Devel. Co.; dir. Patrons State Bank & Trust, Olathe, Kan. Mem. adv. council U. Mo. Sch. Forestry. Served as lt. comdr. USNR, World War II. Recipient Bronze Star Medal. Mem. Home Builders Assn. Greater Kansas City (dir., pres.), Johnson County (Kan.), Kansas City real estate bds., Nat. Assn. Home Builders (life dir.), Phi Delta Theta. Clubs: Kansas City, Indian Hills Country; Lauderdale Yacht, Ft. Lauderdale; Crown Colony (Chub Cay, Berry Islands Bahamas); Ocean Reef (Key Largo, Fla.). Home: 9162 Riggs Lane Overland Park KS 66207 Office: 6909 Nall Av Prairie Village KS 66208

TAYLOR, RAY JEFFERSON, mag. pub.; b. Waltersburg, Pa., Mar. 30, 1918; s. Emmanuel Ray and Bessie (Newcomer) T.; student U. Pitts., 1954-55, Bus. Tng. Coll., Pitts., 1949; m. Georgia Muriel Paris, July 4, 1940; children—Judith (Mrs. Richard Joseph Massabny), Terri Lee, Thomas Jefferson. Vice pres., gen. mgr. Beaver County Times (Pa.), 1953-59; gen. mgr. No. Va. Sun, Arlington, 1960-63; editor, gen. mgr. Washington World mag., 1963-66; editor, gen. mgr., dir. pub. relations Nat. Grange Mag., Washington, 1966-68; editor, pub., owner Rural Am. mag., Arlington, 1968—; v.p. marketing Rural Am. Marketing Corp., Washington, 1970-71; v.p., dir. Publs., Inc., Arlington, 1966—; editorial, pub. cons. Machinery Dealers Nat. Assn., Washington, 1969-71; adminstr. United Grange States Ins. Trust, 1971—; gen. mgr. Contractors Equipment Locator System, 1972—. Sec. treas. Community Leader Tng. Assos., Washington, 1968—; mem. Arlington Com. 100, 1962—. Bd. dirs. Community Leader Inst., Washington. Served with USAAF, 1944-45. Recipient various awards for editorial excellence, Pa., Va. press assns., 1957-63. Mem. Nat. Press Club, Advt. Club Met. Washington, Nat. Grange. Author: (with Richard L. Henschel) A Primer: U.S. Government (5 vols.), 1965-66, also editor. Home: 6207 Lee Hwy Arlington VA 22205 Office: 6207 Lee Hwy PO Box 445 Arlington VA 22210

TAYLOR, RAYMOND MASON, lawyer, librarian; b. Washington, N.C., Jan. 1, 1933; s. Thaddeus Raymond and Mary Ada (Mason) T.; A.B. in Polit. Sci., U. N.C. at Chapel Hill, 1955, J.D., 1960; m. Evelyn Rachel High, Apr. 3, 1965; 1 dau., Elizabeth Lee. Staff reporter Washington Daily News., summers 1952, 54; adminstrv. asst. Civil Def. Orgn., Winston-Salem and Forsyth County, N.C., 1955; adminstrv. intern City Winston-Salem, summer 1958; admitted to N.C. bar, 1960; U.S. Supreme Ct. bar, 1970; research asst. to justice Supreme Ct. N.C., 1960-61; asso. firm Gardner, Connor & Lee, Wilson, N.C., 1961-64; adj. instr., then adj. prof. bus. law Atlantic Christian Coll., Wilson, 1962-64; marshal, librarian Supreme Ct. N.C., 1964—; spl. lectr., econs. N.C. State U., 1967—; dir. N.C. Law Research Facilities Study, 1970. Mem. library services com. Am. Bar Found., 1969—. Sec. Southeastern Area council Am. Jr. Red Cross, 1949-50, study visitor to Europe, 1950; chmn. cultural affairs com. Wilson (N.C.) Jr. C. of C., 1963-64; N.C. rep. civil def. unit Nat. Def. Exec. Res., 1967-70. Democratic precinct chmn. Beaufort County, N.C., 1954-57; parliamentarian Wilson County Dem. Exec. Com., 1962-64; mem. Beaufort County Dem. Exec. Com., 1954-57, N.C. 2d Solicitorial Dist. Dem. Exec. Com., 1962-64. Served with AUS, 1955-57. Recipient awards editorial, news and feature writing U. N.C. Press Club, 1955, award hist. feature writing N.C. Soc. County and Local Historians, 1955, named Tar Heel of the Week, 1971. Mem. Am. (mem. spl. com. law book pub. practices 1970-72), N.C., Wake County bar assns., N.C. State Bar (chmn. spl. com. law book publs. and rev. bd 1971), Am. Assn. Law Libraries (certified law librarian, 1968—; co-chmn. com. relations with pubs. and dealers 1970—), Scribes, Order Golden Fleece (pres. 1958-59), Pi Sigma Alpha, Phi Delta Phi. Presbyn. Club: N.C. State Faculty (Raleigh). Author: History of the North Carolina Supreme Court Library, 1969; also articles. Asst. editor Tar Heel Barrister, 1958-59; mem. student bd. editors N.C. Law Rev., 1960. Home: 3073 Granville Dr Raleigh NC 27609 Office: 500 Justice Bldg PO Box 1841 Raleigh NC 27602

TAYLOR, RICHARD POWELL, lawyer; b. Phila., Sept. 13, 1928; s. Earl Howard and Helen (Martin) T.; student Cornell U., 1946-48; B.A., U. Va., 1950, J.D., 1952; m. Barbara Jo Anne Harris, Dec. 19, 1959; 1 son, Douglas Howard Martin. Admitted to Va. bar, 1952, D.C. bar, 1956; law clk. Judge Armistead M. Dobie, U.S. Ct. Appeals 4th Circuit, 1952-53, practiced in Washington, 1956—; asso. firm Steptoe and Johnson, 1956-61; partner, 1962—; sec., corp. counsel Slick Corp., 1963-69, asst. sec., 1969-72, dir., 1965-68; sec., corp. counsel Slick Indsl. Co., 1963—; sec., dir. Slick Indsl. Co. Can. Ltd., 1966-72; gen. counsel Corsair Air Cargo System, Inc., 1969—, sec., 1969-72, dir., 1972—. Served to lt. (j.g.) Air Intelligence, USNR, 1953-56. Mem. Am., Fed., Fed. Power, D.C., Va. bar assns., Order of Coif, Raven Soc., Chi Phi, Delta Theta Phi. Republican. Episcopalian (vestryman). Clubs: International, Capitol Hill, Congressional Country. Home: 6007 Corewood Lane Sumner Washington DC 20016 Office: 1250 Connecticut Av NW Washington DC 20036

TAYLOR, ROBERT ELLIOTT, psychologist; b. Barre, Vt., May 6, 1931; s. Harold Elliott and Hazel (Locke) T.; B.A., U. Tenn., 1956, M.A., 1957, Ph.D., 1961; m. A. Catharine Parisi, Dec. 28, 1950; children—Jennifer Lyn, Johnathan Elliott. Prof., Radford (Va.) Coll., 1960-62; asst. prof. U. Ga., Athens, 1962-67; psychologist Avalon Psychiat. Clinic, Athens, 1966-68; individual practice clin. psychology, Macon, Ga., 1968—; adj. prof. Mercer U., Macon, 1968—; cons. Macon Hosp., 1969—. Served with USMCR, 1952-54. Diplomate Am. Bd. Profl. Psychology. Mem. C. of C., Ga. Human Relations Council, Am. Acad. Psychotherapists, Am., So., Ga. psychol. assns., Am. Civil Liberties Union. Contbr. to profl. jours. Home: 4518 Beechwood Dr S Macon GA 31204 Office: Live Oaks 2437 Vineville Av Macon GA 31204

TAYLOR, ROBERT L., judge; b. Embreeville, Tenn., Dec. 20, 1899; s. Alfred Alexander and Florence Jane (Anderson) T.; Ph.B., Milligan Coll., 1921; student Vanderbilt Law Sch., 1922-23; LL.B., Yale, 1924; m. Florence Fairfax McCain, May 27, 1933; children—Ann, Robert. Admitted to Tenn. bar, 1923; practiced law, Johnson City, 1924-49; U.S. judge Eastern Dist. of Tenn., 1949—. Mem. Tenn. State, Am., Fed. bar assns., Am. Judicature Soc., Corby Ct., Sigma Alpha Epsilon, Phi Delta Phi. Mem. Christian Ch. Home: 3567 Talahi Dr Knoxville TN 37919 Office: Federal Bldg Knoxville TN 37902

TAYLOR, ROBERT TIECHE, entomologist; b. San Diego, June 29, 1932; s. Clifford Harris and Hazel Marie (Gobar) T.; B.S., Okla. State U., 1954, M.S., 1957, Ph.D., 1960; m. Ellen Clare McAulay, Apr. 11, 1964; children—Suzanne Clare, Kathryn Marie. Engaged in vector control Tulsa City-County Health Dept., summers 1956, 57, 60; engaged in malaria project Pan Am., Health Orgn., Bogota, Colombia, 1960-61; with U.S. Navy Pub. Works, Washington, 1961-63; with malaria project AID, State Dept., Port-au-Prince, Haiti, 1963-65; research entomologist USPHS, Savannah, Ga., 1965—. Served with Med. Service Corps, AUS, 1954-56. Mem. Entomol. Soc. Am., Am. Mosquito Control Assn., Am. Soc. Tropical Medicine and Hygiene, Royal Soc. Tropical Medicine and Hygiene. Contbr. articles to profl. jours. Home: 6 Glen Eden Ct Savannah GA 31406 Office: Box 2167 Savannah GA 31402

TAYLOR, RONALD WAITMAN, petroleum engr.; b. Ashland, Ky., Apr. 11, 1922; s. Henry Martin and Bessie (Warman) T.; B.S. in Petroleum Engring., U. Tex., 1947; m. Jessie Elsie Meyers, June 1, 1947; children— Randolph W., Joanna. Petroleum engr. Gulf Oil Corp., Crane, Tex., 1947-49; gas engr. Warren Petroleum Co., Tulsa, 1949-50; petroleum engr. Sinclair Oil & Gas Co., Enid, Okla., 1951-68, U.S. Geol. Survey, New Orleans, 1968-71, head gas processing group, 1971—. Served with USAAF, 1944-46; CBI. Registered profl. engr., Okla. Mem. Soc. Petroleum Engrs. Methodist (past mem. bd. stewards, charge lay leader 1957-58, ch. sch. supt.). Mason. Home: 400 Heritage Av Gretna LA 70053 Office: 3301 N Causeway Blvd Metairie LA 70002

TAYLOR, ROY ARTHUR, congressman; b. Vader, Wash., Jan. 31, 1910; s. Arthur A. and Lola (Morgan) T.; A.B., Maryville (Tenn.) Coll., 1931; law license Asheville (N.C.) U., 1936; m. Evelyn Reeves, May 8, 1932; children—Alan F., Toni R. (Mrs. John F. Robinson). Admitted to N.C. bar, 1936, practiced in Asheville and Black Mountain, 1936-60; mem. N.C. Legislature from Buncombe County, 1947-49, 51-53; atty. Buncombe County, 1949-60; mem. 86th-87th Congresses 12th Dist. N.C., mem. 88th-92d Congresses 11th dist. N.C.; mem. Sci. and Astronautics Com., House Fgn. Affairs Com.; chmn. nat. parks and recreation subcom. House Com. Interior and Insular Affairs. Served to lt. (s.g.) USNR, 1943-46. Baptist (deacon). Lion (dist. gov. 1951-52). Home: 110 Connally St Black Mountain NC 28711 Office: House Office Bldg Washington DC 20515

TAYLOR, RUTH E. PETERSON (MRS. CLOYD VERON TAYLOR), home economist; b. Olivia, Tex., Feb. 23, 1923; d. Charley Emil and Ellen (Cavallin) Peterson; B.S., N. Tex. State U., 1944; M.S. U. Md., 1967; m. Cloyd Veron Taylor, Aug. 22, 1945; children—Mary Elizabeth, Cloydia Opal, Cloyd Veron. Tchr. home econs. high sch., Arlington County, Va., 1962-64; mgmt. tng. Marriott Hot Shoppes, Washington, 1965-66; program asst. Dairy Council Met. Washington, 1967—; tech. assistance specialist Volt Information Scis., Inc., Washington, 1969—. Leader, Girl Scouts, Frankfurt, Germany, 1957-59, Arlington County, Va., 1959-60. Mem. Am. Home Econs. Assn., D.C. Dietetic Assn. (chmn. pub. relations 1969-70), Home Economists in Bus., D.C. Pub. Health Assn., Phi Delta Gamma. Home: 2631 N Kenmore St Arlington VA 22207 Office: 1511 K St NW Washington DC 20005

TAYLOR, THEODORE WALTER, govt. ofcl.; b. Berkeley, Cal., Dec. 22, 1913; s. Walter Penn and Mary (Fairchild) T.; B.A., U. Ariz., 1935; M.A., Syracuse U., 1938; intern Nat. Inst. Pub. Affairs, 1936-37; Ph.D., Harvard, 1960; m. Jean Esther Shippey, Sept. 6, 1941; children—Terry Jean (Mrs. Jack H. Schwartz), Lynn (Mrs. Virgil K. Nelson), Travis Theodore, Christine Esther (Mrs. Nicholas Van Brunt). Adminstrv. officer Rural Electrification Adminstrn., 1936-40; adminstrv. asst. to dir. extension service Dept. Agr., 1940-42; exec. officer Office Territories and Island Possessions, Interior Dept., 1946-50, chief br. mgmt. planning, Bur. Indian Affairs, 1950-56, dep. commr. Bur., 1966-70, asst. to commr., 1970—; Fed. Exec. fellow Brookings Instn., 1970-71 moblzn. officer, def. electric power Office Asst. Sec. Water and Power, Interior Dept., 1956-59; asst. to sec. Smithsonian Instn., 1959-66; vis. prof. pub. adminstrn. U. So. Cal., summer 1954; guest lectr. George Washington U., Am. U.; mem. critical issues and decisions com. Dept. Agr. Grad. Sch., 1964—. Chmn. Arlington County Sch. Bd., 1968; campaign chmn. Arlingtonians Better County, 1958, 62-64, vice chmn., 1959; mem. adv. com. youth govs. conf. YMCA, 1966—, chmn., 1968; pres. Arlington County Council P.T.A.'s, 1956, bd. mgrs., citizenship chmn. Va. Congress. 1961-63. Served to lt. comdr. USNR, 1942-46. Mem. Am. Soc. Pub. Adminstrn., Am. Polit. Sci. Assn. Democrat. Unitarian (chmn. trustees 1963). Home: 706 N Frederick St Arlington VA 22203 Office: 1951 Constitution Av NW Washington DC 20242

TAYLOR, THOMAS KAUFFMAN, airline exec.; b. Manilla, P.I, (parents U.S. citizens), Dec. 2, 1915; s. Reuben Chapman and Katherine (Kauffman) T.; A.B., Amherst Coll., 1937; LL.B., Washington U., 1940; m. Jane Woods Butler, Apr. 8, 1942; children—Thomas Kauffman, Katherine Stuart, Jennifer Woods. Admitted to Mo. bar, 1940; asso. Fordyce, White, Mayne, Williams & Hartman, St. Louis, 1940-41; joined Trans World Airlines, Washington, 1946, v.p., 1951—, spl. asst. to pres., 1959-60, v.p. govt. affairs, 1960—. Served as lt. col., squadron comdr., Heavy Bombardment Group, USAAF, 1941-46; mil. air attache U.S. Embassy, Prague, 1945-46. Decorated D.F.C., Air Medal, 10 oak leaf clusters. Mem. Psi Upsilon. Clubs: Metropolitan, Chevy Chase, Burning Tree (Washington). Home: 5800 Bent Branch Rd Washington DC 20016 Office: Trans World Airlines 1000 16th St NW Washington DC 20036

TAYLOR, WILLIAM HALL, ednl. adminstr.; b. Miami, Fla., Sept. 16, 1937; s. William Edwin and Frances Hope (Melsom) T.; B.Music Edn., Fla. State U., 1958, M.S., 1964; edn. specialist Ind. U., 1971; m. Constance Rita Schiavoni, Sept. 6, 1970; 1 dau., Katherine Frances. Tchr., Dade County (Fla.) Schs., 1958-59, Mentor (O.) Schs.,

1959-60; media specialist Dade County (Fla.) Schs., Miami, 1961—. Mem. Assn. for Ednl. Communications and Tech., Phi Mu Alpha Sinfonia, Kappa Kappa Psi. Lutheran. Home: 9840 N Kendall Dr Miami FL 33156 Office: 10655 SW 97th Av Miami FL 33156

TAYLOR, WILLIAM L., dir. U.S. Commn. on Civil Rights. Office: US Commn Civil Rights 1121 Vermont Av NW Washington DC 20427*

TAYLOR, WILLIAM MCLEAN, assn. exec.; b. nr. Toccoa, Ga., May 27, 1928; s. Richard McLean and Mayme (Smith) T.; student U. Ga., 1960-62; m. Virginia Ann Robertson, Oct. 19, 1963; 1 son, Kevin McLean. Tour mgr. promotion dept. Louisville Courier Jour. & Times, 1946-52; editorial dir. Wing Publs., Inc., Columbia, S.C., 1964-68; pub. relations, publicity mgr. Charlotte (N.C.) C. of C., 1968—. Served with AUS, 1950-52. Mem. Charlotte Pub. Relations Soc., Kappa Alpha. Contbr. articles to profl. publs. Home: 4725 Woodlark Lane Charlotte NC 28211 Office: 222 S Church St Charlotte NC 28211

TAYLOR, WILLIAM REED, JR., textile co. exec.; b. Cleve., Jan. 29, 1918; s. William Reed and Katherine M. (Kelley) T.; B.S., Mass. Inst. Tech., 1940; m. Elizabeth M. Bricker, Dec. 28, 1940 (dec. Aug. 1969); 3 children; m. 2d, Mary Cecilia Leary, Dec. 21, 1969; 4 adopted children. Student engr. Chrysler Corp., Highland Park, Mich., 1940-41; project engr. Perfection Stove Co., Cleve., 1946-48; with Universal Wire Spring Co., Bedford, O., 1948-61, quality control mgr., 1950-53, supt., 1953-57, mgr. main plant, 1957-61; pres., chief engr. Geometric Spring Co., Cleve., 1961-66; prodn. control and personnel mgr. Jackson Products Co., Tampa, Fla., 1966-67, pres., 1968-71; pres. Gallagher Textile Mills, Inc., Tarpon Springs, Fla., 1971—. Served with AUS, 1941-46. Presbyn. Club: Carrollwood Country (Tampa). Patentee spring mfg. machinery. Home: 10702 Carroll Lake Dr Tampa FL 33618 Office: 425 E Spruce St Tarpon Springs FL 33589

TAYLOR, WILLIAM REGINALD, JR., feed co. exec.; b. Elkins, W.Va., Aug. 17, 1930; s. William Reginald and Melissia Lorene (Moore) T.; student Tex. Tech. U., Lubbock, 1949; m. Molly Margaret Wegenhoft, Aug. 4, 1950; children—Melissia Kay, Terry Lyn, William Reginald III. Self-employed cattle order buyer, speculator, feeder, Houston, 1950-61; cattle feeder, co-owner Sealy Feed Yard (Tex.), 1961-70, cattle feeder, co-mgr. Sealy Feed Yard, Inc., 1970—; dir. Citizens State Bank, Sealy. pres. Sealy Beef Feeders, Inc., 1970—. Committeeman, Houston Livestock Show, since 1970—. Chmn., Tax Equalization Bd., 1970-71; dep. sheriff Austin County, 1968—; mem. speakers adv. com. Tex. Ho. of Reps., 1970—. Bd. dirs. Sealy Med. Center. Mem. Sealy C. of C., Future Farmers Am. (hon. mem. Sealy chpt.). Stephen F. Austin Golf Assn. Democrat. Methodist. Home: 103 Briar Circle Sealy TX 77474 Office: Box 668 Sealy TX 77474

TAYLOR, WINSTON HOWARTH, ch. ofcl.; b. Brunswick, Neb., Oct. 24, 1921; s. Milo Elmer and Jessie May (Howarth) T.; student Willamette U., 1938-43; B.B.A., Tulane U., 1947; m. Betty Frances Terroy, Sept. 9, 1946; children—Alan W., Hope C., Brian D., Meredith E., Graham A. Reporter, news editor Ore. Statesman, Salem, 1939-43, 47-53; dir. pub. relations and promotion San Francisco Area, Methodist Ch., 1953-60; dir. Washington Office, Commn. on Pub. Relations and United Meth. Information, 1960—; lectr. pub. relations Am. U., 1966-67, instr. journalism U. Md., 1971-72. Served with AUS, 1943-46; ETO. Mem. Religious Pub. Relations Council (past nat. pres.). Club: Nat. Press. Home: 1014 Woodside Pkwy Silver Spring MD 20910 Office: 100 Maryland Av NE Washington DC 20002

TAZEWELL, CALVERT WALKE, ret. air force officer, author, historian; b. Wilmington, Del., Apr. 13, 1917; s. Calvert W. and Sophie (Goode) Tazewell; student Air Corps Tech. Sch., 1940, Air Tactical Sch., 1948, Sophia U., Tokyo, 1951, Air Command and Staff Sch., USAF Air. U., 1952, Ind. U., 1956; m. Beverly Mae LaCour, Jan. 14, 1943 (div. Apr. 1959); children—Lyn Diane, Patricia Marie, Beverly Ann; m. 2d, Belle Gordon, July 7, 1959 (div.); 1 son, William Bradford. Pvt., Va. N.G., 1934-35; radio technician, San Antonio, 1936-37; pvt., USAC, 1937, m/sgt. weather observer and forecaster, 1941; commd. 2d lt., U.S. A.A.F. (by direct appointment while overseas), 1942, advanced through grades to lt. col.; Airways and Air Communications Service; comml., multi-engine pilot; as communications specialist on U.S.A.F. meteorol. flight, flew over North Pole, 1947; during World War II developed and supervised for USAAF pioneer worldwide weather communications system, which principles and techniques have been accepted by World Meteorol. Orgn. and Internat. Civil Aviation Orgn.; apptd. officer Regular Army, 1947; transferred to Air Force, 1948; comdr. 1951st AAGS Squadron, Nagoya, Japan, 1950-51; dep. dir. plans and requirements Hdqrs. 1808th AACS Wing, Tokyo, Japan, 1951-52; comdr. 1300th Student Squadron, Great Falls, Mont., 1953-54; 818th AC & W Squadron, Randolph, Tex., 1955-56, Kangnung Air Base, Korea, 1957, Takaoyama Air. Sta., Japan, 1958; dir. communications-electronics 314th Air div. Oson, Korea, 1956-57. Duluth Air Def. Sector, 1958-59; ret., 1959; civil def. coordinator Dade County, Fla., 1961; chmn. Met. Dade County Pub. Library Adv. Bd., 1963-64; instn N.Y.U., 1962-63, Old Dominion U., 1964-65. Trustee Assn. for Preservation Va. Antiquities, 1967-69. Decorated Bronze Star. Mem. Norfolk (1st pres., founder), Va. hist. socs., Common Cause, Am. Civil Liberties Union, UN Assn., Air Force Assn. Am. Radio Relay League, World Tapes for Edn., Am. Assn. State and Local History, Va. History Fedn. (chmn. organizing com., 1st pres. 1967-69), Soc. Archtl. Historians, Newcomen Soc. Amateur radio sta. operator, 1936—. Address: 520 Oak Grove Rd Norfolk VA 23505

TEACHEY, GUY BURTON, sup. schs.; b. Rosehill, N.C., June 8, 1908; s. John Burt and Rosa May (Best) T.; A.A., Wingate Jr. Coll., 1926; A.B., U. N.C., Chapel Hill, 1936, A.M., 1945; m. Anna Marie Cashwell, June 26, 1933; children—Anna Marie, Guy Philip. Tchr., athletics coach, Sampson County Schs., Clinton, N.C., 1926-34, prin., 1935-42; prin. high schs., Clinton and Asheboro, N.C., 1943-47; supt. Asheboro (N.C.) City Schs., 1947—. Trustee Ferree Ednl. and Welfare Fund, 1957—, pres. 1964—. Recipient Citizen of the Year award, Civitan Club, Asheboro, 1963. Mem. N.E.A., N.C. Assn. Educators, Am. Assn. Sch. Adminstrs., Asheboro C. of C. (past dir.), Phi Beta Kappa, Phi Delta Kappa. Democrat. Baptist. Home: 613 South Park St Asheboro NC 27203 Office: 1126 South Park St Asheboro NC 27203

TEAGUE, C.P., supt. schs. Supt. schs., Harris County (Tex.). Office: 6515 Irvington St Houston TX 77022*

TEAGUE, CLIFTON EUGENE, diversified industry exec.; b. Salado, Tex., Sept. 26, 1923; s. Clifton Clifford and Jo L. (Lisenbe) T.; grad. high sch.; m. Estella Hargis, Aug. 14, 1944; children—Stellagene (Mrs. Joe Max Shelton), Dianna (Mrs. Richard Curtis), Mike, Pat, Connie Sharon. With Teague & Goodman, Denison, Tex., 1946-49, C.C. Teague & Son Constrn. Co., Inc., Sherman, Tex., 1949-61; co-founder, v.p. Texoma, Inc., mfr. earth drilling equipment, 1957-67; pres. Teague Industries, Inc., 1961—; dir. G.W. Murphy Industries, Inc., Houston, Texoma Nat. Bank, Sherman, Texoma Savs. Assn., Sherman. Bd. dirs. Salvation Army, chmn. bd. 1970-71. Served with USNR, 1942-46. Methodist (trustee). Mason (Shriner), Kiwanian. Clubs: Civitan, Glen Lakes Country, Lancers, Golf Executives (Dallas); Woodlawn Country (Sherman). Home: 808 Western Hills Sherman TX 75090 Office: PO Drawer G Sherman TX 75090

TEAGUE, EDWARD LINDELL, JR., athletic dir.; b. Washington, Dec. 14, 1921; s. Edward L. and Virginia (Simmers) T.; student N.C. State U., 1940-43; A.B., U. N.C., 1946, M.A., 1947; postgrad. U. Md., 1953-54; m. Rita Mae Smith, Apr. 7, 1945; children—Peggy Diane, Joanne Rita. Asst. football coach Guilford Coll., 1947-49, head coach, dir. athletics, 1949-50; backfield coach U. Md., 1952-56, U. N.C., 1956; head football coach The Citadel, Charleston, S.C., 1957-65, dir. athletics, 1966—, asso. prof. phys. edn., 1957—. Served to 1st lt. USMCR, 1943-46; PTO; to maj., 1950-51; Korea. Named S.C. Coach of Year, 1960, So. Conf. Coach of Year, 1961. Mem. Am. Assn. Health, Phys. Edn. and Recreation, Am. Football Coaches Assn., Coll. Athletic Bus. Mgrs. Assn., Nat. Assn. Coll. Dirs. Athletics, Phi Delta Kappa. Kiwanian (past pres., dir. Charleston). Author: (with Wm. C. Brown) Handbook of Football Scouting and Film Analysis, 1953; The Unbalanced Line Open End T, 1964. Home: 8D The Citadel Charleston SC 29409

TEAGUE, HYMAN FARIS, pub. co. exec.; b. San Angelo, Tex., Jan. 14, 1916; s. John Henry and Minnie (Gauldin) T.; B.A., McMurry Coll., 1935, postgrad., 1940; postgrad. Hardin-Simmons U., 1935-36; m. Sophia Golda Harvey, Dec. 26, 1944; children—Carl Robin, Alan Cole. Tchr. pub. schs. Tex., 1935-43; with The Steck Co. (name changed to Steck-Vaughn Co., 1965), Austin, Tex., 1946—, v.p., 1965, pres., 1965— also dir. Served with USNR, 1943-46. Mem. Assn. Am. Pubs., Nat. Council Tchrs. English. Democrat. Baptist. Rotarian. Home: 4906 Rollingwood Dr Austin TX 78746 Office: 807 Brazos St Austin TX 78701

TEAGUE, JAMES OTIS, accountant; b. Bluff Dale, Tex., Jan. 19, 1923; s. James O. and Lora (Falls) T.; student U. Okla, 1943; B.B.A., Tex. Tech. U., 1948; m. Betty Pritchard, Apr. 8, 1949; children—Jerry, David. Instr. Tex. Technol. Coll., 1953-59; sr. partner James Teague & Co., C.P.A.'s, Lubbock, Tex., 1963—; pres. Teague, Inc., Lubbock, 1958—; sec. Exec. House, Inc., Pres., Far West Found., Lubbock, 1960—. Bd. dirs. Lubbocks Boys Club. Served with inf. AUS, 1944-45. C.P.A., Tex. Mem. Am. Inst. C.P.A.'s. Lion (pres. 1954-55). Home: 3536 34th St Lubbock TX 79410

TEAGUE, OLIN EARL, congressman; b. Apr. 6, 1910; s. James Martin and Ida (Sturgeon) T.; student A. and M. Coll. of Tex., 1928-32; m. Freddie Dunman, Dec. 30, 1932; children—James M., John O., Jill Virginia. Sta. supt. U.S. Post Office, College Station, Tex., 1932-40. Elected, 1946, to fill unexpired term of Luther A. Johnson, as mem. 79th Congress, 1945-47, 6th Tex. Dist., mem. 80th to 92d Congresses, 6th Tex. Dist., chmn. house com. vet. affairs, mem. house com. astronautics and space scis., com. on standards of ofcl. conduct. Served to col. 314th Inf., 79th Div., AUS, World War II. Decorated Silver Star with 2 clusters, Bronze Star with 1 cluster, Purple Heart with 2 clusters, Combat Infantryman's Badge, Army Commendation Ribbon (U.S.); Croix de Guerre with palm (France). Democrat. Baptist. Lion. Home: 6015 Massachusetts Av Woodacres MD 20901 Office: House Office Bldg Washington DC 20525

TEAGUE, SARAH ANN CRUMBLEY (MRS. DONALD WAYNE TEAGUE), journalist; b. Holly Pond, Ala., Aug. 17, 1938; d. James Burr and Alma (Reid) Crumbley; B.A., Howard Coll., 1959; m. Donald Wayne Teague, Feb. 20, 1960. Asst. in pub. relations Howard Coll., Birmingham, Ala., 1959-64; fashion editor Birmingham Post-Herald, 1964—. Co-chmn. state publicity Birmingham Festival Arts, 1963-64; nat. sec. Howard Coll. Alumni Assn., 1963-64; mem. U. Alumni Assn. Scholarship Com., 1964-67; mem. Birmingham's Fall Fashion Time Com., 1964—. Mem. Chi Omega, Sigma Delta Chi. Baptist. Home: 1429 S 28th St Birmingham AL 35205 Office: 2200 4th Av N Birmingham AL 35202

TEAGUE, THOMAS SWANN, educator; b. High Point, N.C. Dec. 9, 1937; s. Thomas Carrick and Ethel (Swaim) T.; A.A., Mars Hill Coll., 1958; B.Mus., Fla. State U., 1961, M.Mus., 1962, Mus.D., 1969; m. Rebecca Holder, June 24, 1960 (div.); children—Julia Leigh, Thomas David. Asst. prof. music Carson-Newman Coll., Jefferson City, Tenn., 1962-69, asso. prof., 1969—, dir. opera, 1965—. Recitalist, opera and oratorio performer. Recipient Malcolm Miller award for Outstanding Student Projects Knoxville Jour., 1965. Mem. Nat. Assn. Tchrs. of Singing; Phi Kappa Lambda, Phi Mu Alpha. Democrat. Baptist. Author: Diction Manual for Singers, 1966. Home: Route 1 Jefferson City TN 37760

TEAGUE, WILLIAM CHANDLER, music dir.; b. Gainesville, Tex., July 8, 1922; s. John Abner and Martha Leo (Chandler) T.; student Gainesville Jr. Coll., 1938-39, So. Meth. U., 1939-41; Mus. B., Curtis Inst. Music, 1948; m. Lucille Ridinger, Sept. 5, 1943; children—Lynda Gayle, William Chandler. Mem. faculty Episcopal Acad., Overbrook, Pa., 1945-48; dir. music St. Mark's Episcopal Ch., also prof. music Centenary Coll., Shreveport, 1948—; concert artist, 1955—, tours throughout Europe, Eng., 1966, 69, 72. Mem. concerto contest com. Shreveport Symphony Soc.; mem. Commn. Ch. Music, Diocese of La., 1949, Liturgical Commn.; adviser Camp Hardtner Choir Camp, 1950; adv. com. 4th Province Conf. Ch. Music, 1951—; mem. Shreveport Cultural Affairs Com. Bd. dirs. Shreveport Community Concerts; asso. trustee Evergreen Conf. Center. Served with USAAF, 1942-45. Named Shreveport Outstanding Musician of Year, 1969; recipient Cultural award Shreveport Jour., 1969, Shreveport Music Tchrs. Assn., 1970. Mem. Am. Guild Organists (dean North La. chpt., S.W. regional chmn. 1969—, nat. council 1970—), Hymn Soc. Am., Am. Assn. U. Profs., La. Music Tchrs. Assn., Music Tchrs. Nat. Assn., Am. Cathedral Organists and Choirmasters Assn., Phi Mu Alpha. Episcopalian. Home: 547 Broadmoor Blvd Shreveport LA 71105

TEARS, CLAUDE FREDERICK, JR., engring exec.; b. Cambridge, Mass., May 13, 1919; s. C. F. and Gwendolyn (Jones) T.; B. Chem., Cornell U., 1940; postgrad. Syracuse U., 1941, Columbia, 1942-44; m. Ruth E. McCulley, May 25, 1945 (div.); children—Claude Frederick III, Lisa Michele. Control chemist Semet-Solvay Co., 1941-42; process engr. Celanese Corp. Am., 1942-44, Kellex Corp., 1944-45; project engr. Bahrein Petroleum Co., 1945-47; chief engr. Process Engrs., Inc., 1947-51; v.p. process and project engring. Tears Engrs., Dallas, 1951-59, exec. v.p., 1959-64, pres., 1964-66, dir., 1951—, chief engr. Chem. Producers Corp., Dallas, 1966-69, v.p. engring., 1970—. Tex. chess champion, 1950, 56; mem. U.S. chess team for World Corr. chess Olympiades III and IV, 1958-66; N. Am. champion Flying Scot Class Yacht, 1971. Engrs. Mem. Am. Inst. Chem. Engrs. (sr.), Am. Petroleum Inst. Home: 8626 Inwood Rd Dallas TX 75209

TEASLEY, EDGAR WILLIAM, assn. exec.; b. Toccoa, Ga., Oct. 7, 1912; s. Edgar Carl and Pearly (Brown) T.; A.B. in Econs., George Washington U., 1936; m. Margaret Pitney, Sept. 15, 1939; children—Stewart P., Russell W. Exec. trainee W.R. Grace & Co., N.Y.C., 1936-41; gen. mgr., owner radio sta. WTNT, Augusta, Ga., 1947-49; self-employed land developer, home builder, realtor, Greenville, S.C., 1950-63; exec. v.p. Home Builders Assn., Greenville, 1963—. Trustee Home Builders Ins. Trust, Home Builders Self Insurers Fund, Home Builders Pension Fund.; bd. dirs. Greenville Housing Found. Served with USNR, 1941-46. Recipient 8 awards as exec. v.p. Home Builders Assn. Greenville. Mem. Am. Soc. Assn. Execs., Nat. Assn. Home Builders (life dir., econ. adviser), Home Builders S.C. (dir.). Presbyn. (chmn. bd. deacons). Editor, pub. Home Building Newsletter, 1962—. Home: 8 Sunset Dr Greenville SC 29605 Office: 702 E McBee Av Greenville SC 29601

TEBO, HEYL GREMMER, educator; b. Atlanta, Oct. 17, 1916; s. Clarence Decker and Olna Maudest (Patterson) T.; A.B., Oglethorpe U., 1937, M.A., 1939; D.D.S., Emory U., 1947; m. Ruth Elizabeth Davidson, Feb. 14, 1940. Instr., Dental Br. U. Tex., Houston, 1947-50; asst. prof. U. Ala. Dental Sch., Birmingham, 1950-52; asst. chief dental service VA Hosp., Houston, 1952-61; prof. U. Tex. Dental Br., Houston, 1962—. Cons. VA Hosp., Houston, 1962—; asso. mem. U. Tex. Grad. Sch. Biomed. Scis., Houston, 1971—. Sec., Vol. Fire Dept., West University Pl., Tex., 1952-62. Served to capt., AUS, 1940-44. Mem. Am. Dental Assn., Internat. Assn. Dental Research, Am. Acad. Dental Radiography, Am., So. assns. anatomists, Assn. Mil. Surgeons, Am. Assn. Phys. Anthropologists, S.C.V. (past comdr.), Pi Kappa Phi. Home: 5822 Queensloch Dr Houston TX 77035

TEDDER, KENNETH ALLEN JOE, mfg. co. exec.; b. Rockwood, Tenn., Oct. 30, 1922; s. Thomas Charles and Ruth Dexter (LaRue) T.; student U. Tenn., 1940; U. Cal. at Berkeley, 1943-44; m. Elizabeth Louise Nickle, Oct. 24, 1942; children—Jodie (Mrs. Robert Millard Stamey), Claudia (Mrs. Barry Steven Owens). Salesman, Herbert & Nickle Furniture Co., Knoxville, Tenn., 1945-49; owner, mgr. Henshaw Furniture Hosp., Knoxville, 1949-55; salesman Covert Textiles, High Point, N.C., 1955-59; salesman Fulton Cotton Mills, Atlanta, 1959-68, sales mgr., 1968-72; mdse mgr. Bibb Co., Macon Ga., 1972—. Served with AUS, 1943-45. Decorated Purple Heart. Mem. Christian Ch. Mason. Home: 230 Stone Mill Trail Atlanta GA 30328 Office: Bibb Co Macon GA 30008

TEDDLIE, STELLA MAYE HARWELL (MRS. HORACE TEDDLIE), educator; b. Cedar Hill, Tex.; d. Josiah Clayton and Myrtle Mae (Trees) Harwell; B.A., U. Wyo., 1945; postgrad. So. Meth. U., 1953-56, 63—; m. Horace Teddlie, Apr. 1, 1926; children— Albert Harwell, Merritt Bonar. Binding librarian Dallas Pub. Library, 1934-42; tchr. pub. schs., Okla., Colo., Wyo., Tex., 1944-53, Dallas, 1953-56, 60—. Mgr. Preston Center Travel Office, Dallas, 1956-57, Dallas Travel Service, 1957-60. Chmn. City Blood Bank for Tchr. of Dallas. Chmn. bd. dirs. Thorp Spring Christian Coll. Mem. N.E.A. (textbook com. for Dallas schs.), Tex. Tchrs. Assn., Dallas Classroom Tchrs. Assn. (chmn. 1970-72), Phi Kappa Phi, Psi Chi, Alpha Delta Kappa (charter Kappa chpt. 1956; internat. transp. chmn. 1957—; organizer Mexico City chpt. 1963). Democrat. Mem. Ch. of Christ. Clubs: Dallas Export-Import, Zonta (program chmn. Dallas 1958-59). Author: (handbook) Practical Handicraft, 1942. Home: 2718 Overcrest St Dallas TX 75211

TEELE, ARTHUR EARLE, educator; b. Vaughan, N.C., Nov. 11, 1910; s. George Washington and Cora (Williams) T.; A.B., N.C. Coll., 1934; A.M., Cornell U., 1941, Ph.D., 1953; m. Florazelle Swayze, Dec. 11, 1937; children—Synthia Florabeale, Arthur Earle. Instr., chmn. dept. social studies Warren County Tng. Sch., Wise, N.C., 1934-39; ednl. therapist. VA Hosp., Roanoke, Va., 1946-50; prof. edn., history, head dept. edn. St. Augustine's Coll., 1953-54; prof., chmn. dept. edn. Prairie View (Tex.) A. and M. Coll., 1954-57; prof., head dept. secondary edn. Fla. A. and M. U., Tallahassee, 1957-70, dir. prins., suprs. workshop 1964-66, prof., asso. dean div. grad. studies, 1970—; dir. Hardee County Curriculum Workshop, 1960; dir. Hampton Jr. Coll. Workshop, 1962; mem. research council Coop. Coll. Projects (Land Grant TVA), 1963-64. Mem. United Fund steering com. Fla. A. and M. U., 1961-67. Bd. dirs. Leon County United Fund, 1962-69, N.E. Fla. Summer Camp, Jacksonville, 1966-69; pres. Coll. Terrace Community, 1963-68. Served with USAAF, 1943-45. Recipient Grant-in-Aid for Research, Cornell U., 1952; named Distinguished Alumnus, N.C. Coll., 1960. Mem. N.E.A., Assn. Supervision and Curriculum Devel., Fla. Edn. Assn., Nat. Assn. Secondary Sch. Prins., Tallahassee Frontiers Internat. (pres. 1972), Kappa Alpha Psi (dir.), Phi Delta Kappa, Kappa Delta Pi. Club: Tallahassee (pres.). Contbr. to various publs. in field. Home: 620 Howard Av Tallahassee FL 32304

TEELE, RAY PALMER, profl. engr.; b. Washington, July 12, 1903; s. Ray P. and Mary (Hazard) T.; B.S. in Elec. Engring., U. Mich., 1927; M.S. in Physics, George Washington U., 1929; m. Marion Beth Johnson, Apr. 12, 1927; 1 dau., Audrey (Mrs. Ronald A. Ryder). With Nat. Bur. Standards, Washington, 1923-65, physicist-in- charge research on photometry, 1965; cons. profl. engr., Washington, 1966—; cons. Am. Assn. Motor Vehicle Adminstrs. Fellow Illuminating Engring. Soc., Optical Soc. Am., Washington Acad. Scis.; mem. Illuminating Engring. Soc. Gt. Britain, Soc. Automotive Engrs., Inst. Traffic Engrs. (affiliate). Address: 3713 Jenifer St NW Washington DC 20015

TEETER, ROBERT LANSDOWNE, corp. exec.; b. Dallas City, Ill., Jan. 14, 1919; s. Loipaid Carl and Minnie (Lansdowne) T.; B.S., Kan. State U., 1940; M.S., Va. Poly. Inst., 1941; J.D., U. Va., 1951; m. Sara Etheredge, June 12, 1943; children—Alan Robert, Sara Joan; m. 2d, Catherine DeVries, Apr. 20, 1963; children—Douglas Andrew, Susan Roberta. With Tenn. Eastman Corp., Kingsport, 1941-48; chem. div. mfg. engr. Gen. Electric Co., Pittsfield, Mass., 1951-52; mgr. long range planning Chemstrand Corp., Pensacola, Fla., 1952-56; asst. dir. corporate planning Reynolds Metals Co., Richmond, Va., 1956-72; founding alternate dir. Aluminium Del Caroni, Caracas, Venezuela, 1962-66; asst sec. Indsl. Metals Co., 1969—. Vice-chmn. Va. State Council Higher Edn. Va., 1970—, chmn. Gov.'s appointees positions catalog com., 1970; mem. Va. delegation Edn. Commn. of States, 1972—. Budget dir. Republican Com. Va., 1968-72, treas., 1972—. Mem. Va. Bar, Nat. Def. Exec. Res., Am. Inst. Chem. Engrs., Am. Chem. Soc., Sigma Xi, Phi Kappa Phi, Pi Mu Epsilon, Phi Lambda Upsilon, Delta Theta Phi. Home: 1604 Pump Rd Richmond VA 23233

TEETER, THOMAS ALLEN, librarian; b. Dumas, Ark., Oct. 4, 1943; s. Charles Ruskin and Neva Katherine (Taylor) T.; B.S., U. Ark., 1965; M.L.S., U. Miss., 1967, Ed.D., 1971; m. Carolyn Flossie Umsted, July 30, 1967. Social studies tchr. Little Rock Pub. Sch. Dist., Little Rock Central High Sch., 1965-66, head librarian, 1966—. Grad. asst. in secondary edn. U. Miss., 1971. Mem. N.E.A., Assn. for Ednl. Communication and Tech., Am., Ark. library assns., Ark. Edn. Assn., Phi Delta Kappa. Home: 30 Nottingham Rd Little Rock AR 72205 Office: Little Rock Central High Sch 14th and Park Sts Little Rock AR 72202

TEETS, FRANK DAVID, agrl. co. exec.; b. Minot, N.D., Mar. 23, 1936; s. Miles Francis and Esther (Olsen) T.; B.S., Stetson U., 1961; m. Carolyn Sue Crawford, Aug. 2, 1958; children—Frank David, James Crawford, Kelly Sue, Rebecca Leeann. Staff accountant W.O. Daley & Co., Orlando, Fla., 1961-64; sec., gen. mgr., dir. South Bay Growers, Inc. (Fla.), 1964—; dir. Thomas Bros., Inc., Fla. Lettuce, Inc., Sobay Crispheart, Inc., Paul Eskew & Assos., Inc. Pres., Belle

Glade Beautification Com., 1967. Bd. dirs. Glades Day Sch., Pahokee, Fla. Served with USCGR, 1953-57. Mem. Fla. Celery Exchange (dir.), Fla. Council Farmer Coops. (v.p. 1968), Council Farmer Coops. (treas. 1968), Pi Kappa Alpha. Republican. Elk. Home: 116 SE 5th St N Belle Glade FL 33430 Office: PO Box 56 South Bay FL 33493

TEFERTILLER, KENNETH RAY, educator; Ph.D., U. Ill. Chmn. dept. agrl. econs. Inst. Food and Agrl. U. Fla., Gainesville. Office: U Fla Gainesville FL 32601*

TEIPEL, JOHN ALBERT, civil engr.; b. Dallas, Nov. 8, 1923; s. Albert Henry and Mary Frances (Bland) T.; student Tex. A. and M. U., 1941-42; B.S. in Civil Engring., So. Meth. U., 1947; postgrad. Command and Gen. Staff Coll., 1959; m. Ellen Louise Townsend, June 21, 1943; children—John Randolph, Ellen Lorraine (Mrs. Richard P. Evans), Philip Andrew. Civil engr. Tex. Hwy. Dept. and City of Dallas, 1947-52; civil engr. Hyden Engring. Co., Dallas, 1953-61; lt. col., bn. comdr. 49th Armored Div., Tex. N.G., 1961-62; dep., then asst. dir. pub. works, dir. Dept. Streets and Sanitation Services, Dallas, 1963—. Comdg. officer Dallas Police Res., 1953-59. Bd. dirs. City Employees Credit Union, Dallas. Served with AUS, 1942-45; ETO. Fellow Am. Soc. C.E. (pres. Dallas br., state dir.); mem. Tex. Pub. Works Assn. (pres. 1972). Mason (master). Club: Bass. Contbr. articles to profl. jours. Home: 5835 Sunnywood Dallas TX 75228 Office: 2721 Municipal Dallas TX 75215

TELESCA, FRANCIS EUGENE, architect; b. Scranton, Pa., Oct. 22, 1921; s. Joseph J. and Bernetta (Bocchiccio) T.; B.Arch. summa cum laude, Catholic U. Am., 1953; m. Dianne Willis, July 31, 1968; children—Celeste (Mrs. Robert Stokes), Anthony, Cheryl, Glenn. Designer-draftsman, project architect Robert M. Little, Miami, Fla., 1953-54; architect Rufus Nims, Miami, 1954-55; chief architect Rader & Assos., Miami, 1955-59; pvt. practice architecture, Miami, 1959-63; partner, Greenleaf/Telesca, engrs. and architects, Miami, 1964—; sec. Greenleaf Enterprises, Inc. Mem. Nat. Com. on Architecture for Commerce and Industry, 1965—. Mem. Fla. Planning and Zoning Assn., 1963-72; mem. South Fla. Hosp. Council, 1963-70; mem. Inst. Urban Affairs, U. Miami, 1965-66; mem. citizens adv. com. South Fla. Bldg. Code Survey, 1965-66; mem. archtl. adv. com. Miami-Dade Jr. Coll., 1967-69. Bd. dirs. South Fla. Interprofl. Council, 1966-68; bd. dirs., pres. Coconut Grove Assn., 1961-63, Grove House, 1962-63. Served with AUS, 1940-45, 50-51; ETO. Decorated Bronze Star medal; recipient spl. citation Am. Assn. Sch. Adminstrs., 1969, Grand Nat. award Nat. Community Fallout Shelter Competition, 1964. Mem. A.I.A. (pres. Fla. chpt. 1965, dir. 1966-68, award of merit 1968), Coconut Grove C. of C. (dir. 1960-65), Phi Eta Sigma. Roman Catholic. Home: 7299 SW 79th St Miami FL 33143 Office: 1451 Brickell Av Miami FL 33131

TEMPLE, FUTRELLE LEE, educator; b. Nettleton, Miss., Apr. 20, 1912; s. Arthur L. and Lee (Minga) T.; B.S., U. Ala., 1937, M.A., 1941; student Harvard, 1951-52; Ed.D., Columbia, 1953; m. Mattaline Matthews, July 23, 1939; children—Margaret Karen, Futrelle Lee. Tchr., Fairview High Sch., Cullman, Ala., 1936-38; tchr., Sylacauga (Ala.) High Sch., 1938-43, prin., 1943-51; dir. instrn., Sylacauga, 1952-53; prof. edn. U. Ala., 1953—, head dept., 1962—. Chmn. Ala. Com. Secondary Schs., 1963-65, Ala. Course Study Com., 1966—. Mem. So. Assn. Colls. and Schs. (exec. com. 1959-62), Am. Assn. Sch. Adminstrs., Assn. Supervision and Curriculum Devel., Nat. Soc. Study Edn., N.E.A., Phi Delta Kappa, Kappa Delta Pi. Rotarian (pres. Sylacauga 1947-48). Author: (with others) Power Politics and the Teacher, 1957. Home: 12 Arcadia Dr Tuscaloosa AL 35401 Office: Graves Hall University AL 35486

TEMPLE, GRAY, clergyman; b. Lewiston, Me., Mar. 13, 1914; s. Charles Hosea and Eleanor (Gray) T.; A.B., Brown U., 1935; B.D., Va. Theol. Sem., 1938, D.D., 1961; D.D., U. of 1961; m. Maria Drane, Jan. 29, 1940; children—Gray, Robert Brent, Charles Adams. Ordained priest P.E. Ch., 1939; rector, Rocky Mt., N.C., 1942-53, Charlotte, N.C., 1953-56, Columbia, S.C., 1956-61; bishop of S.C., 1961—. Successively mem. standing com., exec. council and bd. exam. chaplains P.E. Diocese N.C., 1942-56; successively mem. standing com., exec. com. and bd. exam. chaplains P.E. Diocese S.C., 1956-61; del. Gen. Conv. P.E. Ch., 1949-52, 55, 58; mem. nat. exec. council P.E. Ch. U.S.A., 1970—. Vice pres. East Carolina council Boy Scouts Am., 1950-53. Chmn. trustees Porter Acad.; trustee Voorhees Coll., St. Mary's Sch., Raleigh, York Orphanage, Ch. Home Ladies; trustee, mem. exec. council Kanuga Conf. Center. Home: 1000 S Main St Summerville SC 29483 Office: PO Drawer 2127 Charleston SC 29403

TEMPLE, JAMES PITTS, physician; b. Sylacauga, Ala., June 28, 1927; s. William Frank and Mary Hannah (Pitts) T.; student Howard Coll., 1945, 47; B.S., Auburn U., 1950; postgrad. Huntingdon Coll., 1955; M.D., U. Ala., 1959; m. Alice Fay Shepherd, June 22, 1947; children—Linda Fay, James Pitts. Intern, Carroway Meth. Hosp., Birmingham, Ala., 1959-60; practice medicine, Alexander City, Ala., 1960—; mem. staffs Russell Hosp., Alexander City, East Tallapoosa Hosp., Dodeville, Ala. Pres., Marble City Nursing Home, Sylacauga, 1966—, Temple Med. Clinic, Alexander City, 1968—. Served with USAAF, 1945-47. Mem. Am. Acad. Gen. Practice, Tallapoosa County Med. Soc. (v.p. 1970-71), A.M.A., Beta Beta Beta, Rho Chi. Home: 916 Pineview Dr Alexander City AL 35010 Office: PO Box 268 Alexander City AL 35010

TEMPLE, KEITH ROE, cartoonist; b. Glasgow, Scotland, Feb. 11, 1899 (came to U.S. 1919, naturalized 1925); s. Edward and Lily (Roe) T.; J.D., Loyola U., New Orleans, 1927; m. Anice Phillips, Feb. 13, 1935. Reporter-artist The Times-Picayune, New Orleans, 1919-22, editorial cartoonist, 1923-67; artist New Orleans Item, 1922. Admitted to La. bar, 1927. Served with 2d Australian Bn., 1916-18. Decorated Victory medals (Gt. Britain, Australia). Mem. La. Bar Assn. Home: 1906 Napoleon Av New Orleans LA 70115

TEMPLE, WINNIE LAVENIA, dietitian; b. Killeen, Tex.; d. John Thomas and Fannie (Dockray) Temple; B.S. in Nutrition, Tex. Technol. Coll., 1940; pvt. tutoring, Sinaloa, Mexico, 1931. Asst. dietitian Lubbock Gen. Hosp., 1933-40, chief dietitian, 1941-43; dietetic intern Grassland Hosp., 1941; dietitian Coll. Food Service, Tex. Technol. Coll., 1946; dir. dietetics Scott and White Hosp. and Clinic, Temple, Tex., 1946-70; head nutrition therapy and edn. VA Hosp., Waco, 1970—. Served to lt. M.C. AUS, 1943-46. Mem. Am., Tex. (state pres. 1965-66, state del. 1967-69, state exec. bd. 1955—), Central Tex. dietetic assns., State Nutrition Council, St. Mary Altar Soc., Am. Assn. U. Women, Cath. Daus. Am. Roman Catholic. Home: 2501 West Av Z Temple TX 76501 Office: VA Hosp Waco TX 76703

TEMPLETON, CHARLES CLARK, chemist; b. Houston, Oct. 4, 1921; s. David H. and Miriam (Clark) T.; B.S. in Chemistry, La. Poly. Inst., 1942 M.S., U. Wis., 1947, Ph.D., 1948; m. Ann Hathaway Lewis, Dec. 23, 1944; children—Charles Clark, Robert Dudley, John Foster, Thomas Wofford. Instr. chemistry U.Mich., 1948-50; with exploration and prodn. research div. Shell Devel. Co., Houston, 1950—, research asso. in chemistry, 1963—. Mem.-at-large, dist. commr. Sam Houston Area council Boy Scouts Am., 1956—. Served to lt. USNR, 1942-46. Recipient Turner prize Electrochem. Soc., 1951. Mem. Am. Chem. Soc., Soc. Petroleum Engrs., Sigma Xi, Phi Lambda Upsilon, Phi Kappa Phi, Alpha Chi Sigma. Democrat. Presbyn. (elder). Mason. Contbr. articles to profl. lit. Home: 6119 Reamer St Houston TX 77036 Office: PO Box 481 Houston TX 77001

TENER, GEORGE EVANS, land developer; b. Edgeworth, Pa., May 5, 1917; s. Alexander Campbell and Marion (Clement) T.; B.A., Yale, 1940; student Fgn. Service Inst., 1951-52; m. Patricia Ann Buehner, Apr. 13, 1946 (div. Jan. 1962); children—Roberta Harrison (Mrs. James G. Kekam), Jenifer Evans; m. 2d, Anne Powell Potts Faber, Oct. 11, 1966. With State Dept. 1949-54, vice consul Am. Consulate Gen., Naples, Italy, 1949-51, 2d sec., sec. of embassy, Manila, P.I., 1952-54; security analyst J. & W. Seligman & Co., N.Y.C., 1956-63; dir. Aircraft Engine Parts, Inc.; now pres. Middleburg Lake, Inc. (Va.) Served from vol. to 1st lt. Am. Field Service, World War II. Mem. Va. Angus Assn., Orange County Hunt Assn. Democrat. Episcopalian. Clubs: University (N.Y.C.); Metropolitan (Washington); Potomac Valley Yale (pres.). Home: Ardarra Middleburg VA 22117

TENISON, WILLIAM JEROME, JR., architect; b. Nashville, Apr. 28, 1933; s. William J. and Katherine (Wade) T.; B.S., Ga. Inst. Tech., 1961, B.Arch., 1962; m. Marcia Carolyn Boulware, Sept. 6, 1958; children— Katherine Louise, William J. III, Marcia Carolyn, Melissa Ann. Architect in tng. Hart, Freeland & Roberts, Nashville, 1962-63, 1965, designer, 1965, designer, project architect, Jackson, Tenn., 1967-69, partner, 1969—; archtl. tng. Swensson & Kott, Nashville, 1963-64. Bd. dirs. Jackson Symphony Assn., bd. advisers Vocational Tng. Sch. at McKenzie (Tenn.). Served with USN, 1952-56. Mem. A.I.A. (sec.-treas. West Tenn. sect. 1968-69; pres. 1970-71), Jackson Art Assn. Episcopalian (pres. Churchmen's Club 1968-69). Club: Exchange (Jackson). Home: 417 Wallace Rd Jackson TN 38301 Office: Peoples Protective Life Towers PO Box 212 Jackson TN 38301

TENNANT, BILLY GLENN, health ofcl.; b. Atmore, Ala., Aug. 15, 1918; s. Andrew and Mollie (Collins) T.; student pub. health U. Fla., 1947-48; m. Evelyn Givhan, June 2, 1938; children—Glenn Allen, Cynthia Ann, Susan Patricia. Finance officer WPA, Pensacola, Fla., 1941-42; dir. environmental health Escambia County Health Dept., Fla., 1946—. Adviser, Escambia County Plumbing and Gas Control Bds., 1953—. Mem. Escambia County Community Council, 1957-60; pres. State Fla. Sanitarians Registration Bd., 1960, sec., 1961—. Served with USNR, 1942-45. Recipient Good Govt. award Jr. C. of C., 1953; Outstanding Sanitarian award U.S., 1955, State Fla., 1958-59. Mem. Fla. Assn. Sanitarians (pres. 1954-55), County Environmental Health Dirs. (chmn. 1963), Fla. Pub. Health Assn. (pres. 1971), Nat. Assn. Sanitarians. Mason (Shriner). Home: 4 Teakwood Dr Pensacola FL 32506 Office: 2251 N Palafox St Pensacola FL 32502

TENNANT, DAISY MAE ELMORE, poet; b. Senatobia, Miss., Aug. 27, 1910; d. John Charlie and Nora (Wimberly) Elmore; student U. Tex., 1930, Odessa (Tex.) Evening Coll., various periods, Rutherford Bus. Coll., 1967; m. Tracy W. Tennant, Feb. 17, 1934 (div. 1945); children—Nancy Jo (Mrs. James E. Stiles), Sharon Annora (Mrs Mitchell R. Gause). Part time sec. to chmn. bd., chief exec. officer, office mgr. Ormand Industries, Inc., Odessa, Tex., 1955-64, Dallas, 1964—; office mgr. Main Lafrentz & Co. Poetry workshop leader Odessa Evening Coll. 1957-59; poetry chm. Odessa Coll. Writer's Roundup, 1957-63; Spl. adv. com. services Women's dept. Tex. Bank and Trust Co., Dallas, 1966—; judge various poetry contests. Recipient numerous poetry awards, including Hadra Meml. award, 1965, Chapbook award, 1963, Globe Peace award, 1966, Lyric award, 1966, Grand Prix award Nat. Fedn. State Poetry Socs., 1966, Old South award, 1967, Hurley Meml. award, 1967, and many others. Mem. Poetry Soc. Am., Nat. Fedn. State Poetry Socs., Acad. Am. Poets (affiliate), Poetry Soc. Tex. (rec. sec. 1968—, chmn. Tex. Poet's Meml. Collection Baylor Coll., 1966—, program chmn. 1967—; treas. 1969), Writer's Workshop (pres. Odessa 1961-62), Shakespeare Club (v.p. Odessa Coll. 1962), Avalon World Arts Acad., Vachel Lindsay Assn., Compatriots Dallas. Author books of verse: Shifting Sands, 1954, Miss Fitts and Miss Cellany, 1960; contbr. poems to anthologies, including Anthology of American Poetry, 1959; Avalon Anthologies, 1962; National Federation Anthology, 1968; also to newspapers, mags., radio, television. Home: 7131 Casa Loma St Dallas TX 72514 Office: LTV Tower Dallas TX 75202

TENNANT, HARRY LARENZE, editor; b. Seymour, Ia., Aug. 17, 1909; s. Frank E. and Myrtle (Tennant) Rouse; B.A., State U. Ia., 1933; postgrad. U. Cal. at Berkeley, 1936; m. Margaret Alice Free, Feb. 14, 1942. Reporter, S.W. Newspress, Los Angeles, 1934; pub. relations Shuberts Theatrical Co., Los Angeles, San Francisco, 1935-38; writer U.P.I, Omaha, Lincoln, Neb., Phila., 1940; city editor Ames (Ia.) Daily Tribune, 1941; corr. Chgo.-N.Y. Jours. of Commerce, Washington, 1945-50; editor Watson Publs., Washington, 1952—; U.S. editorial dir. Interavia Pubs., Geneva, 1955-69; editor Cahners Publs., Washington, 1965—; editor Biomed. News, Washington, 1971—. Served with AUS, 1942-45. Mem. Nat. Space Club, White House, State Dept. corrs. assns., Aviation and Space Writers Assn., Nat. Space Writers Assn., Aero Club. Club: Nat. Press. Contbr. articles to profl. jours. Home: 3705 Mill Creek Rd Haymarket VA 22069 Office: Nat Press Bldg Washington DC 20004

TENNANT, RALPH BOYD, dentist; b. Gaffney, S.C., Sept. 8, 1929; s. Boyd Bryan and Ellen Christine (Fincher) T.; student U. Fla., 1951-52, U. Miami, 1955-56; A.A., Charlotte Coll., 1957; D.D.S., Emory U., 1961; m. Charlotte Ross Walker, May 2, 1952; children—Cynthia Ruth, Christine Elizabeth, Ralph Boyd II, Georgia Noel. Individual practice dentistry, Temple Terrace, Fla., 1961—. Golf coach King High Sch., 1966-71; pres. Community Health Services Assn., 1971-72; mem. Hillsborough County Adv. Com. for Gov. Reuben Askew, 1971-72. Served with USMCR, 1952-54. Recipient Coach of the Year award Fla. Athletic Coaches Assn., 1969, Distinguished Service award Fla. Coaches Assn., 1970. Mem. Am. Soc. Dentistry for Children, Am. Dental Assn., West Coast Dist., Hillsborough County (bd. mem. 1967) dental socs., Temple Terrace C. of C. (dir. 1963-65), Delta Sigma Delta. Clubs: Optimist (pres. 1964-65) (Temple Terrace, Fla.). Home: 11008 Ridgedale Rd Temple Terrace FL 33617 Office: 5202 Busch Blvd Temple Terrace FL 33617

TENNEY, GEORGE EDWARD, JR., food co. exec.; b. Mt. Pleasant, Ark., Dec. 14, 1919; s. George Edward and Ruth Eileen (Pew) T.; student U. Ark., summer 1941; B.S. in Chemistry, Coll. of Ozarks, 1942; m. Grace Phillips, Dec. 20, 1942; children—George Edward III, Phillip Clark, John Miller. County supr. USPHS, Crittenden and Monroe counties, Ark., 1947-50; salesman, asst. sales mgr., sales mgr., asst. to pres. Mountaire Corp., North Little Rock, 1953-69, pres., 1969—; pres. Mountaire Kitchens, Inc., Springhill, La.; dir. Beehive Poultry, Inc., Salt Lake City. Served to 1st lt. AUS, 1942-46, 51-53; CBI. Mem. Nat. Broiler Marketing Assn., Southeastern Egg and Poultry Assn. (pres.), Ark. Poultry Processors Assn. (past pres.), United Comml. Travelers, Am. Legion, V.F.W. Methodist (trustee). Mason. Home: 5020 Oaklawn Dr North Little Rock AR 72116 Office: 124 E 5th North Little Rock AR 72114

TENNISON, CHARLES WILLIAM, plastic surgeon; b. Dallas, Aug. 13, 1908; s. Harrison B. and Addie (Nix) T.; B.S., So. Meth. U., 1931; M.D., Baylor U., 1933; m. Kathleen Buchanan, Aug. 17, 1935; children—Charles Buchanan, William Thomas. Intern Baylor U. Hosp., 1933-34; tng. plastic surgery under Dr. J. T. Mills, Dallas, 1934-38; pvt. practice, San Antonio, 1938-44, 46—; asso. prof. clin. surgery Baylor U. Postgrad. Sch., 1947—; lectr. plastic surgery Tex. U. Postgrad. Sch., 1954—; chief plastic surgery service Santa Rosa Med. Center, Robert B. Green Meml. Hosp. Cons. Brooke Army Hosp., Lackland Air Force Hosp., surgeon gen. USAF, 1959-65. Dir., Western Res. Corp., Dallas. Served to lt. comdr., M.C., USNR, 1944-46. Diplomate Am. Bd. Plastic Surgery. Mem. Am. Soc. Plastic and Reconstructive Surgery (pres. 1962), Am., Tex. (past pres.) socs. plastic surgeons, San Antonio (past pres.) socs. plastic surgeons, San Antonio (past pres.), Southwestern, Tex. surg. socs., Bexar County Med. Soc. (past pres.), Am. Assn. Cleft Palate Rehab., A.C.S., Soc. Air Force Clin. Surgeons (hon.), Phi Chi. Club: San Antonio Country. Home: 221 Primrose St San Antonio TX 78209 Office: Medical Profl Bldg San Antonio TX 78212

TEPPER, MORRIS, govt. ofcl.; b. Jerusalem, Palestine, Mar. 1, 1916 (came to U.S. 1922; naturalized 1926); s. Benjamin and Anna (Goldman) T.; B.A., Bklyn. Coll., 1936, M.A., 1938; Ph.D., Johns Hopkins, 1952; m. Sandra Levin; children—Andrew S., Bradford M. Research meteorologist U.S. Weather Bur., Washington, 1946-51. chief severe local storms research unit, 1951-59; dep. dir. Earth Observation programs, dir. meteorology NASA, Washington, 1959—; tchr. fluid mechanics, mem. phys. sci. com. U.S. Dept. Agr. Grad. Sch., 1952-59. Served with USAAF, 1943-46. Recipient Meissinger award Am. Meteorol. Soc., 1950, Distinguished Alumni award of honor Bklyn. Coll., 1961, NASA Execptional Service medal, 1966, Spatiales Gold medal Centre National D'Etudes, 1972. Mem. Am. Meteorol. Soc., Am. Inst. Aeros. and Astronautics, Washington Acad. Scis. Home: 107 Bluff Terrace Silver Spring MD 20902 Office: 400 Maryland Av SW Washington DC 20546

TERRELL, CHARLES OLIVER, physician; b. Quincy, Ill., Oct. 9, 1935; s. Hoydt Brooks and Ina Marie (Hamner) T.; B.S. in Medicine, U. Ill., 1956, M.D., 1960; m. Frances Ann Pfeiffer, Dec. 27, 1958; children— Charles Oliver, Gregory Allen, Susan Marie. Intern, Tampa (Fla.) Gen. Hosp., 1960-61; resident anesthesiology U. Tex., Galveston, 1963-65; anesthesiologist anesthesia dept. Med. Center Clinic, Pensacola, Fla., 1965; practice medicine specializing in anesthesiology, Pensacola, 1965—; chief anesthesia dept. Sacred Heart Hosp., Pensacola, 1969—. Served with USAF, 1961-63. Diplomate Am. Bd. Anesthesiology. Fellow Am. Coll. Anesthesiologists; mem. A.M.A., Fla., Escambia County med. socs., Am., Fla. socs. anesthesiologists, Internat. Anesthesia Research Soc. Methodist (ofcl. bd.). Home: 1221 Durnford St Pensacola FL 32503 Office: 1750 N Polafox St Pensacola FL 32501

TERRELL, GEORGE EDMOND, pub. relations exec.; b. Guthrie, Okla., May 20, 1923; s. George E. and Zenna (Denham) T.; B.A., Okla. A. and M. Coll., 1950; m. Billie Jean Howard, Feb. 6, 1944; children—Susan Kay, George Edmond III. Various positions with newspapers, 1947-54; advt. asst. Southwestern Bell Telephone Co., Dallas, 1954-56, advt. supr., 1956-57, gen. information asst., St. Louis, 1957-58, gen. advt. asst., 1958-60, gen. information supr., 1961-64, customer relations mgr., 1964-65, pub. relations mgr., 1965-66, gen. information mgr., 1966-68, gen. pub. relations mgr., Oklahoma City, 1968—; pub. information supr. Am. Tel. & Tel., N.Y.C., 1960-61. Chmn. pub. relations com. United Appeal Greater Oklahoma City, 1970, author Appeal film, 1970, 71. Bd. dirs. Jr. Achievement Greater Oklahoma City, 1969-71, sec., 1970-71, chmn. fund drive, 1972. Served with AUS, 1942-46; ETO; to capt., 1950-53. Decorated Bronze Star medal, Purple Heart with cluster. Mem. Pub. Relations Soc. Am. (chpt. v.p.), Oklahoma City C. of C., Sigma Delta Chi. Club: Men's Dinner, Press (v.p. Oklahoma City 1970-71), The Greens Golf and Racquet, Petroleum. Home: 2920 Rosewood Lane Oklahoma City OK 73120 Office: 707 N Robinson St Oklahoma City OK 73126

TERRELL, TOL, hosp. adminstr.; b. Merit, Tex., Jan. 25, 1916; s. Burl Toliver and Mary Julia (Swift) T.; A.B., Austin Coll., Sherman, Tex., 1937; m. Grace Hopson Moody, Aug. 28, 1937; children—Charles, Mary Nelle (Mrs. Don Cummins), Hal and Suzanne (Mrs. James Mitchell) (twins). Adminstr., Wilson N. Jones Hosp., Sherman, 1937-39, Harris Hosp., Ft. Worth, 1939-48, Shannon W. Tex. Meml. Hosp., San Angelo, Tex., 1948—. Bd. dirs. Blue Cross-Blue Shield of Tex., 1943—. Recipient Service award N.W. Tex. Hosp. Assn., 1957, Meritorious Service award Austin Coll., 1959, Gold Medal award Am. Coll. Hosp. Adminstrs., 1964. Fellow Am. Coll. Hosp. Adminstrs. (regent 1952-58, pres. 1961-62); mem. Am. (chmn. council 1946-47, trustee 1952-58, pres. 1957-58), Tex. (treas. 1942-44, trustee 1945-48, pres. 1946-47, Earl M. Collier award distinguished hosp. adminstrn. 1966) hosp. assns. Episcopalian. Home: 3328 Lindenwood Ct San Angelo TX 76901 Office: 9 S Magdalen St San Angelo TX 76901

TERRIS, BRUCE JEROME, lawyer; b. Detroit, Aug. 3, 1933; s. Charles Zachary and Ruth (Singer) T.; A.B. summa cum laude, Harvard, 1954, LL.B. magna cum laude, 1957; postgrad. Georgetown U., 1957-60; m. Shirley Duval, Aug. 1958; children—Elizabeth, Jessica. Admitted to D.C. bar; asst. to solicitor gen., Washington, 1958-65; asst. dir. Nat. Crime Commn., 1965-67; asst. to Vice Pres. U.S., 1967-68; cons. crime, poverty, legal service to poor, Washington, 1967; vis. prof. law Cath. U. Am., Washington, 1967-68; exec. dir. Anacostia Assistance Corp., 1968-69; cons. crime, poverty, law, housing, urban problems, 1969—; sr. atty. Center on Law and Social Policy, 1969-70; now individual practice law. Chmn., Nat. Conf. on Law and Poverty, 1965; mem. campaign staff Robert Kennedy, 1968; chmn. Washington Dem. central com., 1968-72. Mem. Phi Beta Kappa. Contbr. articles to profl. jours. Home: 1855 Shepherd St NW Washington DC 20011*

TERRY, ALICE (MRS. WILLIAM C. DIFFENDERFER), artist; b. N.Y.C.; d. Leon and Rose (Smithline) Terry; B.A. cum laude, Pembroke Coll., 1945; m. Benjamin Franklin Johnson V, 1951 (dec. Feb., 1967); children—Leon Axel, Susan Patricia, Benjamin Franklin VI; m. 2d; William C. Diffenderfer; Jan. 17, 1970. One-man shows Krannert Mus., Urbana, Ill., 1961, Fleishman Gallery, N.Y.C., 1960, Hacker Gallery, N.Y.C., 1961, Rose Fried Gallery, N.Y.C., 1963, Wesleyan Coll., 1966, U. Miami 1966, Fla. Presbyn. Coll., 1968, Fla. Presbyn. Coll., 1970, 72, Edison Jr. Coll., 1970, exhibited group shows Guggenheim Mus., N.Y.C., 1964, Whitney Mus., N.Y.C., 1954, Martha Jackson Gallery, N.Y.C., 1960, 1st and 2d religious banner exhibits, also Cranbrook Acad., Lock Haven Art Center, 1972, St. Petersburg Mus. Fine Arts, 1972; represented in permanent collections N.Y.U., Wesleyan Coll., Guggenheim Mus.; Home: 7530 SW 35th St Miami FL 33155

TERRY, AUBREY EUGENE, physician; b. Leighton, Ala., Sept. 9, 1927; s. William Steve and Ludie (Nichols) T.; B.S., U. Ala., 1951, M.D., 1955; m. Hettie Butler, Dec. 24, 1948; 1 dau., Lesa Butler. Intern, Lloyd Noland Hosp., Fairfield, Ala., 1955-56; resident Johns Hopkins Hosp., Balt., 1960-61; practice medicine specializing in pediatrics, Russellville, Ala., 1956—; mem. staff N. Ala. Hosp., Russellville. Mem. Gov.'s and Pres.'s Coms. on Employment Handicapped, 1965—. Served with USNR, 1945-47. Recipient A.H. Robbins award for community service, 1968-69. Mem. Franklin County (past pres., chmn. bd. censors), Ala., So. med. assns., A.M.A.,

Am. Acad. Pediatrics, Ala. Diabetes Assn., Ala. Heart Assn., Am. Legion, Bear Creek Watershed Assn., C. of C. (pres.). Baptist (deacon). Club: Civitan. Home: 1 Signore Dr Russellville AL 35653 Office: 230 Coffee St Russellville AL 35653

TERRY, EDWARD DAVIS, educator; b. Eclectic, Ala., May 19, 1927; s. William Jefferson and Venola (Davis) T.; student Nat. U. of Mex., 1951; B.S., U. Ala., 1949, M.A., 1953; Ph.D., U. N.C., 1958; m. Marilyn Faye Landers. Asst. prof. Spanish, So. Meth. U., Dallas, 1958-62; asst. prof. Romance langs. U. Tenn., Knoxville, 1962-64; asso. prof. Romance langs. U. Ala., University, 1964-70, prof., 1970—, dir. Latin Am. studies program, 1966-72. Vis. prof. U. Tenn., 1969; instr. Spanish, Sullins Coll., Bristol, Va., 1953-55; with accounting dept. Tela R.R. Co. (Honduras), 1949-50. Served with AC, AUS, 1945-46. Mem. Latin Am. Studies Assn., Modern Lang. Assn. (mem. selection com. for scholar's library), Am. Assn. U. Profs., Southeastern Conf. Latin Am. Studies (sec.-treas. 1970—, editor South Eastern Latin Americanist 1970—), Sigma Delta Pi, Beta Gamma Sigma. Editor Artists and Writers in the Evolution of Latin America, 1969. Editorial bd. Revista de Estudios Hispanicos, U. Ala. Press, 1966—. Home: PO Box 1911 University AL 35486 Office: Dept Romance Langs University AL 35486

TERRY, ESTHER NEWTON (MRS. RAYMOND LEE TERRY), educator, civic worker, realtor; b. Kirbyville, Tex., Sept. 30, 1908; d. Francis Jefferson and Emma Josephine (Clark) Newton; B.A., McNeese State Coll., 1955; M.A., Northwestern State Coll., Natchitoches, La., 1956; postgrad. La. State U., 1957, U. Ark., 1958; m. Raymond Lee Terry, Aug. 19, 1933; 1 dau., Emma Susanne (Mrs. Lon Hugh Gowan). Formerly classroom tchr. Beauregard Parish Sch. Bd.; tchr. English, home econs. Singer (La.) High Sch., 1928-29, Merryville, La., 1929-33, DeRidder (La.) Schs., 1933—; reporter, corr. DeRider Enterprise, 1966—; mem. Toledo Bend Bd. Realtors; 1969—. Mem. Beauregard Parish Sch. Bd., 1968—. Named Woman of Year, DeRidder, 1961, One of Top Five in La., in Forestry, 1962; Outstanding Civic work, DeRidder C. of C., 1963, Citizen of Year, 1965; Outstanding Civic Leaders of Am., 1967. Mem. La. Fedn. Bus. and Profl. Women's Club (pres. 1964-65), Am. Assn. U. Women, DeRidder Gardenettes, Lovely La. Tourist Assn., N.E.A., La. Tchrs. Assn., Am. Legion Aux., U.D.C., La. Travel Promotion Assn. (dir.), Delta Kappa Gamma. Democrat. Mem. Order Eastern Star (worthy matron 1961-63). Home: Glendale Rd DeRidder LA 70634 Glendale Rd DeRidder LA 70634 Office: 116 N Pine St DeRidder LA 70634

TERRY, GEORGE ALVIN, bank exec.; b. Oneida, Tenn., Dec. 19, 1926; s. William Claude and Paralee Long (Cowan) T.; student Auburn U., 1943, Ala. U., 1944; B.A., U. Tenn., 1950; m. Sarah Ellen Winn, June 9, 1950; children—Stephanie Rhea, Saralee Winn, Sereessa Louise, Rachel Cowan. Vice pres. Terry Motor Co., 1950-60, v.p., 1950—; part owner, mgr. Ben Franklin Store, Sparta, Tenn., 1960—; v.p. First Trust and Savs. Bank, Oneida, 1963—. Mem. Nat. Com. for Support Pub. Schs., 1961—; dir. fed. and state surplus property for State of Tenn., 1972—; active P.T.A., Hillbrook Camp, Knoxville, Tenn. Mem. Tenn. Ho. of Reps., 1957-59, Tenn. Senate, 1961-65. Bd. dirs. Mid-South Youth Camp, Henderson, Tenn. Served to 2d lt. AUS, 1943-46. Mem. Conservation League, Am. Legion, Nat. Trust for Historic Preservation, Smithsonian Assos., Lambda Chi Alpha. Republican. Kiwanian. Home: Lafayette and Cooper Sts PO Box 432 Oneida TN 37841 Office: PO Box 432 Main St Oneida TN 37841

TERRY, JOHN VERLIN, educator; b. Hagerstown, Ill., Oct. 8, 1920; s. William Bergen and Clester (Hopkins) T.; B.A., John Brown U., 1949; M.B.A., U. Ark., 1966; L.H.D., Linda Vista Bapt. Coll. and Sem. (San Diego), 1967; m. Fern Nadine Stradley, Feb. 14, 1942; children—John Mark, Joan Elizabeth, Luanne, Clay Thomas. Ordained to ministry Bapt. Ch., 1946; pastor chs. Tex., Ark., 1948-58; asst. to pres. Peterson Industries, Decatur, Ark., 1958-62; head bus. dept. John Brown U., Siloam Springs, Ark., 1966-70, head div. devel., 1971—. Guest lectr. U. Ark., 1966—; prin. firm John V. Terry & Assos., Siloam Springs, 1969—. Mem. exec. com., bd. dirs. Ark. Council Econ. Edn., 1968—; commr. Edn. Commn. U.S., 1969—; chmn. adv. council Small Bus. Adminstrn., Ark., 1970—. Served with AUS, 1942-44; PTO. Mem. Am., So., econ. assns., Southwestern Social Sci. Assn., Ark Coll. Tchrs. Econs., Bus. (pres. 1969), Modern Woodmen Am., Beta Gamma Sigma. Contbr. articles to profl. jours. Home: 1242 W Jefferson St PO Box 28 Siloam Springs AR 72761

TERRY, LAWRENCE ELWIN, feed mill exec.; b. nr. Marion, Ala., Nov. 23, 1933; s. Jade Lee and Mary Louise (Jackson) T.; A.A., Marion Inst., 1959; m. Erva Louise Griffin, Aug. 22, 1958 (div. Mar. 1968); 1 dau., Erva Katherine. Mgr., Griffin Bros. Feed Mill., 1958-70; owner, operator Terry Feed Mill, Marion Ala., 1970—. Served with USNR, 1952-56. Mem. V.F.W. (dist. comdr. 1969). Club: Civitan. Home: 208 South St Marion AL 36756 Office: Box 427 Marion AL 36756

TERRY, MARSHALL NORTHWAY, JR., univ. adminstr., author; b. Cleve., Feb. 7, 1931; s. Marshall N. and Margaret (Carpenter) T.; student Amherst Coll., 1949-50, Kenyon Coll., 1950-51; B.A., So. Methodist U., 1953, M.A., 1954; m. Antoinette Barksdale, Sept. 5, 1953; 1 dau., Antoinette Ansley. Teaching fellow English, So. Meth. U., Dallas, 1953-54, lectr. English, 1954-55, dir. pub. relations, lectr. English, editor Mustang, 1957—; free lance writer, 1955-56; copywriter, publicist Bloom Advt., Dallas, 1956-57. Mem. Am. Coll. Pub. Relations Assn., Am. Alumni Council, Delta Kappa Epsilon. Methodist. Club: Press (Dallas). Author: (novel) Old Liberty, 1961; also stories, articles, book revs. in various publs. Home: 2709 Amherst St Dallas TX 75225

TERRY, OLIN BRYAN, advt. agy. exec.; b. Mineral Wells, Tex., Dec. 15, 1929; s. Olin Asbury and Nancy (Bryan) T.; B.A., So. Methodist U., 1950; m. Dorothy Kale, Mar. 2, 1956; 1 son, Steven Wayne. Asst. program dir. sta. KIXL, Dallas, 1949-53; dir. sta. WFAA-TV, Dallas, 1954-56; prodn. mgr. sta. KFJZ-TV, Ft. Worth, 1957-60; operations mgr. sta. WJBK-TV, Detroit, 1960-61; radio/TV dir. Bloom Advt., Dallas, 1961-64; v.p. radio/TV Glenn Advt., Dallas, 1965—. Office: 4700 Republic Bank Tower Dallas TX 75201

TERRY, ONA JOY WALTON (MRS. ALBERT M. TERRY), educator; b. Houston, Nov. 13, 1921; d. John Henderson and Ruby (Young) Walton; student Rice Inst., 1938; B.S., U. Houston, 1942, M.S., 1945; postgrad. U. So. Cal., 1956, Tex. Christian U., 1951, 52, 61, U. Colo., summers 1952-55, Colo. State U., 1959; m. Albert M. Terry, Apr. 12, 1946; 1 dau., Sharon C. (Mrs. Cress). Analytical chemist Eastern States Petroleum Co., 1942-45, Continental Oil Co., 1945-46; tchr. pub. schs. Tex., 1949-58; asso. prof. organic chemistry Tarleton State Coll., Stephenville, Tex., 1958—. Tech. writer Volt Tech. Corp., summer 1969. Mem. Am. Chem. Soc., Am. Assn. U. Profs., Tex. Assn. Coll. Tchrs., Kappa Delta Pi. Author: General Chemistry - Problems and Equations, 1960. Home: PO Box 446 Granbury TX 76048 Office: Phys Scis Dept Tarleton State Coll Stephenville TX 76401

TERRY, SANFORD TOMPKINS, JR., broadcasting co. exec.; b. Richmond, Va., June 1, 1913; s. Sanford Tompkins and Ruby May (James) T.; grad. high sch.; m. Betsy Virginia Lyons, Apr. 24, 1942; children—Sandra, Betty Carol, Sanford T., III. Technician, sta. WRVA, Richmond, 1933-41, research and devel. mgr., 1945-54, chief engr. sta. WRVA-TV, 1954-69; tech. operations mgr. WWBT-TV (formerly WRVA-TV), Richmond, 1969—. Served to capt. AUS, 1943-45. Decorated Bronze Star medal. Designer electronics equipment for broadcasting. Home: 8504 Three Chopt Rd Richmond VA 23229 Office: Station WWBT PO Box 12 Richmond VA 23201

TERZICK, PETER EDWARD, labor union exec.; b. Rossland, B.C., Can., July 12, 1904; s. Edward and Martha (Radovich) T.; came to U.S., 1922, naturalized, 1929; student U. Wash., 1923-25, Ind. U. extension, 1954; m. Hazel Hawkins, July 2, 1935; 1 dau., Jane Ellen. Journalist-editor Union Register, Seattle, 1936-43; editor The Carpenter, ofcl. publ. United Brotherhood Carpenters and Joiners of Am., 1943—, gen. treas. union, 1961—. Adv. com. N. Central region U.S. Forest Service, 1955-60; mem. Marion County (Ind.) Health and Welfare Council, 1955-61; pres. Ind. Assn. Adult Edn., 1957-58. Recipient Freedom Found. award, 1950; Industry Coop. award Forest Products Industry Assn. Mem. Internat. Labor Press Assn. (pres. 1958-59), Am. Forestry Assn. (regional v.p.), Pi Kappa Phi. Lutheran. Clubs: Nat. Press, Nat. Capitol Democratic (Washington). Author: What is Brotherhood 1957; I am a Building Tradesman, 1963. Home: 417 Northwest Dr Silver Spring MD 20901 Office: 101 Constitution Av NW Washington DC 20001

TESHER, FREDERIC KAY, dentist; b. N.Y.C., Feb. 1, 1929; s. Louis and Daisy Dorothy (Klauber) T.; student U. Fla., 1947-48, U. Miami, 1949; D.D.S., U. Md., 1954; m. Helen Hergert, Jan. 7, 1955; children—Lawrence, Robin. Resident anesthesiology Univ. Hosp., Balt., 1947-59; attending anesthesiologist Mt. Sinai Hosp., 1959-60; pvt. practice dentistry, Hollywood, Fla., 1960—; dir. Good Samariton, Inc. Dental cons. Miami Dolphins Profl. Football Team, 1966—. Served with USNR, 1954-56. Mem. Am. Dental Soc. Anesthesiologists, Anesthesiology Research Soc., Am. Dental Assn., East Coast, Fla. dental socs. Contbr. articles to profl. jours. Home: 605 N 14th Av Hollywood FL 33021 Office: 3911 Hollywood Blvd Hollywood FL 33021

TESTERMAN, JACK DUANE, univ. adminstr.; b. Marietta, Okla., Dec. 13, 1933; s. Jesse D. and Lillie (Holt) T.; A.A., Murray Jr. Coll., 1953; B.A., Okla. State U., 1955, M.S., 1957; Ph.D., U. Tex., Austin, 1972; m. Lou Donaghe, Feb. 12, 1953; children—Kenny Ray, Sherri Gail, Jay Darrell; m. 2d, Edwyna Pace, Aug. 30, 1968. Research statistician Jersey Prodn. Research, Tulsa, 1957-62; statistician Phillips Petroleum, Bartlesville, Okla., 1962-63; prof. math., statistics U. Southwestern La., Lafayette, 1963—, registrar, 1965—; dir. institutional research, 1970—. Mem. Am. Statis. Assn., Internat. Platform Assn., Math. Assn., La. Acad. Scis., Assn. Computing Machinery, Data Processing Mgmt. Assn., Sigma Xi, Pi Mu Epsilon, Phi Theta Kappa, Phi Delta Kappa, Omicron Delta Epsilon. Address: Box 940 Lafayette LA 70501

TESTERMAN, MAURICE KENDALL, educator; b. Roanoke, Va., Nov. 19, 1924; s. Glenn H. and Nila Brown (Umberger) T.; B.S. with honors, Va. Poly. Inst., 1944, M.S., 1947, Ph.D. 1950; m. Ellen Jane Jolly, Mar. 18, 1965; 1 son Lawrence Kendall. Instr., Kan. State U., 1950-51; asst. prof. U. Ark., Fayetteville, 1951-53, asso. prof., 1954-59; prof., head dept. electronics and instrumentation U. Ark. Grad. Inst. Tech., Little Rock, 1959—, asso. dir. research coordinator, 1970—. Cons. Baldwin Electronics, Inc., Little Rock, 1958—, Avco Electronics Div., Tulsa, 1963-70, NASA Lunar Planning Team, 1965-68. Mem. Gov's Indsl. Task Force on Elec. Industry, 1966-70. Gov's Sci. and Tech. Council, 1969-70. Served with USNR, 1944-46. Mem. Am. Chem. Soc., Am. Soc. Engring. Edn., Instrument Soc. Am., Am. Soc. Mass Spectrometry. Sigma Xi, Phi Lambda Upsilon. Contbr. articles to profl. jours. Patentee in field. Home: 20 Nob Hill Cove Little Rock AR 72205 Office: 12th and McAlmont Sts PO Box 3017 Little Rock AR 72203

TETEL, MARCEL, educator; b. Paris, France, Oct. 11, 1932; came to U.S., 1947, naturalized, 1952; B.A., U. Chattanooga, 1954; M.A., Emory U., 1956; Ph.D., U. Wis., 1961; postgrad. U. Florence, 1957-58; m. Joan Lieberman, June 16, 1957; children—Jocelyn Beth, Marc Jeffrey. Mem. faculty dept. French and Italian, Duke, Durham, N.C., 1960—, prof. 1968—. Fulbright fellow, Italy, 1957-58, 66-67; Am. Council Learned Socs. grantee, 1963; Guggenheim fellow, 1970. Mem. Modern Lang. Assn., Am. Assn. Tchrs. French, Am. Assn. Tchrs. Italian, Renaisance Soc. Am., Societe des Amis de Rabelais, Southeastern Renaissance Conf., South Atlantic Modern Lang. Assn. Author: Etude sur le comique de Rabelais, 1964; Francois Rabelais, 1967; Rabelais et l'Italie, 1969; Pirandella Enrico IV, 1971; Themes, Language and Structure in Marguerite de Navarre's Heptameron, 1973. Home: 1804 Woodburn Rd Durham NC 27705

TEUNISSON, JOHN HENRY, civil engr.; b. Monticello, Miss., Feb. 12, 1911; s. John Henry and Rilla (Reed) T.; B.S., Miss. State U., 1933; m. Beth Murphy, Nov. 29, 1946; 1 dau., Elizabeth (Beth) Ann. Project engr. Miss. State Hwy. Dept., Jackson, 1933-41, 45-49; city engr. City of Greenville, Miss., 1949—. Pres. S. Delta Econ. Devel. Dist., 1967—. Served to maj., C.E., AUS, 1941-45. Decorated Bronze Star with oak leaf cluster. Mem. Miss. Soc. Profl. Engrs. (v.p. 1964-68), Am. Soc. C.E. (dir. mid south sect. 1953-54), Am. Pub. Works Assn. (Miss. rep. 1958-68), Alpha Tau Omega, Scabbord and Blade. Presbyn. (elder). Home: 1285 Kirk Circle Greenville MS 38701 Office: 340 Main St Greenville MS 38701

TEVERBAUGH, HAROLD G., chem. co. exec.; b. Oklahoma City, July 21, 1920; s. Lon Eugene and Olive May (Townsend) T.; B.S. in Chem. Engring., Okla. State U., 1948; m. Betty Lou Neil, July 24, 1942; children—Harold Neil, Jack Lon, Monte Jay. Chief engr. Sunray DX, Tulsa, 1948-53; v.p., dir. Tex. Natural Gasoline Corp., Tulsa, 1953-60; exec. v.p. Union Tex. Petroleum div. Allied Chem. Corp., Houston, 1961-68, pres., 1968—. Served with USAAF, 1942-45. Mem. Am. Inst. Chem. Engrs., Am. Petroleum Inst., Nat. Assn. Profl. Engrs., Nat. Petroleum Refiners Assn., Ind. Petroleum Assn. Am., Natural Gas Processors Assn., Phi Gamma Delta. Presbyn. Home: 12523 Overcup Dr Houston TX 77024 Office: 3000 Richmond Av Houston TX 77006

THACHER, JOHN SEYMOUR, museum dir.; b. N.Y.C., Sept. 5, 1904; s. John Seymour and Frances (Lake) T.; A.B., Yale, 1927; Ph.D., U. London (Eng.), 1936. Mem. editorial staff World's Work mag., 1928-29; asst. to dirs. Fogg Mus. Art, Harvard, 1936-40, asst. dir., 1940-46; acting dir. Dumbarton Oaks, Washington, 1945-46, dir., 1946—. Trustee Assos. in Fine Arts, Yale, 1953—; exec. com., treas. Byzantine Inst., 1952—; trustee Internat. Exhbn. Found.; bd. dirs. Am. Nat. Opera Co. Served to lt. comdr. USNR, 1943-45. Decorated chevalier Legion of Honor (France), 1946; cavalier Al merito Repubblica Italiana, 1954; knight Order of George I (Greece), 1966. Fellow Pierpont Morgan Library; mem. Henry Focillon Soc. Am., Internat. Inst. Conservation Mus. Objects, Am. Assn. Museums, Coll. Art Assn. Episcopalian. Clubs: Cosmos (Washington); University, Century (N.Y.C.). Contbr. profl. jours. Home: 1735 32d St NW Washington DC 20007 Office: 1703 32d St NW Washington DC 20007

THACKER, HENRY RAY, govt. ofcl.; b. Petersburg, Va., May 29, 1928; s. Thomas Milton and Mary (Campbell) T.; B.S., Va. Poly. Inst., 1949, M.S., 1953, Ph.D., 1965; m. Bettye Louise Best, Dec. 19, 1953; children—Deborah, David Ray, Mary. Instr., Va. Poly. Inst., 1955-56; asst. prof. Ala. Poly. Inst., 1956-59; asso. prof. Auburn (Ala.) U., 1959-63; acting chief program devel. and reports unit Susquehanna Field Sta., Chesapeake Bay-Susquehanna River Basins Project, Fed. Water Pollution Control Adminstrn., 1964-65, chief, 1965-66, acting dir. Susquehanna Field Sta., 1966-67, dir. research and devel. programs Middle Atlantic region, Charlottesville, Va., 1967-71; research adminstr., div. tech., Office of Research and Monitoring, Environmental Protection Agy., Washington, 1971—. Served from 2d lt. to 1st lt. AUS, 1950-52: capt., 1961-62. Registered profl. engr., Va., Ala. Mem. Am. Soc. C.E., Am. Soc. Engring. Edn., Water Pollution Control Fedn., Am. Water Works Assn., Sigma Xi, Chi Epsilon. Home: 100 Powhatan Circle Carrsbrook Charlottesville VA 22901 Office: Environmental Protection Agy 4th and M Sts Washington DC 24060

THACKER, MARION JOSEPH, accountant; b. Dayton, Va., Feb. 7, 1917; s. Albert M. and Lessie (Showalter) T.; student Shenandoah Coll., 1936-38; B.S.C., Nat. Bus. Coll., Roanoke, Va., 1941; m. Leah J. Boyts, June 22, 1941; children—Linda Sue, Gary Joe, David Ray. Tax accountant Va. Pub. Service Co., Alexandria, 1941-43; bursar Nat. Bus. Coll., 1946-50; staff accountant Leslie A. Kimble & Co., C.P.A.'s, Roanoke, 1950-54; individual practice accounting M.J. Thacker, C.P.A., Roanoke, 1954—. Prof. advanced accounting Nat. Bus. Coll., 1954-62, dir., 1963-72; prof. accounting Roanoke Coll., Salem, Va., 1963-68. Bd. dirs. Va. United Methodist Pensions, Inc., Richmond. Served with Finance Dept., AUS, 1943-46. C.P.A., Va. Mem. Am. Inst. C.P.A.'s, Va. Soc. C.P.A.'s, Am. Accounting Assn., Nat. Assn. Accountants, Roanoke C. of C. Methodist (trustee, supt. Sunday sch.; trustee). Clubs: Heights (pres. 1961); Spring Run Swim (treas. 1966-67) (Roanoke). Home: 2467 Livingston Rd SW Roanoke VA 24015 Office: Coulter Bldg Roanoke VA 24011

THAGARD, THOMAS WERTH, judge; b. Greenville, Ala., Apr. 10, 1902; s. James Lee and Minnie (Roach) T.; B.S., Auburn U., 1924; LL.B., Cumberland U., 1929; m. Beverly Preuit, July 5, 1934; children—Thomas Werth, Josephine Thagard. Admitted to Tenn. bar, 1929, Ala. bar, 1929; practiced in Greenville, 1929-52; judge Circuit Ct., 1952-69, presiding judge Ala. Ct. Civil Appeals, Montgomery, 1969—. Chmn. Legislative Council Ala., 1951. County solicitor, Butler County, Ala., 1931-46; mem. Ala. Ho. of Reps., 1946-50; mem. Ala. Senate, 1950-52. Bd. dirs. L.V. Stabler Meml. Hosp.; mem. Walter O. Parmer Scholarship Bd. Mem. Ala. Assn. Circuit Judges (pres.). Democrat. Methodist. Rotarian. Home: 411 Balaclava Dr Greenville AL 36037 Office: State Ct Civil Appeals PO Box 1206 Montgomery AL 36102

THALHIMER, MORTON GUSTAVUS, motion picture theatre exec., real estate cons.; b. Richmond, Va., Oct. 17, 1889; s. Gustavus and Pauline (Lonerstad) T.; student Wharton Sch., U. Pa., 1908-12; m. Ruth Wallerstein, Oct. 11, 1920; children—Margaret T. (Mrs. Jason R. Lewis), Morton G. With Joseph Louchenthal Co., Phila., 1909-10; v.p. Raab & Co., Realtors, Richmond, 1911-12; pres. Morton G. Thalhimer, Inc., Richmond, 1913-60, chmn. bd., 1960—; pres. Neighborhood Theatre of Va., Richmond, 1926-65, chmn. bd., 1965—; dir. emeritus United Va. Bank-State Planters, Spotless Co.; dir., past pres. Broad-Grace Arcade Corp.; dir. Theatre Owners of Am.; dir. emeritus Williamsburg Restoration, Inc.; mem. Commn. on Arts and Humanities, Commonwealth of Va., 1969—. Bd. dirs., v.p. Firemans Mut. Aid Assn., 1924—; dir., chmn. bd. dirs. Richmond Meml. Hosp.; bd. dirs., past pres. Sheltering Arms Hosp., Will Rogers Meml. Hosp., Sarnac Lake, N.Y.; trustee, v.p. Va. Mus. Fine Arts; trustee Historic Richmond Found.; adv. bd. Va. Home, YWCA. Served to capt. U.S. Army, 1917-19. Mem. Richmond Bd. Realtors (past pres.), Va. Real Estate Assn. (past pres.), Am. Soc. Real Estate Counselors, Am. Inst. Real Estate Appraisers, Nat. Assn. Real Estate Bds., Inst. Real Estate Mgmt., Internat. Real Estate Fedn., Va. Motion Picture Assn. (past pres.), Nat. Assn. Theatre Owners, Columbia Assos. Club: Lakeside Country (past pres.). Home: 4 Paxton Rd Richmond VA 23226 Office: 1013 E Main St Richmond VA 23206

THARPE, ROBERT HOLLIS, mortgage banker; b. Moultrie, Ga., Sept. 16, 1912; s. Elijah Mercer and Maude (Mathews) T.; B.S.C., Ga. Inst. Tech., 1934; m. Kathryne Brooks, Aug. 17, 1935; children—Robert Hollis, Mercer McCall II. With mortgage loan dept. Met. Life Ins. Co., 1935-46; pres., chmn. bd. Tharpe & Brooks, Inc., Atlanta, 1947—, also chief exec. officer; dir. Redfern Foods Corp. Chmn. Ga. Ports Authority. Trustee Ga. Inst. Tech. Athletic Assn., Ga. Tech. Found., Darlington Sch., Rome, Ga. Served to lt. comdr. USNR, 1942-45. Mem. Mortgage Bankers Assn. Am. (pres. 1960-61), Atlanta Mortgage Bankers Assn. (past pres.), Phi Delta Theta. Methodist (steward). Clubs: Capital City, Piedmont Driving, Peachtree, Commerce (Atlanta); Columbus (Ga.) Country; Oglethorpe Country (Savannah, Ga.). Home: 665 W Paces Ferry Rd NW Atlanta GA 30305 Office: 728 W Peachtree St NW Atlanta GA 30308

THARPE, ROBERT MAURICE, dentist; b. Utica, Miss., June 29, 1935; s. Robert Powhatan and Armelda (Greene) T.; B.S., Tenn. State U., 1957; D.D.S., Howard U., 1961; m. Lynn Marie Howell, June 10, 1966; children—Robert Maurice, Jason Howell. Gen. practice dentistry Med. Assos. Clinic, Memphis, 1963—. Chmn. financial com. South Dist., Chickasaw council Boy Scouts Am., 1967-68; mem. Founders Club of Goodwill Boys Am., 1971-72; col. Gov. B. Ellington's staff, 1968-71. Served as capt., Dental Corps, USAF, 1961-63. Mem. Am., Tenn. dental assns., Shelby County (v.p.), Memphis dental socs., Nat. Assn. Dentists, Acad. Gen. Dentistry, Assn. Mil. Surgeons, N.A.A.C.P., Omega Psi Phi. Baptist. Mason. Home: 1632 Joanne St Memphis TN 38111 Office: 1324 Mississippi Blvd Memphis TN 38106

THARPE, WILLIAM LEE, paper co. exec.; b. Chipigy, Fla., Aug. 11, 1919; s. Charles and Luvonia (Creamer) T; B.S., Western Ky. State U., 1948; m. Frances Arnold, Apr. 11, 1944; children—William Blalne, Arnold Craig. Gen. mgr. St. Joe Paper Co., Jacksonville, Fla., 1949-65; cons. St. Regis Paper Co., Atlanta, 1965; pres. Birmingham Packaging Corp. (Ala.), 1965—; Jackson Packaging Corp. (Miss.), 1965—. Served with USAAF, 1941-45. Mem. N.A.M., Ala. Assn. Industries, C. of C. Lion. Clubs: Chase Lake Country, The Club. Home: 325 Shenandoah Dr Birmingham AL 35226 Office: 1701 31st Pl SW Birmingham AL 35201

THARRINGTON, BRUCE HIGHT, supt. schs.; b. Louisburg, N.C., Nov. 16, 1909; s. William Henry and Margaret Florence (Hight) T.; A.B., U. N.C., 1932, M.A., 1940, postgrad., 1957; m. May Frances Turner, July 20, 1935; 1 dau., Nancy (Mrs. John E. Boyd). Tchr.-coach, Cameron, N.C., 1933-36; prin. Bell Sch., 1936-40, Apex. Sch., 1940-45, Winecoff Sch., 1945-53; supt. Surry County Schs., 1953-55; prin. Pilot Mountain Sch., 1955-57; supt. Mount Airy City Schs., 1957—. Pres. United Fund, 1962-63. Bd. dirs. Salvation Army, Handicapped Children. Mem. C. of C. (mem. bd. 1960-64). Methodist (chmn. adminstrv. bd. 1971-72). Mason, Lion. Club: Civitan. Home: 207 Robin Rd Mount Airy NC 27030 Office: PO Drawer 710 Mount Airy NC 27030

THAXTON, CARLTON JAMES, librarian; b. Tucson, May 23, 1935; s. Carl Newton and Daisy (Conard) T.; A.B., U. Ga., 1957; M.S., Fla. State U., 1958; m. Donna Jean Bradley, Aug. 25, 1957; children—James Bradley, Carl Stanton. Dir. Coastal Plain Regional Library, Tifton, Ga., 1958-60, 61-68, Kingsport (Tenn.) Pub. Library, 1960-61; dir. div. pub. library services Ga. State Dept. Edn., Atlanta, 1968—; instr. library sci. U. Ga. Sch. Edn. at off campus centers in Albany and Tifton, 1960—. Mem. Am., Ga., Southeastern library assns. Democrat. Methodist. Home: 3207 Oxbridge Way Lithonia GA 30058 Office: 156 Trinity Av SW Atlanta GA 30303

THAXTON, JAMES RALPH, ret. coll. pres.; b. Griffin, Ga., Mar. 23, 1901; s. James Reece and Frances Louise (Jones) T.; A.B., U. Ga., 1921, A.M., 1924; diplome, U. Grenoble, France, 1922; Ph.D., U. Ind., 1937; m. Helen Clarkson, Dec. 30, 1922; children—James Edwin, William Herlot. High sch. teacher, Griffin, 1921; instr. Romance langs. U. Ga., 1922, adjunct prof., 1923, asso. prof., 1926, prof., 1939, dean Co-ordinate Coll (women's jr. coll., U. Ga.), 1941-43, prof. history, 1942-48; dir. admissions 1943-48; registrar, U. Ga., 1945-48; acting pres. Ga. State Woman's Coll., 1948-49, pres. Valdosta State Coll., 1949-66, pres. emeritus, 1966—; ednl. cons., 1966—. Dir. March of Dimes campaign 8th Congl. dist., 1950, co-dir., 1951. Mem., pres. Valdosta Bd. Edn.; dir. Ga. Sch. Bd. Assn. Mem. So. Hist. Assn., Am. Assn. Tchrs. Spanish, Am. Assn. Collegiate Registrars, Com. on Uniform Curriculum, Ga. Coll. Assn., Chmn. of Com. on Evaluation of Vet. Edn. So. U. Conf., Am. Assn. Teachers of French, South Atlantic Modern Lang. Assn., Assn. Ga. Colls. (pres. 1953, v.p. 1954), Ga. Edn. Assn. (pres. coll. div. 1955), Pi Kappa Phi, Phi Beta Kappa, Phi Kappa Phi, Kappa Delta Pi, Alpha Chi, Phi Eta Sigma. Mem. Disciples of Christ Ch. Democrat. K.P., Kiwanian (lt. gov. Ga. dist.). Address: 305 E Jane St Valdosta GA 31601

THAYER, LLOYD YATES, supt. schs.; b. Troy, N.C., June 28, 1911; s. Whitmund Lafayette and Theodocia Ernest (Leach) T.; A.A., Wingate Jr. Coll., 1929; A.B., Wake Forest Coll., 1931, M.A., 1939; Ed.D., U. N.C., 1957; m. Georgia Griffin, Aug. 12, 1942. Tchr., Union County (N.C.) Pub. Schs., 1931-35, prin., 1935-37; prin. Wake County (N.C.) Pub. Schs., 1937-39; prin. High Point (N.C.) Pub. Schs., 1939-59, dir. instrn, 1959-60, asst. supt. schs., 1960-68, asso. supt. schs., 1968—. Mem. N.C. Textbook Commn., 1957-61. Bd. dirs. Family Service Bur., Tb Assn.; trustee Wingate Coll., 1968—, chmn. scholarship com., 1968—. Recipient Distinguished Service award High Point Jr. C. of C., 1946, Kiwanis Internat., 1964, Certificate of Appreciation Nat. Assn. Secondary Sch. Prins., 1956. Mem. Am. Assn. Sch. Adminstrs., N.C. Edn. Assn. (pres. div. prins. 1955-56, state pres. 1961-62), Horace Mann League (N.C. pres. 1962-63), Phi Delta Kappa. Home: 1601 Country Club Dr High Point NC 27262 Office: 900 English Rd High Point NC 27260

THAYER, PAUL, diversified co. exec.; b. Henryetta, Okla., Nov. 23, 1919; s. Bill Ernest and Opal Marie (Ashenhurst) T.; student U. Wichita, 1937-38, U. Kan., 1939-41; m. Margery Schwartz, Feb. 14, 1947; 1 dau., Brynn. Pilot, Trans World Airlines, 1945-47; chief exptl. test pilot Chance Vought Corp., 1948-50, sales mgr., 1951, sales and service mgr., 1952-54, v.p. sales and service, 1954-58, v.p. Washington operations, 1958-59, v.p., gen. mgr. Vought Aeros. div., 1959-63, pres., 1963; chief flight test Northrop Aircraft Co., 1950-51; sr. v.p. Ling-Temco-Vought, Inc., Dallas, 1963, exec. v.p., 1964, chmn. bd., pres., chief exec. officer, 1970—; pres. LTV Aerospace Corp., Dallas, 1965-70. Served from ensign to lt. comdr., USNR, 1941-45. Decorated D.F.C., Air medal with nine oak leaf clusters; recipient Distinguished Service award sec. navy, 1962. Mem. Soc. Exptl. Test Pilots (chmn. membership com.), Phi Gamma Delta. Home: 10200 Hollow Way Dallas TX 75229 Office: PO Box 5000 Dallas TX 75222

THAYER, ROBERT HELYER, diplomat; b. Southboro, Mass., Sept. 22, 1901; s. William Greenough and Violet (Otis) T.; grad. St. Mark's Sch., 1919; student Amherst Coll., 1918-19; A.B., Harvard, 1922, LL.B., 1926; m. Virginia Pratt, Dec. 26, 1926; children—Robert Helyer, Sally Sears, Stephen Badger. Admitted to N.Y. bar, 1926; with Cadwalader, Wickersham & Taft, 1926-29, 47-49; asso. counsel pub. service law investigation N.Y. State, 1929; asso. counsel fed. bankruptcy laws investigation So. Dist. N.Y., 1929; with Donovan, Leisure, Newton & Lumbard, 1929-32, mem. firm, 1932-37; asst. dist. atty. N.Y. County, 1937-41, chief indictment br., 1938-41; asst. N.Y. State commr. housing 1946; commr. against discrimination N.Y. State, 1949-51; asst. U.S. Ambassador to France, 1951-54; officer charge Western European affairs, Operations Coordination Bd., 1954-55; U.S. minister to Rumania, 1955-58; asst. sec. of state Dept. of State, 1958-61; asso. dir. gen. Am. Field Service Internat. Scholarships, 1961-65, dir. govt. relations, 1965—; cons. to sec. of state, 1961—. Asst. to John Foster Dulles, UN Charter Conf., San Francisco, 1945. Candidate for Congress from Bklyn., 1946. Bd. dirs. N.Y. Philharmonic Soc., 1935-55; bd. mgrs. N.Y.C. Mission Soc., 1941-55; bd. dirs. Fgn. student Service Com., Washington Performing Arts, Internat. House; trustee, bd. dirs. AFS Internat. Scholarships; trustee St. Mark's Sch., 1940—, Nat. Trust Historic Preservation. Served from lt. comdr. to comdr. USNR, 1941-45. Mem. N.Y. bar Assn., Audubon Soc. (dir.), Fgn. Policy Assn., Washington Inst. Fgn. Affairs, English Speaking Union (v.p.). Clubs: Somerset (Boston); Racquet and Tennis, Coffee House, Harvard (N.Y.C.): Porcellain (Cambridge, Mass.); Metropolitan (Washington). Home: 3010 O St NW Washington DC 20007 Office: 1616 H St NW Washington DC 20006

THAYER, ROLLIN HAROLD, poultry scientist, educator; b. St. Francis Mission, S.D., Dec. 30, 1916; s. Chester Arthur and Albertina Frederica (Manthey) T.; B.S. in Agr., Okla. State U., 1940; M.S. in Poultry Nutrition, U. Neb., 1942; Ph.D. in Animal Sci., Wash. State U., 1955; m. Ruth Marie Robinson, Aug. 30, 1944; 1 son, Chester Arthur II. Asst. prof. poultry sci. Okla. State U., Stillwater, 1943-46, asso. prof., 1946-55, prof., 1955—. Ralston Purina research fellow, 2 years; mem. Ralston Purina Research Fellowship Awards Com., 1959-61, 71-73. Mem. Stillwater Library Bd., 1959—, v.p., 1968—. Bd. dirs. United Fund, Stillwater, 1966-69; bd. dirs. YMCA, Stillwater, 1967—, v.p., 1970, pres., 1971. Recipient Outstanding Tchr. award Okla. State U. Coll. Agr., 1961. Fellow A.A.A.S., Okla. Acad. Sci.; mem. Am. Inst. Biol. Scis., Poultry Sci. Assn., World Poultry Sci. Assn., Am. Inst. Nutrition, Okla. Feed Mfrs. Assn. (hon.), Stillwater C. of C. (dir. 1968—, v.p. 1970), Sigma Xi (pres. 1971-72), Phi Kappa Phi, Phi Eta Sigma, Alpha Zeta. Presbyn. (elder). Kiwanian (pres. Stillwater 1959, lt. gov. div. 16 Tex.-Okla. dist. 1962). Editor: Bridging the Gap in Nutrition. Research on feed and nutrient intake in chickens and turkeys, feeding of estrogen to market poultry, metabolism studies of turkeys and laying hens. Home: 105 N Stallard St Stillwater OK 74074

THEIS, PAUL ANTHONY, pub. relations exec.; b. Fort Wayne, Ind., Feb. 14, 1923; s. Albert Peter and Josephine Mary (Kinn) T.; B.A., Notre Dame U., 1948; B.S., Georgetown U., 1949; m. Nancy Wilbur, Aug. 21, 1971. Reporter, Fairchild Publs., 1951-53; Washington corr. Newsweek Mag., 1953-54; exec. asst. U.S. congressman, 1955-57; pub. relations dir. Nat. Republican Congl. Com., Washington, 1957—. Served with USAAF, 1943-45; ETO. Decorated Air medal with two clusters. Mem. Pub. Relations Soc. Am., Nat. Press Club. Club: Capitol Hill (Washington). Author: (with William L. Steponkus) All About Politics. Editor: (with Edmund L. Henshaw, Jr.) Who's Who in American Politics. Inventor: (with Donald M. Zahn) Hat in The Ring Game. Home: 38 Ivy St SE Washington DC 20003 Office: 300 New Jersey Av SE Washington DC 20003

THERIOT, ROY RAOUL, lawyer, state ofcl.; b. Erath, La., June 26, 1914; s. Lastie and Emerite (Barras) T.; student U. Southwestern La., 1933-35; LL.B., Tulane U., 1939; D. of Worldly Wisdom (hon.), Boswell Inst., 1966; m. Helen Roberts, June 7, 1947; children—Barbara Ellen, Roy Raoul, Samuel Houston. Admitted to La. bar, 1939, since practiced law in Abbeville; mayor, Abbeville, 1954-60; comptroller State of La., 1960—. Dist. chmn. Vermillion Parish, Evangeline council Boy Scouts of Am., 1949-51; La. pres. March of Dimes, 1964, chmn. Acadian com., 1965—; past pres. Bayou council Girl Scouts U.S. Served with USAAF, 1942-46. Decorated Legion d'Honneur (France). Mem. La. Bar Assn., Nat. Assn. State Auditors, Comptrollers and Treas., Am. Legion. Democrat. Roman Catholic. Lion (dist. gov. 1949-50). Home: 406 S Louisiana Av Abbeville LA 70510 Office: State Comptroller's Office Baton Rouge LA 70804

THEUS, HAROLD C., judge; b., 1915; Th.B., Bethany-Nazarene Coll.; J.D., U. Okla. Admitted to Okla. bar, 1948, U.S. Supreme Ct. bar, 1952; county judge, Oklahoma County, 1961-66, 7th dist. judge Okla., 1966—, judge Okla. Ct. Appeals, 1969-71; presiding judge Okla. Ct. Criminal Appeals, 1971—. Served with USAF, 1932. Home: 3324 NW 62d St Oklahoma City OK 73112 Office: Courthouse 321 Park Av Oklahoma City OK 73102

THIBAUT, JOHN WALTER, educator; b. Marion, O., Apr. 30, 1917; s. Ralph Gooding and Marie (Walter) T.; A.B., U. N.C., 1939; Ph.D., Mass. Inst. Tech., 1949; m. Ann Elliot Hommann, Jan. 5, 1944; children— Constantia, Charles. Instr. philosophy U. N.C., Chapel Hill, 1941-42, asso. prof. psychology, 1953-55, prof., 1955-62, Alumni Distinguished prof., 1962—, chmn. psychology dept., 1960-66; research asso. U. Mich., 1948-49; asst. prof. psychology Boston U., 1949-51; lectr., research asso. Harvard, 1951-53; bd. dirs. Social Sci. Research Council, 1966-69. Served to 1st lt. AUS, 1942-46. Fellow Center For Advanced Study Behavioral Scis. Stanford, 1956-57, USPHS Spl. fellow Sorbonne, Paris, 1963-64. Fellow Am. Psychol. Assn., Soc. for Psychol. Study Social Issues. Author: (with Harold Kelley) The Social Psychology of Groups, 1959. Editor: Jour. Exptl. Social Psychology, 1965-70. Contbr. profl. jours. Home: 1004 Highland Woods Chapel Hill NC 27514

THIEDEMAN, DOUGLAS JOHN, dentist; b. Lansing, Mich., Oct. 17, 1940; s. John Herman and Marjorie Irene (Finkhouse) T.; student Western Reserve U., 1958-60; D.D.S., U. Mich., 1964; m. Bette Ann Johnson, June 15, 1963; 1 dau., Michelle Lynn. Pvt. practice dentistry, Boynton Beach, Fla., 1966-69; staff dentist VA Hosp., Salisbury, N.C., 1969—. Served to capt. AUS, 1964-66. Mem. Am. Dental Assn., Rowan County Dental Soc., Sigma Chi, Psi Omega. Republican. Episcopalian (lay reader 1968-69). Office: VA Hosp 1601 Brenner Av Salisbury NC 28144

THIELE, MILDRED DORCAS BRADFORD (MRS. WALTER H. THIELE), nurse; b. Walnut, Miss.; d. Blythe Thompson and Ellen (Davis) Bradford; diploma in nursing Bapt. Hosp., Memphis, 1938; student U. Mich., 1940; B.S., U. Wash., 1950; m. Walter H. Thiele, Apr. 15, 1968. Pub. health nurse, Miss., 1938-40; head nurse to chief nurse VA hosps., Jackson, Miss., Grand Island, Neb., N.Y.C., Chgo. Mpls., Lake City, Fla., Gainesville, Fla., 1945-69. Served to capt. U.S. Army Nurse Corps, Korean War. Recipient commendation Dir. VA Hosp., Grand Island, 1953. Mem. Am., Fla (chmn. membership com., 1968, dir.) nurses assns., Bus. and Profl. Womens Club Lake City (past pres.), Alpha Tau Delta. Republican. Episcopalian. Club: Ponte Vedra (Fla.) Address: 5347 Noble Circle S Jacksonville FL 32211

THIELE, WALTER HENRY, ret. hosp. adminstr., govt. ofcl.; b. Frankfort, Germany, Oct. 13, 1905 (came to U.S. 1906, naturalized 1916; s. Ludwig A. and Henrietta Maria (Braam) T.; student U. Mich., 1926-28; Ohio State U., 1928-29; U. Basle, 1929-30; M.D., U. Heidelberg, 1932; m. Anne P. Pfeffer, Sept. 17, 1934 (dec. June, 1965); 1 son, Richard Frederick; m. 2d, Mildred D. Bradford, 1968. Intern St. John's Hosp., Nyack (N.Y.) Hosp., 1933-34; resident St. Elizabeths Hosp., Washington, 1934-35; internist Lake City, Ia., also chief medicine Fayetteville (N.C.) VA Hosp., 1934-52; dir. Atlanta VA Hosp., 1952-60, Lake City VA Hosp., 1960-66, Clarksburg (W.Va.) VA Hosp., 1966-67. Served to col., M.C., AUS, 1942-47. Mem. Am. Hosp. Assn., A.M.A., Phi Gamma Delta. Episcopalian. Mason (K.T., Shriner), Rotarian. Home: 5347 Noble Circle S Jacksonville FL 32211

THIES, AUSTIN COLE, utility co. exec.; b. Charlotte, N.C., July 18, 1921; s. Oscar Julius and Blanche (Austin) T.; B.S. in Mech. Engring., Ga. Inst. Tech., 1943; m. Marilyn Joy Walker, June 26, 1945; children—Austin Cole, Robert Melvin, Marilyn Leone. With Duke Power Co., Charlotte, 1946—, mgr. steam prodn., 1963-65, asst. v.p., 1965-67, v.p. prodn. and operation, 1967-71, sr. v.p. prodn. and transmission, 1971—, also dir. Chmn. prodn. com., chmn. engring. and operating div. Southeastern Electric Exchange; chmn. tech. adv. com. Carolinas Va. Nuclear Power Assos. Served with USNR, 1943-46. Decorated Purple Heart. Mem. Edison Electric Inst., Charlotte C. of C., Am. Soc. M.E. (past chmn. Piedmont Carolina sect.), N.C. Soc. Engrs. (v.p.), Charlotte Engrs. Club, Pollution Control Assn., Am. Nuclear Soc., Nat. Rifle Assn. (life), Kappa Sigma. Presbyn. (elder). Rotarian (dir., pres. North Charlotte). Clubs: Cowans Ford Country, Charlotte Executives, Charlotte Ga. Institute Technology (past pres.), Charlotte Rifle and Pistol (past pres.), Charlotte City. Home: 2429 Red Fox Trail Charlotte NC 28211 Office: 422 S Church St Charlotte NC 28201

THIESS, GEORGE HENDERSON, mfg. co. exec.; b. St. Louis, Mo., Oct. 25, 1930; s. Jack and Elva Joy (Brashears) T.; B.S., Washington U., 1958; children—Eric, Suzanne; m. Grace Linda Funk, Apr. 30, 1970; 1 son, Michael. Engr. research dept. Sperry Microwave Electronics Co., Clearwater, Fla., 1958-60; mem. tech. staff apparatus research dept. Tex. Instruments, Inc., Dallas, 1960-63; dir. research and devel. Microwave Physics Corp., Garland, Tex., 1963-66; research scientist S.W. Center Advanced Studies, Dallas, 1966; pres., chmn. bd. Electro Data, Inc., Garland, 1966-71; pres., chmn. bd. Electro Research, Inc., 1971—. Mem. Dallas Leadership Council, 1969-70. Served with USAF, 1951-55. Mem. Am. Phys. Soc., I.E.E.E., Assn. Old Crows, Am. Ordnance Assn., Internat. Platform Assn., Dallas Guild Watchmakers, Tex. Watchmakers Assn., La. Retail Jewelers Assn. (hon.). Inventor electronic wristwatch. Contbr. articles to profl. jours. Home: 6431 Northaven Dallas TX 75230 Office: 418 Yale St Garland TX 75042

THIGPEN, CALVIN HERRITAGE, physician; b. Greenville, N.C., Jan. 7, 1924; s. Zeno Edward and Carrie Bertha (Wilkins) T.; B.S. in Chemistry with distinction, Va. State Coll., 1953; M.D. (Lincoln Found grantee), U. Va., 1962; m. Vera Belle Crawford, Dec. 25, 1947; children—Calvin Herritage, Vera Karen. Tchr., Hopewell, Va., 1953-58; cosmetics chemist, plant mgr. Stuart Products Co., Richmond, Va., 1957-58; intern Med. Coll. Va., 1962-63; individual practice medicine, Petersburg, Va., 1962—; asso. coll. physician Va. State Coll., Petersburg, 1964—. Mem. Planning and Zoning Commn. Hopewell, Va., 1967-70, Hopewell Sch. Bd., 1970—; mem. adv. com. U.S. Army, Ft. Lee, Va., 1970—. Mem. Democratic Com., Hopewell, 1965—. Bd. dirs. Salvation Army, Petersburg. Served to 1st lt. AUS, 1944-49; ETO. Mem. Hopewell C. of C., Old Dominion Med. Soc. (exec. com. 1965—), Sigma Pi Sigma, Beta Kappa Chi. Episcopalian. Club: National Guardsmen (Richmond, Va.). Home: 1830 Arlington Rd Hopewell VA 23860 Office: 133 Harrison St Petersburg VA 23803

THIGPEN, GEORGE EDWARD, ednl. adminstr.; b. Huhtsville, Tex., May 16, 1916; s. John R. and Margaret P. (Burnett) T.; B.S., Sam Houston State Coll., 1939; M.E., U. Houston, 1951; m. Joyce Hines, June 18, 1942; children—George Michael, David Hines. Tchr. Grand Saline (Tex.) Ind. Sch. Dist., 1939-41; math. tchr. Tomball Ind. Sch. Dist., 1946-47; prin. high sch., Pearland, 1947-51; prin. El Campo (Tex.) Ind. Sch. Dist., 1951-53; supt., 1953—. Mem. legislative council U. Tex. Interscholastic League. Served with USNR, 1941-45. Mem. C. of C. (dir.), Am., Tex. assns. sch. adminstrs., Am. Legion, V.F.W. Mason. Lion. Home: 816 Av 1 El Campo TX 77437 Office: 700 W Norris El Campo TX 77437

THIGPEN, JAMES RAY, carpet and rug co. exec.; b. Wayne, Ark., Nov. 4, 1923; s. Samuel James and Bertha Miller (Warner) T.; student N.W. La. State U., 1940-42; m. Elinor Jane Doerr, Sept. 28, 1922; children—James Ray, Ronald H. Exec. trainee Herpolsheimers Dept. Store, 1946-47, buyer, 1947-49, mng. dir. staff, 1949-50; salesman Wunda Weve Carpet Co., 1953-56, dist. mgr., 1956-61, v.p. sales, 1961-65; v.p. marketing Patcraft Co., 1965-69; v.p. sales West Point Pepperell, carpet and rug div., Dalton, Ga., 1969—. Served to capt. USAAF, 1942-46. Decorated Air medal. Mem. Sigma Tau Gamma. Republican. Methodist. Elk. Club: Dalton Golf and Country. Home: 113 Tibbs Rd Dalton GA 30720 Office: PO Box 1208 Dalton GA 30720

THIGPEN, SAMUEL GRADY, author; b. Lake Como, Miss., Aug. 19, 1890; s. Samuel Forrest and Julia (Arledge) T.; B.S., Miss. Coll., 1912; m. Lorena Tate, Apr. 27, 1917; children—Monroe Tate, (dec.), Samuel Grady, Anna Lynn (Mrs. Charles R. Holloway). Founder, pres. Thigpen Hardware Co., Picayune, Miss., 1919-72; pub. Thigpen's Store News, 1924—; chmn. bd. 1st Nat. Bank. Trustee Crosby Meml. Hosp. Mem. Miss. Retail Hardware Assn., C. of C. Baptist. Mason. Author: Pearl River: Highway to Gloryland; Next Door to Heaven; A Boy in Rural Mississippi; Ninety and One Years; Work and Play in Grandpa's Day‡

THIGPEN, SILAS FORREST, JR., merchant, city ofcl.; b. Bay Springs, Miss., Jan. 2, 1907; s. Samuel F. and Julia C. (Arledge) T.; student La. State U., 1928; m. Tattie Mae Smith, Oct. 21, 1932; 1 dau., Tommiann (Mrs. Ronald V. Henagan). Mcht., farm supply, 1929—; mayor, Bay Springs, Miss., 1940—. Mem. Miss. Geol. Survey Bd., 1956; v.p. exec. com. Miss. Municipal Assn., 1963-65, pres., 1965—. Bd. trustees sch. system, 1935-57. Recipient Gov.'s award, 1963; plaque for work as chmn. Geol. Survey Bd., 1970-71. Mem. Retail Mchts. Assn., Miss C. of C. (chmn. com. marine resources, chmn. com. study govtl. purchasing procedures), Nat. League Cities (com. govt. and administrn.), Miss. Seedmens Assn. Baptist. Mason, Rotarian. Address: Bay Springs MS 39422

THISTLETHWAITE, JOHN RICHMOND, editor, publisher; b. Washington, La., July 16, 1918; s. John R. and Charlotte (Frere) T.; student U. Southwestern La., 1935; B.A., Tulane U., 1939; m. Patricia Ann Norman, May 11, 1950; children—John Richmond, Edward Barry, Duncan Frere, Geoffrey Norman, Scott Douglas. Editor, Pub. Daily World, Opelousas, La., 1939—. Mem. La. Coordinating Council for Higher Edn. Bd. dirs. Council for a Better La. Served to major USMC, 1942-46. Mem. La. Press Assn. (pres. 1959-60), Sigma Delta Chi, Delta Kappa Epsilon. Republican. Methodist. Elk. Club: Boston (New Orleans). Home: 705 S Court St Opelousas LA 70570 Office: 137 S Market St Opelousas LA 70570

THOBURN, ROBERT, dentist; b. Phila., Dec 23, 1909; s. Robert and Barbara (Tunstall) T.; student U. Fla., 1929-30; D.D.S., Atlanta-So Dental Coll. (name changed to Emory U. Dental Sch.), 1934; m. Marguerite Emma Steele, June 2, 1936; children—Robert and Thomas Edward (twins), Barbara Kaye (Mrs. Richard M. Davies), Donald William. Individual practice dentistry, Daytona Beach, Fla., 1934—; mem. dental staff Halifax Dist. Hosp. Fla. del. Am. Dental Assn., 1952—; mem. Fla. Bd. Dentistry, 1958-69, also chmn., 1961, 66. Dir. South Peninsula Taxpayers Assn., 1953-55; commr. South Peninsula Zoning Bd., 1953-55; mem. South Peninsula Appeal Bd., 1957-58; area chmn. merit program fund drive Emory U., 1967-69. Fellow Am. Coll. Dentists (chmn. Fla. sect. 1959-60), Fla. Dental Assn. (hon.; historian 1946-60, pres. 1954-55); mem. Am. Dental Assn. (council on dental edn. 1966—), Central Dist. Dental Soc. (legislative com.), Fla. Bd. Dentistry (certificate merit 1969), Volasia County Dental Soc. (life, past pres.), Am. Acad. History Dentistry (pres. 1958-59), Delta Sigma Delta, Lambda Chi Alpha. Presbyn. (deacon, elder). Mason. Author (with Helen S. Haines) 75 Years of Dentistry-History of the Florida State Dental Society, 1960. Home: 1908 S Peninsula Dr Daytona Beach FL 32018 Office: 227 Orange Av Daytona Beach FL 32014

THOM, CORCORAN, JR., banker; b. Nahant, Mass., July 7, 1907; s. Corcoran and Mary Huntington (Lay) T.; student Friend's Sch., Washington, 1912-18, Middlesex Sch., Concord, Mass., 1918-24; B.S., Harvard, 1928; m. Eliza Hutchinson Mitchell, June 20, 1936. With Riggs Nat. Bank, Washington, 1928—, now sr. v.p. Life trustee, treas. Corcoran Gallery Art, 1948—; dir. Children's Hosp.; treas. Air Force Aid Soc., 1948—. Served as 1st lt. to lt. col. U.S. A.A.F., 1942-45; PTO. Decorated Air medal. Mem. Assn. Res. City Bankers, Washington Bd. Trade, Newcomen Soc., Washington Jr. C. of C. (pres. 1935-36). Clubs: University, Metropolitan, Alfalfa, Burning Tree, Chevy Chase (Washington). Home: 4456 Springdale NW Washington DC 20016 Office: 1503 Pennsylvania Av Washington DC 20005

THOMAN, JOHN RICHARD, cons. engr.; b. Columbus, O., Aug. 11, 1920; s. Albert and Clara (Krug) T.; B.S., Case Inst. Tech., 1942; m. Alice Duvall, Feb. 10, 1945; children—Barbara E. (Mrs. T. H. Howell), John R., Patricia A., Daniel P. Commd. officer USPHS, 1944-67, chief san. engr. U.S. Operations Mission to Ethiopia, 1951-57, mem. Imperial Ethiopian Med. adv. bd. of Health, Div. of Water Supply & Pollution Control, Washington 1949-51, 57-59, regional program dir., Atlanta, 1959-64, dir. Southeast Water Lab., Athens, 1963-69; regional dir. Southeast region Fed. Water Quality Adminstrn., 1966-70; acting regional adminstr. Environmental Protection Agy., 1970-71; mgr. Engring.-Sci., Inc., Atlanta, 1971—. Lectr. civil engring. U. Fla., 1963-67; research asso. U. Ga., 1966-68. Diplomate Am. Acad. San. Engrs. Fellow Am. Soc. Civil Engrs.; mem. Am. Water Works Assn., Water Pollution Control Fedn., Am. Pub. Works Assn., A.A.A.S., Tau Beta Pi, Theta Tau, Sigma Alpha Epsilon. Registered profl. engr., D.C., Ga. Home: 1176 Hampton Hall Dr Atlanta GA 30319 Office: 14 Perimeter Center East Atlanta GA 30346

THOMAS, ALAN TOY, chem. engr.; b. Louisville, May 15, 1921; s. M(oses) A(lan) and Ruth (Lacefield) T.; B. Chem. Engring., U. Louisville, 1943, M. Chem. Engring., 1947, Ph.D., 1964; m. Joycelyn Jane Markert, Mar. 18, 1945; children—Thomas Douglas, Tucker Craig. With Brown-Forman Distillers Corp., 1943—, apprentice supr., tech. supr., research engr. and statistician, research asso., project and devel. engr., asst. to the v.p. dir. prodn., 1943-64, asst. dir. prodn., 1964—. Lectr. math. U. Louisville, 1957-59, lectr. bus. mgmt., 1964—. Registered profl. engr., Ind. Fellow A.A.A.S.; mem. Am. Chem. Soc., Am. Mgmt. Assn., Am. Math. Soc., Operations Research Soc. Am., Distillers Feed Research Council, Inst. Mgmt. Sci., Am. Soc. Quality Control, Inst. Math. Statistics, N.Y. Acad. Sci., Phi Lambda Upsilon, Sigma Xi. Presbyn. Contbr. articles to profl. jours. Home: RR 3 Box 86 Anchorage KY 40223 Office: PO Box 1080 Anchorage KY40223

THOMAS, ARCHIE EDWIN, physician; b. Nixburg, Ala., 1898; M.D., Vanderbilt U., 1924. Intern, Tenn. Coal and Iron Co. Employees Hosp., Fairfield, Ala., 1924, Walter Reed Hosp., Washington, 1925-26; clin. tng. Chgo. Lying-In Hosp., 1931-32; chief service St. Margaret's Hosp., Montgomery, Ala.; mem. staff Jackson Hosp., Profl. Center Hosp. (both Montgomery); cons. obstetrics and gynecology Maxwell AFB Hosp., Montgomery, Bapt. Hosp., Montgomery. Diplomate Am. Bd. Obstetrics and Gynecology. Fellow A.S.C.; mem. A.M.A., Am. Coll. Obstetricians and Gynecologists, Central Assn. Obstetricians and Gynecologists, Ala. Med. Assn. (pres.), So. Med. Assn. Office: 331 S Ripley St Montgomery AL 36104*

THOMAS, BENJAMIN HAWES, furniture co. exec.; b. Maceo, Ky., Dec. 10, 1907; s. Joseph Alexander and Mary Ann (Hawes) T.; student Western Ky. Tchrs. Sch., 1927, Bowling Green Coll. Commerce, 1931-32; m. Corinna Marie Robertson, Feb. 1937; children—Mary Marie (Mrs. Clifford Fuller), Bonnie (Mrs. Parvin Bishop), Patsy (Mrs. Joseph Galanti). Property accountant Gen. Motors Corp., Pontiac, Mich., Detroit, 1929-31; cost accountant Ken-Rad Tube & Lamp Corp., Owensboro, Ky., 1932-41; controller, asst. gen. mgr. Eck Miller Transfer Co., Owensboro, 1941-54; controller A & H Truck Line, 1954-56; controller, dir. traffic Murphy-Miller, Inc. subsidiary of Kroehler Mfg. Co., Owensboro, 1956—. Family partner cattle and farming operation. Instr., Jr. Achievement, 1959-60. Served with Ky. Militia, 1942-45. Mem. Nat. Furniture Traffic Assn. (dir.), Owensboro Traffic Mens Assn., Sheriffs Assn. (hon. life), Delta Nu Alpha. Democrat. Baptist. Elk, Odd Fellow. Home: Pleasure Point Rd Route 1 Maceo KY 42355 Office: 931 Wing Av Owensboro KY 42301

THOMAS, BERT L., retail stores exec.; b., 1918; married. With Winn-Dixie Stores, Inc., Jacksonville, Fla., 1946—, v.p. mfg., warehouse and delivery, 1952-65, pres., dir., 1965—. Office: 5050 Edgewood Ct Jacksonville FL 32203*

THOMAS, CHARLES MITCHELL, engr.; b. Wytheville, Va., Jan. 18, 1892; s. Charles Benton and Elizabeth (Crockett) T.; B.S. with distinction in Civil Engring., Va. Poly. Inst., 1913; m. Sue L. Hurt, Feb. 23 (dec. Feb. 1938); 1 dau., Elizabeth Crockett (Mrs. Talmadge Lloyd Jones, Jr.); m. 2d, Mildred M. Coulter, Sept. 23, 1939; 1 dau., Diane Coulter. With U.S. Coast and Geodetic Survey (name changed to Nat. Oceanic and Atmospheric Adminstrn.), 1922-52, comdr. GUIDE, Suisin Bay (Cal.) operations, 1941-42, supr. So. Dist. hdqrs., New Orleans, 1946, Southeastern rep., 1946-52; engr. Savannah River project E.I. duPont Co., 1952-53; Southeastern rep. Vitrified Clay Pipe Assn., 1954—; with Bell Labs., Inc., Orlando, Fla., 1955-72; liaison officer Civil Aero. Adminstrn., Atlanta, 1946-52. Served with U.S. Navy, 1918-20, with USNR., 1942-45. Registered profl. engr. and surveyor, Ga. Mem. Ga. Assn. Registered Land Surveyors (co-founder, charter and life mem.), Am. Soc. C.E. (life), Soc. Am. Mil. Engrs. (dir. Atlantic post; life mem.), Navy League U.S. (mem. Coast Guard affairs com. Atlanta council), Am. Congress Surveying and Mapping, Ga. Soc. Architects and Engrs. (life), Soc. Automotive Engrs. (past chmn. membership com.), Am. Legion. Presbyn. (elder). Mason, Rotarian (charter mem. West End Atlanta club, chmn. four-way test com. 52 yrs.). Author: Compass Surveying and the Simplified Calculation of Farm Areas, 1915. Patentee simplified time charts of world, 1924. Home: 294-A Peachtree Hills Av NE Atlanta GA 30305 Office: 550 Glenn St SW Atlanta GA 30312

THOMAS, CHELKUZIL THOMAS, educator; b. Kerala, India, Sept. 3, 1910; s. Geevargis and Annamma (Thoma) T.; B.D., Serampore Coll., 1939; M.A., Calcutta U., 1942; Ph.D., Hartford Sem. Found., 1961; m. Achamma Mathew, June 10, 1943; children—George, Mathai, John. Came to U.S., 1958, naturalized, 1968. Asst. prof., asso. prof., prof. JCS Theol. Sem., Charlotte, N.C., 1961-69; prof. philosophy Pfeiffer Coll., Misenheimer, N.C., 1969—. Vis. prof. U. N.C., Charlotte, summer 1968, 69, spring 1970, 71. Civil servant Govt. of India, New Delhi, 1942-56; co-dir. Confs. for Diplomats, 1955; rep. Nat. Christian Council of India, 1956-58. Mem. N.C. Philos. Soc., Assn. for Asian Studies, Am. Acad. Religion, English-Speaking Union. Author: Appearance and Reality in Samkara and F.H. Bradley, 1964. Home: 2048 Coniston Pl Charlotte NC 28207

THOMAS, MRS. CLARENCE A., investment bus. exec.; b. Cleburne, Tex., July 17, 1914; d. Martin Coppage II and Florence (Campbell) Sanders; student U. Tex. 1931-33, Tex. Woman's U., 1933-34, U. Tex. at Arlington 1948-49; m. E. O. Nichols, June 2, 1935 (div. Aug. 1947); 1 dau., Judy Nichols (Mrs. Gerald J. Roberts, Jr.); m. 2d, Clarence A. Thomas, Oct. 29, 1950. Tchr., therapeutic dietitian, also interior decorator Plainview (Tex.) Sanitarium, 1941-47; owner, dir. Food Services, Carters Cafeteria, Ft. Worth, 1950-60; asso. exec. investments Carter Investments, Fort Worth, 1950—; owner, operator ranch. Active A.R.C., Jr. League, Art Assn. Mem. Internat. Platform Assn., Kappa Alpha Theta. Mem. Ch. of Christ. Clubs: Kappa Alpha Theta Mothers, North Texas Riding. Home: 3601 Wooten Dr Ft Worth TX 76133 Office: 109 1/2 Main St Ft Worth TX 76102

THOMAS, COLIN GORDON, JR., educator, Iowa City, July 25, 1918; s.; Colin G. and Eloise (Brainerd) T.; B.S., U. Chgo., 1940, M.D., 1943; m. Shirley Forbes, Sept. 14, 1946; children—Karen, Barbara, James G., John F. Intern, U. Ia. Hosp., 1943-44, resident in surgery, 1944-45, 47-50, asso. in surgery, 1950-51, asst. prof., 1951-52; asst. prof. surgery U. N.C., Chapel Hill, 1952-55, asso. prof., 1955-61, prof., 1961—, chmn. dept. surgery, 1966—. Served with M.C. AUS, 1945-47. Diplomate Am. Bd. Surgery. Mem. A.M.A., A.C.S., Am. Thyroid Assn., Am. Assn. Cancer Research, Durham-Orange County Med. Soc., Soc. U. Surgeons, So. Soc. Clin. Research, Am., So. surg. assns., N.Y. Acad. Scis., Am. Assn. U. Profs., Halsted Soc., Soc. Exptl. Biology and Medicine, Soc. Internat. de chirurgie, Allen Whipple Surg. Soc., Womack Surg. Soc., Soc. Surg. Chairmen, Nat. Bd. Med. Examiners (Surgery), Soc. for Surgery Alimentary Tract, Alpha Omega Alpha. Editoral bd. Rev. Surgery. Contbr. numerous articles to med. jours. Home: Morgan Creek Rd Chapel Hill NC 27514 Office: NC Meml Hospital Chapel Hill NC 27514

THOMAS, DAN ANDERSON, univ. dean; b. Ooltewah, Tenn., Oct. 1, 1922; s. Daniel Bryson and Blanche (Sylar) T.; B.S., U. Chattanooga, 1945; Ph.D., Vanderbilt U., 1952; m. Margaret Elizabeth Glaze, Mar. 19, 1944; children—Roger Nelson, Rebecca Lynn. Asst. prof. physics U. South, 1949-51; research physicist U.S. Naval Ordnance Lab., White Oak, Md., 1951-52; asso. prof. physics Rollins Coll., 1952-57, prof., 1957-63, chmn. div. sci. and math., 1956-59, dir. grad. program physics, 1959-63; dean faculty, prof. physics Jacksonville (Fla.) U., 1963-67, prof. physics, v.p. and dean faculties, 1967—; cons. U.S. Navy Underwater Sound Reference Lab., Orlando, Fla., 1953-63. Mem. adv. com. student sects. Am. Inst. Physics, 1963-68; del. Am. Council on Edn., 1968—; mem. Fla. Fulbright Com., 1963-68. AEC fellow, 1947-48; Danforth Asso., 1958-62. Served with USNR, World War II. Fellow A.A.A.S. (mem. council 1961-63); mem. Am. Assn. U. Profs. (exec. com. Fla. 1961-63), Am. Assn. Physics Tchrs., Acoustical Soc. Am., Am. Phys. Soc., Am. Conf. Acad. Deans, Conf. Acad. Deans of So. States, So. Conf. Deans Faculties and Acad. Vice Pres.'s, Fla. Acad. Sci. (pres. 1958), Fla. Audubon Soc. (bd. dirs. 1957-60), Sigma Xi, Alpha Soc., Blue Key, Omicron Delta Kappa, Sigma Pi Sigma, Kappa Sigma. Clubs: University; Meninak (dir.). Contbr. profl. jours. Home: 3272 University Blvd N Jacksonville FL 32211

THOMAS, DANIEL HOLCOMBE, judge; b. Prattville, Ala., Aug. 25, 1906; s. Columbus Eugene and Augusta (Pratt) T.; LL.B., U. Ala., 1928; m. Dorothy Manning Quina, Sept. 26, 1936; children—Daniel H., Merrill Pratt. Admitted to Ala. bar, 1928; practiced in Mobile, 1929-51; asst. solicitor Mobile Country, Ala., 1932-39; U.S. dist. judge, Mobile, 1951—; now chief judge. Vice pres., mem. exec. bd. Mobile Area Council, Boy Scouts of Am., 1961-66, pres., 1967-68. Trustee Ala. State Dept. Archives and History. Served to lt. USNR, 1943-45. Mem. Am. Bar Assn., Phi Delta Theta, Phi Delta Phi. Methodist. Clubs: Internat. Trade (dir.), Mobile Country (dir.). Home: 13 Dogwood Circle Mobile AL 36608 Office: US Ct House Mobile AL 36602

THOMAS, DAVID DUVAL, found. exec.; b. New Castle, Tex., Feb. 19, 1913; s. David Dismukes and Lena Myrtle (Wisdom) T.; student U. Tenn., 1929-32, George Washington U., 1953-57; m. Dorothy Frances Clark, Sept. 1, 1937; children—Lena Frances, David Clark. With CAA, 1938-59, dir. Office Air Traffic Control, 1956-59; with FAA, 1959-70, asso. adminstr. programs, 1963-65, dep. adminstr., 1965-70; pres. Flight Safety Found., Arlington, Va., 1970—. Recipient Meritorious Service award Dept. Commerce, 1953, Medalion award Air Traffic Control Assn., 1963, Laura Taber Barbour Air Safety award, 1963, Pres. U.S. award distinguished civilian service, 1963; Civil Service League award, 1967; Rockefeller Pub. Service award, 1967; Monsanto Air Safety award, 1967, Exceptional Service award FAA, 1965. Mem. Am. Inst. Aero. and Astronautics, Air Traffic Control Assn. Mem. Ch. of Christ (deacon). Home: 3909 Rose Lane Annandale VA 22033 Office: 1800 N Kent St Arlington VA 22209

THOMAS, DIANE, journalist. Editorial asso. Atlanta Mag., 1970—. Office: 1104 Commerce Bldg Atlanta GA 30302

THOMAS, ELMER KOEHLER, bank exec.; b. Oklahoma City, Feb. 19, 1933; s. Wilfred Smith and Miriam Helen (Koehler) T.; B.A., U. Okla., 1954, LL.B., 1954; LL.M., So. Meth. U., 1957; m. Joanna Champlin, Nov. 24, 1956; children—Betsy, Toby, Brooke, Andrew. Admitted to Okla. bar, 1954; law clk. for fed. judge, Oklahoma City, 1956-57; atty. Bohanan, Barefoot & Lee, Attys., Oklahoma City, 1957-59; v.p., trust officer First Nat. Bank & Trust Co., Enid, Okla., 1959-67, pres., 1967—; dir. Enid Realty Co., First Nat. Bank, Banfield Packing Co. (all Enid). Bd. dirs. Dillingham Found., Enid, Bass Meml. Bapt. Hosp., Enid, Okla. Med. Research Found., Oklahoma City. Served to capt. AUS, 1954-56. Mem. Phi Delta Theta, Phi Alpha Delta. Democrat. Presbyn. Rotarian. Home: 2450 Sherwood Enid OK 73701 Office: 201 N Grand St Box 1469 Enid OK 73701

THOMAS, ERNEST SAWAYA, II, mfg. exec.; b. Jackson, Miss., Aug. 8, 1937; s. Ernest Sawaya and Esmer (Joseph) T.; B.S., U. Notre Dame, 1959; m. Margo Saba, July 28, 1962; children—Deborah Lynn, Sharon Marie, Ernest David, John Joseph. Sec. treas. Capitol Mfg. Co., Norman Shirtmakers, Jackson, 1960—. Served with AUS, 1959-60. Elk, Rotarian (dir.) Home: 1973 Aztec Dr Jackson MS 39211 Office: I-55 South Byram Exit Jackson MS 39212

THOMAS, FAY MATHEW, bank ofcl.; b. Creston, Ia., July 9, 1890; s. Lincoln and Fannie Elizabeth (Brenanstal) T.; m. Willa Mae Adams, July 19, 1919; children—Clinton L., Jean-Faye. Mgr. Richmond (Va.) Cafeterias, Inc., 1920-22; gen. mgr. United Hotels Corp. Cafeterias, Toronto, Montreal, Can., 1922-25; mgr. Cavalier Hotel, Virginia Beach, Va., 1925-27; gen. mgr. Hotel Roanoke (Va.), 1927-29, Hotel Patrick Henry, 1929-32, Exchange Buffet Corp., N.Y.C., 1932-35; v.p., gen. mgr. Hotel Carter, Cleve., 1935-39; asst. to pres. Hotel New Yorker, N.Y.C., 1939-41; v.p., gen. mgr. Hotel Roosevelt, New Orleans, 1941-42, Hotel Book—Cadillac, Detroit, 1942-52; v.p. for bus. devel. Nat. Bank Ft. Lauderdale, Fla., 1955-72; dir. Key Biscayne Hotel and Villas, Miami, Jacksonville Coach Co., Jacksonville, Fla. Col. Civil Air Patrol, 1941-50, Mich. wing comdr., Midwest regional comdr., then mem. nat. exec. com.; dir. funding bd. Internat. Swimming Hall of Fame. Served with U.S. Army, World War I. Mem. Am. Legion, D.A.V., Mil. Order World Wars, Detroit Bd. Commerce, So., Ohio, Ft. Lauderdale (hon. life). Detroit hotel assns., Mich. Aeros. and Space Assn. (hon. life). Mason. Clubs: Detroit Athletic; Aero of Michigan (hon. life); Wings (N.Y.C.); Army and Navy (Washington); Ft. Lauderdale (Fla.) Lauderdale Yacht (dir.); Lago Mar Country. Home: 1750 E Las Olas Blvd Fort Lauderdale FL 33301

THOMAS, FRANK ALMERINE, JR., coll. pres.; b. Atlanta, Jan. 14, 1924; s. Frank Amerine and Lois Opal (Hall) T.; student Auburn U., 1942-43, Duke, 1943-44; B.S. in Mech. Engring., Purdue U., 1947; M.S. in Mech. Engring., Ga. Inst. Tech., 1949, Ph.D., 1958; m. Dorothy Mary Havens, June 9, 1947; children—Sarah Lou, Nancy Ann, Frank Almerine III. With Cal. Cotton Mills, 1942, Buckeye Cotton Oil Co., 1942, Hollingsworth Whitney Co., 1942-43; engr. W.A. Roger Industries, 1947; indsl. hygienist Ga. Dept. Pub. Health, 1947-49, AEC, 1949-51; successively instr., asst. prof., research asso. Ga. Inst. Tech., 1951-58; prof. mech. engring., head dept. Lamar State Coll. Tech., Beaumomt, Tex., 1958-62, head dept. indsl. engring, 1962-64, prof. indsl. engring., 1964-65, prof. mech. engring., 1965—, dean engring., 1961-67, v.p. acad. affairs, 1967-69, pres., 1969—. Bd. dirs. Beaumont chpt. A.R.C., 1967, St. Elizabeth Hosp., No. Jefferson County United Appeals; campaign chmn., bd. dirs. No. Jefferson County chpt. Am. Heart Assn; trustee Baptist Hosp. S.E. Tex., 1967. Served to 2d lt. USMCR, 1943-46. Registered profl. engr., Ga., Tex. Mem. Am. Soc. M.E. (chmn. Sabine sect. 1962-63, sr. del. region X 1969—, sec. regional dels. conf. 1961), Nat., Tex. socs. profl. engrs., Am. Soc. for Engring. Edn., Gulf Coast Engring. and Sci. Soc. (dir.), Lamar Honor Soc., Young Bus. League, Beaumont C. of C. (dir. 1970—), Sigma Xi, Pi Tau Sigma, Kappa Sigma, Alpha Phi Omega, Phi Kappa Phi, Phi Eta Sigma. Baptist (deacon). Rotarian. Author tech. papers. Home: 102 Redbird Lane Beaumont TX 77710

THOMAS, FRED WESLEY, govt. ofcl.; b. Florence, Ala., Feb. 7, 1912; s. Jesse Reeder and Ella (Chandler) T.; B.S. in Civil Engring., Ga. Sch. Tech., 1934; M.S. in San. Engring., Harvard, 1940; m. Carolyn Louise Bishop, Oct. 19, 1941; children—Linda (Mrs. Jerre Wayne Gist), Sandra (Mrs. Earl Everett Pugh), Laura Jane. Environmental engr. in gen. sanitation and water and sewage treatment TVA, Muscle Shoals, Ala., 1935-51, dir. air pollution studies and control program, chief air quality br., 1951—. Served as sr. san. engr. USPHS, 1941-43. Registered profl. engr., Ala.; diplomate Environmental Engring. Intersoc. Bd. Mem. Am. Indsl. Health Assn., Am. Pub. Health Assn., Am. Soc. C.E., Delta Omega. Presbyn. Contbr. articles to profl. jours. Home: 1020 Olive St Florence AL 35630 Office: River Oaks Bldg Muscle Shoals AL 35660

THOMAS, GEORGE HERBERT, radio broadcasting co. exec.; b. Zwolle, La., Aug. 10, 1904; s. Henry Herbert and Evie George (Woods) T.; student N.W. State Coll., Natchitoches, La., 1926-27; m. Katherine Florence Porter, Dec. 7, 1933; 1 dau., Joan Katherine (Mrs. Charles W. Brakefield). Hotel mgr., Shreveport, La., Ft. Smith, Ark., Lafayette, La., 1929-44; owner, dir., radio sta. KVOL, Lafayette, 1935-64; owner, pres. radio sta. KANE, New Iberia, La., 1946—; pres. New Iberia Broadcasting Co.; dir. Evangeline Broadcasting Co. (Lafayette), 1935-64; charter mem. bd. dirs. Guaranty Bank & Trust Co. (Lafayette). Active A.R.C., chmn. Lafayette Parish chpt., 1958-60; mem. adv. bd. Salvation Army, Lafayette, 1948-60. Mem. Lafayette Recreation Commn., 1940-56, 57-62, chmn., 1948-56; bd. dirs. S.W. La. Rehab. Center, 1960-62; bd. dirs. Lafayette area Safety Council. Recipient Bronze Plaque award Lafayette City Ofcls., 1959; named King of S.W. La. Mardi Gras, Lafayette, 1960. Hon. life mem. Nat. Recreation Assn.; mem. Nat. La. (pres. 1952-53) assns. broadcasters, Radio Broadcast Pioneers, Am., La. (pres. 1957-58, dir.), So., Western senior golf assns. C. of C., La. Hotel Assn. (pres. 1941-42). Methodist. Shriner. Clubs: Oakbourne Country (pres. 1969) (Lafayette); Dallas Country (Dallas). Home: 1228 Myrtle Pl Lafayette LA 70501 Office: 450 E Main New Iberia LA 70560

THOMAS, H. ASHTON, physician, med. assn. exec., b. 1903; M.D., Tulane U., 1929. Intern Charity Hosp., New Orleans, 1929-30, then resident, sr. vis. surgeon. Diplomate Am. Bd. Otolaryngology. Mem. A.M.A., So. Med. Assn., La. State Med. Soc. (sec.-treas.), Am. Acad. Ophthalmology and Otolaryngology, Am. Rhinologic Soc., Am. Acad. Facial, Plastic and Reconstrn. Surgeons. Office: La State Med Soc 1700 Josephine St New Orleans LA 70113

THOMAS, HARRY EUGENE, city ofcl.; b. Memphis, Dec. 29, 1913; s. Hal A. and Cassie E. (Womack) T.; student Watkins Inst., 1936-40; m. Betty Margaret Smith, Apr. 10, 1943. Area price dir. U.S. OPS, 1949-51; truck and fleet sales mgr., Truex Chevrolet Co., Jackson, Tenn., 1951-53; sales exec. WDXI-TV, 1953-56; exec. dir. Jackson Housing Authority, 1956—. Chmn. Madison City chpt. A.R.C., 1964-66; pres. Jackson-Madison County Health and Welfare Assn., 1958-59. Served with AUS, World War II; ETO. Decorated 5 battle stars, Bronze Star with oak leaf cluster, Combat Infantryman's badge. Baptist. Mason (Shriner). Home: Old Humbolt Rd Jackson TN 38301 Office: 258 Elm St PO Box 3188 Jackson TN 38301

THOMAS, HENRY COFFMAN, physicist, educator; b. Sacramento, Ky., Dec. 29, 1918; s. William Howard and Winifred (Coffman) T.; B.S., Western Ky. State Coll., 1943; M.S., Vanderbilt U., 1948, Ph.D., 1950; m. Martha S. Massie, Jan. 3, 1944; 1 dau., Elisabeth Lee. Grad. fellow Vanderbilt U., 1946-49; asst. prof. physics dept. Miss. State U., 1949-51, asso. prof., 1951-55; asso. prof. Bradley U., 1955-56, chmn. physics dept., 1956-58; chmn. physics dept. Tex. Technol. Coll., 1958—; part-time staff Oak Ridge Nat. Lab. Served to 1st lt. USAAF, World War II. Decorated Air medal with cluster. Mem. Am. Phys. Soc., Sigma Xi, Sigma Pi Sigma. Home: 2110 55th St Lubbock TX 79412

THOMAS, HERBERT REX, govt. ofcl.; b. Riverside, Cal., Apr. 13, 1913; s. Louis Joseph and Anna (Corson) T.; student Chaffey Coll., 1930-33; B.S., U. Cal. at Berkeley, 1935, Ph.D., 1941; m. Martha Katherine Hunter, Apr. 2, 1940; children—Stephanie, Douglas. Plant pathologist U.S. Dept. Agr., Lafayette, Ind., 1937-43, Beltsville, Md., 1946-54, agrl. research adminstr., Washington, 1954-56, asst. dir. crops research div., Beltsville, 1956-65, dir. crops research div., 1965-70, dep. adminstr., Washington, 1970—. Cons., Dept. State, Nat. Acad. Sci. Served with USAAF, 1943-46. Mem. Am. Phytopathol. Soc., Washington Bot. Soc. (pres. 1968). Rotarian (pres. 1971). Home: 3907 Beechwood St Hyattsville MD 20782 Office: US Dept Agr Agr Research Service Washington DC 20250

THOMAS, HORACE REYNOLDS, dentist; b. Etowah, Tenn., Sept. 10, 1906; s. Horace William and Mary Elizabeth (Reynolds) T.; D.D.S., Emory U., 1929; postgrad. U. Tenn., 1960, 66; m. NeeNah Marilyn Billingslea, Oct. 2, 1928; children—Mary Anne (Mrs. Ed Long), Lillian (Mrs. Harold Coker), NeeNah T. Pvt. practice dentistry, Athens, Tenn., 1929-42, 46—. Served from 1st lt. to capt. Dental Corps, AUS, 1942-46. Recipient Bronze plaque City Park Sch. Camp, 1971. Mem. Com. 100, C. of C. Kiwanian. Home: Cedar Springs and Keith Lane Athens TN 37303 Office: White St Fisher Bldg Athens TN 37303

THOMAS, JAMES DAVID, educator; b. Holliday, Tex., July 20, 1910; s. William Albert and Angie Belle (Wisdom) T.; A.B., Abilene Christian Coll., 1943; M.A., So. Methodist U., 1944; Ph.D., U. Chgo., 1957; m. Mary Katherine Payne, Feb. 22, 1931; children—Deborah (dec.), Hannah (Mrs. Dwayne Kissick), John Paul. Asst. city mgr. Lubbock, Tex., 1939-42; minister Northwest Ch. Christ, Chgo., 1945-49; prof. Bible, Abilene (Tex.) Christian Coll., 1949—, head dept., 1970—, lectureship dir., 1952-70; pub., owner, mgr., editor Bibl. Research Press, Abilene, 1958—; staff writer Gospel Adv., 20th Century Christian. Mem. adv. council Am. Bible Soc. Mem. Am. Acad. Religion, S.W. Philos. Soc., Am. Sci. Affiliation, Evangelical Theol. Soc., Soc. Bibl. Lit. (sect. pres. 1967-68). Mem. College Church of Christ (elder 1969—). Kiwanian (dir. 1967-68, program dir. 1968). Mem. editorial bd. Restoration Quar. Home: 774 EN 15th St Abilene TX 79601

THOMAS, JAMES EDWARD, lawyer; b. Maryville, Tenn., Nov. 19, 1918; s. H. Charles and Mary Alice (Mills) T.; B.A., Maryville Coll., 1941; LL.B. cum laude, Harvard, 1948; m. Jean White, Aug. 15, 1941; 1 son, James Edward. Admitted to Ga. bar, 1950; practiced in Atlanta, 1948—; asso firm Alston, Miller & Gaines, 1948-53, partner, 1954—. Dir. Citizens and So. Bank of Sandy Springs (Ga.). Trustee Lovett Sch., Atlanta. Served to capt. AUS, World War II; maj. U.S. Army Res. ret. Decorated Bronze Star medal. Mem. Am., Ga., Atlanta bar assns. Republican. Episcopalian. Clubs: Atlanta Lawyers, Commerce, Cherokee Town Country. Home: 5 Westchester Sq So 238 15th St NE Atlanta GA 30309 Office: Citizens and So Nat Bank Bldg Atlanta GA 30303

THOMAS, JERRY, pres. Fla. senate; b. West Palm Beach, Fla., Apr. 30, 1929; s. Larry A. and Irene (Lee) T.; A.A., Palm Beach Jr. Coll., 1949; B.S., Fla. State U., 1951, postgrad., 1952; M.E., Fla. Atlantic U.,

1968; m. Jeannie Hair, Nov. 21, 1951; children— Robbie, Larry, Kenny, Jerry, Cindy. Chmn. bd. dirs., pres. Gen. Financial Systems, Inc., Riviera Beach, Fla., 1963—; mem. Fla. Ho. of Reps., 1960-64; mem. Fla. Senate, 1964—, pres., 1970—. Chmn., pres. United Capital Corp., First Nat. Bank & Trust Co. of Lake Worth, Capital Leasing Corp.; chmn. bd. First Marine Bank & Trust Co. of Riviera Beach, First Nat. Bank & Trust Co. of Jupiter/Tequesta, First Comml. Bank of Live Oak, Marine Nat. Bank of Jacksonville, Congress Nat. Bank of Palm Springs, First Community Bank of Boca Raton, Peoples Bank of Gainesville, Tri-City Bank of Palm Beach Gardens; former adminstr. dir. Fla. Securities Commn.; Palm Beach chmn. U.S. Savs. Bond Div., 1961—. Bd. dirs. Children's Home Soc. of Fla., South Fla. Fair and Exposition. Served with USMCR, 1952-54, also USNR. Mem. Greater West Palm Beach, No. Palm Beach County chambers commerce, Am. Legion. Presbyn. (elder 1963-66). Home: Rt 1 Box 19960 Jupiter FL 33458 Office: First Marine Bank & Trust Co Box 9787 Riviera Beach FL 33404

THOMAS, JOE, sports exec. Exec. asst. to pres., dir. player personnel Miami (Fla.) Dolphins. Office:*

THOMAS, JOE RAY, supt. schs.; b. Lindsay, Okla., Mar. 30, 1934; s. Aldridge Dunwood and Azalee (Bost) T.; B.S., East Central State U., Ada, Okla., 1955; M.S., Okla. State U., 1961; m. Jo Nita Franklin, June 1, 1955; children—Joe Ray, Tanya, Mark, Terri, Lance. Classroom tchr., Mound Valley, Okla., 1955-59; teaching prin., Glencoe, Okla., 1959-63; supt. schs., Granite, Okla., 1963—. Instl. rep. Kicking Bird council Boy Scouts Am., 1967-72; mem. Greer County Health Bd., 1967-72. Mem. N.E.A., Am., Okla. assns. sch. adminstrs., Okla. Sch. Bus. Ofcls. Assn., Okla. Edn. Assn., Greer County Edn. Unit. Mem. Ch. of Christ (deacon 1967—). Lion. Address: Box 98 Granite OK 73547

THOMAS, JOHN CAMPBELL, lawyer; b. Detroit, Feb. 28, 1928; s. William John and Belle Bernetta (Thompson) T.; B.B.A., U. Mich., 1950, J.D., 1953; m. Margaret Yvonne Stults, Sept. 1, 1951; children—John Campbell, Jeffrey F., Laurel A., Lynda D., Lisa B. Admitted to Mich. bar, 1954, Fla. bar, 1968, mem. legal staff Chrysler Corp., Detroit, 1953-60; trust officer Detroit Bank & Trust Co., 1960-66; v.p., sr. trust officer 1st Bank & Trust Co., Boca Raton, Fla., 1966-71; practiced in Boca Raton, 1971—. Chmn. bd., pres. J. Thomas Boca Raton, Inc. Lectr. Fla. Atlantic U., Boca Raton, 1968—. Served with AUS, World War II. Mem. Am., Fla., Mich. bar assns., Boca Raton C. of C., Chi Phi. Presbyn. Clubs: Boca Raton; University of Mich. (Ann Arbor). Home: 1400 NW 4th Ct Boca Raton FL 33432 Office: First Bank Bldg Boca Raton FL 33432

THOMAS, JOHN HANSFORD, JR., physician; b. Greenville, Va., June 19, 1909; s. John Hansford and Ella Blanche (Burnett) T.; student Washington and Lee U., 1927-30; M.D., U. Va., 1934; m. Mary Johnston Lasley, June 19, 1941; children—Gail (Mrs. Richard Charles Zug), Sarah (Mrs. DuPont Guerry IV), Mary Lasley, John Hansford III, Thomas Randall. Intern, Balt. City Hosps., 1934-35; practice medicine specializing in family medicine, Greenville, 1936—; mem. staff Kings Daus. Hosp., Staunton, Va. Mem. adv. bd. Va. Nat. Bank. Mem. U. Va. Devel. Fund Com., 1966—. Chmn. local com. Democratic party, 1971. Mem. Am., World, So., Va. med. assns., Augusta County Med. Soc. (pres. 1944), Sigma Alpha Epsilon, Phi Beta Pi. Presbyn. (trustee). Clubs: Staunton Cotillion; Windmill Point (Va.) Yacht; Irvington, Cheasapeake (Irvington, Va.); Circus Saints and Sinners (Staunton). Address: Meddock Greenville VA 24440

THOMAS, JOHN PELHAM, educator; b. Ashby, Ala., Apr. 18, 1922; s. John Pelham and Rebecca Jane (Hudson) T.; B.S., Auburn U., 1946; M.A.T., U. Va., 1961; Ph.D., U. S.C., 1965; m. Beulah Marie Hawks, Sept. 23, 1945; children—Sarah Jane, Susan Marie, Nancy Lynn, Mary Elizabeth, Martha Louise, James Paul. With Agrl. Extension Service, Auburn U., 1946-52; farmer, Opp, Ala., 1953-59; tchr. Covington County (Ala.) Schs., 1955-59, Tuscaloosa City Schs., 1959-60; mem. faculty U. N.C., Charlotte, 1964-67; prof., head math. dept. Western Carolina U., Cullowhee, N.C., 1967—. Served with USMCR, 1943-45. Baptist. Home: Route 67 Box 35B Cullowhee NC 28723

THOMAS, JOHN RUSSELL, textile co. exec.; b. Alexander City, Ala., Aug. 1, 1937; s. Russell and Crawford (Anthony) T.; B.S. in Textile Engring., Ga. Inst. Tech., 1960; postgrad. U. Ala., 1961; m. Francis Tate Jordan, Dec. 8, 1962; children—Russell L., John Jordan. Textile engr. Russell Mills, Inc., Alexander City, 1964-70, v.p., 1970—; dir. 1st Nat. Bank, Alexander City, Cotton States Life, Tuscaloosa, Ala., Russell Lands, Inc., Alexander City. Mem. Bd. Edn. Alexander City, 1970—. Bd. dirs. Central Ala. Rehab. Center, Montgomery. Served to 1st lt. AUS, 1962-64. Baptist. (deacon). Clubs: The Club (Birmingham); Willow Point Golf and Country (Alexander City). Home: 107 N Central Av Alexander City AL 35010

THOMAS, JOHN SULLIVAN, JR., optometrist; b. Griffin, Ga., June 8, 1925; s. John Sullivan and Nell (Moore) T.; diploma North Ga. Jr. Coll., 1944; D. Optometry, So. Coll. Optometry, 1949; m. Billie McMinn, Dec. 25, 1948; children—1 son, David Moore. Individual practice optometry, Thomson, Ga., 1949—; v.p. First Fed. Savs. & Loan, Thomson, 1963—, also dir. Served with USMCR, 1945-46. Decorated Purple Heart. Named Ga. Optometrist of Year 1960. Mem. Am., Ga. optometric assns., Omega Delta, Sigma Alpha Sigma, Beta Sigma Kappa. Baptist (deacon). Kiwanian (pres. 1953). Clubs: Belle Meade Country, Thomson Field Archers. Home: 416 Lee St Thomson GA 30824 Office: Knox Shipping Center Thomson GA 30824

THOMAS, JOHN WADE, real estate exec.; b. Lindsay, Okla., Jan. 11, 1907; s. Robert Allen and Ida Pauline (Wade) T.; Life Teaching Certificate, Central State Coll., Okla., 1927; m. Lois Maurine Griffin, May 25, 1929; children—Robert Allen, Jan Maxine (Mrs. Don Boyington). Tchr. schs. Grady County, Okla., 1926-28; tchr., prin. high sch. Mulhall, Okla., 1929-30; owner John W. Thomas & Co., Edmond, Okla., 1930—; dir. 1st Nat. Bank Edmond, local Fed. Savs. & Loan Assn. Oklahoma City; mem. Edmond Indsl. Trust. Active Boy Scouts Am., 1930—. Recipient citation Pres. Harry S. Truman for duties performed World War II, 1945; Silver Beaver award Boy Scouts Am., 1949; Distinguished Student award Central State U. Edmond, 1965. Mem. Alumni Assn. Central State U. (pres. 1969), Edmond C. of C. (pres. 1937), Okla. Real Estate Assn. (pres. 1960, Realtor of Year 1962), Nat. Assn. Real Estate Brokers (v.p. 1963). Methodist (trustee Okla. Conf., pres. trustees 1972). Mason (Shriner), Kiwanian (pres. club 1952). Home: 317 E 7th St Edmond OK 73034 Office: PO Box 70 Edmond OK 73034

THOMAS, LAVERNE BANDY (MRS. NEIL EUGENE THOMAS), educator; b. Godley, Tex., Dec. 5, 1922; d. Isaac Lee and Edna (Phelps) Bandy; student Abilene Christian Coll., 1946-47; B.S., U. Houston, 1952, M.Ed., 1958; Ph.D., Tex. Womans U., 1963; m. Neil Eugene Thomas, July 19, 1946; children—Sandra Kay, Neil E. II, Cynthia Ann, Teresa Lee. Sec. Monsanto Chem. Co., Texas City Tex., 1951-52; head dept. home Econs. Magic Valley Christian Coll., Albion, Ida., 1958-61; asst. prof., textile research Tex. Womans U., Denton, 1964-67; asst. prof. home econs. Colo. State Coll., Greeley, 1962-64; asso. prof., chmn. textiles and clothing dept. Ohio U., Athens, 1967-68, asso. prof. U. Okla., 1968-71; asso. prof. Fla. State U., Tallahassee, 1971—. Served with USNR, 1943-46. Mem. Am. Soc. for Testing Materials, Am. Assn. Textile Chemists and Colorists, Am. Home Econs. Assn., Coll. Profs. Textiles and Clothing, Sigma Xi, Phi Upsilon Omicron. Home: 1445 Oldfield Dr Tallahassee FL 32303

THOMAS, LEE BALDWIN, mfg. exec.; b. Alma, Neb., Sept. 17, 1900; s. Rees and Fannie (Baldwin) T.; B.B.A., U. Wash., 1923; m. Margaret Thomas, 1924; children—Lee Baldwin, Margaret Ellen (Mrs. Wallace Dunbar), Susan Jane (Mrs. A. Scott Hamilton). Advt. mgr. Ernst Hardware Co., Seattle, 1923-24, sales mgr., 1926-29; buyer R. H. Macy Co., N.Y.C., 1924-25; dir. home goods merchandising Butler Bros., Chgo., 1929-41; pres. Ekco Products Co., Chgo., 1941-47, Am. Elevator & Machine Co., Louisville, 1947-48; chmn. bd. Vermont Am. Corp. and subsidiaries, Am. Saw & Tool Co., Louisville, Vt. Tap & Die Co., Lydonville, Vt., Multi Metals, Inc., Louisville, DeLuxe Saw & Tool Co., Louisville and High Point, N.C.; chmn. bd. Thomas Industries, Inc. and subsidiaries; dir. Citizens Fidelity Bank & Trust Co. Bd. dirs. Honey Locust Found., Louisville. Mem. N.A.M. Clubs: Skokie County (Glencoe, Ill.); Owl Creek Country (Anchorage, Ky.); Harmony Landing Country (Prospect, Ky.); Pendennis (Louisville); Union League, Mid-day (Chgo.); Lake Region Country (Winter Heaven, Fla.); Florida Mountain Lake (Lake Wales, Fla.). Home: Evergreen Rd Anchorage KY 40223 Office: 207 E Broadway Louisville KY 40202

THOMAS, NOAH OSCAR, JR., real estate co. exec.; b. Center, Tex., Dec. 10, 1907; s. Noah Oscar and Mary (Beckham) T.; A.B., Baylor U., 1930. Vice pres. Travis-Edwards, Inc., Shreveport, 1956—. Pres., Shreveport Civic Opera Assn., 1958-; mem. Shreveport Met. Planning Commn., 1955-56, Downtown Devel. Commn., 1966-69. Bd. dirs. Schumpert Meml. Hosp., Shreveport. Served with USNR, 1942-46. Recipient Outstanding Citizenship award City Council Shreveport, 1955. Mem. Shreveport C. of C., Order Cincinnati, S.A.R. Clubs: Shreveport; Tulsa. Home: 17 Dudley Sq Shreveport LA 71104 Office: Beck Bldg Shreveport LA 71101

THOMAS, PAT FRANKLIN, Democratic state chmn.; b. Quincy, Fla., Nov. 21, 1933; s. Pat and Verna (Peacock) T.; grad. U. Fla.; m. Mary Ann Jolley; children—Anne Jolley, John Pat. Service rep. Fla. Farm Bur., 1960-62; owner Gen. Ins. Agy., 1962—; Democratic state committeeman, Gadsden County, Fla., 1966—; chmn. Dem. Exec. Com., Fla., 1966—, organizing chmn. delegation Dem. Conv., Chgo., 1968. Served with AUS, Korean War. Named one of five Outstanding Man of Fla., Fla. Jr. C. of C., 1968. Mem. Fla., Gadsden County assns. ins. agts., Quincy Jr. C. of C. (one of Five Outstanding Young Men 1967), Quincy C. of C. (mgr.), Am. Legion, Am. Cancer Soc., Blue Key, Alpha Gamma Rho. Presbyn. Mason (32 deg., Shriner), Rotarian. Club: Sawano Country (Quincy). Home: Hwy 90 Quincy FL 32351 Office: PO Box 488 Quincy FL 32351

THOMAS, PAYNE EDWARD LLOYD, publisher; b. Balt., May 11, 1919; s. Charles C. and Nanette (Payne) T.; m. Judith Pedersen; children—John Fuller, Michael Payne, Peter Charles. Founder, dir. Thomas Found. and its memorials; Edward Waldron Payne Library, Harvey Cushing Hall, Chapel of Margaret and Charles Crankshaw; exec. v.p. Charles C. Thomas, Pub., Springfield, Ill., 1942-48, editor-in-chief sci., tech., med. depts., 1948-55, pres., 1955—. Presbyn. Clubs: Tavern (Chgo.); Island Bay Yacht (Springfield, Ill.); Engineers (N.Y.C.); Lauderdale Yacht (Ft. Lauderdale, Fla.). Home: 10 Island Bay Lane Lake Springfield Springfield IL 62707 also 66 Isla Bahia Dr Harbor Beach Ft Lauderdale FL 33316Office: 301-327 E Lawrence Av Springfield IL 62703 also 735 N Atlantic Blvd Ft Lauderdale FL 33304

THOMAS, ROBERT EGGLESTON, corp. exec.; b. Cuyahoga Falls, O., July 28, 1914; s. Talbott E. and Jane S. (Eggleston) T.; B.S. in Econs., Wharton Sch. Finance, U. Pa., 1936; m. Barbara Darcey, Nov. 12, 1949; children—Robert E., Jr., Barbara A. Asst. to gen. mgr., sec., mgr. r.r. investments Keystone Custodian Funds, Boston, 1936-53; v.p. The Pennroad Corp., N.Y.C., 1953-59; chmn. exec. com., dir. M.-K.-T. R.R., 1956-65; pres., chief exec. officer, dir. mem. exec. com. MAPCO Inc., 1960—; mem. exec. com., dir. Perkin-Elmer Corp.; dir. Nat. Bank Tulsa, Founders Financial Corp., Tampa, Fla., Equity Oil Co., Salt Lake City. Mem. Transp. Assn. Am. (dir.), Am. Petroleum Inst. (dir.), Newcomen Soc. Episcopalian. Clubs: N.Y. Yacht, Links, Metropolitan (N.Y.C.); Chicago; Down Town (Boston); Englewood (N.J.); Tulsa, Summit, So. Hills Country (Tulsa); Kansas City (Mo.). Home: 2870 E 33d St Tulsa OK 74105 Office: 1437 S Boulder Av Tulsa OK 74119

THOMAS, ROSS ELMORE, author; b. Oklahoma City, Feb. 19, 1926; s. J. Edwin and Laura (Dean) T.; B.A., U. Okla., 1949. Reporter, Daily Oklahoman, Oklahoma City, 1943-44; pub. relations dir. Nat. Farmers Union, 1952-56; pres. Stapp, Thomas & Wade, Inc., Denver, 1956-57; reporter, Bonn, Germany, 1958-59; rep. Patrick Dolan & Assos., Ltd., Ibadan, Nigeria, 1959-61; cons. U.S. Govt., 1964-66. Served with inf. AUS, 1944-46. Recipient Mystery Writers Am. award for best 1st mystery, 1966, Edgar award, 1967. Author: The Cold War Swap, 1966; The Seersucker Whipsaw, 1967; Cast a Yellow Shadow, 1967; The Singapore Wink, 1969. Address: 420 4th St SE Washington DC 20003

THOMAS, ROY WELDON, elec. contractor; b. nr. Mt. Airy, N.C., Jan. 10, 1929; s. John Samuel and Annie (Mathis) T.; grad. high sch.; m. Mary Magdalene Blackard, Dec. 23, 1950; 1 dau., Mary Lynn. With Floyd S. Pike Elec. Contractor, Inc., Mt. Airy, 1947—, v.p., 1963—, also dir.; dir. Mt. Airy Hosiery Mill, Mt. Airy Aviation. Served with AUS, 1946-47. Mason. Club: Mount Airy Country. Home: 513 Ridgeway Mount Airy NC 27030 Office: 418 Smith St Mount Airy NC 27030

THOMAS, WARREN MILNER, mech. engr.; b. La Jolla, Cal., Sept. 2, 1920; s. Warren wilkinson and Laura (Milner) T.; B.S., U. Kan., 1942; m. Amy Lee Hill, Apr. 8, 1944; children—David Warren, Gregory Lee, Nancy Ruth. With Phillips Petroleum Co., Bartlesville, Okla., 1942—, mgr. mech. design br., engring. dept., 1956—. Dir. 66 Fed. Credit Union, 1956-65; pres. P.T.A., Bartlesville, 1964-65. Precinct chmn. Republican Party, 1950-57. Registered profl. engr., Okla. Mem. Am. Soc. M.E., Am. Nat. Standards Inst. (com., group chmn. 1965—), Nat., Okla. (chpt. v.p. 1960) socs. profl. engrs., Am. Petroleum Inst. (sec. piping subcom. 1965—), Tau Beta Pi, Sigma Tau, Pi Tau Sigma, Delta Tau Delta. Methodist (ofcl. bd. 1965-69). Lion. Home: 1455 Valley Rd Bartlesville OK 74003 Office: Phillips Petroleum Co Bartlesville OK 74003

THOMAS, WAYNE ELVIN, lawyer; b. Silverton, Tex., Feb. 16, 1928; s. Zerrell and Bertha (Edwards) T.; B.A., West Tex. State U., 1947; LL.B., U. Tex., 1951; m. Mary Hodges, Sept. 26, 1947; children—David Wayne, Shyla, Trent Hodges. Admitted to Tex. bar, 1951; partner firm Thomas and Burdett, Hereford, Tex., 1951—. Dist. committeeman Boy Scouts of Am., 1954-56; chmn. United Fund, 1963-64; chmn. Indsl. Devel. Com., 1967-68. Pres., Deaf Smith County Hosp., 1957, dir., 1954-67; pres. West Tex. Ex-Students, Inc., 1966, dir., 1963-67; mem., chmn. coordinating bd. Tex. Coll. and Univ. Systems, 1969—. Served to 1st lt. USAF, 1951-52. Fellow Am. Coll. Probate Counsel, Tex. Bar Found.; mem. Tex. State Bar, Am. Bar Assn., Am. Judicature Soc., Deaf Smith County C. of C. (pres. 1965), Order of Coif, Delta Theta Phi (pres. 1950-51). Baptist. Contbr. articles in field to profl. jours. Home: 206 Sunset Dr Hereford TX 79045 Office: 116 S 25 Mile Av Hereford TX 79045

THOMAS, WILLIAM FRED, telephone co. exec.; b. Thomston, Ala., Oct. 31, 1913; s. Earl Gaines and Stella (Holt) T.; B.S., Auburn U., 1936; m. Dorothy Perkins, Oct. 17, 1942; children—Dorothy E., Frances Susan. Elec. engr. So. Bell Telephone Co., Columbus, Ga., 1937-47; pres. Elmore Coosa Telephone Co., Eclectic, Ala., 1947—. Cons. engr. J. B. McCrary Engring. Corp., 1950—. Served with AUS, 1942-46. Decorated Bronze Star Medal. Republican. Methodist. Address: Ecletic AL 36024

THOMAS, W(ILLIAM) LAMAR, city ofcl.; b. Atlanta, July 16, 1927; s. Marvin L. and Louise (Stewart) T.; student Ga. Inst. Tech., 1946-50; student Northwestern U. Traffic Inst., 1954; m. Pat Blackmon, Oct. 13, 1947; children—Michael Lamar, Penny. Asst. to traffic engr. transp. engring. sect. Ga. Power Co., Atlanta, 1946-49; asst. traffic engr. City Atlanta, 1950-58; traffic engr. City of Orlando, Fla., 1958—. VIP panel Cherokee Jr. High P.T.A., 1965—, pres. 1964-65; mem. Orange County Citizens Safety Council, 1958—; mem. exec. bd. Central Fla. council Boy Scouts Am. Bd. dirs. YMCA Southeastern br.; Miss Fla. Pagent, Christmas Parade Fla. Citrus Open. Served with USN, 1945-46. Mem. Orlando Jr. C. of C. Mason (32 deg., Shriner). Home: 514 Topaz Way Orlando FL 32806 Office: City Hall Orlando FL 32801

THOMAS, WILLIAM MARION, dentist; b. Troy, Ala., Oct. 19, 1928; s. Norman Marion and Jewel (Tadlock) T.; B.S., U. Ala., 1950, D.M.D., 1954; m. Hilda Smith, Mar. 14, 1964; children—Norma Wilynn, William Marion, Kimberly Jewel, James Norman. Practice of dentistry, Troy, Ala., 1954—; mem. staff Edge Meml. Hosp. Mem. Selective Service Bd., 1969—. Served with Dental Corps, USNR, 1954-56. Mem. Am., Ala. dental assns., Third Dist. Dental Soc., Acad. Gen. Dentistry, C. of C., Am. Legion, Psi Omega, Alpha Epsilon Delta. Democrat. Baptist (deacon). Moose, Lion (pres. 1969). Home: 200 Monroe Dr Troy AL 36081 Office: 541 Elm St Troy AL 36081

THOMASON, BERENICE MILLER, microbiologist; b. Birmingham, Ala., Mar. 10, 1924; d. Henry Herbert and Lillian (Martin) Miller; student Huntingdon Coll., 1941-43; B.S., Ga. State Coll., 1960; m. Earl Luther Thomason, Dec. 4, 1944 (div. June 1948); 1 son, Thomas Stephen. Med. technologist War Dept., Sta. Hosp., Ft. Benning, Ga., 1943-45; pub. health technologist Muscogee County Health Dept., Columbus, Ga., 1948-51; bacteriologist Communicable Disease Center, Atlanta, 1951-53, 3d Army Med. Lab., Ft. McPherson, Ga., 1953-54; microbiologist Communicable Disease Center, Atlanta, 1954-61, research microbiologist, 1961—. Mem. DeKalb Humane Soc., 1967—. Mem. Am. Soc. for Microbiology, Research Soc. Am., Ga. Conservancy, Nat. Wildlife Assn. Research on devel. immunofluorescent techniques for rapid detection of pathogenic bacteria. Contbr. articles in field to profl. jours. Home: 4202 Hambrick Way Stone Mountain GA 30083 Office: Center for Disease Control Atlanta GA 30333

THOMASON, JOHN MELVIN, physician; b. Olanta, S.C., Nov. 18, 1935; s. Eddie Houston and Kate Goodwin (Ordiorne) T.; B.S., Clemson U., 1958; M.D., Med. U. S.C., 1965; m. Martha Elizabeth Bruce, June 20, 1958; children—Katherine Kim, Karen Bruce, Kristie Elizabeth. Landscape constrn. Jack Clark Co., Charlotte, N.C., 1958-59; tchr. Charleston (S.C.) Pub. Schs., also football coach, 1960-61; intern Meml. Hosp., Savannah, Ga., 1965-66; gen. practice medicine Bruce Hosp., Florence, S.C., 1966—; mem. med. staff Saunders Hosp., McLeod's Infirmary. Mem. Florence City Park Commn. Served with AUS, 1959-60; mem. Res. Mem. S.C. Med. Assn., Florence County Med. Soc., Alpha Kappa Kappa. Lion. Home: 1170 S Edisto St Florence SC 29501 Office: 514 S Dargan St Florence SC 29501

THOMASON, SAMUEL HAWTHORNE, sch. adminstr.; b. Fountain Inn, S.C., July 2, 1911; s. Samuel Walter and Ruby (Thompson) T.; B.Ed., U. S.C., 1936; M.Ed., Furman U., 1959; postgrad. Marshall U., summer 1957, Oak Ridge Inst. Nuclear Sci., summer 1958, U. Colo., summer 1963, Furman U., 1970-72; m. Mary Pack Miller, Oct. 24, 1940; 1 son, Samuel Boyce. Tchr. sci. Simpsonville (S.C.) High Sch., 1936-37, Abbeville (S.C.) High Sch., 1937-40, 54-58, Parker High Sch., Greenville, S.C., 1940-41, Paris High Sch., Taylors, S.C., 1941-43, also prin.; supr. vocational edn. Greenville (S.C.) County vets. program, 1946-54; supr. sci. Sch. Dist. Greenville County, 1959—; supr. sci. practice tchr. Western Carolina U., summers 1960-63, instr. sci. workshop, 1967. Served with USAAF, 1943-45. Mem. Nat. Sci. Tchrs. Assn., Nat. Sci. Suprs. Assn., A.A.A.S., Assn. Supervision and Curriculum Devel., Nat. Assn. Geology Tchrs., S.C. Sci. Assn. Home: Rt 2 Millerwood Greenville SC 29607 Office: 420 N Pleasantburg Dr Greenville SC 29606

THOMASSON, LYLE WORTHINGTON, dentist; b. Creek, Tex., Nov. 10, 1919; s. Russell Burton and Opal (Coon) T.; student Baylor U., 1938-40; D.D.S., Tex. U., 1943; m. Elizabeth Dean, Dec. 25, 1942; children—Jan (Mrs. James Craig Thompson), Lyle W., John Russell. Practice dentistry specializing in oral surgery and orthodontics, Crockett, Tex., 1945—; dir. Lyle's Meat Packing Plant, Crockett, Lyle's Mobile Home Mfg., Crockett. Served with USNR, 1943-45. Mem. Tex. (Order of Good Fellow), Brasos Valley dental assns. Lion, Mason. Home: 405 N Grace St Crockett TX 75835 Office: PO Box 837 Old Rusk Rd Crockett TX 75835

THOMASSON, REGINALD ROBERT, educator; b. Warren, Ark., Oct. 10, 1913; s. Robert Finn and Winnie L. (Foster) T.; B.S., S.C. State Coll., 1936, B.A., 1940; M.A., Cal. State Coll. at Los Angeles, 1955; postgrad. U. Cal. at Los Angeles, summers 1953-54, U. So. Cal., 1957-65; student Kansas City Conservatory of Music, 1935; m. Carmen Hermene Sulton, June 12, 1945; 1 dau., Carmen Regina. Band dir. S.C. State Coll., Orangeburg, 1936—; also adjudicator, clinician and guest condr. for region, 1950—. Choir dir. St. Luke United Presbyn. Ch.; founder S.C. Assn. High Sch. Bandmasters, 1950. Recipient Founder's award, 1961. Mem. Nat., S.C., edn. assns., Am. Assn. U. Profs., Coll. Band Dirs. Nat. Assn., Music Educators Nat. Conf., Alston Wilkes Soc. (dir.), Kappa Alpha Psi, Phi Mu Alpha Sinfonia, Kappa Kappa Psi. Presbyn. (elder, mem. men's council 1951—). Original composition Evening Song adopted as school song, S.C. State Coll., 1939. Home: 1312 Russell St SE Orangeburg SC 29115

THOMBS, DAVID DAWSON, physician; b. Woodbury, N.J., Feb. 24, 1938; s. Charles Raymond and Sylvia (Timmins) T.; A.B., Amherst Coll., 1959; M.D., Vanderbilt U., 1963; m. Susanne Reynolds, Apr. 27, 1963; children—Susan, Dawson. Intern, asst. resident Vanderbilt Hosp., Nashville, Tenn., 1963-65; resident Cin. Childrens Hosp., 1965-66; chief resident pediatrics Vanderbilt Hosp., Nashville, 1966-67; practice medicine, specializing in pediatrics, Nashville, 1969—; asst. dir. pediatric ambulatory care unit Vanderbilt U. Hosp., 1969-71. Served to lt. comdr., M.C., USNR, 1967-69. Diplomate Am. Bd. Pediatrics. Mem. Nashville Acad.

Medicine, Tenn. Med. Assn., Davidson County Pediatric Soc. Home: 4506 Wayland Dr Nashville TN 37215 Office: 1924 Church St Nashville TN 37203

THOMPSON, ALBERT THEODORE, JR., cons. engr.; b. Wisconsin Rapids, Wis., Sept. 1, 1918; s. Albert Theodore and Lula (Yokes) T.; B.S., U. Tex., 1948, M.S., 1949; m. Constance Jo MacDonald, June 8, 1947 (div. Aug. 1967); children—Philip Norstaad, Tracey Ellen, Teresa Ann, Martha Louise. Jr. engr. U.S. Engring. Dept., 1940-42; with Tex. Health Dept., 1948-56; cons. engr., 1956—; owner C-T-E Labs., Utilities Service Co., San Antonio, Thompson Enterprises. Dir. Tech., Operational, Profl. Services, Inc. Served from 2d lt. to capt., AUS, 1942-46. Registered profl. engr., Tex., N.M. Mem. Nat., Tex. Socs. profl. engrs. Home: 2618 Nacogdoches Rd San Antonio TX 78217 Office: Perrin-Beitel Rd PO Box 6825 San Antonio TX 78209

THOMPSON, ALMON ORVILLE, dentist; b. Spring Grove, Minn., Dec. 14, 1926; s. Almon A. and Olga M. (Jossendahl) T.; B.A., B.S., U. Minn., 1950, M.S., 1953, D.D.S., 1954; m. Doris Elaine Tweito, July 20, 1952; 1 dau., Beth Ann. Pvt. practice dentistry, Palm Beach Fla., 1954-67, West Palm Beach, Fla., 1967—. Sec.-treas. Woehler Research Group, 1969-71; mem. Atlantic Coast Dental Research Clinic, 1964—. Pres., Town Council Haverhill, Fla., 1959-69. Served with AUS, 1944-45, USAF, 1952-54. Mem. Am., Fla dental assns., So. Acad. Clin. Nutrition, Flad. Acad. Dental Practice, Atlantic Coast Dist., Palm Beach County (pres. 1970-71) dental socs., Lauritzen Study Club. Mason (32 degree, Shriner), Lion. Club: Palm Beach Yacht. Home: 285 Barcelona Rd West Palm Beach FL 33401 Office: 2407 N Flagler Dr West Palm Beach FL 33407

THOMPSON, BEN ERSKINE, JR., savs. and loan exec.; b. Florence, S.C., Dec. 26, 1922; s. Ben E. and Mary (Hubbard) T.; student Ind. U., 1961-62; m. Martha Rose Wertz, Jan. 25, 1943; children—Martha Jean, John Benjamin. Field rep. Security Life & Trust Co., Winston-Salem, N.C., 1941-42, 45-52; asst. sec. First Fed. Savs. and Loan Assn. of Indiana River County, Vero Beach, Fla., 1953-56, v.p., sec., 1957-67, exec. v.p., mgr., 1967-70, pres., 1970—, also dir. Dir. United Fund, 1961—, Indian River County Library Assn., 1966—. Served with USAAF, 1942-45. Mem. Vero Beach C. of C. Lutheran. Kiwanian. Home: 2806 Atlantic Blvd Vero Beach FL 32960 Office: 2045 14th Av Vero Beach FL 32960

THOMPSON, BEVERLEY VENABLE, JR., steel co. exec.; b. Ft. Worth, Dec. 2, 1919; s. Beverley Venable and Anna Mae (Armstrong) T.; grad. Woodberry Forest Sch., 1937; student U. Va., 1937-38, Tex. Christian U., 1938-40; m. Betty Jo Copeland, Dec. 29, 1959; children—Beverley Venable III, Melissa Margaret. Vice pres. Tex. Aviation Co., 1946-47; with Tex. Steel Co., Ft.Worth, 1947—, v.p., 1952-65, pres., 1965—, dir., 1952—; dir. Liberty Mfg.Co., Perfection Ice Scoring Machine Co., Continental Nat. Bank, Ft. Worth. Pres., gen. mgr. Tex. Ednl. Assn., 1965—. Bd. dirs. Tex. Bur. for Econ. Understanding. Served to capt. USAAF, 1941-46. Decorated Air medal. Mem. Steel Founders Soc. Am. (dir. 1958-60), N.A.M. (dir. 1967—, regional v.p. 1968—), Newcomen Soc., Tex. Council for Econ. Edn. (dir. 1970—), Tex. Mfrs. Assn., Sigma Alpha Epsilon. Republican. Episcopalian. Clubs: Rivercrest Country, Ft. Worth, Shady Oaks Country, Steeplechase (Ft. Worth). Home: 6300 Curzon St Fort Worth TX 76116 Office: 3901 Hemphill St Fort Worth TX 76110

THOMPSON, BUFORD DALE, horticulturist; b. Lake Wales, Fla., Oct. 22, 1922; s. Sheldon Stringer and Bonnie (Durrance) T.; B.S. in Agr. with honors, U. Fla., 1948, M.S., 1949, Ph.D., 1954; m. Margaret Virginia Cody, Aug. 20, 1944; children—Margaret D., James G., Michael L. Asst. horticulturist Agrl. Expt. Stas., Inst. Food and Agrl. Scis., U. Fla., Gainesville, 1948-60, asso. prof., asso. horticulturist, 1960-66, prof., horticulturist, 1966—. Served to capt. AUS, 1943-46; ETO. Mem. Am. Soc. Hort. Sci. (Vaughan award 1962), Am. Soc. Plant Physiologists, Fla. Hort. Soc., Caribbean Region Hort. Soc. Club: University Florida Alumni (pres.). Home: 725 NW 40th Terrace Gainesville FL 32601

THOMPSON, CARSON R., leather co. exec.; b. Wilson, Okla., Feb. 10, 1939; s. Silas and Della (Wood) T.; B.S. in Social Sci., Tex. Wesleyan Coll., 1962; m. Charlotte Ann Arwine, Dec. 26, 1959; children— Shelley, Susan. With Tandy Leather Co., Fort Worth, 1957—, warehouse mgr., 1964-70, mdse. mgr., leather buyer, 1970—. Baptist. Lion. Home: 600 Thompson Dr Saginaw TX 76079 Office: 1001 Foch St Fort Worth TX 76107

THOMPSON, CHARLES BENJAMIN, JR., civil engr.; b. Auburn, Neb., Oct. 22, 1917; s. Charles Benjamin and Thelma Tolinda (Call) T.; B.S. in Civil Engring., U. N.M., 1940; M.S., State U. Ia., 1948; m. Kathryn Lois Hanlan, Aug. 3, 1938; children—Charles Hugh, Carolyn Louise, Marilyn Kay. Clk. Woods Bros. Constrn. Co., Omaha, 1935-38; insp., dept. roads and irrigation State Neb., Lincoln, 1940; jr. insp. ordinance material, War Dept., St. Louis Ordnance Dist., 1941, jr., asso., sr., chief insp. ordnance material, St. Louis Ordnance Plant, 1941-43; civil engr. Horner & Shifrin, cons. engrs., St. Louis, 1943; ordnance engr., indsl. specialist, indsl. engr., tech. editor War Dept. Office, Chief of Ordnance, Washington, 1943-46; asst. prof. civil engring. U. N.M., Albuquerque, 1948-51; sr. engr. N.M. Interstate Stream Commn., Santa Fe, 1951-53; chief, tech. div. N.M. State Engr. Office, 1953-58; civil engr.-planner, Litchfield Whiting Bowne Assos., Bangkok, Thailand, 1958-59; hydraulic engr. U.S. Study Commn.-Texas, Houston, 1959-61; water resources engr. U.S. State Dept., AID, Washington, 1961—. Registered profl. engr. Alaska, Ariz., Colo., D.C., N.M., Md., Okla., Tex., La., Miss., Mass. Fellow Am. Soc. C.E.; mem. Internat. Commn. Irrigation and Drainage, Internat. Assn. for Hydraulic Research, Permanent Internat. Assn. Navigation Congresses, Am. Ordnance Assn., Nat. Soc. Profl. Engrs., Internat. Commn. on Large Dams, Internat. Water Supply Assn., Am. Legion, Sigma Tau, Chi Epsilon. Methodist. Author numerous manuals, reports and tech. papers. Address: 2629 S Lynn St Arlington VA 22202 Office: US Dept State AID SER ENGR Washington DC 20523

THOMPSON, CHARLOTTE ANNE, librarian; b. Lansing, Mich., Nov. 10, 1909; d. James Herbert and Mary Elizabeth (Ardis) Thompson; student Hollins Coll., 1927-30; A.B., U. Mich., 1931, A.B. in L.S., 1932, summer student, 1944; M.S. in L.S., Columbia, 1955. Librarian, U. Tampa (Fla.), 1933-70; head spl. collections div. Merl Kelce Library, U. Tampa, 1970—. Mem. Am., Fla., Southeastern, Hillsborough County (pres. 1964-65) library assns., Am. Assn. U. Women, P.E.O., Zeta Tau Alpha, Delta Kappa Gamma. Democrat. Presbyn. Clubs: Pilot, Woman's (Tampa). Home: Bayshore Towers 4015 Bayshore Blvd Tampa FL 33611

THOMPSON, CLARK WALLACE, legislative cons.; b. LaCrosse, Wis., Aug. 6, 1896; s. Clark Wallace and Jessie Marilla (Hyde) T.; student U. Ore., 1915-17; m. Libbie Moody, Nov. 16, 1918; children—Libbie (dec.), Clark Wallace. Treas. Am. Nat. Ins. Co., Galveston, Tex., 1919-20; pres. Clark W. Thompson Co., 1920-32; sec.-treas. Cedar Lawn Co., 1927-34; formerly pub. relations counsel Am. Nat. Ins. Co., Nat. Hotel Co., Moody interests; now dir. Washington operations Tenneco, Inc. Mem. 73d Congress (filled unexpired term of Clay S. Briggs), 80th-89th Congresses, 9th Tex. Dist.; now legislative cons. Served with M.C., U.S. Army, 1917-18; organized and comd. 15th Bn., Marine Corps Res.; on active duty, 1940-46; with 2d Marine Div., and other units in S.W. Pacific area; ret. as col., 1946; grad. Naval War Coll. Mem. Galveston C. of C. (past pres.), Am. Legion, V.F.W., Phi Delta Theta. Democrat. Episcopalian. Mason (32 deg., Shriner), Eagle, Red Man. Clubs: George Town (Washington); Artillery (Galveston, Tex.); Army and Navy, 1925 F Street (Washington). Home: 1616 Driftwood Lane Galveston TX 77550 also 3301 Massachusetts Av NW Washington DC 20008 Office: Solar Bldg 1000 16th St Washington DC 20036

THOMPSON, CLARK WALLACE, JR., investment exec.; b. Galveston, Tex., Aug. 28, 1919; s. Clark Wallace and Libbie (Moody) T.; B.B.A., U. Tex., 1947; m. Rosalie Anne Meador, Aug. 30, 1941; 1 dau., Anne Meador (Mrs. F. J. Whitley, Jr.). With Arthur Anderson & Co., Houston, 1947-56, partner, 1956-61; personal investment mgmt., Houston, 1961—; now also dir. Southwestern Savs. Assn., Houston. Mem. accounting adv. com. U. Tex., Austin, 1958—. Mem. adv. com. Salvation Army; trustee Northwood Inst., Midland, Mich.; steering com. Texas Futures, Austin. Served to capt. AUS, 1943-46. Mem. Am. Inst. C.P.A.'s, Fat Stock Show Assn., Beta Theta Pi, Beta Alpha Psi. Democrat. Episcopalian. Clubs: Houston Country, Houston; Houston. Home: 4911 Tilbury Dr Houston TX 77027 Office: Post Oak Tower Houston TX 77027

THOMPSON, CLYDE CLINTON, dentist; b. Thompson, Ark., Mar. 30, 1898; s. Edwin Staton and Lucy Ardelia (Hall) T.; D.D.S., Vanderbilt U., 1919; m. Oza Grace Leeper, Nov. 20, 1920; children—Betty Anne (Mrs. George Clark Reed), Margaret Ellen (Mrs. J.T. Sharp), Clyde Clinton. Dentist, DeQueen, Ark., 1919—, partner with son, 1949—. Dir. 1st Nat. Bank DeQueen. Leader, Caddo Area council Boy Scouts Am., 1923-68, mem. council, 1926-68; mem.-at-large nat. council, 1962, 63; mem. Sch. Bd. DeQueen, 1931-40, pres., 1935-40. Chmn., Sevier County Republican Central Com., 1932-45; mem. Rep. State Com., 1945-63. Recipient Silver Beaver award Boy Scouts Am., 1948. Fellow Am. Coll. Dentists (vice-chmn. for Ark.); mem. Ark. (life mem., pres. 1936), S.W. Dist. (sec. 1921-30), Am. (life) dental assns., Am. (champion 1931), Ark. (champion 1933) dental golf assns., Phi Kappa Sigma, Psi Omega. Republican. Baptist (deacon). Mason (32 degree, K.T.), Rotarian (pres. DeQueen Club 1936). Club: DeQueen Country. Home: 619 Vandervoort Av DeQueen AR 71832 Office: 111 N 4th St DeQueen AR 71832

THOMPSON, COURNEL WESLEY, ednl. adminstr.; b. Cuthbert, Tex., Sept. 30, 1924; s. Wesley Lonso and Mary Louisa (Brown) T.; B.S., Hardin Simmons Coll., 1948, M.Ed., 1950; Ed.D., U. Tex., 1967; m. Norma J. Marlow, June 4, 1947; children—Michael Wesley, Randall M. Head coach, Pittsburg, Tex., 1946-49, High sch. prin., 1949-52, supt. schs., 1953—. Served with USNR, 1942-46; PTO. Mem. Am., Tex. assns. sch. adminstrs., Tex. Tchrs. Assn., Mid-Tex. Schoolmen's Assn., Pittsburg C. of C. (v.p. 1966-69). Methodist (steward). Rotarian. Home: 113 King St Pittsburg TX 75686 Office: Quitman St Pittsburg TX 75686

THOMPSON, DAN FOX, elec. products mfg. co. exec.; b. Savannah, Ga., Mar. 15, 1920; s. Levy John and Mary Alice (Fairchild) T.; student U. Ill., 1951; B.S., Air Force Inst. Tech., 1954; m. Jane Thomas, Feb. 22, 1964; children—Dan Fox, John Phillip, Merri Lynn, Gay Elizabeth, Jan. Served to col. USAAF, then USAF, 1939-64; organized, trained and equipped the first Air Force unit to teach advanced instrument flying techniques, 1943-44; planned and implemented the first multiple count down procedure for Missile launches Cape Canaveral, 1957-62; mem. original team to recover five million dollars in Spanish Galleon treasure, 1964; devel. engr. IBM, Cape Canaveral, Fla., 1964-68; v.p., dir. Real Eight Co., Inc., elec. products, Melbourne, Fla., 1968—. Adv. oceanography curriculum Brevard Community Coll., 1969-70. Decorated Legion of Merit. Mem. Cape Canaveral chpt. Tech. Socs., Missile Range and Space Pioneers, Inc. (pres. 1970-71), Ret. Officers Assn. Clubs: Eau Gallie Yacht (Indian Harbour Beach, Fla.), PAFB Officers Patrick AFB, Fla.). Home: 117 Cat Cay Lane Indian Harbour Beach FL 32937 Office: PO Box 460 Melbourne FL 32901

THOMPSON, DONALD RICHARD, banker; b. Sioux Falls, S.D., July 21, 1921; s. Burt W. and Anna (Freese) T.; B.A., Augustana Coll., Sioux Falls, 1943; J.D., U. Chgo., 1949; m. June Ruth Randall, Feb. 26, 1946; children—Marcia, Kim and Jan (twins), Susan. Trust officer Fla. Nat. Bank & Trust Co., Miami, 1950-60; with First Nat. Bank Miami, 1960—, exec. v.p. charge trust and investment div., 1966—; chmn. bd. Southeast Bank Deerfield Beach (Fla.). served with USNR, 1943-46. Mem. Am., Fla. (chmn. trust div. 1970-71) bankers assns., Corp. Fiduciaries Assn. S.E. Fla. (pres. 1962-63), Estate Planning Council Greater Miami (pres. 1967-68), Fla., Dade County bar assns. Republican. Rotarian. Clubs: Miami; Riviera Country (Coral Gables, Fla.). Home: 7721 SW 53d Pl Miami FL 33143 Office: PO Box 2500 Miami FL 33101

THOMPSON, DONNELL MILBURN, candy mfg. co. exec.; b. Ft. Worth, Jan. 27, 1930; s. Hugh Donnell and Mary Katherine (Shook) T.; student Tarrant County Jr. Coll., 1968—; m. Patsy Genelle Thomas, Jan. 3, 1948; children—Pat, Mike, Marlyss, Malaree, Catha. With Pangburn Co., Inc., Ft.Worth, 1949—, mgr. materials supply, 1952-56, purchasing mgr., 1956—. Committeeman, Ft. Worth Young Life Campaign, 1964—. Served with USNR, 1947-50. Mem. Nat. Assn. Purchasing Mgmt., Ft. Worth Purchasing Mgmt. Assn. (past pres., past nat. dir.). Baptist. Home: 2656 S Kingsbury Av Fort Worth TX 76118 Office: PO Box 65 Fort Worth TX 76101

THOMPSON, DOUGLAS HERSCHEL, JR., state ofcl.; b. Alexandria, Va., Aug. 8, 1942; s. Douglas Herschel and Ruth (Burdette) T.; B.S. in Bus. Adminstrn., U. Fla., 1965; m. Sara Parks. Legislative auditor State of Fla., Gainesville, 1966-72; exec. dir. Fla. State Bd. of Accountancy, Gainesville, 1968, 72. Div. chmn. United Way; mem. Alachua County Charter Commn.; chmn. Heart Fund, 1972. C.P.A., Fla. Mem. Inst. C.P.A.'S, Fla. Inst. C.P.A.'s., Gainesville Jr. C. of C. (dir.), U. Fla. Alumni Assn. (pres. elect). Rotarian. Methodist. Home: 1817 NW 23d St Gainesville FL 32601 Office: 1204 NW 13th St Gainesville FL 32601

THOMPSON, EDWARD FRANKLYN, banker; b. Memphis, Aug. 21, 1907; s. Frank and Ellen (Gardner) T.; B.A., Southwestern U., Memphis, 1929; M.B.A., Harvard, 1931; grad. certificate Am. Inst. Banking, 1942; m. Ethel McWhorter, Apr. 25, 1936; children—Ellen (Mrs. Curtis E. Kelly), Earl Fincher, Doyle McWhorter. With Union Planters Nat. Bank, Memphis, 1931—, asst. v.p., 1943-56, v.p., 1956—. Instr., Am. Inst. Banking, 1932-71; lectr. and course coordinator Sch. Banking of the South, Baton Rouge, 1952-70. Pres. Tenn.-Ark.-Miss. council, Girl Scouts Am., 1963-65. Mem. Am., So. finance assns., Memphis Security Dealers Assn. (pres. 1955), The Egyptians (sec.-treas. 1965-71), Capleville. Methodist. (lay leader 1968-71, trustee 1961—). Mason. Clubs: Capleville Community (v.p. 1971), Exchange, Harvard (chmn. schs. and scholarship com. 1957-71) (Memphis), Olive Branch Country (Olive Branch, Miss.). Home: 6257 Holmes Rd Germantown TN 38138 Office: PO Box 387 Memphis TN 38101

THOMPSON, EDWARD K(RAMER), editor and pub.; b. Mpls., Sept. 17, 1907; s. Edward T. and Bertha E. (Kramer) T.; A.B., U. N.D., 1927, H.H.D., 1958; m. Marguerite M. Maxam, May 14, 1927 (div.); children—Edward T., Colin R.; m. 2d, Lee Eitingon, Apr. 1, 1963. Editor Foster Co. Independent, Carrington, N.D., 1927; city editor Fargo (N.D.) Morning Forum, 1927; picture editor, asst. news editor Milw. Jour., 1927-37; asso. editor Life, 1937-42, asst. mng. editor, 1945-49, mng. editor 1949-61, editor, 1961-68; spl. asst. to Sec. State, 1968; editor, pub. Smithsonian (Instn.) mag., Washington, 1969—. Served to lt. col. USAAF, 1942-45, Decorated Legion of Merit; Order Brit. Empire; named to N.D. Hall Fame, 1968, Editor of Year, Nat. Press Photographers Assn., 1969. Mem. Phi Beta Kappa, Phi Delta Theta, Sigma Delta Chi. Home: 1601 28th St NW Washington DC 20007 Office: Smithsonian Institution Washington DC 20560

THOMPSON, EUGENE GLENN, entomologist; b. Oklahoma City, Oct. 14, 1937; s. Thomas Benjamin and Thelma Flodal (Dabney) T.; A.A., Cameron State Coll., 1957; B.S., Okla. State U., 1959, M.S., 1964; postgrad. U. Neb., 1959-60, Ohio State U., 1962; m. Vivian Mildred Hamm, June 1, 1957; children—Howard Thomas, Melissa Ann. Entomology student trainee U.S. Dept. Agr., Waco, Tex., 1956-57, Stillwater, Okla., 1957-59, entomologist, Lincoln, Neb., 1959-60; med. entomologist U.S. Army, Korea, 1960-61, Walter Reed Army Inst. Research, Washington, 1961-63, Army Med. Field Service Sch., Fort Sam Houston, Tex., 1963-66, Thailand, 1966-67, U.S. Army Med. Field Service Sch., Fort Sam Houston, 1967—; distbr. Amway products, 1970—. Pack committeeman Alamo council Cub Scouts Am., 1970—. Nat. Indian scholar, Am. Missionary Assn., 1955-59. Mem. Entomol. Soc. Am., Am. Mosquito Control Assn., Dodd Field Protestant Men of Chapel (pres. 1969—), Sigma Xi, Phi Sigma, Phi Theta Kappa. Home: 4107 Monaco St San Antonio TX 78218 Office: Preventive Med Div USAMFSS BAMC Fort Sam Houston TX 78234

THOMPSON, FRANCIS COLEMAN, metal mfg. co. ofcl.; b. Delhi, La., Oct. 29, 1941; s. Clyde Coleman and Vera Frances (Nolan) T.; B.S., U. La. Tech., 1963, M.S., 1971; m. Marilyn Bryant, Sept. 4, 1962; children—Todd, Brant. Tchr., Monroe (La.) City Sch. System, 1963-64; with Delhi Mfg. Corp., 1964—, asst. mgr., 1964-68, bus. mgr., 1968—, also dir. Mem. La. Library Bd., 1970—, Richland Parish Library Bd., 1968—; mem. Richland Parish Sch. Bd., 1968—. Bd. dirs. Richland Parish Retarded Children's Assn. Apptd. col. on La. gov's staff. Mem. Jr. C. of C. (v.p. 1966). Presbyn. (asst. treas.). Lion (regional dir. 1968), Mason. Home: 108 Shady Lane Delhi LA 71232 Office: Illinois Av Delhi LA 71232

THOMPSON, FRANK B., business exec.; b. Louisville, 1895; grad. U. Mich., 1917. Chmn. Glenmore Distilleries Co., Louisville. Home: 501 Lightfoot Rd Louisville KY 40207 Office: 660 S 4th St Louisville KY 40222

THOMPSON, FRANK HODGE, transp. co. exec.; b. Stephens, Ark., Aug. 9, 1921; s. Robert Herbert and Irene (Hodge) T.; student Ouachita Bapt. U., 1940-43; m. Lurline Turbeville, Feb. 23, 1944; children— Celia (Mrs. Artie Gregory), Carolyn, Frank Hodge. Agt., terminal mgr. Wheeling Pipe Line, Inc., Helena, Ark., 1952-58; pres., Frank Thompson Transport, Inc., El Dorado, Ark., 1958—. Chmn., Union County FHA Com., 1966-69, Union County Devel. Council, 1964—. Bd. dirs. Union County Soil and Water Conservation Dist., Meth. Found. Ark. Served to capt., cav. AUS, 1943-46; PTO. Mem. Recipient Soil Conservation award Goodyear Co., 1965; named Union County Farm Family of Year, Ark. Power & Light Co. and El Dorado C. of C., 1967. Mem. Ark. Bus and Truck Assn., C. of C. U.S. Democrat. Methodist (mem. bd. laity 1970-72). Home: Route 5 Box 240 El Dorado AR 71730 Office: Paxton Rd PO Box 29 El Dorado AR 71730

THOMPSON, FRANK MAY, airline co. exec.; b. Indpls., Sept. 26, 1923; s. Frank D. and June (May) T.; B.A., U. Va., 1950; M.B.A., Harvard, 1952; m. Betsy Craig Smith, Sept. 6, 1952; children—Craig, Kerry, Amy, Jay. City reporter Dun & Bradstreet, Inc., N.Y.C., 1950; with Gen. Electric Co., 1952-56; mgmt. cons. McKinsey & Co., Inc., N.Y.C., 1956-61; dir. personnel and indsl. relations Bulova Watch Co., Inc., N.Y.C., 1961-64; v.p. Am. Express Co., N.Y.C., 1964-68; v.p. personnel relations Eastern Airlines, 1968—; dir. Lawrence Tufts Co., Briarcliff, N.Y. Instr. extension div. Sch. Indsl. and Labor Relations, Cornell U., 1959-62. Served with USMCR, 1942-46. Mem. Am. Mgmt. Assn., Indsl. Mgmt. Club. Clubs: Harvard Business School of N.Y.; Harvard of Westchester (N.Y.). Home: 4510 Santa Maria Coral Gables FL 33146 Office: Eastern Airlines Internat Airport Miami FL 33148

THOMPSON, GEORGE ALFRED, JR., county govt. ofcl.; b. Providence, Feb. 21, 1909; s. George Alfred and May Josephine (Heath) T.; B.S., R.I. State Coll., 1932, M.S., 1934; m. Elisabeth Sorensen Willard, Apr. 24, 1939; 1 dau., Joann Elisabeth. With R.I. Dept. Agr., 1932-38, U.S. Dept. Agr., 1938-42, USPHS, 1942-53; dir. Jefferson County Mosquito Control Dist., Nederland, Tex., 1953—. Cons. entomologist. Served with USPHS, 1942-53. Mem. Am. Registry Certified Entomologists, Sci. Research Soc. Am. Contbr. articles to profl. jours. Home: 2313 Av B Nederland TX 77627 Office: Box 194 Nederland TX 77627

THOMPSON, GERALD ELLISON, supt. schs.; b. Hubbard, Tex., Nov. 4, 1909; s. Oscar Scott and Mary (Kitura) T.; A.B., Trinity U., 1932; M. Ed., Tex. U., 1942; m. Louise Baird, June 29, 1935; children—Barry Baird, Gerald Dan. Coach, tchr., Pecos, Tex., 1932-34; prin. Kermit (Tex.) High Sch., 1934-48; supt. schs., Kermit, 1948—. Served from ensign to lt. comdr. USNR, 1942-45. Mem. C. of C. (pres.), Tex. Tchrs. Assn. (past pres.), Am., Tex. (past pres.) assns. sch. adminstrs., N.E.A., Am. Legion. Methodist. Mason, Lion (dist. gov.). Home: 848 Jeffee St Kermit TX 79745 Office: 701 S Poplar St Kermit TX 79745

THOMPSON, GUY PATRICK, electronic engr.; b. Guston, Ky., Mar. 17, 1921; s. Joseph Albert and Eva (Ritchie) T.; B.S., U. Ky., 1949; m. Helen Dean Cummings, Aug. 25, 1944; children—Guy P., Susan Gail, Alan Ray, Theresa Joan. Design engr. General Electric Co., Schenectady, 1951-53; process engr., Owensboro, Ky., 1953-58; process engr. Am. Printing House for the Blind, Louisville, 1958; electronic engr. Army Missile Command, Huntsville, Ala., 1958—. Active Boy Scouts Am. Served with USNR, 1942-45. Registered profl. engr., Ala. Mem. Nat. Geographic Soc., Assn. U.S. Army, Scabbard and Blade. Democrat. Roman Catholic. Home: 10005 Lily Flagg Circle Huntsville AL 35803 Office: AmsmI-RFL Redstone Arsenal AL 35803

THOMPSON, HERMAN ORA, pharmacist, educator; b. Earl Park, Ind., Jan. 21, 1911; s. Ora and Dora T. (Linzbach) T.; B.S., U. N.C., 1937; M.S., Purdue U., 1940, Ph.D., 1944; m. Wilora (Billie) Pike, Mar. 18, 1939; children—Beverly Carol (Mrs. Rudy Watkins Barker), Herman Ora. Practicing pharmacist, N.C., 1937-38; med. service rep. Eli Lilly Co., Durham, N.C., 1938-39; grad. teaching asst. Purdue U., Lafayette, Ind., 1940-43; asst. prof. pharmacy U. Ga., Athens, 1944-45; asso. prof. pharmacy, hosp. pharmacist U. Ill., Chgo., 1945-46; asso. prof. pharmacy U. N.C., Chapel Hill, 1946-51, prof., 1951—. Mem. Am., N.C. pharm. assns., Acad. Pharm. Scis., Am.

Chem. Soc., E. Mitchell Sci. Soc., N.Y. Acad. Sci., Am. Assn. Colls. Pharmacy, Sigma Xi, Rho Chi. Home: 900 Xtopher Rd Chapel Hill NC 27514

THOMPSON, HOWARD ELLIOT, coll. pres.; b. Dobbs Ferry, N.Y., Mar. 4, 1914; s. Harry E. and Anna (French) T.; student Pa. State U., 1934-35; B.S., Springfield (Mass.) Coll., 1938; M.A., Ohio State U., 1940; Ph.D., U. N.C., 1952; m. Helen L. West, Feb. 13, 1939; children—Toni L., C. Scott, Prof., head dept. athletics Cedarville (O.) Coll., 1939-41; dir. health and phys. edn. Bethlehem Central Schs., Albany, N.Y., 1941-43; dir. athletics and phys. edn. Plattsburgh (N.Y.) Schs., 1946-50; prof., head div. health and phys. edn. Mo. State Tchrs. Coll., Kirksville, 1952-53, dir. athletics, 1952-53; prin. Wilkes Central High Sch., North Wilkesboro, N.C., 1953-62; supt. schs. Chapel Hill, N.C., 1962-65; pres. Wilkes Community Coll., Wilkesboro, N.C., 1965—; prof. Grad. Sch. Western Caroline U., summers 1955, 62, Appalachian State U., summer 1956, N.C. Central U., summer 1963, U. N.C., spring 1963. Chmn. Plattsburgh City Youth Commn.; edn. com. Appalachian Regional Commn. adv. council Community Coll.; bd. visitors Western Carolina U. Served from ensign to lt. comdr. USNR, 1943-46. Decorated Philippine Liberation Medal. Mem. No. N.Y. Coaches Assn. (chmn. 1946-50), N.W. Carolina Prins. Assn. (pres.), N.C. Assn. Educators, Am. Assn. Sch. Adminstrs., N.C. Assn. Community Coll. Presidents (chmn.), So. Assn. Secondary Schs. and Colls. (central reviewing com.), C. of C. (dir.), V.F.W. (past post comdr.), Am. Legion, Phi Delta Kappa. Methodist. Home: Country Club Rd Wilkesboro NC 28697

THOMPSON, JACK WINSTON, mech. engr.; b. Dallas, Aug. 12, 1925; s. Willis Elmer and Opal (Loftis) T; student Tex. A. and M. U., 1943-44; B.S., So. Meth. U., 1949; m. Bettye Jeanne Decatur, Feb. 16, 1947; children—Sharon Layne, Jon Randall, Susan Gay, Jay Rodger. Draftsman C. Wallace Plumbing Co., Dallas, 1947-49; sales engr. Tex. Distbrs., Inc., Dallas, 1949-51; gen. mgr., chief engr. Fagan Air Conditioning Co., Little Rock, 1951-59; v.p., mgr., chief engr. Natkin & Co., Lincoln, Neb., 1959-64; exec. v.p. George Linskie Co., Inc. (merged with Sam P. Wallace Co., Inc. 1971), Dallas, 1964—, now v.p., mgr. Dallas br. Mem. com. North Tex. Contractors Assn. 1968—; chmn. mech. code com. city of Dallas, 1968—; past pres., v.p., mem. Constrn. Employees Council N. Tex., 1968-70; mem. Dallas Plumbing/Mech. Code Adv. and Appeals Bd., 1971-73; budget com. United Fund, Little Rock, 1958; circus sales mgr. Boy Scouts Am., Little Rock, 1959, troop com., Lincoln, 1963-64. Democratic precinct chmn. Dallas County, 1968—; mem. Dallas County Dem. Exec. Com., 1968—; dir. Dem. Com. Responsible Govt., Dallas, 1969—; Justice of peace, Pulaski County, Ark., 1954-58. Served to 1st lt. AUS, 1944-47. Registered profl. engr., Tex., Ark., Neb., Ia. Mem. Am. Soc. Heating, Refrigerating and Air Conditioning Engrs. (dir.; regional chmn., past chmn. bd., pres., sec. Ark. chpt., past treas., Distinguished Service award 1971, sec. Neb. chpt.), Mech. Contractors Assn. Dallas (dir. 1972—, v.p. 1967, pres. 1968), Am., Tex. (dir.) mech. contractors assns., Am. Soc. M.E. (charter mem., past vice chmn. Ark. sub.-sect.), Nat., Ark., Tex. socs. profl. engrs., Former Students Assn. and Aggie Club Tex. A. and M. U., Alumni Assn. So. Meth. U. Dallas C. of C. Baptist. Mason (32 deg., K.T., Shriner, Jester), Rotarian. Clubs: Las Colinas Country (Irving, Tex.); Engineers (Dallas)‡

THOMPSON, JAMES ALLEN, racing exec.; b. Harper, Kan., May 10, 1903; s. Zachariah Caleb and Lydia Katherine (Gwinn) T.; student Harper Coll., 1916-24 children by previous marriage—Anita Mae (Mrs. Homer Vanbeber), Glenna Deanne (Mrs. Jack Delametter), Richard Eugene, Brian Andre; m. 3d, Eula Williams, Jan. 23, 1960. Bookkeeper, Hazel-Atlas Glass Co. Okla., Blackwell, 1925-27; clk. M.-K.-T. R.R. Co., Parsons, Kan., 1924-30; with Phillips Petroleum Co., Bartlesville, Okla., 1930-68, sec. to pres., 1938-51, sec. to chmn. bd., 1951-68, sec. to exec. com., 1954-68; pres., dir. Racing Enterprises, Inc., 1968—; co-owner Thompsons' Antiques, Bartlesville, Okla. Mem. Bartlesville C. of C. Republican. Mem. Disciples of Christ. Mason (32 degree, K.T., Shriner, Jester). Club: Hillcrest Country. Home: PO Box 605 Bartlesville OK 74003 Office: Racing Enterprises Inc Bartlesville OK 74003

THOMPSON, JAMES GRANT, physician; b. Carthage, Miss., 1902; M.D., U. Tenn., 1931. Intern, U.S. Marine Hosp., New Orleans, 1931-32; postgrad. course skin and cancer unit N.Y. Postgrad. Med. Sch., 1935-36; resident in dermatology N.Y.C. Hosp., Welfare Island, 1939-40; mem. staff Miss. Bapt. Hosp., Doctors Hosp., St. Dominics Hosp., Hinds Gen. Hosp., Univ. Hosp. (all Jackson); cons., mem. attending staff VA Hosp., Jackson; clin. prof. medicine and chief dermatology sect. dermatology U. Miss. Diplomate Am. Bd. Dermatology. Mem. A.M.A., So. Med. Assn., S.E. Dermatol. Soc., Am. Acad. Dermatology, Pan Am Med. Assn., Internat. Soc. Tropical Dermatology, Soc. Investigative Dermatology. Office: 710 E Fortification St Jackson MS 39201*

THOMPSON, JAMES HOWARD, librarian; b. Memphis, Aug. 20, 1934; s. Curtis Barnabas and Clara (Terry) T.; B.A., Southwestern U., 1955; M.A. (fellow, Ford Found. fellow), U. N.C., 1957, Ph.D., 1961; M.S. (fellow), U. Ill., 1963; m. Margareta Ortenblad, Nov. 24, 1961; children—Ralph, Anna, Howard. Cataloger, bibliographer Duke, 1963-65; asst. prof. history U. Southwestern La., Lafayette, 1965-66, U. Colo., Boulder, 1966-68; dir. house undergrad. library, lectr. dept. history U. N.C., Chapel Hill, 1968-70, dir. libraries, lectr. dept. history, Greensboro, 1970—. U. Colo. grantee, Eng., 1967. Mem. Am., Southeastern, N.C. library assns., Am. Hist. Assn., Phi Beta Kappa, Beta Phi Mu. Home: 1911 Fountain Ridge Chapel Hill NC 27514 Office: Jackson Library U NC Greensboro NC 27412

THOMPSON, JOHN P., business exec.; b. Dallas, Nov. 2, 1925; s. Joe C. and Margaret (Philp) T.; B.B.A., U. Tex., 1948; m. Mary Carol, June 5, 1948; children—Mary Margaret, H. Douglas, John P. With The Southland Corp., Dallas, 1948—, now pres.; dir. 1st Nat. Bank Dallas, Dr. Pepper Co. Bd. dirs. Presbyn. Hosp., U. Dallas. Office: 2828 N Haskall St Dallas TX 75204

THOMPSON, JOHN WILLIAM, JR., broadcasting and pub. co. exec.; b. Washington, Sept. 15, 1914; s. John W. and Elizabeth (Noyes) T.; B.A., Princeton, 1932-36; m. Muriel Gill Webb, June 29, 1938; children—Anthony J., Muriel E. (Mrs. Willis Patterson Young), Joan W. Reporter, Washington Evening Star, 1936-51, asst. city editor, 1951-57, asst. mng. editor, 1957, asso. editor, 1957-63, v.p., 1963—, dir., 1949—; pres., dir. Evening Star Broadcasting Co., WLVA, Inc., Lynchburg, Va., 1965—, WCIV, Charleston, S.C., 1966—; v.p. Washington Star Syndicate, 1965—; dir. Acacia Mut. Life Ins. Co., Nat. Permanent Fed. Savs. & Loan Co., Riggs Nat. Bank; chmn. bd. Fed. Home Loan Bank, Greensboro, N.C., 1959-69. Bd. dirs., past pres. D.C. Soc. Crippled Children: trustee Washington Hosp. Center, George Washington U. Served to capt. AUS, 1941-45. Decorated Bronze Star medal. Mem. Met. Washington Bd. of Trade (dir., past pres.), White House Corrs. Assn. Clubs: Chevy Chase; Metropolitan, Princeton, Broadcasters, Alfalfa (Washington). Home: 4605 Langdrum Lane Chevy Chase MD 20015 Office: 225 Virginia Av SE Washington DC 20003

THOMPSON, KATHLEEN, educator; b. Goodwater, Ala., Feb. 18, 1920; d. Aldrich R. and Urbie (Bailey) Thompson; B.S., U. Ala., 1942; postgrad. Ala. Coll., Montevallo, 1942, U. Tenn., summers 1954-55; M.S., Pa. State U., 1961. Tchr. vocational home econs. Liberty High Sch., Pickens County, Ala., 1942-44; with Coop. Extension Service Auburn U.-USDA, 1944—, asst. home demonstration agt., Randolph, Walker and Calhoun counties, 1944-46, home demonstration agt., Pickens County, 1946-47, asso. home demonstration agt., St. Clair County, 1947-48, home demonstration agt., Fayette County, 1948-52, specialist in clothing and handicraft Auburn U. (Ala.), 1952-69, specialist in clothing, 1969—; cons. State Maid of Cotton; appeared on ednl. TV sta. Auburn U.; adviser Fayette County Home Demonstration Council. Mem. Am. (past com. chmn.), Ala. (com. chmn.) home econs. assns., Bus. and Profl. Womens Club Fayette (past pres.). Contbr. chpt. to Consumers All, The Yearbook of Agriculture, 1965. Contbr. articles to profl. publs. Home: Route 1 Goodwater AL 35072 Office: Coop Extension Service Auburn U Auburn AL 36830

THOMPSON, KINDRED ALLISON, JR., textile co. exec.; b. Cochran, Ga., Oct. 16, 1899; s. Kindred Allison and Mary (Mullia) T.; student Mercer U., 1922; m. Jessie Wade, Apr. 17, 1926; 1 son, Allison Wade. Vice pres. Cochran Cotton Mill, 1923-33; v.p., sec. treas. Fitzgerald Cotton Mills (Ga.), 1934—; exec. v.p. Fitzgerald Mills Corp., 1945—; exec. v.p. Fitzgerald Textile Mills Inc., 1968—. Served with U.S. Navy, 1918. Home: 101 S Merrimac Dr Fitzgerald GA 31750 Office: Rte 1 Fitzgerald GA 31750

THOMPSON, LEE BENNETT, lawyer; b. Miami, Indian Terr., Mar. 2, 1902; s. P.C. and Margerie Constance (Jackson) T.; B.A., U. Okla., 1925, LL.B., 1927; m. Elaine Bizzell, Nov. 27, 1928; children—Lee Bennett, Jr., Ralph Gordon, Carolyn Elaine. Admitted to Okla. bar, 1927, since practiced in Oklahoma City; mem. firm Cantrell, Douglass, Thompson & Wilson; spl. justice Okla. Supreme Ct., 1967-68; sec., gen. counsel Mustang Fuel Corp. and other corps. Past sec. Masonic Charity Found. Okla.; chmn. Okla. County chpt. A.R.C., 2 terms; chmn. resolutions com. Nat. A.R.C. Conv., 1953. Served from capt. to col., AUS, 1940-46; PTO. Decorated Legion of Merit; recipient Distinguished Service citation U. Ala., 1971. Fellow Am. Bar Found., Am. Coll. Trial Lawyers; mem. Oklahoma City C. of C. (past dir.), Oklahoma City Jr. C. of C. (past pres.), U.S. Jr. C. of C. (past dir. and v.p.), Oklahoma City Symphony Orch. (past dir.), Oklahoma City. Community Fund (past dir.), Okla. County (past pres.), Am. (ho. of dels.), Okla. (pres. 1972) bar assns., U. Okla. Alumni Assn. (past mem. exec. com.), U. Okla. Meml. Student Union (pres.), Okla. City Zool. Soc. (past dir.), Am. Judicature Soc., Mil. Order World Wars, Mil. Order Carabao, Am. Legion, Beta Theta Pi (past v.p., trustee), Phi Beta Kappa. Democrat. Mem. Christian Ch. (past elder). Mason (Shriner, Jester, 33 deg.), Rotarian (past pres.). Clubs: Seventy Five, Men's Dinner (past mem. exec. com.), Beacon, Oklahoma City Golf and Country. Home: 539 NW 38th St Oklahoma City OK 73118 Office: First Nat Bldg Oklahoma City OK 73102

THOMPSON, LEROY, JR., army res. officer, radio engr.; b. Tulsa, July 7, 1913; s. LeRoy and Mary (McMurrain) T.; B.S. in Elec. Engring., Ala. Poly Inst., 1936; m. Ola Dell Tedder, Dec. 31, 1941; 1 son, Bartow McMurrain. Commd. 2d lt., U.S. Amy Res., 1935, advanced through grades to col., 1963; signal officer CCC, 1936-40; radio engr. Officer Hdqrs. 4th C A., 1941, signal officer OSS, Burma, 1945, signal officer Hdqrs. OSS, China, 1945, radio engr., tech. liaison officer, Central Intelligence Group, CIA, 1945-50; chief radio br. Hdgrs. FEC, Tokyo, 1950-53, chief radio engring br. Signal C Plant Engring. Agy., 1953-55; radio cons. to asst. dir. def. research and engring. communications, 1960-62; pvt. research and devel. on communication and related problems, 1963—; owner Thompson Research & Exptl. Devel. Lab. Licensed profl. radio engr., Ga. Mem. I.E.E.E. (sr.), Vet. Wireless Operators Assn., Am. Radio Relay League, Nat. Rifle Assn., Res. Officers Assn., Am. Motorcycle Assn., Nat. Wildlife Fedn. Baptist. Home: 6450 Overlook Dr Alexandria VA 22312

THOMPSON, LIBBIE MOODY (MRS. CLARK W. THOMPSON), civic worker; b. Galveston, Tex., Nov. 22, 1897; d. William Lewis and Libbie Rice (Shearn) Moody; student Holton-Arms, Washington, 1915; m. Clark W. Thompson, Nov. 16, 1918; children—Clark W., Libbie (Mrs. James I. Stansell) (dec.). Former dir. YWCA, Galveston chpt. A.R.C.; founding mem. chancellor's council U. Tex.; nat. bd. Med. Coll. Pa., also mem. pres.'s assos.; mem. fine arts commn. U.S. Dept. of State; adv. council fine arts, mem. chancellor's com. U. Tex. Mem. Colonial Dames, Daus. Republic of Tex., Am. Legion Aux., Am. Newspaper Women's Club, League Women Voters (past dir.), Huguenot Soc., U.D.C., Soc. Sponsors USN (life), Magna Charta Dames, Plantagenet Soc., Opera Soc. of Washington, Smithsonian Assos. (life), Salvation Army Aux. Washington (life), Friends Kennedy Center (a founder), Order Washington, Friends Rosenberg Library, UN Assn. U.S.A., Jr. League (hon. life), Order of Washington, Descs. of Most Noble Order of Garter. Clubs: Women's Nat. Democratic, Sulgrave, 1925 F Street, George Town (Washington); Galveston Artillery. Home: 1616 Driftwood Lane Galveston TX 77550 also 3301 Massachusetts Av NW Washington DC 20008

THOMPSON, LOLA MAE COOPER (MRS. WILBURN B. THOMPSON), librarian; b. Sicily Island, La., Mar. 5, 1920; d. Roy Lee and Mae (Bass) Cooper; B.A., U. Southwestern La., 1940, B.S. in L.S., La. State U., 1947; m. Wilburn B. Thompson, June 13, 1961; 1 son, Kelly Roy. Tchr., Catahoula Parish Sch. Bd., Manifest, La., 1941-46; librarian Vivian (La.) High Sch. Library, 1947-48, Ouachita Parish High Sch., Monroe, La., 1948-49; dir. extension E. Baton Rouge Parish Library, 1949-53; librarian LaSalle Parish Library, Jena, La., 1953-58; librarian St. Mary Parish Library, Franklin, La., 1958—. Mem. Am., La. library assns., Bus. and Profl. Women's Club. Home: 1705 Pine St Franklin LA 70538 Office: Box 194 Franklin LA 70538

THOMPSON, LORIN ANDREW, JR., univ. pres.; b. Greeley, Colo., Jan. 23, 1902; s. Lorin Andrew and Annie (Hertzog) T.; B.A., Ohio State U., 1923, M.A., 1924, Ph.D., 1927; m. Dorothy Wright, Jan. 24, 1924 (dec. 1937); children—Margaret E. (Mrs. Donald McNamara), Joan (Mrs. Philip N. Libby, Jr.); m. 2d, Amelia Harney, Aug. 13, 1938; children—Sylvia L. (Mrs. Graham A. Carlton, Jr.), William O., Richard F., Ellen M. (Mrs. Earl Pfeffer), Winifred H. prof. psychology Ohio Wesleyan U., 1927-34; dir. research Regional Dept. of Econ. Security, Cin., 1934-40; dir. Va. Population Study, Richmond, 1940-44; dir. Bur. of Population and Econ. Research, U. Va., 1944-66; prof. Grad. Sch. Bus. Adminstrn., U. Va., 1958—; pres. George Mason U. Fairfax, Va., 1966—. Chmn. Charlottesville Planning Commn. Fellow A.A.A.S., Am. Psychol. Assn.; mem. Am. Statis. Assn., Am., So. econ. assns., Population Assn. Am., Assn. U. Burs. Bus. and Econ. Research (pres. 1957). Author: Interview Aids and Trade Tests for Employment Offices, 1935; Trends and Prospects of Unemployment Compensation in Va., 1953; also other works. Contbr.: The Urban South, 1955; Handbook of Applied Psychology, 1950. Home: 1521 Oxford Rd Charlottesville VA 22903 Office: Office of Pres George Mason U Fairfax VA 22030

THOMPSON, LOUIS CLIFFORD, aerospace engr.; b. Chgo., Aug. 13, 1921; s. Clifford James and Christobel (Sawin) T.; student Fla. So. Coll., 1946-47, George Washington U., 1947-50; B. Mech. Engring., U. Fla., 1957; m. Evelyn King, Apr. 12, 1952; children—Linda Carol, Peggy Lewis, Daniel Duke. Research and devel. program mgr. Bur. Ships, Washington, 1953-56; chief research engr., test lab. Marshall Space Flight Center, Redstone Arsenal, Ala., 1957-62, chief, test office Saturn V program office, 1962-63, chief, mfg. br. S-IC Stage office, 1963-66, asst. chief S-IC Stage project mgr., 1966—. Served with AUS, 1942-45. Decorated D.F.C., Air medal. Registered profl. engr., Ala. Mem. Nat. Soc. Profl. Engrs., Instrument Soc. Am. (sr.), Am. Soc. M.E. U. Fla. Alumni Assn. Methodist. Contbr. articles to profl. publs. Home: 5100 Panorama Dr SE Huntsville AL 35801 Office: I-V-S-IC Marshall Space Flight Center Redstone Arsenal AL 35812

THOMPSON, LUTHER JOE, clergyman; b. Watertown, Tenn., Nov. 9, 1918; s. Eli Wilson and Lucille Smith (Neal) T.; A.B. summa cum laude, Carson-Newman Coll., 1941; Th.M., So. Bapt. Theol. Sem., 1945; Ph.D., U. Edinburgh, 1951; m. Mary Evelyn Wingo, Aug. 23, 1945; children—Joseph Mark, Luther Kent. Ordained to ministry Bapt. Ch., 1938; student pastor, 1938-45; pastor 1st Bapt. Ch., Springfield, Tenn., 1945-50, McAlester, Okla., 1950-54, Calvary Bapt., Jackson, Miss., 1954-60, 1st Bapt. Ch., Chattanooga, 1960-68, 1st Bapt. Ch., Richmond, Va., 1968—. Vis. preacher Ridgecrest and Glorieta Bapt. assemblies; Gheens lectr. preaching So. Bapt. Theol. Sem., Louisville; guest preacher USAF, Spiritual Life Confs., 1965. Mem. Gov.'s Adv. Com. in Pub. Welfare, Chattanooga, 1964-68, Mayor's Com. for Community Improvement, 1963-68. Bd. dirs., exec. com., adv. bd. Richmond Bapt. Assn. Recipient George Washington Honor medal for outstanding sermons, 1960, 64. Author: Monday Morning Religion, 1961; Through Discipline to Joy, 1966. Home: 8905 Highfield Rd Richmond VA 23229 Office: Monument and Boulevard Richmond VA 23220

THOMPSON, MARGUERITE MYRTLE GRAMLING (MRS. RALPH B. THOMPSON), librarian; b. Orangeburg, S.C., Apr. 23, 1912; d. Thomas Laurie and Rosa Lee (Stroman) Gramling; B.A. in English cum laude, U. S.C., 1932, postgrad., 1937; B.A. in Library Sci., Emory U., 1943; m. Ralph B. Thompson, Sept. 17, 1949 (dec. Oct. 1960). Tchr. English pub. high schs., S.C., 1932-43; librarian Rockingham (N.C.) High Sch., 1943-45, Randolph County (N.C.) Library, Asheboro, 1945-48, Colleton County (S.C.) Library, Walterboro, 1948-61; chief librarian Florence (S.C.) County Library, 1961—. Sec. com. community facilities, services and instns. Florence County Resources Devel. Com., 1964-67; vice chmn. Florence County council on Aging, 1968-70, corr. sec., 1971, exec. bd., 1972. Mem. A.L.A. (council 1965—), Southeastern, S.C. (pres. 1960, chmn. assn. handbook revision com. 1967-69, sect. co-chmn. com. standards for S.C. pub. libraries 1966-68, fed. relations coordinator 1972-73) library assns., Delta Kappa Gamma (state scholarship chmn. 1967—, internat. scholarship com. 1970—; 2d v.p. 1971-73), Florence County Hist. Soc., Greater Florence C. of C. (div. vice chmn. 1968; women's div. chmn. 1969-70), Southeastern Regional Conf. Women in Chambers Commerce (dir. 1970-71), Florence Lit. Club (pres. 1970-72, v.p. 1972—). Methodist (chmn. ch. library com. 1965-71, chmn. com. ch. history, 1968-69). Club: Florence Literary (sec. 1964-66). Home: 1012 Woodstone Dr Florence SC 29501 Office: 319 S Irby St Florence SC 29501

THOMPSON, MARVIN CULLUM, ins. co. exec.; b. Dallas, May 11, 1924; s. Robert William and Llora (Cullum) T.; student So. Methodist U., 1941-43; B.S. in Econs., U. Pa., 1944; m. Elizabeth Burgher, Mar. 12, 1949; children—Barbara, Lynda, Marvin Cullum, Beth, Robert Cedric. With Home Ins. Co., N.Y.C., 1944, Standard Accident Co., Detroit, 1945; partner Kirkpatrick-Thompson Co., Dallas, 1946-57; mem. faculty Dallas Coll., So. Methodist U., 1954-58; sec. United Fidelity Life Ins. Co., Dallas, 1957, v.p., 1958-60, exec. v.p., 1960, pres., 1961—; dir., mem. exec. coms. Nat. Bank Commerce, Dallas, Byerly Foods, Inc., Dallas, S.W. Title Ins. Co., Dallas. Treas., Park Cities' Dads' Club. Bd. dirs. Met. YMCA, 1968—, chmn. finance com., 1970—; bd. dirs. Citizens' Traffic Commn. Mem. Dallas Council on World Affairs, Central Bus. Dist. Assn., Young Presidents Orgn., Cotton Bowl Council, Newcomen Soc., So. Methodist U. Alumni Assn. (exec. com.). Presbyn. Clubs: City (dir., chmn. membership com.), Idlewild, Dallas Country (Dallas). Office: 1025 Elm St Dallas TX 75202 Home: 3612 Beverly Dr Dallas TX 75205

THOMPSON, MARY ANN, lawyer; b. Nashville, Nov. 3, 1934; d. William Terry and Gladys (Mitchell) Thompson; student U. Chattanooga, 1954-58; LL.B., Cumberland U., 1960, J.D., 1969. Office mgr. Lookout Beverages, Inc., Chattanooga, 1961-63; admitted to Tenn. bar, 1961; asso. counsel Provident Life & Accident Ins. Co., Chattanooga, 1963—; dir. Provident Employees Credit Union. Bd. dirs., Big Sisters, Big Bros., Inc., Orange Grove Day Care Center; active Nat. Retarded Children's Assn., Tenn. Retarded Children's Assn., Chattanooga Retarded Children's Assn. Mem. Am., Tenn., Chattanooga-Hamilton County Bar Assn., Zonta Internat., Alpha Lambda Delta, Pi Gamma Mu, Iota Tau Tau (dean Zeta chpt. 1959-60). Republican. Episcopalian. Home: Marmons Dr Rd 2 Box 248 Harrison TN 37341 Office: Provident Life & Accident Ins Co Fountain Square Chattanooga TN 37402

THOMPSON, MILTON STRONG, orthopedic surgeon; b. Newbury, Mass., Oct. 26, 1901; s. Milton Strong and Abigail Adams (Johnson) T.; A.B., Harvard, 1924, M.D., 1931; m. Elizabeth Paige, Jan. 20, 1940; 1 dau., Phoebe (Mrs. Robert K. Neesham); (stepchildren) Mary (Mrs. James Donald), Caroline Howe (Mrs. George Erwin). Intern Boston City Hosp., Boston, 1931-33, Mass. Gen. Hosp. and Children's Hosp., Boston, 1933-35; grad. asst. Harvard Med. Sch., Mass. Gen. Hosp., 1936-40; chief orthopedic service Me. Gen. Hosp., 1940-46; commd. maj. M.C., U.S. Army, 1941, lt. col. 1944, col., 1949; chief orthopedic service Brooke Gen. Hosp., Ft. Sam Houston, 1946-53; cons. USAREUR, 1953-56, Walter Reed Army Hosp., Washington, 1956-58; ret., 1958; prof. orthopedic surgery Baylor U. Grad. Sch., 1949-53; vis. prof. forensic orthopedics Sch. Law, U. Tex., 1959-62, clin. prof. orthopedics, 1967—. Spl. lectr. Georgetown U., 1956-58; cons. AID, Formosa, 1962. Pres., Easter Seal Soc., San Antonio, 1968. Bd. dirs. Rogerson House, Boston, 1934-65. Diplomate Nat. Bd. Med. Examiners, Am. Bd. Orthopedic Surgery. Fellow A.C.S. Royal Soc. Medicine (London), Am. Acad. Orthopedic Surgeons, I.C.S., Am. Assn. Surgery Trauma, Am. Orthopedic Assn., Internat. Soc. Orthopedics and Traumatology. Clubs: Argyle, Oak Hills Country (San Antonio); Army and Navy (Washington); Harvard (N.Y.C.). Contbr. articles to med. jours. Home: 441 Burr Rd San Antonio TX 78209 Office: Nix Profl Bldg San Antonio TX 78205

THOMPSON, RALPH BURNHAM, educator; b. Grand Rapids, Mich., Mar. 28, 1912; s. Karl Owen and Maud (Burnham) T.; student Antioch Coll., 1930-34; B.S., Miami U., 1935; M.B.A., Western Reserve U., 1942; Ph.D., U. Tex., 1952; m. Helen Elizabeth Kindig, Aug. 24, 1940; 1 son, Timothy Alan. Instr. La. State U., 1942-43, Western Res. U., 1946-47; asst. prof. U. Tex., 1947-52; asso. prof., 1952-54; editor Southwest Research Inst., 1954-55; asso. prof. U. Fla., Gainesville, 1955-60; prof., 1960—; vis. prof. U. Ill., Chgo., 1966-67.

Served with AUS, 1943-46. Mem. Am. Marketing Assn., So. Marketing Assn. (pres., 1967), Alpha Delta Sigma, Delta Sigma Pi, Gamma Sigma. Author: (with George Breen) Effective Selling, 1950. Editor: Bus. and Econ. Dimensions, 1965—. Home: 1209 NW 43d St Gainesville FL 32601

THOMPSON, RALPH GORDON, lawyer; b. Oklahoma City, Dec. 15, 1934; s. Lee Bennett and Elaine (Bizzell) T.; B.B.A., U. Okla., 1956, LL.B., 1961; m. Barbara Irene Hencke, Sept. 5, 1964; children—Lisa, Elaine and Marie (twins). Admitted to Okla. bar, 1961; spl. agt. Office of Spl. Investigations, 1957-60; gen. practice with Cantrell, Douglass, Thompson & Wilson, Oklahoma City, 1961—; mem. Okla. Ho. of Reps., 1966-70, asst. minority floor leader, 1969-70; spl. justice supreme ct. Okla., 1970-71. Mem. Okla. Crime Commn., 1968-70, gov.'s council on narcotics and drug abuse, 1968-70. Republican nominee for lt. gov. Okla., 1970; Okla. co-chmn. Friends of Richard Nixon, 1971—. Trustee Okla. Bar Found., 1966-70; pres., Okla. Young Lawyers Conf., 1965; Chmn. bd. dirs. A.R.C., 1970—, vice chmn., 1968-70. Served as lt. USAF, 1957-60; maj. Res. Named Oklahoma City's Outstanding Young Man, 1967; one of three Outstanding Oklahomans, 1968. Mem. Am., Okla., Oklahoma County bar assns., Beta Theta Pi, Phi Alpha Delta. Episcopalian. Home: 1109 Huntington Oklahoma City OK 73116 Office: First Nat Bldg Oklahoma City OK 73102

THOMPSON, ROBERT BROCK, hematologist, oncologist, educator; b. Sarnia, Ont., Can., June 24, 1929; s. Howard Bell and Margaret (McDonald) T.; M.D., U. Western Ont., 1953; Masters in Human Biology, U. Paris, 1971; pupil immunology Dr. G. Mathe, Paris, France, 1970-71; m. June Margaret Cutt, Apr. 20, 1957; children—Robert Brock, Arthur Cameron, Bruce Warren Charles, Phyllis Margaret. Intern Victoria Hosp., London, Can., 1953-54; resident Victoria Hosp., 1954-58, Mt. Auburn Hosp., Cambridge, Mass., 1958-59, Eugene Talmaldege, Augusta, Ga., 1959-61; practice medicine, specializing in clin. pathology, hematology, Jackson, Miss., 1963-72; mem. staff U. Miss. Hosp.; asst. dir. clin. labs. U. Miss., 1963-71; instr., Med. Coll of Ga., 1962-63; asst. prof. clin. lab. scis. U. Miss. Med. Center, Jackson, 1963-68, dir. med. oncology clinic, asso. prof., 1968-72; dir. immunohematology Scott White Clinic, Temple, Tex., 1972—, also mem. dept. internal medicine. Scoutmaster, Boy Scouts of Am., 1965-71. Served with RCAF, 1954-58. Mem. Order of Arrow. Home: PO Drawer 1285 Temple TX 76501 Office: Scott White Clinic Temple TX 76501

THOMPSON, ROBERT EUGENE, physician; b. Jackson, Miss., Dec. 10, 1930; s. Robert Lamar and Gladys Aletrice (Cooper) T.; B.S., Tulane U., 1952, M.D., 1955; m. Mary Susan Auguste Sherwood, June 5, 1954; children— Jeffrey Robert, Nanette Kathleen, Virginia Ann. Intern, Charity Hosp. of La., 1955-56; gen. practice medicine, 1956—; with Toccoa (Ga.) Clinic Med. Assos., 1958—, sr. partner, 1959—, chmn. exec. com., 1970. Pres., Ampo, Inc.; dir. Franklin Discount Co. Chmn., United Fund, 1963, Salvation Army Adv. Bd., 1964; v.p. Little League Council, 1970. Trustee Toccoa Housing Authority; trustee, chmn. Library Bd. Served to capt. USAF, 1956-58, Named Jaycee Outstanding Young Man of Year, 1964. Diplomate Am. Bd. Family Practice. Mem. A.M.A., Am. Acad. Family Practice. Presbyn. (deacon, elder). Lion. Home: 175 Pine Valley Dr Toccoa GA 30577 Office: 800 E Doyle St Toccoa GA 30577

THOMPSON, S. FLETCHER, legislator, lawyer; b. College Park, Ga., Feb. 5, 1925; s. R. Standish and Mary (Spencer) T.; A.B., Emory U., 1948; LL.B., Woodrow Wilson Coll. Law, 1957; m. Kathryn Cochran, Nov. 23, 1946; children—Charles Lawrence, Deborah Jean. With Equitable Life Assurance Soc., 1949-50; asst. S.E. mgr. Asso. Aviation Underwriters, 1953-58; now pres. Aero. Ins. Agy.; practice law, 1959—; mem. 90th to 92d Congresses from 5th dist. Ga. Served with M.C., AUS, 1943, USAAF, 1943-46, Air Rescue Service, 1950-53. Decorated Air medal. Mem. Nat. Aviation Trades Assn. (past nat. v.p.), Internat. Lawyer Pilots Bar Assn. (dir.), Sigma Delta Kappa. Rotarian. Club: Lakeside Country (past dir., v.p.). Home: 2631 Hogan Rd East Point GA 30344 Office: Longworth Bldg Washington DC 20515

THOMPSON, SAMUEL ARCH, ret. schs. supt.; b. Harper, Kan., Sept. 16, 1901; s. Zachariah Caleb and Lydia K. (Gwinn) T.; student Harper Coll., 1921-23; B.S., Okla. State U., 1925; M.S., Kan. State U., 1935; LL.D., Okla. Christian Coll., 1966; m. Hildreth Ann Shideler, June 15, 1929; children—Jacquelin J. (Mrs. Phil A. Martin), Sue Ann Charlotte. Tchr. Blackwell (Okla.) Pub. Schs., 1925-35; prin. Sr. High Sch., Blackwell, 1935-48; prin. Sr. High Sch., McAlester, Okla., 1948-50; supt. pub. schs., McAlester, 1950-71. Pres. Educator's Finance Co., 1965. Pres. United Fund, 1957-60. Named Pittsburg County Man of the Year, 1958. Mem. Okla. Edn. Assn. (pres. 1967), C. of C. (pres. 1960), Mason, Rotarian (pres. 1954-55). Home: PO Box 507 McAlester OK 74501

THOMPSON, SOPHUS, univ. dean; b. nr. Hatton, N.D., Mar. 13, 1902; s. Christopher and Ida (Anderson) T.; B.S., N.D. State U., 1925; postgrad. U. Minn., Ia. State U.; m. Dagny H. Aasgaard, Dec. 29, 1926; children—Sophus Aasgaard, Erik Grinde. Jr. engr. Ill. Dept. of Hwys., 1924-26; instr. civil engring. U. Ark., 1926-28; asst. prof. civil engring. So. Meth. U., Dallas, 1928-32, asso. prof., 1932-34, prof., chmn. civil engring. dept., 1934-64, dean of engring., 1964-67; pres. Thompson, Abney & Schoeller, Cons. Engrs., 1967-69; staff specialist Forrest & Cotton Inc., Cons. Engrs., Dallas, 1969—. Cons. engr., Dallas, 1940—. Fellow Am. Soc. C.E. (Tex. pres. 1964-65), Am. Assn. Engring. Edn., Nat. Soc. for Profl. Engrs.; mem. Am. Concrete Inst., Technical Club Dallas. Contbr. articles in field to profl. jours. Home: 2936 Dyer St Dallas TX 75205

THOMPSON, THOMAS BUNNELL, architect; b. San Antonio, Jan. 28, 1907; s. Arthur G. and Laura P. (Preusser) T.; B.S., Tex. A. and M. U., 1930; M.Arch., Cranbrook Acad. Art (Bloomfield, Mich.), 1944; m. Beatrice Syers, 1930 (div. 1958); children—Thomas B., Sue (Mrs. Thomas Petree). Draftsman, L. Harrington Co., San Antonio, 1925-31; mem. firm Boese & Thompson, Architects, San Antonio, 1931-34, Noonan & Thompson & Krocker, San Antonio, 1946-59; architect Nat. Park Service, Austin, Tex., 1934-37; prof., dept. architecture Tex. A. and M. Coll., College Station, 1938-46; architect T.B. Thompson, San Antonio, 1960-61; asst. commr. for devel. PHA Washington, 1961-66: dir. housing devel. div. Housing Assistance Adminstrn., Washington, 1966-68, archtl. adviser to adminstrn., 1968-71; archtl. cons., 1971—. Mem. City Planning Commn., San Antonio, 1955-56, State Com. on Aging, 1960-61, Tex. Govs. Adv. Com., 1960; del. White House Conf. on Aging, 1961. Mem. A.I.A., Nat. Assn. Housing and Redevel. Ofcls. Author: (with Marie C. McGuire) Housing for the Elderly, 1957. Address: 1745 N St NW Washington DC 20036

THOMPSON, THOMAS HAZZARD, newspaper editor; b. Amarillo, Tex., Jan. 27, 1909; s. Aubrey J. and Blanche (Thomas) T.; B.A., U. So. Cal., 1932; M.A., La. State U., 1939; m. Helen Burgess, Sept. 6, 1946; children—Suzanne Keys, Thomas Lycurgus, Sheila Ward. Former mem. faculty La. State U., then tchr. Amarillo pub. schs.; with Amarillo Globe-News, 1941—, bus. editor, 1946-54, edition of the Globe Times, 1954-60, editor Globe-Times, 1961—; mem. Pulitzer Jury, 1962. Mng. partner Thompson Bros. Investments; dir. Globe-NEWS Pub. Co., Bank of the Southwest, Amarillo; v.p. Atchison (Kansas) Globe. Served to lt. comdr. USNR, 1942-45; PTO. Recipient of the Texas Headliner's award, 1960; newspaper recipient Pulitzer Gold medal award, 1960. Mem. Amarillo C. of C. (past dir.), Sigma Delta Chi. (Texas Man of Year award 1960). Episcopalian. Clubs: Amarillo (past pres.); Palo Duro (past dir.); Nat. Press (Washington). Author short stories. Home: 1220 Rusk St Amarillo TX 79107 Office: Globe-News Pub Co 9th and Harrison St Amarillo TX 79107

THOMPSON, WARREN E., scientist; b. Joliet, Ill., June 15, 1930; s. David E. and Edna M. (Templeton) T.; student Joliet Jr. Coll., 1947-49; B.S., U. Wis., 1951; M.A., Harvard, 1953, Ph.D., 1956; m. Ellen E. Coon, June 9, 1962; children—Barbara E., Douglas J. Fulbright scholar Kamerlingh Onnes Lab., Leiden, Netherlands, 1955-57; postdoctoral fellow, instr., asst. prof. chemistry U. Cal. at Berkeley, 1957-59; asst. prof. chemistry Case Inst. Tech., Cleve., 1959-65; sci. adminstr. Office Internat. Programs, NSF Washington, 1965—. Mem. Am. Chem. Soc., A.A.A.S., Sigma Xi, Phi Lambda Upsilon. Contbr. articles in field to profl. jours. Home: 4509 Amherst Lane Bethesda MD 20014 Office: 1800 G St NW Washington DC 20550

THOMPSON, WILLIAM BERT, ednl. adminstr.; b. Columbus, Miss., Nov. 5, 1920; s. Samuel David and Lucy (Daves) T.; B.S., U. Miss., 1947, M.A., 1950, Ed.D., 1968; m. Mary Etta Powell, June 5, 1949; children—William J., Lelon David, Mary Anne. Tchr. history, coach S.D. Lee High Sch., Columbus, 1947; prin. Amory Elementary Sch., 1948-49, Aberdeen Jr.-Sr. High Sch., 1950-55, Greenville High Sch., 1956-60; asst. supt. Greenville (Miss.) Pub. Schs., 1960-64, supt., 1965—. Mem. Miss. Accrediting Com., 1955-61; mem. Pres. Nixon's Commn. on Sch. Finance, 1970-72. Served with AUS, 1942-45. Mem. N.E.A., Assn. for Supervision and Curriculum Devel., Miss., Greenville edn. assns., Miss. Assn. Sch. Adminstrs. (pres. 1971-72), Miss. Assn. Sch. Supts., Miss. Prins. Assn. (pres. 1956-57), Pi Delta Kappa. Home: 263 Bermuda Dr Greenville MS 38701 Office: Box 749 Greenville MS 38701

THOMPSON, WILLIAM BLAINE, JR., railroad ofcl.; b. Falls Church, Va., Aug. 22, 1917; s. William Blaine and Catherine Elizabeth (Foley) T.; A.A., U. Fla., 1940; m. Margaret Louise Covey, Dec. 5, 1958; children— William Blaine III, Holland McTyeire, Gayle Tigert. Asst. cashier Fla. Nat. Bank, Jacksonville, 1940-48; asst. to v.p. Fla. Power and Light Co., 1949; self-employed pub. relations cons., 1952-58, also v.p. Riddle Air Lines; asst. to v.p. Assn. Am. Railroads, 1958-60, 64—, pres. Fla. East Coast Ry. Co., 1961-64, now dir.; pres., dir. Fla. East Coast Hwy. Dispatch Co., 1961—; dir. Fla. Nat. Bank and Trust Co., Miami. Sec., asst. treas. Am. Taxpayers Assn., 1963—. Served to lt. col. USMCR, World War II, Korea. Mem. Am. Legion. Club: Seminole (Jacksonville, Fla.). Home: 2729 S Ives St Arlington VA 22202 Office: Transportation Bldg 17th and H Sts NW Washington DC 20006

THOMPSON, WILLIAM JOEL, county agt.; b. Cragford, Ala., Apr. 5, 1914; s. William Abb and Zula (Alford) T.; student So. Union Jr. Coll., 1935-36; B.S., Auburn U., 1939, M.S., 1952, postgrad., 1957-62; m. Arminda Howell, Dec. 20, 1941. Vocational agr. tchr. Blount County Bd. Edn., Oneonta, Ala., 1939-46, Jefferson County Bd. Edn., Birmingham, Ala., 1946-54; asst. county agt. Auburn U., Jefferson, Walker, Shelby Counties, 1954-71; county extension chmn., Cleburne County, Heflin, Ala., 1971—. Recipient Distinguished Service award Nat. County Agts. Assn., 1972. Mem. Phi Delta Kappa, Epsilon Sigma Phi. Kiwanian. Clubs: Buxahatchee Country (Calera, Ala.); Civitan (pres. Warrior, Ala. 1951-52). Home: PO Box 158 Heflin AL 36264

THOMPSON, WILLIAM LESTER, chem. co. exec.; b. Midland, Tex., Dec. 18, 1932; s. William Lester and Mamie (Jordan) T.; B.S. in Electronic Engring., Tex. Tech. Coll., 1957; postgrad. So. Meth. U., 1957-59; m. Barbara Dillen, July 5, 1953; 1 son, Marc Bradford. Communciations engr. City of Lubbock, Tex., 1955-57; electronic engr. Tex. Instruments Inc., Dallas, 1957-59, tech. marketing engr., 1959-61, marketing mgr. Germanium Products div., 1961-65; exec. v.p. Thermalloy Inc., Dallas, 1965-69, now dir.; pres. Bradford Industries, Dallas, 1969-70, also dir; v.p. operations LTV Edn. Systems Inc., Dallas, 1970—; Thermalloy Plastics Inc.; Served with USN, 1951-55. Registered profl. engr., Tex. Mem. A.A.A.S., I.E.E.E., Tau Beta Pi, Eta Kappa Nu, Kappa Kappa Psi. Developer thermafilm dielectric film; inventor thermacote thermal joint compound. Home: 819 Lockwood Dr Richardson TX 75080 Office: 500 Fidelity Union Tower Bldg Dallas TX 75201

THOMPSON, WILLIAM REID, power co. exec.; b. Durham, N.C., Aug. 13, 1924; s. William Reid and Myrtle (Siler) T.; B.S., U.N.C., 1948; LL.B., Harvard, 1949; m. Mary Louise Milliken, Aug. 16, 1952; children—Mary Elizabeth, William Reid III, John Milliken, Susan Siler. Admitted to N.C. bar, 1949; with firm Barber and Thompson, Pittsboro, 1949-58; judge Superior Cts. N.C., 1958-60; asso. gen. counsel Carolina Power & Light Co., 1960-63, v.p., gen. counsel, 1963-67, exec. v.p., 1967—; mem. Raleigh City bd. N.C. Nat. Bank. Vice pres. Wake County chpt. N.C. Symphony Orch.; dist. chmn. Boy Scouts Am. Mem. N.C. Gen. Assembly from Chatham County, 1955-57. Bd. dirs. Raleigh United Fund. Served to lt. (j.g.) USNR, 1943-45. Mem. Am., N.C. bar assns., Phi Beta Kappa, Delta Kappa Epsilon. Democrat. Methodist (tchr. men's Bible class). Club: Carolina Country (Raleigh). Home: 2425 Glenwood Av Raleigh NC 27608 Office: 336 Fayetteville St Raleigh NC 27601

THOMPSON, WILLIAM TALIAFERRO, JR., educator, physician; b. Petersburg, Va., May 26, 1913; s. William Taliaferro and Ann C. (McIlwaine) T.; A.B., Davidson Coll., 1934; M.D., Med. Coll. Va., 1938; m. Jessie G. Baker, June 21, 1941; children—William Taliaferro III, Addison Baker, Jessie Ball. Intern 4th med. service Boston City Hosp., 1938-40; asst. resident Mass. Gen. Hosp., 1940-41; resident Med. Coll. Va., 1941, mem. faculty, 1946—, prof., chmn. dept. medicine, also chief med. services hosps., 1959—; mem. staff McGuire Clinic-St. Luke's Hosp., 1946-54; chief medicine service McGuire VA Hosp., 1954-59. Chmn. bd. mgrs., mem. med. adv. bd. Alfred I. DuPont Inst. and Nemours Found., 1962—; med. adv. bd. Greenbrier Clinic. Pres., Va. Assn. Mental Health, 1955-57, Richmond Bd. Housing and Hygiene, 1952-59. Bd. dirs. Meml. Guidance Clinic, 1950-59; trustee Collegiate Sch., 1952-69, pres., 1965-67; trustee Davidson Coll., 1965—, Mary Baldwin Coll., 1959-64. Served to maj. M.C., AUS, 1941-46. Diplomate Am. Bd. Internal Medicine. Fellow A.C.P. (chmn. Va. sect. 1961, gov. for Va. 1971—); mem. Am. Clin. and Climatological Assn., N.Y. Acad. Scis., Am. Fedn. Clin. Research, So. Soc. Clin. Investigation, Richmond Acad. Medicine (pres. 1972), Phi Beta Kappa, Alpha Omega Alpha, Omicron Delta Kappa, Kappa Sigma. Presbyn. Clubs: Country of Virginia, Commonwealth (Richmond). Contbr. med. jours. Home: 4602 Sulgrave Rd Richmond VA 23221

THOMPSON, WILLIAM VAN, oil co. exec.; b. Hartshorne, Okla., Oct. 25, 1907; s. James Oliver and Birdie (Hawkins) T.; m. Mary Elizabeth Cram, Sept. 6, 1932; 1 son, William Van. From dist. supt. to mgr. exploration prodn. and land and lease activities Southern Union Gas Co., N.M. and Dallas, 1938-54; exec. v.p. Aztec Oil & Gas Co., Dallas, 1954-61, pres., 1961—, also dir.; dir. Independent Natural Gas Co. Registered profl. petroleum engr., Tex., N.M. Mem. Am. Petroleum Inst., Ind. Natural Gas Assn., Am. Gas Assn., N.M. Oil and Gas Assn., Tex. Ind. Petroleum Assn., Nat. Petroleum Council. Clubs: Preston Trail Golf; Dallas Athletic, Petroleum, Brook Hollow Golf (Dallas). Home: 2917 Amherst Dr Dallas TX Office: First Nat Bank Bldg Dallas TX 75202

THOMPSON, WINIFRED GRACE, govt. ofcl.; b. Windsor, N.C., Mar. 7, 1913; d. William R. and Merle (Nelson) Thompson; student Shepherd Coll., 1931-33; B.A. in Edn., George Washington U., 1950; M.S.W., Catholic U. Am., 1952. Counselor girls Indsl. Home Sch., Washington 1937-42, chief counselor girls, 1946-48; organizer Jr. Village, Washington, 1948, supt., 1948-53; exec. dir. Commrs. Youth Council, Washington, 1953-54; gen. supt. D.C. Children's Center, Laurel, Md., 1954-65; dep. dir. Welfare Instl. Services, Washington, 1965-66; dir. D.C. Dept. Pub. Welfare, 1966-71, now dep. dir. social services D.C. Dept. Human Resources. Served with WAC, 1942-45. Recipient Outstanding Citizen of D.C. award D.C. League Women Voters, 1952; Woman of Year award for Zeta Phi Beta, 1955; Citizenship award for meritorious service to community B'nai B'rith, 1957; Ann. award delinquency and crime control conf. Health and Welfare Council, Nat. Capitol Area, 1964. Mem. Nat. Assn. Social Workers, Child Welfare League, Nat. Assn. for Mental Deficiency, Am. Pub. Welfare Assn., Nat. Conf. Supts. of Tng. Schs. Club: Soroptimist. Baptist. Home: 3701 Thornton Pkwy Oxon Hill MD 20022 Office: Dist Bldg 14th and E Sts NW Washington DC 20004

THOMS, HAROLD HERMAN, broadcasting exec.; b. Indpls., July 9, 1899; s. George Rudolph and Matilda (Goth) T.; B.S., Purdue U., 1921; m. Meredith Selene Jelks, Dec. 18, 1925; children—Matilann Selene (Mrs. Nathaniel C. W. Gennett, Jr.). Pres. Arlington-Fairfax Broadcasting Co., Arlington, Va., 1948—; pres. The Thoms Broadcasting Cos., Greensboro, N.C., 1956—; pres. Thoms Cablevision, Asheville, N.C., 1967—; pres. sta. WANC-TV, Asheville, N.C., 1953—; pres. Thoms Services Corp., Thoms Radio-TV Enterprises, CATV Inc., Thomsland, Inc., CATV Engring. Services, Inc.; mem. exec. com. Radio Advtg. Bur.; pres. N.C. CATV Assn. Bd. dirs., pres. Asheville Orthopedic Hosp. and Rehab. Center. Served with USNR, 1918. Recipient N.C. Rehab. Assn. pub. service award, 1971, Sertoma Club Service to Mankind award, 1971. Clubs: Am. Business (pres. 1935-36), Asheville Country, Biltmore Forest Country. Address: 75 Scenic Hwy Asheville NC 28804

THOMSEN, CHARLES EDWIN, architect; b. Paris, France, Apr. 3, 1931 (came to U.S. 1947, naturalized 1953); s. James W. and Stella Hanoka (deWyet) T.; A.B., Columbia, 1953, B. Arch., 1960; m. Joyce Eleanor Carroll, Aug. 9, 1958; children—Natalie Mai, Christian T. Alexander. Project mgr. William Lescaze, Architect, N.Y.C., 1962-64; project mgr. Edelbaum & Webster, Architects, N.Y.C., 1964-65; asso. editor A.I.A. Jour., Washington, 1965, exec. dir., N.Y., 1965-66; dir. exptl. parks program N.Y.C. Dept. Parks, 1966-67; spl. asst. for design U.S. Dept. Housing and Urban Devel., Washington, 1967—; mem. architects' adv. com. N.Y.C. Housing and Redevel. Bd., 1965-66; chmn. demonstration, research N.Y.C. Com. on Beautification, 1964-67. Mem. governing com. Bklyn. Children's Mus. Served with U.S. Army, 1953-55. Recipient Mayor's citation service to pub. N.Y.C., 1961. Mem. A.I.A. (chpt. dir., chmn. N.Y. chpt. urban and regional planning com. 1972—), Soc. Archtl. Historians, Alumni Assn. Columbia Sch. Architecture (past dir.), Am. Arbitration Assn., Internat. Platform Assn., Am. Soc. Planning Ofcls., Sigma Nu. Clubs: Columbia Rowing, Lake Anne Tennis (mem. gov. com. 1969—), Columbia University, Reston Golf and Country. Contbr. articles to profl. jours. Home: 11535 Links Dr Reston VA 22070

THOMSEN, WELLS HAMLEN, financial cons.; b. Cleve., Oct. 26, 1912; s. Mark Lawrence and Mary Louise (Hamlen) T.; A.B., Oberlin Coll., 1934; M.B.A., Harvard, 1936, M.P.A., 1943; m. Anna-Kathrine Hickok, Sept. 15, 1935; 1 dau., Wendy Hamlen; m. 2d, Katherine Burch, Apr. 18, 1946. Prodn. scheduling and mgmt. incandescent lamp div. Gen. Electric Co., 1936-41; Littauer fellow Harvard, 1942-43; fed. budget exam. Exec. Office of the President, Bur. of the Budget, 1943-53; dir. Office of Analysis and Review, Dept. Navy, 1953-63, dep. dir. Offices Program Appraisal and Mgmt. Information, 1964-65; dir. logistics review Office Asst. Sec. Navy, 1965-72; pvt. municipal financial cons., 1972—. Recipient Distinguished Civilian Service Award (Navy). Mem. Am. Soc. for Pub. Adminstrn., Soc. Logistics Engrs. Club: Woodlawn Country. Home: 217 Virginia Av Alexandria VA 22302

THOMSON, EARL JOHN JOSEPH, profl. engr.; b. Caron, Sask., Can., Dec. 16, 1906; s. William Forsyth and Edna Browning (Keller) T.; student Wesley Coll., U. Man., 1925-27; B.E.E., U. Marquette, 1934; m. Lois Lunsford, Oct. 20, 1936; children—Judith Kae (Mrs. Charles Gutke), Don Cameron. Surveyor, drafter City of Moose Jaw, Sask., Can., 1924-29, asst. city engr., 1929-31, acting city engr., 1934; draftsman, asst. engr. Burns & McDonnel Engring. Co., Kansas City, Mo., 1935-36, resident engr., 1936-39, asso. engr., 1939-42, prin. engr., 1942-47, partner, Miami, Fla., 1947-71, v.p., 1971—, Registered profl. engr Mo., Kan., Miss. Fellow Am. Soc. C.E.; mem. Nat., Mo. socs. profl. engrs., Soc. Am. Mil. Engrs., Am. Pub. Works Assn., U.S. Coast Guard Aux., U.S. Power Squadron, Sigma Phi Delta. Mason (32 deg., Shriner). Clubs: Coral Gables Country, Ocean Reef. Home: 115 Bayshore Ct Punta Gorda Isles Punta Gorda FL 33950 Office: 2671 SW 27th Av Miami FL 33133

THOMSON, JACK WADDELL, JR., lawyer; b. New Orleans, Dec. 5, 1921; s. Jack Waddell and Nancy (Morrison) T.; LL.B., Tulane U., 1951; m. Fannie Favalora, Aug. 25, 1951; children—Peter Michael, Leslie Arden. Admitted to La. bar, 1951; asso. Clay & Coleman, 1951-58; partner Clay, Coleman, Dutrey & Thomson, New Orleans, 1958—. Treas. New Orleans chpt. Young Audiences, 1965—. Mem. Bd. Zoning Adjustments, New Orleans, 1960-65. Trustee M. Louise Burguieres Found. Served with USAAF, 1942-45. Mem. Order of Coif, Phi Delta Phi. Episcopalian. Home: 2018 Dublin St New Orleans LA 70118 Office: 321 St Charles Av New Orleans LA 70130

THOMSON, JAMES MCILHANY, lawyer; b. New Orleans, Aug. 9, 1924; s. Paul J. and Gretchen (Bigelow) T.; B.A., Va. Mil. Inst., 1947; LL.B., U. Va., 1950; m. Sarah Jennings, Nov. 15, 1952; children—Sally J., Teresa L. Admitted to Va. bar, 1951, since practiced in Alexandria; mem. profl. staff U.S. Senate Jud. Com., 1951-52; partner firm Clarke, Richard Moncure & Whitehead, 1953-63, Thomson, Gannon, Thomas & Cacheris, 1965-67; mem. Va. Ho. of Dels., 1955—, majority leader, 1968—; founder, chmn. City Bank & Trust Co. Alexandria, 1964-71; dir. Dominion Nat. Bank, 1972—, Dominion Bankshares Corp., 1969—; founder, sec., dir. Fidelity Savs. & Loan assn., Alexandria, 1961-64, 72—. Mem. adv. bd. George Mason Coll. Served with USMCR, World War II. Recipient Distinguished Service award Jr. C. of C., 1955. Mem. Am. Va., Alexandria bar assns., Am. Legion, Alexandria C. of C., S.A.R., S.C.V., Forty and Eight, Civitan, Beta Theta Pi. Eagle, Odd Fellow. Home: 801 N Pitt St Apt 1101 Alexandria VA 22314 Office: 201 N Washington St Alexandria VA 22314

THOMSON, WILLIAM ALEXANDER, JR., dentist; b. Hattiesburg, Miss., June 22, 1928; s. William Alexander and Monroe Joseph (Tate) T.; student Va. Poly. Inst., 1946-48; B.Engring., Vanderbilt U., 1951; postgrad. U. So. Miss., 1961-62; D.D.S., U. Tenn., 1965; certificate orthodontics U. Pa., 1967. Mech. engr. Chance Vought Aircraft Corp., Dallas, 1951-52, Freeport Sulphur Co., Port Sulphur, La., 1952-53, 56-61; dentist Fla. State Bd. Health, Sarasota, 1965-66; pvt. practice dentistry specializing in orthodontics, Hattiesburg, Miss., 1968—. Served to lt. (j.g.) C.E., USNR, 1953-56. Mem. Am., Miss. dental assns., Am. Assn. Orthodontists, So. Soc. Orthodontists, Richard Doggett Dean and Marguerite Taylor Dean Hon. Odontological Soc., Delta Sigma Delta. Kiwanian (chmn. achievement com. 1971-72)

THORMAN, DAVID FREDERICK, architect; b. El Paso, Tex., July 17, 1938; s. Otto Henry and Adela Field (Wallwork) T.; B.A., Rice Inst., 1960, B.Arch., 1965; m. Merilee Joan Anderson, Apr. 16, 1966; 1 dau., Caillouet Fayre. Mgmt. planning specialist Caudill Rowlett Scott, Houston, 1969, project mgr., 1968-69, mgmt. cons., 1970—. Served with USNR, 1961-64. Mem. Rice U. Archtl. Alumni Assn. (pres. 1969). Home: 2308 South Blvd Houston TX 77006 Office: 1111 W Loop S Houston TX 77027

THORNBERRY, (WILLIAM) HOMER, judge; b. Austin, Tex., Jan. 9, 1909; s. William Moore and Mary Lillian (Jones) T.; B.B.A., U. Tex., 1932, LL.B., 1936; LL.D., Gallaudet Coll.; m. Eloise Engle, Feb. 24, 1945; children—Molly, David Homer, Kate. Admitted to Tex. bar, 1936, since practiced in Austin; dist. atty. 53d Jud. Dist., Travis County, Tex., 1941-42. Mem. city council, Austin, 1946-48; mayor pro tem, 1947-48; mem. Tex. Ho. of Reps., 1937-40; mem. 81st to 88th Congresses, 10th Tex. Dist., resigned 1963; U.S. dist. judge Western Dist. Tex., 1963-65; judge 5th circuit U.S. Ct. Appeals, 1965—. Served with USNR, 1942-46. Recipient Silver Beaver, Boy Scouts Am., 1948; named Distinguished Alumnus U. Tex., 1965. Mem. Am., Tex. Travis County bar assns., Order Coif. Democrat. Methodist. Mason (32 deg., K.C.C.H., Shriner), Kiwanian. Home: 1403 Hardouin St Austin TX 78703 Office: US Court House Austin TX 78701

THORNDIKE, CHARLES JESSE (CHUCK), cartoonist; b. Seattle, Wash., Jan. 20, 1897; s. Charles Adelbert and Hortense Victoria T.; ed. De Koven, Tacoma, 1913-14, Moran Sch., Seattle, 1914-15. U. Wash., 1919-20, U. Cal., 1920-22; m. Anne Lee; 1 dau., Barbara Ann. Began as cartoonist 1916; successively with San Francisco Bulletin, Animated Cartoon Film Corp., New York Herald-Tribune Syndicate, Van Tine Syndicate; art dir. for Gen. Motors Corp., Forbes Magazine, A.M. Walzer Co., Dover, N.J.; artist for Fox Films, United Artists, Universal and Ednl. Films; has conducted cartoon classes in N.Y. City for 3 yrs.; on radio programs "Cartoon Club of the Air." "Behind the Cartoon"; mem. adv. bd. Washington School of Art; sr. visual information specialist USN, 1941—; art dir. OAS. Served in USMC. 1918-19. Mem. Pi Kappa Alpha. Democrat. Episcopalian. Author several books relating to field of interest, 1937—; latest being: Susie and Sam in Silver Springs, 1949; Susie and Sam at Rock City, 1950; New Secrets of Cartooning, 1957; How to Enjoy Good Health, 1966. Originator of newspaper syndicate feature: Oddities of Nature, writer syndicated newspaper feature, World of Tomorrow. Contbr. cartoon to Coll. Humor, Sat. Eve. Post, New Yorker, etc. Lectr. schs. and clubs. Home: 11660 Canal Dr North Miami FL 33161

THORNELL, JACK RANDOLPH, photographer; b. Vicksburg, Miss., Aug. 29, 1939; s. Benjamin O. and Myrtice (Jones) T.; ed. pub. schs.; m. Carolyn Wilson, June 12, 1964; 1 dau., Candice. Photographer, Jackson (Miss.) Daily News, 1960-64, A.P., 1964—; assigned Dominican Republic, 1965, Selma, Ala., 1965, Democratic Nat. Conv., 1968. Served with AUS, 1958-60. Recipient Pulitzer prize for news photography of shooting of James Meredith, 1967; Headliners Photography award, 1967. Home: 5236 Utica St Metarie LA 70002 Office: 3800 Howard St New Orleans LA 70160

THORNTON, BOB M., educator; b. Atlanta, Apr. 24, 1932; student David Lipscomb Coll., Samford U.; B.S., Auburn U., 1959, M.S., 1960; Ed.D. (fellow), Duke, 1965; m.; 2daus. Tchr. Am. history and gen. bus. Central High Sch., Phoenix City, Ala., 1959-60; tchr. Am. history and math., dean men Hewitt-Trussville (Ala.) High Sch., 1960-61; psychometrist Ala. Inst. for Deaf and Blind, Talladega, 1961; instr. U. Ala., Gadsden, 1961; asst. prof. psychology and edn. Jacksonville (Ala.) State U., 1961-63; grad. asst. Bur. Testing and Guidance Duke U., Durham, N.C., 1963-64, grad. asst. to chmn. edn. dept., 1964-65, instr., 1965; chmn., prof. psychology Valdosta (Ga.) State Coll., 1965-67; prof. edn. U. West Fla., 1967—, acting chmn. profl. edn., 1967; also substitute tchr. pub. schs. Pensacola, Fla. area. Edn. cons. Fla. County Bds. Edn.; psychol. cons. Inst. for Personality and Abilities Testing, Champaign, Ill., Personnel Psychology Center, N.Y.C., Lowndes County (Ga.) Bd. Edn., N.C. Dept. Social Welfare, Calhoun County (Ala.) Bd. Edn.; psychol. examiner N.C. Dept. Disability Determination; chief cons. Fla. Community Colls., Drug Edn. Sec. Pensacola City Council-Escambia County Commrs. Drug Abuse Com.; chmn. Pensacola City-Escambia County Com. on Drug Abuse Research and Evaluation; dir. Operation Prevention; regional coordinator Fla. Dept. Edn. Drug Abuse Edn. Program; mem. region 1 Drug Abuse Council Fla. Dept. Health and Rehab.; Ga. rep. to Internat. com. on sociometry Negro-White relations 1st Internat. Congress Sociometry and Social Psychology, Prague, Czechoslovakia. Bd. dirs. Lowndes County Mental Health Assn., 1965-67. Served with USNR, 1952-54. Mem. N.E.A., Ga., Southeastern psychol. assns., Nat. Council for Social Studies, Am. Assn. U. Profs., Assn. Supervision and Curriculum Devel., Am. Psychol. Assn., Psy Chi, Kappa Delta Pi, Phi Delta Kappa, Delta Sigma Phi (pres. 1956-57). Evangl. Author: The Psychology Of The Individual, 1967. Contbr. book revs. to Jour. of Thought. Contbr. articles to psychol. jours. Home: 129 Eufaula St Gulf Breeze FL 32561

THORNTON, CHARLES DEWANE, govt. ofcl.; b. Brownsville, Pa., Mar. 3, 1915; s. De Wane and Sadie (McCune) T.; B.S., U. Pitts., 1939; postgrad. U. Rochester, 1940-41, U. Tenn., 1946; D.Sc., Ind. Inst. Tech., 1957; m. Dakota Wheeler, Oct. 14, 1935; children—D. Darlene (Mrs. David F. Sutter), Charles De Wane, Constance D. (Mrs. Edward J. Frautschi), Janice (Mrs. Richard T. Olsen), Holly V. Tech. asst. Source and Fissionable Materials accountability to chief, Office Operations Analysis and Planning, U.S. AEC, 1948-56; tech. asst. to v.p. Internat. Tel. & Tel., 1965-67, v.p. indsl. labs., 1958-60, N. Am. tech. dir., 1960-63; exec. v.p., dir. Clevepak Corp., 1967-70; chmn. Thornton Industries, Inc., Kingston, Tenn., 1966—, cons. tech. mgmt. group, 1970; dir. div. nuclear materials safeguards AEC, Washington, 1970—. Dir. Venture Systems, Inc., Whitehall, Pa.; trustee Stamford Investment Fund. Cons. U.S. AEC, 1956—, mem. adv. com. on nuclear safeguards, 1966—; mem. Communications Panel; mem. 1966 White Ho. Conf. on Internat. Cooperation. Fellow A.A.A.S., Am. Inst. Chemists; mem. Am. Chem. Soc., Am. Nuclear Soc., Inst. Nuclear Materials Mgmt., Operations Research Soc. Am., Wilderness Soc., Pa. Soc. Home: 404 Chesapeake Dr Great Falls VA 22066 Office: US AEC Washington DC 20545

THORNTON, J. EDWARD, lawyer; b. Starkville, Miss., Nov. 25, 1907; s. Marmaduke Kimbrough and Annie (Knox) T.; A.B., Miss. Coll., 1928; LL.B., Harvard, 1933; m. Mary Belle Quinn. Admitted to Ala. bar, 1934, Mass. bar, 1936; asst. circuit solicitor, Jefferson County, 1936-39; asst. gen. counsel Ala. Dept. Revenue, 1939-42; mem. firm Vickers, Leigh & Thornton, Mobile, Ala., 1945-56, Thornton & McGowin, Mobile, 1956—; mem. Spl. Supreme Ct. Ala., 1967-68. Mem. adv. com. on proposed new appellate rules Supreme Ct. of Ala., 1972; mem. Mobile area adv. council Comprehensive Health Planning, 1970—. Mem. Ala. Democratic Com., 1950-54. Served to lt. comdr. USNR, 1942-45. Fellow Am. Bar Found.; mem. Am. (ho. dels., state del. for Ala. 1958-59), Ala. (pres. 1963-64, chmn. com. jurisprudence and law reform 1951-63, chmn. sect. practice and proc. 1969-72), Mobile (pres. 1955, editor bull. 1966—) bar assns., Am. Law Inst., Jud. Conf. for 5th Circuit U.S., Selden Soc., Mobile Arts Council (1st pres. 1956), English-Speaking Union (pres. Mobile 1960-61), Mobile Opera Guild (pres. 1963-65), Mobile Chamber Music Soc. (pres. 1972), Mobile C. of C., Scribes. Baptist. Clubs: Athelstan, Internat. Trade. Contbr. articles to profl. publs. Address: PO Box 23 Mobile AL 36601

THORNTON, JOHN CARMAN, architect; b. Sturgis, Mich., Nov. 27, 1888; s. James Braithwait and Julia (Carman) T.; B.Arch., U. Mich., 1913; m. Barbara Mae Irvine, Apr. 8, 1916; children—James Irvine, Kenneth George. Draftsman, John Graham, 1914-15; archtl. engr. Detroit Edison, 1916-38, architect, 1938-53; self-employed as architect, Royal Oak, Mich., 1953-65; cons. on masonry and plaster problems and fire safety, Royal Oak, 1953-65, St. Petersburg, Fla., 1965—. Mem. Mich. Bldg. Safety Council, 1951-55; trustee Royal Oak Safety Council, 1958-64; mem. adv. com. to Mich. State Fire Marshal, 1958-62; chmn. home safety conf. Washington, 1956. Recipient Alex Dow award for research Detroit Edison Co., 1952. Mem. A.I.A. (Gold medal Detroit chpt. 1962, chmn. com. human safety 1954-61), Suncoast Gem and Mineral Soc., Nat. Safety Council (dir. 1957), Nat. Fire Protection Assn. (safety to life com. 1959-65), Am. Standards Assn. (chmn. study com. 1950-53), Alpha Rho Chi. Republican. Baptist (chmn. bd. trustees 1926-27). Mason. Club: High Twelve (Royal Oak, St. Petersburg). Home: 6909 9th St S St Petersburg FL 33705

THORNTON, O. FRANK, state ofcl.; b. Mullins, S.C., July 26, 1905; s. O.F. and Lucendia (Cooper) T.; LL.B., U. S.C., 1928; m. Rosa Waring, Aug. 19, 1933; children—Rosa (Mrs. J.M. Cherry, Jr.), Frances C. (Mrs. H. Shelton, Jr.). Admitted to S.C. bar, 1928, practiced in Clover, 1930-50; editor Clover Herald, 1931-50; sec., bus. mgr. Salisbury-Spencer Baseball Club, Piedmont League, 1927-29; city atty. Clover, 1940-50; mem. S.C. Ho. of Reps., 1935-36, reading clk. of Ho., 1936-50; sec. of state S.C., Columbia, 1950—. Chmn. S.C. fund drive Crippled Children's Soc., 1960-61. Mem. S.C. Election Bd., 1940-50; mem. County Democratic Exec. Com., 1940-50. Bd. dirs. United Fund Richland-Lexington Counties, Travelers Aid Soc. Mem. Nat. Assn. Secs. of State (pres. 1959-60). Methodist. Elk, Mason, Lion (dir. 1961-62, 66-67). Home: 712 Arbutus Dr Columbia SC 29205 Office: Wade Hampton Office Bldg Colubia SC 29202

THORNTON, PERCY, JR., judge; b. Clinton, N.C., Apr. 4, 1921; s. Percy Haywood and Mamie (Darden) T.; student Campbell Coll., 1938-39; A.A., George Washington U., 1949, J.D., 1952; m. Estelle Byrd, Mar. 29, 1945; children—William Byrd, Pamela Lee, Marsha Darden. With CIA, 1946-56; admitted to Va. Bar, 1953; partner firm Owens & Thornton, Manassas, Va., 1956-68; judge 16th Judicial Circuit Va., Manassas, 1968—; acting commonwealth atty. Prince William County, Va., 1958. Dir. Piedmont Fed. Savs. and Loan Assn., 1972—. Atty. Prince William Hosp., 1960—, various other civic orgns., 1962—; mem. No. Va. Community Coll. Bd., 1970. Bd. dirs. sta. WNVT, 1972—. Served with USNR, 1942-45. Decorated Purple Heart. Mem. Am., Va. (8th dist. com. 1964-67), various local bar assns., Phi Alpha Delta. Democrat. Baptist (lay preacher). Kiwanian. Designer, builder contemporary homes. Home: PO Box 416 Briarmont Estates Manassas VA 22110 Office: 9302 Peabody St Manassas VA 22110

THORNTON, SUE BONNER, librarian; b. nr. Fairfield, Tex.; d. John Carder and Mary (Bonner) Thornton; A.B., U. Okla., 1920. A.B. in L.S., 1938, Mus.B. in Piano, 1921; M.A., Columbia, 1932; postgrad. U. Hawaii, summer 1936. Music supr. Okla. pub. schs., 1921-25; head music dept. Northeastern State Coll., Tahlequah, Okla., 1925-32, librarian, 1932—. Freestone county chmn. hist. markers and landmarks Tex. Hist. Survey Com. Mem. N.E.A., A.L.A., Daus. Am. Colonists, Colonial Dames 17th Century (rec. sec. Okla. state chpt.), Nat. Soc. Magna Charta Dames, Tahlequah C. of C., United Ch. Women Tahlequah (chmn. 1960), D.A.R. (chmn. good citizens com. for state 1958-60), Huguenots of S.C., U.S. Daus. War 1812, Daus. Colonial Wars, Ams. Royal Descent, Colonial Order of Crown, Platagenet Soc., Tex. Federated Women's Clubs (chmn. edn. dept.) Order of Washington, Soc. Descs. Order of Garter, P.E.O., Okla., Tex. geneal. socs., Tex. Hist. Found., Tex., Southwestern Cattle raisers assns., Alpha Gamma Delta. Democrat. Presbyn. (pres. local women's dept. 1965—). Clubs: Dallas Garden, History (Fairfield), Pan American Round Table, Freestone County Country. Home: Fairfield TX 75840

THORNTON, WILLIAM E., astronaut; b. Faison, N.C., Apr. 29, 1929; ed. U. N.C.; m. Elizabeth Jennifer Fowler; two sons. Dir. electronics div. Del Mar Engring. Labs., Los Angeles, 1956-62; instr. U. N.C. Med. Sch., 1963-64; intern Wilford Hall, USAF Hosp., Lackland AFB, San Antonio, 1964-65; with aerospace med. div. Brooks AFB, San Antonio, 1965-67; scientist-astronaut NASA, 1967—. Address: Manned Spacecraft Center NASA Houston TX 77058*

THOROUGHMAN, JAMES CHANSLOR, physician; b. Ferguson, Mo., Aug. 25, 1904; s. James C. and Hattie (Manget) T.; B.S., Emory U., 1924, M.D., 1927, M.S., 1935; m. Verna Elizabeth Scarborough, May 6, 1929; children— Margaret (Mrs. James A. Callahan), James Chanslor, Thomas Vernon. Intern, Grady Meml. Hosp., Atlanta, 1927-28, resident, 1928-29; chief of surgery Changchow (China) Gen. Hosp., 1930-36; supt., chief of surgery Soochow (China) Hosp., 1936-40, 46-50; chief surgery VA Hosp., Augusta, Ga., 1951-53; clin. prof. surgery Med. Coll. Ga., Augusta, 1951-53; chief surgery VA Hosp., Atlanta, 1953-69; prof. surgery Emory U. Sch. Medicine, 1953-69; staff Lee County Hosp., Opelika, Ala., 1969—. Served to maj. M.C., AUS, 1942-46. Diplomate Am. Bd. Surgery. Fellow A.C.S., So. Surg. Assn., Southeastern Surg. Congress; mem. Ga. Surg. Soc., Assn. Mil. Surgeons, Assn. VA Surgeons (pres. 1968-69), Phi Beta Kappa, Alpha Omega Alpha, Sigma Alpha Epsilon, Alpha Kappa Kappa. Home: 1023 B Northside Terrace Apts Opelika AL 36801 Office: 121 N 29th St Opelika AL 36801

THORP, MITCHELL LEON, merchant, lawyer; b. Knoxville, Tenn., July 1, 1910; s. Benjamin J. and Mollie (Gerber) T.; student Knoxville Bus. Coll., 1929; LL.B., U. Balt., 1934; m. Hilda Rose Rapport, Mar. 20, 1942; children—Stephanie (Mrs. Jay Meiselman), Allan, Marjorie. Admitted to Md. bar, 1935; pres. Thorp & Co., Johnson City, Tenn., 1940—, Thorp, Inc., 1950—, E. Tenn. Enterprises, 1954—; chmn. Johnson City Indsl. Commn., 1965-68; pres. T & T Devel. Corp., 1968—. Vice-mayor, city commr., Johnson City, 1965-69; pres., chmn. Johnson City Yankees (farm club of N.Y. Yankees), 1963-67. Del. Democratic Nat. Conv., 1964. Dist. chmn. Am. Cancer Soc. Recipient Nat. Merit Award, Little League Baseball. Mason (Shriner). Rotarian. Elk. Home: 1312 Iris Av Johnson City TN 37601 Office: Millard & Elm St Johnson City TN 37601

THORPE, DAY, newspaper writer; b. Lawrence, Kan., May 16, 1913; s. Merle and Lillian (Day) T.; B.A., Yale, 1936; m. Barbara Corrigan, Oct. 7, 1950; children—Anna Livia Plurabelle, Merle III, Day, Jr. Editor Bethesda (Md.) Journal, 1939-42; press censor Office of Censorship, 1942-45; music and book critic, Evening Star, Washington, 1953—. Founder, gen. mgr. Opera Soc. Washington, 1956-61. Clubs: Chevy Chase, Metropolitan (Washington); Blue Hill Country (Blue Hill, Me.). Home: 10201 Kindly Ct Gaithersburg MD 20760 Office: Evening Star Newspaper Washington DC 20003

THORPE, JACOB OLIVER, dentist; b. Charlotte, N.C., Oct. 2, 1924; s. Jacob Hoots and Sara Elizabeth (Simpson) T.; A.A., Belmont Abbey Coll., 1948; D.D.S., Georgetown U., 1953; m. Dorothy Marie Heinz, Nov. 20, 1943; children—John Oliver, William Dennis, Mary Elizabeth. Dental health officer Mecklenburg County Health Dept., Charlotte, 1953-54; pvt. practice dentistry Randolph Med. Center, Charlotte, 1955—; mem. dental staff Charlotte Meml. Hosp., 1954—, instr. clin. dentistry, 1954—, chief staff dental div., 1964-66; mem. dental staff Mercy Hosp., Charlotte, 1954—. Mem. dental adv. com. Central Piedmont Community Coll., Charlotte, 1964—; research cons. Pelton & Crane Dental Mfg. Co., Charlotte, 1968—. Pres., Mecklenburg County unit Am. Cancer Soc., 1970-71; active YMCA, United Appeal. Served to maj. Dental Corps, USAAF, 1943-45; PTO. Mem. Am. Dental Assn., Am., N.C. socs. dentistry for children, Dental Found. N.C., N.C. Soc. Dental Anesthesiology (pres. 1967), Am. Inst. Oral Scis., So. Acad. Periodontology, N.C., Charlotte (pres. 1969) dental socs., N.C. Cath. Laymans Assn., N.C. Assn. Professions, N.C. Pub. Health Assn., Charlotte C. of C., Charlotte Execs. Club, Georgetown U., Belmont Abbey Coll. alumni assns., Delta Sigma Delta, Phi Theta Kappa, Omicron Kappa Upsilon. Republican. Roman Catholic. Club: Catawba County Country (Newton, N.C.) Home: 3951 Arbor Way Charlotte NC 28211 Office: 1928 Randolph Rd Charlotte NC 28207

THORPE, MARION DENNIS, univ. pres.; b. Durham, N.C., Sept. 25, 1932; B.A. in Psychology magna cum laude, N.C. Coll. at Durham (now N.C. Central U.), 1957, M.A. in Psychology, 1958; Ph.D. in Adminstrv. Ednl. Services, Mich. State U., 1961; postgrad. U.S. Mcht. Marine Acad., 1965, U.S. Dept. Def. Staff Coll., 1965; m. Lula Glenn; children—Pamela Monique, Marion Dennis. Grad. asst. Mich. State U., 1959-60, asst. instr. ednl. psychology, 1959-61; asst. prof., then asso. prof. psychology N.C. Coll., 1961-65; asst. dir., then dir. Neighborhood Youth Corps, Office Field Operations, Dept. of Labor, Washington, 1965-66, nat. leader Job Devel. Task Force, Washington, 1966; asst. dir. N.C. Bd. Higher Edn., 1966-67; v.p. Central State U., Wilberforce, O., 1967-68; pres. Elizabeth City (N.C.) State U., 1968—. Mem. Nat. Lab. for Higher Edn.; mem. Citizens Adv. Com. Edn. Professions Devel. Act, adv. com. to N.C. Gen. Assembly, 1970; mem. Pres. Nixon's N.C. Com. Pub. Edn.; chmn. edn. com. Mayor's Growth Center Devel. Com., Elizabeth City, 1971; commr. Edn. Commn. States; mem. Appalachian Regional Student Internship program. Mem. Durham Com. Negro Affairs, 1961, Durham Community Planning Council, 1962, Action for Durham Devel. Com., 1962, Mayor's Com. Jobs for Vets., Elizabeth City. Bd. dirs. Manpower Devel. and Tng. Project, Wilberforce, 1967, Martin Luther King Scholarship Com. Woodrow Wilson Found., United Fund., So. Regional Edn. Bd. Mem. N.C. Assn. Colls. and Univs. (mem. com. govtl. relations; mem. exec. com.), Assn. Eastern N.C. Colls. (past mem. exec. com.), Am., N.C. psychol. assns., Am. Personnel and Guidance Assn., So. (commr.), Am. Assns. state colls and univs., Alpha Kappa Mu, Psi Chi,Omega Psi Phi. Home: 1201 Parkview St Elizabeth City NC 27909

THRAILKILL, BENJAMIN EDWARD, JR., dentist; b. Chester, S.C., May 25, 1923; s. Benjamin Edward and Mary (Hall) T.; B.S., Clemson Coll., 1947; D.D.S., Med. Coll. Va., 1954; m. Peggy Braddy, Nov. 26, 1955; children— Benjamin Edward III, William Robert. Pvt. practice dentistry. Hemingway, S.C., 1954—. Mem. regional adv. com. Health Services and Mental Health Adminstrn., Dept. Health, Edn. and Welfare, 1971—. Mem. troop com. Pee Dee Area council Boy Scouts Am., 1956-63. Vice-chmn. Williamsburg County Republican party, 1965-70, chmn., 1970—. Served with inf. AUS, 1943-46. Decorated Purple Heart, Bronze Star medal (2). Mem. Am., S.C. dental assns., V.F.W., Am. Legion, Delta Sigma Delta. Methodist. Club: Civitan (pres. 1958). Address: Box 518 Hemingway SC 29554

THRAILKILL, WARREN MARCUS, accountant; b. Waycross, Ga., Oct. 11, 1920; s. Vesper Houston and Clara Beatrice (Gaylor) T.; B.S. in Accounting, U. Ala., 1947; diploma Command and Gen. Staff Coll., 1971; m. Mary Louise Pogue, Mar. 21, 1947; children—Katherine Louise (Mrs. Charles Duncan), Margaret Allan, Warren Marcus. With Price, Waterhouse & Co., C.P.A.'s, N.Y.C., 1947-48, Arnold, Keller & Smith, C.P.A.'s, Birmingham, Ala., 1948-53, George C. Baird & Co., C.P.A.'s, Augusta, Ga., 1953-56; with So. Elec. Steel Co., Birmingham, 1956-58; prof. St. Bernard Coll., Cullman, Ala., 1958-62; v.p.-treas. King Pharr Canning Operations, Inc., Cullman, 1962-70; self-employed C.P.A., Cullman, 1970—. Tchr., Cullman Coll., 1968—. Bd. dirs. Tennessee Valley council Boy Scouts Am., Girl Scouts N. Ala.; trustee Cullman Hosp., 1968—, vice chmn., 1970—. Served to lt. col. AUS, 1942-45. Mem. Am. Inst. C.P.A.'s, Ala., Ga. socs. C.P.A.'s, Cullman County C. of C., Am. Legion, Assn. U.S. Army, Res. Officers Assn., Sigma Phi Epsilon, Beta Alpha Psi. Methodist (past chmn. bd. stewards). Rotarian Home: 606 1st SE Cullman AL 35055 Office: PO Box 1054 Cullman AL 35055

THRALL, GORDON FISH, govt. atty.; b. Jamestown, N.Y., July 28, 1923; s. Clyde Lowell and Beulah Mae (Fish) T.; A.B., Alfred U., 1949; LL.B., Baylor U., 1953; m. Betty Jane Shamburger Roberts, Sept. 25, 1964; 1 dau., Jenifer Jane. Admitted to Tex. bar, 1953, U.S. Supreme Ct., 1957, D.C. bar, 1958, others; law clk. Fed. Ct. E. Tex., 1953-54; asst. dist. atty. Dallas County, 1954-55; asso. mem. firm Phinney & Hallman, Dallas, 1955-56; asst. atty. gen. Tex., 1956-57; atty. adviser-examiner ICC, Washington, 1957-59; asst. gen. counsel Tex. State Bar, Austin, 1959-61; county atty. Reagan County, Tex., 1961—; pvt. practice law, Big Lake, Tex., 1961—. Vice pres. Concho Valley council Boy Scouts Am., 1968-69, chmn. Permian Basin dist., 1966, 67; Easter Seal rep. Reagan County, 1968—; mem. adv. bd. Office Econ. Opportunity, 1968-70. Bd. dirs. Permian Basin Hist. Soc., 1968—. Served with AUS, 1943-46. Mem. S.A.R., (pres. 1968-69), Tex. State Bar (unauthorized practice law com., vice chmn. 1963-66), Am., Tex., Tom Green County, Trans-Pecos bar assns., Am. Judicature Soc., Big Lake C. of C. (pres. 1962, 69), Phi Delta Phi, Delta Sigma Phi. Baptist (deacon, exec. bd. Tex. gen. conv. 1965-70). Mason (Shriner), Lion. Home: 508 Plaza Big Lake TX 76932 Office: Courthouse Annex Big Lake TX 76932

THREADGILL, JOHN LEWIS, architect; b. Boston, Ala., May 17, 1934; s. James R. and Eva I. (Addison) T.; B.S., U. Ky., 1960; m. Paula Owens, Aug. 27, 1953; children—Cindy Lea, Barbra Lynne, John Lewis. Partner, Perkins Threadgill & Assos., Harlan, Ky., 1960-67;

individual practice John L. Threadgill architect and engr., Harlan, 1967—. Mem. A.I.A., Constrn. Specifications Inst., Council Ednl. Facilities Planners, Nat., Ky. socs. profl. engrs., Harlan County Jr. C. of C. (pres. 1966). Mason (K.T.), Kiwanian, Odd Fellow. Club: Harlan County Shrine. Address: PO Box 979 Harlan KY 40831

THREATTE, JAMES WILSON, sch. adminstr.; b. Pave, Ga., May 17, 1910; s. Julius Barton and Mary Leila (West) T.; B.S., Ga. State Coll. for Men, 1932; postgrad. Duke, summer 1939; M.A., Mercer U., 1944; m. Mary Reynolds, Sept. 17, 1932; children—Babs (Mrs. Frank Gudger), Quay (Mrs. Jimmy Allen). Tchr., coach Lanier County High Sch., Lakeland, Ga., 1932-41; prin. Cedar Grove Sch., Laurens County, 1941-42, Morgan Sch., Calhoun County, 1942-45; supt. schs. Lanier County, Lakeland, 1949—. Hon. life mem. Future Farmers Am., 1950—. Mem. Ga. Edn. Assn., N.E.A., Sch. Adminstrs. Ga. (pres. 1962), 8th Dist. Sch. Adminstrs. (sec. 1960-62). Baptist (deacon). Lion. Home: E Main St Lakeland GA 31635 Office: Valdosta Hwy Lakeland GA 31635

THREEWITTS, ALBERT JUSTICE, banker; b. Littleton, N.C., Jan. 24, 1934; s. John Edwin and Betty Lee (Whitehead) T.; A.B., East Carolina U., 1959; m. Marilyn Jeanette Harmon, Nov. 10, 1962; children—David Albert, John Harmon. Bank examiner U.S. Comptroller of Currency, Richmond, Va., 1959-65; with So. Nat. Bank of N.C., Lumberton, 1965—, v.p., 1969—. Served with AUS, 1953-55. Mem. Robert Morris Assos. Lutheran. Elk. Home: 402 Roslyn Dr Lumberton NC 28358 Office: 500 N Chestnut St Lumberton NC 28358

THRIFT, CHARLES TINSLEY, JR., coll. pres.; b. Kenbridge, Va., Apr. 11, 1911; s. Charles Tinsley and Nell (Webb) T.; A.B., Duke, 1930, A.M., 1932, B.D., 1933; Ph.D., U. Chgo. (fellow in church history, 1934-36), 1936; D.D., Southwestern U., 1965; m. Ruth King, June 30, 1934; children—Ruth Nell, Helen Sue, Mary King. Prof. religion, dir. religious life Southwestern U., Georgetown, Tex., 1936-39; prof. religion Fla. So. Coll., Lakeland, 1940—, v.p. coll., 1946-57, acting pres., 1957, pres., 1957—; vis. prof. Garrett Bibl. Inst., Northwestern U., summer 1946, Emory U., summer 1949, 52, Perkins Sch. Theology, So. Meth. U., 1952. Mem. Meth. Gen. Conf., 1960, 64, Bd. Edn., 1960—. Certification com. So. Regional Edn. (Fla.), 1949—. Mem. Fla. Conf. Meth. Ch.; dean Fla. Pastors' (Meth.) Sch., 1945-60. Mem. Am. Soc. Church History, Southeastern Hist. Soc. (Meth.) (sec. 1944-48), Fla. Assn. Colls. and Univs. (mem. exec. com., 1945-53, v.p., 1949-50, pres., 1950-51), Fla. Hist. Soc. (dir. 1944-46, v.p. 1952-54, pres. 1954-56), Fla. Acad. Scis., Phi Beta Kappa, Omicron Delta Kappa, Kappa Delta Pi, Pi Gamma Mu. Author: The Trail of the Florida Circuit Rider, 1944; Through Three Decades at Florida Southern College; 1955; A Study of Theological Education in The Methodist Church, 1956. Contbr. The Florida Story to Fla. papers. Editor: Marshaling Florida's Resources, 1945. Contbr. to religious, ednl. and hist. publs. Home: 48 Lake Hollingsworth Dr Lakeland FL 33801

THUN, EUGENE WILLIAM, architect; b. Wharton, N.J., Dec. 13, 1924; s. Max O. and Eugenia Sofia (Krook) T.; B Arch., Syracuse U., 1950; m. Angelita Maldonado Lema, Feb. 24, 1964; children—Peter, Richard, Angelique, Christine. Asso. architect D. Wentworth Wright, Basking Ridge, N.J., 1950-54; individual practice as architect, Basking Ridge, N.J., 1954-60, San Juan, P.R., 1960—. Chmn. Community Devel. Centers, 1970-72; mem. tax and econ. planning com., Bernards Twp., N.J., 1957-59. Served with AUS, 1943-46; PTO. Mem. A.I.A. (dir. P.R. chpt. 1970-72), Coll. Engrs. and Architects P.R., Tau Sigma Delta, Sigma Upsilon Alpha, Sigma Phi Epsilon. Prin. archtl. works include Chico Park, Old San Juan Garage. Home: Torre Alta PH4 Calle Mejico Hato Rey PR 00917 Office: Banco Economias Bldg 1504 Hato Rey PR 00917

THUNBERG, PENELOPE HARTLAND, govt. ofcl.; b. Stoneham, Mass.; B.A. in Econs., Brown U., 1940, LL.D., 1966; M.A., Ph.D., Radcliffe Coll.; m. Howard E. Thunberg. Mem. faculty Wells Coll., Mt. Holyoke Coll., Brown U.; internat. economist, staff President's Council Econ. Advisers, 1951-53, rep. interagency internat. econ. programs, 1963-64; econ. research analyst Soviet Bloc internat. econ. activities CIA, 1954-65, dep. chief internat. div., 1962-65; commr. U.S. Tariff Commn., 1965-70; mem. Bd. Nat. Estimates, CIA, 1970—. Recipient Fed. Woman's award Civil Service. Office: Washington DC 20505

THUNE, JEANNE RUTHERFORD (MRS. LELAND E. THUNE), psychologist; b. Jacksonville, Fla.; d. Don and Mayhoward (Austin) McEachern; student Montreat Jr. Coll., 1936-38; B.A., George Peabody Coll., 1940, M.A., 1954; Ph.D., Vanderbilt U., 1960;; m. Leland E. Thune, May 26, 1963; children—Charles H. III, Miriam A (Mrs. Carl William Moebius III), Robert W. (by previous marriage). Counseling psychologist Tng. Sch. for Delinquent Boys, Jordonia, Tenn., 1954-55; research asst., teaching fellow Vanderbilt U., Nashville, 1956-58; asso., prof. psychology Belmont Coll., Nashville, 1958-61; clin. intern, staff psychologist VA Hosp., Murfreesboro, 1961-63; research psychologist Sr. Citizens, Inc., Nashville, 1963-71; clin. psychologist, student health services Vanderbilt U., 1971—. Dir. research on interracial prejudice. Mem. adv. bd. Nashville Artists Guild. Mem. Am., Southeastern, Tenn. psychol. assns., Gerontol. Soc., Sigma Xi. Democrat. Presbyn. Contbr. articles to profl. jours. Home: 3948 Woodlawn Dr Nashville TN 37205 Office: 1801 Broadway Nashville TN 37203

THURMAN, MARION AUGUSTUS, banker; b. Sycamore, Ala., May 27, 1899; s. Augustus Jefferson and Lillie Lee (Thomas) T.; student pub. schs.; m. Alma Baldwin, June 14, 1928; children—James Marion, Mortimer Jefferson. With First Nat. Bank in Sylacauga (Ala.), 1920—, dir., 1940—, pres., 1949-66, vice chmn. bd. dirs., 1966—. Past chmn. Sylacauga Civil Service Bd., dir. Coosa-Ala. River Improvement Assn.; bd. dirs. Sylacauga Family Service Bur., 1949—, chmn., 1952-60; treas. Sylacauga Mut. Concert Assn.; treas. Sylacauga dist. Meth. Chs. N. Ala. Conf. Past chmn. Sylacauga Hosp. bd.; bd. dirs. Meth. Children's Home, Selma. Mem. C. of C. (dir.). Methodist. Rotarian (past pres.). Home: 207 S Broadway Sylacauga AL 35150 Office: 31 N Broadway St Sylacauga AL 35150

THURMAN, MARJORIE CLARK (MRS. ROSS H. THURMAN), mem. Democratic Nat. Com.; b. Atlanta, June 17, 1928; d. Henry Clay and Jessie Early (Boynton) Clark; student Emory U., 1945-46; LL.B., Atlanta Law Sch., 1949, LL.M., 1950; m. Ross H. Thurman. Nov. 20, 1948; 1 dau., Sandra Lynn. Admitted to Ga. bar, 1949; since practiced in Atlanta; asso. firm Leachman, King & Thurman, 1954—. Ga. mem. Young Democratic Com., 1957-63; pres. Fulton County Young Democrats, 1958-61; Ga. dir. women's activities Young Democrats Am., 1958-61, gen. counsel, 1959-61; mem. Dem. Nat. Com. for Ga., 1963—; del. Dem. Nat. Conv., 1964, 68. Del. NATO Exchange Young Polit. Leaders, 1961; mem. Gov.'s Com. on Status of Women; bd. dirs. Atlanta Council Internat. Visitors. Mem. Am., Ga., Atlanta bar assns., Nat. Ga. assns. women lawyers, Am. Assn. UN, League Women Voters, Bus. and profl. Women's Club, C. of C., Internat. Platform Assn. Methodist. Clubs: Nat. Lawyers, Atlanta Equity. Home: 5450 Glenridge Dr NE Atlanta GA 30305 Office: Bank of Ga Bldg Atlanta GA 30305

THURMOND, STROM, U.S. senator; b. Edgefield, S.C., Dec. 5, 1902; s. John William and Eleanor Gertrude (Strom) T; B.S., Clemson Coll., 1923, LL.D., 1961; LL.D., Bob Jones U., 1948, Presbyn. Coll., 1960; Dr. Mil. Sci., The Citadel, 1961; D.Humanities, Trinity Coll., 1965; Litt.D., Cal. Grad. Sch. Theology, 1970; m. Jean Crouch, Nov. 7, 1947 (dec. Jan. 1960); m. 2d, Nancy Moore, Dec. 22, 1968; 1 dau., Nancy Moore. Tchr. in S.C. schs., 1923-29; supt. edn., 1929-33; admitted to S.C. bar, 1930; city atty., county atty.; state senator, 1933-38; circuit judge, 1938-46; gov. S.C., 1947-51; mem. Thurmond, Lybrand & Simons, 1951-55; U. S. senator, 1954—. Del. Democratic Nat. Conv., 1932, 36, 48, chmn. S.C. delegation and nat. committeeman), 52, 56, 60; chmn. S.C. delegation Republican Nat. Conv., 1968, del., 1972; States' Rights Dem. candidate for Pres., 1948. Served with U.S. Army, 1st Army, ETO and PTO; attached to 82d Airborne Div. for invasion of Europe, 1942-45; ret. maj. gen. U.S. Army Res. Decorated 18 medals and awards, including Legion of Merit, Bronze Star medal with V., Purple Heart, Presdl. Distinguished Unit Citation, 5 battle stars (U.S.), Croix de Guerre (France), Order of Crown (Belgium). Past trustee Winthrop Coll. (S.C. Coll for Women). Mem. Am. Bar Assn., Res. Officers Assn. (past nat. pres.; Minuteman of Year award 1971), Am. Legion (nat. def. com.), Mil. Govt. Assn. (past nat. pres.), numerous other vets., civic and fraternal orgns. Baptist. Republican. Office: Senate Office Bldg Washington DC 20510 Home: Aiken SC 29801

THURSTEN, RUBEN LOUIS, sch. counselor; b. Waynesville, Mo., May 11, 1908; s. Charles William Louis and Myrtle May (Luter) T.; B.S., Murray (Ky.) State Coll., 1930, M.A., 1958; Ed.D., George Peabody Coll., 1962; m. Barbara Kaiser McClurg, Jan. 13, 1967; children—Louis, Rose, Charles Michael. Pub. safety officer TVA, 1941-42; sch. supt., Grandrivers, Ky., 1938-41, 43-44; tchr. U.S. Air Force, Ramney, P.R., 1959-60; men's counselor L'Ans Creuse High Sch., Mt. Clemens, Mich., 1960—. Pres. C.I.O. Union, Calvert City, Ky., 1953-54. Mem. Am. Personnel and Guidance Assn., Nat. Vocational Guidance Assn., Mich. Edn. Assn., Mich. Psychol. Assn., Mich. Personnel and Guidance Assn., Am. Civil Liberties Union, Kappa Delta Pi, Phi Delta Kappa. Mason. Club: Hi Twelve (Mt. Clemens). Home: care Raish Jones RFD Calvert City KY 42029 Office: 322 N Gratiot St Mt Clemens MI 48043

THUSS, LOUISE BENEDICT (MRS. WILLIAM GETZ THUSS), civic worker; b. Nashville, Feb. 8, 1899; d. Chauncey B. and Sara (Byrns) Benedict; student Ward-Belmont Coll., 1916; Vanderbilt U., 1920; m. William Getz Thuss, Sept. 25, 1923; children—William Getz, Chauncey Benedict, Robert Wilkey. Organizer, 1st pres. Vis. Nursing Assn., Birmingham, Ala., 1937, bd. dirs., 1937-43, 49-55; bd. mgrs. Mercy Home, 1930—, pres., 1953-55, treas., 1964-68; mem. Jefferson County Coordinating Council, 1950—, pres. children's com. 1929-30; mem. spl. com. on juvenile delinquency Jefferson County Assn. for Mental Health, 1960—, mem. planning com., 1963-64; mem. edn. com. Jefferson County unit Am. Cancer Soc.; past v.p. Radio-TV Council; mem. Home Garden Club; active A.R.C., 1942—; charter mem. U. Hosp. Aux., Cauldron Lit. Club; pres. Jefferson County Med. Soc. Woman's Aux., 1952-53, bd. dirs., 1956-62, hon-mem., 1965—, Community Service award, 1967; pres. Ala. Med. Assn. Woman's Aux., 1955-56, bd. dirs., 1956-62 hon. mem., 1967—; mem. nat. bd. dirs. A.M.A. Woman's Aux., 1954-57, 1st v.p. nat. membership chmn., 1960-61, nat. pres., 1962-63, bd. dirs., 1963-64, nat. chmn. 1972 Golden Anniversary; 1st v.p. So. Med. Assn. Woman's Aux., 1963-64, pres., 1965-66; charter mem., v.p. U.S. sect. Internat. Coll. Surgeons Woman's Aux., 1958-60, 61-63, pres., 1963-64, bd. dirs., chmn. Southeastern region, 1958-60; charter mem., 2d v.p. Southeastern Surg. Congress Woman's Aux., 1960-61, Ala. councilor, 1955-62, chmn. luncheons Women's Com. of 100 for Birmingham, corr. sec., 1967-68, bd. dirs., 1968—, 1st v.p., 1970, pres., 1972-73; steering com. Comprehensive mental Health Planning Com. 1964-65; mem. Salvation Army, v.p. women's aux., 1967-68; bd. dirs. Birmingham Festival of Art. Recipient certificates of appreciation numerous orgns., 1962-70. Mem. Birmingham Art Mus. Birmingham Art Assn. corr. sec. for bd. 1966-68), Birmingham Music Club, Arlington Hist. Assn. (v.p. 1968-71; pres. 1972), Ala. Opera Assn., Family Counseling Assn. Jefferson County, Am. Assn. U. Women, Birmingham Jr. League (sustaining), Internat. Platform Assn., Ala. Consumers Assn., English Speaking Union, Kenmore Hist. Soc., Nat. Hist. Assn., Nat. Trust for Hist. Preservation, Am. Heritage Soc., Birmingham Bot. Soc., Common Cause, Ala. Pro-Am., Kappa Alpha Theta. Methodist. Home: 2837 Southwood Rd Birmingham AL 35223

THUSS, WILLIAM GETZ, JR., physician; b. Birmingham, Ala., Nov. 18, 1924; s. William and Louise (Benedict) T.; M.D., U. Md., 1948; Sc.D. (fellow) U. Cin., 1956; m. Gene Bradley Connell, Jan. 22, 1949; children— Pamela Connell, William G. III, Gene Bradley. Intern, New Haven and Grace-New Haven Community Hosps., Yale, 1948-49; resident in pathology Baylor U., VA Hosp., 1949-50; asso. clin. prof. pub. health and epidemiology, chief, occupational med. sect. Med. Coll., Ala., 1956—. Aviation med. examiner FAA, 1961—; pvt. practice specializing in occupational medicine, Birmingham, 1956—. Served to lt. (j.g.) M.C., USNR, 1951. Mem. A.A.A.S., Indsl. Med. Assn., Indsl. Hygiene Assn., Assn. Tchrs. Preventive Medicine, Acad. Occupational Medicine, Am. Pub. Health Assn., N.Y. Acad. Sci., Royal Soc. Health. Address: Thuss Clinic 2124 4th Av S Birmingham AL 35233

THWEATT, GEORGE BOOKER, constrn. co. exec.; b. Little Rock, Sept 22, 1926; s. Charles B. and Mable (Smith) T.; B.S., U. Ark., 1949; m. Elizabeth Walker, Aug. 12, 1948; children—Kay, Steve. With Ben M. Hogan Co., Inc., Little Rock, 1949—, sec.-treas., 1964—; dir. Ark. Travelers Baseball, Little Rock; pres. R.T., Inc., Little Rock, 1968—; sec.-treas. C.R.T., Inc., 1968—. Served with USNR, 1944-46. Mem. Kappa Sigma. Mason (Shriner). Home: 507 Valley Club Circle Little Rock AR 72203 Office: 1100 Fairpoint St Little Rock AR 72202

THWING, RAILTON CLARE, constrn. co. exec.; b. San Antonio, May 14, 1921; s. James Marvin and Lillie (Childress) T.; B.S., Tex. A. and M. U., 1943; m. Lillian Alma Needles, Feb. 19, 1949; children—James Roland, Dale David, William Hollis. With Loyd W. Richardson Constrn. Corp., Aransas Pass, Tex., 1946—, mng. partner, 1958-60, pres., 1960—; dir. Portland Savs. & Loan Assn. (Tex.). Vice pres. Gulf Coast council Boy Scouts Am., 1966-68, council pres., 1969-71. Mem. City Council Aransas Pass, 1963—. Served to capt. AUS, 1943-45; ETO. Mem. C. of C. (pres. 1962). Methodist. Moose. Clubs: Knife and Fork, Propeller (Corpus-Christi); 20-30 (Aransas Pass). Home: 1059 S McCampbell St Aransas Pass TX 78336 Office: 1054 S Rife St Aransas Pass TX 78336

TICE, DOUGLAS OSCAR, JR., lawyer; b. Lexington, N.C., May 2, 1933; s. Douglas Oscar and Lila (Wright) T.; B.S., U. N.C., 1955, LL.B., 1957; m. Janet N. Capps, Feb. 28, 1959; children—Douglas Oscar III, Janet E. Exec. sec. N.C. Jud. Council, Raleigh, 1958-59; admitted to N.C. bar, 1957; practiced in Raleigh, 1959-61; atty. Office Regional Counsel, U.S. Internal Revenue Service, Richmond, Va., 1961-70; sec., counsel Carlton Industries, Inc., Richmond, 1970—. Served with AUS, 1957-58. Mem. Am., N.C., bar assns., N.C., Va. state bars, Civil War Round Table Richmond (pres. 1968), S.C.V., Va. Hist. Soc., N.C. Lit. and Hist. Soc., Confederate Meml. Lit. Soc. Presbyn. Club: Sertoma (pres. 1968-69). Home: 7901 Three Chopt Rd Richmond VA 23229 Office: 2111 N Hamilton St Richmond VA 23230

TIDBALL, CHARLES STANLEY, physiologist, educator; b. Geneva, Switzerland, Apr. 15, 1928 (parents Am. citizens); s. Charles Taylor and Adele (Desmaison) T.; diploma Choate Sch., 1946; student Worcester Poly. Inst., 1946-47; B.A. in Chemistry, Wesleyan U., 1950; M.S. in Pharmacology, U. Rochester, 1952; Ph.D. in Physiology, U. Wis., 1955; M.D., U. Chgo., 1958; m. Mary Elizabeth Peters, Oct. 25, 1952. Asst. in physiology U. Wis., Madison, 1953-55, U. Chgo., 1955-58; rotating intern Madison Gen. Hosp., 1958-59; physician Mendota (Wis.) State Hosp., 1959; with George Washington U., Washington, 1959—, asst. research prof. physiology, 1959-63, asso. prof., acting chmn. dept. physiology, 1963-64, prof., 1964-65, chmn. physiology dept., 1964-71, Henry D. Fry prof. physiology, 1965—, research prof. medicine, 1972—; mem. faculty Am. Youth Found. Confs., 1967—. Cons. Washington VA Hosp., 1966-69, VA Center, Martinsburg, W.Va., 1960-62, Smith Kline and French Labs., Phila., 1964-66, NASA, Washington, 1964-65, FDA. Washington, 1966-68. Bd. dirs. Half Way House for Women, Washington, 1965-67; bd. dirs. Camp Letts (YMCA), Washington, 1968—, chmn., 1972—. USPHS spl. fellow in gastroenterology, 1960-61; recipient USPHS research career devel. award, 1961-63, Brandenburg Intern award Madison Gen. Hosp., 1959; (with Dr. Marie M. Cassidy) Sci. Achievement award Washington Acad. Scis., 1967. Fellow Washington Acad. Scis.; mem. A.A.A.S., Biophys. Soc., Am. Physiol. Soc. (rep. to pub. information com. Fedn. Am. Socs. Exptl. Biology 1965-70, sec., treas., gastrointestinal sect. 1965-68, chmn. 1968-69), Am. Gastroenterological Assn., Digital Equipment Computer Users Soc., Assn. for Devel. of Instructional Systems, Cathedral Choral Soc., Canoe Cruisers Assn. Republican. Episcopalian. Contbr. articles to profl. jours. Mem. editorial bd. American Jour. Physiology, Jour. Applied Physiology, 1967-69. Home: 2831 49th St NW Washington DC 20007

TIDBALL, (MARY) ELIZABETH PETERS (MRS. CHARLES S. TIDBALL), educator; b. Anderson, Ind., Oct. 15, 1929; d. John Winton and Beatrice (Ryan) Peters; B.A., Mt. Holyoke Coll., 1951; M.S., U. Wis., 1955, Ph.D., 1959; m. Charles S. Tidball, Oct. 25, 1952. Teaching asst., dept. physiology U. Wis., 1952-55, 58-59; research asst. anatomy dept. U. Chgo., 1955-56, research asst. physiology dept., 1956-58; USPHS post-doctoral fellow NIH, Bethesda, Md., 1959-61; staff pharmacologist Hazleton Labs., Falls Church, Va., 1961; cons., 1962; asst. prof. pharmacology dept. The George Washington U., 1962-64, asso. prof., physiology dept., 1964-70, research prof. physiology dept. George Washington U. Med. Center; 1970-71, prof., 1971—. Mem. faculty Am. Youth Found. Confs., 1967—. Cons. FDA, 1966-67. Mem. Nat. Acad. Scis. Adv. Com. Tng. Programs and Fellowships, 1972—; rep. D.C. Commn. Status of Women, 1972—; asso. sci. coordinator sci. assos. tng. program Food and Drug Adminstrn., 1966-67. Trustee Mt. Holyoke Coll., 1968—, vice chmn. bd., 1972-73. Shattuck fellow, 1955-56; Mary E. Woolley fellow Mt. Holyoke Coll., 1958-59; USPHS post-doctoral fellow, 1959-61. Mem. A.A.A.S., Am. Physiol. Soc., Histamine Club, Sigma Delta Epsilon, Sigma Xi, Mt. Holyoke Alumnae Assn. (dir. 1966-70). Episcopalian. Contbr. articles to profl. jours. Home: 2831 49th St NW Washington DC 20007 Office: 1339 H St NW Washington DC 20005

TIDMORE, WILLIAM EWING, air pollution control engr.; b. Collinsville, Ala., Apr. 17, 1900; s. William John and Allie (Albright) T.; B.S., Ga. Sch. Tech., 1930; postgrad. U. Heidelberg; m. Mildred Victoria Jordan, Oct. 25, 1935; children—Anne, William Ewing. Student engr. Ala. Power Co., Anniston, 1925-30, supt. installation and service Automatic Coal Burning Corp., Atlanta, 1931-40; dir. Smoke Abatement Bur. City of Atlanta, 1940-52, air pollution control engr., 1952—. Mem. adv. bd. State Fire Commr., 1949-63, asst. dist., neighborhood commr. Boy Scouts Am., 1955-65. Served to lt. col. AUS, 1940-45. Registered profl. engr., Ga. Mem. Ga. Architect and Engrng. Soc., Air Pollution Control Assn. (dir. 1950-53), Ga. Tech. Alumni Assn., C. of C. (mem. life quality steering com.), Res. Officers Assn., Ret. Officers Assn. Methodist. Author: (with Silver Burdette) People Use the Earth, 1967. Home: 1097 Amsterdam Av NE Atlanta GA 30306 Office: City Hall Atlanta GA 30303

TIDWELL, BILLIE DEE, banker; b. Denton, Tex., Aug. 24, 1927; s. George D. and Willie E. (Miller) T.; student Draughon's Bus. Coll., 1946-47, LaSalle U., 1950-52, Banking Sch., So. Methodist U., 1961; m. Ava Ruth Smith, Apr. 22, 1950; children—Karen Sue, Lana Kay. Bookkeeper, Frederick Implement Co. (Okla.), 1946-51; cashier 1st Nat. Bank, Frederick, 1954—, also dir. Treas. Frederick Sch. Dist., 1963—. Served with AUS, 1952-54. Mem. Bank Adminstrv. Inst., Frederick C. of C. (pres. 1967), Frederick Future Farmers Am. Mem. Ch. of Christ. Rotarian. Home: 404 Circle Dr Frederick OK 73542 Office: 200 W Grand St Frederick OK 73542

TIDWELL, DONAVON DUNCAN, clergyman, educator; b. Iredell, Tex., Feb. 16, 1906; s. Charles L. and Fannie Stell (Harris) T.; B.A., Howard Payne Coll., 1931; Th.M., Southwestern Bapt. Theol. Sem., 1936, Th.D., 1940; m. Thelma Turner, Apr. 30, 1930; children—David, Truett. Student pastor Spurlin, Center Valley, Pleasant Valley, Duffau, Clairette, Spring Creek, Thurber, Valley Grove, Oak Dale, Cresson, 1926-38; ordained to ministry Baptist Ch., 1925; pastor 1st Bapt. Ch., De Leon, Tex., 1938-41, Walnut St. Bapt. Ch., Carbondale, Ill., 1941-44; instr. ch. history Bapt. Foundation, So. Ill. Normal U., Carbondale, 1941-44; prof. Bible and Greek Hannibal-La Grange Coll., Hannibal, Mo., 1944-46; prof. Bible and Greek Howard Payne Coll., Brownwood, Tex., 1946-63, chmn. div. religion, 1957-62, research prof. religion, 1962-63; chmn. div. Christianity, Houston Bapt. Coll., 1963-71. Mem. Am. Acad. Religion (pres. S.W. sect. 1954), Tex. Bapt. Bible Tchrs. (pres. 1953), So. Bapt. Hist. Soc. (v.p., 1942-44). Mason (33 deg., K.T.). Author: A History of the Baptists in Erath County, Tex., 1937; Freemasonry in Brownwood, 1966; A History of the Baptists of Iredell (Texas), 1968; A History of Gray Lodge 329 A.F. & A.M., Houston, Texas, 1870-1970. Editor The Tex. Free-Mason, 1970—. Home: 3702 Castle St Waco TX 76710

TIDWELL, HAZEL ELIZA HAWPE (MRS. MARION LEONARD TIDWELL), anesthetist; b. Anadarko, Okla.; d. Charlie Bartlett and Addie Allen (Kesterson) Hawpe; student Southwestern Jr. Coll., Keene, Tex., 1923; grad. Boulder (Colo.) Sanitarium and Hosp., 1924, Western Res. U. Hosp. Sch. Anesthesia, 1927; m. Marion Leonard Tidwell, Feb. 5, 1946. Supt., Brown Hosp., Mexia, Tex., 1924-35; adminstr., anesthetist Christoffer, Edgar & Willford Hosp., Mexia, 1937-62; anesthetist Gen. Mexia Hosp., also Mexia State Sch. Hosp., 1963—. Anesthetist, A.R.C., 1963—. Recipient Woman of Year award Mexia Bus. and Profl. Women's Club, 1963. Mem. Am., Tex. State nurses assns. Seventh Day Adventist. Mem. Order Eastern Star. Home: 817 Holly Lane Mexia TX 76667

TIDWELL, JAMES CHARLES, mfg. co. exec.; b. Louisville, Sept. 9, 1928; s. Charles Raymond and Lucile (Sanders) T.; B.S., Tri-State Coll., 1950; m. Dorothy Isabel Lorenz, Apr. 24, 1954; children—David Edward, Nancy Sue. With CTS Corp., various locations, 1950—, v.p. sales and engring., Paducah, Ky., 1969-71, v.p., gen. mgr., 1971—. Vice pres. Paducah McCracken County

Community Chest, 1967—; v.p. St. Mary High Sch. P.T.A., 1970-71, pres., 1971-72; mem. Paducah Labor-Mgmt. Com., 1971—, Mayors Com. for Paducah Progress, 1971—; mem. health studies adv. com. Paducah-Tilghman Area Vocational Sch., 1971-72. Served with AUS, 1951-53. Named Duke of Paducah, Ky. col. Mem. Am. Loudspeaker Mfrs. Assn. (pres., dir. 1971-72). Democrat. Roman Catholic. Lion. Club: Rolling Hills Country. Home: 128 Vine St Paducah KY 42001 Office: 1565 N 8th St Paducah KY 42001

TIDWELL, JAMES HAROLD, supt. schs.; b. Brilliant, Ala., Oct. 21, 1928; s. James Monroe and Reatha (Cochran) T.; B.S., Livingston State U., 1952; M.S., U. Ark., 1961; m. Willie Evelyn Adams, Jan. 8, 1951; children—James Thomas, Mitchell Edwin, Steven Leslie. Coach, tchr., Laurel, Miss., 1951-53, Dermott, Ark., 1953-55; coach, tchr., Star City, Ark., 1955-59, supt. schs., 1959-67; adminstrv. asst., Pine Bluff, Ark., 1967-68; supt. schs., Dumas, Ark., 1968—. Served with USNR, 1946-48. Mem. S.E. Ark. Schoolmasters Club (pres. 1960-61), S.E. Ark. Athletic Assn. (pres. 1961-62), Ark. Edn. Assn. (coordinating chmn. S.E. Ark. 1959-60), N.E.A., Am. Assn. Sch. Adminstrs. Club: Optimist (lt. gov. 1965-66) (Star City, Ark.). Home: 114 N College St Dumas AR 71639 Office: 315 S Adams St Dumas AR 71639

TIDWELL, OSCAR CROMWELL, dentist; b. Nashville, June 15, 1914; s. Oscar Cromwell and Corene (Mebane) T.; B.A., Vanderbilt U., 1936; D.D.S., U. Tenn., 1940; m. Mary Louise Lea, May 1, 1948; children—Percie Corene, Mary Louise Lea, Oscar Cromwell. Gen. practice dentistry, Nashville, 1946—; mem. staff Jr. League Home for Crippled Children, Nashville. Dental rep. United Givers Fund, 1951-53; chmn. dental sect. Heart Fund drive, 1955; dental mem. council Community Agy., 1961. Bd. dirs. St. Augustines Chapel, Vanderbilt U. Served to maj. AUS, 1941-45. Mem. Am. (del. 1967—, mem. council 1965-67), Tenn. (v.p. 1960-61; sec. 1967—) dental assns., Nashville Dental Soc. (pres. 1955-56), Pierre Fauchard Acad., Am. Coll. Dentists, Soc. Mil. Surgeons, A.A.A.S., C. of C., Alpha Tau Omega, Psi Omega. Kiwanian. Club: Belle Meade. Contbr. articles to profl. jours., hist. quar. Home: 905 Westview Av Nashville TN 37205 Office: Midstate Med Center Nashville TN 37203

TIDWELL, ROBERT EARL, ednl. adminstr.; b. Blount Springs, Ala., July 21, 1883; s. Robert and Nannie (Graves) T.; B.S., U. Ala., 1905; A.M., Columbia, 1925, supts. diploma, Tchrs. Coll., 1925; LL.D., Birmingham-So. Coll., Ala., 1923, U. Ala., 1927; m. Bessie Sargent, July 6, 1906 (dec. Apr. 1928); m. 2d, Bessye Veach, Feb. 3, 1930. Prin. Ensley High Sch., Birmingham, Ala., 1906- 12; supt. Tenn. Coal, Iron & R.R. Co. Schs., Birmingham, 1912-18; dir. tchr. tng. State Dept. Edn., Montgomery, Ala., 1918-27; asst. state supt. edn., Ala., 1920-27, state supt. edn., 1927-29; dean extension div. and prof. edn. U. Ala., 1930-54, emeritus; asst. to pres. Stillman Coll., 1954, acting dean, 1957-60, prof. edn., chmn. div. social sci., coordinator of self-study, 1964; lectr. edn. Summer Tng. Sch., Halifax, N.S., 1928. Mem ednl. survey groups; mem. dept. supervision and curriculum devel.; chmn. Ala. War Tng. Com., World War II; mem. U.S. Armed Forces Inst. Com on Tng.; cons. on teaching by TV Ala. Dept. Edn. U. Ala. Extension Center Bldg. named for him, 1954. Mem. Ala. Ednl. Assn., N.E.A. (exec. com. dept. rural edn.), Nat. U. Extension Assn. (pres. 1947-48), Nat. Soc. Study Edn., Am. Assn. Adult Edn., Am. Assn. Sch. Adminstrs., Phi Beta Kappa. Phi Delta Kappa, Kappa Delta Pi, Kappa Phi Kappa, Kappa Sigma. Democrat. Baptist. Mason, Rotarian (del. to Japan 1961). Clubs: University, University. Author ann. reports State Bd. Education of Ala., 1927-30, Ala. Unified Equalization Ednl. Program 1927, Teacher Training in Alabama; Planning Improvement in Rural Living through the Schools; Adult Education in a Free Society, 1955; also articles in mags. Travelled India, Egypt, Israel, Jordan. Home: 1602 Alaca Pl Tuscaloosa AL 35401

TIEDEMANN, ALBERT WILLIAM, JR., chemist; b. Balt., Nov. 7, 1924; s. Albert William and Catherine (Madigan) T.; B.S., Loyola Coll., Balt., 1947; M.S., N.Y.U., 1949; Ph.D., Georgetown U., 1958; m. Mary Therese Sellmayer, Apr. 6, 1953; children—Marie Therese, Donna Elise, Albert William III, David Lawrence. Teaching fellow N.Y.U., 1947-50; instr. chemistry Mt. St. Agnes Coll., 1950-55; chief chemist Emerson Drug div. Warner Lambert Pharm. Co., Balt., 1955-60; analytical supr. Hercules Powder Co., Allegany Ballistics Lab., Cumberland, Md., 1960-68; tech. service supt. Hercules Inc., Radford, Va., 1968-72; dir. Div. Consol. Labs., Commonwealth of Va., Richmond, 1972—. Served to lt. (j.g.) USNR, 1943-46. Fellow Am. Inst. Chemists; mem. Am. Mgmt. Assn., Am. Chem. Soc., Am. Soc. Quality Control, U.S. Naval Inst., Naval Res. Assn. (dist. pres. 1954-57; nat. v.p. 1962-63, 65-69; Nat. Meritorious Service award 1971). Home: 3026 Lofton Rd SW Roanoke VA 24018 Office: Div Consolidated Labs 1 N 14th St Richmond VA 23219

TIEDEMANN, JOHN GEORGE, psychologist; b. Washington, Dec. 12, 1927; s. Berthold Diedrich and Eula (Gootee) T.; student U. Del., 1945-46, 48-50; A.A., George Washington U., 1951; B.A., 1953, M.S., 1954; Ph.D., Am. U., 1961; m. Sheila Mary Sloan, Apr. 27, 1957; children—Patricia Ann, John Scott. Research asst. Human Resources Research Orgn., Washington, 1952-53; intern Mansfield State Hosp., 1954-55; sch. psychologist pub. sch. system, Washington, 1955-61; supervising psychologist Army Behavioral Sci. Research Lab., Washington, 1961-68; sr. research officer employee relations dept. U.S. Postal Service, Washington, 1968—. Lectr. D.C. Tchrs. Coll., Washington, 1958-59; teaching asst. Am. U., Washington, 1957-61. Pres., mem. bd. Tempo ABC-Ft. McNair Fed. Credit Union, 1963-69. Served with USNR, 1946-48. Mem. Am., D.C. (treas. 1963-67), psychol. assns., Kappa Alpha, Psi Chi. Contbr. articles to profl. jours. Home: 2938 McKinley St NW Washington DC 20015 Office: US Postal Service 13th St and Pennsylvania Av NW Washington DC 20260

TIEMANN, ARTHUR EDMUND, statistician; b. Boston, June 5, 1918; s. Harry and Sarah (Sisson) T.; B.A., Harvard, 1939; postgrad. Am. U., 1940-41, 47-50; m. Riboline Youngwitz, Apr. 19, 1944; children—Robert Michael, David Jeremy, Zachary Jon. Econ. analyst industry div. Bur. of Census, Washington, 1946; bus. specialist Nat. Housing Authority, 1946-47; statistician U.S. Dept. Navy, Washington, 1947-62; planning officer FAA, Washington, 1962-66; sr. statistician World Bank, Washington, 1966—; lectr. statistics George Washington U., 1960-68. Pres. Montgomery (Md.) Jewish Community, Inc., 1957-58, 67-68. Served to capt. AUS, 1941-46. Decorated Bronze Star medal. Mem. Am. Statis. Assn., Operations Research Soc. Am., Internat. Statis. Inst. Office: 1818 H St NW Washington DC 20433

TIGER, BUFFALO, mem. Fla. Commn. Human Relations; chief Miccosukee Indian Tribe. Mem. Nat. Tribal Chairmen's Assn. (Southeastern rep.). Address: Miccosukee Indian Reservation Dade County FL 32309 also Fla Commn Human Relations Tallahassee FL*

TILFORD, JAMES DEAN, JR., aviation exec.; b. Boston, Jan. 15, 1921; s. James Dean and Helen Morewood (Ferguson) T.; student Princeton, 1939-41; m. Emily Jane Meyer, June 22, 1946; children—James Dean III, Diana Leigh, Richard Ferguson. With Nat. Airlines, 1941, 46-60, sta. agt., Norfolk, Va., 1946-47, Tampa, Fla., 1947-48, sta. mgr., Marianna, Fla., 1948-50, West Palm Beach, Fla., 1950-54, sales mgr., Palm Beach, Fla., 1954-60; partner Palm Beach Aviation, Lantana, Fla., 1958-61, partner 1960-61; partner Aviation Sales & Service, Inc., Palm Beach, 1961-62; pres., owner Tilford Flying Service, West Palm Beach, 1962—. Commr., Palm Beach Shores, Fla., 1958-59, head Palm Beach Community Chest Dr. 1961; bd. dirs. Palm Beach Civic Assn., 1961—, Internat. Flying Fellowship of Rotarians. Nat. Air Transp. Confs., 1968—, chmn. bd., 1970—. Served to maj. USAF, Mem. Nat (dir. 1965-67), Fla. (pres. 1964-65) aviation trades assns., C. of C. (dir. 1957-66), Internat. Flying Farmers, Aircraft Owners and Pilots Assn., Airline Passengers Assn. (nat. adv. council 1971—), Nat. Pilots Assn., Sportsman Pilots Assn., Nat. Bus. Aircraft Assn., Nat. Air Taxi Conf. Rotarian. Clubs: Islander (pres. 1959), Everglades, Sailfish of Fla. (Palm Beach, Fla.); Home: 266 Southland Rd Palm Beach FL 33480 Office: PO Box 713 Palm Beach Internat Airport West Palm Beach FL 33402

TILLERY, DON EDWARD, oral surgeon; b. Phenix City, Ala., Oct. 14, 1927; s. William Henry and Thelma (Sanders) T.; B.S. in Pharmacy, Auburn U., 1950; D.D.S., Emory U., 1957; m. Sarah Ellen Regan, Sept. 1, 1952; children—Nancy Suzanne, Don Edward, James Regan. Asso. prof. pharmacy Med. Coll. S.C., Charleston, 1950-51; med. service rep. Upjohn Co., Miami, Fla., 1951-52; intern oral surgery Jackson Meml. Hosp., Miami, 1957-58; practice oral surgery, Coral Gables, Fla., 1958-60, Winter Park, Fla., 1961—; chief oral surgery and dental dept. Winter Park Meml. Hosp., 1965—; pres., dir. Tilco Internat., Inc., Winter Park, Indian River Marine Basin, Inc., Melbourne, Fla.; treas., dir. Gateway Med. Arts Center, Winter Park; adv. bd. Security Fed. Savs. & Loan, Winter Park; dir. Barnett Mall Bank, Winter Park. Mem. Central Fla. Devel. Com., 1969. Mem. Civil Service Bd. Winter Park, 1969. Bd. dirs. Orange County unit Am. Cancer Soc., 1965—; pres., 1969-70, bd. dirs. Fla. dir., 1969, mem. exec. com., 1970—; bd. dirs. Central Fla. Heart Assn., 1967-70, Winter Park Community Chest, 1969-72, Central YMCA, 1971-72. Served with USNR, 1946-48. Mem. Am., Southeastern, Fla. (pres. 1967-68) socs. oral surgeons, Internat. Assn. Oral Surgeons (founding fellow), Am., Fla. dental assns., Central Dist., Orange County dental socs., Winter Park C. of C. (dir. 1968), Psi Kappa Alpha, Psi Omega, Omicron Kappa Upsilon, Rho Chi. Presbyn. Clubs: Winter Park Racquet. Home: 1621 Via Tuscany Winter Park FL 32789 Office: 800 Morse Blvd Winter Park FL 32789

TILLERY, FRANK, dentist; b. Opelika, Ala., Sept. 16, 1904; s. John Walter and Clara Josephine (Smith) T.; student Auburn U., 1927, 28; D.D.S., Emory U., 1932; m. Bernice Claire O'Neall, Apr. 20, 1946. Practice dentistry, Columbus, Ga., 1932—. 1st lt. U.S. Dental Corps Res., World War II; mem. examining bd. Selective Service, World War II; lt. col. Gov.'s Staff Ga., 1967-70, Ala., 1971—. Hon. fellow, Ga. Dental Assn. (treas. 1937-46); mem. Western Dist. (pres. 1943-44), Am. (life) dental assns., Xi Psi Phi. Methodist. Rotarian. Home: 25-A Country Club Apts Columbus GA 31906 Office: 205 Empire Bldg Columbus GA 31901

TILLERY, MARGIE FREEMAN (MRS. LEE ROY TILLERY, JR.), banker; b. West Point, Ga., Aug. 9, 1921; d. Arthur Roy and Sadie (Clem) Freeman; grad. LaGrange (Ga.) Bus. Coll., 1939; student U. Ga., 1946-47; m. Lee Roy Tillery, Jr., July 19, 1947; 1 son Roy Lewis. Sec., Callaway Mills, LaGrange, Ga., 1939-47; legal sec. Cantey & Huff, Attys., West Point, 1947-48; bookkeeper First Nat. Bank, West Point, 1949-50; mgr. bus. office Valley Med. Group, Langdale, Ala., 1950-55; asst. cashier Valley Nat. Bank, Lanett, 1956-63; cashier Citizens Nat. Bank, Shawmut, Ala., 1963—. Early treatment edn. chmn. West Point area Am. Cancer Soc. Sec., bd. dirs. United Fund, Inc., West Point. bd. dirs. Troup County unit Am. Cancer Soc., Goodwill Industries, Inc., West Point, United Fund, Inc., West Point. Named Key Banker, Chambers County, Ga. Mem. Nat. (membership chmn. Central Ala., v.p. So. region 1972-73), Ala. assns. bank women, Bank Am. Inst. Banking, Beta Sigma Phi. Mem. Christian Ch. Clubs: West Point Junior Woman's (charter mem.), Contemporary. Home: 400 E 4th St West Point GA 31833 Office: Citizens Nat Bank of Shawmut PO Box 708 Shawmut AL 36876

TILLEY, RICE M., lawyer; b. Huntsville, Tex., Aug. 28, 1899; s. J.R. and Lillie Tilley; tchrs. certificate Sam Houston State Tchrs. Coll., 1919; LL.B., U. Tex., 1922; m. Lucille Kelly, Dec. 29, 1932; children—Rice M., Nancy S. Admitted to Tex. bar, 1921; practiced law in Corsicana, Tex., 1922-27; asst. atty. gen. Tex., 1927-29, 1st asst. atty. gen., 1929-30; legal adviser State Senate, 1931; practice law, Ft. Worth, 1931—. Chmn. Am. Cancer Soc.; active Infantile Paralysis Found., Red Cross, others; chmn., pres. dir. various civic and charitable instns. Chmn., del. Democratic State Conv., 1944; chmn. Dem. Nat. Conv., 1944. Served with U.S. Army, 1918. Recipient Presdl. award Outstanding Service, Selective Service Bd., 1956. Home: 3565 Bellaire Dr N Fort Worth TX 76109 Office: Ft Worth Nat Bank Bldg Fort Worth TX 76102

TILLEY, RICE MATTHEWS, JR., lawyer; b. Ft. Worth, June 21, 1936; s. Rice M. and Lucille (Kelly) T.; grad. Phillips Andover Acad., 1954; B.A., Washington and Lee U., 1958; LL.B., So. Meth. U., 1961; LL.M., N.Y.U., 1962; m. Clara Susan Bagby, June 11, 1960; children—Marisa Lynn, Angela Ainsworth, Lisa Scott. Admitted to Tex. bar, 1961; shareholder Law, Snakard, Brown & Gambill, Ft. Worth, 1964—. Bd. dirs. Civic Music Assn. Ft. Worth, 1965-69, v.p., campaign chmn., 1966, 67; bd. dirs. Lena Pope Home, 1966—, pres., 1970-71; bd. dirs. Casa Manana Mus., Inc., 1969—; bd. dirs. Future Ft. Worth 1969—; bd. dirs. Easter Seal Soc. Crippled Children and Adults Tarrant County, Tarrant County Assn. Mental Health, Van Cliburn Found., Arts Council, Ft. Worth Opera Assn.; bd. dirs. Ft. Worth and Tarrant County unit Am. Cancer Soc., exec. v.p., 1969. Served to 1st lt. arty. AUS, 1962-64. Recipient Matthews, Fisher, Budd and Sands award for excellence in writing in field of taxation So. Meth. U. Law Sch., 1961. Mem. Am. Judicature Soc., Am., Ft. Worth-Tarrant County bar assns., State Bar Tex., Ft. Worth Jr. Bar, Tarrant County All-Sports Assn. (dir. sec. 1966), Ft. Worth Bus. and Estate Council (v.p. 1967; pres. 1969-70), Beta Theta Pi, Phi Alpha Delta. Mem. Disciples of Christ Ch. Home: 44 Valley Ridge Rd Fort Worth TX 76107 Office: Fort Worth Nat Bank Bldg Fort Worth TX 76102

TILLINGHAST, BURETTE STINSON, JR., educator; b. Spartanburg, S.C., May 11, 1930; s. Burette Stinson and Bessie (Farley) T.; B.A., Wofford Coll., 1954; M.A., George Peabody Coll., 1955; Ed.D., Fla. State U., 1961; m. Josephine Wood, Aug. 31, 1952; children—Tom Wood, Sam Wood. Tchr., counselor schs., Nashville, 1955-56; psychologist Tenn. Dept. Edn., 1956; sch. psychologist Brevard County (Fla.) Schs., 1956-58; guidance dir. Gadsden County (Fla.) Schs., 1959-60, sch. psychologist, 1960-61, supr. guidance, 1961-62; asst. prof. edn. U. Va., 1962-65, asso. prof., 1965-67; prof. edn. in counseling, guidance U.S. Ala., Mobile, 1967—. Served with USN, 1948-52. Mem. Am. Psychol. Assn., Am. Personnel and Guidance Assn., Nat. Council on Measurement in Edn., Assn. for Counselor Edn. and Supervision, Nat. Vocational Guidance Assn., Phi Beta Kappa, Pi Gamma Mu, Phi Delta Kappa. Contbr. articles to profl. jours. Home: 1011 Woodside Dr E Mobile AL 36608

TILLIS, C(ECIL) RICHARD, educator; b. Jacksonville, Fla., Mar. 31, 1931; s. Andrew Carlysle and Hazel (Tillis) T.; B.S., Fla. State U., 1960, M.S., 1964; m. Rosalyn Brantley; children—Marcia Jeralyn, G. Brantley. Tchr. biology Bay County High Sch., Panama City, Fla., 1961; curriculum writer Fla. State U., Tallahassee, 1962-63; prof. biology Ferrum (Va.) Coll., 1964-66; dir. Pine Jog Conservation Edn. Center, West Palm Beach, Fla., 1966—; asst. prof. biology Fla. Atlantic U., Boca Raton, 1969—. Cons. nature centers throughout S.E., state cons. environmental edn. Mem. Fla. Gov.'s Conf. on Environmental Quality, 1967, Gov.'s Com. on Natural Resource Use Edn., 1967, Gov.'s Conf. on Water Quality, 1971; chmn. bd. sci. advisers Fla. Wildlife Fedn.; mem. Leon County Adv. Council for Environmental Edn.; del. UNESCO Internat. Environmental Tchr. Edn. Conf. mem. gov.'s Keep Fla. Beautiful Com. Bd. dirs. Tallahassee Jr. Mus. Served with AUS, 1950-53. Decorated Purple Heart. Mem. A.A.A.S., Assn. Interpretive Naturalists, Fla. Wildlife Fedn. (v.p.), Am. Inst. Biol. Scientists, Southeastern Assn. Biologists, Fla. Outdoor Writers Assn., Audubon Soc. Home: 2812 Roscommon Dr Tallahassee FL 32303 Office: Knott Bldg Tallahassee FL 32301

TILLMAN, SETH PHILLIP, govt. ofcl.; b. Springfield, Mass., Aug. 26, 1930; s. Samuel and Rose (Austin) T.; A.B., Syracuse U., 1951, M.A., 1952; M.A., Fletcher Sch. Law and Diplomacy, 1956, Ph.D., 1959. Instr. polit. sci. Mass. Inst. Tech., Cambridge, 1956-58, asst. prof., 1958-60; cons. Senate Com. on Fgn. Relations, U.S. Senate, Washington, 1961—; lectr. European diplomacy Johns Hopkins U. Sch. Advanced Internat. Studies, Washington, 1964—. Served with AUS, 1952-54. Mem. Am. Polit. Sci. Assn. Home: 1527 44th St NW Washington DC 20007 Office: Com on Fgn Relations US Senate Washington DC 20510

TILSON, HUGH BOB, oral surgeon; b. Plainview, Tex., Jan. 13, 1937; s. Dennis J. and Ruth (Teague) T.; B.S., W. Texas State Coll., 1959; D.D.S., Baylor U., 1962; M.S., U. Okla., 1962; m. Carol Frances Kimbrough, June 2, 1959; children—Dennis Ashley and William Bradley (twins), Lori D'Lynn. Intern, resident U. Okla. Med. Center, 1962-65; pvt. practice oral surgery asso. of Dr. James E. Bauerie, 1965-70; asso. prof., chmn. dept. oral surgery U. Tex. Dental Sch., San Antonio, 1970—; head div. oral surgery U. Tex. Med. Sch., San Antonio. Diplomate Am. Bd. Oral Surgery. Fellow Am. Coll. Dentists; mem. Am., Tex. dental assns., San Antonio Dist. Dental Soc., Am., S.W. socs. oral surgeons, Delta Sigma Delta. Contbr. articles in field to profl. jours. Home: 4102 Greensboro San Antonio TX 78229 Office: 7703 Floyd Curl Dr San Antonio TX 78229

TILTON, WEBSTER, JR., sales exec.; b. St. Louis, Sept. 11, 1922; s. Webster and Eleanor (Dozier) T.; student St. Marks Prep. Sch., 1936-40, Pawling Prep. Sch., 1940-42; master brewers degree, U.S. Brewers Acad., 1949; m. Grace Drew Wilson, Feb. 14, 1948 (div. Oct. 1959); 1 son, Webster III; m. 2d, Nancy McBlair Payne, Jan. 5, 1963. Asst. brewing technologist F&M Schaffer Brewing Co., Bklyn., 1948-52; factory sales rep. Cole Steel Equipment Co., N.Y.C., 1957-68; dist. sales mgr. Scantlin Electronics, Inc., Washington, 1968-70; sales rep. Comml. Washer's Dryer Sales Co., Washington, 1970—. Served from cadet to chief mate, USNR, 1942-45. Episcopalian. Home: 3719 Fulton St NW Washington DC 20007 Office: 715 Investment Bldg Washington DC 20005

TIMMERMAN, JOHN HODGES, dentist; b. Hartsville, S.C., Mar. 12, 1940; s. Washington Price and Margaret Griffin (Jordan) T.; student Clemson U., 1958-61; D.D.S., Med. Coll. Va., 1965; m. Jewel Garland Hoffmeyer, July 28, 1962; children—Marian Jordan, John Hodges, Jr. Pvt. practice dentistry, Chesterfield, S.C., 1965-66, Columbia, S.C., 1968—. Dir. Riverland Corp.; dir., sec. bd. dirs. Carolina Enterprises Columbia, Inc. Active Boy Scouts Am. Served to capt. Dental Corps, AUS, 1966-68. Mem. Am. Soc. Dentistry for Children (exec. com. S.C. chpt. 1971-72), Am., S.C. dental assns., Greater Columbia Dental Soc., S.C. Nitrous Oxide-Oxygen Analgesia Soc., Clemson U., Med. Coll. Va. alumni assns. Baptist (deacon 1969-72). Clubs: Country of Lexington (Lexington, S.C.); Greater Columbia Clemson. Home: 727 Westover Rd Columbia SC 29210 Office: 1513 Morninghill Dr Columbia SC 29210

TIMMERMAN, ROBERT PHINIZY, textile co. exec.; b. Warrenville, S.C., Nov. 9, 1920; s. Clarence Simpson and Addie (Arthur) T.; B.S. in Textile Chemistry, Clemson U., 1941; m. Maxine Watts, June 6, 1946; children—Deborah Ann, Susan Kay. With Graniteville Co. (S.C.), 1945—, asst. v.p., 1958-62, v.p., 1962-68, pres., chief exec. officer, 1968—, also dir.; chmn. bd. C.H. Patrick & Co., Greenville, S.C., Kenville, Inc., Lilesville, N.C.; mem. adv. bd., also finance com. Citizens and So. Nat. Bank, Augusta, Ga. Mem. council assos. Wofford Coll., Spartanburg, S.C.; mem. exec. council Ga.-Carolina council Boy Scouts Am.; v.p. Augusta Jr. Achievement. Trustee J.E. Sirrine Found.; bd. dirs. pres. Gregg-Graniteville Found.; chmn. trustees Gregg Found.; chmn. bd. dirs. Community Services, Graniteville. Served to maj. USAAF, World War II. Mem. Am. Textile Mfrs. Inst. (dir., exec. bd., numerous coms.), S.C. Textile Mfrs. Assn. (dir., chmn. com. safety and health), Am. Apparel Mfrs., Assn., S.C. C. of C. (dir.), Am. Legion, Mason. Clubs: Exchange (Graniteville); Augusta Nat. Golf, Goshen Plantation Country, Augusta Country, Pinnacle (Augusta, Ga.); Midland Valley Country (Aiken, S.C.); Ponte Vedra (Ponte Vedra Beach, Fla.). Home: 607 Laurel Dr Aiken SC 29801 Office: Graniteville Co Graniteville SC 29829

TIMMONS, PAT FRANCIS, lawyer; b. Texarkana, Ark., Nov. 26, 1917; s. Pat F. and Janet (Spidel) T.; B.A., Baylor U., 1939; J.D., South Tex. Coll., 1947; m. Clara Virginia Penick, Aug. 25, 1940; children—Claire Janet, Patrick F., Terence P. Pub. accountant P. F. Timmons, Houston, 1940-45; staff counsel Superior Oil Co., Houston, 1945-49; tax counsel Transcontinental Gas Pipeline Corp., Houston, 1950-57; admitted to Tex. bar, 1947; practice in Houston, 1957—. Dist. com. mem. Boy Scouts Am., 1965-66. C.P.A., Tex. Mem. Tex. Soc. C.P.A.'s, Am. Inst. C.P.A.'s, State Bar Tex., Am. Bar Assn. Home: 7706 Woodway St Houston TX 77042 Office: 1220 Southwest Tower Houston TX 77002

TIMMONS, WILLIAM EVAN, govt. ofcl.; b. Chattanooga, Dec. 27, 1930; s. Owen Walter and Doris (Eckenrod) T.; grad. Baylor Mil. Acad., Chattonooga, 1949; B.S. in Fgn. Service, Georgetown U., 1959; postgrad. George Washington U., 1959-61; m. Mimi Bakshian, Sept. 28, 1966; children—Karen Leigh, Kimberly Anne, William Evan. Aide to U.S. Senator Alexander Wiley, 1955-62; adminstrv. asst. to U.S. Rep. William Brock, 1963-69; dep. asst. to President Richard M. Nixon, 1969—. Exec. dir. Tenn. Republican Com., 1962; mgr. Brock campaigns, 1962, 64, 66, 68; dir. congl. relations Nixon-Agnew campaign, 1968; co-ordinator Nixon for Pres., Rep. Nat. Conv., Miami, Fla., 1968; mem. exec. com. Nat. Conv., Miami, Fla., 1968; mem. exec. com. Nat. Young Reps., 1965-67; mem. faculty Nat. Rep. campaign workshops, 1963-69. Served with USAF, 1951-55. Named Outstanding Young Rep. of Year Nat. Rep. Com., 1965. Mem. Am. Legion, Chattanooga C. of C. Mason. Home: 9501 Newbold Pl Bethesda MD 20034 Office: White House Washington DC 20501

TIMONER, ELI, business exec.; b. N.Y.C., Dec. 12, 1928; s. Benjamin J. and Rae Frances (Edelman) T.; student U. Ill., 1946-48; B.B.S., U. Miami, 1950; m. Elissa Doane, Dec. 4, 1966; 1 dau., Pamela June. Buyer, Federated Dept. Stores, N.Y.C., 1950; owner Laura Lee Candies, Miami, Fla., 1951-61; pres. Giffen Industries, Inc., Miami,

1961-—, dir. 20 subsidiary corps.; mem. adv. bd. Pan Am. Bank, Mem. Democratic Young Leadership Council. Bd. dirs. U. Miami, Greater Miami Jewish Fedn.; trustee Timoner Family Found. Trust. Mem. Iron Arrow, Omicron Delta Kappa. Jewish religion (dir. temple). Home: 2121 N Bayshore Dr Miami FL 33137 Office: 3235 NW 62d St Miami FL 33147

TINDAL, ROBERT (TAYLOR), educator, engr.; b. Columbia, S.C., Nov. 22, 1912; s. George and Cora (Taylor) T.; B.S. in Civil Engring., The Citadel, 1933; M.S., Ga. Inst. Tech., 1950; postgrad. U. Miami, U. Me., U. Mont., U. Tex.; m. Charlotte Capers Smith, Oct. 19, 1935; children—Charlotte Capers, Robert Taylor. Second engr. U.S. Coast and Geodetic Survey, 1933-34; asst. supervising engr. WPA, 1935-36, Charleston County, S.C., 1938-39; marine engr. Charleston Shipbldg. & Dry Dock, 1941-46; prof. civil engring., U. Miami, 1946-55, U. Ala., 1955-57, U. Tex., 1957-58, U. S.C., 1960-67, Ga. Inst. Tech., 1949-50, Rensselaer Poly. Inst., 1958-60; engr. S.C. Pollution Control Authority, Columbia, 1967-—. Cons. Miami Sewer Project, Lockheed Aircraft Corp., Maurice F. Connell Assn., Internat. Paper Co., USPHS. N.Y. State Health Dept., Rensselaer County Health Dept., radiol. safety during atomic tests. Explorer adviser, Boy Scouts Am. Served 1st lt., U.S. Army, inf., 1936-38, Air Corps, 1940-41. Registered profl. engr., Ala., Fla., S.C., Tex. Mem. Am. Soc. C.E., Nat. Soc Profl. Engrs., Am. Soc. Engring. Edn., Am. Pub. Health Assn., Am. Water Works Assn., Water Pollution Control Fedn., U.S. Pub. Health Service Reserve (sr. san. engr.), Jr. C. of C. Kiwanian. Research in radioactivity detection in and removal from natural waters, insecticides and detergents-detection in and removal from natural waters. Patentee in field. Home: 358 Molasses Lane Mt Pleasant SC 29464 Office: 2600 Bull St Ext Columbia SC 29201

TINDALL, CHARLES W., JR., business exec.; b., 1926; B.B.A., U. Mo., 1950; married. With Price Waterhouse & Co., C.P.A.'s, Houston and Dallas, 1950-66; v.p., treas. Tandy Corp., Fort Worth, Tex., 1966-—. Served with USMCR, 1944-46. C.P.A., Tex. Office: 2727 W 7th St Fort Worth TX 76107*

TINGLE, WILLIAM ANDRE, interior designer; b. Henderson, N.C., Oct. 22, 1926; s. John Noah and Josephine (Rock) T.; grad. Va. Commonwealth U. Sch. Interior Design, 1950; postgrad. Advanced Execs. Inst., Northwestern U., 1962; m. Margaret Martin, June 10, 1950; children—William Andre, Mary Lynn, James Martin. Decorator, Thalheimers, Richmond, Va., 1947-51; pres., dir., gen. mgr., chief designer Reid & Cutshall, Inc., Roanoke, Va., 1952-69; pres., dir. William Tingle & Assos., Inc., Roanoke, 1969-—; designer Tompo Homes, Inc., Roanoke, 1967-—, Creative Constrn. & Devel. Corp., Roanoke, 1969-—; pres. Contract Interiors Inc. div. Gen. Med., Inc., Richmond, 1971-—. Lectr., U. Va. Extension, 1953-57, Roanoke Coll., 1968-71, So. Retail Furniture Assn., High Point, N.C., 1969; guest speaker numerous radio and television shows. Pres., P.T.A., Roanoke, 1962-63 1968-—, Roanoke Council Garden Clubs, 1964-68; adv. bd. Color and Fashion for Living, 1967-70. Del. to conv. Republican party, 1971. Served with USAAF, 1944-46. Mem. Roanoke Mchts. Assn., Advt. Club Roanoke Valley, C. of C., Downtown Roanoke Retail Mchts. Assn., Am. Inst. Interior Designers. Methodist (ofcl. bd. 1955-60). Contbr. articles to retail publs. Address: 100 Randolph Circle College Park Ashland VA 23005

TINGLEY, GLENN VINCENT, clergyman; b. Fields Corner, O., July 31, 1901; s. Nelson Eugene and Edith G. (Gage) T.; student Los Angeles Sem., 1915-20, Los Angeles Pacific Coll., 1919-20; A.B., Mt. Vernon U., 1942, Th.B., 1942; D.D., Christ Sem., 1944; m. Elva Eunice Allen, Sept. 10, 1921; children—Ruth Eunice (Mrs. Bruce Teer), Pauline Elsie (Mrs. John Thomas Sawyer), Alice Mae (Mrs. William Schafer), Marjorie (Mrs. Herman Cano), Peggy Glenn Iris (Mrs. Richard Barker), Glenn Vincent. Ordained to ministry, Christian and Missionary Alliance, 1926; pastor Birmingham Gospel Tabernacle, 1929-56; pres. Birmingham Bible Inst., 1930-50; pastor Alliance Ch., Rochester, N.Y., 1956-60; pres. Radio Revival, Inc., 1929-—; pastor Fort Payne; Ala., 1969-—; pres. Courier Broadcasting Service, Inc., 1944-51, Fair Haven Conf. Grounds, Birmingham, Ala., 1952-60. Evangelist interdenominational crusades various countries, 1959-—; conf. speaker for The Evang. Alliance Mission, Aruba and Curacas, 1961; speaker Slovak Bapt. Union of Europe, 19 countries, 1954, Oriental Missionary Soc. in Greece, 1954; evangelist Christian and Missionary Alliance, Lebanon, Syria, Jordan in Ivory Coast. French West Africa, 1954, nat. evangelist, 1963-64; crusades in Peru, Colombia, Japan, Hong Kong, Philippines, Singapore, Malaysia, Israel. Pres. DeKalb County Mental Health Assn., 1967-68, 71-72. Trustee Toccoa Falls Bible Coll. Mem. Christian and Missionary Alliance, Nat. Religious Broadcaster (dir. 1941-61), Rochester Ministers Fellowship (pres. 1957-58), Rochester Fedn. Chs. (dir. 1957-58), Fort Payne Ministerial Assn., Pastors' Assn. Ft. Payne (pres. 1972). Home: Chalkville Rd Trussville AL 35173 also 309 NW 21ST St Fort Payne AL 35967 also 14th St and Grand Av NW Fort Payne AL 35967 Office: PO Box 1928 Birmingham AL 35201

TINKLE, LON (JULIEN LON TINKLE), educator, editor; b. Dallas, Mar. 20, 1906; s. James Ward and Mary (Gardenhire) T.; A.B., So. Meth. U., 1927, A.M., 1932; Diplome de phonetique, Sorbonne, U. Paris, 1933; grad. student Columbia, 1936, 37; LL.D., St. Mary's U., 1963; m. Maria Ofelia Garza, Dec. 27, 1939; children—Jon Richard, James Alan, Anthony Robert. Instr., asst. prof., then prof. French and comparative lit. So. Meth., U., 1932-—; guest prof. Columbia, summer 1947; asst. lit. editor Dallas News, 1942-47, lit. editor, 1947-—. Vice pres. Margo Jones Theatre in the Round, Dallas, 1945-57; mem. bd. Dallas Mus. Fine Arts, Dallas Civic Music Assn., Dallas Friends of Library. Decorated Palmes Academiques (France); recipient Faculty Achievement award So. Meth. U,, 1959; prize Tex. Inst. Letters, 1959; Book award Sons Republic of Tex., 1959. Mem. Philos. Soc. Tex., Tex. Inst. Letters (pres. 1949-52), C. of C. Democrat. Mem. Christian Ch. Author: (with C. F. Zeek) Les Deux Idoles; 13 Days to Glory; The Alamo, 1958; The Story of Oklahoma, 1962; The Valiant Few, 1964; The Key to Dallas, 1965; Mr. De, 1970. Co-editor: The Cowboy Reader, 1959. Home: 3615 Amherst St Dallas TX 75225

TINNELL, LEONARD EDWARD, accountant; b. Stamps, Ark., Oct. 4, 1916; s. Oscar H. and Gertrude (Tisdale) T.; grad. Internat. Accountants' Soc., Inc., Chgo., 1944; m. Jewell Orleans Wright, Mar. 16, 1935; children—Myrna Evelyn (dec.), James Edward, Sharon Diaine. Comptometer operator to gen. auditor Lion Oil Co., El Dorado, Ark., 1934-49; sec.-treas. Wheeling Pipe Line, Inc., 1949-51, Newell-White Motors, 1949-51; asst. to v.p. Lion Oil Co., El Dorado, 1951-55; asst. to v.p. to dir. supply and transp. Monsanto Chem. Co. - Lion Oil Co., 1955-60, personnel mgr., accounting dept. Monsanto Chem. Co., St. Louis, 1960-67; gen. mgr. Bear Brand Roofing, Inc., Bearden, Ark., 1967-—; dir. Citizen's Bank, Bearden. accounting cons. El Dorado, 1940-—. Sec. El Dorado Water & Sewer Commn., 1951-60. Pres. Jr. C. of C., El Dorado, 1944-46. Mem. Am. Inst. C.P.A'S., La. Tank Truck Carriers, Inc., Ark. Purchasing Agts. Assn. (v.p.), Ark. C. of C., Asphalt Roofing Mfrs. Assn., Nat. Assn. Purchasing Agts. (vice chmn. dist. 7, pub. relations, 1958-60). Mem. Ch. of Jesus Christ of Latter-day Saints (pres. Ark. dist. 1952-60; patriarch state 1969-—). Home: PO Box 358 Bearden AR 71720 Office: Bear Brand Roofing Inc Beardin AR 71720

TINNIN, HELEN LOU, community health scientist; b. Austin, Tex., Feb. 1, 1933; d. Hugh and Mattie May (Carter) Tinnin; A.B., U. Cal. at Berkeley, 1952, M.P.H., 1961; Ph.D., Ohio State U., 1964. Pharm. mfrs. rep. Pfizer Lab. of N.Y., Youngstown, O., 1952-54, Ayerst Labs of N.Y., Birmingham, Ala., 1954-59; instr. personal and community health Ohio State U., 1961-63; health edn. cons., project dir. Tri-Agy. Health Edn. Council, Canton, O., 1963-64; asst. prof. preventive medicine and pub. health, cons. scientist Univ. Hosp. and Clinics, U. Ala. Med. Center, 1964-66; asso. prof. health edn. and asst. to dean program planning U. Tex. Grad. Sch. Biomed. Scis., Tex. Med. Center, Houston, 1966-67; prof. community health and med. practice U. Mo. Med. Sch., Columbia, 1967-71; exec. dir. health professions program Forsyth Health Planning Council, also prof. community medicine Bowman Gray Sch. Medicine, Wake Forest U., Winston-Salem, N.C., 1971-—. Cons. Westinghouse Learning on Population Dynamics, Program Methodology U. Mo. Regional Med. Program, Health Service Research sect. U. Mo. Med. Sch. Adviser youth groups Episcopal Ch. Mem. Assn. Am. Med. Colls., Am. Assn. U. Profs., N.C. Pub. Health Assn., Soc. Pub. Health Educators, Am. Sch. Health Assn., Council on Med. Television, Assn. Tchrs. Preventive Medicine, Am. Pub. Health Assn., Assn. Sch. Allied Health, Am. Assn. U. Women, League Women Voters. Home: 2934-B St Mark's Rd Winston-Salem NC 27103 Office: Bowman Gray School of Medicine Allied Health Bldg 1990 Beach St Winston-Salem NC 27103

TINSLEY, MILTON REUBEN, photography studio exec.; b. Welch, W.Va., Oct. 13, 1909; s. Addison Fishburn and Laura Alice (Childress) T.; student Marshall U., 1928-31; m. Bernice Imogene Carroll, Aug. 22, 1931; 1 dau., Carroll P. (Mrs. Edward Carpenter). Owner, pres. Creative Arts Studio, Inc., Washington, 1940-70; pres. Creative Arts Equipment Corp., Washington, 1965-70, Still Photo Prodn., Inc., Washington, 1970-—, pres., owner James R. Dunlop, Inc., Washington, 1971-—. Trustee Goodwill Industries; bd. dirs. Welfare of Blind. Mem. Assn. U.S. Army (adviser 1966-—). Presbyn. (elder 1965-—). Mason, Kiwanian. Clubs: Congressional Country (Bethesda, Md.); Deltona (Fla) Country. Home: 8500 River Rd Bethesda MD 20034 also 1242 Feather Dr Deltona FL 32763 Office: 2321 4th St NE Washington DC 20002

TINSLEY, NORMA ELISE ROBINSON (MRS. JAMES MADISON TINSLEY), mfg., wholesale co. exec.; b. Shreveport, La., July 18, 1909; d. James Malcolm and Effie (Estes) Robinson; A.B. magna cum laude, Centenary Coll., 1930; postgrad. U. Colo., 1931; m. James Madison Tinsley, Apr. 26, 1943; 1 son, James Robinson. Asso. prof. English, psychology Dodd Coll., Shreveport, 1930-41; mng. partner Robinson-Tinsley Co., Shreveport, 1936-—. Sec., Little Theater Guild, 1936-37; mem. com. Preservation Fort Hudson Battlefield, 1959-61; mem. Soc. Preservation Fort Del., 1959-61. Named hon. Ky. Col., hon. Ky. Adm. Mem. U.S., Shreveport chambers commerce, L'Alliance Francaise, La., N. La. hist. assns. (mem. bd. 1959-61, sec. 1959), Internat. Platform Assn., Am. Assn. U. Women (hospitality chmn. Shreveport br. 1969-72), Ky. Hist. Soc., Centenary Coll. Alumni Assn. (chpt. bd. dirs. 1965-67). Chi Omega (Shreveport chpt. pres. 1935-37), Alpha Chi, Pi Gamma Mu. Baptist. Home: 1039 Sheridan Av Shreveport LA 71104 Office: 2101 Seymour St Shreveport LA 71104

TINSTMAN, ROBERT MECHLING, corp. exec.; b. Johnstown, Pa., Apr. 4, 1928; s. Carl C. and Irene (Mechling) T.; B.S. in Archtl. Engring. Pa. State U., 1950; M.A. in Govtl. Adminstrn., U. Pa., 1955; m. Shirley Mae Overall, June 6, 1953; children—Robert O., Torre R., Tracy D. Asst. city mgr., Kansas City, Mo., 1954-59; mgr. Downtown Com., Kansas City, Mo., 1959-60; city mgr., Abilene, Tex., 1960-63, Oklahoma City, 1963-67, Austin, Tex., 1967-69; v.p., gen. mgr. E.E. Stuessy Co., Inc., Austin, 1969-—. Trustee Oklahoma City Airport Trust, 1963-67, Oklahoma City Municipal Improvement Authority, 1963-67; bd. dirs. Tex. Municipal League, 1962-63. Served with AUS, 1951-54. Mem. Internat. City Mgrs. Assn., Am. Soc. Pub. Adminstrn., Municipal Finance Officers Assn., Am. Pub. Works Assn., Tau Beta Pi, Sigma Tau, Alpha Rho Chi, Scarab. Home: 104 Canyon Circle W Austin TX 78746 Office: PO Box 340 Austin TX 78767

TIPS, CHARLES R., builder; b. Seguin, Tex., June 5, 1892; s. Charles Edward and Mary Ella (Gallaher) T.; grad. West Tex. Mil. Acad., 1908; B.A., U. Tex., 1912; m. Hazel Woodward, Dec. 23, 1915; children—Mary Louise (Mrs. James Thomas Bagby), Hazel (Mrs. Edward Tarry Watkins), Eugenia (Mrs. Harvey Henry Cross), David. Founder City of Three Rivers, Tex.; colonizer surrounding terr., 1913; organizer, pres. First State Bank, Three Rivers, 1914-17; v.p. First Nat. Bank, Seguin, Tex., 1914-32, Dallas Joint Stock Land Bank, 1919-23; pres. Okla.-Tex. Joint Stock Land Bank, 1923-27; pres. Three Rivers Glass Co., 1922-37; developer Mason Park Terrace, Houston, 1937-39, Cedar Crest Country Club Dist., Tips Park Addition, Cedar Crest Indsl. Park, Central Indsl. Park, Cedar Crest Shopping Center, Dallas; pres. Home Owners Internat,; v.p. Overseas Agys., Harvey Cross Assos., Inc., N.Y.C.; pres. Ambassador Hotel Co., Dallas, Golden Triangle Land Co., Tex. Del. White House Conf. on Aging, 1961; mem. Tex. Civil War Centennial Commn.; pres. Tex. Hist. Survey Com. Del. Democratic Nat. Conv., 1932. Pres. Tex. Hist. Found. Col. U.S. Army Res., ret. Decorated Bronze Star Medal for service China and CBI, 1943, 44. Mem. Philos. Soc. Tex., Sons Republic Tex. (pres.), Knights of San Jacinto (comdr.). Mil. Order World Wars (Dallas pres.), Am. Legion (a founder 1919), Am. Assn. Retired Persons (v.p.), Order of Alamo, Phi Gamma Delta. Episcopalian (sr. warden). Mason (33 deg., Shriner, K.T.). Author: Care of the Aging in Europe. Address: 1312 S Ervay St Dallas TX 75215

TIPTON, JOHN AIAN, oil co. exec.; b. Arma, Kan., Nov. 25, 1914; s. William Edward and Eunice (Siple) T.; grad. high sch.; m. Edna Fay Tracy, Sept. 6, 1941. Asst. field man Halliburton Oil Well Cementing Co., 1943-45; field supt. Sharples Oil Corp., 1945-56; prodn. and drilling supt. Amarillo Oil Co. (Tex.), 1956-—. Mem. Am. Inst. Mining, Metall. and Petroleum Engrs., Am. Petroleum Inst. Mason (Shriner), Rotarian. Clubs: Tascosa Country, Amarillo (Tex.). Home: 3609 Memory Lane Amarillo TX 79109 Office: Plaza 1 Amarillo TX 79105

TIPTON, JOHN PEARSON, dentist; b. Ft. Worth, Aug. 11, 1907; s. Robert Wheller and Jenney Emerson (Pearson) T.; student Tex. Christian U., 1926-27, U. Houston, 1927-28; D.D.S., U. Tex., 1932; m. Helen Elizabuth Cohagan, June 3, 1937; children—Julianne (Mrs. Alvin Kershick Cochran), Emily Jean (Mrs. Frank Dean Roberts). Practice gen. dentistry, Ft. Worth, 1932-—. Served with USCGR, 1942-45. Mem. Am., Tex. (certificate of appreciation 1960) dental assns., Tarrant County Dental Soc., Tarrant County Dental Assts. Assn. (hon.), Xi Psi Phi. Democrat. Episcopalian (mem. vestry 1951-53). Mason. Club: Optimist (Ft. Worth). Home: 6401 Yorkshire Fort Worth TX 76119 Office: 3028 Lubbock St Fort Worth TX 76109

TIPTON, RAY ANDERSON, state ofcl.; b. Anniston, Ala., Nov. 3, 1913; s. Anderson W. and Leila (Powell) T.; A.B., U. Ala., 1935, M.A., 1936, postgrad., 1938; postgrad. U. Fla., 1947-55, Columbia U., 1958; m. Emogene Hall, June 18, 1939; 1 son, Ray Anderson. Tchr. DeKalb County High Sch., Ft. Payne, Ala., 1936-42; tchr. Marietta (Ga.) High Sch., 1937-42, prin., 1942; prin. Ft. Myers (Fla.) High Sch., 1946-51; sales rep. A.M. Kidder Co., Ft. Myers, 1952; supt. schs., Ft. Myers, 1953-60; sr. specialist surveys Fla. Dept. Edn., Tallahassee, 1960-62; sch. adminstrn. specialist, exec. sec. Fla. Assn. County Supts., Fla. Edn. Assn., Tallahassee, 1962-68; exec. asst. Fla. Dept. Edn., exec. sec. Fla. Assn. Dist. Sch. Supts., Tallahassee, 1968-—. Mem. Royal Palm council Boy Scouts Am., 1954-60. Bd. dirs. United Fund, 1954-60, Salvation Army, 1955-60, A.R.C., 1950-60. Served to lt. col. USAAF, 1942-46. Mem. N.E.A., Fla. Edn. Assn., Assn. Secs. State Assn. Sch. Adminstrs. (pres., 1969-70), Am. Assn. Sch. Adminstrs. (chmn. Eastern conf., 1971), Phi Beta Kappa, Phi Eta Sigma, Pi Mu Epsilon, Phi Delta Kappa, Omicron Delta Kappa. Methodist. Kiwanian, Rotarian. Home: 1101 Waverly Rd Tallahassee FL 32303 Office: 125 MJ Fla Dept Edn Tallahassee FL 32304

TIPTON, STUART GUY, trade assn. exec.; b. Knightstown, Ind., Dec. 26, 1910; s. Guy Stuart and Bessie (Walters) T.; A.B., Wabash Coll., 1932; J.D., Northwestern U., 1935; m. Lorraine Arnold, May 15, 1937; children—Susan, Judith, Ann, Patience. Admitted to Ind. bar, 1935, D.C. bar, 1940; atty. legislative sect. Office of Gen. Counsel, Treasury Dept., Washington, 1936-38; atty. CAA, Washington, 1938-40, asst. gen. counsel, 1940-44; gen. counsel Air Transport Assn., Washington, 1944-55, pres., 1955-—. Trustee Holton-Arms Sch., Bethesda, Md. Clubs: Internat., Nat. Aviation, Metropolitan, Capitol Hill (Washington); Wings (N.Y.C.); Congressional Country, Burning Tree (Bethesda). Home: 11761 Glen Rd Potomac MD 20854 Office: 1709 New York Av NW Washington DC 20006

TITLOW, GEORGE ALLEN, carpet co. exec.; b. Charleston W.Va., Feb. 23, 1935; s. Fred Harrison and Maureen Chaifin (Boyer) T.; B.S., U. N.C., 1963; postgrad. Emory U., 1964-65; m. Peggy Ann Baugh, Sept. 3, 1969; children—George Allen, Mary Craig. Sr. corporate trust officer First Nat. Bank, Atlanta, 1963-70; pres. O.N. Jonas Co., Inc., Dalton, Ga., 1970-—; dir. City Dodge, Inc., Atlanta, Ga. Sch. Book Depository, Coca Cola Co., Palo Alto, Cal., Daytona Linen Supply Co. (Fla.), City Leasing Co., Atlanta. Chmn., United Appeal, 1964; active Atlanta High Mus. Art, Boy Scouts Am., Jr. Achievement. Mem. Carpet and Rug Inst., Soc. Financial Analysts. Democrat. Club: Cherokee Country, Atlanta Athletic; Dalton (Ga.) Country. Home: 854 W Paces Ferry Rd Atlanta GA 30327 Office: PO Box 1128 Dalton GA 30720

TITUS, FRANK LLOYD, clergyman; b. Deposit, N.Y., Aug. 15, 1906; s. Lloyd Clarke and Sadie (Couse) T.; A.B., Syracuse U., 1930; student Delancey Div. Sch., Buffalo, 1932, Coll. of Preachers, Washington, 1937; grad. Command and Gen. Staff Coll., Ft. Leavenworth, 1952; grad. advanced course Chaplain Sch., Ft. Slocum, N.Y., 1957; m. Frieda Burlingame, Nov. 24, 1926; children—Donald Frederick, Marilyn (Mrs. Ernest Seaton, Jr.). Ordained to ministry Episcopal Ch., 1933; curate Trinity Ch., Watertown N.Y., 1932-35; rector Emmanuel Ch., Little Falls, N.Y., 1935-40; overseas sec. Nat. Council Episcopal Ch., 1946-50; rector Holy Cross Ch., Miami, Fla., 1952-65, Calvary Ch., Indian Rocks Beach, Fla., 1965-—. Dean Miami Episcopal Deanery, 1957-65; hon. canon St. Luke's Cathedral, Orlando, 1967-68; canon St. Peter's Cathedral, St. Petersburg, 1969; mem. standing com. Diocese of So. Fla., 1960-61, 71, mem. diocesan council, 1970-71, mem. com. of the statee of ch., 1961-64; del. Episcopal Gen. Conv., 1970. Bd. dirs. Florence Crittenton Home Dade County, 1962-65; trustee Windham House, N.Y., 1948-50; dir. promotion Diocese of So. Fla., 1953-56, trustee, 1966-70; mem. citizens adv. com. Miami, 1963-65. Bd. dirs. chmn. Allupatah YMCA, bd. mgrs., 1963-64; bd. dirs. Greater Miami YMCA, 1954-65. Mem. Aux. Fla. Hwy. Patrol, 1960-65. Served as chaplain, lt. col. AUS, 1940-46, PTO; lt. col. Res. (ret.). Mem. Greater Miami Ministerial Assn. (treas. 1961-62, pres. 1962-63), Miami Clericus, Am. Legion, 40 and 8, Acad. Religion and Mental Health, Navy League (chaplain Miami chpt. 1964-65), Mil. Order World Wars (chaplain), Res. Officers Assn., Holiday Isles C. of C. (dir. 1970-71), Ret. Officer's Assn. Democrat. Mason (Shriner), Elk, Kiwanian (v.p. Largo 1968, 71). Author: Cross on My Collar, 1955; Oil From the Beard of Aaron, 1961; Descendants of Selah Titus, 1971. Contbr. numerous articles to mags. Home: 107 25th St Belleair Beach FL 33535 Office: 1615 1st St Indian Rocks Beach FL 33535

TITUS, GEORGE FRANCIS, accountant; b. Clarendon, Pa., Jan. 2, 1898; s. Smith Luther and Mary Frances (McBride) T.; B.S., U. Okla., 1927; M.S., Columbia, 1928; postgrad. Harvard Grad. Sch. Arts and Sci., 1932, Yale, 1933; m. Edna Mae Brown. Accountant various accounting firms, N.Y.C., 1928-32; chief field auditor, Dept. Agr., 1934-35; financial analyst, Dept. Internal Revenue, 1935-40; chief auditor Dept. Navy, Phila., 1941-45, mem. Navy Contract Renegotiation Bd., 1945-46, chief accountant Pearl Harbor Naval Shipyard Hawaii, 1947-49, dep. controller Mil. Sea Transport Service N.Y., 1949-50; financial analyst ECA, 1950-53; deptl. internal auditor, Treasury Dept., Washington, 1953-63; former prof. econ. history Southeastern U.; now ret. Mem. Am. Inst. C.P.A.'s, Yale Engring. Assn., Acacia, Chi Beta. Home: 4501 Arlington Blvd Arlington VA 22203

TKACH, WALTER ROBERT, physician; b. LaBelle, Pa., Feb. 9, 1917; s. Joseph and Irene (Leschak) T.; B.S., Pa. State U., 1941; M.D., U. Pitts., 1945; m. Helen Gladys Weller, June 27, 1939; 1 son, John R. Commd. 1st lt. U.S. Army, advanced trhough grades to maj. gen. USAF, 1972; assigned Hdqrs. Japan. 1946-48; Pentagon staff duty, then asst. physician to Pres. Eisenhower, 1953-61; dep. surgeon SAC, 1961-65, PACAF, 1965-68; comdg. surgeon 7th Air Force, Vietnam, 1968; physician to Pres. Richard Nixon, 1968-—. Decorated Legion of Merit, Bronze Star, Air medal, USAF Commendation medal. Mem. A.M.A., Aerospace Med. Assn., Assn. Mil. Surgeons U.S., Soc. USAF Flight Surgeons, Fed. Hosp. Inst. Alumni Assn., Air Force Assn., alumni assns. U. Pitts., Pa. State U. Home: 4784 Command Lane Andrews Air Force Base MD 20331 Office: The White House Washington DC 20500

TOBIASSEN, THOMAS JOHAN, state legislator, mech. engr.; b. Omaha, Nov. 21, 1931; s. Thoralph Johan and Goldie (Marie) T.; B.S., Ohio State U., 1959; postgrad. U. Fla., 1967-68; m. Audrey I. Neumann, Nov. 27, 1959; children—Thomas Johan, Todd Johan. Sr. engr. Monsanto Co.; mem. Fla. Ho. of Reps., 1968-—. Served with C.E., AUS, 1953-55. Mem. C. of C., Sigma Chi. Republican. Lutheran. Kiwanian. Patentee in field. Address: 811 Woodbine Dr Pensacola FL 32503

TOBIN, JOHN PATRICK, educator; b. N.Y.C., Apr. 5, 1927; s. William Francis and Mary (Howell) T.; B.A., Miami U., Oxford, O., 1955; M.S. (United Aircraft asst.), Rensselaer Poly. Inst., 1963; M.A., Fla. State U., 1967; m. Elizabeth Jean Breitenbucher, May 25, 1957; children—John William, Jean Diana. Engr., Frigidaire Corp., Dayton, O., 1956-57; sr. analytical engr. Pratt & Whitney Aircraft Co., East Hartford, Conn., 1957-64; instr. Edison Jr. Coll., Ft. Myers, Fla., 1967-—, pres. faculty senate, 1971-—. Pres. bd. dirs. Cornerstone; chmn. bd. Parole and Probation Vol. Bd.; bd. dirs. S.W. Fla. Self Help Housing. Served with USMCR, 1945-49, 50-52. Mem. Fla. Assn. Pub. Jr. Colls. (past chpt. pres., dist. chmn., del. faculty affairs commn.), Am. Assn. U. Profs., Fla. Philos. Assn., Phi Delta Kappa. Unitarian. Home: 2278 Chandler Av Fort Myers FL 33901

TOBUREN, LAWRENCE RICHTER, transp. co. exec.; b. Cleburne, Kan., July 11, 1915; s. Edward Franklin and Anna Fredericks (Richter) T.; student U. Denver, 1937-41; m. Ella Joyner Brame, Dec. 16, 1942; children—Lawrence Richter, William Brame, Luanne Brame, Gwendolyn Brame. Dispatch clk., dispatcher Continental Airlines, Denver, 1943-48; dispatcher Pacific Intermountain Express, Denver, 1948-52, dir. dispatch, Oakland, Cal., 1952-57, Western region operations mgr., 1957-58; with Pilot Freight Carriers, Inc., Charlotte, N.C. and Winston-Salem, N.C., 1958—, dir. operations, 1963-67, v.p. operations, 1967-71, exec. v.p., 1972—. Served with USAAF, 1942-43. Mem. Equipment Interchange Assn. (dir.). Republican. Methodist. Home: Route 1 Wedge Dr Pfafftown NC 27040 Office: N Cherry Extension and Polo Winston-Salem NC 27102

TODD, EDWARD LAWRENCE, entomologist; b. Eureka, Kan., Mar. 24, 1922; s. Eddie Linsey and Lela (Cook) T.; A.B., U. Kan., 1947, M.A., 1948, Ph.D., 1950; m. Roberta Faye McCullough, Aug. 3, 1945; children—Judith Kay (Mrs. Curtis Bruce Willis), Richard Edward, Jill Anne. Asst. scientist USPHS, Atlanta, 1951-52, sr. asst. scientist, 1952; entomologist, research entomologist U.S. Dept. Agr., Washington, 1953—, investigations leader Lepidoptera, 1965—. Served to 1st lt. AC, AUS, 1942-45; ETO. Decorated Air Medal with four oak leaf clusters, D.F.C. Home: 6820 Kingwood Dr Falls Church VA 22042 Office: Nat Mus Natural History Washington DC 20560

TODD, EDWARD PAYSON, govt. ofcl.; b. Newburyport, Mass., Jan. 26, 1920; s. Glendon Forrest and Stella May (Cashman) T.; B.S., in Physics, Mass. Inst. Tech., 1942; Ph.D., U. Colo., 1954; m. Barbara Adams Wright, June 17, 1950; children—Glendon Gardner, Nathaniel Adams, Charles Payson. Research physicist United Shoe Machinery Corp., Beverly, Mass., 1946-49; supr. applied research Pitney Bowes, Inc., Stamford, Conn., 1954-57; tech. dir. Upper Air Lab., U. Colo., Boulder, 1957-63; asso. program dir. for atmospheric scis. NSF, Washington, 1960-61, program dir. for aeronomy, atmospheric scis. sect., also NSF-Nat. Center Atmospheric Research liaison, Washington, 1963-65, acting head atmospheric scis. sect. Math. and Phys. Scis. div., 1963-64, spl. asst. to asso. dir. for research, 1965-66, dep. asso. dir. for research, 1966-70, dep. asst. dir. for research, 1970—. Mem. Falls Church (Va.) Sch. Bd., 1968—. Served to capt. Signal Corps, AUS, 1942-46. Recipient Distinguished Service award NSF, 1971. Mem. Am. Geophys. Union (council mem. 1970—), Am. Meteorol. Soc. Home: 312 Van Buren St Falls Church VA 22046 Office: NSF 1800 G St NW Washington DC 20550

TODD, EUGENE ALLAN, educator; Ed.D., U. Houston. Asso. prof. edn., chmn. dept. secondary edn. U. Fla., Gainesville. Office: U Fla Gainesville FL 32601*

TODD, FRANK LESESNE, brick mfg. exec.; b. Hendersonville, N.C., Jan. 18, 1922; s. John Haywood and LeNorah (Bennett) T.; B.S., Wake Forest U., 1943, LL.B., 1948, J.D., 1970; m. Betty Anne Drysdale, Oct. 23, 1948; children—Frank Lesesne, Barbara Anne, John Bruce, Elizabeth Drysdale. Admitted to N.C. bar, 1948; practiced in Hendersonville, N.C., 1948-55; pres. Fletcher Brick Co., Hendersonville, 1955-64; pres. Moland-Drysdale Corp., Hendersonville, 1964—; dir. Northwestern Bank, Hendersonville and North Wilkesboro, N.C. Chmn. Hendersonville Planning and Zoning Bd., 1965-69; commr. Hendersonville, 1969—; mayor pro tem, Hendersonville, 1969—. Trustee, Montreat Anderson Coll., Flat Rock Playhouse; bd. visitors Western Carolina U. Served to lt. USNR, 1943-46. Mem. N.C. Bar Assn., N.C. Brick and Tile Assn. (dir. 1964—), Structural Clay Products Inst. (dir. 1966-69), Phi Alpha Delta, Lambda Chi Alpha. Presbyn. Elk, Kiwanian. Clubs: Etowah (N.C.) Golf (pres., also owner); Hendersonville Country. Address: PO Box 2150 Hendersonville NC 28739

TODD, JUNIUS LEONARD, real estate broker; b. Rome, Ga., June 22, 1921; s. Clarence A. and Julia (Reece) T.; student pub. schs.; m. Sarah Joyce Cox, May 1, 1944; children—Julia Mayre, Junius Lee, Jane Elizabeth, John Leonard. Real estate broker, pres., owner J.L. Todd Auction Co., 1948-&3; pres., owner J.L. Todd Co.; pres. Sutosa Corp., Gilmer Estates; dir. Nat. City Bank, State Mut. Ins. Co. Mem. Rome Real Estate Bd., named Realtor of Year, 1964. Mem. army adv. com. council Boy Scouts Am.; charter mem. YMCA; mem. gov.'s staff State of Ga. Trustee Thornwood Sch.; bd. dirs. Coosa Valley Vocational Sch., Boys Clubs. Recipient Golden Boy award Boys Club, 1961. Me. C. of C., Nat. Real Estate Assn., Nat., Tenn., Ga. auctioneers assns., Farm Bur., Floyd County Wildlife Assn., Ga. Sportsmen's Fedn., Ga. Assn. Real Estate Bds., Baptist. Elk, Kiwanian. Club: Coosa Country. Home: 15 Mimosa Dr Rome GA 30161 Office: 531 Broad St Rome GA 30161

TODD, STANLEY EARL, dentist; b. Detroit, Feb. 10, 1923; s. Earl B. and Oca (Logsdon) T.; student U. Eastern Ky., 1940-41; D.M.D., U. Louisville, 1949; m. Esta Newman, June 21, 1946; children—Stanley Earl, Rebecca Newman. Pvt. practice dentistry, Richmond, Ky., 1949—. pres. Ken Rich, Inc.; dir. Bank of Richmond. City commr. Richmond, 1969-71. Bd. dirs. Ky. River Foothill Council. Served with USAAF, 1943-45. Mem. Pierre Fauchard Acad., Am., Ky. dental assns., Beta Delta, Psi Omega. Republican. Mem. Christian Ch. (chmn. bd. 1969-70). Club: Exchange (Richmond). Home: 304 Barnes Mill Rd Richmond KY 40475 Office: 527 W Main St Richmond KY 40475

TODD, THOMAS CARMEL, ednl. adminstr.; b. Dotham, Ala., Jan. 9, 1929; s. Alda Thomas and Ada Estelle (Tharp) T.; B.S., Troy State U., 1955; M.S., Fla. State U., 1957; m. Betty Henderson, Aug. 17, 1950; children—Thomas Edward, Teri Jan. Prin., Telogia (Fla.) Sch., 1955-57, Ponce de Leon Elementary Sch., Clearwater, Fla., 1957-63; supt. schs. Bay County, Panama City, Fla., 1966—. Mem. Bay County Council on Aging, 1970-71. Served with AUS, 1951-53. Decorated Air medal. Recipient Good Govt. award Panama City Jr. C. of C., 1969. Mem. Fla. Assn. County Sch. Supts. (pres. 1971-72), Lynn Haven C. of C. (pres. 1968-69), Kappa Delta Pi, Phi Delta Kappa. Democrat. Baptist. Mason, Elk, Lion. Home: Box 777 Lynn Haven FL 32444 Office: PO Drawer 820 Panama City FL 32401

TOERNER, PAUL EMILE, constrn. co. exec.; b. Creole, La., Oct. 1, 1926; s. Earl Eugene and Eucharist Katherine (Theriot) T.; grad. high sch.; m. Edna E. Hale, Feb. 15, 1947; children—Paula (Mrs. Richard Metts), Richard, William, Katherine, Marie. Splicer, So. Bell, Lake Charles, La., 1949-55; supt. Lindsey Constrn., 1955-58; splicer U.S. Govt., Ft. Polk, La., 1959-61; splicer, supt. Burnup & Sim Inc., West Palm Beach, Fla., 1961-70, v.p., 1970—. Served with paratroopers AUS, 1945-49. Mem. Tampa C. of C. Democrat. Methodist. Mason, Moose. Home: 10465 Acme St West Palm Beach FL 33406 Office: 2011 Okeechobee Blvd West Palm Beach FL 33401

TOLAR, JOHN NEEDHAM, lawyer; b. Ocala, Fla., Apr. 14, 1912; s. John N. and Adeline Virginia (Eminisor) T.; student U. Fla., 1930-31; LL.B., Columbus U., 1937, LL.M., 1938; J.D., Catholic U. Am., 1967; m. Marye N. Walker, July 2, 1941. Admitted to D.C. bar, 1937, Fla. bar, 1940, U.S. Supreme Ct. bar, 1957; clk. Fed. Home Loan Bank, 1933-38; sec. to personnel com. HOLC, 1938-39; with Pub. Works Adminstrn., 1939-40; spl. agt. Dept. of Agr., 1940-46; instl. property specialist War Assets Adminstrn., 1946-48; practice, Ft. Lauderdale, Fla., 1948—. Mgr. local campaign for Gov. Collins of Fla. Pres. bd. trustees Presbytery of South, Synod of Fla., 1956-69; mem. permanent jud. commn., United Presbyn. Ch., U.S.A., 1962-67. Served as officer USAAF, 1942-45. Mem. Am. Bar Assn., Fla. Bar. Home: 2124 Middle River Dr Fort Lauderdale FL 33305 Office: Bayview Bldg Fort Lauderdale FL 33304

TOLBERT, C. WYNNE, lawyer; b. Maysville, Mo., May 14, 1917; B.A., U. Neb., 1939; J.D., Georgetown U., 1947. Admitted to Va. bar, 1947, D.C. bar, 1948, since practiced in Arlington, Va. Mem. Arlington County (pres. 1956-57), Va., Am. bar assns., Va. State Bar (pres. 1971-72), Delta Theta Phi. Address: Box 708 Arlington VA 22216*

TOLEDO-MORELL, JOSE ANTONIO, educator; b. Camuy, P.R., May 1, 1922; s. Jose and Juana (Morell-Rivera) Toledo-Rodriguez; student Coll. Agrl. and Mechanics Arts U. P.R., 1947-52, N.Y. U., 1961-62; m. Monserrate Feria Vilanova, Jan. 3, 1955; children—Freya Monserrate, Roxana Lis. Faculty depts. gen. and civil engring. U. P.R., Mayaguez, 1952—, prof., 1968—, dir. engring. materials lab., 1952-53, acting dir. tech. inst., 1967-68, asst. dir. gen. engring dept., 1970—. Cons. pvt. industry, govt. Served with AUS, 1943-46. Mem. Colegio de Ingenieros, Arquitectos y Agrimensores de P.R. Am. Soc. C.E., Nat. Geographic Soc., Casino de Mayaguez. Roman Catholic. Clubs: Exchange, Deportivo del Oeste, Camuy Country, Camuy Shooting. Home: 24 Caparra St Mayaguez PR 00708 Office: Gen Engring Dept U PR College Station Mayaguez PR 00708

TOLER, WILLIAM FRANKLIN, dentist; b. Washington, La., July 23, 1924; s. Thomas Maxwell and Alice (Voltz) T.; B.S., U. Southwestern La., 1949; D.D.S., Loyola U., 1954; m. Juanita Joy Francez, June 10, 1950; children—Pamela (Mrs. Warren David Albarado), William Franklin, Francezca, William Franklin III, Robin, Thomas, Theodore, Johnice. Pvt. practice dentistry, Washington, La., 1954-59, Opelousas, La., 1959-69, Birmingham, Ala., 1969—. Postgrad. student instr. Birmingham, 1969—. Served with AUS, 1945-46. Diplomate Am. Prosthetic Bd. Mem. Am. Dental Assn., 7th Dist. (v.p. 1964), St. Landry Parish (sec. 1956-58) dental 7th Dist. (v.p. 1964), St. socs., C. Victor Vignes Odontological Soc., Delta Zigma Delta (plaque for outstanding service Zeta chpt. 1951). Roman Catholic. Home: Old Washington Rd Washington LA 70570 Office: 340 W Worth St Opelousas LA 70570

TOLHURST, JOAN GAULENE (MRS. JAMES HAMILTON TOLHURST), pub. relations exec.; b. New Orleans, Aug. 3, 1934; d. Byard Alfred and Marie (Grivas) Gaulene; B.S., Loyola U., New Orleans, 1958; m. James Hamilton Tolhurst, June 8, 1957; 1 dau., Evann Marie. Pub. relations asst. Loyola U., New Orleans, 1958-60; freelance publs., pub. relations programs, New Orleans, 1960-64; pub. relations dir. La. chpt. Arthritis Found., New Orleans, 1964-65, New Orleans Area United Fund, 1965-70; asst. dir. Touro Infirmary, New Orleans, 1971—. Pub. relations adv. com. United Community Funds and Councils of Am., 1969, pub. relations dirs. com., 1968. Mem. Internat. (nat. v.p.-at-large 1968-69), So. (v.p. 1967-68) councils indsl. editors, New Orleans Press Club (v.p. 1968-70), Pub. Relations Soc. Am., Phi Beta. Home: 83 Flamingo New Orleans LA 70124 Office: 1401 Foucher St New Orleans LA 70115

TOLLESON, SHERWELL KLAWYN, educator; b. nr. Boaz, Ala., Mar. 19, 1935; s. Alvin Roy and Lesse (Avery) T.; student Snead Jr. Coll., 1953-55; B.S., U. Ala., 1958, M.A., 1962, Ph.D., 1964; m. Barbara Ann McCreless, Sept. 1, 1957; children—Andrea Jon, Klawyn Seth, Thomas Avery. Secondary sch. tchr. Morgan County, Ala., 1956-57, Marshall County, Ala., 1958-61; Nat. Def. Edn. Act fellowship for doctoral study U. Ala. in edn. and counseling psychology, 1961-64; chmn. psychology and guidance dept. Tenn. Tech. U., 1964—, prof. psychology, 1964—; cons. in psychology. Mem. N.E.A., Am., Tenn. personnel and guidance assns., Assn. Counselors, Educators, Suprs. (pres. 1969-70), Assn. Measurement and Evaluation in Guidance, Nat. Soc. Study Edn., Tenn. Edn. Assn. Phi Delta Kappa, Kappa Delta Pi. Methodist. Contbr. articles in field to profl. jours. Address: Tenn Tech U Cookeville TN 38501

TOLLETT, CHARLES AMOS, educator; b. Crossville, Tenn., July 29, 1936; s. George Franklin and Jane Scott (Effie) T.; B.S., Carons-Newman Coll., 1956; M.S., U. Miss., 1963; M.A., George Peabody Coll., 1964; postgrad. U. Tenn., 1971; m. Donna Jane Hammons, dec. 25, 1963; children—Kara Michelle, Rachel Lea, Kellye Jane. Tchr., Cumberland County (Tenn.) Schs., 1957-62; asst. prof. Miss. State Coll. for Women, 1963-64; supt. Cumberland County Schs., 1964-68; asst. dir. Tenn. Appalachia Ednl. Coop., 1969-70; exec. sec. Tenn. Sch. Bds. Assn., 1970—; asst. prof. edn. U. Tenn., Nashville, 1970—; dir., chmn. bd. Livingston, Byrdstown, Jamestown & Cookeville Devel. Corp., Mem. Tenn. Adv. Council for Vocational Tech. Edn. Mem. Nat. Sch. Pub. Relations Assn., Am., Tenn. assns. sch. adminstrs., Tenn. United Orgns. for Edn. (chmn. 1971—), Tenn. Congress Parents and Tchrs. (bd. mgrs. 1970—). Baptist. Home: 2321 Castlewood Dr Nashville TN 37214

TOLLEY, AUBREY GRANVILLE, psychiatrist, state ofcl.; b. Lynchburg, Va., Nov. 15, 1924; s. Aubrey Thomas and Nonnie Isabell (Pinion) T.; student Duke, 1942-43; M.D., U. Va., 1952; m. Jeannette Leigh Poindexter, Mar. 21, 1947; children—Barbara Leigh, Stuart Granville, Leslie Carroll, Anna Catherine. Intern, St. Elizabeth's Hosp., Washington, 1952-53; resident psychiatry U. Va. Med. Sch., Charlotteville, 1953-56; instr. dept. psychiatry U. N.C. 1956-61, asst. prof., 1961-66; dir. residency edn. John Umstead Hosp., Butner, 1966-67; dir. profl. tng. and edn. N.C. Dept. Mental Health, Raleigh, 1967-72, asst. commr., 1972—; dir. psychotherapy Dorothea Dix Hosp., Raleigh, 1961-67; cons. psychiatry VA Hosp., Fayetteville, 1956—. Served with USNR, 1943-46. Diplomate in psychiatry Am. Bd. Psychiatry and Neurology. Mem. A.M.A., Am. Psychiat. Assn., N.C., Durham-Orange County med. socs., N.C. Neuropsychiat. Assn. Home: 1504 Halifax Rd Chapel Hill NC 27514 Office: Dept Mental Health 325 N Salisbury St Raleigh NC 27611

TOLSON, CLYDE ANDERSON, govt. ofcl.; b. nr. Laredo, Mo., May 22, 1900; s. James William and Joaquin Miller (Anderson) T.; student Cedar Rapids (Ia.) Bus. Coll., 1917-18; A.B., George Washington U., 1925, LL.B., 1927. Confidential sec. to Secs. of War Newton D. Baker, John W. Weeks, Dwight F. Davis, 1919-28; admitted to D.C. bar, 1928, U.S. Supreme Ct. bar, 1935; spl. agt., FBI, U.S. Dept. Justice, 1928, asst. dir., 1930, asst. to dir., 1938, asso. dir., 1947—. Recipient alumni achievement award George Washington U., 1947, Pres.'s award for distinguished fed. civilian service, 1965. Mem. Sigma Nu, Phi Delta Phi. Baptist. Mason. Address: 4936 30th Pl NW Washington DC 20008

TOMA, THOMAS JEFF, dentist; b. Brinkman, Okla., Feb. 3, 1917; s. George A. and Martha (Kouri) T.; B.S., Okla. U., 1939; D.D.S., U. Mo., 1947; m. Betty Jo Farris, Nov. 22, 1953; children—Jeffery Taft, Kory John, Barry Timothy. Property mgr. Retail Food Market, 1940-42; pvt. practice dentistry, Sapulpa, Okla., 1947-51, Bell, Cal., 1953-69, Weatherford, Okla., 1969—. Vice-pres., sec. Bell Med. Center, Inc., 1955-68. Chmn., Liberty Amendment Com. Okla., 1970-71, Support your Local Police Com., 1970—, Ams. of Lebanese-Syrian Ancestry for Am., 1963-67; unit pres. Bring the Nation's Freedom United Repub. Cal., 1963-64. Chmn. S.E. area fund raising com. Joe Shell for Gov., Los Angeles County, 1962; mem. state central com. Republican party, 1964-66; dir. Am.-Arab Cal. Rep. Assembly, 1964-70. Bd. dirs. Am.-Arab Anti-Communist Com. Served with Dental Corps, USAAF, 1942-44. Mem. Pure Water Assn. Am., John Birch Soc., Assn. Am. Dentists, C. of C., Okla. U. Alumni Assn. (life), Am. Dental Assn., Xi Psi Phi. Greek Orthodox. Author: The Mark of Moscow, 1964; An Americanist Opinion, 1967. Cons. editor Pyramid Mag., 1967. Home: 821 Oak Dr Weatherford OK 73096 Office: 617 Washita St Weatherford OK 73096

TOMLIN, JACK, city ofcl.; b. Fort Worth, Apr. 24, 1922; s. J. P. and Rena Elizabeth (Littlefield) T.; student FBI Nat. Acad., 1953; m. Marion Lois Hart, Dec. 20, 1950; children—Gail Leslie, Dale Wesley. Patrolman, Police Dept., Odessa, Tex., 1948, sgt., 1948-52, lt., 1952-53, dep. chief, 1953-56, asst. chief, 1956-69, chief police, 1969—. Bd. dirs. Boys Clubs Odessa. Served with USNR, 1940-46, 50-52. Mem. Internat. Assn. Chiefs Police, Am. Legion, Tex. Police Assn., Tex. Police Chiefs Assn., Tex. Municipal League, Tex. South Plains and Eastern N.M. Peace Officers Assn. (pres. 1968), Tex. Sheriffs' Assn. Democrat. Baptist. Mason, Eagle, Moose, Lion. Home: 1634 E Everglade St Odessa TX 79760 Office: 221 N Lee St Odessa TX 79760

TOMLINSON, LAMBUTH, pub. co. exec.; b. Ft. Worth, July 22, 1923; s. Douglas and Mary (Capers) T.; B.S. in Commerce, Tex. Christian U., 1943; m. Mary Jean Vance, Aug. 28, 1943 (div. 1968); children—John Douglas, Jean Elizabeth; m. 2d, Sally McClanahan Redwine, Sept. 30, 1968; stepchildren—Julia Ann Redwine, Jimmy Redwine. With All-Ch. Press, Ft. Worth, 1939—, dir., 1959—, pres., 1960—. Newspaper tech. cons. Jackson (Miss.) State-Times, 1954-55; pres., S.W. Sch. Printing, Sam Houston State Coll., 1959-61. Pres. Joint Bd. Christian Chs. Tarrant County, 1960-62; mem. Zoning Board Adjustment, City of Ft. Worth; 1st mayor Edgecliff, Tex., 1951-52. Trustee St. Joseph's Hosp., Tarrant County Mental Health-Mental Retardation Center; bd. dirs. Fort Worth Downtown Assn., 1962-63. Served with USAAF, 1942-45. Decorated Air medal. Mem. Christian Ch. (elder). Clubs: Ft. Worth; Colonial. Home: 4912 Stacey Fort Worth TX 76132 Office: 1200 W Berry St Fort Worth TX 76110

TONAHILL, JOE HALBERT, lawyer, banker; b. Hughes Springs, Tex., Nov. 4, 1913; s. Joseph Emmett and Annie (Crump) T.; student U. Tex., 1938; LL.B., Washington Coll., 1941; m. Violett Smith, Mar. 31, 1941; children—Mildred, Rebecca, Susan, Smithy, Joey, Anne. Admitted to Tex. bar, 1941; practiced in Jasper, Tex., 1946—; mem. firm Fisher & Tonahill, 1946-56. Chmn. bd. 1st Nat. Bank, Jasper, Tex., 1960—; lectr. U. Tex., 1952-63. City atty., Jasper, Tex., 1947—. Served with USNR, 1942-45. Mem. Am. Trial Lawyers Assn. (bd. govs. 1955-56), Nat. Assn. Defense Lawyers in Criminal Cases, State Bar Tex. (dir. 1958-61, sect. chmn. 1961-62), Internat. Acad. Trial Lawyers, Tex. Assn. Plaintiffs Attys. (pres. 1951-52), Am., 1st Judicial Dist. (pres. 1951) bar assns., Internat. Soc. Barristers (dir. 1965), Am. Judicature Soc., Am. Legion, Delta Kappa Epsilon, Sigma Nu Phi. Episcopalian. Mason (Shriner). Clubs: Lions. Contbr. numerous articles in field to profl. jours. and books. Home: Kirbyville Hwy Jasper TX 75951 Office: Tonahill Bldg Jasper TX 75951

TONER, JOSEPH STANLEY, govt. adminstr.; b. Cleve., Jan. 19, 1917; s. Abraham and Esther (Rose) T.; B.A., U. Minn., 1939; grad. student pub. adminstrn., Syracuse U., 1940; m. Rebecca Gilson Brown, Jan. 14, 1949; children—John Gilson, Eric Spencer, Andrew Weir. Newswriter, CBS, 1946; editorial asso. Pub. Adminstrn. Clearing House, 1946-47, asst. to dir., 1947-50; program analyst HHFA, 1950-52; exec. sec. Mut. Security Agy., 1952, FOA/ICA, 1952-55, White House Disarmament Staff, 1955-58; sec.-treas. Devel. Loan Fund, 1958-61; exec. sec. AID, 1961-62; dir. AID mission to Cyprus, also counselor embassy for internat. devel., 1962-64; director U.S. AID mission to Nepal, 1964-67; dir. Office Personnel Adminstrn., AID, 1967-70; dir. AID mission to Turkey, also minister counselor of Embassy, 1970—. Served to capt. AUS, 1941-46. Mem. Am. Soc. Pub. Adminstrn., Soc. Internat. Devel. Author: Educational Preparation for Public Administration, 1948-49, 1949; How Good is Your Annual Report, 1948; also articles. Office: AID care Dept of State Washington DC 20523

TONIETTE, SALLYE JEAN, physician; b. Sulphur, La.; d. Eugene Augusta and Sallye (Tanner) Toniette; student John McNeese Jr. Coll., 1946-47; B.S., La. State U., 1949; tchrs. certificate La. State U., 1950, M.D., 1955. Intern, Crawford W. Long Meml. Hosp., Emory U., Atlanta, 1955-56, resident obstetrics and gynecology, jr., sr., chief residencies, 1956-59; practice obstetrics and gynecology, Sulphur, 1959—; bd. dirs. Holly Hill Nursing Home; mem. med. staff W. Calcasieu Cameron, 1959—. Bd. dirs. Calcasieu Parish Cancer Soc. 1963-67. Named Woman of Distinction, Calcasieu Parish Police Jurors-Bus. and Prof. Women's Club of West Calcasieu, 1969. Fellow Am. Coll. Obstetrics and Gynecology; mem. Am., So. med. assns., La., Calcasieu Parish med. socs., La. Wildlife Fedn., Am. Quarter Horse Assn., Assn. Am. Physicians and Surgeons, Alpha Chi Omega, Beta Tau Mu, Iota Sigma Pi, Phi Theta Kappa. Democrat. Methodist. Contbr. articles to profl. jours. Home: 301 W Verdine St Sulphur LA 70663 Office: 521 Cypress St Sulphur LA 70663

TOOLE, GEORGE HENRY, govt. ofcl., transp. cons.; b. Boston, July 26, 1903; s. Patrick Henry and Cora Isabel (Fox) T.; LL.B., Suffolk U., 1929; LL.M., Calvin Coolidge Law Sch., 1924; B.C.S., Benjamin Franklin U., 1945; certificate Indsl. Coll. Armed Forces, 1957; B.S. in Transp., Southeastern U., 1957, M.S. in Transp., 1958; B.Sc. in Econs. with honours, U. London, 1970; m. Kathleen Virginia Gibbons, Apr. 18, 1940. Seaman, purser on steamers to West Indies and S.A.; admitted to Mass. bar, various U.S. adminstrv. commns.; legal adviser Spanish Consulate at Boston, 1929-39; life commr. Supreme Ct. Nfld., 1936, Supreme Ct. S. Africa, 1937, Supreme Ct. of New Zealand, 1938, High Ct. of Judicature of India, 1939; consul of Belgium at Boston, 1932-43; acting Consul of Grand Duchy of Luxembourg, 1932-43; shipping coordinator U.S. Naval Air Station, Quonset Point, R.I., 1941-42; transp. cons. Office Chief of Transp., War Dept., Washington, 1943-46, chief Atlantic Gulf Coasts Cargo sect., 1950-51; engaged in ocean shipping, N.Y.C., 1946-50; mem. export control investigation staff Office Internat. Trade, Dept. of Commerce, Washington, 1951-53; traffic control supr. for U.S. Army, Europe, with hdqrs. at La Rochelle, France, 1953-54; chief, fgn. shipping br. Gen. Services Adminstrn., 1954-56; examiner U.S. Maritime Adminstrn., Washington, 1956-62; chief div. econ. analysis Fed. Maritime Commn., 1962-65, asst. dir. Office Transport Econs., 1965-68, econ. adviser, 1968—; mem. Inter-agency Com. of Fgn Trade Statistics, Exec. Office Pres., 1963—; prof. transp. Southeastern U., Washington, 1957-63, asst. dean Sch. Transp., 1958-63; lectr. internat. transp. Georgetown U. Sch. Fgn. Service, 1960-64. Mem. planning com. Ocean Shipping Mgmt. Inst., Am. Univ., 1962-66. Recipient award for services in field of marine operations War Dept. Feature writer The Mast mag., Bklyn., 1947—, Marine News, N.Y.C., 1951—. Fellow Am. Geog. Soc., Royal Geog. Soc. (London), Royal Econ. Soc. (London); mem. Brit. Inst. Internat. and Comparative Law; mem. Am. Soc. Traffic and Transp. (treas. and gov. D.C. chpt. 1959-66), Naval Hist. Found., Am. Econ. Assn., Econ. History Soc., Nat. Planning Assn., Transp. Research Forum,

Inst. Transport, Am. Acad. Polit. Sci., U.S. Naval Inst., Am. Soc. of Interat. Law, Nat. Aviation Club, Fed. Aviation Club. Author of various monographs on legal and maritime subjects. Home: 9218 Brian Dr Vienna VA 22180 Office: Fed Maritime Commn Washington DC 20573

TOOMBS, KENNETH ELDRIDGE, librarian; b. Colonial Heights, Va., Aug. 25, 1928; s. Garnett Eldridge and Susie W. (Bryant) T.; A.A., Tenn. Wesleyan Coll., 1950; B.S., Tenn. Poly. Inst., 1951; M.A., U. Va., 1955; M.L.S., Rutgers U., 1956; student La. State U., 1961-63; m. Ada Teresa Hornsby, Aug. 29, 1949; children—Susan Elizabeth, Cheri Lynn, Teresa Ann. Reference asst. Alderman Library, U. Va., 1954-55; research asst. Grad. Sch. Library Sci., Rutgers U., 1955-56; mem. staff and faculty La. State U., 1956-63, asst. dir. charge pub. service, 1962-63; dir. libraries, prof. library sci. U. Southwestern La., 1963-67; dir. libraries U. S.C., Columbia, 1967—. Chmn. librarians sect. La. Coll. Conf., 1965-67; mem. Bd. La. Library Examiners, 1966-67. Treas., Wesley Found.; v.p. Am. Field Services Internat. Scholarships. Danforth asso., 1967—. Served to 1st lt. AUS, 1946-47, 51-53. Mem. Am. (life), La. (parliamentarian 1962-63, 66-67), Southeastern, Southwestern library assns., Am. Assn. U. Profs. (sec.), La. Hist. Assn., La. Tchrs. Assn. Mason. Kiwanian. Methodist. Contbr. articles profl. jours. Editor Bull. La. Library Assn., 1959-62; mng. editor Southwest La. Jour., 1963-67. Home: 16 Garden Springs Rd Columbia SC 29209

TOOMEY, ROBERT E., hosp. adminstr.; b. Cambridge, Mass., Mar. 18, 1916; s. Daniel J. and Catherine (Shanley) T.; B.S., Harvard, 1940; M. Ed., Boston U., 1941; M.S., Columbia, 1951; LL.D., Clemson U., 1968; m. Laurette Creighton, Oct. 9, 1943; children—Robert Creighton, Carole Laurett, Richard Kirk, Jeanette Elizabeth. Tchr., coach Browne & Nichols Sch., Cambridge, 1940-42; psychologist VA, Detroit, 1946-49; adminstrv. asst. Roosevelt Hosp., N.Y.C., 1951-52; dir. North Country Hosps., Gouverneur, N.Y., 1952-53; asst. dir., Greenville (S.C.) Gen. Hosp., 1953; gen. dir. Greenville Hosp. System, including Greenville Gen. Hosp., Allen Bennett Meml. Hosp., Greer, S.C., Hillcrest Hosp., Simpsonville, S.C. and Roger Huntington Nursing Center, Greer, William G. Sirrine Hosp., Marshall Pickens Hosp.; Med.-Surg. Hosp., Rehab. Inst., Greenville, 1954—, sec. bd. trustees, 1971—; vis. lectr. Clemson U., 1969—. Pres. Carolinas-Virginias Hosp. Conf., 1957-58; bd. dirs. S.C. Hosp. Service Plan, 1957-70; mem. Gov. S.C. Com. Nursing, 1963, S.C. Study Com. on Alcohol and Drug Addiction, 1963—, S.C. Bd. Health Hosp. Adv. Council, 1964; sec. Com. for Med. Sch. in Greenville, 1962—; mem. com. planning and implementation Nat. League Nursing, 1966— mem. Regional Med. Program Nat. Review Com., 1971-75, Gov.'s S.C. Spl. Health Services Study Com., 1971, S.C. Planning Com. Nursing Edn., 1971-72. Trustee United Fund Greenville County, 1963-66; chmn. trustees Episcopal Day Sch., Greenville, 1959; bd. dirs. Greenville Community Council, 1966—. Served with AUS, 1942-46. Fellow Am. Coll. Hosp. Adminstrs. (council regents 1964-71, chmn. ednl. planning com. dist. III, 1966); mem. Am. (ho. of dels. 1959-63; mem. spl. com. provision health care goals 1970; trustee 1971-74), S.C. (pres. 1957-58, 70; trustee 1955-59, 61-70) hosps. assns., Greenville C. of C. Contbr. to profl. jours. Home: 702 Crescent Av Greenville SC 29601 Office: 100 Mallard St Greenville SC 29601

TOPAZIO, VIRGIL WILLIAM, educator; b. Middletown, Conn., Mar. 27, 1915; s. Concetto and Coradina (Rizzo) T.; B.A., Wesleyan U., 1943; M.A., Columbia U., 1947, Ph.D., 1951; m. Juwil E. Child, July 28, 1941. Lectr. Columbia U., 1947-48; instr. U. Rochester, N.Y., 1948-51, asst. prof., 1951-56, asso. prof., 1956-59, prof., 1959-65; prof., chmn. dept. Rice U., Houston, 1965—, dean humanities and social scis., 1967—, acad. v.p., 1969—. Served with AUS, 1945-46. Fulbright vis. lectr., France, 1964-65. Mem. Modern Lang. Assn., Am. Assn. U. Profs., Am. Assn. Tchrs. French. Author: The Background and Development of D'Holbach's Moral Philosophy, 1956; Voltaire, 1966. Home: 717 Creekside Lane Houston TX 77024 Office: 236 Rayzor Hall Houston TX 77001

TOPP, ALEXANDER JOSEPH, JR., mfg. co. exec.; b. Chgo., Oct. 5, 1917; s. Alexander J. and Mary Magdalene (Schoenbeck) T.; student DePaul U., 1935-41; m. Anne Irene Patterson, July 19, 1941; children—Alexander Joseph III, Terrence P. Auditor, Kraft Foods, 1938-44; v.p. Simmons Engring. Co., Mpls., 1944-47; pres. Suburban Launderers &Cleaners, Anoka, Minn., 1947-50; textile mgr. Kraft Co., Waukegan, Ill., 1950-56; with Red Kap Industries, Nashville, 1956—, dir. research and devel., 1964-68, v.p. marketing, 1968—. Pres., Northbrook (Ill.) Recreation Commn., 1961-68. Named Rotary Man of Year, Northbrook, 1956. Mem. Nat. Inst. Dry Cleaning, Inst. Indsl. Launderers, Linen Supply Assn. Am. Clubs: Germania (Chgo.); Thorngate Country (Deerfield, Ill.); Brentwood (Tenn.) Country; Nashville City; Bay Hill Country (Orlando, Fla.). K.C. Home: 5433 Camelot Rd Brentwood TN 37027 Office: 749 Massman Dr Nashville TN 37210

TOPPING, MARVIN WOODROW, ednl. cons.; b. Poquoson, Va., July 17, 1911; s. Joseph and Amelia (Bunting) T.; B.A., Randolph-Macon Coll., 1932; S.T.B., Boston U., 1936, postgrad., 1937-39; m. Louise E. Marshall, Dec. 3, 1938; children—John Marvin, Jean Carol. Dir. admissions, pub. relations Union Coll., Barbourville, Ky., 1943-47; dir. pub. relations Med. Coll. Va., 1947-50; exec. dir. Am. Coll. Pub. Relations Assn., Washington, 1950-56; vice chancellor Neb. U., 1956-57; asst. dir. devel. George Washington U., 1957-62; founder, pres. Coll. & Univ. Personnel Cons., Washington, 1962—. Contbr. articles to profl. publs. Pioneer 1st ann. Survey Philanthropy to Higher Edn. Home: 9909 E Bexhill Dr Kensington MD 20795 Office: 1629 K St NW Washington DC 20006

TORCHIA, JAMES SANTO, orthodontist; b. Pittsburg, Kan., May 21, 1932; s. James D. and Edith (White) T.; B.S., Kan. State U., 1954; D.D.S., U. Mo., 1957, M.S.D., 1959; m. Anna Mae Saporito, June 20, 1953 (div. Sept. 1967); children—Pamela, Mike, Teresa. Individual practice orthodontics, Tulsa, 1959—. Diplomate Am. Bd. Orthodontics. Mem. Am. Assn. Orthodontists, Am. Dental Assn., Okla. (past pres.), Tulsa (pres. 1965) orthodontic socs., Okla. Soc. Dentistry for Children (past pres.). Lion (pres. 1969-70).Home: 6126 S Lakewood St Tulsa OK 74105 Office: 4828 S Peoria Tulsa OK 74105

TORGERSEN, PAUL ERNEST, coll. dean; b. N.Y.C., Oct. 13, 1931; s. Elnar and Francis (Hansen) T.; B.S., Lehigh U., 1953; M.S., Ohio State U., 1956, Ph.D., 1959; m. Dorothea Zuschiag, Sept. 11, 1954; children— Karen Elizabeth, Janis Elaine, James Einar. Instr., Ohio State U., 1956-59; asst., then asso. prof. Okla. State U., 1959-67; prof., head dept. indsl. engring. Va. Poly. Inst., 1967-70, dean Coll. of Engring., 1970—. Served to 1st lt. USAF, 1953-55. Recipient Outstanding Tchr. award Okla. State U., 1963, Distinguished Alumnus award Ohio State U., 1971. Mem. Am. Inst. Indsl. Engring. (editorial bd. 1967-—), Am. Soc. Engring. Edn. (chmn. I.E. div. 1966-67), Alpha Pi Mu (nat. regional dir. 1962—). Author: (with W. J. Fabrycky) Operations Economy, 1966; A Concept of Organization, 1968; (with I. T. Weinstock) Management: An Integrated Approach, 1972; (with W. J. Fabrycky and P. M. Ghare) Industrial Operations Research, 1972. Home: 1510 Palmer Dr Blacksburg VA 24060

TORGERSON, RAY GERALD, banker; b. Chgo., Apr. 16, 1915; s. Edward Geohegan and Rose Elizabeth (Ekstrom) T.; student Crane Jr. Coll., 1933, Northwestern U., 1936-39, North Park Coll., 1938; m. Virginia Margaret MacDonald, June 21, 1941; children—Keith Richard, Peter Ray. Clk., Continental Ill. Nat. Bank, Chgo., 1933-36; creditman Comml. Credit Co., 1936-46; spl. rep., 1946-49; v.p. Mchts. Acceptance Co., 1949-56, pres. 1956-58; v.p., treas. Paine Lumber Ltd., Oshkosh, Wis., 1958-59; v.p. Nat. Acceptance Co. of Am., Chgo., 1959-60, sr. v.p., 1960-62, also dir.; pres., chief exec. officer, dir. Tex. Western Financial Corp., Dallas, 1962—; dir. Main St. Nat. Bank, Dallas, Transp. Tech. Inc., Dallas, Acme Fence & Iron Co., Norman, Okla. Served to maj. AUS, 1942-46. Democrat. Presbyn. Clubs: City, Cipango (Dallas). Home: 4338 Goodfellow Dr Dallas TX 75229 Office: Adolphus Tower Dallas TX 75202

TORKANOWSKY, WERNER, conductor; b. Berlin, Germany, Mar. 3, 1926; s. Abraham and Herta (Cohn) T.; student Jerusalem U., 1942-46, pupil Pierre Monteux, 1955-61; m. Teresa Viera, Nov. 15, 1954; children— Maria (former marriage), David. Came to U.S., 1948, naturalized, 1952. Violinist in Israel, 1943-47; chamber music and soloist appearances in U.S., 1948—; guest condr., Boston, Phila., Mpls., San Francisco, Rochester and St. Louis orchs.; mus. dir., condr. New Orleans Philharmonic, 1962—; condr. Spoleto Festival of Two Worlds, 1957, 58, 66; condr. operas and ballets in U.S., 1954—. Bd. regents Xavier U., New Orleans, 1966—. Named Hon. Citizens of New Orleans, 1963. Home: 5326 Prytania St New Orleans LA 70115 Office: 605 Canal St New Orleans LA 70130

TORN, THELMA MARY (MRS. ELMORE RURAL TORN), librarian; b. Granger, Tex., June 29, 1908; d. Arnold A. and Mary (Cervenka) Spacek; student Southwestern U., 1925-27, U. Tex., 1927-28; m. Elmore Rural Torn, June 25, 1929; children— Elmore Rural, Patricia Ann (Mrs. G.K. Alexander, Jr.). Tchr. pub. schs., Waterloo, Williamson County, Tex., 1928-29; librarian Taylor (Tex.) Pub. Library, 1948-51; records librarian Austin (Tex.) Pub. Library, 1951-55. Alternate del. Republican Nat. Conv., 1952; dist. committeewoman Tex. Rep. Exec. Com., 1953-56; Rep. nominee as presdl. elector, 1960. Mem. Friends of Taylor Library (treas. 1959-60), Tex. U. Ex-Students Assn. Clubs: Garden Study (dir., founding pres. 1940-42) (Longview, Tex.); Austin (Tex.); Taylor Country, Womans Study (Taylor). Mem. People-to-People Tour, Europe, 1956; travelled S.E. Asia, Middle East, 1965. Home: 1320 Howard St Taylor TX 76574

TORRE, MOTTRAM PETER, social psychiatrist; b. New Orleans, Feb. 6, 1919; s. Peter and Juanita (Mottram) T.; B.S., Tulane U., 1940, M.D., 1943; M.P.H., Columbia U., 1949; m. Elizabeth Lassiter, Apr. 13, 1957. Intern, Phila. Gen. Hosp., 1947; resident Pa. Hosp., 1944, Payne Whitney Hosp., 1947; vis. Fulbright prof. U. Paris Sch. Medicine, 1949-50; psychiat. cons. on selection and tng. of overseas personnel Dept. Def. USPHS, Washington, 1953-54; asso. in psychiatry Columbia U. Coll. Phys. and Surg., 1955-59; psychiat. cons. to med. service UN, N.Y.C., 1955-62; chief psychiat. out-patient dept. St. Luke's Hosp., N.Y.C., 1955-56, asst. attending psychiatrist, 1955-61; spl. cons. World Fedn. for Mental Health, London, Eng., 1956-58, asst. dir., 1958-61, project dir., 1958-63; lectr. Coll. City N.Y., 1959-61, prof., 1961-63, acting chmn., 1961-62; vis. lectr. Tulane U., 1963-64, lectr., 1964, asso. clin. prof. Sch. Pub. Health, 1971—; psychiat. cons. La. Bd. Health, 1964-66; chief mental health program Jefferson Parish Health Unit, New Orleans, 1964-66; asso. dir. Touro Community Mental Health Center, New Orleans, 1966-67; dir. tng. and research DePaul Community Mental Health Center, 1967-69, chief community psychiatry, 1969—. Vice pres. Research Inst. for the Study of Man; pres. Human Potential Research Inst. Served to lt. (j.g.) USNR, 1945-46. Nat. Inst. Mental Health fellow, 1958. Diplomate Am. Bd. Psychiatry and Neurology. Mem. World Fedn. for Mental Health (asst. dir. 1958-61), Am. Psychiat. Assn. (chmn. pub. health com. 1967-69), Group for Advancement Psychiatry (chmn. internat. relations com. 1961-67), Delta Tau Delta. Home: 806 Esplande Av New Orleans LA 70116 Office: 1040 Calhoun St New Orleans LA 70118

TORRES, ISRAEL, oral surgeon; b. El Paso, Tex., Sept. 5, 1934; s. Francisco Mendoza and Manuela (Gallardo) T.; B.S., Tex. Western Coll., 1958; D.D.S., U. Tex., 1963; m. Karen Hensley, Aug. 22, 1970; children—Michael, Stanley, Dianna. Oral surgery intern Meth. Hosp., Houston, 1963-64; oral surgery resident Hermann Hosp., Houston, 1964-65, Ben Taub Hosp., Houston, 1965-66; practice dentistry specializing in oral and maxillofacial surgery, El Paso, Tex., 1966—. Served with USNR, 1952-55. Diplomate Am. Bd. Oral Surgery. Mem. Internat. Assn. Oral Surgeons, Am., S.W., Tex. socs. oral surgeons, Am., Tex. dental assns., El Paso Dist. Dental Soc. Home: 10200 Donway Pl El Paso TX 79925 Office: 2101 N Oregon St El Paso TX 79902

TORRES, PETER, JR., lawyer; b. San Antonio, Dec. 2, 1933; s. Peter and Lola (Whitten) T.; B.A. cum laude, St. Mary's U., 1957, LL.B., 1963; m. Yolanda Parga, June 3, 1958; children—Denise Yvonne, Peter Alan, Tina Cheryl, Paul Andre. Tchr. history and civics Edgewood High Sch., San Antonio, 1957-60; admitted to Tex. bar, 1963, since practiced in San Antonio. Mem. San Antonio city council, 1967-71. Served with USMCR, 1951-54. Mem. Tex., San Antonio bar assns., Tex., San Antonio (dir. 1968—) trial lawyers assns., Tex. (dir. 1965), San Antonio (dir. 1964-65) civil liberties unions. Methodist. Home: 414 North Dr San Antonio TX 78215 Office: 708 Brooklyn Av San Antonio TX 78215

TORRES-AGUIAR, MANUEL AUGUSTO, psychiatrist; b. Fajardo, P.R., May 29, 1920; s. Francisco and Aurora (Torres) A.; B.S.A., U. P.R., 1941, M.S.S., 1944; M.D., Creighton U., 1950; m. Irma Isabel Diaz, Nov. 13, 1944; children—Irmarilis I., Manuel A., Roberto H., Maritza A. Pub. health office, Lares, P.R., 1951-52; psychiat. resident Neb. Psychiat. Inst., U. Neb., 1952-55; staff psychiatrist Norfolk (Neb.) State Hosp., 1955-56; co-dir. social psychiatry project, Social Sci. Research Center, U. P.R., 1956-59, asst. prof. clin. psychiatry, Sch. Medicine, 1956-60, prof. hosp. adminstrn., asso. prof. psychiatry, dir. Univ. Hosp., asst. dean Med. Sch. U. P.R., 1960-62; dep. sec. health Commonwealth of P.R., 1957-60, sec., 1967-69, regional dir. Health and Welfare, 1960-62. Asst. supt., med. dir. Rio Piedras Psychiat. Hosp., 1962-65; cons. comprehensive mental health planning, 1965-67. Diplomate Am. Bd. Psychiatry and Neurology. Mem. P.R. Med. Assn., Am. Psychiat. Assn., P.R. Pub. Health Assn. Democrat. Roman Catholic. Club: Exchange (pres. 1962). Home: Violeta 164 Urb San Fco Rio Piedras PR 00927 Office: Darlington Bldg Rio Piedras PR 00925

TORRES-GAZTAMBIDE, JAIME, architect; b. Las Marias, P.R., Aug. 22, 1930; s. Jaime and Celeste (Gaztambide) T.; B.Arch., U. Miami, 1957; m. Carmen Lydia Vincenty, Dec. 28, 1960; children—Esther Marie, Cristina, Jaime. Architect, various archtl. firms, 1958-61; organizer Jaime Torres-Gaztambide & Asso., Hato Rey, P.R., 1961—; dir. A &E Design & Specifications Cons. Served with USNR, 1950-53. Mem. A.I.A., P.R. Inst. Architects. Home: 263 Columbia St Rio Piedras PR 00927 Office: Tchrs Assn Bldg Hato Rey PR 00918

TORRES-MACHIN, ARTURO, physician; b. San Lorenzo, P.R., May 12, 1928; s. Arturo and Carmen (Machin) T.; B.A., U. Va., 1948, M.D., 1952; m. Rosa Julia Borges, Mar. 28, 1953; children—Arturo, Gerardo, Alexis, Amaury. Intern, San Juan (P.R.) City Hosp., 1952-53; practice medicine specializing in obstetrics and gynecology, Mineral Wells, Tex.; mem. Ryder Meml. Hosp., Humacao, P.R.; dir. Yabucoa Municipal Hosp., 1958-64, Policlinica Torres, Yabucoa, 1969—; med. adviser Union Carbide, Yabucoa, 1970—. Dir. Oriental Fed. Savs., Humacao. Pres., San Antonio Abad High Sch., P.T.A., Humacao, 1970-72; mem. Industrialization Com. Yabucoa, 1965-67; pres. Planning Bd. Commn., 1960-70; examiner Local Draft Bd., 1960-72. Served to capt. AUS, 1956-58. Mem. Farmers P.R. Soc., Cattlesales Soc., Phi Beta Pi. Roman Catholic. Lion. Home: 14 Munoz Rivera Yabucoa PR 00767 Office: 33 Munoz Rivera Yabucoa PR 00767

TORRES RIGUAL, HIRAM, asso. justice Supreme Ct. of P.R. Office: Av Ponce de Leon Parada 8 Puerta de Tierra PR 00906*

TOSTENGARD, STANFORD ORVIND, pipeline co. exec.; b. Dovray, Minn., Sept. 1, 1922; s. Gilbert and Ruth Olive (Hager) T.; B.A. cum laude, St. Olaf Coll., 1947; M.B.A. with distinction, Harvard, 1949; m. Ardyce Aws, Sept. 3, 1950; children—Stephen, Anne. With Gulf Oil Corp., Pitts., 1949-50, Houston, 1951-59, area foreman, New Orleans dist., 1959-61, dist. mgr., 1961-64; v.p., dir., mgr. operations Gulf Refining Co., Houston, 1964—; dir. Laurel Pipe Line Co., West Tex. Gulf Pipe Line Co., Cherokee Pipe Line Co., Toronto Pipe Line Co., Okan Pipeline Co., Gulf Oil Communications Co. Vice chmn. bd. regents Tex. Luth. Coll., Seguin. Served with AUS, 1943-46. Mem. Am. Petroleum Inst., Mid-Continent Oil and Gas Assn., Houston C. of C. Lutheran (pres. ch. 1971—). Clubs: Houston; Myerland (Houston). Home: 5006 Lymbar St Houston TX 77035 Office: Gulf Bldg PO Box 2100 Houston TX 77002

TOTTEN, HERMAN LAVON, coll. dean; b. Van Alstyne, Tex., Apr. 10, 1938; s. Derrell Scott and Dulvi (Sims) T.; B.A., Wiley Coll., 1961; M.L.S., U. Okla., 1964; Ph.D. (So. Edn fellow), 1966 Tchr. Marshall (Tex.) Pub. Schs., 1961-62; asst. to registrar Wiley Coll., Marshall, 1962-63, librarian, prof. L.S., 1966-70, dean of coll., 1970-71; asst. dean. Coll. L.S., U. Ky., 1971—. Mem. Harrison County (Tex.) Progressive Voters League. Am. Council on Edn. fellow, 1970-71. Mem. A.L.A., Southeastern, Ky. library assns., Assn. Am. Library Schs., Beta Phi Mu, Phi Delta Kappa, Alpha Phi Alpha. Home: 175 Malabu Dr Apt 1 Lexington KY 40503

TOUCHSTONE, CARL ALEXANDER, orthodontist; b. Crowley, La., July 14, 1940; s. Carlisle Bayard and Mary Kathleen (Hunt) T.; student U. So. Miss., 1959-61; D.D.S., U. Tenn., 1964, M.S., 1966; m. Patricia Ann McOwen, Oct. 29, 1966; children—Alex, Bradley. Individual practice orthodontics, Kingsport, Tenn., 1966-67, Memphis, 1967—. Scoutmaster Chickasaw council Boy Scouts Am., 1967-72. Served with AUS, 1958-59. Mem. Am. Dental Assn., Am. Assn. Orthodontists, Begg Soc. Orthodontists, So. Soc. Orthodontists, Richard Doggett Dean and Marguerite Taylor Dean Hon. Odontological Soc., Omicron Kappa Upsilon, Pi Kappa Pi, Phi Eta Sigma, Omicron Delta Kappa, Delta Sigma Delta. Optimist. Home: 3631 Shady Hollow Lane Memphis TN 38116 Office: 3333 Hwy 51 S Memphis TN 38116

TOUPS, HERMAN THOMAS, real estate investor grocer; b. Luling, La., Dec. 18, 1921; s. Wilson T. and Laura (Mongrue) T.; grad. high sch.; m. Florence Ryan, May 2, 1942; children—Florence Patricia, Herman Thomas, Evelyn Frances. Operator, Am. Oil Co., Texas City, Tex., 1938-47; owner Toups Ice Service, Texas City, 1947—; pres. Polar Ice & Food Co., LaMarque, Tex., 1955—, Toups Realty, Texas City, 1961—; Served with USAF, 1942-46, Mem. Tex., Galveston County (pres. 1964-65, v.p. 1967—) retail grocers assns., C. of C. (dir. 1963-64). Roman Catholic. Rotarian. Home: 1805 11th St N Texas City TX 77590 Office: 1002 Main St La Marque TX 77568

TOURTELLOTTE, MILLS CHARLTON, mech. elec. engr.; b. Great Falls, Mont., Dec. 16, 1922; s. Nathaniel Mills and Frances (Charlton) T.; B.S., Ill. Inst. Tech., 1947, M.S., 1952; m. Dorothy Gray, Sept. 26, 1947; children—Jane Frances, Kathryn Louise, Thomas Nathan. Co-op. engr. student Acme Steel Co., Riverdale, Ill., 1940-43; engr. Automatic Electric Co., Chgo., 1947-49, Inland Steel Co., East Chicago, Ind., 1952-56; asst. chief engr. Gulf States Tube Corp., Roseberg, Tex., 1956—; pres. Fabricators, Inc., 1967. Vice chmn., then chmn. Fort Bend County Program Bldg. Com., 1967-70. Mem. Tex. Republican Com., Fort Bend County, 1962—. Sec., South Lyon (Mich.) Citzen's Adv. Com., 1960; mem. Gary (Ind.) Symphony Orch., 1941-43; leader 4-H Electric Club, 1964-69; pres. Ft. Bend County 4-H Adult Leaders Assn., 1965-68. Vice chmn. bd. dirs., chmn. music com. Federated Ch., Harvey, Ill. Served with USNR, 1944-46. Recipient award for tech. article Welded Steel Tube Inst., 1964; Friend of 4-H award, Ft. Bend County, 1968. Registered profl. engr., Ill., Mich., Tex. Mem. Am. Soc. M.E., Assn. Iron and Steel Engrs., V.F.W. (post adj. 1964-68, quartermaster 1968-70), Tex. (chmn. edn. com. 1968-69), Nat. socs. profl. engrs., Am. Soc. for Engring. Edn. (chmn. relations with industry com. Houston chpt. 1968-69). Methodist. Patentee in field. Home: 1114 Inwood Dr Richmond TX 77469 Office: PO Box 952 Rosenberg TX 77471

TOUSSIENG, POVL WINNING, child psychiatrist; b. Nysted, Denmark, Sept 5, 1918 (came to U.S. 1949, naturalized 1963); s. Povl W. and Ingeborg (Hansen) T.; M.D., U. Copenhagen, 1945. Intern, Denmark 1945-46, Frederiksborg County Central Hosp., Kansas City, Mo., 1949-50; gen. practice medicine, Denmark, 1946-49; fellow Menninger Sch. Psychiatry, Topeka, 1950-53, John Harper Seeley fellow in child psychiatry Menninger Found., Topeka, 1953-55, mem. staff, 1955-65; cons. Kan. Boys Indsl. Sch., Topeka, 1957-61; asso. prof. child psychiatry and pediatrics U. Okla. Med. Center, Oklahoma City, 1965-69, prof., 1969—; clin. dir. Youth Counseling and Child Devel. Center, Oklahoma City, 1966—; pres. bd. Paseo Center Inc., 1970—. Served with Royal Danish Navy, 1943, 45-46. Fellow Am. Psychiat. Assn., Am. Orthopsychiat. Assn. (bd. 1968-71); mem. Soc. for Research in Child Devel., Midcontinent Psychiat. Assn., Med. and Correctional Assn. Contbr. articles to profl. jours., textbooks. Home: 4500 N Lincoln St Oklahoma City OK 73105

TOWER, JOHN GOODWIN, U.S. senator; b. Houston, Sept. 29, 1925; s. Joe Z and Beryl (Goodwin) T.; A.B. in Polit. Sci., Southwestern U. Tex., 1948, also LL.D.; M.A. in Polit. Sci., So. Meth. U., 1953; student London Sch. Econs. and Polit. Sci. U. London, 1952-53; LL.D., Howard Payne Coll., Alfred U.; m. Joza Lou Bullington, Mar. 21, 1952; children—Penelope, Marian, Jeanne. Announcer radio sta. KFDM, Beaumont, Tex., 1948, KTAE, Taylor, Tex., 1948-49; ins. agt., Dallas, 1950-51; asst. prof. polit. sci. Midwestern U., Wichita Falls, Tex., 1951-60; U.S. senator from Tex., 1961—, mem. banking, housing and urban affairs, armed services, joint def. prodn. coms. Del., Republican nat. convs., 1956, 60, 64, 68, 72, mem. platform com., 1960, 64, 68, 72, chmn. tax delegation, 1972, chmn. senatorial campaign com., 1969-70. Trustee So. Meth. U., Southwestern U. Enlisted man USNR, World War II, PTO. Mem. Am. Polit. Sci. Assn., S.W. Social Sci. Assn., Tex. Hist. Soc., Am. Legion, U.S. Naval Inst., Am. Assn. U. Profs., Kappa Sigma.

Methodist. Kiwanian, Mason (32 deg., Shriner). Home: Wichita Falls TX 76302 Office: Old Senate Office Bldg Washington DC 20510

TOWERS, CHARLES LOREN, oil co. exec.; b. Watertown, S.D., July 3, 1913; s. Charles Leslie and Netley (Swanson) T.; B.A., U. So. Cal., 1937; m. Jean Alberta Bristow, June 25, 1938; children—Donna Jean (Mrs. Samuel G. Friedman), Mary Larraine (Mrs. John H. Ralston). With Shell Oil Co., 1937—, mgr. Atlanta marketing div., 1961-64, v.p. So. marketing region, 1964—. Bd. sponsors Atlanta Symphony Orch., 1963—, mem. exec. com., pres., 1965—, v.p.; trustee Atlanta Arts Alliance, 1965—, vice chmn.-symphony, 1969—; trustee Oglethorpe Coll., 1965—, chmn. bd., 1969—. Presbyn. Mason (Shriner). Clubs: Capital City, Commerce, Piedmont Driving (Atlanta). Home: 4014 Paces Ferry Rd NW Atlanta GA 30322 Office: 230 Peachtree St NW Atlanta GA 30303

TOWLER, MARTIN LEE, physician; b. Hockley, Tex., Sept. 18, 1910; s. Ernest William and Ellen (Shoquist) T.; M.D., U. Tex. Sch. Medicine, 1935; m. Hetta G. Jockusch, Sept. 28, 1940; children—Hetta E., Martin H., Julie G., Sally J., William L. Intern, resident John Sealy Hosp., Galveston, Tex.; resident Colo. Gen. Hosp., Denver; practice medicine, specializing in neurology and psychiatry, Galveston, 1946—; prof. dept. neurology and psychiatry U. Tex. Med. br., Galveston, 1946—, dir. dept. EEG, 1947—. Served with AUS, 1942-46. Home: 5115 Av T Galveston TX 77550 Office: 200 University Blvd Galveston TX 77550

TOWLES, DONALD BLACKBURN, newspaper exec.; b. Lawrenceburg, Ky., Sept. 10, 1927; s. Joseph Sterling and Marjorie (Blackburn) T.; A.B., U. Ky., 1948; m. Geraldine Gooch, Dec. 20, 1947; children—Sally Blackburn, Rebecca Neale. Asst. dir. Ky. div. publicity and editor In Kentucky mag., Frankfort, 1948-55; asst. dir. pub. service and promotion dept. Courier-Jour. and Louisville Times, Louisville, 1956-66, dir. pub. service and promotion, 1966-71, dir. circulation, 1971—. Served with AUS, 1952-54. Mem. Internat. Newspaper Promotion Assn. (pres. so. region 1969-70, dir. 1968-71), Ky. Press Assn. (dir.). Mem. Christian Ch. (elder). Home: 3536 Norbourne Blvd Louisville KY 40207 Office: 525 W Broadway Louisville KY 40202

TOWNSEND, FRANK MARION, physician; b. Stamford, Tex., Oct. 29, 1914; s. Frank M. and Beatrice (House) T.; student San Antonio Coll., 1931-32, U. Tex., 1932-34; M.D., Tulane, U., 1938; m. Gerda Eberlein, 1940 (div. 1944); 1 son, Frank M.; m. 2d, Ann Graf, Aug. 21, 1951; 1 son, Robert N. Intern, Polyclinic Hosp., N.Y.C., 1939-40; commd. 1st lt. M.C., U. S. Army, 1940, advanced through grades to lt. col., 1946; resident instr. pathology Washington U., 1945-47; trans. to USAF, 1949, advanced through grades to col., 1956; instr. pathology Coll. Medicine U. Neb., 1947-48; asso. pathologist Scott & White Clinic, Temple, Tex., 1948-49; asso. prof. pathology Med. br. U. Tex., Galveston, 1949-59; dir. labs. USAF Hosp., Lackland AFB, 1950-54; cons. pathology, chief cons. group Office Surgeon Gen. Hdqrs. SAF, Washington, 1954-55, cons., 1955-63; dep. dir. Armed Forces Inst. Pathology, Washington, 1955-59, dir. 1959-63, now cons. vice comdr. aerospace med. div. Air Force Systems Command, 1963-65; ret., 1965; practice medicine specializing in pathology, San Antonio, 1965—; dir. labs. San Antonio State Chest Hosp., 1965-72; clin. prof. pathology U. Tex. Med. Sch., San Antonio, 1969-72, prof., chmn. dept. pathology, 1972—; cons. Nat. Aeros. and Space Adminstrn., 1967—. Mem. adv. bd. cancer WHO, 1958—; mem. adv. council Civil War Centennial Commn., 1960-65. Mem. adv. com. South Tex. region Pop Warner Jr. Football, 1965—. Bd. dirs. Alamo Area Sci. Fair, 1967—. Decorated D.S.M., Legion of Merit; recipient Founders medal Assn. Mil. Surgeons, 1961, George Patton Meml. award Jr. Football San Antonio, 1964. Diplomate Am. Bd. Pathology. Fellow A.C.P., Coll. Am. Pathologists (regional commr. lab. inspection and accreditation 1971—), Am. Soc. Clin. Pathologists, Aerospace Med. Assn. (H.G. Moseley award 1962); mem. A.M.A. Internat. Acad. Aviation and Space Medicine, Internat. Acad. Pathology, Am. Assn. Pathologist and Bacteriologists, Am. Soc. Exptl. Pathologists, Tex. Med. Assn., Bexar County Med. Soc., Tex. Soc. Pathologists. Club: Torch. Contbr. articles to med. jours. Home: 10406 Mt Marcy Dr San Antonio TX 78213 Office: Dept Pathology U Texas Med School 7703 Floyd Curl Dr San Antonio TX 78229

TOWNSEND, GEORGE ROWE, realtor; b. Bennettsville, S.C., Dec. 23, 1922; s. Arthur Douglas and Jayne (Rowe) Townsend; grad. U. Pa. Sch. X-ray Technicians, 1941. X-ray technician, Florence, S.C. 1941-43, Army hosps., Camp Croft and Ft. Jackson, S.C., 1943-45; chief x-ray technician, Florence, 1945-52; sec. Dept. Army, Salzburg, Austria and Frankfurt, Germany, 1952-53; sec. Nat. Security Council, Washington, 1954-56, J.P. Stevens Co., Wallace, S.C., 1956; chief x-ray technician Marlboro County Gen. Hosp., Bennettsville, S.C., 1956-58; sec. Redstone Arsenal, Huntsville, Ala., 1958-59, Litchfield Beach, Inc., Litchfield Beach, Pawley's Island, S.C., 1959-63; owner Townsend Real Estate Co., Pawley's Island, 1963—; pres., owner Indigo House, Ltd., 1963—. Sec., Litchfield Beaches Homeowners Assn., 1966-69; sec.-treas. Midway Vol. Fire Dept., 1961—. Mem. Georgetown County Bd. Realtors (sec.-treas. 1967-69), Nat. Assn. Real Estate Bds., Myrtle Beach and Grand Strand C. of C. Episcopalian. (pres. Ch. Women 1957-58, vestry 1969, mem. Altar Guild 1963—). Home: Litchfield Beach Pawley's Island SC 29585

TOWNSEND, HAROLD LEE, lawyer; b. Fayetteville, N.C., July 13, 1922; s. Harold Lee and Helen M. (Monroe) T.; B.A., Wake Forest Coll., 1943; LL.B., U. Va., 1948; m. Iris Bear, Sept. 4, 1965; children—Harold Lee III, Linda Ann, Ann Smith, Bruce Lewis. Admitted to Va. bar, 1948; atty. at law, Emporia, Va., 1948—. Mayor Emporia, 1952-56; commonwealth atty. Greensville County, Va., 1956-64. Named Boy Scout Man of Year, 1969. Mem. Am., Va. (bd. dirs. 1968-70), Richmond trial lawyers assns., Va. State Bar, N.Y. Trial Lawyers Assn., Emporia C. of C. (dir. 1949—), Am. Judicature Soc. Home: 802 Brunswick Av Emporia VA 23847 Office: 300 S Main St Emporia TA 23847

TOWNSEND, JAMES LAVALLE, journalist; b. Lanett, Ala., July 5, 1932; s. L.C. and Mary Lou (Pitts) T.; student U. Ala., 1951-54; m. Virginia Huchingson, Jan. 15, 1955; adopted children—Paige Ann, Mary Melissa. Free lance mag. writer, 1954-61; founder, editor Atlanta Mag., 1961-67; founder New Orleans, Cin. mags. tchr. creative writing Emory U., Atlanta, 1962—, Atlanta ed. Penitentiary, 1962—; journalist, mag. writer, editorial cons., 1967—. Adv. bd. trustees Ga. State Coll.; bd. dirs. Big Bros. Assn., Salvation Army, Leukemia Soc. Served with AUS, 1952-53. Named Outstanding Young Man in Community, Northside Jr. C. of C., Atlanta, 1962, Outstanding Young Man in Bus., Atlanta Jr. C. of C., 1962, Outstanding Young Man in Am., 1963; recipient Benjamin Franklin award Atlanta Club Printing House Craftsmen and Printing Industry Atlanta, 1963. Address: 1619 Ansley Lane NE Atlanta GA 30324

TOWNSEND, JAMES LESTER, JR., architect; b. Orangeburg, S.C., Mar. 13, 1939; s. James Lester and Lucile (Boltin) T.; B.Arch., Clemson U., 1962; m. Patricia Ann Files, Oct. 13, 1963; children—Jill, Chris, James. Architect, v.p. McMillan, Bunes, Townsend & Bowen, Architects-Engrs., Greenville, S.C., 1968—. Mem. Guild for Religious Architecture, A.I.A., Greenville Council Architects (sec. 1971). Club: Poinsett Sertoma (dir. Greenville, v.p. 1971-72). Prin. archtl. works include: Meth. Home, Orangeburg; Greenville City Hall Complex. Home: 231 E Avondale Greenville SC 29609 Office: Daniel Bldg Greenville SC 29602

TOWNSEND, JAMES ROWLAND, banker; b. Dallas, June 13, 1921; s. James Pinckney and Amelia Jessamine (Ward) T.; B.S., North Tex. State U., 1942; LL.B., U. Tex., 1948; postgrad. So. Methodist U., 1957; m. Jane Rhea Gustafson, Aug. 20, 1953; children—Craig Pinckney, Rebecca Rhea, Thomas Neal. Admitted to Tex. bar, 1948; mem. firm Sanders, Lefkowitz & Green, Dallas, 1948-53; mem. law dept. Stanolind Oil & Gas Co., Ft. Worth, 1953-56; atty. TXL Oil Corp., Dallas, 1956-62; v.p., trust officer Merc. Nat. Bank Dallas, 1962—. Worker fund drives United Fund, Am. Cancer Soc. and others; pres. P.T.A. Hotchkiss Sch., Dallas, 1966; chmn. troop Com. Circle Ten council Boy Scouts Am., 1967-69. Active precinct affairs Dallas Democratic Com., 1952-56, 68. Bd. dirs. YMCA East Dallas, 1964-68. Served with USAAF, 1942-46. Mem. State Bar Tex., Dallas Bar Assn. (v.p., 1953), Southwestern Legal Found., Dallas Assn. Petroleum Landmen (1960-61), Dallas Estate Council. Conglist. (deacon). Mason. Home: 6108 Joyce Way Dallas TX 75225 Office: PO Box 5415 Dallas TX 75222

TOWNSEND, J(OEL) IVES, educator; b. Greenwood, S.C., Aug. 20, 1920; s. Joel Ives and Emma Chiles (Cothran) T.; B.S., U. S.C., 1941; postgrad. U. Cal. at Berkeley, 1948-49; Ph.D., Columbia, 1952. Asst. prof. zoology U. Tenn., Knoxville, 1952-60; prof. genetics U. Rio Grande do Sul, Porto Alegre, Brazil, 1954; asst. prof. biology Med. Coll. Va., Va., Commonwealth U., Richmond, 1960-62, asso. prof. biology, 1962—. Served to lt. USNR, 1942-46. Fellow A.A.A.S.; mem. Am. Soc. Naturalists, Soc. Study Evolution, Genetics Soc. Am., Am. Genetic Assn., Assn. Southeastern Biologists, Nature Conservancy, Defenders of Wildlife, Va. Hist. Soc., Am. Eugenics Soc., Am. Assn. U. Profs. (pres. Va. conf. 1971-72), Nat. Trust for Historic Preservation, Wilderness Soc., Huguenot Soc., Phi Beta Kappa, Sigma Xi. Presbyn. Research on population genetics of man and trop. Drosophila. Office: Dept Genetics Box 33-MCV Station Richmond VA 23219

TOWNSEND, PAUL SCOTT, petroleum co. exec.; b. Jewett, O., Jan. 20, 1923; s. Leon Fredrick and Wilma Alberta (Shambaugh) T.; student Canton Bus. Coll., 1941-42, Washington and Jefferson Coll., 1943-44; B.S.C., Ohio U., 1948; postgrad. U. Ky., 1959, Syracuse U., 1960; m. Janet Evonne Johnson, Aug. 6, 1949; 1 dau., Darla Lavonne. With Ashland Oil, Inc. (Ky.), 1948—, asst. tax mgr., 1960-65; tax mgr., 1965-70, dir. taxes, 1970—. Instr., U. Ky. at Ashland, part time, 1960-61. Mem. Boyd County Cancer Assn., 1966—. Served with 84th div. AUS, 1943-46. Recipient medals. Mem. Ky. Oil and Gas Assn. (Merit award 1969, chmn. tax com. 1965—), Ky. Petroleum Council (Appreciation award 1969, chmn. tax com. 1965—), Ky., Ashland chambers commerce, Am. Inst. Real Estate Appraisers (dir. 1969—), Am. Petroleum Inst. (adv. com. excise taxation 1966—), W.Va. Petroleum Assn. (chmn. tax com. 1965-70, Outstanding Service award 1969). Ky. col. Methodist. Home: 2925 Forgey St Ashland KY 41101 Office: 1401 Winchester Av Ashland KY 41101

TOWNSEND, RICHARD MARVIN, city mgr.; b. White Plains, N.Y., Dec. 28, 1933; s. B. Richter and Frances (Mills) T.; B.A., Cornell U., 1955, M.P.A., 1956; m. Joanne Schwartz, Apr. 25, 1959; children—Drue, Brent, Merric. With City Corpus Christi, Tex., 1956—, city mgr., 1968—. Mem. Tex. Performance Certification Bd., 1971—. Pres. Corpus Christi dist. mission bd. United Methodist Ch., 1965-68; trustee St. Luke's United Meth. Ch., 1966-69. Mem. Internat. City Mgrs. Assn., Am. Soc. Pub. Adminstrn. Author articles. Home: 4425 Bluefield Dr Corpus Christi TX 78413 Office: PO Box 1622 Corpus Christi TX 78403

TOWNSEND, ROBERT GLENN, JR., physician; b. Grayson, Ky., Aug. 30, 1929; s. Robert Glenn and Lois Juanita (Jackson) T.; student U. Ky., 1949-50; B.S., Wake Forest U., 1957; M.D., U. Louisville, 1961; m. Mina Jean Hensley, Aug. 2, 1958; children—Susan Elizabeth, Robert Glenn III, Neil Hensley. Intern, Indpls. Gen. Hosp., 1961-62; partner J. Q. Stovall Meml. Hosp., Grayson, 1962-64; practice gen. medicine, Raeford, N.C., 1964—; partner family practice medicine, Raeford, 1964—. Bd. dirs. Southeastern Econ. Devel. Commn., 1967—, vice chmn., 1970—; bd. dirs. N.C. Cancer Inst., Lumberton, N.C. Served with USAF, 1951-56. Diplomate Am. Bd. Family Practice (charter). Mem. N.C., Hoke County (pres. 1966-68) med. socs., Am., N.C. Acads. family practice, Raeford-Hoke C. of C. (pres. 1966-67), Alpha Omega Alpha, Sigma Phi Epsilon. Methodist (steward 1966—). Home: 313 W Elwood Av Raeford NC 28376 Office: 116 Campus Av Raeford NC 28376

TOWNSEND, THATCHER LOVEJOY, JR., banker; b. Greensboro, N.C., Apr. 11, 1932; s.Thatcher Lovejoy and Eileen (Martin) T.; B.S., U. N.C., 1954; M.B.A., Northwestern U., 1957; m. Marian Faison, Sept. 15, 1956; children—Thatcher Lovejoy III, Allyn. With Wachovia Bank & Trust Co., Winston-Salem, N.C., 1957—, v.p. internat. dept., 1962—; pres. Wachovia Internat. Investment Corp., 1966—; dir. Fomento de Inversiones, S.A., Mexico City, Mexico, Bow Valley Industries, Ltd., Decca Resources Ltd., Sunningdale Oils, Ltd. (all Calgary, Alta., Can.). Served with AUS, 1954-56. Mem. N.C. World Trade Assn. (dir. 1970—). Methodist. Club: Old Town Country (Winston-Salem). Home: 701 Wellington Rd Winston-Salem NC 27106 Office: PO Box 3099 Winston-Salem NC 27102

TOWNSEND, WILLIAM THOMAS, JR., educator; b. Cartersville, Ga., Feb. 22, 1918; s. William Thomas and Elizabeth (Conyers) T.; student North Ga. Coll., 1935-37; A.B. J., U. Ga., 1939, M.Ed., 1948; Ed.D., U. No. Colo. Coll., 1961; postgrad. Northwestern U.; m. Julia Killen Redmond, June 22, 1941; children—Julia Elizabeth (Mrs. Nik Breitweiser), William Thomas III. Prin. Cochran (Ga.) High Sch., 1939-40, Richland (Ga.) High Sch., 1946-48, Pelham (Ga.) High Sch., 1948-51, Cass High Sch., Cassville, Ga., 1952-54, Treutlen High Sch., Soperton, Ga., 1954-59; owner, mgr. City Fuel Oil Co., Albany, Ga., 1951-52; supt. Sch. Dist. 103, Weld County, Colo., 1959-60; fellow U. No. Colo., 1960-61; asso. prof. sch. adminstrn. Trinity U., San Antonio, 1961-63; prin. S.W. DeKalb High Sch., Decatur, Ga., 1963-71; headmaster Providence Day Sch., Charlotte, N.C., 1971-72; prin. Manchester (Ga.) High Sch., 1972—. Owner, Ednl. Cons. Service, Decatur, Ga., 1963—. Served with AUS, 1940-46; maj. Res., now ret. Mem. Am. Assn. Sch. Adminstr., Nat. Assn. Secondary Sch. Prins., Phi Delta Kappa Kappa Delta Pi. Kiwanian (pres. 1968-69). Home: 307 Pacific St Manchester GA 31816 Office: Manchester High Sch Manchester GA 31816

TOY, HAROLD DWIGHT, research instn. ofcl.; b. Kittanning, Pa., Oct. 3, 1917; s. Wilbur J. and Sarah B. (Bowser) T.; grad. Air Force Inst. Tech., 1942; Dr. Environmental Sci. (hon.), Antrim, N.H., 1970; m. Irene Elizabeth Ditmore, Dec. 18, 1941; 1 son, Harold James. Aerospace engr. Weapons Guidance Systems Research and Devel., Avionics Lab., Air Research Devel. Command, Dayton, O.; 1951-58; mgr. reliability engring. Kollsman Instrument Co., Elmhurst, N.Y., 1958-60; chief flight research project br. Manned Spacecraft Center, NASA, Houston, from 1961, then project mgr. natural resources program space sci. application; pres., dir. Environmental Resources Assos., Inc., Houston; now pres. Nat. Alpha Research Assos., Inc.; v.p. research and devel. Motivation Research Center; with office of dir., parks div. Tex. Parks and Wildlife, Austin. Cons. Mexican Space Council. Mem. Tex. Gov.'s Com. Land Use and Environmental Control, Gov.'s Adv. Com. Youth Secretariat Program. Bd. dirs. YMCA. Served as warrant officer USAAF, 1939-45. Mem. Am. Astronautical Soc., Am. Inst. Aero. and Astronautics, I.E.E.E., Houston Jr. C. of C. (sustaining), A.A.A.S. Rotarian. Home: 500 S Congress St 124 Austin TX 78704 Office: Tex Parks & Wildlife Reagan Bldg Austin TX 78701

TRACEY, JOHN PAUL, lawyer; b. Norwalk, Conn., Nov. 2, 1935; s. Edward J. and Clara (Hammond) T.; B.A., U. Vt., 1958; LL.B., Georgetown Law Center, 1960; m. Susan Jane Hagist, Sept. 7, 1963; children—John Edward, Evan Lane. Admitted to Conn. bar, 1961, D.C. bar, 1961; asso. Hedrick and Lane, Washington, 1961-67; asst. dir. Am. Bar Assn., Washington, 1967-72, asso. dir., 1972—. Mem. Am., D.C. bar assns. Home: 5609 Harwick Rd Washington DC 20016 Office: 1705 DeSales St Washington DC 20036

TRACEY, MINNIE B., educator; b. Battle Creek, Mich.; d. Edward J. and Minnie (Atkinson) Tracey; student Coe Coll., 1919-21, A.B., U. Mich., 1924; M.S.C., U. Denver, 1935; postgrad. U. Chgo., summer, 1938, Ph.D., Ohio State U., 1948. Tchr., Oakridge High Sch., Royal Oak, Mich., 1924-26, Mazon (Ill.) High Sch., 1929-30, Universal Inst., Ft. Wayne, Ind., 1929, Kinman Bus. U., Spokane, Wash., 1930-31, Clifton (Ariz.) High Sch., 1931-37; asst. prof. secretarial sci. Ala. Coll., Montevallo, 1937-44; asst. prof. bus. adminstrn. Wittenberg Coll., Springfield, O., 1946-48; asso. prof. marketing Drake U., Des Moines, 1948-51; prof. marketing La. Poly. Inst., Ruston, 1951—. Mem. La. Tchrs. Assn., S.W. Social Sci. Assn., Am. Marketing Assn., Nat. Council for Small Bus. Mgmt. Devel., Delta Kappa Gamma (past pres.), Am. Assn. U. Women (past pres.). Contbr. articles to profl. jours. Home: Roosevelt Dr Ruston LA 71270

TRACY, DON, author; b. New Britain, Conn., Aug. 20, 1905; s. Wilbur Clinton and Charlotte (Fuller) T.; student pub. schs.; m. Carolyn Boyd Herring, June 14, 1929. Mem. faculty Syracuse U., 1956-60. Mem. Pi Delta Epsilon (hon.). Author: Chesapeake Cavalier, 1950; Streets of Askelon, 1951; The Duck That Flew Backward, 1952; Crimson is the Eastern Shore, 1953; The Amber Fire, 1954; Second Try, 1954; Roanoke Renegade, 1954; Caroline Corsair, 1956; Cherokee 1957; On the Midnight Tide, 1967; No Trespassing, 1961; The Hated One, 1962; (with James Street) Pride of Possession, 1960; The Big Brass Ring, 1963; Bazzaris, 1965; Fun and Deadly Games, 1967; Look Down on Her Dying, 1968; The Reluctant Rebel, 1968; Last Boat Out of Cincinati, 1970. Club: Clearwater (Fla.) Country. Address: 2137 Capri Dr Clearwater FL 33515

TRACY, ROBERT EMMET, bishop; b. New Orleans, Sept. 14, 1909; s. Robert Emmet and Margaret Agnes (Cahill) T.; D.D., Notre Dame Sem., New Orleans, 1932, LL.D., 1959. Ordained priest Roman Cath. Ch., 1932; asst. pastor St. Leo the Great Ch., New Orleans, 1932-46; chaplain Newman Club, Tulane U.-Newcomb Coll., 1941-46; dir. Confrat. Christian Doctrine, Archdiocese New Orleans, 1937-46; chaplain La. State U. Newman Club, 1946-59; nat. chaplain Nat. Newman Clubs, 1954-56; pastor St. Mary Madgalen Ch., Abbeville, La., 1959-60; dean Abbeville Deanery, 1959-60; pastor Our Lady of Fatima Parish, Lafayette, 1960-61; dean Fatima Deanery, 1960-61; consultor Diocese of Lafayette, La., 1959-61; apptd. Titular Bishop of Sergentza and Aux. Bishop of Lafayette, 1959; apptd. 1st bishop of Baton Rouge, 1961. Mem. Phi Kappa Theta. Home: Our Lady of the Lake Hosp Baton Rouge LA 70802 Office: PO Box 2682 Baton Rouge LA 70821

TRACY, THOMAS A., exec. sec. Nat. Mediation Bd. Address: 1230 16th St NW Washington DC 20572*

TRACY, WARREN FRANCIS, librarian; b. Richmond, Ind., Nov. 26, 1914; s. Timothy Leo and Eleanor (Moore) T.; B.A., Earlham Coll., Richmond, 1938; B.S. in L.S., Western Res. U., 1940; M.A., U. Chgo., 1953, Ph.D., 1958; m. Georgia Garber, May 24, 1941; 1 son, Warren Francis. Dir. Henry County (Ind.) Library Demonstration, 1940-41; asst. librarian Knox Coll., 1946-47, Northwestern State Coll. La., Natchitoches, 1947-51; librarian Coe Coll., 1954-62; librarian, chmn. dept. library sci. U. So. Miss., Hattiesburg, 1962—. Chmn. coll. sect. Ia. Library Assn., 1958, chmn. com. grad. library sch., 1962. Pres. Parent's Assn.-Youth Symphony Orch., Hattiesburg, 1962—. Served to 1st lt. AUS, 1941-46. Mem. Am., Miss. library assns., Phi Delta Kappa, Phi Kappa Phi (charter). Presbyn. Author articles in field. Home: Lake Serene Route 4 Hattiesburg MS 39401

TRAGER, EARL ADAM, geologist; b. South Bend, Ind., June 17, 1893; s. Christian Nicholas and Mary (Raffensperger) T.; student Mich. Agrl. Coll., 1913-14, U. Neb., 1914-15, S.B., U. Chgo., 1917; m. Martelle Wickliffe, Mar. 12, 1932; children—Earl Adam, Mary Frances (Mrs. Robert Burns Moore). Chief sub-surface geologist Empire Gas & Fuel Co., Bartlesville, Okla., 1917-20; chief subsurface geologist Marland Oil Co., Ponca City, Okla., 1920-21, chief geologist, Mexico, 1921-25, chief geologist research dept., 1925-26; chief geologist Earl Oliver & Co., Ponca City, 1926-28, Skelly Oil Co., Tulsa, 1928-30; cons. geologist, Tulsa, 1930-32; chief naturalist div., chief geologist Nat. Park Service, Washington, 1932-40; v.p. Bell & Howell, Chgo., 1940-42; chief liasion officer WPB, U.S. Bur. Mines, 1942-46; pres. Color Craft, Washington, 1946-48; chief geologist Sinclair Petroleum Co., Panama, Africa, Can., 1948-50; sr. geologist Fed. Power Commn., Washington, 1950-55; chief geologist H. Zinder & Assos., Houston, 1955-57; pres. Earl Trager & Assos., Inc., 1957-60; research, technologist inhalation therapy and visual edn. S.W. Med. Sch., Parkland and Woodlawn Hosps., 1960-68, Cardio Pulmonary Inst., Inc. of Meth. Hosp., Dallas, 1960—. Mem. Dallas Council on World Affairs, 1959—. Recipient 1st prize for best med. film Am. Coll. Chest Physicians, 1967. Mem. Am. Assn. Petroleum Geologists, Sigma Nu. Republican. Presbyn. Mason (Shriner), Kiwanian. Contbr. articles to profl. jours. Home: 4526 Glenleigh Dr Dallas TX 75220 Office: Meth Hosp Box 5999 Dallas TX 75222

TRAHAN, HAROLD GEORGE, physician; b. Maurice, La., Sept. 17, 1923; s. Ernest Gustave and Laura (Trahan) T.; B.S., U. Southwestern La., 1942; M.D., La. State U., 1945; m. Bertha Lee Broussard, Dec. 19, 1943; children—Donna (Mrs. Richard Putnam), Harold George, Catherine (Mrs. Weston P. Miller), Henry, Lolette, Thomas. Intern, New Orleans Charity Hosp., 1945-46; gen. practice medicine, Maurice, 1949—; staff Abbeville (La.) Gen. Hosp. Mayor, Village of Maurice, 1950-62. Served to capt. AUS, 1946-48. Mem. A.M.A., La., Vermilion Parish med. socs., La. Acad. Gen. Practice. Address: PO Box 156 Maurice LA 70555

TRAIN, RUSSELL ERROL, govt. ofcl.; b. Jamestown, R.I., June 4, 1920; s. Charles R. and Errol C. (Brown) T.; A.B., Princeton, 1941; LL.B., Columbia, 1948; m. Aileen Bowdoin, May 27, 1954; children—Nancy, Emily, C. Bowdoin, Errol. Admitted to D.C. bar, 1949; atty. staff joint com. on internal revenue taxation, U.S. Congress, 1949-53; clk. com. on ways and means U.S. Ho. of Reps., 1953-54, minority advisor, 1955-56; asst. to sec., head legal adv. staff Treas. Dept., 1956-57; judge U.S. Tax Ct., 1957-65; pres., trustee Conservation Found., Washington, 1965-69; under sec. Dept. Interior, 1969-70;

chmn. Council on Environmental Quality, 1970—. Served from 2d lt. to maj. F.A., AUS, 1941-46. Episcopalian. Clubs: Metropolitan (Washington); Chevy Chase (Md.); Princeton, Century (N.Y.C.). Home: 3101 Woodland Dr NW Washington DC 20008 Office: 722 Jackson Pl NW Washington DC 20506

TRAINA, PAUL JOSEPH, govt. ofcl.; b. N.Y.C., Mar. 8, 1934; s. Peter and Mary (Panepinto) T.; B.C.E., Manhattan Coll., 1955; M.S., U. Mich., 1960; m. Mary Ann Delehanty, Oct. 8, 1955; children—Peter, Kenneth, Jeanmarie, Julie Ann, Marie. Chief water resource studies region IV, USPHS, Atlanta, 1960-63; chief southeast comprehensive water pollution control, southeast region Fed. Water Pollution Control Adminstrn., Atlanta, 1963-67; dir. tech. programs, Athens, Ga., 1967-71; dir. water programs Environmental Protection Agy. Region IV, Atlanta, 1971—. Officer, lt. comdr. USPHS, 1955-67. Mem. Am. Soc. C.E., Water Pollution Control Fedn., N.Y. Acad. Sci. Home: 2366 Wood Creek Ct Tucker GA 30084 Office: 1421 Peachtree St Atlanta GA 30309

TRAINOR, GEORGE EDWARD, automobile co. exec.; b. Providence, Aug. 23, 1928; s. George Edward and Helena Regina (Gill) T.; student Md. U., 1948-49, Harvard and Boston U. Summer Sch., 1951, Georgetown U. Dental Sch., 1951-52; B.A. in Journalism and Pub. Relations, George Washington U., 1953; m. Agnes J. Epple, Aug. 22, 1953; children—Sharon Irene, Brenda Jane. With Armed Forces Security Agy., 1952; reporter Washington Post, 1952-53; bur. asst. and feature writer NEA Service, Inc., Scripps-Howard Newspapers Feature Service, 1953-54; reporter news dept. Ford Motor Co., 1954-55, pub. relations field rep., Cleve., 1955-58, sr. pub. relations field rep., N.Y.C., 1958-59, mgr. pub. relations, Washington, 1959-62, European pub. and govtl. affairs mgr., Brussels, Belgium, 1962-65, asst. pub. relations mgr. Ford div., 1965-67, regional pub. relations mgr., Washington, 1967—. Asso. professorial lectr. journalism George Washington U., 1967—; cons. internat. and nat. pub. affairs, parking industry, alcoholic beverage industry. Bd. dirs. Colonials, George Washington U. Served with USMCR, 1945-48. Recipient Extraordinary and Distinguished Service award Colonials, George Washington U., 1962; Alumni Service award George Washington U., 1971. Mem. Pub. Relations Soc. Am. (accreditation bd. 1970-71), Sigma Nu. Clubs: University, George Washington U., National Press (Washington). Home: 2731 N Randolph St Arlington VA 22207 Office: 815 Connecticut Av NW Washington DC 20006

TRALINS, S(ANDOR) ROBERT, author; b. Balt., Apr. 28, 1926; s. Emanuel and Rose (Miller) T.; student Eastern Coll., 1950-51, John Hopkins, 1949; m. Sonya Lee Mandel, Sept. 2, 1945; children—Myles Jay, Alan Harvey. Freelance writer mag. fiction and jour. essays, studies, articles, 1945-54. Served with USMCR, 1943-45. Mem. Sci. Fiction Writers Am. Author numerous books including: Pleasure Was My Business, 1961; Dynamic Selling, 1962; Squaresville Jag, 1965; Beyond Human Understanding, 1966; The Cosmozoids, 1966; Clairvoyant Strangers, 1968; Cairo Madam, 1969; Black Brute, Runaway Slave and Slave's Revenge, 1969; ESP Forewarnings, 1969; Song of Africa, 1969; Panther John, 1970; Clairvoyant Women, 1970; The Mind Code, 1972; Supernatural Warnings, 1972. Address: 440 E Dilido Dr Miami Beach FL 33139

TRAMMEL, CHARLES BUFORD, JR., savs. and loan exec.; b. Washington, N.C., Nov. 13, 1927; s. Charles B. and Annie (Hurst) T.; A.A., Mars Hill Coll., 1946; B.B.A., Wake Forest Coll., 1951; student N.C. State Coll., 1949, Ind. U., 1962; m. Sarah Hamrick, Oct. 12, 1952 (dec. Nov. 1962); children—Lucy Dawn, Sarah Beth, John Charles; m. 2d, Kate Harris, Sept. 12, 1964; 1 dau., Anna Alexander. Adjuster, Wachovia Bank & Trust Co., Salisbury, N.C., 1951; examiner Fed. Home Loan Bank, Greensboro, N.C., 1951-54; v.p., sec.-treas. Elkin-Jonesville Bldg. & Loan Assn., Elkin, N.C., 1954-70, chief exec. officer, 1962-70; exec. v.p., mng. officer First Fed. Savs. & Loan Assn., Hendersonville, N.C., 1970—. Co-chmn. United Fund, Elkin, N.C., 1962; finance chmn. Henderson-Transylvania County dist. Daniel Boone council Boy Scouts Am. Bd. dirs. Henderson County United Fund, Hendersonville C. of C. Trustee Mars Hill Coll. Served with USNR, 1946-48. Mem. N.C. Assn. Realtors, Baptist. Kiwanian (dir. 1963-66), Rotarian (dir. Henderson County). Home: PO Box 291 Hendersonville NC 28739 Office: 1125 White Pine Dr Hendersonville NC 28739

TRAMONTE, DOMINICK SAM, JR., apparel co. exec.; b. Galveston, Tex., Nov. 16, 1932; s. Dominick Sam and Ida (Jenkins) T.; LL.B., U. Tex., 1958; B.S. in Commerce cum laude, St. Edward's U., 1954; m. Rosalee Fewell, Aug. 25, 1956; children—Dominick Sam III, Mary Catherine, Christopher Joseph, Sharon Marie. Admitted to Tex. bar, 1958; sr. partner Tramonte & Tramonte, Attys. at Law, Galveston, 1958—; pres. Tray-Dart, Inc., Galveston, 1959—, Indcom, Inc., Galveston, 1962—; pres., chmn. bd. Dickson-Jenkins Mfg. Co., Ft. Worth, 1969—. Chmn., Galveston Traffic Adv. Com., 1963—; pres. UNICO Nat., 1960-64. Bd. dirs. Del Barto-Tramonte Found. Named Outstanding Young Man of Am., Montgomery (Ala.) C. of C., 1966. Fellow Am. Mgmt. Inst.; Mem. Am. Apparel Mfrs. Assn., Western Apparel and Equipments and Mfrs. Assn. (award 1972, v.p. 1971—), Ft. Worth C. of C., Galveston C. of C. (chmn. housing com. 1971—, dir.). K.C. (4 deg.), Lion. Home: 2623 Christopher St Galveston TX 77550 Office: 2127 Broadway Galveston TX 77550 also 202-08 St Louise Av Ft Worth TX 76101

TRANSUE, DONALD WALTER, oral surgeon; b. Tamaqua, Pa., Aug. 10, 1930; s. Walter and Dorothy (Roth) T.; B.S., East Stroudsburg State Coll., 1952; D.D.S., U. Pa., 1960, postgrad. 1960-61; postgrad. resident in oral surgery Bryn Mawr Hosp., 1961-62, Pa. Hosp., Phila., 1962-64; m. Michele Bonneau Goyette, May 22, 1965; children—Stephanie, Jacqueline, Donald Walter II. Oral surgeon, Miami, 1964—, Coral Gables, Fla., 1968—. Pres., Progress Club of Miami, 1971-72. Bd. dirs. Hearing and Speech Center, Coral Gables, Papanicolaou Cancer Research Inst. at Miami. Served with USCGR, 1952-56. Diplomate Am. Bd. Oral Surgeons. Mem. Am., Fla. (pres. elect 1971-72) socs. oral surgeons, Am., Fla., Fla. East Coast, South Dade, Miami (sec. 1971-72) dental socs., Greater Miami Dental Study Group (sec. 1971-72). Kiwanian (chmn. physically handicapped youth com. 1969-70). Home: 7740 SW 70th St Miami FL 33143 Office: Huntington Med Bldg 168 S E 1st St Miami FL 33131 also 147 Alhambra Circle Coral Gables FL 33134

TRAPOZZANO, VINCENT RUDOLPH, dentist; b. Jersey City, Aug. 15, 1903; s. Vincent and Maria (Juliana) T.; student Valparaiso U., 1923-25, Northwestern U., 1925-27; D.D.S. (fellow in prosthodontics), Med. Coll. Va. Sch. Dentistry, 1931; m. Ruby Fisher Hutchins, Oct. 12, 1960; 1 dau., Barbara (Mrs. James Gerald Simmons). Practice dentistry, Jersey City, 1935-38, N.Y.C., 1939-44, Portsmouth, Va., 1944-45, Phila., 1946-48, New Port Richey, Fla., 1948-54, St. Petersburg, Fla., 1954—. Instr. Med. Coll. Va. Sch. Dentistry, 1931-33; head prosthodontics dept. N.Y. U., 1933-44, U. Pa., 1945-48; dir. postgrad. courses U. Pa., 1945-48; cons. prosthodontia dept. med. and surgery VA Central office, Washington, Fed. Bldg., St. Petersburg, Fla., Bay Pines (Fla.) Med. Center. Diplomate Am. Bd. Prosthodontics. Fellow Royal Soc. Health London (Eng., hon.), Greater N.Y. Acad. Prosthodontics, A.A.A.S., Am. Coll. Prosthodontists; mem. Am. Dental Assn., Fla. Dental Soc., Acad. Denture Prosthetics, Fla. Prosthetics Soc., Fla. Cleft Palate Assn., Xi Psi Phi, Omicron Kappa Upsilon. Mason (Shriner), Elk. Clubs: St. Petersburg Yacht, Wyoming Antelop (St. Petersburg). Author: (with M.G. Swenson) Complete Dentures, 1940. Editor: Review of Dentistry for State Board Examinations, 1960. Contbr. articles to profl. jours. Home: 1909 Brightwaters Blvd St Petersburg FL 33704 Office: 3900 Central Av St Petersburg FL 33711

TRASK, JOHN MAURICE, JR., banker; b. Wilmington, N.C., Oct. 12, 1935; s. John Maurice and Flora Murphy (Graham) T.; A.B., Davidson Coll., 1958; M.B.A., Harvard, 1964; m. Caroline Whitehead Clark, Apr. 15, 1961; children—John Maurice III, Carolina Clark, Samuel Clark, Patrick Graham. Asst. dir. alumni pub. relations dept. Davidson (N.C.) Coll., 1959-60; mgr. Kane Island Farms, Beaufort, S.C., 1960-62; pres. Beaufort Broadcasting Co., 1964—, First Carolina Bank, Beaufort, 1971—; dir. W.S. Clark & Sons, Inc., Tarboro, N.C. Vice pres. Beaufort County Open Land Trust, 1971—; chmn. Lowcountry Regional Planning Commn., 1970-71, mem., 1970—; mem. City Planning Commn. Beaufort, 1967-69; chmn. fine arts com. Beaufort Mus., 1969—. Alternate del. Democratic Nat. Conv., 1968; Trustee Francis Marion Coll., Florence, S.C. Coll. Charleston (S.C.), 1970—, Davidson Coll., 1970—. Served to 1st lt. AUS, 1958-59. Mem. Davidson Coll. Alumni Assn. (pres. 1969-70). Home: PO Box 1063 Beaufort SC 29902 Office: PO Box 230 Beaufort SC 29902

TRAUGHBER, CHARLES EDWARD, traffic exec.; b. Irvin, Ky., June 19, 1923; s. Barney Edward and Ann K. (Lamb) T.; student Ind. U., 1957-60; m. Clara M. Clunie, June 10, 1945; children—Stephen Lee (dec.), Michael Edward, Pamela Ann. Dispatcher, Pa. R.R., Louisville and Indpls., 1940-46, chief clk., 1946-52; rate compiler Central and So. Motor Freight Tarriff Bur., Louisville, 1952-59, exec. asst., 1959-62, gen. mgr., 1962-65; asst. gen. traffic mgr. Tube Turns Div., Chemetrom Corp., Louisville, 1965-69, gen. traffic mgr., 1969—. Dist. chmn., mem. exec. bd., v.p. George Rogers Clark Council, Boy Scouts Am., New Albany, Ind., 1952-65. Served with USNR, 1941-42. Mem. Louisville Transp. Club, Ky. World Commerce Council. Presbyn. (elder). Mason. Home: 1650 Coes Lane New Albany IN 47150 Office: 28th and Broadway PO Box 987 Louisville KY 40201

TRAUTMAN, JOHN R., dir. Leprosarium, USPHS Hosp., Carville, La. Address: USPHS Hosp Carville LA 70721*

TRAUTSCHOLD, JEROME FRANCIS, furniture co. exec.; b. Waco, Tex., Mar. 11, 1909; s. Charles Martin and Marie Antoinette (Muhl) T.; grad. parochial schs.; m. Wilma Ann Adam, Oct. 23, 1930; children— Jeannette (Mrs. William E. Brown), Jerome Francis, Marilyn (Mrs. John B. Tolle). With C.M. Trautschold Co., Inc., Waco, Tex., 1926—, sec. bd. dirs., 1934—, v.p., 1966—. Bd. dirs. Lighthouse for Blind; bd. dirs. Providence Hosp. Adv. Bd., Waco, 1970—, 2d v.p., 1971—. Decorated knight Equestrian Order Holy Sepulchre. Roman Catholic. Clubs: Serra, Ridgewood Country. Home: 2515 Arroyo Rd Waco TX 76710 Office: 1500 Franklin Av Waco TX 76703

TRAVIS, CHARLES JUNIOR, furniture mfg. co. exec.; b. Newton, N.C., May 20, 1935; s. Charles Ralph and Shirley Kate (Stallings) T.; B.A., Lenoir Rhyne Coll., 1958; postgrad. N.C. State U., 1965; m. Shelby Jean Crawford, Dec. 4, 1954; children—Jeffrey Todd, Kevin Charles. Indsl. engr. Hickory Fry Furniture Co., Hickory, N.C., 1961-63; area coordinator Indsl. Extension Service Sch. Engring., N.C. State U., Raleigh, 1963-68; mgmt. cons. Henderson, Lindsay & Michaels Inc., Greenville, S.C., 1968-69; plant mgr. Hibriten Chair Co., Lenoir, N.C., 1969-72, also dir.; dir. mfg. Stanley Furniture Co. div. Mead Interior Furnishings, 1972—; sec.-treas., dir. B & K Frame Co., Hickory. Chmn., Cancer Crusade, Hickory, 1971; vice chmn. adv. com. Caldwell Community Coll., Lenoir, 1970, chmn. adv. com., 1971; mem. N.C. Adv. Council on Vocational and Tech. Edn., 1972—. Pres., Young Democratic Club, Catawaba County, 1971. Served with AUS, 1953-55. Mem. Am. Inst. Indsl. Engrs. (sr., program chpt. chmn. 1970, pres. 1972). Baptist. Moose. Author: Product Cost Estimating and Feasibility Guide, 1966. Contbr. articles to trade jours. Home: 1065 20th Av NW Hickory NC 28601 Office: 346 3d Av NW Hickory NC 28601

TRAVIS, NEVENNA TSANOFF (MRS. DON C. TRAVIS), realtor; b. Houston, Apr. 16, 1916; d. Radoslay Andrea and Corrinne (Stephenson) Tsanoff; B.A. with distinction, Rice Inst., 1936; M.A., U. Wis., 1938; m. Don C. Travis, June 13, 1940; children—Neven Don Tsanoff, Andrew David Tsanoff. Asso., Bob Bright, Austin, Tex., 1955-57, Ann Miller Crockett, Austin, 1957-66; owner N. T. Travis Real Estate, Austin, 1966—. Pres. P.T.A. Am. Dependents Sch., Berlin, Germany, 1952-53. Charter bd. dirs. Tex. System Natural Labs., Inc., sec. bd. 1967-69, treas., 1969—. Recipient Salesman of Yr. 1962 award Austin Real Estate Bd., 1963. Mem. Austin Real Estate Bd. (pres. women's council 1962), Nat. Assn. Real Estate Bds. (women's council), Soc. Certified Master Brokers and Certified Master Salesmen (mem. bd. dirs. 1961-64; sec.-treas. 1964; pres. 1965), Tex. Assn. Realtors (chmn. edn. promotion commn. 1963, historian 1964-69), University Ladies, Pan-Am. Round Table, Phi Beta Kappa. Address: 900 Bluebonnet Lane Austin TX 78704

TRAWICK, HENRY PHILIPS, JR., lawyer; b. Balt., July 20, 1926; s. Henry Philips and Margaret (Porterfield) T.; student N.C. State Coll., 1946-48; LL.B., U. Fla., 1950; m. Louise Jones, Dec. 20, 1949. Admitted to Fla. bar, 1950, practiced in Lakeland, 1951-56, Sarasota, 1956—; mem. firm Millican & Trawick 1966—. Vice chmn. Fla. Law Revision, 1967-69, chmn. 1969-72; atty. Sarasota County Sch. Bd., 1961-65. Served with USAAF, 1944-45. Mem. Am., Sarasota County bar assns., Fla. Bar. Home: 2300 Sunnyside Lane Sarasota FL 33579 Office: 2051 Main St Sarasota FL 33577

TRAWICK, JACK DURWARD, wholesale distbg. co. exec.; b. Brownwood, Tex., Dec. 17, 1932; s. Evans Ramah and Josephine (Harwell) T.; B.S., U.S. Mil. Acad., 1955; M.S., U. Tex., 1961, Carnegie Inst. Tech., 1964; m. Virginia Hallum, June 18, 1955; children—Jack David, Virginia Adele, Roy Hallum. Cons. engr. Frank T. Drought, engrs., San Antonio, 1958-59; comptroller, dir. operations San Antonio Fair, Inc., HemisFair 68, 1965-68; v.p., gen. operations mgr. Straus Frank Co., San Antonio, 1968—. Packmaster, Alamo Area council Boy Scouts Am., 1965-68; chmn. adminstrn. com. Straus-Frank Co. Profit-Sharing and Pension Trust, 1971—. Bd. dirs. Alamo council Camp Fire Girls. Served to 1st lt. AUS, 1955-58. Recipient Lillian Gilbreth Mgmt. award U. Tex., 1961. Mem. Tex. Mfrs. Assn. (chmn. nat. affairs com. 1972-73), San Antonio C. of C. (chmn. urban improvements com. 1967), Sigma Iota Epsilon. Methodist. Kiwanian. Home: 707 Firefly Dr San Antonio TX 78216 Office: 1964 S Alamo St San Antonio TX 78292

TRAWICK, JOHN DAVID, JR., physician; b. Louisville, May 20, 1911; s. John David and Emma (Kendrick) T.; B.S., U. Louisville, 1933, M.D., 1936; m. Vesta Margaret Irwin, Mar. 21, 1946; children—Margaret Jane (Mrs. Robert Keith Egnor), Nancy Kathleen, John Irwin, David Roy. Intern, Louisville Gen. Hosp., 1936-37, resident internal medicine, 1937-40; commonwealth fellow psychiatry Henry Phipps Psychiat. Clinic, Johns Hopkins Hosp., Balt., 1940-43; practice medicine specializing in psychiatry, Louisville, 1946—; mem. staff Our Lady of Peace, Ky. Bapt. hosps.; clin. prof. psychiatry U. Louisville, 1969—. Fellow A.C.P., Am. Psychiatry Assn., Am. Coll. Psychiatrists; mem. A.M.A., So. Psychiatry Assn. (past pres.), Central Neuropsychiat. Assn., Assn. for Research in Nervous and Mental Disease. Home: 89 Indian Hills Trail Louisville KY 40207 Office: 332 W Broadway Louisville KY 40202

TRAWICK, WILLIAM GEORGE, educator; b. Sandersville, Ga., Aug. 16, 1924; s. George Thomas and Ruth (Turk) T.; B.S., Ga. Sch. Tech., 1948; Ph.D., Ga. Inst. Tech., 1955; m. Margaret Gheesling, Aug. 7, 1948; children—Robert Jesse, Charles David. Chemist, Union Carbide Chem. Co., Oak Ridge, 1954-58; asso. prof. chemistry La. Poly. Inst., Ruston, 1958-61; prof. chemistry, Ga. State U., Atlanta, 1961—, chmn. dept. chemistry, 1962—. Mem. Ga. Sci. and Tech. Commn. Served with Signal Corps, AUS, 1943-46. Mem. Am. Chem. Soc. (program chmn. Ga. sect. 1968, chmn. 1969, exec. com. 1970—), Am. Assn. Clin. Chemists, Ga. Acad. Sci., Danforth Asso., A.A.A.S., Sigma Xi. Baptist (deacon). Home: 2479 Burnt Leaf Lane Decatur GA 30033 Office: 33 Gilmer St SE Atlanta GA 30303

TRAYLOR, DONALD REGINALD, educator; b. Shreveport, La., Aug. 14, 1937; s. Guy Kirby and Eva (Hunt) T.; B.A., U. Tex., 1959; M.S., Auburn U., 1960, Ph.D., 1962; m. Jacqueline Pearson, June 4, 1959; children— Chapman Parker, Kirby Russell, Pearson Hunt. Asst. prof. math. Auburn (Ala.) U., 1962-63; asst. prof. math. U. Houston, 1963-65, asso. prof. math., 1966—, chmn. dept. math., 1965-69, prof. math., 1971—. Adminstrv. intern Am. Council on Edn., 1971. Mem. Am. Math. Soc., Math. Assn. Am., Sigma Xi, Phi Kappa Phi, Pi Mu Epsilon, Phi Alpha Theta. Contbr. articles to profl. jours. Home: 510 Lombardy St Sugar Land TX 77478

TRAYLOR, ORBA FOREST, lawyer, economist, educator; b. Providence, Ky., June 16, 1910; s. Eddie Ewing and Dillie (Stuart) T.; B.A., Western Ky. U., 1930; M.A., U. Ky., 1932, Ph.D., 1948; J.D., Northwestern U., 1936; m. Josephine Zananiri, Nov. 17, 1945; children—Joseph Marion, Robert Forest, John Christopher. Head dept. econs. Ashland Coll., 1935-36; legal asst. trust dept. 1st Nat. Bank, Chgo., 1936-37; asso. prof. econs. and sociology Western Ky. U., 1938-40; research asst. Bur. Bus. Research, U. Ky., 1939; research dir. Ky. Legislative Council, 1939-41; admitted to Ky. bar, 1941; dir. research and statistics Ky. Dept. Welfare, 1941; asso. econ. analyst div. tax research U.S. Treasury Dept.,1942; acting chief accounting UNRRA, Balkan Mission, 1944-45; asst. prof. econs. and bus. U. Denver, 1946-47, U. Mo., 1947-50; tax specialist, asst. econ. commr. ECA, Greece, 1950-53; coordinator exec. devel. programs Ordnance Corps, Dept. Army, 1954; pub. finance expert UN, also lectr. financial adminstrn. Inst. Pub. Adminstrn., Egypt, 1954-56; exec. asst. to lt. gov. Ky. Legislative Research Commn., Frankfort, 1956-58; commr. finance State of Ky., Frankfort, 1958-59; dir. finance Office High Commr. Ryukyu Islands, 1960-64, dir. econ. affairs, 1964-65; prof. econs. and pub. adminstrn. U. Ala., Huntsville, 1965—, chmn. dept. bus. and pub. adminstrn., 1966-68, chmn. econs., 1968-70. Cons. operations research Johns Hopkins, 1957-61; fiscal cons. various orgns.; vis. lectr. econs. various univs. and colls.; lectr. U. Md. Far East Div., 1960-65; sr. adviser Bank of Ryukyus, 1960-65; Joint Fgn. Investment Bd., 1964-65; chmn. bd. Ryukyuan Devel. Loan Corp., 1960-65, Joint Petroleum Bd., 1960-65; counsellor Oak Ridge Asso. Univs., 1966-67. Mem. Ala. Edn. Study Commn. Financial Task Force, 1968-69. Served with AUS, 1942-46; lt. col. Res. (ret.). Mem. Am., So. econ. assns. Am. Soc. for Pub. Adminstrn. (council 1967—), Am., Ky. bar assns., Nat. Tax Assn. (dir. 1971-73), Res. Officers Assn., Beta Gamma Sigma, Delta Sigma Pi. Rotarian. Editorial Bd.: Pub. Adminstrn. Rev., 1972—. Contbr. articles to profl. publs. Address: U Ala PO Box 1247 Huntsville AL 35807

TRAYNHAM, WADE LANIER, dentist; b. Hampton, Va., Sept. 5, 1906; s. William Henry and Lilly (Tuck) T.; student Randolph-Macon Coll., 1925-28; D.D.S., Med. Coll. Va., 1932; m. Irene Sigler, June 5, 1935; children—Mary (Mrs. Robert F. Brosnan), Wade L., Benjamin L. Practice gen. dentistry, Phoebus, 1932-68, Hampton, 1932-40, 68—. Med. adviser Selective Service System, 1948—; mem. Elizabeth City County Electoral Bd., 1938-59, Hampton Sch. Bd., 1959-62, vice chmn., 1962-64; vice chmn. Eastern dist. Boy Scouts Am., 1944, chmn. Peninsula dist., 1945. Trustee Zeta Lodge Inst., Ashland, Va. Served to 1st lt. Dental Corps, AUS, 1941. Recipient Civic Community Service award, 1969, Dixie Hosp. award, 1972. Mem. Am., Peninsula (pres.), Va. dental socs., Am. Boxwood Soc., Kappa Alpha, Psi Omega. Methodist (trustee, chmn. adminstrv. bd.). Rotarian, Elk. Developer several dwarf boxwood cultivars. Home: 103 S Bowood St Hampton VA 23369 Office: 90 S Boxwood St Hampton VA 23369

TREADO, PAUL ALBERT, physicist; b. Ironwood, Mich., Mar. 6, 1936; s. Albert Isaac and Elizabeth (Gerard) T.; B.S., U. Mich., 1958, M.S., 1959, Ph.D., 1961; m. Jean Ann Butterer, Feb. 5, 1959; children— Christopher, Todd, Patrick, Daniel, Kerstin, Colin. Instr., U. Mich., 1961; asso. prof. Georgetown U., Washington, 1962—; cons. specialist in nuclear physics U.S. Navy Dept., 1962—. Cons., High Voltage Engring. Corp., Burlington, Mass., U. W.Va., Canberra Industries, Middletown, Conn., Oak Ridge Tech. Equipment Corp. Mem. Am. Phys. Soc., A.A.A.S., N.Y. Acad. Sci., Sigma Xi, Tau Beta Pi, Phi Kappa Phi. Roman Catholic. Author: (with W. Bygrave and J. Lambert) Accelerator Nuclear Physics, 1970. Home: 828 Loxford Terrace Silver Spring MD 20901

TREECE, RAYMOND JOSEPH, coll. pres.; b. Louisville, Mar. 2, 1912; s. Joseph Martin and Catherine (Glenn) T.; student St. Charles Coll., 1930-32; A.B., Catholic U., 1934, M.A., 1935 Asst. rector Cathedral, Louisville, 1939-50; asso. editor Record, Louisville, 1947-50; instr. Nazareth Coll., Louisville, 1939-50; v.p. Bellarmine Coll., Louisville, 1950-72, pres., 1972—. Dir. radio and television Louisville Archdiocese, 1947-67; archdiocesan consultor Liturgical Commn. of Archdiocese, 1965-67. Mem. So. Assn. Coll. and Univ. Bus. Officers. K.C. (4 deg.). Author: In Praise of Mary. Home: 1 Lenihan Hall Bellarmine Coll Louisville KY 40205

TREEN, DAVID CONNER, lawyer; b. Baton Rouge, July 16, 1928; s. Joseph Paul and Elizabeth (Speir) T.; B.A., Tulane U., 1948, LL.B., 1950; m. Dolores Yvonne Brisbi, May 26, 1951; children—Jennifer Anne, David C. and Cynthia (twins). Admitted to La. bar, 1950; with firm Deutsch, Kerrigan & Stiles, New Orleans, 1950-51; v.p. Simplex Mfg. Corp., New Orleans, 1952-57; mem. firm Beard, Blue, Schmitt & Treen, New Orleans, 1957—. Republican candidate for Congress from 2d Congl. dist. La., 1962, 64, 68, candidate gov., 1972; del. Nat. Rep. Conv., 1964, 68, chmn. La. delegation, 1968, 72, mem. Rep. State Central Com., 1962—; chmn. Jefferson Parish exec. com., 1962-67; chmn. met. polit. action council La. Rep. party, 1966—; Rep. nat. committeeman, 1972—. Served as 1st lt. USAF, 1951-52. Mem. La. Bar Assn., Order of Coif, Phi Delta Phi, Kappa Sigma. Methodist. Clubs: Metairie (La.) Country. Home: 430 Dorrington Dr Metairie LA 70005 Office: 833 Howard Av New Orleans LA 70113

TREGO, LAWRENCE ORLIN, clothing co. exec.; b. Woodward, Okla., July 25, 1921; s. George Laverne and Leatress Lovilla (Wright) T.; student U. Okla., 1939-40; m. Mary Ellen Oates, Jan. 13, 1940; children— Orlin Denney, Terry Dean. With Trego's, Inc., retail men's wear, Woodward, Okla., 1940—, pres., 1948—; v.p. Trego's

Westwear, Inc., Woodward, 1948—; owner Trego's, Enid, Okla., 1954—, Trego's Emporium, Cripple Creek, Colo., 1970—; co-owner Woodward Disposal Co., 1970—; pres. Okla. N.W., Inc., 1963. Vice pres. Gt. Salt Plains council Boy Scouts Am., 1971. Democratic precinct chmn., Woodward, 1971. Served to lt. AUS, 1944-45. Mem. Okla. Retail Mchts. Assn. (v.p. 1968-71), Okla., Woodward (pres. 1958-59) chambers commerce. Mem. Christian Ch. Mason, Elk; mem. Order Eastern Star (past patron). Home: 1805 18th St Woodward OK 73801 Office: 817 Main St Woodward OK 73801

TREICHLER, RAY, agrl. chemist; b. Rock Island, Ill., Sept. 10, 1907; s. Wallace and Pearl (Cushman) T.; B.S., Pa. State U., 1929, M.S., 1929; Ph.D., U. Ill., 1939; m. Kathryn Amelia Blakeley, June 13, 1942. Asst. state chemist Tex. Agrl. Expt. Sta., Tex. A. and M. Coll., College Station, 1929-40; chief Chem. and Biochem. Research Labs., Fish and Wildlife Service, U.S. Dept. Interior, Laurel, Md., 1941-44; chief biol. activities research and devel. div. Office Q.M. Gen., U.S. Army, 1945-53; chief toxic agts. br. Chem. Corps Research and Devel. Comd., Army Chem. Center, Md., 1953-56; asst. to dir. Med. Research Directorate, Chem. Warfare Labs., 1956-58; research adminstr. Services and Support Group, Provisional USAF, 1958-68; mem. staff tech. application H.D. Hudson Mfg. Co., 1968—; vis. scientist U. Ill., Urbana, 1940-41. Fellow N.Y. Acad. Sci., A.A.A.S., Am. Soc. Microbiology; mem. Liebig Chem. Soc., Am. Chem. Soc., Am. Inst. Chemists, Am. Inst. Biol. Scis., Entomol. Soc. Am., Mosquito Control Assn., Am. Soc. Agrl. Engrs., Sigma Xi, Gamma Sigma Delta, Theta Upsilon Omega. Mason. Research in food tech., prevention deterioration, chemistry and formulations fungicides, germicides and pesticides, dissemination systems. Contbr. articles on vitamins, basal energy and endogenous nitrogen metabolism, nutrition, composition fishery products, toxic compounds, prevention material deterioration. Home: 4740 Connecticut Av NW Washington DC 20008 Office: H D Hudson Mfg Co 1625 I St NW Washington DC 20006

TREIRES, JAMES JOHN, govt. ofcl.; b. Johnstown, Pa., Nov. 7, 1924; s. John Elias and Pagona Georgia (Grumbos) T.; B.S., U. Pa., 1947, postgrad. Law Sch., 1947-48; m. Kathryn Jean Costas, Mar. 2, 1946; children—John James, Louis James, Athena Diane. Planning asst. Budd Mfg. Co., Phila., 1948-49; research analyst Gallup & Robinson Research, Princeton, N.J., 1949-50; labor economist Bur. Labor Statistics, U.S. Dept. Labor, Washington, 1950-62; sr. economist Econ. Devel. Adminstrn., Dept. Commerce, Washington, 1962-67; chief manpower forecasting Office Civilian Manpower Mgmt., Dept. Navy, Washington, 1967—. Vis. lectr. manpower trends and occupational outlook to various Eastern colls., 1965, 66. Pres. Claremont Citizens Assn., Arlington, Va., 1963. Served with AUS, 1943-45. Decorated Purple Heart; recipient Superior Performance award Bur. Labor Statistics, 1961. Mem. Am. Econ. Assn., Am. Personnel and Guidance Assn., Nat. Vocational Guidance Assn. Mem. Greek Orthodox Ch. (trustee 1971). Author: Treires for President, 1964. Contbr. articles to various publs. Home: 4916 S 25th St Arlington VA 22206 Office: Dept Navy OCMM Washington DC 20390

TREISTER, KENNETH, architect, artist; b. N.Y.C., Mar. 5, 1930; s. Arthur and Anita (Weinberg) T.; student U. Miami (Fla.), 1948-49; B.Arch., U. Fla., 1953; m. Helyne Bressler, Jan. 31, 1954; children—Charles, Alan, Eliot. One man shows include Mirell Gallery, Miami, Fla., 1964, 66, 67; exhibited in group shows at Greenwich Gallery, N.Y.C., Columbus (Ga.) Mus. Fine Arts, Lowe Art Gallery, Coral Gables, Fla., Houston Contemporary Art Mus., Atlanta High Mus.; represented in permanent collections at Norton Gallery, Palm Beach, Fla., Miami (Fla.) Mus. Modern Art; Fla. Supreme Ct. Bldg. individual practice architecture, Miami, 1957—. Lectr., dept. architecture U. Miami, 1965-66. Chmn. Citizens Adv. Com., Miami, Fla., 1965-67. Bd. dirs. Am. Jewish Com., Dade County Conf. on Urban Affairs, Friends of U. Miami Library. Served with USNR, 1953-57. Recipient 1st prize Nat. Ceramic Exhibit, Lowe Art Gallery, 1953, award elementary sch. design Nat. Assn. Sch. Adminstrs., 1966; Nat. Merit award for chapel Temple Israel Greater Miami, Guild Religious Architecture, 1968; Gold medal for design low-rise elderly housing S.E. Regional Conf. Housing and Urban Devel., 1968. Mem. A.I.A., Guild Religious Architecture, Richard J. Nautra Inst., Blue Dome Soc., Fla. Sculpture Soc., So. Assn. Sculptors, Zeta Beta Tau. Contbr. articles in field to profl. jours. Home: 3660 Battersea Rd Coconut Grove Miami FL 33133 Office: Kenlen Bldg 1460 Brickell Av Miami FL 33131

TRENT, CLAUDE LEON, real estate exec.; b. Sulphur Springs, Tex., Sept. 19, 1926; s. Claude Edwin and Mamie Lee (McDonald) T.; B.S., E. Tex. State U., 1950; m. Ruth Landers, Apr. 1, 1950; children—Scott Lee, Sherri Lynn. With Billy Underwood Co., Dallas, 1954-65, v.p., 1956-65; v.p. Beck Cos., Dallas, 1965-67; v.p. Grove & Trent Constrn. Co., Houston, 1967-68; sr. v.p. Hill Cos., Dallas, 1968—; dir. Hilco Constrn. Corp., Hill Financial Corp., Dallas. Active YMCA. Served with AUS, 1944-46, 61-62. Mem. Dallas C. of C., Dallas Home and Apt. Bldgs. Assn., (pres. apt. builders div. 1971). Baptist. Mason (32 deg.). Office: LTV Tower Dallas TX 75201 Home: 3763 Northhavan St Dallas TX 75229

TRENT, DARRELL MELVIN, govt. ofcl.; b. Neosho, Mo., Aug 2, 1938; s. Clarence M. and Ruth (Cananaugh) T.; A.B., Stanford, 1961; postgrad. Internat. Law Sch., Hague, Netherlands, 1962; Columbia, 1964; m. June Yeardye, Dec. 27, 1964. Pres., Asso. Stores, Inc.; owner, mgr. Trent Enterprises, 1963-69; dep. asst. to Pres., White House, Washington, 1969—. Club: Union League of N.Y.C. Home: 501 W Quincy St Pittsburg KS 66762 Office: The White House Washington DC 20500

TRENT, EVA MAE MANES (MRS. HORACE MAYNARD TRENT), mathematician; b. Bloomfield, Ind., Mar. 11, 1909; d. Charles Edgar and Eliza (Abrams) Manes; A.B., Ind. U., 1930, postgrad., 1931; postgrad. Miss. State U., 1936-37; m. Horace Maynard Trent, July 29, 1933; children—Marilyn (Mrs. Jerome Roger Grunkemeyer), Sandra (Mrs. Charles J. Rothwell). Counselor, Westminster Found., Bloomington, Ind., 1930-31; rate procedures analyst Pub. Service Co. Ind., Indpls., 1931-33; instr. math. Ind. U., Bloomington, 1934; instr. edn. Miss. State U., State College, 1937; mathematician U.S. Naval Research Lab., Washington, 1956—. Mem. Philos. Soc. Washington, Sci. Research Soc. Am., Acoustical Soc. Am., Internat. Oceanographic Found., Zeta Tau Alpha, Gamma Zeta (hon. installation initiate). Contbr. articles in field to profl. jours. Research in atmospheric electricity and its relation to meteorology; U.S. Naval research reports. Home: 413 Tennessee Av Alexandria VA 22305 Office: US Naval Research Lab Washington DC 20390

TRENTIN, JOHN JOSEPH, med. scientist, educator; b. Newark, Dec. 15, 1918; s. Joseph and Angelina (Lavaggi) T.; B.S. (Alan Nutt Meml. scholar 1939), Pa. State Coll., 1940; A.M. (John W. White fellow), U. Mo., 1941, Ph.D., 1947; m. Charline Jenkins, Aug. 29, 1946; children—Jane Louise, Ann Marie. Postdoctoral fellow Yale Med. Sch., 1948-51, instr. dept. anatomy, 1951-52, asst. prof., 1952-54; asso. prof. dept. anatomy Baylor U. Coll. Medicine, Houston, 1954-58; prof., acting chmn. dept. anatomy, 1958-60, prof., head div. exptl. biology, dept. surgery, 1960—; asso. prof. U. Tex. Dental Branch, part-time 1954-60; cons. biology U. Tex. M.D. Anderson Hosp. and Tumor Inst., 1958-62; mem. com. for med. research VA Hosp., Houston, 1960-65. Mem. nat. organizing com. 10th Internat. Cancer Congress, Internat. Union against Cancer, Nat. Head Scis., 1967-70; Mem. adv. com. on pathogenesis of cancer Am. Cancer Soc., 1958-60; bd. dirs. Am. Assn. Cancer Research; mem. com. on tissue transplantation NRC, 1960-70; mem. bd. sci. counsellors Nat. Cancer Inst., 1963-67, chmn., 1965-67; mem. spl. animal leukemia ecology studies com. NIH, 1964-67. Served with AUS, 1942-46. Recipient Esther Langer-Bertha Teplitz award for cancer research Ann Langer Cancer Research Found., 1963; Golden Plate award Am. Acad. Achievement, 1965. Mem. Am. Assn. Immunologists. Am. Assn. for Cancer Research (editorial com. 1970—), N.Y. Acad. Scis., Radiation Research Soc., Soc. for Exptl. Biology and Medicine, Am. Soc. for Exptl. Pathology, A.A.A.S., Am. Assn. Lab. Animal Sci., Am. Soc. Microbiology, Transplantation Soc., Assn. for Gnotobiotics. Roman Catholic. Editorial bd. Transplantation jour., 1962-71; editorial adv. bd. Transplantation Proceedings, 1968—. Contbr. numerous articles to med. jours., also chpts. in books. Home: 4609 Waycross Dr Houston TX 77035

TRENTON, RUDOLPH W., educator; b. Rome, Italy, Aug. 27, 1913; s. Stephen and Frieda Weil; Dr.jur., U. Rome, 1936; Dr.rer.pol., U. Turin (Italy), 1938; postgrad. Columbia, 1947-48; m. Marybeth Langston, May 27, 1947; children—Eloise, Stephen W. Came to U.S., 1939, naturalized, 1942. With Am. Export Co., N.Y.C., 1946-47; faculty Okla. State U., Stillwater, 1948—, prof. econs., 1953—. Dir. Standard Milling Co., Kansas City, Mo. Regional rep. Joint Council Econ. Edn., N.Y.C., 1965—. Served with AUS, 1941-45. Recipient Kazanjian award Kazanjian Found., 1962. Mem. Am., So. (v.p. 1954) econ. assns. Author: Basic Economics, 1964. Home: 1007 Lakeridge Av Stillwater OK 74074

TREUCHEL, ROBERT HERMAN, hotel and restaurant co. exec.; b. Balt., Jan. 27, 1930; s. Herman John and Edna Amelia (Gerken) T.; B.S., U. Md., 1951; m. Lois Helena Koenig, May 9, 1959; 1 son, Robert Paul. Operating mgr. Montgomery Ward Co., Balt., 1951-56; mem. staff labor relations mgmt. Lever Bros. Co., N.Y.C., 1956-59; adminstr. personnel Fair Lanes, Inc., Balt., 1959-62; adminstrv. v.p. Marriott Corp., Washington, 1962—. Served with CIC, AUS, 1953-55. Mem. Nat. Restaurant Assn., Am. Mgmt. Assn., Washington Bd. Trade. Republican. Lutheran. Mason. Home: 14217 Cantrell Rd Silver Spring MD 20904 Office: 4701 Sangamore Rd Washington DC 20016

TREUTING, THEODORE FRANCIS, educator, physician; b. New Orleans, Dec. 26, 1917; s. Henry Louis and Lydia (Waldo) T.; B.S., Tulane U., 1937, M.D., 1941. Instr. to asso. prof. Tulane U. Sch. Medicine, 1948-63, prof. medicine and psychiatry, 1963—; mem. med. review team, La. State Dept. Pub. Welfare, 1958—; psychiat. cons. blind div. La. Dept. Pub. Welfare, 1961—. Bd. dirs. Family Service Soc. New Orleans, 1950-63. Fellow A.C.P.; mem. A.M.A., A.A.A.S., N.Y. Acad. Scis., Am. Psychosomatic Soc., Am. Diabetes Assn., Pan Am. Med. Assn., Am. Heart Assn., Alpha Omega Alpha. Democrat. Lutheran. Contbr. articles in field to profl. jours. Home: 931 Gov Nicholls St New Orleans LA 70116

TREVINO, ELIZABETH BORTON DE, author; b. Bakersfield, Cal., Sept. 2, 1904; d. Fred Ellsworth and Carrie (Christensen) Borton; B.A., Stanford, 1925; m. Luis Trevino Gomez, Aug. 10, 1935; children—Luis Federico, Enrique Ricardo. Lectr., 1942—; corr. Religions News Service, 1940—; staff writer Caminos del Aire, 1960—, also free-lance writer, journalist; hon. lectr. Am. Inst. Fgn. Trade, 1960. Recipient medal Kansas City (Mo.) Women's Commn., 1961; named hon. Texan, 1963. Mem. Author's Guild Am., Am. Hispanic Soc., Phi Beta Kappa, Theta Sigma Phi. Author: (juveniles) Our Little Ethiopian Cousin, 1935, Our Little Aztec Cousin, 1934; About Bellamy, 1940; A Carpet of Flowers, 1955; Nacar, the White Deer, 1963; I, Juan de Pareja (Newbery medal 1966) 1965; Casilda of the Rising Moon, 1966; Turi's Poppa, 1968; Here is Mexico, 1970; Beyond the Gates of Hercules, 1971; (adult books) Memoirs: My Heart Lies South, 1953; Where the Heart is, 1962; (novels) Even as you Love, 1957; The Greek of Toledo, 1959; Fourth Gift, 1966; House on Bitterness Street, 1970. Home: Av Pres Lopez Matos 308 Cuernavaca Mexico Office: Apartado 827 Cuernavaca Morelos Mexico

TREVINO, FELIX B., city ofcl; b. San Antonio; ed. Trinity U.; married; 3 children. Owner, operator Trevino Peinting Co., San Antonio; mem. San Antonio City Council. Chmn. Jobs for Progress, Inc.; formerly pres. Bishop's Catholic Council for Spanish-speaking; pres. elementary and high sch. Parent-Tchr. Councils; formerly chmn. bldg. fund Our Lady of Guadalupe Sch.; vice chmn. South Central dist. Boy Scouts Am. Served with AUS, World War II; ETO. Mem. San Antonio C. of C. (chmn. Sister Cities conv. com.), Am. Legion, Optimists, Holy Name Soc. Address: 3147 W Kirk St San Antonio TX 78226*

TREVINO, LEE BUCK, profl. golfer; b. Dallas, Dec. 1, 1939; s. Joe and Juanita (Barrett) T.; ed. pub. schs.; m. Claudia Ann Fenley, Aug. 24, 1964; children—Lesley Ann, Tony Lee. Head profl. Hardy's Driving Range, Dallas, 1961-65; asst. profl. Horizon Hills Country Club, El Paso, Tex., 1966-67; chmn. bd. Lee Trevino Enterprises, Inc.; touring profl., 1967—; tournament winner Tex. Open 1965, 66, N.M. Open, 1966. U.S. Open, 1968, 71, Hawaiian Open, 1968, Tucson Open, 1969, 70, Nat. Airlines Open, 1970, World Cup, 1969, 71, Brit. Open, 1971, Canadian Open, 1971, Danny Thomas Memphis Classic, 1971, Sahara Internat., 1971, Tallahassee Open, 1971; 6th ofcl. money winner, 1968, 1st money winner, 1970; 1st golfer to have scored four sub-par rounds in U.S. Open Competition, 1968; co-holder of all time low scoring record U.S. Open Competition. Hon. chmn. Christmas Seal campaign, 1969, 70, Nat. Sports Ambassador, 1971; hon. chmn. Trans Pecos Tb and Respiratory Disease Assn.; grand marshal Sun Carnival Parade, 1969-70, 71-72; mem. Pres.'s Conf. on Phys. Fitness and Sports; mem. sports com. Nat. Multiple Sclerosis Soc. Served with USMC, 1956-60. Named Profl. Athlete of Year, 1970, Profl. Golf Assn. Player of Year, 1971, Golf mag. Player of Year, 1971, Sportsman of Year Sports Illus. mag., 1971, Internat. Sports Personality of Year Brit. Broadcasting Assn., 1971, A.P. Male Athlete of Year, 1971; recipient Ann. Hickok Belt award, 1971, Gold Tee award, 1971. Star TV golf program. Home: 10020 Eastridge Dr El Paso TX 79925 Office: PO Box 26854 El Paso TX 79926

TRIBBE, FRANK CALVERT, govt. ofcl., lawyer; b. Ironton, Mo., Feb. 3, 1914; s. Frank A. and Mary (Calvert) T.; student George Washington U., 1935-36; LL.B., Southeastern U., 1940, LL.M., 1941; m. Judith N. Grey, July 22, 1955; 1 son, Alan Maxwell. Admitted to Ark., D.C. bars, 1940, Supreme Ct. bar, 1943; investigator WPA, 1935-40; atty. Office Q.M. Gen., U.S. War Dept., 1940-41; chief litigation officer Office Chief of Engrs., U.S. Dept. of Army, 1941-54; asst. gen. counsel U.S. Information Agy., Washington, 1954—. Spl. editor govt. contracts Research Inst. Am., 1940-43. Served with Judge Advocate Gen., AUS, World War II. Mem. Fed. Bar Assn., Nat. Geog. Soc., Am. Soc. for Psychical Research, Am. Soc. Internat. Law Parapsychol. Assn. Baptist. Club: Nat. Lawyers. Home: 3000 Connecticut Ave NW Washington DC 20008 Office: 1750 Pennsylvania Av NW Washington DC 20547

TRIBBLE, EDWIN, editor; b. Jefferson, Ga., May 13, 1907; s. James E. and Susan (Thompson) T.; ed. Mercer U., 1928; m. Emily Winship Cunningham, Feb. 10, 1930; 1 dau., Emily (Mrs. Franklin A. Hart, Jr.). Reporter, then city editor Macon (Ga.) Telegraph, 1927-33; mem. editorial staff Washington Star, 1933—, city editor, 1949-58, Sunday editor and book editor, 1958—; lectr. journalism Am. U., 1951—. Served with AUS, 1942-46. Home: 3115 Foxhall Rd NW Washington DC 20016 Office: 225 Virginia Av SE Washington DC 20003

TRIBBLE, HAL, editor; b. Anderson, S.C., Jan. 11, 1915; s. James Cowan and Belle (Saylors) T.; B.A. in journalism, U. S.C., 1938; m. Eleanor Hodges, June 6, 1939; children—Michael, Hal Hodges, Anina, Vicki, Elize. Editor Horry County News, 1934-35; reporter Anderson Daily Mail, 1938; editor The Car Owner, 1939-40; city hall reporter, polit. reporter, columnist The Charlotte (N.C.) Observer, 1941-51, asso. editor, 1952-60; editor Asheville (N.C.) Citizen, 1960—. Served as lieut. (j.g.), USNR, 1944-45; PTO. Mem. C. of C., V.F.W., N.C. Editorial Writers (pres. 1957, mem. exec. com.), Am. Soc. Newspaper Editors. Democrat. Presbyn. Clubs: Asheville Country, Mountain City. Home: 3 Hillcrest Rd Asheville NC 28804 Office: The Asheville Citizen Asheville NC 28802

TRIBLE, WILLIAM MACLOHON, otolaryngologist; b. Washington, July 3, 1924; s. George Barnett and Letha (MacLohon) T.; A.B., Princeton U., 1943; M.D., George Washington U., 1950; M.S., U. Pa., 1956; m. Elizabeth Stuart Henley, Feb. 3, 1956; children—Letha MacLohon II, George Barnett II, Elizabeth Henley, Annadelia Stuart. Surg. intern George Washington U. Hosp., 1950-51; resident otolaryngology Children's Hosp., Phila. 1952; asst. resident, resident otolaryngology Manhattan Eye, Ear and Throat Hosp., 1952-54; fellow tumor surgery of head and neck, 1954-55; asso. otolaryngology Hahnemann Hosp., 1956-58, chief otolaryngology, 1958; attending otolaryngology Sibley Hosp., 1956-58, chief radical head and neck surgery, 1958-59, chief rhinolaryngology, 1960-62, clin. asst. prof. otolaryngology Howard U. and Freedmens Hosp., 1959-66; clin. asst. George Washington U. Sch. Medicine, 1956-58, asso., 1956-60, clin. asst. prof., 1961—; chief otolaryngology Washington Hosp. Center, 1972—; attending staff D.C. Gen., Doctors, Suburban, Arlington hosps.; cons. VA Hosp., U.S. Naval Hosp.; asso. Childrens Hosp. Served in AUS, 1943-46; ETO. Diplomate Am. Bd. Otolaryngology. Fellow A.C.S., Am. Acad. Ophthalmology and Otolaryngology; mem. Am. Laryngol. Assn., Am. Laryngol., Rhinol. and Otological Soc., Am. Soc. Head and Neck Surgery, Am. Bronchoesophagological Assn., Nu Sigma Nu. Republican. Episcopalian. Clubs: Metropolitan, Army-Navy, Chevy Chase Country. Home: 1515 31st St NW Washington DC 20007 Office: 1234 19th St NW Washington DC 20036

TRICE, ETHEL PRESTON WILLIAMS (MRS. WILLIAM HENRY TRICE, JR.), educator; b. New Orleans, Aug. 12, 1921; d. Preston B. and Ethel (Roan) Williams; B.S., La. State U., 1941; M.S. 1946; Ed.D., George Peabody Coll., 1961; student Southwestern Bapt. Theol. Sem., 1944; m. William Henry Trice, Jr., July 22, 1943 (dec. Oct. 1946); 1 son, William Henry III. Dir. women's phys. edn. Hardin-Simmons U., Abilene, Tex., 1942-43, 47-52, McMurry Coll., Abilene, 1952-54; asso. prof. health and phys. edn. Middle Tenn. State U., Murfreesboro, 1955-60, N.E. La. State Coll., Monroe, 1960-63; chmn. women's div. health, phys. edn. and recreation U. Ark., Fayetteville, 1963-65, chmn. div. health edn., 1965—. Mem. Ark Democratic Com. Bd. dirs. Ark Tb Assn., United Fund, Fayetteville; Southeastern area adv. council A.R.C., 1966-69, bd. dirs., 1963-70, chmn. Co. chpt., 1964-65. Mem. A.A.H.P.E.R. (research and devel. commn. 1966-68, So. dist. v.p. for recreation 1964-65, pres. 1970-71, dir. 1963-67, 69—; exec. council sch. health div. 1969—; exec. council recreation div. 1963-67, sch. health research and devel. commn. 1966-68), N.E.A., Ark Assn. Health, Phys. Edn. and Recreation (v.p. 1964-65), Ark. Pub. Health Assn. (exec. council 1967-69) Ark. Edn. Assn., Am. Pub. Health Assn. (research council 1970—), Royal Soc. Health, Am. Sch. Health Assn., Am. Assn. U. Women, Alpha Delta Kappa, Alpha Omicron Pi. Episcopalian. Mem. Order Eastern Star. Club: Altrusa. Home: 828 Skyline Dr Fayetteville AR 72701

TRICE, REGINALD ROBERTS, life ins. co. exec.; b. Thomaston, Ga., Feb. 28, 1907; s. Zack T. and Pearla (Harp) T.; student Harvard Bus. Sch., 1928, Mercer U., 1932, So. Meth. U. Ins. Sch., 1958; m. Frankie Raines, Feb. 17, 1932; children—Fabia R. (Mrs. John F. Rogers, Jr.), Regina R. (Mrs. Jack M. Hawkins). Wholesale distbr. oils and gasoline, 1926-55; div. mgr. Sinclair Oil Corp., 1955-57; chmn. bd. Piedmont So. Life Ins. Co., 1957—; pres. So. Life Ins. Co. Ga., Atlanta, 1957—, also dir., chmn. exec. and finance coms.; pres. Land Developers, Inc.; dir. First Nat. Bank & Trust Co., Macon, Ga., Southern Bell Tel. & Tel. Co. Cons. gasoline and oil marketing; past pres. Altamaha River Devel. Assn., Macon Area Devel. Corp. Past adviser Girl Scouts Am., Macon. Dir. Macon-Bibb County Planning Bd.; mem. Ga. Legislature, 1940-50; chmn. State Hwy. Bd. Ga.; chmn. bd. trustees, Wesleyan Coll.; mem. Com. of 100 Emory U. Mem. Ga. Ind. Oilmen's Assn. (past pres.), Macon C. of C. (past pres.). Methodist (past supt. church sch.; past chmn. stewards). Kiwanian (past pres. Macon). Home: 4860 Forsyth Rd Macon GA 31204 Office: 1197 Peachtree St NE Atlanta GA 30309

TRICHEL, MILTON CLARENCE, JR., lawyer, educator; b. Shreveport, La., Apr. 7, 1908; s. Milton Charles and Lillian (Hall) T.; B.S., Centenary Coll., 1930; J.D., Columbia, 1932; m. Frances Lou Martin, Mar. 29, 1938; children—Milton Charles II, Neil Martin, Frances Eileen, David Glynn. Admitted to La. bar, 1933; with firm Foster, Hall, Barret & Smith; sr. partner Smith, Trichel, Malsch & Ballard, Shreveport, 1966—. Instr. bus. law Centenary Coll., Shreveport, 1946—. Mem. task force on guardianship Pres.'s Com. on Mental Retardation; originator Ltd. Legal Guardianship Plan, La., N.Y., W. Va.; co-organizer, 1st pres. Presbyn. Found. of La. Bd. dirs. Booker T. Washington Nursing Home, Shreveport Beautification Found., Nat. Assn. Retarded Children; v.p., bd. dirs., chmn. guardianship com. La. Assn. Retarded Children; co-organizer, 2d pres. Evergreen Presbyn. Vocational Sch.; trustee Noel Found.; trustee Newton & Rosa Smith charitable trust, Shreveport, 1956—; co-planner Garland Episcopal Youth Center. Served to lt. (s.g.) USNR, World War II. Mem. local, state, nat. bar assns. Presbyn. Author legislation for retarded children. Contbr. articles to profl. jours.; author handbook on mental retardation. Home: 184 Ockley Dr Shreveport LA 71105 Office: Slattery Bldg PO Box 294 Shreveport LA 71102

TRIGO-GARCIA, GENEROSO, educator; b. Coruna, Spain, Oct. 15, 1937; s. Trigo and Garcia (Carmen) T.; B.A., Sto de Compostela, Spain, 1958; M.A., Salamanca U., 1960, Ph.D., 1966. Faculty, Cath. U., P.R., Ponce, 1966-68; prof. social sci. dept. U. P.R., Mayaguez Campus, 1968—. Mem. Philosophy Assn. P.R., U. Prof. U.S. and P.R., Ontoanalitycal Assn. Home: Darlington 902 Mayaguez PR 00708

TRIMBLE, LEE SHACKLEFORD, JR., librarian; b. Griffin, Ga., Mar. 14, 1923; s. Lee Shackleford and Effie May (Hutcheson) T.; student U. Fla., 1941-43, Duke, 1943-44; A.B. Journalism, B.A., U. Ga., 1949; M.L.S., Emory U., 1952; m. Mary McKinley Cobb, Dec.

22, 1947; children—Lee Shackleford III, Katherine M., Carlisle C., May H. Head librarian Willow Br. Library, Jacksonville, Fla., 1952-53, Southside Br. Library, 1953-55; dir. Beaufort-Hyde-Martin Regional Library, Washington, 1955-59; dir. Dalton Regional Library (Ga.), 1959—. Pres., P.T.A., 1961-62, v.p. county-wide, 1962-65; active Can Help Telephone Counseling. Served with USMCR, 1943-46. Mem. Ga. (treas. 1962-65), Southeastern library assns., Sigma Chi. Democrat. Presbyn. Home: 206 W Hawthorne St Dalton GA 30720 Office: 101 S Selvidge St Dalton GA 30720

TRIPLETT, EARL HARRISON, banker; b. Greenville, Miss., Aug. 25, 1924; s. Ethel Earl and Myrtle (Harrison) T.; B.S., Miss. State U., 1948; grad. La. State U. Sch. Banking South, 1963; m. Lura Johnson, June 28, 1947; children—Lura Nell, Earl Harrison, Melanie, Rebecca, Charner Edward. Gen. mgr. Mentone Plantation, Greenville, 1948-54; div. controller Mohasco Industries, 1954-59; treas. Memphis Trust Co. and Affiliated Cos., 1959—, chmn., pres., 1967—; pres. Memphis Bank & Trust Co., 1965—; chmn. 1st Nat. Bank, Southaven, Miss., 1967—. Treas. Chickasaw council Boy Scouts Am., 1964-65; pres. Exchange Club, 1961-62. Bd. dirs. United Neighbors, Goodwill Industries; trustee devel. com. Lambuth Coll., Memphis State U. Devel. Found. Served with inf. AUS, 1943-46. Decorated Purple Heart, Silver Star. Mem. Am. (state legis. com. 1969—), Tenn. (chmn. state bank div. 1968-69) bankers assns., Downtown Assn. (dir. 1968-71), Memphis C. of C., Execs. Club Memphis. Kiwanian. Club: University (Memphis). Home: 282 Perkins Ext Memphis TN 38117 Office: 44 N 2d St Memphis TN 38103

TRIPLITT, RUPERT ANTON, food co. exec.; b. Cisco, Tex., Jan. 23, 1918; s. John William and Ethel Mabel (Limroth) T.; B.B.A., Tex. Tech. U., 1941; grad. Advanced Mgmt. Program Harvard, 1958; m. Katharine Andrews, Oct. 30, 1948; children—Rupert Anton, Mabel Claire, Tom Andrews, Katharine Pearce. Salesman, asst. dist. sales mgr. Tom's, Lubbock, Tex., 1939-41; food broker Sanborn-Holmes, N.Y.C., 1946-47; mem. sales staff Toms Food Ltd., Columbus, Ga., 1947-50, sales mgr., 1951-53, v.p. sales, 1958—; also dir.; pres. Columbus Tom's Sales, 1970—; dir. 1st Fed. Savs. & Loan Assn., 4th Nat. Bank, Columbus, Chattahoochee Valley Fair. Mem. Columbus Met. Airport Commn., 1966—; pres. Jr. Achievement, 1958-59. Trustee Walter Alan Richards Found., Columbus. Served to lt. comdr. USNR, 1942-46; ETO, CBI. Mem. Peanut Butter Mfrs. and Nut Salters Assn. (past pres.). Baptist (deacon). Rotarian. Clubs: Columbus Country, Green Island. Home: 2730 Averett Dr Columbus GA 31906 Office: 900 8th St Columbus GA 31902

TRIPP, DAVE CHARLIE, ednl. cons.; b. Colfax, Ia., Nov. 7, 1910; s. Charlie S. and Cora Myrtle (Byers) T.; B.A. No. Ia. U., 1931; M.S., Drake U., 1949; postgrad. U. Ia., 1951-52, Ill. State Normal U., 1962; m. Violet LaVerne Alberts, Oct. 8, 1938; 1 dau., Barbara Ann (Mrs. Allan Harrison). Tchr., Delta (Ia.) Pub. Schs., 1931-34, Monroe Jr. High Sch., Mason City, Ia., 1939-44, Fort Dodge (Ia.) Jr. Coll., 1946-47, Pillsbury Acad., Owatonna, Minn., 1947-48; prin. high schs., Rienbeck, Ia., 1948-51, Clarion, Ia., 1951-53, Atlantic, Ia., 1953-56; ednl. cons. Sci. Research Assos., Inc., Chgo., 1953, 56—. Tchr. vocational and ednl. guidance Stetson U., 1966-67. Served to lt. USNR, 1944-46. Mem. Internat. Reading Assn., Am. Ednl. Research Assn., Internat. Platform Assn., Nat. Council on Measurement in Edn., Phi Delta Kappa, Phi Beta Alpha. Mason; mem. Order Eastern Star, Elk. Address: Apt A-1 1935 S Conway Rd Orlando FL 32806

TRIPP, JOHN ALOYSIUS, architect; b. St. Louis, Oct. 8, 1925; s. George Washington and Ella Frances (Broeker) T.; student U. Miami, 1945-48; m. Sally Frances Hand, Jan. 27, 1946; children—Tim Kenneth, Jane (Mrs. Thomas A. Gribbin III). Partner, Tripp & Skrip, architects and planners, A.I.A., Miami, Fla., 1953—. Mem. City of Miami Housing Appeals Bd., 1962-64; mem. City Council West Miami, 1952-58, pres., 1952. Served to lt. USAAF, 1943-45. Mem. A.I.A. Club: Coral Reef Yacht (commodore 1972-73). Home: 1600 S Bayshore Lane Miami FL 33133 Office: 2973 Coral Way Miami FL 33133

TRIPP, THEODORE LAWTON, trailer mfg. co. exec.; b. New Haven, Apr. 23, 1914; s. Walter Ernest and Carolyn Greenleaf (Furbish) T.; student Furman U., 1932-34, Nat. Advt. Inst., 1936-38; m. Paula Louise Jones, June 4, 1941; children—Theodore Lawton, Sherry, Alan, Susan. Advt. sales mgr. R.H. Donnelly Advt. Corp., 1936-49; motel owner, 1950-56; v.p. Miller Trailers, Inc., Bradenton, Fla., 1952—. Mayor, City of Anna Maria, Fla., 1952-54; chmn. City Zoning Adjustment Bd., 1954—. Served with Signal Corps, AUS, World War II; ETO. Named hon. Ky. col. Mem. Nat. R.R. Piggyback Assn. (dir. allied div.), Anna Maria C. of C. (pres. 1956-58). Episcopalian (vestryman). Lion (past pres. Anna Maria). Home: 903 N Shore Dr Anna Maria FL 33501 Office: 333 6th Av Bradenton FL 33505

TRISDALE, RAYMON, librarian; b. Gainesboro, Tenn., Sept. 11, 1916; s. George F. and Emma (Pharris) T.; student Tulsa U., 1947-49; B.A., U. Okla., 1951; m. Elizabeth Dow, 1951. Librarian, Wakeeney (Kan.) High Sch., 1951-56, Hays (Kan.) High Sch., 1956-58; regional demonstration librarian Mo. State Library, Jefferson City, 1958-59; asst. librarian Keokuk (Ia.) Pub. Library, 1959-60; head librarian Ft. Madison (Ia.) Pub. Library, 1960-61; chief open lit. area Tech. Library, White Sands Missile Range, N.M., 1961-71; chief Logistics Library, Ft. Lee, Va., 1971—. Pres. Miss. Valley Film Co-op, Quincy, Ill., 1961. Served with 90th Inf. Div., AUS, 1942-46. Decorated Purple Heart. Mem. N.E.A., A.L.A., Am. Legion, V.F.W. Democrat. Mem. Ch. of Christ. Mason, Lion. Home: 15017 Horseshoe Bend Dr Chester VA 23831 Office: Logistics Library Fort Lee VA 23801

TRIVIGNO, PAT, artist, educator; b. N.Y.C., Mar. 13, 1922; s. Canio and Agnes (Nardi) T.; B.A., Columbia, 1943, M.A., 1946; m. Helen M. Kohl, Mar. 1, 1944; children—Stephen, Michele. Prof. art Tulane U., New Orleans; one-man shows at Saidenberg Gallery, N.Y.C., Rose Fried Gallery, Seligmann Gallery, N.Y.C.; exhibited in group shows at Whitney Mus., Art Inst. Chgo., Palace of Legion of Honor, San Francisco, Bklyn. Mus., Guggenheim Mus., N.Y.C. Trustee Delgado Mus., New Orleans. Served with AUS, 1943-46; ETO. Home: 1831 Marengo St New Orleans LA 70115

TRIZNA, FRANK BENEDICT, dentist; b. Newark, Jan. 23, 1932; s. Frank Michael and Gertrude (Mileski) T.; student Fairleigh Dickinson U., 1956-58, M.S.D., 1964; D.D.S., U. Pa., 1962; m. Dona Buckner, Dec. 27, 1969; children—Frank Martin, Dane Forrest (dec.). Practice dentistry specializing in orthodontics, Pompano Beach, Fla., 1964—. Served with USNR, 1952-56. Mem. Am., Fla. dental assns., Atlantic Coast, Broward County dental socs., Am. Assn. Orthodontists, Fla. Orthodontic Soc., So. Soc. Orthodontists, Greater Miami Acad. Orthodontists, Am. Soc. Dentistry for Children, Stomatological Soc., U. Pa. Cryer Soc., Pompano Beach C. of C., Eta Sigma Sigma, Omicron Kappa Upsilon. Democrat. Roman Catholic. Lion. Club: Lauderdale Athletic, Pompano Beach Optimist. Home: 370 N W 35th St Boca Raton FL 33432 Office: 2323 NE 26th Av Pompano Beach FL 33062

TROCHE, ALFONSO, petroleum co. exec.; b. San Juan, P.R., Oct. 18, 1937; s. Ildefonso and Dora (Rivera) T.; B.S., N.Y. U., 1959; postgrad. (Community Service Soc. fellow), Columbia, 1959-60; m. Myrtha Ortiz, Feb. 7, 1959; children—Marta Doris, Peggy Ann, Denisse Yvette. Asst. press sec. Office of Mayor City N.Y., 1966-68; pub. relations asst., pub. relations mgr. Esso Standard Oil Co., San Juan, 1968-70, sales supr., 1970—, retail sales mgr., 1971—. Pub. relations cons. Sec. Edn., San Juan, 1968. Served with capt. AUS, 1960-66. Recipient bronze medal for outstanding achievement with Spanish community N.Y.C., City N.Y., 1968. Mem. Pub. Relations Soc. Am., Am. Mgmt. Assn., C. of C. P.R. Lion. Club: Overseas Press (asso. mem. San Juan). Home: C5 Calle Los Frailes Urb Los Frailes Guaynabo PR 00657 Office: GPO Box 4269 San Juan PR 00936

TROGDON, WILLIAM OREN, coll. pres.; b. Anadarko, Okla., Nov. 1, 1920; s. Otis H. and Anna (Jackson) T.; B.S., Okla. State U., 1942; Ph.D., Ohio State U., 1949; m. Altha Florene Tucker, Aug. 2, 1942; children—Stephen William, Patricia Ann. Asst. agronomist, soil scientist Blackland Expt. Sta., Temple, Tex., 1948-49; chmn. dept. agr., dir. soils lab. Midwestern U., Wichita Falls, Tex., 1949-53; agronomist Olin Mathieson Chem. Corp., Houston, 1953-58; prof., head dept. soil and crop scis. Tex. A. and M. Coll., Coll. Sta., 1958-63; exec. v.p. Best Fertilizers Co., Plainview, Tex., 1963-65; dir. agronomy and market devel. Occidental Agrl. Chem. Corp., N.Y.C., 1965-66; pres. Tarleton State Coll., Stephenville, 1966—. Cons. agronomy, 1958-63. Served with AUS, 1942-46. Mem. Am. Soc. Agronomy, Crops Sci. Soc. Am., Soil Sci. Soc. Am., Internat. Soil Sci. Soc. Research on fertilizers, water quality for irrigation, soil fertility, crop mgmt., turf. Home: PO Box 1039 Tarleton Sta Stephanville TX 76401 Office: Tarleton College Stephenville TX 76401

TROTTER, DONALD WAYNE, editor; b. York, Ala., Feb. 19, 1939; s. Israel Leonidas and Hazel (Jackson) T.; A.A., Hinds Jr. Coll., 1959; B.A., U. So. Miss., 1961; m. Gloria Lynn Gillenwater, Dec. 26, 1964; 1 son Gregory Scott. Reporter Jackson (Miss.) Daily News, 1962; editorial writer, asso. editor, mng. editor Bristol (Va.) Herald Courier, 1962-66; instr. journalism U. So. Miss., 1964-65; adminstrv. asst. to Rep. William C. Wampler, 9th Dist. VA., 1967; mng. editor Bristol Herald Courier, 1967-69; urban affairs editor Comml. Appeal, Memphis, 1969-70, urban affairs editor, 1970—. Bd. dirs. Campus Conservative Inc. Served with AUS, 1960. Recipient Freedom Found. Editorial Writing award, 1963. Mem. Memphis Press Club (chmn.), Memphis Gridiron Show, Inc. (exec. chmn.), Omicron Delta Kappa, C. of C. Republican. Baptist. Club: Memphis Press (officer). Home: 1797 St Henry's Pl Memphis TN 38116 Office: Memphis Pub Co Memphis TN 38101

TROTTER, FALLON, exec. editor Mobile (Ala.) Press-Register. Office: 304 Government St Mobile AL 36602*

TROTTER, ROBERT WILLIAM, physician; b. Chattanooga, Oct. 14, 1927; s. Lester Samuel and Gertrude (Cox) T.; B.S., U. Chattanooga, 1952; M.D., U. Tenn., 1954; m. Sadie Sue Eldredge, June 18, 1951; children— Patricia Sue, Jane Ida, Robert William, Nancy Carol. Intern, Crawford W. Long Meml. Hosp., Atlanta, 1954-55; resident Univ. Hosp. and Hillman Clinic Med. Coll. Ala., Birmingham, 1955-59; practice medicine, specializing in surgery, Athens, Tenn., 1959—; mem. staff Epperson Hosp. Mem. McMinn County Bd. of Edn., 1963-71. Bd. dirs. Epperson Hosp., 1961—. Diplomate Am. Bd. Surgery. Fellow A.C.S.; mem. A.M.A. Home: 1208 Woodacres Dr Athens TN 37303 Office: Box 625 Medical Center Athens TN 37303

TROTTER, WARREN KINGSBURY, agrl. economist; b. Largo, Fla., July 12, 1922; s. Guthrie and Lois (Kilgore) T.; B.S., U. Fla., 1947, M.S., 1952; Ph.D., Cornell U., 1955; m. Jane Juanita Havener, June 30, 1950; children—Robert Warren, Lo Ann Leslee. Agrl. economist Farmer Co-op. Service, U.S. Dept. Agr., Washington, 1955-58, Econ. Research Service, Peoria, Ill., 1958-65, Richard B. Russell Agrl. Research Center, Econ. Research Service, Athens, Ga., 1968—; prof. marketing Auburn (Ala.), 1965-66; leader utilization econ. research group Econ. Research Service, U.S. Dept. Agr., Washington, 1966-68. Served with AUS, 1943-46. Decorated Bronze Star medal. Mem. Am. Agrl. Econ. Assn., Am. Marketing Assn. Home: Route 2 Colbert GA 30628 Office: PO Box 5677 Athens GA 30604

TROTTER, WILLIAM EDMUNDSON, II, restaurateur; b. Crowley, La., Aug. 27, 1936; s. James M. and Wahneta (Chigley) T.; student Loyola U., New Orleans, 1954-55, Tulane U., 1955-56, La. State U., 1956-57 children— Melissa, Wahneta, William, Deidre; m. Greta Joyce Rabalais, Apr. 17, 1971. Pres., William Trotter & Son, Rice Brokerage, Crowley, 1957-63; v.p. Self Service Restaurants, Inc., New Orleans, 1963-69, chmn. bd., 1969—; pres. Evangeline Downs, Inc., Lafayette, La., 1970—. Mem. New Orleans Tourist and Conv. Commn., 1971—, Delgado-Albania Plantation Commn., 1970—. Roman Catholic. Home: 1 Cromwell Pl New Orleans LA 70118 Office: 4820 Bradley Dr New Orleans LA 70121

TROTTER, WILLIAM PERRY, lawyer; b. Manchester, Ga., Nov. 2, 1919; s. McKie Massenburg and Tudor (Perry) T.; B.A., Vanderbilt U., 1941; LL.B., U. Ga., 1947; m. Julia Thomason, Aug. 5, 1950; children—Jefferson W., William P. Admitted to Ga. bar, 1947, since practiced in La Grange; sr. partner firm Trotter & Duncan, 1963—; atty. Assn. County Commnrs. Ga., 1962—. Mem. Ga. Senate from 37th Dist., 1951-52, 57-58, Ho. of Reps. from Troup County, 1959; dir. Ga. Dept. Pub. Safety, 1959-61; mem. Dem. Nat. Com. for Ga., 1961-71. Chmn. Ga. Police Acad. Bd., 1961-71. Served to maj. USAAF, World War II. Decorated Air medal. Mem. Am., Ga. bar assns. Home: 323 Lane Circle La Grange GA 30240 Office: La Grange Bank Bldg La Grange GA 30240

TROUTMAN, EDWIN GLENN, physician; b. Olathe, Kan., July 31, 1927; s. Edwin Glenn and Maude Roxanne (Seaton) T.; student U. Ariz., 1944-45, 46-47; M.D., U. So. Cal., 1952; m. Mary Olena Flesher, Sept. 4, 1949, children—Clinton Edwin, David Glenn. Intern, resident Barlow Sanatorium, Los Angeles, 1951-54; resident 1st Med. Div. Bellevue Hosp., N.Y.C., 1955,56; teaching resident fellow Nat. Tb. Assn., Am. Trudeau Soc., 1955, 56; practice medicine, specializing in internal medicine, Ft. Worth, 1961—; mem. staff numerous Ft. Worth hosps.; instr. medicine U. So. Cal., 1954; instr. medicine U. Tex. Med. Br., 1957-59, asst. prof. medicine, 1959-61, asst. to dean of medicine 1957-59, med. dir. outpatient dept., asst. dir. for planning, 1959-60; clin. asst. prof. medicine U. Tex. Southwestern Med. Sch., 1961—; dir. med. edn. and research Harris Hosp., Ft. Worth Found., Ft. Worth, 1961-65; pres. Tex. Allergy Labs., Inc., Med. Computers, Inc., Doctors Operational Computer Service, Inc.; med. dir. Computer Labs. Service, Inc Bd. dirs. Ft. Worth-Tarrant County Heart Assn., N. Tex. Respiratory Disease Assn., Served with USNR, 1945-46. Mem. Am. Diabetes Assn., Am., Tex. State, Tarrant County med. assns., Am. Thor. Soc. Republican. Author various articles pub. in profl. jours. Home: 2026 Ward Parkway Fort Worth TX 76110 Office: 712 7th Av Fort Worth TX 76104

TROUTMAN, MARCUS LLOYD, dentist; b. Iredell County, N.C., Aug. 7, 1882; s. Jacob Calwell and Margaret Louise (Troutman) T.; D.D.S., Atlanta So. Dental Coll., 1917; m. Sudie Steele, May 24, 1911; children— Thelma Marjorie (Mrs. James Augustis Peeler), Julis Beatrice (Mrs. Odis Bennett Summers), Sudie Christine (Mrs. H. Wylie M. Yarborough). With Internal Revenue Dept., Statesville, N.C., 1908-14; practice dentistry, Kannapolis, N.C., 1917—; mem. dental staff Cabarrus Hosp., 1954—. Active P.T.A., YMCA. Mem. Am., Cabarrus dental socs. Rotarian, Mason (Shriner); mem. Order Eastern Star. Republican. Lutheran. Home: 317 S Main St Kannapolis NC 28081 Office: PO Box 162 104 West A St Kannapolis NC 28081

TROWBRIDGE, CYRUS PFEIFFER, judge; b. Ottawa, Ill., Aug. 24, 1928; s. Cyrus Pomeroy and Doris (Merner) T.; B.A., Denison U., 1950; J.D., U. Va., 1953; m. Doris Bittinger, Apr. 4, 1953; children—Teri Anne, Leslie Ellen. Admitted to Va. bar, 1952, Fla. bar, 1956; practiced in Stuart, Fla., 1956-60; circuit judge 19th Circuit of Fla., Stuart, 1960—. Exec. officer group 15 Civil Air Patrol. Served to 1st lt. Judge Advocate Gen. Corps. AUS, 1953-56. Mem. Martin County Bar Assn. (pres. 1960), Martin County C. of C. (dir.), USCG Aux., Scribes. Conglist. Mason. Clubs: Rotary, Stuart Sailfish (trustee). Contbr. to legal and flying publs. Home: 1925 Harbor Point Rd PO Box 445 Stuart FL 33494 Office: Martin County Court House Stuart FL 33494

TROY, CARL WILLIAM, profl. engr.; b. St. Clair, Mich., Aug. 1, 1908; s. John William and Magdalena (Wulf) T.; student U. Detroit, 1927-31; B.S., Chrysler Inst. Engring., 1945; M.S., U. Tenn., 1966; m. Myrtle Muller Bettridge, Dec. 29, 1971. Tool engr., tech. specialist Chrysler Corp., Detroit, 1941-45; owner Sales and Service Agy., Paw Paw, Mich., 1945-55; office engr. John G. Hoad & Assos., Inc., Ypsilanti, Mich., 1955-59; mech. engr. Commonwealth Assos., Inc., Jackson, Mich., 1959-61; sr. contracts engr. TVA, Knoxville, 1961—. Registered profl. engr., Ill., Mich., Ohio, Pa., Tenn. Mem. Am. Soc. M.E., Nat., Tenn. socs. profl. engrs., Knoxville Tech. Soc. Roman Catholic. Home: Route 7 Landoak Lane Concord TN 37720 Office: Union Bldg Knoxville TN 37902

TROYER, RONALD DARREL, physician; b. Bristol, Ind., Nov. 20, 1936; s. Ottis Stanley and Grace Evelyn (Garver) T.; student Fla. State U., 1954-55, U. Fla., 1955-57; M.D., U. Miami, 1962; m. Tammy McGill, May 3, 1958 (div. May 1968); children—Michael Scott, Sherri T., Shelly L.; m. 2d, Nancy Jean Gallo, June 18, 1971. Intern USAF Hosp. Carswell, Ft. Worth, 1962-63; gen. med. officer USAF McCoy AFB, Fla., 1963-66; gen. practice medicine, Sarasota, Fla., 1966—; mem. staff Sarasota Meml. Hosp., 1966-67; coll. physician New Coll., Sarasota, 1967-71. Served to capt., USAF, 1962-66. Recipient Merit certificate Indigent Patient Care, Sarasota, 1968. Mem. Am., Fla. med. assns., Sarasota County Med. Soc., Alpha Kappa Kappa, Phi Delta Theta. Clubs: Boating, Model Airplane (Sarasota). Home: 2408 S Brink Av Sarasota FL 33580 Office: 1953 8th St Sarasota FL 33577

TRUE, CLARENCE HARVEY, civil engr.; b. Boston, Jan. 20, 1893; s. Judson B. and Deborah (Cliff) T.; student Franklin Union, 1910-14, Tufts Coll., 1915; m. Laura E. Robertson, Aug. 13, 1917; children—Mildred, Robert, William, Stanley, Bruce. With Panama Canal Co., 1915-17, Am. Ship Bldg. Corp., 1918-21, Am. Bridge Co., 1922-25; civil engr. Panama Canal Co., U.S. Govt., Balboa, C.Z., 1930-55; structural engr. Ingalls Iron Works, Birmingham, Ala., 1956-58; Rader engr., Miami, Fla., 1959-62; with Weed Johnson, Architect, Miami, 1962-66; with pub. works dept. Coral Gables, Fla., 1965—. Instr. nav. C.Z. Jr. Coll. Extension Div., 1944-46, instr. engring., 1947. Fellow Am. Soc. C.E. Author: Navigation and Astronomic Data, 1948. Home: 1417 Ortega Av Coral Gables FL 33134 Office: Pub Works City Hall Coral Gables FL 33134

TRUE, ROY JOE, lawyer; b. Shreveport, La., Feb. 20, 1938; s. Collins B. and Lula Mae (Cady) T.; student Centenary Coll., 1957; B.S., (scholar), Tex. Christian U., 1961; LL.B. (scholar), So. Meth. U., 1963, postgrad., 1968-69; m. Patsy Jean Hudsmith, Aug. 29, 1959; children—Andrea Alane, Alyssa Anne, Ashley Alisbeth. Admitted to Tex. bar, 1963; practiced in Dallas, 1963—; pres. Invesco Internat. Corp., 1969-70. Bus. adviser, counselor Mickey Mantle, 1969—. Served with AUS, 1956. Mem. Am., Dallas bar assns., Phi Alpha Delta. Editorial bd. Southwestern Law Jour., 1962-63. Home: 4606 Beverly Dr Dallas TX 75209 Office: LTV Tower Dallas TX 75201

TRUELSON, JULIUS GEORGE, III, supt. schs.; b. Dallas, Sept. 18, 1913; s. Julius George and Dorathea (Vandergriff) T.; B.B.A., Tex. Christian U., 1935, M.A., 1939; grad. student U. Colo., N. Tex. State U.; m. Ann Louise Nelson, Aug. 12, 1939; children—Judith Ann, Julius George IV. Tchr., Riverside Jr.-Sr. High Sch., 1936; prin. N. Hi Mount Elementary, also Diamond Hill Jr.-Sr. High Sch., 1947-58; asst. bus. mgr. Ft. Worth pub. schs., 1959-60, asst. supt., 1960-66, supt. schs., 1966—. Chmn. Nat. Acad. Sch. Execs. of Am. Assn. Sch. Adminstrs.; bd. dirs. Ednl. Mgmt. Informational Services; chmn. Tex. Textbook Com. for 1969, Tex. Council Econ. Edn., Tex. Edn. Agy. Served to lt. (j.g.) USNR, 1943-46. Mem. Tex., Am. assns. schs. adminstrs., Tex. Tchrs. Assn., Ft. Worth Adminstrs. Assn. Mem. Disciples of Christ Ch. Kiwanian (pres. Downtown Ft. Worth 1969). Home: 3805 Harlanwood St Fort Worth TX 76109 Office: 3210 W Lancaster St Fort Worth TX 76107

TRUETTNER, WILLIAM H., asso. curator 18th and 19th century paintings and sculpture Nat. Collection Fine Arts. Home: 6702 Hillcrest Pl Chevy Chase MD 20015 Office: 8th and G Sts Washington DC 20560*

TRULL, FRANCIS HAROLD, publisher; b. Rock Hill, S.C., June 11, 1915; s. Lee Roy and Leila Florence (Furr) T.; ed. pub. schs., spl. courses; m. Elizabeth Claire Ammons, May 27, 1934; 1 dau., Jean Andree (Mrs. William Bryan Jennings). Asst. sec.-treas. Charlotte (N.C.) Observer, 1941-56; controller, asst. sec.-treas. Knight Pub. Co., Charlotte, 1956-69, treas., asst. sec., controller, 1969—; treas., asst. sec. Observer Transp. Co., Inc.; pres. Frank Investment Co., Inc. Active Mint Mus. Art, United Community Service activities; treas. Observer Charities. Trustee Charlotte News Empty Stocking Fund. Mem. Inst. Newspaper Controllers and Finance officers (past dir.), Charlotte C. of C. Democrat. Methodist. Mason (Shriner). Clubs: Charlotte City, Carmel Country. Home: 3320 Selwyn St Charlotte NC 28209 Office: 600 S Tryon St Charlotte NC 28201

TRULUCK, JAMES PAUL, JR., dentist; b. Florence, S.C., Feb. 6, 1933; s. James P. and Catherine (Nesmith) T.; D.D.M., U. La., 1958; m. Kay Bowen, July 26, 1958; children—James P. III, David Bowen, Catherine Ann. Pvt. practice dentistry, Lake City, S.C., 1960—; dir. Palmette Bank & Trust Co.; mem. staffs Lower Florence County Hosps. Chmn., Greater Lake City Recreation Commn., 1965—. Del., Republican Conv., 1968. Trustee Florence Mus. Served with USAF, 1958-60. Mem. Am., Pee Dee dental assns., Am. Soc. Dentistry for Children, Am. Soc. Clin. Hypnosis, Delta Sigma Delta, Blue Key. Lion. Home: 114 E Main St Lake City SC 29560 Office: 125 Epps St Lake City SC 29560

TRULUCK, REMBERT SCARBOROUGH, printing exec.; b. Sumter, S.C., Sept. 5, 1910; s. W.Z. and Susan (Boyce) T.; student Internat. Corr. Schs.; m. Mary Frances Scruggs, Sept. 3, 1932; children—Rembert, Georgia J. (Mrs. James M. Cook). Supt., Williams Printing Co., Spartanburg, S.C., 1928-34; supr. pressroom John H. Harland Co., Atlanta, 1934-35; supt. Keys Printing Co., Greenville, S.C., 1944-45, Jacobs Press, Clinton, S.C., 1941-47; owner, operator Truluck Printing Co., Clinton, 1947—. Pres.,

Greater Clinton Community Chest, 1961—; finance chmn. Laurens Assn. Bapt. Assembly, 1955, v.p. brotherhood, 1956-57; organizer Cub Scout pack Boy Scouts Am., Clinton, 1942, cubmaster, 1942-43. Named Citizen of Year, City of Clinton, 1958. Mem. Am., Carolinas printing industries, Clinton C. of C. (pres. 1948-49). Baptist (chmn. bd. trustees). Lion (pres. Clinton 1959-60, dist. gov. 1958-59; mem. bd. internat. counsellors 1959—). Author: Papa and Me, 1965. Home: 104 Woodrow Dr Clinton SC 29325

TRULY, RICHARD H., astronaut; b. Fayette, Miss., Nov. 12, 1937; s. James B. and S. S. Truly; B. Aero. Engring., Ga. Inst. Tech., 1959; m. Colleen Hanner; children—Richard Michael, Daniel Bennett, Lee Margaret. Commd. ensign U.S. Navy, 1959, advanced through grades to lt. comdr.; assigned Fighter Squadron 33, 1960-63; served in U.S.S. Intrepid, U.S.S. Enterprise; astronaut Manned Orbiting Lab. Program, U.S. Air Force, 1965-69; astronaut NASA, 1969—. Office: NASA Manned Spacecraft Center 2101 NASA Rd 1 Houston TX 77001

TRUMAN, LOUIS WATSON, ret. army officer, state ofcl.; b. Kansas City, Mo., June 20, 1908; s. Ralph Emerson and Nancy Louise Truman; student Southwest Mo. State Coll., B.S., U.S. Mil. Acad., 1932; grad. Nat. War Coll., 1949; LL.D., Drury Coll., 1967; m. Margaret Stevenson, June 24, 1934. Commd. 2d lt. inf., U.S. Army, 1932, advanced through grades to lt. gen., 1962, ret., 1967; a.d.c. comdg. gen. Hawaiian Dept., 1941-42, chief of staff 84th Inf. Div., 1944-45, asst. div. comdr., 1945; comdg. officer 223d Inf., 40th Div., 1952-53; asst. div. comdr. 2d Inf. Div., 1953; chief of staff and dep. comdg. gen. 3d U.S. Army, 1953-55; asst. chief of staff Hdqrs. Allied Forces So. Europe, Naples, Italy, 1955-56; chief Mil. Assistance Adv. Group Pakistan, 1956-58; comdg. gen. 4th Inf. Div., Ft. Lewis, Wash., 1958-60, dept. chief staff plans, operations and tng. Hdqrs. Continental Army Command, Fort Monroe, Va., 1960-62; dep. comdg. gen., 1962-63; comdg. gen. VII Corps, Stuttgart, Germany, 1963-65; comdg. gen. 3d Army, Ft. McPherson, Ga., 1965-67; now exec. dir. Ga. Dept. Industry and Trade. Sec. U.S. delegation UN, 1946-47, Army mem. joint strategic plans group of the Joint Chiefs of Staff, 1949-52. Decorated D.S.M., Silver Star with oak leaf cluster, Legion of Merit with oak leaf cluster, Bronze Star Medal with 3 oak leaf clusters, Commendation ribbon with 2 clusters, Asiatic-Pacific Campaign medal with 1 star, Eruopean-African-Middle Eastern campaign medal with 3 stars, Korean Service medal with 3 stars, also numerous other medals (U.S.), Legion of Honor, Croix de Guerre (France), Order of Leopold, Croix de Guerre (Belgium), Order of Orange Nassau (Netherlands). Mason (Jester, Shriner), Rotarian. Home: 3648 Peachtree Rd NE Atlanta GA 30319 Office: Trinity-Washington Bldg Atlanta GA 30334

TRUMBO, CHARLES BASS, lawyer; b. Fayetteville, Ark., Feb. 23, 1935; s. Donald and Juanita (Bass) T.; B.S. in Bus. Adminstrn., U. Ark., 1957, LL.B., 1959; m. Carolyn Kay Wells, Aug. 20, 1955; children—Jay Hamilton, Carolyn Bass. Admitted to Ark. bar, 1959, since practiced in Fayetteville; city atty., Fayetteville, 1961-65; dep. pros. atty. Washington County, 1963-66. Lectr. bus. law U. Ark. Sch. Bus. Adminstrn., 1959—. Pres. Boy Land of Ark., 1969-71. Mem. Washington County Democratic Central Com. 1968—. Chmn. bd. dirs. Fayetteville Creative Sch., 1970-71; bd. dirs. Washington County Sch. for Retarded Children. Served as 2d lt. AUS, 1957. Recipient Distinguished Service award Fayetteville Jr. C. of C., 1969; names One of 10 Outstanding Young Men in Ark., 1969. Mem. Ark., Washington County (pres. 1965-66) bar assns., Fayetteville C. of C. Episcopalian. Home: 925 Kings Dr Fayetteville AR 72701 Office: 31 E Center Fayetteville AR 72701

TRUMP, J. LLOYD, educator, assn. exec.; b. Elkhart, Ind., Dec. 11, 1908; s. Lloyd Samuel and Ruby (Lambert) T.; A.B., DePauw U., 1929; A.M., U. Chgo., 1935, Ph.D., 1943; m. Martha Mary Magill, Aug. 30, 1931. Tchr., prin. Jefferson Twp. Sch., Goshen, Ind., 1929-36; supt. city sch., Marengo, Ill., 1936-37; tchr. and adminstrv. asst. U. of Chgo. High Sch., 1937-40; edn. cons. Nat. Youth Adminstrn., Ill., 1940-41; prin. Horace Mann Sch., Gary, Ind., 1941-44; supt. Twp. High Sch., Waukegan, Ill., 1944-47; faculty mem., head tchr. placement U. Ill., Urbana, 1947-60, chmn. div. sch. adminstrn., 1955-60; asso. sec. Nat. Assn. Secondary Sch. Prins., 1960—, dir. nat. study staff utilization, 1956-63, dir. nat. adminstrv. internship project, 1963-69, dir. nat. model sch. project, 1969—, dir. nat. insts. for secondary sch. adminstrs., 1971—. Fulbright lectr., Pakistan, 1953-54. Mem. research adv. council U.S. Office Edn. Coop. Research Program, 1960-63. Mem. Nat. Soc. for Study of Edn., N.E.A., Nat. Assn. Secondary Sch. Prins., Am. Ednl. Research Assn., Phi Delta Kappa. Presbyterian. Author: Management of Extracurriculum Activities, 1944; The Junior College, 1946; New Horizons for Secondary School Teachers, 1957; Images of the Future—A New Approach to the Secondary School, 1959; New Directions to Quality Education, 1960. Co-author: The American Secondary School, 1952; Focus on Change—Guide to Better Schools, 1961; Focus on the Individual—A Leadership Responsibility, 1965; The Present is Prologue, 1966; Secondary School Curriculum Improvement, 1968. Editor: Education for Freedom, 1950; Education During World Transition, 1951. Contbr. articles to mags. Lectr. U.S., W. Germany, Scandinavia, Netherlands, Eng. Home: 5525 Potomac Av NW Washington DC 20016 Office: 1201 16th St NW Washington DC 20036

TRUNDLE, BENTON MCMAHAN, JR., farmer; b. Boyd's Creek, Tenn., Dec. 24, 1934; s. Benton McMahan and Kathleen Elizabeth (Hammer) T.; B.S., U. Tenn., 1957, postgrad., 1971; postgrad. Va. Poly. Inst., 1964; m. Margaret Andrew Ogle, July 16, 1961. Asst. county agt. Va. Agrl. Extension Service, Blacksburg, 1959-64; farmer, Sevierville, Tenn., 1965—; indsl. arts tchr. Sevier County Bd. Edn., Sevier County High Sch., 1971—. Dir. Sevier Farmers Coop. Bd., 1968—. Mem. Sevier County Livestock Assn. (dir. 1968—), Sevier County Farm Bur. (dir. 1968-70), Alpha Gamma Rho, Alpha Zeta, Kappa Kappa Psi. Presbyn. (deacon 1965—). Lion. Club: Boyd's Creek Community. Address: Route 10 Sevierville TN 37862

TRUSSELL, CHARLES TAIT, journalist; b. Balt., May 9, 1925; s. Charles Prescott and Beatrice (Tait) T.; B.A. in Journalism, Washington and Lee U., 1949; m. Woodley Grizzard, Dec. 27, 1953; children—Galen Tait, Thomas Marshall. Reporter, St. Petersburg (Fla.) Times, also writer Congl. Quar. News Features, 1949-54; reporter Wall St. Jour., 1954-56, Washington Evening Star, 1956; asso. editor Nation's Business mag., 1956-64, mng. editor, 1964-69; sr. editor Congl. Quarterly Inc., 1969-70; dir. pub. relations, advt. Investment Co. Inst., 1970-72; columnist Lakeland Ledger, 1972—; freelance writer, 1972—; producer documentary record album The Best of Washington Humor, 1963. Bd. dirs. Washington div. Am. Health Found. Served with USNR, 1944-46. Recipient Loeb Spl. Achievement award for mags. U. Conn., 1961. Mem. Washington Assembly (exec. com. 1961-65, chmn. 1965), White House Corr. Assn., Sigma Delta Chi, Beta Theta Pi. Clubs: Nat. Press (Washington); Gibson Island; Lakeland (Fla.) Yacht and Country. Editor: (with others). Successful Management, 1964; (with Paul Hencke) Dear NASA Please Send Me a Rocket, 1964. Home: 2414 Woodley Av Lakeland FL 33803

TRYGGVASON, EYSTEINN, educator; b. Iceland, July 19, 1924; s. Tryggvi Sigtryggsson and Unnur Sigurjonsdottir; Cand. Real., U. Oslo (Norway), 1951; Fil. Lic., U. Uppsala (Sweden), 1961; m. Gudny Jonsdottir, Nov. 11, 1954; children—Throstur, Kristinn, Gudrun. Came to U.S., 1962. Head geophys. sect. Icelandic Meteorol. Service, Reykjavik, Iceland, 1952-62; asst. prof. geophysics U. Tulsa, 1962-64, asso. prof., 1964-67, prof., 1967—. Mem. Am. Geophys. Union, Seismological Soc. Am., Am. Meteorol. Soc., Soc. Exploration Geophysicists. Home: 1746 S Darlington St Tulsa OK 74112 Office: U Tulsa Tulsa OK 74104

TRYON, LAWRENCE EDWIN, lawyer; b. Channahon, Ill., Nov. 25, 1899; s. Allison and Mary (Alexander) T.; student Salt City Bus. Coll., Hutchinson, Kan., 1919, LaSalle Extension U., 1920-28, Northwestern U., 1931; m. Mary A. Bradshaw, Apr. 12, 1925; children—Myrna Jewell (Mrs. Monte L. Thomas), Allison Charles, Mary Kathryn (Mrs. Delbert Carter); m. 2d, Eugenia Shaw, June 11, 1963. Admitted to Okla. bar, 1929; county judge Texas County, Okla., 1931-36, county atty., 1937-38; practice law, Guymon, Okla., 1938—; dir. City Nat. Bank & Trust Co., Guymon. Pres. Guymon Meml. Hosp., 1949-72. Republican candidate Supreme Ct. Okla., 1960; del. Rep. Nat. Conv., 1960, mem. Com. Order of Bus. Served with U.S. Army, World War I. Mem. Am., Okla. bar assns. Methodist (pres. trustees, del. gen. conf. 1936). Mason (32 deg., K.T., Shriner), Lion (dist. gov. 1947-48). Home: 6044 Sunset Dr Guymon OK 73942 Office: Profl Bldg Guymon OK 73942

TSCHOEPE, THOMAS, bishop; b. Pilot Point, Tex., Dec. 17, 1915; s. Louis and Catherine (Sloan) T.; student St. Thomas Sch. Pilot Point, 1930, Pontifical Coll. Josephinum, Worthington, O., 1943. Ordained priest Roman Catholic Ch., 1943; asst. pastor in Ft. Worth, 1943-46, Sherman, Tex., 1946-48, Dallas, 1948-53; adminstr. St. Patrick Ch., Dallas, 1953-56; pastor St. Augustine Ch., Dallas, 1956-62, Sacred Heart Cathedral, Dallas, 1962-65; bishop of San Angelo, Tex., 1966-69, Dallas, 1969—. Home: 3915 Lemmon Av Box 19507 Dallas TX 75219

TUBB, LESLIE, dentist; b. Aberdeen, Miss., Dec. 10, 1921; s. Napoleon and Agnes (Davidson) T.; B.S., U. Miss., 1948; D.D.S., Baylor U., 1951; m. Louise Maxcy, Oct. 26, 1943. Practice dentistry, Oxford, Miss., 1953—. Bd. dirs. local chpt. Am. Heart Assn. Served with USAF, 1942-53; Korea, ETO. Mem. Am., Miss., N.E. Miss. dental assns., Omicron Kappa Upsilon, Delta Sigma Delta. Republican. Baptist (deacon 1958-60). Mason, Lion. Home: Campground Rd Oxford MS 38655 Office: 713 S Lamar Blvd Oxford MS 38655

TUBBS, HARRY AUGUSTUS, physician; b. Richmond, Va., Sept. 3, 1914; s. William Johnston and Ruth Churchill (Rennie) T.; student U. Tenn., 1930-33, 34-35; M.D., Med. Coll. Va., 1939; m. Joan Ellis, June 11, 1939 (dec. Sept. 1970); children—Charles Gordon, Elisabeth (Mrs. Frank Schmalstieg). Intern, Scott and White Hosp., Temple, Tex., 1939-40; practice medicine specializing in family practice, Fredericksburg, Tex., 1946-52, Post, Tex., 1952—; mem. staff Garza Meml. Hosp., Post; courtesy staff W. Tex. Hosp., Lubbock; med. dir., lab. dir. Med. Center & Lab., Post, 1956—. Pres., Med. Center Found., 1964—; city health officer Post, 1965—; med. cons. Post Ind. Schs., 1970—. Served with AUS, 1940-46; PTO. Mem. Tex. Acad. Gen. Practice (v.p. 1967, med. liaison officer Tex. Tech. U. Sch. Medicine 1970—), A.M.A., So., Tex. med. assns., Lubbock-Crosby-Garza Med. Soc., Am. Acad. Gen. Practice (award 1969), Am., Tex. diabetes assns. Contbr. articles to profl. jours. Home: 415 N Av M Post TX 79356 Office: 111 N Av I Post TX 79356

TUCK, GRAYSON EDWIN, natural gas transmission exec.; b. Richmond, Va., May 11, 1927; s. Bernard Okly and Erma (Wiltshire) T.; B.S., U. Richmond (Va.), 1950; m. Rosalie Scroggs, June 6, 1947; children—Janice Lorraine, Kenneth Edwin, Carol Lynn. Payroll clk., cost clk. Gen. Baking Co., Richmond, 1948-51; jr. accountant Commonwealth Natural Gas Corp., Richmond, 1951-55, sr. accountant, 1956-57, accounting supr., 1957-58, asst. treas., 1959-62, asst. sec., asst. treas., 1963-64, treas., asst. sec., 1965—; sec.-treas. Air Pollution Control Products Inc., Richmond, 1970—; asst. treas., asst. sec. Commonwealth Gas Distbn. Corp., Richmond, 1969—. Troop sec. Boy Scouts of Am., 1965-69. Served with USNR, 1945-46. Mem. Nat. Assn. Accountants (past asso. dir.), Systems and Procedures Assn. Am. (past treas.). Presbyn. (deacon). Home: 2923 Oakland Av Richmond VA 23228 Office: 200 S 3d St Richmond VA 23219

TUCKER, ALLAN, univ. adminstr.; b. Calgary, Alta., Can., Sept. 29, 1921; s. Frank and Nellie (Chester) T.; B.A., U. Toronto (Ont., Can.), 1943, M.A., 1946; Ph.D., U. Mich., 1952; post-doctoral U. London (Eng.), summer 1955; D.Sc. (hon.), Fla. Inst. Tech., 1971; m. Rebecca Cope Kimber; children—Edwin K., David G. Came to U.S., 1946, naturalized, 1952. Mem. faculty dept. biology Mich. State U., East Lansing, 1946-64, prof., 1963-64, asst. dean advanced grad. studies, asst. to v.p. research, 1959-64; vice chancellor for acad. affairs State U. System Fla., Tallahassee, 1964—, also chmn. council acad. vice presidents, 1964—. Chmn. edn. com. Fla.-Colombia Alliance, 1969—; mem. commn. accreditation service experiences Am. Council Edn., 1969—; sci. adviser to U. Ryukyus, Okinawa, 1953-55, cons. to univ. pres., 1957-59. Mem. exec. com. Gov.'s Commn. for Quality Edn. Fla., 1967; mem. panel to select NATO postdoctoral sci. fellows Nat. Acad. Scis., 1969-71; mem. grad. edn. cost com. Council Grad. Schs. U.S., 1969-71, cons. to council, 1969—. Recipient Leadership certificate Adult Edn. Assn. U.S.A., 1971. Mem. Am. Assn. Higher Edn., Nat. Univ. Extension Assn. (mem. nat. com. on govt. relations 1971—), Adult Edn. Assn. U.S.A. (mem. nat. com. on external degrees 1971), Sigma Xi. Author: Pigment Extraction as a Method of Quantitative Analysis of Phytoplankton, 1949; The Relation of Phytoplankton Periodicity to the Nature of the Physico-Chemical Environment, 1957; Attrition of Graduate Students at the Ph.D. Level, 1964; Decentralized Graduate Administration with Centralized Accountability, 1965; also articles. Home: 2301 Delgado Dr Tallahassee FL 32304

TUCKER, BARNEY ALDEN, fertilizer co. exec.; b. Greeneville, Tenn., Oct. 15, 1915; s. Gilbert Bruce and Mattie (Ottinger) T.; B.S., U. Tenn., 1937; m. Shirley June Warfield Keplar, July 3, 1942; children— Alice, Sarah. High sch. instr., Vonor, Tenn., 1937-38; salesman Knoxville Fertilizer Co. (Tenn.), 1938-48, mgr., London, Ky., 1948-55, v.p., 1955-59; v.p. Jackson Wholesale Co., 1956—; pres. London Motor Car Co. (Ky.), 1957-61, Clay Country Farm Service, Inc., 1954-62, Russell Farm Supply (Ky.), 1957—; v.p. Dean Planters Warehouse, Inc., 1956—; pres., gen. mgr. Burley Belt Fertilizer Co., Lexington, 1962—, Burley Belt Chem. Co., London, 1967—, Southeast Chem. Co., London, 1967—, Laurel Warehousing Co., 1971—; dir. First Nat. Bank, London, Cin. br. Fed. Res. Bank of Cleve., 1961-67. Trustee, v.p. Ky. Ind. Coll. Found., 1955-65; dir. Asso. Industries Ky., 1959—. Pres., Ky. Plant Food Council, 1962-64; mem. Gov.'s Commn. on Agr., 1964—. Served from pvt. to maj. F.A., AUS, 1941-46; PTO. Decorated Bronze Star. Mem. A.I.M., Ky. C. of C. (pres. 1956-57, life dir.), London-Laurel County Devel. Assn. (pres. 1950-51), Southeastern Community Devel. Assn. (pres. 1957-58), Am. Legion, V.F.W., Res. Officers Assn. (pres. Ky. dept. 1951-52). Baptist. Home: 1628 Richmond Rd Lexington KY 40502 Office: Cleveland Rd Lexington KY 40505 also Warehouse St London KY 40741

TUCKER, BENJAMIN NORRIS, judge; b. Senatobia, Miss., June 30, 1913; s. Benjamin Archer and Bessie Agnes (Cinnamond) T.; student Southeastern La. Coll., 1929-31; B.A., La. State U., 1931, LL.B., 1935; m. Dorothy Ann Chauvin, Sept. 15, 1955; children—Judith (Mrs. Frank William Lloyd III). Admitted to La. bar, 1935; practice law, Hammond, La., 1935-63; judge 21st Jud. Dist. La., 1963-70, Ct. of Appeal, 1st Circuit, 3d Dist. La., 1970—. Mem. State Bd. Tax Appeals, 1955-56, Edward Douglass White Meml. Commn., 1952-56; pres. Hammond United Givers Fund, 1960-61. Bd. dirs. A.R.C. Mem. La., 21st Jud. Dist. bar assns., Southeastern La. Dairy Festival Assn., La. Coll. Alumni Assn. (pres. 1939), Delta Kappa Epsilon, Tau Kappa Epsilon, Phi Delta Phi. Democrat. Baptist. Mason, Rotarian (pres. 1958-59). Home: 800 General Patton St Hammond LA 70401 Office: PO Box 1346 Hammond LA 70401

TUCKER, CHARLES CLEMENT, artist; b. Greenville, S.C., Sept. 13, 1913; s. Charles Earl and Myrtle (Clement) T.; student N.Y. Art Student League, 1933-38; m. Virginia Eugenia Smith, Feb. 24, 1954. One man shows at Miami Beach Art Center, Asheville (N.C.) Mus., Hickory (N.C.) Mus., Statesville (N.C.) Mus., Civic Art Gallery, Greenville, N.C., Little Art Gallery, Asheville; exhibited in group shows at Met. Mus. (N.Y.C.), many others throughout U.S.; represented in permanent collections at Capitol Bldg. (Washington), St. Vincent Coll., Wingate Coll., Hickory Mus., Crossnore Coll., U. N.C., Mint Mus. of Art, Charlotte, N.C., Mass. Inst. Tech., numerous others. Served with AUS, 1942-45. Recipient 1st award, N.C. Nat. Exhibit, 1958, 59; Directors award, Council Am. Artist Socs. Nat. Exhibition, N.Y., 1966, Charlotte-Mecklenburg Artist of Year award, 1968, Popular Prize, I.P.A., 1970. Mem. Allied Artists Am., Art Student League N.Y. (life), Am. Artist Profl. League, Western N.C. Conservative Artists, Guild Charlotte Artists (past v.p.), Atelier Conservative Artists (past pres.), Nat. Arts Club (N.Y.C.), Atelier Club (N.Y.C.), Internat. Platform Assn., Hudson Valley Art Assn. Home: 3621 Arborway Dr Charlotte NC 28211

TUCKER, CHARLES IRVING, dentist; b. Greenville, Miss., Feb. 12, 1940; s. Enoch Irving and Frances Myrtle (Huff) T.; D.D.S., Loyola U., New Orleans, 1965; student La. State U., 1958-61; m. Penelope Louise Hutchinson, Aug. 23, 1962; children—Elizabeth Louise, Charles Irving. Practice dentistry, Ferriday, La., 1967—. Served with USAF, 1965-67. Mem. Ferriday Jr. C. of C. (v.p. 1970-71), Natchez, 5th Dist. dental socs., Am., La. dental assns., Ferriday C. of C., Xi Psi Phi. Methodist (adminstrv.). Rotarian. Club: Ferriday Country. Home: 325 Woodland Av Ferriday LA 71334 Office: Huntington Plaza Ferriday LA 71334

TUCKER, DAISY SNELLGROVE (MRS. WILLIAM C. TUCKER), librarian; b. Pinckard, Ala., Dec. 11, 1912; d. LaFayette and Jessie (Bryant) Snellgrove; grad. Columbus (Ga.) City Hosp. Sch. Nursing, 1934; student U. Ga., 1952; m. William Clifford Tucker, Jan. 12, 1935 (dec. Apr. 1961); children—William Clifford, Frances (Mrs. Eugene Dobson, Jr.). Librarian Ledger-Enquirer Newspapers, Columbus, Ga., 1952—; book review editor Columbus Enquirer, 1954—; head research dept. Ledger-Enquirer, 1952—. Mem. Gov.'s Adv. Com. Mental Instns., 1959-62; bd. dirs. Muscogee Mental Health Assn., 1957—, Ga. Assn. Mental Health (sec.). Recipient Cup of Hope award Ga. Assn. Mental Health, 1958. Mem. C. of C. Baptist. Club: Country (Columbus). Home: 1915 Wildwood Av Columbus GA 31906 Office: Ledger-Enquirer Newspapers Columbus GA 31902

TUCKER, HOUSTON CLAY, coll. dean; b. Nashville, Nov. 26, 1915; s. Houston C. and Lillian (Johnson) T.; B.S., U.S. Naval Acad., 1939; M.A., George Peabody Coll., 1956; Ph.D., Vanderbilt U., 1960; m. Dorethe Pigg, June 23, 1941; children—Susan (Mrs. Hugh E. Wilson III), Clark. Engaged in sales and accounting Pigg and Parsons, Columbia, Tenn., 1946-53; mem. faculty Middle Tenn. State Coll., Murfreesboro, 1956—, prof. English, dir Sch. Arts and Scis., 1962-65, dean Sch. Arts and Scis., 1965—, Sch. Liberal Arts, 1971—. Served to lt. comdr. U.S. Navy, 1939-46. Decorated Submarine Combat insignia with star. Mem. Modern Lang. Assn. Am., S. Atlantic Modern Lang. Assn., Tenn. Philos. Soc. Home: 1020 E Clark Blvd Murfreesboro TN 37130

TUCKER, HOWARD MCKELDIN, investment banker; b. Washington, Apr. 1, 1930; s. Howard Newell and Bessie (McKeldin), T.; grad. Staunton Mil. Acad., Va., 1949; B.A., U. Va., 1954; m. Julia Merrell, Jan. 23, 1952; children—Deborah N., Mark Merrell, Alexander McKeldin, Howard David. With investment-trust dept. J.P. Morgan & Co., Inc., N.Y., 1955-59, Morgan Guaranty Trust Co., 1959; Mackall & Coe, Washington, investment bankers and mems. N.Y. Stock Exchange, 1959-69, Mason & Co., Inc., 1969-70, Legg, Mason & Co., Inc., 1970—. Mem. balance-of-payment task force U.S. Treasury. Chmn. Washington Cathedral Fund Dr., 1964-65; bd. dirs. Washington area, Council Chs., Washington Cathedral Chpt., 1967—; trustee Nat. Cathedral Sch. for Girls. Served with USNR, 1950-55. Chartered financial analyst. Mem. Washington Soc. Investment Analysts, Beta Theta Pi. Republican. Episcopalian (vestryman). Club: Metropolitan (Washington). Home: 800 Dolley Madison Blvd McLean VA 22101 Office: 1100 17th St NW Washington DC 20036

TUCKER, JACK NORRIS, state senator, lawyer; b. Charleston, Miss., May 15, 1921; s. Harry Randolph and Lucy (Rolph) T.; grad. Holmes Jr. Coll., 1942; B.A., U. Miss., 1948, LL.B., 1950, J.D., 1968; m. Pattye Sue Williams, Sept. 12, 1948. Admitted to Miss. bar, 1950; pvt. practice law Tunica, 1950—; mem. Miss. Senate, 1960—. Commr. election Tunica Co., Miss., 1952-56, chmn. bd., 1952-56; dir. Miss. Heart Assn., 1952-56, 60-64; chmn. Tunica Heart Fund, 1952—; lay-del. Miss. to Am. Heart Assn., 1960-61; chmn. Tunica County Heart Council, 1961—; Boy Scout commr. Tunica County. Served from ensign to lt. (j.g.), USNR, 1942-46; USNR (ret.). Mem. Am., Tunica, Coahoma County bar assns., Miss. State Bar Am. Legion, V.F.W., Delta Kappa Epsilon, Phi Delta Phi. Democrat. Methodist. Rotarian. Home: PO Box 826 Tunica MS 38676

TUCKER, KENNETH WAYNE, contracting co. exec.; b. nr. Pell City, Ala., July 2, 1927; s. Thomas Keaton and Sarah (Gambell) T.; grad. high sch.,; m. Anna Lou Meehan, Nov. 1948 (dec. Dec. 1960); 1 dau., Teresa Jean; m. 2d, Betty Ann Colvin, Nov. 22, 1964; children— Toni Celeste, Terri Ann, Tracy Leigh. Supr., Southeastern Contracting Co., Birmingham, Ala., 1950-57; partner T. & H Constrn. Co. Huntsville, Ala., 1957-59, Tucker Bros. Contracting Co., Birmingham, 1959-70, Pell City, 1970—; pres. Tucker Equipment Co., Birmingham, 1965-70, Pell City, 1970—; v.p. Tucker Enterprises, Birmingham, 1967-70, Pell City, 1970—. Served with USMCR, 1945-48. Mem. Am. Gas Assn., Am. Water Assn., Pell City C. of C. (pres. 1968, dir. 1969). Methodist. Mason (Shriner), Lion. Clubs: Pell City Country (v.p. 1961-73); The Club (Birmingham). Home: Route 1 Box 196 Cropwell AL 35054 Office: PO Box 648 Pell City AL 35125

TUCKER, MILDRED ALYENE, county ofcl.; b. Altus, Okla., Oct. 10, 1921; d. Jasper Milton and Loraine (Taylor) Tucker; student Lippers Bus. Coll., 1958; spl. course Wayland Bapt. Coll., 1958-67.

Am. Tobacco Co., 1915-29, dir., 1958—; with subsidiary Am. Suppliers, Inc., 1929—, v.p., 1957-58, pres., 1958—, also dir. Clubs: Pinnacle (N.Y.C.); Richmond Country, Commonwealth (Richmond, Va.). Home: 5 Paxton Rd Richmond VA 23226 also The Puritan, 1244 S 4th St Louisville KY 40203 Office: 2401 E Main St Richmond VA 23223

TURNER, GEORGE PEARCE, cons., devel. co. exec.; b. Dallas, Aug. 22, 1915; s. Fred Horatio and Florence (Phillips) T.; student U. Tex., Austin, 1932-33, 35-36, 40-41, So. Meth. U., 1934; B.A. cum laude, U. So. Cal., 1962, M.S. summa cum laude Internat. Pub. Adminstrn., 1966; m. June Lori Haney, Feb. 4, 1943; children—Bruce Haney, Brian Phillips, Mark Richardson. Pvt. practice designer, archtl. Los Angeles, 1946-48, prin. Lieberg & Turner, cons. engrs., Pasadena, Cal., 1947-48, Radiant Heat Engring., Inc., Pasadena, 1948-53; exec. asst. to dir. fgn. subsidiaries The Flour Corp., Ltd., Los Angeles, 1953-54; mem. staff Coast Fed. Savs. Loan Assn., Los Angeles, 1954-55; exec. asst. to the exec. v.p. Holmes & Narver, Inc., Los Angeles, 1955-61, Southwestern Engring. Co., Los Angeles, 1962; pres., treas. Fomento e Inversiones Quisqueyanos, C. por A., Dominican Republic; cons. OAS, 1963-68; dir. projects, programming and tech. matters OAS mission to Dominican Republic, 1965-67, ind. cons. devel. econs., 1962—; pres. Haney Devel. Corp., Washington, 1964—. Adviser, Presdl. Commn. for Program Immediate Action, Dominican Republic; adviser Liga Municipal Domincana; mem. Tripartite Mission Direct Tech. Assistance to Govt. of Peru; projects programmer Nat. Planning Inst., Peru; Spl. adviser Superintency for Devel. of N.E., Recife, Brazil; adviser Spl. OAS Task Force to establish Integrated Problem Tech. Assistance to Countries Latin Am. Mem. Los Angeles, La Canada chambers commerce, Soc. Internat. Devel., Internat. Studies Assn., Soc. for Applied Anthropology, Delta Phi Epsilon, Alpha Sigma Lambda. Presbyn. Author: An Analysis of the Economy of El Salvador, 1961; The Alliance for Progress: Concept Versus Structure, 1966; also profl. publs. Home: 4701 Willard Av Chevy Chase MD 20015 Office: Haney Devel Corp 815 15th St NW Washington DC 20005.

TURNER, GISELA KRAUSE, physician; b. Dortmund, Germany; d. Arthur and Elisabeth (Eckardt) Krause; student U. Muenster (Germany), 1941-42, Strassbourg U. (France), 1942-44; M.D., Heidelberg U. (Germany), 1947; m. Samuel R. Turner, July 10, 1970; children (by previous marriage) Stephen Arthur, Ralph Eckardt. Intern Hillcrest Med. Center, Tulsa, 1963-64; resident Vanderbilt U. Hosp., Nashville, 1964-67; practice medicine, specializing in anesthesiology, Nashville, 1967—; mem. staff Vanderbilt U. Hosp.; instr. anesthesiology Vanderbilt U., 1967-69, asst. prof., 1969-70. Mem. Am. Soc. Anesthesiologists, Anesthesia and Analgesia Research Soc., Am. Med. Womens Assn. Home: 2133 E 59th Pl Tulsa OK 74105

TURNER, HENRY LATHROP, III, financial cons.; b. Cin., July 30, 1931; s. Henry Lathrop Jr. and Nancy (Bosart) T.; B.S., U. Ky., 1954; m. Clara Hoskins, Sept. 24, 1954; children—Catherine (Mrs. Daniel Jonathan Foster), Jacqueline Rae, Lucy Elizabeth, Henry Lathrop IV. Ins. agt. Phoenix Mut. Life Ins. Co., Lexington, Ky., 1957-60, Orlando, Fla., 1962-68; pres. Physicians' Adminstrv. Services, Winter Park, Fla., 1968—. Investment cons., 1966—; exec. dir. Nat. Assns. Profl. Corps., Washington, 1969—. Served to 1st lt. USAF, 1955-57. C.L.U. Recipient Certificate Estate Planning and Pensions C.L.U. Am. Coll., 1968. Mem. Assn. Advanced Life Underwriters, Am. Assn. C.L.U.'s (v.p. Central Fla. chpt.), Estate Planning Council, Am. Inst. for Econ. Research. Republican. Mem. Christian and Missionary Alliance Ch. Club: University (Orlando). Pioneer in devel. profl. corps. Home: 810 Juanita Rael Winter Park FL 32789 Office: 807 Morse Blvd Winter Park FL 32789

TURNER, JAMES ALEXANDER, JR., lawyer, accountant, educator; b. Kingstree, S.C., Dec. 15, 1937; s. James Alexander and Alice (Ballentine) T.; B.S., U. N.C., 1961; J.D., U. S.C., 1966; m. Betty Morris, June 29, 1963; children—James Alexander III, William Townsend. Accountant, S.D. Leidesdorf & Co., Greenville, S.C., 1961-63; pvt. practice James A. Turner, Jr., C.P.A., Columbia, S.C., 1963-66, 68-71; admitted to S.C. bar, 1966; tax atty. S.D. Leidesdorf & Co., Greenville, S.C., 1966-68; asst. prof. indsl. mgmt. Clemson (S.C.) U., 1968—; dir. Turner Lumber Co., LeMoyen, La., Pres., Berkeley County Young Republicans, 1964; del. Young Rep. Nat. Conv., 1965. C.P.A., S.C. Mem. S.C. Assn. C.P.A.'s (exec. com. 1971), Am. Inst. C.P.A.'s, Am., Nat. assns. accountants, S.C. Bar Assn., S.A.R. (chpt. pres. 1969-71), S.C. Beta Alumni Corp. Sigma Phi Epsilon (pres. 1970—). Presbyn. Clubs: Green Valley Country (Greenville). Home: Route 2 Box 273A Seneca SC 29678 Office: PO Box 303 Clemson SC 29631

TURNER, JAMES EDWIN, farmer; b. Chuckatuck, Va., Nov. 5, 1909; s. William Robert and Ivey Ruth (Johnson) T.; student pub. schs.; m. Mamie Elizabeth Gilliam, Oct. 10, 1931; children—James Edwin, Richard L. Farmer, Carrollton, Va., 1931-65; partner Turner & Turner, Carrollton, 1965-70; pres. Turner Farms, Inc., Carrollton, 1970—; dir. Bank Smithfield (Va.). Treas., Carrollton Vol. Fire Dept., 1965-71; county fire warden, 1945—; mem. Pub. Welfare Dept., 1956—; mem. electoral bd., 1970-71. Named Outstanding Man of Year, Carrollton Ruritan Club, 1970. Mem. Agrl. Stblzn. and Conservation Com. (recipient award certificates), Farm Bur., So. States Tidewater Petroleum, So. States Co-op., Isle of Wight Farmers Co-op. Methodist (trustee). Club: Carrollton Ruritan. Home: RFD 1 Box 219 Carrollton VA 23314 Office: PO Box 56 Carrollton VA 23314

TURNER, JESSE H., assn. exec. Vice-chmn. N.A.A.C.P., Memphis. Office: 213 S Main St Memphis TN 38106*

TURNER, JOE DOWERY, ret. mining engr.; b. Adger, Ala., May 29, 1902; s. Henry and Alie (Turner) T.; B.S. in Mining Engring., B.S. in Mining Geology, U. Ala., 1926; postgrad. U. Denver, 1952-54; m. Fannie Mildred Thompson, July 2, 1938. Mining engr. Sloss-Sheffield Co., Bessemer, Ala., 1927-28, Woodward Iron Co., 1928-37, U.S. Geol. Survey, Denver, 1937-44; dist. mining supr. McAlester, Okla., 1944-52, regional mining supr. Denver, 1952-54, chief br. mining operations, Washington, 1954-72. Mem. Joseph A. Holmes Safety Awards Com. Registered profl. engr., Ala., D.C. Mem. Am. Inst. Mining, Metall. and Petroleum Engrs., Fed. Profl. Assn., Nat. Soc. Profl. Engrs., Am. Inst. Profl. Geologists, Soc. Am. Mil. Engrs., Ala. Soc. Profl. Land Surveyors, Am. Congress Surveying and Mapping, Gamma Sigma Epsilon. Mason (K.T., Shriner). Home: 836 Linbard Lane Birmingham AL 35226

TURNER, JOHN BUNYAN, devel. co. exec.; b. Davis, Okla., Aug. 27, 1921; s. Joh Bunyan and Bertha Elizabeth (Bollen) T.; B.S., Okla. State U., 1948; postgrad. Northwestern U., 1965; m. Melba Roudebush, Sept. 24, 1943; children—Cynthia Ann (Mrs. Charles Peyton Ripley), Richard Allan, Mark Edward. Jr. engr. Humble Oil & Refining Co., 1948-56, supervising engr. prodn. dept., 1956-60, engr. sect. head gen. services dept., Houston, 1959-63, coordinator Bayport indsl. devel., 1963-65, mgr. land mgmt. dept., 1965—; pres., Friendswood Devel. Co., Houston, 1966—. Mem. adv. bd. Center for Municipal Legal Studies, Southwestern Legal Inst., 1969—; commr. Tex. Indsl. Commn., 1971—. Trustee Urban Land Inst., Humble Cos. Found. Served to capt. AUS, 1943-46. Decorated Purple Heart. Mem. Am. Petroleum Inst., Greater Houston Builders Assn., Petroleum Club Houston, Clear Lake C. of C. (dir. 1969-71). Methodist (trustee 1959—). Club: Riverbend Country (pres. 1970-71) (Sugar Land, Tex.). Home: 6243 Del Monte St Houston TX 77027 Office: 800 Bell Av PO Box 2180 Houston TX 77001

TURNER, KENNETH AUSTIN, judge; b. Memphis, Mar. 9, 1928; s. William Robert and Pearl (Gwin) T.; student U. Tenn., 1947-49; LL.B., Memphis State U., 1959; m. Mary Sue Ballard, Feb. 6, 1948; 1 dau., Carole Joyce. Wih Memphis Police Dept., 1950-63, detective capt.; juvenile ct. judge, Memphis, 1964—. Served with USMCR, 1946-47, 50-51. Mem. Tenn. Council Juvenile Ct. Judges (pres. 1967-68), Phi Alpha Delta Mason (32 deg.). Home: 1972 Kirby Pkwy Memphis TN 38117 Office: 616 Adams Av Memphis TN 38105

TURNER, LELAND STANFORD, utility exec.; b. Dallas, Nov. 5, 1926; s. Leland Standord and Jessie Fay (Sweatt) T.; B.S. in Civil Engring., Tex. A. and M. U., 1948; J.D., So. Methodist U., 1957; m. Donetta Mae Johnson, Jan. 17, 1947; children—Leland, Susan, Marcia, Ellen, Julia. With Dallas Power & Light Co., 1948—, exec. v.p., 1966-67, dir., 1964—, pres., chief exec., 1967—; dir. Tex. Utilities Co. Pres., dir. Community Council Greater Dallas; v.p., dir. Children's Med. Center; bd. dir. S.M.U. Found. Sci. and Engring., State Fair of Tex., United Fund Met. Dallas, Dallas Citizens Council; trustee Presbyn. Hosp. of Dallas, Southwestern Med. Found. Served with AUS, World War II. Mem. Am., Tex. bar assns., Dallas C. of C. (v.p., dir.), Dallas Salesmanship Club, Delta Theta Phi. Presbyn. Clubs: Dallas Athletic, City (dir.). Home: 7111 Cliffbrook Dallas TX 75240 Office: 1506 Commerce St Dallas TX 75201

TURNER, LOYD LEONARD, business exec.; b. Claude, Tex., Nov. 5, 1917; s. James Richard and Maude (Brown) T.; B.A., Baylor U., 1939, M.A., 1940; postgrad. U. Pa., 1940-42; m. Lee Madeleine Barr, Apr. 13, 1944; children—Terry Lee, Loyd Lee. Instr., U. Pa., 1940-42; pub. relations coordinator Consol. Vultee Aircraft Corp., San Diego, 1946-48, dir. pub. relations, Ft. Worth, 1948-53; asst. to pres. Ft. Worth div. Gen. Dynamics Corp., 1953-71, dir. pub. affairs Convair Aerospace div., Ft. Worth, 1971-72; exec. asst. to chmn. bd. and pres. Tandy Corp., Ft. Worth, 1972—. Pres., Ft. Worth Pub. Library Bd., 1958-63; v.p. Ft. Worth Bd. Edn., 1962-65, pres., 1965-71; mem. exec. com. Tex. Assn. Sch. Bds., 1966-71, v.p., 1970-71; mem. steering com., council big city bds. Nat. Sch. Bds. Assn., 1967-69, mem. Gov's Com. on Pub. Sch. Edn., 1966-69; pres. Tex. Council Maj. Sch. Dists., 1968-69. Bd. dirs. Tarrant County chpt. A.R.C., 1956-59, Tex. Com. Pub. Edn., 1961-69. Bd. dirs. Pub. TV Found. North Tex., 1970—. Served with USAAF, 1942-46. Named Library Trustee of Year, Tex. Library Assn., 1961, Pres. of Best Bd. of Large Sch. Systems in U.S., N.E.A., 1968; recipient citation Air Force Assn., 1962; Leadership award West Tex. C. of C., 1966, 69. Mem. Pub. Relations Soc. Am., Aviation Space Writers Assn., Air Force Assn., Navy League U.S., Nat. Mgmt. Assn., Advt. Club Ft. Worth, Friends Ft. Worth Library (v.p. 1971—), Ft. Worth C. of C., Ft. Worth Art Assn., Baylor U. Council for Instnl. Devel., Baylor U. Ex-Students Assn. (dir. 1958-61), Sigma Delta Chi (pres. Ft. Worth 1961-62). Baptist. Rotarian (dir. Fort Worth). Clubs: Knife and Fork (dir. 1963-66, pres. 1965-66), Colonial Country; Press of Fort Worth. Author: The ABC of Clear Writing, 1954. Home: 3717 Echo Trail Fort Worth TX 76109 Office: 2727 W 7th St Fort Worth TX 76107

TURNER, REX ALLWIN, coll. pres., clergyman; b. Corner, Ala., Feb. 13, 1913; s. Elijah Jesse and Mary Ellen Odessa (Fikes) T.; student U. Ala., 1929-30, Jacksonville State U., 1933-34; A.B., Samford U., 1936; M.S., Auburn U., 1946, Ed.D., 1955; LL.B., Jones Law Sch., 1952; m. Opal Shipp, Dec. 24, 1931; children—June Jacqulin (Mrs. Jesse C. Long), Mary Ellen (Mrs. Phillip D. Hargis), Rex Allwin. Ordained to ministry Ch. of Christ, 1932; prin. Mount High elementary schs., Blount County, Alabama, 1935-36, also instr. city system ofschs., Tarrant, Ala.; minister, Montgomery, Ala., 1936-42; co-founder Ala. Christian Coll., Montgomery 1942, co-pres., 1942-48, pres., 1948—; former minister Panama St. Ch. of Christ, Montgomery. Mem. Am. Assn. Sch. Adminstrs., Am. Assn. U. Profs., Assn. Higher Edn., Am. Assn. Curriculum Devel., Nat. Assn. Secondary Principals, Kappa Delta Pi, Phi Delta Kappa, Sigma Delta Kappa, Staff writer for Gospel Advocate. Author: Milestones in the Restoration Movement, 1955; Principles of School Law and Applications to Alabama's Public School System, 1955. Home: 10 Watson Circle Montgomery AL 36109 Office: Atlanta Hwy Montgomery AL 36109

TURNER, RICHARD JACKSON, physician; b. Franklin Springs, Ga., Feb. 12, 1930; s. John Martin and Olivia (Jackson) T.; M.D., U. Ga., 1957; m. Sylvia Nell Moak, Feb. 8, 1958; children—Olivia, Richard, Jennifer. Intern, Macon City Hosp., 1958; sr. asst. surgeon USPHS, Los Angeles, 1958-60; gen. practice medicine specializing in surgery, Clayton, Ga., 1960—. Served with USCGR, 1958-60. Mem. Am. Geriatric Soc., Am. Soc. Abdominal Surgeons, Jr. C. of C. Rotarian. Home: Box 504 Clayton GA 30525 Office: Box 746 Clayton GA 30525

TURNER, ROSCOE WILSON, dentist; b. Marion, Ill., June 13, 1905; s. William L. and Martha Ellen (Brothers) T.; student So. Ill. U., 1925-30; D.D.S., Washington U., St. Louis, 1934; m. Neva E. Fulenwider, Nov. 21, 1925; 1 son, Louis E. Tchr. pub. schs., Ill., 1924-30; practice dentistry, St. Louis, 1934-69; clin. instr. Washington U. Dental Sch., St. Louis, 1942-45; real estate investor, Palm Beach County, Fla., 1959—; pres. Lou-Jon, Inc.; sec. Shoe House, Inc. Mem. Am., Mo. dental assns., St. Louis Dental Soc. Republican. Baptist. Mason (Shriner), Rotarian. Home: 998 SW 7th St Boca Raton FL 33432

TURNER, SAMUEL ROLAND, physician; b. Columbus, Ga., Sept. 5, 1921; s. Samuel Roland and Annie Laurie (Fuller) T.; B.A., Vanderbilt U., 1948, M.A., 1949, M.D., 1951; children—LeAnne (Mrs. John M. Burnett, Jr.), James Winborn, Andrew Roland; m. Gisela Krause, July 10, 1970. Intern, Vanderbilt U. Hosp., 1951-52; resident, 1952-54; anesthesiologist Hillcrest Med. Center, Tulsa, 1954-66; pvt. practice anesthesiology Doctors Hosp., Tulsa, 1966-67; anesthesiologist Asso. Anesthesiolgists, St. Francis Hosp., Tulsa, 1967—, teaching staff, 1967—. Bd. dirs. Miss Okla. Pageant; trustee Okla. Blue Shield. Served with USNR, 1941-44. Mem. Am., Okla. (pres. 1961-62) socs. anesthesiologists, Tulsa County Med. Soc. (pres. 1965-66), Okla. (trustee, 1st chmn. 1965-69), So. (Okla. counselor 1968—) med. assns., Beta Theta Pi, Phi Ch. Home: 2133 E 59th Pl Tulsa OK 74105 Office: 4815 S Harvard St Tulsa OK 74135

TURNER, THOMAS ALEXANDER, airport adminstr.; b. Jackson, Tenn., Apr. 1, 1903; s. Thomas Alexander and Martha (Fleming) T.; B.S., U.S. Naval Acad., 1924; M.S., Mass. Inst. Tech., 1930; postgrad. Naval War Coll., 1950; m. Charlotte Milstead Barksdale, Jan. 11, 1926; children—Thomas A., Elizabeth B. (Mrs. Howard Thomas Murley). Commd. ensign USN, 1924, advanced through grades to capt., 1943; comdr. Naval Air Sta., Pautuxent River, Md., 1948-50, Naval Air Bases, Mariannas, Pacific, 1950-54; ret., 1954; head coll. math dept. Marion (Ala.) Inst., 1954-55; mgr., exec. dir. Airport Authority, Jackson, Miss., 1955—. Decorated Legion Merit. Registered profl. engr., Miss. Mem. Am. Soc. C.E., Am. Meteorol. Soc., Am. Assn. Airport Execs. (exec. mem.), Newcomen Soc. Episcopalian. Mason (Shriner), Rotarian. Home: 768 Belhaven St Jackson MS 39202 ffice: PO Box 1832 Jackson MS 39205

TURNER, THOMAS RICHARD, physician; b. Arp, Tex., May 19, 1917; s. Leonard W. and Rosamond (Dean) T.; B.A., Baylor U., 1938, M.D., 1941; M.S., U. Minn., 1945; m. Donnie Martha Goodner, Aug. 29, 1941; children—Nancy Ethel (Mrs. James Clay Lang), Ann Rosamond (Mrs. Robert Wood Jordan), Richard Leonard. Intern, Baylor U. Hosp., Dallas, 1941-42; fellow Mayo Clinic, Rochester, Minn., 1942-45, resident asso. Springer Clinic, Tulsa, 1945-47, partner, 1947-60; pvt. practice medicine specializing in neurology and psychiatry, Tulsa, 1960—; mem. staff St. John's, Hillcrest, St. Francis hosps. (all Tulsa). Diplomate Am. Bd. Psychiatry and Neurology. Fellow Am. Psychiat. Assn.; mem. A.M.A., Am. Acad. Neurology, Am. Med. Electroencephalographic Assn., Central Neurol. Psychiat. Assn., So. Psychiat. Assn., So. Med. Assn. (life), Beta Beta Beta, Alpha Chi, Alpha Epsilon Delta. Clubs: Oaks Country, Summit. Home: 1831 E 31st Pl Tulsa OK 74105 Office: 3102 S Harvard Av Tulsa OK 74135

TURNER, TOM E., broadcasting exec. Pres. KBUC, KBUC-FM, San Antonio. Office: 3259 E Commerce St San Antonio TX 78220*

TURNER, WILLIAM LINDSAY, state ofcl.; b. Rocky Mount, N.C., June 25, 1923; s. William Lindsay and Bettie (Joyner) T.; B.S., N.C. State U., 1948, M.S., 1949; D.Pub. Adminstrn., Harvard, 1953; m. Marjorie Windle, Sept. 7, 1946; children—Ann Windle, William L. Farm mgt. specialist N.C. State U., Raleigh, 1948-55, in charge extension farm mgmt., 1956-62, asst. bus. mgr., 1962-63, bus. mgr., 1963-65, adminstrv. dean for univ. extension, 1965-69; dir. N.C. Dept. Adminstrn., Raleigh, 1969—. Chmn., Nat. Task Force on Continuing Edn. Unit, 1968—; N.C. rep. to Coastal Plains Regional Commn., 1969—, to Appalachian Regional Commn., 1969—; treas. Gov.'s Fine Arts Council, 1969—. Div. chmn. United Fund Drive, 1969. Bd. dirs. N.C. Marine Sci. Council, N.C. State U. Student Aid Assn. Served with AUS, 1943-45. Recipient Distinguished Service award N.C. Farm Mgrs. and Rural Appraisers Assn., 1962. Mem. Am. Farm Econs. Assn., Am., N.C. socs. farm mgrs. and rural appraisers, Am. Soc. for Pub. Adminstrn., Raleigh C. of C. Clubs: Raleigh City, Rotary.Home: 3337 Thomas Rd Raleigh NC 27607 Office: Box 1351 Raleigh NC 27602

TURNER, WILLIAM WILSON, hosp. exec.; b. Valley Mills, Tex., Apr. 21, 1916; s. Will S. and Nettie A. (Vickrey) T.; B.B.A., Baylor U., 1938; postgrad. Northwestern U., 1939; m. Wilma David, Feb. 22, 1945; 1 dau., Elizabeth Ann. Bus. mgr. Hillcrest Meml. Hosp., Waco, Tex., 1941-47; asst. adminstr. Meml. Bapt. Hosp., Houston, 1947-50; adminstr. Bapt. Hosp., Alexandria, La., 1950-54, Miss. Bapt. Hosp., Jackson, 1954-55; adminstr. Meml. Hosp. System, Houston, 1955-63, exec. dir., 1963-71, pres., 1971—. Dir. Group Hosp. and Life Ins. Co., Blue Cross-Blue Shield of Tex. Served to lt. USNR, 1942-45. Fellow Am. Coll. Hosp. Adminstrs.; mem. Am. Protestant Hosp. Assn., Tex. Hosp. Assn. (trustee 1961-69, treas. 1969, pres. 1971). Bapt. Hosp. Assn. (pres. 1954, trustee 1961-64, 69-71), C. of C., Union Bapt. Assn., Tex. League for Nursing, Delta Sigma Pi. Baptist (deacon). Home: 7730 Pagewood St Houston TX 77042 1100 Louisiana St Houston TX 77002

TURRENTINE, GORDON HENRY, banker, chamber commerce exec.; b. Houston, Dec. 11, 1907; s. Robert Emmett and Emma Kate (Campbell) T.; B.A., Rice U., 1928; m. Margie Wilmer Thiel, Nov. 28, 1929; 1 dau., Noelie Margaret. With Houston Press, 1927-39; research dir. City of Houston, 1940; staff mgr. Houston C. of C., 1941-47, gen. mgr., 1954-70, cons., 1970—; v.p. South Tex. Nat. Bank, Houston, 1948-54; vice chmn. Lockwood Nat. Bank of Houston, 1957—. Served with USAAF, 1942-45; MTO. Mem. Am. C. of C. Execs., So. Assn. C. of C. Execs., Tex. C. of C. Mgrs. Rotarian. Contbr. articles to various publs. Home: 3406 Linkwood Dr Houston TX 77025 Office: PO Box 53600 Houston TX 77052

TURSI, RAFFAELE, hotel exec.; b. Brindisi, Italy, Mar. 31, 1933; s. Luigi and Candida (Dorigo) T.; ed. Marco Visconti Coll. (Italy), Pittman's Sch. English and Comml. Sci. (Eng.); grad. in English, Cambridge U. (Eng.); m. Anunciacion Garasa Lamua, Oct. 24, 1958. Restaurant mgr. Carlton Beach Hotel, Bermuda, 1962-66; food and beverage mgr. Holiday Inn, Freeport, Bahamas, 1966-67; resident mgr. Oceanus Hotels, Bahamas, 1967-69; gen. mgr. Grand Bahama Hotel and Country Club, West End, Bahamas, 1969-71; mng. dir. Indies House Hotel, Freeport, 1971—. Dir., Freeport/Lucaya Tourist and Conv. Bd. Mem. Am. Mgmt. Assn., Bahamas Hotel Assn., Am. Hotel-Motel Assn., Am. Hotel Sales Mng. Assn., Airline Passengers Assn. Address: Indies House Hotel PO Box 455 Freeport Bahamas

TUSH, MASON LEE, distilling co. exec.; b. Louisville, Dec. 26, 1918; s. John Otha and Elsa Louise (Stein) T.; A.B., U. Louisville, 1941; M.B.A. (scholar), Northwestern U., 1946; m. Anna Lucille Coldiron, June 24, 1946; children—Lesleigh Ann, Mason Lee, John William, Patti Lynn. Dir. marketing research Reynolds Metals, Louisville, 1946-48; asst. prof. econs. U. Louisville, 1948-50; dir. promotion Ky. C. of C., Louisville, 1950; with Brown-Forman Distillers Corp., Louisvile, 1951—, v.p., area dir., 1966-69, v.p., 1966—; with Joseph Garneau Co., Louisville, 1951—, exec. v.p., 1969-71, dir. marketing, 1971—, pres., 1972—, also dir.; dir. Benchmark Group, Los Angeles. Mem. psychiat. counsel Norton Meml. Infirmary Psychiat. Clinic, Louisville, 1971—. Served to maj., finance dept. AUS, 1941-46. Decorated Bronze Star. Mem. Mensa (v.p. 1963), Recioto Soc. Verona (Italy), Res. Officers Assn., Sales Exec. Council, Chevalier Chaine des Rotisseurs. Mason (32 deg.). Home: 6358 Limewood Circle Louisville KY 40222 Office: PO Box 1080 Louisville KY 40201

TUTHILL, BURNET C(ORWIN), musician; b. N.Y., 1888; A.B., M.A., Columbia; Mus.M., Coll. Music, Cin.; Mus.D. (hon.), Chgo. Mus. Coll., Southwestern Coll.; m. Helen Hersey, 1917; m. 2d, Ruth Wood, 1930; 2 daus. Condr., Columbia U. Orch., 1909-13; asst. condr. N.Y. Oratorio Soc., 1914-16; condr. People's Choral Union, N.Y.C., 1913-16, Plandome Singers, 1918-22, U. Cin. Glee Clubs, 1922-30, Southwestern Singers, 1935-59, Memphis Symphony Orch., 1938-46; chief fine arts sect. Shrivenham Am. (Army) U., Eng., 1945; gen. mgr. Cin. Conservatory, 1922-30; dir. music Southwestern Coll., Memphis, 1935-59; rep. Waddell & Reed, Inc., 1959-72; composer Concertos for clarinet, string bass, tenor sax, trombone, and orch.; Fantasy Sonata for clarinet and piano, Big River for women's chorus and orch.; sonatas for violin, viola, trumpet, alto and tenor sax, flute, oboe with piano, ensemble music for winds, string quartet, clarinet quintet, others. Founder, Soc. Publ. Am. Music, 1919, treas., 1919-49. Co-founder Nat. Assn. Schs. Music, 1924, sec., 1924-59. Contbr. articles to musical publs. Home: 295 Buena Vista Pl Memphis TN 38318

TUTTLE, CHARLES HUME, supt. schs.; b. Pineola, N.C., Feb. 21, 1913; s. Charles Lee and Mary (Dula) T.; A.B., Lenoir Rhyne Coll., 1936; M.A., Appalachian State Tchrs. Coll., 1951, postgrad., 1952; postgrad. Ind. U., 1953, Yale, 1954, N.C. State Coll., 1958, Western Carolina Coll., 1961; m. Nettie Estelle Moss, Oct. 9, 1937; 1 son, Charles Allen. Tchr. math., coach Claremont (N.C.) High Sch.,

1936-41, prin., 1946-57; prin. Mountain View High Sch., Hickory, N.C., 1941-43; dir. guidance services Catawba County Schs., Hickory, 1957-63, asst. supt., 1964—. Served with USNR, 1943-46. Mem. N.E.A., N.C., Catawba County edn. assns., Am., N.C. personnel and guidance assns. Lion (past pres., zone chmn.). Address: 1004 1st St SW Hickory NC 28601

TUTTLE, FREDERICK BURTON, educator, govt. ofcl.; b. New Haven, July 12, 1908; s. Burton L. and Alta M. (Carter) T.; B.A., Yale, 1930, Ph.D., 1942; postgrad. U. So. Cal., George Peabody Coll., U. Mich.; m. Mary Emily Armstrong, Sept. 3, 1936; children—Frederick Burton, James, Allen, Margaret Emily. Tchr. and prin. New Haven Pub. Schs., 1930-46; adviser edn. CAA, Washington, 1946-49; supt. schs., Westerly, R.I., 1949-52; dir. summer session, dir. placement, prof. edn. State U. Coll., Plattsburgh, N.Y., 1952-58, asso. dean, dir. grad. studies, 1958-63; dep. dir. ednl. programs NASA, 1963-70, dir. ednl. programs, 1970—; vis. prof. U. R.I., George Washington U., R.I. Coll. Edn. Ednl. cons. Nat. Aeronautic and Space Adminstrn.; adviser edn. N.Y. State Bur. Aviation. Served as 1st lt. USMC, World War II. Recipient certificate of service Nat. Celebration, Fiftieth Anniversary of Powered Flight; citations N.Y. State Assn. Elementary School Prins. for service to edn. in N.Y.; Plattsburgh Rotary Club for service to community; Plattsburgh Alumni Assn. for service to Coll. Mem. Am. Assn. Sch. Adminstrs., Nat. Sci. Tchrs. Assn., S.A.R., Order Founders and Patriots, N.E.A., Nat. Council Social Studies. Episcopalian. Mason, Lion. Editor: Aviation Education Reports, 1949, 50; aviation edn. number. Nat. Elementary Prin., New Haven Tchrs. Jour., Sci. Edn. in Space Age. Contbr. periodicals. Home: 9229 Forest Haven Dr Alexandria VA 22309

TUTTLE, RALPH GODFREY, operations analyst; b. Spokane, Wash., Nov. 1, 1912; s. John Freemont and Mae (Godfrey) T.; B.S., U. Wash., 1935; postgrad. Cath. U., 1944-45, George Washington U., 1952-55; m. Alice Wood, May 24, 1934; 1 son, Rand Wood. Operations analyst USAF, 1951-58; naval architect USN Bur. Ships, 1942-50; supervising operations analyst FAA, 1958-60; adv. operations analyst IBM Fed. Systems Div., 1960-63; operations research analyst Naval Research Lab., Washington, 1963—. Founder, pub. Cheverly (Md.) Citizen. Recipient Meritorious Civilian Service award U.S. Navy, 1951. Registered profl. engr., D.C. Mem. Operations Research Soc. Am., Washington Operations Research Council. Home: 6203 Landon Lane Bethesda MD 20034 Office: 4555 Overlook Av SW Washington DC 20390

TUTTLE, RICHARD CAROL, engr.; b. Springfield, Mo., Dec. 24, 1906; s. Ulysses Grant and Bessie (Patterson) T.; student in Geology, Tulsa U., 1938-44; m. Lettie Evelyn Nicholson, Mar. 29, 1926; children— Lelia (Mrs. Tom Brown), Richard R., Willard N. With Sinclair Oil Co., Tulsa, 1927-43, successively draftsman, in pipeline, engring., refining, geol., and liaison geol.-geophys. depts.; chief geophysicist, head exploration Sunray Oil Co., Tulsa, Okla., 1943-45; pvt. cons. practice, Tulsa, Ada, Okla., 1945-58; head drafting and design and math. Tulsa Tech. Coll., 1960-62, later evening class tchr., now head drafting and design; design engr. Douglas Aircraft, 1962-70. Author profl. papers articles profl. jours. Home: 1915 S Yorktown St Tulsa OK 74104 Office: 2525 E 21st Tulsa OK 74114

TUXHORN, SCOTT EDWARD, state ofcl.; b. Enid, Okla., Mar. 4, 1928; s. Marvin Edward and Edna Marie (Hockenberry) T.; B.S., Northwestern State Coll., 1951, M.Ed., 1958; Ed.D., Okla. State U., 1967; m. Dolores Marie Fitzpatrick, Apr. 19, 1952; children—Harriet Ann, Tux Delbert Charles, Marvin Edward. Tchr., Syracuse Kan. pub. schs., 1951-54; prin. Corwin Grade Sch., 1954-56; prin. Helena (Okla.) pub. schs., 1956-58, supt., 1958-62; state rep. Alfalfa County, 1962-64; supt. Jet pub. schs., 1964-69; chmn. Okla. Bd. of Pub. Affairs, 1969; Okla. Supt. of pub. instrn., 1970-71; dep. dir. Dept. Health, Edn. and Welfare, Dallas, 1971—. Chmn. Alfalfa County Republican Com., 1969—, state committeeman, since 1970—. Served with AUS, 1946-47. Mem. Okla. N.W. Dist. Sch. Adminstrs. (pres. 1960-61), Alfalfa County Edn. Assn. (dir.), C. of C. (pres. 1961). Mem. Christian Ch. Mason, Lion (dir.). Home: 1329 Carriage Dr Irving TX 75062 Office: 1114 Commerce St Dallas TX 75202

TWADDELL, GERALD ERVIN, educator; b. Dayton, Ky., Mar. 23, 1943; s. Ervin S. and Kathryn L. (Schoepf) T.; B.A., Sem. St. Pius, 1963; postgrad. Grand Seminaire St. Sulpice, Paris, France, 1963-67; Dip.Et.Fr., Universite de Strasbourg, 1965; postgrad. U. Cin., 1969—. Ordained priest Roman Cath. Ch., 1967; faculty French Sem. St. Pius X, Erlanger, Ky., 1967— prof. philosophy, 1969—, acad. dean, 1970—; tchr. Holy Cross High Sch., Covington, Ky., 1967-69. Mem. Am., Am. Cath. philos. assns., Am. Assn. for Higher Edn. Home: Sem St Pius X Erlanger KY 41018

TWISDALE, HAROLD WINFRED, dentist; b. Roanoke Rapids, N.C., Apr. 28, 1933; s. James Robert and Elma (Smith) T.; B.S., U.N.C., 1955, D.D.S., 1958; m. Barbara Ann Edmonds, Aug. 2, 1958; children—Harold Winfred, Leigh Ann. Individual practice dentistry, Charlotte, N.C., 1961—; mem. dental staff Meml. Hosp., 1961—, head dept. dental prosthetics, 1964-66. Pres. Charlotte Telecasters, Inc., 1965—, Va. Telecasters, Inc., 1966, Augusta Telecasters, Inc., 1966-69, Durham-Raleigh Telecasters, Inc., 1966-70, Memphis Telecasters, Inc., 1966—. partner Twisdale & Steel Assos., 1965-70; proprietor Twisdale Enterprises, 1965—; gen. mgr., pres. WCTU-TV, Charlotte, 1967-69; pres. TV Presentations, Inc., 1967-69; gen. mgr., operator WATU-TV, Augusta, Ga., 1968-69. Mem. N.C. Dental Found., 1958—; transp. chmn. Miss N.C. Pageant, 1965. Trustee Boys Home, Lake Waccomaw, N.C., 1966. Served to capt. USAF, 1958-60. Recipient Certificate of Merit Charlotte Jr. C. of C., 1962, 63, Spoke award, 1962, Sparkplug award, 1963, 64, 65, 66. Mem. Am., Southeastern (founder, pres.) analgesia socs., Am., N.C. (mem. fed. dental service com. 1970—), Charlotte (chmn. dental soc. radiation study com. 1970—), Second Dist. dental socs., N.C. Dental Soc. Anesthesiology, Charlotte Analgesia Study Club, U.N.C. Dental Alumni Assn., Delta Sigma Delta, Lambda Chi Alpha. Democrat. Methodist. Home: 5732 Doncaster Dr Charlotte NC 28211 Office: PO Box 12685 4421 Central Av Charlotte NC 28205

TWITTY, FRANK STARLING, lawyer; b. Camilla, Ga., Aug. 29, 1907; s. Thomas Baker and Tennie E. (Wood) T.; LL.B., Mercer U., 1928; m. Margaret Elisabeth Almand, Aug. 5, 1929; children—Margaret Leah (Mrs. Charles R. Adams, Jr.). Admitted to Ga. bar, 1928; gen. practice Camilla, 1928—; atty. city of Camilla, 1935—; atty. for Mitchell County; sr. mem. firm Twitty & Twitty; dir. Planters & Citizens Bank, Camilla Logging Co. Mem. Ga. Ho. of Reps., 1945-64. Mem. Ga. State (life mem.), Camilla (past pres., dir.) chambers commerce, Am., Ga., Mitchell County bar assns., Am. Judicature Soc., Delta Theta Phi. Mason (Shriner), Rotarian (dist. gov. 1954-55). Home: 72 Scott St Camila GA 31730 Office: 52 E Oakland Av Camilla GA 31730

TWYMAN, JOSEPH PASCHAL, univ. pres.; b. Prairie Hill, Mo., Nov. 21, 1933; s. William L. and Hazel (Dry) T.; B.A., U. Mo. at Kansas City, 1955, M.A., 1959, Ph.D., 1962; m. Patricia Joanne Harper, July 26, 1953; children—Mark Kevin, Patricia Lynn. Asst. prof., then asso. prof. Okla. State U., 1960-66, asso. dir. Research Found., 1965-66; dir. research U. Mo. at St. Louis, 1966-67; v.p. U. Tulsa, 1967-68, pres., 1968—; cons. in field, 1960—. Mem. adv. panel Southwestern Coop. Ednl. Lab., 1967-68; mem. Okla. Bicentennial Commn., 1970—; adv. bd. Tulsa Opera, 1968—, St. John's Hosp., Tulsa, 1969—. Bd. dirs. Okla Council Econ. Edn., 1968—, Tulsa Community Chest, 1968—, Tulsa Civic Ballet, 1968—, Arts Council Tulsa, 1970—, Thomas Gilcrease Inst. Am. History and Art, 1970—; trustee Undercroft Montessori Sch., Tulsa, 1967—, Children's Med. Center, Tulsa, 1968; Hillcrest Med. Center, Tulsa, 1969—; mem. exec. com. Frontiers of Sci. Found. Okla., 1968—; bd. dirs. Tulsa Mental Health Assn., 1967—, Mid-Continent Research and Devel. Council, 1967-69. Ford Found. grantee, 1963-66, U.S. Office Edn. grantee, 1958-60, 61-62, 62-63, 64-65, 64-66. Mem. A.A.A.S., Am. Acad. Polit. and Social Sci., Phi Delta Kappa, Omicron Delta Kappa. Presbyn. Rotarian. Clubs: Tulsa, Southern Hills, University and Summit (Tulsa). Author: (with others) The Concept of Role Conflict, 1964; also articles. Home: 1775 E 31st St Tulsa OK 74105

TYER, ARNOLD JEROME, engring. co. exec.; b. McCrory, Ark., Sept. 23, 1923; s. John William and Mary (Love) T.; student Hendrix Coll., 1946-47, Little Rock U., 1948-49; B.S. in Civil Engring., U. Ark., 1951; m. Johnnie Mae Sandago, June 8, 1947; children— David, Lee Ann, John, Paul. Party chief T.J. Fricke Engr., Stuttgart, Ark., 1951-52, constrn. engr. Marion L. Crist & Assos., Inc., Little Rock, 1952-56, roject engr., 1956-58, mem. firm, 1958-68, pres., 1968—. Served with F.A., AUS, 1943-46; ETO. Mem. Am. Water Works Assn., Am. Soc. C.E., Nat., Ark. Socs. profl. engrs., Cons. Engrs. Council Ark. (pres. 1966-67, nat. bd. dirs. 1968-69), Ark. Pollution Control Fedn., Ark., Little Rock chambers commerce. Methodist. Home: 1500 Mountain Dr Little Rock AR 72204 Office: 4324 W Markham St Little Rock AR 72205

TYLER, CARL HAMILTON, dentist; b. Springdale, Ky., Jan. 25, 1896; s. Charles Duncan and Addie T. (Ritter) T.; D.D.S., U. Louisville, 1920; m. Dewey Lee Arnsparger, Jan. 2, 1922. Dentist, Mental Retarded State Inst., 1920-28, Eastern State Mental Hosp., 1924-28; practice dentistry, Lexington, Ky., 1928—. Mem. Acad. Internat. Dentistry, Internat. Coll. Dentistry, Pierre Fauchard Acad., Blue Grass Dental Soc. (Distinguished award for Outstanding Contbr. to Profession 1969, pres. 1943-44). Mem. Internat. Coll. Dentists. Democrat. Mem. Christian Ch. Mason. Club: Lexington Country, Pyramid, Optimist (life). Home: 1306 Fontaine Rd Lexington KY 40502 Office: First Nat Bank Bldg Lexington KY 40507

TYLER, JAMES HOGE, III, banker; b. Norfolk, Va., May 21, 1910; s. Heth and Nellie (Serpell) T.; A.B., Washington and Lee U., 1931, LL.B., 1933; m. Mabel C. Burroughs, June 24, 1936; children—Elizabeth Calvert, Eleanor Howe. Admitted to Va. bar, 1932, practiced with Mann & Tyler, Norfolk, 1933-55; dir. United Va. Bank-Seaboard Citizens Nat. Bank, 1937—, gen. counsel, 1943-55, chmn. bd., 1969—; pres. Seaboard Citizens Nat. Bank, 1956-67, chmn. bd., 1967-69; chmn. bd. United Va. Bankshares; dir. F.A. Royster Guano Co. Rep. to Va. Legislature, 1942-46, mem. Senate, 1946-47. Mem. C. of C. (pres. 1954-55). Home: 4137-T First Court Rd Virginia Beach VA 23455 Office: PO Box 3127 Norfolk VA 23514

TYLER, JOHNNIE MAE WEEKS, ret. educator, civic worker; b. Ozark, Ala., July 28, 1913; d. John Calvin and Lena Lee (Boyett) Weeks; B.S. in Edn., Troy State Coll., 1946; postgrad. Auburn U., 1955-57; diploma in Christian tng. Baptist Sunday Sch. Bd., Nashville, 1961; m. Saxon DeWitt Dykes, Sr., Sept. 23, 1933 (div. Oct. 1963); children—Saxon DeWitt, Catherine Malissa (Mrs. J. D. Nolin Jr.); m. 2d, William Deval Barefoot, Nov. 25, 1964 (dec. Oct. 1968); m. 3d, E. J. Tyler, June 12, 1969. Tchr. elementary schs. Barbour county, Dale county, Ozark, Ala., 1940-69, 6th group Emma P. Flowers Elementary Sch., Ozark Ala., 1955-69, ret., 1969. Grey lady Dale county chpt. A.R.C., Ozark, 1942-44, 1st aid instr., 1942-69; instr. Civil Def., Ozark, 1963-69; civil Def. coordinator for Ariton, Ala. Notary Pub., Justice Peace, Barbour county, 1963-64. Founding fellow So. Soc. Geneologists; mem. Tex. Geneal. Soc. (historian), Fedn. Womens' Clubs (chmn. Dale County 1949-51), Beta Sigma Phi. Baptist (librarian ch. 1963—). Clubs: Clio Study (pres. 1956-57), Progressive Study (Clio) (pres. 1959-60); Maud Martin Study (Ozark). Contbr. papers to tech. lit., book reviews Ch. Paper Monthly Publ., Clio, 1963. Home: Route 2 Box 168 Ariton AL 36311

'TYLER, STEPHEN ALBERT, educator, anthropologist; b. Hartford, Ia., May 8, 1932; s. Guy Earle and Beatrice Virginia (Slack) T.; B.A., Simpson Coll., Indianola, Ia., 1957; M.A. (Ford Found. fellow), Stanford, 1962, Ph.D., 1964; m. Martha Sue Grosskop, June 15, 1962. Asst. prof. anthropology U. Cal. at Davis, 1964-67; asso. prof. anthropology Tulane U., New Orleans, 1967-70; prof. anthropology and linguistics, chmn. dept. Rice U., Houston, 1971—. Served with USAF, 1952-56. Fellow Am. Anthrop. Assn.; mem. Linguistic Soc. Am., Assn. for Asian Studies, Audubon Soc., Nat. Trust Historic Preservation, Am. Camelia Soc. Author: Koya: An Outline Grammar, 1969; India, The Anthropological Perspective, 1972. Editor: Cognitive Anthropology, 1969; Concepts and Assumptions in Contemporary Anthropology, 1969. Asso. editor Annual Reviews, Inc., Anthropology. Home: 3106 Bluebonnet St Houston TX 77025

TYNES, VICTOR HORACE, dentist; b. Ivandale, Va., Aug. 20, 1915; s. Joseph Walter and Lucy Jane (Rich) T.; B.S., N.C. A. and T. State U., 1940; D.D.S., Howard U., 1950; m. Hazel Estelle Ferguson, June 12, 1948; children—Victor Horace, Myron Kevan. Practice dentistry, Greensboro, N.C., 1952-53; pub. health dentist Dental Health Div., State Bd. Health, Raleigh, N.C., 1953-56, Guilford County Health Dept., Greensboro, 1956—. Instr. English, dir. publicity N.C. A. and T. State U., 1940-43, lectr., 1956—. Active YMCA. Served with AUS, 1943-45; ETO; to capt. Dental Corps, AUS, 1950-52. Mem. Am., N.C. pub. health assns., Nat. Dental Assn., Old North State Dental Soc. (pub. dir. 1953-59), Greensboro Med. Soc., N.A.A.C.P., Alpha Kappa Mu. Baptist (trustee). Home: 1117 Benbow Rd Greensboro NC 27406 Office: PO Box 4264 Greensboro NC 27406

TYRE, WILLIAM HOWARD, devel. co. exec.; b. Frostproof, Fla., Mar. 11, 1936; s. R. H. and Margaret Tyre; B.A., Fla., State U,, 1960; m. Jill Lee Sovilla, Apr. 21, 1962; children—Ashley Howard and Wesley Lee (twins). Salesman, Liberty Nat. Life Ins. Co., Stuart, Fla., 1961-63; asst. city mgr. West Palm Beach Fla., 1964-66, city mgr., 1966-69; v.p. Perini Land & Devel. Co., West Palm Beach, 1969— Vice pres. Boys Club Am., 1970—; co-chmn. Heart Fund, 1970—; coach Babe Ruth Baseball, 1966, 67; mem. adv. bd. West Palm Beach Municipal Auditorium. Bd. dirs. United Fund, Gulf Stream Goodwill Industries, Nelle Smith Residence for Girls, A.R.C. Served with AUS, 1954-57. Mem. Fla. State U. Alumni Assn. (past dir.), Sigma Phi Epsilon. Democrat. Methodist. Kiwanian. Home: 1517 43d St West Palm Beach FL 33407 Office: 714 Chillingworth St West Palm Beach FL 33407

TYRER, JOHN LLOYD, headmaster; b. Brockton, Mass., Jan. 16, 1928; s. Lloyd Perkins and Dorothy (Nicholson) T.; A.B., Bowdoin Coll., 1949; M.A., Middlebury Coll., 1959; m. Jeanne Irene Dunning, June 7, 1952; children—Alison Jane, John Lloyd, David Dunning, Jill Anne. Tchr., Wilbraham (Mass.) Acad., 1949-53; tchr., adminstr. Hill Sch., Pottstown, Pa., 1953-64; headmaster Asheville (N.C.) Sch., 1964—. Mem. Greater Asheville Council, 1966—. Bd. dirs. Asheville Country Day Sch., 1965-68, St. Genevieve/Gibbons Hale Sch., 1971—, Council for Religion in Ind. Sch., 1970—, Ind. Ednl. Services, 1970—. Served with AUS, 1946-47. Mem. Theta Delta Chi. Episcopalian. Rotarian (dir. Asheville 1967—). Club: Biltmore Forest Country (Asheville). Address: Asheville Sch Asheville NC 28806

TYRRELL, JOHN FRANCIS, textile co. pres.; b. Troy, N.Y., Dec. 3, 1925; s. John Edward and Mary Agnes (O'Brien) T.; B.B.A., Siena Coll., 1948; m. Theresa M. Catellier, July 18, 1949; children—Patricia, John, Mary Beth. Cost accountant Arrow Co., Troy, 1948-68; controller Alatex, Inc., Andalusia, Ala., 1968-70; pres. E-Z Mills, Inc., Cartersville, Ga., 1971— (all subsidiaries Cluett, Peabody & Co., Inc.). Served with AUS, 1943-45. Mem. Nat. Knitwear Mfrs. Assn. Republican. Roman Catholic. K.C. Home: 1468 Wimbledon Dr NW Kennesaw GA 30144 Office: 1 Johnson St Cartersville GA 30120

TYRRELL, WILLIAM PATRICK, agriculturist; b. Oak Park Ill., Oct. 21, 1916; s. William Carroll and Marion (Kelley) T.; B.S., Purdue U., 1939, M.S., 1942; m. Ruth E. Evans, Oct. 23, 1940; children—Patrick T., Kathy J., William C., Timothy J., Sally E., Julia, Rosemary, Daniel C. Tchr. vocational agr. pub. sch., Galveston, Ind., 1939-41; apprentice cattle buyer Wilson & Co., Chgo., 1942; asso. extension livestock specialist U. Tenn., Knoxville, 1946-63, extension animal husbandman, 1963-70, prof., leader animal sci. research, 1970—. Active Cardinal Mindszenty Found., St. Louis, 1969—. Served to 1st lt. USMCR, 1942-46. Named col. a.d.c. Gov.'s Staff, 1970; Man of Year in service to Upper South agr. Progressive Farmer mag., 1971. Mem. Tenn. Livestock Assn. (sec. 1954-63, Recognition award 1968), So. Beef Conf. (co-chmn. 1971), Nat. Block and Bridle Club (hon.), Nat. Assn. County Agrl. Agts., Am. Soc. Animal Sci. (chmn. animal sci. extension sect., 1971), Tenn. Charolais Assn., Am. Farm Bur. Fedn., Gamma Sigma Delta. Roman Catholic. K.C. (4 deg.). Clubs: P-Mans (Lafayette, Ind.); Century (Knoxville). Home: 8608 Gleason Rd Knoxville TN 37919 Office: PO Box 1701 Knoxville TN 37901

TYSON, JOHN CAIUS, III, judge; b. Montgomery, Ala., Oct. 7, 1926; s. John Caius and Virginia Bragg (Smith) T.; student Gulf Coast Mil. Acad., Gulfport, Miss., 1942-43, The Baylor Sch., Chattanooga, 1943-44; B.S., also LL.B., U. Ala.; m. M. Mae Martin Bryant, Sept. 27, 1967; stepchildren-Mary Harmon McClellan, T. Marc McClellan. Admitted to Ala. bar, 1951, since practiced in Montgomery; asso. Jones, Murray & Stewart, 1951; individual practice, 1952-56; asso. C. H. Wampold, Jr. in gen. practice law, 1956-60; asst. atty. gen. State of Ala., 1959-71; asso. judge Ala. Ct. Criminal Appeals, 1972—; developer Beaumont Estates; dir. Smith & Tyson, Inc. Lectr. continuing legal edn. program U. Ala. Active A.R.C., United Appeal. Served with USCG, 1944-46. mem. Res., 1947-52. Mem. Am., Ala., Montgomery County (exec. com. 1963) bar assns., Am. Judicature Soc., S.A.R. (past pres. Montgomery County chpt., 1st v.p. Ala.), Soc. Pioneers Montgomery (past pres., dir.), Am. Legion, C. of C. Democrat. Episcopalian (vestryman 1957-61, 69-72. Mason (K.T., Shriner). Kiwanian. Clubs: Montgomery Country, Beauvoir (Montgomery). Contbr. to Ala. Lawyer. Home: 3114 Jasmine Rd Montgomery AL 36111 Office: Ala Court Criminal Appeals 316 Judicial Bldg Montgomery AL 36101

UBERALL, HERBERT MICHAEL STEFAN, educator, scientist; b. Neunkirchen, Austria, Oct. 14, 1931; s. Michael and Stefanie (Hacker) U.; Ph.D., U. Vienna (Austria), 1953; Ph.D., Cornell U., 1956; m. Colette Bry, Sept. 23, 1957; children—Bernadette, Bertrand. Came to U.S., 1953, naturalized, 1963. Staff mem. Signal Corps Engring. Labs., Ft. Monmouth, N.J., 1953-54; research asst. Cornell U., Ithaca, N.Y., 1954-56; research fellow Nuclear Physics Research Lab., U. Liverpool, Eng., 1956-57; Ford Found. fellow CERN, Geneva, Switzerland, 1957-58; research physicist Carnegie Inst. Tech., Pitts., 1958-60; asst. prof. U. Mich., Ann Arbor, 1960-64; asso. prof. Catholic U., Washington, 1964-65, prof. physics, 1965—. Cons. Naval Research Lab., Washington, 1966—. Fellow Am. Phys. Soc.; mem. Acoustical Soc. Am., Am. Assn. U. Profs. Author: Electron Scattering from Complex Nuclei, 1971. Contbr. articles in field to profl. jours. Home: 6100 Landon Lane Bethesda MD 20034 Office: Physics Dept Catholic U Washington DC 20017

UCHIN, ROBERT ALLEN, endodontist; b. Phila., Apr. 19, 1933; s. Harry and Doris (Goodman) U.; student Franklin and Marshall Coll., 1951-53; D.D.S., Temple U., 1957; m. Marlene Nedman, June 20, 1954; children—Andrew, Richard, Carol. Research teaching fellow dept. endodontics Temple U. Sch. Dentistry, Phila., 1957-60; pvt. practice endodontics, Ft. Lauderdale, Fla., 1960—. Co-chmn. endodontic sect. Dental Research Clinic, Miami, 1961—; clin. asso. U. Fla. Sch. Dentistry, Gainesville, 1970—. Trustee Vanguard Sch., Haverford, Pa.; chmn. bd. dirs. Vanguard Sch., Ft. Lauderdale, Fla. Served to capt., Dental Corps, USAF, 1957-59. Mem. Am. Assn. Endodontists (treas. 1971-72), Fedn. Dentaire Internationale, Am. Dental Assn., A.A.A.S., So. Endodontic Study Group (past pres.), Alpha Omega. Jewish religion (pres. congregation 1967-69). Rotarian (pres. 1969-70). Home: 281 SW 63d Av Plantation FL 33314 Office: Bayview Bldg 1040 Bayview Dr Fort Lauderdale FL 33304

UFEN, CHARLES HENRY, economist; b. Norderney, Germany, Dec. 27, 1921; s. George Juergens and Adeline (Speth) U.; came to U.S., 1928, naturalized, 1931; A.B., U. N.C., 1950, M.A., 1963, postgrad., 1963-68, 70-71; m. Diane Gere Deppen, July 7, 1950; children— Marya, Geer, Sarah. Bank examiner Fed. Deposit Ins. Corp., 1952-60; instr., lectr. dept. econs. N.C. State U., Raleigh, 1961-64, asst. prof., 1964-70, economist Center for Urban Affairs and Community Services, 1971—, lectr. dept. econs., 1971—. Research cons. Fed. Res. Bank Richmond, 1963, Econ. Devel. Adminstrn., 1968-69. Served with AUS, 1942-46. Decorated Bronze Star medal. Mem. Am., So. econ. assns., Am., So. finance assns., Phi Eta Sigma, Delta Phi Alpha. Home: 4208 Rowan St Raleigh NC 27609

UHL, NORMAN PAUL, psychologist, educator; b. Bklyn., May 3, 1935; s. Norman P. and Pauline (Gould) U.; B.S., Roanoke Coll., 1957; M.A., U. Md., 1963, Ph.D. (Nat. Def. Edn. Act fellow), 1964; m. Jean I. Henderson, Oct. 10, 1959; children—Steven, Gregory, Jennifer, Kathryn. Electronic engr., project leader Dept. Def., 1957-60, cons., 1960-64; research coordinator, lectr. U. Md., 1963-65; prof. psychology and edn. Emory U., Atlanta, 1965-69, cons., 1969-70, dir. testing and evaluation, 1966-69; research psychologist Ednl. Testing Service, Durham, N.C., 1969-70; prof. psychology, asso. dir. research and evaluation N.C. Central U., Durham, 1970—; cons. Atlanta Pub. Schs., 1967-69. Research cons. several edni. instns. Prin. or co-prin. investigator on grants from U.S. Office Edn., Esso Ednl. Found., Ford Found. Area chmn. ann. fund raising campaign, Roanoke Coll., 1968-70, 71-72. Served with AUS, 1959. Recipient Dept. Def. Nat. Performance awards, 1960, 61. Mem. Am. Psychol. Assn., Am. Ednl. Research Assn., Assn. for Computing Machinery, Psychometric Soc., Southeastern Soc. for Multivariate Exptl. Psychologists, Am. Assn. for Higher Edn. Author 2 books; contbr. articles to profl. jours. Home: Route 1 Box 419 Chapel Hill NC 27514 Office: NC Central U Durham NC 27707

UHR, ROBERT JONES, gas co. exec.; b. San Antonio, Sept. 15, 1910; s. Robert Frederick and Alvina Augusta (Tampke) U.; B.S. in Elec. Engring., Tex. A. and M. U., 1933; m. Margaret T. Richter, Sept. 15, 1936; children—Barry Wayne, Bonnie (Mrs. Richard E. Denson). Jr. engr. San Antonio Pub. Service Co., 1933-41; div. engr. United Gas Co., New Braunfels, Tex., 1945-55, dist. mgr., 1955—; dir. Guaranty State Bank, New Braunfels, Tex. Bd. dirs. New Braunfels Indsl. Found. Served with USAAF, 1941-46. Recipient Friend of 4-H award, 1971. Mem. S. Tex. (dir. 1967-70), Comal County (dir. 1960-63, 69-71), chambers commerce. Mem. Ch. of Christ (mem. council 1966-72). Home: PO Box 723 New Braunfels TX 78130 Office: PO Box 471 New Braunfels TX 78130

UHRIG, PAUL JACOB, dentist; b. Richmondale, O., Oct. 17, 1924; s. Adam and Lena (Oyer) U.; student Ohio U., 1946-48; Grad. Dental Lab. Technologist, Ohio State U., 1950; D.D.S., St. Louis U., 1959; m. Barbara Armstrong, Mar. 11, 1947; children—Paul Jacob, Nicholas Scott. Instr., St. Louis U. Sch. Dentistry, 1950-59; dental intern, Belle Glade, Fla., 1959-60; dir. instl. dental services, Fla. State Hosp., Chattahoochee, 1960—; dir. dental services Div. Mental Health, Div. Retardation, Div. Youth Services, Div. Corrections, 1960—; v.p. med. staff Fla. State Hosp. Council, 1971—. Served with USNR, 1943-46; PTO. Named Outstanding Instr., St. Louis U. Sch. Dentistry, 1959. Mem. Am., Fla., Fla. N.W. Dist. dental assns., Psi Omega. Episcopalian. Rotarian. Home: Doctor's Dr Fla State Hosp Chattahoochee FL 32324 Office: PO Box 4 Fla State Hosp Chattahoochee FL 32324

UITERWYK, JAN CHRISTIAAN, shipping exec.; b. Amsterdam, Netherlands, May 16, 1915; s. Daniel and Dina Cornelia (Verhagen) U.; B.A., U. Amsterdam, 1938; m. Maria Alberts, Oct. 4, 1939; children—Robert Hendrik, Jan Daniel, Hendrik. Came to U.S., 1949, naturalized, 1955. Clk., Wels Van Hasselt, Amsterdam, 1935-36; sec. to pres. Klisser & Citroen, Amsterdam, 1936-37; v.p. Alberts & Morel, Amsterdam, 1937-40, exec. v.p., 1940-49, pres., N.Y.C., 1949-52; dept. mgr. W.R. Grace & Co., N.Y.C., 1952-54; br. mgr. Maurice Pincoffs Co., Tampa, Fla., 1954-56; pres. Jan C. Uiterwyk Co., Inc., Tampa, 1956—; pres., chmn. bd. dirs. Jan C. Uiterwyk Co., New Orleans, 1963—, N.Y.C., 1965—, Houston, 1966—, Chgo., 1967—; pres., dir. Uiterwyk Shipping, Ltd., Nassau, Bahamas, 1964—; dir. Capital Nat. Bank, Tampa. Past pres. Girls Club, Tampa. Mem. C. of C. Presbyn. Clubs: Palma Ceia Golf and Country, Carrollwood Country, University (Tampa); Plimsoll (New Orleans). Home: 10000 Lindelaan St Tampa FL 33618 Office: 715 E Bird St Tampa FL 33604

ULINSKI, BRONISLAUS IGNATIUS, electric vehicle mfg. exec.; b. Buffalo, Apr. 26, 1902; s. Ignatius and Marcella (Butkiewicz) U.; student pub schs.; m. Lorraine J. Carlson, June 17, 1939; children—Mary Ann (Mrs. Calvin Norris Hansen), Richard, Priscilla (Mrs. Fred Rinehart Klunk). Machine designer Automatic Transp. Co., 1922-31; chief engr. McKeown Co., Buffalo, 1932-33; chief engr. Automatic Transp. Co., Chgo., 1933-51, dir. engring. 1951-56, dir. devel. and design, 1956-65; project mgr. Advanced Engring. Center, Eaton Yale & Towne, Inc., Phila., 1965-67; pres. Creative Engring. Consultants, Palm Beach, Fla., 1967-72, Volt-Mobile Co., Palm Beach, 1972—. Registered profl. engr., Ill. Mem. Soc. Automotive Engrs. Patentee in field. Home: 211 Kenlyn Rd Palm Beach FL 33480 Office: 211 Komlym Rd Palm Beach FL 33480

ULMER, RAY E., judge Pinellas County, India Rocks Beach, Fla.*

ULMER, ROBERT PARKE, educator; b. Williamsport, Pa., Apr. 22, 1922; s. Clarence Hyman and Margaret (Parke) U.; B.S., Kutztown State Coll., 1950; M.Ed., Pa. State U., 1951, Ed.D., 1966; m. Sarah Anne Sleppy, Dec. 29, 1949; children—Debra Anne, Dale Robert. Tchr. art Pub. Schs., Mount Carmel, Pa., 1950-53, Bloomsburg, Pa., 1953-56; prof. art Bloomsburg State Coll., 1956-63, chmn., 1959-63; prof. art East Tenn. State U., Johnson City, 1964-70, chmn. dept., 1966-70; Fuller E. Callaway prof. Ga. Southwestern Coll., Americus, 1970—. Bd. govs. J. Carroll B. Reese Mus., 1966-70, mem. exec. com., 1966-70. Served with USAAF, 1943-46. Mem. Pa. State Art Edn. (pres. 1957), Tenn. State Art Edn. Assn. (pres. 1968-69), Ga. Art Edn. Assn. (regional v.p., 1972), Ga. Assn. Edn. Southeastern Arts Assn. (dir. 1968-69), Nat. Art Edn. Assn. (rep. assembly 1967-69), Phi Delta Kappa, Kappa Delta Pi. Lutheran (vestryman 1966-69). Home: 2020 Rose Av Americus GA 31709

ULMER, SHIRLEY SIDNEY, educator; b. North, S.C., Apr. 15, 1923; s. Shirley S. and Anna R. (Reed) U.; B.A. cum laude, Furman U., 1952; M.A., Duke, 1954, Ph.D., 1956; m. Margaret Anel Lipscomb, Mar. 18, 1946; children—Margaret, William, Susan, John, Mary. Rockefeller fellow Duke, 1952-53, instr. polit. sci., 1954-55, Ottis Greene fellow, 1955-56; instr. U. Houston, summer 1956; mem. faculty Mich. State U., 1956-63, asso. prof. polit. sci., 1960-63, chmn. dept., 1961-62; prof. polit. sci., chmn. dept. U. Ky., 1963—. Served with USAAF, 1942-45; PTO. Decorated Air medal with 4 clusters; named Ky. col., 1966. Mem. Am. (editorial asso. rev. 1963—), So. (exec. council 1965-68, v.p. 1966-67, editorial bd. jour. 1965—) polit. sci. assns., Midwest (editorial bd. jour. 1963-64), Ky. (v.p. 1966-67) confs. polit. scientists, Inter-Univ. Consortium Polit. Research (exec. council 1966-67, council chmn. 1967-68), Phi Beta Kappa. Contbr. profl. jours. Editor: Introductory Readings in Political Behavoir, 1961; Political Decision Making, 1969. Home: Lexington KY 40504

ULMER, STANLEY THAD, rubber products co. exec.; b. Oak Creek, Colo., July 8, 1912; s. Charles Edward and Amy Louise (Hale) U.; student Akron U., 1930; m. Dorothy Maud Palmer, Nov. 20, 1941; children— Philip, Sally, (Mrs. Larry N. Hedges). Salesman Keener Automotive Sales Co., 1930-41; with B. F. Goodrich Co., Miami, Okla., 1941—, plant mgr., 1959—; dir. First Nat. Bank. Trustee Miami Bapt. Hosp., 1960-62; bd. dirs. Boy Scouts Am. Mem. C. of C. (dir. 1960-72). Home: 1630 Washington Dr Miami OK 74354 Office: 1000 Goodrich Blvd Miami OK 74354

ULRICH, GUSTAV MCLAUGHLIN, town mgr.; b. Cortland, N.Y., Oct. 3, 1931; s. Gustav H. and Rebecca (McLaughlin) U.; student U. N.H., 1949-51; B.E.E., N.C. State U., 1954; M.Pub. Adminstrn., Syracuse U., 1962; m. Marit Gammelsrod, Mar. 28, 1959; children—Helene, Gustav McLaughlin. Planner City of Greensboro, N.C., 1962-63, adminstrv. asst. to city mgr., 1963-66; town mgr. Town of Kernersville, N.C., 1966-70; dep. dir. Model City Dept., City of Winston-Salem, N.C., 1970-71; town mgr. Town of Garner, N.C., 1971—. Served with USAF, 1955-58. Mem. N.C. City and County Mgrs. Assn., Internat. City Mgmt. Assn., Am. Soc. Pub. Adminstrn. Democrat. Universalist. Home: 1209 Edgebrook Dr Garner NC 27529 Office: Rand Mill Rd Garner NC 27529

ULSETH, ROBERT NORMAN, physician; b. Grand Forks, N.D., June 21, 1930; s. Sigurd and Teressa Edith (Lamphere) U.; B.S., U. Ill., 1952, M.D., 1954; m. Georgiana Klecka, July 19, 1952; children—William, James, Mary Therese, Robert, Gregory, Christopher, Anne Catherine. Intern, St. Mary's Hosp., West Palm Beach, Fla., 1954-55; resident in neurology Brooke Army Hosp., San Antonio, 1956-58; gen. practice medicine, West Palm Beach, Fla., 1955-56, 58—; mem. active staff Good Samaritan Hosp., West Palm Beach; faculty U. Fla. Coll. Medicine, 1971—. Served with AUS, 1956-58. Diplomate Am. Bd. Family Practice (charter). Roman Catholic. Club: Lake Worth Civitan (pres. 1971-72). Home: 7131 W Lake Dr West Palm Beach FL 33406 Office: 6215 S Dixie St West Palm Beach FL 33405

UMPIERRE-SUAREZ, ENRIQUE, lawyer; b. San Juan, P.R., Oct. 12, 1941; s. Francisco and Felicia (Suarez) U.; B.C.E., Coll. Agr. and Mech. Arts, 1964; LL.B., U. P.R., 1970; m. Aglae Suarez, Mar. 20, 1965; children—Aglae, Enrique II, Denise Marie, Liza Margarita. Project engr. P.R. Water Resources Authority, 1965-68; pres. El Morro Equipment Rental, 1967—; cons. engr. V.M. Garcia Assos., 1969—; admitted to P.R. bar, 1970; counsellor, atty. at law Enrique Umpierre-Suarez, San Juan, 1970—; dir. Golden Mile Restaurants. Precinct pres. Popular Democratic party P.R., 1968—, senatorial dist. rep. to central council, 1968—. Mem. Am. Soc. C.E. (sec.-treas. San Juan chpt. 1968), Inst. Architects, Engrs. and Surveyors P.R. (sec. bd. dirs. 1970-71). Home: 603 El ferrol Apts Hato Rey PR 00918 Office: PO Box 5003 San Juan PR 00936

UNDERCOFLER, HIRAM K., asso. justice Ga. supreme ct.*

UNDERHILL, GARY MADISON, credit agy. exec.; b. Richmond, Va., Jan. 20, 1910; s. Ira Dixon and Roselynne E. (Terrell) U.; student U. Richmond, 1929-30; B.S., U. Va., 1932; m. Sarah Jane Reed, Dec. 28, 1936; children—Sarah Reed, Gary M., Thurlow R. Stenographer, clk. So. & C. & O. Rys., Richmond, 1926-28; sec. to pres. Bank of Va., Richmond, 1928-29, asst. to pres., 1932-36, asst. v.p., 1937-44, sec. to Ernest Woodruff, Atlanta, 1936-37; exec. dir. Consumer Bankers Assn., 1945-48; exec. v.p. Charter Bank, Phila., 1948-49; v.p. Girard Trust Bank, Phila., 1949-52; pres., dir. First Nat. Bank of Raleigh (N.C.), 1952-59; sr. v.p. N.C. Nat. Bank, Charlotte, 1959-66; exec. v.p. Bus. Devel. Corp. N.C., Raleigh, 1966—. Served as lt. USNR, 1944-45. Mem. Kappa Sigma, Alpha Kappa Psi, Phi Beta Kappa. Episcopalian. Home: 3111 Eton Rd Raleigh NC 27608 Office: 401 Oberlin Rd Raleigh NC 27605

UNDERHILL, WILLIAM AMORY, lawyer; b. Basinger, Fla., Feb. 21, 1910; s. Wilford Perry and Martha Mabel (Alderman) U.; LL.B., John B. Stetson U., 1936; LL.D., 1969. Admitted to Fla. bar, 1936, D.C. bar, 1952, U.S. Supreme Ct. bar, 1946; practicing lawyer, Deland, Fla., 1936-42, pros. atty., 1940-42; with Dept. Justice, Washington, 1946-52, spl. atty. alien property sect., claims div., 1946-47, spl. atty. vets. affairs sect., 1947, spl. atty., spl. asst. to atty. gen., Office Dept. Atty. Gen., 1947-48, 1st asst. to asst. atty. gen. in charge anti-trust div., 1948-50, acting asst. atty. gen., 1950-51, 1st asst. to dep. atty. gen., 1951, acting dep. atty. gen., 1951, asst. atty. gen. charge lands div., 1951-52; now practicing in Washington, and DeLand, Fla.; spl. counsel to comptroller of Fla., Washington. Asso. dir. Young Democrats Am., 1946. Bd. overseers, Stetson U. Law Sch., St. Petersburg, Fla.; trustee St. Leo (Fla.) Coll., Bert Fish Testamentary Trust. Served to lt. comdr. USNR, 1942-45. Recipient George Washington Honor medal award Freedoms Found., Valley Forge, 1970, Ben C. Willard award Stetson Lawyers Assn., 1970. Mem. Deland (pres. 1938), Fla. State (v.p. 1939) jr. chambers of commerce, Bar Assn. D.C., Am., Fed. bar assns., Fla. Bar, Fla. Council 100, Stetson U. Alumni Assn. (pres. 1971), Mil. Order World Wars, Am. Legion, Phi Alpha Delta, Pi Kappa Phi, Theta Alpha Phi. Elk, Mason (K.T.). Home: 145 N Garfield Av DeLand FL 32720 Office: PO Box 66 DeLand FL 32720also 1625 K St NW Washington DC 20006

UNDERWOOD, BENJAMIN HAYES, hosp. adminstr.; b. Savannah, Ga., Mar. 10, 1942; s. Frank Callaway and Marion Elizabeth (Hayes) U.; B.B.A., U. Ga., 1964; m. Judith Kay Burdine, Aug. 31, 1963; children—Ashley Hayes, Benjamin Hayes. Asst. adminstr., purchasing agt. Northside Manor Hosp., Atlanta, 1965-67; adminstr. Met. Psychiat. Center, Atlanta, 1967—; mem. exec. com., dir. Family Learning Centers, Inc.; v.p., dir. Burdine Enterprises, Inc. Served with USAF, 1966, 68-69. Mem. Am. Hosp. Assn., Assn. Mental Health Adminstrs., Am. Soc. Hosp. Pub. Relations Dirs., Am. Soc. Hosp. Purchasing Agts., Hosp. Financial Mgmt. Assn., Ga. Hosp. Assn., Atlanta C. of C. Club: Chattahoochee Plantation (Atlanta). Home: 6520 Whispering Lane NE Atlanta GA 30328 Office: 811 Juniper St NE Atlanta GA 30308

UNDERWOOD, DAVID MILTON, security co. exec.; b. Houston, Mar. 5, 1937; s. Milton Ramon and Catherine (Fondren) U.; grad. Phillips Acad., Andover, Mass., 1954; B.A., Yale, 1958; postgrad. Inst. Investment Banking, Wharton Sch. Finance, U. Pa., 1969; m. Lynda Knapp, Nov. 21, 1964; children—David Milton, Catherine F., Duncan Knapp. With Morgan Stanley & Co., N.Y.C., 1962; with Underwood, Neuhaus & Co., investment bankers, Houston, 1962—, v.p., 1966—, dir., 1968—; pres. Feliciana Corp., Houston, 1966—; dir. Fannin Bank, Pano Tech Exploration Co. (both Houston). Adv. com. U. Houston, Coll. Bus. Adminstrn., 1966—. Trustee, Fondren Found., Meth. Hosp., Kinkaid Sch. Served to capt. AUS, 1958-60, 61-62. Decorated Army commendation medal. Mem. Zeta Psi. Republican. Episcopalian Clubs: Houston Country, River Oaks Country, Bayou, Ramada, Houston, Allegro, Sarabande, University (Houston); Yale (N.Y.C.). Home: 3645 Willowick Rd Houston TX 77019 Office: 724 Travis St Houston TX 77002

UNDERWOOD, JAMES WILBUR, realtor; b. Sebastopol, Miss., May 5, 1921; s. R. Marvin and Della(Shealy) U.; student Draughn's Bus. Coll., 1938-39, U. Mich., 1946, U. Tenn., 1947, U. Ill., 1958, U. Va., 1966; m. Martha Varnado, May 16, 1943; children—Thomas Madison. Pres., J.W. Underwood & Co., Jackson, Miss., 1948—; chmn. bd. Underwood Ins. Agy., Inc., Homestead Savings & Loan Assn., Jackson, Miss.; dir. Deposit Guaranty Nat. Bank, Jackson, Miss. Pres. United Givers Fund, Jackson, 1960; pres. Andrew Jackson council Boy Scouts Am., 1962. Vice-pres. bd. trustees Jackson (Miss.) Pub. Schs., 1967-72. Bd. dirs. Goodwill Industries; trustee, chmn. exec. com. Miss. Bapt. Hosp. Served with USNR, 1942-45. Mem. Nat. Assn. Home Builders (life, dir. 1946—), Miss. Real Estate Assn., Jackson Real Estate Bd., Jackson Home Builders Assn. (pres. 1949-50), Jackson C. of C. (pres. 1960). Kiwanian. Club: Jackson Country (v.p. 1963—). Home: 6049 Woodlea Rd Jackson MS 39206 Office: PO Box 54 Jackson MS 39205

UNGAR, GEORGES, scientist; b. Budapest, Hungary, Mar. 30, 1906; s. Alexandre and Julia (Barec) U.; D.Sc., U. Paris, 1934, M.D., 1939; m. Alberte Levillain, Oct. 2, 1937; 1 dau., Catherine Anne. Asst. prof. physiology U. Paris, 1934-37; head Lab. Exptl. Med., Paris, 1937-39; Chem. Warfare Lab., French Army, 1939-40; mem. research unit Ministry of Home Security, Oxford, Eng., 1941-44; lectr. U. London, 1944-47; research asso. Northwestern U., Chgo., 1948-53; dir. dept. pharmacol. U.S. Vitamin and Pharmaceutical Corp., N.Y., 1954-62; prof. pharmacology Baylor U. Coll. of Medicine, 1963—; sci. adviser to French Embassy, London, 1945-47; Claude Bernard Prof. U. Montreal, 1948; dir. Inst. Comparative Biology, San Diego, 1962-63; sec. Histamine Club, 1957-69. Fellow A.A.A.S., Royal Soc. Medicine, London, N.Y. Acad. Medicine; mem. Am., Brit., French physiol. socs., Soc. for Endocrinology, Soc. Gen. Systems Research, Internat. Soc. for Neurochemistry, Soc. for Neurosci., Sigma Xi. Contbr. articles in field to profl. jours. Author: Physiological and Pathological Role of Histamine, 1937; Excitation, 1963; Molecular Mechanisms in Memory and Learning, 1970. Discoverer antihistamine drugs, 1937; oral antidiabetic drug, 1957; chem. transfer of memory, 1965. Home: 1800 Holcombe Blvd Houston TX 77025

UNGERMAN, IRVINE E., lawyer; b. Leavenworth, Kan., May 12, 1908; s. William and Rachel (Ettleman) U.; LL.B., Washburn U., 1930; m. Hanna Friedberg, Apr. 13, 1929; children—Maynard I., Rowena Mae (Mrs. David T. Iola). Admitted to Okla. bar, 1930; since practiced in Tulsa; mem. firm Ungerman, Grabel, Ungerman and Leiter, 1930—. Gen. counsel, dir. Boulder Bank & Trust Co. Pres. Tulsa Hebrew Sch., 1949-51; pres. Okla. Bd. Corrections, 1971—. Bd. govs. Washburn U. Law Sch. Fellow Am. Coll. Trial Lawyers; mem. Internat., Am., Okla., Tulsa County bar assns., Am. Judicature Soc., Nat. Assn. Def-Counsel, Am. Trial Lawyers Assn., Am. Comml. Law League. Club: Meadowbrook Country (sec. 1952-65), University. Jewish religion (pres. congregation). Home: 2230 E 39th St Tulsa OK 74105 Office: Wright Bldg Tulsa OK 74103

UNKOVIC, CHARLES M., educator; b. Pitts., Mar. 14, 1922; s. Kosto and Josephine (Polic) U.; B.A., U. Pitts., 1950, M.A., 1951, Ph.D., 1961; m. Marian R. Gotkiewicz, Sept. 3, 1955; children—Blair, Joseph Conrad. Asst. field dir. A.R.C., New Cumberland, Pa., 1951-52; mem. probation staff Allegheny County Juvenile Ct., Pitts., 1952-57; dir. social service Western State Penitentiary, Pitts., 1957-61; asst. prof. sociology Duquesne U., Pitts., 1961-62; asso. prof. sociology State Coll., Shippensburg, Pa., 1962-63, Bowling Green (O.) State U., 1963-66, Cleve. State U., 1966-68; prof., chmn. dept. sociology Fla. Tech. U., Orlando, 1968—. Dir. research Community Action for Youth, Cleve., 1966-67; project dir., various federally funded projects; chmn. adv. council Fla. Probation and Parole Commn; chmn. com. for establishing an Inst. of Police Adminstrn. at Fla. Tech. U.; Fla. del. 1970 White House Conf. on Children and Youth. Served with AUS, 1942-45. Recipient award for service in control of alcoholism Fla. Tech. U.; Community Service award Fla. Parole and probation Commn., 1970; Good Samaritan award Edgewood Boys' Ranch, 1971, others. Mem. Crime and Delinquency Soc., Am., So. sociol. socs., Am. Sociol. Assn., Am. Assn. Mental Deficiency, Am. Correctional Assn., Bibliog. Soc. Author: Hazelwood Survey 1962; The Larc Lane School for Retarded Children, 1965; The Dilemma in Standardizing Report Cards for the Trainable Mentally Retarded, 1966; Culturally Deprived Teen-Ager, 1966; Configurational Approach to Program Evaluation, 1967; (with George Kaluger) Psychology and Sociology: An Integrated Approach, 1969; also articles. Editor Bootstraps, 1970. Home: 3015 Saratoga Dr Orlando FL 32806

UNTERKOEFLER, ERNEST, bishop; b. Phila., Aug. 17, 1917; s. Ernest L. and Anna Rose (Chambers) U; A.B., Cath. U. Am., 1940, S.T.L., 1944, J.C.D,, 1950. Ordained priest Roman Cath. Ch., 1944; asst. pastor Richmond, Va., 1944-47, 50-60, Arlington, Va., 1947-50, sec. Richmond Diocesan Tribunal, 1954-60; moderator Council Cath. Women, 1956-61; chancellor Richmond Diocese, 1960-62, vicar gen., 1962-64, papal chamberlain, 1961; aux. bishop Richmond, titular bishop Latopolis, 1962-64; bishop of Charleston (S.C.), 1965—. Sec., U.S. Cath. Bishops Meeting, 1963; asst. sec. adminstrv. bd. Nat. Cath. Welfare Conf. (now U.S. Cath. Conf.), 1963-66, sec., mem. com. on budget and finance, adminstrv. bd., 1966-69; sec. Nat. Conf. Cath. Bishops, 1966-69, mem. com. for dept. internat. affairs, 1971—, ad hoc com. on women in church and society, 1971—; mem. Nat. Conf. Cath. Bishops' Commn. for Ecumenical and Interreligious Affairs, 1965-69, cons., 1969—, chmn. sub-commn. for dialogue with Presbyn. and Reform Roman Catholic-Anglican Joint Sub-Commn. on Theology of Marriage, 1967—; chmn. Bishops' Com. on Permanent Diaconate, 1968-71; dir. Center for Applied Research in the Apostolate, 1969—, pres., 1972—. Mem. alumni bd. govs. Cath. U. Am. Recipient Pax Christi award St. John's U., 1970. Home: 114 Broad St Charleston SC 29401 Office: 119 Broad St Charleston SC 29401

UPSHAW, JEFFERSON DAVIS, JR., physician; b. Louise, Miss., July 19, 1929; s. Jefferson Davis and Christine (Ferguson) U.; B.S., U. Ala., 1950; M.D., Johns Hopkins U., 1954; m. Grace Hall, July 3, 1953; children— Grace Christine, Jefferson Davis III, Henry Walker. Intern medicine Johns Hopkins Hosp., Balt., 1954-55, asst. resident medicine, 1955-56, 57-59, fellow in medicine, 1959-60, chief resident pvt. med. service, 1960-61; clin. asst. prof. medicine, then asso. prof. U. Tenn. Coll. Medicine, Bapt. Meml. Hosp., Memphis, 1964—, also dir. intern tng. Served to capt. USAF, 1956-58. Fellow A.C.P.; mem. Memphis Acad. Internal Medicine (v.p.), Johns Hopkins Med. and Surg. Assn., Am., Tenn., Memphis, Shelby County med. assns., Am. Soc. Internal Medicine, Phi Beta Kappa, Sigma Xi, Omicron Delta Kappa, Sigma Pi Sigma, Alpha Epsilon Delta, Alpha Omega Alpha, Methodist. Clubs: University, Chickasaw Country (Memphis). Home: 6225 Green Meadows St Memphis TN 38138 Office: 1080 Madison Av Memphis TN 38190

UPSHER, SIDNEY PHELPS, motor freight co. exec.; b. Oklahoma City, July 31, 1923; s. Albert Edward and Florence Elizabeth (Hollingsworth) U.; B.A., U. Okla., 1947, LL.B., 1948; m. Betty Lou Lee, Oct. 8, 1970; children (by previous marriage)—Meridith (Mrs. Patrick O. Glenn), Leslie, Kathy, Elaine; stepchildren—Laurie, Lisa, Lynn Davis. Admitted to Okla. bar, 1948; practiced in Oklahoma City, 1948-51; exec. v.p., sec., dir. Lee Way Motor Freight, Inc., Oklahoma City, 1952—. Mem. trucking industry negotiation com. Nat. Teamster's Negotiations, 1964-67; dir. Will Rogers Bank & Trust Co. Mem. city council, Nichols Hills, Okla., 1966-70, vice mayor, 1970—. Pres. bd. dirs. United Appeal; trustee, pres. Mummers Theatre, Inc.; trustee, sec. Casady Sch. Served with USAF, World War II. Decorated D.F.C., Air medal with three oak leaf clusters. Mem. Motor Carrier Lawyers Assn., Okla. Bar Assn., Phi Gamma Delta, Phi Eta Sigma, Phi Alpha Delta. Episcopalian. Home: 1210 Larchmont Lane Oklahoma City OK 73116 Office: 3000 W Reno St Oklahoma City OK 73108

UPTHEGROVE, WILLIAM RELD, metallurgist, educator; b. Ann Arbor, Mich., Nov. 10, 1928; s. Clair and Hazel Katherine (Platt) U.; B.S.E. in Metallurgy, U. Mich., 1950, M.S., 1954, Ph.D., 1957; m. Margot Jeanne Mowatt, July 11, 1953; children—Amy Elizabeth, David Clair, Thomas Reid, Bruce Warren, Michael John. Mem. faculty U. Okla., 1956-62, chmn. Sch. Metall. Engring, 1956-62, asst. prof., 1956-60, asso. prof. metall. engring., 1960-62; supr. powder metallurgy Internat. Nickel Co. Research Lab., Bayonne, N.J., 1962-64; prof., chmn. dept. mech. engring. U. Tex., Austin, 1964-70; dean Coll. Engring., U. Okla., Norman, 1970—. Materials cons. to industry Served to lt. (j.g.) USNR, 1950-53. Registered profl. engr., Okla., Tex. Mem. Am. Soc. M.E., A.A.A.S., Metall. Soc., Am. Soc. Metals, Inst. Metals (London, Eng.), Sigma Xi, Tau Beta Pi, Phi Lambda Upsilon. Phi Kappa Phi, Pi Tau Sigma, Phi Gamma Delta. Contbr. articles profl. jours. Home: 3941 Warwick Dr Norman OK 73069

UPTON, THOMAS GRAYDON, govt. ofcl; b. Salem, Mass., Mar. 26, 1908; s. George and Lorna (Graydon) U.; A.B., Harvard, 1931, student Bus. Sch., 1931-32; m. Ann Cheshire Nash, Apr. 30, 1942; children—Ann Appleby, Joseph Cheshire, Bryan Graydon, George Upton 2d. With Bank of Manhattan Co., 1932-40, rep. in London, Eng., 1936-40; engaged in investment bus., N.Y.C., 1946-50; v.p. fgn. dept. Phila. Nat. Bank, 1950-58; asst. sec. of treasury, also U.S. exec.

dir. Internat. Bank Reconstrn. and Devel., Internat. Finance Corp., Internat. Devel. Assn., 1958-60; exec. v.p. Inter. Am. Devel. Bank, 1961-71, sr. adviser, 1972—; dir. Loan Devel. Fund, 1959-60. Chmn. Mayor Com. Port Promotion, Phila., 1957-58, Phila. Port Bur., 1957-58. Bd. dirs. Population Reference Bur., Pan Am. Devel. Found., Fund for Multinational Mgmt. Edn. Served to lt. col. AUS, 1940-46. Mem. Bankers Assn. Fgn. Trade (pres. 1957). Clubs: Harvard (N.Y.C.); Metropolitan (Washington). Home: 817 Bulls Neck Rd McLean VA 22101 Office: Inter Am Devel Bank Washington DC 20577

URBAN, FRANCIS STANISLAW, economist; b. Iwanowka, Poland, May 16, 1926; s. Stanislaw and Anna (Korzec) U.; B. Comm., Nat. U. Ireland, 1951; M.A., U. Strasbourg, France, 1954, Diplome en Hautes Etudes Europeenes, 1955; m. Euphemia-Maria Sierman, Dec. 12, 1963; children—Brigitta-Annemarie, Theresa-Elizabeth. Came to U.S., 1956, naturalized, 1965. Lectr. bus. adminstrn. St. Patrick Coll., Karachi, Pakistan, 1957-58; prof. econs. Rangoon U., Burma, 1959-62; instr. math. econs. St. Michael's Coll., Santa Fe, N.M., 1963-65; asst. prof. econs. U. Albuquerque, 1965-66; economist, U.S. Dept. Agr., Washington, 1966—. Lectr. statistics and math. econs. Grad. Sch. U.S. Dept. Agr., 1966—. Served with Polish Army, 1942-48. Recipient Univ. Grant, U.K. Ministry Edn., 1948. Mem. Am. Econ. Assn. Author: Wartime Manpower Mobilization, 1961. Home: 4108 Jewel St Alexandria VA 22312 Office: Fgn Demand and Competition Div Econ Research Service US Dept Agr Washington DC 20250

URBAN, GILBERT WILLIAM, banker; b. Silver Lake, Minn., Oct. 20, 1928; s. William and Alice (Polak) U.; B.B.A., U. Minn., 1949; m. Elvera Mattson, Feb. 23, 1954; children—Lisa Alice Marie, LeAnn Kay. Sr. accountant Price, Waterhouse & Co., Chgo., 1949-50; chief accountant Cal. Bank, Los Angeles, 1950-51; asst. controller 1st Nat. Bank, Mpls., 1951-63, controller, 1963-69; v.p., cashier La. Nat. Bank, Baton Rouge, 1969—; instr. U. Minn. Evening Sch., 1956-69; instr. Nat. Assn. Bank Auditors and Controllers Sch., U. Wis., 1960-63, sr. class sect. leader, 1963—; instr. La. State U., 1970—, chmn. dept. controllership Bank Adminstrn. Inst., 1970; course coordinator Banking Sch. of South, 1970—. Mem. Beta Alpha Psi, Alpha Kappa Psi. Lutheran. Office: 451 Florida St Baton Rouge LA 70801

URBINA, PEDRO YVO JOSE, corp. cons., lawyer; b. Trujilo, Venezuela, Apr. 2, 1898; s. Pedro Y.J. and Josefa (Delgado) U.; LL.B., Nat. U., 1921, postgrad., 1922-23; LL.M., 1922, Master Patent Law, 1922; J.D., George Washington U., 1968;; m. Emily Frances Grigg, May 19, 1923; children—Pepita L. (Mrs. Kenneth M. Kauffman), Pedro Yvo Jose (dec.). Came to U.S., 1919, naturalized, 1922. Admitted to D.C. bar, 1922, Mass. bar, 1928; clk. U.S. Govt. Interior Dept. Bur. Indian Affairs, Washington, 1919-22, law clk., 1922-27; atty. Law Dept. United Fruit Co., Boston, 1927-64, cons. atty., 1965—. Served with USCG Temp. Res., 1942-44. Decorated Medal of Liberty. Mem. Am. Bar Assn. Clubs: National Lawyers (Washington); New Orleans Athletic; University (Boston). Home: The Thames Apt 205 2825 St Charles Av New Orleans LA 70115

UREKE, GEORGE, assn. exec.; b. Chgo., Mar. 19, 1919 John S. and Linca (Rusu) U.; B.S., U. Md., 1959; M.B.A., George Washington U., 1960; postgrad. Am. U., 1961—; m. Anna Mary Lupei, Nov. 9, 1940; children—Margaret Ann, Donald Dean, Brenda Lee. Commd. lt. USAF, 1942, advanced through grades to lt. col., 1963; ret., 1965; pilot flight instr. and tng. officer, 1942-50, flight comdr. B-47 Stratojet, 1951-55, squadron comdr. intelligence, 1956-60, information officer Dept. Def., 1960-65; ednl. dir. Investment Bankers Assn. of Am., Washington, 1965-71, sec., treas., 1971—; v.p. Jake Barcroft Recreation Center; dir. Inst. of Investment Banking, Washington, 1967-71; mem. adv. bd. Hamilton Bank & Trust Co., Falls Church, Va., 1967—. Asso. profl. lectr. George Washington U., 1961-65; lectr. indsl. Coll. of Armed Forces, 1967-70. First v.p. Barcroft Recreation Center, Inc., 1969—. Bd. dirs. Lake Barcroft Community Assn., 1960-63. Decorated D.F.C., Air medal with oak leaf clusters. Mem. Nat. Aero. Assn., Am. Mgmt. Assn., Aircraft Owners and pilots Assn., Air Derby Assn., Am. Soc. Assn. Execs. Baptist. Mason. Club: University (Washington). Home: 3604 Tallwood Terrace Falls Church VA 22041 Office: 425 13th St NW Washington DC 20004

URETZ, LESTER ROBERT, lawyer; b. Chgo., Jan. 10, 1922; s. Louis A. and Bertha (Simon) U.; A.A., Wilson Jr. Coll., Chgo., 1941; J.D., U. Chgo., 1948; m. Miriam Herman, June 9, 1966; children by previous marriage—Leslie, Laurie, Richard, Andy. Admitted to Ill. bar, 1948, D.C. bar, 1951, also U.S. Supreme Ct.; trial atty. fed. Security Agy., 1948-51, Dept. Health, Edn. and Welfare, 1952-53; with Internal Revenue Service, 1953-69, dir. refund litigation div., 1963-64, asst. to chief counsel, 1964-65. dep. chief counsel, 1965-66, chief counsel, 1966-69; partner firm of Cohen & Uretz, Washington, 1969—; speaker in field, 1955—. Exec. v.p. Galesburg Soy Products Co. (Ill.), 1951-52. Served with USAAF, 1942-45; China. Decorated Legion of Merit, Presdl. citation. Mem. Am., Fed., D.C. bar assns. Author articles in field. Home: 3226 Broad Branch Terrace NW Washington DC 20008 Office: 1730 M St NW Washington DC 20036

URMEY, MARY LOUISE SMITH, assn. exec.; b. Nicholsville, Ala., Sept. 14, 1906; d. George Milton and Mattie Emily (Dixon) Smith; student U. Tenn., 1938-41, George Washington U., 1947-48; m. Frank Winepark Urmey, Nov. 15, 1947. Various secretarial, research aide positions, Birmingham, Ala., Knoxville, Tenn., also Washington, 1930-57; exec. sec. Assn. ICC Practitioners, Washington, exec. editor ICC Practitioners' Jour., 1958—, also editorial supr. manuals and other documents ICC Practitioners. Mem. Bus. and Profl. Women's Club D.C. Democrat. Protestant. Home: 405 Valley Brook Dr Falls Church VA Office: Interstate Commerce Commn Bldg Washington DC

URODA, CLEMENT FREDERICK, banker; b. Betina, Jugoslavia, Nov. 24, 1910; s. Jack and Simica (Bilich) U.; grad. high sch.; m. Helen Julia Tacquard, Apr. 15, 1936; children—James Clement, Mary Ann (Mrs. Ronnie J. Anderson), Julia Clementine (Mrs. William L. Young). With First Nat. Bank, Galveston, Tex., 1929-58, asst. cashier, 1942-50, cashier, 1950-58, v.p., cashier, 1958; v.p., asst. comptroller First Hutchings-Sealy Nat. Bank, Galveston, Tex., 1958-59, v.p., auditor, 1959—. Roman Catholic. K.C., Lion. Home: 4817 Av O Galveston TX 77550 Office: PO Box 1500 Galveston TX 77550

URQUHART, SAMUEL LESTER, savs. and loan exec.; b. Norfolk, Va., Feb. 7, 1915; s. Samuel Lawrence and Eva Marion (Lester) U.; B.S., Wilberforce U., 1939; m. Edith Naomi Bedgood, Apr. 3, 1942; 1 dau., Sharon Lynelle. Pvt. practice pub. accounting, Newport News, Va., 1940—; v.p., mgr. Community Savs. & Loan Assn., 1957—. Mem. Newport News-Hampton Bd. Realtors. Chmn. area div., orgn. and extension com. Boy Scouts Am., 1957-59. Served with AUS, 1943-46. Mem. Peninsula C. of C., Nat. Soc. Pub. Accountants, Nat. Bus. League, Nat. Assn. Real Estate Brokers, V.F.W. (past post comdr.), Omega Psi Phi. Baptist. Mason (Shriner). Club: 533 (Richmond, Va.). Home: 1347 26th St Newport News VA 23607 Office: 1512 27th St Newport News VA 23607

URRY, DAN WESLEY, biochemist; b. Salt Lake City, Utah, Sept. 14, 1935; s. Herbert William and Emma Irene (Swaner) U.; B.A., Ph.D., U. Utah, 1964; m. Janet Ruth Mills, July 3, 1958 (div. July 1970); children—Weston Daniel, Douglas Whitmore, David William. Post doctoral fellow U. Utah, 1964, corp. fellow Harvard, 1964-65; vis. investigator Chem., Biodynamics Lab., U. Cal. at Berkeley, 1965-66; asso. mem. Inst. Biomed. Research, Chgo., 1965-69, mem. 1969-70; prefessorial lectr. U. Chgo., 1967-70; prof. biochemistry, dir. div. molecular biophysics U. Ala. Med. Center, Birmingham, 1970-72, dir. lab. molecular biophysics, 1972—. Mem. Am. Chem. Soc. (Gt. Lakes area div. chmn. biochemistry, 1969—), Am. Soc. Biol. Chemists, A.A.A.S., Sigma Xi, Phi Beta Kappa, Phi Kappa Phi, Phi Eta Sigma. Editor: Spectroscopic Approaches to Biomolecular Conformation. Editorial bd. Research/Devel. mag., 1969—, Biochimica Et Biophysica Acta, 1972—. Research on biomolecular conformation and its relationship to biol. function, e.g., biol. calcification and atherosclerosis, ion transport, structure of biomembranes, antibiotics. Home: 2423 Vestavia Dr Birmingham AL 35216 Office: U Ala University Sta Birmingham AL 35294

USDANE, WILLIAM MILLER, govt. ofcl.; b. Seattle, July 29, 1914; s. Louis and Jennie (Miller) U.; B.A., U. Wash., 1936, M.A., 1940; Ph.D., N.Y.U., 1955; m. Bernice Stusser, Dec. 5, 1943; children—Lynn (Mrs. David Millard), Mark. Vocational adviser VA, Seattle, 1946-50; dir. vocational rehab. Inst. for Crippled and Disabled, N.Y.C., 1950-56; prof. rehab. counseling, San Francisco State Coll., 1956-63; div. chief research and demonstration, Dept. Heatlh, Edn. and Welfare Social and Rehab. Service, Washington, 1963-69; dir. office of research Dept. of Labor, Washington, 1969-70; asst. commr. rehab. services adminstrn. Dept. Health, Edn. and Welfare, Washington, 1970—. Pres. Woodly House, Washington, 1968-69; mem. research bd. Easter Seal Found., Nat. Soc. for Crippled Children and Adults, 1963—. Served with AUS, 1942-45. Fulbright sr. research fellow London Sch. Econs., U. London, 1962-63. Mem. Am. Psychol. Assn. (pres. div. Contbr. articles to profl. jours. Home: 931 6th St SW Washington DC 20024 Office: Dept of HEW 330 C St SW Washington DC 20201

USDIN, GENE LEONARD, physician, psychiatrist; b. N.Y.C., Jan. 31, 1922; s. I. L. and Eva (Miller) U.; student U. N.C., 1939-40, U. Fla., 1940-41; B.S., Tulane U., 1943, M.D., 1946; m. Cecile Weil, Nov. 8, 1947; children—Cecile Catherine, Linda Ann, Steven William, Thomas Michael. Intern Touro Infirmary, New Orleans, 1946-47; jr. asst., asst. resident psychiatry Cin. Gen. Hosp., 1949-51; fellow psychiatry, Tulane Sch. Medicine, 1951-52; pvt. practice psychiatry, New Orleans, 1952—; asst. prof. clin. psychiatry Tulane Sch. Medicine, 1959-62, asso. prof. clin. psychiatry, 1962-67; asso. prof. clin. psychiatry La. State U. Sch. Medicine, 1967—; prof. psychiatry Notre Dame Sem., 1969—; chief div. neurology and psychiatry Touro Infirmary, New Orleans, 1962-66, dir. psychiat. services, 1966-71; sr. vis. psychiatrist at DePaul & Charity Hosps.; past chmn. psychiat. cons. com. Am. Bar Found. Asst. examiner Am. Bd. Psychiatry and Neurology, 1956—. Trustee United Fund Greater New Orleans, 1966-70. Served to lt. (j.g.) USNR, 1947-49. Diplomate Am. Bd. Neurology and Psychiatry, Am. Bd. Legal Medicine. Fellow Am. Psychiat. Assn. (chmn. com. psychiatry and law 1964-68, com. on ethics 1970—), Am. Coll. Psychiatrists (bd. regents 1967-70), So. (v.p. 1965-66, pres. elect 1972-73), La. (past pres.) psychiat. assns., Acad. Psychosomatic Medicine, Am. Psychosomatic Soc., New Orleans Soc. Psychiatry and Neurology (past pres.), Group Advancement Psychiatry (chmn. com. psychiatry and law 1963-67, trustee, 1970—), mem. Am., So. (bd. regents 1969-72, chmn. 1971-72) med. assns., Am. Acad. Forensic Scis., La. (chmn. com. mental health), Orleans Parish med. socs., Nat. Assn. Mental Health (profl. adv. council). Rotarian. Author articles in field, Editor in chief Psychiatry Digest, 1964-71; bd. editors Mental Hygiene, 1969—, Clin. Medicine, 1965-71, Med. Digest, 1965-71; editor books: Psychoneurosis & Schizophrenia, 1966; Practical Lectures in Psychiatry for the Medical Practitioner, 1966; Adolescence: Care and Counseling, 1967; Perspectives on Violence, 1972; The Psychiatric Forum, 1972. Editor (with Peter A. Martin and A.W. Sipe) A Physician in the General practice of Psychiatry, 1970. Home: 3 Newcomb Blvd New Orleans LA 70118 Office: 1522 Aline St New Orleans LA 70115

USRY, CHESTER A., U.S. dist. dir. of Internal Revenue*

USRY, HERBERT MILTON, hosp. adminstr.; b. Dallas, May 20, 1917; s. Lee Milton and Maude Mae (Goss) U.; B.A. in Social Sci., Howard Payne Coll., Brownwood, Tex., 1945; B.S. in Hosp. Adminstrn., Okla. Bapt. U., 1961; m. Irene Rothell, May 11, 1940; 1 son, William. Commd. 1st lt. U.S. Army, 1945, advanced through grades to maj., 1955; chaplain, 1945-57; ret., 1957; credit and collections mgr. Grand Valley Hosp., Pryor, Okla., 1957-58, adminstrv. asst., 1958-59, asst. adminstr., 1959-62, adminstr., 1962—. N.E. rep. Bapt. Found. Okla. Mem. Am. Coll. Hosp. Adminstrs., Acad. Med. Adminstrs., Protestant Hosp. Assn. Mason, Rotarian. Home: Route 2 Box 23 Adair OK 74330 Office: 1111 E Center St Pryor OK 74361

USRY, LUTHER WALLACE, realtor; b. Gadsden, Ala., Sept. 2, 1913; s. Henry H. and Eliza (Bryant) U.; A.B., Samford U., 1937; m. Lillian Ruth Royal, Oct. 5, 1932; 1 dau., Charlotte Jane (Mrs. Max Seldon Bobo). Ordained to ministry Bapt. Ch., 1935; pastor Bellevue Bapt. Ch., Gadsden, 1935-46, James Meml. Bapt. Ch., Gadsden, 1946-54; broker Harris-Usry, Co., Gadsden, 1964—; now owner Usry Realty Co., Gadsden. Mem. Ala. Real Estate Bd. (dir. 1965—, finance com. 1967—), Gadsden Real Estate Bd. (pres. 1966—, dir. 1967—), Etowah Bapt. Assn. (mem. exec. com. 1935-54, clk., treas., 1949-54), Ala. Real Estate Assn. (dir. 1969), C. of C. Mason. Home: 147 Washington Circle Gadsden AL 35901 Office: 1137 Forrest Av Gadsden AL 35901

USRY, MILTON FRANKLIN, JR., educator; b. Mineola, Tex., Aug. 31, 1931; s. Milton Franklin and Emma Lucille (Weaver) U.; B.B.A., Baylor U., 1952; M.B.A., U. Houston, 1959; Ph.D., U. Tex., 1964; m. Dona Esther White, Nov. 25, 1951; children—Milton Wayne, Mark Lester. Accountant, Shell Chem. Co., Houston, 1955-59; asst. prof. accounting U. Houston, 1959-61; regents prof. accounting Okla. State U., Stillwater, 1961—. Served with AUS, 1952-54. Arthur Anderson & Co. doctoral fellow, 1963. C.P.A., Tex., Okla. Mem. Am. Accounting Assn., Am. Inst. C.P.A.'s, Beta Gamma Sigma, Beta Alpha Psi, Alpha Chi, Delta Sigma Pi. Mason. Author: Capital-Expenditure Planning and Control, 1966. Cons. editor: Cost Accounting-Planning and Control (Matz and Curry), 1967, 72. Home: 1015 W Knapp St Stillwater OK 74074

UTLEY, CLIFTON GARRICK, TV corr.; b. Chgo., Nov. 19, 1939; s. Clifton Maxwell and Frayn (Garrick) U.; B.A., Carleton Coll., 1961; postgrad. Free U. Berlin (Germany), 1962-63. TV corr. news dept. NBC, 1963—, aasignments in Brussels, Belgium, 1963-64, Vietnam, 1964-65, Chicago, 1966, N.Y.C., 1966, and in Berlin, Germany, 1966-68, chief bur., Paris, France, 1968-70, Washington, 1970—. Served with AUS, 1961-62. Office: 4001 Nebraska Av NW Washington DC 20016

UTLEY, FREDA, author, lectr.; b. London, Eng., Jan. 23, 1898; d. Willie Herbert and Emily (Williamson) Utley; B.A., first class honors in History, London U., 1923, M.A. with distinction, 1925; m. in in Russia, Arcadi Berdichevsky, 1928; 1 son, Jon Basil. Naturalized Am. citizen, 1950. Research fellow London Sch. Econs., 1926-28; spl. corr. Manchester Guardian Comml. in Japan, 1928-29; lived in Russia, 1930-36, working as sr. sci. worker Inst. of World Economy and Politics, Acad. Scis., Moscow; spl. corr. London News Chronicle, China war zone, 1938; resident in U.S., 1939—; econ. adviser to Starr, Park, Freeman, Inc., N.Y.C., 1940-44; cons. to Chinese Supply Commn., 1944-45; accredited corr. Readers Digest in China, 1945-56, Germany, 1948. Adv. council dept. politics Princeton, 1941-47. Dir. Am.-China Policy Assn., Inc. Author: Lancashire and the Far East, 1931; Japan's Feet of Clay, 1936; Japan's Gamble in China, 1937; China at War, 1939; The Dream We Lost, 1940; Last Chance in China, 1946; Lost Illusion, 1948; The High Cost of Vengeance, 1949; The China Story, 1951; Will the Middle East Go West, 1957; Odyssey of a Liberal, Memoirs, 1970. Home: 1611 21st St NW Washington DC 20009

UTTERBACK, DONALD DESMOND, oil and mining co. exec.; b. Edmore, Mich., Aug. 18, 1904; s. Chelsey Chalmers and Margaret (Henderson) U.; B.S., U. Ill., 1930, M.S., 1932, Ph.D., 1936; m. Naomi Wyninger, July 23, 1936; 1 dau., Beverly June (Mrs. Eldridge). Sr. geologist Tex. Co., New Orleans, 1936-46; dist. geologist Houston Oil Co. Tex., 1946-51; v.p. exploration Freeport Oil Co., New Orleans, 1951-60, geol. cons., 1960—; v.p. exploration and devel. Basic Resources Internat. Ltd., Toronto, Ont., Can., 1969—. Served to maj. AUS, 1942-46. Fellow Geol Soc. Am., Am. Assn. Petroleum Geologists, Soc. Exploration Geophysicists, Soc. Ind. Profl. Earth Scientists, Am. Inst. Profl. Geologists, Petroleum Club New Orleans (past sec.). Home: 2223 Palmer Av New Orleans LA 70118 Office: Pere Marguette Bldg New Orleans LA 70112

UTTERBACK, MARTHA, museum curator; b. San Antonio, July 11, 1930; d. Charles Dewey and Ruby (Howard) Utterback; B.A. summa cum laude, Trinity U., 1952; student Inst. Design, Chgo., 1956. Curator natural history Witte Mus., San Antonio, 1952-54; civilian security service with USAF, 1954-56; tchr. English, art, San Antonio and Dallas, 1956-58; curator art Witte Mus., 1958—. Bd. dirs. San Antonio Civil Liberties Union, San Antonio Art League. Mem. Am. Assn. Museums, UN Assn. U.S.A., Inc. Home: 414 Ira Av San Antonio TX 78209 Office: 3801 Broadway San Antonio TX 78209

UVACEK, EDWARD, JR., agrl. economist; b. Newark, Sept. 12, 1930; s. Edward and Julia (Lukasik) U.; grad. Seton Hall, 1948; B.S., Rutgers U., 1952, M.S., 1956; Ph.D., Tex. A. and M. U., 1967; postgrad. U.S. Dept. Agr. Grad. Sch., 1958; m. Beatrice Greer, Apr. 18, 1959; children—Debra Theresa, Cynthia Ann, Edward Eugene. Agrl. economist, research div. U.S. Dept. Agr., Washington, Los Angeles, 1956-59; commodity analyst Armour & Co., Chgo., 1959-61; specialist livestock marketing, agrl. extension service, Tex. A. and M. U., College Station, 1961-63, asso. prof. and extension livestock marketing specialist, 1967—; dir. Western Research Inst., College Station, 1960—. Econ. livestock cons. AID, Panama, 1962, Korea, 1963; testified as expert witness Nat. Commn. on Food Marketing, 1965, Nat. Adv. Commn. on Food and Fiber, 1966. Award Trustee Livestock Merchandising Inst., 1971. Served to 1st lt. USAF, 1952-54. Mem. Am., Western agrl. econs. assns., Internat. Assn. Agrl. Economists, Am. Marketing Assn.Home: 1001 Pershing Dr College Station TX 77840 Office: Dept Agrl Econs Tex A and M U College Station TX 77840

UXER, JOHN ELMO, ednl. adminstr.; b. Garrison, N.M., Mar. 31, 1924; s. John and Myrtle Alice (Albright) U.; B.S., N.M. State U., 1949, M.A., 1951, Edn. Specialist, 1962, Ed.D., 1967; m. Wyvonia Oleta Stroud, Aug. 19, 1944; children—John Elmo, Dell Anne. Tchr., House, N.M., 1950-51, Carlsbad, N.M., 1953-54, Artesia, N.M., 1954-57; dir. guidance and counseling, Artesia, N.M., 1957-59, dir. instrn., 1959-61; supt., Jal, N.M., 1961-65; asst. prof. N.M. State U., Las Cruces, N.M., 1966-67; exec. dir. Legislative Finance Com., N.M. Legislature, 1967-68; exec. dir. Region XIX Edn. Service Center, El Paso, Tex., 1968—. Cons. N.M. State Dept. Edn., 1965-68; mem. adv. commn. Tex. Edn. Agy., 1968—; mem. Gov's. Land Use Com., N.M., 1962-63. Bd. dirs. Armed Forces YMCA. Served with USNR, 1942-46, AUS, 1951-53. Decorated Purple Heart, Bronze Star medal; recipient Distinguished Alumnus award Coll. Edn., N.M. State U., 1971. Mem. Am. Personnel and Guidance Assn., N.E.A., Am. Sch. Counselors Assn., Am. Assn. Sch. Adminstrs., Assn. Higher Edn., Tex. State Tchrs. Assn., Tex. Assn. Sch. Adminstrs., N.M. State U. Alumni Assn. (pres.-elect 1972), Phi Delta Kappa. Baptist. Kiwanian, Rotarian. Home: 6404 Westwind St El Paso TX 79912 Office: PO Box 10716 El Paso TX 79997

UZZELL, MINTER, educator; b. Baird, Tex., Aug. 6, 1909; s. Minter Womack and Ada Estelle (Cooke) U.; A.A., Wayland Baptist Coll.; A.B., Hardin Simmons U., 1930; Th.M., S.W. Bapt. Theol. Sem., 1933; Th.M., Berkeley Bapt. Div., 1937; M.A., U. Tulsa, 1951, P.D.E., 1952, Ed.D., 1954; m. Pauline Dykes, Nov. 14, 1937; children—Carol Sue (Mrs. Rex Wayne Kay), Carey Lee. Ordained to ministry Bapt. Ch., 1928; pastor Tex., Ida., Washington, Cal., Okla., 1928; tchr. pub. schs., Muskogee, Okla., 1945-47; asso. sec. YMCA, Ga. Inst. Tech., 1947-48; instr. Bacone Coll., 1949-59; prof. English, Northeastern State Coll., Tahlequah, Okla., 1959—, formerly dean of students. Active A.R.C. Served with AUS, 1941-45, 53; ETO. Mem. Am. Assn. U. Profs., Nat., Okla. edn. assns., Assn. for Higher Edn., Am. Legion, Res. Officers Assn., Cherokee Hist. Soc., Phi Lambda Chi, Phi Delta Kappa, Kappa Delta Pi. Democrat. Baptist. Kiwanian. Home: 269 Redbud Lane Tahlequah OK 74464

UZZELL, WILLIAM EGBERT, beverage co. exec.; b. Louisburg, N.C., Aug. 11, 1912; s. William Egbert and Alice (Jackson) U.; B.S in Commerce, U. N.C., 1932; m. Francis E. Hill, Dec. 31, 1938; children— Gretchen, Catherine. Asst. mgr. Sears Roebuck & Co., Chattanooga and Jackson, Miss., 1932-37; dist. mgr. Nehi Corp., Nashville, 1938-46, dept. head, Columbus, Ga., 1946-50, asst. sales mgr., 1950-55, gen. sales mgr., 1955-57; v.p. sales Royal Crown Cola Co., Columbus, 1957-60, v.p., dir. marketing, 1961-65, pres., 1965-69; chmn., chief exec. officer Royal Crown Cola Internat., Ltd., 1969-70, spl. adviser to pres., 1970—; dir. 1st Nat. Bank, Columbus, Ga. Trustee Birmingham-So. Coll., Nat. Inf. Mus. Assn. Served to lt. USNR, 1942-45. Baptist. Rotarian. Home: 2919 Fleetwood Dr Columbus GA 31906 Office: 10th St and 10th Av Columbus GA 31902

VAA, NORMAN AUSTIN, computer systems analyst; b. Poulsbo, Wash., Sept. 10, 1925; s. Edwin Knute and Ida Sophia (Larson) V.; student Purdue U., 1944-45; B.A. in Math., U. So. Cal., 1959; M.S. in Operations Analysis, U.S. Naval Postgrad. Sch., 1962; m. Beatrice Lorraine Stigers, Dec. 27, 1945; 1 dau., Catherine (Mrs. Michael Jon McMinn). Commd. ensign U.S. Navy, 1945, advanced through grades to lt. comdr., 1965; systems analyst IBM Corp., Washington, 1965-68, Honolulu, 1968-71, Arlington, Va., 1971—. Mem. Operations Research Soc. Am., Data Processing Mgmt. Assn., Nat., Hawaii rifle assns. Office: 1601 N Kent St Arlington VA 22209

VACCA, JOHN JOSEPH, broadcasting exec.; b. Chgo., Apr. 7, 1922; s. John Joseph and Caroline (Bain) V.; student Northwestern U., 1940-42, Internat. Corr. Schs., 1950-54; m. Alice Isabel Ure, May 2, 1944; children—John Joseph, Dawn Susan, Kim Frances. Editor, Midwest Times, Chgo., 1940-41; with prodn. dept. NBC, Radio, 1946-47; news dir. sta. KECK, Odessa, Tex., 1947-49, chief announcer, 1948-49; program mgr. KOSA-Radio, Odessa, 1949-55, sta. mgr. KOSA-TV, 1955-61, gen. mgr., 1962-72; v.p., dir. Trigg Vaughn Stas., Inc., Odessa, 1962-67; sec. Odessa Broadcasting Co., 1950-72; v.p., asst. sec. Doubleday Broadcasting Co., 1967—; gen. mgr. KDTV, Dallas, 1972—. Bd. dirs. Odessa Community Chest, 1964-72, Better Bus. Bur., 1956—; campaign maj. A.R.C., 1951—; publicity adviser Ector County chpt. Nat. Found. for Infantile Paralysis, 1949-72; campaign coordinator Civic Music Assn., 1950—; sponsor, adviser Permian Playhouse, 1959-72, v.p., dir., 1971-72. City councilman, Odessa, 1962-64. Bd. dirs. Am. Cancer Soc. Served with USAAF, 1942-46. Recipient Zeus award Epsilon Sigma Alpha, 1971. Mem. Tex. AP Broadcasters Assn., Advt. Club Odessa (pres. 1960-61, dir., 1960-63), C. of C. (publicity adviser 1950-72), Holy Name Soc. Roman Catholic K.C. (sec. Odessa 1950-51). Home: 3900 Harry Hines Blvd Dallas TX 75219

VACHON, REGINALD IRENEE, educator; b. Norfolk, Va., Jan. 29, 1937; s. Rene Albert and Regina (Galvin) V.; student U.S. Naval Acad., 1954-55; B.S., Auburn U., 1958, M.S., 1960; Ph.D., Okla. State U., 1963; LL.B., Jones Law Sch., 1969; m. Mary Eleanor Grigg, Jan. 16, 1960; children—Reginald Irenee, Eleanor Marie. Engr., Hayes Aircraft Co., Birmingham, Ala., summer 1958; research and devel. engr. E.I. duPont Co., Orange, Tex., 1960; sr. engr. Thiokol Chem. Corp., Huntsville, summer 1963; aerospace engr. Marshall Space Flight Center, Huntsville, summer 1964, aerospace technologist, summer 1965; asso. prof. mech. engring. Auburn (Ala.) U., 1963-65, alumni asso. prof. mech. engring. dept. 1965-67, alumni prof., 1967—. Served to 2d lt. C.E., AUS, 1960-61. Ford Forgiveable Loan Fellow, 1962-63. Mem. Am. Soc. M.E., Am. Soc. for Engring. Edn., Am. Inst. Aero. and Astronautics, Nat., Nat. Soc. Profl. Engrs., A.L.A., Ala. Bar, Am. Bar Assn., Sigma Xi, Omicron Delta Kappa. Home: 116 Miller Av Auburn AL 36830

VADAKIN, JAMES CHARLES, educator; b. Lima, O., Mar. 8, 1924; s. James Charles and Grace (Miller) V.; B.A., Denison U., 1946; M.B.A., Harvard, 1947; Ph.D., Cornell U., 1952; m. Mary Ann Willoughby, Sept. 8, 1946; 1 son, Jeffrey J. Mem. faculty U. Miami (Fla.), 1947—, prof. econs., 1957—, chmn. dept., 1961—, coordinator Cuban Econ. Research Project, 1961—; arbitrator labor-mgmt., 1950—; frequent speaker. Mem. panel arbitrators Fed. Mediation and Conciliation Service; mem. Fed. Ser. Impasses Panel. Served with USNR, 1942-46. First hon. mem. Personnel Assn. Miami, 1954. Mem. Nat. Acad. Arbitrators (bd. govs.), Am. Arbitration Assn., Am. So. econ. assns., Phi Kappa Phi, Omicron Delta Kappa, Lambda Chi Alpha. Club: Harvard (Miami). Author: Family Allowances, 1958; Children, Poverty and Family Allowance, 1968; also articles. Home: 1450 Ancona Av Coral Gables FL 33146

VADEN, LEWIS H., state treas. Va.*

VAETH, JOSEPH GORDON, govt. ofcl.; b. N.Y.C., Feb. 12, 1921; s. Joseph Anthony and Sara (Billard) V.; A.B., N.Y.U., 1941; m. Joanne Corell, Dec. 30, 1950; 1 son, Gordon Corell. Instr., Adm. Billard Acad., New London, Conn., 1941-42, Lawrenceville (N.J.) Sch., 1946-47; project engr., tech. programs officer U.S. Naval Tng. Device Center, 1947-54, head new weapons and systems div., 1954-58; tech. staff mem. for man-in-space Advanced Research Projects Agy., Def. Dept., 1958-60; mgr. Washington operations Reflectone Electronics, Inc., 1960-62; asst. to dir. Nat. Weather Satellite Center, U.S. Weather Bur., 1962-63, mgr. TIROS operational satellite system engring. div., 1963-66, dir. system engring. Nat. Environmental Satellite Center, Environmental Sci. Services Adminstrn., 1966-70; dir. system engring. Nat. Environmental Satellite Service, Nat. Oceanic and Atmospheric Adminstrn. Commerce Dept., 1970—. Mem. British Interplanetary Soc. U., S. Naval Inst., The Lighter-than-air Soc. Episcopalian. Club: Army and Navy (Washington). Author: Weather Eyes in the Sky, 1965; 200 Miles Up, 1951; Graf Zeppelin, 1958; To the Ends of the Earth, 1962; Langley: Man of Science and Flight, 1966; The Man Who Founded Georgia, 1968; also numerous articles. Contbr. Ency. Brit. Home: 3000 Tennyston St NW Washington DC 20015 Office: Nat Environmental Satellite Service Washington DC 20233

VAGT, JOHN PAUL, coll. dean; b. Jackson, Minn., Nov. 28, 1923; s. John and Dora (Wick) V.; B.A., N. Tex. State U., 1949; M.L.S., U. Tex., 1953; m. Mary Evelyn Hooker, July 29, 1951; children—Janice Evelyn (Mrs. George Smith), Kathryn Juliana. Asst. librarian Tarleton State Coll., 1949-51; librarian, Howard County Jr. Coll., 1953-61, Odessa Coll., 1961-64; dir. libraries Midwestern U., 1964-67; dean learning resources Tarrant County Jr. Coll., Fort Worth, 1967—. Served with AUS, 1945-47. Mem. Am. Assn. Edn. and Communications Tech., Am. Assn. Higher Edn., Am., Tex. library assns., Phi Delta Kappa. Contbr. articles to profl. jours. Home: 3313 Jamestown Dr Fort Worth TX 76119 Office: 5301 Campus Dr Fort Worth TX 76119

VAHLE, CORNELIUS WENDELL, JR., research co. exec.; b. Tracy, Minn., July 15, 1932; s. Cornelius Wendell and Gertrude (Gilronan) V.; B.A., St. Johns U., Collegeville, Minn., 1954; M.A., Cath. U. Am., 1957; Ph.D., Georgetown U., 1967; m. Helen Kate Curry, Feb. 8, 1958; children—Maria, Stephen, Tom More, Peter. Historian, Nat. Park Service, 1958-60; examiner U.S. Bur. of Budget, Washington, 1960-66; v.p. Operations & Policy Research, Inc., Washington, 1966—; mng. editor World Affairs, 1969—; editor Perspective, 1972—. Pres. Queen of Peace Credit Union, 1963-65. Served with AUS, 1954-56. Home: 5536 N 18th St Arlington VA 22205 Office: 4000 Albermarle St NW Washington DC 20016

VAIL, CHARLES CONRADY, JR., indsl. relations exec.; b. N.Y.C., Oct. 19, 1933; s. Charles Conrady and Virginia (Snow) V.; B.A., Roanoke Coll., 1955; M.S., Radford Coll., 1968; m. Mary Paula Pilkenton, Dec. 22, 1960; children—Charles Conrady III, Elizabeth Risen. Indsl. relations trainee Old Dominion Candies, Roanoke, Va., 1957-60; guidance counsellor Roanoke pub. schs., 1960-64; exec. v.p., treas. Roanoke Valley Industries, 1964—, Indsl. Learning Corp. of Va. Co-chmn. Cancer Crusade, Met. Roanoke Valley, 1967, chmn., 1968. Bd. dirs. Am. Cancer Soc., Roanoke Valley, Va. Coll. Placement Assn. Mem. Nat. Indsl. Council, Nat. Assn. Mfrs. Edn., Am. Soc. Personnel Adminstrs., Personnel Assn. Roanoke, Am. Soc. Assn. Execs. Home: 2614 Richelieu Av SW Roanoke VA 24014 Office: Colonial-Am Bldg Roanoke VA 24011

VAIL, EDWIN GEORGE, scientist; b. Toledo, July 25, 1921; s. Jay Coy and Bernice (Hauman) V.; B.Sc., U. Toledo, 1947; M.Sc., Ohio State U., 1948, Ph.D., 1953; m. Mary Janet McFarland, Nov. 27, 1946; children—Edwin Jay, Thomas Clair, Michael Andrew, Valerie Ann, Richard Austin. With aero. systems div. USAF, Wright Patterson AFB, O., 1951-64; chief human engring. Hamilton Standard, Windsor Locks, Conn., 1964-69; research physiologist Navel Ship Research and Devel. Lab., Panama City, Fla., 1970—. Active Boy Scouts Am. Served with AUS, 1951-55. Decorated Air medal with three oak leaf clusters. Mem. Aerospace Med. Assn., Sigma Xi, Alpha Epsilon Delta. Mem. Ch. of Christ. Mason. Contbr. articles to profl. jours. Home: 4502 Vista Lane Lynn Haven FL 32444 Office: Naval Ship Research and Devel Lab Panama City FL 32401

VALAZQUEZ, GONZALO, librarian, lawyer; b. Caguas, P.R., Nov. 25, 1905; s. Antonio and Francusca (Lerdo) V.; B.Edn., U. P.R., 1928, LL.B., 1940; M.L.S., Columbia, 1934; m. Ana Rosa Castro, Jan. 6, 1935. Asst. librarian U. P.R., 1928-43, asso. librarian, 1944-55; admitted to P.R. bar, 1941; library supr. P.R. Dept. Edn., 1955-56; dir. library div. P.R. Dept. Edn., 1957—. Mem. A.L.A., P.R. Bar Assn., P.R. Acad. Arts and Scis., Internat. Cataloging Com., Agrupacion Cubana Jose Toribio Medina (hon.). Author: Complicion de encabezamientos de materia para catalogos diccionarios, 1948; Classification Scheme for the University of Puerto Rico Law Library, 1947; La Bibliograffa en Puerto Rico, La Habana, 1955. Editor: Anuario Bibliografico Puertorriquenio, 1948—. Home: 908 Marti Santurce PR 00907 Office: Box 3127 GPO San Juan PR 00936

VALDEZ-SABATER, FERNANDO ARTURO, physician; b. Azua, Dominican Republic, May 4, 1927; s. Adriano and Ana Consuelo (Sabater) V.; M.D., U. Santo Domingo, 1956; m. America Ana Franco, Mar. 15, 1958; children— Fernando A., Ana Yanilsa, Harold Valdez Franco. Intern, Hosp. Jose Maria Cabral y Baez, Santiago, Dominican Republic, 1955-56, Paterson (N.J.) Gen. Hosp., 1957-58; resident All Souls Hosp., Morristown, N.J., 1959-60; gen. practice medicine, Salinas, P.R., 1969—; dir. Hosp. Municipal, Juana Diaz, P.R., Hosp. Municipal, Salinas, P.R., Unidad Salud Publica, Salinas. Bd. dirs. A.R.C., Salinas, 1965. Mem. Am. Acad. Family Physicians, Asociacion medica Americana y de P.R., Casa del Medico de Ponce. Mason, Lion. Home: Urbanizacion Salimar A-4 1 Salinas PR 00751 Office: Palmer esquina Union Salinas PR 00751

VALDIVIA, JOSE FRANCISCO, JR., food co. exec.; b. Sancti-Spiritus, Las Villas, Cuba, Jan. 4, 1932; s. Jose F. and Elena A. (Jimenez) V.; Litt.B., Colegio De La Salle, Havana, Cuba, 1949; LL.B., U. Havana, 1954; m. Teresa Hernandez, Feb. 4, 1956; children—Teresita, Jose Frank, Maria Elena. Came to U.S., 1961, naturalized, 1967. Admitted to Cuban Nat. bar, 1954; practiced in Sancti-Spiritus, Cuba, 1954-61; adminstr. fgn. affairs Scott-Mattson Farms, Inc., 1961-70, S. P.R. Sugar Co., 1967-70; v.p. corporate affairs Gulf Western Food Products Co., Ft. Pierce, Fla., 1970—, also dir. subsidiaries, Bahamas, P.R., Costa Rica, Dominican Republic. Mem. Inter-Am. Bar Assn., Am. Soc. Internat. Law. Roman Catholic. Club: Pelican Yacht (Ft. Pierce). Home: 4017 Greenwood Dr Fort Pierce FL 33450 Office: Professional Bldg Fort Pierce FL 33450

VALENTI, JACK JOSEPH, motion picture exec.; b. Houston, Sept. 5, 1921; B.A., U. Houston, 1946; M.B.A., Harvard, 1948; m. Mary Margaret Wiley, June 1, 1962; children—Courtenay Lynda, John Lyndon, Alexandra Alice. Co-founder, formerly exec. v.p. Weekley and Valenti, Inc., advt.; spl. asst. to Pres. Johnson, 1963-66; pres. Motion Picture Assn. Am., Inc., 1966—. Dir. Trans World Airlines. Bd. dirs. Am. Film Inst., Corp. for Pub. Broadcasting; trustee John F. Kennedy Center for Performing Arts. Served as pilot USAAF, 1942-45. Decorated D.F.C., Air medal with 5 clusters; named Outstanding Young Man of Houston, 1956. Author: Bitter Taste of Glory, 1971. Home: 1600 Eye St NW Washington DC 20006

VALENTINE, FOY DAN, clergyman; b. Edgewood, Tex., July 3, 1923; s. John Hardy and Josie (Johnson) V.; B.A., Baylor U., 1944; Th. M., Southwestern Baptist Theol. Sem., 1947, Th.D., 1949; D.D., William Jewell Coll., 1966; m. Mary Louise Valentine, May 6, 1947; children—Mary Jean, Carol Elizabeth, Susan Foy. Ordained to ministry Bapt. Ch., 1942; dir. Bapt. student activities colls. of Houston, 1949-50; pastor First Bapt. Ch., Gonzales, Tex., 1950-53; dir. Christian life commn. Bapt. Gen. Conv. Tex., 1953-60; exec. sec.-treas. Christian life commn. So. Bapt. Conv., 1960—, chmn. So. Bapt. inter-agy. council, 1965-67; Willson lectr. applied Christianity Wayland Bapt. Coll., 1963; Christian ethics lectr. Bapt. Theol. Sem., Ruschlikon-Zurich, Switzerland, 1966. Mem. commn. religious liberty and human rights Bapt. World Alliance, 1966—; trustee Protestants and Other Ams. United for Separation of Church and State; bd. dirs. Bapt. Joint Com. Pub. Affairs, Interpreter's House, mem. Nashville Met. Human Relations Commn., 1966—. Mem. Am. Soc. Christian Ethics, Com. So. Churchmen. Democrat. Author: Christian Faith in Action 1956; Believe and Behave, 1964; Citizenship for Christians, 1965; The Cross in the Marketplace, 1966; Peace Peace, 1967; Where the Action is: Studies in James, 1969; also articles. Home: 6354 Torrington Rd Nashville TN 37205 Office: 460 James Robertson Pky Nashville TN 37219

VALENTINE, JOHN PHILLIP, hosp. adminstr.; b. Evanston, Ill., Jan. 11, 1923; s. Frank B. and Margaret P. (Barbutt) V.; B.A., San Francisco State Coll., 1957; M.B.A., Syracuse U., 1958; D.Bus. Adminstrn., George Washington U., 1965; m. Gloria Margo Nelson, Aug. 16, 1948; 1 son, James A. Enlisted as pvt. U.S. Army, 1943, advanced through grades to col., 1970; comdr. Litter Bearer Platoon, 1943-44, Ambulance Co., 1944-45, Collecting Co., 1945-46; exec. officer 25th Med. Bn., 1950-51; exec. officer U.S. Army Hosp., Kyoto, Japan, 1951-53; comptroller Office Surgeon, Hdqrs. Presidio San Francisco, 1953-57, Office Surgeon, Hdqrs. 5th Army, Chgo., 1957-60; spl. asst. to comptroller Office Surgeon Gen., Dept. Army, Washington, 1960-65; dir. U.S. Army-Baylor U. Program in Health Care Adminstrn., 1965-68; dir. dept. adminstrn. U.S. Army Med. Field Service Sch., Brooke Army Med. Center, 1965-69; adminstr. Loudoun Meml. Hosp., Leesburg, Va., 1970—. Bd. dirs. A.R.C. Decorated Bronze Star medal with two oak leaf clusters, Army Commendation medal with three oak leaf clusters. Mem. Am. Acad. Med. Adminstr., Am. Coll. Hosp. Adminstr., Am. Pub. Health Assn., Assn. U.S. Army, Assn. U. Programs in Hosp. Adminstrn. (mem. exec. com. 1967-70), Armed Forces Mgmt. Assn., Am. Mgmt. Assn., Am., Tex. hosp. assns., Alamo Hosp. Div. (v.p. 1965-69). Home: Cattail Ordinary Route 1 Box 468 Leesburg VA 22075 Office: 70 W Cornwall St Leesburg VA 22075

VALERIANI, RICHARD GERARD, news broadcaster; b. Camden, N.J., Aug. 29, 1932; s. Nicholas and Christine (Camerota) V.; B.A., Yale, 1953; student U. Pavia (Italy), 1953-54; m. Coralee Svec Hall, Jan. 22, 1965. Reporter, The Trentonian, Trenton, N.J., 1957; with A.P., 1957-61, corr., Havana, Cuba, 1959-61; with NBC-TV News, 1961—, corr., Washington, 1965—. Served with AUS, 1955-56. Recipient Overseas Press Club award best radio reporting, 1965. Mem. Elihu Soc. Home: 432 St SW Washington DC 20024 Office: 4001 Nebraska Av NW Washington DC 20016

VALIUNAS, ANDREW VYTAUTAS, economist; b. Kaunas, Lithuania, Oct. 20, 1927; s. Domas and Maria (Peciulis) V.; B.A., U. Tuebingen, 1950, M.A., 1950, Ph.D., 1958; m. Colette Rejanne Ducrocq, Oct. 24, 1957. Came to U.S., 1951, naturalized, 1954. Co-founder Vesta G.m.b.H., import-export co., Tuebingen, Germany, 1947-51; research specialist, aerospace engr. Library of Congress, 1958-67; internat. economist Office Econ. Research, U.S. Tariff Commn., Washington, 1967—. Served with USAF, 1952-56; maj. U.S. Army Res. Mem. Am. Econ. Assn., Res. Officers Assn. Author: The Finance Policy of Lithuanian Republic, 1918-40, 1950; The Sovietization of Lithuanian Economy, 1940-41, 1958. Home: 2032 Belmont Rd NW Washington DC 20009 Office: 8th and E Sts NW Washington DC 20436

VALLADARES O., RENE, architect, constrn. co. exec.; b. Guatemala City, Guatemala, July 17, 1926; s. Rodolfo and Carmen (Ortiz) V.; grad. Nat. Inst. Guatemala; B. Scis. and Letters, U. St. Carlos, 1944; Architecture, U. Autonoma de Mexico, 1946-50; postgrad. Tulane U., 1953-55; m. Imelda R. Bueno, Apr. 7, 1951; children— Rodolfo, Oscar, Lizette, Rene, Imelda. Came to U.S., 1952, naturalized, 1959. Partner, Cummins-Valladares, New Orleans, 1959-60; prin. Rene Valladares O., A.I.A. Assos., New Orleans, 1960-65, Miami, 1965—, Valladares & Assos., gen. contractors, Coral Gables, Fla., 1965—. Archtl. consultants and planners Spanish and Latin Am. affairs A.I.A., Nat. Council Archtl. Registration Bds., 1964—. Hon. consul Guatemala to Jefferson, La., 1960-68; attache to Embassy Guatemala, Mexico City, 1950-51; consulate Guatemala in San Francisco, 1951-52. Served to lt. USAF, 1944-45. Mem. A.I.A., Amateur Fencers League Am. (dir. Fla. Gold Coast div. 1970-71). Mason. Club: Country (Coral Gables). Prin. archtl. works include Alvin Calendar Field Weather Radar Sta., New Orleans, Metropolitan Bank, Metairie, La., Mary Star of the Sea Ch., Diocese Nassau. Home: 290 SW 71st Av Miami FL 33144 Office: PO Box 971 Coral Gables FL 33134

VALLECILLO, MANUEL I., supermarket exec.; b. San Juan, P.R., 1914; B.B.A., U. P.R., M.B.A., Northwestern U., 1938; LL.B., U. P.R., 1944; m. Mem. faculty U. P.R., 1938-45, comptroller, 1945; pvt. practice law, 1945-63; exec. v.p., gen. counsel Pueblo Supermarkets Inc., 1960—, also dir. sec., dir. Asso. Fed. Hotels Internat. Inc. Sec., dir. Hosp. San Jorge, San Jorge Research Inst. Home: 467 Sarado Corazon Santurce PR 00915 Office: GPO Box 3288 San Juan PR 00936*

VALLIANOS, LIMBERIOS, coastal engr.; b. N.Y.C., July 19, 1936; s. Spyros and Monte (Livanis) V.; B.S., Poly. Inst. Bklyn., 1958, postgrad., 1961-62; diploma Hydraulic Engr. with distinction, Internat. Course in Hydraulic Engring., Delft, Netherlands, 1968; m. Stella Yasmine Voudiotis, June 15, 1958; children—Alexander Spyros, Tanya Maria. Engr., TVA, Knoxville, Tenn., 1958-59, USPHS, Washington, 1959-60, Reno, 1960-62, Nussbaumer Clark & Velzy-Cons., N.Y.C., 1962-63; chief coastal engring. sect. U.S. Army C.E., Wilmington, N.C., 1963—. Cons. coastal engring. Served with USPHS, 1959-62. Recipient Outstanding Performance award U.S. Army C.E., 1966. Registered profl. engr., N.C. Mem. Am. Soc. C.E., Internat. Assn. for Hydraulic Research, Chi Epsilon. Club: Wilmington Engineering. Home: 1618 Robert E Lee Dr Wilmington NC 28401 Office: PO Box 1890 Wilmington NC 28401

VALLOTTON, WILLIAM WISE, surgeon educator; b. Valdosta, Ga., Nov. 26, 1927; s. Joseph Edward and Mattie (Rouse) V.; A.B., Duke, 1947; M.D., Med. Coll. Ga., 1952; postgrad. Harvard; 1956; m. Hulda Roberta Jones, Sept. 3, 1950; children—Stephen Ralph, Amie, Mark Hugh, William Wise. Intern, U. Wis., 1952-53; resident ophthalmology Duke U., 1953-55, instr., 1953-55, asso., 1955-56, asso. prof. ophthalmology Med. Coll. S.C., Charleston, 1958-65, prof., 1965—, dir. residency program ophthalmology, 1960—, chmn. dept. ophthalmology, 1966—. Cons., USN Hosp., Charleston, 1962—, State Hosp. S.C., Columbia, 1963—, U.S. Vets. Hosp., Charleston, 1966—; faculty home study Am. Acad. Ophthalmology and Otolaryngology. Vice pres. Vallorbe, Inc., Valdosta, Ga., 1955—. Served to lt. M.C., USNR, 1956-58. Diplomate Am. Bd. Ophthalmology. Fellow A.C.S.; mem. S.C. Eye and Ear Assn. (pres. 1965), Charleston Duke Alumni Assn. (past pres.), Assn. Research in Ophthalmology (chmn. S.E. sect. 1966—), Pi Kappa Phi, Alpha Kappa Kappa, Alpha Omega Alpha. Republican. Methodist. Elk. Research in ophthalmology. Home: 15 Broughton Rd Charleston SC 29407

VALLS, CARLOS FRANCISCO, oral surgeon; b. Ponce, P.R., June 23, 1923; s. Carlos H. and Maria Teresa (Sanjurjo) V.; B.A., Poly. Inst. P.R., 1948; postgrad. Columbia, 1949-50; D.D.S., Loyola U., 1956, postgrad., 1956-59; postgrad. Interam. U. Sch. Law, 1970-72; m. Julie Ahedo, Aug. 16, 1947. Pvt. practice oral surgery, Hato Rey, P.R., 1959—; tchr. oral surgery Sch. dentistry U. P.R., 1959-67, asso. prof., 1969—; chief oral surgery sect. Tchrs. Hosp., 1959—; attending oral surgeon U. Hosp., 1961-67; cons. oral surgeon Fondo del Seguro del Estado, 1960-68. Served with AUS, World War II. Recipient award of oral surgery Chgo. Dental Sch., 1956, Mosby Scholastic Book award, 1956. Mem. Assn. Ednl. Communications and Tech., Nat. Assn. Ednl. Broadcasters, Soc. Oral Surgeons P.R. (v.p. 1968-72), Colegio de Cirujanos Dentistas P.R. Contbr. articles to profl. jours. Home: 53 Atlantic View Isla Verde Santurce PR 00913 Office: 730 Ponce de Leon Hato Rey PR 00918

VALLS, RALPH, customhouse broker; b. Laredo, Tex., Mar. 24, 1909; s. Antonio and Rafaela (Mendiola) V.; grad. high sch.; m. Clotilde Withoff, May 24, 1934; 1 son, Richard R. Farmer, San Rafael Farm, 1928-41; insp. Customs Service, 1941-48; farmer, Laredo, 1948-50; customhouse broker, Laredo, 1950—, Galveston, Tex., 1960—, Houston, 1967—, Corpus Christi, Tex., 1960—; pres. Ralph Valls & Son, Inc., Corpus Christi, 1968—; ocean freight forwarder, 1964—; founding dir. Gulf Internat Trader (now Houston Bus. Jours.), Houston, 1964—. Lectr. internat. trade Del Mar Coll., Corpus Christi. Mem. Tex. Internat. Trade Assn. (dir. 1965, 66, 68, 71, 72). Republican. Roman Catholic. Rotarian. Club: Propellers. Home: 4601 Jarvis St Corpus Christi TX Office: Katz Bldg Corpus Christi TX 78403

VAN AALTEN, JACQUES, artist, b. Antwerp, Belgium, Apr. 12, 1907 (father Am. citizen); s. Jacob and Marianna (de Wind) Van A.; grad. N.A.D., 1930; student Art Students League N.Y.C., 1932-34, Grande Chaumiere, Paris, France, 1955, Tulane U., 1970-71; m. Miriam Truebell, Apr. 29, 1939. Executed fresco mural Straubenmuller Textile High Sch., N.Y.C., 1938-39; exhibited one man shows Gallery Circle, New Orleans, 1960, Le Petit Theatre du Vieux Carre, New Orleans, 1961, Norton Gallery, Palm Beach, Fla., 1963, Delray (Fla.) Playhouse, 1963, Galerie van Aalten, Palm Beach, Fla., 1963-64, Rockport (Mass.) Art Assn., 1965; exhibited in group shows including N.A.D., 1930, Whitney Mus., N.Y.C., 1940, Beaux Arts, N.Y.C., 1940, Detroit Inst. Art, 1946, Delgado Mus. Art, New Orleans, 1958-59, Rockport Art Assn., 1962-71; represented in permanent collections at Capitol Bldg., Baton Rouge Vatican collection, Rome, Italy, Religious Ministry Bldg., Jerusalem, also pvt. collections U.S. and abroad. Instr., Nassau Conservatory Art, Rockville Center, N.Y., 1940, Van Aalten Studio Sch., Detroit, 1944-47. Recipient Suydam medal, 1930; Tiffany Found. scholar, 1930. Mem. Rockport Art Assn. (life), Art Students League N.Y. (life), Isaac Delgado Mus. Art Assn. Address: 825 Ursulines St New Orleans LA 70116

VANAMAN, RICHARD HENRY LEROY, clergyman; b. Harrisburg, Pa., Nov. 29, 1913; s. Lester Eugene and Sarah (Coxeter) V.; A.B., Dickinson Coll., 1946; S.T.B., Wesley Theol. Sem., Washington, 1951, M.Div., 1971; S.T.M., Colo. Bible Coll. and Sem., 1955; m. Jean Betty Haupt, Nov. 30, 1934; children—Patricia (Mrs. J.A. Schultz), Sara (Mrs. C.C. Morris). Ordained to ministry Methodist Ch., 1948; minister Meth. Chs., Dillsburg, Wellsville,

Bendersville (all Pa.), Hampton, Salem Center (both N.H.), 1941-51; minister Episcopal Chs., Harrisburg, Pa., Stuttgart, Tollville (both Ark.), Franklin, Portsmouth, (both Va.), South Miami, Lake Placid, Sebring (all Fla.), Holly Springs, Miss., Woodville, Miss., 1951-—; former rector St. Paul's Ch., Woodville; vicar St. Elizabeth's Ch., Zephyrhills, Fla., 1970-—; book reveiw editor Hampton Union and Rockingham County (N.H.) Gazette, 1946-49; personnel dept. UGI, N.Y. Life Ins. Co., Nat. Radio Inst. Mem. bd. examining chaplains Diocese of Miss.; mem. dept. stewardship Diocese of So. Fla.; mem. com. Christian social relations Diocese of Southwest Fla., 1971-—. Active Boy Scouts Am. Mem. Am. Ch. Union, Lake Placid (pres.), Nat. Geog. Soc., Holly Springs (v.p.) ministerial assns., Alphia Chi Rho. Mason, Odd Fellow, Lion, Rotarian; mem. Order Eastern Star. Clubs: Ruritan, Civitan. Home: PO Box 1115 Zephyrhills FL 33599

VAN APPLEDORN, MARY JEANNE, educator, musician; b. Holland, Mich., Oct. 2, 1927; d. John and Elizabeth (Rinck) van Appledorn; Mus.B., Eastman Sch. Music, U. Rochester, 1948, Mus.M., 1950, Ph.D., 1966. Piano debut Carnegie Recital Hall, N.Y.C., 1957; chmn. dept. music lit. and music theory Tex. Tech. U., Lubbock, 1952-—, founder, dir. Symposium of Contemporary Music, 1952-72. Mem. Mu Phi Epsilon, Alpha Chi Omega, Delta Kappa Gamma (Scholar, 1959-60). Presbyn. Author: Keyboard Singing and Dictation Manual, 1968. Composer various piano and organ selections. Home: 1629 16th St Lubbock TX 79401

VAN ARSDALE, DOROTHY LANGFORD THAYER (MRS. STUART FRANK VAN ARSDALE), art gallery and exhbn. service exec.; b. Malden, Mass., Jan. 14, 1917; d. Arthur Langford and Dorothy (Clark) Thayer; B.S., Simmons Coll., 1938; m. Howard Charles Pritham, Aug. 31, 1939 (div. Sept. 1947); children—Howard George, Eleanor (Mrs. Serge Liros); m. 2d, Stuart Frank Van Arsdale, Aug. 25, 1951 (dec. July 1958); 1 son, Stuart Frank. Sec., Filene's, Boston, 1946-48; exec. sec. Macy's, N.Y.C., 1948-51; sec. John Fox, pub. Boston Post, 1952-54, spl. promotions Boston Post, 1954-55; exec. sec. N.E. Industries, Boston, 1957-60, adminstrv. asst., 1960-62, treas., 1960, also dir.; financial mgr. Smithsonian Travelling Exhbn. Service, Washington, 1962-64, chief, 1964-70; pres. Dorothy T. Van Arsdale Assos., traveling exhbn. service and gallery, Clermont, Fla., 1970-—. Decorated Knight Order Dannebrog (Denmark). Mem. Am. Assn. Museums, Internat. Council Museums, Simmons Coll. Alumni Assn., Clermont C. of C. Home: 1676 Bowman St Clermont FL 32711 Office: 830 Montrose St Clermont FL 32711

VAN ARSDEL, WILLIAM CAMPBELL, III, pharmacologist; b. Indpls., June 27, 1920; s. William Campbell and Mabel (Hedde) Van A.; student Ind. U., 1939-40; B.A., Ore. State Coll., 1949, M.S., 1951, Ph.D., 1959; M.S., U. Ore., 1954. Lab. technician, product control lab. U.S. Rubber Co., Indpls., 1941-43, shift supr., 1943-45; teaching fellow zoology, research fellow animal sci. Ore. State Coll., 1954-59, asst. in animal physiology, 1959-63; pharmacologist FDA, Washington, 1963-—. Mem. Under Water Soc. Am. (dir. 1962), Ore. Assn. Underwater Instrs., (chmn. 1963), Ore. Council Skin Diving Clubs (pres. 1962), Atlantic Skin Diving Council (v.p. 1967), Health, Edn. and Welfare Employees Assn. (dir. 1965-—, pres. 1968), A.A.A.S., Japan-Am. Soc. Washington, Ore. State Soc. Washington, Nat. Rifle Assn. Am., N.Y. Acad. Scis., Sigma Xi. Clubs: Sea Beavers (pres. 1959) (Corvallis, Ore.); Washington Athletic Toastmasters International. Editor HEW AND YOU, 1965-—. Home: 1000 6th St SW Washington DC 20024 Office: 200 C St SW Washington DC 20204

VAN AUSDAL, JAMES SAMUEL, dentist; b. Pensacola, Fla., July 6, 1921; s. James Samuel and Mary (Hicks) Van A.; student Auburn U., 1939-41; D.D.S., Ind. U., 1944; m. Dorothy Inez Carmack, June 6, 1950; children—Diane, Linda, Martha. Intern Indpls. City Hosp., also Fla. State Hosp., 1944-45; asso. with Dr. Fred M. York, 1945-46; pvt. practice restorative and preventive dentistry, St. Petersburg, Fla., 1946-—. Chmn. dental health adv. com. St. Petersburg Jr. Coll. Mem. Am., Fla. dental assns., West Coast Dist., Pinellas County dental socs., Fla. Prosthodontic Seminar, Fla. Acad. Dental Practice Adminstrn., So. Acad. Periodontology, So. Acad. Clin. Nutrition, Acad. One Hundred, L.D. Pankey Dental Found. Research on restorative preventive dentistry methods. Home: 442 22d Av S E St Petersburg FL 33705 Office: 3820 5th Av N St Petersburg FL 33713

VAN BROCKLIN, NORMAN MACK, profl. football coach; b. Parade, S.D., Mar. 15, 1926; s. Mack and Ethel (Johnson) Van B.; B.S., U. Ore., 1950, M.S., 1951; m. Gloria May Schiewe, Mar. 22, 1947; children—Karen Jan, Lynne Ann, Judith Lee. Profl. football player Los Angeles Rams, 1949-57, Phila. Eagles, 1958-60; head coach Minn. Vikings, 1961-69; now head coach Atlanta Falcons. Baseball coach Little League, Raleigh Hills, Ore., 1958. Pres. Easter Seal Drive, 1964, Athletes for Kennedy, 1960. Served with USNR, 1943-46. Named All-Am., U. Ore., 1948, Pro-Football Player of Year, 1960, Pro-Bowl Coach, 1962. Mem. Wheaties Sports Fedn., Kappa Sigma, Phi Epsilon Kappa. Democrat. Author: Passing, Punting, Kicking, 1960. Office: care Atlanta Falcons Atlanta GA 30309

VAN CAMP, JAMES RICHARD, lawyer; b. Orange, N.J., June 11, 1940; s. Robert and Thelma (Walters) Van C; A.B., Christian Coll., 1962; LL.B., Wake Forest U., 1965; m. Mary Sue McPhatter, Aug. 19, 1962; children—Ashley Sue, James Richard, Quinton Page. Admitted to N.C. bar, 1965; partner Seawell, Pollock, Fullenwider, Van Camp &Robbins, Carthage, 1965-—; adminstr. Gov.'s Com. on Law and Order, 1969-70; mem. N.C. com. on Law and Order, 1971-—; gen. counsel N.C. Rescue Squads, also Vass Community Devel. Corp. Active Boy Scouts Am. Dir., gen. counsel Humane Soc. Mem. Moore County Bar Assn. (sec.-treas.), Delta Sigma Phi, Phi Delta Phi. Democrat. Episcopalian. Home: 435 Country Club Dr Southern Pines NC 28327 Office: PO Box 277 Carthage NC 28327

VANCE, CHARLES FOGLE, mfg. co. exec.; b. Winston Salem, N.C., Dec. 31, 1892; s. Joseph Addison and Adelaide Jane (Fogle) V.; M.E., Lehigh U., 1915; m. Margaret Vaughn, Dec. 22, 1920; children—Charles Fogle, Lulu Hall (Mrs. William W. Fetzer). Pres., gen. mgr., chmn. bd. J.A. Vance Co., mfrs. sawmill machinery and metal stampings, Winston Salem, 1930-62, now ret. Mem. N.C. Soc. Engrs., Winston Salem Engrs. Club., Sigma Nu. Clubs: Twin City, Forsyth Country. Home: 1129 W 4th St Winston Salem NC 27101

VANCE, JAMES LAKEY, govt. ofcl.; b. Akron, O., Apr. 6, 1936; s. Roy M. and Margaret (Lakey) V.; B.A., Allegheny Coll., 1958; M.A., U. Tenn., 1966; m. Carol Ann Pheteplace, Aug. 30, 1957; children—Lawrence Pheteplace, Constance Ann. Chief operations div. U.S. Air Force Security Service, Wakkanai Air Station, Japan, 1962-65; chief electronic warfare activities Air Force Spl. Communication Center, Kelly AFB, Tex., 1966-69; dir. analysis, dep. asst. sec. of def., Pentagon, Washington, 1969-—. Served to major USAF, 1958-70. Mem. Am. Polit. Sci. Assn., Pi Sigma Alpha. Author: The Japanese People and Democracy, 1966. Home: 4600 N 3d St Arlington VA 22203 Office: 3C200 Pentagon Washington DC 20310

VANCE, NINA ELOISE WHITTINGTON, theatrical exec.; b. Yoakum, Tex.; d. Perry and Minerva (Dewitt) Whittington; B.A., Tex. Christian U.; postgrad. U. So. Cal., Columbia, Am. Acad. Dramatic Art. Dir. Players Guild, Houston, 1944-46; founder, permanent dir., artistic dir. Alley Theatre, Houston, 1947-—; guest dir. Arena Stage, Washington, Playhouse-in-the-Park, Phila. Participant Am. Assembly meeting Asian-Am. Assembly, Kuala Lumpur, Fedn. Malaya; adv. com. Nat. Cultural Center; adv. com. on arts U.S. Adv. Commn. Edni. and Cultural Affairs. Recipient grant English Speaking Union, 1958; Matrix award for contbn. to field of fine arts Theta Sigma Phi; Personal Dir.'s grant for travel and study Ford Found. Home: 1400 Hermann Dr Houston TX 77004 Office: Alley Theatre 615 Texas Av Houston TX 77002

VANCE, ROBERT MERCER, banker; b. Clinton, S.C., July 9, 1916; s. Robert Berly and Mary Ellen (Bailey) V.; B.S., Davidson Coll., 1937; m. Virginia Sexton Gray, Dec. 27, 1949; children—Mary Bailey, Robert Mercer, Russell Gray. Paymaster, Lydia Cotton Mills, Clinton, 1937-41; with M.S. Bailey & Son, Bankers, Clinton, 1946-—, pres., 1948-—; dir., asst. treas. Clinton Cotton Mills, 1948-58, v.p., 1956-58, pres., treas., 1958-70; dir., asst. treas. Lydia Cotton Mills, Clinton, 1948-58, v.p., 1953-58, pres., treas., 1958-70; pres., treas. Clinton Mills, Inc., 1964-—; dir. Clinton Cottons, Inc., N.Y.C., 1948-—, v.p., asst. treas., 1953-58, treas., 1958-—; dir. Textile Hall Corp., Greenville, S.C. Pres. Community Chest Greater Clinton, 1958; mem. nominating com. United Community Services S.C., 1959; trustee exec. com. Ednl. Resources Found., 1965; mem. State Adv. Commn. on Higher Edn., 1965-67; mem. State Commn. on Higher Edn., 1967-—, chmn., 1968-—. Bd. visitors Davidson (N.C.) Coll., 1959-62; trustee, chmn. bd. Presbyn. Coll., Clinton, 1953-67; trustee, sec. bd. Thornwell Orphanage, Clinton, 1959-67; trustee Inst. Textile Tech., Charlottesville, Va., S.C. Found. Ind. Colls. Served with Signal Corps, AUS, 1941; served to lt. USNR, 1941-46. Named Man of Year, Clinton Lions Club, 1955. Mam. Am. Textile Mfrs. Inst. (dir. 1965-68), Am. (v.p. 1953-55), S.C. (pres. 1963-64) bankers assns., S.C. Textile Mfrs. Assn. (dir. 1965-—), S.C. Textile Assn. (pres. 1967-68), Am. Legion, S.C. State (dir. 1959-60), Clinton (dir. 1951-54) chambers commerce, Kappa Alpha. Presbyn. (elder 1958-—). Mason (Shriner), Moose, Kiwanian. Clubs: Lakeside Country (Clinton); Poinsett (Greenville, S.C.); Piedmont (Spartanburg, S.C.). Home: 311 S Broad St Clinton SC 29325 Office: 211 N Broad St Clinton SC 29325

VANCE, ROBERT SMITH, democratic state party chmn.; b. Talladega, Ala., May 10, 1931; s. Harrell Taylor and Mae (Smith) V.; B.S., U. Ala., 1950, J.D., 1952; LL.M., George Washington U., 1955; m. Helen Rainey, Oct. 4, 1953; children—Robert Smith, Charles R. Partner firm Callaway & Vance, Birmingham, Ala., 1956-—. Lectr., Cumberland Sch. Law, Samford U., 1967-69. Chmn., Ala.Dem. party, 1966-—. Served to lst lt. AUS, 1952-54. Mem. Am., Ala., Birmingham bar assns., Omicron Delta Kappa, Beta Gamma Sigma, Delta Chi. Episcopalian. Home: 2824 Shook Hill Rd Birmingham AL 35223 Office: 933 Frank Nelson Bldg Birmingham AL 35203

VANCE, ROY NEWTON, JR., lawyer; b. Paducah, Ky., Nov. 14, 1921; s. Roy Newton and Mary (Bryan) V.; LL.B., U. Ky.; m. Enleen Hamilton, Oct. 20, 1949; children—Linda Barton, Teresa Louise, Roy Newton III. Admitted to Ky. bar, 1946; practiced in Paducah, 1946-70; commr. Ct. of Appeals of Ky., Frankfort, 1970-—. Vice pres., gen. counsel Paducah Bank & Trust Co. County atty. McCracken County, Ky., 1949-53; commonwealth atty. 2d Jud. Dist. of Ky., 1953-57. Chmn. bd. trustees Paducah Community Coll. Served to 1st lt., Signal Corps, AUS, 1942-46. Home: 1041 Algonquin St Frankfort KY 40601 Office: Capitol Bldg Frankfort KY 40601

VANCE, WILLIAM FORD, city commr.; b. nr. Hattiesburg, Miss., Dec. 20, 1909; s. Angus Nicholson and Carrie Pearl (Ford) V.; grad. high sch.; m. Anna Sue Lacey, Oct. 28, 1944; children—Gene Ford, Cindy Sue (Mrs. Gerald J. Kersh). Safety patrolman Miss. Hwy. Dept., 1941-43, 45-46; owner-mgr. Vance Dairy, 1947-56; sheriff, tax collector Forrest County, Miss., 1956-60; pres. Fla. Vance Corp., v.p. Brokers Devel. Corp., sec.-treas. Deep South Investments, Hattiesburg, Miss., 1960-—; city commr., Hattiesburg, 1969-—. Served with USNR, 1932-36, USAAF, 1943-45. Decorated Bronze Star medal with oak leaf cluster, Air medal with four oak leaf clusters. Mem. Am. Legion, V.F.W., Aircraft Owners and Pilots Assn. Democrat. Methodist. Elk, Rotarian. Home: 1205 Windsor Dr Hattiesburg MS 39401 Office: City Hall Hattiesburg MS 39401

VANCE, WILLIAM SILAS, educator; b. Paradise, Tex., Feb. 14, 1901; s. Edward F. and Mary (Gunn) V.; A.B., Baylor U., 1922; A.M., Harvard, 1927; Ph.D., Chgo., 1941; m. Eleanor Graham, Nov. 22, 1945; children—Eleanor Margaret, Dale Lines. Asst. prof. English, Westminster Coll. (Pa.), 1926-28; asst. prof. English, Baylor U., 1929-31; instr. Northeastern U. (Mass.), 1932-36; asso. prof. English, Howard Coll. (Ala.), 1936-40; prof. English, Edinburg Coll. (now Pan-Am. U.) 1941-46, 56-—; head dept. speech, journalism and English, Northwestern State Coll., Alva, Okla., 1946-56. Mem. Am. Assn. U. Profs., N.E.A., Nat. Council Tchrs. English. Author: Carlyle and Whitman, monograph, 1944. Contbr. numerous scholarly, profl. and popular mags. Home: 109 Austin Blvd Edinburg TX 78539

VAN CLEAVE, ROBERT FRANKLIN, geophysicist; b. Indpls., Apr. 28, 1911; s. Benjamin F. and Almeda (Cline) Van C.; student DePauw U., 1928-30; A.B., Wabash Coll., 1933; M.S., U. Okla., 1935; m. Doris Thibodeaux, Apr. 10, 1938; children—Nancy Elizabeth, Margaret Anne, Robert Hamilton. Computer, Western Geophys. Co., Tulsa, 1935-37; supr., party chief Nat. Geophys. Co., Dallas, 1937-46; regional geophysicist, dist. geophysicist Atlantic Refining Co., Dallas, 1946-51; partner Interstate Exploration Co., Tulsa, 1951-59; v.p., chief geophysicist Austral Oil Co., Houston, 1960-—. Mem. Soc. Exploration Geophysicists, Am. Assn. Petroleum Geologists, Petroleum Club Houston, Sigma Xi. Club: Houston. Home: 12426 Woodthorpe Lane Houston TX 77024 Office: Humble Bldg Houston TX 77002

VAN CLEEF, ELMER BOOTH, civil engr.; b. Gainesville, Fla., Apr. 22, 1927; s. Clinton Booth and Elsie (Hansen) Van C.; B.S., U. Fla., 1950; m. Mary E. Kindt, Oct. 17, 1952; children—Clinton Kindt, Timothy Mark, David Keith, James Lawrence, Jeffrey Paul. Engr., State Dept. Transp., Winter Park, Fla., 1957-—. Committeeman, Central Fla. council Boy Scouts Am., 1965-69. Served with USNR, 1945-46. Registered profl. engr., Fla. Mem. Nat. Soc. Profl. Engrs., Fla. Engring. Soc. (publs. com. Central Fla. chpt. 1969-70). Democrat. Mem. Ch. of Christ. Home: 4108 Seybold Av Orlando FL 32808 Office: 931 Morse Blvd Winter Park FL 32789

VAN CLEVE, RUTH GILL, govt. ofcl.; b. Mpls., July 18, 1925; d. Raymond S. and Ruth (Sevon) Gill; student U. Minn., 1943; A.B. magna cum laude, Mt. Holyoke Coll., 1946; LL.B., Yale, 1950; m. Harry R. Van Cleve, Jr., May 16, 1952; children—John Gill, Elizabeth Webster, David Hamilton. Intern, Nat. Inst. Pub. Affairs, 1946-47; admitted to D.C. and Minn. bars, 1950; atty. Dept. Interior, 1950-54, asst. solicitor, 1954-64, dir. Office Ters., 1964-69; atty. Fed. Power Commn., 1969-—. Recipient Fed. Woman's award, 1966, Distinguished Service award Dept. Interior, 1968. Mem. Phi Beta Kappa, Unitarian. Home: 4400 Emory St Alexandria VA 22312 Office: 441 G St NW Washington DC 20426

VANDELL, ROBERT FRANK, educator; b. Bklyn., June 22, 1928; s. Robert Frank and Marjorie Drew (Pritchett) V.; B.S., Yale, 1950; M.B.A., Harvard, 1952, D.Bus. Adminstrn., 1958; m. Margaret Wheeler Edwards, Sept. 4, 1954; children—Robert Charles, Barbara Drew, Warren Edwards. Asst. prof. Harvard Bus. Sch., 1958-61, asso. prof., 1961-65; prof. bus. adminstrn. U. Va. Grad. Sch. Bus. Adminstrn., Charlottesville, 1965-—; v.p., dir. Mgmt. Analysis Center, Inc.; dir. Landmark Communications, Inc., No. Research and Engring. Co. Served to 1st lt. Finance Corps, AUS, 1952-54. Episcopalian (treas. 1969-70). Author: (with Coleman) Case Problems in Finance, 1954; (with Vancil) Cases in Capital Budgeting, 1954. Home: 1438 Grove Rd Charlottesville VA 22901

VANDENBERGH, JOHN GARRY, biologist; b. Paterson, N.J., May 4, 1935; s. Garry and Johanna (Hofstede) V.; B.A., Montclair State Coll., 1957; M.S., Ohio U., 1959; Ph.D., Pa. State U., 1962; m. Barbara Ann Doll, June 8, 1958; children—David John, Michael Paul. Research biologist NIH, La Parguera, P.R., 1962-65; research scientist N.C. Dept. Mental Health, Raleigh, 1965-—. Adj. asso. prof., dept. zoology N.C. State U., 1965-—, cons. Nat. Inst. Mental Health, 1969-—; mem. adv. com. Nat. Primate Centers, 1970-—. USPHS predoctoral fellow, 1961-62. Mem. Animal Behavior Soc. (program officer 1967-70), A.A.A.S., Am. Soc. Mammalogists, Internat. Soc. Primatology, Sigma Xi. Contbr. articles to profl. jours. Office: Box 7599 Raleigh NC 27602

VANDERHOLT, JAMES FREDERICK, clergyman, sch. supt.; b. Beaumont, Tex., Sept. 4, 1932; s. Charles Edward and Helen Elizabeth (Donahue) V.; student St. Mary's Sem., Houston, Catholic U., 1964, U. Notre Dame, 1966, St. Mary's U., 1967; M.Ed., Our Lady of Lake Coll., 1968. Ordained priest Roman Catholic Ch., 1957. Supt. schs. Diocese of Beaumont, 1967-—, counsultor, 1970-—; pastor St. Mary's Ch., Port Arthur, Tex., 1971-—. Chmn. div. edn. Tex. Catholic Conf., 1970-—. Pres., Manpower, Edn. and Tng., Inc., 1967-70. Nat. Cath. Edn. Assn. Rotarian. Address: 528 Augusta St Port Arthur TX 77640

VANDER HORST, JOHN, bishop; b. Orange, N.J. Jan. 10, 1912; s. Elias and Ella Virginia (Cole) Vander H.; B.S., Princeton, 1935; student St. Stephens House, Oxford, Eng., 1935-36; student Va. Theol. Sem., 1938; D.D., U. South, 1955, Va. Sem., 1955; m. Helen Gray Lawrence, Apr. 17, 1940; children—Helen Lawrence, John, Ella Cole. Allston. Ordained to ministry P.E. Ch., 1938; rector in Howard County, Md., 1938-42, Macon, Ga., 1942-45, Phila., 1945-51, St. Paul's Ch., Chattanooga, 1951-54; suffragen bishop Tenn., 1954-61, bishop coadjutor, 1961, diocesan bishop, 1961-—. Home: 6000 Hillsboro Rd Nashville TN 37215 Office: 528 100 Oaks Tower Nashville TN 37204

VANDERLYN, CHARLES PIERRE, economist; b. The Hague, Holland, May 30, 1929; s. Martin and Dina (Abas) Mendels; B.S., U. Md., 1953; M.B.A., U. City N.Y., 1962; m. Barbara Ellen Tilghman, May 26, 1962; children— Peter Mark, Nancy Tilghman, Derek Whitnall. Market research analyst Knoll Assos., N.Y.C., 1962-64, Kendall Co., N.Y.C., 1964-65; mgr. marketing services Earle M. Jorgensen Co., Phila., 1965-67; economist Office Emergency Preparedness, Washington, 1967-68; program analyst/economist Environmental Protection Agy., Washington, 1968-—. Served to 1st lt. USAF, 1953-55. Mem. Am. Marketing Assn., Soc. Govt. Econs., Assn. Pub. Program Analysis, Am. Econ. Assn., Res. Officer's Assn., Lambda Chi Alpha. Home: 5202 Pommeroy Dr Fairfax VA 22030 Office: Environmental Protection Agy Office of Air and Water Programs Washington DC 20460

VANDERPOOL, WYNANT DAVIS, JR., architect; b. Morristown, N.J., Apr. 12, 1914; s. Wynant Davis and Cornelia Grinnell (Willis) V.; A.B., Princeton, 1936, M.F.A., 1940; m. Ann West Wheeler, Jan. 22, 1965; children— Wynant Davis III, Helena, Madeleine. Designer, J.H. and W.C. Ely, architects, Newark, 1940-42; design, adminstrn. Faulkner, Stenhouse, Fryer & Faulkner, architects, Washington, 1965-68; partner Faulkner, Fryer & Vanderpool, architects, Washington, 1968-—. Vice-pres. Potomac br. Commn. Fine Arts; mem. Bd. Archtl. Consultants for Georgetown; pres. Historic Georgetown Inc., Washington, 1971-—. Trustee Found. Preservation Historic Georgetown, Holland Soc. N.Y. Served to lt. USNR, 1942-45. Mem. A.I.A., Century Assn. Episcopalian (jr. warden 1972). Club: Mid-Ocean (Tuckerstown, Bermuda). Home: 1330 30th St NW Washington DC 20007 Office: 2000 L St NW Washington DC 20036

VANDERVEEN, JOHN EDWARD, nutritionist; b. Prospect Park, N.J., May 13, 1934; s. William John and Lena (Rapp) V.; B.S., Rutgers, The State U., 1956; Ph.D., U. N.H., 1961; m. Ernestine Neuhardt, June 3, 1967. Nutritionist, USAF Sch. Aerospace Medicine, Brooks AFB, Tex., 1964-—. Served to lst lt. USAF, 1961-64. Recipient McLester award Assn. Mil. Surgeons, 1967. Mem. Am. Inst. Nutrition, Am. Inst. Clin. Nutrition, Am. Inst. Food Tech., Am. Chem. Soc., Aerospace Med. Assn., Am. Dairy Sci. Assn., Assn. Mil. Surgeons, Sigma Xi. Presbyn. Home: 100 Kings Crown E San Antonio TX 78233 Office: Box 35306 Brooks Air Force Base TX 78235

VAN DER VOORT, AITCHESON BOWMAR, economist; b. Dunkirk, N.Y., Mar. 15, 1926; s. Henry Ferdinand and Emily (Bowmar) Van Der V.; B.A., Princeton, 1949; M.A., Georgetown U., 1955. Mfrs. rep. Voorhis-Tiebout Co., Red Hook, N.Y., 1949-50; economist Nat. Income div. U.S. Dept. Commerce, Washington, 1955-56; economist Machinery and Allied Products Inst., Washington, 1957-—. Instr. econs. Smith Coll., Northampton, Mass., 1956-57. Mem. Alexandria Council Human Relations, 1970-—; active The Hopkins House Assn., Alexandria, Va. Mem. Arlington County Democratic Com., 1965-67. Served to 1st. lt. USMCR, 1944-46, 50-52. Mem. Am. Econ. Assn., Nat. Assn. Bus. Economists, Am. Statis. Assn., Internat. Platform Assn., Acad. Polit. Sci., Nat. Economists Club. Asso. editor Capital Goods Review, 1970-—. Home: 5021 Seminary Rd Alexandria VA 22311 Office: 1200 18th St NW Washington DC 20036

VAN DE VATE, DWIGHT, JR., educator; b. Rochester, N.Y., Feb. 25, 1928; s. Dwight and Helen Lucille (Hagood) Van de V.; student Mass. Inst. Tech., 1945-46, U. Rochester, 1948; B.A. with honors, Wesleyan U., 1952; M.A., Yale, 1953, Ph.D., 1956; m. Nancy Jean Hayes, June 9, 1952; children—Katherine, Barbara, Dwight III. Asst. prof. philosophy U. Miss., 1955-60, asso. prof., 1960-63; asst. prof. philosophy Fla. State U., 1963-64; asso. prof. philosophy Memphis State U., 1964-65, prof., 1965-66; prof. philosophy U. Tenn., Knoxville, 1966-—. Served with USNR, 1946-48. Mem. Am. Philos. Assn., So. Soc. Philosophy and Psychology (pres. 1970), Phi Beta Kappa. Editor: Persons, Privacy, and Feeling: Essays in the Philosophy of Mind, 1970. Home: 5610 Holston Hills Rd Knoxville TN 37914 Office: Dept Philosophy U Tenn Knoxville TN 37916

VAN DE VYVER, HUBERT LOUIS JOHN AUGUSTE, physician; b. Antwerp, Belgium, June 26, 1931; s. Leon Charles and Marie Louise (Van Mosueck) Van de V.; B.S., U. Louvain, Belgium, 1954, M.D., 1958; m. Bernice Pezolkowski, Feb. 10, 1959; children—Elizabeth, Janine, Katia, Paul-Luc, Mes. Came to U.S., 1961. Intern Mercy Hosp., Pitts., 1957-58; asso. anesthesiologist West Penn Hosp., Pitts., 1961-69; anesthesiologist St. Elizabeth and Bapt.

Hosps., Beaumont, Tex., 1969—. Fellow Am. Coll. Anesthesiologists. Home: 2405 Ashley St Beaumont TX 77702 Office: 3155 Stagg St Beaumont TX 77701

VAN DIEPEN, WILLIAM TOWEND, fruit co. exec.; b. Jamaica, Nov. 25, 1912; s. Rudolf Glenn and May Louise (Townend) van D.; B.S.A., U. Toronto, 1935; M.Sc., La. State U., 1937; m. Virginia E. Adams, Sept. 17, 1938; children—Joan Elizabeth, Patricia Gail, Lona Lynn, William Adams, Susan Louise. Came to U.S., 1960, naturalized 1963. With United Fruit Co., 1937—, asst. v.p. agrl. operations, 1961-62, dir. research, 1962-63, v.p., dir. research, 1962—; spl. research devel. and prodn. bananas, plant diseases and insect protection, tropical soils and fertilizers, corp. mgmt.; research devel. and prodn. cacao and palm oil. Mem. Am. Soc. Hort. Sci., Phytopathology Soc., Soc. Agronomy, Soil Sci. Soc., Am. Mgmt. Assn. Home: 12 Whiting Rd Wellesley Hills MA 02181 Office: 321 St Charles St New Orleans LA 70130

VANDIVER, FRANK E(VERSON), author; b. Austin, Tex., Dec. 9, 1925; s. Harry Shultz and Maude Folmsbee (Everson) V.; privately ed.; M.A. (Postwar Rockefeller fellow in Humanities, 1946-47, Rockefellow fellow in Am. Studies, 1947-48), U. Tex., 1949; M.A., Oxford U., Eng., 1963; Ph.D. Tulane U., 1951; m. Carol Sue Smith, Apr. 19, 1952; children—Nita, Nancy, Frank. Apptd. historian, San Antonio, Army Service Forces Depot, Civil Service, 1945, Air U., 1951; prof. history La. State U., summers 1954-57; asst. prof. history Washington U., 1952-55; asst. prof. history Rice U., 1955-56, asso. prof., 1956-58, prof., 1958—, chmn. dept. history and polit. sci., 1962-63, 68-69, Harris Masterson, Jr., chair in history, 1965—, acting pres., 1969-70, provost, 1970—; Harmsworth prof. Am. history Oxford U., 1963-64; vis. prof. history U. Ariz., 1961; master Margarett Root Brown Coll., Rice U., 1964-66, chmn. humanities research council Rice U., 1966-68. Harmon lectr. Air Force Acad., 1963; Walter P. Webb lectr. U. Tex., Arlington, 1967. Mem. Nat. Council on Humanities, 1971—. Adv. council Civil War Centennial Commn. adv. com. office Chief of Mil. History, Dept. Army, 1970—. Recipient research grants Am. Philos. Soc., 1953, 54, 60; Guggenheim fellow, 1955-56; Carr P. Collins award Tex. Inst. Letters, 1957; Huntington library research grant, 1961; Harry S. Truman award, 1965; Jefferson Davis award Confederate Meml. Lit. Soc., 1971; Fletcher Pratt award N.Y. Civil War Round Table, 1971. Mem. Philos. Soc. Tex., Am., So. (asso. editor jour. 1959-62) hist. assns., Tex. Inst. Letters (pres. 1961-63), Jefferson Davis Assn. (pres.; chmn. adv. bd. editors of papers), Soc. Am. Historians (councillor), Civil War Round Table (Chgo.), Phi Beta Kappa. Editor: The Civil War Diary of General Josiah Gorgas, 1947; Confederate Blockade Running Through Bermuda, 1861-65, Letters and Cargo Manifests, 1947; Proceedings of First Confederate Congress, 4th Session, 1954; Proceedings of Second Confederate Congress, 1959; A Collection of Louisiana Confederate Letters; new edit. of J. E. Johnston's Narrative of Military Operations; new edit. J. A. Early's Civil War Memoirs; The Idea of the South, 1964. Author: Ploughshares Into Swords: Josiah Gorgas and Confederate Ordnance, 1952; Rebel Brass: The Confederate Command System, 1956; Mighty Stonewall, 1957; Fields of Glory (with W. H. Nelson), 1960; Jubal's Raid, 1960; Basic History of the Confederacy, 1962; Jefferson Davis and the Confederate State, 1964; John J. Pershing, 1967; Their Tattered Flags, 1970; also hist. articles. Home: 6134 Chevy Chase Houston TX 77027

VANDIVIERE, H(ORACE) MAC, physician, educator; b. Dawsonville, Ga., Mar. 26, 1921; s. Lewis A. and Luna P. (Castleberry) V.; A.B., Mercer U., 1941; M.A., U. Mich., 1944; M.D., U. N.C., 1960; m. Margaret Reynolds, June 5, 1941 (dec. Feb. 1967); children—Christopher, Martin Mac; m. 2d, Irene Graham Melvin, Mar. 23, 1968. Instr., U. Mich., 1944-46; asst. prof. Mercer U., 1946-48; dir. spl. services lab. Ga. Dept. Pub. Health, 1948-51; dir. dept. research N.C. Sanatorium System, Chapel Hill, 1951-67; asst. prof. Duke, 1965-68; med. dir. Haitian Am. Tb Inst., Chapel Hill, also Jeremie, Haiti, 1962—, pres., 1965—; clin. asso. prof. U. N.C. Sch. Pub. Health, 1967—; asso. prof. U. Ky., Lexington, 1967-71, prof., 1971—; dir. Tb. div. Ky. Health Dept., 1971—. Cons. infectious diseases Sante Publique Dept., Republic of Haiti, 1966—. Vice-chmn. Ky. Comprehensive Health Planning Tb Study Com., 1969-70. Decorated, Pres. of Haiti, 1963. Fellow Am. Pub. Health Assn., Am. Geriatrics Assn.; mem. Nat Tb and Respiratory Disease Assn., Am., Ky. (pres. 1970-71) thoracic socs., A.M.A., Ky., N.C. med. assns. Editor: (with others) Bahama International Conference on Burns, 1964. Contbr. articles to profl. jours. Home: 3429 Brookhaven Rd Lexington KY 40502

VAN DRIEM, GEORGE HENRI, physician; b. Djakarta, Indonesia, Feb. 4, 1924; s. Pieter Cornelius and Maria Frederika (Brouwer) Van D.; M.D., State U. Leiden, Netherlands, 1953; m. Felicitas Louise van Vianen, June 3, 1953; children—George Louis, Felix Henri. Came to U.S., 1956, naturalized, 1963. Intern, Johnston-Willis Hosp., Richmond, Va., 1953-54; resident chest diseases Piedmont Sanatorium, Burkeville, Va., 1954-55; resident psychiatry Eastern State Hosp., Williamsburg, Va., 1957-58; family practice medicine, Toano and Williamsburg, 1958—; staff physician Community Hosp., Williamsburg. Bd. dirs. Va. div. Am. Cancer Soc. Fellow Royal Soc. Health, Am. Coll. Angiology, Am. Geriatric Soc.; mem. Am. Thoracic Soc., A.M.A., Assn. Fgn. Med. Grads., Netherland-Am. Med. Assn., Va., James City County-Williamsburg med. socs. Home: PO Box 198 Toano VA 23168 Office: Toano Clinic Rt 60 Toano VA 23168

VAN DUSEN, CLARENCE RAYMOND, educator, author; b. Elkhart, Ind., Nov. 9, 1907; s. Owen and Caroline (Bolster) Van D.; A.B., Ind. U., 1931; M.A., U. Mich., 1932, D.S., 1937; postgrad. U. Chgo., U. Miami, U. Fla.; m. Norma Louise Rankin, Aug. 1, 1940; 1 dau., Susan Lyn. From instr. to asst. prof. Mich. State U., 1937-42; chmn. dept. speech, dir. Speech and Hearing Clinic, U. Miami, 1946-61; dean instrn. Brevard Jr. Coll., 1961-64; pres. Golden Hills Acad., Ocala, Fla., 1964-65, chmn. faculty, Monroe Jr. Coll. 1965-66; dir. speech and hearing clinic Miss. State Coll. for Women, Columbus, 1966-68, coordinator grad. studies in speech, 1968—. Served to maj. AUS, 1942-46. Fellow Am. Speech and Hearing Assn.; mem. Speech Communication Assn., Mich. Speech Correction Assn. (past pres.), Fla. Speech Assn. (past pres.). Democrat. Conglist. Rotarian. Author: Training the Voice for Speech, 1943, rev. 1953; While You Were Away; (with Howard Van Smith) The New Speech-O-Gram Technique for Persuasive Public Speaking, 1962; (with Harvey Cromwell) Oral Approach to Phonetics, 1969. Contbr. articles to profl. jours. Home: 900 5th Av S Columbus MS 39701

VAN DUSEN, RICHARD CAMPBELL, govt. ofcl.; b. Jackson, Mich., July 18, 1925; s. Bruce Buick and Helen (Campbell) Van D.; B.S., U. Minn., 1945; LL.B., Harvard, 1949; m. Barbara Congdon, June 28, 1949; children— Amanda, Lisa, Katherine. Admitted to Mich. bar, 1949; asso. firm Dickinson, Wright, McKean & Cudlip, Detroit, 1949-57, partner, 1958-62, 64-68; mem. Mich. Ho. of Reps. from Oakland County, 1954-56; legal adviser to gov. Mich., 1963; under sec. housing and urban devel., 1969—. Dir. Automobile Inter-Ins. Exchange. Del. Mich. Constl. Conv., 1961-62. Trustee Cranbrook, Kingswood and Brookside Shcs., 1966—; bd. dirs. Boys Republic, 1957—. Served with USNR, 1943-46. Mem. Am., Detroit (bd. dirs. 1965-69) bar assns., State Bar Mich., Econ. Club Detroit, Automobile Club Mich. (bd. dirs.). Republican. Episcopalian. Home: 8300 Burdette Rd Bethesda MD 20034 Office: 451 7th St Washington DC 20410

VAN DYK, ROBERT FALLIS, dentist; b. Louisville, June 22, 1920; s. Frederick John and Viola Daisy (Cummins) Van D.; A.B., Hope Coll., 1941; D.D.S., Loyola U., Chgo., 1950; m. Linda Lee Covert, Nov. 26, 1948; children—Deborah L., Kathleen C., Kerry Jo, Dianne M., Gretchen A., Dirk C. Commd. 1st lt. U.S. Army, 1949, advanced through grades to col., 1967; dep. dental surgeon 2d U.S. Army, 1961-65; dep. dental surgeon, preventive dentistry officer, Europe, 1965-68; dental surgeon, Berlin, Germany, 1968-69, Fort Belvoir, Va., 1969—. Labor mgmt. cons., chief negotiator for mgmt. against Govt. Unions, Fort Belvoir, Va., 1969—. Pres., Council for Retarded Children, Heidelberg, Germany, 1966-68; pres., founder Berlin Council for Handicapped Children, 1968; pres. Council for Handicapped Children, Fort Belvoir, 1969—. Served with AUS, 1941-46. Decorated Legion of Merit, Bronze Star, Army Commendation medal. Mem. Am. Dental Assn., Am. Soc. Preventive Dentistry, Assn. U.S. Army, Assn. Mil. Surgeons U.S., Nat. Assn. Retarded Children, No. Va. Dental Soc., Delta Sigma Delta. Contbr. articles to profl. pubs. Home: 3408 Wessynton Way Alexandria VA 22309 Office: Dental Surgeon Fort Belvoir VA 22060

VAN DYKE, GENE, geologist, ind. oil operator; b. Normal, Ill., Nov. 5, 1926; s. Harold and Ruby (Gibson) Van D.; student U. Ill., 1946, Okla. State Coll., 1947; B.S. in Geol. Engring., U. Okla., 1950; m. Theresa Connelly, Dec. 8, 1952; children—Karen, Scott, Janice, Katherine. Geologist, Kerr-McGee Oil Co., Oklahoma City, 1950; chief geologist S. D. Johnson, Wichita Falls, Tex., 1950-51; pvt. practice geologist, ind. oil operator, Wichita Falls, 1951-58; partner Van Dyke & Mejlaender, ind. oil, gas producers, Houston, 1960-62; owner Van Dyke Oil Co., 1962—. Mem. Houston Land men's Assn., Am. Assn. Petroleum Landmen, Am. Assn. Petroleum Geologists, Houston, New Orleans, Alberta geol. socs., C. of C. Clubs: Houston Petroleum, Houston, Houston Racquet, University, Athletic, Houston; New Orleans Petroleum. Home: 11100 Meadowick St Houston TX 77024 Office: Southwest Tower Bldg Houston TX 77002

VAN DYKE, WILLIAM LAWSHE, JR., tobacco co. exec.; b. Tampa, Fla., Sept. 16, 1921; s. William L. and Marie (Eliot) Van D. div.; children—William L. III, Jess Michael, Melene Marie. With Havatampa Cigar Co., 1945—, sec., 1947—, v.p., 1966—, also mem. exec. com.; mgr. Eli Witt div., Tampa, 1949—. Mem. Tampa Coml 100. Served to lt. USNR, 1942-45. Mem. Ye Mystic Krewe of Casparilla, Sigma Alpha Epsilon. Methodist. Club: University (Tampa). Home: Box 696 Route 1 Lutz FL 33549 Office: 612 Eunice St Tampa FL 33602

VAN GELDER, DAVID WILLIAM, physician; b. Grand Rapids, Mich., 1913; M.D., Rush Med. Sch., Chgo., 1938. Intern, Milwaukee County (Wis.) Gen. Hosp., 1938-39; jr. resident Children's Mem. Hosp., Chgo., 1941-42, sr. resident, 1942-43; resident contagious diseases Cook County Hosp., Chgo., 1940-41; resident in pediatrics Ill. Soldiers and Sailors Children's Hosp., Normal, 1939-40; fellow adolescent medicine Children's Hosp., Washington, 1967; mem. pediatric staff Charity Hosp., New Orleans, Our Lady of the Lake Hosp., Baton Rouge Gen. Hosp.; prof. pediatrics Tulane U. Served with USNR, 1944-46. Diplomate Am. Bd. Pediatrics. Fellow Am. Acad. Pediatrics (dist. chmn.); mem. A.M.A. Office: 888 Tara Blvd Baton Rouge LA 70806*

VAN HAEFTEN, CARL FREDERICK, fgn. service officer; b. Santa Cruz, Cal., Jan 12, 1923; s. Karel August Rudolf and Anna Bartholda (Faure) van H.; B.S., Royal Coll. Tropical Agr., The Netherlands, 1945; m. Dorothy G. Wolthuis, Aug. 30, 1946 (div. 1968); children—Karel A.R., Linda, Eileen; m. 2d, Roberta K. Taylor, Oct. 31, 1969. Investigator, U.S. Mil. Intelligence Unit, The Hague, 1946-47; German youth activities officer U.S. Army, Augsburg, 1947-48; edn. adviser 2d Armored Cav. Regt., Augsburg, 1948-50; chief information and edn. 2d Air Div., Landsburg, Germany, 1950-51; fgn. student adviser Coll. Agr., U. Me., 1952-53; agrl. tng. specialist U.S. mission to European Regional and Other Orgns., 1953-54; chief agrl. tng. br. Europe and Latin Am., FOA, 1954-56; dep., and acting chief div. econ. assistance to Spain for food and agr., 1956-60; dir. program econ. assistance for food and agr., Cambodia, 1960-63, Morocco, 1964-65; asst. dir. U.S. AID mission to Vietnam, 1965-68, spl. asst. war on hunger, Washington, 1968—. Served with Underground Resistance Movement in Holland, World War II. Decorated U.S. Medal of Freedom 1946; Vietnam Agrl. medal, 1968. Home: 2840 Linden Lane Falls Church VA 22042 Office: AFR CWA Dept State AID Washington DC 20523

VAN HERPE, LEO B(RYANT), surgeon; b. Bklyn., Oct. 19, 1929; s. Leo J. and Thelma (Kirkendall) Van H.; B.S., Am. U., 1951; M.D., George Washington U., 1955; m. Ann Dieffenbach, June 11, 1955; children—Michael, Christopher, Sandra, Leslie, Pamela. Mem. staff orthopedics Henry Ford Hosp., 1958-62; gen. practice orthopedic surgery Washington, 1962—; asso. prof. orthopedic surgery Georgetown U., 1962—; dir. Childrens Orthopedic Programs Georgetown U., 1962—; med. dir. Kiwanis Crippled Children's Clinic, 1969—; cons. in orthopedic surgery U.S. Naval Hosp., Bethesda, Md. Served as lt M.C., USNR, 1955-58. Fellow A.C.S.; mem. Am. Acad. Orthopedic Surgery, Washington Orthopedic Club (sec.-treas. 1967, pres. 1968). Republican. Episcopalian. Office: 2520 L St NW Washington DC 20006

VAN HERSH, WILLIAM, investment exec.; b. Memphis, May 10, 1920; s. William and Temple Whiten (Cox) Van H.; student So. Law U., 1941-42, U. Tenn., 1943; m. Dorothy Martin, Nov. 3, 1944; children—William Hayes, Pamela (Mrs. Ronald L. Hall), Deborah K., Thomas Null. Partner Collins & Frreman, 1944-47; owner Van Hersh Real Estate &Ins. Corp., 1947-61; vice chmn. bd. Mid Continent Corp., 1961-66; pres., chmn. bd. Bill Van Hersh Enterprises, Memphis, 1966—; chmn. bd. Ark. Motel Corp., Am. Fidelity, Inc.; vice chmn. bd. Music Mountain Water Co.; pres., chmn. bd. Oak Forest Meml. Gardens. Dir. Boys Town. Rep. Tenn. Legislature, 1957-61; mem. Democratic Exec. Com., 1957-60; commr. Memphis and Shelby County Auditorium; chmn. County Utilities Commn. Named outstanding young man of Memphis, 1951, outstanding Jaycee of Memphis and Tenn., 1952. Cons. Health, Edn. and Research Found., Nat. Council Sr. Citizens. Mem. Memphis Bd. Realtors, Nat., Tenn. assns. realtors. Democrat. Baptist. Elk, Mason (Shriner). Clubs: Palm Bay, Jockey, Racket (Miami); Tennessee, Summit (Memphis). Home: 475 N Highland St Memphis TN 38122 Office: 96 N 3d St Memphis TN 38103

VAN HORN, LAWRENCE VINCENT, steel co. exec.; b. Galena, Kan., Aug. 12, 1913; s. Rob Roy and Pearl May (Page) Van H.; B.S. in Bus. Ed., Central State U., Edmond, Okla., 1935; m. Doretha Lucille Howerton, Aug. 25, 1934; children—Brooke A., Grayson P., Reece M. With Capitol Steel & Iron Co., Oklahoma City, 1935—, chmn. bd., pres., 1963—; dir. Stock Yards Bank; adv. dir. Shepherd Mail State Bank. Mem. adv. bd. Mercy Hosp. Asst sec. Asso. Industries Okla. Mem. Am. Inst. Steel Constrn. (dir. 1966—), C. of C. (dir.). Kiwanian (pres. 1965). Home: 7601 Dorset Dr Oklahoma City OK 73116 Office: 1726 S Agnew St Oklahoma City OK 73108

VAN HOY, JAMES HAROLD, business exec., mgmt. cons.; b. nr. Garden City, Mo., Apr. 6, 1891; s. Waldo Pleasant and Lutie Dell (West) Van H.; student pub. schs.; m. Inez G., Dec. 19, 1968. Salesman to so. div. mgr. Bird & Son, Inc. of E. Walpole, Mass., Sanford, Fla., 1919-58; pres., dir. Smith Lumber Co., Albany, Ga., East Albany Lumber Co., Flint Homes, Inc., Fernandina (Fla.) Lumber & Supply Co., Amelia Investment Co., Fernandina; dir. Chase & Co., Sanford; pres., dir. East Coast Lumber & Supply Co., Ft. Pierce, Fla.; sec.-treas., dir. Peninsula Paint & Plastic Mfrs., Inc., Sanford; 1st v.p. 1st Fed. Savs. & Loan Assn. Sanford. Chmn. bond holders com. City of Sanford. Democrat. Baptist. Club: River (Jacksonville, Fla.). Home: 900 Magnolia Av Sanford FL 32771

VAN JACKSON, WALLACE MERIWEATHER, librarian; b. Richmond, Va., May 6, 1900; s. William and Jeanette (McKenzie) Van J.; B.A., Va. Union U., 1934; B.L.S., Hampton Inst., 1934; A.M., U. Mich., 1935; grad. student U. Chgo., 1939-41; m. Ruth Mae Taylor, Dec. 29, 1924; children— Thomas Winfield, Marjorie B., Taylor William. Vice prin. Higgs Roanoke Inst., 1923-24; editor Richmond Voice, 1925-26; prin. Scottsville (Va.) Colored Graded Sch. 1926-27; librarian Va. Union U., 1927-41; prof. library sci. Atlanta U., 1941-42, univ. librarian, 1942-47; pub. affairs officer U.S. Legation, Monrovia, Liberia, 1947-49; librarian Tex. So. U., 1949-54, Va. State Coll., 1954-62; acquisitions librarian Nat. Library Nigeria, 1962-64; library dir. Va. State Coll., 1964-68; librarian Mary Holmes Coll., West Point, Miss., 1968-69; asst. to librarian Hampton Inst., 1969-71. Decorated Star of Africa (Liberia). Mem. Nigerian, Miss. library assns., Am. Tchrs. Assn., A.L.A. (council 1956—). Assn. Coll. and Reference Librarians, N.A.A.C.P., Delta Sigma Chi, Alpha Phi Alpha. Editorial bd. Phylon mag., 1942-47. Contbr. articles profl. publs. Address: 20400 Loyal Av Ettrick VA 23802

VAN LANDINGHAM, LEANDER SHELTON, JR., patent lawyer; b. Memphis, July 15, 1925; s. Leander Shelton and Bertha (Shumaker) Van L.; B.S. in Chemistry, U. N.C., 1948, M.A. in Organic Chemistry, 1949; J.D., Georgetown U., 1955; m. Henrietta Adena Stapf, July 5, 1959; children—Ann Henrietta, Leander Shelton III. Patent advisor Dept. Navy, Washington, 1953-55; admitted to D.C. bar, 1955, since pvt. practice in Washington. Cons. patent, trademark and copyright law, chem. patent matters, 1955—. Served with USNR, 1943-46, 1951-53. Mem. Am. Chem. Soc., Sci. Assn., Am., D.C., Fed. bar assns., Am. Patent Law Assn., Am. Judicature Soc., Sigma Xi, Phi Alpha Delta. Methodist. Home: 10726 Stanmore Dr Potomac Falls Potomac MD 20854 Office: 2233 Wisconsin Av NW Washington DC 20007

VANLOH, HAROLD CARL, funeral home and ins. exec.; b. Iowa Park, Tex., Dec. 28, 1907; s. Charles Peter and Martha Katherine (Mueller) VanL.; student Draughons Bus. Coll., 1924-25; m. Gwinn Elizabet Brumley, Nov. 25, 1935; children—Jerry Jack, Charles Kenneth. Vice-pres. Farmers State Bank, Burkburnett, Tex., 1925-40; cashier First Nat. Bank, Burkburnett, 1940-43; pres. Owens-Brumley Funeral Homes and Ins., Wichita Falls, Tex., 1943—; pres. First Savs. & Loan, 1960-65, Astro Drilling & Producing Co.; dir. First Nat. Bank, Burkburnett. Mem. Burkburnett City Council; mem. Burkburnett Parks and Recreation Bd., 1966-67; former mem. City-County Welfare Bd. Mem. Tex. State Assn. Mut. Ins. Cos. (v.p. 1956-57, 60-61, pres. 1966-67), Burkburnett C. of C. (dir. 1943-62, v.p. 1961-62), Clara (Tex.) Ex Students Assn. (pres. 1958). Democrat. Lutheran. Rotarian. Clubs: Wichita (Tex.); Wichita Falls (Tex.) Country; Burkburnett Swim (pres., dir.). Home: 311 E 6th St Burkburnett TX 76354 Office: 914 Scott St Wichita Falls TX 76301

VAN MOL, LOUIS JOHN, SR., mgmt. cons.; b. Antwerp, Belgium, Aug. 4, 1909; s. Joseph and Jeanette (Hazen) Van M.; brought to U.S., 1913, naturalized, 1918; student Purdue U., 1927-29, Lewis Inst., Chgo., 1928, U. Tenn., 1938-39, 47-48; m. Evelyn Ramsay, June 8, 1938; children—Cynthia Jeanne (Mrs. Gordon T. Smith), Louis John, Stephen Ramsay, Gordon Knox. Civil engr., C., M., St.P. & P. R.R., 1929-32, U.S. Geol. Survey, Dept. Interior, 1932-34, U.S. Biol. Survey, USDA, 1934-36; civil engr. TVA, 1936-41, personnel classification officer, 1941-46, chief personnel standards staff, 1946-47, asst. to dir. personnel, 1947-50, chief standards and analysis br., 1950-52, asst. dir. personnel, 1952-54, chief budget officer, 1954-55, asst. gen. mgr., chief budget officer, 1955-61, gen. mgr., 1961-70; mgmt. cons., 1970—. Mem. Pub. Personnel Assn. (dir. 1950-53, vice chmn. So. region 1950), Am. Soc. Pub. Adminstrn., Tech. Soc. Knoxville, Pi Kappa Alpha. Presbyn. (elder). Club: Holston Hills Country (Knoxville). Address: 1309 Avonmouth Rd Knoxville TN 37914

VANN, LOYD FRANK, architect; b. Miami, Fla., June 26, 1911; s. Jessie Frank and Mary Augusta (Bunnell) V.; B.S., Ga. Inst. Tech., 1932; m. Carolyn Sue Dorothy, May 22, 1934; 1 dau., Nancy (Mrs. John Nichols). Draftsman, designer Paist & Steward, Architects, Miami, 1932-37; pvt. practice architecture, Miami, 1937-40, 46—; dir. Midtown Bank of Miami. Mem. Met. Dade County Contractors Examining Bd., 1957-60; mem. Bd. Rules and Appeals, Dade County, 1967—. Served to lt. col. C.E., AUS, 1940-46. Baptist. Kiwanian. Important works include Granada Presbyn. Ch., Coral Gables, Fla., Univ. Christian Ch., South Miami, 1st Bapt. Ch., Avon Park, Fla. Home: 2935 Seminole St Miami FL 33133 Office: 101 NW 12th Av Miami FL 33128

VAN NESS, MARVIN LEONARD, pump mfg. exec.; b. Welsh, La., Dec. 1, 1903; s. Marvin Brown and Alice Elizabeth (Archer) van N.; student Asbury Coll., 1922-24, McKendree Coll., 1925-26, Rice Inst. Tech., 1926-27; m. Mabel Guzman, Apr. 26, 1929; 1 son, Joseph Leonard. Machinist, Tex. Co., Port Arthur, Tex., 1929-30, Welsh (La.) Machine Shops, 1930-50; owner Lo-Lift Pump Co., Inc., Welsh, 1951-66, pres., mgr., 1966—; owner, operator van Ness Bldgs., Welsh, 1950—; owner, mgr. Lady Fair, Welsh. Alderman, Welsh, 1959-62. Bd. dirs. La. Intracoastal Seaway Assn., 1967, Welsh Gen. Hosp., 1957-60. Lion (pres. 1950, dep. dist. gov. 1953). Home: 602 E South Welsh LA 70591 Office: 208 N Railroad Av Welsh LA 70591

VANNIER, MARYHELEN, educator, author; b. Decatur, Ill., June 18, 1915; d. William H. and Maude (Rockwood) Vannier; B.A., James Millikin U., 1938; M.A., Tchrs. Coll., Columbia, 1943; Ed.D., N.Y.U., 1950. Dir. womens phys. edn. Drake U., Des Moines, 1940-42, St. Lawrence U., Canton, N.Y., 1948-50, Wellesley High Sch., 1940-41; dir. women's health and phys. edn. So. Meth. U., Dallas, 1950—. Mem. Internat. Congress Phys. Edn. Tchrs. Girls and Women, Nat. Conf. Research in Therapeutic Recreation, Am. Sch. Health Assn., A.A.H.P.E.R., Am. Assn. U. Profs., Park and Recreation Assn., Nat. Assn. Phys. Edn. Coll. Women. Author: Teaching Physical Education in Elementary Schools, 1968, 5th edit., 1972; Methods and Materials in Recreation Leadership, 1966; Individual and Team Sports for Girls and Women, 1969; Physical Activities for College Women, 1968; Physical Activities for the Handicapped, 1972; many others; articles in profl. jours. Home: 7006 Stefani St Dallas TX 75225

VAN NOSTRAND, ROBERT GAIGE, research co. exec.; b. Oneida, N.Y., Nov. 28, 1918; s. George Peyton and Mildred (Gaige) Van N.; B.S., Mo. Sch. Mines, 1942, M.S., 1949; Ph.D., U. N.C., 1953; m. Colette Marie Regnault, June 19, 1962; children—Chantel, Jean Pierre, Thierry, Dominique, Eric, Gregory. Sr. research geophysicist

Magnolia Petroleum Co., Dallas, 1952-56; geophys. supr. Mobil Oil Francaise, Paris, France, 1956-57; chief geophysicist Prepa, Paris, 1957-61; gen. mgr. Exploration Geophysique Roger, Paris, 1961-62; with Alexandria Labs., (Va.), 1962—, mgr. labs., 1971; dir. Computer Cartography, Washington. Served to maj. AUS, 1942-47. Mem. Soc. Exploration Geophysics, Am. Geophys. Union. A.A.A.S., Seismological Soc. Am., European Assn. Exploration Geophysics. Contbr. articles to profl. pubs. Editor: Society of Exploration Geophysics, 1966-67. Home: 1424 Kingston Av Alexandria VA 22302 Office: Box 334 Alexandria VA 22313

VANNOY, JOELLENE, nutritionist; b. McLean, Tex., Aug. 30, 1910; d. John Brown and Cora (Mills) Vannoy; B.S., Tex. Tech., 1931; M.A., Columbia, 1936, Ed.D., 1963. Tchr. home econs. McLean (Tex.) High Sch., 1931-33, Plainview (Tex.) High Sch., 1934; home demonstration agt. Stanton, Tex., 1935, Roby, Tex., 1937-38, Crowell, Tex., 1939-41; foods, nutrition specialist Ark. Agr. Extension Service, Little Rock, 1942-45; regional home economist Wheat Flour Inst., Chgo., 1946-55; nutritionist Millers Nat. Fedn., Washington, 1958-63; nutritionist, home economist Wheat Assos., U. S.A., Inc., Bulgur Assos. Inc., 1964-69; pub. health nutritionist D.C. Dept. Pub. Health, 1969—. U.S. technician First World Agrl. Fair, New Delhi, India, 1959-60. Mem. Am. Acad. Polit. and Social Scis., Am. Home Econs. Assn., Am. Dietetic Assn., Am. Pub. Health Assn., Am. Sch. Food Service Assn., Am. Women in Radio and Television, Nat. Acad. TV Arts Scis., Internat. Platform Assn., Kappa Delta Pi, Pi Lambda Theta. Mem. Christian Ch. Helped develop nutrition edn. programs in mass communications Colombia, S. Am. Egypt, India, Pakistan, The Philippines, Hong Kong, Taiwan, Vietnam, Thailand, 1958—. Home: 1330 Massachusetts Av NW Washington DC 20005 Office: 1221 M St NW Washington DC 20005

VANOCUR, SANDER, news corr.; b. Cleve., Jan. 8, 1928; student Northwestern U., also London (Eng.) Sch. Econs.; m. Edith Pick, Mar. 3, 1956; children—Nicholas, Christopher. Formerly news corr. with Manchester (Eng.) Guardian, BBC, CBS News, N.Y. Times; now with NBC News, formerly White House corr., now roving network polit. reporter. Served with AUS, 1952-54. Home: 3122 Ordway St Washington DC 20008 Office: 4001 Nebraska Av NW Washington DC 20016

VAN OSTENBERG, PAUL ROGER, dentist; b. Grand Rapids, Mich., Aug. 30, 1941; s. Don Henry and Leonora Franciscus (Rylaarsdam) Van O.; A.A., St. Petersburg Jr. Coll., 1961; student U. Fla., 1961-62; B.A., U. So. Fla., 1963; D.D.S., Med. Coll. Va., 1967. Chief dentist Catawba Sanatorium, Va. State Dept. Health, Roanoke, 1967-68; instr. dept. pediatrics U. Va. Sch. Medicine, Charlottesville, 1968-71, asst. prof. dept. pediatrics, dir. dental services Children and Youth Center, clin. staff, 1971—; vis. dentist, prof. staff U. Va. Hosp., 1971—. Bd. dirs. Chesapeake Dist. Found. for Handicapped and Retarded Children, Camp Saponi. Recipient outstanding service award Charlottesville Civitan Club, 1969-70. Mem. Am., Va. dental assns., Shenandoah Valley Dental Soc. (relief com. 1971), Am. Soc. Preventive Dentistry, Am. Soc. Dentistry for Children. Presbyn. Club: Civitan (treas. 1969—) (Charlottesville, Va.). Home: 104 12th St NW Box 3404 Charlottesville VA 22903 Office: University Va Hospital Box 267 Charlottesville VA 22903

VAN OVERBERGHE, ROBERT, Belgian diplomat; LL.D., M. Polit. Scis., U. Ghent (Belgium); m. 1 child. Consul gen. of Belgium to the southeastern U.S., Atlanta. Home: 397 Blanton Rd NW Atlanta GA 30342 Office: Peachtree Center South 225 Peachtree St NE Atlanta GA 30303

VAN RYSWYK, CARL WAYNE, elec. engr.; b. Otley, Ia., June 4, 1938; s. Pete and Nellie (Brandenhorst) Van R.; B.S., U. Tex., 1963, M.S, 1969; m. Shirley Elaine Walker, Sept. 30, 1957; children—Carla Jo, Jeffrey Wayne, Craig Wesley, Chris Walker. Asst. engr. White Instruments, Inc., Austin, Tex., 1963-66, chief engr., 1966—. Cons., Millard Research Assos., Austin, Internat. and Pan Am. Inst. Social Sci. and Ednl. Research, Austin. Bd. dirs. Austin Assn. Retarded Children, treas., 1970-71, pres., 1971-72; bd. dirs. Pan Am. Inst. Social Sci. and Ednl. Research. Baptist (Sunday sch. dir. 1968-70). Home: 606 Brookhaven Trail Austin TX 78746 Office: PO Box 698 Austin TX 78767

VAN SANT, GEORGE MONTGOMERY, educator; b. State College, Pa., Nov. 20, 1927; s. Edward Raguet and Beatrice Nordica (Show) Van S.; A.B., St. John's Coll., Annapolis, Md., 1948; M.A., U. Va., 1955, Ph.D., 1958; m. Peggy Ann Hutchinson, Sept. 12, 1953; children—Edward D., Mary M. Ednl. researcher Nat. Council of Protestant Episcopal Ch., N.Y.C., 1948-49; dir. printing St. John's Coll., 1949-50; information officer Va. Hwy. Research Council, 1956-58; asst. prof. to prof. philosophy Mary Washington Coll. of U. Va., 1958—, chmn. dept., 1969—. Pres. Va. Mus. Fine Arts, Fredericksburg, 1961; v.p. Fredericksburg Cotillion, 1962, 69. Mem. Fredericksburg Democratic Com., 1965-71. Bd. dirs. Fredericksburg Area United Givers Fund, 1969-71. Served with USMC, 1945-46, 50-53; col. Res. Decorated Bronze Star, Purple Heart; Nat. Sci. Found. fellow, 1961. Mem. Am., Va. (pres. 1964) philos. assns., U. Va. Raven Soc., Omicron Delta Kappa. Episcopalian. Contbr. articles profl. jours. Home: 1407 Washington Av Fredericksburg VA 22401

VAN SICKLE, RAYBURN JEFFERSON, physician; b. nr. Greenville, Tex., Nov. 7, 1899; s. Miles William and Margaret Pairlee (Lavender) Van S.; student Harvard Radio Sch., 1917, N.Y.C. Coll. Radar Sch., 1918; A.A., Wesley Coll., Greenville, 1920; grad. Portsmouth (Va.) Pharmacy Sch., U.S. Naval Med. Sch., Washington, 1924; M.D., Baylor U., 1930; m. Lina Hardin Glover, July 2, 1933. Intern, Worley Hosp., Pampa, Tex., 1930-31; practice medicine, Pampa, 1930-31, Longview, Tex., 1931—; resident Cook County Hosp., Chgo., 1933, Polyclinic, N.Y.C., 1934, Mayo Bros., Rochester, Minn., 1935-36; v.p. staff Gregg County Hosp. Served with USN, 1917-19, 21-25. Mem. A.M.A., Tex., Gregg County med. socs., Phi Rho Sigma. Mason (Shriner). Home: 814 Charlotte Dr Longview TX 75601 Office: 100 E Methvin St Longview TX 75601

VAN SKIKE, ROBERT BRUCE, JR., lawyer; b. Bradenton, Fla., Nov. 12, 1929; s. Robert Bruce and Ethel (Byrd) Van S.; A.B., Duke, 1951; J.D., Stetson U., 1955. Admitted to Fla. bar, 1956; asso. Burket, Smith & Bowman, Sarasota, Fla., 1956-57; gen. practice Sarasota, 1958—. Trustee New Coll.; dist. dir. Met. Opera Assn. for Fla. Fellow Am. Coll. Probate Counsel; mem. Am., Fla., Sarasota County bar assns., Chi Phi, Phi Delta Phi. Democrat. Presbyn. Home: 2612 Mulberry Terrace Sarasota FL 33579 Office: Van Skike Bldg Sarasota Fl 33577

VAN SMITH, HOWARD, writer; b. San Francisco, Apr. 6, 1910; s. Arthur Lockwood and Florence (Garrettson) S.; student Pennington Prep., 1927-29, Franklyn Union, 1936-37; m. Anne McCarron, June 21, 1938 (div. 1965); children—Garrett, Parris, Antony, William; m. Micheline Mathews, Nov. 26, 1965. Staff reporter N.Y. Times, 1930-32; free-lance writer, 1933-35; heating and hydraulics engr., 1935-42; civilian engr. Air Force, Warner-Robins Airfield, Ga., 1942-44; reporter Orlando Sentinel, 1944; Sunday editor Miami Daily News, 1945-57, spl. writer, 1957-65; spl. writer Ft. Lauderdale (Fla.) News, 1965—; lectr. U. Miami, 1948-54. Recipient Pulitzer prize for nat. reporting, 1959, meritorious award Fla. Pub. Health Assn., 1959; Service to Mankind award, 1961; N.Y. U. fellow, 1970—. Author (with Dr. C. Raymond Van Dusen) The New Speech-O-Gram Technique for Persuasive Public Speaking, 1962. Florida Gardening Writer of the Year, 1970. Adviser (TV documentary) Harvest of Shame (named to TV Hall of Fame. Contbr. articles, short stories to nat. mags. Home: 736 SW 14th Av Fort Lauderdale FL 33312 Office: Ft Lauderdale News Fort Lauderdale FL 33302

VAN STONE, LORNE FREDERICK, mgmt. cons.; b. Cairo, Ill., Nov. 2, 1906; s. Lorne Disraeli and Adelaide (Mitchell) Van S.; student Tex. A. & M., 1933; U. Houston, 1938; m. Carmen Elizabeth, June 5, 1929; children— Lorne Frederick, Janice (Mrs. L. B. Hedrick). Salesman, J.E. Rogers, Inc., Houston, 1926-33; mgr. bakery supply dept. Rogers Grain Co., 1933-36; v.p., sales mgr. S. Tex. Feed Co., 1936-38; pres., gen. mgr. Uncle Johnny Mills, Inc., 1938-59; exec. v.p., gen. mgr. United Salt Corp., 1960-65; pres. Lorne F. Van Stone Assos., mgmt. cons. and orgn. devel., 1966—; exec. v.p., dir. C.E. Kaiser Co., 1966—; sec.-treas., dir. Standley Inc., 1948— (all Houston); founder, pres. Lorne F. Van Stone Assos. (U.K.) Ltd., London, Eng., 1970—; pres. Matrex Corp., 1969—; treas. V Inc., 1971; dir. Stillwagon Enterprises, 1969—. Chmn. salt com. for agr. Salt Inst. U.S. and Can., 1964-65; chmn. S.W. Area Conf. Indsl. Relations, 1965. Active various local fund raising campaigns; past mem. adv. coms. U. Houston, U. Kan., Tex. A. & M. U. Bd. dirs. Met. YMCA, Houston, 1964-68, Eye Inst., 1958-68. Mem. Houston C. of C. (past chmn. research com., mem. 1972), Tex. Mfrs. Assn. (dir. 1956-60, chmn. retirement plan and trust fund com. 1963-67, treas. 1961-62), Houston Sales Execs. Club. (life mem., past pres.), Salt Producers Assn. (chmn. agrl. com.), Better Bus. Bur. (life mem., past pres. Houston), Am. (past dir.), Midwest (past dir.), Tex. (pres. 1948, 54) feed mfrs. assns., Execs. Assn. Houston (past pres.), S.W. Sales and Marketing Execs. Assn. (mem. council). Presbyn. (ruling elder). Clubs: Salesmanship of Houston (life mem., past pres.), Houston Farm and Ranch (pres. 1956-57), Houston Yacht (commodore 1959-60). Home: 2736 Werlein St Houston TX 77005

VAN SWEARINGEN, EARL CORNELIUS, color process co. exec.; b. New Cumberland, W.Va., Apr. 2, 1904; s. Clarence Chapman and Carrie Cornelia (Carmen) Van S.; student Cleve. Sch. Art, 1923-24; grad. Cin. Acad. Art, 1926; postgrad., Grand Central Art Sch., N.Y.C., 1933; m. Phyllis Margueritte Andrews, May 18, 1925; children—Barbara Ellen (Mrs. William H. Loescher), Earl Cornelius, Phyllis Margueritte (Mrs. J. Brooks Vallentine). Art dir. J. Walter Thompson Advt. Agy., N.Y.C., Buenos Aires, Argentina, 1928-31; free-lance artist and color cons., N.Y.C., 1931-51; with Batten, Barton, Durstine, Osborn, Inc., advt. agy., N.Y.C., 1953-57; creative dir. A. Asch Co., outdoor advt. agy., N.Y.C., 1958-68; pres. Color Monitor Corp., N.Y.C., 1968-71; pres. Van Swearingen Corp. Fla., 1971—. Instr. art and painting Grand Central Art Sch., N.Y.C., 1938-40. Recipient Scoutmaster's key Siwanoy Council Boy Scouts Am., Crosley Television Poster award, 1955, Four Roses Poster award, 1962, citation for inventing new printing technique (Van Swearingen Reprodn. Process) Printing Industries of Met. N.Y., 1966. Mem. Soc. Illustrators. Clubs: Orienta Beach and Yacht (Mamaroneck, N.Y., commodore 1967-69, ret. commodore emeritus); Cape Coral Yacht and Racquet (Cape Coral, Fla.). Author: Pictorial Perspectives, 1939; How To Decorate Your Own Home, 1953; inventor E.C. Van Swearingen Reprodn. Process for printing or painting, universal color casting system, 1954, patentee Eng., Can., U.S. Address: 5714 Driftwood Pkwy Cape Coral FL 33904

VAN VACTOR, DAVID, composer, flutist; b. Plymouth, Ind., May 8, 1906; s. David Ellsworth and Matilda (Fernstermacher) Van V.; Mus. B., Northwestern U., 1928, Mus.M., 1935; student l'Ecole Normale, Paris, summer, 1931; m. Mary Virginia Landreth, May 28, 1931; children—Adriaen, David Landreth. Flutist, Chgo. Symphony Orch., 1931; instr. theory of music Northwestern U., 1935-47; composer, 1928—; asst. condr. Kansas City Philharmonic, 1943-47, also head composition dept. Conservatory of Music, 1945-47; founder condr. Allied Arts Orch. of Kansas City, 1945-47; condr. Knoxville Symphony Orch.; prof. dept. fine arts U. of Tenn., 1947—. Guest condr. Nat. Symphony Orch. of Chile, 1945; vis. prof. U. Chile (S.A.); guest condr. Philharmonia Orch. London, 1954; guest condr., flute soloist Palmengarten Orch., Frankfort, Germany, 1961, 62; artist in residence, guest condr. orchs. of Chile, under auspices U.S. Dept. State, 1965. Mem. Am. Wind Quintet League Composers touring Central and S. Am., summer 1941; former mem. conf. bd. Asso. Research Council Com. on Internat. exchange of Persons. Recipient hon. mention for "The Masque of the Red Death" (full orchestra) in Gustavus Swift competition, 1935; 1st award for "Symphony in D" (full orchestra) N.Y. Philharmonic-Symphony competition, 1938; 1st award for "Quintet with Flute, Two Violins, Viola and Cello," Soc. for Publ. of Am. Music, 1941; "Overture to a Comedy No. 2" won 1942 Juilliard Publ. award; Northwestern University Alumni Merit award, 1950. Has composed for full orchestra and chamber orchestra, also chorals and chamber music; works played by Chgo., Rochester, Atlanta, Chattanooga, Pitts., Kansas City, Indpls., San Francisco, Knoxville, Nat. symphony orchs., N.Y. Philharmonic, Cleveland, Phila., St. Louis orchs.; composed under commn. Louisville Orch., Fantasy, Chaconne, Allegro; New Light Composition for Chorus and Orchestra, 1959. Author: Every Child May Hear, 1960. Fulbright Research fellow, Frankfort, Germany, 1957-58. Guggenheim fellow, 1957-58. Mem. Wranglers, Phi Mu Alpha Sinfonia (hon.), Phi Kappa Lambda. Clubs: Arts, Cliff Dwellers (Chgo.) Home: 2824 Kingston Pike Knoxville TN 37910

VAN VLEET, DAVID EDWARD, dentist; b. Sharon, Conn., Dec. 16, 1931; s. Henry Lee and Edna Zoe (Cassidy) Van V.; student Agrl. and Tech. Inst., Canton, N.Y., 1949-51, Duke U., 1955-57; D.D.S., U. N.C., 1961; m. Norma June Husted, Nov. 17, 1951; children—Nancy Lynn, David Eric, Lee Morris. Pvt. practice gen. dentistry, Durham, N.C., 1963—; pres., chmn. bd. V & H, Inc., 1970—. Served with USAF, 1951-55, 61-63. Mem. Delta Sigma Delta. Methodist (steward 1971—). Kiwanian. Home: 202 E Markham St Durham NC 27701 Office: 624 Gary St Durham NC 27703

VAN WAZER, JOHN ROBERT, educator, chemist; b. Chgo., Apr. 11, 1918; s. John Robert and Florence (Johnson) Van W.; B.S., Northwestern U., 1940; M.A., Harvard, 1941, Ph.D., 1942; m. Mary Elizabeth Ballou, July 15, 1940; 1 dau., Mary Elizabeth. Chemist, Eastman Kodak Co., Rochester, N.Y., 1942-44, group leader, Oak Ridge, 1944-46; phys. chemist Rumford Chem. Works, Providence, 1946-49; head physics research Gt. Lakes Carbon Corp., Morton Grove, Ill., 1949-50; sr. scientist Monsanto Co., Anniston, Ala., 1950-51, sr. scientist, asst. research dir., Dayton, O., 1952-57, sr. scientist, St. Louis, 1957-68, research dir., 1965-68; prof. chemistry Vanderbilt U., Nashville, 1968—. Mem. Am. Chem. Soc., Soc. Rheology, A.A.A.S., N.Y. Acad. Sci., Gesellschaft deutscher Chemiker, Chem. Soc. (London), Am. Recorder Soc., Assn Am. Chamber Music Players, Phi Beta Kappa, Sigma Xi, Alpha Chi Sigma. Club: University (Nashville). Author books in field: contbr. numerous articles to profl. jours. Home: 1121 Ridgeview Dr Nashville TN 37220

VAN WRIGHT, AARON, JR., coll. dean; b. Port Arthur, Tex., Oct. 3, 1932; s. Aaron and Lou (Patterson) Van W.; B.A., Huston-Tillotson Coll., 1953; postgrad. U. Wis., 1956-58; M.A., Columbia, 1961; Ed.D., U. Okla., 1965; m. Evelyn Doris Meredith, July 12, 1963; children—Angela, Aaron III, Alexander. Band dir., pub. schs., Beaumont, Tex., 1953; Port Arthur, 1955-61; instr. music therapy Manhattan (N.Y.) State Hosp., 1961; asso. prof. music theory Winston-Salem (N.C.) State U., 1965-66; chmn. dept. music, dir. div. fine arts Hampton Inst., 1966-69; acad. dean Tex. Coll., Tyler, 1969—. Active Boy Scouts Am. Trustee Tex. Coll. Day Care Center. Served with AUS, 1953-55. Mem. N.A.A.C.P., Phi Mu Alpha, Phi Delta Kappa, Omega Psi Phi. Mason. Contbr. articles to profl. jours. Home: 1403 S Academy St Tyler TX 75701

VAN WYK, JUDSON JOHN, med. educator; b. Maurice, Ia., June 10, 1921; s. John Cornelius and Amelia (Menning) Van W.; A.B., Hope Coll., 1943; postgrad. in Biochemistry (fellow) St. Louis U., 1943-44; M.D. (Henry Strong Dennison scholar), Johns Hopkins U., 1948; m. Persis R. Parker, June 8, 1944; children—Judith Parker, Persis Allen, Peter Menning, Judson John. Intern, resident pediatrics Johns Hopkins Hosp., 1948-50, Cin. Children's Hosp., 1950-51; investigator Nat. Heart Inst., 1951-53; fellow in endocrinology Johns Hopkins Med. Sch., 1953-55; asst. prof. pediatrics U. N.C. Sch. Medicine, 1955-59, asso. prof., 1959-62, prof. pediatrics, 1962—; cons. in endocrinology Womack Army Hosp., Ft. Bragg; vis. scientist Karolinska Institutet, Stockholm, Sweden, 1968-69. Med. adv. bd. Human Growth, Inc., 1968—, chmn. com. on research, 1970—; mem. tng. grants com. Nat. Inst. Arthritis & Metabolic Diseases, 1967—; mem. endocrine study sect. NIH, 1971—. Served with USPHS, 1951-53. Recipient Career Research award USPHS, 1962, John and Mary Markle Scholar in Med. Sci., 1957-62. Diplomate Am. Bd. Pediatrics. Fellow Am. Acad. Pediatrics; hon. mem. Peruana Sociedad Pediatrica, European Pediatric Endocrine Soc.; mem. Endocrine Soc., Am. Thyroid Assn., Soc. for Pediatric Research, Am. Pediatric Soc., So. Soc. Clin. Investigation. Presbyn. Contbr. chpts. to books. Editorial bd. Jour. Clin. Endocrinology and Metabolism, 1956—, Pediatrics, 1969—. Research in sex differentiation, abnormalities of growth and development. Home: 1020 Highland Woods Chapel Hill NC 27514

VARADY, GABOR GEORGE, accountant; b. Szentes, Hungary, July 23, 1921; s. Gabor K. and Elizabeth (Zsoldos) V.; grad. Royal Ludovika Acad., Budapest, Hungary, 1942; student U. Econ. and Tech. Scis., Budapest, 1947, 48; M.B.A., U. Tex., 1952; m. Antoinette Marquis, June 9, 1951; children—Andrew Gabor, Barbara Antoinette. Came to U.S., 1950, naturalized, 1953. With Price Waterhouse & Co., C.P.A.'s, 1952-68; partner Alexander Grant & Co., C.P.A.'s, 1969—; past pres. Houston Estate and Financial Forum. Served as 1st lt. F.A., Royal Hungarian Army, 1944-45. Mem. Tex. Soc. C.P.A.'s (sec. 1969-70, v.p. 1972-73), Am. Inst. C.P.A.'s. Home: 6919 Hartland St Houston TX 77055 Office: care Alexander Grant & Co Century Bldg Houston TX 77002

VARDYS, V. STANLEY, educator; b. Berzoras, Lithuania, Sept. 2, 1924; s. Stasys and Karolina (Budrys) V.; came to U.S., 1949, naturalized, 1955; student U. Tuebingen (Germany), 1945-49; B.A., Carroll Coll., 1951; M.A., U. Wis., 1953, Ph.D., 1958; m. Anna Nijole Rimkus, Apr. 15, 1955; children—Ina M., Elizabeth R., Ruta K., Vytautas S. Faculty U. Wis. at Milw., 1955-68, instr. polit. sci., 1955-58, asst. prof., 1958-64, asso. prof., 1964-68; prof. polit. sci. U. Okla., Norman, 1968—, dir. Munich (Germany) Center for Russian Lang. and Soviet Area Studies, 1968—, chmn. Russian studies com., 1968—. Research grantee Am. Council Learned Socs., 1966-67. Mem. Am. Assn. U. Profs., Am. Polit. Sci. Assn., Am., S.W. (sec.-treas. 1969-70, pres. 1970-71) assns. for advancement Slavic studies, Assn. for Advancement of Baltic Studies (pres. 1970-71), Baltic Research Inst. (corr. U. Bonn Germany), Lions Internat. Editor, contbg. author: Lithuania under the Soviets, 1965; Karl Marx: Scientist Revolutionary Humanist, 1971. Contbr. to books and jours. Home: 1719 Hollywood St Norman OK 73069

VARENA, CHARLOTTE MARIE, bus. exec.; b. Atlanta, Apr. 23, 1902; d. Alfred A. and Albertine (Tuchscherer) Varena; grad. high sch. Asst. cashier Bank of Sebring, also 1st Nat. Bank, Sebring, Fla., 1920-29; sales, traffic mgr. Gregg Maxcy, Inc., Sebring, 1929-48; exec. sec. Maxcy Securities, Inc., Sebring, 1948-60, mgr., sec., treas., 1960—; dir., sec. Cypress Gardens Citrus Products, Inc., Winter Haven, Fla., 1960—. Active community civic functions. Recipient Honor Plaque, Sebring Bus. and Profl. Women's Club, 1932. Mem. Fedn. Bus. & Profl. Women's Clubs. Home: 11 Micco Av PO Box 344 Sebring FL 33870 Office: Maxcys Securities 29 N Ridgewood Dr Box 344 Sebring FL 33870

VARNER, JEANNETTE JOHNSON, ret. librarian; b. Selma, Ala., Aug. 12, 1909; d. Chester Earle and Ruby Jeannette (West) Johnson; B.A., U. Ala., 1930, M.A., 1931; Ph.D., U. Va., 1938; m. John Grier Varner, Apr. 29, 1939. French tchr. Blue Mountain (Miss.) Coll., 1937-39; Spanish tchr. Fairfax Hall Jr. Coll., Waynesboro, Va., also U. Va. extension div., 1941-43; librarian, English tchr. Centro Venezolano-Americano, Caracas, Venezuela, 1943-47; head reference librarian Austin (Tex.) Pub. Library, 1948-71. Am. Philos. Soc. travel grantee, Spain, 1954. Mem. Am., Southwestern, Tex. library assns., Real Academia de Ciencias, Bellas Letras y Nobles Artes de Cordoba (corr.), Latin Am. Studies Assn., Alpha Delta Pi. Democrat. Episcopalian. Editor, translator: (with John Grier Varner) The Florida of the Inca (Garcilaso de la Vega), 1951. Contbr. (with John Grier Varner) to Ency. Americana, 1955. Home: 2510 Jarratt Av Austin TX 78703

VARNER, JOHN GRIER, historian, educator; b. Mt. Pleasant, Tex., Mar. 30, 1905; s. John Grier and Leila Ada (McConnell) V.; B.A., Austin Coll., 1926; M.A., U. Va., 1932, Ph.D., 1940; m. Jeannette Johnson, Apr. 29, 1939. DuPont teaching fellow U. Va., Charlottesville, 1930-38; asst. prof. English, Washington and Lee U., Lexington, Va., 1938-43; dir. Centro Venezolano-Americano, Caracas, 1943-47; asst. cultural attache Am. embassy, Mexico City, Mexico, 1947; prof. English, U. Tex., Austin, 1947—. Dept. State lectr., S.Am. and C.Am., 1951-52. Am. Philos. Soc. grantee, U. Tex. Research Council grantee, Spain, 1954. Mem. Real Academia de Ciencias, Bellas Lectas y Nobles Artes (corr., Cordoba, Spain). Democrat. Presbyn. Club: Headliners (Austin). Author: English Grammar for Venezuelans, 1946; El Inca: The Life and Times of Garcilaso de la Vega, 1968. Editor, translator (with wife): The Florida of the Inca, 1951. Home: 2510 Jarratt Av Austin TX 78703*

VARNER, KINCH MORGAN, JR., banker; b. Union Springs, Ala., Jan. 7, 1915; s. Kinch Morgan and Estelle Eugenia (McGowen) Varner; student Chillicothe Bus. Coll., 1933-35, La. State U., 1953-56; m. Anne Robison, June 20, 1939; 1 son, Kinch Morgan III. Cashier, dir. First Nat. Bank, Union Springs, Ala., 1936-53; asst. v.p. Birmingham Trust Nat. Bank, 1953-56; v.p. Union Bank &Trust Co., Montgomery, 1956-60; pres., dir. First Nat. Bank, Auburn, 1960—; dir. Birmingham br. Fed. Res. Bank, Nixon Real Estate, University Agy. Pres., Auburn Indsl. Devel. Bd., 1962-70; mayor, Union Springs, Ala., 1952. Bd. dirs. Ala. 4-H Club; state treas. Ala. div. Am. Cancer Soc., 1968-71. Served to 2d lt. AUS, 1944-46. Mem. Auburn C. of C. (pres. 1968), Auburn Downtown Mchts. Assn. (bd. dirs. 1968-71).

Lion (dist. gov. 1951-52), Mason. Home: 634 Cary Dr Auburn AL 36830 Office: PO Box 2149 Auburn AL 36830

VASEK, RICHARD JIM, educator; b. Wharton, Tex., June 23, 1935; s. James F. and Albina (Zapalac) V.; student Wharton County Jr. Coll., 1954-56; B.S., Tex. A. & M. U., 1958, M.Ed., 1960, Ed.D., 1967; m. Lou Ann Ponder, Oct. 29, 1955; children—Jeffrey, Donna, Blake, Carole, Laura. Instr. Ft. Worth Pub. Schs., 1958-59; instr. Ark. A. and M. Coll., College Heights, 1959-60; asst., asso. prof. Miss. State U., 1960-66, 68-70, prof., head dept. indsl. and occupational edn., 1970-—, research U.S. Office of Edn., 1966-67; cons. indsl. arts curriculum in pub. schs. Mem. Am. Indsl. Arts Assn. (state rep.) Miss. Indsl. Arts Assn. (pres., bd. mem.), Am. Council on Indsl. Arts Tchr. Edn., Miss. Edn. Assn., Iota Lambda Sigma (pres.). Roman Catholic. Contbr. articles in field to profl. jours. Home: 208 Woodlawn St Starkville MS 39759 Office: Drawer NU State Coll MS 39762

VASS, SIFFREIN M., bus. exec. Pres., gen. mgr. Ford Motor de Mexico. Address: Ford de Mexico Ford Motor Co SA Reforma No 333 Mexico City Mexico Ford de Mexico Ford Motor Co SA Reforma No 333 Mexico City Mexico*

VASSALLO, EDWARD ANDREW, tobacco co. exec.; b. Ardmore, Pa., July 20, 1916; s. Andrew Martin and Ragnhild Marie (Nielsen) V.; student Pa. State U., 1934-36; m. Mickey Lucile McCollum, Mar. 4, 1950; children— Andrea Hamilton, Allison Hood. With Campbell Soup Co., Camden, N.J., 1939-57; gen. sales mgr., exec. v.p., 1954-57; dir. marketing, mng. dir., dep. chmn. Campbell's Soups Ltd., U.K., 1957-69; v.p. research and devel. R.J. Reynolds Tobacco Co., Winston Salem, N.C., 1969-70, now v.p., dir.; v.p. R.J. Reynolds Industries, 1970-71; chmn. bd. RJR Foods. Mem. parents council Stratford Coll. Bd. govs. Greenacre Sch. for Girls, Banstead, Eng. Served to capt. USAAF, 1942-46. Decorated Air medal, Bronze Star, 2 Presdl. citations. Mem. Research Inst. U.S., English Speaking Union, Dirs. Inst. Gt. Britain, Grocers Inst. Gt. Britain, C. of C., Am. Legion. Episcopalian. Rotarian. Club: Old Town Country, Bermuda Run Country (Winston Salem); Hunstanton Golf, King's Lynn Golf (U.K.). Home: 2000 Virginia Rd Winston Salem NC 27104 Office: RJR Building 4th and Main Sts Winston Salem NC 27102

VASSALLO, PAUL, librarian; b. Marsa, Malta, Aug. 3, 1937; s. Salvatore and Josephine V.; B.A. in Polit. Sci., Wayne State U., 1959, postgrad., 1959-61; M.A. in L.S., U. Mich., 1962. With Library of Congress, Washington, 1961-—, asst. chief serial record div., chief Congl. reference div., 1968-—; asst. to dean Sch. Library and Information Services, U. Md., 1967-68. Recipient Meritoriuous Service award Library of Congress, 1966. Mem. A.L.A., Spl. Library Assn., Am. Soc. for Information Sci. Author: (with others) American Library Association List of International Subscription Agents. Home: 8150 Lakecrets Dr Greenbelt MD 20770 Office: Library of Congress Washington DC 20540

VASWANI, NARI KALACHAND, govt. engr.; b. Huderabad, India, Mar. 16, 1920; s. Kalachand H. and Ganga K. (Bhojwani) V.; B.Engring., Bombay U., India, 1943; M.S., Wis. U., 1959; Ph.D., Roorkee U., India, 1964; m. Menghi A. Thadani, June 26, 1948; children—Roma (Mrs. Prem Malkani), Bulbul. Exec. engr. railways, bldg. engr. Indian Railways, 1943-54; prof. Roorkee U., India, 1954-65; mem. Va. Hwy. Research Council, Charlottesville, Va., 1965-—. U.S. fellow, 1958-59. Fellow Am. Soc. C.E.; mem. India Road Congress, Am. Soc. Testing Materials, Soc. Soil Mechanics and Found. Engrs., Inst. Engrs., Sigma Xi. Author: Highway Engineering; Railway Engineering; Airport Engineering. Contbr. articles to profl. pubs. Home: 1006 Glendale Rd Charlottesville VA 22901 Office: 3817 University Station Charlottesville VA 22903

VATH, JOHN, broadcasting exec. Sta. mgr., gen. mgr. WSMB, New Orleans. Office: 901 Canal St New Orleans LA 70112*

VATH, JOSEPH G., clergyman; b. New Orleans, Mar. 12, 1918; ed. Notre Dame Sem. Ordained priest Roman Catholic Ch., 1941; named titular bishop of Novaliciana and aux. of Mobile-Birmingham (Ala.), 1967. Office: 400 Government St Mobile AL 36606*

VAUGHAN, DAVID ROSS, investment co. exec.; b. Augusta, Ga., June 13, 1931; s. George Marion and Virginia Martha (Moore) V.; student Presbyn. Coll., 1948-52; B.A., Vanderbilt U., 1953; postgrad. Ga. State U., 1956; m. Nancy Finley, Dec. 17, 1952; children— David Ross, Daniel, Judith, James. With Mut. Benefit Life Ins. Co., 1956-63; 1st v.p., dir. Financial Service Corp. Internat., Atlanta, 1963-72; pres. Balanced Financial Service, Inc., life ins. agy.; v.p. FSC Properties, Inc., 1969-72; pres. LTP Services Inc., 1972-—; dir. Transp. Tech., Inc. Chmn. Decatur Bapt. Towers; trustee So. Bapt. Annuity Bd. Served to lt. (j.g.) USNR, 1953-55. Mem. Million Dollar Round Table (life), Nat. Assn. Life Underwriters, Assn. Advanced Life Underwriters, Atlanta Estate Planning Council, Pi Kappa Alpha. Republican. Baptist (deacon). Home: 77 E Andrews Dr NW Apt 160 Atlanta GA 30305 Office: Suite 516 100 Colony Sq Atlanta GA 30309

VAUGHAN, JAMES THURMAN, JR., lawyer; b. Hubbard, Tex., Sept. 15, 1927; s. James T. and Johnnie Iola (Orr) V.; B.S., Tex. Christian U., 1950; J.D., So. Meth. U., 1957; m. Henrietta Ann Aikman, Aug. 5, 1950 (div.); 1 dau., Leigh Ann. Exec. dept. Gulf Oil Corp., Ft. Worth, 1950-54; pvt. practice, Dallas, 1957-—; gen. counsel Wrather Oil Interests, Eldorado Oil & Gas, Inc., Sovereign Devel. Corp., Sovereign Oil & Gas, Inc., Williams & Wagner Constrn. Co., Inc., Williams & Wagner Investments, Inc. Served with AUS, 1945-47. Mem. Am., Tex., Irving, Dallas bar assns., Tex. Trial Lawyers Assn., Dallas Assn. Petroleum Landmen, State Bar Tex., Ind. Petroleum Assn. Am., Southwestern Legal Found., Delta Theta Phi. Democrat. Baptist. Mason (Shriner). Home: 1008 Hadrian Irving TX 75060 Office: Eldorado Bldg 2929 Cedar Spring Rd Dallas TX 75219

VAUGHAN, KENNETH DOYLE, coll. pres.; b. Highway Highlands, Cal., June 6, 1928; s. Olin B. and Florence (Scott) V.; B.S., W.Tex. State U., 1949, M.Ed., 1953; m. Melba Ruth Grady, July 29, 1949; children— Linda Sue, Stephen Doyle. Tchr., Borger Ind. Sch. Dist., 1949-52; tchr. Clarendon (Tex.) Jr. Coll., 1952-53, pres., 1961-—; prin. Clarendon Ind. Sch. Dist., 1952-60; tchr. Amarillo (Tex.) Ind. Sch. Dist., 1960-61. Mem. Tex. Tchrs. Assn., Am. Assn., Sch. Adminstrs., Tex. Jr. Coll. Adminstrs. Assn., Tex. Jr. Coll. Tchrs. Assn. Mason. Home: PO Box 925 Clarendon TX 79226 Office: PO Box 986 Clarendon TX 79226

VAUGHAN, ROSWELL FAIRBANKS, III, investment banker; b. San Antonio, June 30, 1938; s. Roswell Fairbanks and Helen Stuart (McFarland) V.; B.A., Duke U., 1960; postgrad. N.Y. U., 1961; m. Ann Blake Campbell, Aug. 14, 1965; children—Ann Blake, Helen Stuart. Exec. trainee Irving Trust Co., N.Y.C., 1960-61; with Rauscher Pierce Securities Corp., Houston, 1961-—, v.p., 1969-—; dir. Intermedco, Houston, Wiener Corp., New Orleans. Bd. dirs. Nat. Cystic Fibrosis Research Found. Mem. Houston Soc. Financial Analysts, Duke U. Alumni (v.p. 1968-—). Episcopalian (asso. vestry 1966-67, lay reader 1967-—). Clubs: Houston Country, Houston. Home: 5629 Longmont St Houston TX 77027 Office: 901 First City Nat Bank Bldg Houston TX 77002

VAUGHAN, STUART (JOHN WALKER VAUGHAN), theatrical dir.; b. Terre Haute, Ind., Aug. 23, 1925; s. John Harwood and Pauletta (Walker) V.; B.A., Ind. State Coll., 1945; M.A., Ind. U., 1946; studied acting with Harold Clurman, 1954-56; m. Gladys Regier, 1948 (div. 1960); m 2d, Helen Quarrier, 1960 (dec. 1963); m. 3d, Anne Thompson, 1965. Profl. acting debut with touring co., 1946; tchr. speech drama Ind. State Tchrs. Coll., 1947-48; dir., actor various stock and repertory cos., N.Y.C., St. Augustine, Fla., Erie, Pa., Nassau, Bahamas, Old Orchard Beach, Me., N.Y. Shakespeare Festival, others, 1948-58; became artistic dir. Phoenix Theatre, N.Y.C., 1958, Seattle Repertory Theatre, 1963; producing dir. Repertory Theatre New Orleans, 1966-—; dir. The Lady's Not for Burning, Omnibus, NBC-TV, 1958. Recipient Vernon Rice award, also Village Voice Off-Broadway award for direction N.Y. Shakespeare Co., 1958. Rockefeller artist-in-residence grantee Stanford, 1947; Fulbright grantee for study Brit. repertory theatres, 1949-50; Ford Found. dirs. grantee in Europe, 1961-62. Mem. The Players, Soc. Stage Dirs. and Choreographers, Actors Equity Assn. Co-editor: The Bantam Shakespeare, 1961. Home: 716 St Philip St New Orleans LA 70116 Office: 546 Carondelet St New Orleans LA 70130

VAUGHAN, WALTER WRIGHT, banker; b. Dracut, Mass., Dec. 25, 1932; s. Walter Wright and Margaret Grace (Ryan) V.; student U. Notre Dame, 1950-53, U. Md., 1970; m. Sarah Louise Vance, Jan. 10, 1959; children— Walter Wright III, Daniel Thomas. Asst. treas. Am. Security & Trust Co., Washington, 1956-63, v.p., 1967-—; v.p. Mt. Vernon Nat. Bank & Trust Co., Annandale, Va., 1963-67. Faculty, Grad. Sch. Consumer Banking, 1970-—; mem. adv. com. 5th Fed. Reserve Dist., 1969-—. Vice pres. Annandale Little League, 1972-73. Bd. dirs. Annandale Boys Club. Served with USMCR, 1953-56. Recipient Distinguished Service award Jr. C. of C., 1959; named Young Man of the Year Jaycees, 1959-60. Mem. Consumer Bankers Assn. (dir. 1971-—). Home: 4016 Iva Lane Fairfax VA 22030 Office: 7th and Massachusetts Av NW Washington DC 20001

VAUGHAN, WILLIAM ROGERS, JR., tobacco co. exec.; b. South Boston, Va., Jan. 10, 1918; s. William Rogers and Mary (Turnbull) Vaughan; student Hampden Sydney Coll., 1936-37; m. Martha Glanville Haymes, June 13, 1942; children—William Rogers III, Sara Dillard, Martha Haymes. With Export Leaf Tobacco Co., 1937-—, supr. leaf processing, Richmond, Va., 1968-69, dir. leaf processing, 1970, v.p. charge leaf processing, 1970-—. Bd. dirs. United Givers Fund, Halifax County, Va., 1963. Served with USNR, 1942-45. Mem. Tobacco Assn. U.S. Episcopalian. Clubs: Halifax County Country (bd. dirs., v.p., 1962-64), Meadowbrook Country. Home: 3500 Traylor Dr Richmond VA 23235 Office: Lombardy and Leigh Sts Richmond VA 23212

VAUGHN, BETTY JEAN, physician; b. Birmingham, Ala., Aug. 19, 1932; d. William Howard and Rose (Barton) Vaughn; B.A., Huntingdon Coll., 1952; M.D., Med. Coll. Ala., 1956 Intern Mt. Sinai Hosp., Miami Beach, Fla., 1956-57; resident obstetrics, gynecology Jackson Meml. Hosp., Miami, Fla., 1957-60; resident U. Miami Sch. Medicine, 1960, instr., 1960-66; practice medicine, specializing in obstetrics and gynecology, Coral Gables, Fla., 1966-69; dir. maternal, infant care project Dade County Dept. Pub. Health, Miami, 1966-71, former chief consumer care; clin. asst. prof. obstetrics and gynecology Sch. Medicine, U. Miami; asso. project dir. Maternal and Infant Care Project S15, Family Planning Project 704 and Children and Youth Project 636; now med. dir. Orange County Maternity and Infant care and Family Planning Project, Orlando. Diplomate Am. Bd. Obstetrics and Gynecology. Fellow Am. Coll. Obstetrics and Gynecology; mem. Am., Fla. pub. health assns., So., Fla., Orange County med. assns., Internat. Platform Assn. Office: 1026 W Central Blvd Orlando FL 33805

VAUGHN, EARL WRAY, judge, lawyer, former state legislator; b. Reidsville, N.C., June 17, 1928; s. John H. and Lelia (Foster) V.; A.B., U. N.C., 1950, LL.B., 1952; m. Eloise Freeland Maddry, Dec. 20, 1952; children—Mark, John, Stuart, Rose. Admitted to N.C. bar; atty. Draper, N.C., 1953-—; solicitor Leaksville Recorder's Ct., 1958-60; mem. N.C. Ho. Reps., 1960-69, speaker, 1967-69; judge N.C. Ct. Appeals, 1969-—. Dir. So. Plastics Engring. Corp. Bd. mgrs. Council State Govts., 1963-69. Chmn. Pub. Utilities Com., 1963-65. Bd. trustees Rockingham Coll. Served with inf. AUS, 1946-47. Mem. Phi Delta Phi. Home: 3312 Felton Pl Raleigh NC 27608 Office: 1 W Morgan St Raleigh NC 27602

VAUGHN, ERASMUS ROSCOE, educator; b. Monroe, Tenn., May 22, 1900; s. James Francis and Rebecca (Phillips) V.; A.B., Transylvania U., 1926, M.A., 1926; B.D., Vanderbilt U., 1944; postgrad. U. Ky., 1928-29; m. Emma Juan Bell, Sept. 25, 1928; children—George Clay, Ann Stoddard (Mrs. Jere Calvin Robertson), James Erasmus. Head edn. dept. Mt. Berry Coll., 1927-28; supt. Stinnett Settlement Sch., Ky., 1928-34; social sci. and Bible tchr. Livingston Acad., 1936-41; supt. Orlinda (Tenn.) Schs., 1941-46; prin. RoEllen Sch., Dyersburg, Tenn., 1950-56, Western High Sch., Hickman Ky., 1956-58; tchr. history, English, Lowes (Ky.) High Sch., 1958-—; pastor Disciples Chs., Livingston, Pa., Sturgis, Ky., 1934-36. Chmn. Prins. Study Council Tenn., 1950-56; chmn. Crippled Children Camp Program. Recipient Honored Minsters Pin of Disciples, Christian Ch., 1969. Mem. Nat., Ky. edn. assns., Nat. Platform Assos., Pi Kappa Delta, Sigma Upsilon. Lion, Rotarian, Kiwanian. Contbr. articles to profl. jours. Home: 827 W Broadway Mayfield KY 42066

VAUGHN, HUBERT ARNOLD, banker; b. Corbin, Ky., July 30, 1912; s. Jack Lewis and Ollie Mae (Black) V.; student Eastern Ky. U., 1932-35, Ohio State U., 1958; m. Clara Gibson, Feb. 7, 1936; children—Hubert Byron, Judith Ann, Jerry (Mrs. George Litton Kline). With Jellico Grocery Co., Inc., various locations, 1935-68, mgr., Somerset, Ky., 1941-60, mgr. Oneida, Tenn., 1960-68; adminstr. customer service 1st Trust & Savs. Bank Oneida, Tenn., 1969-—; also dir.; dir. Oneida Water & Sewer Works, 1969-—. Mem. Scott County C. of C. (dir. 1961-64, treas. 1962-64). Kiwanian, Modern Woodman Am. Home: 638 N Main St Oneida TN 37841 Office: 226 S Main St Oneida TN 37841

VAUGHN, ROBERT DONALD, army officer; b. Iola, Kan., Mar. 27, 1925; s. Ralph Herbert and Alice (Dille) V.; B.A., U. Md., 1954; M.B.A., U. Ala., 1960; postgrad. Command and Gen. Staff Coll., 1964, Nat. War Coll., 1970; m. Ruthe Irene De Bow, Aug. 23, 1946; children— Marta Kristine, Robert Donald, John Patrick. Commd. 2d lt. U.S. Army, 1950, advanced through grades to col., 1970; commissary officer SHAPE, 1951-54; co. comdr., 1955-56; adviser MAAG, Iran, 1957-58; staff officer Inventory Control Point, Germany, 1960-63; chief Civil Schs. Program, 1964-67; bn. comdr. support command comdr. G-4, 1st Cav. Div., Vietnam, 1967-68; monitor M-16 Rifle, 1968; dep. comdr. Atlanta Gen. Depot, 1970-71; comdr. Burtonwood Army Depot, U.K., 1971-—. Decorated Legion of Merit, Bronze Star medal with oak leaf cluster, Air medal. Mem. Nat. Honor Soc., Beta Gamma Sigma. Democrat. Presbyn. (deacon 1969-—). Home: 1516 N Greenbrier St Arlington VA 22205 Office: Burtonwood Army Depot APO NY 09075

VAUGHN, WILLIAM ANDREW, librarian; b. Russellville, Ark., Feb. 13, 1934; s. Worth William and Helen Ruth (Bowden) V.; B.S., Ark. Poly. Coll., 1955; M.Ed., U. Ark., 1956; M.A., George Peabody Coll., 1957; m. Marian Joan Sacrey, Dec. 19, 1954; children—Kirk William, Mark Andrew. Head librarian Ark. Poly. Coll. Library, Russellville, 1957-—. Mem. library com. Dept. Higher Edn., 1968-—; exec. dir. Nat. Library Week in Ark., 1966. Chmn. Wesley Found., 1968. Mem. Am., Ark. library assns., Pi Gamma Mu. Methodist. Mason (32 deg.), Lion. Home: 812 N El Paso Av Russellville AR 72801

VAZQUEZ, RAFAEL MAXIMIANO, diplomat of Argentina; b. San Nicolas, Argentina, Oct. 12, 1919; s. Recaredo and Juana (Maiztegul) V.; ed. law, U. LaPlata (Argentina), 1943; m. Graciela Miro, Apr. 22, 1957; children—Graciela Montes, Roxana, Juana, Maria de Lourdes, Annabella. With pub. service Province of Buenos Aires, 1940-49; joined Argentina Fgn. Service, 1949; 2d sec. embassy, Oslo, Norway, 1949-53; consul Cardiff, U.K., 1953-56; assigned Fgn. Office, 1956-58; 1st sec. embassy, New Delhi, India, 1958-59; counsellor embassy, Dublin, Ireland, 1959-62; dir. comml. promotion Fgn. Office, 1962-64; consul gen., New Orleans, 1964-69; organizer 1st permanent exhbn. Argentine products outside Argentina, New Orleans, 1967; minister embassy, Washington, 1969-71; consul gen., N.Y.C., 1971-—. Decorated Order St. Olaf (Norway). Club: Metropolitan (Washington). Office: 1600 New Hampshire Av NW Washington DC 20036

VEACH, JOHN BEMIS, JR., lumber co. exec.; b. Pitts., July 21, 1927; s. John Bemis and Jane Craig (Miller) V.; A.B., Yale U., 1949; m. Jean Smith Trainer, June 23, 1951; children—John Bemis III, Margaret Hastings. With Bemis Hardwood Lumber Co., Robbinsbille, N.C., 1952-—, sec., dir., 1965-—, pres., 1965-—; exec. v.p., dir. Veach May Wilson, Inc., Alcoa, Tenn., 1965-—; pres. dir. Veach Wilson Oil Co., Robbinsville, N.C., 1969-—. Bd. Trustees Meml. Mission Hosp., Asheville Chamber Music Series. Served with AUS, 1950-52. Mem. N.C. Forestry Assn. (dir. 1970-—), Appalachian Hardwood Mfgs., Inc. (trustee 1970-—), Appalachian Lumbermen's Club (past pres.), Forest Products Research Soc. (past chmn. sect.). Episcopalian (sec. exec. council diocese Western N.C.). Rotarian. Clubs: Biltmore Forest (N.C.) Country; Mountain City Asheville, N.C.). Home: 316 Vanderbilt Rd Ashville NC 28803 Office: PO Box 5857 Asheville NC 28803

VEATCH, ELLIS HARRY, govt. ofcl.; b. Chgo., Oct. 25, 1911; s. Harry Oral and Amelia (Hillebrand) V.; A.B., Miami U., Oxford, O., 1934; m. Mary Maxine Alspach, July 13, 1941. With WPA, 1934-40; chief procedures and distbn. sect. Office Civil Def., 1941-42; with Bur. of Budget (now Office of Mgmt. and Budget), 1942-—, dep. chief mil. div., 1957-61, chief div., 1961-70, chief Nat. Security Programs div., 1970-—. Served with USNR, 1943-45. Mem. Am. Soc. Pub. Adminstrn., Phi Delta Theta. Club: Army-Navy Country (Arlington, Va.). Home: 1580 Mount Eagle Pl Alexandria VA 22302 Office: Exec Office of President Bur of Budget Washington DC 20503

VEAZEY, JOHN HOBSON, physician; b. Van Alstyne, Tex., June 27, 1901; s. James and Malta Augusta (Blassingame) V.; student Austin Coll., 1918-22; M.D., U. Tex., 1926; m. Elizabeth May Chandler, Mar. 14, 1935; children—Samuel James. Intern Sherman (Tex.) Hosp., 1926-28; pvt. practice medicine, Madill, Okla., 1929-35, Ardmore, Okla., 1935-—; one of founders, one of partners Med. Arts Clinic, Ardmore, Okla., 1952-—; pvt. practice internal medicine, Ardmore, 1957-—; chief staff Meml. Hosp., So. Okla., 1958-—; mem. staff Ardmore (Okla.) Hosp. Co-chmn. profl. div. United Fund, 1969. Mem. Am., Okla. State (council 1944-56) med. assns., Carter-Love-Marshall Med. Soc. (pres. 1955), Ardmore C. of C. (dir., v.p.), Am. Soc. Internal Medicine. Presbyn. (trustee). Mason. Home: 305 D St SW Ardmore OK 73401 Office: 921 14th St NW Ardmore OK 73401

VEGA, JUAN BAUTISTA, tribal chieftain; b. Cozumel Island Yucatan, Mexico, June 24, 1889; s. Gerarda and Maria (Cen) V. stepson Ruperto Loria; stepson Florintino Cituk (Mayan chief); reared as a Mayan, Yucatan; translator, sec. to chief; sec. of Saint, supreme Mayan religious authority, 1918-—, also custodian Maya holy book; mem. council of chiefs, 1919-—, now head chief Mayans, Mexico. Served as gen. Mayan Army, during war between Mexican govt. and Mayans. Address: Chumpon Quintana Roo Mexico*

VEGHTE, JACK, ins. agy. exec.; b. Schenectady, May 24, 1935; s. Charles and Ruth (Wurz) V.; B.S., Fla. State U., 1957; m. Nancy Ford, June 8, 1957; children—Melissa, John, Richard, David. Founder, chief exec. officer Veghte Ins. Agy., Clearwater, Fla., 1958-—; dir. 1st Fed. Savs. & Loan, Clearwater, 2d Nat. Bank Clearwater. Chmn. March of Dimes, 1965. Kiwanian. Clubs: Carlouel Yacht, East Bay Country, Casado. Home: 1341 Eastfield Dr Clearwater FL 33516 Office: 601 S Lincoln Av Clearwater FL 33516

VEILLON, EDWARD WARNER, ins. agt.; b. Eunice, La., Sept. 11, 1940; s. E. A. and Myrtle (Andrus) V.; student Tulane U., 1958-59; B.S., La. State U., 1962; m. Ann Bordelon, July 10, 1966. Vice pres. E. A. Veillon Agy., Inc., ins., real estate, 1965-69, pres., 1969-—; v.p., mgr. Val Realty Corp., 1966-—; dir. 1st Fed. Savs. & Loan Assn., Tri-Parish Bank & Trust Co. Served as 1st lt. U.S. Army, 1962-64. Recipient Jaycee Presdl. citation, 1969; named Outstanding Chmn., 1970, Eunice Outstanding Young Man, 1970. Hon. life mem. 8th U.S. Cav. Mem. Eunice C. of C. (dir., past v.p.), Delta Sigma Phi. Democrat. Roman Catholic. Rotarian. Home: 130 Pinecrest Dr Eunice LA 70535 Office: 220 S 2d St Eunice LA 70535

VELCHOFF, WILLIAM, city ofcl.; b. Rayville, La., Jan. 6, 1927; s. Stephen Nidelco and Nila Bell (Roberts) V.; grad. high sch.; m. Esther Louise Hassebrock, Dec. 20, 1952; children—Larry W., William, James G., Nila Kay. Bank teller First Nat. Bank & Trust Co., Vicksburg, Miss., 1946-49; served with USN, 1945-46, USAF, 1949-68; city sec., City of San Angelo, Tex., 1968-—. Home: 3225 Cornell Av San Angelo TX 76901 Office: PO Box 1751 San Angelo TX 76901

VELDHUIS, MATTHEW KERMIT, ret. govt. ofcl.; b. Big Timber, Mont., Dec. 17, 1906; s. John George and Dora B. (Scholten) V.; B.S., Mont. State U., 1929; Ph.D., Ia. State U., 1934; m. Elizabeth Lane Falson, Apr. 19, 1940; children—John Frank, Elizabeth Falson (Mrs. Edwin Ames Green), Mary Isabell. Asst. chemist Mont. Agrl. Expt. Sta., Bozeman, Utah, 1929-30; chemist in charge Food Fermentation Lab., U.S. Dept. Agr., Agrl. Research Service, Raleigh, N.C., 1930-39, Fruit and Vegetable Products Lab., Pullman, Wash., 1939-44, lab. chief, Winter Haven, Fla., 1944-72. Recipient Superior Service award U.S. Dept., 1946. Mem. Am. Chem. Soc. (sect. chmn. 1942-43), Inst. Food Technologists (sect. chmn. 1947-48). Rotarian. Clubs: Winter Haven. Home: 648 Av I NW Winter Haven FL 33880

VELDMAN, DONALD JOHN, educator; b. Grand Rapids, Mich., Dec. 24, 1931; s. Harold E. and Pearl (Paalman) V.; B.A., Hope Coll., 1953; Ph.D., U. Tex., 1960; m. Janet Lou Soeter, Dec. 17, 1955; children— Audrey Ann, Catherine Sue, Gregory John, Stuart Randolph. Asst. prof. U. Tex., Austin, 1961-64, asso. prof., 1964-69, prof. ednl. psychology, 1969-—, coordinator assessment div., research and devel. center for tchr. edn., 1965-—. Statis. research cons., 1960-—. Served with AUS, 1953-55. Fellow Am. Psychol. Assn., Mem. Am. Ednl. Research Assn., Assn. for Computing Machinery,

Psychometric Soc. Author: Fortran Programming for the Behavioral Sciences, 1967; (with Robert K. Young) Introductory Statistics for the Behavioral Sciences, 1965. Contbr. articles to profl. jours. Home: 3007 Savoy Pl Austin TX 78731

VELLER, MARGARET PAXTON, physician; b. Beaver Dam, Ky., Dec. 14, 1925; d. Darrell K. and Gladys (Myers) Veller; B.A., Vanderbilt U., 1947, M.D., 1950. Intern, resident Vanderbilt U. Hosp., Nashville, 1950-54; pvt. practice, 1954—. Mem. Am., Miss. (com. maternal and child welfare 1956-73) med. assns., Adams County Med. Soc., Natchez Assn. of Commerce, Miss. Obstet. and Gynecol. Soc., Natchez-Adams County C. of C., Phi Beta Kappa, Alpha Omega Alpha. Baptist. Club: Pilgrimage Garden. Home: 28 S Circle Dr Natchez MS 39120 Office: Natchez Med Clinic 49 Sgt S Prentiss Dr Natchez MS 39120

VELZ, RICHARD ANTHONY, pharm. co. exec.; b. Lagrangeville, N.Y., Aug. 21, 1911; s. Robert and Mary R. (Suwarrow) V.; B.S., Coll. William and Mary, 1936; m. Anya Mishtowt, Aug. 19, 1961. Dir. pub. relations Coll. William and Mary, 1936; corr. A.P., U.P., 1937-39; mem. editorial staff Richmond News Leader, 1936-39; pres., gen. mgr. Colonial Music Corp., Williamsburg, Va., 1939-41; prodn., program dir. Radio Station WRNL, Richmond, Va., 1945-48; adminstr. Va. Mus. Fine Arts, Richmond, 1955-58; dir. pub. relations A.H. Robins Co., Richmond, 1958—, asst. to pres., 1953-70, asst. v.p., 1967-70, v.p., 1970—. Vice-pres., mem. exec. com. Richmond Soc. Prevention Cruelty to Animals, 1968—. Bd. dirs. Richmond Symphony, Nat. Tobacco Festival, Richmond Thanksgiving Festival, Inc., Richmond Foster Home Com. Served to comdr. USNR, 1941-45, 48-53; now capt. Res. ret. Recipient meritorious pub. service citation Sec. Navy, 1963, commendation, 1954, Navy League Scroll of Honor, 1964. Mem. Pharm. Mfrs. Assn. (chmn. pub. relations sect. 1970-71), Pub. Relations Soc. Am. (chpt. bd. dirs. 1960-62), Va., Richmond (dir. 1972) chambers commerce, Central Richmond Assn., Va. Mfrs. Assn., Pub. Relations com. YMCA, Am. Ordnance Assn., Ret. Officers Assn., Am., Va. pharm. assns., Naval Acad. Found., Richmond Pub. Relations Assn. (pres. 1960-61), Better Business Bur. (pres. 1962-63), Navy League U.S. (region pres. 1962-67, U.S. Naval Inst., Res. Officers Assn. (chpt. pres. 1965-66), Naval Res. Assn., Alpha Kappa Psi, Pi Delta Epsilon, Phi Delta Gamma, Tau Kappa Alpha, Phi Kappa Tau. Presbyn. (ruling elder 1966—), chmn. bd. deacons 1962-65). Clubs: Rotunda (pres. 1969-70) (Richmond); Press Club of Va. (v.p. 1958-60); Nat. Press (Washington). Home: 307 N Allen Av Richmond VA 23220 Office: 1407 Cummings Dr Richmond VA 23220

VENABLE, AUSTIN LEWIS, historian; b. Wetumpka, Ala., May 15, 1902; s. William E. and Susan Roberta (Allen) V.; A.B., U. Ala., 1925, A.M., 1929; student U. Chgo., 1930; Ph.D., Vanderbilt U., 1937; m. Nell E. Smith, Dec 21, 1930. Teaching fellow Vanderbilt U., 1935-37; instr. U. Ark., 1937-40, asst. prof., 1940-45; asso. prof. U. Ala., 1954—. Mem. Ala. Centennial Commn. Recipient Social Sci. Research grant-in-aid; grant U. Ala. Research Com. Mem. Orgn. Am. Historians, Ala. Hist. Assn., Old South Hist. Soc. (pres. 1964-66), S.A.R. (pres. 1972) Am. Hist. Assn., English-Speaking Union (dir. 1963-66), Ala. Acad. Sci., Phi Alpha Theta, Kappa Delta Pi, Pi Kappa Alpha, Kappa Phi Kappa. Club: University. Author monographs, book reviews; editor hist. jours., other publs. Home: Hickory Hill Jasmine Hill Rd Wetumpka AL 36092 Office: 229 Ten Hoor Hall University AL 35486

VENABLE, JOHN HEINZ, physician, state ofcl.; b. Atlanta, Dec. 5, 1908; s. Gus Foute and Josephine (Heinz) V.; B.S., Emory U., 1929, M.D., 1933; M.P.H., Tulane U., 1951; m. Louise Ware, Dec. 18, 1934; children—John Heinz, Linda (Mrs. William A. Webb). Faculty, Emory U., 1929-46; commr. health Dalton (Ga.)-Whitfield Health Dept., 1947-50, Griffin (Ga.)-Spalding County Health Dept., 1950-52; dir. tng. Ga. Dept. Pub. Health, Atlanta, 1952-60, dir. dept., 1960—. Mem. Med. Assn. Ga., A.M.A., Ga. Pub. Health Assn., Assn. State and Territorial Health Officers (past pres.), Conf. State and Provincial Health Authorities N.Am. (past pres.), Phi Beta Kappa, Omicron Delta Kappa, Delta Omega. Home: 2418 Howell Mill Rd Atlanta GA 30318 Office: 47 Trinity Av SW Atlanta GA 30334

VENABLE, NELL SMITH (MRS. AUSTIN L. VENABLE), educator, clubwoman; b. Butler County, Ala., Nov. 24, 1904; d. William Ward and Elizabeth (Presley) Smith; B.A., U. Ala., 1930; M.A., Vanderbilt U., 1953; m. Austin L. Venable, Dec. 21, 1930. Instr., Coll. of Ozarks, 1943; tchr. Sidney Lanier High Sch., Montgomery, Ala., 1955—. Mem. Nat., Ala. (v.p. social studies dept. 1958-60), Montgomery (curriculum steering com. 1959-61, chmn. high sch. div. 1959-60) edn. assns., Classroom Tchrs. Assn., Am. Assn. U. Women (exec. bd. 1955-59), Montgomery County Joint Legislative Council (pres. 1955-57), D.A.R. (corr. sec. 1960-64), Old S. Hist. Soc. (corr. sec. 1961-62, 64-66), English-Speaking Union, Mortar Bd., Phi Beta Kappa. Episcopalian. Home: Hickory Hill Jasmine Hill Rd Wetumpka AL 36092 Office: 1756 S Court St Montgomery AL 36005

VENABLE, ROBERT VANCE, coal co. exec.; b. Economy, Pa., Aug. 11, 1903; s. William Walton and Ann Randolph (Sterrett) V.; student W. Va. U., 1922-26; m. Lois Chapman Smith, July 6, 1942; children—Chloe Randolph (Mrs. Joseph S. Sinisi), Melissa Lynn. Gen. supt. H. E. Harman (Va.) Coal Corp., 1940-53; gen. supt. Feds Creek Coal Co., Harman, 1945-53, gen. mgr., 1953-67, pres., 1966—. Mem. Grundy Town Council, 1963—. Mem. Am. Inst. M.E., Beta Theta Pi. Rotarian. Home: 318 Riverside Dr Grundy VA 24614 Office: Biggs KY 41515

VENEMAN, JOHN G., govt. ofcl.; b. Corcoran, Cal., Oct. 31, 1925; s. John G. and Bertha (Van Konynenburg) V.; ed. Ariz. State Coll., 1944, U. Tex., 1944-45; m. Nita D. Bomberger, July 22, 1947; children—Ann Margaret (Mrs. Machado), John Gerrit, Jane Elizabeth. Supr., Stanislaus County, 1959-62; mem. Cal. Assembly, 1962-69; mem. Cal. Social Welfare Bd., 1964-69; under sec. Dept. Health, Edn. and Welfare, 1969—; key adminstrn. spokesman, welfare reform and health legislation, 1969—. Lectr. New Sch. for Social Research, 1972. Cal. chmn. Robert Finch for lt. gov., 1966. Served with USNR, 1944. Named Young Man of Year, Modesto Jr. C. of C., 1960. Mem. Cal. C. of C., Am. Legion. Presbyn. Elk. Club: Commonwealth (San Francisco). Address: 330 Independence Av SW Washington DC 20201

VENEZKY, DAVID LESTER, chemist; b. Washington, Sept. 12, 1924; s. Benjamin and Anna (Marks) V.; B.S., George Washington U., 1948; Ph.D. (Eastman Kodak fellow), U. N.C., 1962; m. Evelyn L. Gaver, Sept. 3, 1950; children—Donna Lynn, Mark Edward. Phys. sci. aid, Geol. Survey, Washington, 1948-49; organic chemist Naval Research Lab., Washington, 1949-55; instr. U. N.C., Chapel Hill, 1958-60; asst. prof. Auburn (Ala.) U., 1960-62; research chemist, head inorganic polymer sect. Naval Research Lab., Washington, 1962-69, head reaction mechanisms sect., 1969—. Served with USNR, 1944-46. Mem. Am. Chem. Soc., Sigma Xi, Alpha Chi Sigma. Home: 8707 Bradgate Rd Alexandria VA 22308 Office: Naval Research Lab Washington DC 20390

VENN, GRANT, govt. ofcl.; b. Seattle, Mar. 1, 1919; s. Roy William and Vera Patience (Masters) V.; student U. Wash., 1937-38; B.S., B.Ed., Wash. State U., 1941, M.Ed., 1947, Ed.D., 1951; student U. Minn., summers 1949-50; m. Olga M. Tobia, Aug. 2, 1962; children—Victoria Susan, John Jeffrey, Deborah Elizabeth. Tchr. vocational agr., Sedro Woolley, Wash., 1941-42; guidance dir. Pullman (Wash.) pub. schs., 1946-47; dir. guidance curriculum Yakami (Wash.) pub. schs., 1948-49; asst. supt. schs., Bellevue, Wash., 1949-51; asst. prof. edn. Wash. State U., 1951-52; supt. schs., Othello, Wash., 1952-56; supt. schs., Corning, N.Y., 1956-60; pres. Western State Coll., Gunnison, Colo., 1960-62; dir. of field tng., Peace Corps., 1962-63; cons. Am. Council on Edn., Washington, 1963; supt. Wood County Schs., Parkersburg, W.Va., 1963-66; asso. commr. edn. U.S. Office of Edn., Dept. Health, Edn. and Welfare, Washington, 1966—; dir. Nat. Acad. for Sch. Execs., Washington, 1970—; Calloway prof. edn. Ga. State U., Atlanta, 1972—. Pres. N.Y. State Council Econ. Edn., 1959-60; cons. N.Y. State Citizens Com. Pub. Schs., 1957-60; panelist White House Conf. Edn., 1965; chmn. resolution com. Am. Assn. Sch. Adminstrs., 1965-66. Mem. Nat., Colo. edn. assns., Colo. Assn. Sch. Adminstrs., Phi Kappa Phi, Phi Delta Kappa. Alpha Zeta, Psi Chi. Rotarian. Author: Man, Education and Work, 1964. Home: 9039 Sligo Creek Pkwy Silver Spring MD 20901 Office: US Office of Education 400 Maryland Av SW Washington DC 20202

VENTURA, JACK SAL, economist; b. N.Y.C., Dec. 21, 1943; s. Jose and Mathilde (Algranti) V.; A.B., Columbia Coll., 1964; A.M., U. Pa., 1965; Ph.D. (Univ. fellow), Georgetown U., 1970; m. Stephanie Joan Leavitt, May 29, 1966; children—Daniel Reuben, Jerome Hosea. Economist, sect. of research ICC, Washington, 1965—, chief carrier analysis br., sec. of research Bur. Econs., 1970—. Mem. Am. Econ. Assn., Econometric Soc., Transp. Research Forum, Phi Epsilon Pi. Jewish religion. Home: 1025 Chiswell Lane Silver Spring MD 20901 Office: Interstate Commerce Commn Washington DC 20423

VERGNE ROIG, PEDRO J., bldg. mgmt. exec., educator; b. Rio Piedras, P.R., Mar. 3, 1918; s. Juan P. and Sixtita (Roig) Vergne; B.S., U. P.R., 1943;M.A., U. Md., 1943; m. Olga Marini, Jan. 25, 1941; children—Pedro J., Ada Lorraine. Economist in charge Fish and Wildlife Service, U.S. Dept. Interior, 1945-47; asso. prof., dir. social sci. dept. U. P.R., 1947-49; exec. dir., Municipal Housing Authority, Mayaquez, P.R., 1950, tech. dir. slum clearance and urban redevel., Ponce, P.R., 1952; gen. mgr., gen. sales mgr. Cerveceria India, Inc., 1951; gen. mgr., gen. sales mgr. Cerveceria Real, Inc., 1952-54; asst. exec. dir. P.R. Ports Authority, San Juan, 1953-57; treas. Fajardo Eastern Sugar Assos., Caguas, also Eastern Lighterage Co. a subsidiary, 1957-61; pres. gen. mgr. Bldg. Mgmt. Corp. P.R. 1961—; pres. P. Vergne Roig & Assos., mgmt. cons., 1961—; asso. prof., chmn. dept. mgmt. and bus. law U. P.R., 1961—; pres. Coop. Devel. Co., 1969—. Adminstr. Coop. Devel. Adminstrn., 1969—. Mem. Am. Mgmt. Assn., P.R. C. of C., Gamma Sigma Delta, Phi Eta Mu. Democrat. Roman Catholic. Contbr. articles to profl. jours. Home: 1-9 Geranio Rio Piedras PR Office: Town House 2 Rio Piedras PR

VERINK, ELLIS DANIEL, JR., educator; b. Peking, China, Feb. 9, 1920; s. Ellis Daniel and Phoebe (Smith) V.; B.S., Purdue U., 1941; M.S., Ohio State U., 1963, Ph.D., 1965; m. Martha Eulala Owens, July 4, 1942; children—Barbara Ann, Wendy Susan. Engr. devel. div. Aluminum Co. Am., New Kensington, Pa., 1946-59, mgr. chem. and petroleum indsl. sales, Pitts., 1959-62; prof. metall. and materials engring. U. Fla., Gainesville, 1965—. Cons. Aluminum Assn. on corrosion and desalination, 1966—. Served with USNR, 1941-46. Named Man of Year, New Kensington-Arnold Jr. C. of C., 1955. Registered profl. engr., Pa., Fla. Mem. Nat. Assn. Corrosion Engrs. (dir.), Am. Inst. Mining, Metall. and Petroleum Engrs., Am. Soc. for Metals, Am. Welding Soc., Nat. Soc. Profl. Engrs., Electrochem. Soc., Am. Soc. for Testing and Materials, Sigma Xi, Tau Kappa Epsilon, Sigma Tau, Tau Beta Pi, Phi Lambda Upsilon, Alpha Sigma Mu. Presbyn. Mason, Kiwanian. Contbr. articles to profl. jours. Home: 4401 NW 18th Pl Gainesville FL 32601

VERITY, GEORGE LUTHER, lawyer; b. Oklahoma City, Jan. 3, 1914; s. George H. and Mae (Tibbals) V.; LL.B., Okla. U., 1937; m. Ellen Van Hoesen, Mar. 18, 1939; children—George Luther II, Grover Steven, David Webster, Mark Sidney. Admitted to Tex. bar, 1937, Okla. bar, 1939, N.M. bar, 1957; practiced in Wichita Falls, Tex., 1939-40, 46-48, Oklahoma City, 1948-57, Farmington, N.M., 1957-64; partner firm Brown & Verity, Oklahoma City, 1948-57, Verity, Burr, Cooley & Jones, Farmington, 1957-64, Brown, Verity & Brown, Oklahoma City, 1964-71, Brown, Verity, Brown & Baker, 1971—; v.p., sec., dir. Met. Investment Co.; sec.-treas., dir. Progress Life & Accident Ins. Co.; pres., dir. Big D Chem. Co. Trustee Rocky Mountain Mineral Law Found., 1961-64. Served to capt. USAAF, 1941-46; PTO. Decorated Purple Heart. Mem. Am., Okla. bar assns., State Bar N.M., State Bar Tex., Acacia. Mason, Elk, Rotarian. Home: 7107 Brentwood Terrace Oklahoma City OK 73102 Office: 1st Nat Bldg Oklahoma City OK 73102

VERMILLION, WILLIAM HERMAN, educator; b. Oak Park, Ill., Feb. 6, 1937; s. William Herman and Dorothy (Harter) V.; B.A., Northwestern U., 1959; M.S., Purdue U., 1961, Ph.D., 1964; m. Eleanor Jean Browning, Aug. 27, 1960; children—Michael William, Vicki Lynn, David Buford. Asst. prof. David Lipscomb Coll., Nashville, 1963-66, chmn. psychology dept., 1964-72, asso. prof. psychology, 1966-70, prof., 1970-72; asso. prof. psychology Middle Tenn. State U., Murfreesboro, 1972—. Mem. aftercare com. Nashville Mental Health Assn., 1967-68. Mem. Am., Tenn., Southeastern psychol. assns. Mem. Ch. of Christ. Home: 1014 Whitehall Rd Murfreesboro TN 37130

VERNBERG, FRANK JOHN, educator; b. Fenton, Mich., Nov. 6, 1925; s. Sigurd A. and Edna (Anderson) V.; A.B., DePauw U., 1949, M.A., 1950; Ph.D., Purdue U., 1951; m. Winona M. Bortz, Sept. 7, 1945; children— Marcia Lynn, Eric Morrison, Amy Louise. Prof. zoology Duke U., Marine Lab., Beaufort, N.C., 1951-69. Baruch prof. marine ecology, dir. Belle W. Baruch Coastal Research Inst., U. S.C., Columbia, 1969—; vis. prof. U. Coll. West Indies, Jamaica, 1957-58, U. Sao Paulo (Brazil), 1965. Program dir. in exptl. analytical biogeography of sea Internat. Biol. Program, 1967—; mem. com. on manned orbital research lab. Am. Inst. Biol. Scis.-NASA, 1966—. Served with USNR, 1944-46. Guggenheim fellow, 1957-58; Fulbright-Hayes fellow, 1965. Mem. Am. Soc. Zoologists (sec.-treas. div. comparative physiologists 1959-61, edn. com. 1966—), Ecol. Soc. Am. (chmn. com. physiol. ecology 1960—, mem. council 1965-67), A.A.A.S. (mem. coop. com. on teaching sci. and math. 1967). Spl. editor Am. Zoologist, 1963. Contbr. articles to profl. jours., chpts. to books. Home: 6515 Eastshore Rd Columbia SC 29206

VERNER, ARTHUR CHARLES, banker; b. Enoree, S.C., May 14, 1917; s. Charlie Van and Flora (Duncan) V.; B.S., Clemson Coll., 1938; m. Myrna Gaignat, Mar. 28, 1947; children—Paige, Dean, Kay. Asst. supt. Calhoun Mills, Calhoun Falls, S.C., 1938-41; asst. to v.p. Ely-Walker Co., St. Louis, 1946-47; mgr. Gaignat Enterprises, Tahoka, Texas, 1946-56; exec. v.p. First Nat. Bank, Tahoka, 1956-61, pres., 1961-64; exec. v.p., dir. First Nat. Bank, Lubbock, 1964, pres., 1964—; dir. TIME Freight, Inc.; charter dir. Plains Cotton Growers, Inc. Vice chmn. Salvation Army, Tahoka, 1956—; chmn. advance gifts div. United Fund, 1965; exec. bd. Meth. Hosp., Lubbock; vice chmn. pattern gifts div. St. Mary of Plains Hosp. Served to maj. AUS, 1942-45. Mem. C. of C. (past pres.). Clubs: Lions, Holiday, Lubbock, Lubbock Country. Home: 4602 17th St Lubbock TX 79416 Office: First Nat Bank 1500 Broadway Box 1241 Lubbock TX 79408

VERNEZOBRE, ERNEST FRANCISCO, physician; b. Havana, Cuba, Dec. 4, 1927; s. Francisco and Ysabel (Metz) V.; B.S., Inst. Secondary Edn., Havana, 1945; D. Medicine and Surgery, U. Havana, 1952; m. Diana E. Michael, Dec. 26, 1962; children—Diana Isabel, Rhonda Louise. Came to U.S., 1961, naturalized, 1968. Rotating intern Univ. Hosp., Havana, 1953-54, resident obstetrics and gynecology, 1955-57; cons. gynecology Tb Hosp., Las Villas, Cuba, 1957-59; med. dir. St. Emily Hosp., Havana, 1959-60; nat. dir. Orgn. State Hosps., Cuba, 1957-58; rotating intern Riverside Hosp., Newport News, Va., 1961-62; staff physician Tb Hosp., San Antonio, 1963-64; family practice medicine, Midland, Tex., 1966—; mem. staff Midland, Meml., Parkview hosps., Midland; chief staff Parkview Hosp., 1971, chief medicine, 1972. Prof. U. Havana, summers 1954-55; prof. practical obstetrics 9th Nat. Med. Congress, 1955. Decorated officer Charles J. Finlay Nat. Merit Order (Cuba). Diplomate Am. Bd. Family Practice. Fellow Am. Acad. Angiology, Am. Acad. Family Practice; mem. Am., Pan Am., So., Tex. med. assns., Am., Tex. acads. gen. practice, Am. Acad. Geriatrics, Am. Coll. Emergency Physicians, Am., Tex. thoracic socs., Am., Tex. diabetes assns., Pan Am. Cancer Soc., Tex. Heart Assn., Midland County Med. Soc. Lion. Club: Downtowners (Midland). Home: 3300 Ma-Mar Midland TX 79701 Office: 1802 W Wall St Midland TX 79701

VERNON, LACY SINKFORD, granite co. exec.; b. Fries, Va., Aug. 17, 1931; s. Troy J. and Minnie E. (Bond) V.; bus. adminstrn. grad. Draughon's Bus. Coll., 1957; advanced cost accounting grad. Internat. Accountants Soc., 1959; m. Annie Lee Collins, Dec. 22, 1951; children—Terry E., David L., Penny E. With N.C. Granite Corp., Mt. Airy, 1957—, exec. v.p., 1972—. Bd. dirs., treas. United Fund Greater Mt. Airy, 1963-69. Served with Security Agy., AUS, 1951-55. Mem. Moravian Ch. Elk. Club: Western Square Dance. Home: 131 Peace Haven Circle Mount Airy NC 27030 Office: Box 151 Mount Airy NC 27030

VERNON, ROBERT ORION, geologist; b. Montevallo, Ala., Mar. 29, 1912; B.S., Birmingham So. Coll., 1935; M.S., U. Ia., 1938; Ph.D. in Geology, La. State U., 1941. Asst. geologist U. Ia., 1935-38, La. State U., 1938-39; resident geologist Fla. State Geol. Survey, 1938-40, asst. state geologist, 1941-43, asso. state geologist, 1946-53, asst. dir., 1953-58, dir., 1958—. Mem. participating faculty Fla. State U., 1955—, mem. adv. com. water data for pub. use, 1964—. Served with USNR, 1943-46. Fellow Am. Geol. Soc.; mem. Assn. Petroleum Geologists, Am. Water Works Assn., Assn. State Geologists (pres. 1967-68), Am. Inst. Mining, Metall. and Petroleum Engrs. Home: 744 Du Parc Circle Tallahassee FL 32303 Office: Bur Geology Div Natural Resources Box 631 Tallahassee FL 32302*

VERROSS, WILLIAM JOHN, paper co. exec.; b. Chgo., Apr. 14, 1921; s. William Mels and Martha (Fraser) V.; B.Chem. Engring., Ohio State U., 1943; m. Marjorie Frances Cottier, Sept. 14, 1946; children— William E., Thomas S., Robert P., Victoria A. Block plant supt. U.S. Gypsum Co., S.I., N.Y., 1946-47; research engr. Westvaco Corp., N.Y.C., 1947-55, prodn. supt., 1955-60, div. prodn. mgr., 1961-66; v.p. gen. mgr. Interstate Paper Corp., Riceboro, Ga., 1966—; v.p. Liberty Dairy, Hinesville, Ga., 1969—; pres. Newport Timber Corp., Riceboro, 1967— Chmn., Covington (Va.) Planning and Zoning Commn., 1954-56; mem. Covington Sch. Bd., 1957-60, Liberty County (Ga.) Hosp. Authority, 1968-70. Vice chmn. Charleston County Republican party, 1966; chmn. Liberty County Rep. party, 1968. Served with C.E., AUS, 1942-46. Mem. T.A.P.P.I., Paper Industry Mgmt. Assn. (Community Service Award 1969), Liberty County C. of C. (pres. 1967). Home: 512 Martin Rd Hinesville GA 31313 Office: Interstate Paper Corp Riceboro GA 31323

VERTER, HERBERT SIGMUND, educator; b. N.Y.C., Jan. 30, 1936; s. Louis and Bessie (Hochberg) V.; B.S., City Coll. N.Y., 1956; M.A., Harvard, 1957, Ph.D., 1960; postgrad. Imperial Coll. London, 1961; m. Mona Ellen Cowen, July 10, 1960; children—Bradford J., Michael Pippincott, Geoffrey Hantzentrantz Preston, Justine. Teaching asst. Harvard, 1956-60, Imperial Coll. London, 1961; asst. prof. chemistry Central Mich. U., Mount Pleasant, 1961-66; asso. prof. Inter-Am. U. P.R., 1966-67, prof. chemistry, chmn. dept. 1967—. Chief scientist ad honorum P.R. Nuclear Center, Mayaguez, 1967—; chmn. med. sch. adv. com., 1966—. Mem. Am. Chem. Soc., Sigma Xi, Phi Beta Kappa. Author: Oxidation of Aldehydes and Ketones, 1969. Contbr. articles to profl. jours. Home: PO Box 1031 San German PR 00753

VESS, DAVID MARSHALL, educator; b. Birmingham, Ala., Nov. 4, 1925; s. David Walker and Eulalia (Kerby) V.; A.B., Howard Coll., 1948; M.A., Vanderbilt U., 1950; postgrad. (Gen. Edn. Bd. fellow Rockefeller Found.), Harvard, 1950-52; Ph.D., U. Ala., 1965; m. Jean Buchanan, Dec. 30, 1948; 1 son, John Buchanan. Instr., Howard Coll., 1949-50, asst. prof., 1957-65; dir. Americanism, Am. Legion, 1952-57; asso. prof. Samford U., Birmingham, 1965-67, prof. European history, 1967—, dir. Jan. term, 1969, head dept. history and polit. sci., 1970—, chmn. div. social scis., 1970—. Editorial cons. Am. Assn. Ophthalmology, 1967—; CBS news elections analyst Ala., 1964-66. Bd. mem. Five Points YMCA, 1962-66. Served with USNR, 1943-46; PTO. Mem. Am., So. hist. assns., Ala. Acad. Sci., Societe francaise d'histoire d'outre mer (Paris), Am. Legion, Ala. State Council for Social Studies, Kappa Alpha, Omicron Delta Kappa, Pi Gamma Mu, Phi Alpha Theta. Republican. Baptist. Home: 1140 N Shadesview Terrace Birmingham AL 35209

VEST, ALVIN FRANK, ednl. adminstr.; b. Charleston, Ark., Nov. 6, 1919; s. Robert Frank and Ida (Nolen) V.; B.S., U. Ark., 1948, M.S., 1952, diploma of advanced study, 1965; m. Norma Flanagan, Aug. 8, 1947; children—Terence Stephen, Randall Edward and Ronald Frank (twins). Tchr. vocational edn. Ratcliff High Sch., 1948-53; supt. County Line High Sch., 1953-65; dir. vocational sch., Ozark, Ark., 1965—. Mayor, Ratcliff, Ark., 1951-54. Pres. County Line Indsl. Found., Branch, Ark., 1956-58. Dir. Western Ark. Econ. Devel. Dist., 1967—. Served with USAAF, 1941-45, PTO. Mem. Ozark C. of C., Nat., Ark. edn. assns., Alpha Gamma Rho. Methodist, Mason. Home: 1008 West College St Ozark AR 72949 Office: Box 214 Ozark AR 72949

VETTER, HAROLD JOHN, psychologist; b. Buffalo, Mar. 31, 1926; s. Harold J. and Gladys (Bates) V.; B.A. summa cum laude, U. Buffalo, 1949; Ph.D., U. Buffalo, 1955; m. Virginia Rose, Apr. 24, 1964. Instr. psychology U. Buffalo, 1952-54; staff psychologist, psychiat. clinic Erie County Ct., 1954-55; lectr. overseas program U. Md., 1955-63, lectr., 1964-69; asso. prof. criminology Fla. State U., Tallahassee, 1969-71. Cons. editor Internat. Textbook Co., Scranton, Pa. Served with USNR, 1942-46. Mem. Am. Psychol. Assn., Linguistic Soc. Am., Phi Beta Kappa, Psi Chi. Author books, including: Language Behavior in Schizophrenia, 1968; Language Behavior and Communication, 1969; Language Behavior and Psychopathology, 1969; Psychology of Abnormal Behavior, 1972. Asso. editor Jour. Psycholinguistic

Research, 1969—. Home: 4370 LaSalle New Orleans LA 70115 Office: Dept Psychology Loyola U New Orleans LA 70118

VETTER, RICHARD CORTRIGHT, oceanography exec.; b. Homer Mich., Apr. 17, 1923; s. Earnest Hunt and Cynthia (Rising) V.; B.A., Albion Coll., 1949; M.S., Scripps Inst. of Oceanography, 1951; m. Betty Ruth McGee, Sept. 4, 1951 (div.); children—David Bruce, Richard Dean, Robert Alan; m. 2d, Sylvia C. Haidari. Instr., U. Cal. Far East Extension Div., 1951; oceanographer Office of Naval Research, Washington, 1951-57; exec. sec. Nat. Acad. Scis. Com. on Oceanography, Washington, 1957-70, exec. sec. Ocean Affairs Bd., 1971—. cons. oceanographic edn., 1965-67. Served with AUS, 1943-45. Mem. Marine Tech. Soc., Nat. Oceanographic Soc. (dir.), Am. Oceanography A.A.A.S., Am. Geophys. Union, Am. Soc. Limnology and Oceanography. Contbr. articles in field to profl. jours. Office: 2101 Constitution Av NW Washington DC 20418

VIA, WILLIAM FREDRICK, JR., educator; b. Ironton, O., Dec. 27, 1920; s. William Fredrick and Margret Lucille (Smith) V.; student Ohio Wesleyan U., 1938-40; D.D.S., Ohio State U., 1945; M.S., U. Mich., 1953; m. Dorothy Fay Oshanic, July 28, 1947; children—Sara Elizabeth, Judy. Faculty, Ohio State U., Columbus, 1947-51, U. Cal. at San Francisco, 1951-52; guest lectr. U. Detroit, 1957-67; mem. sr. staff Henry Ford Hosp., Detroit, 1953-67; faculty U. Conn., Storrs, 1968-69; prof. Sch. Dentistry, U. N.C., Chapel Hill, 1969—; cons. dental radiography Womack Gen. Hosp., Ft. Bragg, N.C., 1970. Served as lt. USNR, 1945-47. Fellow Am. Acad. Pedodontics, Am. Coll. Dentists, A.A.A.S., Am. Acad. Dental Radiology; mem. Am., N.C. dental assns., Internat. Assn. Dental Research, Am. Coll. Radiology, Omicron Kappa Upsilon. Editor Jour. Dentistry for Children, 1952-56, Jour. Oral Surgery, 1958-63. Home: 810 Indian Springs Rd Chapel Hill NC 27514

VICHAS, ROBERT PAUL, educator; b. Ft. Lauderdale, Fla., Sept. 26, 1936; s. Peter and Idalene L. (Cooper) V.; B.S., La. State U., 1965; M.A., U. of Ams., Mexico City, 1966; Ph.D., U. Fla., 1967; postgrad. Inst. Hautes Etudes Internationales, 1971-72; m. Dolores Flores Castellon, June 26, 1965. Rep. Dun & Bradstreet, Inc., N.Y.C., 1958-63; asst. prof. econs. and finance East Carolina U., 1967-68; asso. prof. econs. West Ga. Coll., 1968—. Vis. prof. U. Jose Simeon Canas (San Salvador); cons. to Choice. Recipient award Dept. of State, 1970. Mem. Am. Econ. Assn., Am. Finance Assn., Assn. Edn. in Internat. Bus., Am. Soc. Psychical Research, Southeastern Conf. Latin Am. Studies, United Comml. Travelers, Betta Gamma Sigma. Author: The Economy of Nicaragua. Editor, contbr.: (with W. Moore) Coeval Economics, 1970. Home: PO Box 1266 Coral Gables FL 33134 Office: IUHEI Case Postale 53 1211 Geneva 21 Switzerland

VICIEDO, EUSEBIO PERDOMO, biochemist; b. Havana, Cuba, Aug. 14, 1901; s. Mariano and Luisa (Perdomo) V.; B.S., Matanzas Inst., 1918; Ph.Dr., Havana U., 1922; m. Serafina Rodriguez, Mar. 22, 1935; 1 dau., Isis (Mrs. Julio Arrendondo). Came to U.S., 1961, naturalized, 1967. Asst. biochemist Iturrioz Laborat, Havana, Cuba, 1925-30; dir. Plasencia Laborat, Havana, 1932-45, Zimotecnica Corp., Havana, 1945-52; researcher in microbiology Cuban Research Inst., Havana, 1957-61; microbiologist Arroyo Pharm. Corp., 1961-64, Atlas Yeast Corp., P.R., 1964-66, Bacardi Corp., San Juan, P.R., 1966—. Prof. applied microbiology U. Oriente, Cuba, 1953-59. Recipient Gold medal Escuela de Quimica RR.PP. Dominicos Cuba, 1959. Mem. Am. Chem. Soc., Soc. Indsl. Microbiology, Soc. Applied Bacteriology. Home: 585 Independencia St Hato Rey PR 00918 Office: PO Box 3549 San Juan PR 00936

VICK, ROBERT EDWARD, lawyer; b. Greenville, Ky., Aug. 2, 1918; s. Robert Emory and Ethel (Murphey) V.; student Western Ky. State Coll., 1937-39; LL.B., U. Ky., 1948; m. Geneva Carpenter, June 8, 1946; children—Robert Edward, Ralph Dennis, Frances Annette. With W. G. Duncan Coal Co., Greenville, 1936-37; admitted to Ky. bar, 1948; practiced in Greenville, 1948-51; mem. firm Donan and Vick, 1956—. Served with U.S. Army, 1941-46, 1951-56, 61-62; served to lt. col. Res. ret. Decorated Silver Star, Bronze Star medal. Mem. Greenville Indsl. Devel. Corp. (sec. 1961-62), Am., Ky. bar assns., Am. Judicature Soc., U. Ky. Alumni Assn., Am. Legion, V.F.W. (past comdr.), C. of C. (former sec.-treas.). Methodist. Democrat. Kiwanian. Club: Civitan (past pres., sec.-treas.). Home: 148 N Main St Greenville KY 42345 Office: 110 E Court Sq Greenville KY 42345

VICKERS, FRANK DOW, educator; b. Sebastian, Fla., Aug. 25, 1936; s. Frank Cox and Estelle (Lassiter) V.; B.S., U. Fla., 1958, M.S., 1959, Ph.D., 1964; m. Nona Kralik Warner, June 4, 1960. Asst. prof. indsl. and systems engring. U. Fla., Gainesville, 1964-67, asso. prof., 1967-71, asso. prof. computer and information scis., 1971—. Mem. I.E.E.E., Am. Soc. for Engring. Edn., Assn. for Computing Machinery, Sigma Xi, Tau Beta Pi, Sigma Tau, Alpha Pi Mu. Home: 6500 NW 18th Av Gainesville FL 32601

VICKERS, FRANK NORMAN, physician; b. Hattiesburg, Miss., Mar. 2, 1931; s. Hawkins Ladson and Elizabeth Rose (Gibson) V.; B.A., So. Meth. U., 1952; M.D., Emory U., 1956; m. Elizabeth Ann Dwyer, Dec. 14, 1957; children—Sarah Ellen, Marie, Frank Norman. Intern, New Eng. Center Hosp., Boston, 1956-57; resident internal medicine Tulane U.-Charity Hosp. of La., New Orleans, 1959-61; resident gastroenterology U. Louisville Sch. Medicine, 1961-62, instr. medicine, sect. gastroenterology, 1962-64, asst. prof. medicine, 1964-65; practice medicine, specializing in gastroenterology, Pensacola, Fla., 1965—; mem. staff Baptist Hosp., Univ. Hosps., Pensacola; chief internal medicine Pensacola Ednl. Program, 1967. Served as lt. M.C., USNR, 1957-59. Mem. A.C.P., Am. Soc. Gastrointestinal Endoscopy, Am. Coll. Gastroenterology, Am. Fedn. Clin. Research, Fla. Soc. Internal Medicine (pres. 1971-72), Escambia County Med. Soc. (sec. 1971). Home: 281 Beacon Rd Pensacola FL 32503 Office: 14 W Jordan St Pensacola FL 32501

VICKERS, LEWIS, JR., banker; b. Douglas, Ga., Nov., 1924; s. Lewis and Emma (McEachern) V.; B.S., U. Fla., 1949, B.A., 1950; postgrad. The Citadel, 1943, Sch. Banking of South, La. State U., 1955-57; m. Mary Alice Ingram, Mar. 3, 1972. Proof clk. Union Trust Co., St. Petersburg, 1941-42; asst. v.p. First Nat. Bank, Greenville, 1952-57; v.p. S.C. Nat. Bank, Greenville, 1957-58; sr. v.p. S.C. Nat. Bank, Florence, 1959-63, exec. v.p., 1963—; pres. Gangplank, Inc., 1968—. Chmn. Florence County Indsl. Commn., 1961-70. Mem. adv. council Sch. of Banking, La. State U., 1958-59, trustee, 1958-64; mem. civilian adv. bd. Shaw AFB, 1963—; chmn. bd. trustees All Saints Day Sch.; trustee James Jones Trust Fund, Florence. Served with AUS, 1943-46. Named Man of Year, Florence, 1961. Mem. S.C. Bankers Assn. (exec. council 1971-72), S.C. (dir.), Florence (past pres.) chambers commerce, V.F.W. Episcopalian (vestryman 1967-69). Clubs: Florence (S.C.) Country, Kiwanis. Home: 706 A-King Av Florence SC 29501 Office: 1509 Cherokee Rd Florence SC 29501

VICKERS, THOMAS FRANCIS, constrn. co. exec.; b. Houston, June 11, 1943; s. Thomas F. and Betty Jane (Patton) V.; B.A., Southwestern U., 1965; LL.B., U. Tex., 1968; m. Zelda Sue Bitner, Oct. 25, 1964; children—Thomas Francis IV, Stephan Joseph. Exec. v.p. Pecan Valley Properties, San Antonio, 1968-69; pres. Tom Vickers Enterprises, Inc., real estate and constrn., San Antonio, 1969—. Mem. planning session com. San Antonio Capitol Bond Issue, 1970; mem. exec. com. San Antonio Bicentennial Celebration, 1971. Justice of peace, 1971—. Bd. dirs. Alamoa Area council Boy Scouts Am., 1970-72, dist. chmn., 1970—; bd. dirs. Festival San Jacinto Assn., 1971. Mem. Tex. (state v.p. 1971—), San Antonio (dir. 1971—) apt. assns., San Antonio Homebuilders Assn., San Antonio Golf Assn. (dir. 1970—), Phi Delta Theta. Rotarian. Home: 4510 Pecan Grove St San Antonio TX 78223 Office: PO Box 23276 San Antonio TX 78223

VICTOR, LEONARD BAKER, pathologist, educator; b. Schenectady, N.Y., Aug. 3, 1934; s. Austin and Matilda (Baker) V.; A.B., N.Y.U., 1953; M.D., U. Brussels (Belgium), 1960; T.M.D., Royal Inst. Tropical Medicine, 1960; m. Rona E. Kogan, Dec. 25, 1966; children— Brian Hyde, Sarah Ruth. Rotating intern U. Buffalo, Gen. and Children's hosps., 1960-61; resident in pathology U. Rochester, Strong Hosp., 1961-65; practice medicine specializing in pathology, Rochester, 1965-67, Nashville, 1968—; dep. med. examiner, sr. instr. U. Rochester, 1965-67; cons. State Hosp., Rochester, N.Y., 1966-67; asso. prof. pathology Meharry Med. Coll., Hubbard Hosp., Nashville, 1968—, dir. multitest screening operations, 1968—; asso. prof. pathology in biomed. engring., Vanderbilt U., Nashville, 1969—. Mem. physicians' com. United Giver's Fund, Nashville, 1968-69. Served as 1st lt. USAF, 1964-65. Diplomate Am. Bd. Pathology. Fellow Am. Soc. Clin. Pathologists, Coll. Am. Pathologists; mem. Tenn. Med. Assn., Tenn. Soc. Pathologists, Nashville Acad. Medicine. Home: 1809 Hillmont Dr Nashville TN 37215 Office: 1005 18th Av N Nashville TN 37208

VICTORY, GENE C., leasing co. exec.; b. Leonard, Tex., Nov. 19, 1934; s. Green F. and Avis Dee (Treadway) V.; student So. Meth. U., 1964; m. Pauline Lawrence, May 12, 1957; children—David, Chris. Chief accountant Nortex Oil & Gas Corp., Dallas, 1962-64; treas. Gandy-McAuley Inc., oil and gas producers, 1964-66; v.p. financial Kingwood Oil Co., Oklahoma City, 1966-72; v.p. finance Public leasing Corp., Oklahoma City, 1972—. Cons. oil and gas accounting. Served with USAF, 1954-57. Mem. U.S., Oklahoma City chambers commerce, Petroleum Accountants Soc. Dallas and Oklahoma City (1st v.p. 1969-70, dir. 1967-70). Baptist (mem. finance com. 1967-69)

VIDUNA, ROBERT JAMES, metal container mfg. exec.; b. Cicero, Ill., June 25, 1923; s. James Albert and Frances (Stepanek) V.; B.S. in Mech. Engring., Gen. Motors Inst. Tech., 1945; environmental engring. certificate U. Tex., 1970; m. Grayce I. Vander Schaaf, Oct. 25, 1946; children—Robert James, Mark R., David B. With Gen. Motors Corp., 1941-48; indsl. engr. Continental Can. Co., Chgo., 1948-50, indsl. master mechanic, Elwood, 1950-54, asst. plant mgr., St. Louis, 1954-55, mfg. engr., 1955-58, prodn. engr., San Francisco, 1959-61, mgr. prodn. engring. So. metal div., Tampa, Fla., 1961-67, div. mgr., Atlanta, 1967-71, regional mgr. engring., Atlanta, 1971—; v.p., treas. R.J. Trebor, Inc., 1964—. Pres. Carrollwood Civic Assn., 1965-66. Served to 1st lt. AUS, 1944-46. Named Boss of Year, Am. Bus. Women's Assn., 1964. Registered profl. engr., Mo., Fla., Ga. Mem. Nat. Soc. Profl. Engrs., Fla. Engring. Soc. (chpt. sec. 1965-66), Am. Soc. Tool Engrs., Am. Soc. Plant Engrs., Am. Soc. M.E. Mason (Shriner). Office: 2 Executive Park West NE Atlanta GA 30329

VIEBIG, VAN RICHARD, JR., certified pub. accountant; b. Houston, June 11, 1940; s. Van Richard and Hulda (Alexander) V.; B.A. cum laude, Rice U., 1962 Sr. accountant Voelkel, Simons & Co., C.P.A.'s, Houston, 1962-65; tax and financial adminstr. Jack C. Pollard Enterprises, Houston, 1965—. Lectr. accounting Rice U., 1968—; Served with USCGR, 1962. Mem. Am. Inst. C.P.A.'s, Tex. Soc. C.P.A.'s Am. Accounting Assn., Tex. Bill of Rights Found., Am. Civil Liberties Assn., Phi Beta Kappa. Episcopalian. Home: 4408 Acacia Bellaire TX 77401 Office: 2419 Fannin St Houston TX 77002

VIERA-MARTINEZ, ANGEL, Puerto Rican congressman; b. Gurabo, P.R., Nov. 18, 1915; s. Nieves Viera and Alejandrina Martinez; LL.B., U. P.R., 1940; m. Gladys Villeneuve, Dec. 22, 1952; children—Angel, Harry. Admitted to P.R. bar, 1941; pvt. practice law, San Juan, 1941-46; asst. dist. atty., San Juan Dist., 1946-49, dist. atty., 1949-55; pvt. practice law, San Juan, 1955-69; mem. P.R. Ho. of Reps., 1969—, now speaker. Rep., New Progressive Party, Electoral Bd. Commonwealth of P.R., 1968—. Mem. Am. Bar Assn., Bar Assn. P.R., Am. Judicature Soc. Home: 1213 Lucchetti St Santurce PR 00907 Office: Ho of Reps Capitol Bldg San Juan PR 00903

VIERLING, BERNARD JULIUS, govt. ofcl.; b. Bakersfield, Cal., Dec. 27, 1914; s. Bernard Julius and Elizabeth J. (Wilcox) V.; B.S. in Mech. Engring., Stanford, 1936; m. Martha Jane Peairs, July 20, 1939; children—Lawrence Bernard, Bruce Wilcox, Karen Jane. Engr., Douglas Aircraft Co., 1936-39; chief engr., dir. engring. and maintenance Pa.-Central Airlines, 1939-47; pres. Aircraft Advisors, Inc., Washington, 1946-48, Aircraft Supply Corp., Washington, 1948-54, Helidusters, Inc., Washington, 1950-52; partner Aircraft Supply Co., Washington, 1954-62; dir. systems maintenance service FAA, 1962-65, dep. dir. supersonic transp. devel., 1965-69, acting dir. supersonic transp. devel. Dept Transp., 1969-70, dep. dir., 1970-71, dir. Morgantown Personal Rapid Transit System Devel., 1971—. Recipient Nat. award for economy achievement Pres. Johnson, 1964. Mem. Nat. Aero. Assn., Air Force Assn., Phi Gamma Delta. Clubs: Nat. Aviation (life; bd. govs. 1954—, v.p. 1954-56, pres. 1956-58, gov. emeritus 1967), Aero (Washington); Belle Haven Country (Alexandria); Lakeview Country (Morgantown, W.Va.). Home: 647 Oakland Terrace Alexandria VA 22302 Office: 400 7th St Av SW Washington DC 20590

VILA-BALZAC, MANUEL ANTONIO, constrn. co. exec.; b. Rio Piedras, P.R., June 8, 1926; s. Joaquin Vila-Mayo and Irene Vila Balzac; B.S., U. Ky., 1950; m. Doris C. Schnitzler, Jan. 28, 1950; children—Patricia Ann (Mrs. Richard Mohon), Peggy Jo. Asst. plant engr. Kawneer Co., Lesington, Ky., 1950-51; estimator James E. Smith & Sons, Inc., Louisville, 1951-54, chief estimator, 1967—, v.p., 1967—; estimator George Blanford Co., Louisville, 1955-61. Chmn. Shively Park Commn., 1969, 70-71. Republican. Roman Catholic (dir. athletic assn. 1970-71). Home: 3446 Janell Rd Shively KY 40216 Office: 7308 Grade Lane Louisville KY 40219

VILLA, DINO SECONDO, govt. ofcl.; b. N.Y.C., Mar. 11, 1920; s. Henry A. and Antoinette (Marzocchi) V.; B.S., Cornell U., 1942; postgrad. Am. U., 1946-48; m. Christine Ceva, Apr. 15, 1950; children—Christopher, Richard. Various adminstrv. positions Fgn. Trade Div., Bur. Census, Dept. Commerce, Washington, 1945—, chief, 1963—. Served with USNR, 1943-45. Mem. Am. Statis. Assn., Am. Econ. Assn., Am. Marketing Assn. Home: 12517 Arrow Park Dr Tantallon MD 20022 Office: Fed Office Bldg No 3 Washington DC 20233

VILLAREJO, OSCAR MILTON, educator; b. Milw., May 3, 1909; s. Oscar Felipe and Isabel (Gonzalez) V.; B.A., George Washington U., 1947, M.A., 1949; postgrad. U. Birmingham (Eng.), 1948; Ph.D., Columbia, 1953; m. Mary Patricia Holan, Mar. 28, 1945. Instr. English, George Washington U., 1947-49, asso. professorial lectr. English, 1972—; instr. English, Spanish and French, New Lincoln Sch., N.Y.C., 1949-52; head dept. English, asst. prof. Nasson Coll., Springvale, Me., 1954-55; asst. prof. English and Spanish, Tex. Luth. Coll., Seguin, 1955-56; chmn. div. humanities, asst. prof. So. State Coll., Magnolia, Ark., 1956-57; asst. prof. English, Memphis State U., 1957-59; asso. prof. English, Wis. State U. at Stevens Point, 1959-60; prof. English, Glassboro (N.J.) State Coll., 1960-64; asso. prof. Spanish, C.W. Post Coll. of L.I. U., 1964-66, Georgetown U., 1966-70; vis. prof. comparative lit. U. Md., 1970-71; mem. faculty dept. English and fgn. langs. Grad. Sch. of U.S. Dept. Agr., Washington, 1971—; cons.; pub. speaker. Del. Ruben Dario World Centenary Observance, Los Angeles, 1967, World Shakespeare Congress, Vancouver, 1971. Served with USMCR, 1943-45. Vice chmn. nat. edn. com. Nat. Confederation Am. Ethnic Groups, Washington, also chmn. Washington-Balt. Acad. Council. Mem. Am. Platform Assn., U.S. Naval Hist. Found., Modern Lang. Assn., Am. Polar Soc., Am. Renaissance Soc. Author: Dr. Kane's Voyage to the Polar Lands, 1965. Mem. editorial bd. of Circulo, 1969—. Contbr. articles to lit. jours. Home: 4213 Jenifer St NW Washington DC 20015 Office: Coll Gen Studies George Washington U 2003 G St NW Washington DC 20006

VILLAVASO, STANLEY STRICKLAND, paper co. exec.; b. Port Arthur, Tex., Oct. 30, 1915; s. William Joseph and Nancy Estelle (Strickland) V.; student pub. schs.; m. Anita Josephine Gaudet, Oct. 30, 1935; children—Stanley Alfred, Eric John, Gerard Joseph, Joy Therese (Mrs. Doval A. Dixon, Jr.), Alfred Gaudet. Mgr., Kennedy Print Shop, Baton Rouge, 1954-57; resident salesman Butler Paper Co., Baton Rouge, 1957-62; resident salesman Alco-Columbia Paper Co., Baton Rouge, 1962-65, br. mgr. 1965-68, v.p., div. mgr., 1968—, also dir. Mem. Baton Rouge C. of C., Baton Rouge Assn. Bus. & Indsl. Editors, Grafik I, Advt. Club Baton Route (v.p. 1967), Sales and Marketing Execs. K.C. (grand knight 1957-58). Club: Sherwood Forest Country. Home: 10563 Ranchwood Dr Baton Rouge LA 70815 Office: 5757 Adams Av Baton Rouge LA 70806

VILLEMARETTE, TERRY JAMES, social worker; b. New Orleans, May 18, 1939; s. James Joseph and Amy (Firmin) V.; student U. Southwestern La., 1957-61; B.A., La. State U., 1962, M.S.W., 1964; m. Janette Mary Ponthieux, June 8, 1963; 1 son, Keith. Caseworker Forest Glen Mental Health Center, 1964-65; case supr. Hosp. Improvement Project, Pineville, La., 1965-68, asst. coordinator, 1968-70, coordinator, 1970—. Mem. Nat. Assn. Social Workers (pres. 1970-71), Acad. Certified Social Workers, Rapides Parish Council Social Agys. (pres. 1965-67), La. (adminstrv. v.p. 1969-70, internal v.p. 1970—), Marksville (regional v.p. 1968-69) Jr. C. of C. K.C. Home: PO Box 474 Marksville LA 71351 Office: PO Box 31 Pineville LA 71360

VILLEPONTEAUX, LORENZ AIMAR, JR., social worker; b. Charleston, S.C., Sept. 1, 1935; s. Lorenz Aimar and Mary (Laurey) V.; A.B., Coll. Charleston, 1958; M.S.W., Tulane U., 1964; m. Anne Louise Bellinger, Dec. 27, 1957; children—Mary Antonia, Virginia Anne, Laura Marian, Elizabeth Laurey. Probation counselor Charleston Juvenile Ct., 1959-60; dir. probation Rock Hill (S.C.) Juvenile Ct., 1961-62; dir. Horizon House, Charleston, 1964-67; instr. psychiat. social work, dept. psychiatry Med. U. Hosp., Charleston, 1967—. Chmn. adminstrv. bd. Charleston Area Mental Health Center, 1969-70. Mem. Nat. Assn. Social Workers (pres. coastal Carolina chpt. 1966-68), Acad. Certified Social Workers, Am. Orthopsychiat. Assn., Alumni Assn. Coll. Charleston (pres. 1969-70, mem. exec. com. 1964—). Democrat. Home: 91 Logan St Charleston SC 29401 Office: 80 Barre St Charleston SC 29401

VIMONT, RICHARD ELGIN, lawyer; b. Lexington, Ky., Aug. 3, 1936; s. Richard Thompson and Christine (Anderson) V.; B.S., U. Ky., 1958, J.D., 1960; m. Marie Salyer, Sept. 10, 1960; children—Richard Thompson II, Margaret Anderson. Admitted to Ky. bar, 1960; since practiced in Lexington, Ky.; now partner Anggelis and Vimont; vis. prof. bus. law Transylvania Coll., 1963; tennis coach U. Ky., 1963-71. Chmn. bd. Eastern State Hosp., 1970-71. City commr., Lexington, 1972—; mem. Regional Crime Council, 1972—. Mem. Ky. State Tennis Assn. (pres. 1960-62), Patterson Literary Soc., Jr. C. of C., Phi Delta Phi, Sigma Alpha Epsilon. Mem. Christian Ch. (elder). Home: 564 Grantchester St Lexington KY 40505 Office: 139 Market St Lexington KY 40507

VINCENT, C. (CHARLES) GEOFFREY, journalist; b. London, Eng., Apr. 14, 1920; s. Charles Bassett and Edith (Vialls) V.; came to U.S., 1928, naturalized, 1942; student U. Buffalo, 1938-39, Washington U., St. Louis, 1947-50; m. Mary Amy Loy, Apr. 12, 1947 (dec. July 1964); children—Wendy Anne, Christopher Loy; m. 2d, Adele Judith Bagnall, Apr. 24, 1965; 1 dau., Mary Jane. Copy boy Buffalo Evening News, 1937, reporter, feature writer, 1939-42; copy editor, feature editor St. Louis Star-Times, 1946, 48-51; copy editor N.Y. Herald Tribune, N.Y.C., 1951-54, asst. night editor, 1954-56; writer News of Week in Review, N.Y. Times, N.Y.C., 1956-61; pub. relations exec. BBDO-Internat., London, 1961-62, Benton & Bowles, London, 1962-63; asso. editor, contbr. N.Y. Times Mag., N.Y.C., 1963-65; Sunday editor Courier-Jour. & Times, Courier-Jour. and Louisville Times Co., Louisville, 1965—. Sec. Louisville Com. on Fgn. Relations. Served with C.I.C., AUS, 1942-46. Mem. English-Speaking Union, Am. Assn. Sunday and Feature Editors (pres. 1970-71). Home: 3900 Fallen Timber Dr Louisville KY 40222 Office: 525 W Broadway Louisville KY 40202

VINCENT, CLARK EDWARD, sociologist; b. Otis, Colo., May 13, 1923; s. Ralph Ellory and Lillian May (Auld) V.; A.B., U. Cal. at Berkeley, 1949, M.A., 1950, Ph.D. (fellow Nat. Inst. Mental Health, Univ. fellow), 1952; m. Roseann Wagoner, Dec. 27, 1955. From instr. to asst. prof. family sociology U. Cal. at Berkeley, 1952-59; asso. prof. State U. Ia., 1959-60; scientist adminstr. Nat. Inst. Mental Health, 1960-64; prof. sociology Bowman Gray Sch. Medicine, 1964—, dir. Behavioral Scis. Center, 1966—. Cons. to tng. and manpower resources br. Nat. Inst. Mental Health, 1964-65, Agy. for Internat. Devel., Dept. State, 1969-71; spl. cons. to com. on family life Nat. Council Chs. Christ in U.S., 1963-66. Fellow Am. Assn. Marriage Counselors (pres. 1973—, exec. bd.), Am. Sociol. Assn., Soc. Sci. Study Sex; mem. Nat. Council Family Relations (chmn. counseling sect. 1961-62, exec. bd., 1962-65, pres. 1964-65). Author: Readings in Marriage Counseling, 1957; Unmarried Mothers, 1961. Compiler, editor Human Sexuality in Medical Education and Practice, 1968. Editor: Psychological Aspects of Medical Training, 1971. Contbr. numerous articles profl. publs. Home: 4408 Woodlark Ct Clemmons NC 27012

VINCENT, HOWARD LOUIS, economist; b. White Plains, N.Y., Jan. 9, 1937; s. Louis and Lena (Bernardi) V.; B.S., Syracuse U., 1960, M.A., 1965; m. Suellen Long, May 7, 1966 (separated 1971); children—Scott, Greg. Operations analyst N. Am. Rockwell, Los Angeles, 1961-63; economist NSF, Washington, 1963-65, U.S. Office Edn., Washington, 1965-71, Office of Sec., U.S. Dept. Labor, Washington, 1971—, spl. assignments to Office of Sec. Dept. Health, Edn. and Welfare, 1970—. Mem. Am. Econ. Assn., Am. Statis. Assn. Home: 13204 Parson Lane Fairfax VA 22030 Office: Office of Evaluation Asst Sec for Planning Evaluation and Research US Dept Labor 14th and Constitution Av Washington DC 20270

VINCENT, LLOYD DREXELL, coll. adminstr.; b. DeQuincy, La., Jan. 7, 1924; s. Samuel and Lila (Dickerson) V.; student Rice U., 1946-47, 49-50; B.S., U. Tex. (Austin), 1952, M.A., 1953, Ph.D., 1960; m. Johnell Stuart, Aug. 30, 1947; children—Drexell Stuart, Sandra. Asst. prof. U. Southwestern La., 1953-55, asso. prof., 1956-58; instr. Tex. A. and M. U., 1955-56; NSF Sci. faculty fellowship U. Tex., 1958-59; research scientist Tex. Nuclear Corp., Austin, 1959-60; prof., dir. physics dept. Sam Houston State U., 1960-65, asst. to pres., 1965-67; pres. Angelo State U., San Angelo, Tex., 1967—. Co-owner, mgr. ACME Glass Corp., Baytown, Tex., 1947-49; physics cons., India, summer 1966. Served to 2d lt. USAAF, 1942-45. Fellow Tex. Acad. Sci., mem. Am. Phys. Soc., Am. Assn. State Colls. and Univs. (state rep. 1972-73), Am. Assn. Physics Tchrs. (sect. chmn. 1965-67), Sigma Xi, Sigma Pi Sigma. Democrat. Baptist. Rotarian. Home: 2602 Live Oak St San Angelo TX 76901

VINCIGUERRA, JOHN VINCENT, govt. ofcl.; b. Akron, O., Nov. 5, 1916; s. Andrew and Carmela (Linsalata) V.; A.B. in Econs., Akron U., 1939; student Ohio State U. Law Sch., 1939-41, John Marshall Sch. Law, 1947; LL.B., George Washington U., 1950. With U.S. Govt. service, 1941—; with AEC, 1947—, asst. dir. safeguards div. internat. affairs, 1960, dir. div. contracts, 1960-64, acting asst. gen. mgr., 1964, exec. asst. to gen. mgr., 1964-66, asst. gen. mgr. adminstrn., 1966—. Served with AUS, 1941-45. Recipient Outstanding Service award, 1958, Sustained Superior Performance award, 1960, Distinguished Service award, 1971 (all from AEC). Home: 10509 Montrose Av Bethesda MD 20014 Office: AEC Washington DC 20545

VINES, DWIGHT DELBERT, coll. dean; b. Jonesboro, La., Sept. 27, 1931; s. Dwight N. and Bessie (Barlow) V.; student Fla. State U., 1950-51; B.S., Northwestern State Coll., 1957; M.B.A., La. State U., 1958; D.B.A., U. Colo., 1966; m. Frances Imogene Varnado, June 4, 1956; children—Michael Allen, Timothy Wayne, David Ray. Sales rep. Burroughs Corp., Shreveport, La., 1956-57; instr., asst. prof. N.E. La. U., Monroe, 1958-63, prof. mgmt., 1964—, dean Coll. of Bus., 1964—. Bus. and mgmt. cons., 1960—. Chmn. bus. adminstrn. div. Conf. of La. Colls. and Univs. Served with USAF, 1950-55. Mem. So. Mgmt. Assn., Southwest Acad. Mgmt., La. Tennis Assn., Omicron Delta Kappa, Pi Sigma Epsilon (nat. dir.), Phi Kappa Phi, Sigma Iota Epsilon, Beta Gamma Sigma, Pi Omega Pi, Pi Kappa Delta, Delta Sigma Pi. Lion. Club: Chauvin Racquet (dir.). Home: 707 Lakeshore St Monroe LA 71201 Office: University Av Monroe LA 71201

VINES, JERRY LANDON, banker; b. Comanche, Tex., Sept. 27, 1933; s. Landon Oral and Mable (Mills) V.; student Tarleton State Coll., 1952; Agr. degree, Tex. Tech U., 1955; m. Isla Sue Barret, June 18, 1954; children—Landon, Jim, John. With Tex. Agrl. Extension Service, 1959-68; with Comanche Nat. Bank, 1968—, v.p., 1969—. Dir. Leon-Bosque Resource Devel. and Conservation Bd., 1971-72. Served to 1st lt. USAF, 1955-59. Mem. Comanche C. of C. (pres. 1970-71). Methodist (mem. ofcl. bd. 1971—). Elk, Kiwanian (pres. 1967), Lion. Home: Route 2 Box 5 Comanche TX 76442 Office: 200 W Central Comanche TX 76442

VINEYARD, EDWIN EARLE, coll. pres.; b. Wright City, Okla., Aug. 30, 1926; s. John R. and Bess (Chronister) V.; B.S., Okla. State U., 1949, M.S., 1951, Ed.D., 1955; m. Imogene Mankin, Nov. 6, 1946; children— Louis Ray, Edwin Roy. Jr. high sch. prin., Beggs, Okla., 1949-51; high sch. prin., Mannford, Okla., 1951-52, Davis, Okla., 1952-54; dir. counseling Panhandle State Coll., Goodwell, Okla., 1955-58; dean students, chmn. dept. edn. and psychology Southwestern State Coll., Weatherford, Okla., 1958-61; prof. edn. Okla. State U., Stillwater, 1961-65; pres. No. Okla. Coll., Tonkawa, 1965—. Dir. Service Bank Tonkawa. Mem. Am. Psychol. Assn., Am. Personnel and Guidance Assn. Baptist (deacon 1956-70). Lion, Kiwanian. Author: (with Harold W. Massey) The Profession of Teaching, 1961. Home: 202 S Pine St Tonkawa OK 74653

VINSON, JAMES RICHARD, educator; b. Wichita Falls, Tex., July 6, 1937; s. Ray R. and Helen L. (Henderson) V.; B.B.A, Hardin-Simmons U., 1963, M.A., 1964; M.A., U. Houston, 1968, Ph.D., 1968; m. Martha Ann McGlothing, Sept. 1, 1961; children—Jennifer Ann, Jeffery James. Teaching fellow Hardin-Simmons U., Abilene, 1963-64, prof. econs., 1967—, dir. econ. research, 1968—; econ. cons., 1964—. Mem. Am., So. econ. assns., So. Finance Assn., Nat. Council U. Research Adminstrs., Western Travel Research Assn., Western Regional Sci. Assn. Mason. Home: 2441 Swenson St Abilene TX 79601

VINSON, LEWIS CHARLESTON, educator; b. Pineville, La., Sept. 24, 1921; s. Joseph W. and Helen (Elton) V.; A.B., La. Coll., 1939A.M., La. State U., 1947; postgrad. Tulane U. Prin., Wise Sch., Alexandria, La., 1939-40; teacher Tioga (La.) High Sch., 1940-42; grad. asst. La. State U., Baton Rouge, 1945-47, instr. dept. social sci., 1947-48; asst. prof. psychology Furman U., Greenville, S.C., 1948-49; supr. student tchrs. in social studies, lab. sch., La. Poly. Inst., Ruston, La., 1949-52; asst. prin. Pineville (La.) Elementary Sch.; head dept. social studies John McDonogh Sr. High Sch., New Orleans; coordinator econ. edn. for New Orleans Pub. Sch., now supr. social studies; also TV series Our Econ. Pattern. Bd. dirs. La. Council on Econ. Edn. Served with AUS 1942-45. Mem. Am. Assn. Univ. Profs., Am. Assn. for Supervision and Curriculum, Nat., La. (dir.) councils for social studies, La. Council on Econ. Edn., N.E.A., La. Edn. Assn., Psi Chi, Sigma Delta Pi, Alpha Chi, Phi Delta Kappa, Kappa Delta Pi. Club: Kiwanis. Home: 924 Royal St New Orleans LA 70130 Office: 731 St Charles Av New Orleans LA 70130

VINSON, NELSON, lawyer; b. nr. Birmingham, Ala., July 25, 1923; s. Fred David and Laura (Nelson) V.; student U. Ala., 1941-43, LL.B., 1949; m. Leila Terry Walker, Aug. 11, 1951; children—Hughes Nelson, William Terry. Admitted to Ala. bar, 1949; county dist. atty., Hamilton, Ala., 1949-50; judge Marion County Superior Ct., Hamilton, 1950-59; practice law, Hamilton, 1959—. Mem. Ala. Bd. Bar Commrs., 1968—. Served with AUS, 1943-46. Mem. U. Ala. Alumni Assn. (pres. Marion County chpt. 1954-58), Bar Assn. Ala. (pres. jud. circuit 1958-60), Ala. Bar Assn., Delta Chi. Methodist. Home: Military Rd Hamilton AL 35570 Office: Court Square Hamilton AL 35570

VINSON, RALPH NICHOLAS, cartoonist; b. nr. Trinity, Tex., Oct. 19, 1916; s. Ralph Magee and Leafy (Pruitt) V.; student Tex. A. and M. Coll. and Sam Houston State Coll., 1934-37, Chgo. Acad. Fine Arts, 1938, Tex. Acad., 1953-54; m. Dorothy Leah Ramey, July 27, 1939. Editorial cartoonist Pasadena (Tex.) Daily Citizen, 1960, Fort Worth Star-Telegram, 1963-64, New Orleans States-Item, 1964—. Served with USNR, 1943-45. Mem. Assn. Am. Editorial Cartoonists, New Orleans Press Club. Methodist. Mason. Home: 324 Arlington Dr Metairie LA 70001 Office: 615 North St New Orleans LA 70130

VINSON, THOMAS GLENN, banker; b. Everton, Ark., Sept. 19, 1923; s. Franklin S. and Chleola J. (Elam) V.; student Draughons Bus. Coll., 1941-42, S.W. Mo. State U., 1942, So. Meth. U., 1960-63; m. Reba Faye Young, Jan. 11, 1946; children—Thomas A., Judy Nanette (Mrs. Allen M. Tucker, Jr.). Cashier, Comml. Bank, Harrison, Ark., 1947-55; pres., dir. First Nat. Bank, Batesville, Ark., 1955—. Bd. dirs. White River Med. Assn. Served with USAAF, 1942-46. Decorated Purple Heart, Air medal with three oak leaf clusters. Mem. Ark. Bankers Assn. (exec. bd. 1960-63), Batesville C. of C. (pres. 1967). Methodist. Mason, Rotarian. Home: 18th St Batesville AR 72501 Office: 250 S Broad St Batesville AR 72501

VINT, JESSE LEE, JR., rig and equipment co. exec.; b. Yuma, Ariz., Feb. 24, 1919; s. Jesse Lee and Nora (Verser) V.; student Kan. U., 1941-46; m. Wanda Pauline Harrod, Oct. 23, 1970; children (by previous marriage)—Jesse Lee III, William Mitchell, Alan Richard; stepchildren—Terry Steele, Carolyn Joy, Susan Kay, Cheryl Ann. Draftsman, Texaco, Inc., Tulsa, Okla., 1936-40; draftsman, design engr. Beech Aircraft, Wichita, Kan., 1940-47; design engr. Unit Rig & Euipment Co., Tulsa, Okla., 1947-48, project engr., 1948-53, chief engr., 1953-54, v.p. engring., 1954-55, v.p. sales, 1955-56, pres., 1956—. Mem. Newcomer Soc., Okla. C. of C. (dir. 1971—). Nat. (state dir. 1969-70), Okla. State (pres. 1968-69) skeet shooting assns. Home: 3721 E 46th Pl Tulsa OK 74135 Office: PO Box 3107 Tulsa OK 74101

VINZANT, CAREY TRUETT, clergyman, former coll. pres.; b. Burns, Miss., July 4, 1904; s. Albert Johnson and Mary Grace (Broadfoot) V.; A.B., Miss. Coll., Clinton, 1926; M.S.T., So. Bapt. Theol. Sem., 1930; D.D., Mercer U., 1948; m. Marian McGinty, Aug. 28, 1935; children—Marianne, Carey Lamar. Ordained to ministry, Baptist Ch., 1926; pastor The Hill Ch., Augusta, Ga., 1931-38, First Ch., Sandersville, 1939-44, First Ch., Fitzgerald, 1945-52; pres. Tift Coll., Forsyth, Ga., 1952-69. Mem. exec. com. Ga. Bapt. Conv., 1940-52, pres. exec. com., 1946-51; pres. Ga. Bapt. Sunday Sch. Conv., 1946-47; mem. Sunday Sch. bd. So. Bapt. Conv., 1945-52. Pres. Ga. Found. for Ind. Colls., 1964-65; v.p. So. Bapt. Assn. Colls., 1964-65; mem. Ga. Higher Edn. Assistance Corp.; mem. Gov.'s Commn. on Student Financial Aid. Bd. dirs. Ga. Scholarship Commn. Mason. Address: 255 Tift College Dr Forsyth GA 31029

VIORST, JUDITH (MRS. MILTON VIORST), author; b. Newark; ed. Rutgers U.; m. Milton Viorst; children—Anthony, Nicholas, Alexander. Formerly fashion model, Seventh Av., N.Y.C.; formerly editor children's books. Mem. Phi Beta Kappa. Author: Projects: Space, 1962; 150 Science Experiments Step-By-Step, 1963; The Natural World, 1965; The Changing Earth, 1967; The Village Square, 1967; Sunday Morning, 1968; It's Hard to Be Hip over Thirty and Other Tragedies of Married Life, 1968; Ill Fix Anthony, 1969; (with Milton Viorst) The Washington D.C. Underground Gourmet, 1970; Try It Again, Sam, 1970; People and Other Aggravations, 1971; The Tenth Good Thing About Barney, 1971; Yes, Married, 1972; Alexander and the Terrible, Horrible, No Good, Very Bad Day, 1972. Address: 3432 Ashley Terrace NW Washington DC 20008

VIORST, MILTON, journalist, author; b. Paterson, N.J., Feb. 18, 1930; s. Louis and Betty (Levine) V.; B.D., Rutgers U., 1951; M.A., Harvard, 1954; M.S., Columbia, 1955; postgrad. U. Lyon; m. Judith Stahl, Jan 30, 1960; children—Anthony Jacob, Nicholas Nathan. Washington corr. N.Y. Post, 1961—; freelance writer. Served to 1st lt. USAF, 1952-54. Author: Liberalism: A Guide to Its Past, Present and Future in American Politics, 1963; Hostile Allies: The Story of Roosevelt and de Gaulle; An Anthology of the Great Documents of Western Civilization. Contbr. to Harper's Nation, Reporter, New Republic, Science, others. Home: 3432 Ashley Terrace NW Washington DC 20008*

VISER, FESTUS JUSTIN, educator; b. Memphis, June 11, 1920; s. Eugene Y. and Janie (Jetton) V.; B.S., Memphis State U., 1942; M.S., N.Y.U., 1950, M.B.A., 1952, Ph.D., 1958. Asst. prof. econs. U. Notre Dame, 1950-51; lectr. econs. Bernard M. Baruch Sch., 1951-55; asso. prof. econs. N.Y.U., 1955-65; prof. econs. Memphis State U., 1965—, dir. M.L. Seidman Meml. Town Hall Lectures. Spl. econ. cons. Gov. Nelson Rockefeller campaign, 1958. Treas., financial officer, bd. regents Barth House, Memphis. Mem. Am. Statis. Soc., Am., So. econs. assns., Am., So. finance assns. Contbr. articles to profl. jours. Home: 79 Lynnfield Rd Memphis TN 38117

VITELLO, JOHN RALPH, pub. relations exec.; b. Rochester, N.Y., July 27, 1929; s. Anthony and Josephine (Cornelia) V.; B.B.A, U. Houston, 1954, M.B.A., 1955; m. Alisbel Mills, Aug. 22, 1958. Exec. dir. Tex. div. Am. Cancer Soc., Houston, 1958-63; dir. pub. relations, spl. projects coordinator 15 hosps. Sisters of Charity of Incarnate Word, Houston, 1963—. Cons. pub. relations, fund raising, Houston, 1963—. Mem. pres.'s council U. Houston, 1967—; exec. dir. St. Joseph Hosp. Found., Houston, 1965—; asst. sec., dir. St. Bernardine Hosp. Found., San Bernardino, Cal., 1970—, St. Mary's Long Beach Hosp. Found., 1970—. Served with AUS, 1955-57. Mem. Nat. Assn. Hosp. Devel. Dirs. (named outstanding devel. dir. 1971), Am. Tex. (bd. dirs. 1970) socs. hosp. pub. relations dirs., Pub. Relations Soc. Am., Sigma Chi. Rotarian. Home: 1812 Albans St Houston TX 77005 Office: 6400 Lawndale St Houston TX 77023

VITOLS, MINTAUTS MICKEY, hosp. supt., psychiatrist; b. Liepaja, Latvia, July 25, 1921; s. Fricis and Sophia (Karlsons) V.; student Med. Sch. Latvia, 1944; Dr.Med., U. Hamburg (Germany), 1947; M.D. U. N.C., 1956; m. Edith Timermanis, May 15, 1943; children—Wilbur M., Sandra E. Came to U.S., 1949, naturalized, 1955. Resident psychiatry Center Research, Tng. and Treatment, dept. psychiatry U. N.C. Med. Sch., 1957-61; sr. med. officer Brit. Control Commn., Germany, 1947-49; staff physician, chief service John Umstead Hosp., Butner, N.C., 1949-55; supt. Cherry Hosp., Goldsboro, N.C., 1956—; mem. faculty U. N.C. Sch. Medicine 1961-&3, clin. asst. prof., 1963—; psychiat. cons. 4th TAC Hosp., S. J. AFB, 1965. Named Tarheel of Week, News and Observer Newspaper, Feb. 1958. Diplomat Am. Bd. Psychiatry, Fellow Am. Psychiat. Assn.; mem. Am., Wayne County, Seaboard med. assn., N.C. Neuropsychiat. Assn. (v.p.). Contbr. profl. jours. Address: Cherry Hosp Goldsboro NC 27530

VIZQUERRA ELQUERA, CARLOS, Peruvian diplomat. Consul gen. from Peru, Miami, Fla. Address: Seybold Bldg Miami FL 33132*

VIZZINI, SALVATORE, city ofcl.; b. Pitts., Nov. 29, 1926; s. Samuel Anthony and Lillian Antonette (Wolfe) V.; student pub. schs., Chgo. Law Enforcement Acad., Washington, 1953-54; m. Marginell DeLoach, Mar. 5, 1949; 1 son, Samuel J. Spl. agt. Dept. Air Force, 1951-53, Fed. Bur. Narcotics, Italy, France, Greece, Syria, Turkey, Lebanon, Thailand, Cuba, P.R., U.S., 1953-66; spl. cons. on organized crime U.S. Senate Select Com. To Investigate Organized Crime and Law Enforcement, 1968-69; chief police City of South Miami (Fla.), 1967—. Served with USMC, 1944-50; PTO; CBI. Recipient Spl. Services award U.S. Treasury Dept., 1956, 61, 62, 64, Outstanding Law Enforcement award 20th Dist. Jr. C. of C., 1967, Fla. Gov.'s medal for outstanding law enforcement, 1968. Mem. Internat. Assn. Chiefs Police, Fla. Police Chief's Assn., Dade County Chiefs Police. Home: 6231 SW 58th St South Miami FL 33143 Office: Chief of Police City Hall South Miami FL 33143

VLADIMIR, ANDREW NEAL, advt. exec.; b. New Rochelle, N.Y., Feb. 6, 1932; s. Irwin Alfred and Geraldine (Schulman) V.; grad. Hotchkiss Sch., 1949; student Trinity Coll., Dublin, 1949-50; B.A., Yale, 1954; m. Donna Lynne Perlman, Oct. 9, 1965; children—Allison, Andrea, Jennifer, Thomas Irwin, Alexander. Radio-TV dir. Gotham-Vladimir Advt., N.Y.C., 1954-55, v.p., 1958-60; sales mgr. WAPA-TV, San Juan, P.R., 1955-56; v.p., gen. mgr. Gotham-Vladimir P.R., 1956-58; dir. plans Ruder & Finn, N.Y.C., 1960-61; pres. Vladimir Internat., San Juan, P.R., 1962-65; v.p. Norman Craig & Kummel, N.Y.C., 1965-66; v.p. Kenyon & Eckhardt of Mexico, 1966-67; pres. Vladimir & Evans, Miami, 1967—. Mem. alumni bd. Yale, 1964-69. Mem. Alpha Delta Sigma. Clubs: Standard, Jockey, Advertising (dir.) (Miami); Yale (N.Y.C.). Author: Puerto Rico - The New Life, 1965; Ryder's Family Highway Guide - Handbook of Truck Drivers Secrets, 1969. Home: 421 Gerona St Coral Gables FL 33146 Office: 2801 Ponce de Leon Av Coral Gables FL 33134

VLADIMIR, MAR FRANZ-JOSEF KONRAD, clergyman, educator; b. Germany, July 15, 1914; s. Vladimir Nicolaevich Balnius and Anna (Krevic) Hohenstaufen; B.A., U. Prague, 1939; M.A., Cal. State Coll., 1954; LL.D., Philathea Coll., 1959; Ph.D., Glastenberg, 1963; m. Bernice F. Cannon, May 28, 1943. Ordained priest Catholic Apostolic Ch.; minister counseling Methodist Ch., 1955-57; counselor, 1957-66; prof. Orthodox Catholic Theol. Sem., 1967-70; prof. Academia Unita Divinatis, 1970—. Pres. Latin Am. Religious Crusade. Herald-marshal Internat. Coll. Arms Noblesse. Decorated Star and Cross Acad. Achievemant; knight Grand Cross Order Guadelupe; grand master Teutonic Order of Levant; chancellor sovereign Sacred Religious and Chivalric OrderSt. Thomas Acon. Home: Plaza Principal Malinalco Mexico

VOAS, ROBERT BRUCE, scientist, govt. ofcl.; b. Evanston, Ill., Feb. 21, 1928; s. William Henry and Florence (Williams) V.; Ph.B., U. Chgo., 1946; B.A., U. Cal. at Los Angeles, 1948, M.A., 1951, Ph.D., 1953; m. Carolyn Sylvia Merry, Apr. 11, 1953; children—David William, Jeanette Merry. Research psychologist U.S. Navy Electronics Lab., 1953-54; astronaut training officer NASA, 1958-64; dir. Life Sci. Lab., Litton, Inc., 1964-65; dir. field selection, dep. dir. office selection Peace Corps, 1965-68; chief Program Devel Div. OAC, Nat. Hwy. Safety Bur., Washington, 1968—. Served with USNR, 1954-61. Fellow Am. Psychol. Assn.; mem. Human Factors Soc. Episcopalian (vestryman 1967-69). Home: 1766 Proffit Rd Vienna VA 22180 Office: 6th and D Sts SW Washington DC 22180

VOCELLE, CHARLES, lawyer; b. St. Marys, Ga., Sept. 4, 1923; s. James T. and Mary Della (Schmitt) V.; A.A., U. Fla., 1947; J.D., U. Miami, 1950; m. Betty Paige Todd, Feb. 4, 1948; children—Charlene, Douglas. Admitted to Fla. bar, 1950; practiced law, Miami, Fla., 1950-60, Lake City, Fla., 1961—; spl. asst. atty. gen. Fla., 1955-60; lectr. U. Miami, 1950-52; pres. Bishop Motels, Inc., 1964—. Vol. lectr. Lake City Jr. Coll. and Forest Ranger Sch., 1962—. Mem. Com. of 100. Young Democratic nat. committeeman for Fla., 1953. Served with USMCR, 1942-45. Hon. life mem. Young Dem. Club of Dade County (pres. 1954), Fla. Pest Control Assn.; mem. Lake City, Columbia County, 3rd Jud. Circuit, Am. bar assns., Fla. Bar, Lake City-Columbia Country C. of C. (dir. 1965-66), Delta Theta Phi. Kiwanian (pres. 1965). Author of Fla. Pest Control Act of 1959. Home: 825 Evergreen Av Lake City FL 32055 Office: State Exchange Bank Bldg Lake City FL 32055

VOCELLE, JAMES THOMAS, lawyer; b. St. Marys, Ga., Jan. 10, 1897; s. Lucien M. and Jane Elizabeth (Vance) V.; LL.B., Atlanta Law Sch., 1916; m. Mary Della Schmitt, May 12, 1920; children—James Thomas, Mary Delena (Mrs. William D. Shettig), Charles Lucien, Louis B., Angelique (Mrs. Earnest A. Bednar), Marguerite (Mrs. George Siebert, Jr.). Admitted to Ga. bar, 1916, Fla. bar; pvt. practice, St. Mary's, Ga. 1916-24, Vero Beach, Fla., 1924—; city atty., Vero Beach. Parole commr., 1941-45; state beverage dir., 1945-49; chmn. Indsl. Commn., 1953-61. Served with U.S. Army, 1917-18. Recipient Vercelli medal, 1952. Mem. Am., Fla. bar assns., Am. Legion, Woodmen of World. Democrat. Roman Catholic. K.C. (4 deg.), Rotarian. Home: 2635 Carissa Dr Vero Beach FL 32960 Office: 1245 20th St Vero Beach FL 32960

VOERG, ALFRED HOWARD, food co. exec.; b. Cleve., Mar. 27, 1922; s. George H. and Ella Mae (McKenna) V.; ed. parochial and service schs.; m. Betty Lorraine Wintering, Jan. 15, 1944; children—Mary Ann (Mrs. Richard F. Kerr), James, John, Richard. Mgr. order dept. Pa. Rubber & Supply Co., Cleve., 1941-47; dir. purchases Dairypak, Inc., Cleve., 1947-62; dir. purchases milk carton div. Diamond Nat. Corp., Cleve., 1963; salesman Consol. Paper Co., Cleve., 1964-65; dir. purchases J. D. Jewell, Inc., Gainesville, Ga., 1966—; cons. milk carton div. Crossett Paper Co., 1962. Served with USNR, 1943-46. Home: 5315 River Mill Circle Marietta GA 30060 Office: 311 Green St Gainesville GA 30501

VOGEL, HENRY CHARLES, lawyer; b. East Chester, N.Y., Nov. 21, 1920; s. Henry William and Ann (Kealy) V.; LL.B., U. Miami, 1951. Admitted to Fla. bar, 1951; partner Morrissey & Vogel, Miami, 1951-65; pvt. practice law, Miami, 1965—; dir., legal adviser Leesburg Freezer Corp., (Fla.), 1953—, Auburndale Freezer Corp. (Fla.), 1954—, Plymouth Cold Storage, Inc., 1955—, Am. Materials Co. Fla., Miami, 1959—, Presto Paint Corp., Miami, 1961—. Rep., S. Fla. Vet. Med. Assn., Inc. Served in USMCR, 1941-46. Mem. Fla. Bar, Kappa Sigma, Delta Theta Phi. Democrat. Roman Catholic. K.C., Moose, Kiwanian. Home: 6780 SW 70th Av Miami FL 33143 Office: City Nat Bank Bldg Miami FL 33130

VOGEL, HENRY ELLIOTT, physicist, educator; b. Greenville, S.C., Sept. 16, 1925; s. Henry Lamprecht and Alice (Cousins) V.; B.S., Furman U., 1948; M.S., U. N.C., 1950, Ph.D., 1962; m. Barbara Argyle Gladden, Aug. 16, 1953; children—Alisabeth, Henry L. II, Barbara Alice, Susan Marie. Instr. dept. physics Clemson (S.C.) U., 1950-52, asst. prof. physics, 1952-59, asso. prof., 1959-65, prof., 1965-67, prof. and head physics dept., 1967-71, prof., dean Coll. Phys., Mathematical and Biol. Scis., 1971—. Served with AUS, 1943-45. Decorated Purple Heart. Mem. Am. Phys. Soc., Am. Vacuum Soc., Am. Assn. Physics Tchrs., Sigma Xi, Sigma Pi Sigma. Home: 207 Lark Circle Clemson SC 29631

VOGT, WELDON EDWIN, psychologist, educator; b. Cordell, Okla., Aug. 26, 1921; s. Edwin Eli and Bertha (Kosanke) V.; student Okla. A. and M. Coll., 1941; B.S., U. Corpus Christi, 1952; M.R.E., Southwestern Bapt. Theol. Sem., 1954, D.R.E., 1961, Ed.D., 1971; m. Helen Hardaway, Dec. 28, 1941; children—Janice Kay, Katherine Ann. Instr. advanced electronics N.A.T.T.C., Corpus Christi, 1943-46; instr. electronics U. Corpus Christi, 1947-52; vocational therapist USPHS Hosp., Ft. Worth, 1953-57; minister edn. Gambrell St. Bapt. Ch., Ft. Worth, 1957-62, Bellmead First Bapt. Ch., Waco, Tex., 1962-65; prof. psychology Ouachita Bapt. U., Arkadelphia, Ark., 1965—; psychologist Ark. Childrens Colony, 1969—; dir. Vol. Probation Officers Program, Arkadelphia. Cons. vocational guidance So. Bapt. Sunday Sch. Bd., Nashville. Served with USNR, 1943-46. Mem. Mental Health Assn., Assn. for Learning Disabilities. Club: Civitan (Arkadelphia). Home: 1080 Phelps Circle Arkadelphia AR 71923

VOGTLE, ALVIN WARD, JR., electric utility exec.; b. Birmingham, Ala., Oct. 21, 1918; s. Alvin Ward and Ollie (Stinger) V.; B.S., Auburn U. 1939; LL.B., U. Ala. 1941; m. Kathryn Drennen Apr. 20, 1945

Sec., Green Machinery Co., Plainview, Tex., 1941; sec., dep. county clk. Hale County, Plainview, 1942-52, county clk., 1952—. Active in Community Chest Drive. Recipient ribbons in fair competitions for art work. Mem. Plainview Bus. and Profl. Women's Club (pres. 1960-61, corr. sec. 1965-66, dir. 1970-72, 2d v.p. 1967-68, parliamentarian 1968-69, bull. editor), Art Guild Assn., Las Camaradas (pres. 1961-62, v.p. 1963-64, 67-68, sec.-treas. 1965-66), League Women Voters. Democrat. Presbyn. (sec. Sunday Sch.). Home: 508 W 10th St Plainview TX 79072 Office: Box M Plainview TX 79072

TUCKER, NORMAN TAYLOR, owner oil tool inspection co.; b. Mineola, Tex., Jan. 30, 1923; s. Uriah Taylor and Vera Ellen (Mitchell) T.; grad. high sch.; m. Betty Joyce Macoy, Oct. 3, 1942; children—Linda Joyce (Mrs. Robert Ernest Smith, Jr.), Patricia Sue. With Kaiser Shipbldg. Co., Portland, Ore., 1943-45; self-employed, Quitman, Tex., 1945-51; insp. Western Inspection Co., Odessa, Tex., 1951-55; dist. mgr. Sperry Western, Inc., Lafayette, La., 1955-62; owner La. Inspection Service, Lafayette, 1962—. Mem. Gulf Coast Oil Center Golf Assn. (dir.), Am. Petroleum Inst., Petroleum of Lafayette. Club: Acadian Hills Country (Lafayette). Home: 106 Maurice St Lafayette LA 70501 Office: PO Box 52351 Lafayette LA 70501

TUCKER, ROBERT CINNAMOND, librarian; b. Senatobia, Miss., Oct. 16, 1915; s. Benjamin A. and Bessie Agnes (Cinnamond) T.; A.B., La. State U., 1936, B.S. in L.S., 1937, M.A., 1941; Ph.D., U. N.C., 1958; m. Mary Kent Seagle, February 19, 1966. Asst. reference librarian La. State U. Library, 1937-40, asst. order librarian, 1941-42; librarian Furman U., 1947—, chmn. faculty, 1968-70. Served as tech. sgt., USAAF, 1942-45; exec. librarian XXIV Corps, Korea, 1946-47. Mem. A.L.A., S.C. (pres. 1956), S.E. library assns., Am. Assn. U. Profs., S.C. Hist. Assn. (sec.-treas. 1962-69), Phi Kappa Phi, Beta Phi Mu. Baptist. Home: 117 Broughton Dr Greenville SC 29609

TUCKER, ROYSTER MILTON, JR., telephone co. exec.; b. High Point, N.C., May 31, 1931; s. Royster Milton and Nell (Hayden) T.; B.S. in Elec. Engring., Duke, 1953; m. Martha Alice Renfro, June 19, 1954; children— Martha Nell, Royster Milton III. With North State Telephone Co., High Point, 1955—, v.p., 1959—. Served with USNR, 1953-55. Mem. U.S. (dir. 1968-71), N.C. (pres., dir. 1960—) ind. telephone assns., High Point C. of C. (dir. 1965). Rotarian. Home: 1223 Devonshire Av High Point NC 27260 Office: North State Telephone Co 111 N Main St High Point NC 27260

TUGGLE, CHARLES SUMMEY, dentist; b. Stone Mountain, Ga., Aug. 7, 1899; s. Hilliard Cherry and Lena Brantley (Hodo) T.; B.A., Emory U., 1916; D.D.S., Atlanta So. Dental Coll., 1919; m. Bertie Louise Britt, July 20, 1917; children—Charles Summey, James Britt, H. Cherry. Practice dentistry, Stone Mountain, 1919-70; pres. Tuggle Investments, 1925-70; chmn. Tuggle Found., 1940-70; dir. Tuggle Enterprises. Active city, county govtl. adminstrn. Decorated Congl. Merit award. Life mem. Am., Ga. dental assns. Mason. Home: 6150 E Ponce deLeon Av Stone Mountain GA 30083 Office: 5234 W Mountain St Stone Mountain GA 30083

TUGGLE, MARY STUART WILSON (MRS. HUGH PEARSON TUGGLE), clinician; b. Keysville, Va., Sept. 23, 1920; d. Monroe Osborne and Mary Stuart (Goss) Wilson; B.A., Randolph Macon Woman's Coll., 1941; M.D., U. Md., 1944; m. Hugh Pearson Tuggle, Sept. 17, 1947; children—Monroe, Stuart (Mrs. Roland C. Harkleroad), Sue, Sally. Rotating intern Garfield Meml. Hosp., Washington, 1945; resident in pediatrics Grady Hosp., Atlanta, 1946; gen. practice medicine, Keysville, 1946—; surgeon So. Ky., 1946-55; clinician Maternal and Child Health Clinic, Charlotte County, Va., 1946-71; asso. staff Southside Community Hosp., Farmville, Va. Med. examiner Charlotte County, Va., 1962—; med. adviser Charlotte County A.R.C., Selective Service Bd., Charlotte County. Chmn. scholarship bd. Keysville Woman's Club, 1958-71. Bd. dirs. United Fund, Charlotte County. Mem. Va., Charlotte County (pres. 1969-71), 4th Dist. med. socs., So. Med. Assn. Methodist (sec. adminstrv. bd. 1965-71). Mem. Order Eastern Star (matron 1963-64). Home: PO Box 297 Keysville VA 23947 Office: King St Keysville VA 23947

TUGGLE, RICHARD WILFRED, tobacco. co. exec.; b. Blackstone, Va., Feb. 23, 1917; s. Douglas Longstreet and Sue Edward (Armstrong) T.; B.A., Coll. William and Mary, 1938; m. Charlotte Scott Booker, July 19, 1941; children—Pattie A., Richard Wilfred, Edward A. With Universal Leaf Tobacco Co., Inc., Richmond, Va., 1946—, asst. traffic mgr., 1947-50, asst. treas., 1950-59, asst. v.p., 1959-67, v.p., 1967—; dir. Inta-Roto, Inc., Richmond. Bd. dirs. South Richmond-Chesterfield County YMCA, Ch. of Good Shepherd Sch. Served to capt. USAAF, 1942-46. Mem. Leaf Tobacco Exporters Assn. (exec. com. 1969-71), Phi Beta Kappa, Omicron Delta Kappa, Kappa Alpha. Episcopalian. Club: Willow Oaks Country (Richmond). Home: 5111 New Kent Rd Richmond VA 23225 Office: PO Box 25099 Richmond VA 23260

TULLOCH, GEORGE SHERLOCK, biologist; b. Bridgewater, Mass., Aug. 3, 1906; s. Douglas James and Irene (Settle) T.; B.S., U. Mass., 1928; M.S., Harvard, 1929, Ph.D., 1931; m. Dorothy Gorton Gooch, Sept. 17, 1931; children—George, James Douglas. Asst. entomologist Mass., 1930; entomologist Fairbanks Exploration Co. (Alaska), 1931; instr. Bklyn. Coll., 1932-35, asst. prof., 1935-44, asso. prof., 1944-52, prof., 1952-62, chmn. dept., 1962-65, prof. emeritus, 1965—; research biologist Arctic Aeromed. Lab., Seattle, 1965-67, Sch. Aerospace Medicine Brooks AFB, Tex., 1967-69; pres. G.S. Tulloch & Assos., San Antonio, 1970—. Chief entomologist Mass. Dept. Pub. Health, 1939; investigator Yellow Fever Lab., Rockefeller Found., Brazil, 1940-41. Served from lt. to lt. comdr. USNR, 1942-46; comdr. Res. Mem. A.A.A.S., Am. Soc. Parasitologists, Entomol. Soc. Am., Bklyn Entomol. Soc. Episcopalian. Mason. Club: Cambridge Entomology. Home: 4919 Pecan Grove San Antonio TX 78222 Office: 4614 Sinclair Rd San Antonio TX 78222

TULLOCH, LYNN HARDYN, mathematician; b. Belton, Tex., Apr. 23, 1907; s. John Henry and Annie Laurie (Andrews) T.; A.B., Baylor U., 1928; grad. study U. Tex., 1930-31, Ph.D., 1965; M.A., Brown U., 1932; grad. study U. Pitts., 1951. Instr. math. Baylor U., 1928-30; head dept. Victoria Ja. Coll., 1934-37, Ranger Jr. Coll., 1937-38, San Antonio Jr. Coll., 1938-46; asso. prof. S.W. Tex. State Coll., 1946-57, prof. 1957—. Served from pvt. to staff sgt. USAAF, 1942-45. Decorated Legion of Merit. NSF faculty fellow U. Tex., 1957-58. Mem. Am., Indian math. socs., Math. Assn. Am., A.A.A.S., Tex. Acad. Sci., Canadian Math. Congress, Soc. Indsl. and Applied Math., Math. Soc. France, Sigma Xi, Kappa Epsilon Alpha. Home: 804 Lyndon B Johnson Dr San Marcos TX 78666

TULLOS, FRANK NORMAN, research specialist; b. Eudora, Ark., Oct. 14, 1914; s. Matthew and Alla (Bonner) T.; B.S., La. State U., 1936; m. Goldie Maxine Haley, May 23, 1936; children—Bryan H., Norma L. (Mrs. Bobbie K. Culpepper), Nona B. Exploration geophysics Humble Oil Co., Houston, 1936-41, geophysics research, 1945-72, now sr. research specialist; applied physics research Johns Hopkins, 1941-45. Mem. I.E.E.E., Am. Acoustical Soc., Soc. Exploration Geophysics. Baptist. Contbr. to profl. publs. Patentee in field of electronics and acoustics. Home: 7435 Ashburn St Houston TX 77017

TULLOS, JOHN BAXTER, banker; b. Morton, Miss., Dec. 3, 1915; s. William Baxter and Mell (Roberts) T.; student Miss. Coll., 1934, Am. Inst. Bank, Jackson, Miss., 1936-40, Sch. Banking South, La. State U., 1955-57; m. Maxine Stone, Sept. 20, 1941. With First Nat. Bank, Jackson, 1935—, now exec. v.p., cashier; sec. First Capital Corp.; faculty Sch. Banking South La. State U.; dir. Bank of Wesson (Miss.). First pres. Miss. Jr. Bankers Assn.; mem. Miss. Valley World Trade Council, 1965—; mem. La.-Miss. Regional Export Expansion Council div. U.S. Dept. Commerce, 1967—; treas. Col. Money in Miss. Assn., 1965—. Chmn. budget com. United Givers Fund, 1964. Served with AUS, World War II. Mem. Miss. Bankers Assn. Methodist. Lion. Club: Jackson Country. Home: 5155 Wayneland Dr Jackson MS 39211 Office: PO Box 291 Jackson MS 39205

TULLY, CHRISTOPHER CARL, JR., dentist; b. Charleston, W.Va., May 30, 1939; s. Christopher Carl and Virginia Bell (Tully) T.; B.S. in Chemistry, Morris Harvey Coll., 1962; M.S. in Biochemistry, W.Va. U., 1965, D.D.S., 1969; m. Judith Ann Fox, Aug. 29, 1959; children— Christopher Carl III, Karen Lynn, Deborah Ann. Practice dentistry, Morgantown, W.Va., 1969; North Augusta, S.C., 1969—. Chmn., North Augusta area Nat. Childrens' Dental Health Week, 1972; dental coordinator United Fund, 1970-71; mem. North Augusta Area Hosp. Planning Com., 1971, Alcohol and Drug Referral Com., 1971; chmn. North Augusta Am. Cancer Soc., 1970-72; chmn. judges com. Miss North Augusta-Miss S.C., 1970; coach Optimist Basketball League, 1969-71, Football League, 1970, Baseball League, 1969-71. Mem. Am., S.C. dental assns., Augusta Dental Soc., W.Va. Dental Alumni Assn., Jr. C. of C., Sigma Nu, Delta Sigma Delta. Republican. Methodist. Lion. Club: North Augusta Booster. Home: 1864 Lodgepole Av North Augusta SC 29841 Office: 501 A East Martintown Rd North Augusta SC 29841

TUNSTALL, GEORGE LUCILLE HAWKINS, educator; b. Thurber, Tex., Jan. 17, 1922; d. Harry and Ruth (Martin) Hawkins; B.S., U. Colo., 1943; M.S., Wayne State U., 1959, Ph.D., 1963; m. William Neal Brown, Jan. 19, 1944 (div. Mar. 1946); m. 2d, Edward Haney Tunstall, June 19, 1947 (div. Apr. 1962); children—Ruth Neal, Leslie Diane. Med. tech. U. Colo. Med. Sch., Denver, 1943-45, Presbyn. Hosp. Colo., Denver, 1946-47, Evang. Deaconess Hosp., Detroit, 1950-52, Sinai Hosp. Detroit, 1952-55, Brent Gen. Hosp., Detroit, 1955-58; research teaching asst. biology dept. Wayne State U., 1958-62; asst. prof. Delta Coll., University Center, Mich., 1963-65; asso. prof. Saginaw Valley Coll., University Center, 1965-67; chmn. biology dept. Bishop Coll., Dallas, 1967-71; asso. dir. United Bd. for Coll. Devel., Atlanta, 1971—. Ednl. cons. Saginaw (Mich.) C. of C., 1966-67, Nat., State, Regional confs., N.A.A.C.P., 1965-67. Active Girl Scouts Am., 1952-62; edn. chmn. Mich. Conf. N.A.A.C.P. brs., 1964-67, pres. Bay City br. 1965-67); exec. sec. Human Relations Commn. Bay City, 1965-67; trustee Mich. Tb. Respiratory Disease Assn., 1965-67; mem. personnel com. YWCA, 1966-67, mem. nominating com. exec. bd., 1967; exec. com. Bay City chpt. Ship Hope, 1966-67. Mem. Bay City Bus. Profl. Women's Club, Am. Soc. Microbiology, Am. Soc. Clin. Pathologists, Mich. Acad. Sci. Arts Letters, A.A.A.S., Am. Inst. Biol. Sci., Am. Soc. for Cell Biology, N.Y. Acad. Scis., Am. Assn. U. Women, Am. Assn. U. Profs., Am. Acad. Polit. Social Sci., Sigma Xi, Alpha Kappa Alpha. Methodist. Contbr. articles profl. jours. Home: 2209 Campbellton Rd SW Atlanta GA 30311

TUNSTILL, GARLAND ALBERT, cons. in finance and govt. relations; b. Eastland County, Tex., Nov. 16, 1901; s. William Austin and Eula (Compton) T.; LL.B., Cumberland U., Lebanon, Tenn., 1923; m. Clover Dell Hill, Feb. 23, 1937 (dec. July 1972). Admitted to Tex. bar, 1924; practice law, Ft. Worth, 1924-26; ind. oil operator, Houston, 1926-40; bus. economist and entrepreneur, 1941-47; financial and govt. relations cons., 1948—. Precinct chmn. Republican party, 1954—. Mem. com. on sociol. conditions in South, Tulane U. Bd. dirs., cons. Movimiento Pro Federacion Americana. Mem. Tex. Bar Assn. Christian Scientist. Author: (essay) Can the Monroe Doctrine Bring Peace and Prosperity to the Americans (in library of James Monroe Meml. Found., Fredericksburg, Va.). Home: 2017 Esperanza Houston TX 77023 Office: PO Box 12846 Houston TX 77017

TURBEVILLE, GUS, coll. pres.; b. Turbeville, S.C., Jan. 20, 1923; s. William Jasper and Ila Lucile (Morris) T.; B.A., Vanderbilt U., 1944; M.A., La. State U., 1946; Ph.D., Mich. State U., 1948; m. Joanne Beverly Johnson, June 7, 1950; children—David Baxter, William Jackson, II, Sara Ellen. Head dept. sociology U. Minn., Duluth, 1948-53; pres. Northland Coll., Ashland, Wis., 1953-61; pres. Hurkos Found., Waukesha, Wis., 1961-62; chmn. dept. sociology and anthropology U. Wis., Superior, 1962-69; pres. Coker Coll., Hartsville, S.C., 1969—. Bd. dirs. Wis. Found. Ind. Colls., 1955-61, S.C. Found. Ind. Colls., 1969—; trustee St. Joseph's Hosp., Superior, Wis., Upper Middle West Regional Ednl. Lab., Mpls. Served with AUS, 1943. Named 1 of Nation's 10 Outstanding Young Men, U.S. Jaycees, 1958. Mem. Am. Sociol. Assn., So. Sociol. Soc., Nat. Geographic Assn., Psi Chi, Pi Gamma Mu, Kappa Alpha. Mem. Soc. Friends. Rotarian. Author (with T. Lynn Smith) Social Problems, 1955; (with Francis A. Soper) If you Smoke, What Have You, 1970. Contbr. articles to profl. and scientific jours. Home: 222 E Home Av Hartsville SC 29550

TURK, JAMES CLINTON, lawyer, state senator; b. Ronaoke, Va., May 3, 1923; s. James Alexander and Geneva (Richardson) T.; A.B., Roanoke Coll., 1949; LL.B., Washington and Lee U., 1952; m. Barbara Duncan, Aug. 21, 1954 children—Ramona Leah, James Clinton, Robert Malcolm Duncan, Mary Elizabeth, David Michael. Admitted to Va. bar, 1952; mem. firm Dalton, Poff & Turk, Radford, Va., 1952—; dir. 1st & Mchts. Nat. Bank of Radford; mem. Va. Senate, 1959—, minority leader. Trustee Radford Community Hosp., 1959—. Served with AUS, 1943-46. Mem. Order of Coif, Phi Beta Kappa, Omicron Delta Kappa. Baptist (deacon). Home: 1002 Walker Dr Radford VA 24141 Office: First and Mchts Nat Bank Bldg Radford VA 24141

TURLINGTON, RALPH D., state representative; b. Gainesville, Fla., Oct. 5, 1920; B.S., B.A., U. Fla.; M.B.A., Harvard, 1942; m. Ann Gellerstedt; children—Donald, Katherine. Engaged in ins. bus.; mem. Fla. Ho. of Reps., 1950—, chmn. finance and taxation com. Del. Democratic Nat. Conv., 1968. Served with AUS, World War II, Korea. Mem. Am. Legion, V.F.W. Baptist. Elk. Club: Exchange. Home: 117 NE 16th Av Gainesville FL 32601*

TURNAGE, AARON CALHOUN, JR., san. engr.; b. Farmville, N.C., Jan. 30, 1928; s. Aaron Calhoun and Maybell (Flanagan) T.; B.C.E., N.C. State Coll., 1952; m. Vivian Taylor, Feb. 10, 1951; children—Sheila, Michael Aaron, Alison. Asst. city engr. Rocky Mount, N.C., 1952-53; city engr., Jacksonville, N.C., 1954-55, city mgr. Selma, N.C., 1956-58; regional san. engr. N.C. Dept. of Water Resources, Greenville, 1958—. Served with USNR, 1946-48. Mem. Water Pollution Control Fedn. Mem. Christian Ch. Democrat. Home: RFD 2 Box 54 Farmville NC 27828 Office: PO Box 499 Greenville NC 27834

TURNBULL, JAMES FRANKLIN, realtor; b. New Orleans, June 15, 1920; s. James Franklin and Pauline (Lefson) T.; B.A., Tulane U., 1940; m. Helen Ferrandou, Feb. 9, 1942; children—Carol Helen (Mrs. Redditt), Catherine Ann (Mrs. David Snyder). Realtor, Gertrude Gardner, Inc., New Orleans, 1936—, v.p., appraiser, auctioneer, 1965—; head real estate dept. Smither & Co., 1963-65. Head real estate dept. Tulane U., New Orleans, 1968—. Served with USNR, 1941-46, 51-53. Mem. S.A.R., Am. Inst. Real Estate Appraisers (Residential Mem. designation 1968, dir. appraisal div. real estate bd. 1969—, chmn. 1971-72), Soc. Real Estate Appraisers (Sr. Real Property Appraiser designation 1972), Nat. Assn. Real Estate Bds., Nat. Inst. Real Estate Brokers, La. Realtors Assn., Real Estate Bd. New Orleans, Real Estate Bd. Jefferson. Club: Pendennis (sec. 1969-70). Home: 4527 S Tonti St New Orleans LA 70125 Office: 7934 Maple St New Orleans LA 70118

TURNBULL, WILLIAM S., lawyer; b. Richmond, Va., Mar. 15, 1924; s. Nathaniel and Marguerite (Massie) T.; student U. Fla., 1946-48; LL.B., John B. Stetson U., 1949; m. Shirley Eileen Wells, Sept. 4, 1948; children—Laurie Eileen, William S. Admitted to Fla. bar; precinct committeeman Orange County Democratic Exec. Com. (Fla.), 1954-66, chmn., 1963-67; mem. Fla. Dem. Exec. Com., 1966, chmn. 5th dist.; del. Dem. Nat. Conv., 1968, 72; Dem. nat. committeeman, Fla., 1968-72. Served to ensign, USNR, 1942-45, lt. comdr. Res. ret. Mem. Am., Fla. (chmn. real property sect.), Orange County bar assns., Sigma Alpha Epsilon. Address: 125 South Ct 32801 Orlando FL 32800

TURNER, AARON LYNN, educator; b. Seagraves, Tex., May 2, 1931; s. John Karr and Effie Beatrice (Smith) T.; student Tex. Technol. Coll., 1948-50; B.A., Harding Coll., 1956; M.Ed., U. Ark., 1958, Ed.D., 1963; postgrad. (fellow) U. Chgo., 1963; m. Doris Alene Combs, July 10, 1953; children—Stephen Lynn, Laura Ann. Supt. schs., St. Paul, Ark., 1956-59; tchr. jr. high sch., Hobbs, N.M., 1959-61; grad. asst. U. Ark., 1961-62; coordinator off-campus centers, 1962-66; prof. ednl. adminstrn., dir. East Tex. Sch. Study Council, East Tex. State U., Commerce, 1966—. Mem. exec. com. Asso. Pub. Sch. Systems, 1967-69, Nat. Sch. Deve. Council, 1969—, vice chmn. 1970-71. Served with USNR, 1951-54. East Tex. State U. faculty research grantee, 1969-70. Mem. N.E.A., Am., Tex. assns. sch. adminstrs., Tex. Tchrs. Assn., Tex. Assn. Coll. Tchrs., Phi Delta Kappa. Mem. Ch. of Christ (elder 1968—), Mng. editor: Catalyst for Change, 1971. Home: 2826 Laurel Lane Commerce TX 75428

TURNER, BESSYE LEE TOBIAS, educator; b. Liberty, Miss.; d. Aaron and Bessie (Smith) Tobias; A.B., Rust Coll., 1939; M.A. in English, Columbia, 1954, M.A. in Speech, 1964. Tchr. English, Burglund High Sch., 1939-44; clk. Internal Revenue, 1945-48; tchr. English drama coach Alexander High Sch., 1950-55; asst. prof. English, dir. dramatics Alcorn A. and M. Coll., 1955-62; asst. prof. English, So. U., Baton Rouge, 1962-63; asst. prof. English and Speech Tex. So. U., Houston, 1963-68; asst. prof. Miss. Valley State Coll., 1968—. Cons., Phelph Stokes Project, Natchez, Miss., 1955-58; co-ordinator Communication Workshop, Natchez City Sch. System, 1961-62; cons. English and lit. Miss. Tchrs. Assn.; drama judge, cons. Big Eight Dramatic Tournament, 1958-62. Recipient Speech award R.C. Speech Club, Holly Springs, Miss., 1938; certificate merit La Librae, Centro Studi EScambi Internazionali e Accademia Leonardo da Vinci, XXI Rassegna Intenazionaili D'Arte, 1972. Mem. Am. Assn. U. Profs., N.E.A., Speech Assn. Am., Nat. Council Tchrs. of English, Conf. Coll. Composition and Communication, Smithsonian Assos., Centro Studi e Scambi Internat. (hon. rep.), Alpha Kappa Alpha, Kappa Delta Pi. Mem. Order Eastern Star. Methodist. Contbr. poems: La Librae: An Anthology of Poetry for Living, 1969, Quaderni di Poesia, 1971, 72. Home: 829 Wall St McComb MS 39648

TURNER, CARROLL GLENN, communications exec.; b. El Campo. Tex., June 17, 1909; s. Earl Kirby and Ethel (Van Cleve) T.; E.E., Finlay Engr., 1933; m. Mary W. Turner; children—Robert W. and Carolyn (Mrs. Malford Hierholzer) (twins). Illumination and elec. engr. Kansas City Power & Light Co., 1931-46; regional mgr. Gen. Electric Co., Kansas City, Mo., 1946-52; v.p., gen. mgr. Communications Engring. Co., Houston, 1952-63; pres. Radio Radio Dispatch, Inc. (Tex.), 1963-68, dir.; pres. Mobile Radio, Inc. Served with AUS, 1942-46; lt. col. Res. Decorated Bronze Star medal. Registered profl. engr. Mem. I.E.E.E. (sr.), Houston Engring. and Sci. Soc. Mason (Shriner). Inventor electronic device for controlling linear voltage. Home: 1412 Azalea Dr Rosenberg TX 77471 Office: 208 S Houston St Wharton TX 77488

TURNER, CHARLES FRANKLIN, chem. co. exec.; b. Lake City, S.C., Mar. 26, 1939; s. James Alexander and Alice (Ballentine) T.; B.A., Furmar U., 1962; m. Joanne Elizabeth Greene, June 11, 1960; 1 son, Charles Franklin. Marketing mgr. Cryovac div. W.R. Grace Co., plastics, food packaging, Duncan, S.C., 1969—; dir. Turner Lumber Co., LeMoyen, La., Served with AUS, 1962-64. Mem. S.A.R. (state pres. 1971-72), Travelers Rest Jr. C. of C. (pres. 1968-69). Home: Route 3 Greenville SC 29609 Office: PO Box 464 Duncan SC 29334

TURNER, ELBERT DAYMOND, JR., educator; b. Gainesville, Fla., Nov. 15, 1915; s. Elbert D. and Lena (Baird) T.; B.A. with honors, Davidson Coll., 1937; M.A., U. N.C., 1939, Ph.D., 1949; m. Irma Aboy, Aug. 2, 1945; children—Carmen Irma (Mrs. Joseph Lipe), Ana Maria, Victoria, Elbert D. III, Rosa. Teaching fellow U. N.C., 1937-38, part-time instr. 1938-39; instr. Ga. Tchrs. Coll., 1939-41; instr. Spanish, U. N.C., 1946-49; asst. prof. U. Del., 1949-58, dir. lang. lab., 1955-66, asso. prof. modern langs., 1958-61, prof. modern languages, 1961-66; prof., chmn. dept. fgn. langs. U. N.C., Charlotte, 1966-71, dir. grad. studies, 1970—; vis. prof. NDEA Inst., Utah State U., 1963-64, Utah State U., Oaxaca, Mexico, summer 1966; cons. pub. schs. Del., 1951-52, 56, Delaware Dept. Pub. Instrn., 1959-66, Memphis State U., 1967-70, Profl. Child Care Centers, Inc., 1969—. Chmn. test devel. Nat. Spanish Exams., 1965—. Served from 1st lt. to lt. col. AUS, 1941-46; col. Res. Fellow Southeastern Inst. Medieval and Renaissance Studies, 1968. Mem. Am. Assn. Tchrs. Spanish and Portuguese, Assn. for Latin-Am. Studies, Am. Council on Teaching Fgn. Langs., Modern Lang. Assn. Am., S. Atlantic Modern Lang. Assn., Instituto de Literature Iberoamericana, Phi Beta Kappa, Delta Sigma Pi, Eta Sigma Phi, Sigma Phi Epsilon. Republican. Presbyn. Club: Charlotte Swimming. Author: Gonzalo Fernandez de Ovideo y Valdes: An Annotated Bibliography, 1967. Contbr. to various profl. publs. Mem. adv. bd. N.C. Fgn. Lang. Tchr., 1970—. Home: 233 Fenton PL Charlotte NC 28207

TURNER, ERNEST CRAIG, educator; b. West Jefferson, N.C., June 15, 1927; s. Ernest Craig and Martha Louise (Cooper) T.; B.S., Clemson U., 1948; Ph.D., Cornell U., 1953; m. Janet Rae Reed, Aug. 1, 1953; children—Marilyn Layton, Edgar Craig, Douglas Reed. Asso. prof. entomology Va. Poly. Inst. and State U., Blacksburg, 1953-65, prof. entomology, 1965—. Served with AUS, 1946-47. Home: 1413 Locust Blacksburg VA 24060

TURNER, GEORGE LUTHER, tobacco co. exec.; b. Fall Creek, Va., July 20, 1899; s. Edgar Hayden and Birdie Katherine (Carter) T.; m. Wilson Hodges, Sept. 11, 1926; children—Sarah Katherine (Mrs. Benjamin W. Mears, Jr.), Helen (Mrs. W. Tayloe Murphy, Jr.). With

(dec.); children—Kathryn D., Anne Moore (Mrs. Bryan Baldwin), Alvin Ward, III; m. 2d, Rachael Giles, 1966; children—Bryant Wade, William Patrick, Rachael Giles, Robert Jackson. Admitted to Ala. bar, 1941; asso. Martin, Vogtle, Balch & Bingham and predecessor firms, Birmingham, 1945-50, mem. firm, 1950-62; exec. v.p., dir. Ala. Power Co., 1962-65; pres. So. Electric Generating Co., 1960-62, dir., 1962—; exec. v.p. The So. Co., 1966-69, pres., dir., 1969—; chmn. bd., dir. So. Services Inc.; dir. Seaboard Coast Line Industries, Inc., Protective Life Ins. Co., Ala., Ga., Gulf, Miss. power cos. Vice chmn. Edison Electric Inst., mem. exec. com. Power Systems Coordination div., chmn. budget com., mem. exec. com.; mem. regional adv. com. Fed. Power Commn.; bd. visitors Emory U. Trustee Com. for Econ. Devel., Tax Found. Served from 2d lt. to capt. USAAF, 1941-45. Mem. Newcomen Soc. Eng., Newcomen Soc. N.Am., Soc. Colonial Wars, The Conf. Bd., S.A.R., Ala. Hist. Assn., Am. Legion, Sigma Nu. Episcopalian. Clubs: The Club, Downtown, Birmingham Country (Birmingham); Piedmont Driving, Peachtree Golf, Capital City (Atlanta); Augusta Nat. Golf. Home: Batesville Rd Route 2 Woodstock GA 30188 Office: 64 Perimeter Center E Atlanta GA 30346

VOIGT, EDDIE DARRELL, city ofcl.; b. Lockhart, Tex., Aug. 5, 1942; s. Aubrey Lee and Delta (Williams) V.; B.B.A., S.W. Tex. U., 1964; m. Peggy Wilson, Mar. 27, 1964; children—Dee Wilson, Vicki Lee. Prodn. mgr. Central Soya Tex., 1964-65; asst. city mgr., Lockhart, 1965-67, city mgr., 1967—. Partner Lockhart Bus. Properties, 1969—. Mem. S. Tex., (dir. 1970-71), Lockhart, Lockhart Jr. (v.p. 1968-69) chambers commerce. Lion. Club: Business Men's (Lockhart). Home: 912 Vogel Dr Lockhart TX 78644 Office: 308 W San Antonio St Lockhart TX 78644

VOITLE, ROBERT BROWN, educator; b. San Francisco, July 20, 1919; s. Robert Brown and Nancy (Hoag) V.; A.B., Harvard, 1949, A.M., 1950, Ph.D., 1954; m. Dorothy Morris, July 10, 1946; children—Jane Sybilla, Nancy Elena. Teaching fellow Harvard, 1951-52; instr. English U. N.C., Chapel Hill, 1952-53, asst. prof., 1954-58, asso. prof., 1959-63, prof., 1964—. Served with AUS, 1944-46. Mem. Internat. Soc. 18th Century Studies, Milton Soc. Am., Johnson Soc. London, Modern Language Assn. Am., Conf. British Studies. Club: Sports Car Am. Author: Samuel Johnson the Moralist, 1961. Home: 307 Country Club Rd Chapel Hill NC 27514

VOKES, HAROLD ERNEST, univ. prof.; b. Windsor, Ont., Can., June 27, 1908; s. Albert John and Beatrice Mary (Howlett) V.; A.B., Occidental Coll., 1931, Ph.D., U. of Calif., 1935; m. Gertrude Dutton Lawrence, Mar. 1, 1932 (div. 1958); children—Gertrude Ann, Rosina B., Frances E., Arthur W.; m. 2d, Emily Hoskins, 1959. Asst. geologist, Ill. State Geol. Survey, 1936-37, asst. curator, 1937-41; asso. curator, invertebrate paleontology Am. Museum of Natural History, 1941-43; sr. geologist U.S. Geol. Survey, 1943-45; asso. prof. geology Johns Hopkins U., 1945-46, prof., 1946-56; prof., dept. geology Tulane U., 1956—; geol. cons. MSA, Philippines, 1952-53. Mem. Internat. Commn. on Zool. Nomenclature, 1944—; Guggenheim Meml. Found. fellow, 1940. Fellow Geol. Soc. Am., Paleontological Soc. (pres. 1951), Internat. Paleontological Union; mem. Am. Assn. Petroleum Geologists, Malacological Soc. London, Phi Beta Kappa, Sigma Xi. Contbr. numerous articles on geology and paleontology. Home: 2501 Audubon St New Orleans LA 70125 Office: Tulane U New Orleans LA 70118

VOLCKER, PAUL A., govt. ofcl.; b. Cape May, N.J., Sept. 5, 1927; s. Paul A. and Alma Louise (Klippel) V.; A.B. summa cum laude, Princeton, 1949; M.A., Harvard, 1951; student London (Eng.) Sch. Econs., 1951-52; m. Barbara Marie Bahnson, Sept. 11, 1954; children— Janice, James. Economist, Fed. Res. Bank N.Y., 1952-57, Chase Manhattan Bank, 1957-61; with Treasury Dept., 1961-65, dep. under sec. monetary affairs, 1963-65; v.p. dir. planning Chase Manhattan Bank, N.Y.C., 1965-68; under sec. of treasury for monetary affairs, 1969—. Dir., Fed. Nat. Mortgage Assn., Overseas Pvt. Investment Corp. Mem. Council on Fgn. Relations. Home: 2936 Cleveland Av NW Washington DC 20008 Office: 3312 Main Treasury Bldg Washington DC 20220

VOLK, WESLEY AARON, educator; b. Mankato, Minn., Nov. 23, 1924; s. Albert Lee and Della (Buelow) V.; B.S., U. Wash., 1948, M.S., 1949, Ph.D., 1951; m. Rose Marjorie Keller, Feb. 24, 1945 (dec. July 1966); children—Pamela Lee, Bradley George; m. 2d, Joan Ryan Franke, Jan. 25, 1969; stepchildren—Fritz Royden Franke, Kurt August Franke. Asst. prof. microbiology Sch. Medicine, U. Va., Charlottesville, 1951-56, asso. prof., 1956-64, prof., 1964—. Served with USNR, 1943-46. Fellow Am. Acad. Microbiology; mem. Am. Soc. Biol. Chemists, Am. Soc. Microbiology. Home: 1706 Yorktown Dr Charlottesville VA 22901

VOLKER, JOSEPH FRANCIS, univ. pres.; b. Elizabeth, N.J., Mar. 9, 1913; s. Francis Joseph and Rose G. (Hennessy) V.; D.D.S., Ind. U., 1936; D.Sc., 1970; A.B., U. Rochester, Carnegie fellow in dentistry, 1938, M.S., 1939, Ph.D., 1941; D.Sc., U. Med. Scis., Thailand, 1967, U. Ala., 1970, Ind. U., 1970; D. honoris causa, Lund U., Sweden, 1968; m. Juanita Berry, Feb. 6, 1937; children—Joseph Francis, Juanita Ann, John Berry. Dental intern Mountainside Hosp., Montclair, N.J., 1936-37; asst. prof. biochemistry U. Rochester, 1941-42; prof. clin. dentistry Dental Sch., Tufts Coll., 1942-47, dean, 1947-48; dean Sch. Dentistry, U. Ala., 1948-62, v.p. health affairs, 1962-68, exec. v.p., 1968-69, pres., 1969—, dir. research and grad. study Med. Center, 1955-65; dir. Ariz. Med. Sch. Study, 1960-61; dental specialist to Thailand, 1951; mem. Unitarian Service Com.'s med. teaching mission to Czechoslovakia, 1946, Germany, 1948. Decorated Order of White Lion (Czechoslovakia); comdr. Order of Crown (Thailand); Order of Falcon (Iceland); fellow in dental surgery Royal Coll. Surgeons Eng., 1962; recipient Hinman Distinguished Service medal, 1970. Mem. Soc. Exptl. Biology and Medicine, Am. Dental Assn., Am. Chem. Soc., Internat. Assn. Dental Research, Inst. of Medicine, Nat. Acad. Scis., Sigma Xi, Omicron Kappa Upsilon, Alpha Omega Alpha. Home: 4101 Altamont Rd Birmingham AL 35213 Office: University Station Birmingham AL 35233

VOLMAR, PETER JON, architect; b. Northport, L.I., N.Y., Feb. 6, 1938; s. Paul George and Lucille Grace (Bailey) V.; B.Arch., U. Fla., 1962 ; m. Judith Elliott, Aug. 25, 1958 (div.); children—Jon Robie, Julie Ellen. Designer Harvard & Jolly, 1961-63; asso. architect C. Randolph Wedding & Assos., 1963-71; pvt. practice architecture, St. Petersburg, Fla., 1971—; archtl. cons. St. Petersburg Waterfront Re-devel., 1964; works include 1st Fed. Savs. & Loan Assn. Annex, Sheen residence, John Knox Apartments, Fla. Power Corp. Hdqrs. Mem. St. Petersburg Young Reps. Club. Recipient award A.I.A., 1961, 64, county archtl. awards, 1969, 71. Mem. A.I.A., St. Petersburg Assn. Architects, Archtl. Prescast Assn., Gargoyle. Presbyn. Club: St. Petersburg Yacht. Home and office 11440 1st St E Treasure Island FL 33706

VOLPE, JOHN ANTHONY, sec. of transp.; b. Wakefield, Mass., Dec. 8, 1908; s. Vito and Filomena (Benedetto) V.; grad. Wentworth Inst., 1930; hon. degrees St. Michael's Coll., Northeastern U., Suffolk U., Stonehill Coll., Merrimack Coll., Am. Internat. Coll., Lowell Tech. Inst., Boston U., Southeastern Mass. Tech. Inst., U. Mass., Anna Maria Coll., Brandeis U., Butler U., Salem State Coll., L.I. U., Calvin Coolidge Coll. Liberal Arts, Lesley Coll., Oblate Coll., So. U., Niagara U., U. So. Cal., Ohio State U.; m. Jennie Benedetto, June 18, 1934; children—Jean (Mrs. Roger H. Rotondi), John Anthony. Founder, John A. Volpe Constrn. Co., Malden, Mass., 1933, pres., 1933-60, chmn. bd., 1960-69; mem. Mass. Commn. Pub. Works, 1953-56; fed. hwy. adminstr., 1956-57; gov. Mass., 1961-63, 65-69; U.S. sec. of transp., 1969—. Dep. chmn. Mass. Republican Com., 1950-53. Treas., adv. bd. Don Orione Home For Aged, East Boston. Served to lt. comdr. USNR, 1943-45. Decorated knight of Malta, knight grand cross Order Merit Republic Italy, knight comdr. with star Equestrian Order Holy Sepulchre Jerusalem; recipient People to People Town Affiliation award, 1966; named Constrn.'s Man of Year, 1970. Mem. Soc. Am. Mil. Engrs. (past pres.), Asso. Gen. Contractors Am. (past. pres.), Mass. Asso. Gen. Contractors (past pres.), Greater Boston C. of C. (past pres.), Sons Italy in Am., Am. Legion, Nat. Govs. Conf. (chmn. 1967-68). Elk. Home: Watergate East Washington DC 20037 Office: Secretary of Transportation 400 7th St SW Washington DC 20590

VOLPE, ROBERT WOODARD, rig and equipment mfg. co. exec.; b. Chgo., Dec. 3, 1923; s. Lewis Philip and Inez (McGinity) V.; student Knox Coll., 1941-43; B.S. in E.E., Northwestern U., 1947; m. Jean Ellyn Manley, May 31, 1947; children—Catherine, Barbara, Robert, Patricia. Engr., product planner Gen. Electric Co., Erie, Pa., 1947-67; mgr. product planning Unit Rig & Equipment Co., Tulsa, 1967—, asst. to pres., 1969—. Served with AUS, 1943-45. Recipient Cordiner award Gen. Electric Co., 1965. Mem. I.E.E.E. (mining industry com. 1968—), Soc. Automotive Engrs., Am. Inst. Mining, Metall. and Petroleum Engrs. Home: 3728 S Braden Pl Tulsa OK 74135 Office: PO Box 3107 Tulsa OK 74101

VOLTA, ARMAND JOSEPH, govt. ofcl.; b. N.Y.C., July 30, 1915; s. Carlo and Erminia (Giacchero) V.; B.A., Bklyn. Coll., 1937, M.A., 1941; m. Emma Massoni, Apr. 20, 1947; children—Richard, Carlo, Armand. Instr. math. Bklyn. Coll., 1936-39; jr. marine engr., naval architect U.S. Maritime Commn., Dept of Commerce, Washington, 1942-43, 46-47; mathematician Navy David Taylor Model Basin, Carderock, Md., 1947-50; dir. computation office U.S. Navy, Oceanographic Office, Washington, 1950—. Served with USNR, 1943-46. Home: 3300 Roslyn Av Washington DC 20028 Office: US Navy Oceanographic Office Washington DC 20390

VON AVERY, HENRY LINTON, govt. ofcl.; b. Little Rock, Aug. 17, 1910; B.A., U. Minn., 1932; M.Ed., St. Louis U., 1949; m. Janice Y. Robinson, June 21, 1961. Supr. surveys and adult edn. Urban League, St. Louis, 1933-34; caseworker Citizens Comm. on Relief and Unemployment, St. Louis, 1934-35; sr. tchr. W.P.A., Kinloch, Mo., 1936-38; sr. interviewer Mo. State Employment Service, St. Louis, 1938-41; sr. employment security dep. U.S. Employment Service, St. Louis, 1942-44; information officer O.P.A., St. Louis, 1944-46; dir. community orgn. Urban League, St. Louis, 1946-56; chief of relocation sect., community services supr., housing project mgr. St. Louis Housing and Land Clearance Authorities, 1956-63; employemnt security adv. Bur. of Employment Security, Chambersburg, Pa., 1963; wage hour adv. U.S. Dept. of Labor, Washington, 1964, regional indsl. tng. adv., St. Louis, 1965-68, nat. indsl. tng. adv., Washington, 1968—. Mem. Acad. Certified Social Workers, Nat. Assn. Social Workers, Am. Acad. Polit. and Social Sci., Polit. Sci. Assn., N.A.A.C.P., Am. GI Forum, Alpha Phi Alpha. Home: 7400 9th St Washington DC 20012 Office: 14th and Constitution Sts Washington DC 20210

VON BRAUN, WERNHER, engr.; b. Wirsitz, Eastern Germany, Mar. 23, 1912; s. Baron Magnus and Emmy (von Quistorp) Von B.; student Inst. Tech., Zurich, Switzerland, 1930; B.S., Inst. Tech., Berlin, Germany, 1932; Ph.D., U. Berlin, 1934; D.Sc. U. Ala., St. Louis U., U. Pitts., Canisius Coll., Clark U., Tech. U., Berlin, Germany, Nat. U. Cordoba, Argentina, Fla. Inst. Tech., Wagner Coll., Emory U., Ia. Wesleyan Coll., Butler U., Bradley U., S.D., Rollins Coll.; LL.D., U. Chattanooga, Pepperdine U., Pa. Mil. Coll., Adelphi Coll., William Jewell Coll., Iona Coll.; Ph.D. in Space Sci. (hon.), Fla. Inst. Tech.; m. Maria Von Quistorp, Mar. 1, 1947; children—Iris, Margrit, Peter. Came to U.S., 1945, naturalized, 1955. Asst. to prof. Oberth, 1930, experimenting with small liquid fuel rocket motors, Berlin-Ploetzensee; founding mem. Rocket Field Berlin, small rocket exptl. sta., sponsored and financed by German Rocket Soc., 1930; liquid fuel rocket expert German Ordnance Dept., Kummersdorf, 1932-37; tech. dir. German Rocket Research Center. Peenemuende, Baltic Sea, 1937-45; responsible for devel. first large liquid fuel rocket (V-2), A. A. Guided Missile Wasserfall, 1937-45. With U.S. Dept. Def., Ordnance Dept., as tech. adviser to White Sands Proving Grounds, also project dir. Ft. Bliss, Tex., 1945-50. Chief Guided Missile Devel. Div., Redstone Arsenal, Huntsville, Ala., 1950-56; dir. Devel. Operations Div., Army Ballistic Missile Agy., Huntsville, Ala., 1956-60; dir. NASA George C. Marshall Space Flight Center, Huntsville, Ala., 1960-70, dep. asso. adminstr. NASA, Washington, 1970-72; corporate v.p. engring. and devel. Fairchild Industries, Germantown, Md., 1972—; specialist in rocket design devel. large liquid fuel rockets and guided missiles, devel. large space boosters and vehicles. Recipient Distinguished Civilian Service award Dept. Def., 1957, Dr. Robert Goddard Meml. Trophy, 1958; Distinguished Civilian Service award 1959; award Aerospace Elec. Soc. and Am. Astonautical Soc., 1965; Louis W. Hill space transp. award Am. Inst. Aeros. and Astronautics, 1965, Wilhelm Boelsche medal Kosmos Soc., 1967, Langley medal Smithsonian Instn., 1967, medal for distinguished service (2) NASA, 1969; Exner medal Austrian Gewerbeverein 1969; Nat. Hall of Fame, 1969; named Engr. of Century, Hobby mag., 1966, Man of Year Am. Soc. M.E., 1967, Indsl. Research Mag., 1969, A.P., 1967. Hon. fellow Brit. Interplanetary Soc., Am. Inst. Aeros. and Astronautics; fellow Am. Astronautical Soc.; hon. mem. Norwegian Interplanetary Soc. (Oslo, Norway), Austrian Astronaut. Soc., German Soc. for Aviation and Space Travel (Munich, Germany), Hermann Oberth Soc. (Hannover, Germany), Hellenic Astronautical Soc. (Athens, Greece), German Soc. Aviation and Space Medicine; mem. Nat. Acad. Engring., Internat. Acad. Astronautics. Author: The Mars Project, 1953; co-author: Physics and Medicine of the Upper Atmosphere, 1952; Space Medicine, 1952; Across the Space Frontier, 1952; Conquest of the Moon, 1953; The Exploration of Mars, 1956; Project Satellite, 1958; First Men to the Moon, 1960; (with Frederick I. Ordway III) History of Rocketry and Space Travel, 1966; Space Frontier, 1967, rev. edit., 1971. Contbr. articles to profl. journals and mags. Club: Explorers (N.Y.C.). Home: Alexandria VA Office: Fairchild Industries Germantown MD 20767

VON BROCK, ROBERT CARL, educator; b. Danville, Ill., June 28, 1926; s. Walter F. and Mildred M. (Smith) Von B.; B.S., Northwestern U., 1951, M.A., 1952, Ph.D., 1962; m. Mary Louise Boone, Aug. 18, 1951; children—Ann, Nancy, Mary Boone, Susan. Tchr., Highland Park, Ill., 1952-57; prin., Glen Ellyn, Ill., 1957-63; asso. prof. edn. La. State U., 1963-68, prof., 1968—. Cons. Washington Parish Sch. Bd.; mem. task force for edn. Goals for La.; mem. com. edn. Baton Rouge Goals Congress. Served with USNR, 1944-49. Mem. N.E.A., Am. Assn. Sch. Adminstrs., Nat. Orgn. for Legal Problems in Edn., Phi Delta Kappa. Contbr. articles profl. jours. Home: 435 Castle Kirk St Baton Rouge LA 70808

VON BUELOW, CARL WERNER, plastic co. exec.; b. Alhambra., Cal., Mar. 2, 1925; s. Ernest Theadore and Anna Marie (Stybr) von B.; B.S., U. So. Cal., 1949; m. Alice Cecile Rankin, Apr. 24, 1954; children— Peter David, Carl Eric, Anna Marie, Mary Beth. Regional sales mgr. Honeywell Co., 1952-56; v.p. Holiday Plan of Home Merchandising, Tulsa, 1956-61; mgr. engring. and sales Johns-Manville Corp., St. Louis, 1961-63; merchandising mgr. plastic products div. Monsanto Co., St. Louis, 1963-66; dir. marketing Vinylex Corp., Knoxville, Tenn., 1967—. Troop com. chmn. Smokey Mountain council Boy Scouts Am., 1971-72. Mem. Central Republican Com. Knox County, 1970—. Bd. dirs. Univ. Acad., St. Louis, 1966-67. Served with USNR, 1943-44. Mem. Sales and Marketing Execs. Assn. (pres. Knoxville) Sertoma Internat., Producers Council, Phi Sigma Delta, Delta Sigma Phi. Author: How to Penetrate the Home Building Market, 1963. Home: 513 Nobscot Knoxville TN 37919 Office: 3600 Pleasant Ridge Rd Knoxville TN 37921

VON DER LEHR, WILLIAM NORMAN, educator; b. Petersburg, Ind., June 9, 1927; s. Norman Henry and Sarah Elizabeth (Crown) Von Der L.; A.B., Wabash Coll., 1951; D.D.S., Loyola U., Chgo., 1955; M.A. in Teaching, The Citadel, 1971; m. Mary Anne Knight, Aug. 19, 1950; children— Beth Anne, Loraine Kay, John Norman. Gen. practice dentistry, Rochester, Ind., 1955-69; asst. prof. dentistry Med. U. S.C., Charleston, 1969-71; asso. prof. dentistry La. State U. Sch. Dentistry, New Orleans, 1971—. Mem. Fulton County Library Bd., 1962-69, pres., 1968. Served with USNR, 1945-46, AUS, 1946-48. Mem. Am., La. dental assns., Kappa Sigma, Omicron Kappa Upsilon, Alpha Sigma Nu, Blue Key. Methodist (trustee 1964-67, pres. 1967). Kiwanian (pres. 1960). Contbr. articles to profl. jours. Home: 8310 Lomond Rd New Orleans LA 70126

VON DREHLE, FRANK RAYMOND, furniture, paper and packaging mfg. co. exec.; b. High Point, N.C., May 8, 1928; s. Charles William and Rose Elizabeth (Koester) Von D.; B.S., High Point Coll., 1950; postgrad. Harvard, 1968; m. Patsy Mae Murphy, July 2, 1950; children— Vicki, Raymond, Steve, Terri, Marie, Kim. Sales rep. sch. jewelry Josten's Inc., Owatonna, Minn., 1950-51; sales rep. course paper jobber Spaugh Paper Co., High Point, 1951-53; sales rep. sch. jewelry Josten's, Inc., Owatonna, 1953-57; sales rep. Cellu-Products Co., Patterson, N.C., 1957-61, v.p. sales, 1961-63, v.p. marketing, 1963-71, exec. v.p. marketing, 1971—, also dir., pres. Widdington, Inc. div. Cellu-Products Cedartown, Ga., 1967-70; dir. Hermitage Cabinet Shop, Inc., Cedartown, Ga., Phyl-Pat Inc., Rome, Ga., 1966-67. Mem. Am. Mgmt. Assn., Nat. Broiler Council (marketing com. 1970—). Elk, Moose, Kiwanian. Home: 425 5th Av Pl NE Hickory NC 28601 Office: Roby-Martin Rd Patterson NC 28661

VON HOFFMAN, NICHOLAS, newspaperman; b. N.Y.C., Oct. 16, 1929; s. Carl and Anna (Bruenn) von H.; grad. Fordham Prep. Sch., 1948; m. Ann Byrne, 1950; children—Alexander, Aristodemos, Constantine. Asso. dir. Indsl. Area Found., Chgo., 1954-63; mem. staff Chgo. Daily News, 1963-66; columnist Washington Post, 1966—. Author: Mississippi Notebook, 1964; Multiversity, 1966; We Are The People Our Parents Warned Us Against, 1968; Left at The Post, 1970.

VONK, PAUL KENNETH, coll. adminstr.; b. Grand Rapids, Mich., July 6, 1913; s. Gerrit and Elizabeth (Dykema) V.; B.A., Calvin Coll., 1935; M.A., U. Mich., 1939; Ph.D., Duke, 1959; m. Idalee Wolf, Sept. 2, 1941; children—Idalee Claire, Paul Kenneth. Mem. faculty U. Miami (Fla.), 1948-63, prof. philosophy, 1956-63; dir. honors programs, 1958-60, dean Univ. Coll., 1960-63; v.p. acad. affairs, prof. philosophy Parsons Coll., Fairfield, Ia., 1963-65; v.p. acad. affairs, dean faculty, prof. philosophy, U. West Fla., 1965-67; pres. Oglethorpe Coll., Atlanta, 1967—. Served to lt. comdr. USNR, 1942-45. Member Am., Fla. (past sec.-treas.) philos. assns., So. Soc. Philosophy Religion (past pres.), So. Humanities Conf. (exec. com.), Fla. Edn. Assn. (chmn. higher edn. com.), Nat. Soc. Study Edn. Co-author: Introduction to College, 1958. Home: 5355 Timber Trail NE Atlanta GA 30305

VON MENDELSSOHN, FELIX, psychiatrist; b. Dresden, Germany, Aug. 11, 1918; s. Robert Georg and Gerta Maria (Clason) von M.; M.D., U. Lausanne (Switzerland), 1943; m. Hildegard Tammert, May 17, 1949; children—Constance F., Thomas F., Bettina E. Came to U.S., 1950, naturalized 1956. Asst. psychiatrist Thurgauische Heilanstalt, Muensterlingen, Switzerland, 1944-50; intern Cedars of Lebanon Hosp., Los Angeles, 1951-52; resident Western State Hosp., Washington, 1952-54, U. Mich., 1954-55, Del. State Hosp., 1955—; asst. clin. dir. William A. White Service, St. Elizabeths Hosp., Nat. Inst. Mental Health, Washington, 1961-65; practice medicine specializing in psychiatry, Washington, 1965—; clin. asso. prof. psychiatry Georgetown U., 1962—. Served to lt. col. M.C., AUS 1955-60. Diplomate Am. Bd. Psychiatry and Neurology. Mem. Am. Psychiat. Assn., Pan Am. Med. Soc., A.M.A., N.Y. Acad. Scis. Author: This Is Psychiatry, 1964. Contbg. author: Encylopedia on Mental Health, 1963. Research and publs. heredity and psychiatry, drugs, psychiat. tng. Home: 2705 N Upshur St Arlington VA 22207 Office: 5185 MacArthur Blvd Washington DC 20016

VON MERING, OTTO OSWALD, educator; b. Berlin, Germany, Oct. 21, 1922; s. Otto O. and Henriette (Troeger) von M.; grad. Belmont Hill Sch., 1940; B.A. in History, Williams Coll., 1944; Ph.D. in Social Anthropology, Harvard, 1956; m. Shirley Ruth Brook, Sept. 11, 1954; children—Gretchen, Karin, Gregory. Came to U.S., 1939, naturalized, 1954. Instr. Belmont Hill Sch., Belmont, Mass., 1945-47, Boston U., 1947-48, Cambridge Jr. Coll., 1948-49; research asst. lab. social relations Harvard, 1950-51, Boston Psychopathic Hosp., 1951-53; Russell Sage Found. fellow, N.Y.C., 1953-55; asst. prof. social anthropoloby U. Pitts., 1955-60, asso. prof., 1960-65, prof., 1965-71, prof. anthropology U. Fla., Gainesville, 1971—; lectr. Sigmund Freud Inst., Frankfurt, Germany, 1964, Pitts. Psychoanalytical Inst., 1960—, Interuniversity Forum, 1967—; cons. Westinghouse Research Co., Pitts., 1972—; cons. mental hosps.; tech. adviser Maurice Falk Med. Fund. Fulbright vis. lectr., 1962-63; Richard-Merton guest prof. Heidelberg U., Germany, 1962-63; Am. Anthrop. Assn. vis. lectr., 1961-62; research grantee Wenner-Gren Found., N.Y., 1962-63, Am. Philos. Soc., 1962-63; vis. prof. Dartmouth Coll., 1970-71. Nat. Inst. Mental Health spl. research fellow, 1971-72. Fellow Am. Anthrop. Assn., Am. Sociol. Assn., A.A.A.S., Am. Gerontol. Soc., Acad. Psychosomatic Medicine, Am. Ethnological Soc.; mem. Human Ecology Soc., Assn. Am. Med. Colls., Am. Fedn. Clin. Research, Am. Pub. Health Assn., Am. Psychiat. Assn. Author: Remotivating the Mental Patient, 1957; A Grammar of Human Values, 1961; (with Mitscherlich and Brocher) Der Kranke in der Modernen Gesellschaft, 1967; (with Kasdan) Anthropology In the Behavioral and Health Sciences, 1970; also articles in field. Corr. editor: Jour. Geriatric Psychiatry; asso. editor: Ethnology. Home: 818 NW 21st St Gainesville FL 32601

VON OESEN, (ANNA) ELAINE, librarian; b. Wilmington, N.C., Sept. 6, 1913; d. Martin and Adeline (Behrens) von Oesen; A.B., Lenior Rhyne Coll., 1938; B.A. in L.S., U. of N.C., 1940, M.A., 1951. Asst. librarian Rockingham County Library, Leaksville, N.C., 1940-42; dir. libraries, Walker County, Lafayette, Ga., 1942-43; chief librarian Camp Davis, N.C., 1943-44; instr., asst. prof. library sci. U.

N.C., Chapel Hill, N.C., 1947-52; field librarian N.C. Library Commn., Raleigh, 1952-56; head extension div. State Library, Raleigh, 1956-65, asst. N.C. state librarian, 1965—, also acting N.C. state librarian. Mem. Am., Southeastern (pres. 1968-70) library assns., Am. Assn. State Libraries (sec. 1961-62), N.C. Adult Edn. Assn. (mem. exec. bd. 1958-68), N.C. Library Assn. (chmn. com. on orgn. 1961-66), Beta Phi Mu, Alpha Psi Omega. Democrat. Lutheran (sec. ch. council 1964-67, 69-71). Home: 201 D Boylan Apts Raleigh NC 27603 Office: 109 E Jones St Raleigh NC 27601

VON RICHTER, ZOYA KLEMENTINOVSKI (MRS. NICHOLAS VON RICHTER), librarian; b. Moscow, Russia, Aug. 2, 1905; d. Paul N. and Sole (de Mareche) Klementinovski; ed. langs., lit. Inst. J.J. Rousseau, Lausanne, Switzerland, 1922; m. Randolph Dickins, Sept. 2, 1923 (dec. 1947); children—Randolph Dickins, Zoya (Mrs. Hillard E. Miller, Jr.); m. 2d T. Lothrop Stoddard, Jan. 4, 1944 (dec. May 1950); children—Theodore L., Mary Alice (Mrs. Arthur J. Smith); m. 3d, Nicholas A. von Richter, Apr 20, 1959 (Dec. Nov. 1971). Asst. librarian, specialist on Slavic material Library of Cong., Washington, 1951-70; now ret. Guest artist Walter Reed, also Bethesda Naval hosps. Chmn. entertainment com., treas. Tolstoy Found., 1946-50. Russian Orthodox. Clubs: Fairfax Hunt; Austrian-American. Home: 2500 Que St NW Washington DC 20007 Office: Library of Congress Washington DC 20025

VON STROEBEL, JAMES-MICHAEL, govt. ofcl.; b. Milw., Dec. 14, 1927; s. George Harvey and Margaret Elizabeth (Sullivan) von S.; student Marquette U., 1945-46, 48-49, U. Iberoamericana (Mexico City), 1954; B.S., Georgetown U., 1955, postgrad., 1955-57 Asst. dean U. Iberoamericana, 1955-56; internat. economist Bur. Internat. Commerce, U.S. Dept. Commerce, Washington, Brazilian affairs, 1957-63, Argentine affairs, 1963-66, Central Am., Panamanian and Dominican Republic affairs, 1966-71, Venezuelan affairs, 1971—. Served with AUS, 1950-52. Mem. Soc. Internat. Devel., Am. Polit. Sci. Assn., Am. Acad. Polit. and Social Sci., Acad. Polit. Sci., Internat. Economists Club Washington, Delta Phi Epsilon. Roman Catholic.Home: 4550 Klingle NW Washington DC 20016 Office: Am Republics Div OICR Bur Internat Commerce US Dept Commerce Washington DC 20230

VONTRESS, CLEMMONT EYVIND, educator; b. Bowling Green, Ky., Apr. 22, 1929; s. Benjamin and Elizabeth (Brown) V.; B.A., Ky. State Coll., 1952; M.S., Ind. U., 1956, Ph.D., 1964; student State U. Ia., 1962-63. Instr. English, So. U., Baton Rouge, 1956-57; tchr. English, George Washington High Sch., Indpls., 1957-58; dir. guidance Crispus Attucks High Sch., Indpls., 1958-65; prof. psychology Atlanta U., summer 1965; tchr. English U.S. Army Edn. Center, Germany, 1954-55; prof. edn. Howard U., Washington, 1965-69; prof. edn. George Washington U., Washington, 1969—. Cons. U.S. Labor Dept., 1966-68, numerous govtl. agys., 1968—. Served with AUS, 1953-55. Mem. Nat. Capital Area Personnel and Guidance Assn. (pres. 1970-71), Am. Personnel and Guidance Assn., Nat. Vocational and Guidance Assn., Am. Assn. U. Profs., Phi Delta Kappa. Author: Counseling Negros. Contbr. numerous articles in field to profl. jours. Editorial bd. Personnel and Guidance, Negro Jour. Edn. Home: 2641 Naylor Rd SE Washington DC 20020

VON TUNGELN, GEORGE ROBERT, educator; b. Golconda, Ill., July 18, 1931; s. Cecil Ernest and Rachel (Wright) von T.; B.S., So. Ill. U., 1951, M.S., 1956; Ph.D., U. Ga., 1973; m. Marilyn Ruth Burris, Nov. 5, 1955; children—Stuart Lee, Cheryl Rae, Brenda Sue, Sonya Gay, Eric Wade. Asst. mgr. exptl. farms So. Ill. U., Carbondale, 1951-52, grad. research asst., 1954-56, Pa. State U., 1956-58; asst. prof., asso prof. Clemson U., 1958—. Served with AUS, 1952-54. Mem. Am. Agrl. Econ. Assn., S.C. Acad. Sci., Assn. So. Agrl. Workers, Gamma Sigma Delta. Baptist. Home: 200 Holly Clemson SC 29631

VON WERSSOWETZ, MURIEL ELIZABETH WILFORD (MRS. ARTHUR J. VON WERSSOWETZ), physician; b. Tzeliutsing, Sze, China, Feb. 1, 1914; d. Edward C. and Claudia (Gaviller) Wilford; M.E.L., Ont. Ladies Coll., Whitby, 1932; M.D., U. Toronto, 1938; m. Arthur J. von Werssowetz, Oct. 3, 1940 (dec. June 1962); children—Diana (Mrs. William F. Kelsay), Arthur J. Intern, St. Micheals Hosp., Toronto, Ont., 1938-39; resident St. Josephs Hosp., Hamilton, Ont., 1939-40; part-time clinician Chattanooga-Hamilton County (Tenn.) Health Dept., 1941-62, clinician, dir. maternal and child health, 1962—. Mem. Cath. Charities, 1963—; v.p. Newman Club Found., Chattanooga, 1966-67. Mem. A.M.A., Chattanooga-Hamilton County Med. Soc., Am., Tenn. pub. health assns., Cath. Bus. Women's Club (past pres.), Chi Omega Mothers Club (v.p. 1962-63), Lambda Chi Alpha Mother's Club (pres. 1967-68). Club: Altrusa (past pres.). Home: 3412 Alta Vista Dr Chattanooga TN 37411 Office: 921 E 3d St Chattanooga TN 37403

VOORHIES, MARGERY ELNORA FELDER (MRS. MARCEL J. VOORHIES, JR.), realtor; b. Baton Rouge, Mar. 25, 1918; d. Louis Edward and Grace (Kugler) Felder; student La. State U., 1934-37; m. Marcel J. Voorhies, Jr., Sept. 23, 1938; children—Stephen, Sherrie, David, Debbie (Mrs. Clay R. Mahaffey). Real estate salesman Hearin-Collens, ins., real estate, mortgage loans, Baton Rouge, 1956-64; realtor, partner McAndrew-Voorhies Agy., Baton Rouge, 1964—. Mem. Nat. Assn. Real Estate Bds. (La. pres. women's council 1969), Baton Rouge Bd. Realtors (pres. women's council 1965; mem. salesmen's award com. 1970), Federated Clubs of La. (state pres. 1948), Delta Gamma Alumni (pres. 1954). Roman Catholic. Clubs: Quota (house chmn. 1967, 68), Les Liseuses Book, Baton Rouge Country, Epochal Study (pres. 1946). Home: 2626 Dalrymple Dr Baton Rouge LA 70808 Office: 4261 Perkins Rd Baton Rouge LA 70808

VOS, BERT JOHN, pharmacologist; b. Bloomington, Ind., Sept. 18, 1908; s. Bert John and Rene (Moelker) V.; A.B. cum laude, Ind. U., 1930; Ph.D., U. Chgo., 1934, M.D., 1937; m. Elizabeth Aughey, Oct. 1, 1944; children—Elizabeth Louise, Margaret Anne. Instr., U. Chgo., 1939; with FDA, Dept. Health Edn. and Welfare, Washington, 1939-70, dep. dir. div. pharmacology, 1961-65, dir. div. toxicological evaluation, 1965-68, dep. dir. div. pharmacology and toxicology, 1968-69, dep. dir. div. toxicology, 1969-70; pvt. cons. in pharmacology, 1970—. Recipient Superior Service award Dept. Health, Edn. and Welfare, 1959, Outstanding Service award, 1963. Mem. Am. Soc. Pharmacology and Exptl. Therapeutics, Soc. Exptl. Biology and Medicine, Phi Beta Kappa, Sigma Xi. Home: 6444 Linway Terrace McLean VA 22101

VOSBECK, WILLIAM FREDERICK, JR., architect; b. Mankato, Minn., May 13, 1924; s. William Frederick and Gladys (Anderson) V.; student Notre Dame U., 1943, Cornell, 1945; B.Arch., U. Minn., 1947; m. Elizabeth Just, Aug. 2, 1947; children—Lee, William Frederick III, Lynn, James Stephen. Partner Vosbeck & Ward, Alexandria, Va., 1957-62, Vosbeck & Vosbeck, 1962-66; mng. partner Vosbeck, Vosbeck, Kendrick, Redinger, archts., engrs., planners, Alexandria, 1966—; dir. United Va./ 1st & Citizens Bank, Alexandria, Va. Electric Power Co., Richmond. Pres. bd. dirs. Alexandria Hosp., 1966, Sr. Citizens Service, Alexandria, 1969. Served with USMCR, 1942, 50. Recipient Meritorious Service citation Pres.'s Com. on Employment of Handicapped, 1968. Fellow A.I.A. (pres. 1971); mem. Va. C. of C. (bd. dirs. 1970-71, recipient bus. and civic leadership citation 1969), Va. Assn. Professions, Washington Acad. Sci. (Nat. Capitol award for achievement in architecture 1959), Alexandria Jr. C. of C. (Key man award 1960). Architect Tavern Sq. Urban Renewal Project, Alexandria, 1968, Woodrow Wilson Rehab. Center, Staunton, 1965. Home: 7512 Fort Hunt Rd Alexandria VA 22307 Office: 720 N St Asaph St Alexandria VA 22314

VOSBURGH, FREDERICK GEORGE, editor, writer; b. Johnstown, N.Y., Sept. 16, 1904; s. John Ross and Alice (Baker) V.; A.B., Syracuse U., 1925; grad. study George Washington U., 1938-39; m. Doris Kennedy, Jan. 2, 1929 (div. 1948); children—Richard Kennedy, Alan Frederick; m. 2d Valerie Paterson, May 28, 1949. Reporter Syracuse (N.Y.) Jour., 1922-24, Syracuse Post-Standard, 1925-26. Asso. Press, N.Y. City and Washington, 1927-33, covering sports, later nat. and fgn. affairs including U.S. Senate, Dept. State, Roosevelt campaign trip, 1932, World Econ. Conf., London, Eng., 1933; joined editorial staff Nat. Geog. Mag. 1933, asst. editor, 1951-56, sr. asst. editor, 1956, asso. editor, 1957-67, editor, 1967-70, ret., 1970. Served to lt. col. USAAF, overseas, 1942-45. Mem. Nat. Geog. Soc. (v.p. 1958-70, trustee 1962—), Phi Beta Kappa. Clubs: Cosmos, Overseas Writers, Nat. Press. Home: 8500 W Howell Rd Bethesda MD

VOSBURGH, VALERIE PATERSON (MRS. FREDERICK G. VOSBURGH), editor; b. Colchester, Eng., Feb. 14, 1912; d. George and Caroline (Malins) Paterson; student parocial schs.; m. Frederick G. Vosburgh, May 28, 1949. Came to U.S., 1948, naturalized, 1958. With pub. relations office A.R.C., London, Eng., 1943-46; with Mirror Features, London, 1946-48, English-Speaking Union, N.Y.C., 1948-49, London Times, Washington, 1950-51; with Am. Psychiat. Assn., Washington, 1951—, editor Hosp. and Community Psychiatry, 1962—, staff, 1964-70. Home: 8500 W Howell Rd Bethesda MD 20034 Office: Am Psychiat Assn Washington DC 20006

VOSKUYL, ROGER JOHN, assn. exec.; b. Cedar Grove, Wis., May 16, 1910; s. Anthony and Jennie (Baden) V.; A.B., Hope Coll., Mich., 1932; A.M., Harvard, 1934, Ph.D., 1938; m. Gertrude Joan Schaap, Aug. 13, 1935; children—Ruth Jane, Howard. Instr. and asst. prof. chemistry Wheaton (Ill.) Coll., 1938-42, asso. prof. and prof. chemistry, 1944-47, dean, 1947-50; pres. Westmont Coll. (Cal.), 1950-68; research chemist Manhattan Project, 1943-44; exec. dir. Council Advancement of Small Colls., 1968—. Bd. dirs. Community Chest. Mem. Am. Chem. Soc., N.E.A., Sigma Xi. Rotarian. Author chpt. in Modern Science and Christian Faith, 1948. Contbr. articles on deuterium chemistry in chem. jours. Home: 5100 Dorset Av Chevy Chase MD 20015 Office: One Dupont Circle NW Washington DC 20036

VOSS, CHARLES HENRY, JR., elec. engring. educator; b. Kiangyen, China, Sept. 28, 1926 (parents Am. citizens); s. Charles Henry and Mathilde (Easley) V.; B.S. in Elec. Engring., La. State U., 1949, M.S. in Elec. Engring., 1956; Ph.D. in Elec. Engring., N.C. State Coll., 1963; m. Elizabeth Ann Brown, July 24, 1954; children—Elizabeth Ann, Charles Henry III. Asst. chief engr. Sta. WJBO-WBRL-FM, Baton Rouge, 1950-53; div. transmission engr. So. Bell Telephone Co., New Orleans, 1953-54; instr. elec. engring. La. State U., Baton Rouge, 1954-56, asso. prof., 1962-67, prof., 1967—; instr. N.C. State Coll., Raleigh, 1957-61. Served with USNR, 1944-46, Ford Found. fellow, 1961-62; Research Council faculty fellow, 1965. Mem. I.E.E.E., Am. Soc. for Engring. Edn., Sigma Xi, Phi Eta Sigma, Phi Kappa Phi, Eta Kappa Nu, Tau Beta Pi. Home: 5823 Clematis Dr Baton Rouge LA 70808

VOSSBERG, CARL AUGUST, elec. mfg. co. exec.; b. Woodhaven, N.Y., July 16, 1918; s. Carl A. and Katherine B. (Duerr) V.; B.E.E., Coll. City N.Y., 1946; M.S., Columbia, 1948; m. Elizabeth E. Moniz, Apr. 16, 1942; children—Kathleen (Mrs. Kermit Rose), Betty (Mrs. Robert Lee Macauley), Carl August III. Chief engr. Standard Electronics Research Corp., N.Y.C., 1942-47; v.p. Indsl. Gauges Corp., Englewood, N.J., 1947-49; pres. Electron Machine Corp., Umatilla, Fla., 1946-70, chmn. bd., 1946—; pres. Corinthian Yacht Corp., Tarpon Springs, Fla., 1968-70, Tri-Yacht, Inc., Umatilla, 1969—. Patentee in field. Home: PO Box G Umatilla FL 32784 Office: PO Box M Umatilla FL 32784

VOUDOURIS, JOHN LOVARD, county ofcl.; b. Austin, Tex., Mar. 19, 1938; s. Nick and Jettie (Thomason) V.; student San Antonio Jr. Coll., 1956-57, U. Tex., 1957-59; m. Sharron Ann Moore, May 9, 1963; children— Mike, Pam, Cindy and Sandy (twins). With weights and measures dept. Tex. Hwy. Dept., 1958-60; pres. Austin Maintenance Service, Inc., 1960—; county commr. Travis County, Precinct 3, Austin, 1969—. Dir. Greater South Austin Jr. Football League. Named as One of Five Most Outstanding Young Businessmen in Austin, 1967, 68, 69, 70. Mem. Austin Livestock Assn. (dir.), S.W. County Commrs. Assn., Austin, Temple chambers commerce. Rotarian. Clubs: Oak Hill (Tex.) Optimist Austin Civitan, South Austin Civic Gardenia. Home: Star Route A-Box 760 Austin TX 78710 Office: Route 5 Box 94-T Austin TX 78710 also 1922 S 1st St Austin TX 78704

VOURNAS, GEORGE CHRISTIAN, lawyer; b. Greece, Feb. 25, 1897; s. Christian John and Anastasia (Sioris) V.; came to U.S., 1914, naturalized, 1924; LL.B., Nat. U., 1919; m. Helen Petrow, Sept. 14, 1944; children—Anastasia, Vasiliky. Admitted to D.C. bar, 1924, since in pvt. practice, Washington; counsel Consular Office of Greek Embassy, 1927-40. Served from capt. to maj. AUS, 1943-45. Mem. Am., D.C. bar assns., Am. Soc. Internat. Law, Order Ahepa (nat. pres. 1942-45). Democrat. Clubs: 1925 F Street, University (Washington); Congressional Country. Home: 4000 Cathedral Av NW Washington DC 20016 Office: 1750 K St NW Washington DC 20006

VOYLES, CHARLES NORMAN, ednl. adminstr.; b. Okemah, Okla., Apr. 27, 1928; s. Roy Curtis and Trula Grace (McBrayer) V.; B.S., Okla. State U., 1952, M.S., 1953; m. Mary Claudette Morton, Dec. 27, 1952; children—Tracy Lynn, Trent Morton. Asst. publs. editor Okla. State U., Stillwater, 1953-61, publs. editor, 1961-67, asso. dir. pub. information, extension editor, 1967—. Served with USAF, 1946-49. Recipient Pioneer award Am. Assn. Agrl. Coll. Editors, 1957. Mem. Am. Assn. Agrl. Coll. Editors (dir. 1968-71, v.p. 1971-72), Alpha Zeta, Phi Kappa Phi, Kappa Tau Pi. Democrat. Baptist (ch. moderator 1970-71, deacon 1956—). Home: 1101 Brown Av Stillwater OK 74074

VRENIOS, ANASTASIOS, lyric tenor; b. Turlock, Cal., Aug. 24, 1940; s. Nicholas and Despina (Vastis) V.; B.Mus., U. Pacific, 1962; M. in Voice, Ind. U., 1965, postgrad., 1965-67; m. Elizabeth Anne Kirkpatrick, July 14, 1963; children—Nicholas Andreas, Christopher Louis. Appeared with Washington Opera and Symphony, spring 1967; leading artist Spoleto (Italy) Festival of Two Worlds, summer 1967; leading tenor Am. Nat. Opera Co., touring throughout U.S.; London debut, Royal Albert Hall, 1968; lead tenor roles Phila. Lyric Opera, Am. Opera Soc., Milw. Opera, San Francisco Spring Opera, and others, 1968. Grad. Asst. in voice Ind. U., 1962-67; appeared on TV in La Rondine; recorded Les Huguenots, 1969. Nat. winner student auditions, Nat. Fedn. Music Clubs, 1960; 1st place winner Auditions of Air, WGN-TV- Ill. Opera Guild, 1967. Mem. Am. Guild Mus. Artists. Greek Orthodox. Home: 6628 32d St NW Washington DC 20016

V'SOSKE, THADDEUS CASIMER, carpet mfg. co. exec.; b. Grand Rapids, Mich., Feb. 4, 1901; s. Stanislav and Mary (Kerstyn) V'S.; student Grand Rapids Jr. Coll.; m. Vesta Searls, Nov. 17, 1935. Pres., V'Soske Shops, Inc., V'Soske, Inc., Kent Carpet Corp., V'Soske Ltd., V'Soske-Joyce Ltd., Ireland. Clubs: Bankers, San Juan, Top of The First, Dorado Beach Golf. Address: Box 457 Vega Boja PR 00763

WACHENDORF, GEORGE, writer, editor; b. South Haven, Mich., June 10, 1927; s. George and Edith (Hlinka) W.; student Mich. State U., 1945; B.S. in Journalism, U. Ill., 1949; m. Beth Clement, July 3, 1953; children—Skye, Nicholas, Clare, Wendy, Lorie. Reporter, editor Democrat, Davenport, Ia., 1949-51; telegraph editor News-Gazette, Champaign, Ill., 1951; asst. news editor New Orleans Item, 1951-53; asst. make-up editor San Francisco Examiner, 1953-55; copy desk chief European Stars and Stripes, 1955-57; copy desk chief Fla. Times-Union, Jacksonville, 1957-58, bus. editor, 1966—; telegraph editor, news editor Jacksonville Journal, 1958-66. Free lance writer, reporter, 1949—; mem. North Fla. Small Bus. Adv. Council, 1967-68. Mem. New Orleans CIO Council, 1955. Pres. Duval County (Fla.) Young Democrats, 1963-64, state committeeman, 1961-63, county committeeman, 1966-70. Served as staff sgt. AUS, 1945-46. Named Fla. Bus. Writer of Year, State Comptroller's Competition, 1967, runnerup, 1968. Mason (32 deg., Shriner). Home: 4228 Camellia Circle W Jacksonville FL 32207 Office: PO Box 1949 Jacksonville FL 32201

WACHS, MELVIN WALTER, govt. ofcl.; b. Detroit, Dec. 5, 1930; s. Harry H. and Gussie (Max) W.; B.A., U. Mich., 1952, M.A., 1954; Ph.D., Am. U., 1968; student U. Detroit, 1951, U. Chgo., 1955, Cornell U., 1954-56, Wayne State U., 1952; m. Eulene Shari Rattner, Sept. 6, 1953; children—Alan L., Laura A., Amy R. Research, teaching asst. Cornell U., Ithaca, N.Y., 1954-57, U. Mich., Ann Arbor, 1954; asst. prof. polit. sci., chmn. Asian studies Western Mich. U., Kalamazoo, 1959-62; asso. dir. Exec. Insts., Office of Career Devel., U.S. Civil Service Commn., Washington, 1962-64, asso. dir. for ednl. resources, 1964-66; coordinator planning, programming and budgeting, acting chief planning br. Nat. Inst. Mental Health, USPHS, Chevy Chase, Md., 1966-68; vis. prof. polit. sci. U. Okla., 1965—, State U. N.Y. Maritime Coll., 1967-68, So. Ill. U., 1972—; dir. community devel. tng. div., U.S. Dept. Housing and Urban Devel., Washington, 1968-71, sr. program officer Office State and Local Mgmt. Assistance, 1971-72; with Office of Planning and Mgmt. Assistance, 1972—. Staff, Panel on Sci. and Tech. Manpower, Pres. Sci. Adv. Com., 1964-67; cons. Office Sci. and Technology, Exec. Office of the Pres., 1964-68. Mem. Fed. Interagy. Com. on Edn., 1968—; coordinator, Maritime adminstrn. mgmt. and tech. programs U.S. Dept. of Commerce, 1966-71; mem. Nat. Allied Health Professions Council, U.S. Dept. Health, Edn. and Welfare, 1968—, dir. implementation for social services and welfare reform, Community Services Adminstrn., 1972; mem. staff Presdl. Task Force on Exec. Devel., 1966-69. Ford Found. fgn. area fellow, 1956-58; Social Sci. Research Council fellow, 1955; Carnegie fellow, 1962-64. Mem. Am. Pub. Health Assn., A.A.A.S., Pi Kappa Phi. Home: 4832 Drummond St Chevy Chase MD 20015 Office: US Dept of Housing and Urban Devel Washington DC 20410

WACHTEL, ANDREW STEPHEN, physician; b. Jersey City, July 12, 1924; s. Alvy E. and Ina Pearl (Neher) W.; student Kingswood Jr. Coll., Springfield, Va., 1940-42; B.A., Greenville Coll., 1946; postgrad. Ga. Sch. Tech., Atlanta, Vanderbilt U., Tulane U.; M.D., Baylor U., 1950; m. Dorothea Steele, Aug. 2, 1946; children—Andrew Stephen, Christopher Steele, Alisa Kay. Gen. med. practice Owosso, Mich., 1954-57; staff physician VA Hosp., Lexington, 1960-61; acting chief, Acute Intensive Treatment Service, VA Hosp., Lexington, 1961; dir. Mental Health Center, Oak Ridge, 1961-64; supt. Eastern State Psychiat. Hosp., Knoxville, 1964-66; Asso. prof. psychiatry Meml. Research Hosp., U. Tenn., 1962, asso. prof. psychology, 1963, prof. psychology (part-time), 1966—, asso. prof. psychiatry U. Tenn. Hosp., 1962-66; clin. asso. prof. Vanderbilt U., Nashville, 1969—; pvt. practice, 1966—. Served to capt. AUS, 1951-54. Diplomate Am. Bd. Psychiatry. Fellow Am. Acad. Psychosomatic Medicine; mem. A.M.A., A.A.A.S., Am. Acad. Gen. Practice, Am. Psychiat. Assn., Am. Orthopsychiat. Assn., Assn. Advancement Psychotherapy, Am. Hosp. Assn. Contbr. articles in field to profl. jours. Home: 2117 Belcourt Av Nashville TN 37202

WACHTEL, LEO MICHAEL, JR., physician; b. Savannah, Ga., Oct. 5, 1912; s. Leo Michael and Beulah (Weil) W.; A.B., Emory U., 1934; M.D., Jefferson Med. Coll., 1938; m. Helen Ross Dixon, Jan. 7, 1941; children— Leo Michael III, John Dixon. Intern St. Vincent's Hosp., Jacksonville, Fla., 1938-40, now staff mem.; practice family medicine Jacksonville, 1940—; mem. staff St. Lukes, Baptist Meml., Univ. hosps. (all Jacksonville). Dir., Blue Shield Fla., 1956-59, 63—, treas., 1963-72. Mem. Fla. Bd. Health, 1963-70. Trustee Bolles Sch., Jacksonville, 1956-64. Mem. Duval County Med. Soc. (pres. 1957), Am. (del. 1960—), Fla. (pres. 1957) acads. gen. practice, Fla. Med. Assn. (pres. 1960), Jacksonville Area C. of C. (dir. 1963-65). Presbyn. (elder). Home: 4521 Ortega Blvd Jacksonville FL 32210 Office: 2708 St Johns Av Jacksonville FL 32205

WACKENHUT, GEORGE RUSSELL, security services exec.; b. Phila., Sept. 3, 1919; s. William Henry and Frances (Hogan) W.; student U. Pa. Wharton Evening Sch., 1937-38, State Tchrs. Coll., West Chester, Pa., 1938-41; B.S., U. Hawaii, 1942; postgrad. Temple U., 1946; M.Ed., Johns Hopkins U., 1949; m. Ruth Johann Bell, Apr. 8, 1944; children—Janis Lynn (Mrs. John P. Thorsen), Richard Russell. Dir. phys. edn. profl. program tchrs. tng. Johns Hopkins, 1946-50; civilian cons. recreational sports br. Office Spl. Services, U.S. Army, Washington, 1950-51; spl. agt. FBI, 1951-54; dir. personnel, security and safety Giffin Industries, Inc., Miami, Fla., 1954; pres., chmn. bd. Spl. Agt. Investigators, Inc., Spl. Agts. Security Guards, Inc., Security Services Corp. (all Miami), 1954-60, Wackenhut Corp., Coral Gables, Fla., 1960—, Wackenhut Services, Inc., Coral Gables, 1960—, Wackenhut Protective Systems, 1966—; dir. fgn. subsidiaries. Mem. Fla. Sec. State's Pvt. Investigative, Guard and Patrol Adv. Com., 1963-67, chmn., 1963-64; dir. Fla. Gov.'s War on Crime, 1967-70; mem. law enforcement council Nat. Council on Crime and Delinquency, 1971—. Bd. visitors U.S. Army Mil. Police Sch., 1972—. Served with AUS, 1941-45. Mem. Soc. Former Spl. Agts. FBI, Inc., Am. Soc. for Indsl. Security, Am. Inst. Mgmt. (presidents council 1964-66). Christian Scientist. Clubs: Kings Bay Yacht and Country (dir. Miami 1963-64), Ocean Reef. Home: 7795 SW 122d St Miami FL 33156 Office: 3280 Ponce de Leon Blvd Coral Gables FL 33134

WACKS, VIRGIL QUINTON, film producer; b. St. Charles, Va., May 1, 1906; s. William Blanton and Allie Mae (Harber) W.; student Bluefield Coll., 1928-30; photography degree N.Y. Inst. Photography, 1933; m. Jauree Elizabeth McElroy, Nov. 16, 1946; children—Virgil Quinton, Mitchell Rawlin. Owner, Virgil Q. Wacks Agy., producer TV shows, spl. film features for TV and theaters, Pennington Gap, Va., 1960—; owner, operator Lee County Agrl. Fair, Pennington Gap,

1945-63, Lee Block Plant, Inc., 1945-72; v.p. Southwestern Va. R.R. Co., 1972-—, Knoxville Sox Baseball Club, 1972-—. Nat. chmn., promoter Nat. Press Day Celebration, Cumberland Gap Nat. Hist. Park, 1970-—. Mayor, City of St. Charles, Va., 1931-33. Bd. dirs. Lee County Community Action Orgn., Lonesome Pine Devel. Corp., Lee Indsl. Commn. Served with USNR, 1944-45. Recipient Acad. award U.P., 1941; named to Frank D. Lawrence Baseball Hall of Fame, Norfolk, Va., 1950. Mem. Mountain States League Profl. Baseball (pres. 1946-54), Lee County C. of C. (pres. 1970-72, exec. dir. 1970-72), Am. Legion (post comdr. 1955). Mason. Club: Civitan (Pennington Gap). Producer films, author articles on snake-handling religious cult in St. Charles, Va. for nat. mags., 1940; producer, promoter Earl Hobson Smith Outdoor Dramas including Trail of Lonesome Pine, Valley Forge, Old Smokey, Davey Crockett, Daniel Boone, others; producer, host weekly TV travel show WKPT-TV, WJHL-TV. Home: Duff St Pennington Gap VA 24277 Office: Main St Pennington Gap VA 24277

WADDELL, KENNETH LEE, hosp. adminstr.; b. Concord, N.C., Nov. 20, 1932; s. Robert Lee and Rose E. (Fulmer) W.; B.S., Wake Forest U., 1954; postgrad. U. N.C., 1954-55, U. Richmond, 1955-56; M.H.A., Med. Coll. Va., 1958; children—Teresa, Patricia, Elizabeth, Nancy. Asst. adminstr. Roanoke (Va.) Meml. Hosp., 1961-62; adminstr. Loudoun Meml. Hosp., Leesburg, Va., 1962-65; adminstr. Waddell Hosp. and Clinic, 1965-—; clinic dir. Galax Med. Center, 1966-—; adminstr. Galax Gen. Hosp., 1967-—; v.p. Waddell Hosp.; sec.-treas. Galax Gen., Twin County Community hosps. Adminstr., Blue Ridge council Boy Scouts Am., 1958-61; chmn. March of Dimes, 1964; div. chmn. United Fund, 1965-—. Bd. dirs. Loudoun chpt. A.R.C.; trustee Twin County Community, Galax Gen. hosps. Recipient Past Pres.'s award Roanoke Area Hosp. Council, 1969. Fellow Am. Coll. Hosp. Adminstrs., Nursing Home Adminstrs.; mem. Am., Va. (dir.) hosp. assns., Hosp. Financial Mgmt. Assn., Carroll-Grayson C. of C. Home: 115 Painter St Galax VA 24333 Office: 112 Painter St Galax VA 24333

WADDELL, MARIE LANDUA (MRS. ROBERT S. WADDELL, JR.), educator; b. Somerville, Tex.; d. Edward H. and Pearl (Taylor) Landua; B.A., Howard Payne Coll., 1939; M.A., Scaritt Coll., 1942; m. Robert S. Waddell, Jr., Apr. 10, 1952; children—Robert Shawn and Marita Kim (twins). Dir. music and edn. Spruce St. Meth. Ch., Morgantown, W.Va., 1942-43; tchr. English to fgn. born Am. Trade Orgn., 1943-45; instr. dept. English, So. Meth. U., Dallas, 1946-47, Arlington State Coll., 1947-52; faculty U. Tex., El Paso, 1954-—, asst. prof. English, 1960-—, dir. Freshman English, 1971-—. Mem. Modern Lang. Assn., Tex. Assn. Coll. Tchrs., Am. Assn. U. Profs., Alpha Chi, Alpha Lambda Delta. Republican. Episcopalian. Author: 10 Steps in Writing the Research Paper, 1965; The Art of Styling Sentences. Home: 812 Fairway Circle El Paso TX 79922

WADDELL, ST. JOHN, newspaper editor; b. Memphis, July 3, 1896; s. St. John and Ada Elizabeth (McCroskey) W.; grad. Phillips Acad., Andover, Mass., 1914; B.A., Yale, 1917; m. Pauline Townsend, July 1, 1924; 1 dau., Irma (Mrs. Erich W. Merrill). Engaged in farming Quitman County, Miss., 1919-21; reporter Memphis Comml. Appeal, New Orleans Times Picayune, N. China Press, Shanghai, 1921-23; exec. asst. to mayor, city commnr., City of Memphis, 1923-28; ins. broker, 1929-33; reporter, bus.-real estate editor Comml. Appeal, 1934-41, asst. mng. editor, 1946-59, mng. editor, 1959-61, asso. editor, 1961-—; financial cons. WPB, 1941-42. Chmn. Memphis Com. Freedoms Found., 1962-—. Served to 1st lt. arty., U.S. Army, 1917-19; AEF in France and Germany; served to maj. inf., AUS, 1942-46; ETO. Mem. Am. Press Inst., Mil. Order World Wars, Am. Legion, Zeta Psi. Mem. Christian Ch. (Disciples of Christ). Clubs: Yale, Press, Lions (past pres., dir.) (Memphis). Home: 265 Buena Vista Pl Memphis TN 38112 Office: 495 Union Av Memphis TN 38103

WADDELL, SUE, educator; b. Big Stone Gap, Va.; d. Tipton David and Georgia (Roller) Waddell; student Mary Washington Coll., 1938-40; B.S., U. Tenn., 1942, M.S., 1955 Sec., TVA, Knoxville, Tenn., 1942-53; tchr. Oak Ridge High Sch., 1953-59; asst. prof. bus. and office edn. Sch. Commerce and Business Adminstrn., U. Ala., 1959-—. Named Sec. of Year, Ala. chpt. Nat. Secs. Assn., 1967. Mem. Nat. Collegiate Assn. for Secs. (nat. sec. 1965), So. Bus. Edn. Assn. (Tenn. state rep. 1955-59, vice-chmn. coll. and u. sect. 1964, chmn. 1965, asst. news editor, 1960, 66), Nat. Secs. Assn., Ala. Bus. Edn. Assn. (sec. 1965), Alpha Xi Delta (v.p. 1965), Delta Pi Epsilon (v.p. 1954, pres. 1955). Baptist. Home: Claymont Apts Tuscaloosa AL 35401

WADDLE, BRADFORD AVON, cotton researcher, educator; b. Greenville, Tex., Jan. 26, 1920; s. Hillard Carl and Edna (Taylor) W.; B.S., Tex. A. and M. U., 1942, M.S., 1950; Ph.D., Purdue U., 1954; m. Wanda Lou McGee, July 7, 1945. Cotton research asst. Tex. A. and M. U., 1938-42, 46-48, student asst., 1948-50; XR fellow Purdue U., 1950-51; chmn. cotton research U. Ark., Fayetteville, 1951-—, prof., 1956-—. Cotton cons. Monsanto; past chmn. Nat. Cotton Improvement Council. Mem. Fayetteville Appeals Bd., 1968-—. Served to maj. USMCR, 1942-46. Mem. Am. Soc. Agronomy, Am. Genetic Assn., Sigma Xi, Gamma Sigma Delta. Methodist (trustee). Home: 805 Crest St Fayetteville AR 72701

WADDY, JOSEPH CORNELIUS, U.S. dist. judge; A.B. cum laude, London (Pa.) U., 1935; LL.B. cum laude, Howard U., 1938; m. Elizabeth Hardy Gregg, Apr. 19, 1941; children—Joseph Cornelius. Admitted to D.C. bar, 1939; mem. firm Houston, Waddy, Bryant and Gardner, and predecessors, Washington, 1939-62; asso. judge domestic relations br. Municipal Ct. D.C., 1962-67; judge U.S. Dist. Ct. for D.C., 1967-—; adj. prof. Howard U. Sch. Law, 1966-67. Mem. citizens adv. council to D.C. Commnrs., 1958-62, chmn., 1961-62; chmn. bd. trustees Washington Action for Youth, 1962-64; trustee, v.p. United Planning Orgn., 1964-67; trustee Lincoln U., 1960-—. Served with AUS, 1944-46. Recipient Meritorious Pub. Service award D.C. Govt., 1962; named Alumnus of Year, Elks, 1963. Mem. Am., Nat., Washington bar assns., Bar Assn. D.C., Nat. Lawyers Club, Alpha Phi Alpha. Democrat. Conglist. Home: 1804 Upshur St NE Washington DC 20018 Office: U S Court House Constitution Av and John Marshall Pl NW Washington DC 20001

WADE, CAMPBELL MARION, JR., radio astronomer; b. Elizabethtown, Ky., Nov. 25, 1930; s. Campbell Marion and Alice (Cates) W.; A.B., Harvard, 1951, A.M., 1955, Ph.D., 1957; m. Mary Jane Elizabeth Stewart, July 21, 1956; children—Karen Elizabeth, Stewart Conrad, David Campbell, Richard Sanders. Research officer Commonwealth Sci. and Indsl. Research Orgn., Sydney, Australia, 1957-59; staff scientist Nat. Radio Astronomy Obs., Green Bank, W.Va., Charlottesville, Va., 1960-—, research in galactic and extragalactic radio astronomy. Vis. prof. Am. Astron. Soc.'s program, 1965-—. Mem. county planning commn. Pocahontas County, W.Va., 1963-65. Bd. dirs. Greenvale, Inc., 1962-65. Served with AUS, 1950-51. Mem. Am. Astron. Soc., Internat. Astron. Union, Internat. Sci. Radio Union. Adv. editor: Soviet Astronomy (English translation), 1969-—. Home: Tall Pines Route 5 Charlottesville VA 22901

WADE, CHARLES BYRD, JR., tobacco co. exec.; b. Morehead City, N.C., July 8, 1915; s. Charles Byrd and Elizabeth (Ormond) W.; A.B., Duke, 1938; m. Margaret Patterson, July 26, 1942; children—Ruth E., Mary M., Charles Byrd III. With R. J. Reynolds Tobacco Co., Winston-Salem, N.C. (name now R.J. Reynolds Industries, Inc.), 1938-—, asst. personnel mgr., 1946-47, asst. supr. mfg., 1949-—, dir., 1955-—, v.p., 1959-70, sr. v.p., 1970-—; dir. Duke Power Co., Hennis Freight Lines; bd. mgrs. Wachovia Bank and Trust Co., Winston-Salem. Mem. adv. council personnel adminstrn. Nat. Indsl. Conf. Bd.; chmn. Urban Redevel. Commn. Winston-Salem; pres. Old Salem Inc. Alderman, Winston-Salem, 1950-51; chmn. bd. Duke, 1969-71. Trustee Salem Coll., Brevard Coll.; bd. dirs. N.C. Citizens Assn. Served from pvt. to maj.; AUS, World War II. Decorated Legion of Merit. Mem. U.S. (bus. relations com.). Winston-Salem (dir.) chambers commerce. Am. Mgmt. Assn. (personnel planning council). Methodist. Clubs: Forsyth Country (Winston-Salem); University (N.Y.C.). Home: 756 Pine Valley Rd Winston-Salem NC 27106 Office: R J Reynolds Tobacco Co Winston-Salem NC 27101

WADE, DAVID, govt. ofcl.; b. Jacksonville, Ark., Dec. 18, 1910; s. Thomas Howell and Mable (Corder) W.; B.S., U. Ark., M.D., 1938; m. Hazel Keenzel, Dec. 9, 1934; 1 dau., Sharon (Mrs. Robert A. Shoop). Intern St. Vincent's Infirmary, Little Rock, 1938-39; resident Galveston (Tex.) State Psychopathic Hosp., 1939-42; practice medicine specializing in psychiatry, Austin, Tex., 1945-67; supt. Galveston State Psychopathic Hosp., Austin State Sch., Rusk State Hosp., 1942-44; asst. commr. pub. welfare, 1967-69; dir. comprehensive health planning Gov's. Staff, Austin, 1969-70; commr. Tex. Dept. Mental Health and Mental Retardation, 1970-—. Served to maj. M.C., AUS, 1951-52. Fellow Am. Psychiat. Assn. Home: 3215 Exposition Blvd Austin TX 78703 Office: PO Box 12668 Austin TX 78701

WADE, DAVID, state govt. ofcl.; b. Homer, La., June 15, 1911; s. Ed and Ola (Crowe) W.; ed. La. Tech. Inst.; m. Marie King, Sept. 28, 1943; 1 dau., Kay (Mrs. MacLeod). Joined USAAF, 1935, advanced through grades to lt. gen. USAF, with USAF Security Service; dep. comdr. 93d Bomb Wing; comdr. 57th Air Div., 303d Bomb Wing, 92d Bomb Wing; chief staff SAC, comdr. 1st Missile Div., 8th Air Force, 2d Air Force, ret., 1967; dir. instns., adj. gen., dir. Dept. Pub. Safety La., 1967-71; adj. gen. State of La., 1971-—; guest speaker in field. Decorated D.S.M., D.F.C., Soldier's medal, Legion of Merit, Air medal with oak leaf clusters. Home: 5 Jackson Barracks New Orleans LA 70117 Office: Hdqrs Bldg Jackson Barracks New Orleans LA 70140

WADE, DWIGHT ROBERT, real estate dealer; b. Sevierville, Tenn., Mar. 14, 1907; s. Robert Ira and Mary Victoria (Atchley) W.; student Maryville Coll., 1924-26, U. Tenn., 1926-28; m. Kate Reagan, June 25, 1939; children—Dwight Robert, Kenneth R., Gary R., Sidney P. Tchr. sch., Greenbrier, Sevier County, Tenn., 1928-29; mng. partner Wades Dept. Store, 1929-69; v.p., dir. Morris Bolling Ford Sales, Clinton, Tenn., 1942-—; dir. Sevier County Bank. Served with USNGR, 1924-26. Mem. Kappa Sigma. Democrat. Baptist. Lion. Home: 114 Joy St Sevierville TN 37962 Office: 118 Bruce St Sevierville TN 37862

WADE, LENNIS PRESTON, engring. co. exec.; b. Lynchburg, Va., June 30, 1933; s. Lennis Bob and Dolah (Carey) W.; B.C.E., Va. Poly. Inst. and State U., 1955, postgrad., 1955-56; m. Jett Gale Preble, July 1, 1955; children—Gale Preble, Larke Lizzette, Stephanie Preston. Instr. applied mechanics Va. Poly. Inst. and State U., Blacksburg, 1955-56; engr. Wiley & Wilson Engrs., Architects, Planners, Lynchburg, 1958-—, partner, 1969-—. Pres. Sandusky Elementary Sch. P.T.A., 1965-66. Served to lt. USAF, 1956-58. Recipient The Societas Cincinnatorum Instituta award, 1955. Mem. Arnold Air Soc., Va. Poly. Inst. and State U. Alumni Assn. (pres. Lynchburg chpt. 1966-67), Va. Soc. Profl. Engrs. (state pres. 1970-71), Nat. Soc. Profl. Engrs., Va. Assn. Professions, Tau Beta Pi, Chi Epsilon, Omicron Delta Kappa, Scabbard & Blade. Presbyn. (deacon 1967-69, elder 1970-—). Clubs: Pershing Rifles, Cotillion. Home: 3908 Peakland Pl Lynchburg VA 24503 Office: 2310 Langhorne Rd Lynchburg VA 24501

WADE, LOUIS ALLISON, lawyer; b. Vero Beach, Fla., Dec. 1, 1934; s. Troy Lee and Maggie Lou (Harris) W.; B.B.A. cum laude, U. Ga., 1957, LL.B. magna cum laude, 1959; m. Martha Jane Bush, Dec. 19, 1954 (div. 1971); children—Louis Allison, Karla Jane, Charles Errol; m. 2d, Kathryn Ware, 1972. Admitted to Ga. bar, 1958; partner Gambrell, Russell, Killorin, Wade & Forbes, Atlanta, 1957-—. Mem. exec. com. hdqrs. bd. Ga. YMCA, 1967-—. Mem. Am., Atlanta bar assns., State Bar Ga., Am. Judicature Soc., Blue Key, Phi Beta Kappa, Phi Delta Phi, Phi Kappa Phi, Beta Gamma Sigma. Clubs: Commerce, Lawyers, Cherokee Town and Country (Atlanta); N.Y. Athletic. Home: 620 Peachtree St NE Atlanta GA 30303 Office: First Nat Bank Tower Atlanta GA 30303

WADE, MARY CARROLL (MRS. RICHARD R. WADE), govt. ofcl.; b. Rome, Ga., Sept. 1, 1909; d. Seaborn Rosa and Dollie (Hill) Carroll; B.A., Maryville Coll., 1931; postgrad. U. of South, summer 1938; M.A. George Washington U., 1948; Ed.D., Am. U., 1970; m. Richard Rudolph Wade, Apr. 1, 1967. Tchr., Hawkins County, Tenn., 1934-36, Pittman Center, Tenn., 1936-37, Meigs County, Tenn., 1937-38, Chattanooga, 1938-42; clk.-typist War Dept., Washington, 1942-43; library asst. Library of Congress, 1943-44; planner Govt. Printing Office, Washington, 1944-67, planner-in-charge, 1967-72, chief marginally punched continuous forms specifications sect., 1972-—. Cons. psychologist Alexandria Vocational Rehab. Dept., 1954-57. Active A.R.C., U.S.O., United Givers Fund; troop leader Girl Scouts U.S.A., Chattanooga. Recipient Distinguished Service award U.S.O., 1946; certificates of merit and hon. award U.S. Govt. Printing Office, 1962, 63, Superior Service award, 1964, 1967, 1968. Mem. Soc. Personnel Adminstrn., Nat. Vocational Guidance Adminstrn., Am. Personnel and Guidance Assn., Nat. Rehab. Assn., Forms Mgmt. Council U.S. Capitol Hist. Soc., George Washington Univ., Maryville Coll. alumni assns., Pub. Personnel Assn., Franklin Tech. Soc., Washington Club Printing House Craftsmen, Am., Va., D.C. psychol. assns., Columbian Women, Washington Litho. Club, Govt. Printing Office Fed. Women's Program (chmn. 1972-73), Kappa Delta Epsilon, Psi Chi, Phi Delta Gamma (chpt. pres. 1957-58, nat. council rep. 1968-72). Presbyn. Clubs: George Washington University, Americana, Toastmistress (sec. 1972, treas. 1972-73); Fairfax County Business and Professional Women's. Home: 614 Bashford Lane Alexandria VA 22314 Office: US Govt Printing Office Washington DC 20401

WADE, PAUL HARRY, hosp. adminstr.; b. Phenix City, Ala., Feb. 15,, 1926; s. Paul Hamilton and Barbara Elizabeth (Barr) W.; student Mercer U., 1944-45; grad. summa cum laude, Franklin Sch. Sci. and Arts, 1951; m. Juanita Walker, Sept. 5, 1952; 1 son, Gregory Scott. Adminstr. Harriman (Tenn.) City Hosp., 1952-—. Trustee Oakridge Regional Mental Health Center, 1971. Mem. Tenn. Hosp. Assn. (trustee 1966-69), Am. Coll. Hosp. Adminstrs., Am. Hosp. Assn. Mason (32 deg.), Rotarian (pres. 1965-66). Home: 526 Cumberland St Harriman TN 37748 Office: 412 Devonia St Harriman TN 37748

WADE, WILLIAM IRL, JR., physician; b. Mena, Ark., Sept. 20, 1938; s. William Irl and Wilson (Anderson) W.; student Little Rock Jr. Coll., 1957-59, Little Rock U., 1956-59; M.D., U. Ark., 1963; m. Wanda Lee Bates, Jan. 12, 1963; children—Cynthia Carolyn, Arthur Colin. Intern, USPHS and Charity Hosp., New Orleans, 1963-64; resident USPHS Hosp., San Francisco, 1965, asst. chief Out-Patient Clinic, 1965; practice medicine, specializing in general practice, Little Rock, 1966-—; mem. staffs St. Vincents Hosp., Baptist Hosp., Meml. Hosp.; family practice preceptorships U. Ark., 1970-72; asso. staff unit family practice U. Ark. Med. Center, 1971-72. Gen. practice state rep. Am. Cancer Soc., 1972; program physician Upward Bound project Philander Smith Coll., 1970-72; vol. physician Office Econ. Opportunity, 1971. Served to lt. comdr. USPHS, 1963-66. U. Ark. fellow, 1961; USPHS grantee, 1962. Mem. A.M.A., Am., Ark. (program com. 1969-71) acads. gen. practice, Pulaski County Gen. Practicioners Soc. (sec. 1971-72), Little Rock Jr. C. of C., Phi Theta Kappa. Episcopalian. Clubs: Caduceus, Razorback. Editor: Ark. Gen. Practicioners Newsletter, 1970-72. Home: & Office: 424 N University St Little Rock AR 72205

WADLEY, DONALD ELWIN, architect; b. El Dorado, Ark., July 24, 1926; s. Charles Elwin and Gladys (Deason) W.; student Northeast La. State Coll., 1946-48, La. State U., 1948-49; m. Peggy Jean Cobb, Mar. 24, 1950; 1 son, Daniel Elwin. Draftsman, W.K. Stubbs, architect, Monroe, La., 1952-55, L.G. High, engr., 1955-59; draftsman H.H. Land, architect, 1959-63, architect 1963-69; propr. D.E. Wadley, architect, 1970-—. Served with USNR, 1945-46. Mem. A.I.A. (chpt. pres. 1970), La Architects Assn. (past bd. dirs.). Mason. Club: Optimist. Home: 2010 Valencia St Monroe LA 71201 Office: 512 Ouachita Bank Bldg Monroe LA 71201

WADSWORTH, JOSEPH ALLISON CANNON, physician; b. Charlotte, N.C., Mar. 22, 1913; s. Joseph Allison Cannon and Mary (Henkel) W.; B.S., Davidson Coll., 1935; M.D., Duke, 1939; m. Martha Toms Buchanan, June 27, 1942; children—Martha (Mrs. George H. Rathman, Jr.), Mary (Mrs. Thomas S. White III), Joseph Allison Cannon III. Intern Bellevue Hosp., N.Y.C., 1939-42; resident Inst. Ophthalmology, Columbia Presbyn. Hosp., N.Y.C., 1945-48; pvt. practice ophthalmology, N.Y.C., 1949-56; attending ophthalmologist Presbyn. Hosp. and Vanderbilt Clinic, 1959-65; attending surgeon Roosevelt Hosp., 1961-64; asso. clin. prof. ophthalmology Columbia, 1959-65; prof. ophthalmology, chmn. dept. Duke Med. Center, 1965-—; cons. VA Hosp., Durham, Watts Hosp., Durham; spl. research ophthalmol. pathology. Bd. visitors Davidson Coll. Served as flight surgeon USAAF, 1942-45. Diplomate Am. Bd. Ophthalmology. Mem. A.C.S., Am. Acad. Ophthalmologists and Otolaryngologists, Am. Ophthalmol. Soc., Nat. Bd. Med. Examiners, N.Y. Acad. Medicine, Verhoeff Soc., Assn. U. Profs. Ophthalmology (chmn. com. continuing edn.), Nat. Soc. Prevention Blindness, Human Betterment League N.C., Sigma Xi, Sigma Alpha Epsilon, Omicron Delta Kappa, Alpha Omega Alpha, Nu Sigma Nu, Sigma Upsilon. Kiwanian. Home: 1532 Pinecrest Rd Durham NC 27706

WADSWORTH, PHILIP ADRIAN, educator; b. Youngstown, O., Dec. 2, 1913; s. Roscoe Conkling and Avis (Hamersly) W.; A.B., Yale, 1935, Ph.D. (fellowship for study in France 1938), 1939; m. Charlotte Louise Riley, Feb. 28, 1942; children—Adrian R., Avis H. (Mrs. Michael Rumney). Instr., then asst. prof. French, Yale, 1939-42, 45-50; asso. prof. Northwestern U., 1950-54; prof. French, U. Ill., 1954-64; prof. French, chmn. dept. dean humanities Rice U., 1964-65, prof. French, 1965-—. Mem. Civil Rights Found. Served to comdr. USNR, 1942-45, 52-53. Guggenheim fellow, 1949-50. Mem. Modern Lang. Assn., Am. Assn. Tchrs. French, Modern Lang. Tchrs. Assn. Author: The Novels of Gomberville, 1942; Young La Fontaine, 1952; Poesies de Tristan l'Hermite, 1962. Home: 2114 McClendon St Houston TX 77025

WADSWORTH, TERRY MICHAEL, architect; b. Nogales, Ariz., Aug. 15, 1936; s. Chet Winston and Mary Carmine (McCormick) W.; B.A., Tex. A. and M. U., 1959; m. Nancy D. Boring, Aug. 15, 1959; children—Michael David, Melanie Dawn. Draftsman, office mgr. Bennie Gonzales, architect, Phoenix, 1961-63; project architect Barnes, Landers, Goodmony, Youngblood, Austin, Tex., 1963-68; partner Scudder & Wadsworth, Austin, 1968-—. Served with AUS, 1959-61. Mem. A.I.A., Tex. Soc. Architects, Constrn. Specifications Inst. (pres. 1968, honor award, 1969, 70). Club: Capitol City A. and M. Home: 5903 Tumbling Circle Austin TX 78731 Office: 800 West Av Austin TX 78701

WAGERS, LYMAN ELLSWORTH, orthodontist; b. Bright Shade, Ky., July 27, 1922; s. Floyd and Myrtle (Peters) W.; student U. Ky., 1938-40; D.M.D., U. Louisville, 1943; postgrad. Ohio State U., 1950-52; m. Lois Hall, Feb. 21, 1942; children—David, Lyman Ellsworth, Susan. Gen. practice dentistry, Falmouth, Ky., 1946-47, Lexington, Ky., 1947-52; pvt. practice orthodontics, Lexington, 1952-—. Clin. instr. orthodontic dept. U. Ky. Health Center, 1969-—. Sec. Ky. Med. Found., 1959; pres. Ohio State U. Orthodontic Alumni Found., 1965. Served to capt., Dental Corps, AUS, 1943-46. Recipient Distinguished Service award Ohio State U. Orthodontic Alumni Found., 1969. Diplomate Am. Bd. Orthodontics. Fellow Am. Coll. Dentists, Internat. Coll. Dentists; mem. Am. Assn. Orthodontists, Am., Ky. (pres. 1959-60) dental assns. Club: Country (Lexington). Home: 1040A Armstrong Mill Rd Lexington KY 40502 Office: 1636 Nicholasville Rd Lexington KY 40503

WAGES, ORLAND JACK, clergyman, librarian; b. Canton, Tex., Aug. 2, 1915; s. Homer DeWitt and Della (Crabtree) W.; student Tex. Tech. Coll., 1936-39; B.S. in L.S., Stephen F. Austin State Coll., 1954; M.S. in L.S., E. Tex. State Coll., 1958, postgrad., 1960-63; m. Alice Ella Humphreys, Aug. 31, 1956. Librarian, instr. speech Jacksonville (Tex.) Coll., 1951-59; asst. librarian, instr. library sci. E. Tex. State Coll., Commerce, 1959-63; librarian, extension instr. library sci. Bridgewater (Va.) Coll., 1963-—; extension instr. U. Va., 1967-—. Ordained to ministry Baptist Ch., 1951; pastor chs. in Maaydelle, Tex., 1953-57, Edom, Tex., 1957-59, Jackson, Tex., 1959-63, Fulks Run, Va., 1963-64, Virginia Av. Bapt. Ch., Harrisonburg, Va., 1967-69. Served to capt. with USAAF, 1940-48. Mem. A.L.A., Southeastern, Va. (editor Va. Librarian 1965-69) library assns., Am. Ednl. Research Assn., Christian Librarians Fellowship (pres. 1967-69), Ministerial Assn., Shenandoah Valley Folklore Soc., Rockingham Hist. Soc., Nat. Geneal. Soc., Phi Delta Kappa. Democrat. Clubs: Civitan (v.p. Jacksonville 1958-59), Rotary (pres. Bridgewater 1966-67). Author: Church Librarian's Handbook, 1961. Home: 210 W Bank St Bridgewater VA 22812 Office: Bridgewater College Bridgewater VA 22812

WAGGONER, WILLIAM JOHNSON, lawyer; b. Salisbury, N.C., Oct. 13, 1928; s. James Martin and Julia (Johnson) W.; A.B., U. N.C., 1951, LL.B., 1954; m. Martha Anne Garwood, Aug. 8, 1953; children—William Johnson, Ellen Christine, David Garwood. Admitted to N.C. bar, 1954; asst. U.S. Atty for Western Dist. of N.C., 1957-59; partner Waggoner, Hasty and Kratt, Charlotte. Mem. Republican Speakers Bur., 1959-—; gen. counsel Mecklenburg Republican Exec. Com., 1963-—. Served with AUS, 1946-47. Mem. C. of C., Nat. Assn. Sch. Bd. Attys., Kappa Alpha. Club: Hornet Toastmasters (past pres.). Mem. Am., N.C. Fed. bar assns., N.C. State Bar, Am. Trial Lawyers Assn. Lutheran (bd. deacons). Home: 6511

Newhall Rd Charlotte NC 28211 Office: 723 Law Bldg Charlotte NC 28202

WAGGONNER, JOSEPH DAVID, JR., congressman; b. Plain Dealing, La., Sept. 7, 1918; s. Joe David and Elizzibeth (Johnston) W.; B.A., La. Poly. Inst., 1941; m. Mary Ruth Carter, Dec. 14, 1942; children—Carol Jean, David. Mem. 87th-92d Congresses, 4th Dist. La. Mem. Bossier Parish Sch. Bd., 1954-61, pres., 1956-57; mem. La. Bd. Edn., 1960-61. Pres. United Sch. Com. La., 1961, La. Sch. Bds. Assn., 1961. Served to lt. comdr. USNR, World War II, Korea. Mem. Am. Legion, 40 and 8, Kappa Sigma. Democrat. Methodist. Mason (33 deg., Shriner), Elk, Lion. Home: Plain Dealing LA 71064 also 2111 Jefferson Davis Hwy Arlington VA Office: House of Representatives Washington DC 20515

WAGLEY, BETTY SUE, educator; b. Eastland, Tex., May 1, 1932; d. Virgil Rufus and Amy (Johnson) Wagley; B.S., Tex. Woman's U., 1953, M.S., N. Tex. State U., 1964. Tchr., Ector County Ind. Schs., Odessa, Tex., 1953-66; instr. modern math., devel. reading Odessa Coll., 1964-66; ednl. cons. Scott, Foresman & Co., Dallas, 1966—. Mem. Ector County Classroom Tchrs. (past sec.), Tex. Tchrs. Assn. (past sec., treas. Ector County), Tex. Council Tchrs. Math., Internat. Reading Assn., Nat. Council Tchrs. English, Tex. Womans U. Alumni Assn., Delta Kappa Gamma, Kappa Kappa Iota. Baptist. Home: 3623 Dawn St Odessa TX 79762 Office: 11310 Gemini Lane Dallas TX 75229

WAGLEY, MARJORIE IRENE CORLEY (MRS. ALTON CADE WAGLEY), educator; b. Florien, La., Nov. 4, 1914; d. Luther Franklin and Nancy (Miller) Corley; B.A., Northwestern U., 1936., U. Houston, 1950; postgrad. S.W. Tex., State Coll., 1946; Brigham Young U., 1958; m. Alton Cade Wagley, Jan. 16, 1937; children—Margie Katherine (Mrs. Gene Barry), Alton Carlin. Tchr. pub. schs., Sabine Parish, La., 1936-42, Beaumont, Tex., 1945-53; dir. spl. edn. S. Parks Sch., Beaumont, 1953—. Dir. Services Unlimited, Beaumont, Mem. N.E.A., Tex. Tchrs. Assn., Council Adminstrs. Spl. Edn. (sec. 1967-69), Council for Exceptional Children, Texas Council for Exceptional Children (pres. 1966; membership chmn. 1967—), Delta Kappa Gamma. Baptist. Club: Soroptimist (charter; corr. sec.), local pres. 1972-73) (Beaumont, Tex.). Author: Organizing and Administering Special Education. Home: PO Box 206 Nome TX 77629 Office: 1025 Woodrow St Beaumont TX 77705

WAGLOW, IRVING FREDERICK, educator; b. Plainfield, N.J., Sept. 21, 1915; s. Casper Frederick and Mary (Giese) W.; B.S., Springfield Coll., 1941, M.Ed., 1948; Ed.D., N.Y.U., 1964; m. Jean Ten Broeck Swalm, Jan. 24, 1942; 1 son, Richard Frederick. Asso. phys. dir. YMCA, Montclair, N.J., 1941-42; chmn. dept. phys. edn. U. Fla., 1958-71, prof. phys. edn., 1946—. Served with USAAF, 1942-46. Recipient Founders Day award, N.Y.U., 1965, Honor award Fla. Assn. Health, Phys. Edn. and Recreation, 1970. Mem. Nat. Coll. Phys. Edn. Assn. for Men, A.A.H.P.E.R., Am. Assn. U. Profs., Phi Delta Kappa, Tau Kappa Epsilon. Author: Social Dance for Students and Teachers, 1953; (with D.K. Stanley) Physical Education Activities Handbook, 2d ed., 1966. Home: 4 SW 23d St Gainesville FL 32601

WAGNER, AUBREY JOSEPH, engr., govt. ofcl.; b. Hillsboro, Wis., Jan. 12, 1912; s. Joseph M. and Wilhelmina (Filter) W.; B.C.E. magna cum laude, U. Wis., 1933; LL.D. (hon.), Newberry Coll., 1966; D.Pub. Adminstrn., Lenoir Rhyne Coll., 1970; m. Dorothea J. Huber, Sept. 9, 1933; children—Audrey Grace, Joseph Michael, James Richard, Karl Edward. Various positions hwy. engring., surveying, soil erosion control; with TVA, 1934—, beginning as engring. aide, successively jr. hydraulic engr., asst. hydraulic engr., asso. nav. engr., nav. engr., asst. chief river transp. div., acting chief and chief nav. and transp. br., asst. gen. mgr., 1951-54, gen. mgr., 1954-61, became dir., 1961, chmn. bd., 1962—. Mem. Breeder Reactor Corp., 1972—, also vice chmn. Com. domestic water nav. projects and nat. policy Pres.'s Water Resources Policy Commn., 1950; mem. Pres.'s Appalachian Regional Commn., 1963-65, Pres.'s Council Recreation and Natural Beauty, 1965-69; Pres.'s Cost Reduction Council, 1968-69; mem. engring. adv. com. Tenn. Technol. U., 1968—; mem. Tenn. Gov.'s Sci. Adv. Com., 1968-70; mem. nat. adv. council 1974 World Energy Conf., 1971—; mem. adv. com. 1972 UN Conf. Human Environment, 1971—; mem. sr. utility steering com. AEC, 1971—; mem. FPC Exec. Adv. Com. Nat. Power Survey, 1972—; lectr. agr. and natural resources session Salzburg Seminar in Am. Studies, 1968. Mem. nat. council Boy Scouts Am. Recipient Silver Beaver award Boy Scouts Am., 1956, Dougherty award U. Tenn., 1969. Mem. Tenn. Archeol. Soc., Ft. Loudoun Assn., Beta Gamma Sigma, Tau Beta Pi, Chi Epsilon, Phi Kappa Phi, Phi Eta Sigma, Lambda Chi Alpha (Order Achievement 1970), Scabbard and Blade. Lutheran (mem. exec. council Luth. Ch. Am. 1962-70, bd. theol. edn. 1970-72). Home: 403 New Spranicle Bldg Knoxville TN 37902 Office: TVA Knoxville TN 37902

WAGNER, FRANCIS STEPHEN, librarian, historian;; b. Krupina, Czechoslovakia, Feb. 28, 1911; s. Ferenc and Maria (Miko) W.; high sch. techr.'s diploma summa cum laude, U. Szeged, 1935, coll. tchr.'s diploma summa cum laude, 1937, Ph.D. summa cum laude, 1940; m. Irene Trefny, Feb. 2, 1947; 1 dau., Christina Maria Teresa. Came to U.S., 1949, naturalized, 1956. Prof. history, Slavic and Hungarian langs. and lit. Budapest (Hungary) State Coll., 1938-45; Slavic specialist Ministry Fgn. Affairs, Budapest, 1945-46; head, Hungarian Consulate Gen., Bratislava, Czechoslovakia, 1946-48; mem. staff Library of Congress, Washington, 1953—. Lectr. in field, 1938—. Mem. Am. Hist. Assn., Am. Studies Assn., Civil War Round Table D.C., Washington Philos. Club, Internat. Platform Assn., Helicon Soc. Author: First Period of Slovak Nationalism, 1940; Cultural Revolution in East Europe, 1955; Szechenyi and the Nationality Problem in the Hapsburg Empire, 1960; The Hungarian Revolution in Perspective, 1967; Toward a New Central Europe, 1970. Mem. adv. bd. Historical Abstracts: Bibliography of the World's Periodical Lit., 1971—; mem. editorial bd. in charge fgn. areas Survey America: History and Life; book revs. sect. editor Studies for a New Central Europe. Contbr. articles, book revs. to profl. jours., mags. Home: 4610 Franklin St Kensington MD 20795 Office: Library of Congress Washington DC 20540

WAGNER, FRED, pres. Union Equity Coop. Exchange. Address: Union Equity Coop Exchange 10th and Willow Sts Enid OK 73701*

WAGNER, FREDERIC EMIL, oil and gas co. exec.; b. Waco, Tex., Aug. 14, 1920; s. Frederic Emil and Ernestine (Clements) W.; student North Tex. Agrl. Coll., 1941-42, So. Methodist U., 1943-45; B.S., U. Tex., 1946; m. Ellen Marie Seay, Mar. 14, 1964; children—Jory Watner, Hilda. Pres. chmn. bd. Williams & Wagner Constrn. Co., Dallas, 1946—. Williams & Wagner Investments, Inc., Dallas, 1946—, Eldorado Oil & Gas, Inc., Dallas, 1956—, Sovereign Oil &Gas, Inc., Dallas, 1965—, Airport Realty Corp., Dallas, 1969—. Chmn.bd. Treasure Island Municipal Dist. Brazoria County, 1968-69; active Dallas Opera Guild. Recipient Distinguished Service award Nat. Exchange Club, 1956. Mem. Council Sci. Socs., Am. Soc. Photogrammetry, Photogrammetry Soc. London, Soc. Petroleum Engrs., Am. Inst. Mining, Metall. and Petroleum Engrs., Petroleum Engrs. Club Dallas, U.S. Power Squadron, USCG Aux., Tex. Thoroughbred Breeders Assn. (pres. 1963-64, 68-69), Horsemen's Benevolent Protective Assn., Nat. Rifle Assn., Nat. Skeet Shooting Assn., Cal. Thoroughbred Breeders Assn. Clubs: Brookhaven Country, Hollow Golf, 21 Turtle, Braniff Internat. Council, Admiral's, Cipango (Dallas); Pala Mesa (Cal.) Golf. Author: Aircraft Lofting Practice, 1943. Home: 8801 Jourdan Way Dallas TX 75225 Office: 2929 Cedar Springs Rd Dallas TX 75219

WAGNER, HILMAR ERNEST, educator; b. Rowena, Tex., Mar. 1, 1929; s. Hilmar Herman and Frances Cecelia (Fowler) W.; B.S., Tex. Tech. U., 1949; M.A., Sul Ross State Coll., 1952; Ed.D., N. Tex. State U., 1967; m. Alpha Louise Brand, Dec. 26, 1951; children—Lisa, Andi, Sheila, Rusty. Band dir. Rochester (Tex.) High Sch., 1949-51, DeLeon (Tex.) High Sch., 1951-52, Fredericksburg (Tex.) High Sch., 1954-58; asso. prof. music Tarleton State Coll., Stephenville, Tex., 1959-66; asso. prof. curriculum and instrn. U. Tex., El Paso, 1966—. Cons. Headstart Supplementary Tng. Program, 1968—, cons. curriculum com. Loretta Acad., El Paso, 1969—. Served with AUS, 1952-54. Named Outstanding Faculty Mem. Sch. Edn., publs. staff U. Tex. at El Paso, 1969-70. Mem. Tex. Tchrs. Assn., N.E.A., Assn. Student Teaching, Assn. Supervision and Curriculum Devel., Kappa Delta Pi, Phi Delta Kappa, Kappa Kappa Psi. Author: (with J. Paulson) Let's March, 1959; (with B. Evans) The Cost of a High School Education, 1970; The Song Flute, 1968. Contbr. articles to profl. jours. Home: 8408 Edgemere Blvd El Paso TX 79925

WAGNER, KIP LOWELL, historian, researcher; b. Montgomery, O., Dec. 4, 1905; s. William H. and Clara E. (Kuhns) W.; student pub. schs., Ohio; D.Sc., Westminster Coll., New Wilmington, Pa., 1966; m. Alice Louise Stocker, Apr. 4, 1931; 1 son, Thomas Lee. Self employed historian researcher Mexico, Barcelona, Madrid, Sevilla, London and Paris pertaining to 1715 Spanish Plate Fleet, 1951-71; chief research Civil Service, Wright AFB, Dayton, 1938-44; pres., chmn. bd. Real 8 Corp., 1960-70; owner, operator research library Foul Anchor Archives. Pres. Wabasso P.T.A., 1951-54; scoutmaster Gulf Stream council Boy Scouts Am., 1951-54; Mgr. Little League Baseball, 1951-54. Recipient Diving award of Year, 1962; plaque for Treasure Hunter of 1962. Mason. Author: Pieces of 8, 1966. Home: 1 Sunset Blvd Sebastian FL 32958

WAGNER, LULAMAY WILSON (MRS. CHARLES EARL WAGNER), state ofcl.; b. Alexandria, La., Sept. 25, 1916; d. Charles Oscar and Mary Lou (Stracener) Wilson; grad. Alexandria Bus. Coll., 1940, Alexandria Acad. Beauty Culture, 1938; m. Charles Earl Wagner, Aug. 22, 1942; 1 dau., June (Mrs. William David Roland, Jr.). Mgr. D. H. Holmes Beauty Salon, Baton Rouge, 1943-44; owner Maison de Beaute, Alexandria, La., 1945—; spl. agt. Dept. Pub. Safety, La., 1960—; hon. atty. gen., Baton Rouge, 1960—. Mem. La. Bd. Cosmetology, 1960-64, 68—, vice chmn., 1964—. Recipient War Bonds Sales award New Orleans, 1942. Mem. Nat.-Interstate Council State Bds. Cosmetology, Nat. Assn. Cosmetology Sch., Nat. Hairdressers and Cosmetologists Assn., Inc., Internat. Platform Assn. Baptist. Mem. Order Eastern Star. Home: 2033 White St Alexandria LA 71301 Office: La Office Bldg Civic Center New Orleans LA 70112

WAGNER, RALPH PATTERSON, investment co. exec.; b. Beatrice, Neb., Aug. 22, 1893; s. William Henry and Cordelia Harriet (Scherer) W.; B.S. in Civil Engring., B.S. in Elec. Engring., U. Neb., 1917; m. Mary Eleanor Houston, Nov. 20, 1924 (dec.); 1 dau., Eleanor Patterson. With Cities Service Co., N.Y.C., 1920-29, Niagara Mohawk Power Co., Albany, N.Y., 1929-56; pres., dir. South Tex. Devel. Co., Albany, 1957—; Sotexco, Inc., Albany, 1971—; with Wytax Corp., Albany, 1957—, pres., 1965—, dir., 1957—; v.p., dir. Triton Corp., Albany, 1964—; dir. Conroy, Inc., San Antonio, Heartland Devel. Co., Albany, Heartland Leasing Corp., Albany. Bd. dirs. Morton Plant Hosp., Clearwater, Fla., 1963-69; bd. dirs., pres. Albany Med. Center Hosp., 1948—, Huntington's Chorea Found., N.Y.C., 1967—; bd. dirs. Albany Med. Coll., 1949—, v.p., 1949-57. Served with U.S. Army 1917-42. Mem. Sigma Tau. Club: University (Albany). Home: 1408 S Betty Lane Clearwater FL 33516 Office: 46 Beaver St Albany NY 12207

WAGNER, VERNON LESLIE, JR., film co. exec.; b. New Orleans, July 4, 1936; s. Vernon Leslie and Jean Margaret (Byrne) W.; B.S., Tulane U., 1957; postgrad., 1961-63; M.S., U. Va., 1958; m. Patricia Edith Cole, Apr. 8, 1959; children—Christopher Lee, Gretchen Steele, John Marshall, Stephanie Keller. Chemist, Shell Oil Co., Norco, La., 1956-57; research chemist Freeport Nickel-Sulphur Co., Braithwaite, La., 1959-62; pvt. cons., New Orleans, 1962—, with Kalvar Corp. film mfg. New Orleans 1962—, v.p. research and devel., 1970—; partner Asso. Ideas, Inc., New Orleans, 1963—. Active in civic and polit. activities. Served with USMCR, 1954-62. Recipient Oscar Lee Putnam fellowship Tulane U., 1955-57; award Am. Inst. Chemists, 1957. Mem. T.A.P.P.I., Soc. Photog. Scientists and Engrs., Am. Inst. Aeros. and Astronautics, Sigma Xi, Phi Eta Sigma. Club: Chemists (N.Y.C.). Patentee in field. Home: 508 Short St New Orleans LA 70018 Office: 909 S Broad St New Orleans LA 70125

WAGNER, WILSON ORR, physician; b. Dallas, July 21, 1915; s. James Ernest and Lottie Mellisa (Hart) W.; B.S., U. Tex. at Austin, 1937, M.D., at Galveston, 1942; m. Lucille Pelham, Oct. 18, 1947; children—Joan, Wilson Orr. Intern U.S. Naval Hosp., Corpus Christi, Tex., 1942-43; Nat. Naval Med. Center, Bethesda, Md., 1945; gen. practice medicine and surgery, Carrollton, Tex., 1946—; mem. staff Brookhaven Gen. Hosp., Farmers Branch, Tex., also past pres., mem. exec. com., mem. staff Meth. Hosp., Dallas. Pres., owner Security Investment Corp., Carrollton, 1965—, Master Electronics, Inc., Carrollton, dir., part owner 1st Security Bank & Trust Co., Carrollton. Served with USNR, 1942-46. Mem. Dallas County Med. Sco., Tex. Med. Assn., Am. Acad. Gen. Practice. Clubs: Brookhaven Country, Lancers (Dallas). Home: 13531 Crestmoor St Dallas TX 75234 Office: 1301 Elm St Carrollton TX 75006

WAHLHEIM, CHARLES ARTHUR, newspaper exec.; b. Rock Island, Ill., July 15, 1931; s. Charles J. and Martha (Gruske) W.; student St. Ambrose Coll., 1949-51, Augustania Coll., 1952; m. Jacqueline A. Stuart, Oct. 23, 1954; children—Patricia Jean, Teresa Marie, Charles Joseph, Peter Thomas, Paul Steven. Prodn. mgr. South Bay Daily Breeze, Torrance, Cal., 1961-65, cons. to pub., 1965-66; operations dir. Sacramento Union, 1966-67, asst. to pub., 1967-69, v.p., gen. mgr., 1969-70; v.p. operations Harte-Hanks Newspapers, Inc., San Antonio, 1970—, also dir. Bd. dirs. Met. YMCA, Sacramento. Served with AUS, 1951-52; Korea. Mem. Am. Legion, Sierra Club. Home: 211 Village Circle San Antonio TX 78232 Office: 711 Navarro PO Box 269 San Antonio TX 78206

WAHLQUIST, JACK RAINARD, ins. co. exec.; b. Omaha, Oct. 10, 1933; s. Kenneth Dudley and Dot (Sesler) W.; B.A. magna cum laude, Yale, 1955; LL.B. cum laude, U. Tex., 1958; m. Elizabeth Jean Bailey, July 8, 1960; children—Laura Alice, Elizabeth Jennifer. With Gt. Nat. Life Ins. Co., Dallas, 1951-69, v.p., sec., 1964-67, exec. v.p., 1967-69; admitted to Tex. bar, 1953; v.p. United Internat. Corp., Dallas, 1969-70, also pres., then chmn. bd. Transport Life Ins. Co., Dallas; v.p. planning and policy services Southland Life Ins. Co., Dallas, 1970—. Bd. dirs. Dallas Theatre Center, 1968-72. Fellow Life Office Mgmt. Assn.; mem. Tex., Dallas, Am. bar assns., Ins. Club, Phi Delta. Clubs: Chapparal, Yale (pres. 1965-67) (Dallas). Home: 6468 Waggoner Rd Dallas TX 75230 Office: PO Box 2220 Dallas TX 75221

WAID, LUTHER PINKNEY, judge; b. nr. Boaz, Ala., Mar. 2, 1915; s. Luther Pinkney and Roxie (Bynum) W.; student Tenn. Wesleyan Coll., 1933-34; LL.B., U. Ala., 1939; m. Louise Griffith, July 2, 1953. Admitted Ala. bar, 1939, pvt. practice, Guntersville, Ala., 1939-41, Oneonta, 1946-51, 65-67; pros. atty., Blount County, 1949-51; dist. atty., 1951-59; circuit judge, 1959-65; dist. atty. 30th Jud. Circuit, 1967-71, circuit judge, 1971—. Chmn., Oneonta Housing Authority, 1949-55, mem. commn., 1955-59. Served from pvt. to 1st lt. AUS, 1941-46. Mem. Marshall County (pres. 1941), Blount County (sec. 1949-52, pres. 1970-71) bar assns., Am. Legion, C. of C. (dir. 1951-53). Democrat. Mason. Club: Civitan (pres. Oneonta 1950-51, gov. Ala. dist. N. 1956-57). Home: 407 4th Av W Oneonta AL 35121 Office: Courthouse Oneonta AL 35121

WAIGHT, ARTHUR ALVIN, JR., city ofcl.; b. Hamilton, Tex., May 24, 1927; s. Arthur Alvin and Thelma (Jenkins) W.; student Panhandle A. and M. Coll., 1949-51, FBI Nat. Acad., 1964; m. Mary Joanne Updike, Nov. 24, 1960; children—John Arthur, Paul Matthew. Mem. Tex. Hwy. Patrol, 1951-61; chief of police, City of Borger, Tex., 1961—. Served with USMCR, 1945-49. Mason, Rotarian (pres. club 1972-73). Home: PO Box 721 Borger TX 79007 Office: 615 Weatherly St Borger TX 79007

WAINSHAL, HAROUZI, housing devel. exec.; b. Jerusalem, Israel, Apr. 15, 1932 came to U.S. 1963, naturalized, 1971.; s. Matityah and Zina (Stein) W.; B.S. in Civil Engring., cum laude, Technion, Israel Inst. Tech., 1955; m. Yael Wasser, Sept. 23, 1962; children— Ron, Ruth, Tamar. Project engr. City of Jerusalem, 1956-58; adminstr., tech. dir. Israel Standards Inst., 1958-60; project engr., Iran, 1960-61, Israel, 1961-62; operations mgr. Hampton Devel. Corp., San Juan, P. R., 1963-66; exec. v.p. Devel. Internat. Corp., Coral Gables, Fla., 1966-72, dir., 1969-72. Pioneer reinforced concrete modular systems. Home: 11001 SW 75th Ct Miami FL 33156 Office: 999 S Bayshore Dr Suite 1610 Miami FL 33131

WAINWRIGHT, BILL C., savs. and loan assn. exec.; b. Tampa, Fla., Nov. 20, 1913; s. Truby L. and Mabel A. (Britt) W.; B.S. in Bus., U. Fla., 1937; LL.B., Atlanta Law Sch., 1947; postgrad. U. Ind., 1956, Dartmouth, 1963; m. Rebecca Ann Bethel, June 27, 1942; children—Rebecca Ann, Bill C. Pres., Atlanta Fed. Savs. & Loan Assn., 1945—, also dir., mem. exec. com.; dir. United Family Life Ins. Co. Mem. Atlanta Bd. Edn., 1966-69, pres., 1968-69; pres. Atlanta Traffic and Safety Council, 1967, Northside Hosp., 1964-65. Served as lt. col. AUS, 1941-46. Mem. Am. Savs. and Loan Inst. (nat. pres. 1961), Ga. Savs. and Loan League (pres. 1959), Atlanta C. of C. (dir. 1963-65), Lambda Chi Alpha (nat. dir.). Home: 3200 Downwood Circle NW Atlanta GA 30327 Office: 20 Marietta St NW Atlanta GA 30303

WAITS, JULIA CAROLYN, sch. adminstr.; b. Greenville, Miss., Jan. 1, 1935; d. Hilton and Mildred (Barnard) Waits; B.A., U. Miss., 1956, M.Ed., 1960, student Sch. Law, 1963-64. Field sec. Phi Mu, Memphis, 1957; panhellenic adviser, asst. dean women U. Miss., Oxford, 1957-66, community program planning specialist, U. Extension, Oxford, 1966-67; asst. dean women, La. State U., Baton Rouge, 1967—. Tchr. U. Miss., 1961-63. Vice pres. League Women Voters, Oxford, Miss., 1967. Bd. dirs. A.R.C., Lafayette County. Mem. Am. Assn. U. Women (Miss. treas. 1965), Nat. Assn. Women Deans and Counselors, Mortar Bd. (sect. dir.), Phi Mu. Home: 1290 Park Blvd Baton Rouge LA 70806

WAITS, THOMAS POPE, dentist; b. nr. Oxford, Miss., July 13, 1935; s. Tommy Alfred and Thelma (Hawkins) W.; D.D.S., U. Louisville, 1960; B.S., Miss. Coll., 1956; m. Sara Maloy Hodges, May 19, 1968. Pvt. practice dentistry, Gulfport, Miss., 1962-63, Bruce, Miss., 1962—. Mem. Calhoun County Com. Mental Health, 1968—; chmn. Calhoun County Heart Fund, 1967—; guardian Pushmataha Area council Boy Scouts Am., 1968; chmn. Bruce Rotary Club Kidney Found. Col., Gov. John B. Williams staff, 1968-72, Gov. Bill Waller staff, 1972—. Served to capt. USAF, 1960-62. Mem. Am., N.E. Miss. dental assns., Bruce C. of C. Delta Sigma Delta. Republican. Baptist. Home: McSwyn St Bruce MS 38915 Office: Calhoun St Bruce MS 38915

WAKEFIELD, DUANE DARIEL, assn. exec.; b. Grimsley, Tenn., Apr. 2, 1936; s. Horace Maynord and Trannie (Stephens) W.; B.S., U. Tenn., 1960; m. Velma Mae Ramsey, July 4, 1967; children—Nancy, Dariel, Michael. Tchr., Knox County Sch. System, 1960-61; ins. agt. State Farm Ins. Co., 1961-63; ins. adjuster Markel Ins. Co., 1963-64; tchr., coach Roane County Sch. System, 1964-69; exec. sec. Livingston (Tenn.) C. of C., 1969—. Cons. Livingston Area Vocational Sch., 1969-72. Bd. dirs. Upper Cumberland Devel. Dist. Served with AUS, 1954-57; ETO. Mem. Tenn. Assn. C. of C. Execs., Jr. C. of C. (pres. 1965). Lion. Home: Golf Course Rd Livingston TN 38570 Office: PO Box 354 Livingston TN 38570

WAKEHAM, HELMUT RICHARD RAE, tobacco co. exec.; b. Hamburg, Germany, Apr. 15, 1916; s. Rae G. and Augusta (Beiss) W.; B.A., U. Neb., 1936, M.A., 1937; Ph.D., U. Cal. at Berkeley, 1939; m. Kathleen Ferguson, June 22, 1939; children—Stuart, Susan, Rosemary. Research chemist Standard Oil Co. Cal., 1939-41, So. Regional Research Lab., U.S. Dept. Agr., 1941-47; research asso. Inst. Textile Tech., Charlottesville, Va., 1947-49; project head chem.-physics sect. Textile Research Inst., also research dir., 1949-56; dir. Ahmedabad (India) Textile Industries Research Assn., 1956-58; staff asst. for research to v.p. Philip Morris, Inc., 1958-59, dir. research and devel., 1959-61, v.p., dir. research and devel., 1961-65, v.p. corporate research and devel., 1965—. Mem. Sci. Commn. of CORESTA, internat. tobacco research orch., 1966—; gen. chmn. CORESTA/TCRC meeting, Williamsburg, Va., 1972; mem. program com. Nat. Conf. Adminstrn. Research Committee; member of general adv. com. Textile Research Inst., 1961—. Fellow Am. Inst. Chemists, Textile Inst. (Great Britain); mem. Am. Chem. Soc. (chmn. local program sect. 1943-45), Fiber Soc. (program chmn., councilor 1950-55), A.A.A.S., Am. Inst. Physics. Home: 8901 Brieryle Rd Richmond VA 23229 Office: PO Box 26583 Richmond VA 23261

WAKEMAN, FREDERIC, writer; b. Scranton, Kan., Dec. 26, 1909; s. Don Conklin and Myrtle (Evans) W.; A.B., Park Coll., Parkville, Mo. 1933; m. Margaret Keys, June 1, 1934; children—Frederic, Jr., Sue, Don. Began as advt. copywriter, later becoming account exec. for advt. agency; free-lance radio script writer and radio exec. Served as lt., U.S.N.R., 1942-43. Author: Shore Leave; 1943; The Hucksters, 1946; Saxon Charm, 1947; The Wastrel, 1949, Mandrake Root, 1953; The Fabulous Train, 1955; Deluxe Tour, 1956; Virginia Q, 1959; Fault of the Apple, 1960; A Free Agent, 1962; The Flute Across the Pond, 1966‡

WALBRIDGE, WILLARD EUGENE, tv broadcasting co. exec.; b. Pa., Mar. 11, 1913; s. Peter D. and Anna (Higbee) W.; A.B., U. Mich., 1936; m. Marietta H. Arner, Nov. 15, 1941; 1 son, Peter F. Salesman Detroit Edison, 1936-39, radio sta. WWJ, Detroit, 1939-43; mgr. sta. WWJ-TV, Detroit, 1946-53; exec. v.p. and gen. mgr. sta. WJIM, Lansing, Mich., 1953-54, KTRK-TV Houston, 1954-70; sr. v.p.

Capital Cities Broadcasting Corp., Washington, 1970—. Bd. dirs. Houston Conv. and Visitors Council, Am. Cancer Soc., Salvation Army, A.R.C., Florence Crittenton Home, Houston Grand Opera Assn., Fat Stock Show, Soc. for Performing Arts. Served from ensign to lt. with USNR, 1943-46. Decorated Silver Star medal. Mem. Nat. Assn. Broadcasters (chmn. bd. 1969-71, dir.). Home: 3460 Piping Rock Lane Houston TX 77027 Office: Box 12 Houston TX 77001 also 1629 K St NW Washington DC 20006

WALD, CARL EDWARD, govt. ofcl.; b. Bridgeport, Conn., Mar. 9, 1917; s. Robert Edward and Margaret (Gregory) W.; B.C.S., Northeastern U., 1939; m. Ruth Jane Canterbury, Dec. 20, 1943; 1 dau., Pamela (Mrs. Jack S. Wagner). Asst. treas. Grotty Bros., Inc., Boston, 1944-50; project planner AEC, Washington, 1950-52; mgr. U.S. Gen. Accounting Office, Washington, 1952-64; project mgr. Gen. Services Adminstrn., Washington, 1964—. Dir. Marva Assos., Silver Spring, Md., 1967-70. C.P.A., N.Y. Mem. Am. Inst. C.P.A.'s, N.Y. State Soc. C.P.A.'s, Fed. Govt. Accountants Assn. Home: 6047 Belleview Dr Falls Church VA 22041 Office: 18th and F Sts NW Washington DC 20405

WALDECK, RUBY B. WEEDELL (MRS. CARL G. WALDECK), club woman, educator; b. Tacoma, Wash., Apr. 13, 1896; d. Peter Andrew and Emmaline (Locke) Weedell; B.A., U. Minn., 1918; M.A., Washington U., 1936; m. Carl G. Waldeck, Dec. 22, 1920; children—Carl R., Beatrice Ann (Mrs. H.E. Beresford). Tchr. history Auston (Minn.) High Sch., 1918-19, Tacoma (Wash.) High Sch., 1919-20. Profl. book reviewer and lectr., also pvt. research work in Library of Congress; research work on old Fairfax County courthouses and early Fairfax County Ct., Fairfax County Planning Commn. Mem. Mayor's Adv. Com. Mem. Am. Assn. U. Women, Internat. Platform Assn., Heritage Soc. Fairfax County, Fairfax County Hist. Soc., Kappa Rho. Episcopalian. Clubs: Centreville Garden; Rocky Run Garden. Home: 1008 Lynn St SW Vienna VA 22180

WALDEN, CHARLES ROY, sociologist, writer; b. Diamond Springs, Cal., Nov. 16, 1931; s. Richard Vern and Florence (Gardner) W.; student San Francisco State Coll., 1949-50; B.A., U. Fla., 1958; student U. Louisville, 1967-68; m. Elaine Agnes Gocek, Sept. 26, 1953; 1 dau., Lisa Maria. Reporter Kansas City (Mo.) Times, 1958-59; reporter, editorial writer Chattanooga Times, 1959-65; editorial writer Louisville Courier-Jour., 1965-69; with Ky. Commn. on Human Rights, Louisville, 1969—. Served with USNR, 1950-54. Mem. Am. Sociol. Assn., Sigma Delta Chi. Home: 44 Eastover Ct Louisville KY 40206 Office: 600 W Walnut St Louisville KY 40203

WALDEN, CLARKE, lawyer; b. Macon, Ga., Oct. 31, 1926; s. Walter Clell and Rossie (Hendrix) W.; B.S., U.S. Mcht. Marine Acad., 1947; B.S. in Bus. Adminstrn., U. Fla., 1951, LL.B., 1952; m. Minnie Louise Tubbs, May 28, 1955; children—Mary Lou, Mark C., Paul Ashley. Mcht. ships officer Moore-McCormack Lines, Inc., N.Y.C., 1947-48; admitted to Fla. bar, 1952; practiced in Dania, 1954—; city atty., 1955—. Dir. Dania Bank. Mem. South Broward Hosp. Dist., 1966—, chmn., 1968. Served to lt. USNR, 1952-53. Mem. Am., Fla. bar assns., Dania C. of C. (dir.), Navy League, Sigma Phi Epsilon, Phi Alpha Delta. Mason (Shriner), Rotarian (past pres.). Club: Propeller. Home: 1502 SW 3d Av Dania FL 33004 Office: Dania Bank Bldg Dania FL 33004

WALDEN, JOHN CLAYTON, educator; b. Clinton, Ill., Sept. 15, 1928; s. Carter Branstetter and Trella Bernice (Bell) W.; A.B., U. Cal. at Los Angeles, 1952; M.A., Cal. State Coll. at Los Angeles, 1957; Ph.D., Claremont Grad. Sch., 1966; m. Shirley Gail Butterfield, Feb. 1, 1952; children—Deanne Carol, Kirk Allen. Tchr. pub. schs., Redlands, Cal., 1952-53; tchr. Monrovia (Cal.) Unified Sch. Dist., 1953-56, jr. high sch. prin., 1956-66; prof. ednl. adminstrn. Auburn (Ala.) U., 1966—, head dept. ednl. adminstrn. and supervision, 1970—. Cons. to sch. dists. in southeast. Pres. Family Service Agy., Monrovia, Cal., 1963. Served with USN, 1946-48. Recipient outstanding young man award Monrovia (Cal.), Jr. C. of C., 1963. Mem. Nat., Ala. edn. assns., Am., Ala. assns. sch. adminstrs., Am. Ednl. Research Assn., Nat. Orgn. Legal Problems of Edn., Am. Assn. University Profs., Nat. Conf. Profs. Ednl. Adminstrn., Phi Delta Kappa, Phi Kappa Tau. Kiwanian. Sect. editor Educational Administration Abstracts, 1969-71. Home: 132 Carter St Auburn AL 36830

WALDENVILLE, DAVID BAIRD, chemist; b. Aspinwall, Pa., Apr. 24, 1923; s. John Weldon and Jennie (Sime) W.; B.S., Ariz. State U., 1953; m. Bettie Vinson, Aug. 7, 1947; children—Cathy Gray, John David, Suan Jane, Nancy Jo. Cryogenic engr AEC, Pacific Test Area, 1953-54; research chemist Continental Oil Co., Ponca City, Okla., 1954-55; corrosion engr. Tretolite Co., St. Louis, 1955-59; microbiologist Buckman Labs., Memphis, 1959-61; sales mgr. chem. div. Baroid div. Nat. Lead Co., Houston, 1961-67; indsl. water chemist Western Chem. Co., Kansas City, Mo., 1967-69; founder, pres., water pollution control chemist and engr. Waste Treat, Inc., Oklahoma City, 1969—, also chmn. bd.; v.p., dir. Sunburst Products Inc., Oklahoma City, 1971—. Served to 1st lt. AUS, 1941-47; ETO Registered profl. engr., Okla. Mem. Nat., Okla. socs. prof. engrs., Okla. Water and Pollution Control Assn., Water Pollution Control Fedn. Patentee high rate oxidizing cell and tower, automatic dry enzyme feeder, purification process of pulp waste water. Home: 3420 Orerholser Dr Bethany OK 73008 Office: 7501 N Broadway Extension Oklahoma City OK 73116

WALDO, TOMMY RUTH BLACKMON (MRS. SELDEN FENNELL WALDO), educator; b. Dallas, Jan. 14, 1916; d. Gulie Hargrove and Mary Lee (Craig) Blackmon; B.A., Agnes Scott Coll., 1938; M.A., U. Fla., 1955, Ph.D., 1961; m. Selden Fennell Waldo, Oct. 28, 1941 (dec. Nov. 1950); children—George Selden (dec.), Andrew Blackmon. Grad. asst. U. Fla., Gainesville, 1952-55; instr., 1955-61, asst. prof. English, 1961—, now asso. prof.; pvt. tchr. piano and organ, 1938-55; organist Holy Trinity Episcopal Ch., Gainesville, 1941-42; asso. organist First Bapt. Ch., 1943-58, organist, 1958—. Dir., v.p. League Women Voters, 1947-50. Mem. S. Atlantic Modern Lang. Assn., Fla., Gainesville music tchrs. assns., Southeastern Renaissance Conf., Phi Beta Kappa, Delta Kappa Gamma, Sigma Alpha Iota. Democrat. Baptist. Contbr. articles to profl. jours. Home: 719 NE 1st St Gainesville FL 32601

WALDRON, CHARLES EMMETT, ednl. adminstr.; b. N.Y.C., Aug. 2, 1920; B.S., St. John's U., 1942, J.D., 1946; LL.M., N.Y. U., 1948 Admitted to N.Y. State bar, 1946; atty. firm Waldron & King, Wantagh, N.Y., 1948-64; asst. prof. law Catholic U. P.R., 1964-67, asso. prof. law, acting dean law sch., 1967-68, dean law sch., 1968—. Mem. Am. Bar Assn., Catholic Lawyers Guild, Am. Trial Lawyers Assn., Phi Alpha Delta. Address: Sch Law Catholic Univ Ponce PR 00731*

WALDROP, DENNIS WINFRED, dentist; b. Benton, Tenn., May 6, 1928; s. John Aubrey and Lola (Mitchell) W.; B.S., U. Tenn., 1954, D.D.S., 1955; m. Janie Lee Florance, Dec. 24, 1949; 1 dau., Patricia Ann. Post exchange officer, sales mgr. Army and Air Force Exchange Service, 1946-50; oral surgeon, dental adminstr. Central State Hosp., and dental cons. Petersburg (Va.) Tng. Sch., 1963-64; pvt. practice dentistry, specializing in oral surgery, Colonial Heights, Va., 1965—; dir. Colonial Beach (Va.) Shopping Center; founder, v.p. Historyland and Playground, Inc., Colonial Beach, 1963—. Served to lt. col. Dental Corps., AUS, 1955-63. Mem. Am. Dental Assn., Va. Philadelphia County dental socs., Federation Internationale Dentaire, Assn. Mil. Surgeons U.S., Assn. Advancement Gen. Anesthesia in Dentistry, Am. Legion, Omicron Kappa Upsilon, The Deans Soc., Psi Omega, Pi Kappa Alpha. Home: 201 Winston Av Colonial Heights VA 23834 Office: 129 Temple Av Colonial Heights VA 23834

WALDROP, LEWIS ANTHONY, civil engr.; b. Atlanta, Jan. 10, 1941; s. Lewis and Dorothy Lenora Jane (Strickland) W.; B.Civil Engring., Ga. Inst. Tech., 1963, postgrad., 1970-71; m. Eleanor Rebecca Barron, Mar. 3, 1962; children—Eleanor Dee, Liesl Annette. Civil engr. TVA, 1963-64; pres. Lewis Waldrop Contractor, Inc., Marietta, Ga., 1964-67; project engr. Hensley-Schmidt, Inc., cons. engrs., Marietta, 1967-69; v.p. Guillebeau, Britt & Waldrop, Inc., Decatur, Ga., 1969—. Pres. Ga. Baptist Conf. for Deaf, 1971-72. Registered profl. engr., Ga., Ark., Va. Mem. Ga. Soc. Profl. Engrs. (treas. Dekalb chpt. 1971-73), Cons. Engrs. Council, Am. Soc. C.E. (asso.), Ga. Water and Pollution Control Assn., Water Pollution Control Fedn., Chi Epsilon (treas. Ga. Inst. Tech. Chpt. 1962-63). Baptist (trustee). Home: Ross Rd Lithonia GA 30058 Office: 4279-H Memorial Dr Decatur GA 30032

WALDROP, ROBERT GLEN, city ofcl.; b. Parrish, Ala., Oct. 27, 1913; s. Robert G. and Mattie (Williamson) W.; B.S., Samford Coll., 1946; m. Louise Wright, May 18, 1940; children—Jane and Jean (twins). Pharmacist, Merck & Co., 1955; with Liberty Nat. Life Ins. Co., 1955—; mayor, Homewood, Ala., 1968—. Served with AUS, 1943-46. Mem. Birmingham Assn. Life Underwriters (v.p. 1967). Mason, Elk, Lion (pres. 1968). Home: 230 Lucerne St Homewood AL 35209 Office: City Hall Homewood AL 35209

WALES, BILL BARTLETT, oil co. exec.; b. Wink, Tex., Nov. 8, 1927; s. Bartlett Adkinson and Vera (Robinson) W.; B.Arch., Tex. A. and M. U., 1950; m. Elizabeth Fay Waters, Apr. 21, 1951; children—Charissa Lynn, William Bartlett, James Steven. Archtl. draftsman Lynn A. Evans, architect, Corpus Christi, Tex., 1950-51; archtl. planner Engrs. Associated, Corpus Christi, 1951-52; prin. Bill B. Wales, designer, Corpus Christi, 1952; archtl. job chief Kruger & Assos., Santa Fe, 1954-56; chief draftsman Hank Avery architect, Midland, Tex., 1956-58; contract rep. J & C Drilling Co., Corpus Christi, 1959-65, mgr., Refugio, Tex., 1965—, v.p., 1970—; sec. Refugio Enterprises, 1965—. Chmn. Mustang dist. Gulf Coast council Boy Scouts Am., 1966-68, mem., 1968—; mem. lay adv. bd. Refugio Meml. Hosp., 1967—; pres. Refugio Primary Elementary P.T.A., 1967-68, mem., 1968—. Served to lt., inf., AUS, 1952-54: Korea. Mem. A.I.A., Am. Assn. Oilwell Drilling Contractors, V.F.W. Lion (dist. gov., 1968-69). Home: 103 Dunbar St Refugio TX 78377 Office: 115 Purisima St Refugio TX 78377

WALESKI, ALEXANDER FRANK, sch. adminstr.; b. Chgo., Feb. 8, 1915; s. Alexander Frank and Henrietta Stefanie (Kovalowski) W.; B.A., Randolph-Macon Coll., 1939; M.A., U. N.C., 1949; m. Dorothy Eleanor Wickham, Dec. 26, 1939; 1 son, Arthur Frank. Tchr., coach Southampton County Sch. Bd., Franklin, Va., 1934-41, Henrico County Sch. Bd., Richmond, Va., 1941-43; mem. faculty Augusta Mil. Acad., Ft. Defiance, Va., 1943-45; tchr., coach Martinsville (Va.) City Sch. Bd., 1945-51; prin. Henry County Sch. Bd., Martinsville, Va., 1951—. Mem. N.E.A., Va., Henry County (pres. 1955) edn. assns., Va. High Sch. League (sec., past pres. Blue Ridge Dist., past pres. Piedmont dist. Baptist. Kiwanian (pres. 1957), Lion (charter mem. Martinsville). Home: Office: Box 511 Martinsville VA 24112

WALFORD, BESS PATERSON, librarian; b. Richmond, Va.; d. Charles Paterson and Bessie (Williams) Walford; B.A., Westhampton Coll., 1939; B.S. in L.S., Drexel Inst. Tech., 1940 Librarian, Mathews County High Sch. 1940-41; supr. libraries Va. Dept. Mental Hygiene and Hosps., 1941-45; librarian post library 3, Fort Meade, Md., 1945-46, med. and tech. library VA Richmond Regional Office, 1947-49, Fed. Res. Bank of Richmond, Va., 1949-59, Philip Morris U.S.A., Research Library, 1959—. Mem. Va. Library Assn. (chmn. spl. libraries div. 1955-57, pres. 1961-62), Spl. Libraries Assn. (vice chmn. financial div. 1957-58; co-chmn. bus.-finance div. 1958-59, mem. govtl. relations com. 1964-67, chmn. 1968-70; div. liaison officer 1970-72; pres. Va. chpt. 1969-70. Home: 3908 Chamberlayne Av Richmond VA 23227 Office: 4201 Commerce Rd Richmond VA 23261

WALHAY, ROBERT DAVIES, assn. exec.; b. Chgo., May 3, 1925; s. Ward and Audrey (O'Neil) W.; B.A., Mich. State U., 1950; postgrad., London Sch. Econs., 1951; m. Ellen Church, Nov. 22, 1951. Corr., editor Reuters News Agy., London, Eng., 1951-53; editor Am. Daily, London, 1953-54; engaged in pub. relations A.R.C., Washington, 1954—, asst. dir., 1971—. Information officer League Red Cross Socs. Hungarian Refugee Relief, Vienna, Austria, 1956-57, Cuban Refugee Program, 1962-63. Served with AUS, 1943-46; PTO. Mem. Sigma Delta Chi. Home: 7300 Rollingwood Dr Chevy Chase MD 20015 Office: 17th & D Sts N W Washington DC 20006

WALKER, ANTONIO MACEO, banker, ins. co. exec.; b. Indianola, Miss., June 7, 1909; s. Joseph Edison and Lela E. (O'Neal) W.; A.B., Fisk U., 1930; M.B.A., N.Y.U., 1932; postgrad. U. Mich., 1935; L.H.D., Wilberforce U., 1959; m. Harriette Ish, June 8, 1938; children—Patricia (Mrs. Harold Shaw), Antonio Maceo, Harriette L. Pres. Tri-State Bank, Memphis, 1946—, also chmn. bd.; pres. Universal Life Ins. Co., Memphis Mortgage Co. Mem. Tenn. Adv. Com. Civil Rights; mem. Nat. Citizens Com., 1964-65; mem. Memphis Transit Authority, 1961-64; chmn. Fisk U. Centennial Alumni fund raising devel. campaign, 1961-65; mem. Anti-Inflation Com. Pres. Truman, 1946; mem. Memphis Community Relations Com., 1959-65. Bd. dirs. Shelby United Neighbors, Pres. Kennedy Meml. Library Fund, Lauderdale br. YMCA; trustee Fisk U. Mem. Nat. Ins. Assn. (past pres.). Democrat. Mem. Christian Ch. Home: 1255 S Parkway E Memphis TN 38106 Office: 480 Linden St Memphis TN 38103

WALKER, SISTER CATHERINE, educator, psychologist; b. Bartlesville, Okla.; d. Ethan Allen and Lula Mae (Kuhn) Walker; B.A., Our Lady of Lake Coll., 1942, B.S. in L.S., 1947; M.A., Cath. U. Am., 1951; Ph.D., Northwestern U., 1955. Jr. high sch. tchr., Alexandria, La., 1941-46; critic tchr. Demonstration Sch., Our Lady of Lake Coll., San Antonio, 1941-46, prin., dean of girls Demonstration Sch., 1946-53, prof. edn. Grad. Sch. Edn., 1955—, dir. student personnel services, 1955-63, dir. counselor edn., 1958—, chmn. grad. edn., 1970—. Guidance cons. Nat. Cath. Edn. Assn., 1968—; exec. sec. Archdiocesan Guidance Council, 1967—; bd. mgrs. United Colls. San Antonio, 1970—; cons., speaker, panelist at local, state and nat. profl. meetings. Mem. Nat. Cath. Guidance Conf. (dir. 1962-66), Am., Tex. (conv. coordinator 1968) personnel and guidance assns., Tex. Assn. Counselor Educators and Suprs. (sec.-treas. 1967-69, exec. bd. 1970—), Tex. Assn. Rehab. Counselors (sec. 1970—); San Antonio Women Deans and Counselors (pres. 1962-63), South Tex. Personnel and Guidance (pres. 1968-69, exec. bd. 1968), Pi Lambda Theta. Mem. editorial bd. The Cath. Counselor, 1958-60, asso. editor, 1960-62, chmn. editorial bd. and staff, 1962-65. Contbr. articles to profl. jours. Address: 411 SW 24th St San Antonio TX 78285

WALKER, CHARLS EDWARD, govt. ofcl.; b. Graham, Tex., Dec. 24, 1923; s. Pinkney Clay and Sammye (McCombs) W.; B.B.A., U. Tex., 1947, M.B.A., 1948; Ph.D., U. Pa., 1955; m. Harmolyn Hart, June 24, 1949; children—Carolyn, Charls E. Instr. finance U. Tex., Austin, 1947-48, asst. prof., 1950-53, asso. prof., 1954; instr. finance Wharton Sch., U. Pa., Phila., 1948-50; financial economist Fed. Reserve Bank, Phila., 1953; economist, v.p., econ. adv. Fed. Reserve Bank, Dallas, 1954-61; economist Republic Nat. Bank, Dallas, 1955-56; asst. to Sec. of Treasury, Dallas, 1959-61; exec. v.p. Am. Bankers Assn., N.Y.C., 1961-69; under sec. of Treasury, Washington, 1969-72, dep. sec. of Treasury, 1972—. Served to 2d lt. USAAF, 1942-45. Editor: The Bankers Handbook, 1966. Home: 1661 Crescent Pl NW Washington DC 20009 Office: Main Treasury Bldg Washington DC 20220

WALKER, COURTENAY JOHN, state govt. ofcl.; b. Cin., July 25, 1930; s. Kenneth Maxwell and Clara Vivien (Brehmer) W.; student Eastern Ky. State Coll., 1948-51; B.A. with honors, U. Cin., 1956; M.A., U. Va., 1958; m. Victoria Shryock, Dec. 27, 1963; 1 step-dau., Nancy Pamela Stratton; 1 dau., Roxanna. Report clk. C. & O. R.R., Covington, Ky., summers 1947-55; research analyst Legislative Research Commn., Commonwealth of Ky., Frankfort, 1956-57, 59-65; research asso. Ky. Council on Pub. Higher Edn., 1965-66; research specialist Ky. Legislative Research Commn., 1966-71, asst. dir. for gen. assembly, 1971—. Served with USAF, 1951-54. Home: 547 Chinook Trail Frankfort KY 40601 Office: State Capitol Frankfort KY 40601

WALKER, DALE LEE, coll. adminstr.; b. Decatur, Ill., Aug. 3, 1935; s. Russell Dale and Eilleen Mary (Guysinger) W.; B.A. in Journalism, U. Tex. at El Paso, 1962; m. Alice McCord, Sept. 30, 1960; children—Dianne, Eric, Christopher, Michael, John. TV newsman KTSM News, El Paso, 1962-66; dir. news and information service U. Tex., El Paso, 1966—. Served with USNR, 1955-59. Mem. Nat. Hist. Soc., Am. Soc. World War I Aero Historians, Am. Coll. Pub. Relations Assn. Author: (with Richard O'Connor) The Lost Revolutionary, 1967; The Fiction of Jack London, 1972; also articles. Home: 4569 Skylark Way El Paso TX 79922

WALKER, DANIEL JOSHUA, JR., lawyer; b. Gibson, N.C., Nov. 27, 1915; s. Daniel Joshua and Annie (Hurdle) W.; A.B., U. N.C., 1936, J.D., 1948; m. Sarah Elizabeth Nicholson, June 14, 1941. Claim dept. Barnwell Bros. Trucking Co., Burlington, N.C., 1936-42; admitted to N.C. bar, 1948; clk. Superior Ct., Alamance County, Graham, N.C., 1948-53; partner Long, Ridge, Harris & Walker, Graham, 1953-67; county atty. Alamance County, Graham, 1964—, county mgr., 1971—; sr. mem. firm Walker Harris, Graham, 1967-71. Mem. Human Relations Council, Alamance County, 1963-71, chmn., 1970. Pres., Alamance County Young Democratic Club, 1950; chmn. Alamance County Dem. Exec. Com., 1956-58; mem. N.C. Dem. Exec. Com., 1958-66. Trustee Tech. Inst. of Alamance, 1964-71; bd. dirs. Alamance County United Fund, Cherokee council Boy Scouts Am., Community YMCA, Burlington; trustee Presbyn. Found., Presbyn. Ch. U.S., 1969—, mem. Exec. Com., 1971—; mem. council Orange Presbytery, 1972—. Served with AUS, 1942-46. Decorated Bronze Star medal. Mem. Am. Judicature Soc., Burlington-Alamance C. of C., Am., N.C., Alamance County bar assns., N.C. Assn. County A Hys. (v.p. 1971, pres. 1972 named county atty. of yr. 1971), Phi Alpha Delta. Democrat. Presbyn. (elder; trustee ch.). Home: 215 Long Av Graham NC 27253 Office: 124 West Elm Graham NC 27253

WALKER, DAVID, judge; b. Lufkin, Tex., Aug. 7, 1931; s. Howard and Ethel (Cruse) W.; B.B.A., Sam Houston State U., 1952; LL.B., S. Tex. Coll. Law, 1959; m. Virgia Jewell Lindsey, Jan. 10, 1953; children—George, Frank, Dorothy, Larry, Carol. Engaged in real estate bus., Lufkin, 1954-59; admitted to Tex. bar, 1959, practiced in Lufkin, 1959-69; city atty. Lufkin, 1964-69; judge 159th Jud. Dist. for Angelina County (Tex.), 1969—. Pres., Lufkin Bd. Realtors, 1956. Pres. Angelina County Sch. Bd., 1961-66. Trustee Angelina Coll., Lufkin, 1966-69, sec., 1968-69. Mem. Angelina County Bar Assn. (pres. 1969). Kiwanian (pres. Lufkin 1968). Home: Route 2 Box 519-x Lufkin TX 75901 Office: Courthouse Sq Lufkin TX 75901

WALKER, DAVID BROWN, educator; b. Phila., Jan. 14, 1926; s. David Brown and Margaret (Thomson) W.; Am. Inst. Banking scholar Rutgers U., 1950; postgrad. U. Birmingham (Eng.), 1951-52; M.B.A., Temple U., 1953 Controller, Indsl. Products Co., Phila., 1949-55; faculty Pierce Coll., Phila., 1950-54; asst. prof. Ursinus Coll., Collegeville, Pa., 1958-63, Antioch Coll., Yellow Springs, O., 1966—. Vis. prof. Howard U., Washington, 1967—. Audit com. Yellow Springs Fed. Credit Union, since 1966—. Served with AUS, World War II; ETO. Mem. Am. Accounting Assn., Geog. Soc. Phila., Am. Assn. U. Profs., St. Andrew's Soc. Phila. Delta Pi Epsilon, Alpha Sigma Phi. Author: (with others) 200th History of St. Andrew's Society of Philadelphia, 1947. Home: PO Box 349 1500 Massachusetts Av NW Washington DC 20005

WALKER, DEE BROWN, judge; b. Royse City, Tex., Dec. 3, 1912; s. Dee Alexander and Lela Blanche (Jones) W.; LL.B., So. Meth. U., 1935; m. Ruthe Elizabeth Edwards, Mar. 28, 1942; children—Susan Hays, Stephen Craig; m. 2d, Anna Lee Gandy, Sept. 13, 1952. Admitted to Tex. bar, 1935; atty. Tex. Fire & Casualty Underwriters, 1935-36, Standard Accident Ins. Co., 1936-41, Glens Falls Indemnity Co., 1941-42; gen. practice law, Dallas, 1946-59; atty. Southland Life Ins. Co., 1959-63; judge 162d Jud. Dist. Ct. Dallas County, 1963—. Mem. Dallas County Dem. Com., 1952-63. Trustee Dallas Pub. Library; v.p., dir., trustee Royse City Cemetery Found., Chisholm Cemetery Found., Cottonwood Cemetery Found. Served from pvt. to 1st lt. AUS, 1942-46. Mem. Am., Dallas bar assns., State Bar Tex., Dallas County Criminal Bar Assn., Am. Judicature Soc., Southwestern Legal Found., So. Meth. U. Alumni and Law Sch. Alumni Assn., Res. Officers Assn., Local History and Geneal. Soc. Dallas (pres. dir. 1963-65), S.A.R. (past pres. Dallas), Am. Legion, Mil. Order World Wars, D.A.V., V.F.W., Soc. Colonial Wars, Sons Confederate Vets., Phi Alpha Delta. Mem. Christian Ch. Mason (K.T., 33 deg., Shriner), Lion. Home: 5918 Vanderbilt Dallas TX 75206 Office: 162d Dist Ct House Dallas TX 75202

WALKER, DENSON, broadcasting exec. Sta. mgr. WFAA, Dallas. Office: Communications Center Dallas TX 75202*

WALKER, DONALD LEE, chem. co. exec.; b. Bandana, Ky., Aug. 11, 1934; s. Richard and Lottie (Berry) W.; Asso. Sci., Paducah Community Coll., 1955; m. Eva M. Lofton, Dec. 30, 1955; children—Michael Lee, Linda Gaye. Engr., Air Reduction Chem. Co., Calvert City, Ky., 1960-70, Air Products Chem. Co., Calvert City, 1971—; prin. Walker & Assos., cons. engrs., Paducah, Ky., 1968—. Served with AUS, 1957-59. Registered profl. engr., Ky., Ohio, N.J. Mem. Am. Soc. M.E. Baptist (deacon). Home: Route 1 Bruce Av Paducah KY 42001 Office: PO Box 97 Calvert City KY 42029

WALKER, DORA FOGARTY (MRS. HAROLD FRANCIS WALKER), librarian; b. New Haven, June 4, 1905; d. James Augustine and Grace (Hyland) Fogarty; B.S., Columbia, 1930; M.A., Yale, 1956; diploma U. Conn., 1962; m. Harold Francis Walker, June 28, 1937 (dec. Nov. 1953); children—John James, Margaret Grace

(Mrs. Edward Stowell Gaffney), Elizabeth Rose (Mrs. Armand Catelli), Francis Edward. Elementary sch. tchr., West Haven, Conn., 1923-29; training tchr. Danbury State Coll., 1930-42; reading tchr. Haley Sch., West Haven, 1952-57; library tchr. Bailey Jr. High Sch., West Haven, 1957-63; library head West Haven (Conn.) High Sch., 1963-71, sch. library cons., 1957-71. Adminstrv. asst. Col. Park Sch., West Haven, 1951-52; spl. state cons. part-time, 1964-68; asst. prof. So. Conn. State Coll., New Haven, part-time, 1960-69; rol. library cons. St. Luke's Sch., Lake Worth, Fla. Water safety chmn. A.R.C., West Haven, 1967-71. Mem. Conn. (pres. 1961-62), New Eng. sch. library assns., Nat. Council Parents and Tchrs. (West Haven v.p. 1956-57), Conn., West Haven edn. assns., Am. Assn. U. Women, Nat. Ret. Tchrs. Assn. Contbr. articles publs. Home: 2811 S Garden Dr Apt 105 Lake Worth FL 33460

WALKER, ESPER LAFAYETTE, JR., civil engr.; b. Decatur, Tex., Sept. 22, 1930; s. Esper Lafayette and Ruth (Mauldin) W.; B.S., Tex. A. and M. U., 1953; B.H.T., Yale, 1958; m. Sara Lynn Dunlap, Oct. 2, 1955; children—William David, Annette Ruth. Design engr. Tex. Hwy. Dept., Austin, 1956-57; dir. Dept. Traffic Engring., High Point, N.C., 1958-63; v.p. Wilbur Smith & Assoc., Houston, 1963—. Served to 1st lt. C.E., AUS, 1953-56. Registered profl. engr., Tex., S.C. Mem. Nat., Tex. socs. profl. engrs., Inst. Traffic Engrs. (past pres.). Methodist Home: 14216 Kellywood Lane Houston TX 77024 Office: 1535 West Loop S Suite 200 Houston TX 77027

WALKER, ESTELLENE PAXTON, librarian; b. Bristol, Va., Sept. 13, 1911; d. John Camp and Willie (Ropp) Walker; B.A., U. Tenn., 1933; B.S. in Library Sci., Emory U., 1935. Head county dept. Lawson McGehee Library, Knoxville, Tenn., 1935-41; post librarian, Fort Jackson, S.C., 1941-45; materials supply librarian Army Spl. Services, ETO, 1945-46; dir. S.C. Library Bd., 1946-70; librarian S.C. State Library, 1970—. Mem. adv. com. on library services program U.S. Office Edn., 1956-57; mem. S.C. Adv. Com. Adult Edn.; S.C. Com. Welfare Children and Youth; sec. Interdepartmental Council State Agys.; del. White House Conf. Children and Youth 1960. Bd. dir. S.C. State Library Bd. Mem. A.L.A. (council mem. 1952-56, adv. com. recruiting project 1962—), S.C. (v.p. 1971—), Southeastern (chmn. county and regional library sect. 1940) library assns., Am. Assn. State Libraries (past pres.), S.C. Council Common Good. Caroliniana Soc., Phi Kappa Phi. Editor: S.C. Library Bull., 1946-56. Contbr. articles library, ednl. periodicals. Office: SC State Library 1500 Senate St Columbia SC 29201

WALKER, EVELYN, ednl. TV exec., educator; b. Birmingham, Ala.; d. Preston Lucas and Mattie (Williams) Walker; A.B., Huntingdon Coll., 1927; postgrad. Cornell U., 1927-29; spl. courses U. Ill., 1955; M.A., U. Ala., 1963. Speech instr. Phillips High Sch., Birmingham, Ala., 1930-34; head speech dept. Ramsay High Sch., Birmingham, 1934-52; head instructional TV programming services, Birmingham Pub. Schs., 1969—; staff producer Birmingham Ednl. TV Studios, for Ala. Ednl. TV network, 1954—, acting program dir., 1959; Miss Ann, broadcaster of daily children's program, WSGN Radio, Birmingham, 1946-57. Cons. Governor's Ednl. TV Legislative Study Commn., 1953. Mem. Def. Adv. Com. Women in Services, 1959-62, Recall to Duty, 1971; bd. dirs. Mental Health Assn., 1960-62, Freedom Ednl. Found., Festival of Arts, 1965—; bd. dirs., Women's Com. of 100, sec., 1968-71; internat. competition chmn. Festival of Arts Creative TV, Radio; mem. Birmingham Adv. Com. on Women in Services, co-chmn. TV and radio Gov.'s Adv. Bd. to State Safety Com., 1965—. Nat. del. Asian-American Women Broadcasters Conf., 1966. Recipient alumnae achievement award Huntingdon Coll., 1958, Festival of Arts, Spl. Silver Bowl, Ednl. TV Award, 1962; Educator's Medal Award, Freedoms Found. at Valley Forge, 1963, 68, 69, 70, Nat. Headliner award Theta Sigma Phi, 1965; named Tops in our Town, Birmingham News, 1957, Top TV award Regional A.R.C. Assn., 1964; named State Woman of Achievement, Ala. Bus. and Profl. Clubs, 1964, Birmingham's Woman of Yr., 1965; Ala.'s Woman of Year, Progressive Farmer's Mag., 1967. Mem. (Ala.), Birmingham edn. assns., Birmingham Tchrs. Club, Nat. Assn. Ednl. Broadcasters, Am. Women in Radio and TV (pres. 1959-60) (area trustee nat. ednl. found. bd.). Am. Assn. U. Women, Nat. League Am. Penwomen, Huntingdon Coll. Alumnae Assn. (internat. pres. 1961-63), Ala. Hist. Assn., Arlington Hist. Soc., Ala. Animal League (dir.), Magna Charta Dames (sec.-treas. 1963-64), D.A.R. (state TV chmn. 1962-64), U.S. Daus. 1812 (state TV chmn. 1963-64), Colonial Dames 17th Century, Daus. Am. Colonists (state TV chmn., 2d v.p. local chpt. 1962—), Ams. Royal Descent, Plantagenets Society, Royal Order Garter, Royal Order Crown, Bot. Soc., Art Mus. Aux., Symphony Women, Women for Patriotic Events, Ala. Dist. Exchange Clubs (hon. life, bronze plaque 1969), Salvation Army Aux., Delta Delta Delta, Theta Sigma Phi (local pres. 1958), Delta Kappa Gamma. Methodist. Clubs: Birmingham Country; Press; Altrusa, Downtown (Birmingham); The Club. Home: 744 Euclid Av Birmingham AL 35213 Office: care ETV 2015 N 7th Av Birmingham AL 35203

WALKER, FRANCIS CHARLES, psychologist; b. nr. Galesburg, Ill., Feb. 1, 1926; s. Ivan Banks and Hazel Anna (Weiler) W.; B.A., Bradley U., 1949, M.A., 1950; m. Donna Jean Bender, Sept. 1, 1946; children—Gregory C., Taffy Dee (Mrs. Michael W. McCauley). Vocational appraiser Personnel Services Assos., Peoria, Ill., 1949-50; personnel counselor Caterpillar Tractor Co., Peoria, 1950-55; indsl. psychologist Byron Harless and Assos., Tampa, Fla., 1955; indsl. relations cons. Sangamo Electric Co., Springfield, Ill., 1955-60; sec., dir. administrv. service Byron Harless, Schaffer, Reid & Assos, Tampa, 1960-69; v.p. Rutenberg Homes, Inc., Belleair Bluffs, Fla., 1969-70; indsl. psychologist Frank Walker Assos., Tampa, Fla., 1970—. Tchr. eve. div. Bradley U., 1951-53, Springfield Jr. Coll., 1956. Mem. Bd. Edn., Richwoods Township, Peoria, 1951-55; Republican precinct committeeman, 1967-68, twp. chmn., 1953-54, dis. chmn., 1967-68. Served with USAAF, 1944-46. Mem. Am., Ill., Southeastern, Fla. (pres. elect. 1971), Tampa Bay (pres. 1965-66) psychol. assns. Presbyn. (clk. of session 1964-67, 71—). Clubs: University, Exchange (Tampa). Home: 215 S Hesperides St Tampa FL 33609 Office: 1111 N Westshore St Tampa FL 33607

WALKER, HAROLD WILLIAM, news corr.; b. Darlington, S.C., July 2, 1933; s. Harold Winston and Betty Augusta (Abernathy) W.; B.A., Denison U., 1954; postgrad. Maxwell Sch. Pub. Affairs, Syracuse U., 1960-63; m. children—Stephen, Alison, Sarah. Unemployment ins. examiner N.Y. State Employment Service, N.Y.C., 1958-59; asst. editor N.Y. State Dept. Mental Hygiene, Albany, 1959-61, N.Y. State Edn. Dept., Albany, 1961-63; news reporter WTOP-TV, Washington, 1963-68; news corr. CBS News, Washington, 1968—; adj. prof. journalism Columbia, summer 1969. Served with AUS, 1954-58. Recipient Emmy award Nat. Acad. TV Arts and Scis., 1969. Mem. Blacks in Broadcasting, Am. Fedn. TV and Radio Artists.Home: 3800 Alton Pl NW Washington DC 20016 Office: 2020 M St NW Washington DC 20036

WALKER, HARRY, athletic orgn. exec. b. Pascagoula, Oct. 22, 1918; s. Ewart and Flossie (Vaughn) W.; student pub. schs.; m. Dorothy Fulmer, Mar. 17, 1941; children—Carole Diane, Mary Sharon, Barbara Anne. Profl. baseball player with St. Louis Cardinals, Phila. Phillies, Chgo. Cubs, Cin. Reds; coach, mgr. St. Louis Cardinal Orgn.; mgr. Pitts. Pirates; now mgr. Houston Astros. Served with AUS. Decorated Bronze Star, Purple Heart. Author: How to Bat. Office: care Houston Astros Houston TX 77058

WALKER, HARRY GREY, judge; b. Ovett, Miss., Sept. 30, 1924; s. Chester A. and Ina (Mangum) W.; LL.B., U. Miss., 1952; m. Carrie Thorne Lang, Apr. 4, 1953; children—Harry Grey, Fred Wallace. Admitted to Miss. bar, 1952; practiced in Gulfport; judge Harrison County Ct., 1964-68; circuit judge 2d dist., 1968-72; asso. justice Miss. Supreme Ct., 1972—. Mem. Miss. Ho. of Reps., 1964. Trustee Cerebral Palsy Assn. Gulf Coast, Good Samaritan Tng. Center. Served with USCG, 1942-44. Mem. Am. Bar Assn., Miss. State Bar, D.A.V., Am. Legion, Paralyzed Vets. Am., Phi Alpha Delta, Kappa Alpha. Democrat. Methodist. Elk. Clubs: Gulfport Yacht, Magnolia Hunting. Home: 12-53d St Circle Gulfport MS 39501 Office: Courthouse Gulfport MS 39501

WALKER, JACOB ALLEN, JR., lawyer; b. Opelika, Ala., Aug. 5, 1920; s. Jacob A. and Emma Lilliam (Pearson) W.; A.B., Harvard, 1942, LL.B., 1948; m. Jane Cole, June 22, 1957; children—Jacob III, Mary Lillian. Admitted to Ala. bar, 1949; practiced in Opelika; mem. firsm Walker & Walker, 1949-61, Walker & Hill, 1961-69, Walker, Hill, Gullage and Adams, 1969—. Dir. Opelika Nat. Bank. Served with AUS, 1943-46. Meth. Home: 1110 Collinwood St Opelika AL 36801 Office: Walker Bldg 205 S 9th St Opelika AL 36801

WALKER, JAMES LORENZO, state legislator; b. Marco, Fla., Nov. 1, 1920; s. Forrest Walker and Adnie (Prine) W.; grad. diesel engr. Hemp Hill Diesel Sch.; m. Marguerite Louise Lanier, Jan. 3, 1942; children—Barbara Anne, Carolyn Sue. Mem. Fla. Ho. of Reps., 1956—, speaker pro tem, 1967—; dir. First Nat. Bank Naples. Past pres. Collier City TB and Health Assn. Mem. Collier County Republican Com., 1950-56. Bd. dirs. Naples Community Hosp. Served with AC, AUS, 1943-46. Mem. Am. Legion (past post comdr.). Mem. Church of God. Home: 1537 Gordon Dr Naples FL 33940*

WALKER, JAMES LYNN, JR., state ofcl.; b. Greenville, S.C., May 14, 1924; s. James Lynn and Ruth (Reaves) W.; student Furman U., 1941-44, 46-48; m. Josephine Breazeale, June 21, 1955; children—Anna Reaves, James Lynn III, and Sallie Mills Walker. With editorial dept. Greenville News, 1941-68, successively reporter, legislative corr., asst. city editor, 1941-55; city editor, 1955-68; asst. dir. pub. relations S.C. Hwy. Dept., 1968-72, dir. pub. relations, 1972—. Served from pvt. to staff sgt. inf. AUS, 1944-46; ETO. Decorated Purple Heart, Bronze Star medal. Mem. Sigma Alpha Epsilon. Home: 1124 Greenridge Lane Columbia SC 29210 Office: SC Hwy Dept PO Drawer 191 1100 Senate St Columbia SC 29202

WALKER, JAMES WHITTENBURG, publishing co. exec.; b. Clayton, N.M., Nov. 10, 1935; s. Basil Eugene and Annie (Whittenburg) W.; B.B.A., U. Tex., 1958; m. Patricia Ann Roberts, Nov. 28, 1959; children—Frances Ann, James Whittenburg, Reid Samuel, Patrick Paul. Reporter, Amarillo (Tex.) Globe News, 1959-62, oil editor, 1962—, asst. to pres., 1967—. Pres., Amarillo United Way, 1971, campaign chmn., 1970. Bd. dirs. Amarillo YMCA, pres. 1968; bd. dirs. Children's Rehab. Center, chmn. 1966-67; bd. dirs. Camp Fire Girls of Amarillo, Panhandle Sci. Fair. Mem. Assn. Petroleum Writers (pres. 1971-72), Tex. Daily Newspaper Assn. (dir. 1971-73), Panhandle Producers and Royalty Owners Assn. (exec. com. 1968-71), Amarillo C. of C. (dir. 1968-71), Phi Gamma Delta, Phi Delta Phi. Democrat. Presbyn. (elder 1967-70). Clubs: Amarillo, Amarillo Country. Home: 6306 Jameson St Amarillo TX 79106 Office: Box 2091 Amarillo TX 79105

WALKER, JAMES WILLIAM, dentist; b. nr. Reidsville, N.C., Aug. 14, 1933; s. Robert Franklin and Lena (Brooks) W.; student Elon Coll., 1955-56, 58, East Carolina U., 1958-59, N.C. State U., 1965; D.D.S., U. N.C., 1969; m. LaVisa Chrismon Walker, Aug. 22, 1958; children—Kenan Bryant, Gregory Franklin. With Martin Furniture Co., Reidsville, N.C., 1950-69, So. Bell Tel. and Tel. Co., Reidsville, 1951-53, Grome Furniture Co., Greensboro, N.C., 1959-60, B.F. Goodrich Co., Reidsville, 1960, Pat Brady Stores, 1960-63, Walker Am. Service, 1962-64; individual practice gen. dentistry, Madison, N.C., 1969—; cons. staff Annie Penn Meml. Hosp., Reidsville, N.C. Chmn. Rockingham County Sch. Merger Study Com., 1971. Served with AUS, 1956-58. Mem. Am., Rockingham County, N.C., 3d Dist. dental assns., Little League Assn. (dir. 1970-72), Xi Psi Phi. Rotarian. Home: 506 W Hunter St Madison NC 27025 Office: 111 E Decatur St Madison NC 27025

WALKER, JOHN ALEXANDER, retail co. exec.; b. Phila., June 10, 1922; s. John Anthony and Dorothy (Morrison) W.; student Muhlenburg Coll., 1941-42, U. Pa., 1942-43, Northwestern U., 1944; m. Beryl Audrey Linehard, Apr. 21, 1966; children by previous marriage—Lynn (Mrs. Phil Riker), Dorothy (Mrs. Robert Moynihan), Gail, Debbie, Mary. Dist. mgr. Hotpoint distbg. div. Gen. Electric Co., Chgo., 1946-58; exec. v.p. Lowe's Companies, Inc., North Wilkesboro, N.C., 1958—, also dir.; dir. Lowe's Profit-Sharing Plan and Trust, Lowe's Charitable & Trust Found., Northwestern Security Life Ins. Co., Phoenix, Wilkes Devel. Corp., Alleghany S. A. Mem. plywood adv. council Chgo. Bd. Trade, 1970—; mem. bus. adv. council Appalachian State U., Boone, N.C., 1970-71; Chmn. North Wilkesboro Housing Authority, 1966-71. Chmn. N.C. Republican Finance Com., 1968-71; mem. Republican Nat. Finance Com., 1969-72; Rep. candidate for lt. gov. of N.C., 1972. Served to lt. USNR, 1942-46. Mem. N.C. Home Builders Assn., Nat. Assn. Home Builders, Phi Kappa Sigma. Presbyn. (deacon). Mason (Shriner), Elk. Clubs: Oakwoods Country, Roaring Gap, Blowing Rock Country. Contbr. articles to profl. jours. Home: 104 Coffey St North Wilkesboro NC 28659 Office: Hwy 268 E North Wilkesboro NC 28659

WALKER, JOHN REX, banker; b. St. Louis, July 22, 1922; s. Virgil Sylvester and Genevieve (Hart) W.; Student U. Kan., 1941-43, Washington U., St. Louis, 1951-52; m. Mary Fearn Tucker, Aug. 5, 1950; 1 son, Mark Evan. Staff accountant H. Stoller & Co., C.P.A.'s, Dallas, 1946-48; asst. gen. ledger accountant Hunt Oil Co., Dallas, 1948-50; with Ernst & Ernst, C.P.A.'s, 1950-65, mgr., Ft. Worth, 1956-65; sr. v.p. adminstrv. div. Ft. Worth Nat. Bank, 1965—. Mem. faculty Southwestern Grad. Sch. Banking, So. Methodist U., 1968—. Served with AUS, 1943-46, 50-52. Recipient John Burnis Allred award Tex. Soc. C.P.A.'s, 1952. C.P.A., Tex. Mem. Am. Inst. C.P.A.'s, Tex. Soc. C.P.A.'s (sec. Tex. 1963-64, pres. Ft. Worth 1962-63), Nat. Assn. Accountants (pres. Ft. Worth 1961-62), Ft. Worth Bus. and Estate Council (treas. 1965-66), Assn. for Systems Mgmt. (pres. Ft. Worth chpt. 1968-69), Am. Mmgt. Assn., Ft. Worth Art Assn., Am. Inst. Banking, Alpha Tau Omega. Baptist. Mason (Shriner). Rotarian (pres. North Ft. Worth 1970-71). Clubs: Colonial Country. Author: Bank Costs for Decision Making, 1970. Home: 3840 Arroyo Rd Ft Worth TX 76109 Office: PO Box 2050 Ft Worth TX 76101

WALKER, JOHN T., bishop; b. Barnesville, Ga., 1925; A.B., Wayne U., 1951; B.D., Va. Theol. Sem., 1954; m. Rosa Maria Flores; 3 children. Rector, St. Mary's Ch., Detroit, 1955-57; tchr. St. Paul's Sch., 1957-66; canon Washington Cathedral, 1966-71; suffragan bishop Diocese of Washington, 1971—; tchr. Bishop Tucker Theol. Coll., Mukono, Uganda, 1964-65. Del. gen. conv. Episcopal Ch., 1970. Trustee, Washington Hosp. Center, Meridan House Found., Potomac Sch., Milton (Mass.) Acad., Va. Theol. Sch. Home: 3409 Woodley Rd Washington DC20016 Office: Washington Cathedral Mount Saint Albans Washington DC 20016

WALKER, KATHARINE DEAN (MRS. WILEY B. WALKER), musician; b. El Dorado, Ark., Apr. 19, 1937; d. Marion Taylor and Ruth (Cannon) McCollum; B.Mus. Edn., Okla. City U., 1961; m. Wiley Bruce Walker, Sept. 15, 1957 children—Wiley Christopher, Marion Bruce, Scott Cannon. Percussionist, Oklahoma City Symphony Orch., 1957-67, Lyric Theatre, 1964—; instr. percussion Central State Coll., 1963-64, Oklahoma City U., 1963-72, Cameron State Coll., 1971—. Mem. Delta Zeta, Pi Kappa Lambda. Home: 10424 Lyndon Rd Oklahoma City OK 73120

WALKER, KENNETH ROLAND, ednl. adminstr.; b. Syracuse, Ind., Apr. 12, 1928; s. Carl and Laura Mae (Ford) W.; B.A., Goshen Coll., 1949; M.A., Ind. U., 1950, Ph.D., 1952; M.Ed., U. Ark., 1964; m. Marylou Evelyn Neff, Sept. 10, 1950; children—Elizabeth Ann, Mary Susan. Asso. prof. history and polit. sci. Ark. Poly Coll., Russellville, 1958-64, prof., 1965—, asst. acad. dean, 1958-69, head history dept., 1965-69, chmn. liberal arts div., 1969-70, dean sch. arts and scis., 1970—. Liaison officer USAF Acad. for Ark., 1964-69, liaison officer coordinator, 1969—. Chmn. Pope County Easter Seal Campaign, 1969—. Served to capt. USAF, 1952-58. Mem. Ark. Dean's Assn. (pres. 1966-67), Ark. Edn. Assn. (pres. dept. higher edn. 1963-64), Ark. Dept. Higher Edn., Orgn. Am. Historians, Southwestern Social Studies Assn., Phi Alpha Theta, Kappa Delta Pi. Methodist. Author: Days the Presidents Died, 1966; The History of the Middle West, 1972. Contbr. articles to profl. pubs. Home: Route 2 Box 43 Russellville AR 72801

WALKER, LILLIAN WALKER, ins. exec.; b. Meridian, Miss., May 8, 1923; d. Rudolph Blanche and Elizabeth (George) Walker; grad. Meridian Jr. Coll.; m. Edward E. Walker, May 25, 1942; children—Edward T., Betti H. Owner Baton Rouge Agy., 1956—; sec. Southland Concessions, Inc., mem. La. Ho. of Reps., 1964-72, chmn. contingent com., 1964-72; mem. exec. com. Baton Rouge Ins. Exchange Capt. bldg. fund dr. YMCA, Baton Rouge, 1959; bd. dirs., treas. Audubon council Girl Scouts; pres. La. Assn. for Retarded Children, 1960; mem. La Commn. Status Women; So. Central region v.p. Nat. Assn. Retarded Children; mem. La. Baton Rouge assns. retarded children; bd. dirs. Baton Rouge chpt. Nat. Arthritis Found. Del., Nat. Democratic Conv., 1960. Named Louisianian of Year, La. Assn. Broadcasters, 1964, Baton Rouge First Lady of Year Beta Sigma Phi, 1966; Nike award La. Fedn. Bus. and Profl. Women's Clubs; Man of the Quarter award, Am. Assn. Mental Deficiency; Pub. Ofcl. award. La. Assn. Retarded Children. Mem. Nat. Order Women Legislators, Nat. Soc. State Legislators, Am. Legion Aux., La Assn. Ins. Agts., Baton Rouge Bus. and Profl. Women's Club (past pres.), La. State U. Alumni Fedn. (hon.). Club: Zonta (v.p.) (Baton Rouge). Presbyn. (capt. bldg. fund dr); Home: 655 Cora Dr Baton Rouge LA 70815 Office: 4750 North Blvd Baton Rouge LA 70806

WALKER, LYNN WESLEY, librarian; b. Okeechobee, Fla., Aug. 30, 1928; s. Benjamin Franklin and Neva Gertrude (Williams) W.; B.A., U. Fla., 1950; M.A., Fla. State U., 1953; m. Joyce Roberta Orr, June 9, 1950; children—John Michael, Richard Allen, Jacqueline Lynne. Cataloger U. Tenn. Library, 1950-52; sci. cataloger U. Fla. Libraries, Gainesville, 1952-53, sci. reference librarian, 1953-54, librarian engring. and physics library, 1954-66; dir. libraries Fla. Tech. U., Orlando, 1966—. Tchr. courses in library sci. and engring. graphics U. Fla., 1953-57; cons. microfilm retrieval systems. Mem. Fla. Library Study Commn., 1970—; chmn. State Adv. Council on Libraries, 1971—; v.p. Fla. Assn. Amateur Athletic Union, 1971-73; active YMCA. Mem. Am., (councillor 1971—), Southeastern, Fla. (pres. 1970-71) library assns., Nat. Microfilm Assn., Beta Phi Mu. Democrat. Episcopalian. Contbr. articles to profl. pubs. Home: 640 Berwick Dr Winter Park FL 32789 Office: PO Box 25000 Orlando FL 32816

WALKER, MARK ANTHONY, judge; b. Covington, Tenn., Sept. 3, 1908; s. Mark Anthony and Ella (Simonton) W.; B.S., U. Tenn., 1931; student U. Tenn. Coll. Law, 1930-31, U. Wis. Sch. Law, 1934; m. Lulie Reynolds Eddins; children—Mark Anthony, Nathalie Eileen, Lawrence Eddins. Admitted to Tenn. bar, 1935; practiced in Covington, 1935-46; circuit judge 16th Jud. Circuit of Tenn., 1946-67; presiding judge Ct. Criminal Appeals, State Tenn., 1967—. Mem. Tenn. Ho. of Reps., 1939-42. Mem. Tenn. Democratic Exec. Com., 1940-43; v.p. Tenn. Young Dem. Club, 1946. Served with USNR, 1942-46; comdr. Res. Mem. Am. Bar Assn., Bar Assn. Tenn., Am. Judicature Soc., Kappa Sigma. Presbyn. Mason (Shriner). Address: 315 S Main St Covington TN 38019

WALKER, MICHAEL NEAL, architect; b. Ft. Worth, Mar. 29, 1941; s. R. N. and Thelma Louise (Fuller) W.; B.Arch., Tex. A. and M. U., 1964 With Matt E. Howard Assos., architect, Houston, 1964-65, Denny & Starnes, architects, 1965-67, Denny & Ray, 1967—. Vice-pres. Harris County Young Republicans, 1967. Bd. dirs. Nat. Pollution Control Conf. and Exposition, Theater under Stars, 1970-73; trustee Tex. Air and Water Resources Found. Mem. A.I.A. (chpt. treas. 1972—), Houston Jr. C. of C. (pres. 1970-71). Home: 3818 Brook Woods St Houston TX 77018 Office: 3914 Fairhill Dr Houston TX 77042

WALKER, ORVILLE CALVIN, educator; b. Roby, Tex., Apr. 20, 1912; s. Ocle C. and Emma (Westerfeldt) W.; A.B., Howard Payne Coll., 1933; LL.B., U. Tex., 1936; postgrad. U. Chgo., So. Meth. U.; children—Jack, Jill. Admitted to Tex. bar, 1936; briefing clk. Supreme Ct. Tex., 1936-42; gen. practice San Antonio, 1951-55; prof. law St. Mary's U., San Antonio, 1955—. Mem. rules adv. com. Supreme Ct. Tex. Served with AUS, 1943-46. Mem. Am. Arbitration Assn., Phi Delta Phi, Pi Kappa Delta. Methodist. Contbr. articles to profl. publs. Home: 2302 Blanton Dr San Antonio TX 78216

WALKER, RHEY, II, physician; b. Hillsboro, Tex., May 19, 1924; s. Lawrence Lara and Rose (Grimes) W.; student Hillsboro Coll., 1940-41, Tex. A. and M. Coll., 1941, 43, North Tex. Coll., 1943, Central Mo. Coll., 1943, 44; M.D., Baylor U., 1947; m. Betty Goodwin, June 23, 1947; children—Laneri, Tama. Intern, Ind. U. Med. Center, Indpls., 1947-48; resident internal medicine Meth. Hosp. Southwestern Med. Sch., Dallas, 1948-49, Jefferson Davis Hosp., Houston, 1949-50; practice medicine, specializing in internal medicine, Houston, 1954—; asso. prof. internal medicine, pulmonary diseases Baylor U. Coll. Medicine, Houston, 1963— attending physician pulmonary diseases Houston VA Hosp., Houston, 1954—; attending Hermann Hosp., Houston, 1954—; asso. St. Lukes Episcopal Hosp., Houston, 1954—; courtesy and asst. St. Joseph, Meth. hosps. (both Houston); chief medicine 12 Oaks Hosp., 1967, vice chief staff, 1968, chief of staff, 1970-71. Sec.-treas. Houston Diabetes Assn., 1959-60, bd. dirs., 1960—, pres., 1965-66; chmn. Diabetes Detection Drive, 1963; mem. spl. com. aging Community Council Houston, 1958—; mem. exec. com. Meml. Bapt. Hosp. S.W.; mem. Community Council and United Fund Com. Served to lt. (j.g.) USNR, 1943-47; to capt. AUS, 1950-54. Mem. Tex. Med. Assn., Am., Tex. diabetes assns., Am. Heart Assn., Postgrad. Med. Assembly South Tex., Tex. Soc. Aging (charter), Tex. Thoracic Soc., Houston

Soc. Internal Medicine, Alumni Assn. Tex., Hind Hagar Soc., Phi Beta Pi, Alpha Phi Alpha. Republican. Clubs: Doctor's (Houston); Internat. Contbr. articles to med. jours. Home: 5319 S Braeswood Houston TX 77035 Office: 3735 Drexel St Houston TX 77027

WALKER, RICHARD DAVID, educator; b. Washington, Feb. 19, 1931; s. Stanton and Amelia (Ramseyer) W.; B.S., U. Md., 1953; M.S., Purdue U., 1955, Ph.D., 1961; m. Alice Patricia Davis, June 6, 1953; children—Patricia Vawn, Jean Brianne, Sharyl Elise. Instr., Purdue U., 1957-61; asst. prof. civil engring. Va. Poly. Inst. and State U., Blacksburg, 1961-62, asso. prof., 1962-68, prof., 1968-—, head. dept., 1970-—. Mem. Montgomery County Republican Com., 1964-—. Served to 1st lt. USAF, 1955-57. Mem. Am. Soc. Testing and Materials (com. sec. 1970-—), Hwy. Research Bd., Am. Concrete Inst., Am. Soc. C.E., Am. Soc. Engring. Edn., Sigma Xi, Chi Epsilon, Phi Sigma Kappa. Presbyn. (chmn. bd. deacons 1970-71). Author: (with R.D. Krebs) Highway Materials, 1971. Home: 701 Broce Dr Blacksburg VA 24060

WALKER, ROBERT B., supt. schs. Supt. Fairfax (Va.) City Schs. Address: 400 Jones St Fairfax VA 22030*

WALKER, ROBERT KIRK, lawyer, city ofcl.; b. Jasper, Tenn., May 22, 1925; s. Jerry A. and Clemmie (Turner) W.; student U. South, 1943-44; LL.B., U. Va., 1948; m. Miriam Joyce Holt, Aug. 11, 1945; children—Robert Kirk, Marilyn Joy, James Holt. Admitted to Va., Tenn. bar, 1948; practice law, Chattanooga, 1949-—; partner firm Strang, Fletcher, Carriger, Walker & Hodge, 1955-—; gen. counsel Tenn. Credit Union League, Chattanooga, 1956-—; spl. counsel, atty. gen. Tenn. Depts. Ins., Banking and Hwys., 1968-71; sec.-treas., dir. McLaughlin Devel. Co., Chattanooga, 1959-—; sec., dir. Southland Fabrics, Inc., Chattanooga, 1959-—; sec. Pepsi Cola Bottling Co. Chattanooga; dir. Lutex Chem. Corp., 1971-—; sec. TCUL Service Corp., 1970-—. Exec. bd. Hamilton County Law Enforcement Commn., 1962-67; vice chmn. adv. bd. U. Tenn. Govt.-Industry-Law Center, 1965-66; bd. advisers on criminal justice act U.S. 6th Jud. Circuit, 1965-66; mem. Tenn. Law Revision Commn., 1970-71; mayor of Chattanooga, 1971-—. Exec. bd. Cherokee Area council Boy Scouts Am., 1958-—, commr., 1959-60, mem.-at-large nat. council, 1966-—, v.p., 1967-69, recipient Silver Beaver, 1966, v.p., 1966-69; exec. bd. Chattanooga Area Heart Assn., 1966-—; vice chmn. Bible in Pub. Schs., 1969-71; bd. dirs. Chattanooga Urban Coalition, 1968-71; adv. com. Chattanooga-Hamilton County Health Dept., 1969-71 pres. McCallie Sch. Patrons Assn., 1967-68. Trustee Shepherd Hills Pool Inc.; bd. dirs. Tenn. Municipal League, Allied Arts Council, Chattanooga-Hamilton County Regional Planning Commn., Met. Council for Community Services, Chattanooga Area Regional Council of govts. Served with USNR, 1943-46; to lt., 1951-52; Korea. Recipient citizenship award Chattanooga Realtors, 1966; George Washington Honor Medals Freedoms Found., 1966, 67, 68, Prin. award, 1969; Service to Mankind award Sertoma Internat., 1969; Outstanding Salesman at Large award Chattanooga Sales and Marketing Execs., 1969; Citizen of Year Chattanooga Edn. Assn., 1970. Fellow Am. Bar Found.; mem. Tenn. (v.p. 1963-64, pres.-elect, 1964-65, pres. 1965-66, bd. govs. 1966-67), Chattanooga (pres. 1962-63, gov. 1959-64) bar assns., Chattanooga C. of C. (bd. dirs. 1969-—), Nat. Conf. Bar Presidents, Am. Law Inst., Estate Planning Council Chattanooga (exec. bd. 1960-62), Tenn. Def. Lawyers Assn., U.S. Jud. Conf. Sixth Circuit (life mem.), Order of the Coif, Sigma Nu Phi. Baptist (deacon, dir. Home Mission Bd. So. Bapt. Conv. 1969-—). Optimist (past pres. and past lt. gov. dist. 11, Man of Year, 1956). Club: Mountain City. Home: 3019 Brownwood Dr Chattanooga TN 37404 Office: Municipal Bldg Chattanooga TN 37402

WALKER, ROBERT V., savs. and loan assn. exec.; b. Pitts., Nov. 26, 1917; s. William Homer and Valeria (Trubey) W.; Student Rollins Coll., also U. Miami (Fla.); m. Barbara Alice Tickell, Jan. 19, 1947; children—Alice Anita, Robert Lawrence, Roy Joseph. With First Fed. Savs. & Loan Assn., Miami, Fla., 1938-—, exec. v.p., gen. mgr., 1955-66, pres., 1966-—. Mem. task force FHLBB, 1961-62. Bd. dirs., mem. exec. com. citizens bd. U. Miami, 1966-67; trustee Fla. Presbyn. Coll., 1965-—. Served with USAAF, World War II. Mem. Fla. Savs. and Loan League (pres. 1949-50). Home: 9300 NE 4th Av Miami Shores FL 33138 Office: 100 NE 1st Av Miami FL 33132

WALKER, RONNIE DERRAL, hosp. adminstr.; b. Sayre, Okla., Nov. 10, 1943; s. Henry Charles and Seaneth Myrtle (Leddy) W.; B.S. in Accounting, Southwestern State Coll. 1966; m. Glenda Carol Moore, Mar. 7, 1970; children—Dana Gayle, Robert Kevin. Asst. mgr. Spot Restaurant, Weatherford, Okla., 1966; asst. adminstr. Southwestern Meml. Hosp., Weatherford, 1966-68, adminstr. Weatherford Hosp. Authority, 1968-—. Mem. Custer County Profl. Adv. Bd., 1970-—; mem. Western Okla. Tb and Respiratory Disease Bd., 1971-—; mem. Southwestern State Coll. Nursing Program Planning Com., 1969-—. Mem. Weatherford Rescue Squad, 1967; dir. Civil Def., 1970-—. Named Outstanding Sr. Man, Phi Beta Lambda, 1966. Mem. U.S. Weatherford chambers commerce, Okla. Hosp. Assn. (instl. mem.). Kiwanian (dir. Weatherford). Home: 1214 Lark St Weatherford OK 73096 Office: 215 N Kansas Weatherford OK 73096

WALKER, RUEL CARLILE, judge; b. Cleburne, Tex., Feb. 26, 1910; s. William Ruel and Nette Tate (Baker) W.; student Austin Coll., 1927-29; B.A., U. Tex., 1931, LL.B., 1934; m. Virginia Sansom, Apr. 20, 1935; children—Virginia Anne, Sara Elisabeth, William Ruel. Admitted to Tex. bar, 1934; legal investigator Office of Atty. Gen. Tex., 1934; gen. civil law practice, partner Walker & Baker, Cleburne, 1934-43, 46-54; state rationing atty. OPA, 1943-44; asso. justice Supreme Ct. Tex., Austin, 1954-—. Served with USNR, 1944-46. Mem. Am. Bar Assn., State Bar Tex., Am. Judicature Soc., Order of Coif, Phi Beta Kappa, Phi Delta Phi, Delta Kappa Epsilon. Democrat. Methodist. Home: 2419 Wooldridge Dr Austin TX 78703 Office: Box 12248 Capitol Sta Austin TX 78711

WALKER, THURMOND OTTO, physician; b. Winnsboro, S.C., Dec. 9, 1932; s. Tally Otto and Vera (Canady) W.; B.S., U. S.C., 1954; M.D., Med. U. S.C., 1958; m. Barbara Ellen Hiller, Nov. 24, 1969; children— Thurmond Otto, Leslie. Intern, Columbia Hosp. of Richland County, S.C., 1958-59; staff physician S.C. State Hosp., Columbia, 1959-60; practice medicine, specializing in family practice, Columbia, 1960-—; mem. staffs Columbia Hosp., Bapt. Hosp., Providence Hosp., Lexington County Hosp., Medicenter Hosp., Forest Hills Hosp.; vol. team physician Irmo High Sch., Columbia, 1961-62, 66-68; team physician Stop Polio Oral Vaccine campaign, 1963-64; participating physician Blue Cross-Blue Shield, 1963; dir. Dutch Fork Investment Corp., Columbia. Fellow Am. Geriatrics Soc., Royal Soc. Health; mem. Am. Acad. Family Practice, Am., S.C. med. assns., Columbia Med. Soc., Assn. Family Practitioners of Central S.C., Heat Assn., Phi Rho Sigma. Democrat. Lutheran. Elk, Lion. Club: University of South Carolina Roundhouse. Home: 262 Sandhurst Rd Columbia SC 29210 Office: 1204 Greenville Circle Columbia SC 29210

WALKER, TOM LEWIS, computer co. exec.; b. Fort Cobb, Okla., Mar. 7, 1935; s. Alfred Swain and Helen Margaret (Hewitt) W.; B.B.A, U. Okla., 1956; m. Charmion Ann Whittle, June 21, 1956; children—Sabrina Lynn, David Craig. With data processing div. IBM Corp., various locations, Tex., 1959-69, resident mgr., Midland, 1964-65, marketing mgr. S.W. Tex., 1965-67, asst. dist. mgr., Dallas, 1967-69; sr. v.p. Nat. Sharedata Corp., Dallas, 1969-70, exec. v.p., 1970-—. Served with AUS, 1956-59. Mem. Am. Mgmt. Assn., Data Processing Mgmt. Assn., Okla. Alumni Assn., Kappa Sigma. Methodist. Rotarian. Home: 7139 Midcrest St Dallas TX 75240 Office: Sharedata Corp 1 Main Place Dallas TX 75250

WALKER, VINCENT JOHN, constrn. co. exec.; b. Mpls., Sept. 12, 1915; s. Oscar John and Mary Agnes (Fitzpatrick) W.; B. in Mech. Engring., U. Minn., 1940; m. Mary Geneveve Hoch, Oct. 23, 1943; children— William V., Robert F., Teresa (Mrs. Richard St. John). Sales engr. Brown Steel Tank Co., Mpls., 1940-41; design engr. Phillips Petroleum Co., Bartlesville, Okla., 1941-47; project design engr. Celanese Corp., Bishop, Tex., 1947-52; v.p., chief engr. S.I.P., Inc., Houston, 1952-—; also dir.; dir. Walker-Hoch, Inc., Bellaire, Tex. Neighborhood commr. Sam Houston area Boy Scouts Am., 1941. K.C. Home: 5009 Mimosa St Bellaire TX 77401 Office: 5304 Old Spanish Trail Houston TX also: PO Box 26266 Houston TX 77032

WALKER, WALTER WINGFIELD, judge; b. Eatonton, Ga., Mar. 11, 1907; s. Hampton C. and Clara (Anderson) W.; student U. Ga., 1924; A.B., Mercer U., 1928, LL.B., 1933; m. Nan Starr, Oct. 2, 1941; children—Starr (Mrs. Lee Ingalls), Claire, Walter Wingfield. Admitted to Ga. bar, 1933, since practiced in Eatonton; solicitor Putnam County Ct., 1950-52, judge, 1952-—; atty. Rural Electric Adminstrn., 1940-—, Farmers & Mchts. Bank, 1940-—, Fed. Land Bank, 1941-—. Supt., Putnam County Schs., 1938. Served with USNR, 1942-45; lt. comdr. Res. Mem. Ga. Bar Assn. Methodist (chmn. bd. trustees). Kiwanian (lt. gov. Ga. 1938). Home: 303 N Madison Av Eatonton GA 31024 Office: Jefferson Eatonton GA 31024

WALKER, WILLIAM ALEXANDER, physician; b. Chester, S.C., Nov. 1, 1894; s. William Alexander and Jannie Harriet (Anderson) W.; B.A., Meharry Med. Sch., 1923, M.D., 1927; m. Ada Louise Givens, June 1, 1941. Pvt. practice gen. medicine, Lewisburg, Tenn., 1927-59, 62-—; dir. phys. medicine VA Hosp., Tuskegee, Ala., 1959-62; mem. staffs Brown's Hosp., Gordon's Hosp., Taylor's Hosp. (all in Lewisburg, Tenn.). Mem. Tenn. Med. Assn., Nat. Med. Assn., Marshall County Med. Soc., Am. Acad. Gen. Practice, N.A.A.C.P., Omega Psi Phi. Democrat. Methodist. Mason (32 deg.). Home: 435 4th Av N Lewisburg TN 37091 Office: 419 4th Av N Lewisburg TN 37091

WALKER, WILLIAM MAY, circuit judge; b. Crawfordville, Fla., May 2, 1905; s. Nat R. and Alice (Tully) W.; J.D., Samford U., 1927; m. Pansy Mavis Crosby, Feb. 22, 1937; children—William May, Joseph Stanley. Admitted to Fla. bar, 1927; practiced in Tallahassee, 1927-40; judge Leon County Ct., 1933-40, 2d Jud. Circuit Ct., Tallahassee, 1940-—. Mem. examining bd. Fla. Parole Commn., 1960. Mem. Fla. Bar, Am., 2d Jud. Circuit, Tallahassee bar assns., Am. Judicature Soc., Fla. Circuit Judges Conf. (past pres.), Tallahassee C. of C. (past dir.), Woodmen of World. Seminole Boosters, Talwar Grotto, Phi Alpha Delta. Democrat. Baptist (deacon). Mason (32 deg., Shriner), Lion (past Tallahassee pres., past Fla. dep. dist. gov.). Home: 405 Pinewood Dr Tallahassee FL 32303 Office: County Courthouse Tallahassee FL 32301

WALKER, WILLIAM RALPH, supt. schs.; b. Ruth, Miss., Feb. 1, 1926; s. Rufus Royd and Leedie Ella (Stewart) W.; B.A., Presbyn. Coll., 1949; M.Ed., U. Tenn., 1953; m. Bertha Rella Prewitt, June 24, 1949; 1 dau. Janella Kaye. Tchr., coach Bradley Central High Sch., 1949-69; supt. schs. Bradley County Schs., Cleveland, Tenn., 1969-—. Served with USCGR, 1943-45. Home: 2605 N Henderson St Cleveland TN 37311 Office: PO Box 399 Cleveland TN 37311

WALKINGSTICK, BENJAMIN THACKER, JR., banker; b. Tahlequah, Okla., Oct. 29, 1930; s. Benjamin Taylor and Theone Leah (Grove) W.; B.B.A., U. Okla., 1952; m. Jerry Marshall, June 10, 1952; children—Judith Ann, Jeffrey T., Janet Lee. Gen. ins. agt., Tulsa, Okla., 1954-63; pres. Union Nat. Bank of Chandler, Okla., 1963-—; dir. Kin-Ark Corp., Tulsa. Bd. dirs. Lincoln County Indsl. Devel. Authority, Deep Fork Watershed Assn. Served with USAF, 1952-54. Mem. Chandler C. of C. (pres. 1965-66), Lion (pres. 1970-71). Home: 242 Marshall Dr Chandler OK 74834 Office: 1001 Manvel St Chandler OK 74834

WALKINGSTICK, HOWARD CHANDLER, social worker; b. Tahlequah, Okla., Jan. 7, 1915; s. Simon R. and Rebecca (Chandler) W.; B.A., George Washington U., 1946; M.S.W., U. Denver, 1949; postgrad. U. Chgo., 1955. With Bur. Indian Affairs, 1935-70, dir. social work Western Okla., Kan. and Tex., 1952-70; asst. supr. group work cons., coordinator, specialist in a service tng. Bur. Children's Services, Dept. Instns., Social and Rehab. Services, Okla. Social Service System, Oklahoma City, 1970-—; asst. prof. U. Okla., 1963. Mem. Okla. Registration Bd. Social Workers, 1965-71; bd. dirs. Okla. Health and Welfare Assn., 1964-—; Mental Health Assn., 1961-—; Okla. del. to White House Conf. Children and Youth, 1960, 70. Staff tchr. 4th Army Hdqrs., Ft. Sam Houston, Tex. Mem. Okla.'s Com. on Handicapped, 1959-—, Com. on Ethnic Minority Groups, Council on Social Work Edn. Served as staff sgt., AUS, 1943-46. Recipient Distinguished Service award Dept. of Interior, 1967. Mem. Am. Soc. Pub. Adminstrn., Nat. Assn. Social Workers, Okla. Health and Welfare Assn. (pres. 1967-68, recipient Distinguished Service award 1967), Tau Kappa Epsilon. Methodist. Mason (32 deg.), Kiwanian. Home: 122 Moore Country Club Dr Holdenville OK 74848 Office: Dept Insts Social and Rehabilitative Services Oklahoma City OK

WALL, JOHN E., govt. ofcl.; b. Benson, N.C., Dec. 29, 1910; s. John Edgar and Bessie M. (Duncan) W.; A.B., U. N.C., 1933; m. Sarah Farmer, Feb. 21, 1935; children—Mary Linda (Mrs. Emerson Scarborough), Janie Leigh (Mrs. Wilson R. Carter). Asst. collector Internal Revenue Service, Greensboro, N.C., 1950-54, asst. dist. dir., 1954-59, dist. dir., 1959-—. Mem. budget com. Greensboro United Fund, 1965-68, chmn. budget com., 1968, bd. dirs., mem. exec. com., 1967-68. Mem. Greensboro Fed. Execs. Assn. (pres. 1967-68). Kiwanis (pres. 1969-70, div. lt. gov. 1972-73). Democrat. Baptist. Home: 1102 Hammel Rd Greensboro NC 27408 Office: 320 Federal Pl Greensboro NC 27402

WALL, MARY K(ATE), lawyer; b. Bertram, Tex., Aug. 7, 1912; d. James Francis and Rosalthe (Lawhon) Parker; B.A., U. Tex., 1932, LL.B., 1934; m. Hubert S. Wall, Oct. 18, 1947. Admitted to Tex. bar, 1934; sec. State Tax Bd., 1935-36, Tex. Employment Commn., 1936-37; statistician Tex. Dept. Pub. Safety, 1937-42; briefing atty. Supreme Ct. of Tex., 1942-50; asst. atty gen. Tex., 1950-62; research asso. Tex. Legislative Council, 1962-63; asst. atty. gen. State Tex., 1963-67; dir. elections div. Sec. of State's Office, 1967-70, Legislative Council, 1970-—. Mem. Order of Coif, Phi Beta Kappa. Home: 2903 Breeze Terrace Austin TX 78722 Office: care Tex Legislative Council Capitol Station Austin TX 78711

WALL, WILLIAM HENRY, JR., dentist; b. Albany, Ga., Mar. 17, 1937; s. William Henry and Hallie Rebecca (Walker) W.; B.S., U. Ga., 1959; D.D.S., Emory U., 1963, postgrad. 1966-67; m. Barbara Kay Thompson, June 22, 1963; children—William Henry III, Patricia Camille, Stephen Braxton, Kimberly Paige. Intern oral surgery Jackson Meml. Hosp., Miami, Fla., 1965-66; resident oral surgery Duval Med. Center, Jacksonville, Fla., 1967-68; pvt. practice dentistry, specializing in oral surgery, Decatur, Ga., 1968-—. Asso. clin. instr. oral surgery Emory U. Sch. Dentistry, 1968-—. Served with USAF, 1963-65. Mem. Am., Ga., Southeastern socs. oral surgeons, Am. Dental Assn., No. Dist., 5th Dist. dental socs., Chi Phi, Psi Omega. Rotarian. Club: Druid Hills Golf (Decatur). Inventor Wall universal fracture splint used in treating fractured jaws. Home: 3797 Briargreen Ct Atlanta GA 30340 Office: 1275 McConnell Dr Decatur GA 30033

WALLACE, BURMA MORGAN, librarian; b. Eva, Ala., May 13, 1929; d. J. Fred and Bertha (Gregory) Morgan; B.S., U. Ala., 1950, M.A., 1965; m. James B. Wallace, July 7, 1950. Librarian, Jefferson County Bd. Edn., Ala., 1950-52, Birmingham Bd. Edn., 1952-54, Misses Howard's Sch. for Girls, Birmingham, 1954-55, Jefferson County Bd. Edn., Ala., 1955-65; dir. library Jefferson State Jr. Coll., Birmingham, 1965-—. Ednl. Devel. and Professions Act grantee, 1970. Mem. Ala., Ala. Jr. Coll. library assns., Ala. Edn. Assn., Alpha Beta Alpha. Home: 1516 2d Place N W Birmingham AL 35215 Office: 2601 Carson Rd Birmingham AL 35215

WALLACE, CARL S., govt. ofcl.; b. Ontario, Wis., Sept. 27, 1918; s. David Wallace and Mae (McQueen) W.; Ph.B., U. Wis., 1943; m. Marian E. Jones, Feb. 22, 1941; children—Carl S., Mary Ann. Mgr. Wausau (Wis.) office Wis. Employment Service, 1951-53, Stevens Point (Wis.) Area C. of C., 1953-64; adminstrv. asst. to U.S. rep. Melvin Laird, 1965-68; spl. asst. to sec., also dep. sec. def., 1969-—. Served with AUS, 1943-45. Decorated Bronze Star (2). Mem. Am. Legion. Republican. Methodist. Elk, Kiwanian. Home: 8315 Ashwood Dr Alexandria VA 22303 Office: Dept of Defense The Pentagon Washington DC 20301

WALLACE, GEORGE CORLEY, gov. Ala.; b. Clio, Ala., Aug. 25, 1919; s. George C. and Mozell (Smith) W.; LL.B., U. Ala., 1942; m. Lurleen Burns, May 23, 1943 (dec. 1968); children—Bobbie Joe, Peggy Sue, George Corley, Janie Lee; m. 2d, Cornelia Ellis Snively, Jan. 4, 1971; stepchildren—Jim, Josh. Admitted to Ala. bar, 1942; asst. atty. gen. Ala., 1946-47; mem. Ala. Legislature from Barbour County, 1947-53; judge 3d Jud. Dist. Ala., 1953-58; pvt. practice, Clayton, Ala., 1958-62; gov. of Ala., 1963-66, 71-—. Sponsor Wallace Act for state trade schs., 1947. Bd. dirs. Ala. Tb Assn. Served with USAAF, 1942-45; PTO. Mem. Am. Legion, V.F.W., Disabled Am. Vets. Democrat. Methodist (past Sunday sch. tchr. and supt.). Mason (Shriner), Moose, Elk; mem. Order Eastern Star, Modern Woodmen of World. Club: Civitan. Home: 1142 S Perry St Montgomery AL 36104

WALLACE, HARMON, city ofcl. Fire chief, Jackson, Miss. Office: City Hall Jackson MS 39505*

WALLACE, H(ARRY) JAY, city planner; b. Pencoyd, Pa., July 7, 1894; s. Harry Eugene and Mary (Brubaker) W.; B.S., Pa. State Coll., 1916; postgrad. Harvard, 1917-18; m. Maude Eldecia West, Feb. 21, 1937 (dec. Jan. 1967). Land devel. planner, Atlanta, 1919-27, 38-43; directed mapping Atlanta, 1927-30; resident engr. Castle Harbour Hotel Devel., Bermuda, 1930-32; asso. regional planner, TVA, 1933-37; asst. planning engr. City of Atlanta, 1943-64; cons. City Atlanta Dept. Planning, 1965-—. Served with AC, U.S. Army, 1918-19. Registered profl. engr., Ga. Mem. Phi Kappa Phi. Presbyn. Mason. Author: (with others) Scenic Resources of the Tennessee Valley, 1937. Prepared maps of Atlanta for U.S. Bur. Census, 1950, 1960, 70. Home: 710 Peachtree St NE Atlanta GA 30308 Office: City Hall Atlanta GA 30303

WALLACE, JACK EUGENE, pharmacologist; b. Harrisburg, Ill., Jan. 5, 1934; s. Harry H. and Ruby V. (Burroughs) W.; B.S., So. Ill. U., 1955, M.A., 1957; Ph.D., Purdue U., 1961; m. Verla Ann Standerfer, Aug. 14, 1955; children—Michael Eugene, Kimberly Ann. Supervisory pharmacologist USAF, chief forensic toxicology USAF Sch. Aerospace Medicine, Brooks AFB, Tex., 1962-72; pharmacologist Bexas County Hosp. and U. Tex. Med. Sch., San Antonio, 1972-—; dir. research and devel. S.W. Bio-clin. Labs., San Antonio, 1969-—; clin. prof. U. Tex. Med. Sch., San Antonio, 1967-72. Served with USAF, 1962-64. Recipient Sci. Achievement award USAF, 1966. Fellow Am. Inst. Chemists, Am. Acad. Forensic Scis.; mem. Am. Chem. Soc., Sigma Xi, Phi Lambda Upsilon. Contbr. articles profl. jours. Home: 5414 Keystone Dr San Antonio TX 78229 Office: Dept Pathology U Texas Med School San Antonio TX

WALLACE, JAMES OLDHAM, librarian; b. San Antonio, Sept. 22, 1917; s. James Vance and Violet Edyth (Oldham) W.; A.A., San Antonio Coll., 1936; B.A., St. Mary's U., 1938, M.A., 1940; B.S. in L.S., Our Lady of the Lake Coll., 1950; m. Lillie Ruth Franklin, July 23, 1948; children—Carolyn, E. Frances, Thelma. Tchr., Natalia (Tex.) Independent Sch. Dist., 1940-41, Los Angeles Heights, San Antonio, 1941-42; clk. Kelly AFB, 1942-43; certifying officer Randolph AFB, 1943-49; tchr., librarian Lanier High Sch., San Antonio, 1949-50; asst. librarian San Antonio Coll., 1950-51, librarian, 1951-—. Lectr., Our Lady of the Lake Coll., 1953-55; cons. Office of Edn., Baker & Taylor Co. Trustee, Baptist Meml. Hosp., San Antonio, 1965-67. Named Tex. librarian of year Tex. Library Assn., 1969; boss of year Mission City chpt. Am. Business Women's Assn., 1971. Mem. San Antonio Hist. Assn. (pres. 1970-71), Nat. Soc. Study Edn., Nat. Microfilm Assn., Assn. Ednl. Communications and Tech., Am. Assn. U. Profs., Am. (council 1967-71, constn. and bylaws com. 1970-72), Tex. (chmn. dist. 8, 1970), Southwestern (local arrangements com. 1962), Bexar (pres. 1951-52), library assns., Assn. Coll. and Research Libraries (exec. bd. 1960-63, 67-71, standards com. 1966-73, jr. coll. standards revision com. 1966-72), Am. Assn. Jr. Colls. (joint com. with A.L.A. 1966-70), Council Research and Acad. Libraries (pres. 1966-68), Collector's Inst., Am. Soc. Eighteenth Century Studies, Tex. Assn. Ednl. Tech., Tex. Jr. Coll. Tchrs. Assn., Librarians in Service to San Antonio. Author: In the Shadow of His Hand, 1961. Home: PO Box 13041 San Antonio TX 78213 Office: 1001 Howard St San Antonio TX 78284

WALLACE, MILTON JAY, lawyer; b. Passaic, N.J., Dec. 17, 1935; s. Mark and Regina (Tenny) W.; B.B.A. cum laude, U. Miami, 1956, LL.B., 1959; m. Patricia Radin, July 7, 1963; 1 son, Mark D. Pub. accountant Harry L. Davis, Miami, Fla., 1956-57; office mgr. Lee Constrn. Co., 1957-59; admitted to Fla. bar, 1959; practiced in Miami, 1959-—; gen. counsel Fla. Securities Commn., Tallahassee, 1965-68; chmn. bd. Computer Controls Corp., 1968-70; chmn. bd. dirs. Nat. Properties, Inc., 1966-—; dir. Consurgico Corp., Brickell Bank, Southeastern Surg. Supply Co. Judge, City of Miami, 1962-63; asst. atty. gen. State of Fla., 1965-70. Mem. adv. bd. Salvation Army; treas. Miami Philharmonic Soc., 1961-65, v.p., 1966-68, dir., 1961-—. Guest lectr. N.Am. Securities Adminstrn., 1966. Served with AUS, 1954-55. Mem. Am., Fla., Dade County bar assns., Fla. Inst. C.P.A.'s C. of C. Clubs: Tip Top Bay, Kings Bay Yacht and Country, Jockey. Home: 10650 SW 65th Av Miami FL 33156 Office: 2138 Biscayne Blvd Miami FL 33137

WALLACE, RAYMOND BYRD, JR., paper co. exec.; b. Richmond, Va., Mar. 11, 1938; s. Raymond Byrd and Martha (Latane) W.; B.A., Hampden-Sydney Coll., 1960; m. Douglas Louise Laughon, June 5, 1964; children—Douglas Louise, Lee Bristow. With Cauthorne Paper Co., Inc., 1961—, sales rep., 1961-64, asst. v.p., 1964-67, v.p., 1967—. Mem. Richmond., Republican City Exec. Com., 1966-70. Bd. dirs. Richmond Area Inter Club Council, Team of Progress, Richmond Community Mental Health and Retardation Services Bd. Mem. Richmond Printing House Craftsmen. Clubs: Civitan of Richmond (pres. 1970-71, dir. 1966—), Richmond First (membership com. 1970). Home: 2012 Hanover Av Richmond VA 23220 Office: PO Box 2059 Richmond VA 23216

WALLACE, SARAH LESLIE, librarian; b. Kansas City Mo., Oct. 28, 1914; d. Leslie Linn and Mary Louise (Shortall) Wallace; A.B. Coll. St. Catherine, 1935, B.S. in L.S., 1936 With Mpls. Pub. Library, 1936-63, pub. relations officer, 1958-63; publs. officer Library of Congress, Washington, 1963—. Instr. Coll. St. Catherine, 1944-60. Recipient St. Joan of Arc award Jr. Catholic League Mpls., 1963, Horace Hart award Edn. Council of Graphic Arts Industry, 1969. Mem. A.L.A. (membership chmn. 1962-68), D.C. Library Assn., Franklin Tech. Soc., Am. Inst. Graphic Arts, Fed. Editors Assn., Delta Phi Lambda, Kappa Gamma Pi. Author: So You Want To Be a Librarian, 1963; Definition: Library, 1961. Author, illustrator: Promotion Ideas for Small Public Libraries, 1953; Patrons Are People, 1956. Editor Quarterly Jour. Library of Congress, 1964. Home: 8705 Jones Mill Rd Washington DC 20015 Office: 10 1st St SE Washington DC 20540

WALLACE, VIRGINIA WILSON (MRS. PAUL MACLELLAN WALLACE), club woman, educator; b. Waterloo, Ia., July 6, 1905; d. Edwin C. and Ellen (Cheseborough) Wilson; student U. Sask., 1926; B.A., U. Ia., 1930; M.A., U. Louisville, 1948; postgrad. Ind. U., 1950-55; m. Paul Maclellan Wallace, July 17, 1930; 1 dau., Mary Wallbridge. Instr. U. Louisville, 1946-48; instr., lectr. Ind. U. Extension, 1948—. Mem. lit. com. Women's Club, 1942—; mem. Arts Club, Monday Afternoon Club, Internat. Order St. Luke; mem. Ky. Opera Assn., 1955—, Jr. Art Gallery, 1950—, Women's Assn. Louisville Orch., 1949—; active A.R.C., 1944—; mem. Frontier Nursing Assn., 1935—, Jr. League, 1933—; mem. hostess com. Farmington Found., 1961—; mem. women's bd. Norton Meml. Infirmary, 1961—; mem. research com. George Rogers Clark Found., 1961—; bd. dirs. Young Artists Promotions. Mem. Am. Assn. U. Profs., Am. Assn. U. Women, Nat. Soc. Colonial Dames of Am., Rotary-Anne, Internat. Platform Assn., Friends of Camphill Movement, Pi Beta Phi. Episcopalian (charter mem. ch. 1945). Author articles in Coll. English, 1953. Clubs: Pendennis; Hurstbourne Country. Home: 4110 Lime Kiln Lane Louisville KY 40222

WALLACH, MERRILL FRANKLIN, physician; b. Long Beach, Cal., Oct. 19, 1933; s. Charles and Wretha Pearl (Merrill) W.; Ampla cum laude, U. Tex., 1964, M.D., 1964; m. Marilyn Louise Miller, May 7, 1971. Rotating intern John Sealy Hosp., Galveston, Tex., 1964-65; gen. praclce medicine and surgery, Ft. Worth, 1965-66, Cisco, Tex., 1966-70, Baird, Tex., 1971—; mem. staffs Northwest Hosp., Ft. Worth, Eastland (Tex.) Meml. Hosp., Graham Hosp., Cisco, Tex., Callahan County Hosp., Baird, Tex.; med. dir. Operation Headstart, Cisco, 1966-70; city health officer City of Cisco, 1966-69. Served with USAF, 1952-56. NIH fellow, 1963. Mem. A.M.A., Am. Geriatrics Soc., Am., Tex. acads. gen. practice, So., Tex. med. assns., Alumni Assn. U. Tex., V.F.W., Theta Kappa Psi. Home: PO Box 956 Baird TX 79504 Office: 643 Vine St Baird TX 79504

WALLEN, IRVIN EUGENE, govt. ofcl.; b. Afton, Okla., Oct. 4, 1921; s. Stuvie C. and Mittie (Hames) W.; B.S., Okla. State U., 1941, M.S., 1946; Ph.D., U. Mich., 1950; m. Dorothy Wiehe, Feb. 12, 1945; children—Karen Kaye (Mrs. Douglas Lofgren), Gary Lee, Kathy Lynn, Shelley Jean, Mark Edward. Instr. zoology Okla. State U., Stillwater, 1948-52, asso. prof., 1952-56; asst. dir. sci. teaching improvement program A.A.A.S., Washington, 1956-57; aquatic biologist AEC, Germantown, Md., 1957-62; dir. office environmental scis. Smithsonian Instn., Washington, 1962-71; spl. asst. for marine programs, dir. Ft. Pierce (Fla.) bur. Smithsonian Instn., 1971—; dir. Harbor Branch Found. Lab., Ft. Pierce, 1971—; mem. corp. Woods Hole (Mass.) Oceanographic Instn., 1967—, tech. assistance bd. Link Found., N.Y.C., 1969-71. Vis. prof. zoology Asia Found., Pakistan, 1960, 63. Trustee Taiping Found., Atlantic Found., Harbor Branch Found., Link Found., bd. dirs. Iran Found. Served with USNR, 1941-45. Decorated Air Medal (Navy); recipient Smithsonian Inst. Outstanding Service award, 1967. Mem. Am. Soc. Linmology and Oceanography (pres. 1971—), A.A.A.S. (council 1963-71), Sigma Xi. Author: (with Roy W. Jones) Biological Science Notebook, 1952. Contbr. chpt. to textbook; also contbr. articles to profl. jours. Home: 1035 33d St Vero Beach FL 32960 Office: RR 1 Box 194-C Fort Pierce FL 33450

WALLER, CHARLIE ERVIN, life ins. exec.; b. Shady Dale, Ga., May 2, 1908; s. Charlie George and Emma Irene (Cook) W.; student Ga. Ala. Bus. Coll., 1927; m. Doris L. Thomas, Sept. 18, 1932; children—Doris Annelle (Mrs. Samuel Spencer Swilling, Jr.), Leland Ervin. Cashier, Inter-Ocean Ins. Co., Jacksonville, Fla., 1927-36; pres. Profl. Ins. Corp., 1937-51; gen. agt. Am. Health Ins. Co., Atlanta, 1952—; pres. First Am. Corp., 1956—, Atlantic and Pacific Life Ins. Co., 1959—. Mason (32 1/2). Home: 2272 Street deVille NE Atlanta GA 30345 Office: 1430 W Peachtree St NW Atlanta GA 30309

WALLER, ERNEST NOLAN, educator; b. Oxford, Miss., Sept. 29, 1928; s. Ralph Ernest and Myrtle Inez (Briscoe) W.; B.B.A., U. Miss., 1957, M.B.A., 1957; m. Mattie Louise White, Apr. 17, 1957; children—Terry Nolan, Judy Louise, Melinda Kay. Research asso. Bur. Bus. and Econ. Research, U. Miss., Oxford, 1957-64, asst. prof. econ. re search, 1964—. Editor, Miss.'s Bus., 1960—. Served with AUS, 1951-52. Hon. col. staff Gov. Miss. Mem. Beta Gamma Sigma. Baptist. Author (with Raymond Curtis and Walter Primeaux, Jr.) Personal Income in Mississippi Counties, 1970, also articles. Home: Route 1 Box 220 Oxford MS 38655

WALLER, HERBERT S., clergyman; b. Memphis, Oct. 23, 1914; s. Jacob and Helen (Schlesinger) W.; B.A., U. Cin., 1935, M.A., 1937; B. Hebrew, Hebrew Union Coll., 1939, M. Hebrew Lit. cum laude, 1939, D.D., 1964; Th.D., So. Baptist Theol. Sem, 1949; m. Sylvia Steinberg, Spet. 14, 1938; 1 son, David. Rabbi, 1939; rabbi Temple B'nai Isr. Columbus, Ga., 1939-47, Congregation Adath Isr, Louisville, 1947—. Moderator weekly inter-faith panel Sta. WLKY-TV; Jewish Chautauqua Soc. resident lectr. theology Bellarmine Coll., Louisville; Ky. chmn. nat. Rabbinical Council Am. combined campaign for Hebrew Union Coll.-Jewish Inst. Religion, also mem. bd. alumni overseers, mem. nat. recruitment com.; mem. Am. bd. World Union for Progressive Judaism; mem. com. on ch. and state Central Conf. Am. Rabbis. Mem. Ky. Council on Human Relations; lectr. speakers bur. Nat. Council Christians and Jews; active Louisville Community Chest, A.R.C. Bd. dirs., pres. Louisville Bd. Edn., 1960-66; bd. dirs. Lincoln Found., Blue Cross Hosp. Plan. Mem. Am. Jewish Com., Assn. Moral and Spiritual Values, Community Concert Assn., Phi Beta Kappa. Kiwanian; mem. B'nai B'rith. Club: Conservation. Home: 612 Cressbrook Dr Louisville KY 40206 Office: 834 S 3d St Louisville KY 40203*

WALLER, SAMUEL CARPENTER, lawyer; b. Augusta, Ga., May 3, 1918; s. Harcourt E. and Josephine (Carpenter) W.; A.B., Princeton, 1940; LL.B., Harvard, 1948; m. Anna Bacon Maxwell, Apr. 18, 1952; children— Anna M., Laura G., Amelia C. Admitted to Ga. bar, 1947, since practiced in Augusta; mem. firm Cumming, Nixon & Eve, 1948-51; partner firm Cumming, Nixon, Yow, Waller & Capers, 1951—; city atty. City of Augusta, 1964-69. Dir. Ga. R.R. Bank & Trust Co. Mem. Nat. Conf. of Commrs. on uniform state laws, 1965-72. Pres., Augusta Library, 1956-58; mem., sec. Augusta Coll. Found. Mem., Augusta City Council, 1950-56; Mem. Richmond County (Ga.) Democratic Exec. Com., 1962—, chmn., 1962-66. Served to capt. with AUS, 1941-45, now maj. Res. Decorated Bronze Star medal. Mem. State Bar Ga. (bd. govs. 1967—), Am., Augusta (pres. 1971-72) bar Assns., Harvard Law Sch. Assn. Ga. (pres. 1960-61). Episcopalian (sr. warden; registrar Diocese of Ga.). Kiwanian. Clubs: Augusta Country, Pinnacle. Home: 600 Gary St Augusta GA 30904 Office: Ga R R Bank Bldg Augusta GA 30902

WALLER, THOMAS RICHARD, paleontologist, geologist; b. Chgo., July 18, 1937; s. Thomas Theodore and Ann (Blank) W.; B.S., U. Wis., 1959, M.S., 1961; Ph.D., Columbia, 1966; m. Carolyn Ruth Nalbach, Sept. 5, 1959; children—John Steven, Lynn Marie. Geologist, Mobile Oil Co., Caracas, Venezuela, summer 1959; asso. curator U.S. Nat. Museum, Smithsonian Instn., Washington, 1966—. Mem. Geol. Soc. Am., Paleontol. Soc., Soc. Systematic Zoology, A.A.A.S., Sigma Xi, Alpha Delta Phi. Research on systematics, evolution, and biostratigraphy of tertiary mollusks. Home: 9807 Holmhurst Rd Bethesda MD 20034 Office: Dept Paleobiology Smithsonian Inst Washington DC 20560

WALLER, TRAVIS WINSTON, health equipment co. owner; b. Trinity, Tex., Sept. 30, 1921; s. Grady Cooper and Ioma Elizabeth (Dunlap) W.; student Sam Houston State U., 1946, U. Houston, 1946-47, U. Tex., 1947-48; m. Mary Eleanor Shivers, July 14, 1962. Clk., First Nat. Bank, Trinity, 1940-41; seismograph computer Universal Exploration Co., Houston, 1941-42; clk. Dept. Navy, Washington, 1948-50; inventory control clk. HOMCO, Corpus Christi, Tex., 1951; comptroller asst. United Gas Corp., Houston, 1951-52; jr. clk. Texaco, Inc., Houston and Dallas, 1952-59, sr. clk., 1959-63; membership salesman Am. Automobile Assn., Dallas, 1964; v.p. State Nat. Bank, Lovelady, Tex., 1964-65, pres., 1965-67; owner Physical Aids Service, Crockett, Tex., 1967—. Asst. scoutmaster Trinity Troop council Boy Scouts Am., 1939-40. Trustee Crockett Pub. Library, 1969—; bd. dirs. Houston County Cancer Crusade, 1967-70, chmn., 1967-68, v.p., 1969-70. Served with AUS, 1942-45. Presbyn. (ruling elder 1969-71). Lion (pres. 1966-67, dir. 1967-68), Rotarian (pres. 1970-71). Club: Spring Creek Country (Crockett, Tex.). Office: 704 E Goliad PO Box 628 Crockett TX 75835

WALLER, WILLIAM, gov. Miss; b. Oxford, Miss., Oct. 21, 1926; B.S., Memphis State U., 1948; LL.B. U. Miss., 1950. Admitted to Miss. bar, 1950, U.S. Dist Ct., 1951, U.S. Ct. Mil. Appeals, 1966, U.S. Supreme Ct.; mem. firm Waller & Fox, Jackson, Miss.; dist. atty. 7th Circuit Dist. Miss., 1960-68; gov. Miss., Jackson, 1971—. Mem. Am., Hinds County bar assns., Miss State Bar, Am. Judicature Soc., Am. Trial Lawyers Assn., Nat. Dist. Attys. Assn. Office: Office of the Governor Capitol Bldg Jackson MS 39201

WALLERSTEIN, MORTON LUDWIG, lawyer; b. Richmond, Va.; s. Joseph and Clara (Ullmann) W.; B.A., U. Va., 1911; LL.B., Harvard U., 1914; m. Ruth Cohn, Sept. 1, 1919; children—Elizabeth, Catherine, Morton Ludwig. Mem. firm Wallertein, Goode, Dobbins & Shuford; asst. to atty. gen. of Va., 1914-16; asst. counsel Va. Tax Bd. 1916-17; counsel P.W.A., 1933-36. Exec. sec. League Va. Municipalities, 1921-41, counsel, 1941-59; regional chmn. Nat. Resources Planning Bd.; mem. Va. Planning Bd., 1938-46, chmn., 1933-38. Served as ensign USNR, U.S.S. Minnesota, 1917-19. Named Distinguished Citizen, Richmond Jewish Community Council, 1957; Outstanding Services, League Va. Municipalities, 1959. Past pres. Am. Municipal Assn., Am. Soc. Planning Ofcls. (life mem.). Mem. Am. Law Inst., Delta Sigma Rho. Democrat. Jewish religion. Mason (Shriner). Author articles on regional and state planning; atty. gen. opinions. Home: 1601 Pope Av Richmond VA 23227 Office: Travelers Bldg Richmond VA 23202

WALLEY, W. W., physician; b. Richton, Miss., Aug. 2, 1916; s. Joe and Octavia Jane (Smith) W.; B.S., U. Miss., 1946; M.D., U. Pa., 1950; m. Eletha Green, June 7, 1943; children—Eletha Jane (Mrs. Danny Wayne Jenkins), Charlotte Ann, Joseph Claude, W. W., Jr. Intern, U. Ala. Med. Center, 1950-51; pvt. practice of gen. medicine, Waynesboro, Miss., 1951—; mem. staff Wayne Gen. Hosp., chief staff, 1970-71; chmn. bd. Wayne County Funeral Homes, Inc., 1971—. Dist. chmn. Boy Scouts of Am. Alderman, vice mayor City of Waynesboro, 1969—. Served to capt. M.C., AUS, 1941-46, ETO Named Alumnus of Year, Jones County Jr. Coll., 1967. Mem. Miss. State Med. Assn. (past v.p.) C. of C. Mason (Shriner), Rotarian (past pres.). Home: 606 South St Waynesboro MS 39367 Office: 804 Mississippi Dr Waynesboro MS 39367

WALLING, DENNIS, basketball coach W. Tex. State U. Office: Athletic Dept W Tex State U Canyon TX 79015*

WALLIS, CARLTON LAMAR, librarian; b. Blue Springs, Miss., Oct. 15, 1915; s. William R. and Tellie (Jones) W.; A.B., Miss. Coll., 1936; A.M., Tulane U., 1946; B.L.S., U. Chgo., 1947; m. Mary Elizabeth Cooper, Feb. 22, 1944; 1 son, Carlton Lamar. Tchr. pub. schs., Miss., 1936-41; instr. Tulane U., 1941-42; librarian Rosenberg Library, Galveston, Tex., 1947-55, Richmond (Va.) Pub. Library, 1955-58; dir. Memphis Pub. Library, 1958—. Bd. dirs. Great Books Found. Served with AUS, 1942-46. Mem. A.L.A., Tex. (pres. 1952-53), Southeastern (chmn. pub. libraries div. 1960-62, chmn. nominating com. 1962-64), Tenn. (pres. 1969) library assns. Presbyn. (ruling elder). Clubs: Egyptians, Holly Hills Country. Author: Libraries in the Golden Triangle. Home: 365 Kenilworth St Memphis TN 38112 Office: 1850 Peabody Av Memphis TN 38104

WALLIS, ERNEST MARTIN, shoe co. exec.; b. Hamburg, Germany, Aug. 7, 1921; s. Alfred and Janina (Abarbanel) W.; brought to U.S., 1936, naturalized, 1942; student Heinrich Herz Real Gymnasium, Hamburg, 1936; grad. Holderness Sch., Plymouth, N.H., 1937; A.B., Coll. City N.Y., 1941; m. Joan Oettunger, Jan. 13, 1947; children—Jeffrey Allan, David Andrew, Deborah Joy. Mgr., Slty. Importing Co., Inc., Cambridge, Mass., 1946-48; v.p. Embo Casual Footwear Corp., Boston, 1948-63; pres. Marlboro Footwear Co., 1963-65; became regional sales mgr. Eversharp Pen Co., 1965; now pres. Wallis Sales, Inc., Miami. Treas., Parents Blind Children, Inc.; del. Mass. Council for the Blind, Boston; chmn. shoe div. Boston Evening Clinic and Hosp. Served as technician 5th grade, 267th F.A. Bn., AUS, 1942-45, ETO. Decorated Bronze Star, Am. Service medal, European, African, Middle Eastern Service medal with 4 stars, World War II Victory Medal. Mem. Boston Power Squadron (dir. lt. comdr., pub. relations officer), Dale Carnegie Internat. (v.p. Boston chpt.), 210 Assos. (Boston), A.I.M. Clubs: Pleasant Park Yacht; Racquet (Miami), Newton Yacht. Editor: Boston Light. Address: 4730 E 10th Lane Hialeah FL 33013

WALLS, CARMAGE, newspaper pub.; b. Cordele, Ga., Oct. 28, 1908; s. Benjamin G. and Anna D. (Byrd) W.; ed. pub. schs., Orlando, Fla.; m. Odessa Lee Dobbs, June 7, 1928 (div.); children—Lee, Thomas, Jean; m. 2d, Martha Ann Williams, Jan. 2, 1954; children—Cooper, Lissa. Bus. mgr. Orlando Daily Newspapers, Inc., 1934-40; pub. Macon Telegraph-News, 1940-47; pres. Gen. Newspapers, Inc., Gadsden, Ala., 1945-59, Gen. Advt. Service, Inc., Atlanta; pres. So. Newspaper, Inc., Montgomery Ala., 1951-69, The Advertiser Co., 1963-69, now owner Walls Investment Co.; chmn. bd. J and P Publs., Inc., Greensboro; dir. Franklin (La.)-Banner-Tribune, Valley Times News, West Point, Ga., Cleveland (Tenn.) Newspapers, Inc. Morgan City Review (La.), Galveston (Tex.) News, Texas City (Tex.) Sun, Altus (Okla.) Times-Democrat, Laredo (Tex.) Newspapers, Inc., Houma (La.) Newspapers, Inc., Jasper (Ala.) Newspapers, Inc., Beaumont (Tex.) Enterprise Co., Inc., Clearwater (Fla.) Newspapers, Inc. Pres. Macon Area Devel. Commn., 1944-45, Gadsden Area Devel. Com., 1951, Macon C. of C., 1944. Trustee Birmingham (Ala.)-So. Coll. Mem. Sigma Delta Chi. Methodist. Home: Route 7 148 Bell Rd Montgomery AL 36109 Office: Walls Investment Co PO Box 7278 Montgomery AL 36107

WALLS, MARTHA ANN WILLIAMS (MRS. B. CARMAGE WALLS), newspaper exec.; b. Gadsden, Ala., Apr. 21, 1927; d. Aubrey Joseph and Inez (Cooper) Williams; student pub. schs., Gadsden; m. B. Carmage Walls, Jan. 2, 1954; children—Byrd Cooper, Lissa Williams. Sec.-treas., So Newspapers, Inc., Montgomery, Ala., 1954-67, also dir.; pres., dir. Walls Newspapers, Inc., Montgomery, 1967-70; pres. So. Newspapers, Inc., Baytown, Tex., 1970—; sec.-treas. Summer Camps, Inc., Guntersville, Ala., 1954-69, also dir.; v.p., dir. Dixie Newspapers, Inc., Gadsden, Ala., Fort Payne (Ala.) Newspapers, Inc., Scottsboro (Ala.) Newspapers, Inc.; dir. Bay City (Tex.) Tribune, Angleton (Tex.) Times, Henderson (Tex.) News, Herald-Coaster, Rosenberg, Tex., Coastal Publs., Inc., Alvin (Tex.) Sun, Brenham (Tex.) Banner, Brazosport Facts, Freeport, Tex., Terrell (Tex.) Tribune, Enterprise (Ala.) Ledger, Reidsville (N.C.) Newspapers, Inc., McKinney (Tex.) Courier-Gazette, LaMarque (Tex.) Times. Bd. dirs. Montgomery (Ala.) Acad. Methodist. Home: Walhaven RFD 7 148 Bell Rd Montgomery AL 36109 Office: PO Box 7278 Montgomery AL 36107

WALNER, ARTHUR H., sci. analyst cons.; b. N.Y.C., Nov. 25, 1928; s. Jack and Anna (Sherman) W.; B.S., Coll. City N.Y., 1951; postgrad. Stevens Inst. Tech., 1951-52, Columbia, 1958, N.Y. U., 1965-66; m. Beverly Block, Apr. 26, 1952; children—Tandi Gwenn, Debra Helene, Phyllis-Jo. Chief quality control Picatinny Arsenal, Dover, N.J., 1951-55; cons. statis. head Applied Sci. Lab., U.S. Naval, Bklyn., 1955-67; dir. operations planning div. Met. Police Dept., Washington, 1967-68; operations analyst Gen. Services Adminstrn., Washington, 1968-71; asst. dir. operational planning Cost of Living Council, 1971-72; sr. program analyst Environmental Protection Agy., 1972—. Cons. in crime analysis and resource planning, 1968—. Mem. Operations Research Soc. Am., Quality Control Soc. Am., Am. Statis. Soc. (div. dir. 1956-67), Internat. Criminology Soc., Internat. Biographers World. Home: 11215 Oak Leaf Dr Silver Spring MD 20901 Office: 401 M St SW Washington DC 20460

WALRAVEN, HAROLD CLAY, JR., dentist; b. Atlanta, May 18, 1928; s. Harold C. and Martha Turner (Jones) W.; B.S., U. Ga., 1950; D.D.S., Emory U., 1954; m. Billie Frances Trunkey, Dec. 27, 1952; children—Terry Frances, Caren Leslie. Med. technician Ga. Bapt. Hosp., Atlanta, 1952; research fellow Emory U., 1952-54, instr., research asso., 1954-69; individual practice gen. dentistry, Atlanta, 1954—. Cons. ceramic engring. Ga. Inst. Tech., 1962—. Mem. Ga. Bd. Dental Examiners, 1969—, pres., 1970—. Dir. Northside Bus. Assn., 1960-65, v.p., treas., 1959-60. Head dental div. United Appeal, 1960, 61, 63, Am. Cancer Soc., 1962, 64, 66, Heart Fund, 1966, 67, 69. Served with AUS, 1945-47. Fellow Am. Coll. Dentists; hon. fellow Ga. Dental Assn.; mem. Interprofl. Council Ga., No. Dist. Dental Soc., Am. Dental Assn., Amateur Athletic Union (officer, committeeman nat. gymnastic championships 1969), Sphinx, Gridiron. Contbr. articles to profl. jours. Patentee coupling agts. Home: 3253 Rilman Dr NW Atlanta GA 30327 Office: 1957 Howell Mill Rd NW Atlanta GA 30318

WALSH, CORNELIUS STEPHEN, co. exec.; b. N.Y.C., Dec. 27, 1907; s. William Francis and Frances (Murphy) W.; student Eastman-Gaines Sch., 1924-25; m. Edwyna Lois Senter, May 1, 1930; children—Jane Linda, Richard Stephen, Suzanne Patricia. With Dyson Shipping Co., Inc., 1925-27, Interocean Steamship Corp., 1928-30; sec. States Marine Corp., N.Y.C., 1931-38, v.p., 1938-53, pres., 1953-65, dir., 1950-65; pres., dir. States Marine Corp. Del., N.Y.C., 1946-65; chmn. Waterman S.S. Corp., N.Y.C., 1965—, Waterman Industries Corp., 1965—, Hammond Leasing Corp., N.Y.C., 1967—; mem. adv. bd. Mfrs. Hanover Trust Co., N.Y.C. Mem. Met. Mus. Art, Soc. Four Arts Palm Beach (Fla.). Mem. Far East-Am. Council Commerce and Industry (dir.), Soc. Naval Architects and Marine Engrs. (asso.), Japan Soc. (dir.), Am. Bur. Shipping. Clubs: Wall Street, Yacht, Metropolitan Opera, Fifth Avenue, Downtown Athletic (N.Y.C.); Seawanhaka Corinthian Yacht (Oyster Bay, L.I., N.Y.); Pine Valley Golf (Clementon, N.J.); Everglades, Bath and Tennis, Beach, Seminole Golf (Palm Beach, Fla.); Bathing and Tennis, Golf and Country (Spring Lake, N.J.). Home: 220 El Bravo Way Palm Beach FL 33480 Office: Waterman Steamship Corporation 345 Park Av New York City NY 10022

WALSH, F. HOWARD, oil producer, rancher; b. Waco, Tex., Feb. 7, 1913; s. P. Frank and Maude (Gage) W.; B.B.A., Tex. Christian U., 1933; m. Mary D. Fleming, Mar. 13, 1937; children—Richard F., F. Howard, D'Ann E. (Mrs. William F. Bonnell), Maudi (Mrs. George C. Porter, III), William Lloyd. Self employed in oil prodn. and ranching, 1942—; pres. Walsh & Watts, Inc.; dir. First Nat. Bank of Ft. Worth; partner Manor Properties. Mem. Tex. Jud. Qualifications Commn. Pres. The Walsh Found.; trustee Southwestern Baptist Theol. Sem., Tex. Christian U.; bd. dirs. So. Baptist Found.; v.p. The Fleming Found. Recipient Valuable Alumnus award Tex. Christian U., 1967; Spl. Recognition for support of ranch tng. program. Tex. Christian U.; med. bldg. S.W. Bapt. Theol. Sem. named for Mary D. and F. Howard Walsh; named Patron of Arts in Ft. Worth, 1970. Mem. Tex.-Mid-Continent, West-Central Tex., North Tex. oil and gas assns., Ind. Petroleum Assn. Am., Tex. Ind. Producers and Royalty Owners, Internat. Charolais Assn. Clubs: Garden of the Gods (Colorado Springs); Colorado Springs Country, Steeplechase, Fort Worth, Ridglea, Rivercrest and Colonial Country, Shady Oaks Country. Home: 2425 Stadium Dr Fort Worth TX 76109 also 1801 Culebra Colorado Springs CO 80907 Office: First Nat Bank Bldg Fort Worth TX 76102

WALSH, GEORGE PAT, food co. exec.; b. Amarillo, Tex., Dec. 17, 1928; s. William D. and Mary (Ellis) W.; student Amarillo Coll., 1949, 56, 65; m. Bobbye Jo Oakley, Aug. 25, 1947; children—Bill Pat, Robbye Jo, Jeffrey Paul. Gen. mgr. Walsh Food Stores No. 3, Amarillo, 1951-56; sales mgr., dealer franchise mgr. Walsh Food Service, Amarillo, 1956-62, gen. mgr., 1962—; v.p. Artic Frozen Foods, Inc., 1962—. Mem. Amarillo Bd. City Devel., 1971; chmn. Council Child Care Agys., 1971; pres. Catholic Family Service, Inc., Amarillo, 1969-70. Mem. Nat. Inst. Locker and Freezer Provisioners (pres., 1968), Amarillo Execs. Assn. (pres., 1971), Frozen Food

Council (pres. 1971), Roman Catholic. K.C., Kiwanian. Club: Serra. Home: 1002 Bowie St Amarillo TX 79102

WALSH, GWENDOLYN ELROY, educator; b. Cambridge, Mass., Mar. 19, 1925; d. Chesley and Elizabeth (Furey) Elroy; diploma Bouve Boston Sch. Phys. Edn. and Phys. Therapy, 1946; B.S., Tufts U., 1946; postgrad. San Jose State Coll., 1961, Stanford, 1962; M.Ed., U. Va., 1967; m. Douglas F. Walsh, Sept. 24, 1950 (div. July 1962); children— Kevin Douglas, Robyn Elizabeth. Tchr., Abbot Acad., Andover, Mass., 1946-50, Katherine Delmar Burke Sch., San Francisco, 1951-58, San Carlos (Cal.) High Sch., 1958-62; asst. prof. phys. edn. Mary Baldwin Coll., Staunton, Va., 1962—, co-chmn. dept. phys. edn., 1969—, dance dir., 1962—. Tchr. swimming and canoeing New Eng. summer camps, 1943-49; tchr. Project Opportunity, summer 1969; choreographer Oak Grove Summer Theater, Verona, Va., 1964-67; tchr. fencing Waynesboro YMCA, 1966—. Mem. Am. Assn. U. Profs., Am. Assn. U. Women, Am. Fencers League of Am. (Va. sec.-treas. 1967-68, nat. dir., 1969-70), Am., Va. assns. health, phys. edn. and recreation, So. Assn. Health, Phys. Edn. and Recreation for Coll. Women, Kappa Delta Pi. Club: Blue Ridge Fencers (pres. 1968-70) (Waynesboro, Va.). Episcopalian. Home: 340 E Beverley St Staunton VA 24401

WALSH, JOHN BREFFNI, govt. ofcl.; b. Bklyn., Aug. 20, 1927; s. George Patrick and Margaret Mary (Rigney) W.; B.E.E. summa cum laude, Manhattan Coll., 1948; M.S., Columbia, 1950; postgrad. N.Y.U., 1954-62; m. Marie Louise Leclerc, June 18, 1955; children—George Breffni, John Leclerc, Darina Louise. Asst. in elec. engring. Manhattan Coll., 1947-48; asst. in elec. engring. Columbia, N.Y.C., 1948-49, instr., 1949-51, asst. prof. elec. engring., 1953-58, asst. dir. Electronics Research Labs., 1958-66, lectr. math., 1959-61; asst. chief radar systems br. Rome (N.Y.) Air Devel. Center, 1951-52, chief air def. systems lab., 1952-53, tech. dir. Directorate Intelligence and Reconnaissance, 1953; dep. for research Office Asst. Sec. Air Force, Washington, 1966-71; spl. asst. to President's sci. adviser, sr. mem. NSC staff, Washington, 1971-72; dep. dir. def. research and engring., Washington, 1972—. Cons. to various govt. and indsl. orgns., including Office Dir. Def. for Research and Engring., Army Research Office, Advanced Research Projects Agy., 1953-66. Mem. Cresskill (N.J.) Planning Bd., 1964-66. Served with AUS, 1946-47. Recipient Exceptional Civilian Service award Dept. Air Force, 1969, Meritorious Civilian Service award Dept. Def., 1971, citation of honor as outstanding Air Force civilian employee of year Air Force Assn., 1971. Registered profl. engr., N.Y. State, N.J. Fellow I.E.E.E.; mem. N.Y. Acad. Scis., Sigma Xi, Eta Kappa Nu. Author: (with K. S. Miller) Introductory Electric Circuits, 1960, Elementary and Advanced Trigonometry, 1962; Electromagnetic Theory and Engineering Applications, 1960; also chpts. in books. Contbr. articles to tech. jours., Ency. Americana. Home: 7803 Birnam Wood Dr McLean VA 22101 Office: Pentagon Washington DC 20301

WALSH, LEONARD PATRICK, U.S. judge; b. Superior, Wis., Mar. 10, 1903; s. William and Margaret (Murphy) W.; ed. U. Minn., LL.B., Nat. U.; m. Bronia Kaczensky, Dec. 1964; children—William L., Dorothy Lynn (Mrs. Michael Karpew, Jr.); 1 stepson, Tobey W. Kaczensky. Admitted to D.C. bar, 1933, also U.S. Supreme Ct.; gen. practice law, Washington, 1936-53; instr. George Washington Sch. Edn., 1929-36; chief judge Municipal Ct. D.C., 1953-59; judge U.S. Dist. Ct., Washington, 1959—; professorial lectr. George Washington U. Sch. Law, 1956-64. Chmn. D.C. Armory Bd., 1944-53, Met. Police Boys Club. Mem. Bar Assn. D.C. (pres. 1951-52, dir.), Phi Delta Phi. Home: 4625 Rockwood Pky Washington DC 20016 Office: US Dist Ct Washington DC 20001

WALSH, MARY D. FLEMING (MRS. F. HOWARD WALSH), club woman; b. Whitewright, Tex., Oct. 29, 1913; d. William and Anna Maud (Lewis) Fleming; B.A., So. Meth. U., 1934; m. F. Howard Walsh, Mar. 13, 1937; children—Richard, Howard, D'Ann (Mrs. William F. Bonnell), Maudi (Mrs. George C. Porter III), William Lloyd. Vice pres. F. H. Walsh Investment Co.; partner The Walsh Co. Commr., Tex. Fine Arts Commn. Bd. dirs. Lloyd Shaw Found.; pres. Fleming Found.: v.p. Walsh Found.; bd. dirs. Van Cliburn Internat. Piano Competition, 1964-67, Am. Field Service, 1960-64; v.p., bd. dirs. Fort Worth Opera, 1961, 65, 66. Recipient Civic First Lady of Fort Worth award Altrusa Club, 1968; named Patron of Arts in Fort Worth, 1970. Mem. Tex. League Composers (hon. life mem. Ft. Worth guild), Ft. Worth Boys Club, Ft. Worth Children's Hosp., Woman's Club, Jewel Charity Ball, Ft. Worth Pan Hellenic (Pres. 1940), Opera Guild, William Edrington Scott Theatre Guild, Chi Omega (Pres. 1935-36). Baptist. Clubs: Fidelite, Rejebian, Chi Omega Mothers, Kappa Sigma Wives and Mothers, Bankers, Wives, Dinner Dance, Roundelay (founder 1946). Home: 2425 Stadium Dr Fort Worth TX 76109 also 1801 Culebra Av Colorado Springs CO 80907

WALSH, RALPH (PAT) AUGUSTUS, II, broadcasting co. exec.; b. Oklahoma City, Apr. 4, 1932; s. Ralph Augustus and Mary Phyllis (Proffitt) W.; student U. Okla., U. Ark.; m. Bobbie Jean Hill, May 24, 1958; children—Mary, Ralph Augustus, Amy. With KGHI radio, Little Rock, 1957-58, KAJI radio, Little Rock, 1958; successively sales mgr., asst. mgr., mgr., gen. mgr. KAAY radio, Little Rock, now pres.; dir. Electric Memory Corp. Chmn. bd. Opportunity Group; bd. dirs. Little Rock Unlimited Progress, Little Rock YMCA. Served with AUS, Germany. Mem. Ark. Advt. Fedn., Little Rock C. of C., Sales and Marketing Execs. Internat., Ark. Broadcasters Assn. Presbyn. (deacon). Clubs: Little Rock, Capital. Home: 208 Hiawatha St Little Rock AR 72205 Office: 1425 W 7th St Little Rock AR 72203

WALSH, TRAVIS, mng. editor Tulsa World. Office: 315 S Boulder Av Tulsa OK 74102*

WALSH, WILLIAM EDWARD, JR., lawyer; b. Washington, Pa., Nov. 10, 1909; s. William Edward and Christine (Bochers) W.; student U. Miami, 1927-30, U. Fla., 1930-31, Cumberland U., 1932; m. Natalie Aiken Brooks, Apr. 30, 1951; children—Christine Laury, William Edward III. Admitted to Fla. bar, 1933, since practiced in Miami; pvt. practice, 1933-42; mem. firm Walsh & Walsh, 1946-54, Walsh, Simmonite, Budd & Walsh, 1954-65, Walsh & Walsh, 1965-69, Walsh, Nottebaum & Laks, 1969—. Pres., Key Biscayne Improvement Assn. Served as lt. AUS, 1942-46. Mem. Fla. Bar, Dade County Bar Assn., Mil. Order World Wars. Democrat. Lion (dir. Key Biscayne). Home: 662 Woodcrest Rd Key Biscayne FL 33149 Office: Alfred I du Pont Bldg 169 E Flagler St Miami FL 33131

WALSTON, VIRGIL ALFRED, civil engr.; b. Palestine, Tex., Dec. 20, 1903; s. William Watts and Nora (Featherstone) W.; student Tex. A. and M. U., 1923-26; B.C.E., U. Houston, 1953; m. Dorothy May Darden, July 15, 1928; children—Dorothy Jean (Mrs. Charles W. Alcorn, Jr.), Virgil Alfred, Jr., Sally Darden (Mrs. Sweeney J. Doehring, Jr.). Chainman civil engring. dept. Mo. Pacific R.R., Palestine, Tex., 1926-27, rodman, 1927-29; with Humble Oil & Refining Co., Houston, 1929-68, office sr. supervising engr. Hqrs. Civil Engring. Dept., Houston, 1948-56, regional engr. Southwest Region, 1964-65, sr. tech. adv., Chief Prodn. Engr.'s staff, 1965-68, ret., 1968; now owner Walston Engring. & Realty Co.; engring. cons. Alyeska Pipeline Service Co., Houston, 1969—. Mem. Am. Petroleum Inst., Am. Congress on Surveying and Mapping, Am. Soc. Civil Engrs., Nat., Tex. socs. profl. engrs, Tex. Surveyors Assn., Tex. State Bd. Registration for Public Surveyors (past mem., chmn. bd. 1967-68), Nat., Houston bds. realtors. Baptist. Mason. Home: 3609 Overbrook Lane Houston TX 77027 Office: 3272 Westheimer Rd Houston TX 77006

WALSWORTH, MARGARET WINCHELL (MRS. CHARLIE F. WALSWORTH), librarian; b. Roanoke, La., Oct. 7, 1908; s. Clifton and Nellie (Berry) Winchell; student Ind. Central Coll., 1926-27, 28-29; B.A., U. Ill., 1930, B.S. in L.S., 1931; m. Charlie F. Walsworth, Jan. 27, 1940 (dec. Nov. 1956). With Bobbs-Merrill Pub. Co., Indpls., 1932-35; librarian extension div. Indpls. Pub. Library 1935-38; asst. librarian Tri-Parish Library, Winnfield, La., 1938-40; librarian Catahoula Parish Library, Harrisonburg, La., 1952-55, Natchitoches (La.) Parish Library, 1955-56, Vermillion Parish Library, Abbeville, La., 1956—. Mem. A.L.A., La. Library Assn., Delta Kappa Gamma. Republican. Presbyn. Home: 507 Guegnon St Abbeville LA 70510 Office: 200 North St Abbeville LA 70510

WALTER, EDWIN D., retail exec.; b. Winnsboro, La., May 1, 1918; s. Edward Dixon and Hattie Louise (Fay) W.; student La. Tech. Coll., 1935-36; Tulane U., 1936-37; m. Yvonne Godfrey, Feb. 20, 1944; children—Gay (Mrs. James E. Swindell), Ellen Dee. Owner, mgr. Walter's Dept. Store, Winnsboro, 1969—; dir. Franklin State Bank & Trust Co., Winnsboro, Southwestern Wholesale Co., Shreveport, La. Served to 1st lt. AUS, World War II; PTO. Mem. Winnsboro Franklin C. of C. (pres. 1965-66). Methodist (chmn. ofcl. bd. 1953-58). Club: Twin Oaks Country (Winnsboro). Home: 409 Prairie St Winnsboro LA 71295 Office: 705 Prairie St Winnsboro LA 71295

WALTERS, CALVIN OTIS, JR., diversified co. exec.; b. Savannah, Ga., Jan. 31, 1936; s. Calvin Otis and Mary (Zellner) W.; B.S., Emory U., 1957; m. Jo-Helen Holman, Apr. 11, 1959; children—Helen, Calvin Otis III, Catherine. Chemist, Savannah Foods & Industries, 1957-60, tech. supt., 1960-63, asst. refinery mgr. Everglades br., 1964-66; with Southdown, Inc., Houston, 1966—, pres., chief operating officer Southdown Lands, Inc., 1970—, corp. v.p., 1971—. Instr. Armstrong U., Savannah, 1960-63. Mem. Sugar Industry Technologists (bd. dirs. 1966-70), Am. Sugar Cane League, Am. Soc. Sugar Cane Technologists, Internat. Soc. Sugar Cane Technologists, Sugar Assn., Inc. (v.p., bd. dir. 1970). Methodist. Lion, Rotarian. Contbr. profl. jours. Home: 11910 Broken Bough St Houston TX 77024 Office: 950 Tenneco Bldg Southdown Inc Houston TX 77002

WALTERS, CHARLES RUFUS, textile co. exec.; b. Newton, N.C., Apr. 29, 1907; s. Martin E. and Laura (Scroggs) W.; A.B., Erskine Coll., 1927, LL.D., 1972; LL.B., Fordham U., 1935; J.S.D., N.Y.U., 1938; m. Ruth K. Moore, 1967; children—Anne I. (Mrs. Frederick Richards II), Margaret M., Charles R. With Chase Manhattan Bank, N.Y.C., 1929-46; v.p. Abney Mills, Greenwood, S.C., 1947-60; dir. Internat. Div., London, Eng., Burlington Industries, Inc., Greensboro, N.C., 1961-63; pres. Kenneth Mills, Walhalla, S.C., 1964, 67; gen. mgr. Cone Mills Corp., Walhalla, 1967-71; chmn. bd. dirs. Hartness Bottling Works, Spartanburg, S.C., 1964-71, Pepsi Cola Bottling Co., Burlington, N.C., 1968-71, Pepsi-Cola Bottling Co., Durham, N.C., 1969-71, Pepsi Cola Bottling Co., Forest City, N.C., 1970-71; pvt. practice law, Abbeville, S.C., 1971—. Pres. Greenwood Community Chest, 1954-55. Pres. Greenwood YMCA, 1958; trustee, bd. counsellors Erskine Coll., Due West, S.C. Served to lt. col. USAAF, 1942-46. Home: Clemson House Clemson SC 29631 Office: PO Box 926 Abbeville SC 29620

WALTERS, ELEANOR BOYD, mathematician, educator; b. Gunnison, Miss., Mar. 28, 1914; d. Jerry Edward and Loudie (Boyd) Walters; B.S. in Edn., Delta State Coll., 1934; M.A., Duke, 1939; Ed.D., Tchrs.; Coll., Columbia, 1956. Tchr. math. Shelby Consol. Sch., Shelby, Miss., 1934-38, Hernando (Miss.) High Sch., 1939-41, Pensacola (Fla.) High Sch., 1941-43; grad. asst. in math. Duke, 1938-39; asso. prof. math. Delta State Coll., Cleveland, Miss., 1943-55, prof., 1955—, acting head dept. math., 1948-55; head dept. 1955—. Mem. adv. com. on secondary math., adv. com. on arithmetic Miss. Dept. Edn., 1960—; math. cons. various Miss. schs., 1961—. Fellow A.A.A.S.; mem. Am. Math. Soc., Math. Assn. Am., Nat. Council Tchrs. Math. (Miss. rep.), Miss. Acad. Scis., Am. Assn. U. Women (v.p. Miss. div. 1959-61, nat. conv. com., 1963, implementation com. 1963-64, br. v.p. 1958-64, sec. S.E. Central region 1963-64, v.p. 1967-71, chmn. nat. conv. com. 1965), Delta Kappa Gamma, Kappa Delta Pi, Pi Gamma Mu. Democrat. Methodist. Home: 1804 Delta State Coll Cleveland MS 38732

WALTERS, FREDERICK J(AMES), mgmt. cons.; b. N.Y.C., Feb. 18, 1906; s. Frederick J. and Laura Patricia (O'Connor) W.; A.B., Princeton, 1927; m. Virginia Cross, Jan. 18, 1934; children—Rosa Lee (Sister Marie Virginia O.P.), Virginia (Mrs. R. M. Stormont), Frederick James (dec.), James Anthony. With Gen. Motors Corp.,1927-45; mem. exec. staff Gen. Electric Co., 1945-46; v.p. Hotpoint, Inc., 1946-52, Packard Motor Car Co., 1952-53; pres. Fred Walters Oldsmobile, Atlanta, 1953-62; asso. in charge Boyden Assos., Inc., 1962-69, v.p., 1969—. Guest lectr. Ga. Inst. Tech., U. Ga., Ga. State U. Mem. Small Bus. Adminstrn. Adv. Council for State of Ga. Roman Catholic. Clubs: Union League (N.Y.C.); Capital City, Princeton. Author: Handbook for District Representatives, 1939; A Summary of Veterans' Reemployment Rights, 1944. Home: 4418 Davidson Av NE Atlanta GA 30319 Office: 1738 Lenox Towers Atlanta GA 30326

WALTERS, GEORGE MERLE, aluminum co. exec.; b. Akron, O., Jan. 29, 1919; s. George Dewey and Ruth (Mitchell) W.; B.B.A, Western Res. U.; m. Helen J. Cerny, May 6, 1943; children—Robert E., Lucille G., Donald M. With Ernst & Ernst, Cleve., 1945-65, partner, 1960-65; controller Reynolds Metals Co., Richmond, Va., 1965-71, v.p. finance, 1971—. Served with USAAF, 1942-45. C.P.A., Ohio, Va. Mem. Am. Inst. C.P.A.'s, N.Y., Ohio, Va. socs. C.P.A.'s. Presbyn. Clubs: Country of Va. (Richmond); University (N.Y.C.); Deep Run Hunt (Manakin, Va.); Rappahannock Yacht (Irvington, Va.); Internat. (Washington). Home: 8908 Norwick Rd Richmond VA 23229 Office: Reynolds Metals Co 6601 W Broad St Richmond VA 23218

WALTERS, HERBERT SANFORD, banker, Dem. nat. committeeman; b. Leadville, Tenn., Nov. 17, 1891; s. John Milo and Lula (Franklin) W.; student Carson Newman Coll., Jefferson City, Tenn., 1907-08, Castle Heights, 1909-10, U. Tenn., 1917; m. Sarah Buckman Lockridge, July 23, 1928. Engring. dept. C.M. & St. P. Ry., Milw., 1911-14, Ill. Central R.R., Chgo., 1914-16; partner, Harrison, Walters & Prater, Morristown, Tenn., 1926, pres. Walters & Prater, Inc., gen. contractors, 1922—, Hamilton Nat. Bank, Morristown, 1946—, dir., 1933—, chmn. bd., 1936-45; commr. State Dept. Hwys., and Pub. Works, Nashville, 1934-35; v.p., Concrete Materials, Inc., 1947—; dir. Tenn. Natural Gas Lines, Inc., Hamilton Nat. Bank, Knoxville, Hamilton Nat. Assos. Mem. Democratic Nat. Com., from Tenn., 1945-47, 56—; mem. Tenn. Dem. Exec. Com., 1934-47, chmn., 1940-44, 53—; mem. U.S. Senate, 1964. Chmn. Morristown Water & Electric Light Commrs., 1944-47; trustee King Coll., Bristol, Tenn., treas. King Coll. endowment funds; trustee U. Tenn., Knoxville, 1962—, mem. devel. cpuncil, 1955—. Mem. Morristown C. of C. (pres. 1945). Presbyn. Mason, Elk, Kiwanian. Home: 620 W 2d North St Morristown TN 37814 Office: Hamilton Nat Bank Bldg Morristown TN 37814

WALTERS, HOYLE SAGER, wholesale co. exec.; b. Danville, Va., May 9, 1924; s. Archie Hoyle and Mabel Cathryn (Lindsay) W.; B.S., Va. Commonwealth U., 1950; m. Ruby G. Merriman, Nov. 20, 1948; children—Wendra Leigh, Joanne. Salesman, Welmont Electric Corp., 1949-52; advt. mgr. Goldberg Co., Inc., Richmond, Va., 1952-54, territory mgr., 1952-63, sales mgr., 1963-64, v.p. sales, 1964—; v.p. 7200 Corp., 1963—. Served with AUS, 1943-46; ETO. Lutheran (v.p. council 1964-65). Home: 4301 Shirley Rd Richmond VA 23225 Office: 1905 Westmoreland St Richmond VA 23230

WALTERS, JOHN SHERWOOD, newspaperman; b. Junction City, Ark., May 15, 1917; s. John Thomas and Cora (McBride) W.; B.A., La. Tech. Inst., 1939; M.A., La. State U., 1941; m. Claire Dailey, June 1, 1941; children—Elizabeth Claire, Mary Dailey (dec.). Editor Ruston (La.) Daily Leader, 1940; reporter Baton Rouge Morning Advocate, 1941; rating examiner Jacksonville Naval Air Sta., 1941-42; reporter Fla. Times-Union, Jacksonville, 1943, 44-53, city editor, 1953-60, exec. editor Times-Union Jacksonville Jour., 1960—; asst. prof. journalism La. Tech. Inst., 1943-44. Chmn. Duval County chpt. A.R.C. Mem. Am. Soc. Newspaper Editors, Fla. Soc. Newspaper Editors (pres. 1971-72), Alpha Lambda Tau, Sigma Delta Chi. Democrat. Methodist. Rotarian (pres. 1971-72). Clubs: Timuquana Country, River, University. Home: 1750 Dogwood Pl Jacksonville FL 32210 Office: Jacksonville Times Union Jour 1 Riverside Dr Jacksonville FL 32201

WALTERS, JOHNNIE MCKELVER, govt. ofcl.; b. nr. Hartsville, S.C., Dec. 20, 1919; s. Tommie Ellis and Lizzie Lee (Grantham) W.; A.B., Furman U., 1942; LL.B., U. Mich., 1948; m. Donna Lucile Hall, Sept. 1, 1947; children—Donna Dianne, Lizbeth Kathern, Hilton Horace, John Roy. Admitted to Mich. bar, 1948, N.Y. bar, 1955, S.C. bar, 1961; atty. office of chief counsel Internal Revenue Service, Washington, 1949-53; atty., asst. mgr. tax div. of law dept., Texaco, Inc., N.Y.C., 1953-61; partner firm Geer, Walters & Demo, Greenville, S.C., 1961-69; asst. atty. gen. tax div. Dept. of Justice, Washington, 1969-71; commr. Internal Revenue, Washington, 1971—. Bd. dirs. Greenville United Fund. Served with USAAF, 1942-45. Decorated Air medal with oak leaf clusters, Purple Heart medal, D.F.C. Mem. Am. (taxation sect.), S.C., Greenville (S.C.) County bar assns., Greater Greenville C. of C. (dir.), Greenville Little Theater (dir.), Greenville Symphony Assn. (dir.). Rotarian (pres. 1968-69). Home: 1327 Oberon Way McLean VA 22101 Office: IRS 1111 Constitution Av Washington DC 20224

WALTERS, LAMAR L., assn. exec. Exec. v.p. La. State C. of C. Address: Capitol House Hotel Baton Rouge LA 70821*

WALTERS, MELVIN REYNOLDS, wholesale trade exec.; b. Hays, Kan., Dec. 27, 1937; s. Leo and Ida (Polifka) W.; A.B., Fort Hays State Coll., 1959; M.S., Kan. State U., 1960; J.D., U. Tulsa, 1967; m. Ellen Schmidt, Aug. 10, 1960; children—Cheryl Ann, David John. Staff accountant Continental Oil Co., Ponca City, Okla., 1961-63; sr. accountant Service Pipe Line Co., Tulsa, 1963-69; sec. treas. Union Petroleum Corp., Tulsa, 1969—. Served with AUS, 1960-61. C.P.A., Okla. Mem. Okla., Tulsa County bar assns., Okla. Soc. C.P.A.'s, Tulsa Jr. C. of C., Delta Theta Phi. Home: Office: PO Box 1649 Tulsa OK 74101

WALTERS, SCOTT, JR., lawyer; b. Atlanta, Sept. 17, 1924; s. Scott and Mae Belle (Hogan) W.; student Ga. Tech., 1941, Ga. State U., 1946-47, 50-51; J.D., Mercer U., 1950; m. Edith L. Stamps, Aug. 10, 1946; children—Scott Andrew, Linda Catherine. Admitted to Ga. bar, 1950; practiced in East Point, Ga., 1950—; mem. firm Scott Walters, 1950-51, 57—, Walters & Roberts, 1951-57; mem. adv. bd. Comml. Bank, 1948-50; justice of peace, East Point, 1953-64. Mem. Gov.'s Staff, 1963-64. Mem. Fulton County Republican Exec. Com., 1964-72, vice chmn., 1970-72, gen. counsel, 1966-67; chmn. East Point Rep. Exec. Com., 1968-71, gen. counsel, 1968-72. Served with USAAF, 1942-45. Mem. Am., Ga., Atlanta (chmn. family law sect. 1967-68) bar assns., Atlanta Legal Aid Soc., Lawyers Reference Panel, Am. Judicature Soc., Am. Trial Lawyers Assn., Am. Legion, V.F.W., Mercer, Ga. State U., Ga. Inst. Tech. alumni assns., Phi Alpha. Baptist. Lion. Home: 2984 Arrowood Dr East Point GA 30344 Office: 1442 Cleveland Av East Point GA 30344

WALTNER, ARTHUR WALTER, educator; b. Moundridge, Kan., Nov. 28, 1914; s. Peter A. and Lydia (Wedel) W.; A.B., Bethel Coll., 1938; M.S., Kan. State U., 1942; Ph.D., U. N.C., 1949; m. Nellie Louise Laird, Apr. 10, 1941; children—Ann Beth, Linda Ruth. Asst. prof. N.C. State U., Raleigh, 1948-53, asso. prof., 1953-56, prof. physics, 1956—; cons. govt., indsl. labs.; exchange scientist A.B. Atomenergie, Stockholm, Sweden, 1952-53; participant Internat. Atomic Energy Agy., Vienna Symposium Pulsed Neutron Research, Karlsruhe, Germany, 1965. Fellow Am. Phys. Soc.; mem. A.A.A.S., Am. Nuclear Soc. Contbr. articles to profl. jours. Home: 1204 Westmoreland Dr Raleigh NC 27609

WALTON, AUBREY GREY, bishop; b. Clarksdale, Miss., June 20, 1901; s. Charles Barron and Carrie Mae (Eddins) W.; B.A., Hendrix Coll., 1928, D.D., 1946; B.D., Duke, 1931, D.D., 1962; LL.D., Centenary Coll., 1963; LL.D., So. Meth. U., 1966; m. Mildred Henry, Sept. 17, 1930; children—Mildred (Mrs. Robert Ziegler), James Macon. Ordained to ministry Meth. Ch., 1931; pastor in Ark., 1931-44, in First Ch., Little Rock, 1944-60; consecrated bishop, 1960; bishop of La. area, New Orleans, 1960—. Mem. World Meth. Council, 1951-61; del. ecumenical confs., Springfield, Mass., 1947, Oxford, 1951, Lake Junaluska, 1956, London, 1966; del. gen. confs., 1952, 56; del. S. Central jurisdictional confs., 1948, 52, 56, 60, chmn. jurisdictional council, 1956-60; mem. gen. bd. missions Meth. Ch., 1952-56, 60—; pres. Television, Radio and Film Commn., Meth. Ch., 1964—; ofcl. visitor in S. and Central Am., 1960—. Trustee Hendrix Coll., 1944-60, So. Meth. U., 1960—. St. Paul Sch. Theology, Kansas City, Mo., 1961—, Centenary Coll., Shreveport, 1960—, Dillard U., 1960—, Meth.-Home Hosp., New Orleans, 1960—. Home: 4002 St Charles Av New Orleans LA 70115 Office: American Nat Bank Bldg New Orleans LA 70130

WALTON, CLARENCE, univ. pres.; b. Scranton, Pa., June 22, 1915; s. Leo and Mary (Southard) W.; B.A., U. Scranton, 1937; M.A., Syracuse U., 1938; Ph.D., Cath. U., 1951; m. Elizabeth Kennedy, June 1, 1946; children—Thomas Michael, Mary Elizabeth. Social sci. instr. Duquesne U., 1940, dean sch. bus. adminstrn.,1954-58; asso. dean, prof. Columbia U. Grad. Sch. Bus., 1958-64, dean Sch. Gen. Studies, 1964-68; pres. Cath. U. Am., 1968—; prof., chmn. dept. history and polit. sci. U. Scranton, 1946-53; Penfield fellow Inst. Advanced Internat. Studies, Geneva, Switzerland, 1951-52; vis. prof. U. Buenos Aires, summer 1961, U. Cal. at Berkeley, 1963-64, Ore. State U., summer 1969. Dir. Lincoln Life Ins. of N.Y., 1964-68. Mem. sch. bd., Scranton 1948-52; chmn. Pres.'s panel on non-pub. edn., 1969-72; mem. Nat. Commn. on Sch. Finance, 1969-72. Served as lt. (s.g.) USNR, 1940-46; with Naval Intelligence, communications officer U.S.S. Wisconsin. Mem. Am. Econ. Assn., Am. Cath. Hist. Assn., Acad. Polit. Sci., A.I.M. Author: Big Government and Big Business, 1968; Corporate Social Responsibilities, 1967; Ethos and The

Executive, 1969; Business and Social Progress, 1971. Contbr. profl. jours. Home: care Cath U Am Washington DC 20017

WALTON, CONRAD GORDON, architect; b. Houston, June 18, 1928; s. John Edward and Evelyn Lucille (Gordon) W.; B.S. (Walsh scholar), Rice U., 1951; postgrad. U. Houston, 1955; m. Rilda Ellen Akin, Dec. 10, 1954; children—Conrad Gordon, Evelyn Coleman, Roberta Agnes. Asso. mem. firm. Hamilton Brown & Assos., Houston, 1960-61; chief supt. Welton Becket & Assos., Houston, 1961-63; partner Alexander, Walton & Hatteberg, Houston, 1963-68; owner Conrad G. Walton, Houston, 1968—. Co-owner subdiv. Holiday Oaks, Lake Somerville, Tex., 1964—; registered fallout shelter analyst Def. Dept., 1966—. Pres. Woodrow Wilson Elementary P.T.O., Houston, 1969-70; chmn. Troop 345, Roberts Sch., Boy Scouts Am., 1960-71. Republican precinct chmn., 1964-71. Served with AUS, 1952-54; Korea. Mem. A.I.A. (treas. 1968), Tex. Soc. Architects, Constrn. Specifications Inst., Houston C. of C. (civic affairs com.). Methodist. Optimist. Architect U. Houston Arch. Bldg. addition, 1969. Home: 9014 Springview Houston TX 77055 Office: 3203 Mercer St Houston TX 77027

WALTON, DEWITT TALMAGE, JR., dentist; b. Macon, Ga., May 25, 1937; s. DeWitt Talmage and Jimmie A. (Braswell) W.; B.S., Howard U., 1960, D.D.S., 1961; m. Joan Granville Robinson, June 11, 1960; children—Jimmie Alisa, Gwen Noel, Gayle Nicole. Practice dentistry, Macon, 1963—. Mem. Bibb County Bd. Edn., Macon, 1969—; mem. Mayor's Com. on Manpower Devel., 1969—. Bd. dirs. Ga. Council on Human Relations, United Cerebral Palsy Center Macon. Served with Dental Corps, AUS, 1961-63. Named Citizen of Year, Omega Psi Phi, 1971. Mem. Am., Ga., Central Dist., Nat. dental assns., Macon Acad. Medicine and Dentistry, Fedn. Dentaire Internat;, Am. Soc. Dentistry for Children, Nat. Rehab. Assn., A.A.A.S., N.A.A.C.P., C. of C. Presbyn. Mason. Home: 2988 Malibu Dr Macon GA 31201 Office: 591 Cotton Av Macon GA 31201

WALTON, G(EORGE) STOKES, lawyer; b. Helena, Ga., Jan. 3, 1906; s. Merrel Callaway and Lucy (Smith) W.; A.B., Mercer U., 1927, J.D., 1929; m. Dorothy Corinne DuPree, Aug. 27, 1930; children—Dorothy (Mrs. Carroll D. Smith III), Marian A. (Mrs. Douglas M. Duggan). Admitted to Ga. bar, 1929, practiced Macon, 1929-33; atty. legal dept. Fed. Land Bank (Farm Credit Adminstrn.) of Columbia, S.C., 1933-43; gen. practice law, La Grange, Ga., 1943-54; mem. Allen & Walton, 1945-47; city atty., La Grange, 1949-54; mem. Matthews, Walton, Smith, Shaw & Maddox, Rome, Ga., 1954—. Trustee Shorter Coll., 1954-58; bd. dirs. LaGrange Community Chest, 1950-54. Fellow Am. Coll. Probate Counsel; mem. Am. Judicature Soc., Am., Ga., Rome (pres. 1961) bar assns., C. of C., S.A.R., Delta Theta Phi, Delta Sigma Pi.Democrat. Baptist. Mason. Clubs: Coosa Country, Kiwanis (pres. 1959), Prince. Asst. in compilation Code of Ga. of 1933. Home: 28 Crestwood Dr Rome GA 30161 Office: First Nat Bank Bldg Rome GA 30161

WALTON, JAMES RICHARD, textile co. exec.; b. Lafayette, Ala., Dec. 13, 1931; s. William Ora and Lynda (Tatum) W.; B.S., Vanderbilt U., 1955; LL.B., Harvard, 1958; m. Phyllis Anne Phair, July 2, 1960; children—Katherine Elizabeth, Allison Anne, James Richard. Admitted to Ala. bar, 1958, Tex. bar, 1959; practiced in Houston, 1958-62; legal counsel, asst. sec. West Point Mfg. Co. (Ga.), 1962-65; legal counsel, asst. sec., dir. indsl. and community relations West Point Mfg. Co. div. West Point-Pepperell, Inc., 1965-66, v.p. personnel services, 1966-71, v.p. personnel and pub. affairs, 1971—. Bd. dirs. George H. Lanier Meml. Hosp., Jr. Achievement of Chattahoochee-Lee, Ala. Safety Council, So. Indsl. Relations Council. Served with USAF, 1951-54. Mem. Am., Ala., Tex. bar assns., Ala. C. of C. (dir.). Methodist. Rotarian. Home: 1705 Rosemont St West Point GA 31833 Office: PO Box 366 West Point GA 31833

WALTON, JOHN B., JR., broadcasting exec. Pres. KBUY, Fort Worth. Office: Seminary S Shopping Center PO Box 2049 Fort Worth TX 76101*

WALTON, MRS. LADY BOGGS, librarian; b. nr. Scottsville, Va., Dec. 5, 1909; d. Walter Francis and Melissa (Frame) Boggs; B.S., Longwood Coll., Farmville, Va., 1935; postgrad. William and Mary, 1939, U. Va., 1953; m. Leslie H. Walton, Aug. 17, 1940. Tchr. Mt. Tabor Sch., Buckingham County, Va., 1927-28, 29-32, Oak Grove Sch., Gilmer County, W.Va., 1928-29, Warren Sch., Albemarle County, Va., 1932-33, Greenwood High Sch., Albemarle County, 1933-35, 51-53, Scottsville High Sch., 1935-47; librarian at Albemarle High Sch., Charlottesville, Va., 1953-63, Greenbrier Sch., Charlottesville, 1963—. Recipient Rotary Fgn. Travel fellowship for tchrs., 1968. Mem. Am. (mem. recruitment com.), Va. (past chmn. recruitment com., sch. corr. Va. Librarian, 2d v.p., 1st v.p., pres.-elect 1965, pres. 1966) library assns., Nat., Va. edn. assns., Nat. Council English, Math. and Social Studies, Pi Gamma Mu, Kappa Delta Pi, Delta Kappa Gamma (chpt. v.p.). Baptist. Home: RFD 1 Crozet VA 22932 Office: Greenbrier Dr Charlottesville VA 22901

WALTON, LEON JERL, dentist; b. Walton's Store, Va., Feb. 15, 1893; s. Joel William and Emma Eva (Johnson) W.; sUdent William and Mary Acad., 1910-11, William and Mary Coll., 1911-13; D.D.S., Med. Coll. Va., 1919; m. Flora Mildred Rasmussen, July 24, 1921; 1 dau., Nancy (Mrs. George C. Herring, Jr.). Mem. faculty Sch. Dentistry, Med. Coll. Va., 1919-20. Served with U.S. Army, 1916-18. Fellow Am. Coll. Dentists; mem. Am., Va. (pres. 1950). Piedmont County (pres. 1924) dental assns., Xi Psi Phi, Sigma Phi Epsilon, Omicron Kappa Upsilon. Clubs: Roanoke Round Table, Roanoke Country. Home: 2903 Rosalind Av SW Roanoke VA 24014 Office: 713 Shenandoah Bldg Roanoke VA 24011

WALTON, PAUL N., lumber and wood products co. exec.; b. Dallas, Aug. 10, 1930; s. Paul N. and Anna (Miller) W.; student A. and M. Bus. Sch., 1947-51, So. Meth. U. Law Sch., 1952-53; m. Beverly C. Piper, Feb. 14, 1952; children—Roseann, Scott. Sales mgr. The Sam A Wing Co. Inc., Dallas, 1952-56; div. mgr. Keller Industries Inc., Miami, Fla., 1956-61; exec. v.p. Wing Industries Inc., 1961-69, pres., 1969—, also dir.; officer, dir. Gen. Forest Products, Inc., Nat. Pacific Inc., Metro Bus. Systems Inc., Metro Bus. Leasing Inc. Home: 7235 Tophill Lane Dallas TX 75240 Office: 2929 N Kinsley St Garland TX 75040

WALTON, WILLIAM B(OWEN), lawyer, motel exec.; b. Pine Bluff, Ark., Jan 24, 1920; s. William Bowen and Katherine (Walters) W.; LL.B., Memphis State U., 1942; m. Geneva Louise Chase, Oct. 21, 1944; children—William B., Richard Russell, Katherine Louise, Geneva Chase. Admitted to Tenn. bar, 1942; practiced in Memphis, 1946-55; exec. v.p. Holiday Inns, Inc., Memphis, 1955-69, pres., 1969—, also dir., mem. exec. com. Mem. Exec. Com. Mayor's Prayer Breakfast. Bd. dirs. Shelby United Neighbors; trustee Hutchison Sch., Memphis State U. Found.; trustee, Memphis chmn. Freedoms Found. at Valley Forge. Served with USAF, 1943-46. Kiwanian. Home: 2710 Forest Hill Rd Germantown TN 38038 Office: 3742 Lamar Av Memphis TN 38118

WALZ, ROBERT BRADSHAW, educator; b. Ashdown, Ark., Sept. 27, 1918; s. Joe and Lolla (Bradshaw) W.; A.A., So. State Coll., 1939; student La. State U., fall 1941; B.A., Henderson State Coll., 1941; M.A., U. Tex., 1952, Ph.D., 1958; m. Curtistine Alice Parsons, Apr. 28, 1951. Grad. asst. La. State U., Baton Rouge, 1941-42; jr. supr. Lone Star Ordnance Corp., Texarkana, Tex., 1942-43; tng. officer VA, Little Rock, Ark., 1946; instr., acting dept; head Texarkana (Tex.) Coll., 1947-51; teaching fellow U. Tex., Austin, 1951-55; instr., asst. prof. history East Tex. State Coll., Commerce, 1955-58; prof. history So. State Coll., Magnolia, Ark., 1958—. Served with USAAF, 1943-45. Mem. Orgn. Am. Historians, So., Ark. (mem. ofcl. bd. 1963—, pres. 1968-70) hist. assns., Kappa Delta Phi, Phi Alpha Theta. Democrat. Methodist. Contbr. articles in field to profl. jours. Home: 1502 N Jackson St Magnolia AR 71753

WAMMOCK, HOKE, surgeon; b. Soperton, Ga., Jan. 7, 1906; s. Benjamin L. and Ida (Bell) W; student U. Ga., 1922-24; M.D., Med. Coll. Ga., 1928; postgrad. U. Pa., 1944-45; m. Virgene Marie Scherer, Sept. 16, 1936; children—Richard Hoke, Lydia Marie (Mrs. William Lee Thompson). Intern, St. Luke's Hosp., Jacksonville, Fla., 1928-29; resident Jeanes Hosp., Phila., 1929-32, asst. surgeon, 1932-42, chief of staff, 1942-45; asst. instr. U. Pa., 1946-48; prof., chmn. dept. oncology and surgery Med. Coll. Ga., Augusta, 1948-62; dir. Enoch Callaway Cancer Clinic, LaGrange, Ga., 1962—. Liaison fellow Oak Ridge Inst. Nuclear Studies, Med. Coll. Ga., 1950-56; cons. Milledgeville (Ga.) State Hosp., 1950-62, VA Hosp., Augusta, 1949-62, Ft. Gordon (Ga.) Army Hosp., 1951-62. Pres., Augusta Community Concert Assn., 1960-62, LaGrange Mut. Concert Assn., 1963-64, 64-65. Diplomate Am. Bd. Surgery. Fellow A.C.S. (liaison fellow Ga. chpt. 1962-63); mem. Am. Cancer Soc. (dir. Ga. div.), Med. Assn. Ga. (subcom. cancer 1961—), Southeastern, Ga. (past pres.), Hawthorne (past pres.) surg. socs., Am. Radium Soc., Soc. Head and Neck Surgeons, A.M.A., Am. Assn. for Cancer Research, Am. Assn. for Cancer Edn. (charter), Sigma Xi, Alpha Omega Alpha. Rotarian. Contbr. to med. jours. Home: 771 Lakewood Dr LaGrange GA 30240 Office: Enoch Callaway Cancer Clinic Vernon Rd LaGrange GA 30240

WAMPLER, WILLIAM CREED, congressman; b. Pennington Gap, Va., Apr. 21, 1926; s. John Sevier and Lillian (Wolfe) W.; B.S., Va. Poly. Inst.; postgrad. U. Va. Law Sch.; m. Mary Elizabeth Baker, Aug. 29, 1953; children—Barbara Irene, William Creed. Owner, operator furniture and carpet bus., Bristol, Va.; mem. Congress from 9th Va. Dist., 1953-54, mem. 90th-92d Congresses. Formerly spl. asst. to gen. mgr. AEC. Pres., Young Republican Fedn. Va.; chmn. 9th Dist. Rep. Com., 1965. Bd. visitors Emory and Henry Coll. Served with USNR, 1943-46. Mem. Am. Legion, 40 and 8, Sigma Nu Phi. Home: 812 Long Crescent Dr Bristol VA 24201 Office: 323 Cannon House Office Bldg Washington DC 20515

WAMPLER, WILLIAM DAVID, food co. exec.; b. Hinton, Va., Apr. 9, 1928; s. Charles Weldon and Zola Estelle (Huffman) W.; student Bridgewater Coll., 1946-48; B.S., Va. Poly. Inst., 1950; m. Bonnie Lou May, Sept. 22, 1951; children—Melinda May, William David, Charles Weldon II, Suzanne. Partner in charge Sunny Slope Hatchery, Harrisonburg, Va., 1950-69, Charles W. Wampler & Sons, Harrisonburg, 1950-72; sec., treas. Massanutten Hatchery, Inc., Harrisonburg, 1955-69; partner in charge Farley-Wampler Bros., Harrisonburg, 1964-69; partner Wampler-Bryan Co., Harrisonburg, 1954-69; v.p. head hatchery div. Wampler Foods, Inc., Hinton, 1969—; pres. Rockingham County Sheep and Wool Producers Assn., 1964-67; dir. Staunton Prodn. Credit Assn., Staunton Fed. Land Bank assn. Mem. poultry adv. com. U.S. Sec. Agr., 1961; mem. exec. com. Va. Future Farmers Am., 1949-50; pres. Va. 4-H, 1948-49. Pres. P.T.A., 1962-63. Recipient Distinguished Service award Va. Poultry Fedn., 1962. Mem. Va. Turkey Assn. (pres. 1961-62), Va. Poultry Fedn. (pres. 1965), Nat. Turkey Fedn. (pres. 1966), Va. Angus Assn. (dir. 1965), Va. Charolais Assn. (dir. 1969-72), Southeastern Poultry and Egg Assn. (state v.p. 1967), C. of C. (dir. 1966—), Farm Bur. Assn., Tau Kappa Alpha, Alpha Zeta, Omicron Delta Kappa. Mem. Ch. Brethren (mem. ch. bd. 1967). Democrat. Elk. Club: Block and Bridle (Blacksburg, Va.); Dayton Ruritan (pres. 1955). Home: Route 6 Box 114 Harrisonburg VA 22801 Office: Wampler Foods Inc PO Box 31 Harrisonburg VA 22801

WANG, KUNG-LEE, economist, operations analyst, govt. ofcl.; b. Pei-Tai-Ho, Hopei, China, Aug. 12, 1925; s. Cheng-Fu and Funghin (Liu) W.; B.A., Yenching U., 1947; M.A., Brown U., 1950; M.B.A., Columbia, 1958; M.P.A., Harvard 1965; m. Christine Wen, Aug. 15, 1959 (div.); 1 son, Christopher Ching-Yu. Came to U.S., 1947, naturalized, 1954. Accountant in charge fiscal mgmt. Bushwick Hosp., Bklyn., 1952-55; economist, civilian and mil. operations analyst, internat. affairs C-E-I-R, Inc., Washington, 1955-60, cons., 1960-61; chief quantitative econ. group, research coordinator quantitative econs. div. econ. analysis Bur. Mines, U.S. Dept. Interior, Washington, 1961—. Cons. Asian econ. affairs Research Analysis Corp., McLean, Va., 1961-68; dir. Internat. Data Applications, Inc., 1969-71; econ. operations adviser to ministry econ. affairs, Republic of China, 1969-71; cons. operation research office Johns Hopkins, Bethesda, Md., 1960-61; ethnic adviser U.S. Office Equal Opportunity, 1972—. Pres., chmn. bd. dirs. Civic League of Brookmont, 1963-64; coordinator Chinese-American Leadership Council, 1971—. Pres. Rho Psi Found., Inc., 1966—. Nat. Inst. Pub. Affairs fellow, 1965. Mem. Am. Inst. Mining, Metall. and Petroleum Engrs., Am. Soc. Pub. Adminstrn., Regional Sci. Assn., Am. Econ. Assn., Assn. Asian Studies, Assn. Study Soviet-Type Economics, A.A.A.S., Inst. Mgmt. Scis., Rho Psi. Chinese Christian Ch. Contbr. articles to profl. publs. Home: 1940 Dundee Rd Rockville MD 20850 Office: Div Econ Analysis U S Bur Mines Washington DC 20240

WANN, MARIE LOUISE DIMARIO (MRS. HARRY ARTHUR WANN), govt. ofcl.; b. N.Y.C., Dec. 13, 1911; d. Peter and Louise (Vandenhoeck) DiMario; B.A., Hunter Coll., 1931; M.A., Columbia U., 1934, Ph.D., 1943; m. Harry Arthur Wann, Oct. 9, 1942 (dec. May 1965). Tchr. math. N.Y.C. high schs., 1932-35; statistician N.Y.C. Dept. Health, 1935-39; statistician U.S. Govt., 1939—, statistician exec. office of pres. Bur. Budget, 1967-69, chief math. statistician Division of Statis. Policy, Exec. Office Pres. 1969—; tchr. math. and statistics; lectr. N.Y.U., Seton Hall Coll., Am. U., Queens Coll., George Washington U. fellow A.A.A.S. Mem. Am. Statis. Assn., Am. Math. Soc., Author: Dependent Baggage, 1955. Contbr. articles to profl. jours. Home: 3457 S Leisure World Blvd Silver Spring MD 20906 Office: New Exec Bldg Washington DC 20503

WANNAMAKER, ALLEN EDWARD, radio sta. exec.; b. St. Matthews, S.C., Jan. 27, 1914; s. William Pou and Ida (Bradham) W.; student pub. schs., St. Matthews; m. Mildred Patterson, Nov. 11, 1939; children—Allen Edward, Robert Laurens, Mildred Morris; m. 2d, Dorothy F. Warren; stepchildren—Lew, Dorothy. With Watson Industries Wilson, N.C., 1937-52; v.p., gen. mgr. N.C. Broadcasting Co., Sta. WBIG, Greensboro, 1952-66; v.p. N.C. Broadcasting Co., Inc., Greensboro, 1955-66, pres., 1966—. Mem. adv. com. FCC, 1960—. Mem.-at-large Greensboro Community Council, 1961-63; adv. bd. Salvation Army, Greensboro, 1963-65; mem. No. Piedmont Area Devel. Assn.; sales com. Piedmont Four-H Fat Stock Show, 1962-65. Bd. dirs. N.C. Heart Assn., 1961-65, Gen. Greene council Boy Scouts Am., 1962—, Greensboro Gens. Boosters Club, 1962-63; bd. dirs., exec. bd. United Fund of Greater Greensboro, 1962—; pres. Jr. Achievement, Greensboro, 1966, bd. dirs., 1968; mem., chmn. pub. relations commn. Greensboro Citizens for Greensboro Coll. Bd. dirs. U.N.C. at Greensboro. Recipient award United Fund of Greater Greensboro, 1962. Mem. Nat. (N.C. membership liaison committeeman), N.C. (pres. 1956, v.p. 1957), assns. broadcasters Tobacco network (past pres.), Greensboro Mcht. Assn. (trade promotion com. 1961-65, dir. 1963—), Greensboro C. of C. (dir. 1964—, pres. 1968), Better Bus. Bur. (pres. 1962), Greensboro Advt. Club (past pres.), Piedmont Triangle Advt. Club com. 1962, dir. 1965—), Broadcast Pioneers. Republican. Methodist. Rotarian (mem. community service com., chmn-club service). Home: 3302 Watauga Dr Greensboro NC 27410 Office: PO Box 20204 Greensboro NC 27420

WANSLEY, HAL BRANTLEY, utility exec.; b. Carnesville, Ga., Jan. 26, 1913; s. John Wesley and Mary (McCarter) W.; B.S., U. Ga., 1934; m. Leona Ruth Simpson, Dec. 1, 1934 (dec. June 1965); children—Hal Brantley, James Wesley, John David; m. 2d, Ruth Dunaway Montgomery, July 9, 1966; children Kim (Mrs. L.W. Simmons), Karen (Mrs. W.B. Kennedy), Katie Montgomery. Plant accounting clk. Ga. Power Co., Atlanta, 1937-46, asst. plant accountant, 1946-53, asst. comptroller, 1953-58, asst. to v.p. finance, 1958-62, v.p., 1962-63, v.p., comptroller, 1963-67, financial v.p., dir., 1967—. Served to capt. USMCR, 1942-46. Mem. Edison Electric Inst., Southeastern Electric Exchange, Financial Execs. Inst. Methodist. Clubs: Lions (past pres.), Civic (past pres.), Commerce (Atlanta). Home: 628 Park Lane Decatur GA 30330 Office: 270 Peachtree St Atlanta GA 30303

WARBURTON, LAWRENCE HENRY, JR., lawyer; b. San Diego, Sept. 6, 1926; s. L. H. and Estellane (Smith) W.; student Coll. Pacific-Stockton, 1945, U. Cal. at Berkeley, 1945-46; B.B.A., U. Tex. at Austin, 1949, LL.B., 1950; m. Jeanelle Golden, Sept. 3, 1955; children—Patrick Allison, William Perry, Lane Golden. Admitted to Tex. bar, 1950; individual practice law, Freer, Tex., 1950-54; asst. atty. gen., Tex., 1954-55; asst. dist. atty. 79th Judicial Dist. Tex., 1955-60; partner firm Perkins, Davis, Oden & Warburton, Alice, Tex., 1960—. Mem. exec. bd. Gulf Coast council Boy Scouts Am., 1960—; pres., campaign chmn. United Fund, 1960-62. Served with USNR, 1944-46. Named 1 of 5 Outstanding Young Texans, Tex. Jr. C. of C., 1960; recipient Silver Beaver award Boy Scouts Am., 1968. Mem. State Bar Tex. (mem. grievance com. for dist. 14-A 1968-69, mem. com. on profl. efficiency and econ. research 1968-69, dir. 1969-72), Coastal Bend Bar Assn. (pres. 1960), Am. Bar Assn., Am. Judicature Soc., Tex. Trial Lawyers Assn., Alice C. of C. (dir., v.p. 1965-66), Alpha Phi Omega (pres. Tex. Alpha chpt. 1949), Sigma Phi Epsilon. Rotarian (pres. 1966). Methodist. Contbr. articles law jours. Home: 1120 Arcadia St Alice TX 78332 Office: Alice Nat Bank Bldg Alice TX 78332

WARBURTON, RALPH JOSEPH, architect; b. Kansas City, Mo., Sept. 5, 1935; s. Ralph Gray and Emma Frieda (Niemann) W.; B.Arch., Mass. Inst. Tech., 1958; M.Arch., Yale, 1959, M.C.P., 1960; m. Carol Ruth Hychka, June 14, 1958; children—John Geoffrey, Joy Frances. With various archtl., planning and engring. firms Kansas City, Mo., Boston, N.Y.C., Chgo., 1952-64; asso., chief of planning Skidmore, Owings & Merrill, Chgo., 1964-66; spl. asst. for urban design U.S. Dept. Housing and Urban Devel., Washington, 1966-72, cons., 1972—; adviser to Govt. Iran, 1970; prof. architecture, chmn. dept. archtl. engring. U. Miami, Coral Gables, Fla., 1972—; sr. partner Ferendino, Grafton, Spillis, Candela, Coral Gables, 1972—; lectr., critic, design juror, 1965—. Chmn. community future com. Lake Barcroft Community Assn., 1971-72; mem. Met. Housing and Planning Council of Chgo., 1965-67; mem. exec. com. Yale Arts Assn., 1965-70. Skidmore, Owings & Merrill Traveling fellow Mass. Inst. Tech., 1958; vis. fellow Inst. for Architecture and Urban Studies, N.Y.C., 1972—; recipient W. E. Parsons medal Yale, 1960. Mem. A.I.A. (housing and urban design coms.), Am. Inst. Planners, Nat. Assn. Housing and Redevel. Ofcls., Nat. Trust for Hist. Preservation (mem. principles and guidelines com. 1967), Am. Soc. Landscape Architects (hon. mem., chmn. design awards jury 1970-72), Am. Soc. Planning Ofcls., Internat. Fedn. Housing and Planning, Am. Soc. Heating, Refrigeration and Air Conditioning Engrs. (mem. urban environment task force), Am. Inst. Interior Designers (hon. mem.). Christian Scientist. Mason. Clubs: Mass. Inst. Tech., Yale, Cosmos (Washington). Asso. author: Man-Made America: Chaos or Control, 1963. Editor: New Concepts in Urban Transportation, 1968; Housing Systems Proposals for Operation Breakthrough, 1970; Focus on Furniture, 1971. Contbr. articles to profl. jours. Mem. adv. panel Industrialization Forum Quar. Home: 6910 Veronese St Coral Gables FL 33124 Office: Dept Architecture and Archtl Engring U Miami Coral Gables FL 33124

WARD, BENJAMIN PORTER, ret. naval officer, educator; b. LaFayette, Ind., July 2, 1897; s. Harry Van Devanter and Nellie Clara (Armbruster) W.; B.S., U.S. Naval Acad., 1919; M.S., Columbia U., 1927; m. Mary Ellen Estes, May 6, 1928; 1 son, Benjamin Porter. Commd. ensign USN, 1919, advanced through grades to capt., 1942, ret., 1950; asso. prof. mech. engring. Auburn U., Auburn, Ala., 1950-68, emeritus, 1968—. Decorated Victory Medal, World War I and World War II. Registered profl. engr., N.Y., Washington. Mem. Am. Soc. Naval Engrs., Am. Soc. M.E., Soc. Naval Architects and Marine Engrs., U.S. Naval Acad. Alumni Assn., Pi Tau Sigma. Mason. Clubs: N.Y. Yacht (N.Y.C.); Ponte Vedra (Fla.); Saugahatchee Country (Auburn, Ala.). Home: 815 S College St Auburn AL 36830

WARD, FRANK PELOUZE, physician; b. Lumberton, N.C., Oct. 24, 1916; s. Archibald Floyd and Elizabeth May (Davis) W.; student Wake Forest Coll., 1937-39, 39-41; M.D., Med. Coll., U. S.C., 1943; m. Mary Alice Batson, June 29, 1940; children—Frank Pelouze, Mary Alice (Mrs. Robert Farnham III), Sarah Margaret (Mrs. Heutis Pennington Whiteside, Jr.), Kathryn Gray. Intern, Henry Ford Hosp., Detroit, 1943, resident, 1944; practice medicine, specializing in internal medicine, Lumberton, N.C., 1944—; mem. staff Southeastern Gen. Hosp., chief staff, 1952-54, chief medicne, 1945-69; cons. Bladen County Hosp., Columbus County Hosp.; founding sr. partner, pres. Lumberton Med. Clinic, 1951—; pres., sr. partner Balarah Ltd., real estate investment co. for med. bldgs., 1963—; asst. medicine Duke U. Med. Center, 1953. Cons. to architect and adminstr. Southeastern Gen. Extended Care Facility and Intensive Care Unit, 1968-70. Bd. dirs. N.C. Heart Assn., 1951-53. Diplomate Am. Bd. Internal Medicine. Fellow A.C.P., Am. Coll. Chest Physicians; mem. A.M.A., N.C., Fifth Dist., Robeson County (pres. 1948) med. socs., Am. Soc. Internal Medicine, Internat. Soc. Internal Medicine, Am. Heart Assn., Am. Diabetic Assn., Lumberton C. of C. (bd. dirs. 1967-71). Democrat. Baptist (deacon 1953-72). Home: 1005 Riverside Blvd Lumberton NC 28358 Office: 395 W 27th St Lumberton NC 28358

WARD, GEORGE FRANKLYN, nursery exec.; b. Washington, Jan. 4, 1917; s. William Franklin and Annie Belle (Gardner) W.; student U. Fla., 1934-36; B.S., Auburn U., 1938; m. Mary Ellen Heitch, Oct. 19, 1940; children—Deborah (Mrs. William Hileman), Marcia L., William Robert. Airport engr. CAA, Columbus, O., 1938-43; owner, operator Peninsular Aero. Corp., Tampa, Fla., 1945-48, Ward Aero Service, Lake Wales, Fla., 1948-50; with Ward's Nursery, Inc., Avon Park, Fla., 1950—, pres., dir. Waverly Growers Coop. (Fla.), Avon Citrus Bank, 1958—; Scoutmaster, Boy Scouts Am., 1958-68; pres.

Ridge Area Assn. Retarded Children, 1957-58, Fla. Assn. Retarded Children, 1958-60, Avon Park P.T.A., 1962-63; mem. Highlands County Sch. Bd., 1968. Bd. dirs. So. Fla. Jr. Coll., Avon Park, 1965-67, Nat. Assn. Retarded Children, 1963-65. Served with AUS, 1943-45. Recipient Silver Beaver award Boy Scouts Am., 1961. Mem. Fla. Citrus Mut. (dir. 1954-56), Ridge Lime and Avocado Growers (v.p. 1955-62). Episcopalian. Rotarian. Home: Lake Lotela Avon Park FL 33825 Office: PO Box 850 Avon Park FL 33825

WARD, GEORGE TRUMAN, architect; b. Washington, July 24, 1927; s. Truman and Gladys Anna (Nutt) W.; B.S., Va. Poly. Inst., 1951, M.S., 1952; postgrad. George Washington U., 1966; m. Margaret Ann Hall, Sept. 10, 1949; children—Carol Ann, Donna Lynne, George Truman, Robert Stephen. Archtl. draftsman Charles A. Pearson, Radford, Va., 1950; head archtl. sect. Hayes, Seay, Mattern, Radford and Roanoke, 1951-52; with Joseph Saunders & Assos., Alexandria, Va., 1952-57, asso. architect, 1955-57; partner Vosbeck-Ward & Assos., Alexandria, 1957-64, Ward & Hall &Assos., Springfield, Va., 1964—; dir. United Va. Bank of Fairfax (Va.). Pres. Lake Montclair Devel., Inc., Springfield, 1964—, chmn. Lake Montclair Assos., 1964—; bd. mgrs. Country Club Lake, Prince William County, Va., 1968—. Pres. P.T.A. Burke (Va.) Sch., 1970-71. Bd. mgrs. Fairfax (Va.) County YMCA, 1964—. Served with AUS, 1946-47. Registered profl. architect Va., Md., D.C., W.Va., Ohio, N.J., Del., Pa., Tenn., Ga., N.C., N.Y. Mem. A.I.A. (corp.), Guild for Religious Architecture, Va. Assn. Professions, Va. C. of C., Tau Sigma Delta, Omicron Delta Kappa, Phi Kappa Phi, Pi Delta Epsilon. Baptist (deacon). Mason (Shriner, K.T.). Home: 9600 Burke View Av Burke VA 22015 Office: 6320 Augusta Springfield VA 22150

WARD, GERALD CHARLES, educator; b. Babcock, Wis., Dec. 16, 1901; s. Charles Eugene and Minnie Olive (Jones) W.; B.S. in Civil Engring. with honors, U. Wis., 1929, C.E., 1955; M.S., Northwestern U., 1960; m. Sarah Augusta Hardy, June 19, 1930; children—Charles Eugene Willoughby, Robert Leigh. Instr. civil engring. U. Wis., 1929-30; coll. editorial rep. McGraw-Hill Book Co., N.Y.C., 1930-33; salesman Wisco Hardware Co., Madison, Wis., 1933-37; comml. rep. Better Roads mag., Chgo., 1937-40; commd. 2d lt. C.E., U.S. Army, 1930, advanced through grades to col., 1955; assigned to Office Chief A.C., 1940-42; mem. Hdqrs. 12th Air Force, Casablanca, French Morocco, 1942-43; assigned to Hdqrs. U.S. Air Force, Pentagon, 1943-49; apptd. to regular U.S. Air Force, 1947; assigned to Office Sec. Def., Washington, 1949-51; assigned to Joint Allied Mill. Assistance Group, London Eng., 1951-52; assigned to Hdqrs. Allied Air Forces, Central Europe, Fontainebleau, France, 1952-55; ret., 1955; editor Better Roads mag., Chgo., 1955-56; lectr. civil engring. Northwestern U., Evanston, Ill., 1956-66; asst. prof. Coll. Engring., Fla. Technol. U., Orlando, 1968-69, asso. prof. civil engring., 1969—. Decorated White Double-headed Eagle (Yugoslavia). Registered profl. engr., Wis., Md. Fellow Am. Soc. C.E. (life mem.); mem. Am. Legion, Ret. Officers Assn., Nat. Assn. Uniformed Services, Air Force Assn., Acacia, Tau Beta Pi, Phi Kappa Phi, Chi Epsilon. Republican. Mason. Clubs: Cercle National des Armees de Terre, de Mer and de l'Air (Paris, France); Naval Officers (Orlando). Author: Study Guide for Engineering Graphics, 1971. Patentee Gizmohr, small mech. computer for solving certain math. and phys. relations concerning stresses and strains inside body of engring. material which is subject to a stated system of loads. Home: 2466 Whitehall Circle Winter Park FL 32789

WARD, HAROLD WALTON, pub. relations officer; b. Nanticoke, Pa., Nov. 26, 1905; s. Edwin Alexander Kerry and Myrtle (Garrison) W.; student Girard Coll., Phila., 1923, Temple U., 1925-26, Bucknell U., 1933-36; m. Betty Mandeville, Aug. 17, 1929; children—Constance Elizabeth (Mrs. Maurice E. Woolard), Edwin Mandeville. Columnist, gen. assignments Wilkes-Barre (Pa.) Record, 1930-37; legislative corr. A.P., Harrisburg, Pa., 1937-42, Washington, 1942-44, labor writer, 1944-51; pub. relations officer United Mine Workers Welfare and Retirement Fund, Washington, 1951—. Mem. Nat. Press Club, Pub. Relations Soc. Am., A.A.A.S., Am. Med. Writers Assn. Home: 13200 Layhill Rd Silver Spring MD 20906 Office: 907 15th St NW Washington DC 20005

WARD, JAMES EVERETT, librarian; b. Dardanelle, Ark., Apr. 10, 1934; s. Norman E. and Nellie I. (Ross) W.; B.A., Hendrix Coll., 1954; M.Ed., U. Ark., 1956, Ed.D., 1962; M.L.S., George Peabody Coll., 1968; m. Betty Jo Wells, Dec. 20, 1964; children—Bradlee Milton, David Everett. Tchr., Carlisle (Ark.) High Sch., 1955-57, Rogers (Ark.) High Sch., 1959-60; chmn. dept. health, phys. edn. and recreation, dir. athletics Central Meth. Coll., Fayette, Mo., 1961-63; asso. prof. dept. health, phys. edn. and recreation David Lipscomb Coll., Nashville, 1963-71, dir. library, 1966—. Served with AUS, 1957-59. Mem. A.L.A., Southeastern, Tenn., Middle Tenn. library assns., A.A.H.P.E.R., Tenn. Assn. Health, Phys. Edn. and Recreation, Tenn. Coll. Phys. Edn. Assn., Phi Delta Kappa, Kappa Delta Pi, Beta Phi Mu. Lion. Home: 3710 Rosemont Av Nashville TN 37215 Office: Crisman Meml Library David Lipscomb Coll Nashville TN 37203

WARD, JAMES M., broadcasting exec. Exec. v.p. WLAC, Nashville. Office: 161 4th Av N Nashville TN 37219*

WARD, JAMES MYRON, newspaper editor; b. Montrose, Miss., Jan. 7, 1919; s. William Joseph and Myra (Anderson) Ward; student Millsaps Coll., 1937-41; m. Bobbye Terry Ward, Dec. 11, 1941; children—Patricia, James Myron, Myra Annette. With Jackson (Miss.) Daily News, 1932—, beginning as carrier boy, successively part-time photographer, part-time reporter, photographer and reporter, city editor, mng. editor, 1932-57, editor, 1957—. Formerly mem. Miss. Agrl. and Indsl. Bd. Served as USAAF, World War II. Decorated Air medal with 9 clusters. Mem. Miss.-La. Mng. Editors Assn., Jackson C. of C., A.P. Mng. Editors Assn., Am. Legion, V.F.W., Am. Soc. Newspaper Editors, Lambda Chi Alpha, Sigma Delta Chi. Clubs: Rotary, Press (past pres.)(Jackson). Home: 327 Naples Rd Jackson MS 39206 Office: 311 E Pearl St Jackson MS 29201

WARD, JAY THOMAS, ins. co. exec.; b. Abilene, Tex., Dec. 27, 1919; s. Joe Thomas and Hilda (Faulke) W.; student Abilene Christian Coll., 1938-40; B.B.A., U. Tex., 1948; m. Jean Marilyn Savage, Sept. 4, 1948; children—Andrea Jean, Angela Ellen. Vice pres. Southland Life Ins. Co., Dallas, 1948—. Served with AUS, 1940-45. C.P.A., Tex. Fellow Life Office Mgmt. Assn.; mem. Tex. Soc. C.P.A.'s (dir. 1967-70, pres. Dallas chpt. 1972-73). Contbr. articles to profl. jours. Home: 9641 Fieldcrest Dr Dallas TX 75238 Office: Southland Center Dallas TX 75201

WARD, JOHN FRANKLIN, supt. schs.; b. Rogers, Tex., May 12, 1937; s. J.F. and Addie (Kemp) W.; B.S., Sam Houston State U., 1959, M.Edn., 1963; m. Mollye Frances Miller, Mar. 16, 1957; children—Donna Gay, Jeffrey Lee, Anthony John. Asst. prin. Lufkin (Tex.) Jr. High Sch., 1964-66; dir. curriculum and instrn. Lufkin Ind. Sch. Dist., 1966-67; supt. schs. Friendswood (Tex.) Ind. Sch. Dist., 1967—. dir. Friendswood Bank. Treas. Boys Scout Troop 446, 1969-71. Bd. dirs. Community Chest. Mem. Tex. Tchrs. Assn., Tex. Adminstrs. Assn., Am. Assn. Sch. Adminstrs., C. of C. (dir. 1970-71). Baptist. Mason. Home: 605 Falling Leaf St Friendswood TX 77546 Office: 302 Laurel Dr Friendswood TX 77546

WARD, JOHN LEWIS, editor; b. Damascus, Ark., Dec. 17, 1930; s. Roy Wilson and Mamie Lillian (Richardson) W.; student State Coll. Ark., intermittently, 1950-60; B.A., U. Ark., 1968; m. Betty Sue Chandler, Feb. 1, 1957; children—Jennifer Kay, Barry Wilson. Reporter, Log Cabin Democrat, Conway, 1956-58, mng. editor, 1972—; editor, editorial feature page Ark. Democrat, Little Rock, 1958-64; dir. pub. relations Winthrop Rockefeller, Gov. of Ark., 1964-71. Dir. Rockefeller for Gov. campaign, Ark., 1968. Mem. Am. Assn. Polit. Cons., Pub. Relations Soc. Am., Ark. Inst. Politics (adv. bd.), Sigma Delta Chi. Home: 3 Post Oak Dr Conway AR 72032

WARD, JUDSON C(LEMENTS), JR., coll. dean; b. Marietta, Ga., Apr. 13, 1912; s. Judson Clements and Bertie (Arnold) W.; A.B., Emory U., 1933, M.A., 1936; Ph.D., U. of N.C., 1947; student Columbia, 1943, American U., 1945; m. Susan-Jane Weyant, Apr. 3, 1946; children—Peter, Michael, Rebecca, Jonathan. Tchr. English and history Fitzgerald (Ga.) High Sch., 1934-37; instr. social scis. Ga. Tchrs. Coll., 1939-40; instr. dept. of history Birmingham-Southern (Ala.) Coll., 1940-42; pres. Ga. Tchrs. Coll., 1947-48; asst. chancellor Univ. System of Ga., 1948; dean Coll. of Arts and Scis., Emory U., 1948-57, v.p., dean of faculties, 1957-70, exec. v.p., dean faculties, 1970—. Dir. Decatur Fed. Savs. & Loan Assn. Trustee Wesleyan Coll., Morris Brown Coll., Pace Acad. Served as 2d lt. F.A., U.S. Army, 1942; instr. dept. econs., govt. and history, U.S. Mil. Acad., 1943-46. Mem. So. Hist. Assn., Phi Beta Kappa, Omicron Delta Kappa. Kappa Phi Kappa, Sigma Pi. Democrat. Home: 1534 Emory Rd NE Atlanta GA 30306

WARD, LEW O., oil producer; b. Oklahoma City, July 24, 1930; s. Llewellyn Orcutt and Addie (Reisdorph) W. II; student Okla. Mil. Acad. Jr. Coll., 1948-50; B.S., Okla. U., 1953; m. Myra Beth Gungoll, Oct. 29, 1955; children—Casidy Ann, William Carlton. Dist. engr. Delhi-Taylor Oil Corp., Tulsa, 1955-56; partner Ward-Gungoll Oil Investments, Enid, Okla., 1956—; owner L.O. Ward Oil Operations, Enid, 1963—; v.p. 1420 Lahoma Rd. Inc., Enid, 1967—, also dir.; dir. Terrane Corp., Pulse Mag. Vice chmn. Indsl. Devel. Commn., Enid, 1968—. Active YMCA. Chmn., Garfield County Republican Com., 1967-69. Bd. dirs. Okla. Polit. Action Com. Served as 1st lt. C.E., AUS, 1953-55. Registered profl. engr., Okla. Mem. Am. Inst. Mining and Metall. Engrs., Okla. Ind. Petroleum Assn. (dir.), Ind. Petroleum Assn. Am. (dir.), C. of C. (dir., indsl. devel. com. 1970-72), Am. Bus. Club (pres. 1964), Order Ky. Cols., Alpha Tau Omega. Methodist. Mason (Shriner), Rotarian. Clubs: Metropolitan Dinner (dir. Enid), Falcon Century, Toastmasters (pres. Enid 1966), Senate. Home: 1621 Indian Dr Enid OK 73701 Office: 1420 Lahoma Rd Enid OK 73701

WARD, (MARY) LUCILE PARRISH (MRS. JACK CHRISTOPHER WARD), club woman; b. Campbellton, Fla.; d. William Albritton and Emma (Hughes) Parrish; B.A., Ala. Coll., 1931; postgrad. Huntingdon Coll., 1937, Wayne U., 1944; m. Jack Christopher Ward, Dec. 2, 1934. Tchr. pub. schs., Abbeville, Ala., 1931-35, Montgomery, 1935-39, Charlotte, N.C., 1945-48. Orientation chmn. Nat. Fedn. Music Clubs, 1963-65, bd. dirs., 1965—, chmn. edn. dept., 1965-69, v.p. in charge southeastern region, 1969, also life mem., mem. 75th anniversary stamp com., 1972; pres. S.C. Fedn. Music Clubs, 1959-63, Guild of Greenville Symphony, 1964-65; bd. dirs. Greenville Symphony Assn., 1957-59, 64-65; chmn. music and arts com. Greenville County Found., 1965—; mem. S.C. Arts Commn., 1967-68; mem. nat. adv. council Brevard (N.C.) Music Center, 1969—. Named Woman of Year—Music Greenville Piedmont Newspaper, 1960. Mem. Fountain Inn Music Club (life), Delta Omicron (state alumnae chmn. 1965-68, pres. Piedmont alumni chpt. 1967-68, province pres. 1968—), Longview Garden Club (pres. 1953-54), Music Club (Greenville, pres. 1957-59), Greenville Garden Club (pres. 1968-70), Greenville Woman's Club, Garden Club S.C. (life). Methodist. Home: Altamont Rd Paris Mountain Greenville SC 29609

WARD, MARVIN, supt. Winston-Salem Bd. Edn. Address: Winston-Salem Bd Edn Box 2513 Winston-Salem NC 27102*

WARD, NEWELL JAY, JR., investment counselor, farmer; b. N.Y.C., Oct. 30, 1917; s. Newell Jay and Ethel (Conderman) W.; student U. Va., 1940, Columbia U., 1942; m. Bettina Belmont, June 29, 1939; children—Daniel Sands, Daphne. Owner, Newmary Farms, thoroughbred horse and cattle operation, Middleburg, Va., 1946—; owner Newell J. Ward, Jr., investment counsel, 1967—; v.p., dir. Middleburg Nat. Bank. Master foxhounds Middleburg Hunt, 1946-72. Mem. Loudoun County Planning Commn., 1948-59. Bd. dirs. Loudoun-Fauquier Health Center. Served to maj. cavalry AUS, 1941-46. Decorated Bronze Star with palm; Croix de Guerre (France); Resistance Medal (Italy). Mem. Nat. Steeplechase and Hunt assn. (steward 1958-62, chmn. hunt's com. 1961-64), Goose Creek Assn. (sec. 1969-72), Masters of Foxhounds Assn. Am. (dir. 1970—); Clubs: Racquet and Tennis (N.Y.C.); Montego Bay Yacht (Jamaica). Home: Newmary Farms Middleburg VA 22117

WARD, PAUL, justice; b. Batesville, Ark., Feb., 1891; s. William J. and Mollie (Churchill) W.; A.B., Ark. Coll.; LL.D., U. Okla.; m. Rebecca Young, Aug. 1, 1924 (dec. 1934); children—Paul (dec.), John D., William V.; m. 2d, Inarea McKenzie, 1938; 1 dau., Jane. Admitted to Ark. bar; mayor, Batesville, 1922; judge 8th Chancery Dist., 1940-49; justice Ark. Supreme Ct., 1950—. Partner Ideal Baking Co., Royal Crown Bottling Co. Mem. Ark. Senate, 1931-37. Served as lt., U.S. Army, World War I. Methodist. Mason (32 deg., Shriner). Club: River Dale Country. Home: 312 Del Rico Little Rock AR 72205 Office: Supreme Court Little Rock AR 72201

WARD, ROBERT, composer, conductor; b. Cleve., Sept. 13, 1917; s. Albert E. and Carrie (Mollenkopf) W.; B. Mus., Eastman Sch. Music, 1939; certificate, Julliard Grad. Sch. Music, 1946; m. Mary Raymond Benedict, June 19, 1944; children—Melinda, Johanna, Jonathon, Mark, Timotny. Student composition with Bernard Rogers, Howard Hanson, Frederick Jacobi, Aaron Copland; in conducting with Albert Stoessel and Edgar Schenkman; mng. editor, mem. bd. Galaxy Music Corp. until 1967, dir., 1967—; exec. v.p. Highgate Press, 1967—; pres. N.C. Sch. Arts, Winston-Salem, 1967—. Mem. music com. Henry St. Settlement. Served with AUS, 1942-46. Decorated Bronze Star medal; recipient MacDowell Colony fellow, 1938; Juilliard Pub. Award, 1942; Alice M. Ditson fellow, Columbia, 1944;, 000 grant, Am. Acad. Arts and Letters. 1946; Guggenheim fellow; 1950, 51, 66-67. Mem. Nat. Inst. Arts and Letters. Composer: 1st Symphony, 1942; Hush'd Be the Camps Today, 1943; Second Symphony, 1947; Third Symphony, 1951; Fourth Symphony, 1958; Divertimento for Orchestra, 1961; Earth Shall Be Fair, 1960; He Who Gets Slapped (Pantaloon), (opera in 3 acts); The Crucible (opera in 4 acts; recipient Pulitzer Prize in music 1962); Hymn and Celebration (for orchestra), 1962; Music for Celebration, 1963; The Lady From Colorado (opera in 2 acts), 1964; Let the Word Go Forth, 1965; Sweet Freedom's Song (cantata), 1965; Hymn To The Night, 1966; First String Quartet, 1966; Concerto for Piano and Orchestra, 1968. Contbr. articles and revs. to Modern Music, Juilliard Rev., Nat. Fedn. Music Clubs Mag. Home: Winston-Salem NC 27102 Office: NC School of Arts Winston-Salem NC 27102

WARD, SIDNEY CHARLES, lawyer; b. Evanston, Ill., Mar. 3, 1929; s. Taylor D. and Helen (Bloss) W.; student Oberlin Coll., 1947-49; B.S., Lawrence Coll., 1951; postgrad. U. Wis., 1951-53; J.D., U. Fla., 1957; m. Sarah C. Spencer, June 27, 1952; children—Julia H., Taylor D., Caroline J., Elizabeth S., Katherine B. Admitted to Fla. bar, 1957; dir., gen. counsel Trust Co. of Fla.; lectr. Trustee Goodwill Industries Central Fla.; bd. dirs. Loch Haven Art Center, Edgewood Boys Ranch, Orange County chpt. Am. Cancer Soc., treas., bd. dirs. Central Fla. chpt. Fellowship of Christian Athletes. Mem. Am. Bar Assn., Beta Theta Pi, Phi Delta Phi. Presbyn. Author: Florida and Federal Estate and Tax Planning, other texts. Home: 1420 Via Tuscany Winter Park FL 32789 Office: Hartford Bldg Orlando FL 32801

WARD, S(OLOMON) KELLY, dentist; b. Weathersby, Miss., Oct. 21, 1897; s. William Robert and Mary Elizabeth (Stringer) W.; B.A., Miss. Coll., 1923; D.D.S., Emory U., 1928; m. Jimmie Davis Holmes, May 12, 1946. Prin., Hollandale (Miss.) High Sch., 1924-25; practice gen. dentistry, Taylorsville, Miss., 1928—. Miss. dir. Vets.' Farm and Home Bd., 1960-64. Alderman, City of Taylorsville, 1940-48; chmn. Smith County Democratic Com., 1960. Served with USN, 1918-19. Recipient certificates of appreciation, Pres. Roosevelt, 1942-44, Pres. Truman, 1945. Mem. LaSociete des Quarante Hommes et Huit Chevaux, Chef de Gar Locale, Grande de La Porte, Grande Cheminot, Grande Conducteur, LaGrande Medicin, Am. Dental Assn., Am. Legion, Miss. Hist. Soc., V.F.W., Miss. Cattlemen's Assn., Delta Sigma Delta. Mason (Shriner, K.T.), Lion; mem. Order Eastern Star. Address: Taylorsville MS 39168

WARD, WALLACE CLYDE, physician; b. Ryland, N.C., Oct. 26, 1905; s. William Caleb and Adrian (Twine) W.; student Wake Forest Coll., 1925-29; B.S., U. Louisville, 1929, M.D., 1931; m. LaRene Romig, Aug. 8, 1946; children—Wallace Clyde, Thomas Richard, Timothy Laurence. Intern, U. Louisville, 1931-32, City Meml. Hosp., Winston-Salem, N.C., 1932-33; resident Charity-Hosp., New Orleans, 1933-34, Cooke County, Chgo., 1938; gen. practice medicine, Pineville, N.C., 1934-38, Raleigh, 1939-43, 46—; mem. staffs Rex Hosp., Wake Meml. Hosp. Alderman Pineville, N.C., 1935; redman, Pineville. Served to maj. M.C., AUS, 1943-46. Mem. Am., Tri-State, N.C., Wake County (pres. 1966-67), So. med. socs., Raleigh Acad. Medicine (pres. 1969-70), Gen. Practioners of Raleigh (pres. 1965), C. of C., N.C. Wildlife Fedn., Phi Rho Sigma. Baptist. Home: 1429 Canterbury Rd Raleigh NC 27608 Office: 235 Bryan Bldg Raleigh NC 27605

WARD, WALTER LEROY, JR., banker; b. Homer, La., Mar. 30, 1902; s. Walter Leroy and Virginia (Madden) W.; student Tulane U., Washington and Lee U.; m. Naomi Terry, Sept. 10, 1966; children (by previous marriage)—Walter Leroy III, Swan Sullivan. Chief clk. La. Banking Dept., 1923-27; engaged in bond and brokerage bus., also mem. New Orleans Cotton Exchange, 1928-31; bank examiner La., 1934-39; with Fidelity Nat. Bank, Baton Rouge, 1939—, pres., 1954-60, chmn. bd., 1960—. Mem. bd. Greater Baton Rouge Port Commn., 1962—, Downtown Baton Rouge Assn., 1962—, Baton Route Better Bus. Bur., 1942—. Bd. dirs. Baton Rouge Little Theatre, 1960—, Baton Rouge Parish Library, 1960-62; mem. La. State U. Found. Mem. Financial Pub. Relations Assn. (past bd. dirs.), Am., La. bankers assns., La. State Sr. Golf Assn. (bd. dirs.), Baton Rouge C. of C. (bd. dirs., exec. com. econ. devel. council). Clubs: Baton Rouge Country (bd. dirs.), Rotary, City, Boston (New Orleans). Home: 3939 Churchill Av Baton Rouge LA 70808 Office: 440 3d St Baton Rouge LA 70821

WARD, WILLIAM FRANKLIN, physician; b. Sumter, S.C., June 16, 1935; s. William Franklin and Mellie Anne (Wells) K.; student Bob Jones U., 1953-55; B.S., U. S.C., 1957; M.D., Med. Coll. S.C., 1961; m. Patricia Lane Fogle, Aug. 27, 1960; children—William Franklin III, Frederick Wells, Darrin Robert. Rotating intern Columbia (S.C.) Hosp., 1961-62; staff physician med.-surg. unit, S.C. State Hosp., Columbia, 1962-63; gen. practice medicine, West Columbia, S.C., 1963—. Springdale, S.C., 1968—; mem. staffs Lexington County Hosp., West Columbia Hosp., So. Baptist Hosp., Providence Hosp., Columbia Hosp., (all Richland and Lexington County); sec. Lexington County Hosp., 1971; sch. physician Columbia Bible Coll., 1968—; team physician Airport High Sch., 1968—. Mem. Regional Health Planning Council, 1970—; mem. Drug Abuse Council of Richland-Lexington Counties 1971—; mem. Lexington County Ambulance Commn., 1970—; chmn. Springdale Health Forum, 1971. Bd. dirs. Mid Carolina Council on Alcoholism, 1965-70, Brookland Plantation. Served with M.C., AUS, 1966-68. Mem. A.M.A., So. Med. Assn., Christian, S.C., Columbia med. socs., Am. Acad. Gen. Practice, Am. Heart Assn., Nat. Rehab. Assn., West Columbia C. of C. Baptist (deacon 1965—). Optimist (dist. lt. gov. Cayce-West Columbia 1971—). Home: 1108 Baywater Dr West Columbia SC 29169 Office: 3114 Platt Springs Rd Springdale West Columbia SC 29169

WARD, WINFRED O'NEIL, physician; b. Exmore, Va., Sept. 28, 1933; s. Marvin Omar and Ruth (Kellam) W.; B.S., Coll. of William and Mary, 1954; M.D., Med. Coll. Va., 1958; m. Anne Sexton Martin, June 21, 1958; children—Anne Elizabeth, Susan Terry, Oma. Intern, Mercy Hosp., Springfield, O., 1958-59; practice gen. medicine and psychoanalysis through hypnosis, Franklin, Va., 1961—; mem. staff Southampton Meml. Hosp., chief of staff, 1968-70. Mem. Franklin Hwy. Safety Council, 1968, Gov.'s Council on Mental Health, 1965—. Chmn., Franklin Republican City Com., 1965-67, 68-70; vice chmn. 4th Dist. Rep. Com., 1968-70. Bd. dirs. Southampton Meml. Hosp. Served with USNR, 1959-61. Mem. Am. Acad. Gen. Practice, A.M.A., So., Tri-County (pres. 1969-70) med. socs., Med. Soc. Va., Nat. Acad. Med. Hypnosis (charter mem., treas. 1972—), Assn. Advancement Ethical Hypnosis, Internat. Platform Assn. Home: 908 N High St Franklin VA 23851 Office: Southampton Med Bldg Franklin VA 23851

WARDELL, ANTHONY WENTWORTH, govt. ofcl.; b. Bklyn., Jan. 11, 1932; s. Raymond and Constance (Jackson) W.; B.S., Ga. Inst. Tech., 1954; M.S., Chrysler Inst. Engring., Detroit, 1959; m. Emily Ayers, Mar. 21, 1954; children—Linda Marie, Mark Douglas. Automotive engr. Chrysler Corp., Detroit, 1957-59; reliability engr. Brown Engring. Co., Inc., Huntsville, Ala., 1959-60; sr. reliability engr. Lockheed Ga. Co., Atlanta, 1960-63; asst. chief System Safety Office, NASA Manned Spacecraft Center, Houston, 1963—. Served as lt. (j.g.) USN, 1954-57. Recipient Sustained Superior Performance award NASA, 1967, Superior Achievement awards NASA, 1968, 69. Registered profl. engr., Ga. Mem. Tau Beta Pi, Pi Tau Sigma, Phi Eta Sigma, Phi Kappa Phi. Contbr. articles to profl. jours. Home: 18307 Blanchmont Lane Houston TX 77058 Office: Mail Code NS NASA-Manned Spacecraft Center Houston TX 77058

WARDEN, EDWARD, lawyer, banker; b. Mt. Pleasant, Pa., May 15, 1907; s. Eugene C. and Pleasant (Glessner) W.; B.S., Washington and Jefferson Coll., 1928; LL.B., Duquesne U., 1931; Litt. M., U. Pitts., 1951; m. Emily Bryce, Jan. 30, 1933; children—Mary Bryce, James Bryce, Gerard Bryce. Clk., 1st Nat. Bank, Pitts., 1929-34, asst. trust officer, 1934-37, trust officer, 1937-39, v.p., trust officer, 1939-46; v.p. Peoples First Nat. Bank and Trust Co. (merger 1st Nat. Bank and Peoples Pitts. Nat. Bank), 1946-60; v.p. Pitts. Nat. Bank (merger Peoples First Nat. Bank and Trust Co. and Fidelity Trust Co.),

1960-72; pvt. practice law, Pinehurst, N.C., 1972; dir. Washington Steel Corp. Mem. Am., Pa., Allegheny County bar assns., Phi Delta Theta, Phi Delta Phi, Pi Delta Epsilon, Phi Alpha Theta. Republican. Episcopalian. Clubs: Pinehurst (N.C.) Country; Duquesne, Fox Chapel Golf (Pitts.); Pike Run Country (Jones Mills, Pa.); Laurel Valley Golf, Rolling Rock (Ligonier, Pa.). Address: 32 Quail Hill Pinehurst NC 28374

WARDEN, FRANCIS MARION, clergyman, educator; b. Pueblo, Colo., Jan. 17, 1904; s. Henry Clay and Rosalie (Forbes) W.; A.B., U. Denver, 1929; B. Th., So. Baptist Sem., 1931, Th.M., 1932, Ph.D., 1938; postgrad. U. Chgo., 1931, Baylor U., 1964, East Tex. State U., 1964; m. Ruth Watson, Aug. 31, 1929. Ordained to ministry Baptist Ch., 1928; pastor First Baptist Ch., Brighton, Colo., 1928-29, Upper Alton (Ill.) Baptist Ch. 1939-42, First Baptist Ch., Union, S.C., 1946-49, First Baptist Ch., Jefferson City, Tenn., 1949-57; chmn. and prof. religion and Greek, East Tex. Baptist Coll., Marshall, 1957-72. Guest prof. religion, Carson-Newman Coll., Jefferson City, Tenn., 1955-56. Mem. Pulpit Supply and Interim Pastorates, 1957-72. Served as chaplain, USAAF, 1942-45. Home: 1401 N Fulton St Marshall TX 75670

WARDEN, PHILLIP L., journalist; b. Trenton, Mo., Nov. 3, 1912; s. L. A. and Jessica Marie (Thomas) W.; A.B., Park Coll., 1934; B.J., U. Mo., 1936; m. Helen Marie Sproul, June 9, 1937; children—Pamela (Mrs. Thomas L. Coit), Philip S., Randy. Reporter, Trenton Republican-Times, 1934-35, The Packer, Kansas City, Mo., also Chgo., 1936-40; financial news reporter Chgo. Tribune, 1940-42, Washington corr., 1942—. Mem. standing com. corrs. Congl. Press Galleries, 1963-64. Served to lt. USNR, 1944-46. Mem. Park Coll. Alumni Assn. (pres. Washington area 1947-50). Methodist. Club: Nat. Press (Washington). Home: 7104 Park Terrace Dr Alexandria VA 22310 Office: 1750 Pennsylvania Av NW Washington DC 20006

WARDLAW, CHARLES DAVID, land surveyor; b. Lafayette, Ga., Feb. 20, 1939; s. Samuel Fariss and Effie Rose Ella (Stanfield) W.; student U. Wis. Extension, 1963-64, U. Tenn., evenings 1970-71; m. Shirley Delona Howard, June 26, 1959; children—Delona Rena, Karen Elaine. Hwy. project engr. State Hwy. Dept. Ga., Lafayette, 1958-70; self-employed bldg. contractor, real estate salesman, archtl. draftsman, Lafayette, 1970—; apptd. surveyor Walker County, 1970—. Served with AUS, 1962-64. Mem. Surveying and Mapping Soc. Ga. Home: 1112 Chota Circle Lafayette GA 30728 Office: 205 W Villanow St Lafayette GA 30728

WARDLEY, JAMES ALAN, accountant; b. Connellsville, Pa., Apr. 16, 1935; s. John Kenneth and Ruth (Weaver) W.; student LaSalle Extension U., 1951-57; B.B.A., U. Tenn., 1956, postgrad., 1968—; m. Molly Laraine Napier, June 8, 1963; children—Linda Gayle, David Kenneth, James Alan II, Marc Scott, Charla Alisha. Jr. accountant, Peat, Marwick, Mitchell & Co., C.P.A.'s, Memphis, 1956-57, sr. accountant, 1957-58; sr. accountant Joe E. Henry & Co. C.P.A.'s, Knoxville, Tenn., 1958-60, partner, 1960-61; partner, dir. John R. Fiser, Inc., Knoxville, 1961-70, controller, 1961-68, v.p., 1968-70; pres. Nova, Inc., Knoxville, 1970—. C.P.A., Tenn. Mem. Tenn. Soc. C.P.A.'s, Am. Inst. C.P.A.'s, Nat. Assn. Home Builders, Delta Sigma Pi (pres.), Beta Alpha Psi (treas.), Sigma Nu (treas.). Republican. Home: Route 5, 9136 Carlton Circle Concord TN 37720 Office: 6910 Kingston Pike Knoxville TN 37919

WARE, CHARLES ARTHUR, ins. exec.; b. Dunnsville, Va., Jan. 20, 1921; s. Catesby and Lila Constance (Maddox) W.; student Lynchburg Coll., 1938-40, William and Mary Coll., 1940-41, U. Ga., 1941-42, Ins. Inst. Am., 1943-44, Columbia U., 1944-45; m. Jeanne Elizabeth Barbour, Oct. 7, 1950; children—Charles Arthur, Keville Barbour, Elizabeth Jeanne. Map clk. Hartford Fire Ins. Co., Atlanta, 1941-42; underwriter Great Am. Ins. Group, N.Y.C., 1943-45, insp., Washington, 1945-46; v.p. South Boston Ins. Agy., Inc. (Va.), 1947-55, pres., 1955—; pres. Randolph Motor Inn, South Boston, 1963—, chmn. bd., 1972; v.p. McDaniel Real Estate Co., Inc., Richmond, 1967—, Ware Oil Co., Dunnsville, Va., 1959—. Sec.-treas. Martinsville Convalescent Home, Inc., 1965—. Sec. South Boston Electoral Bd., 1960-62, South Boston Planning Commn., 1963—. Mem. Halifax County C. of C. (treas., 1954-58), Va. Hotel and Motel Assn. (bd. dirs. 1966—), So. Innkeepers Assn. (bd. dirs. 1970—, v.p. 1971—), South Boston and Va. Retail Mchts. Assn. (bd. dirs. 1970—), South Boston Bd. Ins. Underwriters (bd. dirs. 1957, pres. 1960). Presbyn. (deacon). Rotarian. Home: 1412 Hodges St South Boston VA 24592 Office: 325 Main St South Boston VA 24592

WARE, JAMES WARREN, III, dentist; b. Euharlee, Ga., Feb. 9, 1934; s. James Warren, Jr. and Alma Doris (Nelson) W.; A.B., Shorter Coll., 1956; D.D.S., Emory U., 1960; m. Susie M. Clanton, Aug. 29, 1959; children—Doris Elizabeth, Pamela Anne, John Nelson. Practice dentistry, Carrollton, Ga., 1962-63, Trion, Ga., 1963—; dir. 1st Nat. Bank Chattooga County, Ga. Adviser, Chattooga County Cancer Soc., 1969—. Mem. adv. bd. Shorter Coll., 1971—. Served with USNR, 1960-62. Mem. Am., Ga. dental assns., N.W. Dist. Dental Soc., Xi Psi Phi. Baptist. Rotarian. Home: 1 Greenmeadow Dr Trion GA 30753 Office: Trion Community Hospital Trion GA 30753

WARE, JOHN THOMAS, state senator; b. Chattanooga, Nov. 14, 1931; s. James E. and Marguerite (McQue) W.; student U. Fla., 1949-50; B.S. in Pub. Adminstrn., Fla. State U., 1957; J.D., Stetson Coll. Law, 1961; m. Doris Gregory; children—G. Scott, Stacey, Sheryl, Sheila, Steve. Admitted to Fla. bar, since practiced in St. Petersburg; city atty. St. Petersburg Beach, Fla., 1967. Mem. Fla. Ho. of Reps., 1964-66, 68-70; mem. Fla. Senate, 1970—. Served with USNR, 1950-54; Korea. Mem. St. Petersburg, Fla., Am. bar assns., Fla. Acad. Trial Lawyers, Lambda Chi Alpha. Home: 211 Sunset Dr N St Petersburg FL 33710 Office: Security Fed Bldg 2600 9th St St Petersburg FL 33704*

WARE, LOIS PHILIP, educator; b. Longview, Tex.; d. John Allen and Horace (Flanagan) Ware; B.A., U. Tex., 1917; M.A., 1924, Ph.D., 1931. Tchr. pub. schs., Tex., 1917-21; tutor English, U. Tex., Austin, 1921-24, instr. English, 1924-49, asst. prof. English, 1949-67. Mem. Modern Lang. Assn., South Central Modern Lang. Assn., Am. Assn. U. Profs., D.A.R., Magna Charta Dames, Sovereign Colonial Soc. Ams. Royal Descent, U.D.C., Daus. Am. Colonists, Plantagenet Soc., Descendants of Knights of the Garter, Order of Crown, Phi Beta Kappa. Baptist. Contbr. articles to profl. publs. Home: 2512 San Gabriel Austin TX 78705

WARE, RAY MILLER, educator; b. Nicholasville, Ky., May 11, 1929; s. Frank E. and Mary (Miller) W.; B.S., U. Ky., 1950, M.B.A., 1956, Ph.D., 1963; m. Susan Davenport, Jan. 31, 1961; 1 son, Steven Douglas. Staff accountant Kelley & Galloway, C.P.A.'s, Ashland, Ky., 1956-57, Yeager, Ford & Warren, C.P.A.'s, Lexington, Ky., 1957-58, Jere E. Sullivan, C.P.A., Lexington, 1958-60; prof. econs. Transylvania Coll., Lexington, 1961—. Served with USAF, 1951-55. C.P.A., Ky. Mem. Am., So. econ. assns., Am., So., Midwest finance assns. Mem. Christian Ch. Club: Aquatic. Author: The Balance of Payments, 1965; International Economics, 1971. Contbr. articles to profl. jours. Home: 3521 Greentree Rd Lexington KY 40502

WARF, J. HOWARD, state ofcl.; b. Maury County, Tenn., Sept. 13, 1904; B.S., Middle Tenn. State Coll.; M.A., George Peabody Coll. for Tchrs.; m. Martha Josephine Kisler, 1932. Successively tchr. elementary and secondary schs., asst. prin., prin., supt. Lewis County Schs.; now commr. of edn., State of Tenn. Mem. Tenn. Edn. Assn., N.E.A., Am., Tenn. assns. sch. adminstrs. Methodist. Office: State Capitol Nashville TN 37219*

WARFEL, HARRY REDCAY, publisher; b. Reading, Pa., Mar. 21, 1899; s. Wyatt W. and Kate (Recay) W.; A.B., Bucknell U., 1920, A.M., 1922; A.M., Columbia, 1924; student U. of N.C., 1924-25; Ph.D., Yale, 1932, Sterling Research fellow, 1934-35; m. Ruth Evelyn Farquhar, Apr. 15, 1922 (dec. 1961); m. 2d, Elizabeth Warner Sturges, June 11, 1962. Master St. John's School, Manlius, N.Y., 1920-21; instr. English Bucknell U., 1921-25, asst. prof., 1925-34, asso. prof., 1934-35, adminstrv. officer, 1946-47; prof. English U. Md., 1935-44; officer cultural program Dept. of State, 1943-46, chief book, library sect. 1944-45, adv. libraries and publs., 1945, asst. chief Internat. Exchange of Persons, 1946; prof. English, head dept. Pa. Mil. Coll., 1947-48; prof. English U. of Fla., 1948-69; vis. prof. several univs. and colls.; Fulbright lectr., Philipps U., Marburg, Germany, 1953-54; dir. Guaranty Fed. Savs. & Loan Assn. of Gainesville. Has been ofcl. del. several internat. confs.; dir. Humanities Center for Liberal Edn., 1957—. Recipient Alumni Award for Meritorious Achievement, Bucknell U., 1958. Mem. Coll. English Assn. (pres. 1957), nat., state and local profl. orgns. Author or co-author several books and texts; latest being: Letters of Noah Webster, 1952; Studies in Walt Whitman's Leaves of Grass, 1954: American Novelists of Today, 1951; American English in its Cultural Setting (with D. J. Lloyd), 1956; Uncollected Letters of James Gates Percival, 1959; Language: A Science of Human Behavior, 1962. Cons. editor Am. Book Co., 1942-55; editor, owner Scholars' Facsimiles and Reprints, 1948—. Home: 1605 NW 14TH Av Gainesville FL 32601*

WARFIELD, GRACE LUCILLE JACOBSON (MRS. WALTER S. WARFIELD), educator, editor; b. Albert Lea, Minn., Feb. 27, 1910; d. John and Anna-Cena (Larsen) Jacobson; B.S., U. Minn., 1930, M.A., 1958, specialist in edn., sch. psychology services, 1962; m. Walter S. Warfield, Apr. 16, 1948; children—James D., Patricia Ann (Mrs. Bertram A. Coppock, Jr.), Wendy S. English tchr., Garden City, Minn., 1930-33; prodn. asst. U. Minn. Press, 1952-55; tchr. mentally retarded, Mpls., 1955-61; sch. psychologist, coordinator classes for mentally retarded-handicapped, 1962-65; prin. Dowling Sch. for Crippled Children, Mpls., 1965-66; asst. editor Exceptional Children, The Council for Exceptional Children, Washington, 1966-68, asst. exec. dir. editor, 1968—. Mem. N.E.A., Council for Exceptional Children, Ednl. Press Assn. Am., Am. Assn. Mental Deficiency, Nat. Assn. Sch. Psychologist. Democrat. Author: (with Harriet Blodgett) Understanding Mentally Retarded Children, 1959. Free-lance copy editor Jour. of Counseling Psychology, 1952-62. Home: 7614 16th St NW Washington DC 20012 Office: 1411 Jefferson Davis Hwy Jefferson Plaza Arlington VA 22202

WARFIELD, ROBERT EDGAR, JR., banker; b. Atlanta, Oct. 5, 1924; s. Robert Edgar and Mattie Alice (Bragg) W.; student U. Ga. Extension, 1947-50; m. Elaine Grace Bennett, Apr. 18, 1945; children—Robert L., Janice I. Chief clk. Fulton Nat. Bank, Atlanta, 1946-50; asst. v.p. Bank of Zephyrhills (Fla.), 1953-56; pres., dir. 1st Nat. Bank & Trust Co. Eustis (Fla.), also Bank of Mt. Dora (Fla.), 1965—; dir. Citizens Nat. Bank Leesburg (Fla.), Burnett Finance Co., DeLand, Fla., Brown Sugar Corp., Pahokee, Fla., W.M. Igou, Inc., Eustis; pres. Heard Broadcasting, Inc., Leesburg, 1965—. Pres., Eustis Little League, 1959, Lake County unit Am. Cancer Soc., 1969—; Lake County chmn. A.R.C., 1963; pres. Lake-Sumter Community Mental Health Center, 1969—; treas., exec. com. Waterman Meml. Hosp. Assn., 1965—; pres. N.E. Lake County Hosp. Dist., 1967—. Served with USNR, 1941-45, 51-52. Mem. Fla. Bankers Assn. (dir. 1971—), Bank Adminstrn. Inst. (pres. 1961), Eustis C. of C. (dir. 1960). Republican. Baptist (tchr. Sunday sch.). Mason, Elk. Club: Pine Meadows Golf & Country (past pres., dir. 1960—). (Eustis, Fla). Home: 1310 E Crooked Lane Dr Eustis FL 32726 Office: 100 N Bay St Eustis FL 32726

WARGA, GERZSON, polit. scientist, diplomat, statistician; b. Budapest, Hungary, Nov. 10, 1913; s. Gerzson and Irene (Molnar) W.; Dr. Polit. Sci., Royal Pazmany U. (Budapest, Hungary), 1938; student U. Dijon (France), 1936, U. Wash., 1950-52; m. Anna Lisa Brunsson, Apr. 15, 1943; 1 son, Anders. Came to U.S., 1949, naturalized, 1956. Joined Hungarian Fgn. Ministry, 1938; served in Bucharest, Rumania, 1940-43, Ankara, Turkey, 1943-45, Budapest, 1946-47, Stockholm, Sweden, 1947-48; coll. instr. U.S. Army Lang. Sch., Monterey, Cal., 1952-57; statistician, projections and forecasting U.S. Internal Revenue Service, Washington, 1966—. Mem. Am. Statis. Assn., Am. Acad. Polit. and Social Sci. Home: 4206 Leland St Chevy Chase MD 20015 Office: 1111 Constitution Av Washington DC 20224

WARING, JOHN ALFRED, research writer, cons.; b. San Francisco, Dec. 30, 1913; s. John A. and Mary (Wheeler) W.; student pub. schs. Yachting, marine editor Chgo. Tribune, 1934-47; editor Kellogg Messenger, Kellogg Switchboard & Supply Co., Chgo., 1945-49; research cons. Baxter Internat. Econ. Research Bur., Inc., investment counselling, N.Y.C., 1951-52; research asst. marketing research dept. Fuller, Smith & Ross, Inc., advt., N.Y.C., 1953; research writer, cons. Twentieth Century Fund, N.Y.C., 1953-54; research cons. Ford Motor Co., Dearborn, Mich., 1955; chief researcher Internat. Fact Finding Inst., Lawrence Orgn., pub. relations cons., N.Y.C., Washington, 1957-58; lectr. on energy, tech. and history World Power Conf., Montreal, 1958, First Energy Inst., Am. U., Washington, 1960, Nat. Archives, Washington, 1962, Smithsonian Mus. History and Tech., Washington, 1968; research cons. PARM Project, Nat. Planning Assn., Washington, 1961-62; cons. Sci., Tech. and Fgn. Affairs Seminar, Fgn. Service Inst., U.S. Dept. State, 1965; cons. U.S. energy statistics Smithsonian Instn., U.S. Bur. Census, 1960—; research cons. Program of Policy Studies in Sci. and Tech., George Washington U., 1967-68; del. U.S. commn. UNESCO Conf., San Francisco, 1969; inaugural lectr. Future of Sci. and Soc. in Am. Seminar U.S. Civil Service Commn., Washington, 1970; editorial cons. Nat. Acad. Enging., Washington, 1971; research cons., analyst Seminar Sch., Indsl. Coll. Armed Forces, Ft. Lesley J. McNair, Washington, 1958—. Mem. Soc. History of Tech. (charter), History Sci. Soc., Technocracy Inc., A.A.A.S., Washington Acad. Scis., Phi Beta Kappa Assn. in D.C., Internat. Soc. Gen. Semanties, Am. Humanist Assn., Washington History Sci. Club., Washington Ethical Soc. Contbg. editor: Progressive World Mag., 1962—; technol. trends editor The Futurist Mag., 1968—. Contbr. chpts to books; compiler statis. tabulations. Home: 8502 Flower Av Takoma Park MD 20012 Office: Seminar Sch Indl Coll Armed Forces Fort Lesley McNair Washington DC 20315

WARING, THOMAS R(ICHARD), newspaper editor; b. Charleston, S.C., May 30, 1907; s. Thomas Richard and Laura Campbell (Witte) W.; student Porter Mil. Acad.; A.B., U. of South, 1927; LL.D., The Citadel, 1959; D.C.L., (hon.) U. of South, 1961; m. Clelia Peronneau Mathewes, Sept. 23, 1933 (dec. July 1967); children—Mary Randolph (Mrs. Robert E. Berretta), Thomas. Reporter, N.Y. Herald Tribune, 1929-31. News and Courier, Charleston, 1927, city editor, 1931-42, mng. editor, 1942-51, editor, 1951—; sec., dir. News & Courier Co., Evening Post Pub. Co. Bd. govs. Carolina Plantation Soc., 1950-51. Mem. Am. Soc. Newspaper Editors, Carolina Art Assn. (dir. 1935-50), Charleston C. of C. (dir. 1947-48), St. Cecilia Soc., Phi Beta Kappa, Alpha Tau Omega. Episcopalian. Clubs: Carolina Yacht (commodore 1944), Rotary (dir. 1952-53) (Charleston, S.C.). Home: 10 Atlantic St Charleston SC 29401 Office: 134 Columbus St Charleston SC 29403

WARING, WILLIAM WINBURN, pediatrician, educator; b. Savannah, Ga., July 20, 1923; s. Antonio Johnston and Sue (Winburn) W.; grad. Hotchkiss Sch., 1942; student Yale, 1942-43; M.D., Harvard, 1947; m. Nell Pape Williams, July 19, 1952; children—William Winburn, Benjamin Joseph Williams, Antonio Johnston, Peter Ayraud, Patrick Houstoun. Intern, Children's Hosp., Boston, 1947-48, Johns Hopkins Hosp., Balt., 1948-49; resident Johns Hopkins Hosp., 1949-52; pvt. practice, Jacksonville, Fla., 1954-56; faculty Tulane U., Sch. Medicine, New Orleans, 1957—, prof. pediatrics, 1965—, lectr. physiology, 1966—; v.p. gen. med. and sci. adv. council Nat. Cystic Fibrosis Research Found., 1967—; sr. vis. physician Charity Hosp. La., New Orleans; vis. physician New Orleans Crippled Children's Hosp.; dir. New Orleans Cystic Fibrosis Clinic, Tulane Pediatric Pulmonary Lab.; chief pulmonary diseases sect. pediatrics Tulane U., 1969—. Cons. handicapped children's services La. Dept. Health, 1964—. Bd. dirs. Tb Assn. Greater New Orleans, Vis. Nurses Assn. Served to capt. M.C., AUS, 1952-54. Recipient USPHS Career Devel. award, 1963-67; various research grants. Diplomate Am. Bd. Pediatrics. Fellow Am. Acad. Pediatrics (chmn. diseases of chest 1970-71), Am. Coll. Chest Physicians; mem. Am. Assn. for Inhalation Therapy (asso. med. cons. editor Inhalation Therapy 1967—), Cystic Fibrosis Club (pres. 1968, v.p.), La. Tb and Respiratory Disease Assn., La., Am. (v.p. 1972) thoracic socs., So. Soc. Pediatric Research (pres.), La., New Orleans pediatric socs., Orleans Parish Med. Soc. Roman Catholic. Clubs: Boston, New Orleans Country, So. Yacht, Wyvern (New Orleans). Contbr. articles to profl. jours. Home: 6120 Marquette Pl New Orleans LA 70118 Office: Sch Medicine Tulane U 1430 Tulane Av New Orleans LA 70112

WARKENTIN, JOHN, psychotherapist; b. Hamburg, Germany, June 18, 1913; s. Abraham and Elizabeth (Unger) W.; came to U.S., 1923; Ph.D., U. Rochester, 1938; M.D., Northwestern U., 1942; m. Linda Brown, June 26, 1938 (dec. 1970); children—Marilyn (Mrs. John Hasler), James B., Pamela A., William J.; m. 2d. Elizabeth Valerius, Nov. 27, 1971. Intern Chgo. Wesley Meml. Hosp., 1942-43; resident Walter Reed Army Hosp., Oakridge Hosp., Lawson VA Hosp., Menninger Found., Pa. Hosp., 1943-52; chief neuropsychiatry sect. Lawson VA Hosp., Atlanta, 1946-49; asst. prof. psychiatry Emory U., Atlanta, 1949-53; practice medicine, specializing in psychotherapy, Atlanta, 1953—. Served with AUS, 1943-46. Fellow Am. Psychiat. Assn., Am. Othopsychiat. Assn., Am. Psychol. Assn.; mem. Am. Acad. Psychotherapists (pres. 1960-61), Ga. Psychiat. Assn. (pres. 1966-67). Founding editor Voices: The Art and Science of Psychotherapy. Contbr. articles in field to profl. jours. Home and Office: 2905 Peachtree Rd NE Atlanta GA 30305

WARLICK, WILSON, judge; b. Newton, N.C., Mar. 8, 1892; s. Thomas M. and Martha Elizabeth (Wilson) W.; B.S., Catawaba Coll., 1910, LL.D. (hon.), 1936; LL.B., U. N.C., 1913 (pres. Law Sch. 1912-13); m. Kittie Reed Hipp, Oct. 24, 1925; children—Martha Redd (Mrs. William Brame), Thomas Wilson. Admitted to N.C. bar, 1913; practiced law, Newton, 1913-30; judge Superior Ct., 16th Jud. Dist., 1930-48; U.S. dist. judge Western Dist. N.C. since 1949. Chmn. N.C. Probation Commn, 1937—. Served as lt., G-2, A.E.F., Adj. Gen. Dept., World War I. Mem. N.C. Bar Assn., S.A.R., Am. Legion, 40 et 8, Alpha Tau Omega, Phi Delta Phi. Democrat. Presbyn. (elder). Mason. Club: Catawba Country. Office: Court House Bldg Newton NC 28658

WARMAN, MARY KATHERINE OCKERMAN, ednl. adminstr.; b. Burgin, Ky., Sept., 1924; d. Everett Listen and Jenny Katherine (Scifres) Ockerman; student, U. Md., 1959-62; M.A. in Edn., Murray State U., 1962-67, Ed.S. in Sch. Adminstrn., 1972; m. James A. Warman, Apr. 5, 1942 (div. June 1962); children—James A., Everett Michael, Jenny Katherine, Arthur Louis. Substitute tchr. Hopkins County Bd. Edn., Madisonville, Ky., 1962-63; tchr. Outwood Hosp. and Sch., Dawson Springs, Ky., 1963-65, asst. prin., 1965-67, prin., 1967-69, instnl. program dir., 1969-72; unit dir., Oakwood, Somerset, Ky., 1972—. Mem. Am. Assn. Mental Deficiency, Am. Speech Assn., Internat. Platform. Assn., Ky. Personnel and Guidance Assn., Ky. Assn. Tchr. Edn., N.E.A., Bus. Profl. Women's Club, Kappa Delta Pi. Address: 603 W Columbia St Somerset KY 42501

WARNDORF, EUGENE ROBERT, plastics mfg. co. exec.; b. Covington, Ky., Jan. 27, 1933; s. Eugene Joseph and Claea (Frey) W.; student Villamadonna Coll., 1956-57, U. Cin., 1958-61; m. Beverly Jean Burkhart, Mar. 2, 1957; 1 dau., Kellie Jean. Pres., Bellevue O.H.M. Inc. (Ky.), 1959—, also chmn. bd.; pres., dir. Thermocor Chem. and Mfg. Co., Erlanger, Ky., 1965-72; pres. Continental Plastics Inc., Covington, Ky., 1972—, also dir; pres., dir. Acrylo-Craft Mfg. Inc., Sharonville, Ohio, v.p., dir. J. G. Roth Inc., bd. dirs Campbell County Youth Club Inc. Served with USAF, 1952-56. Recipient Distinguished Service awards K.C., 1967, V.F.W., 1968, Outstanding Airmen award of month 1956; named Ky. col. Mem. Soc. Plastics Engrs., Soc. Cosmetic Chemists, V.F.W. (honor degree 1965, comdr. 9th dist. 1968, chmn. Ky. dept. 1969, life), Am. Legion, Cath. War Vets., Newport Shopping Center Mchts. Assn. (v.p., dir. 1969—), Fraternal Order of Police. K.C., Elk. Club: Dayton (Ky.) Golf. Research on water filtration systems, radar height finders, active chem. formulations. Home: 34 Haywood Ct Ft Thomas KY 41075 Office: 3208 Dixie Hwy Erlanger KY 41018

WARNER, ADDISON WHEELOCK, oil producer; b. Geneva, Ill., June 5, 1899; s. Henry Dimock and Harriette King (Young) W.; student Dartmouth, 1917; B.S., Stanford, 1922; m. Helen Christopher, Dec. 25, 1924; children— Ann Wheelock (Mrs. Kimball), Addison Wheelock. Mgr. investor's aid dept. Chgo. Jour. Commerce, 1922-26; mgr. statis. dept. Stevenson, Perry & Stacy, 1926-27; sales mgr. Robert Stevenson & Co., 1927-28; gen. mgr. Kissell, Kinnicutt & Co., Chgo., 1929-30; sr. partner Addison Warner & Co., 1930-38, pres., 1938-43; now oil producer, also chmn. bd., pres. Imco Dog Food. Bd. dirs. Chgo. Area Project, 1934-53; trustee Union League Boys' Club, 1933-53, pres., 1938-40; chmn. finance com., trustee South Side Boys' Club, 1938-53. Served as flying cadet, U.S. Army, 1918-19; apptd. 2d lt., A.S.S. Res. Corps, 1919. Mem. Order Founders and Patriots Am., Chgo. Stanford Alumni Assn. (pres. 1938-47), S.A.R., Mayflower Soc., Chi Psi. Clubs: Adventurers, Union League (Chgo.); Petroleum (Ft. Worth). Address: 4512 Ester Dr Fort Worth TX 76114

WARNER, ALBIN PAUL, educator; b. Chgo., July 11, 1923; s. Roman and Rose (Meger) W.; B.S., U. Ill., 1948, M.S., 1949; Ph.D., U. Mich., 1952; m. Kathleen May Doyle, Feb. 9, 1948; 1 son, Thomas Paul. Instr. physiol. anatomy and phys. edn. U. Ill., Urbana, 1947-49, extension instr., 1951-54; instr. phys. edn. U. Mich., Ann Arbor, 1949-51; dir. health and phys. edn. Champaign (Ill.) Community Schs., 1951-53; prof., dir. DePaul U. Coll. Phys. Edn., Chgo., 1953-62; prof., head dept. health, phys. edn. and recreation Okla. State U., Stillwater, 1962—; prof. grad. sch. Millikin U., 1952. Served with

USAAF, 1942-46. Mem. Am., Okla. assns. for health, phys. edn. and recreation, Nat. Coll. Phys. Edn. Assn. for Men, Am. Council Adminstrs. in Health, Phys. Edn. and Recreation, Am. Coll. Sports Medicine. Rotarian (pres. 1966-67), Club: Stillwater Golf and Country. Editorial bd. Physical Educator. Home: 2323 W 9th St Stillwater OK 74074

WARNER, CLARENCE E., chmn. Okla. Rep. Com.; b. Booker, Tex., Oct. 31, 1938; s. Virgil O. and Mabel (Arnett) W.; B.A., Kan. State Tchrs. Coll., 1960; M.S., Okla. State U., 1966; m. Ona C. Oldfield, June 5, 1960; 1 dau., Catharine Lynette. Instr. Sterling Coll., 1963; asst. prof. chemistry Phillips U., Enid, Okla., 1963-68. Chmn. Okla. Edn. Council, 1967-68. Chmn. Garfield County (Okla.) Young Republicans, 1965, 66; Rep. precinct chmn. Garfield County, 1965-68; 6th dist. chmn. Okla. Young Rep. Fedn., 1967-68; Rep. state committeeman Garfield County, 1967-68; chmn. Okla. Rep. Com., 1969—; adminstrv. asst. to congressman, 1969. Served to capt. Okla. N.G., 1957—. Mem. Am. Chem. Soc., Am. Assn. U. Profs., Lambda Delta Lambda, Kappa Mu Epsilon, Phi Lambda Upsilon, Alpha Kappa Lambda. Methodist. Home: 11201 Dover Ct Surrey Hills Yukon OK 73099*

WARNER, GEORGE DEWEY, JR., lawyer; b. Greenwood, Miss., Nov. 7, 1929; s. George Dewey and Louise (Coleman) W.; B.S., Miss. State U., 1951; J.D., U. Miss., 1955; m. Nancy Amanda Wilson, Feb. 14, 1970; 1 dau., Elizabeth; children by previous marriage— Deborah, Louanne, Dewey, Cole. Admitted to Miss. bar, 1955; practiced in Meridian, Miss., 1955—; mem. firm Harvey B. Ray, 1966—; dist. atty., Meridian, Miss., 1964-72. Prof. law Meridian Jr. Coll., 1955— Served with USAF, 1951-53, 61-62. Home: 3234 Poplar Springs Dr Meridian MS 39301 Office: 1000 20th Av Meridian MS 39301

WARNER, JACK WESTERVELT, paper co. exec.; b. Decatur, Ill., July 28, 1917; s. Herbert David and Mildred (Westervelt) W.; B.B.A., Washington and Lee U., 1940; m. Elizabeth Turner Butler, Aug. 26, 1939; children— Jonathan Westervelt, David Turner. With Gulf States Paper Corp., Tuscaloosa, Ala., 1946—, exec. v.p., 1950-57, pres., 1957—, chmn., 1959—; dir. So. Ry. System; pres. Warrior Tombigbee Devel. Assn., 1957-60; dir. City Nat. Bank Tuscaloosa. Pres. YMCA Met. Tuscaloosa, 1971; Chmn. bd. Ala. Council Econ. Edn.; pres. Ala. Hunter-Jumper Assn.; dir. Ala. C. of C. Trustee Washington and Lee U. Served with AUS, 1941-45; CBI. Named Man of Year, Ala. Council for Nat. Mgmt. Assn., 1960, Sigma Alpha Epsilon, U. Ala., 1960. Mem. Tuscaloosa C. of C. (pres 1963-64), Am. Forestry Assn., Newcomen Soc. N.Am., Omicron Delta Kappa, Sigma Alpha Epsilon. Rotarian. Clubs: Indian Hills Country, Tuscaloosa Country. Home: 11 Pinehurst St Tuscaloosa AL 35401 Office: PO Box 3199 Tuscaloosa AL 35401

WARNER, JEFF EMANUEL, orgn. exec.; b. Thomasville, N.C., Nov. 18, 1929; s. Robert Vance and Mamie (Miller) W.; B.S., E. Carolina Coll., 1951; m. Mary Lois Jester, Dec. 20, 1950; children—Jeff E., Mary MacDonald. Tchr. pub. schs., Wilmington and Thomasville, N.C., 1951-57; mgr. Thomasville C. of C., 1957-59; exec. mgr. Martinsville (Va.) Henry County C. of C., 1959-60; dist. mgr. Southeastern div. C. of C. of U.S., Jacksonville, Fla., 1960-61; mgr. pub. affairs dept. Greensboro (N.C.) C. of C., 1961-66; exec. v.p. Danville (Va.) C. of C., 1966—. Sec.-treas. Danville Indsl. Devel., Inc., Danville Area Devel. Found.; dir. Roman Eagle Meml. Home. Lion. Home: 207 London Bridge Dr Danville VA 24541 Office: 635 Main St Danville VA 24541

WARNER, JOHN W., lawyer, educator; b. Amarillo, Tex., June 4, 1936; s. Arthur Greeley and Janet (Miller) W.; B.A., Tex. A. and M., 1958; LL.B., U. Tex., 1962; m. Judith Diane Mumma, Dec. 30, 1961; children—Michael, Sandra Kay, Melanie, Patricia. Admitted to Tex. bar, 1962; gen. practice law, Pampa, 1962—; instr. Dale Carnegie Inst., Tex. and Okla., 1964—; municipal ct. judge, 1963-68; atty., county atty., 1969—. Dist. commr. Boy Scouts Am., 1967-70. Incorporator Pampa Youth Council, Inc., 1968—, Southwest Indian Orgn., Inc., 1969. Named Adult Leader of Year, Pampa High Sch. Key Club, 1966, Pampa Outstanding Young Man, 1969. Mem. Am. Trial Lawyers Assn., Am., Gray County bar assns., State Bar Tex., Pampa Jr. C. of C. (pres. 1969-70, state legal counsel 1970-71). Methodist. Club: Democratic (pres. 1963) (Gray County). Home: 2111 Dogwood Pampa TX 79065 Office: 119 E Kingsmill St Pampa TX 79065

WARNER, RONALD LEE, nutritionist; b. Tulsa, May 31, 1941; s. Leland Ward and Burlah Eleanor (Bird) W.; B.S., U. Mo., 1963, M.S., 1965; Ph.D., U. Ky., 1969; m. Betty Angeline Gibson, June 5, 1971. Cons. nutritionist Ralston-Purina, St. Louis and Atlanta, 1969-71; nutritionist Farr Better Feed Co., Hereford, Tex., 1971—; instr. U. Mo., 1964-66. Ralston-Purina Summer fellow, 1962. Mem. Am. Soc. Animal Sci., Sigma Xi (asso.), Gamma Sigma Delta, Phi Eta Sigma, Alpha Zeta. Contbr. articles profl. jours. Home: 718 Thunderbird St Hereford TX 79045 Office: Progressive Rd Hereford TX 79045

WARNKEN, DONALD EUGENE, civil engr.; b. Tulsa, Sept. 12, 1932; s. Merle O. and Velma (Young) W.; B.S., U. Tulsa, 1955; postgrad. U. Kan., summer 1966; m. Twyla M. Dreiling, Aug. 18, 1956; children—Dean, David, Duane. Jr. petroleum engr., Pan Am. Petroleum Corp., Vivian, La., 1955-57, Monroe, La., 1959-60; petroleum engr. William H. Pine, Okmulgee, Okla., 1960-62; water resources planner C.E., Tulsa, 1962—. Planning asso. tng. program for water resources planners Bd. Engrs. Rivers and Harbors, Washington, 1970-71. Served with AUS, 1957-59. Registered profl. engr., Okla. Mem. Nat., Okla. socs. profl. engrs. Am. Water Resources Assn., Am. Inst. Planners. Home: 4030 S 92d E Av Tulsa OK 74145 Office: PO Box 61 Tulsa OK 74102

WARNOCK, WILLIAM SHELEY, banker; b. Gonzales, Tex. Mar. 21, 1897; s. William Joseph and Josephine Cecelia (Sheley) W.; ed. high sch., El Paso; m. Catherine Hoffpauir, Apr. 14, 1941; children—William Sheley, Richard Francis, Arnon Scott, Mary Malissa. With Rio Grande Bank & Trust Co., 1914-18, City Nat. Bank, El Paso, Tex., 1919-23, Peyton Packing Co., 1924, Thurston & Grider, accountants, 1925, First Nat. Bank of Nogales, Ariz., 1926-28; with El Paso Nat. Bank, 1928—, exec. v.p., 1957-62, vice chmn. bd., 1962—, also dir.; dir. El Paso Hotel Co.; past dir. El Paso br. Fed. Res. Bank of Dallas. Past mem. bd. dirs. El Paso chpt. A.R.C., El Paso Community Chest. Served to 2d lt., F.A., U.S. Army, 1918. Mem. El Paso C. of C. (past v.p., treas., dir.). Roman Catholic. Elk. K.C. (4 deg.). Clubs: El Paso Country (past pres., treas., dir.), El Paso. Home: 4248 Ridgecrest Dr El Paso TX 79902

WARNS, HOWARD EUGENE, lawyer; b. Corning, N.Y., Sept. 25, 1921; s. Howard Otten and Olive (Lomison) W.; LL.B., U. Fla., 1948; m. Marjorie A. Owens, Aug. 20, 1946; children—Thomas Eugene, Patricia Ann, Beverly Louise. Admitted to Fla. bar, 1948; gen. practice. St. Petersburg, 1948—; part owner Owosso Hotel, 1954—; municipal judge City of St. Petersburg, 1964—. Hon. life dir. All Children's Hosp., St. Petersburg, 1955—, pres., 1964-65. Served to lt. USNR, 1942-46. Mem. Am., St. Petersburg bar assns., Fla. Bar, Am. Legion, Nat. Sojourner, Trial Lawyers Assn. Democrat. Methodist. Mason, Elk. Home: 7321 2d Av S St Petersburg FL 33707 Office: Hall Bldg St Petersburg FL 33701

WARR, C(LIFFORD) MICHAEL, evangelist, clergyman; b. Ellijay, Ga., Oct. 23, 1918; s. Clifford William and Dorothy O'Delia (Kincaid) W.; A.B., Mercer U., 1944; B.D., Southwestern Bapt. Theol. Sem., 1947, M.Ed., 1957; m. Sara Nelle Vaughn, Sept. 3, 1946; 1 son, Daniel Lee. Accountant, Home Owners Loan Corp., Atlanta, 1936-40; ordained to ministry Bapt. Ch., 1941; asso. pastor Met. Bapt. Ch., Washington, 1947-48; pastor Luther Rice Meml. Bapt. Ch., Washington, 1948-53, Coll. Av. Bapt. Ch., Fort Worth, 1953-57, First Bapt. Ch., Rock Hill, S.C., 1957-68; So. Bapt. evangelist, Atlanta, 1968-71; pastor Jackson Hill Bapt. Ch., Atlanta, 1971—. Guest tchr., numerous churchwide and area wide Bible confs. Trustee Southwestern Bapt. Theol. Sem., 1949-54, Midwestern Bapt. Theol. Sem., 1961—; pres. Pastors Conf., Rock Hill, 1961-62, Fort Worth, 1955-56. Mem. York County Bapt. Assn. (moderator 1963-64), Blue Key. Address: 1403-7 Ponce de Leon Av NE Atlanta GA 30307

WARREN, ALEXANDER, III, agr. packing co. exec.; b. Haines City, Fla., Apr. 11, 1927; s. Alexander and Mabel (Keeter) W.; B.A.S., U. Fla., 1950; m. Elsie Claire Recker, June 27, 1951; children—Alexander Warren IV, Stephen R., Kathern K. Trainee DiGeorgio Fruit Corp., N.Y.C., 1950-53; asst. sales mgr. Lucerne Park Fruit Assn., Winter Haven, Fla., 1953-55, sales mgr., 1955-58; sales mgr. Pipping Packing Co., Winter Haven, 1958-59; mgr. Warren Brothers Citrus Growers Partnership, Haines City, 1958-71; gen. mgr. Warren Estate Citrus Groves, Haines City, 1963-70; founder, pres. Warren Brothers Packing, Inc., Haines City, Fla., 1965—; dir. State Bank, Haines City, 1968-71. Dist. chmn. Gulf Ridge council Boy ScouS Am., 1956-58, mem. exec. bd., 1957-71. Served with USNR, 1944-45. Mem. C. of C., Alpha Tau Omega. Presbyn. (deacon). Elk, Mason, Rotarian. Home: 1150 N Lake Otis Dr Winter Haven FL 33880 Office: PO Box 55 Cypress Gardens FL 33880

WARREN, EUGENE ROLFE, lawyer; b. Forrest City, Ark., Sept. 29, 1910; s. Oliver N. and Sula (Snyder) Warren; LL.B., U. Ark., 1933; m. Betty S. Owen; 1 dau., Dawne (Mrs. Victor G. Attwood). Admitted to Ark. bar, 1933; asso. House, Moses & Holmes, 1933-45; partner Bailey, Warren & Bullion, 1946-58, Warren & Bullion (all Little Rock), 1958—; gen. counsel Ark. Med. Soc., 1948—, Ark. Med. Bd., 1948—, Ark State Bd. Pharmacy, 1962—, Ark Edn. Assn., 1950—, Classroom Tchrs. Assn., 1950—. Dir. Pulaski Heights Bank of Little Rock, Ark. & Ozarks Ry., Transp. Properties, Inc., Ark. Motor Coaches, Ltd., Inc. Served to lt. USNR, 1944-46. Mem. Am., Ark. bar assns., Am. Law Inst., Am. Legion, Central Ark. Camellia Soc. (pres. 1959-60), Kappa Alpha, Phi Alpha Delta. Episcopalian (pres. Epis. Churchmen of Ark. 1958-59). Mason. Home: 7724 W Markham St Little Rock AR 72205 Office: Tower Bldg Little Rock AR 72201

WARREN, FOREST GLEN, economist; b. Kouts, Ind., Dec. 15, 1913; s. Joseph Allen and Mary (Philpott) W.; B.S., Purdue U., 1937; Ph.D., U. Ill., 1945; m. Olive Louise Lauterbach, Nov. 17, 1942; children—Mary Anne, Richard Henry. Asst. to mgr. Grassmer Land Co., Kouts, Ind., 1932-33; asst. in agrl. econs. U. Ill., Urbana, 1937-41; economist Lend Lease Adminstrn. and Fgn. Econs. Adminstrn., 1942-45, U.S. Dept. Commerce, 1945-60; sr. economist Export-Import Bank U.S., Washington, 1960-66; economist U.S. Dept. Agr., Chgo., 1941-42, agrl. economist in charge farm mortgage credit research, Washington, 1966—. Pres., Warren Lands, Inc., Kouts, 1948—. Mem. Am., Am. Farm econ. assns., Am. Soybean Assn., Nat. Econ. Club, Ceres, Sigma Xi, Gamma Sigma Delta, Alpha Chi Rho. Methodist. Club: Blue Ridge Mountain Country (Harpers Ferry, Va.). Contbr. articles to profl. publs. Home: 216 Lawton St Falls Church VA 22046 Office: US Dept Agr 500 12th St SW Washington DC 20024

WARREN, FRANK EDWARD, newspaper exec.; b. Navasota, Tex., Dec. 29, 1919; s. William S. and Myra (Otts) W.; B.B.A., S. Tex. Coll. Commerce, 1948; m. Mildred Ellen Guinn, Nov. 14, 1941; children—Cynthia Lea, Richard Alan. Staff mem. Houston Chronicle Pub. Co., 1937-50, chief accountant, 1950-52, asst. sec.-treas., controller, 1952-58, sec.-treas., 1958-65, became exec. v.p., gen. mgr., 1965, now pres., dir.; dir. Belfort State Bank, Rusk Corp. Served with USAAC, 1942-45. C.P.A., Tex. Mem. Tex. Soc. C.P.A.'s Presbyn. Home: 11615 Windy Lane Houston TX 77024 Office: 512-20 Travis Houston TX 77002

WARREN, FRED BYERS, statistician; b. Jewell County, nr. Courtland, Kan., July 21, 1929; s. Ronald Homer and Ellen (Morlan) W.; B.S., Kans. State U., 1951; M.E.S., N.C. State Coll. at Raleigh, 1967; m. Wanda Mae Archer, Dec. 28, 1956; children—Mary Louise, Joseph William, Ronald Archer. Statistician, U.S. Dept. Agr., Washington, 1955-67, math. statistician, 1967—. Served with USAF, 1951-55. Mem. Am. Statis. Assn. Methodist. Home: 4916 Bristow Dr Annandale VA 22003 Office: S Agrl Bldg Washington DC 20025

WARREN, FREDERICK MARSHALL, ret. army officer, judge; b. Newport, Ky., Aug. 23, 1903; s. William Ulysses and Katherine (Lampe) W.; A.B., LL.B., LL.M., LL.D., U. Cin.; m. Peggy Beaton, Feb. 20, 1926; 1 son, Frederick Marshall. Various positions with lumber and millwork cos., 1926-32; police judge, Southgate, Ky., 1932-35; admitted to Ky. bar, 1935; city atty., Southgate, 1935-40, 46-49; city solicitor, Newport, 1950-52; county judge, Campbell County, 1954-58; cons. to under sec. army, 1958; spl. asst. to asst. sec. army for manpower personnel and res. forces, 1959; recalled to active duty as maj. gen. U.S. Army, 1959; chief U.S. Army Res. and ROTC Affairs, 1959-63; circuit judge 17th Jud. Dist. Ky., Newport, 1964—. Field rep. Alcoholic Beverage Control Bd. Ky., 1949; mem. U.S. Army Gen. Staff com. N.G. and army res. policy, 1953-56; mem. res. forces policy bd. Dept. Def., 1958-59. Served to col. AUS, 1941-46. Decorated D.S.M., Silver Star, Bronze Star, Army Commendation medal (U.S.); Croix de Guerre (France, Belgium). Mem. Am., Ky., Campbell County (past pres.) bar assns., Am. Legion, V.F.W., D.A.V., Assn. U.S. Army, Res. Officers Assn. (past nat. v.p.), Mil. Order World Wars. Mason, Elk. Home: 20 Crow Hill Fort Thomas KY 41075 Office: Courthouse Newport KY 40272

WARREN, GEORGE CARLTON, JR., baking co. exec.; b. Metter, Ga., Oct. 8, 1925; s. George Carlton and Hessie (Harper) W.; student Northwestern U. Inst. Mgmt., 1962; children—George Carlton III, Nancy Ann. Salesman, supr. Colonial Baking Co., Augusta, Ga., 1946-51, supr., Gulfport, Miss., 1951-52, sales mgr., Columbus, Ga., 1952-54, Chattanooga, 1954-56, gen. mgr., 1960-61; sales service rep. Campbell Taggart, Inc., Dallas, 1956-60, dir. sales service, 1961-65, v.p. sales and advt., 1965-70, sr. v.p. sales and advt., 1970—. Mem. Dallas Sales and Marketing Execs. Methodist. Mason. Home: 10006 Regal Park Lane Dallas TX 75230 Office: PO Box 2640 Dallas TX 75221

WARREN, GEORGE FRANCIS, JR., editor; b. Snow Hill, N.C., Sept. 12, 1934; s. George Francis and Mary (McRae) W.; student U. N.C., 1952-55; m. Mary Lou Jones, June 24, 1956; children—William Duncan, Mary McRae, George Francis III. Reporter-photographer Reidsville (N.C.) Rev., 1956-58; Thomasville reporter High Point (N.C.) Enterprise, 1958-60; asst. city editor, 1961-64; Sunday editor Goldsboro (N.C.) News-Argus, 1964-66; mng. editor Kinston (N.C.) Daily Free Press, 1966-71; copy editor Durham (N.C.) Morning Herald, 1970-71, state editor, 1971—. Vice pres. Warren & Mewborn, Inc., Snow Hill, 1955—. Pres. Goldsboro Urban Renewal Citizens Orgn., 1966; v.p. Reach the South Vietnamese People, 1965; mem. High Point All American City Com., 1963, Goldsboro Ballet Bd., 1965; chmn. Kinston Area Outward Bound Sch. Com., 1967; pres. N.C. Soc. for Autistic Children, 1969-72. Dir. High Point Young Democratic Club, 1964. Recipient Spot News award, 1961, N.C. Press. Assn., Resolution City Problems award, 1964. Mem., pres. Wayne Lit. Soc. 1964-65. Episcopalian. Home: Rt 7 Farrington Rd Durham NC 27707 Office: Market St Durham NC 27701

WARREN, GERALD LEE, govt. ofcl.; b. Hastings, Neb., Aug. 17, 1930; s. Hie Ellis and Linnie (Williamson) W.; A.B., U. Neb., 1952; m. Euphemia Florence Brownell, Nov. 5, 1965; children—Gerald Benjamin, Euphemia Brownell. Reporter Lincoln (Neb.) Star, 1951-52; reporter, asst. city editor San Diego Union, 1956-61; bus. rep. Copley News Service, 1961-63; city editor San Diego Union, 1963-68, asst. mng. editor, 1968-69; dep. press sec. to Pres. Nixon, 1969—. Served to lt. (j.g.) USNR, 1952-56. Mem. Sigma Delta Chi, Sigma Nu. Republican. Episcopalian. Home: 3412 O St NW Washington DC 20007 Office: The White House Washington DC

WARREN, ILA FERN, social worker; b. Peoria, Ia.; d. John Wesley and Lillie L. (Hess) Warren; B.A., Penn Coll., 1928; M.A., U. Chgo. Sch. Social Service Adminstrn., 1950. Tchr., Community High Sch., Dakota, Ill., 1928-37; homefinding cons. Children's Service League, Springfield, Ill., 1939-46; supr. Children's Div., Family and Children's Service, Mpls., 1946-49; supr. Child Guidance Bur., East St. Louis, Ill., field instr. George Warren Brown Sch. Social Work, St. Louis, 1950-54; cons. Mental Health div. Tex. Dept. Health, Austin, vis. tchr. Snyder Pub. Schs., 1954-58, cons. psychiat. worker Central Office, 1958-65; adminstrv. cons. Community Services div. Tex. Dept. Mental Health and Retardation, 1965-69, coordinator Title XIX, 1969—. Bd. dirs. Austin-Travis County Mental Health Assn. Mem. Nat. Assn. Social Workers (del. Tex. council, pres. Tex. state council 1968-70), Acad. Certified Social Workers. Methodist (ofcl. bd.). Home: 5005 Manor Rd Apt 101 Austin TX 78723 Office: Capitol Sta Box S Austin TX 78711 also 4405 N Lamar Blvd Austin TX 78711

WARREN, JEFFREY COLE, govt. ofcl.; b. Gadsden, Ala., May 1, 1937; s. Alden Cole and Elizabeth McNeil (Andrews) W.; B.A., Samford U., 1958; m. Frances Pugh, Feb. 16, 1963; 1 son, Ryan Earl. Staff writer Newport News (Va.) Daily Press, 1962-63, Ledger-Star, Norfolk, Va., 1963-66; dir. pub. relations Blount Bros. Corp., Montgomery, Ala., 1966-69; dep. exec. asst. to Postmaster Gen., Washington, 1969-71, exec. asst., 1971—. Mem. del. assembly United Appeal, Montgomery, Ala., 1967-68; exec. com. Southwest Fairfax (Va.) Citizens Assn., 1970-71. Dep. finance dir. Jim Martin for Gov. of Ala., 1966. Served to lt. USNR, 1959-62. Recipient Gold Medal award, Silver Medal award Montgomery Indsl. Editors Assn., 1968. Mem. Pub. Relations Soc. Am., Montgomery Indsl. Editors Assn. (v.p. 1967-68). Republican. Episcopalian. Home: 11526 Fairfax Station Rd Fairfax Station VA 22039 Office: 1200 Pennsylvania Av Washington DC 20060

WARREN, JOHN LEAMING, ret. air force officer; b. Holdenville, Okla., Nov. 6, 1906; s. Frank L. and Annie G. (Leaming) W.; student U. Mo., Okla. U., 1923-26; LL.B., Cumberland U., 1928; m. Shelagh D. MacKey, Apr. 30, 1949; 1 dau., Valery Anne. Admitted to Okla. bar, 1928; mem. law firm Warren & Warren, Holdenville, 1928-40. Served with USAF, 1940-63, ret. Decorated Legion of Merit, Republic Korea Mil. Merit Choongmoo medal. Mem. S.A.R., Okla. Bar Assn., Kappa Alpha, Episcopalian. Club: St. Petersburg Yacht. Home: 858 Placido Way St Petersburg FL 33704

WARREN, JULIAN BENJAMIN, lawyer; b. Culverton, Ga., June 22, 1909; s. Lindsay C. and Louise (Rosser) W.; B.Ph., Emory U., 1931, LL.B., 1933; m. Martha Malone, June 30, 1936; children—Ann Malone, Frances Lynn. Prin., Hogansville High Sch., 1929-30; admitted to Ga. bar, 1934; gen. practice Atlanta, 1934, Griffin, Ga., 1934-37, Monticello, 1937—; atty. City of Monticello, 1965—, Jasper County, 1968—; v.p., also chmn. bd. Bank of Monticello; v.p. Alcovy North Inc; dir Monticello-Jasper County Devel. Corp. Jasper County Devel. Co., Inc. Served with AUS, 1944-46. Mem. Am., Ga. bar assns., Am. Judicature Soc., Comml. Law League Am., Am. Legion (state comdr. 1952-53), Tau Kappa Alpha. Home: 39 Forsyth St Monticello GA 31064 Office: Greene St Monticello GA 31064

WARREN, L(EWIS) COY, petroleum co. exec.; b. Canyon, Tex., Dec. 10, 1922; s. Lewis Alfred and Ruth (Miles) W.; B.S., U. Tex., 1948; m. Alice Slicker, May 1944 (dec. Sept. 1959); children—Connie, Austin, Greg; m. 2d, Elizabeth Gene Austin, July 1, 1968. Geologist, Stanolind Oil & Gas Co., Midland, Tex., 1948-49; cons. geologist, Cisco, Tex., Abilene, Tex., 1949-54; pvt. pracIce geology firm, Abilene, 1954-64; v.p. exploration Laco Oil Co., Abilene, 1964—; dir. Citizens Nat. Bank, Abilene. Served with USAAF, 1943-46. Decorated Air medal, 4 Bronze Star medals. Mem. Am. Assn. Petroleum Geologists, Am. Inst. Profl. Geologists, Ind. Petroleum Assn. Am., Am. Geol. Inst., West Central Tex. Oil and Gas Assn., Am. Inst. M.E., Abilene Geol. Soc. (v.p.), Petroleum Club (dir.). Presbyn. Home: 1817 Woodridge Dr Abilene TX 79605 Office: Citizens Bank Bldg 402 Cypress Abilene TX 79604

WARREN, LINDSAY C., JR., lawyer, state legislator; b. Washington, N.C., Oct. 8, 1924; B.S., U. N.C., 1948, J.D., 1951. Admitted to N.C. bar, 1951; mem. N.C. Senate, 1963—. Mem. Goldsboro (N.C.) Sch. Bd., 1959-62. Trustee Wayne County Meml. Hosp. Mem. N.C. Bar Assn. (pres. 1969—), N.C. State Bar, Phi Delta Phi, Order of Coif. Address: PO Box 1616 Goldsboro NC 27530*

WARREN, MATTHEW FORREST, assn. exec.; b. Pueblo, Colo., Aug. 12, 1918; s. Marshall Henry and Lola Maude (Gentry) Matts; ed. Kan. State Coll. of Architecture, 1937; m. Dorothy Florence Meeks, Aug. 2, 1940; children—D. Sharon, Marcia Louise, Kenneth W. Information officer Anglo-Am. Carribbean Commn., Dept. State, Washington, 1944-45; news commentator Mut. Broadcasting System-WOL, 1945-46; program mgr. Arlington-Fairfax Broadcasting Co., Arlington, Va., 1946-50; dir. news and pub. affairs Dumont-Metromedia Corp. Washington 1951-62; dir. pub. affairs Evening Star Broadcasting Corp.-WMAL, 1962-64; bur. chief Broadcast div. RKO Gen. Corp., 1964-67; nat. dir. pub. relations Goodwill Industries of Am. Inc., 1968—; pres. Warren Properties, 1961—; cons. Motion Picture sect. Johns Hopkins Applied Sci. Labs., Balt., 1966—; contractor, producer dir. USIA Voice of Am., 1957—; dir. Citizen's Band Radio Operators Nat., 1969—. Mem. Donaldson Run Citizens Assn. Mem. Pres.'s Nat. Indsl. Adv. Bd., FCC, 1966—. Served with C.E., AUS, 1941-44. Recipient Award for Exceptional Public Service in Broadcasting, Sylvania, 1957; Emmy Award for best locally produced television Documentary (Child Beating), 1964. Mem. Pub. Relations Soc. of Am., Am. Mgmt. Assn., Nat. Assn. Real Estate Bds., Nat. Pub. Relations Council Health and Pub. Welfare Services. Baptist. Club: Nat. Press (Washington). Producer 39 half-hour documentaries for TV on Aspects of Washington, 1963-64; moderator of Georgetown University Forum TV and Radio program nationally syndicated, 1953-61. Home: 3806 N 25th St Arlington VA 22207 Office: 9200 Wisconsin Av Washington DC 20014

WARREN, VARINA TAYLOR (MRS. PAUL DESHA WARREN), dentist; b. North Wilkesboro, N.C., Jan. 24, 1898; d. William Andrew and Carrie Lee (Jones) Taylor; student Queens Coll., 1915, N.C. Coll. for Women, 1916, 17; D.D.S., Vanderbilt U., 1922; m. Paul Desha Warren, Sept. 18, 1923; children—Paul Desha, William Bonner. Instr., Vanderbilt U. Dental Sch., 1922-24; dentist Tenn. Sch. for Blind, Nashville, 1922-24, practice dentistry, Huntsville, Ala., 1924—. Mem. Nat. (life), Ala. dental assns., N. Ala. Dental Soc. (pres.), Am. Legion Aux. Presbyn. (tchr. Sunday sch.). Club: Altrusa (pres. 1952-53). Home: 1003 Ward Av Huntsville AL 35801 Office: Times Bldg Huntsville AL 35801

WARREN, WILSON F., police officer, C. of C. exec.; b. Prescott, Ark., June 1, 1918; s. Richard Cunningham, Sr., and Florence (Alethia) W.; ed. Sam Houston State U.; m. Florence E. Lloyd, Jan. 22, 1942; 1 son, Lloyd Michael. Police officer, Dallas, 1945—, sta. supr. S.E. patrol dist., 1966—; exec. v.p. Wilmer (Tex.) C. of C.; tchr. U.S. Army Res. Sch., Dallas Police Acad. Mem. Dallas Police Assn. (dir.). Served with AUS, World War II. Decorated Bronze Star, Silver Star, Purple Heart. Mason (Shriner). Home: 237 Walnut Dr Wilmer TX 75172 Office: 6500 Bexar St Dallas TX 75215

WARSHAW, BERTRAM SAUL, cons. civil engr.; b. Bklyn., Mar. 15, 1928; s. Benjamin David and Anna (Wald) W.; B.C.E., Ga. Inst. Tech., 1949; M.S.C.E. U. Miami, 1973; m. Sandra Stein, Sept. 15, 1955; children—Andrew Van, Randy Ladd, Job Lee, Jolie. Area engr. E. I. duPont de Nemours & Co., Savannah River Plant, 1951-53; chief structural insp. Connell & Rader Asso., Miami, 1953-56; structural designer Morton R. Fellman, Cons. Engrs., Miami, 1956-57; structural engr. Jules P. Channing & Asso., Cons. Engr., Miami, 1957-58; staff structural engr. Giller, Payne & Waxman, Miami, 1958-59; pvt. cons. engr. and planner, Miami, 1959—. Active Adult Edn. Program, Dade County, Fla.; asso. structural engr. City Coral Gables, 1963-69; pres. Bertram S. Warshaw & Assos. Inc., cons. engrs., 1969—. Chmn. City Miami Housing Bd. Appeals, 1964-68; chmn. Dade County Bd. Rules and Appeals; v.p. Transp. Terminals Am. Mem. Am. Soc. C.E., Nat. Soc. Profl. Engrs., Fla. Engring. Soc., S.C. Soc. Engrs., Soc. Am. Mil. Engrs., Am. Concrete Inst., N.J. Soc. Profl. Planners, Greater Miami Opera Guild. Club: King's Bay Yacht and Country (Miami, Fla.). Co-patentee in field thin shell concrete constrn. Contbr. articles profl. engring. jours. Home: 4361 Mayfair Dr Miami FL 33133 Office: 1000 NW 57th Av Miami FL 33126

WARTERS, JAMES CARSON, columnist; b. Knoxville, Tenn., Jan. 14, 1928; s. Richards and Kit (Carson) W.; B.S., U. Tenn., 1952; m. Susan Beasley Lyle, Apr. 30, 1955; children—James Carson, Susan Lyle. Reporter, Bristol (Va.) Herald-Courier, 1953; corr. U.P.I., Knoxville, Tenn., 1953-58, bur. mgr., Jacksonville, Fla., 1959-61; asso. editor Howard Publs., Jacksonville, 1961-62; sports columnist Daytona Beach (Fla.) News-Jour. 1962-66; city editor Morning Jour. Daytona Beach, 1966-68; county sports editor Orlando (Fla.) Sentinel Star, 1968-69, sports columnist, 1969—. Served with AUS, 1946-47. Mem. Kappa Sigma. Democrat. Presbyn. Kiwanian. Club: University. Home: 228 Annie St Orlando FL 32806 Office: Sentinel Star Bldg 633 N Orange Av Orlando FL 32802

WASCOM, EARL RAY, city ofcl.; b. Corbin, La., Nov. 26, 1930; s. Charles Wickliffe and Carrie (Coburn) W.; B.S., Southeastern La. Coll., 1956; postgrad. U. Colo., 1959; M.S. in Botany, La. Poly. Inst., 1962; Ph.D., La. State U., 1967; m. Gloria Dean Allen, May 26, 1951; children—Gary Kenneth, Pamela Lynn. With Ethyl Corp., Baton Rouge, 1951-55; field engr. Catalytic Constrn. Co., Baton Rouge, 1957-58; mem. faculty Southeastern La. Coll., Hammond, 1958—, prof. biology, 1967—, also head dept.; mayor, Corbin, La., 1964—. Park ranger Nat. Park Service, Gatlinburg, Tenn., summers, 1956, 57. Bd. dirs. Sci. Fair, Region 8, La., 1961-65. Bd. dirs. Wesley Found. at Southeastern La. Coll. Served with USNR, 1951. Mem. La. Acad. Scis., Assn. Southeastern Biologists, Am. Soc. Plant Taxonomists, Ecol. Soc. Am., Bot. Soc. Am., La. Tchrs. Assn., Phi Kappa Phi. Democrat. Methodist (chmn. ofcl. bd. 1963-66). Mason (Shriner). Home: Route 2 Box 14 Corbin LA 70724 Office: Southeastern La Coll PO Box 814 Hammond LA 70401

WASDEN, WILEY ANDERSON, JR., Republican nat. committeeman, investment adviser; b. Millen, Ga., Jan. 23, 1937;; s. Wiley Anderson and Katherine (Carr) W.; ed. U. Ga.; m. Mary Bell Harrison, Aug. 30, 1958; children—Wiley Anderson III, Robert Hancock, Mary Bell. Formerly asst. trust officer Citizens and So. Nat. Bank, Savannah, Ga.; treas., dir. Abercorn Investors, Inc.; v.p., dir. Savannah Oxygen and Supply Co.; gen. partner Adams & Wasden Enterprises; pres. Wiley A. Wasden Co. Mem. county and dist. Rep. exec. coms.; an organizer 1st Rep. primary, Savannah; chmn. Ga. State Rep. Com., 1969—. Formerly chmn. bd. trustees Savannah Country Day Sch.; treas. Girl Scout Council Inc.; mem. Mayor's Youth Opportunity Council. Served from pvt. to sgt. AUS, 1956-63. Mem. Ga. Alumni Soc. (past dist. v.p.). Address: 80 Dolan Dr/Grimball Pt Savannah GA 31406

WASHBURN, WILCOMB EDWARD, historian; b. Ottawa, Kan., Jan. 13, 1925; s. Harold Edward and Sidsell Marie (Nelson) W.; grad. Phillips Exeter Acad., 1943; A.B., summa cum laude, Dartmouth, 1948; M.A., Harvard, 1951, Ph.D., 1955; m. Lelia Elizabeth Kanavarioti, July 14, 1951; children—Harold Kitsos, Edward Alexandros. Teaching fellow history and lit. Harvard, 1954-55; fellow Inst. Early Am. History and Culture, Williamsburg, Va., 1955-58; instr. Coll. William and Mary, 1955-58; curator div. polit. history Smithsonian Instn., U.S. National Mus., Washington, 1958-65, chmn. dept. Am. studies, 1965—; professorial lectr. Am. U., 1961-63, adj. prof., 1963—. Cons. in research Grad. Sch. Arts and Scis., George Washington U., 1966—. Civil information and edn. officer Toyama Mil. Govt. Team, Toyama Prefecture, Japan, 1946-47. Served with USMCR, 1943-46, 51-52. Fellow Am. Anthrop. Assn.; mem. Am. Soc. Ethnohistory (past pres.), Soc. History Discoveries (past pres.), Am. Studies Assn. (past pres. Chesapeake chpt.), Columbia Hist. Soc. (1st v.p.), Colonial Soc. Mass., Am., So., Western, Va., N.H. hist. assns., Am. Antiquarian Soc., Nat. Congress Am. Indians, Assos. John Carter Brown Library, Archaeol. Inst. Am. Assos. James Ford Bell Library Internat. Soc. Study Symbols, Orgn. Am. Historians, Philos. Soc. Washington, Nat. Trust Historic Preservation, Am. Polit. Sci. Assn., A.A.A.S., Japan-Am. Soc. Washington (bd. trustees), Am. Assn. Museums, Conf. Brit. Studies, Anthrop. Soc. Washington, Internat. Studies Assn., Phi Beta Kappa. Club: Cosmos (Washington). Author: The Governor and the Rebel: A History of Bacon's Rebellion in Virginia, 1957; Red Man's Land/White Man's Law: A Study of the Past and Present Status of The American Indian, 1971. Editor: The Indian and the White Man, 1964. Contbr. articles profl. jours. Home: 2338 Massachusetts Av NW Washington DC 20008 Office: Smithsonian Instn Washington DC 20560

WASHINGTON, EMERY, clergyman; b. Palestine, Ark., Feb; 27, 1935; s. Booker T. and Fannie Mae (Norrington) W.; B.A., Philander Smith Coll., 1957; M.Div., Va. Theol. Sem., 1961; postgrad. Ark. State U., 1966-67; m. Alice Marie Bogard, Oct. 1, 1965; children—Ekila Denese, Marie Antoinette, Emery. Ordained to ministry Episcopal Ch., 1961; vicar in charge Christ Ch. Mission, Forrest City, Ark., 1961-71, St. Andrew's Mission, Pine Bluff, Ark., 1961-66; chaplain U. Ark. at Little Rock, 1971—, lectr., 1971. Chaplain, Christ Ch. Sch., 1961-66; lectr. U. Ark., Fayetteville, 1969; mem. exec. council, canon Episcopal Ch., Diocese of Ark. Mem. Ark. Com. for Disadvantaged, 1971; mem. Ark. Council on Human Relations, 1969—; mem. Ark. Bd. Edn., 1969—, President's Ark. Adv. Com. on Pub. Edn., 1970—. Active Rockefeller and Fulbright campaigns, 1968; exec. dir. St. Francis County Com. for Better Representation, 1969-70. Recipient Bishop's award as outstanding clergyman, 1970. Mem. N.A.A.C.P., Alpha Phi Alpha. Home: 3711 High Dr Little Rock AR 72206 Office: PO Box 6120 Little Rock AR 72206

WASHINGTON, ISAIAH EDWARD, sch. adminstr.; b. nr. Augusta, Ga., Oct. 19, 1908; s. Edward and Sallie (Walker) W.; A.B., Paine Coll., 1937; M.S., Temple U., 1948; Litt.D., Allen U., 1959; m. Justine Wilkinson, Dec. 25, 1940. Tchr. elemn. schs., Augusta, Ga., 1937, prin., 1938, secondary prin., 1964—. Dir. Gwinnett St. Investment Corp., 1962—; tech. assistance specialist Community Action Program, 1966—. Bd. dirs. YMCA, 1958—, chmn. bd., 1965—; dir. Ga.-Carolina council Boy Scouts Am., 1965—. Mem. Am. (regional v.p. 1963-66), Ga. (pres. 1943-45) tchrs. assns., Augusta-Richmond County Voters League, Omega Psi Phi, Sigma Pi Phi. Mason, Elk. Home: 1228 Kent St Augusta GA 30901 Office: 1300 Gwinnett St Augusta GA 30901

WASHINGTON, JAMES AARON, JR., judge D.C. Superior Ct.; b. Asheville, N.C., Feb. 17, 1915; s. James Aaron and Vivian B. (Alston) W.; A.B., Howard U., 1936; LL.B. magna cum laude, 1929; LL.M., Harvard, 1941; m. Ada V. Collins, Jan. 4, 1936; children—Grace C. Alexander, Eleanor J. (Mrs. Ernest Jackson), Vivian A. (Mrs. James Johnson), James Aaron III, Stephen C., Michael G. Atty. Justice Dept., 1942-46; prof. law Howard U., 1946-61, vice dean Sch. Law, 1958-61, Langston prof. law, 1966—, dean, 1969; chmn. D.C. Pub. Ser. Commn.; 1961-66; gen. counsel Transp. Dept., 1969-71; asso. judge Superior Ct., D.C., 1971—. Mem. D.C. Mem. legal staff N.A.A.C.P.; chmn. health and welfare council Model Cities Com.; chmn. police community relations Inst. Nat. Conf. Christians and Jews; chmn. Reconstrn. and Devel. Corp.; mem. com. on legal aid Ct. of Appeals; mem. Com. for Implementation of Pres.'s Report on D.C. Crime. Bd. dirs. Neighborhood Consumer Information Center; trustee Washington Inst. for Quality Edn. Contbr. articles to profl. jours. Home: 14212 Northgate Dr Silver Spring MD 20906 Office: 400 7th St SW Washington DC 20596

WASHINGTON, LEONARD SYLVESTER, JR., librarian; b. New Orleans, July 8, 1924; s. Leonard Sylvester and Olivia Willard (Baranco) W.; B.A., So. U., 1947; M.A., U. Mich., 1949, M.A. in L.S., 1957; m. Earlena Williams, May 25, 1960; children—Alfred, Alvin, Valeria. Instr., Lanston U., 1949-56; reprodn. supt. Engring. Research Inst., U. Mich., 1956-59; librarian So. Univ., New Orleans, 1959—. Served with AUS, 1943-45. Mem. Am., La. library assns., Alpha Phi Alpha. Roman Catholic. Home: 6708 Pauline Dr New Orleans LA 70126 Office: 6400 Press Dr New Orleans LA 70126

WASHINGTON, WALTER E., mayor; b. Dawson, Ga., Apr. 15, 1915; s. William L. and Willie Mae (Thornton) W.; A.B., Howard U., 1938, LL.B., 1948; postgrad. Am. U., 1939-43; LL.D. (hon.), Fisk U., 1968, Georgetown U., 1968, Catholic U., 1969, Boston U., 1969, George Washington U., 1970, Princeton, 1970; L.H.D., Bishop Coll., Dallas, 1970; m. Bennetta Bullock, Dec. 26, 1941; 1 dau., Bennetta (Mrs. Jules-Rosette). Admitted to D.C. bar, 1948, U.S. Supreme Ct., bar, 1952; ofcl. Nat. Capital Housing Authority, 1941-66, exec. dir., 1961-66; chmn. N.Y.C. Housing Authority, 1966-67; mayor-commr. D.C., 1967—. Mem. adv. bd. U.S. Conf. Mayors; vice chmn. Nat. League Cities; mem. ins. panel Nat. Adv. Commn. Civil Disorders. Vice pres. United Community Funds and Councils Am.; past pres. Washington Home Rule Com., Washington Urban League. Trustee, Kennedy Center for Performing Arts; bd. dirs. Washington Council Chs., Nat. Capital Area council Boy Scouts Am., United Planning Orgn., Big Bros. Recipient Career award Nat. Civil Service League, Distinguished Achievement award Howard U.; Nat. Conf. Christian and Jews award; Nat. Bar Assn. award; Washington Archdiocesan award; Community Service award Health and Welfare Council. Mem. Am. Bar Assn., Order of Coif. Clubs: Cosmos, Nat. Lawyers, Federal City (Washington); City (N.Y.C.). Home: 408 T St NW Washington DC 20001 Office: Dist Bldg 14 and E Sts NW Washington DC 20004

WASILEWSKI, VINCENT THOMAS, trade assn. exec.; b. Athens, Ill., Dec. 17, 1922; s. Alex and Anna (Gillespie) W.; A.B. in Polit. Sci., U. Ill., 1948, J.D., 1949; m. Patricia Callery, June 17, 1950; children—Jan, Susan, Catherine, Terese, Thomas, James. Admitted to Ill. bar, 1950; mem. staff Nat. Assn. Broadcasters, Washington, 1949—, v.p. govt. affairs, 1960-61, exec. v.p., 1961-65, pres., 1965—. Mem. U.S. Nat. Commn. for UNESCO, 1956-60. Served with USAAF, 1942-45. Decorated D.F.C. with oak leaf cluster, Air medal with oak leaf cluster. Mem. Advt. Fedn. Am. (bd. dirs.), Fed. Communications Bar Assn., Am. Bar Assn., Am. Judicature Soc., Internat. Radio and TV Soc., Order of Coif, Sigma Phi Epsilon, Phi Kappa Phi, Phi Alpha Delta. Roman Catholic. Clubs: Internat. (Wasington); Congressional Country (Potomac, Md.). Home: 6608 Bay Tree Lane Falls Church VA 22041 Office: 1771 N St NW Washington DC 20036

WASSERMAN, JACK, lawyer; b. N.Y.C., Feb. 20, 1913; s. Samuel and Sabina (Hoffman) W.; A.B., Coll. City N.Y., 1932; J.D. cum laude, Harvard, 1935; m. Marie Krempa, June 7, 1941; children— Lorraine De Vera, Michael Owen. With Harvard Legal Aid Soc., 1934-35; admitted to N.Y. bar, 1936; practiced law in N.Y.C., 1936-41; atty. Bd. of Immigration Appeals, 1941-42; sr. atty. Alien Enemy Control Unit, 1942-43; mem. Bd. Immigration Appeals, 1943-46; atty. Alien Enemy Litigation Sect., 1946-47; now partner firm Wasserman & Parker. Asst. gen. counsel Citizens Com. on Displaced Persons, 1947-48; past nat. pres. and legislative rep. Assn. Immigration and Nationality Lawyers. Mem. Bars U.S. Supreme Ct., Bd. of Immigration Appeals, ICC, FCC, Am., N.Y. State, Fed., Internat. bar assns., Nat. Lawyers Club, Am. Trial Lawyers Assn., Internat. Law Assn., Phi Beta Kappa. Author: Immigration Law and Practice. Contbr. articles on immigration and citizenship to mags. Home: 4405 Sedgwick St Washington DC 20016 Office: Warner Bldg Washington DC 20004

WASSERMAN, ROBERT, leather co. exec.; b. St. Joseph, Mo., Feb. 13, 1934; s. Sam and Dorothy Jean (Horwitz) B.; B.S., Washington U., St. Louis, 1955; m. Shirley Anna Mandel, Dec. 25, 1955; children—Natalie, William, Marli. With Lyntone Belts, Inc., Oklahoma City, 1959—, sales mgr., 1968-69, v.p., 1969—, also pres. Lyntone Belts P.R., Inc., Yabucoa, 1971—. Served to lt. (j.g.) Supply Corps, USNR, 1958-59. Vice pres. Okla. Jewish Community Council, 1970. Jewish religion (dir. synagogue). Mem. B'nai B'rith. Home: 2533 NW 60th St Oklahoma City OK 73118 Office: 45 NW 41st St Oklahoma City OK 73118

WASSON, HAROLD PARDEE, ret. educator; b. Barberton, O., Feb. 13, 1902; s. Richard and Josephine (Hill) W.; B.E.E., Ohio State U., 1924; M.A., Columbia, 1932; M.A., Montclair (N.J.) Tchrs. Coll., 1949; m. Alice Ruth Fasig, Dec. 27, 1927 (dec.); 1 son, Harold Pardee; m. 2d, Ethel I. Lindsley, Oct. 1, 1964. Sales engr. Lincoln Elec. Co., 1924-27; math., sci. tchr. Delta (O.) High Sch., 1927-28; math., phys. edn. tchr. Blume High Sch., Wapakoneta, O., 1928-31; math. tchr. Friends Sch., Bklyn., 1931-34; math., phys. edn. tchr East Orange (N.J.) High Sch., 1934-42; asso. prof. math. Newark (N.J.) Coll. Engring., from 1942, now ret.; substitute tchr. Coral Shores Sch., Tavernier, Fla. Served with research projects Army Ordnance, 1943-44. Wasson Athletic Field at Newark Coll. Engring. named in his honor, 1966. Mem. Math. Assn. Am., Math. Assn. N.J., Am. Soc. Promotion Engring. Edn., Am. Assn. U. Profs., Varsity O Assn., Omicron Delta Kappa, Theta Xi. Republican. Presbyn. Club: Torch (Essex County pres. 1963-64). Designer Wasson aperture, a shooting aid. Home: Box 15 Vacation Village FL 33071

WATERFIELD, HARRY LEE, newspaper exec.; b. Calloway County, Ky., Jan. 19, 1911; s. Burnett and Lois (Burton) W.; B.A., Murray (Ky.) State U., 1932; m. Laura Ferguson, June 1, 1933; children—Rose Gayle (Mrs. Robert Hardy), Mrs. Nancy Waterfield Dudgeon, Harry Lee II. Pres., chmn. bd. Investors Heritage Life Ins. Co., Ky. Investors, Inc.; chmn. bd. Investors Heritage Life Ins. Co. Ohio, Investors Heritage Life Ins. Co. of the South; engaged in community newspaper bus., 1932—; pub. Hickman County Gazette, 1934—; farmer, breeder Shorthorn cattle, 1944—; mem. Ky. Ho. of Reps., 1938-47, 50-51, speaker, 1944-46; lt. gov. Ky., 1955-59, 63-67. Chmn. Ky. Legislative Research Commn., 1955-59, 63-67, Ky. Disabled Ex-Servicemen's Bd., 1955-59. Mgr. Kilgore campaign for Democratic nomination Gov. Ky., 1943; Ky. chmn. Roosevelt-Barkley campaign, 1944; dir. orgn. Ky. Dem. Com., 1944-47, sec., 1956-60. Mem. Ky. Press Assn. (past pres.), Farm Bur., Clinton C. of C. Mem. Christian Ch. Mason, Rotarian. Home: Clinton KY 42031 Office: 200 Capital Av Frankfort KY 40601

WATERMAN, JEREMIAH COLWELL, govt. ofcl.; b. Westfield, N.J., Jan. 18, 1904; s. Marcus Butler and Grace Elizabeth (Hampson) W.; A.B., Princeton, 1926; J.D., Columbia, 1931; m. Mary M. Fager, Sept. 1, 1926; children—Suzanna (Mrs. Howard K. Gray), Judith (Mrs. Owen P. Jacobsen). Atty. So. Pacific Co., 1931-45, asst. gen. atty., 1945-51, gen. atty., 1951-66; counsel Steptoe & Johnson, 1966-70; commr. D.C. Pub. Ser. Commn., 1971—, chmn., 1971—; chmn. Washington Met. Area Transit Commn., 1971—. Mem. Zoning Bd. Appeals, Mamaroneck, N.Y., 1950, Councilman, Mamaroneck, 1951-59; mem. D.C. Republican Com., 1964-70, vice-chmn., 1969-70. Mem. Am., D.C. bar assns., N.Y. County Lawyers Assn., Phi Delta Phi. Clubs: Nat. Press, Metropolitan, Captiol Hill (Washington). Home: 2807 O St NW Washington DC 20007 Office: 1625 I St NW Washington DC 20006

WATERS, JOHN MAYO, JR., city ofcl.; b. Arapahoe, N.C., Aug. 1, 1920; s. John Mayo and Lela (Bell) W.; student N.C. State U., 1938-39; B.S., U.S. Coast Guard Acad., 1942; postgrad. U. Miami, 1959-61; m. Peggy O'Neal, Jan. 9, 1945; children—Peggy Ann, John Stephen. Commd. ensign U.S. Coast Guard, 1942, advanced through grades to capt., 1964; coast guard officer, 1942-68, chief search and rescue, 1964-66, chief aviation, 1967; chief div. emergency services Nat. Hwy. Safety Bur., 1967-68; ret., 1968; dir. Pub. Safety, jacksonville, Fla., 1968-70, chief operating officer, 1970—. Mem. Internat. Assn. Fire Chiefs, Internat. Assn. Police Chiefs, Am. Soc. Safety Engrs., Am. Legion, V.F.W., Navy League, Am. Acad. Orthopedic Surgeons (com. on injuries 1968—), N.E. Fla. Heart Assn. (exec. bd. 1969—, pres. 1971), Nat. Acad. Sci. (emergency med. services com. 1969—), A.C.S. (com. trauma 1969—), D.A.V. Rotarian. Author: Rescue at Sea, 1966; Bloody Winter, 1967. Contbr. articles to profl. jours. Home: 4911 Water Oak Lane Jacksonville FL 32210 Office: City Hall Jacksonville FL 32202

WATERS, LOUIS ALBERT, banker; b. Beeville, Tex., July 28, 1938; s. William Berry and Lola Mae (Smith) W.; B.A., Rice Inst., 1960; B.S. in M.E., Rice U., 1962; M.B.A., Harvard, 1966; m. Wanda Lyn Phears, June 5, 1962; children—Louis Albert, Laurel Ann. Asso. mem. firm Hornblower, Hemphill, Noyes & Weeks, N.Y.C., 1966-67; v.p. Underwood, Neuhaus & Co., Houston, 1967-69; chmn. Browning-Ferris Industries, Inc., Houston, 1969—, also dir.; chmn. Fannin Bank, Houston, 1970—. Mem. Am. Soc. M.E., Harvard Bus. Sch. Club Houston. Clubs: Houston, Warwick. Office: Fannin Bank Bldg Houston TX 77025

WATERS, VINCENT FREDERICK, pub. co. exec.; b. Poquetanuck, Conn., Feb. 10, 1904; s. Douglas Henry and Catherine Elizabeth (Flynn) W.; m. Jerry Wheeler, Mar. 10, 1947; children—Claudia Leigh, Douglas V. F., John Douglas. Supt. of erection Maxson Automatic Machinery Co., Westerly, R.I., 1923-28, 30-32; insp., acting mgr., exec. tng. and insp. dept. Sears Roebuck & Co., Memphis, 1928-29; fieldman Memphis Power & Light Co., 1929-30; plant engr. Wrenn Paper Co., Middletown, O., 1933-36; research engr. Champion Paper & Fibre Co., Hamilton, O., 1936-38; tech. asst. sec. T.A.P.P.I., N.Y.C., 1938-43; gen. mgr. Ernest H. Abernethy Pub. Co., Inc., Atlanta, 1943—, editor So. Pulp and Paper Mfr. mag. Served as cons. WPB, World War II. Registered profl. engr., Ga. Mem. Canadian Pulp and Paper Assn., Ga. Engring Soc. (chmn publs. com. 1945-47), Nat. (chmn. publs. com. 1953-57), Ga. (chmn. publs. com. 1948-53; dir. 1948-50; pres. Atlanta chpt. 1949) socs. profl. engrs., Am. Soc. M.E., T.A.P.P.I. (dir. 1963-66), Am., So. insts. mgmt., Paper Industry Mgmt. Assn. Clubs: Atlanta Athletic, Ansley Golf, Atlanta Athletic Yacht and Golf. Author: (with others) Industrial Waters for Pulp, Paper and Paperboard Manufacture, a monograph, 1942; The Manufacture of Pulp and Paper, 5 vols. of textbooks, 1938-49; Pulp and Paper Manufacture, 4 vols., 1950-55. Contbr. articles to trade jours. Home: 1635 Friar Tuck Rd NE Sherwood Forest Atlanta GA 30309 Office: 75 Third St NW Atlanta GA 30308

WATERS, VINCENT S., clergyman. Ordained priest Roman Cath. Ch., 1931; bishop of Raleigh, N.C., 1945—. Address: 15 N McDowell St Raleigh NC 27603*

WATERS, WILLIAM ALFRED, physician; b. Offerle, Kan., Oct. 27, 1912; s. Earl Evans and Willie Lou (Berry) W.; B.S., Okla. A. and M. Coll., 1933; M.D., U. Okla., 1947; m. Ruth Louise Whitcomb, Jan. 25, 1939. Office salesman, mgr. Oilwell Supply Co., Cushing and Ada., Okla., 1934-36; materials warehouseman Standard Oil Co., Venezuela, 1936-42; intern, Wesley Hosp., Oklahoma City, 1947-48; resident Meth. Hosp., Lubbock, Tex., 1953-54; practice medicine specializing in gen. medicine and surgery, Odessa, Tex., 1948-51, Lubbock, 1953-54, Tulsa, 1954—; mem. staffs Hillcrest Med. Center, Tulsa, Drs. Hosp., Tulsa, St. Francis Hosp., Tulsa. Served with AUS, 1942-46, with M.C., 51-53. Mem. Am., Tulsa County med. assns., Am. Acad. Gen. Practice, Am. Soc. Clin. Hypnosis, Am. Legion, Kappa Alpha. Republican. Mem. Christian Ch. Inventor floss attachment for electric toothbrush, air conditioned helmet. Home: 3648 E 49th St Tulsa OK 74135 Office: 5950 E 31st St Tulsa OK 74135

WATKINS, A.J., lawyer; b. Austin, Tex., July 27, 1924; s. Beda D. and Juel (Roper) W.; B.A., U. Tex., 1948; LL.B., Harvard, 1951; m. Jean Voss, May 11, 1946; children—Gregory Lee, Rebecca Lynn. Admitted to Tex. bar, 1951; briefing atty. Supreme Ct. Tex., 1951-52; asso. Baker, Botts, Shepherd & Coates, Houston, 1952-63; partner Baker, Heard, Elledge, & Watkins, Houston, 1963-66, Watkins & Hamilton, Houston, 1966—. Lectr. trial tactics U. Houston Sch. Law, 1967. Mem. Juvenile Adv. Council, Spring Br.-Meml., 1966—. Served with USMCR, 1943-45. Mem. Am., Harris County bar assns.,

State Bar Tex., Internat. Assn. Ins. Counsel (v.p. casualty ins. com. 1965-66), Tex. Assn. Def. Counsel, Houston C. of C. Methodist. Home: 13002 Indian Creek St Houston TX 77024 Office: Main Bldg Houston TX 77002

WATKINS, CARLTON GUNTER, pediatrician; b. Wilmington, N.C., Aug. 25, 1919; s. Edison Lee and Maysie (Gunter) W.; A.B., U. N.C., 1939; M.D., Washington U., St. Louis, 1943; m. Charlotte Jean Metcalf, Mar. 21, 1943; children—Lloyd Dixon Hollingsworth, Carlton Gunter, Mary Melissa, Charlotte Lou. Successively rotating intern, asst. resident, resident pediatrics St. Louis City Hosp., 1943-45; resident pediatrics Duke Hosp., 1945-46; pvt. practice, Charlotte, N.C., 1946-51, 53-—; chmn. dept. pediatrics Charlotte Meml. Hosp., 1958-61, 63-67; founder, 1963, since sr. mem. Charlotte Pediatric Clinic. Mem. Charlotte Mecklenburg Bd. Edn., 1966-—; pres. N.C. Family Life Council, 1966. Served to capt. M.C., AUS, 1951-53. Fellow Am. Acad. Pediatrics; mem. A.M.A., N.C., Mecklenburg County med. socs., N.C., Charlotte (founder, 1st sec. 1950, pres. 1962) pediatric socs., N.C. P.T.A. (life), Alpha Kappa Kappa. Clubs: Old Catawba, Myers Park Country (Charlotte). Contbr. articles med. jours. Home: 5915 Quail Hollow Rd Charlotte NC 28210 Office: 1700 Abbey Pl Charlotte NC 28209

WATKINS, CHARLES MALCOLM, govt. ofcl.; b. Malden, Mass., Mar. 12, 1911; s. Charles Hadley and Lura Burgess (Woodside) W.; B.S., Harvard, 1934; m. Joan Beatrice Jockwie, June 10, 1962. Curator, Wells Hist. Mus., Southbridge, Mass., 1936-42, Old Sturbridge Village, Sturbridge, Mass., 1946-48; asso. curator, div. ethnology Smithsonian Instn., Washington, 1948-57, curator, div. cultural history, 1957-68, curator div. preindsl. history and chmn. dept. cultural history, 1968-—. Mem. adv. com. Garvan Collection, Yale U., New Haven; chmn. adv. council archaeology Hampton (Va.) Assn. Arts and Humanities; cons. Oakland (Cal.) Mus.; adviser Gunston Hall, Lorton, Va. Served with USAAF, 1942-46. Recipient Smithsonian Reserach Found. grant. Mem. Am. Assn. Museums, Soc. Archtl. Historians, Soc. Hist. Archaeology, Nat. Trust Hist. Preservation, Cal. Hist. Soc., Pioneer Am. Soc. (bd. dirs.), Soc. Preservation New Eng. Antiquities. Unitarian. Author: The Cultural History of Marlborough, Virginia, 1968. Contbr. profl. jours. Home: 11441 Washington Plaza West Reston VA 22070 Office: Smithsonian Instn Washington DC 20560

WATKINS, CLYDE ATER, supt. sanatorium; b. Aberdeen, Miss., July 24, 1916; s. Guy Hartwell and Clyde (Ater) W.; B.A., U. Miss., 1936; M.D., Tulane U., 1940; m. Helen Pere, July 1, 1942; children—Helen, Clyde Ater, Mary Margaret, Sara Beth, Carol. Intern Charity Hosp., New Orleans, 1940-41; physician Vol. Ordnance Works, Chattanooga, 1942-45; resident chest diseases and internal medicine Miss. State San., Sanatorium, Miss., 1945-47, mem. med. staff, 1947-57, supt., 1957-—. Pres. Miss. Tb Assn., 1961. Mem. Am. Thoracic Soc., A.M.A., Central Med. Soc. Miss. (pres. 1961), Kappa Alpha, Phi Chi Fellow Am. Coll. Chest Physicians. Office: Miss State Sanatorium Sanatorium MS 39112

WATKINS, DAVID ALBIN, oil co. exec.; b. Tolar, Tex., Apr. 9, 1912; s. Edward Izatus and Ida (Wood) W.; student Walton Sch. Commerce, Internat. Accounting Soc., 1942-43; m. Naomi Ruth Ashley, July 5, 1934; children—Linda Jean, Nancy Ruth, Doris Anne. Accountant, Cosco Oil Co., Ft. Worth, 1936-39; accountant Cosden Petroleum Corp., Big Spring, Tex., 1939-44, office mgr., Wynnewood, Okla., 1944-45 with Kerr-McGee Oil Industries, Inc., Oklahoma City, 1945-—, controller, 1951-61, treas., 1961-—. Mem. Oklahoma City C. of C., Ind. Petroleum Assn. Am., Am. Petroleum Inst., Mid-Continent Oil and Gas Assn., Am. Mgmt. Assn., Financial Execs. Inst., Okla. Soc. Financial Analysts. Methodist (trustee). Mason. Home: 3104 Thorn Ridge Rd Oklahoma City OK 73120 Office: Kerr-McGee Bldg Oklahoma City OK 73102

WATKINS, JERRY WEST, oil co. exec.; b. Vernon, Tex., Dec. 10, 1931; s. Terrell Clark and Daisy (West) W.; student Hendrix Coll., 1949-50, La. Poly. Inst., 1950-51; LL.B., U. Ark., 1954; m. Elizabeth Jill Cole, Sept. 3, 1955; children—Jennifer Leigh, Jay West, Julie Elizabeth. Admitted to Ark. bar, 1954; law clk. Supreme Ct. Ark., 1954-55; with Murphy Oil Corp., El Dorado, Ark., 1955-—, sec., gen. atty., 1966-71, sec., gen. counsel, 1971-—. Mem. Ark. Bd. Law Examiners, 1969-—. Mem. Am., Ark., Union County bar assns., Am. Soc. Corporate Secretaries. Home: 111 Watkins Dr El Dorado AR 71730 Office: 200 Jefferson Av El Dorado AR 71730

WATKINS, LEVI, coll. pres.; b. Montgomery, Ky., Jan. 15, 1911; s. Adam and Sallie Emma (Darden) W.; B.S., Tenn. A. and I. Coll., 1933; M.A., Northwestern U., 1940; LL.D., Ark. Baptist Coll., 1958; m. Lillian Bernice Varnado; children—Annie Marie, Emma Pearl, Levi, Doristine Louise, Donald Varnado, James Allison. Tchr., asst. prin. Townsend High Sch., Winchester, Tenn., 1933-34; asst. to supt. Hopkinsville (Ky.) colored schs., 1934-35; tchr., asst. prin. Burt High Sch., Clarksville, Tenn., 1935-40; supervising prin. Douglass schs., also adminstrv. asst. to dean Parsons (Kan.) Jr. Coll., 1940-48; vis. summer instr. Ala. State Coll., 1945-48, adminstrv. asst. to pres., 1948-53; founding pres. Owens Coll., Memphis, 1953-59; bus. officer Ala. State Coll., 1959-62, bus. mgr., 1962, acting pres., 1962, pres., 1963-—. Mem. Sears, Roebuck Scholarship Rev. Com., Memphis, 1956-59. Div. chmn. Tukabatchee Area council Boy Scouts Am., 1950-52; mem. Greater Memphis Race Relations Com., 1956-59, Montgomery (Ala.) City Commnr. Com. Community Affairs, 1964-—; Bd. dirs. Parsons Community Chest, 1941-48; bd. dirs., exec. dir. Parsons Community Service Fund, 1940-48, Montgomery chpt. A.R.C., 1965-—. Recipient Mayor Memphis Key to City, 1954. Mem. N.E.A. (life), Am. (life), Ala. tchrs. assns., Alpha Kappa Mu, Sigma Pi Phi, Alpha Phi Alpha. Baptist. Mason. Home: 1101 Thurman St Montgomery AL 36104

WATKINS, MARTIN DAVID, JR., govt. ofcl., real estate devel.; b. Westminster, S.C. Jan. 11, 1922; s. Martin David and Mary (Cobb) W.; B.S., Clemson A. and M. Coll., 1942; m. Betty Brockman, Sept. 30, 1945; children—Mignon Montgomery, Rose Greer, Martin David III, William Brockman. Vets. agr. tchr. Westminster (S.C.) High Sch., 1947-51; rural mail carrier U.S. Post Office, Westminster, 1951-53, postmaster, 1953-—. Dir. Bank of Westminster, Westminster Indsl. Corp. Adv. trustee Westminster Area Schs. Mem. Commn. Pub. Works; mem., past vice chmn. and dir. Oconee County Planning Commn.; pres. Friends of Library; past chmn. A.R.C., dir. Oconee County chpt., 1963-—; pres. Oconee County Meml. Hosp., Lila Doyle Chronic Hosp.; vice chmn. S.C. Devel. Bd.; bd. dirs. Oconee Assembly; dir. Oconee County Tb Assn., Piedmont Tb Assn.; pres. Westminster Swimming Pool Assn.; coordinator, also v.p. SC Apple Festival Assn; chmn. United Fund campaign, 1970-—. Served from 2d lt. to capt., AUS, 1942-46; Res. ret. Decorated Silver Star Medal, Purple Heart, Bronze Star medal. Mem. Am. Legion (past comdr., dist. comdr.), Blue Ridge Art Assn. (pres.), Nat. Assn. Postmasters (pres. S.C. chpt. 1964; nat. v.p. 1972; recipient Olin D. Johnston award 1970), Oconee County Livestock Assn., Oconee County Hist. Soc., C. of C. (pres., dir.). Presbyn. (deacon). Rotarian (past pres.). Club: Westminster Recreation (pres.), Oconee County Country (past pres.). Home: 612 Mimosa Rd Westminster SC 29693 Office: Corner Winsor and Lucky Sts Westminster SC 29693

WATKINS, NORRIS WILLIAM,, banker; b. Columbia, S.C., Aug. 23, 1930; s. Augustus Samuel and Eva Ann (Taylor) W.; A.B., Lenoir Rhyne Coll., 1956; m. Sybil Cline, Sept. 5, 1953; children—Charlotte Ann, Norris William, Maria Susan, Bradley Steven, Brian Todd. Trainee Wachovia Bank & Trust Co., Winston-Salem, N.C., 1956-60; tech. adv. Lowes Co., Inc., North Wilkesboro, N.C., 1960-61; asst. to pres. Fed. Intermediate Credit Bank, Columbia, 1961-65; v.p. 1st Nat. Bank S.C., Columbia, 1965-—. Mem. adv. bd. Midlands Tech. Inst., Columbia. Served with AUS, 1951-53. Club: Spring Valley Country. Home: 7522 Millbrook Rd Columbia SC 29204 Office: Box 111 Columbia SC 29202

WATKINS, RALPH AUSTIN, state legislator; b. Hertha, Kan., July 26, 1902; s. Henry Franklin and Effie (Harrah) W.; grad. pub. schs.; m. Genevra Lavon Nance, Oct. 2, 1926; 1 son, Russell Austin. Mem. Okla. Ho. of Reps., 1958-—, chmn. labor relations com., 1963-69, mem. govtl. reform com., 1967-68, mem. legal and fiscal advisory com., 1963-68, mem. revenue and taxation com., 1958-68, mem. ways and means com., 1963-68. Comml. pilot. Bd. dirs. El Reno (Okla.) United Fund; dir. Boy Scouts Am. Mem. Brotherhood of R.R. Signalmen (gen. chmn., sec. 1952-67, Soaring Soc. Am. (gov. Okla. 1950-58), El Reno C. of C., Aircraft Owners and Pilots Assn. Democrat. Mason (32 deg.). Kiwanian. Home: 1414 W Shuttee St El Reno OK 73036 Office: State Capitol Oklahoma City OK 73105

WATKINS, WILLIAM LAW, lawyer; b. Anderson, S.C., Dec. 26, 1910; s. Thomas Franklin and Agnes (Law) W.; A.B., Wofford Coll., 1932; LL.B., U. Va., 1933; m. Frances Sitton, Oct. 23, 1937; children—Sarah (Mrs. Allen S. Marshall), Anna (Mrs. Alexander C. Hattaway III), Elizabeth (Mrs. Anderson Mills Kinghorn, Jr.), Jane (Mrs. Roger W. Mudd). Admitted to S.C. bar, 1933; since practiced in Anderson; mem. firm Watkins & Prince, 1936-46, Watkins & Watkins, 1946-54, Watkins, Vandiver & Freeman, 1954-64, Watkins, Vandiver, Kirven & Long, 1964-67, Watkins, Vandiver, Kirven, Long & Gable, 1968-—. Dir. Palmetto State Life Ins. Co., Perpetual Bldg. & Loan Assn.; adv. bd. S.C. Nat. Bank. Mem. S.C. Ho. of Reps., 1935-36; mem. S.C. Probation, Parole and Pardon Bd., 1954-69. Trustee Presbyn. Coll., Clinton, S.C., Anderson County Hosp. Assn. Served with AUS, 1942-46. Decorated Bronze Star with oak leaf cluster. Fellow Am. Coll. Trial Lawyers; mem. Am., S.C., Anderson bar assns., Phi Beta Kappa, Sigma Alpha Epsilon. Presbyn. Rotarian. Home: 317 North St Anderson SC 29621 Office: 500 S McDuffie St Anderson SC 29621

WATLAND, CHARLES DUNTON, educator; b. Albert Lea, Minn., Apr. 26, 1913; s. Albert O. and Myrtie Georgiana (Jorgensen) W.; A.B., Swarthmore Coll., 1934; M.A., U. Minn., 1937, Ph.D., 1953; postgrad. U. Mex., 1938, Nat. U. Chile, 1940. Jr. instr. Johns Hopkins, 1939-41; instr. Goucher Coll., Towson, Md., 1945-46; asst. prof. Spanish and comparative literature Union Coll., Schenectady, N.Y., 1946-55, asso. prof., 1955-62; asso. prof. Marquette U., Milw., 1962-66; prof. U. S.C., Columbia, 1968-—. Recipient certificate of honor Govt. Nicaragua, 1956, title and medal of knight comdr. Order Ruben Dario, Nicaragua, 1967. Inter-Am. Exchange fellow Nat. U. Chile, 1940. Mem. Am. Assn. U. Profs., Modern Lang. Assn., Am. Assn. Tchrs. Spanish and Portuguese. Author: Poet Errant, biography Ruben Dario, 1965, La Formacion Literaria de Ruben Dario, 1967. Contbr. articles to profl. jours. Home: 2330 Terrace Way Columbia SC 29205

WATLINGTON, JOHN FRANCIS, JR., banker; b. Reidsville, N.C., Mar. 23, 1911; s. John Francis and Frances (Byers) W.; A.B., Washington and Lee U., 1933; m. Margaret Jones, Feb. 22, 1947; children—John Francis III, Anne Wilson. With Wachovia Bank & Trust Co., Winston-Salem, N.C., 1933-—, successively transit clk., asst. cashier, asst. v.p., v.p., sr. v.p., 1933-56, pres., 1956-—, also chmn. Charlotte office, 1946-56; dir. Colonial Stores, Inc., Piedmont Natural Gas Co., Inc., Piedmont Airlines, Inc., Ga. Pacific Corp., Mass. Mut. Life Ins. Co., Akzona Corp., Carolina Power & Light Co. chmn. Wachovia Corp. Mem. N.C. Bd. Conservation and Devel. Trustee Tax Found., Union Theol. Sem.; chmn. bd. visitors Bowman Gray Sch. Medicine. Mem. Res. City Bankers Assn. (past v.p., dir.), C. of C. (pres. 1953, 58-59, dir. 1957), N.C. Citizens Assn. (dir.). Presbyn. Home: 2020 Virginia Rd Winston-Salem NC 27104 Office: Wachovia Bldg Box 3099 Winston-Salem NC 27102

WATSON, ABBIE I., ret. pub. health nurse; b. Greenville, Mich., July 27, 1905; d. Alfred T. and Effie (Henry) Watson; R.N., Harper Hosp. Sch. Nursing, Detroit, 1929; B.S. in Pub. Health Nursing, Wayne U., 1947; M.S. in Nursing Edn., Western Res. U., 1948. Clinic nurse outpatient dept. Harper Hosp., 1930-33; staff nurse, supr. Vis. Nurse Assn., Detroit, 1933-35, 38-42; supr. Tulare County Health Dept., Visalia, Cal., 1935-38; adminstrv. chief nurse, capt. Army Nurse Corps, AUS, 1942-46; exec. dir. Instructive Vis. Nurse Assn., Richmond, Va., 1948-57; dir. bur. pub. health nursing Instructive Vis. Nurse Assn. and City of Richmond, 1952-57; dir. bur. pub. health nursing pub. health div. Health and Hosp. Corp. of Marion County, Indpls., 1957-61; chief bur. pub. health nursing pub. health dept. Govt. D.C., 1961-65; dir. pub. health nursing Met. Health Dept., Nashville, 1965-72. Mem. nursing services com. D.C. chpt., A.R.C., 1960-61; spl. services dept. D.C. Tb Assn., 1961-—. Fellow Am. Pub. Health Assn. (past vice chmn., past research chmn. pub. health nursing sect. So. br.), Am. Sch. Health Assn., Royal Soc. Health (London); mem. Am. Nurses Assn., Nat. League Nursing (past chmn. program planning com. pub. health nursing biennial conv.), D.C. Pub. Health Assn. (1st v.p., chmn. constn. and by-laws com.). Contbr. articles to profl. publs. Address: 530 Av K NE Winter Haven FL 33880

WATSON, ALBERT, lawyer; b. Sumter, S.C., Aug. 30, 1922; s. Claude A. and Eva (Clark) W.; LL.B. U. S.C., 1950; m. Lillian Williams, May 24, 1948; 3 children. Admitted to S.C. bar, 1950; mem. S.C. Gen. Assembly, 1955-58, 60-62; mem. 88th-91st Congresses 2d Dist. S.C. Served with USAAF, 1942-46. Republican. Baptist. Mason (Shriner), Lion. Office: House Office Bldg Washington DC 20515

WATSON, ALLAN RYAN, clergyman; b. Sumter, S.C., Aug. 30, 1922; s. Claude A. and Eva (Clark) W.; A.A., North Greenville Jr. Coll., 1941; B.A., Furman U., 1943; Th.M., So. Bapt. Theol. Sem., 1949, postgrad., 1949-51; m. Betty Carter, June 27, 1947; children—Carol, Deborah, David. Teaching fellow So. Bapt. Theol. Sem., 1949-51; ordained to ministry Bapt. Ch., 1947; pastor Northwood Bapt. Ch., West Palm Beach, Fla., 1951-60, Calvary Bapt. Ch., Tuscaloosa, Ala., 1960-—. Speaker, WP-TV, West Palm Beach, 1953-60, WCFT-TV, Tuscaloosa, 1967-—; chaplain U. Ala. Crimson Tide Football Team, 1963-—; condr. worship service U.S. Pres. Nixon, White House, Washington, 1969: pres. Bapt. Home for Boys, Tuscaloosa, 1969-70. Mem. charter revision com. City of West Palm Beach, 1955-57; mem. Mayor's Adv. Bd., Tuscaloosa, 1966-—. Bd. dirs., pres. Mental Health Assn. Tuscaloosa; bd. dirs. Retarded Childrens Assn., Tuscaloosa, Head Start Program, Tuscaloosa, Boys Club, Tuscaloosa. Served with USNR, 1943-46; PTO. Named Outstanding Citizen, West Palm Beach City Commn., 1959, Tuscaloosa News, 1967. Mem. Fla. (v.p. 1955-56), Ala. (adminstrn. com. 1964-68), So. (Sunday sch. bd. 1964-—) Bapt. convs., Pi Kappa Phi. Republican. Mason, Rotarian. Contbr. articles to Bapt. publs. Home: 276 Cedar Crest Tuscaloosa AL 35401 Office: 1131 10th St Tuscaloosa AL 35401

WATSON, ARTHUR CHOPIN, Democratic nat. committeeman; b. Natchitoches, La., Dec. 15, 1909; s. Arthur William and Eugenie (Chopin) W.; B.A., Spring Hill Coll.; LL.B., Tulane U.; m. Marion Eugenia Hickman, Apr. 27, 1935; children—Marion (Mrs. O.J. Vienvenu), Saidee (Mrs. Guy R. Newell), Eugenie Chopin. Admitted to La. bar, 1933; partner firm Watson, Murchison, Crews & Arthur, 1933-—; pres. Progressive Savs. and Loan Assn., 1964-—; chmn. bd. Exchange Bank & Trust Co., 1966-—. Mem. La. Ho. of Reps., 1940-44; chmn. Dem. State Central Com., 1968-—; chmn. La. delegation to Dem. Nat. Conv., 1960. Named Man of Yr., Natchitoches C. of C., 1966. Mem. Am., La. (gov. 1956-58; House Del. 1959-67) bar assns., Jr. Bar La. (pres. 1942-43), Order of Coif, Kappa Sigma, Phi Delta Phi. Address: PO Box 226 Natchitoches LA 71457*

WATSON, BILLY RAY, petroleum exec.; b. Snyder, Tex., Aug. 29, 1928; s. William Miles and Ava Jewel (Sorrells) W.; student Tex. Tech. U., 1948-49; B.B.A., Sul Ross Coll., 1952; m. Delores Earle McCright, July 11, 1952; children—Barry Ray, Brad Allan, Bambi Leigh. With accounting dept. Texas Co., Midland, 1952-55; with Lynes, Inc., packers, Midland, Tex., 1955, Oklahoma City, 1955-56, Duncan, Okla., 1956-61, Healdton, Okla., 1961-62, Midland, 1962; owner Watson Packer Service, Monahans, Tex., 1963; pres. Watson Packer, Inc., 1970-—; owner, operator Three-B Oil Co., Monahans, 1965-—; partner C & W Mfg., Sweetwater, Tex., 1970-—; dir. Boomer's Wire Line Service, Monahans, sec.-treas., 1970-—. Bd. dirs. Monahans Indsl. Found. Served with AUS, 1946-48. Mem. Am. Inst. Mining Engrs. (vice chmn. 1969), Ind. Petroleum Assn. Am. Mem. Ch. of Christ (Sunday sch. tchr.). Rotarian (v.p.). Patentee in petroleum field. Home: 1000 S Franklin Monahans TX 79756 Office: Box 756 Monahans TX 79756

WATSON, CHARLES ANDREW, banker; b. Dallas, Nov. 20, 1934; s. C. W. and Mary M. (Watson) W.; certificates numerous data processing tech. schs.; grad. Southwestern Grad. Sch. Banking, So. Methodist U., 1970-72; m. Marilyn R. DeLong, Sept. 17, 1954; children—Karen, Richard, Cary. With data processing operations Tex. & Pacific R.R., 1952-57; data processing programming Mobil Oil Co., Dallas, 1957-65; data processing mgmt. and cons. Diversa Inc., 1965-67; data processing mgmt. 1st City Nat. Bank, Houston, 1967-70, v.p. gen. adminstrn., 1970-—. Instr. computer programming Rutherford Met. Bus. Inst., 1962-66. Office: 1111 Fannin St Houston TX 77002

WATSON, DONALD GEORGE, dentist; b. Birmingham, Ala., Dec. 11, 1933; s. John Edward and Elinor (Robinette) W.; B.S., U. Ala., 1957, D.M.D., 1961, orthodontic certificate, 1966; m. Sandra Sue McCallum, Aug. 28, 1965; 1 son, Donald George. Dir. indigent children's orthodontics Med. Center U. Ala., Birmingham, 1966-68; pvt. practice orthodontics, Florence, Ala., 1968-—. Instr., clinician Dental Sch. U. Ala., parttime, 1968-—. Served with AUS, 1953-55, to capt. Dental Corps, 1962-64. Mem. Am. Assn. Orthodontists, So. Soc. Orthodontists, Ala. Soc. Orthodontists, Am., Ala. dental assns., Tri-Cities Dental Soc. (pres. 1970-71), Kappa Sigma, Omicron Kappa Upsilon. Methodist. Home: & Office: 228 W Tennessee St Florence AL 35630

WATSON, FRANK LIPSCOMB, govt. ofcl.; b. Alderson, Okla., Apr. 4, 1902; s. Frank L. and Emma (Seymour) W.; A.B., U. Okla., 1923, LL.B., 1925; M.E., Miss. State U., 1952; m. Julia Ella Watson, Apr. 10, 1956; children—Emma M., Ursula A. Admitted to Okla. bar, 1925; practiced in McAlester, Okla., 1925-36; atty. Pittsburgh County, Okla., 1930-36, asst. U.S. dist. atty. Eastern Dist. Okla., 1936-42; chief ministry justice sect. Office Mil. Govt. U.S., Berlin, Germany, 1946-47; prof. law Miss. State U., 1947-67; legislative aide to majority leader U.S., Ho. of Reps., Washington, 1967-—. Mem. Okla. Ho. of Reps., 1927-29. Served to col. USAAF, 1942-46. Home: 101 G St SW Washington DC 20024 Office: U S Capital Bldg Washington DC 20515

WATSON, FRED ROGER, city ofcl.; b. Lenoir, N.C., June 3, 1943; s. Lloyd Wilburn and Marylee Victoria (Chester) W.; B.S. in Civil Engring., N.C. State U., 1965; m. Ruth Roosevelt Hunt, June 9, 1964; children—Mary, Dana. Survey party chief, asst. resident engr. N.C. State Hwy. Commn., 1965-68; asst. city engr. city of Gastonia, N.C., 1968-69, city engr., 1969-—. Mem. Am. Soc. C.E., Nat. Soc. Profl. Engrs., Inst. Traffic Engrs., Am. Pub. Works Assn. Home: 1439 Lynhurst Dr Gastonia NC 28052 Office: PO Box 1748 Gastonia NC 28052

WATSON, GEORGE ELDER, III, zoologist; b. N.Y.C., Aug. 13, 1931; s. George Elder and Forsyth (Patterson) W.; B.A., Yale, 1953, M.S., 1961, Ph.D., 1964; m. Louisa Carter Johnson, Dec. 10, 1966; 1 dau., Elisabeth Carter. Sci. collector Peabody Mus., Yale, New Haven, 1953-55; with Smithsonian Instn., Washington, 1962-—, curator Nat. Mus. Natural History, 1966-—, chmn. dept. vertebrate zoology 1967-—. Asso. dept. pathobiology Sch. Hygiene Johns Hopkins, 1969-—. Mem. Audubon Naturalist Soc. (dir.). Author: A Preliminary Field Guide to the Birds of the Indian Ocean, 1963; Seabirds of the Tropical Atlantic Ocean, 1967. Contbr. profl. jours. Home: 4323 Cathedral Av NW Washington DC 20016 Office: Dept of Vertebrate Zoology Smithsonian Institution Washington DC 20560

WATSON, GEORGE FRANKLIN, librarian; b. Luning, Nev., Feb. 20, 1918; s. George Franklin and Nellie Evangeline (Hill) W.; grad. McKay Bus. Coll., 1939; grad. USN Sch. Journalism, 1955; B.S. in Bus. Edn. (Div. of Surveys and Field Service fellow) Peabody Coll., 1960, M.L.S., 1962; m. Mary Virginia Gooch, July 21, 1965. With USN, 1935-57, chief petty officer, submarines, 1941-57, PTO, Korea, 1951-57; tchr. bus. edn. Hampton (Va.) High Sch., 1960-61; head inter-agy. relations and stacks State Library div. Tenn. State Library and Archives, Nashville, 1962-65; head librarian N.E. State Jr. Coll., Rainsville, Ala., 1965-66; dir. library Columbia (Tenn.) State Community Coll., 1966-—. Decorated Letter of Commendation. Mem. Assn. for Preservation Tenn. Antiquities, Am., Tenn., Southeastern library assns., Williamson County Hist. Soc. (pres. 1970-71). Elk, Mason (K.T.). Club: Civitan (Rainsville, Ala.). Home: Executive House B-17 Franklin TN 37064 Office: Columbia State Community Coll Columbia TN 38401

WATSON, HAROLD FRANCIS, educator; b. Milford, Pa., Apr. 2, 1895; s. John Calvin and Adda (Cole) W.; A.B., N.Y.U., 1918, A.M., 1920; Ph.D., Columbia, 1931; m. Martha Hoyt Tucker, Aug. 23, 1924 (dec. Mar. 2, 1961); children—Robert Francis, Stuart Tucker; m. 2d, Elizabeth White, June 26, 1969. Instr. English, N.Y.U., 1918-19, Hedding Coll., 1919-21; asst. prof. English, U. Me., 1922-24; vis. prof. U. W.Va., summer 1929; prof. English, chmn. div. lang. and lit. Simpson Coll. 1924-55, chmn. div. humanities, 1955-—, chmn. faculty council and dean, 1959, prof. emeritus English. Mem. tech. adv. com. on English Ia. Assn. Coll. Pres., 1928; gen. sec. Ia. Colls. Conf. on English, 1939-41; sec. Ia. Authors Club, 1944-46. Mem. Modern Lang. Assn., Augustan Soc., Heraldry Soc. (Brit.), Phi Beta Kappa, Lambda Chi Alpha, Pi Kappa Delta, Alpha Psi Omega. Mason (32 deg.). Author: The Sailor in English Fiction and Drama, 1550-1800, 1931; Writing for Freshmen (with L.W. Smith), 1930; Adventures in Contemporary Reading (with L. W. Smith), 1932; Coasts of Treasure Island, 1969. Joint editor: Types and Times in

English Literature, Book I, 1940. Contbr. articles to profl. jours. Home: 518 E Ash St Fayetteville AR 72701

WATSON, JACK CROZIER, judge; b. Jonesville, La., Sept. 17, 1928; s. Jesse Crozier and Gladys (Talbot) W.; B.A., U. Southwestern La., 1949; LL.B., La. State U., 1956; m. Sue Carter, Dec. 26, 1958; children—Carter, Wells. Admitted to La. bar, 1956; practiced in Lake Charles, La., 1956-64; mem. firm Watson & Watson, 1960-64; prosecutor City of Lake Charles, 1960; asst. dist. atty. 14th Jud. Dist. La., 1961-64; dist. judge 14th Jud. Dist. La., Lake Charles, 1964—. Served to 1st lt. USAF, 1950-54. Mem. Am., La., S.W. La. bar assns., Nat. Council Juvenile Ct. Judges (pres. La. council 1969-70), Am. Legion, Blue Key, Sigma Alpha Epsilon, Phi Delta Phi, Pi Kappa Delta. Home: 311 Shell Beach Dr Lake Charles LA 70601 Office: PO Box 3209 Lake Charles LA 70601

WATSON, JAMES CHESTNUT, physician; b. Trenton, N.J., June 16, 1936; s. Reed and Grace (Chestnut) W.; B.A., Lincoln U., 1958; M.D., Howard U., 1964; M.P.H., U. Tex., 1970; m. Pauline Kathryn Thomas, Apr. 1, 1961; children—Jamie Lyn, Juliette Grace, Paula Elise, Debra Patrice. Intern, Meml. Hosp., South Bend, Ind., 1964-65; practice medicine, specializing in gen. practice, Houston, 1967-69, 1969—; aviation med. examiner FAA, 1970—; asst. prof. community medicine Baylor Coll. of Medicine, 1970—; asst. chief community medicine service Harris County Hosp. Dist., 1971—; mem. active staff Riverside Gen. staff Hosp.; asst. attending physician Harris County Hosp. Served with USAF, 1965-67. Mem. Am., Tex. pub. health assns., Nat. Med. Assn., Houston Med. Forum, Omega Psi, Phi. Democrat. Episcopalian. Home: 5339 Trail Lake Dr Houston TX 77045 Office: 8803 Scott St Houston TX 77051

WATSON, JOHN (HENRY), educator; b. Fultz, Ky., May 21, 1915; s. James H. and Cora (Wilson) W.; B.A., Morehead State U., 1952; M.S., Miss. State U., 1958, M.A., 1961, Ph.D., 1963; m. Katheryn Jeanette Sigrest, Aug. 13, 1954; children—Connie Lou (Mrs. Kenneth Caudill), John Duffy, Katheryn Cecilia, Elizabeth Lauren. Commd. officer U.S. Air Force; various adminstrv. and staff positions, 1941-55, ret. lt. col. 1960; asst. prof. air sci. A.F., R.O.T.C., Miss. State U., State College, 1955-60, instr. sociology, 1960-62; Thomas L. Bailey, prof., head dept. sociology and anthropology, 1967-70; prof. anthropology, chmn. dept. Murray (Ky.) State U., 1970—; prof., head dept. sociology Western Ky. U., 1962-67. Mem. Ky. adv. com. Edn. for Social Services and Demonstration Project for the Recruitment of Social Workers. Served as officer Civilian Conservation Corps, 1938-39. Decorated European and Korean Campaign medals, Belgian Feurragere. Fellow Nat. Sci. Found.; mem. Am. Assn. U. Profs., Am., Sociol. Assns., Anthropologists and Sociologists (pres.), Ret. Officers Assn. (pres. chpt.), Phi Alpha Theta, Alpha Kappa Delta. Democrat. Presbyn. Home: 814 Olive St Murray KY 42071

WATSON, JOHN RAYMOND, structural engr.; b. San Juan P.R., Sept. 7, 1935; s. Edward C. and Stella (Hemsley) W.; B.S.C.E., U. P.R., 1957, B.S., 1958; M.S. in Civil Engring., Mass. Inst. Tech., 1959; m. Brunilda de Jesus Silva, Dec. 28, 1957; 1 son, John Raymond. Instr. gen. and civil engring. U. P.R., Mayaguez, 1957-60; v.p., gen. mgr. Prescon Caribe, Inc., San Juan, 1960-64; asso. Schimmelpfennig, Ruiz & Gonzalez, Rio Piedras, 1964-65; pvt. practice cons. structural engr., Rio Piedras, 1965—; exec. dir. P.R. Hwy. Authority, 1969—. Mem. Nat. Com. Am. Citizenship, 1966—. Mem. Am. Concrete Inst., Am. Soc. C.E., P.R. Soc. Structural Engrs., P.R. Inst. Engrs., Architects and Surveyors, Am. Assn. State Hwy. Ofcls., Internat. Bridge, Tunnel, Turnpike Assn., Sigma Xi, Nu Sigma Beta. Mem. New Progressive Party. Episcopalian. Club: Nat. Exchange (dist sec. 1967-68). Home: 1303 Los Patricios Condominium Guaynabo PR 00920 Office: Hwy Authority Cobian Center Santurce PR 00908

WATSON, JOHN ROBIN, landscape illuminator; b. Temple, Tex., Feb. 22, 1922; s. J. Elmer and Florence Catherine (Granger) W.; B.A. in Landscape Architecture, Tex. A. and M. U., 1943, M.A., 1947; postgrad. Sorbonne U., France, 1945-46; study with Andrew Dasberg, Taos, N.M., 1954; m. Mary Adele Aspoas, Nov. 2, 1963; children—Suzanne Elizabeth, John Shannon. Lighting designer Gen. Electric's Nela Park, Cleve., 1948-52; owner, pres. John R. Watson Landscape Illumination, Dallas and Houston, 1953—. Served with AUS, 1942-45. Recipient Design award Nat. Soc. Interior Designers, 1965. Mem. Illuminating Engring. Soc. Mason. Clubs: Brookhollow Golf, T Bar M Racquet (Dallas); Argyle (San Antonio). Contbr. articles to mags. and newspapers. Pioneer field of landscape illumination; lighting designer for 6 Flags over Tex., 6 Flags over Ga., 6 Flags over Mid-Am., Tex. Pavillion at N.Y. World's Fair; African Veldt-Bush Gardens, Fla., Hemisfair, Gulf States Paper Corp. Oriental Garden complex, Pepsico, others. Home: 4110 Cochran Chapel St Dallas TX 75209 Office: 2517 Carlisle St Dallas TX 75201

WATSON, MARTIN TRUETT, dentist; b. Detroit, June 5, 1932; s. Martin Pascal and Pauline Lelia (Price) W.; student Piedmont Coll., 1949-51; A.B., Emory U., 1953; postgrad. U. Ga., 1956; D.D.S., U. Md. Dental Sch., 1960; m. Cornelia Jane Roach, June 25, 1955; 1 dau., Jane Marie. Pvt. practice dentistry, Royston, Ga., 1960—; mem. staff Cobb Meml. Hosp., Royston, 1961—, v.p. staff, 1964, 70. Chmn. Franklin County Headstart Dental Care, 1968-71; vol. dentist So. Bapt. Missionary, villages Honduras, May 14-22, 1971. Mem. Am. Dental Assn., Nat. Fedn. Ind. Bus. Inc., Royston C. of C., Ga. Dental Assn., Clark County Dental Soc., Delta Tau Delta. Baptist. Served with AUS, 1954-56. Home: 421 Johnson St Royston GA 30662 Office: 421 Franklin Springs Royston GA 30662

WATSON, MICHAEL CUNNINGHAM, physician; b. Ridge Spring, S.C., Jan. 15, 1926; s. Joseph Calhoun and Aurelia C. (Cunningham) W.; B.S., Clemson U., 1949; M.D., U. S.C., 1953; m. Mary Carolyn Tatum, Sept. 1, 1956; children—Mary Elizabeth, Michael Cunningham, Caroline Nicholson, Joseph Calhoun, John Tatum, Aurelia Cunningham. Intern, Maumee Valley Hosp., Toledo, 1953-54; gen. practice medicine, Bamberg, S.C., 1954—; sch. physician Carlise Mil. Sch., 1956—; county health officer, 1966—; mem. staff Bamberg County Meml. Hosp., 1954—, chief of staff 1956, 66. Sec., Bamberg Sch. Bd., 1964-70; vice chmn. Bamberg County Mental Health Assn., 1971; mem. med. adv. commn. Lower Savannah Regional Planning Commn., 1968—, Task Force on Instruction of S.C. Edn. Assn., 1969; mem. gen. bd. Nat. Council Chs., 1964—, mem. gen. assembly, 1964; del. World Council Chs., Uppsula, Sweden, 1968. Sec., treas. Bamberg County Republican Com., 1968. Bd. dirs. United Fund, 1966—; trustee Methodist Home, Orangeburg, S.C., 1970—. Served with USMCR, 1943-45; PTO. Mem. A.M.A., S.C., So. Edisto med. assns., Am. Acad. Gen. Practice. Methodist (chmn. minimum salary commn. S.C., 1964—; dist. steward 1960—; med. adviser, mem. com. for overseas relief 1964—). Home: Charleston-Augusta Rd Bamberg SC 29003 Office: North St Bamberg SC 29003

WATSON, MURRAY, JR., lawyer, state legislator; b. Mart, Tex., May 14, 1932; s. Murray and Ethel (Bryson) W.; B.B.A., Baylor U., 1952, J.D., 1954; Asso. degree in applied sci. (hon.), Tex. State Tech. Inst., 1970; m. Greta Candace Warren, Aug. 15, 1959; children—Millicent, Marcus Warren. Admitted to Tex. bar, 1955, U.S. Supreme Ct. bar; practice law in Mart, 1955-59, 61-62, Waco, 1959-61, 62—; asso. feed, seed and farming bus. with father, 1949-54, 1963—; prof. bus. law Baylor U., 1959-60; asso. Jones, Boyd, Westbrook & Lovelace, Waco, 1962-67, Watson & Weed, Waco, 1967-71, Watson & Kennedy, 1971—. Vis. instr. McLennan Community Coll., 1967-68; prof. adminstrv. law Baylor Sch. Law, 1969-70. Pres., dir. Central Tex. Indsl. Devel. Council. Bill clk., Tex. Ho. of Reps., 1955; mem. Tex. Ho. of Reps., 1957-62; mem. Tex. Senate, 1963-73; mem. Tex. Legislative Council, 1965. Bd. dirs. Central Tex. Museum, 1962—, pres., 1965-67, v.p., 1967-71; bd. dirs. McLennan Tb Assn., Christmas Seal chmn., 1966. Recipient Distinguished Service award Waco Jr. C. of C., 1963, citation appreciation Tex. Assn. Mental Health, 1963, Distinguished Service award Vocational Agrl. Tchrs. Assn. Tex., 1964, Outstanding Citizenship award Mart C. of C. and Agr., 1964, Outstanding Service to Handicapped award Tex. Rehab. Commn. and President's Council to Employ the handicapped, 1970, many other service awards, gov. for a day, July 12, 1969. Mem. State Bar Tex., Waco-McLennan County, Waco Jr. bar assns., Mart, Waco chambers commerce, Tex. and S.W. Cattle Raisers Assn., McLennan County Farm Bur., Tex. State Firemen and Fire Marshals Assn. (hon. life), Waco Jr. C. of C. (dir. 1958-60, 65—), Order Artus, Delta Sigma Pi, Phi Alpha Delta. Methodist. Mason (Shriner), K.P., Lion, Kiwanian; mem. Order Eastern Star. Contbr. articles to profl. jours. Home: 308 Texas Av Mart TX 76664 Office: 820 Lake Air Dr Waco TX 76710

WATSON, ROBERT HARMON, coal mining co. exec.; b. Eckmond, W.Va., Oct. 28, 1920; s. John Thomas and Ethel Lee (Keister) W.; student Hiwassee Coll., 1938-39, Va. Poly. Inst., 1939-40, U. Ky., 1940-41; m. Oma Lee Hall, July 4, 1943; 1 son, Robert Harmon. With Stonega Coal & Coke Co., 1941; office at mine Blue Diamond Coal Co., Knoxville, 1942, asst. office mgr., 1942-48, compensation adjuster, 1948-53, in charge of safety dept., Knoxville, 1953-58, corp. sec. 1958-60, dir., 1960—, adminstrv. v.p., 1961-68, v.p. operations, 1968—. Served with USAAF, 1942-45. Decorated D.F.C., Air medal with 5 oak leaf clusters. Methodist. Mason. Home: 1409 Autumn Lane Knoxville TN 37912 Office: 6305 Kingston Pike Knoxville TN 37919

WATSON, ROMULUS SAUNDERS, lawyer, accountant; b. Swan Quarter, N.C., Nov. 15, 1920; s. Romulus Saunders and Ruby (Tunnell) W.; B.S., N.C. State U., 1942; LL.B., U. N.C., 1952; postgrad. N.Y. U., 1954; m. Statia Kowalski; children—Valerie, Marion. Admitted to N.Y. bar, 1953, N.C. bar, 1955; practiced in Charlotte, N.C., 1957—. Served as lt. USNR, 1942-46. C.P.A., N.C., S.C. Mem. Am. Inst. Attys.-C.P.A.'s (asso. dir. 1969—). Home: 3500 Colony Rd Charlotte NC 28211 Office: Bank of North Carolina Building Charlotte NC 28202

WATSON, THOMAS EDWARD, JR., social scientist; b. Hazlehurst, Miss., Mar. 13, 1930; s. Thomas Edward and Jamie (Storie) W.; A.B., U. Ga., 1952; postgrad. Georgetown U., 1953; m. Linda Landrum, July, 1972; children—by previous marriage—David Randolph, Valerie. Prodn. mgr. advt. Fetty/Hundemer Assos., Baton Rouge, 1960-62; asst. pub. relations officer La. Dept. Hwys., 1962-64; free lance writer, pvt. cons., 1965-66; asst. dir. advt. promotions La. Dept. Commerce and Industry, 1966-68; pub. relations, program devel. and analysis exec. La. State Econ. Opportunity Office, 1968-71; human resources planner and organizer La. Planning Dist. 3, Convent, 1971—. Served to capt. USAF, 1946-48, 52-60. Dept. Housing and Urban Devel. fellow U. Okla., 1972-73. Mem. State Information Reps. La. (past pres.), Am. Legion, V.F.W. Scabbard and Blade. Arnold Air. Soc. Club: Press Baton Rouge (dir., past v.p.). Contbr. articles to profl. jours. Home: 2806 Main St Baton Rouge LA 70802 Office: St James Community Action Agy PO Box 87 Convent LA 70723

WATSON, WILLIAM, educator; b. Clydebank, Dunbartonshire, Scotland, Jan. 5, 1917 (came to U.S. 1963); s. Thomas and Jessie (Brockett) W.; B.A., Cambridge U. (Eng.), 1947, M.Sc., 1949; Ph.D., Manchester U., Eng., 1952; m. Pamela Eugenie Matthews, Feb. 9, 1949; children—Hamish Brockett, Calum Macfarlane, Angus Clark. Anthropologist, Med. Research Council of U.K., 1948-51; research fellow Rhodes-Livingstone Inst., Zambia, 1951-56; prof. anthropology Manchester U., 1956-63; prof. anthropology U. Va., Charlottesville, 1963-69; chmn. dept. sociology U. Okla., 1969—. Cons. sociologist Med. Research Council of U.K., 1959-63; mem. Youth Service Devel. Council of U.K., 1960-63. Served with RAF, 1939-45. Decorated D.F.C. Fellow Assn. Social Anthropologists of U.K.; mem. African Studies Assn., Royal African Inst., Brit. Sociol. Assn., Am. Sociol. Assn. Author: Tribal Cohesion in a Money Economy, 1958; Sociology in Medicine, 1962; also articles. Home: 1847 Rolling Hills St Norman OK 73069 Office: 455 W Lindsay Norman OK 73069

WATSON, WILLIAM MARVIN, oil co. exec. Formerly exec. asst. to pres. Lone Star Steel Co., Dallas; then spl. asst. to Pres. Johnson, also former postmaster gen.; pres. Occidental Internat. Corp., 1969—; sr. v.p., dir. Occidental Petroleum Corp., 1971—; dir. Sulphur Export Corp., Nat. Liberty Corp. Trustee Scott and White Meml. Hosp., Scott, Sherwood and Brindley Found.; bd. dirs. Mt. Vernon Coll., Billy Graham Evangelistic Assn., Baylor U. Council for Instl. Devel.; bd. devel. Hardin-Simmons U. Past chmn. Tex. Democratic Exec. Com. Home: 15060 Corona del Mar Pacific Palisades CA 90272 also 100 Hughes Circle Daingerfield TX 75638

WATSON, WILLIAM THOMAS, educator; b. Hampton, Ark., Aug. 6, 1931; s. Leonard H. and Temple (Benson) Watson; B.S., So. State Coll., 1953; M.A., U. Ark., 1960; m. Jimmie Rae Freeland, June 20, 1953; children— William Thomas, Keith Barrett. Coach, Warren (Ark.) High Sch., 1953-54, 57-59, Crossett (Ark.) High Sch., 1960-64, So. State Coll., Magnolia, Ark., 1964—. Served with AUS, 1954-56. Named All Star High Sch. Coach, 1959; Coach of Year, Nat. Assn. Intercollegiate Athletics 1967. Baptist. Optimist. Home: 1202 Dogwood Magnolia AR 71753

WATSON, WILLIAM WOOD, lawyer; b. Cohasset, Mass., July 19, 1924; s. Robert Clifford and Roxy (Green) W.; A.B., Duke, 1947, LL.B., 1950; postgrad Harvard Program for Mgmt. Devel., 1962. Admitted to D.C. bar, 1951; atty. U.S. Dept. Labor, Washington, 1951-56, NLRB, Washington, 1956-58; atty. Chesapeake and Potomac Telephone Cos., Washington, 1958-66, gen. atty., 1966—. Served with USNR, 1943-46. Mem. Am., Fed., Fed. Communications, D.C. bar assns. Home: 4000 Tunlaw Rd NW Washington DC 20007 Office: 1710 H St NW Washington DC 20006

WATT, ANNIE LILLIAN MANN (MRS. JOHN REID WATT), civic worker; b. Hephzibah, Ga., Aug. 20, 1918; d. David Gilbert and Gertrude (Clark) Mann; A.B. magna cum laude, Ga. Wesleyan Coll., 1941; postgrad. U. Tex., 1960-61; m. Quentin Jauquet, Nov. 7, 1942 (div. 1960); children—David, Catherine, Madeleine; m. 2d, John Reid Watt, May 4, 1962. Tchr. Cochran (Ga.) High Sch., 1941-42, Tinsley Sch., Macon, Ga., 1959-60; librarian Dill Sch., also Casis Sch., Austin, Tex., 1960-62. Bd. dirs. Austin Mental Health Assn., 1963-69, pres., 1967-68; bd. dirs. Tex. Assn. Mental Health, 1966-67; mem. steering com. The Listening Ear, 1968-70; co-chmn. speakers bur. Internat. Hospitality Com., 1963-65, unit. chmn., 1966, mem. adv. com., 1963-69; Fiesta ticket chmn. Laguna Gloria Art Mus., 1963, 64; unit auction chmn. KLRN, ednl. TV, 1969; bd. dirs. University YWCA, 1964-69, trustee, 1968-69; bd. dirs. Tex. Assn. Emotionally Disturbed Children, 1968-69, sec. bd., 1969-71; vice chmn. Austin Mayor's Commn. on Status Women, 1970-71. Recipient 1st prize, non-pub. authors class Ga. Writers Assn., 1956. Mem. D.A.R. (chpt. corr. sec. 1950, del. nat. conv. 1952), Phi Delta Phi. Democrat. Unitarian (pres. Women's Alliance 1963-64; pres. bd. trustees 1969-71, del. gen. assembly 1969, 70). Clubs: Wesleyan Alumnae (pres. San Antonio 1950, 53, 54, pres. Augusta, Ga., 1956-57), Austin Woman's Westwood Country (Austin). Home: 77 E Andrews Dr NW Atlanta GA 30305

WATT, GRAHAM WEND, city mgr.; b. Elizabeth N.J., Oct. 23, 1926; s. William Harrison and Carolyn (Wend) W.; A.B. in Econs., Washington Coll., 1949; M. Governmental Adminstrn., Fels Inst., U. Pa., 1951; m. Mary Aldridge Irish, Sept. 10, 1949; children—Terrence Graham, Laurie Frederika. Various positions City of Kansas City (Mo.), 1950-55; adminstrn. asst. to city mgr., 1955-58; city mgr. City of Alton (Ill.), 1958-62, City of Portland, Me., 1962-67, City Dayton, O., 1967-70; dep. mayor Washington, 1970—; lectr. So. Ill. U., 1958-61. Mem. Public Ofcls. Adv. Council to U. S. Office Econ. Opportunity, 1966-68; mem. adv. com. on urban devel. to Sec. U.S. Dept. Housing and Urban Devel., 1967-68; chmn. Educating Urban Adminstrs. Project, 1971-72; participant White House Conf. on Health, 1966; bd. dirs. Met. Washington Council Govts., v.p., 1971; mem. Pub. Service Commn. D.C.; bd. dirs. Nat. Center for Voluntary Action, Washington Met. Area Transit Authority; adv. council Washington urban semester Am. U., 1970—; del. mem. governing bd. Council State Govts., 1971—. Served with USNR 1944-46. Recipient Mgmt. Innovation award Internat. City Mgmt. Assn., 1969, alumni citation Washington Coll., 1970; recipient Man of Yr. award Wharton grad Bus. Club Washington, 1971. Mem. Internat. City Mgmt. Assn. (bd. 1969-70, pres. 1971-72), Com. on Edn. for Pub. Adminstrn., Am. Pub. Works Assn. (editorial com.), Am. Soc. Pub. Adminstrn. Municipal Finance Officers Assn. of U.S. and Can., Nat. Fire Protection Assn. (com. fire dept. orgn. 1962-68), Fels Inst. Alumni Assn. (pres. 1966-67). Episcopalian. Contbr. articles to various profl. jours. Home: 3001 Veazey Terrace NW Washington DC 20008 Office: District Bldg 14th and E Sts NW Washington DC 20004

WATT, JOHN REID, educator; b. Seattle, Nov. 15, 1914; s. Paul Harris and Roberta (Frye) W.; B.S., U. Wash., 1937, M.A., 1942; postgrad. Harvard, 1937-39; M.S., U. Tex., 1956, Ph.D., 1960; m. Elizabeth Craven, Nov. 25, 1939 (dec. 1961); children—John David, Louisa Catherine, Madeleine Megan; m. 2d, Lillian Mann, May 4, 1962. Instr. econs. U. Tex., Austin, 1941-43, instr. mech. engring., 1943-46, asst. prof., 1948-52, asso. prof., 1952—; vis. asso. prof. Ga. Inst. Tech., Atlanta, 1971-72, prof., 1972—. Cons., dir. L.C. Frye Corp., Seattle, 1948—. Mem. Am. Assn. U. Profs. (chpt. v.p. 1949), Tex. Assn. Coll. Tchrs. (chpt. acting pres. 1954), Am. Soc. Heating, Refrigeration and Air Conditioning Engrs. (chpt. v.p. 1958), Am. Inst. Indsl. Engrs. (chpt. pres. 1967), Tex. Social Sci. Club (pres. 1967), Am. Soc. M.E., Am. Soc. Engring. Edn., Nat. Soc. Profl. Engrs., Am. Hosp. Assn., Hosp. Mgmt. Systems Soc., Sigma Xi, Phi Gamma Delta. Democrat. Unitarian. Club: Harvard Alumni (chpt. pres. 1967). Author: Evaporative Air Conditioning, 1963. Contbr. articles to profl. jours. Home: 77 E Andrews Dr NW Atlanta GA 30305

WATT, WILLIAM JOSEPH, coll. dean; b. Carbondale, Ill., Dec. 15, 1925; s. Philip Clement and Ella (Dickey) W.; student U. Mich., 1943; B.S. in Chemistry U. Ill., 1949; M.S., Cornell U., 1951, Ph.D., 1956; m. Helen Stevens Gravatt, Sept. 1, 1956; children—John Gravatt, Phyllis Cary, William Joseph. Asst. prof. chemistry Davidson (N.C.) Coll., 1951-53; mem. faculty Washington and Lee U., 1955—, prof. chemistry, 1965—, asso. dean of coll., 1968-71, dean, 1971—; vis. prof. NSF Inst. High Sch. Tchrs., Ala. Coll., summers 1959-61, U. Va., summers 1964-66. Summer research participant Cornell U., 1956; Oak Ridge Nat. Lab., 1957, 58, U. Va., 1962. Pres. Rockbridge chpt. Va. Mus. Fine Arts, 1963-65; bd. dirs. Rockbridge Concert Theater Series, 1960—, pres., 1971. Served with AUS, 1944-46. Mem. Am. Chem. Soc., N.Y. Acad. Scis., A.A.A.S., Va. Acad. Sci., Societe Chimique de France, Phi Eta Sigma, Alpha Chi Sigma. Democrat. Presbyn. Contbr. to profl. jours. Home: 7 Providence Pl Lexington VA 24450

WATTERS, JULIAN ALBURTUS, III, investment co. exec.; b. Mobile, Ala., June 10, 1929; s. Julian Alburtus and Madelyn (Pritchett) W.; student U. Ala., 1947-51; m. Patricia Turner Jackson, Sept. 1, 1948; children— Julian Alburtus IV, Patricia duMont, Debra Jackson. Pres., dir. Internat. Investments Inc., Butler, Ala., 1960, Demopolis Constrn. Co., Inc.; v.p. Butler Ins. Agy.; owner Butler Broadcasting Co.; dir. First Nat. Bank of Butler, C.F. Littlepage Lumber Co., Inc., Butler; owner farm. Pres., chmn. Southwestern Devel. Corp. Del. Democratic Nat. Conv., 1960. Mem. Ala. Forest Products Assn., Ala. Cattlemen's Assn., Choctaw County C. of C. (exec. com. 1967-69), U. Ala. Nat. Alumni (v.p. 1965-66), Sigma Nu. Episcopalian. Lion (past pres. Butler). Clubs: Mobile Country, Athelstan (Mobile); Downtown, Northwood, (Meridian, Miss); Demopolis (Ala.); Pensacola (Fla.) Yacht; Choctaw Country. Home: PO Box 2 Lavaca AL 36911 Office: PO Box 705 Butler AL 36904

WATTERSON, BRUCE CARTER, dentist; b. Chase City, Va., Oct. 26, 1939; s. George Shual and Ennis James (Carter) W.; B.A., U. Richmond, 1963, postgrad. 1963-64; D.D.S., Med. Coll. of Va., 1968; m. Juanita Rawls, June 17, 1961; children—Scott Hunter, James Carter. Research technician Med. Coll. of Va., 1958-60, med. technologist, 1961-68; practice of dentistry, Norfolk, Va., 1968-70, Virginia Beach, 1970—; with Virginia Beach Health Dept., 1969—. Mem. Am., Va., Va.-Tidewater dental assns., Virginia Beach Dental Soc., Virginia-Tidewater Dental Study Club, Psi Omega. Home: 4060 Richardson Rd Virginia Beach VA 23455 Office: 760 Independence Blvd Virginia Beach VA 23455

WAUGH, JOHN DAVID, educator; b. Charleston, W. Va., Sept. 20, 1932; s. Oran and Jewel (DeWees) W.; B.S., U. S.C., 1954; postgrad. Notre Dame U., 1957-58; M.S., Yale, 1964; m. Margaret Williamson, June 12, 1954; children—Debra Margaret, Donna Carol, John David. Stress analyst structural design Bendix Co., South Bend, Ind., 1957-58; prof. engring. U. S.C., Columbia, 1959—, asso. dean engring., 1968—. Cons. engr., 1960—; chmn. Southeastern Conf. on Theoretical and Applied Mechanics, 1964-66; mem. adv. com. Richland Tech. Edn. Center. Served to lt. USNR, 1954-57. NSF faculty fellow, 1962. Mem. Am. Soc. for Engring. Edn. (v.p. 1966-67), Am. Soc. C.E. (dist. sec. 1962), Sigma Xi, Tau Beta Pi, Phi Kappa Sigma, Omicron Delta Kappa. Methodist. Kiwanian. Home: 1512 Whipporwill Dr West Columbia SC 29169 Office: Coll Engring Univ SC Columbia SC 29208

WAUGH, KENNETH WILBERT, ednl. adminstr.; b. Blairstown, Mo., Dec. 17, 1919; s. Neal Dow and Stella (Reith) W.; B.S., Central Mo. State Coll., 1947; M.A., Colo. State Coll. Edn., 1952; Ed.D., Ind. U., 1959; m. Jean Frances Higbee, Dec. 19, 1948; children—Michael Deane, Patricia Jeane. Prin., Piper (Kan.) High Sch., 1948-50; supt. schs., Piper, 1950-52; dir. div. guidance and pupil personnel service Ind. Dept. Edn., 1954-56; prof. edn. West Tex. State U. Canyon, 1956-59, dir. student personnel service, 1959—. Coordinator diagnostic and evaluation services Penhandle Ednl. Service Orgn., 1966—; ednl. and counseling cons. Neighborhood Youth Corps, 1966—; dir. Tex. Cripple Children's Camp, 1968—. Bd. dirs. Tex. div. Am. Cancer Soc. Served with AUS, 1942-46. Named Tex.

Panhandle Educator of Year, 1969. Mem. Am., Tex. (dir.) personnal and guidance assns., Assn. Counselor Edn. and Adminstrn., Student personnel Assn. for Tchr. Edn., N.E.A., Tex. Tchrs. Assn., C. of C. (edn. com. 1964-65), Phi Delta Kappa. Lion (dist. gov. 1967-68, local pres. 1964-65). Author: Diagnosing Learning Disorders, 1970. Home: 2514 12th Av Canyon TX 79015

WAX, GEORGE LOUIS, lawyer; b. New Orleans, Dec. 6, 1928; s. John Edward and Theresa (Schaff) W.; LL.B., Loyola U. of South, 1952, B.C.S., 1960; m. Patricia Ann Delaney, Feb. 20, 1965; children—Louis Jude, Joann Olga. Admitted to La. bar, 1952, practice, New Orleans, 1954—. Served with USNR, 1952-54. Mem. Am., La., New Orleans bar assns., Am. Legion. Roman Catholic. Kiwanian. Clubs: New Orleans Athletic, Suburban Gun and Rod, Pendennis. Home: 5635 Pratt Dr New Orleans LA 70122 Office: Nat Bank Commerce New Orleans LA 70112

WAY, LULA ROSETTA, educator; b. nr. Mt. Pleasant, Mich., Dec. 3, 1912; d. C.O. and Nellie (Meginley) Way; B.S., George Peabody Coll. Tchrs., 1940, M.A., 1941; Ed.D., Mich. State U., 1958. Tchr. rural schs., Mich., 1931-36, Okemos Consol. Sch. (Mich.), 1936-39; tchr. social studies Pioneer Sch., W. Carrol Parish, La., 1942-45; elementary supr. campus sch. Neb. State Coll., 1945-49, jr. high sch. supr., 1951-54, prof. edn., 1954-62; prof. psychology, dir. psychol. reading clinic Florence (Ala.) State U., 1962—. Dir. N.E. Ala. Head Start tng. program, 1968—. Bd. dirs. Colbert Lauderdale Child Study Center, Florence, Ala., 1966—; pres. bd. Muscle Shoals (Ala.) Area Retarded Children, 1965-68; bd. dirs. Ala. Assn. Retarded Children, 1966—. Named Neb. Outstanding Tchr. of Year, 1956; recipient Civic award for work with retarded children, 1969. Mem. P.T.A. (mem. Neb. planning bd. 1945-52), N.E.A. Delta Kappa Gamma. Baptist. Author: (with Elizabeth Woolridge) Let's Play Arithmetic, 1960. Contbr. articles profl. jours. Home: 515 Sherwood Ct Florence AL 35630 Office: Box 502 Florence AL 35630

WAY, NATHAN EMERAN, govt. resource agy. exec.; b. Marion, S.D., June 4, 1903; s. Fred E. and Magdalena M. (Ashenbrucker) W.; B.S., U. S.D., 1926; postgrad. U. Tenn., 1939-42; m. Hazel Marie Pugh, Sept. 15, 1935; children—Nathan Emeran, Richard Allan. Structural steel detailer, checker Am. Bridge Co., Phila., 1926-29; structural designer Albert Kahn, Inc., Detroit, 1929-30, Allied Engrs., Inc., Jackson, Mich., 1930-31; design engr. Dakota Engring. Co., Mitchell, S.D., 1933; chief of party U.S.C.G. Survey, Sioux Falls, S.D., 1934; chief draftsman S.D. Hwy. Comm., Pierre, 1934-36; structural engr. TVA Div. of Design, Knoxville, 1936-59, asst. to mgr. TVA Office of Engring. Design and Constrn., 1959-68; dir. The Trail of Tears drama for Cherokee Nat. Hist. Assn., Tahlequah, Okla., 1969. Active Boy Scouts Am. Registered profl. engr. Tenn. Fellow Am. Soc. C.E. (past pres. Tenn. Valley sec.); mem. Tech Soc. Knoxville (past pres.), Scabbard and Blade, Delta Tau Delta. Roman Catholic. Home: Route 3 Williams RD Concord TN 37720

WAYNE, ALAN, educator; b. N.Y.C., June 18, 1909; s. Adolph Otto Johann and Martha (Horvath) Wiesenburg; B.S., Coll. City N.Y., 1931, M.S. in Edn., 1937; postgrad. Columbia, 1945-49, (A.A.A.S. Secondary Sch. fellow) N.Y.U., 1961-68; m. Muriel Rothstein, Aug. 25, 1934; children—Linda (Mrs. Paul Richard Weiss), Susan (Mrs. Lance Kelvin McKee). Tchr. math. and sci. Rhodes Sch., N.Y.C., 1930-45; tchr. math. James Fenimore Cooper Jr. High Sch., N.Y.C., 1940-45, Williamsburg Vocational High Sch., N.Y.C., 1945-51; asst. prin., supr. math. and sci. Eli Whitney Vocational High Sch., N.Y.C., 1951-72 (on leave). Adj. instr. math. Cooper Union, N.Y.C., 1949-67, adj. asst. prof., 1967-72; instr. math. edn. N.Y.U., 1950-51, Yeshiva U. Grad. Sch., 1959-61; adj. asst. prof. math. Queensborough Community Coll., N.Y.C., 1965-72; editorial cons. vocational-indsl. edn. State U. N.Y., 1949-57; mem. curriculum devel. coms. N.Y.C. Bd. Edn., 1950-70. Committeeman, N.Y. County Democratic Com., 1940. Mem. Sch. Sci. and Math. Assn., Council Supervisory Assns., Am. Assn. U. Profs., Am. Math. Soc., Soc. for Indsl. and Applied Math., Math. Assn. Am., Nat. Council Tchrs. Math., Assn. Tchrs. Math. N.Y.C. (pres. 1948-50); exec. bd., historian 1951-71), Assn. Tchrs. Math. N.Y. State (charter, county chmn. 1951-72), Math. Chmns. Assn. N.Y.C. (v.p. 1971-72), Epsilon Pi Tau. Club: N.Y. Riddlers (pres. 1952). Author: Basic Mathematics I, 1951; Basic Mathematics II, 1954; (with Olivo) Basic Applied Science, 1957; (with Bold) Number Systems, 1971. Editor: Metals Technology, 1955. Home: 7209 Lakeshore Dr Holiday FL 33589

WAYNE, GLENN ANTHONY, newspaper researcher; b. Passaic, N.J., May 25, 1930; s. Anthony and Gladys (Hasbrouck) W.; B.S., Johns Hopkins, 1953; M.B.A., N.Y. U., 1956; m. Louise Ott, Feb. 11, 1961; children— Kimberly Ann, Stephen David, Lori Beth. Research analyst Sullivan, Stauffer, Colwell & Bayles, N.Y.C., 1957-60; research analyst, supr. Thomas J. Lipton, Inc., Englewood Cliffs, N.J., 1960-65; staff cons. 1st Research Corp., dir. Gore Newspapers Co., Ft. Lauderdale, Fla., 1967—. Served with AUS, 1953-55. Mem. Am. Marketing Assn., Nat. Assn. Home Builders (econ. adviser 1967—). Home: 3919 Grant St Hollywood FL 33021 Office: 10 N New River Dr East Ft Lauderdale FL 33302

WEABER, GEORGE HAWN, physician; b. Binger, Okla., May 13, 1940; s. Ivan John and Helen (Hawn) W.; B.S., U. Okla., 1962, M.D., 1966. Intern, Baptist Meml. Hosp., Oklahoma City, 1966-67; resident in anesthesiology Parkland Meml. Hosp., Dallas, 1967-69; practice in anesthesiology, Cooper, Graham, Weaber, Arlington, Tex., 1969—; mem. staff Arlington Meml. Hosp., 1969—, Arlington Community Hosp., 1969—. Owner, Green Leaf Art Gallery, 1970—. Fellow Am. Coll. Anesthesiologists; mem. Am., Tex. Socs. anesthesiologists, Tarrant County Med. Assn., Okla. U. Alumni Assn., Delta Kappa Epsilon, Phi Beta Pi. Republican. Conglist. Home: 909 Live Oak Lane Arlington TX 76012 Office: 308 West Park Row Arlington TX 76010

WEAR, JENNINGS DARREL, wholesale co. exec.; b. Houston, Ark., June 23, 1909; s. Oscar Allen and Josie Myrtle (Nix) W.; grad. Chillicothe Bus. Coll., 1928; m. Edna Lee Hester, June 6, 1969; children by previous marriage—JoAnn, (Mrs. Kenneth L. Hatter), Marilyn Yvonne (Mrs. Arthur V. Johnston). With Earl Brothers & Co., Morrilton, Ark., 1928-30; v.p. E.E. Mitchell Co., 1932-40; with Semmes Motor Co., 1940; exec. v.p., treas. F. C. Stearns Hardward Inc., Hot Springs, Ark., 1940—; v.p., treas. F. C. Stearns Real Estate, Inc., 1948—. Sec., Hot Springs Municipal Water System, 1954-70; pres. Garland County Indsl. Devel. Corp., 1956-59. Bd. dirs. Ouachita Meml. Hosp., pres. 1954-55. Mem. Hot Springs C. of C. (pres. 1951-52), U. S. C. of C. (membership com. 1968-69). Mason (32 deg., Shriner), Lion (pres. 1948-49), Rotarian (treas. 1957-72). Home: 808 Woodlawn Av Hot Springs AR 71901 Office: PO Box 940 Hot Springs AR 71901

WEAR, PAT WATERFIELD, educator; b. Murray, Ky., Sept. 25, 1915; s. Linn Boyd and Edna (Hood) W.; B.S., Murray State U., 1939, M.A., 1948; Ed.D., U. Ky., 1956; m. Nedra Bayne Vannoy, June 18, 1940; children— Linda B. (Mrs. Larry K. Blair), Pat Waterfield II. Secondary sch. tchr., Lone Oak (Ky.) High Sch., 1939-42; tour leader Mammoth (Ky.) Cave Nat. Park, 1942-43; prin. Earlington (Ky.) High Sch., 1946-47; vis. prof. Union Coll., Barbourville, Ky., summer 1950; prof. edn. Berea Coll., 1950-61, chmn. dept., 1962—, dir. pre-service program Nat. Tchr. Corps, summer 1966; cons. in field, 1964—. Mem. nat. conf. fgn. policy for educators State Dept., 1967. Served with inf. AUS, 1943-46. Mem. Ky. Assn. Colls., Seconary and elementary Schs. (pres. 1959-60), Ky. Assn. Supervision and Curriculum Devel. (pres. 1969-70), Nat. (life; bd. dirs. dept. rural edn. 1967), Ky. (planning bd. 1960-68, pres. higher edn. assn. sect. 1969-70), Central Ky. (chmn. higher edn. sect. 1966-67) edn. assns., So. Assn. Colls. and Schs. (chmn., Ky. policy com. project opportunity), Am. Assn. Colls. Tchr. Edn. (instl. rep. 1963—, state liaison officer 1972—), Am. Assn. U. Profs., Phi Delta Kappa, Kappa Delta Pi, Phi Kappa Phi. Mem. Disciples of Christ Ch. Contbr. profl. jours. Home: 101 Van Winkle Dr Berea KY 40403

WEARE, BUEL FELLOWS, publishing exec.; b. Morton Park, Ill., Dec. 29, 1902; s. Ely and Mary (Fellows) W.; A.B., Princeton, 1925; M.B.A., Harvard, 1927; m. Nora Borden, Sept. 23, 1938; 1 dau., Mary Owen (Mrs. Paul G. Birdsall). In newspaper work, since 1930; with Des Moines Register and Tribune, 1930-40; mgr., N.Y. Herald Tribune Syndicate, 1946-50; pres. European edit. N.Y. Herald Tribune (Paris), 1950-53; pub. Congressional Quar., also Editorial Research Reports, 1954—. Served from 1st lt. to col. AUS, 1941-45; in Office of Q.M. Gen., Washington, 1941-42; chief of exec. div., Office of Chief Q.M., Communications Zone hdqrs., Europe, 1942-45. Hon. sec. Howard County Hunt, 1956-66. Mem. Phi Beta Kappa. Republican. Episcopalian. Home: Glenwood MD 21738 Office: 1735 K St NW Washington DC 20006

WEATHERALL, JOHN THEODORE, dentist; b. Port Arthur, Tex., July 13, 1924; s. Cyrus Theodore and Flora (Hooper) W.; student Tex. A. and M. U., 1942-43, Northwestern U., 1943, Harvard, 1943-44, Lamar U., 1946, Tex. U., 1946-47; D.D.S., U. Tex., 1951; m. ArrNell Lesikar Boelsche, Aug. 29, 1959. Pvt. practice dentistry, Texas City, Tex., 1953—; dir. Texas City Nat. Bank. Mem. exec. bd. Bay Area council Boy Scouts Am., 1970. Bd. dirs. Tex. Dental Polit. Action Com. Served with AUS, 1943-46, 50-53. Decorated Bronze Star medal. Fellow Am. Coll. Dentists; mem. Am., Tex. dental assns., 9th Dist. Dental Soc. (pres. 1960-61), Texas City C. of C. (dir. 1970—), U. Tex. Dental Br. Alumni Assn. (dir. 1968—), Xi Psi Phi. Presbyn. Mason (Shriner), Rotarian. Home: 1425 19th Av N Texas City TX 77590 Office: 1124 14th St N Texas City TX 77590

WEATHERBY, JOHN JOSEPH, engring. co. exec.; b. Memphis, May 27, 1903; s. Marion M. and Ida (Clifton) W.; B.S., Auburn U., 1925; m. Mae Phillips, Oct. 20, 1923; children—Marion Mae (Mrs. Bernard W. Craig), Mary Frances (Mrs. Jack O. Shaw), Doris (Mrs. Almer C. Engle), Jean (Mrs. Robert F. Craig). Chemist, Am. Agrl. Chem. Co., Atlanta, 1925-26, Dow Chem. Co., Mildland, Mich., 1926-29; plant mgr. Jones Chem. Co. subsidiary of Dow Chem. Co., Shreveport, La., 1930-33; chem. engr. Ark. Fuel Oil Co., Shreveport, 1933-37; chief process engr. to mgr. gas and oil div. Stearns Roger Corp., Denver, 1937-59; pres. Weatherby Engring. Co., Houston, 1959—. Recipient Recognition award Natural Gas Processors Assn., 1971. Fellow A.A.A.S.; mem. Am. Inst. Chem. Engrs., Nat. Soc. Profl. Engrs., Tex. Mfrs. Assn., Houston Engring. and Sci. Soc. Houston C. of C. Rotarian. Clubs: Cherry Hills Country (Denver); Brae-Burn Country (Houston). Contbr. to profl. jours., also chpt. to Ency. Chem. Process Equipment. Home: 7923 S Braeswood Blvd Houston TX 77071 Office: Box 36680 Houston TX 77036

WEATHERBY, LOIS MAXINE FLETCHER (MRS. JOSEPH NORMAN WEATHERBY), civic worker; b. Temple, Tex.; d. Omar Lester and Sarah Belle (McDonald) Fletcher; A.A., Ward-Belmont Coll., 1928; B.A. in English, Tex. U., 1930; postgrad. Mary Hardin Baylor Coll., 1931-32, Howard Payne Coll., 1950-51; m. Joseph Norman Weatherby, Feb. 23, 1933; children—Joseph Norman, Sarah Maxine (Mrs. Homer Hilton Stephens). Gray lady Vol. Service, A.R.C., 1942-46; officer, mem. bd. Women's Missionary Union First Bapt. Ch., 1965-69; regent Mary Garland chpt. D.A.R., 1957-60; sec. Hon. Phillip Livingston chpt. Daus. Am. Colonists, 1963-65; charter mem. Feur de Lis chpt. Huegenot Soc. (Austin, Tex.); corr.-sec. Maj. James McGregor chpt. Colonial Dames of XVIII Century (Dallas); mem. San Antonio County chpt. Nat. Soc. Magna Charta Dames, Sovereign Colonial Soc. Am. Royal Descent, Soc. Descs. Knights Most Noble Order of Garter, Plantagenet Soc., Colonial Order of Crown (all Phila.), Sterling C. Robertson chpt. Daus. Rep. of Tex. (Waco), Jr. Service League; charter mem., div. chmn. Women's Aux. Brownwood (Tex.) Community Hosp., 1968—; organizing sr. pres. Tejas Soc. Children Am. Revolution, 1944—; mem. bd. Brownwood Civic Music Assn., 1955-69; officer Women's Assn. Brownwood Country Club, 1950—. Recipient Gen. D. MacArthur Acad. Freedom medal Howard Payne Coll., 1968. Mem. Tex. Ex-Student Assn., Am. Assn. U. Women (past officer), Ashbel Lit. Soc., Brown County Hist Soc., Clan Donald Soc. Tex., Pi Beta Phi (Dallas mother's club). Rotary Ann. (div. chmn. 1967-69). Clubs: Knife and Fork, Investment, Junior 20th Century Study (Brownwood). Home: 2110 Belmeade St Brownwood TX 76801

WEATHERFORD, WILLIS DUKE, educator; b. Weatherford, Tex., Dec. 1, 1875; s. Samuel L. and Margaret (Turner) W.; B.S., Weatherford Coll., 1895; B.A., Vanderbilt U., 1899, M.A., 1900, Ph.D., 1907; LL.D., Berea Coll., 1955, U. N.C., 1962; m. Julia McCrory Weatherford, May 27, 1915 (dec.); 1 son, Dr. Willis Duke. Internat. student sec. YMCA, 1901-19, pres. YMCA Grad. Sch., Nashville, 1919-36; pres. Blue Ridge Coll., Inc., 1906-44; head dept. religion and philosophy Fisk U., 1936-46. Dir. Am. Cast Iron Pipe Co. Mem. bd. trustees Berea Coll., 1915—, also pres. bd.; dir. of adminstrn. So. Appalachian Studies, chmn. bd. Bd. dirs. Berea Coll. Mem. A.A.A.S., Am. Acad. of Polit. and Social Sci., Tenn. Acad. Sci., Phi Beta Kappa, Pi Gamma Mu, Phi Kappa Phi, Alpha Tau Omega. Methodist. Author numerous books on lit., religion, race, 1909-25; later books: (with Charles S. Johnson) Race Relations, 1934; Life Sketch of James Brownson Dunwoody De Bow, 1935; The American Churches and the Negro, 1937; Analytical Index of De Bows Review, 1946; Pioneers of Destiny, 1955. Co-author, editor: Religion in the Appalachian Mountains, 1955; Educational Opportunities in the Appalachian Mountains, 1955; co-author: Life and Religion in Southern Appalachia. Home: Black Mountain NC 28711 Office: Berea Coll Berea KY 40403

WEATHERLY, OWEN MILTON, educator; b. nr. Sumter, S.C., Oct. 5, 1915; s. Francis Marion and Eda Bell (Best) W.; A.A., North Greenville Jr. Coll., 1943; B.A. cum laude, Furman U., 1947; M.A., U. Chgo., 1950, Ph.D., 1952; m. Myra Sloan, June 21, 1948; children— Pamela, Marcia, Jan. Ordained to ministry Baptist Ch., 1942; pastor Beech Island (S.C.) Bapt. Ch., 1946-47; dir. youth activities 1st Bapt. Ch., Berwyn, Ill., 1949-50; pastor 2d Bapt. Ch., Richmond, Va., 1952-58, 1st Bapt. Ch., Phila., 1958-64; tchr. lang. arts and social studies Evergreen Park (Ill.) Central Sch., 1951-52; asso. prof. religion and philosophy High Point (N.C.) Coll., 1964-67, prof., 1967—. Served with USAAF, 1943-46. Decorated Purple Heart. Mem. Am. Philos. Assn., N.C. Philos. Soc., Am. Acad. Religion. Author: The Fulfillment of Life, 1959; The Ten Commandments in Modern Perspective, 1962; Help your Minister to Do His Best, 1965. Home: 1605 Chatham Dr High Point NC 27260

WEATHERLY, TRAVIS EUGENE, ednl. adminstr.; b. Potts Camp, Miss., May 24, 1925; s. Anderson and Mattie Jane (Caviness) W.; student Northwest Miss. Jr. Coll., 1949-50; B.S., Miss. State Coll., 1951, M.S., 1952; postgrad. U. Ga., 1969-70; m. Peggy Joyce Pierce, Aug. 7, 1953; children—Travis Eugene, Edward Anderson. Tchr., Pascagoula (Miss.) High Sch., 1952-57; vocational tchr. Corinth (Miss.) High Sch., 1958-61; draftsman Tyrone Hydraulics, Corinth, 1961-65, sales adminstr., 1965-66; asst. dir. DeKalb Area Tech. Sch., Clarkston, Ga., 1966-69, dir., 1969-72; asst. to pres. DeKalb Community Coll., 1972—. Mem. edn. professions devel. adv. com. U. Ga., 1971—. Served with USAAF, 1943-45. Decorated Air medal with 4 oak leaf clusters. Mem. Am., Ga. vocational assns., DeKalb Assn. Educators, Ga. Assn. Educators, Nat. Council Local Adminstrs. Mason. Editor: DeKalb Assn. Educators News, 1971-72. Home: 314 Fond du Lac Dr Stone Mountain GA 30083 Office: 555 N Indian Creek Dr Clarkston GA 30021

WEATHERS, BAILEY GRAHAM, physician; b. Shelby, N.C., Dec. 8, 1895; s. John Davidson and Mary Louise (Styers) W.; B.S., Wake Forest Coll., 1927; M.D., Med. Coll. Va., 1929; m. Ora Bumgardner, Dec. 31, 1922; children—Ruth Ann (Mrs. Carl Irvin Grigg), Bailey Graham, John Lewis, Jerry Davidson. Intern, Cook County Gen. Hosp., Chgo., 1935; gen. practice medicine, Stanley, N.C., 1929—; mem. staff Gaston Meml. Hosp., Gastonia, N.C. Served with 30th Arty. Div., U.S. Army, 1917-18. Named Dr. of Yr., Gaston County Med. Soc., 1952, Man of Yr., City of Stanley, 1969. Mem. A.M.A., N.C., Gaston County med. socs., Am. Acad. Gen. Practice (charter mem.). Baptist. Lion (charter mem., 1st pres. Stanley club). Home: 601 Hwy 27 S Stanley NC 28164 Office: 222 S Main St Stanley NC 28164

WEATHERS, BAILEY GRAHAM, JR., physician; b. Stanley, N.C., Apr. 12, 1932; s. Bailey Graham and Ora Edith (Bumbardner) W.; B.S., Wake Forest Coll., 1953; postgrad. So. Bapt. Theol. Sem., 1953-56; M.D., Med. Coll. Va., 1960; m. Wanda Gail Dahmer, Feb. 14, 1970; children by previous marriage—Bailey Graham III, David Gardner, Robert Alfred; 1 foster son, Steven Ray Layell. Intern, Moses H. Cone Hosp., Greensboro, N.C., 1960-61; gen. practice medicine, Farmington, N.C., 1961-67, Stanley, N.C., 1967—; mem. staff Garrison Gen. Hosp., Gastonia, N.C. Profl. artist, 1967—; exhibited paintings and sculpture in shows at Gallery Contemporary Art, Winston-Salem, 1968, 69, Mint Mus. Art, 1968, Festival in the Park, Charlotte, 1969, 70, N.C. Mus. Art, 1970. Mem. Am. Acad. Gen. Practice, A.M.A., N.C., Gaston County med. socs., N.C. Asso. Artists, Gaston County Art Assn., Theta Chi. Home: 301 W Chestnut St Stanley NC 28164 Office: 222 S Main St Stanley NC 28164

WEAVER, BARRY ROLAND, resource analyst; b. Tulsa, Okla., Nov. 11, 1933; s. Carmen and Ruby (Trent) W.; B.A., U. Ark., 1955; postgrad. U. N.C., 1956-57. Corr. instr. in Am. History, U. Ark., Fayetteville, 1955-56; research asst. Inst. for Research in Social Sci., Chapel Hill, N.C., 1956-57; exec. dir. Human Engring Lab., Tulsa, 1958-64; sr. test adminstr. Johnson O'Connor Research Found., N.Y.C., 1965; resource analyst Office of Emergency Preparedness, Exec. Office of the Pres., Washington D.C., 1965-70. Mem. U. Ark. Traffic Bd., 1953-54. Trustee Human Engring Lab., asst. treas., 1959-63; trustee Johnson O'Connor Research Found. Inc., asst. treas., 1959-63; trustee Human Engring Lab., Ontario, asst. treas., 1959-64; trustee Fundacion de Investigaciones Johnson O'Connor, Mexico, 1962-65. Served with AUS, 1957. Named Honorary Citizen, Little Rock, Ark., 1963. Mem. Sierra Club, Wilderness Soc., Met. Washington Coalition for Clean Air (chmn. study strategy com. 1968-70), The Nature Conservancy, Friends of the Earth, Ark. Audubon Soc., Soc. for Environmental Stblzn., The Ozark Soc., Am. Collegiate Polit. League (pres. 1952-53), Phi Alpha Theta Author tech. reports: Princeton University Aptitude Differences, 1963, Roman Catholic Colleges and Universities, 1963, Research Thesis of the American History Survey, 1964. Editor: Item-by-Item Study of English Vocabulary, 1961. Contbr. to various publs. Address: Eagle's Rest Route 2 Springdale AR 72764

WEAVER, CHARLES EARL, electronic engr., cons.; b. Xenia, O., Aug. 23, 1906; s. Charles Lucian and Sylvia (Turner) W.; diploma Radio Inst. Am., 1926; m. Edith Elizabeth Johnson, July 5, 1928; 1 dau., Janet W. (Mrs. Robert William Tarleton). With Am. Tel. & Tel. Co., Columbus, O., 1928-42, Point Reyes, Cal., 1942-47, tech. asst., N.Y.C., 1947-54; electronic engr. Western Electric Co., Inc., Winston-Salem, N.C., 1954-59; electronic engr. USAF, Andrews AFB, Md., 1954-59, sr. engr., Griffiss AFB, Rome, N.Y., 1959-64; sr. engr. Bell Telephone Labs., Whippany, N.J., 1964-68; communications system cons., 1968—. Def. Communications Agy. rep. U.S. Prep. Group for Internat. Tel. and Tel. Consultative Com., 1963. Mem. I.E.E.E. (asso.), Am. Radio Relay League, Armed Forces Communication and Electronic Assn. Patentee in field. Address: 2161 Sarazen Dr Dunedin FL 33528

WEAVER, DON MELVIN, supt. schs.; b. Temple, Tex., Nov. 8, 1932; s. Leonard Harold and Vivian Edith (Armagost) W.; B.S., Tex. A. and M. Coll., 1957, M. Ed., 1966; m. Janice Ann Taliaferro, Dec. 30, 1957; children—Daryle Don, Ray Lavelle. Tchr. Huckabay, Tex., 1959-63, Priddy, 1963-65; prin. Balmorhea, Tex., 1966-68; supt. schs. Bledsoe (Tex.) Independent Sch. Dist., 1968—; pres. and mgr. Bledsoe Nat. Gas Co., 1968—, Bledsoe Water Supply Corp., 1968—. Served with AUS, 1957-59. Mem. Am. Assn. Sch. Adminstrs., Tex. State Tchrs. Assn., Tex. Assn. Sch. Adminstrs. Baptist. Home: Box 85 Bledsoe TX 79314 Office: Box 85 Bledsoe TX 79314

WEAVER, GEORGE HOMER, mfg. co. exec.; b. Sapulpa, Okla., Jan. 17, 1924; s. John Homer and Lucille Lillian (Bunch) W.; B.A., U. Tulsa, 1948, B. in Mus. Edn., 1950, M. Edn., 1951; m. Jaxine Helen Yeagle, Dec. 23, 1951; children—Lori A., Joni A., Tami A. With Liberty Glass Co., Sapulpa, 1956—, dir. marketing, 1968—, sales mgr., 1969—. Served with AUS, 1941-43: ETO. Decorated Purple Heart. Mem. Phi Mu Alpha, Sigma Phi Epsilon. Clubs: Harvard, Oaks Country (Tulsa). Home: 3707 S Florence Pl Tulsa OK 74105 Office: PO Box 520 Sapulpa OK 74066

WEAVER, HERBERT, educator; b. Brewton, Ala., July 28, 1905; s. Levi P. and Anne (Holladay) W.; A.B., Birmingham-So. Coll., 1926, M.A., 1935; Ph.D., Vanderbilt U., 1941; m. Blanche Henry Clark, Mar. 5, 1944. Tchr., Ala. secondary schs., 1926-35; teaching fellow Vanderbilt U., 1936-40; asso. prof. history Ga. Tchrs. Coll., 1940, prof., chmn. dept., 1942-49; mem. faculty Vanderbilt U., 1949—, prof. history, 1952—, chmn. dept., 1962-67. Served to maj. USAAF, 1942-46. Mem. Am., Miss. Valley, So. hist. assns., Tenn. Hist. Soc., Kappa Phi Kappa, Pi Gamma Mu. Methodist. Clubs: Old Oak, University. Author: Mississippi Farmers, 1850-1860, 1945. Editor: Correspondence of James K. Polk. Contbr.: History United States Air Force in World War II, 1948-58. Mem. editorial bd. Jour. So. History, Tenn. Hist. Quar. Home: 3718 Brighton Rd Nashville TN 37205

WEAVER, JAMES ELMER, JR., steel co. exec.; b. Dallas, Nov. 27, 1934; s. J. Elmer and Virginia (West) W.; student Tex. Technol. Coll., 1951-54, So. Meth. U., 1954; m. Marilyn Lewis (div.); children—Kitra Kay, Keith Mitchell, Kirsten Ray; stepchildren—Joseph L., Jefferson L., R. Christopher Smith. Salesman, Weaver Iron Works, Inc., Dallas, 1959-63, v.p., 1963-64, pres., 1964—; mgr. S.W.A.K. Co., Irving,

Tex., 1967—. Mem. Irving Planning and Zoning Commn., 1964-69, chmn., 1969; pres. Irving Assn. for Retarded Children, 1969-70. Served to capt. USAF, 1954. Mem. Tex. (outstanding local pres. 1962-63, outstanding state chmn. 1963-64), Irving (officer of year 1965-66; v.p. 1965-66) jaycees, Irving C. of C. (dir. 1962-63), Dallas Exec. Assn., Alpha Tau Omega. Republican. Methodist. Mason, Elk, Kiwanian. Office: 3302 Pluto St Dallas TX 75212

WEAVER, JOHN B., ins. co. exec.; b. Staunton, Va., Mar. 5, 1925; s. Charles Dwight and Edna (Sayers) W.; student Dunsmore Bus. Coll., 1947; B.S. in Bus. Adminstrn., U. Richmond, 1951; m. Addie Jane Samples, Oct. 17, 1952. Jr. accountant Leach, Calking & Scott, Richmond, Va., 1951-54; audit clk. Life Ins. Co. Va., Richmond, 1954-60, asst. to treas., 1960-64, asst. treas., 1964-68, treas., 1968—. Served with USNR, 1943-46. Fellow Life Office Mgmt. Assn. Inst. Methodist (treas. 1969). Home: 3105 Comet Rd Richmond VA 23229 Office: 914 Capitol St Richmond VA 23209

WEAVER, JOHN WILSON, oil co. exec.; b. York, Pa., Sept. 7, 1924; s. Norman H. and Grace A. (Sheffar) W.; B.S., Drexel U., 1953; m. Jean T. Schneeman, Sept. 3, 1950; children—Lee Ann, Michael. Engr., Standard Oil Co. Cal., Perth Amboy, N.J., 1953-55; sales rep. Cal. Crude Oil Sales Co., N.Y.C., 1955-61; with Standard Oil Co. Ky., Louisville, 1961—, v.p. supply and distbn., 1967-70, exec. v.p., 1970—; dir. Plantation Pipe Line Co., Atlanta. Mem. Ky., Louisville (ambassador) chambers commerce, Am. Waterways Conf., Ohio Valley Improvement Assn. Mason (Shriner). Clubs: Audubon Country, Pendennis (Louisville). Home: 608 Yancy Lane Louisville KY 40207 Office: PO Box 1446 Louisville KY 40201

WEAVER, JOSEPH DUDLEY, physician; b. nr. Winton, N.C., Sept. 11, 1912; s. Jesse Robert and Claudia C. (Hall) W.; B.S., Howard U., 1934, M.D., 1938; m. Rossie Mae Phenis Clay, Apr. 22, 1958; children—Jesse Robert, Patricia (adopted), Claudia. Intern Freedmen's Hosp., Washington, 1938-39; pvt. practice medicine Hartford, N.C., 1939-46, Ahoskie, 1946—; owner, operator Weaver Clinic, Ahoskie; active staff Roanoke Chowan Hosp.; asst. nat. med. dir. Elks. Bd. dirs. N.C. chpt. So. Christian Leadership Conf. Served from 2d lt. (Res.) to 1st lt. M.C., AUS, 1942-44. Named Dr. of Year, Old North State Med. Soc., 1963. Mem. Ahoskie C. of C., Eastern N.C. Med., Dental and Pharm. Soc., Old North State, Hertford County med. socs., Nat. Med. Assn., Med. Soc. State N.C., A.M.A., Am. Geriatric Soc., Nat. Rehab. Assn., Kappa Alpha Psi, Beta Kappa Chi. Democrat. Baptist, Mason (32 deg.). Club: Ambassador (pres. 1948—). Home: RFD 2 256-D Ahoskie NC 27910 Office: 111 N Maple St Ahoskie NC 27910

WEAVER, JOSEPH UPTON, physician, ret. army officer; b. Bolivar, Mo., Nov. 27, 1904; s. John Wiley and Mattie (Upton) W.; A.B., Washington U., 1926; M.D., St. Louis U., 1931; M.P.H., U. N.C., 1959; m. Grace Lida Short, Apr. 2, 1932; children—Joseph Upton, John S. Commd. 1st lt., U.S. Army, 1931, advanced through the grades to col., 1944, ret., 1958; Intern Sta. Hosp., Ft. Sam Houston, Tex., 1931-32, resident in orthopedics, 1932-34; dep. chief Health and Welfare Sect. Supreme Comdr. Allied Powers, Tokyo, Japan, 1945-46, chief, 1946-48; dep. comdr. and comdr. Walter Reed Army Med. Center, Washington, 1948-53; chief surgeon U.S. Army Forces, Austria, 1954-55; comdg. officer U.S. Med. Tng. Center, Ft. Sam Houston, Tex., 1956-57; chief surgeon XVIII Airborne Corps and Ft. Bragg, Ft. Bragg, N.C., 1957-58; dir. Vance County Health Dept., Henderson, N.C., 1959—, also Warren County Health Dept. and Granville County Health Dept., Oxford, N.C. Decorated Legion of Merit with oak leaf cluster. Fellow Am. Pub. Health Assn.; mem. Am. Coll. Hosp. Adminstrs., A.M.A., N.C. Tb Assn. (dir). Home: 855 Park Av Henderson NC 27536 Office: PO Box 824 Henderson NC 27536

WEAVER, JUNIUS VADEN, steel co. exec.; b. Colonial Heights, Va., June 22, 1927; s. Thomas Joseph and Daisy Dean (Vaden) W.; B.S., Va. Poly. Inst., 1954; m. Frances Elizabeth McKnight, Nov. 27, 1954; children—Martha Ann, Mary Elizabeth, Joseph David. Sales engr. Wallace & Tiernan, Inc., Roanoke, Va., 1954-55; field engr. Am. Bridge Co., Roanoke, Chgo., Lynchburg, Va., 1955-59; design engr., sales engr. Montague-Betts Co., 1959-66; pres. J.V. Weaver Steel Co., Lynchburg, 1967—. Served with USAAF, 1945-47. Registered profl. engr., Va., N.C. Mem. Nat., Va. socs. profl. engrs. Methodist (trustee). Pioneer staggered truss system for constrn. high rise bldgs. Home: 1412 Nelson Dr Lynchburg VA 24502

WEAVER, KENNETH, physician; b. Whitetop, Va., Dec. 4, 1933; s. Grover Cleveland and Violet (Baldwin) W.; B.S., U. N.C., 1956, MD., 1960; m. Shelby Jean Davis, June 17, 1967; children by previous marriage—Teresa, Janice, Beverly, Pamela, Cynthia. Intern, USPHS, Boston, 1960; med. officer in charge USPHS Indian Hosp., Cherokee, N.C., 1961-64; practice family medicine, Waynesville, N.C., 1964-70; resident obstetrics and gynecology U. Ark. Med. Center, Little Rock, 1970—; chief staff Haywood County Hosp., Waynesville, N.C., 1970. Pres. Haywood chpt. Am. Cancer Soc., 1969; mem. N.C. Gov.'s Study Commn. for Cause and Control of Cancer, 1970-71. Served to maj. USPHS, 1960-64. Mem. A.M.A., N.C., Haywood County med. socs. Inventor in field. Home: 8910 Cloverhill Rd Little Rock AR 72205

WEAVER, LESTER CLARK, assn. exec.; b. Chesaning, Mich., Oct. 5, 1907; s. Arza Aerold and Leota Susan (Crane) W.; student Emmanuel Missionary Coll., 1926; B.A., Central State Tchrs. Coll., 1928; m. Marian Carolyn Lewis, May 18, 1928; children—Patricia Ann (Mrs. Claude L. Duvoisin), Richard L. Commd. U.S. Air Force, 1942, advanced through grades to lt. col., 1959; flight instr., command pilot at numerous AFB; insp. gen. 64th Air Div., Nfld., Can.; base comdr. McConnell AFB, Kan., now ret.; exec. dir. Greater Plantation (Fla.) C. of C., 1963—. Decorated Air medal; recipient Outstanding Community Service award Wichita C. of C., 1959, Man of Year award West Broward Jr. C. of C., 1967, Outstanding Citizen award Civitan Club Plantation, 1970. Home: 5580 SW 2d Ct Plantation FL 33314 Office: 3877 W Broward Blvd Plantation FL 33312

WEAVER, LUCIUS STACY, coll. pres.; b. Lenoir, N.C., Oct. 29, 1904; s. Charles Clinton and Florence (Stacy) W.; A.B., Duke U., 1924, LL.D., 1971; A.M., Columbia, 1932; Litt.D. (hon.), High Point Coll. 1959; m. Elizabeth Hallyburton, Aug. 1, 1926; children—Charles Horace, Lucius Stacy, Walter Parker. Prof. Rutherford Coll., N.C., 1924-32, pres., 1932-33; pres. Mountain Park N.C. Jr. Coll., 1933-34; prin. Jonesville (N.C.) Pub. Schs., 1934-41; supt. Statesville (N.C.) City Schs., 1941-47, Durham (N.C.) City Schs., 1947-57; pres. Meth. Coll., Fayetteville, N.C., 1957—. Sec. Gov's Commn. on Revision Pub. Sch. Law; vice chmn. Gov.'s Commn. on Pub. Sch. Finance, mem. Gov.'s Commn. Ednl. TV; mem. gen. bd. edn., chmn. jurisdictional com. Methodist Ch.; chmn. State Com. for Evaluation Tchr. Edn. Mem. Am. Assn. Sch. Adminstrs., N.E.A., N.C. Edn. Assn. (past state pres.), Horace Mann League (pres.). Democrat. Methodist (dist. lay leader). Mason, Kiwanian (past pres., past lt. gov.). Author of various papers on ednl. and religious topics. Home: 1717 Raeford Rd Fayetteville NC 28305

WEAVER, MACON LENNY, U.S. atty.; b. Huntsville, Ala., Jan. 6, 1919; s. James W. and Pearl (Brown) W.; LL.B., U. Ala., 1950; m. Flora Virginia Waddell, Sept. 13, 1942; children—Teri Jean, Ricky Ann, Lennie Sue. Admitted to Ala. bar, 1950; pvt. practice, Huntsville, 1950-57; circuit solicitor, 1957-61; U.S. dist. atty. No. Dist. Ala., 1961—. Served to 1st lt. AUS, 1941-45; ETO. Decorated Purple Heart; recipient George Siebels Traffic Safety award Huntsville Jr. C. of C., 1953, Key Man award, 1952. Mem. Am., Ala., Madison County bar assns., Nat. Assn. Pros. Attys., V.F.W. (life; past post comdr.), Phi Alpha Delta. Clubs: Huntsville Sertoma; Vestavia Lions. Home: 2404 Gladstone Dr Huntsville AL 35811 Office: PO Box 195 Birmingham AL 35202

WEAVER, ORDE RICHARD, petroleum co. exec.; b. Orchard, Neb., Apr. 26, 1913; s. George A. and Mae Stella (Knapp) W.; B.S., Neb. State Coll., 1936; M.A., U. Neb., 1946; m. Ann Mae Burkman, Jan. 30, 1970; children—John Charles, Jayne Lonelle. Chief insp. Neb. Def. Corp., Wahoo, 1942-46; mgr. quality control Dept. Army, Ordnance Corps., Neb. Ordnance Plant, Wahoo, 1946-50; mgr. quality control and inspection Nat. Gypsum Co., Wahoo, 1951-54; mgr. quality control Rocket Fuels div. Phillips Petroleum Co., McGregor, Tex., 1954-57, dir. quality control div., Bartlesville, Okla., 1957—. Fellow Am. Soc. Quality Control (v.p. 1970-71, dir. midwest conf. bd. 1959—, Edward J. Oakley award 1971); mem. Phi Delta Kappa. Republican. Presbyn. Mason, Kiwanian. Author: EVOP in Operation, 1966. Home: PO Box 1281 Bartlesville OK 74003 Office: 15 C-1 Phillips Bldg Bartlesville OK 74004

WEAVER, PATSY JEAN, ednl. adminstr.; b. Waterloo, Ark., May 30, 1932; d. Luther P. and Vida (Polk) Weaver; B.S., So. State Coll., Magnolia, Ark., 1954; M.Ed., U. Ark., 1957; postgrad. Auburn U., 1959, 60, U. Ala., 1961-62. Tchr. Harmony Grove High Sch., 1954-55, Camden High Sch., 1955-61; asst. dean of women So. State Coll., Magnolia, Ark., 1962-67, dean of women, 1967—. Mem. Nat., Ark. assns. women deans and counselors, N.E.A., Ark. Edn. Assn., Am., Ark. personnel and guidance assns., Am., Ark. coll. personnel assns., Am. Assn. U. Women, Delta Kappa Gamma. Baptist. Home: 1725 Dogwood Dr Magnolia AR 71753

WEAVIL, JAMES COLON, retail store exec.; b. Winston-Salem, N.C., July 21, 1921; s. Ernest Edgar and Vada Belle (Hastings) W.; grad. high sch.; m. Barbara Louise Chambers, Sept. 6, 1947; 1 dau., Michelle. Salesman Vick Paint Co., Winston-Salem, 1938-42, 45-50; field supr. British Am. Tobacco Co., Caracus, Venezuela, 1950; with Ed Kelly Inc., Winston-Salem, 1950—, gen. mgr., 1951—, v.p., 1955—. Served with USMCR, 1942-45, 50-51. Mem. Winston Salem Retail Mchts. Assn. (bd. dirs., 1969-70). Methodist. Mason. Home: 619 Banner Av Winston-Salem NC 27107 Office: 1122 S Main St Winston-Salem NC 27101

WEBB, ALLAN WAYNE, hotel exec.; b. Electra, Tex., Jan. 6, 1921; s. Clarence Andrew and Ruth Ophelia (Mitchell) W.; student U. Ill., 1946; m. Lois Anges Carr, Nov. 3, 1942; children—Richard Alan, Terry Lee. Commd. 2d lt. USAF, 1942, advanced through grades to lt. col., 1962; combat pilot, 1944-45; mgr. Officers Club, Europe, 1957-62; squadron flight leader Forbes AFB, Kan., 1956-58, Dover AFB, Del., 1962-64; ret., 1964; mgr. Pharaoh Country Club, Corpus Christi, Tex., 1966-68; v.p., gen. mgr. Sheraton-Marina Inn, Corpus Christi, 1968—. Bd. dirs. Community Concerts, 1970—. Decorated D.F.C., Air medal with 8 oak leaf clusters. Mem. Corpus Christi Hotel-Motel Assn. (bd. dirs. 1971-72), V.F.W. Mason, Rotarian. Home: 46 Townhouse Lane Corpus Christi TX 78412 Office: 300 N Shoreline St Corpus Christi TX 78401

WEBB, ALVIN BURGESS, univ. ofcl.; b. Cumberland, Ky., Sept. 28, 1932; s. J.A. and Susannah (Holbrook) W.; B.S. with honors, Pikeville Coll., 1961; M.A. with honors, U. Ky., 1965. Prin., Letcher County Bd. Edn., Whitesburg, Ky., 1953-55; secondary tchr. Jenkins (Ky.) Ind. Sch. Dist., 1961-64; area resource specialist U. Ky. Coop. Extension Service, Prestonsburg, 1965-67, pub. affairs specialist, Prestonburg, also Whitesburg, Ky., 1967—. Pres., Black Oak Coal Co., Mayking, Ky., 1958—. Police judge pro tem City of Jenkins, 1962-64. Mem. Nat., Ky., Jenkins (past pres.) edn. assns., Nat. County Agt. Assn., Jr. C. of C. (nat. dir. 1967-68). Baptist. Author pamphlets: (with Jack Reeves) Kentucky Constitutional Revision, 1965; Public Affairs Citizenship, 1969. Home: 313 Madison St Whitesburg KY 41858 Office: Box 126 Whitesburg KY 41858

WEBB, CHARLES GALLOWAY, civil engr.; b. Montague, Tex., Aug. 28, 1899; s. Atticus and Mattie (Fugitt) W.; student Columbia, 1919; B.S. in Civil Engring., Rice Inst., 1922; postgrad. Okla. U., 1922-25, Oklahoma City U., 1922-25; m. Anna Eleanor Asmussen, Feb. 27, 1932. With W. R. Grimshaw Constrn. Co., Tulsa, 1929-48, v.p., sec., to 1948; propr. Charle G. Webb Cons. Engr., Tulsa, 1948—. Served with Inf. U.S. Army, 1918. Registered profl. engr. Fellow Constrn. Surveyors Inst.; mem. Am. Soc. C.E. Democrat. Methodist. Mason (Shriner); mem. Order Eastern Star. Home: 15975 E 12th St Tulsa OK 74108 Office: 1437 E 3d St Tulsa OK 74120

WEBB, DAVID ALKEN, librarian; b. Greenwood, S.C., June 3, 1917; s. Charles and Rebecca Connor (Aiken) W.; A.B., U. S.C., 1939, Emory U., 1940; A.M., U. Mich., 1947; postgrad. U. Chgo., 1951-53, Ph.D., 1963; m. Ruth Hammerle, Aug. 14, 1948; children—Christopher Lee, Rebecca Ann. Asst. library Ga. Sch. Tech., 1940-42; librarian Technol. Inst., Northwestern U., 1947-48; asso. librarian Rice Inst., Houston, 1948-51; instr. grad. library sch. U. Chgo., 1952-53; dir. libraries, also prof. library sci. N. Tex. State U., Denton, 1953—, dir. library service dept., 1953-67. Served with AUS, 1942-45. Mem. A.L.A., Assn. Coll. and Reference Libraries, Tex., Southwestern library assns., Tex. Council Library Edn. (chmn. 1954-56), Am. Assn. U. Profs., Tex. Assn. Coll. Tchrs. Home: 1214 Clover Lane Denton TX 76203

WEBB, DONALD WAYNE, investment co. exec.; b. Tampa, Fla., Sept. 5, 1914; s. Jeptha L. and Bertha (Bryan) W.; student Norman Coll., 1932, Bus. U. Tampa, 1933; m. Winifred Wilson, 1932; children—Bryan, Angela (Mrs. Willard L. Galloway). Pres., Webb Bros. Dairy, Sweetwater Creek, Fla., 1944-59; founder Import Motor Parts Co., 1959, pres., 1959—; dir. Sunstate Builders, Inc., Tampa, 1962—; dir., mem. loan com. Carrollwood State Bank; dir., financial adviser Fowler Av. Property, Warehouses, Hanna Av., Cyprus St., Church Av. Past pres. Hillsboro County Civic Assn.; press Saddleback Improvement Assn.; bd. dirs. N.W. Hillsboro Basin. Webb scholar U. Tampa, 1971. Mem. Krewe of Venus, Minaret Soc. Methodist. Home: Route 2 Box 722 Lutz FL 33549 Office: 10301 N Dale Mabry Tampa FL 33618

WEBB, EMMA S. (MRS. C. W. WEBB), lawyer; b. Bible Grove, Ill.; d. John Edward and Pauline (Blattner) Stullken; student Blinn Meml. Coll., Brenham, Tex., 1908-10; LL.B., U. Tex., 1923; m. Charles Wilson Webb, July 27, 1917 (dec. 1961); children—Jackson S., Mary Lynn (Mrs. Ray L. Starnes) (dec.). Pub. sch. tchr., 1910-17; admitted to Tex. bar, 1923; partner Webb & Webb, 1923-60, Webb, Webb & Meridith, 1960—. Elgin School tax collector, 1932-46. Vice chmn. Bastrop County com. Tex. State Hist. Survey Com., 1963—; mem. Tex. Hist. Found., 1965—; mem. Elgin Centennial History Com., 1970—. Trustee Elgin Sch., sec. 1925-29. Named Citizen of Year Elgin C. of C., 1959. Mem. Bastrop County (pres.), Tex. State bar assns., Am. Judicature Soc., Tex. State Fedn. Women's Clubs (legal adviser 1925-27), P.T.A., Am. Legion Aux. (pres. 1952-53), Tex. Law Rev. Assn., Bastrop County Hist. Soc., U.D.C., Bastrop County Fedn. Women's Clubs (pres. 1924-26, 1930-32), Kappa Beta Pi. Democrat. Methodist. Mem. Order Eastern Star (life). Club: Elgin New Century (pres. 1929-31, 43-45; life mem. 1968). Home: 710 N Av C Elgin TX 78621 Office: 34 N Av C Elgin TX 78621

WEBB, ERNEST PACKARD, publisher; b. Junta, W.Va., Aug. 30, 1907; s. Robert Moses and Josephine (Harvey) W.; student advt. Internat. Corr. Schs., 1946-48, Alexander Hamilton Bus. Sch., 1948-52. Artist, Mountain State Engraving Co., 1929, Huntington Engraving Co. (W. Va.), 1930, Charleston Engraving Co. (W.Va.), 1931; owner, mgr. Profl. Art Studio, Roanoke, Va., 1931-40; v.p., treas. Roanoke Engraving Co., 1940-48; pres. Va. Engraving Co., Richmond, 1947—; v.p. Dixie Engraving Co., Roanoke, 1961—; pres. W. & H. Corp., Richmond, 1968—. Served with USAAF, 1942-45. Mem. Va., Richmond chambers commerce, Internat. Craftsman's Club. Republican. Baptist. Clubs: Richmond Industrial, Willow Oaks Country, Westwood (Richmond). Home: 2000 Riverside Dr Richmond VA 23225 Office: 2003 Roane St Richmond VA 23222

WEBB, GEORGE C., banker; b. Nashville, Nov. 10, 1910; s. Thomas Dwight and Cora (Crockett) W.; B.A., Vanderbilt U., 1932; m. Peggy Alexander, May 18, 1935; 1 son, Vance Alexander. With Nat. Life &Accident Ins. Co., Nashville, 1932-43; with Union Planters Bank, Memphis, 1945—, now exec. v.p., dir. Pres. Memphis Cotton Carnival Assn., 1956; Tenn. chmn. Am. Cancer Soc. crusade, 1962. Served with USNR, 1943-45. Decorated Bronze Star. Mem. Assn. Res. City Bankers. Home: 57 Wychewood Rd Memphis TN 38117 Office: 67 Madison Av Memphis TN 38101

WEBB, HUBERT JUDSON, scientist, state ofcl.; b. nr. Aiken, S.C., June 8, 1911; s. George R. and Carrie (McCrackan) W.; B.S., Clemson Coll., 1933; Ph.D., Cornell U., 1938; m. Emma Irene McGregor, July 3, 1937;children—Linda (Mrs. Joseph A. Martin), George McGregor, Kennith Edward (dec.). Chief chemist Clemson Coll., 1938-51, dean grad. sci., 1951-55, head agrl. chem. research, 1955-65; dir. environmental health labs. S.C. Bd. Health, Columbia, S.C., 1965-69; asso. dir. S.C. Pollution Control Authority, Columbia, 1969-70, exec. dir., 1970—. Fellow A.A.A.S.; mem. Am. Chem. Soc., Am. Soc. Bacteriology, Am. Water Works Assn. (Fuller award 1963), Water Pollution Control Fedn., Sigma Xi, Phi Kappa Phi, Alpha Zeta, Gamma Sigma Delta. Home: 2025 Rolling Hills Rd Columbia SC 29210 Office: 1321 Lady St S Columbia SC 29211

WEBB, JAMES EDWIN, lawyer; b. Granville County, N.C., Oct. 7, 1906; s. John Frederick and Sarah (Gorham) W.; A.B., U. N.C., 1928; student George Washington U. Law Sch., 1933-36, LL.D., 1961; LL.D., U. N.C., 1949, Syracuse U., Colo. Coll.; Sc.D., U. Notre Dame, 1961, also other hon. degrees; m. Patsy Aiken Douglas, May 14, 1938; children—Sarah Gorham, James Edwin. Exec. asst. to undersec. of treasury, 1946; dir. Bur. Budget, 1946-49; undersec. of state, 1949-52; dep. gov. Internat. Bank for Reconstrn. and Devel. and IMF, 1949-52; pres., gen. mgr. Republic Supply Co., 1953-58, chmn. bd., 1958-60; adminstr. NASA, 1961-68; practice law, Washington, 1968—; dir. Kerr-McGee Oil Industries, Inc., Oklahoma City, Sperry-Rand Corp., Gannet Co., Rochester, NY. Trustee Com. for Econ. Devel.; trustee, past pres. Frontiers of Sci. Found. Okla.; chmn., pres. Urban Studies; treas. Nat. Acad. Pub. Adminstrn; bd. dirs., former chmn. Meridian House Found.; regent Smithsonian Instn. Served as comdg. officer 1st Marine Air Warning Group, 1944-45; lt. col. Marine Corps Res. Recipient NASA Distinguished Service Medal, Collier Trophy, 1968; Goddard Meml. Trophy, 1971; N.C. Pub. Service award, 1971; Medal of Freedom from Pres. L.B. Johnson, 1968. Mem. Am. Soc. Pub. Adminstrn. (pres. 1966-67), Nat. Geog. Soc. (trustee 1966—), Am. Polit. Sci. Assn., Soc. Advancement Mgmt., Am. Bar Assn., Bar Assn. D.C., Acad. Polit. Sci., Phi Beta Kappa, Phi Delta Phi. Democrat. Presbyn. Mason. Clubs: University, Brook (N.Y.C.); University, Chevy Chase, Metropolitan, Alfalfa (Washington). Home: 2800 36th St NW Washington DC 20007 Office: 1771 N St NW Washington DC 20036

WEBB, JAMES KENNETH, dentist; b. Smithville, Tenn., Mar. 7, 1941; s. Thomas Benton and Gladys Gertrude (Gray) W.; B.S., Tenn. Tech., 1962; D.D.S., U. Tenn., 1965; m. Elizabeth Faye Taylor, Sept. 1, 1962; 1 dau., Martha Gray. Pvt. practice dentistry, Pulaski, Tenn. 1968—. Chmn. Giles County March of Dimes, 1970-71. Bd. dirs. Giles County Mental Health, Giles County Mental Retardation. Served to lt. USPHS, 1965-67. Mem. Am., Tenn., 6th Dist. dental socs., Giles County C. of C. (dir.), Xi Psi Phi. Baptist. Rotarian (treas. 1971-73). Home: 109 Tollgate St Pulaski TN 38478 Office: 604 E College St Pulaski TN 38478

WEBB, JAMES MURRAY, architect; b. Aguascali entes, Mexico, Jan. 23, 1908; s. Ray Hickey and Martha Murrah (Barkofay) W.; student Pomona Coll., Cal., 1929-30; A.B. U. Cal. at Berkeley, 1936; M.City Planning, Mass. Inst. Tech., 1946; m. Barbara Gray Henderson Kelly, Nov. 28, 1956. Designer, Warren C. Perry, architect, San Francisco, 1937-39, William W. Wurstler, architect, San Francisco, 1939-42; pvt. practice architecture and planning, Chapel Hill, N.C., 1949—; planning cons. Appalachian State U., Boone, N.C., 1957—; prof. dept. city and regional planning U. N.C., Chapel Hill, 1947—. vis. prof. planning U. Cal. at Berkeley, spring, 1961. Mem. Chapel Hill Appearance Commn., 1964—. Served with AUS, 1942-43. Mem. A.I.A., Am. Inst. Planners, Am. Assn. U. Profs. Prin. archtl. works include campus plan Appalachian State U., 1971. Home: 110 Cameron Ct Chapel Hill NC 27514 Office: 201 E Rosemary St Chapel Hill NC 27514

WEBB, JAMES SJOBERG, hosiery co. exec.; b. Macon, Ga., Dec. 2, 1931; s. Jesse Tatum and Dura (Brooks) W.; B.S., (Faculty scholar), U. Tenn., 1956, J.D. summa cum laude, 1956; m. Nina Josephine Holt, June 30, 1956; 1 son, James Sjoberg. Admitted to Tenn. bar, 1956; practiced in N.Y.C., 1956-57, Cleveland, Tenn., 1960-63; asso. Mudge, Stern, Baldwin & Todd, N.Y.C., 1956-57; atty. Bowaters So. Paper Corp., Calhoun, Tenn., 1960-61; partner Bell, Whitson, Painter & Webb, Cleveland, Tenn., 1962-63; v.p. Charleston Hosiery Mills, Cleveland, 1963—. Trustee Cleveland (Tenn.) Day Sch.; bd. dirs. Bradley-McMinn County Jr. Achievement. Served as capt. USAF, 1957-60. Mem. Tenn. Mfrs. Assn. (mem. indsl. relations com. 1969—), Cleveland Assos. Industries (pres. 1971—), Cleveland-Bradley County C. of C. (pres. 1969), Cleveland Indsl. Personnel Club (pres. 1968), Order of Coif, Omicron Delta Kappa, Phi Delta Phi, Delta Sigma Pi, Phi Gamma Delta. Republican. Episcopalian (vestryman 1969). Kiwanian, Elk. Club: Cleveland (Tenn.) Golf and Country. Editor-in-chief Tenn. Law Review, 1955-56. Home: Annandale Park Cleveland TN 37311 Office: 465 1st St SW Cleveland TN 37311

WEBB, JOHN COTHER, mfg. co. exec.; b. Dayton, O., Dec. 29, 1914; s. John Basil and Estelle (Williams) W.; B.A., Oxford U., 1938; B.S. in Elec. Engring., N.Y.U., 1942; m. Gloria Bernal Atristain, Dec. 29, 1951, (dec. 1968); children—John Robert, Gerard Michael. Vice pres. Ferro-Cart Corp. of Am., 1941-44; dir. sales Maguire Industries, 1944-46; chmn. Magnetic Core Corp.; pres. Electro-Metall. Products Inc., 1948-67, Fritzal Corp., Ft. Pierce, Fla., John C. Webb & Assos., Ft. Lauderdale, Fla.; v.p. Fair-Rite Corp., 1951-67; dir. Faradyne Electronics Corp. Mem. Broward Council of 100. Mem. Ossing C. of C. (past pres.), Metals Powder Industry Fedn. (past pres.), I.E.E.E.

Clubs: Lions, Ardsley Country, Beach, Rotary (dir.). Author: The New Rubaiyat and Other Verse, 1968. Home: 2782 NE 5th St Pompano Beach FL 33062 Office: PO Box 23039 Fort Lauderdale FL 33307

WEBB, JOSEPH ELIJAH, JR., state ofcl.; b. Aiken, S.C., Mar. 6, 1908; s. Joseph Elijah and Sadie (Whetstone) W.; B.S., Clemson U., 1932; M.S., Ohio State U., 1934; M.P.H., U. N.C., 1954; m. Lois Alice Carter, Nov. 22, 1936; children—Patricia (Mrs. James B. Hendershot), Jane (Mrs. Charles Ivey), Joseph R. Entomologist dept. entomology State of Ga., 1934-41; commd. lt., Med. Service Corps, U.S. Army, 1941, advanced through grades to col., 1961, ret., 1963; pub. health environmentalist Ga. Dept. Pub. Health, Clayton, 1966—. Med. entomology cons. to NATO, U.S. Army, London, Eng., 1957; chmn. U.S. Armed Forces Pest Control Bd., 1961-63. Recipient certificate of achievement Army Surgeon Gen., 1962. Mem. Entomol. Soc. Am., Am. Pub. Health Assn., Am. Mosquito Control Assn., Nat. Malaria Soc. Mason (Shriner), Lion. Home: Box 784 Clayton GA 30525 Office: Box 327 Clayton GA 30525

WEBB, JULIAN, state senator; b. Bryomville, Ga., Oct. 2, 1911; s. Vester Otis and Flossie (Woodruff) W.; A.B., LL.B., Mercer U., 1932; m. Jo Smith, Sept. 25, 1935; children—Joanna (Mrs. Henry Clayton Custer), Julianna (Mrs. Robert Edward Cheshire III). Admitted to Ga. bar, 1932, practiced in Augusta until 1933; in legal dept. Farm Credit Adminstrn., 1933-42; practice law, Donalsonville, 1943—; Donalsonville (Ga.) city atty., 1945—; mem. Ga. Senate, 1963—, asst. floor leader, 1963, floor leader, 1964; pres. pro tem, 1967—; mem. Ga. Constn. Revision Commns., 1963, 69; mem. Ga. Bar Disciplinary Bd., 1964-67. Trustee, chmn. So. Ga. Home for Aging Ams. Mem. Am., Ga. (bd. govs.), Pataula Circuit bar assns., Am. Judicature Soc., State Disciplinary Bd., C. of C. (dir.), Blue Key, Sigma Pi, Phi Alpha Delta. Democrat. Methodist. (chmn. Thomasville dist. trustees, del. world conf. 1966). Mason (Shriner), Lion (pres. 1945). Address: 208 E 3d St Donalsonville GA 31745

WEBB, OTTIS CECIL, well drilling co. exec.; b. Belden, Miss., Aug. 9, 1914; s. John Wesley and Maggie (Simmons) W.; grad. high sch.; m. Doris Elaine Bost, Mar. 11, 1937; children—Ottis Cecil, Johnny Bost, David Lynn, Susan Lavern. Partner, J.W. Webb & Sons, Belden, and predecessor firm, 1931-60, sole owner, 1960-64, inc., 1964, pres., chmn. bd., 1964—; chmn. bd. So. Well Supply Co., Inc., Memphis, 1968—; dir. Lee Investments, Inc., Col., gov.'s staff State of Miss., 1968—. Recipient recognition award for service to ground water industry Tom Hunt Co., 1969; Ruby Citation award Driller, 1966. Mem. Miss. Water Well Contractors Assn. (pres. 1958, 69; dir.). Methodist (sec.-treas. 1966—, steward 1947—). Mem. Nat. Water Well Contractors Assn. (ins. com. 1960-64). Address: Box 88 Belden MS 38826

WEBB, RALPH GARNETT, television exec.; b. Whitesboro, Tex., Apr. 25, 1927; s. G. Ralph and Inez (Richards) W.; student Parsons (Kan.) Jr. Coll., 1949, Pathfinder Radio-Television Sch., Kansas City, Mo., 1950; m. Doris Elaine Watson, Dec. 22, 1951; children—James Ralph, Gayle Elaine. Announcer radio sta. KLKC, Parsons, 1948-49, WDAF, Kansas City, Mo., 1949-50, KSET, El Paso, Tex., 1950; program dir. radio sta. KELP, El Paso, 1952-53; producer, dir. sta. KTSM-TV, El Paso, 1953-55; program operations mgr. KWTX Broadcasting Co., Waco, Tex., 1955—. Cons., film producer athletic dept. Baylor U. 1959—; radio and TV adviser Tex. Radio and Film Commn. of Meth. Ch. Mem. Drug Abuse Council, Waco. Bd. dirs. Lions Crippled Camp, Kerrville, Tex.; past bd. dirs. Goodwill Industries McLennan County, March Dimes Waco, Little League Waco; publicity dir. Heart O'Tex. Boy Scouts Scout-o-rama; Past chmn. bd. McLennan County Nat. Found.; mem. council instl. devel. Baylor U.; mem. adv. council Environmental Control, Waco; adv. council VA on Jobs for Returning Vets., Waco. Served with USNR, 1944-46, 50-52. Mem. Alpha Epsilon Rho. Republican. Methodist. Lion. Club: Woodland West Country (dir.). Home: 3900 W Waco Dr Waco TX 76710 Office: 4520 Bosque Blvd Waco TX 76710

WEBB, ROBERT BECK, telephone co. exec.; b. Chapin, Ia., Oct. 12, 1921; s. Chester G. and Grace (Beck) W.; A.A., Waldorf Jr. Coll., 1940; B.C.S., Am. Inst. Bus., 1948; postgrad. U. Kan., 1965; m. Norma Jean Totten, June 15, 1947; children—Mary Ellen, James Totten. Gen. accountant Ia. Continental Telephone Co., Grinnell, 1948-53; with Fla. Telephone Corp., Ocala, 1953—, sec., comptroller, asst. treas., 1963—, v.p. finance, 1969—. Campaign chmn. Marion County (Fla.) United Appeal, 1968. Served with USAAF, 1942-45. Mem. Am. Soc. Corporate Secs., Fla. Telephone Assn. (sec.-treas. 1967), Marion County C. of C., Marion County Com. of 100. Methodist. Kiwanian (pres. Ocala 1966)

WEBB, ROBERT DELWIN, supt. schs.; b. Brownfield, Tex., Mar. 22, 1926; s. Robert E. and Iris (Brannan) W.; B.S., Tex. Technol. Coll., 1949, M.S. in Edn., 1950, Ed.D., 1967; m. Barbara Ann Crowe, Dec. 28, 1954; children—Rhonda Suzanne, Melissa Ann. Tchr. Littlefield (Tex.) Pub. Schs., 1950-51; prin. Brownfield (Tex.) Pub. Schs., 1951-54, curriculum dir., 1955-63; supt. schs., Abernathy, Tex., 1963—. Served with USNR, 1944-46. Mem. West Tex. C. of C. (dir., mem. edn. com. 1963-64), Tex. Tchrs. Assn. (dist. pres. 1971-72), Tex. Assn. Sch. Adminstrs. (chmn. for N.E.A. relations 1971-72). Baptist. Mason (32 deg.), Lion (pres. 1966-67). Home: PO Box 778 Abernathy TX 79311

WEBB, ROBERT ELDRIDGE, journalist; b. Gulfport, Miss., Oct. 9, 1928; s. Otho Barney and Ola (Reagan) W.; B.J., U. Mo., 1949; postgrad. Tulane U., 1951, Yale, 1958, Ariz. State U., 1962; m. Sara Virginia Patton, June 2, 1956; children—John Robert, Mary Virginia. Reporter, Tampa Times, 1949, New Orleans States, 1949-55; with Jackson (Miss.) State Times, 1955-62; statehouse reporter Ariz. Jour., Phoenix, 1962-63; reporter Cin. Enquirer, 1963-64, edn. writer, 1964-66, asst. city editor, 1966-67, polit. writer, columnist, 1967-69, corr., chief Washington Bur., 1969—. Sec., Enquirer Middle Mgmt. Bd., 1969, chmn., 1969—; lead writer, lead researcher Enquirer's Govt.-In-Crisis project, 1969. Served with AUS, 1950-51. Mem. Ky. Cols., Sigma Delta Chi (a founder Queen City chpt. 1967, pres. 1967-69, Miss. chpt. pres. 1958-59), Tau Kappa Epsilon (nat. pub. relations com. 1965—). Methodist (steward). Kiwanian. Office: Nat Press Bldg Washington DC 20004

WEBB, ROBERT LEE, chem. co. exec.; b. Topeka, Nov. 19, 1926; s. Floyd William and Laura Leona (Arnold) W.; B.S., Washburn U., 1949; m. Mary Elizabeth White, Jan. 25, 1952; children—Robert, Brigitte. Chemist, IH Milling Co., Topeka, 1949-50; research chemist Glidden Co., Jacksonville, Fla., 1950-57, mgr. research and devel. labs., 1957-59, prodn. mgr., 1959-61, asst. tech. dir., 1961, dir. devel., 1961-62; v.p. cons.-research chemistry Terpene Research Inst., Jacksonville, 1962-64; with Union Camp Corp., Jacksonville, 1964, gen. mgr. Terpene and Aromatics div., 1968—. Served with USNR, 1944-46. Mem. Am. Chem. Soc. Luth. Contbr. articles to profl. publs. Patentee in field. Home: 2479 Holly Point Rd E Orange Park FL 32073 Office: 2051 Lane Av N Jacksonville FL 32205

WEBB, ROBERT S., city ofcl.; b., 1925; student Tex. A. and M. U.; LL.B., South Tex. Coll. Law. Admitted to bar, 1953; councilman City of Houston. Address: Office of City Councilmen City Hall Houston TX 77002*

WEBB, ROBERT WATKINS, physician, educator; b. Chickasha, Okla., Jan. 25, 1906; s. Napoleon B. and Mary Elizabeth (White) W.; B.A., So. Meth. U., 1926; M.D., Tulane U., 1933; grad. Washington D.C. Sch. Psychiatry, 1952, Washington D.C. Psychoanalytic Inst., 1952; m. Elisabeth M. Nutting, Sept. 13, 1952. Intern Hotel Dieu Hosp., New Orleans, 1933-34; resident Pa. Hosp. Mental and Nervous Diseases, Phila., 1934-36, Inst. Pa. Hosp., 1936; asso. physician Silver Hill Found., New Canaan, Conn., 1936-37, resident Payne-Whitney Psychiat. Clinic, N.Y. Hosp., 1937-38; clin. asso. prof. psychiatry Southwestern Med. Sch., Dallas, 1953—; pvt. practice, Dallas, 1939-41, 52—; sr. attending staff physician Parkland Hosp., Dallas, 1953—. Trustee Dallas Art Assn.; bd. dirs. Dallas Theater Center. Served with M.C., AUS, 1941-46. Mem. A.M.A., Internat., Am. psychoanalytic assns., Am. Coll. Psychiatrists, Am. Coll. Psychoanalysts, Tex. Neuropsychiat. Assn., Am., So. psychiat. assns. Home: 5530 Farquhar Lane Dallas TX 75209 Office: 4338 Lemmon Av Dallas TX 75219

WEBB, VAN WYCK HOKE, ins. and railroad exec.; b. Raleigh, N.C., Feb. 18, 1915; s. Alexander and Lydia Maverick (Hoke) W.; B.S., U. N.C., 1936; m. Anna Fawcett Tomlinson, Mar. 22, 1947; children—Van Wyck Hoke, Mary Lovelace, Anna Tomlinson. Teller, N.C. Nat. Bank, Raleigh, 1937-39; spl. agt. N.C. Fire Ins. Rating Bur., Raleigh, 1939-41; state agt. N.Y. Underwriters Ins. Co., Raleigh, 1941-50; asso. mgr. ins. dept. Wachovia Bank & Trust Co., Winston-Salem, N.C., 1950-56; v.p. Dupree & Webb, Inc. Ins., Raleigh, 1956-69, pres., 1969—; v.p. N.C. R.R. Co., Raleigh, 1960—; dir. Troxler Electronic Labs., Raleigh. Bd. dirs. YMCA, 1968—. Served to lt. comdr. USNR, 1942-46; ATO, ETO, PTO. Mem. Ind. Ins. Agts. N.C. (pres. 1965-66, bd. dirs. 1956-67), Chartered Property and Casualty Underwriters, Sigma Alpha Epsilon. Democrat. Episcopalian. Kiwanian. Clubs: City, Carolina Country, Raleigh. Home: 2518 Wake Dr Raleigh NC 27608 Office: 336 Fayetteville St Raleigh NC 27601

WEBB, WILLIAM YATES, economist; b. Shelby, N.C., Oct. 12, 1910; s. Edwin Yates and Willie (Simmons) W.; student Wake Forest U., 1928-29; A.B. with honors in Econs., Columbia, 1932, M.A. in Econs., 1933; postgrad. fellow in econs. Duke, 1933-34, N.Y.U., 1934-35, 36-37, Brookings Instn., 1935-36,; m. Laura Mae Brown, Oct. 12, 1941; 1 dau., Shirley Webb (Mrs. Moses N. McCall). Economist, tin investigating com. U.S. Ho. Reps., 1934; economist Bituminous Coal Consumers Counsel Dept. Interior, 1937-40; economist, chief oil and gas sect. Census Bur., 1940-42; economist WPB, 1942; economist, indsl. engr. Office Naval Material, 1946-51; indsl. specialist Munitions Bd., Dept. Def., Washington, 1951-53, indsl. specialist Office Asst. Sec. Def., 1954-61; vulnerability analyst Office Civil Def., 1961-65, Office of Sec. Def., 1965-69. Served to comdr. USNR, 1942-46. Mem. Am. Econ. Assn., Am. Inst. Mining, Metall. and Petroleum Engrs., Am. Ordnance Assn., Am. Statis. Assn., Nat. Conf. State Socs. (past pres.), Navy League, Roanoke Island Hist. Soc., N.C. Soc. of Washington (past pres.), Res. Officers Assn., Columbia U., Duke, Wake Forest alumni assns., Kappa Alpha, Pi Gamma Mu. Methodist. Clubs: Kenwood Golf and Country (Bethesda, Md.), Nat. Economists. Contbr. articles and book revs. to profl. jours. Home: 3614 Warren St NW Washington DC 20008

WEBBER, WILLIAM TEMPLE, JR., banker; b. Texarkana, Tex., Oct. 3, 1931; s. William Temple and Asa Love (Wheeler) W.; grad. Choate Sch., 1949; B.A., Washington and Lee U., 1954; m. Barbara Chase, June 18, 1954; children—William Temple III, Dianne Chase, Christopher Wheeler, David Falconer. Dist. mgr. Temple Lumber Co., Lufkin, Tex., 1954-60; asst. cashier Tex. Nat. Bank, Houston, 1960-64; sr. v.p. So. Nat. Bank, Houston, 1964—; dir. Bank of Harris County. Mem. Houston C. of C. Episcopalian. Clubs: River Oaks Country (Houston); Lakewood Golf (Point Clear, Ala.). Home: 3714 Inwood St Houston TX 77019 Office: PO Box 2529 Houston TX 77001

WEBSTER, BURNICE HOYLE, physician; b. Leeville, Tenn., Mar. 3, 1910; s. Thomas Jefferson and Martha Anne (Melton) W.; B.A. magna cum laude, Vanderbilt U., 1936, M.D., 1940; m. Georgia Kathryn Foglemann, May 6, 1939; children—Brenda Kathryn, Phillip Hoyle, Adrienne Elise. Intern St. Thomas Hosp., Nashville, 1940-42, resident, 1942-43; practice medicine, specializing in chest disease, Nashville, 1943—; mem. staff St. Thomas, Bapt., Nashville Gen. hosps.; cons. VA Hosp.; asso. in medicine Vanderbilt Med. Sch., 1943—; prof. anatomy Gupton-Jones Sch. Mortuary Sci., 1941-43. Served with USPHS. Fellow Am. Coll. Chest Physicians, Am., Internat. colls. angiology; mem. Am. Cancer Soc. (dir.), A.M.A., Am. Thoracic Soc., So. Med. Soc., Tenn. Med. Assn., Nashville Acad. Medicine. Research in mycotic and parasitic diseases. Home: Valley Brook Rd Nashville TN 37215 Office: Mid-State Med Center Nashville TN 37203

WEBSTER, DONALD ALBERT, internat. trade and investment cons.; b. Rochester, N.Y., Dec. 9, 1930; s. Albert Charles and Madeline (Vandenbush) W.; B.A., Hamilton Coll., 1953; M.A., Johns Hopkins, 1955; m. Helen Long, Mar. 29, 1959; Asst. to asst. adminstr. Gen. Services Adminstrn., Washington, 1959-61; minority economist Joint Econ. Com., U.S. Congress, Washington, 1962-68; domestic policy coordinator, Key Issues Com., Nixon-Agnew Campaign Com., Washington, 1968; asst. to sec. U.S. Treasury Dept., Washington, 1969-70, dep. asst. sec. for internat. affairs, 1970-71; asst. dir. council on Internat. Econ. Policy, White House, 1971; pres. Webster, Johnson & Stowell, Inc., Washington, 1971—. Served to lt. (j.g.) USNR, 1956-59. Mem. Am. Econ. Assn., Nat. Economists Club. Club: Capitol Hill. Home: 4615 Sedgwick St NW Washington DC 20016 Office: 733 15th St NW Washington DC 20005

WEBSTER, GEORGE DRURY, lawyer; b. Jacksonville, Fla., Feb. 8, 1921; s. George D. and Mary Gaines (Walker) W.; B.A., Maryville Coll., 1941; LL.B., Harvard, 1948; m. Ann Kilpatrick, May 3, 1952; children—Ann Walker, George Drury, Hugh Kilpatrick. Admitted to Ga. bar, 1950, D.C. bar, 1952; atty. tax div. Dept. Justice, 1949-51; practice law, Washington, 1951—; now partner Marmet and Webster; lectr. tax. insts.; adviser U.S. C. of C., 1959—; dir. 1st Western Financial Corp. Nat. dir. Lawyers for Nixon-Agnew, 1968; nat. co-chmn. Lawyers to Re-elect the Pres., 1972. Bd. dirs. Maryville Coll.; trustee U.S. Naval Acad. Found. Served to lt. USNR, 1942-46. Mem. Am. Law Inst., Am. Bar Assn. (council), Nat. Assn. Execs. Club. Clubs: Chevy Chase (Md.); Harvard (N.Y.C. and Washington); Metropolitan, Capitol Hill (Washington). Author: Associations and the IRS, 1966; Business and Professional Political Action Committees, 1968; The Law of Associations, 1971. Home: 5305 Cardinal Ct Washington DC 20016 also Webster Angus Farm Rogersville TN Office: 1822 Jefferson Pl NW Washington DC 20036

WEBSTER, JAMES EPPS, motion picture exec.; b. Evansville, Ind., Mar. 6, 1919; s. Robert Byrd and Nancy Elizabeth (Roberts) W.; student Colo. State Coll., 1937-38, U. Tenn., 1939; B.A., U. Chattanooga, 1934; m. Elizabeth Thatcher, May 23, 1944; children—Katherine (Mrs. Ted Rose), James L., Lynn. Propr. Running Eagle Trading Post, Bluewater, N.M., 1937-43; with field advt. dept. Proctor & Gamble Co., Cin., 1939-42; asst. mgr. Firestone Stores, Inc., Knoxville, Tenn. 1942; mgr. Rock City Gardens, Lookout Mountain, Tenn., 1945-47; propr. mgr. Lookout Mountain Photo Shop (Tenn.), 1947-50; pres. Camera Mart, Chattanooga, 1950-51; propr. Webster Visual Sales Co., Chattanooga, 1951-65; pres. Continental Film Prodns. Corp., Chattanooga, 1951—, also dir. Served to 1st lt., USAAF, 1943-45. Mem. Soc. Motion Picture and Television Engrs., Aircraft Owners and Pilots Assn., Yucatan Exploring Soc. Clubs: Underwater Archeology and Explorations of Mexico (Mexico City), Fairyland Country (dir. 1960-63), Belle Monte (Lookout Mountain); Explorers of Am. (N.Y.C.); U.S. Polo (Chattanooga). Episcopalian. Home: 1502 Peter Pan Rd Lookout Mountain TN 37350 Office: 2320 Rossville Blvd Chattanooga TN 37408

WEBSTER, RONALD ARTHUR, lawyer, county ofcl.; b. nr. Oliver Springs, Tenn., Dec. 21, 1938; s. Paris Guthrie and Myrtle (Hill) W.; B.S., U. Tenn., 1960, J.D., 1962; m. Dianne Sharp Webster, 1967. Admitted to Tenn. bar, 1963, since practiced in Knoxville; asso. firm Frantz, McConnell, Seymour, 1963-65, Webster & Webster, 1965—; city trial atty. Knoxville, 1965-67; mem. Tenn. Ho. of Reps., 1965-68; now atty. gen. Knox County, Knoxville. Chmn. atty.'s div. East Tenn. Heart Fund, 1964-65. Mem. Knox County Republican Exec. Com., 1960—; mem. Tenn. Rep. Exec. Com.; mem. Knox County Young Republican Club. Mem. Am., Tenn., Knoxville bar assns., Am. Trial Lawyers Assn., Sigma Chi, Phi Delta Phi, Tau Kappa Alpha. Baptist. Mason. Clubs: Dean Hill, Senators Country. Home: 4120 Maloney Rd Knoxville TN 37920 Office: Criminal Ct Bldg Knoxville TN 37902

WECHSBERG, HENRY, dentist; b. Germany, June 29, 1919 (came to U.S. 1935, naturalized 1941); s. Edward and Sara (Kaufmann) W.; D.D.S., Washington U., 1951; m. Florence Orin, Aug. 18, 1945; children—Orin, Wendy. Pvt. practice dentistry, Miami, Fla., 1951—. Served with CIC, AUS, 1942-45. Recipient award Am. Acad. Dental Medicine. Fellow Royal Soc. Health; mem. Am., Fla., East Coast Dist. dental assns., South Dade Dental Soc., Alpha Omega, Omicron Kappa Upsilon. Jewish religion (temple dir.). Mem. B'nai B'rith. Home: 11031 SW 60th Ct Miami FL 33156 Office: 3542 Coral Way Miami FL 33145

WEDAMAN, THOMAS HAYNE, JR., elec. engr.; b. Aiken, S.C., Oct. 17, 1937; s. Thomas Hayne and S. Carolyn (Holston) W.; B.E.E., Ga. Inst. Tech., 1961; M.B.A., Fla. State U., 1971; m. Ann Grainger Williams, Oct. 16, 1964; children—Michael Hayne, David Grainger. Project engr., aerospace services div. Pan Am. World Airways, Patrick AFB, Fla., 1965—. Scoutmaster, Boy Scouts Am., Satellite Beach, Fla., 1964—. Served with USAF, 1962-65. Registered profl. engr., Fla. Presbyn. Mason. Home: 478 Kale St Satellite Beach FL 32935 Office: Mail Unit 706 Patrick AFB FL 32925

WEDDING, CHARLES RANDOLPH, architect; b. St. Petersburg, Fla., Nov. 16, 1934; s. Charles Reid and Marion (Whitaker) W.; student McCallie Sch., 1950-52; B.Arch., U. Fla., 1957; m. Audrey Whitsel, Aug. 18, 1956; children—Daryl Leigh, Douglas Randolph, Dorian Blair. Apprentice draftsman, architect Harvard & Jolly, A.I.A., St. Petersburg, Fla., 1957-58, 60; individual practice C. Randolph Wedding, A.I.A., St. Petersburg, 1960—. Bd. dirs. Jr. Achievement, St. Petersburg, 1967-68; chmn. bd. Canterbury Sch., 1969-72; chmn. urban renewal Citizen's for Better St. Petersburg, 1965, Bldg. Dept. Survey Team, 1966—; chmn. architects and engrs. United Fund, St. Petersburg, 1965, 66. Trustee Mus. Fine Arts, St. Petersburg, All Children's Hosp., 1970-73. Served to 1st lt. AUS, 1958-60. Recipient Best Multi-Family Housing in Pinellas County award, 1964-68, 65-69; Best Residential Structure award, 1965-69; Outstanding Comml. Structure award, 1964-68, 65-69, Merit Design award Fla. Assn. Architects, 1966. Mem. A.I.A., St. Petersburg Assn. Architects (pres. 1964-66), Com. of 100 (chmn. 1971-72), Suncoasters, C. of C. (treas.), Phi Delta Theta. Episcopalian (vestryman). Rotarian. Home: 990 31st Av NE St Petersburg FL 33703 Office: 2901 58th Av N St Petersburg FL 33714

WEDGE, ERNEST ALPHONSE, ednl. adminstr.; b. Leominster, Mass., July 1, 1912; s. Alphonse and Hannah Elizabeth (O'Neill) Gouin; A.B. cum laude, Amherst Coll., 1935; postgrad. Harvard, 1937; M.A., Columbia, 1954. Asst. headmaster Milw. U. Sch., 1954-56; headmaster Am. Sch., Paris, France, 1956-62, St. John's Sch., San Juan, P.R., 1964—. Served to lt. USNR, 1942-45, 50-52. Mem. Phi Gamma Delta. Home: 66-68 Condado St Santurce PR 00907 Office: 1466 Ashford Av Santurce PR 00907

WEDGE, M.C., airline exec.; b. Parkersburg, W.Va., Mar. 29, 1917; s. Dencil and Dorothy (Gerlach) W.; grad. Boeing Sch. Aeros., Oakland, Cal., 1939; m. Verona Willis, Apr. 5, 1946; children—Michael Lloyd, Linda Lou. Operator flying sch., Gallipolis, O., 1937-38; 1st officer United Airlines, Denver, 1939-40; capt. Pan Am. Airlines, Miami, Fla., 1941-42; capt., dir. flight tng., asst. operations mgr. Nat. Airlines, Inc., Miami, 1942-62, v.p. flight operations, 1962—; pres. Simultrain, Inc., Miami, 1962—. Served as capt. RAF, 1940-41. Mem. Soaring Soc. Am., Quiet Birdmen, Aerobatic Club Am. Club: OX 5. Home: 9360 SW 164th St Miami FL 33157 Office: PO Box 2055 AMF Miami FL 33159

WEDLER, FREDERICK CHARLES OLIVER, textile co. exec.; b. Pitts., Jan. 30, 1903; s. Frederick George and Lee (Wilson) W.; student U. Fla., 1960; grad. exec. program, U. N.C., 1959; m. Mary Louise Wadsworth, Sept. 7, 1934; children—Frederick Charles Oliver II, Margaret Wadsworth. With E.I. duPont deNemours & Co., Inc., 1930-35, Am. Viscose Corp., 1937-47; with Burlington Industries, Inc., 1947—, v.p., 1964—. Vice pres. Greensboro council Boy Scouts Am., 1960-63; mem. missions com. Episcopal Diocese N.C., 1956—. Served with AUS, 1942-45. Recipient Sir Samuel Salvage award Am. Viscose Corp., 1940. Clubs: Carolina Sailing (Henderson, N.C.); Greensboro Country. Patentee chem. and mech. processing textiles. Home: 2317 Princess Anne Rd Greensboro NC 27408 Office: Box L-1 Greensboro NC 27402

WEEKS, CHARLES, JR., pub. co. exec.; b. Palo Alto, Cal., Apr. 25, 1919; s. Charles and Mary Alice (Johnson) W.; student U. Fla., 1936-38; m. Patricia Anne Blair, Apr. 7, 1949; children—Patricia Alice, Charles Blair, Clayton Brian, Phyllis Anne. Prin., Fla. Airmotive, Inc., Lantana, Fla., 1946-50; v.p., dir. Perry Publs., Inc., West Palm Beach, Fla., 1950-69; asst. sec., dir. Perry Oceanographics, Inc., Riveria Beach, Fla., 1969—; dir. Underseas Engring., Inc., Riviera Beach, Sub/Marine Equipment Co., Riviera Beach, Higgins-McArthur/Longino & Porter, Inc., Atlanta, The Longport Co., Inc., Atlanta, Palm Beach Cable TV Co., Palm Beach Gardens, Fla., Martin County Cable Co., Inc., Stuart, Fla., Perry Bldg. Systems, Inc., Riviera Beach; v.p., dir. Bahama Publishers Ltd., Freeport, Bahamas, 1961—. Mem. Planning and Zoning Bd., Lantana, 1962-65. Served to 1st lt., pilot, USAF, 1943-46; ETO. Decorated Air medal. Recipient Pilot Safety award Nat. Bus. Aircraft Assn., 1970. Mem. Quiet Birdmen. Episcopalian. Democrat. Clubs: Manalapan, LaCoquille (Manalapan, Fla.); Handersonville (N.C.) Country. Home: PO Box 3411 Lantana FL 33462 Office: 100 E 17th St Riviera Beach FL 33404

WEEKS, GEORGE COMPTON, newspaperman, free lance writer; b. Traverse City, Mich., Aug. 1, 1932; s. Donald C. and Juanita, (Magdanz) W.; B.A., Mich. State U., 1954; m. Mollie Rae McKinley, Jan. 26, 1957; children—Julie Rae, Donald Jay. With UPI, 1954—, legislative corr., Lansing, Mich., 1954-55, state capital bur. chief, polit. writer, Lansing, 1958-60, diplomatic reporter, Washington, 1960-66, fgn. editor, 1966—. Served with AUS, 1955-57. Mem. White House Corrs. Assn., State Dept. Corrs. Assn., Overseas Writers, Nat. Press Club, Mich. Outdoor Writers Assn., Am. Newspaper Guild, Sigma Delta Chi, Sigma Alpha Epsilon. Contbr. to Handbook of African Affairs. Britannica Book of the Year, Living History Yearbook, Africa Report, various periodicals. Home: 5011 N 14th St Arlington VA 22205 Office: National Press Bldg Washington DC 20004

WEEKS, HARRY CURTIS, lawyer; b. Arlington, Tex., Sept. 25, 1890; s. W.C. and Ella (Potter) W.; student Carlisle Mil. Acad., 1902-06, Hanover Coll., 1909, U. Tex., 1906-11; m. Ethel Gill, Nov. 26, 1912 (dec.); 1 son, Harry Curtis; m. 2d, Mrs. Martha Cantey Teas, Feb. 9, 1952 (dec.). Admitted to Tex. bar, 1915, practiced in Witchita Falls and Ft. Worth; sr. mem. Weeks, Bird, Appleman, 1937—. Mem. Newcomen Soc. N.Am., State Bar Tex., Am., Ft. Worth bar assns., Ft. Worth Art Assn., Beta Theta Pi. Episcopalian. Clubs: Shady Oaks Country, Ft. Worth, River Crest Country (Ft. Worth); Petroleum (Dallas). Home: 5444 Byers St Fort Worth TX 76107 Office: Fort Worth Nat Bldg Fort Worth TX 76101

WEEKS, LAWRENCE MICHAEL, aerospace exec.; b. Aububon, Ia., Oct. 18, 1921; s. Leo Elliot and Bonnie Agnes (Eagen) W.; B.S., Ia. State U., 1943; M.S., Washington U., 1950; m. Gloria Ramona Partney, Oct. 27, 1945; children—Michele (Mrs. William E. Bader), Renee. Mgr. advt. design McDonnell Douglas Corp., Robertson, Mo., 1943-60; group dir. Aerospace Corp., El Segundo, Cal., 1960-66; asst. gen. mgr. IBM Electronics Systems Center, Owego, N.Y., 1966-69; v.p., gen. mgr. LTV Aerospace Corp., Dallas, Tex. div. Vought Missiles and Space Co., 1969—; cons. Def. Sci. Bd. Recipient applied mechs. award Am. Soc. Testing and Materials, 1942. Asso. fellow Am. Inst. Aeros. and Astronautics; mem. Navy League, Air Force Assn., Assn. Old Crows, Am. Ordnance Assn., Tau Beta Pi, Phi Kappa Phi, Pi Mu Epsilon. Presbyn. Club: Las Colinas Country (Irving, Tex.). Home: 6103 Shadycliff St Dallas TX 75240 Office: PO Box 6267 Dallas TX 75222

WEEMS, CARL CLINTON, educator; b. Chattanooga, Apr. 18, 1912; s. Edward W. and Georgia (McCrory) W.; student Paine Coll., 1932-35; A.B., Fisk U., 1938, M.A., Ariz. State U., 1949; Ed.D., U. Denver, 1961; postgrad. U. So. Cal., 1949-54; m. Evis LaFay Biggins, Oct. 28, 1950. Mem. Fisk U. Jubilee Singers, Nashville, 1936-42; tchr. pub. schs., Phoenix, 1946-48; asst. prof. edn. Tex. So. U., 1949-51; edn. adviser U.S. Army, Munich, Germany, 1951-54; asst. prof. edn. Prairie View A. and M. Coll., 1954-56, prof. edn., 1965-66, prof. edn. dir. Upward Bound Project, 1966-68; prof., dir. financial aids Huston-Tillotson Coll., Austin, Tex., 1968-71, exec. v.p., 1971—. Research asso. Bur. Edn. Research, U. Denver, 1959-60. Mem. Jr. Police Commn., Phoenix, 1947-48. Bd. dirs. West Side br. Boys Clubs, Phoenix, 1946-47. Served with USAAF, 1942-46. Mem. Am. Assn. Sch. Adminstrs., Am. Assn. U. Profs., Phi Delta Kappa, Kappa Delta Pi, Omega Psi Phi. Democrat. Methodist. Mason (33 deg.). Home: 1807 Astor Pl Austin TX 78721

WEEMS, GEORGE MACDUFF, lawyer; b. Ames, Ia., Oct. 10, 1901; s. Julius Buel and Lila Chapin (Fletcher) W.; student Randolph-Macon Coll., 1920-21, 22-23; B.S. in Commerce, U. Va., 1925, M.S. in Commerce, LL.B., 1928; postgrad Harvard, 1928-29; m. Ella Elizabeth Talley, June 26, 1941; 1 dau., Susan Archer. Admitted to Va. bar, 1928; practiced in Ashland, Va., 1932—; pres. Hanover Nat. Bank of Ashland (Va.), 1945-61, chmn. bd., 1961—. Pres., Woodland Cemetery Co., Ashland, 1940—. Treas. Hanover County, Va., 1935—. Mem. Va. State Bar, Va. Bar Assn., Treas. Assn. Va., Alumni Assn. U. Va., Farm Bur. Hanover County. Baptist (former trustee; deacon). Kiwanian. Home: 905 S Center St Ashland VA 23005 Office: 116 N Center St Ashland VA 23005

WEEMS, JOHN EDGAR, coll. pres.; b. Nashville, Feb. 23, 1932; B.S., George Peabody Coll., 1953, M.A., 1956, Ed.D., 1965; m. Frankie Gooch; children—John Mark, David Van, Nancy Carol. Successively mem. exec. tng. program Proctor-Gamble Co., Louisville; asst. prof. bus. adminstrn., dir. admissions, dean students, dir. placement Atlantic Christian Coll., Wilson, N.C.; dean admissions, also registrar Ky. Wesleyan Coll., Owensboro; dean admissions and records Middle Tenn. State U., Murfreesboro, later v.p. finance and adminstrn.; pres. Meredith Coll., Raleigh, N.C., 1972—. Statis. cons. Ohio Valley Conf.; cons. tchr. edn. Nat. Council on Accreditation Tchr. Edn. Commr. Jr.-Pro Football League. Mem. Delta Pi Epsilon, Delta Sigma Phi. Contbr. articles to profl. jours. Address: Meredith Coll Raleigh NC 27602

WEGE, WILLIAM RICHARD, educator; b. Shawano, Wis., Mar. 31, 1926; s. William John and Helen (Jensen) W.; D.D.S., Marquette U., 1952; M.S. (Nat. Inst. Dental Research fellow), U. Ala., 1967; postgrad. Samford U., 1966-67, (NIH Spl fellow) Med. Coll. Ga., 1967-68; m. Doris Mae Mohr, Sept. 2, 1950; children—William E., Donna M., Linda J. Practice gen. dentistry, Rothschild, Wis., 1952-64; asso. prof., dir. dental radiology Med. Coll. Ga., Augusta, 1967—, dir. continuing edn., Sch. Dentistry, 1971—. Cons. U.S. Army, Ft. Gordon, Ga., 1971—, VA Hosp., Augusta, 1968—, Ft. Jackson, S.C., 1967—. Pres., Am. Cancer Soc., 1970—. Served with USAAF, 1944-45. Fellow Am. Coll. Dentists; mem. Am. Dental Assn., Am. Acad. Dental Radiology (treas. 1968—), Internat. Assn. Dental Research (pres. 1971-72), Am. Assn. Dental Schs. (chmn. radiology sect. 1971-72), Am. Legion, Alpha Phi Omega. Home: 8130 Sir Galahad Dr Evans GA 30809 Office: 1120 15th St Med Coll Ga Augusta GA 30902

WEGER, MARVIN LOUIS, physician; b. Newport News, Va., May 24, 1932; s. Maurice A. and Jenny Florence (Goldberg) W.; A.B., U. Pa., 1954; M.D., Med. Coll. Va., 1958; m. Shelia Barbara Tuchmann, June 16, 1956; children—Lawrence Moss, Margaret Alice, Stuart Yves. Intern, Stuart Circle Hosp., Richmond, Va., 1958-59; resident Richmond (Va.) Meml. Hosp., 1959-60; practice medicine, specializing in family practice, Richmond, 1960—; owner Parham Med. Center; mem. staff St. Mary's Hosp.; v.p. Med. Planning Corp., 1970-72; partner Med. Park Assos.; organizer Va. Capital Bank. Bd. dirs. Richmond Hebrew Day Sch. Diplomate Am. Bd. Family Practice. Fellow Richmond Acad. Gen. Practice, (pres. 1968). Jewish religion (bd. dirs. temple). Mason (32 deg., Shriner). Club: Richmond Stamp. Home: 10007 River Rd Richmond VA 23233 Office: Parham and Quioccasin Rd Richmond VA 23229

WEHLE, VICTOR OTTO, judge; b. N.Y.C., June 19, 1902; s. Henry J. and Marie (Kuehne) W.; LL.B., Cornell U., 1924; m. Irma E. Anschuetz, Sept. 10, 1932; children—James H., Mary (Mrs. James E. Lewallen), Margaret (Mrs. Leonard Lund), Irma (Mrs. Albert Stephens). Admitted to Fla. bar, 1926; asst. city atty. St. Petersburg, Fla., 1926-28; practice law, St. Petersburg, 1928-45; circuit judge 6th Circuit of Fla., St. Petersburg, 1945-54, 64—; prof. Stetson U. Coll. Law, 1954—. Bd. dirs. Elks Crippled Children's Hosp., Am. Legion Crippled Children's Hosp. Recipient Jr. C. of C. Distinguished Service award, 1945. Mem. Am. Bar Assn., Fla. Bar, Am. Trial Lawyers Assn., Acad. Fla. Trial Lawyers. Lutheran. Mason, Elk, Kiwanian. Home: 920 15th Av North St Petersburg FL 33704 Office: County Bldg St Petersburg FL 33701

WEIBEL, DALE ELDON, educator; b. DeWitt, Neb., Dec. 14, 1920; s. Oscar Warren and Clara (Mathews) W.; B.S., U. Neb., 1942, M.S., 1947; Ph.D., Ia. State U., 1955; m. Ardith M. Hackman, Aug. 21, 1942; children—Kathryn, Claudia, Louise, Joyce. Research agronomist USDA, Kan. State U., 1947-53, Tex. A. & M., 1953-58; asso. prof. agronomy Okla. State U., 1958-61, prof., 1961—; cons. U.S. AID Sorghum prodn. Philippine Islands, 1966-67. Served to lt. USAAF, 1942-46. Mem. Am. Soc. Agronomy, Crop Sci. Soc. Am., Farm House, Phi Kappa Phi, Sigma Xi, Gamma Sigma Delta, Alpha Zeta. Home: 721 S Ridge Rd Stillwater OK 74074

WEIDNER, LARRY WAYNE, physician; b. Shattuck, Okla., Nov. 14, 1938; s. Bill and Sarah (Repp) W.; student Southwestern State Coll., 1956-59; M.D., U. Okla., 1963; m. LuVana Sue Chaney, Oct. 27, 1962; children—Larry Wayne, Bryan. Intern, St. Anthony Hosp., Oklahoma City, 1963-64; gen. practice medicine, Buffalo, Okla., 1964—; partner Hudson-Weidner Clinic, Coldwater, Kan., 1969—; med. flight examiner FAA, 1967—. Pres. Harper County Airport Trust Authority, 1969—; mem. Buffalo Municipal Airport Authority, 1967—, Active Boy Scouts Am. Mem. Am., Okla. med. assns., N.W. Counties med. assns. (v.p. 1968-69), Am. Acad. Gen. Practice, Buffalo C. of C. (pres. 1969-70), Phi Beta Pi, Beta Beta Beta. Republican. Methodist. Home: PO Box 301 Buffalo OK 73834 Office: Hwy 64 Buffalo OK 73834

WEIGESTER, WILLIAM FREDERICK, lawyer; b. Troy, Pa., Jan. 19, 1894; s. William and Susie Jerusha (Smiley) W.; B.S., Pa. State U., 1918; J.D., George Washington U., 1925; m. Margaret Eleanor Ayres, Nov. 24, 1937. Admitted to D.C. bar, 1926; with Standard Oil Devel. Co. (now Esso Research & Engring. Co.), 1927-54, mgr. Washington office, 1936-54; lawyer with Dept. Justice, Washington, 1954-65. Mem. Am., Inter-Am. (chmn. sect. on patents, trademarks and copyrights 1950-54) bar assns., Bar Assn. D.C. (chmn. com. on relations with Inter-Am. Bar Assn. 1950-54, chmn. com. on patents), S.A.R., Newcomen Soc. N.Am., Sigma Phi Epsilon. Mason (Shriner). Clubs: Chevy Chase, Metropolitan, Burning Tree, Nat. Press (Washington). Home: 3133 Connecticut Av Washington DC 20008

WEIGLE, LESTER J., sec. Humble Oil and Refining Co. Address: 800 Bell Av Houston TX 77002*

WEIHE, RUDOLPH GEORGE, dentist; b. Chgo., June 11, 1913; s. Emil Christian and Elsie Ellen (Gerbing) W.; B.S., U. Ill., 1939, D.D.S., 1941; m. Starr Culver, Oct. 20, 1967; children—Sally (Mrs. Louis L. Wheeler), R. Geoffrey, Bruce. Pvt. practice dentistry, Oak Park, Ill., 1941-60, St. Petersburg, Fla., 1960—. Clin. instr. prosthetics Coll. Dentistry, U. Ill., 1941-47. Mem. budget com. United Fund, Oak Park, Ill., 1955-60. Trustee, Mound Park Hosp. Found., St. Petersburg, sec., 1964—, asso. dir. div. gerontological research, 1970—. Fellow Fla. Acad. Scis.; mem. Fla. Dental Assn. (trustee 1971—, ho. dels. 1971—), Pinellas County Dental Soc. (bd. dirs. 1970—, chmn. ins. council 1967—), West Coast Dental Soc., Emphysema Research Assn. (bd. dirs. 1965—), Gerontological Soc., Fedn. Dentaire Internat., A.A.A.S., U. Ill. Dental Alumni Assn. (pres. 1960-61), Theta Delta Chi. Lutheran. Clubs: St. Petersburg Yacht, Lakewood Country (St. Petersburg). Home: 4726 Sunrise Dr S St Petersburg FL 33705 Office: 415 45th Av S St Petersburg FL 33705

WEIL, A. SIGMUND, wholesale druggist; b. Winona, Minn., Aug. 22, 1901; s. Eugene I. and Lillian (Morrell) W.; B.S. in Elec. Engring., Ga. Sch. Tech., 1922; postgrad. Emory U.; m. Lucy Cawthon, Mar. 20, 1944 (dec. Nov. 1958); m. 2d, Celeste Dunson, Nov. 25, 1960. Pres. Fed. Savs. & Loan Assn., Fla., 1924-42; chmn. bd. Cawthon-Coleman Drug Co., Selma, 1944—; pres. Embassy Dinner Club, Inc., Acme Underwriters, Inc., Versine Co. Bd. dirs. Sturdivant Mus. Served from lt. to capt. AUS, 1942-44. Mem. Ala. Pharm. Assn. Episcopalian. Mason (Shriner), Elk, Rotarian. Club: Selma Country. Home: 605 Lapsley St Selma AL 36701 Office: Hwy 22E Selma AL 36701

WEIMER, RAE O., educator; b. Mason City, Neb., Nov. 2, 1903; s. Curtis E. and Kitty (Foster) W.; student Kearney (Neb.) State Coll., 1922-25; m. Ruth Meister, Nov. 5, 1942; children—Rae O., Helen Ann. Reporter Moline (Ill.) Dispatch, 1925; reporter-state editor Marion (O.) Star, 1925-26; sports editor and telegraph editor Olean (N.Y.) Herald, 1926-27; state editor Fort Wayne (Ind.) Journal-Gazette, 1927-28, state editor Akron (O.) Beacon Jour., 1928-30, asst. city editor, 1931-33; asst. city editor Akron Times-Press, 1934-35, news editor, 1936-38; city editor Buffalo (N.Y.) Times, 1938-39; copy desk Cleve. Press, 1939-40; asst. mng. editor PM, N.Y.C., 1940-46, mng. editor, 1946-48; The Weimer Orgn., pub. relations, Columbus, O., 1948-49, pres., 1955-57; station mgr. ednl. TV sta. WUFT; dir. Sch. Journalism, U. Fla., 1949-54, dir. Sch. of Journalism and Communications, 1954-67, dean Coll. Journalism and Communications, 1967-68, dean emeritus, prof. journalism, spl. asst. to pres. univ., 1968—. Past mem. So. Regional Edn. Bd. TV Com.; nat. research committee of Am. council for Better Broadcasts. Quill and Scroll chpts. in Palm Beach and Tampa named for him. Mem. Nat. Assn. Ednl. Broadcasters, Fla. Soc. Editors, Assn. Profl. Broadcasting Edn., Assn. for Edn. in Journalism, Am. Assn. Schs. and Depts. Journalism (pres. 1965-66), Sigma Delta Chi, Alpha Delta Sigma, Kappa Tau Alpha, Alpha Epsilon Rho, Blue Key (hon.) Presbyn. kiwanian. Home: 2042 NW 7th Lane Gainesville FL 32601

WEINBERG, BENJAMIN LOUIS, lawyer; b. Pinewood, S.C., Oct. 26, 1926; s. Benjamin Louis and Susan (Hodge) W.; student Ga. Inst. Tech., 1943-45, 47-48; A.B., U. Ga., 1950, J.D., 1952; m. Vera Juanita Rowland, Apr. 8, 1950; children—Mary Thomas, Benjamin Louis III. Admitted to Ga. bar, 1952, since practiced in Atlanta; asso. firm Thomas Jefferson Long and successor firm Long, Weinberg & Ansley, sr. partner, 1960—. Active various charity drives. Served to lt. USNR, 1945-47. Mem. Am., Ga., Atlanta (pres. 1969-70, exec. com. 1965—) bar assns., Lawyers Club Atlanta, Phi Beta Kappa, Phi Kappa Phi, Lambda Chi Alpha. Club: Commerce. Home: 491 Peachtree Battle Av NW Atlanta GA 30305 Office: Equitable Bldg Atlanta GA 30303

WEINBERG, ELLSWORTH ARTHUR, lawyer; b. Marlington, W.Va., Oct. 19, 1912; s. Joseph Lionel and Helen (Webb) W.; A.B., U. Balt., 1935; LL.B., So. Meth. U., 1936; m. Mary Caroline Larimore, Aug. 14, 1946; children—Mary Pamela (Mrs. Michael McManus), Ellsworth Arthur. Admitted to Tex. bar, 1936, since practiced in Dallas. Dir. Lumar, Inc., SMC Industries, Inc. Dist. commodore USCG Aux., 1960-62, nat. commodore, 1964-66. Bd. mgmt. Town North br. Dallas YMCA. Served with USNR, 1941-45. Mem. Am., Tex., Dallas bar assns., Am. Judicature Soc. Republican. Episcopalian. Home: 6035 Meadowcrest Dr Dallas TX 75230 Office: Republic Nat Bank Tower Dallas TX 75201

WEINBRECHT, STANDAU ERNST, lawyer; b. Terre Haute, Ind., Oct. 11, 1924; s. Albert M. and Amelia (Standau) W.; student Rose Poly. Inst., 1942-43, Ind. State Tchrs. Coll., 1950-51; student U. Chgo., 1951-52, J.D., 1955; m. Ruby Mae York, Nov. 22, 1956. Admitted to Ind. bar, 1955; pvt. practice Terre Haute, 1955-58; appellate litigation atty. NLRB, Washington, 1958-62, chief legal research and spl. projects br., 1963—. Atty., Selective Service Bd., 1956-58. Served with AUS, 1946-49. Mem. Am. Bar Assn., Am. Soc. for Information Scis., Indsl. Relations Research Assn., U. Law Sch. Alumni Assn., Am. Acad. Polit. and Social Sci., Assn. for Computing Machinery. Home: 8107 Touchstone Terrace McLean VA 22101 Office: 1717 Pennsylvania Av NW Washington DC 20570

WEINBRECHT, MRS. STANDAU (RUBY YORK WEINBRECHT), librarian; b. Spartanburg, S.C., Mar. 19, 1927; d. Tyre Jenkins and Mae (Rollins) York; B.A., Mary Washington Coll., U. Va., 1948; M.A., George Peabody Coll., 1950; postgrad. Grad. Library Sch., U. Chgo., 1954-55; m. Standau E. Weinbrecht, Nov. 22, 1956. Acquisitions librarian Vassar Coll. Library, Poughkeepsie, N.Y., 1950-52; regional post librarian U.S. Army Library Service, Japan, 1952-54; asst. prof. library sci., reference librarian Ball State Coll., Muncie, Ind., 1955-56; chief readers services, asst. prof. library sci. Ind. State Coll., Terre Haute, 1956-58; cataloging editor 3d edit. Union List of Serials, Library of Congress, Washington, 1959-60, sr. decimal classifier Decimal Classification Office, 1960-63; librarian Office Distbn. Services, Bus. and Def. Services Adminstrn., Dept. Commerce, Washington, 1963-65, editor Marketing Information Guide, 1965-67, chief tech. information div., Equal Employment Opportunity Commn., 1967-72; librarian, Mary Washington Coll. Fredericksburg, Va., 1972—. Recipient Achievement certificate Dept. of Army, 1952, 54. Mem. Corcoran Art Gallery, Nat. Trust Historic Preservation, Am., D.C. (editor D.C. Libraries), Va., Southeastern library assns., Assn. Coll. and Research Libraries, Jr. Mems. Round Table (pres. D.C. 1960-61, exec. bd. 1961-62), Potomac Valley Regional Processing Assn., Am. Acad. Polit. and Social Sci., Am. Assn. U. Profs., Am. Assn. U. Women, Internat. Platform Assn., Alumnae Assn. Mary Washington Coll. of U. Va. (pres., chmn. bd. dirs. 1970—), Am. Marketing Assn., Alpha Phi Sigma, Pi Gamma Mu. Contbr. profl. jours. Home: 8107 Touchstone Terrace McLean VA 22101

WEINER, HAROLD, psychologist; b. Bklyn., Mar. 28, 1932; s. Max and Lillian (Weinstein) W.; B.B.A., Coll. City N.Y., 1953; M.A., U. Md., 1956, Ph.D., 1960; m. Zelda Iris Weiner, June 6, 1959; children—Eric, Kevin, Karen. Dir., Behavioral Research Lab., Am. Inst. for Research, Washington, 1956-61; dir. Operant Conditioning Lab., St. Elizabeth Hosp., Washington, 1961-69 acting asso. for research, 1971—; chief, sect. on operant behavior Nat. Inst. Mental Health, Washington, 1969—; clin. prof. psychiatry George Washington U., 1969—; pvt. practice as behavior therapist, 1972—. Served with AUS, 1954-56. Fellow A.A.A.S., Am. Psychol. Assn. Home: 20 Maplewood Ct Greenbelt MD 20770 Office: St Elizabeth Hosp Washington DC 20032

WEINER, MORTON DAVID, bus. exec.; b. Balt., Aug. 19, 1922; s. Max and Rose (Wolfe) W.; B.S., Towson State Coll., 1942; grad. exec. program, U. Cal. at Los Angeles, 1959; m. Joan M. Maggin; children—Bruce, Susan, Lori, Julie, Jeffrey. Pres. Weiner & Kane, Inc., Ins. brokers, Los Angeles, 1946-56, 60-62; v.p. A.S.R. Products Corp., Los Angeles, 1956-59, also pres. subsidiary Com-Air Products Co. and chmn. subsidiary U.S. Relay Co.; pres. Service Mgmt. Corp., mgmt. cons., Los Angeles, 1956-62; pres., chief operating officer, dir., mem. exec. com. AVNET, Inc., N.Y.C., 1963-69; pres. Morton D. Weiner & Co., investment bankers, N.Y.C., 1969-70; chmn. bd. Nat. Investors Life Ins. Cos., 1970—; pres. Norin Corp., North Miami, Fla., 1970—; chmn. bd., exec. v.p. Norris Grain Co., 1970—; dir. U.S. Life Holding Corp., 1968-70. Served to capt., Signal Corps, AUS, 1942-46; CBI. Mem. N.A.M. Mason (Shriner). Office: 12100 NE 16th Av North Miami FL 33161

WEINGARTEN, ERIC, clin. psychologist; b. Vienna, Austria, Dec. 2, 1925 (came to U.S. 1939, naturalized 1944); s. Leo and Lotte (Schickler) W.; B.S., Coll. City N.Y., 1948; M.A., U. Ky., 1951, Ph.D., 1954. Clin. psychologist VA Hosp., St. Louis, 1954-55; supervisory clin. psychologist VA Hosp., Perry Point, Md., 1955-61; chief clin. psychologist North East Mental Health Clinic, Washington, 1961-68; chief psychology services Rehab. Center for Alcoholics, Occoquan, Va., 1968—. Served with AUS, 1944-46. Decorated Bronze Star, Purple Heart; recipient Superior Performance award VA, 1961. Mem. Am., Md. psychol. assns. Home: 5375 Duke St Alexandria VA 22304 Office: Rehab Center for Alcoholics Occaquan VA 22125

WEINKLE, JULIAN, educator; b. Atlanta, Nov. 19, 1924; s. Carl and Esther (Silver) W.; A.B., U. N.C., 1947; M.A., U. Miami, 1965, Ph.D., 1970; m. Mary Norma Levine, June 29, 1947; children—Martin Jeanne, William, Andrew, James, Thomas, Katherine. Dir. store operations, dir. Carls Markets, Inc., Miami, Fla., 1947-50, exec. v.p. operations, dir., 1950-54; pres. Family Investors, Inc., Miami, 1954-70; chmn. bd. dirs. Bank of Dade County, Miami, 1962-69; mem. faculty Center for Advanced Internat. Studies, U. Miami, research scientist Inst. Inter-am Studies, 1966—; asst. prof. history U. Miami, 1970—. Pres. citizens bd. U. Miami, 1963-65; founder Mt. Sinai Hosp. Dir. United Health Found. of United Fund, Dade County, 1963—; trustee, lectr. Greater Miami Opera Guild. Served to lt. (j.g.) USNR, 1942-46. Mem. Phi Kappa Phi, Phi Alpha Theta. Jewish religion. Rotarian. Clubs: Standard, Royal Palm Tennis, Coconut Grove Sailing. Miami Yacht. Asso. editor Jour. Interam. Studies and World Affairs, 1968—. Contbr. articles to profl. jours. Home: 130 Arvida Pkwy Coral Gables FL 33156

WEINSTEIN, ALLEN ISAAC, linguistic scientist, govt. ofcl.; b. Bklyn., Feb. 7, 1933; s. Louis H. and Harriette (Siegel) W.; B.A., Columbia, 1955, M.A., 1956; Ph.D., State U. N.Y. at Buffalo, 1966; postgrad. U. Wash., 1962; m. Claire Frant, June 9, 1954; children—Lynette Hope, Howard Lawrence. Instr. German, State U. N.Y. at Buffalo, 1959-64, lectr. German, 1964-65, asst. prof. German, 1965-66; linguistic scientist Dept. State, Washington, 1966—. Served with AUS, 1956-58. Fellow Am. Anthrop. Assn., A.A.A.S.; mem. Am. Assn. U. Profs., Linguistic Soc. Am. Author: (with E. Mayer) Deutsche Stunden, 1964. Home: 6236 23d St N Arlington VA 22205 Office: Fgn Service Inst Dept State Washington DC 20520

WEINSTEIN, RAYFORD LEE, physician; b. Lumberton, N.C., Feb. 5, 1911; s. Harry and Yetta (Weinstein) W.; student U. N.C., 1928-29; B.S. magna cum laude, Wake Forest Coll., 1932, M.D., 1934; M.D., Jefferson Med. Coll., 1936; m. Hilda Harris, Mar. 30, 1941 (div. 1952); 1 son, Alan Barry; m. 2d, Nov. 27, 1957 (div. June 1959). Intern Lying in Hosp., Phila., South Pacific Gen., St. Francis, St. Johns, French hosps., all San Francisco, 1934-36, Meml. Hosp., Danville, Va., 1936-37; individual practice medicine, San Francisco, 1934-36, Danville, 1936-37, Fairmont, 1938—; owner, chief Weinstein Clinic, Fairmont, N.C., 1938—. Farmer, realtor, automobile dealer; owner R.L.W. Ranch, grocery store, filling sta., barber shop, beauty shop, blacksmith and machine shop, syrup and grist mill, feed mill, horse and pony ranch, timber bus., realty and constrn. bus., numerous other businesses. Fellow Internat. Acad. Proctology, Internat. Coll. Surgery, N.Y. Acad. Sci.; mem. A.M.A.,

Am. Geriatric Soc., Am. Assn. Plastic Surgery, N.C., Robeson County, 5th Dist. med. socs., Internat. Coll. Angiology, World Med. Assn., So., Israel, Tri-State med. assns., N.Y. Acad. Sci., Nat. Fed. Wildlife Fedn., Theta Kappa Psi. Republican. Jewish religion. Mason (Shriner), Elk, Moose; mem. order Eastern Star. Clubs: Civitan, Horseless Carriage Am.; Robeson County Wildlife. Home: Route 2 Box 294 Rowland NC 28383

WEINTRAUB, JOSEPH, lawyer; b. Waynesboro, Ga., Dec. 10, 1904; s. Sigmond and Anne (Goodman) W.; student U. Va., 1922-25, N.Y. U., 1925-26; m. Hortense Katz, Jan. 27, 1929; children—Joanne, Michael. Admitted to Fla. bar, 1927, U.S. Dist. Ct., 1927, Supreme Ct. of U.S., 1937; practiced law, Miami, since 1927, head law firm Weintraub, Martin, Schwartz & Spector and predecessor firm, Miami, Fla., 1943—; organized Am. Title & Ins. Co., 1936, pres., 1940-56, dir. 1936—, chmn. bd. 1956—; pres., dir. Gibson Security Corp., 1936—; chmn. bd. Pan Am. Bank of Miami Beach, 1965—, Tex. Title Guaranty, Inc., Atico Financial Corp., 1962—, Comercial Aseguradora, S.A. of Guatemala, Columbia Title Ins. Co., Continental Corp., Continental Ins. Co. N.Y., Fidelity & Casualty Co. N.Y., Seaboard Fire & Marine Ins. Co. N.Y. Bd. dirs. United Fund Dade County, Miami Heart Inst., Crime Commn. Greater Miami; v.p. citizens bd. U. Miami, Opera Guild Miami, Dade County Research Found. Mem. Miami-Dade C. of C., Dade County (v.p., 1939-40, dir. 1938-41), Fla., Am. bar assns., Am. Judicature Soc. Jewish religion. Mason (Shriner), Rotarian. Elk. Clubs: Wall Street (N.Y.C.); Westview Country (pres.), Variety. Home: 108 W Rivo Alto Dr Rivo Alto Island Miami Beach FL 33139 Office: 901 NE 2d Av Miami FL 33132

WEINTRAUB, MICHAEL, lawyer, finance co. exec.; b. Miami, Fla., June 5, 1938; s. Joseph and Hortense (Katz) W.; B.A., U. Va., 1960, J.D., 1963; m. Barbara Posthumus, Sept. 5, 1968; 1 stepdau., Lori Ellen Anderson. Admitted to Fla. bar; partner firm Smathers & Thompson, Miami, 1963—; v.p. Atico Financial Corp., Miami, 1967—, also dir.; Pan. Am. Bancshares, Inc., 1969—, also dir.; dir. Pan Am. Bank of Miami. Mem. Citizens Adv. Bd. Variety Childrens Hosp.; bd. dirs. Miami Heart Inst., A.R.C. Mem. Am., Dade County bar assns., Am. Judicature Soc. Clubs: Westview Country; Ocean Reef Country. Home: 3370 Devon Rd Miami FL 33133 Office: 150 SE Third Av Miami FL 33131

WEINTRAUB, SIGMUND, hotel owner; b. N.Y.C., Mar. 4, 1918; s. Abraham and Pauline (Ritter) W.; student Embry Sch. Aviation, 1942; m. Marjorie Cohen, Nov. 5, 1949; children—Paul H., Steven G., Stuart R., Peter B. Mgr., Weintraub's Grocery, Bklyn., 1938-42; night mgr. Netherland Hotel, Miami Beach, Fla., 1945-46, mgr., 1946-51, owner, 1951—. Served with USAAF, 1942-45. Decorated Air medal with cluster. Mem. Miami Beach South Shore Hotel Assn. (pres. 1967-68), Miami Beach, Miami chambers commerce, Am. Hotel and Motel Assn. Home: 3011 Royal Palm Av Miami Beach FL 33140 Office: 1330 Ocean Dr Miami Beach FL 33139

WEIR, CLAYTON J., lawyer; b. McGregor, Ia., July 31, 1901; s. Ithiel and Christina (Tweet) W.; LL.B., Cumberland U., 1931; J.D., Cumberland Sch. Law Samford U., 1969; m. Eva Mae Pate, Dec. 5, 1922; children—Imogene, James. Admitted to Fla. bar, 1931, since practiced in Groveland; also ins. and real estate positions. Mayor, mem. Town Council, Groveland, 1932-40, also former city atty. Democrat. Methodist. Mason, Elk, Kiwanian. Home: Groveland FL 32736

WEIR, JOHN HOWARD, real estate and banking exec.; b. Binghamton, N.Y., Jan. 18, 1925; s. Milton N. and Mildred L. (Young) W.; student pub., pvt. schs.; m. Jamesena H. Hardee, Aug. 31, 1950; children— Deborah Suzanne, John Howard. Gen. mgr. M. N. Weir & Sons, Inc., Boca Raton, Fla., 1952-58, 61-68; v.p., gen. mgr. Arvida Corp., 1958-61; exec. v.p., dir. Boca Raton Nat. Bank, 1961—. v.p., treas., dir. Castleton Industries, Inc., 1968-69; pres. Boca Raton Plaza, Inc., 1962—; sec., dir. Fla. Bancgrowth, Inc., 1963—; partner Milton N. Weir & Sons; pres., dir. Citizens Nat. Bank, Boca Raton; vice-chmn., dir. Fidelity Nat. Bank, Pompano Beach, Fla. Trustee, vice chmn. Boca Raton Community Hosp. Served with USNR, 1943-46. Mem. Am. Legion, Bankers Club of N.Y. Republican. Presbyn. Mason. Clubs: Miami (Fla.); Wings (N.Y.C.); Royal Palm Yacht and Country (Boca Raton). Home: 272 Coconut Palm Rd Boca Raton FL 33432 Office: 855 S Fed Hwy Boca Raton FL 33432

WEIR, WILLIAM DONALD, econ. analyst; b. Itasca, Tex., Nov. 21, 1925; s. William Calvin and Helen (Downard) W.; B.S., U.S. Naval Acad., 1949; M.B.A., Xavier U., 1960; m. Marilyn Anne Parke, June 4, 1949; children—Andrew M., David A., Holly E., Heather H. Test engr. Tex. Power & Light Co., Dallas, 1954-55; operations analyst Gen. Electric Co., Cin., 1956-59; bus. analyst Martin Co., Balt., 1959-63; econ. analyst Center Naval Analyses, Washington, 1963—, dir. cost analysis div., 1966—. Served with USNR, 1949-54. Home: 7110 Beechwood Dr Chevy Chase MD 20015 Office: Center for Naval Analyses 1401 Wilson Blvd Arlington VA 22209

WEISERT, JOHN JACOB, educator; b. Louisville, Dec. 18, 1914; s. John Jacob and Laura Elizabeth (Krug) W.; B.A., U. Louisville, 1936; M.A. (Carl Schurz fellow), Columbia, 1938, Ph.D., 1948; Carnegie fellow U. Chgo., 1955-56; m. Anita Bartley Boss, Sept. 7, 1962. Instr., U. Tenn., 1947-48; asst. prof. U. Louisville, 1948-51, 53-56, asso. prof., 1956-62, prof., 1962—, chmn. dept. modern langs., 1963-71, editor Library Rev., 1962—; asst. prof. Pa. State Coll., 1951-53. Served to capt., AUS, 1942-46. Recipient Woodcock medal U. Louisville, 1936. Mem. Modern Lang. Assn. Am., S.Atlantic Modern Lang. Assn., Am. Assn. Tchrs. German. Cin. Hist. Soc., J.B. Speed Art Mus., U. Louisville Library Assos. (pres. 1962-65). Club: Filson (Louisville). Author: The Dream in Gerhart Hauptmann, 1949, Last Night at Macauley's, 1951. Home: 1819 Harvard Dr Louisville KY 40205

WEISMILLER, EDWARD RONALD, educator, writer; b. Monticello, Wis., Aug. 3, 1915; s. Jacob and Georgia (Wilson) W.; student Swarthmore Coll., 1931-32; B.A., Cornell Coll., 1938, D.Litt., 1953; student Merton Coll., Oxford (Eng.) U., 1938-39, D.Phil., 1950; M.A., Harvard, 1942; m. Frances Merewether Power, June 15, 1941; children—Sara Stuart (Mrs. Kenneth Chaffee), Georgia Louise (Mrs. Emmet R. Sargeant, Jr), Peter Wilson, Charles Edward, Mary Luverne. Teaching fellow English, Harvard, 1940-43; mem. faculty Pomona Coll., 1950-68, prof. English, 1958-68; prof. English, George Washington U., 1968—; Fulbright prof. U. Leiden (Netherlands), 1957-58. Served to 1st lt. USMCR, 1943-46; ETO. Decorated Bronze Star; Medaille de la Reconnaissance Francaise. Rhodes scholar, 1938-39, 48-50; Guggenheim fellow, 1946-47, 47-48; fellow Fund Advancement Edn., Ford Found., 1953-54; research award Am. Council Learned Socs., 1963-66, 69, Am. Philos. Soc., 1966, 69; research fellow Folger Library, 1965; Spl. Research grantee Rockefeller Found., 1965-66; sr. fellow in letters Center for Advanced Studies, Wesleyan U. Conn., 1967-68. Mem. Phi Beta Kappa. Author: (poems) The Deer Come Down (Yale Series Younger Poets), 1936; (poems) The Faultless Shore, 1946; (novel) The Serpent Sleeping, 1962; also articles. Contbr. The Lyric and Dramatic Milton, 1965. Home: 2400 Virginia Av NW Washington DC 20037

WEISS, ARDEN OSCAR, govt. ofcl.; b. Belleville, Ill., Feb. 26, 1939; s. Oscar William and Flora Adeline (Wilderman) W.; B.S., U. Ill., 1961, M.S., 1966; m. Caroline Louise Martin, Feb. 24, 1962; children—Paul Arden, Stewart William, Scott Andrew, Caroline Elizabeth. Planning and design engr. Ill. Soil Conservation Service, 1957-65; systems design engr. Quaker Oats Co., 1965-67; sr. water resources cons. McDonnell Douglas Corp., 1967-68; dir. systems engring. div. Tex. Water Devel. Bd., Austin, 1968-71; nat. assessment leader Water Resources Council, Washington, 1971—. Served with AUS, 1957. Home: 1566 Crofton Pkwy Crofton MD 21113 Office: 2120 L St NW Washington DC 20037

WEISS, ARMAND BERL, economist; b. Richmond, Va., Apr. 2, 1931; s. Maurice Herbert and Henrietta (Shapiro) W.; B.S. in Econs., Wharton Sch. Finance U. Pa., 1953, M.B.A., 1954; D.B.A., George Washington U., 1971; m. Judith Bernstein, May 18, 1957; children—Jo Ann Michele, Rhett Louis. Commd. ensign U.S. Navy, 1954, advanced through grades to lt.; spl. asst. to auditor gen. Navy, 1964-65; resigned, 1965; sr. economist Center for Naval Analyses, Arlington, Va., 1965-68; project dir. Logistics Mgmt. Inst., Washington, 1968—; sr. v.p. Weiss Pub, Co., Inc., Richmond, Va., 1960—; vis. lectr. George Washington U., 1971. Chmn. U.S. delegation, session chmn. NATO Symposium on Cost-Benefit Analysis, The Hague, Netherlands, 1969, NATO Conf. on Operational Research in Indsl. Systems, St. Louis, France, 1970; pres. Nat. Council Assns. Policy Scis., 1971—; chmn. adv. group Def. Econ. Adv. Council, 1970—. Sr. v.p. George Washinton U. Sch. Bus. and Govt. Doctoral Assn., 1968-69; del. Pres.'s Mid-Century White House Conf. on Children and Youth, 1950; scoutmaster Japan, U.S., leader World Jamborees, France, Can., U.S., 1945-61; U.S. del. Internat. Conf. on Operations Research, Dublin, Ireland, 1972; mem. bus. com. Washington Nat. Symphony Orch., 1968—. Fellow A.A.A.S.; mem. Operations Research Soc. Am. (chmn. meetings com. 1969-71; chmn. cost-effectiveness sect. 1969-70), Washington Operations Research Council (editor newsletter 1969—; sec. 1971-72, pres.-elect 1972-73), Internat. Inst. Strategic Studies (London), Inst. for Mgmt. Sci., Am. Econ. Assn., Am. Accounting Assn., Wharton Grad. Sch. Alumni Assn. (exec. com.), Am. Acad. Polit. and Social Sci. Jewish religion (pres. temple). Club: Wharton Grad. Sch. Washington (sec. 1967-69, pres. 1969-70). Editor Cost-Effectiveness Newsletter, 1966-70, Operations Research/Systems Analysis Today, 1971—; asso. editor Operations Research, 1971—; co-editor various pamphlets. Home: 6516 Truman Lane Falls Church VA 22043 Office: 4701 Sangamore Rd Washington DC 20016

WEISS, JEFFREY J., wholesale trade co. exec.; b. Bklyn, July 13, 1943; s. Louis M. and Miriam (Solow) W.; student Miami Dade Jr. Coll., 1961-63; m. Glenda Joyce Penner, June 26, 1965; children—Lara J., Gina J. Pres., chmn. bd. Atlantic Industries, Inc., Miami, Fla., 1965—; chmn. bd., v.p. Exposition Corp. of Am., Miami, 1968—; dir. Underwriters Financial of Fla., Inc. Cons. Church Community Unions Nat., Inc., 1971—. Mem. Direct Selling Assn. of Am. Home: 8500 SW 85th St Miami FL 33143 Office: 720 NW 27th Av Miami FL 33125

WEISS, MARTIN, marine geologist; b. N.Y.C., Jan. 21, 1919; s. Emil and Helen (Fogel) W.; B.S., Coll. City N.Y., 1948; M.S., U. Mich., 1951, Ph.D., 1954; student Cooper Union, 1939-41; m. Irene Fogel, Aug. 21, 1949; children—Philip M., Lesley Lea, Ronald Jay. Geologist, U.S. Geol. Survey, Washington, 1953-63; oceanographer Nat. Oceanographic Data Center, Washington, 1963—, head geosci. br., 1964-68, staff oceanographer, 1968-72; marine geologist Nat. Geophys. and Solar Terrestrial Data Center, 1972—. Instr., grad. sch. U.S. Dept. Agr. 1964—. Served to maj. A.C., U.S. Army, 1942-46. Decorated Bronze Star. Fellow Geol. Soc. Am.; mem. Am. Geophys. Union, Geol. Soc. Washington, Paleontological Soc. Washington, Internat. Assn. Math. Geologists, Sigma Xi. Home: 3710 Prado Pl Fairfax VA 22030 Office: Nat Geophysical and Solar Terrestrial Data Center NOAA Dept Commerce Rockville MD 20852

WEISS, SANFORD, welfare agy. exec.; b. Cleve., Dec. 29, 1906; s. Morris H. and Rose (Weiss) W.; A.B., Adelbert Coll., 1929; LL.B., Western Res. U., 1931, M.S. in Social Admistrn., 1943; m. Viola Wolfson, Nov. 25, 1943. Intake worker, office mgr. Cuyahoga County (O.) Relief, 1930-41; probation officer Cuyahoga County Juvenile Ct., 1943-45, children's caseworker, regional rep., Bellefaire, Cleve., 1945-50; exec. dir. Jewish Children's Home Service, New Orleans, 1951—. Treas., Cleve. Indsl. Union Council, 1936-37. Bd. dirs. New Orleans Social Welfare Planning Council, 1963-67. Mem. Nat. Assn. Social Workers (nat. social action commn. 1965-69; pres. southeastern La. chpt. 1965-67), Nat. Conf. Jewish Communal Service, La. Welfare Conf. Mem. B'nai B'rith (bd. dirs. New Orleans). Author monograph: (with wife) Follow-up Study of Children Released from Residential Treatment Centers, 1969. Home: 4014 Chestnut St New Orleans LA 70115 Office: 5342 St Charles Av New Orleans LA 70115

WEISSBACH, HERBERT, biochemist; b. N.Y.C., 1932; B.S., Coll. City N.Y.; Ph.D., George Washington U., 1957. With Nat. Heart Inst., 1953—, acting chief Lab. of Clin. Biochemistry, 1968—. Recipient award Am. Soc. Biol. Chemists, Superior Service award U.S. Dept. Health, Edn. and Welfare, 1968, award in enzyme chemistry Am. Chem. Soc., 1970. Mem. A.A.A.S., Am. Soc. for Pharmacology and Exptl. Therapeutics, Am. Soc. Microbiology. Contbr. articles to profl. jours. Editor Jour. Pharmacology and Exptl. Therapeutics, Archives of Biochemistry and Biophysics. Office: Nat Heart Inst 5204 Cedar Lane Bethesda MD 20014*

WEISSING, LOUIS, judge; b. Tampa, Fla., Aug. 4, 1925; s. Louis and Kathryn (Fitzpatrick) S.; LL.B., U. Fla., 1953; m. Lois I. McGeachy, Jan. 6, 1951; children—Andrew Michael, Matthew Douglas, Christopher Todd, Steven Scott. Admitted to Fla. bar, 1953; asst. county solicitor, Broward County, Fla., 1954-57; judge Criminal Ct. Record, Broward County, 1957-59; judge Ct. of Record, Broward County, 1959-66; circuit judge 17th Jud. Circuit, 1966—. Served with AUS, 1943-47. Decorated Bronze Star medal, Purple Heart; recipient Outstanding Young Man award Ft. Lauderdale Jr. C. of C., 1961. Mem. Am. Legion, 40 and 8, D.A.V., Blue Key, Civil and Criminal Ct. of Record Judges Assn. (pres. 1963). Democrat. Home: 551 NW 66th Av Plantation FL 33313 Office: Court House Fort Lauderdale FL 33301

WEISSLER, ALFRED, chemist; b. N.Y.C., Mar. 13, 1917; s. Joseph and Gladys (Sobel) W.; B.S. cum laude, Coll. City N.Y., 1936; M.S., U. Wis., 1938; Ph.D., U. Md., 1946; m. Pearl Goldman, May 30, 1941; children—Lenore Eve, Frederic Bennett, Robert Charles. Chemist, Naval Research Lab., 1942-51; chief chemistry br. Office Ordnance Research, 1951-54; chemist, pub. health analyst NIH, 1954-62; phys. chemistry program chief Air Force Office Sci. Research, 1962-67; asst. dir. phys. scis. research FDA, Bur. Sci., Washington, 1967-70, dir. div. colors and cosmetics, 1970—. Adj. asst. prof. U. Md., 1946-52; adj. prof. Am. U., 1961-68; chmn. phys. scis. departmental com. U.S. Dept. Agr. Grad. Sch., 1965—. Fellow Acoustical Soc. Am. (pres. D.C. chpt. 1967), A.A.A.S., Wash. Acad. Scis.; mem. Am. Chem. Soc., Am. Phys. Soc., Biophys. Soc. Am., Philos. Soc. Washington. Contbr. articles to profl. jours. Home: 5510 Uppingham St Chevy Chase MD 20015 Office: 200 C St SW Washington DC 20204

WEITZ, PAUL JOSEPH, astronaut; b. Erie, Pa., July 25, 1932; s. Paul Joseph and Violet (McClymont) W.; B.S. in Aero. Engring., Pa. State U., 1954; M.S. in Aero. Engring., U.S. Navy Postgrad. Sch., Monterey, Cal., 1964; m. Suzanne Margaret Berry, June 23, 1956; children—Matthew, Cynthia. Commd. ensign U.S. Navy, 1954, advanced through grades to comdr., 1968; naval aviator, 1956, with various squadrons, 1956-65; astronaut NASA Manned Spacecraft Center, Houston, 1966—. Decorated Air medal with 4 gold stars, Navy Commendation medal; Sec. Navy Commendation for Achievement. Mem. Beta Theta Pi. Mason. Home: NASA MSC Code CB Houston TX 77058

WEITZMAN, STANLEY HOWARD, ichthyologist; b. Mill Valley, Cal., Mar. 16, 1927; s. John Howard and Iva (Hager) W.; A.B., U. Cal. at Berkeley, 1951, M.A., 1953; Ph.D., Stanford, 1960; m. Marilyn Jean Sohner, Feb. 7, 1948; children—Earl David, Anna Lisa. Instr. anatomy Stanford, 1957-62; asso. curator fishes Smithsonian Instn., Washington, 1963-67, curator fishes, 1967—. Served with USNR, 1945-46. Mem. Am. Soc. Ichthyologists and Herpetologists (editorial bd. 1965-71, gov. 1970—, treas. 1972—), Am. Fisheries Soc., Soc. Study Evolution, Soc. Systematic Zoology, A.A.A.S., Sigma Xi. Research and publs. on osteology and evolution of teleost fishes, S.Am. freshwater fishes, deep-sea oceanic fishes. Home: 8704 Hidden Hill Lane Potomac MD 20854 Office: Div of Fishes Smithsonian Instn Washington DC 20560

WELCH, JAY J., physician; b. Smithfield, Ill., Sept. 19, 1916; s. Alan Richard and Mabel Lee (Hinckle) W.; B.S., U. Ill., 1938; M.B., Northwestern U., 1942, M.D., 1943, M.S., 1949; m. Esther Apperson, Mar. 2, 1946; 1 dau., Sheila (dec.). Intern Wesley Meml. Hosp., Chgo., 1942-43, resident internal medicine, 1946-49; internist Collins-Bellas Clinic, Peoria, Ill., 1953-54, Glenn-Maguire Clinic, Canton, Ill., 1954-58, Greer Clinic, Houston, 1958-59; practice medicine specializing in internal medicine, Houston, 1959—; clin. asso. prof. medicine Baylor U., 1958-66; chief internist medicine Houston Meml. Hosp. Chmn. bd. dirs. H. Lowrie, Inc.; mng. partner Houston Assos. II. Served with AUS, 1943-46, 49-50, 50-52. Fellow A.C.P.; mem. Am. Soc. Internal Medicine, Am. Inst. Parliamentarians, Fulton County Med. Soc. (pres. 1957), Tex. Soc. Internal Medicine (pres. 1971), Phi Beta Kappa, Alpha Kappa Kappa, Phi Eta Sigma, Phi Lambda Upsilon. Clubs: Houston Toastmasters (area gov. internat. 1957), Houston Yacht, Plaza (Houston). Home: 4539 Shetland Pl Houston TX 77027 Office: Memorial Professional Bldg Houston TX 77002

WELCH, LOUIE, mayor; b. Lockney, Tex., Dec. 9, 1918; s. Gilford E. and Nora (Shackelford) W.; B.A. magna cum laude, Abilene Christian Coll., 1940; m. Iola Faye Cure, Dec. 17, 1940; children—Guy Lynn, Gary Dale, Louie Gilford, Shannon Austin, Tina Joy. Organized Welch Industries, Inc., Houston 1955, pres., 1955—, pres. Louie Welch & Co., Inc., real estate and investment brokers; mayor City of Houston, 1963—. Vice pres. League of Tex. Municipalities, 1957-58, pres., 1958-59, mem. legislative com., 1956—. Councilman at large City of Houston. Bd. dirs. Abilene Christian Coll. Mem. Tex. Mayors and Councilmens Assn. (pres. 1958-59), Nat. League Cities (v.p.), U.S. Conf. Mayors, Tex. Constrn. Council (mem. exec. council 1960), Automotive Wholesalers of Tex. Home: 5013 Happy Hollow Houston TX 77018 Office: Mayor's Office City Hall Houston TX 77002

WELCH, NATHAN LEE, supt. schs.; b. Abilene, Tex., Jan. 21, 1922; s. Lynton Horace and Beulah (Smith) W.; B.S., W. Tex. State U., 1947, M.Ed., 1953; postgrad. Tex. Tech., 1966—; m. Roberta Walker, Mar. 4, 1944; children—Derrith Lee, Vicki Dawnelle. Prin. elementary sch., Witharral, Tex., 1946-47, Vega, Tex., 1947-48; asst. coordinator Childress (Tex.) County Vocational Sch., 1948-51; tchr. jr. high sch., Abernathy, Tex., 1951-52; prin. River Rd. Ind. Sch. Dist. Amarillo, Tex., 1952-56; supt. Booker (Tex.) Ind. Sch. Dist., 1956-60, McLean (Tex.), 1960-64; supr. Kress (Tex.) Ind. Sch. Dist., 1964—. Dir. Credit Union Swisher County, 1967—, pres., 1968. Served with USAAF, 1942-46. Mem. Tex., Swisher County tchrs. assns. Mason, Lion (pres. 1967-68). Home: 311 Ripley St Kress TX 79052

WELCH, PORTER PRATHER, banker; b. Lexington, Ky., Dec. 29, 1925; s. Dexter Nathan and Myrtle (Farmer) W.; student Fugazzi Bus. Coll., 1950, Am. Inst. Banking, 1953; m. Betty Jane Price, Jan. 4, 1947; 1 dau., Kathy Ann (Mrs. C. Noel Hall). With Woodford Bank & Trust Co., Versailles, Ky., 1953—, 1st. v.p. 1960-69, pres., 1969—, also dir. Sec. United Fund, Versailles, 1954—; treas. Woodford County Meml. Hosp. Mem. Versailles C. of C. (sec.-treas. 1956—). Kiwanian (pres. 1955). Club: Woodford Hills Country (treas. 1968-71). Home: 241 Morgan St Versailles KY 40383 Office: 101 N Main St Versailles KY 40383

WELDEN, JAMES LEE, clergyman; b. Senoia, Ga., Aug. 24, 1916; s. George Lee and Susie Ella (Thompson) W.; grad. Reinhardt Jr. Coll., 1938; B.S., U. Ga., 1946; B.D., Emory U., 1950; m. Lucy Margaret Tinsley, Nov. 4, 1945; children—Patsy (Mrs. John W. Simmons), James Lee, Gary Tinsley. Ordained to ministry Methodist Ch., 1945; supply pastor Athens (Ga.) Circuit, 1945-46; pastor Gate City Mills, East Point, Ga., 1946-48, Red Oak (Ga.) Meth. Ch., 1948-52, Oak Grove Meth. Ch., Decatur, Ga., 1952-56, 1st Meth. Ch., Jonesboro, Ga., 1956-62, Park St. Meth. Ch., Atlanta, 1962-67, 1st Meth. Ch., Monroe, Ga., 1967-71, Bethany Meth. Ch., Smyrna, Ga., 1971—. Dist. missionary sec. Decatur-Oxford dist. N. Ga. Conf. Meth. Ch., 1955-56, sec.-treas. Bd. Social and Econ. Relations, 1954-55, sec.-treas. Bd. Hosp. and Homes, 1962-71, dist. missionary sec. Griffin dist., 1960-61, vice chmn. Bd. Social Concerns, 1964—, rep. to Ga. Council Chs., 1964—, pres. Ga. Council Chs., 1969-71, sec. Decatur-Oxford dist. conf., 1952-56, sec. Griffin dist. conf., 1957-61; bd. dirs. Ga. Meth. Fed. Credit Union, 1960—, pres., 1970—. Mem. Gov.'s Youth Opportunity Council, 1970—; pres. Council on Human Relations, Atlanta, 1950-55. Bd. dirs., an organizer Sr. Citizens Met. Atlanta, 1965-67. Served with AUS, 1942-45. Recipient Citation of Merit, Ga. Gerontology Soc., 1967. Mem. Ga. Congress Parents-Tchrs. (hon. life mem.), Reinhardt Coll. Alumni Assn. (pres. 1968-69, bd. dirs. 1964-69), Ga. Assn. Pastoral Care (bd. dirs. 1964-67), Woman's Soc. Christian Service (hon. life mem.). Democrat. Mason. Club: Exchange (pres. Jonesboro 1960). Home: 3585 Hicks Rd SW Marietta GA 30060 Office: 741 Hurt Rd SW Smyrna GA 30080

WELDON, JACK GERARD, broadcasting co. exec.; b. N.Y.C., Aug. 2, 1911; s. John B. and Katherine (Osmond) W.; student Columbia, 1929-31; m. Ann Blain, Sept. 11, 1937; children—Ann Stuart (Mrs. Frederick Praither), John Blain. Announcer various radio stas., N.Y.C., 1927-34; announcer, salesman WDBJ, Roanoke, Va., 1934-39, program dir., 1939-46; exec. v.p., gen. mgr. Old Dominion Broadcasting Corp., WWOD, Lynchburg, 1946-52; exec. rep. A.P., 1952, regional membership exec., 1954-58; gen. mgr. WAIR, Winston-Salem, N.C., 1952-53; sales mgr. WSUN radio, St. Petersburg, Fla., 1958-66; local/regional sales mgr. WLCY-TV, Largo, Fla., 1966—. Tchr. broadcasting, writing, acting, prodn. U. Va. Extension Div., 1942-44. Bd. dirs. Leisure Manor Retirement Facility, 1960-65. Recipient Printer's Ink AFA Silver Medal award, 1965. Mem. Am. Advt. Fedn. (2d lt. gov. 4th dist. Fla.), Advt. Club (pres. 1965-66). Presbyn. (treas. 1963-65). Home: 5025 39th St S St

Petersburg FL 33711 Office: WLCY-TV 11450 Gandy Blvd St Petersburg FL 33702

WELDON, WILSON OSBOURNE, editor, clergyman; b. Camden, S.C., Mar. 15, 1911; s. John Wesley and Leila (Wilson) W.; B.A., U. S.C., 1931; B.D., Duke, 1934; D.D., High Point Coll., 1952; m. Margaret Hammond Lyles, July 19, 1939; children—Nanci Leila (dec.), Wilson Osbourne, Alice Adelaide. Ordained to ministry Meth. Ch., 1938; pastor Meth. chs., China Grove, N.C., 1938-42, High Point, N.C., 1942-48, Meml. Meth. Ch., Thomasville, N.C., 1948-52, 1st Meth. Ch. Gastonia, N.C., 1952-58, Myers Park Meth. Ch., Charlotte, N.C., 1958-63, West Market St. Meth. Ch., Greensboro, N.C., 1963-67; editor Upper Room, Nashville, 1967—. Del., Meth. Ecumenical Conf., Oxford, Eng., 1951, World Meth. Conf., London, Eng., 1966, Denver, 1971, Gen. Conf. Meth. Ch., 1956, 60, 64, 68, 70, 72, Meth. S.E. Jurisdictional Conf., 1952, 56, 60, 64, 68, 72; mem. Gen. Bd. Evangelism, 1960-67; mem. Am. exec. com. World Meth. Council, 1967—. Trustee Greensboro Coll., Scarritt Coll., Nashville, Duke, Junaluska Assembly, Lake Junaluska, N.C. Mem. Lake Junaluska Assos. (pres. 1968—). Mason (32 deg., K.T., Shriner), Rotarian. Author: Thrill of Christian Living, 1966; Discoveries in the Lord's Prayer, 1968; APlain Man Faces Trouble, 1971. Editor: When Fires Burn. Compiler: Breakthru. Home: 1900 Richard Jones Rd Nashville TN 37215 Office: 1908 Grand Av Nashville TN 37203

WELK, WILLIAM GEORGE, govt. ofcl., econ. cons.; b. Trieste, Italy, Jan. 5, 1907 (came to U.S. 1929, naturalized 1934); s. Francis and Theresa (Graf) W.; Dr. Econs. and Comml. Sci., U. Trieste, 1928; M.A., Harvard U., 1932, Ph.D., 1933. Prof. econs. Coll. St. Thomas, St. Paul, Minn., 1933-39; sr. and prin. comml. policy analyst U.S. Tariff Commn., Washington, 1939-43; br. and div. chief UNRRA, 1944-46; sect. chief and economist Internat. Bank for Reconstrn. and Devel. (World Bank), 1947-51; br. chief and econ. adviser ECA and Mut. Security Adminstrn., 1951-53; economist, chief Near East and South Asia div., v.p., contract administrn, Export-Import Bank U.S., Washington, 1953-71; econ. cons., 1971—. Lectr. in internat. econs. Grad. Sch., Howard U., Washington, part time 1968-72. Mem. Am. Econ. Assn., Nat. Economists Club. Club: Cosmos (Washington). Author: Fascist Economic Policy: An Analysis of Italy's Economic Experiment, 1938; Italian Commercial Policy and Foreign Trade, 1922-1940, 1941, also numerous articles and book revs. Home: 1734 P St NW Washington DC 20036

WELLER, JOHN ALBERT, banker; b. Havana, Cuba, Sept. 29, 1918; s. Albert George and Gladys Eileen (Oates) W.; came to U.S., 1955; naturalized, 1960; B.A. in Bus. Adminstrn., Queen's U., 1943; m. Hedalia Gou, Dec. 12, 1944; children—John Albert, Edward, Gladys. Asst. accountant Bank of Nova Scotia, Havanna, Cuba, 1937-46; comml. and polit. adviser Brit. Embassy, Caracas, Venezuela, 1947-55; with First Nat. Bank of Miami (Fla.), 1958—, sr. v.p., 1970—. Fellow Canadian Bankers Assn.; mem. Bd. Internat. Trade, Bankers Assn. for Fgn. Trade, Nat. Fgn. Trade Council, Latin C. of C. Office: 100 Biscayne Blvd S Miami FL 33131

WELLINGER, (PEARL) KITTY BRITTINGHAM, librarian; b. Pittsville, Md.; Sept. 24, 1909; d. William Henry and Effie (Jones) Brittingham; A.B., Western Md. Coll., 1931; B.S., Madison Coll., 1951; m. Karl E. Wellinger, Dec. 12, 1932. Tchr. Pittsville High Sch., 1932-33; tchr., then tchr. librarian Margaret Brent High Sch., Helen, Md., 1933-41; sec. to mgr. Naval Powder Factory Hotel, Indian Head, Md., 1941-44; recreation social hostess War Dept. ASF, 4th Service Command, Camp Wheeler, Ga., 1944-45; tchr. Alexandria (Va.) pub. schs., 1947-50, librarian, 1950—. Mem. exec. bd. Charles Barrett Sch. P.T.A., 1963; mem. Alexandria Hosp. Corp. Mem. Alexandria Bus. and Profl. Women's Club (mem. exec. bd. 1958-59, 64), Nat., Va. edn. assns., Am., Va. library assns., Assn. Childhood Edn. Internat., Defenders of Wildlife, Edn. Assn. Alexandria. Democrat. Methodist. Club: Zonta (mem. exec. bd.). Home: 7925 Ft Hund Rd Alexandria VA 22308 Office: 1115 Martha Custis Dr Alexandria VA 22302

WELLINGTON, JAMES ELLIS, educator; b. Arlington, Mass., July 9, 1921; s. William Edward and Jessie (Dennett) W.; A.B., Dartmouth, 1948; M.A., Boston U., 1950; Ph.D., Fla. State U., 1956; m. Mary Canfield Grier, July 22, 1952; children—Georgia Grier, Anne Ross. Instr. dept. English U. Neb., 1950-53; teaching asst., instr. English, Fla. State U., 1953-56; instr., asst. prof. English, U. Miami, Coral Gables, Fla., 1956-63, asso. prof., 1963-70, prof., 1970—. Lang. cons., 1958—. Served with USNR, 1941-46. Mem. Modern Lang. Assn., Renaissance Soc. Am., Malone Soc., Am. Assn. U. Profs., South Atlantic Modern Lang. Assn., Southeastern Renaissance Conf., Augustan Reprint Soc., Delta Upsilon. Democrat. Anglo-Catholic. Author: Alexander Pope's Epistles to Several Persons, 1963; Pope's Eloisa to Abelard, with the Hughes Letters, 1965. Home: 4615 Santa Maria St Coral Gables FL 33146 Office: Dept English U Miami Coral Gables FL 33124

WELLS, ALFRED EUGENE, supt. schs.; b. Springtown, Tex., Oct. 11, 1909; s. Alfred W. and Lillie (Roberts) W.; B.A., Abilene Christian Coll., 1931; M.A., Colo. State Coll. Edn., 1936; m. Zieta Guest, July 11, 1932. Classroom tchr., coach, prin., Albany, Tex., 1931-33; prin. elementary sch., Gladwater, Tex., 1933-40, supt. schs., 1940-42; dir. elementary schs., Gladwater, 1933-40, supt. schs., 1940-42; dir. elementary schs., San Angelo, 1942-45; supt. schs., Sonora, 1945-50; dir. curriculum and instrn., Abilene, 1950-51, supt. schs., 1951—; tchr. summers East Tex. State Tchrs. Coll., 1936-42, Southeastern La. Normal Sch., 1943, Northwestern La. Normal Sch., 1943, San Angelo Jr. Coll., 1944, U. Tex., 1965. Mem. Tex. Elementary Adv. Com., 1936-40; mem. adv. com. Tex. Bd. Edn., 1936-38; chmn. Tex. Textbook Com., 1956; chmn. Tex. Bd. Examiners for Tchr. Edn., 1958-64. Vice pres. Gregg County Tb Assn., chmn. leadership tng. Chisholm Trail council Boy Scouts Am., 1951—. Bd. dirs. West Tex. Rehab. Center, Abilene United Fund. Mem. N.E.A., Tex. Tchrs. Assn. (exec. com. 1963-70, dist. pres.), Am., Tex. (past mem. exec. com., past dist. pres.) assns. sch. adminstrs., Classroom Tchrs. Assn., Tex. Elementary Prins. and Suprs. Assn., Nat., Tex. assns. supervision and curriculum devel., Tex. P.T.A. (life), Abilene C. of C. (past dir.). Mem. Ch. of Christ (dir. ch. music). Lion (pres. 1966). Home: 686 Westwood St Abilene TX 79603 Office: Box 981 Abilene TX 79604

WELLS, BENJAMIN B(AXTER), govt. ofcl., health services adminstr.; b. Rockdale, Tex., Jan. 23, 1912; s. William Monroe and Mary Elizabeth (Baxter) W.; B.S., Baylor U., 1931, M.D., 1935; Ph.D. (Mayo Found. fellow), U. Minn., 1941; m. Minnie England, Jan. 7, 1935; children—Benjamin Baxter, Howard Ernest, Flora (Mrs. Robert A. Conley). Intern, Scott and White Meml. Hosp., Temple, Tex., 1935-36; fellow Mayo Clinic, Rochester, Minn., 1939-41; investigator Carnegie Instn., Cold Spring Harbor (N.Y.) Lab., 1941-42; prof. medicine U. Ark., 1946-53, dean Sch. Medicine, 1948-53; v.p., chief editor W.B. Saunders Pub. Co., Phila., 1953-54; prof. medicine Creighton U. Sch. Medicine, Omaha, 1954-57; dean, U. Cal. at Irvine Med. Sch., 1962-63; dep. chief med. dir. VA, Washington, 1970—. Served with AUS, 1942-46. Decorated Legion of Merit. Diplomate Am. Bd. Internal Medicine. Mem. Am. Soc. Clin. Pathologists, Soc. Exptl. Biology and Medicine, Am. Fedn. Clin. Research, Royal Soc. Health, Sigma Xi, Alpha Omega Alpha. Author: Clinical Pathology, 1950, 3d edit., 1967; (with Todd and Sanford) Clinical Diagnosis by Laboratory Methods, 1953, (with Davidson), 1962. Contbr. articles to profl. jours. Home: 1213 Forestwood Dr McLean VA 22101 Office: 810 Vermont Av NW Washington DC 20420

WELLS, CHARLES W(ESLEY), bus. exec.; b. Petersburg, Va., Oct. 6, 1893; s. Beauregard Lee and Bessie (Adams) W.; student pub. and pvt. schs.; m. Laura Booth Tucker, Oct. 7, 1924. Pres. Petersburg Holding Corp., 1942—, Mt. Erin Corp., 1948—; pres. Sycamore Shopping Center, Inc., 1956; owner Wells Realty. Served with Armed Forces, World War I. Mem. Am. Legion. Mason (Shriner), Kiwanian. Home: 1622 Westover Av Walnut Hill Petersburg VA 23803 Office: 36-40 S Union St Box 790 Petersburg VA 23803

WELLS, CLARENCE HENRY, architect; b. Denver, Nov. 17, 1926; s. Thomas Patterson and Mary Elizabeth (Mitze) W.; B.Arch., U. Denver, 1951; m. Carole Jeannine Perkins, Dec. 29, 1951; children—Clare D., T. Jeffrey, Peter J., Robert B. Designer, Evans & Lincoln, Oakland, Cal., 1953-56; partner Turpin & Wells, Monroe, La., 1956-61, Wells & Parker, Monroe, 1961—. Bd. dirs. YMCA, 1966—. Served with AUS, 1945-46. Mem. A.I.A. (pres. Monroe chpt. 1963), La. Architects Assn. (dir. 1963). Lion (dir. North Monroe 1971). Home: 2706 Point Dr Monroe LA 71201 Office: 1011 N 9th St Monroe LA 71201

WELLS, CLAUDIA MAE ELLIS (MRS. JOHN W. WELLS), educator, dietician; b. Reform, Ala., Apr. 25, 1911; d. Leven Handy and Mary (Sibley) Ellis; B.S. in Home Econs. (fellow), U. Ala., 1931, M.S., 1933; m. John Walter Wells, Sept. 10, 1935; 1 son, John Walter. Dietician U. Ala., 1931-33; tchr. home econs., sci. Ala. high schs., 1942-50; tchr. sci. Marietta (Ga.) High Sch., 1950-53, head sci. dept., 1953-56; instr. biology U. Ga. Center, Marietta, 1953-56; asst. prof. nutrition and food sci. U. Ky., 1956—. Research projects (with others): Effect of Ionizing Radiation on Storage Life and Quality of Certain Vegetables and Fruits, contract Q.M. Food and Container Inst. Armed Forces, 1962, Quality Evaluation of Frozen Vegetables, 1964, Quality of Frozen Whole Strawberries as Affected by Addition of Citric Acid, 1968, both agrl. expt. sta. U. Ky.; Nutritional Inter-relationship Minerals and other Nutrients, So. Regional Nutrition, 1968; also paper 60th Annual Conv. Assn. So. Agrl. Workers, Inc., Memphis, 1963. Organizer Ga. Sci. Fairs, 1954-56, Lafayette (Ky.) High Sch. Band Club and Central Ky. Youth Orch. Assn., 1956-58; active A.R.C., Y.W.C.A., P.T.A. (Ala., Ga., Ky.); sponsor Baptist Student Union U. Ky., 1964; asso. Young Peoples Dir., mem. Bapt. Tng. Union, Community Missions div. Woman's Missionary Union (chmn. 1963-64), Elkhorn (Ky.) Assn.; mem. faculty councils, study coms. U. Ky. Mem. Nat., Am., Ga. ednl. assns., Biology Tchrs. Am., Inst. Technologists, Inst. Food Technologists (historian Bluegrass sect. 1965-71), Am., Ky. home econ. assns., Am., Ky. (pub. relations chmn. 1968-71), Bluegrass (v.p. 1963-64, pres. 1964-65) dietetic assns., Sigma Xi. Clubs: Science Clubs Am., Delta Zeta. Contbr. articles to profl. jours. Home: 924 Maywick Dr Lexington KY 40504

WELLS, CLYDE OTAMUS, JR., orthodontist; b. Spartanburg, S.C., Aug. 23, 1926; s. Dr. Clyde Otamus and Allene (Chapman) W.; B.S., Wofford Coll., 1948; D.D.S., U. Md., 1952; m. Margaret Ezell, July 23, 1949; children—Margaret Allene, Janet Alice, Tina Chapman. Preceptor, 1952-54; individual practice orthodontics, Spartanburg, 1954—. Chmn. bd. dirs. Spartanburg Speech and Hearing Clinic, 1962-67. Chmn. Spartanburg Airport Commn., 1963-71. Bd. dirs. Glendale Acad., 1970—. Served with USNR, World War II. Mem. Spartanburg Dental Study Group, Am., S.C., Piedmont dental assns., S.C., Am., Fla. orthodontic assns., So. Soc. Orthodontists, Pierre Fauchard Acad. Methodist. Clubs: Spartanburg Country, Spartanburg Gun, Piedmont (Spartanburg). Home: 1195 Partridge Rd Spartanburg SC 29302 Office: 641 E Main St Spartanburg SC 29302

WELLS, DAMON, JR., investment co. exec.; b. Houston, May 20, 1937; s. Damon and Margaret Corinne (Howze) W.; B.A., magna cum laude, Yale, 1958; B.A., Oxford U., 1964, M.A., 1968; Ph.D., Rice U., 1968. Owner, chief exec. officer Damon Wells Interests, Houston, Tex., 1958—. Bd. dirs. Child Guidance Center of Houston; trustee Christ Ch. Cathedral Endowment Fund. Mem. Am., So. hist. assns., Am. Assn. State and Local History, English-Speaking Union (nat. dir. 1970—, v.p. Houston br. 1966—), Phi Beta Kappa, Pi Sigma Alpha. Episcopalian. Clubs: Coronado, Houston Country, Houston; Garden of the Gods (Colorado Springs, Colo.), Yale (N.Y.C.). Author: Stephen Douglas: The Last Years, 1857-1861, 1971. Home: 2929 Buffalo Speedway Houston TX 77006 Office: 3810 Westheimer Rd Houston TX 77027

WELLS, ERNEST HATTON, aerospace technologist, space scis.; b. Crossville, Tenn., Aug. 1, 1921; s. Noah and Chloe (Burges) W.; B.S. in Elec. Engring., Tenn. Tech. U., 1951; m. Signa Faye Stinnett, Dec. 15, 1954; children—David Allen (dec.), William Ernest, Ronald Eston, Robert Lawrence. Instr. radio Tenn. Tech. U., 1947-48; project engr. electronics Airplane & Marine Instruments, Inc., Clearfield, Pa., 1951-53; engr. mine detection ERDL, with research on Greenland Ice Cap, Ft. Belvoir, Va., 1953-55; engr. electronics, radar hdqrs. USMC, Washington, 1955-57; engr. Army Ballistic Missile Agy., Redstone Arsenal, Huntsville, Ala., 1957-62; aerospace technologist NASA, Huntsville, 1962—, former planetary astronomer, exptl. physicist solar research, staff Nuclear and Plasma Physics Lab., now research scientist, environmental sci. Laser Scatter Physics & Astrophysics Lab. Served with USAAF, 1943-46. Decorated Bronze Star with oak leaf cluster. Registered profl. engr., Tenn. Sr. mem. I.E.E.E. Author: Astronomy Finds the Days of Creation; also numerous tech. reports. Home: 712 Kilkenny St U Highland Huntsville AL 35805 Office: NASA MSFC Space Scis Lab S & E-SSL Marshall Space Center AL 35812

WELLS, GERMAINE CAZENAVE, owner Restaurant Arnaud's, New Orleans. Address: 801-29 Bienville St New Orleans LA 70112*

WELLS, JACK HUBERT, ice mfg. co. exec.; b. Forest Park, Ga., Sept. 15, 1907; s. Emmett Jackson and Mary Frances (Smith) W.; grad. high sch.; m. Mozelle Virginia Moore, Dec. 24, 1927; children—Joel Tommie, Roger Lynn, Carlton Lee, Andrew Michael. With Purity Ice Mfg. Co., Forest Park, 1930—, pres., 1946-68, chmn. bd., 1952—; dir. Bank Forest Park. Mem. So. Ice Exchange (pres. 1962-63), Ga. Ice Mfrs. Assn. (pres. 1962-63), Nat. Ice Assn. (bd. dirs. 1961-66, hon. Life). Baptist (deacon) Kiwanian, Moose. Club: Lakeshore Country. Home: 4775 Courtney Dr Forest Park GA 30050 Office: 964 Main St Box 605 Forest Park GA 30050

WELLS, JOHN HART, ednl. adminstr.; b. Union Level, Va., Dec. 5, 1934; s. Walter James and Vela (Floyd) W.; lit. diploma Ferrum Jr. Coll., 1955; A.B., Atlantic Christian Coll., 1957; M.A., Longwood Coll., 1963; postgrad. U. Va., 1957-70, William and Mary Coll., 1969-71; m. Gladys Rose George, June 27, 1960; children—David Errol, Laura Anne. Prin., tchr. Boydton (Va.) Elementary Sch., 1957-59; tchr. Buckhorn Elementary Sch., Union Level, 1959-63; prin. LaCrosse (Va.) Elementary Sch., 1963-67; dir. instrn. Lunenburg County Pub. Schs., Victoria, Va., 1967—. Served with AUS, 1959-60. Mem. Mecklenburg Edn. Assn. (past treas.), Roanoke River Archeol. Chpt. (past pres.), Archeol. Soc. Va. (dir.). Baptist (deacon). Kiwanian. Home: Box 436 Park Av Victoria VA 23974 Office: Drawer X Victoria VA 23974

WELLS, LEONARD MILTON, city ofcl.; b. Covington, Okla., Nov. 29, 1902; s. Eli Newton and Nancy Jane (Elliott) W.; student Okla. State U., 1922-25; m. Marguerite Hale, Aug. 5, 1928; children—Willia Jane (Mrs. Robert L. Cummins), Robert Milton. Insp., Okla. Hwy. Dept., Okla., 1925-26; partner Wells & Son, Enid, 1926-31; engr. Enid Water Plant, 1931-48; supt. water prodn. City of Enid, 1948-60, dir. pub. works, 1960—. Bd. dirs. Kaw Dam Assn., 1957-72. Mem. Am. Water Works Assn. (pres. Okla. 1967-68, recipient Samuel A. Greeley Local Govt. Service award 1972), Am. Pub. Works Assn., Sigma Nu. Baptist. Rotarian. Home: 409 S Hoover St Enid OK 73701 Office: City Hall Enid OK 73701

WELLS, MARCUS, retail trade co. exec.; b. Charleston, W.Va., Apr. 11, 1908; s. Joseph Wolfe and Anna (Valinsky) W.; B.S.C., U. Cin., 1935; m. Minette Stern, June 3, 1930; children—Richard Allan, Jerry Ames. Div. mdse. mgr. Allied Stores, Cin., 1932-36, Marks-Isaacs, New Orleans, 1936-37; asst. gen. mdse. mgr. Wolff &Mark Co., San Antonio, 1937-40; regional mgr. Sally Frocks, Little Rock, 1940-46; divisional mdse. mgr. E.S. Levy & Co., Inc., Galveston, Tex., 1946—, v.p., 1971—; also dir. Mem. mid-mgmt. com. Galveston Jr. Coll., 1969-72, res. instr., coordinator mid-mgmt., 1971—; chmn. adult edn. Bay Area council Boy Scouts Am., 1949-50; pres. Am. Council for Judaism Galveston, 1951-52. Mem. C. of C. (higher edn. com), Phi Beta Delta. Jewish religion. Mason (32 deg., Shriner). Home: 4527 Av N 1/2 Galveston TX 77550 Office: 2227 Central Plaza Galveston TX 77550

WELLS, MILDRED, social worker; b. Huntsville, Ala., Oct. 18, 1905; d. Earl C. and Lela (Lyne) Wells; B.A., H. Sophie Newcomb Coll., 1924; postgrad. Tulane U., 1924-25, William and Mary Sch. Social Work, 1939-40. Tchr. English Katherine Bress Sch., New Orleans, 1924-27; social worker A.R.C. Mil. Naval Welfare, Vets. Hosp., Algiers, Alexandria, La., 1927-32; with Fed. Emergency Relief Adminstrn., La., 1932-36; La. Dept. Pub. Welfare, Natchitoches, 1936-39, Shreveport, 1946-59, pub. welfare dir., 1944-72, research disaster worker; mil. and naval welfare field dir. A.R.C., 1940-44. Mem. Nat. Am. Pub. Welfare Com. Ageing, 1957-59; regional chmn. La. Conf. Social Welfare, 1952; state rep. to Conf. So. Social Work Execs., Blue Ridge, N.C., 1951, mem. exec. council, 1952-54; chmn. disaster relief A.R.C., 1953-54; mem. bd. dirs. Community Council, 1954-59; sec. Am. Cancer Soc., 1952-56; chmn. relocation com. Shreveport Slum Clearance; mem. bd. La. State Health Council, 1959; mem. welfare com. of Survey of Shreveport's Negro Community (won Am. Cities award by Council Social Agys., 1952). 1950-51; mem. Nat. Speakers Service Community Health and Welfare Councils, 1964; sec. Nat. Council Local Pub. Welfare Adminstrs.; mem. Council on Alcoholism, 1962-64; sec. Tb League, 1963-64; del. Internat. Congress Against Tb, Munich, Germany, 1965; mem. bd. Cath. Charities Alexandria Diocese, Alcoholism Information Center, 1972; mem. White House Conf. on Children and Youth. Recipient Community Service award, 1967. Mem. Am. Assn. U. Women, Acad. Certified Social Workers, Pub. Welfare Dirs. Assn. (pres. 1962-64), Am. Assn. Social Workers (chmn. local chpt. 1948), Bd. Social Service Exchange (pres. 1957-59), Council Social Agys. (chmn. case conf. com. 1953-54). Clubs: Social Work Executives (chmn. 1950), Altrusa (local pres. 1949, 66-67). Died July 28, 1972. Home: 643 McCormick St Shreveport LA 71104

WELSH, RONALD ARTHUR, pathologist; b. Houston, Oct. 13, 1926; s. Leo Arthur and Octavia (Franssen) W.; A.B., U. Tex., 1947, M.D., 1950; m. Mary Jeanne Duncan, June 23, 1950; children—Mary J., William A., James D. Intern, USPHS Hosp., New Orleans, 1950-51; resident USPHS Hosp., Balt., 1951-55; practice medicine, specializing in pathology, New Orleans, 1957—; mem. staff Charity Hosp., New Orleans; pathologist Orleans Parish Coroners Office, 1961—, Charity Hosp., 1957—, USPHS Hosp., Galveston, Tex., 1955-57; cons. in pathology VA Hosp., New Orleans, Earl K. Long Hosp., Baton Rouge; asst. prof. La. State U. Sch. Medicine, New Orleans, 1957-59, asso. prof., 1959-62, prof., 1962—. Bd. dirs. La. div. Am. Cancer Soc.; del. dir. Am. Cancer Soc., 1968-70. Served with USNR, 1944-46; served with USPHS 1950-57. Mem. Am. Assn. Pathologists and Bacteriologists, Am. Soc. Exptl. Pathology, Internat. Acad. Pathology, Coll., Coll. Am. Pathologists, Am. Soc. Clin. Pathology. Research in electron microscopy, pathology of tumors. Home: 2429 Octavia St New Orleans LA 70115 Office: 1542 Tulane Av New Orleans LA 70112

WELSH, WILLIAM JOSEPH, librarian; b. Weatherly, Pa., Nov. 15, 1919; s. Edward C. and Mary A. (Doheny) W.; A.B. in Philosophy, U. Notre Dame, 1940, student law, 1940-41; m. Winifred Hatfield, Oct. 21, 1950; children—Douglas B., James F. With Library of Congress, 1947—, dir. processing dept., 1968—; cons. in field, 1965—. Served to maj. USAAF, 1941-47. Recipient Melvil Dewey award, 1971. Mem. A.L.A. (chmn. fed. library com. task force acquisition library materials and correlation fed. library resources, 1965-70; mem. various coms.). Contbr. articles in field. Home: 4805 Edgefield Rd Bethesda MD 20014 Office: Library of Congress Washington DC 20540

WELT, LOUIS GORDON, physician, educator; b. Elizabeth, N.J., Sept. 6, 1913; s. Sigmund and Hattie (Gordon) W.; B.A., N.Y.U., 1934; M.D., Yale, 1938; m. Mary Patton, Oct. 14, 1959; children—Robert Gray Sigmund, Frederick Gordon Patton. Intern, New Haven Hosp., 1938-39; resident, 1939-41; instr. Yale, 1941-42, clin. instr., 1946-48, USPHS fellow, 1948-49, asst. prof., 1949-52; pvt. practice medicine, Willimantic, Conn., 1946-47; chief reserach sect. VA Central Office, Washington, 1947-48; asso. prof. U. N.C. Sch. Medicine, Chapel Hill, 1952-54, prof., 1954-69, chmn. dept. medicine, 1965—, Alumni Distinguished prof., 1969—. Served with AUS, 1942-46. Decorated Bronze Star medal. Mem. A.M.A., Am. Soc. Clin. Investigation, Sigma Xi, Alpha Omega Alpha. Home: 614 Morgan Creek Rd Chapel Hill NC 27514

WELTIN, WILLIAM LAWRENCE, advt. exec.; b. Chgo., Dec. 2, 1936; s. John Merle and Garnett (Russell) W.; A.B., Dartmouth, 1958; postgrad. Sch. Journalism, U. Mo., 1961-63; m. Feriba Ann Berry, June 17, 1961; children—Laurie Ann, Kimberly Garnet. Copywriter Leo Burnett Co., Chgo., 1963; account exec. Needham, Harper & Steers, Inc., Chgo., 1963-66; v.p., dir. Henderson Advt., Greenville, S.C., 1966-70; pres. Weltin Advt. Agy., Atlanta, 1971—. Vice pres. Greater Atlanta Arts Council, 1969—. Served as capt. USMCR, 1958-61. Mem. Am. Assn. Advt. Agys. (chmn. 1970), Sigma Alpha Epsilon, Kappa Tau Alpha, Alpha Delta Sigma. Republican. Presbyn. Clubs: Cherokee Town and Country, Internat. Golf, Downtown Atlanta. Home: 1060 Huntcliff Trace NW Atlanta GA 30338 Office: 100 Colony Sq Atlanta GA 30309

WELTNER, CHARLES LONGSTREET, lawyer; b. Atlanta, Dec. 17, 1927; s. Philip and Sally Cobb (Hull) W.; A.B., Oglethorpe U., 1948; LL.B., Columbia, 1950; m. Juanita McK. Lynn; children by previous marriage—Elizabeth Shirley, Philip II, Susan Martin, Charles Longstreet. Admitted to Ga. bar, 1949; pvt. practice in Atlanta, 1950—; mem. 88th-89th Congresses 5th Dist. Ga. Served to capt. AUS, 1955-57. Democrat. Presbyn. Author: Southener, 1966. Home: 1105 E Rock Springs Rd NE Atlanta GA 30303 Office: 1st Nat Bank Bldg Atlanta GA 30303

WENTZ, EARLE JERRY, JR., apparel co. exec.; b. Kannapolis, N.C., June 4, 1913; s. Earle Jerry and Jennie (Safrit) W.; A.B., Duke U., 1936; m. Merle Horne, May 25, 1940; children—E. Russell, John Wade. Supt. depts. P.H. Hanes Knitting Co., Winston-Salem, N.C., 1936-54; asst. gen. mgr. Roanoke Mills, Inc. (Va.), 1954-64, gen. mgr. all divs., 1954—, dir., 1955-64, v.p., 1955-64; v.p. mfg. Pannill Knitting Co., Inc., Martinsville, 1965—. Bd. dirs. Jr. Achievement, Roanoke, Va., chmn. bd., 1961-62.; bd. dirs. Roanoke Valley Industries. Methodist. Club: Chatmoss Country (Martinsville, Va.). Home: 1202 Sam Lions Trail Martinsville VA 24112 Office: PO Box 5151 Cleveland Av Martinsville VA 24112

WENZE, IRA HARMON, physician; b. Brunswick, Ga., Dec. 10, 1932; s. Frank Smith and Ethel (Jurshial Ponder) W.; B.S., Morehouse Coll., 1954; M.S., U. Mich., 1958; M.D., Meharry Med. Coll., 1967; m. Alberta Brown, Oct. 9, 1961; children—Cornelia, Ira II, Don and Darnell (twins). Instr. biology Fla. A. and M. U., Tallahassee, 1958-63, acting chmn. dept., summer 1963; intern Menorah Med. Center, Kansas City, Mo., 1967-68, resident internal medicine, 1968-69; practice gen. medicine Fort Lauderdale, Fla., 1969—; mem. staff Broward Gen. Med. Center, Fort Lauderdale, Plantation Gen. Hosp., Fort Lauderdale; med. dir. Sweeting Nursing Home, Fort Lauderdale, 1971—, Broward County Sheriff's Dept., Fort Lauderdale, 1971. Served with M.C., AUS, 1954-56. Mem. A.M.A., Alpha Phi Alpha, Beta Kappa Chi. Democrat. Baptist. Home: PO Box 9303 Fort Lauderdale FL 33310 Office: 1429 NW 6th St Fort Lauderdale FL 33311

WERMUTH, ANTHONY LEWIS, social scientist; b. Phila., June 1, 1915; s. Paul Charles and Susan Aloysius (Manga) W.; B.S., U.S. Mil. Acad., 1940; postgrad. Army Command and Gen. Staff Coll., 1944, Army War Coll., 1958-59, Mass. Inst. Tech., 1966-67; M.A., Columbia, 1951, George Washington U., 1961; Ph.D., Boston U., 1971; m. Charlotte J. Malinowski, July 24, 1940; children—Philip (dec.), Anthony Lewis, Marianne N. Commd. 2d lt., inf., U.S. Army, 1940, advanced through grades to col.; asst. prof. English U.S. Mil. Acad., 1946-50; co. and bn. comdr. World War II; bn., regiment comdr., Korea, 1956-57; mem. faculty Army War Coll., 1959-62. brigade comdr., Germany, 1963-64; staff officer hdqrs. U.S. Army in Europe, Germany, Hdqrs. SHAPE, Paris; mil. asst. to chmn. Office Sec. Def.; ret. 1966; now dir. social sci. studies Westinghouse Electric Corp., Center for Advanced Studies, Falls Church, Va. Decorated D.S.M. Mem. Internat. Inst. for Strategic studies (London), Am. Polit. Sci. Assn., Am. Acad. Polit. and Social Sci., Acad. Polit. Sci., U.S. Naval Inst., Assn. U.S. Army, World Future Soc., Interuniv. Seminar on Armed Forces and Soc., Internat. Studies Assn., others. Home: 6544 Bay Tree Ct Falls Church VA 22041 Office: Westinghouse Center for Advanced Studies and Analyses 6521 Arlington Blvd Falls Church VA 22042

WERNER, ELDON A., utilities co. exec.; b., 1904 With Brockton Edison Co., 1926-30, Ponce Electric Co., 1930-32, Stone & Webster, 1932-34, El Paso Electric Co., 1934-39; with Gulf States Utilities Co., Beaumont, Tex., 1939—, personnel mgr., 1945-58, v.p., 1958-65, exec. v.p., 1965-66, pres., 1966—, also dir.; dir. 1st Security Nat. Bank Beaumont, Baton Rouge City Nat. Bank. Office: 285 Liberty Av Beaumont TX 77701

WERNER, RICHARD ALLEN, entomologist; b. Reading, Pa., Feb. 20, 1936; s. Roy Martin and Hazel Sarah (Rightmyer) W.; B.S., Pa. State U., 1958, B.S. in Entomology, 1960; certificate Kutztown State Coll., 1961; M.S., U. Md., 1965; Ph.D., N.C. State U., 1968. Forester, U.S. Forest Service, Roseburg, Ore., 1957-59, research entomologist, Juneau, Alaska, 1961-64, research entomologist, Research Triangle Park, N.C., 1965—. Vice pres. Research Triangle Park Fed. Employees Credit Union, 1971—; v.p. Research Triangle Park Fed. Employees Recreation Assn., 1967-68, sports chmn., 1970-71. Active Boy Scouts Am., 1966—. Mem. Soc. Am. Foresters, Entomol. Soc. Am., Ga. Entomol. Soc., Tau Phi Delta, Phi Sigma. Contbr. articles to profl. publs. Home: 310 Brandywine St Chapel Hill NC 27514 Office: Box 12254 Forestry Sciences Lab Research Triangle Park NC 27709

WERNER, STANLEY PATRICK, dentist, educator; b. Memphis, Tenn., Sept. 19, 1938; s. Paul Ulrich and Lilla Ruth (Whitehead) W.; student Memphis State U., 1956-57, 59-62; D.D.S. (USPHS fellow), U. Tenn., 1965, M.S. in Orthodontics, 1968; m. Joy Humphries, May 5, 1962; children—Scott Patrick, Kelly Lynn. Instr. U. Tenn. Coll. Dentistry, 1965—; practice of dentistry, specializing in orthodontics, Memphis, 1968—. Served with AUS, 1957-59. Recipient award Internat. Coll. Dentists, 1965. Mem. Am., Memphis dental socs., Tenn. Dental Assn., Memphis Dental Legion, Memphis Soc. Dentistry for Children (sec. treas. 1971—, v.p. 1972) So., Tenn. socs. orthodontists, Am. Assn. Orthodontists, Delta Sigma Delta, Lambda Chi Alpha, Omicron Kappa Upsilon. Republican. Episcopalian. Home: 6227 Lochlevin Cove Memphis TN 38138 Office: 6209 Poplar St Memphis TN 38138

WERNICK, GERALD IRWIN, dentist; b. Watertown, N.Y., Feb. 13, 1934; s. Henry B. and Deborah F. (Fried) W.; grad. Emory U., 1955, D.D.S., 1959; postgrad. endodontics Boston U., 1961-62; m. Violet Konig, Aug. 19, 1956; children—Barbara, Sharon, Jeffrey. Endodontist, Miami Beach, Fla., 1962—; chmn. dept. endodontics Mt. Sinai Hosp., Miami Beach, 1963—. Co-chmn. endodontic sect. Dade County Dental Research Clinic, 1964—; cons. VA Hosp., Miami, 1970—. Served to lt. USNR, 1959-61. Diplomate Am. Bd. Endodontists. Mem. Am. Dental Assn., Am. Assn. Endodontists (editor 1969-71), Fla. Bd. Dentistry (asst. sec.-treas. 1969—), Miami Beach Dental Soc. (pres. 1970-71), Fla. Soc. Endodontists (pres. 1969-72), Fla. Dental Assn., Fla. Acad. Practice Mgmt., N.Y. Acad. Sci., Alpha Omega, Alpha Epsilon Pi. Mason (Shriner). Home: 9375 Balada St Coral Gables FL 33156 Office: 333 Arthur Godfrey Rd Miami Beach FL 33140

WERTS, LEO ROBERT, ednl. cons.; b. Wren, O., Feb. 7, 1905; s. Jess J. and Else (Slyh) W.; B.A.S., George Williams Coll., Chgo., 1929, L.H.D., 1969; Ph.B., U. Chgo., 1930; m. Frances Moan, May 24, 1948; 1 dau., Barbara Carolyn. Sec. YMCA, Van Wert, O., also Chgo., 1924-32; vocational adviser, dir. vocational service Ill. State Relief Adminstrn., 1932-35; supr., dir. Ill. State Employment Service, 1935-41; manpower specialist OPM, WPB, War Manpower Commn., 1941-45; manpower, labor adviser, dir. manpower div. U.S. Mil. Govt., Germany, 1945-49; U.S. rep. manpower directorate Allied Control Council, Germany, 1946-48; asso. dir. Office Internat. Labor Affairs, Dept. Labor, 1949-50, dep. exec. dir. Def. Manpower Adminstrn., 1950-53, mem. adv. bd. econ. growth and stability, 1953, spl. asst. Sec. Labor, 1953; dep. asst. sec. of labor for manpower, 1954; dep. asst. sec. for internat. labor affairs, 1956-59; asst. sec. of labor for adminstrn., 1962-71; with The Manpower Inst., 1971—; manpower cons. Govt. India, 1959-60; tech. adv. Sec. Labor, ILO Confs., 1950-52. Home: 4819 Cumberland Av Chevy Chase MD 20015 Office: Mampower Inst Washington DC 20236

WERTZ, SPENCER KIEFER, educator; b. Amarillo, Tex., Oct. 27, 1941; s. Ralph Everitt and Pauline (Tressler) W.; B.A., Tex. Christian U., 1965, M.A., 1966; postgrad. Eliot Coll., U. Kent, Canterbury, Eng., 1965; Ph.D. (Kingfisher Coll. fellow), U. Okla., 1970; m. Linda Lee Loflin, Aug. 12, 1967. Instr. in philosophy Austin Coll., Sherman, Tex., 1969; instr. Tex. Christian U., Fort Worth, 1969-71, asst. prof., 1971—. Mem. Am., North Tex., N.M. philos. assns., Am. Assn. U. Profs., Southwestern Philos. Soc., Assn. Symbolic Logic, Mind Assn., Phi Sigma Tau. Club: Ridglea Country (Fort Worth). Contbr. articles to profl. jours. Home: 6712 Woodstock Rd Fort Worth TX 76116

WESLEY, GEORGE RANDOLPH, educator; b. Houston, July 31, 1931; s. George and Flora (Black) W.; B.A., U. Houston, 1957; M.A., U. Denver, 1959, Ph.D., 1965 m. children—Lynda Jacqueline, Charles Edward, Phyllis Michelle, Carla Cassandra; m. 2d, Ingrid Grace Kremer, 1963. Instr., Northeastern Jr. Coll., Sterling, Colo., 1961-63; prof. psychology Appalachian State U., Boone, N.C., 1963-66, 67—; asst. prof. psychology Meml. Nfld. (Can.), St. John's, 1966-67; prof. psychology U. Me. at Ft. Kent, summers 1970-71. Cons. New River Mental Health Center, Boone, 1967-69, Hosp. of Mental and Nervous Diseases, St. Johns, 1966-67, Wilkes County (N.C.) schs., 1970—, N.C. Juvenile Evaluation and Correction Center, Swannanoa, N.C., 1971—. Served with AUS, 1952-54. Mem. Am. Assn. U. Profs. (br. v.p. 1968-69), Nat., N.C. edn. assns., N.C. Psychol. Assn., Am. Mensa, Phi Delta Kappa, Kappa Delta Pi, Beta Beta Beta, Gamma Sigma Epsilon. Author: Educational Psychology Revisited, 1970; The U.S. of A. and other Writings, 1971; A Primer of Misbehavior, 1972. Home: Route 3 Box 308 Boone NC 28607*

WESLEY, JAMES WYATT, JR., broadcasting exec.; b. Atlanta, Sept. 5, 1933; s. James Wyatt and Nellie (Johnson) W.; B.S., Ga. Inst. Tech., 1955; m. Mary Phillips, Mar. 20, 1954; children—Alan, David. Announcer, radio sta. WSB Cox Broadcasting Corp., Atlanta, 1955-57; CBC salesman WSB Radio, Atlanta, 1958-62, local sales mgr., 1963-65; sta. mgr. WIOD, Miami, Fla., 1965-66, gen. mgr., 1966—. Mem. Greater Miami Broadcasters Assn. (pres. 1968-69; award 1969), Econ. Soc. Fla. (sec. 1969-70), Fla. (pres. 1971-72), Nat. assns. broadcasters. Methodist. Home: 4700 Adams St Hollywood FL 33021 Office: 1401 N Bay Causeway Miami FL 33138

WESLEY, RICHARD HAL, bus. exec.; b. Detroit, July 1, 1918; s. Hal E. and Annette (Fordon) W.; grad. Wayne State U., 1943, Wash. U., 1949; m. Christine Bailey, July 28, 1954; children—Richard Hal II, Phyllis. Geologist party chief Union Mines Devel. Corp., 1943-44; sales, marketing engr. Socony Mobile Oil Co., West Africa div., 1944-46; cons. geologist, geophysicist, Detroit, also Ft. Worth, 1949-57; mfg. research engr. Gen. Dynamics Corp., Ft. Worth, 1957-60; pres. Electro Hydraulics Corp., Ft. Worth, 1960-67, Gen. Hefco Corp., Ft. Worth, 1967—; founder Electro Hydraulic Research Corp., Ft. Worth, 1963—; pres. Delta Research Corp., Houston, Magnetic Arts Corp., Eagle Pass, Tex., 1971—; v.p. HERF Industries, Inc., Little Rock, 1972—. Mem. Soc. Exploration Geophysicists, Am. Inst. Mining and Metall. Engrs., Am. Geophys. Union, Seismol. Soc. Am., Soc. Econ. Pateontologists and Mineralogists, Am. Soc. Metals, Am. Soc. Tool and Mfg. Engrs. Inventor, patentee in high energy rate forming field, also in capacitor discharge application in mining; research and devel. in petroleum recovery, sewage purification, agr., air pollution abatement. Home: 14715 Barry Knoll Houston TX 77024 Office: PO Box 79020 Addicks Branch Houston TX 77079

WEST, AUBREY IVAN, oil well service co. exec.; b. Pitkin, La., Aug. 20, 1927; s. Lee and Susie (Sweet) W.; student U. Southwestern La., 1947-50; m. Christy Belle Langley, July 29, 1950; children—Christiann, Denise, Llona. Accountant and cost analyst Glaser Constrn. Co., Lafayette, La., 1950-51; with Sladco, Inc., Eunice, La., 1951—, pres., gen. mgr., chief exec. officer, 1970—; with Harris Well Service, Inc., Eunice, 1951—, pres., gen. mgr., chief exec. officer, 1970—. Bd. dirs. Acadiana Health Planning Council. Served with AUS, 1945-47. Mem. Nat. Assn. Oilwell Servicing Contractors (v.p. 1971-72), Eunice Jr. C. of C. (pres. 1963-64), Am. Legion (dist. vice comdr. 1955-56). Democrat. Mason, Lion (pres. 1954-55). Home: 340 Great Slave Av Eunice LA 70535 Office: Drawer 949 Eunice LA 70535

WEST, BEN, lawyer; b. Columbia, Tenn., 1911; A.B., Vanderbilt U., 1934; J.D., 1930. Admitted to Tenn. bar, 1932, since practiced in Nashville; dist. atty. gen. pro tem 12th Judicial Dist., 1942; asst. dist. atty. gen. 10th Judicial Dist., 1934-44. Pres., Tenn. Municipal League, 1957, Pan Am. Assn. Tenn., 1963-67; v.p. Nat. Safety Council, 1964-69; pres. Am. Municipal Assn., 1957. Mem. 6th Congl. Dist. Democratic Exec. Com., 1942, 44, 46; vice chmn. for Middle Tenn., State Dem. Exec. Com., 1946; vice mayor, Nashville, 1947-51, mayor, 1951-63; mem. Tenn. Senate, 1949-51. Mem. nat. bd. Urban America, 1966-69. Mem. Am., Tenn., Nashville (dir., 1st v.p. 1942-45) bar assns. Office: Commerce Union Bank Bldg Nashville TN 37219*

WEST, CHARLES RICHARD, editor; b. Cleburne, Tex., Sept. 14, 1912; s. Charles Robertson and Mary Elizabeth West; B.J., U. Tex.,1934, M.Journalism and Polit. Sci., 1935; m. Betsy Page, Feb. 2, 1940; children—Richard, Elliott, George. Reporter, Dallas News, 1935-36, asst. agrl. editor, 1936-40; writer A.P., 1940-43; spl. writer Dallas News, 1943-44, mem. editorial staff, 1944—, editor editorial page, 1960-69, editorial dir., 1969—; radio commentator sta. WFAA, Dallas, 1948-65. Recipient 1st prize editorial awards Tex., 1947, 51, 62, 64, annual award Americanism, So. Meml. Assn., 1960, also 11 awards for excellence in editorial direction and writing, 1945-61. Mem. Am. Acad. Polit. Sci., Phi Delta Theta, Sigma Delta Chi. Methodist. Clubs: Dallas Press, Dallas Critic. Author: Fair Comment and Criticism, A Defense in Libel. Home: 4537 Belfort Av Dallas TX 75205 Office: Dallas Morning News Dallas TX 75221

WEST, CLAUDE OTIS, retail co. exec.; b. Minden, La., Aug. 26, 1927; s. Herman O. and Gladys (Tatum) W.; B.B.A., La. State U., 1949; postgrad. N.Y. U., 1953-54; m. Leatrice Mae David, Sept. 3, 1946; children—Sandra Lee (Mrs. James M. Jackson), Peggy Ann (Mrs. Charles Waters), Claudia Jane. Asst. mgr. West Bros., Springhill, La., 1949-51, Bastrop, 1951-52, Stuttgart, Ark., 1952-53, Homer, La., 1953, buyer Gen. Office, DeRidder, La., 1953-56, buyer, v.p. West & Co. of La., Inc., Minden, 1956-65, pres., 1965—; pres. Gibson Products Co. of Camden, Inc., Camden, Ark., 1964—; pres. Gibson Products Co. of Greenwood, Inc., Greenwood, Miss., 1965—; pres. West's Gibson Products Co., Inc., Minden, 1966—; pres. Gibson's Shopping Center of Benton, Inc., Benton, Ark., 1968—; developer West Plaza Shopping Center, Minden, 1966. Dir., Peoples Bank, Minden. Mem. commn. Minden City Airport, 1969—. Sec., treas., West Found., 1957—. Pres. Bossier-Webster Fair and Forrest Festival, 1959; pres. Minden Edn. Found., 1966-67; v.p. Minden Parents League, 1969; mem. exec. bd. Norwela council Boy Scouts Am. Bd. dirs. Glenbrook Sch. Served with USNR, 1945-46. Mem. La. (dir. 1961), Minden (pres. 1960; chmn. long range planning com. 1968-71), U.S. chambers commerce, Am. Legion (post comdr. 1962; club pres. 1964), Lambda Chi Alpha. Baptist (deacon 1957—). Mason, Lion (dir. 1959). Clubs: Minden Tennis and Aquatic (dir. 1968-69), Minden Exchange, One Hundred, Louisi-anne Booster, Pine Hills Country (Minden); Metropolitan Dinner (Greater Shreveport, La.), Holiday In Dixie Ambassadors (Shreveport), Minden Ambassadors. Home: 1110 Madison Av Minden LA 71055 Office: PO Drawer G Minden LA 71055

WEST, DICK SHEPPARD, journalist; b. Merkel, Tex., Dec. 26, 1920; s. Henry Clay and Grace (Sheppard) W.; B.A., Trinity U., San Antonio, 1942; m. Louise Parker Knight, Aug. 23, 1949; children—Larry K., Rebecca M., Forrest A., George T. Reporter, Corpus-Christi (Tex.) Caller-Times, 1942, 46; with U.P.I., 1947—, mem. Washington bur., 1952—, author syndicated column The Lighter Side, 1960—. Served with AUS, 1942-45. Author: The Backside of Washington, 1961. Home: 3039 Crane Dr Falls Church VA 22042 Office: United Press Internat Nat Press Bldg Washington DC 20004

WEST, EDWARD HAMILTON, bishop; b. Birmingham, Ala., July 25, 1906; s. Edward Hamilton and Clarine (Buell) W.; B.A., Birmingham So. Coll. 1926, LL.D., June, 1956; M.A., U. Ida., 1933; B.D., Va. Theol. Sem., 1931, D.D., 1949, U. South, 1948; m. Charlotte Matthews, Aug. 29, 1933; children—Edward Hamilton, Margaret, John Matthews. Ordained to ministry Episcopal Ch., 1931; minister-in-charge St. Agnes, Sandpoint, Ida., St. Mary's, Bonners Ferry, Ida., 1931; rector St. Marks, Moscow, Ida., 1932-35, St. Paul's Ch., Augusta, Ga., 1940-48; chaplain Episcopal students Chapel of Incarnation, U. Fla., 1935-40; elected and consecrated Bishop Coadjutor of Fla., 1948; became Bishop of Fla., 1956; mem. Nat. Council Episcopal Ch., 1945-47, dep. gen. conv., 1943, 1946, Provincial Council, chmn. coll. work, 1944-46, chmn. Forward in Service, dept. Christian edn., 1942-46; mem. standing com. Diocese of Ga., 1944-46. Mem. Sigma Alpha Epsilon. Rotarian. Clubs: Timuguana Country, Ponte Vedra (Jacksonville). Home: 4949 Vandiveer Rd Jacksonville FL 32210 Office: 325 Market St Jacksonville FL 32202

WEST, ELMER GORDON, fed. judge; b. Hyde Park, Mass., Nov. 27, 1914; s. William Albert Howard and Edith Louise (Hall) W.; student Northeastern U., 1934-35, Lamar Jr. Coll., 1935-36; B.S., La. State U., 1941, LL.B., 1942; m. Viola Kay Cayard, Oct. 30, 1942; children—Roger Gordon, Dan Edward. Accountant, Stone & Webster, 1937-42; admitted to La. bar, 1942; mem. firm Long & West, Baton Rouge, 1946-50, Kantrow, Spaht, West & Kleinpeter, and predecessor, Baton Rouge, 1950-61; U.S. dist. judge Eastern Dist. Ct. La., 1961-68, chief judge, 1968—. Atty., La. Revenue Dept., 1946-48, La. inheritance tax collector, 1948-52; asst. prof., spl. lectr. La. State U. Law Sch., 1947-48; mem. Jud. Conf. U.S., 1971—. Served to lt. USNR, 1942-45. Mem. Am., La., East Baton Rouge bar assns., Am. Judicature Soc., Internat. Assn. Ins. Counsel, Nat. Assn. Compensation Claimants Attys., Alpha Tau Omega, Phi Delta Phi. Episcopalian. Mason. Home: 2629 Lakeshore Dr Baton Rouge LA 70808 Office: Fed Ct Bldg Baton Rouge LA 70801

WEST, FRANCIS THORNTON, window and door mfg. co. exec.; b. Salem, Va., Feb. 6, 1920; s. Thomas Fendol and Bentley (Wysor) W.; student Roanoke Coll., 1937-38; m. Nina Penn Moir, Oct. 5, 1940 (div.); children—Suzanne (Mrs. Louis L. Guy, Jr.), Nina (Mrs. James M. Guy), Francis Thornton, Bentley Wysor; m. 2d, Eleanor Eastwick Seeley, May 1, 1970. Sales rep. for several cos., 1938-49; owner West Window Corp., 1949-65; pres. West Window Corp., 1965—; pres. Franklin Finance Co., Inc., Rocky Mount, Va. Lay del. Diocese Southwestern Va. to Anglican Congress; lay dep. Epis. Gen. Conv.; mem. Diocesan Exec. Bd. Mem. Martinsville City Council, 1966—; vice mayor, Martinsville 1968-72, mayor, 1972—; chmn. adv. com. Patrick-Henry Coll. of U. Va., 1962-71. Mem. C. of C. (pres. 1961-62). Episcopalian. Mailing Address: 1012 River Forest Pl Martinsville VA 24112 Office: Drawer 3071 Industrial Park Martinsville VA 24112

WEST, HAROLD DADFORD, JR., physician, naval officer; b. Nasvhille, Sept. 12, 1938; s. Harold Dadford and Jessie (Penn) W.; B.S., Tenn. A. and C. State U., 1959; M.D., Meharry Med. Coll., 1964; m. Carole Vivian Baltimore, Dec. 28, 1960; children—Harold Dadford III, Tonya Rene. Commd. ensign M.C., U.S. Navy, 1960, advanced through grades to lt. comdr., 1968; intern U.S. Naval Hosp., San Diego, 1965-66, resident orthopedic surgery, 1966-70; med. officer submarine tender U.S.S. Nereus, 1966-67; mem. part-time staff Kaiser Found. Hosp., La Mesa, Cal., 1970-71; mem. courtesy staff U.S. Naval Hosp., Yokosuku, Japan, 1970-71, Camp Pendelton, Cal., 1971—. Mem. Soc. Mil. Surgeons, Soc. Mil. Orthopedic Surgeons, Soc. of Upper Tenth, Alpha Ph Alpha, Alpha Omega Alpha, Beta Kappa Chi. Home: 3519 Geneva Circle Nashville TN 37209 Office: U S Naval Hosp Camp Pendleton CA 92055

WEST, JAMES EDWIN, lawyer; b. Greenwood Junction, Okla., May 9, 1928; s. Dudley G. and Dollye (Quinn) W.; J.S.D., U. Ark., 1952; m. Doris Ann Stevenson, July 24, 1950; children—Carolyn Sue (Mrs. James Richard Wagner), Janice Evonne. Admitted to Ark. bar, 1952; since practiced in Ft. Smith; law clk. U.S. Dist. Judge, 1952-58; asso. Daily & Woods, 1958-61, partner, 1961-70; partner Daily, West, Core & Coffman, 1970—. Chmn. Sebastian County March of Dimes, 1963; chmn. Girls Club Summer Camp Program, 1965. Served with USMCR, 1946-47. Mem. Am., Ark. (pres.-elect 1972-73), Sebastian County (pres. 1961) bar assns., Ark. Bar Found. (pres. 1968), Conf. Local Bar Assns. (pres. 1964-65). Baptist. Club: Fort Smith Toastmasters (pres. 1966). Vice pres. Ark. Law Rev., 1969—. Home: 3201 S Dallas Fort Smith AR 72901 Office: Merchants Bank Bldg Fort Smith AR 72901

WEST, JAMES KING, educator; b. Keysville, Va., Sept. 13, 1930; s. Charles Thomas and Pearl (Crawley); W.; student U. Richmond, 1947-49, U. Va., 1950-51; B.A., Lynchburg Coll., 1951; B.D., So. Theol. Sem., 1954; Ph.D., Vanderbilt U., 1961. Ordained to ministry Baptist Ch., 1954, United Ch. Christ, 1964; parish minister, Va. and Tenn., 1957-60; prof. religion and philosophy Catawba Coll., Salisbury, N.C., 1962—. Lilly grantee Vanderbilt U., 1959-60. Mem. Am. Schs. Oriental Research, Soc. Bibl. Lit., Am. Acad. Religion. Author: Introduction to the Old Testament, 1971; (with Donald J. Selby) Introduction to the Bible, 1971. Contbr. articles to profl. jours., Ency. Brit. Office: Box 116 Catawba Coll Salisbury NC 28144 Home: 320 W Corriher St Salisbury NC 28144

WEST, JAMES LEROY, business exec.; b. Gravity, Ia., May 28, 1903; s. Edgar and Anna (Heatherington) W.; student Grinnell Coll., 1919-22, St. Louis U. Sch. Commerce, 1925-26; m. Eunice Pearl East, Jan. 6, 1937. Salesman, Seiberling Rubber Co., Ft. Worth, also Abilene, Tex., 1927-30; mgr. Hinckley-Tandy Leather Co., Houston, 1930-41, partner, 1941-50; dir. Tandy Leather Co., Ft. Worth, 1951-55, v.p., 1955-57, pres., 1957—; pres., dir. Tandy Corp., Wilmington, Del., 1964—; dir. Continental Nat. Bank. Mem. Ft. Worth Sales Mgrs. Club, Tex. Mfrs. Assn. (State pres. 1968), Newcomen Soc. (honoree 1968). Presbyn. Mason. Home: 6371 Lansdale St Fort Worth TX 76116 Office: 2727 W 7th St Fort Worth TX 76107

WEST, JAMES WATT, newspaperman; b. Prattville, Ala., Aug. 3, 1908; s. James Watt and Martha Malissa (Wilson) W.; student U. Tenn., 1927-28; J.D., Nashville, YMCA Law Sch., 1934; LL.D., Augusta Law Sch., 1958; m. Helen Lunn, June 23, 1928; children—James W., Margery, William. Reporter Nashville Banner, 1926, 29-37, Knoxville Dispatch, 1927-28, Nashville Tennessean, 1928; mng. editor Raleigh Times, 1937-38, mng. editor Kansas City Jour., 1938-40; gen. mgr. Kingsport (Tenn.) Times-News, 1940-53;

bus. mgr., advt. dir. for Newspaper Printing Corp. (Augusta Chronicle, Augusta Herald), Augusta, Ga., 1953-54, v.p., gen. mgr. Southeastern Newspapers, Inc., 1955-57, pres.; treas., 1957-58; v.p. Augusta Newspapers, Inc., 1955-58, Radio Augusta, Inc. (radio and TV stas. in Augusta), 1955-58; gen. mgr. Citizens Pub. Co. Jackson State (Miss.) State Times, 1958-59; editor, pub. Laurel Leader-Call, Miss., 1959—; v.p. Ind., Inc., div. Thomson Newspapers. Newspaper Typographer, designed Kingsport Times and Kingsport News (winners of NEA and Ayer citations for best typography in class); also Jackson State Times citation. Chmn. Sullivan County Infantile Paralysis Campaign, Employ Physically Handicapped, R.C. campaign in Richmond County, 1956. Recipient Jr. C. of C. award. Served Comm. Bn. Hdqrs. Classification, Tank Destroyers, F.A., AUS, 1944-45. Received De-Molay Legion of Honor; Herrick award for editorial writing, 1966; certificate of merit for editorials Am. Bar Assn., Miss. Agr. Editor's award, 1968. Pres., Tenn. Press Assn., 1947-48 and instituted Tenn. Election Law Reform Campaign. Mem. tech. adv. bd. Inst. Newspaper Controllers. Mem. Ga. Newspaper Advt. Execs. Assn. (treas. 1956), Laurel C. of C. (pres. 1962). Democrat. Mem. Ch. of Christ. Elk. Author: Manual for State Reporters, 1936. Contbr. articles to trade publs. and picture mags. Admitted to Tenn. bar, 1934; to U.S. Supreme Ct., 1943. Nat. judge newspaper typography. Lecturer on journalism subjects. Home: Sherwood Dr Laurel MS Office: Laurel Leader-Call 130 Beacon St Laurel MS

WEST, JOHN CARL, gov. S.C.; b. Camden, S.C., Aug. 27, 1922; s. Shelton J. and Mattie (Ratterree) W.; LL.B. magna cum laude, U.S.C., 1948; m. Lois Rhame, Aug. 29, 1942; children—John Carl, Douglas Allen, Shelton Anne. Admitted to S.C. bar, 1948; former atty. firm West Holland, Furman and Cooper, Camden; mem. S.C. Hwy. Commn., 1948-52, vice chmn., 1952; mem. S.C. Senate, 1954-62; lt. gov. S.C., 1967-70, gov., 1970—. Vice-chmn. So. Gov.'s Conf., 1971-72. Chmn., United Cerebral Palsy Dr., S.C., 1964. Trustee Coker Coll. Served with AUS, 1942-46. Mem. Am. Legion, C. of C., Phi Beta Kappa. Presbyn. (deacon, elder). Kiwanian. Office: State House Columbia SC 29201

WEST, JULIAN RALPH, govt. ofcl.; b. Hot Springs, S.D., Dec. 12, 1915; s. Joseph C. and Helen E. (Nason) W.; B.S. in Liberal Studies, U. Okla., 1969; m. Marvel E. Knorr, May 1, 1937; children—Stuart J., R. Bruce, Judy E. (Mrs. Jerome H. Hagedorn). Engaged in pub. accounting, 1946-49; audit policy div. Office Sec. Def., Arlington, Va., 1962-67, chief, procurement audit div., 1967—. Served with USAF, 1949-62. C.P.A., Cal. Mem. UN Assn. U.S.A., Am. Inst. C.P.A.'s, Accounting Research Assn., Am. Soc. Mil. Comptrollers, Nat. Contract Mgmt. Assn., Fed. Govt. Accountants Assn., Am. Accounting Assn. Am. Automobile Assn., Airline Passengers Assn., Smithsonian Assos. Clubs: Admirals; Ambassadors; National Travel; Americana. Mem. Christian Ch. (elder). Home: 3317 Old Dominion Blvd Alexandria VA 22305 Office: Office Asst Sec Def (Comp) 1111 N 19th St Arlington VA 22209

WEST, LOUIS CARLTON, petroleum co. exec.; b. Glasgow, Ky., Aug. 9, 1933; s. Thomas Scott and Velma A. (Ary) W.; A.A., San Antonio Jr. Coll., 1952; B.S., Trinity U., 1956; m. Johnney Ruth Vorpahl, Sept. 22, 1964. Founder, partner and mgr. West Oil Co., San Antonio, Tex., 1958—; founder, sec. treas. West Petroleum Corp., San Antonio, 1963—, also dir. Mem. South Tex. Muscular Dystrophy Assn. Republican. Baptist. Home: Route 4 Box 24 Seguin TX 78155 Office: Alamo Nat Bldg San Antonio TX 78205

WEST, RHEA HORACE, JR., educator; b. Loudon, Tenn., Oct. 5, 1920; s. Rhea Horace and Verna (Quillen) W.; B.S. in Accounting, U. Tenn., 1947; postgrad. (Sloan fellow, Mass. Inst. Tech. fellow), Mass. Inst. Tech., 1959-60, 63, Case Inst. Tech., summer 1960; Ph.D., U. Ala., 1964. Asso. prof. mgmt. Wake Forest Coll., 1950-51; budget and reports analyst AEC, Oak Ridge, 1951-55; teaching fellow U. Ala., Tuscaloosa, 1956-57; asst. prof. mgmt. U. Ark., Fayetteville, 1957-59; Sloan teaching intern Mass. Inst. Tech., Cambridge, 1959-60; asso. prof. econs. Carson-Newman Coll., Jefferson City, Tenn., 1960-65; prof. mgmt. Ga. State Coll., 1965-70; prof. mgmt., dir. grad. studies Auburn (Ala.) U., 1970—; mgmt. cons.; cons. Cape Kennedy and Huntsville (NASA), Lockheed Aircraft Co., U.S. Civil Service Commn., others. Active Center for Study Democratic Instns., Atlanta High Mus. Art. Served with AUS, 1943-46. Mem. Am. Accounting Assn., Am. Mgmt. Assn., Am. Soc. Personnel Adminstrn. (nat. dir. industry edn. com. 1958-60), Inst. Mgmt. Scis., Soc. Advancement Mgmt., Acad. Mgmt., Soc. Sloan Fellows, Am. Assn. U. Profs., Am. Legion, Opelinka C. of C., Am. Ordnance Assn., A.A.A.S., Am. Inst. Aeros. and Astronautics, Am. Inst. Decision Scis., N.Y. Acad. Scis., Internat. Platform Assn., UN Assn. U.S., Newcomen Soc. N.Am., Sigma Iota Epsilon, Alpha Kappa Psi (dist. dir. 1965—), Alpha Phi Omega, Kappa Phi Kappa. Baptist. Kiwanian (pres. 1965). Clubs: Mass. Institute Technology Harvard Faculty. Book rev. editor Personnel Adminstr., 1960—. Contbr. numerous articles and book revs. to profl. publs. Home: 4819 Skyline Dr Knoxville TN 37914 Office: 212 Thach Hall Auburn U Auburn AL 36830

WEST, WALTER PRESTON, coll. adminstr.; b. Hopkinsville, Ky., Sept. 16, 1916; s. Robert Cary and Clyde (Carroll) W.; B.A., Maryville Coll., 1938; M.A., George Peabody Coll. for Tchrs., 1948; postgrad. Ia. State U., 1949-50; m. Rowena Sims Grimes, July 2, 1961; stepchildren—Linda Jeanne Grimes, Janet Ellen Grimes. Tchr.-coach Russellville (Ky.) schs., 1938-42; high sch. prin. Russellville, 1946-48, Beattyville, Ky., 1948-49; supr. instrn. schs., Calhoun County, Ia., 1949-50; dir. news service, asst. prof. edn. Florence (Ala.) State Coll., 1950-53; bus. mgr. Highland Park Presbyn. Ch., Dallas, 1953-55; dir. Evening Sch., dir. admissions, asso. prof. edn. Trinity U., San Antonio, 1955—, asst. dean., 1970—. Served from ensign to lt USNR, 1943-46. Mem. Assn. Coll. Admission Counselors, Pi Gamma Mu, Pi Kappa Delta. Presbyn. (elder). Home: 3602 LaSabre Dr San Antonio TX 78218

WEST, WILLIAM BEVERLEY, III, lawyer; b. Ft. Worth, Feb. 5, 1922; s. William Beverley, Jr., and Ella Louise (Moore) W.; B.A., U. Tex., 1942, LL.B., 1948; Indsl. Adminstr., Harvard Grad. Sch. Bus. Adminstrn., 1943; LL.M., Columbia, 1949; grad. Command and Gen. Staff Sch. Admitted to Tex. bar, 1949; practiced in Ft. Worth; asst. U.S. atty., No. Dist of Tex., 1953; 1st asst. U.S. atty., 1957-58, U.S. atty., 1958-61; exec. asst. to asst. atty. gen., Lands Div., Dept. of Justice, 1961-63; partner Clark, West, Keller, Sanders & Ginsburg, Dallas, 1963—; faculty Acad. Am. and Internat. Law, Southwestern Legal Found., Police Acad. Southwestern Law Enforcement Inst., 1965—. Chmn. div. criminal justice adminstrn. Southwestern Legal Found., 1958—, research fellow, 1965; mem. adv. bd. Southwestern Law Enforcement Inst., Dallas, 1959—. Served from pvt. to capt., AUS, 1942-46. Decorated Bronze Star medal. Fellow Tex. Bar Found.; mem. Inst. Jud. Adminstrn. N.Y.C., State Jr. Bar of Tex. (dir., 1955-56), Am. (chmn. sect. jud. adminstrn. 1970-71, ho. of dels. 1971—), Fed. bar assns., Am. Judicature Soc., Delta Tau Delta, Phi Alpha Delta, Pi Sigma Alpha. Episcopalian. Clubs: Fort Worth; Nat. Lawyers (Washington); Northwood Country (Dallas). Home: 3701 Turtle Creek Dr Dallas TX 75219 Office: 1st Nat Bank Bldg Dallas TX 75202

WEST, WILLIAM GARRETT, clergyman, educator; b. nr. Princess Anne, Md., Mar. 25, 1913; s. John William and Lenier R. (Garrett) W.; B.A., Lynchburg Coll., 1937; B.D., Yale, 1940, Min. of Div., 1944, S.T.M., 1947, Ph.D., 1949; m. Doris Ewers, June 13, 1938; children—Robert G., Laurie (Mrs. W. Benjamin Johnston). Ordained to ministry Christian Ch., 1937; minister Melrose Av. Christian Ch., Roanoke, Va., 1935-37, Weldermere Beach Community Ch., Melford, Conn., 1937-46, Old Stone Ch., East Haven, Conn., 1940-48, First Christian Ch., Chattanooga, 1948—; faculty Vanderbilt U. Sch. Religion, Pub. Speaking and Homiletics, 1948-53, U. Chattanooga, 1966-68, U. Tenn. at Chattanooga, 1968—. Civilian chaplain 429 Air Base, New Haven, 1942-45; chaplain Chattanooga Scottish Rite Soc. and Alhambra Shrine, 1953; chaplain Chattanooga Police Assn., 1950-58; religious news reporter radio sta. WDEE, 1950—. Gen. chmn. Chattanooga Roundtable Nat. Conf. Christians and Jews, 1954-55; mem. panel of scholars Disciples of Christ or Christian Chs., 1956-62; del. Chs. of Christ in Gt. Britain, 1957, 3d Assembly World Council Chs., New Delhi, 1961. Gen. chmn. Chattanooga Mayor's Com. on UN Day, 1951-52; mem. Council of Community Forges, 1954-60; v.p. Chattanooga Psychiat. Clinic. Bd. dirs. Chattanooga Pub. Library, Disciples Found. at Vanderbilt, Chattanooga Area Found. for Research, Tng., Treatment and Teaching in Mental Health Disciplines, Inc. Mem. Tenn. Assn. Christian Chs. (past pres.), Tenn. Tennis Assn. (past pres.), So. Lawn Tennis Assn. (past mem. exec. com.). Kiwanian. Home: 203 Hillcrest St Chattanooga TN 37411

WEST, MRS. WILLIAM G., ch. and club woman; b. Lynchburg, Va., May 29, 1913; d. Alexander Lee and Laura (Burch) Ewers; B.S., Longwood Coll. 1932; student Lale Div. Sch., 1938-40; m. William G. West, June 18, 1938; children—Robert G., Laurie Lee. Tchr. pub. schs., Lynchburg, 1934-38; dir. vacation ch. schs., Lynchburg, 1937, Milford, Conn., 1938-40; Old Stone Congl. Ch., East Haven, Conn., 1943-47; tchr. pvt. schs., New Haven, 1938-40. Chaplain Kosmos Women's Club, Chattanooga, 1957-58, chmn. state and gen. fedn., 1958-59; chmn. by-laws and Parliamentarian Brainerd Garden Club, Chattanooga, 1956-57; dist. chaplain, Tenn. Fedn. Garden Clubs, 1955-57, state chaplain, 1956-57; dir. worship State Bd. Tenn. Christian Women's Fellowship, 1958-59; mem. nat. nominating com. United Christian Missionary Soc., Indpls., 1956, 63; fraternal del. Internat. Conv. Christian Chs. to Chs. Christ Gt. Britain, 1957; accredited visitor 3d Assembly World Council Chs., New Delhi, India, 1961. Home: 203 Hillcrest Av Chattanooga TN 37411

WESTABY, JANICE RUTH, educator; b. Madison, S.D., Nov. 1, 1921; d. John Roy and Marcia (Eldred) Westaby; B.S. in Nursing, U. Minn., 1946, M.P.H. in Health Edn., 1950. Pub. health nurse, Fillmore County, Minn., 1946-47, Josephine and Union Counties, Ore., 1947-49; health edn. cons. Ore. Bd. Health, 1951-53, dir. home safety program, 1953-57; sr. pub. health educator N.Y. State Dept. Health, 1957-61, dir. accident prevention program, 1961-62; asso. prof. pub. health adminstrn. Sch. Pub. Health, U. N.C., Chapel Hill, 1962—, program dir. accident control grad. program, dep. head dept. health adminstrn. sch. Pub. Health, 1971—, also dir. study motorcycle injuries. Co-prin. investigator Rockland County Child Injury Prevention project USPHS, 1959-64; co-dir. Demonstration Project on Integration Accident Prevention in Total Patient Care, Washington County, N.Y., 1962; cons. Accident Study Group, Syracuse, N.Y., 1962—; chmn. conf. Injury Control and Emergency Health Services; mem. Council Disease Prevention and Control. Fellow Am. Pub. Health Assn.; mem. N.C. Pub. Health Assn., Nat. Safety Council (chmn. home conf. 1967-69, dir. 1964—; v.p. homes, 1970—, Delta Omega. Methodist. Contbr. articles to profl. jours. Home: 129 Woodland Dr Cary NC 27511 Office: Sch Pub Health Chapel Hill NC 27514

WESTALL, WILLIAM GLADSTONE, civil engr.; b. Celo, N.C., July 14, 1904; s. Theodore and Hattie Ellen (Autrey) W.; student Wake Forest Coll., 1923-25; C.E., George Washington U., 1934; m. Bethea C. Yeck, Nov. 3, 1932; 1 son, William Grant. Commd. 2d lt. C.E., U.S. Army, 1926, advanced through grades to lt. col. U.S. Air Force, 1951; ret., 1955; asst. mgr. paving bur. Portland Cement Assn., 1955-66; quality control engr. H.B. Zachry, San Antonio, 1967-68; cons. engr., Largo, Fla., 1968—. Decorated Army Commendation medal. Fellow Am. Soc. C.E. Contbr. articles profl. jours.; sect. to McGraw-Hill Handbook of Heavy Construction (Hobbs and Havers), 1971. Home and office: 1700 S Indian Rocks Rd Largo FL 33540

WESTBERRY, ELVIS CLINTON, civil engr.; b. Estelle, S.C., May 29, 1914; s. Clinton and Ethel (Parker) W.; student Internat. Corr. Schs., 1939-43; extension courses U. Fla., 1943, various seminars; m. Margaret Houck, Dec. 12, 1939 (div. Feb. 1945); 1 dau., Melinda (Mrs. Melinda Westberry Warren); m. 2d, Mary Deonacea Safritis, Apr. 12, 1947 (div. Mar. 1966); children—Laurence Elvis, Bianca (Mrs. Douglas Castleberry), Eugenia (Mrs. Robert Ziegler), Candace Marie, Sibyl Ann; m. 3d, Erna Bernice Morris, Apr. 8, 1967. Apprentice carpenter Local 627, Jacksonville, Fla., 1933-38; archtl. draftsman Kapalow Engring. Co., Inc., Memphis, 1935-42; apprentice shipfitter, draftsman St. Johns River Shipbuilding Co., 1942-43, liaison coordinator, naval architect's dept., 1943-45; individual practice small home designing, Mandarin, Fla., 1945-50; draftsman, designer Thomas N. Evans, Jr., Jacksonville, 1949-58, George O. Holmes, Jacksonville, 1951-52; sr. draftsman, engring. dept. Nat. Container Corp., Jacksonville, 1952-58; structural designer Evans & Hammond, Inc., Jacksonville, 1958-65; with Dow Chem. Co., Titusville, Fla., 1965-70, engring. technician, 1967, engr., 1967-70; with Pan Am. Airways, Kennedy Space Center, Fla., 1970—. Registered profl. engr., Fla. Home: Route 1 Box 413 Titusville FL 32780 Office: Pan Am Airways Hdqrs Bldg Kennedy Space Center FL 32899

WESTBROOK, JAMES AUGUSTUS, san. engr.; b. Rocky Mount, N.C., Sept. 19, 1914; s. John Hardy and Ella Blount (Boney) W.; B.S., U. N.C., 1936; M.S., Harvard, 1937; m. Frances Curry Westbrook, Jan. 27, 1944. San. engr. N.C. Bd. Health, Raleigh, 1937-50; with USPHS, various locations, 1950—, san. engr., Denver, 1964-66, Atlanta, 1966—. Instr. Sch. Pub. Health, U. N.C., Chapel Hill, 1937-50. Diplomate Am. Acad. Environmental Engrs., Fellow Am. Soc. C.E. Methodist. Club: Farmington Country (Charlottesville, Va.). Home: 989 Winding Creek Trail NW Atlanta GA 30328 Office: 50 7th St Room 404 Atlanta GA 30323

WESTBROOK, WILLIAM JERRY, judge; b. Trion, Ga., June 22, 1938; s. Wilmer Carlyle and Dorothy Madalyn (Colbert) W.; student Furman U., 1958; LL.B., J.D., Woodrow Wilson Coll. Law, 1961; m. Judy Gail Woodall, Apr. 29, 1967; 1 son, William J. II. Clk., Gulf Oil Corp., 1959-61; admitted to Ga. bar, 1961, U.S. Supreme Ct., 1971; individual practice law, Summerville, Ga., 1964—; judge State Ct., Chattooga County, Ga., 1966-70, 71—. Sec., Ray's, Inc., Trenton, Ga., 1967—. Served with AUS, 1961-63. Mem. Ga. Bar Assn. (bd. govs. 1968-70, 71—), Chattooga County Jr. C. of C. Mason. Office: Box 427 Summerville GA 30747

WESTER, JOHN GAY, elec. engr.; b. Mineral Wells, Tex., Aug. 27, 1935; s. S. Gay and Juanita (Johns) W.; B.S., U. Tex., 1960; m. Dianne Williams, May 7, 1971; children by previous marriage—Linda, Gerald, Julie, Patrick, Glenn James. Engr., Westinghouse Electric Co., Balt., 1960-63; program mgr. airborne infrared mapper and tactical information processing and interpretation system Tex. Instruments, Dallas, also Austin, Tex., 1963—. Served with USCGR, 1953-57. Registered profl. engr., Tex. Mem. Nat., Tex. socs. profl. engrs. Patentee film devel. by laser. Home: 2610 18th St Plano TX 75074 Office: PO Box 6015 Dallas TX 75222

WESTERHOUSE, ROBERT ALLEN, computer co. exec.; b. Eudora, Kan., Feb. 13, 1935; s. Allen H. and Elfrieda Elizabeth (Schlegle) W.; B.S. in E.E., U. Kan., 1962. Tech. rep. Gen. Electric Co., Europe, 1962-65; systems analyst Philco-Ford, 1965-66; regional applications mgr. Sci. Data Systems, 1966-67; v.p. operations Com-Share So., Inc., 1967, v.p. marketing, 1967-68, exec. v.p., 1968-69; pres. Computer Complex, Inc., Houston, 1969-70, chmn. bd., pres., 1970—, also dir. Served with USAF, 1953-57. Mem. I.E.E.E., Assn. Data Processing Service Orgns., Assn. Computing Machinery. Clubs: Houston, The Houston. Home: 819 Edgewick Ct Sugarland TX 77478 Office: SW Freeway Houston TX 77036

WESTERMAN, HERMAN WILLIAM, chem. co. exec.; b. Bellville, Tex., Jan. 10, 1917; s. Herman and Lula (Viereck) W.; student Draughon's Bus. Coll., 1935-36;; m. Helen Frances Jircik, July 1, 1938; children—Barbara (Mrs. Glenn Shirley Richards), Eric Lane. With Swift & Co., Houston, 1936, Acme Fast Freight, Houston, 1936-41; with Dow Chem. Co., Freeport, Tex., 1941—, So. region traffic mgr., 1965—; exec. v.p., dir. Quintana Enterprises, Inc., Freeport, 1968—; pres., dir. Growman Corp., Lake Jackson, Tex., 1971—; partner Eagle Devel. Co., Lake Jackson, 1971—. Traffic cons. Brazos Harbor Nav. Dist., Freeport, 1952-64. Mem. Am. Soc. Traffic and Transp., S.W. Shippers Adv. Bd. (chmn. chems. and explosives com. 1956—), Tex. Indsl. Traffic League. Club: Houston Traffic. Home: 210 Oak Dr PO Box 576 Lake Jackson TX 77566 Office: Drawer K Freeport TX 77541

WESTFALL, DEAN PAUL, internat. trade ofcl.; b. Akron, O., May 18, 1920; s. Donald Edmond and Rissa May (Black) W.; student Hammel Bus. Coll., 1938-39, Actual Bus. Coll., 1946-47, Internat. Corr. Schs., 1949-51; m. Pauline Kornas, Aug. 22, 1941; children—Richard Dean, John Thomas, Shirley Anne. Dept. mgr. waste control and methods investigation Goodyear Aircraft Corp., Akron, 1941-42, 45-46; warehouse contractor War Surplus Adminstrn., Dallas, 1946; asst. indsl. engr. Luscombe Aircraft Co., Garland, Tex., 1946-47; traffic mgr., purchasing agt. Moncreif-Lenoir, Houston, 1947-52; owner Mgmt. & Cons. Services, Houston, 1952-60; port dir., mgr. indsl. park Warren County Port Commn., Vicksburg, Miss., 1960-66; cons. on water traffic, 1949-66; regional mgr. Nissho-Iwai Am. Corp., 1966—. Mem. Warren County Indsl. Com., 1964-66; mem. Nat. Def. Exec. Res. Mem. Warren County Republican Exec. Com., 1964—. Served with AUS, 1942-45. Decorated Bronze Star. Mem. Vicksburg C. of C., Miss. Rivers and Harbors Assn., Nat. Def. Transp. Assn., Am. Assn. Port Authorities, Central Miss. Traffic Club, Delta Nu Alpha. Presbyn. Kiwanian. Home: 3511 Graceland St Memphis TN 38116 Office: PO Box 13226 Memphis TN 38113

WESTFALL, LEAHN RECTOR, supt. schs.; b. Shawnee, Okla., Dec. 5, 1923; s. Iva Almus and Stella Ethel (Stephens) W.; B.S., Okla. State U., 1944, M.S., 1949, Ed.D., 1958; m. Eloise J. Hart, July 14, 1945; children—Darrell, Karen (Mrs. Bud W. Mullen), Bradley. Prin., Carney, Okla., 1945-49; supt. schs., Orienta, Okla., 1949-51, Greenfield, 1951-55, Canton, 1955-62, Weatherford, 1962-64, Artesia, N.M., 1964-69; supt. schs., Shawnee, Okla., 1969—. Chmn. United Fund, Weatherford, 1963, Artesia, 1967. Served with USNR, 1944. Mem. Am., Okla. assns. sch. adminstrs., N.E.A., Shawnee Edn. Assn., Okla. Secondary Sch. Activities Assn. (v.p. 1963-65). Mason, Kiwanian. Home: 9 Turkey Knob Shawnee OK 74801 Office: 10th and Harrison Sts Shawnee OK 74801

WESTFALL, ROBERT MADISON, educator; b. Buckhannon, W.Va., Apr. 19, 1919; s. Ira Burton and Ida Cathrine (Lowe) W.; student George Washington U., 1950, Am. U., 1950-51; B.S., W.Va. Wesleyan Coll., 1963; m. Dorothy May Trippett, Mar. 30, 1942; children—Ann Ruth, Robert Harrison, Sheri Lee. Commd. ensign U.S. Navy, 1942, advanced through grades to lt. comdr., 1946; asst. supt. naval aero. photog. exptl. lab., 1948-49, officer in charge photog. interpretation center, 1949-50, asst. head research and devel. dept., 1950-51, photog. officer naval ordnance test sta., 1951-53, operations officer motion picture dept., 1955-57, photog. officer photog. squadrons, 1953-55, 57-59, tng. aids officer Naval Air Sta., Pensacola, Fla., 1960-62; ret., 1962; tchr. Escambia High Sch., 1963-65, Brownsville Jr. High Sch. and Pensacola Jr. Coll., 1963-72, Geggs Ednl. Center, 1969—. Mem. Soc. Motion Picture and TV Engrs., Am. Soc. Photogrammetry, Soc. Photog. Scientists and Engrs., Escambia Edn. Assn., N.E.A., Nat. Assn. Pub. Sch. Adult Educators, Fla. Adult Edn. Assn., Nat., Fla. (dist. dir.), Escambia County (past pres.) councils tchrs. math., Escambia Math. Tchrs. Assn. Club: Navy League (Pensacola, Fla.). Home: 705 Wayne Av Pensacola FL 32507

WESTFALL, VERNON DALE, aircraft co. exec.; b. Troy, O., Mar. 24, 1920; s. John and Edith Mary (Poorman) W.; Aero. Engr., West Coast U., 1941; m. Barbara Mary Rose, Mar. 3, 1951; 1 son. Michael Todd. Test pilot Hartzell Propeller Co., 1944-47; airline pilot Trans World Airlines, 1947-50; engring. flight test agt. CAA, 1951-53; flight test engr. Northrop Aircraft, 1954-55; chief flight test Cessna Aircraft, 1956-57; v.p. operations Airline Tng., Inc., 1958; dir. sales Lockheed Ga. Co., Marietta, 1959—; pres. Flight Engring. Labs., 1954—; dir. Cargo Masters Inc. Block chmn. Atlanta Republican Com. 1964. Mem. Am. Inst. Aeros. and Astronautics, Instrumentation Soc. Am., Soc. Automotive Engrs. Lutheran (elder 1953-68). Home: 420 N Harbor Dr Atlanta GA 30328 Office: 86 S Cobb Dr Marietta GA 30060

WESTLING, RALPH FORD, purchasing agt.; b. Taylor, Tex., Jan. 6, 1927; s. Frank Albert and Nell Ann Ray (Ford) W.; B.A., U. Tex., 1951, postgrad., 1952; m. Georgia Rose Bailey, Jan. 21, 1956; 1 son, Mark Ford. Office staff Graybar Elec. Co., Inc., San Antonio, 1952-56; purchasing foreman Ed Friedrich, Inc., San Antonio, 1956-61; office mgr. Todd-Ford, Inc., San Antonio, 1962-65; purchasing agt. Steck-Warlick, Austin, Tex., 1966—. Served with AUS, 1944-47. Mem. Purchasing Mgmt. Assn. Austin (pres. 1971), Austin C. of C., Lambda Chi Alpha. Club: Longhorn (Austin). Home: 2710 Pinewood Terrace Austin TX 78757 Office: 8000 Shoalcreek Blvd Austin TX 78767

WESTMAN, RAGNAR THEOPHILE, govt. ofcl., physician; b. Kramfors, Sweden, Oct. 2, 1905 (came to U.S. 1912, naturalized 1919); s. Nils Theodore and Ida (Wedin) W.; B.S. magna cum laude, Hamline U., 1927; M.B., U. Minn., 1930, M.D., 1931; M.P.H., Johns Hopkins, 1936, Dr.P.H., 1939; m. Gladys E.R. Magiera, Oct. 4, 1932. Intern Mpls. Gen. Hosp., 1931; practice medicine, specializing in preventive medicine and pub. health, Washington, 1932—; epidemiologist Div. Pub. Health, Mpls., 1932-37; dir. health, Bay County, Mich., 1937-38, Kansas City, Kan., 1939-41; sr. surgeon USPHS, 1941-47, served as acting dir. health, New Orleans, 1942-43, acting commr. health, Seattle, 1943-45; acting dir. health Calcasieu Parish and City of Lake Charles (La.), 1945; investigator USPHS Dist. Office, Kansas City, Mo., 1946; dep. area med. dir. VA, St. Louis, now dir. profl. inquiries VA Central Office, Washington, 1947—; prof., head dept. hygiene and pub. health U. Kan. Med. Sch., 1939-41. Recipient So. Minn. Med. Assn. Gold medal, 1930; Rockefeller Found. fellow. Fellow Am. Pub. Health Assn.; mem. A.M.A. Am. Coll. Preventive Medicine, Assn. Mil. Surgeons U.S., A.A.A.S., Kappa Phi, Alpha Omega Alpha, Delta Omega. Home: 1401 Blair Mill Rd Silver Spring MD 20910 Office: US VA Central Office 810 Vermont Av NW Washington DC 20420

WESTROPE, MARTHA R., psychologist; b. Gaffney, S.C., May 19, 1922; d. Gordon Robert and Hannah (Brown) Westrope; B.S., Winthrop Coll., 1942; M.A., U. N.C., 1944; Ph.D., State U. Ia., 1952; 1 adopted son, Ashley. Psychologist U. Hosps., Iowa City, 1947; clin. psychologist Spartanburg (S.C.) Mental Hygiene Clinic, 1949, 50; chief psychologist S.C. Mental Health Div., Mental Health Commn., 1952-53; chief clin. psychologist Richland County Mental Health Clinic, Columbia, S.C., 1953-55; research psychologist Psychiat. Inst., U. Md., 1955; head psychology sect., psychiatry Med. Sch., U. Miami, 1956-57; chief psychologist Greenville Mental Health Clinic, S.C. Mental Health Commn., 1957-60; individual practice, 1960—; cons. psychologist Clemson (S.C.) Agr. Coll.; vis. lectr. Furman U., 1958-57; instr. Greenville Tech. Edn. Center, 1968; cons. research psychologist, evaluation projects Greenville Community Council, 1957-60, Juvenile Ct., 1957-60. S.C. rep. on So. Regional Edn. Bd. original steering com. on psychol. resources in the South 1953; mem. Greenville Assn. for Retarded Children, 1968; cons. Spartanburg Mental Health Clinic, 1971—. Men. Am., S.C. (rep. to nat. orgn. 1953-54) psychol. assns., Greenville Mental Health Assn., Bus. and Profl. Women's Club, Sigma Xi. Home: Route 2 Darien Way Greenville SC 29607 Office: 101 Chapman St Greenville SC 29605

WESTRUP, ROGER BO, assn. exec.; b. Helsingborg, Sweden, Mar. 10, 1923 (came to U.S. 1949, naturalized 1953); s. Carl Albrekt and Elly (Kennedy) W.; student Svalof, Sweden, 1944-45, U. Houston, 1957-63; m. Nancy H. Links, Oct. 25, 1953; children—Diana Lisa, Carl Eric, John Anders. Asst. to agrl. attache Swedish Embassy, London, 1946-48; exec. trainee Foley Bros., Houston, 1951-53; store mgr. Meyer Bros., Bellaire, Tex., 1953-56; mgr. C. of C., Bellaire, 1956—. Tchr. Swedish lang. Swedish Consulate, Houston, 1962-64. Mem. Aux. Police Div., Bellaire, 1954-65. Bd. dirs. S.W. YMCA, Houston, 1960—. Served with Swedish Army, 1943-45. Recipient Outstanding Service awards Bellaire Lions, 1959, S.W. YMCA, 1966, South Tex. C. of C. Outstanding Mgrs. Award, 1968-69. Mem. South Tex (San Antonio dir.; asso. mgr. 1963—), Tex. (editor News 1968-69; dir.), chambers commerce, C. of C. Mgrs. and Secs. Assn. South Tex. (pres. 1966-67), C. of C. Mgrs. and Secs. Assn. East Tex. (pres. 1969-70), Gulf Coast C. of C. Mgrs. Assn. (charter, pres. 1968-69), Swedish Am. Culture Soc. (pres.). Lion. Home: 5100 Grand Lake St Bellaire TX 77401 Office: 6510 S Rice St Bellaire TX 77401

WETHERILL, MELVIN HOWARD, lawyer; b. Lake Charles, La., Oct, 28, 1908; s. John Nathaniel and Katherine (Green) W.; LL.B;, Tulane U., 1932, J.D., 1969; m. Claire Winona Chafin, Apr. 12, 1932. Admitted to La. bar, 1933; practiced in Lake Charles, 1933—; municipal atty., Vinton, La., 1933-59; asst. dist. counsel Home Owners Loan Corp., 1935-36; asst. dist. atty. 14th Judicial Dist. La;, 1936, 48-53; atty. for tax collector Calcasieu Parish, La., 1940-41, 42-43, 46-48; spl. asst. to atty. gen. La., 1941; mem. firm Jones, Kimball, Patin, Harper, Tete & Wetherill and predecessor firm, 1953—. Served with AUS, 1943-45; PTO. Mem. Am., La., S.W. La. bar assns., Sigma Alpha Epsilon. Democrat. Methodist. Lion. Home: 613 W McNeese St Lake Charles LA 70601 Office: Gulf Nat Bank Bldg Lake Charles LA 70601

WETZOLD, WILLIAM WOLDEMAR, textile co. exec.; b. Rotschau, Saxony, Germany, Dec. 11, 1907; s. Woldemar Arthur and Ida Selma (Kessler) W.; B.S. in Textile Engring., Coll. Engring. for Textile Industry, Reichenbach, Germany, 1924; m. Frieda Lydia Koegler, May 14, 1932; 1 son, William Arthur. Came to U.S., 1929, naturalized, 1938. Asst. textile engr; J. Lambrette, Reichenbach, Germany, 1924-27; textile plant supt, F. Claviez, Schoenberg, Germany, 1927-29; supr. Forstmann Wollen Co., Passaic, N.J., 1931-51, plant supt., 1951-57; plant mgr. J. P. Stevens & Co., Inc., Allendale, S.C., 1957—. Group mem. Wool Research Textile Research Inst;, Princeton, N.J., 1954-55. Lion. Author: (with others) von Bergens Wool Handbook, Vol. II, Part 1, 1969. Patentee in field. Home: Bluff Rd Allendale SC 29810 Office: PO Box 647 Allendale SC 29810

WEXLER, HARVEY JOSEPH, airline exec.; b. N.Y.C., Apr. 25, 1928; s. Samuel and Etta (Saunders) W.; B.S., N.Y.U., 1947; M.B.A., Harvard, 1950. Dir. internat. services Air Transport Assn., Washington, 1958-63; asst. to chmn. bd. Slick Corp., 1963-65; v.p. Continental Airlines, 1965—. Financial and econ. cons., 1950-52; econ. adviser Senate Aviation Sub-Com., 1959-62. Served to capt. USAF, 1952-58. Clubs: Harvard (N.Y.C.); Army-Navy, Harvard Business School (Washington). Home: 2401 Calvert St NW Washington DC 20008 Office: 1025 Connecticut Av NW Washington DC 20006

WEXLER, LEWIS POPE, tire co. exec.; b. Johnson City, Tenn., Nov. 7, 1936; s. Daniel Benjamin and Marie Eloise (Pope) W.; B.A., Washington and Lee U., 1958; student Program Mgmt. Devel., Harvard, 1965; m. Martha Hayes Patton, June 20, 1959; children—Lewis Pope, Lillian, Harrison, Susan. Budget mgr. Goodyear Tire & Rubber Co., Memphis, 1959, budget mgr., asst. store mgr., Nashville, 1959-61; store mgr. Alcoa, Maryville, Tenn., 1961; with Free Service Tire Co., various locations, 1962—, pres., Biltmore and Asheville, N.C., 1970-71, pres. all affiliates, Johnson City, 1971—; dir. 1st Peoples Bank, Johnson City. Bd. dirs. United Fund, 1969, Boys Club, 1969. Methodist. Kiwaian, Elk. Club: Hurtleigh. Home: 106 Belmeade Circle Johnson City TN 37601 Office: 126 Buffalo St Johnson City TN 37601

WEXLER, WILLIAM ABE, orgn. ofcl., optometrist; b. Toledo, July 16, 1913; s. Isadore and Yetta (Leffner) W.; student Toledo U., 1934-35; D. Optometry, So. Coll. Optometry, Memphis, 1937; m. Dorothy M. Levy, July 18, 1937, (dec.); children—Allan V., Edward I., Raymond H.; m. 2d, Osnat Itelson, May 24, 1971. Practice optometry, Savannah, Ga., 1938—. Vice pres. Levy Jewelers. Vice chmn. recreation commn. United Community Services, Savannah, 1946-48; commr. Coastal Empire council Boy Scouts Am., 1944-48; chmn. United Jewish Appeal, 1951-56; chmn. Israel Bond Com., 1957-63; co-chmn. World Conf. Jewish Orgns., 1965-71, chmn., 1971—. Alderman, Savannah, 1946-47. Pres., bd. dirs. Savannah Jewish Community Council, Savannah Jewish Community Center; v.p. Nat. Jewish Welfare Bd., 1969—, also bd. dirs. So. sect.; bd. dirs. UN Assn., Meml. Found. Jewish Culture, Am. Friends Hebrew U.; v.p. Leo W. Levi Hosp., Nat. Jewish Hosp.; mem. nat. council Boy Scouts Am. Named Outstanding Man of Year, Savannah Jewish War Vets, 1955. Mem. Am., Ga. optometric assns., Conf. Presidents Maj. Jewish Orgns. (pres. 1970—), Am. Optometric Found. Mason (Shriner); Mem. B'nai B'rith (internat. pres.; mem. internat. council). Home: 623 E 49th St Savannah GA 31402 Office: 139 Bull St Savannah GA 31402

WEYHRAUCH, ERNEST EMIL, librarian; b. N.Y.C., July 20, 1926; s. Frederick and Martha (Ingber) W.; B.A., Washington Sq. Coll., 1945-51; M.S., Columbia, 1959; postgrad Coll. City of N.Y., 1955-57, Ind. U., 1965-66; m. Mary Ekris, July 8, 1955; children—Ernest Christopher, Anne Martha. Tech. asst. N.Y. Pub. Library, 1952-55; tchr. pub. schs., N.Y.C., 1955-57; cataloger, asst.; edn. librarian, chief circulation Bklyn. Coll. Library, 1957-64; edn. librarian Ind. U., 1964-66; dir. libraries Eastern Ky. U., Richmond, 1966—. Mem. Am., Southeastern, Ky. (v.p., pres. elect 1972-73) library assns., Ky. Hist. Soc., Madison County Hist. Soc., Nat., Ky. rifle assns. Contbr. articles to profl. mags. Home: 211 Ridgeway Richmond KY 40475 Office: Eastern Ky University Richmond KY 40475

WEYMAN, EDWARD BRUNSON, banker; b. Midland, Tex., Feb. 1, 1933; s. Alexander Coffin and Alma (Brunson) W.; B.B.A., Tex. Technol. Coll., 1954, postgrad., 1955; grad. certificate Am. Inst. Banking, 1965; m. Diana Lynn David, June 7, 1968; children—David Scott, Laura Lynn. With 1st Nat. Bank, Midland, 1959—, v.p., 1968—; mgr. Weyman Enterprises, 1969—. Chmn. Midland County Vets. Land Bd., 1969—. Bd. dirs. Arthritis Found. Served to lt. (j.g.) USNR, 1955-59, comdr. Res. Mem. Midland County Livestock Assn (dir. 1968-71), Robert Morris Assn., Midland Hist. Soc. (dir.), S.A.R., Res. Officers' Assn., Naval Res. Assn., Tex. Tech. Ex-student Assn., Naval Supply Corps Alumni Assn., Naval Inst., Midland C. of C. (chmn. cultural com. 1970-71), Sigma Alpha Epsilon. Methodist. Rotarian. Home: 2818 Marmon St Midland TX 79701 Office: 301 Wall St Midland TX 79701

WEYSSER, JOHN LOUIS GALLUS, mining engr.; b. Nutley, N.J., Feb. 12, 1910; s. John R.G. and Helen (Konstan) W.; B.S, in Mining Engring., Lehigh U., 1931, E.M., 1937; m. Miriam Bullock, Apr. 23, 1931. Instr. mining engring. Pa. State U., 1931-34; research mining engr. Lehigh Navigation Coal Co., Lansford, Pa., 1934-39, cost engr;, 1938-39, project mgr., 1945-48; asst. prof. mining engring. U. Ill., 1939-41; tech. adviser WPB, Washington, 1941-42, tech. adviser 1942-43, chief, coal-mining sect., 1943-45; gen. mgr. Lehigh Materials Co., Lansford and N.Y.C., 1948-51; cons. mining engr., Sun City Center, Fla., 1951—. Cons., Def. Solid Fuels Adminstrn., Washington, 1951, various mining cos. U.S., 1951-53, UN Korean Reconstrn. Agy., Dai Han Coal Corp., Korea, 1953-54, ICA, Washington, 1955; minerals adviser Govt. Pakistan, Karachi, 1956-57; v.p. Pierce Mgmt. Corp., Scranton, Pa., 1959-67; co-gen. mgr. Dai Han Coal Corp., Seoul, Korea, 1959-64; coal industry adviser Republic of Korea, 1964-67; resident chief engr. Paul Weir Co., Zonguldak, Turkey, 1969-70. Commr., Panther Valley council Boy Scouts Am., 1936-37, pres., 1938-39; chmn. Carbon County (Pa.) chpt. A.R.C., 1937. Recipient citation for assistance to U.S. Army in devel. coal mines in Alaska, Sec. War, 1943; citation WPB, 1945; Premier's citation for contbn. to econ. devel. Korea, 1963; letter of Appreciation, Gov. Dan Han Coal Corp., 1967. Registered profl. engr., Ky., Pa. Mem. Am. Inst. Mining, Metall. and Petroleum Engrs., Nat. Soc. Profl. Engrs., Ill. Mining Inst., Rocky Mountain Coal Mining Inst., Lehigh U. Alumni Assn., Korean Mining Inst. (hon.), Sigma Gamma Epsilon (hon.), Theta Xi. Republican. Episcopalian. Club: Seoul (Korea) Country. Author: Underground Mine Haulage, 1952, Pennsylvania Anthracite Mining Guidance Standards, 1954, also articles. Developer longhole anthracite mining method. Home and office: 1501 Hartwick Dr Sun City Center FL 33570

WHALEN, ROBERT STANBURY, marine co. exec.; b. St. Paul, Dec. 27, 1916; s. Andrew J. and Jane (O'Brien) W.; student U. Ill., John Marshall Law Sch., 1934-39; m. Elinor M. Hayman, Oct. 3, 1941; children—Robert s., Judith (Mrs. Donald F. Zimmer); Barbara Jane, Nancy Patricia. Salesman, Nat. Cash Register Co., 1938-41; asst. chief insp. Buick Aviation Div., 1941-45; gen. sales mgr. Maypole Boats Co., 1945-47; v.p., dir. sales Rodi Chris Craft, 1947—; pres. Chris Craft Sales Center, Inc., 1971—. Mem. Mayor's Marine Adv. Com., Ft. Lauderdale; gov.'s rep. to Fla. Boating Council; chmn. Broward County Commn., 1970; mem. Narcotics Guidance Council. Dir. Ft. Lauderdale Beach Hosp. Mem. Gt. Lakes Boat Dealers Assn. (v.p.), Central Marine C. of C. (past pres.), Navy League (chpt. v.p.), Fla. State Assn. County Commrs. (dir.), Sigma Nu. Clubs: Lions (past pres.), Coral Ridge Yacht (past commodore). Home: 622 Middle River Dr Fort Lauderdale FL 33304 Office: Box 1660 Fort Lauderdale FL

WHALEY, BEN SCOTT, lawyer; b. Edisto Island, S.C., June 28, 1909; s. William James and Martha Elizabeth (Bailey) W.; A.B., The Citadel, 1929, LL.D., 1970; LL.B., U. S.C., 1932, J.D., 1970; postgrad. Nat. U., 1934-35; m. Emily Wharton Fishburne, Dec. 15, 1934; children—Emily Fishburne (Mrs. J.D. Balentine), Anne Sinkler (Mrs. Fredric V.S. LeClercq), Martha Elizabeth (Mrs. Julian Calhoun Adams). Admitted to S.C. bar, 1932, Fed. Dist. Ct. bar, 1932, Ct. Appeals 4th Circuit bar, 1938, Ct. Claims bar, 1937; sec., law clk. to Senator James F. Byrnes, 1934-37; asst. U.S. dist. atty. Eastern Dist. S.C., Charleston, 1938-47, U.S. dist. atty., 1947-54; sr. partner firm Barnwell, Whaley, Stevenson & Patterson, Charleston, 1951—. Sec.-treas., dir., gen. counsel. Edisto Beach Devel. Co. Mem. S.C. Ho. of Reps., 1930-33. Trustee, Historic Charleston Found., 1946—, pres., 1955-69, gen. counsel, 1969—. Wisdom Award of Honor, 1972. Fellow Internat. Acad. Trial Lawyers, Am. Coll. Trial Lawyers; mem. Am., S.C. (pres. 1967-68) bar assns., Am. Judicature Soc., Hibernian Soc., St. Andrew's Soc. (past pres.), S.C. Soc. Episcopalian (past jr. and sr. warden). Elk (past exalted ruler Charleston). Clubs: Snee Country, Charleston. Charleston Rifle, Carolina Yacht Home: 58 Church St Charleston SC 29402 (Charleston) Office: 120 Meeting St Charleston SC 29402

WHALING, ANNE, educator; b. Houston, Mar. 30, 1914; d. Horace Morland and Annie Byrd (Ward) Whaling; B.A., So. Meth. U., 1933, M.A., 1934; Ph.D., Yale, 1946. Cataloger, specialist in music, fgn. langs. So. Meth. U., 1947-55; tchr., English dept. Arlington State Coll., 1955, instr., 1955-57, asst. prof., 1957-60, asso. prof., 1960-68; asso. prof. English, U. Tex. at Arlington, 1968-71, prof., 1971—. Program annotator for chamber music series Dallas Mus. Fine Arts, 1956—; bd. dirs. Dallas Chamber Music Soc., 1954—; chmn. Pro Musica, Dallas, 1960-62. Recipient Decima Lantern award, So. Meth. U., 1933; named Woman of Achievement, So. Meth. U. Assn., 1968. Mem. Am. Studies Assn. Tex. (councilor 1961-62), South Central Modern Lang. Assn., Am. Assn. U. Women (chmn. fellowship com. Dallas br. 1959-64), Music Library Assn., Phi Beta Kappa, Sigma Tau Delta, Delta Kappa Gamma. Methodist. Home: 3320 Daniels Av Dallas TX 75205 Office: Dept English U Tex Arlington TX 76010

WHANG, SANG YOUN, communications co. exec.; b. Korea, Oct. 16, 1931; s. Andrew Chaikyung and Hyun Sook (Kim) W.; came to U.S., 1951; B.S. in E.E. summa cum laude, Poly. Inst. Bklyn., 1956, M.S. in E.E., 1966; m. Mary Alice Pai, Dec. 25, 1955; children—Jeanne, Stephen, Peter. Instr., Poly. Inst. Bklyn., 1956-60; v.p., chief engr. SEG Electronic Co., Inc., Bklyn., 1960-64; tech. specialist Milgo Electronic Co., Miami, 1964-68; v.p., tech. dir. Internat. Communications Corp., 1968—; cons. Compucon Contact Lens Co., Queens, N.Y., 1958—. Bd. dirs. Miami area Korean Student Fund, 1970—. Recipient Presdl. Citation and Medal for Pub. Service, Republic of Korea, 1970. Mem. Korean Assn. of Miami (pres. 1965-70, hon. pres. 1970—), Tau Beta Pi, Eta Kappa Nu. Democrat. Methodist. Patentee bowling pin setting machine, cornea measuring device, contact lens, electronic filter, data transmission equipment (Modem). Home: 8445 SW 148th Dr Miami FL 33158 Office: 7620 NW 36th Av Miami FL 33147

WHARRAM, KENNETH JONES, physician; b. Painesville, O., Jan. 25, 1915; s. Rutherford Hayes and Theresa Louise (Heider) W.; B.S., Ohio U., 1937; M.D., Ohio State U., 1941; m. Pauline L. Davis, Nov. 12, 1955; children—Kay (Mrs. James A. Johnson), Nancy (Mrs. Stephen G. Johnson), Stephen Paul. Intern, Springfield (O.) City Hosp., 1941-42; practice of medicine, Harlingen, Tex., 1946-55, Lockney, Tex., 1955-57, Nocona, Tex., 1957—; mem. staffs Major Clinic Hosp., Nocona, Bowie (Tex.) Meml. Hosp. Mem. city council, Nocona, 1962—. Served to lt. comdr. M.C., USNR, 1942-46. Mem. A.M.A., Am., Tex. acads. gen. practice, Tex. Med. Assn., County Med. Soc. Elk, Mason. Home: 303 Carolyn Rd Nocona TX 76255 Office: Box 207 Nocona TX 76255

WHARTON, HUNTER POISAL, labor union exec.; b. Martinsburg, W.Va., Oct. 20, 1900; s. John Jacob and Anne Lee (Gordon) W.; student Carnegie Inst. Tech., 1920-22; LL.D., Fordham U., 1966; m. Lydia Marie Koller, May 13, 1925. With Douglas of Pitts., contractors, 1922-30; with Internat. Union Operating Engrs., 1930—, gen. sec.-treas., 1958-62, gen. pres., 1962—; v.p. bldg. constn. trade dept. AFL-CIO, 1962—, v.p. metal trades dept., 1962—; v.p. AFL-CIO, 1965—; dir. Union Labor Life Ins. Co. Vice pres, Nat. Safety Council, 1963—; mem. labor adv. bd. Office Emergency Planning, 1965—, Dept. Health, Edn. and Welfare, 1965—; bd. dirs. Nat. Com. Employment Youth. Bd. dirs. Soc. Prevention Blindness, Big Bros. Am. Recipient several awards Nat. Safety Council. Elk, Eagle (pres. 1937-39; Murray-Greene award 1963, Eagles Hall of Fame award 1966), Knight of Malta (post comdr. 1925). Home: 4805 Wellington Dr Chevy Chase MD 20015 Office: 1125 17th St NW Washington DC 20036

WHARTON, PORTER, JR., oil co. exec.; b. Elkhart, Ind., Sept. 25, 1922; s. Porter Estle and Clara (Rodewald) W.; A.B., Ind. U., 1949; m. Barbara Dee Dearmin, May 28, 1949; children—Porter III, Sally Dee, Thad Dearmin. Advt. salesman, home bldg. editor Elkhart Truth, 1949-52; pub. relations, advt. exec. Miles Labs., Inc., 1952-59; dir. pub. relations Kerr-McGee Oil Industries, Inc., Oklahoma City, 1960-62, dir. pub. relations, corp. advt., 1962—. Chmn. pub. relations com. United Fund of Elkhart County, 1958-59. Bd. dirs. Elkhart Symphony Soc., 1954-59, treas., 1959. Served with USAAF, 1943-46. Mem. Okla. Petroleum Council, Ind. Natural Gas Assn., Ind. Petroleum Assn. Am., Mid-Continent Oil and Gas Assn., Assn. Petroleum Writers, Okla. Pub. Relations Assn., Sigma Pi. Clubs: Twin Hills Golf and Country; Oklahoma City Press Club, Petroleum Club Oklahoma City. Home: 6702 Trenton Rd Oklahoma City OK 73116 Office: Kerr-McGee Bldg Oklahoma City OK 73102

WHATLEY, JAMES ARNOLD, univ. adminstr.; b. Calvert, Tex., Feb. 26, 1916; s. James Arnold and Mabel (Peel) W.; B.S., Tex. A. and M. U., 1936; M.S., Ia. State U., 1937; Ph.D., 1939; m. Dorothy Crawford, Sept. 9, 1939; children—Barbara (Mrs. David R. Friels), William Arnold. Faculty, Okla. State U., Stillwater, 1939—, prof. animal sci., 1948—, asso. dir. agrl. expt, sta., 1964-68, dir., 1968—, dean Agrl. Coll., 1968—. Served from 2d lt, to maj. AUS, 1941-46; ETO. Recipient Don M. Tyler award Okla. State U., 1963. Mem. Am. Soc. Animal Sci., Sigma Xi, Alpha Zeta, Phi Sigma. Kiwanian (pres. Stillwater 1966). Home: 2221 W 8th St Stillwater OK 74074

WHEAT, JERRY D., pub. utility exec.; b. Sonora, Tex., Jan. 20, 1929; s. James Floyd and Veda Mae (Seaton) W.; B.S. in Phys. Edn. and Math., Howard Payne Coll., 1951; M.B.A. in Personnel Mgmt., So. Meth. U., 1963; m. Billie Hicks, Sept. 4, 1948; children—Jerry Danniel, Tanya Kay. Tchr., coach Brownwood (Tex.) Ind. Sch. Dist., 1951-52; with Lone Star Gas Co., 1952—, dir. personnel, adminstrn. and information, 1967—; cons. in field, 1954—. Trustee Dallas Ind. Sch. Dist., 1966-70. Chmn. county towns div. Dallas County United Fund, 1966-68; co-chmn. maj. div. campaigns Meth. Hosp., Presbyn. Hosp., Baylor Hosp., Boy Scouts Am., Am. Cancer Soc., 1959-69. Precinct chmn. Dallas County Democratic Exec. Com., 1959-65. Trustee Howard Payne Coll.; bd. dirs. Am. Cancer Soc., Tex. 4-H Youth Devel. Found., Devel. Council Golden Gate Bapt. Theol. Sem., San Francisco. Baptist (deacon 1954-69, Sunday sch. dept. supt. 1954-69). Home: 2010 Riverway Dr Dallas TX 75217 Office: 301 S Harwood St Dallas TX 75201

WHEAT, JOSIAH, lawyer; b. Woodville, Tex., Dec. 21, 1928; s. J.E. and Ruby (Rotan) W.; LL.B., U. Tex., 1952; m. Glendale Richter, July 12, 1952; children—Julia, Beth, Josiah, Jennifer. Admitted to Tex. bar, 1952, since practiced in Woodville; partner Wheat, Wheat & Stafford; county atty. Tyler County, 1955-56; city atty. Woodville, 1960—. Dir. 2d Dist. Tex. bar, 1964-67, chmn. com. on water law, mem. legislative com., 1968—, pres., 1969-70. Mem. Gov.'s Adv. Com. Tex. Indsl. Council, 1955-56, Nat. Water Commn. U.S.; v.p., asst. to pres., chmn. River Authority Panel, pres. Tex. Water Conservation Assn.; pres. Tyler County Dogwood Festival; pres. Deep East Tex. Devel. Council, 1970-71. Bd. dirs. Lower Neches Valley Authority, 1959-70, asst. counsel, 1970—. Served with AUS, 1953-54. Named Man of Month, East Tex. C. of C., 1968. Fellow Tex. Bar Found. (dir.); mem. Tex. City Attys. Assn. (past dir.), Am. (spl. com. on environmental law), 88th Jud. (past pres.) bar assns., Woodville and East Tex. C. of C. Mason (chmn. com. on titles; deeds and civil law Tex. grand lodge). Address: PO Box 156 Woodville TX 75979

WHEATLEY, ELMER DURWOOD, dentist; b. Haskell, Tex., Jan. 25, 1937; s. Elmer Cecil and Mamie Bernice (Mapes) W.; student Tex. Tech. Coll., 1955-56, North Tex. State Coll., 1956-58; D.D.S., U. Tex., 1962; m. Clara Elaine Petty, Aug. 30, 1958; children—Travis Ray, Vesta Marie. Individual practice dentistry, Wichita Falls, Tex., 1962—. Dental cons. Wichita County Health Unit, 1962—, North Tex. Rehab. Center, 1971—; staff dental cons. Bethania Hosp., 1963—. Chmn. 4H and Future Farmers Am. Beef Show, 1963, 64; mem. sci. fair judges com., 1966, 68, 70; mem. Cub Scouts pack com. Northwest Tex. Boy Scouts Am., 1971. Bd. dirs. North Tex. Rehab. Center. Mem. Am., Tex. (dist. dental health chmn. 1964-65, 69-70) dental assns., Wichita Dist. Dental Soc., Wichita Falls Jr. C. of C. (v.p. 1965), Phi Kappa Sigma, Delta Sigma Delta. Baptist. Club: Metropolitan (dir. 1971) (Wichita Falls). Home: 2700 Speedway St Wichita Falls TX 76308 Office: 1620 11th St Wichita Falls TX 76301

WHEATLEY, EUGENE AUSTIN, JR., physicist; b. Cin., Aug. 12, 1928; s. Eugene Austin and Grace (Appleton) W.; M.E., U. Cin., 1951, M.S. in Physics, 1954; m. Dolores Gerhardt, June 9, 1956 (div. Dec. 1965); m. 2d, Carol Betty Houck, Nov. 7, 1969. Controls systems engr. Gen. Electric Co., Evendale, O., 1955-58; staff mem. nuclear rocket div. Los Alamos Sci. Lab., 1958-61; asst. sr. engr. NERVA nuclear rocket div. Aerojet Gen. Azusa, Cal;, 1961-63; staff mem. AC spark plug div. Gen. Motors, El Segundo, Cal., 1963-64; prin. engr. Saturn V flight evaluation working group Boeing Co., Huntsville, Ala., 1964-69; cons. Code Research Corp., Huntsville, Ala., 1970; sr. engr. Skylab, Martin Marietta Corp., Huntsville, 1971—. Mem. Am. Phys. Soc., Am. Nuclear Soc., Am. Soc. M.E., Am. Inst. Aeros. and Astronautics, Internat. Platform Assn., Pi Tau Sigma. Club: Ala.

Internat. Country (Point Aquarius). Contbr. articles in field to profl. jours. Home: 1619 Drake Av SE Huntsville AL 35802 Office: Martin Marietta Corp 201 Pinehurst Dr Huntsville AL 35807

WHEATLEY, REUBEN, govt. ofcl.; b. St. Thomas, V.I., Oct. 6, 1925; s. O.S. and Anna W.; grad. Rider Coll. (N.J.), 1951; m. Juel Petersen, Dec. 22, 1956; children—Russell, Paul Byron, Torrance, Bertram. With V.I. Dept. Finance, 1951—, dir. tax div., 1951-60, asst. commr., 1960-66, commr., 1966—. Served to master sgt. AUS, 1944-46. Mem. U.S. V.I. Jr. C. of C. (past pres.), Jr. C. of C. Internat. (senator). Methodist. Mason. Home: 27 Havensight Box 546 St Thomas VI 00801 Office: Dept of Finance PO Box 2515 St Thomas VI 00801

WHEATON, ELIZABETH LEE, educator; b. Sherman, Tex.; d. Percival King and Minerva Fay (Ratzel) Fulton; student Rice Inst., 1920-21, San Angelo Coll., 1949-51; certificate S.W. Tex. State Coll., 1922, Kansas City-Horner Conservatory, 1929; B.S., McMurray Coll., 1952; postgrad. A. and I. Coll., 1953-54; m. Grant Wiltsie Wheaton, Dec. 23, 1923. Tchr. pub. schs., Texas City, Tex., 1922-24; tchr. speech, 1922-29, voice and speech, 1929-47; reporter, soc. editor Texas City Sun, 1930-36; corr. Galveston (Tex.) News, 1934; dir. The Texas City Hour, radio sta. KGBC, 1947; elementary tchr. La Feria (Tex.) Pub. Schs., 1952—; tchr. voice, speech, 1956-57; originator, writer, dir., master Story Book Time TV series sta. KRGV-TV, 1957; mem. staff S.W. Writers Conv., Corpus Christi, Tex., 1954—. Mem. Composers, Authors and Artists Am. (chpt. pres.; mem. nat. pub. com. 1960), Tex. Woman's Press Assn., Tex. State Tchrs. Assn., Tex. Poetry Soc., Tex. Inst. Letters, Am. Legion Aux. (pres. LaFeria unit 1960), Tex. State Dept. Music (chmn. 1960), Lower Rio Grande Valley Hist. Soc., Community Concert Assn. (bd. dirs. Harlingen chpt., chmn. La Feria com. 1969—), Poetry Soc. Am. (charter; sec. Lower Rio Grande Valley chpt.), Am. Budgerigar Soc., Tex. Bird Breeders and Fanciers Assn., Tex. Southmost Bird Assn. (sec. 1962), Delta Kappa Gamma (chmn. publicity com.). Author: Mr. George's Joint, 1941; Texas City Remembers, 1948; also poems, articles, revs. in various mags., newspapers. Home: Valley Vista Box 1026 La Feria TX 78559 Office: Sam Houston Sch La Feria TX 78559

WHEATON, GRANT WILTSIE, journalist; b. Kewanee, Ill., Apr. 27, 1895; s. Jeremiah Grant and Myrtle Mable (Hubbard) W.; student Draughan's Bus. Coll., Galveston, Tex., 1920, McMurray Coll., Abilene, Tex., 1951-52; m. Elizabeth Lee Fulton, Dec. 23, 1923. Various positions from sec. to v.p., gen. mgr. to corporate sec., asst. gen. mgr. Texas City (Tex.) Terminal Ry. Co., 1922-48; sec. Terminal Indsl. Land Co., 1943-48; asso. E. Gordon Perry Real Estate, Ins. Agy., San Angelo, Tex., 1948-51; owner Valley Vista Farm, La Feria, Tex., 1953—; originator, mgr., editor Suez Scribblings San Angelo, 1950-51; field editor H. L. Peace Publs., New Orleans, 1953-57; free lance writer, 1957—; staff lectr. Southwestern Writers Conf., Corpus Christi, Tex., 1956-60. Treas. March Dimes, Texas City, 1936-38; dir. La Feria March of Dimes, 1959-66, dir. Cameron County chpt., 1961-67. Served wtih F.A., U.S. Army, 1917-18. Decorated Silver Star medal, Purple Heart. Mem. Lower Rio Grande Valley Hist. Soc., La Feria C. of C., La Feria Live Stock Club, Am. Budgerigar Soc., Tex. Bird Breeders and Fanciers Assn., Tex. Southmost Bird Breeders Assn. (past pres.), Am. Legion, Vets. World War I. Presbyn. (elder). Mason (Shriner), Rotarian. Club: Tip-O-Tex Exhibition Budgie. Contbr. to newspapers, non-fiction mags. Address: Valley Vista Box 1026 La Feria TX 78559

WHEELEN, THOMAS LEO, educator; b. Gardner, Mass., May 30, 1935; s. Thomas Leo and Kathryn Elizabeth (McGrath) W.; student Fordham U., 1953-54; B.B.A. cum laude, Boston Coll., 1957; M.B.A., Babson Coll., 1961; D. Bus. Adminstrn., George Washington U., 1969; m. Margaret A. Doyle, June 25, 1966; children—Kathryn, Thomas Leo II, Richard. Grad. teaching asst. Babson Coll., 1960-61; teaching fellow George Washington U., 1965-68; mfg. tng. program Gen. Electric Co;, 1961-64, systems programmer, 1964-65; asst. prof. McIntire Sch. of Commerce, U. Va., 1968-71, asso. prof., 1971—. Served to lt. USNR, 1957-60. Mem. Am. Mgmt. Assn., Am. Hosp. Assn., Assn. Systems Mgmt., Acad. Mgmt;, Alpha Kappa Psi, Beta Gamma Sigma. Co-editor: Developments in Management Information Systems, 1972. Contbr. articles in field to profl. jours. Home: 404 Westmoreland Ct Charlottesville VA 22901

WHEELER, CHARLES LOVELACE, state ofcl.; b. Upton, Ky., July 30, 1925; s. Joe J. and Ruby (Talley) W.; A.B., Western Ky. State U., 1949; profl. degree So. Regional Tng. Program in Pub. Adminstrn., 1950; m. Patton Galloway, Jan. 12, 1957; children—Barendina Mary, Charles Galloway. Research editor Ky. Legislative Research Commn., 1950-56, dir., 1960-63; research editor Ohio Legislative Service Commn., 1956-58; asst. dir. Ohio Dept. Pub. Welfare, 1959; spl. asst. to Gov. N.C., 1964; dir. N.C. State Commn. Higher Edn. Facilities, Raleigh, 1965—. Sec., N.C. Commn. Interstate Coop., 1964—; vice chmn. Com. State Ofcls. on Suggested State Legislation Council of State Govts., 1962-72; cons. Adv. Commn. on Intergovtl. Relations, 1968—. Trustee Kittrell Coll. Served with AUS, 1943-46. Mem. Assn. Exec. Dirs. Higher Edn. Facilities Commns. (nat. sec. 1967-68, nat. vice chmn. 1968-69, chmn. 1970—, dir.), Council of State Higher Edn. Agys. (nat. chmn. 1970-71), Nat. Com. Support Pub. Schs. Home: 3211 Burns Pl Raleigh NC 27609 Office: 320 W Jones St Raleigh NC 27602

WHEELER, CLARENCE JOSEPH, JR., physician; b. Dallas, Sept. 25, 1917; s. Clarence Joseph and Sadie Alice (McKinney) W.; B.S. in Math., So. Meth. U., 1941, B.A. in Psychology, 1946; M.D., Johns Hopkins, 1950; m. Alice Freels, Dec. 6, 1942 (dec.); children—Stephen Freels, Clarence Joseph III, Robert McKinney, Thomas Michael, David Ritchey; m. 2d, Jean Grant Faucett, Mar. 2, 1968. Intern Johns Hopkins Hosp., Balt., 1950-51; resident surgery Barnes Hosp., St. Louis, 1951-54; thoracic surgery fellow U. Wis. Hosps., Madison, 1954-55; instr. surgery, 1955-56; practice medicine specializing in gen. and thoracic surgery, Houston, 1956—; clin. instr. surgery Baylor Coll. Medicine, Houston, 1957—; lectr. surgery U. Tex. Postgrad. Med. Sch., Houston, 1957—; mem. active staff Herman Hosp., Houston, 1958—, mem. cardio-vascular research team, 1960—; mem. active staff St. Luke's Hosp., Houston, 1958—, St. Joseph's Hosp., Houston, 1958—, Meml. Hosp., Houston, 1959— Tex. Children's Hosp., Houston, 1960—, Meth. Hosp., 1960—, Ben Taub City-County Hosp., Jefferson Davis Hosp.; now attending active staff Gordon Hosp., Lewisburg, Tenn. sr. med. office Thua Thien Province, South Vietnam, 1968-70; chief surgery Hue Central Hosp., S. Vietnam, 1968-70; mem. courtesy staff all peripheral outlying hosps.; sr. attending staff Lindley Hosp., Duncan, Okla. Treas. Samuel Clark Ree Sch., P.T.A., Houston, 1959-61; mem. bd. Salvation Army Boys Club, Houston. Served to capt. USMCR, 1942-45; PTO; comdr. USNR, 1968-70. Decorated D.F.C. (3), Air medal, Purple Heart, Navy Commendation medal, Bronze Star, Vietnamese Medal of Health, Vietnamese Medal of Social Welfare. Diplomate Am. Bd. Surgery. Fellow A.C.S., Am. Coll. Chest Physicians; mem. Am., Tex., So., Indsl. med. assns., Harris County, St. Louis med. socs., Am., Tex. thoracic socs., Nat. Tb Assn., Am. Assn. History Medicine, Am., Tex., Houston heart assns., A.A.A.S., Johns Hopkins Med. and Surg. Soc., Southwestern Surg. Congress, Tex. Anti-Tb Assn., Houston Gastroenterological Soc., Houston Surg. Soc., Postgrad Med. Assembly S. Tex., Am. Cancer Soc., Am. Coll. Angiology, Am. Soc. Abdominal Surgeons, Marine Corps Res. Officers Assn., Nat. Geog. Soc., Kappa Sigma, Phi Chi, Phi Eta Sigma, Kappa Mu Epsilon, Psi Chi. Clubs: International; Elks Golf and Country (Duncan, Okla.). Home: Route 6 Box 256 A Summer Pl Rd Lewisburg TN 37091 Office: Gordon Hosp 101 3d Av N Lewisburg TN 37091

WHEELER, CLYDE ARLIE, JR., oil co. exec.; b. Laverne, Okla., Mar. 12, 1921; s. Arlie Clyde and Lulu G. (Rector) W.; student Wichita U., 1946, Friends U., 1948; B.A., Okla. State U., 1947, M.A. in Polit. Sci., 1950; m. Barbara Ann Dodd, Aug. 23, 1953; children—Barbara Ruth, Clyde Arlie III, Jane Dodd. Teaching fellow Okla. State U., 1949-50; exec. sec. U.S. Congressman Page Belcher, Enid, Okla., 1951-54; confidential asst. Sec. of Agr. Ezra Taft Benson, Washington, 1954-57, spl. asst., 1957-59; staff asst. Pres. Eisenhower, Washington, 1959-60; became v.p. pub. affairs and pub. relations Sunray DX Oil Co., Tulsa, 1961; now dir. govt. relations Sun Oil Co., Washington. Nat. committeeman Okla. Young Republican Fedn., 1952-54; v.p. Nat. Fedn. Young Republicans, 1953-54; U.S. Congressional candidate, 6th Dist. Okla;, 1960. Bd. dirs. Indian Nations council Boy Scouts of Am., Jr. Achievement, Salvation Army; bd. govs. Okla. State U. Devel. Found., Hillcrest Assos. Served with AUS, 1942-43; served to lt. (j.g.) USNR, 1943-45. Mem. Okla. State Regents for Higher Edn. (dir. 1964-73), Okla. Pub. Expenditures Counsel, Mid-Continent Oil & Gas Assn., Okla. State C. of C. Clubs: Washington Golf and Country, Carlton, Army-Navy. Home: 1512 Laburnum St McLean VA 22101 Office: Sun Oil Co 1800 K St NW Washington DC 20006

WHEELER, FRANKLIN, profl. engr.; b. Painesville, O., July 30, 1927; s. Willard Alonzo and Flossie (Rundell) W.; B.S., Okla. State U., 1953; postgrad. U. Tulsa, 1963-65; m. June Blair, Aug. 5, 1951; children—Lucinda Jane, Franklin Lee, Pamela Sue. Control chemist Diamond Alkali Co., Cleve., 1946-47; field petroleum engr. Texaco, Inc., Fairfield, Ill., 1951-56; reservoir petroleum engr. Atlantic Refining Co., Tulsa, 1956-59; staff petroleum engr. Skelly Oil Co., Tulsa, 1959,—, organizer, instr. Formation Evaluation Sch., 1965—. Guest lectr. U. Tulsa, 1968-69. Chmn., Tulsa County Republican Precinct, 1964-68. Served with AUS, 1945-46. Mem. Internat. Soc. Profl. Well Log Analysts (pres. 1966-67), Nat. Soc. Profl. Engrs., Am. Inst. Mining, Metall. and Petroleum Engrs., Tulsa Geneal. Soc., C. of C. Baptist (deacon). Home: 4919 E 26th Pl Tulsa OK 74114 Office: 1430 S Boulder St Tulsa OK 74102

WHEELER, JACK REED, govt. ofcl.; b. Conneaut, O., Jan. 4, 1921; s. Walter W. and Naomi (Entsminger) W.; B.A., Rollins Coll., 1953; postgrad U. Miami (Fla.), 1955-57; m. Phyllis J. Gibson, June 26, 1946; children—Ardella Ann, James Walter, Edward Reed. Auditor, Fla. Auditing Dept., 1953-57; budget dir. Clk.-Auditor, Broward County, Ft. Lauderdale, Fla., 1957-64; clk. Circuit Ct., Broward County, Ft. Lauderdale, 1964—. Served with AUS, 1942-46. Mem. Fla. State Finance Officers Assn. (past pres.), Fla. Clks. Assn. (pres. 1970-71), Am. Legion, V.F.W. Mason (Shriner), Elk, Kiwanian. Home: 4541 SW 34th Av Fort Lauderdale FL 33312 Office: PO Box 1540 Fort Lauderdale FL 33301

WHEELER, JAMES PAUL, lawyer; b. Edgewood, Tex., Nov. 21, 1936; s. Hansel Cleburn and Gladys Inez (Barber) W.; A.A., Paris Jr. Coll., 1957; B.A., in Math., U. Tex., 1959; J.D., So. Meth. U., 1966; m. Patricia Ann Johnson, Mar. 3, 1960; children—Keith Paul, James Patrick, Harlan Clark, Sherri Catherine. Analyst, Western Geophys. Co., Shreveport, La., 1959; engring. mgmt. Tex. Instruments, Inc., Dallas, 1959-68; v.p., sec., dir. Spectronics, Inc., Richardson, Tex., 1968—; admitted to Tex. bar, 1967; pvt. practice law, Mesquite, Tex., 1968—; dir. Wheeler & Lovelace, Optical Services Co., Joy Lynn, Inc. Judge, Corporate Ct. City of Mesquite, 1970. Mem. State Bar Tex., Am. Bar Assn., Dallas Criminal Bar, Mesquite Bar Assn., Optical Soc. Tex., Mesquite C. of C. (chmn. pub. affairs com. 1971), Mesquite Friends of Library (pres. 1970, bd. dirs.). Democrat. Baptist. Lion. Home: 4721 Shands Dr Mesquite TX 75149 Office: 3318 Hwy 67 E Mesquite TX 75149

WHEELER, MARSHALL RALPH, educator; b. Carlinville, Ill., Apr. 7, 1917; s. Ralph Adelbert and Hester Mae (Ward) W.; student Blackburn Coll., 1935-37; B.A., Baylor U., 1939; postgrad. Tex. A. and M. U., 1939-41; Ph.D. (NRC fellow), U. Tex., 1947; m. Linda Carol Lackner, May 10, 1966; children—Sandra (Mrs. Lee King, Jr.), Karen, Carson. Instr. zoology U. Tex., Austin, 1947-51, asst. prof. 1951-55, asso. prof. 1955-61, prof., 1961—. Gosney fellow Cal. Inst. Tech. Served with USNR, 1941-45. NSF, NIH research grantee. Mem. Entomol. Soc. Am. (editor Annals 1970—), Genetics Soc. Am., Soc. Study Evolution, S. W. Assn. Naturalists (pres. 1961), Am. Soc. Naturalists, Soc. Systematic Zoology, Am. Hemerocallis Soc. Editor: Studies in Genetics, 1960—. Home: 1313 Ardenwood Rd Austin TX 78722

WHEELER, MARY (MRS. RONALD W. WHEELER, JR.), educator; b. Bloomington, Ind., Feb. 27, 1919; d. Claude Elmer and Cordelia (Jones) Cogswell; B.S., Tex. Christian U., 1938, postgrad., 1940-41; M.A., E. Tex. State U., 1963, Ph.D., 1969; m. Ronald W. Wheeler, Jr., Aug. 5, 1938; children— Wendelyn Florence (Mrs. E. D. White), Marilyn Anne (Mrs. Jon D. Kindred), Gregg Alan, Carol Kay (Mrs. John A. Klevecz), Ronald Scott. Employed Frederick Broadcasting Co., radio sta. KTAT, 1948-62, program dir., women's editor, 1948-62, acting mgr., 1950-51, 61-62, bus. mgr., 1956-62; instructional specialist audio-visual edn. E. Tex. State U., Commerce, 1966-68, dir. ednl. TV services, asst. prof. audio-visual edn., 1968—. Pres. Teen Town Adult Council; dir. Tillman County Day Nursery. Mem. Am., S.W., Tex. psychol. assns., Tex. Assn. Ednl. Tech., Tex. Ednl. TV Assn. (prodn. chmn. 1970-71), curriculum chmn. 1971-72, sec.-treas. 1972-73), Nat. Assn. Ednl. Broadcasters, Tex. Assn. Coll. Tchrs., Okla. Broadcasters Assn., Philharmonic Music Club (pres. 1957-58), Okla. Fedn. Music Clubs, Past Pres.'s Assembly, C. of C., Univ. Dames (pres.), Tex. Personnel and Guidance Assn., Psychology Club, Mortar Bd., Psi Chi. Mem. Christian Ch. Clubs: Webb Hill Country, Sand Hills Golf and Country; Fort Worth Woman's, Afflatus Culture (rec. sec. 1965-67; pres. 1969-71). Home: 2810 Tanglewood Dr Commerce TX 75428 Office: Audio-Visual Center E Tex State U Commerce TX 75428

WHEELER, MAURICE AULICK, dentist; b. Hazard, Ky., Sept. 17, 1908; s. Peter Taylor and Leora Obra (Aulick) W.; student Georgetown Coll., 1926-29, Transylvania Coll., 1932; D.D.S., U. Louisville, 1934; m. Helen Margaret Brashear, Oct. 6, 1936; children—Jayne (Mrs. John A. Package), James M., Susan (Mrs. James M. Dodson). Pvt. practice dentistry, Hazard, Ky., 1934-42, 46-49, Lexington, Ky., 1949—. Served with AUS, 1942-46; lt. col. Res. ret. Mem. Res. Officers Assn. (pres. Hazard chpt. 1946-48), U.S. Mil. Order World Wars (pres. Lexington chpt. 1964). Ret. Officers Assn., Am., Ky. dental assns., Bluegrass, Ky. Mountain (pres. 1937) dental socs., Delta Sigma Delta. Republican. Moose, Lion. Home: 1620 Clayton St Lexington KY 40502 Office: 239 Walton Av Lexington KY 40502

WHEELER, ROBERT MARRET, gen. contractor; b. Ridgway, Pa., May 13, 1906; s. Robert N. and Ida M. (Marret) W.; B.E. in Civil Engring. magna cum laude, Vanderbilt U., 1927; LL.B., YMCA Law Sch., 1935; m. Elizabeth Burton Hibbs, Oct. 6, 1934; children—Elizabeth H. (dec.), Alice M. (Mrs. W.E. Norteman, Jr.), Mary Burton. Engr., Concrete Steel Co., Milw., 1927; estimator So. Cut Stone Co., Bowling Green, Ky., 1927-29; sec.-treas. Tanksley-Drumright Cut Stone Co., Nashville, 1929-36; supt. constrn. WPA, Nashville, 1936; engr. estimator, supt. Foster & Creighton Co., 1936-38; engr., partner Hibbs, Parrent & Wheeler, architects, 1938-41; engr., estimator F.N. Thompson, Charlotte, N.C., 1941-42; estimator, project mgr. Grannis, Higgins, Thompson & McDevitt Co., Blackstone, Va., 1942-44; engr. F.N. Thompson, Charlotte, 1944-45; gen. mgr. The Wearn Lumber Co., 1945-50; chief engr. Interstate Constrn. Co., 1950-51; owner R. Marret Wheeler Co., gen. contractors, 1951—. Admitted to Tenn. bar. Registered profl. engr., Tenn., N.C. Mem. Am. Soc. C. E., Engring. Assn. Nashville, Charlotte Engrs. Club (pres. 1951), C. of C., Asso. Gen. Contractors, N.C. Soc. Engrs., Constrn. Specifications Inst., Tau Beta Pi. Presbyn. Mason (32 deg. Shriner), Kiwanian. Clubs: Myers Park Country, Charlotte Athletic; Highlands Country; Pinehurst Country; Country of the Mountains. Home: 1919 Cassamia Pl Charlotte NC 28211 Office: 513 S Tryon Charlotte NC 28202

WHEELER, ROGER MILTON, corp. exec.; b. Boston, Feb. 27, 1926; s. Sidney S. and Florence W. (Kendall) W.; student Mass. Inst. Tech., 1943-44, Notre Dame U., 1944-45; B.S., Rice U., 1945-46; m. Patricia Jane Wilson, Sept. 6, 1946; children—Roger Milton, Pamela, David, Lawrence, Mark. Engrs., Gulf Oil Co., 1946-47, Standard Oil Co. Ohio, 1947-48; pres. Standard Magnesium & Chem. Co., 1949-64; gen. mgr. magnesium projects Kaiser Aluminum & Chem. Co., 1964-65; chmn. bd. Telex, Inc., Tulsa, 1965—, Continental Industries, Tulsa, 1958—; pres. Am. Magnesium Co.; dir. City Nat. Bank, Tulsa. Served with USNR, 1943-46. Mem. Magnesium Assn. (pres.), Young Pres. Orgn. Author papers in field. Home: 1957 E 41st St Tulsa OK 74105 Office: Telex Inc 41st and Sheridan Sts Tulsa AZ 74105

WHEELER, RONALD WENDELL, JR., educator; b. Ft. Worth, June 1, 1914; s. Ronald Whitehead and Kathryn (McMillion) W.; B.A., Tex. Christian U., 1936, M.A., 1940; postgrad. Kilgore Jr. Coll., 1937-38, So. Meth. U., 1938-39, U. Tex., 1940-42, Harvard, 1942-43; Ed.D., U. Okla., 1959; m. Mary Florence Cogswell, Aug. 5, 1938; children—Wendelyn Florence (Mrs. Edwin D. White), Marilyn Anne (Mrs. Jon D. Kindred), Gregg Alan, Carol Kay (Mrs. John A. Klevecz), Ronald Scott. Dir. ofcl. guide band Tex. Central Centennial Expn., Dallas, 1936; music supr., dir. bands Salem Consol. Schs., nr. Troup, Tex., 1936-39; dir. mus. therapy USPHS Hosp., Ft. Worth, 1939-42; partner, gen. mgr. Radio Sta. KTAT, Frederick, Okla., 1948-62, owner, pres., 1956-62; instr. dept. psychology and spl. edn. E. Tex. State U. at Commerce, 1961-62, asst, prof., 1962-64, asso. prof., 1964-69, prof., 1969—, dir. reading lab., 1963—. Area III adviser S.W. Ednl. Developmental Lab. Pres. Tillman County Mental Health Assn., 1958-61. Bd. dirs. Wesley Found., E. Tex. State U. Served to capt. USNR, 1942-48, 50-51. Named commodore Okla. Navy, 1953, adm. of fleet, Okla., 1958. Mem. Am., Southwestern, Tex. psychol. assns., Res. Officers Assn. (liaison officer Greater Dallas chpt.-E. Tex. State U.), N.E.A., Tex. Tchrs. Assn., Tex. Soc. Coll. Profs. Edn., Tex. Assn. Coll. Tchrs. (chpt. pres. 1965-67; mem. state nominating com. state chmn. research com. faculty and classroom, mem. state exec. com. 1968-69), Assn. Higher Edn., Tex. Christian U. Ex-Students Assn., Tex. Christian U. Ex-Letterman's Assn., N.E. Tex. Schs. Men's Club, Lambda Chi Alpha (faculty adviser), Tex. Student Edn. Assn. (faculty adviser), Student Nat. Edn. Assn. (faculty adviser), Am. Legion (post comdr.), V.F.W., Okla. Broadcasters Assn. (dir. 1959-61), C. of C. (pres.), Phi Delta Kappa, Psi Chi. Mem. Christian Ch. (Sunday sch. supt., mem. ch. bd.). Clubs: Webb Hill Country, Sand Hills Golf and Country. Author: Read with Speed; co-author: Reading Laboratory Handbook. Contbr. articles profl. jours. Home: 2810 Tanglewood Dr Commerce TX 75428

WHEELER, WARREN ELWELL, physician; b. Youngstown, O., 1909; M.D., Harvard, 1933. Intern, Mass. Gen. Hosp., Boston, 1934-35; intern Children's Hosp., Boston, 1933-34, 35-36, resident, 1936-37; prof. chmn. dept. pediatrics U. Ky. Diplomate Am. Bd. Pediatrics. Mem. Am. Pub. Health Assn., Am. Acad. Pediatrics, Soc. Pediatric Research, Am. Pediatric Soc. (pres.), Am. Soc. Microbiologists. Office: Univ Kentucky Med Center Lexington KY 40506*

WHELAN, JOSEPH GERALD, govt. ofcl.; b. Olean, N.Y., Jan. 1, 1921; s. Richard Joseph and Catherine (Conway) W.; B.A. with honors in History, Trinity Coll., 1948; Ph.D. in History, U. Rochester, 1959; m. Anne Marie Downey, Dec. 28, 1948; children—Timothy James, Terrence J., Joanne, Christopher. Sr. specialist in internat. affairs Fgn. Affairs div. Congl. Research Service, Library of Congress, Washington, 1952—. Served with USNR, 1941-46. Mem. Am. Hist. Assn., Am. Assn. for Advancement Slavic Studies, Am. Polit. Sci. Assn. Contbr. numerous articles Am. fgn. policy, Soviet affairs and internat. relations to profl. and Congl. publs. Home: 10912 Fairchester Dr Fairfax VA 22030 Office: Fgn Affairs Div Congl Research Service Library of Congress Washington DC 20540

WHELCHEL, CLARENCE ANTHONY, banker; b. Dawsonville, Ga., Sept. 9, 1899; s. Jeff D. and Margaret (Boone) W.; student Ga. Sch. Tech., 1920-24; m. Sibyl Esther Aiken, June 28, 1923; 1 dau., Sibyl Ann (Mrs. C. W. Nestor, Jr.). Pub. accountant, Gainesville, Ga., 1929-32; examiner Fed. Res. Bank of Atlanta, 1932-39; v.p. Commerce Union Bank, Columbia, Tenn., 1939-44; pres., chmn. bd. First Farmers & Mchts. Nat. Bank, Columbia, 1944—; dir. Nashville br. Fed. Res. Bank Atlanta, 1959-61. Mem. Columbia Pub. Service Commn., 1943-49. Trustee Maury County Hosp., Columbia. Episcopalian. Home: 408 Wahella Way Columbia TN 38401 Office: 816 S Garden St Columbia TN 38401

WHELESS, THOMAS OMEGA, physician; b. Louisburg, N.C., Sept, 7, 1918; s. Frank Williams and Dona (Purnell) W.; B.S., Wake Forest U., 1939; M.D., Bowman Gray Sch. Medicine, 1943; m. Ruth Lois Brown, Sept. 1, 1945; children—Thomas Omega, Evelyn Kay. Intern, N.C. Bapt. Hosp., Winston-Salem, 1943-44, resident, 1944-45; pvt. practice gen. medicine, Louisburg, N.C., 1947—; instr. obstetrics and gynecology Bowman Gray Sch. Medicine, N.C. Bapt. Hosp., Winston-Salem, 1943-45; mem. staff Franklin Meml. Hosp., Louisburg; med. adviser Local Draft Bd., 1950—; instr. of nurses Franklin Meml. Hosp., Louisburg, 1968—. Bd. trustees Franklin Meml. Hosp., 1951-53. Served with M.C., AUS, 1945-47. Mem. A.M.A., N.C., Franklin County med. socs. Club: Green Hill Country (Louisburg). Home: 106 John St Louisburg NC 27549 Office: 948 N Main St Louisburg NC 27549

WHIDDON, DURELL, lawyer; b. Ashford, Ala., Apr. 11, 1926; s. Freddie Joel and Willie Lee (King) W.; B.A., U. Ala., 1950, LL.B., 1951; m. Martha Kate McGriff, Aug. 3, 1956; children—Bobby P. Hamil, Lisa, Linda. Admitted to Ala. bar, 1951; mem. firm Halstead, Whiddon & Woodham, Abbeville, Ala., Headland, Ala., 1952—. Exec. dir.Headland Housing Authority, 1959—. Dep. dist. atty. Henry County, Ala., 1957—. Served with AUS, 1946-47. Mason, Kiwanian. Home: 101 Whitten St Headland AL 36345 Office: 36 Main St Headland AL 36345 also 19 Kirkland St Abbeville AL 36310

WHIDDON, FREDERICK PALMER, univ. pres.; b. Newville, Ala., Mar. 2, 1930; s. Samuel Wilson and Mary (Palmer) W.; A.B., Birmingham So. Coll., 1952; B.D. cum laude, Emory U., 1955, Ph.D. in Philosophy, 1963; m. June Marie Ledyard, June 14, 1952; children—Charles Wilson, John Tracy, Karen Marie and Keith Frederick (twins). Grad. asst. Inst. Liberal Arts, Emory U;, 1955-56; asst. prof. philosophy, dean students Athens (Ala.) Coll., 1957-58; dir. Mobile Center U. Ala., 1960-63; pres. U. South Ala., Mobile, 1963—. Dir. Home Savs. & Loan Assn., Mchts. Nat. Bank, Mobile. Chmn., Marine Environmental Scis. Consortium. Bd. dirs. Mobile chpt. A.R.C., Mobile Opera Guild. sec. Mobile Area Found. Pub. Higher Edn.; mem. Mobile Arts Council; adv. com. Mobile Infirmary Sch. Nursing. Named Outstanding Young Man of Year, Ala. Jr. C. of C., 1964. Mem. Mobile C. of C. (dir.). Methodist (steward). Kiwanian (dir. Mobile). Home: 4518 Kingsway Dr Mobile AL 36608

WHIDDON, GENE AUSTIN, lumber co. exec.; b. Lenox, Ga., July 30, 1928; s. Oscar Ray and Mary Alma (Rutherford) W.; student U. Fla., 1946-47; student Broward Bus. Coll., 1947-48, hon. Asso. Bus. Adminstrn., 1962; m. Angelyn Sylvia Gatlin, May 19, 1950; children—Tari Lynn, Gene Austin, Michael Scott. Salesman, Causeway Lumber Co., Inc., Fort Lauderdale, 1950-53, asst. to mgr., 1953-55, sec., treas., gen. mgr., 1955-70, pres., gen. mgr., 1970—; pres. Causeway Lumber Co. of Boca Raton, Inc. (Fla.), 1970—; pres., gen. mgr. Alray Supply, Inc., 1962—; dir. First Nat. Bank, Fort Lauderdale. Chmn. Broward Met. area Nat. Alliance Businessmen, 1972—; mem. Fla. Local Govt. Study Commn., 1972—. Campaign dir. United Fund of Broward County, Fort Lauderdale, 1963, pres., 1964. Bd. dirs. Broward County Citizens Safety Council, 1966-71, A.R.C., Opera Guild of Fort Lauderdale; chmn. bd. dirs. Broward Community Coll. Found.; trustee Stetson U., 1969—; vice chmn. Broward County Adv. Com. to Gov., 1971—. Served with USAF, 1948-50. Named One of Five Outstanding Young Men, Jr. C. of C., Fort Lauderdale, 1960-61; Boss of the Year award PBX Club of Broward County, 1964; Boss of the Year award Fort Lauderdale chpt. Nat. Secretaries Assn., 1965-66; Liberty Bell award Law-Day, Broward County Bar Assn., 1965; Layman of the Year award Kiwanis, 1967; recipient Top Mgmt. award Fort Lauderdale Sales and Marketing Execs. Club, 1965. Mem. Fla. Lumber and Bldg. Material Dealers Assn. (bd. dirs.; pres. 1968-69), Fla.; State (exec. com. 1970-72), Greater Fort Lauderdale (pres. 1969-72) chambers commerce, Aircraft Owners and Pilots Assn., Christian Businessmen's Com., Execs. Assn. of Fort Lauderdale, Feramo Grotto, Broward Builders Exchange (pres. 1956-57), Gold Key of Nova U. Baptist (deacon, 1955-72, chmn. 1959-60), Kiwanian (pres. 1969-70), Mason (Shriner). Clubs: Metropolitan Dinner (Greater Fort Lauderdale); Lauderdale Yacht, Propeller (Fort Lauderdale), The One Hundred (Broward County, Fla.). Home: 1131 SW 9th Av Fort Lauderdale FL 33315 Office: 2627 S Andrew Av Fort Lauderdale FL 33315

WHIGHAM, E. L., supt. schs. Dade County (Fla). Office: 1410 NE 2d Av Miami FL 33132*

WHINERY, ROBERT, engring. co. exec.; b. N.Y.C., Oct. 24, 1922; s. Samuel Brent and Mabel (Riker) W.; student Newark Coll. Engring., 1940-43; B.M.E., Cornell U., 1944; m. Helen Tarbox McEvoy, Nov. 27, 1948; children—Pamela (Mrs. Keneth H. Knowles), Patricia, Sharon, Elizabeth, Andrew. Engr., Standard Oil Devel. Co., Bayway, N.J., 1946-53; sales engr. Mason-Neilan Regulator Co., N.Y.C., 1953-56; br. mgr. Jay Instrument & Splty. Co., Louisville, 1956-59; owner, pres. Whinery Engring. Co., Louisville, 1959—. Served with USNR, 1943-46. Registered profl. engr., Ky. Republican. Episcopalian. Club: Owl Creek Country. Home: PO Box 27 Anchorage KY 40223 Office: PO Box 107 Anchorage KY 40223

WHIPPLE, ALLEN P., real estate co. owner; b. Tampa, Fla., Dec. 21, 1926; s. Allen Pugh and Evelyn (Taylor) W.; B.A., Emory U., 1950; m. Elinor Trunnell, June 15, 1949; children—Allen Metts, Elinor Lane, Laura Amelia. Founder, owner Whipple Realty & Ins. Co., Perry, Ga., 1955—. Campaign mgr. Mayor of Perry, 1967. Mem. exec. bd. Boy Scouts Am., 1971—. Served with USNR, 1944-46. Named One of Five Outstanding Young Men of Ga., 1958. Mem. Perry Bd. Realtors, Ga. Farm Brokers Inst., Perry Jr. C. of C. (pres. 1957-58), Emory U. Alumni Assn. (pres. 1969-70), Ga. Assn. Real Estate Brokers (dir. 1958-62). Methodist. Mason (32 deg., Shriner). Home: 810 Forrest Hill Rd Perry GA 31069 Office: 1010 Ball St Perry GA 31069

WHIPPLE, PAUL WARREN, mgmt. cons.; b. Tonganoxie, Kan., Jan. 21, 1915; s. John Godfrey and Ola (Bull) W.; student Colo. Sch. Mines, 1932-34; B.A. cum laude in English, Willamette U., 1941; M.A. in Pub. Administrn., Am. U., 1950; m. Irma Stark, Nov. 20, 1948; children—Sara Elizabeth, Laura Melanie. Mgmt. analyst U.S. Govt., Washington, 1946-1955, War Dept., 1946-47, Weather Bur., 1947-50, Dept. Agr., 1950-52, Navy Dept., 1952-55; sr. systems analyst Bur. Naval Personnel, Washington, 1955-59; data systems coordinator State of Ore., Salem, 1959-61; computer systems analyst FAA, Washington, 1961-63; data systems cons. HHFA, Washington, 1963-64; asst. mgmt. officer D.C. Govt., Washington, 1964-69, asst. for planning Office Budget and Exec. Mgmt., 1969-72; dir. policy services Nat. Center for Prosecution Mgmt., Washington, 1972—. Served with USAAF, 1942-46; MTO. Mem. Am. Soc. for Pub. Adminstrn., A.A.A.S., Am. Polit. Sci. Assn., Internat. Platform Assn. Unitarian. Club: Torch (pres. 1970-71) (Washington). Contbr. articles profl. jours. Home: 3619 Everett St NW Washington DC 20008 Office: 1900 L St NW Washington DC 20036

WHISNANT, ISAAC EDWARD, lawyer; b. Clover, S.C., July 22, 1920; s. Isaac Elcana and Emma Grace (Johnson) W.; student St. Mary's U., San Antonio, 1957-59; B.A., U. Md., 1961; J.D., U. Fla., 1965; m. Verna Fae Ray, Aug. 14, 1952; children—William Robert, Sarah Ray. Commd. 2d lt. U.S. Army, 1942, advanced through grades to lt. col., 1951; ret., 1962; admitted to Fla. bar, 1965; v.p., trust officer 1st Nat. Bank of Bradenton (Fla.), 1965-72; practice law, Bradenton, 1972—. Bd. dirs. Fla. West Coast Symphony Orch., 1968-70, Manatee County Soc. Crippled Children and Adults, Happiness House, Manatee County Family YMCA. Decorated Bronze Star. Mem. Am., Fla., Manatee County bar assns., Delta Theta Phi. Presbyn. (elder). Mason, Kiwanian (past dir.). Home: 5611 10th Av Dr W Bradenton FL 33505 Office: 802 12th St W Bradenton FL 33505

WHISNANT, MANLY DOWELL, educator; b. Morganton, N.C., June 13, 1900; s. Thedore W.C. and Mary E. (Chapman) W.; B.A., U. N.C., 1927; m. Pearl B. Jones, Dec. 23, 1929. Athletic coach, phys. edn. instr. Gastonia (N.C.) High Sch., 1927-31, Hoosac (N.Y.) Sch. for Boys, 1931-33, Bath (N.C.) High Sch., 1933-34; prin. Belhaven (N.C.) High Sch., 1934-40; supt. Thompson Orphanage, Charlotte, N.C., 1940-65; pres. Meck Co., 1954-65; dir. F. C. X. Mem. Beaufort County Commn., 1969—; active 4-H leadership. Bd. dirs. N.C. Farm Bur., 1955-65, v.p., 1965-69. Mem. Farm Mgrs. and Rural Appraisers (pres. 1945-71). Democrat. Rotarian (pres. Charlotte club 1961). Address: 519 Riverside Dr Belhaven NC 27810

WHITAKER, JOHN KING, educator; b. Burnley, Eng., Jan. 30, 1933; s. Ben and Mary (King) W.; B.A., U. Manchester, 1956; M.A., John Hopkins U., 1957; Ph.D., Cambridge U., 1961; m. Sally Bell Cross, Aug. 24, 1957; children—Ann Elizabeth, Jane Claire, David John. Came to U.S., 1967. Lectr., prof. U. Bristol, 1960-67; prof. econ. U. Va., Charlottesville, 1967—. Home: 1615 Yorktown Dr Charlottesville VA 22901

WHITAKER, WILLIAM M., JR., radio exec.; b. Blackey, Ky., Aug. 8, 1917; s. William M. and Callie (Caudill) W.; student Alice Lloyd Jr. Coll., Pippa Passes, Ky., 1937-39, Morehead (Ky.) State Coll., 1939-40, 50-52; m. Hazel Dean Hicks, Jan. 4, 1941; 1 son, William M. III. Elementary tchr., Letcher County, Ky., 1939-41; retail mcht., feeds and fertilizer wholesaler, 1941-43; welder insp. Willow Run Bomber Plant, Mich., 1943-44; coal mining co-owner, foreman Caudill & Whitaker Coal Co., Blackey, 1945-49; livestock buying and selling, Morehead, 1950-55; gen. mgr. radio sta. WMOR, 1955—; bldg. constrn., Morehead, 1960—. Mem. Ky. Broadcasters Assn. (past pres.), Morehead C. of C. Democrat. Baptist. Optimist, Lion. Home: Route 1 Forest Hills Subdiv Morehead KY 40351 Office: Radio Sta WMOR Morehead KY 40351

WHITBECK, FRANK LYNN, JR., ins. co. exec.; b. Oklahoma City, Feb. 29, 1916; s. Frank Lynn and Myrtle May (Alexander) W.; Student George Washington U., 1934-35, 36-38, U. Okla., 1935-36, LL.B., Oklahoma City U., 1938, postgrad. 1939-42; m. Beverly Robinson Butterfield, Dec. 26, 1938; 1 son, Frank Butterfield; Agy. asso. Mid-Continent Life, Oklahoma City, 1938-42; agy. sec., v.p., dir. agys. Union Life Ins. Co., Little Rock, 1942-55; founder Pioneer Western Life Ins. Co., Little Rock, 1955, pres., chief exec. officer, 1955-62, (co. name changed to Am. Found. Life Ins. Co., 1962), chmn. bd., chief exec. officer, 1962—. Sec., Ada Thompson Home for the Aged, 1966—; co-founder Ark. Council on Econ. Edn., 1962, chmn; 1965-66; mem. spokesman Ark. Econ. Expansion Study Commn., 1963—. Del., Democratic state and nat. convens., 1950—; treas. Ark. Dem. Com. Vice pres. Catholic High Sch. Edn. Enrichment Endowment Fund, 1970—; v.p., bd. dirs. Met. YMCA, 1971—; bd. dirs. Nat. Council Family Financial Edn. Served to 1st lt. Transp. Corps, AUS, 1942-46; PTO, ETO, C.L.U. Mem. Life Ins. Agy. Mgmt. Assn. (bd. dirs. Hartford, Conn., 1954-55; chmn. agy. mgmt. conf. 1953-54), Ark., Pulaski County bar assns., Ark. (bd. dirs.), Little Rock chambers commerce, Mng. Gen. Agts. (chmn. 1955—), Phi Eta Sigma, Alpha Kappa Psi, Beta Gamma Sigma. Democrat. Episcopalian (vestryman 1949—; sr. warden 1953-57). Mason (32 deg., Shriner). Clubs: Little Rock, Capital, Little Rock Country, Space Age Investment (pres. 1970—) (Little Rock). Home: 2 Glenridge Rd Little Rock AR 72207 Office: 1020 W 4th St Little Rock AR 72201

WHITCOMB, HAROLD WILLIAM, textile exec.; b. Concord, N.H., May 18, 1899; s. Alec Clark and Grace (Silver) W.; B.S., U. N.H., 1926, LL.D., 1964; LL.D., Catawba Coll., 1965; m. Margaret Shaw Marnoch, Oct. 12, 1929. Asst. gen. mgr. Sulloway Hosiery Mills, Franklin, N.H., 1926-36; divisional v.p. Fieldcrest Mills div., Marshall Field & Co., 1936-53; v.p. Fieldcrest Mills, Inc., 1953, pres., 1953-65, now chmn. bd. and exec. com.; dir. Fanny Farmer Candy Shops, Inc., Dibrell Bros., Inc., Danville, Va., Carolina & Northwestern R.R. Trustee Rockingham Community Coll., Wentworth, N.C., Morehead Meml. Hosp., Eden, N.C.; dir. Med. Found. N.C., Inc.; pres. mem. bd. N.C. Textile Found., Inc. Mem. Am. Textile Mfrs. Inst. (pres. 1968—), Phi Kappa Phi, Phi Psi, Theta Chi. Episcopalian. Mason, Rotarian. Clubs: Meadow Greens Country; The Country of N.C. (Pinehurst). Home: Highland Dr Eden NC 27288 Office: Eden NC 27288

WHITCOMB, RICHARD TRAVIS, research scientist; b. Evanston, Ill., Feb. 21, 1921; s. Kenneth Fredrick and Gladys (Travis) W.; B.S. with high distinction in Mech. Engring., Worcester Poly. Inst., 1943. D.Eng. (hon.), 1956. Aero. research scientist NASA, Langley Research Center (formerly NACA, Langley Aero. Lab.), 1943—, asst. head 8-foot transonic tunnels br., 1948-58, head 8-foot tunnels br., 1958—. Recipient Exceptional Service award USAF; Collier Trophy for achievement in aviation Nat. Aero. Assn., 1954; Distinguished Service medal NACA, 1956. Mem. Inst. Aero. Sci. Home: 46 Lakeshore Dr Hampton VA 23366 Office: Langley Research Center Langley Field VA 23365

WHITCOMB, ROBERT FAY WRIGHT, cons.; b. Topeka, Feb. 8, 1896; s. George Herbert and Jessie Elvira (Wright) W.; B.A., Washburn U., 1915; M.A., U. Colo., 1940; m. Louise Brewer, Nov. 9, 1927 (dec. 1963); children—George Herbert, Julia Mac Nair (Mrs. John A. Glass); m. 2d, Edith A. Ramsay, 1964. With Fidelity Trust Co., Kansas City, Mo., 1916; fgn. service officer First Nat. City Bank N.Y., assigned Panama, Shanghai, Java, P.I., Japan, Argentina; pvt. bus., 1933-41; staff fgn. funds control U.S. Treasury, 1942-43; loan officer Export-Import Bank of Washington, Brazil, 1943-58; fgn. service officer ICA, 1958-60, adviser Korean Reconstrn. Bank; lectr. devel. banking topics, various Korean univs.; econ. cons. econ. devel., devel. banking, Ecuador, Pakistan, Cyprus, 1961—; staff Checchi & Co., Washington, 1961—; contbr. report on exporter credit financing Senate Com. on Banking and Currency, hearings on Export-Import Bank, 83d Congress; econ. survey, Peru, and World-wide pvt. investment survey, 1963-65. Decorated Officer Brazilian Order So. Cross. Mem. Kappa Sigma, Pi Gamma Mu. Episcopalian. Contbr. articles to Korean publs. Home: 6340 31st St Washington DC 20015

WHITCOMB, STANLEY PAGE, JR., land developer; b. Waltham, Mass., July 31,, 1940; s. Stanley Page and Jeannie (Lees) W.; B.S., Babson Coll., 1961; student U. Miami (Fla.), 1965-66; m. Nancy Dee Hellmich, July 2, 1966; children—Frederick C.D., Stanley P. III, Scott Edward. Accountant, Price Waterhouse & Co., Boston, 1961-65; dir. financial services Nat. Airlines, Miami, Fla., 1965-67; controller Coral Ridge Properties subsidiary Westinghouse Corp., Ft. Lauderdale, Fla., 1967-69; exec. v.p. Realtec Inc., Ft. Lauderdale, 1969-71, pres., 1972—, also dir.; pres., treas. Corporate & Profl. Services, Inc., Sarasota, Fla., 1965—; pres., dir. Sapphire Valley Devel. Corp., 1971—, Connestee Falls Devel. Corp., 1971—; pres., dir. Lake Keowee Devel. Corp., 1972—; v.p., dir. Valley Forge Corp., 1971—. Mem. Mass., N.Y. socs. C.P.A.'s, Am. Inst. C.P.A.'s, Nat. Assn. Accountants, Greenville, Ft. Lauderdale Chambers Commerce, Am. Land. Devel. Assn., Financial Execs. Inst., Alpha Kappa Psi. Republican. Christian Scientist. Home: 9404 NW 36th Ct Coral Springs FL 33060 also 206 Fairview Av Greenville SC 29601 Office: 3101 N Federal Hwy Ft Lauderdale FL 33306 also 110 Perimeter Rd Greenville SC 29605

WHITCOMB, WESLEY WYMAN, editor, publisher; b. Powellton, Ill., July 28, 1922; s. Grover Farnum and Ella (Bright) W.; student U. Ia., 1941, Drake U., 1942; B.S., Tulane U., 1949, M.S., 1950. Psychologist, Man-Ser Personnel Service, Dallas, 1950-52, Sinclair Oil & Refining Co., Houston, 1952-54; activities dir. Foley's, Houston, 1954-56; editor, pub. Houston's Jour. Soc. Fine Arts, Houston Town and Country mag., 1956—; engaged in advt., pub. relations, McAllen, Tex., 1972—. Served with USNR, 1942-45. Mem. Tex. Press Assn., C. of C., Sigma Alpha Epsilon, Sigma Delta Chi. Home: 520 N 15th St McAllen TX 78501 Office: Suite 4 Valley Fed Bldg 120 S Broadway McAllen TX 78501

WHITE, BYRON R., asso. justice U.S. Supreme Ct.; b. Ft. Collins, Colo., June 8, 1917; grad. with honors, U. Colo., 1938; Rhodes scholar, Oxford (Eng.) U.; grad. Yale Law Sch.; m. Marion Stearns; children—Charles, Nancy. All-Am. halfback U. Colo., 1937, later played with Pittsburgh Steelers, Detroit Lions of Nat. Profl. League; clk. Chief Justice U.S. Supreme Ct., 1946, 47; dep. atty. gen. U.S., 1961-62; asso. justice U.S. Supreme Ct., 1962—. Chmn. Nat. Citizens for Kennedy, 1960. Served with USNR, World War II; PTO. Mem. Order of Coif, Phi Beta Kappa, Phi Gamma Delta. Home: McLean VA 22101 Office: Supreme Ct US 1 1st St NE Washington DC 20543

WHITE, CARL LUTHER, JR., city ofcl.; b. San Marcos, Tex., July 6, 1931; s. Carl L. and Mildred (Waller) W.; B.B.A., S.W. Tex. State U., 1958; M.B.A., St. Mary's U., 1968; m. Wilma Joyce, June 1, 1956; children—Tammy, Stacey, Wesley. Controller, Del Rio Loan Co. (Tex.), 1954-57; budget dir. City of San Antonio, 1957-68, asst. finance dir., 1968-71, dir. finance, chief financial officer, 1971—. Prof. accounting San Antonio Coll., 1968—. Mem. Municipal Finance Officers Assn. U.S. and Can., Urban and Regional Information Systems Assn., Nat. Accountants Assn. Lion. Club: Toastmasters. Home: 310 Blaze St San Antonio TX 78218 Office: City Hall San Antonio TX 78218

WHITE, CHARLES ALEXANDER, variety store exec.; b. Greenville, N.C., Sept. 3, 1899; s. Samuel Tilden and Annie (Sheppard) W.; student Mars Hill Coll., 1913, Randolph-Macon Acad., 1914-15, U. N.C., 1916-18; m. Nancy Rogers Lay, June 23, 1925; children—Samuel Tilden II, Barbara Sheppard (Mrs. A. Ward Peacock), Charles Alexander, Elizabeth Atkinson (Mrs. Robert F. Clayton), George Lay, Anna Louise (Mrs. Errol Haun). Ins. adjuster N.J. Fidelity & Plate Glass Ins. Co., N.Y.C., 1919-23; asso. Thomas A. Edison, Inc., East Orange, N.J., 1924-25, Hassell-Dupree Co., Miami, Fla., 1925-26; owner brokerage Charles A. White, Greenville, 1927-29; partner, mgr.-buyer White's Stores, Inc., Greenville, 1930—, pres., 1966—; treas. Carolina Mills Fabrics, Inc. Comdr., Civil Def., Greenville, 1942-55; chmn. Pitt County chpt. N.C. Symphony Soc., 1947-50; mem. adv. bd. East Carolina U. Summer Theatre, 1964-65, 66-68, East Carolina U. Artists Series, 1967-70, chmn., 1971-72; v.p. Pitt County United Fund, 1966-67. Bd. dirs. East Carolina U. Sch. Music Fund, 1971-72. Mem. Greenville (pres. 1952, dir. 1950-60, 64), N.C. (dir. 1966-72) mchts. assns., C. of C. (pres. 1960; dir. 1957-63, 64), Pitt County Hist. Soc. (pres. 1968-70). Episcopalian. Rotarian. (pres. 1951-52, dir. 1948-56, 65-66). Club: Greenville Music (pres. 1949). Home: 425 W Longmeadow Rd Greenville NC 27834 Office: 601-607 Dickinson Av Greenville NC 27834

WHITE, CHARLES DENNY, clergyman; b. High Point, N.C., Mar. 3, 1914; s. John Charles and Mayme (York) W.; A.B., High Point Coll., 1939, D.D., 1959; B.D., Duke, 1947; m. Julia Lucille Everhart, June 6, 1939 (dec.); children—Charles Denny, Delbert Leon Welch, Judith (Mrs. George W. Ramsey III), LaDean (Mrs. Richard Giles), Zenda R. Welch, David L.; m. 2d, Cornelia Thompson Welch, Mar. 24, 1962. Ordained to ministry Meth. Ch., 1944; pastor All Meth. Ch., Winston Salem, N.C., 1938-41, First-West End Ch., Thomasville, N.C., 1941-43, Duke's Chapel, Durham, N.C., 1943-47, Biltmore Ch., Asheville, N.C., 1947-52, First Meth. Ch., Mt. Holly, 1952-57, Trinity Meth. Ch., Kannapolis, 1957-62, First Meth. Ch., Asheboro, 1962-67; dist. supt. Gastonia Dist., 1967—; Sec., Western N.C. Conf. Meth. Ch., 1952-68, Southeastern Jurisdictional Conf., 1960-68; sec. gen. Conf. United Meth. Ch., 1968-71. Trustee Greensboro Coll.; bd. mgrs. Meth. Home, Charlotte. Mason, Lion, Rotarian. Address: 1540 Westbrook Circle Gastonia NC 28052

WHITE, CHARLES MAXWELL, physician; b. Phila., Dec. 12, 1927; s. Charles Johnson and Anne (Maxwell) W.; student Emory U., 1944; B.S., U. Miami, 1946; M.D., U. Pa., 1951; m. Rosemary Patricia Fischer, Aug. 26, 1950; children—Cynthia Laurice, Pamela Anne; m. 2d, Josephine P. Wood, Apr. 16, 1971; stepchildren—Janet Lee, Richard Allen, James William. Intern, Jackson Meml. Hosp., Miami, Fla., 1951-52; resident VA Hosps., Coatesville, Pa. and Phila., 1952-55, U. Cal at Los Angeles, 1957; psychoanalytic trainee Los Angeles Inst. for Psychoanalysis, 1957-63; instr. psychiatry U. Cal. at Los Angeles, 1957-63; practice medicine, specializing in psychiatry, Beverly Hills, Cal., 1957-63, Coral Gables, Fla., 1963—; mem. staffs Jackson Meml. Hosp., Miami, Cedars of Lebanon, Miami; clin. instr. psychiatry U. Miami Sch. Medicine, 1964-68, clin. asst. prof., 1968—. Mem. Internat. Oceanographic Found. Served with USNR, 1955-57. Diplomate Nat. Bd. Med. Examiners, Am. Bd. Psychiatry and Neurology. Mem. A.M.A., Fla., Dade County med. assns., Fla., South Fla. psychiat. socs., Am. Psychiat. Assn., N.S. Lawn Tennis Assn., Sigma Chi, Phi Chi. Clubs: Palm Bay, University, Royal Palm Tennis (Miami). Home: Box 528 Islamorada FL 33036 Office: 33 Giralda Av Coral Gables FL 33134

WHITE, CHARLIE MARSHALL, supt. schs.; b. Snyder, Tex., Jan. 1, 1930; s. Willie Marion and Mary Ruth (Waddell) W.; B.S., Howard Payne U., 1952; M.Ed., Tex. Tech U., 1958, postgrad., 1968; m. Monte Faye Murphree, June 5, 1948; children—Charlie Marshall, Bobby, Sarita. Tchr., coach, Hermleigh Independent Schs., Tex., 1952-54; coach, New Deal, Tex., 1954-55; coach, asst. prin., Plainview, 1955-63; supt. schs., O'Donnell, Tex., 1963-64, Petersburg, 1965-68, Dimmitt, 1968—. Advancement chmn. Haynes Dist. Boy Scouts Am., 1963. Bd. dirs. YMCA, Plainview, Tex., 1957. Life mem. N.E.A. (dist. membership chmn. 1970-71), Tex. Parent Tchrs. Assn.; mem. Tex. Tchrs. Assn., Am., Tex. assns. sch. adminstrs., Castro County Tchrs. Assn., Panhandle Sch. Leaders Assn. Baptist. Mason, Lion (v.p. 1964). Home: 609 Cleveland St Dimmitt TX 79027 Office: 1505 Western St Dimmitt TX 79027

WHITE, DAVID MEADE, JR., state justice; b. Richmond, Va., Mar. 10, 1918; s. David Meade and Bessie (Turner) W.; student McGuire's Univ. Sch., Richmond, 1931-34, Hampden-Sydney Coll., 1934-36; LL.B., U. Richmond, 1939; m. Carolyn McEldowney, Sept. 11, 1942; children—David Meade III, Carolyn McEldowney. Admitted to Va. bar, 1939; sr. partner firm White, Roberts, Cabell and Paris, Richmond, 1939-68; judge 37th U.S. Jud. Circuit Va., 1968—; prof. U. Richmond, 1947; substitute judge Richmond Juvenile Ct., 1952-68; commr. in chancery, 1949-68; commr. accounts Chesterfield County, 1957-68. Mem. Chesterfield Bd. Welfare, 1958-68. Bd. regents Lincoln Meml. U. Named Richmond's Outstanding Young Man of Year, Richmond Jr. C. of C., 1950. Mem. Am., Va., Richmond (pres. 1962-63), Chesterfield (pres. 1965-66) bar assns., Phi Gamma Kappa, Beta Gamma Sigma, Sigma Chi, Phi Delta Theta. Clubs: Country of Virginia, Bull and Bear (Richmond); Four Seasons (Lanexa, Va.). Home: Route 1 PO Box 102B Moseley VA 23120 Office: Judge's Office Chesterfield Courthouse Chesterfield VA 23832

WHITE, DONALD BURDETT, hotel co. exec.; b. St. Petersburg, Fla., Sept. 22, 1933; s. Amos Burdett and Kathryn (Moran) W.; grad. St. Petersburg Jr. Coll., 1952; B.S., Fla. State U., 1956. With Jack Tar Hotels, Galveston, Tex., 1956-60, mgmt. trainee, 1956-58, traveling accountant, 1958-60; with Internat. Inn, Tampa, Fla., 1960-66, resident mgr., 1961-66; asst. mgr. Hawaiian Village Motel, Tampa,

1966-67, gen. mgr. 1967—. Mem. Tampa C. of C., Fla., Tampa motel and hotel assns., Fla. Motel and Resort Assn. (v.p., 1968-69), Sigma Pi Epsilon. Democrat; Roman Catholic. Home: 3113 B Carlton Arms Dr Tampa FL 33614 Office: 2522 N Dale Mabry Tampa FL 33607

WHITE, DONALD KNOX, educator; b. East Point, Ga., Aug. 29, 1917; s. Charles Walker and Jennie Belle (Millwood) W.; B.C.S., Ga. State U., 1941; postgrad. U. Ga., 1941, Emory U., 1941; m. Helen Shirley Hyde, May 31, 1947; children—Donald Knox, William Hyde, Barbara Louise. Head audio-visual extension service Div. Gen. Extension U. System Ga., Atlanta, 1936-41; asso. visual information specialist USAAF, Maxwell Field, Ala., Washington, N.Y.C., 1941-42; exec. v.p. Nat. Audio-Visual Assn., Fairfax, Va., 1946-71; sr. scholar Center Advanced Study Tech. in Edn., U.S. Internat. U., San Diego, Cal., 1971-72; dep. supt. for Congl. relations Cal. Dept. Edn., Washington, 1972—. Cons. USIA, 1951-52, U.S. Office Edn., 1969—; chmn. Audio-Visual Commn. on Pub. Information, 1959; mem. D.C. Vocational Rehab. Adv. Council, 1968-70; mem. internat. copyright adv. com. U.S. Dept. of State, 1970-72. Bd. dirs. Electronics for Edn., Inc., 1963-64. Served from 2d lt. to maj. USAAF, 1942-46. Recipient Spl. Service award Nat. Audio-Visual Assn., 1965; Service plaque Rochester Audio-Visual Assn., 1966; Tiger Club award Audio-Visual Edn. Assn. Cal., 1967. Mem. Assn. for Ednl. Communications and Tech., N.E.A., Am. Assn. Sch. Adminstrs., Alpha Kappa Psi, Kappa Phi Kappa. Episcopalian. Club: Country of Fairfax. Home: 4832 Prestwick Dr Fairfax VA 22030

WHITE, ELBERT ASA, III, pediatrician; b. Corinth, Miss., July 17, 1935; s. Elbert Asa and Mabel (Spencer) W.; A.B., Vanderbilt U., 1957, M.D., 1960; m. Anna Marie Wright, July 22, 1962; children—Laura Spencer, Elbert Asa, John Weston. Intern, Vanderbilt Med. Center, Nashville, 1960-61, resident, 1963-65, chief resident, 1965-66; practice medicine specializing in pediatrics, Corinth, 1966—; staff Magnolia Hosp., Corinth, N.E. Miss. Hosp., Booneville; cons. in pediatrics Project Head Start, N.E. Miss., 1967—. Partner, Radio Corinth, WWTX, 1967—. Founder, Alcorn County Assn. for Handicapped Children, Corinth, 1968; treas. Corinth Theatre-Arts, 1968—, also bd. dirs. Served with M.C., USAF, 1961-63. Named Corinth's Outstanding Young Man, 1969. Diplomate Am. Bd. Pediatrics. Fellow Am. Acad. Pediatrics. Kiwanian (pres. Corinth 1969-70). Home: 1410 Pine Rd Corinth MS 38834 Office: 705 Shiloh Rd Corinth MS 38834

WHITE, ELLISON FRED, physician; b. Brookhaven, Miss., Apr. 7, 1916; s. Ellison Fred and Myrtle (Greer) W.; B.A., Miss. Coll., 1937; student U. Miss., 1938-40; M.D., U. Tenn., 1942; M.S. in Medicine (fellow Mayo Found. 1944-47), U. Minn., 1947; m. Olive Ruth Joneson, Jan. 7, 1950; children—Joyce, Ruth, Victor, Greer, Ellen, Susan, Mark, Paul, Martha, and Barbara. Intern, Baptist Hosp., Memphis, 1942-43; staff physician at Firland Sanatorium, Seattle, 1947-48; supt., med. dir. Middle River Sanatorium, Hawthorne, Wis., 1948-50, Wis. State Sanatorium, Wales, 1950-55; supt. Harlingen (Tex.) State Tb Hosp., 1955-63; med. dir. So. Wis. Colony and Tng. Sch., Union Grove, 1963-68; practice internal medicine specializing in chest diseases, Houston, Miss., 1968—; mem. staff Houston Hosp.; cons. in clin. investigation N. Miss. Research Found. Mem. A.A.A.S., Am. Thoracic Soc., Am. Assn. on Mental Deficiency, A.M.A., Alumni Assn. Mayo Grad. Sch. Medicine, Miss., N.E. Miss. med. socs., Alumni Assn. Mayo Grad. Sch. Med., Alpha Omega Alpha, Phi Chi. Club: Exchange. Home: 105 White Dr Houston MS 38851 Office: 553 E Madison St Houston MS 38851

WHITE, ETHYLE HERMAN (MRS. S. ROY WHITE), artist; b. San Antonio, Apr. 10, 1904; d. Ferdinand and Minnie (Simmang) Herman; ed. pvt. schs., instrs.; m. S. Roy White, Mar. 3, 1924; children—De Lois Eileen (Mrs. William Marion Mohrle), Patsyruth (Mrs. Henry Wheeler). Exhibited numerous one-man, group shows, Tex.; represented pub. collections in U.S., pvt. collections in Switzerland, Germany, Sweden. Del. Internat. Com. Centro Studi E. Scambi Internationali. Mem. Anahuac Fine Arts Group, San Antonio, Beaumont, Galveston, Houston art leagues, Daus. Republic Tex., Nat. League Am. Pen Women. Episcopalian. Clubs: Fine Arts (Anahuac); Artist and Craftsmen (Dallas); Conservative Arts (Houston). Author, illustrator: Arabella. Author: Poet's Hour. Home: PO Box 176 Anahuac TX 77514

WHITE, FABER ALLEN, farm implement dealer; b. Greenbrier, Ark., Aug. 2, 1905; s. James Walter and Della (Griffin) W.; B.A., State Coll. Ark., Conway, 1924; m. Mary Catherine Ward, Mar. 5, 1932; children— Mary Alma (Mrs. Joe Carter Thomas), Faber Allen. Mgr., Osceola (Ark.) Motor Co., 1925-40; pres., gen. mgr. Missco, Inc., Osceola, 1940—; dir. Planters Bank, First Nat. Bank in Osceola. Chmn. Osceola chpt. A.R.C., 1944-50; mem. N.E. Ark. council Boy Scouts Am., 1946-52; mem. Osceola Sch. Bd., 1948-66; chmn. Housing Authority, Osceola, 1960—. Mem. City Council, Osceola, 1928-36; county judge Mississippi County, Ark., 1951-53. Chmn. bd. dirs. Ark. State Hosp.; bd. dirs. Methodist Childrens Home, Little Rock; mem. Ark Adv. Bd., Little Rock; trustee Cotuit Trust, Wesson Fund, Wesson (Ark.) Holdings. Served with Ark. N.G., 1920-23. Named Man of Year, Osceola, 1942. Democrat. Methodist. Mason (Shriner), Rotarian. Clubs: Five Lakes Outing (pres.), Osceola Country. Home: 847 W Semmes Av Osceola AR 72370 Office: 501 S Walnut St Osceola AR 72370

WHITE, GEORGE MALCOLM, architect; b. Cleve., Nov. 1, 1920; B.S., M.S., Mass. Inst. Tech., 1942; M.B.A., Harvard, 1948; LL.B., Case Western Res. U., 1960. Pvt. practice architecture, Cleve., 1948-71; architect of the Capitol, Washington, 1971—. Fellow A.I.A. (mem. exec. com. Cleve. chpt. 1962-63, 66-67, mem. nat. ins. com. 1960-69, chmn. nat. ins. com., 1966, 67, mem. nat. documents review com. 1966-69, chmn. nat. documents review com. 1968-69, nat. v.p. 1969—), Architects Soc. Ohio (dir. 1963, 66-67). Address: 1231 Potomac St Washington DC 20007*

WHITE, GEORGE PHILLIPS, lawyer; b. Centreville, Ala., Aug. 4, 1915; s. James Bailey and Berta (Jones) W.; LL.B., U. Ala., 1939; m. Betty Ann Poag, Nov. 28, 1952; children—George P. III, Allison, Rachel. Admitted to Ala. bar, 1939; with Employers Liability Assurance Corp., 1940-43; practice law in Centreville, 1946—; dist. atty. Bibb County, 1965—; pres. Abstract Co., Inc.; sec. Centreville Oil Co., Inc., Belcher Motor Co., Inc. Sec., treas. Bibb County Democratic Exec. Com. Served from ensign to lt. Naval Air Force, USNR, 1943-46; PTO. Decorated Presdl. Unit Citation, 5 battle stars. Mem. 4th Jud. Circuit Bar Assn. (past pres.), Ala. Bar Assn., U. Ala. Alumni Assn. (pres. Bibb County chpt. 1962). Presbyn. Home: 116 Ceder St Centreville AL 35042 Office: 132 Courtsquare E Centreville AL 35042

WHITE, HARRY THOMAS, photographer; b. Spartanburg, S.C., Sept. 5, 1930; s. Jimmie A. and Clara (Cothran) W.; student N.Y. Inst. Photography, 1947; student journalism U. N.C., 1950; m. Lillian Ruth Hughes, Mar. 15, 1949; children—Diane Elizabeth, Karen Patryce, Thomas Harry. With editorial staff Spartanburg Herald Jour., 1947-50; organized B. & B. Studios, Inc., Spartanburg, 1950, pres., gen. mgr., 1962—. Pres. Kaminers Art and Frame Co., Spartanburg, 1965—. Recipient awards including Nat. Art League award, 1948, S.C. Press Assn. award, 1949. Mem. Photog. Soc. Am., Nat. Press Photographers Assn. Mem. United Methodist Ch. (lay leader). Mason (32 deg. Shriner). Club: Sertoma. Photog. works in traveling photog. exhbns. Home: 230 Cart Dr Spartanburg SC 29302 Office: 268 E Main St Spartanburg SC 29302

WHITE, HENRY CORNELUIS, banker; b. Cadiz, Ky., Aug. 28, 1912; s. John Preston and Martha Grace (Burnett) W.; grad. Vanderbilt U., 1934; postgrad. Bowling Green Bus. U., 1934-35; m. Betty Lewis Hopson, Dec. 15, 1938; 1 son, John Preston III. Owner, operator Henry C. White Chevrolet Co., Cadiz, 1935-65, White Lake Farm, 1941—; mgr. Trigg County Farmers Bank Br., 1971—, also dir.; dir. Cadiz R.R. Co., 1941—. Mem. Cadiz City Council, 1940-52, 66—. Baptist. Home: Box 71 Cadiz KY 42211 Office: Trigg County Farmers Bank Br Main St Cadiz KY 42211

WHITE, JACK NOBLE, sch. adminstr., clergyman, musician; b. Weatherford, Tex., Apr. 25, 1938; s. James F. Cody and Jen (Noble) W., Sr.; B.Mus., Tex. Christian U., 1961; postgrad. Union Theol. Sem., 1962, (fellow) Westminster Choir Coll., 1968; M.A., U. S. Ala., 1972; m. Johanna Parrott, Aug. 2, 1959; children—Stephanie Jeanne, Alicia Kirsten. Organist, choirmaster All Saint's Episcopal Ch., Ft. Worth, 1959-66, St. Paul's Episcopal Ch., Mobile, Ala., 1966—; minister of youth, 1972—; dir. mus. Ft. Worth Country Day Sch., 1963-66; asst. headmaster St. Paul's Day Sch., Mobile, 1966-69, headmaster, 1969-72. Mem. joint commn. on ch. music Episcopal Ch., 1960—, sec., 1963—, cons. radio-tv, films dept., 1964-67, cons. on prayerbook revision, 1966—. Bd. dirs. Mobile Symphony, Civic Music Assn., Mobile. Mem. Am. Guild Organists, Nat. Assn. Episcopal Schs. Composer: Omnes Gentes, Plaudite, 1968; Destin, 1970; Come Let Us Sing, 1971; Be Joyful, Songs for the Jesus Generation, 1972. Contbr. articles to periodicals. Home: 309 Brawood Dr Mobile AL 36608

WHITE, JAMES JOHNSON, banker; b. Yorktown, Ark., Sept. 8, 1903; s. James Johnson and Mary Virginia (McGehee) W.; student Ark. Tech. Coll., 1922-23, 25-26, 26-27, 27-28, Miss. State Coll., 1928-30; m. Beulah Rogers, July 13, 1934; 1 dau., Virginia (Mrs. John J. Joiner). Tchr., Ark. State Coll., Jonesboro, 1930-31, Yellville (Ark.) High Sch., 1931-35; county agt. Phillips County Extension Service, Helena, Ark., 1935-44; pres. Helena Nat. Bank (Ark.), 1944—; dir. Memphis br. Fed. Res. Bd. St. Louis, Arkla Chem. Corp., Shreveport, La., Phillips County Farm Bur., Helena, Farmers Oil & Supply, Helena, Delta Fertilizer Co., Helena. Pres. Phillips County Fair Assn., 1942-43. Mem. Helena-W. Helena Indsl. Commn. (pres. 1959-60), Phillips County Farmers Assn. (pres. 1936-54), Phillips County C. of C. (bd. dirs. 1940-71), Ark. Agrl. Council (bd. dirs. 1940-71). Mason (Shriner). Home: 34 Waverly Wood St Helena AR 72342 Office: 302 Cherry St Helena AR 72342

WHITE, JAMES ROY, architect; b. Crowley, La., Jan. 21, 1907; s. James Edgar and Mary Joe (White) W.; B.Arch., U. Tex., 1929; m. Mary Elmer Scurlock, Sept. 1, 1930; children—James Roy, Mary Jo (Mrs. James E. Fielder). Gen. practice architecture, Austin, Tex., 1929—; asso. Hugo F. Kuehne, Giesecke, Kuehne & Brooks, 1929-50, Kuehne, Brooks & Barr, Brooks & Barr, 1950-64; partner Brooks, Barr, Graeber & White, 1964—. Bd. dirs. Austin Heritage Soc., Austin Heritage Found., Inst. for Advanced Environmental Studies. Recipient Architecture of Merit award Tex. Soc. Architects, 1959, citation Austin Heritage Soc., 1968, certificate of commendation Am. Assn. State and Local History, 1969, First Honor award Tex. Soc. Architects, 1970. Mem. A.I.A., Tex. Soc. Architects, Nat. Trust for Hist. Preservation, Tex. Fine Arts Assn., Tex. Hist. Assn., Tex. Hist. Found., Travis County Hist. Survey Com., Alpha Rho Chi. Episcopalian. Clubs: Austin Country, Citadel. Author: The Restoration of the Birthplace of President Lyndon B. Johnson, 1964; Limestone and Log, 1968. Important works include Huston-Tillotson Coll. Bldgs., St. David's Episcopal Ch., Austin Pub. Schs., Restoration Work for Pres. & Mrs. Lyndon B. Johnson, Lyndon B. Johnson State Park, Labor Bldg., Washington, U.S. Embassy, Mexico City. Home: 1403 Gaston Av Austin TX 78703 Office: Perry Brooks Bldg Austin TX 78701

WHITE, JAMES WHITCOMB RILEY, publisher; b. Halls, Tenn., Feb. 20, 1919; s. John Lee and Lorene (Mitchell) W.; grad. high sch.; m. Nell Ruth Burnette, Feb. 21, 1943; children—James Timothy, JoMarilyn (Mrs. Stephen Koslow), Gerald Harvey. Pub., Weakley County Press, Martin, Tenn., 1947-63, So. Standard, McMinnville, Tenn., 1955—, Smithville (Tenn.) Rev., 1963—, Warren County Tribune, McMinnville, 1968—; pres. WBMC Radio, McMinnville, 1964—; dir. First Nat. Bank, McMinnville. Pres., Warren County-McMinnville, A.R.C., 1958-64. Served with AUS, 1943-45. Mem. Tenn. Press Assn. (pres. 1952-53). Home: 620 W Main St McMinnville TN 37110 Office: Morford St McMinnville TN 37110

WHITE, JERALD RAYMOND, ednl. adminstr.; b. Hominy, Okla., July 4, 1915; s. John William and Opal (Privett) W.; B.Ed., Shenandoah Coll. and Conservatory of Music, 1954; M.Ed., U. Va., 1959, Cert. Advanced Grad. Study in Sch. Adminstrn., 1969; m. Una Vass, Mar. 12, 1938. 1 son, Jerald Raymond Jr. Band dir. Roanoke (Va.) City Schs., 1941-58; asst. prin. Jefferson Sr. High Sch., Roanoke, 1958-61, prin., 1961-66; gen. supr. instrn. Culpeper (Va.) County Schs., 1967-69, dir. instrn., 1969—. Served with AUS, 1945-46. Mem. Phi Delta Kappa. Baptist (deacon, tchr. Sunday sch. 1967—). Mason (Shriner). Rotarian (dir. 1970, chmn. program and music 1971). Home: 2130 Mountain Run Lane Culpeper VA 22701 Office: N Main St Extension Culpeper VA 22701

WHITE, JOHN C., state ofcl.; b. Newport, Tex., Nov. 26, 1925; s. E. H. White; grad. Tex. Technol. U.; postgrad. Tex. A. and M. U.; m. Wynelle Watson; children—John Richard, Edward, Russell, Kay Lynn, Jake Rayburn, Craig. Head agr. dept. Midwestern U., Witchita Falls, Tex., until 1951; commr. of agr., Tex., 1950—. Recipient Outstanding Nat. Leader in Agr. award Fed. Land Bank, 1968; Merit award Govt. France, 1969. Mem. So. Assn. Commrs. and Secs. Agr., Nat. Assn. State Dept. Agr., Optimists. Democrat. Home: 2321 Hartford Rd Austin TX 78703 Office: PO Drawer 12847 Austin TX 78711

WHITE, JOHN FRANKLIN, accountant; b. Oklahoma City, Mar. 1, 1944; s. John Franklin and Edith Margaret (Carter) W.; student Little Rock U., 1961-63; B.B.A., N. Tex. State U., 1965; m. Rita Mae Hubbard, June 6, 1964; children—Sandy Lynn, Kari Kyle. With Cullum Companies, Inc., 1964—, chief accountant, 1966-69, treas. subsidiary Page Drugs, Inc., 1969-70, asst. treas. parent co., Dallas, 1970-71, controller subsidiaries A. W. Cullum & Co., Inc., Tom Thumb Stores, Inc., Page Drugs, Inc., 1971—. C.P.A., Tex. Mem. Tex. Soc. C.P.A.'s. Home: 3321 Whippoorwill St Irving TX 75060 Office: 2533 Hawes St Dallas TX 75235

WHITE, JOHN HENRY, oil exec.; b. Maxton, N.C., Feb. 2, 1918; s. William H. and Alma (Stewart) W.; student Southeastern Bus. Coll., Florence, S.C., accounting Walton Sch. Commerce, Chgo.; m. Jane Hanlon, Dec. 31, 1941; children—Sally Hanlon (Mrs. Charles F. Greer), Nancy Hanlon, Peggy Hanlon. All depts. Am. Bakeries, Inc., Florence, 1934-36; accountant Swift & Co., Florence and Charleston, S.C., 1936-38; cost accountant Am. Tobacco Co., Charleston, 1939-41; with Hewitt Oil Co., Charleston, 1944—, successively accountant, sec.-treas., v.p., gen. mgr. 1944-53, dir., pres., 1953—; pres., chmn. bd. Palm Oil Co., 1957—; sec.-treas. Coastal Terminals, Inc., Fort Sumter Oil Co., Universal Oil Equipment & Supply Co.; acquired controlling interest in Hewitt Oil Marketing Co. (now Port Oil Co.), 1954, pres., chmn. bd.; pres. chmn. bd. Palm Oil Co., 1957—, Sanape Realty Corp.; chmn. bd. Gas-Up, Inc;, Wilson Tire Co.; dir. So. Petroleum Co., United Mortgage Investments, Inc., Standard Am. Life Ins. Co., Port Lubricants Co., East Oil, Inc., S.C. Nat. Bank, Charleston. Commr. 9th dist. S.C. Hwy. Dept., 1966—; mem. Charleston County Indsl. Commn., 1965—. Mem. bd. Charleston Community Chest, 1955-56; mem. exec. com. Charleston Devel. Bd., 1956-58; dir. United Fund, chmn. spl. div. drive, 1958; mem. Greater Charleston Auditorium commn.; bd. dirs. YMCA. Dir. Nat. Oil Jobbers Council, 1948—, chmn., 1954—, mem. exec. com., 1959-60, bd. dirs. exec. com., 1961-62; mem. Nat. Petroleum Council, 1952. Served as auditor USN at Charleston Shipyard and Drydock Co., 1941-44. Mem. S.C. Oil Jobbers Assn. (pres. 1950, dir. 1964—), Am. Petroleum Inst., C. of C. (dir.; dir. hwys. and bridges com. for Greater Charleston Area 1957—), S.C. Hist. Soc. Roman Catholic. Elk. Clubs: Charleston Country, Carolina Yacht, Hibernia Soc., Lions. Contbr. to petroleum jours. Home: Castle Pinckney Dr James Island Charleston SC 29407 Office: Port Oil Co PO Box 372 Charleston SC 29412

WHITE, JOHN HOXLAND, JR., mus. ofcl.; b. Cin., Nov. 10, 1933; s. John Hoxland and Sarah Christine (Seebaum) W.; B.A., Miami (O.) U., 1958. Mus. aid Smithsonian Instn., Washington, 1958, asst. curator, 1958-67, curator in charge div. transp., 1967-69, chmn. dept. industries, 1969—. Bd. dirs. R.R. Advancement Information Law Found., Nat. Capitol Mus. Transp. Mem. Assn. Pvt. R.R. Car Owners (dir. 1971—), Soc. History Tech. (adv. council 1971—). Author: Cincinnati Locomotive Builders, 1965; American Locomotives 1830-1880: An Engineering History, 1968. Mem. editorial bd. Bus. History Rev., 1969—; editor Bull. Ry. and Locomotive Hist. Soc., 1970—. Contbr. articles to profl. jours. Office: Nat Mus History and Tech Smithsonian Instn 14th St and Constitution Av Washington DC 20560

WHITE, JOSEPH MALLIE, physician, univ. dean; b. Dallas, Dec. 4, 1921; s. Joseph M. and Vada (VonderBurke) W.; B.S., So. Methodist U., 1944; M.D., Southwestern Med. Sch., 1947; M.Sc., U. Ia., 1950; m. Colleen Dennis, Nov. 25, 1950; children—Cynthia Ann, Jennifer Sue. Intern Denver Gen. Hosp., 1947-48; resident anesthesiology U. Ia., 1948-51; practice medicine specializing in anesthesiology; instr. anesthesiology U. Ia., 1950-51; asst. prof. anesthesiology U. Wash., Seattle, 1954-56; prof., head dept. anesthesiology U. Okla. Med. Center, 1956-65, prof. anesthesiology U. Okla., 1965-68, asso. dean research affairs, 1960-64, asso. dir., asso. dean, 1964-67, dean med. faculty, 1967-68; prof. anesthesiology U. Tex. Med. Branch, Galveston, 1968—, v.p. for acad. affairs, dean medicine, 1968—; cons. anesthesiology Oklahoma City VA Hosp., 1956-68, Indian Health Service, 1956-68, NIH, 1964-68, Nat. Library Medicine, 1965-68, USPHS Hosp., Galveston, 1968—. Mem. medicine and osteopathy ednl. improvement grants rev. com., div. health manpower NIH, USPHS, 1967—. Served to capt. M.C., AUS, 1952-54; Korea, Japan. Decorated Bronze Star medal; recipient 1st Distinguished Alumnus award Southwestern Med. Coll., U. Tex., 1968. Diplomate Am. Bd. Anesthesiology; Mem. A.M.A. (council on med. edn. 1969—), Am. Soc. Anesthesiologists, Sigma Xi. Editor: Clinical Anesthesia, 1966. Contbr. articles to sci. jours. Home: 1416 Harbor View St Galveston TX 77550

WHITE, JOSHUA WARREN, JR., paper co. exec., state legislator; b. Norfolk, Va., Aug. 27, 1916; s. J. Warren and Emily (Johnston) W.; B.A., Washington and Lee U., 1939; m. Dorothy Lee Winstead, Aug. 30, 1939; children—Joshua Warren, Dorothy Lee, William Carr, Emily Johnston. With Old Dominion Paper Co., Norfolk, 1946—, treas., 1946—, pres., 1946—; dir. Va. Nat. Bank, Norfolk. Mem. mcht. adv. bd. Union Bay-Camp Paper Corp., N.Y.C., 1959; chmn. mcht. adv. bd. Internat. Paper Co., N.Y.C., 1962. Pres., Young Democratic Clubs Va., 1946; treas., mem. 2d Dist. Dem. Com., 1967—; mem. Ho. of Dels., Va. State Legislature, 1962—; mem. So. Regional Edn. Bd., 1962-69. Bd. dirs. United Communities Fund, Tidewater Cancer Soc., Norfolk Gen. Hosp.; trustee Tidewater Va. Devel. Council; treas. Edgewater Turney Home for Boys and Girls, 1970—, also bd. dirs. Served as lt. comdr. USNR, 1941-45: PTO. Mem. Nat. (past dir.), Southeastern (past pres.) paper trade assns., Navy League (dir. Hampton Roads council), Norfolk C. of C., Presbyn. (past deacon.). Clubs: Norfolk Yacht and Country, Norfolk German; Virginia (Norfolk); Cedar Point Country (Portsmouth, Va.); Princess Anne Country (Virginia Beach, Va.). Home: 1206 Graydon Av Norfolk VA 23507 Office: 3600 Progress Rd Norfolk VA 23502

WHITE, LENDELL AARON, microbiologist; b. Sabetha, Kan., Nov. 10, 1926; s. Leonard Aaron and Della C. (Graham) W.; B.A., U. Kan., 1951, M.A., 1955; student Washburn U., 1948-49; m. Helen June Rhodes, Sept. 5, 1948; children—Charles Leonard, Peggy Ann. Bacteriologist, Kan. State pub. Health Labs., Topeka, 1951-53; research asst. U. Kan., Lawrence, 1953-54; supervisory research microbiologist Center for Disease Control, Atlanta, 1955—. Dist. commr. Atlanta area council Boy Scouts Am., 1967-70, asst. council commr., 1970—. Recipient Silver Beaver award Boy Scouts Am. Served with USNR, 1944-46. Mem. Am. Soc. Microbiologist, Sci. Research Soc. Am. Methodist. Lion. Home: 2534 Wilson Woods Dr Decatur GA 30033 Office: 1600 Clifton Rd Atlanta GA 30333

WHITE, LEONARD ALOYSIOUS, JR., educator; b. Joplin, Mo., June 23, 1933; s. Leonard Aloysious and Louise Clare (Schorgl) W.; B.B.A, Rockhurst Coll., 1954; M.S., St. Louis U., 1961, Ph.D., 1963; m. Katherine C. Kirk, Sept. 28, 1957; children—Linda, Paula, Dale, Thomas, Leslie. Instr., St. Louis U., 1961-63, asst. prof., 1963-65; asso. prof. U. Ark., Fayettesville, 1965-70, prof., 1970—, head dept. econs., 1971—; cons. antitrust cases, 1965—. Served with USNR, 1954-58. Recipient NSF Grant, Purchasing Agents Grant. Mem. Am., Midwest, So. econ. assns., S.W. Social Sci. Assn. Home: 2595 Manor Dr Fayetteville AR 72701

WHITE, LEWIS CHARLES, govt. ofcl.; b. Morrison, Ill., Dec. 27, 1915; s. Lewis Woody and Reka (Laman) W.; ed. high sch., Holland, Mich.; m. Lillian May Ard, Nov. 26, 1936; children—Daniel Lyman, Paul Judson. Personnel officer, civilian personnel sect. Hdqrs. SCAP, Dept. Army, Tokyo, Japan, 1946-54; personnel officer U.S. Operations Mission, New Delhi, India, 1954-56; regional personnel officer ICA, Washington, 1956-58; exec. officer U.S. Operations Mission to Iran, Tehran, 1958-61; personnel office AID, Washington, 1961-65; exec. officer U.S. AID Mission to Afghanistan, Kabul, 1965-67, asst. dir. mgmt., 1967-68; dep. dir. fgn. service personnel Office Personnel and Mgmt., AID, Washington, 1968—. Named Civic Leader of Am., 1968. Episcopalian. Mason. Club: Am. Home: 6427 16th St Alexandria VA 22307 Office: US AID Dept State Washington DC 20523

WHITE, LOUISE RUFFIN (MRS. MORRIS EDWARD WHITE), civic worker; b. Como, Miss., Apr. 24, 1898; d. Robert and Kate (Weller) Ruffin; A.B., Miss. State Coll. for Women, 1916; postgrad. Peabody Coll., 1917; m. Morris Edward White, Oct. 8, 1920; children—Louise (Mrs. William Caldwell Cooke), Frances

(Mrs. James Klay), Martha (Mrs. Dan Blalock, Jr.). Tchr. math., Aberdeen, Miss., 1917-18, Tarrytown, N.Y., 1918-20. Pres. P.T.A., Tampa, Fla., 1930-32; bd. dirs. YMCA, Tampa, 1932-38, treas., 1933; mem. Tb Bd., Tampa, 1938-41, treas., 1938; treas. Def. Council, Tampa, 1941-46, chmn. county nutrition, 1941-46; mem. Children's Home Bd., Tampa, 1946-56, pres., 1951-52; pres. Chiselers of U. Tampa, 1961-62; mem. Golfview Garden Circle Book Club, Tampa Symphony Club, Tampa Yacht Club, Palma Ceia Golf Club, Rotary Ann, Hillsboro County Bar Aux. (pres. 1963-64), Colonial Dames Am., Inner Wheel Club Lampa U.S.A. Democrat. Episcopalian. Home: 916 Golfview Av Tampa FL 33609

WHITE, MABLE D(UNN) (MRS. EDGAR R. WHITE), painter; b. Charlotte, N.C.; d. John A. and Fannie Covington (Stogner) Dunn; student art under Mrs. Milton Sullivan, Greenville Coll. Women, 1937, 38; m. Edgar R. White, Apr. 20, 1920 (dec. June 15, 1970); children—Bruce B., Ralph R. (dec.). Painter in home studio, 1938—; exhibits in various civic groups; owner, mgr. Olde Brick Motel, Dunnellon, Fla. Chmn. Nat. Art Week S.C., 1945-48. Mem. Am. Artist Profl. League, Fla. Fedn. Arts, Fla., Jacksonville art assns. Baptist. Club: Womens (Dunnellon). Office: PO Box 866 Dunnellon FL 32630

WHITE, MORRIS EDWARD, lawyer; b. Yazoo City, Miss., Aug. 13, 1892; s. Andrew and Fannie (Middleton) W.; B.S., U. Miss., 1913, M.A., 1915, LL.B., 1915; m. Louise Ruffin, Oct. 8, 1920; children—Louise (Mrs. W. C. Cooke), Frances Ruffin (Mrs. James B. Klay), Martha Moris (Mrs. Daniel S. Blalock, Jr.). Admitted to Miss. bar, 1915; practiced in Columbus, 1915-17; mem. firm Bell & White, Greenville, 1919-25; admitted to Fla. bar, 1925, since practiced in Tampa; mem. firm Shackleford, Brown, White & Tillman, 1925-28, Mabry, Reaves, Carlton & White, 1930-44, Fowler, White, Gillen, Yancey & Humkey, 1944-59, Fowler, White, Gillen, Humkey & Trenam, 1959, now mem. firms Fowler, White, Gillen, Humkey, Kinney & Boggs, Tampa, Fowler, White, Humkey, Burnett, Hurley & Banick, Maimi. Mem. Hillsborough County Def. Council, 1941-42; bd. dirs. U.S.O., 1941-45; chmn. Hillsborough County Port Authority, 1945-48; pres. Tampa Community Chest, 1938. Served to capt. U.S. Army, 1918. Mem. Am., Fla., Hillsborough County bar assns., Internat. Assn. Ins. Counsel, Maritime Law Assn. U.S., Am. Judicature Soc., Am. Legion (past post comdr.). Episcopalian. Mason (33 deg., Shriner). Clubs: University, Palma Ceia Golf and Country, Tampa Yacht and Country, Rotary (past pres.; dist. gov. internat. 1948-49). Home: 916 Golfview Av Tampa FL 33609 Office: First Fed Bldg Tampa FL 33602

WHITE, NOAH WESLEY, ins. co. exec.; b. McKinney, Tex., Oct. 29, 1924; s. Noah and Cecil Vance (Meador) W.; student So. Meth. U., 1946, Tex. Christian U., 1947-48; m. June Wight, July 3, 1943; children— Carolyn (Mrs. Ronald D. Scott), William Wesley. With Agrl. Workers Mut. Auto Ins. Co., Fort Worth, 1948—, asst. sec., 1948-52, treas., dir., 1952-60, v.p., treas., 1960—; v.p. Nat. Farm Life Ins. Co., 1947—. Served with A.C., AUS, 1943-46. Mem. Tex. Christian U. Alumni Assn. Methodist. Elk. Home: 4421 Ridgeton Rd Fort Worth TX 76116 Office: 6001 Bridge St Fort Worth TX 76101

WHITE, ORLANDO HOMER, coll. exec.; b. Charleston, S.C., Mar. 23, 1928; s. Homer S. and Mattie M. (McWhite) W.; B.S., Sc. State Coll., 1953; postgrad. N.Y.U., 1959-61; LL.D., Allen U., 1970; m.Marion Lelia Brown, Nov. 24, 1956; children—Orlando Homer, Lesylee Maurelia Aleson. Acting bus. mgr. Voorhees Coll., Denmark, S.C., 1953, bur. mgr., 1954—, accountant, purchasing agt., supr. non-acad. personnel, 1954—. Mem. Nat., So. assns. coll. and univ. bus. officers, Omega Psi Phi. Episcopalian. Club: Kahine Investment (pres.). Address: Voorhees Coll Denmark SC 29042

WHITE, PAUL JENNINGS, textile co. exec.; b. Greenville, S.C., Apr. 8, 1918; s. Charles Robert and Annie Lou (Wiggs) W.; grad. Draughan's Bus. Coll., 1939; B.S. in Textiles with honors, Clemson U., 1949; m. Thelma Farrar Mason, July 21, 1943; children—Paul Jennings, Philip Mason. With J.P. Stevens & Co., Inc., Milledgeville, Ga., 1935—, gen. overseer dept. Dunean plant, Greenville, S.C., 1946-51, supt. Greer (S.C.) plant, 1951-57, mgr. Victor plant, Greer, 1957-62, mgr. Greer and Victor plants, 1962-63, group mgr. 4 plants, 1963-66, asst. gen. mgr. 4 plants, 1966-67, gen. mgr. 4 worsted menswear plants, 1967—, mem. new plant and equipment com., 1969—. Active YMCA. Served with USMCR, 1942-46. Recipient Citizen of Year award Woodmen of World, 1967. Mem. Greer C. of C. (v.p. 1969; bd. dirs. 1966-69), Phi Kappa Phi. Republican. Baptist. Club: Greenville County Textile. Home: Peachtree Dr Greer SC 29651 Office: Box 159 Greer SC 29651

WHITE, RALPH KIRBY, educator, social sci.; Ph.D., Stanford, 1937. Supr., Pub. Opinion Research, USIA, 14 yrs.; now prof. social psychology George Washington U., Washington. Contbr. to profl. jours. Home: 560 North St NW Washington DC 20001*

WHITE, RICHARD CRAWFORD, congressman; b. El Paso, Tex., Apr. 29, 1923; s. James Crawford and Lela (Mueller) W.; B.A., U. Tex., 1946, LL.B., 1949; m. Katherine Huffman, Dec. 18, 1949 (dec. Mar. 1972); children—Rodrick James, Richard Whitman, Raymond Edward. Admitted to Tex. bar, 1949; trial atty., El Paso, 1949-64; mem. 89th-92d congresses from 16th Dist. Tex. Active civic and vets. orgns. Mem. Tex. Ho. of Reps., 1955-58; chmn. El Paso County Democratic Com., 1962-64. Served with USMCR, World War II; PTO. Mem. El Paso County Bar Assn., State Bar Tex., Phi Alpha Delta, Sigma Alpha Epsilon. Episcopalian. Club: 89th Democratic Congress (dir.). Home: 146 US Courthouse El Paso TX 79901 Office: Cannon House Office Bldg Washington DC 20515

WHITE, ROBERT MAYER, govt. ofcl.; b. Boston, Feb. 13, 1923; s. David and Mary (Winkeller) W.; B.A., Harvard, 1942; certificate, Mass. Inst. Tech., 1944, M.S., 1949, Sc.D., 1950; m. Mavis Seagle, Apr. 18, 1948; children—Richard Harry, Edwina Janet. Project scientist, gen. circulation project Atmospheric Analysis Lab., Air Force Cambridge Research Center, 1950-52, chief large scale processes br., 1952-58, chief meteorol. devel. lab., 1958-59; research asso. Mass. Inst. Tech., 1959; asso. dir. research dept. Travelers Ins. Co., 1959-60; pres. Travelers Research Center, Inc., 1960-63; chief U.S. Weather Bur., 1963-65; adminstr. Environmental Sci. Services Adminstrn., Dept. Commerce, 1965—. Mem. Commn. Marine Sci., Engring. and Resources; mem. Interagy. Com. Oceanography, Interagy. Group Internat. Aviation, Meteorol. Satellite Program Rev. Mem. exec. com. Daniel and Florence Guggenheim Found. Mem. sci. adv. bd. USAF. Served to capt. USAAF, World War II. Mem. Am. Meteorol. Soc. (councilor 1965-67, chmn. planning commn.), Nat. Acad. Engring., Am. Geophys. Union (exec. com.), Royal Meteorol. Soc., Sci. Research Soc. Am., World Meteorol. Orgn. (exec. com., permanent U.S. rep., chmn. U.S. Ad Hoc com.), Fed. Council Sci. and Tech., U.S. Power Squadron (bd. govs.), Sigma Xi. Contbr. articles to profl. publs. Address: care Ralph Cooler Box 160 Ridgeland SC 21236

WHITE, SAMUEL HARVEY, JR., hosp. dir.; b. Ethel, Miss., July 11, 1934; s. Samuel H. and Kathleen (Barnes) W.; B.S., Miss. Coll., 1954; postgrad. Miss. State U., 1954-55; m. Martha Jo Sumrall, June 29, 1961; children—Katherine McLaurin, Isabel Ingram. Sr. accountant Peat, Marwick, Mitchell & Co., Jackson, Miss., 1957-62; chief accountant Sch., Pictures, Inc., Jackson, 1962-64; asst. treas. Lamar Life Ins. Co., Jackson, 1964-66; asst. dir. Univ. Hosp., Jackson, 1966—. Treas., Jackson Men's Y Club, 1966; mem. budget com. Greater Jackson United Givers Fund, 1969. Served with USNR, 1955-57. C.P.A., Miss. Mem. Am. Inst. C.P.A.'s, Miss. Soc. C.P.A.'s (chpt. pres. 1967), Hosp. Financial Mgmt. Assn. (chpt. treas. 1969). Kiwanian (chmn. finance com. 1965). Home: 5901 Medallion Dr Jackson MS 39211 Office: 2500 N State St Jackson MS 39216

WHITE, SID JOHNSTONE, state ct. ofcl.; b. Clearwater, Fla., Sept. 20, 1930; s. Jack F. and Mary Carr (Westbrook) W.; B.A., U. Va., 1955; LL.B., Stetson Coll. of Law, 1960; m. Pat Wolff, May 4, 1952; children—Elizabeth Ann, Sid J. Admitted to Fla. bar, 1960; spl. asst. to Atty. Gen., 1960-61; research aide to justice Fla. Supreme Ct., 1961-64, apptd. clk., 1964—. Served with USMC, 1950-52. Mem. Fla. Bar Assn. Home: Box 486 Monticello FL 32344 Office: Supreme Ct Bldg Tallahassee FL 32304

WHITE, THOMAS NICHOLAS, govt. ofcl.; b. Gorizia, Italy, May 25, 1938; s. Nicholas M. and Olga (Fodor) W.; B.A., George Washington U., 1962, M.A., 1965, postgrad., 1966—; m. Julie Ahlman, Sept. 11, 1971. Research asso. Research & Microfilm Publs., Inc., Washington, 1965-68; research asst. George Washington U., 1966; social sci. analyst U.S. Civil Rights Commn., Washington, 1967; edn. research, planning asso. Washington Pub. Schs., 1968, asst. to asst. supt. for planning and devel., 1969—; cons. Dept. Edn., Commonwealth of P.R., 1971. Intercollegiate soccer coach George Washington U., Washington, 1964-69. Mem. Am. Polit. Sci. Assn., Am. Acad. Polit. and Social Scis. Home: 2000 N St NW Washington DC 20036 Office: 415 12th St NW Washington DC 20004

WHITE, THOMAS SKINNER, JR., securities co. exec.; b. Hertford, N.C., Dec. 21, 1910; s. Thomas Skinner and Mattie (Toms) W.; B.S., U. N.C. at Chapel Hill, 1933; grad. Wharton Sch. Finance U. Pa., 1955; m. Mary Frances Council, June 6, 1942; children—Thomas Skinner III, Carlyle Council, Mary Frances. With Liggett & Myers Tobacco Co., Richmond, Va., 1946-50, Eastern sales mgr., 1950-52; with 1st Securities Corp., Durham, N.C., 1952—, sr. v.p., 1968-70, exec. v.p., 1970—; dir. Durham Herald Co., Inc. Mem. U. N.C., Chapel Hill Ednl. Found., 1952. Vice chmn. adjustments, Durham, 1960. Trustee N.C. Wesleyan Coll., Rocky Mount, 1970—. Methodist (trustee). Kiwanian. Clubs: Hope Valley Country, Tobac, Durham City; Country N.C. (Pinehurst). Home: 804 Hermitage Ct Durham NC 27707 Office: 1st Securities Corp Durham NC 27702

WHITE, THURMAN JAMES, univ. ofcl.; b. Ponca City, Okla., Nov. 7, 1916; s. Charles L. and Winona Faye (Enfield) W.; A.B., Phillips U., 1936; M.S., U. Okla., 1941; Ph.D., U. Chgo., 1950; m. Corrine Laura Hartson, June 13, 1939; children—Sue Ann, Charles Frank. Instr. prison edn. U. Okla., 1937-39, supr. Statewide Mus. Service, 1940-42, dir. audio-visual edn., 1942-46, asst. dir. extension div., 1946-47, acting dir., 1947-48, dir., 1949-50, dean extension div. 1950—, dean Coll. Continuing Edn., 1961—, now v.p. univ., exec. sec. Film Council of Am., 1946-47, bd. trustees, 1950. Mem. Def. Adv. Com. Edn. Armed Forces, 1957-60; exec. vice chmn. 1961 White House Conf. on Aging; mem. UNESCO Com. for Advancement of Adult Edn., mem. nat. adv. council Adult Basic Tchr. Tng. Program, 1966; mem. Pres.'s Nat. Adv. Council on Extension and Continuing Edn.; mem. White House Conf. on Internat. Cooperation, 1965, White House Conf. on Edn., 1965, mem. commn. acad. affairs Am. Council Edn. Bd. dirs. Gt. Books Found., Center Study Liberal Edn. Adults. Mem. N.E.A., Ednl. Screen (mem. editorial bd. 1947-50), Adult Edn. Assn. U.S.A. (pres. 1965-66), C. of C., Okla. Congress Parents and Tchrs. (state bd. mgrs., 1942—), Okla. Edn. Assn., Am. Legion, Okla. Mental Health Assn. (1st v.p.), Nat. U. Extension Assn. (chmn. liberal edn. com., chmn. on Extension Services in Armed Forces, rep. Am. Council on Edn., 1958-60, pres. 1960-61), S.W. Adult Edn. Assn. (exec. com.), Okla. Adult Edn. Assn., Phi Beta Kappa, Phi Delta Kappa, Psi Chi, Pi Kappa Alpha. Clubs: Internat. (Washington); Rotary. Editor: Adult Education. Contbr. articles ednl. jours. Home: 1105 Woodland Dr Norman OK 73069

WHITE, WALTER NYACK, hosp. and nursing home administr.; b. Cagayan, Philippines, Jan. 5, 1933 (came to U.S. 1937); s. Matthew James Walter III and Rita True (Rothgeb) W.; student Otterbein Coll., 1951-53; B.A. in Psychology, U. Va., 1956; postgrad. Med. Coll. Va. Sch. Hosp. Adminstrn., 1958-60; m. Joyce Woodard, Aug. 17, 1962; children—Kenneth Nyack, Kimberly True. Adminstrv. resident U. Va. Hosp., Charlottesville, 1960-61, adminstr. Children's Rehab. Center, 1961-63, adminstrv. asst., 1963-65; adminstr. R.J. Reynolds-Patrick County Meml. Hosp., 1965-69; adminstr. Page Meml. Hosp., Luray, Va., 1969-71; adminstr. Nursing Pavilion, Point Village, Christian and Missionary Alliance Found., Ft. Myers, Fla., 1971; now with Hillhaven, Inc., Tacoma, Wash. Chmn., Charlottesville-Albermarle Com. on Employment Physically Handicapped, 1963-65; mem. Ednl. TV Authority, Patrick County, Va., 1966-69, chmn., 1967-69; pres. Page County unit Am. Cancer Soc., 1970-71; past pres. Piedmont Tb and Respiratory Disease Assn.; past mem. curriculum devel. com. Lord Fairfax Community Coll. Served with USNR, 1956-58; 1st lt. Res., 1958-64. Mem. Am. Coll. Hosp. Adminstrs., Am. Hosp. Assn., Am. Acad. Med. Adminstrs., U. Va., Otterbein Coll., Med. Coll. Va. alumni Assns., Am., Va. hosp. assns., Am., Fla. nursing home assns. Home: 2636 Wisteria Pl Sarasota FL 33579

WHITE, W(ALTER) PRESTON, JR., lawyer; b. Lynchburg, Va., Apr. 19, 1923; s. Walter Preston and Virginia (Candler) W.; B.S., U. N.C., 1946, J.D., 1949; m. Kathryn Mary Whittle, Oct. 12, 1951; children—Edith Rebecca, Amy Patricia. Admitted to N.C. bar, 1949, Fla. bar, 1961, Ga. bar, 1969; gen. practice, Concord, N.C., 1949-51; spl. atty. Office of Chief Counsel, Internal Revenue Service, Washington, 1951-53, Birmingham, Ala., 1953-56, Jacksonville, Fla., 1956-58, asst. regional counsel, Jacksonville, 1958-62; partner Dowling, White & Mooers, 1962-68; staff asst. to regional counsel Internal Revenue Service, Atlanta, 1968—. Served to 2d lt. AC, OUC, 1942-46. Mem. Am., Jacksonville, N.C., Fed. bar assns., Fla. Bar, Phi Kappa Sigma, Delta Sigma Pi, Delta Theta Phi. Presbyn. Kiwanian. Home: 6851 Roswell Rd NE Atlanta GA 30328 Office: 275 Peachtree St Atlanta GA 32201

WHITE, WILBER SIDNEY, JR., dentist; b. Beaumont, Tex., Mar. 15, 1922; s. Wilber Sample and Florence Viola (Lloyd) W.; A.A., Lamar Jr. Coll., 1941; B.S., Sam Houston State Tchrs. Coll., 1943; Certified in Meteorology, U. Cal. at Los Angeles, 1944; D.D.S., Baylor U., 1950; m. Margaret Culver, June 5, 1949; children—Susan, Mary Katherine, Marilyn, Patricia, David, John, Paul, Sarah. Practice of dentistry, Beaumont, Tex., 1950—; dir. dental clinic City Health Clinic, 1967—; chmn. adv. com. Lamar Sch. Dental Hygiene, 1969—. Bd. dirs. Tex Found. Dental Health and Edn., Tex. Dental Plans, Inc., Citizens Nat. Dental Plan. Served to capt. A.C., AUS, 1943-47; CBI. Fellow Am. Coll. Dentistry; mem. Am. Dental Assn. (mem. council dental health 1971—, alternate ho. dels. 1972—, del. nat. health council), Tex. Dental Assn. (chmn. council dental health 1969-70; v.p. 1971—), Sabine Dist. Dental Soc. (pres. 1963, gen. chmn. spring clinic meetings 1963—), Am. Acad. Gen. Practice, Internat. Assn. Orthodontists, Tex. Pub. Health Assn., Chgo. Dental Soc. (asso.). Methodist. Mason (K.T., Shriner). Clubs: Sertoma (pres. 1963) Optimist (pres. 1954, lt. gov. 1958) Bus. and Profl. (pres. 1962) (Beaumont). Home: 3495 Kenwood Dr Beaumont TX 77706 Office: PO Box 5453 Beaumont TX 77702

WHITE, WILLIAM EARLE, lawyer; b. Dinwiddie County, Va., Aug. 19, 1898; s. William R. and Annie E. (Hone) W.; B.A., U. Richmond, 1917; postgrad. Harvard, 1919-20; m. Marian L. Molloy, Apr. 23, 1924; children—Marian Molloy (Mrs. P. T. Distanislao), William Earle, Stephen Graham. Admitted to Va. bar, 1920; gen. practice law, Petersburg, 1921—; mem. firm White, Hamilton, Wyche & Shell. Chmn. bd. Delta Oil Co.; dir., mem. exec. com. Commonwealth Gas Distbn. Corp. Fellow Am. Coll. Trial Lawyers, Am. Bar Found.; mem. Am., Va. State (pres. 1963-64), Petersburg bar assns., Am. Judicature Soc. Democrat. Baptist. Mason. Home: 2014 Woodland Rd Petersburg VA 23803 Office: 20 E Tabb St Petersburg VA 23803

WHITE, WILLIAM ERLE, bus. exec.; b. Brooken, Indian Ter., Oct. 13, 1907; s. Walter Alexander and Lily May (Oldham) W.; student pub. schs.; m. Emma Marietta Cosper, Oct. 30, 1930; children—Marilyn (Mrs. L. J. Onstott), Carolyn (Mrs. David Brown). Bookkeeper Highway Garage, Henryetta Okla., 1925-27; salesman Okla. Tire & Supply Co., Tulsa, 1927-30, mgr. El Reno, Okla., 1930-33; pres. dir. White Stores, Inc., Wichita Falls, Tex., 1942-69; chmn. bd., dir. Merc. Credit Corp., 1938—; pres., dir. Eureka Life Ins. Co. Am., 1953—, Beacon Nat. Ins. Co., Wichita Falls, Tex.; dir. M.-K.- T. R.R. (St. Louis), Coleman Co. (Wichita); chmn. bd. 1st Wichita Nat. Bank. Dir. Meth. Hosp., Dallas, Bethania Hosp., Wichita Falls, Wichita Falls Boys' Club, Midwestern University. Mem. Retail Furniture Assn. Tex. (dir.). Methodist. Mason. Home: 3200 Hamilton Blvd Wichita Falls TX 76808 Office: 2600 Midwestern Pkwy Wichita Falls TX 76307

WHITE, WILLIAM SMITH, journalist; b. DeLeon, Tex., May 20, 1907; s. John Van Dyke and Lucia Alberta (Smith) W.; student U. Tex., 1923-26; m. Irene Mason (div. 1945); m. 2d, June McConnell, Apr. 12, 1945; children—Lucia Stanton, Ann Victoria. Successively corr., feature writer, editor, war editor, assault war corr. A.P., 1926-45; Washington staff N.Y. Times, 1945—, senate corr., 1953-56, chief congl. corr., 1956-58, nationally syndicated polit. columnist, 1958; Washington corr. Harper's mag. 1957-58, contbg. editor, 1958-62; regents prof. U. Cal., Berkeley, 1957-58. Served with inf. AUS, 1942. Recipient Pulitzer prize in letters, 1955. Mem. Overseas Writers, Sigma Delta Chi. Clubs: Century (N.Y.C.); Nat. Press, Metropolitan, Cosmos (Washington). Author: The Taft Story, 1955; Citadel: The Story of the U.S. Senate, 1957; Majesty and Mischief: A Mixed Tribute to F.D.R., 1961; The Professional: Lyndon B. Johnson, 1964; Home Place, 1963; The Responsibles, 1972. Contbr. mags. Address: 2101 Connecticut Av NW Washington DC 20008

WHITED, SAM THOMPSON, govt. ofcl.; b. White Bluff, Tenn., July 3, 1909; s. Samuel Stephen and Elizabeth (Thompson) W.; B.E. in Civil Engring., Vanderbilt U., 1932; m. Hazel Inez Speight, Nov. 28, 1937; 1 son, Sam Thompson. Engr., Tenn. Planning Commn., Nashville, 1934-37, chief clk., 1937-39, personnel technician, 1939-42, dep. dir., 1942-48, 49-55, 59-61, dir., 1948-49, acting dir., 1955-59, acting commr., 1961-63, dep. commr. personnel dept., 1963—. Mayor, White Bluff, Tenn., 1937-41; mem. Dickson County Planning Commn., 1968—. Served from pvt. to capt., AUS, 1942-46. Mem. Pub. Personnel Assn., Am. Legion Democrat. Methodist. Elk. Home: White Bluff TN 37187 Office: Cordell Hull Bldg Nashville TN 37219

WHITEFIELD, NORMAN WAINWRIGHT, educator; b. Sinton, Tex., Feb. 18, 1921; s. Emmit C. and Mable (Howland) W.; B.A., Abilene Christian Coll., 1947; M.A., U. Denver, 1954; postgrad. Case Western Res. U., 1966-68; m. Joyce Fulbright, Dec. 7, 1943. Instr., Abilene (Tex.) Christian Coll., 1948-58, prof., head dept. art, 1958—. Bd. dirs. Abilene Fine Arts Mus. Served with USAAF, 1943-45. Decorated Air medal. Mem. Coll. Art Assn., Soc. for Aesthetics. Mem. Ch. of Christ. Home: 610 E N 19th St Abilene TX 79601

WHITEHEAD, CLAY THOMAS, govt. ofcl.; b. Neodesha, Kan., Nov. 13, 1938; s. Clay Bell and Helen (Hinton) W.; B.S., Mass. Inst. Tech., 1960, M.S., 1961, Ph.D., 1967. Tech. aide Bell Telephone Labs., Murray Hill, N.J., 1958-59, sr. tech. aid, 1960; cons. to RAND Corp., Santa Monica, Cal., 1961, 62, 63, organizer policy research program on health services, 1967-69; teaching asst. Mass. Inst. Tech., Cambridge, 1962-63, lectr., 1966-67; mem. Pres.-elect's Task Force on Budget Policies, Washington, 1968-69; spl. asst. to Pres., Washington, 1969-70; dir. Office Telecommunications Policy, Washington, 1970—. Cons. to Bur. Budget, Washington, 1966-68. Served from 1st lt. to capt., AUS, 1963-65. Mem. Sigma Xi, Tau Beta Pi, Eta Kappa Nu. Office: 1800 G St NW Washington DC 20504

WHITEHEAD, ELLIS, linen supply co. exec.; b. Rockmart, Ga., Oct. 3, 1910; s. Claude E. and Willie May (Phinizy) W.; B.S. in Textile Engring., Ga. Inst. Tech., 1932; m. Louise Miller, July 8, 1940; children—Jon, Tanya. Plant supt. Pepperell Mfg. Co., Lindale, Ga., 1933-45; pres. Whitehead Laundry and Cleaners, Inc., Dalton, Ga., 1945-52, Whitehead Woven Wire, Inc., Covington, Ga., 1951-54; owner, operator Whitehead Linen Supply, Dalton, 1952—; dir., chmn. trust com. 1st Nat. Bank, Dalton, pres., Whitfield Indsl. Park, Dalton, 1957—, Ga. Linen Service, Rome, 1957—. Pres. Jr. Achievement Dalton, 1967-68. Mem. Whitfield County Democratic Exec. Com., 1948-54. Chmn. bd. trustees Dalton Jr. Coll. Found. Recipient citation for service to organized recreation Mayor and Council City Dalton, 1963, Lay award Ga. Recreation Soc., 1962. Mem. Linen Supply Assn. Am. (dir., treas. 1966-69), Southeastern Linen Supply Assn. (pres. 1960-61), Dalton C. of C. (pres. 1951-52). Presbyn. (chmn. bd. deacons). Rotarian (pres. 1966-67). Club: Dalton Golf and Country. Home: 606 S Thornton Av Dalton GA 30720 Office: 1024 Dozier St Dalton GA 30720

WHITEHEAD, H(ARRIS) THORNTON, banker; b. Townsend, Va., Aug. 26, 1918; s. Claude Douvault and Nora (Elliott) W.; B.C.S., Strayer Coll., 1940; m. Karlotta Jacob, May 18, 1962. With Union Trust Co., Washington, 1941—, auditor, 1951-60, comptroller. 1960-64, v.p., comptroller, 1965-70, sr. v.p., 1971—. Mem. Am., D.C. bankers assns., Am. Inst. Banking, Internat. Platform Assn., Washington Bd. Trade, Phi Theta Pi. Republican. Presbyn. Club: Internat. (Washington). Home: 6534 Renwood Lane Annandale VA 22003 Office: 15th and H Sts NW Washington DC 20005

WHITEHEAD, LUCIE KEBLINGER (MRS. LAURENCE WHITEHEAD), assn. exec.; b. Clyde, Tex., Jan. 24, 1896; d.Thomas White and Alma (Kendrick) Keblinger; A.B., Trinity U., 1917; postgrad. U. Cal., U. Wis.; M.A., Columbia, 1921; grad. study Vassar Inst. Euthenics, Va. U.; m. Laurence Conner Whitehead, July 30, 1925; children—Lucie Jean (Mrs. Francis Stanley Bourne), Mary Ann (Mrs. Arthur Bartlett Hague, Jr.). Asso. prof. history and econs. Kidd-Key Coll., Sherman, Tex., 1921-22, Sul Ross State Coll., Alphine, Tex., 1922-23; Sam Houston State Coll., 1923-24; mgr., owner twenty farms in Tex., 1935—. Pres. San Antonio YWCA, 1968—; mem. Tex. adv. com. for organizing new YWCA's, mem. nat. pub. affairs com., participant internat. seminar in connection with UN Commn. Status of Women; vice chmn. bd. dirs. Peninsular Playhouse, Inc., mem. Alumni Council, charter mem. Taylor Fine Arts Center, Trinity U.; asso. San Antonio Symphony Soc.; active Community Welfare and Tex. Social Welfare Orgns. Mem. League Women Voters, Comal County, San Antonio conservation socs., Am. Assn. U. Women, P.E.O., Rotary Wives. Presbyn. Home: 280 Tuxedo Av San Antonio TX 78209

WHITEHEAD, RICHARD HOLMES, univ. ofcl.; b. Largo, Fla., July 9, 1917; s. James George and Janie (Taylor) W.; B.A., U. Fla., 1940, postgrad., 1954-56; grad. certificate in meteorology Cal. Inst. Tech., 1942; m. Martha Dallas Colson, Sept. 29, 1941; children—Carolyn Jo (Mrs. Robert Griffin Harrell), Karen Louise (Mrs. Wayne Lawrence Martin), Barbara Anne (Mrs. Jimmie Melvin Brunson), Shirley Jean. Chief clk. Registrar's Office, U. Fla., Gainesville, 1938-42, asst. registrar, 1946-52, asso. registrar, 1952-65, dean admissions, registrar, 1965—. Served to maj. USAAF, 1942-46. Mem. Am., Fla. (past pres.) assns. collegiate registrars and admissions officers, Assn. Coll. Admission Councillors, Fla. Assn. Ednl. Data Processors, Phi Kappa Phi, Alpha Phi Omega, Phi Gamma Delta. Mem. Ch. of Christ (bishop). Kiwanian. Club: Optimist (past pres.). Home: 923 NW 21st Terrace Gainesville FL 32601

WHITEHEAD, THOMAS HILLYER, univ. dean emeritus; b. Maysville, Ga., Sept. 5, 1904; s. Asa Hillyer and Clara (Comer) W.; B.S., U. Ga., 1925; M.A., Columbia, 1928, Ph.D., 1930; m. Dorothy Simms, Dec. 19, 1931; children—Thomas Hillyer, John Simms. Head sci. dept. Athens (Ga.) High Sch., 1925-27; asst. in chemistry Columbia, 1927-30; asst. prof., asso. prof. U. Ga., Athens, 1930-39, prof. chemistry, 1939—, asso. dean, 1967-68, dean Grad. Sch., 1968-72, dean emeritus, 1972—. Cons., AEC, Aiken, S.C., McGraw-Hill Informations System, U.S. Office of Edn. Served with AUS, 1942-46, 51-52. Mem. A.A.A.S., Sigma Xi, Phi Kappa Phi, Phi Lambda Upsilon, Chi Psi. Democrat. Methodist. Kiwanian (pres. 1958). Home: 236 Henderson Av Athens GA 30601

WHITEHOUSE, ULYSSES GRANT, II, chemist, educator; b. Henderson, Ky., July 27, 1917; s. Ulysses Grant and Rosa (Leascher) W.; B.S. magna cum laude, U. Ky., 1940, M.S. magna cum laude (Sullivan Meml. fellow), 1941; M.S. (Chem. Research fellow), U. Ia., 1959; postgrad. (research fellow) Carnegie Inst. Tech., 1948-50; Ph.D. in Chemistry magna cum laude (Dow fellow, Am. Petroleum Inst. fellow), Tex. A. and M. U., 1953, Ph.D. in Oceanography, 1955; m. Doris Yvonne Sheets, Dec. 21, 1954; 1 son, Ulysses Grant III. Research supr. U.S. Rubber Co., Williamsport, Pa., 1942-43; asso. research dir. Carbide & Carbon Chems., Brook, N.J., 1945-47; research scientist div. war research Columbia, N.Y.C., 1943-45; prof., research dir. electron microscopy and colloid sci. Tex. A. and M. U., College Station, 1953—, research project dir., oceanography and colloid chem. cons. Found., 1953—. Dir. research projects NIH, 1959—, Office Naval Research, 1953—, NSF, 1958—, Am. Petroleum Inst., 1951-53; cons. U.S. Corps Engrs., 1954—, Tex. Indsl. Commn., 1960—. Recipient Distinguished Service award Manhattan Project, 1945. Fellow A.A.A.S., Am. Inst. Chemists; mem. Am. Chem. Soc. (tour lectr. 1968-72), Am. Petroleum Inst., Assn. Atomic Scientists, Electron Microscope Soc. Am., Geochem. Soc. Am., Soc. Limnology and Oceanography, Lenshawks Photog. Soc., Profl. Photograhers Assn., N.Y. Acad. Sci., Phi Beta Kappa, Sigma Xi, Phi Kappa Phi, Sigma Pi Sigma, Phi Lambda Upsilon, Omicron Delta Kappa, Alpha Chi Sigma. Moose. Club: Brazos Valley Kennel (pres. Bryan 1968-70). Contbr. numerous articles on colloid chemistry, clay mineralogy, phys. chem. to profl. publs. Pioneer colloid chem. interactions in saline waters; biomed. research. Home: 4309 Nagle St Bryan TX 77801 Office: Electron Microscopy Div Tex A and M U College Station TX 77843

WHITEHURST, CLINTON HOWARD, JR., economist, educator; b. Richmond, Va., May 29, 1927; s. Clinton Howard and Elizabeth (Leech) W.; B.S., Fla. State U., 1957, M.A., 1958; Ph.D., U. Va., 1962; m. Marion Ard, Mar. 2, 1957; children—Elizabeth Leech, Clinton Howard III. Asst. prof. Clemson (S.C.) U., 1960-63, asso. prof., 1963-68; prof., 1968—, head dept. indsl. mgmt., 1964—; cons. on econometrics, regional econs., transp. econs. to govtl. agys. Served with U.S. Mcht. Marine, 1944-53. AUS, 1953-55. Mem. Am., So. econ. assns., S.C. Acad. Sci., Inst. Mgmt. Scis., U.S. Naval Inst., Am. Inst. Indsl. Engrs., S.A.R., Phi Kappa Phi, Pi Sigma Alpha. Republican. Contbr. articles to profl. jours. Editor, Clemson U. Rev. Indsl. Mgmt. and Textile Sci., 1967. Home: Box 47 Clemson SC 29631

WHITEHURST, GEORGE WILLIAM, congressman; b. Norfolk, Va., Mar. 12, 1925; s. Calvert Stanhope and Laura (Tomlinson) W.; B.A., Washington and Lee U., 1950; M.A., U. Va., 1951; student W. Va. U., 1956-57, Ph.D., 1962; m. Jennette Seymour Franks, Aug. 24, 1946; children— Frances Seymour (Mrs. James Fitzgerald), Calvert Stanhope. Mem. faculty Old Dominion U., 1950-68, dean students, prof. history, 1963-68; news analyst sta. WTAR-TV, 1962-68; mem. 91st-92d Congresses, 2d Dist. Va. Past mem. Mayor Norfolk Commn. Crime and Delinquency, Tidewater Council Health and Welfare, Norfolk Council Alcoholism. Past pres. Norfolk chpt. Am. Assn. UN, Norfolk Forum; past chmn. Am. Cancer Soc. crusade in Norfolk. Served with USNR, 1943-46. Decorated Air Medal with oak leaf cluster. Mem. Am. Hellenic Ednl. and Philanthropic Assn., Fleet Res. Assn. (hon.), Am. Legion, V.F.W., Delta Upsilon. Methodist (past chmn. bd.). Lion, Rotarian. Home: 7320 Glenroie Av Norfolk VA 23505 also 2300 S 24th St Arlington VA 22206 Office: Cannon House Office Bldg Washington DC 20515

WHITELEY, KENNETH CHARLES, lawyer; b. Kelton, Tex., Jan. 27, 1933; s. Charley and Laura Rachel (Carothers) W.; B.B.A., Tex. Tech. U., 1955; J.D., So. Meth. U., 1961; m. Martha Ann Ogle, Jan. 29, 1954; children— Karen Jan and Sharon Ann (twins), Jonathan Mark. Engr., writer Gen. Dynamics, Fort Worth, 1957-61; admitted to Tex. bar, 1961; practiced in Hurst, 1964—; asst. dist. atty., Fort Worth, 1961-64; pvt. practice, 1964-69; with firm Whitely & Boring; Hurst; 1969—. Municipal judge, Hurst, Tex., 1965—. Served with AUS, 1955-57. Mem. Am., Tex., Fort Worth Tarrant County, N.E. Tarrant County (pres. 1969), Arlington (sec.-treas. 1964) bar assns., Municipal Judges Assn., Hurst-Bedford-Euless C. of C. (dir. 1969). Lion. Home: 1700 Brown Trail Hurst TX 76053 Office: 300 Bedford Rd Hurst TX 76053

WHITEMAN, HAROLD BARTLETT, JR., coll. pres.; b. Nashville, Apr. 22, 1920; s. Harold Bartlett and Emma Morrow (Anderson) W.; student Montgomery Bell Acad., 1937-34, Taft Sch., 1934-37; A.B., Yale, 1941, Ph.D., 1958; M.A., Vanderbilt U., 1950; m. Edith Uhler Davis, July 13, 1946; children—Bartlett, Maclin, Priscilla. Adminstrv. asst. Pan Am. Airways Africa, Ltd., 1941-42; instr. Taft Sch., 1946-47, trustee, 1950-55; teaching fellow Vanderbilt U., 1947-48; asst. dean freshmen, dean undergrad. affairs, 1948-54; dean of freshmen Yale, 1954-64, lectr. in history, 1956-64, asst. to pres., 1964-67; asst. chancellor N.Y. U., 1967-69, vice chancellor, 1969-71, prof. govt. and internat. relations, 1966-71; pres. Sweet Briar Coll., 1971—. Bd. dirs. Episcopal Ch. Found.; trustee, Hollins Coll., chmn. bd. trustees Berkeley Div. Sch. Served as maj. in USAAF, 1942-46. Mem. Phi Beta Kappa, Delta Kappa Epsilon, Scroll and Key. Author: Neutrality 1941, 1941. Editor: Charles Seymour, Letters from the Paris Peace Conf., 1965. Home: Sweet Briar Coll Sweet Briar VA 24595

WHITENACK, HAROLD WILLIAM, constrn. co. exec.; b. Portland, Ind., Mar. 30, 1915; s. Grant and Blanche (Wise) W.; grad. high sch.; m. Virginia Stults, May 15, 1939; children—Marjorie Sue (Mrs. Roger Johnson), Lindia Jane Haughmeir. Supt. Portland Forge & Foundry (Ind.), 1939-52; plant mgr. Walker Forge, Racine, Wis., 1952-57; plant mgr. Dietz Forge, DeKalb, Ill., 1957-62; mgr. Diamond Acres Inc., Lead Hill, Ark., 1962-67; owner, mgr. Whitenack Constrn., Diamond City, 1967—. Mem. Home Builders Ark. (pres. 1970, 71). Mason. Home: Box 103 Lead Hill AR 72644 Office: Box 164 Diamond City AR 72644

WHITESEL, THEODORE LEWIS, educator; b. Charleston, Ill., Nov. 2, 1907; s. John Allen and Ida (Newby) W.; B.Ed., Eastern Ill. U., 1931; B.S., U. Ill., 1932, M.S., 1934, Ph.D., 1952; postgrad. Cornell U., 1946, U. Mich., summers 1946, 47, N.Y. U., summer 1952; m. Cora Hoffpauir, Dec. 23, 1961 (dec. July 1962). Accountant, No. N.J., 1936-40; asst. prof. econ. Parsons Coll., 1940-41; instr. indsl. engring. adminstrn. Cornell U., 1941-46; asst. prof. indsl. and engring. adminstrn., 1949-50; asst. prof. econs. U. Ark., 1946-48, U. Detroit, 1948-49; asst. prof. econs. U. Ill., 1951-52; asso. prof. finance Mont. State U., 1952-55; asso. prof. econs. Winona State Coll., 1955-58; asso. prof. econs. and finance La. Poly. Inst., 1958-62; asso. prof. econs. and finance U. Tex., Arlington, 1962-67, prof., 1967—. Instr. engring. sci. mgmt. War Tng. program U.S. Office Edn., N.Y., 1942-45. Faculty Research fellow in econs. Ford Found., summer 1960. Mem. Am., So., Western econ. assns., Am. Finance Assn., Am. Accounting Assn., Am. Assn. U. Profs., Assn. for Evolutionary Econs., Southwestern Social Sci. Assn., Phi Kappa Phi, Beta Gamma Sigma, Kappa Delta Pi, Alpha Kappa Psi. Home: 1821 Kenwood Terrace Arlington TX 76010

WHITESELL, JAMES EDWIN, coll. dean; b. Buchanan, Va., Nov. 21, 1909; s. William James and Cora Estelle (Brubaker) W.; A.B., Randolph-Macon Coll., 1930; M.A., Harvard, 1931, Ph.D., 1935; m. Lyla Virginia Bergdoll, Apr. 27, 1936; children—James Thomas, Carolyn Virginia. Instr., English, Northwestern U., 1935-39; asst. prof. Mary Washington Coll., U. Va., 1939-44; asso. prof. U. S.C., Columbia, 1946-49, prof. English, 1949-66; dean Sch. Arts and Scis. Va. Commonwealth U. (formerly Richmond Profl. Inst.); 1966—. Served to lt. USNR, 1944-46. Mem. Am. Assn. U. Profs. (chpt. pres. 1950-51, sec.-treas. S.C. conf. 1958-60, sec.-treas. S.E. region 1960-63), Modern Lang. Assn., Am. Dialect Soc., Nat. Council Tchrs. English, Coll. English Assn., S. Atlantic Modern Lang. Assn. (exec. com. 1965-68), Ga. S.C. Coll. English Assn. (pres. 1964-65), Blue Key, Phi Beta Kappa (pres. chpt. 1959-60), Sigma Upsilon, Omicron Delta Kappa. Co-founder, co-editor Explicator, 1942-54, mng. editor, 1954—; co-editor The Explicator Cyclopedia, Vol. 1: Modern Poetry, Vol. 2: Traditional Poetry, Vol. 3: prose; compiler The Explicator Cumulative Index, Vols. I-XX. Home: 3241 Archdale Rd Richmond VA 23235

WHITESELL, ROBERT WESLEY, social worker; b. Durham, N.C., Dec. 5, 1927; s. Robert Banks and Eula (Walters) W.; A.B., Houghton Coll., 1953; M.S. in Social Work, Richmond Profl. Inst., 1964; m. Agnes Julia Bonesteel, Dec. 20, 1950; children—Carol Elaine, David Robert, Paul Wesley, Elena Marta. Probation officer, supt. juvenile detention home Guilford County Domestic Relations Ct., Greensboro, N.C., 1957-63; coordinator services to children and alcoholics Mecklenburg County Mental Health Clinic, Charlotte, N.C., 1964-67; unit clin. social worker VA Hosp., Salisbury, N.C., 1967—. Field instr. U. N.C., 1966-70. Served with USNR, 1946-48, 53-55. Mem. Nat. Assn. Social Workers, Acad. Certified Social Workers. Home: 5849 Charing Pl Charlotte NC 28211 Office: 1601 Brenner Av Salisbury NC 28144

WHITESIDE, E. W., ednl. adminstr.; b. Moscow, Ark.; grad. Ark. State Coll; A.B., Lincoln U.; postgrad. Talledega Coll., U. Cin., U. Pa., U. Chgo., U. Ky., M.Ed., Pa. State U. Tchr., coach pub. schs., Augusta, Ga.; tchr. pub. schs., Paducah, Ky.; prin. Paducah Pub. Schs., now asst. dir. curriculum and guidance Paducah Pub. Schs. Mem. Paducah's Mayor's Com. for Indsl. Harmony, Paducah Housing Commn., Paducah Redevel. Program, Ky. Bd. Edn., Paducah Adv. Com. on Aging Mems., mem. adv. bd. Salvation Army, Paducah; mem. Paducah Human Rights Commn., mem. appeal bd. SSS; commr. Boy Scouts Am., Paducah; active numerous other civic orgns. Past mem. bd. dirs. McCracken County chpt. A.R.C.; past mem. bd. dirs., treas. Paducah-McCracken County Mental Health Assn.; trustee Paducah Community Coll. Served with U.S. Army. Recipient certificate of appreciation for service to SSS, 1971; named Duke of Paducah, Ky. col. Mem. N.E.A., Ky. (past dir.), 1st Dist. (organizer, past pres.) tchrs. assns., Ky., Paducah edn. assns., Ky. Ednl. Suprs. Assn., Am. Legion (past post comdr.), Kappa Alpha Psi. Baptist. Mason (32 deg.). Club: Paducah Teachers (founder, past pres.). Office: Board of Education Adminstrv Bldg Paducah KY 40601

WHITEWAY, HOWARD EARLE, steel co. exec.; b. Oak Park Ill., May 1, 1927; s. William Earl and Ivy Mae (James) W.; B.A., Westminster Coll., 1950; m. Sue Adelaide Sperry, July 1, 1950; children—Ralph, Paula, Nan. Vice pres. sales Corey Steel Co., Chgo., 1951-66, also dir.; exec. v.p. Jenks Metals Inc., Miami, 1966-69; pres., owner Asso. Steel Co. of Houston, 1969—. Pres. Oak Brook Sch. Bd., 1965. Served with AUS, 1945-46. Mem. Steel Service Center Inst. (pres. Central States chpt. 1965-66, Fla. chpt. 1968-69, v.p. Tex. chpt. 1970-71). Rotarian. Home: 11907 Memorial St Houston TX 77024 Office: 7211 Av B Houston TX 77011

WHITFIELD, CARROLL JULIAN, farm implement mfg. co. exec.; b. nr. Cairo, Ga., Feb. 24, 1931; s. Charles and Carolyn Amanda (Bryant) W.; student Middle Ga. Coll., 1948-49; B. M.E., Ga. Inst. Tech., 1955; m. Laura Susan Gandy, Dec. 27, 1955; children—Amanda Susan, Julia Carol, Miles Gandy. Design engr. Chemstrand Corp., textile machinery mfg., Pensacola, Fla., 1955-56, Timber Fabrications, pre-fabricated truss prodn., Perry, Fla., 1956-57; project engr. Lilliston Corp., farm implements mfg., Albany, Ga., 1957-67; v.p., dir. Kelley Mfg. Co., farm implements, Tifton, Ga., 1967—. Served with AUS, 1956. Mem. Am. Soc. M.E., Am. Soc. Agrl. Engrs., Tau Beta Pi, Pi Tau Sigma. Baptist. Patentee in field. Office: Kelley Mfg Co South Industrial Park PO Box 1145 Tifton GA 31794

WHITFIELD, JACK DUANE, aero. engr.; b. Paoli, Okla., May 16, 1928; s. Lloyd Vernon and Ethel Mae (Wigley) W.; B.S., U. Okla., 1951; M.S., U. Tenn., 1960; m. Marcheta Rae Steward, Sept. 11, 1949; children—Donna Rae, Jeffrey Dwayne, Karen Sue. Engr., Consol. Vultee Aircraft Corp., Daingerfield, Tex., 1951-54; with ARO, Inc., Arnold AFB, Tenn., 1954—, chief von Karman Gas Dynamics Facility, 1968—. Cons. Nat. d'Etudes et de Recherches Aeronautiques, adv. group Aero. Research and Devel., Paris, France, 1960; cons. VITRO/Smith Corp., N.Y.C., 1963. Troop treas. Middle Tenn. council Boy Scouts Am., 1966—; active P.T.A. Served with AUS, 1946-48. Recipient Gen. H. H. Arnold award for contbns. to aerodynamic testing by Tenn. sect. Am. Inst. Aero. and Astronautics, 1968. Mem. Am. Inst. Aero. and Astronautics (sec., treas. 1961-62). Methodist. Lion. Club: Ozarks Wildlife (Little Rock, Ark.). Contbr. articles in field to profl. jours. Home: 506 Edgewood Dr Tullahoma TN 37388 Office: ARO Inc von Karman Gas Dynamics Facility Arnold AFB TN 37389

WHITLEDGE, CLYDE OWEN, computer tape co. exec.; b. Sayre, Okla., Dec. 5, 1921; s. Clarence Othar and Myrta Jay (York) W.; A.A., Sayre Jr. Coll., 1942; B.S. in M.E., U. Okla., 1949; postgrad. So. Meth. U., 1957; m. Kathryn Lucille Kennedy, Apr. 14, 1949; children— Dru Alan, Dana Ann. Air conditioning engr. Lone Star Gas Co., 1949-51; mgr. mfg. missile div. Tex. Instruments, 1951-63; pres. M-H Equipment Co., 1963-65; mgr. mfg. Stanray Corp. div. Traveler Boat Co., 1965-66; chief engr. Magnetic Tape Systems, Geotech. Corp., 1966-67; sr. v.p. Graham Magnetics Mfg., Inc., Graham, Tex., 1967—. Served to lt. (j.g.) USNR, 1942-46. Mem. Okla. U. Alumni Assn., C. of C. (mem. ednl. com. 1969-72; mem. indsl. com. 1969-71), Nat. Soc. Profl. Engrs. Unitarian. Mason. Club: Graham Country. Home: 921 Cherry St Graham TX 76046 Office: Graham TX 76046

WHITLOCK, FRED HENRY, mathematician; b. Winston-Salem, N.C., June 17, 1936; s. Henry Fred and Luvenia (Edwards) W.; B.S., N.C. A. and T. State U., 1959; m. Barbara Hill, Nov. 2, 1962; children—Carlton Fred, Kenneth Henry, Jacquelyn Ewaugh. Mathematician, sci. programmer NASA, Goodard Space Flight Center, Greenbelt, Md., 1962—. Mem. D.C. Young Democrats, 1964-68; mem. S.E. Washington Young Democrats, 1964-68. Served with AUS, 1959-62. Mem. Math. Assn. Am., Assn. for Computing Machinery, Nat. Urban League, Anacostia Civic Assn. Author: Orbit Prediction Accuracy Theory, 1963; Interplanetary Trajectory Encke Method Program, Manual 1, 1967, Manual 2, 1967, Manual for IBM OS/360, 1970; also articles in field. Home: 166 Chesapeake St SW Washington DC 20032 Office: Code 642 Bldg 1 Goodard Space Flight Center Greenbelt MD 20771

WHITLOCK, JAMES EDWARD, state legislator, savs. and loan exec.; b. Lebanon, Ky., Jan. 20, 1934; s. Robert Henry and Carrie (Benningfield) W.; student Bellarmine Coll., 1952-53; B.S., U. Ky., 1960; m. Barbara M. Hazard, Jan. 2, 1956; children—James Edward, Vincent Murrell, Elizebeth, Stephen. Owner real estate, gen. ins. agy., Lebanon, 1961-65; mem. Ky. Ho. of Reps., 1962-68, chief clk., 1968-70; pres., dir. Taylor County Fed. Savs. and Loan Assn., Campbellsville, Ky. Mem. Ky. Bldg. and Loan Legislative Com. Served with USMCR, 1954-58. Mem. Am. Legion, Lebanon Jr. C. of C. K.C. Home: 407 Lebanon Av Campbellsville KY 42718 Office: 1st and Broadway Campbellsville KY 42718

WHITLOCK, JAMES WILLIAM, ednl. adminstr.; b. Pulaski, Tenn., July 25, 1921; s. Cecil Ray and Mary Ruth (Phillips) W.; B.S., U. Tenn., 1949; M.A., George Peabody Coll., 1952, Ed.D., 1955; m. Dorothy Louise Long, June 1, 1945; children—Lawrence, Cathy. Tchr., Tullahoma (Tenn.) city schs., 1949-52; prin. Elkton High Sch., 1952-54; with Tenn. State Dept. Edn., 1955-58; prof. edn. Peabody Coll., Nashville, 1958-61; asso. dir. div. surveys and field service U.S. Office of Edn., 1961-62; dir. div. surveys and field service George Peabody Coll. for Tchrs., Nashville, 1962—; cons. Trustee, Harding Place Children's Home, 1965-69, Mid-State Educators Credit Union, 1965—. Served with USMCR, 1941-45. Mem. Nat. Council Ednl. Facility Planners, N.E.A., Am. Assn. Sch. Adminstrs., Assn. Sch. Bus. Ofcls.; Tenn. Edn. Assn. Author: Automatic Data Processing in Education, 1960; Jobs and Training for Southern Youth, 1962; Educational Data Systems, 1964. Home: 5947 Lone Meadow Rd Nashville TN 37205 Office: Box 164 Peabody Coll Nashville TN 37203

WHITLOCK, (JUDY) MARY ELLEN JENKINS (MRS. DOUGLAS WHITLOCK), social worker; b. Brownville, Neb., Sept. 3, 1906; d. John Crisler and Mabel (Sapp) Jenkins; student Sullins Coll., 1923-24, Ferris Inst., 1924—; A.B., Ind. U., 1927; m. Douglas Whitlock, June 18, 1929; children—Douglas Whitlock II, Marilyn (Mrs. Robert E. Long), Sandra (Mrs. Theodore G. Driscoll, Jr.). Case worker Children's Aid Soc., Detroit, 1927-28, head adoption dept., 1928-29; case supr. Asso. Charities Washington, 1929-32. Mem. Women's Inaugural Com., Washington, 1953, 57. Chmn. women's com. Devereux Found., Devon, Pa., 1959-61. Mem. League Republican Women, Nat. Fedn. Rep. Women. Bd. dirs. Family Service Assn. of Am., Goodwill Industries Assn., Mental Health Assn., Vis. Nurse Assn. Trustee Family and Child Services, Washington, 1951-65, 1st v.p., 1962-65; v.p. Episcopal Ch. Women of Washington, 1963, pres., 1969-72. Recipient award Alpha Omicron Pi, 1963, award Diocese of Loash. Mem. Ind. Soc. of Washington (mem. exec. bd. 1932—; recipient award 1962), Indiana U. Alumni Assn., Alpha Omicron Pi. Republican. Episcopalian (vestry-woman 1968-71). Clubs: Little Garden (pres. 1938-40), Wednesday (pres. 1940-42) (both of Sandy Spring, Md.); International Neighbors (1st pres. 1956-57, sec. 1969—) (Washington); Women of St. Thomas (pres. 1960-62). Home: 2550 Massachusetts Av NW Washington DC 20008

WHITLOW, ETHOLENE RAMSEY (MRS. HOMER P. WHITLOW), educator; b. Franklin County, Va., Aug. 6, 1910; d. Benjamin F. and Lillie (Hodges) Ramsey; student Coll. William and Mary; m. Homer P. Whitlow, Jan. 21, 1933; children—Berger M., Benjamin H., Mary Sue (Mrs. Arthur P. Burgess), D. Ramsey. Tchr., Snow Creek Sch., Martinsville, Va. 1948-58, became prin., 1959; later tchr. Callaway Elementary Sch., Rocky Mounty, Va., now tchr. Sontag Elementary Sch., Franklin County, Va. Mem. Va., Franklin County (v.p. 1962-64) edn. assns., N.E.A., Internat. Platform Assn. Methodist. Home: RFD 2 Rocky Mount VA 24151

WHITLOW, HUBERT HENRY, JR., librarian; b. Atlanta, Ga., Feb. 16, 1930; s. Hubert Henry and Ruby Lee (Simmons) W.; B.A., Emory U., 1951, M.L.S., 1956; M.A., U. Fla., 1967. Asst. catalog humanities librarian U. Ga., Athens, Ga., 1956-58; social scis. librarian, 1958-60; res. librarian Emory U., Atlanta, 1961-62, chief serials and binding dept., 1962-64, chief circulation dept., 1964-66, documents librarian, 1966-67, chief circulation dept., 1967-70; librarian Floyd Jr. Coll., Rome, Ga., 1971—. Served with USAF, 1951-55. Home: Rt 3 Rome GA 30161 Office: Floyd Junior Coll Library PO Box 789 Rome GA 30161

WHITMAN, AINSLEY ABBOTT, librarian; b. Pomona, Cal., Sept. 22, 1912; s. William Ainsley and Margaret (Abbott) W.; B.A., San Jose State Coll., 1935; B.S., La. State U., 1936; m. Joyce Bruner Whitman. Librarian, Rayne (La.) High Sch., 1935-37, Poinsett County Library, Harrisburg, Ark., 1937-39; asst. librarian La. Library Commn., Baton Rouge, 1939-40; library asst. San Jose State Coll., 1940-42; librarian Cal. State Poly. Coll., 1946-49, Coll. of Agr., U. Ga., 1949-50, Willamette U., 1950-55, Central State Coll., 1955-57; asst. librarian Jacksonville State Coll., 1957-62; librarian U. N.C. at Asheville, 1962—. Served with M.C., AUS, 1942-46. Mem. N.C., Am., Southeastern library assns., Am. Assn. U. Profs. Democrat. Episcopalian. Home: College Park Apts Asheville NC 28804 Office: D Hiden Ramsey Library Univ of NC Asheville NC 28801

WHITMAN, HOWARD, journalist; b. Cleve., May 6, 1914; s. Lawrence Alvin and Bettie (Goldman) W.; A.B. magna cum laude Western Res. U., 1935; m. Suzanne Marcia Desberg, Mar. 9, 1938;

children—Constance Marcia, Kenneth Jay. Mem. staff N.Y. Herald Tribune, Paris edition, 1936, London Daily Express, 1936-37, N.Y. Daily News, 1937-45; war corr. E.T.O., World War II; specialist on articles on social problems since 1945. Mem. commn. mental health edn. Internat. Congress on Mental Health, 1948; lectr. sex edn., mental health, social problems. Pres. Grand Bahama Mental Health Assn., 1968-69. Comdr. Grand Bahama Boating Squadron, 1968-69. Joint winner Profl. Journalism award for pub. service for series articles in Collier's, Terror In Our Cities, Sigma Delta Chi, 1949-50; winner Partents' mag. book award, 1948-49; winner Freedoms Found. award for the article The Truth About Patriotism, 1952, for TV series A Time to Remember, 1956, for TV program The Flag, 1970; Blakeslee award Am. Heart Assn., 1956; TV award Nat. Assn. Mental Health, 1957; First award for program Nervous Tension, Ohio State U. Inst. for Radio and TV, 1961. Clubs: Saugatuck Harbor Yacht (commodore 1965), Palm Beach Nat. Golf. Author: Let's Tell The Truth About Sex, 1948; Terror in the Streets, 1951; A Reporter in Search of God, 1953; Success Is Within You, 1956; A Brighter Later Life, 1961; The Sex Age, 1962; syndicated news series: Vandalism, 1953, The Divorce Dilemma, 1954; Parenthood Without Hokum, 1955; Keeping Our Sanity, 1957: Our Moral Crisis, 1958; Our Drinking Habits, 1958; New Frontiers in Living, 1959; Your Middle Years, 1961; Making Marriage More Rewarding, 1962; Don't Be Nervous, 1963; The American Way of Love, 1964; Our Family Crisis, 1968; appeared NBC-Television series Howard Whitman Talks, 1953; News of Medicine and Health, NBC-TV, 1956; roving editor NBC-TV Home Show, 1957; Dumont television series Probe, 1957-58; Collier's series The Struggle for our Children's Minds, 1954; Better Homes and Gardens series America's Moral Crisis, 1957; commentator WPTV, Palm Beach, 1970. Producer nat. TV series Medical Special Events, 1958-61; News of Your Life, NBC-TV, 1962-64; NBC radio Emphasis, 1964-66, NBC Monitor, 1967-70; News About You, 1970; also nationally syndicated newspaper spls., 1971. Address: 2165 Ibis Isle Rd Palm Beach FL 33480

WHITMER, KENNETH SWEET, ophthalmologist; b. Dayton, O., Jan. 23, 1910; s. Rollo R. and Winifred (Ball) W.; A.B., Miami U. (Oxford, O.), 1931; M.D., Ohio State U., 1936; m. Marcia Ann Butcher, Sept. 14, 1968; children—Cynthia Ann (Mrs. William Thomas), Patricia, Kenneth Sweet, Carl N. Intern, Jackson Meml. Hosp., 1936-39; resident Detroit Reciving Hosp., 1939-40; pvt. practice medicine specializing in ophthalmology, Miami, Fla., 1940—; mem. staff Childrens, Victoria, Coral Gables hosps., cons. VA Hosp., Miami; clin. prof. ophthalmology U. Miami Sch. Medicine, Served to maj. USAAF, World War II. Mem. Am. Assn. Opthalmology (trustee), Alpha Kappa Kappa, Sigma Chi. Presbyn. Kiwanian (bd. dirs.). Home: 2000 Tigertail St Miami FL 33133 Office: 550 Brickell Av Miami FL 33133

WHITMIRE, BOYCE AUGUSTUS, lawyer; b. Brevard, N.C., Oct. 21, 1905; s. William P. and Annie (Floyd) W.; student U. N.C., 1924-26, Wake Forest U., 1926-28; m. Hazel Patricia Bean, July 1, 1929; children—Boyce Augustus, Jr., William F., Guy P., John F., James T., Patricia L. Admitted to N.C. bar, 1928, since practiced in Hendersonville. Past pres. Hendersonville YMCA. Mem. Henderson County Bd. Edn., 1963-69; mem. N.C. Ho. of Reps., 1959-61; mem. N.C. Senate, 1961-63; mayor, Hendersonville, 1969—. Trustee Western Carolina U., 1963—. Baptist. Mason, Lion (pres. 1946), Elk (exalted ruler 1943-44, pres. N.C. assn. 1946-47). Home: 201 Ewbank Dr Hendersonville NC 28739 Office: 4th Av W Hendersonville NC 28739

WHITMIRE, CHARLES DANIEL, pub. accountant; b. Shepherd, Tenn., July 10, 1921; s. William Madison and Mintie (Lingerfelt) W.; grad. McKenzie Bus. Coll., 1950; m. Bonnie Bryan, Apr. 7, 1944; children— Alfred, Hayden, Charline (Mrs. Larry T. Elliott). Clk.-typist U.S. Civil Service, 1946; office mgr. Electric Power Coop., Iuka, Miss., 1948-52; office mgr. Hydratane Gas Co., Athens, Tenn., 1953-55; staff accountant W.W. Stribling & Co., C.P.A.'s, 1955-60; sales service mgr. Carpet Mill, Dalton, Ga., 1960-65; treas. World Carpets, Inc., 1965-71; owner C.D. Whitmire and Co., C.P.A.'s, Dalton, 1971—. Served with USAF, 1939-45. C.P.A., Ga. Mem. Am. Inst. C.P.A.'s, Ga. Soc. C.P.A.'s Office: 126 W Gordon St Dalton GA 30720

WHITMORE, ALDEN WILCHER, ednl. adminstr.; b. Broadway, Va., Feb. 16, 1919; s. Allen Wilcher and Kitty (Aldhizer) W.; B.Ed., U. Va., 1943, M.Ed., 1953, Ed.D., 1969; m. Marjorie Evelyn Foltz, Jan. 2, 1942; 1 son, Alden Wilcher. Tchr. social studies, coach, Albemarle and Rockingham Counties, Va., 1946-52; prin. elementary and secondary schs., Amherst County, Va., 1954-56; supervising prin. Lexington (Va.) Pub. Schs., 1956-60; prin. Lexington High Sch., 1960-66; gen. supr. Danville (Va.) City Schs., 1968—. Served with AUS, World War II. Decorated Bronze Star medal. Mem. Va., Nat., Danville (pres.) edn. assns., Kappa Delta Pi, Phi Delta Kappa. Baptist (dir. Sunday sch. 1971, deacon 1972—). Club: Lions Internat. (pres. 1964-65, dir. 1962-64, 71—). Home: 110 Briarcliff Pl Danville VA 24541 Office: 313 Municipal Bldg Danville VA 24541

WHITMORE, JOHN EDWIN, banker; b. Tucumcari, N.M., Dec. 17, 1907; s. John Elias and Margaret (Neafus) W.; student U. N.M., 1926-29; LL.B., Jefferson U., 1937; m. Clara Bauman, Mar. 28, 1942; children— John Edwin III, Maria, James C., Margaret. Admitted to Tex. bar, 1937; with Tex. Commerce Bank, Houston (formerly Tex. Nat. Bank Commerce), 1945—, pres., 1965-69, chmn. bd., chief exec. officer, 1969—; chmn. bd. dirs. Tex. Commerce Bancshares, Inc.; dir. Houston br. Fed. Res. Bank of Dallas, Gordon Jewelry Co. Trustee Baylor Coll. Medicine. Served to lt. comdr. USNR, 1942-45. Mem. Res. City Bankers Assn., Tex. Bar Assn., Houston C. of C. (dir.), Pi Kappa Alpha. Democrat. Presbyn. Mason. Clubs: Houston, Ramada, River Oaks Country (Houston). Home: 704 W Friar Tuck Lane Houston TX 77024 Office: 712 Main St Houston TX 77002

WHITMORE, STEPHEN BOYD, govt. ofcl.; b. Boonton, N.J., July 2, 1913; s. Leonard Cecil and Florence (Boyd) W.; grad. N.Y. State Mcht. Marine Acad., 1933; m. Margaret E. Vollmer, June 1, 1950; children— Gail (Mrs. Howard Langford), Stephen T., R. Neale. Career officer Grace, Farrell, Alcoa S.S. Cos., 1933-56; constrn. engr. Carrier Corp., Atlanta, 1956-61, Gen. Services Adminstrn., Atlanta, 1961-65; regional facilities mgr. Environmental Protection Agy.-Region IV, Atlanta, 1971—. Clubs: United States Figure Skating Assn. (Eastern com. 1967—, figure skating judge 1964—, ice dancing judge 1967—), Atlanta Figure Skating (dir.) Home: 340 Dogwood Dr Athens GA 30601 Office: 1421 Peachtree St NE Atlanta GA 30309

WHITNER, GEORGE CRABTREE, banker; b. Jacksonville, Fla., June 27, 1923; s. John Addison and Eleanor (Crabtree) W.; B.S., U. N.C., 1947; m. Virginia Hilyard, Dec. 3, 1955; children—Banta H., Virginia, Eleanor, John A. Field supt. Whitner & Lawrence, Inc., Fire & Casualty Gen. Agts., 1947-57; agy. supt. N.Y. Underwriters Ins. Co., 1957-58; v.p. Fla. Nat. Bank Jacksonville, 1958—, dir., 1968—, vice chmn., 1972—. Treas., Am. Cancer Soc., 1960-63; pres. Speech & Hearing Center, 1966, Fla. Jr. Coll. at Jacksonville Found., Inc., 1972. Bd. dirs. Travelers Aid. Served to lt. (j.g.) USNR, 1943-46. Mem. Meninak Internat. (treas., dir. Jacksonville 1969—). Clubs: River, Timuquana Country (Jacksonville). Presbyn. Office: 214 Hogan St Jacksonville FL 32202

WHITNEY, ADELBERT GRANT, merc., ins. co. exec.; b. Lowell, Mass., July 25, 1917; s. Adelbert Howard and Julia (Sheehan) W.; B.S. in Bus. Adminstrn., Boston U., 1940; m. Lillian Ritch DeArmon, Nov. 17, 1950; children—Julia Woodley, Adelbert Grant, Frank DeArmon. Asst. to v.p. Belk Stores, Charlotte, N.C., 1946-52, asst. to pres., 1952-55; v.p., sec.-treas. Belk Stores Ins. Reciprocal, Belk Underwriters, Inc., Charlotte, 1950-58, exec. v.p., sec-treas., 1958—; sec.-treas. Archdale Mut. Ins. Co., 1962-65, exec. v.p., sec.-treas., 1965—; gen. mgr. ins. dept. Belk Stores, 1951—; sec., mem. exec. com. Belk Stores Services, Inc., 1959-68, v.p., 1964-68; v.p., sec.-treas. Providence Realty Corp., Charlotte, 1950-63, pres., 1959-60, pres., treas., 1964—; v.p. Queen City Investors, Inc., Charlotte, 1959-62; sec. Thrifty Investors, Inc., Charlotte, 1961-62. Mem. exec. com. Arthritis and Rheumatism Found., Charlotte, 1959-60, dir., 1959-60; v.p. Mecklenburg council Boy Scouts Am., 1962-66; chmn. N.C. U.S.O., 1959—; spl. gifts chmn. N.C. div. Am. Cancer Soc., 1967; program chmn. Charlotte Bi-Centennial Celebration Com., 1968. Bd. dirs. Mecklenburg Citizens Better Libraries, 1967—; bd. dirs. Charlotte Council on Alcoholism, Goodwill Industries Charlotte, Inc., N.C. Multiple Sclerosis Soc., Festival in the Park; chmn. promotional activities planning com. Downtown Charlotte Assn. Served as officer AUS, World War II. Recipient Distinguished Service award Jr. C. of C., 1952; named Charlotte Young Man of Year, 1952; recipient Silver Beaver award Boy Scouts Am., 1956, Soldiers Medal for Heroism U.S. Army; elected to Exec. and Profl. Hall Fame, 1966 mem. selection com., 1967—; recipient Distinguished Service award Charlotte Exchange Club, 1967. Mem. Am. Soc. Ins. Mgmt. (pres. Carolinas chpt. 1963-64, nat. v.p. conf. activities 1965-66, 1st v.p. 1966-67, pres. 1967-68, Man of Yr. award, Pres.'s award 1971), Am. Mgmt. Assn., Nat. Assn. Ind. Insurers (v.p., 1953-67), U.S. (mem. ins. com. 1967-69), Charlotte chambers commerce, Am. Legion, Carolina Carrousel (hon.), Jr. Achievement, Inc., Royal Soc. Knights Carrousel (pres. 1954-64, chmn. governing council 1964-68), Soc. 1st Div. Inf., Assn. U.S. Army, Am. Found. Religion and Psychiatry (gov. 1959—), French Fgn. Legion (hon.). Presbyn. (elder). Mason (33 degree, Shriner), Lion. Clubs: Boston University Alumni of the Carolinas, Executives (pres. 1963-64), Myers Park Country, Charlotte City, Goodfellows (Charlotte). Home: 684 Colville Rd Charlotte NC 28207 Office: 308 E 5th St Charlotte NC 28202

WHITNEY, J. WILBUR WAYNE, JR., investment exec.; b. Tulsa, Mar. 22, 1926; B.S., Tulsa U., 1949; m. Blanche Tiffany, Jan. 17, 1947; children—David Michael, Diann Tiffany, J. Wilbur Wayne III. Dist. petroleum engr. Magnolia Petroleum Co., Electra, Tex., 1949-55; gen. prodn. supt. Helmerich & Payne, Inc., Tulsa, 1955-61; pres. Whitney Operating Co., Whitney Engring. Co., Tulsa, 1961-64; pres., dir. White Shield Corp., Tulsa, 1966-70; pvt. investments, 1971— dir. Utica Sq. Nat. Bank, Tulsa. Served with inf. AUS, 1945-46. Mem. Soc. Petroleum Engrs., Am. Petroleum Inst., Ind. Petroleum Assn. Am.,Okla. Ind. Producers Assn. (dir.). Home: 3021 S Wheeling St Tulsa OK 74114 Office: 1804 First Nat Bldg Tulsa OK 74103

WHITNEY, JOHN EDWARD, educator; b. Casper, Wyo., July 6, 1926; s. Gary M. and Harriett (Whitney) W.; A.B., U. Cal., Berkeley, 1947, M.A., 1948, Ph.D., 1951; Ph.D., U. Cambridge (Eng.), 1956; m. Barbara Laundrie, June 11, 1949; children—Karen, Kathleen, Eric, Emily, Brian. Research asso. Cedars of Lebanon, Los Angeles, 1951-52, U. Cal., Los Angeles, 1952-54, U. Cambridge (Eng.), 1954-56; mem. faculty U. Ark., Little Rock, 1959—, prof. physiology, head dept., 1962—. Served with USNR, 1944-45. Mem. Am. Physiology Soc., Soc. Exptl. Biology and Medicine, Endocrine Soc., A.A.A.S., Sigma Xi, Alpha Omega Alpha. Home: 7016 Rockwood St Little Rock AR 72207

WHITNEY, RANDALL BROOKS, physician; b. Selma, Ala., July 13, 1933; s. Edwin George and Wanda Livesay (Hess) W.; B.S., Tulane U., 1955, M.D., 1959; m. Martha Carole Bowden, Dec. 21, 1963; children—Aubrey Mark, Lisa Claire, Robin Laurel. Intern, Duval Med. Center, Jacksonville, Fla., 1959-60; resident in gen. practice San Bernardino County (Cal.) Hosp., 1963-65; pvt. practice medicine, Mount Dora, Fla., 1965—. Pres., Parent-Tchr. Orgn., 1969-70. Bd. mgmt. Duval Home for Mentally Retarded, Deland, Fla., 1970—. Recipient Distinguished Service award Mt. Dora Jr. C. of C., 1969. Mem. A.M.A., Fla., So. med. assns., Lake County Med. Soc., Mt. Dora C. of C. (pres. 1969). Democrat. Presbyn. Rotarian. Home: 351 W 10th St Mount Dora FL 32757 Office: 1100 Morningside Dr Mount Dora FL 32757

WHITSEL, TRAVIS SEWELL, mgmt. cons.; b. Jackson County, Miss., Aug. 13, 1890; s. Nelson Brown and Myrtle (Sewell) W.; B.S. in Mech. Engring., Purdue U., 1911; m. Irene Tracy, June 11, 1921 (dec. Aug. 1930); children—Travis Sewell, Ruth (Mrs. Norman E. Westphal), Audrey (Mrs. Randolph Wedding), Cynthia (Mrs. William Borden), Joyce (Mrs. Frank W. Bean); m. 2d, Gertrude Ann Louise Van Hermann, Aug. 12, 1933. Rancher nr. Ft. Stockton, Tex., 1904-45; fireman C.I. & L. R.R. Co., 1911-14; tchr. pub. schs., Laketon, Ind., 1914-15; with Union Spl. Machine Co., Chgo., 1919-61, v.p. sales, 1940-61; pvt. practice as mgmt. cons., Chgo. Served to capt. U.S. Army, 1916-19. Mem. Underwear Inst., Internat. Assn. Clothing Designers, Am. Assn. Apparel Mfs. (past chmn. tech. adv. com.), Textile Hall Fame. Clubs: Burning Tree (Washington); Capitol City (Atlanta); Lake Shore (Chgo.); St. Petersburg (Fla.) Yacht; Lakewood Country. Address: 2901 58th Av N St Petersburg FL 33714

WHITSON, BILL JOSEPH, city ofcl.; b. nr. Newport, Tenn., Aug. 8, 1938; s. James Garland and Bessie Mae (Denton) W.; student Carson-Newman Coll., 1955-56; m. Betty Hicks, Aug. 26, 1956; 1 son, Russell. Mem. research dept. staff Alcoa Aluminum, Cleve., 1957-58; salesman Kickliter Ford, Inc., Newport, 1959-65; mgr. Newport Chrysler-Plymouth, 1966-67; city recorder, city judge, Newport, 1967—. Chmn. Cocke County Young Republican Club, 1971—. Baptist. Kiwanian, Moose. Home: 205 Sequoyah Dr Newport TN 37821 Office: Box 390 Newport TN 37821

WHITSON, JAMES NORFLEET, JR., diversified co. exec.; b. Clinton, Okla., Mar. 14, 1935; s. James Norfleet and Georgia (Webb) W.; B.B.A., Tex. Tech. Coll., 1957; m. Lyda Lee Gibson, Apr. 19, 1956; 1 son, James Mark. Field accountant Texfel Petroleum Corp., Monshans, Tex., 1957-59; accountant Wickett Refining Co., Monahans, 1959-60; accounting supr. LTV, Inc., Dallas, 1960-63, asst. to treas., 1963-66, asst. treas., 1966-67, asst. dir. financial plans, 1967-68; v.p. finance LTV Ling Altec, Inc., Dallas, 1968—; dir. Tamar Electronics Industries, Inc. Mem. Alpha Tau Omega. Home: 9758 Wisterwood St Dallas TX 75238 Office: PO Box 30385 Dallas TX 75230

WHITT, DONALD EDWARD, supt. schs.; b. Muenster, Tex., June 22, 1937; s. William Buford and Nomie (Bowles) W.; student Arlington State Coll., 1955-57; B.S., Tex. A. and M. U., 1959; postgrad. E. Tex. State U., 1964; M.Ed., N. Tex. State U., 1966, postgrad., 1966—; m. Geraldine Ann Geary, Aug. 30, 1959; children—Daniel, Andrea, Carter, Douglas. Tchr. Grapevine (Tex.) Pub. Schs., 1960-66, adminstrv. asst., 1966-68, asst. supt., 1968-70; supt. schs. Kennedale (Tex.) Pub. Schs., 1970-72, Wylie (Tex.) Pub. Schs., 1972—. Mem. Am., Tex. assns. sch. adminstrs., Tex. Tchrs. Assn., Tarrant County Supt. and Prins. Assn., Kennedale C. of C. (dir.), Phi Delta Kappa, Alpha Zeta. Mason. Home: Box 666 Wylie TX 75098 Office: Box 490 Wylie TX 75098

WHITT, JIMMY LEE, real estate broker; b. Carmen, Ky., Mar. 16, 1934; s. Ertel L. and Elmo (Coleman) W.; B.S. in Mech. Engring., U. Ky., 1957; m. Shirley Anne Arrington, Aug. 18, 1956; children—Jennifer Anne, Melissa Jayne. Mech. engr. Somet Solvay div. Allied Chem. and Dye Corp., Tralee, W.Va., 1957; plant layout engr. Sperry Piedmont div. Sperry Rand Corp., Charlottesville, Va., 1959-61; plant mgr. E. R. Carpenter Co., Richmond, Va., 1961; owner gen. contracting bus., Charlottesville, 1961-65; gen. mgr. Frank A. O'Neill Constrn., Charlottesville, 1965-69; v.p., dir. Blue Ridge Bldg. and Devel. Co., Charlottesville, 1965-69; owner Whitt & Co., real estate, 1969—. Served with USAF, 1957-59. Registered profl. engr., Ky. Mem. Home Builders Assn. (nat. dir. 1963-66), Blue Ridge Home Builders Assn. (1st pres. 1963-65, state dir. 1963-66). Presbyn. Home: Whispering Pines RFD 3 Box 460 Charlottesville VA 22901 Office: 2248 Ivy Rd Charlottesville VA 22903

WHITT, LONNIE WELDON, cosmetic co. exec.; b. Medina, Tenn., Dec. 17, 1923; s. Thomas Clifford and Emma Jane (Blackwell) W.; student W. Tenn. Bus. Coll., Jackson, 1946-47, Memphis Coll. Accountancy, 1950-54; m. Annie B. Jones, Dec. 14, 1946; children—Lonnie Franklin (dec.), Danny Wayne. Accountant, Firestone Tire & Rubber Co., Memphis, 1948-49; exec. v.p., dir. J. Strickland & Co., Memphis, 1961—; pres. Comml. Towel & Uniform Co., Memphis, 1961-65; exec. v.p., dir. Hoyt Co., Inc., Memphis, 1961—; exec. v.p., dir. Beauty Creations, Inc., Memphis, 1961—; v.p., dir. Elco Co., Inc., Memphis, 1961—, The Loreco Co., Memphis, 1961—. Past dirs. Jr. Achievement, Inc. Served with AUS, 1943-45. Decorated Bronze Star medal. Baptist. Home: 2893 Signal Memphis TN 38127 Office: 1400 Ragan St Memhis TN 38106

WHITTAKER, LEON, educator; b. Benton, La., Oct. 7, 1927; s. Osborne and Mamie (Owens) W.; B.S., Grambling Coll., 1949; M.A., Mich. State U., 1956; Ed.D., Wash. State U., 1966; m. Clarice Jordan, June 8, 1952; children—Lino Gerard, Leona Marie, Sharon Ann, Eric Durand. Tchr., Bossier Parish Sch. Bd., 1949-50, 52-55; counselor, dir. placement Grambling (La.) Coll., 1956-70, dean students, prof. edn., 1970—. Cons. Coll. Placement Services, Inc., 1968—. Served with AUS, 1950-52. Mem. Am. Psychol. Assn., Am. Personnel and Guidance Assn., Phi Delta Kappa, Alpha Phi Omega. Mem. Christian M.E. Ch. (steward, lay leader). Mason (Shriner). Home: PO Box 422 Grambling LA 71245

WHITTEMORE, FRANK JACKSON, investment banker; b. Morgan County, Tenn., Jan. 11, 1918; s. Frank and Annie (Penn) W.; B.A., U. N.C., LL.B., 1942; m. Valor M. Snyder (div.); 1 son, Stephan Rand; m. 2d, Ann M. Seaman; step-children—Derek Letz, Jon Letz, Paula Letz. Various positions family interest in tobacco, comml. banking, savs. & loan assn., mortgage co., farming, ranching, 1939—; exec. v.p., dir. Kassler & Co., mortgage bankers, Denver, 1945-56; pres. dir. Franklin Investment Co., Denver, 1956-62; dir., chmn. bd. Met. Co., other land devel., bldg. cos., 1956—; v.p., asst. to exec. v.p. Douglas L. Elliman & Co., N.Y.C.; asso. Ben G. McGuire & Co., Houston, 1965—; chmn. Intebon Corp., Wilmington, Del.: pres. Met. Mortgage Co., Houston, Franklin Investors, Houston; dir. Continental Corp., Franklin Financial, Peachtree Mortgage Corp., Atlanta. Cons. various corps., State of Fla., 1963. Served to lt. comdr. USNR, 1942-45. Mem. Am. Savs. and Loan Inst. (pres. 4th dist. 1942), Mortgage Bankers Assn. (pres. Colo. 1955), Internat. Soc. Real Estate Appraisers (pres. Denver 1954), Mil. Order World Wars. Episcopalian (vestryman). Contbr. articles various publs. Office: PO Box 42177 Houston TX 77042

WHITTEMORE (EDWARD) REED, II, educator, writer; b. New Haven, Sept. 11, 1919; s. Edward Reed and Margaret Eleanor (Carr) W.; A.B., Yale, 1941; student Princeton, 1945-46; m. Helen Lundeen, Oct. 3, 1952; children— Catherine Carr, Edward Reed III, John Lundeen and Margaret Goodhue Whittemore. Mem. faculty Carleton Coll., 1947-67, prof. English, 1962-67, chmn. dept., 1962-64; program asso. Nat. Inst. Pub. Affairs, 1966—; editor Carleton Miscellany, 1960-64; cons. in poetry Library of Congress, 1964-65; Bain-Swiggett lectr. Princeton U., 1967—; prof. U. Md., 1968—. Served to capt. USAAF, 1941-45. Mem. Assn. Lit. Mags. Am. (dir. 1961—). Author: Heroes and Heroines, 1947; An American Takes a Walk, 1956; The Self-Made Man, 1959; The Boy From Iowa, 1962; The Fascination of the Abomination, 1963; Poems, New and Selected, 1967; From Zero to the Absolute, 1967. Editor: Furioso, 1939-53; Browning, 1960. Home: 3509 Macomb St NW Washington DC 20016 Office: 1825 K St Washington DC 20006

WHITTEMORE, ROBERT CLIFTON, educator; b. Lockport, N.Y., Feb. 1, 1921; s. Clifton Houghton and Zelia Florence (Duke) W.; B.A., Yale, 1949, M.A., 1951, Ph.D., 1953; m. Dorothy Jane Gordon, June 15, 1959; stepchildren—Stanley Allen Lawton, Shirley Anne Lawton. Instr., Yale, 1950-52; mem. faculty Tulane U., prof. philosophy, 1963—, also dean Univ. Coll., 1968—. Served with AUS, 1942-45. Mem. Am. Philos. Assn., Metaphys. Soc. Am., So. Soc. Philosophy and Psychology, Southwestern Philos. Conf., Indian Philos. Congress. Episcopalian. Author: Makers of the American Mind, 1964. Home: 7521 Dominican St New Orleans LA 70118

WHITTEN, DOLPHUS, JR., univ. pres.; b. Hope, Ark., June 20, 1916; s. Dolphus and Annie Tyree (Logan) W.; B.A., Ouachita Coll., 1936; M.A., U. Tex., 1940, Ph.D., 1961; postgrad. Western Res. U.; LL.D; McMurry Coll., Abilene, Tex., 1964; m. Marie Braden, May 1, 1939; 1 dau., Suzanne (Mrs. H. Robert Guy). High Sch. tchr. and prin., Ark. pub. schs., 1936-42; prin. Hope Jr.-Sr. High Sch., 1945-47; dir. extension and placement services, asso. prof. history Henderson State Tchrs. Coll., Arkadelphia, Ark., 1947-58; adminstrv. dean Oklahoma City U., 1958-61, adminstrv. v.p., 1961-70, acting pres., 1962-63, 69-70, pres. 1970—. Bd. dirs. Community Council Oklahoma City Symphony Soc., Okla. Rehab. Assn., Civic Music Assn., Okla. Health Scis. Assn.; Frontiers of Sci. Found. Served with USAAF, 1942-45; lt. col. Res. Mem. Assn. Field Services Tchrs. Edn. (past pres.), Okla. Edn. Assn., Am. Hist. Assn., UN Assn. (dir.), Okla. Zool. Soc. (dir.), Okla. Council Chs., Newcomen Soc., Alpha Chi (past pres. region II), Gamma Mu, Phi Alpha Theta. United Methodist. (ofcl. bd.; bd. edn. Okla. conf., jurisdictional bd. edn., gen. bd. publs., gen. commn. ecumenical affairs). Rotarian. Home: 2501 N Blackwelder St Oklahoma City OK 73106

WHITTEN, JAMIE LLOYD, congressman; b. Cascilla, Miss., Apr. 18, 1910; s. Alymer Guy and Nettie (Early) W.; student lit. and law depts. U. Miss., 1926-31; m. Rebecca Thompson, June 20, 1940. Prin. pub. sch., 1931; elected Miss. Legislature, 1931; dist. atty. 17th Dist. of Miss., 1933, reelected, 1935, 39; mem. 77th-92d Congresses from 2d Miss. Dist. Mem. Beta Theta Pi, Phi Alpha Delta, Omicron Delta Kappa. Democrat. Mason. Home: Charleston MS 38921 also 5804 Nebraska Av Washington DC 20015

WHITTENBURG, JOE DANIEL, newspaper exec.; b. Pelmons, Tex., Feb. 19, 1918; s. George Allen and Lillie (Archer) W.; grad. high sch.; m. Wanda Jeanne Smith, Oct. 9, 1937; children—Joe Daniel, Wanda Jeanne. Pres., MM Cattle Co., Amarillo, Tex., 1949—; with Globe-News Pub. Co., 1952-72, v.p., 1937-72, also dir.; dir. Avalanche-Jour. Pub. Co., Plains Radio Broadcasting Co., Spool Oil Co. (all Amarillo). Served with AUS, 1942-45. Presbyn. Club: Hundred (Amarillo). Home: 2 Greenwood Lane Amarillo TX 79109 Office: 305 W 9th Av Amarillo TX 79101

WHITTINGTON, PAUL ELVIN, govt. ofcl.; b. Guthrie, W.Va., Oct. 1, 1908; s. James Elvin and Georgianna (Ballard) W.; student W.Va. Inst. Tech., 1928-30, George Washington U., 1941-45; m. Helen Beatrice Tucker, Aug. 27, 1938; children—Judith A. (Mrs. Zar), Dorothy L. Engr., City of Charleston (W.Va.), 1930; engr. W.Va. Dept. Engring., Charleston, 1932-33; mech. engr. Union Carbide and Carbon Co., South Charleston, W.Va., 1934-38, Havens & Emerson, Cleve., 1939; with U.S. Army Materiel Comd., Washington and Natick, Mass., 1939—, mech. engr., Washington, 1966—. Mem. Research Soc. Am. (chpt. pres. 1964, mem. coms.), Psi Delta, Phi Zeta Kappa. Unitarian (bd. sessions ch.). Mason (32 deg.). Patentee life support system for space exploitation including moon walks, other spl. Army equipment. Home: 9208 Forest Haven Dr Alexandria VA 22309 Office: Hdqrs US Army Materiel Command Bldg T-7 Gravelly Point Washington DC 20315

WHITTINGTON, TONY BURNICE, ednl. adminstr.; b. Amarillo, Tex., Mar. 21, 1940; s. Claude Burnice and Velda Marjorie (Grounds) W.; B.B.A. in Advt., Tex. Technol. Coll., 1963, M.Ed. in Higher Edn., 1971; m. Judith Lynn Prideaux, Jan. 21, 1967. Asst. dir. pub. relations Children's Hosp., Columbus, O., 1968-69; housing mgr. Tex. Technol. U., Lubbock, 1969—. Served to capt. USAF, 1963-68; Vietnam. Mem. Pub. Relations Soc. Am., Columbus Jr. C. of C. Home: 3520 41st St Lubbock TX 79413

WHITTLESEY, EDWARD DEMING, assn. exec.; b. Old Mystic, Conn., May 21, 1905; s. Frederick Averill and Elizabeth (Weiant) W.; B.A., Coll. of Emporia, 1931; grad. Pulitzer Sch. of Journalism, 1935; postgrad. Tchr.'s Coll., 1930, Columbia U., 1933, Western Res. U., 1937-39; m. Helen Marie Miller, Dec. 25, 1928; children— David Edward, Wayne Averill. Reporter, Emporia (Kan.) Gazette, 1925-26; editor asst. Keller Pub. Co., N.Y.C., 1927; rewrite man Cleve. News, 1928; editor Lakewood (O.) Courier, 1929-30; dir. publicity, lectr. journalism and advt. Coll. Emporia, 1931-33; pres. Whittlesey Pub. Co., N.Y.C. (now Research Inst. of Am.), 1934-36; dir. publicity Western Res. U., Cleve., 1937-44, U. Denver, 1945-49, U. Fla., Gainesville, 1949-55, Fla. State U. at Tallahassee 1955-60; fund raiser Ketchum, Inc., Pitts., 1960-62; bond sales coordinator South Miami (Fla) Hosp., 1967-69; devel. officer Papanicolaou Cancer Research Inst., Miami, 1962-63, 1969—; dir. Research Services, Inc., Denver, 1947—. Recipient Ad of the Year, Denver Advt. Club, 1946, 47, 48. Mem. Pub. Relations Soc. Am. 1950-56, pres. Fla. chpt. 1957), Am. Coll. Pub. Relations Assn. (pres. 1944; Distinguished Service award 1948), Fla. Pub. Relations Assn. (pres. 1954), Nat. Soc. of Fee Appraisers (sec. Miami chpt. 1970), Omicron Delta Kappa, Sigma Delta Chi, Alpha Delta Sigma, Sigma Chi. Kiwanian, Rotarian, Elk. Clubs: Hollywood Stamp (Hollywood, Fla.); Miami Beach Executive, Miami-Dade Civitan Pres. 1972-73). Home: 2210 Alton Rd Miami Beach FL 33140 Office: 1155 NW 14th St Miami FL 33136

WHITTON, GILBERT MARSHALL, JR., county agrl. agt.; b. Albany, Mo., Mar. 2, 1922; s. Gilbert Marshall and Susan Louvina (Trimm) W.; A.A.B., Kansas City Jr. Coll., 1950; B.S. in Agr., U. Fla., 1955, M.A., 1957; m. Helen E. Vermeulen, Nov. 23, 1945 (div. Sept. 1966); children—Thomas Clemmens, Marsha Susan. Asst. county agt., U.S. Dept. Agr., Largo, Fla., 1957-63, asso. agt., 1963-64, county agent 1964—; weekly and daily TV program, WLCY, St. Petersburg, 1965; writer daily newspaper columns Clearwater Sun, 1957—, St. Petersburg Evening Ind., 1958—. Served with USNR, 1940-45, 1947-52. Recipient citation for outstanding service, WDAE Radio Sta., Tampa, Fla., 1965; citation for service beyond normal job affiliation Fla. West Coast Gulf Course Supts. Assn., 1967; fellowship award for advanced study Fla. Agrl. Council, 1955. Mem. Fla. Turf Grass Assn. (bd. dirs. 1965—), Fla. Nurserymen and Growers Assn., Phytopathology, Helminthological Soc., Pinellas County Horticulture Club, Pinellas County Rose Soc. Methodist. Mason. Home: PO Box 267 Largo FL 33540

WHITTON, PAUL LEWIS, retail co. exec.; b. Appleby, Tex., Aug. 2, 1909; s. Lewis Alexander and Mary Elmira (Ward) W.; B.S., Stephen F. Austin U., 1930; M.Ed., U. Tex., 1935; m. Robbie Katherine Morton, Feb. 20, 1942; children—Paul Lewis, Linda Kay (Mrs. James Martin Hill), James Morton. Tchr., prin., supt. pub. schs., Tex., 1930-66; pres. Miller's Visual Aids, Inc., Fort Worth, 1966—. Served with A.C., AUS, 1942-45. Mem. Tex. Assn. Sch. Adminstrs. (life), Scholarship Soc. of South. Democrat. Methodist. Mason. Club: Optimist (Ft. Worth). Home: 3913 Clayton Rd E Fort Worth TX 76116 Office: 100 N University Dr Fort Worth TX 76107

WHITWORTH, VIRGIL LEE, photo-geologist; b. Nevada, Mo., Feb. 29, 1896; s. Robert Lee and Cora (Robertson) W.; B.S. in Geology, Mo. Sch. Mines, 1923; refresher course in multiplex machines, 1950. With Roxana (now Shell) Oil Co., 1923-26, Simms Oil Co. (now Tidal Oil), Dallas, 1926-28, Henry L. Doherty & Co., Ft. Worth, 1928-30; chief geologist Tex., Deep Rock Oil Co., Ft. Worth, 1930-31; with Continental Oil Co., Ft. Worth, 1936-42; cons. geologist to Brazilian Govt. and introduced photo-geology to Brazil while with Drilling and Exploration Co. in Brazil, 1946-48, photo-geology for co. in West Tex. area, 1948-49; cons. geologist Washington, 1950-53, Abilene, Tex., 1953-55; with Saxon Exploration Co. and Allison, Prestridge & Anderson Co., 1953-55; engaged in photogeology, Cal., 1955-57; now cons. photogeology, U.S., Can., Alaska; asso. L.B. Oils, Ltd., Can.; cons. Shacron Oil Corp., Photogravity Co., Inc., Houston; with Amuedo & Ivy in cons. capacity; geomorphologist, lectr. in field. Discover oil fields, Tex., oil and gas fields Alta., Can., Tex. Served as capt. Photog. Intelligence, USAAF, 1942-45; CBI. Mem. Am. Assn. Petroleum Geologists, A.A.A.S., Am. Soc. Photogrammetry, Abilene (Tex.) Petroleum Club, Houston Geol. Soc., Internat. Platform Assn., Pi Kappa Alpha. Christian Scientist. Mason (Shriner). Club: Castille (Houston). Houston House 1617 Fannin St Houston TX 77002 Office: Photogravity Co Inc Adair Center 6440 Hillcroft St Houston TX 77017

WHORTON, GARY PAUL, banker; b. New Bern, N.C., Oct. 26, 1943; s. Elmo and Margaurite (Hardy) W.; student South Ga. Coll., 1963; m. Marcia O. Babbitt, Mar. 25, 1967; 1 dau., Jennifer Ann. Teller, 1st Nat. Bank, Brunswick, Ga., 1963-64; bookkeeper 1st Nat. Bank, Merritt Island, Fla., 1965-66; head bookkeeper South Seminole Bank, Fern Park, Fla., 1966; cashier Am. Nat. Bank & Trust, St. Petersburg, Fla., 1967-69, Hendry County Bank, Labelle, Fla., 1969; exec. v.p., dir. Beach Nat. Bank, Ft. Myers Beach, Fla., 1970—. Bd. dirs. Ft. Myers Beach Library Tax Dist., 1971. Served with AUS, 1963-64. Mem. Ft. Myers Beach C. of C. (dir. 1971). Home: PO Box 4059 Fort Myers Beach FL 33931 Office: 2525 Esterow Blvd Ft Myers Beach FL 33931

WHYTE, JAMES LUCAS, publishing co. exec.; b. Highland Park, Mich., Feb. 18, 1927; s. Horace Brittain and Ardelia Mirinda (Lucas) W.; student Albion Coll., 1946-48, Grand Rapids Jr. Coll., 1946-47, Miami Law Sch. 1949-50; B.A., U. Miami, 1951; m. Doris Lucile Newburn, Dec. 17, 1949; children—Michael Brittain, Martha Jean, James Newburn. Reporter, sports editor Hollywood Sun-Tattler, 1951-54, editor, asst. pub., 1954-66; editorial writer Miami (Fla.) News, 1953-54; v.p., gen. mgr. Savannah (Ga.) News-Press, 1966—; pres. Shamrock Aircraft Leasing, Inc., Savannah, since 1970—. Bd. dirs. Savannah chpt. A.R.C. Trustee Savannah Sci. Mus., 1967—. Served with AUS, 1945-46. Mem. Am. Soc. Newspaper Editors, Savannah C. of C. (dir. 1967-69), Assn. U.S. Army. Presbyn. (elder 1967—). Clubs: Savannah Golf, Savannah Inn and Country, Chatham. Home: 128 Winchester Dr Savannah GA 31404 Office: 111 W Bay St Savannah GA 31401

WHYTE, WILLIAM, journalist; b. Jersey City, Oct. 28, 1933; s. William James and Elizabeth (Richmond) W.; B.S., Rutgers U., 1957; m. Bonnie Patricia Smith, Apr. 20, 1963. With U.S. Dept. Agr., Washington, 1957—, editor Agrl. Situation, 1960-64, Employee Newsletter, 1965-67, originator, editor Report on Actions for a Better Environment, Response, 1971—, pesticide information officer, also Great Plains program information officer. Cons., contbr. Ency. Americana Yearbook, 1964-68. Mem. Fed. Editors Assn. (pres. 1963-64). Club: Nat. Press (Washington). Home: 1615 Greenbrier Ct Reston VA 22070 Office: US Dept Agr INF Washington DC 20250

WHYTE, WILLIAM GEORGE, steel co. exec.; b. Chgo., Sept. 14, 1915; s. Robert James and Georgia (Kirby) W.; B.S. in Commerce, U. Ill., 1937; postgrad. Journalism Sch., Northwestern U., 1938; m. Margaret Elizabeth Paine, Feb. 6, 1943; children—William Kirby, Roger James. Pub. relations dept. Western Electric Co., Chgo., 1937-41; pub. relations rep. U.S. Steel Corp., Chgo., 1946-49, staff asst. office of chmn., U.S. Steel, 1949-51, asst. dir. pub. relations, Chgo., 1951-52, asst. to v.p., Washington, 1952-57, asst. v.p., Washington, 1957-63, v.p., 1963—. Vice pres., chmn. finance com. Nat. Capitol Area council Boy Scouts Am.; v.p. membership and finance Fed. City Council. Trustee Am. U. Served from 2d lt. to col. AUS, 1941-46, with 3d Army, ETO. Decorated Legion of Merit, Bronze Star (U.S.); Croix de Guerre (France). Mem. Nat. Security Indsl. Assn. (past pres. Washington), Am. Iron and Steel Inst., Am. Soc. Naval Engrs., Am. Ordnance Assn., U.S. C. of C. (dir., chmn. pub. affairs com.). Republican. Methodist. Clubs: Carlton, Chevy Chase, Burning Tree, 1925 F Street, Metropolitan (Washington); Pine Valley Golf (Clementon, N.J.); Rolling Rock (Ligonier, Pa.). Home: 5124 Rockwood Pkwy Washington DC 20016 Office: 1625 K St NW Washington DC 20006

WICK, ROBERT EDWARD, airline co. exec.; b. Canova, S.D., Oct. 5, 1910; s. Peter Thorbergson and Maude (Gleason) W.; B.A., U. Minn., 1937; m. Helen Victoria Ohlund, Oct. 28, 1939; children—Peter L., Robert E., Janice Therese. Spl. agent F.B.I., 1942-59, insp., 1959-65, asst. dir., 1965-67; mgr. pub. relations Pan American World Airways, Inc., 1967—. Mem. Pub. Relations Soc. Am., Internat. Assn. Chiefs of Police, Sigma Delta Chi. Clubs: Nat. Press, Nat. Aviation, Aero (Washington). Episcopalian. Home: 2219 N Military Rd Arlington VA 22207 Office: 815 Fifteenth St NW Washington DC 20005

WICKENBERG, CHARLES HERBERT, newspaper editor; b. Charleston, S.C., Apr. 5, 1923; s. Charles Herbert and Lois (McAteer) W.; student The Citadel, 1942, U. N.C., 1945, U. S.C., 1946, Am. Press Inst. Columbia U., 1963; m. Margaret Smith Gall, Feb. 11, 1951; children— Elizabeth Caroline, Nancy Ross, Margaret Ann. Staff corr. U.P. Raleigh, N.C., 1946-47, Memphis, 1947—, Columbia, S.C., 1947-48, Mpls.-St. Paul, 1948-49; polit. writer News & Courier, Charleston, 1949-51; exec. sec. to gov. of S.C., 1954-57; S.C. bur. chief Charlotte (N.C.) Observer, 1958-62; govt. affairs editor The State, Columbia, 1962-63; exec. news editor The State-Columbia (S.C.) Record, 1963—. Trustee St. Mary's Jr. Coll., Raleigh; bd. dirs. Salvation Army. Served with USMCR 1942-45, 1950-52. Mem. A.P. Mng. Editors Assn., Am. Soc. Newspaper Editors, Columbia (pres.-elect) C. of C., Assn. U.S. Army, Sigma Delta Chi (S.C. pres. 1963), Sigma Nu (pres. 1946), Omicron Delta Kappa (pres. 1946). Episcopalian (sr. warden 1957-62). Club: Forest Lake Country. Home: 4540 Fernwood Rd Columbia SC 29206 Office: Box 1333 Columbia SC 29202

WICKENS, DONALD LEE, civil engr.; b. Oklahoma City, Aug. 11, 1934; s. Claude Preston and Idora (Wainscott) W.; B.S., Okla. State U., 1957, M.S., 1961, postgrad., 1961; m. Sylvia Ann Knopp, Aug. 25, 1957; children—Julia Ann, Donna Sue. Grad. asst. Okla. State U., 1960-61; structural engr. Hudgins Thompson Ball, Oklahoma City, 1961-65; chief structural engr. v.p. Benham-Blair & Affiliates, Oklahoma City, 1965—; v.p. Acad. Computing Corp., Oklahoma City, 1968-70. Served from lt. to capt., USAF, 1958-60. Registered profl. engr., Okla., Tex., Ark. Mem. Am. Concrete Inst. (sec.-treas. 1972), Prestressed Concrete Inst., C. of C., Phi Delta Theta (sec. 1956), Chi Epsilon, Sigma Tau. Lutheran (councilman 1969—). Mason. Author: (with James W. Gillespie) Design of a Concrete Rigid Frame Bridge, 1960; Analysis of Folded Plate Structures by the Carry Over Method, 1961. Home: 6504 N Omaha St Oklahoma City OK 73116 Office: 6323 N Grand Blvd Oklahoma City OK 73116

WICKER, SEABORN RICHMOND, JR., realtor; b. Abita Springs, La., June 19, 1933; s. Seaborn Richmond and Lula (Corbin) W.; B.B.A., La. State U., 1956; m. Jean Brown, Dec. 19, 1951; children—Debbie Leigh, Michael Keith, Brent Alton. Pres., Baton Rouge Millwork Inc., 1959-62; Archtl. Millwork, Inc., Baton Rouge, 1962-66, Realty Mart, Inc., Baton Rouge, 1966—; instr. real estate sales Baton Rouge YMCA. Commr. Baton Rouge Capital Regional Planning Commn. Vice-pres., bd. dirs. La. Realtors Assn. Found. Served with USNR, 1952-55. Mem. Nat. Inst. Real Estate Brokers (state chmn. 1971, regional v.p. 1972), La. Realtors Assn. (edn. com. 1970-72). Mason (32 deg.). Author: How to Know if You Are Motivated, 1970; Formula for Achievement, 1970; Want to Sell Every Listing You Take, 1971. Home: 1046 Wooddale Blvd Baton Rouge LA 70806 Office: 1739 Wooddale Blvd Baton Rouge LA 70806

WICKER, THOMAS CAREY, JR., judge; b. New Orleans, Aug. 1, 1923; s. Thomas Carey and Mary (Taylor) W.; B.B.A., Tulane U., 1944, LL.B, 1949; m. Lilliemae Hansen, Dec. 20, 1946 (div. June 1965); children—Thomas Carey III, Catherine Anne; m. 2d, Veronica Jean Di-Carlo Dec. 10, 1965. Admitted to La. bar, 1949; law clk. La. Supreme Ct., New Orleans, 1949-50; asst. U.S. Atty., 1950-53; practiced in New Orleans, 1953-72; mem. firm Simon, Wicker & Wiedemann, 1953-67; partner firm Wicker, Wieldemann & Fransen, 1967-72; dist. judge Jefferson Parish (La.), 1972—. Vice chmn. com. on pattern jury instrns. La. Supreme Ct. Served from ensign to lt. (j.g.), USNR, 1944-46. Mem. Am., La. (chmn. jr. bar sect. 1958-59, gov. 1958, mem. ho. of dels. 1960—, law reform com., chmn. com. on continuing legal edn. 1968, 69), New Orleans (chmn. jr. bar com. 1957-58), Jefferson Parish, Criminal Cts. (exec. com.) bar assns., La., Orleans (mem. bd.) assns. def. counsel, Tulane U. Alumni Assn. (past pres.), Am. Judicature Soc., Order of Coif, Beta Gamma Sigma, Pi Kappa Alpha. Democrat. Episcopalian. Rotarian (pres. 1971-72). Clubs: Metairie (La.) Country; Young Men's Business, Toastmaster's (pres. 1969), Touchdown (past pres.), Green Wave (v.p. 1967—) (New Orleans). Home: 3700 Cleveland Pl Metairie LA 70003 Office: New Courthouse Bldg Gretna LA 70053

WICKER, THOMAS GREY, newspaperman; b. Hamlet, N.C., June 18, 1926; s. Delancey David and Esta (Cameron) W.; A.B. in Journalism, U. N.C., 1948; Nieman fellow, Harvard, 1957-58; m. Neva Jewett McLean, Aug. 20, 1949; children—Cameron McLean, Thomas Grey. Exec. dir. Southern Pines (N.C.) C. of C., 1948-49; editor Sandhill Citizen, Aberdeen, N.C., 1949; mng. editor The Robesonian, Lumberton, N.C., 1949-50; pub. information dir. N.C. Bd. Pub. Welfare, 1950-51; copy editor Winston-Salem (N.C.) Jour., 1951-52, sport editor, 1954-55, Sunday feature editor, 1955-56, Washington corr., 1957, editorial writer, city hall corr., 1958-59; asso. editor Nashville Tennesseean, 1959-60; mem. staff Washington bur. N.Y. Times, 1960—, chief bur., 1964—, asso. editor N.Y. Times, 1968—. Served to lt. (j.g.) USNR, 1952-54. Mem. Soc. Nieman Fellows. Author: (pseudonym Paul Connolly) (novels) Get Out of Town, 1951, Tears Are For Angels, 1952, So Fair, So Evil, 1955; (under own name) (novels) The Kingpin, 1953, The Devil Must, 1957, The Judgment, 1961; (non-fiction) Kennedy Without Tears, 1964; also contbr. articles to nat. magazines, chpts. to books. Home: 3333 Cleveland Av NW Washington DC 20008 Office: 701 K St NW Washington DC 20006

WICKER, WILLIAM JENNINGS, hosp. adminstr.; b. Newberry, S.C., Dec. 25, 1918; s. Lawrence Pope and Alice (Jennings) W.; B.S., Newberry Coll., 1940; m. Inez Louise McMordie, Mar. 8, 1945; children—Julia Anna, William Jennings. Lab. technician County Meml. Hosp., Newberry, S.C., 1950-55; adminstr. Allendale County Hosp., Fairfax, S.C., 1955—. Served with M.C., AUS, 1941-45; ETO. Mem. Am. Soc. Clin. Pathologists. Methodist. Mason, Lion. Home and office: Box 218 Fairfax SC 29827

WICKWAR, WILLIAM HARDY, polit. scientist, educator; b. London, Eng., May 22, 1903; s. John William and Rose (Hardy) W.; B.A., U. London, 1924, M.A., 1926; student U. Paris, 1927-28, Heidelberg U., 1931; m. Margaret Beauchamp, May 19, 1934; 1 son, Vincent Beauchamp. Lectr. London Sch. Econs., 1937; asst. prof. Rockford Coll., 1938-43; asso. prof. Conn. Coll. for Women, 1943-44; prof. govt. Hamilton Coll., 1946-49; social affairs officer UN, N.Y.C., 1948-65; prof. polit. sci. U. S.C., Columbia, 1965-71; dir. planning Richland County Hosp., Columbia, 1972—; vis. prof. Am. U. Beirut, 1961-62; lectr. Grad. Sch. Pub. Adminstrn., N.Y. U., 1962, 63. Cons. UN, 1966—, State Econ. Opportunity Office, 1966, State Bd. Health, 1967, State Dept. Mental Health, 1968. Adviser, Govt. Lebanon, 1954-55, Govt. Ivory Coast, 1969; dir. regional seminar for govts. in S.E. Asia, Bangkok, 1959; leader community devel. study tour Africa, 1960; interim dir. S.C. Econ. Opportunity Bd., 1967. Mem. Plainsboro (N.J.) Planning Commn., 1953; pres. UN Fed. Credit Union, 1952; chief world food program sect. UN, N.Y.C., 1963-65; vice chmn. Columbia Area Community Mental Health Bd., 1971. Served as social welfare officer UNRRA, 1944-46. Recipient Rockefeller Found. fellowship, 1927-31. Mem. Internat. Inst. Adminstrv. Scis., Am. Soc. Pub. Adminstrn., Am. Polit. Sci. Assn. Club: British Schools and Universities (N.Y.). Author: The Struggle for the Freedom of the Press, 1928; Baron d'Holbach, 1935; Social Services, 1936, 2d edit., 1948; Public Services, 1938; Modernization of Administration in the Near East, 1963; Anti-poverty in South Carolina, 1967; Health in South Carolina, 1968; Criminal Policy in South Carolna, 1968; Community Mental Health in South Carolina, 1969; Political Theory of Local Government, 1970; 300 Years of Development Administration in South Carolina, 1970; Administration of Public Social Programs, 1971. Home: 914 Gregg St Columbia SC 29201

WIDDECKE, HENRY AUGUST, JR., banker; b. Bryan, Tex., Jan. 10, 1916; s. Henry August and Josephine (Baker) W.; B.B.A., U. Tex. at Austin, 1938; m. Rogerina Clay, Aug. 20, 1940; children—Patricia (Mrs. Kenneth Edward Linton), Suzanne. Personnel dept. Fed. Reserve Bank, Dallas, 1946-48; v.p. First Nat. Bank, Kansas City, Mo., 1948-53; v.p. The Fort Worth Nat. Bank, 1953—; dir. Curtis Mathes Mfg. Co., Dallas. Bd. dirs. YMCA, pres., 1972—. Served to lt. comdr. USNR, 1942-45. Mem. Merit System Council, State of Tex. (chmn. 1969), Am. Inst. Banking, Phi Gamma Delta, Beta Alpha Psi. Methodist. Home: 4108 Warnock Ct Fort Worth TX 76109 Office: 800 Main St Fort Worth TX 76102

WIDEMAN, RONALD, dentist; b. Homer, La., May 9, 1932; s. Yandell and Nena Houston (Plant) W.; D.D.S., Baylor U., 1957; m. Bettye A. Steakley, Sept. 1, 1956; children—David, Kathy Ann, Betsy Lynn, Craig. Practice of dentistry, Dallas, 1959—. Served with AUS, 1957-59. Mem. Am., Tex. dental assns., Dallas County Dental Soc., Acad. Psychosomatic Medicine. Mem. Bible Ch. (deacon 1963-66). Club: Royal Oaks Country (Dallas). Home: 3509 Greenbrier St Dallas TX 75225 Office: 311 Preston Royal Med Center Dallas TX 75230

WIDGER, WALTER LEWIS, psychiat. social worker; b. Boston, Oct. 28, 1919; s. Arthur Dunham and Emma (Mykkanen) W.; A.A., Valley Forge Mil. Acad. Jr. Coll., 1939; B.S., Trinity U., 1954; M.S.W., Worden Sch. Social Service, 1957; m. Gloria Elizabeth Ramirez, Feb. 2, 1955; 1 dau., Barbara Ann. Psychiat. caseworker U. Okla. Med. Center, 1957-58; caseworker Family Service Galveston, Tex., 1959-61, Family Service Dallas, 1962-64; dir. social service State Hosp., Big Spring, Tex., 1964—. Faculty, Howard County Jr. Coll., Big Spring, 1965—. Pres., Credit Union, Big Spring, 1966-68. Bd. dirs. Maco Stewart Post, Galveston, Tex., 1958-60. Served with USMCR, 1941-45. Recipient Meritorious Service award Big Spring State Hosp., 1968. Mem. Big Spring Health and Welfare Assn. (co-founder, first chmn. 1966-67), Am. Hosp. Assn., Tex. Pub. Employees Assn., Nat. Rehab. Assn., Nat. Assn. Social Workers, Nat. Acad. Certified Social Workers. Presbyn. Home: Gail Route Box 3 Big Spring TX 79720 Office: Big Spring State Hosp PO Box 231 Big Spring TX 79720

WIDMER, ERNEST CLYDE, cost analyst; b. Daytona Beach, Fla., Mar. 31, 1929; s. Ernest John and Edith (Booth) W.; student Fla. State U., 1951; m. Martha Elizabeth Hunter, Dec. 21, 1951; children—Robert Frederick, Charles Glenn, Jennifer Lynn. Partner, Ernest J. Widmer & Son, Daytona Beach, 1951-67; with FHA Dept. Housing and Urban Devel., 1967—, constrn. cost analyst, 1969—. Mem. Nat. Builders Econ. Council, 1957-59; South Daytona Planning and Zoning Bd., 1958-62; pres. Halifax Children's Mus., 1958, Mus. Arts and Scis., 1959, 60. Mem. Am. Malacological Union, Internat. Oceanographic Found., Daytona Beach Area C. of C. (award 1968, mem. coms. 1961-63). Home: PO Box 814 2360 Holly Leaf Lane Orange Park FL 32073 Office: Peninsula Plaza 661 Riverside Av Jacksonville FL 32204

WIDNER, WILLIAM RICHARD, educator; b. nr. Three Brothers, Ark., Apr. 24, 1920; s. Walter Elum and Rena (Long) W.; A.B., Eastern N.M. U., 1942; postgrad Cornell U., 1943; M.S., U. N.M., 1948, Ph.D., 1952; m. Edna Holcombe, Aug. 17, 1962; children—William Richard, Barbara. Research asst. radiobiology Los Alamos U. Cal., 1948-50; teaching asst. biology U. N.M., Albuquerque, 1950-52; indsl. hygienist Sandia Corp., Albuquerque, 1952-55; tchr. Albuquerque Indian Sch., 1955-56; prof. biology Howard Payne Coll., Brownwood, Tex., 1956-59, Baylor U., Waco,

Tex., 1959-—. Served with USNR, 1942-46; mem. Res. Fellow Tex. Acad. Sci.; mem. A.A.A.S., Nat. Rifle Assn. Baptist. Mason (32 deg., Shriner). Home: 111 Turtle Creek Dr Waco TX 76710

WIDSTROM, NEIL WAYNE, research geneticist; b. Hecla, S.D., Nov. 11, 1933; s. John William and Tena Henrietta (Frohling) W.; B.S., S.D. State U., 1959, Ph.D., 1962; m. Virginia Rose Elder, Sept. 4, 1960; children—Gerald Allen, Jeffrey Lee. Postdoctoral fellow Dept. Genetics, N.C. State U., Raleigh, 1963-64; research geneticist So. Grain Insects Research Lab., U.S. Dept. Agr., Tifton, Ga., 1964-—. Pres. P.T.A., 1971-72. Served to cpl. USMCR, 1954-56. Mem. Am. Soc. Agronomy, Genetics Soc. Am., Am. Geneticists Assn., Entomology Soc. Am., Am. Inst. Biol. Sci., A.A.A.S., Gideons Internat. (chaplain 1971), Luth. Laymen's League (bd. govs. Fla-Ga. dist. 1968-—), Am. Contract Bridge League, Sigma Xi, Gamma Sigma Delta. Lutheran (elder 1970-71). Contbr. articles in field to profl. jours. Home: Route 4 Box 127A Tifton GA 31794 Office: Tifton GA 31794

WIELAGE, ROBERT CECIL, architect; b. Evanston, Ill., Apr. 28, 1929; s. Marcus Francis and Ada Mary (Bartstra) W.; student U. So. Cal., 1947-48, U. Miami (Fla.), 1948-49; B.S., Ga. Inst. Tech., 1953; m. Marian Dee Connelly, Dec. 21, 1952; children—Marcus Francis, Rosemary Wells, Robert Simmons. Mem. firm Robert Wielage Architect, Tampa, Fla., 1954-66, Walker & Wielage Architects, Tampa, 1966-68, Wielage & McKenna Architects & Planners, Tampa, 1968-—. Bd. govs. Tampa Bay Art Center, 1968-69. Served to 1st lt. AUS, 1946-56. Mem. A.I.A., Soc. Coll. and Univ. Planning, Fla. Assn. Architects (recipient various awards), Constrn. Specifications Inst. Clubs: Palma Ceia Golf, Commerce. Home: 3103 Euclid Av Tampa FL 33609 Office: 5440 Mariner Dr Tampa FL 33609

WIENER, FREDERICK BERNAYS, lawyer; b. N.Y.C., June 1, 1906; Ph.B., Brown U., 1927; LL.B., Harvard, 1930; LL.D., Cleve.-Marshall Law Sch., 1969. Admitted to R.I. bar, 1931, D.C. bar, 1938; asst. solicitor U.S. Dept. Interior, 1934-37; spl. atty., spl. asst. to atty. gen. U.S., 1937-41; asst. to solicitor gen. U.S., 1945-48; reporter to Com. of U.S. Supreme Ct. on Revision of Rules, 1953-54; lectr. George Washington U., Washington, 1951-52, professional lectr., 1952-56. Served to col. AUS, 1941-45. Recipient Bicentennial Medallion, Brown U., 1965; Guggenheim fellow, 1962. Fellow Internat. Acad. Trial Lawyers (dir. 1970-71); mem. Am., N.Y.C. bar assns., Bar Assn. D.C., Judge Advs. Assn. (pres. 1958), Selden Soc. (council 1961-—), Mil. Order Fgn. Wars (past comdr.-gen.), Mil. Order Carabao (historian). Author: Practical Manual of Martial Law, 1940; Effective Appellate Advocacy, 1950; Briefing and Arguing Federal Appeals, 1961; Civilians Under Military Justice, 1967. Home: 922 24th St NW Washington DC 20037 Office: 1750 Pennsylvania Av NW Washington DC 20006

WIENER, SAMSON, lumber co. exec.; b. Shreveport, La., Dec. 27, 1907; s. Eli and Selma (Loewenstein) W.; B.A., U. Mich., 1928; m. Fan Gardner, Mar. 12, 1939; children—Thomas Eli, Nancy (Mrs. Leon A. Mellow). With Angelina County Lumber Co., Keltys, Tex., 1928-32; co-organizer Wiener Lumber Co., Dallas, 1934, pres., gen. mgr., 1955-—, also dir.; v.p., dir. Mellow's Board and Brush, 1966-—, Board and Brush of Mesquite, 1969-—; chmn. bd., dir. Sola Investment Corp., Shreveport, La.; dir. Angeline & Neches River R.R. Co., Lufkin, Tex., Lufkin Industries. Trustee Tex. Scottish Rite Hosp. for Crippled Children, v.p., 1967-—; bd. dirs. Dallas Crime Commn.; pres. Dallas Big Brothers, 1954-55, bd. dirs.; bd. dirs. Big Brothers Am.; pres. Dallas Big Brothers Found., 1967-69. Recipient Lumberman of Year award Lumbermen's Assn. Tex., 1963; Brotherhood award Nat. Conf. Christians and Jews, 1968. Mem. Lumbermen's Assn. Tex. (pres. 1969-70), Nat. Lumber and Bldg. Material Dealers Assn. (pres. 1969-70), North Dallas C. of C. (bd. dirs. 1968-70), Sigma Alpha Mu. Mason (33 deg. Shriner), Rotarian (pres. Park Cities-Dallas 1950-51); mem. B'nai B'rith. Jewish religion. Clubs: Columbian (sec. 1940). Home: 4408 Lorraine Av Dallas TX 75205 Office: PO Box 35125 Inwood and Maple Avs Dallas TX 75235

WIESENBURG, KARL, lawyer; b. L.I., N.Y., Aug. 1, 1911; s. Adolph Johann and Martha Mary (Horwath) W.; student pub. schs., N.Y.C.; m. Denise Higginbotham, Dec. 23, 1939; children—Karl, Denis Alan, Martha Ann, Anirah Denise. Admitted to Miss. bar, 1933; practiced in Pascagoula, Miss., 1934-—; city atty., Pascagoula and Ocean Springs, 1951-55. Chmn., Pascagoula Democratic Exec. Com., 1950-55; del. Nat. Dem. Conv., Chgo., 1956, Los Angeles, 1960, Miami, 1972. Mem. Miss. Ho. of Reps., 1956-64. Pres., Pascagoula Port Commn., 1939-42, Jackson County chpt. A.R.C., 1947-48. Bd. dirs. Nat. Rivers and Harbors Congress. Served with USCGR, 1929-34, to lt. col. Signal Corps, AUS, 1942-46. Decorated Bronze Star medal. Mem. Fed., Am., Miss., Jackson County (pres.) bar assns., Am. Judicature Soc., Pascagoula C. of C. (dir.), Miss. Rivers and Harbors Assn., V.F.W. (state comdr. 1948-49), Am. Radio Relay League. Roman Catholic (pres. parish council). Kiwanian (past pres.). Home: 525 Spanish Av Pascagoula MS 39567 Office: 3106 Canty St (Box 26) Pascagoula MS 39567

WIESNET, DONALD RICHARD, research hydrologist; b. Buffalo, Feb. 7, 1927; s. Charles Anthony and Rose Elizabeth (Hildenbrand) W.; student Syracuse U., 1946-47; B.A., U. Buffalo, 1950, M.A., 1951, postgrad. 1951-52; postgrad. U. Ariz., 1964-65; m. Evelyn Elaine Jordan, Dec. 27, 1952; children—Andrew J., Elizabeth A., Peter C., Ellen E. Geologist U.S. Geol. Survey, Washington, 1952-60; geohydrologist, Washington, also Tucson, Boston, 1960-67; oceanographer, research hydrologist U.S. Naval Oceanographic Office, Washington, 1967-71; sr. research hydrologist NOAA, Environmental Satellite Service, 1971-—. Served with USNR, 1944-46. Fellow Geol. Soc. Am.; mem. A.A.A.S., Geol. Soc. Washington, Glaciological Soc., Am. Soc. Photogrammetry, Nat. Water Resources Council (mem. com. hydrology 1968-71). Research and publs. on geology, geohydrology, remote sensing and coastal oceanography, geologic cartography. Home: 601 McKinley St NE Vienna VA 22180 Office: 3737 Branch Av SE Washington DC 20031

WIESS, RICHARD THOMAS, dentist; b. Phila., Dec. 31, 1930; s. Louis Charles and Mary Catherine (Dugan) W.; B.A., U. N.C., 1952; D.D.S., 1959; m. Evelyn Adair Beasley, Dec. 22, 1953; children—Sandra Adair, Evelyn Dugan, Mary Julia. Practice dentistry, DeFuniak Springs, Fla., 1959-—. Cons. dental hygiene program Pensacola (Fla.) Jr. Coll., 1966-69. Served with USNR, 1952-54. Recipient Best in Show award Walton County Art Show, 1969; 3d place award Bay County Art Show (Fla.), 1970. Mem. Northwest Dist. Dental Soc. (pres. 1969-70), Am. Dental Assn., Fla. Dental Assn., Zi Psi Phi, Kappa Sigma Phi. Presbyn. Lion. 1 Home: S 2d St DeFuniak Springs FL 32433 Office: Circle Dr DeFuniak Springs FL 32433

WIETING, DAVID LEE, elec. co. exec.; b. Chgo., Sept. 12, 1933; s. Frank J. and Marie (Steeg) W.; B.S., U. Tulsa, 1956; m. Roberta Hill, Sept. 12, 1958; 1 son, Jerry Michael. Dist. petroleum engr. Pure Oil Co., Madill, Okla., 1956-61; asst. design group engr., test condr. Gen. Dynamics/Astronautics, Altus, Okla., 1962-65; mgr. facilities and utilities Gen. Electric Co., Bay St. Louis, Miss., 1965-—. Served with AUS, 1957. Registered profl. engr., Okla. Mem. Nat., Okla. socs. profl. engrs., Am. Inst. Mining, Metall. and Petroleum, Engrs., Pi Epsilon Tau. Club: Optimist. Home: Bay Royale Apts 3 Bay St Louis MS 39520 Office: Gen Electric Co MTSD Bay St Louis MS 39520

WIGGINS, ARTHUR WALTER, banker; b. Nashville, Ga., Oct. 6, 1923; s. Oscar Kibbe and Frances (Eldridge) W.; B.S., U. Tampa, 1952; m. Mary Louise Cuddy, Jan. 22, 1956; children—Frances, Arthur Walter, William. Dist. sales mgr. Nat. Airlines, Phila., 1952-57, Northeast Airlines, Tampa, 1957-64; v.p. 1st Nat. Bank Tampa, 1964-—. Bd. dirs. Am. Cancer Soc. Hillsborough County, 1968-—, Gulf Ridge council Boy Scouts Am., 1969-—. Served with AUS, 1941-45. Decorated Bronze Star. Mem. Bank Marketing Assn., Sales and Marketing Execs. Tampa (bd. dirs.). Lion. Home: 214 Bonnie Brae Temple Terrace FL 33617 Office: 416 Franklin St Tampa FL 33602

WIGGINS, BEN T., state ofcl.; b. Augusta, Ga., Nov. 19, 1920; student Spartanburg Jr. Coll., U. Ga., Atlanta Law Sch.; m. Muriel Redfern (dec.); 2 daus. Admitted to Ga. bar, practiced in Toccoa; mem. Ga. Ho. of Reps., 1951-54; exec. sec. to Gov. of Ga., 1955-57; mem. Ga. Pub. Service Commn., 1957-—, vice chmn., 1965-—. Chmn. com. on communications Nat. Assn. Regulatory Utility Commrs., 1962-—, also mem. exec. com. Vice pres. Upper Chattahoochee Devel. Assn.; upper region chmn. Chattahoochee River Basin Devel. Commn. Bd. dirs. Greater Atlanta chpt. Leukemia Soc. Am., Inc., Atlanta Council Campfire Girls. Served with USAAF, World War II; ETO. Mem. Ga. Bar Assn., Atlanta Gridiron Soc., Sigma Delta Kappa. Methodist. Mason (Shriner). Address: 244 Washington St SW Atlanta GA 30334

WIGGINS, CLIFTON ALLEN, sch. adminstr.; b. Savannah, Ga., June 21, 1912; s. Samuel Sr. and Wilhelmina (Ford) W.; B.S. in Social Studies, Savannah State Coll., 1947; M.A. in Sch. Adminstrn., Atlanta U., 1955; m. George Alma Hayes, Feb. 7, 1938; children—Drusilla Deanna (Mrs. Jimmy Lee Rucker), Ima Wilhemina (Mrs. Sanford Burney, Jr.), Clifftena Allette, Clifton Allen. Asst. prin. Rosenwald Indsl. Sch., Screven, Ga., 1937-41; prin. Clyo High Sch. (Ga.), 1949-56, Central High Sch., Springfield, Ga., 1956-66, Riceboro (Ga.) Elementary Sch., 1966-70; dir. Title I, ESEA, Liberty County Schs., Hinesville, Ga., 1970-—. Mem. Selective Service Bd. Recipient Certificate of Merit for Outstanding Bravery, A.R.C., 1939. Mem. N.E.A., Ga. Tchrs. and Edn. Assn. (treas. region 8), Effingham County Tchrs. Assn., Effingham County Prins. Council, Region 8, Ga. prins. councils. Baptist (financial sec.). Mason, Odd Fellow. Home: 1112 W 42d St Savannah GA 31401 Office: Liberty County Bd Edn PO Box 93 Hinesville GA 31313

WIGGINS, JAMES CECILASSN, educator; b. Live Oak, Fla., Apr. 7, 1925; s. Benjamin F. and Mamie (Skeen) W.; B.S. in Phys. Edn., U. Fla., 1950, M.Ed., 1951; m. Gloria Jean Bender, Aug. 4, 1946; children—James Cecil,Jon Henry. Head phys. edn. dept., athletic dir., head football and track coach Cherokee Jr. High Sch., Orlando, Fla., 1950-—; instr. Seminole Jr. Coll., Sanford, Fla., part-time 1968-69. Served with USNR, 1944-46. Mem. Fla. Assn. for Health, Phys. Edn. and Recreation (pres. 1968-69), Orange County Coaches Assn. (pres. 1954), Orange County Phys. Edn. Assn. (pres. 1961), Orlando High Sch. Athletic Assn. (v.p. 1967). Methodist (ofcl. bd. 1960-66; tchr. Sunday sch. 1962-67). Home: 3316 Hargill Dr Orlando FL 32806

WIGGINS, NORMAN ADRIAN, coll. pres.; b. Burlington, N.C., Feb. 6, 1924; s. Walter James and Margaret (Chason) W.; A.A., Campbell Coll., 1948; B.A., Wake Forest Coll., 1950, LL.B., 1952; LL.M. (Harlan Fiske Stone fellow), Columbia, 1956, J.S.D., 1964; LL.D., Gardner-Webb Coll., 1972; m. Mildred Harmon, Apr. 14, 1948. Admitted to N.C. bar, 1952; asst. trust officer Planters Nat. Bank & Trust Co., Rocky Mount, N.C., 1952-53, asso. trust officer, 1953-55; mem. faculty Wake Forest Coll., Winston-Salem, 1956-67, prof. law, 1962-67, gen. counsel 1964-67; pres. Campbell Coll., Buies Creek, N.C., 1967-—. Mem. faculty Cannon Trust Sch., Brevard (N.C.) Coll., 1961-—, Nat. Trust Sch., Southwestern U., 1961-—; mem. drafting com. N.C. Gen. Statutes Commn., 1958-67; pres. N.C. Assn. Colls. and Univs., 1971-72; mem. long range planning com. So. Baptist Conv.; mem. faculty Southeastern Trust Sch., 1970-— mem. Gov.'s Com. on Law and Order, chmn. Task Force Com. on Adjudication. Chmn. trust faculty Southwestern Grad. Sch. Banking, So. Meth. U., 1965-67, bd. dirs., 1967-—; pres. N.C. Found. Ch.-Related Colls., 1969-70. Served with USMCR, 1943-47. Recipient Distinguished Service award Campbell Coll., 1964, Distinguished Alumnus award Phi Alpha Delta, 1966. Mem. N.C. State Bar, N.C. Bar Assn., Nat. Assn. Coll. and Univ. Attys. (exec. bd. 1967-—, 2d v.p.), Jay Waugh Evangelistic Assn. (pres. 1965-—), Nat. Assn. Coll. and Univ. Attys. (pres. 1972-73), Wake Forest Alumni Assn. (chpt. pres. 1954-—), Campbell Coll. Alumni Assn. (v.p. 1958-62). Baptist. Democrat. Author: Wills and Administration of Estates in North Carolina I-II, 1964. Contbr. articles to legal periodicals. Home: Box 127 Buies Creek NC 27506

WIGGINS, RICHARD HENRY, educator; b. Sinton, Tex., Sept. 29, 1912; s. Henry Wesley and Sallie (Beard) W.; B.A. in Journalism, La. State U., 1934, M.A., 1936; Ph.D. in Mass Communications, U. Ia., 1964; m. Louise Hubert Dugas, Dec. 18, 1935; children—Louise A. (Mrs. Howard K. Sommers), Mona B. (Mrs. Peter H. Perkins), Richard Henry. Editor, The Reveille, Baton Rouge, 1933-34; mem. faculty La. State U., Baton Rouge, 1935-72, instr., 1935-38, asst. prof., 1938-46, asso. prof., 1946-64, prof. journalism, 1964-72, prof. emeritus, mgr. La. State U. printing office 1948-70, bus. mgr. Daily Reveille and Gumbo, 1937-70. Reporter Morning Adv., Baton Rouge, 1934; staff A.P., Little Rock, 1935; graphic arts cons. Mem. adv. bd. St. Albans Chapel, Baton Rouge, 1964-67. Mem. Am. Assn. Edn. in Journalism, Printing Hist. Soc., Scabbard and Blade, Sigma Delta Chi, Omicron Delta Kappa, Phi Kappa Phi, Pi Alpha Mu, Pi Sigma Alpha. Democrat. Episcopalian. Contbr. articles to profl. publs. Mem. editorial bd. Visible Language. Home: 751 DuBois Dr Baton Rouge LA 70808

WIGGINS, RICHARD LLOYD, civil engr.; b. Bronson, Tex., June 23, 1937; s. Richard Louis and Gertrude (Stewart) W.; student Arlington State Jr. Coll., 1956-58; B.S. with honors, So. Meth. U., 1962; m. Lavonne Patricia McGowen, Apr. 12, 1957; children—Janet Faye, Robin Jill, Rebecca Colleen. Engr., Tex. Power & Light Co., Dallas, 1962-70, Indsl. Generating Co., Rockdale, Tex., 1970-71, adminstrv. asst. to v.p., Dallas, 1971-—. Cons. structural, found. design to industry. Mem. canvas com. So. Meth. U. sustentation drive, 1967. Registered profl. engr., Tex. Mem. Am. Soc. C.E., Nat., Tex. socs. profl. engrs., Sigma Tau, Chi Epsilon. Baptist. Home: 10817 Ridge Spring Dr Dallas TX 75218 Office: Indsl Generating Co 1512 Commerce St Dallas TX 75201

WIGGINTON, JOHN TALBOT, judge; b. Miami, Fla., May 4, 1908; s. Junius T. and Florence (Frederick) W.; J.D., U. Fla., 1932; m. Jane Emily Graham, Apr. 9, 1933; children—Nan Emily (Mrs. A.H. Tebault, Jr.), John Klein. Admitted to Fla. bar, 1932; practiced in Milton, Fla., 1932-44, Tallahassee, 1944-57; atty. U.S. Dept. Justice, Milton, 1936-45, Fla. Bd. Adminstrn., Tallahassee, 1945-49; judge 1st Dist. Ct. Appeal, Tallahassee, 1957-—. Mem. Fla. Bar (past pres.), Sigma Alpha Epsilon. Rotarian (past pres.). Home: 1221 Betton Rd Tallahassee FL 32303 Office: Supreme Ct Bldg Tallahassee FL 32302

WIGGS, ASHTON PARKER, educator; b. Pine Level, N.C., Sept. 28, 1928; s. Jasper Joseph and Lucille (Parker) W.; A.B., Atlantic Christian Coll., 1955; postgrad. U. N.C., summer 1956; M.A., E. Carolina U., 1958; m. Jean Vaughan, Aug. 21, 1955; 1 son, Russell Ashton. Forman, Bright Leaf & Burley Tobacco Co., Smithfield, N.C., 1948-50; tchr. Needham Broughton High Sch., Raleigh, N.C., 1956; prin W. Bertie High Sch., Lewiston, N.C., 1957-59; asst. prof. bus. Atlantic Christian Coll., Wilson, N.C., 1960-—. Republican precinct chmn., 1968-—; mem. Wilson County Rep. Exec. Com., 1968-—. Bd. dirs. United Fund. Served with AUS, 1951-52. Mem. Am. Accounting Assn., Am. Assn. U. Profs., V.F.W., Phi Delta Gamma. Presbyn. (deacon). Mason, Rotarian (pres. Wilson club). Home: 1701 Anderson St Wilson NC 27893 Office: Wilson NC 27893

WIGHTMAN, JOSEPH, coll. adminstr.; b. County of Dorset, Eng., May 18, 1916; s. Joseph and Maud (Pomeroy) W.; B.A., St. Johns Coll., Oxford U., 1938, M.A., 1945; Ph.D., U. S.C., 1961; m. Elaine Taylor, Aug. 5, 1942; children—Robert Mark, Sarah Rosalind. Tchr. Forest Sch., London, Eng., 1938-40, Ilford Grammar Sch. Essex, Eng., 1946-50; head history dept. Weymouth (Dorset, Eng.) Sch., 1950-55, 56-57; guest prof. Erskine Coll., Due West, S.C., 1955-56, prof., dept. history, 1957-63, acad. dean, 1963-66, pres., 1966-—. Served with Brit. Army, 1940-46. Mem. Am. Hist. Assn., S.C. Hist. Assn. Home: PO Box 308 Due West SC 29639 Office: Erskine Coll Due West SC 29639

WILBUR, OSCAR MILTON, JR., physician; b. Bangor, Me., Apr. 15, 1921; s. Oscar Milton and Mary (Wentworth) W.; B.A., U. Me., 1944; M.D., Boston U., 1946; m. Louise Wells, Nov. 16, 1946; children—Mary Crosby, Anne Lawton. Intern Rochester (N.Y.) Gen. Hosp., 1946-47; asst. resident internal medicine Mt. Alto VA Hosp., Washington, 1949-50; asst. resident in pathology, resident in pathology Johns Hopkins Hosp., Balt., 1950-55; asso. pathologist Augustana Hosp., Chgo., 1956; pathologist Hibbing, Minn., 1956-61, Pueblo, Colo., 1962-64, Buffalo, 1965-68, Savannah and Americus, Ga., 1968-70; instr. pathology Johns Hopkins Sch. Medicine, 1950-55; asst. clin. prof. pathology U. Colo. Sch. Medicine, 1962-64, State U. N.Y. at Buffalo Med. Sch., 1965-68; asst. prof. pathology Emory U. Sch. Medicine, 1971-—. Served to capt. M.C., AUS, 1947-49. Diplomate in path. anatomy, clin. pathology Am. Bd. Pathology. Fellow Am. Soc. Clin. Pathologists, Coll. Am. Pathologists; mem. Internat. Acad. Pathology, Johns Hopkins Med. and Surg. Assn., A.M.A., Am. Assn. Blood Banks, Ga., Atlanta med. socs., Ga. Assn. Pathologists. Republican. Episcopalian. Contbr. papers to Bull. Johns Hopkins Hosp., 1953, 54, 55. Home: 804 Edgewood Av NE Atlanta GA 30307 Office: Grady Meml Hosp Atlanta GA 30303

WILBUR, PAUL FRANK, architect; b. Blackwell, Okla., Mar. 1, 1936; s. Orval E. and Edra (Frazier) W.; B.Arch., Okla. State U., 1959; m. Joan Carol Meade, June 2, 1957; children—Mark, Perry, Beth. Field supr. Stowers & Boyce, Little Rock, 1959-63; partner Wilbur, Butcher & Assos., Architects, Rogers, 1963-—. Mem. region 7 archtl. adv. bd. Gen. Services Administrn., 1971-—. Mem. Rogers Planning Commn., 1963-71, chmn., 1969-70; mem. Rogers Bd. Adjustments, 1965-71. Mem. A.I.A. Methodist. Rotarian. Home: 121 N 7th St Rogers AR 72756 Office: 116 1/2 W Walnut St Rogers AR 72756

WILCOX, ARTHUR MANIGAULT, newspaper editor; b. Phila., May 2, 1922; s. John Walter and Caroline (Manigault) W.; B.S., Ga. Inst. Tech., 1943; m. Katharine Moore McMurray, Nov. 24, 1944; children—Margaret Moore, Arthur Manigault, Priscilla McMurray, Robert Manigault. Reporter, Charleston (S.C.) Eve. Post, 1946-52, city editor, 1952-57, editor, 1968-—; asst. editor Charleston News and Courier, 1957-68; dir. Eve. Post Pub. Co. Curator S.C. Hist. Soc., 1957-60. Trustee Charleston Museum, 1968-—. Served with USNR, 1943-46. Mem. Am. Soc. Newspaper Editors, St. Cecilia Soc., Soc. Colonial Wars. Mem. P.E. Ch. (vestry 1954-59, 62-66). Clubs: Charleston, Carolina Yacht (Charleston). Home: 86 Lenwood Blvd Charleston SC 29401 Office: 134 Columbus St Charleston SC 29402

WILCOX, DAVID BERTELL, cosmetic mfg. co. exec.; b. Liberty, Mo., May 18, 1930; s. David Bertell and Mary Gertrude (Banks) W.; B.S. in Econs. with high honors, U. Ill., 1956; m. Betsy Ross, Aug. 15, 1955; children—Mary Lou, Julie, Ruth. Mgr. municipal services dept. 1st Nat. Bank, Memphis, 1961-65; asst. sec., treas., controller Graham & Warren, Inc., advt. agy., 1965-67, sec., treas., controller, 1967-70; sec., treas., controller Mitchum Co., 1967-70; asst. sec., treas., controller Mitchum-Thayer, Inc., Paris, Tenn., 1970-71, v.p. adminstrn., 1971-—; dir. Puryear Community Devel. Corp., 1967-—; trustee Mitchum Pension and Profit Sharing Fund, 1967-—. Commr., City of Paris, 1970-—; mem. coms. Henry County Ct. Budget, 1968-—, fiscal study com., 1971-—, airport com., 1967-69; pres. Paris Little Theater, 1969; dist. chmn. Boy Scouts Am., 1970-71, bd. dirs. West Tenn. council; bd. dirs. Paris-Henry County Youth Center. Served with USNR, 1948-52. Mem. Henry County Plant Mgmt. Assn. (chmn. 1969), Paris C. of C. (treas. 1969-72, dir.), Beta Gamma Sigma, Sigma Iota Epsilon, Chi Gamma Iota. Elk. Home: 307 Jackson St Paris TN 38242 Office: 2700 W Wood St Paris TN 38242

WILCOX, REX EUGENE, journalist; b. Portland, Ore., May 26, 1915; s. Ralph James and Lida (Riches) W.; student U. Wis., 1939-41, U. Ill., 1942-43, U. Chgo., 1958-59; m. Doris Lucile Haney, July 27, 1937; children—James Hamilton, John Patrick. Pub. relations worker So. Cal. Edison Co., Los Angeles, 1946-52; asst. to editor Ft. Smith (Ark.) Times Record, 1952-59; editor, columnist, lectr. Natchez (Miss.) Times, 1959-61; city editor, editorial writer Palm Beach Post, West Palm Beach, Fla., 1961-70, Palm Beach Times, 1970-—. Mem. Internat. Platform Assn., Sigma Delta Chi. Republican. Episcopalian. Mason. Home: 5826 Church Circle W West Palm Beach FL 33405 Office: 2751 S Dixie St West Palm Beach FL 33405

WILCUT, BERT EDWARD, aviation co. exec.; b. Sloan, Ia., Nov. 18, 1901; s. Rasmer Dupree and Iva (Shannon) W.; B.A., S.W. Tex. State Coll., 1927. Mgr. credit dept. Service Finance Corp., San Antonio, 1930-40; pres., gen. mgr. San Antonio Aviation, Inc., 1946-—, designer, mfr. Palomino aircraft, 1965-—. Coordinator aviation dist. 3-B, Tex. Aero. Commn., San Antonio, 1960-—. Served with USAAF, 1943-45. Mem. Exptl. Aircraft Assn. Republican. Mason (Shriner). Club: Pecan Valley Country (San Antonio). Home: 3451 E Southcross San Antonio TX 78223 Office: Hanger 10 Stinson Field San Antonio TX 78214

WILDER, ALICE FITCH, mem. Republican Nat. Com.; b. Richmond, Va., Jan. 1, 1904; d. Francis Burt and Alice (Riedeman) Fitch; A.B., U. S.C.; m. Marion Archer Wilder, July 16, 1938; children—Marion Archer, Mary Alice (Mrs. Hastings Wyman, Jr.). Headmistress, Aiken Day Sch., 1935-55; dir. curriculum Mead Hall, Aiken, 1955-62; polit. organizer Aiken County, S.C., 1958-—; mem. Rep. Nat. Com. for S.C., 1960-—. Home: 1535 Forest Hill Av Aiken SC 29801

WILDER, FRANKLIN, lawyer; b. Ft. Smith, Ark., Aug. 18, 1913; s. Solon F. and Mary (Miles) W.; LL.B., U. Ark., 1936; m. Bernice Marley, July 17, 1941; children—Franklin M., Sheila Ann, Robert Seab. Admitted to Ark. bar, 1936; practiced in Ft. Smith, 1936-42, 46-—; spl. agt. FBI, 1942-45; chancery and probate judge, Ft. Smith,

1955-60. Pres. Sebastian County Mental Health Assn., 1959-60, Churchmen of Western Ark., 1960. Mem. Internat., Am., Ark. bar assns., Am. Trial Lawyers Assn. Methodist. Author: Immortal Mother (biography Susanna Wesley, Mother of Methodism), 1967; Father of the Wesleys, 1971. Home: 6302 Duncan Rd Fort Smith AR 72901 Office: Mchts Bank Bldg Fort Smith AR 72901

WILDER, JAMES SAMPSON, JR., clergyman, coll. pres.; b. Washington, Apr. 4, 1919; s. James Sampson and Leah Mae (McElfish) W.; B.A., Emory U., 1941; B.D. (Leopold Schepp Found. scholar 1942-43, 43-44), Yale U., 1944; Ph.D. (Leopold Schepp Found. fellow 1946-48), New Coll., U. Edinburgh (Scotland), 1948; postgrad. Mansfield Coll., Oxford (Eng.) U., 1947, U. Zurich (Switzerland), 1948; m. Louise Summers, Mar. 18, 1947; children—James Sampson III, Robert Coke, Anne Shannon. Ordained to ministry Methodist Ch., 1944; pastor in Tenn., 1944-45; conf. youth dir., 1945-46; pastor First Meth. Ch., Gatlinburg, Tenn., 1948-52, Magnolia Av. Meth. Ch., Knoxville, Tenn., 1952-59, Brainerd Meth. Ch., Chattanooga, 1959-62; pres. Lambuth Coll., Jackson, Tenn., 1962—. Pres., dir. Leisure Lands, Inc.; dir. Nat. Bank of Commerce. Prod. weekly worship service, His Word, sta. WATE-TV, Knoxville, 1953-54; prod., moderator pub. forums on current community questions, also Pastor's Study, sta. WRGP-TV, Chattanooga, 1962; del. Meth. Ch. to World Christian Youth Conf., Oslo, Norway, 1947; mem. So. Regional Edn. Bd., 1967—. Pres. Tenn. Coll. Assn., 1966-67, Jackson Symphony Assn., 1965-67, Tenn. Coll. Assn., 1966-67; v.p. Affiliated Colls. of Tenn., Inc., 1965-66; chmn. W. Tenn. Health Planning Com., 1970—. Recipient First City Maker award Jackson C. of C., 1966. Mem. Kappa Alpha. Rotarian. Contbr. articles and lesson materials to ch. publs. Home: 450 Roland Av Jackson TN 38301

WILDER, ROBERT EDWIN, ins. exec.; b. Marche, Ark., Sept. 28, 1918; s. Harry C. and Elta (Rice) W.; student pub. schs.; m. June C. Bolick; children—Thomas Brett, Robert Edwin II. Founder, pres., chmn. bd. Nat. Am. Life Ins. Co., Baton Rouge, 1955—, also dir.; pres., chmn. bd. Nat. Am. Corp., 1955-65, 1st Colonial Corp. Am., 1965—; pres. Norris Ins. Shares, Chgo., Exec. Nat. Life Ins. Co., Chgo., Ala. Sch. Supply, Inc., Ala. Granite, Inc.; chmn. bd. Nat. Investors Life Group, Little Rock. Mem. exec. bd. Istrouma Area Council, Boy Scouts of Am., 1964—. Served with USNR, Mem. Nat. Assn. Life Companies, La. Insurers Assn., Nat. Assn. Left-handed Golfers (pres. 1964-70). Baptist. Mason (Shriner). Clubs: Arrowhead Country, Sherwood Forest Country. Contbr. articles to profl. jours. Address: 2566 Woodley Rd Montgomery AL 36111

WILDERMUTH, JOE HENRY, architect; b. Pulaski County, Ind., July 6, 1897; s. Elias and Olive (Herrick) W.; student U. Ariz., 1917-18; B.A., U. Ill., 1920; postgrad. real estate valuation U. Chgo., 1935; m. Madeleine Havens, Jan. 5, 1923; children—Richard Lee, Dorthy Ann (Mrs. Mike Vekasi). Architect pub. schs., Gary, Ind., 1921-39; prin. Joe H. Wildermuth & Co., Architects, 1921-46, Wildermuth & Wildermuth, Gary, Ind., 1946-60, Joe H. Wildermuth Emeritus, Marathon Shores, Fla., 1960—; pres. Washington & 7th Corp., 1931—, Vesta Ct. Corp.; with Gary Fed. Savs. & Loan Assn., 1935-60, v.p., pres., 1958-61. Chief appraiser, asst. mgr. Fed. Home Owners Loan Corp., N.W. Ind., 1933-37; chmn. FHA N.W. Ind., 1934-40; mem. fed. com. sch. house design Interior Dept., 1933-44; chmn. Ind. Bd. Architects, 1933-45. Del., Democratic Ind. Conv., 1932, 36, 40. Served with U.S. Army, 1917-18. Mem. A.I.A., Ind. Soc. Architects (v.p. 1934-36), Am. Legion, Nat. Assn. Real Estate Appraisers, Sigma Chi, Alpha Rho Chi. Elk. Author: Real Estate Valuation, 1934; Treatise on School House Design, 1935. Home: Treasure Cove 12601 Overseas Hwy Marathon Shores FL 33052 Office: PO Box 2676 Marathon Shores FL 33052

WILDS, JOHN W., city editor States-Item, New Orleans. Address: 601-625 North St New Orleans LA 70140*

WILEY, FORREST PARKS, biologist, chemist; b. Weldon, N.C., Nov. 1, 1937; s. Joseph Weldon and Georgia (Parks) W.; B.S., Tuskegee Inst., 1966; m. Gloria Jean Chisholm, Dec. 18, 1961; children—Joseph Lamar, John Lamont. Letterflex field engr. W.R. Grace & Co., Washington Research Center, Clarksville, Md., 1967—; dir. research New Ventures, Inc., 1970—. Bd. dirs. Washington-Tuskegee Housing Found. Mem. Nat. Geog. Soc., Bot. Soc. Am., Am. Soc. Plant Physiologists, Am. Inst. Biol. Scis. Patentee in field. Home: 8408 Barron St Washington DC 20012 Office: Washington Research Center Clarksville MD 21029

WILEY, JOSEPH BRANTLEY, judge; b. Birmingham, Ala., Oct. 25, 1922; s. Clarence C. and Lillian (Brantley) W.; A.B., U. Ala., 1947, LL.B., 1949; m. Mary Ann Conrad, Mar. 19, 1949; children—Joseph Brantley, Elizabeth Henderson, James Conrad. Admitted to Ala. bar, 1949; practiced in Troy, Ala., 1949—; city judge, Troy, 1961—; exec. dir. Troy Housing Authority, 1968-71; dir. Troy Broadcasting Corp., Citizens Bank of Troy. Chmn. Choctowhatchee Regional Library, Indsl. Devel. Bd., Troy, 1960-61. Bd. dirs. Pike County Mus. Assn. Served to lt. (j.g.) USNR, 1943-46. Mem. Am., Ala. bar assns., Phi Delta Phi, Sigma Alpha Epsilon. Rotarian (pres. Troy, 1965-66). Home: 312 Flavia Circle Troy AL 36081 Office: 123 Madison St Troy AL 36081

WILHOLD, GILBERT ANTHONY, aero. engr.; b. East St. Louis, Ill., Dec. 9, 1934; s. Gilbert O. and Bernice (Petroski) W.; B.S., St. Louis U., 1957; postgrad. U. Ala., 1960-62; m. Juanita O. Martinez, June 6, 1957; children—Joseph A., Gilbert A., Sherrie G. Engr., McDonnell Aircraft Corp. Mo., 1957-60; engr. Chrysler Corp. Ala., Huntsville, 1960-62; with Marshall Space Flight Center, NASA, 1962—, analytical and theoretical acoustics tech. asst., lab. dir., 1963-66, dep. br. chief unsteady gas dynamics, 1966—. Recipient certificate of recognition Marshall Space Flight Center, 1968; Outstanding Service award NASA, 1969. Registered profl. engr., Ala. Mem. A.A.A.S., Acoustical Soc. Am. Home: 2604 Pitkin Lane Huntsville AL 35810 Office: Marshall Space Flight Center AL 35812

WILKERSON, JOHN P., lawyer; b. Cuthbert, Ga., Nov. 7, 1918; s. Walter McLendon and Viola (Joyner) W.; student U. Ga., 1946-47; grad. USAAF tech. sch. aircraft engring. Yale, 1945; LL.B., Stetson U., 1949; m. Sarah; m. Sarah Terrill Morris, June 14, 1950; children—Ann Terrill, John Morris, Sarah, Mary. Insp. engring. dept. Brewster Aero. Corp., L.I., N.Y., 1940-43; admitted to Ga. bar, 1948, Fla. bar, 1949; mem. firm Wilkerson & Wilkerson, Atlanta, 1949-51; practiced in Eustis, Fla.; judge municipal ct. Eustis, 1957-59; atty. Town of Tavares (Fla.), 1957-59; citrus grower. Active civic orgns. Served as capt. USAAF, World War II. Mem. Am., Ga., Lake Sumter (pres. 1953-55) bar assns., Fla. Bar, Nat. Hist. Soc. (founder), Republican. Phi Alpha Delta. Episcopalian. Mason (Shriner), Rotarian. Home: 505 S Center St Eustis FL 32726 Office: Suite 2 Eustis Prof Bldg Eustis FL 32726

WILKERSON, WILLIAM, dentist; b. Madill, Okla., Dec. 21, 1917; s. Olen and Nina (Bennett) W.; student N. Tex. State U., 1940, Tex. A. and M. Coll., 1941; D.D.S., Baylor U., 1947; m. Cleo K. Vickers, June 29, 1968; children—Craig, Damon. Pvt. practice dentistry, Grapevine, Tex., 1947—. Mem. council, Flower Mound, Tex., 1961-67, mayor, 1967—. Served with AUS, 1941-43. Mem. Am., Tex. dental assns. Home: Box 176 Route 1 Box 56F Flower Mound TX 76051 Office: 1701 W College St Grapevine TX 76051

WILKERSON, WOODROW WILSON, state ednl. ofcl.; b. Prince Edward County, Va., Apr. 29, 1913; s. John Henry and Betty Maude (Young) W.; B.A. magna cum laude, Hampden-Sydney Coll., 1934, M.A., Coll. William and Mary, 1938; Ed.D., U. Md., 1952; m. Dorothy Price, Sept. 1, 1937; children—Carrington Cabell, Elizabeth Claire (Mrs. Stephen C. Starbuck), Dorothy Swann. Tchr. English, Latin and gen. sci. Lunenburg County, Va., 1934-36; prin. Dillwyn High Sch., Buckingham County, Va., 1936-38, King William (Va.) High Sch., 1938-40, Marion High Sch., Smyth County, Va., 1940-45; asst. supr. secondary edn. Va. Dept. Edn., 1945-47, supr. secondary edn., 1947-57, dir. tech. edn., 1957-58, dir. secondary edn., 1958-60, supt. pub. instrn., 1960—. Commr. from Va. to Edn. Commn. of the States. Hon. life mem. Va. P.T.A., 1962. Mem. So. Assn. Colls. and Secondary Schs. (exec. sec. Va. 1952-57, chmn. central reviewing com. pub. schs., commn. secondary edn. 1956-57), Nat. Assn. Suprs. and Dirs. Secondary Edn. (pres. 1954-55), Nat. Assn. Secondary Sch. Prins., Council Chief State Sch. Officers, State Council Higher Edn. (ex-officio), Phi Delta Kappa (Distinguished Service award 1961), Phi Kappa Phi, Omicron Delta Kappa, Sigma Chi. Methodist. Kiwanian. Home: 914 Ridgetop Rd Richmond VA 23229 Office: State Office Bldg Richmond VA 23216

WILKES, CHARLES LATIMER, lawyer; b. Washington, Mar. 7, 1929; s. James Claiborne and Edna (Cross) W.; A.B., Dartmouth, 1950; LL.B., George Washington U., 1954; m. Norma Paige Fitchett, July 17, 1956; children—Charles Latimer, Douglas Hallett, David Claiborne, Karen Elizabeth. Admitted to D.C. bar, 1954, Mich. bar, 1958; practiced in Washington, 1954-57, 60—, Saginaw, Mich., 1958-60; mem. firm Wilkes & Artis, 1954-57, 60—. Dir. Columbia Fed. Savs. & Loan Assn., Washington. Mem. D.C. Hackers License Appeal Bd., 1962—; mem. Nat. Capitol Area council Boy Scouts Am., 1969—. Mem. Capitol Hill club Republican party. Trustee Fed. City Council, Washington, 1969—, Washington City Orphan Asylum, 1971—; bd. dirs. Met. Washington YMCA and YMCA Found., 1969—. Named Leader of Year, YMCA Met. Washington, 1970. Mem. Bar Assn. D.C., Am. Bar Assn., Barristers, Delta Tau Delta. Republican. Methodist. Mason (32 deg., Jester). Clubs: University, Dartmouth, Lawyers (Washington), Congressional Country. Home: 1004 Woburn Ct McLean VA 22101 Office: 1401 K St NW Washington DC 20005

WILKES, EUGENE PEIRCE, editor emeritus; b. Biloxi, Miss., Aug. 9, 1885; s. George W. and Laurie (Chidsey) W.; ed. Biloxi pub. schs.; m. Loretta V. Voivedich, Oct. 1, 1910; children—Josephine (Mrs. Reicker), Mrs. Robert A. Miller, Walter J. With Biloxi-Gulfport Daily Herald, 1898-70, pres. until 1970; editor Daily Herald Biloxi, also Gulfport. Chmn. Harrison County Pkwy. Commn., pres. Harrison County Devel. Commn., 1963-69; active Boy Scouts Am., 43 years; mem. Gulf Islands Seashore Adv. Commn., 1972. Named Outstanding Citizen of Biloxi, Lions, 1935; recipient Laurel Wreath award, 1966, Council cup Boy Scouts Am., 1936. Mem. So. Newspaper Pubs. Assn. (dir.). Rotarian (hon.). Home: 217 Fayard St Biloxi MS 39530

WILKEY, MALCOLM RICHARD, judge; b. Murfreesboro, Tenn., Dec. 6, 1918; s. Malcolm Newton and Elizabeth (Gilbert) W.; A.B., Harvard, 1940, LL.B., 1948; m. Emma Secul Depolo, Dec. 21, 1959. Admitted to Tex. bar, 1948, N.Y. bar, 1963, U.S. Supreme Ct. bar, 1952, Ct. of Appeals, D.C. Circuit, 1958; with Butler Binion Rice & Cook, 1948-54, 61-63; U.S. atty. So. Dist. Tex., 1954-58, asst. atty. gen. U.S., 1958-61, sec., asso. gen. counsel, Kennecott Copper Corp. 1963-67, sec., gen. counsel, 1967-70; judge U.S. Ct. Appeals, D.C. Circuit, 1970—. Del. Republican Nat. Conv., 1960. Served from 2d lt. to lt. col. AUS, 1941-45. Fellow Am. Bar Found.; mem. Am., Inter-Am. bar assns., Internat. Law Assn., Assn. Bar City N.Y., Am. Law Inst., Phi Beta Kappa, Delta Sigma Rho. Club: Harvard. Home: 540 N St SW Washington DC 20024 Office: US Ct Appeals Washington DC 20001

WILKINS, BENJAMIN HARRISON, JR., mfg. co. exec.; b. Nashville, May 28, 1899; s. Benjamin Harrison and Jane Bryan (Weeden) W.; B.S., Ga. Inst. Tech., 1921; m. Mary Boyers McQuiddy, June 29, 1935. With Tenn. Overall Co., Inc., Tullahoma, 1922—, pres., treas., 1941—; with Tenn. Glove Co., Inc., Tullahoma, 1922—, treas., pres., 1941—; dir. 1st Nat. Bank Tullahoma. Served with U.S. Army, 1918-19; to lt. col. USAAF, 1942-46. Mem. Am. Legion (past comdr.), V.F.W. (past comdr.), Tullahoma C. of C. (past pres.), So. Garment mfrs. Assn. (pres. 1956-57). Episcopalian. Mason (Shriner). Club: Tullahoma Golf and Country. Home: 408 N Atlantic St Tullahoma TN 37388 Office: 401 N Atlantic St Tullahoma TN 37388

WILKINS, JUDD RICE, microbiologist; b. Chgo., Dec. 12, 1920; s. Lewis Morris and Maude Edith (Wells) W.; B.S., U. Ill., 1946, M.S., 1947, Ph.D., 1950; m. Mary Helen Steinman, Jan. 25, 1950; children—Louise Edith, Ralph Martin. Asst. prof. microbiology U. S.D. Med, Sch., 1950-51; research investigator Upjohn Co., Kalamazoo, 1951-57; project scientist Booz Allen Applied Research, Inc., Bethesda, Md., 1957-64; head dept. microbiology Eye Research Found., Bethesda, 1964-66; biol. research officer Langley Research Center, NASA, Hampton, VA, 1966—. Served with AUS, 1943-45. Mem. Am. Soc. for Microbiology, Sigma Xi. Episcopalian. Kiwanian (dir. Bethesda 1966). Research on effect of gravity on growth of microorganisms; devised math. model of incubation period of infectious diseases. Patentee continuous recording nephelometer and antibiotic combinations. Home: 313 Beechmount Dr Hampton VA 23369 Office: NASA Langley Research Center Hampton VA 23365

WILKINS, MAURICE LAYNE, aerospace engr.; b. Fayetteville, Ark., Apr. 7, 1941; s. Woodrow and Marion (Phillips) W.; B.S. in Mech. Engring., U. Ark., 1963; m. Estell Gentry, Feb. 1, 1964; children—Scott Allen, Stacy Layne, Aerospace engr. Oklahoma City Air Materiel Area, Tinker AFB, Okla., 1963—. Recipient Silver Zero Defects award Ocama, 1967, Gold Zero Defects award, 1969. Registered profl. engr., Okla. Mem. Soc. Profl. Engrs. and Scientists Tinker AFB, Tinker Mgmt. Club. Baptist. Home: 3701 Greenway Terrace Del City OK 73115 Office: Tinker AFB OK 73145

WILKINS, RAOUL WHEELER, architect; b. Charlottesville, Va., Aug. 18, 1921; s. John William and Evelyn (Wheeler) W.; B.S., U. Va., 1950 children (by previous marriage)—Susan Wheeler, Virginia (Mrs. W. Todd), William Widdifield; m. 2d, Sandra Leigh Sandlin, Aug. 1, 1970. Draftsman, Ballou & Justice, architects, Richmond, Va., 1950-52, Walford & Wright, architects, Richmond, 1952-57; architect Raoul Wheeler Wilkins, Maidens, Va., 1959—. Past. dir. Duntreath Community Assn. Served with Combat Engrs., AUS, 1942-45. Registered architect, Va., Tenn., N.C., Md. Mem. A.I.A., Am. Registered Architects, Confederate Hist. Soc. Eng., S.C.V., Order Stars and Bars, Nat. Steeplechase and Hunt Assn., Am. Legion, U. Va., Greenbrier Mil. (past dir.) alumni assns., Alpha Rho Chi. Democrat. Methodist. Club: Kallikrates, Deep Run Hunt. Spl. works include shopping centers, apt. projects. Home: Pavilion Hill Maidens VA 23102 Office: Route 6 at 522 S Maidens VA 23102

WILKINS, RICHARD COWAN, oil co. exec.; b. Warren, Pa., Aug. 31, 1908; s. Percy Waters and Hariett (Cowan) W.; B.S. in Petroleum Engring., Pa. State U., 1931; m. Sally Lou Darr, Oct. 28, 1938; children—Linda Lou (Mrs. John C. White), Richard Cowan. Engr., geologist Texaco, La., 1931-33, field engr., 1933-35, drilling, prodn. field supt., 1935-46; supt. J.C. Hawkins & Delta Drilling Co., La., Tex., Miss., 1946-50; part owner W. Hawkins Drilling Co., Hawkins-Wilkins Prodn. Co., Houston, 1950-60; cons., ind. oil operator, Houston, 1960-64; eastern regional mgr. Dyna-Drill Co. div. Smith Internat., Houston, 1965—. Mem. Alpha Tau Omega. Mason. Club: Houston. Home: 1225 Wood Hollow Dr Houston TX 77027 Office: Cullen Bank Center 600 Jefferson St Houston TX 77002

WILKINS, ROBERT PEARCE, lawyer; b. Jesup, Ga., Sept. 10, 1933; s. Ransome Little and Sarah (Pearce) W.; B.S., U. S.C., 1953, LL.B., 1954; LL.M., Georgetown U., 1957; m. Rose Truesdale, Jan. 7, 1956; children—Robert Pearce, Chisolm Wallace, Sarah Ruth, Rose Anne. Admitted to S.C. bar, 1954; atty. Office Gen. Counsel Sec. Army, Washington, 1956; trust officer First Nat. Bank S.C., Columbia, 1957-60; practiced law, 1960-64; partner firm McLain, Sherrill & Wilkins, Columbia, 1964-68, McKay, Sherrill, Walker, Townsend & Wilkins, Columbia, 1969—; pres. Sandlapper Press, Inc., 1967—, pub. Sandlapper, Mag. of S.C., 1968—, editor, 1968-69. Del., Spl. Liaison Tax Com. Southeastern Region, 1967-70; exec. com. Richland County Republican Com., 1960-64; sec.-treas. Richland County Rep. Club, 1960. Bd. dirs. Central Tb-RD Assn.; trustee Sch. Dist. 1, Lexington County, S.C. Served with AUS, 1954-55. C.L.U., S.C. Mem. Am. (chmn. valuation subcom., estate and gift tax com., taxation sect. 1967—, vice chmn. service and assistance to law student div. com. gen. practice sect. 1971—), S.C. (tax coordinating com. 1968-70), Richland County bar assns., Columbia Jr. C. of C. (sec.-treas. 1958-59), Columbia Estate Planning Council (pres. 1964-65), Am. Y-Flyer Yacht Racing Assn. (area v.p. 1971), Omicron Delta Kappa, Sigma Chi. Clubs: Columbia Sailing (dir. 1968-71), Columbia Tip-Off (dir. 1968—, pres. 1971-72). Author: Drafting Wills and Trust Agreements in South Carolina. Contbr. articles to publs. Home: Route 7 Lexington SC 29072 Office: 1340 Bull St Columbia SC 29201

WILKINS, RUTH LOIS, mus. curator; b. Boston, Nov. 20, 1926; d. Abraham and Harriett (Olive) Strauss; B.A., Wellesley Coll., 1948 children—Peter Dana, Michael Paul. Adminstrv. asst. Everson Mus. of Art, Syracuse, N.Y., 1959-65, curator of collections, 1966-70; cons. Mus. of Am. China Trade, Milton, Mass., 1971—; curator edn. Kimbell Art Mus., Ft. Worth, Tex., 1971—. Recipient Post Standard Woman of Achievement in Arts award, 1968. Co-author: China Trade Silver for the Anglo-American Market, 1971. Editor: American Painting from 1830, 1965; Chinese Art from the Cloud Wampler and other collections, 1968; Everson Dedication, 1968; What is an Art Museum, 1970; American Ship Portraits and Marine Painting, 1970. Home: 308 Ridglea Village 6035 Westridge Lane Fort Worth TX 76116 Office: Kimbell Art Mus Will Rogers Rd W Fort Worth TX 76107

WILKINS, WILLIAM THOMAS, JR., polit. party ofcl.; b. Cotton Plant, Ark., Jan. 17, 1940; s. William Thomas and Sue Ellen (Brown) W.; student Millsaps Coll., 1958-60; B.Pub. Administrn., U. Miss., 1962, M.A., 1966; m. Martha Ann Huddleston, Aug. 18, 1961; children—Martha Ellen, William Thomas IV. Part-time research asst. U. Miss. Bur. Research in Bus. and Govt., 1961-62; field rep., dir. research Miss. Republican Com., Jackson, 1962-64, exec. dir., adminstrv. asst. to state chmn., 1964—. Exec. dir. So. Assn. Rep. State Chmn., 1969—, So. Rep. Conf., 1969, 71. Mem. Am. Polit. Sci. Assn., Am. Assn. Polit. Consultants, Kappa Sigma, Delta Sigma Phi, Pi Sigma Alpha. Presbyn. Home: 4820 Northampton Dr Jackson MS 39211 Office: PO Box 1178 Jackson MS 39205

WILKINS, WILLIE THOMAS, JR., dentist; b. Durham, N.C., Dec. 10, 1929; s. Willie Thomas and Ida (Boddie) W.; B.S., N.C. Agr. and Tech. State U., 1949; postgrad. Howard U., 1949-50, D.D.S., 1960; postgrad. in oral surgery Georgetown U., 1960-61; m. Burma Louise Whitted, June 23, 1962. Oral surgery intern D.C. Gen. Hosp., Washington, 1960-61; practice dental surgery, Greensboro, N.C., 1961—; chmn. dental affairs L. Richardson Meml. Hosp., Greensboro; active staff Moses Cones Meml. Hosp., Greensboro; staff Evergreen Hosp., Greensboro. Served with AUS, 1952-54; Korea. Recipient Valuable Contbn. award D.C. Dental Soc., 1961. Fellow Am. Sch. Health Assn. (governing council), Royal Soc. Health, Intercontinental Biog. Assn.; mem. Am., Nat. dental assns., N.C. Dental Soc., Am. Acad. Gen. Dentistry, N.C. Acad. Sci., Am. Soc. Geriatric Dentistry, A.A.A.S., Am. Dental Soc. Anesthesiology, Soc. Advancement Dental Anesthesia, Fedn. Dentaire Internat., Greensboro C. of C. Mem. A.M.E. Ch. (chmn. bd. trustees 1963—). Club: Health. Author: Stabilizing of Replanted or Loose Teeth, 1963. Home: Route 6 Box 198 Greensboro NC 27405 Office: 1607 Asheboro St Greensboro NC 27406

WILKINSON, CHARLES BURNHAM, govt. ofcl.; b. Mpls., Apr. 23, 1916; s. Charles P. and Edith (Lindbloom) W.; B.A., U. Minn., 1937; M.A., Syracuse U., 1940; m. Mary Shifflett, Aug. 29, 1938; children—Charles P., James G. Asst. football coach Syracuse U., 1937-41, U. Minn., 1941-42; asst. football coach U. Okla., 1946-47, athletic dir., head football coach, 1947-64; spl. cons. to Pres. Kennedy on phys. fitness, 1961-64, now spl. cons. to Pres. Nixon. Pres., Am. Football Coaches Assn., 1959; pres. Lifetime Sports Found., 1965-68. Republican candidate for U.S. Senate from Okla., 1964; mem. Rep. Nat. com. for Okla. Named Coach of Year, Am. Football Coaches Assn., 1949, A.P., 1950; named to Football Hall of Fame. Home: PO Box 910 Norman OK 73069 Office: The White House Washington DC 20500

WILKINSON, GLEN ANDERSON, lawyer; b. Ogden, Utah, Apr. 17, 1911; s. Robert Brown and Cecilia (Anderson) W.; B.S., Brigham Young U., 1934; J.D. with honors, George Washington U., 1938; m. Katherine McKinnon, Apr. 26, 1943; children—Frederick McKinnon, Malcolm Glen, Richard Claude, Charles Symmes. Admitted to D.C. bar, 1938; law clk. Bd. Tax Appeals, Washington, 1938-40; asst. corp. counsel D.C., 1940-42, asso. firm Ernest L. Wilkinson, Washington, 1946-51; partner firm Wilkinson, Cragun & Barker, Washington, 1951—; gen. counsel Arapahoe Indian Tribe, Am. Soc. Travel Agts., Inc., N.Y.C. Dir. Camperdown Co., Piedmont Plush Mills & Commodity Warehouse Corp., Greenville, S.C., HAR Corp., Washington. Mem. governing bd. Gen. Alumni Assn., 1968—, treas., 1970-71; mem. adv. council Nat. Law Center, George Washington U., 1968—. Served to lt. col. AUS, 1942-46. Decorated Legion of Merit. Mem. George Washington U. Law Assn. (pres. 1966-68), Bar Assn. D.C. (chmn. com. on Ct. of Claims 1964-66, ann. banquet com. 1969), Am. Bar Assn., Am. Judicature Soc. Republican. Mem. Ch. of Jesus Christ of Latter-day Saints. Home: 4308 Forest Lane NW Washington DC 20007 Office: 1616 H St NW Washington DC 20006

WILKINSON, HOWARD CHARLES, coll. pres.; b. Katy, Tex., June 23, 1918; s. Leroy and Carrie (Hoyt) Wilkinson; A.B., Southwestern U., 1939, D.D., 1963; M.Div., Duke, 1942; m. Juanita Scott, June 24, 1947; children—Scott Russell, Melinda Faye, Barbara Gail, Fleeta Mae. Ordained to ministry Methodist Ch., 1942; asso.

minister First Ch., Charlotte, N.C., 1942-47; minister Haywood St. Ch., Asheville, 1947-49, First Ch., Lexington, N.C., 1949-56, Central Ch., Shelby, N.C., 1956-57; chaplain Duke U., Durham, N.C., 1957-72; pres. Greensboro (N.C.) Coll., 1972—. Chmn. Inter-Conf. Commn. on Student Religious Work in N.C., 1956-60; chmn. Western N.C. Meth. Conf. Bd. Trustees, 1956-69; chmn. trustees Camp Tekoa, 1954; pres. Lexington (N.C.) Ministerial Assn., 1951. Pres. Lexington chpt. A.R.C., 1952; dir. Lexington United Fund, 1954-56; v.p. Cleveland County chpt. A.R.C., 1957. Bd. dirs. Found. for Research on Nature of Man, 1969-72. Named Young Man of the Year 1951, Lexington, N.C.; recipient George Washington Honor medal Freedoms Found. at Valley Forge, 1964. Mem. N.C. Council Chs., Fellowship of Reconciliation, Fellowship of So. Churchman, Nat. Assn. Coll. and Univ. Chaplains (exec. com. 1961—, chmn. southeastern sect. 1965-66), Durham City-Wide P.T.A. Council (pres. 1965-67). Mason. Rotarian (pres. Durham 1962-63). Contbr.: Effective Prayers; Parapsychology Today. Home: Box 222 Greensboro NC 27402

WILKINSON, JAMES RALPH, mfrs. rep.; b. Albion, Mich., May 28, 1921; s. Ralph Eugene and Bessie (McLain) W.; student Mich. State Coll., 1940-41; m. Patricia Elaine Hallett; children—Tracy, Leslie, Kathy, Robert, Vickie, Randi, Donald, Kelly, Penny. Nat. service mgr. Lonergan Mfg. Co., Albion, 1946-49; nat. service mgr. Kitchen Machine div. Toledo Scale Co., 1949-55, sales mgr., Fla., 1955-59; mfrs. rep. kitchen equipment, Plantation, Fla., 1959—; pres. Gene Burel Assos., Inc., Atlanta, 1971—. Republican precinct committeeman, 1964-68; mem. Broward Rep. Exec. Com., 1964-68. Served with USMCR, 1941-45. Mem. Fla. United Numismatists, Orders and Medals Soc. Am., Orders and Medals Research Soc. Eng., Mil. Collectors Club of Can. Baptist. Contbr. articles to profl. jours. Home: 4210 SW 3d St Plantation FL 33314

WILKINSON, NORMAN MEANS, lawyer, banker; b. Greenwood, Ark., Oct. 26, 1910; s. William Norman and Mary Myrtle (Means) W.; B.A., U. Ark., 1931; LL.B., Cumberland U., 1933; J.D., Samford U., 1969; m. Betty Jean Forbus, June 13, 1953; children—Norman, Stanhope, Susan, Edward. Admitted to Ark. bar, 1933; individual practice law, Greenwood, 1933—; cashier Farmers Bank, Greenwood, 1935-55, pres., 1955—. Mem. Gen. Assembly Ark., 1933-42, speaker Ho. of Reps., 1941; city atty., 1970—. Mem. Sebastian County Bd. Edn., 1950—, Ark. Banking Bd., 1948-49, Ark. Bd. Edn., 1949-55, Ark. Indsl. Devel. Commn., 1970-71. Sec., Sebastian County Democratic Central Com., 1950—. Trustee Banking Sch. South, La. State U.; bd. dirs., Sparks Regional Med. Center and Found., Fort Smith, 1971—. Served to lt. comdr. USNR, 1942-46. Decorated Purple Heart. Mem. Ark. Bankers Assn. (pres. 1970-71), Blue Key, Lambda Chi Alpha. Mason. Author: History of Sebastian County, Arkansas, 1961. Home: 404 W Sycamore Greenwood AR 72936 Office: Farmers Bank 5 Hackett Rd Greenwood AR 72936

WILKINSON, REYMOND WALLACE, oil co. exec.; b. Baton Rouge, June 10, 1927; s. Earl V. and Maydea (Mixon) W.; B.S. in Geology, La. State U., 1949; m. Betty Pecora, Jan. 29, 1949; children—Reymond Neal, Dona Lynn. Seismologist, Keystone Exploration Co., Houston, 1950-52; geophysicist La. Oil Exploration Co., Inc., New Orleans, New Iberia, La., 1952-66, Getty Oil Co., New Orleans, 1966—; also active in real estate investment and devel., So. La. 1966—. Served with USNR, 1945-46: PTO. Mem. New Orleans Geologic Soc., Southeastern Geophys. Soc., Soc. Exploration Geophysicists (gen. chmn. internat. meeting 1970), Permian Basin Geophys. Soc. Mason. Home: 2412 Dartmouth Dr Midland TX 79701 Office: PO Box 1231 Midland TX 79701

WILKINSON, RONALD STERNE, historian; b. Chgo., Feb. 16, 1934; s. Maurice Sterne and Florence Marie (Colby) W.; B.A., Mich. State U., 1960, Ph.D., 1969; Ryder scholar, U. London, 1960; Woodrow Wilson fellow, Harvard, 1960-61; Fulbright scholar, Univ. Coll., London, 1965-66; postgrad. Inst. Hist. Research, London, 1965-66. Instr., rare book librarian Mich. State U., 1963-70; dir. Entomol. Reprint Specialists, Pubs., East Lansing, Mich., 1968-69; manuscript historian Library of Congress, Washington, 1970—. Fellow Linnean Soc. London, Royal Entomol. Soc. London; mem. History of Sci. Soc., Brit. Soc. for History of Sci., Soc. for History of Alchemy and Early Chemistry, Soc. for Bibliography of Natural History, A.A.A.S. Editor: The Michigan Entomologist, 1966-71. Contbr. articles to profl. jours. Home: 228 9th St NE Washington DC 20002 Office: Library of Congress Washington DC 20540

WILKOFF, LEE JOSEPH, microbiologist; b. Youngstown, O., Oct. 17, 1924; s. Irving and Adelaide (Nichol) W.; student North Park Coll., 1942-44; B.S., Roosevelt U., 1948; Ph.D. (Frank G. Logan fellow), U. Chgo., 1963; m. Meryl Louis Traub, Oct. 17, 1953, 1 son, Jay Foster. Biochemist, VA Hosp., Hines, Ill., 1952-54; research asst. dept. medicine U. Chgo., 1954-60; USPHS trainee, 1961-62; dir. microbiol. labs. Woodard Research Corp., Herndon, Va., 1963-64; sr. microbiologist So. Research Inst., Birmingham, Ala., 1964-70, head cell biology div., 1970—. Mem. A.A.A.S., Am. Soc. Microbiology, Soc. for Gen. Microbiology, N.Y. Acad. Scis., Soc. for Exptl. Biology and Medicine, Am. Assn. for Cancer Research, Sigma Xi. Contbr. articles to profl. jours. Home: 1813 Old Creek Trail Vestavia Hills AL 35216 Office: 2000 9th Av S Birmingham AL 35205

WILKS, STANLEY NEAL, systems analyst; b. London, Eng., Oct. 25, 1932; s. Samuel Stanley and Gena (Orr) W. (parents Am. citizens); B.A., North Tex. State Coll., 1955; postgrad. Cambridge (Eng.) U., 1955-56, Am. U., 1969—; M.A., Columbia, 1961; m. Jocelyn Wilkins, June 28, 1958; children—Elizabeth Anne, Christine Jocelyn, Victoria Lynn, Jeffrey Neal. Mathematician, Nat. Security Agy., Washington, 1956-58; lab. supr. IBM, N.Y.C., 1959-61; program analyst Internat. Electric Corp., Paramus, N.J., 1961-63; sr. analyst Decision Systems, Inc., Paramus, 1963-64; operations research scientist, computer systems specialist System Devel. Corp., Falls Church, Va., 1964-71; computer systems analyst Naval Command Systems Support Activity, Washington, 1971—. Served with AUS, 1956-58. Mem. Am. Statis. Assn., Assn. Computing Machinery. Home: 3240 N Abingdon St Arlington VA 22207 Office: Code 20.1 Bldg No 196 Washington Navy Yard Washington DC 20390

WILKS, WILLIAM TAYLOR, univ. adminstr.; b. Berea, Ky., Jan. 11, 1911; s. William Pugh and Mamie (Powell) W.; B.S., Auburn U., 1930, M.S., 1935; Ed.D., Columbia, 1949, postgrad., 1955; m. Gurley Bright, Nov. 26, 1935; 1 dau., Laura Elizabeth. Tchr. sci., Cullman (Ala.) High Sch., 1930-36, Tallassee (Ala.) High Sch., 1936-41, Montgomery (Ala.) High Sch., 1941-42, tchr. sci. Goddard Coll., Plainfield, Vt., 1942-43, 46-47; asst. prof. physics Auburn (Ala.) U., 1943-44; head physics dept. Marion (Ala.) Mil. Inst., 1944-46, asso. prof., 1947-55, prof., head dept., 1955-68; v.p. acad. affairs Troy (Ala.) State U., 1968—. Chmn., Selective Service Bd. 1953-68, Troy Housing Authority, 1967—. Trustee Pike Tchrs. Credit Assn. Fellow Ala. Acad. Sci., A.A.A.S.; mem. Ala. Edn. Assn., Troy Tchrs. Assn. (pres. 1952-53), Nat. Sci. Tchrs. Assn. (state dir. 1956-65), Phi Kappa Phi, Kappa Phi Kappa, Kappa Delta Pi, Phi Delta Kappa. Rotarian. Contbr. profl. jours. Home: 202 Highland Av Troy AL 36081

WILL, EDWIN EUGENE, supt. schs.; b. Mt. Jackson, Va., July 22, 1909; s. Lewis Miller and Ada Florence (Grim) W.; B.A., Bridgewater Coll., 1931; M.A., U. Va., 1942; m. Anna Mae Pope, Sept. 5, 1944; children—Sharon, David. Tchr., coach pub. schs. Northampton County, Va., 1931-32, Rockingham County, Va., 1932-37; prin. Timberville Sch., Rockingham County, 1937-49; supt. pub. schs. Bath County, Va., 1949-60; asst. supt. schs. Hampton, Va., 1960-61; supt. Brunswick County, Lawrenceville, Va., 1961—. Mem. Rockingham County Edn. Assn. (pres., 1941-46), Va. Edn. Assn. (v.p. 1946-51), Bridgewater Coll. Alumni Assn. (pres. 1952), Brunswick County C. of C. (pres. 1967), Va. Assn. Sch. Adminstrs. (sec.-treas. 1968), Va. High Sch. League (Va. chmn. 1949-50), Phi Delta Kappa. Rotarian (pres. 1963-64), Mason, Lion (pres. 1964-65). Home: 306 Turnbull St Lawrenceville VA 23868 Office: Box 26 Lawrenceville VA 23868

WILL, ERWIN HOGE, ret. utility exec.; b. Richmond, Va., Jan. 8, 1900; s. Fritz and Eda Louise (Briel) W.; B.S., Va. Poly. Inst., 1922; D.Sc., Hampden-Sydney Coll.; m. Virginia Wilroy Simpson, Apr. 23, 1927; children—Joyce Virginia (Mrs. William P. Hooten), Erwin Hoge. With engring. dept. Va. Electric & Power Co., 1922-26, asst. supt., 1926-28, mgr. Suffolk Dist., 1928-35, gen. mgr. operations, 1947-50, v.p., 1950-54, v.p., gen. mgr. 1954, dir., 1955, pres., 1956-58, chmn. exec. com., vice chmn. bd., 1958-60, chmn. bd., 1960-72; gen. supt. El Paso Electric Co., 1935-42, pres., dir., 1942-47; past pres. Carolinas Va. Nuclear Power Assos., Inc.; dir. Ethyl Corp., Va. Chems., Inc., Central Nat. Bank of Richmond, Central Nat. Corp., Surveyor Fund, Inc. Past Pres. Va. Mus. Fine Arts. Served with C.E., U.S. Army, 1918. Mem. Newcomen Soc., Omicron Delta Kappa, Chi Psi, Pi Tau Sigma, Tau Beta Pi. Mason. Clubs: Commonwealth, Forum (Richmond Va.); Country of Va. Home: 6161 River Rd Richmond VA 23226

WILLARD, ANNE OLDHAM, phys. therapist; b. Cleve., Aug. 4, 1916; d. John Lorraine and Olga Caroline (Wellington) Oldham; B.A., Rollins Coll., 1940; postgrad. U. Wis., 1942-44, U. Pa., 1959; m. Leland Henry Willard, June 8, 1945 (dec. Nov. 1960); children—Dorothy Ann, Byron Keith, David. Phys. therapist Dr. Charles Graybill Meml. Hosp., Lawton, Okla., 1951-53, State of Ala., Gadsden, 1954-57; chief phys. therapist Crippled Children's Soc., Ft. Worth, 1957-60; pvt. practice phys. therapy, Mineral Walls, Tex., 1960-61; head phys. therapist Flow Meml. Hosp., Denton, 1961-71; chief phys. therapist Collin Meml. Hosp., McKinney, Tex., 1971—. Served to 1st lt. AUS, 1940-46. Mem. Nat. Wildlife Fedn., Denton Humane Soc., Greater Dallas Great Dane Club, Alpha Phi. Episcopalian. Mem. Order Eastern Star. Club: Soroptimist. Home: Box 850 Denton TX 76201 Office: Phys Therapy Dept Collin Meml Hosp McKinney TX

WILLARD, GARRY AARON, editor; b. Utica, N.Y., May 9, 1904; s. Edwin Herbert and Cora (Blair) W.; grad. high sch.; m. Mary Cook Skinner, Aug. 6, 1927; children—Garry Aaron, Nancy Jane, Mary Blair. Editor Boonville (N.Y.) Herald, 1918-36, Leaksville (N.C.) News, 1937-43; co-pub. Danville (Va.) Comml. Appeal, 1943-50; staff Jour. Messenger, Manassas, Va., 1951—, editor, gen. mgr. 1951—; v.p. Prince William Pub. Co., Inc., Manassas, 1954—; dir. 1st Va. Bank. Mem. Va. Press Assn. (pres. 1969-70), Greater Manassas C. of C. (dir.), Sigma Delta Chi. Mason, Kiwanian. Club: Evergreen Country. Home: 9200 Battle St Manassas VA 22110 Office: 9102 Center St Manassas VA 22110

WILLARD, HENRY KELLOGG, II, city ofcl.; b. Washington, Aug. 11, 1926; s. Henry Augustus and Abby Fuller (Hooker) W.; grad. Choate Sch., 1944; B.A., Yale, 1950; m. Louise Phelps Brooks, Sept. 1, 1950; children— Henry Augustus III, John Brooks. Intelligence officer CIA, Washington, 1950-52; v.p. Am. Security & Trust Co., Washington, 1952-71 (on leave of absence); Presdl. appointee Washington City Council, 1971—. Trustee Equitable Life Ins. Co., Washington, 1970—. Chmn. finance com. Republican party Washington, 1968-71; mem. Rep. Nat. Finance Com., 1970-71; alternate del. Rep. Conv., 1968. Served with USNR, 1944-46. Clubs: Chevy Chase, Metropolitan (Washington); Nantucket (Mass.) Yacht. Home: 2731 31st Pl NW Washington DC 20008 Office: City Hall 14th & E Sts NW Washington DC 20004

WILLARD, RUDOLPH HAROLD, educator; b. Jersey City, Mar. 9, 1893; s. Joel Gilman and Mary Sophronia (Brown) W.; Ph.B., Yale, 1913; m. Marion Britton Rafferty, Oct. 22, 1924; 1 son, Frank Gilman. Engr., Westinghouse Electric and Mfg. Co., East Pittsburgh, Pa., 1913-18; engr., plant supt. Tenn. Furniture Corp., Chattanooga, 1919-23; various positions, 1924-36; cons. engr., Ridgewood, N.J., 1936-51; vis. prof., cons. N.C. State U., Raleigh, 1952—. Scoutmaster Chattanooga council Boy Scouts Am., 1922-25. Served with Signal Corps, AUS, 1918. Mem. Sigma Xi. Mason. Club: Torch (Raleigh). Author 2 textbooks on furniture tech., 1958, 62; monthly columnist Furniture Design and Mfg. mag., 1960-71. Patentee steel side rail for beds. Home: S-2 Raleigh Apts Raleigh NC 27605

WILLARD, WILLIAM B(RADLEY), banker, estate mgr.; b. Washington, Aug. 17, 1904; s. Henry Kellogg and Helen Wilson (Parker) W.; A.B., Dartmouth, 1926; m. Florence Fatio Keys, Jan. 12, 1929; children—Helen Parker (Mrs. John C. Chapin), Amie Keys (Mrs. Huntington T. Block), William Bradley. Clk., Nat. Met. Bank, Washington, 1926-30; v.p. Nat. Savs. & Trust Co., Washington, 1934-54; trustee Estate of H.K. Willard, Washington, 1926—; mgr., cashier Bank of Guam, 1945-46; chmn. exec. com., dir. Nat. Savs. & Trust Co. Dir. Nat. Capital Area Council Boy Scouts Am., 1937-42, treas., 1941-42; dir. Legal Aid Soc., Washington, 1951-57; pres. Helen Parker Willard Found.; trustee Phi Gamma Delta Ednl. Found. Served with USNR, World War II; now capt. Res. Decorated Bronze Star medal. Mem. Newcomen Soc. N.Am., Oldest Inhabitants D.C., Naval Order U.S., Washington Bd. Trade. Presbyn. (past trustee, treas.). Clubs: Burning Tree, Chevy Chase, Metropolitan. Home: 2615 31st St Washington DC 20008 Office: 509 Walker Bldg 734 15th St NW Washington DC 20005

WILLE, (ROLAND) FRANK, lawyer, govt. ofcl.; b. N.Y.C., Feb. 27, 1931; s. Frank Joseph and Alma (Schutt) W.; grad. Phillips Acad., Andover, Mass., 1947; A.B. cum laude, Harvard, 1951, LL.B. cum laude, 1956; LL.M. in Taxation, N.Y.U., 1960; m. Barbara Bowen McIntosh, July 2, 1969. Admitted to N.Y. bar, 1956; asso. firm Davis Polk Wardwell Sunderland & Kiendl, N.Y.C., 1956-60; asst. counsel to gov. State of N.Y., Albany, 1960-62, 1st asst. counsel, 1962-64; supt. banks State of N.Y., N.Y.C., 1964-70; chmn. Fed. Deposit Ins. Corp., Washington, 1970—, mem. com. on interest and dividends, 1971—. Adv. mem. N.Y. State Joint Legislative Com. on Interstate Co-op; ex officio mem. N.Y. Job Devel. Authority, N.Y. Urban Devel. Corp., 1968-70. Mem. N.Y. County Republican Com., 1959-61. Served to lt. (j.g.) USNR, 1951-54. Mem. N.Y. State Bar Assn., Assn. Bar City N.Y. Home: 3507 Springland Lane NW Washington DC 20008 Office: 550 17th St NW Washington DC 20429

WILLEFORD, GEORGE, chmn. Tex. Rep. Com.; b. Dallas, Oct. 23, 1921; s. George and Joy Brenner W.; B.S., Tex. A. and M. U., 1943; M.D., U. Tex., 1946; m. Ann Jennings, Mar. 27, 1948; children—George III, Allison Ann, Joy Hale. Practice medicine, specializing in pediatrics, Austin, Tex. Chmn., Cameron County Republican Com., 1960-62, 66-70; exec. committeeman Rep. Exec. Com, 1962-66; chmn. Region Three, Tex. Rep. Com., 1970—, state chmn., 1970—. Served to capt., M.C., USAF, 1946-49. Diplomate Am. Bd. Pediatrics. Mem. Am., Tex. med. assns., Tex. Pediatric Assn., Am. Acad. Pediatrics, Cameron County (Tex.) Farm Bur., Phi Rho Sigma. Episcopalian. Rotarian. Author: Medical Word Finder, 1966. Address: 1404 Gaston Av Austin TX 78703*

WILLETT, CLARENCE HUNTER, former broadcasting co. exec.; b. Pollock, La., June 16, 1906; s. William P. and Adelia Elizabeth (Walker) W.; student La. Coll., 1924-26; m. Louise Jackson, May 4, 1926; 1 son, Clarence Hunter. With Guaranty Corp., Baton Rouge, 1937—, pres., 1961-71; dir. Guaranty Corp., Guaranty Income Life, Guaranty Broadcasting; v.p., treas. Guaranty Income Life Ins. Co., 1946-71; treas. Guaranty Broadcasting Corp., 1961-71. Mem. Nat. Assn. Pub. Accountants (charter), Baton Rouge C. of C. Methodist. Home: 646 Nelson St Baton Rouge LA 70808 Office: 929 Government St Baton Rouge LA 70802

WILLETT, EUGENE PATRICK HENRY, lab. exec.; b. Shawnee, Okla., Dec. 6, 1909; s. Eugene Jerome and Ophelia (Linz) W.; student Belmont Abbey Coll., 1928; m. Carolyn Brockway Chappelle, June 21, 1939, (dec. Jan. 1964); children—Eugene Brockway, Carol Louise, William Charles; m. 3d, Ruby Lee Lester, Mar. 14, 1972. Instrument man, surveyor, chief of party U.S. Engrs. Corps, N.C., S.C., 1929-32, concrete insp., Tuscaloosa (Ala.) Lock and Dam, 1936-38; timber cruiser, chief of party U.S. Forest Service, 1933-36; asst. concrete engr., concrete engr. Harza Engring. Co., 1938-41; concrete engr. U.S. Navy, Charleston, S.C., Bklyn., 1941-43, E.I. DuPont de Nemours, Hanford (Wash.) Engr. Works, 1943-45; engr. Ala. Hwy. Dept., 1946-50; concrete cons. Govt. El Salvador, 1951-53; co-founder, co-owner Dixie Labs, Inc., Mobile, Dothan, Ala., Columbus, Ga., 1953—. Mem. C. of C., Am. Soc. Testing Materials, Am. Concrete Inst., Better Bus. Bur., Baldwin County Hist. Soc., Eastern Shores Art Assn., Am. Welding Soc. Democrat. Roman Catholic. Clubs: Fairhope Yacht, Lake Forest Yacht and Country. Home: 1211 Middlering Rd Mobile AL 36608 Office: 604 Loeffler St PO Box 7387 Mobile AL 36607

WILLETT, JAMES F., assn. exec. Treas., Am. Automobile Assn. Office: 15th and Pennsylvania Av NW Washington DC 20013*

WILLETTS, FREDERICK, JR., savs. and loan exec.; b. Wilmington, N.C., June 4, 1925; s. Frederick and Eleanor (Harriss) W.; student U. N.C., 1943, U. Ind., 1950-52; m. Helen Messick, June 25, 1948; children— Frederick III, Margaret, Elizabeth. With Coop. Savs. and Loan Assn., Wilmington, 1946—, asst. loan officer, 1946-47, sec., 1947-59, treas., 1947—, exec. v.p., 1959-63, pres., 1964—; pres. N.C. Savs. & Loan League; dir. Am. Mortgage Ins. Co., Raleigh, N.C. Dir. Boys Brigade Clubs Am., Wilmington, 1959-70. Bd. dirs. YMCA, Wilmington. Served with USAAF, 1943-46; PTO. Mem. U.S. Savs. and Loan League (mem. legislative com.), Greater Wilmington C. of C. (pres. 1966), Sigma Alpha Epsilon. Democrat. Episcopalian. Rotarian. Clubs: Carolina Yacht, Surf (Wrightsville Beach, N.C.), Cape Fear Country (Wilmington, N.C.). Home: 703 Windson Dr Wilmington NC 28401 Office: Coop Savs and Lan Assn 201 Market St Wilmington NC 28401

WILLEY, MALCOLM MACDONALD, sociologist, univ. adminstr.; b. Portland, Me., Nov. 13, 1897; s. Carlton Bartlett and Helen Marr (Macdonald) W.; A.B., Clark U., 1920, L.H.D., 1945; A.M., Columbia U., 1921, Ph.D., 1926; LL.D., U. Me., 1952; m. Nancy Burnham Boyd, Feb. 6, 1924 (div.); m. 2d, Betty Washburn, Aug. 1, 1955 (dec. June 1962); m. 3d, Delores T. Miller, Sept. 7, 1963; 1 son, Anil; stepchildren—Christine, George, Dolores. Instr. sociology, Dartmouth, 1923-24, asst. prof., 1924-27; asso. prof. U. Minn., 1927-29, prof., 1929-34, univ. dean and asst. to pres., 1934-43, v.p. acad. adminstrn., 1943-63; ednl. cons. Ford Found., U. Calcutta (India), 1963-68; prof., chmn. dept. sociology Maryville (Tenn.) Coll., 1968-70, 72—; acad. exec. officer, 1970-72. Vis. lectr. sociology U. Chgo., winter 1929-30. Mem. U.S. Nat. Commn. for UNESCO, 1953-59; investigator Pres. Research Com. on Social Trends, 1931, and author (with S.A. Rice) sect. on communication in com. report; dir. studies for Com. on Effect of Depression and Recovery on Higher Edn., Am. Assn. U. Profs., 1934-35; Mem. com. on faculty research fellowships, 1950-56, mem. P. and P. com., 1952-56, 59-63, Social Sci. Research Council, dir., 1950-63, chmn. bd. dirs., 1959-63; mem. sci. adv. com. specialized personnel Nat. SSS, 1949-52. Dir. Midwest Inter-Library Corporation (chmn. bd. 1958-59). Bd. dirs. Calcutta YMCA, 1966-68, NSF, 1960-63. Fellow Am. Sociol. Soc., A.A.A.S.; mem. Newcomen Soc., several profl. assns. Club: Cosmos (Washington). Author and co-author several books in field, 1926-68; (with J. Arthur Branch) Self Study Manual for Indian Colleges and Universities, 1968. Contbr. to profl. jours. Home: 310 Broady Lane Maryville TN 37801 Office: Maryville Coll Maryville TN 37801

WILLIAMS, ADALIA FUTRELL (MRS. R. E. WILLIAMS), club woman; b. Woodland, N.C., Nov. 5, 1908; d. Julian Linwood and Adalia (Tayloe) Futrell; A.B., Guilford Coll., 1928; postgrad. Duke, 1934, U. N.C., 1936; m. Robert Edgar Williams, July 21, 1935. Tchr., Wayne County Schs., Goldsboro, N.C., 1928-30; tchr., elementary librarian Princeton (N.C.) High Sch., 1931-45; tchr. Snow Hill (N.C.) High Sch., 1950-51. Leader Girl Scouts U.S.A., 1947-51, mem. Wayne County council, 1947-52, v.p. Coastal Carolina council, 1952-61; mem. Am. Legion Aux., 1935—, chmn. poppy drive, 1954; historian N.C. Dental Aux., 1956-57, 5th Dist. Dental Aux., 1953-55; pres. Wayne County Dental Aux., 1953; bd. dirs. N.C. Dental Aux., 1956-57; historian Guilford Coll. Alumni Assn., 1957-58, treas., 1958-59, pres. Wayne County chpt., 1959-60, mem. exec. com., 1963-64; active in fund drives for Community Chest, Polio, A.R.C.; bd. dirs. United Fund, 1954; charter mem. Wayne Meml. Hosp. Aux.; program chmn. Bus. and Profl. Womens's Club, 1955, pres., 1959-60; mem. exec. com. Guilford Coll., 1965-66. Mem. Wayne County Hist. Soc., Delta Kappa Gamma (sec. chpt. 1950-51). Clubs: Toastmistress (treas. 1961), Pilot (dir., pres. 1965-66), Women's (exec. bd. 1951-52) (Goldsboro). Contbr. articles to ednl. publs. Home: 1405 E Mulberry St Goldsboro NC 27530

WILLIAMS, ADDISON LE CLERQ, lawyer; b. Denver, Nov. 13, 1900; s. George and Jennie F. (Andre) W.; A.B., U. Colo., 1921, LL.B., 1925; m. Mary T. Hosie, Oct. 7, 1926; 1 dau., Mary Jeanette; m. 2d, Jessie H. Jones, Mar. 26, 1971. Admitted to Fla. bar, 1926; asso. firm Shepard & Wahl, Cocoa, Fla., 1926; mem. firm Pleus, Williams & Pleus, Orlando, Fla., 1927-40; practiced law, 1940-42; mem. firm Johnson & Williams, Orlando, 1942-55, Williams & Chapman, Orlando, 1955—. Pres. McCory Holding Co., 1955—, McCory Properties, Inc., 1955—. Pres. Orlando Jr. Coll., 1944-57, chmn. bd. trustees, 1957-70. Mem. Am., Orange County (pres. 1944) bar assns., Fla. Bar, Orlando C. of C., Phi Kappa Tau, Phi Alpha Delta. Presbyn. Club: Executives (Orlando). Home: 700 Daniels Av Orlando FL 32801 Office: McCory Bldg Orlando FL 32801

WILLIAMS, ARTHUR MIDDLETON, JR., elec. utility exec.; b. Charleston, S.C., Sept. 16, 1914; s. Arthur Middleton and Katherine (Ward) W.; B.S. in Textile Chemistry, Clemson U., 1936; LL.B. magna cum laude, U. S.C., 1942; m. Katherine Murphy, Nov. 4, 1943; children—Katherine Elizabeth (Mrs. Mahon), Patricia LaBruce (Mrs. Boykin), Elizabeth Middleton. Joined U.S. Army, 1936, served in cav.

until 1938; trans. to inactive duty, 1938-42; active duty with armored forces, 1942-43; ret., 1943; admitted to S.C. bar, 1942, U.S. Supreme Ct. bar; practice in Columbia, S.C., 1943-44; with S.C. Electric & Gas Co., Columbia, 1944—, sr. v.p., 1961-66, pres., 1966—, also chief exec. officer, dir.; tchr. law U. S.C. Law Sch., 1943-48; dir. S.C. Nat. Bank, Columbia, Liberty Corp. Chmn. S.C. Employment Security Commn. System Council, 1950-56; mem. Gov. S.C. Fiscal Survey Commn., 1955; mem. So. Govs.' Conf. Peacetime Uses Nuclear Energy, 1955-59, So. Interstate Nuclear Bd. Exec. Com., 1959-63; sec. S.C. Nuclear Energy and Space Commb., 1962-63; mem. bd. sch. commnrs. Dist. 1, Richland County, S.C., 1958-71; former mem. Greater Columbia Council on Human Relations; mem. S.C. Com. on Human Affairs. Past pres. U.S.C.-Bus. Partnership Found.; bd. dirs. United Fund for Community Services, Columbia and Richland County, 1955-58, pres., 1956; bd. dirs. Richland County chpt. A.R.C., 1945-48, Family Welfare Assn. Richland County, 1950-55, Columbia U.S.O., 1948-51; bd. dirs. Carolinas United, 1959-62, exec. com., 1959-62; trustee Porter Gaud Sch., Charleston, 1966-68, Converse Coll. Recipient Feedoms Found. award, 1950. Mem. Am., S.C. (v.p. 5th jud. circuit 1954), Richland County bar assns., Columbia C. of C. (bd. dirs. 1951-57, 61-64, pres. 1955, nat. counselor 1956), S.C. C. of C. (bd. dirs. 1963-66, v.p. 1966, pres. 1968, chmn. bd. 1969), Southeastern Electric Exchange (v.p. 1967, pres. 1970), N.A.M. (dir.), Phi Beta Kappa, Scabbard and Blade, Blue Key, Phi Psi, Beta Gamma Sigma, Sigma Nu. Episcopalian (past vestryman). Clubs: Palmetto (pres. 1967-71), Columbia Sailing. Cotillion, Quadrille, Tarantella, Pine Tree Hunt, Centurian, Forest Lake (Columbia); Spring Valley Country; Carolina Yacht (Charleston); Winyah Indigo (Georgetown). Home: 861 Abelia Rd Columbia SC 29205 Office: 328 Main St Columbia SC 29201

WILLIAMS, ARVIN SAMUEL, sch. adminstr.; b. Appalachia, Va., Nov. 7, 1920; s. Irvin Patrick and Cleo Hattie (Blankenship) W.; B.S., Milligan Coll., 1942; M.A., George Washington U., 1967; m. Emma Keren Mauck, Aug. 13, 1949; 1 dau., Lucy Ellen. Tchr., coach Norton (Va.) High Sch., 1941-42; tchr., coach, registrar, athletic dir., dir. devel., exec. v.p., v.p., pres. Randolph-Macon Acad., Front Royal, Va., 1947—. Served with USAAF, 1942-47. Mem. Front Royal C. of C. (1st v.p.). Methodist. Kiwanian. Address: Randolph-Macon Acad Front Royal VA 22630

WILLIAMS, ASBURY HAMILTON, physician; b. Lake City, S.C., Oct. 24, 1937; s. Eugene Mood and Emera Alyne (Rogers) W.; B.S., Furman U., 1959; M.D., Med. U. S.C., 1963; m. Peggy Rae Kenney, Aug. 9, 1959; children— Asbury Hamilton, Peggy Laura, Suzanne Elizabeth. Intern, Columbia Hosp., Richland County, S.C., 1963-64; practice medicine, Lake City, 1964—; mem. staff Lower Florence County Hosp.; asso. staff McLeod's Infirmary, Saunder's Meml., Williamsburg County hosps. Bd. dirs. Lower Florence County Hosp. Mem. A.M.A., S.C., Florence County, Pee Dee med. assns., Am. Acad. Family Practice, Jr. C. of C. (pres. 1969-70). Republican. Baptist (deacon 1967-70). Home: Lockewood Estates Lake City SC 29560 Office: 101 John St Lake City SC 29560

WILLIAMS, AUDREY ARTHUR, JR., architect; b. Dallas, Mar. 25, 1925; s. Audrey Arthur and Helen Myrtle (Stark) W.; B.S. in Archtl. Constrn., Tex. Agrl. and Mech. U., 1951; m. Martha Louise Thomas, July 2, 1943; 1 dau., Sally Ann (Mrs. James Richard Hewell, Jr.). Architect, Art Williams Jr. & Assos., Architects, Dallas, 1954—. Owner, Art Williams Jr. Interiors; owner Motor Hotel Consultants; pres., dir. Standard Constrn. Co. Waco (Tex.), Am. Motor Inns, Inc., Americana Mortgage & Leasing Corp.; designer numerous bldgs. including motor hotels, restaurants. Served with USAF, 1942-45; ETO. Mem. Nat., Am. insts. architects, Constrn. Specification Inst., Tex. Soc. Architects. Republican. Home: 14140 Rawhide Parkway Dallas TX 75234 Office: 2880 LBJ Freeway Dallas TX 75234

WILLIAMS, BEN FORREST, JR., curator, art mus.; b. Lumberton, N.C., Dec. 24, 1925; s. Ben Forrest and Mamie (Britt) W.; A.B. in Art and Edn., U. N.C., 1949, grad. tchrs. certificate, 1951; A.A. in Art Criticism and History Art, George Washington U., 1945-47; postgrad. Corcoran Sch. Art, 1942-45, Nat. Sch. Art, 1941-42, Ecole de Louvre (France), 1957, Netherlands Inst. for Art History, 1964; m. Margaret Click, July 2, 1955. Designer U.S. Navy Dept., Washington, 1944-46; color lithographist Nat. Gallery, Washington, 1946; instr. art Corcoran Sch. Art, Washington, 1945-46; instr. art Chapel Hill (N.C.) pub. schs., 1947-48, Ferree Sch. Art, Raleigh, N.C., 1950-52; dir. exhbns. Person Hall Art Gallery, Chapel Hill, 1948-49; exhbn. asso. N.C. State Art Gallery Raleigh, 1950-56; curator art N.C. Mus. Art, Raleigh, 1956—; exhibited paintings and sculpture, Nat. Mus. Art, 1945, Corcoran Gallery, 1945, Phillips Gallery, 1946 (all Washington), Atlanta Art Assn., 1947, Va. Mus., Richmond, 1946, Va. Intermont Gallery, Bristol, 1947, Jacques Seligmann Galleries, N.Y.C., 1948; Weatherspoon Gallery, Greensboro, 1948—, Person Hall Art Gallery, Chapel Hill, 1948-49, Asheville Art Mus., 1949, with Am. Fedn. Arts throughout U.S., 1947. Recipient 1st prize and Painting award, Southeastern Annual Exhibit, Atlanta Art Assn., 1947; 1st Painting award, Washington Art Fair, 1946; 1st prize, Corcoran Sch. Art, 1945, and others. Contbr. articles on art, conservation to profl. jours. Home: 2813 Mayview Rd Raleigh NC 25607 Office: NC Mus of Art Raleigh NC 27601

WILLIAMS, BEN T., judge; b., 1911; LL.B., U. Okla. Admitted to Okla. bar, 1933; practiced in Pauls Valley; now asso. justice Supreme Ct. of Okla. Office: State Capitol Bldg Oklahoma City OK 73105*

WILLIAMS, BERT, lawyer, city ofcl. Mayor of El Paso, Tex.; was city alderman, 2 yrs., asst. city atty., 5 yrs. Office: City Hall El Paso TX 79901*

WILLIAMS, BILL J., dentist; b. Boone, N.C., Mar. 2, 1939; s. Warren Wilson and Elizabeth (Rucker) W.; student U. N.C., 1957-59, Lees McRae Coll., 1959-60, Pfeiffer Coll., 1964; A.B., U. N.C., 1969. Electroceramic researcher Charlotte Chem. Labs. (N.C.), 1964-65; pub. health dentist, Mecklenberg County, Charlotte, 1969; instr. dental hygiene dept. Community Coll. Central Piedmont, Charlotte, 1969—; pvt. practice dentistry, Charlotte, 1970—. Mem. Am. Dental Assn., N.C., 2d Dist., Charlotte dental socs. Baptist. Club: Tega Cay Country. Home: 2500-18-C Eastway Dr Charlotte NC 28205 Office: 2513 Westerly Hills Dr Charlotte NC 28208

WILLIAMS, BRUCE HAROLD, govt. ofcl.; b. McMahan, Tex., Aug. 12, 1913; s. Lawrence and Sadie (Garner) W.; B.S., S.W. Tex. Tchrs. Coll., 1934; M.Ed. in Ednl. Adminstrn., U. Tex., 1938; Ed.D. in Ednl. Adminstrn., George Washington U., 1951; m. Lora Pooley, July 28, 1934; children—Patricia Jo. Robert O'Neal, James Lawrence. Prin. pub. schs., Leesville, Tex., 1934-37, Prairie Lea, Tex., 1937-41, pub. high schs., Kennedy, Tex., 1941-42; instr. San Antonio Cadet Center, Kelly Field, 1942-43, U. Tex., Austin, 1943; tng. specialist Bur. Naval Personnel, Washington 1946-55; asst. dir. Office Information, U.S. Office Edn., Washington, 1955-63, asst. dir. civil def. edn. br., 1966-68, chief civil def. edn. br., 1968-71, dir. div. survey operations Nat. Center Ednl. Statistics, 1971—. Pres. Masonville Heights Civic Assn., 1958-59; del. Fairfax County Fedn. Civic Assns. Served with USNR, 1943-46. Mem. Am. Assn. Sch. Adminstrs., Am. Coll. Pub. Relations Assn., Adult Edn. Assn. U.S.A., Am. Acad. Polit. and Social Sci., Alpha Chi, Phi Delta Kappa. Baptist. Author: Damage Controlman, 1947; Progress of Public Education in the U.S.A., 1956-57. Home: 7406 Austin St Annandale VA 22003 Office: Office of Edn US Dept of Health Edn and Welfare Washington DC 20201

WILLIAMS, CARLISLE MISTER, JR., county ofcl.; b. Painter, Va., June 27, 1937; s. Carlisle M. and Evelyn (Hickman) W.; student Coll. William and Mary, 1955-56; A.A., Goldey Beacom Jr. Coll., 1958; A.B., E. Carolina U., 1960; m. Dolly Evans Taylor, June 15, 1958; children— Carlisle M. III, Valerie T. Jr. accountant Leatherbury-Broache, Accomac, Va., 1960; accountant Eastern Shore News, Inc., Onancock, Va., 1960-62; bus. mgr. clk. Accomack County Sch. Bd., Accomac, 1962-66, county adminstr. Accomack County, 1966—. Lectr. accounting Eastern Shore Community Coll., 1971—. Sec.-treas. Cedar Island Bridge and Beach Authority, 1968—; coordinator Accomack County Hwy. Safety Commn., 1968—; mem. Com. for Better Schs., 1966-68; dir. Civil Def. for Accomack County, 1971—; chmn. Eastern Shore unit Salvation Army, 1971—. Mem. Va. Assn. County Adminstrs., Onley Recreation Assn., Va., Eastern Shore (pres. 1967-68) jaycees, Eastern Shore C. of C. (dir.), Phi Sigma Pi. Methodist (adminstrv. bd.). Clubs: Eastern Shore Yacht and Country (Onancock). Home: 22 Sturgis St Onnancock VA 23417 Office: County Office Bldg Accomac VA 23301

WILLIAMS, CHARLES DANA, supt. schs.; b. Frankston, Tex. Mar. 26, 1916; s. James Kinny and Frances Eugenia (Woods) W.; B.S., Stephen F. Austin Coll., 1940, M.A., 1947; m. Lou Mangham, Aug. 9, 1935; children—Mary Ann (Mrs. William T. Baker, Jr.), Donna Lynne, Bettye Lou. Supt. schs. Corpus Christi, Tex. Mem. Hale-Aikin Com., White House Conf. Children and Youth, Tex. Com. Edn. and Welfare. Mem. N.E.A. (bd. dirs.), Tex. Tchrs. Assn. (past pres.), P.T.A. (life). Methodist (steward). Rotarian. Home: 713 Gregory Dr Corpus Christi TX 78412 Office: 515 N Caranhua St Corpus Christi TX 78401

WILLIAMS, CHARLES IVAN, dentist; b. Dallas, Dec. 29, 1943; s. John Groce and Emma Virginia (Fox) W.; student So. Meth. U., 1961-63, Arlington State Coll., summers 1961-63, Dental Sch. U. Tex., 1963-65; D.D.S., Baylor U., 1967; m. Mary Catherine Hollingsworth, Nov. 25, 1965; children—Charles Ivan II, Rachel Dawn. Gen. practice dentistry, Mexia, Tex., 1967—; mem. staff Gen. Mexia Hosp., sec. staff, 1969-71. Mem. Jr. C. of C. (dir.), Am., Tex. dental assns. Mem. Ch. of Nazarene. Rotarian. Home: 508 N Canton St Mexia TX 76667 Office: 214 N Sherman St Mexia TX 76667

WILLIAMS, CHARLES OLIVER, JR., dentist; b. Greensboro, N.C., Sept. 1, 1939; s. Charles Oliver and Amy (Groves) W.; student U. N.C., 1957-61, Elon Coll., 1961, Wake Forest Coll., 1961, Guilford Coll., 1961; D.M.D., U. Louisville, 1966; m. Nancy Jane McIntosh, July 31, 1965; children—Cristin McIntosh, Charles Oliver III. Practice gen. dentistry, Winnsboro, S.C., 1966—; asso. mem. staff Fairfield Meml. Hosp., Winnsboro. Editor-in-chief S.C. Dental Jour., 1970—, State Publs. Chmn., Nat. Children's Dental Health Week, Fairfield County, 1967; chmn. profl. div. United Fund, Fairfield County, 1967-68; mem. Fairfield County Mental Health Assn., 1970—; spl. lectr., cons. forensic dentistry S.C. Criminal Justice Acad., Columbia. Bd. dirs. Fairfield County Boy Scouts Am. Recipient Dental Editors award Ohio State U., Am. Dental Assn., 1970. Mem. Am., Central Dist., S.C. (Ho. of Dels. 1968—) dental assns., A.A.A.S., Nat. Rehab. Assn., Fairfield Jr. C. of C. (past v.p.), Am. Soc. Dentistry for Children, Southeastern Acad. Prosthodontics, Am. Assn. Dental Editors, Mid-Carolina Dental Study Acad., Federation Dentaire Internat., Royal Soc. Health (Gt. Britain), Order Ky. Cols., Delta Sigma Delta (Nat. Lit. Excellence award 1966). Episcopalian (past sr. warden). Clubs: Winnsboro Cotillion, Fairfield Country (Winnsboro). Home: 203 Carlisle Ct Winnsboro SC 29180 Office: 204 E Washington St Winnsboro SC 29180

WILLIAMS, CLARENCE RUSSELL, educator; b. Clarksville, Ark., Dec. 1, 1921; s. Solen Ethel and Nancy (Russell) W.; B.A., Coll. of Ozarks, 1948; M. Music Edn., U. Okla., 1950; Ed.D., U. Ark., 1967; m. Katala Ann Green, May 28, 1948; children—Anitra Sharane, Russell Greenlee. Choral music dir. pub. schs., Van Buren, Ark., 1949-59, instr. oil painting, 1949-60; pvt. practice as profl. photographer, Ozark, Ark., 1959-61; asst. prof. music and speech Coll. of Ozarks, Clarksville, Ark., 1960-65, asso. prof., 1966—; on leave as dir. Harrison Regional Arts and Crafts Center, from 1967, now dir. Ednl. Research and Devel. Center, Harrison. Served to 1st lt. USMCR, 1942-46. Recipient Innovative Project award Pres. Nixon's Adv. Council on Supplementary Centers and Services, 1971. Mem. N.E.A., Music Educators Nat. Conf., Ark. Edn. Assn., Nat. Art Edn. Assn., Ark. Art Center, Phi Delta Kappa. Democrat. Presbyn. Rotarian. Home: Route 1 Ozark AR 72949 also 11 Hawthorne Dr Harrison AR 72601 Office: Sch Adminstrn Bldg Harrison AR 72601

WILLIAMS, CLAUDE DOWELL, ret. educator; b. Abbott, W.Va., July 3, 1899; s. Jason Lunceford and Effie (McCue) W.; B.S., W.Va. Wesleyan U., 1922; Ph.D. (Henry D. Sharpe fellow), Brown U., 1932; m. Mildred Frances Harne, July 8, 1923; children—James Allen, Peter Mong. Tchr. gen. sci. Buckhannon (W.Va.) High Sch., 1922-24, chemistry and physics, sr. high, 1924-28; tchr. sci., basketball coach Providence Country Day Sch., 1932-38; prof. biology, head sci. dept. Rider Coll., Trenton, N.J., 1938-44; head sci. dept. Manlius (N.Y.) Sch., 1944-64, Blue Ridge Sch., Dyke, Va., 1964-71. Summer research various marine biol. labs. Served with U.S. Army, 1918. Westinghouse fellow Mass. Inst. Tech., summer 1949. Mem. Nat. Sci. Tchrs. Assn., N.E.A., N.Y. Acad. Sci., Va. Ind. Sch. Sci. Assn., Va. Sci. Tchrs. Assn., Sigma Xi. Address: 313 Lincoln Av Smyrna Beach FL 32069

WILLIAMS, CLAYTON WHEAT, oil co. exec.; b. Fort Stockton, Tex., Apr. 15, 1895; s. Oscar Waldo and Sallie (Wheat) W.; B.S., Tex. A. and M. U., 1915; m. Chicora Lee Graham, Sept. 10, 1928; children—Clayton Wheat, Janet (Mrs. Robert W. Pollard). With Chino Copper Co., Santa Rita, N.M., 1916-17; elec. engr. Oil Belt Power Co., Eastland, Tex., 1919; county surveyor Pecos County, Tex., 1920; hwy. engring., N.M., Tex., 1921-24; chief engr. Texon Oil & Land Co. and Group No. One Oil Corp., Santa Rita, Tex., 1924-28; ind. oil operator, 1928—; owner, operator 1st ice plant and water works, Crane, Tex., 1927-35; partner ranch, Pecos County, Tex., 1935-54; v.p., dir. Olix Industries (formerly USM Oil Co.), Austin, Tex., 1960—. County commr. Pecos County, 1935-40, 43-50; life mem. Pecos County Sheriff's Possee, 1950—. Tex. Hist. Assn. (life). Served to 2d lt. U.S. Army, 1917-19. Mem. C. of C., Am. Legion, Tex., W. Tex., Fort Stockton (life) hist. assns. Methodist. Lion, Mason. Author: Never Again, 3 vols., 1969. Home: PO Box 546 Fort Stockton TX 79735 Office: Corner Rooney and 1st St Fort Stockton TX 79735

WILLIAMS, CLIFTON CURTIS, JR., astronaut; b. Mobile, Sept. 26, 1932; s. Clifton Curtis and Gertrude (Medicus) W.; student Spring Hill Coll., 1949-51; B.M.E., Auburn U., 1954; m. Jane Elizabeth Lansche, July 1, 1964. Commd. 2d lt., USMC, 1954, advanced through grades to maj., 1963; naval aviator, 1956-60; test pilot Naval Air Test Center, Patuxent River, Md., 1960-63; astronaut Manned Space Flight Center, NASA, Houston, 1963—. Home: Dickinson TX 77539 Office: Manned Space Flight Center NASA Houston TX 77058

WILLIAMS, DAN C., life ins. exec.; b. Brenham, Tex., Feb. 22, 1913; s. Dan C. and Harriet (Wilkins) W.; B.S. in Petroleum Engring., U. Tex., 1935; m. Carolyn Carpenter, June 18, 1936; children—Carolyn, Harriet, Suzanne. With Magnolia Petroleum Co., 1935, asst. dist. petroleum engr. to asst. chief petroleum engr.; engaged in ind. oil bus.; dir. Southland Life Ins. Co., Dallas, 1944—, successively v.p., 1st v.p. and chmn. investment com., pres., 1953-68, chmn. exec. com., 1968—. Dir. State Fair Tex.; chmn. big gifts div. County Cancer Campaign; mem. coordinating bd. Tex. Colls. and Univs.; mem. devel. bd. U. Tex.; pres. Am. Life Conv.; dir. Heart Assn., Community Chest, Tb Assn., county chpt. A.R.C., Met. Opera Assn., Symphony Orch., Dallas Citizen Council (all Dallas); past pres. bd. dirs. County United Fund; bd. govs. Am. Nat. Red Cross; bd. regents U. Tex. System. Mem. Am. Inst. Mining, Metall. and Petroleum Engrs., C. of C., Cotton Bowl Athletic Assn. (dir.), Cotton Bowl Council (dir.). Presbyn. (elder). Clubs: Dallas, Insurance, Petroleum, City, Dallas Country, Northwood Country, Chaparral, Los Colinas Country. Home: 3711 Lexington Av Dallas TX 75201 Office: PO Box 2220 Dallas TX 75221

WILLIAMS, DAVID WILLARD, educator; b. Venedocia, O., Aug. 20; s. David W. and Elizabeth J. (Morgan) W.; B.S.A., Ohio State U., 1915; M.Sc., U. Ill., 1916; postgrad. A. and M. Coll. Tex., 1923, postgrad. U. Chgo., summers, 1927-28; Ingeniero Agronomo, U. Coahuila, Mexico, 1957; LL.D., Austin Coll., 1957; m. Magdalene Rees, Aug. 18, 1921; children—Margaret Ann (Mrs. Walter W. Cardwell, Jr.), Ruth Elizabeth (Mrs. Bruce B. Lawrence), David Willard. Extension animal husbandman U.S. Dept. Agr., Clemson Agrl. Coll., 1917-19; asso. prof. A. and M. Coll. Tex., 1919-20, prof., 1920-22, head dept. animal husbandry, 1922-46, v.p. for agr., 1946-48, vice chancellor for agr., 1948-58, acting pres., 1956-57, vice chancellor emeritus, 1962—. Cattle rancher, 1932-72; cons. U. Ceylon, 1958-62; dir. Bryan Bldg. & Loan. Dept. supt. Southwestern Expn. and Fat Stock Show, 1920-43, chmn. adv. com., 1946-58; Am. Soc. Animal Prodn. rep. Internat. Livestock Breeding Congress, Zurich, Switzerland, 1939; agrl. cons. ECA, Germany, 1949; personnel cons. Fgn. Agr. Service, 1949-58; instnl. rep. Ark., White, Red River Interagy. Com., 1951-58; mem. U.S.-Mexico Joint Tech. Agr. Exchange Com., 1951; cons. to Morocco for AID, 1962; councilor Tex. A. and M. Research Found.; cons. Rockfeller Found., Colombia, 1951; cons. ICA, East Pakistan Agr. and Edn.; cons. agr. Escuela Superior De Agricultura, Mexico, 1954. Hon. v.p. State Fair Tex. Served with CWS, 1918, lt. col. U.S. 1943, 46. Fellow A.A.A.S., Tex. Acad. Sci., Am. Soc. Animal Sci.; mem. Tex. Southwestern Cattle Raisers Assn., Am. Soc. Animal Prodn. (past pres.), Tex. Agrl. Workers Assn., Am. Quarter Horse Breeders Assn. (past adv. com.), Bryan C. of C. (past pres.), Ceylon Assn. Advancement Sci. (pres. agr. sect. 1958-59), Nat. Collegiate Athletic Assn. (past v.p. councilman at large), Southwest Athletic Conf. (past pres.), Am. Legion, Sigma Delta Chi, Alpha Gamma Rho (past pres. Ohio), Lambda Gamma Delta. Presbyn. (elder). Mason, Rotarian. Clubs: Nat. Block and Bridle, Saddle and Sirloin (past pres. Ohio). Author: Beef Cattle in the South, 1941; co-author: Livestock and Poultry, 1925; Agriculture in the Southwest, 1940. Home: 500 Fairview St College Station TX 77840

WILLIAMS, DONALD LEE, architect; b. Louisville, July 5, 1935; s. Benjamin John and Lucille (Clark) W.; B.S. in Civil Engring., U. Ky., 1957; B.Arch. cum laude, U. Ill., 1962; Diploma Architecture, Ecole de Beaux Arts, Fountainbleau, France, 1962; M.S. in Community Devel., U. Louisville, 1970; m. Betty Ann Owen, Jan. 28, 1956; children—Vicki Lynn, Donald Lee II, Benjamin Jon III. Engr., Convair Corp., Ft. Worth, 1957; asso. McCullock, Bickel, architects, Louisville, 1962-66; v.p. DEGA, Inc., Louisville, 1966—. Asst. dir. Urban Studies Center, U. Louisville, 1968—, adj. asst. prof., 1971—. Chmn. Louisville Mayor's Adv. Com. for Community Devel., 1968-70, Nat. Task Force on Environment, Phila., 1968-70, Citizens Met. Planning Council, Louisville, 1965-67. Served to capt. USAF, 1957-60. Ryerson fellow, Europe, 1964. Mem. A.I.A. (chmn. nat. com. regional devel. 1970), Am. Inst. Planners (asso.). Democrat. Presbyn. (elder, chmn.). Prin. works include: Village West, Louisville, 1968. Home: 1535 Tyler Park Dr Louisville KY 40204 Office: 505 S 3d St Louisville KY 40402

WILLIAMS, DONALD SHAND, architect; b. Patchogue, N.Y., Apr. 30, 1930; s. Walter H. and Florence (Shand) W.; B.Arch., Rensselaer Poly. Inst., 1952; m. Eleanor Jean Kent, June 15, 1952; children—Kent Scott, Karen Shand. Designer, N.Am. Aviation, Los Angeles, 1952-53, Frederick P. Weidersum, Valley Stream, N.Y., 1953-55, Daniel Perry, Port Jefferson, N.Y., 1955-56; partner Wakeling, Levison, Williams & Walker, Clearwater, 1956-71, Williams & Walker, 1971—. Mem. Clearwater City Commn., 1967—, Pinellas County Charter Commn., 1971—; sec.-treas. Pinellas Transit Authority, 1970—. Mem. A.I.A., C. of C. (v.p. 1965), Alpha Theta Omega. Republican. Rotarian. Home: 1931 Ripon St Clearwater FL 33516 Office: 1445 Court St Clearwater FL 33516

WILLIAMS, DUDLEY RIDAULT, lawyer; b. Martinsville, Va., June 19, 1939; s. Harry Pemberton and Ruth (Thomas) W.; B.A., Howard U., 1961, J.D., 1964; m. Katherine Ann Crowe, Oct. 25, 1969. Admitted to D.C. bar, 1966; partner firm Luck & Williams, Washington, 1966-67; exec. dir. D.C. br. N.A.A.C.P., Washington, 1967-68; dep. dir. D.C. Law Students in Ct., Washington, 1969, dir., 1969—. Legal adviser Pride, Inc., Washington, 1968—; cons. United Planning Orgn., Washington. Mem. S.E. Community Local Devel. Corp., Washington Urban League. Mem. Nat., D.C., Washington bar assns., Jud. Conf. of D.C. Circuit. Democrat. Home: 1209 33d Pl SE Washington DC 20019 Office: 635 F St NW Washington DC 20001

WILLIAMS, E. PAUL, banker; b. Jackson, O., July 24, 1909; s. E. Pratt and Jenny May (Williams) W.; student Washington and Lee U., 1926-28; J.D., U. Ky., 1933; m. Elizabeth Ann DeHart, Mar. 11, 1941; 1 dau., Suzanne. Admitted to Ky. bar, 1934; practiced in Ashland, 1934-42; with 2d Nat. Bank, Ashland, 1946—, exec. v.p., trust officer, 1951-62, pres., 1962—, also dir.; dir. Mayo Arcade, Collins & Mayo Collieries, Ky. Physicians Mutual. Former mem. Regional Adv. Com. on Banking Policies; dir. Fed. Res. Bank of Cleve., Cin. Bd. dirs. Ky. State Tech. Services; nat. asso. Boys Club Am.; adv. dir. Kings Daus. Home for Aged; mem. exec. com. nat. bank div. Am. Bankers Assn.; chmn. bd. Pikeville Coll., commr. Ky. Indsl. Devel. Found.; commr. Ky. Savs. Bonds. Served with AUS, World War II. Named Boss of Year, 1962. Mem. Am. (govt. relations council), Ky. (past pres.) bankers assns., Ky. C. of C. (treas., dir.), Am. Legion, Sigma Nu. Episcopalian. Mason. Clubs: Kiwanis, Bellefonte Country. Home: 620 Amanda Furnace Dr Ashland KY 41101 Office: 1544 Winchester Av Ashland KY 41101

WILLIAMS, EARL CRANSTON, JR., state ofcl.; b. Corbett, Md., Dec. 26, 1920; s. Earl Cranston and Mildred Cecelia (Nimmo) W.; B.S. in Civil Engring., U. Md., 1950; postgrad. Yale, 1954-55; m. Billie Leona Harris, Mar. 11, 1945; children—Andrea (Mrs. Preston Rotier Perkerson), Linda (Mrs. Stephen Stuart Putney, Janet, Earl Cranston III. With Wichita Falls Pub. Works Dept., 1950-52, city traffic engr., 1952-59; chief traffic engring. div. Montgomery County, Md., 1959-62; state traffic engr. Tenn. Dept. Hwys., Nashville, 1962—. Served with USAAF, World War II. Registered profl. engr., Tenn., Tex. Fellow Am. Soc. C.E.; mem. Inst. Traffic Engrs. (pres. So. sect.

1969-70), Hwy. Research Bd., Am. Assn. State Hwy. Ofcls. (nat. joint com. on uniform traffic control 1963—). Nat. (pres. North Central Tex. chpt. 1958-59), Tenn. socs. profl. engrs. Home: 3629 Central Av Nashville TN 37205 Office: 317 Highway Bldg Nashville TN 37219

WILLIAMS, EARL RAY, educator, economist; b. Granite, Okla., Dec. 7, 1938; s. Bert A. and Minerva (Leonard) W.; B.S., Okla. State U., 1961, M.S., 1963; Ph.D., U. Tenn., 1968; m. Susie Dobson Williams, Sept. 6, 1961; children—Terry, Connie. Teaching, research asst. Okla. State U., Stillwater, 1962; vol. Peace Corps, Colombia, S.Am., 1963-65; asst. agrl. econs. U. Tenn., Knoxville, 1965-68; asst. prof., chmn. dept. econs. Northeastern State Coll., Tahlequah, Okla., 1968-70, asso. prof., 1970, chmn. bus. div., 1971—. Mem. Air N.G., 1961-63. Mem. Am., So. econ. assns., Southwestern Social Sci. Assn., Tahlequah C. of C., Gamma Sigma Delta. Methodist (adminstrv. bd., finance com.). Home: 1016 N Cedar Tahlequah OK 74464

WILLIAMS, EDWARD BENNETT, lawyer; b. Hartford, Conn., May 31, 1920; s. Joseph Barnard and Mary (Bennett) W.; A.B. summa cum laude, Coll. Holy Cross, 1941, S.J.D., 1963; LL.B., Georgetown U., 1945; LL.D., Loyola Coll., 1967, Georgetown U., 1968, Fairfield U., 1968, Loyola U., Chgo., 1970, Albertus Magnus Coll., 1971, St. Joseph's Coll., Phila., 1971; Lincoln Coll., 1972; m. Dorothy Adair Guider, May 3, 1946 (dec. May 1959); children—Joseph Barnard, Ellen Adair, Peter Bennett; m. 2d, Agnes Anne Neill, June 11, 1960; children—Edward Neill, Dana Bennett, Anthony Tyler, Kimberly A. Admitted to D.C. bar, 1944, since practiced in Washington; sr. partner firm Williams Connolly & Califano, 1971—; gen. counsel Georgetown U., 1949—, Internat. Brotherhood Teamsters, 1958—; prof. criminal law and evidence Georgetown U. Law Sch., 1946-58; guest prof. U. Frankfurt (Germany), 1954, vis. lectr. Yale Law Sch., 1970—. Pres. Washington Redskins, profl. football team, 1965—, Williams Properties, Washington, 1961—. Mem. Chief Justice's Com. on Ct. Facilities and Design, 1971—. Served with USAAF, 1941-43. Mem. Am. (chmn. spl. com. on crime prevention and control 1970-71, D.C. (v.p. 1950, 55-56, Lawyer of Year award 1966) bar assns., Am. Coll. Trial Lawyers (regent), Internat. Acad. Trial Lawyers (dir.), U.S. Jud. Conf. (adv. com. on fed. rules of evidence 1965—). Democrat. Roman Catholic. Author: One Man's Freedom, 1962; You in Trial Law, 1963. Home: 8901 Durham Dr Potomac MD 20854 Office: Hill Bldg Washington DC 20006

WILLIAMS, EDWARD EARL, profl. engr.; b. Rogers, Ark., Mar. 3, 1932; s. Leslie Edward and Jessie (Baldwin) W.; B.S., U. Ark., 1957, M.S., 1960; m. Camilla Ann Harris, Nov. 24, 1971; children—Jennifer Jo, Edward Earl, Nat Allen, Stephanie Darlene. Various positions, Kan., La., 1958-64; sr. design engr. Boeing Co., Huntsville, Ala., 1965-66; sr. staff engr. Sperry Rand Corp., Huntsville, 1965-66; div. head engring. techs. State Tech. Inst., Memphis, 1967-68; tchr. indsl. tech. Ala. A. and M. U., Huntsville, 1968-71; engr. elec. design div. So. div. Naval Facilities Engring. Command, Charleston, S.C., 1971—. Profl. engring. cons. edn., govt., industry. Served with USAF, 1949-53. Registered profl. engr., La., Tex., Okla. Mem. Am. Soc. Engring. Edn., Nat., Ala. socs. profl. engrs., Internat. Platform Assn., V.F.W., Pi Mu Epsilon, Eta Kappa Nu, Tau Beta Pi. Contbr. articles to profl. jours. Office: Electrical Design Div So Div Naval Facilities Engring Command PO Box 10068 Charleston SC 29411

WILLIAMS, EDWARD KENT, architect; b. Lynchburg, Va., July 2, 1934; s. Edward and Fenton (Kent) W.; B.Arch., U. Va., 1962; m. Emily Louise McMullen, Mar. 15, 1955; children—Jane, Kent, Beth. Draftsman, Strang & Childers, Annandale, Va., 1962-65, asso., 1965-67; project architect Allen J. Dickey, Arlington, Va., 1967-70, Beery & Rio, Annandale, 1970—. Mem. Fairfax (Va.) Planning Commn., 1967—, chmn., 1969; mem. No. Va. Regional Planning Commn., 1967-69. Served with USAF, 1953-57. Mem. A.I.A. Club: Civitan (Fairfax). Home: 12216 Quinque Lane Clifton VA 22024 Office: 4215 Evergreen Lane Annandale VA 22003

WILLIAMS, EMIL OTTO NOLTING, utility co. exec.; b. Richmond, Va., July 1, 1909; s. Langbourne Meade and Susanne Catherine (Nolting) W.; B.A., U. Va., 1931; m. Mary Binford Hobson, Apr. 11, 1934; children—E. Otto Nolting, John Langbourne, Julien Hobson. Vice pres., pres. Va. Central Ry., Fredericksburg, Va., 1932-41; pres. Bottled Gas Corp. Va., Richmond, 1941—, also dir.; dir. Commonwealth Natural Gas Corp., Richmond Fredericksburg & Potomac R.R. Bd. dirs. Christian Children's Fund, Children's Home Soc. Va.; chmn. bd. govs. St. Christopher's Sch., 1966-68. Served from 1st lt. to capt., Transp. Corps, AUS, 1942-45. Mem. Nat. (dir., pres. 1961), Va. (dir., founder) liquified petroleum gas assns., Phi Kappa Sigma. Episcopalian (trustee, vestryman). Clubs: Country of Va., Commonwealth, Rotunda, Richmond German, Richmond Hundred (Richmond). Home: 6601 River Rd Richmond VA 23229 Office: 1701 Brook Rd Richmond VA 23260

WILLIAMS, EMILY RUTH, wholesale co. exec.; b. Rocky Mount, N.C., Oct. 6, 1919; d. George Marvin and Elsie Mae (Clark) Williams; student Womans Coll. U. N.C., 1936-37. Asst. Bookkeeper John Flanagan Ford Agy., Rocky Mount, 1937-38; sec., treas. Auto Equip. Co., Rocky Mount, 1937-41, prodn. mgr., 1941-71, head contract div., 1960-71; sec., treas. B & W Mfg. Co., Rocky Mount, 1970-71; promoter, mgr. Winstead Auto Parts Warehouse, Rocky Mount, 1971—. Pres. Rocky Mount Pilot Club, 1965-66. Recipient Honor Pilot of Year award, 1966. Mem. Bapt. Bus. Women Roanoke Assn. (pres. 1952). Baptist (librarian 1969-72). Club: Benvenue Country. Home: 616 Marigold St Rocky Mount NC 27801 Office: Box 433 N Washington St Rocky Mount NC 27801

WILLIAMS, ERNEST FRANKLIN, dentist; b. Gallatin, Tenn., Feb. 17, 1917; s. Samuel Watkins and Elizabeth (Franklin) W.; A.B., Ark. Coll., 1938; B.S. in Civil Engring., U. Ark., 1942; postgrad. U. Cal. at Los Angeles, 1943; D.D.S., Washington U., St. Louis, 1950; m. Frances Elizabeth Holloway, June 14, 1948; children—Richard Franklin, Stephen Pryor. Engr., E.I. DuPont Co., Pryor, Okla., 1942; pvt. practice dentistry, Batesville, Ark., 1950—. Mem. Batesville Sch. Dist. Bd., 1969—. Served with USAAF, 1942-46. Mem. Am. Dental Assn., N.E. Ark. Dental Soc. (pres. 1959-60), Sigma Alpha Epsilon, Xi Psi Phi. Methodist. Kiwanian (pres. 1961). Home: 1680 Highland Rd Batesville AR 72501 Office: 359 E Main St Batesville AR 72501

WILLIAMS, ETHEL NAOMI LANGLEY (MRS. LOUIS JOHNSON WILLIAMS), librarian; b. Balt.; d. William Herbert and Carrie Amelia (Sampson) Langley; A.B., Howard U., 1930; B.S. in L.S., Columbia, 1933; m. Louis Johnson Williams, Jan. 13, 1932; 1 dau., Carole Juanita (Mrs. George Jones). Caseworker pub. assistance div. Bd. Pub. Welfare, Washington, 1933-36; searcher Library of Congress, Washington, 1936-40; reference librarian, cataloger Howard U. Library, Washington, 1940-47, librarian Howard U. Sch. of Religion Library, Washington, 1947—. Mem. A.L.A., Am. Theol. Library Assn., D.C. Library Assn., N.A.A.C.P., Washington Urban League. Democrat. Episcopalian. Author: Afro-American Religion: A Bibliography, 1972. Editor: Biographical Directory of Negro Ministers, 1965, 2d edit., 1970. Contbr. weekly book rev. column to Afro-American Newspaper, 1945-46. Home: 1625 Primrose Rd NW Washington DC 20012

WILLIAMS, EVERETT HOLLAND, JR., state ofcl.; b. Jacksonville, Fla., Aug. 7, 1918; s. Everett Holland and Mamie (Whitehead) W.; B.A., U. Fla., 1940; M.S., Johns Hopkins, 1951; m. Bettye Jane Hyatt, July 7, 1942; 1 dau., Patricia A. Statistician, Fla. Bd. Health, Jacksonville, 1940-42, 46-47, dir. vital statistics, 1947—. Served with AUS, 1942-46. Mem. Am., Fla. (sec.) pub. health assns., Am. Assn. Vital Records and Statistics (pres.-elect), Kappa Sigma. Home: 5208 Rollins Av Jacksonville FL 32207 Office: 1217 Pearl St Jacksonville FL 32201

WILLIAMS, FAYETTE CREED, JR., orthodontist; b. Corinth, Miss., June 4, 1933; s. Fayette Creed and Margaret (Schumpert) W.; B.S., U. Tenn., 1955, D.D.S., 1957; m. Mary Elizabeth Phillips, Sept. 3, 1967; 1 dau., Margaret Elizabeth. Resident, U. Ala. Dental Sch., 1957-59; practice dentistry specializing in orthodontics, Tupelo, Miss., 1959—; research asso. U. Ala., 1959-61. Lee County campaign chmn. Tb Christmas Seal drive, 1963-67; Miss. chmn. Project Concern, 1968-69. Named Miss.'s Outstanding Young Man, Miss. Jaycees, 1966. Fellow Am. Coll. Dentists; mem. So. soc. Orthodontists (sec. 1971—), Am. Assn. Orthodontists, Miss. Dental Assn. (editor jour. 1964-69, pres. 1968-69), U. Tenn. Dental Alumni Assn. (pres. 1964-65), Soc. Mayflower Descs. Presbyn. (deacon). Home: 1406 Pinecrest St Tupelo MS 38801 Office: 914 S Gloster St Tupelo MS 38801

WILLIAMS, FRANK EDWARD, physician; b. Talledga, Ala., Nov. 21, 1919; s. Frank Albert and Mauda Albert (Hiett) W.; B.S., Auburn U., 1947; M.D., Hahnemann Med. Coll., 1952. Intern Lloyd Noland Hosp., Birmingham, Ala., 1952-53; gen. practice medicine, Pensacola, Fla., 1954—; mem. staff Sacred Heart Hosp., Baptist Hosp.; staff, chmn. bd. Univ. Hosp. (all Pensacola); med. dir. U. West Fla., Pensacola, 1968—, Pensacola Jr. Coll., 1970—, Westinghouse Corp., Pensacola, 1968—; trustee Excambia Gen. Hosp., Pensacola, 1959—. Mem. Greyhound Found., Pensacola, 1959—. Served to 1st lt. USAAF, World War II. Clubs: Scenic Hill Country. Home: 8880 Scenic Hills Pensacola FL 32504 Office: 100 E Hood St Pensacola FL 32504

WILLIAMS, FRANKLIN BURLEIGH, JR., educator; b. Cobleskill, N.Y., Nov. 21, 1906; s. Franklin Burleigh and Katherine Eldora (Klock) W.; A.B. summa cum laude, Syracuse U., 1931; M.A., Harvard, 1932, Ph.D., 1934, Sheldon Traveling fellow, Eng., 1934-35; m. H. Virginia Kelly, Feb. 1, 1947; children—Virginia Anne, Franklin Thomas. Newspaper reporter Middletown (N.Y.) Times-Herald, 1923-27; instr., tutor English, Harvard, 1935-39; mem. faculty Georgetown U., 1939-68, prof. English, 1960—, chmn. dept., 1959-66. Served with USAAF, 1942-46. Guggenheim fellow, 1955-56. Mem. Am. Assn. U. Profs., Modern Lang. Assn., Nat. Council Tchrs. English, Coll. English Assn., Modern Humanities Research Assn., Bibliog. Soc. (London), bibliog. socs. Am., U. Va., Renaissance Soc. Am., Shakespeare Assn. Am., Malone Soc., Milton Soc., Phi Beta Kappa. Roman Cath. Author: Elizabethan England, 1939; Index of Dedications in English Books before 1641, 1962; also articles. Home: 724 N Emerson St Arlington VA 22203 Office: Georgetown U Washington DC 20007

WILLIAMS, FRANKLIN SPRINGER, educator; b. Cin., Feb. 17, 1912; s. John F. and Eva (Springer) W.; B.S., Kent State U., 1933; M.B.A., U. Chgo., 1944; Ph.D., U. Ark., 1957; m. Elizabeth Corbett Bassett, Aug. 28, 1945; children—Jeffrey Springer, Christopher B.T., Philip F.C. Tchr. pub. schs., Conneaut, O., 1935-39, Mason City High Sch. and Jr. Coll, 1939-41, Youngstown schs., 1941-42; market analyst Chgo. Assn. Commerce, 1944-45, Link Belt Co., 1945-46; instr. U. Ark., 1946-47, asst. prof., 1947-48; asst. prof. Antioch Coll., 1948-49, U. Okla., 1949-53; asst. prof. U. Ark. Sch. Pharmacy, Little Rock, 1953-57, asso. prof., 1957-59, chmn. dept., 1953-59; prof. marketing, mgmt. U. Ark., Fayetteville, 1959-67, prof. mgmt., 1967—. Bus. cons. Cranford Johnson Assos., Little Rock, McClinton Bros. Co., Fayetteville, Calvert-McBride, Ft. Smith, Ark., 1968—; mem. firm Mgmt. Research Assos., Fayetteville, 1964—, cons. Studebaker Corp. Can., 1964-65. Mem. adv. bd. Washington Gen. Hosp., 1967—. Bd. dirs. Econ. Opportunity Agy. Washington County. Mem. Am. Marketing Assn., Acad. Mgmt. Southwestern Social Sci. Assn., Ozark Econ. Assn., Blue Key, Beta Gamma Sigma. Democrat. Unitarian. Home: Knerr Rd PO Box 25 Fayetteville AR 72701

WILLIAMS, FRED ANTHONY, coll. dean; b. Biloxi, Miss., Dec. 28, 1919; s. Fred and Evelyn (Gollott) W.; B.A., Southwestern Assemblies of God Coll., 1953; M.A., So. Methodist U., 1956, B.D. (scholar), 1959, Th.M., 1970; m. Doris Inez Canaan, July 6, 1940; children—Donna Lois, Rhonda Ann. Ordained to ministry Assemblies of God Ch., 1952; asst. pastor 1st Assemblies God Ch., Dallas, 1950-52, pastor, Godley, Tex., 1952-53; pastor Casa View Assembly of God Ch., Dallas, 1953-62; asso. prof. Southwestern Assemblies of God Coll., Waxahachie, Tex., 1958-62; acad. dean South Eastern Bible Coll., Lakeland, Fla., 1962—, registrar, 1962-69, 1969—, mem. adminstrv. bd., 1963—. Registered lobbyist higher edn. Fla. Legislature, 1969—. Served with USNR, 1942-45. Mem. Acad. Deans and Vice Pres.'s Acad. Affairs of So. Assn. Colls. and Schs., Am. Assn. Collegiate Registrars and Admissions Officers, Phi Delta Kappa. Author: The Comrephensive Self-Study Evaluation Report, 1963. Home: 1716 Virginia Ct Lakeland FL 33803

WILLIAMS, GENE, judge; b. Chgo., June 11, 1916; s. George A. and Marie (Lauletta) W.; J.D., U. Miami, 1939; m. Virginia Handley, Apr. 12, 1946; children—Susan, Judy, Gary. Admitted to Fla. bar, 1939; partner firm Williams & Brion, Miami, Fla., 1939-41, Roth &Williams, Miami, 1946-52; asst. states atty. State of Fla., Miami, 1953-55; judge Criminal Ct. of Record, Miami, 1955-66; judge Circuit Ct., Miami, 1966—. Mem. Dade County Bar Assn. (sec. 1951-53), Ct. of Record Judges Assn. Fla. (pres. 1960-62), U. Miami Alumni Assn. (past dir.), U. Miami Law Alumni Assn. (past dir.), Delta Theta Phi, Lambda Chi Alpha. Episcopalian. Home: 9500 SW 60th Ct Miami FL 33156 Office: Dade County Ct House Miami FL 33136

WILLIAMS, GEORGE HOWARD, univ. pres.; b. Hempstead, N.Y., Feb. 12, 1918; s. George R. and Marcella (Hogan) W.; A.B., Hofstra U., 1939, LL.D., 1969; J.D., N.Y.U., 1946, LL.D., 1969; postgrad. Inst. Advanced Legal Studies, U. London (Eng.), 1959; m. Mary Celeste Madden, Nov. 23, 1946; children—Mary Beth, Stephen, Kevin, Jeanne Marie. Asst. to dean N.Y.U. Law Sch., 1946-47, instr., 1948-50, asst. prof., 1950-52, asso. prof., 1952-55, prof., 1956-68; asst. dean N.Y.U., 1958-62, v.p. univ. devel., 1962-66, exec. v.p. planning and devel., 1966-68; pres. Am. U., Washington, 1968—. Trustee Hofstra U., 1961-65, Nat. Center Edn. Politics, 1958-65, Fed. City Council, 1968—. Served to lt. col. AUS, 1941-45. Decorated Silver Star, Legion of Merit, Purple Heart. Mem. Alpha Kappa Delta, Phi Delta Kappa. Author reports, articles. Home: 3300 Nebraska Av NW Washington DC 20016

WILLIAMS, GORDON LEE, civil engr.; b. Galbis, Cuba, Dec. 7, 1910 (parents Am. citizens); s. Noah Kellum and Birdie Fay (Pickett) W.; B.S. in Civil Engring., U. Fla., 1932; m. Ethel Cleo Campbell, June 18, 1933; children—Robert, Sarah (Mrs. Allan J. Finnell), Mary Lou (Mrs. Charles J. Thomas). Jr. to asso. engr. U.S. Bur. Reclamation, Nev., Colo., Cal., 1932-41; asso. engr. TVA, Ocoee and Fontana Dams, Tenn., N.C., 1942-45; hydraulic turbine specialist Gen. Electric Co., Rio de Janeiro, Brazil, 1946-49; planning engr. hydroelectric projects Brazilian Light Co., Sao Paulo, 1949-53; engr. Harza Engring. Co., Chgo., 1954-59; project mgr. Devel. & Resources Corp., N.Y.C., 1960-64, Engring. Cons., Inc., Denver, 1965-66; prin. Gordon L. Williams, Miami, Fla., 1968—. Registered profl. engr., Ill. Fellow Am. Soc. C.E. Supr. constrn. Pahlavi Dam, Iran, 1960-64.‡

WILLIAMS, HAROLD EDWARD, city ofcl.; b. Clermont, Fla., Jan. 27, 1929; s. Henry J. and Mildred (Crews) W.; grad. high sch., Fla.; m. Lily Jean Reed, Mar. 5, 1950; children—Stephen Edward, Mildred Joyce, Sarah Jean. With A&P Tea Co., Jacksonville, Fla., 1948-53; city clk. Palatka, Fla., 1959-61, city mgr. 1961-70; city mgr. Naples, Fla. 1970—. Chmn. Azalea Festival, 1962, 63, dir. United Fund, 1956. Named Outstanding Jaycee, 1962; recipient Good Govt. award Palatka Jr. C. of C., 1966. Mem. Putnam County Hist. Soc. (dir.), Internat., Fla. (pres. 1969-70) city mgrs. assns., Municipal Finance Officers Assn. Democrat. Presbyn. (deacon). Home: 2102 Alamanda Dr Naples FL 33940

WILLIAMS, HARRY JOHN, accountant; b. West Frankfort, Ill., June 21, 1900; s. George Harry and Lydia (Morgan) W.; student U. Ill., 1920-22;; m. Helita Eubanks Durham, Oct. 24, 1922; children—Harry John, Patricia (Mrs. Reynold H. Richaud). With Peat, Marwick, Mitchell & Co., C.P.A.'S, 1922-63, partner, 1943-63; accounting adviser Internat. Finance Corp., 1963-67, accounting cons., 1967—. Instr. City Coll. Law and Finance, St. Louis, 1927, Loyola U. of South, New Orleans, 1935. Chmn., Sea Transp. Industry Com., 1952-63; mem. Petroleum Industry Com., 1948-63, chmn. subcom. accounting procedures, 1955-63; mem. Internat. Com. Accounting Cooperation, 1966-72, treas., 1966-67; mem. accountants div. Nat. Fund for Med. Edn., 1955-64; mem. Trade Mission to Orient, 1961. Bd. dirs. Internat. House, New Orleans, 1958-63. C.P.A., Mo., La. Mem. Am. Inst. C.P.A.'s, La. Soc. C.P.A.'s (pres. 1941-42), Nat. Assn. Accountants (pres. New Orleans 1942-43), New Orleans Power Squadron, Grand Isle Tarpon Rodeo (chmn. boat com. 1958-63), Sigma Lambda Epsilon (hon.). Republican. Presbyn. Mason (K.T.). Clubs: Big Ten Universities (pres. 1938), Pickwick, Southern Yacht, Country (New Orleans). Author pamphlets in field. Home: 309 Opal St New Orleans LA 70124 Office: 1818 H St NW Washington DC 20433

WILLIAMS, HARRY JOHN, JR., accountant; b. Marion, Ill., Mar. 10, 1924; s. Harry John and Helita (Durham) W.; B.B.A., Tulane U., 1948; m. Joanne Elizabeth Schwartz, Nov. 1, 1947; children—Kathleen Anne, Marianne Elizabeth, Barbara Helen, Harry John III. With Peat, Marwick, Mitchell & Co., St. Louis, 1948-53; pvt. practice accounting, New Orleans, 1953—. Chmn., Asso. Regional Accounting Firms, 1969-71. Served with USNR, 1943-46. Mem. Am. Inst. C.P.A.'s, Soc. La. C.P.A.'s (pres. New Orleans chpt. 1964-65, parliamentarian 1971-72, dir. 1964-65, 71—, chmn. numerous coms.), Accounting Research Assn., New Orleans Estate Planning Council (treas. 1970-71), New Orleans Bd. Trade, Greater New Orleans C. of C., Pi Kappa Alpha. Clubs: Pickwick, Southern Yacht, Internat. House (New Orleans). Methodist. Democrat. Editor: La. C.P.A., 1961-62. Home: 6824 Vicksburg St New Orleans LA 70124 Office: Hibernia Bank Bldg New Orleans LA 70112

WILLIAMS, HATCHER CRENSHAW, ednl. adminstr.; b. Oxford, N.C., Nov. 27, 1918; s. John Arrington and Lily Belle (White) W.; A.B., Duke, 1940, M.A., 1949; postgrad. Memphis State U.; m. Jacqueline Ray, Aug. 30, 1944; children—Beverly Royster, John Arrington II, Madge Ray, Margaret Ray. Tchr., Darlington Sch., 1944-53; asst. headmaster, dir. summer session Christchurch Sch., 1953-62; founder, Corolla Acad., Outer Banks, N.C., 1959; asst. headmaster Blue Ridge Sch., Dyke, Va., 1962, headmaster, 1963—. Founder Corolla-in-Eng. Summer Sch., 1964. Bd. govs. Christchurch Sch. Served with USAAF, 1944. Mem. English Speaking Union (dir.). Episcopalian (vestryman) 1959-62). Home and office: Blue Ridge School Dyke VA 22935

WILLIAMS, HENRY JOSEPH, sch. adminstr.; b. Montgomery, Ala., Sept. 8, 1907; s. Richard and Ella W. (Jones) W.; A.B., Ala. State U., 1931; M.A., Columbia, 1967; m. Bertha N. Glover, June 5, 1952; children—Michelle A., Henry J., II. With Birmingham Bd. Edn., 1932—, tchr. Lincoln Elementary Sch., 1932-37, Parker High Sch., 1936-56, prin. Bryant Elementary Sch., 1956-65, Alberta Shields Elementary Sch., 1965—. Active United Appeal, 1954, Heart Fund, 1969, YMCA, 1969. Founder, sec. Progressive Democratic Council, 1945-60. Mem. N.E.A. (life), Nat. Congress Parents and Tchrs., Ala. Tchrs. Assn., Ala. (chmn. citizenship com. 1969-70), Birmingham edn. assns., Prins. Assn., Omega Psi Phi, Phi Delta Kappa. Baptist (deacon). Home: 6215 2d Av S Birmingham AL 35212 Office: 3969 N 14th Av Birmingham AL 35234

WILLIAMS, HENRY LUCIEN, city ofcl.; b. McColl., S.C., Nov. 5, 1916; s. Lucien and Annie (Rogers) W.; student Robinson Bus. Coll., 1936-37; m. Annie Bess Ladd, June 8, 1951; children—Henry Lucien, Helen Ann. With U.S. Post Office, McColl., 1933-36, 37-41; mgr. Western Auto Asso. Store, McColl., 1941-42; supr. file room VA, Columbia, S.C., 1946-48; accountant J.W. Hunt & Co., Columbia, 1948-59; city clk., treas., City of Cayce (S.C.), 1959-62; dir. finance City of Spartanburg (S.C.), 1962—. Bd. dirs. Office Econ. Opportunity, 1967-70. Served with AUS, 1942-46. Recipient Govt. Accounting award State Mcpl. Assn., 1961. Decorated Bronze Star. Mem. S.C. City Clk. and Treas. Assn. (past pres.). Baptist. Home: 107 Lakeview Dr Spartanburg SC 29301 Office: 145 Broad St Spartanburg SC 29301

WILLIAMS, HERMAN DAVID, religious assn. exec.; b. nr. Livingston, Tenn., Aug. 3, 1906; s. Frank and Sarah (Bennett) W.; certificate Ch. of God Bible Inst., N.C., 1940; m. Gertrude Baker, Dec. 18, 1927; children—Edward L., Robert H. Pastor, various chs. Ch. of God, Cal., 1938, Ariz., 1939, N.C., 1940, 44-45, 47-48, Tenn., 1949-50; supt. Ch. of God Home for Children, Kannapolis, N.C., 1946; state overseer chs., Ala., 1941-42, Ala., 1950-54, N.C., 1962-66; gen. sec. Ch. of God, 1954-58, asst. gen. overseer, 1959-62; adminstrv. asst. to pub. Ch. of God Pub. House, Cleveland, Tenn., 1963-65; gen. chmn. gen. bd. edn., coordinator Bible Insts. for Ministerial Enrichment, Ch. of God, Cleveland, 1967—. Chmn. chaplains commn. Nat. Assn. Evangs., 1958-62. Chmn. bd. dirs. Lee Coll., Cleveland, 1952-54, 60-62. Home: 2320 Oakland Dr Cleveland TN 37311

WILLIAMS, HERMANN WARNER, JR., mus. dir.; b. Boston, Nov. 2, 1908; s. Hermann Warner and Helen Chilton (French) W.; A.B., Harvard, 1931, A.M., 1933; Ph.D., Courtauld Inst. of Art, U. London, Eng., 1935; postgrad. Inst. Fine Arts, N.Y.U., 1935-41; m. Alice Barrett Farley, Aug. 30, 1942; children—Susan, Penelope, Richard. Appt. interne Bklyn. Mus. grant of Rockefeller Found., 1935; asst. curator of Renaissance and modern art Bklyn. Mus., 1936; asst. dept. paintings Met. Mus. Art, 1937, asst. curator, 1942; asst. dir. Corcoran Gallery Art, Washington, 1946, dir., sec., 1947-68, dir. emeritus, cons. to bd. trustees, 1968—; adviser to bd. trustees Lauren Rogers Mus., Laurel, Miss., 1970—. Served in AUS, 1942-46, in part, as chief, hist. properties sect., War Dept. Recipient Corcoran Gold medal, 1969. Fellow Co. Mil. Historians; mem. Am. Assn. of

Museums, Am. Soc. Arms Collectors. Unitarian. Clubs: Harvard, Armor and Arms, Century Assn. (N.Y.C.); Cosmos, Harvard (Washington). Author: (with Bartlett Cowdrey) William Sidney Mount, 1944: The Civil War: The Artists' Record, 1961; Mirror to the American Past, A Survey of American Genre Painting 1750-1900, 1972. Contbr. articles on art subjects to art and ednl. publs. Home: 3226 Woodley Rd NW Washington DC 20008 Office: Corcoran Gallery Art Washington DC 20006

WILLIAMS, HIRAM DRAPER, painter, educator; b. Indpls., Feb. 11, 1917; s. Earl Boring and Inez Mary (Draper) W.; B.S., Pa. State U., 1950, M.Ed., 1951; m. Avonell Baumunk, July 7, 1941; children—Curtis Earl, Kim Avonell. Tchr. art U. So. Cal., 1953-54, U. Cal. at Los Angeles, summer 1959, U. Tex., 1954-60; mem. faculty U. Fla., 1960-—, now prof. of art paintings exhibited Pa. Acad. Fine Arts annuals, Whitney Mus. Am. Art bi-annuals, Corcoran Gallery bi-annuals, U. Ill. bi-annuals, Mus. Modern Art exhibitions, also Nordness Gallery, N.Y.C.; represented in permanent exhbns. Mus. Modern Art, Wilmington Art Center, Whitney Mus. Am. Art, N.Y.C., Sheldon Meml. Art Mus. Milw. Art Center, also pvt. collections. Served to capt. C.E., AUS, World War II; ETO. Recipient Tex. Research grant, 1958; Guggenheim fellow, 1962-63. Author: Notes for a Young Painter, 1963; also articles. Address: 2804 NW 30th Terrace Gainesville FL 32601

WILLIAMS, HOSEA LORENZO, religious and civil rights assn. ofcl.; b. Attapaulgus, Ga., Jan. 5, 1926; s. Turner and Lacenia Williams; B.A., Morris Brown Coll., 1951; postgrad. Atlanta U., 1951-52; m. Juanita Terry; children—Barbara Jean, Elizabeth Lacenia, Hosea Lorenzo, Andrea Jerome, Yolanda Felecia. High sch. tch., 1951-52; research chemist U.S. Dept. Agr., Savannah, Ga., 1952-64; bd. dirs. So. Christian Leadership Conf., 1961-64, spl. projects dir., 1964, nat. dir. voter registration and polit. edn., Atlanta, 1964-69, dir. Selma to Montgomery March, 1965, dir. Nat. Summer Community Orgn. and Polit. Edn. Project, 1965-66, coordinator Meredith March, 1966, overall coordinator Poor People's Campaign, Washington, 1968, nat. program coordinator, 1970-—, rep. to Nat. Black Coalitiion, 1970-—, regional v.p., 1970-—. Pres. Chatham County (Ga.) Crusade for Voters, 1961-64, Southeastern Crusade for Voters of Ga., 1962-64; chmn. Nat. Com. for Albany Eleven, 1966-68; mayor Resurrection City, Washington, 1968; mem. adv. council Martin Luther King Jr. Meml. Project, 1970-—. Bd. dirs. Nat. Com. Black Churchmen, Black Adv. Council, Small Bus. Adminstrn. Served with AUS, 1960-65. Recipient Antler Guard award Elks, 1954, Outstanding Achievement award U.S. Dept. Agr., 1956, Civil Achievement in Community and Race Relations award Nat. Alumni Assn. Morris Brown Coll., 1962, Unselfish Pub. Service in Field of Race Relations award Coastal Empire Emancipation Assn., 1962, Cause of Freedom award Ga. Registration Com. and So. Christian Leadership Conf., 1963, Community Service award Delta Sigma Theta, 1963. Mem. D.A.V., V.F.W., Am. Legion, N.A.A.C.P. (Courageous Leadership in Freedom Movement award Savannah br. 1961), Ga. Voters League (co-chmn. 1965-70), Phi Beta Sigma. Presbyn. (deacon 1954-70). Mason, Elk. Clubs: Creative Dancing Dramatics (Atlanta). Home: 8E Lake Dr NE Atlanta GA 30317 Office: 334 Auburn Av NE Atlanta GA 30303

WILLIAMS, HOWARD GLENN, accountant; b. Rocky Mount, N.C., June 1, 1938; s. Charles T. and Lucille (Taylor) W.; A.B., E. Carolina Coll., 1963, postgrad. Grad. Sch. Bus., 1963-64; m. Patsy Ann Edwards, June 17, 1967; 1 son, Charles Edwards. Staff accountant Arthur Andersen & Co., 1964-—, audit mgr., Charlotte, N.C., 1969-—. Served with USNR, 1956-60. Mem. N.C. Soc. C.P.A.'s, Am. Inst. C.P.A.'s, Nat. Assn. Accountants, Phi Sigma Pi. Home: 108 Waycross Dr Charlotte NC 28214 Office: 300 S College St Charlotte NC 28282

WILLIAMS, JACK LESLIE, telephone co. exec.; b. Mineola, Tex., Sept. 14, 1944; s. Charles G. and Della Mae (Suggs) W.; student Tyler Jr. Coll., 1964-65; B.B.A., Stephen F. Austin U., 1967; m. Nancy Grace Walters, May 2, 1970. Finance trainee Gulf States United Telephone Co., Tyler, Tex., 1967-69, treasury asst., 1969-70, asst. to treas., 1970, treas., 1970-—. Mem. Tyler Jr. C. of C. (dir.). Home: 7 Shady Lane Lake Villages Flint TX 75762 Office: 120 S College St Tyler TX 75701

WILLIAMS, JAMES ALEXANDER, lawyer; b. Pine Bluff, Ark., Oct. 30, 1929; s. Absalom Alexander and Kyle (Baggarly) W.; student U. Ark., 1948; B.A., So. Methodist U., 1951, J.D., 1952, M.L.A., 1971; m. Janet L. Bray, Nov. 27, 1953; children—Laura Kay, Victoria Lynn, Diana Leigh. Admitted to Tex. bar, 1952, since practiced in Dallas; mem. firm Touchstone, Bernays & Johnston, 1955-57; partner firm Bailey, Williams, Westpall & Henderson, 1957-—. Bd dirs. Spl. Care Sch.; bd. mgmt. YMCA. Served to lt. USNR, 1952-55. Mem. Am., Dallas bar assns., State Bar Tex., Dallas, Tex. assns. def. counsel, Internat. Assn. Ins. Counsel, Fedn. Ins. Counsel, Am. Bd. Trial Advocates, Soc. Hosp. Attys., Trial Attys. Am., Lambda Chi Alpha, Phi Alpha Delta. Democrat. Methodist. Club: Exchange; Dallas; Brookhaven Country. Home: 9617 Lanshire Dr Dallas TX 75238 Office: 1725 Corrigan Tower Dallas TX 75201

WILLIAMS, JAMES ALLEN, JR., editor; b. Wytheville, Va., Aug. 26, 1907; s. James Allen and Virginia (Tynes) W.; student pub. schs.; m. Dora Emelinee Burgess, June 20, 1928; children—Virginia Elizabeth (Mrs. N.C. Sutherland), Ella Frances (Mrs. Norris Porter), James A. III. Printers devil S.W. Va. Enterprise, Wytheville, 1926-31, mech. supt., 1932-38, advt. mgr., 1938-44, mng. editor, 1944-45, editor, gen. mgr., 1945-46, editor-in-chief, mng. editor, gen. mgr., 1946-—; editor Bland (Va.) Messenger, 1960-—. Bd. dirs. Wythe Community Hosp. Recipient Va. Pub. Relations award, 1968; Freedoms award for editorial, 1969; Resolution for contbn. to state of Va., Va. Legislature, 1969. Mem. 5-State Gt. Lakes to Fla. Hwy. Assn. (pres. 1956-—), Wytheville C. of C. (organizer, pres. 1946-53, dir. emeritus 1968). Baptist (trustee). Kiwanian (membership chmn.). Home: 220 19th St Wytheville VA 24382 Office: 275 W Monroe St Wytheville VA 24382

WILLIAMS, JAMES HOWARD, research exec.; b. Wheat, Tenn., Dec. 19, 1920; s. William Wess and Sallie (Shelton) W.; A.B., Carson-Newman Coll., 1942; M.A., George Peabody Coll., 1947; Ph.D., Vanderbilt U., 1956; m. Mary Helen Mewshaw, Aug. 31, 1946; children—James Howard, Edward Robert, Nancy Jean. Instr., dept. sociology U. S.C., 1950-55; asst. dir. Nat. Inst. Mental Health Project, Vanderbilt U. 1956-58; asst. prof. social welfare and sociology Fla. State U., 1958-61; research dir. Fla. Bur. Alcoholic Rehab., Avon Park, 1961-—. Social sci. cons. City of Columbia (S.C.) Planning Comm., 1950-55. Served to lt. USNR, 1942-46. Mem. N. Am. Assn. Alcohol Programs, So. Sociol. Soc., Soc. for Study of Social Problems, Am. Sociol. Assn. Nat. Rehab. Assn., Population Assn. Am., Fla. Acad. Sci. Kiwanian (pres. Avon Park club 1970-71). Contbr. articles in field to profl. jours. Home: 971 E Cornell St Avon Park FL 33825 Office: PO Box 1147 Avon Park FL 33825

WILLIAMS, JAMES LAWRENCE BASIL, clergyman; b. Colonial Beach, Va., Mar. 1, 1914; s. Hiram Walter Basil and Clara (Denmead) W.; grad., Randolph-Macon Acad., 1931; student Randolph-Macon Coll., Ashland, Va., 1933; B.S., U. Va., Charlottesville, Va. 1936, M.A., 1938; postgrad. U. Minn., Va. Theol. Sem., Frederick Wilhelm U., Bonn, Germany, Am. U., Am. Bible Inst., Kansas City, Mo., D.D., N.Y. U.; m. Jean Rowell McCardell, Sept. 13, 1941; children—Judith Lawrence Barcroft (Mrs. Wisner Washam), Ian Rowell Denmead. Minister-in-charge Immanuel Ch.-on-the-Hill, Va. Theol. Sem., Alexandria, Va., 1947-53; minister Henry Stimson Chapel, Bad Godesberg, Germany, 1953-54; rector Cunningham Chapel Parish, Millwood, Va., 1954-58. Grace Parish, Okla., 1958, St. Basil Ch., Tahlequah, Okla., Bethesda by-the Sea, Palm Beach, Fla.; asso. rector St. Thomas Ch., N.Y.C., Ch. of Holy Spirit, Nice, France; founder, dean Am. Center for theol. studies, Boyce, Va., 1958-—. Thoroughbred bloodstock agt. Stallion Service, Inc. Chmn. White House Conf. Com. on Aging, Okla., 1960; mem. Bishop and Council. Diocese of Okla. Ecumenical Commn. Episcopal Ch., 1960; bd. mem. Overseas Mission Soc. Trustee, Bethel Meml. Assn., bd. dirs. James Monroe Birthplace Assn. Served from ensign to lt. comdr. USNR, 1941-47. Mem. Soc. Cin., S.R., Soc. Colonial Wars, Order Lafayette. Chaplain Flag Inst., Welsh-Am. Soc. (pres.), Soc. Descs. Colonial Clergy Am., Brecknock Soc. (Wales), Nat. Trust Historic Preservation, Va. Breeders Assn., Sertoma, Ruritan, Am. Legion, Phi Delta Theta. Alpha Kappa Psi, Sigma Upsilon. Clubs: Chevy Chase, Metropolitan, Army-Navy-Country (Washington); Muskegee Country; Millwood Country (Boyce, Va.); American (pres.) (Nice, France). Author: An Economic and Social Survey of Westmoreland County, Va., 1935; Minister Without Portfolio, 1954; Contemporary Virginia. Producer TV documentaries This World and the Next, A Dead Certainty. Home: Upshot Boyce Clark County VA Office: 13800 S Biscayne River Dr Miami FL 33161

WILLIAMS, JAMES NEWTON, psychiatrist; b. Richmond, Va., Aug. 29, 1904; s. Samuel Newton and Frances (Kolbe) W.; A.B., Washington and Lee U., 1926; M.D., Med. Coll. Va., 1930; m. Dorothy Henrietta Behle, Aug. 29, 1933; children—James Newton, Dorothy M. Resident psychiatry Med. Coll. Va., Richmond, 1932-35; pvt. practice psychiatry, 1936-—; dir. Va. Bd. Mental Hygiene, Richmond, 1935-41; chief neuropsychiat. service U.S. Naval Hosp., Portsmouth, Va. and Newport, R.I., 1950-—; dir. Portsmouth Area Counseling and Guidance Clinic, 1950-54, Atlantic Mental Hygiene Center, Virginia Beach, Va., 1960; mem. adv. bd. Atlantic Mental Health Center, Virginia Beach, 1960-—, dir.-psychiatrist, 1962-—. Mem. adv. bd. Child and Family Service and Travelers Aid, Portsmouth, 1961-—, Portsmouth Mental Hygiene Assn., 1960-—. Served from lt. to capt., M.C., USNR, 1941-62. Fellow A.C.P., Am. Psychiat. Assn.; mem. A.M.A., Royal Medico Psychol. Assn. (London, Eng.), Med. Soc. Va., C. of C. (exec. bd.). Rotarian (past pres). Contbr. numerous articles to profl. jours. Home: 717 Cardinal Rd Virginia Beach VA 23451 Office: 1876 Wildwood Dr Virginia Beach VA 23454

WILLIAMS, J(AMES) TAYLOR, judge; b. Lynchburg, Va., May 13, 1916; s. William Twyman and Annabel (Lyle) W.; A.B., Hampden-Sydney Coll., 1937; certificate in meteorology Cal. Inst. Tech., 1942; LL.B., Washington and Lee U., 1953; m. Eleanor Kathleen Nuckols, June 11, 1942; 1 dau., Kathleen Eleanor. Tchr. Math Whitmell (Va.) Farm-Life Sch., 1937, Cumberland (Va.) High Sch., 1938, Fishburne Mil. Sch., Waynesboro, Va., 1939-41; admitted to Va. bar, 1953; practiced in Cumberland, 1954-55; commonwealth's atty., Cumberland County, 1956-57; judge Cumberland County Cts., Cumberland, 1957-—. Pres., Cumberland County Indsl. Devel. Corp., 1963-—; chmn. Cumberland County Ct. House Restoration Com., 1968-70. Sec., Cumberland County Democratic Com., 1960-—. Bd. dirs. Cumberland Edn. and Recreation Assn. Served to lt. col. AUS, USAAF, 1941-48; ETO. Mem. Assn. County and Municipal Judges, Va. Bar Assn., 5th Jud. Circuit Bar. Assn. (past pres.), Am. Legion, V.F.W., Va. Farm Bur. Democrat. Presbyn. Mason. Club: Ruritan (Cumberland). Home: US Hwy 60 E Cumberland VA 23040 Office: County Office Bldg Cumberland VA 23040

WILLIAMS, JEAN LOCKWOOD (MRS. DANIEL MORTIMER WILLIAMS), ret. social worker, educator; b. Rockdale, Tex.; d. Henry and Emma J. (Bagley) Lockwood; B.A., M.A. in Econs. and Sociology, U. Tex., 1921; teaching certificate U. Tex. Sch. Social Work and Counseling, 1938; M.S.W., Howard U., 1953; m. Daniel Mortimer Williams, June 14, 1921 (dec. Nov. 1969); children—David Raworth, Jean (Mrs. Ronnie Dugger). Tchr. sch., Tex., 1920; librarian U. Tex., Austin, 1921; mem. research dept. J. Walter Thompson, Pedlar and Ryan, N.Y.C., 1925-29; dist. supr. WPA, Austin, 1938-42; exec. dir. nat. bd. YWCA-U.S.O., Tucson, Orange, Tex., Jacksonville Beach, Fla., 1942-46, YWCA, Alexandria, Va., 1946-52; acting dir. information and referral Health and Welfare Council, Washington, 1952-53; dir. vol. services D.C. Gen. Hosp., Washington, 1954-70. Educator, counselor on family life, pub. schs. Washington, 1947-50; field instr. Howard U., Washington, 1950-51, Nat. Catholic Sch. Social Service, Washington, 1954-65; cons. on vol. social services Dept. State on Bogota Conf., 1962; program chmn. Vol. Conf. Health and Welfare Council, Washington, 1954-62; hon. mem. vol. services div. Hosp. Council of Nat. Capitol Area, 1971-—. Mem. Nat. Assn. Social Workers, Acad. Certified Social Workers, Internat. Platform Assn., Internat. Council on Social Welfare, Nat. Conf. on Social Welfare, D.C. Assn. Mental Health, Md., D.C., Del. hosp. assns., Am. Assn. Group Workers (rep. on Settlement House Study 1952-53), Am. Assn. Ret. Persons, A.R.C., Ch. Women United, Nat. Conf. on Aging, Tex. Soc., U. Tex. ex-students clubs, Mortar Bd., Chi Omega. Democrat. Methodist (chmn. Christian social relations Women's Soc. Christian Service). Home: 1514 17th St NW Washington DC 20036

WILLIAMS, JERRY ALEXANDER, chem. co. exec.; b. Cape Town, South Africa, Oct. 24, 1926; s. William Parkin and Alfa L. (Gunderson) W.; grad. South African Naval Acad., 1943; B.S., U. Ida., 1951; m. Ida-Mae Peterson, Oct. 26, 1946; children—Richard Alexander, Linda Lorene. Came to U.S., 1946, naturalized, 1954. With Shell Chem. Co., N.Y.C., Atlanta, New Orleans, 1951-58, sales supr., 1958-60; with Helena Chem. Co., West Helena, Ark., Memphis, 1961-—, chief exec. officer, chmn. bd. dirs., 1964-—. Served with Royal Navy, 1943-46. Decorated Atlantic Star, African Star. Republican. Christian Scientist. Mason (Shriner). Home: 131 Waring Rd Memphis TN 38117 Office: 100 N Main Bldg Suite 3100 Memphis TN 38113

WILLIAMS, JOHN BARRY, dentist; b. Austin, Tex., May 19, 1928; s. J.B. and Ethyl Lloyd (Clark) W.; B.A., U. Tex., 1948; D.D.S., Baylor U., 1951; m. Marilyn Agnew, June 23, 1951 (div. May 1971); children— John Barry, Marilee. Practice dentistry, Austin, 1954-—. Bd. dirs., treas. Child and Family Service, 1959-61. Served with USAF, 1952-54. Fellow Soc. Oral Physiology and Occlusion; mem. Am., Tex. dental assns., Austin Dist. Dental Soc. (v.p. 1963). Home: 7586 Chevy Chase Austin TX 78703 Office: 17 Med Arts Sq Austin TX 78705

WILLIAMS, JOHN BELL, former gov. of Miss., lawyer; b. Raymond, Miss., Dec. 4, 1918; s. Graves Kelly and Maude Elizabeth (Bedwell) W.; student Hinds Jr. Coll., Raymond, Miss., 1934-36, U. Miss., 1938, Jackson (Miss.) Sch. Law, 1940; m. Elizabeth Ann Wells, Oct. 12, 1944; children—Marcia E., John Bell, Kelly. Admitted to Miss. bar, 1940; practiced in Raymond, 1940-46; pros. atty. Hinds County, 1944-46; mem. 80th-83d congresses from 7th Miss. Dist., 83d-87th congresses from 4th Miss. Dist., 88th-90th congresses from 3d Miss. Dist.; gov. State of Miss., Jackson, 1968-72. Served with USAAF, AUS, 1941-44. Mem. Miss. State Bar Assn., Am. Legion, V.F.W., D.A.V. Democrat. Baptist. Mason. Home: Raymond MS 39154

WILLIAMS, JOHN FRED, ret. personnel dir.; b. Volga, Ky., Sept. 7, 1904; s. James Marion and Jennie (Vaughan) W.; A.B., U. Louisville, 1931; LL.D., Union Coll., Barbourville, Ky., 1945; m. Carrie Bennett Cecil, Mar. 29, 1928; children—John Marion, Jane Florence (Mrs. Howard Van Antwerp III). Tchr., Johnson County, Ky., rural school, 1924-30, Louisville city schs., 1930-31, Johnson County high sch., 1931-34, Paintsville (Ky.) high sch., 1934-35; county supt. Johnson County Schs., 1935-43; supt. pub. instrn. State of Ky., 1944-48; v.p., personnel dir. Ashland (Ky.) Oil and Refining Co., 1948-69; past dir. Ky. Oil & Gas Assn. Past pres. Ky.-Tenn.-Ohio Valley Personnel Relations Conf. Past mem. Ky. Com. Functions and Resources of State Govt. Past chmn. Govs. Citizens Adv. Com. on Highways (Kentucky); past mem. Ky. State Fair Bd., Ky. Adv. Council for Vocational Edn., Ky. Commn. on Pub. Edn. Past mem. bd. regents Ky. State Coll.; past chmn. bd. trustees Eastern State Tchrs. Coll., Western State Tchrs. Coll., Morehead State Tchrs. Coll., Murray State Tchrs. Coll.; past mem. bd. trustees U. Ky.; former sec. State Textbook Commn.; former chmn. Council Pub. Higher Edn. of Ky., State Bd. of Edn. of Ky.; past mem. planning bd. Ky. Edn. Assn.; past mem. bd. trustees Ky. Tchrs. Retirement System. Designated Hon. Ky. Farmer, 1944; received award of merit for outstanding Ednl. Service by Ky. Assn. Colls. and Secondary Schs., 1945. Mem. Ky. Hist. Soc., Phi Delta Kappa. Mason. Club: Filson. Home: 712 Bellefonte-Princess Rd Ashland KY 41101

WILLIAMS, JOHN FREDERICK, chemist; b. York, S.C., May 14, 1923; s. Eddie Meek and Laura (Pegram) W.; B.S. in Chem. Engring., U. S.C., 1944; M.S. in Chemistry, Clemson Coll., 1951; Ph.D. in Chemistry, U. Va., 1954; m. Billie Margaret Lowry, Nov. 9, 1945 (dec. Feb. 1970); children—John Franklin, Frederick Lowry; m. 2d, Katherine Coleman, Aug. 29, 1970. Sr. chemist Liggett & Myers Inc., Durham, N.C., 1954-60, supr. analytical chemistry, 1960-—; dir. Williams Realty Inc., York. Served with USNR, 1944-47. Mem. Am. Chem. Soc., Soc. for Applied Spectroscopy, A.A.A.S., Coblentz Soc., Sigma Xi. Presbyn. (deacon 1958-63, ruling elder 1963-—). Kiwanian. Home: 3732 St Marks Rd Durham NC 27707 Office: Liggett & Myers Inc W Main St Durham NC 27702

WILLIAMS, JOHN OCE, food co. exec.; b. Avery, Tex., Apr. 5, 1936; s. Charley James and Edna Dale (Medford) W.; B.S., East Tex. State U., 1959; m. Sonja Miller, Dec. 29, 1957; children—John Oce, Amy Elizabeth. Grocery clk. Piggly Wiggly, Commerce, Tex., 1955-56; tchr. Edgar Allen Poe Jr. High Sch., San Antonio, 1960-62; salesman Kraft Food Co., Paris, Tex., 1963-68; mgr. Medford's Foods, Avery, 1968-—. Mem. Avery C. of C. (pres. 1971). Methodist. Mason. Home: Route 2 Avery TX 75554 Office: Medford's Foods Box 128 Avery TX 75554

WILLIAMS, JOHN RICHARD, electronic scientist; b. Detroit, May 19, 1919; s. Nicolas and Louise (Keydel) W.; B.S., Wayne State U., 1942; m. Mary E. Hornbeck, Aug. 28, 1971. Electronic scientist Naval Research Lab., Washington, 1942-—. Mem. Nat. Republican Club. Mem. Am. Ordnance Assn. (life), A.A.A.S. (life), I.E.E.E., Air Force Assn., Assn. Old Crows (charter). Presbyn. (deacon). Clubs: Washington Athletic, Potomac Appalachian Trail. Research and devel. in electronic countermeasures for navy. Home: 2111 Jefferson Davis Hwy Arlington VA 22202 Office: Naval Research Lab Code 5741A Washington DC 20390

WILLIAMS, JOHN WILLIAM, bookstore exec.; b. Red Hill, Va., Nov. 24, 1916; s. John William and Louise Gray (Anderson) W.; grad. Tarleton Bus. Coll., 1936; student U. Va., 2 yrs.; grad. LaSalle U., 1947; m. Laura Elizabeth Kegley, Nov. 6, 1937; children—Elizabeth Byrd (Mrs. Charles Cortez Abbott), Martha Hayes (Mrs. Ward W. Anderson). Clk., Anderson Bros. Bookstores, Inc., Charlottesville, Va., 1936-40, asst. gen. mgr., 1940-41, v.p., 1941-62, pres., gen. mgr., 1962-—; asst. sec.-treas. Anderson Realty Corp., Charlottesville, 1938-69, sec.-treas., 1969-—, also dir.; dir. Va. Nat. Bank. Asst. varsity, head freshman boxing coach U. Va., 1941-43, head boxing coach, 1953-—. Mem. Va. Hosp. Bd., 1963-—, vice chmn., 1969; mem. Albemarle County Bd. Pub. Welfare, 1949-61. Mem. Albemarle County Sch. Bd., 1946-49; mem. Albemarle County Bd. Suprs., 1949-64, chmn., 1957-64; a.d.c. to gov. of Va., 1959-—; chmn. SSS, Charlottesville, 1970-—. Pres. Young Democratic Clubs Va., 1953-55; sec. 8th Congl. Dist. Dem. Com., 1956-66; mem. Va. Dem. Central Com., 1956-—, mem. steering com., 1969-—; chmn. 7th Congl. Dist. Dem. Com., 1969. Gen. vice chmn. devel. com. U. Va. Grad. Sch. Bus. Served to 1st lt. AUS, 1943-46, col. Va. State Guard. Mem. Va. Coll. Stores Assn. (pres. 1971-72), Nat. Intercollegiate Boxing Coaches Assn. (pres. 1957), Assn. Va. Counties (pres. 1960), U. Va. Alumni Assn., Albemarle Hist. Soc. (pres. 1969), Am. Legion. Rotarian. Clubs: Monticello Guard, Farmington Country. Home: Meadowbrook Heights Charlottesville VA 22901 Office: 1541 W Main St Charlottesville VA 22901

WILLIAMS, JOHNNY KNOTT, supt. schs.; b. Memphis, May 5, 1926; s. Gladstone and Johnny (Knott) W.; B.S., Ark. State Tchrs. Coll., 1950; M.A., George Peabody Coll., 1953; advanced diploma U. Ark., 1967; m. Edna Earle Stephens, Aug. 23, 1953; children—Stephen Gladstone, Jaye Kay, John David, Edward Allen. Tchr., coach, prin. pub. schs., Dumas, Ark., 1950-53, supt. schs., 1954-58; asst. registrar U. Ark., 1958-63; supt. schs. Paragould, Ark., 1963-65, Blytheville, Ark., 1965-70, Pulaski County Spl. Sch. Dist., Little Rock, 1970-—. Mem. Ark. State Econ. Edn. Council, 1966-70; bd. dirs. YMCA, Blytheville, Ark., 1966-67. Served with USN, 1943-46. Mem. Ark. Sch. Adminstrs. Assn. (treas. 1966-67), Ark. Edn. Assn. (mem. legislative com. 1966-67), Miss. County Sch. Adminstrn. (pres. 1966), Nat. Edn. Assn., Am. Assn. Sch. Adminstrs., Phi Delta Kappa. Methodist (bd. dirs., 1966-69). Club: Rotary. Home: 6424 Tulip Rd Little Rock AR 72209 Office: 924 Marshall Little Rock AR 72204

WILLIAMS, JOSEPH HILL, diversified industry exec.; b. Tulsa, June 2, 1933; s. David Rogerson and Martha Reynolds (Hill) W.; grad. St. Paul's Sch., 1952; B.A., Yale, 1956; postgrad. U. Tex. Sch. Pipeline Tech., 1960; m. Penny Baldwin, Nov. 24, 1956; children—Joseph Hill, Peter B., James C. With Williams Cos., 1958-—, resident mgr., Tehran, Iran, 1965-67, exec. v.p., Tulsa, 1968-70, pres., chief operating officer, 1971-—, also dir.; chmn. bd. Oklahoma City br. Fed. Res. Bank Kansas City; dir. Okla. Natural Gas. Co. Bd. dirs. Tulsa Community Chest. Served to 1st lt. AUS, 1957-58. Mem. Met. Tulsa C. of C. (dir.), Am. Petroleum Inst. (dir.), Urban League (dir.), Young Presidents Orgn. Episcopalian (vestryman). Clubs: Tulsa, Southern Hills Country, Summit, Yale (pres. Tulsa); St. Anthony (N.Y.C.); Houston; Springdale Hall (Camden, S.C.). Office: Nat Bank Tulsa Bldg Tulsa OK 74103

WILLIAMS, KEMPER SAM, JR., lawyer, govt. ofcl.; b. Victoria, Tex., May 21, 1931; s. Kemper S. and Genevieve (Sitterle) W.; A.A., Victoria Coll., 1950; B.B.A., St. Marys U., 1952, LL.B., 1958; m. Patricia Aileen Tuttle, July 14, 1952; children—Cecilia Anne, Mary Patricia, Jane Nancy, Kemper S. III. Admitted to Tex. bar, 1958;

practiced in Victoria, Tex., 1961—; mem. firm Tibiletti and Williams, 1961-63, Tibiletti, Williams and Ritchey, 1963-65, Cullen, Edwards, Williams & Stevenson, 1965—. Mayor, Victoria, Tex., 1963—. Republican County Chmn., 1960-63. Served to 1st lt. AUS, 1952-56. Mem. Tex., Victoria bar assns., Tex. Municipal League (regional pres. 1965-66, 1st v.p. 1968-70, pres. 1970). Roman Catholic. Home: 404 E Loma Vista St Victoria TX 77901 Office: PO Box 2207 Victoria TX 77901

WILLIAMS, KENNETH BURDG, economist; b. Brunswick, Me., Apr. 3, 1910; s. Joseph Abraham and Beulah (Burdg) W.; student S.D. State Coll., 1927-28, Fullerton Jr. Coll., 1929-30; A.B., Stanford, 1932; M.A., George Washington U., 1937; m. Jean Isabel Hawley, Oct. 20, 1934; children—Randall Burdg, Margaret Jean (Mrs. Steven Willis Underwood). Economist, WPA, Washington, 1935-41; economist, adviser to bd. govs. Fed. Res. System, Washington, 1941—. Fellow Am. Statis. Assn. (dir.) A.A.A.S.; mem. Am. Econs. Assn., Indsl. Relations Research Assn., Nat. Assn. Bus. Economists, Artus, Phi Beta Kappa. Mem. Soc. of Friends. Club: Nat. Economists. Home: 4816 Cumberland Av Chevy Chase MD 20015 Office: Fed Res Bd Washington DC 20551

WILLIAMS, KENNETH RAST, univ. pres.; b. Monticello, Fla., Oct. 26, 1908; s. John Franklin and Mary Elizabeth (Bearden) W.; B.S., U. Fla., 1929, M.A., 1932; Ph.D., U. Chgo., 1944; m. Selma Rey Reynolds, June 7, 1934; children—Harriet Virginia, John Franklin. Prin., St. Andrews (Fla.) Elementary Sch., 1929-30; instr. edn. Fla. State Coll. for Women, 1930-36; asst. prof. edn. U. Ga., Athens, 1938-40, dean students, asso. prof., 1940-41, dean Coll. Edn., 1944-46; dir. war tng. programs, prof. Sch. Adminstrn., U. Fla., 1941-43; dir. ednl. adv. staff, dean instrn. USAF Air U., Montgomery, Ala., 1946-51; asso. dir. So. Regional Edn. Bd., Atlanta, 1951-52; mem. Commn. Secondary Edn., Govt. India, 1953-54; cons. Atlanta Bd. Edn., 1953-55, dept. supt. schs., 1956-58; cons. higher edn. Govt. Indonesia, 1955-56; pres. Central Fla. Jr. Coll., Ocala, 1958-60, Dade County Jr. Coll., Miami, 1960-62, Fla. Atlantic U., Boca Raton, 1962—. Mem. Council Rehab. Returning Servicemen and Women, Gainesville, 1941-43; cons. Pres. Roosevelt's Adv. Commn. Edn., 1938-39. Mem. Fla. Council of 100. Bd. dirs. Fla. Mental Health Assn. Recipient Distinguished Service award for civic work Fla. Jr. C. of C., 1944, commendation for meritorious civilian service USAF, 1951, certificate of merit U. Fla., 1953. Mem. Nat., Fla. edn. assns., Fla. Assn. Jr. Colls. (pres. 1960-61), Blue Key, Phi Kappa Phi, Phi Delta Kappa, Kappa Delta Pi, Phi Sigma, Pi Gamma Mu, Alpha Phi Epsilon, Omicron Delta Kappa, Sigma Phi Epsilon. Methodist. Rotarian (pres. Ocala 1957). Home: 2166 Silver Palm Rd W Boca Raton FL 33432

WILLIAMS, LAFAYETTE WESLEY, JR., dentist; b. Valdosta, Ga., Dec. 17, 1937; s. Lafayette Wesley and Ethel Mae (Davis) W.; B.S., Morehouse Coll., 1960; D.D.S., Meharry Med. Coll., 1968; m. Nedra Milicent Huggins, Nov. 28, 1968. Mem. staff Central State Hosp., Milledgeville, Ga., 1968-69; pvt. practice dentistry, Valdosta, 1969—; mem. staff Valdosta Nursing Home, Internat. Nursing Care Center, Valdosta. Mem. Valdosta Black Community Action Group, 1970—. Trustee Lowndes County Progressive Voters League. Mem. Nat., Am. dental assns., Ga., S.W. Dist. dental socs., Valdosta-Lowndes County C. of C., N.A.A.C.P., Beta Kappa Chi, Alpha Phi Alpha. Mason (Shriner, 32 deg.), Elk. Home: 415 Church St Valdosta GA 31601 Office: PO Box 83 Valdosta GA 31601

WILLIAMS, MARGARET HICKS, author, lectr.; b. Pittsfield, Mass.; d. William Cleveland and Margaret (Hughes) Hicks; spl. student Columbia, 1927-29; m. James Bradley Williams, Jr., June, 1927 (div. 1942). Polit. analyst on Europe and USRR., U.S. M.I., 1921-24, Far East, 1924-27; author, traveler, 1928-40; head of spot news sect. (O.G.R.), Exec. Offices of Pres., 1941; editor in chief publs. sect. Press Intelligence, OWI 1942; chief civilian cons. on Brit. Empire in M.I., War Dept., 1943-44; information and liaison officer Europe and Occupied Area, Dept. State, 1944-46; in charge Brit. Commonwealth br. Office Internat. Information and Cultural Affairs, Dept. State, 1946-47, chief No. European-British sect. Office Information and Ednl. Exchange, 1947-48; in charge Brit. Commonwealth and North European sects. Pub. Affairs Overseas Program Staff, Office Asst. Sec. State, 1948-49; pub. affairs adv. Office Brit. Commonwealth and North European Affairs, 1950, cultural affairs adv. Bur. European Affairs, 1951; cultural officer U.S. Fgn. Service, Tokyo, 1951-52, cultural attache Am. embassy, Tokyo, 1952-53, Am. embassy, Manila, 1954-56; spl. asst. Office Chief Cultural Operations (ICS), USIA, 1956, officer in charge cultural planning and coordination for Far East, 1957-59; officer in charge internat. orgn. affairs Bur. Edn. and Cultural Affairs, Dept. State, Washington, 1959-62, asst. to dir. multilateral and spl. activities, 1962-66; spl. asst. to dep. asst. sec. state edn. and cultural affairs, 1966-69; exec. dir. D.C. Women's Com. for Crime Prevention, 1969-70; author, lectr. fgn. affairs, 1970—. Bur. Edn. and Cultural Affairs coordinator Internat. Year Human Rights, 1968; Dept. State rep. to European Conf. on U.S. Cultural Affairs Policy, Copenhagen, 1950; USIA del. to Dept. State Far East and South Asian Regional Conf. Ednl. Exchange, Bangkok, 1957; lectr. U.S. Fgn. Service Inst., 1950; War Dept. Gen. Staff del. to Inst. of Politics, Williamstown, Mass. Recipient Nat. Civil Service League Career Service award for distinguished service, 1958, Meritorius Service Honor medal Dept. State, 1969. Fellow Royal Geog. Soc.; mem. Am. Acad. Polit. Sci., Bus. and Profl. Women's Club (pres. D.C. 1969-70). Clubs: Am. Newspaper Womens, Junior League. Author: Confidential History of Japan (for War Dept. ofcl. use only), 1927. Contbr. articles on internat. relations in mags. and jours. Died Aug. 18, 1972. Home: 2500 Virginia Av Washington DC 20037

WILLIAMS, MARJORIE, astronomer; b. Marshalltown, Ia., Oct. 12, 1900; d. J. Edgar and Anna (White) Williams; B.S., Guilford Coll., 1921; A.M., Smith Coll., 1928; Ph.D., U. Mich., 1942. Asso. prof. astronomy, dir. observatory Smith Coll., 1925-53; astronomer NSF, Washington, 1959-72, ret., 1972. Vol. worker Am. Friends Service Com., Germany, 1948-49. Mem. A.A.A.S., Am. Assn. U. Women, Am. Astron. Soc. Mem. Soc. Friends. Home: 825 New Hampshire Av NW Washington DC 20037

WILLIAMS, MARK BYRD, physician; b. Lexington, Va., Aug. 15, 1913; s. William Twyman and Annabel Preston (Lyle) W.; B.S., Hampden-Sydney Coll., 1935; postgrad. U. Tenn., 1937-38; M.D., Med. Coll. Va., 1943; m. Jane Hertzler Mumper, Aug. 20, 1950. Intern, Stuart Circle Hosp., Richmond, Va., 1943-44, resident, 1944; chief med. service East State Hosp., Williamsburg, Va., 1949-52; gen. practice medicine, Richmond, 1952-70; chief med. service Petersburg (Va.) Tng. Sch. and Hosp., 1970—. Served to capt., M.C. AUS, 1944-46; ETO. Mem. Am. Acad. Gen. Practice, Richmond Acad. Medicine, Med. Soc. Va., A.M.A., Civitan, Chi Phi, Phi Chi. Home: 210 Walnut Blvd Apt 19 Petersburg VA 23803 Office: Petersburg Tng Sch and Hosp Petersburg VA 23803

WILLIAMS, MARVIN DALE, JR., clergyman, librarian, archivist; b. Indpls., Oct. 27, 1935; s. Marvin Dale and Betty (Robison) W.; B.A., Butler U., 1958, M.A., 1963; B.D., Christian Theol. Sem., 1962; M.A., George Peabody Coll., 1963; student Am. U., 1966. Ordained to ministry Disciples of Christ Ch., 1962; pastor Olive Christian Ch., Paragon, Ind., 1959-60; periodicals librarian Christian Theol. Sem., Indpls., 1958-62; cataloger Disciples of Christ Hist. Soc., Nashville, Tenn., 1963-65, head tech. services, 1965, dir. library, 1966—, archivist, 1967—. Lilly Endowment scholar, 1962. Mem. Beta Phi Mu, Theta Phi. Editor: Discipliana, 1965—. Home: 422 Acklen Park Dr Nashville TN 37205 Office: 1101 19th Av S Nashville TN 37212

WILLIAMS, MAX, mgr., coach basketball team, 1938; grad. So. Meth. U., 1960; m. Carolyn Cooper; children—Wayne, Laura. Ins. salesman, 1960-62; pres. constrn. co., 1962-65; metal buyer, 1966; gen. mgr. Chaparrals of Am. Basketball Assn., Dallas, 1967—, coach, 1970—. Address: 2001 McKinney St Dallas TX 75201*

WILLIAMS, MAXIE RAYMOND, supt. schs.; b. Johnsonville, Tenn., Aug. 2, 1918; s. Grover Cleveland and Sarah Frances (Moore) W.; B.S., U. Tenn., 1940; M.S., George Washington U., 1965; m. Mary Sue Waldrop, Aug. 8, 1944; children—Maxie Raymond, Gregory Neal. Commd. 2d lt. USMC, 1941, advanced through grades to col., 1967; assigned East Coast, PTO, N. China, 1940's, Washington, Brazil, 6th Fleet, Mediterranean, 1950's, San Juan, P.R., Army War Coll., Vietnam, 1960-67; ret., 1967; prin. Commonwealth High Sch., San Jaun, P.R., 1968-69; supt. Caribbean Consol. Sch., San Juan, 1969—. Vice pres. Rooney Wholesale, San Juan, 1967-68. Vice pres. Travelers Aid; bd. dirs. Salvation Army, Boys Club. Decorated Navy Cross, Joint Services Commendation medal, Navy Commendation medal, Purple Heart with star. Mem. Am. Assn. U. Profs., Am. Assn. Sch. Adminstr., N.E.A., 2d Marine Assn., Inter Am. Edn. Assn., Mil. Order World Wars, Am. Legion, Pvt. Schs. Assn. P.R., Ret. Officers Assn., U. Tenn., George Washington U. alumni assns., Navy League (v.p., dir.). Rotarian (pres. San Jaun 1971-72). Home: Lakeshore Cond 7A 1 Madrid St Santurce PR 00907 Office: 435 Pedro A Espada Hato Rey PR 00918

WILLIAMS, NOLAN EUGENE, educator; b. Whitener, Ark., Aug. 2, 1923; s. Nolan L. and Rubie (Robertson) W.; B.S., Okla. State U., 1947, M.S., 1948; Ph.D., U. Tex., 1957; m. Madelyn Englert, Aug. 28, 1943; children—Janet Kay (Mrs. Richard T. Roessler), Susan E. (Mrs. Richard M. Mayes, Jr.). Asst. prof. accounting U. Tex., Austin, 1950-51; prof., head accounting U. Ark., Fayetteville, 1951—. Part-time accounting and bus.-cons. service, 1947—; partner Fresh-O-Canning Co., Haskell, Okla., 1941-51; vis. prof. Price Waterhouse & Co., Humble Pipe Line Co., U. Ariz. Bd. dirs. Wesley Found. Served with AUS, 1943-45. Decorated Purple Heart. Danforth fellow, 1952-54. Mem. Am. Accounting Assn. (v.p., exec. com. 1965), Am. Inst. C.P.A.'s (com. on auditing procedures 1965-68, nat council 1967-68, 70—), Ark. Soc. C.P.A.'s, Blue Key, Phi Kappa Phi, Beta Gamma Sigma, Beta Alpha Psi (nat. grand council), Delta Sigma Pi. Methodist (mem. bd.). Lion. Club: Fayetteville Country. Home: 512 Adam St Fayetteville AR 72746

WILLIAMS, PAT PARKER (MRS. M. LEE WILLIAMS), radio commentator, composer; b. Berkeley, Cal., Jan. 27, 1923; d. George and Mildred (Johnston) Parker; student Sullins Jr. Coll., 1940-41; Mus.B., U. Miss., 1943; m. Grayson Headley, Dec. 30, 1946 (dec. 1961); m. 2d, M. Lee Williams, Dec. 18, 1964; 1 son, Philip Lee. Women's dir. radio sta. WNNT, Warsaw, Va., commentator daily women's program, Chat with Pat, now owner radio sta. WNNT AM-FM, pres. 1965—; asst. soc. editor Jackson Daily News, 1943-44. Composer: concerto for piano and orchestra, Rhapsody of Youth, performed by Nat. Air Force Symphony, Washington, Lisner Auditorium, 1947, guest pianst with Nat. Air Force Symphony, 1964; (song) Cotton Picking Blues, featured in several musicals in Miss., Washington; (song) Maid of Cotton, used as theme song Nat. Cotton Council, 1945-51; (song) Lucky X, ofcl. song Chi Omega. Chmn., Red Cross water safety program, Lancaster County, Va., 1950-56; mem. exec. com. Jr. Assembly, Washington; jr. chmn. Home Hospitality Com., Washington, 1943-46; also UN Club activities, Washington, 1943-48. Mem. Am. Women in Radio and Television (dir. Va. 1962-65), Johns Hopkins Women's Aux., Balt. Assembly, Nat. Assn. Am. Composers and Conductors, Salvation Army Aux., Art for Hosps., Inc., Nat. Soc. Arts and Letters (music chmn. Washington chpt. 1964-65), Va. Assn. Broadcasters, Nat. Assn. for Am. Composers, Chi Omega, Delta Beta Sigma, Sigma Alpha Iota, Alpha Psi Omega. Episcopalian. Clubs: Debutante of Miss., Women's (chmn. music div. Lancaster County 1956-60); Indian Creek Women's Golf Assn.; Irvington Garden; Guilford Garden; Elkridge Tennis; Tides Inn Chesapeake; Friday Cotillion; Washington; Mount Vernon (Balt.). Home: 203 Westway Baltimore MD 21212 also tween Times Box 33 Irvington VA 22480 Office: Radio Sta WNNT Warsaw VA 22572

WILLIAMS, PATRICK NEHEMIAH, chmn. V.I. Dem. Com.; b. Christiansted, St. Croix, V.I., Sept. 28, 1928; s. Norman and Ingerborg Cassimeer W.; grad. high sch., 1959; m. Inex Maria Byron, Dec. 21, 1951; children— Glenice Ingerborg, Sharon Maria, Lindel Alphonso, Wayne, Patricia-Ann, Patrick Maurice, Raymond Jerome. Mngr., Alexander Hamilton Supply Hardware, 1959-60, Abramson's Enterprises, 1960; asst. store mgr. Merwin Hardware Inc., 1960-62; mem. V.I. State Senate, 1963-65; cons. V.I. Legislature, 1965—; mem. Traffic Safety Commn., 1966—; chmn. Vocational and Tech. Edn., 1967—; vice chmn. Commn. Aging, 1967—, Comprehensive Health Planning, 1967—. Chmn., Bd. Pub. Ednl. TV, 1969; mem. exec. com. Boy Scouts. Chmn. V.I. Democratic Com., 1966—; del. Dem. Nat. Conv., 1968; now mem. Dem. Nat. Com. Served as cpl., USMCR, 1951-53. Mem. Navy League U.S. (1st v.p. St. Croix Chpt.), Am. Vocational Assn. Roman Catholic. Home: Estate Grove Pl St Croix VI 00850 Office: PO Box 22 Kingshill St Croix VI 00850*

WILLIAMS, PAUL X., judge; b. Booneville, Ark., Feb. 19, 1908; s. Charles X. and Sallie (Cruce) W.; B.A., U. Ark., 1928, LL.B., 1930; m. Elizabeth Hays, May 16, 1935; children—Paul X., Jr., Charles David, Elizabeth (Mrs. Jerry Allen Trowbridge), Sarah Virginia, John Roger. Admitted to Ark. bar, 1930, U.S. Supreme Ct. bar, 1956, U.S. Ct. Mil. Appeals, 1956; practiced in Booneville, 1930-32, 34-42; atty. Ark. Hwy. Dept., Little Rock, 1932-34; chancery and probate judge 14th dist. Ark. 1949-67; U.S. dist. judge Western dist. Ark., Ft. Smith, 1967—. Served with USNR, 1942-46. Home: 815 Kennedy St Booneville AR 72927 Office: US Court House Fort Smith AR 72466

WILLIAMS, POLLY MADDOX, real estate rep.; b. Centre, Ala.; d. Walter Lee and Alma (Estes) Maddox; B.S., Fla. So. Coll., 1957; M.S. Fla. State U., 1960; m. Josiah McKewn Williams, Apr. 27, 1944 (div. 1945); 1 dau., Mary Virginia. Tchr., Tampa, Fla., 1957-59; tchr., counselor, Jacksonville, Fla., 1960-62; counselor, instr. psychology Fla. State U., Tallahassee, 1962-64; counselor West Fulton Sch., Atlanta, from 1964; group leader EOA Project, ENABLE, 1967; now vocational rehab. counselor Ga. Dept. Human Resources. Mem. Mental Health Assn., Druid Hills Art Council; mem. telephone com. Druids Hills Art Council; mem. program planning com., a coordinator world service com. YMCA. Mem. Am. Assn. U. Profs., Nat., DeKalb rehab. counseling assns., Ga. Rehab. Assn., Am. Personnel and Guidance Assn. Am. Assn. U. Women (chmn. legislative study and action group 1970—), Internat. Platform Assn., Fla., Ga. counselors assns., Ga. Writers Club, League Women Voters, DeKalb bd. realtors (asso.), High Mus Art, Beta Beta Beta. Democrat. Christian Scientist, Clubs: Atlanta Sky Lark, Atlantic Ski. Home: 42 Eastwyck Rd Decatur GA 30032 Office: 1793B Cambridge Av College Park GA 30337

WILLIAMS, PRYOR ALLEN, JR., dentist; b. Birmingham, Ala., Oct. 12, 1939; s. Pryor Allen and Florence Annette (Ross) W.; B.A., Vanderbilt U., 1959; D.M.D., U. Ala. Sch. Dentistry, 1963; certificate specialization in orthodontics, 1967; m. Sandra Dale Payne, Aug. 23, 1960; children—Pryor Allen, III, Warren Payne, Ashley. Asso. with Dr. Marion F. Dick, specializing in orthodontics, Birmingham, 1967—. Mem. state exec. com. Republican Party Ala., 1970—, mem. finance com., 1970—. Served with Dental Corps, USNR, 1963-65. Mem. Birmingham Dist. Dental Soc., Am., Ala. dental assns., Ala. Orthodontic Soc., So. Soc. Orthodontics, Am. Assn. Orthodontists, Delta Sigma Delta (chpt. pres. 1969-70). Methodist. Kiwanian. Home: 3225 Bonny View Dr Birmingham AL 35226 Office: 3351 Montgomery Hwy Birmingham AL 35209

WILLIAMS, RALPH EMERSON, ch. ofcl.; b. Branford, Fla., Feb. 28, 1915; s. Edison Wendell and Daisy (Russell) Williams; grad. Lee Coll., Cleveland, Tenn., 1935; postgrad. Beckley (W.Va.) Coll., 1961, Morris Harvey Coll., Charleston, W.Va., 1962; D.D., N.W. Coll., Minot, N.D., 1968; m. Ruth Lee Whittington, June 10, 1937; children—Juanelle (Mrs. John W. Oliver, Jr.), Wendell Long. Ordained to ministry Ch. of God, 1944; youth dir. Ch. of God in N.C., 1939-43, in Ohio, 1943-45, in Tenn., 1945-46; nat. youth dir. Ch. of God, 1946-50; minister in Ft. Lauderdale, Fla., 1950-54; overseer Ch. of God minister in Charlotte, N.C., 1962-64; gen. sec.-treas. Ch. of God, 1964—, mem. supreme council, 1956-60, exec. council, 1962-66, exec. com., 1964—, state supr. Tenn., Chattanooga, 1968—. Pres., W. Coast Bible Coll., Fresno, Cal., 1954-58. Chmn. bd. Lee Coll., Cleveland, Tenn. Home: 7120 McCutcheon Rd Chattanooga TN 37421 Office: 7120 Lee Hwy Chattanooga TN 37421

WILLIAMS, RALPH MAYNARD, oral surgeon; b. Johnson City, Tenn., Sept. 11, 1927; s. Dewey Maynard and Mary Alice (Crumley) W.; B.S., Lincoln Meml. U., 1949; D.D.S., U. Tenn., 1953, postgrad., 1955-56; m. Ann Marie Ryan, Dec. 29, 1955; children—William Joe, Dewey Maynard, Dana Beth. Resident, Univ. Hosp., Oklahoma City, 1953-54, Scott and White Hosp., Temple, Tex., 1954-55; practice oral surgery Bartlesville, Okla., 1956—; mem. staff Jane Phillip-Washington County Med. Center, Bartlesville; vis. staff, Nowata, Okla., 1956—. Chmn. Washington County Republican Com., 1969—. Fellow Internat. Assn. Oral Surgeons; mem. Am., Okla. dental assns., Am., S.W., Midwest, Okla. (pres., 1966-67) socs. oral surgeons, Internat. Acad. Dentistry. Baptist (deacon). Rotarian, Elk. Home: 3432 Hawthorn Ct Bartlesville OK 74003 Office: 3500 State St Bartlesville OK 74003

WILLIAMS, RAY ROBINSON, lawyer; b. Easley, S.C., Mar. 5, 1899; s. G.E.R. and Marinda Jane (Robinson) W.; B.A. magna cum laude, U. S.C., 1923, M.A., LL.B., 1924; m. Genevieve Castleman Groom, Apr. 17, 1929; children—Genevieve Castleman (Mrs. Beecher Allan Bartlett), Mary Ola (Mrs. Horace Lynwood Harper, Jr.), Ray Robinson. Admitted to S.C. bar, 1924, since practiced in Greenville; mem. firm Williams & Henry, 1926—. Chmn. Greenville County Water Arbitration Bd.; mem. Greenville County Marketing Commn.; mem. legal coms. serving state. Chmn. Adv. Council for Blind, S.C., 1957—. Mem. S.C. Ho. of Reps., 1937-40, S.C. Senate, 1941-52. Trustee U. S.C., 1937-48. Recipient certificate of commendation for outstanding service to agrl. marketing in S.C., Clemson Coll. and State Agrl. Marketing Commn., 1960. Mem. Am., S.C., Greenville County (pres. 1957) bar assns., Am. Judicature Soc. Baptist. Home: 110 Vannoy St Greenville SC 29601 Office: Lawyers Bldg 301 E North St Greenville SC 29603

WILLIAMS, RAYMOND AUBREY, JR., lawyer, rancher, oil co. exec.; b. Shreveport, La., June 11, 1924; s. Raymond Aubrey and Lucy (Perkins) W.; grad. N.M. Mil. Inst., 1941-43; B.B.A., So. Meth. U., 1948, J.D., 1949; m. Emily Burt, Feb. 28, 1953 (dec. May 1961); children—Raymond Aubrey III, Holly, Carol, Ralph; m. 2d, Mary Elizabeth Brodnax, May 19, 1963; children—Mary, Robert. Admitted to Tex. bar, 1949; mem. firm Frank C. Bolton, Jr., Longview, 1949-50, George, Russell and Williams, Dallas, 1950-52; atty. Ind. Oil Co. of M.B. Rudman, Dallas, 1952—, gen. mgr., partner 1954—. Town North YMCA, Dallas, 1966—, baseball coach North Dallas C. of C. Little League teams, 1964-68. Bd. dirs. Southwestern Legal Found. Served to capt. AUS, 1943-46. Decorated Bronze Star, Purple Heart; named All-Am. Wildcatter, 1968. Mem. State Bar Tex., Dallas Bar Assn., Am., (dir.), Dallas (1st v.p. 1957—, dir.) assns. petroleum landmen, Tex. Ind. Producers and Royalty Owners, Am. Inst. Mining Metall, and Petroleum Engrs., Dallas Grand Jury Assn., Blue Key, Kappa Sigma, Phi Alpha Delta (pres. 1949—). Methodist. Clubs: Engineers (Dallas), Northwood, Mustang, Chapparal. Editor, Southwestern Law Jour., 1949. Home: 4914 Keyhole Lane Dallas TX 75229 Office: Merc Dallas Bldg Dallas TX 75201

WILLIAMS, RICHARD ROGER, JR., educator; b. Marshall, Tex., May 5, 1917; s. Richard Roger and Odessa (Herron) W.; B.S., Wiley Coll., 1941; M.S., U. Mich., 1950, postgrad., summers 1951-54, 57-58 (spl. grad. fellow Danforth Found.); postgrad. (Ford Found. grantee) North Tex. State U., summer 1970; m. Bernice Lewis, May 17, 1947 (dec. Aug. 1956); 1 son, Richard R. III (dec.); m. 2d, Artie Mosley Price Bennett, Aug. 22, 1957; 1 dau., Kim Aletta Williams; stepchildren—Freddie, Shirley, Teresa. Tchr. math. Galillee High Sch., Hallsville, Tex., 1941-43; instr. math. Wiley Coll., Marshall, 1946-61, asso. prof., 1961—, chmn. dept. math., 1950-69, chmn. div. natural sci. and math., 1953-58, coordinator div., 1962-69, chmn. Tchr. Edn. Council, 1964-70, bus. mgr., 1969—. Ofcl. rep. Am. Assn. Colls. Tchr. Edn. Sustaining mem. East Tex. Area Council Boy Scouts Am. Served with USMCR, 1943-46. Mem. Am. Math. Soc., Am. Assn. U. Profs., Math. Assn. Am., Nat. Inst. Sci., Am. Assn. Sch. Adminstrs., Nat., So. assns. coll. and univ. bus. officers, Beta Kappa Chi, Phi Beta Sigma. Methodist. Co-author: College Algebra, 1956, rev. 1963. Home: 1809 Gatewood St Marshall TX 75670

WILLIAMS, ROBERT EMBERRY, ins. co. exec.; b. Corsicana, Tex., Oct. 9, 1923; s. Robert Henry and Ida Eunice (Honea) W.; B.B.A., So. Meth. U., 1956, M.B.A., 1963; m. Peggy Joyce Bolton, Dec. 23, 1945; children— Richard Dale, Patricia (Mrs. Kenneth Roy Cobler). Enlisted USN, 1946; adminstr., instr. various schs.; ret., 1963; v.p. personnel and tng. Zale Corp., Dallas, 1963-70; dir. human resources Blue Cross-Blue Shield, Dallas, 1970—. Lectr., Dallas County Jr. Coll., 1966-67, Am. Mgmt. Assn. Active United Fund; sponsor Williams award ann. grant to top grad. CPO Acad. USN, Pensacola, Fla., 1968-71; mem. So. Meth. U. Career Hall of Fame. Served with AUS, 1942-45. Mem. Dallas Personnel Assn. (v.p. 1971), Dallas Retail Personnel Assn. (pres. 1967-68), Am. Soc. Personnel Adminstrn., Sigma Iota Epsilon. Club: North Texas Travel Trailer (pres. 1968). Home: 2018 Cooper Dr Irving TX 75061 Office: 2201 Main St Dallas TX 75201

WILLIAMS, ROBERT L(EON), educator, psychiatrist, neurologist; b. Buffalo, July 22, 1922; s. Leon R. and L. Paulyne (Ingraham) W.; B.A., Alfred U., 1944; M.D., Albany Med. Coll., Union U., 1946; m. Shirley Glynn Miller, Feb. 5, 1949; children—Karen, Kevin. Chief neurology and psychiatry Lackland AFB Hosp., USAF, San Antonio, 1952-55; cons. neurology and psychiatry to USAF Surgeon Gen., 1955-58; faculty Coll. Medicine, U. Fla., Gainesville, 1958-72, prof., chmn. dept. psychiatry, 1964-72; prof., chmn. dept. psychiatry Baylor

Coll. Medicine, Houston, 1972—. Mem. faculty various univs. part time 1949-58, including Albany Med. Coll., Columbia Coll. Phys. and Surg., Boston U., U. Tex., Georgetown U. Recipient USAF Certificate Profl. Achievement, USAF Surgeon Gen., 1967. Mem. Am. Psychiat. Assn., Am. Electroencephalographic Soc., Am. Coll. Psychiatrists, Am. Acad. Neurology, A.M.A., Group for Advancement of Psychiatry, others. Author: (with W.B. Webb) Sleep Therapy: A Bibliography and Commentary, 1966. Research and publs. on basic psychophysiology of human sleep. Home: 1744 South Blvd Houston TX 77006

WILLIAMS, ROBERT MARSHALL, JR., civil engr.; b. Wilmington, N.C., Jan. 21, 1927; s. Robert Marshall and Amanda Nutt (Parsley) W.; student U. N.C., 1944, U.S. Mcht. Marine Acad., 1944-45; B.C.E., N.C. State U., 1956; m. Elizabeth Whitehead Taylor, Nov. 25, 1959; children— Elizabeth Whitehead, Robert Marshall III, William Arthur. Office engr. City of Wilmington, 1956-57; gen. engr. U.S. Army Corps Engrs., Wilmington, 1957-62; cons. engr., v.p., sec. John Talbert & Assos., Inc., Wilmington, 1963—. Served as 2d lt., Corps Engrs., U.S. Army, 1946-47; to 1st lt., 1951-53. Mem. Am. Soc. C.E., N.C. Soc. Engrs., Nat. Soc. Profl. Engrs., Profl. Engrs. N.C. (pres. S.E. chpt.), Aircraft Owners and Pilots Assn., Permanent Internat. Assn. Navigation Congresses. Clubs: Carolina Yacht, Cape Fear Country. Home: 1937 Brookhaven Rd Wilmington NC 28401 Office: 916 S 17th St PO Box 3333 Wilmington NC 28401

WILLIAMS, ROBERT MAXWELL, engring. services co. exec.; b. Frostburg, Md., Jan. 10, 1912; s. James Garfield and Myrtle Nina (Davis) W.; student Gen. Motors Inst. Tech., 1930-34; m. Mary Jane Giffin, Aug. 10, 1935; children—Thomas Allan, Linda (Mrs. Frank Leeming). Engr., Gen. Motors Corp., Detroit, 1934-44; chief engr. aviation engine div. Packard Motor Co., Toledo, 1944-48; head engr. Sverdrup & Parcel, Inc., engrs. and architects, St. Louis, 1949-52, asst. to pres., 1952-54; mng. dir. ARO, Inc., Tullahoma, Tenn., 1954-62, pres., 1963—; v.p. Sverdrup & Parcel & Assos., St. Louis, 1962—; dir. 1st Nat. Bank Tullahoma. Dist. chmn. Middle Tenn. council Boy Scouts Am., 1960-71. Asso. fellow Am. Inst. Aeros. and Astronautics; mem. Am. Soc. M.E., Soc. Automotive Engrs., Am. Soc. Metals, Nat. Soc. Profl. Engrs., Tau Beta Pi, Alpha Tau Iota. Mason, Rotarian. Pioneer work in design first Am. turbo-fan engine, 1948. Home: Route 5 Manchester TN 37355 Office: ARO Inc Arnold Air FB TN 37389

WILLIAMS, ROBERT PIERCE, educator; b. Chgo., Oct. 27, 1920; s. Gross Taylor and Cornelia (Pierce) W.; A.B., Dartmouth, 1942; S.M., U. Chgo., 1947, Ph.D., 1949; m. Elizabeth Ranstead, Dec. 20, 1944; children—Robert Eskridge, Scott Ranstead. Asst. in bacteriology U. Chgo., 1946-47, curator bacteriology, 1947-49; instr. U. So. Cal., 1949-51; faculty Coll. Medicine, Baylor U., Houston, 1951—, prof. microbiology, 1963—, acting chmn. dept., 1961-66. Cons. in bacteriology VA Hosp., also M.D. Anderson Hosp., Houston, 1957—; vis. prof. Tex. A. and M. U., 1963—, Pres. Friends Bellaire Library, 1956, Bellaire Library Bd., 1956-58, 72—. Served with AUS, 1943-45. Diplomate Am. Bd. Microbiology. Fellow Am. Acad. Microbiology (charter); mem. A.A.A.S., Am. Chem. Soc., Am. Soc. Microbiology, Soc. Gen. Microbiology Gt. Britain, Photog. Soc. Am., Dartmouth Asso. Alumni (exec. com.), Phi Beta Kappa, Sigma Xi. Democrat. Episcoplian. Author: (with K.L. Burdon) Microbiology, 6th edit., 1968; also papersand abstracts. Research on biosynthesis of bacterial products, growth of bacteria, effects of bacteria and products upon animals. Home: 5122 Brae Burn Dr Bellaire TX 77401 Office: 1200 Morsund Av Houston TX 77025

WILLIAMS, ROBERT W., univ. provost; b. Nashville, Oct. 11, 1922; s. Robert Webb and Helen (Schenck) W.; B.A., Tulane U., 1951, M.A., 1952, Ph.D., 1954; m. Elizabeth Buchanan, Dec. 14, 1942; 1 dau., Elizabeth (Mrs. Shelby Health). Prof. history Brenau Coll., 1954-56; prof. history and govt. Lamar State Coll. Tech., 1957-59; prof. history govt. East Carolina Coll., 1959-64, dean Sch. Arts and Sci., 1965, dean academic affairs, 1965—; mem. com. academic programs N.C. State Bd. Higher Edn.; cons. Bur. Old Age and Survivor Ins. Served with USMCR, 1942-46. Mem. Phi Beta Kappa. Contbr. articles in field to scholastic jours. Home: 103 Dalebrook Circle Greenville NC 27834

WILLIAMS, ROGER DAVIS, surgeon; b. Charlotte, N.C., May 26, 1924; s. Edward Eugene and Lucy C. (Davis) W.; B.S., Duke, 1947, M.D., 1947; M.S., Ohio State U., 1951; m. Martha Jeanne Wiedeman, Sept. 7, 1957; children—Diana Lynn, Roger D., George Monroe. Intern, Duke Hosp., 1947-48; resident Ohio State U. Hosps., 1949-54; asst. prof., asso. prof. Ohio State U., 1955-61, prof. surgery, 1961-65; prof. surgery, chmn. dept. surgery U. Tex., Galveston, 1965-67; practice medicine specializing in surgery, Ft. Lauderdale, Fla., 1968—; mem. staff Broward Gen. Med. Center; clin. prof. surgery U. Miami, Fla., 1968—. Mem. adv. group Easter Seal Found., Ft. Lauderdale, 1969—. Bd. dirs. Am. Cancer Soc., Broward County, Fla. Served with USNR, 1952-53. Decorated Bronze Star medal. Mem. Am., Western, Central Surg. assns., Soc. Univ. Surgeons, Am. Assn. Surgery Trauma, Am. Gastroent. Assn., Soc. Surgery Alimentary Tract. Contbr. articles to profl. jours. Home: 2211 SE 20th St Fort Lauderdale FL 33316 Office: 500 SE 17th St Suite 201 Fort Lauderdale FL 33316

WILLIAMS, ROGER JOHN, chemist; b. Ootacumund, India, Aug. 14, 1893 (parents Am. Citizens); s. Robert Runnels and Alice Evelyn (Mills) W.; B.S., U. Redlands, 1914, D.Sc., 1934; postgrad. U. Cal., 1914-15; M.S., U. Chgo., 1918, Ph.D., 1919; D.Sc., Columbia, 1942, Ore. State Coll., 1956; m. Hazel Elizabeth Wood, Aug. 1, 1916 (dec. 1952); children—Roger John, Janet, Arnold; m. 2d, Mabel Phyllis Hobson, May 9, 1953; 1 son (by previous marriage), John W. Hobson. Research chemist Fleischmann Co., Chgo., 1919-20; asst. prof. chemistry U. Ore., 1920-21, asso. prof., 1921-28, prof., 1928-32; prof. chemistry Ore. State Coll., 1932-39, U. Tex., Austin, 1939—; dir. Clayton Found., Biochem. Inst. Tex., 1941-63. Recipient Mead-Johnson award Am. Inst. Nutrition, 1941; Chandler medal Columbia U., 1942. Fellow A.A.A.S.; mem. Am. Chem. Soc. (pres. 1957, S.W. Region award 1950), Am. Soc. Biol. Chemists, Am. Assn. for Cancer Research, Soc. Exptl. Biology and Medicine, Nat., N.Y. acads. scis., Biochem. Soc. London, Phi Beta Kappa, Sigma Xi, Phi Kappa Phi, Phi Sigma, Pi Kappa Delta, Phi Lambda Upsilon. Methodist. Author or co-author books relating to chemistry; latest: The Biochemistry of B Vitamins (with R. E. Eakin, E. Beerstecher, W. Shive), 1950; Nutrition and Alcoholism, 1951; Free and Unequal, 1953; Biochemical Individuality, 1956; Alcoholism: The Nutritional Approach, 1959; Nutrition in a Nutshell, 1962, You Are Extraordinary, 1967; Nutrition against Disease, 1971. Discoverer pantothenic acid; also made microbiol. study of vitamins, individual metabolic patterns. Office: Clayton Found Biochem Inst U Tex Austin TX 78712

WILLIAMS, SAM HENRY, bank dir.; b. San Augustine, Tex., Jan. 15, 1915; s. Sam Sterling and Jennie Eugene (Henry) W.; student Stephen Austin Coll., 1933; m. Wilda David, Nov. 25, 1943; children—Virginia Ann (Mrs. James Scogin), Bonnie Blue, David S. Salesman, Frito Co., Leesville and Lake Charles, La., 1946-62; pres. Williams Transp. & Storage, Leesville, Lake Charles, 1952—; dir. Mchts. &Farmers Bank, Leesville, 1967—. Mgr. theatre, Leesville, 1946-48; mail contract delivery, 1942-64; pres. Farm Equipment, Inc., 1964—, Am. Moving & Storage, 1968—, Gen. Maintenance & Constrn. Inc., all Leesville, 1968—; owner, operators farms Leesville, La., 1955—, San Augustine, 1954—; owner So. Moving &Storage Co., La. Transfer Co., S.W. Transfer Co., City Transfer Co., Sunshine Transfer Co. Mem. C. of C. Democrat. Roman Catholic. K.C., Mason (K.T.). Home: Texas Rd Leesville LA 71446 Office: 301 N 3d Rd Leesville LA 71446 also 202 Stanton Rd New Llano LA

WILLIAMS, SQUIRE NEEDHAM, JR., lawyer; b. Frenchburg, Ky., Nov. 8, 1917; s. Squire Needham and Mary Lee (Spencer) W.; student Berea Coll., 1935-36; A.B., U. Ky., 1939, LL.B., 1942; m. Doris Ellen Macauley, Aug. 24, 1946; children—Janice Lee, Laura Macauley, Kathryn Doris, Squire Needham III. Admitted to Ky. bar, 1942; practiced in Lexington, Ky., 1945-46, Frankfort, Ky., 1955-59, 69—; atty. War Assets Administrn., 1947; asst. atty. gen. Commonwealth of Ky., 1948-55; Franklin County judge pro tem and trial commr., 1956-57; spl. circuit judge, 1957-59; judge, chief justice Ct. Appeals Ky., 1959-69. Served as aviator USNR, 1942-45. Mem. Am., Ky. bar assns., V.F.W. Democrat. Presbyn. (elder). Club: Frankfort Country (dir.). Home: 120 W Todd St Frankfort KY 40601 Office: 405 McClure Bldg Frankfort KY 40601

WILLIAMS, STAFFORD HOYT, JR., mech. engr.; b. nr. Grundy, Va., Dec. 27, 1939; s. Stafford Hoyt and Alma Gluck (Pettit) W.; B.S., Va. Poly. Inst., 1962, M.S., 1965; m. Lucretia Dawneda Fowler, Dec. 21, 1961; children—Lucretia Gay, Stafford Hoyt III. Jr. engr. Balt. Gas & Electric Co., summer 1962; project engr. U.S. Air Force Research and Tech. div., Wright-Patterson AFB, O., 1964-67; cons. engr., v.p. charge civil engring. Thompson & Litton, engrs., architects, surveyors and planners, Wise, Va., 1967—; dir. Toliad Properties, Inc. Served from 2d lt. to 1st lt., USAF, 1964-67. Mem. Nat. Soc. Profl. Engrs. (chpt. pres.-elect), Am. Soc. Heating, Refrigeration and Air Conditioning Engrs., Cons. Engrs. Council, Pi Tau Sigma. Mem. Ch. of Christ. Home: PO Box 548 Wise VA 24293 Office: PO Box 1307 Wise VA 24293

WILLIAMS, T. HARRY, historian, educator, author; b. Vinegar Hill, Ill., May 19, 1909; s. William D. and Emma (Necollins) W.; B.E., Platteville (Wis.) State Tchrs. Coll., 1931; Ph.M., U. Wis., 1932, Ph.D., 1937. Instr. extension div. U. Wis., 1936-38; instr. W.Va. U., summer 1937; instr. and asst. prof. U. Omaha, 1938-41; mem. faculty La. State U., Baton Rouge, 1941—, prof. history, 1948-53, Boyd prof. history, 1953—; Guggenheim fellow, 1957; Harmsworth prof. Am. history Queen's Coll., Oxford (Eng.) U., 1966-67. Mem. hist. adv. com. Dept. of Army, 1955-60. Recipient Lincoln Diploma of Honor, Lincoln Meml. U., 1956, Nat. Book award for history, biography, 1969, Pulitzer Prize, 1969, La. Lit. award, 1969. Mem. Am. Assn. U. Profs., Am. Mil. Inst., Civil War Centennial Assn. (dir.), Soc. Am. Historians, Am., So. (v.p. 1957-58, pres. 1958-59), Mississippi Valley (exec. com. 1955) hist. assns., Orgn. Am. Historians (pres. 1972-73). Author: Lincoln and the Radicals, 1941; Lincoln and His Generals, 1952; P.G.T. Beauregard, 1955; The Union Sundered, 1963; The Union Restored, 1963. Editor: Selected Writings and Speeches of Abraham Lincoln, 1943; With Beauregard in Mexico, 1956; Abraham Lincoln—Selected Speeches, Messages and Letters, 1957; (with others) A History of the United States, 1959; Americans at War, 1960; Romance and Realism in Southern Politics, 1961; Military Memoris of a Confederate by E. Porter Alexander, 1962; McClellan, Sherman and Grant, 1962; Every Man a King, 1964; Hayes: The Diary of a President, 1964; Hayes of the Twenty-third; The Civil War Volunteer Officer, 1965; Huey Long, 1969. Home: 353 Nelson Dr Baton Rouge LA 70808

WILLIAMS, TALMAGE THEODORE, JR., physicist; b. Atlanta, Jan. 20, 1933; s. Talmage Theodore and Maye (Lamb) W.; B.S., Ga. Inst. Tech., 1955; postgrad. Fla. Inst. Tech., 1965-71; m. Judy Ann Bain, Dec. 15, 1964; 1 dau., Angelyn Patricia. Physicist, E. I. DuPont Co., Aiken, S.C., 1958-62; leader RCA Apollo Ships Evaluation, Patrick AFB, Fla., 1962-68, staff physicist, chief scientist's office RCA Missile Test Project, 1968-72, mgr. land and air systems analysis, 1972; mgr. sci. analysis dept. ITT Fed. Electric Corrp., Cal., 1972—. Served to lt. (j.g.) USNR, 1955-58. Mem. A.A.A.S., Am. Phys. Soc., Am. Inst Physics, Inst. Nav., Sigma Pi Sigma. Contbr. articles to profl. jours. Home: 311 E Bunny Av Santa Maria CA 93454 Office: ITT Fed Electric Corp Vandenberg AFB CA 93437

WILLIAMS, TED, baseball exec. Formerly player Boston Red Sox; now v.p., mgr. Tex. Ranger. Address: Arlington Stadium 1500 Copeland Rd Arlington TX 76010*

WILLIAMS, THOMAS EARL, lawyer; b. Corsicana, Tex., Oct. 21, 1924; s. William Archie and Mildred (Gammill) W.; student Tex. A. and M. U., 1942, 43, 46, N. Tex. State U., 1942, Kan. State Coll., 1943; LL.B., Baylor U., 1954, J.D., 1969; m. Johnnie Frances Reynolds, Nov. 10, 1948; children—Stephen Earl, Randolph Walling, Cynthia Ann, Daniel Zachary. Adjuster, Farm Bur. Ins. Co., Waco, Tex., 1954-56, State Farm Ins. Co., McKinney, Tex., 1957; admitted to Tex. bar, 1955; asst. county atty., McKinney, Tex., 1957-60; criminal dist. atty., McKinney, 1960-64; asst. dist. atty., Dallas, 1963-64; practiced in Athens, Tex., 1965—; city atty. Athens, 1967—. Cons. Gulf States United Telephone Co., City of Chandler, Tex. Organizer, dir. Amigos Internacionales Corp., 1967—. Bd. dirs. Athens Little Theater, 1967-68. Served with USAAF, 1943-48; served to 2d lt. AUS, 1948-50. Mem. State Bar of Tex., Am., Henderson County bar assns., Am. Judicature Soc., C. of C. (dir. 1967—). Baptist. Mason (32 deg.), Kiwanian. Home: 900 Ward Lane Athens TX 75751 Office: 207 E Corsicana St Athens TX 75751

WILLIAMS, THOMAS STANLEY, packaging mfg. co. exec.; b. Evanston, Ill., Sept. 18, 1919; s. Thomas Samuel and Bertha Ella (Zander) W.; B.S., Tex. A. and M. U., 1941; m. Ethel Naomi Boutwell, June 4, 1941; children—T. Samuel, Gretchen (Mrs. William E. Dunn), Molly (Mrs. Richard Tune), Trudi Zander. Pres., gen. mgr. Superior Decals, Inc., Dallas, 1942-48; with Dixico, Inc., Dallas, 1948—, sr. v.p. operations, 1957-64, chmn. exec. com., 1964—; pres. Bancook Maintenance Co., Dallas, 1961—. Mem. Bd. Edn. Dallas Ind. Sch. Dist., 1971—. Mem. Tex. exec. com. Republican party, 1967-69. Trustee Meth. Hosp. Dallas, C.C. Young Meml. Home, Dallas, Denton Wesley Found., N. Tex. State U. and Tex. Womens U. Served with F.A., AUS, 1941-42. Mem. Flexographic Tech. Assn. Methodist. Mason (Shriner, 32 deg.), Lion.‡

WILLIAMS, THOMAS WOLFORD, physician; b. Kansas City, Mo., Nov. 16, 1928; s. Walter E. and Henrietta (Wolford) W.; B.S., Westminister Coll., 1950; M.D., Washington U. Med. Sch., 1954; postgrad. U. Kan., 1966; m. Elizabeth Stewart, Apr. 13, 1967; 1 son, Thomas Wolford. Intern, U.S. Naval Hosp., Portsmouth, Va., 1954-55, resident internal medicine, 1955-56; resident internal medicine U.S. Naval Hosp., Chelsea, Mass., 1956-57; chief resident internal medicine St. Agnes Hosp., Phila., 1960-61; practice medicine specializing in family practice, Etowah, Tenn., 1967—; clin. asst. prof. dept. medicine, div. family practice and ambulatory medicine U. Ala., Birmingham, 1971—; mem. staffs Woods Meml. Hosp., Etowah, chief 1970-71, McMinn Meml. Nursing Home, Etowah, chief, 1970-71. Served with U.S. Navy, 1954-61. Mem. Am., So., Tenn. med. assns., McMinn County Med. Soc. (pres. 1971). Home: Brentwood Dr Etowah TN 37331 Office: Hwy 411 N Etowah TN 37331

WILLIAMS, TURNER NELSON, JR., dairy exec.; b. Buena Vista, Ga., May 12, 1920; s. Turner Nelson and Etta (Lowe) W.; B.S., Auburn U., 1940; m. Winifred Greene, Nov. 11, 1944; children—Robert G., Mary (Mrs. James P. Wardlow), Susan E., Turner Nelson III. Tchr. vocational agr. Marion County High Sch., Buena Vista, Ga., 1946-51; operator Williams Dairy Farm, Ellaville, Ga., 1952—; dir. Wells Dairies Cooperative, Columbus, Ga., 1958—, sec.-treas., 1969—. Owner, mgr. ind. ins. agy., Ellaville, 1957—; dir. Ga. div. Dairymen, Inc., Atlanta, Ga. Milk Producers, Inc. Mem. Schley County Bd. Registrars, 1964-69; chmn. Schley County Bd. Tax Assessors, 1960-70, mem., 1970—; chmn. Schley County Bd. Health, 1969—. Served to 1st lt. 101st Airborne Div., AUS, 1941-46. Mem. Am. Legion. Methodist. Home: Route 2 Ellaville GA 31806 Office: PO Box 404 Ellaville GA 31806

WILLIAMS, TYLER EDWARD, JR., financial mgmt. exec.; b. Chgo., July 10, 1926; s. Tyler Edward and Anne (Salmon) W.; B.S., Ill. Inst. Tech., 1951, M.S., 1956; postgrad. U. Ia.; M.Ed. (Fed. Career Exec. fellow) U. Va., 1972; m. Frances M. Reif, Aug. 27, 1949; children—Tyler Edward III, Michael, Thomas, Margaret, Gerard, Joseph (dec.), John, Mary. Dept. supr. Oscar Mayer & Co., Chgo., 1949-52; indsl. engr. Am. Gage & Machine Co., Chgo., 1952-54; sr. indsl. engr. Bendix Aviation Corp., Davenport, Ia., 1954-55; engr., engring. exec. Ordnance Corps, U.S. Army, Rock Island Arsenal (Ill.), 1955-63, Office Mgmt. and Orgn., Dept. Commerce, Washington, 1963-65; with Office Comptroller Army, Washington, 1965-71, dep. dir. budget and manpower Safeguard System Office, Office Chief of Staff, Dept. Army, 1971—. Served to comdr. USNR, 1944—. Registered profl. engr., Ia., Ind. Mem. Soc. Gen. Systems Research, Am. Soc. Engring. Edn., A.A.A.S., Council Basic Edn., Am. Inst. Indsl. Engrs., Washington Operations Research Soc. Author articles in field. Home: 3312 Prince William Dr Fairfax VA 22030 Office: Office Chief of Staff Hdqrs Dept Army Pentagon Washington DC 20310

WILLIAMS, VICK F(RANKLIN), anatomist; b. Pittsburg, Tex., Apr. 30, 1936; s. Vernon Guinn and Eula (Vick) W.; B.A., Austin Coll., 1958; M.D., U. Tex. Med. Br., 1964, Ph.D., 1964; m. Dorothy Jean Rodina, June 23, 1962; children—Dorothy Jean, Sarah Ellen. Intern in pathology, Charity Hosp. La., New Orleans, 1964-65; instr. in anatomy U. Tex. Southwestern Med. Sch., Dallas, 1965-67, asst. prof. anatomy, 1967-70; asso. prof. anatomy U. Tex. Dental Sch. and U. Tex. Med. Sch., San Antonio, 1970—. Dir. Dynamic Ventures Corp., Dallas. Recipient Borden award for undergrad. research, 1964. Mem. Am. Assn. Anatomists, Am. Soc. for Cell Biology, Electron Microscopy Soc. Am., Cajal Club. Nu Sigma Nu, Sigma Xi. Presbyn. Office: 7703 Floyd Curl Dr San Antonio TX 78229

WILLIAMS, VOLIE ADKINS, JR., judge; b. Sanford, Fla., Jan. 10, 1920; s. Volie Adkins and Mary Elizabeth (Miller) W.; Asso. Sci., Marion Inst., 1938-40; LL.B., Stetson U., 1948; m. Constance Lott, Sept. 5, 1946; children—James Lang, Patricia Lee, Penelope, Donald Neal. Admitted to bar, 1948; spl. asst. Atty. Gen. Fla., 1949; mem. Fla. Ho. of Reps., 1950-55; asst. state atty., 1955-57; judge 18th Circuit Ct., Sanford, Fla., 1957—. Served as capt. USAAF, 1944-46; PTO. Decorated Air medal. Mem. Phi Alpha Delta, Sigma Nu. Democrat. Presbyn. Mason (Shriner). Home: 1203 Washington Dr Sanford FL 32771 Office: Brevard County Courthouse Titusville FL 32780 also Seminole County Courthouse Sanford FL 32771

WILLIAMS, W. ROBERT, state ofcl. Dir., Fla. Bd. Archives and History. Office: 401 E Gaines St Tallahassee FL 32301*

WILLIAMS, WALKER ALONZO, ret. automobile co. exec.; b. Wellington, Mo., June 8, 1901; s. Henry A. and Helen (Walker) W.; student Kan. City Sch. Law, evenings 1921, Kansas City Jr. Coll., evenings, 1921, U. Ill., 1922-23; m. Evelyn Forrester, Sept. 25, 1926; children—Walker Forrester, John Haviland. With traffic dept. Armour Grain Co., Kansas City, Mo., 1920-22; with accounting dept. Am. Can Co., Kansas City, 1924-25; with Kansas City br., Ford Motor Co., 1925-34, asst. br. mgr., Omaha, 1934-39, Kansas City, 1939-41, br. mgr., Salt Lake City, 1941-42, 44-45, Somerville, Mass., 1945-46, Ford sales mgr., Dearborn, Mich., 1946-48, gen. sales mgr. Ford div., 1948-50, v.p. sales and advt. for parent co., 1950-56, v.p., vice chmn. dealer policy bd. for parent co., 1956-58, v.p. parent co., asst. gen. mgr. Lincoln-Mercury div., 1958-61; bus. mgr. Kalunite, Inc., Salt Lake City, 1942-44; ret., 1961. Former mem. Nat. Highway Users Conf. Chmn. Mich. Crusade for Freedom, 1951-52; former mem. Detroit Mayor's Rapid Transit Commn., Detroit Bd. Commerce. Former bd. dirs., gen. chmn. United Found. Detroit; former bd. dirs. Automobile Safety Found. mem. Fla. Atlantic Music Guild, Friends of City Center (N.Y.C.), DeMolay Legion of Honor, Phi Gamma Delta. Clubs: Detroit Athletic; Royal Palm Yacht and Country, Boca Raton Hotel and Club (Boca Raton, Fla.); Vermilion Fairways Golf (Cook, Minn.). Home: 1355 Fan Palm Rd Boca Raton FL 33432

WILLIAMS, WALTER ROLLIN, III, educator; b. Norwood, O., Oct. 2, 1933; s. Walter Rollin and Helen Horton (Coons) W.; student Fla. So. Coll., 1953, Fla. State U., 1956; B.S. in Edn., U. Fla., 1955, M.Ed., 1959; Ed.D., U. Md., 1963; m. Janice Louise Southerland, June 16, 1955; children—Walter Rollin IV, David Southerland. Tchr., Leon High Sch., Tallahassee, 1955-56, Rockville (Md.) Jr. High Sch., 1961-62; faculty indsl. edn. Ga. So. Coll., Statesboro, 1962-66; prof., head dept. indsl. edn. Morehead (Ky.) State U., 1966-67; prof., chmn. dept. indsl. edn. E. Tenn. State U., Johnson City, 1967—. Served with USNR, 1956-57. Mem. Tenn. (pres. 1970-71), Am. (Peace Corps rep. 1964-66) indsl. arts assns., Tenn. Edn. Assn. (pres. dept. higher edn. 1972—), Am. Council Elementary Sch. Indsl. Arts (sec. 1966), Southeastern Indsl. Arts Conf. (pres. 1967-68), Epsilon Pi Tau (dir.), Phi Kappa Phi, Kappa Delta Pi, Phi Delta Kappa, Iota Lambda Sigma. Methodist. Contbr. articles to profl. jours. Home: 1510 Crystal Springs Dr Johnson City TN 37601

WILLIAMS, WESLEY WEEKS, clin. counselor; b. Fort Worth, Dec. 9, 1922; s. Clarence Vernon and Lura Helen (Weeks) W.; B.S., Tex. Wesleyan Coll., 1952; B.D., So. Meth. U., 1955; D. Religion, So. Cal. Sch. Theology, 1967; m. Doris Tinker, Dec. 5, 1942; children—Linda Cheryl (Mrs. Leslie Hotman), John Wesley, Thomas Christian. With labor relations dept. Gen. Motors, Fort Worth, 1946-52; ordained to ministry Meth. Ch., 1952; asso. pastor Meadowbrook Meth. Ch., Fort Worth, 1955-57, 1st Congl. Ch.; pastor 1st Meth. Ch., Grandview, Tex., 1957-59, Eastwood Meth. Ch., Fort Worth, 1959-61; coll. chaplain, asso. prof. religion Tex. Wesleyan Coll., Fort Worth, 1962-71; dir. Hulen Med. Center Counseling Service, Ft. Worth, 1971—. Exec. sec. Fort Worth Religion and Labor Fellowship, 1955-57; mem. Central Tex. Conf. Bd. Hosps. and Homes, 1955-59. Served with AUS, 1942-46. Mem. Am. Assn. Pastoral Counselors, Am. Assn. Coll. and Univ. Profs., Am. Assn. Coll. and Univ. Chaplains, Meth. Assn. U. Profs., Am. Assn. Marriage and Family Counselors. Mason. Club: Ft. Worth Optimist (dir.). Home: 24 Bounty Rd W Ft Worth TX 76116 Office: 3600 Hulen Ft Worth TX 76107

WILLIAMS, WILBERT BROSCO, wholesale trade co. exec.; b. Red Level, Ala., July 29, 1921; s. John Jay and Amie (Cross) W.; B.S. in Accounting, U. Ala., 1950; m. Carolyn Jackson Bryant, Apr. 19, 1947; children—Richard W., Michael J. Spl. agt. in charge intelligence div. Internal Revenue Service, Mobile, Ala., 1948-56; v.p., controller So. Pipe & Supply Co., Inc., Meridian, Miss., 1956—. Mgr., Dixie Youth Baseball, 1957-67, city coordinator, 1967-69. Served with USAAF, 1942-45. C.P.A., Ala., Miss. Mem. Am. Inst. C.P.A.'s, Ala., Miss. socs. C.P.A.'s. Baptist. Clubs: Optimist (v.p. 1960-67), Briarwood Country (Meridian). Home: 5118 Druid Lane Meridian MS 39301 Office: 102 22d Av Meridian MS 39301

WILLIAMS, WINTON HUGH, civil engr.; b. Tampa, Fla., Feb. 14, 1920; s. Herbert DeMain and Alice (Grant) W.; student U. Tampa, 1948; B.C.E., U. Fla., 1959; grad. U.S. Army Res. Asso. Command and Gen. Staff Coll., Ft. Leavenworth, U.S. Army Logistics Mgmt. Center; m. Elizabeth Walser Seelye, Dec. 18, 1949; children—Jan, Dick, Bill, Ann. Constrn. engr. air fields C.E., U.S. Army, McCoy AFB, Fla., 1959-61, Homestead AFB, Miami, Fla., 1961-62; civil engr. C.E., Jacksonville (Fla.) Dist. Office, 1962-65, chief master planning and layout sect., 1965-70; chief master planning and real estate div. Office of Engr. Hdqrs. USARSO, Ft. Clayton, C.Z., 1970—. Troop com. chmn. Boy Scouts Am., Explorer Scouts, Curundu, C.Z. Served with U.S. Army, World War II, Korean War; ETO, Korea; col. Res. Decorated Breast Order of Yun Hi (Republic China); presdl. citation (Republic Korea). Registered profl. engr., Fla., Panama, C.Z., Republic Panama. Mem. Nat. Soc. Profl. Engrs., Am. Soc. C.E., Fla. Engring. Soc., Prestressed Concrete Inst., Res. Officers Assn. (v.p. chpt.), Soc. Am. Mil. Engrs., U. Tampa Alumni Assn. (nat. council), Theta Chi. Presbyn. (bd. ushers). Lion (dir.). Home: Box 771 Curundu Canal Zone Office: Office of the Engineer Ft Clayton Canal Zone

WILLIAMSON, ARTHUR ELDRIDGE, JR., physicist; b. Montgomery, Ala., July 6, 1926; s. Arthur E. and May Ellen (Bray) W.; B.E.P., Auburn U., 1950, M.S., 1951; postgrad. Ga. Inst. Tech., 1959; m. Dorothy Jean Phillips, Oct. 13, 1951; children—Arthur Mark, Paul Steven. Research engr. North Am. Aviation, Inc., Downey, Cal., 1951-52; instr. physics U. Richmond, 1952-53; research physicist Southern Research Inst., Birmingham, 1953-55; asst. prof. physics and research project dir. Ga. Inst. Tech., Atlanta, 1955-59; chief, electro-optics Lab., Research div. Martin Marietta Corp., Orlando, Fla., 1959-69, marketing mgr. research and tech., 1969—. Served with USNR, 1944-46. Mem. Am. Phys. Soc., Am. Optical Soc., Sigma Pi Sigma, Phi Kappa Phi. Methodist. Home: 1670 Algonquin Trail Maitland FL 32751 Office: PO Box 5837 Orlando FL 32806

WILLIAMSON, DONALD GLENN, banker; b. Ft. Worth, July 17, 1935; s. Ernest Lee and Nadine (Minor) W.; B.A., Baylor U., 1957, J.D., 1959; postgrad. Nat. Trust Sch. Northwestern U., 1963-64, Stonier Grad. Sch. Banking Rutgers U., 1965-66; m. Nancy Mary Harrison, July 18, 1959 (div. Apr. 1970). With estate and gift div. Internal Revenue Service, Dallas, 1959-62; v.p., trust officer City Nat. Bank, Wichita Falls, Tex., 1962-67; sr. v.p., trust officer 1st Bank & Trust, Bryan, Tex., 1967-69; v.p., trust officer Nat. Bank Commerce Dallas, 1969—; dir. W.D. Felder & Co., Dallas. Pres. North Tex. Estate Council, 1966-67; v.p. Brazos Valley Estate Council, 1968-69; sec. Dallas Symphony Orch. Guild, 1970-71; mem. council for instnl. devel. Baylor U., 1965-71; mem. counsellors Baylor Law Sch., 1970-71. Mem. exec. com. Brazos County Republican Com., 1968-69. Bd. dirs. Wichita Falls Symphony Orch., 1962-67, pres., 1966-67; bd. dirs. Wichita Falls Ballet Theater, 1965-67, Dallas Estate Council, 1971, Baylor Ex-Students Assn., 1968-70. Recipient Gold Baton award Wichita Falls Symphony Orch., 1967. Mem. Tex., Dallas bar assns., Dallas Assn. Life Underwriters, Dallas Civic Opera Guild, Phi Alpha Delta, Alpha Phi Omega. Baptist. Club: Lancer's (Dallas). Home: 2710 Douglas St Dallas TX 75219 Office: PO Box 2249 Dallas TX 75221

WILLIAMSON, HAROLD LAMAR, furniture co. exec.; b. Cordele, Ga., June 7, 1925; s. Felix Drewry and Ida Florence (Bryan) W.; student Emory U., 1947-48; B.B.A. in Accounting, U. Ga., 1951; m. June Malcom, Apr. 15, 1950; children—Harold Lamar, Malcolm B. Asst. sales mgr. Simmons Co., Atlanta, 1948-57; v.p. Helmly's Furniture Co., Orlando, Fla., 1958—, Clearwater, Fla., 1960—, Tampa, Fla., 1962—, also dir. Served with AUS, 1944-46. Mem. Lambda Chi Alpha. Presbyn. Clubs: Winter Park (Fla.) Racquet; University, Citrus (Orlando). Home: 81 Oakleigh Dr Maitland FL 32751 Office: 2100 E Colonial St Orlando FL 32803

WILLIAMSON, JOHN ALEXANDER, computer co. exec.; b. Birmingham, Ala., Feb. 5, 1918; s. John Kelly and Mary (Lee) W.; A.B., Birmingham-So. Coll., 1939; m. Jean Cochran, Feb. 14, 1948; children—John, Alexander, Linda Sue, Margaret Lee. Mem. parts dept. Gen. Motors Corp., Birmingham, 1935-39; dist. mgr. motor div. Chevrolet, Birmingham, 1945-47; salesman Drennen Motor Co., Birmingham, 1939-40; sales mgr., 1947-56; pres. John Williamson &Assos., mgmt. cons., Birmingham, 1956—; pres., Computerized Automotive Reporting Service, Inc., Birmingham, 1964—, Key Real Estate & Investment Co., 1960—. Bd. dirs. Birmingham Boys' Club, 1964—; chmn. bd. dirs. New Methodist Hosp., 1967—. Served to capt. USNR, 1940-46, 50-52. Decorated Legion of Merit, Silver Star. Methodist. Clubs: The Club, Birmingham Country. Home: 3012 N Woodridge St Birmingham AL 35223 Office: 12 Office Park Circle Birmingham AL 35223

WILLIAMSON, JOHN HENRY, JR., dentist; b. Henrietta, Tex., Sept. 26, 1919; s. John Henry and Zelma (Grimes) W.; B.S., U. Tex., 1942, D.D.S., 1945; m. Marian Irene Broussard, June 20, 1955; 1 son, John Henry III. Asst. mgr. Walgreens, Houston, 1942; instr. U. Tex., 1945-46; pvt. practice dentistry, Galveston, Tex., 1946—. Chmn. adv. com. Galveston Community Coll. Dental Hygiene Sch. Mem. adv. bd. Rainbow Girls. Fellow Am. Coll. Dentists; mem. 9th Dist. Dental Soc. (pres. 1951), Am. Dental Assn., Galveston C. of C., Psi Omega. Baptist. Mason (Shriner). Club: Exchange (Galveston). Home: 7202 Sycamore St Galveston TX 77550 Office: 1025 25th St Galveston TX 77550

WILLIAMSON, JUANITA VIRGINIA, educator; b. Shelby, Miss.; d. John Morris and Alice (McAllister) Williamson; B.A., LeMoyne Coll., 1938; M.A., Atlanta U., 1940; Ph.D., U. Mich., 1961. Tchr. pub. schs., Memphis, 1940-46; instr. English, LeMoyne Coll., Memphis, 1946-53, prof. English, 1953—; vis. prof. English and linguistics Ball State U., 1962-63; cons. Bd. dirs. Bethlehem Center, 1964-67, mem. Tenn. Council on Human Relations, 1962—; exec. com. Conf. Coll. Composition and Communication. Gen. Edn. Bd. fellow, 1949-51; Ford Found. Fellow, 1954-55; Am. Council Learned Socs. grantee, summer 1951; United Negro Coll. Fund fellow, 1960; U.S. Office Edn. grantee; Amistad Found. grantee. Mem. Linguistic Soc. Am., Am. Assn. U. Profs., Modern Lang. Assn., Coll. Lang. Assn., Nat. Council Tchrs. English, Conf. Coll. Composition, Am. Dialect Soc., Am. Assn. U. Women, Phi Lambda Theta, Delta Sigma Theta. Conglist. Co-editor: A Various Language, 1971. Research in the area Negro speech. Home: 1217 Cannon St Memphis TN 38106

WILLIAMSON, MARCOS JOHNSON, real estate appraiser; b. Port Lavaca, Tex., Dec. 18, 1903; s. Marcos and Josephine (Williams) W.; student U. Tex., 1921-23; m. Pearl Irene Lovett, Aug. 22, 1948; 1 dau., Penn Marie. Tchr., coach pub. schs., Victoria, Tex., 1925-30; sports writer, 1930-32; appraiser FCA, 1933-34, 45-46; field dir. A.R.C., 1944-45; valuation engr., chief appraisal div. War Assets Administrn., Gen Services Administrn., Atlanta, 1946-53; v.p. Molton, Allens & Williams, Inc., Birmingham, Ala., 1953-56; owner, mgr. Appraisal Service Co., Birmingham, 1956—. Lectr. appraisal principles U. Ala., 1960, U. Miss., 1958. Recipient citation for A.R.C. work in Battle of Bulge, 9th Armored Div., 1945. Mem. Am. Inst. Real Estate Appraisers, Am. Soc. Appraisers, Am. Soc. Rural Appraisers, Nat. Assn. Ind. Fee Appraisers, Am. Right-of-Way Assn. Methodist (ofcl. bd.). Elks. Clubs: The Club, Mountain Brook Swin and Tennis (Birmingham); Civitan (past dist. gov. Ala.-Miss. dist.). Home: 3125 Ryecroft Rd Birmingham AL 35223 Office: Bldg 6 Office Park Circle Birmingham AL 35223

WILLIAMSON, ROY CARTER, JR., cons. engr.; b. Waco, Tex., Dec. 6, 1932; s. Roy Carter and Nina Sue (Gill) W.; student Baylor U., 1951-53; B.S. in Petroleum Engring. and Geol. Engring., U. Okla., 1956; m. Karen Sylvia Stewart, July 12, 1956; 1 dau., Jana Sue. With Gulf Oil Corp., Monahans, Midland, Odessa, Tex., 1958-67; sr. reservoir engr. Bailey, Sipes, Williamson & Runyan, Inc. (formerly Leibrock, Landreth, Campbell & Callaway), cons. engrs., Midland, 1967-69, partner, v.p., 1969-72; pres. Midland div. Sipes, Williamson & Runyan, Inc., 1972—; v.p. Western Pollution Control, Inc., Midland, 1969—. Active United Fund, Cancer Crusade, YMCA. Served as 1st lt. USAF, 1956-58. Registered profl. engr., Tex. Mem. Soc. Petroleum Engrs. (sec.-treas. Permian Basin sect. 1966-67, program chmn. 1967-69, chmn. 1969-70), Soc. Profl. Well Log Analysts, West Tex. Geol. Soc. Republican. Methodist (chmn. council on ministries 1970—). Home: 6 Chatham Ct Midland TX 79701 Office: Gihls Tower W Midland TX 79701

WILLIAMSON, WILLIAM THOMAS, advt. co. exec.; b. Lakeland, Fla., Oct. 24, 1925; s. William Richter and Florence Elizabeth (Bellwood) W.; student Pa. Acad. Fine Arts, 1945-49; m. Edna Pauline Pledger, June 17, 1950; children—Mary Margaret, William Campbell. Artist, Miller & Rhoads, Richmond, Va., 1949-51; layout artist Hecht Co., Washington, 1951-53; designer Kal, Ehrlich & Merrick, Washington, 1953-62, art dir., 1962-68; art dir. Ehlrich, Linkins & Assos., Washington, 1968-69, v.p., 1969—. Served with USMCR, 1943-45. Mem. Nat. Symphony Orch. Assn. Home: 2419 N Kenmore St Arlington VA 22207 Office: 4926 Wisconsin Av NW Washington DC 20016

WILLIS, BENJAMIN CAWTHON, circuit judge; b. Quincy, Fla., Oct. 7, 1913; s. Lee Lawrence and Etta (Bell) W.; student Emory U., 1930-32; LL.B., U. Fla., 1936; m. Helen Saxon Ausley, Sept. 25, 1940; children—Lee Lawrence II, Benjamin Cawthon. Admitted to Fla. bar, 1936; practiced in Tallahassee, 1936-57; partner firm Messer & Willis, 1942-57; circuit judge 2d Jud. Circuit Fla., Tallahassee, 1957—, presiding judge, 1961-63, 69-71, chief judge, 1971-73. Dir. Blue Shield of Fla., Inc. Served as capt. AUS, 1942-46. Mem. Jr. C. of C. (pres. 1938), C. of C. (pres. 1953), Fla. Bar (gov. 1953-54), Tallahassee Bar Assn., Fla. Hist. Soc. Methodist (mem. ofcl. bd.). Clubs: Cotillion, Exchange (pres. 1958-59). Home: 1504 Hickory Av Tallahassee FL 32303 Office: PO Box 24 Tallahassee FL 32302

WILLIS, CECIL, supt. schs.; b. Austin, Tex., Jan. 12, 1918; B.S., Trinity U., 1949, M.S., 1952; postgrad. U. Okla., 1967, Stanford U., 1968; m. Georgia Roberson. Coach, tchr. Harlandale High Sch., San Antonio, 1939-40, 44-46; football coach, athletic bus. mgr. Trinity U., San Antonio, 1947-50; self-employed businessman, 1950-54; high sch. prin., athletic dir., La Coste, Tex., 1954-55; dir. athletics, coach Huntsville, Tex., 1955-56; supt. schs., Natalia, Tex., 1956-59, New Braunfels, Tex., 1959-61, Brookshire, Tex., 1963-65; supt. schs., Novice (Tex.) Ind. Sch. Dist., 1970-72, Kennedale (Tex.) Ind. Sch. Dist., 1972—; dir. edn. Terr. of Guam, 1962-63. Ednl. spl. Exec. Office of Pres. U.S., 1965-69; manpower devel. specialist U.S. Dept. Labor, 1969-70; ednl. cons. Am. Overseas Sch., Rome, Italy, 1965. Served with USAF, 1941-43. Mem. Am., Tex. assns. sch. adminstrs., N.E.A., Tex. Tchrs. Assn., Tex. Small Sch. Assn. Home: 3516 Wooten Dr Fort Worth TX 76133 Office: PO Box 216 Kennedale TX 76060

WILLIS, DELBERT, newspaper editor; b. Brashear, Tex., Aug. 27, 1914; s. Robert L. and Ella (Ward) Turner; student Harvard, 1949; m. Patricia LeNeve Doss, Jan. 1, 1958; children—Charles Delbert, Danny, Virginia (Mrs. Robert Groom), Priscilla (Mrs. Harold Benefield), Rebecca (Mrs. Jerry Hazelwood). With Ft. Worth Press, 1932—, city editor, 1953-69, mng. editor, 1969-70, editor, 1970—. Adviser Block Partnership; founder Tarrant County Election Bur. Served with inf. AUS, 1942-49; PTO. Decorated Bronze Star medal, Purple Heart; recipient awards for news stories Headliner Club, 1951, 53, 66; Nieman fellow, 1948-49. Mem. Sigma Delta Chi. Club: Ft. Worth Press. Contbr. to mags. and jours. Home: 3731 Westcliff Rd N Ft Worth TX 76109 Office: Ft Worth Press 5th and Jones Sts Ft Worth TX 76102

WILLIS, ERNEST LINWOOD, III, mfg. co. exec.; b. Vicksburg, Miss., Mar. 22, 1940; s. Ernest Linwood and Frances Teresa (Romano) W.; B.S., U. S.C., 1962; m. Martha Caroline Goodale, Feb. 2, 1963; children— Paige, Elizabeth Ernest Linwood IV. Vice pres. Southeastern Steel Co., Florence, S.C., 1962—, also dir.; pres., treas. Willis-Bryce Co., Florence, 1971—; v.p. Mill & Contractors Supply Co., Wilmington, N.C., 1968—; dir. Charleston Supply Co. (S.C.), So. Mill Supply Co., Charleston, Columbia Supply Co. (S.C.), Matthews-Morse Supply Co., Charlotte, N.C., Mill & Contractors Supply Co., Wilmington, N.C., Augusta Mill Supply Co. (Ga.). Trustee James F. Byrnes Acad., Florence. Mem. Am. Soc. C.E., Nat. Soc. Profl. Engrs. Episcopalian. Rotarian. Club: Florence Country. Home: 522 Iris Dr Florence SC 29501 Office: PO Box 989 Florence SC 29501

WILLIS, GUY ROBERTS, dentist; b. Marshallberg, N.C., Sept. 10, 1915; s. Charles Steadman and Alice Gertrude (Davis) W.; student Campbell Coll., 1932-33, U. Md., 1933-35; D.D.S., Georgetown U., 1939; m. Agnes Bell Atkinson, Mar. 8, 1941; children—Gail Roberts (Mrs. Robert Maurice Cannon), Charles Steadman. Pvt. practice gen. dentistry, Washington, 1939-40, Durham, N.C., 1940—; asst. prof. fixed prosthodontics U. N.C., Sch. Dentistry, 1951-52. Mem. N.C. Bd. Dental Examiners, 1965-71, pres., 1967, vice chmn. council Nat. Bd. Dental Examiners, 1971—. Served with USAF, 1955-57. Mem. N.C. (v.p. 1952-53), 3d Dist (pres.) dental socs., Am. Dental Assn., Am. Acad. Dental Practice Adminstrn., Omicron Kappa Upsilon. Democrat. Methodist. Mason. Club: Hope Valley Country. Home: 1034 W Forest Hills Blvd Durham NC 27707 Office: Central Carolina Bank Bldg Durham NC 27701

WILLIS, JAMES, ednl. adminstr.; b. Cairo, Ga., Oct. 2, 1928; s. Prince and Wealthy (Butler) W.; B.S., Savannah State Coll., 1955; M.Ed., Fla. A. and M. U., 1957; postgrad. Atlanta U., summers 1966-68; m. Eula Mae Armstrong, Sept. 18, 1954; children—Talitha Renee, James II. Head football coach, athletic dir., track coach, asst. prin., tchr. 7th grade Monitor High Sch., Fitzgerald, Ga., 1956-59; prin. Beckbranch Elementary Sch., Calvary, Ga., 1959-70; prin. Charlie A. Gray Sch., Moultrie, Ga., 1970—. Lt. col. a.d.c. gov.'s staff, 1971—; mem. Colquitt County Planning Bd., 1972—; dep. registrar Colquitt County, 1972—. Bd. dirs. S. Ga. Agr. Festival. Served with AUS, 1951-52. Mem. Ga., Colquitt County assns. educators, N.E.A., Ga. Elementary Sch. Prins. Assn. Democrat. Baptist. Mason. Club: Moultrie Men's (corr. sec.). Home: 522 2d St NW Moultrie GA 31768

WILLIS, LYNWOOD GRAYSON, architect; b. Savannah, Ga., Sept. 17, 1931; s. Charles Wesley and Valeria (Grayson) W.; B.S., Ga. Inst. Tech., 1956; B.Arch., 1957; m. Jane Thompson, July 7, 1954; children—Ellen Kathleen, Linda Jane, Julia Ann, Ashley Grayson. Partner, Willis & Veenstra, Atlanta and Jacksonville, Fla., 1960—, Willis & Veenstra Investment Co., Atlanta, Jacksonville, 1968; gen. partner Heritage Sq. Apts. of Savannah Ltd. (Ga.), 1970—, other apt. complexes, Augusta, Jacksonville, Orlando, Atlanta. Mem. Com. of 100, Jacksonville, 1965-71. Bd. dirs. Vols. Am., Jr. Achievement, Jacksonville. Mem. Nat. Capital Democratic Club, Washington. Founder, Jacksonville Episcopal High Sch., 1966-67. Served with USAF, 1950-51. Recipient Cleve. Found. Structural Design award, 1957, Distinguished Service award Jacksonville Jr. C. of C., 1966. Mem. A.I.A. (Merit award 1971), Alpha Tau Omega. Democrat. Clubs: University, Quarterback, Deerwood, Ponte Vedre (Jacksonville); West Lake Country (Augusta); Chatham (Savannah). Archtl. works include: Fla. Jr. Coll., 1971, U.S. Post Office, 1971, Bapt. Towers, 1971, Jacksonville Gen. Hosp., 1971 (all Jacksonville); U.S. Post Office and Fed. Office Bldg., Waycross, Ga., 1971. Home: 10411 Deerwood Club Rd Jacksonville FL 32216 Office: 415 E Monroe St Jacksonville FL 32202

WILLIS, MARGARET FRISTOE, librarian; b. St. Louis, Apr. 7, 1906; d. Prior Fristoe and Elva (Moss) Willis; B.A., Washington U., 1928; postgrad. St. Louis Library Sch., 1929, U. Mo., 1937, Ariz. State Coll., 1950. Asst. St. Louis Pub. Library, 1928-37; asst. The Booklist, A.L.A. 1937-42; hosp. librarian Jefferson Barracks, Mo., 1942-44; head circulation dept. Louisville Free Pub. Library, 1944-45; coordinator Library Extension Div., Frankfort, Ky., 1955-57, dir., 1957-62; state librarian Ky. Dept. Libraries, 1962—. Sec. Ky. Bookmobile Project, 1953-55. Mem. A.L.A. (council mem. 1956-63), Bus. and Profl. Women, Am. Assn. U. Women, Southeastern, Ky. (state pres. 1954) library assns. club: Arts (Louisville); Altrusa (Frankfort, Ky.). Author: Adult Study Camps, 1952. Home: 130 W State St Frankfort KY 40601 Office: Berry Hill Frankfort KY 40601

WILLIS, ROBERT ALEXANDER, journalist; b. Atlanta, Oct. 8, 1929; s. William Warner and Bonnie (Alexander) W.; A.B. in Journalism, U. Ga., 1950; M.A. in English, State U. Ia., 1951; postgrad. Army Lang. Sch., 1952; m. Mildred Rita Pasquariello, Nov. 5, 1955; children—Michael Bruce, Paula Christine, Daniel Alexander, Jeffrey Thomas. Newsman, A.P., Charlotte, N.C., 1954-62, N.Y.C., 1962-63; tech. writer IBM, Poughkeepsie, N.Y., 1963-64; reporter Ledger-Star, Norfolk, Va., 1964-66, editorial writer 1966-67, spl. writer, 1968-69; asso. editor editorial pages Roanoke (Va.) Times and World News, 1969—. Part-time lectr. English, Old Dominion Coll., Norfolk, 1964-69. Served with AUS, 1951-54. Democrat. Roman Catholic. Home: 3835 Darlington Rd SW Roanoke VA 24018 Office: 201 Campbell Av SW Roanoke VA 24010

WILLIS, WILLIAM DARRELL, JR., neurophysiologist; b. Dallas, July 19, 1934; s. William Darrell and Dorcas (Chamberlain) W.; B.S., B.A., Tex. A. and M. U., 1956; M.D., U. Tex. Southwestern Med. Sch., 1960; Ph.D., Australian Nat. U., 1963; m. Jean Colette Schini, May 28, 1960. Postdoctoral research fellow Nat. Inst. Neurol. Diseases and Blindness, Australian Nat. U., 1960-62, Istituto di Fisiologia, Universita di Pisa (Italy), 1962-63; asst. prof. anatomy, U. Tex. Southwestern Med. Sch., Dallas, 1963-64, prof., chmn. anatomy, 1964-70; chief, lab. comparative marine neurobiology Marine Biomed. Inst., Galveston, Tex., 1970—; prof. anatomy and physiology U. Tex. Med. Br., Galveston, 1970—. Mem. A.A.A.S., Am. Assn. Anatomists. Am. Physiol. Soc., Soc. Exptl. Biol. Medicine, Biophys. Soc., Soc. for Neurosci., Sigma Xi, Alpha Omega Alpha. Home: 4608 Av O Galveston TX 77550 Office: Marine Biomedical Inst 200 University Blvd Galveston TX 77550

WILLIS, W(ILLIAM) EARL, hosp. exec.; b. Chase City, Va., May 9, 1927; s. William Richardson and Edmonia (Jordan) W.; B.S., Va. Commonwealth U., 1951; postgrad. U. Richmond, 1953-54, Med. Coll. Va., 1955-56; m. Mary Jane Bowers, Mar. 21, 1959; children—Elizabeth Ann, Ros Richardson. Hosp. auditor Bur. Hosps. and Nursing Homes, Va. State Health Dept., 1954-55; asst. adminstr. Roanoke Meml. Hosp., 1957-60; adminstr. Southside Community Hosp., Farmville, Va., 1960-63; adminstr. Gen. Hosp. Virginia Beach, Va., 1963—, v.p., 1969—. Bd. dirs. Windjammer Corp., Birchwood Corp., Medic-Home Health Centers Sch., Ocean Sands Corp. Pres., Tidewater Hosps. Council, 1968; mem. exec. com. Virginia Beach Beautification Commn., 1966—; pres. Cherry-Pearson, Ltd. Bd. dirs. Jobs for Vets., Va. Mayor's Task Force, Norfolk Central YMCA. Served with USNR, 1945-46, 51-52. Fellow Am. Coll. Hosp. Adminstrs.; mem. Va. (sec.-treas. 1971, pres.-elect 1972, mem. exec. com., dir.), Am. hosp. assns., Va. Beach C. of C. (dir., com. of 100), Club: Princess Anne Country (Virginia Beach). Home: 1411 Cherry Lane Virginia Beach VA 23454 Office: 1060 1st Colonial Rd Virginia Beach VA 23454

WILLIS, WILLIAM PASCAL, state ofcl.; b. Anadarko, Okla., Oct. 17, 1910; s. Robert Garnet and Lulu (Wyatt) W.; B.A., E. Central State Coll., Ada, Okla., 1935; M.A., Tulsa U., 1948; m. Zelma M. Bynum, Sept. 19, 1935; children—Diane, Joyce (Mrs. Gerald Browder), Billie Jean (Mrs. Alvon Crosslin), Zelma (Mrs. David Bailey), Herbert, William Pascal, Doak. Prin. Spaulding (Okla.) High Sch., 1935-36, Mill Creek High Sch., 1936-37; mayor, Locust Grove, 1937-44; mem. Okla. Ho. of Reps., 1958—. Owner, operator Willis Merc., Tablequah, 1937-56. Served with AUS, 1944. Recipient Tahlequah Outstanding Citizen award Tahlequah Star Citizen, 1965. Mem. Cherokee Hist. Soc. (bd. dirs.), C. of C. Mason (Shriner), Kiwanian. Address: 1 Valley St Tahlequah OK 74464

WILLS, CARL DURWOOD, city ofcl.; b. Raleigh, N.C., Oct. 10, 1937; s. John Daniel and Geneva Idella (Stell) W.; B.S., N.C. State U., 1962; m. Janet Page Thompson, Aug. 25, 1962; children—Lisa Paige, Carl Durwood, Jane Ashley. With J.M. Thompson Constrn. Co., Raleigh, 1953-59, foreman, 1956-59; engr. trainee N.C. Hwy. Commn., Raleigh, 1962-64; design engr. City High Point, N.C., 1964-67, dir. pub. works, 1967—. Chmn., Downtown Heart Fund, 1968-69, pub. employees sect United Fund, 1967-68; div. chmn. membership campaign YMCA, 1969-70. Registered profl. engr. N.C. Recipient Meade award Am. Soc. C.E., 1962. Mem. Jr. C. of C. (Outstanding Layman of Year, 1969), N.C. Soc. Profl. Engrs., Am. Pub. Works Assn. (pres. N.C. chpt. 1971). Rotarian, Mason, Kiwanian. Home: 508 Spruce St High Point NC 27260 Office: 200 E Commerce St High Point NC 27260

WILLS, DAVID HILARY, radio commentator; b. Wallasey, Eng., May 15, 1904; s. Thomas A. D. and Isobel (Wardlesworth) W.; B.Engring., Liverpool U., 1924, Ph.D., 1927; postgrad. (Commonwealth Fund fellow in econs.), Harvard, 1931-34; m. Virginia Floyd, 1934; children—Nadia, Jonathan Floyd, Susan; m. 2d,

Dorothy Lee Eck, May 8, 1953. Came to U.S., 1940, naturalized, 1944. Jr. engr. Met.-Vickers, Ltd., Eng., 1927-31; asst. chmn. London Daily News, Ltd., 1934-38, finance mgr., 1938-41; mgr. Czechoslovakian Relief Fund News-Chronicle, Prague, 1938-39; editorial writer The Economist, 1934-40; London corr. Christian Sci. Monitor, 1936-40, Washington Post, 1934-37, NBC, 1939-40; dir. information Brit. Supply Council, Washington, 1941-44; commentator radio sta. WMAL, ABC. Washington, 1944-48; chief Washington bur. The Reporter, 1948-50; dir. information IMF, Washington, 1950-52; partner Daveck Assos., Washington, 1952—; commentator fgn. affairs Three Star Extra, NBC, 1953-65. Fellow Royal Econ. Soc. (Eng.), Overeas Writers. Co-author: Total Victory without Atomic War, 1962.Home: 908 Mackall Av McLean VA 22101

WILLS, IRVIN ANDREWS, educator; b. Mendota, Ill., Dec. 21, 1904; s. Edgar Bunker and Margaretta (Moore) W.; B.S., Wheaton Coll., 1927; M.S., State U. Ia., 1932, Ph.D., 1935; m. Ruth Harriet Fisher, July 11, 1934; children—Ruth Elizabeth (Mrs. Paul Perks), Helen Margaret (Mrs. Richard Davis), Paul Irvin. Instr., Valparaiso (Ind.) U., 1927-29; asst. instr. State U. Ia., 1930, asst., 1931, 32-34, research asso., 1934-35; prof. biology John Brown U., Siloam Springs, Ark., 1935—, dean acad. coll., 1935-54, chmn. nat. sci. div., 1954—, recipient 30-year Service pin, 1965. Recipient 20-year Service pin U.S. Weather Bur., 1965, 25-year award Ark. Dept. Higher Edn., 1960. Fellow Am. Sci. Affiliation, A.A.A.S.; mem. Am. Zoologists, Ark. Edn. Assn., Ark. Acad. Sci. (pres. 1941), Creation Research Soc. Rotarian (pres. Siloam Springs 1950). Home: 225 S Holly St Siloam Springs AR 72761

WILLS, JAMES DONALD, mining engr., state ofcl.; b. Prestonsburg, Ky., Aug. 26, 1940; s. Clayton Edward and Ethel Lorena (Conley) W.; B.S. in Mining Engring. (Princess Coals, Inc. scholar), U. Ky., 1963; m. Alberta Belle Pilcher, Dec. 18, 1965; children—Susan Yvette, Carmen Michelle. With Princess Coals, Inc., David, Ky., summers 1959-64; engr., asst. to dir. Ky. Div. Reclamation, Frankfort, 1964-66; hwy. design engr. div. design Ky. Dept. Hwys., Frankfort, 1966-68; profl. engr. Ky. Air Pollution Control Commn., Frankfort, 1968—. Registered profl. engr., Ky. Mem. Jehovah's Witnesses. Home: 120 Compton Dr Apt C-1 Frankfort KY 40601 Office: 275 E Main Frankfort KY 40601

WILLSON, CEDRIC, mfg. co. exec.; b. Mason City, Ia., Oct. 26, 1900; s. John David and Rosalie (Reiniger) W.; student N.Y. U., 1919-21; B.S. in C.E., U. Kan., 1926; m. Lois Elizabeth von Landig, Apr. 28, 1946; children—Donn (Mrs. Charles Fortun) and Drusilla (Mrs. William A. Walker) (twins). Bassoonist, John Philip Sousa's Concert Band, 1922-23; with Gen. Portland Cement Co., Fredonia, Kan., Houston, Dallas, 1927-46, research engr., 1939-42, 43-46; plant mgr. Erle P. Halliburton Inc., Corpus Christi, Tex., 1947-50; v.p. design and constrn. Portland Cement plant, Corpus Christi, 1947-50; v.p. research and devel. Tex. Industries, Inc., Arlington, 1951—. Trustee, exec. com. Dallas Symphony Orch. Assn., 1951—. Fellow Am. Soc. C.E.; mem. Am. Concrete Inst., Expanded Shale, Clay and Slate Inst. (dir.), Dallas Engring. Club, Am. Soc. Testing and Materials (dist. chmn. 1966-68), Nat., Tex. socs. profl. engrs. Clubs: Lancers, Southwest. Contbr. articles to profl. jours. Home: 6720 Willow Lane Dallas TX 75230 Office: Box 400 Arlington TX 76010

WILLSON, DAVID RICHARD, lumber co. exec.; b. Fort Worth, Jan. 9, 1933; s. James McCrory and Mavis Louise (Terry) W.; B.S., N. Tex. State U., 1954; m. Rochelle Ann Leibovitz, July 20, 1954; children—David Blair, Cynthia Faith. Owner, mgr. Willson & Son-Bldg. Materials, Plainview, Tex., 1956—. Scoutmaster, South Plains council Boy Scouts Am., 1968-71, dist. chmn. camping activities, 1959-60; coach Little League Baseball, 1967-70; bd. commrs. Meth. Home, Waco, Tex., 1971. Trustee McMurry Coll., Abilene, Tex., Mt. Sequoiah Meth. Camp, Fayetteville, Ark., Ceta Canyon Meth. Camp, Canyon, Tex. Served with AUS, 1954-56. Mem. C. of C. Lambda Chi Alpha. Methodist. Mason (Shriner), Rotarian, Toastmaster. Home: Box 1178 1106 Ennis St Plainview TX 79072 Office: 700 E 5th St Plainview TX 79072

WILLSON, JAMES MCCORRY, lumberman; b. Boonesville, Tex., Dec. 21, 1887; s. David and Sarah Eugenia (Strange) D.; A.B., Southwestern U., 1912; LL.D., Tex. Wesleyan Coll., 1947; L.H.D. (hon.), McMurry Coll., 1956; m. Mavis Louis Terry, June 14, 1919; children—James McCrorry, Mavis Louis (Mrs. Robert Arnold), Ora Eugenia (Mrs. Will Addis), David R. Owner lumber yard, 1908—; line yard operator Willson & Son, 1916—; established founds. in numerous colls., instns. Mem. Nat. council Boy Scouts Am. Trustee So. Methodist U., 1930-64; trustee McMurray Coll., 1934—, pres. bd., 1951-54; chmn. jurisdictional bd. hosp. and homes Methodist Ch., 1949-54; chmn. bd. edn. N.W. Tex. Meth. Conf., 1952-54; mem. gen. bd. edn. Meth. Ch., 1960-64; trustee, vice chmn. bd. Meth. Western Assembly, 1934-66, Meth. Hosp., Lubbock, Tex. 1954-71; del. Meth. Gen. Conf., 1934, 38, 40, 44, 48, 52, 56, 60, 64, 66, 68, Uniting Conf., 1939. Served with U.S. Army, World War I. Decorated Purple Heart; recipient Silver Beaver award Boy Scouts Am., Top Leadership award Freedoms Found. Valley Forge, 1960. Mem. West Tex. C. of C. (pres. 1971), V.F.W., Am. Legion (dist. comdr.). Mason (Shriner), Rotarian (dist. gov. 1935-36). Home: 820 Kentucky St Floydada TX 79235 Office: 215 E California St Floydada TX 79235

WILLSON, MRS. JAMES M., coll. trustee; b. Vashti, Tex., May 11, 1895; d. Richard Everet and Ora Ann (Jetton) Terry; student Seth Ward Coll., 1912, Southwestern U., 1914, A.B., So. Methodist U., 1916; D.Litt., McMurry Coll., 1962; m. James McCorry Willson, June 14, 1919; children—James McCorry, Mavis Louis (Mrs. Robert Neff Arnold), Ora Eugenia (Mrs. Will Addis), David. Tchr. Tex. pub. high schs., 1916-19; trustee Floydada (Tex.) High Sch., 1940. Trustee Tex. Wesleyan Coll., Ft. Worth, 1948-71, Lydia Patterson Inst., El Paso, Tex., 1948—. Recipient Freedoms Found. award, 1960; named Ky. Colo. Mem. Am. Legion Aux. (vice chmn. Tex. dept. 1947, chmn. 19th dist. 1945-46, chmn. state child welfare com., 1948, mem. state finance com. 1949-51, dist. pres., state Woman's Soc. Christian Service (local pres.). Democrat. Methodist. (dist. sec. young people's supply work). Clubs: Study (pres.), Garden (Floydada). Established (with husband) founds. for youth in various colls. and univs. in S.W. Home: Box 985 Floydada TX 79235

WILMATH, CLIFF HARRY, editor, publisher; b. Hartford, Conn., May 31, 1917; s. Clifford H. and Julia (Collins) W.; student pub. schs., Mass.; m. Irene M. Gowell, Sept. 6, 1942; children—Robert C., Sandra K. Sportswriter Quincy (Mass.) Patriot-Ledger, 1935-36; asst. sports editor Daily News, Quincy, 1936-38; editor Dreadnaught, Quincy, 1938-41; news editor Riviera-Times Daily, Coral Gables, Fla., 1946-47; mng. editor, 1947-48; editor, pub. Mobile Home and Trailer News, Miami, Fla., 1946—, Fla. Trailerite Handbook, 1949—; pres. Holiday Travel Trailer Parks, Inc., Fiesta Key, Fla., 1966—. Mem. Mobile Homes Mfrs. Assn. (hon.), Dealers Nat. Assn. Club: Riviera Country (Coral Gables). Home: 6460 Chapman Field Dr Miami FL 33156 Office: Box 967 Kendall Br Miami FL 33156

WILMER, RICHARD HOOKER, lawyer; b. Washington, Oct. 20, 1892; s. William Holland and Re Lewis (Smith) W.; A.B., Yale, 1915; J.D., Columbia, 1917; m. Margaret Van Dyke Grant, June 2, 1917; children—Richard Hooker, John Grant. Admitted to D.C. bar, 1917, N.Y. State bar, 1929; asso. firm Minor, Gatley & Rowland, Washington, 1919-24, Cravath, de Gersdorff, Swaine & Wood, N.Y.C., Washington, 1924-29, partner, 1929-42; sr. partner firm Wilmer & Broun, Washington, 1946-62, Wilmer, Cutler & Pickering, Washington, 1962—. Chmn. met. area campaign A.R.C., Washington, 1946. Served as 1st lt., CAC, 1917-19, col. CAC, AUS, 1942-46; chief legal advisor Allied Commn. (Italy), 1944. Decorated Legion of Merit with oak leaf cluster; comdr. Order Saints Mauritius and Lazarus (Italy); chevalier Legion of Honor (France). Mem. Soc. of Cin. (past pres. gen.), Am. Legion, Mil. Order World Wars, Am., D.C. bar assns., Bar Assn. City N.Y., Am. Law Inst., Washington Cathedral. Episcopalian. Clubs: Metropolitan, International (Washington); Chevy Chase. Home: 2600 31st St Washington DC 20008 Office: Farragut Bldg Washington DC 20006

WILMOT, WILLIAM VERNON, JR., educator; b. Newark, Sept. 15, 1916; s. William Vernon and Agnes (Reed) W.; A.B., Syracuse U., 1937, M.A., 1939; Ph.D., U. Wis., 1954; m. Clarice Mary King, Sept. 2, 1941; children— Barbara Mary, William Vernon III. Instr. econs. U. Wis., 1946-54, asst. prof., 1954-57; asst. prof. finance U. Ia., 1957-59, prof., chmn. dept. mgmt. and bus. law, 1959-72; prof. bus. and econs. St. Andrews Presbyn Coll., 1972—. Sec.-treas., dir. Order Assos., Inc., Gainesville, Fla., 1966-67. Served to lt. USNR, 1943-46. Mem. Am. Econ. Assn., Acad. Mgmt., Econometric Soc., So. Econ. Assn., So. Mgmt. Assn. (v.p. 1964), Alpha Kappa Psi, Beta Gamma Sigma, Chi Eta Sigma, Sigma Phi Epsilon. Home: Pecan Lane Laurinburg NC 28352

WILNOTY, JOHN JULIUS, sculptor; b. Cherokee, N.C., 1940. Sculptor and carver of subjects from nature and Indian mythology in stone, wood and bone 1960—. Represented in permanent collections Smithsonian Instn. and other mus. Address: Cherokee NC 28719*

WILSON, AGNES JULIET HILDEBRAND (MRS. THOMAS E. WILSON), educator; b. Chapin, S.C., June 11, 1914; d. Benjamin F. and Agnes (Brogdon) Hildebrand; A.B., Allen U., 1935, L.H.D., 1969; postgrad. Atlanta U., 1938; M.Ed., Temple U., 1951; diploma in French, The Sorbonne, Paris, 1955; certificate in French, U. Mo., 1960; postgrad. Rutgers U., 1965; m. Thomas E. Wilson, May 10, 1942 (dec. Jan. 1965). Tchr., Manning, S.C., 1935-39, Carver High Sch., Spartanburg, S.C., 1939-48, rural sch. Sumter County, S.C., 1948-50; tchr. French and journalism Lincoln High sch., Sumter, S.C., 1950—. Mem. religious resources com. YWCA, Sumter, 1949—; mem. planning com. Internat. Christian U. Japan, 1958—; vis. prof. French Morris Coll., Sumter, 1960—. Publicity chmn. Cancer Crusade Sumter County, 1967—. Trustee Barber-Scotia Coll., Concord, N.C. Named S.C. Tchr. of Year, Council of Chief State Sch. Officers and Look Mag., 1969. Mem. N.E.A., Am. Assn. Tchrs. French, S.C. Edn. Assn. (pres. 1972—), Sumter Ministers Wives Alliance (pres. 1968-70), Zeta Phi Beta. Presbyn. (pres. soc. U.P. Women 1951-67, mem. nat. bd. Christian edn. 1958-63, chmn. planning div. Synod of South). Home: PO Box 482 1284 N Main St Extension Sumter SC 29150 Office: Lincoln High Sch Sumter SC 29150

WILSON, ALEXANDER ERWIN, JR., lawyer; b. East Point, Ga., Aug. 26, 1910; s. Alexander Erwin and Evelyn (Smith) W.; A.B., Emory U., 1930, A.M., 1932; m. Constance Dinkler, June 10, 1932; children—Constance Dinkler (Mrs. E. Ralph Paris, Jr.), Alexander Erwin III. Admitted to Ga. bar, 1931, and practiced in Clarkesville, 1930-34; lawyer Home Owners Loan Corp., Atlanta and Washington, 1934-37; atty., H.O.L.C., 1934-37; regional atty. N.L.R.B., 1937-42; practice of law, Atlanta, 1942—; partner Wilson, Wilcox & Wilson, and predecessor firms, 1947—. Chmn. bd. Whitley Constrn. Co. Mem. bd. visitors Emory U. Bd. dirs. Met. Boys Club of Atlanta, 1954—; past pres. Atlanta br. Nat. Cystic Fibrosis Research Found. Mem. Sigma Pi (nat. pres. 1956-58), Am., Ga., Atlanta bar assns., Am. Judicature Soc. Episcopalian. Clubs: Atlanta Athletic (dir. 1963—), Capital City, Peachtree Golf, Piedmont Driving, Commerce (Atlanta). Home: 358 King Rd NW Atlanta GA 30342 Office: 100 Peachtree St NW Atlanta GA 30303

WILSON, BARRY PRESTON, ins. co. exec.; b. Batavia, N.Y., Mar. 16, 1932; s. Wilbur Charles and Gwendolyn Irene (Frey) W.; A.B., Coll. Williams and Mary, 1953; M.A., Cornell U., 1955; m. Mary Louise Hazelgrove, Jan. 20, 1962; children—Nancy Randolph, Anne Bidgood, Terry Jane, Timothy Bland. News editor Va. Gazette, Williamsburg, 1955-56; staff writer Newport News (Va.) Daily Press, 1958-59; news bur. editor Coll. William and Mary, 1959-60; asst. pub. relations mgr. Group Hospitalization, Inc., Washington, 1960-67, pub. relations mgr., 1967-71, v.p. personnel and pub. affairs, 1971—. Served with AUS, 1956-58. Recipient awards Va. Press Assn., 1956, Advt. Club Washington, 1971, Nat. Outdoor Advt. Assn., 1969. Mem. Pub. Relations Soc. Am. (dir. Nat. Capital chpt.), Am. Soc. Hosp. Pub. Relations Dirs., Sigma Alpha Epsilon, Theta Alpha Phi. Democrat. Episcopalian (vestryman). Home: 4125 Village Ct Annandale VA 22003 Office: 550 12th St SW Washington DC 20024

WILSON, BERNARD EDGAR, ins. co. exec.; b. Chattanooga, Feb. 23, 1912; s. Bernard E. and Lillian (Ledford) W.; B.S., Eastern Ky. State, 1936; M.A., U. Ky., 1938; m. Elizabeth Irene Howard, Apr. 20, 1942; children—Bernard E. III, William Gerald. High sch. athletic coach, Harlan, Ky., 1936-39; athletic dir. Union Coll., 1939-46; head basketball coach Coll. William & Mary, 1946-51; with Commonwealth Life Ins. Co., 1951, successively agt., mgr., dir. agys. of home office, 1951-59, br. mgr., 1959; v.p., dir. agys. Appalachian Nat. Life Ins. Co., 1959-61, dir., 1960-61; v.p., dir. agys., sr. v.p., Am. Gen. Life Ins. Co. of Del., 1962-69, dir., 1962—; dir. Life & Casualty, 1971—, Am. Gen. of Okla., 1971—; dir. Am. Gen. Life of Tex. Chmn. exec. com. LIAMA, 1970. Trustee Life Underwriters Tng. Council, 1971. Served from 2d lt. to maj. USAF, 1942-46. Mem. Nat., Nashville assns. life underwriters, Newcomen Soc., Nashville Area C. of C., Sales and Marketing Execs. Assn., Gen. Agts. and Mfrs. Assn., Pa. Soc. Methodist. Kiwanian. Clubs: Hillwood Country; Nashville City; Duquesne; Exchange. Home: 1104 Stonewall Jackson Ct Nashville TN 37220 Office: 159 4th Av N Nashville TN 37219

WILSON, BRYANT ROSS, physician; b. Philadelphia, Miss., Feb. 24, 1900; s. John Marion and Mary Elizabeth (George) W.; student Whitworth Coll., 1920-22, Miss. State Coll., 1925-27; M.S., U. Tenn., 1925, M.D., 1931; postgrad. Miss. U., 1966, 68-69; m. Roberta Wright, Sept. 15, 1944. Practiced medicine with C.H. Harrison, Philadelphia, 1923-31; intern Memphis Gen. Hosp., 1930-32; practice gen. medicine Philadelphia, 1932-33, Carthage, Miss., 1933-64; owner own hosp., 1944-58; mem. bd. Leake County Hosp., Carthage, 1958-64. Served with U.S. Army, World War I, inf. AUS, World War II. Mem. Am., Miss., So. med. assns., Lake County Med. Soc., Chi Zeta Chi, Phi Rho Sigma. Democrat. Methodist. Rotarian. Home: 1304 Hwy 16 W Carthage MS 39051 Office: 111 S Pearl St Carthage MS 39051

WILSON, CHARLES JEFFERSON, physician; b. Eldon, Mo., Sept. 22, 1933; s. Carmy Jefferson and Dora Louisa (Vernon) W.; B.A. in Biology, Berea Coll., 1955; M.D., U. Louisville, 1959; m. Patricia Elaine Johnson, June 8, 1958; children—Doris, Dana, Gregory. Intern, Ky. Baptist Hosp., Louisville, 1959-60; gen. practice medicine, Spruce Pine, N.C., 1960—; chief staff Spruce Pine Hosp., 1964-66. Owner Johnson Nursery, Crossnore, N.C., 1962—. Mem. A.M.A., N.C., Mitchell-Yancey County (pres. 1964) med. socs. Baptist (deacon 1968-71). Kiwanian (v.p. 1970-71, pres. 1971—), Moose. Home: Martha Dr Spruce Pine NC 28777 Office: 112 Hospital Dr Spruce Pine NC 28777

WILSON, CLAUDE RAYMOND, JR., lawyer; b. Dallas, Feb. 22, 1933; s. Claude Raymond and Lottie (Watts) W.; B.B.A., So. Methodist U., 1954, LL.B., 1956, LL.M., 1958; m. Barbara Jean Cowherd, Apr. 30, 1960; 1 dau., Deidra Nicole. Admitted to Tex. bar, 1956, practiced in Dallas, 1956-58, 65—; lawyer Tex. & Pacific R.R. Co., Dallas, 1958-60; sr. trial atty., chief counsel Internal Revenue Service, Washington, 1960-65; mem. firm Golden, Potts, Boeckman & Wilson, Dallas, 1965—. Bd. dirs., treas. St. Phillips Community Center. Mem. State Bar Tex., Am., Dallas (chmn. sect. taxation 1971-72) bar assns., Tex. Soc. C.P.A.'s (dir. Dallas chpt. 1971-72), Delta Sigma Phi, Delta Theta Phi. Republican. Episcopalian. Mason (K.T., 32 degree, Shriner) Clubs: Chaparral, Royal Oaks Country, Dallas Gun. Home: 4069 Hanover Dallas TX 75225 Office: 2300 Republic Bank Tower Dallas TX 75201

WILSON, CREOLA DANIEL, ret. librarian; b. Galax, Va., Dec. 17, 1901; d. Joseph Emory and Mollie (Ward) Daniel; m. Carl Bain Wilson, Dec. 3, 1924; 1 dau., Betty Jean (Mrs. Louis Franklin Bussler). Tchr., Loudoun County (Va.) pub. schs., 1920-24; cataloger Pub. Documents Library, Govt. Printing Office, Washington, 1937-42; librarian U.S. Fish and Wildlife Service, Washington, 1942-44; librarian U.S. Bur. Mines, Washington, 1944-45; subject cataloger, classification specialist Armed Forces Med. Library, Washington, 1945-55; subject cataloger Library of Congress, Washington, 1955-56; asst. librarian St. Elizabeth's Hosp., Washington, 1956-58; subject analyst, chief librarian Def. Documentation Center, Alexandria, Va., 1958-71. Mem. Spl. Libraries Assn. (chmn. Washington chpt. biol. scis. group 1953-54), Med. Library Assn., Loudoun County Hist. Soc. Democrat. Mem. Soc. of Friends. Home: Route 2 Box 103A Leesburg VA 22075

WILSON, DAVID BENJAMIN, hosp. dir.; b. Yazoo City, Miss., Aug. 23, 1913; s. Richard B. and Jennie (Bowman) W.; B.S., U. Miss., 1936; M.D., Emory U., 1938; M.P.H., Yale, 1944; m. Sarah Barry Gillespie, June 20, 1940; children—Sarah Elizabeth (Mrs. Frank Otte), David Benjamin, Jane Tyler (Mrs. Robert W. Fulton). Intern USPHS Hosp., Staten Island, N.Y., 1938-39, Miss. Bd. Health, 1939-40; commd. officer USPHS, 1940-51, asst. dir. Commn. Hosp. Care, Chgo., 1945-46, chief program planning sect. Hill Burton Hosp. constrn. program, 1946-48, asst. med. dir. Alameda County Instns., Oakland, Cal., 1948-50; staff Commn. Hosp. Care, Jackson, Miss., 1951-54; dir. Univ. Hosp., Jackson, 1954—. Commr. Joint Commn. Accreditation Hosps.; bd. govs. Blue Cross Assn.; mem. nat. med. adv. council Dept. Def. Bd. dirs. United Givers Fund Jackson. Served with AUS, 1961-62. Mem. Am. (past pres.), Miss. (past pres.) hosp. assns., Soc. Med. Adminstrs., Miss. Med. Assn., Jackson C. of C. (bd. dirs.), Newcomen Soc. Rotarian (pres. Jackson 1969-70). Club: Capitol City (Jackson). Home: 1267 Belvoir Pl Jackson MS 39202 Office: 2500 N State St Jackson MS 39216

WILSON, DAVID WINSLOW, advt. agy. exec.; b. Kansas City, Mo., May 22, 1939; s. Edward Graham and Anne Elizabeth (Saunders) W.; B.A. cum laude, U. South, 1961; M.S. in Journalism, Northwestern U., 1963; m. Sandra Slough, Aug. 26, 1961; children—Glen Mackie, Heather Louise. Asst. account exec. Marsteller Inc., Chgo., 1962-66, account exec., 1966-67, dir. collateral, 1967; account exec. Shattuck-Roether Frailey & Wilson, Inc., Orlando, Fla., 1967-70, v.p., 1970—, prin., 1971—. Bd. dirs. Fla. Symphony Orch. Mem. Orlando Area Advt. Club (pres. 1970-71, pres. bd. trustees 1971-72), Orlando Area C. of C., South Seminole C. of C., Antique Airplane Assn., Kappa Sigma. Republican. Episcopalian. Club: Citrus (Orlando). Home: 1121 Glengarry Circle Maitland FL 32751 Office: 601 N Ferncreek St Orlando FL 32803

WILSON, D(OYCE) JOE, mfg. co. exec.; b. Denton County, Tex., Jan. 2, 1926; s. Walter John and Maggie Lee (Hindsley) W.; grad. Branch Agrl. Coll. Utah, 1944, Alexander Hamilton Inst., 1953; m. Vivian C. Castleberry, Oct. 14, 1944; 1 dau., Linda C. Vice pres., gen. mgr. Plains Dist. Co., Amarillo, Tex., 1948-58, Air-Tex div. Holly Corp., Dallas, 1958-62; pres., founder Remac Corp., Dallas, 1962-69; gen. mgr. Remac div. Sealed Power Corp., Dallas, 1969—; dir., pres., chief exec. officer Penny-Plus Corp., Dallas, 1970—. Served with USAAF, 1943-45. Mem. Jr. C. of C., 1952-58. Lutheran. Elk. Patentee spl. tools for servicing automobile air conditioning. Home: 1702 Glen Valley St Irving TX 75060 Office: 2920 Anode Lane Dallas TX 75220

WILSON, EDGAR CECIL, orthodontist; b. Harrisville, W.Va., Jan. 26, 1931; s. Oscar Homer and Affa Avis (Huff) W.; B.A., W.Va. U., 1952; D.D.S., U. Md., 1955; certificate orthodontics U. Pitts., 1969; m. Betty Lee Taylor, Aug. 15, 1953; children—Edgar James, Mary Robin. Gen. practice dentistry, Vienna, W.Va., 1957-67, specialist in orthodontics, Roanoke, Va., 1969—; mem. staff Camden-Clark Meml. Hosp., 1962-67. Pres., Roanoke Gideon Camp., 1970-71; mem. adv. bd. Wood County Civil Def. Council, 1964-67. Served to capt. Dental Corps, USAF, 1955-57. Mem. Blennerhasset (past pres.), Roanoke, Piedmont, Va. dental socs., Am. Dental Assn., Va., So., Am. assns. orthodontists, Izaak Walton League, Roanoke Orthodontic Study Club, Psi Omega. Republican. Methodist. Mason (32 deg.), Lion (v.p. 1962). Home: 5719 Brahma Rd SW Roanoke VA 24011 Office: Med Arts Bldg Roanoke VA 24011

WILSON, ERNEST JOHN FREWEN, JR., cons. engr.; b. Lynchburg, Va., June 12, 1920; s. Ernest John Frewen and Mary Dawes (Appleton) W.; B.S., Va. Polytech. Inst., 1941; m. Betty Gray Gillespie, June 15, 1946; children— Ernest John Frewen III, Robert Scott. Jr. engr. Corps Engrs., Norfolk, Va., 1941; engr., asso., partner, mng. partner Wiley & Wilson, Lynchburg, 1946—; dir. Central Va. Devel. Corp., Lynchburg; pres. Wiley & Wilson of N.C., Inc., Winston-Salem, 1967—; sec., dir. W & W Corp., Lynchburg, 1962—. Mem. Lynchburg City Planning Commn., 1949-52, chmn., 1952. Bd. dirs. Piedmont Heart Assn., 1953-62, treas., 1956-61, pres., 1962. Served from 2d to 1st lt., AUS, 1941-46. Mem. Nat. Soc. Profl. Engrs. (chmn. contract deocuments com. 1970-72), Nat. Conf. Lawyers and Profl. Engrs. (co-chmn. 1971-72). Episcopalian. Club: Boonsboro Country (Lynchburg). Home: Route 4 Box 163B Lynchburg VA 24503

WILSON, FRANK MOORE, judge; b. Waco, Tex., June 6, 1908; s. Frank M. and Memrie (Perkins) W.; A.B., Baylor U., 1931, LL.B., 1931, LL.D., 1968; m. Dorothy Ann Tucker, June 1, 1935; children—Martha Fay (Mrs. George C. Witt), Frank M. III. Admitted to Tex. bar, 1931, since practiced Waco. asst. dist. atty. McLennan county. County, 1931-34; mem. firm Darden, Burleson & Wilson, 1931-36, Wilson & Cureton, 1954-59; Justice Ct. Civil Appeals of Tex. Chmn. ins. law sect., chmn. rules com., dir. jud. sect., mem. com. adminstrn. justice, supreme ct. adv. com. State Bar Tex. Instr. law, polit. sci., Baylor U. Chmn. bd. trustees Baylor U.; trustee Waco Library, Waco Schs.; dir. United Charities, Fair Bd.; chmn. Tex. Youth Council, 1957-59. Served as lt. USNR. Fellow Am. Coll. Trial

Lawyers; mem. C. of C. (dir.), McLennan County Bar Assn. (past pres.), Baylor Law Sch. Alumni (past pres.), Am. Bar Assn., Am. Judicature Soc. Baptist (chmn. deacons, teacher men's Bible class). Mason (past master, 32 deg., Shriner). Contbr. articles profl. jours. Home: 2820 Morrow Av Waco TX 76707 Office: Ct House Waco TX 76701

WILSON, FRANK WILEY, judge; b. Knoxville, Tenn., June 21, 1917; s. Frank Caldwell and Mary E. (Wiley) W.; A.B., U. Tenn., 1939, LL.B., 1941; m. Helen E. Warwick, Apr. 6, 1942; children—Frank Carl, William Randall. Admitted to Tenn. bar, 1941, since practiced in Oak Ridge; county atty., Anderson County, Tenn., 1948-50; city atty., Norris, Tenn., 1950-61, U.S. dist. judge Eastern dist. Tenn. So. Div., Chattanooga, 1961-—, chief judge, 1970-—. Vice pres., dir. Bank of Oak Ridge, 1952-63. Pres. Community Chest; mem. Oak Ridge Bd. Edn. Trustee Siskin Meml. Found. Served with USAAF, 1941-46; MTO. Mem. C. of C. (pres.), Am. Legion (comdr.), Order of Coif, Phi Delta Phi, Phi Kappa Phi. Rotarian (past pres.). Home: Stratford Lane Burnham Woods Signal Mountain TN 37377 Office: US Dist Court Chattanooga TN 37402

WILSON, FRED L., textile co. exec.; b. Bakersville, N.C., Dec. 3, 1906; s. Green B. and Lockie (Young) W.; B.S., N.C. State Coll., 1931; m. Anne Lois Hancock, June 2, 1934; children—Jane Hancock, Frederick McRay. With Cannon Mills Co., Kannapolis, N.C., 1931-—, v.p., 1959-70, gen. mgr., 1955-68, sr. v.p., 1971-—, dir. mfg., 1968-—, also dir. Trustee Greater U. N.C. Mem. Newcomer Soc. Clubs: Y Men Internat., Rotary. Home: 600 Nance St Kannapolis NC 28081 Office: Cannon Mills Co Kannapolis NC 28081

WILSON, GEORGE EDWARD, JR., textile co. exec., Republican nat. committeeman; b. Rockwood, Tenn., July 26, 1921; s. George Edward and Madge (Tarwater) W.; grad. Vanderbilt U., 1943; m. Emmie Chalmers Brown, Apr. 26, 1947; children—George Edward III, Emmie N., Madge T. With Roan & Hosiery, Inc., Harriman, Tenn., 1950-—, v.p., sec., 1950-—. Chmn. Tenn. Republican Com., 1963-64; mem. Rep. Nat. Com. for Tenn., 1968-—. Bd. dirs. East Tenn. Children's Hosp., Knoxville Symphony Soc. Served with USCGR, 1943-46. Mem. Tenn. Mfrs. Assn. (v.p., dir.), Nat. Assn. Hosiery Mfrs. (dir.), Am. Legion, V.F.W., Vanderbilt U. Alumni Assn. (dir.), Delta Kappa Epsilon. Presbyn. Elk. Clubs: Cherokee Country, City (Knoxville). Home: 702 Cumberland St Harriman TN 37748 Office: PO Box 431 Harriman TN 37748

WILSON, GEORGE HOWARD, state judge; b. Mattoon, Ill., Aug. 21, 1905; s. George Duncan and Helen Maude (Bresee) W.; A.B., Phillips U., 1926; postgrad. U. Mich. Law Sch., 1926-27; LL.B., U. Okla., 1929, J.D., 1970; grad. Nat. Coll. State Trial Judges U. Nev., 1970; m. Myrna Kathryn Reams, June 26, 1929; children—Jane Kathryn, Sandra Kay, Myrna Lee, George Howard II. Admitted to Okla. bar, 1928, U.S. Supreme Ct., in 1934; practiced in Enid, Okla., 1929-52; spl. agt. FBI, U.S. Dept. Justice, 1934-38; city atty., Enid, 1939-42; mem. 81st Congress (1949-51), 8th Dist. Okla.; superior ct. judge, Garfield County, Okla., 1952-68; presiding dist. judge div. 1, 4th Jud. Dist., 1968-—. Chief judge Okla. Adminstrv. Zone 1, 1967; pres. Okla. Jud. Conf., 1968; chief judge Ct. of Bank Rev., 1971-—; judge panel 1, div. 2 Okla. Appellate Ct. of Criminal Appeals, 1971-—. Dir. Okla. Crime Commn. 1951-52. Former chmn. Cherokee Strip dist. Boy Scouts Am.; former pres. Enid Community Chest; former pres. bd. dirs. YMCA, Enid, 1968. Served as col., judge adv. gen.'s dept., U.S. Army, 1942-46. Commd. commodore by Okla. gov. 1954; recipient Legionnaire of Honor DeMolay. Mem. Am., Garfield County, Okla. bar assns., Am. Legion, Acacia, Phi Delta Phi, Delta Sigma Rho, Order of Coif. Democrat. Presbyn. (elder). Mason (K.T.). Kiwanian (past lt. gov.). Home: 1724 W Cherokee St Enid OK 73701 Office: Ct House Enid OK 73701

WILSON, HAROLD STALETS, lawyer, state senator; b. Chgo., Sept. 28, 1921 s. Harold B. and Luella (Stalets) W.; B.A., U. Chgo., 1943; LL.B., Harvard, 1953; m. Mary Ellen Rusin, Jan. 19, 1963; children—Jennie Ellen, Janice Mary. Owner, operator Harold's Dept. Store, Amsterdam, N.Y., 1952-59; admitted to Fla. bar, 1960, since practiced in Clearwater; mem. firm Harold S. Wilson, 1967-—; mem. Fla. Senate, 1966-—; asst. pub. defender, Pinellas County, Fla., 1963-64; asso. municipal judge Indian Rocks Beach, Fla., 1966; city atty., Safety Harbor, Fla., 1962-65. Served with Signal Corps, AUS, 1943-46. Mem. Am., Fla., Largo, Clearwater bar assns., Pinellas County Trial Lawyers Assn., Delta Sigma Pi. Home: 1406 Maple Forest Rd Clearwater FL 33516 Office: 307 S Osceola Av Clearwater FL 33516

WILSON, HOMER MARVIN, elec. engr.; b. St. Louis, Oct. 3, 1934; s. Homer Marvin and Ogarita (Bailey) W.; student Loughborough Coll., Eng., 1957-58; B.A., Rice U., 1959, B.S. in Elec. Engring., 1960; m. Joy Lee Clark, Mar. 1, 1957. Tech. mgr. Palmer Nuclear Lab., Princeton, 1961, Bonner Nuclear Lab,, Rice U,, 1961-62; v.p. Tech. Enterprises Corp., Houston, 1962-65; pres. H.M. Wilson Co., Houston, 1965-—. Served with AUS, 1955-56. Registered profl. engr., Tex. Mem. I.E.E.E., Soc. Profl. Engrs., Nat. Assn. Corrosion Engrs., Instrument Soc. Am., Aircraft Owners and Pilots Assn. Patentee dual channel well logging system, logging channel disabling circuit, casing collar logging system, well logging system, electrochem. well log, corrosion rate meter, probe assembly for corrosion tests, also others. Home: 8810 Ariel St Houston TX 77036 Office: 11501 Chimney Rock Houston TX 77035

WILSON, HOWARD HAZEN, internat. relations writer; b. La Salle, Ill., July 2, 1908; s. George Alexander and Florence Mellen (Hazen) W.; Ph.B. in History, U. Chgo., 1936, Ph.D. in Internat. Relations, 1941; m. Mary Louise Bennett, Dec.6, 1933; 1 son, Howard Hazen. Asst. economist, internat. econs. U.S. Dept. Commerce, 1942-43; asso. economist U.S. Office Alien Property Custodian, 1943-44; divisional asst. Am. Republics affairs U.S. Dept. State, 1944-46; internat. relations intelligence research Hdqrs. U.S. Air Force, 1951-58, historian, 1958-66 (all Washington). Prof. internat. relations Am. Inst. for Fgn. Trade, 1946-47; lectr. history Am. U., 1950; lectr. internat. law and orgn. Georgetown U., summer 1949; vis. prof. history Shephard Coll., summer 1950. Recipient Honor award Dept. Air Force, 1956. Mem. Am. Soc. Internat. Law, Am. Polit. Sci. Assn., Psi Upsilon. Author 9 books, numerous articles on internat. politics and history (under ofcl. anonymity or security restrictions), 1952-66; bibliography on enemy property control, 1943. Home: 2140 Wyoming Av NW Washington DC 20008

WILSON, J.N. (PETE), supt. schs.; b. Seagraves, Tex., Dec. 17, 1923; s. Edd S. and Ruth W.; m. Jimmie Thomas, Aug. 14, 1947; children—Cynthia (Mrs. Jack Scarborough), Cathy Sue. Prin., coach high sch., Avoca, Tex., 1948-53; bus. mgr., coach Abernathy (Tex.) pub. sch., 1953-62; supt. schs., Petersburg, Tex., 1962-—. Pres. Colokan, Inc., Ulysses, Kan., 1966-67. Served with USMCR, 1943-44. Mem. Hale County Tchrs. (pres. 1961-62), N.E.A., Tex., Am. assns. sch. adminstrs., Tex. State Tchrs. Assn., Univ. Interscholastic League (West Tex. rep. legislative council). Mason, Lion. Home: Box 159 Petersburg TX 79250 Office: Box 160 Petersburg TX 79250

WILSON, JACK ALEXANDER, govt. ofcl.; b. Birmingham, Ala., May 24, 1924; s. Robert Elias and Zula (Alexander) W.; B.S., U. Ala., 1949; postgrad. U. Tenn., 1950-51; M.B.A., Am. U., 1964, postgrad., 1964-—; m. Leda Amick, May 28, 1955; 1 dau., Joan Amick. Salesman, Addressograph-Multigraph Corp., San Francisco, 1949-50; labor economist U.S. Dept. Labor, Bur. Labor Statistics, Atlanta, 1951-53, Bur. Labor Statistics and Bur. Labor-Mgmt. Reports, Washington, 1954-60; supervisory conf. leader Carbide and Carbon Chem. Co., Oak Ridge, 1953-54; industry economist Bus. and Def. Services Adminstrn., U.S. Dept. Commerce, Washington, 1960-65; research asso. Office of Edn., U.S. Dept. Health, Edn. and Welfare, Washington, 1965-—. Lectr. U. Md., College Park, 1967-68, 70-—. Served with AUS, 1943-46; capt. Res. Mem. Am. Econ. Assn., Am. Marketing Assn. (treas. chpt. 1962-63, dir. 1961-62, 63-65), Am. Vocational Assn. Unitarian. Writer various govt. reports. Home: 8511 LaVerne Dr Adelphi MD 20783 Office: 400 Maryland Av SW Washington DC 20202

WILSON, JACK COOK, physician; b. Little Rock, Nov. 10, 1937; s. Jesse Milton and Ruby Faye (Cook) W.; B.A., Hendrix Coll., 1958; B.S. (HEW-NIH fellow), U. Ark., 1961, M.D., 1963; m. Kay Eloise McSpadden, Aug. 30, 1959; children—Jesse, Matthew, Bruce. Intern, Univ., Hosp., Little Rock, 1963-64; physician Cheney, Snow, Wilson, Kerr Clinic, Mountain Home, Ark., 1966-—; chief staff Baxter Gen. Hosp., Mountain Home, 1967-69, dir. labs., 1969-—, bd. dirs., 1967-69. Pres., Pradco, Inc., Mountain Home, 1968-—. Chmn. Baxter County Adv. Health Council, 1968-70, mem., 1971-—; coroner Baxter County, 1971-—. Served with USAF, 1964-66. Mem. Baxter County Med. Soc. (pres., 1967), Ark. Med. Soc. (del. 1971), A.M.A., Am. Acad. Gen. Practice, Alpha Omega Alpha. Rotarian. Home: 910 Russell St Mountain Home AR 72653 Office: 353 E 8th St Mountain Home AR 72653

WILSON, JAMES ROBERT, nitrogen co. exec.; b. Tremont, Miss., Aug. 26, 1932; s. James Gordy and Eva D. (Ledbetter) W.; M.E., Internat. Corr. Schs., 1964; m. Floyce B. Barnett, Mar. 1, 1952; children— Deborah S., James L., Michael S. Trainee, operator Am. Cyanamid Co., New Orleans, 1954-56, product supr., 1956-59, start-up supr. engring. constrn. div., 1959-60; prodn. supr. Am. Cyanamid, 1960-66; product supr. First Nitrogen Corp. (merger CF Industries, Inc.) New Orleans, 1966, supr., safety dir., 1966-69, operations supt., safety dir., Donaldsonville, La., 1969-—; owner, mgr. Wilson's, Inc., Donaldsville and Gonzales, La., 1967-—. Chmn., St. Charles Parish Republican Orgn., 1965. Mem. Nat. Safety Council (exec. com. fertilizer sect.), La. Loss Prevention Assn., Donaldsonville C. of C. Baptist. Mason (Shriner), Rotarian. Club: Riverdale Golf (Donaldsville). Home: 10336 Oliphant Rd Baton Rouge LA 70809 Office: PO Box 468 Donaldsonville LA 70346 also 100 S Wacker Av Chicago IL 60606

WILSON, JAMES WEBER, govt. ofcl.; b. Portland, Ore., Mar. 17, 1912; s. Harry Lewis and Irene (Weber) W.; B.S. in Naval Sci., Wash., 1934, M.B.A. in Marketing and Mgmt., 1952; m. Lucille Deborah Sprague, July 25, 1936; children—Julia Ann (Mrs. William C. Collins), Henry Weber, Harry Sprague. Salesman, Wason Bros. Coffee Co., Seattle, 1935-40; various sales and mgmt. positions, Seattle, 1946-53; asst. prof. marketing U. B.C. (Can.), Vancouver, 1953-58; asso. prof. marketing and bus. adminstrn. Am. U., Washington, 1958-59; bus. analyst Office Mgmt. and Research Assistance, Research Studies div. Small Bus. Adminstrn., Washington, 1959-61; asso. professorial lectr. bus. adminstrn. and marketing George Washington U., Washington, 1959-63, sr. scientist Mgmt. Research Group, 1961-63; trade specialist indsl. devel. br. Bur. Indian Affairs. U.S. Dept. Interior, Washington, 1963-—. Chmn. com. unemployed employables Community Chest, Vancouver, 1956-57. Served with USNR, 1940-45; PTO; now capt. Res. ret. Mem. Interagy. Craft Com., Am. Marketing Assn. (pres. Vancouver 1954), Am. Statis. Assn., Res. Officers Assn., Naval Res. Assn. (nat. pub. information officer 1962), S.A.R., Theta Delta Chi. Home: 5110 Baltimore Av Washington DC 20016 Office: Bur Indian Affairs 1951 Constitution Av Washington DC 20242

WILSON, JAMES WOODFIN, JR., physician; b. Haughton, La., Oct. 28, 1923; s. James Woodfin and Anna Kathleen (Harp) W.; M.D., La. State U., 1948; m. Evoria Anne Dier, June 6, 1954; children—James Woodfin III, Paul Stuart, Roxanne, Barry, Mary Kathleen. Intern Charity Hosp., New Orleans, 1948-49; ships surgeon Alcoa Shipping Co., Miss. Shipping Co., 1949-50; resident internal medicine Confederate Meml. Med. Center, Shreveport, La., 1953-54, chief resident, 1955-56; resident pulmonary disease Essex County Sanitarium, Verona, N.J., 1954-55; practice medicine specializing in internal medicine, Shreveport, 1956-—; chief medicine Schumpert Meml. Hosp., 1971-72; instr. medicine Northwestern Sch. Nursing, 1956-60; clin. asst. prof. medicine La. State U. Med. Sch., Shreveport, 1967-—. Pres., Caddo Heart Council, 1969-70, 70-71, La. Heart Assn., 1970-71. Served to capt. AUS, 1951-52. Fellow A.C.P., Am. Coll. Chest Physicians; mem. Am. Legion, A.M.A., La., (v.p. 1968-71), So. med. socs. Club: Country (Shreveport). Editor: Shreveport Med. Bull., 1960-62. Contbr. articles to profl. jours. Home: 10501 Ellerbe St Shreveport LA 71106 Office: 925 Olive St Shreveport LA 71104

WILSON, JERRY LEE, research engr.; b. Hope, Ark., June 20, 1939; s. Autrey U. and Cornelia (Lewallen) W.; student So. State Coll., 1957-59; B.S., U. Ark., 1961; postgrad. Mass. Inst. Tech., 1964, U. Ariz., 1968; m. Emily Naron, June 5, 1960; children—David Allen, Mark Andrew. Mech. engr. Little Rock C.E., 1961-63; research engr. U.S. Army Mobility Equipment Research & Devel. Center, Ft. Belvoir, Va., 1963-—. Served with AUS, 1957-63. Mem. Am. Soc. Heating, Refrigeration and Air Conditioning Engrs. (asso.), Sci. Research Soc. Home: 5424 Gainsborough Dr Fairfax VA 22030 Office: US Army Mobility Equipment Research and Devel Center Ft Belvoir VA 22060

WILSON, JOHN HUMAN, II, oil co.exec.; b. Denver, Oct. 4, 1927; s. John Human and Harriette Evarista (Fromhart) W.; Petroleum Refining Engr., Colo. Sch. Mines, 1948; m. Mary Florence Ryan, Nov. 28, 1951; children—Mary Catherine, John Human III, James Ryan, Christopher Michael Thomas. Petroleum engr. Fred M. Manning, Inc., Denver, 1948-50; v.p., chief engr. Wilson Exploration Co., Ft. Worth, 1954-—; v.p., dir. Piper Petroleum Co., Ft. Worth, 1956-—. Served with AUS, 1950-53. Registered profl. engr, Tex. Mem. Am. Inst. Mining Engrs., Soc. Exploration Geophysicists, Sigma Alpha Epsilon, Theta Tau. Clubs: Ft. Worth, River Crest Country. Home: 1515 Thomas Pl Fort Worth TX 76107 Office: 1212 W El Paso St Fort Worth TX 76102

WILSON, JOHN JEFF, oil co. exec.; b. Belton, Tex., July 31, 1917; s. Frank William and Edna Alice (Bassel) W.; B.B.A., U. Tex., 1944; postgrad. Tex. Christian U., 1945-46; m. Gayle Roberts, Sept. 17, 1949; children—Wesley, Jeffrey. Accountant, McCammon, Morris, Pickens & Mayhew, Fort Worth, 1945-48; auditor Davidson Drilling Co. and Cascade Petroleum Co., Fort Worth, 1948-61, Davidson Bros. Co., Inc., 1961-71, C.J. Davidson, 1971-—. Instr. accounting Tex. Christian U. Evening Coll., Fort Worth, 1947-48. Precinct chmn. Tarrant County Republican party, 1968-—, del. Tex. Rep. Conv., 1969. Sec., Davidson Family Charitable Found., 1961-—. Chmn. trustees Mary Hardin-Baylor Coll., Belton, Tex., 1968-—. C.P.A., Tex. Mem. Tex. Soc. C.P.A.'s (dir.), Fort Worth Petroleum Soc., Petroleum Accountants Soc., Am. Inst. C.P.A.'s. Baptist (deacon). Home: Route 9 Box 101-A Fort Worth TX 76179 Office: Continental Life Bldg Fort Worth TX 76102

WILSON, JOHN OLIVER, govt. ofcl.; b. St. James, Mo., May 22, 1938; s. John Riffie and Jacquetta (Link) W.; B.A., Northwestern U., 1960; Ph.D. (Rockham Grad. sch. fellow, Ford Found. fellow), U. Mich., 1967; m. Beclee Newcomer, Jan. 26, 1961; children—Beth Anne, Benjamin Duncan. With operations research dept. United Air Lines, Chgo., 1958; staff mem. Met. Planning Commn., Washtenaw County, Mich., 1964, Inst. Pub. Adminstrn., U. Mich., 1966; asst. prof. econs. Yale, 1968-—; dir. Office Planning, Research and Evaluation, Office Econ. Opportunity, Washington, 1969-—. Cons. Midwest Research Inst., Kansas City, 1964-69; dir. Mo. State Tax Study, 1967; cons. Met. Planning Commn., Kansas City Region, 1968; acad. dir. Urban Fellows Program, 1969. Served to lt., USNR, 1960-63. Mem. Am. Econ. Assn. Author: Capital Budgeting and Resource Allocation in Metropolitan Areas, 1967. Home: 1715 Oak Lane Dr McLean VA 22101 Office: 1200 19th St NW Washington DC 20506

WILSON, KEMMONS, realtor and motel co. exec.; b. Osceola, Ark., Jan. 5, 1913; s. Charles and Ruby L. (Hall) W.; grad. high sch.; m. Dorothy Lee, Dec. 2, 1941; children—Spence, Robert, Charles Kemmons, Carol, Betty. Pres., Kemmons Wilson, Inc., residential and comml. constrn., Memphis, 1945-—, Kemmons Wilson Realty Co., Memphis, 1946-—; chmn. bd. Holiday Inns, Inc., 1952-—; vice chmn. Alodex Corp.; dir. Winrock Enterprises. Vice chmn. Medicenters of Am., Inc. Bd. dirs. Memphis State U. Served as flight officer with Air Transport Command, 1942-45. Mem. Chief Execs. Forum, Sportsman Pilots Assn., Home Builders Assn. Memphis (past pres.), Real Estate Bd. Memphis. Methodist (bd. stewards). Mason (Shriner, Jester). Home: 3615 S Galloway Dr Memphis TN 38111 Office: 3742 Lamar Av Memphis TN 38118

WILSON, LEON LANDON, ednl. adminstr.; b. Leslie, Ark., June 15, 1936; s. Zora and Frances Biryal (Matheny) W.; B.S., Memphis State U., 1959, M.A., 1962; Ed.D., U. Ark., 1969; m. Edna M. Jennings, Sept. 3, 1955; children—Ravonda Kay, Kermie Lynn, Ivan Leon, Kenda Beth. Tchr., Marshall (Ark.) Sch. Dist., 1957-59, prin., 1959-62; supt. Leslie (Ark.) Sch. Dist., 1962-65; dir. Ark. Dept. Edn., Little Rock, 1965-69; exec. dir. Central Ark. Ednl. Center, Little Rock, 1969-—. Vis. prof. State Coll. Ark., Conway, 1970-—; cons. Ark. Dept. Edn., 1969-—. Mem. N.E.A., Ark. Edn. Assn., Am. Assn. Sch. Adminstrs., Ark. Sch. Adminstrs. Assn., Phi Delta Kappa. Baptist. Club: Civitan (Little Rock). Contbr. articles to profl. jours Home: 805 N Mellon Little Rock AR 72205 Office: W Markham and Izard Little Rock AR 72201

WILSON, LEONARD WILLIAM, JR., mobile home mfg. co. exec.; b. Clarendon, Tex., Nov. 28, 1925; s. Leonard W. and Vera Gertrude (March) W.; student So. Meth. U., 1947; m. Barbara Edith Young, July 17, 1946; children—Linda (Mrs. Robert Walker), Leonard Gregory. Mgr., Wilson-Young Lumber, Spur, Tex., 1947-49; regional mgr. Chambers, Inc., lumber, Hobbs, N.M., 1949-51; pres. Mathis-Wilson, Inc., gen. contractors, Lubbock, Tex., 1953-60; sec.-treas. Wilson & Wilson, Inc., Lubbock, 1962-—; pres., chmn. bd. Castle Industries, Inc., Lubbock, 1968-—, also dir. Rancher, Red River County, Tex., 1965; owner Carriage House Motel, 1970. Served with USNR, 1943-45. Mem. C. of C. Democrat. Baptist. Mason. Clubs: Lubbock Country, Knife & Fork (Lubbock). Home: 4513 9th St Lubbock TX 79416 Office: 5208 34th St Lubbock TX 79407

WILSON, LYLE LAWRENCE, metal bldg. co. exec.; b. Gillette, Wyo., May 6, 1928; s. Robert Walter and Maude (Shannon) W.; B.S. in Civil Engring., U. Wyo., 1950; M.S. in Civil Engring., Ga. Inst. Tech., 1958; m. Patricia Anne Chittim, Dec. 24, 1948; 1 dau., Shannon Tracey. Design engr. Arctic Contractors, Fairbanks, Point Barrow, Alaska, 1950-52; univ. engr. U. Alaska, College, 1952-54; mem. engring., research, operations and corporate staff Humble Oil & Refining Co., New Orleans, 1957-66; v.p. engring. Am. Bldgs. Co., Eufaula, Ala., 1966-—, also dir.; dir. U.S. Golf Co., Eufaula, Viking Hydraulics Inc., Eufaula. Mem. adv. com. Chauncy Parks State Trade Sch. Served to 1st lt. USAF, 1954-56. Recipient M.A. Ferst Sigma Xi Grad. Research award for outstanding research Ga. Inst. Tech., 1958. Registered profl. engr., La., Ark., Miss., Tex., Ala. Mem. Am. Soc. C.E., Tex. Soc. Profl. Engrs., Am. Inst. Steel Constrn. (S.E. regional adv. com., joint research com. on bolted connections with Metal Bldg. Mfrs. Assn.), Metal Bldg. Mfrs. Assn. (chmn. tech. com.), Sigma Xi, Sigma Phi Epsilon. Republican. Methodist. Lion, Kiwanian. Home: Fox Ridge Rd Eufala AL 36027 Office: PO Drawer A Eufaula AL 36027

WILSON, MARGARET LOUISE BROWN (MRS. JAMES ATCHERSON WILSON, JR.), ret. librarian; b. Muskogee, Okla., Oct. 26, 1899; d. Jacob Brookfield and Margaret (Peyton) Brown; grad. State Normal Sch., Bloomsburg, Pa., 1916-18; B.A., George Washington U., 1927, B.A. in L.S., 1933; m. James Atcherson Wilson, Jr., Aug. 21, 1934; children—James Atcherson III, Margaret Brown. Clk.-typist Office Surgeon Gen., War Dept., Washington, 1918-19; sec. The Come-Back, newspaper, Washington, 1919-21; sec. to U.S. Rep. Benjamin L. Fairchild, from N.Y., Washington, 1922-24, 25-27; sec. A.I.A., Washington, 1924-25; sec., office mgr. Am. Home Econs. Assn., Washington, 1927-36; librarian div. pub. documents U.S. Govt. Printing Office, Washington, 1939-69, chief of library, 1965-69. Mem. George Washington U. Library Sch. Alumni Assn. (v.p. 1936, sec. 1962). Episcopalian. Home: RFD 1 Box 81-B Ashland VA 23005

WILSON, MILLARD FILLMORE, educator; b. Sanderson, Fla., Oct. 16, 1911; s. George Washington and Martha Christopher (Houston) W.; B.E., U. Fla., 1939, M.Ed., 1940; postgrad. Duke, 1941; m. Sigrid Claire Devoire, Dec. 2, 1936. Instr. Andrew Jackson Sch., Jacksonville, Fla., 1940-44, dean of men, 1944-48; asso. prof. commerce Catawba Coll., Salisbury, N.C., 1948-—, dir. placement office, 1948-—, chmn. dept. commerce, 1950. Pres. Rowan County Inter-Civic Council; vice chmn. Rowan County Youth Comm., Rowan County Youth Bd.; mem. nat. speakers bur. Boy Scouts Am., vice chmn. Rowan County council. Named Rowan County Man of Year, 1967. Mem. Am. Acad. Polit. and Social Sci., So. Econ. Assn., Adminstrv. Mgmt. Soc. (pres.), Sales-Marketing Execs. Club (exec. Salisbury), Am. Accounting Assn., Soc. Advt. Mgmt., Acad. Mgmt., Am. Marketing Assn., N.C., Bus. Edn. Council, Internat. Platform Assn., Acad. Certified Adminstrv. Mgrs., Kappa Delta Pi. Christian Scientist. Mason (K.T., Shriner), Lion (pres. Salisbury, zone chmn., dist. gov., internat. counselor). Club: Salisbury Country (dir.). Address: Catawba Coll Salisbury NC 28144

WILSON, NATHAN EDWARD, dentist; b. Elys, Ky., May 5, 1933; s. Edgar and Carrie (Centers) W.; D.D.S., U. Tenn., 1956; m. Bettye Grace Brown, June 21, 1953; children—Nathan Edward, Cindy Elizabeth, Gwynneth Grace, Kevin Warren. Pvt. practice dentistry, Oak Ridge, 1958-—; treas. Lambuth Div. Corp., Oak Ridge, 1972-—. Vice-pres. Oak Ridge High Sch. Band Parents Assn., 1972; exec. council Oak Ridge High Sch. P.T.A. Served with USNR, 1956-58; now comdr. Res. Mem. Am., Tenn. dental assns., Am. Soc. Dentistry for Children, 2d Dist Dental Soc. (exec. council 1972-—), Naval Res. Officers Assn. Methodist. (Sunday sch. tchr. 1972-—). Club: Oak Ridge Country. Home: 100 Oklahoma Av Oak Ridge TN 37830

WILSON, OSCAR MAX, edn. exec.; b. Centre, Ala., Dec. 23, 1932; s. Oscar B. and Jeanette (Coursey) W.; B.S. (Sears Roebuck Found. scholar), Auburn U., 1953; postgrad. George Peabody Coll., 1958; M.S. (NSF fellow), U. Va., 1959; m. Julia Nadine Johnson, Oct. 17, 1954; children—Kathy J., Keith M., Knox C. Tchr. sci. Rome City (Ga.) Schs., 1955-58, sci. coordinator, 1959-60; tchr. sci. TV Ga. Dept. Edn., Atlanta, 1960-64, ednl. TV utilization specialist, 1964-65, adminstr. of utilization, 1965-69, dir. instructional TV, 1970-—; dir. Project VIDAC, 1972-—; pres. Cableways, Inc., Rossville, Ga., 1965. State chmn. instructional TV fixed service com. FCC, 1969-—. Pres. Nat. Council Individual Excellence. Served with AUS, 1953-55. Mem. Nat. Assn. Ednl. Broadcasters (chmn. utilization sect. 1968-70), N.E.A., Ga. Edn. Assn., Nat. Sci. Tchrs. Assn., Ga. Acad. Sci., So. Ednl. Communications Assn. (chmn. instruction div. 1969-71), Ga. Ednl. Media Assn. (dir.), Cedar Bluff High Sch. Alumni Assn. (pres. 1966-67). Methodist (chmn. council on ministries). Mason. Home: 7 Robin St Rome GA 30316 Office: 1540 Stewart Av SW Atlanta GA 30310

WILSON, OWEN DUNCAN, lawyer; b. Enid, Okla., Feb. 8, 1937; s. Rolland O. and Gladys (Kent) W.; B.A., U. Okla., 1959, LL.B., 1961; m. Mary Elizabeth Donnell, Aug. 23, 1958; children—Philip Owen, Angela Christine. Admitted to Okla. bar, 1961; mem. firm Wilson & Wilson, Enid, 1963-—; pres., dir. Wilson Royalty Co., 1963-—. Atty. Enid Sch. Bd., 1970-—. Served to capt. AUS, 1961-63. Mem. Am., Okla., Garfield County (sec. 1964) bar assns., Sons and Daus. Cherokee Strip Pioneers (pres. 1969), Beta Theta Pi. Methodist. Lion. Home: 1931 Huron St Enid OK 73701 Office: 217 N Independence Enid OK 73701

WILSON, PATRICK JAMES, lawyer; b. Idaho Falls, Ida., Nov. 22, 1923; s. Richard Sheridan and Margaret (Hart) W.; student U. Ida., 1941-43; B.S. cum laude, U. Notre Dame, 1947; LL.B., Georgetown U., 1950; m. Adriana Mercado, June 19, 1949; children—Maria Luisa, Margarita Maria, Richard S. Admitted to P.R. bar, 1950, D.C. bar, 1950; law clk. Supreme Ct. of P.R., San Juan, 1950; practiced in Washington, 1951-54, 59-—; asso. firm Ginsberg, Leventhal and Brown, 1951-54; resident partner firm Gadsby & Hannah, P.R., 1959-71; partner Firm O'Neill & Borges, Hato Rey, P.R., 1971-—; exec. Mario Mercado e Hijos, Ponce, P.R., 1954-59. Founding dir. Ponce Fed. Savings & Loan Co. (P.R.). Mem. bd. examiners P.R. bar exam. com. Supreme Ct. of P.R., 1964-65. Served with USMCR, 1942-46. Republican. Roman Catholic. Home: Condominium San Geronimo 860 Ashford Av Santurce PR 00907 Office: Chase Manhattan Bank Bldg Hato Rey PR 00918

WILSON, PRINCE E., univ. admistr.; b. Asheville, N.C., Oct. 22, 1918; s. Isaac N. and Edna (Goins) W.; A.B., Talladega Coll., 1939; A.M., U. Chgo., 1942, Ph.D., 1954; m. Veola Kittles, Aug. 19, 1956; children—Kristal, Sherrill. Tchr., Asheville (N.C.) City Schs., 1939-42, Bennett Coll., Greensboro, N.C., 1943-45; faculty Morris Brown Coll., Atlanta, 1945-62, acad. dean, 1957-62; faculty Central State U., Wilberforce, O., 1962-66, grad. dean, 1963-66; exec. sec. Atlanta U. Center, Inc., 1966-—. Tchr. Tex. So. U., Houston, 1954, 55, So. U., Baton Rouge, 1956, U. Redlands (Cal.), summers 1965-68. Cons., U.S. Commn. on Civil Rights, 1962, Ford Found. sponsored study Tuskegee Inst., Mem. N.A.A.C.P.; mem. citizens adv. com. on Urban Devel. Trustee, United Bd. for Coll. Devel.; bd. dirs. Central Atlanta Progress. Mem. Assn. for Study of Negro Life and History (exec. com. 1963-—), Alpha Phi Alpha. Contbr. articles on Black history. Home: 3343 Cedar Island Dr SW Atlanta GA 30311 Office: 55 Walnut St Atlanta GA 30314

WILSON, R. BAXTER, utilities exec.; b. Yazoo City, Miss., Dec. 11, 1905; s. Richard Baxter and Jennie (Bowman) W.; B.S., U. Miss., 1927; m. Katherine Owen, Sept. 25, 1930; children—Richard Baxter, Miriam (Mrs. Sam D. Knowlton). With Miss. Power & Light Co., Jackson, Miss., 1926-—, beginning as mgr., Edwards, Miss., successively mgr., Cleve., div. mgr., asst. operating mgr., Jackson, asst. gen. mgr., v.p. 1946-54, pres., 1954-—, also dir.; v.p. Middle South Utilities, Inc.; dir., past pres. So. Electric Exchange; dir. Standard Life Ins. Co., Southeastern Electric Exchange, Deposit Guaranty Bank & Trust Co., Magna Am. Corp. Past chmn. Jackson Airport Authority; chmn. Planning Bd. Jackson, past pres., exec. bd. Andrew Jackson council Boy Scouts Am. Trustee So. Research Inst. Birmingham, Miss., Belhaven Coll., Jackson. Named Engr. of Yr. Miss., 1960; recipient 1st Fed. Found. award U. Miss., 1963; Silver Beaver award Boy Scouts Am. Mem. Edison Electric Inst., C. of C. (past pres.), Ole Miss. Alumni Assn. (past pres.), I.E.E.E., Am. Soc. M.E., Miss. Soc. Profl. Engrs., Nat. Assn. Electric Companies, Newcomen Soc. Presbyn. (deacon). Mason (Shriner). Clubs: Boston (New Orleans); Jackson Co., Rotary (past pres.), Capital City Petroleum (Jackson); Metropolitan (N.Y.C.). Home: 3644 Old Canton Rd Jackson MS 39205 Office: Miss Power and Light Co Electric Bldg Jackson MS 39205

WILSON, RAY FLOYD, educator; b. Giddings, Tex., Feb. 20, 1926; s. Fred and Beulah (McCloud) W.; B.S. cum laude, Houston-Tillotson Coll., 1950; M.S., Tex. So. U., 1951, J.D. magna cum laude, 1972; Ph.D., U. Tex., 1953; m. Ruby J. Terry, Nov. 11, 1957 (div.); children—Ray Floyd II, Freddy O., Roy A., Mercedes L. Asso. prof. chemistry Tex. So. U., Houston, 1953-57, prof., 1957-—. Served with USNR, 1944-46. Mem. Am. Chem. Soc., N.Y., Tex. acads. sci., Am. Inst. Chemists, Sigma Xi, Phi Lambda Upsilon, Beta Kappa Chi. Conglist (trustee). Contbr. articles to profl. jours. Home: 3502 Arbor Rd Houston TX 77004 Office: 3201 Wheeler St Houston TX 77004

WILSON, RAYMOND HIRAM, JR., astronomer, govt. ofcl.; b. Gap, Pa., Feb. 14, 1911; s. Raymond Hiram and Agnes (Wright) W.; A.B., Swarthmore Coll., 1931; A.M., U. Pa., 1933, Ph.D., 1935, postgrad. 1950-51, Harvard, summer 1937; m. Irene Gladys Louise Hansing, Aug. 21, 1940; 1 dau., Kristin Marie. Research asso., instr. math. and astronomy at various colls., 1929-40; astronomer, Naval Obs., 1940-42, prin. investigator contracts Office Naval Research, 1949-52; asst. prof. math. and astronomy, also cons. to research inst., Temple U., 1946-51; asst. prof. math. U. Louisville, 1951-54; physicist Naval Research Lab. and Project Vanguard, 1954-58; applied mathematician Goddard Space Flight Center and chief applied math. br., NASA, Washington, 1958-—; profl. lectr. in astronomy Georgetown U., Grad. Sch., 1962-—. Liaison com. mem. div. math. Nat. Acad. Sci. Served to comdr. USNR, 1942-46. Recipient incentive award for patent application, NASA, 1963. Fellow A.A.A.S., Am. Inst. Aeros. and Astronautics; mem. Am. Astron. Soc., Math. Assn. Am., Soc. Indsl. and Applied Math., Rittenhouse Astron. Soc. (pres. 1949), Officers Open Mess, Bolling AFB, Sigma Xi, Sigma Pi Sigma. Episcopalian. Contbr. articles to profl. jours. Patentee in field. Home: 3937 First St SW Washington DC 20032 Office: Code 554 NASA-Goddard Space Flight Center Greenbelt MD 20771

WILSON, RICHARD CARLTON, educator; b. Greenville, N.C., Oct. 13, 1924; s. Richard Clayton and Myrtle (House) W.; student N.Y.U., 1943-44; B.S., East Carolina Coll., 1948; M.A., U. N.C., 1951, Ph.D., 1958; m. Peggy Ann Tucker, Aug. 24, 1952; children—Richard Carlton, Sherrie Tucker. Tchr. elementary and secondary schs., N.C., 1948-53; elementary sch. prin., Rocky Mount, N.C., 1953-57; asso. prof. Fla. State U., 1958-68; prof., dir. reading U. West Fla., Pensacola, 1968-—. Cons. reading and curriculum, 1958-—. Served with AUS, 1943-46. Mem. Fla Reading Council (life, pres.), Nat. Council Tchrs. English, Internat. Fla., Leon (pres. 1966-67) reading assns. Clubs: Scenic Hills Country, Current Topics Rocky Mount (pres. 1956). Author: Individualized Reading-A Practical Approach, 1965; Viewpoints for the Reading Teacher. Editor: Fla. Reading Quar., 1967-71. Contbr. articles to profl. jours. Home: 8901 Scenic Hills Dr Pensacola FL 32504

WILSON, RICHARD LEE, assn. exec., economist; b. Dayton, O., June 29, 1940; s. Roscoe Charles and Elizabeth Lewis (Robinson) W.; B.A., U. Md., 1963; M.B.A., U. Mo., 1967; m. Sue Ellen Hemphill, July 23, 1967; children—Charles Andrew, Michael McCall. Mgr. research dept. Louisville Area C. of C., 1970-—. Served to capt. USAF, 1963-70. Mem. Am. C. of C. Researchers Assn., Am., Ky. chamber commerce execs. assns., Kappa Alpha. Editor: Louisville Area Manufacturers Directory, 1971, 72, Directory Louisville Area Manufacturers Agents, 1971, Louisville Area Shopping Center Directory, 1972, Metropolitan Louisville Market Data, 1972. Home: 7415 Woodhill Valley Rd Louisville KY 40222 Office: 300 W Liberty St Louisville KY 40202

WILSON, ROBERT E. LEE, III, farmer, mayor; b. Memphis, July 27, 1913; s. Robert E. Lee and Natalie (Armstrong) W.; A.B., Yale, 1936; m. Mildred Martin, Dec. 31, 1962; children—Michael, Stephen, Robert, Frank, Diana, Midlred. Pres., Lee Wilson Co., Wilson, Ark., 1950-—, Delta Valley and So. Ry., 1951-—; chmn. bd. Bank of Wilson, 1960-—; mayor City of Wilson, 1950-—; dir. Ark. Power & Light Co., Middle South Utilities, Inc. Justice of peace, Wilson, 1950-—; drainage commr. Mississippi County, Ark., 1952-—. Trustee, U. Ark.; trustee 3 estates for ednl. purposes. Served to capt. AUS, 1941-45. Decorated Bronze Star with two oak leaf clusters. Club: Memphis Country. Home: Wilson AR 72395 Office: Lee Wilson & Co Hwy 61 Wilson AR 72395

WILSON, ROBERT NEAL, educator; b. Syracuse, N.Y., Nov. 15, 1924; s. Robert Marchant and May Eloise (Neal) W.; B.A., Union Coll., 1948; student The Citadel, 1943-44, Trinity Hall, Cambridge, 1945-46; Ph.D., Harvard, 1952; children—Lynda (Mrs. Thomas Twele), Deborah. Research asso. Cornell U., Ithaca, N.Y., 1951-53; mem. staff Social Sci. Research Council, Washington, 1953-56; fellow Center for Advanced Study in Behavioral Scis., Stanford, Cal., 1956-57; lectr. Harvard, 1957-60; asso. prof. Yale, 1960-63; prof., chmn. dept. mental health, Sch. Pub. Health, prof. sociology U. N.C., Chapel Hill, 1963-—. Cons. Nat. Inst. Mental Health, Nat. Inst. Child Health and Human Devel., U.S. Office Edn. Trustee, Easter Seal Research Found. Served with AUS, 1943-46. Fellow Am. Sociological Assn., Am. Pub. Health Assn.; mem. Phi Beta Kappa, Delta Omega. Author: (with Temple Burling and Edith M. Lentz) The Give and Take in Hospitals, 1956, Man Made Plain, 1957, Community Structure and Health Action, 1967, The Sociology of Health, 1970. Editor, contbg. author The Arts in Society, 1964. Editor: (with John A. Clausen and Alexander H. Leighton) Explorations in Social Psychiatry, 1957. Home: 10 Fidelity Ct Carrboro NC 27510

WILSON, ROBERT WAYNE, clergyman; b. San Antonio, Oct. 23, 1932; s. Finis Alexander and Willie Faye (Guthrie) W.; ed. Assumption Sem., San Antonio, 1957; M.S. in Psychology, St. John's U., 1964; postgrad. N.Y.U., 1964-—. Joined Diocese Dallas-Ft. Worth, 1950, ordained priest Roman Cath. Ch., 1957; dean students U. Dallas, 1961-64; dir. vocations Cath. Diocese of Dallas-Ft. Worth, 1964-67; pastor St. Rita's Ch., Ranger, Tex., 1967-70, St. John the Apostle Ch., Ft. Worth, 1970-—; supt. schs. Catholic Diocese of Ft. Worth, 1970-—, pres. senate of priests, 1970-—. Pres. senate of priests Diocese of Dallas-Ft. Worth, 1969-70; chmn. Provincial Conf. Priests' Councils, Province of San Antonio, 1971-72. Mem. Am. Psychol. Assn., Nat. Cath. Edn. Assn. (parliamentarian supt.'s dept. 1970-72). K.C. Club: Glen Lakes Country (Dallas). Author: Book of Liturgical Ceremonies, 1956. Contbr. articles to religious publs. Home: 4608 Vance St Fort Worth TX 76118 Office: PO Box 13186 Fort Worth TX 76118

WILSON, ROLLAND OWEN, lawyer, business exec.; b. Mattoon, Ill., Jan. 25, 1903; s. George Duncan and Helen Maud (Bresee) W.; A.B., Phillips U., 1924; J.D., U. Mich., 1927; m. Gladys Helen Kent, Aug. 3, 1935; 1 stepdau., Helen Lorene (Mrs. Helen Wells Barnes); 1 son, Owen Duncan. Admitted to Okla. bar, 1927, U.S. Supreme Ct. Bar, U.S. Dist. Ct. West Dist. Okla., U.S. Ct. Appeals 10th Circuit; mem. firm Wilson & Wilson, Enid, Okla., 1927-—; atty. in charge legal div. Okla. Dept. Pub. Safety, 1937-38; appellate atty. State Ins. Fund, 1938-39; U.S. naturalization examiner U.S. Dept. Labor, St. Louis, 1939-40, U.S. Dept. Justice, 1940-41; sec.-treas., dir. Wilson Royalty Co., 1928-—. Atty., Enid Sch. Bd., 1963-—. Fellow Am. Coll. Probate Counsel; mem. Am., Okla., Garfield County (pres. 1957-58) bar assns. Presbyn. (elder).Home: 1825 Indian Dr Enid OK 73701 Office: 217 N Independence St Enid OK 73701

WILSON, SAMUEL, JR., architect; b. New Orleans, Aug. 6, 1911; s. Samuel and Stella (Poupeney) W.; B.Arch., Tulane U., 1931; m. Ellen Elizabeth Latrobe, Oct. 20, 1951. Architect office Moise H. Goldstein, 1930-33, Historic Am. Bldgs. Survey in La., 1934-35; architect office Richard Koch, 1935-42, asso., 1945-55, partner Richard Koch & Samuel Wilson, Jr., New Orleans, 1955-—. Lectr. La. architecture Tulane U. mem. exec. bd. New Orleans area council Boy Scouts Am.; mem. bd. Friends of Cabilde, Maison Hospitaliere; mem. Orleans Parish Landmarks Commn., La. Hist. Preservation and Cultural Commn., 1968-71. Served with USCGR, 1942-45. Edward Langley scholar A.I.A., 1938. Fellow A.I.A.; mem. Soc. Archtl. Historians, La. Landmarks Soc. (pres. 1950-56), Christian Women's Exchange (hon.). Roman Catholic. Club: Boston (New Orleans). Author: A Guide to Architecture of New Orleans, 1699-1959; Plantation Houses on The Battlefield of New Orleans, 1965; The Vieux Carre New Orleans, 1969; Bienvilles New Orleans; co-author Baroness Pontalba's Buildings, 1964; The Basilica on Jackson Square, 1965; The St. Louis Cemeteries of New Orleans, 1963; The Cabildo on Jackson Square, 1970; New Orleans Architecture—Lower Garden District, Vol. I. Editor: Impressions Respecting New Orleans (B. H. B. Latrobe), 1951. Contbr. articles to profl. and hist. publs. Home: 1121 Washington Av New Orleans LA 70130 Office: Masonic Temple Bldg New Orleans LA 70130

WILSON, STAN EUGENE, broadcasting exec.; b. Lovilia, Ia., Jan. 26, 1916; s. Frank Martin and Lucy (Clark) W.; B.S., Tex. Christian U., 1940; m. Christine Smith, Aug. 31, 1940; children—Carole Kay (Mrs. Al Pugsley, Jr.), Lucy Lynn (Mrs. Harry Burr III), Cathy Christine. Sales mgr. Radio Sta. WACO, Waco, Tex., 1940-51; gen. mgr. Sta. KRIO, McAllen, Tex., 1951-53; v.p., gen. mgr. Sta. KFDA-AM-TV, Amarillo, Tex., 1953-55; v.p. Tex. State Network, Ft. Worth, 1955-65, pres., 1965-—, also dir.; dir. Radio Corpus Christi, Inc., Va. State Network, Norfolk. Instr. radio and TV dept. Tex. Christian U., Ft. Worth, 1966-67. Bd. dirs. Tarrant Co. chpt. A.R.C., Goodwill Industries, Mental Health Assn., Camp Fire Girls, Casa Manana. Served to lt. USNR, 1943-45. Recipient Betty award Assn. Broadcast Execs., 1969, Tex. Assn. Broadcasters Pioneer award, 1969. Home: 2909 Hartwood St Fort Worth TX 76109 Office: 4801 West Freeway Fort Worth TX 76101

WILSON, WILL, govt. ofcl.; b. Dallas, July 29, 1912; s. Will R. and Kate (Bransford) W.; B.S., Okla. U., 1934; LL.B., So. Meth. U., 1937; m. Marjorie Ashcroft, Nov. 1948; children—Lou Ellen Christian (stepdau.), Will R., III. Admitted to Tex. bar, 1937; trial lawyer civil law firm, Dallas, 1937-41; asst. atty. Gen. Tex., 1941-42; dist. atty., Dallas Co., 1947-50; asso. justice Supreme Ct. of Texas, 1950-56; atty. gen. Tex., 1957; asst. atty. gen. criminal div. Dept. Justice, 1969-—. Selected as one of five dist. attys. in U.S. to advise Nat. Crime Conf., Washington. Feb. 1950. Served as maj., staff 6th Army and I Corps, Australia and New Guinea; exec. officer, 126th F.A., 32nd div. Luzon, P.I.; comdg. officer, 456th F.A. Bn., A.U.S., Biak and Luzon 1943-45; accented surrender forces of Gen. Yamashita. Recipient Law Book award So. Meth. U., 1937; Wyman award Outstanding State Atty. Gen. U.S., 1960. Mem. Dist. and Co. Attys. Assn. Tex. (past pres.), Am. Legion. Vets. Fgn. Wars, 32d Div. Assn., Phi Kappa Psi. Presbyn. Clubs: Northwood Country (Dallas); Westwood Country (Austin). Home: 3207 Bowman Rd Washington DC Office: Dept of Justice Constitution Av and 10th St NW Washington DC 20580

WILSON, WILLIAM EDWARD, rural resources specialist; b. Wedowee, Ala., June 24, 1923; s. James Floyd and Mary Jim (Weathers) W.; B.S., Auburn U., 1949, M.S., 1961; m. Olive Rudine Cooper, May 15, 1946; children—Robert Cooper, Rebecca. Dept. mgr., salesman Guy Hood Feed Seed Fertilizer Co., Gadsden, Ala., 1949-51; farm supt. Ala. Baptist Childrens Home, Troy, 1951-54; asst. county agt. Auburn (Ala.) U. Co-op. Extension Service, 1954-61, specialist in rural resource devel., 1961-—. County fund drive chmn. Girl Scouts U.S.A., 1963-64; city chmn. fund drive A.R.C., 1959; organizer, v.p., dir. Clay County Arts and Crafts League, 1970-—. Bd. dirs. Tallacoosa Highland Lakes Assn., 1969-—, Clay County United Givers Fund, 1967-—; chmn. Clay County chpt. Nat. Found., 1956-—; trustee Clay County High Sch., 1961-65. Served with AUS, 1943-46. Mem. East Central Ala. Planning and Devel. Commn., Ashland Jr. C. of C. (dir., sec. 1957-58, pres., 1958-59), Community Devel. Soc. (a founder 1969), Gamma Sigma Delta, Epsilon Sigma Phi. Baptist (Sunday Sch. dir., chmn. bd. deacons 1969-71). Rotarian. Club: Clay County Country (Ashland). Address: PO Box 485 Ashland AL 36251

WILSON, WILLIAM FIGH, mfg. co. exec.; b. Mart, Tex., June 18, 1919; s. Howard Lee and Georgia Louise (Figh) W.; B.B.A., U. Tex., 1940; m. Ella Burndrett, Sept. 12, 1942; children—Fred Lee, Robert Orr. With Shell Oil Co., various locations, 1940-53, mgr. cost accounting, Houston, 1948-51, chief cost analyst, N.Y.C., 1951-53; with Tenneco Inc., various locations, 1953-—, dir. systems, Houston, 1968-69, adminstrv. v.p. Newport News Shipbuilding & Dry Dock Co. subsidiary (Va.), 1969-—; dir. 1st & Mchts. Nat. Bank, Newport News. Bd. dirs. Riverside Hosp., Newport News, 1970-—. Served with AUS, 1942-43. Mem. Sigma Iota Epsilon, Beta Alpha Phi. Methodist. Clubs: James River Country, Huntington. Home: 160 Yeardley Dr Apt 26 Newport News VA 23601 Office: 4101 Washington Av Newport News VA 23607

WILSON, WILLIS TRENT, dentist; b. Stanley, N.C., Aug. 28, 1902; s. William Henry and Sarah (Ashlin) W.; student Va. Poly. Inst., 1922-23; D.D.S., Med. Coll. Va., 1927; m. Emily Louise Lincke, Oct. 27, 1934; children—Christine Lincke (Mrs. Benjamin Bishop Johnson), Willis Trent, Maurice Lincke. Individual practice dentistry, Hopewell, Va., 1927-—. Mem. adv. bd. Hopewell br. First Mchts. Nat. Bank. Mem. Am., Southside Va. dental assns., Va., Hopewell (pres. 1960) dental socs. Moose (pres. 1958-61, mem. nat. civic affairs com. 1971-72), Kiwanian (pres. 1930). Home: 2713 Walnut St Hopewell VA 23860 Office: 201 State Planters Bldg Hopewell VA 23860

WILSON, WOODROW HOYT, wholesale co. exec.; b. Seminole, Okla., Nov. 30, 1912; s. Edward Lee and Ethel Mae (Mosier) W.; student Oklahoma City U., 1942-43; m. Lou Baney, Dec. 31, 1953; children—Dolores, Carole Sue; 1 adopted son, Jeffery. With Stevens Products Co., Oklahoma City, 1934-46; with Scrivner Boogaart, Inc., Oklahoma City, 1946-—, v.p. J.V. Smith div., 1948-—. Served with AUS, 1944-46; ETO. Mem. Okla. Shippers Assn. (v.p. 1954-—). Mem. Christian Ch. (deacon). Home: 6468 Sterling Dr Oklahoma City OK 73132 Office: 3421 N Walnut St Oklahoma City OK 73105

WILT, PAXTON MARSHALL, tobacco co. exec.; b. Flemingsburg, Ky., Sept. 21, 1908; s. William M. and Mary (Harbeson) W.; student Centre (Ky.) Coll., 1927; B.A., U. Louisville, 1930; m. Virginia Johnson, June 30, 1939; children—Paxton Marshall, Virginia Ann. With Brown and Williamson Tobacco Corp., Louisville, 1932-—, controller, 1959-64, v.p. finance, 1964-70, exec. v.p., 1970-—, also dir., mem. exec. com.; dir. Pocahontas Corp. Chmn. Louisville Manpower Commn. Mem. C. of C., Sigma Alpha Epsilon. Clubs: Hunting Creek Country (Prospect, Ky.); Pendennis (Louisville). Home: 2000 Camargo Rd Louisville KY 40207 Office: 1600 West Hill St Loisville KY 40201

WILTSE, JAMES CORNELIUS, JR., lasers and microwaves engr.; b. Tannersville, N.Y., Mar. 16, 1926; s. James Cornelius and Leah Ida (Showers) W.; B.E.E., Rensselaer Poly. Inst., 1946, M.E.E., 1952; Dr.Eng., Johns Hopkins, 1959; m. Margaret Lucille John, Jan. 27, 1950; children—Linda Margaret, Paul James. Engr., Gen. Electric Co., Schenectady, 1947, 48, 51; instr. Rensselaer Poly. Inst., 1948-51; instr. Johns Hopkins, 1953-54, research asso., 1954-58; research scientist Electronic Communications, Inc., St. Petersburg, Fla., 1959, mgr. microwaves and antennas, 1960-63, dir. advanced devel., 1963-64; prin. scientist, lab. chief Martin Marietta Corp., Orlando, Fla., 1964-68, mgr. electromagnetics dept., 1968-70, mgr. lasers and optics, 1970-72, mgr. electro-optics and microwaves, 1972-—. Instr., Naval Res. Officers Sch., 1966-69. Mem. vis. com. elec. engring. U. Fla., 1969-71; judge Fla. Sci. Fair, Miami, 1968, Winter Park, 1972. Served with USNR, 1943-47. Named Engr. of Year, Orlando div. Martin Marietta Corp., 1970, Author of Year, 1967. Mem. I.E.E.E. (Engr. of Year Orlando 1968, exec. com. Orlando sect.). Club: Bay Hill Country (Orlando). Co-author: Radar Handbook, 1970. Contbr. articles to profl. jours. Home: 8731 Bay Hill Blvd Orlando FL 32811 Office: Box 5837 MP381 Orlando FL 32805

WILWERS, EDWARD MATHIAS, educator; b. Chgo., Feb. 4, 1918; s. Michael and Hermina (Meier) W.; M.F.A., Ohio U., 1951; postgrad. U. Wis., 1958; m. Esther M. Mathiesen, May 17, 1943; children—William S., Wendy C. Accounting dept. C.M. St. Paul & P. R.R., Chgo., 1937-42, Crooks Terminal Warehouses, Chgo., 1942-43, 46-48; designer, gen. sales mgr. Hutcheson Displays, Omaha, 1952-59; advt. mgr. D & H Assos., Ogden, Utah, 1959-60; head dept. art Ark. Poly. Coll., Russellville, Ark., 1960-—. Served with AUS, 1943-46. Fellow Royal Soc. Arts; Southwestern Coll. Art Conf., Am. Assn. U. Profs. (chpt. v.p. 1966). Home: Route 4 Bayou Lane Russellville AR 72801

WIMBERLEY, NORRIS ADRON, JR., physician; b. Starkville, Miss., Mar. 27, 1925; s. Norris A. and Bula (Dalhoff) W.; M.D., Med. Coll. Ala., 1947; M.S., Temple U., 1953; m. Laura Ellen Smith, July 3, 1958; children—Patricia, Vicki, Janet, Norris Adron III, Smith. Intern, Walter Reed Hosp., Washington, 1947, resident, 1948-49;

resident Temple U. Hosp., Phila., 1951-53; practice medicine, specializing in internal medicine, Tyler, Tex., 1953—; asso. prof. mil. sci. and tactics in medicine Temple U., 1951-53; pres. med. staff Med. Center Hosp., Tyler, 1971. Pres. Smith County chpt. Am. Cancer Soc., 1967. Served with M.C., AUS, 1947-53. Diplomate Am. Bd. Internal Medicine. Fellow A.C.P.; mem. Tex. Acad. Internal Medicine, Pi Kappa Alpha, Phi Chi. Methodist. Home: 3711 Bain Circle Tyler TX 75701 Office: 1001 S Fleishel St Tyler TX 75701

WIMBERLY, HARRINGTON, newspaper publisher; b. Hale Center, Tex., June 22, 1901; s. Joe Ed and Margaret (Wilson) W.; A.B., U. Okla., 1924; m. Myrth McCurley, Apr. 22, 1927; children—Janis Myrth, Mary Margaret. Editor, Altus (Okla.) Daily Times-Democrat, 1929—, Duncan (Okla.) Daily Banner. Chmn. Dem. State Com. of Okla., 1944-45; apptd. mem. Fed. Power Commn., 1945. Home: 911 Hillcrest Dr Duncan OK 73533 Office: 23 S 8th Duncan OK also Farragut Bldg Washington DC

WIMBERLY, JOHN HARRY, gas co. exec.; b. Houston, Dec. 6, 1904; s. Stonewall Jackson and Hallie (Holland) W.; student Rice Inst., 1922; B.B.A., U. Tex., 1927; m. Edith Cooney, Oct. 15, 1931; children—Bryan Holland, Lane Mayfield, Thomas Allan. Auditor Houston Natural Gas Corp., 1931-40, treas., 1940-45, v.p., treas., 1945-47, exec. v.p., 1947-55, pres., 1955—, dir., 1940—; exec. v.p., dir. Houston Natural Gas Prodn. Co., 1953-56, pres., 1956-57, chmn. bd., 1967—, also chmn. bd. of subsidiaries; pres. Houston Pipe Line Co., 1956-67, chmn. bd., 1967—; dir. Bank of Tex., Houston, Port City State Bank. Pres. Houston Jr. C. of C., 1936. Trustee S.W. Research Inst., Inst. Gas Tech., St. Luke's Episcopal Hosp. Mem. Am. (past dir., past pres.), So. (pres. 1952) gas assns., Tex. Bur. Econ. Understanding, Tex. Research League (dir.), Tex. Mid-Continental Oil and Gas Assn. Episcopalian (pres. churchmen's assns. 1949). Clubs: Houston Country (past pres.), Texas (Houston). Home: 5421 Sturbridge Dr Houston TX 77027 Office: Houston Natural Gas Bldg PO Box 1188 Houston TX 77002

WIMBERLY, TED B., environmental cons. engr.; b. Kirkland, Tex., Aug. 10, 1917; s. Titus Bennie and Opal (Harris) W.; student Rice U., 1935-38; B.S., U. Tex., 1941; certificate in meteorology U. Chgo., 1942; m. Willie Inez Montgomery, May 31, 1941; 1 son, Ted B. Engr., Bariod Sale div. Nat. Lead Co., Houston, 1941, 45-47; owner W & R Locker Plant, Austin, Tex., 1947-51; owner, engr., cons. Austin Oil & Gas Pub. Co., Tex., 1951-64, now owner; asst. exec. sec. Tex. Air Control Bd., Austin, 1964-70; environmental cons. engr., 1970—. Bd. dirs. Austin YMCA. Served with USAAF, 1941-46. Registered profl. engr., Tex. Methodist. Mason. Club: Austin Civitan (pres. 1956-57). Home: 5010 Strass Dr Austin TX 78731

WIMBERLY, WILLIAM KENNETH, dentist; b. Campti, La., Apr. 16, 1918; s. Henry Olin and Mollie (Blackman) W.; student Northwestern State U., 1936, grad. Emory U., 1940; m. Belle Russell, Apr. 5, 1942; children—Linnye Ruth (Mrs. Lester), Susanne (Mrs. Perot). Individual practice dentistry, Campti, 1940—. Served to capt. Armed Forces. Mem. La. Dental Assn. Baptist (deacon). Mason (Shriner). Home and office: Box 118 Campti LA. 71411

WIMPEY, JOHN ANDREW, state ofcl.; b. Blairsville, Ga., Mar. 16, 1927; s. James LaFayette and Thanie Elvira (Cook) W.; A.B., Mercer U., 1950; M.A., George Peabody Coll. Tchrs., 1950, M.Ed., 1954, Ph.D., 1958; postgrad. Harvard, 1958, Columbia, part-time 1961-64; m. Leta Shelby, Nov. 30, 1949; 1 dau., LeAnn (Mrs. Robert James Hulsey). Prin., Rhine (Ga.) Schs., 1954-56; prof., head dept. social scis. Belmont Coll., 1958-61; asso. prof. edn. The Citadel, 1961-67; dir. tchr. edn. and certification Ga. Dept. Edn., Atlanta, 1967—. Cons. planning research and evaluation Ga. Dept. Edn., 1971—. Served with AUS, 1945-47. Recipient Gov.'s citation, 1945; named Dodge County Tchr. of Yr., 1956. Mem. N.E.A. (life), Nat. Soc. Study Edn., Assn. Higher Edn., Am. Assn. U. Profs., Nat. Assn. State Dirs. Tchr. Edn. and Certification, Danforth Assos., Phi Delta Kappa. Baptist. Kiwanian. Clubs: Exchange (program chmn. 1968-69), Woodvalley Park (Hapeville, Ga.). Contbr. chpt. to Vital Issues in American Education; articles to profl. jours. Home: 2109 LaVista Circle Hapeville Atlanta GA 30354 Office: State Dept Edn Atlanta GA 30303

WIMPRESS, GORDON DUNCAN, JR., coll. pres.; b. Riverside, Cal., Apr. 10, 1922; s. Gordon Duncan and Maude A. (Waldo) W.; B.A., U. Ore., 1946, M.A., 1951; Ph.D., U. Denver, 1958; m. Jean Margaret Skerry, Nov. 30, 1946; children—Wendy Jo, Victoria Jean, Gordon Duncan III. Dir. pub. relations, instr. journalism Whittier (Cal.) Coll., 1946-51; asst. to pres. Colo. Sch. Mines, Golden, 1951-58; pres. Monticello Coll., Alton, Ill., 1959-64, Monmouth (Ill.) Coll., 1964-70, Trinity U., San Antonio, 1970—. Mem. commn. on colls. and univs. North Central Assn. Trustee of Lincoln Acad. Ill.; mem. Ill. State Fulbright Com.; mem. adv. council Pres. Assn. Governing Bds. Univs. and Colls.; mem. Nexus com. Presbyn. Coll. Union. Served to 1st lt. AUS, 1942-45. Decorated Bronze Star. Mem. Am. Coll. Pub. Relations Assn., Am. Alumni Council, Asso. Colls. Ill. (v.p., mem. exec. com.), Pub. Relations Soc. Am., Young Pres.'s Orgn., Newcomen Soc., Nat. Pilots Assn., Aircraft Owners and Pilots Assn., Assn. Am. Colls., Am. Council on Edn., Sigma Delta Chi, Sigma Delta Pi, Sigma Upsilon, Pi Gamma Mu, Sigma Phi Epsilon. Presbyn. Rotarian. Clubs: University (Chgo.); Monmouth Country. Author: American Journalism Comes of Age, 1950. Office: 715 Stadium Dr San Antonio TX 78212

WINCHESTER, CLARENCE FLOYD, educator; b. Chgo., Oct. 14, 1901; s. Leon Alpheus and Nina Pearl (Thompson) W.; B.S., U. Cal. at Berkeley, 1924, M.S., 1935; Ph.D., U. Mo., 1939; m. Maxine Gertrude Kiefer, Sept. 15, 1924 (div. 1938); 1 dau., Maxine Claire (Mrs. Robert Cloon); m. 2d, Alma Elizabeth Tatsch, Sept. 25, 1943; Tchr. pub. schs., Los Angeles, 1924-28, Palo Verde, Cal., 1928-29, Fresno, Cal., 1929-31; research scientist U. N.H., 1931-32, U. Cal. at Davis, 1932-37, U. Mo., 1937-46; asso. prof. U. Fla., 1946-49; agrl. research scientist, Beltsville, Md., 1949-61; nutritionist U.S. Dept. Interior, 1961-66; lectr. Howard U., Washington, 1966—. Served from 1st lt. to capt. AUS, 1942-46. Fellow Intercontinental Biog. Assn., A.A.A.S., Am. Inst. Chemists; mem. Am. Inst. Nutrition, Am. Assn. U. Profs., Assn. Overseas Educators, Am. Soc. Animal Prodn., Sigma Xi, Gamma Sigma Delta, Alpha Chi Sigma, Gamma Alpha. Mason (32 deg.). Home: 2124 Sudbury Pl NW Washington DC 20012 Office: Howard Pl and 4th St NW Washington DC 20001

WINCHESTER, LUCY ALEXANDER, White House social sec.; b. Lexington, Ky., Jan. 11, 1937; d. James Holloway and Lucy (Moulthrop) Alexander; grad. Finch Jr. Coll., 1957; student Villa Torre di Bellosguardo, Florence, Italy, 1959; B.A., U. Ky., 1960; m. 1 dau., Lucy. With protcol office U.S. Mission to UN, 1960; guide UN, N.Y.C., 1961-62; owner, mgr. Alexander Farms, Lexington, 1964-69; social sec. to White House, Washington, 1969—. Home: 4201 Cathedral Av Washington DC 20016 Office: The White House Washington DC 20050

WINDHAM, EULA HEARD, librarian; b. Tifton, Ga.; d. William Guy and Eula Beall (Wilson) Windham; A.B., Ga. State Coll. for Women, 1940; postgrad. So. Baptist Theol. Sem., 1945-47; M.R.E., 1950; M.L.S., Emory U., 1956. Tchr. pub. schs. Tifton, 1940-44; bookkeeper State Nat. Bank, Sheffield, Ala., 1944; caseworker Ga. Dept. Pub. Welfare, Tifton, 1945; state jr. leader Ga. Baptist Sunday Sch. Dept., Atlanta, 1947-55; circulation and reference librarian Hardin-Simmons U., Abilene, 1957-60. asst. librarian, 1960-61; librarian Middle Ga. Coll., Cochran, 1961—. Mem. A.L.A., Tex., Southwestern, Abilene, Ga. (exec. bd. 1963—), Southeastern library assns., Ga. Assn. Jr. Colls. (chmn. library div. 1963, 69), Ga. Assn. Educators (local chmn. 1967), Pilot Internat., Beta Sigma Phi. Clubs: XXI (sec. 1960-61), Cochran Women's. Compiler: Library Handbook, 1962, rev., 1965. Contbr. articles to profl. jours. Office: Middle Ga Coll Cochran GA 31014

WINDHAM, WHIT, judge; b. Millport, Ala., Feb. 6, 1897; s. Reuben Vaughn and Martha (Waldrop) W.; A.B., U. Ala., 1918, LL.B., 1925; m. Lavica Margaret Stapp, Apr. 21, 1920; children—Philip, Stephen. Former mem. firms London, Yancy, Smith & Windham and Smith, Windham, Jackson & Rives; judge Circuit Ct., Birmingham, Ala., 1941—. Office: County Courthouse Birmingham AL 35203

WINDLE, HOUSTON ERASMUS, farmer; b. Aliceville, Ala., Nov. 4, 1897; s. Davis Whitmore and Sammie (Jones) W.; grad. high sch.; m. Mina Nell Huffman, June 2, 1935; children—Jane (Mrs. W. Phelps Young), Bobbie (Mrs. Donald Lambert), Anne (Mrs. Jacob H. Childs, Jr.), Hugh. Farmer, Aliceville, 1925—; cattle rancher, 1940-72; lumber mfr., Aliceville, 1935-58; dir. Aliceville Bank & Trust Co. Pres., Pickens County Livestock Commn., 1965-72. Served with U.S. Army, World War I. Mem. Pickens County Farm Bur. (1st v.p.), Pickens County Cattleman's Assn. Democrat. Methodist. Mason. Address: Olney Rd Aliceville AL 35442

WINESTONE, ROBERT LOUIS, govt. economist; b. Portland, Ore., Nov. 22, 1915; s. Jacob and Lena (Feldman) W.; B.A., U. Ore., 1939, M.A., 1942; postgrad. U. Minn., 1946-47; Ph.D., Northwestern U., 1954; m. Mildred Rosen, Nov. 27, 1944; children—Jerome Alan, Lee Philip. Tchr. pub. high scho., Portland, 1939-42; instr. U. Minn., Mpls., 1946-47, Northwestern U., Evanston, Ill., 1947-50; asst., prof. Coe Coll., Cedar Rapids, Ia., 1950-51; economist U.S. Dept. Commerce, Washington, 1951-53; asso. prof. U. Wichita, 1953-56; economist Rand Corp., Santa Monica, Cal., 1956-65; economist Research Analysis Corp., McLean, Va., 1966-68; econometrician U.S. Dept. Transp., Washington, 1968—. Lectr. U. Cal. at Los Angeles, 1963-65, Los Angeles State Coll., 1964-65. Pres., Pacific Palisades (Cal.) Democratic Club, 1959-61. Served with AUS, 1942-45. Mem. Am. Assn. U. Profs., Am. Econ. Assn., Artus, Phi Delta Kappa. Democrat. Home: 6504 Callander Dr Bethesda MD 20034 Office: 400 7th St SW Washington DC 20591

WINFIELD, JOHN ANDREW, mech. engr.; b. Petersburg, Va., Feb. 10, 1917; s. Bryant Dewees and Rebecca Beeman (Applewhite) W.; B.S. in Mech. Engring., Clemson U., 1940; postgrad. Emory U., 1968; m. Mary Catherine Lennon, Aug. 17, 1946; children—Catherine (Mrs. Ronald Masden), Marcia (Mrs. Sidney Sparrow). Supr., Bethlehem Steel Co. (Pa.), 1940-42; supr., mgr. Clark Bros. Co., Olean, N.Y., 1946-54; plant mgr. Brunner Co., Gainesville, Ga., 1954-55; mgr. tool design, mgr. standard tool gen. dept., mgr. standard tool control dept. Lockheed Ga. Co., Marietta, 1955—. Mem. adv. bd. North Ga. Tech. Sch., 1957-68; Atlanta/Fulton Co. Vocational and Tech. Sch., 1958-68; mem. Ga. gov.'s staff. 1960-64; dep. chief Civil Def., Olean, 1953. Bd. dirs., founder, v.p. Ga. Engring. Found., 1972—. Vernon Woods Devel. Corp., 1960. Served to capt. AUS, 1942-46. Decorated Bronze Star medal. Mem. Soc. Mfg. Engrs. (nat. dir. 1967-71), Lockheed Mgmt. Club. Home: 6434 Cherry Tree Lane Atlanta GA 30328 Office: Dept 44-11 Lockheed Ga Co Marietta GA 30060

WINFIELD, MARY JONES (MRS. JOHN A. WINFIELD), Democratic nat. committeewoman; b. Valdosta, Ga., Jan. 16, 1916; d. Henry Davis and Ethel Mae (Hightower) Jones; student Ga. State Women's Coll., 1934-35, East Carolina U., 1936; m. John Augustus Winfield, June 28, 1935 (dec. Sept. 1971); children—Frances Ann (Mrs. Bowers), Mary Virginia (Mrs. Dowdy), Gloria Jean, John Scott. Dem. chmn. Yeatesville Precinct, N.C., 1958-68; alternate del. Dem. Nat. Conv., 1968; vice chmn. Beaufort County Dem. Com., 1968—; Dem. nat. committeewoman from N.C., 1968—. Mem. local sch. bd.; chmn. Better Schs. Beaufort County, 9 years; spl. chmn. Library Resources; mem. N.C. Bd. Assessment, 1971—; mem. adv. bd. Belhaven Mus.; mem. coll. parallel adv. com. Beaufort Tech. Inst., 1971—. Bd. dirs. Mt. Olive Coll., Tb Assn., Cancer Soc. Named Outstanding Club Woman, 1965, Outstanding Ch. Woman Albemarle Dist., 1966; recipient Atlantic and Pacific Leadership award, 1965, Rural award Rural Electrification Assn., 1968. Baptist (Sunday sch. tchr.). Address: Rural Route 2 Pinetown NC 27865

WINFREE, FLOYD LEONARD, fruit coop. exec.; b. Daytona Beach, Fla., Nov. 10, 1928; s. Floyd and Velma (McPherson) W.; B.S. in Bus. Adminstrn., U. Fla., 1950, postgrad., 1954-55; m. Rita Ann Pruet, Jan. 19, 1957 (div. 1967); 1 dau., Nancy Ann. Staff accountant W. O. Daley & Co., Orlando, Fla., 1955-58; controller Winter Garden (Fla.) Citrus Products Coop., 1958-66; treas. Plymouth (Fla.) Citrus Products Coop., 1966—. Bd. dirs., pres. Fla. Symphony, Orlando; pres., mem. exec. com. Fla. Symphony Assn., Orlando. Served to 1st lt. USAF, 1952-54. C.P.A., Fla. Mem. Sigma Phi Epsilon, Alpha Kappa Psi. Home: 1329 W Yale St Orlando FL 32804 Office: PO Box 367 Plymouth FL 32768

WINFREY, DORMAN HAYWARD, state librarian; b. Henderson, Tex., Sept. 4, 1924; s. Luke Abel and Linnie (Fears) W.; B.A., U. Tex., 1950, M.A., 1951, Ph.D., 1962; m. Ruth Carolyn Byrd, June 12, 1954; children— Laura, Jennifer. Social sci. research asso. Research in Tex. History, Tex. Hist. Assn. at U. Tex., 1946-58; state archivist, 1958-60; archivist U. Tex., 1960-61; dir., librarian Tex. State Library, 1962—. Chmn. State Bd. Library Examiners, 1962—, State Records Preservation Adv. Com.; 1965—. Served with AUS, 1943-46, ETO. Clara Driscoll scholar for research in Tex. history, 1952-54. Fellow Tex. Hist. Assn. (exec. council, pres. 1971—), Soc. Am. Archivists (council), Am. Assn. for State and Local History (council), mem. Tex. Inst. Letters, Philos. Soc. Tex., Am. Assn. State Libraries (planning com.), A.L.A., Tex. Library Assn., Am., Tex., So. hist. assns., Phi Alpha Theta, Pi Sigma Alpha. Mem. Disciples of Christ Ch. Author, editor: Texas Indian Papers, 1825-1843, 1959; Texas Indian Papers, 1844-1845, 1960; Texas Indian Papers, 1946-1859, 1960; A. History of Rusk County, Texas, 1961; Julien Sidney Devereux and His Monte Vendi Plantation, 1964; Indian Papers of Texas and the Southwest, 1825-1916 (5 vols.), 1966; Arturo Toscanini in Texas; The 1950 NBC Symphony Orchestra Tour, 1967; spl. editor Tex. Ency. for Young People, 1964; asso. editor Jr. Historian mag., 1951-58. Home: 6503 Willamette Dr Austin TX 78723 Office: Tex State Library Box 12927 Capitol Sta Austin TX 78711

WINGATE, THOMAS HERRON, editor; b. Charlotte, N.C., Apr. 1, 1912; s. Thomas Edgar and Mary (Severs) W.; A.B. cum laude, Presbyn. Coll., Clinton, S.C., 1930-34; m. Frances Lee Alexander, Aug. 25, 1935; children—Mary Alice (Mrs. Eugene Marshall), Daphne Herron (Mrs. Frederick A. Skidmore, III), Frances Anne (Mrs. James W. Little). Editor, Independent (weekly), Kannapolis, N.C., 1934-42, Daily Independent, 1946-52, 59—; pub. Rutherford County News, 1952-58, state editor Charlotte News, 1958; pres. Kannapolis Pub. Co., Inc., 1965—. Bd. dirs. N.C. div. Am. Cancer Soc. Served with AUS, 1942-46; ETO. Decorated Purple Heart with oak leaf cluster. Rotarian. Presbyn. (elder). Home: 1207 Rogers Lake Rd Kannapolis NC 28081 Office: 123 N Main St Kannapolis NC 28081

WINGER, MAURICE H., business exec.; b. Kansas City, Mo., Dec. 28, 1917; s. Maurice H.; B., William Jewel Coll., 1939; LL.B., Duke, 1942; m. Virginia McNabb, 1940; children—Eric, Stephen. Admitted to N.Y. State bar, 1942, D.C. bar, 1946; asso. firm Sullivan & Cromwell, N.Y.C., 1942, Douglas, Proctor, MacIntyre & Gates, Washington, 1946-48, Debevoise, Plimpton & McLean, N.Y.C., 1948-50; with Export-Import Bank, Washington, 1943-44; sec., asst. gen. counsel Am. Enka Co. (N.C.), 1950-60, gen. mgr. Brand-Rex 1960-64, gen. mgr. Nylon div., 1964-70, v.p., 1966-70, pres., 1970—. Served to 1st lt. USMCR, 1944-46. Recipient Distinguished Service award (Man of Year), Asheville Jr. C. of C., 1953. Office: Am Enka Co Enka NC 28728

WINGERTER, LORAIN FRANCIS, lawyer, judge; b. New Orleans, Sept. 17, 1917; s. Anthony M. and Vera (Voegtlin) W.; A.B., Loyola at New Orleans, 1938, LL.B., 1940; m. Betty Roden, Nov. 14, 1942; children—Donald S., Martin J. Admitted to La. bar, 1940; practiced in New Orleans, 1945—; judge 2d City Ct., New Orleans, 1948—. Instr. Loyola at New Orleans, 1946-47, asst. prof., 1947-48, asso. prof., 1948; sometimes lectr. Served to lt. USNR, 1942-45. Mem. La., New Orleans bar assns., Am. Judicature Soc. Home: 5815 Sutton Pl New Orleans LA 70114 Office: 509 Verret St New Orleans LA 70114

WINGROVE, CHARLES RAY, educator; b. Falmouth, Va., July 27, 1937; s. Floyd Ray and Mary (Houdershelt) W.; B.A., U. Richmond, 1959; M.A. (Ford Behavioral Sci. fellow), U. N.C., 1962, Ph.D., 1964; m. Jane Melissa Smoller, Dec. 18, 1966; 1 son, Benjamin Ray. Grad. asst. U. N.C., 1960-64; asst. prof. U. Ga., Athens, 1964-71; asso. prof. U. Richmond, 1971—. Vis. prof. Emory U., 1966. Named Outstanding Young Man in Am., 1966. Mem. Am., So. (sec.-treas. 1968-70), Ga., Rural sociol. socs., Gerontological Soc., Phi Beta Kappa. Contbr. articles and book revs. to profl. jours. Home: 208 E Brook Run Dr Richmond VA 23233

WINK, HOWARD LAMAR, JR., mech. engr.; b. Boalsburg, Pa., Dec. 29, 1935; s. Howard Lamar and Anna Beamer (Tawney) W.; B.S. in M.E., Pa. State U., 1957; m. Joan Bryant Strohecker, Dec. 24, 1959; children— Christine Lynne, Robert Bruce. Mech. engr. facilities planning Ternstedt div. Gen. Motors Corp., Warren, Mich., 1959-63, sr. design engr. product design, 1963-68; project engr. product engring. Refrigerator Products div. Gen. Electric Co., Louisville, 1968—. Served to 1st lt. Ordnance Corps, AUS, 1957-59. Registered profl. engr., Ky. Mem. Appliance Engring. Soc. (sec. 1971-72), Engring. Soc. Detroit. Clubs: Plantation Country, Sailing (Louisville). Patentee in field. Home: 3614 Breeland Av Louisville KY 40222 Office: Appliance Park Louisville KY 40225

WINKELMAN, HERBERT WILLIAM, accountant; b. Brenham, Tex., Jan. 6, 1902; s. Frederick Henry and Louisa (Jahnke) W.; grad. Blinn Meml. Coll., Brenham, 1918; m. Cordie Louise Dupree, Aug. 4, 1923; 1 dau. Camille (Mrs. F.B. Graham). Accountant, Mattison & Block, Houston, 1920-26; mem. firm J. L. Block & Co., Houston, 1926-29, Winkelman & Tucker, Houston, 1929-33; sr. mem. Winkelman, Davies, Johnson & Watson, and predecessor firm, Houston, 1933—. Mem. Nat., Tex. socs. pub. accountants, Houston Real Estate Bd., Houston Turn Verein. Lutheran. Rotarian. Home: 2102 Bolsover Rd Houston TX 77005 Office: Main Bldg Houston TX 77002

WINKLER, HUGH DONALD, univ. ofcl.; b. Cobden, Ill., Nov. 25, 1932; s. Hugh Stelle and Vesta Marguerite (Schimpf) W.; student So. Ill. U., summers 1952, 53; A.B. magna cum laude, McKendree Coll., 1954; M.S., Ohio U., 1956; m. Edna Azile Thomson, Dec. 21, 1956; children— Donald Thomson, James Randolph. Editorial fellow Meth. Pub. House, Nashville, summer 1954; editor-in-chief Concern Mag., also projects sec. Nat. Conf. Meth. Youth, Nashville, 1955-57; acting dir., instr. communications N.D. State U., 1957-59; dir. information services Randolph-Macon Woman's Coll., 1959-66; dir. pub. relations George Washington U., Washington, 1966—. Cons., speaker, panelist various nat. ednl. confs. Mem. Alexandria City Democratic Com. Recipient 19 Nat. awards for ednl. publs. and pub. relations projects Am. Coll. Pub. Relations Assn., Am. Alumni Council, Ednl. Press Assn., Am. Inst. Graphic Arts. Mem. Am. Coll. Pub. Relations Assn. (dir. dist. workshop 1971), Am. Alumni Council (judge nat. direct mail competition 1968), Ednl. Press Assn. (dir. Washingotn workshop 1969), Pub. Relations Soc. Am., Am. Inst. Graphic Arts, Internat. Platform Assn., Am. Assn. Higher Edn., Sigma Delta Chi. Methodist (chmn. council ministries). Club: Nat. Press. Home: 5543 Gary Av Alexandria VA 22311

WINKLER, THOMAS ROBERT, trade assn. exec.; b. Midland, Mich., Mar. 3, 1930; s. Herman Henry and Cora (Sommerville) W.; B.A., Mich. State U., 1952; m. Virginia Sheila MacDade, Dec. 1, 1957. TV producer, dir. Evening Star Broadcasting Co., 1952; editorial dir. ABC-TV Jimmy Dean Show WMAL-TV, 1961-66; asst. to mgr.-radio code Nat. Assn. Broadcasters, 1966-67, mgr. radio code, 1967—. Bd. dirs. Washington Heart Assn. Mem. Met. Wash. Bd. Trade, Nat. TV Acad. Arts and Scis. (dir., pres. Washington chpt. 1971-73), Vets. Bedside Network (treas. Washington chpt.), Episcopalian. Home: 3730 N Dittmar Rd Arlington VA 22207 Office: 1771 N St NW Washington DC 20036

WINKS, ISLA DALE BROCK, librarian; b. Lamesa, Tex., July 5, 1920; d. William Foster and Helena (Cannon) Brock; spl. student Coll. of S.W., 1967; m. Bernard Leroy Winks, Nov. 12, 1939; children—Barbara Ann (Mrs. Donald Topping), Linda Sue (Mrs. Randall Lee Lippincott). Bookkeeper, Henny Penny Grocery, 1955-57; asst. librarian Gaines County Library, Seminole, Tex., 1958-63, county librarian Seminole Library and Seagraves br., Gaines County, 1963—. Baptist (ch. librarian, 1966-70). Mem. Order Eastern Star (past worthy matron). Club: Seminole Study (pres. 1967). Home: 509 NW Av I Seminole TX 79360 Office: Gaines County Library Seminole TX 79360

WINN, DAN PEACE, judge; b. Douglasville, Ga., Sept. 19, 1921; s. Frank M. and Mary (Peace) W.; student Young Harris Jr. Coll., 1939-40; grad. Emory U., 1948; m. Mildred Marceline, June 1, 1946; children— Darice, Nila, Frank, Nick. Admitted to Ga. bar, 1948; Ct. Appeals, Supreme Ct. Ga., Supreme Ct. U.S.; practiced in Cedartown, 1949—; asst. atty. gen. Ga., 1948; solicitor City Ct. Polk County, 1951-59; solicitor-gen. Tallapoosa Jud. Circuit Ga., 1959-67, judge Superior Ct., 1967—. Mem. Ga. State Constrn. Revision Commn., 1963-64. Bd. dirs. Cedartown Community Fund. Served to 2d lt. USMCR, World War II; PTO. Decorated Air medal, D.F.C. Mem. Ga., Tallapoosa Circuit, Polk County bar assns., Solicitors-Gen. Assn. Ga. (pres.), Nat. Dist. Atty's. Assn., Council Superior Court Judges Ga. (pres.), Am. Legion, V.F.W., Cedartown C. of C. Methodist. Mason. Club: Optimist. Home: 611 Martha Lane Cedartown GA 30125 Office: Polk County Courthouse Cedartown GA 30125

WINN, JOHN FRANCIS, diagnostics co. cons.; b. Springfield, Mo., May 25, 1917; s. John Francis and Virgile (Kelly) W.; B.A., U. Cal. at Los Angeles, 1940; B.S., Colo. State U., 1946, D.V.M., 1948; M.P.H., U. Cal. at Berkeley, 1952; m. Lorrene Whittemore, Sept. 26, 1941; children—Thomas Scott, Carol Jean. Bacteriologist, Los Angeles City Health Dept., 1940-41; with USPHS, 1948-66, dir. biol. reagents program, 1957-66; dir. Biol. Research Nat. Drug Co., 1946; lab. mgmt. cons. Nat. Center for Disease Control, Atlanta, 1967-70, dir. Credit Union, 1962-66, pres., 1964-66; mgr. Beckman Diagnostics, Atlanta, 1970-72, cons., 1972—. Adviser, WHO, 1957-69, Pan Am. Health Orgn., 1959-69. Served with USNR, 1941-45. Recipient Commendation medal USPHS, 1965. Fellow Am. Pub. Health Assn., Am. Acad. Microbiology; mem. Am. Vet. Medicine Assn., Sci. Research Soc. Am., Sigma Xi, Theta Chi. Home: 4903 Leeds Ct Dunwoody GA 30338

WINSETT, MARVIN DAVIS, author, poet; b. Van Alstyne, Tex., Feb. 13, 1902; s. Asa and Lily (Gorrell) W.; student So. Methodist U., 1922-24; L.H.D., Universite Libre (Asie), 1968; m. Hettie Lee Bryant, June 20, 1925; children—Betty Lee (Mrs. Wilbur Ausphera Richerson, Jr.), Janis Sue (Mrs. Roger L. Swain). Asst. furniture buyer Sanger Brothers, Dallas, 1925-28; mgr. El Paso and Abilene Sears Roebuck & Co. stores, 1928-30; established advt. agy. under name Marvin Winsett Advt. Agy., 1930, head, 1930-47, owner, 1952-67, partner Winsett, Gidley & Darley Advt. Agy., 1947-52. Pres. Nat. Fedn. State Poetry Socs., 1964-66; Tex. co-chmn. Nat. Poetry Day Com., 1965-67; chmn. Tex. Council Promotion Poetry, 1965—. Apptd. Poet Laureate of Tex., 1962; recipient Deane Settoon Mernagh Sonnet award, 1957; William Lamar Meml. award, 1958; Oread award, 1959; Margaret Royalty Edwards Poetry day award, 1959. Mem. bd. Civilian Def. Vol. Office, 1942-45. Fellow Royal Soc. Arts (Eng.), Internat.Inst. Arts and Letters (life); mem. Acad. Am. Poets (affiliate), United Poets Laureate Internat. (gold medal and named hon. poet laureate leader 1965), Poetry Soc. Tex. (treas. 1956-61, editor bull. 1962-66, pres. 1962-65), Vachel Lindsay Assn. (adv. bd.), Estranger Academie Francaise de la Poesie (corr.), Chili Appreciation Soc. Internat., Sigma Delta Chi (past sec., treas. Dallas profl. chpt., Key Club mem.), Lambda Chi Alpha. Democrat. Presbyn. Mason (32 deg., Shriner). Club: Dallas Coin. Author: Winding Stairway. A Book of Verse, 1953; Basic Ad Writing, 1954; April Always (verse), 1956; Remembered Earth (verse), 1962; Some Uses of Words, 1969. Contbr. articles and verse to numerous nat. mags. and anthologies Originator Cyclus verse form. Home: 3936 Colgate St Dallas TX 75225

WINSHIP, WADLEIGH CHICHESTER, express co. exec.; b. San Francisco, Oct. 3, 1940; s. Henry Dillon and Anne Eliza (Chichester) W.; student Woodberry Forest (Va.) Sch., 1954-56; grad. Darlington Sch., Rome, Ga., 1959; B.A., U. Ga., 1964; m. Lynne McPherson, Dec. 28, 1970. Exec. trainee G. Hwy. Express, Inc., Atlanta, 1964-68, v.p., 1968—, also dir., mem. exec. com.; pres. SurfAir, Inc., Atlanta, 1970—; dir. Underground Atlanta, Inc. Chmn. transp. com. A.R.C., Atlanta, 1968—. Mem. Am. Trucking Assn. (terminal operations council), Atlanta Air Cargo Assn. (charter), Ga. Bus. and Industry Assn. (dir.), Chi Phi. Clubs: Peachtree Golf, Capital City, The Nine O'Clocks, German, Atlanta City. Home: 3296 Rilman Rd NW Atlanta GA 30327 Office: 2090 Jonesboro Rd SE Atlanta GA 30315*

WINSLOW, FRANCIS EDWARD, lawyer; b. Hertford, N.C., July 7, 1888; s. Tudor Frith and Mary E. (Wood) W.; A.B., U. N.C., 1909, student law sch., 1910; student Columbia Law Sch., 1911; m. Nemmie G. Paris, June 20, 1917; children—Adelaide (Mrs. Oliver Crawley), Mary W. (Mrs. Julian D. Bobbitt), Margaret (Mrs. R. M. Wiley), Francis Edward. Admitted to N.C. bar, 1911, also U.S. Supreme Ct., U.S. Ct. Appeals; mem. firm Battle, Winslow, Scott & Wiley, and predecessor law firms, Rocky Mount, N.C., 1911—. Dir. Planters Nat. Bank and Trust Co., Rocky Mount, N.C. Chmn., The Carolina Charter Tercentenary Commn. Mem. for 4th U.S. Judicial Circuit standing com. on fed. judiciary, Am. Bar Assn., 1956-59; mem. exec. com. Com. for Def. of Constitution by Preserving Treaty Power, 1953—; charter mem. World Peace Through Law Center, Wash., 1963—; mem. Lawyers Com. Civil Rights, 1963—. Trustee Rocky Mount Pub. Library, 1922—, chmn. bd., 1937-47. Fellow Am. Bar Found.; mem. Am. (N.C. del. 1940-47), N.C. (pres. 1937-38), Rocky Mount-Nash County (pres. 1927) bar assns., Am. Law Inst., Am. Judicature Soc. (dir. 1943-52, 58-60), N.C. Lit. and Hist. Soc., N.C. Soc. Preservation Antiquities, N.C. Art Soc., Soc. Cincinnati (pres. N.C. 1956-58, del., tri-ennial conv., Paris, 1959), Phi Beta Kappa, Sigma Nu. Democrat. Episcopalian. Contbr. articles law reviews. Home: 701 Tarboro St Rocky Mount NC 27801 Office: Battle Winslow Scott & Wiley Box 269 Rocky Mount NC 27801

WINSLOW, LEONARD FRANCIS, JR., land co. exec.; b. Phila., Aug. 13, 1931; s. Leonard Francis and Marjorie Elizabeth (Bloomfield) W.; student Washington and Lee U., 1950-53; B.A., U. Richmond, 1954; m. Mary Hobson Hurt, Oct. 2, 1954; children—Mary Elizabeth, Leonard Francis III. Vice pres. Leonard F. Winslow Co., Inc., Richmond, Va., 1956-61; sales mgr. Va. Land Co., Charlottesville, 1961—, v.p., 1965-72, pres., 1972—; pres. Albermarle Hotel, Albermarle Galleries, Charlottesville-West Main St. Corp., North Water Co., Inc.; v.p. Allegany Land Co.; dir. First Va. Bank-Monticello Nat. Vice pres., dir. Charlottesville-Albemarle Bd. Realtors. Chmn. Chris Greene Lake Fund, 1972—. Served with USNR, 1954-55. Mem. Internat. Real Estate Fedn., Blue Ridge Homebuilders Assn., Izaak Walton League (dir.). Nat. Rifle Assn. (life), Sigma Chi. Episcopalian (vestryman). Elk, Kiwanian (dir. 1956-57). Clubs: Farmington Country, Boars Head. Home: Flordon Dr Charlottesville VA 22901 Office: Va Land Co Route 29 N Charlottesville VA 22901

WINSLOW, NICHOLAS SCOTT, econ. cons.; b. Los Angeles, Feb. 24, 1943; s. Benjamin I. and Mary (Scott) W.; B.A., Pomona Coll., 1964; M.B.A., Stanford, 1966; m. Cheryl L. Pyeatt, June 18, 1971; 1 son, Benjamin Scott. Asso., Econ. Research Assos., Los Angeles, 1967, sr. asso., 1969-70, sr. asso. Washington, 1970-71, v.p., mgr. Fla. office, 1971—; gen. mgr. Facts Consol., Los Angeles, 1967-69; v.p., dir. Armada, Inc., Los Angeles, 1968—. Mem. Am. Marketing Assn., Miami C. of C., Miami Internat. Center. Republican. Episcopalian. Home: 1403 Columbus Blvd Coral Gables FL 33134 Office: 5553 NW 36th St Miami Springs VA 33166

WINSTEAD, BASIL MAYO, food store exec.; b. Dresden, Tenn., Dec. 19, 1913; s. William Almerry and Mary (Cunningham) W.; grad. U.S. Armed Forces Inst., Madison, Wis., 1946; m. Thelma Mae Slaven, Dec. 29, 1945; children—Patricia Ann (Mrs. Dennis Finch), Autumn Frances. Store mgr. Piggly Wiggly Corp., St. Louis, 1928-38, auditor, 1938-41; with Safeway Stores, Inc., Washington, 1949—, v.p., div. mgr., 1964—; pres., chmn. bd. Holly Enterprises, Wilkesboro, N.C., 1970—. Bd. dirs. Met. Washington Bd. Trade, Downtown Progress, Washington, Capital Area council Boy Scouts Am. Served to maj. AUS, 1941-49. Decorated Bronze Star medal, ETO medal with 5 battle stars. Mem. Nat. Alliance Businessmen, Washington Conv. and Visitors Bur. Home: 4030 N 27th St Arlington VA 22207 Office: 6700 Columbia Park Rd Landover MD 20785

WINSTEAD, BURLUS RANDOLPH, JR., city ofcl.; b. Ft. Wayne, Ind., Feb. 20, 1931; s. Burlus Randolph and Vivian (Johnson) W.; B.S., U. Ala., 1952, M.B.A., 1958; m. Billie Beasley, Sept. 4, 1962; children—John Fayette, Elizabeth Renee. Accountant, Lybrand, Ross Bros. & Montgomery, Birmingham, Ala., 1958-61; mgmt. cons., Phila., 1962-63; dir. finance City of Birmingham, 1963—. Treas. Jefferson County Civil Def. Corps, 1963—, Birmingham Mus. Art, 1963—, Birmingham Library Bd., 1963—, Jefferson County Dept. Health, 1963—, Birmingham Park and Recreation Bd., 1963—; sec.-treas. Birmingham Water Works Bd., 1969—; treas. Birmingham Bd. Edn., 1963—. Served to lt., Supply Corps, USNR, 1952-55. C.P.A., Ala., Pa. Mem. Am. Mgmt. Assn., Am. Inst. C.P.A.'s, Ala. Soc. C.P.A.'s, Nat. Assn. Accountants, Nat. Municipal League, Nat. Conf. Pub. Employee Retirement Systems, Municipal Finance Officers Assn. U.S. and Can. (state chmn. 1965-71). Mem. Christian Ch. Kiwanian. Home: 1364 Swallow Lane Birmingham AL 35213 Office: City Hall Birmingham AL 35203

WINSTEAD, NASH NICKS, phytopathologist, univ. adminstr.; b. Durham, N.C., June 12, 1925; s. Nash L. and Lizzy (Featherston) W.; B.S., N.C. State U., 1948, M.S., 1951; Ph.D., U. Wis., 1953; m. Geraldine Larkin Kelly, Sept. 17, 1949; 1 dau., Karen Jewell. Asst. prof. plant pathology, Raleigh, 1953-58; asso. prof., 1958-61, prof., 1961—, dir. inst. biol. scis., 1965-67, asst. dir. agrl. exptl. sta., 1965-67, asst. provost, 1967—, Phillip Found. intern acad. adminstrn. Ind. U., 1965-66. Mem. N.C. Council on Higher Edn. for Adults; inst. rep. So. Assn. for Colls. and Schs., 1967—. Bd. dirs. N.C. State U. YMCA, 1963-65. Chmn. interaction between protoplasm and toxicants com. So. Regional Edn. Bd., 1964-65. Served with USAAF, 1943-46. Recipient Sigma Xi research award, 1960. Mem. Am. Phytopath. Soc. (chmn. disease, pathogen physiology com.), Am. Soc. Hort. Sci., Am. Inst. Biol. Scis., N.C. Acad. Sci., Acad. Deans for So. States, A.A.A.S., Sigma Xi, Phi Kappa Phi. Club: Torch Internat. (sec.). Contbr. to profl. jours. Home: 1109 Glendale Dr Raleigh NC 27609 Office: NC State U Raleigh NC 27607

WINSTEAD, PHILIP CONNOR, JR., univ. adminstr.; b. Mullins, S.C., Dec. 10, 1935; s. Philip Connor and Hilda (Renfrow) W.; A.B., Davidson Coll., 1957; M.A., Appalachian State U., 1964; Ed.D., Duke U., 1966; m. Hazel Jenon Wehunt, May 30, 1961; children—Amoret Beth, Hilda Marie, Mary Connor. Tchr., adminstr. McClenaghan High Sch., Florence, S.C., 1957-64; asst. dir. grad. program edn. Rollins Coll., 1966-68; program asso. higher edn. Regional Edn. Lab. for Carolinas and Va., Durham, N.C., 1968-69, acting dir. Sr. Coll. div., 1969-70; asso. dir. sr. coll. div. Nat. Lab. for Higher Edn., Durham, 1970-71; coordinator institutional planning Furman U., Greenville, S.C., 1972—. Mem. Am. Ednl. Research Assn., Assn. for Instl. Research, Am. Assn. Higher Edn., Am. Assn. Sch. Adminstrs., Am. Assn. U. Profs., Kappa Delta Pi. Research coll. and univ. adminstrn. and organization. Home: 107 Old Mill Rd Taylors SC 29687 Office: Furman U Greenville SC 29613

WINSTEAD, WARREN JUDSON, univ. pres.; b. Washington, Nov. 10, 1927; s. Purnell J. and Mellie (Winstead) W.; B.A., U. Richmond, 1950, M.S., 1955; Ed.D., Harvard, 1958; m. Elizabeth Ferguson, Feb. 27, 1959; children—Warren J., John Scott, Elizabeth, Winifred. Edn. dir. U.S. Army Logistics Mgmt. Center, Ft. Lee, Va., 1959-62; dir. edn. U.S. Army, Europe, 1962-64; pres. Nova U., Ft. Lauderdale, Fla., 1964—. Dir. Sterling Nat. Bank, Ft. Lauderdale. Bd. dirs. Inst. of Applied Linguistics, U. Heidelberg, South Fla. Edn. Center, Nat. Ednl. Assos. for Research and Devel., Ft. Lauderdale Pictorial Life Mag., Holy Cross Hosp., ADI Inc.; chmn. bd. L'Academie Montessori, Inc., 1970. Mem. Am. Acad. Polit. and Social Scis., Am. Assn. Sch. Adminstrs., Am. Council on Edn., Am. Soc. for Engring. Edn., Assn. for Higher Edn. Fla. Acad. Sci., Res. Officers Assn. Mason (Shriner). Club: Harvard. Home: Nova U of Advanced Tech Fort Lauderdale FL 33314

WINSTON, LOUIS SIMPSON, dentist; b. Alvin, Tex. Feb. 27, 1893; s. LaFayette Fontaine and Jane Elisabeth (Simpson) W.; A.B., Austin Coll., 1915; D.D.S., Tex. Dental Coll., 1923; postgrad. Dewey Sch. Orthodontia, 1923; m. Dorothy Quincy Mills, July 30, 1927; children—Quincy (Mrs. Eldridge Anthony Helwick), Dorothy Ann. Practice dentistry, specializing in orthodontics, Houston, 1923-48, Sherman, Tex., 1950-54, San Antonio, 1953-63, Schulenburg, Tex., 1968—. Served with USNR, 1917-19. Recipient Meritorious Service award Austin Coll., 1955. Diplomate Am. Bd. Orthodontics; mem. Am. Dental Assn. (life mem.), Houston Dist. Dental Soc. (pres. 1932-33), Am. Assn. Orthodontists (life mem.), Southwestern Soc. Orthodontists (pres. 1933). Presbyn. Kiwanian. Editor, founder monthly publ. of Houston Dist. Dental Soc., 1929. Home: Route 4 Schulenburg TX 78956 Office: 511 Summit St Schulenburg TX 78956

WINSTON, THOMAS JOSEPH, JR., govt. ofcl.; b. Washington, June 25, 1912; s. Thomas and Elizabeth Agnes (Cunniffe) W.; A.B., St. Mary's U., 1935; student N.Am. Coll., Gregorian U., Rome, Italy, 1935-37; J.D., Cath. U. Am., 1940; m. Edna Mae Hill, Nov. 14, 1945; children—Beth Anne Tordella, Lawrence Edward. Admitted to D.C. bar 1940; atty. Bur. Pub. Debt, Office Gen. Counsel of Treasury, 1941-47, asst. chief counsel, 1947-54, chief counsel, 1954—. Home: 104 E Melbourne Av Silver Spring MD 20901 Office: Treasury Dept Washington DC 20220

WINTER, CARLTON VERNON, pedodontist; b. Charleston, S.C., June 11, 1928; s. Carlton Oliver and Ethel (Doniphen) W.; student Coll. Charleston, 1946-47; B.S., U. S.C., 1951; postgrad., Med. U.S.C., 1951-52; D.D.S., Emory U., 1958; M.S., U. N.C., 1959; m. Carrie Cole, June 7, 1952; children—Patti, Carlton Bennett. Pvt. practice pedodontics, Charlotte, N.C., 1960—; mem. staff Charlotte Meml. Hosp. Lectr. pedodontics Dental Intern Program, Dental Asst. Teaching Program, Central Piedmont Community Coll., 1961. Co-chmn. health com. county council P.T.A., 1970-71. Bd. dirs. Bklyn. Day Care Center. Served with AUS, 1952-54. Recipient award Am. Soc. Dentistry for Children, 1958. Diplomate Am. Bd. Pedodontics. Fellow Am. Acad. Pedodontics; mem. Am. Soc. Dentistry for Children, Am., N.C. dental assns., Southeastern Acad. Pedodontics, Charlotte Dental Soc., C. of C., U.S. Power Squadrons, Nat. Skeet Shooting Assn., Pi Kappa Phi, Delta Sigma Delta. Baptist (deacon 1967-70). Rotarian. Clubs: Mecklenburg Wildlife, Lake Norman Yacht, Carmel Country (Charlotte). Home: 1620 Lyndale Pl Charlotte NC 20210 Office: 1613 Mentford Dr Charlotte NC 28219

WINTER, CARRIE BESS COLE (MRS. CARLTON VERNON WINTER), civic worker; b. Lexington, N.C., Mar. 29, 1930; d. Bennett Columbus and Bessie (Smith) Cole; B.S., Appalachian State Thcrs. Coll., 1949; M.S., U.S.C., 1951; spl. grad. student Emory U., 1955; m. Carlton Vernon Winter, June 7, 1952; children—Patricia Ann, Carlton Bennett. Instr., Appalachian State Tchrs. Coll., Boone, N.C., 1950; med. tech. S.C. Bapt. Hosp., Columbia, 1951-52, U.S. Army Hosp., Ft. Jackson, 1952-54; research techn. Communicable Disease Center, USPHS, Atlanta, 1954-55, research bacteriologist, 1955-58, Venereal Disease Exptl. Lab., Chapel Hill, N.C., 1958-60; guest lectr. Sch. Nursing, Sch. Med. Tech., Grady Meml. Hosp., Atlanta, 1957-58; spl. cons. depts. san. engring., pathology, anatomy and microbiology U. N.C., Chapel Hill, 1958-60. Bd. dirs. Family Life Council, Charlotte-Mecklenburg County (N.C.), 1964-70, Bklyn. Day Care Center, 1969—; pres. Starmount P.T.A., 1967-70; sect. chmn. United Arts Fund, 1968; sec. Charlotte Opera Guild, 1966-67, 69-70; pres. Charlotte Nature Mus. Guild, 1968-69, docent, 1966—. Mem. Soc. Am. Microbiology, A.A.A.S., Am. Assn. U. Women (N.C. sec. 1964-67), N.Y. Acad. Sci., Charlotte Dental Aux. (sec. 1963-64, pres. 1967-68), Sigma Xi. Home: 1620 Lyndale Pl Charlotte NC 28210

WINTER, THOMAS SWANSON, editor; b. Teaneck, N.J., Dec. 28, 1937; s. Frank J. and Beulah (Swanson) W.; A.B., Harvard, 1959, M.B.A., 1961. Asst. editor Human Events, Washington, 1961-64, editor, 1964—. Republican. Lutheran. Clubs: Nat. Press Capitol Hill. Home: 323 6th St SE Washington DC 20003 Office: 422 1st St SE Washington DC 20003

WINTER, TRAVIS ALVIN, banker; b. Wellington, Tex., Feb. 25, 1914; s. Jessie Richard and Minnie Mae (Vaughn) W.; student Draughon's Bus. Coll., 1932-33, Internat. Sch. Commerce, 1934; m. Katie Lena Cary, Oct. 30, 1938. With Dept. Agr., Amherst, Tex, 1934-36, office mgr., Muleshoe, Tex., 1943-53; asst. mgr. Farmers Coop. Gin, Amherst, 1936-43; asst. mgr. White's Concrete Pipe, Littlefield, Tex., 1953-58; with 1st Nat. Bank, Amherst, 1958—, cashier, dir., 1966—; partner Duffy Ins. Agy., Amherst, 1966—. Mason. Home: 519 E 13th St Littlefield TX 79339 Office: 1001 Main St Amherst TX 79312

WINTERHOLLER, JAMES VINCENT, JR., civil engr.; b. Wheeling, W.Va., Sept. 10, 1927; s. James V. and Madelon (Moran) W.; B.S., W.Va. U., 1950; m. Doris J. Gray, Dec. 27, 1954; children—Dana Marie, Deanna Lee. Quality control engr. Wheeling Steel Corp., 1950-53; civil engr. Fla. Rd. Dept., Ft. Lauderdale, 1953-58; co-founder, pres. Fla. Testing & Engring. Co., Ft. Lauderdale, 1958—. Registered profl. engr., Fla. Mem. Fla. Engring. Soc., Nat. Soc. Profl. Engrs. Home: 2611 NE 40th St Fort Lauderdale FL 33308 Office: 3555 NW 10th Av Fort Lauderdale FL 33309

WINTERKAMP, GREDERICK HENRY, chem. co. ofcl.; b. Yountstown, O., June 30, 1927; s. Fred and Kathie Dora (Meyer) W.; B.Chem. Engring., M.S., Ohio State U., 1950; m. Lucy Ann Mandry, May 26, 1951; children—Karen Elizabeth, Judith Leigh, Frederick Mandry, Lucy Christine. With DuPont Co., Orange, Tex., 1950—maintenance supt., Belle, W.Va., 1961-64, tech. supt., 1964-67; mech. cal supt., La Porte, Tex., 1969—. Asst. scoutmaster Boy Scouts Am., 1959-64. Mem. Kanawha County Republican City and County Com., Charleston, W.Va., 1967-69. Fellow Instrument Soc. Am. (dir. prodn. processes, standards and practices dept. 1957-61), Tau Beta Pi. Presbyn. (Synod home and family nurture com. 1967-69). Home: 4110 Rolling Green Dr Seabrook TX 77586 Office: DuPont Co Houston Plant Box 347 La Porte TX 77517

WINTERS, LEO, treas. of Okla.; b. Hooker, Okla., Nov. 7, 1922; s. David and Gertrude (Strochin) W.; A.B., Panhandle A and M Coll., Goodwell, Okla., 1950; LL.B., U. Okla., 1957. Admitted to Okla. bar, 1957, since practiced in Oklahoma City; pres. Alaskan Livestock Co., Kodiak, 1956—; lt. gov. State of Okla., Oklahoma City, 1963-67, treas., 1967—. Served as pilot USAAF, World War II. Mem. Am. Quarter Horse Assn. Democrat. Mason (32 deg.). Home: Box 53411 Oklahoma City OK 73105

WINTERS, RICHARD LEE, physician; b. McAlester, Okla., Nov. 12, 1926; s. Marion P. and Ina (Perry) W.; B.S., Souteastern State Coll., 1949; M.D., Okla. U., 1953; m. Joyce Yvonne Creamer, July 7, 1951; children—Richard Bruce, Cynthia Rebecca, Mark Creamer. Intern, Denver Gen. Hosp., 1953-54; resident VA Hosp., Oklahoma City, 1954-55; gen. practice medicine, Poteau, Ikla., 1955—; chief staff Le Flore County Meml. Hosp., Poteau; preceptor U. Okla. Sch. Medicine, 1958—. Vice chmn. Eastern Okla. Hist. Soc., 1971. Served with AUS, 1944-46. Diplomate Am. Bd. Family Practice. Mem. LeFlore Haskell Med. Soc. (pres. 1971), Alpha Omega Alpha, Phi Chi. Mem. Christian Ch. (elder). Mason, Kiwanian. Home: 206 Orville Av Poteau OK 74953 Office: 501 Dewey St Poteau OK 74953

WINTERS, WILLIAM KYRAN, state ofcl.; b. Albany, N.Y., Dec. 28, 1938; s. William H. and Helen G. (Winters) W.; B.S., Utah State U., 1960; M.S., Kan. State U., 1963; m. Anita E. Eberhard, Aug. 15, 1959; children—Heidi Ann, Gary William. Asst. prof. computer sci. U. Mo., Rolla, 1963-66; operations research analyst U.S. Office Edn., Washington, 1966-67; dir. computer assisted registration U. Tenn., 1967-69; dir. information systems Okla. State Regents for Higher Edn., Oklahoma City, 1970—. Cons., U.S. Office Edn., 1967-70, Okla. State Regents for Higher Edn., 1969. Mem. Am. Statis. Assn., Inst. Math. Statistics, Inst. Mgmt. Sci., A.A.A.S., Assn. for Computing Machinery. Home: 3701 Baird Dr Edmond OK 73034 Office: State Capitol Oklahoma City OK 73105

WINTTER, ARCHIE HERMAN, mech. engr.; b. Hueytown, Ala., June 25, 1920; s. John Arnold and Ruth (Kinnett) W.; student Birmingham So. Coll., 1946-47; B.S. in Mech. Engring., Auburn U., 1949; m. Helen Eloise West, Aug. 12, 1950; children—Archie Kent, Helen Sue. With Woodward Iron Co. (Ala.), 1949-53, draftsman, 1950-53; with Fairfield (Ala.) works U.S. Steel Corp., 1953-70, head design draftsman, 1963-70; engr. Woodward Co. div. Mead Corp., 1970-71, chief draftsman, 1971—. Served with USAAF, 1941-45. Decorated Air medal. Registered profl. engr., Ala. Mem. Pi Tau Sigma. Baptist. Home: 507 Charleston Dr Bessemer AL 35020 Office: Woodward Co Woodward AL 35189

WISDOM, JOHN MINOR, judge; b. New Orleans, May 17, 1905; s. Mortimer Norton and Adelaide (Labatt) W.; A.B., Washington and Lee U., 1925; LL.B., Tulane U., 1929; m. Bonnie Stewart Mathews, Oct. 24, 1931; children—John Minor, Kathleen Mathews, Penelope Stewart. Admitted to La. bar, 1929; practiced law as mem. firm Wisdom, Stone, Pigman and Benjamin, New Orleans, 1929-57; judge U.S. Ct. of Appeals, 5th Circuit, 1957—; mem. Multi-Dist. Litigation Panel; part-time prof. law Tulane U., 1938—. Mem. Pres.'s Com. Govt. Contracts. Trustee Washington and Lee U. Served from capt. to lt. col., USAF, 1942-46. Decorated Army Commendation Ribbon, Legion of Merit. Rep. nat. committeeman for La., 1952-57 (mem. exec. com.); chmn. So. Conf. Eisenhower. Past pres. New Orleans Council Social Agys.; treas. Community Chest. Mem. Fgn. Policy Assn. (pres.), Am., La., New Orleans, Inter-Am. bar assns., Am., La. law insts., Order of Coif. Delta Kappa Epsilon, Phi Alpha Delta, Omicron Delta Kappa. Episcopalian. Clubs: Boston, Louisiana (New Orleans); Metropolitan (Washington). Home: 1732 Palmer Av New Orleans LA 70118 Office: 600 Camp St New Orleans LA 70130

WISE, JAMES BERRY, physician; b. Stillwater, Okla., Mar. 15, 1936; s. Paul Conrad and Geneva (Holcomb) W.; B.A., Okla. State U., 1957; M.D., Johns Hopkins, 1961; m. Verena Joss, Sept. 27, 1968; children—Doris Jean, Lee Ann, Ben Paul. Polymer chemist E.I. duPont Co. de Nemours & Co., Inc., Wilmington, Del., 1957; intern, resident Johns Hopkins, 1957-65; postdoctoral research fellow Inst. Ophthalmology, London, Eng., 1965-66; practice medicine, specializing in ophthalmology, Oklahoma City, 1966-67; asst. prof. ophthalmology U. Okla. Med. Sch., Oklahoma City, 1967, asso. prof., 1968—; chief ophthalmology Mercy Hosp., treas. Northwest Eye Physicians Inc. Cons. ophthalmology Oklahoma City VA Hosp. NSF postdoctoral fellow, 1965-66. Diplomate Am. Bd. Ophthalmology. Mem. A.M.A., Okla. State, Oklahoma County med. assns., Am.

Acad. Ophthalmol. and Otolarynology, Johns Hopkins Med. and Surg. Soc. Home: 3401 Hickory Stick Rd Oklahoma City OK 73120 Office: 5700 NW Grand Blvd Oklahoma City OK 73112

WISE, JOHN ELWOOD, ednl. adminstr.; b. Carlisle, Pa., June 6, 1920; s. Jacob William and Lynette Olive (Beetem) W.; B.S., U. Md., 1960; M.A. (fellow) U. Ky., 1964; m. Mary Louise Sympson, Nov. 23, 1949; children—John B., Robert K. Enlisted as pvt., U.S. Army, 1941, advanced through grades to col., 1960; with Dept. Army, Washington, 1951-54, NSA, Washington, 1958-61; dir. Research Found. U. Ky., Lexington, 1961-66; v.p. bus. affairs Med. U. S.C., Charleston, 1967—, asst. prof. adminstrv. medicine, 1967-71. Bd. dirs. S.C. League Nursing, 1967-71. Decorated Combat Infantrymen Badge. NIH grantee 1971-72. Mem. Am. Soc. Personnel Adminstrn., Nat. Assn. Coll. and U. Bus. Officers, Charleston C. of C., Phi Delta Kappa. Mason (Shriner). Home: 446 Wampler Dr Charleston SC 29401

WISE, SIDNEY LEE, publisher; b. Swansea, S.C., Jan. 17, 1924; s. Lee R. and Addie (Hyman) W.; student U. Me., 1942-43; B.J., U. S.C., 1946; M. J., Northwestern U., 1947; m. Agnes B. Delaney, Nov. 24, 1951; children—Sidney Lee II, Charlotte D., Marcus B., Winston W., Marian Olivia, Agnes Terry. Pres. Wing Publs., Inc., Columbia, S.C., 1956—, S.C. Mag. Corp., 1956—, Southeastern Press, Inc., 1959—; editor Carolina Law, 1959—; editor S.C. Mag., 1959—. Pres. Columbia Boys Club Am., 1966—. Served with AUS, 1943-46, 1950-51. Decorated Purple Heart with oak leaf cluster, Bronze Star medal, Silver Star medal. Mem. Columbia C. of C., Am. Legion, Blue Key, Kappa Sigma, Kappa Sigma Kappa. Elk, Moose. Club: Exchange. Home: 6915 Sandy Shore Rd Columbia SC 29206 Office: PO Box 3 Columbia SC 29202

WISE, WES, advt. agy. exec.; b. Shreveport, La., Nov. 25, 1928; s. George Arthur and Myrtle (Hamilton) W.; student N.E. La. U., 1945-46, Kan. State Coll., 1951-52, N.C. State Coll., 1952-53; m. Sally Ann Browning, Sept. 24, 1955; children—Westley, Wynford, Wendy. Broadcaster, KNOE, Monroe, La., 1945-49; baseball broadcaster Liberty Broadcasting System, Dallas, 1949-51; pub. relations dir. Beaumont (Tex.) Baseball Club, 1953-55; sports dir. WFAA-TV, Dallas, 1956-61; news, sports broadcaster KRLD-TV, Dallas, 1961-68; v.p. Underwood Advt., Inc., Dallas, 1969—. Polit. cons. Dallas-Ft. Worth corr. Sports Illustrated Mag., 1960-69; CBS color broadcaster ann. Cotton Bowl Football Classic, 1965-69. Mem. Dallas City Council, 1969-70, mayor, 1971-72. Served with AUS, 1951-53. Mem. Press Club Dallas Found. (past pres.), Sigma Delta Xi. Club: Press (past pres.) (Dallas). Home: 10026 Lakedale Dr Dallas TX 75218 Office: Collum Bldg Dallas TX 75220

WISE, WILLIAM FRANKLIN, apparel mfg. co. exec.; b. Little Mountain, S.C., Aug. 22, 1927; s. James Harold and Vanie (Lake) W.; B.S. in Indsl. Mgmt., Ga. Inst. Tech., 1950; m. Kathleen Skelton, Feb. 8, 1953; children—Phillip, Andrew. Vice pres. sales Wesco Co., Atlanta, 1950-63; v.p., div. mgr. Stone Mfg. Co., Greenville, S.C., 1964—. Served with USNR, 1944-45. Mem. Sales Marketing Execs. Internat. (pres. local chpt.), Phi Sigma Kappa. Lutheran. Home: 209 Terramont Dr Greenville SC 29607 Office: PO Box 3725 Park Pl Greenville SC 29608

WISEBRAM, JOSHUA HENRY, dept. store exec.; b. Atlanta, Aug.9, 1923; s. Elijah and Nora (Rice) W.; B.S., U. N.C., 1948; m. Jeanne D. Witt, June 16, 1946; children—Diane, Steve. With Wisebram's Dept. Store, Inc., Barnesville, Ga., 1948—, gen. mgr., v.p., 1958—; dir. 1st Nat. Bank Barnesville. Pres., Flint River council Boy Scouts Am., 1969-70. Trustee, Gordon Mil. Coll., chmn., 1964-70. 1955—, Served with AUS, 1942-46. Decorated Bronze Star medal; recipient Silver Beaver award Boy Scouts Am., 1965. Mem. Barnesville C. of C., Am. Legion, Phi Beta Kappa. Rotarian (past pres.), Mason (Shriner). Home: 216 Harrell Circle Barnesville GA 30204 Office: 216 Main St Barnesville GA 30204

WISER, RALPH LLOYD, govt. ofcl.; b. Lyndonville, N.Y., June 30, 1910; s. Floyd J. and Alice (Hook) W.; A.B., George Washington U., 1934, J.D., 1938; m. Mae C. Crosby, Sept. 10, 1938; children—Ralph L., Phillip R., Charles S. With CAB, Washington, 1940—, informal complaint and contract examiner, 1940-42, hearing examiner, 1943—, asso. chief examiner, 1968-71, chief examiner, 1971-72, chief adminstrv. law judge, 1972—. Active Boy Scouts Am. Served to lt. USNR, 1943-46. Mem. Am., Active Boy Scouts Am. Fed. bar assns., Delta Theta Phi, Alpha Kappa Psi. Club: Bethesda Country. Home: 3509 Shepherd St Chevy Chase MD 20015 Office: Civil Aeronautics Bd Washington DC 20428

WISER, VIVIAN DORIS, historian; b. Lyndonville, N.Y., June 17, 1915; d. Floyd J. and Alice (Hook) Wiser; A.B., U. Md., 1938, M.A., 1939, Ph.D., 1963; postgrad. George Washington U., 1942-44. Archivist, Nat. Archives, 1943-46, 48-56; historian U.S. Dept. Agr., Washington, 1956—. Recipient Certificate of Merit, U.S. Dept. Agr., 1962; Phi Delta Gamma award to outstanding woman completing Ph.D. requirements U. Md., 1963. Mem. Am. Hist. Assn., Agrl., Md. hist. socs., Am. Soc. Pub. Adminstrn., Orgn. Am. Historians, Soc. Am. Archivists. Author: Records of the Bureau of Agricultural Economics, 1958; (with others) Century of Service: the First 100 Years of the U.S. Department of Agriculture, 1963; writings relevant to farm mgmt. in records Bur. Agrl. Econs. Home: 9522 50th Pl College Park MD 20740 Office: Econ Research Service US Dept Agr Washington DC 20505

WISHCAMPER, ED NUINEZ, editor; b. Oklahoma City, Dec. 30, 1917; s. Alvin Frank and Annie Serilda (Nuinez) W.; B.A., McMurry Coll., 1938, L.H.D. (hon.), 1971; m. Louise Ernestine Smith, Apr. 19, 1941; children—Jan (Mrs. Hubert G. Wardlaw, Jr.), Joe. Reporter, Abilene (Tex.) Reporter-News, 1936-46, news editor, 1946-52, asst. mng. editor, 1952, mng. editor, 1953-68, editor, v.p. editorial, 1968—, dir. Reporter Pub. Co., 1953—. Mem. adv. bd. Salvation Army, 1946—. Trustee, Sunshine Nursery, Abilene; bd. dirs. Taylor County Coliseum, Tex. Election Bur. Served with USNR, 1941-45. Recipient award for citizen contbg. most to pub. edn. Abilene Pub. Schs., 1958, Liberty Bell award Abilene Bar Assn., 1969, Superior Journalism award Tex. Chiropractic Assn., 1971. Mem. Abilene C. of C. (pres. 1970), Am. Soc. Newspaper Editors, W. Tex. Press Assn. (pres. 1955-56), Tex. A.P. Mng. Editors Assn. (pres. 1959). Baptist (deacon 1958-63). Kiwanian (pres. 1969). Home: 1417 Meadowbrook Dr Abilene TX 79603 Office: Box 30 100 block Cypress St Abilene TX 79604

WISHNEFSKY, BRIAN STEPHEN, chemist; b. Fairhaven, Mass., Sept. 2, 1940; s. Jack Isadore and Rebecca (Goldstein) W.; B.S., Southeastern Mass. U., 1962; m. Cynthia Ann Honneyman, Apr. 29, 1961; children—Marci, Aaron, Wendi. Salesman, Uniroyal, Inc., Gastonia, N.C., 1962-71; chemist Gurney Industries, Gastonia, 1971—; owner Mar-Ron Packaging Co. Chmn. ways and means com. Gaston Assn. Retarded Children. Treas., bd. dirs. Gaston Comprehensive Day Care Center for Retarded Children. Recipient Service award N.C. Assn. Retarded Children, 1970. Mem. Delta Kappa Phi. Eagle. Club: Gastonia Sertoma (1st v.p. 1970-71). Home: 615 Honeywood Lane Gastonia NC 28052 Office: 201 E 5th Av Gastonia NC 28052

WISKEMAN, RICHARD HENRY, JR., educator, pub. accountant; b. Akron, O., Feb. 25, 1922; s. Richard Henry and Margaret (Campbell) W.; B.B.A., U. Miami, 1959, M.B.A., 1961; m. Sheila Esther Mary Hardwick, Sept. 20, 1945; 1 son, Richard Henry III. Exec. v.p. Smokeater, Inc., Buffalo, 1949-56; partner Hosken & Wiskeman, C.P.A.'s, Coral Gables, Fla., 1961-62; instr. U. Miami, Coral Gables, 1961-64, asst. prof. accounting, 1964—; gen. practice as C.P.A., South Miami, Fla., 1962-68, merged, became partner Laventhol, Krekstein, Horwath & Horwath, C.P.A.'s, Miami, 1968—; pres. S & D Sales, until 1969; pres., dir. Hetero Investments, Inc., until 1968; sec., dir. Instnl. Investment, Inc., 1962-68; organizer, dir. Mfrs. Nat. Bank Hialeah (Fla.), 1964-66. Bd. assos. South Miami Hosp. Served with USAAF, 1942-46. Mem. Am., Fla. insts. C.P.A.'s, Am. Accounting Assn., Nat. Assn. Accountants (dir. Miami). Presbyn. Mason. Home: 6425 SW 133 Dr Miami FL 33156 Office: 999 S Bayshore Dr Miami FL 33131

WISLAR, GEORGE ROWLAND, investment co. exec.; b. Trenton, N.J., Dec. 12, 1932; s. George Garsed and Marian Beulah (Wakefield) W.; B.A., Yale, 1954; M.B.A., Harvard, 1960; m. Sue Dingman, Dec. 27, 1963; children—Reed W., George G. II, Philip M. Pension adminstr. Bankers Trust Co. N.Y., N.Y.C., 1957-58; registered rep. Kidder, Peabody & Co. N.Y., N.Y.C., 1960-64; with Robinson-Humphrey Co., Inc., Atlanta, 1964—, sr. v.p., dir., 1969—; dir., chmn. exec. com. Nat. Data Corp., Atlanta, 1967—. Served to capt. USMC, 1954-57. Mem. Phi Gamma Delta. Republican. Episcopalian. Clubs: Peachtree Golf, Piedmont Driving, Commerce (Atlanta); University (N.Y.C.). Home: 412 Broadland Rd NW Atlanta GA 30342 Office: Robinson-Humphrey Co Inc Two Peachtree St Atlanta GA 30303

WITHERELL, JULIAN WOOD, research librarian; b. Washington, Aug. 29, 1935; B.A. in History, Bowdoin Coll., 1956; M.A., U. Wis., 1958, Ph.D., 1962. Reference librarian Library of Congress, Washington, 1962-64, Africa specialist, 1964-66, head African sect., 1966—. Publ. survey trips, Africa, Library of Congress, 1963-68. Mem. African Studies Assn., A.L.A., Am. Hist. Assn. Contbr. profl. jours. Home: 7109 Braddock Rd Springfield VA 22151*

WITHERS, BEN TERREL, physician; b. Jasper, Tex., Dec. 18, 1915; s. Bennie Terrel and Bertice (Justice) W.; B.A., U. Tex., 1937, M.D., 1940; M.S., Washington U., 1948; m. Denise H. Crook, Jan. 1, 1944; children—Ellen Elizabeth, Timothy Justice. Intern Jeff Davis Hosp., Houston, 1940-42, resident, 1945-46; postgrad. Barnes Hosp., St. Louis, 1946-47; practice medicine, specializing in ear, nose and throat, Houston, 1947—; mem. staff Hermann Hosp., Meth. Ben Taub Gen., Jefferson Davis, Baptist Meml., St. Josephs hosps.; asst. clin. prof. otolaryngology Baylor Med. Coll., 1947-65, clin. prof., 1965—. Bd. dirs. Houston Speech and Hearing Center; vice chmn. med. div. United Fund Dr., 1953-54. Served from 1st lt. to maj. M.C., AUS, 1942-45. Decorated Bronze Star medal. Fellow A.C.S.; mem. A.M.A., Am. Acad. Otolaryngology, Am. Triological Soc., Am. Otol. Soc., Tex. State, Harris County med. socs., Tex. Ophthal. and Otolaryngol. Soc., Houston Otolaryngol. Soc. (pres. 1957-58), Postgrad. Med. Assembly S. Tex. (pres. 1967-68), Tex. Otolaryngol. Assn. (pres. 1966-68). Episcopalian. Contbr. articles in field to profl. jours. Home: 2211 Troon Rd Houston TX 77019 Office: Hermann Profl Bldg Houston TX 77025

WITHERS, JAMES CLYDE, aircraft co. exec.; b. Buna, Tex., Nov. 5, 1934; s. James William and Vera Idel (Owens) W.; student U.S. Naval Acad., 1952-53; B.S., Am. U., 1956, M.S., 1957, postgrad., 1957-60; m. Helga Tiffany Heppich, Apr. 17, 1969; children—(by previous marriage)—Marc, Chris, Laura. Asst. mgr. materials div. Melpar, Inc., Falls Church, Va., 1954-58; mgr. materials br. Am. Machine and Foundry Co., Alexandria, Va., 1958-61; pres., chief operations officer Gen. Techs. Corp., Reston, Va., 1961—; chmn. bd. Potomac Savs. & Loan Assn. Mem. adv. bd. Va. Poly. Inst., 1969—. Mem. Lakeside Cluster Assn. (pres. 1969-70). Club: Golf and Country (pres. 1970-71) (Reston). Home: 1612 Greenbriar Ct Reston VA 22070 Office: 1821 Michael Faraday Dr Reston VA 22070

WITHERS, K(AY) BALL, lawyer; b. Galveston, Tex., May 19, 1935; s. William Banks and Alledo (Ball) W.; A.B., U. Tex., 1957; LL.B., Harvard, 1960; m. Ann McGivney Hamilton, May 16, 1964; children—Susan McGivney, Pamela Ball. Admitted to Tex. bar, 1960; practiced in Galveston, 1960-61, 62-70; mem. firm Greenberg and Schwartz, 1962-65, Schwartz & Withers, 1965-66, Levy, Levy, Schwab, Coughlin & Withers, 1970—. Alternate judge of Corp. Ct., City of Galveston, 1964-67; local counsel Galveston Housing Authority, 1964—. Bd. dirs. Galveston Little Theatre, 1964-66, Performing Arts Enterprises, 1968-72. Served with AUS, 1961-62. Mem. Am., Tex., Galveston County bar assns., Phi Beta Kappa, Phi Eta Sigma. Home: 3311 Ashton Pl Galveston TX 77550 Office: US National Bank Bldg Galveston TX 77550

WITHERSPOON, JAMES W., lawyer; b. Indianola, Okla., Sept. 20, 1906; s. Ernest and Mary Etta (Stafford) W.; A.B., Montezuma Coll., 1926; LL.B., U. Okla., 1929; m. Margaret Gilliland, July 25, 1930 (dec.); children—Gerald Winfrey (dec.), Eleanor Irene (Mrs. Calvin R. Couch); m. 2d, Elizabeth Womble, Feb. 14, 1959. Admitted to U.S. Supreme Ct. bar, Tex. bar, 1929, since practiced in Hereford; dist. atty., 1933-40, dist. judge, 1940-44; legislative rep. Tex.-N.M. Sugar Beet Growers Assn., now exec. sec. Committeeman state-wide Tex. Hi-Y. Chmn. bd 1st Nat. Bank Herefore; dir. Colo. Beef Producers, Inc., Transport Life Ins. Co., Agri-Basic Corp. Bd. dirs. Tex. A. & M. Coll., 1951-57. Mem. Am. Bar Assn., State Bar Tex., Tex. Assn. Plaintiffs' Attys., Nat. Plaintiffs' Attys. Assn., Am. Judicature Soc., Am. Coll. Probate Counsel, Tex. Bar Found., Am. Trial Lawyers Assn., Nat. Assn. Tax Attys., C. of C., S.A.R., S.C.V., Panhandle Hist. Soc. (dir.), Phi Alpha Delta. Mason (Shriner), Rotarian, Elk. Clubs: Knife and Fork, Amarillo (Hereford). Home: 1712 Plains St Hereford TX 79045 Office: PO Box 1818 Hereford TX 79045

WITHEY, GRAYDON GILLULY, judge; b. Reed City, Mich., June 16, 1910; s. Charles Alan and Helene Rose (Doherty) W.; student pub. schs.; m. Edna B. Leonard, Mar. 9, 1929; children—Sally May (Mrs. Messinger), Joan Gray (Mrs. Patrick Gillespie), Carol Ray (Mrs. Raymond Mackey), James Charles, John Alan. Factory machinist Buick div. Gen. Motors Corp., Flint. Mich., 1928-29; law stenographer, student law office Charles A. Withey, Flint, 1929-33; admitted to Mich. bar, 1933; chief asst. prosecutor, Genesee Co., Mich., 1937-38; practice of law, Flint, 1939-48, 51-52; dep. atty. gen., Mich., 1949-50; judge tax ct. U.S., 1952—. Mem. Am., Mich. Genesee Co. bar assns. Democrat. Elk. Home: 2011 N Quantico St Arlington VA 22205 Office: Tax Court of US Washington DC 20044

WITHROW, JON RICHARD, geologist; b. Seminole, Okla., Jan. 8, 1933; s. Richard Dean and LoLeta (Carroll) W.; student Seminole Jr. Coll., 1950-51; B.S. in Petroleum Engring., U. Okla., 1954, M. Geol. Engring., 1959; postgrad. U. Tex., 1958; m. Carol Ann Ferguson, Nov. 21, 1960 (div. Nov. 1968); 1 stepdau., Ann Todd. Mem. engr. tng. program Humble Oil & Refining Co., Odessa, Tex., 1954, petroleum engr., asst. to dist. engr., Andrews, Tex., 1954-55, Wink, Tex., 1955-56, petroleum engr., Midland, Tex., 1956-57, Houston, 1957, Midland, 1957-58; petroleum engr., geologist Montgomery Oil Co., El Dorado, Ark., 1959-60; self-employed petroleum engr., geologist, Oklahoma City, 1960-62; mgr. geol. and engring. dept. Sarkeys Enterprises, Oklahoma City, 1962-65; mgr. geol. and engring. dept. Sarkeys, Inc., Oklahoma City, 1965-72, v.p., 1966-72; ind. petroleum geol. engr., 1972—. Registered profl. engr., Okla. Mem. Am. Inst. Mining, Metall, and Petroleum Engrs., Am. Assn. Petroleum Geologists, Nat., Okla. socs. profl. engrs., Oklahoma City Geol. Soc., Oklahoma City Tennis Assn., S.A.R., Sigma Nu, Tau Beta Pi, Pi Epsilon Tau. Republican. Methodist. Clubs: Oklahoma City Ski, Oklahoma City Racquet. Home: 6300 NW 63d St Oklahoma City OK 73114

WITT, ROBERT EDWARD, oil co. exec.; b. El Dorado, Ark., June 28, 1909; s. Edward Nathan and Lula Rebecca (Rankin) W.; student Davidson Coll., 1926-27, 29-30, Washington U., St. Louis, 1927-28; A.B., U. Ark., 1934; M.A., 1934; m. Zoe Elizabeth O'Ferrall, Feb. 22, 1938; 1 dau., Zoe Ann. Chemist Lion Oil Co., El Dorado, 1934-36, with asphalt sales dept., 1936-56, mgr. asphalt sales dept., 1956-58; pres. Witt Oil Prodn. Co., Shreveport, La., El Dorado, 1957—. Mem. asphalt subcom. War Petroleum Adminstrn., 1942-44. Pres. El Dorado Community Chest Bd., 1955; chmn. Community Chest Campaign, 1953; pres. Sr. Teen Age Club Bd., 1956, El Dorado Community Concert Assn., 1956, El Dorado Library Bd., 1946-47; bd. dirs., exec. v.p. Shreveport Symphony Soc.; vice chmn. Sewanee All Saints Campaign, 1952-54; chmn. dept. finance exec. council Diocese of Ark., 1953-54, mem. steering com., 1958-64, mem. com. mission extension, 1964-67; dep. gen. conv. Episcopal Ch., 1953, 56. Trustee, mem. exec. com. Sem. of S.W., Austin, Tex.; adv. bd. trustees Warner-Brown Hosp. Mem. Independent Petroleum Assn. Am. (Ark. v.p. 1960-63, exec. com. 1963-66), Assn. Asphalt Paving Technologists, Asphalt Inst. (mem. mgmt. com. Div. III 1950-58), Mid-Continent Oil and Gas Assn. (exec. com.), Shreveport C. of C. Sigma Upsilon. Democrat. Episcopalian. Rotarian (dir.). Clubs: Shreveport, Shreveport Petroleum; Athelstan (Mobile, Ala.). Home: 710 N Madison Av El Dorado AR 71730 Office: Comml Bank Bldg Shreveport LA 71101 also Petroleum Bldg El Dorado AR 71730

WITTE, JOHN JACOB, health ofcl.; b. Passaic, N.J., Mar. 10, 1932; s. John Jacob and Edith (Beswick) W.; A.B., Hope Coll., 1954; M.D., Johns Hopkins, 1959; M.P.H., Harvard, 1966; m. Shelley Gothran, June 28, 1968; children—Kelli Ruth, Nanci Kay, Susan Scott. Intern, Johns Hopkins Hosp., Balt., 1959-60, resident in pediatrics, 1960-62; commd. officer USPHS, 1962; med. epidemiologist Epidemic Intelligence Service, Center for Disease Control, Atlanta, 1962-64, dep. chief. Surveillance sect. epidemiology br., 1964-65, chief field services br., 1966-70, chief immunization br., 1970—. Mem. adv. com. immunization practices USPHS, 1969—. Diplomate Am. Bd. Preventive Medicine. Fellow Am. Coll. Preventive Medicine, Am. Pub. Health Assn.; mem. A.M.A., Ga. Pediatric Soc., Am. Acad. Pediatrics (mem. com. on control infectious diseases 1970—), Commd. Officers Assn. USPHS. Contbr. articles to profl. jours. Home: 4774 W Hampton Dr Tucker GA 30084 Office: Center for Disease Control 1600 Clifton Rd Atlanta GA 30333

WITTEN, VICTOR HERBERT, dermatologist; b. Jacksonville, Fla., Aug. 8, 1916; s. Morris H. and Cecilia W. (Starr) W.; student Washington and Lee U., 1934-35; B.S., Tulane U., 1938, M.D., 1941; postgrad. N.Y. U. Med. Sch., 1946-49; m. Joan Adrienne Kalmine, June 22, 1956 (dec. Aug. 1970). Preceptee, Office of Marion B. Sulzberger, N.Y.C., 1946-49; practice medicine, specializing in dermatology, N.Y.C., 1949-62, Miami, Fla., 1968—; mem. faculty N.Y. U. Med. Sch., 1950-62, asso. clin. prof. dermatology, 1957-62; prof. dermatology U. Miami Sch. Medicine, 1962-68, clin. prof., 1968—; cons. VA Hosp., N.Y.C., 1955-62, Rockefeller Inst., 1957-62. Mem. adv. panel on med. and biol. scis. Office Research and Engring., U.S. Dept. Def., 1962-67; mem. adv. com. on gen. medicine, also chmn. subcom. dermatology to surgeon gen. U.S. Army Med. Research and Devel. Command. 1962-71; mem. commn. on cutaneous diseases Armed Forces Epidemiological Bd., 1968-71. Trustee Dermatology Found. Miami. Served from lt. j.g. to lt. comdr., M.C., USNR, 1942-46. Fellow Am. Acad. Dermatology (v.p. 1969, dir. 1966-69), A.C.P., N.Y. Acad. Medicine, N.Y. Acad. Scis.; mem. Am. Dermatol. Assn., Venezuelan Soc. Dermatology, Venerology and Leprology, Israeli Dermatology Assn., Danish Dermatology Soc., Soc. for Investigative Dermatology, Pan-Am. Med. Assn. (mem. council dermatology sect. 1970—). Author: (with Marion B. Sulzberger and Jack Wolf) Essentials of Diagnosis and Treatment, 1961; (with Rudolf L. Baer) Yearbook of Dermatology, 1955-62. Mem. internat. editorial bd. Excepta Medica, 1955—; mem. editorial adv. bd. Skin and Allergy News, 1969—. Contbr. articles to med. jours. Home: 480 Casuarina Concourse Coral Gables FL 33143 Office: 1150 NW 14th St Miami FL 33136

WITTI, FRITZ PAUL, univ. ofcl.; b. Munich, Germany, May 10, 1925; s. Eugen and Johanna (Breitner) W.; B.A., U. Minn., 1949; m. Jean Eloidie Hermanson, July 1, 1950; 1 dau., Gretchen. Came to U.S., 1929, naturalized, 1938. Corr., Asso. Press, Mpls., Fargo, N.D., Washington, 1952-63; pub. information officer U.S. Office of Edn., Washington, 1963-64; press relations mgr. Am. Cyanamid Co., Wayne, N.J., 196465; news bur. mgr., asso. dir., pub. relations N.Y.U., 1965-66; press officer, dep. dir., dir. pub. information U.S. Dept. Health, Edn. and Welfare, Washington, 1966-68; v.p. devel. and univ. relations Am. U., Washington, 1968—. Served with AUS, 1943-46. Unitarian. Home: Alexandria VA 22313 Office: Nebraska and Massachusetts Avs NW Washington DC 20016

WITTMANN, STEPHAN JOHN, physician; b. Budapest, Hungary, Jan. 7, 1933; s. Anthony and Maria Kathleen (Gyengesi) W.; came to U.S., 1957; student Georgetown U., 1958-60; B.S., U. Md., 1962, M.D., 1966; m. Maria Irsa, Sept. 4, 1965; children—Nicole, Suzann, Nora. Intern Mercy Hosp., Balt., 1966; resident anesthesia U. Va. Hosp., Charlottesville, 1967-69; anesthesiologist Martha Jefferson Hosp., Charlottesville, 1969, Fairfax (Va.) Hosp., 1969-71, Washington Sanitorium, Takoma Park, Md., 1969-71, Manatee Meml. Hosp., Bradenton, Fla., 1971—; asst. chief anesthesia, tchr. resident program Walter Reed Gen. Hosp., Washington, 1969-71. Served as maj. AUS, 1969-71. Mem. Am. Soc. Anesthesiologists, Internat. Anesthesia Research Soc. Home: 719 Hillcrest Dr Bradenton FL 33505 Office: Manatee Memorial Hospital Bradenton FL 33505

WITTNER, TED PHILIP, ins. exec.; b. Tampa, Sept. 17, 1928; s. Jacob and Helen (Goldman) W.; B.S. in Bus. Adminstrn., U. Fla., 1950; m. Sylvia Haller, Apr. 3, 1954; children—Sharyn (Mrs. Richard Jacobson), Pamela Anne. Mgr., Bell Luggage Co., 1953-54; pvt. life ins. agt., 1955-56; gen. agt. Crown Life Ins. Co., St. Petersburg, Fla., 1956-64; pres. Ted P. Wittner & Assos., 1964-67, pres. Wittner & Co., 1968-72 (both St. Petersburg.); pres. Crown Life Brokerage Gen. Agts. Assn., 1968-70, Profit Programs Co., St. Petersburg, 1969—; dir. Nat. Bank St. Petersburg, Para-Med. Enterprises, Inc., St. Petersburg. Mem. Com. of 100; Pinellas County mem. St. Petersburg Civic Adv. Com. Bd. dirs. Pinellas Assn. Retarded Children; bd. dirs., sec.-treas. Menorah Center. Served to 2d lt. USAF, 1950-53. Life and qualifying mem. Million Dollar Round Table. Mem. Gen. Agts. and Mgrs. Conf. (pres. St. Petersburg chpt. 1957), Nat. Assn. Life Underwriters, St. Petersburg Area C. of C. (v.p. 1969-72), Fla. Blue Key. Jewish religion (pres. congregation 1966-68, chmn. bd. 1964-66). Club: Commerce (v.p.) St. Petersburg. Home: 6726 10th Av N St Petersburg FL 33710 Office: 3663 Central Av St Petersburg FL 33713

WITTS, DAVID, lawyer; b. Denton, Tex., Dec. 13, 1920; s. Phillip and Mary (Lee) W.; LL.B., So. Methodist U., 1948; m. Jean Travis, June 21, 1950; 1 dau., Elane. Admitted to Tex. bar, 1948; mem. firm Witts, Lee, Pletcher, Douglass & Casterline, Dallas, 1948—. Dir. Dallas County State Bank, Carrollton, Tex.; chmn. bd. Bank of Mesquite (Tex.), 1971—. Chief counsel, gen. investigating com. Tex. Legislature, 1956-70. Mem. council Scott and White Clinic, Temple, Tex., 1960—. Served with USAAF, 1942-46; Decorated Air medal. Mem. Am. Judicature Soc., State Bar Tex. (chmn. Am. citizenship com. 1950-53), Tex. Hereford Assn., Am. Legion (past comdr.), Phi Alpha Delta. Editor-in-chief Southwestern Law Jour., 1947. Office: 1000 Empire Life Bldg Dallas TX 75201

WITTY, ROBERT GEE, ednl. adminstr.; b. Glasgow, Ky., Oct. 6, 1906; s. Robert Lee and Maude Mae (Lawrence) W.; A.B., Willmette U., 1928; postgrad. Princeton Theol. Sem., 1929; B.D., Asbury Theol. Sem., 1932; Ph.D., U. Fla., 1959; m. Katherine Henderson Hoover, Dec. 24, 1943; children—Mary (Mrs. Marty Span), Robert Maxwell, Edith, Daniel, Ann, Robert Earl Hoover. Ordained to ministry Baptist Ch., 1944; pastor Faith Temple, Jacksonville, Fla., 1935-43, Central Bapt. Ch., 1942-70; pres. Luther Rice Sem., 1966—, dean grad. studies, 1964-66; treas. Bapt. Towers, Inc., Jacksonville, 1969—; Bd. dirs. Fredricksburg Bible Inst.; bd. mission Fla. Bapt. Conv., 1970-73, central com. 1971—. Mem. Pastor's Conf. (pres. 1969-70). Author: Power for Church, 1968; Help Yourself to Happiness, 1969; Church Visitation, 1969; Signs of the Second Coming, 1970. Home: 357 Tidewater Dr Jacksonville FL 32211 Office: 1050 Hendricks Av Jacksonville FL 32207

WIYGUL, GLENN, entomologist; b. Shannon, Miss., Nov. 26, 1940; s. Frank Mitchell and Mabel Stein (Gordon) W.; grad. Itawamba Jr. Coll., 1960; B.S., Miss. State U., 1962, M.S., 1964. Research technologist Boll Weevil Research Lab., State College, Miss., 1964-65, chemist, 1965-66, entomologist, 1966—. Mem. Entomol. Soc. Am., Sigma Xi. Contbr. articles to sci. jours. Home: 9 McKee Trailer Ct Starkville MS 39759 Office: Box 5367 State College MS 39762

WOERNER, NORWOOD KELLER, state ofcl.; b. Omaha, Feb. 8, 1908; s. William Herman and Alice (Meier) W.; B.A., Municipal U., Omaha, 1931; m. Virginia Jane McGuire, Feb. 28, 1946. Statistician, Tex. Hwy. Dept., Austin, 1936-39; chief statistician Tex. Dept. Pub. Safety, Austin, 1939-42, dir. research and statistics, 1946-71; traffic cons. Tex. Commn. on Law Enforcement Officer Standards and Tng., Austin, 1971—; Tex. coordinator project STAR (systems and tng. analysis of requirements), Am. Justice Inst., Austin, 1971—. Instr. Tex. Police Tng. Acad., 1939—. Chmn. nat. com. Uniform Traffic Accident Statistics, 1954-62; chmn. com. on research Tex. Mil.-Civilian Traffic Safety Council, 1960—; mem. Nat. Crime Information Center Devel. Bd., 1967. Served to capt. USAAF, 1942-46; exec. officer Spl. Investigations Detachment Tex. State Guard. Mem. Am. Statis. Assn. (chpt. pres. 1961), Tex. Police Assn., Sheriffs Assn. Tex., Tex. Pub. Employees Assn. (bd. mem. 1964-67), Am. Soc. Pub. Adminstrn. (past chpt. pres.). Mason, K.P. Home: 1400 Ridgemont Dr Austin TX 78723 Office: Box 4087 Austin TX 78776

WOERNER, PERRY MONROE, banker; b. Fredericksburg, Tex., Mar. 5, 1924; s. Charles H. and Mary (Ahrens) W.; B.A., Bob Jones U., 1956; postgrad. Nat. Trust Sch. Northwestern U., 1964; m. Bernice Durst, Aug. 14, 1946; children—Rene Sheldon, Hadley Ross, Gaylon Reese. With Schneider Produce Co., 1941-42, Stehling Brothers Mens Clothiers, 1946-47; program clk. U.S. Agr. Dept., 1949-52, adminstrv. asst., 1956-59; with Fredericksburg Nat. Bank, 1959—, asst. cashier, asst. trust officer, 1961-64, trust officer, 1965— (all Fredericksburg). Chmn. service unit Salvation Army, 1959-70; pres. Gillespie County Am. Cancer Soc., 1962-63. Served with AUS, 1943-46; PTO. Mem. C. of C. (past dir.), S. Central Fedn. Gem and Minerol. Socs. (dir. 1970—), Gillespie County Ministerial Assn. (sec. 1970—). Mem. Emmanuel Gospel Ch. (asso. pastor 1959—). Rotarian. Club: Rockhounds. Home: 407 E College St Fredericksburg TX 78624 Office: 155 E Main St Fredericksburg TX 78624

WOFFORD, CHARLES AUGUSTUS, govt ofcl., judge; b. Atlanta, Nov. 29, 1914; s. James Avery and Ollie Eva (Osborne) W.; LL.B., Atlanta Law Sch., 1943, LL.M., 1945; LL.D., Webster U., 1945; m. Marie Norene Root, July 6, 1936; children—Charles Augustus, Stephanie (Mrs. Roddy Ingraham). Judge municipal Ct., City Atlanta, 1954-58; judge Criminal Ct. Fulton County, 1959-67; judge, Fulton Superior Ct., Atlanta Jud. Circuit, 1967—. Pres., Overland Guaranty and Ins. Agy., Inc. Hon. dir. Atlanta Health Council. Charter pres. Ga. Children's Chiropractic Center; bd. dirs. Joseph B. Whitehead Meml. Boys' Club. Mem. Am., Atlanta bar assns., Atlanta Lawyers Club, State Bar Ga., Fulton County Lawyers Assn., Underwater Soc. Am., Peace Officers Assn. Ga., Rack-N-Cue Soc., Atlanta Law Sch. Alumni Assn. (charter pres.), Old War Horse Lawyers Assn., Sigma Delta Kappa (life mem., officer numerous offices). Mason (K.T., 33 deg.), K.P. (chancellor comdr. 1945), Elk, Eagle, Moose; mem. Order Eastern Star. Clubs: Atlanta Athletic, East Lake Country, Lakeside Country (Atlanta). Home: 636 Virginia Av NE Atlanta GA 30306 Office: Fulton County Ct House 136 Pryor St SE Atlanta GA 30303

WOJCIK, GEORGE PAUL, rubber co. ofcl.; b. Wheeling, W.Va., Apr. 21, 1925; s. Michael and Agnes (Tomasovic) W.; B.S., U. So. Cal., 1950; student Bethany Coll., 1943-44; m. Erin Jean Wade, June 7, 1947; 1 son, Mark Stephen. Accountant Baker Oil Tools, Inc., Los Angeles, 1949-51; sr. cost accountant B.F. Goodrich Co., Los Angeles, 1951-53, supr. accounting, 1953-57, mgr. accounting, Miami, Okla., 1957-66, staff supt., 1966—. Mem. Gov.'s. Mgmt. Study Com. on Efficiency, Okla., 1967. Served with USNR, 1943-47. Mem. Miami C. of C. (dir.). K.C. Club: Miami Golf and Country (pres. 1968-69, dir. 1967-70). Home: 1216 Johnson Dr Miami OK 74354 Office: 1000 Goodrich Blvd Miami OK 74354

WOLF, CLARENCE, JR., stockbroker; b. Phila., May 11, 1908; s. Clarence and Nan (Hogan) W.; student Pa. Mil. Prep. Sch., 1921; grad. Swarthmore (Pa.) Prep. Sch., 1923; m. Alma C. Backhus, Sept. 11, 1942. Founder French-Wolf Paint Products Corp., Phila., 1926, pres. until 1943; admitted to Phila.-Balt. Stock Exchange, 1937; asso. Reynolds & Co., 1944—, rep., Miami Beach, Fla., 1946—, apptd. spl. rep., 1963; dir., vice chmn. bd., mem. exec. com. Am. Cement Corp.; dir. George S. MacManus Co., Rand Broadcasting Co., owners radio and TV stas., also hotels, 1946-68. Pres. Normandy Isles Improvement Assn., Miami Beach, 1952-53; mem. Presidents Council Miami Beach, 1952—. Mem. Alumnus Assn. Pa. Mil. Coll. (Fla. dir. 1961—). Clubs: Penn Athletic (Phila.); Variety, Standard (Miami, Fla.). Home: Seacoast Towers 5151 Collins Av Miami Beach FL 33140 Office: care Reynolds & Co 202 SE 1st St Miami FL 33131

WOLF, ROBERT FORRY, food co. exec.; b. Hellam, Pa., Nov. 5, 1926; s. Spungon Wilson and Edith Irene (Forry) W.; grad. high sch.; m. Jean Collene Libhant, Oct. 28, 1950; children—Michael, Julia, Cindy. Sales and product mgr. Swift & Co., Harrisburg, Pa., 1950-56; dir. meats P.A. & S. Small Co., York, Pa., 1956-58; div. mgr. Anbogast & Bastian, Allentown, Pa., 1958-63; div. mgr. HyGrade Food Products, Richmond, Va., 1963-67; v.p. prodn. and distbn. Hardee's Food Systems, Inc., Rocky Mount, N.C., 1967—. Served with USAAF, 1944-46. Lutheran. Mason. Home & Office: 1233 N Church St Rocky Mount NC 27801

WOLFE, J. SMILEY, banker; b. Savannah, Ga., July 26, 1904; s. Joseph S. and Susie E. (Ridle) W.; ed. Armstrong Coll.; m. Elizabeth Simmons; children—John, Sue. With Citizens and So. Nat. Bank Athens (Ga.), 1940—, exec. v.p., 1962—; dir. E. & S. Nat. Bank, Athens. Pres., Community Chest, 1948-50, Clarke County Bd. Edn., 1960-63, Athens Gen. Hosp., 1964-69. Commr. Clarke County, Ga., 1971. Mem. bd. YMCA, Salvation Army, N.E. Ga. council Boy Scouts Am.; trustee Methodist Childrens Home. Mem. Athens C. of C. (past pres.). Methodist (steward, trustee). Kiwanian (mem. bd.). Home: 210 McWhorter Dr Athens GA 30601 Office: Citizens & So Nat Bank Athens GA 30601

WOLFE, JOHN ALLEN, cons. firm exec.; b. Riverton, Ia., June 3, 1920; s. Asa Allen and Alice (Thomas) W.; Geol. Engr., Colo. Sch. Mines, 1947, M.S., 1954; children—James Perry, Cynthia (Mrs. J.A. Banghart Jr.), m. 2d, Lenora Irvin, 1969. Dir. exploration Ideal Cement Co., Denver, 1948-65; geol cons., P.I., Latin Am., 1965-68; pres. Mineral Resources Cons., Houston, 1968—; partner Schoenike, Wolfe & Assos., Houston, 1970—; v.p., gen. mgr. Lobo Mines, Inc., Manila, Philippines, 1970—. Lectr., cons. in field; mem. Colo. Mining Industry Devel. Bd., 1963-65. Fellow Geol. Soc. Am.; mem. Am. Mining Congress (gov. 1963-65), Colo. Mining Assn. (pres. 1963), Am. Inst. Mining Engrs., Soc. Econ. Geologists, Am. Inst. Profl. Geologists. Republican. Contbr. articles to profl. jours. Home: care Lobo Mines Inc 504 Manila Banking Bldg Makati Rizal Philippines Office: 5133 Richmond Av Suite 1 Houston TX 77027

WOLFE, RICHARD ARLEN, banker; b. Pulaski, Va., Mar. 10, 1936; s. Steine Clarence and Katherine Marie (Ferguson) W.; student Emmanuel Coll., Franklin Springs, Fa., 1953-55, Valencia Jr. Coll., 1970—; m. Vesta Joyce Cole, Nov. 14, 1957; children—Richard Douglas, Ronald Steine. With 1st Nat. Bank Orlando Fla., 1959-68, data processing officer, 1966-67; v.p. Citizens Nat. Bank Orlando, 1968—. Served with USAF, 1955-59. Mem. Orlando Jr. C. of C. (dir. 1970), Data Processing Mgmt. Assn. Republican. Mem. Assembly of God (deacon). Home: 202 E Kaley St Orlando FL 32806 Office: 250 N Orange St Orlando FL 32802

WOLFE, THOMAS LEROY, lawyer; b. Wichita Falls, Tex., Oct. 24, 1928; s. Thomas G. and Virginia (Martin) W.; B.S., U. Va., 1950; LL.B., U. Okla., 1953, M.B.A., 1954; m. Anita Mackenzie, Dec. 31, 1953; children—Thomas T., Melissa J., Megan Mackenzie, Beverly. Admitted to Okla. bar, 1953, Fla. bar, 1958; practiced in Oklahoma City, 1953-54; partner firm Shutts & Bowen and predecessor firms, Miami, Fla., 1958—. Instr. Oklahoma City U., 1954; dir. Hill Bros. Inc., Jerry's, Inc. Mem. South Fla. council Small Bus. Adminstrn.; mem. Miami Com. of 100. Bd. dirs. Guliver Acad. Served to capt. Judge Adj. Gens. Corps, AUS, 1955-58; maj. Res. C.P.A., Okla. Mem. Sigma Phi Epsilon (treas. alumni bd.). Methodist (steward). Clubs: University, Rotary (pres. 1968-69, dir.). Home: 6330 Cellini St Coral Gables FL 33146 Office: 1st Nat Bank Bldg Miami FL 33131

WOLFE, TOWNSEND DURANT, III, arts center exec., educator, artist; b. Hartsville, S.C., Aug. 15, 1935; s. Christian Townsend and Elizabeth (Bryant) W.; student Ga. Inst. Tech., 1954-57; B.F.A., Atlanta Sch. Art, 1958; M.F.A., Cranbrook Acad. Art, 1959; postgrad. Harvard Inst. in Arts Adminstrn., 1970; m. Jane Rightor Lee, Aug. 28, 1968; 1 dau., Zibilla Lee; children by previous marriage— Juliette Fielding, Mary Bryan, Townsend Durant IV. Tchr., Atlanta Art Assn., 1957-59, Memphis Acad. Art, 1959-64, Ark. Arts Center, Little Rock, 1960-64, Scarsdale (N.Y.) Studio Workshop, 1965, Seamen Inst., N.Y.C., 1965; dir. Wooster Community Art Center, Fund for Advancement of Edn., Danbury, Conn., 1966-68; exec. dir. Ark. Arts Center, Little Rock, 1968—; exhibited in one-man shows including Madison Gallery N.Y.C., Memphis Acad. Arts, 1961, U. Ark, Med. Center, Little Rock, 1962, U. Miss. Oxford, 1962, Miss. Art Assn. Jackson, 1963, Ark. State U. Jonesboro, 1964-70, Southwestern U., Memphis, 1964, Wooster Sch., Danbury, Conn., 1966, Hoffman Gallery, 1968, others; exhibited in group shows including U. Miami, 1963, Birmingham (Ala.) Mus. Arts Religious Exhbn., 1966, Mercyhurst Coll. Graphics Exhbn., 1967; Audubon Arts, N.Y.C., 1968, S.C. Tri-Centennial Exhbn., Greenville, 1970; numerous others; Model Cities rep., Little Rock, 1969. Recipient Prize for Painting, Atlanta Art Inst., 1958, purchase prize Okla. Printmakers Soc. Nat. Exhbn., 1961, hon. mention Southeastern Ann. Exhbn., 1962, Popular prize Mid-South Exhbn., 1963, M.J. Kaplan award Nat. Soc. Painters in Casein, N.Y.C., 1965, Framemakers' Watercolor award 17th Ann. New Eng. Exhbn., 1966, award of Merit, Purchase award 57th Nat. Painting Exhbn., Miss. Art Assn., 1967, Silvermine Guild award 18th Ann. New Eng. Exhbn., 1967, numerous others. Represented in collections at Ark. Arts Center, First Nat. Bank Memphis, U. Okla., Ark. State Coll., Memphis Acad. Art, Mint Mus., Charlotte, N.C., N.A.A.C.P., Memphis, Miss. Art Assn., Jackson, Worthen Bank & Trust Co., Little Rock, Middle S. Utilities Corp., New Orleans. Mem. Artists Equity. Rotarian. Home: 2119 S Scott St Little Rock AK 72203 Office: Ark Arts Center MacArthur Park Little Rock AK 72203

WOLFF, ELMER ALBERT, JR., elec. products co. exec.; b. Dallas, Jan. 16, 1930; s. Elmer Albert and Mary (Crumpley) W.; B.S., So. Meth. U., 1952, M.S., 1953; m. Elizabeth Ann Wiggs, June 27, 1956; children—Mary Lou, James R. Franklin. With Tex. Instruments, Inc., Dallas, 1953—, sr. engr., 1955-58, chief engr. Tex. Instruments Ltd., Bedford, England, 1965-67, dept. mgr., Dallas, 1967—. Teaching fellow So. Meth. U., 1952-53. Mem. I E.E.E., Tex. Profl. Engrs. Republican. Home: 317 Sutton St Richardson TX 75080 Office: Semi Conductor Group North Central Expressway Dallas TX 75222

WOLFF, NIGEL O'CONNOR, mus. adminstr.; b. Ickesburg, Pa., Dec. 17, 1916; s. Edward Kenneth and Dorcas (Niles) W.; student Pa. State U., 1933-34, Swarthmore Coll., 1938-39; m. Dorothy Florence Davies, June 8, 1940; 1 son, Stephen South. Lab. technician, asst. dir. antivenin dept. Sharp & Dohme, Inc., Glenolden, Pa., 1935-40; keeper monkey house Phila. Zool. Garden, 1940-41, asst. curator, 1941-43; pub. relations dir. Franklin Inst., Phila., 1944-46; asst. dir. edn., lectr. Fels Planetarium, 1948-50; gen. mgr. C.E.S. Assos., pub. relations, Phila., 1946-48; exec. v.p. Spitz Labs., Inc., Phila., 1950-53; curator Phila. Comml. Mus., 1953-54; dir. Municipal Planetarium, Montevideo, Uruguay, tech. adviser Municipal Zool. Gardens, Montevideo, 1954-58; vol. worker Am. Friends Serv. Com., Gould Farm, Inc., Great Barrington, Mass., 1958-59; dir. sci. projects div. Edmund Sci. Co., Barrington, N.J., 1959-61; dir. Md. Acad. Scis., Balt., 1961-72; dep. dir. Mus. African Art, Washington, 1972—. Pres., Internat. Inst. Phila., 1951-54; treas. Phila. Fellowship Commn., 1952-54. Fellow A.A.A.S. (mem. governing council); Am. Asociacion Meterologica del Uruguay (hon.), Am. Assn. Mus., Md. Archeol. Soc., Balt. Astron. Soc., Balt. Mineral Soc. Home: Stevenson Rd Stevenson MD 21153 Office: 316-318 A St NE Washington DC 20002

WOLFORD, DONALD GARY, oral surgeon, educator; b. Port Clinton, O., Mar. 19, 1943; s. Donald Ralph and Wilma (Miller) W.; B.S. in Chemistry, U. Pitts., 1963; D.D.S., Temple U., 1967. Intern, Parkland Meml. Hosp., Dallas, 1967-68, resident, 1968-70; chief dept. oral surgery Dallas VA Hosp., 1970—; clin. instr. dept. surgery Oral Surgery div. Southwestern Med. Sch., U. Tex., Dallas, 1971—; mem. attending staff Parkland Meml. Hosp., Children's Med. Center, Dallas, John Peter Smith Hosp., Fort Worth. Mem. Am. Dental Assn., Xi Psi Phi. Lutheran. Clubs: Dallas Rugby Football, Calyx. Home: 6616 Winterwood Lane Dallas TX 75240 Office: 4500 S Lancaster St Dallas TX 75216

WOLFORD, FARLEY EDWIN, cons. engr.; b. Honaker, Va., Oct. 19, 1934; s. Kaney Kyle and Elgie Bell (Price) W.; student Bluefield (Va.) Coll., 1952-54; B.S., Va. Polytech. Inst., 1958; M.B.A., Ga. State U., 1969; m. Carl Sayers, Sept. 29, 1956; children—Elaine Carol, Farley Edwin, Craig Foster, Annette Ruth. Cartographic engring. aide TVA, Chattanooga, 1954-55; rodman So. Ry. Co., Knoxville, Tenn., 1955-57, asst. supr., 1958-60, track supr., Jacksonville, Fla., 1960-63; constrn. engr. N.C. Hwy. Commn., Rocky Mount, 1963; engr. Atlantic Coastline R.R. Co., Rocky Mount, 1963-66; engr. planning and design cons. to Met. Atlanta Rapid-Transit Authority; Parsons Brinckerhoff-Tudor-Bechtel, Atlanta, 1966-68; project civil engr. John J. Harte Assos., Atlanta, 1968—. Individual practice cons. engr. Coach, Midget Football League and Little League Baseball, Tucker, Ga., 1970; Webelos leader, committeeman Atlanta Area council Boy Scouts Am., 1968-71, asst. scoutmaster, 1971—. Served with N.G., 1953-54. Registered profl. engr., Ga., N.C. Mem. Am. Soc. C.E. Va. Polytech. Inst. Alumni Assn. Methodist (adminstrv. bd. 1968—). Home: 3976 Camelot Ct Tucker GA 30084 Office: 198 Luckie St NW ALanta GA 30301

WOLFSON, LOUIS, II, business state legislator; b. Miami, Fla., Sept. 19, 1927; s. Mitchell and Francis (Cohn) W.; grad. Berkshire (Mass.) Sch., 1948; B.A., U. Miami, 1952; m. Lynn Rabin, Nov. 21, 1951; children—Lynda Louise, Louis, Francis Jo. With WTVJ-TV, Miami, 1952-58, bus. mgr., 1954-58; Wometco rep., operator WLOS-TV, AM, FM, Asheville, N.C., 1958-59; Wometco rep., operator WFGA-TV, Jacksonville, Fla., 1960-61; owner KVOS-TV, Bellingham, Wash., 1961-62; v.p. charge TV operations Wometco Enterprises, Miami, 1961—, also dir.; dir. Probity Investments of South Africa, Caribbean Bottling Co., Ltd., Nassau Seaquarium, Miami; mem. Fla. Ho. of Reps., 1963—, chmn. legislative auditing com. Past chairman, mem. mgmt. com. Fla. Legislative Council. Bd. dirs. Mitchell Wolfson Charity Found., Wometco Found., Mt. Sinai Hosp. Miami Beach, Children's Cardiac Hosp., Miami; bd. overseers Stetson Coll. Law. Served with USNR, 1944. Mem. Nat., Fla., N.C., Wash. assns. broadcasters, Am., So. insts. mgmt., Miami C. of C., Miami Beach Taxpayers Assn., Television Pioneers, Suwanee River Citizens Assn., Civic League Miami Beach, Navy League. Democrat. Rotarian, Kiwanian, Eagle. Clubs: River (Jacksonville); Footlighters; Standard (Miami); University (Vancouver, B.C., Can.); Executive, Asheville City (Asheville, N.C.); Tiger Bay Political (dir.). Home: 4595 N Meridian Av Miami Beach FL 33140 Office: 316 N Miami Av Miami FL 33128

WOLIN, S. ROGER, airline exec.; b. Rochester, N.Y., Sept. 9, 1909; s. Kief Louis and Ina (Cate) W.; A.B., Union Coll., 1930; m. Dorothy Gibler, Jan. 17, 1946; children—John Anthony, Gregory Chaye, Melissa Conchita. Writer, editor Hearst Newspapers, Rochester, Syracuse, Albany, N.Y., 1929-32; with A.P., Albany, 1932-33. U.P., Washington, 1933-34, Internat. News Service, Washington, 1934-35; pub. relations Pan Am. Airways, Miami, Fla., 1936-41, mgr. pub. relations, Brownsville, Tex., 1941, div. mgr. pub. relations, Mexico City, Mexico, 1942-44, pub. relations mgr. Latin Am. Div., Miami, 1944-64, dir. pub. relations, 1964—. Mem. adv. bd. Biscayne Coll. Mem. Inter-Am. Fla., press assns., Aviation Writers Assn., Internat. Soc. Aviation Writers, Soc. Am. Travel Writers, Pub. Relations Soc. Am., Internat. Pub. Relations Assn., Sigma Delta Chi. Clubs: Nat. Press, Wings; Riviera Country; Coral Gables Country, 200 (dir.). Home: 7677 Ponce de Leon Rd Miami FL 33143 Office: Pan Am Bldg Miami FL 33159

WOLKOMIR, NATHAN TULLY, labor union ofcl.; b. Baku, Russia, Oct. 12, 1909; s. Boris and Rose (Silver) W.; came to U.S., 1912, naturalized, 1917; B.S., N.Y.U., 1929, St. Johns U., 1930, St. Francis Coll., N.Y.C., 1930; M.Ed., St. John's Univ., 1940; D.Ed., U. Ill., 1960; m. Louise Orthelia Shimmin, Mar. 10, 1944; 1 dau., Rhya Natalia. Tchr., N.Y.C., 1940-42; ednl. specialist, tng. command USAAF and USAF, 1942-64; mem. Nat. Fedn. Fed. Employees, 1942—, pres. Ill., 1950-52, nat. pres., 1964—. Chmn. Community Concerts, Rantoul, Ill., 1960, Rantoul Recreation Bd., 1961; pres. Chanute AFB Recreation and Welfare Orgn., 1962; mem. President's Com. Hiring Handicapped, 1965. Police commr., Rantoul, 1962. Mem. Soc. Personnel Adminstrn., Soc. Programmed Instrn., Am. Soc. Pub. Adminstrn., Pub. Personnel Assn., Air Force Assn. Mason, Odd Fellow, Moose. Author: (with others) Modern Airmanship, 1957. Home: 1001 Lamberton Dr Silver Spring MD 20902 Office: 1737 H St NW Washington DC 20006

WOLSKI, EUGENE JOSEPH, physician; b. Balt., Mar. 29, 1938; s. Milton Joseph and Anna Victoria (Regula) W.; B.S., Loyola Coll., Balt., 1959; M.D., U. Md., 1963; m. Anne Pauline Cann, Feb. 4, 1961; children—Eugene Joseph, Edward Stephan, Catherine Virginia, Michael Paul. Rotating intern Union Meml. Hosp., Balt., 1963; pvt. med. practice, Lewisville, Tex., 1968—; med. staff Flow Meml. Hosp., Denton, Tex.; health officer City of Lewisville. Mem. adv. council Lewisville Nat. Bank. Served with USNR, 1963-68. Recipient medal for service in Dominican Republic, 1965. Mem. A.M.A., Tex., So. med. assns., Denton County Med. Soc., Am. Acad. Family Practice, Med.-Surg. Clinic Assn. (dir.). Roman Catholic. Home: 124 Red Oak Lane Flower Mound Farms Lewisville TX 75067 Office: Doctors Clinic 233 Kay Lane Lewisville TX 75067

WOLTER, ALLAN BERNARD, clergyman, educator; b. Peoria, Ill., Nov. 24, 1913; s. Bernard Gregory and Marianne (Strub) W.; B.A., Our Lady of Angels Sem., 1937; postgrad. St. Joseph's Sem., 1941; M.A., Catholic U. Am., 1942, Ph.D., 1947; Sc.D., Quincy Coll., 1967. Joined Chgo.-St. Louis Province of Franciscans, 1934; ordained priest Roman Catholic Ch., 1940; instr. Our Lady of Angels Sem., Cleve., 1943, asso. prof., 1946-51; vis. asso. prof. Franciscan Inst., St. Bonaventure U., Olean, N.Y., 1946-51, prof., 1951-62; vis. prof. Catholic U. Am., Washington, 1962-63, prof., 1963—. Vis. prof. Princeton, 1965, U. Mich., 1967, N.Y.U., 1969; lector generalis Franciscan Inst., St. Bonaventure U., 1954. Mem. Am. Catholic (pres.), Am. philos. assns., A.A.A.S., Philosophy of Sci. Assn., Metaphys. Soc. Am., Mind Assn., Soc. Gen. Systems Research, Washington Philosophy Club. Author: Transcendentals and the Function in the Metaphysics of Duns Scotis, 1946, The Book of Life, 1954, Summula Metaphysicae, 1958, Duna Scotus; Philosophical Writings, 1962, John Duns Scotus, A Treatise on God as First Principle, 1965; editor: (with J.F. Wippel) Medieval Philosophy: From Augustine to Nicholas of Cusa, 1969, Franciscan Series, 1949-51, Franciscan Inst. Publs., 1946-62, Quincy Coll. Publs., 1964; asso. editor New Scholasticism, 1949-52; mem. editorial bd. Ency. Philosophy. Address: Catholic University of America Washington DC 20017

WOLVERTON, JOE B., banker; b. Mart, Tex., May 30, 1918; s. Mary David and Pauline (Benson) W.; student Val. Mil. Inst., 1935-36; B.B.A., U. Tex., 1939; m. Mary Honoure Henry, June 28, 1939; children— Mabry David, Joe Benson, Jr. With Waggoner Nat. Bank, Vernon, Tex., 1939-50, pres., 1950; pres. Wichita Nat. Bank, Wichita Falls, Tex., 1957-60, First Wichita Nat. Bank, 1960—, also dir.; adv. dir. S.W. Nat. Bank, Wichita Falls; dir. First Nat. Bank, Seymour, Tex. Mem. Comptroller of Currency's Nat. Adv. Com. Banking Policies and Practices. Pres. Indsl. Devel. Wichita Falls, Inc. Pres. United Fund Wichita Falls, also mem. exec. com. Bd. dirs. Wichita Falls Boys Club, Wichita Falls YMCA, Tex. Research League. Served with USNR, World War II; PTO. Recipient spl. recognition for outstanding leadership Wichita Falls C. of C. Mem. Am., Tex. (chmn. W. Tex. dist., chmn. legislative com.) bankers assns., U.S., Wichita Falls (past pres.) chambers commerce, Am. Inst. Banking, Sigma Alpha Epsilon. Baptist. Clubs: Wichita Falls Country, Wichita; Longhorn (U. Tex.). Home: 2011 Hampstead St Wichita Falls TX 76307 Office: Box 540 Wichita Falls TX 76307

WOMACK, GEORGE CLEVELAND, bank dir.; b. Natchez, Miss., Sept. 27, 1936; s. Grover Cleveland and Eunice Edna (Richardson) W.; B.S., La. State U., 1959; m. Alma McClure, Sept. 25, 1970. Mgr., Smithland Plantation, Jonesville, La., 1959-64, owner, 1964—; dir. Catahoula Bank, Jonesville, 1963—. Mem. Catahoula Parish Farm Bur., 1962—. Democrat. Baptist. Home: Star Route B Box 45A Jonesville LA 71343 Office: Catahoula Bank Jonesville LA 71343

WOMACK, GEORGE WASHINGTON, IV, elec. supplies co. exec.; b. Greensburg, La., Mar. 21, 1907; s. Robert Emmett and Agnes (Watson) W.; student La. State U., 1923-24; m. Martha Lee Daniel, Nov. 16, 1938; children— Austin Daniel, George Linwood. With Standard Oil Co., Baton Rouge, 1924-27; with circulation dept. New Orleans Times-Picayune, 1927-29; sales rep. Interstate Elec. Co., New Orleans, 1929-34; with Evans Elec. Supply, Inc., Baton Rouge, 1935—, mgr., treas., Lafayette, La., 1946—, also dir. Mem. Evangeline council Boy Scouts Am., Lafayette Hobo Firemen. Mem. Lafayette C. of C., Kappa Sigma. Democrat. Baptist. Mason (32 deg., Shriner), Rotarian. Clubs: Knife and Fork (past v.p.), Oakbourne Country, Lafayette Area Sportsmens (Lafayette). Home: 736 Parkside Dr Lafayette LA 70501 Office: Evans Lane and Scott Rd Lafayette LA 70501

WOMACK, JAMES A., govt. ofcl.; b. Mantee, Miss., Mar. 3, 1923; s. James Alexander and Zada (Kolb) W.; B.A., Miss. Coll., 1948; M.B.E., U. Miss., 1951; M.S. in Social Work, U. Tenn., 1963 Chmn. bus. dept. Clarke Meml. Coll., Newton, Miss., 1948-50; tchr. Oakland (Miss.) High Sch., 1950-51; chmn. bus. edn. dept. Miss. Delta Jr. Coll., Moorhead, 1951; acting asst. prof. office adminstrn. U. Miss., Oxford, 1951-52; instr. Wood Jr. Coll., Mathiston, Miss., 1952-55; office mgr. dean men. tchr. Clarke Meml. Coll,, Newton, Miss., 1955-56; cashier, chmn. bd. dirs. Bank of Mantee, 1956-59; county agt., supr. cons. Miss. Pub. Welfare Dept., Jackson, 1959-65, operational dir., 1966-69, dir. div. research and statistics, 1969-71, exec. dir. programs div., 1971—; supr. Tenn. Dept. Pub. Welfare, Nashville, 1965-66. Mem. Nat. Assn. Social Workers (treas. local chpt. 1967-69, pres.), Am. Pub. Welfare Assn., Miss. Conf. Social Welfare (exec. com. 1966—), Acad. Certified Social Workers, Delta Pi Epsilon, Phi Delta Kappa. Home: 1572 Lowery Lane Jackson MS 39209 Office: PO Box 4321 Jackson MS 39216

WOMACK, MILFORD THORBORN, farmer, bank dir.; b. Manifest, La., May 28, 1928; s. Grover Cleveland and Eunice (Richardson) W.; B.S. in Agr., La. State U., 1952; m. Annie Ruth Webb, Feb. 24, 1951; children—Cleve., Janie, Bill. Mgr. Manifest (La.) Farm, 1954-61, owner, 1965—; owner, mgr. Womack Tractor Co., Jonesville, La., 1961, inc. to W&Y Tractor Co., 1967—; dir. Catahoula Bank, Jonesville, 1956—. Bd. dirs. Farm Bur., 1969-71, Catahoula Parish Fair Assn., 1956-58. Served with AUS, 1952-54; Germany. Democrat. Home: Route 2 Jonesville LA 71343 Office: Mount St Jonesville LA 71343

WOMACK, ROBERT BOYD, mining exec.; b. New Orleans, Sept. 15, 1939; s. Vincent Reid and Mabel Louise (Lorio) W.; B.A., Emory and Henry Coll., 1961; m. Ruth Ann Mullins, May 19, 1958; children—Jenifer Paige, Amanda Lee. Pres. Stamack Mining Corp., Appalachia, Va.; dir. 1st Nat. Exchange Bank. Mem. Selective Service Bd. Vice pres., bd. dirs. Lonesome Pine Hosp. Corp.; mem. bd. visitors Emory and Henry Coll. Mem. Va. Mining Inst. (v.p.). Baptist. Moose. Home: 105 Balsam Lane Oak Ridge TN 37830 Office: Stamack Mining Corp PO Drawer 389 Appalachia VA 24216

WOMBLE, WILLIAM FLETCHER, lawyer; b. Winston-Salem, N.C., Oct. 29, 1916; s. Bunyan Snipes and Edith (Willingham) W.; A.B., Duke, 1937, J.D., 1939; m. Jane Payne Gilbert, Oct. 11, 1941; children—William Fletcher, Jane, Russell G., Ann P. Admitted to N.C. bar, 1939; asso. firm Womble, Carlyle, Sandridge & Rice, and predecessors, 1939-47, partner, 1947—. Mem. N.C. Gen. Statutes Commn., 1953-55, N.C. Bd. Higher Edn., 1955-57, 60-63, N.C. Adv. Budget Commn., 1957-58; campaign chmn. Forsyth County Community Chest, 1948. Mem. N.C. Ho. of Reps., 1953-58, chmn. com. on higher edn., 1957, vice chmn. finance com., 1957. Mem. vis. com. Duke Law Sch.; trustee High Point (N.C.) Coll., Winston-Salem Tchrs. Coll., 1953-55; trustee, pres. Children's Home, Inc. Served to maj. USAAF, 1941-46. Mem. Am. (council mem. Jr. Bar Conf. 1951-52), N.C. (pres. 1966-67), Forsyth County (pres. 1962) bar assns., Winston-Salem C. of C. (pres. 1960-61). Methodist (steward, chmn. bd. 1961-63). Rotarian (pres. 1964). Home: 2027 Virginia Rd Winston-Salem NC 27104 Office: Wachovia Bldg Winston-Salem NC 27102

WOOD, ALFRED MCCREARY, ret. sales exec.; b. Wildie, Ky., Nov. 1, 1896; s. Henry Hugh and Eliza (Stewart) W.; student U. Ky., 1916-17; B.A., Harvard, 1921; m. Mary Swain, Mar. 11, 1958. With Procter & Gamble Co., 1921-61, salesman, gen. salesman, Kansas City, asst. to gen. sales mgr., Cin., sales supr. Phila., gen. sales supr., N.Y. dist. mgr., Boston, spl. assignment, Dallas, 1921-48, div. mgr., Cin., 1949-61. Served with USN, 1918-19; from maj. to lt. col., USAAF, 1942-45. Decorated Bronze Star, Croix de Guerre with palm. Mem. Am. Acad. Polit. and Social Sci., Newcomen Soc. N.Am., Dallas Council World Affairs (dir.), Sigma Alpha Epsilon. Republican. Presbyn. Mason. Clubs: Harvard (Dallas, Boston), Dallas Country, Dallas, Admiral's. Home: 3525 Turtle Creek Blvd Dallas TX 75219 Office: Tower Petroleum Bldg Dallas TX 75201

WOOD, BILLY RAY, supt. schs.; b. Roscoe, Tex., Sept. 19, 1926; s. Henry Elbert and Elize Mae (Webb) W.; B.S., E.Tex. State U., Commerce, 1951, M.Ed., 1956; m. Terry Alene Brookshire, Aug. 20, 1946; children—Terry Darlene (Mrs. Bill Dickey), Rebecca Rae (Mrs. Mike Spikes). Tchr. math. Los Fresnos (Tex.) High Sch., 1946-48, Rockwall Tex., 1949-55; prin. high sch., Rockwall, 1955-58, Ft. Worth, 1958-61; supt. schs., Henrietta, Tex., 1961-72, Memphis, Tex., 1972—. Mem. Gallon Club, A.R.C., 1970—. Served with U.S. Mcht. Marine, 1944-46. Recipient State Distinguished Service award Future Farmers Am., 1969. Mem. Am., Tex. assns. sch. adminstrs., Tex. Tchrs. Assn., Clay County (dir.), Henrietta (past pres.) chambers commerce, Phi Delta Kappa. Kiwanian (past pres., dir.). Home: 714 W Main Memphis TX 79245 Office: Box 460 Memphis TX 79245

WOOD, CHALMERS BENEDICT, fgn. service officer; b. N.Y.C., Dec. 9, 1917; s. Chalmers and Katherine Benedict (Turnbull) W.; grad. St. Mark's Sch., 1936; A.B., Harvard, 1940; m. Barbara A. Lindner, Mar. 7, 1942 (div. May 1967); children—Ramsay, Chalmers; m. 2d, Patricia Houghton, July 2, 1969; children—Felicity, Penelope. Admitted to D.C. bar, 1947; entered U.S. Fgn. Service, 1947; 3d sec. Am. embassy, Brussels, Belgium, 1948-52, 2d sec., Manila, 1952; assigned Dept. State, Washington, 1952, officer charge Greek affairs, 1954-57; 2d sec. Am. embassy, Saigon, 1957-59; officer charge Vietnamese affairs Dept. State, 1959-61, dep. dir. and dir. Viet Nam Task Force, 1961-63; sr. seminar Dept. of State, 1963-64; 1st sec. Am. embassy, London, 1964-66; office dir. Cyprus, Dept. State, 1966-67; sr. province adviser, Binh Dinh, Viet Nam, 1967-69; counselor Am. embassy Wellington, New Zealand, 1970—. Served from pvt. to capt., USAAF, 1940-45. Clubs: Metropolitan (Washington); Brook (N.Y.C.); St. James (London). Home: American Embassy Wellington New Zealand

WOOD, CHARLES HENRY, textile exec.; b. Bklyn., Apr. 12, 1911; s. Matthew Hardenbergh and Mary (Frith) W.; B.A. summa cum laude, Lafayette Coll., 1933; m. Elizabeth Taylor Marsh, Nov. 19, 1933; children—Charles Henry, John Wainwright, Patricia Gretchen (Mrs. James Harrelson). Asst. sec.-treas. Consol. Textile Co., Inc., N.Y.C., 1933-40; asst. controller Esmond Mills (R.I.), 1940-42; sec.-treas. Consol. Textile Co., Inc., 1942-46; controller Blough Mfg. Co., Inc., Harrisburg, Pa., 1946-50; v.p., treas., dir. Oneita Knitting Mills, Andrews, S.C., 1950—. Mem. Nat. Assn. Accountants, Financial Execs. Inst. Mason. Home: Wedgefield Plantation Duck Pond Rd Georgetown SC 29440 Office: Oneita Knitting Mills Andrews SC 29510

WOOD, CLIFF CALVIN, banker; b. Harrison, Ark., Oct. 1, 1903; s. Walker Lee and Emma (Johnson) W.; ed. high sch., Harrison; m. Sarah Mildred Wood, Dec. 18, 1938; children—Mary Jeanette, Cynthia Taylor. Asst. cashier Peoples State Bank, Berryville, Ark., 1925-27, First Nat. Bank, Batesville, Ark., 1928-29; nat. bank examiner Office Comptroller of Currency, 1930-41; v.p. First Nat. Bank of Memphis, 1942-47, Republic Nat. Bank, Dallas, 1948-68; sr. v.p., dir. First Nat. Bank, Little Rock, 1968-70; pres. Union Nat. Bank Little Rock, 1970—, also dir. Bd. dirs. Southwestern Hist. Wax Mus., Dallas. Mem. Ark. Art Center, Am. Inst. Banking. Republican. Methodist. Mason (32 deg.). Clubs: Dallas Country; Little Rock, Little Rock Country, Pleasant Valley Country (Little Rock). Home: 8580 Cantrell Rd Little Rock AR 72207 Office: Union National Bank Union National Plaza Little Rock AR 72201

WOOD, EDWARD LEE, ret. govt. ofcl.; b. Hartfield, Va., Sept. 21, 1908; s. Bernard Lewis and Cora H. (Brown) W.; B.S., Va. Poly. Inst., 1933, postgrad.; postgrad. U. Ark., U. Ga.; m. Charlie Elizabeth Joyner, June 11, 1938; 1 dau., Cora Elizabeth (Mrs. Thomas R. Stark). Asst. entomologist Va. Poly. Inst., 1933-34; asst. county agt. Southampton County, Va., 1934-36; county agt., Amelia County, Va., 1936-55, Norfolk County, 1955-63; became county agt., head dept. agr. City of Chesapeake (Va.), 1963; now ret.; adviser to Chesapeake Drainage Commn.; cons. for lawns and shrubs. Mem. agrl. com. Southeastern Regional Planning Commn., 1958—; mem. Va. Com. on Care. Chm., Chesapeake Democratic Com., 1971-72. bd. 1941-42. Recipient Distinguished Service award Nat. Assn. County Agrl. Agts., 1951. Mem. Nat. Assn. County Agrl. Agts. (profl. improvement com., 1961—, 4-H Club com., 1965—), Va. County Agts. Assn. (past pres., dir.; chmn. prof. improvement com. 1961—), Norfolk (chmn. agr. com. 1970), Chesapeake (dir. 1969-70), chambers commerce, World Affairs Council Greater Hampton Rds. (dir., exec. com. fgn. affairs), Am. Legion (past post comdr.), Navy League of Norfolk, Epsilon Sigma Phi, Squanto. Democrat. Methodist (chmn. bd. stewards). Mason. Kiwanis. Clubs: Ruritan (Amelia and Great Bridge), Amelia Golf (past pres., dir.); Cedar Point. Address: 317 Constance Dr Chesapeake VA 23320

WOOD, ELMER DONOVAN, ret. clergyman; b. Spartanburg, S.C., Aug. 29, 1902; s. David and Sally Selina (Holcombe) W.; B.A., Presbyn. Coll. S.C., 1922; B.D., Columbia Theol. Sem., 1925, M. Div., 1971; postgrad. U. S.C., 1923-24, Princeton Theol. Sem., 1926; m. Sarah Eliza Timmons, Apr. 18, 1925; children—Sally (Mrs. Frank Victor Canfield), Joanna (Mrs. Warner Hale Anthony), Elmer Donovan, Richard H., Kate Sims (Mrs. Romilly Timmins). Ordained to ministry Presbyn. Ch., 1925; pastor in Lockhart, S.C., 1924-25, Villa Rica, Ga., 1925-26, Gt. Falls, S.C., 1927-28, Mulberry St. Presbyn. Ch., Montgomery, Ala., 1928-30, Broad St. Presbyn. Ch., Mobile, Ala., 1930-31, Monroeville, Ala., 1931-35, El Campo, Tex., 1946-54, Columbia, S.C., 1954-55, West Baton Rouge Presbyn. Ch., Port Allen, La., 1957-69. Chaplain Civilian Conservation Corps, 4th Corp area, 1935-41; tchr., coach Monroeville, 1932-34; chmn. evangelism Brazos (Tex.) Presbytery, 1946-54; chmn. com. ministers annuity La. Presbytery, Synod of La., 1957-62, mem. exam. com., 1957-62, clk. ch. extension com., 1957-62, council mem., 1957—; chaplain, El Campo, Tex. Fireman. Served as chaplain, AUS, 1941-46. Mem. Internat. Platform Assn., Am. Legion (chaplain El Campo), S.A.R. Mason, Elk (chaplain El Campo), Rotarian (pres. El Campo 1947-48. Port Allen 1960-61). Builder chs. in El Campo, Port Allen. Home: PO Box 416 3608 Oak Hill St Zachary LA 70791

WOOD, GARNETT ELMER, research chemist; b. Gloucester, Va., Feb. 14, 1929; s. Frank Tucker and Julia (Braxton) W.; B.S., Va. State Coll., 1951, M.S., 1956; Ph.D., Georgetown U., 1966; m. Frances Lorraine Coles, May 23, 1953; children—Garnett Elmer, Kenneth B. Microbiologist, Walter Reed Army Med. Center, Washington, 1956-64; research fellow Georgetown U., Washington, 1964-65; research chemist div. food chemistry FDA, Washington, 1965—. Served to capt. AUS, 1951-53. Mem. Am. Chem. Soc., Am. Oil Chemists Soc., Alpha Phi Alpha. Home: 4020 20th St NE Washington DC 20018 Office: 200 C St SW Washington DC 20204

WOOD, GEORGE MARK, JR., securities co. exec.; b. Montgomery, Ala., Sept. 6, 1925; s. George M. and Mattie Maxwell (Pegues) W.; student Starke U., 1937-41, U. Ill., 1942-43, Auburn U., 1942; B.S., U. Tex., 1946; postgrad. U. Ala., 1946; 1 dau., Meri. Vice pres., sec. George M. Wood & Co., Inc., Montgomery, 1946-72, also dir.; treas. Ausa Corp., dir. Thermal Components, Inc., Montgomery. Chmn. Operation Drug Alert, 1969-70. Bd. dirs. Montgomery Area Mental Health, 1969-72, South Ala. State Fair. Served with USNR, 1942-46, 51-52. Mem. Nat., Ala. security traders assns., Kappa Sigma. Republican. Episcopalian. Kiwanian (pres.). Clubs: Pioneers, Montgomery Country. Home: 2320 E Cloverdale Park Montgomery AL 36106 Office: 8 Commerce St Montgomery AL 36102

WOOD, HARLINGTON, JR., lawyer, govt. ofcl.; b. Springfield, Ill., Apr. 17, 1920; s. Harlington and Marie (Green) W.; A.B., U. Ill., 1942, J.D., 1948; m. Rosemary Miller, June 27, 1945; 1 dau., Alexa. Admitted to Ill. bar, 1948, since practiced in Springfield; spl. asst. atty. gen. of Ill., 1954-58; U.S. atty. So. Dist. of Ill., 1958-61; partner law firm of Wood and Wood, 1961—; chief of ballot security Republican Nat. Com., 1964—; now asso. dep. atty. gen., Washington; minority counsel Ill. Elections Laws Commn. Chmn. pub. transp. study com., City of Springfield, 1957; mem. regional planning commn., Sangamon County, 1957-58; now mem. Ill. Crime Commn.; bd. dirs. Ill. State Race Track Security Police, 1963-65, Abraham Lincoln Assn., Ill. Appaloosa Assn. Pres., Vachel Lindsay House Fund, 1956-62. Served from lt. to maj., Transp. Corps, AUS, 1942-46. Mem. Am., Ill. bar assns., Civil War Round Table. Republican. Home: Main St Waterford VA 22190 Office: Dept of Justice Washington DC 20530

WOOD, JAMES EDWARD, JR., clergyman, educator, author; b. Portsmouth, Va., July 29, 1922; s. James Edward and Elsie (Bryant) W.; A.B., Carson-Newman Coll., 1943; M.A., Columbia, 1949; B.D., So. Bapt. Theol. Sem., 1947, Th.M., 1948, Th.D., 1957; postgrad. U. Tenn., 1943-44, Yale, 1949-50, Naganuma Sch. Japanese Studies, Tokyo, 1950-51; m. Alma Leacy McKenzie, Aug. 12, 1943; 1 son, James E. III. Ordained ministry Bapt. Ch.; pastor chs. Tenn. and Ky., 1942-48; prof. religion and lit. Seinan Gakuin U., Fukuoka, Japan, 1951-55; So. Bapt. Missionary to Japan, 1950-55; prof. history of religions Baylor U., 1955—, dir. honors program for superior students, 1959-62, also dir. J.M. Dawson studies in ch. and state grad. program, 1959—, dir. Baylor U.-Seinan U. Exchange Program, 1971—. Vice chmn. Nat. Com. for Amish Religious Freedom; mem. nat. adv. council Ams. United; mem. Commn. on Religious Liberty and Human Rights Baptist World Alliance; mem. Nat. Com. on Taos Pueblo Claim to Blue Lake area. Bd. dirs. Waco Planned Parenthood, pres., 1972. Mem. So. Bapt. Hist. Soc., Am. Assn. U. Profs. (pres. Baylor chpt. 1959-60), Am. Soc. Ch. History, Am. Acad. Religion, Am. Assn. Profs. Missions, Am. Civil Liberties Union (pres. Waco area), Assn. Asian Studies, Am. Assn. U. Profs., Sponsor Ams. for Pub. Schs., Pi Kappa Delta, Alpha Psi Omega, Phi Eta Sigma. Democrat. Baptist. Rotarian. Author: A History of American Literature: An Anthology, 1952; (with E.B. Thompson and R.T. Miller) Church and State in Scripture, History and Constitutional Law, 1958; The Problem of Nationalism, 1969; Jewish-Christian Relations in Today's World, 1971. Contbr., resource rep. Ency. Christian Missions, 1967. Editor, Contbr.: Church and State, 1960. Editor: Jour. of Ch. and State, 1959—. Contbr.: We Hold These Truths, 1964; The Teacher's Yoke, 1964, also numerous articles scholarly jours. Home: 6112 Summit Ridge Dr Waco TX 76710

WOOD, JAMES MATTHEW, JR., publisher; b. Dade City, Fla., Nov. 7, 1926; s. James Matthew and Vana (Keith) W.; B.A., U. Ala., 1948; m. Martha Maxwell, June 19, 1954; children—James M. III, Frank Maxwell, Keith Farrar, John Christopher. With West Point (Ga.) News, 1948-49, Columbus (Ga.) Ledger; editor LaGrange (Ga.) Daily News, 1951-55, Rural Ga., Millen, 1955-56; editor, gen. mgr. Weekly Star, Atlanta, 1956-57; asso. editor W.R.C. Smith Pub. Co., Atlanta, 1957-62; med. sci. writer dept. psychiatry Emory U., 1962-63; pub. Fayette County News, Fayetteville, Ga. 1963—, Clayton County Jour., Jonesboro, Ga., 1964—, Troup County Herald, Hogansville, Ga., 1965—, Forest Park (Ga.) Free Press, 1969—; pres. Woodprint, Inc., Jonesboro, 1968—. Served with AUS, 1946-47. Methodist. Rotarian. Home: 175-A Route 1 Rex GA 30273 Office: Box 368 Jonesboro GA 30236

WOOD, JAMES POWERS, physician; b. Clinton, Miss., Dec. 29, 1920; s. Arthur Eugene and Anne (Powers) W.; B.A. with distinction, Miss. Coll., 1941; M.D., Tulane U., 1950; m. Carroll Bullock, June 14, 1943; children—James Powers, Anne Carroll, Louise Dampeer, Marshall Bullock. Intern Charity Hosp., New Orleans; gen. practice medicine, Waynesboro, Miss., 1951-53, State Line, Miss., 1953-66, Waynesboro, Miss., 1966—; mem. staffs Wayne Gen. Hosp., Waynesboro, Miss., 1951—, Washington County Hosp., Chatom, Ala., 1953—; trustee Greene County Hosp., Leakesville, Miss., 1958-60. Dir., Consumers Wirebound Box Co., Waynesboro, 1957-58; chmn. bd. AGM Drug Co. Miss., Jackson, Miss.; organizer, chmn. bd. 1st Nat. Bank Way, 1966-68. Chmn. bd. trustees State Line High Sch., 1957-59; mem. Greene County Bd. Edn., 1963-66, Miss. Hosp. Commn., 1964-72, Miss. Oil and Gas Bd., 1970—. Served with USAAF, 1943-46. Decorated Air medal with oak leaf cluster. Hon. col. Miss. Gov.'s staff, 1960-72. Mem. Am., Miss. med. assns., So. Miss. Med. Soc., Miss. Acad. Gen. Practice, Alpha Kappa Kappa. Baptist. Home: McIlwain Dr Waynesboro MS 39367 Office: 709 Chickasawhay St Waynesboro MS 39367

WOOD, JOHN CLINTON, lawyer; b. N.Y.C., Mar. 29, 1918; s. Robert Schofield and Eva Murray (Ketchum) W.; J.D., U. Va., 1943; m. Louise Rebecca Parrish, June 8, 1945; children—John Parrish, Anne Clinton. Admitted to Va. bar, 1943, U.S. Supreme Ct., 1954; practice law, Fairfax, Va., 1943—; dir. Potomac Bank and Trust Co., Fairfax, EZ Communications, Inc. Mem. Town Council, Fairfax, 1952-53; mayor city Fairfax, 1953-64. Chmn. adv. bd. George Mason Coll., 1971—, trustee Coll. Found., 1964—; bd. control No. Va. br. U. Va. Recipient Man of Year award Am. Legion, 1958. Mem. Va. State Bar Assn. (past v.p., past chmn. 10th dist. council), Fairfax County Bar Assn. (past pres.), Raven Soc., Sigma Phi Epsilon. Episcopalian. Rotarian. Mason (Shriner). Clubs: Commonwealth (Richmond); Country (Fairfax); University of Virginia. Bd. editors Va. Law Rev., 1943. Home and office: PO Box 369 Fairfax VA 22030

WOOD, KATHERINE ALICE, social worker; b. Kingsville, Tex.; d. John J. and Katie (Steves) Wood; student Pan Am. Coll., 1927-29; B.S., S.W. Tex. State Coll., 1936; M.Ed., U. Tex., 1939; postgrad. La. State U., 1941; M.S.W., Tulane U., 1950. Tchr. elementary sch. Palm Garden Sch. Dist., Mercedes, Tex., 1930-34, prin. 1934-37; tchr. social sci. Weslaco (Tex.), Ind. Sch. Dist., 1937-42; field worker Dept. Pub. Welfare, Austin, Tex., 1942-46, supr., 1946-50; supr. casework Houston-Harris County chpt. A.R.C., Houston, 1950-70, dir. service to mil. families, 1970—. Field instr. Worden Sch. Social Service Our Lady of Lake Coll., San Antonio, 1951—, Sch. Social Work, U. Houston, also Prairie View A. and M. Coll. Chmn. interagy. communications com. Community Council, Houston, 1956-58. Mem. Altrusa Club (dir. 1972-73), Nat. Assn. Social Workers (chmn. nominating com. San Jacinto chpt., 1963-65), Acad. Certified Social Workers, Nat. Conf. on Social Welfare, Council on Social Work Edn., Tex. United Community Services (state bd. 1972—), Houston Bus. and Profl. Women's Club (1st v.p. 1971-72). Home: 2716 San Jacinto St Apt 8 Houston TX 77004 Office: 2006 Smith St Houston TX 77002

WOOD, MILTON LEGRAND, bishop; b. Selma, Ala., Aug. 21, 1922; s. Milton LeGrand and Roberta (Hawkins) W.; B.A., U. of South, 1943, B.D., 1945, D.D., 1967; m. Ann Scott, May 3, 1949; children—Leigh, Ann, Milton, Roberta. Clin. tng. Norristown (Pa.) State Hosp., 1945-46; ordained priest Episcopal Ch., 1946; rector in Mobile, Ala., 1946-52, Atlanta, 1952-60; dir. Appleton Ch. Home, also archdeacon, Macon, Ga., 1960-63; canon to bishop of Atlanta, 1963-67; suffragen bishop of Atlanta, 1967—. Home: 2765 Normandy Dr NW Atlanta GA 30305 Office: 2744 Peachtree Rd NW Atlanta GA 30305

WOOD, OLIVER GILLAN, JR., educator; b. Greer, S.C., Apr. 27, 1937; s. Oliver Gillan and Grace (McBrayer) W.; B.S. cum laude, U. S.C., 1958, M.A., 1963; Ph.D. (Univ. fellow), U. Fla., 1965; m. Shirley Blackwell, May 30, 1959; 1 son, Brian Jay. Asst. prof. econs. U. S.C., Columbia, 1965-68, asso. prof. econs., 1968—. Cons. several financial instns., 1966—; tchr. C.L.U. course Columbia, 1969-70. Served to lt. (j.g.) USNR, 1959-61; now lt. comdr. Res. Mem. Am., So. econ. assns., Am., So. finance assns., S.C. Acad. Sci., Beta Gamma Sigma, Omicron Delta Epsilon. Methodist (stewardship and finance com. 1968—, adminstrn. bd. 1968—, chmn. stewardship commn.

1969-70). Editor: Business and Econ. Rev., 1969—. Contbr. articles to profl. jours. Home: 4820 Quail Lane Columbia SC 29206

WOOD, RICHARD HARVEY, educator; b. Wellington, South Africa, Apr. 5, 1908 (parents Am. citizens); s. Clinton Tyler and Jennie (Clark) W.; B.A., Princeton, 1930, Ph.D., 1943; m. Frances Anne Manning, Apr. 16, 1937; children—Richard H., Anne S. Dir., Rutgers U. Inst. Mgmt. and Labor Relations, New Brunswick, N.J., 1947-59; prof. internat. devel., dir. Johns Hopkins Inst. Internat. Devel., Washington, 1959-63; chief planning div. Africa Bur., AID, Washington, 1963-64; chief of party U. Pa. at Pahlavi U., Shiraz, Iran, 1964-66; exec. asso. Edn. and World Affairs, N.Y.C., 1966-69; prof. bus. adminstrn. U. Ala., University, 1969—. Mem. Princeton (N.J.) Twp. Com., 1954-56. Home: 109 Woodland Hills St Tuscaloosa AL 35401 Office: Box 6154 University AL 35486

WOOD, ROBERT BENTON, ret. physician; b. Manardville, Tenn., Sept. 3, 1896; s. William Patton and Sara (Gentry) W.; B.A., U. Tenn., 1916; M.D., Vanderbilt U., 1921; m. Mary Elizabeth McCreary, Jan. 23, 1951; children—Sara (Mrs. Robbie Flowers), Robert Benton. Intern, Vassar Bros. Hosp., Poughkeepsie, N.Y., 1921-22, resident, 1922-23; practice medicine specializing in internal medicine, Knoxville, Tenn., 1924-71; mem. courtesy staff St. Mary's Hosp., 1948-71; chmn. dept., prof. medicine U. Tenn. Meml. Research Center Hosp., 1956-66; mem. staffs E. Tenn. Bapt., Ft. Sanders hosps. Mem. Tenn. Pub. Health Council, 1939-53. Recipient Distinguished Service award Knoxville Acad. Medicine, 1965, E. Tenn. Heart Assn., 1968. Diplomate Am. Bd. Internal Medicine. Fellow A.C.P., mem. A.M.A. (del. 1948-56), Am., Tenn. (pres. 1955-56) heart assns. Home: 3604 Lakecrest Dr Knoxville TN 37920

WOOD, ROBERT GARLAND, physician; b. Lithia, Fla., May 1, 1908; s. Robert Garland and Caddie Blanche (Alderman) W.; student U. Fla., 1925-27; M.D., Tulane, 1932; m. Eunice Luella Holzer, June 27, 1933; children—Florence Jane (Mrs. Gary Omar Dotson), Robert Garland III. Intern, So. Bapt. Hosp., New Orleans, 1931-33; practice gen. medicine, St. Cloud, Fla., 1933—; chief med. dept. Osceola Gen. Hosp., Kissimmee, Fla., 1964—; vice chief staff St. Cloud Hosp., 1971-72. Vice pres., dir. Citizens State Bank, St. Cloud, 1945—. Commr., City of St. Cloud, 1954, utilities commr., 1955-57. Mem. Orange County Med. Soc. (v.p. 1946), A.M.A., Fla. Med. Soc., So. Med. Assn. Mason. Home: 700 Florida Av St Cloud FL 32769 Office: 1205 Penn Av St Cloud FL 32769

WOOD, ROBERT HAFNER, county agt.; b. Dewar, Okla., July 28, 1914; s. Rufus Hiram and Della Blanche (Hafner) W.; Asso. in Agr., Connor's State Agrl. Coll., 1935; B.S., Okla. State U., 1937; m. Doris Ellen Watson, June 26, 1939; 1 dau., Doris Roberta (Mrs. Ronny Trueman Smithee). Tchr. vocational agr. Indiahoma Pub. Schs., 1937-40; tchr. agr. jr. high sch. coach Geronimo (Okla.) Pub. Schs., 1940-41; tchr. agr. and sci. Sterling High Sch., 1941; instr. agr. Bur. Indian Affairs Sch., Zuni, N.M., 1941, Albuquerque, 1942, Jones Acad., Hartsborne, Okla., 1942-47, Riverside Indian Sch., 1947-49; farm mgmt. supr., county extension agt. Indian program Cheyenne and Arapaho Reservation Area, Watonga, Okla., 1949—. Served with USNR, 1945. Mem. Am. Legion (comdr. Woodrow Wilson post 1960), N.E.A., Okla. Edn. Assn., Okla. Assn. County Extension Agts. (dir. 1969-71), Watonga C. of C. Mem. Christian Ch. (elder 1942—). Kiwanian, Lion, Rotarian. Home: PO Box 456 Watonga OK 73772

WOOD, RYAN LEE, clergyman; b. Spartanburg, S.C., Feb. 2, 1901; s. David and Sally Selina (Holcombe) W.; B.A., Presbyn. Coll., Clinton, S.C., 1921, D.D., 1950; B.D., Columbia Theol. Sem., Decatur, 1925; m. Mattie Gertrude Timmons, Mar. 15, 1924; children—Ryan Lee, Selina Ellen (Mrs. Ernest Millar Smith), John David, Marion Timmons, Rebecca Holcombe. Prin., athletic coach Williamsburg High Sch., Kingstree, S.C., 1921-22; pastor First Presbyn. Ch., Marion, Ala., 1925-27, Wauchula, Fla., 1927-35, Hyde Park Ch., Tampa, Fla., 1936-42, Meml. Ch., West Palm Beach, 1944-69, Seacrest Blvd. Presbyn. Ch., Delray Beach, Fla., 1969—; human relations counselor Rinker Materials Corp., West Palm Beach, 1969—; instr. N.T., U. Tampa, 1941, instr. O.T., Palm Beach Jr. Coll., 1948. Moderator Synod Fla. 1958-59. Trustee Columbia Theol. Sem.; mem. St. Lucie County bd. Am. Cancer Soc., Ft. Pierce, Fla. Bd. dirs. Palm Beach County chpt. A.R.C. Served from maj. to lt. col., AUS, 1941-44. Mem. Res. Officers Assn., Assn. U.S. Army, Sons Confederate Vets., Ret. Officers Assn., S.A.R. Mason (32 deg.). Kiwanian, Lion. Home: 4600 Sunrise Blvd Fort Pierce FL 33450 Office: 2703 N Seacrest Blvd Delray Beach FL 33444

WOOD, SAM, editor Austin American Statesman. Address: 308 Guadalupe St Austin TX 78767*

WOOD, SANFORD WATTS, educator; b. Winnsboro, La., Aug. 24, 1939; s. Sanford Hudson and Sara Elizabeth (DeMoss) W.; B.A., La. Coll., 1961; Ph.D., Vanderbilt U., 1968; m. Betty Jean Loftin, Jan. 28, 1961; children—Judith Lynn, James Eric, Philip Hudson, Rebecca Gail. Instr. La. Poly. Inst., 1964-68; asst. prof. E. Tex. State U., 1968-71; asso. prof. philosophy U. So. Miss., 1971—. Active Am. Civil Liberties Union. Mem. Am. Assn. U. Profs., So. Soc. Philosophy and Psychology, Southwestern Philos. Assn. Episcopalian. Home: 2807 Prince George Rd Hattiesburg MS 39401

WOOD, THOMAS WESLEY, JR., educator; b. Hugo, Okla., Mar. 16, 1920; s. Thomas W. and Alma Rogers (Daniel) W.; B.A., U. Tulsa, 1951, M.A., 1953; M.S., Northwestern U., 1953; Ph.D., U. Okla., 1966; m. Deloris Gray, May 31, 1968; children—John, Tommy. Prof. history and journalism U. Tulsa, 1954—. Reporter City News Bur. Chgo., 1952-54, Tulsa Daily World, 1954—, Phila. Inquirer, summer 1956, Chgo. Sun-Times, summer 1960. Served with USAAF, 1942-46. Mem. Am. Hist. Soc., So. Hist. Soc., Okla. Press Assn., Tulsa Press Club, Assn. for Edn. in Journalism, Am. Assn. U. Profs., Pi Alpha Mu, Sigma Delta Chi, Phi Alpha Theta. Author: An Outline History of American Journalism, 1961; Editing Handbook, 1960; History of the University of Tulsa, 1935-58; Basic Production Equipment and Processes for Letterpress, 1961. Home: 547 S Gary Pl Apt 1 Tulsa OK 74104

WOOD, VEVA BOEKE (MRS. L.E. WOOD), librarian; b. Kansas City, Oct. 11, 1899; B.A. in English, Baker Coll., 1921; M.Ed., Oklahoma City U., 1938; postgrad. U. Kan., summers 1937, 38, U. Okla., summer 1941, U. Colo., summer 1944; M.L.S., Tex. Womans' U., 1953; m. L. E. Wood. Tchr. English, Waverly (Kansas) High Sch., 1921-25, Burns (Kansas) Consol. High Sch., 1925-27, El Dorado (Kan.) High Sch., 1927-33; instr. English, Oklahoma City U., 1938-41, asst. prof., 1941-43, asso. prof., 1943-49; instr. English, Baylor U., 1949-51, asso. librarian Armstrong Browning Library, 1952-60, librarian, 1960—. Active YWCA. Mem. A.L.A., Tex., Western library assns., Assn. Coll.-Research Libraries, Am. Assn. Univ. Women, Am. Assn. Univ. Profs., Cardinal Key, Zeta Tau Alpha, Beta Phi Mu. Address: 1812 Seneca St Waco TX 76707*

WOOD, WALTER WYVILL, mech. engr.; b. Louisville, Feb. 5, 1928; s. George Twyman and Louise Fairfax (Robertson) W.; B.S. in Mech. Engring., U. Louisville, 1954, M.Engring., 1972; m. Caroline Shelburne Crone, Dec. 29, 1956; children—Victoria Armistead, Walter Wyvill. Product devel. engr. Gamble Bros., Inc., Louisville, 1954-56; sales engr. Air Reduction Sales Co., Louisville, 1956-61; welding engr. Naval Ordnance Sta., Louisville, 1961-62, head prodn. devel. br., 1962-66, head prodn. engring. div., 1966-68, head armament div., 1968—. Bd. dirs. Valley Camp, United Fund Agy. Served with AUS, 1950-52; ETO; lt. col. Res. Registered profl. engr., Ky. Mem. Am. Welding Soc. (past sec., chmn.), Order Ky. Cols., Louisville Engr. and Sci. Councils Soc., Louisville Municipal Harbor Assn., Theta Tau. Democrat. Episcopalian. Home: 209 Kennedy Ct Louisville KY 40206 Office: Southside Dr Louisville KY 40214

WOOD, WILLIAM ANDREW, JR., printing co. exec.; b. Atlanta, Sept. 13, 1919; s. William A. and Naomi (Majors) W.; student U. Ga., 1948; m. Helen C. Kelley, Nov. 19, 1940; children—Elaine (Mrs. Thomas Ira Carlisle), Susan, Shirley, Margaret Kelley. With Foote & Davies div. McCall Printing Co., Doraville, Ga., 1938—, v.p. sales, 1955-69, exec. v.p., 1969—. Bd. dirs. DeKalb County chpt. Am. Cancer Soc. Served with USAAF, 1942-45. Mem. Atlanta C. of C., Atlanta Advt. Club, Commerce Club. Kiwanian. Club: Atlanta Athletic.Home: 2050 Amberwood Way NE Atlanta GA 30345 Office: 3101 McCall Dr Doraville GA 30340

WOOD, WOODSON TAULBEE, lawyer; b. Maysville, Ky., Feb. 24, 1928; s. Donald L. and Evelyn (Taulbee) W.; student U. Mich., 1945-46; LL.B., U. Ky., 1950; m. Mary Betty Bower, Jan. 22, 1952; children—Woodson T., Stockton, Ann, Jane, Mary, Andrew. Admitted to Ky. bar, 1950; practiced in Maysville, 1950-51; mem. firm Wood & Wood, Maysville, 1951-55, Fox, Wood & Wood, 1955—; commonwealth atty., 19th Jud. dist., Ky., 1956—. Served to 1st lt., AUS, 1952-54. Mem. N.Y., Mason County bar assns., Mensa, Am. Legion, Sigma Alpha Epsilon, Phi Alpha Delta. Presbyn. Odd Fellow (grand master Ky.), Moose, Lion. Maysville C. of C. Democrat. Home: Rural Route 1 Maysville KY 41056 Office: State Nat Bank Bldg Maysville KY 41056

WOODALL, LOWERY A., hosp. adminstr.; b. Lincoln County, Miss., June 10, 1929; s. Clem and Ruth (Smith) W.; B.A., U. So. Miss., 1951; postgrad. Basic Inst. Am. Coll. Hosp. Adminstrs., Baylor U., 1956, Advanced Inst., U. Chgo., 1959; m. Margaret Dee Bethany, Feb. 17, 1952; children—Linda Carol, Lowery A., Michelle. Bus. mgr. Miss. Baptist Hosp., Jackson, 1956-58, adminstrv. asst., 1956-58, asst. adminstr., 1958-62; exec. dir. Forrest County Gen. Hosp., Hattiesburg, Miss., 1962—. Dir. 1st Miss. Nat. Bank, Hattiesburg. Pres., Miss. Commn. on Hosp. Care, 1971—. Bd. dirs. Southeastern Hosp. Conf. Fellow Am. Coll. Hosp. Adminstrs.; mem. Hattiesburg Area C. of C. (pres. 1970), Miss. Hosp. Assn. (pres. 1971). Rotarian (dir. 1970—). Club: Hattiesburg Country. Home: 607 Woodbine Lane Hattiesburg MS 39401 Office: Forrest County General Hosp 400 S 28th Av Hattiesburg MS 39401

WOODALL, NORMAN EUGENE, banker; b. nr. Meridian, Miss., June 10, 1916; s. Albert Edward and Annie (Smith) W.; B.S. in Bus. Adminstrn., Miss. State U., 1939; postgrad. Am. Inst. Banking, 1962, Sch. Banking South La. State U., 1964, Command and Gen. Staff Coll., 1955, Indsl. Coll. Armed Forces, 1970; m. Virginia Dale Willard, Aug. 12, 1967. Adjuster Comml. Credit Co., Jackson, Miss., 1939-41; loan examiner RFC, Birmingham, Ala., 1946-55; with First Nat. Bank Birmingham, 1955—, sr. v.p., 1970—. Served with AUS, 1941-46. Decorated Bronze Star, Legion of Merit. Mem. Res. Officers Assn., Assn. U.S. Army, Am. Inst. Banking, Miss. State U. Alumni Assn., Birmingham C. of C., Sigma Chi. Clubs: Exchange (bd. govs. 1960-62, 71-72, sec. 1972-73), The Club, Relay House, Vestavia Country (Birmingham, Ala.). Home: 3422 Loch Ridge Trail Birmingham AL 35216 Office: 1900 5th Av N Birmingham AL 35203

WOODARD, DANIEL JOEL, author; b. Nashville, Feb. 2, 1930; s. Daniel Bennett and Quennie Mozell (Swallows) W.; student George Peabody Coll., 1952-53; B.S., U. Tenn., 1957, J.D. cum laude, 1957; m. Fredericka Novella Horner, Nov. 28, 1953; children—Daniel Joel II, Durenka Sue, Breck Randall. Field claim rep. State Farm Mut. Automobile Ins. Co., Chattanooga, 1957-59; admitted to Tenn. bar, 1957; claim atty. L. & N. R.R., 1959-61; practiced in Chattanooga, 1961-63. Dir. Park Theatre, Chattanooga. Served with USN, 1948-52. Mem. Centenary Players (dir. 1958-63), Center Players (dir. 1963-64), Delta Tau Delta (treas. 1953-54). Methodist. Author plays: The White Cracker, The Voices, Tom Jones, A Change of Luck, The Monkey and the Flag Pole, Serendipity, Pink Angels, Joy Stick Incident. Home: 524 Sharondale Rd Chattanooga TN 37412

WOODARD, JAMES EDWARD, dentist; b. Ardmore, Tenn., Jan. 14, 1918; s. Bernard Hatcher and Bessie (Carter) W.; A.B., Vanderbilt U., 1940; D.D.S., U. Tenn., 1943; m. Dorothy Louise Carter, Sept. 21, 1946; children—Joseph Anderson, Dorothy Louise, Daniel Carter. Gen. practice dentistry, Columbia, Tenn., 1946—. Mem. Maury County Bd. Health; mem. adv. com. Tenn. Mid-South Regional Med. Program, Tenn. Bd. Dentistry, So. Conf. Dental Deans and Examiners. Mem. Maury County Bd. Edn., 1956—, chmn., 1971—. Bd. dirs. Maury County Bd. Mental Health, Maury County Tb and Health Assn., Tenn. chpt. Am. Cancer Soc. Served with AUS, 1943-46. Mem. Am., Tenn. (trustee 1951-54) dental assns., 6th Dist. Dental Soc. (pres. 1949), U. Tenn. Dental Alumni (chmn. bd. trustees), Am. Coll. Dentists, Pierre Fauchard Acad., Southeastern Acad. Prosthodontics, Omicron Kappa Upsilon, Delta Sigma Delta. Methodist (sec. bd. trustees). Kiwanian (pres. Columbia 1954). Home: 906 Hillcrest Av Columbia TN 38401 Office: 208 W 6th St Columbia TN 38401

WOODARD, JOSEPH RAYMOND, educator; b. Spring Hope, N.C., Sept. 28, 1924; s. George Ollie and Mamie Larue (Whitley) W.; B.S., N.C. State U., 1949, M.S., 1960; m. Ellen Joyce Clark, Aug. 15, 1951; Agrl. extension agt., Halifax County, N.C., 1949-57; mem. faculty N.C. State U., Raleigh, 1958—, prof. animal sci., 1962—. Served with USNR, 1944-46. Mem. Am. Soc. Animal Sci., Epsilon Sigma Phi.‡

WOODBERY, D. HOYT, cigar co. exec.; b., 1892; m. With Havatampa Cigar Corp., Tampa, Fla., 1910—, pres., treas., chief exec. officer, mem. exec. com., 1947—; dir. Exchange Nat. Bank Tampa. State Fair, Gasparilla Assn. Address: 609 Cumberland Av Tampa FL 33602*

WOODBRIDGE, DAVID DAVIS, corp. exec.; b. Seattle, Jan. 29, 1922; s. Frederick W. and Florence (Davis) W.; B.S., U. Wash., 1949; postgrad. Mass. Inst. Tech., 1949-50; M.S., Ore. State U., 1951, Ph.D., 1956; m. Mary Ruth Woodard, June 3, 1950; children—David Davis (dec.), Wayne Woodard, Thomas Curtis, Robert Peter. Faculty physics Colo. Sch. Mines. Golden, 1954-57; chief space enrionment br. Army Ballistic Missile Agy., Redstone Arsenal, Ala., 1957-60; dir. exptl. programs Army Rocket and Guided Missile Agy., Red Stone Arsenal, 1960-61; staff scientist Chance Vought Co., Dallas, 1961-62; dir. Univ. Center for Pollution Research, prof., head sci. edn. Fla. Inst. Tech., Melbourne, 1962—; pres. Energy Systems, Inc., Melbourne, 1966-71. Chmn. bd. Nat. Shellfish Processors, Inc., Melbourne. Mem. Am. Meteorol. Soc., Am. Assn. Physics. Tchrs., Solar Energy Soc., Am. Astronaut. Soc., Am. Geophys. Union, Am. Ordnance Soc., A.A.A.S., Am. Inst. Aeros. and Astronautics, Pi Kappa Alpha. Author: Physics of the Atmosphere and Outer Space of Space Science and Engineering, 1965. Home: 1856 Washington Av Melbourne FL 32935

WOODBURY, JAMES HARRY, univ. adminstr.; b. Somerville, Tenn., June 8, 1918; s. James Harry and Mattie Matilda (Anderson) W.; B.S., Memphis State U., 1940; postgrad. U. Miss., 1940-41; m. Ruth Gaskell, Jan. 3, 1941; 1 son, Charles. City hall reporter Memphis Comml. Appeal, 1941-53; partner Archer & Woodbury, Inc., Memphis, 1953-68; dir. pub. service City of Memphis, 1968-71; dir. devel. Memphis State U., 1971—. Pres. Memphis Area Better Bus. Bur., 1965. Chmn. citizen's adv. com. for Shelby County of Tenn. Dept. Pub. Welfare, 1966-68; dir. Memphis Div. Pub. Service. mem. Memphis State Found. Bd.; mem. adv. com. Les Passees Rehab. Center. Bd. dirs. Memphis & Shelby County unit Am. Cancer Soc, Goodwill Industries, Vis. Nurse Assn., Sheltered Occupational Shop. Named outstanding alumnus Memphis State U., 1969. Mem. Memphis State Alumni Assn. (pres. 1968), Pub. Relations Soc. Am. (past pres. Mid South chpt.), Pi Kappa Alpha. Episcopalian. Clubs: Tennessee (v.p. 1969-72), Memphis Press, Kiwanis (Memphis). Home: 247 Deloach St Memphis TN 38111

WOODHAMS, JOHN ARTHUR, physician, educator; b. Irumu, Belgian Congo, July 21, 1926; s. Roy Charles and Beryl (Dewey) W. (parents Am. citizens); B.A., Houghton Coll., 1950; M.D., Western Res. U., 1954; m. Carolyn E. Peebles, Jan. 1, 1968; children by previous marriage—Karen Jean, David Keith, Jonathan Mark. Intern St. Luke's Hosp., Cleve., 1954-55, surg. resident, 1955-59; clin. fellow Am. Cancer Soc., 1957-59; pvt. practice surgery, Cleve., 1959-61, also mem. staff Bedford (O.) Municipal Hosp., St. Luke's Hosp., 1959-67; mem. asso. staff Huron Rd. Hosp., Cleve., also dir. surg. edn., 1961-67; asst. prof. surgery Emory U., also dir. surg. clinics Grady Meml. Hosp., Atlanta, 1968—. Diplomate Am. Bd. Surgery. Fellow A.C.S.; mem. Cleve. Acad. Medicine, Ohio State Med. Soc., Cleve. Med. Library Assn., Cleve. Surg. Assn., Christian Med. Soc., So. Gospel Mission Assn. (dir.). Served as sgt., AUS, 1944-46. Office: Grady Meml Hosp Atlanta GA 30303

WOODHURST, ROBERT STANFORD, JR., architect; b. Abbeville, S.C., July 12, 1921; s. Robert Stanford and Eva (Ferguson) W.; B.Arch., Clemson U., 1942; m. Dorothy Ann Carwile, Aug. 4, 1945; 1 son, Robert Stanford III. Designer, Harold Woodward, Architect, Spartanburg, S.C., 1946-47; asso. architect F. Arthur Hazard, Architect, Augusta, Ga., 1947-54; partner Woodhurst & O'Brien, Architects, Augusta, 1954—; v.p. Southeastern Architects and Engrs., Inc. Mem. Augusta-Richmond County Planning Commn., 1958-68, chmn., 1966-68; mem. Mayor's Adv. Com., 1965-68; mem. Augusta Bldg. Code Bd. of Appeals, 1955-58; financial adviser Jr. League Augusta. Mem. Historic Augusta, Inc., Augusta Museum. Served to capt. USAAF, 1942-46. Decorated Air medal with seven oak leaf clusters, French Croix de Guerre with palms. Mem. A.I.A. (sec. Ga. assn. 1970, dir. 1972), C. of C. Greater Augusta (dir.), Nat. Trust for Historic Preservation, Am. Soc. Planning Ofcls., Constrn. Specifications Inst., V.F.W. Clubs: Kiwanis, Elks, Augusta Country, West Lake Country, Pinnacle. Home: 810 Dogwood Lane Augusta GA 30904 Office: 607 15th St Augusta GA 30901

WOODIN, MARTIN DWIGHT, univ. adminstr.; b. Sicily Island, La., July 7, 1915; s. Dwight E. and Gladys Ann (Martin) W.; B.S., La. State U., 1936; M.S., Cornell U., 1939, Ph.D., 1941; m. Virginia Johnson, Sept. 7, 1939 (dec.); children—Rebecca (Mrs. Albin S. Johnson), Pamela (Mrs. James Cangelosi), Linda (Mrs. Vernon Porter Middleton); m. 2d, Elisabeth Wachalik, Oct. 8, 1968. Mem. faculty La. State U., 1941—, prof. agrl. econs., head dept., 1956-59, dir. resident instrn. Coll. Agr., 1959-60, dean at Alexandria, La., 1960-62, exec. v.p. at Baton Rouge, 1962—. Dep. dir. La. Civil Def. Agy., 1961—; v.p., exec. com. United Givers Baton Rouge, 1962-67. Sec. La. State U. Found., 1962—. Served with USNR, 1942-46; PTO. Mem. Am. Agr. Econ. Assn., Am. Marketing Assn., Am. Legion (post comdr.), Sigma Xi, Omicron Delta Kappa, Phi Kappa Phi, Beta Gamma Sigma, Phi Eta Sigma, Gamma Sigma Delta, Alpha Zeta, Pi Gamma Mu. Presbyn. Elk, Rotarian. Author articles in field. Home: 234 Court St Baton Rouge LA 70803

WOODLAND, DON LYNN, educator; b. Ballinger, Tex., Sept. 3, 1936; s. Tom Blackwell and Rena (Grant) W.; B.B.A., U. Tex. at Austin, 1958, M.B.A., 1959, Ph.D., 1962; m. Molli Ann Howell, June 3, 1960; children—Wendy, Leigh Anne. Economist, Fed. Res. Bank Dallas, 1962-65; financial economist Okla. State U., Stillwater, 1965-68; asso. prof. finance La. State U., Baton Rouge, 1966—. Asst. dir. Sch. Banking of South, Baton Rouge, 1967—; exec. dir. Central Am. Grad. Sch. Banking, San Pedro Sula, Honduras, 1970—. Mem. Am. Finance Assn. Democrat. Methodist. Club: Bocage Racquet. Author: (with Edward Reed) Cases in Commercial Banking, 1970. Home: 774 Castle Kirk St Baton Rouge LA 70808

WOODMANSEE, RICHARD ELLERY, furniture co. exec.; b. Kansas City, Mo., June 18, 1911; s. Joseph Emmett and Blanche M. (Lockridge) W.; A.B., U. Kan., 1932; m. Virginia Lapham, Oct. 6, 1934; children—Richard Scott, Susan (Mrs. James W. Strawn III). City salesman Richards and Conover Wholesale Hardware Co., Kansas City, Mo., 1932-35, furniture and appliance mgr., Oklahoma City, 1935-48; v.p., sales mgr. furniture Frank Lyon Co., Little Rock, 1948—. Mem. budget com. United Fund, 1960—. Bd. dirs. Salvation Army, 1952—, chmn., 1956—; bd. dirs. YMCA; v.p. Frank Lyon Found., 1948—; bd. commdrs. Presbyn. Village, 1966—. Named Man of Year, Furniture Hall of Fame, 1961. Mem. Nat. Wholesale Furniture Assn. (dir., v.p., pres., chmn. bd.), Phi Delta Theta. Presbyn. (treas., deacon, elder, bldg com. 1948—). Rotarian. Club: Pleasant Valley Country (Little Rock). Home: 9 Virginia Lane Little Rock AR 72207 Office: 65th and Scott Hamilton Dr Little Rock AR 72205

WOODRESS, FREDERICK ALBERT, pub. relations cons.; b. St. Louis, Jan. 11, 1923; s. James L. and Jessie (Smith) W.; student Antioch Coll., 1941-43; A.B., 1948; student Washington U., 1946; M.S., U. Ky., 1971; m. Anne Loraine Blackmon, Dec. 31, 1953; 1 dau., Cathy Loraine. Stringer, reporter various Ohio and Mo. newspapers, 1939-48; free-lance writer, 1948-49; pub. relations asst. Methodist Div. Fgn. Missions, 1949; reporter, columnist, entertainment editor Birmingham (Ala.) Post-Herald, 1949-55; owner Fred Woodress, pub. relations cons. firm, 1955-69; asst. to chief adminstr. and pub. affairs dir. U. Ala. Med. Center, 1964-69; dir. pub. relations U. Ky.; Lexington 1969-71; pub. relations cons. Woodress & Myers, Louisville, 1971—. Tchr. advt. Birmingham So. Coll., 1958; information specialist U.S. Salvation Army, Haiti, 1963, La., Ark. Salvation Army, New Orleans, 1965. Served with AUS, 1943-46. Mem. Pub. Relations Soc. Am. (v.p. Ala.-Miss. chpt., Presdl. citation 1968, pres. Ala. chpt., nat. membership chmn.). Episcopalian. Author: Impasse pub. in Best One Act Plays, 1949; (with others) 87th Infantry Division History, 1946. Contbr. articles to mags. Home: 3148 Trinity Rd Lexington KY 40503 Office: Woodress & Myers Commerce Bldg Louisville KY 40202

WOODRING, ALVIN JAMES, hosp. adminstr.; b. Detroit, Sept. 27, 1924; s. Alvin and Jean Houston (Mitchell) W.; B.S., Susquehanna U., 1948; m. Evelyn Ellagene Latimer, Oct. 18, 1952; children—James Latimer, Stephen Alvin. Inventory controller Wiedenman & Co., Bloomsburg, Pa., 1948-49, collection mgr. Sears, Roebuck & Co.,

Greensboro, N.C., 1949-51; asst. adminstr. Anderson (S.C.) Meml. Hosp., 1951-54; adminstr. Fairfield Meml. Hosp., Winnsboro, S.C., 1954-58; asst. dir. U. Fla. Teaching Hosp., Gainesville, 1958-60; adminstr. Tifton (Ga.) County Hosp., 1960-64, Southeastern Ky. Bapt. Hosp., Corbin, 1964—. Served with USAAF, 1942-45. Decorated Air medal with oak leaf cluster, D.F.C. Mem. Am. Coll. Hosp. Adminstrs. Mason. Office: Mitchell St Corbin KY 40701

WOODRUFF, EDWIN CUSHING, geophysicist; b. N.Y.C., July 22, 1926; s. George Percy and Margaret (Neville) W.; student Princeton, 1947-50; B.S. in Geology, Marietta Coll., 1953; A.M., U. Mo., 1954; m. Barbara Anne Brown, June 2, 1957; 1 dau., Anne Elizabeth. With Geophys. Service, Inc., Merced, Cal., 1953; grad. asst. U. Mo., 1953-54; with Shell Oil Co., 1954-71, seismologist, 1955-59, geophysicist, party chief, 1959-65, geophysicist, 1965-69, sr. geophysicist, Midland, Tex., 1969-71; sr. geophysicist Basin Geophysical, Inc., Midland, 1971—. Pres., Lee chpt. Am. Field Service, 1966-68, liaison v.p., 1969-70. Served with USNR, 1944-46. Mem. Permian Basin Aviation Assn. (pres. 1966-67), Am. Assn. Petroleum Geologists, Permian Basin Geophys. Soc. (membership chmn. 1968), W.Tex. Geol. Soc. (geothermal survey chmn.), Am. Petroleum Inst., Gamma Alpha, Delta Upsilon. Unitarian. Kiwanian (sec.-treas.), Toastmaster (pres. 1970). Home: 208 Club Dr Midland TX 79701 Office: 9 Patio Bldg Midland TX 79701

WOODRUFF, F(RANK) NORMAN, gas co. exec.; b. Houston, Sept. 7, 1921; s. Matthew Franklin and Arvie (Weaver) W.; student U. Houston, 1939-42; B.S., U. Tex., 1948; m. Mary Geraldyne Hatcher, Oct. 26, 1963; children—Lockie (Mrs. Donald Mitchell), Frank Norman, Letitia (Mrs. James D. Wilson), Matthew. Tech. clk. Shell Oil Co., Houston, 1940-42; head gas dept. oil and gas div. Tex. R.R. Commn., Austin, 1948-50; reservoir engr. El Paso Natural Gas Co., Houston, 1950-55, mgr. gas proration operations, El Paso, Tex., 1955-71, dir., 1971—. Chmn., Mayor's Engring. Adv. Com., 1968-69; mem. U.S. Nat. Com.-World Energy Conf., 1959—, chmn., 1970-72; chmn. Nat. Energy Forum, 1971—. Served to 1st lt USAAF, 1943-45; PTO. Decorated Air medal with oakleaf clusters. Registered profl. engr., Tex. Fellow A.A.A.S.; mem. Nat. (chmn. com. on engring. preparation 1967-69), Tex. (chmn. profl. engrs. in industry 1966-67, chmn. engring. preparation com. 1967-70) socs. profl. jours., Am. Inst. Mining, Metall. and Petroleum Engrs. (chmn. El Paso sect. 1969-70), Engring. Guidance Council (bd. chmn. 1966—). Methodist. Kiwanian. Clubs: El Paso, El Paso Country. Author: Petroleum Powers Irrigation Systems - Farming Possible in Arid Areas, 1966; Guidance of Precollege Youth—An Engineers Responsibility, 1968. Home: 6317 Westwind Dr El Paso TX 79912 Office: PO Box 1492 El Paso TX 79999

WOODRUFF, GEORGE ROBERT, educator; b. Athens, Ga., Mar. 14, 1916; s. Joseph G. and Mary (Phillips) W.; B.S. in Engring., U. Tenn., 1939; postgrad. U.S. Mil. Acad., 1944-45, Baylor U., 1947-50, U. Fla., 1950-60, U. Tenn., 1961; m. Margaret Artley, Sept. 3, 1942; children— William Robert, Mark Artley, Joseph G., Margaret Elizabeth. Asst. coach U. Tenn., Knoxville, 1941, athletic dir., 1961—; asst. coach U.S. Mil. Acad., West Point, N.Y., 1944-46; line coach Ga. Inst. Tech., Atlanta, 1946; head football coach Baylor U., 1947-50; head football coach, athletic dir. U. Fla., 1950-60. Bd. dirs. U.S. Olympic Com. Served from 2d lt. to maj. C.E. AUS, 1942-46. Named to Savannah (Ga.) Football Hall of Fame, 1965, Coach of Year Fla. Sports Writers Assn., 1952, Southwest Conf. Tex. Sports Writers Assn., 1949, Ga. Hall of Fame, Tenn. Hall of Fame. Mem. Am. Football Coaches Assn., Nat. Assn. Collegiate Dirs. Athletics (exec. com. univ. div.), Nat. Collegiate Athletic Assn. (dist. III rep.), Am. Legion, Alpha Tau Omega. Democrat. Baptist. Home: 7412 Sheffield Dr Knoxville TN 37919

WOODRUFF, WALLACE JACK, comml laundry sales and leasing co. exec.; b. Louisville, Mar. 3, 1918; s. Wallace G. and Ella (Rebsch) W.; B.S., U. Ky., 1946; m. Mildred Marshall Griffin, Mar. 1, 1943; children—John Steven, Elizabeth Anne. With Kawneer Co., Cynthiana, Ky., 1946-66, successively personnel mgr., plant mgr., sales mgr., plant mgr., works mgr., v.p. and gen. mgr. until 1966; gen. mgr. Archl. div. Gen. Bronze Corp., Miami, Fla., 1966-68; v.p. Miller Distbg. Corp., Miami, 1969—. Mem. Miami Com. of 100. Bd. dirs. Ky. Soc. Crippled Children, Asso. Industries Ky. Served with USNR, 1940-45. Decorated D.F.C., Air medal. Mem. C. of C. (dir., pres.), Navy League. Baptist. Home: 2131 S Bayshore Dr Miami FL 33133 Office: 6300 NW 77th Ct Miami FL 33148

WOODS, BOBBY WILLIAM, clergyman; b. Frederick, Okla., Apr. 23, 1930; s. Eugene William and Nellie Allene (Hayter) W.; student Cameron Jr. Coll., 1954-55; B.A., Midwestern U., Wichita Falls, Tex., 1957; B.D., Southwestern Theol. Sem. (Ft. Worth), 1960, Th.D., 1964; m. Bobbie Ann Butcher, July 2, 1948; children—Mark, Debra. Ordained to ministry Bapt. Ch., 1955; pastor First Bapt. Chs., Hollister, Okla., 1957-61, Wynnewood, Okla., 1961-65, Tucumari, N.M., 1965-67, Seminole, Okla., 1967—. Bd. dirs. Bapt. Gen. Conv. Okla., 1968-71. Mem. Seminole C. of C. (bd. dirs. 1971-72). Kiwanian. Author: God's Answer To Anxiety, 1968. Contbr. to profl. jours.; to Zondervan's Pastors Annual, 2 vols., 1970, 71. Home: 2210 Phelps Dr Seminole OK 74868 Office: PO Box 310 Seminole OK 74868

WOODS, CULLEN CURLEE, dentist; b. Ft. Worth, Mar. 29, 1928; s. Dexter Levert and Margaret Faulds (O'Leary) W.; B.A., Vanderbilt U., 1950; D.D.S., U. Tenn., 1957; m. Jimmie Louise Beckham, Sept. 17, 1950; children—Cullen, Patrick, Susan, Timothy. Dentist, Okla. Health Dept., Shawnee, 1958; individual practice dentistry, Oklahoma City, 1958—. Clin. instr. oral surgery U. Okla. Sch. Medicine, 1969—. Mem. Okla. Dental Polit. Action Com., 1970—. Served with USAF, 1950-54. Mem. Internat., Am., Okla. wildlife fedns., Acad. Gen. Dentistry, Am., Okla. dental assns., Okla. County (dir.; Ho. of Dels.), Deans (hon.) dental socs., Smithsonian Inst., Am. Soc. Implantology, Okla. Peace Officers Assn., YMCA, Omicron Kappa Upsilon. Kiwanian (sec.; pres.), Mason (Shriner). Home: 2321 NW 120th St Oklahoma City OK 73120 Office: 2812 W Hefner Oklahoma City OK 73120

WOODS, EDGAR HALL, mfr.; b. Calyx, Miss., Aug. 13, 1913; s. Edgar Hall and Ida (Lyell) W.; B.S., Marion Inst., 1934; A.B., U. Ky., 1935; m. Irma M. Mihalic, Oct. 12, 1955; children—Charles Scott, Elizabeth Callaway. Cotton planter, 1935-41; adminstr. Munitions Bd. of Standards Agy., 1948-50; v.p. John Deere Plow Co., Balt., 1950-56; gen. sales mgr. Ford Tractor & Implement div., Birmingham, Mich., 1956-58; pres. Midland Ford Tractor Co., St. Louis, 1958-64; pres., dir. Preco, Inc., Los Angeles, 1963—; chmn. bd. D.J. Bricker Lincoln Mercury, Hollywood, Cal., Implement Sales Co., Inc., Memphis; pres., chmn. bd. Midland Mfg. Co., Electric Mills, Miss.; pres. Northcote, Inc., Monterey, Cal. Served with USNR, 1942-46. Decorated Purple Heart. Mem. Am. Soc. Agrl. Engrs., Am. Soc. M.E., Kappa Alpha. Clubs: Northwood (Meridian, Miss.); Jonathan (Los Angeles); Capitol City (Atlanta); Army-Navy (Washington). Home and office: Scooba MS 39358

WOODS, EDWARD LAFAYETTE, civil engr.; b. Knoxville, Tenn., Dec. 14, 1933; s. William Orville and Lela Mae (Dyer) W.; A.A., U. N.C., Charlotte, 1960; B.S., N.C. State U., 1962; m. Eloise Delores Isaacs, Mar. 20, 1954; children—Renee, Janice. Asst. design engr. Duke Power Co., Charlotte, N.C., 1959-68; supr. inspections Mecklenberg County Dept. Pub. Works, Charlotte, 1968—. Registered profl. engr., N.C. Mem. Am. Soc. C.E. (sec.), Charlotte Engrs. Club, N.C. Bldg. Insps. Assn. (dir.). Home: 107 Chadmore Dr Matthews NC 28105 Office: PO Box 1516 Charlotte NC 28201

WOODS, G. CECIL, JR., seminary dean; b. June 6, 1922; B.A. magna cum laude, Vanderbilt U., 1942; post grad. in English Lit. Yale, 1947-48, M.S.T., 1958; B.D., Episcopal Theol. Sem., 1953; advanced study in theology, Oxford U., Eng., 1962-64; m. Marie Gager Cartinhour; four children. With Volunteer State Life Ins. Co., Chattannooga, Tenn., 1945-47; instr. English lit. U. of South, Sewanee, Tenn., 1948-50; ordained priest Episcopal Ch., 1954; parish rector Diocese of Tenn., 1953-56; asst. prof. liturgics, patristics, also chaplain Sch. Theology, U. of South, 1958-69; dean Episcopal Theol. Sem., Va., 1969—. Mem. bd. trustees Episcopal Radio-TV Found.; chmn. bd. trustees also chmn. exec. com. Washington Theol. Consortium. Mem. Phi Beta Kappa. Office: 3737 Seminary Rd Protestant Episcopal Theological Seminary Alexandria VA 22304*

WOODS, GILBERT WELCH, civil engr.; b. Lamont, Okla., May 3, 1921; s. Elmer Ervin and Hazel (Welch) W.; B.S. in Civil Engring., Okla. U., 1948; m. Wilma Lounsbury, Sept. 25, 1944; 1 dau., Susan. Designer, Okla. Hwy. Dept., 1948-49; hwy. engr. Bur. Pub. Roads, 1949-51; asst. chief engr. Taft & Williamson, cons. engrs., 1951-56; chief civil engr. J.B. Payne & Assos., cons. engrs., 1956-61; chief engr. Serv-Air Inc., Enid, Okla., 1961-72; dir. civil engring. Northrop Worldwide Aircraft Services, 1972—. Served to 1st lt. USAAF, 1942-48. Decorated D.F.C., Air medal with three oak leaf clusters. Registered profl. engr., Okla., Colo. Mem. Am. Soc. Testing and Materials, Nat., Okla. socs. profl. engrs. Mem. Christian Ch. Lion. Home: 1717 E Maple St Enid OK 73701 Office: Serv-Air Inc Vance AFB Enid OK 73701

WOODS, LLOYD LANDER, chemist; b. Iola, Kan., Mar. 2, 1908; s. Arthur G. and Minnie (Montgomery) W.; A.B., Friends U., 1930; M.S., Kan. State U., 1934, Ph.D., 1944; m. Dora E. Keeton, Aug. 10, 1932; 1dau., Elaine. Prof. St. Augustine's Coll., 1931-48; prof. Tex. So. U., Houston, 1948—, Distinguished prof., 1968—, also head dept. chemistry, chmn. div. natural and phys. scis. Recipient Distinguished Alumni award Friends U., 1968. Fellow Chem. Soc. London, Am. Inst. Chemists, Tex. Acad. Sci.; mem. Am. Chem. Soc., Kan., N.Y. acads. sci., Phi Lambda Upsilon, Beta Kappa Chi. Contbr. articles to chemistry jours. Home: 2706 Barbee St Houston TX 77004

WOODS, PENDLETON, ednl. adminstr., author; b. Ft. Smith, Ark., Dec. 18, 1923 ; s. John Powell and Mabel (Hon) W.; B.A. in Journalism, U. Ark., 1948; m. Lois Robin Freeman, Apr. 3, 1948; children— Margaret, Paul Pendleton, Nancy. Editor, asst. pub. mgr. Okla. Gas & Electric Co., Oklahoma City, 1948-69; dir. Living Legends of Okla., Okla. Christian Coll., Oklahoma City, 1969—. Bd. dirs. Campfire Girls Council, Okla. Jr. Symphony (past pres.), Boy Scout Council; past pres. Oklahoma City Mental Health Clin.; pub. relations chmn. Oklahoma County chpt. A.R.C.; chmn. Western Heritage award Nat. Cowboy Hall of Fame; past pres. Variety Health Center; dir. Am. Freedom Council. Served with AUS, World War II and Korean; lt. col., state historian Okla. N.G. Named Outstanding Young Man of Year, Oklahoma City Jr. C. of C., 1953; Silver Beaver award Boy Scouts Am., 1963. Mem. Soc. Asso. Indsl. Editors (past v.p.), Advt. Fedn. Am. (past dist. dir.), Central Okla. Indsl. Editors (past pres.), Okla. Jr. C. of C. (hon. life; past internat. dir.), Okla. Distributive Edn. Clubs (hon. life), Oklahoma City Advt. Club (past pres.), Sigma Delta Chi, Kappa Sigma (nat. commr. publs.). Author: You and Your Company Magazine, 1950; Myriad of Sports, 1971. Recorded Sounds of Scouting, 1969. Home: 541 NW 31st St Oklahoma City OK 73118

WOODS, POWELL, lawyer; b. Ft. Smith, Ark., Jan. 19, 1922; s. John Powell and Mabel Fairfax (Hon) W.; B.A., U. Ark., 1948; LL.B., U. Ark. at Little Rock, 1950; m. Lola Lavoy Keener, June 18, 1954; children—Lola Lavoy, John Powell. Admitted to Ark. bar, 1950; practiced in Ft. Smith, 1950-58; individual practice law, Siloam Springs, 1958—. City atty., Siloam Springs, 1960-62; municipal judge, Siloam Springs, 1963-64. Sec.-treas. Siloam Springs Salvation Army, 1962—. Served with AUS, 1943-45. Mem. Am., Ark., Benton County bar assns., Comml. Law League, Nat. Rifle Assn., C. of C., N.W. Ark. Geol. Soc., Isaac Walton League. Rotarian. Home: 411 S Britt St Siloam Springs AR 72761 Office: 207 S Broadway Siloam Springs AR 72761

WOODS, ROBERT JAMES, III, computer co. exec.; b. Memphis, Feb. 23, 1937; s. Robert James, Jr., and Mary Virginia (Allen) W.; B.A., Stanford, 1959; m. Margaret Bostic Schreck, June 18, 1960. Accountant Tenn. Gas Transmission, Houston, 1960-61; systems engr. IBM Corp., Tulsa, 1961-67, mgr. data center, Tulsa, 1967-68; v.p. Comptran Computer Corp., Tulsa, 1968—. Served with USAF, 1959. Mem. Kappa Alpha Order. Republican. Episcopalian. Club: Southern Hills Country (Tulsa). Home: 3613 E 49th St Tulsa OK 74135 Office: 4900 S Lewis St Tulsa OK 74105

WOODS, ROSE MARY, govt ofcl.; b. Sebring, O., Dec. 26, 1917; d. Thomas M. and Mary (Maley) Woods; ed. high sch. With Royal China, Inc., Sebring, 1935-43, Office of Censorship 1943-45, Internat. Trading Adminstrn., 1945-47, Herter Com. Fgn. Aid, 1947. Fgn. Service Ednl. Found., 1947-51; sec. to senator, then v.p. Nixon, 1951-61; asst. to Mr. Nixon with firm Adams, Duque & Hazeltine, Los Angeles, 1961-63, firm Nixon, Mudge, Rose, Guthrie & Alexander, N.Y.C., 1963-68; sec. to Pres. Nixon, 1969—. Named one of ten Women of Year, Los Angeles Times, 1961. Home: 2500 Virginia Av NW Washington DC 20037 Office: The White House Washington DC 20500

WOODS, SAMUEL HUBERT, JR., educator; b. Ardmore, Okla., Mar. 10, 1926; s. Samuel Hubert and May (Wilson) W.; student U. Okla., 1943-45; A.B. cum laude, Harvard, 1947, M.A., 1949; Ph.D., Yale, 1956; m. Clara Belle Brown, Aug. 21, 1962. Instr. English, U. Colo., 1949-51, Duke U., 1954-55, Rutgers U., 1955-56; instr. English, Okla State U., 1956-57, asst. prof., 1957-61, asso. prof., 1961-65, prof., 1965—. Mem. Modern, South Central modern lang. assns., Nat. Council Tchrs. English, Am. Assn. U. Profs., Sigma Alpha Epsilon. Democrat. Episcopalian. Author: (with M. Rohrberger, E. Eukore) Introduction to Literature, 1968, (with M. Rohrberger) Reading and Writing about Literature, 1971. Contbr. articles to profl. pubs. Home: 1709 W 3d Av Stillwater OK 74074

WOODS, VELDA VIOLA (MRS. WALTER J. BLACKMON), public accountant; b. Atwater, Cal., June 3, 1915; d. Samuel Simmion and Winnie Viola (Harris) Woods; B.B.A., U. Tex., 1939; m. Walter J. Blackmon, Mar. 15, 1947; 1 dau., Margo Mamie. Accountant, Caller-Times Pub. Co., Corpus Christi, Tex., 1940-44; accountant Carneiro Chumney & Co., C.P.A.'s, 1944-47; partner Collier, Johnson & Woods, C.P.A.'s Corpus Christi, 1947—. Charter mem. Corpus Christi Estate Planning Council, 1947—. Mem. Am. Inst. C.P.A.'s, Tex. Soc. C.P.A.'s. Presbyn. Home: 3370 San Antonio St Corpus Christi TX 78411 Office: Guaranty Bank Plaza Corpus Christi TX 74801

WOODS, WALTER ABNER, consumer research cons.; b. Lingle, Wyo., Jan. 16, 1915; s. James A. and Mazeppa (Israel) W.; A.B., U. Wyo., 1937; M.A., Syracuse U., 1942; Ph.D., Columbia, 1952; student Art Students League, 1946-47; m. Margaret C. Edmiston, June 16, 1955; 1 dau., Dana Jeanne. Field asst. FSA, 1939-42; counseling psychologist Stevens Inst. Tech., 1946-47; research psychologist Pratt Inst., 1947-51; staff pyschologist Fort Hays State Coll., 1951-52; asso. psychology Coll. William and Mary, 1952-55; psychologist, research dir. Nowland & Co., Greenwich, Conn., 1955-57, v.p., 1958-60, sr. v.p., 1960-61; self-employed as consumer research cons., Sparta, N.J., 1961-71; pres. Consultants in Consumer Research, Inc., 1961-68; pres. Products and Concepts Research Internat., 1968—, Island Matrix Corp., 1968—; prof. marketing West Ga. Coll., 1971—. Served to lt. USNR, 1942-46. Mem. Am. Psychol. Assn., Am. Marketing Assn., Internat. Assn. Applied Psychology, Am. Soc. Aesthetics, Internat. Platform Assn. Address: 37 Lynda Circle Carrollton GA 30117

WOODSON, BENJAMIN NELSON, ins. co. exec.; b. Altoona, Kan., June 5, 1908; s. Benjamin Nelson and Mary Ola (Burke) W.; ed. pub. schs., Omaha; m. Grace Mareen Cook, Jan. 25, 1930; 1 dau., Mary Burnett (Mrs. John P. Dennis, Jr.). With U.P. R.R., 1926-27, with Mut. Trust Life Ins. Co., 1928-37; with Life Ins. Agy. Mgmt. Assn., Hartford, Conn., 1937-44, asst. mgr. dir., 1941-44; exec. v.p. Commonwealth Life Ins. Co., Louisville, Ky., 1944-51; mng. dir. Nat. Assn. Life Underwriters, Life Underwriters Tng. Council, 1951-53; v.p., dir., mem. exec. com. Am. Gen. Ins. Co., 1953-64, exec. v.p., 1964-65. pres. 1966—; pres., chmn., and/or dir. all subsidiary cos. Am. Gen. Group; chmn. Variable Annuity Life Ins. Co., Cal.-Western States Life Ins. Co.; dir. Houston Lighting & Power Co. Emeritus mem. internat. bd. electors, Ins. Hall of Fame; a founder, past pres., sec., now life trustee, dir. Life Underwriter Tng. Council; trustee Am. College Life Underwriters, S.S. Huebner Found. for Ins. Edn. Spl. asst. to sec. war, 1947-48; area chmn. U.S. Savs. Bonds drives, 1956-65; pres. Nat. Space Hall of Fame Found. Bd. dirs. United Fund Houston and Harris County, Greater Houston (Bluebonnet) Bowl Assn., Houston Symphony Soc., Jr. Achievement Houston, Community Effort, Inc., Salvation Army, Houston, Texas Research League; gov. advisor Rice U. Recipient John Newton Russell Meml. award Nat. Assn. Life Underwriters, 1963. C.L.U. Mem. Rice U. Assos., Philos. Soc. Tex., Newcomen Soc. N.Am., Houston Council on World Affairs, Tex. Life Conv. (past pres.), Houston C. of C. (pres. 1972-73). Clubs: Houston (pres.) International, River Oaks Country, Ramada, Coronado, Warwick (Houston); Metropolitan (N.Y.C.); Pacific, Oahu Country (Honolulu); Tres Vidas (Acapulco); El Dorado, Palm Desert. Author: More Power to You, 1951; The Set of the Sail, 1963; contbg. author: Life and Health Insurance Handbook, 1959. Home: 3315 Del Monte Dr Houston TX 77019 Office: 2727 Allen Pkwy Houston TX 77019

WOODSON, HENRY LEE, JR., electronics co. exec.; b. Roanoke, Va., Apr. 12, 1908; s. Henry L. and Estelle (Hancock) W.; B.S. in Elec. Engring., Va. Mil. Inst., 1932; m. Dicie May Cassady, July 1, 1950; children—Douglas Lee, James Neal, Patricia Lea. Asst. city mgr., Roanoke, 1937-45; chief maintenance and operations N.W. Pacific area VA, Seattle, 1945-48; engring. rep. G. F. Muth Co., Washington, 1948-52; chief property mgmt., orgn., methods examiner Office U.S. Housing Adminstr., Washington, 1952-55; adminstr., field mgmt. officer USOM, Pakistan, 1955-56; exec. officer, Turkey, 1956-57; mgr. Washington office Bendix Radio div. Bendix Corp., 1957-67, regional mgr. Bendix Communications div., 1967—. Mem. Radio Tech. Commn. for Aeros. Served to lt. col. AUS, 1941-46. Mem. I.E.E.E., Am. Helicopter Soc., Am. Congress Mapping and Surveying, A.A.A.S., Nat. Assn. Housing Ofcls., Internat. City Mgrs. Assn., Am. Marketing Assn., Aero Club Washington, Am. Inst. Aeros. and Astronautics, Nat. Space Club, Armed Forces Communications and Electronics Assn., U.S. Naval Inst., Air Force Assn., Assn. Old Crows, Internat. Platform Assn., Fedn. Aeronautique Internationale, Nat. Security Indsl. Assn., Am. Ordnance Assn., Armed Forces Mgmt. Assn., Navy League U.S., Assn. U.S. Army. Clubs: Army-Navy, MDW Officers, Nat. Aviation, Gaslight. Home: 2401 N Vernon St Arlington VA 22207 Office: 1730 K St NW Washington DC 20006

WOODSON, RICHARD PEYTON, III, ins. co. exec.; b. Albuquerque, Mar. 1, 1923; s. Richard Peyton and Katherine (McMillen) W.; student Phillips Exeter Acad., 1938-41; A.B. cum laude, Princeton, 1949; postgrad. Leland Stanford U., 1949-50; m. Martha Ann Avison, Sept. 18, 1954; children—Sheila Prentice, Richard Peyton IV, Martha Winslow. Sec., treas. Woodson Assos., Inc., Albuquerque, 1950-55; asst. treas. Occidental Life Ins. Co., Raleigh, N.C., 1955-57, treas. 1957-62, v.p., 1959-62, chmn. bd., chief exec. officer, 1962-72, pres., 1968—, dir., 1952—; treas., Occidental Fire & Casualty Co., 1961-63, chmn., 1963—, dir., 1961—; mem. Raleigh bd. mgrs. Wachovia Bank & Trust Co.; dir. Peninsular Life Ins. Co., Brit.-Am. Ins. Co.; pres., dir. Mgmt. Services Corp., 1961—; chmn. bd. Independent Data Processing Corp., 1963—. Past pres. Raleigh Little Theatre; chmn. N.C. Housing Authority, 1969—. Bd. dirs. Shaw U.; bd. visitors Davidson Coll.; bd. dirs. Boys Club Raleigh, Occonecchee council Boy Scouts Am. Served to maj. USAAF, 1943-46. Decorated Air Medal with 3 oak leaf clusters. Mem. Life Office Mgmt. Assn. (chmn. bd. 1968-69), Young Presidents Orgn., Inst. Life Mgmt. (dir.). Presbyn. Clubs: Rotary, Carolina Country; Lyford Cay (Nassau); Country of N.C.; Marco Polo, Princeton, Sky (N.Y.C.). Home: 2805 Lakeview Dr Raleigh NC 27609 Office: 1001 Wade Av Cameron Village Raleigh NC 27605

WOODSON, WARREN BROOKS, athletic dir.; b. Ft. Worth, Feb. 24, 1903; s. William Warren and Jeanette (Brooks) W.; A.B., Baylor U., 1924; B.Phys. Edn., Springfield (Mass.) Coll., 1926; m. Muriel Young, Dec. 23, 1928; 1 dau., Dawn. Dir. phys. edn. San Marcos (Tex.) Acad. 1926-27; dir. phys. edn., head football coach Texarkana (Tex.) Coll., 1927-35, Ark. State Tchrs. Coll., 1935-41; athletic dir., head football coach Hardin-Simmons U., 1941-42, 46-52; head football coach U. Ariz., 1952-56; athletic dir., head football coach N.M. State U., 1958-68; athletic dir. Trinity U., 1968—, head football coach, 1971—. Bd. dirs. Tucson YMCA, 1953-58. Served to lt. comdr. USNR, 1942-45. Named Football Coach of Year Coll. Coaches Am., 1960; named to Helms Athletic Hall Fame, 1959; Warren Woodson Day in N.M. celebrated, 1961; recipient citation of honor for contbns. to coll. football, Football Writers Association of America, 1965. Mem. Am. Football Coaches Assn. (football rules com. 1962-64). Rotarian. Baptist. Originated Wing-T offensive, 1941, Space-T offensive, 1964. Home: 8401 N New Braunfels San Antonio TX 78209

WOODWARD, DANIEL HOLT, educator; b. Ft. Worth, Tex., Oct. 17, 1931; B.A. in Philosophy, U. Colo., 1951, M.A. in English, 1955; Ph.D. in English, Yale, 1957; M.S. in L.S., Catholic U., 1969; m. Mary Jane Gerra. Asst. prof. English, Mary Washington Coll., U. Va., 1957-61, asso. prof., 1961-66, prof., 1966—, librarian, 1969—. Served with AUS, 1952-54. Mem. Modern Lang. Assn., A.L.A., Renaissance English Text Soc., Am. Civil Liberties Union, Phi Beta

Kappa. Club: Grolier. Editor: The Poems and Translations of Robert Fletcher, 1969. Contbr. to profl. publs. Address: 1439 College St Fredericksburg VA 22401*

WOODWARD, FELIX GRUNDY, coll. ofcl.; b. Gallatin, Tenn., Apr. 3, 1903; s. Frederick Augustus and Eliza Keeble (Reid) W.; student U. Wis., 1921-23; B.S., George Peabody Coll., 1928; M.A., Vanderbilt U., 1929; m. Laura Miller, Sept. 12, 1936; children—John Maury, David Reid, Fred Miller. Tchr. English, Lincoln County High Sch., Fayetteville, Tenn., 1923-27; prof. English, Austin Peay State Coll., Clarksville, Tenn., 1929-47, dean faculty, 1947-68, asst. to pres., 1968—; dir. grad. div., 1952—. Mem. Tenn. Joint Com. Higher Edn., Tenn. Adv. Council Tchr. Edn. and Certification. Mem. Middle Tenn. Edn. Assn. (pres. 1961-62), Phi Delta Kappa. Democrat. Presbyn. Home: RR 6 Clarksville TN 37040

WOODWARD, HALBERT OWEN, U.S. dist judge; b. Coleman, Tex., Apr. 8, 1918; s. Garland A. and Helen (Halbert) W.; B.B.A., U. Tex., LL.B., 1940; m. Dawn Blair, Sept. 28, 1940; children—Halbert Owen, Garland Benton. Admitted to Tex. bar, 1941; practice in Coleman, 1949-58; chmn. Tex. Hwy. Commn., 1959-68; U.S. dist. judge No. Dist. Tex., 1968—. Dir. S.W. State Bank, Brownwood, Tex. Bd. dirs. Overall Meml. Hosp., Coleman. Served with USNR, 1942-45; Mem. Am., Tex. bar assns., Am. Judicature Soc., Beta Theta Pi. Home: 4608 11th St Lubbock TX 79416 Office: PO Box 2838 Lubbock TX 79408

WOODWARD, HARRY EVANS, state ofcl.; b. Clifton Forge, Va., Sept. 9, 1916; s. Harry Evans and Hilda Mitchell (Morris) W.; B.A., U. Va., 1940. With Sales Mgmt. Mag., N.Y.C., 1944-65, spl. features editor, 1950-60, sr. editor, 1960-65; dir. pub. relations and advt. Va. Div. Indsl. Devel., Office Gov., Richmond, 1965—. Founding mem. Alleghany Hist. Soc., 1967—. Mem. exec. bd. Richmond Symphony, 1966-68. Mem. Pub. Relations Soc. Am., Richmond Pub. Relations Assn., Va. Writers Club (bd. dirs. 1970—). Episcopalian. Club: 2300. Author: Time of Grace, 1968. Contbr. mags. Home: 3804 Hawthorne Av Richmond VA 23222 Office: Gov's Office Capitol Sq Richmond VA 22219

WOODWARD, KENNETH EMERSON, engring. exec.; b. Washington, Oct. 30, 1927; s. George W. and Mary (Compton) W.; B.M.E., George Washington U., 1949, M.Engring. Adminstrn., 1960; M.S., Md. U., 1953; postgrad. Am. U., 1967—; m. Mary Margaret Eungard, Mar. 29, 1956; children— Stephen Mark, Kristi Lynn. Jr. mech. engr. O.S. Peters Co., 1949-50; mech. engr. Naval Research Lab., 1950-55; mech. engr. Harry Diamond Labs., 1955-61, research and devel. supr., 1961-69, chief reliability assessment, 1969— (all Washington). Bd. dirs. Youth for Christ Greater Washington, 1955-69. Served with AUS, 1946-47. Recipient Exceptional Civilian Service award Dept. Army, 1962; Honors Achievement award Angiology Research Found., 1966. Mem. Am. Soc. M.E., Am. Soc for Artificial Internal Organs. Patentee missile packaging, medicine. Home: 1701 Huntsend Ct Vienna VA 22101 Office: Harry Diamond Labs Dept Army Washington DC 20438

WOODWARD, LESTER ARMAND, oil co. exec.; b. Goodland, Kan., Jan. 31, 1908; s. William A. and Gertrude A. (McDole) W.; A.B., Coe Coll., 1930, LL.D. (hon.), 1966; M.B.A., Northwestern U., 1932, C.P.A., 1932; m. Frances M. Danberg, Aug. 1, 1936; children—Douglas Earl, Russell Clark. Staff, Arthur Andersen & Co., C.P.A.'s Chgo., 1932-40, mgr., 1941-44; treas. Mid-West Refineries, Inc., 1944-45, v.p., 1946-57, pres., 1950-56; financial v.p. Kerr-McGee Oil Industries, Inc., Oklahoma City, 1956-67; senior v.p. Kerr-McGee Corp., 1967—; dir. Moss-American, Inc., Am. Potash & Chemical Corp., also Penn Square Nat. Bank, Kerr-McGee Chem. Corp. Mem. Am. Inst. C.P.A.'s. Unitarian. Clubs: Petroleum, Chandelle, Oklahoma City Country. Home: 1616 Bedford Dr Oklahoma City OK 73116 Office: Kerr-McGee Bldg Oklahoma City OK 73102

WOODWARD, RUPERT CARLETON, librarian; b. nr. Statesboro, Ga., Mar. 4, 1918; s. Guy David and Irene (Stapleton) W.; B.S., George Peabody Coll., 1940, B.L.S., 1947; M.A., La. State U., 1961; m. Angela Mora, Sept. 3, 1950; children—Guy Frederick, Rupert. Order librarian U. Ala. Library, Tuscaloosa, 1948-49; librarian USIS, Latin Am., 1950-54; chief acquisitions librarian La. State U., Baton Rouge, 1954-63; asso. library dir. Tex. A. and M. U., College Station, 1963-66; dir. libraries George Washington U., Washington, 1967—. U.S. del. Conf. Devel. Pub. Libraries in Latin Am., Sao Paulo, Brazil, 1951; cons. Ford Found., Lima, Peru, 1966. Bd. dirs. U.S. Book Exchange Corp., 1969-71. Served with AUS, 1943-46. Mem. D.C. Library Assn. (pres. 1972), Pi Gamma Mu, Phi Delta Kappa, Kappa Phi Kappa; hon. mem. Asociacion Costarricense de Bibliotecarios, San Jose, Costa Rica. Home: 1013 Gelston Circle McLean VA 22101 Office: Goerge Washington University Washington DC 20006

WOODWARD, WARREN STANTON, assn. exec.; b. Uniontown, Pa., Feb. 4, 1919; s. Alexander and Nellie Alice (Stanton) W.; B.S., Syracuse U., 1939; H.H.D., Lincoln Meml. U., 1971; m. Charlotte Ingeborg Lund, Dec. 6, 1938 (dec. Apr. 1962); children—Priscilla Celeste (Mrs. David York), Charlotte Stanton (Mrs. Raymond Czwakiel); m. 2d, Gisela Anna Marie Eichler, Nov. 18, 1962. Pub. relations cons., Clinton, N.Y., owner College Inn, Clinton, 1946-54; pres. Woodward Motors, Inc., Utica, N.Y., 1954-63, Woodward Oil Co., Utica, 1959-61, Precision Hardware Corp., Blauvelt, N.Y., 1964-66; exec. sec. S.A.R., Washington, 1966—, also mng. editor mag. Bd. dirs. Sr. Citizens Program Rockland County, Rockland County (N.Y.) Hist. Area Bd. Rev. Served to lt. USNR, World War II. Decorated comdr. Ordre National (Ivory Coast), comdr. Cross of Merit, Papal Order of Holy Sepulchre. named Hon. Atty. Gen. La., 1964, hon. col. Ky. State Police, 1966; hon. mem. Consul Corps Washington, 1970—. Mem. S.A.R., Am. Soc. French Legion Honor, L'Association Nationale Des Croix De Guerre, Descs. Founders of Hartford (Conn.), Sons and Daus. of Pilgrims, Order Founders and Patriots of S.C.V., Pontifical Tiberina Acad. Rome (fgn. corr.), N.Y. Acad. Scis. Mason (K.T.). Asso. gen. editor Hereditary Register of U.S.A. Address: 2412 Massachusetts Av Washington DC 20008

WOODWARD, WAYNE WILLIAM, librarian; b. Greensburg, Ind., May 4, 1930; s. Arthur Coy and Hazel Prue (Ayres) W.; A.B., Taylor U., 1952; B.D., Asbury Theol. Sem., 1955; M.A., Appalachian State Tchrs. Coll., 1960; M.S. in L.S., U. Ky., 1968; m. Haughtie Corinne Vaughn, Jan. 17, 1956; children—Gail, Karen. Ordained to ministry Methodist Ch., 1956; minister chs. in Western N.C. Conf., 1955-59, 61-65; tchr. Mt. Pleasant (N.C.) High Sch., 1959-61; admistrv. asst. to librarian Asbury Theol. Sem., Wilmore, Ky., 1965-67; librarian Asbury Coll., Wilmore, 1967—. Home: 103 Asbury Av Wilmore KY 40390 Office: Asbury Coll Wilmore KY 40390

WOODWARD, WILLIAM EDWARD, lawyer; b. Port Arthur, Tex., Jan. 13, 1927; s. Fred Wall and Emma (Wolf) W.; B.A., La. State U., 1956, J.D., 1960; m. Hattie Whittington, Aug. 22, 1964; step-children—Willie L., Robert Lee. Admitted to La. bar, 1961; practiced in St. Francisville, La., 1961-62; mem. firm Kilbourne & Woodward, Clinton, La., 1962-66; practiced in Clinton, 1966—. Sec. Silliman Pvt. Sch. Corp., 1965—, bd. dirs., 1966—; chmn. East Feliciana Parish Heart Fund, 1965. Mem., sec. East Feliciana Parish Republican Com., 1967—. Bd. dirs. Marston Recreational Parks, Inc., Silliman Inst. Served with AUS, 1948-54. Mem. La. Bar. Assn., Am. Judicature Soc., Am. Legion, Pi Gamma Mu, Gamma Eta Gamma. Mem. Pentecostal Ch. Mem. Woodmen of World. Home: Race St Jackson LA 70748 Office: St Helena St Clinton LA 70722

WOODWORTH, LAURENCE NEAL, economist; b. Loudenvile, O., Mar. 22, 1918; s. Alfred Ray and Nora (Sheldon) W.; A.B., Ohio No. U., 1940 hon. Dr. Pub. Admin.; M.S. in Govt. Mgt., U. Denver, 1942; Ph.D., N.Y.U., 1960; hon. J.D., Juniata Coll.; m. Margaret Forest Bretz, Sept. 1, 1940; children—Laurence Sheldon, Joseph Ray, Esther Margaret, Melissa Mary. Economist, Joint Congl. Com. Internal Revenue Taxation, 1944-64, chief of staff, 1964—. Pres. Md. Municipal League, 1963-64. Councilman, Cheverly, Md., 1948-59, mayor, 1959-64. Mem. Alpha Phi Gamma, Sigma Phi Epsilon. Methodist. Address: 2810 Crest Av Cheverly MD 20785*

WOODY, THADDEUS BRAXTON, educator; b. Petersburg, Va., June 4, 1901; s. Rufus Milford and Annie (Blanks) W.; B.A., U. Va., 1923; M.A., Ind. U., 1927; postgrad. Northwestern U., 1927-28; m. Dorothy Carlyle Kean, Aug. 7, 1930; 1 son, James Braxton. Instr. French Ind. U., 1924-27, Northwestern U. 1927-28; asst. prof. romance langs. U. Va., Charlottesville, 1928-45, asso. prof., 1945-58, prof., 1958-71, prof. emeritus, 1971—, asst. dean Coll. Arts and Scis., 1957-71. Mem. Am. Assn. Tchrs. French, Phi Beta Kappa, Omicron Delta Kappa. Home: 4 Gildersleeve Wood Charlottesville VA 22903

WOODZELL, STEPHEN R., utility co. exec.; b. Warrenton, Va., Dec. 6, 1908; B.S. in Elec. Engring., George Washington U., 1933; m. Mildred Albright; children—Stephen R., George, Mary Martha. Pres., chief exec. officer Potomac Electric Power Co., Washington. Office: 929 E St NW Washington DC 20004

WOOLDRIDGE, CHARLES WILLIAM, electric utility exec.; b. Ft. Worth, Jan. 14, 1908; s. Clarence Enos and Bulah (Miller) W.; B.S. in Textile Engring., Tex. Tech. U., 1930; m. Evelyn Allred, Aug. 24, 1934; children—Charles William, Robert Allred, John Claren. With Tex. Power & Light Co., 1930—. v.p. engring., purchasing and transp., 1964-67, exec. v.p., dir., 1967—; dir. Met. Savs. and Loan Assn., 1965—. Pres., chmn. bd. Cotton Bowl Athletic Assn., 1963-66, bd. dirs., 1958—; founder, charter pres. Tex. Dogwood Trails, Inc., 1938; co-chmn. Dallas County A.R.C. campaign, 1957. Bd. dirs. Dallas summer Musicals, 1960—; bd. regents Tex. Tech. U., 1947-53, Dallas, YMCA, 1947-57, Dallas County A.R.C., 1954-58, family service Bur., 1942-46. Named to Tex. Tech. Athletic Hall of Honor, 1964; named Tex. Tech. U. Distinguished Engr., 1968. Registered profl. engr., Tex. Mem. Nat., Tex. socs. profl. engrs. Mem. Ch. of Christ (elder, Bible tchr.). Rotarian (pres. Dallas 1947-48, dist. gov. 1939-40). Clubs: Northwood, Dallas, Engineers (Dallas). Home: 5712 Ridgetown Circle Dallas TX 75230 Office: 1511 Bryan St Dallas TX 75201

WOOLDRIDGE, GERTRUDE STEWART (MRS. JETER WITT WOOLDRIDGE), cosmetologist; b. Cin.; d. Lawrence Lee and Mary (Shupe) Stewart; student Va. Poly. Inst., 1957-63, Clinch Valley Coll., 1958-61; m. Jeter Witt Wooldridge, Sept. 19, 1937. Waitress, Sweet Briar Coll. Dining Room, 1931-36; with Cox Dept. Store Beauty Salon, Covington, Va., 1936-38, Thompson's Beauty Salon, Covington, 1938-41; stylist Modern Beauty Salon, Covington, 1941-57, co-owner, mgr., 1942-57. owner, 1957-68, mgr. Sweet Briar Coll. Beauty Salon, 1949-50; tchr. cosmetology Wise County Sch. Bd., Wise County Vocational-Tech. Sch., Wise, Va., 1957-65, Woodbridge (Va.) Sr. High Sch., 1965—. Mem. Va. Bd. Registered Profl. Hairdressers, 1962-72, mem. Nat.-Interstate Council of State Bds. of Cosmetology, 1962—, treas., 1965-67, 69-71, 4th v.p., 1967-68, 3d v.p., 1968-69, pres., 1971-72; mem. Little Theater, Clifton Forge, Va., 1953-57. Mem. N.E.A., Va., Prince William County edn. assns., Am., Va. Vocational assns., No. Va. Indsl. Edn. Club, Wise County (charter mem., pres. 1961-63), Eastern Prince William County (charter mem., pres. 1968-70) Covington (pres. 1955-57), bus. and profl. women's clubs, Eastern Prince County Hairdressers Affiliate (charter mem., pres. 1967-69), Nat., Va. State hairdressers and cosmetologists assns. (Va. parliamentarian 1955-57, 5th v.p. 1957-59, 2d v.p. 1959-61, pres. 1961-62), Internat. Platform Assn. Baptist. Home: PO Box 136 Woodbridge VA 22191 Office: 2201 York St Woodbridge VA 22191

WOOLDRIDGE, P(OWHATAN) JACK, JR., editor; b. Ft. Smith, Ark., July 22, 1918; s. Powhatan Jack and Dolly (Sorrels) W.; student St. John's Sem., Little Rock, 1937-40; m. Margaret Elizabeth Foalden, Aug. 7, 1965; children—Powhatan Jack III, Michelle Leigh; children by previous marriage-Regina Marie (dec.), Deborah Lorraine; stepchildren—Sharon (Mrs. Aubrey Martin), Wayne D. Bowers. With S.W. Am., Ft. Smith; news editor Radio Sta. KARK, Little Rock; reporter Houston Press, 1945-46; copy editor Corsicans (Tex.) Daily Sun, 1945-48; editor A.P., Dallas, 1948-50; information specialist OPS, Washington, 1951-52; copy editor Washington bur. Wall Street Jour., 1953-60; asso. editor Nation's Bus., Washington, 1960-62, mng. editor, 1962-64, editor, 1964—. Mem. Am. C. of C. Execs., White House Corrs. Assn., Sigma Delta Chi. Club: Nat. Press. Home: 11231 Sorrel Ridge Lane Oakton VA 22124 Office: 1615 H St Washington DC 20006

WOOLDRIDGE, WILLIAM CHARLES, supt. schs.; b. Petty, Tex., Oct. 2, 1916; s. William Frank and Ada Mary (Baldridge) W.; A.A., Paris Jr Coll., 1936; B.S., East Tex. State U., 1941, M.S., 1949; m. Stella Irene Parsons, May 15, 1942; children—Patricia (Mrs. Robert Carmack), Victoria Elizabeth, William Charles II. Tchr. high sch., prin. Chicota (Tex.) High Sch., 1938-43; tchr. rural sch., Lamar County, Tex., 1936-38, county sch. supt., 1947-54; supt. schs. DeKalb (Tex.) Ind. Sch. Dist., 1954—. Bd. dirs. Lake Texarkana Water Supply Corp., DeKalb. Indsl. Found., Inc. Served with AUS, 1943-44, USAF, 1944-45, CIC, 1945-46. Named Boss of Year, Am. Bus. Woman's Assn., 1969; recipient Community Service award John H. Moore Am. Legion Post, 1968. Mem. Am., Tex. assns. sch. adminstrs., Tex. Tchrs. Assn. (state exec. com. 1971—), Methodist. Lion. Home: Box 416 DeKalb TX 75559 Office: 152 SW Maple St DeKalb TX 75559

WOOLFLEY, FRANCIS AUGUSTUS, army officer; b. New Orleans, Apr. 30, 1893; s. Franklin Flanders and Mary Florence (Kessler) W.; grad. Inf. Sch., Ft. Benning, Ga., 1926. Command and Gen. Staff Coll., Ft. Leavenworth, Kan., 1935, Army War Coll., Washington, 1938, Chem. Warfare Sch., Edgewood Arsenal, Md., 1938; m. Rosalie Elizabeth Dufour, June 16, 1920; children—Francis Augustus, Rosalie Elizabeth (Mrs. Allen Henry Johness), Horace Louis. Commd. 2d lt. U.S. Army, 1917, advanced through grades to brig. gen., 1943, inf. advisor to Turkish Army and chief of staff U.S. Army Group, Joint Am. Mil. Mission for Aid to Turkey, Ankara, 1949-52, ret., 1953; dir. La. Civil Def. Agy., 1953-56; asst. adj. gen., dir. La. Civil Def. and dir. Office Emergency Planning for La., 1960-64. Decorated Silver Star with oak leaf cluster, Bronze Star with oak leaf cluster, Legion of Merit, Air medal; Croix de Guerre with palm, chevalier Legion of Honor (France); Croix de Guerre with palm (Belgium); Croix de Guerre (Luxemburg). Mem. S.A.R. (past pres. La. Soc.), Soc. Colonial Wars, Soc. War 1812, Mil. Order World Wars (past comdr.), Am. Legion, Civil War Round Table New Orleans (past pres.). Club: Pendennis (New Orleans). Home: 932 Solomon Pl New Orleans LA 70119

WOOLSEY, ROBERT BEDFORD, sch. headmaster; b. Beloit, Wis., Dec. 19, 1917; s. Theodore Dwight and Mary Phoebe (Bedford) W.; B.A., Yale, 1938, Ph.D., 1950; m. Jo Anne Selleck, Aug. 21, 1954; children—Kathryn, Mary, Michael, Robert Bedford. Tchr. Latin, Phillips Acad., Andover, Mass., 1939-43; tchr. classical langs. Yale U., 1946-52; chmn. classics dept. Taft Sch., Watertown, Conn., 1952-63; headmaster Casady Sch., Oklahoma City, 1963—. Cons. to Crippled Children's Program. Bd. dirs. Okla. Halfway House, Youth Counseling and Child Devel. Center, Okla. Sci. and Arts Fedn., Frontiers of Sci. Fedn. Served to 1st lt. USAAF, 1943-46. Mailliard fellow Taft Sch., 1960. Mem. Ind. Schs. Assn. Southwest (pres. 1967, v.p. 1972), The Headmasters Assn., Nat. Assn. Episcopal Schs. (gov. bd. 1967-70), Nat. Assn. Ind. Schs. Clubs: University of Oklahoma Faculty, Oklahoma City Golf and Country; Yale (N.Y.C.), Graduates (New Haven). Contbr. articles to profl. pubs. Address: Box 20390 Oklahoma City OK 73120

WOOTAN, CHARLEY V., educator, research adminstr.; b. Junction, Tex., Oct. 9, 1926; s. Thomas Jefferson and Lilly (Eaton) W.; B.S., Tex. A. and M. U., 1950, M.S., 1951, Ph.D., 1965; m. Doxie Ann Cannon, May 27, 1950; children—Richard Charles, Debra Alice. Research asst. marketing analyst dept. agrl. econs. Tex. A. and M. U., College Station, 1951-53, prof. econs., 1965—; commodity analyst Indsl. Commodity Corp., N.Y.C., 1953-55; livestock marketing analyst, asst. coordinator Western Livestock Marketing Com., Denver, 1955-56; asso. research economist, project leader Tex. Transp. Inst., College Station, 1956-61, head transp. econs. and planning div., 1961-65, asso. dir., research economist, 1965—. Chmn., College Station Planning and Zoning Commn., 1968-69, College Station Recreation Council, 1963-65. Bd. dirs. Progress Assn. College Station. Served with USMCR, 1944-46. Mem. Nat. Def. Transp. Assn., Operations Research Soc. Am., A.A.A.S., Am. Soc. Traffic and Transp., Nat. Adad. Scis., C. of C. (dir.), Sigma Xi, Phi Kappa Phi, Alpha Zeta. Contbr. articles to profl. jours. Home: 1205 Walton Dr College Station TX 77843

WOOTEN, DON, ry. co. exec.; b. Abilene, Tex., June 2, 1922; s. E.O. and Connie (Harris) W.; B.B.A., U. Tex., 1946; m. Maureen Greer, Jan. 27, 1945; children—Karen Elizabeth, Bourdon. Pres., H.O. Wooten Grocer Co., Abilene, 1948-60; exec. v.p. Wooten Properties, Inc., Abilene, 1948-63; pres. Roscoe, Snyer & Pacific Ry. Co., Roscoe, Tex., 1948-58, chmn. bd., chief exec. officer, 1958—; v.p. Tex-Hart, Inc., Hart, Tex., 1963—, Reef Oil Corp., Abilene, 1949—; dir. 1st Nat. Bank Abilene, Abilene Savs. & Loan Assn. Pres. Abilene Council Chs., 1964-65; chmn. fund United Fund Abilene, 1965-65; mem. Com. of 75, U. Tex., 1957-58; v.p., dir. Scurry County United Fund, 1968-70, pres., 1970; mem. Merit System Council State Tex., 1958—; mem. adv. council, law study com. Tex. Dept. Mental Health and Mental Retardation, 1965—. Bd. dirs. Tex. Assn. Mental Health, Tex. Good Rds. Assn., Tex. United Community Services, Abilene Council on Alcoholism, A.R.C. Taylor County, Nat., Tex., Abilene assns. mental health, Abilene YMCA. Served with USAAF, 1942-44. Episcopalian. Home: Bass Ridge Dr Snyder TX 79549 Office: 111 Cypress St Roscoe TX 79545

WOOTEN, M(ARION) FRANK, JR., city ofcl.; b. Charlotte, N.C., Apr. 8, 1906; s. Marion Frank and Lela (McKamey) W.; B.S. in Civil Engring., U. N.C., 1929; postgrad. Rutgers U. Extension, Europe, 1929, U. N.C., 1932-33; m. Estelle Farmer, June 18, 1934; children—William Scott, Robert Frank. Asso. engr. San. Engring. div., Tenn. Dept. Pub. Health, Nashville, 1929-32; state dir., asst. san. engr. N.C. Dept. Pub. Health and USPHS, Raleigh, N.C., 1933-37; engr. dist. office Frigidaire Corp., Roanoke, Va., 1937-38; sales mgr., engr. Wade Mfg. Co., Charlotte, 1938-39; partner Wooten & Wooten, cons. engrs. and architects, Charlotte, 1939-53; partner Wooten, Wooten & Crosby, 1953-55; v.p., treas. Frank Wooten & Assos., Inc., Charlotte and Orlando, Fla., 1956-61; engr. city Maitland, Fla., 1961-62; dir. pub. works city Winter Park, Fla., 1962—. Pres., FEWRO, Inc., Maitland, 1970—. Trustee, Fishburne-Hudgins Ednl. Found., Inc. Registered profl. engr., N.C., S.C., Va., Tenn., Ga., Ala., Miss., Fla. Mem. Inst. Municipal Engring., Nat. (v.p. 1954-55, dir. 1950-53), N.C. (pres. 1950; dir. 1951-52) socs. profl. engrs., Fla. Engring. Soc., Charlotte Engrs. Club (life), Fishburne Alumni Assn. (pres. 1952-56; pres. emeritus 1956—). Methodist (chmn. ofcl. bd., trustee 1960-64). Rotarian. Club: Winter Park University. Home: 930 Pace Av Maitland FL 32751 Office: City Hall Winter Park FL 32789

WOOTEN, SIMEON FRANCIS, JR., banker; b. Tampa, Fla., July 4, 1923; s. Simeon Francis and May (Carter) W.; B.A., U. Fla., 1947; M.B.S., Harvard, 1949; m. Marion McMillin, July 4, 1951; children—Simeon III, Frank, Carter. Landman, Standard Oil Ind., Tulsa, 1951-54; program dir. Apache Corp., Mpls., 1956-58; v.p. Marine Bank & Trust, Tampa, 1958-65, 1st Nat. Bank Fort Lauderdale, Fla., 1967-71; treas. Li'l Gen. Stores, 1965-67; pres. Ocean 1st Nat. Bank Fort Lauderdale, 1971—. Bd. govs. United Fund, 1968-71. Served with AUS, 1943-46, 50-52. Mem. Fla. Bankers Assn., Ft. Lauderdale C. of C., Sigma Alpha Epsilon. Republican. Episcopalian. Home: 1735 SE 8th St Fort Lauderdale FL 33316 Office: 303 S Atlantic Blvd Fort Lauderdale FL 33316

WOOTTON, PERCY, physician; b. Burkeville, Va., June 14, 1932; s. James Edgar and Annie Winston (Carter) W.; B.S., Lynchburg Coll., 1953; M.D. (Florence Smith Found. Med. scholar), Med. Coll. Va., 1957; m. Barbara Jane Pendleton, June 16, 1962; children—Jane Meredith, Madison Pendleton. Intern, Roanoke Meml. Hosp., 1957-58; jr. asst. resident in medicine Med. Coll. Va., 1958-59, asst. resident in medicine, 1959-60, resident in cardiology, 1962-63; practice medicine, specializing in internal medicine and cardiology, Richmond, Va., 1963—; chief medicine Richmond (Va.) Meml. Hosp., 1971—; mem. active staff Johnston Willis, Grace, Stuart Circle, St. Mary's, Retreat for Sick, St. Luke's, Sheltering Arms, Va. Home hosps.; instr. medicine, cardiology Med. Coll. Va., Richmond, 1963—. Physician, Boy Scouts Am., 1963—, Boys Club, Richmond, 1963—. Served to lt. comdr. M.C., USNR, 1960-62. Va. Heart Assn. grantee, 1962-63; Med. Coll. Va. grantee, 1962-63. Fellow Am. Coll. Cardiology; mem. Richmond Soc. Internal Medicine, A.M.A., A.C.P., Am. (mem. clin. council cardiology 1963—), Va. (dir. 1969—), Richmond Area (pres. 1972-73) heart assns., Med. Soc. Va., Richmond Acad. Medicine, Lynchburg Coll. Alumni Assn. (dir. 1964-67), Theta Kappa Psi, Omicron Delta Kappa. Mem. Christian Ch. (deacon 1967—). Mason (Shriner). Clubs: 2300 (dir. 1964-67), Country of Va. (Richmond); Amelia (Va. Country. Home: 509 Tuckahoe Blvd Richmond VA 23226 Office: Profl Bldg Richmond VA 23219

WOOTTON, WILLIAM HOWARD, ins. co. exec.; b. Rockdale, Tex., Nov. 14, 1915; s. Thomas Ballad and Hattie Belle (Wilson) W.; student U. Tex. at Arlington, 1933-35; m. Helen Louise Reynolds, Dec. 14, 1940; 1 dau., Melissa Ann. Asst. cashier Rauscher Pierce & Co., Inc., Dallas, 1947-49, head bookkeeper, 1937-47; with Ins. Co. N. Am., Dallas, 1949—, field payroll auditor, 1949-52, payroll audit supr., 1952—. Pres., M.B. Henderson Dads Club, 1965-66, Band Boosters Club Duncanville, 1970-72. Served with USNR, 1942-45; PTO. Recipient Meritorious Service award Navy Dept., 1963. Mem.

Ins. Auditors Assn. Dallas (pres. 1960), Ins. Auditors Assn. Southwest (pres. 1971). Mem. Christian Ch. (elder). Mason. Home: Route 1 Box 587 Cedar Hill TX 75104 Office: 7900 Carpenter Freeway Dallas TX 75247

WORCESTER, DONALD EMMET, educator; b. Tempe, Ariz., Apr. 29, 1915; s. Thomas Emmet and Maud (Worcester) Makemson; A.B., Bard Coll., 1939; M.A., U. Cal., 1940, Ph.D., 1947; m. Barbara Livingston Peck, July 5, 1941; children—Barbara Livingston and Elizabeth Stuart (twins), Harris Eugene. Lectr., Cal. Coll. Agr., Davis, 1946, U. Cal., 1947; asst. prof. U. Fla., 1947-51, asso. prof., 1951-55, head dept., 1955-59, prof. history, 1955-63; chmn. dept. history Tex. Christian U., Ft. Worth, 1963-72, Lorin A. Boswell prof. history, 1971—, also editor monograph series in history and culture. Vis. prof. U. Madrid, 1956-57. Chmn. bd. U. Press Mgrs., 1961-63. Served from ensign to lt. comdr., USNR, 1941-45. Mem. Authors League Am., Am., Western, So. (v.p. 1972-73) hist. assns., Western Writers Am., N.M. Hist. Soc., Phi Beta Kappa, Phi Alpha Theta (pres. 1961, 62). Author: The Interior Provinces of New Spain, 1786, 1951; also children's books; (with Wendell G. Schaeffer) The Growth and Culture of Latin America, 1956; Sea Power and Chilean Independence, 1962 (Spanish translation 1971); The Three Worlds of Latin America, 1963; (with Maurice Boyd) American Civilization, 1964; (with Robert and Kent Forster) Man and Civilization, 1965; Makers of Latin America, 1966; (with Maurice Boyd) Contemporary America; Issues and Problems, 1968. Mag. editor Hispanic Am. Hist. Rev., 1960-65; gen. editor A Miscellany of History series. Home: Route 2 Box 61 Aledo TX 76008 Office: Texas Christian U Ft Worth TX 76129

WORD, JOHN WILLIAM, supt. schs.; b. Altus, Okla., June 24, 1928; s. Walter Thomas and Lucy Ellen (Sullivan) W.; B.S., Southwestern State Coll., Okla., 1952; M.A., Western State Coll., Gunnison, Colo., 1953-55, Ed.S., 1960; postgrad. U. Okla.; m. Edna Orline Elliott, Aug. 20, 1950; 1 dau., Ann Elizabeth Orline. Prin. high sch., tchr. math. Buffalo (Okla.) Pub. Schs., 1953-61; supt. Waynoka (Okla.) Pub. Schs., 1961-65, Anadarko (Okla.) Pub. Schs., 1965—. Chmn. profl. practices commn. State of Okla., 1965—. Chmn. Buffalo United Fund, 1958. Chmn. Harper County Democratic Com., 1960. Served with AUS, 1946-48, 59-60. Mem. Okla. (v.p. N.W. dist.), Harper and Woods County (pres.) edn. assns., N.W. Dist. Sch. Adminstrs. (pres.). Methodist. Mason, Rotarian. Home: 602 W Broadway Anadarko OK 73005 Office: PO Box 338 Anadarko OK 73005

WORD, L.D., county judge; b., 1916; s.; B.S., J.D., U. Tenn. Admitted to Tenn. bar, 1940; now county judge Knox County. Address: County Courthouse Knoxville TN 37902*

WORDEN, ALFRED MERRILL, air force officer, astronaut; b. Jackson, Mich., Feb. 7, 1932; s. Merrill Bangs and Helen (Crowell) W.; B.S., U.S. Mil. Acad., 1955; M.S., U. Mich., 1963; m. Pamela Ellen Vander Beek, June 9, 1955 (div.); children—Merrill Ellen, Alison Pamela. Commd. 2d lt. USAF, 1955, advanced through grades to lt. col., 1971; stationed at Andrews AFB, Md., 1956-61, USAF/RAF Exchange 1964-65, Edwards AFB, 1965-66, NASA-Manned Spacecraft Center, 1966; command module pilot Apollo 15 flight to moon, July 26-Aug. 7, 1971. Home: 2105 San Sebastian St Houston TX 77058 Office: NASA MSC CB Houston TX 77058

WORK, PETER T., mech. engr.; b. Lake City, Colo., Mar. 7, 1934; s. David Burton and Lydia Julia (Wolf) W.; B.S. in M.E., Colo. State U., 1955; M.B.A., Brigham Young U., 1966; m. Edwyna Dayonne Hurt, Aug. 12, 1956; children—Wayne, Paul, Arlen, Adrian, Irene, Celia, Glen. With Gen. Elec., Tyler, Tex., 1955-64, Louisville, 1966-68; prof., head, air conditioning dept., supr. Engring. Lab., Tex. State Tech. Inst., Waco, 1968-70; owner Work Environment Systems, Denton, Tex., 1970—. Instl. rep. Longhorn council Boy Scouts Am., 1971—; chmn. Engr's Week, E. Tex. chpt. Tex. Soc. Profl. Engrs., 1963. Served to capt. USAF, 1955-58. Registered profl. engr., Tex., Ky. Mem. Am. Soc. Heating, Refrigeration and Air Conditioning Engrs., Am. Soc. M.E. (asso.), Nat., Tex. socs. profl. engrs. Home: 1028 Ector St Denton TX 76201

WORKMAN, DON RAE, banker; b. Plainview, Tex., Feb. 3, 1937; s. C.A. and Elsie Mae (Carpenter) W.; student Lubbock Christian Coll., 1958; B.S., Tex. Tech U., 1960; M.S., Tex. A. and M. U., 1962; m. Almeida Ratliff, Mar. 31, 1961; children—David, Mark. Asst. prof. Tex. A. and M. U., 1962-63; ranch economist State of Tex., 1963-64; v.p., dir. First State Bank, Morton, Tex., 1964-66; v.p. comml. loan dept. First Nat. Bank, Lubbock, Tex., 1966—. Mem. West Tex. Health Planning Council, 1970—; chmn. ABC rodeo, 1971; chmn. state com. Tex. Grain Fed Beef Promotion, 1971; mem. Gov.'s Traffic Safety Council, 1970; team capt. community div. United Fund, 1970. Bd. govs. ABC Clubs Am; bd. dirs. West Tex. Water Inst. Mem. Am. Inst. Banking (econs. instr. 1969—), Ranch Hdqrs. Assn. (chmn. annual meeting day 1970), West Tex. C. of C. (regional v.p. 1970—, bd. dirs. 1960-71), Lubbock C. of C. (steering com. agrl. com. 1970). Contbr. articles to profl. pubs. Home: Route 4 Box 176L Lubbock TX 79410 Office: First National Bank PO Box 1241 Lubbock TX 79408

WORKMAN, WILLIAM DOUGLAS, JR., journalist; b. Greenwood, S.C., Aug. 10, 1914; s. William Douglas and Vivian (Watkins) W.; A.B., The Citadel, 1935, Litt.D., 1969; postgrad. Law Sch., George Washington U., 1935-36; Litt.D., Newberry Coll., 1969; m. Rhea Thomas, June 10, 1939; children—William Douglas III, Dorrill (Mrs. Charles B. Kirbow). Reporter, News and Courier, Charleston, S.C., 1936-39; mgr. Sta. WTMA, Charleston, 1939-40; capital corr. News and Courier, 1946-61, Greenville (S.C.) News, 1956-62; columnist Hall Syndicate, N.Y.C., 1960-62; asso. editor The State, Columbia, S.C. 1963-66, editor, 1966—. News analyst Sta. WIS, Columbia, 1950-62; news analyst, panelist Sta. WIS-TV, 1953-62. Sec., S.C. Constl. Revision Com., 1966-69. Republican nominee for U.S. Senate, 1962. Bd. dirs. Race Relations Information Center, Nashville. Served with AUS, 1941-45. Decorated Legion of Merit. Mem. S.C. Press Assn. (pres. 1971), Assn. Citadel Men (pres. 1952-53). Author: The Case for the South, 1960; The Bishop from Barnwell, 1963; (with others) This is the South, 1959, With All Deliberate Speed, 1957, Southern Schools, Progress and Problems, 1959. Home: 915 Belt Line Blvd Columbia SC 29205 Office: care The State Box 1333 Columbia SC 29202

WORLEY, CHARLIE, state ofcl.; b. Bluff City, Tenn., June 28, 1916; s. Charles E. and Lucy D. W.; grad. Emory and Henry Coll., Emory, Va., 1938; LL.B., U. Tenn., 1941; m. Elizabeth Hickerson, 1942; children—Betsy (Mrs. W.C. Haffner, Jr.), Susan. Admitted to Tenn. bar, 1941; mgr. Bluff City Mills, 1944—; state treas., Tenn., 1967—. Past chmn. Sullivan County Democratic Exec. Com.; past mem. Tenn. State Dem. Exec. Com.; chmn. Tenn. Electoral Coll., 1948. Bd. dirs. Bristol Meml. Hosp. Served to 1st lt. USAAC. Mem. Am. Legion, 40 and 8, Blue Key, Phi Delta Phi, Sigma Chi. Methodist (steward). Elk, Moose, Lion. Address: State Capitol Nashville TN 37219*

WORLEY, JOHN KYLE, geophysicist; b. Detroit, Aug. 31, 1930; s. John Kyle and Virginia (Fox) W.; student Mass. Inst. Tech., 1948-49; B.S., Wayne State U., 1952; m. Mary Frances O'Flynn, Sept. 7, 1955; 1 dau., Gladys Charmaine (Mrs. Charles Edward Dillon). Seismologist, Geophys. Service, Inc., Dallas, 1953-54; party chief Nancy Exploration Co., Houston, 1955-57; party chief Ray Geophys. Div., Houston, 1957-66, program application geophysicist, 1966-72, mgr. nav./gravity/magnetic dept., 1972—. Mem. Soc. Exploration Geophysicists, Aircraft Owners and Pilots Assn. 15402 W Westwood Circle Houston TX 77071 Office: 6909 SW Freeway Houston TX 77036

WORLEY, WYETH HARDY, dentist; b. Shreveport, La., Sept. 22, 1935; s. Wyeth Bodine and Dessie (Bostick) W.; B.S. in Natural Scis., Centenary Coll., 1957, B.S. in Chemistry, 1959; D.D.S., Loyola U., New Orleans, 1963; m. Jackie Dean Champion, Dec. 26, 1954; children—Susan Elizabeth, Hardy Hayes, Dean Lewis. Practice dentistry, specializing in oral surgery, Shreveport, 1966—; clin. prof. Sch. Medicine, La. State U., Shreveport, 1968—. Cons. Barksdale AFB, 1967—. Bd. dirs. Centenary Coll. Diplomate Am. Bd. Oral Surg. Mem. La. (v.p.), S.W., Am. socs. oral surgeons, A.M.A., Am., 4th Dist. dental assns., Kappa Sigma. Republican. Baptist. Home: 558 Longleaf St Shreveport LA 71106 Office: 2751 Virginia St Shreveport LA 71103

WORONIAK, ALEXANDER, economist, edcuator; b. Lviv, Ukraine, Feb. 27, 1918; s. Thomas and Eudoxia (Husar) W.; LL.M., Yohanni Casimiri U. (Lvov, Poland), 1939; M.S., Columbia, 1953, postgrad., 1956-58; m. Maria Zvenyslava Patchovski, Apr. 27, 1943. Asst. prof. Ivan Franko U., Ukraine, 1940-42; cons., 1942-44; legal counselor, welfare officer UNRRA, IRO, Germany, 1946-50; accountant Advance Solvents & Chem. Corp., N.Y.C., 1950-51, Gregory V. Collins & Co., 1953-54, Radio Clinic, Inc., 1954-57; research asst. Grad. Sch. Bus., Columbia, 1957-58; asst. prof. econs. Cath. U. Am., 1958-67, asso. prof. econs., 1967-71, prof., 1971—; lectr. Howard U., 1963-69; research asso. USAF grant, 1964-69; cons. Rio Bermejo Devel. Project, Argentina, 1967-69, Inst. for Def. Analysis, 1970-71, Stanford Research Inst., 1971—, also bus. firms, 1958—. Bronner scholar, 1951; Ford fellow, 1957. Mem. Am. Econ. Assn., Am. Accounting Assn., Nat. Assn. Accountants, Am. Assn. U. Profs., Assn. Comparative Econs., Assn. Study of Soviet Type Economies, Am. Statis. Assn., Pi Gamma Mu. Author: Labor Mediation and Counseling, 1942; Job Descriptions and Specifications, 1943; Integration of Refugees and Displaced Persons into German Economy, 1949; Business Organization and The Transfer of Technology; Experience of the Soviet Union, 1967; Industrial Concentration in Eastern Europe: The Search for Optimum Size and Efficiency, 1969; Problems and Achievements of Soviet Technology Exports, 1969; Technological Transfer in Eastern Europe: Receiving Countries, 1970; A Microeconomic Approach to the Problem of Regionalism in Soviet Business Management, 1971; Ruble Dollar Conversion Ratio Survey, 1972. Co-author: The Feasibility of Developing Transfer of Technology Functions, 1967; The Transfer of Technology to Developing Countries, 1967; Valuing Transfer of Military Acquired Skills to Civilian Employment, 1969; Transfer of Technology Functions Extended: The German Case, 1970. Home: 1435 Geranium St NW Washington DC 20012 Office: Box 254 Cath U Am Washington DC 20017

WORONIN, EUGENIE, educator; b. Voronezh, Russia, Jan. 19, 1905; d. Maxim and Kapitolina (Boldina) W.; M.D., U. Med. Coll. (Russia), 1930; studied voice Conservatory, Kharkov. Russia. Came to U.S., 1950, naturalized, 1955. Physician specializing ears, nose and throat in Russia, 1930-34; founder, chmn. dept. phoniatrics Research Inst. for E.N.T., Voice and Speech, Kharkov, Russia, 1934-41; Russian lang. tchr. U. Syracuse (N.Y.), 1951-64; sr. research fellow, asso. prof. Russian and German, Eastern Ky. U., Richmond, 1964—; tchr. Russian course TV-WHEN, Syracuse, 1960-61. Commd. Ky. col., 1969. Contbr. articles on voice disorders to profl. jours. Office: Eastern Ky U Box 518 Richmond KY 40475

WORRELL, ANNE EVERETT ROWELL (MRS. THOMAS EUGENE WORRELL), newspaper exec.; b. Surry, Va., Mar. 7, 1920; d. Charles Gray and Ethel (Roache) Rowell; student Va. Intermont Coll., 1937-39; m. Thomas Eugene Worrell, Sept, 12, 1941; children—Thomas Eugene. Instr., VIRanch Camp, Bristol, Tenn., 1938-39, dir., 1942, 47-51; sec. Gen. Motors Acceptance Corp., Richmond, Va., Washington, 1939-41; feature writer, fashion editor Bristol Herald Courier, Va. Tennessean, Bristol, 1963—; sec.-treas., dir. Worrell Newspapers, Inc., Bristol, 1958—. Pres., Bristol Border Guild, 1959; mem. Va. Mus., 1960—, Carroll Reece Mus., 1968—. Bd. dirs., sec. Bristol chpt. A.R.C., 1966-70. Presbyn. Home: 117 Shady Lane Bristol TN 37620 Office: 320 Pierce St Bristol VA 24201

WORRELL, THOMAS EUGENE, newspaper pub.; b. Bristol, Va., July 30, 1919; s. Howard Hampton and Hester (Denton) W.; B.S., Wake-Forest Coll., 1940; law student, George Washington U., 1940-41; m. Anne Rowell, Sept. 12, 1941; 1 son, Thomas Eugene. Admitted to Va. bar, 1941; pvt. practice law Bristol, 1941, 1946-49; spl. agt. F.B.I., 1942-46; pres. Worrell Newspapers, Inc.; newspaper pub. as pres. Bristol Newspaper Printing Corp., publishers Bristol Herald Courier and Bristol Va.-Tennessean; officer, dir. Southwest Times, Pulaski, Va., Elizabethton (Tenn.) Starr, Radford (Va.) News Jour., Tri-Cities Newspapers, Florence, Ala., Tri-County News, Spruce Pine, N.C., Sullivan County News, Blountville, Tenn., Daily Mountain Eagle, Jasper, Ala., The Daily Corinthian, Corinth, Miss., Suffolk (Va.) News Herald, News-Topic, Lenoir, N.C., Princeton (W.Va.) Times, Blackburg (Va.) Sun, Altus (Okla.) Times Democrat, Cushing (Okla.) Daily Citizen, Galveston (Tex.) Daily News, Daily Sun, Texas City, Tex., Sun Herald, Winter City; Fla. Republican candidate for Congress from 9th District of Va., 1948; del., sec. com. on credentials Rep. Nat. Conv., Chgo., 1952. Mem. Va. Bar Assn., Va. C. of C. (pres. 1956-58, dir.). Elk, Kiwanian. Home: 117 Shady Lane Bristol TN 37620 Office: 320 Pierce St Bristol VA 24201

WORSHAM, ARCH DOUGLAS, educator; b. Culloden, Ga., Feb. 22, 1933; s. Grover C. and Stella (Douglas) W.; B.S., U. Ga., 1955, M.S., 1957; Ph.D., N.C. State U., 1961; m. Carolyn Howie Jackson, Sept. 9, 1956; children—Robert Douglas, Carol Elizabeth. Extension agronomy specialist crop sci. dept. N.C. State U., 1960-67, asso. prof. crop sci., 1967-69, prof., 1969—. Cons. Environmental Protection Agy.; exec. bd. So. Weed Conf., 1967-68, now editor. Mem. Am. Soc. Plant Physiologists, Am. Inst. Biol. Sci., Weed Sci. Soc. Am. (editorial bd.), Sigma Xi, Phi Kappa Phi, Gamma Sigma Delta. Methodist. Contbr. articles to profl. jours. Home: 1713 Athens Dr Raleigh NC 27606

WORTHAM, LYNDALL FINLEY (MRS. GUS SESSIONS WORTHAM), civic leader, club woman; b. Sherman, Tex., July 22, 1895; d. Alfred Philip and Eudora (Traynham) Finley; B.L., Kidd Key Coll., 1909; B.A., life teaching certificate, U. Tex., 1912; m. Gus Sessions Wortham, Oct. 4, 1926; children—Lyndall Finley (Mrs. Russell George Petersen), Diana Gayle (Mrs. Allen Skeens). Formerly tchr. Richmond (Tex.) Pub. Schs., Scoville Sch., N.Y.C. Rec. sec. YWCA, Houston, 1931-34; bd. dirs. Women in Yellow Aux. Jefferson Davis City-County Hosp., Houston; gray lady A.R.C., Houston; bd. dirs. Houston Garden Club, Houston Symphony, Houston Grand Opera; rec. sec. Harris County Cancer Soc.; pres. bd. dirs. Girlstown U.S.A., Whiteface, Tex.; 2d v.p. Houston Speech and Hearing Soc.; bd. regents U. Houston; charter mem. bd. govs. Am. Found. Religion and Psychiatry, N.Y.C.; bd. dirs., Ballet Found., Houston; trustee Wortham Found., Houston. Recipient Matrix award, Theta Sigma Phi, 1964. Mem. English-Speaking Union (dir. Houston), Colonial Dames Am., Harris County Heritage Soc. (dir.), Tex. Ex-Students, Colleagues of Soc. for Performing Arts, Houston C. of C. (com. for cultural affairs), So. Methodist U. Alumni, Rice U. Assos., Beta Sigma Phi (sponsor-dir. 1935—, mem. Order of Rose 1956), Kappa Kappa Gamma. Democrat. Presbyn. Clubs: Houston Country, Paul Jones, Ramada, Petroleum, Tejas, Coronado, Allegro (Houston). Author: Around the World on a Frayed Shoestring, 1968. Contbr. articles to Houston Chronicle, Dallas News. Home: 1505 South Blvd Houston TX 77006

WORTHINGTON, FRANK SMOOT, r.r. exec.; b. Lake City, Tenn., Oct. 17, 1899; s. James Henry and Margaret Mae (Smoot) W.; student U. Tenn., LaSalle Extension U.; m. Thelma Sams, Aug. 11, 1920; children—Frank Smoot, Thomas Lynn. With So. Ry. Co., 1913—, clk., engr. accountant, draftsman, supr. safety, trainmaster, div. supt., 1954-56, gen. supt. transp., v.p., 1956-63, asst. v.p. operations, Washington, 1963-64, v.p., Chattanooga, 1964—; v.p., dir. Chattanooga Choo Choo Co. Inc.; dir. Cin., New Orleans & Tex. Pacific Ry. Co., Tenn. Valley RR. Mem. Traffic and Transp. Club, C. of C. Mason (Shriner). Rotarian. Clubs: Chattanooga Golf and Country, Mountain City (Chattanooga); Southern and Southwestern Railway; Red Fez. Home: 3810 Rogers Rd Chattanooga TN 37411 Office: 1301 Market St Chattanooga TN 37402

WORTHY, MARVIN NASH, city ofcl.; b. Detroit, Dec. 9, 1924; s. Marvin Olin and Clara (Brooks) W.; student North Ga. Coll., 1942-43, Internat. Corr. Schs., 1951-52. With meter reading dept. Atlanta Gas Light Co., 1942, swimming instr. Sweetwater Park, Ga., 1964-68, asst. mgr., 1965-69; mgr. Lilburn (Ga.) Lions Club Swimming Pool, 1969; city councilman, Lilburn, 1970—; county historian Gwinnett County (Ga.), 1969—; researcher in Ga. geneal. records, 1947-70. Vice chmn. Gwinnett County Republican Com., 1964-66, mem. 9th Ga. Congl. Dist. Rep. Com., 1964-66, 68-70, del. Ga. Rep. Conv., 1964-68. Served with C.E., AUS, 1943-47; ETO. Mem. Gwinnett Hist. Soc. (exec. council 1967-69, now pres.). Lion (hon. Lilburn). Contbr. articles to History of Gwinnett County, Vol. II, 1960. Home: PO Box 333 Decatur Hwy Lilburn GA 30247

WORTZ, CARL HAGLIN, bus. analyst, cons.; b. Ft. Smith, Ark., May 9, 1921; s. Carl H. Wortz and Ed Dell (Haglin) W.; grad. N.M. Mil. Inst., 1940; Sparton Sch. Aeronautics, 1943; B.S. in Bus., U. Ark., 1947; m. Charlotte Wacker, June 29, 1943; 1 dau., Carolyn Jane. Chmn. bd. Wortz Co., cracker and cookie mfg. co., now ret.; cons., bus. analyst. Served with AUS, 1943-46; CBI. Mem. Biscuit and Cracker Mfrs. Assn. (dir.). Sigma Alpha Epsilon. Presbyn. Office: PO Box 45565 Dallas TX 75235

WOYTYCH, ROBERT LUCIEN, govt. ofcl.; b. Annapolis, Md., Oct. 18, 1915; s. Louis J. and Mary (Brady) W.; student George Washington U., 1935-36; B.A., Benjamin Franklin U., 1942; m. Suzanne Lajoye, June 17, 1939; children—Judith Anne (Mrs. Bruce Henry Danielson), Robert Lucien, Suzanne M. With Immigration and Naturalization Service, 1941—, successively officer in charge, Washington, 1948-54, dist. dir., St. Paul, 1956-59, dist. dir., Washington, 1959-60; supervisory immigrant insp. N.W. Regional Office, St. Paul; 1960-64, dist. dir., Miami, Fla., 1964—. Active Little League, Babe Ruth Baseball, Mpls. Served with AUS, 1945-46. Mem. Am. Legion (past post comdr. Cheverly, Md., chmn. fgn. relations Fla. dept. 1968-69), Dade County Assn. Chiefs of Police (chmn. Greater Miami exec. council 1966-67). Home: 7001 SW 16th Ct West Hollywood FL 33023 Office: Fed Bldg 51 SW 1st Av Miami FL 33130

WOZENCRAFT, FRANK MCREYNOLDS, lawyer; b. Dallas, Apr. 25, 1923; s. Frank Wilson and Mary Victoria (McReynolds) W.; B.A. summa cum laude, Williams Coll., 1946; LL.B., Yale, 1949; m. Shirley Ann Cooper, Nov. 25, 1960; children—Frank McReynolds, Ann Lacey, George Wilson. Admitted to Tex. bar, 1950; law clk. U.S. Supreme Ct., Washington, 1949-50; mem. firm Baker & Botts, Houston, 1950-60, partner, 1960-66, 69—. Sec. Tex. Fund, Inc., Houston, 1958-66; asst. atty. gen. charge Office Legal Counsel, Dept. Justice, Washington, 1966-69. Mem. Commn. Polit. Activity Govt. Employees, 1967, Pres.'s Adv. Panel on Ins., 1967-68; vice chmn. Adminstrv. Conf. U.S., 1968-71; U.S. rep. Vienna Conf. on Law of Treaties, 1968. Mem. exec. bd. Sam Houston Area council Boy Scouts Am., 1959-66, 69—; mem. adv. bd. Houston Mus. Fine Arts; chmn. bd. Assn. for Community Television. Trustee Hedgecroft Hosp., 1964-66; bd. dirs. Alley Theatre, 1961-66. Served to capt. AUS, 1943-46. Decorated Bronze Star. Mem. Am. Soc. Internat. Law, Am. Law Inst., Am., Houston, bar assns., State Bar Tex., Order of Coif, Gargoyle, Phi Beta Kappa, Phi Delta Theta, Phi Delta Phi. Episcopalian. Home: 51 E Broad Oaks St Houston TX 77027 Office: 3000 One Shell Plaza Houston TX 77002

WRAIGHT, AARON JOSEPH, geographer, govt. ofcl.; b. St. Louis, July 31, 1913; s. Edward Earl and Sarah Ann (Dowell) W.; A.B., Washington U., St. Louis, 1939, M.S., 1941; Ph.D., Clark U., 1951; m. Esther Lee Ollis, Apr. 6, 1949. Field geographer U.S. Coast and Geodesic Survey, Washington, 1948-53, geographer, 1954-59, chief geographer, 1960—; vis. prof. geography and earth sci. St. Louis U., 1953-54; prof. geography, earth and space sci. Edinboro (Pa.) Coll., 1959-60; prof. geography Anne Arundel Coll., Md., 1963-68; prof., dir. div. phys. scis. Southeastern U., Washington, 1966-68. Chmn. publs. Am. Congress Surveying and Mapping, 1960-63; chmn. U.S. Bd. on Geog. Names, 1970—. Capt. fund dr. Clark U., 1958. Bd. dirs. Nat. Inst. Urbiculture, 1956-57. Recipient Meritorious Service award Dept. Commerce, 1957, Exceptional Service awards Coast and Geod. Survey, 1957, 62. Fellow Royal Geog. Soc.; mem. Assn. Am. Geographers, Nat. Council Geog. Edn., Sigma Xi. Mason (32 deg.). Author: The Field Study of Place, 1954; The U.S. Coast and Geodetic Survey—150 Years of History, 1957; Our Dynamic World, 1967. Author transp. plan for D.C. Research on coastal geography. Home: 5431 Connecticut Av NW Washington DC 20015 Office: US Coast and Geod Survey Washington DC

WRAY, ANDREW JACKSON, ins. exec.; b. Waco, Tex., Jan. 11, 1900; s. Roland Dallas and Minnie (Crow) W.; student Southwestern U., Georgetown, Tex., 1918-20; m. Margaret Culliman, Apr. 14, 1926; 1 dau., Lucie Halm. Chmn. bd. Marsh & McLennan of Tex.; owner Wray Ranch, Columbus, Tex., 1949—. Trustee United Fund; chmn. bd. dirs. Soc. Prevention Cruelty to Animals. Served from 1st lt. to maj. USAAF, 1942-45. Episcopalian. Clubs: Houston Country, Eagle Lake Rod and Gun, Tejas, Bayou, Ramada, Petroleum; Bohemian (San Francisco); Allegro. Home: 3 Remington Lane Houston TX 77005 Office: Bank of Southwest Bldg Houston TX 77002

WRAY, DAVID FRANKLIN, chem. co. exec.; b. Memphis, May 24, 1939; s. Vance Cooper and Louise (Dawson) W.; student Memphis State U.; m. Suzanne Carol Logan, Feb. 21, 1969; children—John David, Carolyn, Janet. Chemist, E.L. Bruce div. Armour & Co., Memphis, 1958-65; v.p. Mars Chem. Corp., Atlanta, 1965-70; pres. Apollo Industries, Inc., Atlanta, 1970—. Served with AUS, 1957-58.

Home: 2263 Coronet Way NW Apt T-2 Atlanta GA 30318 Office: 1401 Ellsworth Industrial Dr NW Atlanta GA 30318

WRAY, ROBERT FREDERICK, city ofcl.; b. Dayton, Ky., Feb. 6, 1935; s. Robert M. and Louise (Rasch) W.; student Va. Poly. Inst., 1953-56; B.S. in Civil Engring., U. Cin., 1959-62; m. Ann Saunders, Nov. 26, 1957; children—Douglas, Louise, Lisa. Asst. engr. W.L. Harper Co., Cin., 1958-60; gen. supt. Eaton Oil Co., Covington, Ky., 1960-64; self-employed as engring. cons., Erlanger, Ky., 1964-68; city mgr. City Covington (Ky)., 1968-71, City of Jacksonville (N.C.), 1971—. Served with USMCR, 1957-59. Mem. Internat. City Mgmt. Assn., Municipal Finance Officers Assn., Ky. Assn. City Mgrs. (v.p. 1968-69). Mem. Christian Ch. Mason. Clubs: Optimist (Covington). Home: 600 River Ct Jacksonville NC 28540 Office: City Hall Jacksonville NC 28540

WRENN, EARLE LEWIS, pediatric surgeon; b. Olive Branch, Miss., Sept. 19, 1924; s. Earle Lewis and Linnie Mae (Wilkins) W.; B.A., U. Miss., 1944; M.D., Johns Hopkins, 1947; m. Lynette Boney, Apr. 28, 1956; children—Edward Howard, John Jeffries, Earle Lewis, Claire Wilkins. Intern dept. surgery Peter Bent Brigham Hosp., Boston, 1947-48; asst. resident pathology Grady Meml. Hosp., Atlanta, 1948-49; asst. resident surgery Univ. Hosp., Columbus, O., 1951-53, Children's Med. Center, Boston, 1953-54; chief resident surgery Children's Hosp., Phila., 1954-55, Children's Med. Center, Boston, 1955-56; asst. clin. prof. dept. surgery U. Tenn., Memphis, also instr. pediatric surgery St. Jude Hosp., Memphis, 1956—; instr. surgery Le Bonheur Children's Hosp., Memphis, 1956—, chief of surgery, 1969—. Served with AUS, 1949-51. Diplomate Am. Bd. Surgeons. Mem. A.C.S., Am. Bd. Gen. Surgery, Am. Acad. Pediatrics, A.M.A. Contbr. articles to med. jours. Home: 205 S Belvedere Blvd Memphis TN 38104 Office: 848 Adams Av Memphis TN 38103

WRENN, THOMAS LOVELL, lawyer, govt. ofcl.; b. Savoy, Tex., Mar. 28, 1905; s. James Thomas and Maud (DeBerry) W.; A.B., Austin Coll., 1927, M.A., 1928; J.D., Nat. U., 1938. Admitted to D.C. bar, 1938; mem. faculty Austin Coll., 1929-32; bus. analyst U.S. Dept. Commerce, 1933-36, chief domestic transp. sect. transp. div., 1936-39; hearing examiner, 1945-50, asso. chief examiner, 1950-67, chief examiner, 1968—. Mem. Am. Bar Assn. D.C., Nat. Aero. Assn., Am. Judicature Soc., Nat. Aviation Club, Nat. Lawyers Club, Sigma Nu Phi. Methodist. Home: 1600 S Eads St Arlington VA 22202 Office: Civil Aeros Bd Washington DC 20428

WRIGHT, ALMA MCINTYRE, publishing co. exec.; b. Knoxville, Tenn., July 31, 1909; d. William Mobry and Theresa (Biagiotti) McIntyre; B.S. in Edn., U. Tenn., 1932; m. Robert Oliver Wright, Feb. 17, 1931; 1 son, Robert Oliver. Writer stories, articles on African violets, house plants, 1947—; editor African Violet mag., 1947-63; exec. dir. African Violet Soc. Am., Inc., 1960-63; pres. Indoor Gardener Pub. Co., Inc., Knoxville, 1963—; editor Gesnerlad-Saintpaulia News, 1963—. Mem. Am. Hort. Soc. (hon. v.p. 1954), African Violet Soc. Am. (hon. life, rec. sec. 1946-48, nat. pres. 1948-49, membership sec. 1953-63), Saintpaulia Internat. (editor publs., rec. sec. 1963—). Editor: Master List of African Violets, 1962; editor for Am., Gesneria Soc. Home: 4752 Calumet Dr Knoxville TN 37919 Office: 1800 Grand Av Knoxville TN 37901

WRIGHT, CARROLL, JR., real estate appraiser and cons.; b. Alexandria, Va., Dec. 10, 1928; s. Carroll and Alice (Barron) W.; B.A., Va. Poly. Inst., 1949; M.A., Am. U., Washington, 1959, postgrad. 1965—; m. Laura Beville Hailey, July 23, 1950; children—Carroll Tilden, Laura Alice. Pres., Carroll Wright, Jr. & Co., real estate appraisal and counseling, Arlington, Va., 1967—; real estate appraiser, broker, market analyst, and cons., Washington met. area, also other areas, 1955—; pres., co-founder Am. Real Estate Appraisal Corp., Washington and Falls Church, Va., 1962-67; pres. Loudoun Land & Devel. Corp. Pres., Community Projects, Inc. Mem. bd. control, George Mason Coll., Fairfax, Va. Served as 1st lt., Inf., AUS, 1950-54; Korea. Mem. Am. Inst. Real Estate Appraisers (pres. Washington met. area chpt. 1971). No. Va. Bd. Realtors, Va. Assn. Assessing Officers (affiliate), Am. Real Estate and Urban Econs. Assn. (affiliate). Rotarian. Club: Washington Golf and Country. Office: 1815 Ft Myer Dr PO Box 9466 Rosslyn Station Arlington VA 22209

WRIGHT, CHARLES ALAN, educator, author; b. Phila., Sept. 3, 1927; s. Charles Adshead and Helen (McCormack) W.; A.B., Wesleyan U., Middletown, Conn., 1947; LL.B., Yale, 1949; m. Mary Joan Herriott, July 8, 1950 (div. Jan. 1955); children—Charles Edward; m. 2d, Eleanor Custis Broyles, Dec. 17, 1955; children—Henrietta, Cecily; stepchildren—Eleanor Custis Clarke, Margot Clarke. Admitted to Minn. bar, 1951, Tex. bar, 1959; law clk. U.S. Circuit Judge Clark, New Haven, 1949-50; asst. prof. law U. Minn., 1950-53; asso. prof. 1953-55; asso. prof. law U. Tex., Austin, 1955-58; prof., 1958-65, McCormick prof., 1965—. Vis. prof. U. Pa., Phila., 1959-60, Harvard, 1964-65, Yale, 1968-69; reporter study div. of jurisdiction between state and fed. cts. Am. Law Inst., 1963-69; mem. adv. com. on civil rules Jud. Conf. U.S., 1961-64, mem. standing com. on rules of practice and proc., 1964—. Trustee St. Stephen's Episcopal Sch., Austin, Tex., 1962-66, Capitol Broadcasting Assn., Austin, 1966—, chmn. bd., 1969—; trustee Austin Symphony Orch. Soc., 1966—, mem. exec. com., 1966-70. Mem. Am. Law Inst. (mem. council 1969—), Am. Bar Assn., Inst. Jud. Adminstrn., Am. Judicature Soc., Order of Coif, Phi Kappa Phi. Republican. Episcopalian (vestryman). Clubs: Country, Headliners (Austin); Yale (N.Y.C.). Author: Wright's Minnesota Rules, 1954; Cases on Remedies, 1955; (with C.T. McCormick and J.H. Chadbourn) Cases on Federal Courts, 5th edit., 1970; Handbook of the Law of Federal Courts, 2d edit., 1970; (with H.M. Reasoner) Procedure—The Handmaid of Justice, 1965; Federal Practice and Procedure; Criminal, 1969; (with A.R. Miller) Federal Practice and Procedures: Civil, 1969. Home: 5304 Western Hills Dr Austin TX 78731

WRIGHT, CHARLES WILLIAM, psychiat. social worker; b. Livingston, Tenn., June 5, 1919; s. Carl W. and Bettie A. (Sewell) W.; B.S., Okla. U., 1949, certificate social work, 1950, M.S.W., 1955; m. Naninna Bambino, Oct. 17, 1942; children—Charles Wayne, Michael Phillip. Caseworker, Oklahoma County Dept. Pub. Welfare, Oklahoma City, 1949; sch. social worker, counselor, spl. edn. tchr. Oklahoma City Schs., 1950-55; juvenile officer Oklahoma County Detention Home, 1955-60, 1st supt., 1958-60; psychiat. social worker Community Mental Health Center, Okla. Mental Health Dept., Norman, 1960—, chief social worker, 1967—. Cons. Social Work Registration Bd. Okla., 1965—; pres. CSH Fed. Credit Union, Norman, Okla., 1964-65, 65-66. Served with AUS, 1941-45; ETO. Decorated Bronze Star. Recipient Distinguished Social Worker award Okla., 1967. Mem. Nat. Assn. Social Workers (past Okla. chmn.), Nat. Conf. Social Welfare, Assn. for Research and Enlightenment, Am. Legion. Unitarian. Club: Civitan (Norman). Home: 221 NW 1st St Moore OK 73160 Office: PO Box 95131 Oklahoma City OK 73109

WRIGHT, CLEO ALVA BUCKNER (MRS. MERRILL CLAIR WRIGHT), civic worker; b. Bertram, Tex.; d. Ira Arthur and Vonnie (Ross) Buckner; B.A. (scholar), U. Houston, 1951; m. Merrill Clair Wright, Apr. 23, 1938. Vice pres. Wright Light, Inc., Houston, 1950-67. Vol. worker hosp. and recreation corps A.R.C., Atlanta, 1942-43, Houston, 1946-48; charter founder sec. Elva A. Wright Aux. to City Tb Hosp., Houston, 1950-52, pres., 1952-53, bd. dirs., 1950-60; mem. Past Pres.'s Bd. Hosp. Auxs., 1950—, sec. Glenbrook Valley Civic Club, 1971—. Mem. Houston Turn Verein Ladies Aux. (historian 1965-66), Woman of Rotary (vol. and publicity chmn. 1964-65), Nat. Hist. Soc. (charter), Turn Verein Ladies Bowling Assn. (pres. 1962-64), Theta Sigma Phi (v.p. 1966-67), Phi Kappa Phi. Club: Caprice Dance (sec. 1970—). Home: 8102 Colgate St Houston TX 77017

WRIGHT, DESSEL TAYLOR, wholesale co. exec.; b. Weakly County, Tenn., Oct. 25, 1926; s. Hubert Barton and Cassie Ann (Harrison) W.; grad. high sch.; m. Relma Jones, Sept. 26, 1947; children—Stephen Taylor, Pamela Ann, Bradley Jones. Owner, operator Dessel T. Wright Co., Martin, Tenn., 1951—; dir. Martin Bank, 1969—, Martin Indsl. Bd., 1966—. Chmn. Heart Fund, 1966-67, Boy Scouts Am. dr., 1962, 63, Girl Scouts Am. dr., 1965, 66; pres. Martin High Booster Club, 1965, 66. Served with USNR, 1944-45. Mem. Weakly County C. of C. (charter; bd. dirs., 1960-62). Mem. Ch. of Christ (deacon). Clubs: U. Tenn. Pace Maker, U. Tenn. Century (Martin); Weakly County Country (Sharon, Tenn.). Home: 507 S McComb St Martin TN 38237 Office: 501 Main St Martin TN 38237

WRIGHT, DON CONWAY, editorial cartoonist; b. Los Angeles, Jan. 23, 1934; s. Charles and Sally (Olberg) W.; ed. pub. schs.; m. Rita Rose Blondin, Oct. 1, 1960. Mem. staff Miami (Fla.) News, 1952-56, 58—, photo editor, 1960-63, polit. cartoonist, 1963—; rep. permanent exhbn. U. Syracuse. Served with AUS, 1956-58. Recipient Pulitzer prize for editorial cartooning, 1965; Freedoms Found. award for editorial cartoon, 1966; also local citations; named Outstanding Person in Communication Media, Young Democrats Fla., 1966. Mem. Am. Assn. Editorial Cartoonists, Sigma Delta Chi. Home: 11725 SW 88th Av Miami FL 33156 Office: 1 Herald Plaza Miami FL 33101

WRIGHT, EDWARD LEDWIDGE, lawyer; b. Little Rock, July 16, 1903; s. Benjamin B. and Katie (Ledwidge) W.; A.B., Little Rock Coll., 1923; LL.B., Georgetown U., 1928; m. Rosemary Tuohey, Oct. 20, 1931; children—Edward Ledwidge, Rosemary, Bridget, Kathleen. Admitted to Ark. bar, 1925, practiced in Little Rock, 1928—; mem. firm Wright, Lindsey & Jennings. Dir., Pulaski Fed. Savs. & Loan Assn., Worthen Bank & Trust Co. Co-draftsman Ark. Probate Code, 1948; chmn. Ark. Bd. Law Examiners, 1938-41; commr. Nat. Conf. Commnrs. Uniform State Laws, 1945-57; mem. 2d Hoover Commn. Legal Task Force. Trustee Southwestern Legal Found., Ark. Blue Cross-Blue Shield. Mem. Am. (state del. 1946-67, chmn. ho. dels. 1962-64, nat. pres. 1970), Ark. (pres. 1957). Pulaski County (pres. 1948) bar assns., Am. Judicature Soc., Am. Law Inst., Internat. Assn. Ins. Counsel. Roman Catholic. K.C. (4 deg.), Knight of Malta. Home: 5011 Hawthorne Rd Little Rock AR 72207 Office: 2200 Worthen Bank Bldg Little Rock AR 72201

WRIGHT, EGBERT ANDERSON, judge; b. Wilmington, N.C., Nov. 17, 1902; s. Oscar Herbert and Linnie (Alderman) W.; LL.B., Atlanta Law Sch., 1933; m. Virginia Gill, July 15, 1922; 1 dau., Virginia Elizabeth (Mrs. Lee Hampton Hume). Admitted to Ga. bar, 1933, practiced in Atlanta, 1933-51; sr. mem. firm Wright, Oxford & Love, 1951-56; asst. county atty. Fulton County, 1948-56; judge Civil Ct. Fulton County, 1956—. Mem. Am., Ga., Atlanta bar assns., Sigma Nu Phi. Baptist. Mason (Shriner). Clubs: Old War Horse Lawyers, Lawyers of Atlanta, Optimist (Atlanta). Home: 3407 Rockhaven Circle NE Atlanta GA 30324 Office: Civil Criminal Ct Bldg Atlanta GA 30303

WRIGHT, EMMETT WOMACK, JR., ednl. adminstr.; b. Atlanta, May 24, 1926; s. Emmett Womack and Frances (Williams) W.; B.A., Furman U., 1950; M.A., Emory U., 1951; m. Betty Wilson, Aug. 27, 1948; children—James Howard, Robert Morris. History tchr. West Fulton High Sch., Atlanta, 1951-52; chmn. history dept., prin. Westminster Schs., Atlanta, 1952-68; curriculum coordinator Woodberry Forest Sch., Orange, Va., 1968-70; headmaster Metairie Park Country Day Sch., Metairie, La., 1970—. Cons. Coll. Entrance Exam. Bd., 1965—; reader Ednl. Testing Service, 1961—. Served with USNR, 1944-46. William Robertson Coe fellow Stanford, 1960. Mem. Orgn. Am. Historians, So. Hist. Assn., Nat. Hist. Soc. Baptist. Author: Political Leadership in America, 1967. Home: 320 Iona St Metairie LA 70005 Office: 300 Park Rd Metairie LA 70005

WRIGHT, ERNIE EDWARD, lawyer, judge; b. Cisco, Ark., Oct. 31, 1915; s. James Robert and Vindie (Williams) W.; A.B., U. Ark., 1938, LL.B., 1940, J.D., 1969; grad. Nat. Coll. State Trial Judges, 1967; m. Alyce Erline Collins, Aug 22, 1941; children—Warren James, Carolyn Doris. Admitted to Ark. bar, 1940, since practiced in Mountain Home, Ark.; city atty., Mountain Home, 1940-41; pros. atty. 16th Dist. Ark., 1943; chancery judge 11th Dist. Ark., 1955—. Mem. Ark. Tax Commn., 1949; chmn. Baxter County chpt. A.R.C., 1946-47; finance chmn. Boone County unit Am. Cancer Soc., 1955-56; mem. Nat. Com. for Support Pub. Schs., 1964—. Served with USAAF, 1944-45. Mem. Ark. Jud. Council (exec. com. 1963, pres. 1967-68), Nat. Conf. State Trial Judges (Ark. del.), Harrison C. of C. (past dir.), Am. Legion (past dist. comdr.). Methodist. Mason, Rotarian (past pres.), Elk. Home: 522 N Cherry St Harrison AR 72601 Office: Court House Harrison AR 72601

WRIGHT, FLETCHER JOHNSTON, JR., physician; b. Fork Union, Va., Oct. 19, 1910; s. Fletcher J. and Anne (Seay) W.; B.S., U. Richmond, M.D., U. Va., 1934; m. Martha Jeanette Andrews, June 29, 1935; children—Fletcher Johnston, Anne Andrews (Mrs. Edouard B. Steele). Intern, U. Va. Hosp., 1934-35; resident Princeton (W.Va.) Meml. Hosp., 1935-37; pvt. practice, Petersburg, Va., 1937—; surg. staff Petersburg Hosp., now Petersburg Gen. Hosp., chmn. staff, 1952. Mem. adv. bd. Petersburg Savs. br., also dir. First & Mchts. Nat. Bank. Dir. Va. Blue Shield, 1959-71, pres., 1961-62; mem. bd. Va. Council Health and Med. Care, 1958-64; mem. Va. Study Commn. on Mental Health, 1964, Va. Commn. for Emergency Planning, 1965-66; v.p. Va. Bd. Health, 1967—. Mem. Petersburg City Council, 1968—, vice mayor, 1970—. Served from capt. to maj. M.C., AUS, 1942-45; ETO. Mem. Petersburg Med. Faculty (pres. 1946), 4th Dist. Med. Soc. (pres. 1949). Med. Soc. Va. (past exec. com. council, speaker ho. of dels., 1960-62, pres. 1962-63), A.M.A., Am. (state dir. 1955), Va. (pres. 1959-60) acads. gen. practice, Kappa Alpha, Phi Beta Pi. Baptist. Mason, Rotarian. Club: Petersburg Country. Home: 1617 Blair Rd Petersburg VA 23803 Office: 49 S Market St Petersburg 23803

WRIGHT, FRANCIS EVERETT, coll. pres.; b. Dequeen, Ark., Apr. 19, 1915; s. Gerden Gate and Ellen (Beesley) W.; A.B., Baylor U., 1942; M.A., Peabody Coll., 1948, Ed.D. (Algier Sullivan scholar) postgrad. Harvard, 1964; grad. IBM Exec. Computer Course, 1969; m. Mildred Cooper, June 5, 1941; 1 dau., Kay (Mrs. William Stuve). Personnel counselor Northwestern State Coll., Natchitoches, La., 1948-50; dean men Baylor U., Waco, Tex., 1950-52; acad. dean Union U., Jackson, Tenn., 1954-63, pres., 1963-67; pres. Jackson State Community Coll., 1967—. Edn. cons. Child Health Centers Am., 1969—; mem. steering com. Baptist edn. study task force So. Baptist Conv.; mem. Tenn. N.G. Scholarship Com., Programmed Learning for Child Health Centers Am. Com.; chmn. Tenn. Community Coll. President's Council, 1970-71. Mem. policy adv. com. Jackson Civil Def., 1963-68; hon. adv. com. Boys Club of Jackson. Bd. dirs. United Fund, pres., 1971; chmn. bd. dirs. Jackson Rainbow Girls; pres. bd. dirs. Jackson Symphony Orch.; bd. dirs. East Jackson Devel. Council, Jackson Arts Council, Jackson Community Concert, Jackson-Madison County chpt. A.R.C., Jackson-Madison County Diabetic Unit Council; trustee Midwestern Theol. Sem., 1965—, mem. exec. com., 1969—. Served from 1st lt. to maj., USAAF, 1943-46. Recipient Grand Cross Colors, Tenn. Rainbow Girls, 1959—. Mem. Nat. Assn. Higher Edn., Am. Sociol. Soc., Nat. Assn. Student Teaching, N.E.A., Am. Assn. Student Personnel Adminstrs., Jackson Area C. of C. (dir.), So. Assn. Jr. Colls. (exec. com.), Tenn. Jr. Coll. Athletic Assn. (exec. com. 1969-70), Tenn., West Tenn. edn. assns., Phi Delta Kappa, Kappa Sigma. Baptist. Rotarian. Club: West Tenn. Executive (Jackson). Home: PO Box 3254 Jackson TN 38301

WRIGHT, GEORGE HERSCHEL, physician; b. Memphis, Jan. 4, 1913; s. James Robin and Lula Lee (Mercer) W.; B.S., La. State U., 1936, M.D., 1940; m. Clara Rebecca Armstrong, Aug. 28, 1941; children—Judy Kaye (Mrs. Timothy Walter), George Herschel, Larry Don, William Randall. Intern, Shreveport (La.) Charity Hosp., 1940-41; gen. practice medicine, New Roads, La., 1946, Hope, Ark., 1946—; mem. staff Hempstead County Meml. Hosp., Hope. Served with AUS, 1942-46. Fellow Am. Acad. Family Physicians; mem. Hempstead County Med. Soc., Ark. Med. Soc., A.M.A., Am. Acad. Gen. Practice. Mason (Shriner). Home: Route 1 Box 344 W Hope AR 71801 Office: PO Box H Hope AR 71801

WRIGHT, HAROLD HANNON, clergyman; b. Watertown, Conn., Oct. 8, 1895; s. Ernest Gilbert and Eva Frances (Hannon) W.; B.A., Yale, 1916, postgrad., 1916-17; postgrad. Chgo. Theol. Sem., 1931-33; m. Mary Elizabeth Ritchey, July 9, 1928; 1 son, Harold Hannon. Ordained to ministry Congl. Ch., 1928; asso., First Congl. Ch., Tucson, 1928-29; pastor Pilgrim Ch., El Paso, 1934-41, First Congl.-Unitarian Ch., Fort Collins, Colo., 1941-60. Moderator S.W. Congl. Conf., 1936; v.p. Unitarian Conf. S.W., 1938; state chmn. social action com. Congl. Ch., 1942-48. Served with F.A. AUS, 1917-19. Mem. Ft. Collins Council Chs. (pres. 1942), Ministerial Alliance (pres. 1944), Phi Beta Kappa, Alpha Chi Rho. Democrat. Mason, Lion. Club: Optimist (El Paso, Tex.). Editor: Thoughts of Mary Ritchey Wright, 1970. Home: 1201 W Main St Durant OK 74701

WRIGHT, HARROLD EUGENE, oil co. exec.; b. Vernon, Tex., Aug. 28, 1924; s. Jess N. and Bess (Buroughs) W.; B.S., Tex. Technol. U., 1944; postgrad. Mass. Inst. Tech., 1945; m. Velma Joyce Overbay, Mar. 2, 1946; children—Arthur Lawrence, Amy Lucile, Bradley Sloan. Cons. engr. Freese & Nichols, Ft. Worth, 1946-47; dist. engr. Hiawatha Oil & Gas Co., Midland, Tex., 1949-51; pres. Mohawk Oil Well Service Co., Alice, 1953—; petroleum engr. San Juan Oil Co., Dallas, 1951-56; v.p. Producing Properties, Inc., 1956-64; owner, pres. Lone Star Aviation Co., 1957—; v.p. San Juan Exploration Co., Longview, Tex.; pres. Swift Operations, Inc., Longview, Tex., Caddo Wells Service, Inc., Thunderbird Tools, Inc.; v.p., dir. Gulf Resources, Inc., 1969—; v.p. San Juan Exploration Co. Precinct chmn. Democratic party; gen. coordinator Dem. Com. for Responsible Govt. and Election of Pro-Connally Precinct Chmn. Registered profl. engr., Tex. Mem. Soc. Petroleum Engrs., Am. Assn. Petroleum Geologists, Am. profl. engrs. Clubs: Engineers, Petroleum Engineers (Dallas). Home: Stoneleigh Terrace Bldg Dallas TX 75235 Office: Swift Bldg Lake Harris Rd Longview TX 75601 also Met Fed Savs Bldg Dallas 75202

WRIGHT, HARVEY RUSSELL, banker; b. Gageby, Tex., June 24, 1926; s. John Thomas and Nola (Jeanette) W.; student W. Tex. State Coll., 1946-47; grad. comml. banking Southwest Grad. Sch. Banking So. Meth. U., 1968; m. children—Marcia Lee, Harvey Russell. Gen. mgr. Nash Supply Co., Wheeler, Tex., 1947-55; br. mgr. Universal C.I.T. Credit Corp., Amarillo, Tex., 1955-64; v.p. Farmers Nat. Bank, Elk. City, Okla., 1964—; also dir. Chmn. United Fund, 1966-67. Bd. dirs. Elk City Rodeo Assn., 1964—. Served with USNR, 1944-46; PTO. Mem. Okla. Bankers Assn., Western Okla. Bankers Assn. (treas. 1970—). Methodist. Lion, Elk, Mason. Club: Elk City Country. Home: Box 253 Elk City OK 73644 Office: Box 507 Elk City OK 73644

WRIGHT, HENRY HALSEY, realtor; b. Rocky Mount, N.C., Sept. 23, 1913; s. Prince Henry and Sarah Halsey (Powell) W.; student Jones Bus. Coll., 1936-37; m. A. Lucille Norton, June 3, 1939; children—Susan (Mrs. Robert Underwood), Henry Halsey. Cashier, bookkeeper Mal Haughton Jr. Co., Jacksonville, Fla., 1937-40; property mgr. Nussbaum & Sons, Jacksonville, 1940-41; v.p. Stockton, Whatley, Davin & Co., Jacksonville, 1941—. Mem. Nat. Assn. Real Estate Bds., Inst. Real Estate Mgmt. (state sec. 1963-72, chmn. 1965-66). Bldg. Owners and Mgrs. Assn. (pres. Jacksonville chpt. 1964-65), Fla. Assn. Realtors (chmn. Fla. Realtor mag. com. 1970), Execs. Assn. Jacksonville (pres. 1952-53, 59, 62), Jacksonville Bd. Realtors (dir. 1962-64), Property Mgrs. Assn. Jacksonville (pres. 1948-49). Home: Box 201F Switzerland Route Green Cove Springs FL 32043 Office: 100 W Bay St Jacksonville FL 32202

WRIGHT, JAMES C., JR., congressman; b. Ft. Worth, Dec. 22, 1922; s. James C. and Marie (Lyster) W.; student Weatherford Coll., U. Tex.; children—Jimmy, Virginia Sue, Patricia Kay, Alicia Marie. Mem. Tex. Ho. of Reps., 1947-49; mayor City of Weatherford (Tex.), 1950-54; mem. 84th-92d congresses from 12th Tex. Dis., regional Democratic whip, chmn. pub. works subcom. on investigations and oversight. Chmn., Commn. on Hwy. Beautification; mem. Ho. of Reps. delegation to U.S. Mexico Interparliamentary Conf., 1963-71. Served with USAAF, World War II. Decorated D.F.C., Legion of Merit; named outstanding young man Tex. Jr. C. of C., 1953. Mem. League Tex. Municipalities (pres. 1953). Democrat. Presbyn. Author: You and Your Congressman, 1965; The Coming Water Famine, 1966; Of Swords and Plowshares, 1968; co-author Congress and Conscience, 1970. Address: House Office Bldg Washington DC 20515

WRIGHT, JAMES FREDRICK, govt. ofcl.; b. Volga, S.D., Aug. 31, 1914; s. James Cady and Clara (Hymes) W.; student U. S.D., 1930-31; Asso. in Adminstrn., Am. U., 1952; m. Eula Page Hockett, Apr. 11, 1950; children—James Oliver, Clara Lynn. Various positions Naval Communications, U.S. Navy Dept., Washington, 1941-48; budget analyst, budget officer Office Navy Comptroller, 1948-53; dep. fiscal dir. Marine Corps, 1953-62, fiscal dir., 1962—. Served with AUS, 1944-46. Mem. Am. Soc. Mil. Comptrollers, Armed Forces Mgmt. Assn. (assso.),V.F.W. Presbyn. Home: Route 2 Sterling VA 22170 Office: Hdqrs USMC Washington DC 23080

WRIGHT, JAMES LEITCH, JR., educator; b. Ashland, Va., Aug. 9, 1929; s. James Leitch and Frances Lee (Bagley) W.; B.S., Va. Mil. Inst., 1950; M.A., U. Va., 1956, Ph.D., 1958; m. Elizabeth Hall Hatcher, Dec. 20, 1955; children—Marshall Felton, Nancy Mann, Margaret Leitch, Helen Lee, Lucy Langhorne. Prof. history Va. Mil. Inst., 1958-61, Randolph Macon Coll., 1961-68, Fla. State U., Tallahassee, 1968—. Served with AUS, 1950-52. Am. Philos. Soc. grantee. Mem. Am., So. hist. assns., Soc. Am. Historians, Fla., Tallahassee hist. socs., Am. Assn. U. Profs., Fla. Anthrop. Soc. Author: William Augustus Bowles, Director General of the Creek

Nation, 1967; Anglo-Spanish Rivalry in North America, 1971. Home: 911 Lothian Dr Tallahassee FL 32303

WRIGHT, JAMES SKELLY, judge; b. New Orleans, Jan. 14, 1911; s. James Edward and Margaret (Skelly) W.; Ph.B., Loyola U., 1931, LL.B., 1934; LL.D., Yale, 1961, U. Notre Dame, 1962, Howard U., 1964; m. Helen Mitchell Patton, Feb. 1, 1945; 1 son, James Skelly. Tchr. high sch. 1931-35; lectr. English history Loyola U., 1936-37; admitted to U.S. Supreme Ct. bar; asst. U.S. atty., New Orleans, 1937-46; U.S. atty. East Dist. La., 1948-49, U.S. dist. judge, 1949-62; U.S. circuit judge for D.C., 1962—. Mem. faculty Loyola U. Sch. Law, 1950-62; James Madison lectr. N.Y.U., 1965; Robert L. Jackson lectr. Nat. Coll. State Trial Judges, 1966; lectr. series on law and free soc. U. Tex., 1967; Frank Irvine lectr. Cornell U., 1968; Brainerd Currie lectr. Duke, 1970; mem. com. on ct. adminstrn., chmn. subcom. on fed. jurisdiction, mem. standing com. rules practice and procedure Jud. Conf. U.S.; observer U.S. State Dept. Internat. Fisheries Conf., London, 1943. Served as lt. comdr. USCGR, 1942-45. Mem. Am., Fed. (pres. New Orleans), La. (gov.), New Orleans bar assns., Bar Assn. D.C., Am. Law Inst., Blue Key, Alpha Delta Gamma (nat. pres.), Phi Delta Phi (hon.). Roman Catholic. Democrat. Home: 5317 Blackistone Rd Washington DC 20016 Office: US Ct House Washington DC 20001

WRIGHT, JAMES TURNER, savs. and loan exec.; b. Bastrop, Tex., Oct. 24, 1939; s. Harlyn T. and Mildred (Nite) W.; B.B.A., Tex. U., 1963; postgrad. Savs. and Loan Grad. Sch., 1968-70; m. Stella Lee Morgan, Sept. 4, 1958; children—Pamela Lynn, James Turner, Robert Turner. Loan collection officer Mut. Savs. & Loan Assn., Austin, Tex., 1960-61; tax auditor Peat, Marwick, Mitchell & Co., C.P.A.'s, Houston, 1963-67; controller, v.p., dir. Bryan Bldg. & Loan Assn. (Tex.), 1967—; dir. Tex. Data Center Bd.; instr. courses Savs. and Loan Inst., 1967-68, Am. Banking Inst., 1968-69. Chmn. Brazos County Easter Seal Campaign, 1969-72. Served with Tex. N.G., 1957-61. C.P.A., Tex. Mem. Am. Inst. C.P.A.'s, Tex. Soc. C.P.A.'s, U.S., Bryan-College Station (v.p., treas.) jr. chambers commerce. Baptist. Club: Texas Aggie Quarterback (Bryan). Home: 3601 Parkway Terrace Bryan TX 77801 Office: Bryan Bldg and Loan Assn Bryan TX 77801

WRIGHT, JIMMY DEAN, librarian; b. Clinton, S.C., Jan. 16, 1934; s. Jake Woodard and Sue Etta (Center) W.; A.A., Spartanburg Jr. Coll., 1960; A.B., Wofford Coll., 1962; M.L.S., Peabody Coll., 1966. Page, Spartanburg County Library (S.C.), 1960-62; librarian Edmunds High Sch., Sumter, S.C., 1962-63; cataloger Wofford Coll., Spartanburg, 1963-64; young adult librarian Spartanburg County Library, 1964-65; asst. librarian Converse Coll., Spartanburg, 1966-67, librarian, 1967—. Cons. book collection Spartanburg Jr. Coll., summer, 1967, adv. circulation, summer 1968. Served with USAF, 1952-56. Mem. Am., Southeastern, S.C. library assns., Am. Assn. U. Profs. Club: Spartanburg Kennel. Home: Box 216 Mayo SC 29368 Office: Converse College Spartanburg SC 29301

WRIGHT, JOHN HERMAN, JR., dentist; b. Hulbert, Okla., Apr. 30, 1934; s. John Herman and Ocie Mae (Disheroon) W.; student U. Okla., 1951-52, Northeastern State Coll., 1952-55; D.D.S., U. Tenn., 1958; m. Patsy Carolyn Hamilton, Oct. 18, 1958; children—Kimberly Kaye, John Herman III, Sylynn Ann. With Okla. State Health Dept., 1958; pvt. practice dentistry, Wagoner, Okla., 1959—; dir. First Wagoner Bank & Trust Co. City councilman, Wagoner, 1960-64; chmn. County Democratic Party 1964-67, dist. coordinator, 1967-70, del. conv., 1964, 68. Bd. dirs. Grand River Dam Authority, vice-chmn., 1971—. Mem. Okla., Am. dental assns., Eastern Dist. Dental Soc., C. of C. Lion. Home: RR 3 Wagoner OK 74467 Office: 1104 W Cherokee St Wagoner OK 74467

WRIGHT, JOHN J(OSEPH), pub. health physician; b. Toledo, Jan. 18, 1903; s.John Francis and Eleanor H. (Kelp) W.; student U. Mich., 1920-23; A.B., Vanderbilt, 1931, M.D., 1935; M.P.H., Johns Hopkins, 1939; m. Lillian Mayfield, Sept. 30, 1939. Interne Vanderbilt Univ. Hosp., Nashville, Tenn., 1935-36; field cons. Tb Control, Tenn. Health Dept., 1936-37, dir. div. vital statistics, 1939-40; health officer Carter-Unicoi Health Dist., Erwin, Tenn., 1937-38; research prof. epidemiology, Sch. Pub. Health, U. N.C., 1940-47, prof. pub. health adminstrn., 1947—, head dept., 1947-62, dir. continued edn. service, 1962—, cons. Armed Services residency tng. program; adminstrn. cons. Fla. Bd. Health, 1960-61. Dir. field epidemiol. studies of syphillis, N.C., 1940-52; mem. exec. staff N.C. State Health Dept. 1940-53, med. cons., Health Pubs. Inst. 1947-53. Diplomate Am. Bd. Preventive Medicine. Fellow Am. Pub. Health Assn.; mem. A.M.A., Am. Venereal Disease Assn. (pres. 1952), Elisha Mitchell Sci. Soc., Am. Coll. Preventive Medicine (charter mem., pres. 1965), Alpha Omega Alpha, Delta Omega. Home: 505 Louvel Hill Circle Chapel Hill NC 27514

WRIGHT, JOHN PEALE, banker; b. Chattenooga, Mar. 27, 1924; s. Robert T. and Margaret (Peale) W.; student Davidson Coll., 1941-43, U. N.C., 1943; B.S. in Phys. Sci., U. Chgo., 1944; M.B.A., Harvard, 1947; m. Ruth Garrison, Sept. 11, 1948; children—Margaret Shapard, John Peale, Ruth Garrison, Mary Ivens. With Am. Nat. Bank & Trust Co., Chattanooga, 1947—, pres., 1962—, also dir. Served to lt. USAAF, 1943-46. Mem. Robert Morris Assos. (past pres.), Tenn. Bankers Assn. (mem. exec. council). Presbyn (elder, treas.). Home: 1331 Scenic Hwy Lookout Mountain TN 37350 Office: 736 Market St Chattenooga TN 37401

WRIGHT, JOHN RICHARD, hotel co. exec.; b. Washington, Jan. 23, 1942; s. John Charles and Gladys Bell (Hartle) W.; student Old Dominion Coll., 1960-66; m. Inabelle Marlene Phillips, Apr. 17, 1965. Owner, operator South Gate Motor Hotel, Inc., Arlington, Va., 1957-61; partner John C. Wright & Son, Leesburg, Va., 1964—; owner, operator Quality Motel Lake Wright, Norfolk, Va., 1964—, Lake Wright Golf Course, 1966—, Country Club Apts., Leesburg, 1970—, Quality Inn, Leesburg, Va., 1972—; sec. Tuscarora, Inc., Leesburg, 1968—. Treas., coach Loudoun County Boy's Midget Football League, Leesburg, 1969—. Bd. dirs. John C. Wright Found. Presbyn. Optimist, Kiwanian. Club: Cosmopolitan (Norfolk). Home: 1 Orr Circle Leesburg VA 22075 Office: PO Box 1338 Leesburg VA 22075

WRIGHT, LOUIS CHARLES, judge; b. Gadsden, Ala., May 14, 1922; s. Louis Clifford and Elizabeth (McBrayer) W.; B.S., Auburn U., 1943; LL.B., U. Ala., 1948; m. Maxine McClendon Wright, Mar. 24, 1944; children— Adele (Mrs. Joseph Miller), Louis Charles II, Dennis McClendon. Admitted to Ala. State bar, 1948; pvt. practice law, Gadsden, Ala., 1948-69; dist. atty. Sixteenth Judicial Circuit Ala., 1955-63; mem. Ala. House Reps., 1967-69; judge Ala. Ct. Civil Appeals, Montgomery, 1969—. Served with USNR, 1943-46. Mem. Ala., Am. bar assns., Ala. Defense Lawyers Assn., Etowah County Bar Assn., V.F.W., Am. Legion. Gadsden C. of C., Phi Alpha Delta. Democrat. Baptist. Mason. Club: Internat. Lions. Home: 2347 Wentworth Dr Montgomery AL 36106 Office: Court of Civil Appeals Judicial Bldg Montgomery AL 36102

WRIGHT, MARGARET BEESLEY JOHNSON (MRS. NEIL HUTCHISON WRIGHT), organist, educator; b. Nashville, Aug. 8, 1918; d. Ben Howard and Sarah (Beesley) Johnson; B.S., Vanderbilt U., 1938; M.A., Peabody Coll., 1941, postgrad., 1946-47; student Ward Belmont Conservatory, 1938-39, Nashville Conservatory, 1932-34, Chgo. Mus. Coll., 1950; m. Neil Hutchison Wright, Aug. 29, 1939; children—Neil Hutchison III, David Quintin. Dir. music Isaac Litton High Sch., 1938, Nashville City Schs., 1939, Bristol (Tenn.) City Schs., 1939-43, A.R.C., CBI Theatre, 1943-45; mem. faculty Middle Tenn. State U., Murfreesboro, 1946—, asso. prof. music, 1947—. Organ recitalist throughout Tenn., Ga., Ala., 1948-72; contralto soloist various choirs, chs., 1939-68; choral adjudicator, condr. choral festivals, Tenn., Ga., 1951-68; lectr., workshop clinician; founder Middle Tenn. State U. Sacred Harp Singers, 1947, dir., 1947-71; chmn. Tenn. folk arts Tenn. Arts Com., 1966-69. Bd. mem. Murfreesboro Community Concerts Assn., 1949-60. Named Outstanding Musician of Tenn., Tenn. Fedn. Music Clubs, 1964. Mem. Music Tchrs. Nat. Assn. (nat. com. orgn. 1970—), Tenn. Music Tchrs. Assn. (v.p. 1967-69, exec. bd. 1965-69, 71-72, nat. com. pvt. tchr. certification 1965—, state exec. bd. 1959—, pres. 1971-72), Music Educators Nat. Conf., Tenn. Music Educators Assn. (state chmn. pvt. tchr. certification 1956-58), Am. Guild Organists (chpt. exec. bd. 1954-66, dean 1958-59), N.E.A., Tenn. Edn. Assn., D.A.R. (chpt. capt. 1948-67), Murfreesboro Arts Council, Harpeth Valley Sacred Harp Assn. (v.p. 1969-71), Phi Beta Kappa, Omicron Psi, Delta Omicron (award 1968), Gamma Phi Beta. Club: Bohannon Music (pres. 1964, 66). Author: Technic and Art of Singing, 1968; Developing Musicianship, 1972. Arranger folk songs including I Gave My Love a Cherry, 1961; The Preacher and the Bear, 1961. Home: 614 Shawnee Dr Murfreesboro TN 37130

WRIGHT, MARVIN EUGENE, JR., librarian; b. Alexandria, La., Sept. 4, 1936; s. Marvin Eugene and Yvonne (Gravel) W.; B.A., Northwestern State Coll., 1959; M.L.S,, La. State U., 1961; m. Diana Jane Smith, Aug. 21, 1963; 1 son, Gene Christopher. Tchr. Port Sulphur (La.) High Sch., 1959-60; reference librarian Queensboro (N.Y.) Pub. Library, 1961-62; librarian Jackson Parish (La.), Jonesboro, 1962-63; dir. Scottsdale (Ariz.) Pub. Library, 1964-65; asst. librarian New Orleans Pub. Library, 1966-67, librarian, 1967—. Mem. New Orleans Jr. C. of C., Young Men's Bus. Club, Phi Kappa Phi. Kiwanian. Home: 2124 Gibson St Gretna LA 70053 Office: New Orleans Pub Library 219 Loyola Av New Orleans LA 70140

WRIGHT, MELTON FISHER, supt. schs.; b. Charleston, S.C., Aug. 9, 1922; s. Harold Edward and Marion (Millar) W.; A.B., Bob Jones U., 1945, LL.D., 1961; M.Ed., U. Va., 1951; m. Betty Gearing, Aug. 31, 1945; children—David G., Frank E. Prin., W.H. Keister Sch., Harrisburg, Va., 1951-56, Harrisburg High Sch., 1956-58; dir. instrn. Frederick County, Va., 1958-66, asst. supt., 1966-68, supt. schs., Winchester, 1968—. Pres., Community Chest, Winchester, 1965. Bd. dirs. Lord Fairfax Community Coll. Kettering Found. fellow, 1970. Mem. Va. Edn. Assn. (pres. 1969), Phi Delta Kappa, Kappa Delta Pi. Club: Stonewall Ruritan (Winchester, Va.). Author: Giant for God, 1951, Into the Light, 1955, Beloved Schoolmaster, 1958, Fortress of Faith, 1960, Thoughts on Education, 1966. Home: PO Box 221 Winchester VA 22601 Office: 36 Whitlock Av Winchester VA 22601

WRIGHT, MURIEL HAZEL, historian; b. Lehigh, Indian Ty.; d. Eliphalet Nott and Ida Belle (Richards) Wright; grad. E. Central State Normal, Ada, Okla., 1912; postgrad. Barnard Coll., Columbia, 1916-17; L.H.D., Oklahoma City U., 1964. High sch. and elementary sch. tchr., Tishomingo, Okla., 1912-13, 13-14; tchr. grade sch., also high sch. prin., Wapanucka, Okla., 1914-18; prin. rural sch., Coal County, Okla., 1918-20, 22-24; hist. researcher, writer state histories and articles Okla. Hist. Soc., 1924—, asso. editor The Chronicles of Oklahoma, 1943-55, editor, 1955—. Mem. hist. adv. panel Gov.'s Council for Cultural Devel., 1964; pres. Nat. Hall of Fame for Famous Am. Indians, 1965—; mem. Okla. bd. geog. names Okla. Geol. Survey, 1965. Recipient Distinguished Service citation U. Okla., 1948; MacDowell Club award, 1948; named Woman of Year, Oklahoma City Bus. and Profl. Women, 1951; named to Okla. Hall of Fame, 1940; Matrix award Theta Sigma Phi, 1941. Mem. Byliners Oklahoma City, Nat. League Am. Pen Women (pres. Oklahoma City br. 1962-64), Am. Historian, Oklahoma City Civil War Round Table (pres. 1963-64), Am. Assn. State and Local History, So., Miss. Valley hist. assns., Soc. Mayflower Descs., U.D.C., D.A.R., Colonial Dames XVII Century, Okla. Hist. Society (hon. life), Okla. Goals (chmn. pub. com. 1969), Theta Sigma Phi, Alpha Gamma Delta, Delta Kappa Gamma (hon.). Presbyn. Clubs: Red Bud, Women's Dinner, Westerner's Indian Terr. Women's Posse. Author: AGuide to the Indian Tribes of Oklahoma, 1951; The Story of Oklahoma, 1929; Our Oklahoma, 1939; The Oklahoma History, 1955; (with J.B. Thoburn) Oklahoma: A History of the State and Its People, 1929; Rambler in Oklahoma, 1956; (W. LeRoy H. Fischer) Civil War Sites in Oklahoma, 1967. Office: Editorial Office Okla Hist Soc Hist Bldg Oklahoma City OK 73105

WRIGHT, NATHALIA, educator; b. Athens, Ga. Mar. 29, 1913; d. Hilliard Carlisle and Elizabeth (MacNeal) Wright; B.A., Maryville Coll., 1933; M.A., Yale, 1938, Ph.D., 1949. Instr. Maryville Coll., 1934-35, 41-47, asst. library, 1940-43, asst. librarian, 1943-48; asst. prof. U. Tenn., 1949-55, asso. prof., 1955-62, prof. English, 1962—. Recipient Willis Tew Prize Yale, 1936, Albert Stanburrough Cook prize in poetry, 1937; grantee Am. Philos. Soc., 1952; Guggenheim fellow, 1953, Am. Assn. U. Women fellow, 1959. Mem. Modern Lang. Assn., Melville Soc., Accademia Internazionale Siculo-Normanna. Author: The Inner Room, 1938; Melville's Use of the Bible, 1949; Horatio Greenough, First American Sculptor, 1963; American Novelists in Italy: The Discoverers, 1965; (with Harold Orton) Questionnaire for the Investigation of American Regional English, 1972; also articles. Editor: Horatio Greenough, The Travels, Observations and Experience of a Yankee Stonecutter, 1958; John Galt, The Life of Benjamin West, 1959; Washington Allston, Lecturers on Arts and Poems and Monaldi, 1967; Washington Irving, Journals and Notebooks, Vol. 1, 1969; Letters of Horatio Greenough, American Sculptor, 1972. Home: 713 Court St Maryville TN 37801

WRIGHT, PETER, labor mgmt. adviser; b. N.Y.C., Jan. 21, 1934; s. Stuyvesant Bayard and Rebecca Addison (Holland) W.; student U. of South, 1952-53, George Washington U., 1953-56, 62-63; m. Carolann Wright, 1956; children—Peter, Andrew S., Edward Stuyvesant. Air force account Underwood Corp., CIA, Washington, 1953-56; with 1st Fed. Savs. & Loan Assn., Alexandria, Va., 1955; asst. exec. mgr. Truck Body & Equipment Assn., 1956-57; owner, operator Bayard's Bend Farm, 1957-61; pres., dir. Bayard's Bend Farms, Inc., 1960—; dir. supervisory tng. U.S. Dept. Agr., 1961-62, organizational and staffing analyst., 1963-66, personnel staffing specialist, chief tech. services section Far East personnel AID, Washington, 1966-68; supervisory personnel officer Office Personnel and Manpower, Washington, 1968; labor-mgmt. adviser Am. Fedn. Govt. Employees, 1968-69, asst. dir. labor mgmt. dept., chief regulations rev., 1969-71; personnel mgmt., labor relations specialist U.S. Dept. Commerce, Rockville, Md., 1971—. Vice pres. Belmont Civic Assn., 1965-66; pres. Mason Neck Citizens' Assn., 1972-73. Campaign mgr. City of Alexandria, 1956; city committeeman, 1955-57; v.p. No. Va. Young Republicans, 1956-57; del. state Rep. conv., 1956; Rep. co-committeeman, 1969-71. Mem. Am. Soc. Pub. Adminstrn., Am. Church Union, Am. Guernsey Breeders Assn., Phila. Assemblies, Old Gaffers' Assn. Episcopalian. Toastmaster (ednl. v.p. 1971-72). Home: 10904 Belmont Blvd Lorton VA 22079 Office: Personnel Div US Dept of Commerce Rockville MD 20850

WRIGHT, R(ALEIGH) LEWIS, neurosurgeon; b. Roanoke, Va., Apr. 16, 1931; s. Raleigh Lewis and Mary Lillian (Major) W.; B.A., U. Richmond, 1951; M.D., Med. Coll. Va., 1955; m. Sarah Bird Grant, Sept. 7, 1963; 1 son, Alexander Grant. Intern, Duke U. Hosp., 1955-56, surg. resident, 1956-57; neurosurg. resident Mass. Gen. Hosp., Boston, 1959-63; practice medicine specializing in neurosurgery, Boston, 1964-70, Richmond, Va., 1970—; mem. staff St. Mary's, Retreat, Richmond Meml., Stuart Circle, Grace hosps., Med. Coll. Va.; faculty Harvard Med. Sch., Boston, 1962-70; asst. clin. prof. neurosurgery Med. Coll. Va., 1970—. Served with M.C., USNR, 1957-59. King Trust Fund fellow, 1963-64. Diplomate Am. Bd. Neurol. Surgery, Nat. Bd. Med. Examiners. Fellow A.C.S.; mem. A.M.A., Am. Fedn. Clin. Research, Harvey Cushing Soc., Congress Neurol. Surgeons, Southern Neurol. Soc., Microcirculatory Soc., English-Speaking Union, Am. Acad. Neurology, Med. Soc. Va. Assn. for Research in Nervous and Mental Diseases, Richmond Acad. Medicine, N.Y. Acad. Scis., Am. Assn. History Medicine. Episcopalian. Author: Postoperative Craniotomy Infections, 1966; Septic Complications of Neurosurgical Spinal Procedures, 1970. Contbr. articles to profl. jours. Home: 3505 Old Gun Rd Midlothian VA 23113 Office: 4908 Monument Av Richmond VA 23230

WRIGHT, RICHARD GLENN, financial cons. co. exec.; b. Palestine Tex., Mar. 30, 1929; s. Robinson H. and Mattie L. (Spruill) W.; student Sam Houston State Coll., 1946-48, U. Houston, 1955-59; m. Grace Marie Everts, Dec. 30, 1948; children—Rebecca Lynn, Edie Anne. Accounting supr. Superior Oil Co., 1949-53; ins. auditor Cravesn Dargan & Co., 1948-49; with Tenneco, Inc., Houston, 1955-68, banking mgr., 1961-64, asst. treas. subsidiary Tenneco Oil Co., 1964-66, treas., 1966-68; asst. treas. Ashland Oil & Refining Co., (Ky.), 1968-71, also internat. treas.; owner, mgr. R.G. Wright and Co., internat. financial consultants, Houston, 1971-72; v.p. finance, treas. Reed Tool Co., Houston, 1972—. Served with AUS, 1953-55. Mem. Am. Petroleum Inst., Am. Mgmt. Assn., U. Houston Coll. Bus Alumni Assn., Nat Assn. Accountants, Internat. Platform Assn. Home: 17906 Canyon Creek St Houston TX 77090 Office: Navigation Bldg Houston TX 77002

WRIGHT, ROBERT BRUCE, govt ofcl.; b. Manila, Philippine Islands, June 18, 1917; s. (parents Am. citizens); Bruce S. and Margarette (Armstrong) W.; A.B., Allegheny Coll., 1940; M.A., Fletcher Sch. Law and Diplomacy, 1941, M.A.L.D., 1942; m. Elizabeth Truman, Apr. 20, 1940; children—Michael B., Anthony T. With Office Asst. Chief, USAAF Intelligence, Washington, 1942-45; economist comml. policy div. U.S. Dept. of State, Washington, 1945-49, asst. chief econ. resources and security div., 1949-51, asst. chief econ. def. div., 1951-56, chief econ. def. div., 1956-61, dir. mut. def. control staff Dept. of State, 1961-65, dir. office of East-West Trade, 1965—. Mem. Phi Beta Kappa, Phi Delta Theta. Home: 212 W Cameron Rd Falls Church VA 22046 Office: Dept of State Washington DC 20525

WRIGHT, ROBERT ERNEST, mfg. co. exec.; b. Oconto, Wis., Nov. 28, 1917; s. Ernest William and Rheua (Nickey) W.; B.S. in Mech. Engring., U. Wis., 1940; m. Janet Christie, Feb. 20, 1943; children—Anne E., William C., Richard C., Robert C. With Monsanto Chem. Co., 1940-51, 64-66, project engr., St. Louis, 1945-47, asst. mgr. design sect., 1947-51, dir. process design, mgmt., internat. engr., 1964-66; with Chemstrand Corp., 1952-64, dir. engring. and devel., Pensacola, Fla., 1958-62, dir. engring., Decatur, Ala., 1962-64; v.p. engring. Wheeling-Pitts. Steel Corp. (formerly Wheeling Steel Corp.) (W.Va.), 1966-69, v.p. corporate devel., 1969-71; chmn. bd. Black Diamond Enterprises, Inc., Bristol, Va., 1972—, also dir. Bank of Wheeling. Bd. dirs. Wheeling Symphony Soc., Inc., Wheeling YMCA, Wheeling Hosp. Mem. Am. Soc. M.E., Am. Inst. Chem. Engrs., Nat. Soc. Profl. Engrs., Am. Iron and Steel Inst., Am. Iron and Steel Engrs. Presbyn. (elder). Office: Box 151 Bristol VA 24201

WRIGHT, ROBERT LEE, educator; b. Wabasso, Fla., Nov. 16, 1938; s. Edward and Alyce Trassel (Broxton) W.; ed. Howard U.; M.L.S., U. Md., 1970; m. Gail Patricia Davis, Sept. 28, 1968; children—Theresa Marie, Robert Broxton. Desk supr., readers' adviser D.C. Pub. Library, Washington, 1964-68; reference librarian, media technologist Fed. City Coll., Washington, 1968-70; lectr., dir. recruitment and spl. programs Sch. Library and Information Sci., U. Md., College Park, 1970—. An organizer N.E. Washington Community Orgn., Lamond-Riggs Community Orgn. Served with AUS, 1962-64. Mem. A.L.A. (black caucas), D.C. Library Assn., Big Bros. Am., Inc., Am. Soc. Information Sci. Home: 312 Nicholson St NE Washington DC 20011 Office: Sch Library and Information Sci U Md College Park MD 20742

WRIGHT, ROBERT ROSS, III, lawyer; b. Ft. Worth, Nov. 20, 1931; s. Robert Ross and Alma (Stewart) W.; B.A. cum laude, U. Ark., 1953, J.D., 1956; M.A. (grad. fellow), Duke, 1954; S.J.D., U. Wis.; m. Jacqueline Sue Stucker, 1955; children—Robert Ross IV, John, David. Instr. polit. sci. U. Ark., 1955-56; admitted to Ark. bar, 1956, Okla. bar, 1970; asso. firm Norton & Norton, Forrest City, Ark., 1956-58; partner firm Norton, Norton & Wright, Forrest City, 1959; asst. sec., asst. gen. counsel Crossett Co. (Ark.), 1960-62; asst. sec. Pub. Utilities Co. Crossett, Triangle Bag Co., Covington, Ky., 1960-62; dir. continuing legal edn. and research, asst. prof. law U. Ark., Fayetteville, 1963-67, prof. law, 1967-70, asst. dean charge Little Rock div., 1965-66; vis. prof. law, spl. asst. to provost U. Ia., 1969-70; dean Coll. Law, dir. Okla. Law Center, prof. U. Okla., Norman, 1970—. Participant, Ark. Conf. Local Bar Assn. Presidents, 1959; commr. Nat. Conf. Commrs. Uniform Laws, 1967-70; chmn. Okla. Center for Criminal Justice, 1971—; chmn. task force for joint devel. Hwy. Research Bd. Chmn. St. Francis County heart dr., 1958; corporate contbns. chmn. United Fund, 1961. Named Ark. Man of Year, Kappa Sigma, 1958. Mem. Am. (dist. membership chmn., 1958-59), Ark. (exec. com. Jr. Bar 1959-60; chmn. legal preceptorship com.), Okla. (vice chmn. legal internship com. 1971-72), St. Francis County (pres. 1959), Washington County, Cleveland County bar assns., Assn. Continuing Legal Edn. Adminstrs. (charter), Okla. Jud. Council (vice chmn.), Order of Coif, Phi Beta Kappa, Omicron Delta Kappa, Phi Alpha Delta. Episcopalian (layreader, former vestryman). Kiwanian (pres. Forrest City 1959, dir. Crossett 1960-61), Rotarian. Club: Fayetteville Country. Author: Arkansas Eminent Domain Digest, 1964; Arkansas Probate Practice System, 1965; The Law of Airspace, 1968; (with J. H. Beuscher) Cases and Materials on Land Use, 1969; Uniform Probate Code Practice Manual, 1972; Model Airspace Code. Home: 1218 Cherry Stone Norman OK 73069

WRIGHT, ROBERT WAYNE, govt. ofcl.; b. Fowler, Kan., Jan. 17, 1919; s. John H. and Carrie E. (VanNorman) W.; student Central Coll., McPherson, Kan., 1938; B.S., U. Kan., 1947; M.S., Ia. State U., 1949; m. Velma L. Smothers, Apr. 30, 1941; children—Lawrence Wayne, David Warren. Clk. U.S. Census Bur., Washington, 1939-42; jr. mgmt. asst. Dept. Air Force, Tinker AFB, Okla., 1950-51, maintenance planner, analyst, 1951-58, logistics planner, 1958—. Bd. dirs. Deaconess Hosp., Oklahoma City, 1955—. Served with USAAF, 1941-45. Mem. Beta Gamma Sigma, Pi Mu Epsilon. Free Methodist. Club: Management (Tinker AFB). Home: 1005 Christine

Dr Oklahoma City OK 73130 Office: OCAMA Tinker Air Force Base OK 73145

WRIGHT, THOMAS HENRY, bishop; b. Wilmington, N.C., Oct. 16, 1904; s. John Maffitt and Josie Young (Whitaker) W.; A.B., U. of South, 1926, D.D., 1946; B.D., Va. Theol. Sem., Alexandria, 1930, D.D., 1946; D.D., Washington and Lee U., 1940, U. N.C., 1965;; m. Hannah Hagans Knowlton, Dec. 1, 1937; children—Thomas Henry, Hannah K., James K., John M. Clk., Standard Oil Co. of N.J., Wilmington, 1926-27; ordained to ministry P.E. Ch., 1929; nat. acting sec. of coll. work P.E. Ch., 1933-34; Episcopal chaplain U. N.C., 1931-32, Va. Mil. Inst., 1934-41, Washington and Lee U., 1934-41; rector Robert E, Lee Meml. Ch., Lexington, Va., 1934-41; dean Grace Cathedral, San Francisco, 1941-43; rector St. Mark's Ch., San Antonio, 1943-45; consecrated bishop Diocese of East Carolina, St. James Ch., Wilmington, N.C., 1945—. Rep. of U.S. to World Christian Student Fed. Meeting, Holland, 1932; regional dir. Ch. Soc. for Coll. Work; asso. mem. Forward movement Commn., P.E. Church; chmn. overseas dept. Nat. Council Episcopal Ch.; pres. 4th province Episcopal Ch., 1968—. Trustee U. of South, Va. Sem. Mem. Sigma Nu (former grand chaplain), Sigma Upsilon, Alpha Phi Epsilon, Omicron Delta Kappa (hon.). Democrat. Contbr. articles to profl. jours. Address: Diocesan House 305 S 3d St Wilmington NC 28401

WRIGHT, THOMAS H(ENRY), JR., chem. mfg. co. exec.; b. Wilmington, N.C., Dec. 19, 1918; s. Thomas Henry and Eleanor (Gilchrist) W.; grad. Woodberry Forest Sch., 1937; A.B. in Chemistry, U. N.C., 1941; m. Margaret Guest Taylor, Aug. 10, 1946 (dec. 1956); children— Margaret T., Thomas H.; m. 2d, Elizabeth Devereux Labouisse, Oct. 9, 1959; children—Elizabeth, Eleanor G. Chmn., Wright Chem. Corp., Acme, N.C., 1959—, Wright Realty Co., 1952—; pres., dir. Shell Island Corp.; dir. Wachovia Bank and Trust Co., Wachovia Corp., Caroline Forest Products. Mem. Wilmington Parking Commn. Bd. dirs. St. John's Art Gallery, Cape Fear Acad., Historic Wilmington Found., Inc.; chmn. Wrightsville Marine Bio-Med. Lab.; trustee Woodberry Forest Sch.; Served to lt. comdr. USNR, 1941-45. Episcopalian (vestryman). Home: 2232 Acacia Dr Wilmington NC 28401 Office: Acme Sta Riegelwood NC 28456

WRIGHT, WALTER LIVINGSTON, III, economist; b. Washington, May 25, 1931; s. Walter Livingston, Jr., and Katharine Hine (Fenning) W.; A.B., Ursinus Coll., 1954; m. Nancy Isabel Fletcher, Nov. 28, 1958. Economist U.S. Fed. Power Commn., Washington, 1958—. Treas. Glover Park Citizens Assn.; del. D.C. Fedn. Citizens Assns. Inc., 1964-67, Am. Fedn. Govt. Employees, 1971. Mem. English Speaking Union U.S., St. Andrews Soc., Middle East Inst., Am. Friends of Middle East, Inc., Am. Econ. Assn. Club: Washington Area Ursinus Alumni (treas.). Home: 3902 W St NW Washington DC 20007 Office: 441 G St NW Washington DC 20426

WRIGHT, WILLIAM CARTER, lawyer, rancher; b. Eagle Pass, Tex., Aug. 6, 1918; s. Ralph Dowell and Daisy (Clemmer) W.; LL.B., U. Tex., 1947; m. Margaret Wheeler, Dec. 10, 1949; children—Ralph, Frank. Admitted to Tex. bar, 1948; practiced in Laredo, Tex., 1948—; asst. dist. atty. Webb County, Tex., 1951-58. Served with USAAF, 1941-45; lt. col. Res. ret. Asst. U.S. Mil. Air Attache, Santiago, Chile, 1944-45. Decorated D.F.C., Air Medal with one oak leaf cluster. Mem. Am., Tex., Laredo bar assns., Tex. Assn. Trial Counsel, Peruvian Paso Horse Assn. (dir.). Republican. Contbr. articles on conservation to nat. mags. Home: Wright Ranch North West Webb County PO Box 1146 Laredo TX 78040 Office: 918 Houston St Laredo TX 78040

WRIGHT, WILSON WALKER, lawyer, state ofcl.; b. Washington, Jan. 26, 1930; s. Chester Maynard and June (Walker) W.; student U. Fla., 1948-52; LL.B., U. Miami, 1954; certificate Fla. State U., 1960; m. Patricia Anne Davis, May 14, 1955; children—Randahl June, Lee Anne. Admitted to Fla. bar, 1954; asst. state's atty. gen. state of Fla., Tallahassee, 1957—. Past pres. Leon County Cancer Soc. Past pres. Young Democrats Leon County; state pres. Young Dem. Clubs Fla., 1961-62. Served from 2d lt. to capt., USAF, 1954-57. Named One of Fla.'s 5 Outstanding Young Men, 1961; recipient Good Govt. award Talahassee Jr. C. of C., 1967. Mem. Am., Fla. Govt. bar assns., Fla. Bar, U.S. (dir.), Fla. (past sec., past editor news), Tallahassee (past pres.) jr. chambers commerce, Sigma Alpha Epsilon, Phi Alpha Delta, Alpha Kappa Psi. Democrat. Kiwanian (charter; dir., pres.), Elk. Contbr. articles to profl. jours. Home: 3375 E Lakeshore Dr Tallahassee FL 32303 Office: 217 S Adams St Tallahassee FL 32304

WRIGLEY, ROBERT LACORAN, JR., economist, govt. ofcl.; b. Logan, Utah, July 5, 1911; s. Robert LaCoran and Esther (Erickson) W.; B.S., Utah State U., 1934, M.S., 1935; Ph.D., U. Chgo., 1942; m. Ada Espenshade. Asst. prof. geography U. N.C., 1942-43; sr. planner Chgo. Planning Commn., 1943-48; econ. geographer U.S. Bur. Census, 1948-54; chief project planning br. Md. Nat. Capital Park and Planning Commn., 1954-59; regional economist Office of Area Devel., U.S. Dept. Commerce, 1959-61; regional economist Area Redevel. Adminstrn., 1961-65; chief dist. and area planning div. Office Devel. Orgns., Econ. Devel. Adminstrn., U.S. Dept. Commerce, Washington, 1965—. Mem. Am. Inst. Planners, Am. Soc. Planning Ofcls., Lambda Alpha. Office: US Dept Commerce Washington DC 20230

WROTENBERY, PAUL TAYLOR, computer co. exec.; b. Pollok, Tex., Apr. 24, 1934; s. Delbert Monroe and Lillie Mae (King) W.; B.S., U. Tex., 1958, M.A., 1962, Ph.D., 1964; m. Janice Neal, May 5, 1954; children—Lori, Byron Nathan. Sr. project mgr. Tracor, Inc., Austin, Tex., 1958-64; mgr. IBM, Dallas, Houston and Washington, 1964-68; sr. v.p. Tracor Computing Corp., Austin, 1968-70; pres., chmn. bd., chief exec. officer United Systems Internat., Dallas, 1970—, also dir. Served with USMCR, 1952-54. Mem. Sigma Xi. Democrat. Unitarian. Club: City (Dallas). Contbr. articles to profl. jours. Home: 3411 Monte Vista St Austin TX 78731 Office: 1025 Elm St Dallas TX 75202

WUERTENBERGER, CHARLES BENSON, constrn. co. exec.; b. Pitts., Dec. 11, 1918; s. Charles Peter and Anna Margaret (Claypoole) W.; student Am. U., Cairo, Egypt, 1935; B.A., U. Pitts., 1940; m. Eleanor Euwer, Apr. 5, 1941; children—Jan (Mrs. Fred L. Cooper, III), Gary Peter. Constrn. foreman Harrison Constrn. Co., Charleston, W.Va., 1946-47; asst. supt. Blythe Bros. Co., Albany, Ga., 1947, constrn. engr., Charlotte, N.C., 1948-51; asst. to constrn. mgr. Atlas Constructors, French Morocco, 1952-53; prin. officer Towhee Constrn. Co., Charlotte, 1953; with Rea Constrn. Co., Charlotte, 1954—, chmn. bd., pres., 1968—; dir. J.A. Jones Constrn. Co., Charlotte. Served to lt. col. USMCR, 1940-45. Recipient Distinguished Service award Nat. Asphalt Pavement Assn., 1963, 70. Mem. Nat. (dir. 1960-63), Carolina (pres. 1967-69) asphalt pavement assns., Pres. Assn., Kappa Sigma (pres. 1938-39). Clubs: Charlotte City, Rolling Hills Country; Port Royal Golf (S.C.); Kannapollis (N.C.) Golf. Home: 5513 Topping Pl Charlotte NC 28209 Office: PO Box 27067 Charlotte NC 28208

WUKASCH, MARTIN CHARLES, state ofcl.; b. Austin, Tex., Feb. 20, 1915; s. George Charles and Emma (Hannusch) W.; B. Chem. Engring., U. Tex., 1941; M.S. in pub. health engring. Ga. Inst. Tech., 1950; m. Winifred Ruth Faubion, Sept. 28, 1937; children—Charles, Kenneth, James, Jan. Analyt. chemist Shell Chem. Co., Houston, 1941-42; ordnance research engr. U.S. War Dept., Washington, 1942-45; environmental health engr. Tex. Health Dept., Austin, 1945-48, chief indsl. hygiene sect., 1948-50, chief engr. div. occupational health and radiation control, 1950-60, dir., 1970—, chief Tex. Radiation Control Agy., 1960-70. Mem. faculty U. Tex. Postgrad. Sch. Medicine, 1960—. Registered profl. engr., Tex.; certified Bd. Health Physics, Safety Profl. Bd. Fellow Am. Pub. Health Assn. (chmn. radiol. health sect. 1972-73); mem. Am. Acad. Environmental Engrs., Health Physics and Safety Profls. (diplomate indsl. hygiene), Tex. Pub. Health Assn., Travis County, Tex. socs. profl. engrs., Austin Council on Alcoholism (v.p. 1960-64), Health Physics Soc., Soc. Nuclear Medicine, Southwestern Soc. Nuclear Medicine (2d v.p. 1969-71), Am. Indsl. Hygiene Assn. Home: 4100 Wildwood Rd Austin TX 78722 Office: 1100 W 49th St Austin TX 78756

WUNDERLICH, GOOLOO SAHIAR (MRS. GENE L. WUNDERLICH), govt. ofcl.; b. Bombay, India, Aug. 21, 1930; d. Hormusji K. and Shirin (Gobhai) Sahiar; B.A., U. Bombay, 1949, M.A., 1951, Ph.D. (research scholar), 1955; postgrad. U. Minn., 1955, (Am. Assn. U. Women internat. scholar) U. Chgo., 1956; m. Gene L. Wunderlich, Mar. 19, 1957; children—Karl A., Roshna E. Came to U.S., 1955, naturalized, 1960. Fellow Population Council, 1955-57; workshop participant Population Reference Bur., Washington, 1956; research asst. Population Research and Tng. Center, Chgo., 1956-57; analytical statistician Tb program USPHS, 1958-61; analytical statistician div. accident prevention USPHS, U.S. Dept. Health, Edn. and Welfare, Washington, 1961-62, survey statistician, nat. center for health statistics, 1962-66, demographer Office Dep. Asst. Sec. for Population Affairs, 1967-72, demographer office Dep. Asst. Sec. Health Policy Devel., 1972—; statistician U.S. Bur. Census, Dept. Commerce, 1966; staff demographer President's Nat. Adv. Commn. on Rural Poverty, 1966-67; staff President's Com. on Population and Family Planning, 1968. Mem. Population Assn. Am., Am. Statis. Assn., Am. Sociol. Assn., Indian Fedn. U. Women, Indian Sociol. Soc. (founder 1953), Am. Pub. Health Assn. Home: 6027 Lomack Ct Alexandria VA 22312 Office: US Dept Health Edn and Welfare 4th St and Independence Av SW Washington DC 20201

WURF, JERRY, labor union ofcl.; b. N.Y.C., May 18, 1919; s. Sigmund and Lena (Tannenbaum) W.; A.B., N.Y.U., 1940; m. Mildred Kiefer, Nov. 26, 1960; children—Susan, Nicholas S., Abigail. Employed in cafeteria, N.Y.C., 1940-43; an organizer local 448 Hotel and Restaurant Employees, 1943, organizer, adminstr. union's Welfare Fund, 1947; organizer in N.Y. for Am. Fedn. State, County and Municipal Employees, 1948-58, exec. dir. dist. council 37, 1959-64, internat. pres., 1964—; lectr. indsl. relations problems Cornell U. Sch. Labor and Indsl. Relations, 1964—; v.p. exec. council, v.p. indsl. union dept. AFL-CIO; pres. council AFL-CIO Unions Sci., Profl. and Cultural Employees, 1967—; mem. exec. bd. maritime trades dept. AFL-CIO. Mem. Fed. Adv. Council on Employment Security; treas. Nat. Trade Union Council for Civil Rights, mem. nat. exec. com. Jewish Labor Com.; mem. Pres.'s Com. on Employment of Handicapped; co-chmn. nat. bd. Workers Def. League; bd. dirs. Norman Thomas Fund, Catalyst; trustee Inst. Politics and Planning; mem. citizens bd. inquiry Nat. Health Services for Am.; mem. exec. com. Com. for Nat. Health Ins., Leadership Conf. on Civil Rights; mem. project adv. com. Washington Center for Met. Studies; co-chmn. urban coalition Panel on Equal Housing Opportunity. Home: 3220 Cleveland Av Washington DC 20005 Office: 1155 15th St NW Madison Bldg Washington DC 20005

WURFEL, SEYMOUR WALTER, educator; b. Denver, Oct. 4, 1907; s. Walter Conrad and Mabel Clair (Seymour) W.; B.A., Pomona U., 1927; LL.B., Harvard, 1930; J.D., Emory U., 1950; m. Violet Elizabeth Mark, July 30, 1932; children—David, Walter. Admitted to Cal. bar, 1930; practiced in San Diego, 1930-40; served from capt. to col., inf. U.S. Army, 1940-60, col. Judge Adv. Gen.'s Corps, 1946-60; prof. law U. N.C., Chapel Hill, 1960. Ford Found grantee, 1963, U.S. Dept. Commerce grantee, 1970-72. Mem. Am., Cal. bar assns., Am. Soc. Internat. Law, Phi Beta Kappa. Author: (with Aycock) Military Law Under the Uniform Code of Military Justice, 1955, Foreign Enterprise in Colombia, Laws and Policies, 1964. Contbr. articles to profl. pubs. Home: 421 Westwood Dr Chapel Hill NC 27514

WURSTER, MARGUERITE RAY SMITH, librarian; b. Ocala, Fla., Sept. 7, 1916; d. William Edward and Inez (Ray) Smith; A.B., U. Fla., 1963; postgrad. U. So. Fla.; m. Hal Crockett Batey, Jr., Feb. 20, 1933 (div. June 1948); children—Hal Smith, Marilyn (Mrs. James Lynn Holeman), Diana Ed (Mrs. David Miller Pettengill); m. Robert Frederick Wurster, June 6, 1965. Library asst., library U. Fla., 1952-58; librarian, div. plant industry Fla. Dept. Agr., Gainsville, 1958-63; asst. to dir. library Fla. Inst. for Continuing U. Studies, Gainesville, 1963-65; asst. dir. Extension Library, U. South Fla., Bay Campus, St. Petersburg, 1965—. Mem. Spl. Libraries Assn. (pres. Fla. chpt. 1970-71), Fla. (chmn. coll. and spl. libraries sect. 1968—), Southeastern Library assns., YWCA, D.A.R., Kappa Delta Pi, Delta Kappa Gamma. Methodist (mem. membership com.). Club: University Women's. Home: 6514 27th Av N St Petersburg FL 33710 Office: U South Fla Bay Campus 845 1st St S St Petersburg FL 33701

WURZ, JOHN ARNOLD, architect; b. Clarksdale, Miss., Feb. 11, 1936; s. Arnold George and Mildred (Whittle) W.; B.S., Ga. Inst. Tech., 1958, B.Arch., 1959; m. Sally Cooper Fortson, Mar. 20, 1958; children—Vaili Elizabeth, Susan Priscilla, John Arnold. Project mgr. Rich's, Inc., Atlanta, 1962-63; project mgr. Heery & Heery Architects & Engrs., Atlanta, 1963-65, asso. architect, 1965-67, partner, 1967—. Dir. Sigma Nu Frat. House Corp. Served as 1st lt. USAF, 1959-62. Registered architect, 17 states. Mem. Atlanta Art Assn., Bldg. Research Inst., Ga. Indsl. Devel. Assn., Ga. Tech. Alumni Assn., A.I.A., Sigma Nu Alumni Assn. Clubs: Cherokee Town and Country, Indian Hills Country. Home: 3723 High Green Dr Marietta GA 30060 Office: 880 W Peachtree St NW Atlanta GA 30309

WYATT, CHARLES HANDFIELD, chem. co. exec.; b. Cin., Feb. 26, 1937; s. Charles Handfield and Margaret (Jones) W.; B.S., Northwestern U., 1959; m. Janet Louise Blair, June 27, 1959; children—Charles, Julia, Lisa. With Carlisle Chem. Works Inc., various locations, 1959-67, salesman, Houston, 1961-66, sales and comml. devel. exec., N.Y.C., 1966-67; sr. tech. sales rep. Hughson Chem. Co., Houston, 1967—. Pres. Wilchester Elementary Sch. P.T.A., Houston, 1970-71; commr. Pee Wee Baseball, 1971. Mem. Nat. Assn. Corrosion Engrs., Houston Coating Soc., Houston Chem. Club, Sabine Coating Soc., So. Rubber Group, Sigma Chi. Republican. Episcopalian. Club: Wilchester. Home: 13410 Queensbury St Houston TX 77024 Office: 2400 W Loop S Houston TX 77027

WYATT, EDWARD AVERY, IV, newspaper editor; b. Petersburg, Va., Mar. 10, 1910; s. Edward Avery and Bessie Sutherland (Spain) W.; A.B., Randolph Macon Coll., 1931; student Harvard, 1939-40; m. Martha V. Seabury, Aug. 31, 1940 (dec. Feb. 1963); children—Edward A. V. Elizabeth. Reporter, News Leader, Richmond, Va., 1930-31; asso. editor, Progress-Index, Petersburg, 1931-39, editor 1940—. Trustee Petersburg Mus. Nieman fellow in journalism, Harvard, 1939-40 Past chmn. Va. State Library Bd.; trustee Mchts. Hope Ch. Restoration Found. Mem. Am. Soc. Newspaper Editors; mem. Phi Beta Kappa, Omicron Delta Kappa, Phi Delta Theta, Soc. Cincinnati. Rotarian. Episcopalian. Author: Along Petersburg Streets, 1943. Co-author: Petersburg's Story, A History, 1960. Contbr. articles on hist. subjects to mags. Editor: Petersburg Imprints, 1786-1876, 1949. Home: 106 S Market St Petersburg VA 23803 Office: The Progress-Index Petersburg VA 23803

WYATT, JOSEPH PAUL, journalist; b. Phila., Oct. 8, 1942; s. Joseph Thomas and Margaret (Duffy) W.; B.A. in Bus. Adminstrn., St. Joseph's Coll., 1964; student U. Ibermericana, Mexico, 1963; m. Martha Villalpando, Aug. 14, 1964; children—Arthur, Theresa Maria. With U.P.I., 1964—, Latin Am. corr., 1965—, now day editor, Mexico City. Mem. Am. Civil Liberties Union. Roman Cath. K.C. Home: Caiz de Oxtopulco 20 Casa 1 Mexico DF 20 Mexico Office: Av Morelos 110 Mexico DF 1 Mexico

WYATT, PHILIP YATEMAN, JR., dentist; b. Charlottesville, Va., Aug. 6, 1907; s. Philip Yateman and Lula (Kersey) W.; student Va. State Coll., 1922-28; D.D.S., Howard U., 1932; m. Minnie Ella Taylor, Oct. 2, 1934; children—Shirley M. (Mrs. Raymond Mundle), Philip Yateman III, Kenneth Mercer. Gen. practice dentistry, Fredericksburg, Va., 1933—, Alexandria, 1957-59; dir. Hazel Hill Apts. Mem. Va. Human Relations Council, 1940—; co-chmn. Fredericksburg Biracial Commn., 1965. Recipient Man of the Year award Omega Phi Psi, 1969; Dentist of the Year award Old Dominion Dental Soc., 1965-69; citation Richmond Civic Council, 1957; certificate of merit Va. Union U., 1957. Mem. Nat. Dental Assn., Old Dominion Dental Soc. (pres. 1954-57, treas. 1957—), Fredericksburg Dental Soc., N.A.A.C.P. (state pres. 1957-58, city pres. 1957—), Va. Bapt. Tng. Union (pres. 1948-58, chmn. bd. dirs. 1958-62), Bapt. Gen. Conv. Va. (sec. bd. dirs. 1946-60), Alpha Phi Alpha. Democrat. Baptist. (chmn. deacon bd. 1940—). Home: 804 Wolfe St Fredericksburg VA 22401 Office: PO Box 393 also 610 Princess Anne St Fredericksburg VA 22401

WYATT, WILLIAM FRANKLIN, JR., apparel co. exec.; b. Burlington, N.C., Dec. 18, 1927; s. William Franklin and Aetna (Walker) W.; B.S., N.C. State U., 1949; m. Peggy Montgomery Von Canon, Oct. 1, 1949; children— Margaret Elizabeth, William Franklin III, John Walker, Kathryn Rebecca. Owner, Beta Hosiery Co., Sanford, N.C., 1942—; with Wyatt Knitting Co., Sanford, 1949—, pres., 1963—. Mem. Sigma Phi Epsilon. Methodist (steward 1949-57). Rotarian (pres. 1964-65), Elk. Clubs: Central Carolina Beagle, Chicora Riders and Saddle (treas. 1971-72), Associate Investors (treas. 1969-70). Home: Route 3 Sanford NC 27330 Office: 1006 Goldsboro Av Sanford NC 27330

WYATT, WILLIAM HENRY, coll. trustee; b. Lorado, Ark., July 26, 1912; s. Stant and Ethel T. (Adams) W.; A.B., Ark. State Coll., 1938; m. Mary Grace Hill, May 29, 1938; children—William Vincent, Ethel Jean, Richard Hill. Chmn. bd. Yarbo Coop. Assn., 1948—; dir. Farmers Soybean Corp., 1952—, Farm Bur. Ins. Co., 1954—. Chmn. Blytheville Bd. Edn., 1963—; mem. Elk Chute Draingage Bd.; pres. Ark. Tb Assn.; pres. Miss. County Tb Assn., 1952-55, YWCA, Blytheville, Ark., 1955-57. Chmn. bd. trustees Ark. State Coll. Mem. Ark. Farm Bur. (dir. 1954—), Methodist (chmn. bd. stewards). Rotarian, (pres. Blytheville 1958-59). Home: 800 W Main St Blytheville AR 72315

WYATT, WILSON WATKINS, lawyer; b. Louisville, Nov. 21, 1905; s. Richard H. and Mary (Watkins) W.; student U. Louisville, 1922-23, LL.B., 1927, LL.D., 1948; LL.D., Knox Coll., 1945; m. Anne Kinnaird Duncan, June 14, 1930; children—Mary Anne, Nancy Kinnaird, Wilson Watkins. Admitted to bar, 1927; began practice at Louisville; with Garnett & Van Winkle, 1927-32; individually, 1933-35; trial atty. City Louisville, 1934; partner law firm Peter, Heyburn, Marshall & Wyatt, 1935-41; mayor Louisville, 1941-45; housing expediter, adminstr. Nat. Housing Agy., 1946; sr. partner law firm Wyatt, Grafton & Sloss, 1947—; lt. gov. Ky., 1959-63; spl. emissary from Pres. U.S. to Pres. Indonesia, 1963. Mem. law faculty Jefferson Sch. Law, 1929-35; dir. Roper Pub. Opinion Research Center, Courier Jour. and Louisville Times Co., WHAS, Inc., Standard Gravure Co., Levy Bros., Inc., Forest Farmers Assn. Spl. rep. Bd. Econ. Warfare, North Africa, 1943; chmn. Louisville Met. Area Def. Council (twice awarded Citation of Merit), 1942-45; pres. Am. Soc. Planning Ofcls., 1943-44, Ky. Municipal League, 1944; pres. Am. Municipal Assn., 1945, Louisville Area Devel. Assn., 1944-45; adv. bd. U.S. Conf. Mayors, 1942-45; v.p. Nat. Municipal League, 1945—; mem. Louisville Sinking Fund Commrs., 1936-38; mem. Louisville Com. on Fgn. Relations (chmn. 1940-41); chmn. Ky. Econ. Devel. Commn., 1960-63. Bd. trustees U. Louisville, 1950-58, chmn. 1951-55; Ky. chmn. Treasury adv. com. U.S. Savs. Bonds Program, 1948-55. First pres. Young Democrats Club, Louisville-Jefferson County; nat. chmn. Jefferson-Jackson Day Dinners, 1948, 49; del.-at-large nat. convs., 1944—; personal campaign mgr. for Stevenson, 1952, mem. Dem. Nat. Com. Ky., 1960-64. Recipient U.S. Treasury distinguished service award. Mem. English Speaking Union U.S. (dir.), Louisville Area C. of C. (pres. 1972), Am., Fed. Communications, Ky. (sec. 1930-34, commr. 1958), Louisville bar assns., Am. Law Inst. Democrat. Presbyn. Rotarian. Clubs: Pendennis, Louisville Country, Harmony Landing Country; Century (N.Y.); Federal City (Washington). Home: 1001 Alta Vista Rd Louisville KY 40205 Office: Marion E Taylor Bldg Louisville KY 40202

WYCHE, HENRY BLANCHARD, banker; b. Hallsboro, N.C., Feb. 23, 1914; s. Joseph Byron and Mary Bailey (Blanchard) W.; B.S., Wake Forest Coll., 1936; postgrad. nat. security forum Air War Coll., 1968, exec. program U. N.C., 1969; m. Georgia Rogers Huntington, June 10, 1939; children—Henry Blanchard, Anne (Mrs. John A. Hinson). Office mgr. agrl. adjustment adminstrn. U.S. Agr. Dept., Whiteville, N.C., 1936-38; with Waccamaw Bank & Trust Co., Whiteville, 1938—, v.p., sr. trust officer, 1960-67, sr. v.p., 1967—; v.p., sec., dir. United Carolina Bancshares Corp., Whiteville, 1970—, Pierce & Co., Hallsboro, N.C., 1958-71, Pierce, Wuche & Co., Hallsboro, 1958-71. Bd. dirs. St. John's Art Gallery, Wilmington, N.C., 1969—, Mgmt. Devel., Inc. U. N.C., 1968—; trustee Southeastern Community Coll., Whiteville, 1965—; regent Southeastern Trust Sch. Campbell Coll., 1970—. Mem. N.C. (dir. 1968-70), Am. camelia socs., N.C. Art Soc., Asso. Artists N.C., Assn. Registered Bank Holding Companies. Democrat. Baptist. Home: 11 Cedar St Hallsboro NC 28442 Office: PO Box 632 Whiteville NC 28472

WYLAND, BEN F., clergyman; b. Harlan, Ia., Mar. 16, 1882; s. Frank and Mary (Griffith) W.; Ph.B., U. Ia., 1905; B.D., Yale, 1908; M.Div., 1971; Litt.D., Edward Waters Coll., 1954; m. Ada D. Beach, Jan. 14, 1909; children—Gordon B., Hugh C., Robert B., Molly G.; m. 2d, Mildred E. Oeschger, May 5, 1955. Ordained to ministry Congl. Ch., 1908; pastor, Worcester, Mass., 1918-20, Lincoln, Neb., 1926-36, Bklyn., 1936-39; radio pastor Sta. KFAB, 1926-36; exchange pastor to Eng., 1933; in charge ch. relations for Herbert Hoover's Campaign, Food for Small Democracies, 1940-41; exec. sec. United Chs. Greater St. Petersburg (Fla.), 1948-56, Fla. Council Racial Cooperation, St. Petersburg, 1956—. Chmn. Com. To Preserve Negro Rights; founder Negro Girls Welfare Home, St. Petersburg, St. Petersburg Helping Hand for Sr. Citizens; chmn. United Negro Coll. Fund. Recipient citation from Maj. Gen. Philip Hayes, 3d Service Command; B'nai B'rith Brotherhood award, St. Petersburg, 1954; recipient Oscar,

Community Chest dr., 1955; citation Met. Council, Inc., 1958; Bethune Cookman Coll., Edward Waters Coll. Mem. Am. Relief Assn. (dir.), Am. Com. Christian Refugees in Bklyn. (exec. sec.), Bklyn. Fedn. Chs., (dir.), Crime Prevention Soc. (dir.), N.Y.C. Assn. Chs. (pres. bd. dirs.), Congl. Ministers (pres.), Americanization Com. (chmn.), Food Commn. (chmn.), Delta Sigma Phi, Alpha Chi Rho. Mason (32 deg., K.T.), Kiwanian. Home: 1898 Shore Dr S St Petersburg FL 33707

WYLY, SAM E., govt. adviser; b. Lake Providence, La., Oct. 4, 1934; s. Charles Joseph and Flora (Evans) W.; B.A., La. Poly. Inst., 1956, Ph.D. (hon.), 1969; M.B.A., U. Mich., 1957; m. Rosemary Acton, May 20, 1960; children—Evan Acton, Laurie Louise, Lisa Ann. Sales rep. Service Bur. Corp., Dallas, 1958-61; area sales mgr. Honeywell Inc., 1961-63; pres., founder Univ. Computing Co., 1963-—, chmn. bd. dirs., 1969-—. Mem. Dallas County Republican Finance Com., 1966-68; Tex. finance chmn. Nixon for Pres. Campaign, 1968; del. Rep. Nat. Conv., 1968; mem. Rep. Nat. Finance Com., 1969-—; mem. Pres.'s Com. on White House Fellows; chmn. Adv. Council for Minority Enterprise, Washington, 1970-—. Served with USAF, 1957-63. Named one of five outstanding young men Tex. Jr. C. of C., 1967, one of ten outstanding young men of Am., U.S. Jr. C. of C., 1968. Mem. Am. Mgmt. Assn., Young Presidents Orgn., C. of C., Phi Kappa Phi, Pi Kappa Delta, Beta Sigma Omicron, Omicron Delta Kappa. Clubs: City of Dallas, Dallas Petroleum. Address: Dept of Commerce 14th St between Constitution Av and E St Washington DC 20230

WYNN, DANIEL W., clergyman, educator; b. Wewoka, Okla., Mar. 19, 1919; s. Phay Willie and Mary (Carter) W.; A.B., Langston U., 1941; postgrad. Eden Theol. Sem., Webster Groves, Mo., 1942-43, D.D., 1959; B.D., Howard U., 1944, A.M., 1945; Ph.D., Boston U., 1954; postgrad. Harvard, 1948-50; spl. student Hebrew U., summer 1963; m. Lillian Robinson, June 4, 1944; children—Marian Danita, Patricia Ann. Ordained to ministry Baptist Ch., 1942; pastor Vt. Av. Jr. Ch., Washington, 1944-45; chaplain, prof. sociology and econs. Ky. State Coll., Frankfort, 1945-46; dean Sch. Religion, Bishop Coll., Marshall, Tex., 1946-53; acting chaplain Tuskegee (Ala.) Inst., 1953-54, chaplain, 1955-65, also prof. philosophy; dean students Langston U., 1954-55; pastor Shiloh Ch., Medford, Mass., 1948-50; asso. dir. dept. ednl. instns. div. higher edn., Bd. Edn., United Methodist Ch., Nashville, 1965-—; ordained elder United Meth. Ch., 1957. mem. Univ. Senate, United Meth. Ch., sec. bd. ministry, registrar Central Ala. Conf. Recipient Distinguished Alumnus award Langston U., 1963. Mem. N.A.A.C.P., Prince Hall Grand, Nat. Assn. Meth. Colls., Am. Assn. Protestant Colls., Am. Council on Edn., Kappa Alpha Psi. Mason (33 deg., Shriner). Author: The N.A.A.C.P. Versus Negro Revolutionary Protest, 1955; The Chaplain Speaks, 1956; Moral Behavior and the Christian Ideal, 1962; Timeless Issues, 1967. Editor: Developing a Sense of Community, 1958; Major Issues in Human Relations, 1961; Nat. Assn. Coll. and U. Chaplains Newsletter, 1960-—. Contbr. articles on religion to Black Ency., various publs. Home: 3926 Drakes Branch Rd Nashville TN 37218 Office: PO Box 871 Bd Edn The United Meth Ch Nashville TN 37202

WYNNE, ELMER STATEN, bacteriologist, educator; b. El Paso, Tex., Oct. 23, 1917; s. P.D. and Mary (Durnell) W.; B.A., U. Tex., 1938, M.A., 1944, Ph.D., 1948; m. Regina Edith Everett, Mar. 4, 1938; children—Edith Jane, Frank Staten. Tutor, U. Tex., Austin, 1939-42, instr., 1946, research asso., 1946-48; asst. prof. U. Okla., 1948-50; research bacteriologist U. Tex., M.D. Anderson Hosp. and Tumor Inst., Houston, 1950-58, asso. prof. Dental Sch., 1958-59; chief microbiology USAF Sch. Aerospace Medicine, Brooks AFB, Tex., 1959-67, sr. microbiologist, 1968-70, ednl. coordinator bioscis. div., 1968-69; asso. prof. St. Philip's Coll., 1970-—. Served with USNR, 1942-46; PTO. Diplomate Am. Bd. Microbiology. Fellow Am. Acad. Microbiology (charter); mem. Am. Assn. U. Profs., Am. Soc. Microbiology, A.A.A.S., Am. Inst. Biol. Scis. Baptist (music dir. 1960-64, 66-67). Contbr. articles to sci. jours. Home: 4826 Hershey Dr San Antonio TX 78220

WYNNE, TODDIE LEE, JR., oil exec.; b. Kaufman, Tex., Nov. 3, 1924; s. Toddie Lee and Imogen (Young) W.; ed. Culver Mil. Acad., Babson Bus. Inst.; m. Martha Jane Smith, July 10, 1948 (dec.); children—Toddie Lee III, Wreno Smith, James Young, Tancy Anne, William Benjamin. With Am. Liberty Oil Co., Dallas, 1948-—, pres., 1962-—; dir. 1st Nat. Bank in Dallas; chmn. bd. New Orleans East, Inc., 1959-—. Chmn. bd. trustees Presbyn. Hosp., 1966-—; dir. Tex. Presbyn. Found., 1966-—, Stillman Coll., 1961-—. Served as 1st lt. inf., AUS, World War II; PTO. Mem. East African White Hunters Profl. Assn., Dallas, Houston petroleum clubs. Presbyn. Club: Idlewild (Dallas). Home: 7037 Turtle Creek Blvd Dallas TX 75205 Office: First National Bank Bldg Dallas TX 75202

YABROFF, ARTHUR, librarian; b. Horicon, Wis., Oct. 17, 1910; s. Benjamin and Rose (Katznelson) Y.; B.A., U. Wis., 1932; B.S. in L.S., Western Res. U., 1937; m. Ethel Walker, June 7, 1941; 1 foster dau., Mary Jane (Mrs. Edward T. Rowe). Auditor, Cook Coffee Co., Cleve., 1932-37; librarian bus. and commerce div. Detroit Pub. Library, 1937-42, bus. dir., 1946-64; chief fiscal services Library Congress, 1964-68, asst. dir. for mgmt. services, 1968-—; mathematician Jam Handy Orgn., Detroit, 1942-43; library bldg. and program cons. Served with USNR, 1943-45. Mem. Mich. Bd. for Libraries, 1951-61, chmn., 1955, 60. Mem. Am. (treas. 1960-64, mem. pub. bd., chmn. com. on program and budget 1970-71), D.C. library assns., Com. 100 Arlington, Va. Home: 2121 Columbia Pike Arlington VA 22204 Office: Library Congress Washington DC 20540

YAGHJIAN, EDMUND, artist, educator; b. Harpoot, Armenia, Feb. 16, 1904; s. Samuel and Sultan (Ajootian) Y.; came to U.S., 1907, naturalized, 1930; B.F.A., R.I. Sch. Design, 1930; postgrad. Art Students League, N.Y.C., 1930-32; m. Dorothy Candy, May 30, 1941; children—Candy, Robin, David, Susy. One man shows Kraushaar Galleries, 1940, Gibbes Art Gallery, 1959, 63, U. Mo., 1945, U. S.C., 1948, Columbia Art Mus., 1945, Dorsey Galleries, 1952, Telfair Acad., 1953, Chafee Mus., 1962, 63, Madison Gallery, 1962, Augusta Mus., 1959, Mint Mus., 1966, Galerie Internationale, 1967, Galerie Fontainebleau, 1965, Ligoa Duncan Gallery, 1966, AGBU Gellery, 1968, Florence Mus., 1969, Carson McKenna Galleries, 1969, Vt. Art Center, 1968, also others exhibited in group shows various mus. U.S.; represented in permanent collections Duke, N.Y. Pub. Library, N.Y. U., High Mus., Atlanta, Montpelier, Birmingham, West Point museums; numerous pvt. collections; head art dept. Great Neck Prep. Sch., 1934-36; instr. Art Students League N.Y., 1938-42; prof. art Edgewood Park Jr. Coll., 1941-44; guest instr. painting U. Mo., 1944-45; head fine arts dept. U. S.C., 1945-66; artist-in-residence U. S.C., 1966-—. Pres., Columbia Artists Guild, 1948-50, Guild S.C. Artists, 1950-51, 59-60. Recipient 1st prizes S.C. Artists, 1946, 47, 61, 63, Purchase award S.C. Artists, 1953, award Merit Guild S.C. Artists, 1954, 62, Purchase prizes, 1955, 58, 62, 63; Arts and Sci. award Univ. S.C., 1967. Mem. Southeastern Coll. Art Assn. (past pres.), Coll. Art Assn., Am. Fedn. Arts, Am. Assn. U. Profs. Home: 1510 Adger Rd Columbia SC 29205

YAMBRUSIC, EDWARD SLAVKO, lawyer; b. Conway, Pa., Mar. 9, 1933; s. Michael Misko and Sylvia Slavica (Yambrusic) Y.; B.A., Duquesne U., 1957; postgrad. Georgetown U., 1959-61; J.D., U. Balt., 1966; postgrad. Cath. U. Am., 1966-—; certificate The Hague Acad. Internat. Law, 1967, 69. Admitted to U.S. Customs Ct., 1970, Md. bar, 1969; practiced before U.S. Immigration and Naturalization Service, N.Y.C., also Washington, 1966-—; copyright atty. Library Congress, U.S. Copyright Office, Washington, 1960-—. Served to capt. AUS, 1957-59. Mem. Internat. Law Assn., Am. Bar Assn., Am. Soc. Internat. Law, Internat. Fiscal Assn., UN Assn., Center for Study Democratic Instns., Croatian Acad. Am., Croatian Cath. Union, Md. Bar Assn., Assn. Attenders Alumni Hague Acad. Internat. Law, Duquesne U. Tamburitzans Alumni Assn., Pi Gamma Mu. Home: 4720 Massachusetts Av NW Washington DC 20016 Office: US Copyright Office Library Congress Washington DC 20540

YANCEY, ASA GREENWOOD, physician; b. Atlanta, Aug. 19, 1916; s. Arthur H. and Daisy L. (Sherard) Y.; B.S., Morehouse Coll., 1937; U. Mich., 1941;; m. Carolyn E. Dunbar, Dec. 28, 1944; children—Arthur H. II, Carolyn L., Caren L., Asa Greenwood. Intern, City Hosp., Cleve. 1941-42; resident Freedmens Hosp., Washington, 1942-45, U.S. Marine Hosp., Boston, 1945; practice medicine specializing in surgery, Atlanta, 1958-—; asso. dean Emory U. Sch. Medicine; mem. staff Hughes Spalding, St. Joseph, Ga. Bapt. hosps.; med. dir. Grady Meml. Hosp.; instr. surgery Meharry Med. Coll., 1946-48; chief of surgery VA Hosp., Tuskegee, Ala., 1948-58; asst. prof. surgery Emory U., 1968-—. Mem. Atlanta Bd. Edn., 1968-—. Trustee Ga. chpt. Am. Cancer Soc. Served to 1st Lt. M.C., AUS, 1942. Diplomate Am. Bd. Surgery. Fellow A.C.S.; mem. Nat. Med. Assn. (trustee 1960-66, editorial bd. jour. 1964-—). Baptist. Contbr. articles to profl. jours. Home: 2845 Engle Rd NW Atlanta GA 30318 Office: Grady Meml Hosp Atlanta GA 30303

YANCEY, CLAUD WALTER, educator; b. Hackett, Ark., Aug. 17, 1916; s. Henry Lee and Johanna (Gist) Y.; student Ark. Poly. Coll., 1935-37; B.S., U. Ark., 1941, M.B.A., 1951; m. Cora Lucille Risley, Jan. 31, 1941; children—Claud Walter, Paul Stanley, Jack Weldon, Linda Lucille. Accounting instr. Mansfield (Ark.) High Sch., 1946-51, 52-54; instr. bus., dept. chmn. Westark Jr. Coll. (formerly Ft. Smith Jr. Coll.), 1954-—. Served with USNR, 1942-45. Mem. Nat., Am. accounting assns., Am. Econ. Assn. Home: Route 1 Mansfield AR 72944 Office: Grand Av and Waldron Rd Fort Smith AR 72944

YANCEY, EDWIN LOVELL, agrl. agt.; b. Wedowee, Ala., Nov. 18, 1934; s. James David and Eula Pearl (Huey) Y.; B.S., N.C. State U., 1956, M. Adult Edn. (Kellogg fellow), 1969; m. Betty Anne Williford, Nov. 16, 1956; children—Betty Lael, Elaine Huey, Edwin Lovell. Asst. agrl. extension agt. Johntson County, Smithfield, N.C., 1956-61; service and sales mgr. Benson Feed Mills (N.C.), 1961-63; agrl. extension agt., Smithfield, 1963-69; county extension chmn. Pitt County, Greenville, N.C., 1969-—. Rec. sec. Pitt County Planning Bd., 1971-—; adviser to bd. dirs. Coastal Plain Devel. Assn., 1969-—; chmn. Pitt County Rural Devel. Panel, 1970-—. Mem. N.C. Assn. County Agrl. Agts. (chmn. East Central dist.), Epsilon Sigma Phi. Methodist. Moose, Kiwanian. Home: 107 Queen Anne's Rd Greenville NC 27834 Office: PO Box 1427 Greenville NC 27834

YANCEY, ROBERT EARL, oil refinery exec.; b. Cleve., July 15, 1921; s. George Washington II and Mary (Gutzwiller) Y.; B.E., Marshall U., 1943; m. Mary Estelline Tackett, July 25, 1941; children—Robert Earl, Susan Carol. With Ashland Oil Inc. (Ky.), 1943-—, process engr., project engr., operating supt., coordinator sales and refining, gen. supt. refineries, 1943-56, v.p. in charge mfg., 1956-59, became adminstrv. v.p., 1959, sr. v.p., 1965-67, chief operating officer, 1967-72, pres. Ashland Chem. Co., 1967-69, chief operating officer, pres. Ashland Petroleum Co., 1969-72, pres. parent co. Ashland Oil, Inc., 1972-—. Mem. Nat. Petroleum Assn. (dir.), Am. Petroleum Inst., Ky. Soc. Profl. Engrs. Home: 102 Lycan Dr Bellefonte Ashland KY 41101 Office: 1409 Winchester Av Ashland KY 41101

YANDLE, THOMAS BRUCE, JR., educator; b. Lyons, Ga., Aug. 12, 1933; s. Thomas Bruce and Mollye Lomita (Thompson) Y.; student Young Harris Coll., 1951-52; A.B., Mercer U., 1955; M.B.A., Ga. State U., 1968, Ph.D., 1970; m. Dorothy King Smith, Aug. 28, 1954; children— Kathryn, Thomas Bruce III, Eric. Accountant, sales mgr. Bearings & Drives, Inc., Macon, Ga., 1952-59, exec. v.p., Atlanta, 1960-67; asst. prof. econs. Clemson (S.C.) U., 1969-—, head dept. econs., 1972-—. Served to 2d lt. AUS, 1956-57. Mem. Assn. Bearing Specialists (dir. 1966-67), Pub. Choice Soc., Am., So. econ. assns., Omicron Delta Epsilon. Methodist (chmn. ofcl. bd. 1967-69). Home: 323 Tamassee Dr Clemson SC 29631

YANDRE, ANN B. MILLER (MRS. E. W. YANDRE), lawyer; b. Chattanooga, Dec. 22, 1897; d. Jeremiah T. and Rachel E. (Callahan) Miller; student Tampa U., Wash. Coll. Law, Am. Inst. Banking, 1938-48; m. Richard D. Morales, June 29, 1921 (dec. 1931); m. 2d, Edward W. Yandre, Mar. 4, 1954 (dec. Sept. 1967). Admitted to Fla. bar, 1946; asso. with husband in gen. practice law, Tampa, Fla., 1921-31; asso. with firm Lewis H. Hill, Jr. & Robert D. Hill, attys., Tampa, 1931-37; legal sec., office (mgr.) trust dept. Exchange Nat. Bank Tampa (Fla.), 1938-48; pvt. practice law, Tampa, 1948-—, Orlando, Fla., 1954-70. Mem. Am., Fla., Tampa, Hillsborough and Orange Counties bar assns., Estate Planning Council Tampa (treas.), Central Fla. Estate Planning Council, Nat. (past state dir.; S.E. regional dir.), Fla. (past sec., past dir., (past pres.), assns. women lawyers, Am. Inst. Banking (pres. Tampa chpt. 1946-—), U.S. Council Bus. and Financial Cons. (asso. counsel), Phi Delta Delta. Presbyn. Clubs: Tampa (Fla.) Yacht & Country; Orlando (Fla.) Country. Address: 2426 Sunset Dr Tampa FL 33609

YANEZ, AGUSTIN, author; b. Guadalajara, Jalisco, Mexico, May 4, 1904; Ph.D., Nat. U. Mexico; m. Olivia Ranurer, Dec. 26, 1938. Dir. pub. edn., rector Nayarit Inst., 1930-31; tchr. Nat. Prep. Sch., Mexico, Nat. U. Mexico, Coll. of Mexico; dir. radio dept. Ministry of Pub. Edn., 1932-34; head dept. libraries and econ. archives Mexican Treasury, 1935-45, coordinator humanities Nat. U. Mexico, 1945. Gov., State of Jalisco, 1953-59. Decorated officer Legion of Honor (France). Mem. Mexican Acad. Lit., El Colegio Nacional. Author: Espejismo de Juchitan, 1940; Flor de Juegos antiquos, 1942, 2d edit., 1958; Genio y figuras de Gualalajara, 1942; Fray Bartolome de las Casas, 1942, 2d edit., 1949; Pasion y convalescencia, 1943; Archipielago de majueres, 1943; El contenido social de la literature inberoamericana, 1944; Esta es mala suerte, 1945; Alfonso Gutierrez Hermosillo y algunos amigos, 1945; El clima espiritual de Jalisco, 1945; Yahualica, 1946; Al Filo del Agua, 1947, 2d edit., 1955; Don Justo Sierra, su vida, sus ideas y su obra, 1950; La Creacion, 1959; Ojerosa y Pintada, 1960; La tierra prodiga, 1960. Address: Mantines de Castro 16 Mexico City DF 18 Mexico

YANG, DAVID WEI-HSEIN, educator; b. Kwei-yang City, Kwei-chow, China, Sept. 13, 1938; s. Shou-chen and Huey-ying (Huang) Y.; LL.B., Nat. Cheng-chi U., 1961; M.A., Atlanta U., 1967; m. Teresa Rong-hwa Tung, Jan. 28, 1967; children—Phoebe Li-huey, Priscilla Li-ning. Came to U.S., 1965. Tchr., Er-chung Middle Sch., Hsin-chu, Taiwan, Republic of China, 1963-65; instr. Ark. A.M. and N. Coll., Pine Bluff, 1967-68, asst. prof., 1968-71, asso. prof. dept. bus. and econs., 1971-—. Exec. dir. Small Bus. Assistance Center, 1971; founder, pres. United Realty Co., 1972-—. Served with Chinese Army, 1961-63. Mem. Nat. Bus. League (local v.p.), U.S. Jr. C. of C. Baptist.

YARBOROUGH, DON, lawyer; b., 1925; B.A., LL.B., U. Tex. Admitted to bar, 1950; practice law, Houston.

YARBOROUGH, KEMP PLUMMER, educator; b. Louisburg, N.C., Apr. 29, 1912; s. William Henry and Eloise (Hill) Y.; B.A., U. N.C., 1933; postgrad. law Wake Forest Coll., 1935-36; M.A., U. S.C., 1950; Ph.D., Columbia, 1963; m. Brigitte Margarete Freiin Roeder von Diersburg, Nov. 15, 1947; children—Victoria (Mrs. Kennedy Poyser), William Andrew, Charles Christopher; Admitted to N.C. bar, 1936; practiced law; Louisburg, N.C.; 1936-41; codification asst. N.C. Dept. Justice, Raleigh, 1941-42; teaching asst. U.S.C., 1948-51; head social studies dept. St. Marys Coll., St. Marys City, Md., 1954-65, dean faculty, 1957-65; asso. prof. Tex. Womans U., Denton, 1965-68, prof. history, 1968-—, chmn. dept. history and govt., 1969-—. Served with AUS, 1942-48, 51-53, maj. Res. ret. Decorated Bronze Star medal. Mem. Am. Assn. U. Profs., Am. Hist. Assn., Acad. Polit. Sci., Phi Beta Kappa; Phi Alpha Theta. Episcopalian.Home: 2522 Emerson Lane Denton Tx 76201

YARBOROUGH, RALPH WEBSTER, lawyer, former U.S. senator; b. Chandler, Tex., June 8, 1903; s. Charles Richard and Nannie Jane (Spear) Y.; student U.S. Mil. Acad., 1919-20, Sam Houston State Tchrs. Coll., 1921; LL.B. with highest honors, U. Tex., 1927; L.H.D., Lincoln (Ill.) Coll., 1965; LL.D., St. Edwards U., 1971; hon. fellow Postgrad. Center Mental Health, N.Y.C., 1965; m. Opal Catherine Warren, June 30, 1928; 1 son, Richard Warren. Admitted to Tex. bar, 1927; engaged in private practice of law, El Paso, 1927-31; assn. atty. gen. Tex., 1931-34; lectr. real property law U. Tex., 1935; dir. Lower Colorado River Authority, 1935; judge 53d Jud. Dist. of Tex., 1936-40; pvt. practice law, Austin, 1941-57, 70-—; U.S. Senator from Tex., 1957-70, delegate Inter-parliamentary Union Confs. including at Palma de Mallorca, Spain, 1967, Lima Peru, 1968, Vienna, Austria, Delhi, India, 1969; mem. com. on appropriations, chmn. senate com. on labor and pub. welfare, 1969-70. Past mem. State Bd. Law Examiners. Former mem. Abraham Lincoln Sesquicentennial Commn.; past mem. exec. bd. National Civil War Centennial Commn.; del. to Interparliamentary Union Conf., 1962, 65, 66. Democratic candidate for gov. of Tex., 1952, 54, 56; del. Dem. Nat. Conv., 1964. Served as lt. col., 97th Inf. Div., AUS, 1943-46. Mem. Am., Travis County (past pres.), El Paso bar assns., State Bar Tex. (past dir.), Am. Law Inst., V.F.W., Am. Legion, Order of Coif, Phi Delta Phi, Acacia. Democrat. Baptist. Mason (Shriner). Contbr. Lincoln for the Ages, 1964; Texas Avenue at Main Street, 1964; Frank Dobie: Man and Friend, 1967; Three Men in Texas, 1967; The Public Lands of Texas: 1519-1970, 1972. Home: 2527 Jarratt Av Austin TX 78703 Office: 721 Brown Bldg Austin TX 78701

YARBROUGH, CLEO CLIFFORD, contractor, realtor, union ofcl.; b. Ada, Ark., Feb. 1, 1920; s. Herman George and Bertie (Harris) Y.; B.A., Hendrix Coll., 1948; M.A., La. State U., 1951; m. Julia Barber, Apr. 15, 1944 (dec. Dec. 1970); children—George Clifford, Laura Ellen. Grad. teaching fellow La. State U., 1948-51; cost analyst Esso Standard Oil Co., Baton Rouge, 1951-58; gen. mgr. Allen-Wallace Constrn. Co., 1958-61; exec. v.p., gen. mgr. Myer Devel. Corp., Baton Rouge, 1961-—; pres. Local 538 Am. Fedn. Musicians, 1960-—; v.p., mgr. Myer-Yarbrough Realty, Inc., 1966-—; ins. agt., 1958-—. Mem. Baton Rouge Bd. Realtors, 1966-—. Coordinator, Baton Rouge Civic Symphony Youth Concerts, 1960-—. Served with AUS, 1940-45. Decorated Bronze Star medal. Mem. Nat. Assn. Homebuilders, Baton Rouge Bd. Realtors; Baton Rouge C. of C., Blue Key, Alpha Chi, Phi Kappa Phi, Beta Gamma Sigma, Phi Lambda Chi, Phi Mu Alpha Sinfonia. Democrat. Methodist. Club: Sherwood Forest Country (Baton Rouge). Author: The Underconsumptionists Critique of Classical Economics, 1951. Composer: Alpha Phi Epsilon Nat. Sorority Song. 1939. Home: 2335 Baywood Av Baton Rouge LA 70808 Office: 7417 Exchange Pl Baton Rouge LA 70806

YARBROUGH, WILLIAM MAX, JR., physician; b. Shreveport, La., Aug. 26, 1937; s. William Max and Hazel (Hubley) Y.; B.S., La. State U., 1960, M.D., 1963; m. Nancy LeRouge, Dec. 27, 1961; children—William Max III, Paul Allen, Janet Anne, Sidney Thomas. Intern, U.S. Naval Hosp., Charleston, S.C., 1963-64; resident neurosurgery La. State U., Charity Hosp., 1967-68, resident in anesthesiology, 1968-70; practice medicine specializing in anesthesiology, New Orleans, 1968-—; asso. dir. dept. anesthesiology Charity Hosp., New Orleans, 1968-—; instr. anesthesiology dept. surgery La. State U. Sch. Medicine, New Orleans, 1971-72, instr. dept. oral surgery, 1971-72. Served with M.C., USNR, 1963-67. Mem. Internat., Am., La. socs. anesthesiologists, A.M.A., Am. Acad. Neurology, La., Orleans Parish med. socs. Club: Vista Shores Country (New Orleans). Home: 6600 Beauregard Av New Orleans LA 70124 Office: Charity Hosp 1532 Tulane Av New Orleans LA 70120

YARD, RIX NELSON, athletic dir.; b. Lakewood, N.J., July 1, 1917; s. George Rix and Lena (Nelson) Y.; B.S., U. Pa., 1941, M.S., 1946, Ed.D., 1956; m. Adra Gehrett, Sept. 12, 1941; children—Rix Nelson, Constance Suzanne. Asst. coach, Denison U., 1946-49, dir. athletics, chmn. dept. phys. edn., 1953-63; asst. coach U. Pa., 1949-53; dir. athletics Tulane U., New Orleans, 1963-—, prof. phys. edn., 1969-—. Bd. dirs. New Orleans Red Cross. Served with USNR, 1941-46; capt. Res. Mem. Nat. Assn. Collegiate Dirs. Athletics (exec. com.), Navy League (dir.), New Orleans Nat. Football Hall of Fame (dir.), A.A.H.P.E.R., Sigma Alpha Epsilon. Republican. Presbyn. Club: Quarterback of New Orleans (dir.), Colonial Country (v.p.). Home: 4820 Page St Metairie LA 70003 Office: Tulane U New Orleans LA 70118

YARDLEY, JONATHAN, journalist; b. Pitts., Oct. 27, 1939; s. William Woolsey and Helen (Gregory) Y.; A.B., U. N.C., 1961; m. Rosemary Roberts, June 14, 1961; children—James Barrett, William Woolsey. Asst. to James Reston, New York Times, Washington, 1961-62; writer, News of Week in Review, New York Times, N.Y.C., 1962-64; editorial writer and book editor Greensboro (N.C.) Daily News, 1964-—. Episcopalian. Home: 223 Elmwood Dr Greensboro NC 27408 Office: Greensboro Daily News Greensboro NC 27420

YARRUT, LOUIS HANO, judge; b. New Orleans, June 15, 1894; s. Abraham and Tillie (Loeb) Yarutzky; LL.B., Tulane U., 1916; m. Eva Levenberg, June 28, 1916; 1 dau., Elise (Mrs. Ralph H. Fishman). Judge, Ct. of Appeals, New Orleans, 1960-—. Dir. Bank of New Orleans, Central Savs. & Loan Assn., United Theatres, Inc. Mem. Orleans Parish Democratic Exec. Com., 1917. Pres., Jewish Community Center; bd. regents Loyla U., Jewish Childrens Home. Served with USCGR, 1919. Mem. Am., New Orleans (past pres.) bar assn., Blue Key, Phi Delta Phi. Jewish religion (trustee synagogue). Home: 293 Audubon Blvd New Orleans LA 70118 Office: 421 Loyola Av New Orleans LA 70112

YATES, CHARLES ROBERT, dentist; b. Wedowe, Ala., Mar. 25, 1937; s. Thomas T. and Pauline (Cofield) Y.; B.S., U. Ala., 1961, D.M.D., 1966; m. Delois Marlene Horton, Sept. 21, 1956; children—Stacy Ann, Charles Robert, Dustin Blake. Practice dentistry, Bessemer, Ala., 1966-—. Treas. Delta Dental Plans of Ala. Pres. Bessemer Leased Housing Authority, 1971-72. Chmn. adv. com.

Park and Recreation Bd., 1971-72. Sec. bd. dirs. YMCA, 1969-72; bd. dirs. Salvation Army; trustee Troy State U., 1969-70. Served with USAF, 1961-62. Mem. Am.; Ala. dental assns.; Birmingham Dist. Dental Soc., Jr. C of C. (v.p. 1967), Omicron Delta Kappa, Psi Omega (v.p. 1965-66). Baptist (deacon). Lion (pres. 1971-72). Home: 716 Millgray Lane Bessemer AL 35020 Office: 802 Memorial Dr Bessemer AL 35020

YATES, DONALD PITT, supt. schs.; b. Cross Plains, Tenn., Jan. 3, 1929; s. William Herman and Azzie Lee (Pitt) Y.; diploma, Martin Coll., 1949; B.S., U. Chattanooga, 1951; M.A., George Peabody Coll., 1952, Ed.S., 1958; Ed.D., U. Tenn., 1968; m. Elsie Arnold, Jan. 1, 1953; 1 dau., Donna Elaine. Tchr., coach, Harriman, Tenn., 1954-56; elementary sch. prin., Rockwood, Tenn., 1956-61, supt. schs., 1961-66; cons. sch. planning lab. U. Tenn., 1966-68; supt. schs., Cleveland, Tenn., 1968—; Served with AUS, 1952-54. Mem. Phi Delta Kappa. Methodist. Lion. Home: 3722 Hillside Dr NE Cleveland TN 37311 Office: 190 Church St Cleveland TN 37311

YATES, EDITH OLIVE COE, club woman; b. McPherson, Kan., Dec. 31, 1890; d. James Buchanan and Christine Matilda (Aelmore) Coe; tchrs. certificate U. Tex., 1909; m. Calder Emmet Yates, Apr. 28, 1917; 1 dau., Mildred (Mrs. Herbert Aden Plummer). Auditor 4th dist. Tex. Fedn. Music Clubs, 1946; pres. Dept. Club, Port Arthur, Tex., 1940-41, Symphony Club, 1929-30, 44-45, Griffing Park Garden Club, 1954-55, Country Club Aux., 1941-42, Past Presidents of Symphony Club; del. to 68th Continental Congress of D.A.R., Washington, 1959. Recipient with Dau. of Outstanding Club Family award Tex. Fedn. Women's Clubs, 1958. Mem. Tex. Hist. Assn., Tex. Fedn. Women's Clubs (dist. parliamentarian 1962-64). Travel in U.S., Europe, Can., Mex., Guatemala. Home: 4200 Griffing Dr Port Arthur TX 77640

YATES, OSCAR WALLACE, JR., county govt. ofcl.; b. Roanoke, Va., Feb. 15, 1931; s. Oscar Wallace and Irene (Frier) Y.; B.S., Va. Poly. Inst., 1953, M.S., 1958; m. Rosa Joan Mitchell, May 31, 1953; children— Deborah Joan, Linda Sue, Jane Lee. Sales engr. Wallace & Tiernan, Inc., Roanoke, Va., 1956-57; civil engr. Wiley & Wilson, Lynchburg, Va., 1957-61; dir. pub. works Prince William County, Manassas, Va., 1961—. Mem. regional san. adv. bd. Washington Met. Council of Govts., 1961—. Served as commd. officer with AUS, 1954-56. Profl. engr., Va., Md., Ky., W. Va., Tenn., D.C. Mem. Va., Am. socs. profl. engrs., Am. Pub. Works Assn., Bldg. Ofcls. Conf. Am., Am. Soc. C.E., Inst. for Municipal Engrs. Baptist. Lion. Home: 9907 Greenview Lane Manassas VA 22110 Office: 9258 Lee Av Manassas VA 22110

YATES, SCOTT TUCKER, dept. store exec.; b. Asheboro, N.C., Feb. 5, 1937; s. Frank Ogburn and Sue Ragland (Tucker) Y.; grad. Woodberry Forest Sch., 1955; A.B., U. N.C., 1959; m. Virginia Alexander Shuford, Feb. 3, 1962; children—Virginia Ogburn, Sue Alexander, Scott Tucker, William Shuford. With Belk Yates Co., Asheboro, 1960—, v.p., gen. mgr., 1968—; also dir.; dir. Wachovia Bank & Trust Co., Asheboro, Greyco, Inc., Asheboro. Bd. dirs. Randolph Hosp., Inc., Asheboro, Hope Harbor, Greensboro, N.C. Served with AUS, 19——. Mem. Asheboro C. of C., Full Gospel Businessmen's Fellowship Internat. (pres. Piedmont chpt. 1966—). Alpha Tau Omega. Episcopalian.‡

YEAGER, ARTHUR JOSEPH, coop. assn. exec.; b. Kurten, Tex., May 8, 1908; s. Joe Charlie and Lena (Herzog) Y.; grad. high sch.; m. Johanna Kehlenbrink, Nov. 28, 1935; children—Grace (Mrs. Olley C. Ashley), Elsie (Mrs. Glenn Dressen), Ruth (Mrs. Harry Bostic), Eldon. Cotton gin operator Opersteny Bros. Gin, Kurten, 1930-41, Ward Moring Gin, Brazos County, Tex., 1941-43; gen. mgr. Producer Coop. Assn., Bryan, Tex., 1943—. Mem. adv. bd. Houston Bank for Coops., 1967-70, adv. bd. Farmland Industries, 1966-72, bd. dirs., 1971—. Rural chmn. Brazos County A.R.C., 1952-54. Mem. Brazos County Sch. Bd., 1955—, v.p., 1971. Named Hon. State Farmer Bryan Future Farmers Am., 1961; recipient 4-H award, 1962. Mem. Bryan Young Farmers (life), Bryan C. of C. (chmn. agrl. com. 1957). Tex. Fedn. Coops. (pres. 1971-72). Tex. Feed Control Service (mem. adv. com. 1965-72). Mem. United Ch. of Christ (pres. ch. council 1955-57). Mason (32 deg.). Home: Route 2 Box 143 Bryan TX 77801 Office: PO Box 1108 Bryan TX 77801

YEAGER, KENNETT WILLIAM, govt. ofcl.; b. Pottstown, Pa., Oct. 16, 1917; s. William A. and Edna Mae (Krout) Y.; B.A., U. Pitts., 1938, M.A., 1940, Ph.D., 1949; student U. Pa., 1941-42, U. Wis., summer 1939; m. Margaret L. Oliphant, Sept. 11, 1948; children—Barbara Louise, Margaret Allison. Instr., polit. sci. and econs. Chatham Coll., Pitts., 1942-43; instr. soc. Kent State U., Ohio, 1946-49; asst. prof. sociology George Washington U., Washington, 1949-51; air research specialist Air Force Intelligence Center, Washington, 1951-63; intelligence operations specialist Def. Intelligence Agy., Washington, 1963—. Lectr. sociology U. Md., Am. U. Served with AUS, 1943-46. Mem. Am., Eastern, D.C. sociol. assns., Am. Acad. Polit. and Social Sci. Home: 1104 N Rochester St Arlington VA 22205 Office: Defense Intelligence Agy Washington DC 20301

YEAGER, TILFORD STEPHEN, hosp. adminstr.; b. Cullman, Ala., Jan. 11, 1919; s. Robert Edward and Mamie Lee (Reese) Y.; ed. U.S. Air U., U. Md. Overseas Br.; m. Anna Mae Lilley, Jan. 9, 1942; children— Harold Stephen, Donald Reese, Constance Gary Laney. Joined USAF as pvt., 1938, advanced through grades to capt., 1960; stationed USAF Hosp., Eglin AFB, Fla., USAF Hosp., Nashville, USAF Hosp., Harlingen AFB, Tex., USAF Dispensary, Kelly AFB, Tex., Kadena AFB, Okinawa, USAF Hosp., Orlando AFB (Fla.), med. materiel specialist Hdqrs. USAF, Europe; ret., 1960; adminstrv. asst. William Booth Meml. Hosp., 1961-64; asst. adminstr. Normandy Osteo. Hosp., 1964-67; adminstr. Heller Meml. Hosp., 1967-68, Highlands Gen. Hosp., Sebring, Fla., 1969—. Chmn. county chpt. A.R.C., 1970. Decorated Bronze Star medal. Mem. Am. Acad. Med. Adminstrs., Am., Fla., Ohio hosp assns. Baptist (deacon 1958—). Kiwanian. Home: 1105 Pasadent Av Sebring FL 33870 Office: 3600 Highlands Av Sebring FL 33870

YEARY, GLENN HILLIS, physician; b. Elmore City, Okla., Sept. 29, 1905; s. Edwin Hannibal and Ruth Alice (McCandlis) Y.; B.S., Okla. U., 1927, M.D., 1929; m. Mary Bell Duval, May 9, 1936; 1 dau., Mary Glenn (Mrs. Samuel C. Goldman). Intern, Kansas City (Mo.) Gen. Hosp., 1929-30; gen. practice medicine, Arma, Kan., 1930-33, Newkirk, Okla., 1933—; mem. staff Ponca City (Okla.) Hosp., 1933—. Mem. A.M.A., Okla. Med. Assn., Kay-Noble Med. Soc., Phi Beta Pi. Home: 704 W 9th St Newkirk OK 74647 Office: 109 S Maple St Newkirk OK 74647

YEH, WALTER HUAL-TEH, educator, composer; b. Shanghai, China, Jan. 7, 1911; s. Ziang Tsung and Pei-Yu (Huang) Y.; came to U.S., 1944, naturalized, 1955; A.B., St. John's U. (China), 1933; grad. summa cum laude Nat. Conservatory of Music (China), 1935; M.A. and Mus. M., Eastman Sch. Music, U. Rochester, 1945; A.M., Harvard, 1948, researcher, 1951-54; Ph.D., U. Rochester, 1949; m. Moong Yue, Aug. 8, 1942; children—Peter Wen-chun, Arthur Cho-ch[illegible]. Prof. flute Nat. Conservatory of Music, China, 1940-44; prof. music, chmn. joint music dept. Allen U., and Benedict Coll., Columbia, S.C., 1954—, chmn. humanities div. Allen U., 1957-60, 63—, chmn. div. fine arts and drama Benedict Coll., 1968-71, 72—. Fellow Internat. Inst. Arts and Letters. Rotarian. Composer: Concerto Grosso in F for Oboe, String Quartet and Harp with String Orchestra, 1944; Symphony in D, 1944; Chinese Suite, 1945; Chinese Symphony, 1948; (madrigal) Come Away, Come Away, Death, 1957; The Cuckoo Chorus, 1958; Hymn for Peace, 1960; And Ruth Said: "Intreat Me Not to Leave Thee," 1962; The Solitary Reaper, 1964; She Never Told Her Love, 1965; This Glorious Christmas Night, 1967; Gloria Patri and Kyrie, 1968; The Pattering Rain, 1968; The Lord's Prayer, 1969; We Shall Overcome, 1970; A Tombstone Epitaph, 1971; Alleuia, May Peace Be on Earth, 1972; Farewell for Ever, 1972; composer orchestral and choral works, other compositions. Home: 710 Heidt St Columbia SC 29205

YEILDING, FRANK BROOKS, JR., savs. and loan co. exec.; b. Birmingham, Ala., Mar. 22, 1904; s. Francis B. and Margana (Bland) Y.; A.B., Birmingham So. Coll., 1925; m. Augusta Gage Smith, Nov. 18, 1925; children— Frank Brooks III, Augusta Gage (Mrs. C. Beaty Hanna). Pres., dir. Jefferson Fed. Savs. & Loan Assn., 1946—; pres. Yeilding Realty Co., 1948—; chmn. bd. Jackson Ins. Agy.; v.p., dir. Internat. Realty Co., Yeilding Bros. Holding Co., sec.-treas. Motel Birmingham, Inc.; dir. Jackson Co., Yeilding's Dept. Store, Perfection Bedding Co., Investors Mortgage Ins. Co. Past trustee Savs. and Loan Found. Mem. Ala. Savs. and Loan League (past pres.), U.S. Savs. and Loan League (pres., past v.p.; past pres. Southeastern group conf.), C. of C. (past dir.), Sigma Alpha Epsilon, Omicron Delta Kappa. Methodist (trustee, past chmn. bd. stewards). Clubs: Birmingham Country, Kiwanis (past pres.), Executives (past pres.) (Birmingham); The Club, Downtown. Home: 3015 Brookwood Rd Birmingham AL 35223 Office: 215 N 21st St Birmingham AL 35203

YELLOTT, KATHLEEN SIGHTLER, business exec.; b. Birmingham, Ala., Feb. 24, 1905; d. Joseph Edward and Ida Lou (Hutchins) Sightler; student Ala. pub. schs.; m. Wendell W. Smith, Dec. 10, 1922 (dec. Nov. 1928); 1 son, Kenneth H.; m. Charles Lewis, Dec., 12, 1929 (div. Feb. 1938); children—John M., James A.; m. Oscar Yellott, July 1, 1939; 1 adopted son, Phillip Allen. Owner nursing home, Birmingham, 1922, Beaumont, Tex., 1933—. Legislative del. Tex. nursing homes, Washington, 1953-56. Mem. Pvt. Hosps. and Clinics, Tex. Hosp. Assn. Home: Route 3 Box 566 Silsbee TX 77656

YELTON, PARIS LELAND, ret. oil distbr., farm implement dealer; b. nr. Shelby, N.C., Jan. 18, 1899; s. William Francis and Rachel Merinda (White) Y.; grad. high sch.; m. Donnis Glaire Gold, June 19, 1935; children—Robert William, Don Leland. Engaged in farming, cotton ginning, Shelby, until 1933; an organizer Lutz-Yelton Oil Co., Shelby, 1933; former exec. Lutz-Yelton Tractor & Truck Co., Lutz-Yelton Transport Co., Auto Inn, Shelby Investment Co., Shelby Oil Co., Lutz-Yelton Coal Co., L-Y Heating & Air Conditioning Co. Mem. State Adv. Com. on Agrl. Tech. Edn., 1960-61; pres. P.T.A., 1953-54; Cleveland County chmn. United Fund, 1947-48; local pres. Heart Assn., 1960-61; gen. chmn. devel. program Gardner-Webb Coll., 1959-60. Mem., vice-chmn. Shelby Sch. Bd., 1955-65. Bd. dirs., pres. Cleveland Meml. Hosp., 1953-54; bd. dirs. Shelby Rescue Squad; bd. advisers Gardner-Webb Coll. Recipient Bronze Plaque, Gardner-Webb Coll., 1960, Certificate of Appreciation, Salvation Army, 1969; named Lion of Year, 1964-65. Mem. Carolinas Equipment Dealers Assn. (dir. 1956-57). Democrat. Baptist (deacon). Mason (Shriner), Lion (past pres.). Club: Cleveland Country (Shelby). Home: 312 Belvedere St Shelby NC 28150 Office: 400 N Lafayette St Shelby NC 28150

YENAWINE, WAYNE STEWART, librarian, educator; b. St. Louis, May 22, 1911; s. Frank S. and May (Lewellyn) Y.; B.S. in Bus. and Pub. Adminstrn., Washington U., 1933; B.S. in L.S., U. Ill., 1934, M.A., 1938, Ph.D., 1955; m. Marjorie Gardner, June 26, 1937; children— Gardner, Philip, Peter, Martin, Bruce. Librarian reserved book room U. Ill., 1934-35, head newspaper div., 1935-36, cataloger, 1936-37, asst. to dir. libraries, 1937-41; asso. dir. libraries U. Ga., 1941-42, acting dir. libraries, 1942-46; librarian Air U., Maxwell AFB, Montgomery, Ala., 1946-48; circulation librarian U. Ill., 1948-56; dir. libraries, also dean Sch. Library Sci., Syracuse U., 1956-65; dir. libraries U. Louisville, 1965-70; dean Coll. Librarianship U.S.C., 1970—. Mem. Gov.'s Com. on Library Devel. in Ky., 1967-70; mem. midwest regional council U.S. Nat. Archives, 1968-70. Mem. A.L.A., Ky., S.C., S.E. library assns., Bibliog. Soc. Am., Am. Assn. U. Profs., Assn. Am. Library Schs. (pres. 1963-64), Manuscript Soc., Am. Assn. Higher Edn., Beta Phi Mu (founder), Sigma Phi Epsilon. Episcopalian. Clubs: Filson, Grolier. Mem. editorial bd. Library Trends, 1952-56; editorial com. Syracuse U. Press, 1957-64. Contbr. profl. jours. Home: 1520 Senate St Apt 20D Columbia SC 29201

YEOMAN, WILLIAM F., athletic coach; b. Elnora, Ind., Dec. 26, 1927; s. Cluade Allen and Anna Lillian Y.; B.S., U.S. Mil. Acad., 1950; m. Alma Jean, July 1, 1950; children—William Vance, Gary Layne, Kathy Ann, Carrie Lynn. With U.S. Army in Europe, 1950-53; asst. football coach Mich. State U., 1954-61; head football coach U. Houston, 1962—. Home: 6237 Willers Way Houston TX 77027 Office: 3855 Holman Houston TX 77004

YERGER, JOHN HENRY, orgn. exec.; b. Reading, Pa., Jan. 4, 1914; s. John Henry and Anna (Long) Y.; A.B., Muhlenberg Coll., 1935; M.S. in Social Service, Boston U., 1942; m. Christine Helen Fegley, June 12, 1937; 1 dau., Pamela Louise. Supr. Pa. Dept. Pub. Assistance, Reading, 1935-40; exec. A.R.C., Boston, Cape Cod, Worcester, Mass., Hudson County, N.J., 1942-50, Niagara Falls (N.Y.) Community Chest, 1950-51; exec. dir. Ottawa (Ont., Can.) Community Chest, 1951-55, United Appeal Met. Toronto (Ont.), 1955-72; v.p. United Way of Am., Alexandria, Va., 1972—. Lectr., Harvard, 1941-42, Clark U., 1946-47, Cornell U., 1950-51, Boston U., 1942, U. Toronto, 1962—; cons. community orgn. to nat. orgns. and U.S. and Canadian cities, 1945—; chmn. nat. com. bus. leaders Canadian Community Funds, 1964—, chmn. nat. com. to improve public relations, 1964; chmn. Internat. Conf. Community Funds and Councils, Los Angeles, 1972. Mem. Mayor's Civic Com., Toronto, 1958—; founder Cape Cod Council, 1943. Bd. dirs. Canadian Welfare Council, Met. Toronto Social Planning Council. Served with USCGR, 1943-45. Decorated Most Venerable Order of Hosp. of St. John of Jerusalem in Brit. Realm; Letters of The Kings At Arms, City Ottawa, Can.; recipient citation A.R.C., 1946, Distinguished Service award United Community Funds, 1959. Fellow Royal Soc. Health; mem. Internat. Platform Assn., Acad. Certified Social Workers, Canadian Assn. Social Workers, United Community Funds and Councils Am. (adv. com. to corps. 1965—), Nat. Assn. Social Workers (chmn. Worcester chpt. 1944-45), Nat. Assn. Fund Raisers, Toronto Bd. Trade, Phi Kappa Tau, Tau Kappa Alpha. Lutheran. Clubs: National Club, Canadian (Toronto); Empire of Canada. Contbr. articles to tech. mags. Home: Apt 1104 N Skyline Towers 5601 Seminary Rd Falls Church VA 22041 Office: 801 N Fairfax St Alexandria VA 22313

YERGER, WIRT ADAMS, JR., ins. co. exec., mem. Republican Nat. Com.; b. Jackson, Miss., Mar. 18, 1930; s. Wirt Adams and Rivers (Applewhite) Y.; B.B.A., U. Miss., 1952; m. Mary Polk Montague, June 9, 1956; children—Wirt Adams III, Mary Montague, Frank M. With Ross & Yerger Ins. Agy., Jackson, 1954—, v.p., 1957, now pres. Founder Miss. Young Republicans, 1956; chmn. Miss. Rep. Com., 1956-66; chmn. So. Assn. Reps., 1961-65, Miss. chmn., 1956—. Served to 1st lt., USAAF, 1952-54. Recipient Distinguished Service award Jackson Jr. C. of C., 1956, 60. C.L.U. Mem. Miss. Assn. Ins. Agts. Rotarian. Home: 2457 E Northside Dr Jackson MS 39205 Office: First Nat Bank Bldg Jackson MS 39205

YGLESIAS, MANUEL ESPINOSA, chmn., mng. dir. Banco de Comercio S.A. Address: Banco de Comercio SA Verustiano Carranza No 44 PO Box 9 Bis Mexico 1 DF Mexico*

YINGLING, DORIS BEAUMONT, nursing sch. adminstr.; b. Balt., Dec. 3, 1918; d. Paul M. and Helen (Beaumont) Yingling; R.N., Union Meml. Hosp., Balt., 1943; B.S., U. Ore., 1944; M.A., U. Md., 1950; Ed.D. 1956; m. Harry Lyons, January 12, 1969. Instr., Sch. Nursing Union Meml. Hosp., 1943-44, instr., supr., 1944-46; cons. Liberty Mut. Ins. Co., Phila., 1946-50; lectr. U. Md., 1950-51; exec. sec. Gov., Md. Commn. Survey of Nursing Needs and Resources 1950-53; dean Orvis Sch. Nursing, U. Nev., 1956-57; dean Sch. Nursing, Va. Commonwealth U., Richmond, 1958—. Mem. Gov. Va. Commn. Higher Edn., 1964, Gov. Va. Com. on Nursing, 1966, Adv. Council Practical Nurse Edn., 1965—, Nursing Scholarship Com. Va., 1962—, task force chronic bronchitis Nat. Tb Assn., 1965; cons. div. hosp. and med. facilities Dept. of Health, Edn. and Welfare, 1967. Mem. Va., Richmond (bd. dirs. 1962-69) personnel and guidance assns., Instructive Vis. Nurse Assn., Nat., Richmond leagues for nursing, Am., Va. nurses assns., Council Practical Nurse Edn. (chmn. evaluation com. 1966-69), Sigma Theta Tau, Phi Kappa Phi, Alpha Sigma Chi. Contbr. articles profl. publs. Home: 7618 Idlewyld Rd Richmond VA 23225

YODER, AMOS, govt. ofcl.; b. Falls City, Neb., Mar. 2, 1921; s. Amos H. and Mildred (Johnson) Y.; B.A., Ohio Wesleyan U., 1942; Ph.D., U. Chgo., 1949; m. Janet Lee Tatman, June 15, 1946; children— James Amos, Barbara Ann, Sally Irene. Jr. econ. editor Bd. Econ. Warfare, Washington, 1942-43; economist, fgn. service officer Dept. State, Washington, also Bangkok, Thailand, Tel Aviv, Israel, 1949—, asst. dep. dir., Washington, 1969-71, acting chief, 1971—. Asso. professorial lect. George Washington U., 1963-64, U. Cal. at Davis, 1964-65. Served with USAAF, 1944-46; ETO, PTO. Recipient Merit Honor award Dept. State, 1967, Meritorious Civilian Service award, 1972. Mem. Nat. Inst. Pub. Affairs, Am. Polit. Sci. Assn., Phi Gamma Delta, Omicron Delta Kappa. Home: 1822 Rupert St McLean VA 22101 Office: Bur Internat Orgn Affairs Dept State Washington DC 20520

YOHN, KENNETH CRAWFORD, physician; b. Dothan, Ala., Nov. 1, 1936; s. Houston Crawford and Julie Lee (Trant) Y.; student Troy State U., 1955-56, Howard Coll., 1956-58; M.D., U. Ala., 1962; postgrad. Naval Aerospace Med. Inst., 1963-64. Intern U.S. Naval Hosp., Portsmouth, Va., 1962-63; student flight surgeon Naval Aerospace Med. Inst., Pensacola, Fla., 1963-64; gen. practice medicine, Eufaula, Ala., 1967—; mem. staff Barbour County Hosp. Served to lt. comdr. M.C., USNR, 1962-67. Decorated Air medal. Mem. Ala. Acad. Gen. Practice (dist. v.p. 1971—), Barbour County Med. Soc. (pres. 1969-71), Eufaula C. of C. (dir. 1971—). Baptist (deacon). Home: 628 Holly Dr Eufaula AL 36027 Office: 108 N Randolph Av Eufaula AL 36027

YOO, YOUNG HYUN, librarian; b. Hongsong, Korea, July 15, 1927; s. Bock Don and Sang Sil (Suh) Y.; LL.B., Korea U., Seoul, 1957; M.A. in L.S., Peabody Coll., 1958; LL.M., Seoul Nat. U., 1960; postgrad. Cath. U. Am., 1964-65, U. Md., 1968; m. Sun Gyu Im, Oct. 25, 1958; children—Mi Young, Tae Young, Dae Jin, Alice. Came to U.S., 1963, naturalized, 1971. Chief, Western books dept. Dongguk U. Library, Seoul, 1955-59; librarian Seoul Nat. U. Coll. Law, 1959-63; mem. staff Far Eastern subject analysis Library of Congress, Washington, 1963—. Lectr. law and library sci. Seoul Nat. U., Yonsei U., Kukhak Coll., Nat. Communications Coll., Korea, 1958-63; mem. translating com. Dewey Decimal Classification, Korean Ministry Edn.-George Peabody Adv. Group, 1958-62; mem. selection com. for library trainees sponsored U.S. Dept. State, Korea, 1959-60; mem. reviewing com. Korean Library Law, 1959; cons. computerized bibliog. system Yale Human Relations Area Files, 1967-70; spl. adviser Far Eastern Research and Publis. Center, 1970—. ICA grantee, 1957-58. Mem. Am., Korean (councillor, mem. tech. com., editor bull. 1958-63) library assns., Korean Soc. Criminal Law and Criminology, Library of Congress Profl. Staff Assn. Author: An Analysis of the Criminal Law of Yi Dynasty of Korea, 1962; (as Grace S. Yoo) Two Korean Brothers, 1970; Wisdom of the Far East: A Dictionary of Proverbs of the Chinese, Japanese and Korean, 1971. Editor: English-Korean Dictionary Romanized, 1962-70. Contbr. chpts. to books, articles to newspapers and mags.

YORDAN, ERNESTO COLON, physician, govt. ofcl.; b. Ponce, P.R., June 24, 1920; s. Ernesto Colon and Belisa (Yordan) Rosich; B.S., U. P.R., 1940; M.D., U. Md., 1943; m. Jacqueline Bennet Colon, Dec. 11, 1943; children—Janice Jacqueline, Jeffrey Ernesto. Intern, Providence Hosp., Detroit, 1944, resident internal medicine, 1945; resident anesthesiology Grad. Hosp., U. Pa., 1949-51; practice medicine, specializing in anesthesiology, Santruce, P.R., 1951—; dir. anesthesia dept. Hosp. de Damas, Ponce, 1951-68, med. dir., 1953-68, dir. respiratory care unit, 1968—; clin. asso. U. P.R. Med. Sch., 1953-59; cons. in anesthesiology Oncologic Clinic, Ponce, 1956-68; attending anesthesiologist St. Lukes Episcopal Hosp., 1951-68, Ponce Dist. Hosp., 1955-62; cons. anesthesiologist Hosp. de la Concepcion, San German, P.R., 1958-68. Mem. State Bd. Med. Examiners, Commonwealth P.R., 1961-65. Pres., State Comprehensive Health Planning Adv. Bd.; bd. dirs. Caribbean Sch., Ponce; organizer, founder, mem. 1st bd. dirs. P.R. Blue Shield Plan. Served with M.C., AUS, 1945-47. Diplomate Am. Bd. Anesthesiology. Fellow Am. Coll. Anesthesiologists, P.R. Med. Assn. (past com. pres., speaker Ho. of Dels.), A.M.A.; mem. Am., Puerto Rican (past pres.) socs. anesthesiologists, So. Dist. Med. Assn. P.R. (past pres.), (hon.) P.R. Dental Assn. Contbr. articles profl. jours. Home: D-6 Sun Valley Bayamon PR 00619 Office: Ponce de Leon Santruce PR 00908

YORK, CHARLES IRVING, govt. ofcl.; b. Washington, Sept. 15, 1925; s. Lamar Watson and Helen (Hall) Y.; student Duke, 1943-44; B. Civil Engring., Cath. U., 1951, M. Civil Engring. cum laude, 1956; postgrad. Mass. Inst. Tech., 1960, U. N.M., 1964; grad. Fed. Exec. Inst.; m. Theresa Marie Fritz, Feb. 12, 1952; children—Stephen, Michael, Eileen, Kathleen, Kevin. Engr., George Hyman Constrn. Co., Washington, 1950-52; engr., project mgr. VA, Dept. of Navy, Air Force Ballistic Missile Div., 1952-62; asst. dir. AEC, Washington, 1962—. Cons. civil engr. ballistic missile and space systems divs. USAF, 1958-62; mem. Fed. Constrn. Council, Bldg. Research Adv. Bd. Various adminstrv. positions Boy Scouts Am., 1959-61; athletic coach Pop Warner League, Cath. Youth Orgn., 1960-62; active various ch. activities, bond drs., blood drs. Served to lt. (j.g.) USNR, 1943-47. Recipient Meritorious Civilian Service medal USAF, 1960, Sustained Superior Service award, 1961; Dept. of Commerce Sci. and Tech. fellow, 1966-67. Registered profl. engr., Vt. Mem. Am. Soc. C.E., Am. Assn. Cost Engrs., Am. Inst. Plant Engrs., Nat. Soc. Profl. Engrs., Sci. Research Soc. Am., Nat. Rifle Assn., Nat. Acad. Sci., Sigma Xi. Club: Senators (Washington). Home: 6012 Kingsford Rd Bethesda MD 20034 Office: AEC Washington DC 20545

YORK, CHRISTOPHER LAFAYETTE, educator; b. Round Rock, Tex., Oct. 20, 1907; s. Milton Garrett and Ida (Holland) Y.; student Mary Hardin-Baylor Coll., 1927-30; B.A., Baylor U., 1931; M.A., U. Tex., 1942, Ph.D., 1950; m. Gertrude James Pudig, June 28, 1942. Tchr. Kyle (Tex.) pub. sch., 1932-34, Longview (Tex.) pub. schs., 1934-39, Gladewater (Tex.) pub. schs., 1939-42; acting curator herbarium, dept. botany U. Tex., 1947-48, research asso., 1948-50; acting head biology dept. Southwestern U., 1950-53; head dept. biology, prof. biology Mary Hardin-Baylor Coll., Boston, Tex., 1953—. Mgr. Tex. Acad. Sci. Collegiate Acad., 1953—. Served to capt. USAAF, 1942-46; lt. col. Res. (ret.). Fellow Tex. Acad. Sci.; mem. Bot. Soc. Am., So. Appalachian Bot. Club, Southwestern Assn. Naturalists, Ret. Officers Assn. (life), Sigma Xi, Phi Sigma, Phi Alpha Theta. Baptist. Democrat. Mason (32 deg. K.T.). Home: 409 W 9th St Belton TX 76513

YORK, E. TRAVIS, JR., univ. provost; b. Mentone, Ala., July 4, 1922; s. E. Travis and Leila (Hixon) Y.; B.S., Auburn U., 1942, M.S., 1946; Ph.D., (research fellow 1946-49), Cornell U., 1949; postgrad. George Washington U., 1957-59; m. Vermelle Cardwell, Dec. 26, 1946; children—Lisa Carol, Travis Loften. Asso. prof. agr. N.C. State Coll., 1949-52, prof., 1952-56, head dept. agronomy, 1953-56; Eastern dir. Am. Potash Inst., 1956-59; dir. Ala. Extension Service, Auburn U., 1959-61; adminstr. Fed. Extension Service, Dept. Agr., 1961-63; provost for agr. U. Fla., 1963—. Bd. dirs. Am. Grassland Council, 1957-59, Ala. Bd. Agr. and Industries also Ala. Bd. Conservation, 1959-61, Fed. Crop Ins. Corp., 1962-63; mem. Am. Food for Peace Council, 1961-62, Freedom from Hunger Com., 1961-62, President's Panel Vocational Edn., 1961-62; adv. bd. Nat. Agrl. Extension Center Advanced Study, 1961-63; chmn. council grad. edn. in agrl. scis. So. Regional Edn. Bd., 1964-66; mem. Pres.' Sci. Adv. Council Task Force on World Food Problems, 1966-67; mem. senate, exec. com. Nat. Assn. State Univs. and Land Grant Colls., 1967-70. Bd. dirs. Nat. 4-H Service Com., 1963—, trustee, mem. exec. com. Nat. 4-H Found., 1968—; mem.-at-large Nat. council Boy Scouts Am., 1962—; dir., pres. Alpha Gamma Rho Edn. Found., 1965—; bd. dirs. So. Interstate Nuclear Bd., 1968—; bd. dirs., planning com. Nat. Center for Voluntary Action, 1970—. Served to capt. AUS, 1943-45. Recipient B.B. Comer award excellence natural sci. Auburn U., 1942; Distinguished Service award Fla. Vet. Med. Assn., 1966; Nat. 4-H Alumni award, 1967; George Washington honor medal award Freedoms Found., 1967; Nat. Partner in 4-H award, 1970. Fellow A.A.A.S., Am. Soc. Agronomy; mem. Assn. So. Agrl. Workers (pres. 1968), Soil Sci. Soc. Am., Crop Sci. Soc. Am., Internat. Soil Sci. Soc., Soil Conservation Soc. Am., Sigma Xi, Phi Kappa Phi, Alpha Zeta, Gamma Sigma Delta, Omicron Delta Kappa, Epsilon Sigma Phi, Alpha Gamma Rho, Blue Key. Baptist. Mason, Rotarian. Club: Cosmos (Washington). Home: 7911 SW 36th Av Gainesville FL 32601

YORK, ROBERT, cartoonist; b. Mpls., Aug. 23, 1909; s. Raymond and Nelle (Johnston) Y.; student Drake U., 1927-28, Cummings Sch. Art, 1928, Chgo. Acad. Fine Arts, 1930; m. Lillian Lossin, Apr. 11, 1936; 1 dau., Robin Lee. Asst. comic strip artist Chicago Tribune, Chgo., 1930-35; polit. cartoonist Nashville Banner, 1936-37, Louisville Times, 1937-43, 45—. Served as sgt. artist, USAAF, 1943-45. Recipient Pulitzer prize, 1956. Home: 3611 Kings Hwy Louisville KY 40220

YORK, THOMAS LUTHER, physician; b. Swannanoa, N.C., Jan. 24, 1926; s. Robert Lee and Annie May (Spivey) Y.; B.S., U. N.C., 1947; M.D., U. Md., 1950; m. Alice Mae Flory, Jan. 7, 1947; children—Thomas Flory, Susan Lynn, Christopher Alan. Intern, USPHS Hosp., Galveston, Tex., 1950; resident in surgery USPHS Hosp., Memphis, 1951; practice medicine specializing in family practice, Corpus Christi, Tex., 1951—; asso. owner Physicians and Surgeons Gen. Hosp., 1967-69; owner, mgr. Everhart Clinic, 1959—; dir. Mercantile Nat. Bank; rancher, farmer, Live Oak County, Tex., 1969—. Chmn. United Fund, 1957. Served with USNR, 1943-45. Mem. Am., Tex., Tex. Indsl. (dir. 1967—) med. assns., Tex. Acad. Gen. Practice (chmn. 1960), Tex. Med. Assts. (state rep. 1960), Live Oak Cattleman Assn., Phi Beta Pi, Kappa Sigma. Kiwanian. Home: 301 Williamson Place Corpus Christi TX 78411 Office: 4541 Everhart St Corpus Christi TX 78411

YOUENS, CYNTHIA TANNER, educator; b. Columbus, Tex., Sept. 7, 1905; d. John Osborne and Phyrne (Claiborne) Tanner; B.S., U. Houston, 1951, M.Ed., 1953; m. Willis George Youens, Feb. 13, 1935; children—Phyrne (Mrs. Philip Bacon), Leonard Claiborne, John Tanner, Phillip Whitfield. Faculty mem. Alief (Tex.) Sch., 1951—. Mem. Internat. Platform Assn., A.A.A.S., Tex. Tchrs. Assn., Tex. Hist. Assn., Women's Aux., Harris County Med. Soc., Kappa Delta Pi. Home: 19 Westlane Houston TX 77019 Office: Alief Sch Alief TX 77411

YOUNCE, DALE RICHARD, educator; b. Foley, Ala., July 3, 1937; s. Dallas Campbell and Nettie Mae (Du kes) Y.; B.A., Miss. Coll., 1959; M.A., Dallas Theol. Sem., 1963, Th.D., 1969; m. Theresa Overstreet, June 10, 1963; children—Dale Richard, Dallas Webster. Instr., Dallas Bible Coll., 1964; instr. Bible and philosophy Frank Phillips Coll., Borger, Tex., 1969—; minister Grace Ch., Wichita Falls, Tex., 1963-68, Faith Covenent Ch., Borger, 1969—. Named an Outstanding Young Man of Am., 1972. Mem. Nat. Assn. Evangelicals, Soc. Bibl. Lit., Tri-Cities Pastors Assn. (pres. 1970). Rotarian. Home: 2000 Lister St Borger TX 79007 Office: PO Box 584 Borger TX 79007

YOUNG, C.W. BILL, congressman; b. Harmarville, Pa., Dec. 16, 1930; m. Marian Ford, children—Pamela Kay, Terry Lee, Kimber. Dist. asst. to Congressman William C. Cramer, 1957-60; senator Fla. Legislature, 1960-70; mem. 92d Congress 8th Dist. Fla., 1970—. Mem. Fla. Constn. Revision Commn., 1965-67; chmn. So. Hwy. Policy Com., 1966-68; del. Rep. Nat. Conv., 1968; chmn. Nixon-Agnew campaign 8th Congl. Dist., 1968; mem. Electoral Coll., 1968. Served to sgt. Fla. N.G., 1948-57. Named One of Outstanding Young Men Am., U.S. Jr. C. of C., 1965, Most Valuable Senator, Capitol Press Corps, 1969. Methodist. Home: 7880 Ridge Rd Seminole FL 33540 also 9001 Captain's Row Alexandria VA

YOUNG, CALVIN LOCKE, utility exec.; b. Marshall, Tex., Feb. 27, 1899; s. Thomas Peters and Katy (Knight) Y.; B.S., Ala. Poly. Inst., 1920, Mass. Inst. Tech., 1922; m. Laura Lee Edwards, Dec. 19, 1925; 1 son, Thomas Peters. Test course, service engr. Gen. Electric Co., 1923-24; with West Tex. Utilities Co., 1924—, beginning as engr.; successively chief engr., v.p., dir., asst. to pres., 1924-55, pres., 1955-65, chmn. bd., 1965—. Mem. I.E.E.E. Democrat. Presbyn. Home: 1602 Sylvan Dr Abilene TX 79605 Office: 1062 N 3d St Abilene TX 79601

YOUNG, CARLOS LOWERY, furniture co. exec.; b. Shelby, N.C., Sept. 13, 1915; s. H. Fields and Nina (Lowery) Y.; B.S., Davidson Coll., 1936; m. Constance Alice Champion, Apr. 30, 1949; children—Carlos Lowery, Edna Anne, Kathleen Alice, Stephen Lewis. Pres., Young Bros. Inc., Shelby, 1938—; partner Young Bros. Bldg. Fund, Shelby, 1950—, also in real estate interests. Mem. Cleveland County Welfare Bd., 1963-67; mem. Gov.'s Adv. Council on Comprehensive Health Planning N.C., 1967—. Bd. dirs. N.C. Mental Health Assn., Nat. Assn. for Mental Health, N.C. Mental Health Research; trustee Gardner-Webb Coll., Boiling Hills, N.C., Asheville (N.C.) Orthopedic Hosp., Southeastern Bapt. Theol. Sem., Wake Forest, N.C. Served to maj. AUS, 1941-46. Decorated Bronze Star medal; recipient Shelby Outstanding Citizen award, 1970; recipient Distinguished Service medal Jaycees, 1949. Baptist (deacon, mem. gen. bd. N.C. conv.). Mason (Shriner). Home: 922 W Sumter St Shelby NC 28150 Office: 215 S Washington St Shelby NC 28150

YOUNG, CHARLIE ROSS, C. of C. exec.; b. Vivian, La., Nov. 2, 1923; s. Lawrence Miller and Maude (Crosley) Y.; student U. Mo.; m. Patsy George, Dec. 25, 1946; children—Barbara Ann, John Bruce. Clk. W. Tex. Utility Co., McCamey, Tex., 1948-50, owner C. & R. Restaurant, 1950-52; mgr. McCamey C. of C., 1952-56; exec. v.p. Plainview C. of C., 1956—. Served with USAAF, 1942-46. Mem. C. of C. Execs. Assn. W. Tex. (pres. 1958-59), Tex. C. of C. Mgrs. Assn. (v.p. 1961-62), Am. Legion. Mason. Home: 1315 Garland Plainview TX 79072 Office: 710 W 5th St Plainview TX 79072

YOUNG, DORCELL, business exec.; b. Carlton, Tex., Apr. 28, 1925; s. Oscar Eugene and Charlie (Burris) Y.; student Am. Inst. Banking, 1946-51; m. Lou Ann Williamson, June 1, 1947; children—Richard Dee, Debra Lee. With Citizens Nat. Bank, Lubbock, Tex., 1946-61; chief exec. officer First Nat. Bank, Wynnewood, Okla., 1961-63; pres., chmn. bd. First Nat. Bank, Denton, Tex., 1963-71; spl. asst. to pres. Lifetime Security Life Ins. Co., Denton, 1971-72; owner Young Volkswagen Inc., Denton, 1972—; engaged in ranching. Served with USAAF, 1943-45. Decorated Air Medal with 3 oak leaf clusters. Kiwanian. Home: Route 2 Box 35B Aubrey TX 76227 Office: Young Volkswagen Inc 2101 University Dr W Denton TX 76201

YOUNG, GALE, physicist; b. Baroda, Mich., Mar. 5, 1912; B.S., Milw. Sch. Engring., 1933; B.S., M.S., U. Chgo., 1936. Asst. in math. biophys. research U. Chgo., 1936-40; head dept. math. and physics Olivet Coll., 1940-42; physicist Manhattan Dist. Project, U. Chgo., 1942-46, Clinton Labs. (Tenn.), 1946-48; tech. dir. Nuclear Devel. Assos., 1948-55; v.p. Nuclear Devel. Corp. Am., 1955-61; v.p. div. United Nuclear Corp., 1961-62; asst. dir. Oak Ridge (Tenn.) Nat. Lab., 1962—. Mem. sci. adv. bd. U.S. Air Force, 1954-58. Fellow Am. Phys. Soc.; mem. Am. Nuclear Soc. Address: Oak Ridge National Laboratory Oak Ridge TN 37831*

YOUNG, GEORGE CRESSLER, judge; b. Cin., Aug. 4, 1916; s. George Phillip and Gladys (Cressler) Y.; student Rollins Coll., 1934; A.B., U. Fla., 1938, LL.B., 1940; postgrad. Harvard Coll. Law, 1947; m. Iris June Hart, Oct. 6, 1951; children—George Cressler, Barbara Ann. Admitted to Fla. bar, 1940; asst. city atty. Winter Haven, Fla., 1941-42; asso. in law firm Smathers, Thompson, Maxwell & Dyer, Miami, Fla., 1947; adminstr., also legislative asst. to Senator George Smathers, Fla., 1948-52; asst. U.S. atty., 1952; partner law firm Knight Kincaid, Young & Harris, 1953-61; U.S. dist. judge Fla., 1961—. Bd. dirs. United Cerebral Palsy Jacksonville, 1953-60. Served from ensign to lt. USNR, 1942-46, ETO, PTO. Mem. Am., Jacksonville (past pres.) bar assns., Fla. Bar (bd. govs. 1961), C. of C. (chmn. nat. affairs com. 1956-57), Phi Beta Kappa, Phi Kappa Phi, Phi Delta Phi, Fla. Blue Key, Sigma Alpha Epsilon. Rotarian. Home: 2424 Shrewsbury Rd Orlando FL 32803 Office: US Ct House Orlando FL 32801

YOUNG, GLEN MURPHY, truck rental co. exec.; b. Tuscaloosa, Ala., Aug. 28, 1924; s. Glenn Jones and Vertrees Elsie (Murphy) Y.; B.S., U. Ala., 1948; m. Patsy Ruth Howard, Feb. 4, 1945; children—Glen Howard, Robert Alan, Patricia Susan. Agt., Internal Revenue Service, U.S. Treasury Dept., Birmingham, Ala., 1948-51; sales mgr. Fairfield Barrell Co., Inc., 1953-55; with Ryder Truck Rental, Inc., 1955—, group v.p. corp. hdqrs., Miami, 1971—, gen. mgr., 1972—; dir. Ryder Truck Rental Ltd., Ryder System N.V.; dir. Ryder System Fed. Credit Union. Republican. Methodist. Home: 9370 Gallardo St Coral Gables FL 33156 Office: 2701 S Bayshore Dr Miami FL 33133

YOUNG, JACK, dentist, educator; b. Ashland, Ky., Aug. 24, 1920; s. Earnest and Eureka Sarah (Seagraves) Y.; A.A., Ashland Jr. Coll., 1940; postgrad. Moorehead State Tchrs. Coll., 1940-42; D.M.D., U. Louisville, 1951; m. Mildred Evelyn Virgin, Sept. 9, 1944; children—Steven Earnest, Peggy Lynn, James Elwood, John Cameron. Intern, Dr. C.O. Van Antwerp, gen. dentistry, Louisville, 1951-52; pvt. practice dentistry, 1952-65; prof., div. chmn. spl. edn. Pensacola Jr. Coll. (Fla.), 1965-71, dean Sch. Health Related Edn., 1971—. Mem. task force Northwest Fla. Comprehensive Health Planning Council. Bd. dirs. Escambia Residences, Inc., Am. Cancer Soc. Served with USNR, 1942-45. Fellow Internat. Coll. Dentists; mem. Am., Fla. dental assns., Louisville Dist., Pensacola, Northwest Fla. Dist. dental socs., Am. Vocational Assn. Author: Outline of Oral and Dental Anatomy, 1964; Dissection Guide for Nurses and Dental Hygienists, 1969. Home: 2080 Galt Rd Pensacola FL 32503

YOUNG, JAMES HARVEY, educator, historian; b. Bklyn., Sept. 8, 1915; s. W. Harvey and Blanche (DeBra) Y.; B.A., Knox Coll., 1937, D. Humane Letters, 1971; M.A., U. Ill., 1938, Ph.D., 1941; m. Myrna Goode, Aug. 25, 1940; children—Harvey Galen, James Walter. Mem. faculty Emory U., 1941—, prof. history, 1958—, chmn. dept., 1958-66; vis. asso. prof. Columbia, 1949-50. Mem. nat. adv. food and drug council FDA, 1964-67; mem. history of life scis. study sect. NIH, 1970—, chmn., 1972—; mem. consumers task force White House Conf. on Food, Nutrition and Health, 1969. Served with AUS, 1943-45. Carnegia Research grantee, 1947; Faculty fellow Fund Advancement Edn., 1954-55; Social Sci. Research Council fellow, 1960-61; grantee USPHS, 1960-65; Guggenheim fellow, 1966-67. Mem. Am., So. hist. assns., Oral History Assn., Orgn. Am. Historians, Am. Studies Assn., Am. Assn. History Medicine, Am. Inst. History Pharmacy (Edward Kremers award 1962). Am. Assn. U. Profs., Phi Beta Kappa, Sigma Xi, Phi Kappa Phi, Omicron Delta Kappa. Conglist. Author: The Toadstool Millionaires, 1961; The Medical Messiahs, 1967. Editor: (with W.A. Beardslee and T.J.J. Altizer) Truth, Myth and Symbol, 1962. Home: 272 Heaton Park Dr Decatur GA 30030 Office: Dept History Emory Univ Atlanta GA 30322

YOUNG, JESS WOLLETT, lawyer; b. San Antonio, Sept. 16, 1926; s. James and Zetta (Alonso) Y.; student Southwestern U., 1944, U. Tex., 1946-49; B.A., Trinity U., 1956; LL.B., St. Marys Sch. Law, 1958; m. Mary Alma Keeter, Apr. 17, 1954; children—Zetta, Imogen. Admitted to Tex. bar, 1957; practiced in San Antonio, 1957—; mem. firm Moursund, Ball and Young, 1965—. Dir., Dean L. Leeper Co., Dallas. County judge, Bexar County, Tex., 1964; city atty., Olmos Park, Tex., 1965—. Precinct committeeman, San Antonio, 1964, 70—; state Democratic committeeman, 1970—. Served with USNR, 1944-46. Mem. Am., San Antonio bar assns., State Bar Tex., Delta Theta Phi. Clubs: Kiwanis, San Antonio Gun (dir. 1958-63). Democrat. Home: 232 Stanford Dr San Antonio TX 78212 Office: Frost Nat Bank Bldg San Antonio TX 78205

YOUNG, JOE GALBRAITH, retail store ofcl.; b. Whitesburg, Tenn., Aug. 22, 1920; s. Fred Johnson and Chassie O'Dell (Walker) Y.; grad. high sch.; m. Virginia Juanita Greenwell, Oct. 15, 1949. With Dobyns Taylor Hardware Co., Kingsport, Tenn., 1940—, buyer, 1950—. Bd. dirs. Community Chest, 1969-71; pres. Kingsport Mchts. Bur., 1962; mem. Mayor's Adv. Bd., 1971—. Served with USAAF, 1942-46. Mem. V.F.W., Am. Legion. Democrat. Methodist. Elk, Moose. Clubs: Metropolitan Dinner, Kingsport Riding (pres. 1965), Civitan. Home: 704 Fleetwood St Kingsport TN 37660 Office: 120 Broad St Kingsport TN 37660

YOUNG, JOE MORRISON, brick co. exec.; b. Wilsonville, Ala., Dec. 30, 1928; s. Eugene Morrison and Emmie Jane (Reinhardt) Y.; B.S., U. Ala., 1951; m. Mary Katherine Chumleyy, July 19, 1951; children—Jon Morrison, Jefferson Chumley, Virginia Murray. Mgmt. trainee Nat. Carbon Co., Columbia, Tenn., 1953-55; chief cost accountant Kingsberry Homes, Ft. Payne, Ala., 1955-58; asst. controller Chattahoochee Brick Co., Atlanta, 1958-59, controller, 1959-61, v.p., 1961-65, exec. v.p., 1965-70, pres., 1970—, dir., 1967—. Served to 1st lt. AUS, 1951-53. Mem. So. Brick and Tile Mfrs. Assn. (v.p. 1970—), Structural Clay Products Inst. (dir. 1970—), Beta Gamma Sigma, Delta Tau Delta. Unitarian. Club: Atlanta City. Home: 2720 Overlook Dr NE Atlanta GA 30345 Office: 3195 Brick Plant Rd NW Atlanta GA 30318

YOUNG, JOHN, congressman; b. Corpus Christi, Tex., Nov. 10, 1916; s. Phillip M. and Catherine J. (Gaffney) Y.; B.A., St. Edwards U., 1937, LL.D., 1961; law student, U. Tex., 1940; m. Jane F. Gallier, Jan. 21, 1950; children—Catherine, Nancy, John, Robert, Mary. Admitted to Tex. bar, 1940; asst. county atty. Nueces County, Tex., 1946; asst. dist. atty. Nueces County, 1947-50; county atty., 1951-52, county judge, 1953-56; mem. 85th-92nd Congresses, 14th dist. Tex., mem. house com. on rules. Served with USNR, 1941-45. Decorated Presidential Unit Citation. Mem. Tex., Nueces County bar assns., U.S. Supreme Ct. Bar, Am. Legion, V.F.W., D.A.V. K.C., Elk, Moose. Address: US Courthouse Corpus Christi TX 78401 Office: House Office Bldg Washington DC 20515

YOUNG, JOHN W, state ofcl.; b. Louisville, May 29, 1916; s. Birch Higgins and Bertha (Lindeman) Y.; ed. U. Louisville, U. Heidelberg (Germany); m. Dorothy M. Mialback, Aug. 28, 1941; 1 son, John W. Brewer, Oertel Brewing Co., 1935-64, engaged in pub. relations, 1964-67; commr. labor Commonwealth Ky., Frankfort, 1967—. Active Protestant Orphans Home, Salvation Army. Ward chmn., Louisville, 1948—; alderman city Louisville, 1962-67, pres. bd., 1965-67. Served with AUS, 1942-45; ETO. Mem. Am. Legion, V.F.W. Republican. Club: Wildwood Country. Home: 3121 McMahan Blvd Louisville KY 40220 Office: State Office Building Frankfort KY 40601

YOUNG, JOHN W., astronaut; b. San Francisco, Sept. 24, 1930; s. William H. Young; B.S. in Aero. Engring., Ga. Inst. Tech., 1952; m. Susy Feldman; children—Sandra, John. Joined U.S. Navy, 1952, advanced through the grades to capt.; test pilot, program mgr. F4 weapons systems projects, 1959-62; then maintenance officer Fighter Squadron 143, Naval Air Sta., Miramar, Cal.; astronaut Project Gemini, NASA, made two man 3 orbit flight Mar. 1965, 2d Gemini flight, 1966, Apollo 10 Lunar orbit flight, May 1969; comdr. Apollo 16 Lunar Landing Mission, Apr. 1972. Fellow Am. Astro. Soc.; mem. Am. Inst. Aeros. and Astronautics, Soc. Exptl. Tests Pilots (asso. fellow). Office: Office Manned Spacecraft Center NASA Houston TX 77058

YOUNG, JOSEPH, newspaper columnist; b. Chgo., Aug. 12, 1918; s. Ben and Rae (Sloman) Y.; student pub. schs., Chgo.; m. Helen Lucille Smith, June 9, 1945; children—Linda, Richard, David, Stephen. Staff, Washington Star, 1942—, syndicated govt. columnist Fed. Spotlight, 1945—. Recipient ann. award for contbg. most to cause of good govt. Soc. Personnel Adminstrn., 1963. Club: Nat. Press. Author: (with Harry Lever) Wartime Racketeers, 1945. Editor: Fed. Employees Almanac, 1954—. Fed. Employees News Digest, 1951—; co-editor Uniformed Services Almanac, 1956—. Home: 1706 Hollinwood Dr Alexandria VA 22307 Office: Washington Star 2d and Virginia Av SE Washington DC 20003

YOUNG, KENNETH EVANS, ednl. adminstr.; b. Toronto, Ont., Can., Mar. 21, 1922; s. John Osborne and Gwendolyn May (Evans) Y.; A.B., San Francisco State Coll., 1943; M.A., Stanford, 1947, Ph.D., 1953; post doctoral fellow, U. Mich., 1959-60; LL.D., U. Nev., 1972; m. Mae Catharine Wittenmyer, July 1, 1945; 1 son, Bruce Kenneth. Instr. journalism and speech San Francisco State Coll., 1946-48; instr. journalism and English, Cal. State Poly. Coll., 1949-50, asst. prof., then asso. prof. and acting dean arts and scis. Kellogg-Voorhis campus, 1951-57; dean faculty U. Alaska, 1957-59; exec. v.p. U. Nev., 1960-64; pres. State U. Coll., Cortland, N.Y., 1964-68; v.p., dir. Washington office Am. Coll. Testing Program, 1968—, also mem. bd. dirs. Served with USAAF, 1943-45. Mem. Am. Assn. Higher Edn., Phi Delta Kappa. Home: 4411 Garfield St NW Washington DC 20007 Office: 1 DuPont Circle NW Washington DC 20036

YOUNG, MARJORIE WILLIS, writer, journalist, lectr.; b. Mansfield, O.; d. John Edgar and Mary Adelle (Reiter) Willis; student agr., Cornell U., 1924, Art Students League, 1925-27, Cooper Union, 1925-27, Columbia, 1927, Sorbonne, U. Paris, 1928-30, Japanese Lang. Sch., Tokyo, 1934-35, Columbia, 1943, N.Y.U., 1944; m. James Russell Young, Oct. 2, 1934; 1 son, Willis Patterson. Columnist in Far East, Internat. News Service, 1938-41; feature writer King Features Syndicate, 1939, Saturday Pictorial Rev., 1941-45; asst. tech. dir. motion picture Behind the Rising Sun, 1943; research dept. Believe It or Not, 1946-48; feature editor and columnist The Sunday Star, Wilmington, Del., 1946-48; promotion dir. David McKay Pub. Co., 1945-48; lectr. Nat. Concert and Artists Corp., 1942-43; feature writer Anderson (S.C.) Independent Tribune, 1949—; feature writer Anderson Daily Mail, 1949—, asso. editor The New South, annual special edition of Daily Mail, 1966—; editor The Safety Jour., Anderson, 1953—; program moderator Decorating for a Holiday, sta. WAIM-TV, 1953—, safety program moderator WAIM-TV, 1953—, program moderator How to Cut and Sew, 1954—; editor Vets. of Safety news page, What's What monthly; dir. Capitol City Communications, Inc. Spl. scroll dir. Chinese War Orphans Relief, 1941-45; publicity dir. Crusade for Children, State of Del., 1948; publicity chmn. S.C. Indsl. Nurses Assn., 1953; dir. S.C. 4-H Club TV Safety Program, 1953. Recipient various awards for safety activities. Mem. U. S.C. Caroliniana Soc., Far East Soc., Writer's Assn. Am., Nat. Recreation Assn., S.C. Recreation Soc. (v.p. and program dir. 1954—), Am. Soc. Safety Engrs. editor S.C. News Letter; chpt. bd. dirs.), Am. Soc. Travel Writers, Garden Writer's Assn., Am. Hort. Council, Vets. Safety Internat., Nat. Press Photographers Assn., D.A.R. Episcopalian. Clubs: Am. Newspaper Women's, Washington Press (Washington); Overseas Press of Am.; Cornell Women's (N.Y.C.). Author: Decorating for Joyful Occasions, 1952; It's Time for Christmas Decorations, 1957; Fodor's Tour Guide of South Carolina, 1966-68, Tour Guide of Georgia, 1966-67. Editor: Textile Leaders, 1963; Japanese American Cook Book, 1972. Home: 2003 Laurel Dr Anderson SC 29621 Office: Anderson Daily Mail Anderson SC 79621

YOUNG, PAUL B., lawyer; b. Malvern, Ark., May 12, 1920; ed. Hendrix Coll., Conway, Ark.; J.D., U. Ark., 1947. Admitted to Ark. bar, 1947, since practiced in Pine Bluff. Mem. Am. (mem. corp., banking and bus. law sect.). Jefferson County, Ark. (jr. bar chmn.

1953, pres. 1971-72) bar assns., Fedn. Ins. Counsel, Phi Alpha Delta. Address: Box 7808 Pine Bluff AR 71601*

YOUNG, RALPH ROWLAND, economist; b. East Orange, N.J., Apr. 4, 1943; s. Rowland Smith and Helen (Hartman) Y.; B.A., U. N.H., 1965; M.A., George Washington U., 1969; m. Judith Corbett, June 19, 1966; 1 dau., Kimberly. Economist, George Washington U., 1968-69; mgmt. analyst, mgmt. officer Fairfax County, Va., 1969—. Served to capt. AUS, 1966-68. Mem. Am. Econ. Assn., Am. Statis. Assn., Omicron Delta Epsilon. Home: 1110 Hillcrest Dr Vienna VA 22180 Office: 4100 Chain Bridge Rd Fairfax VA 22030

YOUNG, ROBERT CAMERON, newspaper corr.; b. Phila., Aug. 14, 1914; s. Howard B. and Effie M. (Adams) Y.; B.A., U. Mich., 1936; m. Mildred Evelyn Wright, Aug. 27, 1938; children—Robert Wright, Peter Adams, Sara Amy. Reporter, Suburban Pub. Co., Oak Park, Ill., 1936-38, City News Bur., Chgo., 1938-40; reporter Chgo. Tribune, 1940-44, corr. Washington bur., 1944—. Mem. Nat. Press Club, Phi Delta Theta. Republican Episcopalian. Home: 3601 Porter ST NW Washington DC 20016 Office: 1750 Pennsylvania Av NW Washington DC 20006

YOUNG, ROBERT LYLE, engring. educator; b. Neoga, Ill., Apr. 3, 1925; s. Max Dryden and Neva (Higgins) Y.; B.S. in Mech. Engring., Northwestern U., 1946, M.S., 1948, Ph.D., 1953; m. Pyllis Eileen Ralston, Aug. 2, 1946 (dec. Aug. 1968); children—Ronald Lyle, Scott Alan; m. 2d, Martha Moore Robertson, Nov. 15, 1969; 1 stepson, Scotland Randolph Robertson. Instr., then asst. prof. Northwestern U., 1948-57; mem. faculty U. Tenn., 1957—, prof. mech. engring., dep. dir. Space Inst., 1961—; cons. USAF, 1957—. Served with USNR, 1943-46. Mem. Am. Soc. M.E., Am. Inst. Aero. and Astronautics, Am. Soc. Engring. Edn., Sigma Xi. Rotarian. Author: (with E.F. Obert) Elements of Thermodynamics and Heat Transfer, 1961; also articles. Home: 108 Wilkins Dr Tullahoma TN 37388

YOUNG, TERENCE O., architect; b. Lubbock, Tex., Jan. 23, 1932; s. Claud Olen and Clara (McClellan) Y.; B.Arch., Tex. Tech. Coll., 1956; m. Ann Raby Miller, June 6, 1957; children—Amy Lynn, Ellen Elizabeth. Designer, draftsman Charles S. Peete, architect, Memphis, 1956-60, Bruce-Russell Assos., architects, Tyler, Tex., 1959-60, D.B. Morrison, architect, Memphis, 1961, F.E. Hall & Assos., engrs. and architects, Greenville, Miss., 1961-64; pvt. practice architecture, 1964-72; facilities design analyst State of Fla.; Tallahassee, 1972—. Bd. dirs. William A. Percy Library, Greenville. Mem. A.I.A. (chpt. pres. 1971). Presbyn. (elder). Elk. Club: Exchange (dist. dir. 1968-70). Home: 2000 N Meridian St Tallahasse FL 32303

YOUNG, VIRGINIA SHUMAN (MRS. GEORGE FENWICK YOUNG), constrn. co. exec., civic worker; b. Norfolk, Va., Sept. 16, 1917; d. Irving George and Myrtle (Tenbrook) Shuman; student pub. schs., Ft. Lauderdale, Fla.; m. George Fenwick Young, Mar. 27, 1937; children—George William, Nancy Anne, Catherine Reta (Mrs. Howard Stayman), (Mrs. John H. Moore). Co-owner, George F. Young Bldg. Constrn. Co., Ft. Lauderdale, Fla.; vice mayor, Ft. Lauderdale, 1971—. Chmn. bd. trustees Broward County Sch. System, 1953-57, mem. bd. pub. instrn., 1958-66, chmn. bd., 1961, 65; pres. Fla. Sch. Bd. Assn., 1965; camp dir. Girl Scouts Am., 1945-46; mem. Gov.'s Com. on Aging, Ft. Lauderdale, 1956, Citizens Tax Council, 1957, Gov.'s Conf. Edn., 1966. Mem. Nat. Sch. Bds. Assn. (legislative com.), Bus. and Profl. Woman's Club, League Women Voters, C. of C. (pres. women's div. 1969-71), Delta Kappa Gamma. Methodist. Clubs: Fort Lauderdale Woman's (pres. 1969-71). Soroptimist. Home: 1101 SE 7th St Fort Lauderdale FL 33301

YOUNGBLOOD, RAY WILSON, pub. co. exec.; b. Tulia, Tex., Feb. 18, 1931; s. Burk Richard and Jenny Lucile (Wilson) Y.; B.B.A., Tex. Tech. U., 1952; postgrad. U. Tex., 1957-58; m. Imogene Price, June 7, 1959; children—Michael Ray, Janet Lynn. Auditor, Peat, Marwick Mitchell & Co., C.P.A.'s, Houston, 1958-65; chief accountant Houston Chronicle Pub. Co., newspaper pub., 1965-66, controller, asst. treas., 1966—; pres. Houston Chronicle Employees Fed. Credit Union, 1970—. Served to 1st lt. USAF, 1952-57. C.P.A., Tex. Mem. Inst. Newspaper Controllers and Finance Officers (bd. dirs. 1971—), Am. Inst. C.P.A.'s, Tex. Soc. C.P.A.'s, Nat. Assn. Accountants, Delta Sigma Pi. Methodist (mem. meml. drive 1967—). Clubs: Exchange (treas. 1971-72), Goodfellows (treas. 1969—, bd. dirs. 1969—). Home: 13626 Pinerock St Houston TX 77024 Office: 801 Texas Av Houston TX 77002

YOUNGBLOOD, SUE DAVIS (MRS. JACK YOUNGBLOOD), govt. ofcl.; b. Corsicana, Tex.; d. Plemon B. and Jimmie (McClendon) Davis; student pub. schs.; m. Jack Youngblood, May 25, 1946; children—Gary Jack, David Alan. Partner, office mgr. Youngblood Ins. Agy., Corsicana, Tex., 1954—. City commr., Corsicana, Tex., 1968-71, mayor, 1971—. Mem. Bus. and Profl. Womens Club. Home: 1000 Dobbins Rd Corsicana TX 75110 Office: 615 W 7th Av Corsicana TX 75110

YOUNGDAHL, LUTHER W., former gov. Minn., judge; b. Mpls., May 29, 1896; s. John Carl and Elizabeth (Johnson) Y.; U. Minn., 1915-16; A.B., Gustavus Adolphus Coll., 1919; LL.B., Minn. Coll. Law, 1921; numerous hon. degrees; m. Irene Annet Engdahl, June 23, 1923; children—Margaret Louise, Luther William Andrew, Paul David. Asst. city atty. Mpls., 1921-23; practiced law with Judge Tifft, 1923-30; judge, Municipal Ct., Mpls., 1930-36; judge Dist. Ct., Hennepin County, Mpls., 1936-42; asso. justice Minn. Supreme Ct., 1942-46; gov. Minn., 1947-51; judge U.S. Dist. Ct. for D.C., 1951—, sr. judge, 1966—. Chmn. com. on adminstrn. probation system in fed. cts. Nat. Jud. Conf., 1963-66. Mem. Pres.'s Commission Law Enforcement and Adminstrn. Justice, 1965-67; mem. adv. council judges Nat. Council on Crime and Delinquency, 1953-71; mem. adv. com. on sentencing and rev. Am. Bar Assn. Project on Minimum Standards for Criminal Justice, 1965—. Bd. dirs. Joint Commn. on Correctional Manpower and Tng. Recipient Grand Cross Royal Order North Star, Finnish Order of Lion. Served in World War I. Author: Ramparts We Watch. Home: 4101 Cathedral Av NW Washington DC 20016 Office: US Courthouse Washington DC 20543

YOUNGER, EDWARD FRANKLIN, JR., lawyer; b. Lynchburg, Va., May 1, 1912; s. Edward Franklin and Grace Schenck (Gilliam) Y.; student Hampden-Sydney Coll., 1929-33; A.B., U. Va., 1934, LL.B., 1937, J.D., 1971; m. Nell English, June 29, 1940; children—Katherine Lee, Edward Franklin III, Grace (Mrs. Sheldon M. Rutter), Goerge English. Admitted to Va. bar, 1937, since practiced in Lynchburg; trustee Wage Earner Plans under Chpt. XIII of Bankruptcy Act, 1965—. Sec.-treas. Reams Co., Rock Creek Colliery Co.; dir. Bank of Central Va. Bd. dirs., mem. exec. com. Spring Hill Cemetery Assn.; bd. dirs. Family Service Central Va.; pres. bd. trustees Va. Bapt. Hosp. Served with AUS, 1944-45. Decorated Bronze Star medal, Combat Inf. badge. Mem. Am., Va., Lynchburg bar assns., U.S. Power Squadron. Baptist. Rotarian. Club: Oakwood Country. Home: 1300 Langhorne Rd Lynchburg VA 24503 Office: 915 1/2 Main St Lynchburg VA 24504

YOUNGER, HAROLD BURRNELL, dentist; b. Morgan, Tex., Sept. 20, 1906; s. Williamson Henry and Stella (McKisick) Y.; D.D.S., Baylor U., 1927; postgrad. So. Methodist U., 1943-44; m. Lois Hortense King, Feb. 21, 1935; 1 dau., Suzanne (Mrs. Aubrey Benjamen/Pinnell, Jr.). Practice dentistry, Dallas, 1927—. Mem. staff Children's Med. Center, Dallas, 1928—, chief dental service, 1935-67, chief emeritus, 1967—; asso. dental research Baylor U., Dallas, 1941-50, lectr., 1957-62, asso. prof., 1962-63, clin. prof., 1963-69; columnist Your Teeth and You, Dallas Morning News, 1960—; mem. Dallas Pub. Health Bd., 1962; chmn. Dallas Health Council, 1956-58; dir. Freeman Meml. Clinic, Dallas, 1953—. Mem. City-County Civil Def. Commn; chief Dallas County (Tex.) Sheriff's Res., 1950—. Bd. dirs. Dallas Council Social Agys., 1956-60, Dallas Community Chest, 1959-60. maj. gen. Tex. State Guard ret. Fellow Am. Coll. Dentists (pres. Tex. sect. 1957-58); mem. Am. (clinician), Tex., Neb. (hon., clinician), Colo. (clinician), N.M. (clinician) dental assns., Dallas County Dental Soc. (pres. 1959-60), Internat. Assn. Dental Research, Am. Acad. Dental Medicine, Southwestern Soc. Dental Medicine (pres. 1953-54), Dallas Dentoecon. Soc., Orgn. of Tchrs. Dental Practice Adminstrn. (pres. 1966-67), Am. Acad. Dental Practice Adminstrn., Omicron Kappa Upsilon, Delta Sigma Delta. Meth. Kiwanian (distinguished service award Dallas 1953, pres. Dallas 1969). Contbr. articles and chpts. to profl. publs. Home: 3615 Fairmount St Dallas TX 75219

YOUNKER, SISTER M. MARGUERITE, educator; b. Paducah, Ky.; d. Henry Francis and Rosa (Poat) Younker; Mus.B., Catholic U. of Am., 1927; Mus.M., Am. Conservatory Music (Chgo.), 1939. Tchr., chmn. dept. music Mt. St. Joseph Jr. Coll., Maple Mount, Ky., 1927-49; tchr. Brescia Coll., Owensboro, Ky., 1949—, chmn. dept. music, 1949—. Mem. bd. dirs. Owensboro Symphony Orchestra. Mem. Nat. Catholic Music Educators Assn., Nat. Music Edn. Assn., Coll. Music Soc., Music Tchrs. Nat. Assn., Ky. Music Tchrs. Assn., Internat. Piano Tchrs. Assn., Am. Musicol. Soc., Ky. Music Educators Assn. Address: 120 W 7th St Owensboro KY 42301

YOUNKIN, CHARLES ROBERT, physician; b. Uniontown, Pa., May 9, 1921; s. John Eli and Henrietta (Shelkey) Y.; B.S., Washington and Jefferson Coll., 1943; M.D., Temple U., 1950; m. Anna Marie Aydam, Feb. 7, 1945; children—John Eric, Paula (Mrs. Robert O'Neill Dosch), Justin Neil. Intern, Hermann Hosp., Houston, 1950-51; gen. practice medicine, Houston, 1951-55; sr. asso., chmn. bd. Hillcroft Med. Clinic and Assn., Houston, 1955—; bd. dirs. Sharpstown Gen. Hosp. Pres. OMY Corp., 1955—. Served to 1st lt. USAAF, 1943-45; ETO. Decorated Air medal with eight oak leaf clusters. Mem. Harris County Med. Soc. (past chmn. bd. censors, mem. exec. com.), Delta Tau Delta, Alpha Kappa Alpha, Phi Chi. Home: 5610 Valerie St Houston TX 77036 Office: 6243 Bissonnet St Houston TX 77036

YOUNT, LAVINIA ANN CAROTHERS (MRS. JAMES L. YOUNT), civic worker; b. Pitts., Feb. 23, 1927; d. James M. and Lavinia (Jones) Carothers; A.B., Vassar Coll., 1948; postgrad. U. N.C., 1948-50, U. Hawaii, 1950; m. James Locke Yount, Sept. 6, 1949; children—Eric C., Jennifer Ann. Tchr., Punahou Sch., Honolulu, 1951-54. Pres. League Women Voters, Polk County, 1962-65, mem. Fla. bd. dirs., 1965-71, 2d v.p., 1969-71; bd. dirs. United Fund, Winter Haven, Fla., 1969-72; bd. dirs., sec. Ridge Sch., Winter Haven, 1968-70. Presbyn. Home: Lake Daisy Rd Route 4 Box 130 Winter Haven FL 33880

YOUNT, THOMAS LEO, precision instrument co. exec.; b. Birmingham, Ala., Mar. 23, 1928; s. Thomas Leo and Hazel Bernice (Felts) Y.; B.Engring., Vanderbilt U., 1952; postgrad. U. Pitts., 1953; m. Jane Wilkerson, Sept. 5, 1953; children—Lee Louise, Margaret, Pamela. Purchasing agt Westinghouse Electric Corp., Pitts., 1952-56; v.p., gen. mgr. Internat. Electronic Industries, Nashville, 1956-61; pres. Ortec, Inc., Oak Ridge, 1961—; v.p. E G & G, Inc., Bedford, Mass., 1970—; dir. The Nucleus Co., Pic-Air, Chem. Separations Corp. (all Oak Ridge), Camp-N-Air, Knoxville, Tenn.; dir., mem. exec. com. Bank Oak Ridge. Bd. dirs. Coop. Sci. Edn. Center, Planned Parenthood Assn.; trustee Oak Ridge Hosp. of Meth. Ch. Indsl. Devel. Bd. Oak Ridge, Coll. Oak Ridge. Served with USNR, 1946-48. Named Young Man of the Year, Oak Ridge C. of C., 1962. Mem. C. of C. (dir. 1971—), Tau Beta Pi, Omicron Delta Kappa. Rotarian (dir. 1967). Home: 109 Canterburg Rd Oak Ridge TN 37830 Office: 100 Midland Rd Oak Ridge TN 37830

YOUNTS, CHARLES ALBERT, dentist; b. Temple, Tex., Nov. 17, 1920; s. Charlie and Bessie Mae (Guinn) Y.; student Temple Jr. Coll., 1945-47, U. Houston, 1947-48; D.D.S., U. Tex., 1952; m. Fayola Lauretta Schneider, June 25, 1942; children—Timothy, Todd, Tana. Pvt. practice dentistry, Humble, Tex., 1952—; dir. Am. Nat. Bank, Humble. City councilman, Humble, 1954-61, city judge, 1961-63; mem. Humble Ind. Sch. Dist., 1968—, pres., 1971. Served with USAAF, 1943-46; PTO. Mem. Am., Tex. dental assns., Houston Dist. Dental Soc. K.C., Lion. Home: 513 Lakeland St Humble TX 77338 Office: 110 S Av E Humble TX 77338

YOUNTS, CHARLES ROLPHI, ret. petroleum exec.; b. Pineville, N.C., July 7, 1895; s. William E. and Eunice (Bell) Y.; grad. Bairds U., 1912; L.H.D., Erskine Coll., 1962; m. Willie Antoinette Camp, March 12, 1930. With Standard Oil Co. of N.J. and affiliates, 1912-60; pres. Plantation Pipe Line Co., 1941-59, chmn. bd., 1960. Past moderator Gen. Synod Asso. Ref. Presbyn. Ch., mem. session, Doraville, Ga., treas. retirement plan. Bd. dirs. Blue Ridge Assembly, Inc.; bd. dirs., pres. Churches Homes for Bus. Girls, Inc., Atlanta; bd. dirs., past chmn. Atlanta chpt. A.R.C.; dir. So. Indsl. Relations Conf.; trustee, treas. Erskine Coll., Due West, S.C.; trustee Met. Atlanta YMCA. Served from pvt. to 1st sgt., U.S. Army, 1917-19. Mem. Newcomen Soc., S.A.R. Mason Clubs: Piedmont Driving, Capital City, Rotary (Atlanta Armin Maier award for 1949-50) (Atlanta). Home: 3018 Habersham Rd NW Atlanta GA 30305 Office: 140 Peachtree St NW Atlanta GA 30303

YU, FRANK, physician; b. Padang, Sumatra, July 9, 1918; s. John W. and Julienne C. (Leonard) Y.; M.D., Aurora U., Shanghai, 1939; m. Charlotte A. Dyer, Dec. 3, 1960; children—Frank Simon, Paula Robbyn. Came to U.S., 1947. Intern St. Mary's Hosp., Shanghai, 1939-40; asso. prof. clin. surgery Aurora U., 1945-47; postgrad. N.Y. Polyclinic, 1947-48; pvt. practice anesthesia, Chattanooga, Tenn., 1950-61, Atlanta, 1961—. Mem. A.M.A., So. Med. Assn., Greater Atlanta, Am., Ga. socs. anesthesiologists, Internat. Anesthesiol. Research Soc., Med. Assn. Ga. Home: 3588 Cochise Dr NW Atlanta GA 30339 Office: 159 Forest Av NE Atlanta GA 30303

YU, JASON CHIA-HSIN, educator; b. Hupei, China, Feb. 5, 1936; s. Ping Shu and Wen Tsing (Hong) Y.; B.S., Nat. Taiwan U., 1957; M.S., Ga. Inst. Tech., 1964; Ph.D., W.Va. U., 1968; m. Dorothy Do-sun, May 29, 1965; children—William, Danny. Came to U.S., 1963. Grad. research asst. Ga. Hwy. Dept., 1963-64; research asso. W.Va. U., 1965-67; sr. research specialist U. Pa., 1967-68, lectr. Civil and Mech. Engring. Sch., 1967-68; asst. prof. civil engring. Va. Poly. Inst. and State U., Blacksburg, 1968-70, asso. prof., 1970—, prin. investigator, co-investigator various research projects, 1968—, program chmn. short course on hwy. safety Va. Poly. Inst. and State U. and Dept. Housing and Urban Devel., 1969, cons. System Sci. div. Tech. Operations, Inc., Alexandria, Va., 1969—, Alexander-John Assos., Mpls., 1970—; lectr. Va. Assn. Traffic Engrs., 1970. Mem. Am. Soc. C.E., Am. Soc. Engring. Edn., Inst. Traffic Engrs., Operations Research Soc. Am., Va. Assn. Traffic Engrs., Hwy. Research Bd. Contbr. articles to profl. jours. Home: 204 Watson Av Blacksburg VA 24060

YURGAITIS, ALEXANDER W., JR., constrn. exec.; b. Front Royal, Va., Sept. 13, 1925; s. Alexander W. and Margaret Elizabeth (Clegg) Y.; student Columbia Tech. Inst., Washington, 1947-48; m. Alice Trigg Swain, Jan. 3, 1951; children—Helen (Mrs. Richard Isley), Diane, Twila, Alexander Thomas. Pres. Yurgaitis Constrn. Co., Inc., Warrenton, Va., 1951—; pres. Yurgaitis Real Estate Co., Bethel Acad. Water Co., Inc.; dir. Peoples Nat. Bank, America, Inc.; pres., dir. Sulphur Springs Investment Co., Inc. Active Boy Scouts Am. Served with USNR, 1944-46; PTO. Mem. Nat. Assn. Realtors, Fauquier Bd. Realtors (pres. 1968-69, dir.), Va. Assn. Realtors (dir. 1968-69). Democrat. Episcopalian. Clubs: Corinthian Yacht (Washington); Virginia Yacht (Urbanna, Va.); Augusta Country (Staunton, Va.); Fauquier Lions (pres. 1962-63); Fauguier Springs Country (chmn. bd. 1971-72). Home: Bethel Academy Rd Warrenton VA 22186 Office: Rt 1 Warrenton VA 22186

YUSK, JANICE ANN WOODS (MRS. JOHN YUSK), physician; b. Knoxville, Tenn., Feb. 27, 1942; d. Raymond Floyd and Inalee (Brooks) Woods; B.S. cum laude, U. Tenn., 1963, M.D., 1966; m. John Yusk, May 8, 1965; children—John David, Lisa Ashley. Intern City Memphis (Tenn.) Hosps., 1967-68; resident in dermatology, 1968-71; pvt. practice medicine, Louisville, 1971—. Mem. Alpha Lambda Delta, Alpha Omega Alpha, Alpha Xi Delta. Home: 5683 B Brett Dr Fort Knox KY 40121 Office: Div Dermatology U Louisville Med Sch Louisville KY 40208

ZABALETA, NICANOR, harpist; b. San Sebastian, Spain, Jan. 7, 1907; s. Pedro and Isabel (Zala) Z.; student Madrid Conservatory Music; studied harp with Marcel Tournier, 1924-28, harmony with Marcel Samuel-Rousseau, counterpoint and fugue with Eugene Cools; m. Graciela Torres, Feb. 22, 1952; children—Pedro, Estela. Came to U.S., 1953. Soloist numerous symphony orchs. including Berlin Philharmonic, Israel Philharmonic, London New Philarmonia, Madrid Nat. Symphony, Paris Orch., Phila. Orch., Tokyo NHK Orch., Budapest Philharmonic, Rome RAI Orch.; performed numerous music festivals at Edinburgh, Venice, Osaka, Berlin, others; also gave 2500 recitals throughout world. Mem. jury Israel 1st Internat. Harp Contest, 1959, Israel 4th Internat. Harp Contest, 1970, Paris 1st Internat. Harp Contest, 1971. Home: 1300 Luchetti Av Santurce PR 00907 Office: PO BOX 886 San Juan PR 00902

ZABIJAKA, VALENTINE, govt. ofcl.; b. Perwo-Marijiwka, Ukraine, Feb. 23, 1933; s. Theodore and Halyna (Kushka) Z.; came to U.S., 1952, naturalized, 1953; B.A., George Washington U., 1960; M.A., George Washington U., 1969; m. Anna M. Rojko, May 25, 1963; children—Natalie H., George T. With demographic surveys div. U.S. Census Bur., Washington, 1960-66; survey statistician, 1960; regional economist econ. devel. div. U.S. Dept. Agr., Washington, 1966—. Served with AUS, 1953-56. Mem. Am. Econ. Assn., Sigma Phi Epsilon. Home: 11017 Lombardy Rd Silver Spring MD 20901 Office: US Dept Agriculture Economic Research Div South Bldg Washington 20250

ZACHARY, HUGH, author; b. Holdenville, Okla., Jan. 12, 1928; s. John F. and Ida Louise (Duckworth) Z.; B.A., U. N.C., 1951; m. Elizabeth Wiggs, Jan. 10, 1948; children—Whitney Leigh (Mrs. Allen Walters), Leslie Beth. Engaged in radio-TV broadcasting, 15 years; free lance writer, 1963—. Pres. Ridge Art Assn., Winter Haven, Fla., 1960-61. Served with 82d Airborne Div., AUS, 1946-48. Author: A Feast of Fat Things, 1968; The Beachcombers Handbook of Seafood Cookery, 1970. Address: Pebble Beach Dr Oak Island NC 28461

ZACHERT, VIRGINIA, psychologist, educator; b. Jacksonville, Ala., Mar. 1, 1920; d. Rev. R. E. and Cora H. (Massee) Zachert; student Norman Jr. Coll., 1937; A.B., Ga. State Woman's Coll., 1940; M.A., Emory U., 1947; Ph.D., Purdue U., 1949. Statistician, Davison-Paxon Co., Atlanta, 1941-44; research psychologist Mil. Contracts, Auburn Research Found., Ala. Polytechnic Inst.; indsl. and research psychologist Sturm & O'Brien, cons. engrs., 1958-59; research project dir. Western Design, Biloxi, Miss., 1960-61; self-employed cons. psychologist, Norman Park, Ga., 1961-71, Good Hope, Ga., 1971—; research asso. med. edn. Med. Coll. Ga. Augusta, 1963-65, asso. prof., 1965-70, prof., 1970—. Mem. adv. bd. Comdr. Gen. ATC, USAF, 1967-70. Served aerologist USN, 1944-46, aviation psychologist USAF, 1949-54. Fellow Am. Psychol. Assn.; mem. Am. Statis. Assn., N.E.A., Sigma Xi. Baptist. Author: (with P. L. Wilds) Essentials of Gynecology-Oncology, 1967, Applications of Gynecology-Oncology, 1967. Home: Rt 1 Good Hope GA 30641 Office: Dept Obstetrics and Gynecology Med Coll Ga Augusta GA 30902

ZACK, ALBERT JOSEPH, labor union ofcl.; b. Holyoke, Mass., Nov. 22, 1917; s. Charles Sumner and Mary (Crean) Z.; ed. pub. schs., N.J.; m. Jane Lillian Nesworthy, May 27, 1939; children—Linda Jane (Mrs. Davis S. Tarr), Allen Young. News editor Springfield (Mass.) Daily News, 1942-46, sta. WSPR, Springfield, 1946-47; pub. relations dir. Ohio CIO Council, Columbus, 1947-52; asst. pub. relations dir. CIO, Washington, 1952-55; asst. pub. relations, dir. AFL-CIO, 1955-57, dir. pub relations, 1957—. Democrat. Club: Nat. Press (Washington). Home: 1380 4th St SW Washington DC 20024 Office: 815 16th St NW Washington DC 20006

ZACK, PETER GEORGE, physician; b. Pine Bluff, Ark., Nov. 28, 1933; s. George and Eugenia (Paschal) Z.; student Tulane U., 1951-53; B.S., U. Ark., 1955; postgrad. Duke, 1955-56; M.D., U. Ark., 1960; m. Ida Gaile Reynolds, Sept. 3, 1957; children—Peter Gregory, Karen Anne. Intern, Meth. Hosp. Dallas, 1960-61; pediatric resident Children's Med. Center, Dallas, 1963-65; pediatric fellow Mead-Johnson Labs., 1964-65; practice medicine specializing in pediatrics Pediatric Center, Wilmington, N.C., 1971—; mem. staff New Hanover Meml. Hosp.; cons. staff Babies Hosp., Wrightsville, N.C., Cape Fear Hosp., Wilmington. Bd. dirs. local Mental Retardation Assn. Served with USNR, 1961-63. Mem. A.M.A., So. Tenn. med. assns., Hanover County Med. Soc., U. Ark. Alumni Assn. Home: 3813 Canterbury Rd Wilmington NC 28401 Office: 1914 Glen Meade Rd Wilmington NC 28401

ZAD, MARTIE STEPHEN, journalist; b. Bridgeport, Conn., Aug. 25, 1927; s. Martin Frank and Christina (Mulch) Zadravec; B.S., U. Md., 1953; m. Katharine E. Elson, Dec. 27, 1956; children—Gina, Martin, Lisa, Karen, Sarah, Stefanie. Sports reporter Washington Post, 1950-63, exec. sports editor, 1963-70, asst. mng. editor sports, 1970—. Served with USNR, 1944-46. Home: 3804 Williams Lane Chevy Chase MD 20015 Office: 1515 L St NW Washington DC 20005

ZAGORIA, SAM, labor relations ofcl.; b. Somerville, N.J., Apr. 9, 1919; s. Nathan and Rebecca (Shapiro) Z.; B.L. in Journalism, Rutgers U., 1941; m. Sylvia Bomse, Dec. 21, 1941; children—Paul, Marjorie (Mrs. David Olds), Ronald. With New Brunswick (N.J.) Daily Home News, 1940-41, N.J. Def. Council, Trenton, 1941-42, Fed. Office Govt. Reports, Newark, 1942; reporter Washington Post, 1946-55; adminstrv. asst. to Senator Clifford P. Case, Washington, 1955-65;

mem. NLRB, Washington, 1965-69; dir. City-County Labor Mgmt. Relations Service, 1970—. Served with USAAF, 1942-45. Nieman fellow Harvard, 1954. Mem. Soc. Nieman Fellows. Rutgers U. Alumni Assn. Jewish religion. Club: Federal City (Washington). Home: 3537 Marlbrough Way College Park MD 20740 Office: 1612 K St NW Washington DC 20006

ZAHASKY, MARY CAMPBELL (MRS. JAMES W. ZAHASKY), dietitian; b. Worcester, Mass.; d. Andrew and Margaret (O'Quinn) Campbell; B.S., State Coll. at Framingham, Mass., 1938; postgrad. N.Y.U., 1941-42, Columbia, 1942-43; m. James W. Zahasky, Mar. 28, 1945; children—May, Jay. Therapeutic and adminstrv. dietitian St. Vincents Hosp., N.Y.C., 1940-43; dietitian U.S. Army, 1943-46; adminstrv. dietitian Meml. Hosp., Worcester, 1946-47; asst. dir. dept. dietetics U. Okla. Health Scis. Center, Oklahoma City, 1947-48, dir. dept. nutrition and dietetics, dietetic internship dir., 1948—. Panel mem. White House Conf. on Food, Nutrition and Health, 1969. Recipient Byliner award Oklahoma City chpt. Theta Sigma Phi, 1962; certificate of award Home Econs. Alumni Assn. Okla. State U., 1963; Recognition Day award Framingham State Coll., 1963. Mem. Am. (past pres.), Okla. (past pres.), Oklahoma City dietetic assns., Am., Okla. home econs. assns., Assn. Schs. Allied Health Professions, Am. Soc. for Hosp. Food Service Adminstrs., Am. Okla. pub. health assns. Contbr. articles to profl. jours. Home: Route 1 Box 58 Oklahoma City OK 73111 Office: PO Box 26901 Oklahoma City OK 73190

ZAHN, JOSIAH HILLMAN, telephone co. exec.; b. Phila., Aug. 6, 1920; s. George W.A. and Mellie (Crawford) Z.; B.S. in Econs., Wharton Sch., U. Pa., 1942; m. Constance Escott Morgan, Aug. 24, 1944; children— Robert Allen, Elizabeth Carroll. With Bell Telephone Co. Pa., 1945-60, Mich. Bell Telephone Co., 1960-61; with C & P Telephone Companies, 1961—; v.p. publ relations, 1966—; dir. Equitable Life Ins. Co. Bd. dirs. Washington Bd. Trade, 1962-67, 69-70; trustee Fed. City Council, 1964—; exec. v.p. Nat. Alliance of Businessmen, 1969-70. Bd. dirs. Doctors Hosp. Research Found., 1969—; adv. bd. George Washington U., 1968-70; trustee, treas. Mt. Vernon Coll., 1968-69; bd. dirs. Health Facilities Planning Council, 1962-69, vice chmn., 1969; trustee Washington Tech. Inst., 1967—. Served to lt. USNR, 1942-45. Mem. Md.-D.C. Utilities Assn. (pres. 1968). Lutheran. Club: University (Washington). Home: 5236 Westpath Way Washington DC 20016 Office: 1710 H St NW Washington DC 20006

ZAHRT, MARTHA LEONARD, indsl. editor; b. Dallas; d. Ernest E. and Lily V. (Bell) Leonard; student U. Chgo.; m. Walter S. Zahrt, Sept. 10, 1935 (div. 1946); 1 dau., Kathleen W. With advt. dept. Carson Pirie Scott & Co., Chgo., 1931; asst. to account exec. N.W. Ayer & Son, Inc., Chgo., 1931-36; researcher part-time market survey Tracy Locke Dawson, advt. agy., Dallas, 1936-38; editor employee newspaper Braniff Internat., Dallas, 1945-54, mgr. publs., 1954-70, dir. publs., 1970—. Nat. chmn. editors com. Savs. Bonds div. U.S. Treasury, 1968-70. Recipient Bronze Medalion S.W. Journalism Forum, 1956; named Editor of Year Dallas Indsl. Editors Assn., 1953. Mem. Greater Dallas Council Chs. (mem. publicity com. 1966—), Internat. Council, Dallas (dir. nat. affairs 1964-65) indsl. editors, Airline Editors Conf., Theta Sigma Phi (Matrix award Dallas chpt. 1966, chpt. pres. 1966—, area dir. 1970). Clubs: Braniff International Management (v.p. 1961), Press (Dallas) (charter, treas. 1957, Best Indsl. Newspaper award 1962). Office: Braniff Internat Braniff Bldg Exchange Park Dallas TX 75235

ZAIN, GEORGE KALIL, advt., promotion, and publicity exec.; b. Tyre, Lebanon, Nov. 1 1888; s. Paul and Mary (Habib) Z.; grad. Friends Sch., Mt. Lebanon, Lebanon, 1906, Pottsdam Normal Sch., N.Y., 1909; m. Rebyl Silver, Feb. 21, 1935. Came to U.S., 1906, later naturalized. Pres., owner Zain Advt. System & Zain Features Syndicate, N.Y.C., 1912-42; civic worker, Coral Gables, Fla., 1937-44; originator, founder, developer Miracle Mile of Coral Gables, Fla., 1944, pres., 1944-46, chmn. bd., 1946-66; adv. cons. newspapers business and cities. Creator, executor Zain Plan of parking to solve Coral Gables, Fla. parking problem, 1950; founder Garden Look, Zain plan of beautification, originator, for cities residential streets and parkways, 1962. Recipient of a permanently installed bronze plaque, City Coral Gables, 1961. Episcopalian. Club: Country of Coral Gables (Fla.). Author spl. articles newspapers. Advocate Communities for Retired. Died Sept. 25, 1966. Office: 220 Miracle Mile Coral Gables FL 33134

ZAIN, REBYL (MRS. GEORGE K. ZAIN), publicity and pub. relations leader; b. nr. Findlay, O., Sept. 7, 1909; d. Peter and Rebecca (Gossman) Silver; student pub. schs.; m. George K. Zain, Feb. 21, 1935 (dec. Sept. 1966). Vice-pres. newspaper campaigns The Zain Advt. System, N.Y.C., 1930-41; publicist varied civic activities Coral Gables, Fla., 1942-44; v.p. charge publicity and promotion Miracle Mile Coral Gables, 1944—, chmn. bd., 1966—; publicity, promotion, pub. relations dir. Zain Plans Beautification Cities downtown shopping sts., 1944—, parking, 1950—, residential sts., pkwys., 1962—. Recipient (with husband) bronze plaque city Coral Gables, Fla., 1961. Episcopalian. Clubs: Coral Gables (Fla.) Country. Home: 700 Biltmore Way Coral Gables FL 33134 Office: 220 Miracle Mile Coral Gables FL 33134

ZAISER, MARION LLEWELLYN BROWN (MRS. ROBERT ALAN ZAISER), writer, civic worker; b. St. Petersburg, Fla., Jan. 12, 1917; d. Llewellyn Chauncey and Marion Edwina (Ames) Brown; B.A., Sweet Briar Coll., 1938; m. Robert Alan Zaiser, Aug. 26, 1939 (dec. Feb. 1947); children—Alan Robert, Kent Ames. Reporter, features, editorials Evening Ind., St. Petersburg, 1938-39; owner, operator copper tooling studio, 1952-54; dir. pub. information South Pinellas County chpt. A.R.C., 1954-56; sec. Equity Holdings, Inc., St. Petersburg, 1961—, also Brown, Zaiser & Brown; partner Marion B. Zaiser & L.C. Brown, citrus grove. Br. dir. Nat. League Am. Pen Women, 1962-66, br. pres., 1964-66, state corr. sec., 1966-67; coordinator Ams. Abroad, Am. Field Service, St. Petersburg, 1962-63; active various community drives; pub. relations chmn., bd. dirs. Christmas Toy Shop, Inc., 1958-61, 68-72, rec. sec., 1970-72; chmn. Jr. Red Cross, 1942-44; mem. pub. information com. A.R.C., 1956—, chpt. bd. dirs., 1971-72; sec. Snell Isle Property Owners Assn., 1963-64; den mother Cub Scouts, 1950-55; mem. diocesan Christian edn. com. Episcopal Churchwomen South Fla., 1952-55; mem. St. Petersburg Mus. Fine Arts, All Children's Hosp., Little Theater, 1938-71, YWCA, Sci. Center; mem. Jr. League, 1938-47. Trustee Canterbury Sch. Fla., 1968—. Recipient Pageant award for best biography, 1960, citation Sigma Delta Chi, 1960. Mem. Stuart Soc., Sweet Briar Alumnae Assn. (class sec. 1958-63), Christmas Belles. Republican. Episopalian (mem. ch. sch. com. 1966-68, sec. vestry 1971-72). Clubs: Nat. Writers, St. Petersburg Yacht, MacDill AFB Officers. Author: The Beneficient Blaze, 1960. Home: 1248 Monterey Blvd St Petersburg FL 33704

ZALAR, CHARLES, govt. ofcl.; b. Franzdorf, Austria, Sept. 10, 1909; s. Joseph and Marianne (Oblak) Z.; B.S., Belgrade U., 1930; B.A., Ljubljana U., 1931, LL.M., 1935, Ph.D., 1936; postgrad. (scholar) Sorbonne, Paris, 1936-38, Rome U., 1941-43; Ph.D., Georgetown U., 1958; m. Minka Verbic, Aug. 16, 1936; 1 son, Gregory. Came to U.S., 1952, naturalized 1957. Fgn. service officer, Belgrade, Vatican, Paris, 1938-52; research analyst Library of Congress, 1952-62; sci. information adminstr. NSF, Washington, 1962-71, fgn. sci. adminstr., 1971— asso. program Washington, 1962-71, fgn. sci. adminstr., 1971— asso. program dir., 1969-72, program dir., 1972—. Cons. internat. law, 1946-52. Mem. French Soc. Comparative Legislation, Am. Polit. Sci. Assn., Am. Soc. Internat. Law, Internat. Polit. Sci. Assn., Am. Mil. Inst., A.A.A.S. Author: Yugoslav Communism, 1961. Home: 4545 Connecticut Av NW Washington DC 20008 Office: 1800 G St NW Washington DC 20550

ZALE, WILLIAM, jewelry co. exec.; b. Shershev, Grodno, Russia, Sept. 9, 1903; s. Sam and Libby (Kruger) Z.; grad. high sch.; m. Sylvia Weinstein, Apr. 21 1929; children—Lew Darrell, Eugene, Theodore Robert. Came to U.S., 1909, naturalized, 1923. With Zale Jewelry Co., Inc. (name now Zale Corp.), Wichita Falls, Tex., 1924—, dir., v.p., Dallas, 1924—; pres. Zale Life Inc. Co. Crusade chmn. Dallas County, hon. State of Tex. chmn. Am. Cancer Soc., 1971; chmn. Zale Found., 1968—; Israel bond chmn. Jewish Welfare Found., Dallas, 1965-67. Jewish religion (pres. congregation 1954-56). Mason (32 deg.). Club: Columbian (Dallas). Home: 6142 Averill Way Dallas TX 75225 Office: 3000 Diamond Park Dallas TX 75247

ZANDALL, RICHARD RUDOLPH, program adminstr. in education; b. Gary, Ind., Jan. 22, 1931; s. Rudolph Richard and Anne (Barlock) Z.; grad. Valparaiso Tech. Inst., 1956; m. Kathleen Margaret Sager, Jan. 31, 1959; children—Mary Ann, Laura Louise, Nancy Marie, Margaret Rose. Customer engr. IBM, Chgo., 1956-59, customer engr. computer instr., 1959-62, customer engring. field mgr., 1962-65, fed. region staff systems rep., Washington, 1965-68, edn. industry marketing staff, 1968-71, program adminstr. in edn., 1971—. Served with USAF, 1951-55. Mem. I.E.E.E., Data Processing Mgmt. Assn. Republican. Roman Catholic. K.C. Home: 11221 Hunting Horn Lane Reston VA 22070 Office: 10401 Fernwood Rd Bethesda MD 20034

ZANDER, RALPH ARTHUR, architect; b. Mpls., Mar. 20, 1914; s. Arthur F. and Margrete (Jensen) Z.; B.Arch., U. Minn., 1937; m. Phyllis Margaret Borget, May 20, 1939; children—Stephen Arthur, Jeffrey Ralph. Product application designer Wood Conversion Co., St. Paul, 1937-38; draftsman, designer Foss & Co., Architects, Fergus Falls, Minn., 1938-41; architect, asso. Kenneth Franzheim, Houston, 1946-59, with Estate of K. Franzheim also pvt. practice, 1959-60; architect, partner Golemon & Rolfe, Houston, 1960—; cons. architect Houston First Fed. Office Bldg., 1960-63, project mgr. Houston Intercontinental Airport, 1963-71. Republican precinct chmn., 1954. Served to maj. AUS, 1941-46. Mem. A.I.A., Tex. Soc. Architects, Scarab. Republican. Roman Catholic. Home: 3819 Portsmouth Houston TX 77027 Office: 5100 Travis St Houston TX 77002

ZANGWILL, WILLARD IRA, govt. ofcl.; b. Pitts., Mar. 18, 1938; s. Bernard Louis and Lillian (Abel) Z.; A.B. magna cum laude in Physics, Columbia, 1959; M.S. in Statistics, Stanford, 1962, Ph.D. in Operations Research, 1965; m. Judith Ruth Heller, June 3, 1959; children— Richard Michael, Monica Laurie. Asso. prof. operations research Sch. Bus. Adminstrn. U. Cal. at Berkeley, 1965-69; dir. ednl. evaluation Office Sec., Dept. Health Edn. & Welfare, Washington, 1969-70; pres. Sullivan Ednl. Systems, Palo Alto, Cal., 1970-71; spl. asst. to asso. commr. U.S. Office Edn., Washington, 1971—. Cons. Rand Corp., 1965-69, IBM, 1965-69, CEIR-Control Data, 1966-69. Served to lt. (j.g.) USNR, 1959-62. Mem. Operations Research Soc., Inst. Mgmt. Sci., Phi Beta Kappa. Author: Nonlinear Programming, A Unified Approach, 1969. Contbr. articles to profl. jours. Home: 3709 Yuma St NW Washington DC 20016 Office: US Office of Edn 7th and D Sts SW Washington DC 20024

ZAPATA, MILTON, state ofcl. Sec. commerce Commonwealth of P.R. Address: Avenida Fernandez Juncos Parada 19 Santruce PR 00908*

ZAPOLEON, MARGUERITE WYKOFF, cons., lectr., author; b. Cin., Aug. 18, 1907; d. Fred Clark and Elizabeth (Voth) Wykoff; B.A., engring. degree, U. Cin., 1928; postgrad. Geneva Sch. Internat. Studies, 1927, N.Y. Sch. Social Work, 1928-29, London Sch. Econ. and Polit. Sci., 1932; M.A., Am. U. 1938; m. Louis B. Zapoleon, Oct. 2, 1937, (dec. Dec. 1969). Began career as vocation counselor in the Cin. Pub. Schs., 1929-35; chief of counseling div. D.C. Employment Center, 1935-39; specialist occupational information and guidance service U.S. Office Edn., 1939-43; tng. specialist Hdqrs. ASF, 1943-44; chief employment opportunities br. Women's Bur., Dept. Labor, 1944-51, spl. asst. occupational outlook service Bur. Labor Statistics, 1951-55, spl. asst. to dir. Women's Bur., 1955-60; cons. on labor econs. and vocational guidance, 1960—; lectr., workshop leader, instr. vocational guidance and occupational research colls., univs., Am. Assn. U. Women adult counseling project, 1965; adv. com., panel asso. Assn. Appraisers Earning Capacity, 1964-70; del. White House Conf. on Aging, 1971. Bd. dirs. Am. Soc. Econometric Appraisers, 1967-70. Mem. Nat. Vocational Guidance Assn. (trustee 1945-51), Council Guidance and Personnel Assn. (v.p. 1947-48), Alliance for Guidance Rural Youth (2d v.p. 1952-60), Am. Personnel and Guidance Assn. (del. to Assembly 1951-60), Am. Econ. Assn., Indsl. Relations Research Assn., Am. Ednl. Research Assns., Nat. Assn. Deans and Counselors of Women. Am. Assn. U. Woman, Nat. League Am. Pen Women, A.A.A.S., Am. Statis. Assn., Internat. Platform Assn., Nature Conservancy (rec. sec. Fla. br. 1972—), Kappa Kappa Gamma (alumni achievement award 1968), Pi Chi Epsilon. Presbyn. Author: (with Louise Moore) Reference and Related Information. Vocational Guidance for Girls and Women, 1941; Community Occupational Surveys, 1942; The College Girl Looks Ahead to Her Career Opportunities, 1956; Occupational Planning for Women, 1961; Girls and Their Futures, 1963; wrongful Death of Housewife and Mother, 1965; Economic Aspects of Counseling Adult Women, 1966; also author of numerous govermental pamphlets on occupations and vocational guidance edn. and tng.; articles in profl. jours. Editor: Vocational Guidance Quar., 1953-54. Home: 816 SE Riviera Isle Fort Lauderdale FL 33301

ZAREMBA, SYLVIA ANNE (MRS. ROBERT E. PRESTON), concert pianist, educator; b. Chicopee, Mass.; d. John and Anna (Szot) Zaremba; B.Mus., artist's diploma, Curtis Inst. Music, Phila., 1947; m. Robert E. Preston, June 4, 1960. Concert pianist; debut at age 10, Town Hall, N.Y.C.; concertized in U.S., Europe, Central and S.Am.; appearances with symphony orchs., N.Y.C., Chgo., Cleve., Phila., San Antonio, Dallas, Oklahoma City, New Orleans; asst. prof., artist-in-residence U. Okla., 1953-60; asso. prof. music Newcomb Coll., Tulane U., New Orleans, 1964—. Rec. artist, 1958—; soloist Am. Symphony Orch., Carnegie Hall, 1966; artist-in-residence N.H. Music Festival, 1970—. Named Outstanding Faculty Woman U. Okla., 1961. Mem. Pi Kappa Lambda, Mu Phi Epsilon. Home: 5870 Sylvia Dr Lakewood North New Orleans LA 70124

ZARSKY, CLIFFORD LOUIS, constrn. co. exec.; b. Woodsboro, Tex., Sept. 9, 1928; s. Louis J. and Beatrice Marie (St. Onge) Z.; B.A., Mary Knoll Coll., 1951; J.D., U. Tex., 1957; m. Joyce Clarice Vicak, Feb. 4, 1961; children—Brion Clifford, Louis John, Karen Clarice. Admitted to Tex. bar, 1957; practiced in Austin, 1957-58, Corpus Christi, 1958—; asso. Arthur Mitchel, Austin, 1957, Corpus Christi, 1958; asst. dist. atty., Nueces County, Tex., 1959-61, 1st asst. dist. atty., 1964-68; with Wood Constrn. Co., Seattle, 1962-64; Cliff Zarsky Texan Homes, Inc., Corpus Christi, 1969—; pres. partner Zarsky & Hill, attys., 1968—. Bd. dirs. Corpus Christi (Tex.) Osteopathic Hosp., 1969. Served with USAF, 1952-54. Mem. Am., Tex., Nueces County bar assns., Tex. (v.p. 1972—), Corpus Christi (pres. 1970-71) builders assns. K.C. Clubs: Serra (dist. gov. 1971-72), Sertoma (pres. 1967) (Corpus Christi). Home: 4701 Sea Island Corpus Christi TX 74815 Office: 3840 S Padre Island Dr Corpus Christi TX 74815

ZARTMAN, LEONARD STORY, lawyer, govt. ofcl.; b. Rochester, N.Y., Sept. 18, 1926; s. Leonard S. and Eva (Cushman) Z.; A.B., Yale, 1948; LL.B., Columbia, 1953; m. Barbara Jean Flower, Aug. 2, 1969; children—(by previous marriage) Lydia Sarah G., Nathaniel S., Dana S., Mary W. Admitted to N.Y. bar, 1953; practiced in Rochester, 1953-68; mem. firm Nixon, Hargrave, Devans & Doyle, 1963-64; atty. Eastman Kodak Co., 1964-68; spl. asst. to Pres. Nixon, 1969; gen. counsel Small Bus. Adminstrn., Washington, 1969—. Served with USNR, 1944-46; as capt. USMCR, 1950-52. Mem. Am., N.Y. State, Fed., Monroe County (N.Y.) bar assns. Home: 2400 Virginia Av Washington DC 20037 also 15 Portsmouth Terrace Rochester NY 14607 Office: 1411 L St NW Washington DC 20416

ZARZAR, NAKHLEH PACIFICO, state ofcl.; b. Bethlehem, Palestine, Jan. 21, 1932; s. Pacifico Y. and Anita Zarzar; B.A., Am. U. Beirut, 1952, M.D., 1956; m. Doris Azzam, Sept. 23, 1957; children—Michael, Nicholas, David. Intern, Am. U. Hosp., Beirut, Lebanon, 1955-56; resident U. N.C., Chapel Hill, 1956-59; clin. dir., family sect. John Umstead Hosp., Butner, N.C., 1959-62, entire hosp., 1962-63, supt., 1964-68; interim supt. Dorothea Dix Hosp., Raleigh, N.C., 1966; dep. commr. N.C. Dept. Mental Health, Raleigh, 1966—. Clin. asso. prof. U. N.C. Fellow Am. Psychiat. Assn., mem. N.C. Neurophychiat. assn., Am., N.C., Wake County med. assns., Alpha Omega Alpha. Contbr. articles to profl. jours. Home: 4727 Wedgewood St Raleigh NC 27612 Office: PO Box 26327 Raleigh NC 27611

ZEEDICK, JOHN FRANCIS IVAN, physician, anesthesiologist; b. Pitts., Feb. 21, 1928; s. Peter Ivan and Annette (Evers) Z.; student Carnegie Inst. Tech., 1946-47; B.S. in Math., U. Pitts., 1950, M.D., 1954; m. Conelia Alice Williams, May 7, 1960; children—John Michael, Laura Ann. Intern Mercy Hosp., Pitts., 1954-55; Berry Plan resident, U.S. Army, (Mercy Hosp.), 1955-57 teaching fellow anesthesiology U. Pitts. Sch. Medicine, 1955-57, instr. anesthesiology, 1959-61; anesthesiologist DeWitt Army Hosp., Ft. Belvoir, Va., 1959, 339th Gen. Hosp. U.S. Army Reserve, Aspinwall, Pa., 1959-61; dir. anesthesia Braddock (Pa.) Hosp., 1961-66, cons., 1967—; lectr. sch. anesthesia, St. Francis Gen. Hosp., Pitts., 1959-70, asst. anesthesiologist, 1959-61, cons. anesthesiologist, 1961-66, anesthesiologist, 1966-70; anesthesiologist Charlotte (N.C.) Meml. Hosp., 1970-72; dir. anesthesia H.J. Thomas Meml. Hosp., South Charleston, W.Va.; asst. vis. prof. anesthesia U. Tenn., 1966; asso. faculty mem. dept. pharmacology, toxicology Duquesne U., Pitts., 1967-70; lectr. Anesthesiology U. N.C. Sch. Medicine, 1970, clin. asso. prof., 1970—. Lectr. med. emergencies Police Acad. Pitts., 1960-70; lectr. symposia hosps., profl. socs., pub. health agys., U.S., Japan, Can., 1958-70. Chmn. anesthesiology panel Hosp. Utilization Project Western Pa., 1963, mem. med. adv. com., 1968-70. mem. adv. bd. Ambulance Attendants Tng. Program Pa., 1963-70; bd. dirs. W.Va. Heart Assn. Served to capt., M.C., AUS, 1957-59; PTO. Diplomate Am. Bd. Anesthesiology. Fellow Am. Coll. Anesthesiologists, Am. Coll. Clin. Pharmacology and Chemotherapy; mem. Am. (certificates appreciation 1960, 63, 67), Pa., Western Pa., N.Y. State (certificates appreciation 1960, 63, 65, 66) socs. anesthesiologists, A.M.A., Pa., Allegheny County (Pa.) med. socs., N.C., Mecklenburg County med. socs., Am. Ordnance Assn., Nat. Fire Protection Assn., Charlotte C. of C., Internat. Anesthesia Research Soc., Pitts. Acad. Medicine, N.Y. Acad. Scis., A.A.A.S., Am. Assn. Inhalation Therapists (hon.), Assn. Advancement Med. Instrumentation, Am. Therapeutic Soc. (affiliate), I.E.E.E. (bio-med. group). Contbr. articles profl. jours. Address: 1417 Mt Vernon Rd Charleston WV 25314

ZEEMAN, HAROLD, cafeteria exec.; b. N.Y.C., May 5, 1910; s. Charles and Anne (Rosenthal) Z.; grad. De Witt Clinton High Sch.; m. Beth Irene Berger, Oct. 4, 1944; 1 dau., Peggy Jill (Mrs. John I. Gordon). Partner Bachrach Printing Co., Mohawk Beef Co., 1945-50, Tropical Cafeteria, 1951-58; partner Biscayne Cafeteria, Miami, Fla., from 1959, pres., 1968—. Pres. Pan-Am. Hotel and Restaurant Exposition. Mem. Fla. Restaurant Assn. (pres.). Home: 251 SW 26th Rd Miami FL 33132 Office: 1917 Biscayne Blvd Miami FL 33129

ZEFF, STEPHEN ADDAM, educator; b. Chgo., July 26, 1933; s. Roy David and Hazel (Sex) Z.; B.S., U. Colo., 1955, M.S., 1957; M.B.A., U. Mich., 1960, Ph.D., 1962. Instr. U. Colo., 1955-57; teaching fellow, instr. U. Mich., 1958-61; asst. prof. accounting Tulane U., New Orleans, 1961-63, asso. prof., 1963-67, prof., 1967—; vis. asso. prof. U. Cal., Berkeley, 1964-65, U. Chgo., 1966; vis. prof. Instituto Tecnologico y de Estudios Superiores de Monterrey (Mexico), 1969, spl. lectr., also hon. sr. Fulbright scholar Monash U., Australia, 1972. Mem. Am. Accounting Assn., (dir. edn. 1969-71), Am. Econ. Assn., Nat. Assn. Accountants, Financial Execs. Inst., Brit. Inst. Mgmt. Author: Uses of Accounting for Small Business, 1962, American Accounting Assn. It's First 50 Years, 1966; Forging Accounting Principles in Five Countries: A History and an Analysis of Trends, 1972. Co-editor: Financial Accounting Theory, 1964, 69. Book rev. editor Accounting Rev., 1962-66. Founder, editor Boletin Interamericano de Contabilidad, 1968-71. Contbr. articles to profl. jours. Home: 2231 Marengo St New Orleans LA 70115

ZEGEL, FERDINAND HRANT, physicist; b. N.Y.C., Nov. 26, 1933; s. Ferdinand Jacob and Elinco (Aghamalian) Z.; B.S., Fairfield U., 1955; M.S., Boston Coll., 1958. Supr. Spectrophotometry Lab., Ansco, div. of Gen. Analine and Film Corp., Binghamton N.Y., 1958-59; research physicist Melpar, div. of Westinghouse Air Brake, Fairfax, Va., 1959-61; project engr. U.S. Weather Bur., Washington, 1961-68, U.S. Army Night Vision Lab., Ft. Belvoir, Va., 1968—; chief spectroscopist Beryllium Internat., Washington, 1960-67. Mem. Am. Physical Soc., Am. Meteorol. Soc., Optical Soc. Am., Soc. for Applied Spectroscopy. Roman Catholic. Contbr. articles in field to profl. jours. Home: 3449 N Randolph St Arlington VA 22207 Office: US Army Night Vision Lab Fort Belvoir VA 22060

ZEIGLER, EUGENE N., lawyer; b. Florence, S.C., July 20, 1921; B.A., U. of South, 1942; LL.B., Harvard, 1949. Admitted to N.C. bar, 1949, since practiced in Florence; spl. judge, 1964, 65. Pres., Florence Museum, 1951-60, Pee Dee Area Big Bros. Assn., 1953-55. Mem. S.C. Senate, 1967—. Mem. Am., Florence County, S.C. bar assns., Am. Judicature Soc., Phi Beta Kappa, Omicron Delta Kappa. Office: 246 W Evans St Florence SC 29501*

ZEIGLER, GEORGE MORRIS, securities co. exec.; b. Pulaski, Tenn., Aug. 10, 1934; s. Denzil H. and Ira Irene (Raines) Z.; B.S., David Lipscomb Coll., 1956; postgrad. U. Md., 1958; m. Sandra Evelyn Lawrence, May 8, 1960; children—George Gavin, Robin Evelyn, Amanda Lawrence. Vice pres. Clark Landstreet Kirkatrick, Inc., 1959-65, First Ala. Securities, Inc., Nashville, 1965-70; pres.

Zeigler, Cline & Holman, Inc., Nashville, 1970-—. Trustee Harpeth Acad., Franklin, Tenn. Served with AUS, 1956-59. Mem. Nashville Assn. Security Traders (dir. 1969-—). Republican. Club: Cumberland (Nashville). Home: Spencer Creek Farm Route 7 Franklin TN 37064 Office: Stahlman Bldg Nashville TN 37201

ZEILSTRA, EDWARD ERNEST, chem. engr.; b. Grand Rapids, Mich., Apr. 4, 1912; s. John Albert and Tena Alida (Moss) Z.; B.S., Calvin Coll., 1934; Asso. Synthetic Rubber Tech., Princeton, 1944; m. Anne Gertrude Mersman, Nov. 14, 1933; children—Linda Kay (Mrs. John J. Kellum), David Edward. Asst. chief rubber chemist Ford Motor Co., Dearborn, Mich., 1934-42; chief rubber devel. engr. John A. Roeblings' Co., Trenton, N.J., 1943-45; rep. midwestern tech. sales Wilmington Chem. Co., 1946; chief chemist Carr Mfg. Co., Bristol, R.I., 1947-52; tech. dir. Lloyd Mfg. Co., Appanaug, R.I., 1952-58; tech. supt. Rhee Elastic, Warren, R.I., 1958-61; chief chemist D.S. Brown Co., North Baltimore, O., 1961-66, Lewis Products Co., Hohenwald, Tenn., 1966-—. Mem. Am. Chem. Soc., Am. Contract Bridge League, Franklin Mint Collectors Soc., Nat. Hist. Soc., Am. Mus. Natural History, Am. Heritage Soc., So. Rubber Group Republican. Mason. Home: Trotwood Apts Columbia TN 38401 Office: Old Swan Rd Hohenwald TN 38462

ZELENY, CHARLES ELLINGSON, psychologist; b. Champaign, Ill., Apr. 24, 1918; s. Charles and Ida (Ellingson) Z.; B.A., U. Ill., 1939, M.A., 1953; m. Marjorie Ann Pfeiffer, Dec. 11, 1950; children—Ann Douglas, Charles Timberlake. Research psychologist Human Resources Research Center, Chanute AFB, Ill., 1949-52; research asst. U. Ill., 1952-54; research psychologist, human factors br. Electronic Warfare Dept., Ft. Huachuca, Ariz., 1954-58, chief of br., 1955-58; program dir. Applied Psychology Corp., Tucson, 1958-63; research psychologist Bendix Corp. Systems Div. Ann Arbor, Mich., 1963-66, project leader, 1965-66; chief of evaluation and selection br., nat. hdqrs. Vols. in Service to Am., Washington, 1966-69, chief vol. placement, 1969-71; policy and program devel. specialist Action Agy., Washington, 1971-—. Served with AUS, 1942-46; capt. Res. Mem. A.A.A.S., Am., D.C. psychol. assns., Soc. for Psychol. Study Social Issues, Alpha Kappa Lambda. Conglist. Home: 6825 Wemberly Way McLean VA 22101 Office: 806 Connecticut Av NW Washington DC 20525

ZELENY, MARJORIE PFEIFFER (MRS. CHARLES ELLINGSON ZELENY), psychologist; b. Balt., Mar. 31, 1924; d. Lloyd Armitage and Mable (Willian) Pfeiffer; B.A., U. Md., 1947; M.S., U. Ill., 1949, postgrad., 1951-54; m. Charles Ellingson Zeleny, Dec. 11, 1950; children—Ann Douglas, Charles Timberlake. Vocational counseling psychologist VA, Balt., 1947-48; asst. U. Ill., Urbana, 1948-50, research asso. Bur. Research, 1952-53; chief psychologist dept. neurology and psychiatry Ohio State U. Coll. Medicine, Columbus, 1950-51; research psychologist, cons., Tucscon, Washington, 1954-—. Mem. Am., D.C. psychol. assns., A.A.A.S., Soc. for Psychol. Study Social Issues, D.A.R., Mortar Bd., Delta Delta Delta, Sigma Delta Epsilon, Psi Chi, Sigma Tau Epsilon. Baptist. Home: 6825 Wemberly Way McLean VA 22101

ZELLER, EMILIO, III, architect; b. Santiago, Dominican Republic, Dec. 13, 1935; s. Emilio, Jr. and Hilda (Cordero Puello) Z.; came to U.S., 1941, naturalized 1953; B.S., Ga. Inst. Tech., 1957, B.Arch., 1957; m. Frances Faye Andrews, Aug. 12, 1962; children— Melanie, Stephanie, Amy. With Beiswenger-Hoch & J. Brooks Haas, Jacksonville, Fla., 1957-62; pvt. practice architecture, Jacksonville, Fla., 1962-—. Campaign coordinator YMCA. Mem. Duval County Republican Exec. Com., 1961-69; v.p. Young Rep. Club, 1968-69; Goldwater campaign chief Duval County, 1964. Served as capt., C.E., AUS, 1958. Mem. A.I.A., Theta Chi. Roman Catholic. Clubs: Georgia Tech. Alumni, University, Baymeadows Racquet; South Jacksonville Sertoma. Home: 1237 Northwood Rd Jacksonville FL 32207 Office: 1000 Riverside Av Jacksonville FL 32204

ZEMAN, WILLIAM J., oil co. exec.; b. Tobias, Neb., May 29, 1906; s. John and Mary (Klasek) Z.; B.A., Central State Coll., Edmond, Okla., 1929; LL.B., U. Okla., 1932; m. Neva M. Shultz, Mar. 26, 1937; children—Joe William, Carolyn Neva. Admitted to Okla. bar, 1932; mem. firm Beets, Zeman & Beets, Oklahoma City, 1933-42; staff atty. Phillips Petroleum Co., Oklahoma City, 1942-43, Bartlesville, Okla., 1943-55, asst. gen. atty., 1955-59, gen. atty., 1959-61, v.p., gen. counsel, mem. exec. com., dir. 1961-—, mem. finance com., 1967-—. Recipient outstanding student alumnus achievement award Central Coll., 1955. Mem. Am., Okla., Washington County bar assns., Ind. Petroleum Assn. Am., Am. Petroleum Inst., Ind. Natural Gas Assn. Am., Mid-Continent Oil and Gas Assn., Order Coif, Phi Delta Phi. Club: Hillcrest Country. Home: 3417 Hawthorn Ct Bartlesville OK 74003 Office: Phillips Bldg Bartlesville OK 74003

ZEMKE, JOHN C(LAUD), hosp. adminstr.; b. Portland, Mich., Sept. 12, 1913; s. Otto Albert and Anna Rosalie (Olsen) Z.; B.S., Ferris Inst., 1938; M.B.A., Rollins College, Winter Park, Fla., 1967; m. Madeline Mary Muck, Oct. 30, 1937; children—Ann Maureen (Mrs. Otis Graham, Jr.), Kathryn Mary (Mrs. Dale Flowers), Margery Jean (Mrs. Dennis Enberg), Penny Sue, Jill Lakin. Comml. tchr., bus. mgr. athletic dept. Van Dyke (Mich.) pub. schs., 1938-41, asst. supt. schs., 1941-43; resident mgr. Peninsular Finance Co., Keller Tractor & Equipment Co., Armada Farm Equipment Co., Armada, Mich., 1943-44; mng. owner sporting goods retail store, Armada, 1944-48; adminstr. Mt. Clemens (Mich.) Gen. Hosp., 1948-63; adminstr. Orlando (Fla.) Gen. Hosp., 1964-—. Cons. Gov.'s Study Com. on Blue Cross Rates; instr. gun safety Mich. Dept. Conservation. Pres. bd. edn., Armada Area Schs., 1944-59. Mem. Fla. (past pres.), Am. (pres.), Mich. (past pres.) osteopathic hosp. assns., Am. Coll. Osteopathic Hosp. Adminstrs., Am. Assn. Hosp. Accountants. Conglist. (deacon). Mason (Shriner, 32 deg.). Club: Lions (past pres.). Home: 2758 Cady Way Winter Park FL 32789 Office: 7727 Lake Underhill Dr Orlando FL 32807

ZENICH, MARGRETT BARTON, information exec.; b. Mead, Okla., Dec. 4, 1915; d. John Dandridge and Inez (Hightower) Barton; B.A., Southeastern State Coll., 1938; postgrad. San Jose State Coll., 1947; B.S. in Library Sci., U. Okla., 1951; spl. student Tex. Western Coll., 1964-65 children—Ruth Ann Linder, Peter Barton Linder, Mary Antoinette Camillo. Tchr., Big Cabin, Okla., 1938-39; Carnegie br. librarian, pub. sch. library, Oklahoma City, 1946-51; spl. services librarian 4th Army White Sands Missile Range, 1951-55, chief tech. library system, 1955-68; chief Sci. and Tech. Information Div., Office of Chief Engrs., Washington. Mem. A.L.A., Spl. Libraries Assn. (sec.-treas. documentation div. 1958-59, pres. Rio Grande chpt. 1967), Am. Assn. Information Sci., Am. Assn. U. Women, PIANC, El Paso County Humane Soc. (dir.), Alpha Phi Sigma. Baptist. Home: 4712 Poplar Dr Alexandria VA 22310 Office: Office Chief Engrs 1000 Independence Av Washington DC 20003

ZENKE, OTTO GEORGE, interior designer; b. Bklyn., May 31, 1904; s. Henry Christian and Susan (Kohler) Z.; student Pratt Inst., N.Y.C., Parsons Sch. Design, N.Y.C. Formerly with Theodore Hofstatter & Co., N.Y.C., B. Altman & Co., N.Y.C., Morrison-Neese, Greensboro, N.C., 1937-50; pres. Otto Zenke, Inc., Greensboro, 1950-—. Mem. Am. Inst. Designers, Interior Decorating and Designing Assn. (Brit.). Club: Greensboro Country. Works pub. in House and Garden, House Beautiful, Interior Design and Interiors, Antiques in Interior Decoration (H. Lionel Williams). Address: 220 S Eugene St Greensboro NC 27401

ZENS, CLARENCE M., editor; b. Racine, Wis., Aug. 17, 1918; s. Henry M. and Elizabeth (Roebling) Z.; student Marquette U., 1936-40; m. Mildred Irene Larson, May 24, 1944; children—Michael Louis, Karen Larson. With Milwaukee Herald-Citizen, 1940-41; news desk, Nat. Catholic Welfare Conf. News Service, Washington, 1945-50, asst. to dir. bur. information, 1950-51; mng. editor The Catholic Standard, Washington, 1951-61; fgn. information specialist, U.S. Dept. Commerce, 1961-64; editor, fgn. commerce weekly Internat. Commerce, Washington, 1964-—. Cons. internat. trade fairs; free lance writer. Bd. dirs. St. John's Mil. High Sch., Marquette U. Sch. Journalism. Served to 1st lt., USAF, 1941-45. Recipient By-Line award Marquette Sch. Journalism, 1961. Mem. Marquette U. Alumni Assn., Men of St. John's. Author: Saints in Crosswords 1958. Contbr. articles to Cath. pubis. Home: 406 A St SE Washington DC 20003 Office: International Commerce US Dept Commerce Washington DC 20230

ZERFOSS, LESTER FRANK, mgmt. cons., educator; b. Mountaintop, Pa., Nov. 2, 1903; s. Clinton and Mabel (Wilcox) Z.; B.A. cum laude, Pa. State U., 1926, M.Ed., 1934, D.Ed., 1958; m. Harriet Mildred Cary, Dec. 21, 1928; children—Patricia Ann (Mrs. Thomas Sibben), Clinton Cary, Robert Williamson. Coll. tchr., pub. sch. adminstr., Pa., 1928-41; supr. design, devel. Gen. Motors Inst., 1942-46; head supervisory devel. Detroit Edison Co., 1946-52; corporate tng. dir. Am. Enka Corp. (N.C.), 1952-59, dir. indsl. relations, mgmt. services, 1952-66, mgmt. cons. for managerial and tech. devel., 1966-—; asso. prof. psychology Asheville-Biltmore Coll., 1966-68; research prof. developmental psychology, dir. mgmt. devel. programs U. N.C. at Asheville, 1968-—. Mem. bd., head mgmt. devel. com. N.C. Personnel Bd., 1966-70; cons. to Gov. for mgmt. devel., 1970-—; mem. Southeastern Regional Manpower Adv. Com., 1966-—, N.C. Adv. Com. for Community Colls. Trustee Brevard Coll., Asheville-Buncombe Tech. Inst. Mem. Am. Mgmt. Assn., Nat. Soc. Advancement Mgmt. (profl. mgr. citation 1962), Am. Soc. Tng. and Devel., Phi Delta Kappa, Kappa Phi Kappa, Kappa Delta Pi, Delta Sigma Phi. Elk, Rotarian. Author: Developing Professional Personnel in Business, Idustry and Government, 1969. Contbr. articles to profl. jours. Home: 910 4th Av W Hendersonville NC 28739 Office: Univ of NC Asheville NC 28801

ZICKEFOOSE, MENDLE SHERMAN, ednl. adminstr.; b. Buckhannon, W.Va., Apr. 15, 1922; s. Issac Sherman and Lillie Blanche (Lanham) Z.; student N.C. State U., 1944; B.S., W.Va. Wesleyan U., 1959; m. Mary Lou McWhorter, Nov. 4, 1948; 1 dau., Suzanne. Profl. football player, Washington Redskins, 1945; comml. financing field rep., credit mgr. personal finance Universal Credit Investment Trust & Asso. Discount Corp., 1946-53; ins. agt. Nationwide Ins. Co., Leesburg, Va., 1953-59; tchr. secondary schs., S. Augustine, Fla., 1959-61; bus. mgr., athletic dir., coach Shenandoah Coll. and Conservatory Music, Winchester, Va., 1961-67, treas., bus. mgr., 1967-—. Mem. So. Assn. Coll. and Univ. Bus. Officers. Mason, Rotarian. Home: 423 W Monmouth St Winchester VA 22601 Office: Millwood Av Winchester VA 22601

ZIEGLER, A(RTHUR), govt. ofcl.; b. Anderson, Ind., June 27, 1917; s. Maurice Robert and Martha (Bortner) Z.; A.B., U. N.C., 1939, M.A., 1941, Ph.D., 1948; m. Martha Coker, June 6, 1946; children—Robert Jackson, David Coker, Daniel Roper. Instr., U. N.C., 1947; faculty biol. scis. Fla. State U., 1948-63; chief univ. relations br. AEC, Bethesda, Md., 1963-—. Served with AUS, 1942-46. Mem. A.A.A.S., Mycol. Soc. Am., Bot. Soc. Am. Home: 5600 Beam Ct Bethesda MD 20034 Office: 7920 Norfolk Av Bethesda MD 20545

ZIEGLER, RONALD LOUIS, govt. ofcl.; b. Covington, Ky., May 12, 1939; s. Louis Daniel and Ruby (Parsons) Z.; student Xavier U., 1957-58; B.S., U. So. Cal., 1961; m. Nancy Lee Plessinger, July 30, 1960; children—Cynthia Lee, Laurie Michelle. Salesman, Proctor & Gamble Distbg. Co., 1961; account rep. J. Walter Thompson Co., 1962-68; press dir. Cal. Republican Central Com., 1961-62; press aide to Richard Nixon in Cal. gubernatorial campaign, 1962; press aide staff Richard Nixon, 1968-69; press sec. to Pres. Nixon, 1969-—. Mem. Sigma Chi. Home: 2008 Fort Dr Alexandria VA 22307

ZIELKE, GEORGE ROBERT, newspaper corr.; b. LaCrosse, Wis., Apr. 15, 1911; s. Otto C. and Hulda (Ulrich) Z.; student LaCrosse Tchrs. Coll., 1928-30; A.B., U. Wis., 1932; m. Ruth Hungate, July 3, 1936; 1 dau., Betty. Reporter-editor LaCrosse (Wis.) Tribune, 1927-36; with Asso. Press, 1936-44; Washington corr. Toledo Blade, Pitts. Post-Gazette, 1944-—. Mem. Sigma Delta Chi, Phi Mu Alpha Sinfonia. Club: Nat. Press (Washington). Home: 503 N Pickett St Alexandria VA 22304 Office: 531 14th St NW Washington DC 20004

ZIESENHEIM, JOSEPH C., state ofcl.; b. Houston, Oct. 4, 1918; B.S., U. Pitts., 1940; M.H.A., Baylor U., 1961. Commd. 2d lt. U.S. Army, 1943; advanced through grades to lt. col., 1961; adj. 27th Med. Tng. Bn., Camp Grant, Ill., 1943-44, Ft. Lewis, Wash., 1944, 250th Gen. Hosp., France, 1944-45, 365th Sta. Hosp., 1946; comdr. med. tng. co. Brooke Army Med. Center, Ft. Sam Houston, Tex., 1950; med. adminstrv. asst. 7th Mobile Army Surg. Hosp., Ft. Jackson, S.C., 1951; troop comdr. med. detachment 5th Gen. Hosp., Germany, 1953; comdg. officer 66th Ambulance Train, Germany, 1955; exec. officer U.S. Army Hosp., Sandia Base, Albuquerque, 1956-59; hosp. mgmt. officer U.S. Army Hosp., Ft. Devens, Mass., 1961-62; exec. officer 121st Evacuation Hosp., Korea, 1962-63; comdg. officer 106th Gen. Hosp., William Beaumont Gen. Hosp., El Paso, 1963-64; ret., 1964; adminstr. Fla. Alcoholic Rehab. Program, Avon Park, 1964-—. Decorated Croix de Guerre with Silver Star (France). Home: 3310 W Lakeview Dr Sebring FL33870 Office: Box 1147 Avon Park FL 33825*

ZIETZ, ROBERT JOSEPH, librarian; b. Menominee, Mich., Sept. 7, 1922; s. Joseph R. and Mary (Eckert) Z.; B.S., Spring Hill Coll., 1949; M. Library, Emory U., 1950; m. Norma Corners, Nov. 2, 1943; children—Suzanne (Mrs. John N. McAtee), Michael, Stephen, Jan, Jennifer, Kristin. Asst. librarian Spring Hill Coll., Mobile, Ala., 1951-61, librarian, 1961-—. Bd. dirs. Mobile Mus. Served with USAAF, 1943-46. Mem. Am., Ala. (pres. 1966-67), Catholic (sect. pres. 1968-—), Southeastern library assns. Co-author: Writing & Research. Home: 4580 Hawthorne Pl Mobile AL 36608

ZIMMERER, CARL EDWARD, editor; b. Niles, Mich., Dec. 15, 1912; s. Charles L. and Eva (Gardner) Z.; A.B. magna cum laude, U. Notre Dame, 1934; m. Alice Balcerzak, Aug. 26, 1940; 1 son, Michael G. Reporter South Bend (Ind.) News-Times and South Bend Tribune, 1930-40, book editor, 1935-40; telegraph editor, asst. news editor Courier-Jour., Louisville, 1940-60, chief wire services, 1960-—. Owner, operator Snappy Filler Service, 1950-—. Served with U.S. Merchant Marine, 1944-45. Roman Catholic. Club: Big Spring Country. Home: 610 Wataga Dr Louisville KY 40206 Office: 525 W Broadway Louisville KY 40202

ZIMMERMAN, HYMAN JOSEPH, physician, educator; b. Rochester, N.Y., July 14, 1914; s. Philip and Rachel (Marine) Z.; A.B., U. Rochester, 1936; M.A., Stanford, 1938, M.D., 1942; m. Kathrin J. Jones, Feb. 28, 1943; children—Philip M., David J., Robert L., Diane E. Intern, Stanford U. Hosp., 1942-43; resident George Washington U. div. Gallinger Municipal Hosp., 1946-48, clin. instr. medicine Sch. Medicine, 1948-51; practice medicine specializing in internal medicine, Washington, 1948-49, Omaha, 1951-53, Chgo., 1953-65; asst. chief med. service VA Hosp., Washington, 1949-51, dir. liver and metabolic research lab., 1965-68, chief med. service, 1971-—; asst. prof. medicine U. Neb. Coll. Medicine, also chief med. service VA Hosp., Omaha, 1951-53; chief med. service West Side VA Hosp., Chgo., also clin. asso. prof. medicine U. Ill. Coll. Medicine, 1953-57; prof., chmn. dept. medicine Chgo. Med. Sch., also chmn. dept. medicine Mt. Sinai Hosp., Chgo., 1957-65; prof. medicine George Washington U. Sch. Medicine, Washington, 1965-68, 71-—; chief med. service Boston VA Hosp., 1968-71; prof. medicine Boston U. Sch. Medicine, 1968-71; lectr. medicine Tufts U. Sch. Medicine, 1968-71; clin. prof. medicine Georgetown U., 1971-—, Howard U., 1971-—. Served to maj., M.C., AUS, 1943-46. Fellow A.C.P.; mem. A.M.A., A.A.A.S., Am. Fedn. Clin. Research, Am. Diabetes Assn., Endocrine Soc., Assn. Study Liver Disease, Am. Soc. Clin. Investigation, N.Y. Acad. Scis., Central Soc. Clin. Research, Soc. Exptl. Biology and Medicine, Chgo. Heart Assn. (gov.), Chgo. Soc. Internal Medicine (past pres.), Am. Gastroent. Assn., Sigma Xi, Alpha Omega Alpha. Address: 50 Irving St NW Washington DC 20422

ZINCK, JAMES HOWARD, dentist; b. Houston, Mar. 29, 1931; s. Howard Abraham and Gertrude Lenard (Lamkin) Z.; student La. State U., 1948-51; D.D.S., Loyola U. South, 1959; m. Jeanne Brulet, Sept. 6, 1952; children—Jean Carol, Julie Ann, Joseph Howard. Pvt. practice dentistry, Lake Charles, La., 1959-65, Austin, Tex., 1965-68, Luling, Tex., 1968-—; dir. Indsl. Corp., Luling, Trustee, Luling Ind. Sch. Dist., 1969-71, v.p., 1970-71. Served with USAF, 1951-54. Research grantee U.S. Govt. Dept. Operative Dentistry, 1958; recipient Certificate of Merit award Am. Acad. Dentistry, 1959. Mem. Am., Tex. dental assns., Guadalupe Valley Dental Soc., C. Victor Vignes Odontological Soc. (v.p. 1958), 7th Dist. Dental Assn. La. (sec.-treas. 1963, pres. 1964), S. Tex. (dir. 1970-71), Luling (dir. 1969-71, pres. 1970) chambers commerce, Luling Thump Assn. (dir. 1969), Alpha Sigma Nu, Omicron Kappa Upsilon, Sigma Alpha Epsilon, Xi Psi Phi. Democrat. Roman Catholic. Lion. Club: Sertoma (Austin, Tex.). Home: 220 Parkview Dr Luling TX 78648 Office: 409 E Crockett St Luling TX 78648

ZINCONE, LOUIS HENRY, educator; b. Richmond, Va., Jan. 4, 1941; s. Louis H. and Alice (Purcell) Z.; B.A., U. Richmond, 1963; Ph.D., U. Va., 1967; m. Maria Taylor, July 27, 1963; children—Mary Maria, Alice Elizabeth. Asst. prof. econs. East Carolina U., Greenville, 1966-69, prof., chmn. dept., 1968-—. Home: 1730 Beaumont Rd Greenville NC 27834

ZINN, CAROLYN JUNE, educator; b. Takoma Park, Md., June 9, 1933; d. Donald Schaeffer and Erma (Sirbaugh) Zinn; B.A., W.Va. U., 1955, M.A., 1955, Ph.D., 1967; postgrad. (Fulbright scholar) Free U. Brussels (Belgium), 1955-56. Publicity dir., advt. copywriter, asst. book prodn. mgr. Wadsworth Pub. Co., Belmont, Cal., 1959-61; adminstrv. asst. to editorial dir. McGraw-Hill Book Co., Inc., Novato, 1961-63; grad. asst. polit. sci. W.Va. U., 1964-67; asso. prof. polit. sci. Elon (N.C.) Coll., 1967-69; vis. prof. polit. sci. U. N.C., Chapel Hill, summer 1969; asst. prof. polit. sci. U. Pa., Uniontown, 1969-71; historian, archivist State of W.Va., 1971-—. Pink Lady, Med. Aux. Alamance County-Meml. Hosp. Mem. Am. Polit. Sci. Assn., Phi Beta Kappa, Mortar Bd., Pi Sigma Alpha, Pi Gamma Mu, Phi Alpha Theta, Pi Delta Phi, Kappa Delta Pi, Delta Gamma. Home: Box 467 Church St Reedsville WV 26547 Office: Capitol 2106 Kanawha Blvd E Charleston WV 25311

ZIPFEL, EDWARD WILLIAM, mech. engr.; b. Oak Harbor, O., June 29, 1909; s. William and Freda Wilhelmena (Meinke) Z.; B.Sc., Heidelberg Coll., 1933; m. Vivian A. Kolath, June 29, 1935 (dec.); children—Diane (Mrs. Louis R. Lee), William Edward. Field engr. U.S. Govt., Port Clinton, O., 1934-35; plant engr. Standard Products, Port Clinton, 1936-51, Am. Synthetic Rubber Corp., Louisville, 1951. City engr. Oak Harbor, 1942-51. Mem. Oak Harbor City Council, 1942-51. Mem. Am. Inst. Plant Engr. (dir., past pres.). Mason. Home: 1134 Audubon Pkwy Louisville KY 40213 Office: 4500 Camp Ground Rd Louisville KY 40201

ZIRKLE, CHARLES RANKIN, surgeon; b. Kingston, Tenn., Nov. 1, 1914; s. G.P. and Clara (Bettis) Z.; A.B., Tusculum Coll., 1937; M.D., Vanderbilt U., 1941; m. Jean B. Collins, Nov. 5, 1945; children—Helen, Ian, Kevin. Intern Deaconness Hosp., Buffalo, 1941-42; resident Vanderbilt Hosp. and St. Thomas Meml. Hosp., Nashville, 1946-50; practice surgery, Knoxville, Tenn., 1950-—. Trustee Tusculum Coll., 1958-—. Served to capt., M.C., AUS, 1942-45. Diplomate Am. Bd. Surgery. Mem. A.C.S., Southeastern Surg. Congress. Democrat. Presbyn. Club: Cherokee Country (Knoxville). Home: 2207 Cherokee Blvd Knoxville TN 37920 Office: Blount Profl Bldg Knoxville TN 37920

ZOGG, RICHARD EDWARD, univ. adminstr.; b. Belleville, Ill., Apr. 29, 1924; s. Adolph Gustav and Adalia Susan (Joerg) Z.; A.A., Blackburn Coll., 1943; B.S., U. Ill., 1947; M.B.A., St. Louis U., 1960; m. Marie Annette Flack, July 10, 1948; children—William David, Janice Louise, Paul Alan, Judith Elaine. Head spectrochem. sect. Sinclair Research Labs., Harvey, Ill., 1947-53; asst. to chmn. bd. Midwest Rubber Reclaiming Co., East St. Louis, Ill., 1953-67; lab. adminstr. Brown & Williamson Tobacco Co., Louisville, 1967-70; dir. health scis. labs. U. Louisville, 1970-—. Tchr. mgmt. Belleville Jr. Coll., 1963-65, St. Louis U., 1960-67, Bellarmine Coll., 1967-70. Vice-chmn. A.R.C., St. Louis Bi-state chpt., 1966-67; St. Clair County publicity chmn. Am. Heart Assn., 1966-67. Served with USNR, 1944-46. Recipient awards Freedom Found., 1961, 62, St. Louis United Fund, 1963, St. Louis Indsl. Press, 1961. Mem. Am. Assn. Spectrographers (chmn. 1952-53), Am. Chem. Soc., Prodn. Control Soc., Indsl. Press Assn., Assn. Multidisciple Edn. Roman Catholic. Author: Rubberized Playgrounds, 1959. Home: 9211 Trentham Lane Louisville KY 40222

ZON, HENRY, pub. relations co. exec.; b. Vilna, Russia, Oct. 9, 1912 (parents Am. citizens); s. Raphael G. and Anna (Puzyriski) Z.; B.A., U. Minn., 1934; postgrad. London Sch. Econs. and Polit. Sci., 1935; m. Mary Woodbridge Goddard, June 14, 1951; 1 son, Calvin Goddard. Washington corr., labor papers, 1936-42; news editor Radio Sta. WQQW, 1946-47; pub. relations dir. CIO Polit. Action Com., 1947-55; research and pub. relations dir. AFL-CIO Com. on Polit. Edn., 1955-59; v.p., sec. Maurer, Fleisher, Zon & Assos., Washington, 1959-—. Served to 1st lt. USAF, 1942-46. Democrat. Club: Nat. Press. Home: 2220 20th St NW Washington DC 20009 Office: 1120 Connecticut Av NW Washington DC 20037

ZORN, EUGENE CHRISTIAN, JR., bank economist; b. N.Y.C., Jan. 17, 1916; s. Eugene Christian and Charlotte (Bode) Z.; B.B.A., Coll. City N.Y., 1937; M.S., Columbia, 1942; m. Elizabeth Orban, Aug. 11, 1956; children—Barbara Jean, Robert Eugene. Dept. mgr., dir. research Am. Bankers Assn., N.Y.C., 1940-60; v.p., economist Republic Nat. Bank, Dallas, 1960-66, sr. v.p., economist, 1966—. Served to capt. USAAF, World War II. Mem. Am. Econ. Assn., Am. Finance Assn., Am. Statis. Assn., Am. Mgmt. Assn., Nat. Economists Club, So. Finance Assn., Financial Mgmt. Assn., Nat. Assn. of Bus. Econ., Southwestern Social Sci. Assn., Newcomen Soc., Beta Gamma Sigma. Clubs: Northwood (Dallas). Home: 4647 Hallmark Dr Dallas TX 75229 Office: Republic Nat Bank Dallas TX 75222

ZORN, WILLIAM EDWARD, city ofcl.; b. Henderson, Tex., Aug. 16, 1911; s. Louis Edward and Margaret (Norvell) Z.; grad. high sch.; m. Hazle Acker, July 4, 1931; children—William Edward, Thomas Lee. Mem. Del Rio Vol. Fire Dept., 1936-51; driver, City Del Rio (Tex.) Fire Dept., 1951-54, chief, 1954—. Instr. Firemen's Tng. Sch., A. and M. U., mem. adv. bd. Tng. Sch., 1971—. Chmn. Val Verde County chpt. A.R.C., 1958—. Mem. Tex. Firemen's and Fire Marshals' Assn. (pres. 1962-63), Wintergarden Firemen's Assn. (pres. 1940). Mason, Order Hermann Sons. Home: 405 W 5th St Del Rio TX 78840 Office: Central Fire Sta PO Box 543 Del Rio TX 78840

ZUBER, JOHN M., banker; b. Fort Wayne, Ind., 1907; LL.B., Ohio State U., 1929; m. Admitted to Ohio bar, 1929; pvt. practice law, 1929-38; v.p. trust dept. Ohio Citizens Trust, Toledo, 1938-45, Am. Nat. Bank, Indpls., 1945-53, Rep. Nat. Bank Dallas, 1953-69; exec. v.p. First City Nat. Bank, Houston, 1969—. Office: 1001 Main St Houston TX 77002

ZUBER, ORAN HAMILTON, finance and investment exec.; b. Bedias, Tex., Oct. 4, 1910; s. James Andrew and Lillian Gertrude (Owens) Z.; student Sam Houston State U., 1931-32; grad. Sales Analysis Inst., Detroit, 1948, Chrysler Corp. Conf. Bus. Mgmt., Detroit, 1949; m. Minnie Marion Cuthbertson, June 1, 1940; children—Zachary H., Leah Kaye (Mrs. Douglas Whitty), Randolph C., Beverly Kaye (Mrs. Lynn Worden). Br. mgr. Universal Credit Co., Houston, 1934-43; sales rep. Gen. Mills Co., Dallas, 1943, Wesson Oil Sales Corp., New Orleans, 1943-44; br. mgr., div. credit mgr., asst. v.p. Comml. Credit Corp., Dallas, 1944-52; v.p. Southwestern Investment Co., Amarillo, Tex., 1952—. Budget com. United Fund, Amarillo, 1965-66; active Operations Drug Alert, Amarillo Area, 1970-72; active Girl Scouts. Bd. dirs. Better Bus. Bur., Amarillo, 1962-63. Mem. Ch. of Christ. Mem. Order of DeMolay (past master counsellor), Kiwanian. Office: 205 E 10th St Amarillo TX 79105

ZUCK, GORDON DARNELL, steel fabricating co. exec.; b. Crawfordsville, Inc., Aug. 25, 1911; s. James Franklin and Charlotte (Darnell); U. Ind., 1924-26; m. Ruth Janet Winter, Apr. 22, 1936; children—Wilma J. (Mrs. Stanley Aulsbrook), David L., Sandra E., Richard D., Susan, Linda, Louis. Advt., sales promotion mgr. Wilson & Bennett Mfg. Co., Chgo., 1932-45; sales mgr. Inland Steel Container Co., Chgo., 1945-47, v.p. 1947-51; pres. Pan American Indsl. Products Co., 1941-46; pres., dir. Vulcan Steel Container Co., Birmingham, Ala., (merger Zucon, Inc., 1963), 1951-65; pres., dir. Zuck Pail & Can Co., Jonesboro, Ga., 1965—, also Atlantic Vulcan Steel Containers, Inc., Peabody, Mass., Vulcan International S.A. Panama, Automated Theatres, Inc.; dir. Vulcan Containers, Inc., Bellwood, Ill., Vulcan Containers, Ltd., Toronto and Vancouver; pres., dir. Vulcan Associated Container Cos., Inc., Birmingham, Ala., Fla. Internat. Motor Speedway, Inc. Clubs: Vestavia Country, The Downtown (Birmingham); Illinois Athletic (Chgo.), Capitol City (Atlanta); Lakeshore Country (Jonesboro, Ga.). Author articles in field. Home: Vestavia Hills AL 35209 also Fort Walton Beach FL 32548 Office: 2824 Linden Av Homewood AL 35209

ZUERCHER, WILLIAM ROBERT, hosp. adminstr.; b. Nampa, Ida., Mar. 31, 1937; s. Elliott Howard and Edna Irene (Roth) Z.; B.A., Goshen Coll., 1958; M.H.A., Duke, 1968; m. Mary Joyce Gingerich, June 14, 1958; children—Melanie Alice, Andrea Elizabeth, Edward William. Asst. bus. mgr. Goshen (Ind.) Coll., 1960-62; adminstr. Brook Lane Psychiat. Center, Hagerstown, Md., 1961-66; asst. adminstr. Harlan (Ky.) Appalachian Regional Hosp., 1968-70, adminstr., 1972—; spl. asst. to pres., 1970—; adminstr. Clover Fork Clinic, Evarts, Ky., 1970—. Dir., chmn. finance com. Mennonite Mut. Aid. Assn., Inc., Goshen, Ind., 1967—; pres. Harlan (Ky.) City P.T.A., 1969-71; dir., treas. Mennonite Mental Health Services, Inc., Akron, Pa., 1967—; mem. Cumberland River Mental Health-Mental Retardation Bd., 1971—; nat. chmn. Goshen Coll. Alumni Fund, 1973. Recipient Leadership and Service citation Family Service Agy., Hagerstown, Md., 1969. Mem. Am. Coll. Hosp. Adminstrs., Assn. for Clin. Pastoral Edn., Ky. Hosp. Assn. (chmn. ednl. steering com. 1971—), C. of C. (mem. task force on community improvement 1971). Presbyn. (trustee 1969-71). Mennonite (mem., vice chmn. health and welfare com. bd. missions 1968—). Kiwanian. Home: 604 S Main St Harlan KY 40831 Office: Martins Fork Rd Harlan KY 40831

ZUHDI, MOHAMED NAZIH, physician; b. Beirut, Lebanon, May 19, 1925; s. Omar and Lutfiye (Atef) Z.; came to U.S., 1950; B.A., Am. U., Beirut, Lebanon, 1946, M.D., 1950; diploma Instituto Brasileiro de Investigatioes Cardiovascularis, Rio de Janeiro children—Omar, Nabil Intern St. Vincent's Hosp., N.Y.C., 1950-51, Presbyn.-Columbia Med. Center, N.Y.C., 1951-52; resident Kings County State U. N.Y. Med. Center, N.Y.C., 1952-56, fellow, 1952-53; resident U. Hosp., Mpls., 1956, Oklahoma City, 1957-58; practice medicine, specializing in cardivocascular and thoracic surgery, Oklahoma City, 1958—; active thoracic Bapt., Mercy, St. Anthony hosps.; mem. intensive care, inhalation therapy coms. Bapt. Meml. Hosp., Oklahoma City; asst. instr. surgery State U. N.Y., 1955-56. Named Hon. Citizen Brazil. Diplomate Am. Bd. Surgery, Am. Bd. Thoracic Surgery. Fellow A.C.S.; mem. Am., Okla. Thoracic socs., Am., So., Okla. med. assns., Internat., Am. colls. angiology, Am. Coll. Chest Physicians, Oklahoma City C. of C., Oklahoma County Med. Soc., Oklahoma City Clin. Soc., Okla. Surg. Assn., Southwestern Sug. Congress, Am. Coll. Cardiology, Am. Soc. Artificial Internal Organs: Soc. Thoracic Surgeons (founder mem.), Internat. Cardiovascular Soc., Okla. Heart Assn., Osler Soc. Research cardiovascular surgery, Am. Assn. Thoracic Surgery, La Sociedad Colombia de Cardiologia (hon.). Contbg. author Cardiac Surgery. Contbr. numerous articles to profl. jours. Home: 2904 Rosewood Lane Oklahoma City OK 73120 Office: 1211 N Shartel Oklahoma City OK 73103

ZUMWALT, ELMO RUSSELL, JR., naval officer; b. San Francisco, Nov. 29, 1920; s. Elmo Russell and Frances Z.; B.S. with distinction, U.S. Naval Acad., 1942; student Naval War Coll., 1952-53, Nat. War Coll., 1961-62; m. Mouza Coutelais-du-Roche; children—Elmo Russell III, James Gregory, Ann F., Mouza C. Commd. ensign U.S. Navy, 1942, advanced through grades to adm., 1970; served with U.S.S. Phelps, Operational Tng. Command Pacific, San Francisco, 1942-43, with U.S.S. Robinson, 1943-45; exec. officer U.S.S. Saufley, 1945-46; exec. officer, navigator U.S.S. Zellars, 1946-48; asst. prof. naval sci. Naval R.O.T.C., U. N.C. at Chapel Hill, 1948-50; comdr. U.S.S. Tills, 1950-51; navigator U.S.S. Wisconsin, Korea, 1951-52; head shore and overseas bases sect. Bur. Naval Personnel, Washington, 1953-55; comdr. destroyer U.S.S. Arnold J. Isbell, 1955-57; lt. detailer, Washington, 1957; spl. asst. for naval personnel Office Asst. Sec. Navy, Washington, 1957-58, exec. asst., sr. aide, 1958-59; comdr. U.S.S. Dewey, 1959-61; desk officer for France, Spain and Portugal Office Asst. Sec. Def. for Internat. Security Affairs, 1962-63, dir. arms control and contingency planning for Cuba, 1963; exec. asst., sr. aide Sec. of Navy, 1963-65; comdr. Cruiser-Destroyer Flotilla Seven, 1965-66; dir. chief naval operations systems analysis group, Washington Office Chief Naval Operations, dep. sci. officer Center Naval Analyses, 1966-68; comdr. U.S. Naval Forces Vietnam, chief naval adv. group, Vietnam, 1968-70; chief naval operations, Washington, 1970—. Decorated D.S.M. with 1 Gold Star, Legion of Merit with Gold Star, Bronze Star with Combat V, SECNAV Commendation Ribbon with combat V, also numerous campaign and area citations, medal; Philippine Republic Presdl. Citation; Vietnamese Chuong My Medal 1st Class, Nat. Order Vietnam 3d Class, Vietnamese Navy Distinguished Service Order 1st class. Home: Admiral's House Naval Obs Washington DC 20390 Office: Office Chief Naval Operations Navy Dept Washington DC 20350

ZUNG, MAX MING-KWAI, physician; b. Hankow, China, Oct. 2, 1922; s. Bate and Rose Yu-sun (Fong) Z.; came to U.S., 1937, naturalized, 1951; B.S., Columbia, 1946, M.D., 1950; m. Madeline Elizabeth Roye, May 1, 1965; children—Robert, Richard, Rebecca, Michael. Research asst. dept. biochemistry Coll. Phys. and Surgs., Columbia, 1942-45; intern Orange (N.J.) Meml. Hosp., 1950-51; resident Columbia Presbyn. Med. Center, N.Y.C., 1951-53; sr. attending dept. anesthesia Providence Hosp., Washington, 1954—; dep. rep. subcom. on anesthesia NRC, 1954-55; mem. staff Washington Sanitarium and Hosp., 1953-55, Suburban Hosp., Bethesda, Md., 1953-55. Bd. dirs. Med. Scis. Research Found. Served with USNR, 1953-55. Diplomate Am. Bd. Anesthesiology. Fellow Am. Coll. Anesthesiology; mem. Md.-D.C. Soc. Anesthesiologists (v.p. 1972—). Mem. Chinese Community Ch. (chmn. ch. council 1964-65). Lion. Home: 4136 N River St Arlington VA 22207 Office: 1150 Varnum St NE Washington DC 20017

ZUNIGA, FRANCISCO, artist; b. San Jose, Costa Rica, Dec. 27, 1912. Exhibited in group shows Expn. Central Am. Art, San Jose, 1935, Arts Club, Chgo., 1942, Phila. Mus. Art, 1943, Casa de Arte, Mexico City, 1945, Knoedler Galleries, N.Y.C., 1945, 3d Sculpture Internat., Phila. Mus. Art, 1949; Musee Nacional, San Jose, 1954, Dept. Tourism, San Salvador, El Salvador, Salon Anual Escultura, Mexico City, 1957, 58, Unst der Mexikaner, Cologne, Germany, 1959, Instituto de Bellas Artes, Mexico City, 1960, Galeria Universitaria Aristos, 1963, Latin Am. Artists Art Alliance, Phila., 1964, Phoenix Art Mus., 1964, Gallery Modern Art, Scottsdale, Ariz., 1966, Expn. Art of Mexico, Montreal, Que., Can., 1968, Museo de Arte Moderno, Mexico City, 1968, Musee Middelheim, Antwerp, Belgium, 1971, Galeria Tasende, Acapulco, Mexico; works represented in permanent collections Museo de Arte Moderno, Mexico City, Riverside Museum, N.Y.C., Phoenix Art Museum, Museo Nacional de Costa Rica, San Jose, Museo de Arte de Ponce, San Juan, P.R. Address: care Jose Ma Tasende Acapulco Mexico*

ZWICK, CHARLES J., banker; b. Plantsville, Conn., July 17, 1926; s. Louis C. and Mabel (Rich) Z.; B.S., U. Conn., 1950, M.S., 1951; Ph.D. in Econs., Harvard, 1954; m. Joan Wallace Cameron, June 21, 1952; children—Robert Louis, Janet Ellen. Prof. econs. U. Conn., 1951-54, Harvard, 1954-56; head logistics dept. RAND Corp., Santa Monica, Cal., 1956-65; with U.S. Bur. Budget, Washington, 1965-69, asst. dir., 1965-68, dir., 1968-69; pres., dir. Southeast Banking Corp., Miami, Fla., 1969—; dir. First Nat. Bank of Miami, Southeast Mortgage Co.; exec. v.p., dir. First Fgn. Investment Corp.; trustee, dir. The RAND Corp., dir. Southeast Services, Inc., Southeast Properties, Inc., Southeast Financial Services Inc., Southeast Data Processing, Compass Finance, S.A., Compass Finance (U.K.) Ltd. Served with AUS, 1946-47. Mem. Operations Research System Am., Econometric Assn. Democrat. Catholic. Author: (with Merton U. Peck, John Stenason and John R. Meyer) The Economics of Competition in the Transportation Industries, 1959. Home: 4210 Santa Maria St Coral Gables FL 33146 Office: 100 S Biscayne Blvd Miami FL 33131

ZWICK, ELMER GEORGE, music co. exec.; b. Cin., May 20, 1907; s. Philip and Anna (Michael) Z.; grad. high sch.; m. Jane Eliz Snyder, Dec. 26, 1933; children—David, Jude, Thomas. Joined Wurlitzer Co., 1925, became store mgr., Ashland, Ky.; pres., owner Zwick Music Co., Ashland, 1939—; dir. Bank Ashland. Mem. adv. bd. Our Lady of Bellefonte Hosp., Ashland, 1958—. K.C., Elk. Home: 1212 Montgomery St Ashland KY 41101 Office: 325 14th St Ashland KY 41101

Who'sWho in America
Biographees of the South and Southwest

The following biographies, which appear in the current edition of *Who's Who in America*, are not included in *Who's Who in the South and Southwest* because of space limitations.

Aaron, Henry
Abadie, Lloyd J.
Abbadessa, John P.
Abbot, Charles G.
Abbot, William W.
Abbott, Lynn D.
Abegg, Roland
Abel, Elle
Abell, Thomas H.
Abels, Jules
Abelson, Philip H.
Abernathy, Maurine H.
Abernathy, Kenneth B.
Abernathy, Tom L.
Abernethy, Cecil E.
Abersfeller, Heinz A.
Abhau, William C.
Abrams, Bernard B.
Aby, Hulette F.
Achenbach, Gerald H.
Achilles, Theodore C.
Achinstein, Asher
Acker, Charles E.
Ackerly, S(amuel) S.
Ackerman, Edward A.
Ackerman, Richard H.
Ackerman, William C(ooper)
Acree, Vernon D.
Adair, Charles W.
Adam, Paul J.
Adamec, Charles J.
Adams, Apollonia F. O.
Adams, Benjamin C.
Adams, Denvel D.
Adams, Edward J.
Adams, Edwin M.
Adams, Frank T., Jr.
Adams, John A. S.
Adams, John B.
Adams, John E.
Adams, John G.
Adams, John H.
Adams J(ohn) W., Jr.
Adams, Joseph P.
Adams, Kenneth S.
Adams, Leonard C.
Adams, Lewis W.
Adams, Nicholson B.
Adams, Paul D.
Adams, Ralph W., Sr.
Adams, Richard N.
Adams, Robert W., Jr.
Adams, Sam
Adams, Walter H.
Adams, William H.
Adams, William J., Jr.
Adamy, Clarence G.
Aderhold, Omer C.
Adkerson, J(oseph) C.
Adkins, John N.
Adkinson, Burton W.
Adler, John H.
Adrian, William L.
Aeck, Richard L.
Agee, Warren K.
Agey, Charles S.
Agnew, Allen F(rancis)
Agnew, Bruce A.
Agnew, Donald C.
Agnich, Fred J.
Ahmann, Mathew H.
Ahoua, Timothee N.
Ahrenholz, H(erman) W.
Ahrens, Maurice R.
Ailes, Stephen
Ainsworth, H. G.
Ainsworth, Stanley H(umphreys)
Airis, Thomas F.
Akers, John M.
Akers, Susan G.
Akers, William W.
Akhurst, Denys O.
Albanese, Naomi G.
Albert, John
Albertoni, Albert E.
Albertson, Fred W(oodward)
Albrecht, George J.
Albright, Arnold D.
Albright, George F.
Albright, Malvin M.
Albright, Raymond J.
Albrittain, John W.
Albritton, Claude C., Jr.
Alden, Douglas W.
Alden, John R.
Alden, Roland H(errick)
Aldewerld, Simon
Aldrin, Edwin E., Jr.
Aleck, Adolph W.
Aleman, Roberto R.
Alexander, Chalmers W.
Alexander, Charles H.
Alexander, Clifford L., Jr.
Alexander, Edward P.
Alexander, George M.
Alexander, Harold B.
Alexander, Irving E(manuel)
Alexander, John D., Jr.
Alexander, Myrl E(arly)
Alexander, Theodore M.
Alexander, (Richard) Thomas
Alexopoulos, Const(antine) J(ohn)
Alfaro, Victor R.
Alford, Frederick F., Jr.
Alford, John M.
Alford, Neill H., Jr.
Al-Ghoussein, Talat
Allan, Denison M.
Allan, Frank N(athaniel)
Allan, J(ohn) H.
Allard, William A.
Allaway, Howard
Allbritten, Leo T.
Allen, Bobbie R.
Allen, Brooke E.
Allen, Charles L.
Allen, Charles L.
Allen, Clarence M.
Allen, Cuthbert E.
Allen, David E.
Allen, Edward L.
Allen, Eliot D.
Allen, George V.
Allen, Herbert
Allen, Jack
Allen, James C(aldwell)
Allen, James E.
Allen, James H.
Allen, James S.
Allen, John H.
Allen, Lafe F.
Allen, Lee N.
Allen, Nicholas E(ugene)
Allen, Raymond B.
Allen, Robert S.
Allen, Turner W.
Allen, Ward P.
Allen, William H.
Allison, John M.
Allison, Noah D.
Allred, John C.
Al-Sowayel, Ibrahim
Alstadt, William R.
Alston, James O.
Alston, Annie M.
Alston, Philip H., Jr.
Alston, Robert A.
Alston, Wallace M.
Alter, Gerald M.
Althouse, H. J.
Altman, Oscar L.
Alvey, Edward, Jr.
Alworth, E. Paul
Alyea, Edwin P.
Amateis, Edmond R.
Ames, Fisher
Ames, Milton B., Jr.
Amisano, Joseph
Ambram, Philip W.
Amussen, Theodore S.
Anders, William A.
Anderson, Arnold H.
Anderson, Carl W.
Anderson, Dillon
Anderson, Donald B.
Anderson, Edward C.
Anderson, Frank A.
Anderson, George W., Jr.
Anderson, Glenn E.
Anderson, Gwen O.
Anderson, H(arry) L.
Anderson, Harry R.
Anderson, Howard C.
Anderson, Howard S.
Anderson, Hugh H.
Anderson, James R.
Anderson, John F.
Anderson, John H., Jr.
Anderson, Leonard G.
Anderson, Martin
Anderson, Norman J.
Anderson, Ralph A., Jr.
Anderson, Richard D.
Anderson, Robbin C.
Anderson, Robert J.
Anderson, Robert N.
Anderson, Roland B.
Anderson, Stanley R.
Anderson, Thomas D.
Anderson, Wallace E.
Anderson, Walter S., Jr.
Anderson, W(illiam) A(rnold) D.
Anderson, William B.
Anderson, William P., III
Anderson, William S.
Anderson, Wilton T.
Andersson, Theodore
Anderton, Farris N.
Andolsek, Ludwig J.
Andree, Richard V.
Andrew, Dean C.
Andrews, Archie M.
Andrews, Frank A.
Andrews, George W.
Andrews, Glenn
Andrews, Jay D.
Andrews, John C.
Andrews, J(ohn) R.
Andrews, Lavone D.
Andrews, Mark E.
Andrews, Mildred M.
Andrews, Robert V.
Andrews, T. Coleman
Andrews, Thelma
Andrews, William H., Jr.
Andreychuk, Theodore
Andy, Orlando J.
Angel, Grover L(aMarr)
Angel, J(ohn) Lawrence
Angell, Warren M.
Angevine, D(aniel) Murray
Anigstein, Ludwik
Anlyan, William G.
Annis, Edward R.
Annis, Morton L.
Ansley, (William) Bonneau
Anson, Charles P.
Anthis, Fay W. (Mrs. Austin F. Anthis)
Anthis, Rollen H.
Anthony, Charles R.
Apple, William S.
Applebee, Frank W.
Appleton, Joseph H.
Appling, Hugh G.
Arand, Louis A.
Arant, William D.
Arbegast, Neil R.
Arceneaux, Thomas J.
Archer, Edmund M.
Archer, Glenn L.
Archie, William C.
Arden, Thomas T.
Ardery, Julia H. S.
Ardery, Philip P.
Arduser, Raymond A.
Arendall, Charles B(aker), Jr.
Arens, Richard
Arensmeyer, Robert M.
Arent, Albert E.
Arlt, Gustave O.
Armbrecht, Frank M.
Armbrecht, William H.
Armistead, Parkes
Armistead, Theus N.
Armstrong, Alfred R.
Armstrong, Allan L.
Armstrong, George E.
Armstrong, George R.
Armstrong, Oliver W. (Jack)
Armstrong, Robert B.
Armstrong, Robert M.
Arnall, Ellis G.
Arnett, Ross H., Jr.
Arnett, William T(obias)
Arnhart, James R.
Arnold, Elting
Arnold, G. Dewey, Jr.
Arnold, James E.
Arnold, Julean
Arnold, Milton W.
Arnold, Remmie L.
Arnold, Robert O.
Arnold, Thurman W.
Arnold, Tom
Arnold, Walter M.
Arrowsmith, Marvin
Arrowsmith, William A.
Arthur, John K. S.
Arutunoff, Armais S.
Asbill, Mac
Aschaffenburg, E. L.
Ash, Robert
Ashabranner, Brent K.
Ashby, Clarence G.
Ashby, Lyle W.
Ashcraft, George C.
Asher, Robert E.
Ashmore, Frank L.
Ashmore, Henry L.
Ashmore, Robert T.
Ashworth, Maynard R.
Astin, Allen V(arley)
Atcheson, James E.
Atherton, Alfred L., Jr.
Atherton, James K.W.
Atkeson, Thomas C(onner)
Atkins, Chet
Atkins, Craig S.
Atkins, Edward J.
Atkins, Irvin M.
Atthakor, Buchana
Attinello, John S.
Atwater, Gordon I.
Atwell, Webster
Atwood, Edward C., Jr.
Atwood, Felix
Atwood, Rollin S.
Aubry, Eugene E.
Aucoin, Clayton V.
Aude, Theodor R.
Aurand, Evan P.
Ausley, Charles S.
Aust, Joe B.
Austern, H(erman) T.
Austin, Burton F.
Austin, Gordon H.
Austin, Harry G.
Austin, John F., Jr.
Austin, John P.
Austin, Tom N.
Austin, Walter J.
Auten, John H.
Autori, Franco
Auxier, George W(ashington)
Auyb, Muhammad
Avalle-Arce, Juan B.
Ave, Paul E.
Avila, Charles F.
Avramovic, Dragoslav
Axelrod, Leonard R.
Axford, Hiram W.
Axman, Laurence H.
Aycock, William B.
Ayer, Hugh M.
Ayers, Archie R.
Ayers, James R., Jr.
Aylor, John H.
Aynesworth, Horace D.
Ayres, John F.
Ayres, Robert M., Jr.
Ayres, William L.
Azhari, Yusuf O.
Azpeita, Mario

Babcock, Frederic
Baber, George W.
Bacon, Donald W.
Bacsik, Joseph G.
Badeau, John L.
Bader, Henri
Badger, James G.
Badouid, John J.
Baer, Ben K.
Baer, Donald G.
Bauer, Herbert R(alph)
Baer, John M(iller)
Bagdikian, Ben H.
Bagwill, John W.
Bailey, Cecil C.
Bailey, Charles E., Jr.
Bailey, Daniel M.
Bailey, Edward W.
Bailey, Frank H.
Bailey, (Edward) J.
Bailey, Joel F.
Bailey, Raymond V.
Bailey, Richard E.
Bailey, Stuart L.
Bailey, Wilford S.
Bain, Chester W.
Baird, Edward R.
Baird, Eugene
Baird, Valliant C.
Baker, Arthur A.
Baker, George C., Jr.
Baker, George E.
Baker, Harold F.
Baker, James E.
Baker, John A.
Baker, Lenox D., Sr.
Baker, Lisle, Jr.
Baker, Paul, Jr.
Baker, Robert C(alhoun)
Baker, Robert E., Jr.
Baker, Roger D(enio)
Baker, Royal N.
Baker, Vernon V.
Baker, W. Browne
Bakke, Oscar
Balancy, Pierre G. G.
Balassa, Bela
Balch, Samuel E.
Baldes, Edward J(ames)
Baldridge, Edgar E.
Baldridge, Howard D.
Baldwin, Charles F.
Baldwin, David M.
Baldwin, Horace S.
Baldwin, J(ohn) T(homas), Jr.
Baldwin, Phillip B.
Bales, Richard H. H.
Baley, James M., Jr.
Balfour, Maxwell W.
Ball, Mary M.
Ball, Norman T(ower)
Ball, Robert P(earl)
Ballance, Paul S.
Ballard, Emerald G.
Ballard, Frederick A.
Ballard, Stanley S.
Ballew, Leighton M.
Bandy, William T., Jr.
Bane, David M.
Bane, Frank
Banerjee, Purnendu K.
Banes, Daniel
Bangoura, Karim
Bangs, John R.
Banister, John R.
Bank, Thodore P., Jr.
Banks, John H.
Banner, James W.
Bannerman, Arthur M.
Bannister, Turpin C.
Banzhaf, John F. III
Barall, Milton
Baranowski, Frank P.
Barber, Arthur W.
Barber, Edward J.
Barbour, Walworth
Barcella, Ernest L.
Barck, Oscar T., Jr.
Barclay, Harriet G. (Mrs. Bertram Donald Barclay)
Barelare, Bruno
Bares, Rudolph, Jr.
Barff, Stafford E. D.
Barger, Herman H.
Barkalow, Frederick S., Jr.
Barkan, Alexander E.
Barkan, Leonard
Barker, Samuel B.
Barksdale, Hiram C.
Barlow, Joel
Barlow, Milton A.
Barnes, Carl B.
Barnes, Kenneth K.
Barnes, William P.
Barnett, Arthur D.
Barnett, Burleigh F.
Barnett, Charles C.
Barnett, Das K.
Barnett, Herman L.
Barnett, Walter M.
Barnett, William R.
Barnette, Newton H.
Barnhardt, William H.
Barnhart, William R.
Barnstone, Howard
Barr, Andrew
Barr, E(rnest) Scott
Barr, J. McFerran
Barr, Joseph W.
Barrett, Clifton W.
Barrett, James E.
Barrett, Joe C(lifford)
Barrett, Linton L.
Barrick, Nolan E.
Barriger, John W.
Barringer, Lewis T.
Barringer, Philip E.
Barritt, Carlyle W.
Barron, Bryton
Barrow, Allen E.
Barrow, George T.
Barrow, John R.
Barrow, William R.
Barrows, Leland (Judd)
Barter, Robert H.
Barthelme, Donald
Bartlett, Charles L.
Bartlett, Chris H.
Bartlett, George R(obert)
Bartlett, Lynn M.
Bartley, Robert T(aylor)
Bartling, Theodore C.
Barton, Eleanor D.
Barton, Fred J.
Barton, Richard F.
Barton, Robert T., Jr.
Barton, Walter E.
Barton, William B.
Barwick, Eugene T(homas)
Basch, Antonln
Baskerville, Jack H.
Basler, Roy P(rentice)

Bass, Allan D.
Bass, Boylston B.
Bass, Lawrence W.
Bass, Perry R.
Bass, Ross
Bassett, Harry H(ood)
Bassett, John E.
Bassin, Jules
Basten, Ray F.
Batcheller, Edgar H.
Bateman, Frank B(race)
Bateman, Fred W.
Bates, A. Allan
Bates, Frederick L.
Bates, John L
Bates, Roger G(ordon)
Bates, William B.
Batrus, Frederick E.
Batson, Blair, E.
Batson, Randolph
Batte, George A., Jr.
Battle, Hyman L.
Battle, Kemp D.
Battle, William C.
Batts, Henry L.
Batzell, Elmer E(llsworth)
Baucum, A.W.
Bauer, Richard H.
Bauer, William C.
Baughman, George F.
Bauhens, George J.
Baukhages, Frederick E(dwin)
Baum, John P(inson)
Baumer, William H.
Bawden, James W.
Baxter, Batsell B.
Baxter, Dana F.
Baxter, Edmund
Baxter, L.C.
Baxter, Robert H., III
Baxter, Samuel N., Jr.
Baxter, Stephen B.
Baxter, William M.
Bayer, Bruce M.
Bayer, Kenneth H.
Baylen, Joseph O.
Baylis, Charles A(ugustus)
Bayton, James A.
Bazelon, David T.
Beaber, James D.
Beach, Earl E.
Beach, Leonard B.
Beach, Walter R.
Beach, William W.
Beadles, Jack A.
Beal, K(enneth) Malcolm
Beale, Betty (Mrs. George K. Graeber)
Beale, Franklin A.
Beall, Arthur C., Jr.
Beall, Carlton G.
Beall, William C.
Beals, Frank L.
Beam, Charles G.
Beam, John G.
Bean, Maurice D.
Bear, Richard S.
Beard, Charles L.
Beard, Joseph W.
Beard, William
Bearden, Walter S., Jr.
Beardslee, William A.
Beasley, L. R.
Beasley, (Delmar) Otis
Beasley, Theodore P.
Beattie, Donald S.
Beaty, Jack
Beaty, Orren, Jr.
Beauchamp, William E.
Beaver, Sandy
Becerra, Carlos S.
Beck, Abe J.
Beck, Clifford K.
Beck, Henry C., Jr.
Beckenbach, Joseph R.
Becker, Charles L.
Becker, Ralph E.
Becker, Ralph S.
Becker, Mrs. William A.
Beckett, Paul L.
Beckham, Clifford M.
Beckham, Walter H., Jr.
Beckler, David Z(ander)
Beckman, Alfred R.
Beckman, Norman
Beckmann, Herbert W. K.
Beckwith, William H.
Beddall, Thomas H., Jr.
Bedsole, Joseph L.
Beebe, Raymond N.
Beelar, Donald C.
Beers, Roland F.
Beers, Thomas M.
Berry, John R(epiogle)
Begg, John M.
Beggs, E(lmore) Dixie
Beggs, James M.
Beggs, Thomas M.

Behr, Lyell C.
Behrens, Egbert F.
Behrman, Jack N.
Beirne, Joseph A.
Beiser, J(oseph) Ryan
Bekkedahl, Norman
Belaval, Emilio S.
Belcher, Alquernon S.
Belcher, Taylor G.
Belden, Clark
Belen, Frederick C.
Belew, Howard H.
Belk, Henry
Belknap, Paul E.
Bell, Alex W.
Bell, Clarence E., Jr.
Bell, Collin W.
Bell, David B.
Bell, Harry H.
Bell, Henry M., Jr.
Bell, James D.
Bell, John H.
Bell, John O(scar)
Bell, L. Nelson
Bell, Major T.
Bell, Wilson B(ryan)
Bellinger, Frederick
Bellino, Carmine S.
Bellman, Russell
Bellows, Everett H.
Beltran, Roberto S.
Bemis, F. Gregg, Jr.
Benbow, Charles F.
Bender, Howard M.
Bender, Morton A.
Bender, Stanley S.
Benedetto, Francis A.
Benedict, Bill C.
Benedict, Wayne L.
Benedum, Thomas R.
Benerito, Ruth R.
Benington, Herbert D.
Benitez, Agustin
Bennett, Carol M.
Bennett, Charles D.
Bennett, Charles L.
Bennett, Earl D.
Bennett, Elmer F.
Bennett, (Silas) Fleming
Bennett, Fred G.
Bennett, Gordon R.
Bennett, H(arry)
Bennett, Harry W., Jr.
Bennett, Henry S.
Bennett, Howard C.
Bennett, J(ames) M.
Bennett, John M., Jr.
Bennett, Joseph A.
Bennett, Miriam F.
Bennett, Newcomb B., Jr.
Bennett, Robert L.
Bennett, Robert L(eo), Jr.
Bennett, Walter H.
Bennett, William T., Jr.
Bennington, Neville L.
Benoit, Emile
Benson, Ezra T.
Benson, Fred J.
Benson, George S.
Benson, Homer L.
Benson, Lawrence K.
Benson, Otis O., Jr.
Benson, Robert D.
Benson, Robert G(reen)
Benson, William A.
Bent, Donn N.
Bent, Willard O.
Bentley, Herschel P., Jr.
Benton, Edward L.
Benton, Thaddeus G.
Bentonelli, Joseph (Joseph Horace Benton)
Bentrup, Maud M. C.
Bentsen, Lloyd (Millard), Jr.
Berckemeyer, Fernando
Berding, Andrew H.,
Berg, Norman A.
Bergaust, Erik
Bergdolt, Volmar E.
Bergen, John V.
Bergeron, Wilbur L.
Bergin, Thomas F.
Bergson, Herbert A.
Berla, Julian E.
Berlin, Seymour S.
Bernal Y Garcia Pimentel, Iganacio
Bernard, Lawrence G.
Bernbaum, Maurice M.
Bernd-Cohn, Max
Berne, Robert M.
Berne-Allen, Allan
Bernheim, Frederick
Bernier, Joseph L(eroy)
Berrian, Albert H.
Berry, Charles A.
Berry, Charles O.
Berry, James D.

Berry, Keehn W.
Berry, Loren M.
Berry, William W.
Berryman, Robert B.
Berson, Robert C.
Berthrong, Donald J.
Bertland, Charles P.
Besch, Everett D.
Besson, Frank S., Jr.
Best, Arthur C.
Betances, Luis R.
Bethel, Carlysle A.
Bette, Mrs. Torrey James
Betts, Austin W.
Betts, Doris J. W.
Betts, Ernest C., Jr.
Betzig, Edward
Beutel, Albert P.
Bevelander, Gerrit
Beyer, Gerhard H.
Beyer, Robert C.
Bibby, Douglas E.
Bickel, Herbert J., Jr.
Bickerstaff, T(homas) A(lton)
Bickam, Jack M.
Biddle, Eric H.
Biddle, James
Biegel, Herman C.
Biemiller, Andrew J(ohn)
Bienfang, Ralph D.
Bienvenu, Bernard J.
Biesele, John J(ulius)
Bigelow, Donald N.
Bigger, Charles P., III
Bigger, Richard A(ndrews)
Biggers, Ray N.
Biggio, Alvin A.
Biggs, Wellington A.
Billing, Fred C.
Billings, Frederic T., Jr.
Billings, William D.
Billingslea, Charles
Billingsley, Hascal S.
Billman, Carl
Bills, Robert E.
Billups, Frederick H.
Billups, W. L.
Binda, H. Jeffrey
Binford, Chapman H.
Bingham, Millicent T. (Mrs. Walter V. Bingham)
Binney, Arthur F.
Binswanger, Millard I.
Birdsall, Guy H.
Birkhead, Kenneth M.
Birnie, Joseph E.
Bisbee, Frank D.
Bishop, Barbara J.
Bishop, Charles E.
Bishop, Luther D.
Bishop, Samuel W.
Bishopric, Karl
Bissett, James R.
Bissinger, Barnard H.
Bitter, John
Bittinger, Donald S.
Bittman, William O.
Bivens, William J(ames)
Bivins, Howard J.
Bixby, J. E.
Bixler, Ray H.
Black, Barron F.
Black, David S.
Black, Eugene
Black, Hugo L.
Black, Martin L., Jr.
Black, Myron L.
Black, Richard B.
Black, Robert B.
Black, Robert E. L.
Black, Robert S.
Black, William B., Jr.
Blackard, Embree H.
Blackburn, David R.
Blackburn, Francis M.
Blackburn, John L.
Blackburn, Paul P., Jr.
Blackie, W(illiam) M(cAlister)
Blackman, Herbert N.
Blackmon, Larry
Blackmun, Harry A.
Blackstock, LeRoy
Blackstock, Robert W.
Blackstone, William T.
Blackwell, Lloyd (Phalti)
Blackwell, William A.
Blades, Brian B.
Blades, William H.
Blair, William D., Jr.
Blair, W(illiam) Frank(lin)
Blair, William M., Jr.
Blaisdell, Warren C.
Blake, Robert O.
Blakely, Newel H.
Blakemore, Neville

Blalock, Jack B.
Blalock, Joseph R.
Blanchard, Lawrence E., Jr.
Blanche, Fred A.
Blanchet, Waldo W. E.
Blanco, Teodora
Blank, Samuel
Blasick, Henry J.
Blatt, Joseph D.
Blatt, Genevieve
Blattner, Russell J.
Blayton, Jessie B.
Blee, Myron R.
Blessey, Walter E.
Blevins, Robert W.
Blick, Charles A.
Blitch, Lorimer H.
Bloch, Charles J.
Block, Ralph
Blocker, Truman, G., Jr.
Blodgett, Hugh C.
Blodgett, Ralph H.
Blossman, Alfred R., Jr.
Blough, Carman G.
Blouin, Francis J.
Blouke, Pierre
Blount, R. A.
Blount, Robert E.
Blount, William H.
Blount, Winton M.
Bloxom, Elliott
Blum, John C.
Blumberg, Joe M.
Blumberg, Richard W.
Blumenauer, Thomas W., Jr.
Blythe, David K.
Blythe, William L.
Boardman, Francis
Boardman, Richard S.
Boatner, Charles K.
Bobbitt, Oliver B., Jr.
Bobbitt, Robert L.
Bochner, Salomon
Bocquet, Philip E(dmund)
Bodenstein, Dietrich H. F. A.
Bodie, Benjamin T.
Bodman, Ralph
Boe, Nils A.
Boehl, Herbert F.
Boehmler, Erwin W.
Boese, Elsie J. M. (Mrs. Herman Lamar Boese)
Bogard, Ben(jamin) T(aylor)
Bogart, Frank A.
Bogdan, Corneliu
Bogdonoff, Morton D.
Boggs, James H.
Boggs, John C.
Bogusch, Edwin R.
Bohan, Merwin L(ee)
Bohannon, Richard L.
Bohlen, Charles E.
Boisen, Harold L.
Bok, Bart J.
Bokat, George
Boles, C. E.
Boling, Edward J.
Bolles, E(dmund) Blair
Bolles, James C.
Bolster, Edward A(ndrew)
Boltz, Gerald E.
Boman, John H., Jr.
Bomar, Steve H.
Bomar, William P.
Bonadio, Frank
Boncher, Hector P.
Bond, Charles R., Jr.
Bond, Horace M.
Bond, Lewis H.
Bond, Niles W.
Bond, Thomas J.
Bond, William R.
Bondurant, Arthur P.
Boner, C(harles) P(aul)
Bonham, Howard B.
Bonner, Francis W.
Bonnyman, George G.
Bonsal, Philip W.
Bontemps, Arna W.
Boochever, Louis C.
Boom, Aaron M.
Boone, (James) Buford
Boone, Walter F.
Boonstra, Clarence A.
Booth, Charles L.
Booth, Robert M., Jr.
Booth, Windsor P.
Boothby, Norman B.
Borders, William D.
Borel, Paul A.
Boren, Benjamin N.
Borg, Alfred F(rancis)
Borman, Frank
Borrego, Edward C.

Borsody, Benjamin F.
Bosch, Gulnar K.
Boshell, Edward O.
Bosserman, Joseph N.
Bostian, C(ary) H(oyt)
Bostick, Edward M.
Boswell, Lorin A.
Boswell, William O.
Bosworth, Edwin C.
Bothwell, Frank E.
Bottoms, John W.
Bottorff, Charles R.
Bottorff, Orville O.
Botts, Guy W.
Boudreaux, Felix J.
Bouker, John G.
Boulenger, Albert L.
Boullioun, Ernest H., Jr.
Boulware, Lemuel R.
Bourdier, James A.
Bourgeois, Andre M. G.
Bourne, Henry C., Jr.
Boutwell, Albert B.
Bouwsma, Oets K.
Bowden, Edwin T.
Bowden, Henry L.
Bowden, Owen C.
Bowdoin, Wilmoth B.
Bowen, Don L.
Bowen, William H.
Bowers, Edward T.
Bowers, Fredson T.
Bowles, Aubrey R(ussell), Jr.
Bowles, Grover C., Jr.
Bowles, Lester L.
Bowling, John W.
Bowman, A. Smith
Bowman, Albert H.
Bowman, George S., Jr.
Bowman, Philip I.
Bowman, Raymond T(omlinson)
Bows, Albert J., Jr.
Bowser, Alpha L.
Box, Cloyce K.
Box, Clyde
Boxley, Arney
Boy, John B.
Boyce, Benjamin
Boyce, Joseph C(annon)
Boyd, Bernard H.
Boyd, Clarence E., Jr.
Boyd, George E.
Boyd, George R.
Boyd, Harold B(uhalts)
Boyd, Howard T.
Boyd, Jack I.
Boyd, James E.
Boyd, John D.
Boyd, Joseph A(ubrey)
Boyd, Maurice
Boyd, Murrell N.
Boyd, Richard F.
Boyd, Robert O.
Boyd, T(homas) Munford
Boyd, William R.
Boye, Frederic W., Jr.
Boyer, Harold E.
Boyer, Perry F.
Boykin, Sam M., Jr.
Boykin, Samuel
Boyko, Edgar P.
Boyle, William A.
Boynton, Willard H.
Bozarth, Howard J.
Brack, Reginald K., Sr.
Bracken, Thomas E.
Braden, Emmett W.
Braden, Thomas W(ardell)
Bradford, James C.
Bradley, Emmett H.
Bradley, Frederick M.
Bradley, Gene E.
Bradley, Hugh W.
Bradley, James T.
Bradley, Lee C., Jr.
Bradshaw, Howard H(olt)
Bradsher, Charles K.
Brady, James H.
Brady, Leslie S.
Brady, Robert F(rederick)
Bramson, Leo
Branch, Harllee, Jr.
Branch, James E.
Branch, Robert L.
Brand, Donald D.
Brand, Louis
Brand, Paul W.
Brandborg, Stewart M.
Brandis, Henry (Parker), Jr.
Brandon, Inman
Brandon, Robert W.
Brandt, Paul H.
Brandt, Raymond P.
Branigan, George F.
Brannen, Teddy R., Jr.
Brannon, Clifton W.

Branscom, William J.
Branscomb, Harvie
Branson, Carl C.
Branson, Herman R.
Branson, Thomas H.
Brantley, Rabun L.
Branton, Wiley A.
Brasfield, Stephen A.
Bratton, James H., Jr.
Brauer, Ralph W.
Braun, Gerhard W.
Braun, Kurt
Brawley, Hiram W. (Bill)
Bray, Richard M.
Bray, Robert S.
Brazeal, Brailsford R.
Breathitt, Edward T.
Brecher, Gerhard A.
Brecht, E(dward) A(rmond) (Jr.)
Breder, Charles M., Jr.
Breecher, Charles H.
Breeden, Robert H.
Breen, John R.
Breen, William J., Jr.
Breeskin, Adelyn D.
Brehm, William K.
Breitenbach, Edward V(ictor)
Brenizer, Addison G., Jr.
Brenkert, Karl Jr.
Brennan, James G.
Brennan, John W.
Brennan, Joseph B(enjamin)
Brennan, William J(oseph), Jr.
Brenner, Robert
Brenner, Edward J.
Brent, Andrew J.
Bresnahan, William A.
Bresnick, Edward
Breuninger, Lewis T.
Brewer, (Marion) Carey
Brewer, John W.
Brewer, William D.
Brice, Ashbel G.
Brickfield, Cyril F.
Bridger, Grover L.
Bridgman, Anna J.
Briggs, Robert L.
Briggs, Wallace N.
Briggs, William P.
Bright, John
Brignone, Carlos S.
Bril, Jacques L.
Brim, Kenneth M.
Brinkhous, K(enneth) M(erle)
Brinkely, A.M., Jr.
Brinkely, Homer L.
Brinton, Edgar H.
Briscoe, Birdsall
Brite, Ralph W.
Britt, Harry M., Jr.
Britten, Milton R.
Broadbent, Sam R.
Broadbent, Smith D., Jr.
Broady, K(nute) O(scar)
Broches, Aron
Brock, Ignatius W.
Brock, James D.
Brock, Pope F.
Brock, William E., Jr.
Brockenbrough, Henry W.
Brockey, Harold
Brode, Wallace R.
Brodie, Henry
Brodsky, Nathan
Broker, Thomas O.
Bromberg, Henri L., Jr.
Bronner, Frederick L.
Brookby, Harry D.
Brooke, F. Dixon
Brooke, Francis J., (3d)
Brooker, Marvin A(del)
Brooks, Charles L.
Brooks, David B.
Brooks, Eugene H.
Brooks, Laurance W.
Brooks, Mary T.
Brooks, Neil
Brooks, Richard B.
Brooks, Robert M.
Brooks, Seth R.
Brooks, Thomas J., Jr.
Broom, Leonard
Brotzen, Franz R.
Brotzman, Donald G.
Broughton, Thomas R. S.
Broullire, John M.
Brown, Alexander J., Jr.
Brown, Aubrey J.
Brown, Aubrey N(eblett), Jr.
Brown, Bernard L.
Brown, Bob M.
Brown, Bruce K.
Brown, Charles P.

Brown, Clair A(lan)
Brown, Darwin C.
Brown, David S.
Brown, Earl I., II
Brown, Eli H., II
Brown, Elizabeth A.
Brown, Frances R.
Brown, Fred
Brown, Gerald A.
Brown, Gladys L. H. (June Brown)
Brown, Grover C.
Brown, Harlan C.
Brown, Herbert L., Jr.
Brown, Horace B., Jr.
Brown, Ivan W., Jr.
Brown, James A.
Brown, James G.
Brown, James S.
Brown, James T.
Brown, James V(incent)
Brown, John E., Jr.
Brown, John L.
Brown, Joseph G.
Brown, Keith S.
Brown, Lester R.
Brown, Lewis D.
Brown, Loy T.
Brown, Morgan C.
Brown, Myrtle I.
Brown, Paul M., Jr.
Brown, Philip B.
Brown, Richard K.
Brown, Richard R.
Brown, Robert D.
Brown, Robert L.
Brown, Robert O.
Brown, Robinson S., Jr.
Brown, Rodgers N.
Brown, Russell W.
Brown, Samuel R., Jr.
Brown, Thomas M.
Brown, Vincent M.
Brown, William O.
Brown, Wood
Browne, Rollin
Browne, Secor D.
Brownlee, Jerry L.
Brownlee, Thomas M.
Brownley, Floyd I., Jr.
Brownstein, Philip N.
Bruce, David K. E.
Bruce, Imon E.
Bruce, John G.
Bruch, Hilde
Brueckheimer, William R.
Bruestle, Beaumont
Bruhn, Joachim
Brummett, Marvin K.
Brundage, Percival F.
Brunenkant, Edward J.
Bruner, William W.
Brunchild, Gordon
Brunn, David J.
Bruns, Carl H.
Bruns, William H.
Brunson, May A.
Bruton, Thomas W.
Bryan, A(lbert) Huges
Bryan, Colgan H.
Bryan, Gordon K.
Bryan, James E.
Bryan, J(oseph), III
Bryan, Joseph M.
Bryan, Joseph S., Jr.
Bryan, Wright
Bryant, Cecil F.
Bryant, Eugene
Bryant, J. C. Herbert
Bryant, James C.
Bryant, William A.
Buchanan, John D., Jr.
Buchanan, Lilian B.
Buchanan, Sam A.
Buchanan, Wiley T., Jr.
Buchanan, William
Buchheim, Robert W.
Buchheister, Carl W.
Buck, Ervin O.
Buck, Hugh Q.
Buck, Thomas R.
Bucke, Emory S.
Buckhout, Clay
Buckingham, David R.
Buckle, John F.
Buckley, Edmond C.
Buckley, Frank W.
Buckner, George W., Jr.
Buckner, Hubbard G.
Bucy, Charles W.
Budd, Philip J.
Budina, Adolph O.
Bueter, Arnold G.
Bugg, James L., Jr.
Buggs, Charles W.
Buhler, John E.
Buie, Bennett F.
Bulkeley, John D.
Bull, Fred W.
Bull, John C.
Bullion, Bruce T.
Bullock, Henry M.
Bullock, Maurice R.
Bulshefski, Veronica
Bultman, Fritz
Bumgarner, John C., Sr.
Bump, Morrison M.
Bunce, William K.
Bunch, Franklin S.
Bunker, Ellsworth
Bunker, George (Maverick)
Bunker, William B.
Bunn, Edward B.
Bunn, George
Bunn, George P., Jr.
Bunnelle, Robert E.
Burbank, Wilbur S.
Burch, George E.
Burch, J(ames) C(harlie) Horton
Burch, Lucius E., Jr.
Burchard, Charles
Burck, Arthur A.
Burdett, William C.
Burdette, Walter J.
Burdick, Alger E.
Burford, Samuel P.
Burge, William L.
Burger, Alfred
Burger, Joseph C.
Burger, Warren E(arl)
Burgess, W(arren) Randolph
Burgin, Richard
Burke, Arleigh A.
Burke, Ellen C.
Burke, Frederic G.
Burke, James G.
Burke, John E(mmett)
Burke, Vincent J.
Burkett, Lowell A.
Burkhalter, George L.
Burkhalter, William M.
Burkhart, Carl, Jr.
Burkhead, Margaret B.
Burkley, George G.
Burlage, Henry M.
Burleson, Ira L.
Burlingme, Mark V.
Burn, Harry T.
Burnam, Paul W.
Burnes, James A.
Burnet, Arthur L., Jr.
Burney, Cecil E(dward)
Burney, Virgil D.
Burns, Arthur E.
Burns, Findley, Jr.
Burns, James P., Sr.
Burns, John H.
Burns, Norman
Burns, Paul Y.
Burns, Robert K.
Burns, Robert O.
Burns, Robert W.
Burnside, M(aurice) G(winn)
Burnum, James H.
Burress, Richard T.
Burrill, Meredith F.
Burroughs, Henry D.
Burroughs, Raymond
Burrows, William F.
Burrows, Charles R.
Burrus, George B.
Burson, Mrs. Phyllis S.
Burt, Alvin V., Jr.
Burt, George D. W.
Burt, Millard P.
Burton, Alexander T(ennille)
Burton, Dwight L.
Burton, Edwin (Welsman)
Burton, Glenn W.
Burton, James B.
Burton, Joe W.
Burton, John F.
Burton, John F.
Burton, Ralph J.
Burts, Charles W.
Busby, Elden B.
Busch, Arthur W.
Busch, Harris
Buschman, Arthur W., Jr.
Buschman, Leonard V.
Bush, Charles K., Jr.
Bush, Dorothy V.
Bush, Ian E.
Bush, John W.
Bush, Millard M.
Bush, Oliver F.
Bush, Peter B.
Bussmann, Charles H.
Busteed, Robert C.
Butcher, Devereux
Butcher, Ernest D.
Butenhoff, Robert L.
Buthod, Arthur P.
Butland, Ralph A.
Butler, Broadus N.
Butler, Chauncey W., Jr.
Butler, Eugene
Butler, George A.
Butler, John P.
Butler, Lee D.
Butler, Ogbourne D., Jr.
Butler, Richard C.
Butler, Roy F.
Butler, T. J.
Butler, William R.
Butterfield, Alexander P.
Butterworth, James D.
Buttle, Edgar A.
Button, Jack B.
Button, Robert Y.
Byerly, Theodore C(arroll)
Byers, Buckley M.
Byers, Edna H.
Byers, Horace R.
Byrd, Charles L.
Byrd, Daniel M., Jr.
Byrd, David H.
Byrd, David L.
Byrd, Elon E(ugene)
Byrd, Hy
Byrd, Isaac B.
Byroade, Henry A.
Byrum, Woodrow R.
Bywaters, Jerry

Cabaniss, J(ames) A.
Cabell, Charles P.
Cabell, Robert G., Jr.
Cabot, John M.
Cabot, Ted
Caddell, John A.
Cahalane, Victor H.
Cahill, Fred V(irgil)
Cahn, Robert
Cain, Robert E.
Cain, Wofford
Caine, Walter E.
Cairns, Huntington
Caldwell, Frank H.
Caldwell, Harry B.
Caldwell, J. Philo
Caldwell, John M.
Caldwell, Lafayette H.
Caldwell, Millard F., Jr.
Caldwell, Robert T.
Caldwell, Turner F., Jr.
Calfee, William H.
Calhoon, Richard P(ercival)
Calhoun, Byron C.
Calhoun, Harold
Calhoun, John A.
Calhoun, John C., Jr.
Calhoun, Lawton M.
Calhoun, Patrick N., Jr.
Calhoun, Walter B.
Callaham, Thomas H.
Callahan, Alston
Callahan, Nicholas P.
Callaway, Carl B.
Callaway, Fuller E., Jr.
Callaway, Howard H.
Callaway, Jasper L.
Callaway, Paul S.
Callaway, William H(oward)
Callcott, Wilfrid H.
Callery, Francis A.
Callicutt, Laurie T.
Callihan, E. L.
Callison, Maston K.
Calver, James L.
Calvert, James H.
Camacho, Alvro M.
Cambre, Roland J.
Camden, (Charles) Carroll
Cameron, Charles C.
Cameron, Charles F(ranklin)
Cameron, Richard R.
Cameron, Turner C., Jr.
Cameron, William K.
Cammack, Cecil C.
Camp, David B.
Camp, Earl D.
Camp, Ehney A., Jr.
Camp, James L., Jr.
Camp, Truman W.
Campbell, Alexander
Campbell, Ben S.
Campbell, Clifford B.
Campbell, Donald A.
Campbell, Donald H.
Campbell, Edmund D.
Campbell, Ernest Q.
Campbell, George W.
Campbell, Harry M.
Campbell, James D.
Campbell, James P., Jr.
Campbell, John M.
Campbell, Joseph
Campbell, Laurence R.
Campbell, Oscar J., Jr.
Campbell, Robert D.
Campbell, Robert F.
Campbell, Thomas N.
Campbell, William B.
Campbell, William W.
Campos, Salos
Canaga, Bruce L., Jr.
Cancellare, Frank E.
Candler, Asa W.
Candler, Samuel C.
Candler, William L.
Canfield, Edward F.
Canfield, Wright
Cannan, Robert K.
Cannon, Charles A.
Cannon, Edward W.
Cannon, Joseph H.
Cannon, William R.
Cano, Joaquin G.
Canter, Jacob
Canter, Milton E.
Cantey, Emory A.
Cantey, James W.
Cantrell, Clyde H.
Cantrell, John H.
Cantrell, Roy H.
Cantwell, Conan
Canup, William C.
Capehart, W. J.
Capers, Gerald M., Jr.
Caplenor, Donald
Caplin, Mortimer M(axwell)
Capp, Glenn R.
Cappon, Lester J.
Capron, William M.
Caram, Angel R.
Caravati, Charles M.
Caraway, Paul W.
Carbaugh, Harry C.
Cardozo, Manoel
Cardozo, Michael H.
Carey, Charles I.
Carey, Francis E.
Carey, Harvey L.
Carey, James B.
Carey, John J.
Carey, John T.
Carey, William D.
Cargill, Henron
Cargill, James N.
Carl, Marion E.
Carlile, Thomas
Carlisle, James M.
Carlitz, Leonard
Carlock, John K.
Carlough, Edward F.
Carlson, Albin E.
Carlson, James G.
Carlson, Karen L.
Carlton, Doyle E.
Carlyle, Irving E.
Carmi, Eugenio
Carmichael, Emmett B.
Carmichael, Hugh T.
Carmichael, James H.
Carmichael, Katherine K.
Carmichael, Mary M.
Carmichael, Stokly
Carmody, John J(oseph)
Carnell, Paul H.
Carney, Price F.
Carnicero, Jorge
Carpenter, Coy C.
Carpenter, Francis W.
Carpenter, John M.
Carpenter, John W., III
Carpenter, Leslie E.
Carpenter, M(alcolm) Scott
Carpenter, Thomas E.
Carr, Archie
Carr, Braxton B.
Carr, Chalmes R.
Carr, Charles A.
Carr, Howard E.
Carr, Isaac N(ewton)
Carr, Oscar C., Jr.
Carr, Waggoner
Carr, William B.
Carraway, Gertrude S.
Carretta, Albert A.
Carrico, James L.
Carriere, Charles M.
Carriere, Joseph M.
Carriger, John S.
Carrington, Alexander B., Jr.
Carrion, Rafael Jr.
Carrol, Louis
Carroll, David S.
Carroll, Edwin W.
Carroll, Francis X.
Carroll, Joseph F.
Carroll, Loren
Carroll, Mollie R.
Carson, David B.
Carson, James
Carson, Samuel O.
Carta, Alvaro L.
Carter, Alan
Carter, Albert E.
Carter, Albert H.
Carter, Ann
Carter, Coleman, Jr.
Carter, Edgar B.
Carter, Edward J.
Carter, Francis B.
Carter, Frank C., Jr.
Carter, George F.
Carter, Harry T.
Carter, Hugh D., Jr.
Carter, Sir John
Carter, John P.
Carter, Lester C.
Carter, Oliver
Carter, Walter C.
Carter, Wendell E.
Carter, William G.
Carter, William T., III
Carter, William W.
Carter, Willis M.
Cartwright, Edwin O.
Cartwright, John P.
Cartwright, William H(olman)
Caruth, William W., Jr.
Carver, Dale R.
Carver, George A.
Cary, Charles O(swald)
Cary, John B.
Casey, Maurice F.
Casey, Ralph E.
Cash, Claybourne A.
Cash, James B., Jr.
Cash, James (Robert)
Cash, William B.
Cashman, John W.
Casler, Harry S.
Cason, Charles M.
Caso Y Andrade, Alfonso
Casper, Joseph J.
Casper, Thomas P.
Caspersen, O(laus) W(estby)
Cass, Millard
Cassels, Louis W.
Cassidy, Helen E.
Cassidy, Patrick F.
Cassidy, Richard T.
Cassidy, William F.
Cassilly, Philip J(acquemn)
Castleman, Samuel T.
Cate, Wirt A.
Cater, Douglass
Cathey, Cornelius O.
Caudill, Harry M.
Caudill, Robert P.
Caudill, William W.
Cauthen, Baker J.
Cavanaugh, Kenneth C.
Caven, Hubbard S.
Cavenaugh, George K.
Caveny, Elmer L.
Cawley, Edward P.
Cawley, Francis R(iggs)
Cayce, Kenneth O., Jr.
Cella, Francis R.
Cerf, Jay H.
Cernick, Clifford
Cerrone, Warren E.
Cestaro, Michael P.
Chadbourn, Philip H., Jr.
Chadenet, Bernard
Chafee, John H.
Chaille, Howard E.
Chalker, James I.
Chamberlain, Alexander S.
Chamberlain, Donad F(rank)
Chamberlin, Wellman
Chambers, David S.
Chambers, Jack H.
Chambers, John C.
Chambers, Justice M(arion)
Chambless, John R.
Champion, John E.
Chandler, Alvin D.
Chandler, Caroline A.
Chandler, R(euben) Carl
Chandler, Wallace L.
Chaney, David W.
Chang, Chieh Chien
Chapelle, Howard I.
Chapin, Aldus H.
Chapin, Edward Y., Jr.
Chapin, William A.
Chaplin, Maxwell
Chapman, Alan J.
Chapman, Charles H., Jr.
Chapman, Christian A.
Chapman, Donald D.
Chapman, Gordon W.
Chapman, Helen (Mrs. Theodore Stillman Chapman)
Chapman, Ione M.
Chapman, James A., Jr.
Chapman, John W., Jr.
Chapman, Joseph E., Jr.
Chapman, Leonard F., Jr.
Chapman, Oscar L.
Chapman, Philip K.
Chappell, Amey
Chappell, Richard A.
Chapman, Robert H.
Charbonnet, Pierre N., Jr.
Charles, Herman E.
Charles, Robert H.
Charrin, Paul J.
Charteris, Leslie
Charters, William A.
Charyk, Joseph V.
Chase, Gilbert
Chase, Nicholas J.
Chatelain, Leon Jr.
Chatham, Hugh G., II
Chatham, James R.
Cheatham, Elliott E.
Cheatham, John M.
Cheatum, Evelyn L.
Checchi, Vincent
Cheek, Leslie, Jr.
Cheney, James S.
Chenoweth, Alice D.
Cherington, Paul W(hiton)
Cherpack, Clifton
Cherry, Ralph W(alter)
Cherry, William W.
Chesarek, Ferdinand J.
Chesnut, Franklin G.
Chess, Edwin R.
Cheston, Charles E.
Chevalier, Douglas
Chew, Woodrow W(ilson)
Chewning, Lewis G.
Cheyney, William J.
Childers, Kenan C., Jr.
Childress, Francis B.
Chiles, Harrell E.
Chiles, John H.
Chillman, James Jr.
Chilton, St. John P(oindexter)
Chilton, Samuel B.
Chinn, Herman I.
Chisholm, Alexander F.
Chisholm, Shirley A. S.
Chow, Shu-Kai
Chrisman, Allen S.
Christenberry, George A.
Christenberry, Robert K.
Christensen, Ernest E.
Christensen, Kenneth S.
Christian, Delos H.
Christian, George E.
Christian, Murray
Christiansen, Edward S., Sr.
Christie, Amos
Christie, M(arion) Francis
Christopher, Paul R.
Christopher, Wilford S.
Chubb, Talbot A.
Church, Donald (Eisenbrey)
Church, Frederick L., Jr.
Churchill, Irving L.
Chworowsky, Martin P(hillip)
Cieplinski, Michel
Cizauskas, Albert C.
Cizik, Robert
Clabaugh, Samuel F.
Clabaugh, Stephen E.
Clague, Ewan
Claiborne, John W., Jr.
Clamann, Hans G.
Clapp, Norman M.
Clapp, Robert T.
Clapp, Verner W.
Clapp, William J.
Clarey, Bernard A.
Clark, Albert P.
Clark, Alfred
Clark, Andy E., Jr.
Clark, Blake
Clark, Carl H.
Clark, Chester W.
Clark, Clare C.
Clark, Clarence C.
Clark, Earl W(esley)
Clark, Edward
Clark, Eliot C.
Clark, Frank D.
Clark, George M(cMurry)
Clark, G(ilbert) Edward
Clark, H. Sol
Clark, Harold F.
Clark, Harold W.
Clark, Harry W.
Clark, J(ames) Ingraham

Clark, James B.
Clark, James H.
Clark, Joe T.
Clark, John C.
Clark, John H., III
Clark, John W., Jr.
Clark, Julian J.
Clark, Kenneth W.
Clark, Leigh M.
Clark, Lloyd M.
Clark, Mark W.
Clark, Pendleton S(cott)
Clark, Ralph L.
Clark, Ramsey
Clark, Randolph L.
Clark, Robert L.
Clark, Samuel F.
Clarke, Beverly L.
Clarke, Bruce C.
Clarke, Ellis E. I.
Clarke, Frank E.
Clarke, Frederick J.
Clarke, Harrison
Clarke, H(arry) J(oseph)
Clarke, J. Calvitt
Clarke, J(ohn) F(rederick) Gates
Clarke, Oldham
Clarkson, Mark H.
Clary, Howard L.
Class, Calvin M.
Class, Maurice M.
Claverie, Louis B.
Clawson, Marion
Claxton, Philander P., Jr.
Clay, Cassius (Muhammad Ali)
Clay, John W.
Clay, Lucius D., Jr.
Clay, William L.
Clay, William M(arion)
Claydon, Sister Margaret
Clayton, Charles T.
Clayton, Claude F.
Clayton, Hugh N.
Claytor, Robert B.
Cleaveland, Frederic N.
Cleere, Albert E.
Cleino, Edward H.
Clem, William W., Jr.
Clement, Besse A.
Clement, Frank G.
Clements, Charles L.
Clements, Charles L., Jr.
Clements, Woodrow W.
Clepper, Henry E.
Cleveland, Robert G.
Cleveland, Theron, C., Jr.
Cleverdon, Ernest G.
Cliett, Charles B.
Cliff, Edward P.
Clifford, Alfred H.
Clifford, Clark M.
Clifford, Frederick B.
Clifford, Stewart H.
Clifton, Chester V., Jr.
Clifton, Ernest S.
Clifton, Joseph W.
Cline, Howard F.
Cline, John H.
Clinesmith, Bruce C.
Cloar, Carroll
Clotworthy, John H.
Cloud, Bruce B.
Clough, Ralph N.
Clowes, Molly (Mrs. Jacques Willy Walsh)
Cluff, Leighton E.
Coates, Albert
Coates, Clarence L., Jr.
Coates, Francis G.
Coatney, G(eorge) Robert
Cobb, Cully A.
Cobb, George H.
Cobb, Lloyd J(oseph)
Cobb, William L(yman)
Cobb, W(illiam) Montague
Coburn, Melville B.
Cochran, Archibald P.
Cochran, George M.
Cocke, Bartlett
Cocke, Erie, Sr.
Cocke, Erie, Jr.
Codd, Leo A.
Cody, Welborn B(utt)
Coe, Paul F.
Coe, William C.
Coerr, Wymberley D.
Coffey, Robert J.
Coffey, Rufus
Coffey, Thomas F., Jr.
Coffin, Lewis C.
Coffin, Robert E.
Coffman, Amos J.
Cogen, Charles
Coggan, Bernard F.
Coggin, Walter A.
Coghill, Calvin E.
Cohan, Avery B.
Cohee, George V.
Cohelan, Jeffery
Cohen, Benjamin V.
Cohen, Edwin S.
Cohen, Isadore T.
Cohen, Lester
Cohen, Manuel F.
Cohen, Sheldon S.
Cohen, Wallace M.
Cohn, Jess V.
Cohn, Marcus
Cohn, Samuel M.
Cohn, Victor E.
Coira, Louis E.
Coke, Henry C., Jr.
Coke, James E.
Coker, Charles W.
Coker, Elizabeth B. (Mrs, James Lide Coker)
Coker, Robert R.
Coker, Samuel T.
Colberg, Marshall R.
Colbert, Charles R(alph)
Colbert, James C.
Colclaser, H. Alberta
Coldwell, Philip E.
Cole, Benjamin R.
Cole, Benjamin T.
Cole, Buster
Cole, David W.
Cole, Fred (Carrington)
Cole, Gordon H.
Cole, James W., Jr.
Cole, Kenneth R., Jr.
Cole, Robert B.
Cole, Robert T.
Cole, Sterling
Cole, Thomas W., Sr.
Cole, Warren H.
Cole, William E.
Colean, Miles L.
Colee, Harold W.
Coleman, Almand R(ouse)
Coleman, A(moss) Lee
Coleman, Edmund B.
Coleman, Henry C.
Coleman, Howard S.
Coleman, J(ohn) Phillips
Coleman, John S.
Coleman, John S.
Coleman, John W., Jr.
Coleman, Samuel O.
Coleman, Wade H(ampton) Jr.
Coleman, Winson
Coles, John W.
Coll, Harry H.
Colley, John L., Jr.
Collie, Marvin K.
Collier, Nell R.
Collins, Arthur S., Jr.
Collins, Charles C.
Collins, Charles D.
Collins, Conrad G.
Collins, Copp
Collins, Frederic W.
Collins, Henry B(ascom)
Collins, James F.
Collins, J(oseph) Lawton
Collins, LeRoy
Collins, Thomas A.
Collins, Thomas H.
Collins, Truman E(dward)
Collins, Vincent P.
Colman, William G.
Colowick, Sidney P.
Colquitt, Landon A.
Colson, Charles W.
Colton, Joel
Columkille, Sister Mary (Colbert)
Colvard, Dean W.
Colvert, Clyde C(ornellus)
Combes, Frank C(harles)
Comer, Donald, Jr.
Compton, Randolph P.
Compton, William R.
Conant, Norman F.
Conder, Joseph M.
Condit, Gex P., Jr.
Condon, Arthur D.
Condon, Martin J., III
Cone, Carl B.
Cone, Clarence N.
Cone, George S., Jr.
Cone, Sydney M., Jr.
Conklin, Clarence R.
Conklin, Harvey H.
Conley, Binford H.
Conley, Eugene
Conlon, James A.
Conn, Jack T.
Connally, Ben C.
Connally, Frederick H.
Connally, Herschel F., Jr.
Connell, John G., Jr.
Connell, Ted C.
Connelly, Charles E.
Connelly, Robert L.
Conner, Forrest E.
Conner, Frederick W.
Conner, Norval W.
Connerat, William S.
Connett, William B., Jr.
Connolly, Charles H.
Connolly, Paul R.
Connolly, Thomas F.
Connor, Albert O.
Connor, George C.
Connor, James T.
Conole, Clement V(incent)
Conrad, Charles, Jr.
Conrad, Harold E(verett)
Conrad, Ivan W.
Conroy, Francis P., II
Conroy, Raymond C.
Considine, James W(illiam)
Consolo, Federico
Constable, Stuart
Conti, Samuel F.
Conway, Daniel E.
Conway, Jack T.
Conway, Theodore J.
Conway, Walter J.
Conwell, H(ugh) Earle
Cook, Cecil N.
Cook, Charles W.
Cook, Earl F.
Cook, Edward W.
Cook, Everett R(ichard)
Cook, James L.
Cook, John L., Jr.
Cook, Mercer
Cook, Ramona G.
Cook, Raymond A.
Cook, Richard W.
Cook, Robert C.
Cook, Robert C(ecil)
Cook, Thomas I.
Cook, Walter R.
Cooke, Dennis H.
Cooke, Don A.
Cooley, Bernard H.
Cooley, James A.
Coolidge, Harold J.
Coombes, Ethel R.
Coon, Carleton S., Jr.
Coon, Milton C., Jr.
Cooney, James P.
Coons, Kenneth W.
Cooper, Albert H.
Cooper, Byron N(elson)
Cooper, Cecil H.
Cooper, Charles G(ray)
Cooper, Chauncey I.
Cooper, Damon W.
Cooper, Donald L.
Cooper, Grace R.
Cooper, Gustav A.
Cooper, John A., Jr.
Cooper, John A. D.
Cooper, Kenneth E.
Cooper, Robert J.
Cooper, Russell M.
Cooper, Samuel I.
Cooper, Thomas L.
Cooper, Weldon
Cooperman, James
Cope, Sydney R.
Copeland, Donald E.
Copeland, James I.
Copeland, Joseph B.
Copeland, Joseph J.
Copeland, Murray M.
Copeland, William G.
Corbett, Jack C.
Corbin, Alvin L.
Corbin, Thomas G.
Corcoran, Thomas G.
Corcoran, Thomas J.
Corey, Stephen M.
Corgan, Joseph A.
Cork, Charles M.
Corle, Frederic W.
Cornelius, Edward G.
Cornett, Richard O.
Corpe, Raymond F.
Corrigan, Leo F(rancis)
Corrigan, Robert F.
Cortada, James N.
Cortright, Edgar M., Jr.
Cory, William L.
Cosgrove, John E.
Cosgrove, John P.
Cosgrove, William B.
Costa, Aubrey M.
Costa, Jasper S.
Costa, Joseph
Costello, Donald P.
Costley, Richard J(oseph)
Cothen, Grady C.
Cothran, Tilman C.
Cothran, William T.
Cotner, Thomas E.
Cottam, Clarence
Cotter, Francis P.
Cottingham, Harold F.
Cotton, Emile L.
Cotton, Norris
Cotton, William D.
Cottone, Benedict P(eter)
Cottrell, David Jr.
Cottrell, Leonard S., Jr.
Cottrell, Will R., Jr.
Couch, Glenn C.
Couch, John N.
Coughlin, Robert L., Jr.
Coulling, Sidney B.
Coulter, E(llis) Merton
Coulter, Kirkley S.
Counts, James C.
Courtenay, Walter R.
Courts, Richard W.
Cousins, William J.
Cover, John H.
Covey, Charles W.
Covey, Milton H.
Covi, Darie A.
Coville, Cabot
Covington, William D.
Cowan, Donald A.
Cowan, Howard S.
Cowan, John C., Jr.
Cowden, Dudley J.
Cowen, Martin L.
Cowger, William O.
Cowley, Luis M.
Cox, Allen, Jr.
Cox, Edward H.
Cox, Edwin
Cox, Edwin L.
Cox, Elmus E.
Cox, Headley M., Jr.
Cox, Hugh
Cox, James M.
Cox, John R.
Cox, Joyce
Cox, Kenneth A.
Cox, Lewis J.
Cox, Robert D.
Coxe, Lewis C.
Coyle, William
Crabb, Cecil V. M. Jr.
Crabill, Ralph E., Jr.
Craf, John R.
Craft, Edward O.
Craft, George S.
Cragg, Henry
Cragun, John W.
Craig, Hardin, Jr.
Craig, James B.
Craig, Mack W.
Craig, (Ellsabeth) May
Craig, Walter
Craighead, Claude C.
Crain, Wilbert O.
Cramer, Leonard F.
Cramer, Robert E.
Crampton, Bruce S.
Crane, Neal D.
Crane, Radford R.
Crary, Albert P.
Crass, Maurice F., Jr.
Crater, Robert W.
Cravens, Carlisle
Cravens, Kathryn
Cravens, Raymond L.
Crawford, B(urnett) Hayden
Crawford, Clarence L.
Crawford, Earl B.
Crawford, Earl R.
Crawford, Ernest S.
Crawford, John C., Jr.
Crawford, Kenneth G.
Crawford, Meridith P.
Crawford, William A.
Creech, Danten D.
Creech, Oscar Jr.
Creel, Joe
Creel, Robert C.
Creer, Philip D.
Creighton, William F.
Crenshaw, Craig M.
Crenshaw, Kirby E.
Crenshaw, Ollinger
Creston, Paul
Crews, Clyde C.
Crimmins, John H.
Criser, Marshall
Crisler, Robert M.
Crispell, Kenneth R.
Critchfield, Jack B.
Crittenden, Christopher
Critz, Harry H.
Crnobrnja, Bogdan
Crocker, Michaux H.
Croft, Herbert S.
Cromer, Voigt R.
Cromiller, Harold L.
Cromley, Allan W.
Cromley, Raymond A.
Croneis, Carey
Cronin, John W.
Cronin, Thomas D.
Cronk, Edwin M.
Cronvich, James A.
Crook, Dorothy (Mrs. C. Sprague Hazard)
Crooker, John H., Jr.
Crooker, John H.
Crosby, Lucius O., Jr.
Crosland, Dorothy M.
Cross, James A.
Cross, James E.
Cross, James U.
Cross, John W(alker)
Cross, Tom G.
Crossette, George
Crossfield, Albert S.
Crossman, Jerome K.
Crouch, Courtney C.
Crouch, Hubert B.
Crow, Duward L.
Crow, Jane H.
Crow, John O.
Crowe, Eugene B.
Crowe, James R.
Crowe, Vincil P.
Crowell, Thomas I.
Crowley, John J., Jr.
Crowther, Harold E.
Crudup, Joslah
Cruikshank, Nelson H.
Crull, Elgin E(nglish)
Crum, James M.
Crumpacker, John W.
Crumpler, Thomas B.
Crutchfield, Robert R.
Crutchfield, William G.
Cruze, Gifford
Cuaron, Alfredo
Cubbage, Thomas L.
Culberson, George W.
Culbert, William E.
Culbertson, Robert E.
Culbreath, Hugh L., Jr.
Cullen, Frederick J.
Cullen, George
Culler, Floyd L., Jr.
Culley, Perry H.
Culligan, Glendy
Culpepper, James H.
Culver, John C.
Cumley, Russell W.
Cumming, Joseph B.
Cummings, Naurice G(rant)
Cummings, Ralph W(aldo)
Cundiff, Edward W.
Cuneo, Ernest
Cuneo, Gilbert A.
Cunha, Tony J.
Cuninggim, Margaret L.
Cunningham, Glenn (Clarence)
Cunningham, Horace H.
Cunningham, Jacques
Cunningham, James E.
Cunningham, Joseph A.
Cunningham, R. Walter
Cunningham, William A., III
Cureton, Edward E.
Curl, Robert F.
Curran, Alice T.
Current, Richard N(elson)
Currie, James S.
Curry, George M.
Curry, Othel J.
Curry, Thomas H.
Curtin, Robert H.
Curtis, Carl T.
Curtis, Doris S. M.
Curtis, Morton L.
Curtis, William R.
Curtiss, John H.
Curtiss, John S.
Cushing, Richard (Golle)
Cushman, Robert E.
Cushman, Robert E., Jr.
Cusic, Wayne N.
Cuthbert, Kenneth N.
Cuthbertson, George R.
Cutini, Gary S.
Cutler, Edward I.
Cutler, Lloyd N.
Cutler, Robert H.
Cutrer, Lewis W.
Cutter, Margot E.
Cuttino, John T.

Daane, James D.
Dabney, Hovey S.
Dabney, Virginius
Dacey, John E.
Dahl, George L.
Dahl, Leo P.
Dahlen, Chester A.
Dainow, Joseph
Dale, Bruce A.
Dale, Edward E.
Dale, William B.
Dale, William N.
D'Alesandro, Thomas Jr.
Dalton, Harry L.
Dame, Lawrence
Dampier, Joseph H.
Daniel, Bill (William P.)
Daniel, Kenneth R.
Daniel, James M.
Daniel, Jacquelin J.
Daniel, Lawrence R., Jr.
Daniel, Lois H.
Daniel, Robert H.
Daniel, Ruby K.
Danieley, James E.
Danielian, Noobar R(éthésos)
Daniels, Dominick V.
Daniels, R(obertson) Balfour
Daniels, Worth B.
Danielson, Wayne A.
D'Antoni, Joseph S.
Darby, William J(efferson), Jr.
Darden, Colgate W., Jr.
D'Arezzo, Joseph P.
D'Arista, Robert A.
Darnell, Carl Jr.
Darrow, Don O(rville)
Dart, Henry P., Jr.
Dart, Raymond O.
Darwent, Basil de Baskerville
Dashner, Lee A.
Daspit, Alexander B.
Dauer, Manning J(ulian), Jr.
Davenport, Gwen (Mrs John Davenport)
Davenport, John S., III
Davenport, Raymond R.
David, Henry
David, Paul T(heodore)
Davidson, Bryant
Davidson, Chalmers G.
Davidson, Charles E.
Davidson, C(row) Girard
Davidson, David I.
Davidson, Floyd F.
Davidson, James J., Jr.
Davidson, Joseph Q.
Davidson, Lloyd J.
Davidson, Lorimer A.
Davidson, Robert F(ranklin)
Davidson, Robert H.
Davidson, Vernon G.
Davidson, Walter H.
Davies, Alfred I.
Davies, Jack
Davies, John S.
Davies, Rodger P.
Davies, Thomas D.
Davies, William D.
Davis, Arthur K., Jr.
Davis, Benjamin O., Jr.
Davis, Bruce G.
Davis, Burke
Davis, Champion M.
Davis, Charles S.
Davis, Darrey A(dkins)
Davis, Edwin A.
Davis, Ellsworth I.
Davis, Finis E.
Davis, Frank W.
Davis, Frederick C.
Davis, Gaylord
Davis, Gene B.
Davis, George M.
Davis, Gifford
Davis, Graham P.
Davis, Harold E(ugene)
Davis, Harold T.
Davis, Harry
Davis, Harry W.
Davis, Henry C.
Davis, Howard
Davis, J. Luther
Davis, James C.
Davis, James F.
Davis, James H.
Davis, James O., Jr.
Davis, Jefferson
Davis, John A.
Davis, John C.
Davis, John E.
Davis, John H(enry), Jr.
Davis, John J.
Davis, John J.
Davis, Kenneth N., Jr.
Davis, Kleffer D.
Davis, Lawrence A.
Davis, Lloyd H.
David, Louis F.
Davis, M. Austin
Davis, Mack P.
Davis, Mendell M.
Davis, Morgan J(ones)
Davis, N(oah) Knowles
Davis Norman S.
Davis, Richard B.

Davis, Robert F.
Davis, Roy W.
Davis, Saville R.
Davis, Sid
Davis, Stephen S.
Davis, Thomas H.
Davis, Thomas K.
Davis, Walter S.
Davis, William C.
Davis, William L.
Davis, W(illiam) True, Jr.
Davis, William V.
Davison, Charles M., Jr.
Davison, Roderic H.
Davison, Vernon G.
Davison, Wilburt C.
Dawalt, Kenneth F.
Dawson, Giles E.
Dawson, Lyle R(amsay)
Dawson, Martha E.
Dawson, William L.
Day, Daniel E.
Day, J(ames) Edward
Day, James V.
Day, James W.
Day, LeRoy E.
Day, Nancy J.
Deakin, James
Dean, Alan L.
Dean, Harris W.
Dean, James W.
Dean, Paul R.
Deane, Frederick, Jr.
Deane, Michael B.
Dearborn, Henry
Dearing, W(arren) Palmer
Deason, Willard
De Bardeleben, Bailey T.
DeBardeleben, Newton H.
Debevoise, Thomas M.
Debrah, Ebenezer M.
De Bremaecker, Jean-Claude
DeBusk, Manuel C.
deButts, Harry A.
De Chant, John A.
Decker, Charles L.
Decker, George H.
Decker, Harold
Decker, Ralph W.
DeCosta, Laier C.
DeCoursey, Elbert
Deener, David R.
de Estavillo, Gregorie G.
Deferrari, Roy J.
Dehoney, William W.
DeHority, Edward H.
Deigert, Robert C.
Deitrick, William H.
de Laittre, John
DeLamater, Edward D.
Delaney, George P.
Delany, Frank J.
Delaup, Paul S.
de la Vergne, Jules K.
Del Canto Schramm, Jorge
Delchamps, Alfred F.
del Mar, Roland H.
Delmore, John R.
Delo, David M(arlon)
DeLoach, Cartha D.
De Long, Earl H.
DeLong, Vaughn R.
Dembling, Paul G.
de Menil, Dominique
DeMere, McCarthy
de Merry del Val, Alfonso
Deming, Olcott H.
Dempsey, William J.
Demuth, Richard H.
Denby, James O.
Dendy, Marhsall C.
Denegre, George
Denfeld, Louis E.
Denham, Harry C.
Denholm, Charles J.
Denius, Franklin W.
Denius, Homer R.
Denman, Leroy G., Jr.
Denney, Walter R.
Dennis, Earl A(ubrey)
Dennis, James L.
Dennis, Joe
Dennis, Wayne
Dennison, Raymond A(lexander)
Dennison, Robert L.
Denny, Ludwell
DeNoyer, John M.
Dent, Albert W.
Dent, John H.
Dent, John W.
Denton, Ira C.
DePalma, Samuel
de Poix, Vincent P.
DePuy, William E.
Derby, Donald
Dermer, Otis C.
Der Nersessian, Sirarple

Derrick, Leland E.
Derry, John A(lvin)
Derryberry, Everett
Derthick, Lawrence G.
Desautels, Claude J.
de Segonzac, Adalbert R.
De Simone, Daniel V.
Dessler, Alexander J.
Detgen, Edward J.
DeuPree, Charles L.
Devin, William A., Jr.
Devine, Frank J.
Devine, Samuel L.
Devor, John W.
DeVore, George W.
de Vyver, Frank T.
Dewar, Henry H. (Hal)
Dewar, Michael J. S.
Dewberry, Lawrence G., Jr.
de Weldon, Felix W.
Dewey, Charles S.
Dewey, Lawrence R.
DeWitt, Bryce S.
DeWolf, L. Harold
Dexter, John B.
Dey, John A(lexander)
Dey, Joseph C., Jr.
Dial, William H.
Diamond, Murray A.
Dickerson, Claude W., Jr.
Dickerson, Norvin K.
Dickert, Herman A.
Dickey, Imogene B.
Dickey, Raymond R.
Dickinson, Alfred J.
Dickinson, Dwight
Dickinson, John B., Jr.
Dickinson, William B., Jr.
Dickinson, William H., Jr.
Dickson, Paul
Dickson, William P., Jr.
Diddle, Albert W.
Diederich, John T.
Diehl, Walter J.
Diem, Bul
Dies, Edward J.
Dietrich, Robert L.
Diettrich, Sigismond de R(uedesheim)
Dietz, James S.
Diez de Medina, Raul
di Furia, Giulio
Diggs, Charles C., Jr.
Diggs, Lemuel W.
Diggs, Walter W.
Dillard, Allyn
Dillard, Hardy C.
Dillard, Robert L., Jr.
Dillard, William E.
Dillaway, Robert B.
Dillon, Jesse W.
Dillon, John A., Jr.
Dimock, Ross A.
Dinbergs, Anatol
Dingell, John D., Jr.
Dinwoodey, Dean
Dismukes, William P(aul)
Disosway, Gabriel P.
Ditzen, Lowell R.
Divers, William K.
Divine, William R.
Diwoky, Roy J.
Dixon, James A.
Dixon, James W., Jr.
Dixon, Thomas F.
Diz, Adolfo C.
Dobbins, Charles G.
Dobbins, Gaines S.
Dobbins, Innes W., Jr.
Dobbs, Hubert L.
Dobbs, R(ufus) Howard, Jr.
Dobrynin, Anatoly F(edorovich)
Dobson, Philip E.
Doby, John T.
Dobyns, Edward P.
Dockeray, James C.
Dodd, Charles G(ardner)
Dodd, Lamar
Dodd, Thomas J.
Dodge, Charles G.
Dodson, Edward G., Jr.
Dodson, Maxie R.
Doggett, Joseph M.
Doherty, Edward W.
Doherty, Richard P.
Dolan, John W., Jr.
Dolan, Margaret B. (Mrs. Charles E. Dolan)
Dolar, Raymond E.
Dole, Robert J.
Dolley, James C.
Dolley, Robert D.
Dollmeyer, Walker G.
Dominy, Floyd E.
Donachie, Robert J.
Donaho, Glynn R.

Donahue, Charles
Donahue, Hayden H.
Donahue, Thomas R.
Donaldson, Lauren R.
Donegan, Thomas J.
Donelson, Lewis R., III
Donovan, Clement H.
Donlan, Charles J.
Donnelley, Dixon
Donnelly, Thomas R., Jr.
Donner, Arvin N.
Donohew, Jack N.
Donohue, F. Joseph
Donohue, James C.
Donovan, James A., Jr.
Donovan, Robert J.
Doole, George A., Jr.
Dooley, Thomas P.
Dooly, Oscar E.
Dorn, Charles M.
Dorsett, James K., Jr.
Dorsey, Earl A.
Dorsey, Hugh M., Jr.
Dorvillier, William J.
Dotterweich, Frank H(enry)
Douglas, John
Douglas, John G(ray)
Douglas, John W.
Douglas, Paul H.
Douglass, H(ilton) L(ee)
Douglass, Robert R(aymond)
Douma, John H.
Dovat, Ernest C.
Dow, John G.
Dow, Robert N., Jr.
Dowd, Thomas N.
Dowdey, Clifford (Shirley), Jr.
Dowdy, George W.
Dowdy, John W.
Dowdy, Lewis C.
Dowgray, John G. L., Jr.
Downer, Samuel F.
Downing, Dera G.
Downs, Thomas J(oseph)
Doyle, Donald E.
Doyle, Edward A.
Doyle, Lee T.
Doyle, Marion W. (Mrs. Henry Grattan Doyle)
Doyle, Wilson K.
Dragnich, Alex N.
Dragstedt, Lester R.
Draine, Donald P.
Drake, Dixie
Drake, Richard B.
Drake, Robert M., Jr.
Drake, William E.
Draper, Earle S.
Draper, Frederick G.
Draper, George W.
Draper, Warren F.
Dratz, Henry M.
Draper, William H(enry), Jr.
Drawdy, Sherman
Dreier, John C.
Drennan, Merrill W.
Dresser, Laurence L.
Drew, Jesse M.
Drewry, John E.
Dreyfous, Felix J.
Dreyfus-Barney, Laura (Mme. L. Dreyfus-Barney)
Drinkard, Donald
Driver, Lottie E.
Driver, Randolph S.
Droste, Edward P.
Drucker, Miriam K.
Drumheller, Joseph
Drumm, Streuby L.
Dublin, Thomas D(avid)
Dubs, Adolph
Ducayet, Edwin J.
Duckett, John W.
Duckworth, Kenton M.
Duckworth, William H.
Ducrest, Willis F.
Duda, Karel
Dudek, Richard A.
Dudley, Francis M.
Dudley, Tilford E.
Duerbeck, Edwin, M.
Duesenberry, James S.
Dufek, George J(ohn)
Duff, Fratis L.
Duff, James H.
Duffey, Frank M.
Duffy, Elizabeth (Mrs. John E. Bridgers, Jr.)
Dufour, Maurice F.
Dugan, Hugh P.
Dugdale, J. M.
Duggan, Ben O., Jr.
Dukas, Peter
Duke, Angier B.

Dulan, Harold A.
Dulles, Eleanor L.
Dumas, Hal S.
Dumont, Donald A.
Dunbar, Charles E., III
Duncan, A. Baker
Duncan, Charles K.
Duncan, George T.
Duncan, John B.
Duncan, John H.
Duncan, John P.
Duncan, Marion M.
Duncan, Phillip A.
Dunford, Ralph E.
Dunham, Charles L.
Dunham, Lowell
Dunkle, David H.
Dunlap, Charles E.
Dunlap, James A.
Dunlap, Robert C.
Dunn, Burton
Dunn, Clark A(llan)
Dunn, Edgar H., Jr.
Dunn, Edward C.
Dunn, James H.
Dunn, R. Roy
Dunn, Richard M., Jr.
Dunn, R. Walter
Dunn, Stephen F.
Dunstan, Florence J.
Dunton, Edward A.
Dunwody, William E., Jr.
Dunwody, William E., IV
DuPont, Alfred V.
DuPre, Henry H., Jr.
DuPuis, Robert N.
Dupuy, Richard E.
Dupuy, Trevor N.
Dupy, John D.
Durand, John D.
Durand, Loyal, Jr.
Durant, Frederick C., III
Durant, John
Durbrow, Elbridge
Duren, William L(arkin), Jr.
Durfee, Harold A.
Durfee, James R.
Durham, Frank L.
Durkee, William C.
Durr, Clifford J.
Dusard, Leo F., Jr
Duson, Curley P.
Dutcher, Clinton H.
Dutton, Donnell W.
Duvall, Evelyn M.
Duvall, Severn P. C.
DuVall, W(allace) O(dell)
Dvornik, Francis
Dwan, Ralph H.
Dybczak, Zbigniew W.
Dye, Stuart F.
Dyer, Everett D.
Dyer, Harry B.
Dyer, Rolla E.
Dyke, James (Parvin)

Eaker, Ira C.
Eakin, Carl T.
Eames, Wilmer B.
Earl, Charles H.
Earl, Lewis H.
Earle, Kenneth M.
Earle, T(homas) T(heron)
Earls, Richard F.
Earnest, Robert C.
Earthman, William F.
Eason, Thaddeus W.
Easterly, Frederick J.
Eastin, Mark E., Jr.
Eastwood, Douglas W.
Eaton, Clement
Eaton, Reginald C.
Eaton, Robert E. L.
Eaves, James C.
Eaves, Robert W.
Ebaugh, Bessie M.
Eberhardt, Homer C.
Eberwine, Vernon G.
Eblen, Amos H.
Echavarria, Hernan
Eckels, Arthur R.
Eckler, A. Ross
Economos, George T.
Eddinger, Lucille A.
Eddy, Dayton W.
Edens, Henry H.
Edge, Arthur B., Jr.
Edge, Findley B.
Edgerton, Henry W.
Edgerton, Justin L.
Edgerton, Norman E.
Edinger, Lois V.
Edlund, Milton C.
Edmonds, Helen G.
Edmondson, Ed
Edmonson, Munro S.
Edmunds, Robert L.
Edson, Peter

Edwards, Billy M.
Edwards, Charles H.
Edwards, Daniel K(ramer)
Edwards, G(ilbert) F.
Edwards, James D.
Edwards, Leverett
Edwards, Marshall H.
Edwards, Roderick Y.
Edwards, Walter A.
Edwards, William F.
Efferson, John N.
Effinger, Robert C.
Efron, Samuel
Egan, John T.
Egger, George E(dward)
Eggleston, John W.
Ehlers, Joseph H.
Ehrlich, Alvin Q.
Eichenbaum, Howard S.
Eidman, Kraft W.
Eifler, Charles W.
Eighmy, Herbert H.
Einkauf, Oscar E., Jr.
Eisch, John J.
Eisenberg, Fillmore B.
Eisenberg, Matthew E.
Eitel, Hubert M.
Ekeberg, John M.
Eklund, John M.
Eklund, Laurence C.
Ekstrom, William F.
Elbrick, Charles B.
El-Dabh, Halim
Elebash, Hunley A.
Elfin, Mel
Eliason, Norman E.
Elkins, James A.
Elkins, James A., Jr.
Elkins, Lloyd E.
Eller, Ernest M.
Elliman, George T.
Elliot, Reed A.
Elliot, Robert S., Jr.
Elliott, John C.
Elliott, John M.
Elliott, Martin A.
Elliott, Robert G.
Elliott, William Y.
Ellis, Clyde T.
Ellis, Leslie L., Jr.
Ellis, R(ichard) A.
Ellis, Sydney T.
Ellis, Tellis B., Jr.
Ellis, Van V.
Ellis, William E.
Ellison, David M., Jr.
Ellison, Fred P.
Ellison, Newell W.
Ellison, Samuel P(orter), Jr.
Elmer, William M.
Elmore, Franklin H.
Elsey, George M.
Elson, Edward L(ee) R(oy)
Elston, Dorothy A.
Ely, Northcutt
Emary, Abdel G.
Embry, Lloyd B.
Emery, Harlan J.
Emery, Stephen A(lbert)
Emiliani, Cesare
Emmanuel, Michel G.
Emrich, Duncan B. M.
Emrick, Edward, Jr.
Enders, Richard W.
Enfield, Clifton W.
Engel, Joseph H.
Engel, Ruben W.
Enger, Walter M.
Engert, Cornelius V. H.
Engler, Henry J., Jr.
Engler, Jean E.
Englert, Roy T.
English, George W(ashington)
English, Spofford G.
Ennis, Thomas G.
Ensey, Lot
Epes, Horace H., Jr.
Eppler, William B.
Epps, Augustus C.
Epps, William M.
Erlandson, Ray S.
Erlewine, John A.
Erly, Robert B.
Ernest, Joseph M., Jr.
Erni, Hans
Ernst, Robert C.
Ervin, Paul R.
Ervin, Robert M.
Erwin, Cyral P.
Erwin, Frank C., Jr.
Erwin, Frank W.
Erwin, William J.
Esenbel, Melih
Eskew, Cletis T.
Eskildson, Hugo N., Jr.
Espinosa, Manuel Y.
Essene, Frank J.

Ethridge, Mark F.
Ethridge, Willie S. (Mrs.)
Etter, Harry S.
Eubanks, Ralph
Eugere, Edward J.
Evans, Andrew J., Jr.
Evans, Benjamin F., Jr.
Evans, Clifford
Evans, David A.
Evans, Elinor L.
Evans, Elwyn
Evans, Frank O.
Evans, Grose
Evans, Hugh M.
Evans, James C.
Evans, William N.
Eve, Henry P.
Eveland, Harmon E.
Evenden, Frederick G(eorge)
Everest, Harvey P.
Everett, Mark R(ueben)
Everett, Roberts
Everett, Sara M.
Everett, Warren S.
Evins, Lucius S., Jr.
Ewbank, John N., Jr.
Ewen, David
Ewers, John C.
Ewing, John A.
Ewing, Oscar R.
Ewing, Richard T.
Ewing, Samuel E.
Exton, Hugh M.
Eyre, John D.
Ezell, John S.
Ezelle, Sam, III

Fable, Robert C., Jr.
Fadner, Frank L.
Fadum, Ralph E(igil)
Fahien, Raymond W.
Fairbank, Henry A.
Fairbanks, Charles H.
Fairley, Francis H.
Falck, Edward
Falk, Eugene H.
Falk, Werner D.
Fama, Sebastian
Fancher, George H.
Fanning, John H(arold)
Fanseen, James F.
Farbach, Carl F.
Faricy, William T.
Faris, Esron M., Jr.
Farley, Philip J.
Farley, Robert J.
Farmer, Frances
Farmer, Guy
Farmer, Thomas L.
Farnsley, Charles (Rowland Peaslee)
Farnsworth, Jerry
Farnsworth, Richard A.
Farrell, John J.
Farrell, John R.
Farrior, Jewel R.
Farris, Milton G.
Farson, William J.
Faruki, Mahmud T.
Farwell, F. Evans
Faubus, Orval E.
Faulk, E. Ward
Faulkner, Claude W.
Faulkner, Elizabeth C.
Faulkner, Rafford L.
Faulkner, (Herbert Winthrop) Waldron
Faunt, Joan S. R.
Favell, Thomas R.
Favrot, Clifford F.
Fawley, John J.
Fay, William M.
Fayer, Mischa H.
Fearey, Robert A.
Featherston, Errett G.
Feaver, John C.
Fee, William E., Jr.
Fehr, Arthur
Fehr, Carl A.
Feibelman, Julian B.
Feibleman, James K.
Feidler, Ernest R(eynold)
Feighner, James W.
Fein, John M.
Feiss, Carl
Feitel, Arthur
Felber, Everett H. F.
Feld, Nicholas
Feldman, Jacob
Feldman, Myer
Feldmann, Edward G(eorge)
Feldt, Harold W.
Fellendorf, George W.
Fellers, James D(avison)
Fellers, Rufus G.
Fels, Rendigs
Fenn, Dan H., Jr.

Fenner, Darwin S.
Fenner, Mildred S. (Mrs. H. Wolcott Fenner)
Fenninger, Leonard D.
Fensterstock, Howard W.
Ferguson, Allen R.
Ferguson, Charles R.
Ferguson, Chester H.
Ferguson, Clarence C., Jr.
Ferguson, Harry
Ferguson, James H.
Ferguson, James S.
Ferguson, John H(oward)
Ferguson, Noel M.
Ferguson, Oliver W.
Ferguson, Phil M.
Ferguson, Rowena
Ferguson, William McL.
Fergusson, Willie E., III
Fernandez, Mariano H.
Ferneau, Elmer F.
Ferrand, Jean C.
Ferre, Gustave A.
Ferre, Maurice A.
Ferris, George M.
Ferst, Robert H.
Fetterman, John D.
Feurt, Seldon D.
Few, Mary R. T. (Mrs. William Preston Few)
Fidel, Edward A.
Fidler, William P.
Field, Frank M.
Field, Lamar
Fielder, Parker C.
Fields, Carl R.
Fields, D. Wallace
Fields, Emmett B.
Fields, Lewis J.
Fields, William S.
Fields, Wilmer C.
Fifield, Harry A.
Fifield, Willard M.
Finch, Edwin P.
Fincher, Myron G.
Findley, Thomas P., Jr.
Fine, Paul C.
Fine, Phil D.
Finerty, John C.
Finger, Harold B.
Finger, Homer E., Jr.
Fink, Arthur E(mil)
Finley, David E.
Finley, Harold E(ugene)
Finley, Jean C.
Finley, States R. G.
Finney, Nat(haniel) S(olon)
Finney, Ruth (Mrs. Robert Sharon Allen)
Finucane, Charles C.
Firfer, Alexander
Fischer, Earl W.
Fischer, George D.
Fischoff, Ephralm
Fishburn, Howard D.
Fisher, Adrian S(anford)
Fisher, Allan C., Jr.
Fisher, Charles H.
Fisher, Edward
Fisher, Granville C.
Fisher, Leslie H.
Fisher, Wilber C.
Fisher, William E.
Fishwick, John P.
Fitch, Alva R(evista)
Fite, Daniel H.
Fite, Gilbert C.
Fitzgerald, Thomas R.
Fitzgerald, William H. G.
Fitzgibbons, Edward S.
Fitz-Hugh, Glassell S.
Fitzpatrick, Berchmans T.
Fitzpatrick, Francis J.
Flanders, Helen H.
Flannery, William L(ouis)
Flavin, Thomas J.
Flax, Alexander H.
Fleece, George A.
Fleischaker, Betty J.
Fleischaker, Joseph
Fleischbein, Margie O. E.
Fleming, Denna F.
Fleming, John W.
Fleming, Mack G.
Fleming, Neal B.
Fleming, Robert H.
Fleming, Robert W.
Fleming, Roger W.
Fleming, Samuel M.
Fleming, William A.
Fleming, William C.
Fleming, William L(eRoy)
Flemming, Harry S.
Fletcher, Albert L.
Fletcher, Arthur A.
Fletcher, C(yril) Scott
Fletcher, Frank U.
Fletcher, Lloyd
Fletcher, R(obert) I(rving)
Fletcher, Thomas W.
Flewellen, William C., Jr.
Flieger, Howard W.
Flinner, Charles F.
Flipse, Mathew J.
Flittie, William J(orgen)
Flom, Edward L.
Flom, Samuel L.
Florio, Lloyd J.
Flory, William E. S.
Flott, Frederick W.
Floyd, Edwin E.
Flynn, Thomas E.
Flynt, Ralph C(omer) M(ichael)
Focke, Arthur B.
Fogel, Ernest J.
Fogle, Richard H.
Folda, Jaroslav T., Jr.
Foley, Arthur D.
Foley, Leo A.
Foley, William E.
Folger, John C.
Folkers, Karl A.
Follett, Dwight W.
Folley, A.J.
Folsom, John R.
Fontaine, Thomas D.
Fonville, Robert E.
Forbes, Douglas W.
Forbes, Theodore M., Jr.
Forbush, Scott E.
Ford, Amos W.
Ford, Frederick W.
Ford, Hamilton
Ford, Jesse H.
Ford, John J.
Ford, John W.
Ford, Rubye L.
Ford, Thomas R.
Foree, Robert L.
Foreman, Edgar F., Jr.
Foreman, Lawton D.
Forest, Herbert L.
Forney, John M.
Forster, William B.
Forsythe, George I.
Fort, Ada
Fort, Rufus E., Jr.
Fortenberry, Charles N.
Forth, Stuart
Foscue, Henry A.
Foster, Charles A.
Foster, David H.
Foster, Gordon W.
Foster, H(arry) Schuyler
Foster, John S., Jr.
Foster, Mark G.
Foster, Rayburn L.
Foster, Thomas A.
Foster, William C.
Foulkrod, Harry E.
Fouracre, Maurice H.
Foust, John W.
Fowle, James L.
Fowle, Wilson F., Jr.
Fowler, Ben B.
Fowler, Charles A.
Fowler, Cody
Fowler, Frederick C., II
Fowler, Harold L.
Fowler, James R.
Fowler, Sister Mary C.
Fowler, Richard G.
Fowler, Samuel B.
Fowlie, Wallace
Fowlkes, Richard W.
Fox, Charles R.
Fox, Edward G.
Fox, Edward J.
Fox, Henry J.
Fox, John G.
Fox, Lawrence A.
Fox, Sidney W(alter)
Francis, Charles I.
Francis, Sir Frank (Chalton)
Francis, John D.
Francis, Muriel B.
Frandsen, Julius
Frank, Isaiah
Frankel, Max
Frankel, Samuel B.
Franklin, Alan D.
Franklin, Bernard W.
Franklin, James B.
Franklin, Joe L., Jr.
Franklin, Joseph L.
Franklin, Omer W., Jr.
Franklin, Richard E.
Franklin, William B.
Franks, Charles L.
Frantz, Harry W.
Frantz, Joe B.
Frasca, John A.
Fraser, Arthur M.
Fraser, Hugh R.
Fraser, Hugh W., Jr.
Frazer, James N.
Frazer, Keener C.
Frazier, James B., Jr.
Frazier, Owsley B.
Frazier, Robert H.
Frear, J(oseph) Allen, Jr.
Freas, Howard G.
Frechtling, Louis E.
Freckleton, Frank R.
Frederick, Anthony P.
Fredericks, J(acob) Wayne
Fredine, C(larence) Gordon
Freedman, Monroe H.
Freedman, Selma G.
Freeman, Frank S.
Freeman, John
Freeman, John D., Jr.
Freeman, John H.
Freeman, Milton V.
Freeman, Monroe E.
Freeman, Nelson W.
Freeman, Orville L(othrop)
Freeman, Paul D.
Freeman, Robert T., Jr.
Freeman, Roger A.
Freeman, William R.
Frei, Emil III
Freitag, Robert F.
Frelinghuysen, Peter H. B.
French, C(harles) C.
French, William W., Jr.
Frensley, Herbert J.
Freret, Douglass V.
Freudenthal, Alfred M(artin)
Freundlich, August L.
Friar, G(eorge) Edward
Frick, Thomas C.
Friday, Herchel H.
Fridge, Benjamin W.
Fridley, Richard M.
Friedel, Samuel N.
Frieden, Earl
Friederich, Werner P(aul)
Friedewald, William (Frank)
Friedkin, Joseph F.
Friedman, Alvin
Friedman, Bayard H.
Friedman, Edmund
Friedman, Herbert
Friedman, Joseph B(ivens)
Friedrich, Jack A.
Friedrichs, George S.
Frierson, John B., Jr.
Friesen, Ernest C., Jr.
Frisard, Emile L.
Fritchey, Clayton
Frith, James R(obert)
Fritzlan, A(ndrew) David
Froehlke, Robert F.
Frohman, Philip H.
Frost, Jack
Frost, M(orris) M(cCampbell)
Frost, Thomas C.
Fry, Thomas A., Jr.
Frye, William W.
Fuhr, Samuel E.
Fuhrman, Ralph E.
Fulgham, Cecil E.
Fulgham, John R., Jr.
Fuller, Edgar
Fuller, Helen
Fuller, R(ufus) Clinton
Fullerton, Richard C.
Fulmer, Daniel W.
Fulton, James S.
Fulton, Robert B.
Fumich, George
Funkhouser, Richard
Fuqua, Don
Fuqua, Herbert B.
Furcron, A(urelius) S(ydney)
Furlong, Edward C., Jr.
Furlong, William R.
Furness, Betty
Furniss, W(arren) Todd
Furr, Roy
Furth, Hans G.
Furtseva, Ekaterina A(lexeyevna)
Futch, Olivia

Gable, G. Ellis
Gabrielson, Ira N.
Gaebelein, Frank E.
Gaffney, M(errill) Mason
Gaffron, Hans
Gage, Robert
Gailey, Franklin B.
Galatzan, Morris A.
Galbraith, Francis J.
Gall, Lawrence H.
Gallington, Ralph O.
Gallman, Waldemar J.
Galloway, George H.
Galloway, James H.
Galvin, Charles O.
Galvin, Hoyt R(ees)
Gamble, Clinton
Gambrell, David H.
Gambrell, E(noch) Smythe
Gammon, Landon H.
Gamser, Howard G.
Ganger, Robert M.
Gantt, Paul H.
Gantz, Hallie G.
Ganus, Clifton L., Jr.
Garber, Paul E.
Garcia-Godoy, Hector
Gardiner, Harold C.
Gardner, Ellis B., Jr.
Gardner, George T.
Gardner, Lucien D., Jr.
Gardner, Paul V.
Gardner, Samuel N.
Garets, Wallace E.
Garin, Vasco V.
Garland, Fred M(cKee)
Garman, Willard H.
Garner, Alto L.
Garner, Mildred M.
Garner, Robert L.
Garner, S(amuel) Paul
Garnett, Richard L.
Garrard, Ralph H.
Garrett, Clyde D(avis)
Garrett, Donald W.
Garrett, Edward R.
Garrett, Ethel S.
Garrett, George P., Jr.
Garrett, Pearson B.
Garrett, R(obert) Norval
Garrick, Isadore E.
Garrigus, W(esley) P(atterson)
Garrison, Lloyd L.
Garrison, Olen B.
Garrison, Weldon S.
Garrison, William C.
Garrou, Louis W.
Garvey, James A.
Garvey, Robert R., Jr.
Garwood, Wilmer St. J.
Gary, Frank B.
Gary, J. V.
Garza, Reynaldo G.
Gaskell, James S., Jr.
Gaskill, Harold V.
Gaston, D. F.
Gaston, David A.
Gatchell, William H.
Gates, Howard P., Jr.
Gates, James E(dward)
Gates, William F., Jr.
Gathright, Joseph R.
Gaud, William S.
Gaudian, Martin F(erdinand)
Gaumnitz, Walter H.
Gautier, Redmond B., Jr.
Gavazzi, Aladino A.
Gavin, Robert L.
Gay, J. Edwin
Gay, Thomas B.
Gay, William S.
Gayle, Gibson, Jr.
Gayler, Noel A. M.
Gaylord, C(harles) N(elson)
Gaylord, Harvey
Gazzolo, Dorothy H.
Gearhart, Lester R.
Gearheart, Ernest T.
Gebhard, Louis A.
Gee, Edward F.
Gee, Samuel E.
Geehan, Robert W(illiam)
Geer, William D.
Gehrig, Leo J.
Gehron, William J.
Geis, Duane V.
Geis, Lawrence R.
Geisert, Wayne F.
Geller, Henry
Geltz, Charles G.
Gemmill, Chalmers L(aughlin)
Gentner, William E., Jr.
Gentry, John T.
George, Claude S., Jr.
Geraghty, John J.
Gerber, Joseph N.
Gerber, William
Gerlach, Arch C.
German, Leslie
Germany, Eugene B.
Gerow, Richard O.
Gerrard, Robert W.
Gerstenfeld, Norman
Gervasi, Frank
Geschickter, Charles F.
Gessler, A(lbert) E(dward)
Geyelin, Philip L.
Geyer, Richard A.
Ghiglione, Angelo F. S.
Ghormley, William K.
Gibbs, Carey A.
Gibbs, Delbridge L.
Gibson, Byron H(all)
Gibson, Charles (Arnold)
Gibson, Elmer J.
Gibson, Foye G.
Gibson, George D.
Gibson, Herbert R.
Gibson, Jerry L.
Gibson, Patrick A.
Gibson, William W.
Gibson Barboza, Mario
Gibson, James O.
Gidney, Ray M.
Gil, Francisco A., Jr.
Gilbert, Ben W.
Gilbreth, Frank B., Jr.
Giles, Julian W.
Giles, Robert E.
Gilford, Dorothy M.
Gilkerson, Yancey S.
Gilkeson, Fillmore B.
Gill, Atticus J.
Gill, Jocelyn R.
Gill, Tom (Thomas Harvey)
Gillem, Alvan C., II
Gillen, William A.
Giller, Edward B.
Gillette, Hyde
Gillette, Norman C., Jr.
Gilliland, Charles E., Jr.
Gilliland, Whitney
Gillingham, William J.
Gillon, John W.
Gills, Joe P.
Gilmer, Howard C(ecll), Jr.
Gilmer, Thomas E(dward)
Gilmore, Eugene A., Jr.
Gilmore, Fred W.
Gilpatric, Donald S.
Gilpin, G. Noble
Gilreath, Esmarch S.
Gilruth, Robert R.
Ginger, Lyman V.
Gingles, Charles H.
Ginnane, Robert W.
Ginsberg, Paul
Ginsberg, Reuben M.
Ginsburg, Charles D.
Girard, Louis J.
Girvin, Eb C.
Givens, Johnnie E.
Givens, Thomas H.
Givens, Willard E.
Gladney, William B(eckett)
Glaser, Milton
Glaser, Vera R. (Mrs. Herbert R. Glaser)
Glass, Bryan P(ettigrew)
Glass, Robert R.
Glasser, Arthur C.
Glasser, Otto J.
Glassie, Henry H.
Glazier, Richard L.
Gleason, Jackie
Gleason, Sarell E.
Gleazer, Edmund J., Jr.
Glenn, Hortense M.
Glenn, James H.
Glenn, John H(erschel), Jr.
Glenn, Wayne E.
Glenn, Wilbur H.
Glennan, T(homas) Keith
Gleysteen, Culver
Glick, Philip M(ilton)
Glitsch, Hans C.
Glock, John W.
Glover, Charles C., Jr.
Glover, Robert O.
Glover, W. J.
Gobbel, James T.
Godard, James M.
Godchaux, Frank A(rea), Jr.
Godchaux, Leon
Godfrey, Arthur
Godfrey, (Edwin) Drexel, Jr.
Godfrey, Horace D.
Godfrey, James L.
Goelz, Paul C.
Goethert, Bernhard (Hermann)
Goglia, Gennaro L.
Goglia, Mario J.
Gohdes, Clarence L. F.
Goin, Lauren J.
Going, Allen J.
Gold, Joseph
Goldburg, Norman M.
Golden, Hawkins
Golden, Ruth S.
Goldfield, Edwin D.
Goldfinger, Nathaniel
Goldhurst, William
Goldman, Joseph B.
Goldner, Joseph L.
Goldsmith, Grace A.
Goldsmith, Jack L(andman)
Goldsmith, Thomas T., Jr.
Goldstein, Max F.
Goldstein, Moise H.
Goldthwaite, Robert
Goldwater, Leonard J.
Golemon, Albert S.
Gomberg, Henry J.
Gonzales, Carlotta (Lahey)
Gonzalez, Richard J.
Gooch, John A.
Goodall, Donald B.
Goodchild, Chauncey G(eorge)
Goode, Richard B.
Goodell, Sol
Goodfellow, Alexander S.
Goodfellow, Millard P.
Goodfellow, Thomas M.
Goodloe, John D., III
Goodman, Benjamin
Goodman, Charles M.
Goodman, Clark D.
Goodman, Leo M.
Goodman, Mary E.
Goodrich, Max
Goodrich, Robert E., Jr.
Goodson, Charles L.
Goodson, James B.
Goodson, Louie A., Jr.
Goodwin, Andrew J.
Goodwin, John E., Sr.
Goodwin, John P.
Goodwin, Leo, Sr.
Goodwin, Paul
Goodwyn, John L.
Goodwyn, Ulysses V.
Goodykoontz, Harry G.
Gordh, George R.
Gordon, Felipe
Gordon, Harry B.
Gordon, Howard H.
Gordon, James B(raund)
Gordon, Joseph E.
Gordon, Joseph H.
Gordon, Kermit
Gordon, Robert L., Jr.
Gordon, Samuel C., Jr.
Gordon, Ulysses S.
Gordon, William E.
Gordon, William T.
Gordy, Walter
Gore, George W(illiam), Jr.
Goren, Charles H.
Gorham, William
Gorman, Cornelius E(ugene)
Gorman, Thomas K.
Gosnell, John A.
Goss, James W.
Gottschalk, Carl W.
Gottschalk, John S.
Gottwald, Bruce C.
Gottwald, Floyd D.
Gould, Gordon T., Jr.
Gould, Michael
Gould, Sylvester E.
Gourley, James E(dwin)
Govan, Mary C. N.
Gozonsky, Moses J.
Graber, Paul J(ames)
Gracy, John S.
Graebner, Norman A.
Graff, William
Graffis, Herb
Grafton, Arthur W.
Gragg, Logan
Graham, Alice M.
Graham, Bruce
Graham, Ford M.
Graham, Gordon M.
Graham, Jackson
Graham, John M., II
Graham, Richard A.
Graham, Thomas
Graham, Walter W., Jr.
Graham, Willis S.
Gralla, Arthur R.
Gram, Harvey B., Jr.
Gramley, Dale H(artzier)
Gramling, Lea G.
Granberry, Edwin P.
Grand, John L(ouis) R(ochon)
Grandy, Cyrus W.
Granger, Shelton B.
Granik, Hannah B.
Granik, Theodore
Grant, Charles L.
Grant, Edward D.
Grant, Harold W.

Grant, Hugh G.
Grant, (James) Inge
Grant, James P.
Grant, Lindsey
Grant, Murray
Grantham, Robert G.
Grattan, C(linton) Hartley
Graver, William J.
Graves, Allen W.
Graves, Benjamin B.
Graves, Charles L.
Graves, Harold N., Jr.
Graves, James M.
Grawemeyer, Henry C.
Gray, Gordon
Gray, James A.
Gray, John E.
Gray, Robert H.
Gray, Warren P.
Gray, Wellington B.
Gray, Willard F.
Gray, W(illiam) Ashley, Jr.
Gray, William L., Jr.
Gray, William P.
Graybiel, Ashton
Grayson, Charles J., Jr.
Grayson, James M.
Grayson, Walton G. III
Greathouse, Glenn A.
Greaves, Thomas G., Jr.
Greeley, Arthur W.
Green, Alice
Green, Cecil H.
Green, Fitzhugh
Green, Fletcher M.
Green, John C(awley)
Green, (Abner) Leon
Green, Leon, Jr.
Green, Marshall
Green, Paul M.
Green, Thomas F(itzgerald)
Green, William C.
Green, William J.
Green, William J.
Greenberg, Howard
Greene, A(lvin) C(arl)
Greene, Francis T.
Greene, George B., Jr.
Greene, James E.
Greene, John W., Jr.
Greene, Joseph N.
Greene, Joseph N., Jr.
Greene, Jule B.
Greene, Lee S.
Greenebaum, Samuel L.
Greenhut, Melvin L.
Greenlief, Francis S.
Greenspan, Martin
Greenwalt, Tibor J.
Greenwood, Erma G.
Greenwood, James, Jr.
Greenwood, James W., Jr.
Greenwood, William F.
Greep, Harry P.
Greer, John J.
Greer, Walter E(ugene), Jr.
Gregg, Donald E.
Gregg, R. Frank
Gregory, Edward W., Jr.
Gregory, John M. M., Jr.
Gregory, Lloyd J.
Gregory, Merrill V.
Gregory, Walton C.
Gremillion, Jack P. F.
Gremillion, (Curtis) Lionel, Jr.
Gresham, Newton
Greulach, Victor A.
Grey, J(ames) D(avid)
Gribbin, John H.
Gribble, William C., Jr.
Grier, William H.
Griffin, Amos C.
Griffin, Angus M.
Griffin, Charles D.
Griffin, George R.
Griffin, Oscar O., Jr.
Griffin, Robert T.
Griffis, Stanton
Griffis, Winford E.
Griffith, Edwin C.
Griffith, Ernest S.
Griffith, Paul H.
Grigg, Charles M.
Grigg, Milton L.
Griggs, Robert S.
Grignon, Henri G.
Grimes, Stephen H.
Grimson, Keith S.
Griner, John F.
Grinter, Linton E.
Grismer, Raymond L.
Grissom, Pinkney
Griswold, Ralph E.
Griswold, Rettig A.
Grollman, Arthur
Gropp, Armin H.

Grose, Peter B.
Groseclose, Elgin
Groseth, Haakon B.
Gross, Gerlad C.
Gross, John B.
Gross, John O.
Gross, Paul M.
Grosslight, Joseph H.
Grosstephan, Arthur R.
Grosvenor, Gilbert M.
Grosvenor, John H.
Grote, Irvine W.
Grovenstein, Erling, Jr.
Grover, Norman L.
Groves, Leslie R.
Grubb, H. Dale
Grubb, Homer V.
Gruene, Hans F.
Gruening, Ernest
Gruenther, Alfred M.
Gruenther, Homer H.
Grumbles, Leland C.
Grunwald, Joseph
Guenther, Carl F.
Guerassimov, Luben N.
Guerin, Dean P.
Guerin, John W.
Guerrero, E. T.
Guest, Raymond R.
Guffin, Gilbert L.
Guilds, John C., Jr.
Guilmartin, James L.
Guinn, Dick H.
Guinn, George E.
Guinn, John A(lonzo)
Gulick, Clarence S.
Gulick, James W.
Gulick, John
Gulledge, Charles G.
Gullette, George A.
Gulley, Halbert E.
Gully, Arnold J.
Gunn, Lewis B.
Gunneng, Arne
Gunter, John W.
Gurney, J(ames) Thomas
Gussman, Herbert
Gustafson, Wesley A.
Guth, Donald J.
Gutheim, Frederick
Gutheim, Robert J.
Guthrie, John C.
Guthrie, Paul N.
Guthrie, Robert L.
Guy, Charles A.
Guy, William G.
Guy, William T(homas), Jr.

Haag, William G.
Haas, Joseph M.
Haas, Paul R.
Habberton, Benjamin G.
Habib, Philip C.
Hacker, Joseph B.
Hackes, Peter S.
Hackley, Howard H.
Hadlow, Earl B.
Hadsel, Fred L.
Haeussermann, Walter
Hagan, Charles B(anner)
Hagan, Thomas W.
Hagan, Wallace W.
Hageman, Elmer L.
Hager, Alice R.
Hager, George P.
Hager, John W.
Hager, Lawrence W.
Haggerty, Bernard J.
Haggerty, Patrick E.
Hahn, August C.
Hah, Frederic H.
Haile, Minasse
Haines, Ralph E., Jr.
Haislip, Wade H.
Halderman, John W(illiam)
Hale, Frank C.
Hale, Frank J.
Hale, Lucius M.
Hale, Nancy
Hale, Oron J(ames)
Hale, William H.
Hall, Dale, L.
Hall, George B.
Hall, John C.
Hall, John L.
Hall, John R.
Hall, Joseph A., III
Hall, Josiah C.
Hall, Miles L., Jr.
Hall, Nicholas D., Jr.
Hall, O. Glen
Hall, Robert D.
Hall, Robert E. L.
Hall, Theo E.
Hall, Warner L.
Hall, Wayne C.
Hall, Wilbur C.
Hall, William C.

Hall, Wilton E.
Halladay, Daniel W.
Hallden, Karl W.
Hallenbeck, George A.
Haller, Ellis M.
Halley, Harry L(ee) S(tuart)
Hallgarten, George W(olfgang) F(elix)
Halliburton, John H.
Hallman, Paul W.
Halsema, James J(ulius)
Hamblet, Julia E.
Hambrick, Marvin K.
Hamel, Charles D.
Hamel, Dana B.
Hamer, Fannie
Hamilton, Charles H.
Hamilton, Earl F.
Hamilton, George E., Jr.
Hamilton, Harold P.
Hamilton, Herbert A.
Hamilton, Hubert E. (Bert), Jr.
Hamilton, James A.
Hamilton, John A.
Hamilton, Robert S.
Hamilton, Robert W.
Hamilton, William H., Jr.
Hamiter, Joe B.
Hamm, Edward F., Jr.
Hamm, William D.
Hamm, William G.
Hammaker, Paul M.
Hammarsten, James F.
Hammer, Carl Jr.
Hammerschmidt, William W.
Hammond, John P.
Hammond, Lewis M.
Hammond, William R.
Hammonds, Oliver W.
Hamon, Jake L.
Hampton, Robert E.
Hand, Charles C.
Hand, John A.
Hand, William E.
Handley, William J.
Hanes, Gordon
Hanes, Pleasant H., Jr.
Haney, Paul P.
Hanft, Frank W(illiam)
Hanger, Franklin M(cCue)
Hanks, Bryan C.
Hanna, Alfred J.
Hanna, Gordon
Hanna, Jane F.
Hannah, Harvey H.
Hannon, Clarence W.
Hannon, William M.
Hannum, Erwin C.
Hansen, Grant L.
Hansen, Hobart G.
Hansen, Ira B.
Hansen, Richard M.
Hansen, Walter
Hanson, Alvin W.
Hanson, Clarence B., Jr.
Hanson, Earl P.
Hanson, Harold P.
Hapala, Milan E.
Haraldson, Wesley C.
Harbaugh, William H.
Harber, W(inford) Elmer
Harbin, John P.
Harbrecht, Paul P.
Harcum, Eugene R.
Hardaway, Elliott
Hardberger, Phillip D.
Hardeman, Ben
Hardeman, William D.
Harden, Komuria A.
Harder, Martha B.
Hardin, Dale W.
Hardin, George C., Jr.
Hardin, Lenard E.
Harding, Bertrand M.
Harding, Harold F.
Harding, Vincent
Hardman, Lamartine G., Jr.
Hardre, Jacques
Hardwick, John H.
Hardy, Glenn W.
Hardy, John S.
Hare, Channing
Hare, Francis H.
Hare, Raymond A.
Hare, William V.
Hargis, William J., Jr.
Hargrave, William L.
Hargrove, James W.
Hargrove, M(erwin) M(atthew)
Hargrove, William R.
Harithas, James
Harker, Hayes E.
Harkins, William G.
Harkness, Richard L.

Harkrader, Carleton A.
Harkrader, Charles J.
Harlan, John F., Jr.
Harland, James P.
Harley, Charles R.
Harfinger, Frederick J., II
Harlin, Maxey B(arlow)
Harlee, Ella F.
Harlow, Bryce N.
Harman, Charles L.
Harmon, Lindsey R.
Harmon, Nolan B.
Harmon, Reginald C.
Harp, Reno S., Jr.
Harper, Charles W.
Harper, Howard V.
Harper, Laura J.
Harper, Robert A.
Harper, Verne L.
Harrar, Ellwood S.
Harrar, Helen J.
Harrell, George F.
Harrell, Linwood P.
Harrell, Morris
Harrelson, Walter J.
Harrer, Gustave A.
Harrill, Ernest E.
Harriman, Edward E.
Harriman, W(illiam) Averell
Harrington, Donald D.
Harrington, Harold E.
Harrington, John C.
Harris, Arthur L.
Harris, Edward A.
Harris, Grady D., Jr.
Harris, Henry W.
Harris, Huntington
Harris, Jerome S.
Harris, Jesse G., Jr.
Harris, John H.
Harris, Julian H.
Harris, Louis C.
Harris, Loyd E.
Harris, Martin
Harris, Milton
Harris, Nell
Harris, Patricia R.
Harris, Robert A.
Harris, Robert J(ennings)
Harris, Rufus C.
Harris, S. Herschel
Harris, Shearon
Harris, Thomas E.
Harris, William A.
Harrison, Albertis S., Jr.
Harrison, Baya M., Jr.
Harrison, Benjamin F., Jr
Harrison, Bertram C.
Harrison, Burr P.
Harrison, C. Bennett
Harrison, Charles T.
Harrison, DeSales
Harrison, Francis M.
Harrison, Ike H(enry)
Harrison, James L.
Harrison, John A.
Harrison, Kenneth S.
Harrison, M(artin) Leigh
Harrison, Milton M.
Harrison, Preston E.
Harrison, Richard A.
Harrison, Richard H.
Harrison, T. Felton, Sr.
Harrison, T(homas) Wade
Harrison, W. Earl
Harrison, W(allace) Benton
Harrison, William H., Jr.
Harrison, William W.
Harriss, J(ulius) Welch
Harriss, Lynn M. F.
Harrold, Orville G., Jr.
Harron, Marion J.
Harsh, David N.
Harshbarger, Boyd
Hart, Charles E.
Harte, Houston
Harte, Houston H.
Hartford, Ellis F.
Hartgraves, Ruth
Hartke, Gilbert V(incent)
Hartke, Vance
Hartley, Lodwick (Charles)
Hartley, Robert W.
Hartman, Louis F.
Hartmann, Paul E.
Hartmann, Robert T.
Hartsfield, William B.
Hartshorn, Herbert H.
Hartshorn, Merrill F.
Hartshorne, Charles
Hartson, Nelson T.
Hartt, Frederick
Hartwell, Stephen
Hartwig, Lawrence E(dward)
Hartzog, George B., Jr.

Harvey, Holman
Harvey, James D.
Harvey, John (Lacey)
Harvey, Mose L.
Harvey, Paul H.
Harvey, Thomas W.
Harvin, Lucius H., Jr.
Harwell, Coleman
Harwell, Kenneth
Harwood, Douglas A.
Harwood, James E.
Haskew, Laurence D.
Haslam, James Y.
Haslanger, Robert U.
Hassler, Francis J.
Hastings, Lawrence V.
Hastings, Wilmot R.
Haswell, Harold A., Jr.
Hatch, Alden
Hatch, Lewis Frederic(k)
Hatch, Winslow R(oper)
Hatcher, Paul G.
Hatchett, Stephen P(inckney)
Hatzfeld, Helmut A.
Haugerud, Howard E.
Hauseman, David N.
Hauser, Charles R(oy)
Hausman, Louis
Havens, Ralph M.
Haverty, Rawson
Hawes, George A.
Hawkins, Francis G.
Hawkins, Osle P., Jr.
Hawkins, Rebecca B.
Hawley, Amos H.
Hawley, Langston T.
Hawn, Charles F.
Hawthorne, Edward W.
Hawthorne, Frank H.
Hay, Isaac K.
Hay, Stephen J.
Hayden, Carlos K.
Hayden, Donald E.
Hayden, Robert E.
Hayes, Charles W.
Hayes, Edwin S.
Hayes, James L.
Hayes, John S.
Hayes, Joseph C.
Hayes, Nathaniel P.
Hayes, Ray H.
Hayes, Robert S.
Haymes, Robert C.
Haynes, F. Boykin
Haynie, Roscoe (George)
Hays, Brooks
Hays, Jack N.
Haywood, Charles F.
Haywood, Egbert L.
Haywood, Theodore J.
Hayworth, Don
Hazel, Michael F.
Hazelet, Craig P.
Head, Jack D.
Head, James A.
Head, Robert J.
Head, Walton O.
Heald, Kenneth C.
Healey, Vincent P.
Healy, Paul F.
Healy, Robert E.
Healy, Sarah L.
Heard, Wilbur W.
Hearin, Robert M.
Hearn, Edell M.
Hearn, George H.
Hearn, Wilfred A.
Heartwell, Charles M., Jr.
Heath, Milton S(ydney)
Heaton, Leonard D(udley)
Heazel, Francis J.
Hebert, Paul M.
Hechtman, Robert A.
Heck, Frank H.
Heckscher, William S.
Hector, Louis J.
Hedlund, Earl C.
Hedlund, Floyd F.
Hedrick, Frederick C., Jr.
Hedrick, Walter R., Jr.
Heeschen, David S.
Heffelfinger, William S(tewart)
Heffernan, John B.
Heffernan, Paul M.
Heflin, Aubrey N.
Heflin, Howell T.
Hefner, Frank K.
Hegner, Casper F.
Heidingsfield, Myron S(amuel)
Heikenen, Harry W.
Heiling, Frank J.
Heinen, Erwin
Heinl, Robert D., Jr.
Heinz, Luther C.
Heiple, Loren R.
Heires, John H.

Heiskell, Augustus L.
Heiskell, John N.
Heisler, Kenneth G.
Heitz, Glenn E.
Hekman, Edward J.
Heldenfels, Frederick W., Jr.
Heller, Frank H.
Heller, Jack I.
Heller, Max
Hellwege, Herbert E.
Helmbold, F. Wilbur
Helmerich, Walter H., III
Helms, Fred B.
Hemphill, William E.
Hempstone, Smith, Jr.
Hemry, Jerome E.
Hemsing, Albert E.
Henderlite, Rachel
Hendershot, James C.
Henderson, Douglas
Henderson, Edwin H.
Henderson, George E.
Henderson, H(erbert) B(lair)
Henderson, Horace E.
Henderson, James J.
Henderson, Lawrence J(oseph)
Henderson, Loy W.
Henderson, Margaret M.
Henderson, Thomas H.
Henderson, Zach S.
Hendl, Walter
Hendon, Robert C.
Hendon, Robert R(andall)
Hendrick, James P.
Hendricks, Charles H.
Hendricks, Donald D.
Hendricks, George L.
Hendricks, Logan B.
Hendrix, Clyde, Jr.
Hendrix, Harold V. (Hal)
Heneman, Harlow J.
Henke, Robert H.
Henkle, Herman H(enry)
Henley, William S.
Henneke, Ben G.
Hennessy, James L.
Hennington, Burnette Y.
Henry, Carl F. H.
Henry, David H., II
Henry, Donald L.
Henry, H. Neely
Henry, Herman L., Jr.
Henry, John B., Jr.
Henry, John C.
Henry, Joseph L.
Henry, Rene P.
Henry, Waights G., Jr.
Henry, Walter L., Jr.
Henry, William O. E.
Hensarling, Paul R.
Henshaw, Francis H(arold)
Henshel, Walter M.
Henson, Chelsea L.
Henson, Elmer D.
Henze, Henry R.
Hepner, Charles K.
Hereford, Frank L.
Herman, George E.
Hernandez, Benigno C.
Herndon, Walter R., Jr.
Heroy, William B.
Herpich, Charles R.
Herrera, Felipe
Herrick, Allyn M.
Herrick, H. T.
Herring, Jack W.
Herrmann, Donald J.
Herrmann, George (Rudolph), III
Herron, Francis W.
Hershey, Jacob W.
Hershman, Jacob E.
Hertzog, Ambrose J(ohn)
Herz, Gerhard
Herzfeld, Karl F.
Herzig, Henry A.
Hess, George K., Jr.
Hess, Stephen
Hess, Walter C.
Hester, Clinton M.
Heston, Walter E.
Heuser, Gustave A.
Heuson, William G.
Hewatt, Willis G.
Hewins, Kenneth F.
Hewitt, Helen M.
Hewitt, Richard M.
Hewitt, William C.
Hewlett, Frank W.
Hexter, David B.
Heymann, Philip B.
Heyward, Alexander S., Jr.
Hiaasen, Carl A.
Hibbs, Richard G.

Hickey, Edward J., Jr.
Hicklin, Robert M.
Hicks, James J.
Hicks, John
Hicks, John D.
Hicks, William N.
Hicks, Wilson
Hiebert, Ray E.
Higbee, Floyd F.
Higginbotham, Fred C., Jr.
Higginbotham, Sanford W.
Highfill, Jester V.
Highsaw, Robert B.
Hightower, John M.
Hightower, William H., Jr.
Hilaly, Agha
Hilborne, Tom G.
Hild, Walther J.
Hildebrand, Ruth M.
Hill, Archibald A.
Hill, B. Harvey
Hill, Donald W.
Hill, Francis W.
Hill, George M.
Hill, James L.
Hill, John C.
Hill, John H.
Hill, Joseph M.
Hill, Lee H.
Hill, Leon W.
Hill, Lister
Hill, Luther L.
Hill, Robert L.
Hill, Samuel R., Jr.
Hill, Thomas B., Jr.
Hillard, James M.
Hillenbrand, Martin J.
Hiller, Charles F.
Hilliard, Isaac
Hilliard, Pauline
Hilliker, Grant G.
Hillman, John W.
Hills, George B.
Hilton, Mary N.
Hiltz, John P., Jr.
Himmelsbach, Clifton K.
Hinckley, Elmer D.
Hine, Gilbert C.
Hines, Charles A.
Hines, Emmett W.
Hines, Gerald D.
Hines, Howard H(arry)
Hines, William M., Jr.
Hinks, Kennett W.
Hinman, Carroll S.
Hinsdale, Kenneth P.
Hinton, William M.
Hintze, Guenther
Hipp, Francis M.
Hirsch, Eric D.
Hirsch, Maurice
Hirschberg, Joseph G.
Hirschowitz, Basil I.
Hirschtritt, Ralph
Hise, A.W.
Hiskey, George R.
Hitch, Robert M.
Hitchcock, Billy
Hittle, James D.
Hjellum, John
Hla Maung, U.
Hoadley, George B.
Hoag, Merritt E.
Hobbs, Charles S.
Hobbs, Edward H.
Hobbs, Grimsley T.
Hobbs, Herschel H.
Hobbs, Horton H., Jr.
Hobbs, Marcus E.
Hobbs, Nicholas
Hobgood, Charles G.
Hobgood, Price
Hobson, Robert C.
Hobson, Robert L.
Hochberger, Simon
Hoche, Philip A.
Hockensmith, Roy D.
Hockersmith, Forest D.
Hockett, Harry G.
Hocking, Richard B. O.
Hoctor, Thomas F.
Hodges, Gus M.
Hodges, James R.
Hodges, Thompson G.
Hodson, Kenneth J.
Hoelscher, Leonard W.
Hoff, Ebbe C.
Hoff, Hebbel E.
Hoff, Syd
Hoff, William J.
Hoffacker, Lewis
Hoffman, Edgar P.
Hoffman, Francis B.
Hoffman, Fred S.
Hoffman, Mark
Hoffman, Michael L.
Hoffmeister, John E.
Hoffstrom, Piercy J. (P.J. Hoff)
Hofheimer, Henry C.
Hofreiter, Charles G.
Hogan, Bartholomew W.
Hogan, Daniel W.
Hogan, H(enry) L(eon), III
Hogan, William R.
Hogard, Earl L.
Hogg, William R.
Hogue, Alexandre
Holaday, Beverly E.
Holaday, Duncan A.
Holbrook, Hollis H.
Holbrook, William D.
Holcomb, George R.
Holden, Donald A.
Holden, John B.
Holden, Raymond T.
Holderness, Haywood D.
Holderness, Howard
Holding, Lewis R.
Holguin, Alfonso H.
Holladay, Wendell G.
Holland, Charles D.
Holland, Jack
Holland, Jerome H.
Holland, Lynwood M.
Holland, Reginald V.
Holland, Robert C.
Holland, William C.
Hollander, Richard I.
Holleman, Frank L.
Holley, Edward G.
Holliday, Raymond M.
Hollis, C(harles) Carroll
Hollis, Samuel B.
Holloman, Delmar W.
Holloway, James L., III
Holloway, Leonard L.
Holloway, William V.
Holly, John P.
Holm, Jeanne M.
Holman, C(larence) Hugh
Holman, William R.
Holmberg, Paul A.
Holmes, Bert (Otis, Jr.)
Holmes, Edward H.
Holmes, Edward M(arion), Jr.
Holmes, Ephrain P.
Holmes, Eugene C.
Holmes, Oliver W.
Holmes, Urban T.
Holmes, Verner S.
Holmesly, Edward S.
Holt, Bryce R(oswell)
Holt, David E.
Holt, D(octor) Dillon
Holt, Ernest H.
Holt, Harry H., Jr.
Holt, Ralph M., Jr.
Holt, Robert L.
Holt, Thad
Holtman, (Darlington) Frank
Holtzclaw, Benjamin C.
Holtzman, Wayne H.
Holtzoff, Alexander
Homer, Porter W.
Honeywell, Charles F.
Hoofnagle, James E.
Hook, Emmett R.
Hooker, Charles W.
Hooker, John J.
Hooker, Richard J.
Hoole, (William) Stanley
Hooper, Edwin B.
Hooper, Gilman S.
Hoover, Calvin B.
Hoover, John P.
Hoover, Joseph S.
Hoover, Linn
Hoover, Sam(uel) R(andolph)
Hope, A(shley) Guy
Hope, Clarence C., Jr.
Hope, Henry R(adford)
Hopkins, Ellie
Hopkins, Everett H(arold)
Hopkins, Frank S.
Hopkins, Garland E.
Hopkins, Howard
Hopkins, John A., Jr.
Hopkins, John I.
Hopkins, Lindsey
Hopkins, Welly K.
Hopla, Cluff E.
Hopps, Howard C.
Horadam, Weyman W.
Horkey, William R.
Horn, Carl, Jr.
Horn, Edward C.
Horn, Friedrich J. M.
Horn, Stanley F.
Horn, Stefan F.
Hornaday, Fred E.
Hornbake, R(alph)
Hornbeak, Mack H.
Horne, John E.
Horne, Josh L.
Horne, Mark D.
Horne, Roman L.
Horner, William L(udwig)
Horrigan, Alfred F.
Horsey, Outerbridge
Horsky, Charles A(ntone)
Hortenstine, Raleigh
Horton, Claude W.
Horton, Kenneth D.
Horton, Ralph, Jr.
Horton, Wade H.
Horvitz, Wayne L.
Horwitz-Barak, Abraham
Hosner, John F.
Hotelling, Harold
Hotz, Robert B(ergmann)
Houchin, John M.
Houck, Calvin B.
Houck, George C.
Hough, Cass S.
Houghton, Woodson P.
Hounshell, Charles D(avid)
Houser, William D.
Housewright, Wiley L.
Housman, Kenneth A.
Houston, Benjamin F.
Houston, Joe B.
Houston, William V.
Hovde, Howard T.
Howard, Alvin H.
Howard, Bushrod B.
Howard, Daggett H.
Howard, Fontaine M.
Howard, Harry N.
Howard, Jack
Howard, John Z.
Howard, Joseph L.
Howard, L(awrence) V.
Howard, Lee M.
Howard, Rhea
Howard, Robert A.
Howard, Robert L.
Howard, Travis G.
Howarth, Thomas
Howell, Arthur
Howell, Benjamin R.
Howell, D(ariel) E(iza)
Howell, John O., Jr.
Howell, William M.
Howell, William T.
Hower, Frank B., Jr.
Hower, Paul A.
Howland, Harold E.
Howland, Richard H.
Howland, William F., Jr.
Howrey, Edward F.
Howsam, Robert B.
Howse, W. L., Jr.
Hoy, Harry E.
Hoy, W(illiam) I.
Hoyt, Robert L.
Hubbard, Charlotte M.
Hubbard, John B.
Hubbard, John R.
Hubbard, Robert M.
Hubbard, Rudolph T.
Hubbell, Lester E.
Hubbert, M(arion) K.
Hubert, Frank W. R.
Hubley, George W., Jr.
Huddleston, George, Jr.
Hudgins, D(aniel) E(dward)
Hudgins, Samuel E.
Hudon, L. Denis
Hudson, Arthur P.
Hudson, Benjamin F., Jr.
Hudson, Bradford B.
Hudson, Hinton G.
Hudson, Jesse T., Jr.
Hudson, N(oel) P.
Hudson, Robert D.
Hudson, William H.
Hudspeth, Emmett L.
Hueber, Francis M.
Huestis, Charles B.
Huff, Gerald B(oone)
Huff, Isaac C., Jr.
Huff, Zachary T.
Huffines, Robert L., Jr.
Huffman, William C.
Hufnagel, Charles A.
Hufty, Page
Huggins, Sara E.
Hughes, Carl W.
Hughes, Eric M(ilton)
Hughes, Frank C.
Hughes, Howard R.
Hughes, James D.
Hughes, James G.
Hughes, Joseph K.
Hughes, Leo
Hughes, Phillip S.
Hughes, William P.
Hughlett, Robert B.
Hugus, Z. Z., Jr.
Huie, William B.
Huie, William O.
Hull, David R.
Hull, James M.
Hull, Robert W.
Hulsey, William H.
Hultgren, Warren C.
Humann, Walter J.
Humbert, R(euben) L.
Hume, David M.
Humes, Bernard J.
Humkey, Walter
Hummel, Arthur W., Jr.
Humphrey, Hubert H., Jr.
Humphrey, Muriel F. B.
Humphreys, Edwin W.
Humphreys, Herbert
Humphreys, James W., Jr.
Humphreys, Ward C.
Hund, James M.
Hunnicutt, Clarence W.
Hunsucker, Robert D.
Hunt, Alma F.
Hunt, Charles B., Jr.
Hunt, Haroldson L.
Hunt, (Everette) H., Jr.
Hunt, Lamar
Hunt, Russell F.
Hunt, Thelma
Hunt, Walter S., Jr.
Hunter, Bynum M.
Hunter, Edwin F., Jr.
Hunter, Frank R., Jr.
Hunter, H(oward) L(ouis)
Hunter, John M.
Hunter, John P., Jr.
Hunter, Kermit H.
Hunter, Louis N.
Hunter, Marshall K.
Hunter, Phelan H.
Hunter, Thomas H(arrison)
Hunter, William A.
Hunter, W(illiam) C.
Huntington, Frances C. (Mrs. William Chapin Huntington)
Huntley, Harlan H.
Huntley, Robert E. R.
Hunton, Eppa, IV
Hurley, Leonard F.
Hurley, Ruby
Hurst, John W.
Hurst, Vernon J.
Hurt, John J., Jr.
Hurwitch, Robert A.
Husband, Arthur K.
Husband, Richard W.
Husted, Ladley
Husted, Walter
Huston, Luther A.
Hutchens, Raymond P.
Hutcheson, Joseph C., III
Hutcheson, Robert H.
Hutchings, Paul R.
Hutchins, Francis S.
Hutchins, Lee M.
Hutchinson, James G.
Hutchison, David W.
Hutchison, Joseph C.
Hutton, Robert F.
Hyatt, James P.
Hyde, G(eorge) O.
Hyde, Henry v.
Hyde, John B.
Hyde, Joseph R., Jr.
Hyde, Roy E.
Hyer, Julien C.
Hyman, Harold M.
Hymon, Mary W. (Mrs. George Jerome Hymon)

Ignatius, Paul R.
Ignico, Robert V.
Ikenberry, Oliver S.
Iler, Frank R.
Illig, Carl
Illig, James M.
Imhoff, John L.
Imhoff, Lawrence E.
Ingalls, Daniel H. H.
Inge, Frederick D.
Ingersol, John E.
Ingerson, (Fred) E.
Ingols, Robert S(malley)
Ingram, Charles C., Jr.
Ingram, Dean
Ingram, Erskine B.
Ingram, Frederic B.
Ingram, George M., III
Ink, Dwight A., Jr.
Ioanes, Raymond A.
Ireland, William C.
Irish, Marian D(oris)
Irons, Edward P.
Irvin, J(oseph) L.
Irvin, Rea
Irvin, William D.
Irvine, Donald G.
Irving, Frederick
Irving, George W., Jr.
Irwin, Wayne
Isaac, Charles M.
Isaacs, Normal E(llis)
Isbell, Harris
Isenbergh, Max
Israel, Larry H.
Ives, H(iram) D.
Ives, Stephen B., Jr.
Ivey, George M., Jr.
Ivey, James B.
Izzard, Wesley S.

Jack, Harold H.
Jackson, Charles P.
Jackson, Donald L.
Jackson, George W.
Jackson, Hezekiah
Jackson, J. Harry
Jackson, Jay M.
Jackson, Joe C.
Jackson, John E.
Jackson, John N.
Jackson, Julian E.
Jackson, Miles M., Jr.
Jackson, Percival W.
Jackson, Robert C.
Jackson, Thomas S.
Jackson, Thomas W(oodrow)
Jackson, Will W.
Jackson, William C. (Decker), Jr.
Jackson, William N.
Jacobansky, Ann M
Jacobs, James A.
Jacobs, Jay W.
Jacobs, J(ohn) R.
Jacobs, Leon
Jacobs, Sydney
Jacobs, Walter B.
Jacobsen, Hugh N.
Jacobson, A(lfred) T.
Jacobson, Dorothy H.
Jacoby, Oswald
Jacoby, Robert B.
Jacome, Rodrigo M.
Jaeger, Leonard H.
Jaenke, Edwin A.
Jaffe, Leonard
Jagels, Charles H.
Jahn, Walter J.
Jahncke, Herbert G.
Jalonick, George W.
James, Edward W.
James, Floyd B.
James, Harold L.
James, Herman B.
James, John V.
James, L. Eldon
James, Louis G.
James, Ralph K.
James, Roy E.
James, William T.
Jameson, Minor S., Jr.
Jamison, Frank S.
Janeway, Ray C.
Janney, Frederick E.
Janow, Seymour J.
Jansson, Karl O.
Jantzen, Alice C.
Jarman, Burnice H.
Jarrard, Jerald O.
Jarrell, John W(illiams)
Jarrett, Thomas D.
Jaslow, Robert I.
Jason, Robert S.
Jaszi, George
Jauchem, Clarence R.
Jayaratne, Merenna F. d.
Jaynes, Lawrence C.
Jayson, Lester S.
Jeffe, Ephraim F.
Jeffe, Huldah C.
Jeffers, Lewis F.
Jeffers, William A.
Jefferson, Thomas B.
Jeffords, Lawrence (Suggs)
Jelks, Joseph W., Jr.
Jenkins, Alfred l.
Jenkins, Dale W.
Jenkins, Daniel E., Jr.
Jenkins, Howard, Jr.
Jenkins, Iredell
Jenkins, John S., Jr.
Jenkins, Joseph A.
Jenkins, Leo W.
Jenkins, Ray H(oward)
Jenkins, Raymond T.
Jenkins, Robert O.
Jenkins, Romilly J. H.
Jenkins, Thomas M.
Jenkins, William M., Jr.
Jenks, George F.
Jenks, Thomas E.
Jenner, William E.
Jennette, Marshall C.
Jennings, Alston
Jennings, Eleanor E. (Mrs. Alvin R. Jennings)
Jennings, Lewellyn A.
Jennings, Paul
Jennings, W. Croft
Jensen, Howard F.
Jernegan, John D(urnford)
Jervey, Harold E., Jr.
Jesse, William H(erman)
Jessup, Claude A.
Jessup, Joe L.
Jett, Thomas S.
Jimenez, Jorge J.
Johanos, Donald
Johns, Jasper
Johns, Lucy I.
Johns, Roe L.
Johnson, Alfred E.
Johnson, Amos N.
Johnson, Andrew
Johnson, Arnold W.
Johnson, Ben(jamin) F(ranklin), Jr.
Johnson, Briard P.
Johnson, Bruce H.
Johnson, Cecil C.
Johnson, Cecil S.
Johnson, Charles B., Jr.
Johnson, Charles C., Jr.
Johnson, Charles E., III
Johnson, David S(imonds)
Johnson, E. Fred
Johnson, Edward E.
Johnson, Edward L.
Johnson, Edwin H.
Johnson, Edwin W.
Johnson, Elliott A(mos)
Johnson, Ellwood W.
Johnson, Elmer D.
Johnson, Eric G.
Johnson, Ernest W.
Johnson, Esther F.
Johnson, Eugene I.
Johnson, Francis S.
Johnson, Franklyn A.
Johnson, Gifford K.
Johnson, Glen R.
Johnson, Glendon E.
Johnson, Harvey L.
Johnson, Henry S., Jr.
Johnson, Herbert H.
Johnson, Howard B.
Johnson, Hubert D.
Johnson, Hunter
Johnson, Irving H. (Mrs. Curtis B. Johnson)
Johnson, Ivan E.
Johnson, James D. (Jim)
Johnson, James E.
Johnson, Jess W.
Johnson, Jesse G.
Johnson, John B., Jr.
Johnson, Kellum
Johnson, Kenneth O.
Johnson, Kimbell
Johnson, Lee H(arnie)
Johnson, Lester
Johnson, Lewis K.
Johnson, Loftin
Johnson, Ludwell H., III
Johnson, Neis C.
Johnson, Raymon D.
Johnson, Raymond E.
Johnson, Rex D.
Johnson, Richard A(braham)
Johnson, Richard C.
Johnson, Richard N.
Johnson, Richard T.
Johnson, Ruth C.
Johnson, Sam H.
Johnson, Ruth C. (Mrs. J. Lee Johnson III)
Johnson, Sam H.
Johnson, Searcy L.
Johnson, Sherman E(llsworth)
Johnson, Stanfield B.
Johnson, Terry W., Jr.
Johnson, Thomas M.
Johnson, Thor
Johnson, U. Alexis
Johnson, Vernon A.
Johnson, Victor S., Jr.
Johnson, Wallace E.
Johnson, Walter H., Jr.
Johnson, Wilfrid E.
Johnson, William L.
Johnson, William L.
Johnson, William W.
Johnson, Zachary T.
Johnston, Clement D.
Johnston, Daniel W.
Johnston, Everett D.
Johnston, Frontis W.
Johnston, George B.
Johnston, George W.
Johnston, Henry R.
Johnston, Joseph F.

Johnston, Means, Jr.
Johnston, Robert A.
Johnston, S(amuel) P.
Johnston, Thomas M.
Johnston, W(illiam) D(rumm), Jr.
Johnstone, Francis E., Jr.
Johnstone, Harry I.
Johnstone, James R.
Johnstone, Robert L.
Johnstone, William C.
Jonassen, Hans B.
Joncich, Micheal J.
Jones, Alfred W.
Jones, Bob, (Jr.)
Jones, Bolling, Jr.
Jones, Booker T.
Jones, Carl A.
Jones, Charles S.
Jones, Claiborne S.
Jones, Dace W.
Jones, Douglas E.
Jones, Edmund L.
Jones, E(dmund) R., Jr.
Jones, Edward M.
Jones, Edward N.
Jones, Edwin L.
Jones, Edwin L., Jr.
Jones, Elmer A.
Jones, Ernest C.
Jones, Everett H.
Jones, F. P., Jr.
Jones, Frank L.
Jones, Galen
Jones, George L., Jr.
Jones, Girault M.
Jones, Gordon
Jones, Halbert M.
Jones, Harry L.
Jones, Harry R.
Jones, Herbert L.
Jones, James H.
Jones, James R.
Jones, Jameson M.
Jones, Joe C.
Jones, Joseph M., Jr.
Jones, Joseph W.
Jones, L. Bruce
Jones, Lawrence B.
Jones, Malcolm G.
Jones, Marshall R.
Jones, Marvin
Jones, Morgan, Jr.
Jones, Nelson
Jones, Oliver H.
Jones, Otis H.
Jones, Ralph W. E.
Jones, Ralph W.
Jones, Raymond A., Jr.
Jones, Robert C.
Jones, Robert E.
Jones, Robert T., Jr. ("Bobby" Jones)
Jones, Roger W.
Jones, Ronald W.
Jones, Rudolph
Jones, Samuel S.
Jones, Taylor
Jones, Thomas H.
Jones, Virginia L. (Mrs. E. A. Jones)
Jones, Walk C., Jr.
Jones, William B.
Jones, William K.
Jones, William N.
Jones, William P.
Jones, Winifred S.
Jones, Wyman H.
Jordan, Bryce
Jordan, Castle W.
Jordan, Charles E.
Jordan, Donald L(ewis)
Jordan, George R.
Jordan, Howard S.
Jordan, Hugh D.
Jordan, William B., Jr.
Jordan, William D.
Jordan, William S., Jr.
Jorden, William J.
Jorgensen, Albert N.
Joslin, Ennis S.
Joslin, G(eorge) S.
Jova, Joseph J.
Joyce, J(ames) W.
Joyner, William T.
Judd, Deane B.
Judd, Frank
Judd, Thomas M.
Judd, Walter H.
Judkins, Wesley P.
Judy, Hubert S.
Julian, Leo S.
Juliana, James N.
Juniper, Walter H.
Junkin, Marion M.
Just, Carolyn R.
Justice, Jack

Kabanda, Celestin
Kafka, Alexandre
Kafka, Maximillian M.
Kafoed, E. J.
Kahler, Elizabeth S. (Mrs. Ervin Newton Chapman)
Kahn, Benjamin M.
Kahn, Edwin L.
Kahn, Reuben L.
Kahn, Robert L.
Kain, Richard M.
Kain, Ronald S.
Kaiser, Fred
Kalmus, Henry P.
Kamarck, Andrew M.
Kamerick, John J.
Kaminstein, Abraham L.
Kamm, Robert W.
Kampelman, Max M.
Kamphoefner, Henry L.
Kamrath, Karl
Kanaly, Earl D.
Kane, Charles J.
Kane, Harnett T.
Kane, Wilbur P.
Kane, Willard W.
Kantor, Harry S.
Kantor, MacKinlay
Kaplan, Benjamin
Kaplan, Sheldon Z.
Kaplowitz, Paul
Karasik, Monroe
Karcher, John C.
Kardiner, Abram
Karl, John J.
Karnes, Houston T(hurman)
Karns, Russell D.
Kasha, Michael
Kashiwa, Shiro
Katz, Abraham
Katz, Eugene R.
Katz, Julius L.
Katzenbach, Edward L., Jr.
Kaufman, Clemens M.
Kaufman, Harold F(rederick)
Kaufman, Herbert
Kaufmann, Cecil D.
Kaufmann, Ralph J.
Kay, Brian R.
Kayser, Elmer L.
Kear, Frank G.
Kearney, Richard D.
Kearns, Amos R.
Keating, L(ouis) C.
Keats, Charles B.
Keats, Theordore E.
Keck, Howard B.
Kee, Sarah J.
Keefe, William C.
Keefer, Richard E.
Keeling, Gerald F.
Keenan, Edward L., Jr.
Keesing, Frans A. G.
Keeton, (Werdner) P.
Keim, Christopher P.
Keith, Nathaniel S.
Keith, Noel L.
Keith, Warren G.
Keith-Lucas, Alan
Kekich, Emil A.
Kelch, David E.
Keleher, Gregory C.
Kellam, William P.
Kelleher, Harry B.
Keller, Charles, Jr.
Keller, H. A.
Keller, Henry, Jr.
Keller, Robert F.
Keller, William L.
Kellermann, Henry J(oseph)
Kelley, Daniel F., Jr.
Kelley, Roger T.
Kelliher, Thomas G.
Kellogg, Charles E.
Kellogg, Frederic H.
Kellogg, Grace (Mrs. Claredon Waite Smith)
Kellogg, Marion K.
Kelly, Balmer H.
Kelly, Cullen J.
Kelly, Edward J.
Kelly, Harry C.
Kelly, James F.
Kelly, James J.
Kelly, James W.
Kelly, John E.
Kelly, John S.
Kelly, Joseph L., Jr.
Kelly, Lawrence V.
Kelly, Luther W., Jr.
Kelly, Stephen J.
Kelly, Thomas P., Jr.
Kelly, William C.
Kelsey, Frances O. (Mrs. Fremont Ellis Kelsey)
Kelsey, John E.
Kelso, John H.
Kemp, Lebbeus C., Jr.
Kemp, Verbon E.
Kemper, Wallace C.
Kempfer, Homer H.
Kempner, Harris L.
Kempner, Walter
Kempton, Rudolf T.
Kendall, Bruce E.
Kendig, Edwin L., Jr.
Kendrew, A(lbert) E.
Kendrick, Baynard H.
Kendrick, Caldwell C.
Kendrick, Douglas B., Jr.
Kenealy, William J.
Kennan, Kent W.
Kennard, William J.
Kenneally, Joseph T.
Kennedy, Clephane A.
Kennedy, Donald S.
Kennedy, John W.
Kennedy, Joseph P.
Kennedy, Matthew W.
Kennedy, Sabe M.
Kennedy, Walter (Wallace)
Kenney, Edward C.
Kenney, John A., Jr.
Kenney, John J.
Kenney, W. John
Kennon, Albert W., Jr.
Kenny, Nicholas N. (Nick Kenny)
Kent, Carleton V., Jr.
Kent, Ernest D.
Kent, Frederick H.
Kent, George C., Jr.
Kent, Glenn A.
Kenworthy, Carroll H.
Keown, William H.
Keppel, John
Kercheville, F(rancis) M(onroe)
Kern, John W.
Kernodle, Rigdon W.
Kerns, Rolland E.
Kerr, Breene M.
Kerr, Hawley C.
Kerr, William L.
Kerwin, Walter T., Jr.
Kesselman, Louis C.
Kessler, Clay J.
Kessler, Karl G.
Ketcham, Bruce V.
Ketchum, Harry W.
Kettle, John J(oseph)
Kettler, Stanton P.
Kevan, Robert A.
Keyserling, Leon H.
Keyserling, Mary D.
Khadduri, Majid
Kibler, David B., III
Kidd, Aubrey V.
Kidd, Charles V.
Kidston, Donald E.
Kiefer, Charles F.
Kieffer, William B.
Kier, Porter M.
Kiernan, Loyd J.
Kiernan, Owen B.
Kiger, Joseph C.
Kilday, Ralph
Kiley, Leo A.
Kilgore, Joe M(adison)
Kilgore, John E., Jr.
Kilgore, William J.
Killinger, George G.
Killorin, Edward W.
Kilpatrick, Arnold R.
Kilpatrick, James J., Jr.
Kilpatrick, Martin E.
Kilpatrick, Samuel J., Jr.
Kim, Dong J.
Kim, Yongjeung
Kimball, Arthur A.
Kimball, Dan A.
Kimball, Solon T(oothaker)
Kimball, Thomas L.
Kimball, Vera F.
Kimble, Kenneth L.
Kimbrough, Verman
Kinard, James C.
Kincaid, Garvice D.
Kincaid, Harry G.
Kincaid, James L.
Kincaid, John F.
Kincheloe, James B.
Kindelsperger, Walter L.
Kindsvater, Carl E.
King, A(rnold) K(imsey)
King, Benjamin C.
King, Ed R.
King, Elmer R.
King, George H.
King, George H., Jr.
King, Huger S.
King, John P., Jr.
King, John Q. T.
King, Joseph L., Jr.
King, Marian
King, Morton B(randon)
King, Preston C., Jr.
King, Richard A.
King, Robert D.
King, Robert L.
King, Spencer B., Jr.
King, Thomas C.
King, Thomas S., Jr.
King, William H.
King, Willis J.
King, Winston L.
Kingery, Dwane
Kingsbury, Gilbert W., Sr.
Kingsley, Joseph T., Jr.
Kingsley, Robert I.
Kiniery, Gladys
Kinkaid, Thomas C.
Kinnard, Harry W. O.
Kinne, Frances B.
Kinney, Andrew J(ohn)
Kinney, Sterling E.
Kinney, Thomas D.
Kintner, Earl W(ilson)
Kipp, Dean C.
Kirby, George F.
Kirby, John P.
Kirby, Thomas A.
Kirby, Thomas M.
Kircher, William L.
Kirchhoff, Donald J.
Kirk, John K.
Kirkby, Arthur M(artin)
Kirkendoll, Chester A., Jr.
Kirkland, James B.
Kirkland, Joseph L.
Kirklin, John W.
Kirkman, Oscar A.
Kirkman, Ralph E.
Kirkpatrick, Charles V.
Kirkpatrick, Evron M(aurice)
Kirkpatrick, John E.
Kirkpatrick, Lyman B., Jr.
Kirkpatrick, Richard B.
Kirksey, Howard G.
Kirrmann, Ernest N.
Kirsner, Robert
Kirwan, Albert D.
Kissick, Harold G.
Kistler, Alan A.
Kistler, Joy W.
Kitchel, George B.
Kitchen, Delmas K.
Kitchin, Alvin P.
Kittleson, Henry M.
Kittrell, Flemmie P.
Kitzmiller, Francis R.
Kjelson, Lee
Klagsbrunn, Hans A(lexander)
Klatte, Eugene C.
Klausmeyer, David M.
Klay, Andor C.
Kleberg, Robert J., Jr.
Kleckner, Albert L.
Kleiler, Frank M.
Klein, William H.
Kleindienst, Richard G.
Kline, Claire B., Jr.
Kline, Gordon M.
Kline, Oral L.
Kling, William
Klingberg, Frank W.
Klocko, Richard P.
Kloeffler, Royce G.
Klontz, Charles E.
Klopp, Calvin T.
Klosinski, Stanley J.
Klosson, Boris H.
Klotz, Herbert W.
Klotz, John W.
Kluge, Ralph W.
Kluttz, Jerry
Knapp, George L., Jr.
Knapp, J(oseph) B.
Knauss, Herman
Knickerbocker, Kenneth L(eslie)
Knight, Dewey
Knight, Eugene H.
Knight, Frances G(ladys)
Knight, Homer L.
Knight, James A.
Knight, James L.
Knight, John L.
Knight, Nathaniel B., Jr.
Knight, Peter O., Jr.
Knight, Vernon
Knight, Walker L.
Knighton, Holmes T(utt)
Knipe, James L.
Knipling, Edward F(red)
Knoblauch, Harold C.
Knochel, John C.
Knoll, Jerry
Knopf, William C., Jr.
Knott, Aubrey K.
Knowles, H(arold) L(oraine)
Knowles, Jack O.
Knowlton, William A.
Knox, Bernard M. W.
Knox, Carl W.
Knox, John
Knox, John M.
Knox, Katharine M.
Knudson, Alvin B. C.
Kobayashi, Riki
Koch, Adolph M.
Koch, Richard
Kocurek, Louis J(oe)
Koehl, George M.
Koehler, John T(heodore)
Koenig, Myron L(aw)
Koeppe, Roger E.
Kohl, John C.
Kohler, Foy D.
Kohler, Karl O., Jr.
Kohlmeyer, Herman S.
Konnecci, Eugene B.
Koop, Theodore F.
Koppanyi, Theodore
Koren, Henry J.
Koren, Henry L. T.
Korn, David
Kornegay, Horace R.
Kortendick, James J.
Korth, Fred
Kosolapoff, Gennady M.
Kossler, Herman J.
Kothe, Charles A.
Kotschnig, Walter M.
Kotz, Nathan K. (Nick)
Kowalski, Frank
Kozy, John, Jr.
Kraft, Christopher C., Jr.
Kramer, Jackson C.
Kramer, Paul J.
Kramer, Robert
Kramer, Russell A.
Kramer, Simon P.
Krampf, Charles E.
Kraner, Thomas E.
Kratt, Emil J.
Kratzer, Myron B.
Krause, Clarence J.
Kreeger, David L.
Kreeger, Joseph P.
Kreps, Clifton H., Jr.
Kresge, Howard S.
Krieg, William L.
Krieger, Robert L.
Krizay, John
Krombein, Karl v.
Kronenberg, Henry H.
Kronheim, Milton S.
Kronzer, Walter J.
Krooth, David L.
Kroyt, Boris
Krueger, Erich G.
Krug, Robert C(harles)
Krumholz, Louis A.
Kruse, H(eeren) Samuel (Eilts)
Krusen, Edward M.
Kubat, Jerald R.
Kubisch, Jack B.
Kucheman, Henry B., Jr.
Kuersteiner, Karl O.
Kuh, Frederick R.
Kuhn, Carl S(ellner)
Kuhn, Charles
Kuhn, Edward W.
Kuhn, Ferdinand
Kulczycki, Lucas L.
Kullerud, Gunnar
Kulski, Wladyslaw W.
Kulynych, Petro
Kunen, James L.
Kuntz, Eugene O.
Kunzig, Robert L.
Kurtz, Stephen G.
Kurzman, Dan
Kurzweg, Hermann H.
Kushner, Daniel S.
Kushner, Lawrence M.
Kuss, Henry J., Jr.
Kuykendall, Jerome K(enneth)
Kuypers, John M.
Kyger, Murray
Kyle, George T.
Kyle, Laurence H.
Kyser, Robert C.

Labadie-Eurite, Juan
Labault, Fernando
Labban, George, Jr.
Laborde, Alden J.
Labouisse, John P(riestley)
Lacey, John A.
Lachs, John
Lacy, Lewis
Lacy, William S. B.
Ladd, Harry S.
Ladd, Mason
Lado, Robert
LaGasse, Alfred B., Jr.
Lagemann, Robert T.
LaGrone, Cyrus W., Jr.
LA Hay, Wauhillau
Lahr, Raymond M.
Laise, Frederic S.
Lallinger, E. Michael
Lambert, Charles F.
Lambert, George H.
Lambert, Jay W.
Lambert, Sam M.
Lambert, Valdemar G.
Lamm, LeRoy B.
Lampert, James B.
Lamsa, George M.
Lancaster, Bruce M.
Lancaster, Robert S.
Lance, Thomas J.
Landers, Frank M.
Landes, J. D.
Landis, E. K.
Landis, Lewis R.
Landiss, Morris P.
Landon, Herman R(obert)
Landon, Kenneth P.
Landstrom, Karl S.
Lane, Alvin H.
Lane, Connie B., Jr.
Lane, Edward H.
Lane, Edward W., Jr.
Lane, George S.
Lane, Hugh C.
Lane, James T.
Lane, John J.
Lane, Samuel O.
Lane, William H.
Laney, James J.
Lang, Cecil Y.
Lang, John A., Jr.
Lang, Richard E.
Lang, Sylvan
Lang, William E.
Lange, Frederick M.
Lange, John D.
Langford, James B.
Langlinais, Joseph W.
Langmuir, Alexander D(uncan)
Langston, Paul T.
Langston, Roy A.
Lanier, Joseph L(amar)
Lanier, Sartain
Lankford, Francis G., Jr.
Lanning, John T.
Lansdale, Edward G.
Lansdell, Sarah W.
Lantaff, William C. (Bill)
Lapham, Maxwell E.
Lapham, Samuel
Lapin, Raymond H.
Lapp, Ralph E(ugene)
Laramore, Don N.
LaRocque, Gene R.
Larrabee, Carroll B.
Larrabee, Harold A.
Larre, Rene J.
Larrick, Thomas
Larsen, Finn J.
Larsen, Stanley R.
Larsh, John E., Jr.
Larson, Clarence E(dward)
Larson, G(odfrey) Edward
Larson, Harold V.
Larson, Jens F.
Larson, Jess
Larson, Paul M.
Larson, Paul S(tanley)
Larson, Roberts B.
Lasater, Hubert L.
Lasley, James B.
Lasser, David
Lasseter, Hewen A(ugustus)
Lassiter, Robert, Jr.
Lasswell, Mary C. G. L.
Lastra-Gonzalez, Carlos J.
Latham, Jean L.
Latham, William P.
Lathrop, Barnes F(letcher)
Latimer, Murray W.
Latta, Gordon E.
Lattu, Onnie P.
Latty, Elvin R.
Lau, Edgar B.
Laufer, Leopold
Laughlin, Charles V.
Lauinger, P(hillp) C(harles)
Laurence, Robert A.
Laurie, James W.
Lautenschlaeger, Lester J.
LaVarre, William
Laverge, Jan

Law, Thomas C., Jr.
Lawrason, F. Douglas
Lawrence, Charles B., Jr.
Lawrence, David
Lawrence, David
Lawrence, John W.
Lawrence, Kenneth M(orrison)
Lawrence, Philip S.
Lawson, George M.
Lawton, Alfred H(enry)
Lawton, George A.
Lawton, Robert O.
Lay, Herman W.
Laylin, John G(allup)
Laymon, Charles M.
Layne, James N.
Lazonby, Joseph L.
Lazzari, Pietro
Leacacos, John P.
Leach, Edward C.
League, Archie W.
Leak, Robert E.
Leake, Gerald
Lear, Floyd S.
Lear, William E.
Learey, Fred D.
Leary, John C.
Leary, Lewis
Leavell, David C(ox)
Leavitt, Ithaman M.
Leavitt, Lewis A.
Leavy, Charles W.
LeBaron, Robert
Lebensohn, Zigmond M.
Lechner, Sister Joan M.
Lecht, Leonard A.
Lee, Addison E.
Lee, Alonzo H.
Lee, Armistead M.
Lee, David B.
Lee, Douglas H. K.
Lee, Frederick B.
Lee, Gus C.
Lee, Lucien T., Jr.
Lee, Mary A.
Lee, Maurice W(entworth)
Lee, Merrill C.
Lee, Milton O.
Lee, Mollie H.
Lee, Ronald B.
Lee, Wallace L.
Lee, William F., III
Lee, William L.
Leech, Robert M.
Leeds, William L.
Leedy, Daniel L.
Leek, Frederick E.
Leen, Dennis M.
Leer, John
Leestma, Robert
Leff, Arthur
Leffingwell, William M.
Leflar, Robert A.
Lefler, Hugh T.
Legates, James E.
Legier, John
Legler, Henry M.
Legner, Wolfram K.
Lehman, Arnold J.
Lehman, John W.
Lehmann, Winfred P.
Lehne, Henry
Lehrer, Robert N(athaniel)
Leichliter, Gould A.
Leiferman, Irwin H.
Leigh, Walter H.
Leinenweber, George L.
Leitner, Howard M.
LeJeune, Francis E.
LeJeune, Michael L.
LeMaistre, Charles A.
Lemann, Thomas B.
Le Matty, Rodger S.
Le May, Geraldine
Lemberger, Ernst
Lemle, Louis G.
Lemm, Walter H.
Lemnitzer, Lyman L.
Lemon, James H.
Lemos, William E.
Lenhart, Robert F.
Lennartson, Nils A.
Lennartson, Roy W.
Lenski, Lois (Mrs. Arthur S. Covey)
Lent, George E.
Leonard, Edward J.
Leonard, Irving A(lbert)
Leonard, Robert H.
Leonard, Rodney E.
Leonard, Will E., Jr.
Leonard, William N.
Leonhart, William
Leslie, Gerald R.
Leslie, John W.
Leslie, John W.
Lesser, Arthur J.
Lesser, Lawrence S(tanley)
Lester, Barnett B.
Lester, Charles T.
Lester, Edward
Lester, Richard G.
Lester, Robert M.
LeSueur, Lawrence E.
Lethbridge, Francis D.
LeTourneau, Roy S.
Leva, Marx
Leven, Stephen A.
Levengood, Claude A.
Levenson, Seymour
Leverenz, Oscar T.
Levey, Gerrit
Levin, Carl
Levin, Harold A.
Levin, Isadore
Levine, Daniel B.
Levine, David L.
Levine, Jay
Levine, Max
Levison, Robert H.
Levy, Babette
Levy, Gilbert J.
Levy, Harold R.
Lewis, Archibald R.
Lewis, Austin W.
Lewis, David M.
Lewis, Edward S.
Lewis, Edward W.
Lewis, Emery F.
Lewis, Floyd W.
Lewis, Frederick D.
Lewis, George R.
Lewis, Hal G(raham)
Lewis, Harold G.
Lewis, Harold R.
Lewis, Harold W.
Lewis, John M.
Lewis, Joseph
Lewis, Joseph H(illard)
Lewis, Mark B.
Lewis, Robert C.
Lewis, Thomas R.
Leyburn, James G.
Lichten, Robert L.
Liddel, Urner
Liddle, Grant W(inder)
Liebelt, Robert A.
Liebenow, Robert C.
Liebman, David I.
Liedtke, William C., Jr.
Lieftinck, Pieter
Lientz, James R.
Liggett, Richard A.
Liggit, Clarence R.
Light, Charles P., Jr.
Light, Rudolph A.
Ligtner, Lee M.
Ligon, Wister H.
Lilley, Tom
Lillie, Ralph D.
Lilliott, Richard W., Jr.
Lilly, James O.
Lilly, William E.
Lincoln, George A.
Lincoln, Lawrence J.
Lindeman, Philip F.
Lindemann, Oscar C.
Linden, Carl H.
Linder, Forrest E.
Lindholm, William L.
Lindley, Ernest K.
Lindsay, Crawford B.
Lindsay, Inabel B.
Lindsey, Edward M.
Lindsey, John M.
Lindsey, Robert S.
Linduska, Joseph P(aul)
Linebarger, Leon W.
Linn, Julius E.
Linowitz, Sol M.
Linsenmayer, Leonard R.
Linton, Calvin D.
Liotta, Domingo
Lippert, Karl M.
Lippincott, Stuart W.
Lippitt, Gordon L.
Lipscomb, Mance
Lipscombe, R. Boone
Lipshy, Ben A.
Lipton, Ronald A.
Liska, George
Liskow, Cullen R.
Lisle, Raymond E.
Litchfield, John T., Jr.
Litke, Arthur L.
Litschgi, Albert B.
Littell, Norman M.
Little, Ivan L.
Little, John P.
Little, John W.
Little, Robert M.
Little, William F.
Littlejohn, Carl W., Jr.
Littlejohn, Charles E., Jr.
Littleton, Isaac T., III
Litton, George W.
Livaudais, Jacques A.
Livesay, Richard E.
Livezey, William E.
Livingood, James W.
Livings, George E.
Livingston, Boynton P.
Livingston, James A., Jr.
Livingston, Johnston R.
Livingston, Otis W.
Ljung, Karl
Lloyd, Arthur Y.
Lloyd, Hermon
Lloyd, Ralph W.
Lock, Frank R.
Locke, Hugh A.
Lockett, Aubrey L.
Lockhart, Bill C.
Lockhart, Ernest R.
Lockhart, Vance E.
Lockmiller, David A.
Lockwood, Mason G.
Lodoen, George O. N.
Lodovichetti, Arthur V.
Loemker, Leroy E.
Loesch, Harrison
Loevinger, Lee
Loflin, Zeke L., Jr.
Loftus, Joseph A.
Logan, Garrett
Logan, John A.
Logan, Margot B.
Logan, Rayford W.
Lohr, Mary M.
Lokey, Charles M.
London, Kurt L.
Londrey, James L.
Long, Augustus C.
Long, Erven J.
Long, E(ugene) Hudson
Long, Gillis W.
Long, Herman H.
Long, Lawrence W.
Long, LeRoy D.
Long, Maurice W(ayne)
Long, Robert C.
Longino, James C., Jr.
Longley, James F.
Lonnquist, John H.
Look, Arnold E.
Looper, Charles E.
Looram, Matthew J., Jr.
Loos, Karl D.
Lord, Anthony
Lord, John F.
Loredo, Pedro
Loren, Elbert A.
Lory, Hillis
Loser, Joseph C.
Lottinville, Savole
Lotz, John
Louchheim, Donald H.
Louchheim, Katie S.
Louchheim, Walter C., Jr.
Loucks, Charles E.
Loucks, William N.
Lourie, Reginald S.
Louviere, William H.
Love, Albert I.
Love, Franklin S.
Loveless, Herschel C.
Lovell, Ernest J., Jr.
Lovell, Malcolm R.
Lovell, Malcolm R., Jr.
Lovett, H(enry) Malcolm
Lovvorn, Wilmer L.
Low, Frank J.
Low, John T(homas) C(uyama)
Low, Lawrence D.
Lowe, Clowney O.
Lowe, Harry
Lowe, Sam F., Jr.
Lowe, Richard B.
Lowery, George H., Jr.
Lowndes, Charles L. B.
Lowrance, Vernon L.
Lowry, Charles W.
Lowry, Kate R.
Lowry, Wallace E.
Loy, Frank E.
Loy, Milton E.
Lubell, Samuel
Lucas, C. Payne
Lucas, Henry L., Jr.
Lucas, J. Richard
Lucas, Jim G.
Lucas, John P.
Lucas, Louis F.
Lucas, Robert W.
Lucas, William F.
Luce, Dwain G.
Lucet, Charles
Luckie, Robert E., Jr.
Ludlow, James M.
Luedecke, Alvin R.
Luedeka, Edwin M.
Lugo, Luis B.
Luhrs, Albert W.
Luikart, Fordyce W.
Luisi, Hector
Luke, Charles D(aniel)
Luke, Norman J.
Luke, Robert A.
Lull, Edward E.
Lumpkin, John H.
Lund, F(ranze) Edward
Lund, Horace O.
Lund, Roy P.
Lund, Wendell L.
Lundahl, Arthur C.
Lundeberg, Philip K.
Lundell, Cyrus L.
Lundquist, Clarence T.
Lunger, Irvin E.
Luper, Oral L.
Lurie, Victor L.
Lush, Gerson H.
Luskin, Harold T.
Luter, Edward R.
Lutes, Dallas D.
Lutkins, LaRue R.
Luton, Johnston E.
Luttrell, A. Lothrop
Luttrell, Everett S.
Lutz, E. Russell
Lutz, Robert E(liot)
Lynbrook, William R.
Lycan, Gilbert L(ester)
Lyda, Wesley J.
Lydman, Jack W.
Lyght, Charles E.
Lykes, James M., Jr.
Lykes, Joseph T., Jr.
Lyle, Guy R.
Lyle, Joseph M., Jr.
Lyman, Carl M.
Lynch, Daniel F.
Lynch, Hugh, Jr.
Lynch, John F.
Lynch, Russell V.
Lynch, William W.
Lyne, Lewis F., III
Lyng, Richard E.
Lynn, Henry S.
Lynn, Kenneth S.
Lyon, George M.
Lyons, Charlton H.
Lyons, Clifford P.
Lyons, Harry
Lyons, Robert D.

Mabry, George L., Jr.
Mabry, William A.
MacArthur, Douglas, II
Macaulay, Hugh H., Jr.
MacCorkle, Stuart A.
MacCracken, William P., Jr.
MacDonald, Frank A.
MacDonald, Torbert H.
MacDonnell, Robert G.
Mace, Charles H.
Mace, David R.
Mace, Howard P.
MacEwen, Harry A(lbert)
MacFarland, Lonsdale P., Jr.
MacGowan, Charles F.
MacGregor, George L.
MacGuire, John T.
Macht, Robert
MacInnes, W. C.
MacIntyre, A(lfonso) Everette
Mack, Carl T.
Mack, Edward J.
Mack, Pauline B.
Mack, Raymond F.
Mack, William P.
Mackaman, Donald H.
MacKay, Donald B.
MacKenzie, Charles A.
Mackey, Howard H.
Mackey, Louis H.
MacKie, Frederick J., Jr.
Mackin, Catherine P.
Mackland, Ray
Mackle, Elliott J.
Mackle, Francis E., Jr.
Mackle, Robert F.
MacLaughlin, Victor J.
Maclay, W(illiam) Dayton
MacLean, Paul R.
MacLeary, Bonnie
Maclellan, H.O.
MacLennan, David A.
MacLeod, Dorothy S. (Mrs. William Murdoch MacLeod)
MacNabb, Richard R.
MacNaughton, Lewis W.
Macnees, James B.
Macon, George W., Jr.
Macy, John W., Jr.
Macy, Josiah N.
Madan, Bal K.
Madden, Wales H., Jr.
Maddlone, Joseph H.
Maddox, Donovan
Maddox, Robert N.
Maddux, Jared
Maddux, Sam, Jr.
Maechling, Charles, Jr.
Magee, Walter H.
Maggiolo, Walter A.
Magill, Robert N.
Magill, Samuel H.
Magner, James A.
Magruder, Carter B.
Magruder, Eugene R.
Maguire, Charlotte E. C. (Mrs. Raymer Francis Maguire)
Maguire, Philip F., Jr.
Mahoney, James W.
Mahood, David
Mahorner, Howard R.
Maisel, Sherman J.
Major, James R.
Major, Randolph T(homas)
Mak, Dayton S.
Makeig, Carl S.
Maki, T(enho) Ewald
Maktos, John
Malek, Fred V.
Malley, John W.
Mallick, Earl W.
Mallison, Richard S.
Mallon, Henry N.
Mallon, John J.
Mallory, Robert L., Jr.
Malloy, John M.
Malone, Frank M.
Malone, Lee H. B.
Malone, Ralph W.
Malone, Wex S.
Maloney, Frank E.
Maloney, John A.
Malott, James P.
Maloy, Richard J.
Mamatey, Victor S.
Manasco, Carter
Manatos, Mike
Mandel, H(arold) George
Mandelstam, Robert S.
Mandil, I. Harry
Manell, Abram E.
Maness, Irving
Mangelsdorf, Paul C.
Manger, William
Manget, Dan T(homas), Jr.
Mango, Cyril A.
Mangrum, John E.
Manhart, Charles D.
Manier, Miller
Manion, Raymond R.
Manire, James M.
Manley, Harold
Manley, Marion I.
Mann, Charles A.
Mann, Geoffrey T.
Mann, Gerald C.
Mann, James H(arold)
Mann, Marvin M.
Mann, Maurice
Mann, Thomas C.
Manning, Ellis W.
Manning, Herbert L(ybrand)
Manning, Hubert V.
Manning, William R.
Manoli, Dominck L.
Manring, Edward R.
Mansfield, John K.
Manship, Charles P(helps), Jr.
Manss, Robert W.
Mantell, Murray I.
Mapes, Charles M.
March, Anthony
Marcus, Edward S.
Marcus, Hyman
Marcy, Carl M.
Mardian, Robert C.
Maren, Thomas H.
Margileth, Andrew M.
Margolin, Bessie
Margolin, Edward
Margrave, John L.
Marilley, Jane E.
Marinho, Ilmar P.
Marino, Samuel J.
Marion, Cecil P., Jr.
Marion, William F.
Mark, David E.
Markee, Joseph E.
Markel, Hazel
Markey, Lucille P.
Markle, Herbert J.
Marks, Sam R.
Marks, Sumter D., Jr.
Markun, Patricia M.
Marlowe, Donald E.
Marmion, William H.
Marney, Leonard C.
Marriott J(ohn) Willard
Marris, William C.
Marsh, Burton W.
Marsh, Quinton N.
Marsh, T(had) N(orton)
Marshall, Charles B.
Marshall, Charles L.
Marshall, J. Howard, II
Marshall, John, Jr.
Marshall, John S.
Marshall, Lawrence M.
Marshall, Samuel F.
Marshall, William J.
Martell, Arthur E.
Martens, Robert J.
Martin, Allie B.
Martin, Boyce F.
Martin, Charles
Martin, Edward T.
Martin, Edwin G.
Martin, Edwin W.
Martin, Farris J., Jr.
Martin, Glen W(ebster)
Martin, Graham (Anderson)
Martin, Guy
Martin, Harold H.
Martin, James E.
Martin, John B.
Martin, John D., Jr.
Martin, John F.
Martin, Lee J.
Martin, LeRoy A.
Martin, Maceo C.
Martin, Mark
Martin, Melbourne L.
Martin, Otis O.
Martin, Paul E.
Martin, Preston
Martin, Samuel M., Jr.
Martin, S(idney) Walter
Martin, Theodore K.
Martin, Thomas B.
Martin, Thomas T.
Martin, William F.
Martin, William H.
Martin, William H.
Martin, William R.
Martin, William T.
Martinez, Guillermo D.
Mase, Darrel J.
Masey, Jack
Mason, Aaron S.
Mason, C. Avery
Mason, David D.
Mason, Frank E.
Mason, Harold T.
Mason, Jesse W.
Mason, John R.
Mason, Martin A.
Mason, Paul W.
Massel, Mark S.
Massey, Mary E.
Massibe, Lazare
Masters, Edward E.
Masterson, Harris
Masterson, Kieber S.
Masterson, William H.
Maston, Thomas B.
Masur, Gerhard S.
Materne, Stewart K.
Mathews, Charles W.
Mathews, Joseph J(ames)
Mathews, L. Ross
Mathews, Robert E.
Mathis, James V.
Mathis, Walter N.
Mathis, William L.
Matlock, Arleigh G.
Matlock, Clifford C.
Matrone, Gennard
Matson, Greta
Matson, Max M.
Matson, Sigfred C.
Matter, Alfred R.
Mattern, Donald H.
Matthew, Robert J.
Matthews, Burnita S.
Matthews, Charles A.
Matthews, David L.
Matthews, Donald R. (Billy)
Matthews, Eugene A.
Matthews, H. Freeman
Matthews, James C.
Matthews, Robert
Matthews, Roy M., Jr.
Matthews, Wilbur L.
Matthews, William L., Jr.
Matthews, Wright
Mattingly, Thomas W.
Mattison, George A., Jr.
Mattison, George G.
Mattox, Richard B.
Mattson, Joe O. P.
Mattson, Vernon L.
Maudlin, C(ecil) V(earl)
Maupin, Armistead J.
Maurer, Richard S(cott)

Moseley, Herbert C.
Moseley, John D.
Moses, Harold F.
Mosher, Edward J.
Mosher, Lloyd W.
Mosley, Donald C.
Mosley, Zack T.
Moss, Emma S.
Moss, James P.
Moss, Joseph A.
Moss, William W., Jr.
Mossman, Mereb E.
Mosso, Lyle D.
Mostow, Elmer
Mott, William C.
Mouly, George J.
Mountcastle, Paul
Mountien, Eisbeth I. E.
Mountrey, Robert W.
Moursund, Albert W., III
Moursund, M. Weddell
Mowrer, Edgar A.
Mowry, George E(dwin)
Moye, Charles A., Jr.
Moyle, Walter G.
Moyler, John, Jr.
Moynihan, daniel P.
Mozley, Samuel
Mudd, Roger H.
Mueller, George E.
Mueller, John F.
Mueller, Walter J(ulius)
Muir, Andrew F.
Muirhead, Peter P.
Muirhead, Samuel J.
Mulcahy, Edward W.
Mullahy, John H.
Mullaney, James
Mullen, Robert R.
Muller, William H., Jr.
Mullin, Eugene F., Jr.
Mulroney, John E.
Multhauf, Robert P.
Munce, Robert J(ohn)
Muncy, Lysbeth W.
Munford, Dillard
Munkki, Olavi
Munn, Cecil E.
Munroe, Johnson F.
Munroe, Pat
Munson, Joseph J.
Munson, Paul L.
Munter, Godfrey L(eon)
Munves, William
Murch, Gerald E.
Murchison, Charles H.
Murchison, John D.
Murfee, Latimer
Murfin, Mark
Murphey, Francis
Murphy, Charles P.
Murphy, Charles S(prings)
Murphy, Gardner
Murphy, George W.
Murphy, Henry C(lifford)
Murphy, James D.
Murphy, James R.
Murphy, John D.
Murphy, John F.
Murphy, Matthew P.
Murphy, Robert D.
Murphy, Robert T.
Murphy, Rupert L.
Murphy, Tom
Murray, Jo (Mrs. William J. Murray, Jr.)
Murray, Raymond L.
Murray, Roderick
Murray, William D.
Murray, William M(ozley), Jr.
Muse, Leonard G.
Muse, Thomas C.
Muse, William T.
Musgrave, Charles R.
Musgrave, F. Story
Muskat, Irving E.
Musselman, Vernon A.
Musser, Marc J.
Mustin, Lloyd M.
Muth, George E.
Myers, Albert G(allatin), Jr.
Myers, Bayard M., Jr.
Myers, Clark E.
Myers, Jack E.
Myers, Orie E., Jr.
Myers, Raymond E(dward)
Myers, Robert J.
Myers, Ronald E.
Myrick, John K.
Myskowski, Walter J.

Nabrit, Samuel M.
Naeser, Charles R(udolph)
Nagel, Charles
Nagler, Benedict
Nagy, Ferenc
Nagy, Janos
Naiden, Neil D.
Nairne, Clayton L.
Nakarai, Toyozo W.
Nall, A(ndrew) W.
Nance, Joseph M.
Nash, Bernard E.
Nash, James P(hilip)
Nash, William
Nash, Woodson M.
Nassikas, James A.
Nassikas, John N.
Nathan, Robert R.
Naugle, John E.
Naumoff, Philip
Neal, Mills F.
Neal, Phil H.
Neal, Roger L.
Neal, William W.
Neary, William H.
Nebergall, Roger E.
Needham, Donald J.
Needham, James J.
Neel, Samuel E.
Neely, Frank H.
Neely, Ralph P.
Neese, C. G.
Nef, John U.
Neff, Zeigel W.
Negley, Glenn
Nehmer, Stanley
Neibel, John B.
Nelles, Maurice
Nelson, Carl R.
Nelson, Curtis A.
Nelson, David
Nelson, Dotson M., Jr.
Nelson, Edward G.
Nelson, Harold S.
Nelson, Ivan
Nelson, John H.
Nelson, Joseph C.
Nelson, Lewis B.
Nelson, Marion M.
Nelson, Richard A.
Nelson, Robert A.
Nelson, Robert O.
Nelson, William A.
Nelson, William S.
Nemec, Frank A.
Nestingen, Ivan A.
Netterville, John T.
Nettleship, Anderson
Neumann, Alfred R.
New, William N.
Newberg, Richard R.
Newcomer, James W.
Newell, Homer E(dward)
Newell, William E.
Newhouse, Norman N.
Newland, Chester A.
Newlin, Dika
Newlove, George H.
Newman, Elliot V.
Newman, George S.
Newman, Guy D.
Newman, Leon E.
Newman, Marcel K.
Newman, Richard K.
Newman, Richard O.
Newman, Robert J.
Newman, William A., Jr.
Newsom, David D.
Newson, Henry W.
Newton, Earle W.
Newton, Frank R., Jr.
Newton, John W.
Ney, Jerome M.
Nicholas, Alan G(ordon), Sr.
Nicholas, Louis T.
Nicholls, William H.
Nichols, Eugene D.
Nichols, Henry L.
Nichols, Louis B.
Nichols, Marvin C.
Nichols, Perry
Nichols, Philip, Jr.
Nichols, Raymond H.
Nichols, Shuford R(einhardt)
Nicholson, Patrick J.
Nicholson, Roy S.
Nicklaus, Jack W.
Nicol, William K.
Nicoud, George A., Jr.
Niederlehner, Leonard
Niedermair, John C.
Nielsen, Aldon D.
Nielsen, Alvin H.
Nielsen, Elner
Nielsen, Niels C., Jr.
Nielsen, Otto R.
Nielson, Oscar H.
Nieset, Robert T.
Nigro, Felix A.
Niles, John J.
Nitze, Paul H.
Noah, Phillips B.
Noble, George B.
Nobles, William L.
Noe, James A.
Noe, Samuel V.
Noël Hume, Ivor
Noer, Rudolf J.
Noggle, Glenn R.
Nolan, Charles P.
Nolan, James P.
Nolan, John L.
Nolan, Philip J.
Nolan, Thomas B., Jr.
Nolan, Thomas B(rennan)
Noland, E(dward) W.
Noland, Lloyd U., Jr.
Nolla, José A(ntonio) B(ernabé)
Nolte, Roger E.
Nooe, Robert S.
Noojin, Ray O.
Noonkester, James R.
Norbeck, Edward
Nordby, Gene M.
Nordness, Nedville E(rving)
Norman, Frank A., Jr.
Norman, George E., Jr.
Norman, Jonathan V. D., Jr.
Norman, Robert C.
Norris, Frank T.
Norris, Frank W.
Norris, Frank W.
Norris, Philip A.
Norris, Richard A.
Norris, Robert H.
North, John R.
North, Robert H.
North, William H.
Northcutt, Jesse J.
Northen, Mary M.
Northrop, Paul A.
Northrup, Doyle L.
Norton, Clarence C.
Norton, Edwin M.
Norton, Ethelbert B.
Norton, Herman A.
Norton, Howard M.
Norwood, Bernard
Norwood, William U., Jr.
Nossiter, Bernard D.
Nourse, Edwin G.
Novack, Ben
Novak, Anthony
Novak, Robert D. S.
Nover, Barnet
Novo, Salvador
Novosal, Paul P.
Nowlin, Charles F.
Nowlin, William F.
Noyes, Blanche
Noyes, William A., Jr.
Nunally, Van D., Jr.
Nunn, Ira H.
Nunnally, Jum C., Jr.
Nusbaum, Charles J.
Nussbaum, Max E.
Nutter, Gilbert W.
Nutter, William H.
Nutting, Charles B.
Nydell, Carl C., Jr.
Nye, Brig. Gen. Francis W.
Nystrom, Harold C.
Nystrom, John W.

Oakes, John C.
Obear, Hugh H.
Oberbeck, Arthur W.
Oberdorfer, Donald, Jr.
Oberdorfer, Louis F.
Oberhelman, Harley D.
Oberlin, David W.
Oberwarth, C(larence) Julian
O'Brian, John L.
O'Brien, Brian J.
O'Brien, Eugene W.
O'Brien, Gerald D.
O'Brien, Leslie J., Jr.
O'Brien, Morrough P.
O'Bryan, Samuel O., Jr.
O'Bryan, William M.
O'Callaghan, Jerry A.
Ochs, Robert D.
Ochsner, Erwin C.
O'Connell, James D.
O'Connor, James B.
O'Connor, James P(atrick)
O'Connor, Lawrence J., Jr.
O'Connor, Ralph S.
O'Connor, Roderic L.
O'Dea, Thomas E.
Odell, Patrick L.
O'Dell, William F.
Oden, Delk M.
Odishaw, Hugh
Odle, Joe T.
Odom, John P.
O'Donnell, William L.
O'Donnell, Emmett, Jr.
O'Donnell, Robert D.
Oehlert, Benjamin H(ilborn), Jr.
Oehmann, Andrew F.
Oehser, Paul H.
Oetjen, Henry
Oettinger, Katherine B.
Oganovic, Nicholas J.
Ogburn, Charlton, Jr.
Ogden, James N.
Ogden, Squire R.
Ogden, William H.
Ogle, Arthur H.
O'Grady, James W.
O'Hara, Eliot
O'Hearn, Joseph A.
Ohin, Alexandre J.
Ohlke, Clarence C.
O'Keefe, Timothy F.
Okun, Arthur M.
Okun, Herbert S.
Olan, Levi A.
O'Leary, John F.
Oleksiw, Daniel P.
Olive, John R.
Olive, Lindsay S(hepherd)
Oliver, Allen L., Jr.
Oliver, Alvin E.
Oliver, Clarence P.
Oliver, Covey T.
Oliver, Henry
Oliver, James R.
Oliver, John
Oliver, William B.
Olmsted, George H.
Olsen, William A.
Olson, John V.
Olson, Loren K.
Olson, Ralph E.
Olson, Robert W.
Olson, Sylvester I(rwin)
Olverson, John B., II
O'Malley, Charles S., Jr.
Omerg, Arthur C.
O'Meara, Andrew P.
O'Meara, Arthur C.
Omer, Daniel O.
O'Neal, F(orest) Hodge
O'Neal, Robert M.
Onebane, Joseph
O'Neill, Frances A(loysius), Jr.
O'Neill, Lewis P.
Oppenheim, Saul C.
Oppenheimer, Monroe
O'Quin, Leon
Oram, James W.
Ordman, Arnold
Orebaugh, Walter W.
Oren, John B.
Orgain, Benjamin D.
Orn, Clayton L.
Orne, Jerrold
Orovitz, Max
Orr, Clyde L.
Orr, Douglas M.
Orr, Kenneth D.
Orr, William F.
Orth, Franklin L.
Ortiz Mena, Antonio
Orton, Stewart
Orwig, James P.
Osberg, James W.
Osborn, David L.
Osborn, Stellanova
Osborne, John
Osborne, Melville E.
Osborne, Robert
Osgood, Robert E.
Osius, Larry C.
Osman, H. E. Ahmed
Osorio, Trinidad
Ossenfort, William F.
Otis, Arthur B.
Otjen, William J.
O'Toole, James L.
Ottenheimer, Gus
Ottman, Robert W.
Otto, Henry J.
Oulahan, George M. C.
Ould, Edward H.
Oulliber, John A. (Jr.)
Oustinoff, Pierre C.
Outlaw, Arthur R.
Outlaw, Edward C.
Outler, Albert C.
Overby, Kermit O(swald)
Overstreet, Noah W.
Overton, Edward F.
Overton, Joseph A., Jr.
Overton, Stanley D.
Owen, Ralph
Owen, Thomas B.
Owens, Hubert B.
Owens, Jack B.
Owens, William A., Jr.
Owings, Ralph S.
Owono, Joseph N.
Owre, J. Riis
Oxford, Clifford
Oxley, John T.
Ozbirn, Mrs. E. Lee (Katie Freeman Ozbirn)

Paarlberg, Don
Pace, Ashley D. W., Jr.
Pace, Thomas A(ndrew)
Pachler, Francis T.
Pachler, William J.
Packard, David
Packer, Leo S.
Packett, Leonard V., Jr.
Padev, Michael A.
Page, Chester H.
Page, George K.
Page, Howard E.
Page, Jerry D.
Page, Richard G., Jr.
Page, Tate C.
Pagin, Renzo
Paglin, Max D.
Paine, Clarence S.
Paine, George P.
Paine, Roger W., Jr.
Paine, Thomas O.
Painter, Thomas W.
Palladino, Ralph A.
Palmatier, Everett D.
Palmby, Clarence D.
Palmer, Archie M(acInnes)
Palmer, Bruce, Jr.
Palmer, Charles F.
Palmer, Donald K.
Palmer, Forrest C.
Palmer, James E., Jr.
Palmer, John R.
Palmer, Richard C.
Palmer, Wayne F.
Pannell, Anne T. G. (Mrs. Henry Clifton)
Panoff, Robert
Papageorge, Evangeline T.
Papale, Antonio E.
Pardo, Arvid
Parelman, Samuel T.
Parham, Frederick D.
Paris, Leonard A.
Parish, Archie G.
Park, Charles R.
Parker, Alexander W.
Parker, Alfred B.
Parker, Andrew
Parker, B. B.
Parker, Blaine F.
Parker, David B.
Parker, Edelen A.
Parker, Edward N.
Parker, Foster
Parker, Frank, Jr.
Parker, George, Jr.
Parker, George F.
Parker, Grady P.
Parker, Herbert M(yers)
Parker, Jameson
Parker, John A.
Parker, John C.
Parker, John W.
Parker, Joseph B., Jr.
Parker, Paul J.
Parker, Richard B.
Parker, Robert O.
Parker, Robert P.
Parker, Roy T.
Parker, Wayne A.
Parker, W(illiam) V(ann)
Parkes, Ed
Parks, Harold F.
Parks, Joseph H.
Parris, James L.
Parrish, Alvin E.
Parrish, Frank J.
Parrish, Herbert C.
Parrish, John R.
Parrish, Linwood G.
Parrish, Wayne W.
Parry, Hugh J. (James Cross)
Parry, Stanley
Parsons, Howard L.
Parsons, Irene
Parsons, Robert B., Jr.
Parsons, Willard H.
Pasewark, William R.
Pastore, Peter N.
Patchin, Zelma
Pate, John R.
Pate, Woodrow W.
Paterson, Neil J.
Patrick, Luke V.
Patrick, Ransom R.
Patrick, Rembert W(allace)
Patrick, Walton R.
Patten, Gerland (Paul)
Patterson, Donald W.
Patterson, Harry W.
Patterson, John M.
Patterson, John M.
Patterson, John S.
Patterson, Joseph A.
Patterson, Joseph J.
Patterson, Paul M.
Patterson, Perry S.
Patterson, Samuel J., Jr.
Pattison, Hal C.
Patton, Ernest
Patton, James G.
Patton, James W.
Patton, Stuart L.
Patton, Wendell M., Jr.
Pauck, Charles E.
Pauck, Wilhelm
Paul, Martin A.
Paul, Norman S.
Paul, William B., Jr.
Pauli, Alvin F.
Pauls, Rolf
Paulsen, Monrad G.
Paulson, Donald L.
Pauly, John E.
Pauly, Paul E(dward)
Pawley, William D.
Paxton, William F., II
Payne, Leon M.
Payne, Melvin M.
Payne, Thomas R.
Payne, Vernon V.
Payne, Wilbur B.
Payne, William A.
Payne, William J.
Payne, William T.
Peabody, Endicott
Peabody, (James) R., Jr.
Peacock, Markham L., Jr.
Peal, Samuel E.
Peal, William H.
Pearce, William M.
Pearle, Stanley C.
Pearson, Clyde C.
Pearson, Drew (Andrew Russell)
Pearson, James B.
Pearson, Rufus J., Jr.
Pechman, Joseph A.
Peck, Harry D., Jr.
Peck, Margaret
Peck, Merton J.
Pedelahore, Joseph E.
Pedersen, Richard F.
Peers, William R.
Peery, Thomas M.
Peet, Raymond E.
Pegg, Carl (Hamilton)
Pellerzi, Leo M.
Pemberton, Harrison J., Jr.
Pendell, Elmer
Pendergrass, Edward J(ulian), Jr.
Pendergrass, Webster
Pendleton, Eugene B., Jr.
Penick, Edward M.
Pennebaker, Gordon B.
Pennekamp, John D.
Pennington, Paul J.
Penz, Anton J.
Peoples, David S.
Pepper, William M., Jr.
Pepperdene, Margaret W.
Pequegnat, Willis E(ugene)
Perez, Gines
Perez Pimentel, Pedro
Perkins, Cyrus L.
Perlin, Irwin E.
Perlis, Leo
Perlmutter, Jack
Perot, H. Ross
Perrine, Laurence
Perry, Charles D.
Perry, Clifford
Perry, John H., Jr.
Perry, Marvin B.
Perry, Percival
Perry, R(ufus) Patterson
Perry, Willie C.
Pershing, John J.
Person, John L.
Persons, John C.
Perusse, Roland I.
Pessel, Adolph J.
Peters, James A.
Peters, James S.
Peters, Ralph M.
Peters, Warren E.
Peterson, Carl R.
Peterson, Charles B., Jr.
Peterson, Dean F., Jr.
Peterson, Esther
Peterson, Frank D.
Peterson, M(endel) L(azear)
Peterson, Merrill D.
Peterson, Oliver A.
Peterson, Walter J.
Petree, Richard W.

Petree, William H.
Petrone, Rocco A.
Petry, Herbert C(harles), Jr.
Petry, Ray C.
Pettaway, C. D.
Pettit, Mason B.
Pettit, Rowland
Pettus, David M.
Petty, Travis H.
Petty, William B.
Pettyjohn, Charles R.
Pfaff, Eugene E(dwin)
Pfahler, Robert D.
Pfeiffer, Ralph A., Jr.
Pflaum, Irving P.
Pfohl, James C.
Phair, George
Phay, John E.
Pheiffer, Chester H.
Phelps, Arthur W.
Phelps, Jewell A.
Phelps, Joseph B.
Phelps, Malcom E.
Phelps, Ralph A., Jr.
Phifer, Kenneth G.
Philipson, Herman L., Jr.
Phillips, Alfredo
Phillips, Cabell B. H.
Phillips, Charles E.
Phillips, David S.
Phillips, Florence L.
Phillips, George O.
Phillips, Gerald C.
Phillips, Guy B., Jr.
Phillips, James D., Jr.
Phillips, John G.
Phillips, John W.
Phillips, Louie M.
Phillips, Loyal
Phillips, Marjorie
Phillips, Nathaniel P.
Phillips, Richard I.
Phillips, Robert Y.
Phillips, Rufus C., III
Phillips, Samuel C.
Phillips, Thomas M.
Phillips, Travis F.
Philos, Conrad D.
Phipps, John H. (Ben)
Phipps, William E., Jr.
Picirilli, Robert E.
Pickens, John K.
Pickering, John H(arold)
Pickering, Laurence G.
Pickering, Thomas R.
Pickett, Barzillai S.
Pickett, Ben B.
Pickett, George B., Jr.
Pickett, George E.
Pickrell, Kenneth L.
Pico, Rafael
Pierce, Charles C.
Pierce, Charles E.
Pierce, Clayton B.
Pierce, Harvey F.
Pierce, Hugh V.
Pierce, Joseph A(lphonso)
Pierce, Lovick
Pierce, Truman M.
Pierce, William S.
Pierpont, Robert M.
Pierson, Earl W.
Pierson, Robert H.
Pigford, Joseph H.
Pigott, Charles M.
Pinder, William C.
Pinkney, James F.
Pinney, Frank L., Jr.
Pinnix, Robert H(enry)
Pinson, Ernest R.
Pinson, Furman B., Jr.
Pinson, Thomas J.
Piper, Alexander R.
Pipes, Samuel W., III
Pipkin, James H(arold)
Piquet, Howard S.
Pirkey, Henry W., Jr.
Pirrung, Gilbert R(obinson)
Pisacano, Nicholas J.
Pisani, Joseph M.
Pistor, Charles H., Jr.
Pitman, Benjamin F.
Pittinger, Charles B.
Pittinger, James H.
Pittman, Julius D.
Pittman, Margaret
Pittman, Melvin A.
Pittman, Steuart L.
Pitts, Thomas J.
Pitts, William R.
Plank, John N.
Plant, Thomas W.
Platig, Emil R.
Plaxico, James S.
Plaza, Galo (Lasso)
Plemmons, W(illiam) H(oward)
Plescoff, Georges
Pletcher, Kenneth E.
Pletta, Dan H.
Plimpton, Russell A.
Ploger, Robert R.
Plotkin, Harry M.
Plough, Abe
Plummer, Curtis B.
Plummer, Frank A.
Plummer, Leonard N.
Plummer, Roger S.
Plummer, William E(dwin)
Plunkett, Robert L.
Plyler, Earle K.
Poag, Thomas E.
Poage, Edwin F.
Poats, Rutherford M.
Pogue, Lloyd W.
Poindexter, Hildrus A.
Poindexter, Robert D.
Polak, Jacques J.
Polanco-Abreu, Santiago
Polevitzky, Igor B.
Polk, Baxter
Pollack, Herbert
Pollack, Herman
Pollack, Irving M.
Pollak, Stephen J.
Pollard, Eric G. F.
Pollard, George M.
Pollard, James B.
Pollard, James J.
Pollin, Abe
Pollock, Lawrence S.
Pomeroy, Edward C.
Poole, Daniel A.
Poole, Frazer G.
Poole, James P.
Poole, John J.
Poor, Charles L.
Poor, Russell S.
Popper, David H.
Porter, Dudley, Jr.
Porter, Fred T.
Porter, Ira J.
Porter, Paul A.
Porter, Paul R.
Porter, William A.
Porterfield, Robert H.
Portwood, Thomas B.
Posey, Thomas E.
Posey, Walter B.
Posgate, James C.
Posner, Victor
Post, Mrs. Merriweather
Post, Troy V.
Poston, Lawrence S., Jr.
Poston, Met R.
Potter, Charles E.
Potter, Edward
Potter, Lester T.
Potter, Philip
Potter, William E.
Potts, Thomas C.
Powell, Benjamin E.
Powell, Benjamin H., IV
Powell, Benton W.
Powell, Beverley E.
Powell, George M.
Powell, Hampton O.
Powell, Herbert B.
Powell, James H.
Powell, Lewis F., Jr.
Powell, Ralph L.
Powell, Richard P.
Power, George W.
Powers, Edward L.
Powers, Edward L.
Powers, George T.,III
Powers, John A. (Shorty)
Powers, Lawrence J.
Powers, Leland E.
Powers, Noyes T.
Powers, Richard
Powers, Samuel J., Jr.
Powley, George R.
Poyner, James M.
Poynter, Juliet J.
Pozen, Walter
Prather, Charles L.
Pratt-Thomas, Harold R.
Predmore, Richard L.
Prentice, Howard A.
Prescott, Wallace S.
Presley, Elvis
Press, William H.
Pressler, Herman P.
Pressly, William L(aurens)
Preston, Edward F.
Preston, Richard J., Jr.
Prewett, Clinton R.
Prewitt, Thomas R.
Price, Alvin A.
Price, C. Hoyt
Price, Charles J.
Price, Daniel O.
Price, Frank J.
Price, Frank (Francis) W.
Price, Harold L.
Price, H(arry) B(orum), Jr.
Price, Harvey E.
Price, Hickman, Jr.
Price, James L., Jr.
Price, Julian P.
Price, Karl R.
Price, Pearl (Mrs. Leon S. Price)
Price, Reynolds
Price, Robert B.
Price-Williams, Douglas R.
Priebe, Elden P.
Priest, A. J. Gustin
Priest, Bill J.
Priest, Melville S.
Prince, David C.
Prince, Gregory S.
Prince, Julius S.
Prindle, Richard A(lan)
Prinosch, Francis J.
Pritchard, Edward K.
Pritchard, Robert
Pritz, Howard W.
Procter, Charles D.
Procter, John E.
Procter, Russell
Proctor, David
Proctor, Russell
Proffitt, David W.
Proffitt, Maris M.
Prothro, Adolphus M.
Provosty, LeDoux R(oger)
Prowell, B. D.
Prunty, Merle (Charles)
Pryor, Joseph E.
Prystowsky, Harry
Puckett, William O.
Pugh, Herbert L.
Puhan, Alfred
Pulitzer, Sam C.
Pullen, William R.
Pulley, Charles H.
Pulver, Wilfrid A. (Dick)
Pumphrey, Fred H.
Purcell, Joe
Purdy, Rob R.
Purse, Victor
Purser, Stuart R.
Pursley, Norman B.
Purvis, George F., Jr.
Purvis, Hugh F.
Puryear, Richard A., Jr.
Pusey, Merlo J.
Pusey, William W., III
Putnam, Walter B.
Puttroff, Paul A.
Pyle, Harold G.
Pyle, Paul W., Jr.
Pyper, William F.
Pyszka, Gerard E.

Quam, Louis O(tto)
Quandt, Douglass P.
Quandt, Russell J.
Quarles, Gilford G.
Quarles, James C.
Quarles, Lawrence R.
Quarles, Robert J.
Quasten, John
Quesada, Elwood R.
Quest, Charles F(rancis)
Quick, Nicholas W.
Quigley, Carroll
Quigley, Howard M(alcolm)
Quill, James B.
Quillian, Joseph D., Jr.
Quillian, Warren W.
Quimby, Thomas H. E.
Quindlen, Eugene J.
Quinlan, William L., Jr.
Quinn, George F.
Quinn, John J.
Quinn, Robert W.
Quinn, William W.
Quittmeyer, Charles L.

Raba, Ernest A.
Raborn, Hubert H.
Race, George J.
Rachford, Henry H., Jr.
Radcliff, Robert H., Jr.
Rademaker, Stanley C.
Rader, Louis T.
Radford, Arthur W.
Radigan, James P.
Radin, George
Radius, Walter A.
Raeder, Oscar J.
Ragon, Heartsill
Ragsdale, Warner B.
Rahdert, Frederick C.
Raine, Phillip
Raines, Richard C.
Rainey, Edward C.
Rainey, Kenneth D.
Rains, Edwin F.
Rainwater, Crawford V.
Ralston, Noel P(rintis)
Ramage, Lawson P.
Ramirez, Mariano H.
Ramm, H(ans) Henry
Ramsaur, Ernest E., Jr.
Ramsay, Louis L., Jr.
Ramsay, Marion L.
Ramsey, Charles S.
Ranard, Donald L.
Rand, Clayton T.
Rand, Robert L.
Randall, Harold M.
Randall, Kenneth A.
Randall, Robert L.
Randolph, John H., Jr.
Randolph, Roger S.
Raney, Dallas P.
Rankin, Hugh F.
Rankin, Jeannette
Rankin, J(oseph) Winfield
Rankin, Raymond C.
Rankin, Robert S.
Rankin, Winton B.
Ransom, Crisler B.
Ranta, Hugo A.
Rapoport, Daniel
Rapp, William F.
Rase, Howard F.
Rash, Bryson B.
Rasmussen, Boyd L.
Rasmussen, Marius P.
Rasor, Robert W.
Rast, John M.
Rathgeber, Lewis W.
Ratliff, Charles E., Jr.
Rauh, Joseph L., Jr.
Ravkind, Edna F.
Ravlin, James N.
Rawalt, Marguerite
Rawles, James W.
Rawlings, Norborne L.
Rawls, Flora H.
Rawls, George C.
Ray, DeWitt T.
Ray, Donald P.
Ray, Elizabeth N.
Ray, George E.
Ray, Jeter S.
Ray, John E., 3d
Ray, Joseph M.
Rayburn, John C.
Raymond, John F.
Rayson, Edwin H.
Rayzor, Jesse N.
Read, Benjamin H.
Read, Clark P.
Read, Henry J.
Read, William E.
Read, Willie H.
Reagin, Ewell K.
Ream, Norman J.
Reardon, Timothy J., Jr.
Reason, Joseph H(enry)
Reaves, Kelsie L.
Rece, Ellis H.
Redd, George N.
Reddell, William J.
Redden, Kenneth R.
Reddick, DeWitt C.
Redding, Robert E.
Redditt, John S.
Redfern, John J., Jr.
Redford, Emmette S.
Redling, William N.
Redman, Hamilton M.
Reece, Mrs. Carroll (Louise Goff)
Reed, Aln R.
Reed, Bevington A.
Reed, Charles H.
Reed, David C.
Reed, George L.
Reed, Henry M., Jr.
Reed, John C.
Reed, J(ohn) F.
Reed, John H.
Reed, John J.
Reed, Kenneth G.
Reed, Revon
Reed, Sidney G., Jr.
Reed, Stanley (Forman)
Reed, Stanley F.
Reed, Victor J.
Reed, Wayne O.
Reed, William L.
Reeder, James P.
Reedy, George E., Jr.
Rees, Charles H.
Rees, Eberhard F. M.
Reese, Jim E.
Reesing, John P., Jr.
Reeves, John E.
Reeves, Thomas J.
Regan, Purdy C.
Regenstein, Louis
Rehder, Harald A.
Rehnquist, William H.
Reich, Eli T.
Reichelderfer, F(rancis) W(ilton)
Reichert, Herbert W.
Reid, Albert C.
Reid, George W.
Reid, John C.
Reid, John T.
Reid, Joseph E.
Reid, Lyne S.
Reid, Paul A.
Reid, Robert N.
Reid, Roger D.
Reidy, Edward M.
Reifman, Alfred
Reiger, Siegfried H.
Reiling, Herman T.
Reilly, Francis X.
Reilly, Gerard D.
Reilly, John R.
Reily, William B., Jr.
Reimer, Rudolph E.
Reinhold, Paul E.
Reinmuth, Oscar W.
Reistle, Carl E., Jr.
Reith, Carl J.
Reitz, J(ulius) W.
Renchard, George W.
Renegar, Horace C.
Renshaw, Edgar F.
Rentzel, Delos W(ilson)
Rephan, Jack
Resor, Stanley R.
Reuben, Odell R.
Reuter, Irving J.
Reuther, Victor G.
Revercomb, Everett E.
Reves, George E.
Rewinkel, Milton C.
Reyner, Anthony S.
Reynolds, Charles W.
Reynolds, Dana D.
Reynolds, David P.
Reynolds, Donald W(orthington)
Reynolds, Edwin L.
Reynolds, Ferris E.
Reynolds, Frank
Reynolds, Frank M.
Reynolds, Jim D.
Reynolds, Joe H.
Reynolds, John O.
Reynolds, Joseph M.
Reynolds, Joshua P.
Reynolds, Mercer, Jr.
Reynolds, Orr E.
Reynolds, Thomas L(ee)
Reynolds, Victor G. F.
Reynolds, Wiley R.
Reynolds, William G.
Rhame, William T.
Rhett, Leigh C.
Rhetts, Charles E.
Rhine, Joseph B.
Rhinelander, Laurens H.
Rhines, Frederick N.
Rhoads, James B.
Rhoads, Webster S., Jr.
Rhode, Robert D(avid)
Rhodes, Daniel D.
Rhodes, Francis M.
Rhodes, Fred B., Jr.
Rhyne, Charles S.
Ribeiro, Lenor S.
Rice, George W.
Rice, H. LaMarr
Rice, Joseph E.
Rice, Leon L., Jr.
Rice, Oscar K(nefler)
Rice-Wray, Edris
Rich, Arthur L.
Rich, Clifford A. L.
Rich, Linvil G.
Richards, Arthur L.
Richards, Benjamin B., II
Richards, James M.
Richards, Karl F.
Richards, Reginald B. J.
Richardson, Arthur P.
Richardson, Sir Egerton R
Richardson, Elliot L.
Richardson, Francis H(arrie)
Richardson, Frank H.
Richardson, James A., III
Richardson, John, Jr.
Richardson, John W., Jr.
Richardson, Robert C., III
Richardson, Rupert N.
Richardson, Walter B.
Richmond, David W.
Richmond, Luther H.
Richter, George H.
Ricketts, Richard D.
Rickey, Harry W.
Rickover, Hyman G.
Ridder, Walter T(hompson)
Ridenhour, Joseph C.
Ridgeway, James F.
Riecken, Henry W(illiam)
Riedel, Alan E.
Rieder, Rudolph C.
Riegel, Oscar W.
Riemondy, Augustus A.
Riepma, Siert F(rederick)
Riesenberg, Saul H.
Riester, Alan D.
Rietz, H. Lewis
Rigby, Fred D.
Rigg, Edgar T.
Riggs, Carl D(aniel)
Riggs, Cecil D.
Rigney, Carl J.
Riley, Donald C.
Riley, Emma J.
Riley, Harris D., Jr.
Riley, Herbert P.
Riley, John R.
Riley, Paul H.
Rill, Woodrow W.
Rimestad, Idar
Rimlinger, Gaston V.
Ringel, Herbert A.
Rioch, David M.
Riordan, Emmet F.
Ripper, C(arl) Harold
Risher, James F.
Risinger, Burton R.
Rist, Leonard B.
Ristow, Walter W(illiam)
Ritchie, Albert E.
Ritchie, Reeves E.
Ritter, Paul O.
Ritter-Aislan, Eduardo
Ritz, Wilfred J.
Ritzenthaler, Arthur B.
Rives, James H.
Rives, Richard T.
Rivet, Charles L.
Rivlin, Alice M.
Rizley, Robert S.
Roach, Frederick E.
Roadman, Charles H.
Robb, Roger
Robbins, Jerome W.
Robbins, Paul H.
Roberson, Virgil O., Jr.
Roberts, Aubrey L.
Roberts, Benny K.
Roberts, Carlisle
Roberts, Carlyle J.
Roberts, Chalmers M.
Roberts, Edward V.
Roberts, Frank L.
Roberts, Granville O.
Roberts, Henry S.
Roberts, Irving
Roberts, James B.
Roberts, John H.
Roberts, Joseph B.
Roberts, (Mary) Juanita D.
Roberts, Kenneth A.
Roberts, Marguerite
Roberts, Maurice A(aron)
Roberts, Ralph S.
Roberts, Richard B.
Roberts, Richmond R.
Roberts, Robert, Jr.
Roberts, Walter K.
Robertson, Alton E.
Robertson, Archibald G.
Robertson, Cary
Robertson, Elgin B.
Robertson, George L.
Robertson, Harry S.
Robertson, J(ames) D.
Robertson, James L.
Robertson, John L.
Robertson, Joseph E.
Robertson, Joseph M.
Robertson, Julian H.
Robertson, Lemuel C.
Robertson, Randal M.
Robertson, Reuben B.
Robertson, Thomas J.
Robertson, Walter S.
Robey, Ralph W.
Robins, E. Claiborne
Robinson, Alice G.
Robinson, Harold
Robinson, Harold N.
Robinson, Henry L.
Robinson, Herbert W.
Robinson, James A.
Robinson, Leonard H.
Robinson, Mary F. M.
Robinson, Paul B.
Robinson, Paul B.
Robinson, Robert A., Jr.
Robinson, Robert M.
Robison, John M(arshall), Jr.
Robson, C(harles) B(askervill)
Roche, Josephine A.
Rock, George D.
Rockstein, Morris
Rockwell, Stuart W.
Rockwell, Theodore, III

Rodgers, Eric
Rodgers, Jack
Rodman, Roland V.
Roe, Arthur S.
Roe, Edward C.
Roebuck, Julian B.
Roedel, Gerhard W. E.
Roenne, Torben H.
Roesler, Robert H.
Roessler, Robert L.
Roettger, Gregory J.
Rogers, Ernest P(aul)
Rogers, Frank W.
Rogers, Gaines M.
Rogers, Gladys P.
Rogers, Grover L.
Rogers, Hamilton
Rogers, James C.
Rogers, James L.
Rogers, John J. W.
Rogers, Mac E.
Rogers, Nathaniel S.
Rogers, Thomas F.
Rogers, Virgil M.
Rogers, Warren J., Jr.
Rogers, William D.
Rogin, Lawrence M.
Rogovin, Mitchell
Rohan, Alexander J.
Rolleston, William F.
Rollins, Robert L., Jr.
Rollins, Steed
Rolnick, Harry
Rolnick, Robert F.
Rolston, Holmes
Romagosa, Elmo L.
Romanowitz, Harry A.
Rommel, Wilfred H.
Ronald, Peter
Ronne, Finn
Rood, Leslie L.
Roodhouse, W. W.
Roose, Kenneth D.
Roosevelt, Archibald B., Jr.
Roosevelt, Kermit
Root, Blake S.
Root, John F.
Ropp, Theodore
Rosberg, David W.
Rose, David J.
Rose, Frank A.
Rose, John C.
Rose, Morris E.
Rose, (Thornton) Turner
Rose, William A.
Roseberg, Carl A.
Rosen, Bernard
Rosen, Martin M.
Rosenbaum, Harold D.
Rosenbloom, Morris V.
Rosenfeld, Eugene
Rosenstein, Claude H.
Rosenweig, Stanley H.
Rosenthal, Aaron
Rosenthal, Jacob
Rosenthal, Jerome M.
Rosenthal, Sol
Rosinger, Kurt E.
Rosow, Jerome M.
Ross, Albert S.
Ross, Bradford
Ross, Claude G. A.
Ross, Herbert H.
Ross, Roy G.
Ross, Sherman
Ross, Stanley R.
Ross, William B.
Ross, William D., Jr.
Rosson, William B(radford)
Rotan, Edward
Roth, Irving
Roth, Robert
Rothenberg, Morris
Rothert, Matthew H.
Rothrock, Addison M(ay)
Rothschild, Louis S.
Rottet, Ralph K.
Rotty, Ralph M.
Rountree, William M.
Rous, John H.
Rouse, Robert L.
Roush, Oliver E.
Rovetta, Charles A.
Rowand, Wilbur H.
Rowe, Charles E.
Rowe, James H., Jr.
Rowe, Mrs. James H., Jr. (Elizabeth Rowe)
Rowe, Robert J.
Rowe, Robert S.
Rowland, Arthur R.
Rowland, Richard C.
Rowland, Robert R.
Rowland, Robert R.
Rowles, Russell R.
Rowlett, Frank B.
Rowley, Craig M.
Rowley, John H.
Rowntree, R(ichardson) H(enry)
Rowsome, Frank H(oward), Jr.
Royall, Kenneth C.
Royer, John E.
Royster, Wimberly C.
Royston, Robert W.
Ruark, Arthur E.
Rubin, Abe
Rubin, de la Borbolla, Daniel F.
Rubottom, Roy R., Jr.
Ruckelshaus, William D.
Rucker, Tinsley W., III
Rucker, Truman B.
Ruckner, Edward A.
Rudd, Gordon W.
Rudder, James E.
Ruddley, John
Ruddock, John Y.
Rudolph, Arthur L. H.
Ruff, Thomas C.
Ruffin, Thomas L.
Ruffin, William H.
Ruge, Nell (Marshall)
Ruggiers, Paul G.
Ruhlen, George
Rumsfeld, Donald
Rundell, Orvis H.
Rundles, Ralph W.
Runge, DeLyle P.
Runk, B(enjamin) F(ranklin) Dewees
Runnells, Clive
Runnels, Richard S.
Rupe, Dallas G.
Ruppenkamp, Wilford K.
Rush, Bert
Rush, Fletcher G., Jr.
Rush, N(ixon) Orwin
Rushing, Reginald
Rushton, William J.
Rushton, William J., III
Rusk, Dean
Russ, Joseph R.
Russell, Austin J.
Russell, Francis H.
Russell, Harold L.
Russell, H(arry) K(itsun)
Russell, Howard H.
Russell, I(saac) Willis
Russell, Marvin W.
Russell, Ralph C.
Russell, Richard J.
Rust, Robert B.
Rustad, Elmer L.
Rustin, John W.
Rutland, John W., Jr.
Rutland, Leon W., Jr.
Rutland, Robert A.
Rutland, Thomas W., Jr.
Ruttenberg, Charles B.
Ruttenberg, Stanley H(arvey)
Ryan, Bryce F.
Ryan, Charles B.
Ryan, John A.
Ryan, John D.
Ryan, John K.
Ryan, Patrick J.
Ryberg, H(erman) Theordore
Ryburn, Francis M., Jr.
Ryder, Claire F.
Ryder, James A.
Ryerson, Joseph L.
Rymer, S. Bradford, Jr.
Rysan, Josef

Saad, Ahmed Z.
Sabiston, David C., Jr.
Sabrosky, Curtis W.
Sachs, Sidney S.
Sackett, Walter W., Jr.
Sackton, Frank J.
Safire, William
Sager, John P.
St. Amant, Clyde P.
St. Clair, Huston
St. John, John
St. Lewis, Roy
Salans, Carl F.
Salant, Walter S.
Saldana, Lino J.
Salinger, Herman
Salisbury, Arthur G.
Salla, Salvatore
Salmon, Kurt
Salsburg, Zevi W.
Saltsman, Daniel L.
Saltzman, Herbert A.
Saltzman, Maurice
Salzman, Herbert
Samford, Yetta G., Jr.
Sample, John G.
Sampson, Francis L.
Sampson, George P.
Sams, J. C.
Sams, Robert S.
Sams, Wiley M.
Samson, Charles H., Jr.
Samuel, John S.
Samuels, J. Clifton
Samuelson, Adolph T.
Samuelson, Albert C.
Sanchez, Allan J.
Sanchez y Sanchez, George I.
Sancho-Bonet, Rafael, Jr.
Sandell, Milton E.
Sanders, Carl E.
Sanders, Clinton L.
Sanders, Earnest E.
Sanders, Frank
Sanders, Harold B., Jr.
Sanders, Paul D. L.
Sanders, Paul H(ampton)
Sanders, Terry B., Jr.
Sanders, Wilbur H.
Sanders, William
Sanders, William K.
Sanderson, Fred H.
Sandifer, Durward V.
Sanditen, Julius
Sandlin, Marlin E.
Sandoval, Hilary J., Jr.
Sandridge, William P.
Sandy, William C.
Sanford, John B., Jr.
Sangster, William M.
Sansom, Richard E.
Santa-Maria, Domingo
Santos, Joao O.
Sapirie, Samuel R.
Saraw, Arnold F.
Sarber, Raymond W.
Sargent, Thomas R., III
Sarpy, Leon
Sarra, Valentino
Sartain, Aaron Q.
Sashoff, Stephan P(encheff)
Satchwell, John L.
Satterfield, John C.
Satterthwaite, Joseph C.
Sauer, Walter C.
Saul, Ralph S.
Saunders, Charles R.
Saunders, Eugene D.
Saunders, James P.
Saunders, Joseph B., Jr.
Saunders, R. Duane
Saunders, Richard P.
Savage, Henry, Jr.
Savage, Wallace H.
Savkar, Dattatraya S.
Sawyer, Alan R.
Sawyer, Bonner D.
Sawyer, Helen A.
Sawyer, Herbert S.
Sawyer, Thomas L.
Saxe, Harry C.
Sayre, Francis B., Jr.
Scaglione, Aldo D(omenico)
Scales, James R.
Scammon, Richard M.
Scarlett, Frank M.
Scates, Hiram S.
Schachtel, Hyman J.
Schade, Arnold F.
Schaefer, Robert E.
Schaefer, Mrs. William B. (Orville Tyler)
Schairer, John F.
Schaub, James H.
Schaufele, William E., Jr.
Scheele, Leonard (Andrew)
Scheer, Julian W.
Scheffer, Walter F.
Scheibel, Kenneth M.
Scheick, William H.
Schell, Braxton
Schellman, Robert H.
Schenk, Peter J.
Schenker, Tillie A.
Scheyven, Baron (Louis)
Schiefen, Robert W.
Schild, Alfred
Schilling, Ralph F.
Schilling, Sylvester P.
Schimmel, Joseph
Schine, J. Myer
Schipper, Gerrit
Schiro, Victor H(ugo)
Schirra, Walter M., Jr.
Schlei, Norbert A.
Schlosstein, Adolph G., Jr.
Schmeltzer, Edward
Schmid, Bernard F.
Schmidt, Carl F.
Schmidt, Frederick H.
Schmidt, L(eon) H(erbert)
Schmidt, Richard M., Jr.
Schmidt, William A.
Schmidt, Wilson E.
Schmidt-Nielsen, Knut
Schmied, Alfred L.
Schmitt, Waldo L.
Schmitz, Wallace B.
Schneider, Hans
Schneider, Louis
Schneider, Wilbert M.
Schnyder, Felix
Schoech, William A.
Schoen, Edward, Jr.
Schoenborn, Edward M., Jr.
Schoeny, Leo J.
Schofield, James R.
Schoggen, Phil
Scholtes, Robert M.
Schooley, Allen H.
Schoon, Owen H.
Schoonover, Irl C.
Schoonover, Kermit
schrank, Auline R.
Schriever, Bernard A(dolf)
Schriver, Lester O.
Schroder, William H.
Schroeder, George W.
Schroeder, Laurence A.
Schroth, Thomas N.
Schubert, Leo
Schuhardt, V(ernon) T(ruett)
Schulman, Robert A.
Schultz, Edward W.
Schultz, Leonard P(eter)
Schultz, Leslie P.
Schultze, Charles L.
Schumann, Fred
Schuster, Stephen A.
Schuyler, William E., Jr.
Schwab, Richard N(ewelt)
Schwartz, Carl H(erbert), Jr.
Schwartz, Charles F.
Schwartz, David B.
Schwartz, Frank L.
Schwartz, Harry S.
Schwartz, Kessel
Schwartz, William S.
Schwartz, Roy M.
Schwarzschild, William H., Jr.
Schwebel, Stephen M.
Schwend, Fred S.
Schwenk, Otto G.
Schwert, George W.
Schwetman, Herbert D.
Scofield, John
Scofield, Robert W.
Scott, Alonzo L.
Scott, Buford
Scott, Cornelius A.
Scott, David W.
Scott, Deroy
Scott, Donald R.
Scott, Glenn A.
Scott, Henry W., Jr.
Scott, H(omer) Vernon
Scott, John I. E.
Scott, John R.
Scott, John T., Jr.
Scott, John W.
Scott, Joseph W.
Scott, Louis A.
Scott, Robert B., Jr.
Scott, Robert C.
Scott, Robert J.
Scott, Roger A.
Scott, Tom B., Jr.
Scott, Walter C.
Scott, Willard P.
Scott, Wilton E.
Scribner, Allison K.
Scribner, Fred C(lark), Jr.
Scudder, Delton L.
Scurlock, Arch C.
Seaborg, Glenn T.
Seabrook, Belford L.
Seacat, Russell H., Jr.
Seagle, William
Seago, Dorothy W.
Seale, Allen T. F.
Sealy, Tom
Searls, David T.
Sears, John P.
Seawell, Leon T., Jr.
Seay, William A.
Secrest, Fred G.
Secrest, James D.
Sedelow, Walter A., Jr.
Seeger, Raymond J.
Seelbach, Louis
Seely, Charles S.
Seeman, Lyle E.
Seger, Joseph L.
Sehrt, Clem H.
Seibert, Florence B(arbara)
Seidman, Harold
Seiferth, Solis
Seigle, John S.
Seigworth, Kenneth J.
Seitchik, Joseph
Selden, Samuel
Seldin, Donald W.
Selecman, Charles E.
Self, James C.
Self, Margaret C.
Self, William K.
Seligmann, Albert L.
Selke, Oscar O., Jr.
Selkirk, George A.
Sellars, W(alter) Bailey
Sellers, James
Sellers, Mark A.
Sells, Leonard L.
Sells, Saul B.
Semer, Milton P.
Sendón, Andrés R.
Senft, Ernest E.
Sensabaugh, Leonidas F.
Senter, William O.
Senti, Frederic R.
Sentner, David
Seretean, Martin B.
Serfass, Earl J.
Servaites, Francis X.
Servies, James A.
Sessions, Cliff
Sessions, Edson O.
Sessions, John M.
Sessoms, Stuart M.
Sessums, Roy T(homas)
Sestanovich, Stephen N.
Settle, Peveril O(zroe)
Settle, William A., Jr.
Setzer, Richard W.
Setzler, Edwin L.
Seufer, Paul E.
Sevcenko, Ihor
Severance, Robert W.
Sevilla-Sacasa, Guillermo
Seward, Doris M.
Seward, Ralph T.
Seward, William W., Jr.
Sewell, Ben G.
Sewell, Frank A(sa)
Sewell, James L.
Sexton, Burton H.
Shackelford, Francis
Shackelford, Virginius R., Jr.
Shackford, Roland H.
Shackleford, Samuel D., Jr.
Shackleford, Thomas M., Jr.
Shackleton, Polly
Shade, Camille S.
Shade, Chester S.
Shafer, W.O.
Shaffer, John H.
Shafroth, Will
Shahan, Ewing P(ope)
Shaheen, Edward L.
Shands, William A.
Shands, William R.
Shank, Clare Brown (Williams)
Shanks, E(ugene) Baylis
Shanley, Bernard M(ichael)
Shannon, Charles V.
Shannon, Howard L.
Shannon, James A.
Shannon, William V.
Shanor, Leland
Shapiro, John L.
Shapiro, Samuel B.
Shapley, Fern R.
Sharer, Robert E.
Sharp, Aaron J.
Sharp, Charles F.
Sharp, Charles S.
Sharp, Edward P.
Sharp, Susie M.
Sharp, Vernon H.
Sharp, William
Shattuck, Roger W.
Shaver, Jesse M.
Shaw, Arnold F.
Shaw, Brackley
Shaw, George B.
Shaw, J(ames) Howard
Shaw, John S., Jr.
Shaw, Milton
Shaw, Russell B.
Shaw, William
Shawn, Edwin M. ("Ted Shawn")
Shea, Francis M.
Shea, John J.
Shea, Joseph W.
Shea, Robert F.
Shea, William L.
Shearer, Ross S.
Shearin, Paul E(dmundson)
Sheehan, Harold W(illiam)
Sheehan, John E.
Sheehan, Mark T.
Sheen, Robert T.
Sheffield, Edward R.
Sheffield, I. M., Jr.
Sheffield, Roy D.
Shelbourne, Roy M.
Sheline, Raymond K.
Shell, George R. E.
Shelley, Edwin A.
Shelly, Chester P.
Shelmire, Bedford
Shelokov, Alexis
Shelton, Edward N.
Shelton, Turner B.
Shepherd, Mark Jr.
Shepherd, Patricia D.
Shepherd, Richard J.
Sheppard, Franklin C.
Sheps, Cecil G.
Sherer, Albert W., Jr.
Sherer, R J.
Sheridan, Edward J.
Sheriff, Hilla
Sherman, Louis
Sherman, Merritt
Sherman, Robert C.
Sherman, William C.
Sherrill, Joseph H.
Sherrill, William W.
Sherrod, (Blackie) William F.
Sherry, William J.
Sherwood, Sidney
Shewmaker, Russell N.
Shields, Murray
Shields, Robert H.
Shifley, Ralph L.
Shillington, James K.
Shillito, Barry J.
Shimoda, Takeso
Shingleton, William W.
Shinkman, Paul A.
Shinn, John C.
Shinowara, George Y(uklo)
Shipp, Kathryn G.
Shippen, Zoe
Shirk, Frank C.
Shirkey, Albert P.
Shirley, David A.
Shirley, Harold C.
Shiskin, Julius
Shive, William
Shiver, Erika M. M. (Mrs. Sam M. Shiver)
Shivers, Allan
Shoaib, Mohamed, H.
Shoemaker, Perry M.
Shollenberger, Lewis W.
Shook, Alfred M., III
Shook, Cleo F.
Shook, John L.
Shor, Franc M. L.
Shores, Louis
Short, Byron E.
Shotzberger, Martin L.
Shoults, A. M.
Shoup, Charles S.
Shoup, David M.
Shreve, Charles E.
Shriner, Ralph L.
Shriver, Harry C.
Shuford, A. Alex,, Jr.
Shuford, Cecil E.
Shuford, Harry A.
Shuler, Thomas G.
Shuler, William R.
Shull, J(ames) Malcolm
Shull, Leon
Shulman, Stephen N(eal)
Shults, Dan S.
Shults, Robert L., Jr.
Shuman, Frederick G.
Shuman, Ronald B.
Shupert, George T.
Shupper, Burton H.
Shure, R(alph) D.
Shurtleff, Miller F.
Shute, John W.
Shytle, John D.
Sias, Azariah B.
Sibley, Charles K.
Sibley, John A.
Sickles, Carlton R.
Siegel, Irving H.
Siegel, John B., Jr.
Siegel, Peter V.
Siepert, Albert F., Jr.
Sievering, Nelso F., Jr.
Sieverts, Frank A.
Sigel, Stanley J.
Sigmon, Richard R.
Sikes, Walter A.
Silber, John R.
Silberman, Lou H.
Silberstein, Joseph A.
Silin, Charles I.
Sill, Gerald D.

Silver, Earl C.
Silver, Francis A.
Silver, Samuel I.
Silver, Solomon
Silvergleid, David
Silverman, Abner D.
Silverman, Alvin M.
Silverman, Shirleigh
Silvey, Joseph K. G.
Simmang, Clifford M.
Simmons, Charles F.
Simmons, Dwight L.
Simmons, Richard M., Jr.
Simmons, Samuel J., Jr.
Simmons, William P., Jr.
Simms, Arthur B.
Simms, John H.
Simms, Richard L., Jr.
Simon, Charlie M. (Mrs. John Gould Fletcher)
Simon, William
Simonds, Albert R.
Simonds, Omar H., Jr.
Simonelli, Charles F.
Simons, Albert
Simonson, Roy W(alter)
Simpson, Donald F.
Simpson, Eugene M.
Simpson, Gordon
Simpson, James A.
Simpson, John D., Jr.
Simpson, Maurice E.
Simpson, Ormond R.
Simpson, Robert E.
Simpson, Robert L.
Simpson, (Robert) Smith
Simpson, William
Simpson, Willis W. (Jerry)
Simrall, Harry C(harles Fleming)
Sims, Edward H.
Sims, James R.
Sinclair, John T., Jr.
Sinclair, Thornton C.
Singer, Derek S.
Singer, Sanford R.
Singer, S(iegfried) Fred
Singleton, W(illard) Ralph
Sinkford, Jeanne C.
Sisco, Joseph J.
Sisk, Glenn N(olen)
Sisler, Harry H.
Sistrunk, James D.
Sitterly, Charlotte M.
Siu, Ralph G.
Sivard, Robert P(aul)
Sizemore, Richard C.
Skaggs, Harvey T.
Skallerup, Walter T., Jr.
Skelton, John F., Jr.
Skelton, Robert B.
Skiles, Elwin L.
Skinner, John L.
Skoufis, Peter J.
Skuce, Walter C.
Slaiman, Donald S.
Slater, John C.
Slaton, William H.
Slaughter, Adolph J.
Sledd, Herbert D.
Sledd, Marvin B.
Sledge, Clarence L.
Slenczynska, Ruth
Slick, Earl F.
Sliepcevich, Cedomir M.
Sliepcevich, Elena M.
Sliger, Bernard F.
Sligh, Frederick H.
Sloan, Arthur W.
Sloan, Frank K.
Sloan, Robert D.
Sloane, Joseph C.
Sloss, Robert L.
Small, Charles H.
Small, Ray
Smart, Jacob E.
Smart, Robert F.
Smathers, Frank, Jr.
Smathers, George A.
Smeltzer, Charles C.
Smiley, Joseph R.
Smiley, Wendell W.
Smith, A. Robert
Smith, Abbot E.
Smith, Alexander G.
Smith, Alexander W., Jr.
Smith, Andrew C.
Smith, Anthony J.
Smith, Ashby G.
Smith, Benjamin J.
Smith, Beverly W., Jr.
Smith, Blake
Smith, Bryan F.
Smith, Burton P.
Smith, Carleton D.
Smith, Carroll N.
Smith, C(harles) Alphonso
Smith, C(harles) Carney
Smith, Charles S., Jr.
Smith, Charles T.
Smith, Chesterfield H.
Smith, Clebert C.
Smith, Clifford E.
Smith, Clyde F(uhrlman)
Smith, Cullen
Smith, Cyril J.
Smith, Dale O.
Smith, David E.
Smith, David T.
Smith, Donald L.
Smith, Douglas
Smith, Douglas R.
Smith, Earl E. T.
Smith, Edward B.
Smith, Edward D.
Smith, Edwin V.
Smith, Elden T.
Smith, Eugene R.
Smith, Forrest M(oseley)
Smith, Frederic H., Jr.
Smith, F(rederick) G(eorge) Walton
Smith, George E.
Smith, Geo(rge) M(cClellan), Jr.
Smith, Glenn J.
Smith, Glenn L.
Smith, Gordon H.
Smith, Guy C.
Smith, Guy D.
Smith, Hale G.
Smith, Harlan J.
Smith, Harry
Smith, Harry M.
Smith, Hedrick L.
Smith, Herbert B.
Smith, Herbert W.
Smith, Hilton A.
Smith, Howard W.
Smith, Hubert W.
Smith, James A.
Smith, Jack G.
Smith, James C.
Smith, James M.
Smith, James R.
Smith, Jessie C.
Smith, J(ohn) B(ertie)
Smith, J(ohn) Denson
Smith, John H(enry)
Smith, John S.
Smith, J(oseph) C.
Smith, Kenneth M.
Smith, Lawrence W.
Smith, LeRoy V.
Smith, Leslie R.
Smith, Levering
Smith, Lloyd H.
Smith, (Charles) Louis
Smith, Luther A.
Smith, Lyman B(radford)
Smith, Marilu C.
Smith, Mary E.
Smith, Matthew D., Jr.
Smith, Mayo E.
Smith, McNeill
Smith, Merriman
Smith, Monroe W.
Smith, Moreland G.
Smith, Nelson
Smith, Norman C.
Smith, Paul C.
Smith, Peter G.
Smith, Richard B.
Smith R(ichard) K(nowles)
Smith, R(obert) Blackwell, Jr.
Smith, Robert H.
Smith, Robert J(ames)
Smith, Robert L.
Smith, Robert N.
Smith, Robert R.
Smith, Rufus B.
Smith, Rufus Z.
Smith, Russell J.
Smith, Selwyn D., Jr.
Smith, Stuart S.
Smith, Tad R.
Smith, T(homas) Lynn
Smith, Mrs. Turner E. (Lella Bunce)
Smith, Waldo E(dward)
Smith, Walter F.
Smith, Walter R.
Smith, Wilburn J., Jr.
Smith, Willard J.
Smith, William B.
Smith, William C.
Smith, William C.
Smith, William H.
Smith, William J.
Smith, William J.
Smith, William T.
Smith, Willis, Jr.
Smith, Willis B.
Smith, Willis E.
Smutz, Morton
Smyth, Philip
Snapp, Roy B.
Snavely, Brant R.
Snavely, Tipton R.
Sneed, Earl
Sneider, Richard L.
Snell, John L.
Snellgrove, Harold S.
Snipes, Wilson C.
Snowden, Frank M., Jr.
Snowden, Obed L.
Snowden, Robert G.
Snyder, Edward P.
Snyder, John W.
Snyder, Philip W.
Snyder, Robert M.
Snyder, Wahl J.
Sobel, Irvin
Sober, Sidney
Soday, Frank J(ohn)
Soedjatmoko
Sohl, Walter W., Jr.
Sokol, Sidney S.
Soldwedel, Bette J.
Solem, Delmar E.
Soler-Favale, Santiago C. S.
Solomon, Richard A.
Solomon, Robert
Solterer, Josef
Solverud, Truman
Somers, James J.
Somerville, Ormond
Sommerlatte, Karl E.
Sonenshein, Nathan
Sonfield, Robert L.
Sonnemann, Harry
Sonnenfeldt, Helmut
Sonnichsen, C(harles L(eland)
Sorenson, Herbert
Sorkin, Martin
Sottile, James, Jr.
Soule, Edgar C. H.
Southard, Frank A(llan)
Southerland, Louis F., Jr.
Southwick, Paul
Souvanlasy, Khamking
Sowell, O. James
Sowers, George F.
Sowers, Joseph C.
Spafford, John L.
Spain, Frank E.
Spain, James W.
Spann, William B., Jr.
Sparer, Phineas J.
Sparks, William J.
Sparrow, Herbert G.
Spatafora, Anthony F.
Spaugh, Rufus A.
Spaulding, Asa T.
Speakman, Edwin A.
Spear, Moncrieff J.
Spearmen, Walter S(mith), Jr.
Spears, Monroe K.
Spears, Robert W.
Spears, William D.
Speck, Marvin L.
Spector, Melbourne L.
Speight, Francis W.
Speirs, Mary
Spence, Harry M.
Spencer, Daniel L.
Spencer, Edgar W.
Spencer, George A.
Spencer, Harry C.
Spencer, Lee B.
Spencer, Samuel
Spencer, Terry W.
Spencer, William A.
Spengler, Joseph J.
Spengler, William F.
Sperling, Godfrey, Jr.
Spicer, George W.
Spicer, William M.
Spiers, Ronald I.
Spies, Emerson G.
Spilhaus, Athelstan
Spilman, Robert H.
Spindle, Richard B., III
Spingarn, Jerome H.
Spingarn, Stephen J.
Spiro, Robert H., Jr.
Spivack, Herbert D.
Spivack, Robert G.
Spivacke, Harold
Spivak, Alvin A.
Spivey, Herman E.
Sponsler, George C., III
Spragens, Thomas A.
Spragens, William H., Jr.
Sprague, Arthur C.
Sprague, Howard B.
Sprague, Irvine H.
Sprague, Robert O.
Springer, Charles E.
Springer, Stanley G.
Springsteen, George S., Jr.
Springer, Charles E.
Springer, Stanley G.
Springsteen, George S., Jr.
Sprowls, Joseph B., Jr.
Spruce, Everett F.
Sprunt, Alexander, Jr.
Sprunt, Douglas H(amilton)
Spurlock, James J.
Squire, Charles F.
Squirru, Rafael
Staacke, H. Fred
Stacey, John M.
Stadler, William L.
Stadtler, John W.
Stage, Thomas B.
Stahl, O(scar) Glenn
Stahlman, E. B., Jr.
Stair, Fred R., Jr.
Stakem, Thomas E., Jr.
Stalling, Bettin
Stallings, C(harles) Norman
Stallings, Frank H.
Stallings, Samuel J.
Stalter, Samuel E.
Stambaugh, John H.
Stamm, Gilbert G.
Stancil, James W.
Standeven, James W.
Stanford, Henry K.
Stangel, Wenzel L.
Stanger, Frank B.
Stanwick, Tad
Stanwix-Hay, Allen T.
Stapp, John P.
Starbird, Alfred D.
Stark, Jeremiah M.
Starling, James H.
Starnes, Julia B.
Starnes, Richard
Starr, Harold W.
Staton, Rocker T., Jr.
Staub, John F.
Stead, Eugene A., Jr.
Steadman, John M.
Steadman, Robert F(oster)
Stedman, John P.
Steel, Marshall T.
Steel, William C.
Steele, Allen M.
Steele, Frank S.
Steele, Horace
Steele, Jack
Steele, James H.
Steele, John L.
Steele, Westbrook
Steele, William O.
Steele, William T., Jr.
Steely, Will F.
Steen, Ralph W.
Steen, Sidney J.
Steere, David D.
Steeves, John M.
Stegenga, Preston J.
Steger, Meritt H.
Steger, William M.
Steglich, Winfred G(eorge)
Stein, Albert H.
Stein, Calvin W.
Stein, Herbert
Steinbach, Warren H.
Steincrohn, Peter J.
Steiner, Bernard S.
Steiner, Gilbert Y.
Steiner, Robert E., III
Steiner, Robert L.
Steinheimer, Roy L., Jr.
Steinhoff, Dan
Steininger, Fred H.
Steinmetz, Maurice
Stell, Lawrence I.
Stellari, Raymond F.
Stellings, Ernest G.
Stembler, John H.
Stempler, Jack L.
Stephan, A(nthony) Stephen
Stephan, Edward C.
Stephens, Jackson T.
Stephens, John C., Jr.
Stephens, Robert G., Jr.
Stephens, Roy M.
Stephens, Stanley G(eorge)
Stephenson, Raymond C.
Stern, Arthur C.
Stern, Edgar B., Jr.
Stern, Edith M.
Stern, John K.
Stern, Julius D.
Stern, Laurence M.
Stern, Philip M.
Sternberg, Daniel A.
Sterne, Augustus H.
Sterne, Mervyn H.
Sterne, Theodore E.
Sterner, James H.
Stetler, C. Joseph
Stetson, Nathaniel
Stevens, Boswell
Stevens, Francis B.
Stevens, George C., Jr.
Stevens, George N.
Stevens, Phineas
Stevens, Preston S.
Stevens, Richard K.
Stevens, Russell B(radford)
Stevenson, Albert H.
Stevenson, Elizabeth
Stevenson, Eric V. C.
Stevenson, Ian
Stevenson, Lionel
Stevenson, O. Roy
Stevenson, Robert E.
Stewart, Charles A.
Stewart, Harris B., Jr.
Stewart, Irvin
Stewart, James W., Jr.
Stewart, James W. H.
Stewart, Jefferson D., Jr.
Stewart, Robert
Stewart, Robert, Jr.
Stewart, Robert E.
Stewart, Robert M.
Stewart, Ross
Stewart, Samuel B.
Stewart, Thomas D.
Stewart, Ward
Stewart, W(ellington) (Buel)
Stewart, William D.
Stickel, Delford L.
Stickler, William H.
Stickley, John L.
Stidham, Wofford H.
Stiemke, Robert E.
Stier, Robert H(ighton)
Stiles, Kenneth
Still, Richard L.
Still, Richard R.
Stillwell, Bertram E.
Stillwell, Erle G.
Stilwell, James J.
Stimmel, Thomas S.
Stirling, Marion
Stoaks, DuVal
Stocker, Arthur F.
Stocking, Collis
Stockton, Gilchrist B.
Stockton, John R(obert)
Stockwell, Oliver P.
Stockwell, Richard E.
Stoessel, Walter J., Jr.
Stohl, Ralph N.
Stokes, Collin
Stokes, George A.
Stokes, Katharine M.
Stokes, Mack (Marion) Boyd
Stoldt, Clarence A.
Stollerman, Gene H.
Stoltzfus, William A., Jr.
Stone, Albert E., Jr.
Stone, Charles T.
Stone, Doris
Stone, Ferdinand F.
Stone, I. F. (Isidor Feinstein)
Stone, John O.
Stone, Leon
Stone, Mode L.
Stone, Paul T.
Stone, Sam P.
Stone, Walker
Stone, Williard E.
Stoneman, Walter G.
Stoner, James R.
Stoothoff, Everett O.
Stopher, Joseph E.
Stophlet, Donald V.
Storck, Roger L.
Storer, George B., Jr.
Storey, Frederick G(eorge)
Storey, Woodrow W.
Storke, Harry P.
Storrs, Robert W., III
Storrs, Thomas I.
Story, Bascom H.
Stoughton, Tom R.
Stout, Arthur W., Jr.
Stout, Hiram M.
Stout, Richard H.
Stovall, Franklin L.
Stover, James H.
Stover, Phil S., Jr.
Stow, Henry L.
Stow, Micollius N.
Stoy, John M(etzger)
Strachan, Paul A.
Straiton, Archie W.
Strand, K(aj) Aa(ge) (Gunnar)
Strange, William E.
Strassburg, Bernard
Stratman, George E.
Stratton, Arbon W.
Stratton, Everett F.
Stratton, James D.
Straumfjord, Jon V., Jr.
Straus, R. Peter
Straus, Robert
Strauss, Lewis L.
Strean, Bernard M.
Street, Clarence P.
Street, Thomas W.
Streeter, Donald C.
Streit, Clarence K.
Stretch, Lorena B.
Strevell, Wallace H.
Strickert, Roland R.
Strickland, William E.
Strickler, Thomas D.
Stringer, Henry D.
Stroh, Robert J.
Strong, Robert C.
Stroup, Russell C.
Stroupe, Henry S.
Strout, Richard L.
Strughold, Hubertus
Stuart, George R. C.
Stuart, Jesse H.
Stuart, Walter B., III
Stuart, William A.
Stubbeman, Frank D.
Stubblefield, Robert L.
Stubbs, Frank M.
Stubbs, Truett T.
Stuckey, Williamson S., Jr.
Stuckwisch, Clarence G.
Stuhlinger, Ernst
Stump, Felix B.
Sturc, Ernest
Styers, James H.
Styles, Paul L.
Suffridge, James A.
Suggs, John T.
Sugihara, Thomas T.
Suitor, Jesse H.
Sukati, Samuel T. M.
Sulaiman, Ali H.
Sullivan, Adele W.
Sullivan, Dabbs
Sullivan, Edward G.
Sullivan, Harold J.
Sullivan, James L.
Sullivan, John L.
Sullivan, John T.
Sullivan, Leonard
Sullivan, Leonor K. (Mrs. John B. Sullivan)
Sullivan, Mark, Jr.
Sullivan, Richard H.
Sullivan, William C.
Sulya, Louis L.
Summerford, Ben L.
Summers, Lionel M.
Sumners, Robert W.
Sunquist, James L.
Suojanen, Waino W.
Suratt, Samuel T.
Surface, Thomas J(ames)
Surles, Alexander D., Jr.
Surrey, Walter S.
Susong, Walter L.
Suss, Frederick T.
Sussex, James N.
Sussman, Jerry
Suter, Cary G.
Suter, Emanuel
Sutherland, James W., Jr.
Sutherland, Matthew R.
Sutherland, Robert L.
Sutherland, William A.
Sutherlin, Johnson B.
Suthon, Walter J., Jr.
Suttle, William W.
Sutton, David N.
Sutton, George M.
Sutton, Hirst
Sutton, Leonard v.
Sutton, Louis V.
Sutton, Reginald M.
Sutton, William J.
Suydam, Henry W., Jr.
Suzuki, Hideo
Swank, Emory C.
Swankin, David A.
Swantz, Alexander
Swatek, Edward J.
Swecker, John P.
Sweeney, J(ames) Shirley
Sweeney, Mary
Sweeney, William R.
Sweeny, Charles A.
Sweet, John H.
Sweigert, Ray L.
Swesnik, Robert M.
Swezey, Robert D.
Swick, Edgar H.
Swidler, Joseph C.
Swift, A(lbert) Ervine
Swift, Clifford J., Jr.
Swigart, Theodore E(arl)
Swihart, James W.
Swim, Allan L.

Swindell, Lewis H., III
Swindler, William F.
Swinford, John W.
Swink, Earl T.
Switosky, Joseph V.
Switzer, Mary E.
Sykes, Roosevelt
Symonds, Gardiner
Synan, Joseph A., Sr.

Tackman, Arthur L.
Tade, George T.
Taft, William H., III
Taishoff, Sol J.
Tait, Edward T.
Talbert, Samuel S.
Talbott, Francis L.
Talbott, Frank, Jr.
Talbott, Frank, III
Taliaferro, Edmund P., Jr.
Taliaferro, Paul E(verett)
Tallamy, Bertram D.
Talley, Bascom D., Jr.
Talley, Ruth G.
Talmage, Roy V.
Tamm, Quinn
Tanberg, Lawrence F.
Tandy, Charles D.
Tanguy, Charles R.
Tann, Beue
Tannenwald, Theodore, Jr.
Tanner, Eugene J.
Tape, Gerald F(rederick)
Tarbell, Dean S.
Tarrant, Paul
Tarver, William S.
Tasca, Henry J.
Taswell, Harold L. T.
Tate, Allen (John Orley)
Tate, Frederick W.
Tate, Mildred T.
Tate, Stonewall S.
Tatum, Finley W.
Tatum, Herbert M(adison)
Tatum, Samuel C.
Taub, Ben
Tauch, Waldine
Tavel, William S.
Taylor, Albert W.
Taylor, Alfred W.
Taylor, Amos E.
Taylor, Benjamin B., Jr.
Taylor, Beverly D.
Taylor, Charles A.
Taylor, Clyde W.
Taylor, David W. A.
Taylor, Donald F.
Taylor, Elliott H.
Taylor, Eugene C.
Taylor, Garland F(orbes)
Taylor, Harold R.
Taylor, Harry G.
Taylor, Harvey G.
Taylor, Henry H., Jr.
Taylor, Hobart, Jr.
Taylor, Irby N.
Taylor, Isaac M.
Taylor, Ivan E.
Taylor, Jay
Taylor, John F.
Taylor, Joseph H.
Taylor, Joseph R.
Taylor, J(oshua) Eugene
Taylor, Lauriston S(ale)
Taylor, Maxwell D.
Taylor, Peter H.
Taylor, Prentiss
Taylor, Robert E.
Taylor, Robert L.
Taylor, Robert P.
Taylor, Rufus L.
Taylor, Thomas K.
Taylor, Vernon F.
Taylor, William J.
Tazi, Abderrahman
Teague, Robert S.
Teal, Gordon K.
Tebeau, Charlton W.
Tedards, Rufus C.
Telesca, Francis E.
Telford, Ira R.
Telkes, Maria
Tellepsen, Howard T.
Telles, Raymond L., Jr.
Temple, Futrelle L.
Temple, William B.
Templeton, Arleigh B.
Templin, Lucinda d.
Tennison, Charles W.
TERHorst, Jerald F.
Terhune, Charles H., Jr.
Terrel, Charles L.
Terrell, Arthur P.
Terrell, Lake E., Jr.
Terrell, Tol
Terretta, Paul
Terry, Raymond V.
Terzick, Peter E.
Tesoro, George A.
Tesseneer, Ralph A., Jr.
Teverbaugh, Harold G.
Thach, John S.
Thacher, Nicholas G.
Thackery, Russell I.
Thaler, Alwin
Thaler, William J.
Thalimer, William B(lum), Jr.
Tharin, Frank C.
Thaxton, James R.
Thaxton, Leslie B.
Thayer, Robert H.
Thayer, William P.
Theis, Frank V.
Theis, J(ohn) William
Therrel, Catchings
Thigpen, Charles C.
Thigpen, Richard E.
Thistlethwaite, Donald L.
Thom, Corcoran, Jr.
Thomas, Andrew J.
Thomas, Arthur E.
Thomas, Bryan R., Jr.
Thomas, C. A.
Thomas, Carla
Thomas, C(larence) D(elmar)
Thomas, David D.
Thomas, Donald S.
Thomas, Earl (Tilman)
Thomas, Frank A., Jr.
Thomas, Gerald W.
Thomas, Helen A.
Thomas, Henry C.
Thomas, Jack E.
Thomas, Jesse W.
Thomas, John N.
Thomas, J(ohn) Warrick
Thomas, Joseph A.
Thomas, Joyce K.
Thomas, Llewellyn H.
Thomas, Marion B.
Thomas, Orville C.
Thomas, Payne E. L.
Thomas, Robert C.
Thomas, Robert E.
Thomas, Roderic B(ruce)
Thomas, William J.
Thomason, James R.
Thompson, Beverley V., Jr.
Thompson, Carey C.
Thompson, Charles C.
Thompson, Charlotte A.
Thompson, Edwin B.
Thompson, Ernest T.
Thompson, Fletcher
Thompson, Floyd L.
Thompson, Graves H.
Thompson, H. Raybourne
Thompson, J. Neils
Thompson, James A.
Thompson, James C.
Thompson, James E.
Thompson, John A(rchie)
Thompson, John M.
Thompson, Kenneth H(erman)
Thompson, Lawrence S.
Thompson, Llewellyn E., Jr.
Thompson, Lorin A., Jr.
Thompson, Milton J.
Thompson, Richard H., Jr.
Thompson, Robert A.
Thompson, Seton H.
Thompson, Standish F.
Thompson, Thomas E.
Thompson, William B., Jr.
Thompson, William R.
Thompson, William T., Jr.
Thompson, William V.
Thompson, Yewell R.
Thomsen, Carl J.
Thomsen, Wells H.
Thomson, James R., Jr.
Thomson, Lewis C.
Thornal, Benjamin C.
Thorndike, Charles J. (Chuck)
Thorne, Henry G., Jr.
Thorne, James R.
Thorne, Thomas E.
Thorning, Joseph F.
Thornley, Fant H.
Thornton, J. L.
Thornton, Spencer P.
Thornton, William N., Jr.
Thornton, Winfred L.
Thorpe, Merle Jr.
Thorsen, Thomas W.
Thorson, Phillip (Thorwald)
Thorsteinsson, Petur
Threadgill, Walter D.
Thresher, Brainerd A.
Thrift, Charles T., Jr.
Throckmorton, John L.
Throop, Allen E.
Thrower, Randolph W.
Thunberg, Penelope H.
Thurman, Henry L., Jr.
Thurman, William G.
Thurman, William T.
Thurston, Carl G.
Thurston, Elliott L.
Thurston, James N.
Thweatt, C. Harold
Tibbitts, Clark
Tietjens, Norman O.
Tihany, Leslie C.
Tilford, Henry J.
Tilford, John E., Jr.
Tiller, Carl W(illiam)
Tiller, Frank M.
Tillman, Sadie W. (Mrs. J. Fount)
Tillson, John C. F. III
Timanus, Hall E., Sr.
Timberg, Sigmund
Timberlake, Clare H.
Timm, Tyrus R.
Timmermann, John R.
Timmons, Bascom N.
Timmons, William E.
Tindall, George B.
Tinoco, Luis D.
Tinsely, Thomas A.
Tinsely, Willa V.
Tinstman, Robert M.
Tipler, Frank J.
Tipton, Samuel R.
Tischer, Robert G.
Tobey, Frank A.
Tobin, Irwin M.
Tobler, John H.
Tobriner, Walter N.
Tocker, Phillip
Todd, Alexander C., Jr.
Todd, Anderson
Todd, Lewis P.
Todman, Terence A.
Toland, Henry S.
Toland, William G.
Tolar, Thomas S.
Tolbert, Charles M.
Tolbert, Stokes M.
Toledano, Ralph d.
Toler, John L.
Tolk, Roy
Toll, Daniel R.
Tollett, Kenneth S.
Tollett, Raymond L.
Tolson, Hillory A.
Tomes, George K.
Tomlin, Daniel O.
Thompkins, Ellsworth
Tompkins, Henry B.
Tompkins, Rathvon M.
Tompsett, Ralph
Toner, Joseph S.
Tonks, Raymond M.
Toombs, Kenneth E.
Topazio, Virgil W.
Toppel, George
Torbert, Horace G(ates), Jr.
Torkanowsky, Werner
Torn, Elmore R.
Toro-Goyco, Efrain
Torrance, Ellis P.
Torrence, Andrew P.
Torrey, Volta W.
Tors, Ivan
Tosch, Charles A., Jr.
Tosteson, Daniel C.
Totten, Arthur I., Jr.
Totten, James W.
Totter, John R.
Toulouse, Robert B.
Tousey, Richard
Toussaint, Paul A.
Touster, Oscar
Tower, Marcus R.
Towers, Charles D.,Jr.
Towery, Twyman L.
Towill, John B.
Towner, Alonzo A.
Townley, Finos J.
Townsend, Francis A.
Townsend, Francis G.
Townsend, Lee H.
Townsend, Shepard V.
Toy, Henry, Jr.
Trabue, Charles C., Jr.
Trace, John R.
Tracht, Lloyd V(otaw)
Tracy, Don
Tracy, Warren F.
Tragen, Irving G.
Trager, George L(eonard)
Train, Robert
Trammell, George T.
Trautman, John A.
Travell, Janet G. (Mrs. John W. G. Powell)
Traxler, Arthur E(dwin)
Traynor, Harry S.
Treadwell, Carleton R.
Treff, Theodore R.
Trelease, Allen W.
Trelogan, Harry C(hester)
Tremaine, Marie
Tremmel, Ernest B.
Tremonti, Joseph B.
Trenam, John J.
Trescott, Paul H.
Tretick, Stanley
Trevillian, Wallace D.
Tribble, Hal
Trice, Ben
Trice, J. Mark
Trice, William E.
Triebe, Edward J(ames)
Trimble, George S.
Trimble, Paul E.
Trimble, Vance H.
Troester, Carl A., Jr.
Trohan, Walter
Trombley, Kenneth E.
Trott, Norman L.
Trotter, Charles L.
Trotter, Samuel E.
Troup, Cornelius V.
Trout, Walter W.
Troutman, Henry B.
Troutman, Robert B(attey)
Trouyet, Carlos
Trudeau, Arthur G.
Trued, Merlyn N.
Trueheart, William C(lyde)
Trueman, William H.
Truesdail, John H.
Truesdell, Frederick D.
Truesdell, Leonard C.
Truett, Fred M.
Trueworthy, Orson W.
Truitt, James M.
Truitt, Robert W.
Trytten, M(erriam) H(artwick)
Tsanoff, Radoslav A.
Tsutsui, Minoru
Tubb, Thomas J.
Tuck, William M.
Tucker, John H., Jr.
Tucker, Morrison G.
Tucker, Robert C.
Tucker, William B(oose)
Tucker, William T.
Tucker, Willis C.
Tuckson, Coleman R.
Tuepker, D. J.
Tufty, Esther V. W.
Tuggle, Kenneth H.
Tugman, Forrest E.
Tulloch, George S.
Tullos, John B.
Tully, Andrew F., Jr.
Tumilty, Howard T(insley)
Tunison, Abram V.
Turlington, Edgar L., Jr.
Turman, James A.
Turman, John P.
Turman, Solon B.
Turnbull, Willard J.
Turner, (Henry) Arlin
Turner, Billie L.
Turner, Bolon B.
Turner, Bridges A.
Turner, Charles W.
Turner, Claude G.
Turner, Don A.
Turner, Edward F., Jr.
Turner, E(dwin) Archer
Turner, Etter M.
Turner, Francis C.
Turner, George L.
Turner, Henry H.
Turner, Herbert D.
Turner, James G.
Turner, John W.
Turner, Leland S.
Turner, Norfleet
Turner, Othel D.
Turner, Richard B.
Turner, William W.
Turney, John R.
Turney-High, Harry H.
Turpin, Robert M.
Turpin, William P.
Tuthill, John B.
Tuttle, Elbert P.
Tuttle, John C.
Tuttle, Lee F.
Tuttle, Magruder H.
Tuve, Merle A.
Twining, Nathan F.
Twitty, Thomas E(skridge)
Tyler, David B(ernard)
Tyler, James H., III
Tyler, Max E.
Tyler, Paul R.
Tyler, William R.
Tyree, David M.
Tyree, Sheppard Y., Jr.
Tyrer, John L.
Tyson, Remer H., Jr.
Tyson, William S(herrod)

Uhl, Alexander H.
Uhrig, Robert E.
Ulich, Willie L.
Ulmer, Herman
Ulmer, Shirley S.
Ulrich, Floyd E.
Umstattd, James G.
Underwood, Milton R.
Underwood, Willis O.
Unger, Sherman E.
Unna, Warren W.
Unruh, Henry C.
Upchurch, Vernon H.
Upleger, Arthur C(hristian)
Upshaw, Preston C.
Upson, Stephen L.
Upton, Arvin E(dward)
Upton, Eldon C., Jr.
Urbanovsky, Elo J.
Uretz, Lester R.
Urmey, Mary L. S.
Usery, Willie J., Jr.
Utley, Freda
Utterback, Martha
Uzzell, William E.

Vadakin, James C.
Vagtborg, Harold
Valazquez, Gonzalo
Valdes, Adolfo
Valdes, Alfonso
Vale, William G.
Valentine, Charles S.
Valeo, Francis R.
Valeriani, Richard G.
Van Arsdall, Robert A.
Van Artsdalen, Ervin R.
Van Buren, Martin L.
van Campenhout, Andre J. L.
Van Caspel, Venita W.
Vance, John K.
Vandemark, Robert G.
Vandenbosch, Amry
Van Derbur, Charles A.
Van der Heuvel, Gerry B.
Van Der Slice, Austin
Vandervoort, Benjamin H.
Van Dusen, Richard C.
Van Dyke, William L., Jr.
Van Evera, Benjamin D.
Van Fleet, D(ick) S(cott)
Van Fleet, James A.
Van Houweling, Cornelius D.
Van Jackson, Wallace M.
VanKrevelen, Alice
Van Mol, Louis J., Sr.
Vannoy, Frank W.
van Overbeek, Johannes
van Pelt, John V., 3d
VanPoole, Thomas B., Jr.
Van Royen, William
Van Ryzin, William J.
Van Sant, Daniel M.
Van Vactor, David
Van Wagenen, Richard W.
Van Winkle, Matthew
Van Zandt, John P.
Van Zandt, Lydia
Vardaman, John W.
Varnedoe, Samuel L.
Vaughan, John G., Jr.
Vaughan, Joseph L.
Vaughey, William M.
Vaughn, James M.
Vaught, Jack T.
Vavala, Domenic A.
Veatch, Ellis H.
Veatch, Ralph W(ilson)
Veletsos, Anestis S.
Venn, Grant
Vereen, William C., Jr.
Verlander, Joseph M.
Verner, Elizabeth O.
Verner, Hugh D.
Verner, James M.
Vernon, Robert O.
Vesecky, Stephen
Vestal, Donald M., Jr.
Vestal, Lucian L.
Vestal, Paul A.
Veth, Kenneth L.
Vickery, Edward D.
Vickery, Katherine
Vicroy, Frank M.
Vigderman, Alfred G.
Viglione, Amy E.
Vigness, David M.
Villarreal, Carlos C.
Villarreal, Jesse J.
Vincent, Harry F.
Vining, (Daniel) Rutledge
Vinson, Bailie W.
Vinson, Bryant F.
Vinson, Fred M., Jr.
Vinzant, Carey T.
Viorst, Milton
Virden, Frank
Vitols, Mintauts M.
Vliet, Rollin D.
Vogel, Harold A.
Vogel, Herbert D.
Vogel, Leroy
Vogt, John W., Jr.
Voigt, Robert N.
Vokes, Harold E.
Volpe, Erminio P.
Volpe, John A.
Volpitto, Perry P.
Volz, Marlin M(ilto)
vom Baur, Francis T.
vom Hofe, Ernst A. L.
Von Arx, Joseph A.
Von Canon, Fred
von Herberg, Mary P.
Vonk, Paul K.
Von Kann, Clifton F.
von Krusenstiern, Alfred
Voorhees, Alan M.
Voorhees, Tracy S.
Voorhis, Harry M.
Voris, Frank B.
Voris, LeRoy
Voskuyl, Roger J.
Voss, Elbert
Vrenios, Anastasios

Wachs, Fred B.
Waddell, St. John
Wade, Albert G., II
Wade, Charles B., Jr.
Wade, F(ranklin) Alton
Wade, Horace M.
Wade, John W(ebster)
Wade, Thomas L., Jr.
Wadlington, Walter J., III
Wadsworth, James J.
Wadsworth, Philip A.
Waechter, Arthur J., Jr.
Wagenheim, Michael B.
Wagner, Carruth J.
Wagner, John P.
Wagner, Robert R.
Wagner, William F.
Wagstaff, Robert M.
Wahl, John H., Jr.
Wahl, Richard A.
Wahrhaftig Felix S.
Wainer, David S., Sr.
Wainhouse, David W.
Wakeham, Helmut R. R.
Wakeland, Henry H.
Wakelin, James H., Jr.
Wald, Haskell P.
Walden, James T.
Waldrop, Frank C.
Waldschmitt, Joseph A.
Walker, Agesilaus W., Jr.
Walker, Andrew J.
Walker, Antonio M.
Walker, Charles E.
Walker, Dean E.
Walker, Edwin A.
Walker, Edwin R.
Walker, Granville T.
Walker, Henry G.
Walker, John B.
Walker, John H.
Walker, J(ohn) Leonard
Walker, John L(uther)
Walker, John M.
Walker, John R.
Walker, Margaret
Walker, Oliver L.
Walker, Oliver M.
Walker, Richard L.
Walker, Robert V.
Walker, Ross H.
Walker, Thomas J., III
Walker, Wesley M.
Walker, William W.
Wall, Frederick T.
Wall, Maurice S.
Wall, William J.
Wallace, Alexander D.
Wallace, Anthony F. C.
Wallace, C. M. Jr.
Wallace, George R.
Wallace, Howard K.
Wallace, Mac D.
Wallace, Travis T.
Wallace, Wayne P.
Walleigh, Robert S.
Waller, (John) Keith
Waller, William
Wallin, Harry N.
Wallner, Woodruff
Wallop, (John) Douglass 3d
Walrath, Laurence K.
Walser, William D.

Walsh, James A
Walsh, James L.
Walsh, John E.
Walsh, Walter W.
Walsh, William B.
Walshe, Woollen H.
Walske, M(ax) Carl, Jr.
Walt, Lewis W.
Walter, George R.
Walter, James W.
Walters, Geoffrey K.
Walters, George M.
Walters, John B., Jr.
Walters, Lawrence M.
Walters, Richard L., Jr.
Walters, Roy N.
Walther, Carl Hugo
Walton, Charles S., Jr.
Walton, Miller
Walton, William
Walvoord, John F.
Wannamaker, William W., Jr.
Wansley, Hal B.
Ward, Alfred D.
Ward, David E.
Ward, Henry D.
Ward, Norvell G.
Ward, Paul L.
Ward, Paul W.
Ward, Robert
Ward, Robert S.
Ward, Thomas G(reydon)
Ward, Virgil S.
Ward, Walter L., Jr.
Ward, William S.
Wardlaw, Frank H., Jr.
Wardlaw, William C., Jr.
Wardle, Robert, Jr.
Wardropper, Bruce W.
Ward-Smith, Kenneth
Ware, Caroline F.(Mrs. Gardiner C. Means)
Ware, Henry H., Jr.
Ware, Jack
Warfel, Harry R.
Warga, Mary E(lizabeth)
Warhover, Robert E.
Warlick, Wilson
Warner, Albert L.
Warner, Arthur E.
Warner, C(harles) A(lbert)
Warner, Harold C.
Warner, Jack W.
Warner, James P.
Warnke, Paul C.
Warnock, William S.
Warren, Eva W.
Warren, Harold O(strander), Jr.
Warren, Katherine
Warren, Lucian C.
Warren, Nina P. M. (Mrs. Earl Warren)
Warren, Robert H.
Warren, W. Dean
Warren, Willis B.
Warthers, Mark
Wartman, William B.
Warwick, Herbert S., Jr.
Washburn, Abbott M.
Washburn, A(lbert) L(incoln)
Washburn, Wilcomb E.
Wasmuth, Thomas C.
Watanabe, Takeshl
Waterman, Jerome A(aron)
Waters, Herbert J.
Waters, Kenneth L.
Waters, Odale D., Jr.
Waters, William H., Jr.
Watkins, Daniel E.
Watkins, David A.
Watkins, Gustav M.
Watkins, Henry V.
Watkins, Jerry W.
Watkins, Levi
Watkins, Mark H.
Watkins, Ralph J.
Watkins, Thomas F.
Watrous, Livingston D.
Watson, Albert, II
Watson, Allan J., Jr.
Watson, Donald S.
Watson, James E.
Watson, Justin T.
Watson, Kenneth N.
Watson, Max P.
Watson, Richard L., Jr.
Watson, Robert C.
Watson, Willard O.
Watt, James
Watt, Ray A.
Watt, William J.
Watters, Frank C(arleton)
Watterson, Joseph
Watts, James W.
Watts, John A(ugustus)

Watts, John C.
Watts, Olin E(thredge)
Watts, Otto O(live)
Watts, Stanley S.
Watzek, Peter F(icke)
Wauchope, Robert
Wayland, Russell G., Jr.
Waymouth, William A.
Weakley, Charles E.
Wear, Pat W.
Weatherbee, Artemus E.
Weathers, Carroll W.
Weathersby, William H.
Weaver, Charles H.
Weaver, Charles S.
Weaver, Earl W.
Weaver, Galbraith M.
Weaver, Herbert
Weaver, James H.
Weaver, Narvin B.
Weaver, Warren E.
Weaver, William C., Jr.
Webb, Charles A.
Webb, Clarence H.
Webb, David A.
Webb, George C.
Webb, Grady, Jr.
Webb, Harry C.
Webb, James P.
Webb, James W.
Webb, John M.
Webb, William E., Jr.
Webb, Wilse B.
Weber, Arnold R.
Weber, C(harles) Swan
Weber, Eugene W(illiam)
Weber, Paul
Webster, Gilbert T.
Webster, Lee D.
Webster, Luther D., Jr.
Webster, Reginald N.
Wedel, Cynthia C.
Wedel, Waldo R(udolph)
Wedler, Frederick C. O.
Weedon, William S.
Weeks, George C.
Weeks, Robert H.
Weens, Heinz S.
Weerasinghe, Oliver
Weersing, Marc C.
Wehr, Allan G.
Wehrli, Robert L.
Weidner, Hermann K.
Weimer, Rae O.
Weinberg, Alvin M.
Weinberger, Caspar W.
Weinel, John P.
Weiner, Arthur E.
Weingarten Bernard L.
Weinmann, John G.
Weinstein, Milton N.
Weinstein, Samuel M(ilton)
Weintal, Edward
Weintraub, Joseph
Weir, Donald W.
Weir, Milton N.
Weisert, John J.
Weisl, Edwin L., Jr.
Weismiller, Edward R.
Weisner, Maurice F.
Weiss, Martin G.
Weiss, Milton
Weiss, Paul
Weiss, Richard A(lexander)
Weiss, Seymour
Weiss, Seymour
Weitzel, Frank H.
Weitzell, Everett C.
Weitzenfeld, Daniel K.
Welch, Ernest R.
Welch, Felix P.
Welch, Frank J.
Welch, James T.
Welch, John A.
Weld, William E., Jr.
Welham, Walter
Wellborn, Alfred T.
Wellman, Harvey R.
Wellons, Alfred E.
Wells, Everett F.
Wells, James E.
Wells, Joel R.
Wells, Leonard N. D., Jr.
Wells, Linton
Wells, Maxwell W.
Wells, William C.
Wells, William C., Jr.
Welsch, Glenn A.
Welsh, J(ohn) Robert
Welsh, Peter C.
Welsh, Wiley A.
Welsh, William J.
Wemyss, William H.
Wende, Ernest A.
Wenger, Don S.
Wengert, Norman I.
Wernert, John J., Jr.

Werthan, Mary J. (Mrs. Albert Werthan)
Wesley, Charles H.
Wessel, Carl J.
Wessenauer, Gabriel O.
West, Arthur L., Jr.
West, Charles R.
West, Elmer G.
West, Felton
West, Harold D.
West, James W.
West, Philip W.
West, Robert H.
West, W(arren) Reed
Westerfield, Samuel Z., Jr.
Western, Forrest
Westfall, Jonathan J(ackson)
Westmoreland, William C.
Westphal, William H.
Wetherald, Charles E.
Wetherby, Lawrence W(inchester)
Wetmore, Alexander
Wetzel, Harold E.
Weyland, Frederick C.
Weyerhaeuser, Vivian O. (Mrs. Frederick K. Weyerhaeuser)
Weymouth, Ralph
Whalen, Richard J.
Whaley, W(illiam) Gordon
Whan, Forest L.
Wharton, Hunter P.
Whatley, Brown L.
Whayne, Tom F.
Whealy, Roger D.
Wheat, Francis M.
Wheat, Tom H.
Wheat, Willis J.
Wheeler, Earle G.
Wheeler, Edward K.
Wheeler, Harman E.
Wheeler, Henry P., Jr.
Wheeler, John D.
Wheeler, John H.
Wheeler, John P., Jr.
Wheeler, Kenneth R.
Wheeler, Raymond M.
Wheeler, Roger M.
Wheeler, T(owson) Ames
Wheeler, Warren E.
Wheelock, John N.
Wheless, N(icholas) Hobson
Whiddon, Frederick P.
Whitaker, Jack E., Sr.
Whitaker, Joe R.
Whitaker, John C.
Whitcomb, Gail
White, Barbara M.
White, Bruce W.
White, Chester W., Jr.
White, Eli G., Sr.
White, Ellison F.
White, Frederick R.
White, George H.
White, Goodrich C.
White, Gordon E.
White, J. H.
White, J. Olin
White, James D.
White, Jean M.
White, Jesse A.
White, Joseph B.
White, Lewis L.
White, Mastin G.
White, Reginald P.
White, Rollie H., Jr.
White, Travis A.
White, Walter S(tanley)
White, Warren T.
White, William D.
White, William E.
White, William R.
White, Wyndham K.
Whitehair, Francis P.
Whitehead, A(sa) Carter
Whitehead, Don
Whitehouse, Albert
Whitehurst, John D.
Whiteman, Marjorie M.
Whitener, Basil (Lee)
Whiting, Albert N.
Whitley, Wyatt C.
Whitlock, Douglas
Whitman, Marcus
Whitman, Reginald N.
Whitman, William M.
Whitman, W(illiam) Tate
Whitmer, Charles A.
Whitmore, Coby (Maxwell Coburn Whitmore)
Whitmore, Frank C., Jr.
Whitmore, John E.
Whitnack, Doris S.
Whitney, Robert S.
Whitsett, Wesley G.

Whitmore, (Edward) Reed, II
Whitten, Dolphus, Jr.
Whitten, Leslie H., Jr.
Whittenburg, Samuel B.
Whittier, Charles T.
Whittington, Dorsey
Whittington, Marvin E.
Whittle, Charles E., Jr.
Whyburn, William M.
Whyte, James P., Jr.
Whyte, William G.
Wickens, Aryness J.
Wicker, John J., Jr.
Wicker, Thomas G.
Wickham, Kenneth G.
Wicks, C(harles) Beaumont
Wiegmann, Fred H.
Wienefeld, Robert H.
Wiener, Samuel G(ross)
Wiener, William B.
Wieseman, Frederick L.
Wiggins, Archibald L. M.
Wiggins, James W.
Wiggins, Walter S.
Wigley, Willard R.
Wilber, Inez E(dith)
Wibur, Cornelia B.
Wilburn, E. Thomas
Wilcox, Francis O.
Wilcox, Walter W.
Wilder, James S., Jr.
Wiles, C(harles) Preston
Wiley, Autrey N.
Wiley, Bell I.
Wiley, William H.
Wiley, William L.
Wilgus, A(lva) Curtis
Wilhelmi, Alfred E.
Wilhoit, James C., Jr.
Wilken, David
Wilkens, Harold L.
Wilkins, George F.
Wilkins, George T.
Wilkins, Robert B.
Wilkinson, J(ames) Harvie, Jr.
Wilkinson, John B.
Wilkinson, Vernon L.
Will, John
Willard, William R.
Willcox, Alfred B.
Willens, Howard P.
Willey, Robert H.
Willi, George
Williams, Alfred H.
Williams, Arthur M., Jr.
Williams, Ashbel C.
Williams, Charles L., Jr.
Williams, Charles P.
Williams, Charles W.
Williams, Cratis D.
Williams, David R., Jr.
Williams, Donald G.
Williams, Douglas E.
Williams, Edward A.
Williams, Edwin G.
Williams, Ernest B., Jr.
Williams, Fielding L.
Williams, Franklin B., Jr.
Williams, George G.
Williams, George M.
Williams, George R., Jr.
Williams, Godwin, Jr.
Williams, Gordon C.
Williams, Harold
Williams, H(enry) Franklin
Williams, Hiram D.
Williams, Jesse W.
Williams, John C.
Williams, John C.
Williams, John F.
Williams, John H.
Williams, John T.
Williams, Joseph J., Jr.
Williams, Judson F.
Williams, Laurens
Williams, Lewis E(benezer)
Williams, Lewis K.
Williams, Malcolm D.
Williams, Marjorie J.
Williams, Maurice J.
Williams, Melvin J(ohn)
Williams, Murat W.
Williams, Preston B.
Williams, Raymond E.
Williams, Reginald L.
Williams, Robert C.
Williams, Robert M.
Williams, Samuel T.
Williams, Stanley B.
Williams, T. Harry
Williams, Walter J.
Williams, Willard F.
Williams, William R.
Williams, William T., Jr.
Williams, Wilson C.

Williamson, Dan H.
Williamson, John D.
Williams, Rene d. V.
Willig, Winston A.
Willingham, Harris E.
Willis, George H.
Willis, Hubert T.
Willis, William H.
Willman, Marilyn D.
Willocks, Robert M.
Wills, Jesse E.
Willson, James H.
Wilmer, Richard H.
Wilner, Morton H.
Wilsdorf, Heinz G. F.
Wilson, Allan M.
Wilson, Allen B.
Wilson, Benjamin A.
Wilson, Charles J., Jr.
Wilson, Charles M.
Wilson, Charles V.
Wilson, C(harles) W(illiams), Jr.
Wilson, Christopher L(umley)
Wilson, Claude L.
Wilson, Coyt T.
Wilson, David B.
Wilson, Donald E.
Wilson, Edward F.
Wilson, Edwin G.
Wilson, Everett K.
Wilson, F(red) Talbott
Wilson, Fred V.
Wilson, George
Wilson, George A.
Wilson, George D.
Wilson, Harwell
Wilson, James L.
Wilson, John B.
Wilson, John B(yron)
Wilson, John C(ullum)
Wilson, John J.
Wilson, Kemmons
Wilson, Leonard S.
Wilson, Logan
Wilson, Malcolm E., Jr.
Wilson, M(athew) Kent
Wilson, Milton
Wilson, R. Baxter
Wilson, Ralph E.
Wilson, Richard L.
Wilson, Robert A.
Wilson, Roy K.
Wilson, Thomas F.
Wilson, Thomas W.
Wilson, Walter K., Jr.
Wilson, Willard M(artin)
Wilson, William H.
Wilson, William L.
Wilson, Winston P., Jr.
Wilson, Paxton M.
Wilt, Paxton M.
Wiman, David W.
Wimberly, Harrington
Wimberly, John H.
Wimer, Arthur G., Jr.
Windham, Charles (Wyatt)
Windsor, H. R. H., The Duke of (Edward Albert Christian George Andrew Patrick David)
Winesanker, Michael M.
Wingfield, Edmund D.
Winn, Albert C.
Winn, Edward B.
Winnacker, Rudolph A(ugust)
Winner, Percy
Winship, Charles T.
Winship, Henry D.
Winslow, Francis E.
Winstead, Raymond L.
Winstead, Samuel G.
Winston, Carey
Winston, Ellen
Winston, James O., Jr.
Winston, Thomas J., Jr.
Winter, Harvey J.
Winter, William E.
Winters, John M., Jr.
Winters, John S.
Winzler, Richard J.
Wirth, Conrad L.
Wirtz, William W.
Wise, George H.
Wise, John H.
Wise, Louis N.
Wise, Parker S.
Wise, Sherwood W.
Wise, Watson W.
Wisenbaker, Thomas C.
Wisner, Elizabeth
Wissemann, Hilmer J.
Withers, Charles D.
Witherspoon, Gibson B.
Witherspoon, Ralph L.
Withrow, Frank B., Jr.

Witman, William, II
Witt, James A.
Witte, Ernest F.
Witten, Carroll L.
Witten, George W. B. (George Witten)
Witten, Harold B.
Wogan, Daniel S.
Wolcott, Fred W.
Wold, Robert P.
Wolf, Stewart G., Jr.
Wolfbein, Seymour L.
Wolfe, Deborah C. P.
Wolfe, Herbert E.
Wolfe, John B(ascom)
Wolfe, William G.
Wolff, Lester L.
Wolff, Reinhold P.
Wolfle, Dael (Lee)
Wolfson, Mitchell
Woll, Joseph A.
Wollan, Ernest O.
Wollenberg, J. Roger
Wollstadt, Paul
Wolper, Marshall
Woltz, Charles K.
Wolverton, Joe B.
Womack, Nathan A.
Womble, Bunyan S.
Wonderley, Anthony W.
Wong, Lin K.
Wood, Ann P(earson)
Wood, Frank B.
Wood, John E., III
Wood, John W. H.
Wood, Laurence I.
Wood, Richard H.
Wood, Richardson K.
Wood, Thomas J.
Woodward, William T., Jr.
Woodbury, Murray C.
Woodhall, Barnes
Woodliff, George F.
Woodrow, Robert H., Jr.
Woods, Frederic J.
Woods, Granville C.
Woods, Leon E.
Woods, William G.
Woods, William S. D.
Woods, William S.
Woodson, Charles S.
Woodson, Warren B.
Woodward, Albert Y.
Woodward, Edward R.
Woodward, Ernest, II
Woodward, Felix G.
Woodward, Fielden
Woodward, Lester A.
Woodward, Lewis K., Jr.
Woodward, Madison T., Jr.
Woodworth, Norval W.
Woody, G. Ray
Woolridge, Charles W.
Wooley, J. B.
Woolf, Jack R.
Woolnough, James K.
Woolsey, Samuel M.
Wooten, Benjamin H.
Worcester, Willis G.
Worden, George M.
Work, Martin H.
Worley, Evelyn L.
Worrell, Lawson, Jr.
Wortham, Gus S.
Wortham, John L.
Worthington, William F.
Worthy, Edmund H.
Wortzel, Arthur I.
Wrape, James W.
Wray, Robert C.
Wright, Benjamin F.
Wright, Charles A.
Wright, Douglas G.
Wright, Ernest L.
Wright, Floyd V.
Wright, Floyd V.
Wright, Hamilton W.
Wright, James E.
Wright, John J(oseph)
Wright, John P.
Wright, Louis B.
Wright, Nathalla
Wright, Samuel L.
Wright, Thomas K.
Wright, W. Marshall
Wright, Willard H(ull)
Wrightsman, Charles B.
Wulfman, Boysie A.
Wulfman, Joseph C.
Wyatt, De Marquis D.
Wyatt, Joseph P.
Wyatt, O. S., Jr.
Wyatt, William H.
Wyckoff, Peter H.
Wydler, John W.
Wyeth, Marion S.
Wyker, John W., Jr.
Wylie, Clarence R., Jr.

Wyanhoff, Louis A.
Wynn, Earl (Raymond)
Wynn, Sproesser
Wynne, Angus G., Jr.
Wynne, Toddie L., Jr.
Wyss, Orville

Yabroff, Arthur
Yager, Joseph A., Jr.
Yaghjian, Edmund
Yameogo, Antoine W.
Yancey, Benjamin W.
Yancey, Clarence L.
Yancey, Patrick H.
Yancey, Robert E.
Yankee, Richard M.
Yarborough, William P.
Yarbrough, James R.
Yates, Chalmers B.
Yater, Wallace M.
Yater, Wallace M.
Yates, Donald N.
Yates, Gerard F.
Yates, Kyle M.
Yeagley, J. Walter
Yeargan, Gordon S.
Yearley, Alexander IV
Yeilding, Brooks, III
Yeilding, Frank B., Jr.
Yenawine, Wayne S.
Yerkes, David N.
Yingling, Doris B.
Ylvisaker, Lenvik
Yochelson, Leon
Yocum, J(ack) H(arlan)
Yoder, Fred R.
Yoder, Hatten S., Jr.
Yoe, Harry W.
Yon, Joseph L.
York, E. Travis, Jr.
York, Robert
Yost, F. Randolph
Yost, Francis L.
Youel, Kenneth
Young, Arthur C.
Young, Arthur W.
Young, Burton O.
Young, Calvin L.
Young, Dana
Young, Franklin W.
Young, Henry B.
Young, James H.
Young, John D.
Young, Kenneth E.
Young, Louise M. (Mrs. Ralph A. Young)
Young, Raymond A.
Young, Robert L.
Young, Samuel D.
Young, Samuel R.
Young, Thomas D.
Young, William T., Jr.
Youngblood, Ovid
Youngdahl, Luther W.
Youngdale, Carl A.
Younger, Edward E.
Yount, Ernest H., Jr.
Yriart, Juan F.
Yudkin, Richard
Yust, Harold R.

Zack, Albert J.
Zahl, Paul A.
Zakhartchenko, Constantine L.
Zale, Morris B.
Zallen, Harold
Zane, Edward R.
Zartman, Leonard S.
Zech, Robert F.
Zeder, Fred M., II
Zeidman, Philip F.
Zelle, Robert K.
Zeman, William J.
Zemke, John C(laud)
Zemp, Wilfred M.
Zenkovsky, Serge A.
Zerbe, Karl
Zielke, George R.
Zim, Herbert S.
Zimmer, William L., III
Zimmerman, Edwin M.
Zinner, Paul
Zirkle, Charles R.
Zook, Donovan Q.
Zuk, William
Zumwalt, Richard D.
zur Burg, Frederick W.
Zurhellen, J(oseph) Owen, Jr.
Zwingle, James L.